~	above a vowel indicates nasalization, as in French *un* (œ̃), *bon* (bɔ̃), *vin* (vɛ̃), *blanc (blɑ̃)*.
χ	*ch* in German *Buch*, *j* in Spanish *Juan*.
ç	*ch* in German *ich*: a (j) sound as in *yes*, said without voice; similar to the first sound in *huge*.
β	*b* in Spanish *Habana*: a voiced fricative sound similar to (v), but made by the two lips.
ʎ	*ll* in Spanish *llamar*, *gl* in Italian *consiglio*: similar to the (lj) sequence in *million*, but with the tongue tip lowered and the sounds said simultaneously.
ɥ	*u* in French *lui*: a short (y).
ɲ	*gn* in French *vigne*, Italian *gnocchi*, *ñ* in Spanish *España*: similar to the (nj) sequence in *onion*, but with the tongue tip lowered and the two sounds said simultaneously.
ɣ	*g* in Spanis[h] ... friction.

Length

The symbol ː denotes length and is shown together with certain vowel symbols when the vowels are typically long.

Stress

Three grades of stress are shown in the transcriptions by the presence or absence of marks placed immediately *before* the affected syllable. Primary or strong stress is shown by ˈ, while secondary or weak stress is shown by ˌ. Unstressed syllables are not marked. In *photographic* (ˌfəʊtəˈɡræfɪk), for example, the first syllable carries secondary stress and the third primary stress, while the second and fourth are unstressed.

List of Abbreviations

abbrev.	abbreviation
adj	adjective
adv	adverb(ial)
approx.	approximate(ly)
Austral.	Australian
Brit.	British
C	century (e.g. **C14** = 14th century)
°C	degrees Celsius
cap(s).	capital initial(s)
cf.	compare
conj	conjunction
E	east(ern)
e.g.	for example
esp.	especially
est.	estimate
etc.	et cetera
fem	feminine
foll.	followed
ft.	foot *or* feet
i.e.	that is
in.	inch(es)
interj	interjection
intr	intransitive
IPA	International Phonetic Alphabet
km	kilometres
m	metre(s)
masc	masculine
N	north(ern)
n	noun
NE	northeast(ern)
no.	number
NW	northwest(ern)
N.Z.	New Zealand
p.	page
pl	plural
Pop.	population
pp.	pages
prep	preposition(al)
pron	pronoun
pt.	point
RP	Received Pronunciation
S	south(ern)
S. African	South African
Scot.	Scottish, Scots
SE	Southeast(ern)
sing	singular
sq.	square
SW	southwest(ern)
tr	transitive
U.S.	United States
vb	verb
vol.	volume
W	west(ern)
wt.	weight

THE TIMES ENGLISH DICTIONARY

General Consultant

J M Sinclair
Formerly Professor, Department of English Language
and Literature
University of Birmingham

THE TIMES ENGLISH DICTIONARY

TIMES BOOKS

HarperCollins Publishers
PO Box, Glasgow G4 0NB

First Edition 2000

1 2 3 4 5 6 7 8 9

ISBN 0 00 472460-7

A catalogue record for this book is available from the British Library.

This edition prepared in conjunction with Market House Books Ltd, Aylesbury, England

Maps specially prepared for The Times Dictionary by Bartholomew Mapping Solutions, Westerhill Road, Bishopbriggs G64 2QT.
www.bartholomewmaps.com

Typographical design by Kerry Aylin
Wrapper design by Dominic Forbes
Style Guide typeset by Helen Newstead

Typeset by Market House Books Ltd, Aylesbury, England

Printed and bound in Great Britain by Caledonian International Book Manufacturing Ltd, Glasgow

Contents

Guide to the Text

Headword

Pronunciation

prenomen (priːˈnəʊmɛn) *n, pl* **-nomina** (-ˈnɒmɪnə) *or* **-nomens.** *U.S.* a less common spelling of **praenomen.**

prenominal (priːˈnɒmɪnᵊl) *adj* **1** placed before a noun, esp. (of an adjective or sense of an adjective) used only before a noun. **2** of or relating to a praenomen.

prenotion (priːˈnəʊʃən) *n* a rare word for **preconception.**

prentice (ˈprɛntɪs) *n* an archaic word for **apprentice.**

prenuptial agreement *n* a contract made between a man and woman before they marry, agreeing on the distribution of their assets in the event of divorce.

preoccupation (priːˌɒkjuˈpeɪʃən) *or* **preoccupancy** (priːˈɒkjupənsɪ) *n* **1** the state of being preoccupied, esp. mentally. **2** something that holds the attention or preoccupies the mind.

preoccupied (priːˈɒkjʊˌpaɪd) *adj* **1** engrossed or absorbed in something, esp. one's own thoughts. **2** already or previously occupied. **3** *Biology.* (of a taxonomic name) already used to designate a genus, species, etc.

preoccupy (priːˈɒkjʊˌpaɪ) *vb* **-pies, -pying, -pied.** (*tr*) **1** to engross the thoughts or mind of. **2** to occupy before or in advance of another. **[C16:** from Latin *praeoccupāre* to capture in advance, from *prae* before + *occupāre* to seize, take possession of**]**

Inflected forms

preordain (ˌpriːɔːˈdeɪn) *vb* (*tr*) to ordain, decree, or appoint beforehand. ▸ **preordination** (ˌpriːɔːdɪˈneɪʃən) *n*

prep (prɛp) *n* **1** *Informal.* short for **preparation** (sense 5) or (chiefly U.S.) **preparatory school.** ◆ *vb* **preps, prepping, prepped. 2** (*tr*) to prepare (a patient) for a medical operation or procedure.

Part of speech

prep. *abbrev. for:* **1** preparation. **2** preparatory. **3** preposition.

preparation (ˌprɛpəˈreɪʃən) *n* **1** the act or process of preparing. **2** the state of being prepared; readiness. **3** (*often pl*) a measure done in order to prepare for something; provision: *to make preparations for something.* **4** something that is prepared, esp. a medicine. **5** (esp. in a boarding school) **5a** homework. **5b** the period reserved for this. Usually shortened to **prep. 6** *Music.* **6a** the anticipation of a dissonance so that the note producing it in one chord is first heard in the preceding chord as a consonance. **6b** a note so employed. **7** (*often cap.*) the preliminary prayers at Mass or divine service.

Sense number

Example

Subject-field label

preparative (prɪˈpærətɪv) *adj* **1** serving to prepare; preparatory. ◆ *n* **2** something that prepares. ▸ **preˈparatively** *adv*

preparatory (prɪˈpærətərɪ, -trɪ) *adj* **1** serving to prepare. **2** introductory or preliminary. **3** occupied in preparation. **4 preparatory to.** as a preparation to; before: *a drink preparatory to eating.* ▸ **preˈparatorily** *adv*

preparatory school *n* **1** (in Britain) a private school, usually single-sex and for children between the ages of 6 and 13, generally preparing pupils for public school. **2** (in the U.S.) a private secondary school preparing pupils for college. ◆ Often shortened to **prep school.**

prepare (prɪˈpɛə) *vb* **1** to make ready or suitable in advance for a particular purpose or for some use, event, etc.: *to prepare a meal; to prepare to go.* **2** to put together using parts or ingredients; compose or construct. **3** (*tr*) to equip or outfit, as for an expedition. **4** (*tr*) *Music.* to soften the impact of (a dissonant note) by the use of preparation. **5 be prepared.** (*foll. by an infinitive*) to be willing and able (to do something): *I'm not prepared to reveal these figures.* **[C15:** from Latin *praeparāre,* from *prae* before + *parāre* to make ready**]** ▸ **preˈparer** *n*

Definition

Idiom or phrase

preparedness (prɪˈpɛərɪdnɪs) *n* the state of being prepared or ready, esp. militarily ready for war. ▸ **preˈparedly** *adv*

prepared piano *n* a piano in which some strings have been damped by having objects placed between them or tuned differently from the rest for specific tonal effect. This process was pioneered by John Cage.

prepay (priːˈpeɪ) *vb* **-pays, -paying, -paid.** (*tr*) to pay for in advance. ▸ **preˈpayable** *adj* ▸ **preˈpayment** *n*

prepense (prɪˈpɛns) *adj* (*postpositive*) (usually in legal contexts) arranged in advance; premeditated (esp. in the phrase **malice prepense**). **[C18:** from Anglo-Norman *purpensé,* from Old French *purpenser* to consider in advance, from *penser* to think, from Latin *pēnsāre* to weigh, consider**]**

preponderant (prɪˈpɒndərənt) *adj* greater in weight, force, influence, etc. ▸ **preˈponderance** *or* **preˈponderancy** *n* ▸ **preˈponderantly** *adv*

preponderate (prɪˈpɒndəˌreɪt) *vb* (*intr*) **1** (often foll. by *over*) to be more powerful, important, numerous, etc. (than). **2** to be of greater weight than something else. **[C17:** from Late Latin *praeponderāre* to be of greater weight, from *pondus* weight**]** ▸ **preˈponderately** *adv* ▸ **preˈponderˌating** *adj* ▸ **preˌponderˈation** *n*

Grammatical information

preposition (ˌprɛpəˈzɪʃən) *n* a word or group of words used before a noun or pronoun to relate it grammatically or semantically to some other constituent of a sentence. Abbrev.: **prep. [C14:** from Latin *praepositiō* a putting before, from *pōnere* to place**]** ▸ **ˌprepoˈsitional** *adj* ▸ **ˌprepoˈsitionally** *adv*

> **USAGE** The practice of ending a sentence with a preposition (*Venice is a place I should like to go to*) was formerly regarded as incorrect, but is now acceptable and is the preferred form in many contexts.

Usage note

Guide to the Text

prepositive (priːˈpɒzɪtɪv) *adj* **1** (of a word or speech element) placed before the word governed or modified. ◆ *n* **2** a prepositive element. ▸ **preˈpositively** *adv*

prepositor (priːˈpɒzɪtə) *or* **prepostor** (priːˈpɒstə) *n Brit., rare.* a prefect in any of certain public schools. [C16: from Latin *praepositus* placed before]

prepossess (ˌpriːpəˈzɛs) *vb* (*tr*) **1** to preoccupy or engross mentally. **2** to influence in advance for or against a person or thing; prejudice; bias. **3** to make a favourable impression on beforehand.

prepossessing (ˌpriːpəˈzɛsɪŋ) *adj* creating a favourable impression; attractive. ▸ **ˌpreposˈsessingly** *adv* ▸ **ˌpreposˈsessingness** *n*

prepossession (ˌpriːpəˈzɛʃən) *n* **1** the state or condition of being prepossessed. **2** a prejudice or bias, esp. a favourable one.

preposterous (prɪˈpɒstərəs) *adj* contrary to nature, reason, or sense; absurd; ridiculous. [C16: from Latin *praeposterus* reversed, from *prae* in front, before + *posterus* following] ▸ **preˈposterously** *adv* ▸ **preˈposterousness** *n*

prepotency (prɪˈpəʊtᵊnsɪ) *n* **1** the state or condition of being prepotent. **2** *Genetics.* the ability of one parent to transmit more characteristics to its offspring than the other parent. **3** *Botany.* the ability of pollen from one source to bring about fertilization more readily than that from other sources.

prepotent (prɪˈpəʊtᵊnt) *adj* **1** greater in power, force, or influence. **2** *Biology.* showing prepotency. [C15: from Latin *praepotens* very powerful, from *posse* to be able] ▸ **preˈpotently** *adv*

Usage label

preppy (ˈprɛpɪ) *Informal.* ◆ *adj* **1** characteristic of or denoting a fashion style of neat, understated, and often expensive clothes; young but classic: suggesting that the wearer is well off, upper class, and conservative. ◆ *n, pl* **-pies. 2** a person exhibiting such style. [C20: originally U.S., from *preppy* a person who attends or has attended a preparatory school before college]

preproduction (ˌpriːprəˈdʌkʃən) *n* **1** preliminary work on or trial production of a play, industrial prototype, etc. ◆ *adj* **2** (of a period, model, etc.) preliminary; trial.

prep school *n Informal.* See **preparatory school.**

Cross-reference

Related word

prepuce (ˈpriːpjuːs) *n* **1** the retractable fold of skin covering the tip of the penis. Nontechnical name: **foreskin. 2** a similar fold of skin covering the tip of the clitoris. [C14: from Latin *praepūtium*] ▸ **preputial** (priːˈpjuːʃəl) *adj*

prequel (ˈpriːkwəl) *n* a film that is made about an earlier stage of a story or character's life because the later part of it has already made a successful film. [C20: from PRE- + (*se*)*quel*]

Pre-Raphaelite (ˌpriːˈræfəlaɪt) *n* **1** a member of the **Pre-Raphaelite Brotherhood,** an association of painters and writers including Rossetti, Holman Hunt, and Millais, founded in 1848 to combat the shallow conventionalism of academic painting and revive the fidelity to nature and the vivid realistic colour that they considered typical of Italian painting before Raphael. ◆ *adj* **2** of, in the manner of, or relating to Pre-Raphaelite painting and painters. ▸ **ˌPre-ˈRaphaelˌitism** *n*

prerequisite (priːˈrɛkwɪzɪt) *adj* **1** required as a prior condition. ◆ *n* **2** something required as a prior condition.

prerogative (prɪˈrɒgətɪv) *n* **1** an exclusive privilege or right exercised by a person or group of people holding a particular office or hereditary rank. **2** any privilege or right. **3** a power, privilege, or immunity restricted to a sovereign or sovereign government. ◆ *adj* **5** having or able to exercise a prerogative. [C14: from Latin *praerogātīva* privilege, earlier: group with the right to vote first, from *prae* before + *rogāre* to ask, beg for]

Etymology

pres. *abbrev. for:* **1** present (time). **2** presidential.

Pres. *abbrev. for* President.

presa (ˈpresɑː) *n, pl* **-se** (-seɪ). *Music.* a sign or symbol used in a canon, round, etc., to indicate the entry of each part. Usual signs: +, :S:, or ※ [Italian, literally: a taking up, from *prendere* to take, from Latin *prehendere* to grasp]

presage *n* (ˈprɛsɪdʒ). **1** an intimation or warning of something about to happen; portent; omen. **2** a sense of what is about to happen; foreboding. **3** *Archaic.* a forecast or prediction. ◆ *vb* (ˈprɛsɪdʒ, prɪˈseɪdʒ). **4** (*tr*) to have a presentiment of. **5** (*tr*) to give a forewarning of; portend. **6** (*intr*) to make a prediction. [C14: from Latin *praesāgium* presentiment, from *praesāgīre* to perceive beforehand, from *sāgīre* to perceive acutely] ▸ **preˈsageful** *adj* ▸ **preˈsagefully** *adv* ▸ **preˈsager** *n*

Derived words

presale (ˈpriːseɪl) *n* the practice of arranging the sale of a product before it is available.

ˌpre-Reforˈmation *adj*
ˌpre-Reˈnaissance *adj*
ˌprereˈtirement *adj*
pre-ˈRoman *adj*
ˌprescienˈtific *adj*

Listed entries

Editorial Staff

EDITORIAL DIRECTOR
Diana Treffry

EDITORIAL CONSULTANT
Alan Isaacs

MANAGING EDITOR
Sheila Ferguson

LEXICOGRAPHERS
Elspeth Summers (Senior Lexicographer)
Ian Brookes **Lorna Gilmour**
Andrew Holmes **Mary O'Neill**

COMPUTER STAFF
Raymond Carrick

USAGE NOTES
John Todd

MARKET HOUSE EDITORS
John Daintith **Elizabeth Martin** **Fran Alexander**
Jonathan Law **Peter Blair**

COMPUTERS
Anne Stibbs

KEYBOARDERS
Jessica Scholes **Sandra McQueen** **Gwynneth Shaw** **Brenda Tomkins**

COMPILER
of *The Times Guide to English Style and Usage*
Tim Austin

CARTOGRAPHY
Bartholomew Mapping Solutions

The Times English Dictionary

Foreword

The Times English Dictionary, in the best tradition of The Times, presents a clear account of the English language as it is used today in Britain and around the world as well as reflecting how the language has changed over time.

As in The Times itself, there is an enormous breadth of coverage. The terms used in disciplines as diverse as mathematics and law, in sports and the arts, in education and health are all included. The whole gamut of the sciences is particularly well represented with terms from the latest research and development in fields like biochemistry and medicine. Computing and the explosion of terms related to the Internet are also covered.

Besides dealing with a broad range of subjects, **The Times English Dictionary** covers the many different varieties of English used around the world from Australia and New Zealand, through India, the Caribbean, Canada, and the United States. As well as separate entries for the different words, different meanings within an entry are clearly labelled, for instance at **blue** see senses 12, 13, and 14. US spellings are shown as variants of the British spelling at the main entry as well as having their own entry. Equivalent terms are shown at the end of some entries, see for instance **hire-purchase**.

Within British English, Scots, Irish, and Welsh words and expressions are included along with a certain amount of English regional dialect, from **grockle** in the Southwest to **stottie** in the Northeast, as well as some Irish and Scots Gaelic words.

Another dimension of the English language is the range of styles, or registers, from the most formal, often Latinate, terms to the most informal, sometimes Anglo-Saxon, expressions. The whole range is represented in the Dictionary, carefully labelled, especially where terms may be considered derogatory, offensive, or taboo. The lexicographer's task is to describe the language as it currently is. The labels reflect current conventions of usage which may differ in different circles. Where there is uncertainty, the lexicographers have tended to adopt a cautious approach.

The Dictionary is organised so that every word that needs an explanation appears as a main entry, or headword, in the single alphabetical list. Derived words whose meaning can easily be deduced from the headword are shown in bold at the end of the entry preceded by an arrowhead (▸). This means that important features of English, like phrasal verbs, eg **buy up**, special uses of plurals, eg **bowls**, and standard expressions, eg **ways and means**, have their own headword entries and are quicker and easier to find.

Pronunciations for all words are shown in the International Phonetic Alphabet, a key for which can be found both on the front endpaper and on page xxiv before the Dictionary.

Parts of speech are shown abbreviated in italics, and where a word can be used as more than one part of speech, the change is signalled by a lozenge (◆). Different senses of a word are numbered in bold sequentially through the whole entry; subdivisions of a sense are marked by bold **a**, **b**, **c**, etc. following the number. Idioms are shown in bold and grouped towards the end.

The history of root words is given in etymologies placed in bold square brackets at the end of the definition(s). When the root word comes from Old English related words are shown; when the root word comes from another language the century when it entered English and the series of sources before that is shown.

A real boon for both general users and crossword puzzle solvers is the unique feature of showing related adjectives where the adjective is related in meaning but not spelling. For instance, where there is a Latinate adjective, like **lapidary** for **gemstone**, which would not easily be found unless you already knew it, this is shown at the noun entry.

There is thus an enormous wealth of information in the Dictionary. But that is not all. Appropriately for The Times, the Dictionary also includes a wide range of encyclopedic material, especially for people and places. So within the alphabetical sequence of the dictionary you will find entries, for instance, for **Baily's beads** and **Beethoven**, and for **Shakespeare**, **London**, and **Londonderry**. The entries for towns, cities, and countries give the latest available population figures as well as salient features. The entries for people include many household names both historical and current and include dates and particular claims to fame. The geographical and biographical entries make the Dictionary an especially good companion to The Times newspaper.

There are two additional special features to **The Times English Dictionary** that make it uniquely helpful and useful. These are world maps and The Times Guide to Style and Usage.

The map section consists of 24 full-colour maps covering all the regions of the world, including details of geographical features and principal place names.

The Times Guide to Style and Usage lays out in alphabetical order of words the rules, the preferred forms, and the house style used by writers for The Times. Following The Times Guide enables our writers to achieve consistency, so that, as a reader, your attention is not jarred by different spellings being used in different articles. It also offers a useful and respected rule book if you so desire. But it is of course only one choice among many offered by the diverse and inclusive nature of the English language. Each person has their own voice that comes through in the way that they write. But if you find you are puzzled about whether a form or construction is 'right' you have the option to follow the ready-made rule book of The Times Guide to Style and Usage or consult the various Usage notes within the body of the Dictionary. These describe current practice often compared or contrasted with former or strict usage, providing information and advice but not usually hard-and-fast rules.

The Dictionary, as described earlier, covers and describes the great variety of English worldwide. Thus it shows a range of variant spellings, all of which are acceptable. The first spelling is usually the one that is most frequently used, but it may sometimes differ from the preferred form in The Times Guide. For example, the Dictionary puts the **~ize** spelling form of verbs first, whereas The Times Guide prefers the **~ise** spelling. The Times Guide to Style and Usage offers a set of rules for one variety of English, within the whole complex and comprehensive nature of English as it is described and explained in **The Times English Dictionary**. Together, along with the maps and the encyclopedic entries in the Dictionary they offer unrivalled information, guidance, and interest to everyone who reads, writes, and uses English in the world today.

Special Consultants

AUSTRALIAN ENGLISH
W S Ramson
Reader in English
Australian National University

BRITISH REGIONAL ENGLISH, URBAN DIALECTS
Harold Orton
Professor Emeritus, Department of English
University of Leeds

CANADIAN ENGLISH
R J Gregg
Formerly Professor, Department of Linguistics
University of British Columbia

Patrick Drysdale
Editor, *A Dictionary of Canadianisms on Historical Principles*

James Arthurs
Professor, Department of Linguistics
University of Victoria

CARIBBEAN ENGLISH
S R R Allsopp
Coordinator, Caribbean Lexicography Project
University of the West Indies, Barbados

EAST AFRICAN ENGLISH
J Kalema
Department of Linguistic Science
University of Reading

INDIAN ENGLISH
R K Bansal
Professor, Department of Phonetics and Spoken English
Central Institute of English and Foreign Languages
Hyderabad

IRISH ENGLISH
R J Gregg
Formerly Professor, Department of Linguistics
University of British Columbia

T de Bhaldraithe
Professor, Department of Irish Dialectology
University College, Dublin

NEW ZEALAND ENGLISH
Ian A Gordon
Professor Emeritus
University of Wellington

SCOTTISH ENGLISH
A J Aitken
Department of English Language
University of Edinburgh
Formerly Editor, *Dictionary of the Older Scottish Tongue*

SOUTH AFRICAN ENGLISH
L W Lanham
Professor, Department of Phonetics and General Linguistics
University of the Witwatersrand

M V Aldridge
Professor, Department of Phonetics and General Linguistics
University of the Witwatersrand

Geoffrey Hughes
Professor, Department of English
University of the Witwatersrand

WEST AFRICAN ENGLISH
J Spencer
Director, Institute of Modern English Language Studies
University of Leeds

PRONUNCIATION
A C Gimson
Formerly Professor, Department of Phonetics and Linguistics
University College
University of London

Specialist Contributors

AERONAUTICS
T C Wooldridge
Angus Boyd
Senior Lecturer in Aerodynamics,
The College of Aeronautics,
Cranfield

ARCHITECTURE; CIVIL ENGINEERING
Bruce Martin

AUSTRALIAN ENGLISH
Steve Higgs
Melbourne Grammar School

BIOGRAPHIES, PLACES
Market House Books
Aylesbury

BROADCASTING, FILM, ETC.
Patrick Leggatt
Chief Engineer, External Relations,
British Broadcasting Corporation

BUSINESS
Alan Isaacs

CHEMISTRY
John Daintith

COMPUTERS
Richard Fryer
Department of Computer Science,
University of Strathclyde

CONSTRUCTION
M J Walker
Construction Industry Research
and Information Association

EARTH SCIENCES
Peter J Smith
Reader in Earth Sciences,
The Open University

ECONOMICS
P Donaldson
Ruskin College, Oxford

EDUCATION
Catherine Playford
Head Teacher of English,
Priestnall School

ENGINEERING
J P Quayle
Editor, *Kempe's Engineering Year-Book*

INDUSTRIAL RELATIONS
Professor Angela M Bowey
Strathclyde Business School,
University of Strathclyde
Alexander Purdie
Scottish College of Textiles,
Galashiels

INFORMATION TECHNOLOGY
Professor Thomas Carbery
Andrew Doswell
Catherine M Young
Department of Information Science,
University of Strathclyde

JUDAISM
Ephraim Borowski
Department of Philosophy,
University of Glasgow

LANGUAGES & PEOPLES
David Kilby
Formerly, Department of Language and Linguistics,
University of Essex

LAW
Richard Latham
Queen's Counsel
Brian Russell Davis
Barrister-at-Law
Sandra Clarke

LIFE SCIENCES
Miranda Robertson
Life Sciences Editor,
Nature
Dr W Gratzer
MRC Cell Biophysics Unit

LINGUISTICS
Professor Yorick Wilks
New Mexico State University

LINGUISTICS AND GRAMMAR
Lloyd Humberstone

LOGIC
Ephraim Borowski
Department of Philosophy,
University of Glasgow

MALAYSIAN ENGLISH
U Yong-ee

MARKETING
Professor M Christopher
Department of Marketing and
Logistics Systems,
Cranfield School of Management

Specialist Contributors

Helen Peck
Research Fellow,
Cranfield School of Management

METALLURGY
Stanley White

MILITARY
Major S R Elliot
Colonel Andrew Duncan
The International Institute
for Strategic Studies

MILITARY AND NAUTICAL TERMS
Cmdr I Johnston RN

PHILOSOPHY
Christopher Sion
Ephraim Borowski
Department of Philosophy,
University of Glasgow

PHYSICAL SCIENCES
R Cutler

PHYSICS
J W Warren
Department of Physics,
Brunel University

PIDGINS AND CREOLES
Loreto Todd
The School of English,
University of Leeds

PLANTS
Sandra Holmes

POP MUSIC
Ingrid von Essen

PRINTING
C H Parsons
Laurence Chizlett

Gerry Riach
Glasgow College of Printing

PSYCHOLOGY
Dr Eric Taylor
Professor Stuart Sutherland
Director, Centre for Research
on Perception and Cognition,
University of Sussex

RAILWAYS
James Barnes

RELIGION
The Rev D Lancashire
University of Essex
Sister Isabel Smyth
Sisters of Notre Dame,Glasgow

RELIGIOUS TERMS
David Bourke
Rev Canon D W Gundry
Chancellor of Leicester Cathedral

SOCIAL WELFARE
Bob Marsden
Harrow Social Services
Department

SOCIOLOGY
Jenny Oswald

SPORT
Stuart Bathgate
Freelance Journalist

STATISTICS
Ephraim Borowski
Department of Philosophy,
University of Glasgow

TOOLS
N J Smail
Associate of the Institute of Marine Engineers

Other Contributors

Jane Bartholomew ANIMALS
Jenny Baster COOKERY; CLOTHING AND FASHION; TEXTILES
Denise Bown PLACE NAMES
Ron Brown JAZZ
Daphne Butler CHEMISTRY
Christopher L Clarke HOROLOGY
Brian Dalgleish METALLURGY
Carolyn Eardley ANTIQUES; FURNITURE; TEXTILES
R J Edwards PSYCHOLOGY
Dennis Exton FILMS, TV, AND RADIO
Rosalind Fergusson BIOGRAPHIES
Ian Fuller PSYCHOLOGY
C Gallon PLANTS
William Gould ETYMOLOGIES
Robert Hine BIOGRAPHIES
Amanda Isaacs BIOGRAPHIES
Cherry McDonald-Taylor EDUCATION; LIBRARY SCIENCE
David Martin PSYCHOLOGY
Mary Marshall CARDS; DANCING AND BALLET
Peter Miller SPORTS
Stewart Murray METALLURGY
Serena Penman ART
H G Procter PSYCHOLOGY
Mark Salad PLACE NAMES
David H Shaw ENGINEERING
Brian Street ANTHROPOLOGY
Andrew Treacher PSYCHOLOGY
Ralph Tyler FILMS, TV, AND RADIO; LITERATURE; MYTHOLOGY; THEATRE; BIOGRAPHIES
Jennifer Wearden ARCHAEOLOGY
Irene Wise BIOCHEMISTRY

Guide to the Use of the Dictionary

The Times English Dictionary is designed to be easy to use so that you can go straight to the word you want. The Guide that follows sets out the main principles on which the Dictionary is arranged and enables you to make full use of the Dictionary by showing the whole range of information that it contains.

1 HEADWORD

All main entries, including place names, biographies, abbreviations, prefixes, and suffixes, are printed in large boldface type and are listed in strict alphabetical order. This applies even if the headword consists of more than one word.

1.1 Order of entries

Words that have the same spelling but are derived from different sources (homographs) are entered separately with superscript numbers after the headwords.

saw[1] (sɔː) *n* **1** any of various hand tools...

saw[2] (sɔː) *vb* the past tense of **see**[1].

saw[3] (sɔː) *n* a wise saying, maxim, or proverb....

A word with a capital initial letter, if entered separately, follows the lower-case form. For example, **Arras** follows **arras**.
Names beginning with **Mc-** are listed in alphabetical order, as if they were spelt **Mac-**. Saints are entered under their Christian names, but places named after saints are all listed alphabetically under **Saint**.

1.2 Place names

If a place has more than one name, its main entry is given at the name most often used in modern English, with a cross-reference at other names. Thus, the main entry for the capital of Bavaria is at **Munich**, with a cross-reference at **München**. If a place name has no current anglicized form, its main entry is at the form of the name used in the official language of the area. Thus, the main entry is at **Brno**, with a cross-reference at **Brünn**. Historical names of importance are also given, with dates where these can be ascertained.

Paris[1] ('pæris; *French* pari) *n*...Ancient name: **Lutetia**.

Volgograd (*Russian* vəlga'grat; *English* 'vɒlgə,græd), *n*...Former names: **Tsaritsyn** (until 1925), **Stalingrad** (1925–61).

Statistical information about places has been obtained from the most up-to-date and reliable sources available. Population figures have been compiled from the most recent census available at the time of going to press. The date of the census is always given. Where no census figure is available, the most reliable recent estimate has been given, with a date.

1.3 Biographical entries

Biographical entries are entered separately from and immediately following place names of the same spelling. They are entered at the surname of the subject or at his or her title if that is the name by which he or she is better known and are grouped under one headword when the spelling of the surname (or title) is identical.
Dates given for literary works are of first publication; dates for dramatic works are of first performance.

1.4 Abbreviations, acronyms, and symbols

Abbreviations, acronyms, and symbols are entered as headwords in the main alphabetical list. In line with modern practice, full stops are not used with symbols (**Ga**), nor for most abbreviations that are either strings of initials (**MA**, **mph**) or contractions (**St**, **Mr**). However, stops are used for an abbreviation of a word that is not a contraction (**Brig.**) and for strings of lower-case initials that could form a word (**c.o.d.**). Alternative forms with stops are only shown for certain standard abbreviations (**e.g.** *or* **eg**) but it can be assumed that nearly all abbreviations are equally acceptable with or without stops.

1.5 Prefixes, suffixes, and combining forms

Prefixes (e.g. **in-**, **pre-**, **sub-**), suffixes (e.g. **-able**, **-ation**, **-ity**), and combining forms (e.g. **psycho-**, **-iatry**) have been entered as headwords if they are still used freely to produce new words in English.

1.6 Plural headwords

Words that have a standard use or uses in the plural may be entered as separate headwords at both singular and plural forms, with a cross-reference to the plural form at the singular entry if other headwords intervene.

affair (ə'fɛə) *n* **1** a thing to be done or attended to...◆ See also **affairs**.

affairs (ə'fɛəz) *pl n* **1** personal or business interests...

1.7 Variant spellings

Common acceptable variant spellings of English words are given as alternative forms of the headword.

capitalize *or* **capitalise** ('kæpɪtəˌlaɪz) *vb*...

2 PRONUNCIATION

Pronunciations of words in this Dictionary represent those that are common in educated speech. They are transcribed in the International Phonetic Alphabet (IPA). A *Key to the Pronunciation Symbols* is printed at the end of this Guide and on the front endpapers. See also the section on pronunciation in the article on *Australian English* by Professor Wilkes on p. xxxiv. The pronunciation is normally given in brackets immediately after the headword.

abase (əˈbeɪs) *vb* (*tr*) **1** to humble...

The stress pattern is marked by the symbols ˈ for primary stress and ˌ for secondary stress. The stress mark precedes the syllable to which it applies.

2.1 Variant pronunciations

When a headword has an acceptable variant pronunciation or stress pattern, the variant is given by repeating only the syllable or syllables that change.

economic (ˌiːkəˈnɒmɪk, ˌɛkə-) *adj* **1** of or relating to...

2.2 Pronunciations with different parts of speech

When two or more parts of speech of a word have different pronunciations, the pronunciations are shown in brackets before the relevant group of senses.

record *n* (ˈrɛkɔːd). **1** an account in permanent form...◆ *vb* (rɪˈkɔːd). (*mainly tr*) **19** to set down in some permanent form...

2.3 Pronunciation of individual senses

If one sense of a headword has a different pronunciation from that of the rest, the pronunciation is given in brackets after the sense number.

conjure (ˈkʌndʒə) *vb* **1** (*intr*) to practise conjuring or be a conjurer. **2** (*intr*) to call upon supposed supernatural forces by spells and incantations. **3** (kənˈdʒʊə) (*tr*) to appeal earnestly or strongly to: *I conjure you to help me*...

2.4 Foreign words and phrases

Foreign words or phrases are printed in boldface italic type and are given foreign-language pronunciations only unless they are regarded as having become accepted in English.

haut monde *French*. (o mɔ̃d) *n*...

2.5 Foreign proper names

Foreign proper names, chiefly place names and biographies, are printed in large boldface roman type. If they do not have widely acceptable conventional English pronunciations, they are given only foreign-language pronunciations.

Milazzo (*Italian* miˈlattso) *n* a port in NE Sicily...

3 INFLECTED FORMS

Inflected forms of nouns, verbs, and adjectives are shown immediately after the part-of-speech label if they are irregular or, in certain cases, if they are regular but might cause confusion.

3.1 Regular inflections

Where inflections are not shown, it may be assumed that they are formed as follows:

nouns. Regular plurals are formed by the addition of *-s* (e.g. *pencils, monkeys*) or, in the case of nouns ending in *-s, -x, -z, -ch,* or *-sh*, by the addition of *-es* (e.g. *losses*).

verbs. In regularly inflected verbs:
the third person singular of the present tense is formed by the addition of *-s* to the infinitive (e.g. *plays*)
or, for verbs ending in *-s, -x, -z, -ch,* or *-sh*, by the addition of *-es* (e.g. *passes, reaches*)
the past tense and past participle are formed by the addition of *-ed* to the infinitive (e.g. *played*)
the present participle is formed by the addition of *-ing* to the infinitive (e.g. *playing*).
Verbs that end in a consonant plus *-e* (e.g. *locate, snare*) regularly lose the final *-e* before the addition of *-ed* and *-ing*.

adjectives. The regular comparatives and superlatives of adjectives are formed by adding *-er* and *-est* to the base (e.g. *short, shorter, shortest*).
Adjectives that end in a consonant plus *-e* regularly lose the *-e* before *-er* and *-est* (e.g. *fine, finer, finest*).

3.2 **Irregular and unfamiliar inflections**

Inflected forms are shown for the following:
Nouns and verbs whose inflections involve a change in internal spelling.

goose[1] (guːs) *n, pl* **geese**...

drive (draɪv) *vb* **drives, driving, drove** (drəʊv), **driven**...

Nouns, verbs, and adjectives that end in a consonant plus *y*, where *y* is changed to *i* before inflectional endings.

augury ('ɔːghʊrɪ) *n, pl* **-ries**...

Nouns having identical singular and plural forms.

sheep (ʃiːp) *n, pl* **sheep**...

Nouns that closely resemble others but form their plurals differently.

mongoose ('mɒŋ,guːs) *n, pl* **-gooses**...

Nouns that end in *-ful*, *-o*, and *-us*.

handful ('hændfʊl) *n, pl* **-fuls**...

tomato (tə'mɑːtəʊ) *n, pl* **-toes**...

prospectus (prə'spɛktəs) *n, pl* **-tuses**...

Nouns whose plurals are not regular English inflections.

basis ('beɪsɪs) *n, pl* **-ses** (-siːz)...

Plural nouns whose singulars are not regular English forms.

bacteria (bæk'tɪərɪə) *pl n, sing* **-rium** (-rɪəm)...

Nouns whose plurals have regular spellings but involve a change in pronunciation.

house (haʊs) *n, pl* **houses** ('haʊzɪz)...

Multiword nouns when it is not obvious which word takes a plural inflection.

attorney-at-law *n, pl* **attorneys-at-law**...

Adjectives that change their roots to form comparatives and superlatives.

good (gʊd) *adj* **better, best**...

Adjectives and verbs that double their final consonant before adding endings.

fat (fæt)...◆ *adj* **fatter, fattest**...

control (kən'trəʊl) *vb* **-trols, -trolling, -trolled**...

Verbs that are regular and do not (as might be expected) double their final consonant before adding endings.

gallop ('gæləp) *vb* **-lops, -loping, -loped**...

Verbs and adjectives that end in a vowel plus *-e*.

canoe (kə'nuː)...◆ *vb*, **-noes, -noeing, -noed**...

free (friː) *adj* **freer, freest**...◆ *vb* **frees, freeing, freed**...

4 **PARTS OF SPEECH**

A part-of-speech label in italics precedes the sense or senses relating to that part of speech.

4.1 **Standard parts of speech**

The standard parts of speech, with the abbreviations used, are as follows:
adjective (*adj*), adverb (*adv*), conjunction (*conj*), interjection (*interj*), noun (*n*), preposition (*prep*), pronoun (*pron*), verb (*vb*).

4.2 **Less traditional parts of speech**

Certain other less traditional parts of speech have been used in this Dictionary. They are as follows:

determiners. Such words as *that, this, my, his*, etc., which used to be classed as demonstrative and possessive adjectives and/or pronouns, have been classified in this Dictionary as determiners. The label *determiner* also replaces the traditional classification for words like *the, a, some, any*, as well as the numerals, and possessives such as *my* and *your*. Many determiners can have a pronoun function without change of meaning, and this is indicated as in the following example:

some (sʌm; *unstressed* səm) *determiner*...**2a** an unknown or unspecified quantity or amount of: *there's some rice on the table; he owns some horses.* **2b** (*as pronoun; functioning as sing or pl*): *we'll buy some*...

sentence connectors. This description replaces the traditional classification of certain words, such as *therefore* and *however*, as adverbs or conjunctions. These words link sentences together rather in the manner of conjunctions; however, they are not confined to the first position in a clause as conjunctions are.

sentence substitutes. Sentence substitutes are words such as *yes, no, perhaps, definitely*, and *maybe*. They can stand as meaningful utterances by themselves. They are distinguished in this Dictionary from interjections such as *ouch, ah, damn*, etc., which are expressions of emotional reaction rather than meaningful utterances.

4.3 Words used as more than one part of speech

If a word can be used as more than one part of speech, the senses of one part of speech are separated from the others by a lozenge (◆).

> **lure** (lʊə) *vb* (*tr*)...**2** *Falconry.* to entice (a hawk or falcon) from the air to the falconer by a lure. ◆ *n* **3** a person or thing that lures...

5 GRAMMATICAL INFORMATION

Grammatical information is provided in brackets and typically in italics to distinguish it from other types of information.

5.1 Adjectives and determiners

Some adjectives and determiners are restricted by usage to a particular position relative to the nouns they qualify. This is indicated by the following labels:

postpositive (used predicatively or after the noun, but not before the noun):

> **ablaze** (əˈbleɪz) *adj* (*postpositive*), *adv* **1** on fire; burning...

immediately postpositive (always used immediately following the noun qualified and never used predicatively):

> **galore** (gəˈlɔː) *determiner* (*immediately postpositive*) in great numbers or quantity: *there were daffodils galore in the park*...

prenominal (used before the noun, and never used predicatively):

> **chief** (tʃiːf)...◆ *adj* **5** (*prenominal*) **5a** most important; principal. **5b** highest in rank or authority...

5.2 Intensifiers

Adjectives and adverbs that perform an exclusively intensifying function, with no addition of meaning, are described as (intensifier) without further explanation.

> **blooming** (ˈbluːmɪŋ) *adv, adj Brit. informal.* (intensifier): *a blooming genius; blooming painful.*

5.3 Conjunctions

Conjunctions are divided into two classes, marked by the following labels placed in brackets:

coordinating. Coordinating conjunctions connect words, phrases, or clauses that perform an identical function and are not dependent on each other. They include *and, but*, and *or*.

subordinating. Subordinating conjunctions introduce clauses that are dependent on a main clause in a complex sentence. They include *where, until*, and *or*.

Some conjunctions, such as *while* and *whereas*, can function as either coordinating or subordinating conjunctions.

5.4 Singular and plural labelling of nouns

Headwords and senses that are apparently plural in form but that take a singular verb, etc., are marked *'functioning as sing'*.

> **physics** (ˈfɪzɪks) *n* (*functioning as sing*) **1** the branch of science...

Headwords and senses that appear to be singular, such as collective nouns, but that take a plural verb, etc., are marked *'functioning as pl'*.

> **cattle** (ˈkætᵊl) *n* (*functioning as pl*) **1** bovid mammals of the tribe *Bovini*...

Headwords and senses that may take either a singular or plural verb, etc., are marked *'functioning as sing or pl'*.

> **bellows** (ˈbɛləʊz) *n* (*functioning as sing or pl*) **1** Also called: **pair of bellows**. an instrument consisting of an air chamber...

5.5 **Modifiers**

A noun that is commonly used as if it were an adjective is labelled *modifier*. If the sense of the modifier can be understood from the sense of the noun, the modifier is shown without further explanation, with an example to illustrate its use.

> **denim** ('dɛnɪm) *n Textiles.* **1a** a hard-wearing twill-weave cotton fabric used for trousers, work clothes, etc. **1b** (*as modifier*): *a denim jacket...*

If the sense of the modifier cannot be understood from the sense of the noun, or if it is related to more than one of the noun senses, its meaning and/or usage is explained separately.

> **key**[1] (kiː) *n*...**24** (*modifier*) of great importance: *a key issue...*

5.6 **Verbs**

The principal parts given are: 3rd person singular of the present tense; present participle; past tense; past participle if different from the past tense.

5.7 **Intransitive and transitive verbs**

When a sense of a verb (*vb*) is restricted to transitive use, it is labelled (*tr*); if it is intransitive only, it is labelled (*intr*). If all the senses of a verb are transitive or all are intransitive, the appropriate label appears before the first numbered sense and is not repeated.

Absence of a label is significant: it indicates that the sense may be used both transitively and intransitively.

If nearly all the senses of a verb are transitive, the label (*mainly tr*) appears immediately before the first numbered sense. An individual sense may then be labelled (*also intr*) to show that it is both transitive and intransitive, or it may be labelled (*intr*) to show that it is intransitive only.

> **carry** ('kærɪ) *vb*...(*mainly tr*) **1** (*also intr*) to take or bear (something) from one place to another: *to carry a baby in one's arms.* **2** to transfer for consideration; take: *he carried his complaints to her superior*...**27** (*intr*) (of a ball, projectile, etc.) to travel through the air or reach a specified point: *his first drive carried to the green.*

Similarly, all the senses of a verb may be labelled (*mainly intr*) and the labels (*also tr*) and (*tr*) introduced before individual senses as required.

When a sense of a verb may be transitive or intransitive, a direct object that would typically follow its transitive use is sometimes shown in brackets. The brackets should be ignored in order to obtain the intransitive use.

> **act** (ækt)...◆ *vb*...**11** to perform (a part or role) in a play...

When the object of the transitive use of a verb constitutes the subject of the intransitive use, this is shown as follows:

> **fire** (faɪə)...◆ *vb*...**25** to discharge (a firearm or projectile) or (of a firearm, etc.) to be discharged...

When the intransitive use of a verb functions with a preposition but the transitive use does not, an equivalent preposition is given in brackets.

> **differentiate** (ˌdɪfəˈrɛnʃɪˌeɪt) *vb*...**2** (when *intr*, often foll. by *between*) to perceive, show, or make a difference (in or between); discriminate.

5.8 **Copulas**

A verb that takes a complement is labelled *copula.*

> **seem** (siːm) *vb* (may take an infinitive) **1** (*copula*) to appear to the mind or eye; look: *this seems nice; the car seems to be running well.*

5.9 **Phrasal verbs**

Verbal constructions consisting of a verb and a prepositional or an adverbial particle are given headword status if the meaning of the phrasal verb cannot be deduced from the separate meanings of the verb and the particle.

Phrasal verbs are labelled to show four possible distinctions:
a transitive verb with an adverbial particle (*tr, adv*); a transitive verb with a prepositional particle (*tr, prep*); an intransitive verb with an adverbial particle (*intr, adv*); an intransitive verb with a prepositional particle (*intr, prep*):

> **turn on**...**4** (*tr, adv*) *Informal.* to produce (charm, tears, etc.) suddenly or automatically.

> **take for** *vb* (*tr, prep*) *Informal.* to consider or suppose to be, esp. mistakenly: *the fake coins were taken for genuine; who do you take me for?*

> **break off**...**3** (*intr, adv*) to stop abruptly; halt: *he broke off in the middle of his speech.*

> **turn on**...**2** (*intr, prep*) to depend or hinge on: *the success of the party turns on you.*

As with the labelling of other verbs, the absence of a label is significant. If there is no label (*tr*) or (*intr*), the verb may be used either transitively or intransitively. If there is no label (*adv*) or (*prep*), the particle may be either adverbial or prepositional.

Any noun, adjective, or modifier formed from a phrasal verb is entered under the phrasal-verb headword. In some cases, where the noun or adjective is more common than the verb, the phrasal verb is entered after the noun or adjective form:

> **breakaway** (ˈbreɪkəˌweɪ) *n* **1a** loss or withdrawal of a group of members from an association, club, etc. **1b** (*as modifier*): *a breakaway faction*...◆ *vb* **break away.** (*intr, adv*)...**4** (often foll. by *from*) to leave hastily or escape.

A cross-reference is given at the main verb when related phrasal verbs are entered as headwords but are separated from it by more than five intervening entries.

> **fit**[1] (fɪt) *vb*...See also **fit in, fit out, fit up. [**C14: probably from Middle Dutch *vitten*]...

6 RESTRICTIVE LABELS

If a particular sense is restricted as to appropriateness, connotation, subject field, etc., an italic label is placed immediately before the relevant definition.

> **hang on** *vb* (*intr*)...**5** (*adv*) *Informal.* to wait or remain: *hang on for a few minutes.*

If a label applies to all senses of one part of speech, it is placed immediately after the part-of-speech label.

> **assured** (əˈʃʊəd) *adj*...◆ *n* **4** *Chiefly Brit.* **4a** the beneficiary under a life assurance policy. **4b** the person whose life is insured....

If a label applies to all senses of a headword, it is placed immediately after the pronunciation (or inflections).

> **con**[1] (kɒn) *Informal.* ◆ *n* **1a** short for **confidence trick. 1b** (*as modifier*): *con man.* ◆ *vb* **cons, conning, conned. 2** (*tr*) to swindle or defraud...

6.1 Usage labels

Slang. This refers to words or senses that are racy or extremely informal. The appropriate contexts in which slang is used are restricted, for example, to members of a particular social group or those engaged in a particular activity. Slang words are inappropriate informal speech or writing.

Informal. This label applies to words or senses that may be widely used, especially in conversation, letter-writing, etc., but that are not common in formal writing. Such words are subject to fewer contextual restrictions than slang words.

Taboo. This label applies to words that are not acceptable in polite use. The reader is advised to avoid the use of such words if he or she wishes to be sure of avoiding social disapproval.

Offensive. This label indicates that a word might be regarded as offensive by the person described or referred to, even if the speaker uses the word without any malicious intention.

Derogatory. This implies that the connotations of a word are unpleasant with intent on the part of the speaker or writer.

Not standard. This label is given to words or senses that are frequently encountered but widely regarded as incorrect and therefore avoided by careful speakers and writers.

Archaic. This label denotes a word or sense that is no longer in common use but that may be found in literary works or used to impart a historical colour to contemporary writing.

Obsolete. This label denotes a word or sense that is no longer in use. In specialist or technical fields the label often implies that the term has been superseded.

The word 'formerly' is placed in brackets before a sense or set of senses when the practice, concept, etc., being described, rather than the word itself, is obsolete or out of date.

A number of other usage labels, such as *Ironic*, *Facetious*, and *Euphemistic*, are used where appropriate.

More extended help on usage is provided in usage notes after certain entries. See section 14 of the *Guide to the Use of the Dictionary*.

6.2 Subject-field labels

A number of italic labels are used to indicate that a word or sense is used in a particular specialist or technical field. Subject-field labels are given either in full (e.g. *Astronomy, Philosophy*) or only slightly abbreviated, so that the full label may be easily understood.

6.3 National and regional labels

Words or senses restricted to or associated with a particular country or region are labelled accordingly. The following labels are the ones most frequently used: *Austral.* (Australian), *Brit.* (British), *Canadian, Caribbean, Irish, N.Z.* (New Zealand), *S. African, Scot.* (Scottish), *U.S.* (United States).

The label *Brit.* is used mainly to distinguish a particular word or sense from its North American equivalent or to identify a term or concept that does not exist in North American English. The North American equivalent may be given in boldface type after the appropriate numbered sense.

Regional dialects (*Scot. and northern English dialect, Midland dialect, etc.)* have been specified as precisely as possible, even at the risk of overrestriction, in order to give the reader an indication of the appropriate regional flavour.

7 MEANING

The meaning of each headword in this Dictionary is explained in one or more definitions, together with information about context, typical use, and other relevant facts.

Where a headword has more than one sense, each sense is given separately and numbered in order to avoid confusion.

Example sentences and phrases illustrating the use of a sense are given at the end of many definitions.

7.1 Order of senses

As a general rule, where a headword has more than one sense, the first sense given is the one most common in current usage.

> **complexion** (kəmˈplɛkʃən) *n* **1** the colour and general appearance of a person's skin, esp. of the face. **2** aspect, character, or nature: *the general complexion of a nation's finances*. **3** *Obsolete.* **3a** the temperament of a person...

Where the editors consider that a current sense is the 'core meaning' in that it illuminates the meaning of other senses, the core meaning may be placed first.

> **competition** (ˌkɒmpɪˈtɪʃən) *n* **1** the act of competing; rivalry. **2** a contest in which a winner is selected from among two or more entrants. **3** a series of games, sports events, etc. **4** the opposition offered by a competitor or competitors...

Subsequent senses are arranged so as to give a coherent account of the meaning of a headword. If a word is used as more than one part of speech, all the senses of each part of speech are grouped together in a single block. Within a part-of-speech block, closely related senses are grouped together; technical senses usually follow general senses; archaic and obsolete senses follow technical senses; idioms and fixed phrases are usually placed last.

7.2 Scientific and technical definitions

Units, physical quantities, formulas, etc. In accordance with the recommendations of the International Standards Organization, all scientific measurements are expressed in SI units (*Système International d'Unités*). Measurements and quantities in more traditional units are often given as well as SI units. The entries for chemical compounds give the systematic names as well as the more familiar popular names.

Plants and animals. When the scientific (Latin) names of phyla, divisions, classes, orders, families, genera, and species are used in definitions, they are printed in italic type and all except the specific name have an initial capital letter. Taxonomic information is always given.

> **moss** (mɒs) *n* **1** any bryophyte of the class *Musci*, typically growing in dense mats on trees...

> **capybara** (ˌkæpɪˈbɑːrə) *n* the largest rodent; a pig-sized amphibious hystricomorph, *Hydrochoerus hydrochaeris*...

8 CROSS-REFERENCES

The main entry is always given at the most common spelling or form of the word. Cross-reference entries refer to this main entry. Thus the entry for **deoxyribonucleic acid** cross-cross-refers to **DNA**, where the full explanation is given.

8.1 Comparisons

Cross-references introduced by the words 'See also' or 'Compare' refer the reader to additional information elsewhere in the Dictionary. If the cross-reference is preceded by a lozenge (◆), it applies to all senses of the headword that have gone before it, unless otherwise stated. If there is no lozenge, the cross-reference applies only to the sense immediately preceding it.

8.2 Variant spellings

Variant spellings (e.g. **foetus**...a variant spelling of **fetus**) are generally entered as cross-references if their place in the alphabetical list is more than ten entries distant from the main entry.

8.3 Alternative names

Alternative names or terms are printed in boldface type and introduced by the words 'Also' or 'Also called'. If the alternative name or term is preceded by a lozenge, it applies to the entire entry.

9 RELATED ADJECTIVES

Certain nouns, especially of Germanic origin, have related adjectives that are derived from Latin or French. For example, *mural* (from Latin) is an adjective related in meaning to *wall*. Such adjectives are shown in a number of cases after the sense (or part-of-speech block) to which they are related.

> **wall** (wɔːl) *n* **1a** a vertical construction made of stone, brick, wood, etc....Related adj: **mural**...

10 IDIOMS

Fixed noun phrases, such as **dark horse**, and certain other idioms are given full headword status. Other idioms are placed under the key word of the idiom, as a separate sense, generally at the end of the appropriate part-of-speech block.

> **ground**[1] (graʊnd) *n*...**21 break new ground** to do something that has not been done before...

11 ETYMOLOGIES

Etymologies are placed in bold square brackets after the definition. They are given for all headwords except those that are derivative forms (consisting of a base word and a suffix or prefix), compound words, inflected forms, and proper names. Thus, the headword **manage** has been given an etymology but the related headwords **manageable** (equivalent to *manage* plus the suffix *-able*), **management** (*manage* plus *-ment*), **manager** (*manage* plus *-er*), **manageress** (*manager* plus *-ess*), etc., do not have etymologies.

Inflected forms such as **saw** (the past tense of *see*) and obvious compounds such as **mothball** are not given an etymology. Many headwords, such as **enlighten** and **prepossess**, consist of a prefix and a base word and are not accompanied by etymologies since the essential etymological information is shown for the component parts, all of which are entered in the Dictionary as headwords in their own right (in this instance, **en-**, **light**, **-en** and **pre-**, **possess**).

The purpose of the etymologies is to trace briefly the history of the word back from the present day, through its first recorded appearance in English, to its origin, often in some source language other than English. The etymologies show the history of the word both in English (wherever there has been significant change in form or sense) and in its pre-English source languages. Since records of both Latin and Ancient Greek exist, it is usually possible to show the actual Latin or Greek form of the source of an English word. In the case of English words of Germanic origin, cognate forms in one or more Germanic languages are shown. These cognate forms are words from the same (lost) Germanic originals, and the chief cognate languages cited are Old Norse, Swedish, Danish, German, Dutch, and Old Saxon.

All the languages and linguistic terminology used in the etymologies are entries in their own right in the Dictionary. Words printed in SMALL CAPITALS refer the reader to other headwords where relevant or additional information, either in the definition text or in the etymology, may be found.

11.1 Dating

The etymology records the first known occurrence (a written citation) of a word in English. Words first appearing in the language during the Middle English period or later are dated by century, abbreviated **C**.

> **mantis**...**[**C17: New Latin, from Greek: prophet, alluding to its praying posture**]**

This indicates that there is a written citation for **mantis** in the seventeenth century, when the word was in use as a New Latin term in the scientific vocabulary of the time. The absence of a New Latin or Greek form in the etymology means that the form of the word was the same in those languages as in English.

11.2 Old English

Native words from Old English are not dated, written records of Old English being comparatively scarce, but are simply identified as being of Old English origin.

> **mar** (mɑː) *vb* **mars, marring, marred....**[Old English *merran*; compare Old Saxon *merrian* to hinder, Old Norse *merja* to bruise]

12 DERIVED WORDS

Words derived from a base word by the addition of suffixes such as *-ly*, *-ness*, etc., are entered in boldface type immediately after the etymology or after the last definition if there is no etymology. The meanings of such words may be deduced from the meanings of the suffix and the headword.

13 LISTED ENTRIES

In English many words are formed by adding productive prefixes such as *non-*, *over-*, *un-*, etc., to existing words. In most cases, the meanings of these words are obvious. Such words are included, without definition, boxed at the foot of the appropriate page in the alphabetical sequence.

14 USAGE NOTES

A brief note introduced by the device **USAGE** has been added at the end of a number of entries in order to comment on matters of usage. These comments reflect current English usage, as well as detailing historical practice.

> **ago** (əˈgəʊ) *adv* in the past: *five years ago; long ago.* [**C14** *ago*, from Old English *āgān* to pass away]
>
> **USAGE** The use of *ago* with *since* (*it's ten years ago since he wrote the novel*) is redundant and should be avoided: *it is ten years since he wrote the novel.*

Pronunciation Key

The symbols used in the pronunciation transcriptions are those of the International Phonetic Alphabet. The following consonant symbols have their usual English values: *b, d, f, h, k, l, m, n, p, r, s, t, v, w, z*. The remaining symbols and their interpretations are listed in the tables below.

English Sounds

ɑ: as in *father* ('fɑ:ðə), *alms* (ɑ:mz), *clerk* (klɑ:k), *heart* (hɑ:t), *sergeant* ('sɑ:dʒənt)

æ as in *act* (ækt), *Caedmon* ('kædmən), *plait* (plæt)

aɪ as in *dive* (daɪv), *aisle* (aɪl), *guy* (gaɪ), *might* (maɪt), *rye* (raɪ)

aɪə as in *fire* ('faɪə), *buyer* ('baɪə), *liar* ('laɪə), *tyre* ('taɪə)

aʊ as in *out* (aʊt), *bough* (baʊ), *crowd* (kraʊd), *slouch* (slaʊtʃ)

aʊə as in *flour* ('flaʊə), *cower* ('kaʊə), *flower* ('flaʊə), *sour* ('saʊə)

ɛ as in *bet* (bɛt), *ate* (ɛt), *bury* ('bɛrɪ), *heifer* ('hɛfə), *said* (sɛd), *says* (sɛz)

eɪ as in *paid* (peɪd), *day* (deɪ), *deign* (deɪn), *gauge* (geɪdʒ), *grey* (greɪ), *neigh* (neɪ)

ɛə as in *bear* (bɛə), *dare* (dɛə), *prayer* (prɛə), *stairs* (stɛəz), *where* (wɛə)

g as in *get* (gɛt), *give* (gɪv), *ghoul* (gu:l), *guard* (gɑ:d), *examine* (ɪg'zæmɪn)

ɪ as in *pretty* ('prɪtɪ), *build* (bɪld), *busy* ('bɪzɪ), *nymph* (nɪmf), *pocket* ('pɒkɪt), *sieve* (sɪv), *women* ('wɪmɪn)

i: as in *see* (si:), *aesthete* ('i:sθi:t), *evil* ('i:v^{ə}l), *magazine* (ˌmægə'zi:n), *receive* (rɪ'si:v), *siege* (si:dʒ)

ɪə as in *fear* (fɪə), *beer* (bɪə), *mere* (mɪə), *tier* (tɪə)

j as in *yes* (jɛs), *onion* ('ʌnjən), *vignette* (vɪ'njɛt)

ɒ as in *pot* (pɒt), *botch* (bɒtʃ), *sorry* ('sɒrɪ)

əʊ as in *note* (nəʊt), *beau* (bəʊ), *dough* (dəʊ), *hoe* (həʊ), *slow* (sləʊ), *yeoman* ('jəʊmən)

ɔ: as in *thaw* (θɔ:), *broad* (brɔ:d), *drawer* ('drɔ:ə), *fault* (fɔ:lt), *halt* (hɔ:lt), *organ* ('ɔ:gən)

ɔɪ as in *void* (vɔɪd), *boy* (bɔɪ), *destroy* (dɪ'strɔɪ)

ʊ as in *pull* (pʊl), *good* (gʊd), *should* (ʃʊd), *woman* ('wʊmən)

u: as in *zoo* (zu:), *do* (du:), *queue* (kju:), *shoe* (ʃu:), *spew* (spju:), *true* (tru:), *you* (ju:)

ʊə as in *poor* (pʊə), *skewer* (skjʊə), *sure* (ʃʊə)

ə as in *potter* ('pɒtə), *alone* (ə'ləʊn), *furious* ('fjʊərɪəs), *nation* ('neɪʃən), *the* (ðə)

ɜ: as in *fern* (fɜ:n), *burn* (bɜ:n), *fir* (fɜ:), *learn* (lɜ:n), *term* (tɜ:m), *worm* (wɜ:m)

ʌ as in *cut* (kʌt), *flood* (flʌd), *rough* (rʌf), *son* (sʌn)

ʃ as in *ship* (ʃɪp), *election* (ɪ'lɛkʃən), *machine* (mə'ʃi:n), *mission* ('mɪʃən), *pressure* ('prɛʃə), *schedule* ('ʃɛdju:l), *sugar* ('ʃʊgə)

ʒ as in *treasure* ('trɛʒə), *azure* ('æʒə), *closure* ('kləʊʒə), *evasion* (ɪ'veɪʒən)

tʃ as in *chew* (tʃu:), *nature* ('neɪtʃə)

dʒ as in *jaw* (dʒɔ:), *adjective* ('ædʒɪktɪv), *lodge* (lɒdʒ), *soldier* ('səʊldʒə), *usage* ('ju:sɪdʒ)

θ as in *thin* (θɪn), *strength* (strɛŋθ), *three* (θri:)

ð as in *these* (ði:z), *bathe* (beɪð), *lather* ('lɑ:ðə)

ŋ as in *sing* (sɪŋ), *finger* ('fɪŋgə), *sling* (slɪŋ)

^{ə} indicates that the following consonant (*l* or *n*) is syllabic, as in *bundle* ('bʌnd^{ə}l) and *button* ('bʌt^{ə}n)

χ as in Scottish *loch* (lɒχ). See also below

əɪ as in Scottish *aye* (əɪ), *bile* (bəɪl), *byke* (bəɪk).

Foreign Sounds

The symbols above are also used to represent foreign sounds where these are similar to English sounds. However, certain common foreign sounds require symbols with markedly different values, as follows:

a *a* in French *ami*, German *Mann*, Italian *pasta*: a sound between English (æ) and (ɑ:), similar to the vowel in Northern English *cat* or London *cut*.

ɑ *a* as in French *bas*: a sound made with a tongue position similar to that of English (ɑ:), but shorter.

e *é* in French *été*, *eh* in German *sehr*, *e* in Italian *che*: a sound similar to the first part of the English diphthong (eɪ) in *day* or to the Scottish vowel in *day*.

i *i* in French *il*, German *Idee*, Spanish *filo*, Italian *signor*: a sound made with a tongue position similar to that of English (i:), but shorter.

ɔ *o* in Italian *no*, French *bonne*, German *Sonne*: a vowel resembling English (ɒ), but with a higher tongue position and more rounding of the lips.

o *o* in French *rose*, German *so*, Italian *voce*: a sound between English (ɔ:) and (u:) with closely rounded lips, similar to the Scottish vowel in *so*.

u *ou* in French *genou*, *u* in German *kulant*, Spanish *puna*: a sound made with a tongue position similar to that of English (u:), but shorter.

y *u* in French *tu*, *ü* in German *über* or *fünf*: a sound made with a tongue position similar to that of English (i:), but with closely rounded lips.

ø *eu* in French *deux*, *ö* in German *schön*: a sound made with the tongue position of (e), but with closely rounded lips.

œ *œu* in French *œuf*, *ö* in German *zwölf*: a sound made with a tongue position similar to that of English (ɛ), but with open rounded lips.

~ above a vowel indicates nasalization, as in French *un* (œ̃), *bon* (bɔ̃), *vin* (vɛ̃), *blanc (blɑ̃)*.

χ *ch* in German *Buch, j* in Spanish *Juan*.

ç *ch* in German *ich*: a (j) sound as in *yes*, said without voice; similar to the first sound in *huge*.

β *b* in Spanish *Habana*: a voiced fricative sound similar to (v), but made by the two lips.

ʎ *ll* in Spanish *llamar, gl* in Italian *consiglio*: similar to the (lj) sequence in *million*, but with the tongue tip lowered and the sounds said simultaneously.

ɥ *u* in French *lui*: a short (y).

ɲ *gn* in French *vigne*, Italian *gnocchi, ñ* in Spanish *España*: similar to the (nj) sequence in *onion*, but with the tongue tip lowered and the two sounds said simultaneously.

ɣ *g* in Spanish *luego*: a weak (g) made with voiced friction.

Length

The symbol ː denotes length and is shown together with certain vowel symbols when the vowels are typically long.

Stress

Three grades of stress are shown in the transcriptions by the presence or absence of marks placed immediately *before* the affected syllable. Primary or strong stress is shown by ', while secondary or weak stress is shown by ˌ. Unstressed syllables are not marked. In *photographic* (ˌfəʊtə'græfɪk), for example, the first syllable carries secondary stress and the third primary stress, while the second and fourth are unstressed.

List of Abbreviations

abbrev.	abbreviation	**N**	north(ern)
adj	adjective	**n**	noun
adv	adverb(ial)	**NE**	northeast(ern)
approx.	approximate(ly)	**no.**	number
Austral.	Australian	**NW**	northwest(ern)
Brit.	British	**N.Z.**	New Zealand
C	century (e.g. **C14** = 14th century)	**p.**	page
°C	degrees Celsius	**pl**	plural
cap(s).	capital initial(s)	**Pop.**	population
cf.	compare	**pp.**	pages
conj	conjunction	**prep**	preposition(al)
E	east(ern)	**pron**	pronoun
e.g.	for example	**pt.**	point
esp.	especially	**RP**	Received Pronunciation
est.	estimate	**S**	south(ern)
etc.	et cetera	**S. African**	South African
fem	feminine	**Scot.**	Scottish, Scots
foll.	followed	**SE**	Southeast(ern)
ft.	foot *or* feet	**sing**	singular
i.e.	that is	**sq.**	square
in.	inch(es)	**SW**	southwest(ern)
interj	interjection	**tr**	transitive
intr	intransitive	**U.S.**	United States
IPA	International Phonetic Alphabet	**vb**	verb
km	kilometres	**vol.**	volume
m	metre(s)	**W**	west(ern)
masc	masculine	**wt.**	weight

The Development of English as a World Language

The Making of English

by David Brazil

English Around the World

by A J Aitken, S R R Allsopp, R K Bansal, D Brazil, R J Gregg, L W Lanham, T H Long, Harold Orton, J M Sinclair, John Spencer, Loreto Todd, and G A Wilkes

Over the last five hundred years, the English language, formerly the language of a mere five or six million people living within the confines of the British Isles, has expanded to become the everyday speech of over three hundred million. Among the results of this expansion is the present status of English as the mother tongue of most of the inhabitants of the vast ethnically diverse society of the United States of America and as the most important second language of some fifty million in Southern Asia and a number of the new nations of Africa. The expansion has, however, for practical purposes been a feature of the most recent of the three major phases of development into which linguistic scholarship customarily divides the recorded history of the language. Although our principle concern here is with that geographical extension that has led to the label 'English' being applied to many simultaneously existing varieties round the world, we can achieve a proper perspective only if we consider briefly the historical dimension of its variation.

'New English' or 'Modern English', which has been so pre-eminently an article for export, is distinguished from the earlier variety, 'Middle English', and the latter from the still earlier variety 'Old English'. The three periods are separated by two watersheds, one associated with the Norman Conquest, and the other with those complex developments to which historians apply the terms Renaissance and Reformation. At each of these times there occurred marked accelerations in the process of continuous change that all living language is subject to. The response of the language to historical pressures resulted on each occasion in the emergence of a form significantly different from that which preceded it, so that Old English must now be learned by the native speaker of English almost as a foreign language, and Middle English, the language of Chaucer and Langland, is today fully intelligible only to the specialist scholar.

Old English was the language of the heathen invaders who began to appear along the Eastern coast of Britain in the third century A.D., and who, after the withdrawal of the Roman legions, settled all but the North and West, where a Celtic language continued to be used. They were by no means homogeneous culturally, speaking different dialects of a common Germanic tongue, and the geographical disposition which tradition assigns to them, the Jutes in the Southeast, the Saxons in Wessex, and the two major divisions of the Angles in the Midlands and the North, set up at the outset many of the regional differences that still persist in the popular speech of the British Isles.

The earliest written records date from after the Christian conversion of the English instigated by Pope Gregory in or around 597. The West Saxon dialect, which is most often used in the texts that survive, acquired a special status as a literary medium. By this time, the warlike habits of the English had, for the most part, given way to agricultural pursuits, and one can create a pleasant, if somewhat romanticized, picture of their agrarian life from a stock of words that have often been spoken of approvingly as 'short', 'simple', and 'Anglo-Saxon' – e.g. *man* and *child*; *eat*, *drink*, and *sleep*; *love* and *hate*; *land*, *harvest*, and *crops*.

Old English had a facility, comparable with that of modern German, for meeting the need for new vocabulary by compounding or redefining existing words: *daisy* is picturesquely derived from 'day's eye' and *nostril* from 'nose hole'. When the conversion to Christianity created new needs, many of these were supplied from indigenous resources. Thus *Easter* was adopted from the pagan vocabulary and applied to the new Christian festival while the compound *godspell* (good news) was preferred to the Latin *evangelium*. Native material did not supply all the needs, however, and it was the Latin of the new clerics that provided the first large-scale input of foreign loans we know of. Apart from words of obvious ecclesiastical significance, like *priest*, *monk*, *hymn*, and *altar*, others like *master* and *grammar*, *plaster* and *fever*, reflect the Church's commitment to learning and medical care.

The arrival of the Vikings, who, until King Alfred's victory in 878, threatened to subjugate the newly Christianized English, resulted in further augmentation of the vocabulary. But the language they spoke, which had a strong influence upon English speech, particularly in the Danelaw, the area lying to the northeast of a line drawn from Chester to London, was closely related to it. The results of its admixture were more subtle and elusive. Pairs of words, differentiated by a single sound, like *skirt* and *shirt*, *whole* and *hale*, have survived. Instead of a quasi-technical vocabulary associated with a new field of interest or endeavour, we have Old Norse borrowings that are every bit as commonplace as native Old English words: *husband*, *ugly*, *call*, *want*, and, most surprisingly, the pronouns *they*, *them*, and *their* to go alongside Old English *he*, *him*, and *her*.

The effects of this kind of merging are not evident until we come to examine texts of the early Middle English period, and its thoroughness is such that we cannot always be sure to which of the two Germanic languages a particular word should be traced.

When William, Duke of Normandy, defeated the English king at Hastings in 1066, he inaugurated a period of rule by French-speaking kings and of pervasive domination by a nobility and clergy whose interests were predominantly in things French. Until King John lost the last of the continental possessions in 1205, Norman French was the language of the Court, of business, and of lay culture, while Latin remained the ecclesiastical language. English seems virtually to have been reduced to the role of a patois. Further contact with France, through royal marriages and through participation in the wider European cultural scene, of which French was the unchallenged medium, ensured that that language retained its privileged position in the upper reaches of society right up to Chaucer's time, but alongside this the thirteenth century saw a gradual reinstatement of English.

By this time, the language had undergone radical changes, some of which can be directly related to the long break in the literary tradition. The elaborate inflection system that had been so conspicuous a feature of Old English, manifested, for instance, in the six different forms of the noun *stan* (stone), may well have been undergoing simplification in the spoken language before the Norman Conquest. Absence of the conservative influences of the written form would undoubtedly accelerate the process: although some vestiges of inflectional endings survive until after Chaucer's time, Middle English is essentially without this refinement. Instead, the relations between content words are specified by a freer use of prepositions. Another change was largely due to the fact that the French-trained scribes, who now replaced those trained in the Old English tradition, introduced new orthographic conventions and in so doing were responsible for much of the inconsistency for which modern English spelling is notorious. New characters — k, g, q, v, w, z — were brought into use. As a consequence, the two pronunciations of Old English 'c' could now be differentiated, as in the modern spelling of *king* (from *cyning*) and *choose* (from *ceosan*). But the retention of 'c' in words like *cat* and its use to represent /s/ in *nice* have left the confusing results: *king*, *can*, *cent*. The characteristic Old English letters þ and ð were gradually replaced by *th*, and the loss of ʒ resulted in the sound it represented (a sound which was itself subsequently lost) being spelt as *gh* in words like *night*, *daughter*, and *laugh*. Finally, because of the similarity of a number of characters such as *u*, *v*, *n*, *m*, and *w* in the Carolingian script used by the scribes, *u* was replaced by *o* in many words like *come*, *son*, and *wonder*.

But by far the most noticeable feature of English, as it re-emerges after the period of the supremacy of French, was the very large number of French words that had been absorbed into the common stock. Many of these can be sorted into sets that correspond with activities in which the indigenous English speakers are thought to have played only minor parts. For instance, they include much of the modern vocabulary of government and law, of ecclesiastical and military matters, of art, learning, and medicine. Other words reflect an upper-class preoccupation with fashion, polite social life, and refined feeding habits. A measure of the degree of assimilation of the new French words is the speed of their occurrence in derivatives, often taking English endings as in *gently* and *gentleness*, and forming hybrid compounds like *gentleman*. The early borrowings were naturally from Norman French, but later the source was predominantly the culturally more prestigious dialect of Central France. The borrowing, at different times, of related words from both dialects provided such differentiated forms as *cattle* and *chattel*, *warden* and *guard*. Generally, the massive accession of loan words seems to have inhibited the language's facility for creating new, self-explanatory compounds, a practice that was not revived extensively until the nineteenth century, when scientific and technological advances generated new needs.

A characteristic of Middle English was its very considerable regional variation. Contemporary writers testify that the speech of one area was frequently unintelligible to inhabitants of another. Amid the confusion, it is possible to distinguish five major areas: the North, extending as far as the Humber; the East and West Midlands, together extending from the Humber to the Thames; the South; and Kent. Each of these is represented in some part of the literary output that has survived, a situation that contrasts with the near monopoly of West Saxon as a literary dialect in the earlier, Old English, period. The end of the fourteenth century, however, saw the rise of Standard English, a result largely of the commercial supremacy of the East Midlands. In particular the growing importance of London as a political, judicial, social, and intellectual centre led to the elevation of one particular variety of the East Midland dialect, namely London English, to a position of prestige that it has enjoyed ever since. It was this dialect that was to be used overwhelmingly when the invention of printing opened up unprecedented opportunities for disseminating the written word.

The printing press was one of the factors that, around 1500, resulted in the second great change in English. The need and the possibility of what we can properly think of as mass circulation placed a high premium on the use of the vernacular. As in other parts of Europe, the latter made incursions into territories in which Latin had formerly held sway: law, medicine, and religion in particular. And one aspect of the revival of interest in classical antiquity was the very considerable translating activity that gave Shakespeare, for instance, with his 'little Latin and less Greek', access to much of the classical heritage. Engagement with Latin and Greek had effects upon English...upon both vocabulary and grammar. The effects on vocabulary were more immediately noticeable and led to a further accession of new words, often those of a learned and polysyllabic kind, which, when carried to excess, earned contemporary castigation as 'inkhorn' terms. In this way, the classical experience may be said to have been a potent instrument of change. Its effect upon grammar, though less immediate, was, by contrast, conservative.

The increasing use of English in more scholarly contexts after 1500 resulted in misgivings about its ability to survive. Compared with the fixity and predictability of Ciceronian Latin — by now a well and truly 'dead' language — it seemed all too subject to change. The desire to 'fix' English, so that matter expressed in it would have the same chances of survival as that expressed in the ancient languages, led to attempts by grammarians to legislate for the user; the basis of their legislation was, understandably, the well-known syntax of Latin. A similar concern for durability and respectability underlay the new preoccupation with orthography. Early spelling reformers, especially printers, sought to replace the largely idiosyncratic practices that had sufficed in the preprinting era with a common system that seemed to them to be related to the sound system in a more consistent way. They were not helped in this enterprise — an enterprise that, incidentally, has continued to exercise the minds of language teachers ever since — by the fact that some of the sounds were themselves currently undergoing major changes. A complex process that led to an altered distribution of all the long vowels of English, known to philologists as the Great Vowel Shift, began in the latter part of the Middle English period but was not completed until after Shakespeare's time. For his audiences *Rome* rhymed with *room*, and *raisin* with *reason*.

In bringing this sketch of the development of English up to the beginning of the Modern English period, we have already reached the stage where its internal history and its external history react upon each other. The astonishing — and as some thought — excessive openness of English to new vocabulary resulted in the adoption of words not only from every major European language, but also from the exotic languages of remoter lands to which it was now being carried. In the following paragraphs we note something of the effects of local languages and local conditions upon the speech of English-speaking settlers across the world; they were felt not only in vocabulary, but in grammar and pronunciation also. An important aspect of the more recent development of British English has been its absorption of features from the new regional varieties to which geographical dispersion gave rise. Since no account of language development, however brief, can legitimately omit reference to attitudes, we must recognize that this last tendency has by no means always been welcomed by purists. And if a desire to protect the home-grown product from the effects of outside interference is questionable, the wish to prescribe standards for the much greater number of people who speak English outside the British Isles is even more so.

In the various forms that Standard English now takes, there are, in fact, only very slight differences in grammar, and the variations in pronunciation — the numerous local accents — represent no insuperable barrier to intelligibility, however forcibly they may impress themselves upon the listener. As for vocabulary, there is a central core of ordinary, most frequently used words that all geographically distinguished varieties of the standard language share. There is also a shared and continually growing lexicon of highly specialized and technical terms. Between these two lies a considerable body of moderately common words and idioms, and it is here that the major national and local distinctions are to be found: Americanisms, Australianisms, Scotticisms, and so on, all having their own peculiarities of usage.

The differences and distinctions we find in the use of English round the world seem hardly likely to wither away. Present conditions seem rather to indicate a gradual increase. Common sense seems to suggest willing acceptance of them as natural and interesting aspects of the language and of the individualities of the people who use it.

The Regional Dialects of England

The question of the existence of a standard pronunciation of English has been the occasion for controversy nowhere more than in the context of discussions of the local and social varieties of the language that coexist within England. Before World War II many believed that a standard form did exist but that it was a class dialect rather than a regional one, flourishing in the public schools, the older universities, the law courts, the higher ranks of the armed forces and the civil service, the BBC, and of course the Royal Court. Having a well-recognized sound system, it was also characterized by the use of a pleasing voice quality, a rhythmical unhurried speech tempo, and a good articulation that was not staccato or too precise and lacked a glottal stop or any trace of regional intonation. This they called 'Received Pronunciation' or RP.

Between the World Wars, linguistic historians recognized the existence of modified forms of RP. Having penetrated into the provinces, the socially prestigious speech of London and the Home Counties was modified by local speech habits, which differed from county to county and even from town to town. These modified varieties have since achieved much greater prominence and standing, partly through changed attitudes to English used in broadcasts and partly through the emergence of an influential group from the provincial grammar schools and universities, who have been inclined to resent the stigmatization of their own regional accents. A widely held belief that any pronunciation is good provided it is intelligible and appropriate to its geographical context has also perhaps helped, though a reaction, in the form of a returning preference for RP, is now discernible.

The sounds of RP vary in their realizations within acceptable limits. They also undergo changes. Recently these changes have been less extensive and have been rather obscured by phonological features of educated London English. Nevertheless, the traditional long /ɔː/ before /s/, /f/, and /θ/, as in *cross*, *off*, and *cloth*, has now given way to the more open vowel /ɒ/; the long /ɑː/ that developed before the same sounds, as in *pass*, *path*, and *chaff*, has been extended by some speakers to other words such as *plastic*, *mass*, and *raffia*; the *-ing* of present participles and verbal nouns (*hunting*, *shooting*) has recovered its /ŋ/; and initial *wh-*, as in *white*, often persists as /hw/.

Among modern trends that seem definitely attributable to the influence of London English is the treatment of the vowels /ɛ/ and /æ/, which, in words like *set* and *sat*, may sound very similar. Many young people in the public eye tend in their speech to retract /æ/ to a type of /a/ similar to a sound long assumed to characterize Northern and Midland English. In so doing they reduce the distinction from the /ʌ/ of *hut*, a sound very similar in quality to /a/. Other London traits involve the pronunciation of /əʊ/ in *boat* rather like /ʊ/, the diphthongization of /iː/ and /uː/, as in *feet* and *boot*, and the representation of /aʊ/ in *mouse* and /aɪ/ in *mice* with an advanced and a retracted first element respectively.

Some of the sounds that serve to differentiate the regional dialects of England can be traced back to Old English. Initial *wh-* is still a vigorous /hw/ in Northumbrian speech; in South Lancashire and the West Midlands a characteristic /g/ ends words like *ring* and *long*; in Northumberland /l/ is clear (like the first *l* in *little*) in all positions, while further south it becomes darker (like the second *l* in *little*) until it almost becomes /ʊ/ in the Home Counties. In the eastern part of the country /r/ before a consonant disappears or is faintly articulated (*farm*, *fort*), in the south and west it is pronounced with the tongue turned back or reverted, and in Northumbria it is characteristically 'throaty' (the Northumberland burr). The pronunication of the *u* of *cup* and *bun* as /ʊ/, as in Standard English *pull*, is a trait commonly found in dialects of much of the north of England (except for the extreme northeast). The absence of initial /h/ is frequently assumed to characterize regional dialects generally; it is, however, still preserved in the extreme north, in East Anglia and Essex, and in Somerset and Wiltshire.

Historical factors have conditioned the lexicon and grammar of the modified forms of Standard English as well as their sounds. Many educated northerners do not hesitate to use local vernacular items like *beck*, *burn*, and *gill* (streams). *Bonny* and *canny* (agreeable) are frequently encountered, as are *body* (a person), *lad*, *lass*, *pikelet* (a crumpet), and *scallion* (a spring onion). The word stock of large parts of Northern England, the East Midlands, and East Anglia was greatly enriched as a result of the Viking invasions. Local words like *band* (string), *lop* (flea), *nay*, *sile*, *stoop* (a post), and *teem* (pour) come from this source. The ubiquity of *bairn* is due to its double descent from both the Old English and the Old Norse word for *child*. The extent of the choice that may be provided by dialectal variants can be illustrated by the variety of the terms *drawing room*, *front room*, *lounge*, *parlour*, and *sitting room*; and tea may be *made*, *brewed*, *mashed*, *scalded*, or *steeped*.

Dialect usages characteristic of the regions also seem sometimes to spread into varieties of the language that are nearer to high prestige forms. Educated Northerners may use expressions like *I'll be away then*; *I want this letter posting*; *The dog wants out*; and *The boy got wrong off* (was punished by) *his father*.

Local historical dialects in England are disappearing faster than ever before, regional peculiarities of pronunciation being supplanted by the sounds of RP or of one of its locally modified varieties. Provincial vocabulary seems, however, more likely to survive, except for the names of things that have themselves become obsolete, such as terms relating to equipment used for thatching, harvesting, or blacksmithing.

The English of Scotland

Until the seventeenth century the national literary and spoken language of Scotland was the Northern English dialect known as Older Scots, the ancestor of the modern dialects of the Lowlands, but with the accession of the Stuarts to the English throne in 1603 this began to give way to Standard English as the language of writing. The use of something approximating to educated Standard English as the spoken language of polite society began a little later. But this new Scottish English was shaped and modified by the native Scots that the gentry and intelligentsia had previously spoken. The distinctiveness of the Scots variety of present-day Standard English is attributable to this underlying native tradition.

Its peculiarites include the free use of a very considerable body of Scots vocabulary. Many words associated with special cultural features of Scottish society, like *laird*, *kirk*, *ceilidh*, and *Hogmanay*, are as likely to be used by anyone who writes or talks of Scotland as they are by a Scotsman and are hardly to be considered peculiarities of Scottish usage. Neither are the many Scotticisms that have passed into general English usage, largely through the influence of Burns, Scott, and Carlyle, such as *cuddle*, *eerie*, *gloaming*, and *greed* (all from Old English) and *clan*, *pet*, *slogan*, and *whisky* (from Gaelic). More peculiarly Scottish are those native locutions with which speakers are apt to pepper their English, especially when adopting an informal or explicitly Scottish role: *He's a right old sweetiewife*; *It's back to auld claes* (old clothes) *and parritch* (porridge) *tomorrow*; *like a hen on a het* (hot) *girdle*; or similarly used 'couthy' words like *dreich*, *peely-wally*, and *scunner*. But in addition to such obvious and deliberate Scotticisms, most Scottish speakers of English also employ usages the Scottishness of which they may be scarcely aware of: *Is that you away then?* (Are you about to leave?); *I put her gas at a peep* (I deflated her); *to come up one's back* (occur to one), and, of course, the ubiquitous preposition *outwith*.

The grammar of spoken Scottish English has one or two minor rules of its own, such as the avoidance of *isn't* and *won't*, for which *'s not* and *'ll not* are regularly substituted, and the use of the form *mines* in *that's mines*.

The variety is most Scottish, however, in its pronunciation. Characteristic forms are /lɛnθ/ and /strɛnθ/ (for *length* and *strength*), and /lʌdʒ/ and /ˈlʌdʒər/ (for *lodge* and *lodger*); the 'full' pronunciation of items like *raspberry*, *Wednesday*, and *tortoise*; and disyllabic versions of words like *elm*, *burn*, and *whirl*. Many sounds, particularly the vowels and *wh-*, *r*, and *l*, have special Scottish pronunciations, and there is an extra consonant, /x/, heard in words like *loch*, *Buchan*, and *Brechin*. Whereas *aunt* and *ant* are usually pronounced alike, *oar*, *or*, and *awe*, which are indistinguishable in the speech of London and certain other kinds of English, are quite distinct in Scots.

Scottish English is exceptional among other kinds of English in having no true long vowels: the vowel in *seed* and *seat* is short. On the other hand, there is marked lengthening of certain vowels in particular positions: the verb *close* ending with /z/ has a much longer vowel than the adjective *close* which ends in /s/. Related to this is the long diphthong in words like *five* and *rise*, which can be compared with the short diphthong in *fife* and *rice*. This last phenomenon, which is observable also in Ulster Scots (Scotch-Irish standard speech), can be shown to result from sound changes occurring around the year 1600.

Apart from the educated Scottish English to which the foregoing notes apply, many other types exist, particularly among rural speakers, who have additional dialect features in their pronuncations. Working-class people in Glasgow and Edinburgh also have features that are widely regarded, by speakers who do not have them, as debased or slovenly. They include pronunciation habits like the tendency to replace noninitial /p/, /k/, or /t/ by the glottal stop, and special usages of vocabulary and grammar: *You'll be away to the bingo, eh, no?*; *She's awfie tattie-peelin* (stuck-up); *I shouldnae never went.* At the other extreme are the varieties of Scottish speech that have been strongly influenced by the RP of the Scottish gentry and by broadcasting, of which the 'Morningside' and 'Kelvinside' types are regarded by many Scots as comical. Yet another set of distinguishing features separates the 'Highland English' and 'Island English' from all these dialects, which share a typically Lowland provenance. The most important of such features are those that derive from speech habits orginally native to Scottish Gaelic and from the fact that English was for so long a 'schoolbook' language in the Highlands and Islands.

The influence of the earlier Celtic tongue is by and large less noticeable in the English used in Wales. However, its effect on Irish English merits greater attention.

The Development of English as a World Language

Irish English

All the varieties of English currently heard in Ireland have their origins in the Elizabethan period. The English that developed in the Pale around Dublin at that time is frequently called Anglo-Irish. It was based mainly on the northwest Midland dialects of England. This was the type of English that, encroaching everywhere on the native Gaelic, spread south and west and as far north as the Ulster border. The survival of Gaelic dialects there stopped its advance and separated it from a northern version of Anglo-Irish, which had similarly originated in the English Midlands but entered Ireland by way of Belfast and the Lagan valley. The differences that are nowadays observable between the northern and southern dialects arise for the most part from differences in the substratum of Gaelic speech.

Similarities include many characteristically Irish vocabulary items that are widely distributed throughout the whole island; *blarney*, *galore*, *slug* (swig, drink), *smithereens*, and *twig* (to understand, find out) are all of Gaelic origin. Some of the special vocabulary — *banshee* and *keen* (lament for the dead), for instance — is naturally related to Irish folk culture and has thus attained wider currency. Syntactic peculiarities shared by North and South are exemplified in: *He is just after finishing his work; She has a desperate cold on her; I have a terrible drooth* (drought) *on me* (I am very thirsty); *I wonder will she go*. All these arise from a literal translation of the Gaelic. Among the distinctive phonological features is the universal retention of final and preconsonantal /r/, which has a semivocalic articulation that seems to have arisen in Elizabethan times. Irish English further agrees in giving the lateral /l/ a 'bright' or 'clear' resonance as in French. 'Pure' long vowels generally occur where many other varieties of English have diphthongs: thus /de:/ is preferred to /deɪ/ as a pronunciation of *day*, and /go:/ to /gəʊ/ for *go*. The vowel in words like *pat* and *mat* is pronounced with the tongue lower in the mouth than in most other regional types. The slight lip-rounding observable everywhere in the Irish English vowel in words like *putt* is paralleled in some Northern English dialects.

Northern Anglo-Irish was considerably influenced by its contacts with Lowland Scottish dialects that were introduced into Ulster during the Jacobean period. The influence has been sufficiently strong to give rise to the expression *Scotch Irish*, used originally in North America to distinguish all types of Ulster accents from the so-called southern Irish brogue. Much of the distinctive vocabulary of the North is of Scottish origin. It includes *byre* (cow house), *corn* (oats), *dander* or *danner* (stroll), *lift* (steal), and *mind* (remember). Ulster speakers resemble some Scots also in pronouncing words like *too* or *prove* with a very advanced central vowel somewhat like that in the French word *tu*.

The southern variety is often distinguished from that of the north by the use of a different dialectal form, or set of forms, for a particular notion. Thus the concept 'left-handed' — including all the social and superstitious implications proper to the Irish environment — is expressed by *clootie*, *flyuggy*, etc., in the north, but by *kittagh*, *kittogue*, etc., in the south. The most conspicuous pronunciation trait of the south is the treatment of the fricatives /θ/ and /ð/, a dental variety of /t/ or /d/ being used at the beginning of words like *thin* and *then*. These sounds are, however, quite distinct from the alveolar /t/ and /d/ that are regularly used in *tin* and *den*. Ulster speakers normally have the usual English fricatives.

An interesting feature of the English of most parts of Ireland is the survival of pronunciations characteristic of earlier stages in the development of the language in England. We can instance /te:/ (*tea*), /'de:sənt/ (*decent*), /kürs/ (*course*), /'lɑ:ndrɪ/ (*laundry*), and /'so:dʒər/ (*soldier*).

American English

The development of English in the United States may be traced in three historical stages. The first of these, the colonial period, dates from the settlement of Jamestown in 1607 (followed shortly, in 1620, by the arrival of the Puritans in New England) to about 1790, the date of the ratification of the Constitution of an independent United States. The settlers in Virginia and New England spoke a seventeenth-century English that was predominantly that of the southern counties of England. Although regional dialects never developed the distinctive characteristics they have in England, some of the local variation that does exist can be traced to this time. Subsequent settlement of the Middle Atlantic States was influenced by the ideals of William Penn, and the population of these areas, in particular colonial Pennsylvania, was less uniformly Anglo-Saxon in origin. The presence there of a large number of immigrants from Ulster and, after an agreement made with Penn in 1683, of Palatinate Germans, has been a factor of continuing linguistic significance.

The second stage of development runs from 1790 to about the time of the Civil War (1860). This period saw two important developments. There was an expansion southwards and westwards from the thirteen original Atlantic colonies, across the Appalachian Mountains that had temporarily confined them, and on to the Pacific. In addition, new waves of immigrants arrived, this time from Ireland, after the famine of 1845, and from Germany after 1848. At the end of this period, the population was still predominantly British by origin, as it had been at the beginning, but it now included a higher proportion of other northern European immigrants.

The most recent phase, from about 1860 to the present, witnessed massive immigration from southern Europe and from the Slavonic countries. This last development seems to have had little effect on American English with the exception of New York and its environs, where certain influences on speech and vocabulary are discernible.

The first of these three periods is responsible for certain archaisms that survive in American English. Forms like *gotten* (the past participle of *get*), *sick*, with its general instead of its restrictive sense, and *I guess* meaning *I suppose*, exemplify this linguistic conservatism, the latter having been standard in England as early as the fourteenth century. Such evidences of conservatism are, however, far less representative than developments that show the facility of the language for innovation. Contemporary American speech differs as much from the language of the colonists as modern British English differs from the seventeenth- and eighteenth-century speech of England.

The vocabulary of American English began to change at first contact with the new environment. Words were borrowed from Native Americans and from other Europeans, and native English words were adapted to new meanings. From the Native American languages came a number of words for flora and fauna and other terms relating to Native American life: *canoe*, *caucus*, *hickory*, *hominy*, *moccasin*, *opossum*, *pecan*, *raccoon*, *skunk*, *squash* (a vegetable marrow), *tapioca*, and *toboggan*. From Dutch settlers the colonists borrowed *boss*, *cookie*, and *coleslaw*, and from the French *chowder* and *bureau*. Perhaps the most famous example of an existing English word being borrowed for a new use is *corn*, a development that occurred when the adjective was dropped from the colonists' original phrase, *Indian corn*. The term *maize* entered British English as a Spanish loan word at the same time as the specialized use of *corn* was becoming established in America.

The pattern of settlement in the seventeenth and eighteenth centuries has left its mark on the dialects of present-day America. Three large speech areas are conventionally distinguished: *Northern* (New England and New York State), *Midland* (Pennsylvania and New Jersey and along the Blue Ridge Mountains south to Georgia), and *Southern* (southern Delaware and Virginia along the Atlantic coast and west to the foothills in the Carolinas and Georgia). Within these large areas, eighteen dialects have been identified. Discussion of the sound patterns of American English involves reference not only to the way they differ from British English but also consideration of how the dialects — at least the three major ones — differ from each other.

The retention of final and preconsonantal /r/, which tends to be dropped in England, for instance, is characteristic of Midland American but is not a feature of Eastern New England or of all Southern dialects. Another feature of American speech, sometimes wrongly assumed to characterize all dialects, is the vowel /æ/ in such words as *fast*, *laugh*, *grass*, etc. In Eastern New England and Virginia, a so-called broad *a* /ɑ/ is often used, the quality of which more closely resembles that of the comparable vowel in southern British English. A distinction that does hold between British English and most American English is in the treatment of *o*, which American English tends to make unrounded as /ɑ/ in such words as *rob*, *stop*, and *hop*. This, like the use of /i:/ in *either* and *neither*, is a survival of the pronunciation that was current in Britain at the time of colonization. Finally, we may note the tendency, which has increased in America in recent years, to pronounce words like *duke*, *new*, and *Tuesday* with /u:/ instead of /ju:/, in sharp contrast with British usage.

Two further characteristics that differentiate much American speech from British may be noted. One is that the Northern American dialects have less variety in pitch-pattern. The second is the preservation of the secondary accent in polysyllabic words, especially those ending in *-ory*, *-ary*, or *-ery*. The contrast with British pronunciation in *ordinary*, *dictionary*, *secretary*, *temporary*, etc., is noticeable in all American speech.

Many specific differences between American and British English were listed by H L Mencken in *The American Language* (first edition 1919). Since the publication of that book, various influences have operated to reduce these differences, among them films, radio, television, and the growth since the 1950s and 1960s of an international youth culture grounded in a common popular music (rock). Most often, resulting changes have been in favour of terminology originating in America. Nevertheless, much of the diversity represented by Mencken's list still exists:

US	UK
apartment	flat
baby carriage	pram
broiled (meat)	grilled
candy	sweets
cookie	biscuit
cotton (absorbent)	cotton wool
daylight-saving time	summer time
druggist	chemist
elevator	lift
installment plan	hire-purchase
oatmeal (boiled)	porridge
second floor	first floor
sidewalk	pavement
spigot (or faucet)	tap
suspenders (men's)	braces
undershirt	vest or singlet
water heater	geyser
checkers (game)	draughts
deck (cards)	pack
gasoline, gas	petrol
hood (car)	bonnet
intermission (theatre)	interval
legal holiday	bank holiday
vacation	holiday
windshield (car)	windscreen

Finally, there are minor differences between preferred spellings. Among them are the American preference for *-er* in *center*, *fiber*, and *theater*; *-or* in *honor*, *color*, *humor*, *-se* instead of *-ce* in *defense* and *offense*; and undoubled intervocalic consonants in certain words such as *jeweler*, *marvelous*, and *traveling*. The majority of these differences are traceable to the lexicographer Noah Webster's interest in spelling reform. Although his earlier writings on the subject argued for radical changes based on phonetic spelling, he gradually modified his view. The system used in his *American Dictionary* (1828) was adopted in America and accounts for most of the distinguishing features of modern American orthography.

Canadian English

The early history of Canadian English resembles that of American English. In the early days of settlement the language used was that of contemporary Britain. Features have persisted from this time, supplying a conservative element in present-day speech. Innovations, subsequently made in response to the new environment, led to differentiation that eventually produced a distinctive brand of English that is said to sound like American to Britons and like British to Americans. After the War of American Independence a political boundary separating Canada from the United States encouraged linguistic differentiation. Since then, the continuous contacts to the south on the one hand and the uninterrupted flow of immigrants to Canada from Britain on the other have maintained cultural and linguistic links with both countries.

Many additions to the lexicon resulted from the contacts the Canadians made with the various indigenous Native American and Inuit peoples, as well as the languages of other groups of settlers from many parts of the Old World. In pioneer days they borrowed many words from Canadian French: *bateau* (flat-bottomed riverboat), *brulé* (area of forest destroyed by fire), *coureur de bois*, *habitant* (a French Canadian, esp. a farmer), *mush* (a command to sled dogs, from French *marche!*), *charivari* or *shivaree*, and *snye* (side channel of a river, from Canadian French *chenail*). More recent borrowings from Canadian French include *anglophone* and *francophone* (referring respectively to English and French speakers) and *tuque* (a long knitted woollen cap, as worn by skiers).

From the Native American languages came many terms, including the following ultimately from Algonquian sources in Eastern and Central Canada: *babiche* (thongs of rawhide), *bogan*, otherwise *pokelogan* or *logan* (a sluggish side-stream), *carcajou*, *caribou*, *kinnikinnick*, *muskeg*, *pemmican*, and *totem*. The contributions of the languages of British Columbia frequently came in through the Chinook Jargon, a Native American-based trade or contact language current in pioneer days west of the Rockies and as far north as the Yukon. Among them were: *chuck* (a body of water), *klahanie* (the great outdoors), *mowitch* (deer), and *tillicum* (friend). The Tlingit language has contributed *hooch*, shortened from *hootchinoo*, which has now passed into general English. From Inuit Canadian English acquired *anorak*, *Inuit*, *komatik*, *malamute*, *mukluk*, *Nanook*, *parka*, *igloo*, and *kayak*.

Educated Canadian English probably still reflects the spoken norms of the eighteenth century to a large extent. It shares with Midland American the conservative habit of articulating final and preconsonantal /r/. Another early feature is the voicing of medial /t/ in words like *better*, *patio*, and *little* (/'bɛdər/, /'pædi:ou/, /'lɪdᵊl/); and yet another is the loss of /t/ following /n/, as in *winter* /'wɪnər/ and *Toronto* /'trɑnou/.

The Canadian vocalic system is on the whole very similar to that of General American, but has normally only ten vowels, as illustrated in the following series of words: *beet*, *bit*, *bait*, *bet*, *bat*, *bought*, *butt*, *boat*, *boot*. The tenth vowel, that of *pull*, is in contrast with that in *pool* (which is the same as that in *boot*). The words *cot* and *caught* usually rhyme in Canada.

Most characteristic, however, is the Canadian treatment of diphthongs. Speakers in England and the U.S. have generally only one type of diphthong in words like *rye*, *ride*, and *right*, namely /aɪ/. Canadians agree for the first two items, but have a different diphthong, [əi], for the third, which occurs in all such cases where the following consonant is voiceless, for instance *ripe*, *hike*, *life*, and *ice*. Similarly, in words like *now*, *loud*, and *lout*, Canadian English resembles other types in having /aʊ/ for the first two, but differs in having [ʌu] for the last.

Americans will also notice that the choice of vowel is different in *docile*, /'dousəil/ not /'dɒsᵊl/, and in *lever*, /'li:vər/ not /'lɛvər/. Britons, on the other hand, will notice the use of /'mɪsᵊl/ instead of /'mɪsaɪl/ for *missile*.

English of the Caribbean

The history of the English language in the Caribbean dates from the settlement of St Christopher (St Kitts) in 1624 and Barbados in 1627. The core of Caribbean English is British English. Modified by the African background of many of its speakers since that first settlement, it has also been subjected to the linguistic influences of French, Spanish, Dutch, and Asian Indian. Portuguese and Chinese have also left their marks. In more recent times, the nearness of the United States, its economic prestige, its cinema and broadcasting, and its Black ethnic and cultural sympathies have produced further considerable effects.

All these ingredients mix to produce local varieties at the social bottom of a continuum, the top end of which is the national form of the standard language we may call *Caribbean English*, the variety aspired to by educated speakers. Vocabulary items show the effect of these many influences well. They include survivals from British dialects such as *fig* (a segment of an orange), *gie* (give), and *kerfuffle*; older English words (*glebe land*, *proven*); and everyday expressions whose use may be related to the influence of the Anglican Church (*beforetime*, *bounden duty*, *whosoever*). From African sources have come such items as *ackee*, *bakra*, *kokobeh*, and *Quashi*, and many calques (literal translations) based on African substructures, such as *cut one's eye on*, *day-clean*, and *forceripe*. Many plant and animal names are of Amerindian origin (*cassava, manatee*, etc.). European elements other than those of British English include, from French, *crapaud* and *dasheen* (from *chou de Chine*), while *pannier* replaces *basket* in many areas. From Dutch come *mawger* and *paal*, and from Spanish *mamaguy* and *mustee* (from *mestizo*). The postslavery immigrations of workers have introduced many Hindu, Muslim, and Chinese terms to do with food, clothing, etc. (*dhoti, chow mein*). Other recent acquisitions have come from informal American English.

The Caribbean life style and culture have produced lexical and idiomatic forms of their own: *Berbice chair, jump-up* (a celebration or dance), *good hair*, etc. Some are now international: *calypso, reggae, steel band, obeah, Rastafarian*. Moreover, in the Caribbean some Standard English words take on different meanings. *Breakfast*, among older people, means the midday meal: *bath* and *bathe* refer chiefly to showering; *galvanize* is used as a noun meaning corrugated iron sheeting; and *wares* regularly means crockery.

The pronunciation of Caribbean English is remarkable for its characteristically wide-ranging intonation patterns, probably the result of early phonological influences from African languages. A peculiarity of the distribution of stress in relation to pitch treatment is illustrated in the pronunciation of a word like *biscuit*, which often is pronounced with the main stress on the first syllable (as in Standard English) but with a higher pitch level in the second. A few of the many distinguishing segmental features may be singled out. There are fewer vowels and diphthongs than in Standard English. The vowel in *fat* is /a/, intermediate between the RP pronunciation of *a* in *fat* and *father*. The RP diphthongs in *bare, beer*, and *bait* are replaced by the same pure vowel /eː/. The vowels in *hot* and *fall* are more open than their RP counterparts. The ending *-ing* is pronounced /ɪn/, and forms of /t/ and /d/ replace the fricatives /θ/ and /ð/.

Nonstandard Caribbean English is a form of creole, noticed in more detail at the end of this article. In it, inflections and tense distinctions may be abandoned, and this, combined with functional shifts in syntax, results in sentences like: *de two son tek de fader car go Georgetown las' night* (the two sons took their father's car and went to Georgetown last night); *dey unfairin you* (they're cheating you). Echoic interjections abound, and language at all levels is enlivened by gestures.

English in Africa

English as a mother tongue was not fully and firmly established on the African continent until the 19th century. Notably instrumental in this process were the 1820 settlers, a group of some four thousand British colonists who took up residence along the eastern borders of the Cape Colony. They were a heterogeneous group representing several social and regional British dialects, but within two generations a distinctive South African English had emerged, in which the original speech variations had coalesced into a more or less uniform dialect characterized particularly by speech habits derived from those of the working and lower middle classes of Southeast England, especially London. For example, the tongue positions for the vowels /æ/ and /ɛ/, being higher and more advanced than they are for RP, reflect even in present-day South African English a feature of later 18th-century London pronunciation that is also evident in the semiliterate phonetic spellings of early colonists: *yis* for *yes, kittle* for *kettle, eksel* for *axle*.

These early colonists adapted themselves to their new environment by borrowing from the already implanted Dutch (later Afrikaans) language and to a lesser extent from the indigenous Bantu languages and Khoisan (Hottentot, etc.).

The early efforts of educators were vigorously in the direction of inculcating the grammar and usage prescribed by the middle-class doctrine of correctness that prevailed in late eighteenth- and nineteenth-century Britain. The grammar of South African English differs little, therefore, from the standard southern British form of the language. In vocabulary and usage the more picturesque colloquialisms and slang words disappeared early on, as did those socially stigmatized features of pronunciation that were probably present in the speech of the settlers.

The industrial changes consequent upon the discovery of gold and diamonds significantly changed linguistic attitudes during the late nineteenth and early twentieth centuries. In the new mining and industrial cities, a high social value was placed upon the RP of the British middle classes, to the detriment of both South African English and other British dialects. This attitude, characteristic of urban rather than rural society, continued to prevail among the most influential groups until World War II. Since then, South African English, which had been preserved in the rural areas of its origin, has once again been heard in all sections of society.

Generally, however, rural society was and has remained predominantly Afrikaner. Since the 1920s, the contact between speakers of English and speakers of Afrikaans has resulted in further vocabulary acquisitions, like *platteland* and *verkrampte*; and pronunciation changes such as the rendering of *sin* and *did* with a vowel like the second one of *enter* are probably due to the same cause. The influence of Afrikaans grammar is evident in locutions like *Will you come with?* and *I will throw you with a stone* (I will hit you with a stone). The influence of Bantu and other indigenous African languages has continued to be comparatively weak.

In addition to the one and three-quarter million Whites and some half-million Indians who use English as a mother tongue in South Africa, several million Africans and Afrikaans-speaking Whites employ it competently as a second language. The Indian population share with the latter groups a distinctive dialect and accent, which makes its own contribution to the richness and vitality of South African English.

West Africa is the first of the regions considered so far in which the chief importance of English is associated with its status as a second language. It has this status for many speakers in The Gambia, Liberia, Sierra Leone, Ghana, Nigeria, and Cameroon. (These states are themselves interspersed between other West African countries that were formerly French colonies and in which French is a lingua franca.) In the first five of these states English is the sole medium of education beyond the first few years of primary school, the main administrative and legislative language, the medium for journalism and broadcasting, and the vehicle for science, technology, large-scale business, and international communication. In the western sector of the Republic of Cameroon it fulfils a similar range of functions, sharing them with French elsewhere in that country. The whole of West Africa is extremely fragmented linguistically, several hundred indigenous languages being in use in the area. In consequence, English serves as a lingua franca for mobile educated West Africans both within and between these states. It is, therefore, de facto, if not always de jure, a national language for each of them and for their combined population of nearly 100 million.

Historically, English was first used along the West African coast as a contact language between English traders and the Africans with whom they had dealings. The first recorded instance of West Africans being taught English was in 1554, when an English merchant from Bristol took back five inhabitants of the Guinea coast to learn the language, later returning with them to act as interpreters. As the slave trade increased in the seventeenth and eighteenth centuries, a pidginized variety of English developed along the coast, used not only between European and African but also among the Africans themselves. Freed slaves were settled in Freetown (Sierra Leone) from the end of the eighteenth century, and in Liberia they brought with them a creolized English developed in the slave plantations of the New World. Pidginized and creolized forms continue to be used today alongside Standard English. The spread of the western type of education through missionary effort and colonial rule from the nineteenth century onwards gradually extended literacy in English, encouraged the use of the standard form, and gave it high prestige.

Some of the terms peculiar to West African English have resulted from calques or loan translations, especially those for institutions or objects of a traditional kind, as for instance *outdooring*, the traditional ceremony of naming a baby on its first appearance out of doors, practised particularly in Ghana. Others are compounds such as *palm wine*, the drink produced by tapping the palm tree, or *head-tie*, a cloth tied in traditional fashion on the heads of women. Some common English words have special collocations and senses: *on seat* means available for consultation, and is normally used of officials; *beento*, used either as a noun or attributively, signifies someone who has studied in Britain. Words borrowed from local languages include *kente*, a handwoven cloth from Ghana. Many words in colloquial use have come from pidginized English: *chop* (food to eat), *pass* (to serve drinks or food), *pickin* (small child — from Portuguese), etc.

The Development of English as a World Language

The pronunciation of English in West Africa is variable, depending on the degree to which the phonetic imprint of the first language has been eradicated. There is thus as yet no stable, homogenous pronunciation. Such general phonetic characteristics as have begun to emerge are mainly distinctive prosodic features relating to syllabification and rhythm.

English is so extensively used in West Africa that slang and colloquial idioms are constantly created and local languages drawn upon for special use. In its written form, however, the language tends to conform to the norms of Standard English. Only in Liberia, which has a long history of contact with the United States, is the American variety preferred to the British.

As an expanding second language, the future development of West African English and the processes whereby it accommodates itself to local needs seem unlikely to follow precisely the pattern of change and adaptation observed among native English-speaking communities. While colloquial English is likely to be marked in varying degrees by the continuing contact with African languages and pidginized English, formal and written usage may be expected to conform to internationally accepted norms, except where creative demands or special semantic needs force the language to extend its resources in particular situations.

The present status of English elsewhere on the African continent can usually be related to the availability or nonavailability of an indigenous language enjoying sufficiently general currency to serve as a lingua franca. In Zambia, for instance, a survey conducted in 1970–71 by the local broadcasting service identified eleven different language groups; in this situation English serves as the language of education and public life in spite of objections by Zambian teachers, academics, and publicists. By contrast, the linguistically homogeneous state of Lesotho, though ranking English as a second official language, uses Sesotho for many official and semiofficial purposes, including its national newspapers. In Malawi, although Chichewa is used as a lingua franca by the majority of the population, English holds a prestigious position among an educated minority. The government of Tanzania has actively promoted the replacement of English by Swahili for all public matters since 1974. In neighbouring Kenya, the very firmly established role of English as a school subject and as a gateway to professional preferment will probably make a similar policy more difficult to implement.

The linguistic complexity that results from the needs — often conflicting ones — for effective communication and the satisfaction of national aspirations makes it difficult to identify particular varieties of English in these countries. It means also that any useful attempt to relate distinctive features, whether of lexis, grammar, or pronunciation, to historical development or the influence of local languages is far beyond the scope of such an introductory article as this.

English in Asia

The situation in Asia is no easier to decribe in summary terms, although the use of English in Asia, as in Africa, is best established in those areas that were formerly part of the British Empire. In the nineteenth century English became the medium of higher education, the language of administration, and the lingua franca among the educated population of the whole of the Indo-Pakistan subcontinent. Since the end of British rule in 1947 it has been in competition to differing degrees, with Hindi in India, with Urdu in Pakistan and, more recently, with Bengali in Bangladesh. In India it has retained the status of associate official language and is still widely used by educated people. In Pakistan it is the language in which the business of government, the higher courts of law, and higher academic studies are normally conducted. Since the political separation of Bangladesh from Pakistan, the teaching and use of English in the former has declined sharply, partly because it is no longer necessary as a link between the two areas of what was formerly a single Muslim state.

The English of India itself shares a number of features with the versions in use in the neighbouring states, all of which resulted ultimately from the influence of the British Raj. Its special vocabulary includes on the one hand words from Indian languages commonly used in English-language books, journals, and newspapers published in India and on the other words that relate particularly to Indian contexts or that have acquired a special form of meaning in India. In the first category are words having mythological, philosophical, or religious reference: *Buddha, Ram, Siva, yoga*, etc. Others are concerned with political activity (*bandh, hartal, Naxalite, satyagraha*), sociology (*adivasi, Harijan, Sarvodaya, Swadeshi*), clothing (*dhoti, sari*), administration (*Panchayat, Pradesh, Zila*), titles (*mahatma, sahib, sardar*), food (*dal, puree, pan*), and music (*sarangi, tabla*). In the second category are, firstly, words like *Anglo-Indian, Aryan, betel, cardamom, caste, chariot, chilli*, and *turban*, and secondly, words and phrases like *Akademi, basic education, Gandhi cap, Congress, gazetted officer, mass leave*, and *quarters*.

The pronunciation of English in India differs from other varieties very considerably. Here, only some of the more noticeable differences can be indicated. For example, vowel length is not maintained consistently. Words like *cot* and *caught* are pronounced alike; the vowels in the two syllables of a word like *butter* have a similar pronunciation; pairs like *shot/short, coat/court*, and *shut/shirt* are distinguished only by the presence of /r/ in the second.

There are also differences in the distribution of stress between Indian English and British varieties. This affects both the occurrence of stressed syllables within words and the way stress is related to word classes: grammatical words like articles, pronouns, auxiliary verbs, and prepositions are sometimes stressed while content words may lack stress. A feature related to this is the intonation pattern, which often imposes different groupings of sentence constituents from those that a speaker of British English would expect, and distributes the emphasis among words in a way that can sound confusing. Another related feature is the tendency for unstressed syllables to retain their 'full' value instead of being reduced to /ə/ or /ɪ/.

Indian speakers often use a weak /ʋ/ for both /v/ and /w/, /p/, /t/ and /k/ are always unaspirated. Dental forms of aspirated /t/ and unaspirated /d/ replace the fricatives /θ/ and /ð/ in words like *thin* and *then*, while the sounds /t/ and /d/ are sometimes retroflex.

Grammatical divergences can be illustrated by the following example from Indian English: *They want that the number should be fixed* (They want the number to be fixed). *Would* is often used where standard usage would have *will*, and there are characteristic differences in the use of the definite article.

Further east, English has an important role in Malaysia and Singapore. In the latter its increasing use in higher education is recognized in the emphasis on bilingualism in schools. In Malaysia its use is still widespread, in spite of its being officially superseded by Bahasa Malaysia as the language used in government offices and official correspondence. The popular tendency to lump together the English of Singapore with that of, for instance, Kuala Lumpur, is probably an oversimplification. Research yet to be undertaken is likely to reveal systematic differences due to the predominant Chinese and Malaysian influences respectively. Vocabulary differences reflect cultural differences — as for example the Chinese custom of giving *red packets* at the Chinese New Year. English is also important as a language of business and administration in Hong Kong, and as a second language in Japan and the Philippines. In the latter two countries the influence of American English may be detected, in contrast with the countries where English is a legacy of the British Empire.

Creoles and Pidgins

English is in fact now used as a lingua franca of business, science, and sport almost everywhere in the world, whether or not it is spoken as a native language. Its status as a world language has been developing for several centuries, and in the process many exotic varieties, widely different from the native tongue of London, have grown up in places where the influence of the source country has been slight. One such language is Neo-Melanesian, the official language of Papua New Guinea, which is in origin an English pidgin, although to the casual listener its English antecedents are no longer apparent.

A pidgin is a trade or vehicular language of limited vocabulary and structure. It arises to facilitate communication between people with no common language, drawing its vocabulary almost exclusively from a single language. There are two types of pidgin: the first is *restricted pidgin*, a minimal contact language like Korean 'Bamboo English' that dies out when contact ceases; the second, *developed pidgin* like Cameroon pidgin, remains in existence after the removal of the contact that initiated it and becomes a lingua franca between indigenous peoples with no mutually intelligible language. The latter type may eventually become the mother tongue of the community and so acquire the status *creole*.

The above process accounts for one of the ways in which a creole may arise. The other is when communities with mutually intelligible languages are kept apart, as was the case with African Blacks in the Americas, who were separated to prevent insurrection. In this situation the community resorts to a pidgin as the only viable lingua franca, and this then becomes a creole.

All the pidgins and creoles examined to date share certain characteristics. They are syntactically simpler than the languages upon which they are based: inflections are minimal, distinctions being made by varying word order; reduplication is common (Jamaica Creole *small-small*, Neo-Melanesian *talk-talk*), as is serial verb structure, giving sentences like this from Cameroon pidgin: *dat chief he woman go start begin teach he*.

Creoles and pidgins based on English exist in all six continents and can be divided into two main groups: *Atlantic* varieties, showing certain West African features, and *Pacific* varieties, related to the English used, especially in the late nineteenth and early twentieth centuries, on the China Coast. While most of the vocabulary comes from English, it also includes Portuguese words such as *savvy* and *piccaninny*, which have passed into Standard English.

Australian English

by G A Wilkes

Australian English offers the opportunity of studying the development of a linguistic community from its beginnings. The settlement established in New South Wales in 1788 inherited the language of England, Scotland, Ireland, and Wales, including its dialect forms, but then began to take a different direction. This was partly because of the new vocabulary supplied by the environment, partly because existing words acquired new senses and applications, and partly because some words, especially those from dialect, survived in Australia while they fell into disuse in their place of origin.

Vocabulary

The first source of the new vocabulary was the language of the Aborigines, adopted to describe things for which there was no counterpart in the countries from which the settlers had come. The Aboriginal languages are responsible for the names of various animals (*kangaroo, dingo, wallaby, wombat*, and the mythical *bunyip*), of birds (*galah, brolga, corella*), of fish (*barramundi, morwong, wobbegong*), of trees (*kurrajong, belah, mallee, mulga*), of natural features (*billabong, gibber, bombora*), and of some artefacts (*boomerang, waddy, dillybag, gunyah*). Some of these terms, like *boomerang*, have become part of international English, and many others, like the expression *point the bone* (to place a jinx on someone), have been adopted into the colloquial language of the White population. Occasionally a word which we assume to be Aboriginal proves on inquiry not to be of Australian origin at all. Thus *bandicoot* is an Indian word, and *goanna* is a corruption of *iguana*. *Emu* comes from the Portuguese word for crane, and *piccaninny*, from the Portuguese word for little, probably reached Australia from the West Indies, as there were several Black convicts among the First Fleet. *Rosella* seems like an Aboriginal term, but is a corruption of Rose Hill, where these brightly coloured parrots were observed.

The convict system itself gave a new meaning to words like *assignment* and *special*, and led to *Botany Bay* being a synonym for New South Wales in England for most of the nineteenth century, although no penal settlement was ever established at Botany Bay. The convicts brought the thieves' slang of England with them so that *shake* in the sense of steal and *scale* in the sense of defraud quickly found a currency in Australian English, which they still share with *school* for a collection of gamblers, *castor* for a hat (now old-fashioned), and *throw off at* in the sense of deride or ridicule, with its variants *sling off at* and *chuck off at*. These are all recorded in the 'Vocabulary of the Flash Language' compiled in 1812 and published in the *Memoirs* of James Hardy Vaux, who was transported to Australia on three separate occasions. The modern slang expression to *give someone the drum*, meaning to convey necessary and reliable information, may be traceable to a convict origin. Vaux lists *drummond* as 'any scheme or project considered to be infallible,...meaning, it is as sure as the credit of the respectable banking-house, Drummond and Co.'

The argot of the convicts was but one of the special vocabularies to take on a fresh life in Australia in the nineteenth century. The others were the various English dialects, the source of many a term that has been regarded as Australian in origin. *Dinkum* comes from a dialect word for hard work, from which it has developed the sense of authentic or genuine; *cobber* comes from the Suffolk word *cob*, to take a liking to someone; *larrikin* is the Warwickshire and Worcestershire word for a mischievous or frolicsome youth; the *bowyangs*, the strings tied around the trouser leg below the knee, that seem so characteristic of the outback, are the *bowy-yanks* of Lincolnshire, a species of leather leggings; and even *wowser*, the term applied to the prudish and censorious, probably comes from the dialect word *wow*, to whine, grumbled, or complain, just as *whinge* and *skite* (from *bletherskite*) derive from Scottish. There is some ground for regarding such words as Australian, as their currency in Australia is less specialized than it is elsewhere, and visitors from the United Kingdom encountering them usually have to ask their meaning. The same holds for *barrack* in the sense of making noisy comment, for *bodgy* as false or sham, for *chiack* as tease or ridicule, *barney* as an argument or disturbance, *dunny* as a lavatory, *skerrick* for a fragment or morsel, and *sollicker* for something large.

With the extension of settlement, new terms naturally arose to describe the new conditions encountered. *Paddock* acquired a specifically Australian sense, as fenced land of any area; a *creek* ceased to be an inlet on the seacoast or an arm of a river and became a general term for a watercourse, and words like *spinney, coppice*, and *dell* disappeared from the Australian vocabulary, as having no obvious application to local conditions. More appropriate terms were *outback, backblocks*, and *back country*, with *stockman, boundary rider*, and *squatter* for those who inhabited those regions, besides, of course, the *swagman* and the *bushranger* — the last giving an additional meaning to *bail up*. It was natural for the conditions and occupations of rural Australia to have such a marked effect on the growth of Australian vocabulary in the nineteenth century. A detailed picture of bush life could be built up just from what it has contributed to our stock of words. The typical sheep or cattle *station* (which is never a 'ranch') would have the *homestead* for the owner or manager, a *jackeroo* or two with good family connections learning *pastoral* management, skilled hands like the *bullock-driver* or the *expert* in the shearing shed, besides the *rouseabout* as a general factotum who if he happened to be the cook's *offsider* would probably be referred to as the *wood-and-water joey*. The *sundowner* or *remittance man* might present himself from time to time, or the swagman *humping his bluey*, like the other itinerant unemployed, on the *wallaby track*.

Outback conditions gave a new meaning to *whaler*, who became a bush nomad avoiding work, as well as an assistant to a bullock-driver; to *banker*, which became a river in flood; to *ropable*, which came to mean enraged; and perhaps to *picnic*, which came to mean a troublesome experience, while possessing its original meaning besides. Necessity produced *sliprails* and *dogleg fences*; *bullock* became the verb for toiling hard; a *mudmap* came into existence as directions for travelling scratched with a stick on the ground. Activities like shearing developed vocabularies of their own (e.g. *bell sheep, cobbler, ringer, drummer*), from which terms like *smoko* (for the break between shifts) and *cut out* (to finish) have gained a much wider distribution. In the twentieth century a playing-field is still referred to as *the paddock*, and tinned meat is sold as *camp pie*.

The gold discoveries of the mid-ninteenth century brought an influx of immigrants, and the terminology of another industry. Few terms seem to have been invented during the gold rush: in that respect the later discoveries in Western Australia, the land of the *dry-blowing* and the *Coolgardie safe*, may have been more fruitful. The importance of the gold rush of the 1850s was rather to give terms like *mullock* (for the debris at the top of the shaft), *fossick, nuggety*, and *duffer* — none of them Australian in origin — a prominence in the Australian vocabulary that they might not otherwise have achieved. The immigrants from North America brought some terms that became established as Australianisms — again by adoption, not origin — especially *digger* (for any miner) and the expressions *up a gumtree* and *stir the possum*. The influx of Chinese gave currency to the derogatory term *chow*.

Evidence for the development of Australian English during the first three quarters of the nineteenth century has to be sought mainly in writings of a 'documentary' kind — the journals of explorers, the dispatches of governors, travel books by English visitors, and the like. But from the 1870s onward imaginative writing in Australia began to reflect the local idiom, tentatively at first in a novelist like 'Rolf Boldrewood' (T A Browne) and then decisively in the work of Henry Lawson, A B Paterson, Steele Rudd, Joseph Furphy, and others of the *Bulletin* school. In these writers we see the discovery of the bush as a literary subject, and an attempt to reproduce the vernacular of the swagman and the bullocky in its natural rhythm and idiom. These writers have left the classic descriptions of the life of the *shed hand*, the *free-selector*, the *cockatoo farmer*; of the methods of rolling a *swag* or making a *damper*; of figures like the *hatter* and the *bush lawyer*; of what is involved in having a *dog tied up* at a *shanty* or in *drinking with the flies*, or suffering from *sandy blight* or *doing a perish* in the *scrub*.

A distinctive language of city life was slower to emerge. Lawson wrote some stories of the *larrikin* and his *push*, and one series about a *bottle-o*, while C J Dennis contributed to the vogue of terms like *shicker* and *bonzer*, now rather old-fashioned. But the anonymous *Sydney Slang Dictionary* (c. 1882) and Cornelius Crowe's *Australian Slang Dictionary* (1895) show that what passed as 'Sydney' and 'Australian' slang at this time was still predominantly English. An exception might be found in a handful of terms with criminal associations, like *bludger*, *drum* (for brothel), *keep nit*, and later *standover*, but even these are in the nature of extensions of existing words. The entries in a dictionary like Crowe's show incidentally that most of the rhyming slang heard in Australia even now is English rather than Australian. Instances of Australian inventions in this field are rare: *on one's pat* for alone (Pat Malone), *babbler* for cook (babbling brook), *oscar* for cash (Oscar Asche, the actor), and more recently *septic* for Yank (septic tank).

The next accession to Australian English came from the First World War. The campaign in France was responsible for *plonk* as a corruption of *vin blanc*, for the verb *souvenir* gaining the extra sense of purloin, for *draw the crabs* as attracting unwelcome attention, especially enemy fire, and for *Woodbine* as an equivalent for Englishman (from the brand of cigarettes). *Furphy* in the sense of a latrine rumour, and later of any unverified report, came from the manufacturer of the water carts around which the soldiers gathered, while they were still in camp in Australia. A useful dictionary of World War I slang was compiled by W H Downing and published in 1919 as *Digger Dialects*. It contains a number of terms, like *two-up* and *heading them*, which did not originate in the war but which became better known as a result of the servicemen's activities. Further examples are *the good oil*, *put the acid on*, *put the hard word on*, *stoush*, and *stonker*.

The Depression that followed the war gave further significance to a word familiar in Lawson's time, *battle*, in the sense of struggling for a livelihood. *Battler* has ever since been almost a commendatory term. *Susso* came to be applied to someone 'on the sustenance' or on the dole; those without means of support risked being *vagged*. The hardship of country dwellers led them to admit rabbits to their diet, as *underground mutton*, even though the rabbit was so despised as a pest. The decision of the New South Wales premier of the time, J T Lang, to make his budget work by 'taxing the tall poppies' made a *tall poppy* anyone with a high income, and later anyone at all who stood out from his fellows.

The distinction between a *battler* and a *tall poppy* illustrates the way in which social differences are progressively reflected in Australian idiom. As early as the 1820s the term *pure merino*, taken rather scornfully from sheep-breeding, had come to designate a colonist who prided himself on his freedom from the convict taint; later it was applied to anyone of an old family who was socially prominent. In the same way *squatter* (derived from American English) became the term for a large landowner, and *pastoralist* and *grazier* acquired overtones of affluence which they do not possess in British English. All were set apart from the *cockatoo*, who still had to scratch the earth for a living — unless he happened to be particularly *well in*. It was no compliment to be described as a *pure merino* or member of the *squattocracy*, still less as a *silvertail*. It is tempting to interpret such usages as evidence of a democratic Australian sentiment emerging, and the interpretation would be valid, though it does not stop short of those of a different race or colour. Thus *chow* was hostile, *Abo* was condescending, and the later *boong* derogatory. The application of *tyke* to Roman Catholics showed that the religious intolerances of the Old World had not been overcome, although *walloper* may be a more congenial word for a policeman than some of those current elsewhere.

Of the words with social or nationalistic overtones, the most interesting is *pommy*. Although its origin is uncertain, immigrants from England in the earlier nineteenth century were already being called *jimmygrants*, or *jimmies* for short. Before the First World War *jimmygrant* had become associated with *pomegranate*, and Xavier Herbert in his autobiography *Disturbing Element* recalls in his childhood jeering at newly arrived migrants in heavy British clothing: 'Jimmygrants, Pommygranates, Pommies!' It has never been a favourable term, as the frequency of combinations like *pommy bastard* and *whingeing pommy* may indicate. But the attitude implied is of such long standing that is has passed into folklore, and mellowed in the process. Lion parks in Australia are supposed to have notices outside giving the prices of admission as 'Adults $5.00; Children $2.00; Poms on bicycles — free.' Further twists to the story, in which the lions eat the bicycles and reject the poms, suggest an attitude with some element of good humour somewhere.

World War II was responsible for more additions to Australian English. Some of them, like *choco* (for chocolate soldier) or *munga* (for food) were revivals from the past, but experience in new theatres of war gave rise to *troppo* (nervously affected by conditions in the tropics) and *jungle juice* (improvised alcoholic drink). To *come the raw prawn*, in the sense of seeking an advantage, trying to impose on someone, dates from the war years, as do *earbasher* and *spine-basher*, with *jack up* for a collective refusal of orders and *pull your head in* for 'come off it.' A *brownout* was a partial blackout, while a *brown bomber* was a serviceman who became a parking policeman after the war, preserving a khaki uniform. The change of uniform has since made him into a *grey ghost*.

Servicemen of World War II had a particular aversion to *lolly water*, the coloured soft drinks which were no alternative to beer. Australian English has an extensive vocabulary concerned with beer. The custom of *shouting*, or taking turns to stand rounds of drinks, was already being remarked upon at the time of the gold rushes, when *sly grog* shops were also doing a brisk trade. They were probably dispensing rum, but *grog*, which in England was a mixture of rum and water, soon became in Australia a general term for beer. Among other terms for it are *turps* and *sherbet*, and (from the container) a *tube* or a *stubby*. The measures in which beer is sold vary confusingly from state to state, and the *pot*, the *middy*, and the *schooner* are glasses of different sizes in different places. A *two-pot screamer* is someone with a limited capacity for it, whatever the size of the glass. The drinker of beer disdains *plonk* and *lolly water* alike, and knows that a *session* is a period of heavy drinking, in which again he will probably be a member of a *school*. To say that someone has been *on it* requires no further explanation, just as a restaurant displaying the sign BYO ('bring your own') does not need to specify what is to be brought.

The more formal additions to Australian English in the twentieth century have come from industrial relations and to some extent from commerce and politics. Examples are *award wage*, *margins*, *penalty rates*, *loading*, *flow-on*, *log of claims*, and less formally *compo* (for workers' compensation) and *sweetheart agreement* for an agreement on wages and conditions negotiated directly between employers and employed, without reference to arbitration. From politics come the *informal vote* for a ballot paper incorrectly marked, *donkey vote* for the marking of preferences simply in the alphabetical order in which the candidates appear on the ballot paper, and *swinging voter* for a member of that percentage of the electorate that can be expected to change allegiance between elections. Australians are often surprised to learn that these expressions are their own. They would, however, recognize the singularity of the *Pitt Street Farmer* or the *Collins Street Farmer*, the professional man in the city who engages in primary production for the tax advantages.

The formation of words by abbreviation and by addition of a diminutive ending in *-ie* or *-o* is a common feature of Australian English. The *bottle-o*, the *milko*, and the *Salvo* go back to the turn of the century, as does the *rabbito*, but the *garbo*, the *metho*, and the *dero* came later. The *schoolie*, the *postie*, and the *trammie* were established by the 1920s, though the habit of taking a *sickie* has grown since, and the *hostie* had to await the development of commercial aviation. Officially she is a flight attendant.

Some misunderstanding can arise from the way in which Australian English has drawn away from British English, when words held in common have come to denote different things. The *never-never* in Australia refers to regions remote from settlement, not to hire-purchase. A *spell* is an interval of rest, not another turn of work. A *scallop* in Australia is not only a shellfish and a dressmaking term, but also a flat slice of potato cooked in batter. *Maggoty* means angry or irritated; *tinned dog* is not what it seems; *snags* are sausages. A *theatre* is commonly a 'picture theatre', or what is elsewhere a *cinema*. A *radiator* may be a portable electric fire, not a fixed heating system, and *Durex* is a brand of adhesive tape. To be *crook* is to be ill, not dishonest, *Hooray* has the meaning of goodbye.

If in the nineteenth century the main influences on the growth of Australian English were conditions in the outback, in the twentieth century the main influences have been the two wars, the Depression intervening, industrial relations — and sport. Australian Rules football, for example, has developed a special vocabulary of its own (e.g. *mark*, *pocket*, *rover*, *the bounce*), besides giving an ambiguity to *kicking a behind* and acquiring the nickname *aerial pingpong* in the states in which it is not the dominant code. In the same way *life-saving*, also of Australian origin, gave rise to such terms as *belt man, lineman, reel man*, and *sweep*. The sport with the most influential role would be horse racing. The *boilover*, the unexpected result due most often to the favourite's not getting a place, goes back to the 1870s, and there have been numerous variations on the theme since — the *roughie* or outsider that wins at long odds, the *monte* or certainty that does not *run a drum*, and so on. Racing in Australia has given a special sense to *firm* and *blow, go for the doctor, urger*, and *mudlark*. The betting systems include the *quinella* and the *trifecta*. *Toey* in the sense of restive or fractious probably derives from the racetrack, together with more common expressions like *on the outer* and *not in the race*. *Picnic races* are meetings held in country areas and regarded as social occasions.

In the twentieth century, as in the nineteenth, Australian English has acquired some of its vocabulary from the names of figures in history, and sometimes in folklore. The system of *Torrens title* was devised by Sir Robert Richard Torrens, premier of South Australia in 1856, as part of a reform in the transfer of land. *Furphy*, as has been mentioned, came from the Furphy works in Shepparton, and *oscar* from the Australian actor Oscar Asche. *Paterson's curse*, the Australian name for viper's bugloss, was named after the gardener in Albury, NSW, from whose garden it was thought to have spread. *Pavlova* was named after the ballerina who visited Australia in 1926 and 1929, although the first recipe for a *Pavlova* is recorded in New Zealand. Dame Nellie Melba sponsored *Melba toast* and *peach Melba*, and made *doing a Melba* an expression for repeated farewell performances.

The derivation of some other phrases that make use of proper names is more uncertain. To have *Buckley's chance*, or *two chances — yours and Buckley's*, is to have no chance at all. This is not altogether appropriate to William Buckley, the convict who absconded in 1803 and lived for thirty-two years with the Blacks, and was pardoned after being found again in 1835, so that he died in his seventies on a government pension. The phrase may be a play on the Melbourne firm of Buckley and Nunn, but no real connection has so far been found. Jimmy Wood may have been a shearer of the 1880s who was never known to shout, so that a solitary drink came to be called a *Jimmy Woodser*. *Blind Freddie*, used as a standard of incompetence or impercipience ('Blind Freddie could see that'), may have been a blind hawker in Sydney in the 1920s, but the documentation is lacking. There is no place on the map called *Woop Woop* or *Bullamakanka* (the country town that is a byword for remoteness and backwardness), and although more than one property has been called 'The Black Stump,' the name may have been derived from expressions like *beyond the black stump* and the *biggest liar this side of the black stump*, rather than the other way round. While it is clear that *Rafferty's rules* are no rules at all, denoting a state of disorder, the identity of the original Rafferty remains unknown.

There are of course many other expressions which certainly belong in Australian English, whose origin cannot be traced. If something is *not worth a bumper*, it is being valued below a discarded cigarette end, but if it is *not worth a cracker*, though the meaning is the same, the nature of the comparison cannot be specified. Is a cracker a firework, the tip of a stock whip, a worn-out horse or cow, or a crust of bread such as was once issued to convicts? Not to have a *brass razoo* is to be penniless, but no coin called a razoo has yet been located: is this a variant of *not a sou*? In the same way one can only conjecture about the origin of the *good oil, tinny* (meaning lucky), and *yike* for an argument or disturbance.

The last particular source of Australianisms that should be mentioned is pidgin. This is the patois that arises in different parts of the world from the linguistic interchange of the indigenous people and the newcomers, so that it becomes a shared language. *Piccaninny*, which is Portuguese in origin, and was current in the West Indies before it was used in Australia, is an example of a word taught to the Aboriginals by the Europeans, which then became a pidgin term. Relatively few pidgin expressions have become a settled part of Australian English. *Mary* as a general term for woman has a regional currency, and so has *pink-eye* for a holiday celebration. *Walkabout* would be the best known of such terms. Used first of the periodic migration of Aboriginals from their usual habitat, it has since been applied to meet-the-people excursions by royalty, as in an informal departure from a set programme. To *go walkabout* is also to lose concentration, especially in a sporting contest.

There is a handful of words in Australian English directly imported from other languages, such as *hoot* for money (from Maori *utu*), and a few others that have arrived unrequested, like *kangaroo court* and *down under*, which no Australian would ever use, except as Americanisms. Most of the vocabulary, however, has been generated within Australia, and most of it is colloquial. Apart from a short list of acronyms like *Anzac*, and the rather technical language of *margins* and *penalty rates* already mentioned, the inventiveness displayed has been in everyday informal speech. This makes contemporary Australian drama, in which the dialogue catches the vernacular idiom, a particularly valuable linguistic source. Often the tone of voice alone will determine whether a model of address like *sport* is a term of insult or of good fellowship. *Dingo* in its standard meaning refers to the Australian native dog, but in its colloquial application to human beings it becomes one of the insults traded by politicians. Some naturalists would say that the implications of cowardice and treachery in such a use of the word are an insult to the animal itself. Certainly the lady who reported that her husband, an English officer in charge of Australian troops, was getting on so well that they had already given him an Australian nickname, was insensitive to the implications of being called 'Dingo Jack'. Some nuances are hard to catch. As a girl's name, *Sheila* was early in the nineteenth century used in Australia as a name for any Irish girl, as a counterpart to *Paddy*. It then came to be applied to women in general — to young sheilas and old sheilas alike — but its peculiarity is that it is a word used by males. Although there is no reflection on a woman's morals in referring to her as a *sheila*, there must be a reflection of some kind, because no woman would apply the term to herself.

Social observers have found it hard to refrain from interpreting Australian idiom as an expression of the Australian character. Does the profusion of terms like *nong, galah, drongo, dill*, and *no-hoper* suggest that the average Australian has no very high expectations of his average compatriot? He is certainly alert to pretence or affectation, to the person who *has tickets on himself* or who *big-notes himself*, or who tries to *come the raw prawn*. A disbelieving attitude comes through in expressions like *break it down* or *fair go*, and potential expressions of enthusiasm tend to occur mainly in the negative: it is more common to be *not shook on* something than to be *shook on* it. But then it may be a *fair cow*. Even positive expressions typically fall short of the ecstatic, as in the reassurance *She'll be right*. This may be a response to an environment that has more often than not presented a hostile aspect to its inhabitants, where those unable to cope *drop their bundle* while others persist in the hope of some day *cracking it*.

Recent international developments, especially in sensitive areas such as race and conservation, have had an effect on Australian English. The term *Aboriginal* can arouse resentment, as having been imposed by Whites on Blacks, who prefer to be named from their own language, for example as *koories* or *murries*. The policy of *multiculturalism* has been developed to overcome such racial tensions, with an emphasis on the diversity of ethnic cultures and at the same time on commitment to Australia as a whole. It does not mean that all cultures are equal, as English remains the language of the mainstream. *Anglo-Australian* has come to distinguish those of Anglo-Celtic descent, in a rough parallel with *Anglo-American*.

The conservation movement has given *wilderness* a positive meaning in Australian English as elsewhere, and *sustainable development* is offered as a policy of reconciling the claims of ecology with the need for commercial exploitation of resources. A *green ban* is a trade union ban on any development which might be considered environmentally harmful, and it can be applied to a historic building as well as to natural features. Although traditionally there has been a reluctance to *dob in*, the Australian expression for informing on someone to the authorities, the success in the various states of telephone campaigns to 'dob in a druggie' may suggest a changed sense of social responsibility.

Pronunciation

In pronunciation, Australian English exhibits differences from Southern British English, just as the English spoken in Scotland or Ireland diverges from Received Pronunciation. These differences are least marked in what phoneticians have designated Cultivated Australian, perhaps used by ten per cent of the population, and most marked in Broad Australian, perhaps used by thirty-five per cent. The majority, of fifty-five per cent, use General Australian, which lies between the two extremes.

Australian English

Users of this dictionary need to be aware of the following Australian variations of the pronunciations specified in it.

In Cultivated Australian, /ɪ/ in an unaccented position (e.g. in *pocket*) is generally replaced by /ə/, so that the distinction still made in Southern British English between *boxes* and *boxers* is not reproduced in Australian speech. In words ending in *-y*, and especially in *-ity*, the final /ɪ/ becomes /i/, so that *capacity* is pronounced /kə'pæsəti/ in Cultivated Australian. There are also differences of stress, as in a word like *hostess*, where the stress in Southern British English is on the first syllable but in Australian speech on the second.

Cultivated Australian may be taken to include what some phoneticians have politely called 'modifed Australian', a conscious effort to imitate British English with occasionally grotesque results, described colloquially as *putting on jam*. Usually the intonation patterns of British English alone are enough to frustrate such attempts. At the other end of the spectrum is Broad Australian, and its characteristics constitute what has been called 'the Australian accent.' It is most readily identified by the presence of six sounds:

/eɪ/ as in *praise*. In Broad Australian this tends towards /ʌɪ/, so that *praise* may be heard (though not by another speaker of Broad Australian) as *prize*.
/əʊ/ as in *dough*. This tends towards /ʌʊ/ in Broad Australian.
/iː/ as in *me*. This tends towards the diphthong /əɪ/.
/uː/ as in *boot*. This tends towards the diphthong /əʊ/.
/aɪ/ as in *buy*. This tends towards /ɒɪ/, so that *buy* may be heard as *boy*.
/aʊ/ as in *house*. This tends towards /æʊ/, sometimes with nasalization.

Earlier explanations of 'the Australian accent' as cockney were prompted by some of these sounds, especially the first, as cockneys were supposed to sing 'Praise him for his grace and favour' as 'Prize him for his grice and fiver.' (On the other hand the Received Pronunciation would sound to a cockney like 'grease and fever,' which in modified Australian it could well become.) While no misunderstandings are likely between two speakers of Broad Australian, they can occur between Broad Australian speakers and others. An American visitor to Oxford formed the impression that the spelling of Brasenose College must be Brisenose, because he had heard it spoken of only by an Australian resident there.

The vowel /ɑː/ as in *part* is in all Australian pronunciations forward of the RP vowel, approximating to /a/, and in Broad Australian it is usually replaced by /æ/ in words like *dance* and *chance*. (A similar change may be occurring in British English, as in this dictionary the first syllable of *translation* is rendered as /æ/, not /ɑː/.) The vowel /ɜː/ as in *bird* is closer in Australian English, so that the English pronunciation may sound to a Broad Australian speaker like *bard*. While a word like *capacity*, pronounced /kə'pæsɪtɪ/ in RP, becomes /kə'pæsəti/ in Cultivated Australian, in Broad Australian it becomes /kə'pæsəteɪ/. This reflects a tendency to give full value to unaccented vowels and diphthongs, which in Southern British English are reduced to /ə/ or /ɪ/. While *accent* and *comrade* may be pronounced /'æksənt/ and /'kɒmrɪd/ in Southern British English, in Australian speech they become /'æksent/ and /'kɒmreɪd/, with the second syllable also receiving stress. This is most obvious in the pronunciation of the days of the week, where in Australian speech *Monday* is not /'mʌndɪ/ but /'mʌndeɪ/.

Although the characteristics of Broad Australian are the most readily identified as marking off the pronunciation of Australian English from RP, in fact Broad Australian, General Australian, and Cultivated Australian are a continuum and cannot be satisfactorily distinguished in terms of social or geographical groupings. Many Australian speakers use this continuum selectively according to the occasion, like politicians in Britain who are able to use a provincial accent in addressing their constituents, but revert to RP in Parliament, or like children everywhere who have one mode of speech for the playground and another in the classroom.

Aa

a *or* **A** (eɪ) *n, pl* **a's, A's,** *or* **As. 1** the first letter and first vowel of the modern English alphabet. **2** any of several speech sounds represented by this letter, in English as in *take, bag, calm, shortage,* or *cobra.* **3** Also called: **alpha.** the first in a series, esp. the highest grade or mark, as in an examination. **4 from A to Z.** from start to finish, thoroughly and in detail.

a[1] (ə; *emphatic* eɪ) *determiner* (*indefinite article;* used before an initial consonant. Compare **an**[1]) **1** used preceding a singular countable noun, if the noun is not previously specified or known: *a dog; a terrible disappointment.* **2** used preceding a proper noun to indicate that a person or thing has some of the qualities of the one named: *a Romeo; a Shylock.* **3** used preceding a noun or determiner of quantity: *a cupful; a dozen eggs; a great many; to read a lot.* **4** used preceding a noun indicating a concrete or abstract thing capable of being divided: *half a loaf; a quarter of a minute.* **5** (preceded by *once, twice, several times,* etc.) each or every; per: *once a day; fifty pence a pound.* **6** a certain; one: *to change policy at a stroke; a Mr Jones called.* **7** (preceded by *not*) any at all: *not a hope.* ◆ Compare **the**[1].

a[2] (ə) *vb* an informal or dialect word for **have:** *they'd a said if they'd known.*

a[3] (ə) *prep* (usually linked to the preceding noun) an informal form of **of:** *sorta sad; a kinda waste.*

a[4] *symbol for:* **1** acceleration. **2** are(s) (metric measure of land). **3** atto-. **4** *Chess.* See **algebraic notation.**

A *symbol for:* **1** *Music.* **1a** a note having a frequency of 440 hertz (**A above middle C**) or this value multiplied or divided by any power of 2; the sixth note of the scale of C major. **1b** a key, string, or pipe producing this note. **1c** the major or minor key having this note as its tonic. **2** a human blood type of the ABO group, containing the A antigen. **3** (in Britain) a major arterial road: *the A3 runs from London to Portsmouth.* **4** (in Britain, formerly) **4a** a film certified for viewing by anyone, but which contains material that some parents may not wish their children to see. **4b** (*as modifier*): *an A film.* **5** mass number. **6** the number 10 in hexadecimal notation. **7** *Cards.* ace. **8** argon (now superseded by **Ar**). **9** ampere(s). **10** Also: **at.** ampere-turn. **11** absolute (temperature). **12** (in circuit diagrams) ammeter. **13** area. **14** (*in combination*) atomic: *an A-bomb; an A-plant.* **15** *Chem.* affinity. **16** *Biochem.* adenine. **17** *Logic.* a universal affirmative categorical proposition, such as *all men are mortal:* often symbolized as **SaP.** Compare **E, I**[2], **O**[1]. [from Latin *a(ffirmo)* I affirm] **18a** a person whose job is in top management, or who holds a senior administrative or professional position. **18b** (*as modifier*): *an A worker.* ◆ See also **occupation groupings.** ◆ **19** *international car registration for* Austria.

Å *symbol for* angstrom unit.

a. *abbrev. for:* **1** acre(s) or acreage. **2** alto. **3** amateur. **4** answer.

A. *abbrev. for:* **1** acre(s) or acreage. **2** America(n). **3** answer.

a', aa, *or* **aw** (ɔ:) *determiner Scot.* variants of **all.**

a-[1] *or before a vowel* **an-** *prefix* not; without; opposite to: *atonal; asocial.* [from Greek *a-, an-* not, without]

a-[2] *prefix* **1** on; in; towards: *afoot; abed; aground; aback.* **2** *Literary or archaic.* (*used before a present participle*) in the act or process of: *come a-running; go a-hunting.* **3** in the condition or state of: *afloat; alive; asleep.*

A1, A-1, *or* **A-one** ('eɪ'wʌn) *adj* **1** in good health; physically fit. **2** *Informal.* first class; excellent. **3** (of a vessel) with hull and equipment in first-class condition.

A4 *n* **a** a standard paper size, 210 × 297 mm. **b** (*as adj*): *an A4 book.* ◆ See also **A sizes.**

A5 *n* **a** a standard paper size (half A4), 148 × 210 mm. **b** (*as adj*): *A5 notepaper.* ◆ See also **A sizes.**

aa[1] ('ɑ:ɑ:) *n* a volcanic rock consisting of angular blocks of lava with a very rough surface. [Hawaiian]

aa[2] *abbrev. for* **ana**[1].

AA *abbrev. for:* **1** Alcoholics Anonymous. **2** anti-aircraft. **3** Architectural Association. **4** (in Britain) Automobile Association. ◆ *symbol for:* **5** (in Britain, formerly) a film that may not be shown publicly to a child under fourteen.

AAA *abbrev. for:* **1** (formerly) *Brit.* Amateur Athletic Association. **2** anti-aircraft artillery. See also **triple A. 3** *U.S.* Automobile Association of America.

Aachen ('ɑ:kən; *German* 'a:xən) *n* a city and spa in W Germany, in North Rhine-Westphalia: the northern capital of Charlemagne's empire. Pop.: 247 923 (1996 est.). French name: **Aix-la-Chapelle.**

Aalborg *or* **Ålborg** (*Danish* 'ɔlbɔr) *n* a city and port in Denmark, in N Jutland. Pop.: 159 980 (1996 est.).

Aalesund (*Norwegian* 'o:ləsun) *n* a variant spelling of **Ålesund.**

aalii (ɑ:'li:i:) *n* a bushy sapindaceous shrub, *Dodonaea viscosa,* of Australia, Hawaii, Africa, and tropical America, having small greenish flowers and sticky foliage. [Hawaiian]

Aalst (a:lst) *n* the Flemish name for **Alost.**

Aalto (*Finnish* 'ɑ:ltɔ) *n* **Alvar** ('alvar). 1898–1976, Finnish architect and furniture designer, noted particularly for his public and industrial buildings, in which wood is much used. He invented bent plywood furniture (1932).

AAM *abbrev. for* air-to-air missile.

A & E *abbrev. for* Accident and Emergency (in hospitals).

A & M *abbrev. for:* **1** Agricultural and Mechanical. **2** Ancient and Modern (hymn book).

A & P (in New Zealand) *abbrev. for* Agricultural and Pastoral (Association, Show, etc.).

A & R *abbrev. for* artists and repertoire.

AAP *abbrev. for:* **1** Australian Associated Press. **2** (in the U.S.) affirmative action program.

Aarau (*German* 'a:rau) *n* a town in N Switzerland, capital of Aargau canton: capital of the Helvetic Republic from 1798 to 1803. Pop.: 15 881 (1990).

aardvark ('ɑ:d,vɑ:k) *n* a nocturnal mammal, *Orycteropus afer,* the sole member of its family (*Orycteropodidae*) and order (*Tubulidentata*). It inhabits the grasslands of Africa, has long ears and snout, and feeds on termites. Also called: **ant bear.** [C19: from obsolete Afrikaans, from *aarde* earth + *varken* pig]

aardwolf ('ɑ:d,wʊlf) *n, pl* **-wolves.** a nocturnal mammal, *Proteles cristatus,* that inhabits the plains of southern Africa and feeds on termites and insect larvae: family *Hyaenidae* (hyenas), order *Carnivora* (carnivores). [C19: from Afrikaans, from *aarde* earth + *wolf* wolf]

Aargau (*German* 'a:rgau) *n* a canton in N Switzerland. Capital: Aarau. Pop.: 528 887 (1996 est.). Area: 1404 sq. km (542 sq. miles). French name: **Argovie.**

Aarhus *or* **Århus** (*Danish* 'ɔrhu:s) *n* a city and port in Denmark, in E Jutland. Pop.: 279 759 (1996 est.).

Aaron ('ɛərən) *n Old Testament.* the first high priest of the Israelites, brother of Moses (Exodus 4:14).

Aaronic (ɛə'rɒnɪk) *adj* **1** of or relating to Aaron, his family, or the priestly dynasty initiated by him. **2** of or relating to the Israelite high priesthood. **3** of or relating to the priesthood in general. **4** *Mormon Church.* denoting or relating to the second order of the Mormon priesthood.

Aaron's beard *n* another name for **rose of Sharon** (sense 1).

Aaron's rod *n* **1** the rod used by Aaron in performing a variety of miracles in Egypt. It later blossomed and produced almonds (Numbers 17). **2** a widespread Eurasian scrophulariaceous plant, *Verbascum thapsus,* having woolly leaves and tall erect spikes of yellow flowers.

A'asia *abbrev. for* Australasia.

Ab (æb) *n* a variant of **Av.**

AB *abbrev. for:* **1** Also: **a.b.** able-bodied seaman. **2** (in the U.S.) Bachelor of Arts. **3** Alberta (Canada). ◆ **4** *symbol for* a human blood type of the ABO group, containing both the A antigen and the B antigen.

ab-[1] *prefix* away from; off; outside of; opposite to: *abnormal; abaxial; aboral.* [from Latin *ab* away from]

ab-[2] *prefix* denoting a cgs unit of measurement in the electromagnetic system: *abvolt.* [abstracted from ABSOLUTE]

aba ('æbə) *n* **1** a type of cloth from Syria, made of goat hair or camel hair. **2** a sleeveless outer garment of such cloth. [from Arabic]

ABA *abbrev. for:* **1** (in Britain) Amateur Boxing Association. **2** American Booksellers Association.

abac ('eɪbæk) *n* another name for **nomogram.** [C20: from French, from Latin ABACUS]

abaca ('æbəkə) *n* **1** a Philippine plant, *Musa textilis,* related to the banana: family *Musaceae.* Its leafstalks are the source of Manila hemp. **2** another name for **Manila hemp.** [via Spanish from Tagalog *abaká*]

aback (ə'bæk) *adv* **1 taken aback. 1a** startled or disconcerted. **b** *Nautical.* (of a vessel or sail) having the wind against the forward side so as to prevent forward motion. **2** *Rare.* towards the back; backwards. [Old English *on bæc* to the back]

abactinal (æb'æktɪn°l) *adj Zoology.* (of organisms showing radial symmetry) situated away from or opposite to the mouth; aboral. ► **ab'actinally** *adv*

abacus ('æbəkəs) *n, pl* **-ci** (-,saɪ) *or* **-cuses. 1** a counting device that consists of a frame holding rods on which a specific number of beads are free to move. Each rod designates a given denomination, such as units, tens, hundreds, etc., in the decimal system, and each bead represents a digit or a specific number of digits. **2** *Architect.* the flat upper part of the capital of a column. [C16: from Latin, from Greek *abax* board covered with sand for tracing calculations, from Hebrew *ābhāq* dust]

Abadan (,æbə'dɑ:n) *n* a port in SW Iran, on an island in the Shatt-al-Arab delta. Pop.: 84 774 (1991).

Abaddon (ə'bæd°n) *n* **1** the Devil (Revelation 9:11). **2** (in rabbinical literature) a part of Gehenna; Hell. [Hebrew: literally, destruction]

abaft (ə'bɑ:ft) *Nautical.* ◆ *adv, adj* (*postpositive*) **1** closer to the stern than to another place on a vessel: *with the wind abaft.* ◆ *prep* **2** behind; aft of: *abaft the mast.* [C13: *on baft; baft* from Old English *beæftan,* from *be* by + *æftan* behind]

Abakan (*Russian* aba'kan) *n* a city in S central Russia, capital of the Khakass Republic, at the confluence of the Yenisei and Abakan Rivers. Pop.: 161 000 (1995 est.).

abalone (,æbə'ləʊnɪ) *n* any of various edible marine gastropod molluscs of the genus *Haliotis,* having an ear-shaped shell that is perforated with a row of respiratory holes. The shells are used for ornament or decoration. Also called: **ear shell.** See also **ormer.** [C19: from American Spanish *abulón;* origin unknown]

abampere (æb'æmpɛə) *n* the cgs unit of current in the electromagnetic system; the constant current that, when flowing through two parallel straight infinitely long conductors 1 centimetre apart, will produce a force between them of 2 dynes per centimetre: equivalent to 10 amperes. Abbrev.: **abamp.**

abandon (ə'bændən) *vb* (*tr*) **1** to forsake completely; desert; leave behind: *to abandon a baby; drivers had to abandon their cars.* **2** **abandon ship.** the order given to the crew of a ship that is about to sink to take to the lifeboats. **3** to give up completely: *to abandon a habit; to abandon hope.* **4** to yield control of or concern in; relinquish: *to abandon office.* **5** to give up (something begun) before completion: *to abandon a job; the game was abandoned.* **6** to surrender (oneself) to emotion without restraint. **7** to give (insured property that has suffered partial loss or damage) to the insurers in order that a claim for a total loss may be made. ♦ *n* **8** freedom from inhibitions, restraint, concern, or worry: *she danced with abandon.* [C14: *abandounen* (vb), from Old French, from *a bandon* under one's control, in one's power, from *a* at, to + *bandon* control, power] ▸ **a'bandonment** *n*

abandoned (ə'bændənd) *adj* **1** deserted: *an abandoned windmill.* **2** forsaken: *an abandoned child.* **3** unrestrained; uninhibited: *wild, abandoned dancing.* **4** depraved; profligate.

abandonee (əˌbændə'ni:) *n Law.* a person to whom something is formally relinquished, esp. an insurer having the right to salvage a wreck.

abapical (æb'eɪpɪkᵊl) *adj Biology.* away from or opposite the apex.

à bas *French.* (a bɑ) *interj* down with!

abase (ə'beɪs) *vb* (*tr*) **1** to humble or belittle (oneself, etc.). **2** to lower or reduce, as in rank or estimation. [C15 *abessen,* from Old French *abaissier* to make low. See BASE[2]] ▸ **a'basement** *n*

abash (ə'bæʃ) *vb* (*tr; usually passive*) to cause to feel ill at ease, embarrassed, or confused; make ashamed. [C14: via Norman French from Old French *esbair* to be astonished, from *es-* out + *bair* to gape, yawn] ▸ **abashedly** (ə'bæʃɪdlɪ) *adv* ▸ **a'bashment** *n*

abate (ə'beɪt) *vb* **1** to make or become less in amount, intensity, degree, etc.: *the storm has abated.* **2** (*tr*) *Law.* **2a** to remove, suppress, or terminate (a nuisance). **2b** to suspend or extinguish (a claim or action). **2c** to annul (a writ). **3** (*intr*) *Law.* (of a writ, legal action, etc.) to become null and void. **4** (*tr*) to subtract or deduct, as part of a price. [C14: from Old French *abatre* to beat down, fell]

abatement (ə'beɪtmənt) *n* **1** diminution or alleviation; decrease. **2** suppression or termination: *the abatement of a nuisance.* **3** the amount by which something is reduced, such as the cost of an article. **4** *Property law.* a decrease in the payment to creditors or legatees when the assets of the debtor or estate are insufficient to meet all payments in full. **5** *Property law.* (formerly) a wrongful entry on land by a stranger who takes possession after the death of the owner and before the heir has entered into possession.

abatis *or* **abattis** ('æbətɪs, 'æbəti:) *n Fortifications.* **1** a rampart of felled trees bound together placed with their branches outwards. **2** a barbed-wire entanglement before a position. [C18: from French, from *abattre* to fell]

abator (ə'beɪtə) *n Law.* a person who effects an abatement.

abattoir ('æbəˌtwɑ:) *n* another name for **slaughterhouse.** [C19: French, from *abattre* to fell]

abaxial (æb'æksɪəl) *adj* facing away from the axis, as the surface of a leaf. Compare **adaxial.**

Abba ('æbə) *n* **1** *New Testament.* father (used of God). **2** a title given to bishops and patriarchs in the Syrian, Coptic, and Ethiopian Churches. [from Aramaic]

abbacy ('æbəsɪ) *n, pl* **-cies.** the office, term of office, or jurisdiction of an abbot or abbess. [C15: from Church Latin *abbātia,* from *abbāt-* ABBOT]

Abbado (ə'bɑ:dəʊ) *n* **Claudio.** born 1933, Italian conductor; principal conductor of the London Symphony Orchestra (1979–88); director of the Vienna State Opera (1986–91), and the Berlin Philharmonic from 1989.

Abbas ('æbəs) *n* **Ferhat.** 1899–1985, Algerian nationalist leader: joined the National Liberation Front (1956); president of the provisional government of the Algerian republic (1958–61).

Abbas I *n* called *the Great.* 1557–1628, shah of Persia. He greatly extended Persian territory by defeating the Uzbeks and the Ottomans.

Abbasid ('æbəˌsɪd, ə'bæsɪd) *n* **a** any caliph of the dynasty that ruled the Muslim empire from Baghdad (750–1258) and claimed descent from Abbas, uncle of Mohammed. **b** (*as modifier*): *the Abbasid dynasty.*

abbatial (ə'beɪʃəl) *adj* of or relating to an abbot, abbess, or abbey. [C17: from Church Latin *abbātiālis,* from *abbāt-* ABBOT; see -AL[1]]

abbé ('æbeɪ; *French* abe) *n* **1** a French abbot. **2** a title used in addressing any other French cleric, such as a priest.

Abbe ('æbɪ; *German* 'a:bə) *n* **Ernst.** 1840–1905, German physicist, noted for his work in optics and the microscope condenser known as the **Abbe condenser.**

abbess ('æbɪs) *n* the female superior of a convent. [C13: from Old French, from Church Latin *abbātissa*]

Abbeville (*French* abvil) *n* a town in N France: brewing, sugar-refining, and carpet industries. Pop.: 24 590 (1990).

Abbevillian (æb'vɪlɪən, -jən) *Archaeol.* ♦ *n* **1** the period represented by Lower Palaeolithic European sites containing the earliest hand axes, dating from the Mindel glaciation. See also **Acheulian.** ♦ *adj* **2** of or relating to this period. [C20: after ABBEVILLE, where the stone tools were discovered]

abbey ('æbɪ) *n* **1** a building inhabited by a community of monks or nuns governed by an abbot or abbess. **2** a church built in conjunction with such a building. **3** such a community of monks or nuns. [C13: via Old French *abeie* from Church Latin *abbātia* ABBACY]

Abbey Theatre *n* an influential theatre in Dublin (opened 1904): associated with it were Synge, Yeats, Lady Gregory, and O'Casey. It was destroyed by fire in 1951 but was rebuilt; it reopened in 1966.

abbot ('æbət) *n* the superior of an abbey of monks. Related adj: **abbatial.** [Old English *abbod,* from Church Latin *abbāt-* (stem of *abbas*), ultimately from Aramaic *abbā* ABBA] ▸ **'abbotˌship** *or* **'abbotcy** *n*

abbrev. *or* **abbr.** *abbrev. for* abbreviation.

abbreviate (ə'bri:vɪˌeɪt) *vb* (*tr*) **1** to shorten (a word or phrase) by contraction or omission of some letters or words. **2** to shorten (a speech or piece of writing) by omitting sections, paraphrasing, etc. **3** to cut short. [C15: from the past participle of Late Latin *abbreviāre,* from Latin *brevis* brief] ▸ **ab'breviˌator** *n*

abbreviation (əˌbri:vɪ'eɪʃən) *n* **1** a shortened or contracted form of a word or phrase used in place of the whole. **2** the process or result of abbreviating.

ABC[1] *n* **1** (*pl in U.S.*) the rudiments of a subject. **2** an alphabetical guide to a subject. **3** (*often pl in U.S.*) the alphabet.

ABC[2] *abbrev. for:* **1** (formerly, of weapons or warfare) atomic, biological, and chemical. **2** Australian Broadcasting Corporation. **3** American Broadcasting Company.

abcoulomb (æb'ku:lɒm) *n* the cgs unit of electric charge in the electromagnetic system; the charge per second passing any cross section of a conductor through which a steady current of 1 abampere is flowing: equivalent to 10 coulombs.

Abd Allah (æbd 'ælə) *n* 1846–99, Sudanese leader; he led the uprising against the Egyptian government of the Sudan; defeated by Kitchener in 1898.

Abd al-Malik ibn Marwan (æbd ʊl'mɑ:lɪk ɪbᵊn 'mɑ:wən) *n* ?646–705 A.D., fifth caliph (685–705) of the Omayyad Arab dynasty. He pacified the Muslim empire and extended its territory in North Africa.

Abdelkader (ˌæbdʊl'kɑ:də) *n* ?1807–83, Algerian nationalist, who resisted the French invasion of Algeria and established (1837) an independent state. He surrendered to the French in 1847.

Abd-el-Krim (ˌæbdʊl'krɪm) *n* 1882–1963, Moroccan chief who led revolts against Spain and France, surrendered before their combined forces in 1926, but later formed the North African independence movement.

Abdias (æb'daɪəs) *n Bible.* the Douay form of **Obadiah.**

abdicate ('æbdɪˌkeɪt) *vb* to renounce (a throne, power, responsibility, rights, etc.), esp. formally. [C16: from the past participle of Latin *abdicāre* to proclaim away, disclaim] ▸ **abdicable** ('æbdɪkəbᵊl) *adj* ▸ **ˌabdi'cation** *n* ▸ **abdicative** (æb'dɪkətɪv) *adj* ▸ **'abdiˌcator** *n*

abdomen ('æbdəmən, æb'dəʊ-) *n* **1** the region of the body of a vertebrate that contains the viscera other than the heart and lungs. In mammals it is separated from the thorax by the diaphragm. **2** the front or surface of this region; belly. Related adj: **coeliac. 3** (in arthropods) the posterior part of the body behind the thorax, consisting of up to ten similar segments. [C16: from Latin; origin obscure] ▸ **abdominal** (æb'dɒmɪnᵊl) *adj* ▸ **ab'dominally** *adv*

abdominal thrust *n* another name for **Heimlich manoeuvre.**

abducens nerve (æb'dju:sənz) *n* either of the sixth pair of cranial nerves, which supply the lateral rectus muscle of the eye. [see ABDUCENT]

abducent (æb'dju:sᵊnt) *adj* (of a muscle) abducting. [C18: from Latin *abdūcent-, abdūcens* leading away, from *abdūcere,* from *ab-* away + *dūcere* to lead, carry]

abduct (æb'dʌkt) *vb* (*tr*) **1** to remove (a person) by force or cunning; kidnap. **2** (of certain muscles) to pull (a leg, arm, etc.) away from the median axis of the body. Compare **adduct.** [C19: from the past participle of Latin *abdūcere* to lead away] ▸ **ab'duction** *n* ▸ **ab'ductor** *n*

Abdul-Hamid II (ˌæbdʊl'hæmɪd) *n* 1842–1918, sultan of Turkey (1876–1909), deposed by the Young Turks, noted for his brutal suppression of the Armenian revolt (1894–96).

Abdullah (æb'dʌlə) *n* 1882–1951, emir of Transjordan (1921–46) and first king of Jordan (1946–51). He joined the Arab revolt against Turkish rule in World War I; assassinated 1951.

Abdullah II *n* born 1962, king of Jordan from 1999, son of King **Hussein.**

Abdul Rahman ('æbdʊl 'rɑ:mən) *n* **Tunku.** 1903–90, Malaysian statesman; prime minister of Malaya (1957–63) and of Malaysia (1963–70).

abeam (ə'bi:m) *adv, adj* (*postpositive*) at right angles to the length and directly opposite the centre of a vessel or aircraft. [C19: A-[2] + BEAM]

abecedarian (ˌeɪbi:si:'deərɪən) *n* **1** a person who is learning the alphabet or the rudiments of a subject. ♦ *adj* **2** alphabetically arranged. [C17: from Late Latin *abecedarius,* from the letters *a, b, c, d*]

abed (ə'bɛd) *adv Archaic.* in bed.

Abednego (ə'bɛdnɪˌgəʊ) *n Old Testament.* one of Daniel's three companions who, together with Shadrach and Meshach, was miraculously saved from destruction in Nebuchadnezzar's fiery furnace (Daniel 3:12–30).

Abel ('eɪbᵊl) *n Old Testament.* the second son of Adam and Eve, a shepherd, murdered by his brother Cain (Genesis 4:1–8).

Abelard ('æbəˌlɑ:d) *n* **Peter.** French name *Pierre Abélard.* 1079–1142, French scholastic philosopher and theologian whose works include *Historia Calamitatum* and *Sic et Non* (1121). His love for Héloïse is recorded in their correspondence.

abele (ə'bi:l, 'eɪbᵊl) *n* another name for **white poplar.** [C16: from Dutch *abeel,* ultimately related to Latin *albus* white]

Abelian group (ə'bi:lɪən) *n* a group the defined binary operation of which is commutative: if *a* and *b* are members of an Abelian group then *ab* = *ba.* [C19: named after Niels Henrik *Abel* (1802–29), Norwegian mathematician]

abelmosk ('eɪbᵊlˌmɒsk) *n* a tropical bushy malvaceous plant, *Hibiscus abelmoschus,* cultivated for its yellow-and-crimson flowers and for its musk-scented seeds, which yield an oil used in perfumery. Also called: **musk mallow.** [New Latin, from Arabic *abu'l misk* father of musk]

Abelson ('eɪbᵊlsən) *n* **Philip.** born 1913, U.S. physical chemist. He created (with Edwin McMillan) the first transuranic element, neptunium (1940).

Abeokuta (ˌæbɪəʊ'ku:tə) *n* a town in W Nigeria, capital of Ogun state. Pop.: 427 400 (1996 est.).

Abercrombie ('æbəˌkrʌmbɪ) *n* Sir **(Leslie) Patrick.** 1879–1957, British town planner and architect, best known for *The County of London Plan* (1943) and *The Greater London Plan* (1944).

Aberdare (ˌæbəˈdɛə) *n* a town in South Wales, in Rhondda, Cynon, Taff county borough. Pop.: 29 040 (1991).

Aberdeen[1] (ˌæbəˈdiːn) *n* **1** a city in NE Scotland, on the North Sea: centre for processing North Sea oil and gas; university (1494). Pop.: 217 260 (1996 est.). **2 City of.** a council area in NE Scotland, established in 1996. Pop.: 219 100 (1995 est.). Area: 186 sq. km (72 sq. miles). ▸ **Aberdonian** (ˌæbəˈdəʊnɪən) *n, adj*

Aberdeen[2] (ˌæbəˈdiːn) *n* **George Hamilton-Gordon,** 4th Earl of. 1784–1860, British statesman. He was foreign secretary under Wellington (1828) and Peel (1841–46); became prime minister of a coalition ministry in 1852 but was compelled to resign after mismanagement of the Crimean War (1855).

Aberdeen Angus *n* a black hornless breed of beef cattle originating in Scotland.

Aberdeenshire (ˌæbəˈdiːnˌʃɪə, -ʃə) *n* a council area and historic county of N Scotland, on the North Sea: became part of Grampian Region in 1975 but reinstated as an independent unitary authority (with adjusted borders) in 1996: rises to the Grampian and Cairngorm Mountains in the SW: chiefly agricultural (esp. sheep and stock raising). Administrative centre: Aberdeen. Pop.: 227 430 (1996 est.). Area 6319 sq. km (2439 sq. miles).

Aberdeen terrier *n* a former name for **Scottish terrier.**

aberdevine (ˌæbədɪˈviːn) *n* a former name for the **siskin** (sense 1), esp. as a cagebird. [C18: of unknown origin]

Aberfan (ˌæbəˈvæn) *n* a coal-mining village in S Wales, in Merthyr Tydfil county borough: scene of a disaster in 1966 when a slag heap collapsed onto part of the village killing 144 people (including 116 children).

abernethy (ˌæbəˈnɛθɪ) *n* a crisp unleavened biscuit. [C19: perhaps named after Dr. John *Abernethy* (1764–1831), English surgeon interested in diet]

aberrant (æˈbɛrənt) *adj* **1** deviating from the normal or usual type, as certain animals from the group in which they are classified. **2** behaving in an abnormal or untypical way. **3** deviating from truth, morality, etc. [rare before C19: from the present participle of Latin *aberrāre* to wander away] ▸ **abˈerrance** *or* **abˈerrancy** *n*

aberration (ˌæbəˈreɪʃən) *n* **1** deviation from what is normal, expected, or usual. **2** departure from truth, morality, etc. **3** a lapse in control of one's mental faculties. **4** *Optics.* a defect in a lens or mirror that causes the formation of either a distorted image (see **spherical aberration**) or one with coloured fringes (see **chromatic aberration**). **5** *Astronomy.* the apparent displacement of a celestial body due to the motion of the observer with the earth.

Aberystwyth (ˌæbəˈrɪstwɪθ) *n* a resort and university town in Wales, in Ceredigion on Cardigan Bay. Pop.: 11 154 (1991).

abet (əˈbɛt) *vb* **abets, abetting, abetted.** (*tr*) to assist or encourage, esp. in crime or wrongdoing. [C14: from Old French *abeter* to lure on, entice, from *beter* to bait] ▸ **aˈbetment** *or* **aˈbettal** *n* ▸ **aˈbetter** *or* (*esp. Law*) **aˈbettor** *n*

abeyance (əˈbeɪəns) *n* **1** (usually preceded by *in* or *into*) a state of being suspended or put aside temporarily. **2** (usually preceded by *in*) *Law.* an indeterminate state of ownership, as when the person entitled to an estate has not been ascertained. [C16–17: from Anglo-French, from Old French *abeance* expectation, literally a gaping after, a reaching towards] ▸ **aˈbeyant** *adj*

abfarad (æbˈfæræd, -əd) *n* the cgs unit of capacitance in the electromagnetic system; the capacitance of a capacitor having a charge of 1 abcoulomb and a potential difference of 1 abvolt between its conductors: equivalent to 10^9 farads.

ABH *abbrev. for* actual bodily harm.

abhenry (æbˈhɛnrɪ) *n, pl* **-ries.** the cgs unit of inductance in the electromagnetic system; the inductance that results when a rate of change of current of 1 abampere per second generates an induced emf of 1 abvolt: equivalent to 10^{-9} henry.

abhor (əbˈhɔː) *vb* **-hors, -horring, -horred.** (*tr*) to detest vehemently; find repugnant; reject. [C15: from Latin *abhorrēre* to shudder at, shrink from, from *ab-* away from + *horrēre* to bristle, shudder] ▸ **abˈhorrer** *n*

abhorrence (əbˈhɒrəns) *n* **1** a feeling of extreme loathing or aversion. **2** a person or thing that is loathsome.

abhorrent (əbˈhɒrənt) *adj* **1** repugnant; loathsome. **2** (when *postpositive,* foll. by *of*) feeling extreme aversion or loathing (for): *abhorrent of vulgarity.* **3** (usually *postpositive* and foll. by *to*) conflicting (with): *abhorrent to common sense.* ▸ **abˈhorrently** *adv*

Abia (æbˈiːa) *n* a state of SE Nigeria. Capital: Umuahia. Pop.: 2 569 362 (1995 est.). Area (including Imo state): 11 850 sq. km (4575 sq. miles).

Abib (*Hebrew* ɑˈbiːb) *n Judaism.* an older name for the month of **Nisan** (Exodus 13:4). [Hebrew *ābhībh* ear of grain, hence the month when grain was fresh]

abide (əˈbaɪd) *vb* **abides, abiding, abode** *or* **abided. 1** (*tr*) to tolerate; put up with. **2** (*tr*) to accept or submit to; suffer: *to abide the court's decision.* **3** (*intr;* foll. by *by*) **3a** to comply (with): *to abide by the decision.* **3b** to remain faithful (to): *to abide by your promise.* **4** (*intr*) to remain or continue. **5** (*intr*) *Archaic.* to dwell. **6** (*tr*) *Archaic.* to await in expectation. **7** (*tr*) *Archaic.* to withstand or sustain; endure: *to abide the onslaught.* [Old English *ābīdan,* from *a-* (intensive) + *bīdan* to wait, bide] ▸ **aˈbidance** *n* ▸ **aˈbider** *n*

abiding (əˈbaɪdɪŋ) *adj* permanent; enduring: *an abiding belief.* ▸ **aˈbidingly** *adv*

Abidjan (ˌæbɪˈdʒɑːn; *French* abidʒɑ̃) *n* a port in the Côte d'Ivoire, on the Gulf of Guinea: the legislative capital (Yamoussoukro became the administrative capital in 1983). Pop.: 2 797 000 (1995 est.).

abietic acid (ˌæbɪˈetɪk) *n* a yellowish powder occurring naturally as a constituent of rosin and used in lacquers, varnishes, and soap. Formula: $C_{19}H_{29}COOH$; melting pt.: 173°C. [C19 *abietic,* from Latin *abiēt-,* from *abiēs* silver fir (the acid originally being extracted from the resin)]

Abigail (ˈæbɪˌgeɪl) *n Old Testament.* the woman who brought provisions to David and his followers and subsequently became his wife (I Samuel 25:1–42).

Abilene (ˈæbəˌliːn) *n* a city in central Texas. Pop.: 108 476 (1996 est.).

ability (əˈbɪlɪtɪ) *n, pl* **-ties. 1** possession of the qualities required to do something; necessary skill, competence, or power: *the ability to cope with a problem.* **2** considerable proficiency; natural capability: *a man of ability.* **3** (*pl*) special talents. [C14: from Old French from Latin *habilitās* aptitude, handiness, from *habilis* ABLE]

Abingdon (ˈæbɪŋdən) *n* a market town in S England, in Oxfordshire. Pop.: 35 234 (1991).

ab initio *Latin.* (æb ɪˈnɪʃɪˌəʊ) from the start.

abiogenesis (ˌeɪbaɪəʊˈdʒɛnɪsɪs) *n* the hypothetical process by which living organisms arise from inanimate matter: formerly thought to explain the origin of microorganisms. Also called: **spontaneous generation, autogenesis.** Compare **biogenesis.** [C19: New Latin, from A-[1] + BIO- + GENESIS] ▸ ˌ**abiogeˈnetic** *adj* ▸ **abiogenist** (ˌeɪbaɪˈɒdʒɪnɪst) *n*

abiosis (ˌeɪbaɪˈəʊsɪs) *n* absence of life. [C20: from A-[1] + Greek *biōsis* a way of living] ▸ **abiotic** (ˌeɪbaɪˈɒtɪk) *adj*

abirritant (æbˈɪrɪtənt) *adj* **1** relieving irritation. ◆ *n* **2** any drug or agent that relieves irritation.

abirritate (æbˈɪrɪˌteɪt) *vb* (*tr*) *Med.* to soothe or make less irritable.

abject (ˈæbdʒɛkt) *adj* **1** utterly wretched or hopeless. **2** miserable; forlorn; dejected. **3** indicating humiliation; submissive: *an abject apology.* **4** contemptible; despicable; servile: *an abject liar.* [C14 (in the sense: rejected, cast out): from Latin *abjectus* thrown or cast away, from *abjicere,* from *ab-* away + *jacere* to throw] ▸ **abˈjection** *n* ▸ **ˈabjectly** *adv* ▸ **ˈabjectness** *n*

abjure (əbˈdʒʊə) *vb* (*tr*) **1** to renounce or retract, esp. formally, solemnly, or under oath. **2** to abstain from or reject. [C15: from Old French *abjurer* or Latin *abjurāre* to deny on oath] ▸ ˌ**abjuˈration** *n* ▸ **abˈjurer** *n*

Abkhaz (æbˈkɑːz) *n* **1** (*pl* **-khaz**) Also called: **Abkhazi, Abkhazian.** a member of a Georgian people living east of the Black Sea. **2** the language of this people, belonging to the North-West Caucasian family.

Abkhazia (æbˈkɑːzɪə) *n* an administrative division of NW Georgia, between the Black Sea and the Caucasus Mountains: a subtropical region, with mountains rising over 3900 m (13 000 ft.); Abkhazian separatists seized control of the region in 1993. Capital: Sukhumi. Pop.: 516 600 (1993 est.). Area: 8600 sq. km (3320 sq. miles). Also called: **Abkhaz Autonomous Republic.**

abl. *abbrev. for* ablative.

ablactation (ˌæblækˈteɪʃən) *n* **1** the weaning of an infant. **2** the cessation of milk secretion in the breasts.

ablate (æbˈleɪt) *vb* (*tr*) to remove by ablation. [C20: back formation from ABLATION]

ablation (æbˈleɪʃən) *n* **1** the surgical removal of an organ, structure, or part. **2** the melting or wearing away of an expendable part, such as the heat shield of a space re-entry vehicle on passing through the earth's atmosphere. **3** the wearing away of a rock or glacier. [C15: from Late Latin *ablatiōn-,* from Latin *auferre* to carry away, remove]

ablative (ˈæblətɪv) *Grammar.* ◆ *adj* **1** (in certain inflected languages such as Latin) denoting a case of nouns, pronouns, and adjectives indicating the agent in passive sentences or the instrument, manner, or place of the action described by the verb. ◆ *n* **2a** the ablative case. **2b** a word or speech element in the ablative case.

ablative absolute *n* an absolute construction in Latin grammar in which a governor noun and a modifier in the ablative case function as a sentence modifier; for example, *hostibus victis,* "the enemy having been beaten".

ablator (æbˈleɪtə) *n* the heat shield of a space vehicle, which melts or wears away during re-entry into the earth's atmosphere. [C20: from ABLATION]

ablaut (ˈæblaʊt; *German* ˈaplaut) *n Linguistics.* vowel gradation, esp. in Indo-European languages. See **gradation** (sense 5). [German, coined 1819 by Jakob Grimm from *ab* off + *Laut* sound]

ablaze (əˈbleɪz) *adj* (*postpositive*), *adv* **1** on fire; burning. **2** brightly illuminated. **3** emotionally aroused.

able (ˈeɪbᵊl) *adj* **1** (*postpositive*) having the necessary power, resources, skill, time, opportunity, etc., to do something: *able to swim.* **2** capable; competent; talented: *an able teacher.* **3** *Law.* qualified, competent, or authorized to do some specific act. [C14: ultimately from Latin *habilis* easy to hold, manageable, apt, from *habēre* to have, hold + *-ilis* -ILE]

-able *suffix forming adjectives.* **1** capable of, suitable for, or deserving of (being acted upon as indicated): *enjoyable; pitiable; readable; separable; washable.* **2** inclined to; given to; able to; causing: *comfortable; reasonable; variable.* [via Old French from Latin *-ābilis, -ībilis,* forms of *-bilis,* adjectival suffix] ▸ **-ably** *suffix forming adverbs.* ▸ **-ability** *suffix forming nouns.*

able-bodied *adj* physically strong and healthy; robust.

able-bodied seaman *n* an ordinary seaman, esp. one in the merchant navy, who has been trained in certain skills. Also: **able seaman.** Abbrevs.: **AB, a.b.**

abled (ˈeɪbᵊld) *adj* having a range of physical powers as specified (esp. in the phrases **less abled, differently abled**).

ableism (ˈeɪbᵊlˌɪzəm) *n* discrimination against disabled or handicapped people.

able rating *n* (esp. in the Royal Navy) a rating who is qualified to perform certain duties of seamanship.

abloom (əˈbluːm) *adj* (*postpositive*) in flower; blooming.

ablution (əˈbluːʃən) *n* **1** the ritual washing of a priest's hands or of sacred vessels. **2** (*often pl*) the act of washing (esp. in the phrase **perform one's ablutions**). **3** (*pl*) *Military informal.* a washing place. [C14: ultimately from Latin *ablūere* to wash away] ▸ **abˈlutionary** *adj*

ably (ˈeɪblɪ) *adv* in a competent or skilful manner.

ABM *abbrev. for* antiballistic missile.

Abnaki (æbˈnɑːkɪ) *n* **1** (*pl* **-ki** *or* **-kis**) a member of a North American Indian people formerly living in Maine and Quebec. **2** the language of this people, belonging to the Algonquian family.

abnegate (ˈæbnɪˌgeɪt) *vb (tr)* to deny to oneself; renounce (privileges, pleasure, etc.). [C17: from Latin *abnegāre* to deny] ▸ ˌ**abneˈgation** *n* ▸ ˈ**abneˌgator** *n*

Abney level (ˈæbnɪ) *n* a surveying instrument consisting of a spirit level and a sighting tube, used to measure the angle of inclination of a line from the observer to another point. [C20: named after Sir William *Abney* (1843–1920), British chemist and physicist]

abnormal (æbˈnɔːməl) *adj* **1** not normal; deviating from the usual or typical; extraordinary. **2** *Informal.* odd in behaviour or appearance; strange. [C19: AB-[1] + NORMAL, replacing earlier *anormal* from Medieval Latin *anormalus,* a blend of Late Latin *anōmalus* ANOMALOUS + Latin *abnormis* departing from a rule] ▸ **abˈnormally** *adv*

abnormality (ˌæbnɔːˈmælɪtɪ) *n, pl* **-ties. 1** an abnormal feature, event, etc. **2** a physical malformation; deformity. **3** deviation from the typical or usual; irregularity.

abnormal psychology *n* the study of behaviour patterns that diverge widely from generally accepted norms, esp. those of a pathological nature.

Abo (ˈæbəʊ) *n, pl* **Abos.** *(sometimes not cap.) Austral. informal, often derogatory.* **a** short for **Aborigine. b** *(as modifier): an Abo reserve.*

Åbo (ˈoːbuː) *n* the Swedish name for **Turku.**

aboard (əˈbɔːd) *adv, adj (postpositive), prep* **1** on, in, onto, or into (a ship, train, aircraft, etc.). **2** *Nautical.* alongside (a vessel). **3 all aboard!** a warning to passengers to board a vehicle, ship, etc.

abode[1] (əˈbəʊd) *n* a place in which one lives; one's home. [C17: n formed from ABIDE]

abode[2] (əˈbəʊd) *vb* a past tense and past participle of **abide.**

abohm (æbˈəʊm, ˈæbˌəʊm) *n* the cgs unit of resistance in the electromagnetic system: equivalent to 10^{-9} ohm.

aboideau (ˈæbəˌdəʊ) *or* **aboiteau** (ˈæbəˌtəʊ) *n, pl* **-deaus, -deaux** (-ˌdəʊz) *or* **-teaus, -teaux** (-ˌtəʊz). (in the Canadian Maritimes) **1** a dyke with a sluicegate that allows flood water to drain but keeps the sea water out. **2** a sluicegate in a dyke. [Canadian French]

abolish (əˈbɒlɪʃ) *vb (tr)* to do away with (laws, regulations, customs, etc.); put an end to. [C15: from Old French *aboliss-* (lengthened stem of *abolir*), ultimately from Latin *abolēre* to destroy] ▸ **aˈbolishable** *adj* ▸ **aˈbolisher** *n* ▸ **aˈbolishment** *n*

abolition (ˌæbəˈlɪʃən) *n* **1** the act of abolishing or the state of being abolished; annulment. **2** *(often cap.)* (in British territories) the ending of the slave trade (1807) or the ending of slavery (1833): accomplished after a long campaign led by William Wilberforce. **3** *(often cap.)* (in the U.S.) the emancipation of the slaves, accomplished by the Emancipation Proclamation issued in 1863 and ratified in 1865. [C16: from Latin *abolitio,* from *abolēre* to destroy] ▸ ˌ**aboˈlitionary** *adj* ▸ ˌ**aboˈlitionism** *n* ▸ ˌ**aboˈlitionist** *n, adj*

abomasum (ˌæbəˈmeɪsəm) *n* the fourth and last compartment of the stomach of ruminants, which receives and digests food from the psalterium and passes it on to the small intestine. [C18: New Latin, from AB-[1] + *omāsum* bullock's tripe]

A-bomb *n* short for **atomic bomb.**

abominable (əˈbɒmɪnəbᵊl) *adj* **1** offensive; loathsome; detestable. **2** *Informal.* very bad, unpleasant, or inferior: *abominable weather; abominable workmanship.* [C14: from Latin *abōminābilis,* from *abōminārī* to ABOMINATE] ▸ **aˈbominably** *adv*

abominable snowman *n* a large legendary manlike or apelike creature, alleged to inhabit the Himalayan Mountains. Also called: **yeti.** [a translation of Tibetan *metohkangmi,* from *metoh* foul + *kangmi* snowman]

abominate (əˈbɒmɪˌneɪt) *vb (tr)* to dislike intensely; loathe; detest. [C17: from the past participle of Latin *abōminārī* to regard as an ill omen, from *ab-* away from + *ōmin-,* from OMEN] ▸ **aˈbomiˌnator** *n*

abomination (əˌbɒmɪˈneɪʃən) *n* **1** a person or thing that is disgusting. **2** an action that is vicious, vile, etc. **3** intense loathing.

abondance *(French* abɔ̃dɑ̃s) *n Cards.* a variant spelling of **abundance** (sense 6).

à bon marché *French.* (a bɔ̃ marʃe) *adv* at a bargain price.

aboral (æbˈɔːrəl) *adj Zoology.* away from or opposite the mouth.

aboriginal (ˌæbəˈrɪdʒɪnᵊl) *adj* existing in a place from the earliest known period; indigenous; autochthonous. ▸ ˌ**aboˈriginally** *adv*

Aboriginal (ˌæbəˈrɪdʒɪnᵊl) *adj* **1** of, relating to, or characteristic of the native peoples of Australia. ◆ *n* **2** another word for an Australian **Aborigine.**

USAGE The use of *Aboriginal* to refer to a person can be offensive and should be avoided.

Aboriginality (ˌæbəˌrɪdʒɪˈnælɪtɪ) *n* the state of being Aboriginal, esp. with regard to having a common Aboriginal culture.

aborigine (ˌæbəˈrɪdʒɪnɪ) *n* an original inhabitant of a country or region who has been there from the earliest known times. [C16: back formation from *aborigines,* from Latin: inhabitants of Latium in pre-Roman times, probably representing some tribal name but associated in folk etymology with *ab origine* from the beginning]

Aborigine (ˌæbəˈrɪdʒɪnɪ) *n* **1** Also called: **native Australian, Aboriginal,** (Austral.) **native,** (Austral.) **Black.** a member of a dark-skinned hunting and gathering people who were living in Australia when European settlers arrived. **2** any of the languages of this people. See also **Australian** (sense 3).

USAGE The use of *Aborigine* to refer to a person can be offensive and should be avoided.

aborning (əˈbɔːnɪŋ) *adv U.S.* while being born, developed, or realized (esp. in the phrase **die aborning**). [C20: from A-[2] + *borning,* from BORN]

abort (əˈbɔːt) *vb* **1** to undergo or cause (a woman) to undergo the termination of pregnancy before the fetus is viable. **2** *(tr)* to cause (a fetus) to be expelled from the womb before it is viable. **3** *(intr)* to fail to come to completion; go wrong. **4** *(tr)* to stop the development of; cause to be abandoned. **5** *(intr)* to give birth to a dead or nonviable fetus. **6** (of a space flight, military operation, etc.) to fail or terminate prematurely. **7** *(intr)* (of an organism or part of an organism) to fail to develop into the mature form. ◆ *n* **8** the premature termination or failure of (a space flight, military operation, etc.). [C16: from Latin *abortāre,* from the past participle of *aborīrī* to miscarry, from *ab-* wrongly, badly + *orīrī* to appear, arise, be born]

abortifacient (əˌbɔːtɪˈfeɪʃənt) *adj* **1** causing abortion. ◆ *n* **2** a drug or agent that causes abortion.

abortion (əˈbɔːʃən) *n* **1** an operation or other procedure to terminate pregnancy before the fetus is viable. **2** the premature termination of pregnancy by spontaneous or induced expulsion of a nonviable fetus from the uterus. **3** the products of abortion; an aborted fetus. **4** the arrest of development of an organ. **5** a failure to develop to completion or maturity: *the project proved an abortion.* **6** a person or thing that is deformed. ▸ **aˈbortional** *adj*

abortionist (əˈbɔːʃənɪst) *n* **1** a person who performs abortions, esp. illegally. **2** a person who is in favour of abortion on demand.

abortion pill *n* a drug, such as mifepristone (RU486), used to terminate a pregnancy in its earliest stage.

abortive (əˈbɔːtɪv) *adj* **1** failing to achieve a purpose; fruitless. **2** (of organisms) imperfectly developed; rudimentary. **3** causing abortion; abortifacient.

ABO system *n* a system for classifying human blood on the basis of the presence or absence of two antigens in the red cells: there are four such blood types (A, B, AB, and O).

Aboukir Bay *or* **Abukir Bay** (ˌæbuːˈkɪə) *n* a bay on the N coast of Egypt, where the Nile enters the Mediterranean: site of the Battle of the Nile (1798), in which Nelson defeated the French fleet. Arabic name: **Abu Qîr** (abuˈkiːr).

aboulia (əˈbuːlɪə, -ˈbjuː-) *n* a variant spelling of **abulia.**

abound (əˈbaʊnd) *vb (intr)* **1** to exist or occur in abundance; be plentiful: *a swamp in which snakes abound.* **2** (foll. by *with* or *in*) to be plentifully supplied (with); teem (with): *the gardens abound with flowers; the fields abound in corn.* [C14: via Old French from Latin *abundāre* to overflow, from *undāre* to flow, from *unda* wave]

about (əˈbaʊt) *prep* **1** relating to; concerning; on the subject of. **2** near or close to (in space or time). **3** carried on: *I haven't any money about me.* **4** on every side of; all the way around. **5** active in or engaged in: *she is about her business.* **6 about to. 6a** on the point of; intending to: *she was about to jump.* **6b** *(with a negative)* determined not to: *nobody is about to miss it.* ◆ *adv* **7** approximately; near in number, time, degree, etc.: *about 50 years old.* **8** nearby. **9** here and there; from place to place; in no particular direction: *walk about to keep warm.* **10** all around; on every side. **11** in or to the opposite direction: *he turned about and came back.* **12** in rotation or revolution: *turn and turn about.* **13** used in informal phrases to indicate understatement: *I've had just about enough of your insults; it's about time you stopped.* **14** *Archaic.* in circumference; around. ◆ *adj* **15** *(predicative)* active; astir after sleep: *up and about.* **16** *(predicative)* in existence, current, or in circulation: *there aren't many about nowadays.* [Old English *abūtan, onbūtan* on the outside of, around, from ON + *būtan* outside]

about-ship *vb* **-ships, -shipping, -shipped.** *(intr) Nautical.* to manoeuvre a vessel onto a new tack.

about turn *or U.S.* **about face** *interj* **1** a military command to a formation of men to reverse the direction in which they are facing. ◆ *n* **about-turn** *or U.S.* **about-face. 2** a complete change or reversal, as of opinion, attitude, direction, etc. ◆ *vb* **about-turn** *or U.S.* **about-face. 3** *(intr)* to perform an about-turn.

above (əˈbʌv) *prep* **1** on top of or higher than; over: *the sky above the earth.* **2** greater than in quantity or degree: *above average in weight.* **3** superior to or prior to: *to place honour above wealth.* **4** too honourable or high-minded for: *above petty gossiping.* **5** too respected for; beyond: *above suspicion; above reproach.* **6** too difficult to be understood by: *the talk was above me.* **7** louder or higher than (other noise): *I heard her call above the radio.* **8** in preference to: *I love you above all others.* **9** north of: *which town lies just above London?* **10** upstream from. **11 above all.** most of all; especially. **12 above and beyond.** in addition to. **13 above oneself.** presumptuous or conceited. ◆ *adv* **14** in or to a higher place: *the sky above.* **15a** in a previous place (in something written). **15b** *(in combination): the above-mentioned clause.* **16** higher in rank or position. **17** in or concerned with heaven: *seek the things that are above.* ◆ *n* **18 the above.** something that is above or previously mentioned. ◆ *adj* **19** mentioned or appearing in a previous place (in something written). [Old English *abufan,* from *a-* on + *bufan* above]

above board *adj* (**aboveboard** *when prenominal*), *adv* in the open; without dishonesty, concealment, or fraud.

ab ovo *Latin.* (æb ˈəʊvəʊ) from the beginning. [literally: from the egg]

Abp *or* **abp** *abbrev. for* archbishop.

abr. *abbrev. for:* **1** abridged. **2** abridgment.

abracadabra (ˌæbrəkəˈdæbrə) *interj* **1** a spoken formula, used esp. by conjurors. ◆ *n* **2** a word used in incantations, etc., considered to possess magic powers. **3** gibberish; nonsense. [C17: from Latin: magical word used in certain Gnostic writings, perhaps related to Greek *Abraxas;* see ABRAXAS]

abrade (əˈbreɪd) *vb (tr)* to scrape away or wear down by friction; erode. [C17: from Latin *abrādere* to scrape away, from AB-[1] + *rādere* to scrape] ▸ **aˈbradant** *n* ▸ **aˈbrader** *n*

Abraham (ˈeɪbrəˌhæm, -həm) *n* **1** *Old Testament.* the first of the patriarchs, the father of Isaac and the founder of the Hebrew people (Genesis 11–25). **2 Abraham's bosom.** the place where the just repose after death (Luke 16:22).

abranchiate (əˈbræŋkɪɪt, -ˌeɪt) *or* **abranchial** *adj Zoology.* having no gills. [C19: A-[1] + BRANCHIATE]

abrasion (əˈbreɪʒən) *n* **1** the process of scraping or wearing down by friction. **2** a scraped area or spot; graze. **3** *Geography.* the effect of mechanical erosion of rock, esp. a river bed, by rock fragments scratching and scraping it; wearing down. Compare **attrition** (sense 4f), **corrasion.** [C17: from Medieval Latin *abrāsiōn-*, from the past participle of Latin *abrādere* to ABRADE]

abrasive (ə'breɪsɪv) *n* **1** a substance or material such as sandpaper, pumice, or emery, used for cleaning, grinding, smoothing, or polishing. ◆ *adj* **2** causing abrasion; grating; rough. **3** irritating in manner or personality; causing tension or annoyance. ▸ **a'brasiveness** *n*

abraxas (ə'bræksəs) *or* **abrasax** (ə'bræsəks) *n* an ancient charm composed of Greek letters: originally believed to have magical powers and inscribed on amulets, etc., but from the second century A.D. personified by Gnostics as a deity, the source of divine emanations. [from Greek: invented word]

abreact (ˌæbrɪ'ækt) *vb (tr) Psychoanal.* to alleviate (emotional tension) through abreaction.

abreaction (ˌæbrɪ'ækʃən) *n Psychoanal.* the release and expression of emotional tension associated with repressed ideas by bringing those ideas into consciousness.

abreast (ə'brest) *adj (postpositive)* **1** alongside each other and facing in the same direction. **2** (foll. by *of* or *with*) up to date (with); fully conversant (with).

abri (æ'bri:) *n* a shelter or place of refuge, esp. in wartime. [French, from Latin *apricum* an open place]

abridge (ə'brɪdʒ) *vb (tr)* **1** to reduce the length of (a written work) by condensing or rewriting. **2** to curtail; diminish. **3** *Archaic.* to deprive of (privileges, rights, etc.). [C14: via Old French *abregier* from Late Latin *abbreviāre* to shorten] ▸ **a'bridgable** *or* **a'bridgeable** *adj* ▸ **a'bridger** *n*

abridgment *or* **abridgement** (ə'brɪdʒmənt) *n* **1** a shortened version of a written work. **2** the act of abridging or state of being abridged.

abroach (ə'brəutʃ) *adj (postpositive)* (of a cask, barrel, etc.) tapped; broached. [C14: from Old French *abrochier* from *a-* to + *brochier* to BROACH[1]]

abroad (ə'brɔ:d) *adv* **1** to or in a foreign country or countries. ◆ *adj (postpositive)* **2** (of news, rumours, etc.) in general circulation; current. **3** out in the open. **4** over a wide area. **5** *Archaic.* in error. [C13: from A-[2] + BROAD]

abrogate ('æbrəuˌgeɪt) *vb (tr)* to cancel or revoke formally or officially; repeal; annul. [C16: from Latin *abrogātus* repealed, from AB-[1] + *rogāre* to propose (a law)] ▸ ˌ**abro'gation** *n* ▸ '**abroˌgator** *n*

abrupt (ə'brʌpt) *adj* **1** sudden; unexpected. **2** brusque or brief in speech, manner, etc.; curt. **3** (of a style of writing or speaking) making sharp transitions from one subject to another; disconnected. **4** precipitous; steep. **5** *Botany.* shaped as though a part has been cut off; truncate. **6** *Geology.* (of strata) cropping out suddenly. [C16: from Latin *abruptus* broken off, from AB-[1] + *rumpere* to break] ▸ **ab'ruptly** *adv* ▸ **ab'ruptness** *n*

abruption (ə'brʌpʃən) *n* a breaking off of a part or parts from a mass. [C17: from Latin *abruptio*; see ABRUPT]

Abruzzi (*Italian* a'bruttsi) *n* a region of S central Italy, between the Apennines and the Adriatic: separated from the former administrative region **Abruzzi e Molise** in 1965. Capital: Aquila. Pop.: 1 270 591 (1996 est.). Area: 10 794 sq. km (4210 sq. miles).

ABS *abbrev. for* acrylonitrile–butadiene–styrene: any of a range of tough copolymers used esp. for making moulded articles.

Absalom ('æbsələm) *n Old Testament.* the third son of David, who rebelled against his father and was eventually killed by Joab (II Samuel 15–18).

ABS brake *n* another name for **antilock brake.** [from German *antiblockier System*]

abscess ('æbses, -sɪs) *n* **1** a localized collection of pus formed as the product of inflammation and often caused by bacteria. ◆ *vb* **2** *(intr)* to form such a collection of pus. [C16: from Latin *abscessus* a going away, a throwing off of bad humours, hence an abscess, from *abscēdere* to go away] ▸ '**abscessed** *adj*

abscise (æb'saɪz) *vb* to separate or be separated by abscission. [C17: from Latin *abscisus*, from *abscīdere* to cut off]

abscissa (æb'sɪsə) *n, pl* **-scissas** *or* **-scissae** (-'sɪsi:). the horizontal or *x*-coordinate of a point in a two-dimensional system of Cartesian coordinates. It is the distance from the *y*-axis measured parallel to the *x*-axis. Compare **ordinate.** [C17: New Latin, originally *linea abscissa* a cut-off line]

abscission (æb'sɪʒən, -'sɪʃ-) *n* **1** the separation of leaves, branches, flowers, and bark from plants by the formation of an abscission layer. **2** the act of cutting off. [C17: from Latin *abscissiōn-*, from AB-[1] + *scissiō* a cleaving]

abscission layer *n* a layer of parenchyma cells, bounded on both sides by cork, that is formed at the base of fruit, flower, and leaf stems and under bark before abscission. As the parenchyma disintegrates the organ becomes separated from the plant.

abscond (əb'skɒnd) *vb (intr)* to run away secretly, esp. from an open institution or to avoid prosecution or punishment. [C16: from Latin *abscondere* to hide, put away, from *abs-* AB-[1] + *condere* to stow] ▸ **ab'sconder** *n*

abseil ('æbsaɪl) *vb (intr)* **1** *Mountaineering.* to descend a steep slope or vertical drop by a rope secured from above and coiled around one's body or through karabiners attached to one's body in order to control the speed of descent. **2** to descend by rope from a helicopter. ◆ *n* **3** an instance or the technique of abseiling. ◆ Also called: **rappel.** [C20: from German *abseilen* to descend by a rope, from *ab-* down + *Seil* rope]

absence ('æbsəns) *n* **1** the state of being away. **2** the time during which a person or thing is away. **3** the fact of being without something; lack. [C14: via Old French from Latin *absentia*, from *absēns* a being away]

absent *adj* ('æbsənt). **1** away or not present. **2** lacking; missing. **3** inattentive; absent-minded. ◆ *vb* (æb'sent). **4** *(tr)* to remove (oneself) or keep away. [C14: from Latin *absent-*, stem of *absēns*, present participle of *abesse* to be away] ▸ **ab'senter** *n*

absentee (ˌæbsən'ti:) *n* **a** a person who is absent. **b** *(as modifier)*: *an absentee voter.*

absenteeism (ˌæbsən'ti:ɪzəm) *n* persistent absence from work, school, etc.

absentee landlord *n* a landlord who does not live in or near a property from which he draws an income.

absente reo (æb'sentɪ 'ri:əu) *Law.* in the absence of the defendant. [Latin, literally: the defendant being absent]

absently ('æbsəntlɪ) *adv* in an absent-minded or preoccupied manner; inattentively.

absent-minded *adj* preoccupied; forgetful; inattentive. ▸ ˌ**absent-'mindedly** *adv* ▸ ˌ**absent-'mindedness** *n*

absent without leave *Military.* the full form of **AWOL.**

absinthe *or* **absinth** ('æbsɪnθ) *n* **1** a potent green alcoholic drink, technically a gin, originally having high wormwood content. **2** another name for **wormwood** (the plant). [C15: via French and Latin from Greek *apsinthion* wormwood]

absinthism ('æbsɪnˌθɪzəm) *n Pathol.* a diseased condition resulting from excessive drinking of absinthe.

absit omen *Latin.* ('æbsɪt 'əumen) may the presentiment not become real or take place. [literally: may the (evil) omen be absent]

absolute ('æbsəˌlu:t) *adj* **1** complete; perfect. **2** free from limitations, restrictions, or exceptions; unqualified: *an absolute choice.* **3** having unlimited authority; despotic: *an absolute ruler.* **4** undoubted; certain: *the absolute truth.* **5** not dependent on, conditioned by, or relative to anything else; independent: *an absolute term in logic; the absolute value of a quantity in physics.* **6** pure; unmixed: *absolute alcohol.* **7** (of a grammatical construction) syntactically independent of the main clause, as for example the construction *Joking apart* in the sentence *Joking apart, we'd better leave now.* **8** *Grammar.* (of a transitive verb) used without a direct object, as the verb *intimidate* in the sentence *His intentions are good, but his rough manner tends to intimidate.* **9** *Grammar.* (of an adjective) used as a noun, as for instance *young* and *aged* in the sentence *The young care little for the aged.* **10** *Physics.* **10a** *(postpositive)* (of a pressure measurement) not relative to atmospheric pressure: *the pressure was 5 bar absolute.* Compare **gauge** (sense 18). **10b** denoting absolute or thermodynamic temperature. **11** *Maths.* **11a** Also: **numerical.** (of a value) having a magnitude but no sign. **11b** (of a constant) never changing in value. **11c** (of an inequality) unconditional. **11d** (of a term) not containing a variable. **12** *Law.* (of a court order or decree) coming into effect immediately and not liable to be modified; final. See **decree absolute. 13** *Law.* (of a title to property, etc.) not subject to any encumbrance or condition. ◆ *n* **14** something that is absolute. [C14: from Latin *absolūtus* unconditional, freed from, from *absolvere.* See ABSOLVE]

Absolute ('æbsəˌlu:t) *n (sometimes not cap.)* **1** *Philosophy.* **1a** the ultimate basis of reality. **1b** that which is totally unconditioned, unrestricted, pure, perfect, or complete. **2** (in the philosophy of Hegel) that towards which all things evolve dialectically.

absolute alcohol *n* a liquid containing at least 99 per cent of pure ethanol by weight.

absolute ceiling *n* the maximum height above sea level, usually measured in feet or metres, at which an aircraft can maintain horizontal flight. Compare **service ceiling.**

absolute configuration *n Chem.* the spatial arrangement of atoms or groups in a chemical compound about an asymmetric atom. See **chirality.**

absolute humidity *n* the humidity of the atmosphere expressed as the number of grams of water contained in 1 cubic metre of air. Compare **relative humidity.**

absolute judgment *n Psychol.* any judgment about a single stimulus, e.g. about the value of one of its properties or about whether it is present or absent. Compare **comparative judgment.**

absolutely (ˌæbsə'lu:tlɪ) *adv* **1** in an absolute manner, esp. completely or perfectly. ◆ *sentence substitute.* **2** yes; certainly; unquestionably.

absolute magnitude *n* the magnitude a given star would have if it were situated at a distance of 10 parsecs (32.6 light years) from the earth.

absolute majority *n* a number of votes totalling over 50 per cent, such as the total number of votes or seats obtained by a party that beats the combined opposition. Compare **relative majority.**

absolute monarchy *n* a monarchy without constitutional limits. Compare **constitutional monarchy.**

absolute music *n* music that is not designed to depict or evoke any scene or event. Compare **programme music.**

absolute pitch *n* **1** Also called (not in technical usage): **perfect pitch.** the ability to identify exactly the pitch of a note without comparing it to another. **2** the exact pitch of a note determined by vibration per second.

absolute temperature *n* another name for **thermodynamic temperature.**

absolute threshold *n Psychol.* the minimum intensity of a stimulus at which it can just be perceived. Compare **difference threshold.**

absolute unit *n* **1** a unit of measurement forming part of the electromagnetic cgs system, such as an abampere or abcoulomb. **2** a unit of measurement forming part of a system of units that includes a unit of force defined so that it is independent of the acceleration of free fall.

absolute value *n Maths.* **1** the positive real number equal to a given real but disregarding its sign. Written $|x|$. Where r is positive, $|r| = r = |-r|$. **2** Also called: **modulus.** a measure of the magnitude of a complex number, represented by the length of a vector in the Argand diagram: $|x + iy| = \surd(x^2 + y^2)$, so $|4 + 3i| = 5$.

absolute viscosity *n* a full name for **viscosity,** used to distinguish it from kinematic viscosity and specific viscosity.

absolute zero *n* the lowest temperature theoretically attainable, at which the particles constituting matter would be in the lowest energy states available; the zero of thermodynamic temperature; zero on the International Practical Scale of Temperature: equivalent to –273.15°C or –459.67°F.

absolution (ˌæbsəˈluːʃən) *n* **1** the act of absolving or the state of being absolved; release from guilt, obligation, or punishment. **2** *Christianity.* **2a** a formal remission of sin pronounced by a priest in the sacrament of penance. **2b** the prescribed form of words granting such a remission. [C12: from Latin *absolūtiōn-* acquittal, forgiveness of sins, from *absolvere* to ABSOLVE] ▸ **absolutory** (æbˈsɒljʊtərɪ, -trɪ) *adj*

absolutism (ˈæbsəluːˌtɪzəm) *n* **1** the principle or practice of a political system in which unrestricted power is vested in a monarch, dictator, etc.; despotism. **2** *Philosophy.* **2a** any theory which holds that truth or moral or aesthetic value is absolute and universal and not relative to individual or social differences. Compare **relativism. 2b** the doctrine that reality is unitary and unchanging and that change and diversity are mere illusion. See also **monism** (sense 2). **3** *Christianity.* an uncompromising form of the doctrine of predestination. ▸ **ˈabsoˌlutist** *n, adj*

absolve (əbˈzɒlv) *vb* (*tr*) **1** (usually foll. by *from*) to release from blame, sin, punishment, obligation, or responsibility. **2** to pronounce not guilty; acquit; pardon. [C15: from Latin *absolvere* to free from, from AB-[1] + *solvere* to make loose] ▸ **abˈsolvable** *adj* ▸ **abˈsolver** *n*

absorb (əbˈsɔːb, -ˈzɔːb) *vb* (*tr*) **1** to soak or suck up (liquids). **2** to engage or occupy (the interest, attention, or time) of (someone); engross. **3** to receive or take in (the energy of an impact). **4** *Physics.* to take in (all or part of incident radiated energy) and retain it without reflection or transmission. **5** to take in or assimilate; incorporate. **6** to accept and find a market for (goods, etc.). **7** to pay for as part of a commercial transaction: *the distributor absorbed the cost of transport.* **8** *Chem.* to cause to undergo a process in which one substance, usually a liquid or gas, permeates into or is dissolved by a liquid or solid: *porous solids absorb water; hydrochloric acid absorbs carbon dioxide.* Compare **adsorb.** [C15: via Old French from Latin *absorbēre* to suck, swallow, from AB-[1] + *sorbēre* to suck] ▸ **abˌsorbaˈbility** *n* ▸ **abˈsorbable** *adj*

absorbance (əbˈsɔːbəns, -ˈzɔː-) *n Physics.* a measure of the light-absorbing ability of an object, expressed as the logarithm to base 10 of the reciprocal of the internal transmittance. See **transmittance.**

absorbed (əbˈsɔːbd, -ˈzɔːbd) *adj* engrossed; deeply interested. ▸ **absorbedly** (əbˈsɔːbɪdlɪ, -ˈzɔː-) *adv*

absorbed dose *n* the amount of energy transferred by nuclear or ionizing radiation to a unit mass of absorbing material.

absorbefacient (əbˌsɔːbɪˈfeɪʃənt, -ˌzɔː-) *Med.* ◆ *n* **1** a medicine or other agent that promotes absorption. ◆ *adj* **2** causing or promoting absorption.

absorbent (əbˈsɔːbənt, -ˈzɔː-) *adj* **1** able to absorb. ◆ *n* **2** a substance that absorbs. ▸ **abˈsorbency** *n*

absorbent cotton *n* a U.S. term for **cotton wool** (sense 1).

absorber (əbˈsɔːbə, -ˈzɔː-) *n* **1** a person or thing that absorbs. **2** *Physics.* a material, esp. in a nuclear reactor, that absorbs radiation or causes it to lose energy.

absorbing (əbˈsɔːbɪŋ, -ˈzɔːb-) *adj* occupying one's interest or attention; engrossing; gripping. ▸ **abˈsorbingly** *adv*

absorptance (əbˈsɔːptəns, -ˈzɔːp-) *or* **absorption factor** *n Physics.* a measure of the ability of an object or surface to absorb radiation, equal to the ratio of the absorbed flux to the incident flux. For a plate of material the ratio of the flux absorbed between the entry and exit surfaces to the flux leaving the entry surface is the **internal absorptance.** Symbol: α Compare **reflectance, transmittance.** [C20: ABSORPTION + -ANCE]

absorption (əbˈsɔːpʃən, -ˈzɔːp-) *n* **1** the process of absorbing or the state of being absorbed. **2** *Physiol.* **2a** normal assimilation by the tissues of the products of digestion. **2b** the process of taking up various gases, fluids, drugs, etc., through the mucous membranes or skin. **3** *Physics.* a reduction of the intensity of any form of radiated energy as a result of energy conversion in a medium, such as the conversion of sound energy into heat. **4** *Immunol.* the process of removing superfluous antibodies or antigens from a mixture using a reagent. [C16: from Latin *absorptiōn-*, from *absorbēre* to ABSORB] ▸ **abˈsorptive** *adj*

absorption costing *n* a method of cost accounting in which overheads are apportioned to cost centres, where they are absorbed using predetermined rates. Compare **marginal costing.**

absorption spectrum *n* the characteristic pattern of dark lines or bands that occurs when electromagnetic radiation is passed through an absorbing medium into a spectroscope. The same pattern occurs as coloured lines or bands in the emission spectrum of that medium.

absorptivity (ˌæbsɔːpˈtɪvɪtɪ, -zɔːp-) *n Physics.* a measure of the ability of a material to absorb radiation, equal to the internal absorptance of a homogeneous plate of the material under conditions in which the path of the radiation has unit length and the boundaries of the plate have no influence.

absquatulate (æbˈskwɒtjʊˌleɪt) *vb* (*intr*) to leave; decamp. [C19: humorous formation as if from Latin]

abstain (əbˈsteɪn) *vb* (*intr;* usually foll. by *from*) **1** to choose to refrain: *he abstained from alcohol.* **2** to refrain from voting, esp. in a committee, legislature, etc. [C14: via Old French from Latin *abstinēre,* from *abs-* AB-[1] + *tenēre* to hold, keep] ▸ **abˈstainer** *n*

abstemious (əbˈstiːmɪəs) *adj* moderate or sparing, esp. in the consumption of alcohol or food; temperate. [C17: from Latin *abstēmius,* from *abs-* AB-[1] + *tēm-*, from *tēmētum* intoxicating drink] ▸ **abˈstemiously** *adv* ▸ **abˈstemiousness** *n*

abstention (əbˈstɛnʃən) *n* **1** a voluntary decision not to act; the act of refraining or abstaining. **2** the act of withholding one's vote. [C16: from Late Latin *abstentiōn-*, from Latin *abstinēre.* See ABSTAIN] ▸ **abˈstentious** *adj*

abstergent (əbˈstɜːdʒənt) *adj* cleansing or scouring. [C17: from Latin *abstergent-, abstergens* wiping off, from *abs-* away, off + *tergēre* to wipe]

abstinence (ˈæbstɪnəns) *n* **1** the act or practice of refraining from some action or from the use of something, esp. alcohol. **2** *Chiefly R.C. Church.* the practice of refraining from specific kinds of food or drink, esp. from meat, as an act of penance. [C13: via Old French from Latin *abstinentia,* from *abstinēre* to ABSTAIN] ▸ **ˈabstinent** *adj*

abstract *adj* (ˈæbstrækt). **1** having no reference to material objects or specific examples; not concrete. **2** not applied or practical; theoretical. **3** hard to understand; recondite; abstruse. **4** denoting art characterized by geometric, formalized, or otherwise nonrepresentational qualities. **5** defined in terms of its formal properties: *an abstract machine.* **6** *Philosophy* (of an idea) functioning for some empiricists as the meaning of a general term: *the word "man" does not name all men but the abstract idea of manhood.* ◆ *n* (ˈæbstrækt) **7** a condensed version of a piece of writing, speech, etc.; summary. **8** an abstract term or idea. **9** an abstract painting, sculpture, etc. **10 in the abstract.** without reference to specific circumstances or practical experience. ◆ *vb* (æbˈstrækt). (*tr*) **11** to think of (a quality or concept) generally without reference to a specific example; regard theoretically. **12** to form (a general idea) by abstraction. **13** (ˈæbstrækt). (*also intr*) to summarize or epitomize. **14** to remove or extract. **15** *Euphemistic.* to steal. [C14 (in the sense: extracted): from Latin *abstractus* drawn off, removed from (something specific), from *abs-* AB-[1] + *trahere* to draw]

abstracted (æbˈstræktɪd) *adj* **1** lost in thought; preoccupied. **2** taken out or separated; extracted. ▸ **abˈstractedly** *adv* ▸ **abˈstractedness** *n*

abstract expressionism *n* a school of painting in New York in the 1940s that combined the spontaneity of expressionism with abstract forms in unpremeditated, apparently random, compositions. See also **action painting, tachisme.**

abstraction (æbˈstrækʃən) *n* **1** absence of mind; preoccupation. **2** the process of formulating generalized ideas or concepts by extracting common qualities from specific examples. **3** an idea or concept formulated in this way: *good and evil are abstractions.* **4** *Logic.* an operator that forms a class name or predicate from any given expression. See also **lambda-calculus. 5** an abstract painting, sculpture, etc. **6** the act of withdrawing or removing. ▸ **abˈstractive** *adj* ▸ **abˈstractively** *adv*

abstractionism (æbˈstrækʃəˌnɪzəm) *n* the theory and practice of the abstract, esp. of abstract art. ▸ **abˈstractionist** *n*

abstract noun *n* a noun that refers to an abstract concept, as for example *kindness.* Compare **concrete noun.**

abstract of title *n Property law.* a summary of the ownership of land, showing the original grant, conveyances, and any incumbrances.

abstriction (æbˈstrɪkʃən) *n* the separation and release of a mature spore from a sporophore by the formation of a septum. This process occurs in some fungi. [C17: from Latin AB-[1] + *strictio* a binding, from *stringere* to bind]

abstruse (əbˈstruːs) *adj* not easy to understand; recondite; esoteric. [C16: from Latin *abstrūsus* thrust away, concealed, from *abs-* AB-[1] + *trūdere* to thrust] ▸ **abˈstrusely** *adv* ▸ **abˈstruseness** *n*

absurd (əbˈsɜːd) *adj* **1** at variance with reason; manifestly false. **2** ludicrous; ridiculous. ◆ *n* **3** *Philosophy.* (*sometimes cap.*; often preceded by *the*) the conception of the world, esp. in Existentialist thought, as neither designed nor predictable but irrational and meaningless. ◆ See also **theatre of the absurd.** [C16: via French from Latin *absurdus* dissonant, senseless, from AB-[1] (intensive) + *surdus* dull-sounding, indistinct] ▸ **abˈsurdity** *or* **abˈsurdness** *n* ▸ **abˈsurdly** *adv*

ABTA (ˈæbtə) *n acronym for* Association of British Travel Agents.

Abu-Bekr (əˌbuːˈbɛkə) *or* **Abu-Bakr** (əˌbuːˈbækə) *n* 573–634 A.D., companion and father-in-law of Mohammed; the first caliph of Islam.

Abu Dhabi (ˈæbuː ˈdɑːbɪ) *n* a sheikdom (emirate) of SE Arabia, on the S coast of the Persian Gulf: the chief sheikdom and capital of the United Arab Emirates, consisting principally of the port of Abu Dhabi and a desert hinterland; contains major oilfields. Pop.: 928 360 (1995 est.). Area: 67 350 sq. km (25 998 sq. miles).

Abu Hanifah (ˈæbuː hæˈniːfə) *n* 700–67 A.D., Muslim theologian and teacher of jurisprudence.

Abuja (əˈbuːdʒə) *n* the federal capital of Nigeria, in the centre of the country. Pop.: 350 100 (1996 est.).

Abukir Bay (ˌæbuːˈkɪə) *n* a variant spelling of **Aboukir Bay.**

abulia *or* **aboulia** (əˈbuːlɪə, -ˈbjuː-) *n Psychiatry.* a pathological inability to take decisions. [C19: New Latin, from Greek *aboulia* lack of resolution, from A-[1] + *boulē* will] ▸ **aˈbulic** *adj*

abundance (əˈbʌndəns) *n* **1** a copious supply; great amount. **2** fullness or benevolence: *from the abundance of my heart.* **3** degree of plentifulness. **4** *Chem.* the extent to which an element occurs in the earth's crust or some other specified environment: expressed in parts per million or as a percentage. **5** *Physics.* the ratio of the number of atoms of a specific isotope in a mixture of isotopes of an element to the total number of atoms present: often expressed as a percentage: *the abundance of neon-22 in natural neon is 8.82 per cent.* **6** Also called: **abondance.** a call in solo whist undertaking to make nine tricks. **7** affluence. [C14: via Old French from Latin *abundantia,* from *abundāre* to ABOUND]

abundant (əˈbʌndənt) *adj* **1** existing in plentiful supply. **2** (*postpositive;* foll. by *in*) having a plentiful supply (of). **3** (of a chemical element or mineral) occurring to an extent specified in relation to other elements or minerals in the earth's crust or some other specified environment. **4** (of an isotope) occurring to an extent specified in relation to other isotopes in a mixture of isotopes. [C14: from Latin *abundant-*, present participle of *abundāre* to ABOUND]

abundantly (əˈbʌndəntlɪ) *adv* **1** very: *he made his disagreement with her abundantly clear.* **2** plentifully; in abundance.

ab urbe condita *Latin.* (æb ˈɜːbɪ ˈkɒndɪtə) the full form of **AUC** (sense a). [literally: from the founding of the city]

A bursary *n N.Z.* the higher of two bursaries available for students entering university, polytechnic, etc. Compare **B bursary.**

abuse *vb* (əˈbjuːz). (*tr*) **1** to use incorrectly or improperly; misuse. **2** to maltreat, esp. physically or sexually. **3** to speak insultingly or cruelly to; revile. **4** (*reflexive*) to masturbate. ◆ *n* (ə'bju:s). **5** improper, incorrect, or excessive use; misuse. **6** maltreatment of a person; injury. **7** insulting, contemptuous, or coarse speech. **8** an evil, unjust, or corrupt practice. **9** See **child abuse. 10** *Archaic.* a deception. [C14 (vb): via Old French from Latin *abūsus,* past participle of *abūtī* to misuse, from AB-[1] + *ūtī* to USE] ▸ **a'buser** *n*

Abu Simbel (ˌæbu: 'sɪmbᵊl) *n* a former village in S Egypt: site of two temples of Rameses II, which were moved to higher ground (1966–67) before the area behind the Aswan High Dam was flooded. Also called: **Ipsambul.**

abusive (ə'bju:sɪv) *adj* **1** characterized by insulting or coarse language. **2** characterized by maltreatment. **3** incorrectly used; corrupt. ▸ **a'busively** *adv* ▸ **a'busiveness** *n*

abut (ə'bʌt) *vb* **abuts, abutting, abutted.** (usually foll. by *on, upon,* or *against*) to adjoin, touch, or border on (something) at one end. [C15: from Old French *abouter* to join at the ends, border on; influenced by *abuter* to touch at an end, buttress]

abutilon (ə'bju:tɪlən) *n* any shrub or herbaceous plant of the malvaceous genus *Abutilon,* such as the flowering maple, that have showy white, yellow, or red flowers. [C18: New Latin from Arabic]

abutment (ə'bʌtmənt) *or* **abuttal** *n* **1** the state or process of abutting. **2a** something that abuts. **2b** the thing on which something abuts. **2c** the point of junction between them. **3** *Architect., civil engineering.* a construction that takes the thrust of an arch or vault or supports the end of a bridge.

abuttals (ə'bʌtᵊlz) *pl n Property law.* the boundaries of a plot of land where it abuts against other property.

abutter (ə'bʌtə) *n Property law.* the owner of adjoining property.

abuzz (ə'bʌz) *adj* (*postpositive*) humming, as with conversation, activity, etc.; buzzing.

abvolt ('æbˌvəʊlt) *n* the cgs unit of potential difference in the electromagnetic system; the potential difference between two points when work of 1 erg must be done to transfer 1 abcoulomb of charge from one point to the other: equivalent to 10^{-8} volt.

abwatt ('æbˌwɒt) *n* the cgs unit of power in the electromagnetic system, equal to the power dissipated when a current of 1 abampere flows across a potential difference of 1 abvolt: equivalent to 10^{-7} watt.

aby *or* **abye** (ə'baɪ) *vb* **abys** *or* **abyes, abying, abought.** (*tr*) *Archaic.* to pay the penalty for; redeem. [Old English *ābycgan* to pay for, atone for, from *bycgan* to buy]

Abydos (ə'baɪdɒs) *n* **1** an ancient town in central Egypt: site of many temples and tombs. **2** an ancient Greek colony on the Asiatic side of the Dardanelles (Hellespont): scene of the legend of Hero and Leander.

abysm (ə'bɪzəm) *n* an archaic word for **abyss.** [C13: via Old French from Medieval Latin *abysmus* ABYSS]

abysmal (ə'bɪzməl) *adj* **1** immeasurable; very great: *abysmal stupidity.* **2** *Informal.* extremely bad: *an abysmal film.* ▸ **a'bysmally** *adv*

abyss (ə'bɪs) *n* **1** a very deep or unfathomable gorge or chasm. **2** anything that appears to be endless or immeasurably deep, such as time, despair, or shame. **3** hell or the infernal regions conceived of as a bottomless pit. [C16: via Late Latin from Greek *abussos* bottomless (as in the phrase *abussos limnē* bottomless lake), from A-[1] + *bussos* depth]

abyssal (ə'bɪsəl) *adj* **1** of or belonging to the ocean depths, esp. below 2000 metres (6500 feet): *abyssal zone.* **2** *Geology.* another word for **plutonic.**

Abyssinia (ˌæbɪ'sɪnɪə) *n* a former name for **Ethiopia.** ▸ ˌ**Abys'sinian** *adj, n*

Abyssinian cat *n* a variety of cat with a long body and a short brown coat with black or dark brown markings.

abyssopelagic (əˌbɪsəʊpɛ'lædʒɪk) *adj* referring to or occurring in the region of deep water above the floor of the ocean.

Ac *the chemical symbol for* actinium.

AC *abbrev. for:* **1** alternating current. Compare **DC. 2** ante Christum. [Latin: before Christ] **3** Air Corps. **4** athletic club. **5** Companion of the Order of Australia. **6** appellation d'origine contrôlée: the highest French wine classification; indicates that the wine meets strict requirements concerning area of production, strength, etc. Compare ***VDQS, vin de pays, vin de table.***

a.c. *abbrev. for* (in prescriptions) ante cibum. [Latin: before meals]

a/c *Book-keeping. abbrev. for:* **1** account. **2** account current.

ACA *abbrev. for* Associate of the Institute of Chartered Accountants.

acacia (ə'keɪʃə) *n* **1** any shrub or tree of the tropical and subtropical mimosaceous genus *Acacia,* having compound or reduced leaves and small yellow or white flowers. See also **wattle** (sense 4). **2 false acacia.** another name for **locust** (senses 2, 3). **3 gum acacia.** another name for **gum arabic.** [C16: from Latin, from Greek *akakia,* perhaps related to *akē* point]

academe ('ækəˌdi:m) *n Literary.* **1** any place of learning, such as a college or university. **2 the grove(s) of Academe.** the academic world. [C16: first used by Shakespeare in *Love's Labour's Lost* (1594); see ACADEMY]

academia (ˌækə'di:mɪə) *n* the academic world.

academic (ˌækə'dɛmɪk) *adj* **1** belonging or relating to a place of learning, esp. a college, university, or academy. **2** of purely theoretical or speculative interest: *an academic argument.* **3** excessively concerned with intellectual matters and lacking experience of practical affairs. **4** (esp. of a schoolchild) having an aptitude for study. **5** conforming to set rules and traditions; conventional: *an academic painter.* **6** relating to studies such as languages, philosophy, and pure science, rather than applied, technical, or professional studies. ◆ *n* **7** a member of a college or university. ▸ ˌ**aca'demically** *adv*

academicals (ˌækə'dɛmɪkᵊlz) *pl n* another term for **academic dress.**

academic dress *n* formal dress, usually comprising cap, gown, and hood, worn by university staff and students.

academician (əˌkædə'mɪʃən, ˌækədə-) *n* a member of an academy (sense 1).

academicism (ˌækə'dɛmɪˌsɪzəm) *or* **academism** (ə'kædəˌmɪzəm) *n* adherence to rules and traditions in art, literature, etc.; conventionalism.

academy (ə'kædəmɪ) *n, pl* **-mies. 1** an institution or society for the advancement of literature, art, or science. **2** a school for training in a particular skill or profession: *a military academy.* **3** a secondary school: now used only as part of a name, and often denoting a private school. [C16: via Latin from Greek *akadēmeia* name of the grove where Plato taught, named after the legendary hero *Akadēmos*]

Academy (ə'kædəmɪ) *n* **the. 1a** the grove or garden near Athens where Plato taught in the late 4th century B.C. **1b** the school of philosophy founded by Plato. **1c** the members of this school and their successors. **2** short for the **French Academy, Royal Academy,** etc.

Academy Award *n* the official name for an **Oscar.**

Acadia (ə'keɪdɪə) *n* **1a** the Atlantic Provinces of Canada. **1b** the French-speaking areas of these provinces. **2** (formerly) a French colony in the present-day Atlantic Provinces: ceded to Britain in 1713. ◆ French name: **Acadie** (akadi).

Acadian (ə'keɪdɪən) *adj* **1** denoting or relating to Acadia or its inhabitants. ◆ *n* **2** any of the early French settlers in Nova Scotia, many of whom were deported to Louisiana in the 18th century. See also **Cajun.**

acajou ('ækəˌʒu:) *n* **1** a type of mahogany used by cabinet-makers in France. **2** a less common name for **cashew.** [C18: via French from Portuguese *acajú,* from Tupi]

acalculia (ˌækæl'kju:lɪə) *n Psychol.* an inability to make simple mathematical calculations. [C20: from A-[1] + Latin *calculāre* to calculate]

acaleph ('ækəˌlɛf) *n Obsolete.* any of the coelenterates of the former taxonomic group *Acalephae,* which included the jellyfishes. [C18: from New Latin, from Greek *akalēphē* a sting]

acanthaceous (ˌækən'θeɪʃəs) *adj* **1** of or relating to the *Acanthaceae,* a mainly tropical and subtropical family of flowering plants that includes the acanthus. **2** having spiny or prickly outgrowths.

acanthine (ə'kænθaɪn, -θi:n) *adj* **1** of or resembling an acanthus. **2** decorated with acanthus leaves.

acantho- *or before a vowel* **acanth-** *combining form.* indicating a spine or thorn: *acanthocephalan.* [New Latin from Greek *akanthos* thorn plant, from *akantha* thorn]

acanthocephalan (əˌkænθəʊ'sɛfələn) *n* **1** any of the parasitic wormlike invertebrates of the phylum *Acanthocephala,* the adults of which have a spiny proboscis and live in the intestines of vertebrates. ◆ *adj* **2** of, relating to, or belonging to the *Acanthocephala.*

acanthoid (ə'kænθɔɪd) *adj* resembling a spine; spiny.

acanthopterygian (ˌækənˌθɒptə'rɪdʒɪən) *adj* **1** of, relating to, or belonging to the *Acanthopterygii,* a large group of teleost fishes having spiny fin rays. The group includes most saltwater bony fishes. ◆ *n* **2** any fish belonging to the *Acanthopterygii.* ◆ Compare **malacopterygian.** [C19: from New Latin *Acanthopterygii,* from ACANTHO- + Greek *pterúgion* fin]

acanthous (ə'kænθəs) *adj* another term for **spinous.**

acanthus (ə'kænθəs) *n, pl* **-thuses** *or* **-thi** (-θaɪ). **1** any shrub or herbaceous plant of the genus *Acanthus,* native to the Mediterranean region but widely cultivated as ornamental plants, having large spiny leaves and spikes of white or purplish flowers: family *Acanthaceae.* See also **bear's-breech. 2** a carved ornament based on the leaves of the acanthus plant, esp. as used on the capital of a Corinthian column. [C17: New Latin, from Greek *akanthos,* from *akantha* thorn, spine]

a cappella (ɑ: kə'pɛlə) *adj, adv Music.* without instrumental accompaniment. [Italian: literally, according to (the style of the) chapel]

Acapulco (ˌækə'pʊlkəʊ; *Spanish* aka'pulko) *n* a port and resort in SW Mexico, in Guerrero state. Pop.: 515 374 (1990). Official name: **Acapulco de Juárez** (*Spanish* de 'xwares).

acariasis (ˌækə'raɪəsɪs) *n* infestation of the hair follicles and skin with acarids, esp. mites. [C19: New Latin. See ACARUS, -IASIS]

acaricide (ə'kærɪˌsaɪd) *n* any preparation for killing acarids.

acarid ('ækərɪd) *or* **acaridan** (ə'kærɪdᵊn) *n* **1** any of the small arachnids of the order *Acarina* (or *Acari*), which includes the ticks and mites. ◆ *adj* **2** of or relating to the order *Acarina.* [C19: from ACARUS]

acaroid ('ækəˌrɔɪd) *adj* resembling a mite or tick. [C19: see ACARUS, -OID]

acaroid gum *or* **resin** *n* a red alcohol-soluble resin that exudes from various species of grass tree, esp. *Xanthorrhoea hastilis,* and is used in varnishes, for coating paper, etc. Also called: **gum accroides.** [C19 *acaroid,* of uncertain origin (apparently not related to ACARUS)]

acarology (ˌækə'rɒlədʒɪ) *n* the study of mites and ticks.

acarpellous *or U.S.* **acarpelous** (eɪ'kɑ:pələs) *adj* (of flowers) having no carpels.

acarpous (eɪ'kɑ:pəs) *adj* (of plants) producing no fruit. [from Greek *akarpos,* from A-[1] + *karpos* fruit]

acarus ('ækərəs) *n, pl* **-ri** (-ˌraɪ). any of the free-living mites of the widely distributed genus *Acarus,* several of which, esp. *A. siro,* are serious pests of stored flour, grain, etc. [C17: New Latin, from Greek *akari* a small thing, a mite]

ACAS *or* **Acas** ('eɪkæs) *n* (in Britain) *acronym for* Advisory Conciliation and Arbitration Service.

acatalectic (æˌkætə'lɛktɪk) *Prosody.* ◆ *adj* **1** having the necessary number of feet or syllables, esp. having a complete final foot. ◆ *n* **2** a verse having the full number of syllables. [C16: via Late Latin from Greek *akatalēktikos.* See A-[1], CATALECTIC]

acaudal (eɪ'kɔ:dᵊl) *or* **acaudate** *adj Zoology.* having no tail.

acaulescent (ˌækɔ:'lɛsᵊnt) *adj* having no visible stem or a very short one.

acauline ('ækɔ:ˌlaɪn) *or* **acaulose** *adj Biology.* having no stem.

ACC (in New Zealand) *abbrev. for* Accident Compensation Corporation.

acc. *abbrev. for:* **1** *Commerce.* acceptance. **2** accompanied. **3** according. **4** *Book-keeping.* account. **5** *Grammar.* accusative.

ACCA *abbrev. for* Associate of the Chartered Association of Certified Accountants.

Accad ('ækæd) *n* a variant spelling of **Akkad.**

Accademia (*Italian* akka'dɛmja) *n* an art gallery in Venice housing a collection of paintings by Venetian masters from the 13th to 18th centuries. Full name: **Galleria dell' Accademia** (*Italian* galle'ria dell akka'dɛmja).

Accardo (*Italian* ak'kardo) *n* **Salvatore.** born 1941, Italian violinist and conductor.

accede (æk'siːd) *vb (intr;* usually foll. by *to)* **1** to assent or give one's consent; agree. **2** to enter upon or attain (to an office, right, etc.): *the prince acceded to the throne.* **3** *International law.* to become a party (to an agreement between nations, etc.), as by signing a treaty. [C15: from Latin *accēdere* to approach, agree, from *ad-* to + *cēdere* to go, yield] ▸ **ac'cedence** *n* ▸ **ac'ceder** *n*

accel. *abbrev. for* accelerando.

accelerando (æk,sɛlə'rændəʊ) *Music.* ◆ *adj, adv* **1** (to be performed) with increasing speed. ◆ *n, pl* **-dos. 2** an increase in speed. [Italian]

accelerant (æk'sɛlərənt) *n Chem.* another name for **accelerator** (sense 3). [C20: from Latin from *accelerāns,* present participle of *accelerāre* to go faster]

accelerate (æk'sɛlə,reɪt) *vb* **1** to go, occur, or cause to go or occur more quickly; speed up. **2** *(tr)* to cause to happen sooner than expected. **3** *(tr)* to increase the velocity of (a body, reaction, etc.); cause acceleration. [C16: from Latin *accelerātus,* from *accelerāre* to go faster, from *ad-* (intensive) + *celerāre* to hasten, from *celer* swift] ▸ **ac'celerable** *adj* ▸ **ac'celerative** *or* **ac'celeratory** *adj*

acceleration (æk,sɛlə'reɪʃən) *n* **1** the act of accelerating or the state of being accelerated. **2** the rate of increase of speed or the rate of change of velocity. Symbol: *a*

acceleration of free fall *n* the acceleration of a body falling freely in a vacuum in the earth's gravitational field: the standard value is 9.806 65 metres per second per second or 32.174 feet per second per second. Symbol: *g* Also called: **acceleration due to gravity, acceleration of gravity.**

accelerator (æk'sɛlə,reɪtə) *n* **1** a device for increasing speed, esp. a pedal for controlling the fuel intake in a motor vehicle; throttle. **2** Also called (not in technical usage): **atom smasher.** *Physics.* a machine for increasing the kinetic energy of subatomic particles or atomic nuclei and focusing them on a target. **3** *Chem.* a substance that increases the speed of a chemical reaction, esp. one that increases the rate of vulcanization of rubber, the rate of development in photography, the rate of setting of synthetic resins, or the rate of setting of concrete; catalyst. **4** *Economics.* (in an economy) the relationship between the rate of change in output or sales and the consequent change in the level of investment. **5** *Anatomy.* a muscle or nerve that increases the rate of a function.

accelerometer (æk,sɛlə'rɒmɪtə) *n* an instrument for measuring acceleration, esp. of an aircraft or rocket.

accent *n* ('æksənt). **1** the characteristic mode of pronunciation of a person or group, esp. one that betrays social or geographical origin. **2** the relative prominence of a spoken or sung syllable, esp. with regard to stress or pitch. Compare **pitch**[1] (sense 28), **stress** (sense 3). **3** a mark (such as ', ˌ, ´ or `) used in writing to indicate the stress or prominence of a syllable. Such a mark may also be used to indicate that a written syllable is to be pronounced, esp. when such pronunciation is not usual, as in *turnèd.* **4** any of various marks or symbols conventionally used in writing certain languages to indicate the quality of a vowel, or for some other purpose, such as differentiation of homographs. See **acute** (sense 10), **grave**[2] (sense 5), **circumflex. 5** (in some languages, such as Chinese) any of the tones that have phonemic value in distinguishing one word from another. Compare **tone** (sense 7). **6** rhythmic stress in verse or prose. **7** *Music.* **7a** stress placed on certain notes in a piece of music, indicated by a symbol printed over the note concerned. **7b** the rhythmic pulse of a piece or passage, usually represented as the stress on the first beat of each bar. See also **syncopation. 8** *Maths.* either of two superscript symbols indicating a specific unit, such as feet (′), inches (″), minutes of arc (′), or seconds of arc (″). **9** a distinctive characteristic of anything, such as taste, pattern, style, etc. **10** particular attention or emphasis: *an accent on learning.* **11** a strongly contrasting detail: *a blue rug with red accents.* ◆ *vb* (æk'sɛnt). *(tr)* **12** to mark with an accent in writing, speech, music, etc. **13** to lay particular emphasis or stress on. [C14: via Old French from Latin *accentus,* from *ad-* to + *cantus* chant, song. The Latin is a rendering of Greek *prosōidia* a song sung to music, the tone of a syllable]

accentor (æk'sɛntə) *n* any small sparrow-like songbird of the genus *Prunella,* family *Prunellidae,* which inhabit mainly mountainous regions of Europe and Asia. See also **hedge sparrow.**

accentual (æk'sɛntʃʊəl) *adj* **1** of, relating to, or having accents; rhythmic. **2** *Prosody.* of or relating to verse based on the number of stresses in a line rather than on the number of syllables. Compare **quantitative.** ▸ **ac'centually** *adv*

accentuate (æk'sɛntʃʊ,eɪt) *vb (tr)* to stress or emphasize. ▸ **ac,centu'ation** *n*

accept (ək'sɛpt) *vb (mainly tr)* **1** to take or receive (something offered). **2** to give an affirmative reply to: *to accept an invitation.* **3** to take on the responsibilities, duties, etc., of: *he accepted office.* **4** to tolerate or accommodate oneself to. **5** to consider as true or believe in (a philosophy, theory, etc.): *I cannot accept your argument.* **6** *(may take a clause as object)* to be willing to grant or believe: *you must accept that he lied.* **7** to receive with approval or admit, as into a community, group, etc. **8** *Commerce.* to agree to pay (a bill, draft, shipping document, etc.), esp. by signing. **9** to receive as adequate, satisfactory, or valid. **10** to receive, take, or hold (something applied, inserted, etc.). **11** *(intr;* sometimes foll. by *of) Archaic.* to take or receive an offer, invitation, etc. [C14: from Latin *acceptāre,* from *ad-* to + *capere* to take] ▸ **ac'cepter** *n*

acceptable (ək'sɛptəbᵊl) *adj* **1** satisfactory; adequate. **2** pleasing; welcome. **3** tolerable. ▸ **ac,cepta'bility** *or* **ac'ceptableness** *n* ▸ **ac'ceptably** *adv*

acceptance (ək'sɛptəns) *n* **1** the act of accepting or the state of being accepted or acceptable. **2** favourable reception; approval. **3** (often foll. by *of)* belief (in) or assent (to). **4** *Commerce.* **4a** a formal agreement by a debtor to pay a draft, bill, etc. **4b** the document so accepted. Compare **bank acceptance. 5** *(pl) Austral. and N.Z.* a list of horses accepted as starters in a race. **6** *Contract law.* words or conduct by which a person signifies his assent to the terms and conditions of an offer or agreement.

acceptant (ək'sɛptənt) *adj* receiving willingly; receptive.

acceptation (,æksɛp'teɪʃən) *n* the accepted meaning, as of a word, phrase, etc.

accepted (ək'sɛptɪd) *adj* commonly approved or recognized; customary; established. ▸ **ac'ceptedly** *adv*

accepting house *n* a financial institution that guarantees a bill of exchange, as a result of which it can be discounted on more favourable terms.

acceptor (ək'sɛptə) *n* **1** *Commerce.* the person or organization on which a draft or bill of exchange is drawn after liability has been accepted, usually by signature. **2** Also called: **acceptor impurity.** *Electronics.* an impurity, such as gallium, added to a semiconductor material to increase its p-type conductivity by increasing the number of holes in the semiconductor. Compare **donor** (sense 5). **3** *Electronics.* a circuit tuned to accept a particular frequency. **4** *Chem.* the atom or group that accepts electrons in a coordinate bond.

access ('æksɛs) *n* **1** the act of approaching or entering. **2** the condition of allowing entry, esp. (of a building or room) allowing entry by wheelchairs, prams, etc. **3** the right or privilege to approach, reach, enter, or make use of something. **4** a way or means of approach or entry. **5** *(modifier)* designating programmes made by the general public as distinguished from those made by professional broadcasters: *access television.* **6** a sudden outburst or attack, as of rage or disease. ◆ *vb* **7** to gain access to; make accessible or available. **8** *(tr) Computing.* **8a** to obtain or retrieve (information) from a storage device. **8b** to place (information) in a storage device. See also **direct access, sequential access.** [C14: from Old French or from Latin *accessus* an approach, from *accēdere* to ACCEDE]

accessary (ək'sɛsərɪ) *n, pl* **-ries,** *adj Law.* a less common spelling of **accessory.** ▸ **ac'cessarily** *adv* ▸ **ac'cessariness** *n*

access course *n* (in Britain) an intensive course of study for people without academic qualifications that enables them to apply for higher education.

accessible (ək'sɛsəbᵊl) *adj* **1** easy to approach, enter, or use. **2 accessible to.** likely to be affected by; open to; susceptible to. **3** obtainable; available. **4** *Logic.* (of a possible world) surveyable from some other world so that the truth value of statements about it can be known. A statement *possibly p* is true in a world W if and only if *p* is true in some worlds accessible to W. ▸ **ac,cessi'bility** *n* ▸ **ac'cessibly** *adv*

accession (ək'sɛʃən) *n* **1** the act of entering upon or attaining to an office, right, condition, etc. **2** an increase due to an addition. **3** an addition, as to a collection. **4** *Property law.* **4a** an addition to land or property by natural increase or improvement. **4b** the owner's right to the increased value of such land. **5** *International law.* the formal acceptance of a convention or treaty. **6** agreement; consent. **7** a less common word for **access** (sense 1). ◆ *vb* **8** *(tr)* to make a record of (additions to a collection). ▸ **ac'cessional** *adj*

accession number *n Library science.* the number given to record a new addition to a collection.

accessorius (,æksɛs'ɔːrɪəs) *n Anatomy.* a muscle or nerve that has an augmenting action.

accessorize *or* **accessorise** (ək'sɛsə,raɪz) *vb (tr)* to add accessories to: *accessorize a plain jacket with feminine jewellery.*

accessory (ək'sɛsərɪ) *n, pl* **-ries. 1** a supplementary part or object, as of a car, appliance, etc. **2** *(often pl)* a small accompanying item of dress, esp. of women's dress. **3** a person who incites someone to commit a crime or assists the perpetrator of a crime, either before or during its commission. ◆ *adj* **4** supplementary; additional; subordinate. **5** assisting in or having knowledge of an act, esp. a crime. [C17: from Late Latin *accessōrius:* see ACCESS] ▸ **accessorial** (,æksɛ'sɔːrɪəl) *adj* ▸ **ac'cessorily** *adv* ▸ **ac'cessoriness** *n*

accessory fruit *n* another name for **pseudocarp.**

accessory nerve *n* either one of the eleventh pair of cranial nerves, which supply the muscles of the head, shoulders, larynx, and pharynx and the viscera of the abdomen and thorax.

accessory shoe *n Photog.* a bracket on top of a camera to which a flash unit or other accessory may be fitted.

access road *n* a road providing a means of entry into a region or of approach to another road, esp. a motorway.

access time *n Computing.* the time required to retrieve a piece of stored information.

acciaccatura (ɑː,tʃɑːkɑː'tʊərə) *n, pl* **-ras** *or* **-re** (-reɪ, -riː). **1** a small grace note melodically adjacent to a principal note and played simultaneously with or immediately before it. **2** (in modern music) a very short appoggiatura. [C18: Italian: literally, a crushing sound]

accidence ('æksɪdəns) *n* inflectional morphology; the part of grammar concerned with changes in the form of words by internal modification or by affixation, for the expression of tense, person, case, number, etc. [C15: from Latin *accidentia* accidental matters, hence inflections of words, from *accidere* to happen. See ACCIDENT]

accident ('æksɪdənt) *n* **1** an unforeseen event or one without an apparent cause. **2** anything that occurs unintentionally or by chance; chance; fortune: *I met him by accident.* **3** a misfortune or mishap, esp. one causing injury or death. **4** Also called: **adjunct.** *Logic, philosophy.* a nonessential attribute or characteristic of something (as opposed to substance). **5** *Metaphysics.* a property as contrasted with the substance in which it inheres. **6** *Geology.* a surface irregularity in a natural formation, esp. in a rock formation or a river system [C14: via Old French from Latin *accident-* chance, happening, from the present participle of *accidere* to befall, happen, from *ad-* to + *cadere* to fall]

accidental (ˌæksɪˈdɛntᵊl) *adj* **1** occurring by chance, unexpectedly, or unintentionally. **2** nonessential; incidental. **3** *Music.* denoting sharps, flats, or naturals that are not in the key signature of a piece. **4** *Logic.* (of a property) not essential; contingent. ◆ *n* **5** an incidental, nonessential, or supplementary circumstance, factor, or attribute. **6** *Music.* a symbol denoting a sharp, flat, or natural that is not a part of the key signature. ► ˌ**acciˈdentally** *adv*

accident insurance *n* insurance providing compensation for accidental injury or death.

accident proneness *n* the unconscious tendency, thought to exist in some people, to involve themselves in a large number of accidents. ► ˈ**accident-ˌprone** *adj*

accidie (ˈæksɪdɪ) *or* **acedia** *n* spiritual sloth; apathy; indifference. [in use C13 to C16 and revived C19: via Late Latin from Greek *akēdia,* from A-[1] + *kēdos* care]

accipiter (ækˈsɪpɪtə) *n* any hawk of the genus *Accipiter,* typically having short rounded wings and a long tail. [C19: New Latin, from Latin: hawk]

accipitrine (ækˈsɪpɪˌtraɪn, -trɪn) *adj* **1** Also: **accipitral** (ækˈsɪpɪtrəl). of, relating to, or resembling a hawk; rapacious. **2** of, relating to, or belonging to the subfamily *Accipitrinae,* which includes the hawks.

acclaim (əˈkleɪm) *vb* **1** (*tr*) to acknowledge publicly the excellence of (a person, act, etc.). **2** to salute with cheering, clapping, etc.; applaud. **3** (*tr*) to acknowledge publicly that (a person) has (some position, quality, etc.): *they acclaimed him king.* ◆ *n* **4** an enthusiastic approval, expression of enthusiasm, etc. [C17: from Latin *acclāmāre* to shout at, shout applause, from *ad-* to + *clamāre* to shout] ► **acˈclaimer** *n*

acclamation (ˌækləˈmeɪʃən) *n* **1** an enthusiastic reception or exhibition of welcome, approval, etc. **2** an expression of approval by a meeting or gathering through shouts or applause. **3** *Canadian.* an instance of electing or being elected without opposition: *there were two acclamations in the 1985 election.* **4 by acclamation. 4a** by an overwhelming majority without a ballot. **4b** *Canadian.* (of an election or electoral victory) without opposition: *he won by acclamation.* ► **acclamatory** (əˈklæmətərɪ, -trɪ) *adj*

acclimatize, acclimatise (əˈklaɪməˌtaɪz), *or* **acclimate** (əˈklaɪmeɪt, ˈæklɪˌmeɪt) *vb* to adapt or become accustomed to a new climate or environment. ► **acˈclimaˌtizable, acˈclimaˌtisable,** *or* **acˈclimatable** *adj* ► **acˌclimatiˈzation, acˌclimatiˈsation,** *or* ˌ**accliˈmation** *n* ► **acˈclimaˌtizer** *or* **acˈclimaˌtiser** *n*

acclivity (əˈklɪvɪtɪ) *n, pl* **-ties.** an upward slope, esp. of the ground. Compare **declivity.** [C17: from Latin *acclīvitās,* from *acclīvis* sloping up, steep] ► **acˈclivitous** *or* **acclivous** (əˈklaɪvəs) *adj*

accolade (ˈækəˌleɪd, ˌækəˈleɪd) *n* **1** strong praise or approval; acclaim. **2** an award or honour. **3** the ceremonial gesture used to confer knighthood, originally an embrace, now a touch on the shoulder with a sword. **4** a rare word for **brace** (sense 7). **5** *Architect.* a curved ornamental moulding, esp. one having the shape of an ogee arch. [C17: via French and Italian from Vulgar Latin *accollāre* (unattested) to hug; related to Latin *collum* neck]

accommodate (əˈkɒməˌdeɪt) *vb* **1** (*tr*) to supply or provide, esp. with lodging or board and lodging. **2** (*tr*) to oblige or do a favour for. **3** to adjust or become adjusted; adapt. **4** (*tr*) to bring into harmony; reconcile. **5** (*tr*) to allow room for; contain. **6** (*tr*) to lend money to, esp. on a temporary basis until a formal loan has been arranged. [C16: from Latin *accommodāre* to make fit, from *ad-* to + *commodus* having the proper measure] ► **acˈcommoˌdative** *adj*

accommodating (əˈkɒməˌdeɪtɪŋ) *adj* willing to help; kind; obliging. ► **acˈcommoˌdatingly** *adv*

accommodation (əˌkɒməˈdeɪʃən) *n* **1** lodging or board and lodging. **2** adjustment, as of differences or to new circumstances; adaptation, settlement, or reconciliation. **3** something fulfilling a need, want, etc.; convenience or facility. **4** *Physiol.* the automatic or voluntary adjustment of the thickness of the lens of the eye for far or near vision. **5** willingness to help or oblige. **6** *Commerce.* a loan, usually made as an act of favour by a bank before formal credit arrangements are agreed.

accommodation address *n* an address on letters, etc., to a person or business that does not wish or is not able to receive post at a permanent or actual address.

accommodation bill *n Commerce.* a bill of exchange cosigned by a guarantor: designed to strengthen the acceptor's credit.

accommodation ladder *n Nautical.* a flight of stairs or a ladder for lowering over the side of a ship for access to and from a small boat, pier, etc.

accommodation platform *or* **rig** *n* a platform or semisubmersible rig specially built or adapted to act as living accommodation for offshore personnel in the oil industry.

accompaniment (əˈkʌmpənɪmənt, əˈkʌmpnɪ-) *n* **1** something that accompanies or is served or used with something else. **2** something inessential or subsidiary that is added, as for ornament or symmetry. **3** *Music.* a subordinate part for an instrument, voices, or an orchestra.

accompanist (əˈkʌmpənɪst, əˈkʌmpnɪst) *or U.S.* (*sometimes*) **accompanyist** (əˈkʌmpəniːɪst) *n* a person who plays a musical accompaniment for another performer, esp. a pianist accompanying a singer.

accompany (əˈkʌmpənɪ, əˈkʌmpnɪ) *vb* **-nies, -nying, -nied. 1** (*tr*) to go along with, so as to be in company with or escort. **2** (*tr; foll. by with*) to supplement: *the food is accompanied with a very hot mango pickle.* **3** (*tr*) to occur, coexist, or be associated with. **4** to provide a musical accompaniment for (a performer). [C15: from Old French *accompaignier,* from *compaing* COMPANION[1]] ► **acˈcompanier** *n*

accomplice (əˈkɒmplɪs, əˈkʌm-) *n* a person who helps another in committing a crime. [C15: from *a complice,* interpreted as one word. See COMPLICE]

accomplish (əˈkɒmplɪʃ, əˈkʌm-) *vb* (*tr*) **1** to manage to do; achieve. **2** to conclude successfully; complete. [C14: from Old French *acomplir* to complete, ultimately from Latin *complēre* to fill up. See COMPLETE] ► **acˈcomplishable** *adj* ► **acˈcomplisher** *n*

accomplished (əˈkɒmplɪʃt, əˈkʌm-) *adj* **1** successfully completed; achieved. **2** expert; proficient.

accomplishment (əˈkɒmplɪʃmənt, əˈkʌm-) *n* **1** the act of carrying out or achieving. **2** something achieved or successfully completed. **3** (*often pl*) skill or talent. **4** (*often pl*) social grace, style, and poise.

accord (əˈkɔːd) *n* **1** agreement; conformity; accordance (esp. in the phrase **in accord with**). **2** consent or concurrence of opinion. **3 with one accord.** unanimously. **4** pleasing relationship between sounds, colours, etc.; harmony. **5** a settlement of differences, as between nations; compromise. **6 of one's own accord.** voluntarily. ◆ *vb* **7** to be or cause to be in harmony or agreement. **8** (*tr*) to grant; bestow. [C12: via Old French from Latin *ad-* to + *cord-,* stem of *cor* heart] ► **acˈcordable** *adj* ► **acˈcorder** *n*

accordance (əˈkɔːdəns) *n* **1** conformity; agreement; accord (esp. in the phrase **in accordance with**). **2** the act of granting; bestowal: *accordance of rights.*

accordant (əˈkɔːdᵊnt) *adj* (*usually postpositive* and foll. by *with*) in conformity or harmony. ► **acˈcordantly** *adv*

according (əˈkɔːdɪŋ) *adj* **1** (foll. by *to*) in proportion; in relation: *salary will be according to age and experience.* **2** (foll. by *to*) on the report (of); as stated (by). **3** (foll. by *to*) in conformity (with); in accordance (with): *everything went according to plan.* **4** (foll. by *as*) depending (on whether). **5** *Not standard.* dependent on: *it's all according where you want to go.*

accordingly (əˈkɔːdɪŋlɪ) *adv* **1** in an appropriate manner; suitably. ◆ *sentence connector.* **2** consequently.

accordion (əˈkɔːdɪən) *n* **1** a portable box-shaped instrument of the reed organ family, consisting of metallic reeds that are made to vibrate by air from a set of bellows controlled by the player's hands. Notes are produced by means of stud-like keys. **2** short for **piano accordion.** [C19: from German *Akkordion,* from *Akkord* harmony, chord] ► **acˈcordionist** *n*

accordion pleats *pl n* tiny knife pleats.

accost (əˈkɒst) *vb* **1** (*tr*) to approach, stop, and speak to (a person), as to ask a question, accuse of a crime, solicit sexually, etc. ◆ *n* **2** *Rare.* a greeting. [C16: from Late Latin *accostāre* to place side by side, from Latin *costa* side, rib] ► **acˈcostable** *adj*

accouchement *French.* (akuʃmɑ̃; *English* əˈkuːʃmɒnt) *n* childbirth or the period of confinement. [C19: from *accoucher* to put to bed, to give birth. See COUCH]

accoucheur *French.* (akuʃœr) *or* (*fem*) ***accoucheuse*** (akuʃøz) *n* an obstetrician or midwife. [literally: one who is present at the bedside]

account (əˈkaʊnt) *n* **1** a verbal or written report, description, or narration of some occurrence, event, etc. **2** an explanation of conduct, esp. one made to someone in authority. **3** ground; basis; consideration (often in the phrases **on this** (**that, every, no,** etc.) **account, on account of**). **4** importance, consequence, or value: *of little account.* **5** assessment; judgment. **6** profit or advantage: *to turn an idea to account.* **7** part or behalf (only in the phrase **on one's** *or* **someone's account**). **8** *Finance.* **8a** a business relationship between a bank, department store, stockbroker, etc., and a depositor, customer, or client permitting the latter certain banking or credit services. **8b** the sum of money deposited at a bank. **8c** the amount of credit available to the holder of an account. **8d** a record of these. **9** a statement of monetary transactions with the resulting balance. **10** (on the London Stock Exchange) the period, ordinarily of a fortnight's duration, in which transactions formerly took place and at the end of which settlements were made. **11** *Book-keeping.* a chronological list of debits and credits relating to a specified asset, liability, expense, or income of a business and forming part of the ledger. **12a** a regular client or customer, esp. a firm that purchases commodities on credit. **12b** an area of business assigned to another: *they transferred their publicity account to a new agent.* **13 call** (*or* **bring**) **to account. 13a** to insist on explanation. **13b** to rebuke; reprimand. **13c** to hold responsible. **14 give a good** (**bad,** etc.) **account of oneself.** to perform well (badly, etc.): *he gave a poor account of himself in the examination.* **15 on account. 15a** on credit. **15b** Also: **to account.** as partial payment. **16 on account of.** (*prep*) because of; by reason of. **17 take account of** *or* **take into account.** to take into consideration; allow for. **18 settle** *or* **square accounts with. 18a** to pay or receive a balance due. **18b** to get revenge on (someone). **19** See **bank account** or **credit account.** ◆ *vb* **20** (*tr*) to consider or reckon: *he accounts himself poor.* [C13: from Old French *acont,* from *conter, compter* to COUNT[1]]

accountable (əˈkaʊntəbᵊl) *adj* **1** responsible to someone or for some action; answerable. **2** able to be explained. ► **acˌcountaˈbility** *n* ► **acˈcountably** *adv*

accountancy (əˈkaʊntənsɪ) *n* the profession or business of an accountant.

accountant (əˈkaʊntənt) *n* a person concerned with the maintenance and audit of business accounts and the preparation of consultant reports in tax and finance.

account day *n* (on the London Stock Exchange) the day on which deliveries and payments relating to transactions made during the preceding account are made.

account executive *n* an executive in an advertising agency or public relations firm who manages a client's account.

account for *vb* (*intr, prep*) **1** to give reasons for (an event, act, etc.). **2** to make or provide a reckoning of (expenditure, payments, etc.). **3** to be responsible for destroying, killing, or putting (people, aircraft, etc.) out of action.

accounting (əˈkaʊntɪŋ) *n* **a** the skill or practice of maintaining and auditing accounts and preparing reports on the assets, liabilities, etc., of a business. **b** (*as modifier*): *an accounting period; accounting entity.*

account payable *n Accounting, U.S.* a current liability account showing amounts payable by a firm to suppliers for purchases of materials, stocks, or services on credit.

account receivable *n Accounting, U.S.* a current asset account showing amounts payable to a firm by customers who have made purchases of goods and services on credit.

accouplement (əˈkʌpᵊlmənt) *n* a timber joist or beam that serves as a tie or support. [C15: French, from *accoupler,* from Latin *copulāre* to COUPLE]

accoutre *or U.S.* **accouter** (əˈkuːtə) *vb (tr; usually passive)* to provide with equipment or dress, esp. military. [C16: from Old French *accoustrer* to equip with clothing, ultimately related to Latin *consuere* to sew together]

accoutrement (əˈkuːtrəmənt, əˈkuːtə-) *or U.S.* **accouterment** (əˈkuːtərmənt) *n* **1** equipment worn by soldiers in addition to their clothing and weapons. **2** (*usually pl*) clothing, equipment, etc.; trappings: *the correct accoutrements for any form of sport.*

Accra (əˈkrɑː) *n* the capital of Ghana, a port on the Gulf of Guinea: built on the site of three 17th-century trading fortresses founded by the English, Dutch, and Danish. Pop.: 949 113 (1988 est.).

accredit (əˈkrɛdɪt) *vb (tr)* **1** to ascribe or attribute. **2** to give official recognition to; sanction; authorize. **3** to certify or guarantee as meeting required standards. **4** (often foll. by *at* or *to*) **4a** to furnish or send (an envoy, etc.) with official credentials. **4b** to appoint (someone) as an envoy, etc. **5** *N.Z.* to pass (a candidate) for university entrance on school recommendation without external examination: *there are six accrediting schools in the area.* [C17: from French *accréditer,* from the phrase *mettre à crédit* to put to CREDIT] ▸ **ac͵crediˈtation** *n*

accrescent (æˈkrɛsᵊnt) *adj Botany.* (of a calyx or other part) continuing to grow after flowering. [C18: from Latin *accrēscere* to continue to grow, from *crēscere* to grow]

accrete (əˈkriːt) *vb* **1** to grow or cause to grow together; be or become fused. **2** to make or become bigger, as by addition. ◆ *adj* **3** (of plant organs) grown together. [C18: back formation from ACCRETION]

accretion (əˈkriːʃən) *n* **1** any gradual increase in size, as through growth or external addition. **2** something added, esp. extraneously, to cause growth or an increase in size. **3** the growing together of normally separate plant or animal parts. **4** *Pathol.* **4a** abnormal union or growing together of parts; adhesion. **4b** a mass of foreign matter collected in a cavity. **5** *Law.* an increase in the share of a beneficiary in an estate, as when a co-beneficiary fails to take his share. **6** *Astronomy.* the process in which matter under the influence of gravity is attracted to and increases the size of a celestial body. **7** *Geology.* the process in which a continent is enlarged by the tectonic movement and deformation of the earth's crust. [C17: from Latin *accretiō* increase, from *accrēscere.* See ACCRUE] ▸ **acˈcretive** *or* **acˈcretionary** *adj*

accretionary wedge *or* **prism** *n Geology* a body of deformed sediments, wedge-shaped in two dimensions or prism-shaped in three dimensions, that has been scraped off the surface of the oceanic lithosphere as it moves downward beneath a continent. The sediments are added to the continental edge.

Accrington (ˈækrɪŋtən) *n* a town in NW England, in SE Lancashire. Pop.: 36 466 (1991).

accrual (əˈkruːəl) *n* **1** the act of accruing. **2** something that has accrued. **3** *Accounting* a charge incurred in one accounting period that has not been paid by the end of it.

accrue (əˈkruː) *vb* **-crues, -cruing, -crued.** (*intr*) **1** to increase by growth or addition, esp. (of capital) to increase by periodic addition of interest. **2** (often foll. by *to*) to fall naturally (to); come into the possession (of); result (for). **3** *Law.* (of a right or demand) to become capable of being enforced. [C15: from Old French *accreue* growth, ultimately from Latin *accrēscere* to increase, from *ad-* to, in addition + *crēscere* to grow]

ACCT *abbrev. for* Association of Cinematograph, Television, and Allied Technicians.

acculturate (əˈkʌltʃə͵reɪt) *vb* (of a cultural or social group) to assimilate the cultural traits of another group. [C20: from AD- + CULTURE + -ATE[1]] ▸ **ac͵culturˈation** *n*

accumbent (əˈkʌmbənt) *adj* **1** *Botany.* (of plant parts and plants) lying against some other part or thing. **2** a rare word for **recumbent.** [C18: from Latin *accumbere* to recline] ▸ **acˈcumbency** *n*

accumulate (əˈkjuːmjʊ͵leɪt) *vb* to gather or become gathered together in an increasing quantity; amass; collect. [C16: from Latin *accumulātus,* past participle of *accumulāre* to heap up, from *cumulus* a heap] ▸ **acˈcumulable** *adj* ▸ **acˈcumulative** *adj* ▸ **acˈcumulatively** *adv* ▸ **acˈcumulativeness** *n*

accumulation (ə͵kjuːmjʊˈleɪʃən) *n* **1** the act or process of collecting together or becoming collected. **2** something that has been collected, gathered, heaped, etc. **3** *Finance.* **3a** the continuous growth of capital by retention of interest or earnings. **3b** (in computing the yield on a bond purchased at a discount) the amount that is added to each yield to bring the cost of the bond into equality with its par value over its life. Compare **amortization** (sense 2). **4** the taking of a first and an advanced university degree simultaneously.

accumulation point *n Maths.* another name for **limit point.**

accumulator (əˈkjuːmjʊ͵leɪtə) *n* **1** Also called: **battery, storage battery.** a rechargeable device for storing electrical energy in the form of chemical energy, consisting of one or more separate secondary cells. **2** *Horse racing, Brit.* a collective bet, esp. on four or more races, in which the stake and winnings on each successive race are carried forward to become the stake on the next, so that both stakes and winnings accumulate progressively so long as the bet continues to be a winning one. **3a** a register in a computer or calculator used for holding the results of a computation or data transfer. **3b** a location in a computer store in which arithmetical results are produced.

accuracy (ˈækjʊrəsɪ) *n, pl* **-cies. 1** faithful measurement or representation of the truth; correctness; precision. **2** *Physics, chem.* the degree of agreement between a measured value and the standard or accepted value for that measurement.

accurate (ˈækjərɪt) *adj* **1** faithfully representing or describing the truth. **2** showing a negligible or permissible deviation from a standard: *an accurate ruler.* **3** without error; precise; meticulous. **4** *Maths.* **4a** (to *n* significant digits) correctly representing the first *n* digits of the given number following the first nonzero digit, but approximating to the nearest digit in the final position: *since* $\pi = 3.14159\ldots$, *the approximation 3.1416 is accurate to 5 significant digits.* **4b** (to *n* decimal places) giving the first *n* digits after the decimal point without further approximation: $\pi = 3.1415$ *is in this sense accurate to 4 decimal places.* [C16: from Latin *accūrātus,* past participle of *accūrāre* to perform with care, from *cūra* care] ▸ **ˈaccurately** *adv* ▸ **ˈaccurateness** *n*

accursed (əˈkɜːsɪd, əˈkɜːst) *or* **accurst** (əˈkɜːst) *adj* **1** under or subject to a curse; doomed. **2** (*prenominal*) hateful; detestable; execrable. [Old English *ācursod,* past participle of *ācursian* to put under a CURSE] ▸ **accursedly** (əˈkɜːsɪdlɪ) *adv* ▸ **acˈcursedness** *n*

accusal (əˈkjuːzᵊl) *n* another word for **accusation.**

accusation (͵ækjʊˈzeɪʃən) *n* **1** an allegation that a person is guilty of some fault, offence, or crime; imputation. **2** a formal charge brought against a person stating the crime that he is alleged to have committed.

accusative (əˈkjuːzətɪv) *adj* **1** *Grammar.* denoting a case of nouns, pronouns, and adjectives in inflected languages that is used to identify the direct object of a finite verb, of certain prepositions, and for certain other purposes. See also **objective** (sense 5). **2** another word for **accusatorial.** ◆ *n* **3** *Grammar.* **3a** the accusative case. **3b** a word or speech element in the accusative case. [C15: from Latin; in grammar, from the phrase *cāsus accūsātīvus* accusative case, a mistaken translation of Greek *ptōsis aitiatikē* the case indicating causation. See ACCUSE] ▸ **accusatival** (ə͵kjuːzəˈtaɪvᵊl) *adj* ▸ **acˈcusatively** *adv*

accusatorial (ə͵kjuːzəˈtɔːrɪəl) *or* **accusatory** (əˈkjuːzətərɪ, -trɪ, ͵ækjʊˈzeɪtərɪ) *adj* **1** containing or implying blame or strong criticism. **2** *Law.* denoting criminal procedure in which the prosecutor is distinct from the judge and the trial is conducted in public. Compare **inquisitorial** (sense 3).

accuse (əˈkjuːz) *vb* to charge (a person or persons) with some fault, offence, crime, etc.; impute guilt or blame. [C13: via Old French from Latin *accūsāre* to call to account, from *ad-* to + *causa* lawsuit] ▸ **acˈcuser** *n* ▸ **acˈcusing** *adj* ▸ **acˈcusingly** *adv*

accused (əˈkjuːzd) *n* (preceded by *the*) *Law.* the defendant or defendants appearing on a criminal charge.

accustom (əˈkʌstəm) *vb (tr;* usually foll. by *to*) to make (oneself) familiar (with) or used (to), as by practice, habit, or experience. [C15: from Old French *acostumer,* from *costume* CUSTOM]

accustomed (əˈkʌstəmd) *adj* **1** usual; customary. **2** (*postpositive;* foll. by *to*) used or inured (to). **3** (*postpositive;* foll. by *to*) in the habit (of): *accustomed to walking after meals.*

Accutron (ˈækjuː͵trɒn) *n Trademark.* a type of watch in which the balance wheel and hairspring are replaced by a tuning fork kept in vibration by a tiny internal battery.

AC/DC *adj Informal.* (of a person) bisexual. [C20: humorous reference to electrical apparatus that is adaptable for ALTERNATING CURRENT and DIRECT CURRENT]

ace (eɪs) *n* **1** any die, domino, or any of four playing cards with one spot. **2** a single spot or pip on a playing card, die, etc. **3** *Tennis.* a winning serve that the opponent fails to reach. **4** *Golf, chiefly U.S.* a hole in one. **5** a fighter pilot accredited with destroying several enemy aircraft. **6** *Informal.* an expert or highly skilled person: *an ace at driving.* **7 an ace up one's sleeve** *or* **an ace in the hole.** a hidden and powerful advantage. **8 hold all the aces.** to have all the advantages or power. **9 play one's ace.** to use one's best weapon or resource. **10 within an ace of.** almost to the point of: *he came within an ace of winning.* ◆ *adj* **11** *Informal.* superb; excellent. ◆ *vb* **12** (*tr*) *Tennis.* to serve an ace against. **13** *Golf, chiefly U.S.* to play (a hole) in one stroke. **14** *U.S. and Canadian.* to perform extremely well or score very highly in (an examination, etc.) [C13: via Old French from Latin *as* a unit, perhaps from a Greek variant of *heis* one]

ACE (eɪs) *n acronym for:* **1** (in Britain) Advisory Centre for Education; a private organization offering advice on schools to parents. **2** Allied Command Europe. **3** angiotensin-converting enzyme. See **ACE inhibitor.**

-acea *suffix forming plural proper nouns.* denoting animals belonging to a class or order: *Crustacea* (class); *Cetacea* (order). [New Latin, from Latin, neuter plural of *-āceus* -ACEOUS]

-aceae *suffix forming plural proper nouns.* denoting plants belonging to a family: *Liliaceae; Ranunculaceae.* [New Latin, from Latin, feminine plural of *-āceus* -ACEOUS]

acedia (əˈsiːdɪə) *n* another word for **accidie.**

ACE inhibitor *n* any one of a class of drugs, including captopril and enalpapril, that cause the arteries to widen by preventing the synthesis of angiotensin: used to treat high blood pressure and heart failure. [C20: from *a(ngiotensin-)c(onverting) e(nzyme) inhibitor*]

Aceldama (əˈsɛldəmə) *n New Testament.* the place near Jerusalem that was bought with the 30 pieces of silver paid to Judas for betraying Jesus (Matthew 27:8; Acts 1:19). [C14: from Aramaic *haqēl demā* field of blood]

acellular (eɪˈsɛljʊlə) *adj Biology.* not made up of or containing cells.

acentric (eɪˈsɛntrɪk) *adj* **1** without a centre. **2** not on centre; eccentric. **3** *Genetics.* (of a chromosome or chromosome fragment) lacking a centromere. ◆ *n* **4** an acentric chromosome or fragment.

-aceous *suffix forming adjectives.* relating to, belonging to, having the nature of, or resembling: *herbaceous; larvaceous.* [New Latin, from Latin *-āceus* of a certain kind; related to *-āc, -āx,* adjectival suffix]

acephalous (əˈsɛfələs) *adj* **1** having no head or one that is reduced and indistinct, as certain insect larvae. **2** having or recognizing no ruler or leader. [C18: via Medieval Latin from Greek *akephalos.* See A-[1], -CEPHALIC]

acer (ˈeɪsə) *n* any tree or shrub of the genus *Acer,* often cultivated for their brightly coloured foliage. See also **maple.**

ACER *abbrev. for* Australian Council for Educational Research.
acerate ('æsəˌreɪt, -rɪt) *adj* another word for **acerose.** [C19: from Latin *ācer* sharp + -ATE[1]]
acerbate ('æsəˌbeɪt) *vb (tr)* **1** to embitter or exasperate. **2** to make sour or bitter. [C18: from Latin *acerbātus,* past participle of *acerbāre* to make sour]
acerbic (ə'sɜːbɪk) *adj* harsh, bitter, or astringent; sour. [C17: from Latin *acerbus* sour, bitter]
acerbity (ə'sɜːbɪtɪ) *n, pl* **-ties. 1** vitriolic or embittered speech, temper, etc. **2** sourness or bitterness of taste.
acerose ('æsəˌrəʊs, -ˌrəʊz) *or* **acerous** *adj* shaped like a needle, as pine leaves. [C18: from Latin *acerōsus* full of chaff (erroneously used by Linnaeus as if derived from *ācer* sharp)]
acervate (ə'sɜːvɪt, -ˌveɪt) *adj Botany.* growing in heaps or clusters. [C19: from Latin *acervātus,* from *acervāre* to heap up, from *acervus* a heap] ▸ **a'cervately** *adv*
acescent (ə'sɛsᵊnt) *adj* slightly sour or turning sour. [C18: from Latin *acēscent-,* from *acēscere* to become sour, from *ācer* sharp] ▸ **a'cescence** *or* **a'cescency** *n*
acetabulum (ˌæsɪ'tæbjʊləm) *n, pl* **-la** (-lə). **1** the deep cuplike cavity on the side of the hipbone that receives the head of the thighbone. **2** a round muscular sucker in flatworms, leeches, and cephalopod molluscs. **3** the aperture in the thorax of an insect that holds the leg. [Latin: vinegar cup, hence a cuplike cavity, from *acētum* vinegar + *-abulum,* suffix denoting a container]
acetal ('æsɪˌtæl) *n* **1** a colourless volatile liquid used as a solvent and in perfumes. Formula: $CH_3CH(OC_2H_5)_2$. **2** any organic compound containing the group $-CH(OR_1)OR_2$, where R_1 and R_2 are other organic groups. [C19: from German *Azetal,* from ACETO- + ALCOHOL]
acetaldehyde (ˌæsɪ'tældɪˌhaɪd) *n* a colourless volatile pungent liquid, miscible with water, used in the manufacture of organic compounds and as a solvent and reducing agent. Formula: CH_3CHO. Systematic name: **ethanal.**
acetamide (ˌæsɪ'tæmaɪd, ə'sɛtɪˌmaɪd) *or* **acetamid** (ˌæsɪ'tæmɪd, ə'sɛtɪmɪd) *n* a white or colourless soluble deliquescent crystalline compound, used in the manufacture of organic chemicals. Formula: CH_3CONH_2. [C19: from German *Azetamid,* from ACETO- + AMIDE]
acetanilide (ˌæsɪ'tænɪˌlaɪd) *or* **acetanilid** (ˌæsɪ'tænɪlɪd) *n* a white crystalline powder used in the manufacture of dyes and rubber and as an analgesic in medicine. Formula: $C_6H_5NHCOCH_3$. [C19: from ACETO- + ANILINE + -IDE]
acetate ('æsɪˌteɪt) *n* **1** any salt or ester of acetic acid, containing the monovalent ion CH_3COO^- or the group CH_3COO-. Systematic name: **ethanoate. 2** *(modifier)* consisting of, containing, or concerned with the group CH_3COO-: *acetate group or radical.* **3** short for **acetate rayon** *or* **cellulose acetate. 4** a sound recording disc composed of an acetate lacquer coating on an aluminium or plastic base: used for demonstration or other short-term purposes. [C19: from ACETIC + -ATE[1]] ▸ **'aceˌtated** *adj*
acetate rayon *n* a synthetic textile fibre made from cellulose acetate. Also called: **acetate.**
acetic (ə'siːtɪk, ə'sɛt-) *adj* of, containing, producing, or derived from acetic acid or vinegar. [C19: from Latin *acētum* vinegar]
acetic acid *n* a colourless pungent liquid, miscible with water, widely used in the manufacture of acetic anhydride, vinyl acetate, plastics, pharmaceuticals, dyes, etc. Formula: CH_3COOH. Systematic name: **ethanoic acid.** See also **glacial acetic acid, vinegar.**
acetic anhydride *n* a colourless pungent liquid used in the manufacture of cellulose and vinyl acetates for synthetic fabrics. Formula: $(CH_3CO)_2O$.
acetify (ə'sɛtɪˌfaɪ) *vb* **-fies, -fying, -fied.** to become or cause to become acetic acid or vinegar. ▸ **aˌcetifi'cation** *n* ▸ **a'cetiˌfier** *n*
aceto- *or before a vowel* **acet-** *combining form.* containing an acetyl group or derived from acetic acid: *acetone.* [from Latin *acētum* vinegar]
acetometer (ˌæsɪ'tɒmɪtə) *n* a device for measuring the concentration of acetic acid in a solution, esp. in vinegar.
acetone ('æsɪˌtəʊn) *n* a colourless volatile flammable pungent liquid, miscible with water, used in the manufacture of chemicals and as a solvent and thinner for paints, varnishes, and lacquers. Formula: CH_3COCH_3. Systematic name: **propanone.** [C19: from German *Azeton,* from ACETO- + -ONE] ▸ **acetonic** (ˌæsɪ'tɒnɪk) *adj*
acetone body *n* another name for **ketone body.**
acetophenetidin (əˌsiːtəʊfə'nɛtɪdɪn) *n* another name for **phenacetin.**
acetous ('æsɪtəs, ə'siː-) *or* **acetose** ('æsɪˌtəʊs, -ˌtəʊz) *adj* **1** containing, producing, or resembling acetic acid or vinegar. **2** tasting like vinegar. [C18: from Late Latin *acētōsus* vinegary, from *acētum* vinegar]
acetum (ə'siːtəm) *n* **1** another name for **vinegar. 2** a solution that has dilute acetic acid as solvent. [Latin]
acetyl ('æsɪˌtaɪl, ə'siːtaɪl) *n (modifier)* of, consisting of, or containing the monovalent group CH_3CO-: *acetyl group or radical.* [C19: from ACET(IC) + -YL] ▸ **acetylic** (ˌæsɪ'tɪlɪk) *adj*
acetylate (ə'sɛtɪˌleɪt) *vb* **1** *(tr)* to introduce an acetyl group into (a chemical compound). **2** *(intr)* (of a chemical compound) to gain or suffer substitution of an acetyl group. ▸ **aˌcety'lation** *n*
acetyl chloride *n* a colourless pungent liquid used as an acetylating agent. Formula: CH_3COCl. Also called: **ethanoyl chloride.**
acetylcholine (ˌæsɪtaɪl'kəʊliːn, -lɪn) *n* a chemical substance secreted at the ends of many nerve fibres, esp. in the autonomic nervous system, and responsible for the transmission of nervous impulses. Formula: $C_7H_{17}NO_3$.
acetylcholinesterase (ə'siːtaɪlˌkəʊliːn'ɛstəˌreɪz,'æsɪtaɪl-) *n* an enzyme in nerve cells that is responsible for the destruction of acetylcholine and thus for switching off excitation of the nerve.
acetylene (ə'sɛtɪˌliːn) *n* **1** a colourless soluble flammable gas used in the manufacture of organic chemicals and in cutting and welding metals. Formula: C_2H_2. Systematic name: **ethyne. 2a** another name for **alkyne. 2b** *(as modifier)*: *acetylene series.* ▸ **acetylenic** (əˌsɛtɪ'lɛnɪk) *adj*
acetylide (ə'sɛtɪˌlaɪd) *n* any of a class of carbides in which the carbon is present as a diatomic divalent ion (C_2^{2-}). They are formally derivatives of acetylene.
acetylsalicylic acid (ˌæsɪtaɪlˌsælɪ'sɪlɪk, ə'siːtaɪl-) *n* the chemical name for **aspirin.**
acey-deucy ('eɪsɪ'djuːsɪ) *n* a form of backgammon.
ACGI *abbrev. for* Associate of the City and Guilds Institute.
ach (ɑːx) *interj Scot.* an expression of surprise, impatience, disgust, etc. Also: **och.**
Achaea (ə'kiːə) *or* **Achaia** (ə'kaɪə) *n* **1** a department of Greece, in the N Peloponnese. Capital: Patras. Pop.: 300 078 (1991). Area: 3209 sq. km (1239 sq. miles). Modern Greek name: **Akhaïa. 2** a province of ancient Greece, in the N Peloponnese on the Gulf of Corinth: enlarged as a Roman province in 27 B.C.
Achaean (ə'kiːən) *or* **Achaian** (ə'kaɪən) *n* **1** a member of a principal Greek tribe in the Mycenaean era. **2** a native or inhabitant of the later Greek province of Achaea. ◆ *adj* **3** of or relating to Achaea or the Achaeans.
Achaean League *n* a confederation of Achaean cities formed in the early third century B.C., which became a political and military force in Greece, directed particularly against Macedonian domination of the Peloponnesus.
Achaemenid (ə'kiːmənɪd, ə'kɛm-) *n, pl* **Achaemenids, Achaemenidae** (ˌækɪ'mɛnɪˌdiː), *or* **Achaemenides** (ˌækɪ'mɛnɪˌdiːz). any member of a Persian dynasty of kings, including Cyrus the Great, that ruled from about 550 to 331 B.C., when Darius III was overthrown by Alexander the Great. [from Greek, after *Akhaimenēs,* name of the founder]
achalasia (ˌækə'leɪzɪə) *n Pathol.* failure of the cardiac sphincter of the oesophagus to relax, resulting in difficulty in swallowing. [New Latin, from A-[1] + Greek *chalasis* relaxation]
acharya (ˌa'tʃærɪə) *n Hinduism.* a prominent religious teacher and spiritual guide. [from Sanskrit, literally: teacher]
Achates (ə'keɪtiːz) *n* **1** *Classical myth.* Aeneas' faithful companion in Virgil's *Aeneid.* **2** a loyal friend.
ache (eɪk) *vb (intr)* **1** to feel, suffer, or be the source of a continuous dull pain. **2** to suffer mental anguish. ◆ *n* **3** a continuous dull pain. [Old English *ācan* (vb), *æce* (n), Middle English *aken* (vb), *ache* (n). Compare BAKE, BATCH] ▸ **'aching** *adj* ▸ **'achingly** *adv*
Achebe (ə'tʃeɪbɪ) *n* **Chinua.** born 1930, Nigerian novelist. His works include *Things Fall Apart* (1958), *A Man of the People* (1966), and *Anthills of the Savannah* (1987).
Achelous (ˌækɪ'ləʊəs) *n Classical myth.* a river god who changed into a snake and a bull while fighting Hercules but was defeated when Hercules broke off one of his horns.
achene *or* **akene** (ə'kiːn) *n* a dry one-seeded indehiscent fruit with the seed distinct from the fruit wall. It may be smooth, as in the buttercup, or feathery, as in clematis. [C19: from New Latin *achaenium* that which does not yawn or open, from A-[1] + Greek *khainein* to yawn] ▸ **a'chenial** *or* **a'kenial** *adj*
Achernar ('eɪkəˌnɑː) *n* the brightest star in the constellation Eridanus, visible only in the S hemisphere. Visual magnitude: 0.6; spectral type: B5; distance: 66 light years. [from Arabic *ākhīr al-nahr,* literally: end of the river, alluding to the star's location in the constellation]
Acheron ('ækəˌrɒn) *n Greek myth.* **1** one of the rivers in Hades over which the souls of the dead were ferried by Charon. Compare **Styx. 2** the underworld or Hades.
Acheson ('ætʃɪsən) *n* **Dean (Gooderham).** 1893–1971, U.S. lawyer and statesman: secretary of state (1949–53) under President Truman.
Acheulian *or* **Acheulean** (ə'ʃuːlɪən, -jən) *Archaeol.* ◆ *n* **1** (in Europe) the period in the Lower Palaeolithic following the Abbevillian, represented by the use of soft hammerstones in hand axe production made of chipped stone, bone, antler, or wood. The Acheulian dates from the Riss glaciation. **2** (in Africa) the period represented by every stage of hand axe development. ◆ *adj* **3** of or relating to this period. [C20: after *St. Acheul,* town in northern France]
à cheval *French.* (a ʃəval) *adv* (of a bet, esp. in roulette) made on two adjacent numbers, cards, etc. [literally: on horseback]
achieve (ə'tʃiːv) *vb (tr)* **1** to bring to a successful conclusion; accomplish; attain. **2** to gain as by hard work or effort: *to achieve success.* [C14: from Old French *achever* to bring to an end, from the phrase *a chef* to a head, to a conclusion] ▸ **a'chievable** *adj* ▸ **a'chiever** *n*
achievement (ə'tʃiːvmənt) *n* **1** something that has been accomplished, esp. by hard work, ability, or heroism. **2** successful completion; accomplishment. **3** *Heraldry.* a less common word for **hatchment.**
achievement age *n Psychol.* the age at which a child should be able to perform a standardized test successfully. Compare **mental age.**
achievement quotient *n Psychol.* a measure of ability derived by dividing an individual's achievement age by his actual age. Abbrev.: **AQ.**
achievement test *n Psychol.* a test designed to measure the effects that learning and teaching have on individuals.
achillea (ˌækɪ'liːə) *n* any plant of the southern temperate genus *Achillea,* with white, yellow, or purple flowers, some species of which are widely grown as garden plants: family *Compositae.* See also **sneezewort, yarrow.** [from ACHILLES, who was credited with discovering medicinal properties in the plant]
Achilles (ə'kɪliːz) *n Greek myth.* Greek hero, the son of Peleus and the sea goddess Thetis: in the *Iliad* the foremost of the Greek warriors at the siege of Troy. While he was a baby his mother plunged him into the river Styx making his body invulnerable except for the heel by which she held him. After slaying Hector, he was killed by Paris who wounded him in the heel. ▸ **Achillean** (ˌækɪ'liːən) *adj*
Achilles heel *n* a small but fatal weakness.

Achilles tendon *n* the fibrous cord that connects the muscles of the calf to the heelbone.

Achill Island ('ækɪl) *n* an island in the Republic of Ireland, off the W coast of Co. Mayo. Area: 148 sq. km (57 sq. miles). Pop.: 2853 (1991).

achimenes (ˌækɪ'miːniːz) *n* any plant of the S American tuberous-rooted perennial genus *Achimenes,* with showy red, blue, or white tubular flowers, some of which are grown as greenhouse plants: family *Gesneriaceae.* [from Latin *achaemenis,* from Greek *achaimenis,* a species of euphorbia]

Achitophel (ə'kɪtəˌfɛl) *n Bible.* the Douay spelling of **Ahithophel.**

achlamydeous (ˌæklə'mɪdɪəs) *adj* (of flowers such as the willow) having neither petals nor sepals. [C19: from Greek *a-* not, without + *chlamys* cloak]

ach-laut ('æklaut, 'æx-) *n* (*sometimes cap.*) *Phonetics.* the voiceless velar fricative sound that is written as *ch* in Scottish *loch* or in German *ach,* often allophonic with the ich-laut. See also **ich-laut.** [from German, from *ach* ah + *Laut* sound]

achlorhydria (ˌeɪklɔː'haɪdrɪə) *n* a marked reduction or virtual absence of free hydrochloric acid from the gastric juice. [C20: New Latin; see A-[1], CHLORO-, HYDRO-]

achondrite (eɪ'kɒndraɪt) *n* a rare stony meteorite that consists mainly of silicate minerals and has the texture of igneous rock but contains no chondrules. Compare **chondrite.** ▶ **achondritic** (ˌeɪkɒn'drɪtɪk) *adj*

achondroplasia (eɪˌkɒndrəʊ'pleɪzɪə) *n* a skeletal disorder, characterized by failure of normal conversion of cartilage into bone, that begins during fetal life and results in dwarfism. [C20: New Latin; see A-[1], CHONDRO-, -PLASIA] ▶ **achondroplastic** (eɪˌkɒndrəʊ'plæstɪk) *adj*

achromat ('ækrəˌmæt) *n* **1** Also called: **achromatic lens.** a lens designed to bring light of two chosen wavelengths to the same focal point, thus reducing chromatic aberration. Compare **apochromat. 2** a person who has no colour vision at all and can distinguish only black, white, and grey. The condition is very rare.

achromatic (ˌækrə'mætɪk) *adj* **1** without colour. **2** capable of reflecting or refracting light without chromatic aberration. **3** *Cytology.* **3a** not staining with standard dyes. **3b** of or relating to achromatin. **4** *Music.* **4a** involving no sharps or flats. **4b** another word for **diatonic. 5** denoting a person who is an achromat. ▶ ˌ**achro'matically** *adv* ▶ **achromatism** (ə'krəʊməˌtɪzəm) *or* **achromaticity** (əˌkrəʊmə'tɪsɪtɪ) *n*

achromatic colour *n Physics.* colour, such as white, black, and grey, that is devoid of hue. See **colour** (sense 2).

achromatin (ə'krəʊmətɪn) *n* the material of the nucleus of a cell that does not stain with basic dyes. Compare **chromatin.**

achromatize *or* **achromatise** (ə'krəʊmətaɪz) *vb* (*tr*) to make achromatic; to remove colour from. ▶ **aˌchromati'zation** *or* **aˌchromati'sation** *n*

achromatous (ə'krəʊmətəs) *adj* having little or no colour or less than is normal.

achromic (ə'krəʊmɪk) *or* **achromous** *adj* colourless.

achy ('eɪkɪ) *adj* **achier, achiest.** affected by a continuous dull pain; aching.

ach-y-fi (ˌaxə'viː, ˌax-) *interj Welsh dialect.* an expression of disgust or abhorrence. [Welsh, probably from *ach, achy* general exclamation of disgust + *fi* I, me]

acicula (ə'sɪkjʊlə) *n, pl* **-lae** (-ˌliː). a needle-shaped part, such as a spine, prickle, or crystal. [C19: New Latin, diminutive of *acus* needle] ▶ **a'cicular** *adj*

aciculate (ə'sɪkjʊlɪt, -ˌleɪt) *or* **aciculated** *adj* **1** having aciculae. **2** marked with or as if with needle scratches.

aciculum (ə'sɪkjʊləm) *n, pl* **-lums** *or* **-la** (-lə). a needle-like bristle that provides internal support for the appendages (chaetae) of some polychaete worms. [C19: New Latin; see ACICULA]

acid ('æsɪd) *n* **1** any substance that dissociates in water to yield a sour corrosive solution containing hydrogen ions, having a pH of less than 7, and turning litmus red. See also **Lewis acid. 2** a sour-tasting substance. **3** a slang name for **LSD.** ◆ *adj* **4** *Chem.* **4a** of, derived from, or containing acid: *an acid radical.* **4b** being or having the properties of an acid: *sodium bicarbonate is an acid salt.* **5** sharp or sour in taste. **6** cutting, sharp, or hurtful in speech, manner, etc.; vitriolic; caustic. **7** (of rain, snow, etc.) containing pollutant acids in solution. **8** (of igneous rocks) having a silica content of more than two thirds the total and containing at least one tenth quartz. **9** *Metallurgy.* of or made by a process in which the furnace or converter is lined with an acid material: *acid steel.* [C17 (first used by Francis Bacon): from French *acide* or Latin *acidus,* from *acēre* to be sour or sharp] ▶ **'acidly** *adv* ▶ **'acidness** *n* ▶ **'acidy** *adj*

acid anhydride *n* another name for **anhydride** (sense 3).

acidanthera (ˌæsɪ'dænθərə) *n* any plant of the African cormous genus *Acidanthera,* cultivated for its graceful tubular white and red or white and purple flowers, often scented: family *Iridaceae.* [from Greek *akis* point + New Latin *anthera* anther, from the shape of the anthers]

acid drop *n* a boiled sweet with a sharp taste.

acid dye *n* a dye in which the chromophore is part of a negative ion usually applied from an acidic solution.

acid-fast *adj* (of bacteria and tissues) resistant to decolorization by mineral acids after staining.

acid-forming *adj* **1** (of an oxide or element) yielding an acid when dissolved in water or having an oxide that forms an acid in water; acidic. **2** (of foods) producing an acid residue following digestion.

acid halide *n* another name for **acyl halide.**

acidhead ('æsɪdˌhɛd) *n Slang.* a person who uses LSD.

Acid House *or* **Acid** *n* a type of funk-based electronically edited disco music of the late 1980s, which has hypnotic sound effects and is associated with hippy culture and the use of the drug ecstasy. [C20: perhaps from ACID (LSD) + HOUSE (MUSIC)]

acidic (ə'sɪdɪk) *adj* **1** another word for **acid. 2** (of an oxide) yielding an acid in aqueous solution.

acidify (ə'sɪdɪˌfaɪ) *vb* **-fies, -fying, -fied.** to convert into or become acid. ▶ **a'cidiˌfiable** *adj* ▶ **aˌcidifi'cation** *n* ▶ **a'cidiˌfier** *n*

acidimeter (ˌæsɪ'dɪmɪtə) *n* **1** any instrument for determining the amount of acid in a solution. **2** another name for **acidometer.**

acidimetry (ˌæsɪ'dɪmɪtrɪ) *n* the determination of the amount of acid present in a solution, measured by an acidimeter or by volumetric analysis. ▶ **acidimetric** (ˌæsɪdɪ'metrɪk) *or* ˌ**acidi'metrical** *adj* ▶ ˌ**acidi'metrically** *adv*

acidity (ə'sɪdɪtɪ) *n, pl* **-ties. 1** the quality or state of being acid. **2** the amount of acid present in a solution, often expressed in terms of pH. **3** another name for **hyperacidity.**

acidometer (ˌæsɪ'dɒmɪtə) *n* a type of hydrometer for measuring the relative density of an acid solution, esp. the acid in a battery. Also called: **acidimeter.**

acidophil ('æsɪdəʊˌfɪl, ə'sɪdə-) *or* **acidophile** ('æsɪdəʊˌfaɪl, ə'sɪdə-) *adj also* **acidophilic** (ˌæsɪdəʊ'fɪlɪk, əˌsɪdə-) *or* **acidophilous** (ˌæsɪ'dɒfɪləs). **1** (of cells or cell contents) easily stained by acid dyes. **2** (of microorganisms) growing well in an acid environment. ◆ *n* **3** an acidophil organism. [C20: see ACID, -PHILE]

acidophilus milk (ˌæsɪ'dɒfɪləs) *n Med.* milk fermented by bacteria of the species *Lactobacillus acidophilus,* used in treating disorders of the gastrointestinal tract.

acidosis (ˌæsɪ'dəʊsɪs) *n* a condition characterized by an abnormal increase in the acidity of the blood and extracellular fluids. ▶ **acidotic** (ˌæsɪ'dɒtɪk) *adj*

acid rain *n* rain that contains a high concentration of pollutants, chiefly sulphur dioxide and nitrogen oxide, released into the atmosphere by the burning of fossil fuels such as coal or oil.

acid rock *n* a type of rock music characterized by electronically amplified bizarre instrumental effects. [C20: from ACID (sense 3), alluding to its supposed inspiration by drug-induced states of consciousness]

acid salt *n Chem.* a salt formed by partial replacement of the acidic hydrogen atoms of the parent acid.

acid soil *n* a soil that gives a pH reaction of below 7.2, found especially in cool moist areas where soluble bases are leached away.

acid test *n* a rigorous and conclusive test to establish worth or value: *the play passed the critic's acid test.* [C19: from the testing of gold with nitric acid]

acidulate (ə'sɪdjʊˌleɪt) *vb* (*tr*) to make slightly acid or sour. [C18: ACIDULOUS + -ATE[1]] ▶ **aˌcidu'lation** *n*

acidulous (ə'sɪdjʊləs) *or* **acidulent** *adj* **1** rather sour. **2** sharp or sour in speech, manner, etc.; acid. [C18: from Latin *acidulus* sourish, diminutive of *acidus* sour]

acid value *n* the number of milligrams of potassium hydroxide required to neutralize the free fatty acid in one gram of a fat, oil, resin, etc.

acierate ('æsɪəˌreɪt) *vb* (*tr*) to change (iron) into steel. [C19: from French *acier* steel, from Latin *aciēs* sharpness] ▶ ˌ**acier'ation** *n*

ACII *abbrev. for* Associate of the Chartered Insurance Institute.

acinaciform (ˌæsɪ'næsɪˌfɔːm) *adj* (of leaves) shaped like a scimitar; curved. [C19: via Latin *acīnacēs,* from Greek *akinakēs* short sword, ultimately from Iranian + -FORM]

aciniform (ə'sɪnɪˌfɔːm) *adj* shaped like a bunch of grapes. [C19: from New Latin *aciniformis;* see ACINUS]

acinus ('æsɪnəs) *n, pl* **-ni** (-ˌnaɪ). **1** *Anatomy.* any of the terminal saclike portions of a compound gland. **2** *Botany.* any of the small drupes that make up the fruit of the blackberry, raspberry, etc. **3** *Botany, obsolete.* a collection of berries, such as a bunch of grapes. [C18: New Latin, from Latin: grape, berry] ▶ **acinic** (ə'sɪnɪk), **'acinous,** *or* **'acinose** *adj*

Acis ('eɪsɪs) *n Greek myth.* a Sicilian shepherd and the lover of the nymph Galatea. In jealousy, Polyphemus crushed him with a huge rock, and his blood was turned by Galatea into a river.

ack-ack (ˌækˌæk) *n Military.* **1a** anti-aircraft fire. **1b** (*as modifier*): *ack-ack guns.* **2** anti-aircraft arms. [C20: British army World War I phonetic alphabet for AA, abbreviation of *anti-aircraft*]

ackee *or* **akee** ('ækiː) *n* **1a** a sapindaceous tree, *Blighia sapida,* native to tropical Africa and cultivated in the Caribbean for its fruit, edible when cooked. **1b** the red pear-shaped fruit of this tree. **2** a sapindaceous tree, *Melicoccus bijugatus,* that grows on some Caribbean islands and is valued for its timber and edible fruit. **3** the green tough-skinned berry of this tree. [C18: of African origin]

ack-emma ('æk'ɛmə) *adv Old-fashioned.* in the morning; a.m. [World War I phonetic alphabet for A, M]

acknowledge (ək'nɒlɪdʒ) *vb* (*tr*) **1** (*may take a clause as object*) to recognize or admit the existence, truth, or reality of. **2** to indicate recognition or awareness of, as by a greeting, glance, etc. **3** to express appreciation or thanks for: *to acknowledge a gift.* **4** to make the receipt of known to the sender: *to acknowledge a letter.* **5** to recognize, esp. in legal form, the authority, rights, or claims of. [C15: probably from earlier *knowledge,* on the model of Old English *oncnāwan,* Middle English *aknowen* to confess, recognize] ▶ **ac'knowledgeable** *adj* ▶ **ac'knowledger** *n*

acknowledgment *or* **acknowledgement** (ək'nɒlɪdʒmənt) *n* **1** the act of acknowledging or state of being acknowledged. **2** something done or given as an expression of thanks, as a reply to a message, etc. **3** (*pl*) an author's statement acknowledging his use of the works of other authors, usually printed at the front of a book.

aclinic line (ə'klɪnɪk) *n* another name for **magnetic equator.** [C19: *aclinic,* from Greek *aklinēs* not bending, from A-[1] + *klinein* to bend, lean]

ACM *abbrev. for* air chief marshal.

acme ('ækmɪ) *n* the culminating point, as of achievement or excellence; summit; peak. [C16: from Greek *akmē*]

acme screw thread *n* a type of screw thread having inclined flat flanks and a flat top and bottom: used in machine tools.

acne ('æknɪ) *n* a chronic skin disease common in adolescence, involving inflammation of the sebaceous glands and characterized by pustules on the face, neck, and upper trunk. [C19: New Latin, from a misreading of Greek *akmē* eruption on the face. See ACME]

acnode ('æk,nəʊd) *n* a point whose coordinates satisfy the equation of a curve although it does not lie on the curve; an isolated point. The origin is an acnode of the curve $y^2 + x^2 = x^3$. [C19: from Latin *acus* a needle + NODE] ▶ **ac'nodal** *adj*

Acol ('ækᵊl) *n Bridge.* a popular British bidding system favouring light opening bids and a flexible approach. [C20: named after a club in Acol Road, London]

acolyte ('ækə,laɪt) *n* **1** a follower or attendant. **2** *Christianity.* an officer who attends or assists a priest. [C16: via Old French and Medieval Latin from Greek *akolouthos* a follower]

Aconcagua (*Spanish* akon'kaɣwa) *n* a mountain in W Argentina: the highest peak in the Andes and in the W Hemisphere. Height: 6960 m (22 835 ft.).

aconite ('ækə,naɪt) *or* **aconitum** (,ækə'naɪtəm) *n* **1** any of various N temperate plants of the ranunculaceous genus *Aconitum,* such as monkshood and wolfsbane, many of which are poisonous. Compare **winter aconite. 2** the dried poisonous root of many of these plants, sometimes used as a narcotic and analgesic. [C16: via Old French or Latin from Greek *akoniton* aconite, monkshood] ▶ **aconitic** (,ækə'nɪtɪk) *adj*

Açôres (ə'sorəʃ) *n* the Portuguese name for (the) **Azores.**

acorn ('eɪkɔːn) *n* the fruit of the oak tree, consisting of a smooth thick-walled nut in a woody scaly cuplike base. [C16: a variant (through influence of *corn*) of Old English *æcern* the fruit of a tree, acorn; related to Gothic *akran* fruit, yield]

acorn barnacle *or* **shell** *n* any of various barnacles, such as *Balanus balanoides,* that live attached to rocks and have a volcano-shaped shell from the top of which protrude feathery food-catching appendages (cirri).

acorn valve *or U.S.* **tube** *n* a small electronic valve, approximately acorn-shaped with small closely-spaced electrodes, used in ultrahigh-frequency applications.

acorn worm *n* any of various small burrowing marine animals of the genus *Balanoglossus* and related genera, having an elongated wormlike body with an acorn-shaped eversible proboscis at the head end: subphylum *Hemichordata* (hemichordates).

acotyledon (ə,kɒtɪ'liːdᵊn) *n* any plant, such as a fern or moss, that does not possess cotyledons. ▶ **a,coty'ledonous** *adj*

acouchi *or* **acouchy** (ə'kuːʃɪ) *n, pl* **-chis** *or* **-chies.** any of several South American rodents of the genus *Myoprocta,* closely related to the agoutis but much smaller, with a white-tipped tail: family *Dasyproctidae.* [C19: via French from a native name in Guiana]

acoustic (ə'kuːstɪk) *or* **acoustical** *adj* **1** of or related to sound, the sense of hearing, or acoustics. **2** designed to respond to, absorb, or control sound: *an acoustic tile.* **3** (of a musical instrument or recording) without electronic amplification: *an acoustic bass; an acoustic guitar.* [C17: from Greek *akoustikos,* from *akouein* to hear] ▶ **a'coustically** *adv*

acoustic coupler *n Computing.* a device converting computer-data signals into acoustic form for transmission down a telephone line, through the handset microphone. See also **modem.**

acoustic feature *n Phonetics.* any of the acoustic components or elements present in a speech sound and capable of being experimentally observed, recorded, and reproduced.

acoustic guitar *n* an ordinary guitar, which produces its normal sound through the sounding board and is not amplified in any way. Compare **electric guitar.**

acoustician (,æku'stɪʃən) *n* an expert in acoustics.

acoustic nerve *n* either one of the eighth pair of cranial nerves, which supply the cochlea and semicircular canals of the internal ear and contribute to the sense of hearing.

acoustic phonetics *n* (*functioning as sing*) the branch of phonetics concerned with the acoustic properties of human speech. Compare **auditory phonetics, articulatory phonetics.**

acoustics (ə'kuːstɪks) *n* **1** (*functioning as sing*) the scientific study of sound and sound waves. **2** (*functioning as pl*) the characteristics of a room, auditorium, etc., that determine the fidelity with which sound can be heard within it.

acoustoelectronic (ə,kuːstəʊ,ɪlek'trɒnɪk) *adj* denoting a device in which electronic signals are converted into acoustic waves, esp. in delay lines, etc. Also: **electroacoustic.** ▶ **a,cousto,elec'tronics** *n*

acpt. *Commerce. abbrev. for* acceptance.

acquaint (ə'kweɪnt) *vb* (*tr*) **1** (foll. by *with* or *of*) to make (a person) familiar or conversant (with); inform (of). **2** (foll. by *with*) *Chiefly U.S.* to introduce (to); bring into contact (with). [C13: via Old French and Medieval Latin from Latin *accognitus,* from *accognōscere* to know perfectly, from *ad-* (intensive) + *cognōscere* to know]

acquaintance (ə'kweɪntəns) *n* **1** a person with whom one has been in contact but who is not a close friend. **2** knowledge of a person or thing, esp. when slight. **3 make the acquaintance of.** to come into social contact with. **4** those persons collectively whom one knows. **5** *Philosophy.* the relation between a knower and the object of his knowledge, as contrasted with knowledge by description (esp. in the phrase **knowledge by acquaintance**). ▶ **ac'quaintance,ship** *n*

acquainted (ə'kweɪntɪd) *adj* (*postpositive*) **1** (sometimes foll. by *with*) on terms of familiarity but not intimacy. **2** (foll. by *with*) having knowledge or experience (of); familiar (with).

acquiesce (,ækwɪ'ɛs) *vb* (*intr;* often foll. by *in* or *to*) to comply (with); assent (to) without protest. [C17: from Latin *acquiēscere* to remain at rest, agree without protest, from *ad-* at + *quiēscere* to rest, from *quiēs* QUIET] ▶ **,acqui'escence** *n* ▶ **,acqui'escent** *adj* ▶ **,acqui'escently** *adv*

USAGE The use of *to* after *acquiesce* was formerly regarded as incorrect, but is now acceptable.

acquire (ə'kwaɪə) *vb* (*tr*) to get or gain (something, such as an object, trait, or ability), esp. more or less permanently. [C15: via Old French from Latin *acquīrere,* from *ad-* in addition + *quaerere* to get, seek] ▶ **ac'quirable** *adj* ▶ **ac'quirement** *n* ▶ **ac'quirer** *n*

acquired behaviour *n Psychol.* the behaviour of an organism resulting from the effects of the environment.

acquired characteristic *n* a characteristic of an organism resulting from increased use or disuse of an organ or the effects of the environment. See also **Lamarckism.**

acquired drive *n Psychol.* a drive, like the desire for money, that has not been inherited but is learned, presumably because it leads to the satisfaction of innate drives.

acquired immune deficiency syndrome *or* **acquired immunodeficiency syndrome** *n* the full name for **AIDS.**

acquired immunity *n* the immunity produced by exposure of an organism to antigens, which stimulates the production of antibodies.

acquired taste *n* **1** a liking for something that is at first considered unpleasant. **2** the thing so liked.

acquisition (,ækwɪ'zɪʃən) *n* **1** the act of acquiring or gaining possession. **2** something acquired. **3** a person or thing of special merit added to a group. **4** *Astronautics.* **4a** the re-establishment of communications between a spacecraft and a ground control station after a temporary blackout. **4b** the process of locating a spacecraft, satellite, etc., esp. by radar, in order to gather tracking and telemetric information. [C14: from Latin *acquīsītiōn-,* from *acquīrere* to ACQUIRE]

acquisition accounting *n* an accounting procedure in which the assets of a company that has recently been taken over are changed from the book value to the fair market value.

acquisitive (ə'kwɪzɪtɪv) *adj* inclined or eager to acquire things, esp. material possessions. ▶ **ac'quisitively** *adv* ▶ **ac'quisitiveness** *n*

acquit (ə'kwɪt) *vb* **-quits, -quitting, -quitted.** (*tr*) **1** (foll. by *of*) **1a** to free or release (from a charge of crime). **1b** to pronounce not guilty. **2** (foll. by *of*) to free or relieve (from an obligation, duty, responsibility, etc.). **3** to repay or settle (something, such as a debt or obligation). **4** to perform (one's part); conduct (oneself). [C13: from Old French *aquiter,* from *quiter* to release, free from, QUIT] ▶ **ac'quitter** *n*

acquittal (ə'kwɪtᵊl) *n* **1** *Criminal law.* the deliverance and release of a person appearing before a court on a charge of crime, as by a finding of not guilty. **2** a discharge or release from an obligation, duty, debt, etc.

acquittance (ə'kwɪtəns) *n* **1** a release from or settlement of a debt, etc. **2** a record of this, such as a receipt.

acre ('eɪkə) *n* **1** a unit of area used in certain English-speaking countries, equal to 4840 square yards or 4046.86 square metres. **2** (*pl*) **2a** land, esp. a large area. **2b** *Informal.* a large amount: *he has acres of space in his room.* **3 farm the long acre.** *N.Z.* to graze cows on the verge of a road. [Old English *æcer* field, acre; related to Old Norse *akr,* German *Acker,* Latin *ager* field, Sanskrit *ajra* field]

Acre *n* **1** ('ɑːkrə). a state of W Brazil: mostly unexplored tropical forests; acquired from Bolivia in 1903. Capital: Rio Branco. Pop.: 455 200 (1995 est.). Area: 152 589 sq. km (58 899 sq. miles). **2** ('eɪkə, 'ɑːkə). a city and port in N Israel, strategically situated on the **Bay of Acre** in the E Mediterranean: taken and retaken during the Crusades (1104, 1187, 1191, 1291), taken by the Turks (1517), by Egypt (1832), and by the Turks again (1839). Pop.: 40 500 (1989 est.). Old Testament name: **Accho** (ɑː'kəʊ). Arabic name: **'Akka** (ɑː'kɑː). Hebrew name: **'Akko** (ɑː'kəʊ).

acreage ('eɪkərɪdʒ) *n* **1** land area in acres. ◆ *adj* **2** *Austral.* of or relating to a large allotment of land, esp. in a rural area.

acred ('eɪkəd) *adj* (*usually in combination*) having acres of land: *a many-acred farm; a well-acred nobleman.*

acre-foot *n, pl* **-feet.** the volume of water that would cover an area of 1 acre to a depth of 1 foot: equivalent to 43 560 cubic feet or 1233.5 cubic metres.

acre-inch *n* the volume of water that would cover an area of 1 acre to a depth of 1 inch; one twelfth of an acre-foot: equivalent to 3630 cubic feet or 102.8 cubic metres.

acrid ('ækrɪd) *adj* **1** unpleasantly pungent or sharp to the smell or taste. **2** sharp or caustic, esp. in speech or nature. [C18: from Latin *ācer* sharp, sour; probably formed on the model of ACID] ▶ **acridity** (ə'krɪdɪtɪ) *or* **'acridness** *n* ▶ **'acridly** *adv*

acridine ('ækrɪ,diːn) *n* a colourless crystalline solid used in the manufacture of dyes. Formula: $C_{13}H_9N$.

acriflavine (,ækrɪ'fleɪvɪn, -viːn) *n* a brownish or orange-red powder used in medicine as an antiseptic and bacteriostat. Formula: $C_{14}H_{14}N_3Cl$. [C20: from ACRIDINE + FLAVIN]

acriflavine hydrochloride *n* a red crystalline water-soluble solid substance obtained from acriflavine and used as an antiseptic. Also called: **flavine.**

Acrilan ('ækrɪ,læn) *n Trademark.* an acrylic fibre or fabric, characterized by strength, softness, and crease-resistance and used for clothing, upholstery, carpets, etc.

acrimony ('ækrɪmənɪ) *n, pl* **-nies.** bitterness or sharpness of manner, speech, temper, etc. [C16: from Latin *ācrimōnia,* from *ācer* sharp, sour] ▶ **acrimonious** (,ækrɪ'məʊnɪəs) *adj* ▶ **,acri'moniously** *adv* ▶ **,acri'moniousness** *n*

acro- *combining form.* **1** denoting something at a height, summit, top, tip, beginning, or end: *acropolis; acrogen.* **2** denoting an extremity of the human body: *acromegaly.* [from Greek *akros* extreme, topmost]

acrobat ('ækrə,bæt) *n* **1** an entertainer who performs acts that require skill, agility, and coordination, such as tumbling, swinging from a trapeze, or walking a tightrope. **2** a person noted for his frequent and rapid changes of position or allegiances: *a political acrobat.* [C19: via French from Greek *akrobatēs* acrobat, one who walks on tiptoe, from ACRO- + *bat-*, from *bainein* to walk] ► **ˌacroˈbatic** *adj* ► **ˌacroˈbatically** *adv*

acrobatics (ˌækrəˈbætɪks) *n* **1** (*functioning as pl*) the skills or feats of an acrobat. **2** (*functioning as sing*) the art of an acrobat. **3** (*functioning as pl*) any activity requiring agility and skill: *mental acrobatics.*

acrocarpous (ˌækrəʊˈkɑːpəs) *adj* (of ferns, mosses, etc.) having the reproductive parts at the tip of a stem. [C19: from New Latin, from Greek *akrokarpos*]

acrocentric (ˌækrəʊˈsentrɪk) *adj* **1** (of a chromosome) having the centromere at one end. ◆ *n* **2** an acrocentric chromosome.

acrocyanosis (ˌækrəʊˌsaɪəˈnəʊsɪs) *n* persistent cyanosis of the hands and feet due to poor circulation of the blood.

acrodont (ˈækrəˌdɒnt) *adj* **1** (of the teeth of some reptiles) having no roots and being fused at the base to the margin of the jawbones. See also **pleurodont** (sense 1). **2** having acrodont teeth. [C19: from ACRO- + -ODONT]

acrodrome (ˈækrəˌdrəʊm) *adj* (of the veins of a leaf) running parallel to the edges of the leaf and fusing at the tip. Also: **acrodromous** (əˈkrɒdrəməs). [from ACRO- + -DROMOUS]

acrogen (ˈækrədʒən) *n* any flowerless plant, such as a fern or moss, in which growth occurs from the tip of the main stem. [C19: from ACRO- + Greek *genēs* born; see -GEN] ► **acrogenic** (ˌækrəˈdʒenɪk) *or* **acrogenous** (əˈkrɒdʒɪnəs) *adj* ► **aˈcrogenously** *adv*

acrolein (əˈkrəʊlɪɪn) *n* a colourless or yellowish flammable poisonous pungent liquid used in the manufacture of resins and pharmaceuticals. Formula: CH_2:CHCHO. [C19: from Latin *ācer* sharp + *olēre* to smell + -IN]

acrolith (ˈækrəlɪθ) *n* (esp. in ancient Greek sculpture) a wooden, often draped figure with only the head, hands, and feet in stone. [C19: via Latin *acrolithus* from Greek *akrolithos* having stone extremities] ► **ˌacroˈlithic** *adj*

acromegaly (ˌækrəʊˈmegəlɪ) *n* a chronic disease characterized by enlargement of the bones of the head, hands, and feet, and swelling and enlargement of soft tissue, esp. the tongue. It is caused by excessive secretion of growth hormone by the pituitary gland. Compare **gigantism.** [C19: from French *acromégalie*, from ACRO- + Greek *megal-*, stem of *megas* big] ► **acromegalic** (ˌækrəʊmɪˈgælɪk) *adj, n*

acromion (əˈkrəʊmɪən) *n, pl* **-mia** (-mɪə). the outermost edge of the spine of the shoulder blade. [C17: New Latin, from Greek *akrōmion* the point of the shoulder, from ACRO- + *ōmion*, diminutive of *ōmos* shoulder]

acronychal, acronycal, *or U.S.* **acronical** (əˈkrɒnɪkᵊl) *adj* occurring at sunset: *the star has an acronychal rising.* [C16: from Greek *akronychos* at sunset, from ACRO- + *nykh-*, *nyx* night] ► **aˈcronychally, aˈcronycally,** *or U.S.* **aˈcronically** *adv*

acronym (ˈækrənɪm) *n* a pronounceable name made up of a series of initial letters or parts of words; for example, *UNESCO* for the *United Nations Educational, Scientific, and Cultural Organization.* [C20: from ACRO- + -ONYM] ► **ˌacroˈnymic** *or* **acronymous** (əˈkrɒnɪməs) *adj*

acroparaesthesia (ˌækrəʊˌpæresˈθiːzɪə) *or U.S.* **acroparesthesia** *n Pathol.* a persistent sensation of numbness and tingling in the hands and feet.

acropetal (əˈkrɒpɪtᵊl) *adj* (of leaves and flowers) produced in order from the base upwards so that the youngest are at the apex. Compare **basipetal.**

acrophobia (ˌækrəˈfəʊbɪə) *n* abnormal fear or dread of being at a great height. [C19: from ACRO- + -PHOBIA] ► **ˌacroˈphobic** *adj*

acropolis (əˈkrɒpəlɪs) *n* the citadel of an ancient Greek city. [C17: from Greek, from ACRO- + *polis* city]

Acropolis (əˈkrɒpəlɪs) *n* the citadel of Athens on which the Parthenon and the Erechtheum stand.

acrospire (ˈækrəˌspaɪə) *n* the first shoot developing from the plumule of a germinating grain seed. [C17: from obsolete *akerspire*, from *aker* EAR[2] + *spire* sprout, SPIRE[1]; the modern form is influenced by ACRO-]

across (əˈkrɒs) *prep* **1** from one side to the other side of. **2** on or at the other side of. **3** so as to transcend boundaries or barriers: *people united across borders by religion and history; the study of linguistics across cultures.* ◆ *adv* **4** from one side to the other. **5** on or to the other side. [C13: *on croice, acros*, from Old French *a croix* crosswise]

across-the-board *adj* **1** (of salary increases, taxation cuts, etc.) affecting all levels or classes equally. **2** *Horse racing.* the U.S. term for **each way.**

acrostic (əˈkrɒstɪk) *n* **a** a number of lines of writing, such as a poem, certain letters of which form a word, proverb, etc. A **single acrostic** is formed by the initial letters of the lines, a **double acrostic** by the initial and final letters, and a **triple acrostic** by the initial, middle, and final letters. **b** the word, proverb, etc., so formed. **c** (*as modifier*): *an acrostic sonnet.* [C16: via French from Greek *akrostikhis*, from ACRO- + *stikhos* line of verse, STICH] ► **aˈcrostically** *adv*

acroter (əˈkrəʊtə, ˈækrətə) *n Architect.* a plinth bearing a statue, etc., at either end or at the apex of a pediment. [C18: from French, from Latin *acroterium*, from Greek *akrōtērion* summit, from *akros* extreme]

acrylic (əˈkrɪlɪk) *adj* **1** of, derived from, or concerned with acrylic acid. ◆ *n* **2** short for **acrylic fibre, acrylic resin. 3** a paint or colour containing acrylic resin. [C20: from ACROLEIN + -YL + -IC]

acrylic acid *n* a colourless corrosive pungent liquid, miscible with water, used in the manufacture of acrylic resins. Formula: CH_2:CHCOOH. Systematic name: **propenoic acid.**

acrylic fibre *n* a textile fibre, such as Orlon or Acrilan, produced from acrylonitrile.

acrylic resin *n* any of a group of polymers or copolymers of acrylic acid, its esters, or amides, used as synthetic rubbers, textiles, paints, adhesives, and as plastics such as Perspex.

acrylonitrile (ˌækrɪləʊˈnaɪtraɪl) *n* a colourless liquid that is miscible with water and has toxic fumes: used in the manufacture of acrylic fibres and resins, rubber, and thermoplastics. Formula: CH_2:CHCN. [C20: from ACRYLIC + NITRILE]

acrylyl (ˈækrɪlɪl) *n* (*modifier*) of, consisting of, or containing the monovalent group CH_2:CHCO-: *acrylyl group or radical.*

a/cs pay. *abbrev. for* accounts payable.

a/cs rec. *abbrev. for* accounts receivable.

act (ækt) *n* **1** something done or performed; a deed. **2** the performance of some physical or mental process; action. **3** (*cap. when part of a name*) the formally codified result of deliberation by a legislative body; a law, edict, decree, statute, etc. **4** (*often pl*) a formal written record of transactions, proceedings, etc., as of a society, committee, or legislative body. **5** a major division of a dramatic work. **6a** a short performance of skill, a comic sketch, dance, etc., esp. one that is part of a programme of light entertainment. **6b** those giving such a performance. **7** an assumed attitude or pose, esp. one intended to impress. **8** *Philosophy.* an occurrence effected by the volition of a human agent, usually opposed at least as regards its explanation to one which is causally determined. Compare **event** (sense 4). ◆ *vb* **9** (*intr*) to do something; carry out an action. **10** (*intr*) to function in a specified way; operate; react: *his mind acted quickly.* **11** to perform (a part or role) in a play, etc. **12** (*tr*) to present (a play, etc.) on stage. **13** (*intr;* usually foll. by *for* or *as*) to be a substitute (for); function in place (of). **14** (*intr;* foll. by *as*) to serve the function or purpose (of): *the glass acted as protection.* **15** (*intr*) to conduct oneself or behave (as if one were): *she usually acts like a lady.* **16** (*intr*) to behave in an unnatural or affected way. **17** (*copula*) to pose as; play the part of: *to act the fool.* **18** (*copula*) to behave in a manner appropriate to (esp. in the phrase **act one's age**). **19** (*copula*) *Not standard.* to seem or pretend to be: *to act tired.* **20 clean up one's act.** to start to behave in a responsible manner. **21 get in on the act.** *Informal.* to become involved in a profitable undertaking or advantageous situation in order to share in the benefits. **22 get one's act together.** *Informal.* to become organized or prepared. ◆ See also **act on, act out, act up.** [C14: from Latin *actus* a doing, performance, and *actum* a thing done, from the past participle of *agere* to do] ► **ˈactable** *adj* ► **ˌactaˈbility** *n*

ACT *abbrev. for:* **1** Australian Capital Territory. **2** advance corporation tax.

Actaeon (ækˈtiːən, ˈæktɪən) *n Greek myth.* a hunter of Boeotia who, having accidentally seen Artemis bathing, was turned into a stag and torn apart by his own hounds.

actant (ˈæktənt) *n Linguistics.* (in valency grammar) a noun phrase functioning as the agent of the main verb of a sentence.

actg *abbrev. for* acting.

ACTH *n* adrenocorticotrophic hormone; a polypeptide hormone, secreted by the anterior lobe of the pituitary gland, that stimulates growth of the adrenal gland and the synthesis and secretion of corticosteroids. It is used in treating rheumatoid arthritis, allergic and skin diseases, and many other disorders. Also called: **corticotrophin.**

actin (ˈæktɪn) *n* a protein that participates in many kinds of cell movement, including muscle contraction, during which it interacts with filaments of a second protein, myosin. [C20: from ACT + -IN]

actinal (ˈæktɪnᵊl, ækˈtaɪnᵊl) *adj* **1** of or denoting the oral part of a radiate animal, such as a jellyfish, sea anemone, or sponge, from which the rays, tentacles, or arms grow. **2** possessing rays or tentacles, as a jellyfish. [C19: see ACTINO-, -AL[1]] ► **ˈactinally** *adv*

acting (ˈæktɪŋ) *adj* (*prenominal*) **1** taking on duties temporarily, esp. as a substitute for another: *the acting president.* **2** operating or functioning: *an acting order.* **3** intended for stage performance; provided with directions for actors: *an acting version of "Hedda Gabler".* ◆ *n* **4** the art or profession of an actor.

actinia (ækˈtɪnɪə) *n, pl* **-tiniae** (-ˈtɪnɪˌiː) *or* **-tinias.** any sea anemone of the genus *Actinia*, which are common in rock pools. [C18: New Latin, literally: things having a radial structure. See ACTINO-, -IA]

actinic (ækˈtɪnɪk) *adj* (of radiation) producing a photochemical effect. [C19: from ACTINO- + -IC] ► **acˈtinically** *adv* ► **ˈactinˌism** *n*

actinide (ˈæktɪˌnaɪd) *n* a member of the actinide series. Also called: **actinon.** [C19: from ACTINO- + -IDE]

actinide series *n* a series of 15 radioactive elements with increasing atomic numbers from actinium to lawrencium.

actiniform (ækˈtɪnɪˌfɔːm) *adj* another word for **actinoid.** [C20: from ACTINO- + -FORM]

actinium (ækˈtɪnɪəm) *n* a radioactive element of the actinide series, occurring as a decay product of uranium. It is used as an alpha-particle source and in neutron production. Symbol: Ac; atomic no.: 89; half-life of most stable isotope, ^{227}Ac: 21.6 years; relative density: 10.07; melting pt.: 1051°C; boiling pt.: 3200 ± 300°C. [C19: New Latin, from ACTINO- + -IUM]

actinium series *n* a radioactive series that starts with uranium-235 and ends with lead-207.

actino- *or before a vowel* **actin-** *combining form.* **1** indicating a radial structure: *actinomorphic.* **2** indicating radioactivity or radiation: *actinometer.* [from Greek *aktino-*, from *aktis* beam, ray]

actinobiology (ˌæktɪnəʊbaɪˈɒlədʒɪ) *n* the branch of biology concerned with the effects of radiation on living organisms.

actinochemistry (ækˌtɪnəʊˈkemɪstrɪ) *n* another name for **photochemistry.**

actinodermatitis (ˌæktɪnəʊˌdɜːməˈtaɪtɪs) *n* dermatitis from exposure to radiation, esp. ultraviolet light or X-rays.

actinoid (ˈæktɪˌnɔɪd) *adj* having a radiate form, as a sea anemone or starfish.

actinolite (ækˈtɪnəˌlaɪt) *n* a green mineral of the amphibole group consisting of calcium magnesium iron silicate. Formula: $Ca_2(Mg,Fe)_5Si_8O_{22}(OH)_2$. [C19: from ACTINO- (from the radiating crystals in some forms) + -LITE]

actinomere (ˈæktɪnəʊˌmɪə) *n* another name for **antimere.**

actinometer (ˌæktɪˈnɒmɪtə) *n* an instrument for measuring the intensity of radiation, esp. of the sun's rays. ▶ **actinometric** (ˌæktɪnəʊˈmɛtrɪk) *or* **ˌacti-noˈmetrical** *adj* ▶ **ˌactiˈnometry** *n*

actinomorphic (ˌæktɪnəʊˈmɔːfɪk) *or* **actinomorphous** *adj Botany.* (esp. of a flower) having radial symmetry, as buttercups; capable of being cut vertically through the axis in any of two or more planes so that the two cut halves are mirror images of each other. See also **zygomorphic.** ▶ **ˈactinoˌmorphy** *n*

actinomycete (ˌæktɪnəʊmaɪˈsiːt) *n* any microorganism of the group *Actinomycetes,* usually regarded as filamentous bacteria. [C20: from ACTINO- + -MYCETE]

actinomycin (ˌæktɪnəʊˈmaɪsɪn) *n* any of several toxic antibiotics obtained from bacteria of the genus *Streptomyces,* used in treating some cancers.

actinomycosis (ˌæktɪnəʊmaɪˈkəʊsɪs) *n* a fungal disease of cattle, sometimes transmitted to man, characterized by a swelling of the affected part, most often the jaw or lungs. Nontechnical name: **lumpy jaw.** ▶ **actinomycotic** (ˌæktɪnəʊmaɪˈkɒtɪk) *adj*

actinon (ˈæktɪˌnɒn) *n* **1** a radioisotope of radon that is a decay product of radium. Symbol: An or ^{219}Rn; atomic no.: 86; half-life: 3.92s. **2** another name for **actinide.** [C20: New Latin, from ACTINIUM + -ON]

actinopod (ækˈtɪnəˌpɒd) *n* any protozoan of the phylum *Actinopoda,* such as a radiolarian or a heliozoan, having stiff radiating cytoplasmic projections.

actinotherapy (ˌæktɪnəʊˈθɛrəpɪ) *n* another name for **radiotherapy.**

actinouranium (ˌæktɪnəʊjʊˈreɪnɪəm) *n* the isotope of uranium that has a mass number of 235.

actinozoan (ˌæktɪnəʊˈzəʊən) *n, adj* another word for **anthozoan.**

action (ˈækʃən) *n* **1** the state or process of doing something or being active; operation. **2** something done, such as an act or deed. **3** movement or posture during some physical activity. **4** activity, force, or energy: *a man of action.* **5** (*usually pl*) conduct or behaviour. **6** *Law.* **6a** a legal proceeding brought by one party against another, seeking redress of a wrong or recovery of what is due; lawsuit. **6b** the right to bring such a proceeding. **7** the operating mechanism, esp. in a piano, gun, watch, etc. **8** (of a guitar) the distance between the strings and the fingerboard. **9** (of keyboard instruments) the sensitivity of the keys to touch. **10** the force applied to a body: *the reaction is equal and opposite to the action.* **11** the way in which something operates or works. **12** *Physics.* **12a** a property of a system expressed as twice the mean kinetic energy of the system over a given time interval multiplied by the time interval. **12b** the product of work or energy and time, usually expressed in joule seconds: *Planck's constant of action.* **13** the events that form the plot of a story, film, play, or other composition. **14** *Military.* **14a** a minor engagement. **14b** fighting at sea or on land: *he saw action in the war.* **15** *Philosophy.* behaviour which is voluntary and explicable in terms of the agent's reasons, as contrasted with that which is coerced or determined causally. **16** *Brit.* short for **industrial action. 17** *Informal.* the profits of an enterprise or transaction (esp. in the phrase **a piece of the action**). **18** *Slang.* the main activity, esp. social activity. ◆ *vb* (*tr*) **19** to put into effect; take action concerning: *matters decided at the meeting cannot be actioned until the following week.* ◆ *interj* **20** a command given by a film director to indicate that filming is to begin. See also **cue**[1] (senses 1, 8). [C14 *accioun,* ultimately from Latin *āctiōn-,* stem of *āctiō,* from *agere* to do, act]

actionable (ˈækʃənəbᵊl) *adj Law.* affording grounds for legal action. ▶ **ˈactionably** *adv*

action at a distance *n Physics.* the supposed interaction of two separated bodies without any intervening medium. In modern theories all interactions are assumed to require a field of force.

actioner (ˈækʃənə) *n Informal.* a film with a fast-moving plot, usually containing scenes of violence.

action painting *n* a development of abstract expressionism evolved in the 1940s, characterized by broad vigorous brush strokes and accidental effects of thrown, smeared, dripped, or spattered paint. Also called: **tachisme.** See also **abstract expressionism.**

action potential *n* a localized change in electrical potential, from −70 mV to +30 mV, that occurs across a nerve fibre during transmission of a nerve impulse.

action replay *n* the rerunning of a small section of a television film or tape of a match or other sporting contest, often in slow motion. U.S. and Canadian name: **instant replay.**

action stations *pl n* **1** *Military.* the positions taken up by individuals in preparation for or during a battle. ◆ *interj* **2** *Military.* a command to take up such positions. **3** *Informal.* a warning to get ready for something.

Actium (ˈæktɪəm) *n* a town of ancient Greece that overlooked the naval battle in 31 B.C. at which Octavian's fleet under Agrippa defeated that of Mark Antony and Cleopatra.

activate (ˈæktɪˌveɪt) *vb* (*tr*) **1** to make active or capable of action. **2** *Physics.* to make radioactive. **3** *Chem.* **3a** to increase the rate of (a reaction). **3b** to treat (a substance, such as carbon or alumina) so as to increase powers of adsorption. **4** *Physiol.* to prepare by arousal (the body or one of its organs (e.g. the brain)) for action. **5** to purify (sewage) by aeration. **6** *U.S. military.* to create, mobilize, or organize (a unit). ▶ **ˌactiˈvation** *n* ▶ **ˈactiˌvator** *n*

activated alumina *n* a granular highly porous and adsorptive form of aluminium oxide, used for drying gases and as an oil-filtering material and catalyst.

activated carbon *n* a porous highly adsorptive form of carbon used to remove colour or impurities from liquids and gases, in the separation and extraction of chemical compounds, and in the recovery of solvents. Also called: **activated charcoal, active carbon.**

activated sludge *n* a mass of aerated precipitated sewage added to untreated sewage to bring about purification by hastening bacterial decomposition.

active (ˈæktɪv) *adj* **1** in a state of action; moving, working, or doing something. **2** busy or involved: *an active life.* **3** physically energetic. **4** exerting influence; effective: *an active ingredient.* **5** *Grammar.* **5a** denoting a voice of verbs used to indicate that the subject of a sentence is performing the action or causing the event or process described by the verb, as *kicked* in *The boy kicked the football.* Compare **passive** (sense 5). **5b** another word for **nonstative. 6** being fully engaged in military service (esp. in the phrase **on active service**). **7** (of a volcano) erupting periodically; not extinct. Compare **dormant** (sense 3), **extinct** (sense 3). **8** *Astronomy.* (of the sun) exhibiting a large number of sunspots, solar flares, etc., and a marked variation in intensity and frequency of radio emission. Compare **quiet** (sense 8). **9** *Commerce.* producing or being used to produce profit, esp. in the form of interest: *active balances.* **10** *Electronics.* **10a** containing a source of power: *an active network.* **10b** capable of amplifying a signal or controlling some function: *an active component; an active communication satellite.* ◆ *n* **11** *Grammar.* **11a** the active voice. **11b** an active verb. **12** *Chiefly U.S.* a member of an organization who participates in its activities. [C14: from Latin *āctīvus.* See ACT, -IVE] ▶ **ˈactively** *adv* ▶ **ˈactiveness** *n*

active centre *n Biochem.* the region in an enzyme molecule in which the reactive groups that participate in its action are juxtaposed.

active galaxy *n* a galaxy that emits usually large amounts of energy from a very compact central source, such as Seyfert galaxies, radio galaxies, and quasars. Also called: **active galactic nucleus.**

active list *n Military.* a list of officers available for full duty.

active service *or esp. U.S.* **active duty** *n* military duty in an operational area.

active transport *n Biochem., physiol.* a process by which molecules are enabled to pass across a membrane from a region where they are in a low concentration to one of high concentration; this requires the expenditure of energy in metabolism and is assisted by enzymes, commonly referred to as pumps.

active vocabulary *n* the total number of words a person uses in his own speech and writing. Compare **passive vocabulary.**

activism (ˈæktɪˌvɪzəm) *n* a policy of taking direct and often militant action to achieve an end, esp. a political or social one. ▶ **ˈactivist** *n*

activity (ækˈtɪvɪtɪ) *n, pl* **-ties. 1** the state or quality of being active. **2** lively action or movement. **3** any specific deed, action, pursuit, etc.: *recreational activities.* **4** the number of disintegrations of a radioactive substance in a given unit of time, usually expressed in curies or disintegrations per second. **5a** the capacity of a substance to undergo chemical change. **5b** the effective concentration of a substance in a chemical system. The **absolute activity** of a substance B, λ_B, is defined as exp (μ_B/RT) where μ_B is the chemical potential.

act of contrition *n Christianity.* a short prayer of penitence.

act of faith *n Christianity.* an act that demonstrates or tests a person's religious beliefs.

act of God *n Law.* a sudden and inevitable occurrence caused by natural forces and not by the agency of man, such as a flood, earthquake, or a similar catastrophe.

act of war *n* an aggressive act, usually employing military force, which constitutes an immediate threat to peace.

actomyosin (ˌæktəʊˈmaɪəsɪn) *n* a complex protein in skeletal muscle that is formed by actin and myosin and which, when stimulated, shortens to cause muscle contraction.

acton (ˈæktən) *n* (in medieval Europe) **1** a jacket or jerkin, originally of quilted cotton, worn under a coat of mail. **2** a leather jacket padded with mail. [C14: from Old French *auqueton,* probably ultimately from Arabic *alqutun* the cotton]

Acton[1] (ˈæktən) *n* a district of the London borough of Ealing.

Acton[2] (ˈæktən) *n* **1 John Emerich Edward Dalberg,** 1st Baron. 1834–1902, English historian: a proponent of Christian liberal ethics and adviser of Gladstone. **2** his grandfather, Sir **John Francis Edward.** 1736-1811, European naval commander and statesman: admiral of Tuscany (1774–79) and Naples (1779 onwards) and chief minister of Naples (1779–1806).

act on *or* **upon** *vb* (*intr, prep*) **1** to regulate one's behaviour in accordance with (advice, information, etc.). **2** to have an effect on (illness, a part of the body, etc.).

actor (ˈæktə) *or* (*fem*) **actress** (ˈæktrɪs) *n* **1** a person who acts in a play, film, broadcast, etc. **2** *Informal.* a person who puts on a false manner in order to deceive others (often in the phrase **bad actor**).

act out *vb* (*adv*) **1** (*tr*) to reproduce (an idea, former event, etc.) in actions, often by mime. **2** *Psychiatry.* to express unconsciously (a repressed impulse or experience) in overt behaviour.

actressy (ˈæktrɪsɪ) *adj* exaggerated and affected in manner; theatrical.

Acts of the Apostles *n* the fifth book of the New Testament, describing the development of the early Church from Christ's ascension into heaven to Paul's sojourn at Rome. Often shortened to **Acts.**

ACTT *abbrev. for* Association of Cinematograph and Television Technicians.

ACTU *abbrev. for* Australian Council of Trade Unions.

actual (ˈæktʃʊəl) *adj* **1** existing in reality or as a matter of fact. **2** real or genuine. **3** existing at the present time; current. **4** (usually preceded by *your*) *Brit. informal, often facetious.* (intensifier): *that music's by your actual Mozart, isn't it?* ◆ See also **actuals.** [C14 *actuel* existing, from Late Latin *āctuālis* relating to acts, practical, from Latin *āctus* ACT]

USAGE The excessive use of *actual* and *actually* should be avoided. They are unnecessary in sentences such as *in actual fact, he is forty-two,* and *he did actually go to the play but did not enjoy it.*

actual bodily harm *n Criminal law.* injury caused by one person to another that is less serious than grievous bodily harm. Abbrev.: **ABH.**

actuality (ˌæktʃʊˈælɪtɪ) *n, pl* **-ties. 1** true existence; reality. **2** (*sometimes pl*) a fact or condition that is real.

actualize *or* **actualise** (ˈæktʃʊəˌlaɪz) *vb* (*tr*) **1** to make actual or real. **2** to represent realistically. ▶ **ˌactualiˈzation** *or* **ˌactualiˈsation** *n*

actually (ˈæktʃʊəlɪ) *adv* **1a** as an actual fact; really. **1b** (*as sentence modifier*):

actually, I haven't seen him. **2** at present. **3** *Informal.* a parenthetic filler used to add slight emphasis: *I don't know, actually.*

actuals ('æktʃuəlz) *n* See **physicals.**

actual sin *n Christianity.* any sin that a person commits of his own free will and for which he is personally responsible. Compare **original sin.**

actuary ('æktʃuərɪ) *n, pl* **-aries.** a person qualified to calculate commercial risks and probabilities involving uncertain future events, esp. in such contexts as life assurance. [C16 (meaning: registrar): from Latin *āctuārius* one who keeps accounts, from *actum* public business, and *acta* documents, deeds. See ACT, -ARY] ▸ **actuarial** (ˌæktʃu'ɛərɪəl) *adj*

actuate ('æktʃuˌeɪt) *vb (tr)* **1** to put into action or mechanical motion. **2** to motivate or incite into action: *actuated by unworthy desires.* [C16: from Medieval Latin *actuātus,* from *actuāre* to incite to action, from Latin *āctus* ACT] ▸ **ˌactu'ation** *n* ▸ **'actuˌator** *n*

act up *vb (intr, adv) Informal.* to behave in a troublesome way: *the engine began to act up.*

acuity (ə'kjuːɪtɪ) *n* **1** keenness or acuteness, esp. in vision or thought. **2** the capacity of the eye to see fine detail measured by determining the finest detail that can just be detected. [C15: from Old French, from Latin *acūtus* ACUTE]

aculeate (ə'kjuːlɪɪt, -ˌeɪt) *or* **aculeated** *adj* **1** cutting; pointed. **2** having prickles or spines, as a rose. **3** having a sting, as bees, wasps, and ants. [C17: from Latin *acūleātus;* see ACULEUS]

aculeus (ə'kjuːlɪəs) *n* **1** a prickle or spine, such as the thorn of a rose. **2** a sting or ovipositor. [C19: from Latin, diminutive of *acus* needle]

acumen ('ækjuˌmɛn, ə'kjuːmən) *n* the ability to judge well; keen discernment; insight. [C16: from Latin: sharpness, from *acuere* to sharpen, from *acus* needle] ▸ **a'cuminous** *adj*

acuminate *adj* (ə'kjuːmɪnɪt, -ˌneɪt). **1** narrowing to a sharp point, as some types of leaf. ◆ *vb* (ə'kjuːmɪˌneɪt). **2** *(tr)* to make pointed or sharp. [C17: from Latin *acūmināre* to sharpen; see ACUMEN] ▸ **aˌcumi'nation** *n*

acupoint ('ækjuˌpɔɪnt) *n* any of the specific points on the body where a needle is inserted in acupuncture or pressure is applied in acupressure. [C19: from ACU(PUNCTURE) + POINT]

acupressure ('ækjuˌprɛʃə) *n* another name for **shiatsu.** [C19: from ACU(PUNCTURE) + PRESSURE]

acupuncture ('ækjuˌpʌŋktʃə) *n* the insertion of the tips of needles into the skin at specific points for the purpose of treating various disorders by stimulating nerve impulses. Originally Chinese, this method of treatment is practised in many parts of the world. Also called: **stylostixis.** [C17: from Latin *acus* needle + PUNCTURE] ▸ **'acuˌpunctural** *adj* ▸ **'acuˌpuncturist** *n*

acutance (ə'kjuːtᵊns) *n* a physical rather than subjective measure of the sharpness of a photographic image.

acute (ə'kjuːt) *adj* **1** penetrating in perception or insight. **2** sensitive to details; keen. **3** of extreme importance; crucial. **4** sharp or severe; intense: *acute pain; an acute drought.* **5** having a sharp end or point. **6** *Maths.* **6a** (of an angle) less than 90°. **6b** (of a triangle) having all its interior angles less than 90°. **7** (of a disease) **7a** arising suddenly and manifesting intense severity. **7b** of relatively short duration. Compare **chronic** (sense 2). **8** *Phonetics.* **8a** (of a vowel or syllable in some languages with a pitch accent, such as ancient Greek) spoken or sung on a higher musical pitch relative to neighbouring syllables or vowels. **8b** of or relating to an accent (´) placed over vowels, denoting that the vowel is pronounced with higher musical pitch (as in ancient Greek), with a certain special quality (as in French), etc. Compare (for a and b) **grave**[2] (sense 5), **circumflex.** **9** (of a hospital, hospital bed, or ward) intended to accommodate short-term patients. ◆ *n* **10** an acute accent. [C14: from Latin *acūtus,* past participle of *acuere* to sharpen, from *acus* needle] ▸ **a'cutely** *adv* ▸ **a'cuteness** *n*

acute accent *n* the diacritical mark (´), used in the writing system of some languages to indicate that the vowel over which it is placed has a special quality (as in French *été*) or that it receives the strongest stress in the word (as in Spanish *hablé*).

acute arch *n* another name for **lancet arch.**

acute dose *n* a total dose of radiation received over such a short period that biological recovery is impossible.

ACW *abbrev. for* aircraftwoman.

acyclic (eɪ'saɪklɪk, eɪ'sɪklɪk) *adj* **1** *Chem.* not cyclic; having an open chain structure. **2** *Botany.* having flower parts arranged in a spiral rather than a whorl.

acyl ('eɪsaɪl) *n* **1** *(modifier)* of, denoting, or containing the monovalent group of atoms RCO-, where R is an aliphatic group: *acyl group or radical; acyl substitution.* **2** an organometallic compound in which a metal atom is directly bound to an acyl group. [C20: from ACID + -YL]

acyl anhydride *n* another name for **anhydride** (sense 3).

acylation (ˌeɪsaɪ'leɪʃən) *n* the introduction into a chemical compound of an acyl group.

acyl halide *n* any derivative of carboxylic acid in which the hydroxyl group has been replaced by a halogen atom. Also called: **acid halide.**

ad[1] (æd) *n* short for **advertisement.**

ad[2] (æd) *n Tennis, U.S. and Canadian.* short for **advantage.** Brit. equivalent: **van.**

AD *abbrev. for:* **1** same as **A.D.** **2** *Military.* active duty. **3** *Military.* air defence.

A.D. *or* **AD** (indicating years numbered from the supposed year of the birth of Christ) *abbrev. for* anno Domini: *70* A.D. Compare **B.C.** [Latin: in the year of the Lord]

USAGE In strict usage, A.D. is only employed with specific years: *he died in 1621* A.D., but *he died in the 17th century* (and not *the 17th century* A.D.). Formerly the practice was to write A.D. preceding the date (A.D. *1621*), and it is also strictly correct to omit *in* when A.D. is used, since this is already contained in the meaning of the Latin *anno Domini* (in the year of Our Lord), but this is no longer general practice. B.C. is used with both specific dates and indications of the period: *Heraclitus was born about 540* B.C.; *the battle took place in the 4th century* B.C.

ad- *prefix* **1** to; towards: *adsorb; adverb.* **2** near; next to: *adrenal.* [from Latin: to, towards. As a prefix in words of Latin origin, *ad-* became *ac-, af-, ag-, al-, an-, acq-, ar-, as-,* and *at-* before *c, f, g, l, n, q, r, s,* and *t,* and became *a-* before *gn, sc, sp, st*]

-ad[1] *suffix forming nouns.* **1** a group or unit (having so many parts or members): *triad.* **2** an epic poem concerning (the subject indicated by the stem): *Dunciad.* [via Latin from Greek *-ad-* (plural *-ades*), originally forming adjectives; names of epic poems are all formed on the model of the *Iliad*]

-ad[2] *suffix forming adverbs.* denoting direction towards a specified part in anatomical descriptions: *cephalad.* [from Latin *ad* to, towards]

Ada ('eɪdə) *n* a high-level computer programming language designed for dealing with real-time processing problems: used for military and other systems. [C20: named after *Ada,* Lady LOVELACE, who worked with Babbage and whose description of his computing machines preserved them for posterity]

adactylous (eɪ'dæktɪləs) *adj* possessing no fingers or toes. [C19: from A-[1] + DACTYL + -OUS]

adage ('ædɪdʒ) *n* a traditional saying that is accepted by many as true or partially true; proverb. [C16: via Old French from Latin *adagium;* related to *āio* I say]

adagio (ə'dɑːdʒɪˌəu; *Italian* a'dadʒo) *Music.* ◆ *adj, adv* **1** (to be performed) slowly. ◆ *n, pl* **-gios.** **2** a movement or piece to be performed slowly. **3** *Ballet.* a slow section of a pas de deux. [C18: Italian, from *ad* at + *agio* ease]

Adam[1] ('ædəm) *n* **1** *Old Testament.* the first man, created by God: the progenitor of the human race (Genesis 2–3). **2 not know (someone) from Adam.** to have no knowledge of or acquaintance with (someone). **3 the old Adam.** the evil supposedly inherent in human nature. **4 Adam's ale** *or* **wine.** water.

Adam[2] *n* **1** *(French* adɑ̃) **Adolphe.** 1803–56, French composer, best known for his romantic ballet *Giselle* (1841). **2** ('ædəm) **Robert.** 1728–92, Scottish architect and furniture designer. Assisted by his brother, **James,** 1730–94, he emulated the harmony of classical and Italian Renaissance architecture. ◆ *adj* **3** in the neoclassical style made popular by Robert Adam.

adamant ('ædəmənt) *adj* **1** unshakable in purpose, determination, or opinion; unyielding. **2** a less common word for **adamantine** (sense 1). ◆ *n* **3** any extremely hard or apparently unbreakable substance. **4** a legendary stone said to be impenetrable, often identified with the diamond or loadstone. [Old English: from Latin *adamant-,* stem of *adamas,* from Greek; literal meaning perhaps: unconquerable, from A-[1] + *daman* to tame, conquer] ▸ **'adamantly** *adv*

adamantine (ˌædə'mæntaɪn) *adj* **1** very hard; unbreakable or unyielding. **2** having the lustre of a diamond.

Adamawa (ˌædə'mɑːwə) *n* a small group of languages of W Africa, spoken chiefly in E Nigeria, N Cameroon, the Central African Republic, and N Democratic Republic of the Congo (formerly Zaïre), forming a branch of the Niger-Congo family.

Adamite ('ædəˌmaɪt) *n* **1** a human being. **2** a nudist, esp. a member of an early Christian sect who sought to imitate Adam. ▸ **Adamitic** (ˌædə'mɪtɪk) *adj*

Adamov *(French* adamɔf) *n* **Arthur.** 1908–70, French dramatist, born in Russia: one of the foremost exponents of the Theatre of the Absurd. His plays include *Le Professeur Taranne* (1953), *Le Ping-Pong* (1955), and *Le Printemps '71* (1960).

Adams[1] ('ædəmz) *n* a mountain in SW Washington, in the Cascade Range. Height: 3751 m (12 307 ft.).

Adams[2] ('ædəmz) *n* **1 Gerry,** full name *Gerrard Adams.* born 1948, Northern Ireland politician; president of Sinn Féin from 1983: negotiated Irish Republican Army ceasefires in 1994–96 and 1997. **2 Henry (Brooks).** 1838–1918, U.S. historian and writer. His works include *Mont Saint Michel et Chartres* (1913) and his autobiography *The Education of Henry Adams* (1918). **3 John.** 1735–1826, second president of the U.S. (1797–1801); U.S. ambassador to Great Britain (1785–88); helped draft the Declaration of Independence (1776). **4 John Couch.** 1819–92, British astronomer who deduced the existence and position of the planet Neptune. **5 John Quincy,** son of John Adams. 1767–1848, sixth president of the U.S. (1825–29); secretary of state (1817–25). **6 Richard.** born 1920, British author; his novels include *Watership Down* (1972), *The Plague Dogs* (1977), and *Traveller* (1988). **7 Samuel.** 1722–1803, U.S. revolutionary leader; one of the organizers of the Boston Tea Party; a signatory of the Declaration of Independence.

Adam's apple *n* the visible projection of the thyroid cartilage of the larynx at the front of the neck.

adamsite ('ædəmˌzaɪt) *n* a yellow poisonous crystalline solid that readily sublimes; diphenylaminechlorarsine. It is used in chemical warfare as a vomiting agent. Formula: $C_6H_4AsClNHC_6H_4$; relative density: 1.65; melting pt.: 195°C; boiling pt.: 410°C. [C20: named after Roger *Adams* (1899–1971), U.S. chemist]

Adam's-needle *n* a North American liliaceous plant, *Yucca filamentosa,* that has a tall woody stem, stiff pointed leaves, and large clusters of white flowers arranged in spikes. It is cultivated as an ornamental plant. See also **Spanish bayonet.**

Adams-Stokes syndrome *n* another term for **heart block.** [C19: named after R. *Adams* (1791–1875) and W. *Stokes* (1804–78), Irish physicians]

Adana ('ædənə) *n* a city in S Turkey, capital of Adana province. Pop.: 1 066 544 (1995 est.). Also called: **Seyhan.**

adapt (ə'dæpt) *vb* **1** (often foll. by *to*) to adjust (someone or something, esp. oneself) to different conditions, a new environment, etc. **2** *(tr)* to fit, change, or modify to suit a new or different purpose: *to adapt a play for use in schools.*

[C17: from Latin *adaptāre,* from *ad-* to + *aptāre* to fit, from *aptus* APT] ▸ **a'daptable** *adj* ▸ **a,dapta'bility** *or* **a'daptableness** *n* ▸ **a'daptive** *adj*

adaptation (,ædəp'teɪʃən, ,ædæp-) *n* **1** the act or process of adapting or the state of being adapted; adjustment. **2** something that is produced by adapting something else. **3** something that is changed or modified to suit new conditions or needs. **4** *Biology.* an inherited or acquired modification in organisms that makes them better suited to survive and reproduce in a particular environment. **5** *Physiol.* the decreased response of a sense organ to a repeated or sustained stimulus. **6** *Psychol.* (in learning theory) the weakening of a response to a stimulus with repeated presentation of the stimulus without reinforcement; applied mainly to innate responses. **7** *Social welfare.* alteration to a dwelling to make it suitable for a disabled person, as by replacing steps with ramps.

adaptor *or* **adapter** (ə'dæptə) *n* **1** a person or thing that adapts. **2** any device for connecting two parts, esp. ones that are of different sizes or have different mating fitments. **3a** a plug used to connect an electrical device to a mains supply when they have different types of terminals. **3b** a device used to connect several electrical appliances to a single mains socket.

adaption (æ'dæpʃən) *n* another word for **adaptation.**

adaptive radiation *n* the development of many different forms from an originally homogeneous group of animals as a result of the increase of the original stock and its spread and adaptation to different environments. This type of evolution occurred in the Tertiary mammals and the Mesozoic reptiles.

Adar (a'dar) *n* (in the Jewish calendar) the twelfth month of the year according to biblical reckoning and the sixth month of the civil year, usually falling within February and March. In a leap year, an additional month **Adar Rishon** (first Adar) is intercalated between Shevat and Adar, and the latter is known as **Adar Sheni** (second Adar). [from Hebrew]

adaxial (æd'æksɪəl) *adj* facing towards the axis, as the surface of a leaf that faces the stem. Compare **abaxial.**

ADC *abbrev. for:* **1** aide-de-camp. **2** analogue-digital converter.

add (æd) *vb* **1** to combine (two or more numbers or quantities) by addition. **2** (*tr;* foll. by *to*) to increase (a number or quantity) by another number or quantity using addition. **3** (*tr;* often foll. by *to*) to join (something) to something else in order to increase the size, quantity, effect, or scope; unite (with): *to add insult to injury.* **4** (*intr;* foll. by *to*) to have an extra and increased effect (on): *her illness added to his worries.* **5** (*tr*) to say or write further. **6** (*tr;* foll. by *in*) to include. ◆ See also **add up.** [C14: from Latin *addere,* literally: to put to, from *ad-* to + *-dere* to put]

ADD *abbrev. for* attention deficit disorder.

add. *abbrev. for:* **1** addendum. **2** addition. **3** additional. **4** address.

Addams ('ædəmz) *n* **Jane.** 1860–1935, U.S. social reformer, feminist, and pacifist, who founded Hull House, a social settlement in Chicago: Nobel peace prize 1931.

addax ('ædæks) *n* a large light-coloured antelope, *Addax nasomaculatus,* having ribbed loosely spiralled horns and inhabiting desert regions in N Africa: family *Bovidae,* order *Artiodactyla.* [C17: Latin, from an unidentified ancient N African language]

added sixth *n* a chord much used esp. in jazz, consisting of a triad with an added sixth above the root. Also called: **added sixth chord.** Compare **sixth chord.**

addend ('ædɛnd, ə'dɛnd) *n* any of a set of numbers that is to be added. Compare **sum** (sense 1). [C20: short for ADDENDUM]

addendum (ə'dɛndəm) *n, pl* **-da** (-də). **1** something added; an addition. **2** a supplement or appendix to a book, magazine, etc. **3** the radial distance between the inner and outer pitch circles of a screw thread. **4** the radial distance between the pitch circle and tip of a gear tooth. [C18: from Latin, literally: a thing to be added, neuter gerundive of *addere* to ADD]

adder[1] ('ædə) *n* **1** Also called: **viper.** a common viper, *Vipera berus,* that is widely distributed in Europe, including Britain, and Asia and is typically dark greyish in colour with a black zigzag pattern along the back. **2** any of various similar venomous or nonvenomous snakes. ◆ See also **death adder, puff adder.** [Old English *nǣdre* snake; in Middle English *a naddre* was mistaken for *an addre;* related to Old Norse *nathr,* Gothic *nadrs*]

adder[2] ('ædə) *n* a person or thing that adds, esp. a single element of an electronic computer, the function of which is to add a single digit of each of two inputs.

adder's-meat *n* another name for the **greater stitchwort** (see **stitchwort**).

adder's-mouth *n* any of various orchids of the genus *Malaxis* that occur in all parts of the world except Australia and New Zealand and have small usually greenish flowers. See also **bog orchid.**

adder's-tongue *n* **1** any of several terrestrial ferns of the genus *Ophioglossum,* esp. *O. vulgatum,* that grow in the N hemisphere and have a spore-bearing body that sticks out like a spike from the leaf: family *Ophioglossaceae.* **2** another name for **dogtooth violet.**

addict *vb* (ə'dɪkt). **1** (*tr; usually passive;* often foll. by *to*) to cause (someone or oneself) to become dependent (on something, esp. a narcotic drug). ◆ *n* ('ædɪkt). **2** a person who is addicted, esp. to narcotic drugs. **3** *Informal.* a person who is devoted to something: *a jazz addict.* [C16 (as adj and as vb; n use C20): from Latin *addictus* given over, from *addīcere* to give one's assent to, from *ad-* to + *dīcere* to say]

addiction (ə'dɪkʃən) *n* the condition of being abnormally dependent on some habit, esp. compulsive dependency on narcotic drugs.

addictive (ə'dɪktɪv) *adj* of, relating to, or causing addiction.

adding ('ædɪŋ) *n* **1** an act or instance of addition. ◆ *adj* **2** of, for, or relating to addition. **3** (in systemic grammar) denoting a bound clause that qualifies the meaning of an antecedent noun rather than of the sentence as a whole. Compare **contingency** (sense 4).

adding machine *n* a mechanical device, operated manually or electrically, for adding and often subtracting, multiplying, and dividing.

Addington ('ædɪŋtən) *n* **Henry,** 1st Viscount Sidmouth. 1757–1844, British statesman; prime minister (1801–04) and Home Secretary (1812–21).

Addis Ababa ('ædɪs 'æbəbə) *n* the capital of Ethiopia, on a central plateau 2400 m (8000 ft.) above sea level: founded in 1887; became capital in 1896. Pop.: 2 316 400 (1994 est.).

Addison ('ædɪsᵊn) *n* **Joseph.** 1672–1719, English essayist and poet who, with Richard Steele, founded *The Spectator* (1711–14) and contributed most of its essays, including the *de Coverley Papers.*

Addison's disease *n* a disease characterized by deep bronzing of the skin, anaemia, and extreme weakness, caused by underactivity of the adrenal glands. Also called: **adrenal insufficiency.** [C19: named after Thomas *Addison* (1793–1860), British physician who identified it]

addition (ə'dɪʃən) *n* **1** the act, process, or result of adding. **2** a person or thing that is added or acquired. **3** a mathematical operation in which the sum of two numbers or quantities is calculated. Usually indicated by the symbol + **4** *Chiefly U.S. and Canadian.* a part added to a building or piece of land; annexe. **5** *Obsolete.* a title following a person's name. **6 in addition.** (*adv*) also; as well; besides. **7 in addition to.** (*prep*) besides; as well as. [C15: from Latin *additiōn-,* from *addere* to ADD]

additional (ə'dɪʃənᵊl) *adj* added or supplementary. ▸ **ad'ditionally** *adv*

additionality (ə,dɪʃə'nælɪtɪ) *n* (in the European Union) the principle that the EU contributes to the funding of a project in a member country provided that the member country also contributes.

Additional Member System *n* a system of voting in which people vote separately for the candidate and the party of their choice. Parties are allocated extra seats if the number of constituencies they win does not reflect their overall share of the vote. See also **proportional representation.**

additive ('ædɪtɪv) *adj* **1** characterized or produced by addition; cumulative. ◆ *n* **2** any substance added to something to improve it, prevent deterioration, etc. **3** short for **food additive.** [C17: from Late Latin *additīvus,* from *addere* to ADD]

additive process *n* a photographic process in which the desired colours are produced by adding together appropriate proportions of three primary colours. Compare **subtractive process.**

addle[1] ('ædᵊl) *vb* **1** to make or become confused or muddled. **2** to make or become rotten. ◆ *adj* **3** (*in combination*) indicating a confused or muddled state: *addle-brained; addle-pated.* [C18 (vb), back formation from *addled,* from C13 *addle* rotten, from Old English *adela* filth; related to dialect German *Addel* liquid manure]

addle[2] ('ædᵊl) *vb Northern English dialect.* to earn (money or one's living). [C13 *addlen,* from Old Norse *öthlask* to gain possession of property, from *ōthal* property]

add-on *n* a feature that can be added to a standard model or package to give increased benefits.

address (ə'drɛs) *n* **1** the conventional form by which the location of a building is described. **2** the written form of this, as on a letter or parcel, preceded by the name of the person or organization for whom it is intended. **3** the place at which someone lives. **4** a speech or written communication, esp. one of a formal nature. **5** skilfulness or tact. **6** *Archaic.* manner or style of speaking or conversation. **7** *Computing.* a number giving the location of a piece of stored information. See also **direct access. 8** *Brit. government.* a statement of the opinions or wishes of either or both Houses of Parliament that is sent to the sovereign. **9** the alignment or position of a part, component, etc., that permits correct assembly or fitting. **10** (*usually pl*) expressions of affection made by a man in courting a woman. ◆ *vb* **-dresses, -dressing; -dressed** *or* (*obsolete or poetic*) **-drest.** (*tr*) **11** to mark (a letter, parcel, etc.) with an address. **12** to speak to, refer to in speaking, or deliver a speech to. **13** (used reflexively; foll. by *to*) **13a** to speak or write to: *he addressed himself to the chairman.* **13b** to apply oneself to: *he addressed himself to the task.* **14** to direct (a message, warning, etc.) to the attention of. **15** to consign or entrust (a ship or a ship's cargo) to a factor, merchant, etc. **16** to adopt a position facing (the ball in golf, a partner in a dance, the target in archery, etc.). **17** to treat of; deal with: *chapter 10 addresses the problem of transitivity.* **18** an archaic word for **woo.** [C14 (in the sense: to make right, adorn) and C15 (in the modern sense: to direct words): via Old French from Vulgar Latin *addrictiāre* (unattested) to make straight, direct oneself towards, from Latin *ad-* to + *dīrectus* DIRECT] ▸ **ad'dresser** *or* **ad'dressor** *n*

addressable (ə'drɛsəbᵊl) *adj Computing.* possessing or capable of being reached by an address. ▸ **'ad,dressa'bility** *n*

addressee (,ædrɛ'siː) *n* a person or organization to whom a letter, parcel, etc., is addressed.

Addressograph (ə'drɛsəʊ,grɑːf, -,græf) *n Trademark.* a machine for addressing envelopes, etc.

adduce (ə'djuːs) *vb* (*tr*) to cite (reasons, examples, etc.) as evidence or proof. [C15: from Latin *addūcere* to lead or bring to] ▸ **ad'ducent** *adj* ▸ **ad'ducible** *or* **ad'duceable** *adj* ▸ **adduction** (ə'dʌkʃən) *n*

adduct (ə'dʌkt) *vb* (*tr*) **1** (of a muscle) to draw or pull (a leg, arm, etc.) towards the median axis of the body. Compare **abduct** (sense 2). ◆ *n* **2** *Chem.* a compound formed by direct combination of two or more different compounds or elements. [C19: from Latin *addūcere;* see ADDUCE] ▸ **ad'duction** *n*

adductor (ə'dʌktə) *n* a muscle that adducts.

add up *vb* (*adv*) **1** to find the sum (of). **2** (*intr*) to result in a correct total. **3** (*intr*) *Informal.* to make sense. **4** (*intr;* foll. by *to*) to amount to.

-ade *suffix forming nouns.* a sweetened drink made of various fruits: *lemonade; limeade.* [from French, from Latin *-āta* made of, feminine past participle of verbs ending in *-āre*]

Adelaide ('ædɪˌleɪd) *n* the capital of South Australia: **Port Adelaide,** 11 km (7 miles) away on St. Vincent Gulf, handles the bulk of exports. Pop.: 1 081 000 (1995 est.).

Adélie Land ('ædɪlɪ; *French* adeli) *n* a part of Antarctica, between Wilkes Land and George V Land: under French sovereignty. Also called: **Adélie Coast.** French name: **Terre Adélie.**

ademption (ə'dɛmpʃən) *n Property law.* the failure of a specific legacy, as by a testator disposing of the subject matter in his lifetime. [C16: from Latin *ademptiōn-* a taking away, from *adimere* to take away, take to (oneself), from *ad-* to + *emere* to buy, take]

Aden ('eɪdᵊn) *n* **1** the main port and commercial capital of Yemen, on the N coast of the **Gulf of Aden**, an arm of the Indian Ocean at the entrance to the Red Sea: capital of South Yemen until 1990: formerly an important port of call on shipping routes to the East. Pop.: 562 000 (1995 est.). **2** a former British colony and protectorate on the S coast of the Arabian Peninsula: became part of South Yemen in 1967, now part of Yemen. Area: 195 sq. km (75 sq. miles).

Adenauer (*German* 'a:dənauər) *n* **Konrad** ('kɔnra:t). 1876–1967, German statesman; chancellor of West Germany (1949–63).

adenectomy (ˌædə'nɛktəmɪ) *n, pl* **-mies. 1** surgical removal of a gland. **2** another name for **adenoidectomy.** [C19: from ADENO- + -ECTOMY]

adenine ('ædənɪn, -ˌni:n, -ˌnaɪn) *n* a purine base present in tissues of all living organisms as a constituent of the nucleic acids DNA and RNA and of certain coenzymes; 6-aminopurine. Formula: $C_5H_5N_5$; melting pt.: 360–365°C.

adenitis (ˌædə'naɪtɪs) *n* inflammation of a gland or lymph node. [C19: New Latin, from ADENO- + -ITIS]

adeno- *or before a vowel* **aden-** *combining form.* gland or glandular: *adenoid; adenology.* [New Latin, from Greek *adēn* gland]

adenocarcinoma (ˌædɪnəʊˌkɑ:sɪ'nəʊmə) *n, pl* **-mas** *or* **-mata** (-mətə). **1** a malignant tumour originating in glandular tissue. **2** a malignant tumour with a glandlike structure.

adenohypophysis (ˌædɪnəʊhaɪ'pɒfɪsɪs) *n* the anterior lobe of the pituitary gland. Compare **neurohypophysis.**

adenoid ('ædɪˌnɔɪd) *adj* **1** of or resembling a gland. **2** of or relating to lymphoid tissue, as that found in the lymph nodes, spleen, tonsils, etc. **3** of or relating to the adenoids. [C19: from Greek *adenoeidēs.* See ADENO-, -OID]

adenoidal (ˌædɪ'nɔɪdᵊl) *adj* **1** having the nasal tones or impaired breathing of one with enlarged adenoids. **2** another word for **adenoid** (for all senses).

adenoidectomy (ˌædɪnɔɪ'dɛktəmɪ) *n, pl* **-mies.** surgical removal of the adenoids.

adenoids ('ædɪˌnɔɪdz) *pl n* a mass of lymphoid tissue at the back of the throat behind the uvula: when enlarged it often restricts nasal breathing, esp. in young children. Technical name: **pharyngeal tonsil.**

adenoma (ˌædɪ'nəʊmə) *n, pl* **-mas** *or* **-mata** (-mətə). **1** a tumour, usually benign, occurring in glandular tissue. **2** a tumour having a glandlike structure.

adenopathy (ˌædɪ'nɒpəθɪ) *n Pathol.* **1** enlargement of the lymph nodes. **2** enlargement of a gland.

adenosine (æ'dɛnəˌsi:n, ˌædɪ'nəʊsi:n) *n Biochem.* a nucleoside formed by the condensation of adenine and ribose. It is present in all living cells in a combined form, as in ribonucleic acids. Formula: $C_{10}H_{13}N_5O_4$. [C20: a blend of ADENINE + RIBOSE]

adenosine monophosphate (ˌmɒnəʊ'fɒsfeɪt) *n* another term for **adenylic acid.** Abbrev.: **AMP.**

adenosine triphosphate *n* the full name of **ATP.**

adenovirus (ˌædɪnəʊ'vaɪrəs) *n* any of a group of viruses that may cause upper respiratory diseases in man. Compare **enterovirus, myxovirus.**

adenylic acid (ˌædə'nɪlɪk) *n* a nucleotide consisting of adenine, ribose or deoxyribose, and a phosphate group. It is a constituent of DNA or RNA. Also called: **adenosine monophosphate.**

adept *adj* (ə'dɛpt). **1** very proficient in something requiring skill or manual dexterity. **2** skilful; expert. ◆ *n* ('ædɛpt). **3** a person who is skilled or proficient in something. [C17: from Medieval Latin *adeptus,* from Latin *adipiscī* to attain, from *ad-* to + *apiscī* to attain] ▸ **a'deptly** *adv* ▸ **a'deptness** *n*

adequate ('ædɪkwɪt) *adj* able to fulfil a need or requirement without being abundant, outstanding, etc. [C17: from Latin *adaequāre* to equalize, from *ad-* to + *aequus* EQUAL] ▸ **adequacy** ('ædɪkwəsɪ) *n* ▸ **'adequately** *adv*

à deux *French.* (a dø) *adj, adv* of or for two persons.

ADFA *abbrev. for* Australian Defence Force Academy.

ADH *abbrev. for* antidiuretic hormone. See **vasopressin.**

adhan (ˌa'ða:n) *n Islam.* a call to prayer. [changed from Arabic *adhān,* literally: announcement]

adhere (əd'hɪə) *vb (intr)* **1** (usually foll. by *to*) to stick or hold fast. **2** (foll. by *to*) to be devoted (to a political party, cause, religion, etc.); be a follower (of). **3** (foll. by *to*) to follow closely or exactly: *adhere to the rules.* [C16: via Medieval Latin *adhērēre* from Latin *adhaerēre* to stick to] ▸ **ad'herence** *n*

USAGE See at **adhesion.**

adherent (əd'hɪərənt) *n* **1** (usually foll. by *of*) *a supporter or follower.* ◆ *adj* **2** sticking, holding fast, or attached.

adhesion (əd'hi:ʒən) *n* **1** the quality or condition of sticking together or holding fast. **2** ability to make firm contact without skidding or slipping. **3** attachment or fidelity, as to a political party, cause, etc. **4** an attraction or repulsion between the molecules of unlike substances in contact: distinguished from *cohesion.* **5** *Pathol.* abnormal union of structures or parts. [C17: from Latin *adhaesiōn-* a sticking. See ADHERE]

USAGE *Adhesion* is the preferred term when talking about sticking or holding fast in a physical sense. *Adherence* is preferred when talking about attachment to a political party, cause, etc.

adhesive (əd'hi:sɪv) *adj* **1** able or designed to adhere; sticky: *adhesive tape.* **2** tenacious or clinging. ◆ *n* **3** a substance used for sticking objects together, such as glue, cement, or paste. ▸ **ad'hesively** *adv* ▸ **ad'hesiveness** *n*

adhesive binding *n Bookbinding.* a style of binding used mainly for paperback books, where the backs of the gathered sections are trimmed and inserted into a cover along with adhesive to hold the pages and cover together. Also called **perfect binding.**

ad hoc (æd 'hɒk) *adj, adv* for a particular purpose only; lacking generality or justification: *an ad hoc decision; an ad hoc committee.* [Latin, literally: to this]

ad hocracy (æd'hɒkrəsɪ) *n* management that responds to urgent problems rather than planning to avoid them.

ad hominem *Latin.* (æd 'hɒmɪˌnɛm) *adj, adv* **1** directed against a person rather than against his arguments. **2** based on or appealing to emotion rather than reason. ◆ Compare **ad rem.** See also **argumentum ad hominem.** [literally: to the man]

adiabatic (ˌædɪə'bætɪk, ˌeɪ-) *adj* **1** (of a thermodynamic process) taking place without loss or gain of heat. ◆ *n* **2** a curve on a graph representing the changes in two characteristics (such as pressure and volume) of a system undergoing an adiabatic process. [C19: from Greek *adiabatos* not to be crossed, impassable (to heat), from A-[1] + *diabatos* passable, from *dia-* across + *bainein* to go]

adiactinic (ˌædɪæk'tɪnɪk) *adj Physics.* denoting a substance that does not transmit radiation affecting photochemically sensitive materials, such as a safelight in a photographic darkroom.

adiaphorism (ˌædɪ'æfəˌrɪzəm) *n* a Christian Protestant theological theory that certain rites and actions are matters of indifference in religion since not forbidden by the Scriptures. [C19: see ADIAPHOROUS] ▸ **ˌadi'aphorist** *n* ▸ **ˌadiˌapho'ristic** *adj*

adiaphorous (ˌædɪ'æfərəs) *adj Med.* having no effect for good or ill, as a drug or placebo. [C17: from Greek *adiaphoros* indifferent, from A-[1] + *diaphoros* different]

adiathermancy (ˌædɪə'θɜ:mənsɪ) *n* another name for **athermancy.** ▸ **ˌadia'thermanous** *adj*

Adie ('eɪdɪ) *n* **Kathryn,** known as *Kate.* born 1945, British television journalist, noted esp. for her frontline reporting of revolutions, wars, etc.

adieu (ə'dju:; *French* adjø) *sentence substitute, n, pl* **adieus** *or* **adieux** (ə'dju:z; *French* adjø). goodbye; farewell. [C14: from Old French, from *a* to + *dieu* God]

Adige (*Italian* 'a:didʒe) *n* a river in N Italy, flowing southeast to the Adriatic. Length: 354 km (220 miles).

Adi Granth (ˌa:dɪ 'grʌnt) *n* another name for **Guru Granth.** [from Punjabi: first book]

ad infinitum (æd ˌɪnfɪ'naɪtəm) *adv* without end; endlessly; to infinity. Abbrev.: **ad inf.** [Latin]

ad interim (æd 'ɪntərɪm) *adj, adv* for the meantime; for the present: *ad interim measures.* Abbrev.: **ad int.** [Latin]

adios (ˌædɪ'ɒs; *Spanish* a'ðjos) *sentence substitute.* goodbye; farewell. [literally: to God]

adipic acid (ə'dɪpɪk) *n* a colourless crystalline solid used in the preparation of nylon. Formula: $HOOC(CH_2)_4COOH$. [C19: from New Latin *adiposus* fat + -IC]

adipocere (ˌædɪpəʊ'sɪə, 'ædɪpəʊˌsɪə) *n* a waxlike fatty substance formed during the decomposition of corpses. Nontechnical name: **grave-wax.** [C19: via French from New Latin *adiposus* fat (see ADIPOSE) + French *cire* wax] ▸ **adipocerous** (ˌædɪ'pɒsərəs) *adj*

adipocyte ('ædɪpəʊˌsaɪt) *n* a fat cell that accumulates and stores fats.

adipose ('ædɪˌpəʊs, -ˌpəʊz) *adj* **1** of, resembling, or containing fat; fatty. ◆ *n* **2** animal fat. [C18: from New Latin *adiposus,* from Latin *adeps* fat]

adipose fin *n* a posterior dorsal fin occurring in the salmon and related fishes.

Adiprene ('ædɪpri:n) *n Trademark.* a polyurethane elastomer with exceptional abrasion resistance and strength.

adipsia (eɪ'dɪpsɪə) *n* **1** complete lack of thirst. **2** abnormal abstinence from drinking. [C20: from A-[1] + Greek *dipsa* thirst]

Adirondack Mountains (ˌædɪ'rɒndæk) *or* **Adirondacks** *pl n* a mountain range in NE New York State. Highest peak: Mount Marcy, 1629 m (5344 ft.).

adit ('ædɪt) *n* an almost horizontal shaft into a mine, for access or drainage. [C17: from Latin *aditus* an approach, from *adīre,* from *ad-* towards + *īre* to go]

Adivasi ('ɑ:dɪˌvɑ:sɪ) *n* a member of any of the aboriginal peoples of India. [Sanskrit, from *adi* beginning + *vasi* dweller]

adj. *abbrev. for:* **1** adjective. **2** *Maths.* adjoint. **3** adjunct. **4** adjourned. **5** *Insurance, banking, etc.* adjustment. **6** Also: **adjt.** adjutant.

adjacent (ə'dʒeɪsᵊnt) *adj* **1** being near or close, esp. having a common boundary; adjoining; contiguous. **2** *Maths.* **2a** (of a pair of vertices in a graph) joined by a common edge. **2b** (of a pair of edges in a graph) meeting at a common vortex. ◆ *n* **3** *Geometry.* the side lying between a specified angle and a right angle in a right-angled triangle. [C15: from Latin *adjacēre* to lie next to, from *ad-* near + *jacēre* to lie] ▸ **ad'jacency** *n* ▸ **ad'jacently** *adv*

adjacent angles *pl n* two angles that have the same vertex and a side in common.

adjective ('ædʒɪktɪv) *n* **1a** a word imputing a characteristic to a noun or pronoun. **1b** (*as modifier*): *an adjective phrase.* Abbrev.: **adj.** ◆ *adj* **2** additional or dependent. **3** (of law) relating to court practice and procedure, as opposed to the principles of law dealt with by the courts. Compare **substantive** (sense 7). [C14: from Late Latin *adjectīvus* attributive, from *adjicere* to throw to, add, from *ad-* to + *jacere* to throw; in grammatical sense, from the Latin phrase *nōmen adjectīvum* attributive noun] ▸ **adjectival** (ˌædʒɪk'taɪvᵊl) *adj*

adjoin (ə'dʒɔɪn) *vb* **1** to be next to (an area of land, etc.). **2** (*tr;* foll. by *to*) to join; affix or attach. [C14: via Old French from Latin *adjungere,* from *ad-* to + *jungere* to join]

adjoining (ə'dʒɔɪnɪŋ) *adj* being in contact; connected or neighbouring.

adjoint ('æd,dʒɔɪnt) *n Maths.* **a** another name for **Hermitian conjugate. b** a generalization in category theory of this notion.

adjourn (ə'dʒɜ:n) *vb* **1** (*intr*) (of a court, etc.) to close at the end of a session. **2** to postpone or be postponed, esp. temporarily or to another place. **3** (*tr*) to put off (a problem, discussion, etc.) for later consideration; defer. **4** (*intr*) *Informal.* **4a** to move elsewhere: *let's adjourn to the kitchen.* **4b** to stop work. [C14: from Old French *ajourner* to defer to an arranged day, from *a-* to + *jour* day, from Late Latin *diurnum,* from Latin *diurnus* daily, from *diēs* day] ▸ **ad'journment** *n*

adjt. *or* **adj.** *abbrev. for* adjutant.

adjudge (ə'dʒʌdʒ) *vb* (*tr; usually passive*) **1** to pronounce formally; declare: *he was adjudged the winner.* **2a** to determine judicially; judge. **2b** to order or pronounce by law; decree: *he was adjudged bankrupt.* **2c** to award (costs, damages, etc.). **3** *Archaic.* to sentence or condemn. [C14: via Old French from Latin *adjūdicāre.* See ADJUDICATE]

adjudicate (ə'dʒu:dɪ,keɪt) *vb* **1** (when *intr,* usually foll. by *upon*) to give a decision (on), esp. a formal or binding one. **2** (*intr*) to act as an adjudicator. **3** (*tr*) *Chess.* to determine the likely result of (a game) by counting relative value of pieces, positional strength, etc. **4** (*intr*) to serve as a judge or arbiter, as in a competition. [C18: from Latin *adjūdicāre* to award something to someone, from *ad-* to + *jūdicāre* to act as a judge, from *jūdex* judge] ▸ **ad,judi'cation** *n* ▸ **adjudicative** (ə'dʒu:dɪkətɪv) *adj*

adjudicator (ə'dʒu:dɪ,keɪtə) *n* **1** a judge, esp. in a competition. **2** an arbitrator, esp. in a dispute.

adjunct ('ædʒʌŋkt) *n* **1** something incidental or not essential that is added to something else. **2** a person who is subordinate to another. **3** *Grammar.* **3a** part of a sentence other than the subject or the predicate. **3b** (in systemic grammar) part of a sentence other than the subject, predicator, object, or complement; usually a prepositional or adverbial group. **3c** part of a sentence that may be omitted without making the sentence ungrammatical; a modifier. **4** *Logic.* another name for **accident** (sense 4). ◆ *adj* **5** added or connected in a secondary or subordinate position; auxiliary. [C16: from Latin *adjunctus,* past participle of *adjungere* to ADJOIN] ▸ **adjunctive** (ə'dʒʌŋktɪv) *adj* ▸ **'adjunctly** *adv*

adjunction (ə'dʒʌŋkʃən) *n* (in phrase-structure grammar) the relationship between a branch of a tree representing a sentence to other branches to its left or right that descend from the same node immediately above.

adjure (ə'dʒʊə) *vb* (*tr*) **1** to command, often by exacting an oath; charge. **2** to appeal earnestly to. [C14: from Latin *adjūrāre* to swear to, from *ad-* to + *jūrāre* to swear, from *jūs* oath] ▸ **adjuration** (,ædʒʊə'reɪʃən) *n* ▸ **ad'juratory** *adj* ▸ **ad'jurer** *or* **ad'juror** *n*

adjust (ə'dʒʌst) *vb* **1** (*tr*) to alter slightly, esp. to achieve accuracy; regulate: *to adjust the television.* **2** to adapt, as to a new environment, etc. **3** (*tr*) to put into order. **4** (*tr*) *Insurance.* to determine the amount payable in settlement of (a claim). [C17: from Old French *adjuster,* from *ad-* to + *juste* right, JUST] ▸ **ad'justable** *adj* ▸ **ad'justably** *adv* ▸ **ad'juster** *n*

adjustment (ə'dʒʌstmənt) *n* **1** the act of adjusting or state of being adjusted. **2** a control for regulating: *the adjustment for volume is beside the speaker.*

adjutant ('ædʒətənt) *n* **1** an officer who acts as administrative assistant to a superior officer. Abbrevs.: **adjt., adj. 2** short for **adjutant bird.** [C17: from Latin *adjūtāre* to AID] ▸ **'adjutancy** *n*

adjutant bird *or* **stork** *n* either of two large carrion-eating storks, *Leptoptilos dubius* or *L. javanicus,* which are closely related and similar to the marabou and occur in S and SE Asia. [so called for its supposedly military gait]

adjutant general *n, pl* **adjutants general. 1** *Brit. Army.* **1a** a member of the Army Board responsible for personnel and administrative functions. **1b** a general's executive officer. **2** *U.S. Army.* the adjutant of a military unit with general staff.

adjuvant ('ædʒəvənt) *adj* **1** aiding or assisting. ◆ *n* **2** something that aids or assists; auxiliary. **3** *Med.* a drug or other substance that enhances the activity of another. **4** *Immunol.* a substance that enhances the immune response stimulated by an antigen when injected with the antigen. [C17: from Latin *adjuvāns,* present participle of *adjuvāre,* from *juvāre* to help]

Adler *n* **1** (*German* 'a:dlər). **Alfred** ('alfre:t). 1870–1937, Austrian psychiatrist, noted for his descriptions of overcompensation and inferiority feelings. **2** ('ædlə). **Larry,** full name *Lawrence Cecil Adler.* born 1914, U.S. harmonica player.

Adlerian (æd'lɪərɪən) *adj* of or relating to Alfred Adler or his ideas.

ad-lib (æd'lɪb) *vb* **-libs, -libbing, -libbed. 1** to improvise and deliver without preparation (a speech, musical performance, etc.). ◆ *adj* (**ad lib** *when predicative*) **2** improvised; impromptu. ◆ *adv* **ad lib. 3** without restraint; freely. **4** *Music.* short for **ad libitum.** ◆ *n* **5** an improvised performance, often humorous. [C18: short for Latin *ad libitum,* literally: according to pleasure] ▸ **ad-'libber** *n*

ad libitum ('lɪbɪtum, -təm) *adj, adv Music.* (to be performed) at the performer's discretion. Often shortened to **ad lib.** [See AD-LIB]

ad litem *Latin.* (æd 'laɪtεm) *adj* (esp. of a guardian) appointed for a lawsuit.

Adm. *abbrev. for:* **1** Admiral. **2** Admiralty.

adman ('æd,mæn, -mən) *n, pl* **-men.** *Informal.* a person who works in advertising.

admeasure (æd'mεʒə) *vb* **1** to measure out (land, etc.) as a share; apportion. **2** (*tr*) to determine the dimensions, capacity, weight, and other details of (a vessel), as for an official registration, documentation, or yacht handicap rating. [C14: *amesuren,* from Old French *amesurer,* from *mesurer* to MEASURE; the modern form derives from AD- + MEASURE] ▸ **ad'measurement** *n*

Admetus (æd'mi:təs) *n Greek myth.* a king of Thessaly, one of the Argonauts, who was married to Alcestis.

admin ('ædmɪn) *n Informal.* short for **administration.**

adminicle (æd'mɪnɪkəl) *n Law.* something contributing to prove a point without itself being complete proof. [C16: from Latin *adminiculum* support]

administer (əd'mɪnɪstə) *vb* (*mainly tr*) **1** (*also intr*) to direct or control (the affairs of a business, government, etc.). **2** to put into execution; dispense: *administer justice.* **3** (when *intr,* foll. by *to*) to give or apply (medicine, assistance, etc.) as a remedy or relief. **4** to apply formally; perform: *to administer extreme unction.* **5** to supervise or impose the taking of (an oath, etc.). **6** to manage or distribute (an estate, property, etc.). [C14 *amynistre,* via Old French from Latin *administrare,* from *ad-* to + *ministrāre* to MINISTER]

administrate (əd'mɪnɪ,streɪt) *vb* to manage or direct (the affairs of a business, institution, etc.).

administration (əd,mɪnɪ'streɪʃən) *n* **1** management of the affairs of an organization, such as a business or institution. **2** the duties of an administrator. **3** the body of people who administer an organization. **4** the conduct of the affairs of government. **5** term of office: often used of presidents, governments, etc. **6** the executive branch of government along with the public service; the government as a whole. **7** (*often cap.*) *Chiefly U.S.* the political executive, esp. of the U.S.; the government. **8** *Chiefly U.S.* a government board, agency, authority, etc. **9** *Property law.* **9a** the conduct or disposal of the estate of a deceased person. **9b** the management by a trustee of an estate subject to a trust. **10a** the administering of something, such as a sacrament, oath, or medical treatment. **10b** the thing that is administered. ▸ **ad'ministrative** *adj* ▸ **ad'ministratively** *adv*

administration order *n Law.* **1** an order by a court appointing a person to manage a company that is in financial difficulty, in an attempt to ensure the survival of the company or achieve the best realization of its assets. **2** an order by a court for the administration of the estate of a debtor who has been ordered by the court to pay money that he owes.

administrator (əd'mɪnɪ,streɪtə) *n* **1** a person who administers the affairs of an organization, official body, etc. **2** *Property law.* a person authorized to manage an estate, esp. when the owner has died intestate or without having appointed executors. ▸ **ad,minis'tratrix** *fem n*

admirable ('ædmərəbəl) *adj* deserving or inspiring admiration; excellent. ▸ **'admirably** *adv*

admiral ('ædmərəl) *n* **1** the supreme commander of a fleet or navy. **2** Also called: **admiral of the fleet, fleet admiral.** a naval officer of the highest rank, equivalent to general of the army or field marshal. **3** a senior naval officer entitled to fly his own flag. See also **rear admiral, vice admiral. 4** *Chiefly Brit.* the master of a fishing fleet. **5** any of various nymphalid butterflies, esp. the red admiral or white admiral. [C13 *amyral,* from Old French *amiral* emir, and from Medieval Latin *admīrālis* (the spelling with *d* probably influenced by *admīrābilis* admirable); both from Arabic *amīr* emir, commander, esp. in the phrase *amīr-al* commander of, as in *amīr-al-bahr* commander of the sea] ▸ **'admiral,ship** *n*

admiralty ('ædmərəltɪ) *n, pl* **-ties. 1** the office or jurisdiction of an admiral. **2a** jurisdiction over naval affairs. **2b** (*as modifier*): *admiralty law.*

Admiralty Board *n* **the.** (formerly) a department of the British Ministry of Defence, responsible for the administration and planning of the Royal Navy.

Admiralty House *n* the official residence of the Governor General of Australia, in Sydney.

Admiralty Islands *pl n* a group of about 40 volcanic and coral islands in the SW Pacific, part of Papua New Guinea, in the Bismarck Archipelago: main island: Manus. Pop.: 35 200 (1995). Area: about 2000 sq. km (800 sq. miles). Also called: **Admiralties.**

Admiralty mile *n* another name for **nautical mile.**

Admiralty Range *n* a mountain range in Antarctica, on the coast of Victoria Land, northwest of the Ross Sea.

admiration (,ædmə'reɪʃən) *n* **1** pleasurable contemplation or surprise. **2** a person or thing that is admired: *she was the admiration of the court.* **3** *Archaic.* wonder.

admire (əd'maɪə) *vb* (*tr*) **1** to regard with esteem, respect, approval, or pleased surprise. **2** *Archaic.* to wonder at. [C16: from Latin *admīrāri* to wonder at, from *ad-* to, at + *mīrāri* to wonder, from *mīrus* wonderful] ▸ **ad'mirer** *n* ▸ **ad'miring** *adj* ▸ **ad'miringly** *adv*

admissible (əd'mɪsəbəl) *adj* **1** able or deserving to be considered or allowed. **2** deserving to be admitted or allowed to enter. **3** *Law.* (esp. of evidence) capable of being or bound to be admitted in a court of law. ▸ **ad,missi'bility** *or* **ad'missibleness** *n*

admission (əd'mɪʃən) *n* **1** permission to enter or the right, authority, etc., to enter. **2** the price charged for entrance. **3** acceptance for a position, office, etc. **4** a confession, as of a crime, mistake, etc. **5** an acknowledgment of the truth or validity of something. [C15: from Latin *admissiōn-,* from *admittere* to ADMIT] ▸ **ad'missive** *adj*

admit (əd'mɪt) *vb* **-mits, -mitting, -mitted.** (*mainly tr*) **1** (*may take a clause as object*) to confess or acknowledge (a crime, mistake, etc.). **2** (*may take a clause as object*) to concede (the truth or validity of something). **3** to allow to enter; let in. **4** (foll. by *to*) to allow participation (in) or the right to be part (of): *to admit to the profession.* **5** (when *intr,* foll. by *of*) to allow (of); leave room (for). **6** (*intr*) to give access: *the door admits onto the lawn.* [C14: from Latin *admittere* to let come or go to, from *ad-* to + *mittere* to send]

admittance (əd'mɪtəns) *n* **1** the right or authority to enter. **2** the act of giving entrance. **3** *Electrical engineering.* the reciprocal of impedance, usually measured in siemens. It can be expressed as a complex quantity, the real part of which is the conductance and the imaginary part the susceptance. Symbol: *y*

admittedly (əd'mɪtɪdlɪ) *adv* (*sentence modifier*) willingly conceded: *admittedly I am afraid.*

admix (əd'mɪks) *vb* (*tr*) *Rare.* to mix or blend. [C16: back formation from obsolete *admixt,* from Latin *admīscēre* to mix with]

admixture (ədˈmɪkstʃə) *n* **1** a less common word for **mixture.** **2** anything added in mixing; ingredient.
admonish (ədˈmɒnɪʃ) *vb (tr)* **1** to reprove firmly but not harshly. **2** to advise to do or against doing something; warn; caution. [C14: via Old French from Vulgar Latin *admonestāre* (unattested), from Latin *admonēre* to put one in mind of, from *monēre* to advise] ▸ **adˈmonisher** *or* **adˈmonitor** *n* ▸ **admonition** (ˌædməˈnɪʃən) *n* ▸ **adˈmonitory** *adj*
ADN *international car registration for* Yemen.
adnate (ˈædneɪt) *adj Botany.* growing closely attached to an adjacent part or organ. [C17: from Latin *adnātus,* a variant form of *agnātus* AGNATE]
ad nauseam (æd ˈnɔːzɪˌæm, -sɪ-) *adv* to a disgusting extent. [Latin: to (the point of) nausea]
adnexa (ædˈnɛksə) *pl n Anat.* adjoining organs, esp. of the uterus. [C19: New Latin: appendages] ▸ **adˈnexal** *adj*
adnominal (ədˈnɒmɪnᵊl) *Grammar.* ◆ *n* **1** a word modifying a noun. ◆ *adj* **2** of or relating to an adnoun.
adnoun (ˈædnaʊn) *n* an adjective used as a noun; absolute adjective. [C18: from Latin *ad* to + NOUN, formed on the model of ADVERB]
ado (əˈduː) *n* bustling activity; fuss; bother; delay (esp. in the phrases **without more ado, with much ado**). [C14: from the phrase *at do* a to-do, from Old Norse *at* to (marking the infinitive) + DO[1]]
adobe (əˈdəʊbɪ) *n* **1a** a sun-dried brick used for building. **1b** *(as modifier): an adobe house.* **2** a building constructed of such bricks. **3** the clayey material from which such bricks are made. [C19: from Spanish]
adobe flat *n Chiefly U.S.* a gently sloping clayey plain formed by a short-lived stream or flood water.
adolescence (ˌædəˈlɛsəns) *n* the period in human development that occurs between the beginning of puberty and adulthood. [C15: via Old French from Latin *adolēscentia,* from *adolēscere* to grow up, from *alēscere* to grow, from *alēre* to feed, nourish]
adolescent (ˌædəˈlɛsᵊnt) *adj* **1** of or relating to adolescence. **2** *Informal.* behaving in an immature way; puerile. ◆ *n* **3** an adolescent person.
Adonai (ˌædɒˈnaɪ, -ˈneɪaɪ) *n Judaism.* a name for God. [C15: from Hebrew: lord; compare ADONIS]
Adonic (əˈdɒnɪk) *adj* **1** (in classical prosody) of or relating to a verse line consisting of a dactyl (—⏑⏑) followed by a spondee (——) or by a trochee (—⏑), thought to have been first used in laments for Adonis. **2** of or relating to Adonis. ◆ *n* **3** an Adonic line or verse.
Adonis (əˈdəʊnɪs) *n* **1** *Greek myth.* a handsome youth loved by Aphrodite. Killed by a wild boar, he was believed to spend part of the year in the underworld and part on earth, symbolizing the vegetative cycle. **2** a handsome young man. [C16: from Latin, via Greek *Adōnis* from Phoenician *adōni* my lord, a title of the god Tammuz; related to Hebrew ADONAI]
adopt (əˈdɒpt) *vb (tr)* **1** *Law.* to bring (a person) into a specific relationship, esp. to take (another's child) as one's own child. **2** to choose and follow (a plan, technique, etc.). **3** to take over (an idea, etc.) as if it were one's own. **4** to take on; assume: *to adopt a title.* **5** to accept (a report, etc.). [C16: from Latin *adoptāre* to choose for oneself, from *optāre* to choose] ▸ **ˌadopˈtee** *n* ▸ **aˈdoption** *n*
adopted (əˈdɒptɪd) *adj* having been adopted: *an adopted child.* Compare **adoptive.**
adoption panel *n Social welfare.* (in Britain) a committee appointed by an adoption agency, such as a local authority, to make recommendations concerning the suitability of prospective adoption cases.
adoptive (əˈdɒptɪv) *adj* **1** acquired or related by adoption: *an adoptive father.* **2** of or relating to adoption. Compare **adopted.**
adorable (əˈdɔːrəbᵊl) *adj* **1** very attractive; charming; lovable. **2** *Becoming rare.* deserving or eliciting adoration. ▸ **aˈdorably** *adv*
adoration (ˌædəˈreɪʃən) *n* **1** deep love or esteem. **2** the act of worshipping.
adore (əˈdɔː) *vb* **1** *(tr)* to love intensely or deeply. **2** to worship (a god) with religious rites. **3** *(tr) Informal.* to like very much: *I adore chocolate.* [C15: via French from Latin *adōrāre,* from *ad-* to + *ōrāre* to pray] ▸ **aˈdorer** *n* ▸ **aˈdoring** *adj* ▸ **aˈdoringly** *adv*
adorn (əˈdɔːn) *vb (tr)* **1** to decorate: *she adorned her hair with flowers.* **2** to increase the beauty, distinction, etc., of. [C14: via Old French from Latin *adōrnāre,* from *ōrnāre* to furnish, prepare] ▸ **aˈdornment** *n*
Adorno *(German* aˈdɔrno) *n* **Theodor Wiesengrund.** 1903–69, German philosopher, sociologist, and music critic. His writings include *The Philosophy of the New Music* (1949) and *Negative Dialectics* (1966).
Adowa (ˈɑːduˌwɑː) *n* a variant spelling of **Aduwa.**
ADP *n Biochem.* adenosine diphosphate; a nucleotide derived from ATP with the liberation of energy that is then used in the performance of muscular work.
Adrastea (əˈdræstɪə) *n* a small satellite of Jupiter, discovered in 1979.
Adrastus (əˈdræstəs) *n Greek myth.* a king of Argos and leader of the Seven against Thebes of whom he was the sole survivor.
ad referendum *adv, adj* subject to agreement by others and finalization of details: *an ad referendum contract.* [Latin]
ad rem *Latin.* (æd ˈrɛm) *adj, adv* to the point; without digression: *to reply ad rem; an ad rem discussion.* Compare **ad hominem.**
adrenal (əˈdriːnᵊl) *adj* **1** on or near the kidneys. **2** of or relating to the adrenal glands or their secretions. ◆ *n* **3** an adrenal gland. [C19: from AD- (near) + RENAL]
adrenal gland *n* an endocrine gland at the anterior end of each kidney. Its medulla secretes adrenaline and noradrenaline and its cortex secretes several steroid hormones. Also called: **suprarenal gland.**
Adrenalin (əˈdrɛnəlɪn) *n Trademark.* a brand of **adrenaline.**
adrenaline *or* **adrenalin** (əˈdrɛnəlɪn) *n* a hormone that is secreted by the adrenal medulla in response to stress and increases heart rate, pulse rate, and blood pressure, and raises the blood levels of glucose and lipids. It is extracted from animals or synthesized for such medical uses as the treatment of asthma. Chemical name: aminohydroxyphenylpropionic acid; formula: $C_9H_{13}NO_3$. U.S. name: **epinephrine.**
adrenal insufficiency *n* another name for **Addison's disease.**
adrenergic (ˌædrəˈnɜːdʒɪk) *adj* releasing or activated by adrenaline or an adrenaline-like substance. [C20: ADRENALINE + Greek *ergon* work]
adrenocorticotrophic (əˌdriːnəʊˌkɔːtəkəʊˈtrɒfɪk) *or* **adrenocorticotropic** (əˌdriːnəʊˌkɔːtəkəʊˈtrɒpɪk) *adj* stimulating the adrenal cortex.
adrenocorticotrophic hormone *n* the full name of **ACTH.**
Adrian (ˈeɪdrɪən) *n* **Edgar Douglas,** Baron Adrian. 1889–1977, English physiologist, noted particularly for his research into the function of neurons: shared with Sherrington the Nobel prize for physiology and medicine 1932.
Adrian IV *n* original name *Nicholas Breakspear.* ?1100–59, the only English pope (1154–59).
Adrianople (ˌeɪdrɪəˈnəʊpᵊl) *or* **Adrianopolis** (ˌeɪdrɪəˈnɒpəlɪs) *n* former names of **Edirne.**
Adriatic (ˌeɪdrɪˈætɪk) *adj* **1** of or relating to the Adriatic Sea, or to the inhabitants of its coast or islands. ◆ *n* **2 the.** short for the **Adriatic Sea.**
Adriatic Sea *n* an arm of the Mediterranean between Italy and the Balkan Peninsula.
adrift (əˈdrɪft) *adj (postpositive), adv* **1** floating without steering or mooring; drifting. **2** without purpose; aimless. **3** *Informal.* off course or amiss: *the project went adrift.*
adroit (əˈdrɔɪt) *adj* **1** skilful or dexterous. **2** quick in thought or reaction. [C17: from French *à droit* according to right, rightly] ▸ **aˈdroitly** *adv* ▸ **aˈdroitness** *n*
adscititious (ˌædsɪˈtɪʃəs) *adj* added or supplemental; additional. [C17: from Latin *adscītus* admitted (from outside), from *adscīscere* to admit, from *scīscere* to seek to know, from *scīre* to know] ▸ **ˌadsciˈtitiously** *adv*
adscription (ədˈskrɪpʃən) *n* a less common word for **ascription.**
adsorb (ədˈsɔːb, -ˈzɔːb) *vb* to undergo or cause to undergo a process in which a substance, usually a gas, accumulates on the surface of a solid forming a thin film, often only one molecule thick: *to adsorb hydrogen on nickel; oxygen adsorbs on tungsten.* Compare **absorb** (sense 8). [C19: AD- + *-sorb* as in ABSORB] ▸ **adˈsorbable** *adj* ▸ **adˌsorbaˈbility** *n* ▸ **adˈsorption** *n*
adsorbate (ədˈsɔːbeɪt, -bɪt, -ˈzɔː-) *n* a substance that has been or is to be adsorbed on a surface.
adsorbent (ədˈsɔːbənt, -ˈzɔː-) *adj* **1** capable of adsorption. ◆ *n* **2** a material, such as activated charcoal, on which adsorption can occur.
adsuki bean (ædˈzuːkɪ) *n* a variant spelling of **adzuki bean.**
adsum (ˈædˌsʊm) *sentence substitute.* I am present. [Latin]
adularescent (əˌdjʊləˈrɛsənt) *adj* (of minerals, such as moonstone) having or emitting a milky or bluish iridescence. [C19: from ADULAR(IA) + -ESCENT] ▸ **aˌdulaˈrescence** *n*
adularia (ˌædjʊˈlɛərɪə) *n* a white or colourless glassy variety of orthoclase in the form of prismatic crystals. It occurs in metamorphic rocks and is a minor gemstone. Formula: $KAlSi_3O_8$. [C18: via Italian from French *adulaire,* after *Adula,* a group of mountains in Switzerland]
adulate (ˈædjʊˌleɪt) *vb (tr)* to flatter or praise obsequiously. [C17: back formation from C15 *adulation,* from Latin *adūlārī* to flatter] ▸ **ˌaduˈlation** *n* ▸ **ˈaduˌlator** *n* ▸ **adulatory** (ˌædjʊˈleɪtərɪ, ˈædjʊˌleɪtərɪ) *adj*
Adullamite (əˈdʌləˌmaɪt) *n* a person who has withdrawn from a political group and joined with a few others to form a dissident group. [C19: originally applied to members of the British House of Commons who withdrew from the Liberal party (1866); alluding to the cave of *Adullam* in the Bible, to which David and others fled (1 Samuel 22: 1–2)]
adult (ˈædʌlt, əˈdʌlt) *adj* **1** having reached maturity; fully developed. **2** of or intended for mature people: *adult education.* **3** regarded as suitable only for adults, because of being pornographic: *adult films.* ◆ *n* **4** a person who has attained maturity; a grownup. **5** a mature fully grown animal or plant. **6** *Law.* a person who has attained the age of legal majority (18 years for most purposes). Compare **infant.** [C16: from Latin *adultus,* from *adolēscere* to grow up, from *alēscere* to grow, from *alēre* to feed, nourish] ▸ **aˈdulthood** *n*
adulterant (əˈdʌltərənt) *n* **1** a substance or ingredient that adulterates. ◆ *adj* **2** adulterating.
adulterate *vb* (əˈdʌltəˌreɪt). **1** *(tr)* to debase by adding inferior material: *to adulterate milk with water.* ◆ *adj* (əˈdʌltərɪt, -ˌreɪt). **2** adulterated; debased or impure. **3** a less common word for **adulterous.** [C16: from Latin *adulterāre* to corrupt, commit adultery, probably from *alter* another, hence to approach another, commit adultery] ▸ **aˌdulterˈation** *n* ▸ **aˈdulterˌator** *n*
adulterer (əˈdʌltərə) *or (fem)* **adulteress** *n* a person who has committed adultery. [C16: originally also *adulter,* from Latin *adulter,* back formation from *adulterāre* to ADULTERATE]
adulterine (əˈdʌltərɪn, -ˌriːn, -ˌraɪn) *adj* **1** of or made by adulteration; fake. **2** conceived in adultery: *an adulterine child.*
adulterous (əˈdʌltərəs) *adj* **1** of, characterized by, or inclined to adultery. **2** an obsolete word for **adulterate** (sense 2). ▸ **aˈdulterously** *adv*
adultery (əˈdʌltərɪ) *n, pl* **-teries.** voluntary sexual intercourse between a married man or woman and a partner other than the legal spouse. [C15 *adulterie,* altered (as if directly from Latin *adulterium*) from C14 *avoutrie,* via Old French from Latin *adulterium,* from *adulter,* back formation from *adulterāre.* See ADULTERATE]
Adult Training Centre *n Social welfare.* a day centre, run by a local authority, for mentally handicapped people to gain work experience.
adumbral (ædˈʌmbrəl) *adj Usually poetic.* shadowy. [C19: from AD- (in the sense: in) + Latin *umbra* shadow]
adumbrate (ˈædʌmˌbreɪt) *vb (tr)* **1** to outline; give a faint indication of. **2** to

foreshadow. 3 to overshadow; obscure. [C16: from Latin *adumbrātus* represented only in outline, from *adumbrāre* to cast a shadow on, from *umbra* shadow] ▸ ˌ**adum'bration** *n* ▸ **adumbrative** (æd'ʌmbrətɪv) *adj* ▸ **ad'umbratively** *adv*

adust (ə'dʌst) *adj Archaic.* 1 dried up or darkened by heat; burnt or scorched. 2 gloomy or melancholy. [C14 (in the sense: gloomy): from Latin *adūstus,* from *adūrere* to set fire to, from *ūrere* to burn]

Aduwa *or* **Adowa** ('ɑːdʊˌwɑː) *n* a town in N Ethiopia: Emperor Menelik II defeated the Italians here in 1896. Pop.: 17 476 (1989 est.). Italian name: **Adua** (a'dua).

adv. *abbrev. for:* 1 adverb. 2 adverbial. 3 adversus. [Latin: against] 4 advertisement. 5 advocate.

ad val. *abbrev. for* ad valorem.

ad valorem (æd və'lɔːrəm) *adj, adv* (of taxes) in proportion to the estimated value of the goods taxed. Abbrevs.: **ad val., a.v., A/V.** [from Latin]

advance (əd'vɑːns) *vb* 1 to go or bring forward in position. 2 (foll. by *on*) to move (towards) in a threatening manner. 3 (*tr*) to present for consideration; suggest. 4 to bring or be brought to a further stage of development; improve; further. 5 (*tr*) to cause (an event) to occur earlier. 6 (*tr*) to supply (money, goods, etc.) beforehand, either for a loan or as an initial payment. 7 to increase (a price, value, rate of occurrence, etc.) or (of a price, etc.) to be increased. 8 (*intr*) to improve one's position; be promoted: *he advanced rapidly in his job.* 9 (*tr*) *Archaic.* to promote in rank, status, or position. ◆ *n* 10 forward movement; progress in time or space. 11 improvement; progress in development. 12 *Commerce.* 12a the supplying of commodities or funds before receipt of an agreed consideration. 12b the commodities or funds supplied in this manner. 12c (*as modifier*): *an advance supply.* 13 Also called: **advance payment.** a money payment made before it is legally due: *this is an advance on your salary.* 14 a loan of money. 15 an increase in price, value, rate of occurrence, etc. 16 a less common word for **advancement** (sense 1). 17 **in advance.** 17a beforehand: *payment in advance.* 17b (foll. by *of*) ahead in time or development: *ideas in advance of the time.* 18 (*modifier*) forward in position or time: *advance booking; an advance warning.* ◆ See also **advances.** [C15 *advauncen,* altered (on the model of words beginning with Latin *ad-*) from C13 *avauncen,* via Old French from Latin *abante* from before, from *ab-* away from + *ante* before] ▸ **ad'vancer** *n* ▸ **ad'vancingly** *adv*

advance corporation tax *n* a UK tax in which a company paying a dividend must deduct the basic rate of income tax from the grossed-up value of the dividend and pay it to the Inland Revenue. Abbrev.: **ACT.**

advanced (əd'vɑːnst) *adj* 1 being ahead in development, knowledge, progress, etc.: *advanced studies.* 2 having reached a comparatively late stage: *a man of advanced age.* 3 ahead of the times: *advanced views on religion.*

advanced gas-cooled reactor *n* a nuclear reactor using carbon dioxide as the coolant, graphite as the moderator, and ceramic uranium dioxide cased in stainless steel as the fuel. Abbrev.: **AGR.**

advance directive *n* another name for **living will.**

Advanced level *n* (in Britain) the formal name for **A level.**

advance guard *n* 1 a military unit sent ahead of a main body to find gaps in enemy defences, clear away minor opposition, and prevent unexpected contact. 2 a temporary military detachment sent ahead of a force to prepare for a landing or other operation, esp. by making reconnaissance.

advance man *n U.S.* an agent of a political candidate or other public figure who travels in advance of the candidate to organize publicity, arrange meetings, and make security checks.

advancement (əd'vɑːnsmənt) *n* 1 promotion in rank, status, etc.; preferment. 2 a less common word for **advance** (senses 10, 11). 3 *Property law.* the use during a testator's lifetime of money or property for the benefit of a child or other person who is a prospective beneficiary in the testator's will.

advance notice *n* See **notice** (sense 6).

advance poll *n Canadian.* (in an election) a poll held prior to election day to permit voters who expect to be absent then to cast their ballots.

advance ratio *n Aeronautics.* 1 the ratio of wind speed along the axis of a rotor or propeller to the speed of the blade tip. 2 the ratio of forward flight speed to the speed of the rotor tip of a helicopter.

advances (əd'vɑːnsɪz) *pl n* (*sometimes sing;* often foll. by *to* or *towards*) personal overtures made in an attempt to become friendly, gain a favour, etc.

advantage (əd'vɑːntɪdʒ) *n* 1 (often foll. by *over* or *of*) superior or more favourable position or power: *he had an advantage over me because of his experience.* 2 benefit or profit (esp. in the phrase **to one's advantage**). 3 *Tennis.* 3a the point scored after deuce. 3b the resulting state of the score. 4 **take advantage of.** 4a to make good use of. 4b to impose upon the weakness, good nature, etc., of; abuse. 4c to seduce. 5 **to advantage.** to good effect: *he used his height to advantage at the game.* 6 **you have the advantage of me.** you know me but I do not know you. [C14 *avantage* (later altered to *advantage* on the model of words beginning with Latin *ad-*), from Old French *avant* before, from Latin *abante* from before, away. See ADVANCE]

advantaged (əd'vɑːntɪdʒd) *adj* in a superior social or economic position.

advantageous (ˌædvən'teɪdʒəs) *adj* producing advantage. ▸ ˌ**advan'tageously** *adv* ▸ ˌ**advan'tageousness** *n*

advection (əd'vɛkʃən) *n* the transference of heat energy in a horizontal stream of gas, esp. of air. [C20: from Latin *advectiō* conveyance, from *advehere,* from *ad-* to + *vehere* to carry]

advent ('ædvɛnt, -vənt) *n* an arrival or coming, esp. one which is awaited. [C12: from Latin *adventus,* from *advenīre,* from *ad-* to + *venīre* to come]

Advent ('ædvɛnt, -vənt) *n Christianity.* the season including the four Sundays preceding Christmas or (in Eastern Orthodox churches) the forty days preceding Christmas.

Advent calendar *n Brit.* a large card with a brightly coloured sometimes tinselled design on it that contains small numbered doors for children to open on each of the days of Advent, revealing pictures beneath them.

Adventist ('ædvəntɪst, 'ædvən-) *n* a member of any of the Christian groups, such as the **Seventh-Day Adventists,** that hold that the Second Coming of Christ is imminent.

adventitia (ˌædvɛn'tɪʃɪə, -'tɪʃə) *n* the outermost covering of an organ or part, esp. the outer coat of a blood vessel. [C19: New Latin, from the neuter plural of Latin *adventīcius;* see ADVENTITIOUS]

adventitious (ˌædvɛn'tɪʃəs) *adj* 1 added or appearing accidentally or unexpectedly. 2 (of a plant or animal part) developing in an abnormal position, as a root that grows from a stem. [C17: from Latin *adventīcius* coming from outside, from *adventus* a coming] ▸ ˌ**adven'titiously** *adv*

adventive (əd'vɛntɪv) *Biology.* ◆ *adj* 1 introduced to an area by chance and not yet established there; exotic. ◆ *n* 2 such a plant or animal. ◆ Also called: **casual.**

Advent Sunday *n* the first of the four Sundays of Advent, and the one that falls nearest to November 30.

adventure (əd'vɛntʃə) *n* 1 a risky undertaking of unknown outcome. 2 an exciting or unexpected event or course of events. 3 a hazardous financial operation; commercial speculation. 4 *Obsolete.* 4a danger or misadventure. 4b chance. ◆ *vb* 5 to take a risk or put at risk. 6 (*intr;* foll. by *into, on, upon*) to dare to go or enter (into a place, dangerous activity, etc.). 7 to dare to say (something): *he adventured his opinion.* [C13 *aventure* (later altered to *adventure* after the Latin spelling), via Old French ultimately from Latin *advenīre* to happen to (someone), arrive] ▸ **ad'ventureful** *adj*

adventure playground *n Brit.* a playground for children that contains building materials, discarded industrial parts, etc., used by the children to build with, hide in, climb on, etc.

adventurer (əd'vɛntʃərə) *or* (*fem*) **adventuress** *n* 1 a person who seeks adventure, esp. one who seeks success or money through daring exploits. 2 a person who seeks money or power by unscrupulous means. 3 a speculator.

adventurism (əd'vɛntʃəˌrɪzəm) *n* recklessness, esp. in politics and finance. ▸ **ad'venturist** *n*

adventurous (əd'vɛntʃərəs) *adj* 1 Also: **adventuresome.** daring or enterprising. 2 dangerous; involving risk. ▸ **ad'venturously** *adv*

adverb ('ædˌvɜːb) *n* a a word or group of words that serves to modify a whole sentence, a verb, another adverb, or an adjective; for example, *probably, easily, very,* and *happily* respectively in the sentence *They could probably easily envy the very happily married couple.* b (*as modifier*): *an adverb marker.* Abbrev.: **adv.** [C15–C16: from Latin *adverbium* adverb, literally: added word, a translation of Greek *epirrhēma* a word spoken afterwards]

adverbial (æd'vɜːbɪəl) *n* 1 a word or group of words playing the grammatical role of an adverb, such as *in the rain* in the sentence *I'm singing in the rain.* ◆ *adj* 2 of or relating to an adverb or adverbial. ▸ **ad'verbially** *adv*

adversarial (ˌædvɜː'sɛərɪəl) *adj* 1 pertaining to or characterized by antagonism and conflict. 2 *Brit.* having or involving opposing parties or interests in a legal contest. U.S. term: **adversary.**

adversary ('ædvəsərɪ) *n, pl* **-saries.** 1 a person or group that is hostile to someone; enemy. 2 an opposing contestant in a game or sport. ◆ *adj* 3 the U.S. term for **adversarial** (sense 2). [C14: from Latin *adversārius,* from *adversus* against. See ADVERSE]

adversative (əd'vɜːsətɪv) *Grammar.* ◆ *adj* 1 (of a word, phrase, or clause) implying opposition or contrast. *But* and *although* are adversative conjunctions introducing adversative clauses. ◆ *n* 2 an adversative word or speech element.

adverse ('ædvɜːs, æd'vɜːs) *adj* 1 antagonistic or inimical; hostile: *adverse criticism.* 2 unfavourable to one's interests: *adverse circumstances.* 3 contrary or opposite in direction or position: *adverse winds.* 4 (of leaves, flowers, etc.) facing the main stem. Compare **averse** (sense 2). [C14: from Latin *adversus* opposed to, hostile, from *advertere* to turn towards, from *ad-* to, towards + *vertere* to turn] ▸ **ad'versely** *adv* ▸ **ad'verseness** *n*

adverse possession *n Property law.* the occupation or possession of land by a person not legally entitled to it. If continued unopposed for a period specifed by law, such occupation extinguishes the title of the rightful owner.

adverse pressure gradient *n Aerodynamics.* an increase of pressure in the direction of flow.

adversity (əd'vɜːsɪtɪ) *n, pl* **-ties.** 1 distress; affliction; hardship. 2 an unfortunate event or incident.

advert[1] (əd'vɜːt) *vb* (*intr;* foll. by *to*) to draw attention (to); refer (to). [C15: from Latin *advertere* to turn one's attention to. See ADVERSE]

advert[2] ('ædvɜːt) *n Brit. informal.* short for **advertisement.**

advertence (əd'vɜːtəns) *or* **advertency** *n* heedfulness or attentiveness. ▸ **ad'vertent** *adj* ▸ **ad'vertently** *adv*

advertise *or U.S.* (*sometimes*) **advertize** ('ædvəˌtaɪz) *vb* 1 to present or praise (goods, a service, etc.) to the public, esp. in order to encourage sales. 2 to make (something, such as a vacancy, article for sale, etc.) publicly known, as to possible applicants, buyers, etc.: *to advertise a job.* 3 (*intr;* foll. by *for*) to make a public request (for), esp. in a newspaper, etc.: *she advertised for a cook.* 4 *Obsolete.* to warn; caution. [C15: from a lengthened stem of Old French *avertir,* ultimately from Latin *advertere* to turn one's attention to. See ADVERSE] ▸ **'adverˌtiser** *or U.S.* (*sometimes*) **'adverˌtizer** *n*

advertisement *or U.S.* (*sometimes*) **advertizement** (əd'vɜːtɪsmənt, -tɪz-) *n* any public notice, as a printed display in a newspaper, short film on television, announcement on radio, etc., designed to sell goods, publicize an event, etc. Shortened forms: **ad, advert.**

advertising *or U.S.* (*sometimes*) **advertizing** ('ædvəˌtaɪzɪŋ) *n* 1 the promotion of goods or services for sale through impersonal media, such as radio or television. 2 the business that specializes in creating such publicity. 3 advertisements collectively; publicity.

advertising agency *n* an organization that creates advertising material, contracts for publication space, and undertakes market research on behalf of its clients.
Advertising Standards Authority *n* an independent UK body set up by the advertising industry to ensure that all advertisements comply with the British Code of Advertising Practice. Abbrev.: **ASA.**
advertorial (ˌædvɜːˈtɔːrɪəl) *n* advertising material presented under the guise of editorial material. [C20: from ADVERT[2] + (EDIT)ORIAL]
advice (ədˈvaɪs) *n* **1** recommendation as to appropriate choice of action; counsel. **2** (*sometimes pl*) formal notification of facts, esp. when communicated from a distance. [C13 *avis* (later *advise*), via Old French from a Vulgar Latin phrase based on Latin *ad* to, according to + *vīsum* view (hence: according to one's view, opinion)]
advice note *n* a document sent by a supplier to a customer to inform him that goods he ordered have been dispatched. It usually gives details such as the quantity of goods and how they have been sent.
advisable (ədˈvaɪzəbᵊl) *adj* worthy of recommendation; prudent; sensible. ▸ **adˈvisably** *adv* ▸ **adˌvisaˈbility** *or* **adˈvisableness** *n*
advise (ədˈvaɪz) *vb* (*when tr, may take a clause as object or an infinitive*) **1** to offer advice (to a person or persons); counsel: *he advised the king; to advise caution; he advised her to leave.* **2** (*tr;* sometimes foll. by *of*) *Formal.* to inform or notify. **3** (*intr;* foll. by *with*) *Chiefly U.S., obsolete in Brit.* to consult or discuss. [C14: via Old French from Vulgar Latin *advīsāre* (unattested) to consider, from Latin *ad-* to + *visāre* (unattested), from *vīsere* to view, from *vidēre* to see]
advised (ədˈvaɪzd) *adj* resulting from deliberation. See also **ill-advised, well-advised.** ▸ **advisedly** (ədˈvaɪzɪdlɪ) *adv*
advisement (ədˈvaɪzmənt) *n Chiefly U.S., archaic in Britain.* consultation; deliberation.
adviser *or* **advisor** (ədˈvaɪzə) *n* **1** a person who advises. **2** *Education.* a person responsible for advising students on academic matters, career guidance, etc. **3** *Brit. education.* a subject specialist who advises heads of schools on current teaching methods and facilities.
advisory (ədˈvaɪzərɪ) *adj* **1** giving advice; empowered to make recommendations: *an advisory body.* ◆ *n, pl* **-ries. 2** a statement issued to give advice, recommendations, or a warning: *a travel advisory.* **3** a person or organization with an advisory function: *the Prime Minister's media advisory.*
advisory teacher *n Brit.* a teacher who visits schools to advise teachers on curriculum developments within a particular subject area.
advocaat (ˈædvəʊˌkɑː, -ˌkɑːt, ˈædvə-) *n* a liqueur having a raw egg base. [C20: Dutch, from *advocatenborrel,* from *advocaat* ADVOCATE (n) + *borrel* drink]
advocacy (ˈædvəkəsɪ) *n, pl* **-cies.** active support, esp. of a cause.
advocate *vb* (ˈædvəˌkeɪt). **1** (*tr; may take a clause as object*) to support or recommend publicly; plead for or speak in favour of. ◆ *n* (ˈædvəkɪt, -ˌkeɪt). **2** a person who upholds or defends a cause; supporter. **3** a person who intercedes on behalf of another. **4** a person who pleads his client's cause in a court of law. See also **barrister, solicitor, counsellor. 5** *Scots Law.* the usual word for **barrister.** [C14: via Old French from Latin *advocātus* legal witness, advocate, from *advocāre* to call as witness, from *vocāre* to call] ▸ ˌ**advoˈcatory** *adj*
Advocate Depute *n* a Scottish law officer with the functions of public prosecutor.
advocation (ˌædvəˈkeɪʃən) *n Scots Law, papal law.* the transfer to itself by a superior court of an action pending in a lower court.
advocatus diaboli *Latin.* (ˌædvəˈkɑːtəs daɪˈæbəˌlaɪ) *n* another name for the **devil's advocate.**
advowson (ədˈvaʊzᵊn) *n English ecclesiastical law.* the right of presentation to a vacant benefice. [C13: via Anglo-French and Old French from Latin *advocātiōn-* the act of summoning, from *advocāre* to summon]
advt *abbrev. for* advertisement.
Adygei *or* **Adyghe** (ˈɑːdɪˌgeɪ, ˌɑːdɪˈgeɪ, ˌɑːdɪˈge) *n* **1** (*pl* **-gei, -geis** *or* **-ghe, -ghes**) a member of a Circassian people of the Northwest Caucasus. **2** the Circassian language, esp. its Western dialect. Compare **Kabardian.**
Adygei Republic *or* **Adygea** (ˌɑːdɪˈgeɪə; *Russian* adɪˈgeja) *n* a constituent republic of SW Russia, bordering on the Caucasus Mountains: chiefly agricultural but with some mineral resources. Capital: Maikop. Pop.: 450 000 (1995 est.). Area: 7600 sq. km (2934 sq. miles).
adynamia (ˌædɪˈneɪmɪə) *n* loss of vital power or strength, esp. as the result of illness; weakness or debility. [C19: New Latin, from A-[1] + *-dynamia,* from Greek *dunamis* strength, force] ▸ **adynamic** (ˌædɪˈnæmɪk) *adj*
adytum (ˈædɪtəm) *n, pl* **-ta** (-tə). the most sacred place of worship in an ancient temple from which the laity was prohibited. [C17: Latin, from Greek *aduton* a place not to be entered, from A-[1] + *duein* to enter]
adze *or U.S.* **adz** (ædz) *n* a heavy hand tool with a steel cutting blade attached at right angles to a wooden handle, used for dressing timber. [Old English *adesa*]
Adzhar Autonomous Republic (əˈdʒɑː) *or* **Adzharia** (əˈdʒɑːrɪə) *n* an administrative division of SW Georgia, on the Black Sea: part of Turkey from the 17th century until 1878; mostly mountainous, reaching 2805 m (9350 ft.), with a subtropical coastal strip. Capital: Batumi. Pop.: 386 700 (1993 est.). Area: 3000 sq. km (1160 sq. miles).
adzuki bean *or* **adsuki bean** (ædˈzuːkɪ) *n* **1** a papilionaceous plant, *Phaseolus angularis,* that has yellow flowers and pods containing edible brown seeds and is widely cultivated as a food crop in China and Japan. **2** the seed of this plant. [*adzuki,* from Japanese: red bean]
æ *or* **Æ** **1** a digraph in Latin representing either a native diphthong, as in *æquus,* or a Greek αι (*ai*) in Latinized spellings, as in *æschylus:* now usually written *ae,* or *e* in some words, such as *demon.* **2** a ligature used in Old and early Middle English to represent the vowel sound of *a* in *cat.* **3** a ligature used in modern phonetic transcription also representing the vowel sound *a* in *cat.*
ae (e) *or* **yae** *determiner Scot.* one; a single. [from Old English *ān*]
ae. *abbrev. for* aetatis. [Latin: at the age of; aged]
A.E. *or* **AE** *n* the pen name of (George William) **Russell.**
AEA (in Britain) *abbrev. for* Atomic Energy Authority.
AE & P *abbrev. for* Ambassador Extraordinary and Plenipotentiary.
AEC (in the U.S.) *abbrev. for* Atomic Energy Commission.
aeciospore (ˈiːsɪəˌspɔː) *n* any of the spores produced in an aecium of the rust fungi, which spread to and infect the primary host. Also called: **aecidospore.** [C20: from AECIUM + SPORE]
aecium (ˈiːsɪəm) *or* **aecidium** (iːˈsɪdɪəm) *n, pl* **-cia** (-sɪə) *or* **-cidia** (-ˈsɪdɪə). a globular or cup-shaped structure in some rust fungi in which aeciospores are produced. [C19: New Latin, from Greek *aikia* injury (so called because of the damage the fungi cause)]
aedes (eɪˈiːdiːz) *n* any mosquito of the genus *Aedes* (formerly *Stegomyia*) of tropical and subtropical regions, esp. *A. aegypti,* which transmits yellow fever and dengue. [C20: New Latin, from Greek *aēdēs* unpleasant, from A-[1] + *ēdos* pleasant]
aedile *or U.S.* (*sometimes*) **edile** (ˈiːdaɪl) *n* a magistrate of ancient Rome in charge of public works, games, buildings, and roads. [C16: from Latin *aedīlis* concerned with buildings, from *aedēs* a building]
Aeëtes (iːˈiːtiːz) *n Greek myth.* a king of Colchis, father of Medea and keeper of the Golden Fleece.
AEEU (in Britain) *abbrev. for* Amalgamated Engineering and Electrical Union.
Aegean (iːˈdʒiːən) *adj* **1** of or relating to the Aegean Sea or Islands. **2** of or relating to the Bronze Age civilization of Greece, Asia Minor, and the Aegean Islands.
Aegean Islands *pl n* the islands of the Aegean Sea, including the Cyclades, Dodecanese, Euboea, and Sporades. The majority are under Greek administration.
Aegean Sea *n* an arm of the Mediterranean between Greece and Turkey.
Aegeus (iːˈdʒiːuːs, ˈiːdʒɪəs) *n Greek myth.* an Athenian king and father of Theseus.
Aegina (iːˈdʒaɪnə) *n* **1** an island in the Aegean Sea, in the Saronic Gulf. Area: 85 sq. km (33 sq. miles). **2** a town on the coast of this island: a city-state of ancient Greece. **3 Gulf of.** another name for the **Saronic Gulf.** ◆ Greek name: **Aiyina.**
Aegir (ˈiːdʒɪə) *n Norse myth.* the god of the sea.
aegis *or U.S.* (*sometimes*) **egis** (ˈiːdʒɪs) *n* **1** sponsorship or protection; auspices (esp. in the phrase **under the aegis of**). **2** *Greek myth.* the shield of Zeus, often represented in art as a goatskin. [C18: from Latin, from Greek *aigis* shield of Zeus, perhaps related to *aig-,* stem of *aix* goat]
Aegisthus (iːˈdʒɪsθəs) *n Greek myth.* a cousin to and the murderer of Agamemnon, whose wife Clytemnestra he had seduced. He usurped the kingship of Mycenae until Orestes, Agamemnon's son, returned home and killed him.
Aegospotami (ˌiːgəsˈpɒtəˌmaɪ) *n* a river of ancient Thrace that flowed into the Hellespont. At its mouth the Spartan fleet under Lysander defeated the Athenians in 405 B.C., ending the Peloponnesian War.
aegrotat (ˈaɪgrəʊˌtæt, ˈiː-; iːˈgrəʊtæt) *n* **1** (in British and certain other universities, and, sometimes, schools) a certificate allowing a candidate to pass an examination although he has missed all or part of it through illness. **2** a degree or other qualification obtained in such circumstances. [C19: Latin, literally: he is ill]
Aegyptus (iːˈdʒɪptəs) *n Greek myth.* a king of Egypt and twin brother of Danaüs.
Ælfric (ˈælfrɪk) *n* called *Grammaticus.* ?955–?1020, English abbot, writer, and grammarian.
-aemia, -haemia, *or U.S.* **-emia, -hemia** *n combining form.* denoting blood, esp. a specified condition of the blood in names of diseases: *leukaemia.* [New Latin, from Greek *-aimia,* from *haima* blood]
Aeneas (ɪˈniːəs) *n Classical myth.* a Trojan prince, the son of Anchises and Aphrodite, who escaped the sack of Troy and sailed to Italy via Carthage and Sicily. After seven years, he and his followers established themselves near the site of the future Rome.
Aeneas Silvius *or* **Sylvius** (ˈsɪlvɪəs) *n* the literary name of **Pius II.**
Aeneid (ɪˈniːɪd) *n* an epic poem in Latin by Virgil relating the experiences of Aeneas after the fall of Troy, written chiefly to provide an illustrious historical background for Rome.
aeolian (iːˈəʊlɪən) *adj* of or relating to the wind; produced or carried by the wind. [C18: from AEOLUS, god of the winds]
Aeolian *or* **Eolian** (iːˈəʊlɪən) *n* **1** a member of a Hellenic people who settled in Thessaly and Boeotia and colonized Lesbos and parts of the Aegean coast of Asia Minor. ◆ *adj* **2** of or relating to this people or their dialect of Ancient Greek; Aeolic. **3** of or relating to Aeolus. **4** denoting or relating to an authentic mode represented by the ascending natural diatonic scale from A to A: the basis of the modern minor key. See also **Hypo-.**
aeolian deposits *pl n Geology.* sediments, such as loess, made up of wind-blown grains of sand or dust.
aeolian harp *n* a stringed instrument that produces a musical sound when a current of air or wind passes over the strings. Also called: **wind harp.**
Aeolian Islands *pl n* another name for the **Lipari Islands.**
aeolian tone *n* the musical tone produced by the passage of a current of air over a stretched string, etc., as in an aeolian harp.
Aeolic *or* **Eolic** (iːˈɒlɪk, iːˈəʊlɪk) *adj* **1** of or relating to the Aeolians or their dialect. ◆ *n* **2** one of four chief dialects of Ancient Greek, spoken chiefly in Thessaly, Boeotia, and Aeolis. ◆ Compare **Arcadic, Doric, Ionic.** See also **Attic** (sense 3).

aeolipile (iːˈɒlɪˌpaɪl) *n* a device illustrating the reactive forces of a gas jet: usually a spherical vessel mounted so as to rotate and equipped with angled exit pipes from which steam within it escapes. [C17: from Latin *aeolīpilae* balls of AEOLUS or *aeolīpylae* gates of AEOLUS]

Aeolis (ˈiːəlɪs) *or* **Aeolia** (iːˈəʊlɪə) *n* the ancient name for the coastal region of NW Asia Minor, including the island of Lesbos, settled by the Aeolian Greeks (about 1000 B.C.).

aeolotropic (ˌiːələʊˈtrɒpɪk) *adj* a less common word for **anisotropic**. [C19: from Greek *aiolos* fickle + -TROPIC]

Aeolus (ˈiːələs, iːˈəʊləs) *n Greek myth*. **1** the god of the winds. **2** the founding king of the Aeolians in Thessaly.

aeon *or esp. U.S.* **eon** (ˈiːən, ˈiːɒn) *n* **1** an immeasurably long period of time; age. **2** *Astron.* a period of one thousand million years. **3** (*often cap.*) *Gnosticism.* one of the powers emanating from the supreme being and culminating in the demiurge. [C17: from Greek *aiōn* an infinitely long time]

aeonian *or* **eonian** (iːˈəʊnɪən) *adj Literary.* everlasting.

aepyornis (ˌiːpɪˈɔːnɪs) *n* any of the large extinct flightless birds of the genus *Aepyornis*, remains of which have been found in Madagascar. [C19: New Latin, from Greek *aipus* high + *ornis* bird]

aer- *combining form.* a variant of **aero-** before a vowel.

aerate (ˈɛəreɪt) *vb* (*tr*) **1** to charge (a liquid) with a gas, esp. carbon dioxide, as in the manufacture of effervescent drink. **2** to expose to the action or circulation of the air, so as to purify. ▸ **aerˈation** *n* ▸ **ˈaerator** *n*

aeri- *combining form.* a variant of **aero-**.

aerial (ˈɛərɪəl) *adj* **1** of, relating to, or resembling air. **2** existing, occurring, moving, or operating in the air: *aerial cable car; aerial roots of a plant.* **3** ethereal; light and delicate. **4** imaginary; visionary. **5** extending high into the air; lofty. **6** of or relating to aircraft: *aerial combat.* ◆ *n* **7** Also called: **antenna.** the part of a radio or television system having any of various shapes, such as a dipole, Yagi, long-wire, or vertical aerial, by means of which radio waves are transmitted or received. [C17: via Latin from Greek *aerios*, from *aēr* air]

aerialist (ˈɛərɪəlɪst) *n Chiefly U.S.* a trapeze artist or tightrope walker.

aerial ladder *n* the U.S. and Canadian term for **turntable ladder.**

aerial perspective *n* a means of indicating relative distance in terms of a gradation of clarity, tone, and colour, esp. blue. Also called: **atmospheric perspective.**

aerial pingpong *n Austral. slang.* Australian Rules football.

aerial top dressing *n* the process of spreading lime, fertilizer, etc. over farmland from an aeroplane.

aerie (ˈɛərɪ, ˈɪərɪ) *n* a variant spelling (esp. U.S.) of **eyrie.**

aeriform (ˈɛərɪˌfɔːm) *adj* **1** having the form of air; gaseous. **2** unsubstantial.

aerify (ˈɛərɪˌfaɪ) *vb* **-fies, -fying, -fied. 1** to change or cause to change into a gas. **2** to mix or combine with air. ▸ **ˌaerifiˈcation** *n*

aero (ˈɛərəʊ) *n* (*modifier*) of or relating to aircraft or aeronautics: *an aero engine.*

aero-, aeri-, *or before a vowel* **aer-** *combining form.* **1** denoting air, atmosphere, or gas: *aerodynamics.* **2** denoting aircraft: *aeronautics.* [ultimately from Greek *aēr* air]

aeroacoustics (ˌɛərəʊəˈkuːstɪks) *n* (*functioning as sing*) the study of the generation and transmittance of sound by fluid flow.

aeroballistics (ˌɛərəʊbəˈlɪstɪks) *n* (*functioning as sing*) the ballistics of projectiles dropped, launched, or fired from aircraft.

aerobatics (ˌɛərəʊˈbætɪks) *n* (*functioning as sing or pl*) spectacular or dangerous manoeuvres, such as loops or rolls, performed in an aircraft or glider; stunt flying. [C20: from AERO- + (ACRO)BATICS] ▸ **ˌaeroˈbatic** *adj*

aerobe (ˈɛərəʊb) *or* **aerobium** (ɛəˈrəʊbɪəm) *n, pl* **-obes** *or* **-obia** (-ˈəʊbɪə). an organism that requires free oxygen or air for respiration. Compare **anaerobe.** [C19: from AERO- + Greek *bios* life. Compare MICROBE]

aerobic (ɛəˈrəʊbɪk) *adj* **1** (of an organism or process) depending on free oxygen or air. **2** of or relating to aerobes. **3** designed for or relating to aerobics: *aerobic shoes; aerobic dances.* ◆ Compare **anaerobic.**

aerobics (ɛəˈrəʊbɪks) *n* (*functioning as sing*) any system of sustained exercises designed to increase the amount of oxygen in the blood and strengthen the heart and lungs. ▸ **aerˈobicist** *n*

aerobiology (ˌɛərəʊbaɪˈɒlɪdʒɪ) *n* the study of airborne microorganisms, spores, etc., esp. those causing disease. ▸ **ˌaerobioˈlogical** *adj* ▸ **ˌaerobioˈlogically** *adv* ▸ **ˌaerobiˈologist** *n*

aerobiosis (ˌɛərəʊbaɪˈəʊsɪs) *n* life in the presence of free oxygen. ▸ **aerobiotic** (ˌɛərəʊbaɪˈɒtɪk) *adj*

aerobraking (ˈɛərəʊˌbreɪkɪŋ) *n* the use of aerodynamic braking in extremely low-density atmospheres in space at hypersonic Mach numbers.

aerodonetics (ˌɛərəʊdəˈnɛtɪks) *n* (*functioning as sing*) the study of soaring or gliding flight, esp. the study of gliders. [C20: from Greek *aerodonetos* tossed in the air, from AERO- + *donētos*, past participle of *donein* to toss]

aerodrome (ˈɛərəˌdrəʊm) *or U.S.* **airdrome** (ˈɛəˌdrəʊm) *n* a landing area, esp. for private aircraft, that is usually smaller than an airport.

aerodynamic braking *n* **1** the use of aerodynamic drag to slow spacecraft reentering the atmosphere. **2** the use of airbrakes to retard flying vehicles or objects. **3** the use of a parachute or reversed thrust to decelerate an aircraft before landing.

aerodynamics (ˌɛərəʊdaɪˈnæmɪks) *n* (*functioning as sing*) the study of the dynamics of gases, esp. of the forces acting on a body passing through air. Compare **aerostatics** (sense 1). ▸ **ˌaerodyˈnamic** *adj* ▸ **ˌaerodyˈnamically** *adv* ▸ **ˌaerodyˈnamicist** *n*

aerodyne (ˈɛərəʊˌdaɪn) *n* any heavier-than-air machine, such as an aircraft, that derives the greater part of its lift from aerodynamic forces. [C20: back formation from AERODYNAMIC; see DYNE]

aeroembolism (ˌɛərəʊˈɛmbəˌlɪzəm) *n* the presence in the tissues and blood of nitrogen bubbles, caused by an abrupt and substantial reduction in atmospheric pressure. See **decompression sickness.**

aero engine *n* an engine for powering an aircraft.

aerofoil (ˈɛərəʊˌfɔɪl) *or U.S. and Canadian* **airfoil** (ˈɛəˌfɔɪl) *n* a cross section of an aileron, wing, tailplane, or rotor blade.

aerogel (ˈɛərəˌdʒɛl) *n* a colloid that has a continuous solid phase containing dispersed gas.

aerogram *or* **aerogramme** (ˈɛərəˌɡræm) *n* **1** Also called: **air letter.** an airmail letter written on a single sheet of lightweight paper that folds and is sealed to form an envelope. **2** another name for **radiotelegram.**

aerography (ɛəˈrɒɡrəfɪ) *n* the description of the character of the atmosphere.

aerolite (ˈɛərəˌlaɪt) *n* a stony meteorite consisting of silicate minerals. ▸ **aerolitic** (ˌɛərəˈlɪtɪk) *adj*

aerology (ɛəˈrɒlədʒɪ) *n* the study of the atmosphere, including its upper layers. ▸ **aerologic** (ˌɛərəˈlɒdʒɪk) *or* **ˌaeroˈlogical** *adj* ▸ **aerˈologist** *n*

aeromechanic (ˌɛərəʊmɪˈkænɪk) *n* **1** an aircraft mechanic. ◆ *adj* **2** of or relating to aeromechanics.

aeromechanics (ˌɛərəʊmɪˈkænɪks) *n* (*functioning as sing*) the mechanics of gases, esp. air. ▸ **ˌaeromeˈchanical** *adj*

aerometeorograph (ˌɛərəʊˈmiːtɪərəˌɡrɑːf, -ˌɡræf) *n Chiefly U.S.* an aircraft instrument that records temperature, humidity, and atmospheric pressure.

aerometer (ɛəˈrɒmɪtə) *n* an instrument for determining the mass or density of a gas, esp. air. ▸ **aerometric** (ˌɛərəˈmɛtrɪk) *adj*

aerometry (ɛəˈrɒmɪtrɪ) *n* another name for **pneumatics.**

aeron. *abbrev. for:* **1** aeronautics. **2** aeronautical.

aeronaut (ˈɛərəˌnɔːt) *n* a person who flies in a lighter-than-air craft, esp. the pilot or navigator.

aeronautical (ˌɛərəˈnɔːtɪkᵊl) *adj* of or relating to aeronauts or aeronautics. ▸ **ˌaeroˈnautically** *adv*

aeronautical engineering *n* the branch of engineering concerned with the design, production, and maintenance of aircraft. ▸ **aeronautical engineer** *n*

aeronautics (ˌɛərəˈnɔːtɪks) *n* (*functioning as sing*) the study or practice of all aspects of flight through the air.

aeroneurosis (ˌɛərəʊnjʊˈrəʊsɪs) *n* a functional disorder of aeroplane pilots characterized by anxiety and various psychosomatic disturbances, caused by insufficient oxygen at high altitudes and the emotional tension of flying.

aeronomy (ɛəˈrɒnəmɪ) *n* the science of the earth's upper atmosphere.

aero-optics (ˌɛərəʊˈɒptɪks) *n* (*functioning as sing*) the study of the effect of aircraft-induced and atmospheric disturbances on the efficiency of laser weapons.

aeropause (ˈɛərəˌpɔːz) *n* the region of the upper atmosphere above which aircraft cannot fly.

aerophagia (ˌɛərəˈfeɪdʒɪə, -dʒə) *n* spasmodic swallowing of air, a fairly common neurotic habit that may lead to belching and stomach pain.

aerophobia (ˌɛərəˈfəʊbɪə) *n* a pathological fear of draughts of air. ▸ **ˌaeroˈphobic** *adj*

aerophyte (ˈɛərəˌfaɪt) *n* another name for **epiphyte.**

aeroplane (ˈɛərəˌpleɪn) *or U.S. and Canadian* **airplane** (ˈɛəˌpleɪn) *n* a heavier-than-air powered flying vehicle with fixed wings. [C19: from French *aéroplane*, from AERO- + Greek *-planos* wandering, related to PLANET]

aeroplane cloth *or* **fabric** *n* **1** a strong fabric made from cotton, linen, and nylon yarns, used for some light aircraft fuselages and wings. **2** a similar lightweight fabric used for clothing. ◆ Also called: **aircraft fabric.**

aeroplane spin *n* a wrestling attack in which a wrestler lifts his opponent onto his shoulders and spins around, leaving the opponent dizzy.

aerosol (ˈɛərəˌsɒl) *n* **1** a colloidal dispersion of solid or liquid particles in a gas; smoke or fog. **2** a substance, such as a paint, polish, or insecticide, dispensed from a small metal container by a propellant under pressure. **3** Also called: **air spray.** such a substance together with its container. [C20: from AERO- + SOL(UTION)]

aerospace (ˈɛərəˌspeɪs) *n* **1** the atmosphere and space beyond. **2** (*modifier*) of or relating to rockets, missiles, space vehicles, etc., that fly or operate in aerospace: *the aerospace industry.*

aerosphere (ˈɛərəˌsfɪə) *n* the entire atmosphere surrounding the earth.

aerostat (ˈɛərəˌstæt) *n* a lighter-than-air craft, such as a balloon. [C18: from French *aérostat*, from AERO- + Greek *-statos* standing] ▸ **ˌaeroˈstatic** *or* **ˌaeroˈstatical** *adj*

aerostatics (ˌɛərəˈstætɪks) *n* (*functioning as sing*) **1** the study of gases in equilibrium and bodies held in equilibrium in gases. Compare **aerodynamics. 2** the study of lighter-than-air craft, such as balloons.

aerostation (ˈɛərəˌsteɪʃən) *n* the science of operating lighter-than-air craft.

aerostructure (ˈɛərəʊˌstrʌktʃə) *n* any separately manufactured unit, component, or section of an aircraft or other vehicle capable of flight.

aerothermodynamics (ˌɛərəʊˌθɜːməʊdaɪˈnæmɪks) *n* (*functioning as sing*) the study of the exchange of heat between solids and gases, esp. of the heating effect on aircraft flying through the air at very high speeds. ▸ **ˌaeroˌthermodyˈnamic** *adj*

aerugo (ɪˈruːɡəʊ) *n* (esp. of old bronze) another name for **verdigris.** [C18: from Latin, from *aes* copper, bronze] ▸ **aeruginous** (ɪˈruːdʒɪnəs) *adj*

aery[1] (ˈɛərɪ, ˈeɪərɪ) *adj Poetic.* **1** a variant spelling of **airy. 2** lofty, insubstantial, or visionary. [C16: via Latin from Greek *aērios*, from *aēr* AIR]

aery[2] (ˈɛərɪ, ˈɪərɪ) *n, pl* **aeries.** a variant spelling of **eyrie.**

Aeschines (ˈiːskəˌniːz) *n* ?389–?314 B.C., Athenian orator; the main political opponent of Demosthenes.

Aeschylus (ˈiːskələs) *n* ?525–?456 B.C., Greek dramatist, regarded as the father of Greek tragedy. Seven of his plays are extant, including *Seven Against Thebes, The Persians, Prometheus Bound*, and the trilogy of the *Oresteia.* ▸ **Aeschylean** (ˌiːskəˈliːən) *adj*

Aesculapian (ˌiːskjʊˈleɪpɪən) *adj* of or relating to Aesculapius or to the art of medicine.
Aesculapius (ˌiːskjʊˈleɪpɪəs) *n* the Roman god of medicine or healing. Greek counterpart: **Asclepius.**
Aesir (ˈeɪsɪə) *pl n* the chief gods of Norse mythology dwelling in Asgard. [Old Norse, literally: gods]
Aesop (ˈiːsɒp) *n* ?620–564 B.C., Greek author of fables in which animals are given human characters and used to satirize human failings. ► **Aeˈsopian** *or* **Aeˈsopic** *adj*
aesthesia *or U.S.* **esthesia** (iːsˈθiːzɪə) *n* the normal ability to experience sensation, perception, or sensitivity. [C20: back formation from ANAESTHESIA]
aesthete *or U.S.* **esthete** (ˈiːsθiːt) *n* a person who has or who affects a highly developed appreciation of beauty, esp. in poetry and the visual arts. [C19: back formation from AESTHETICS]
aesthetic (iːsˈθɛtɪk, ɪs-) *or U.S. (sometimes)* **esthetic** *adj also* **aesthetical** *or U.S. (sometimes)* **esthetical. 1** connected with aesthetics or its principles. **2a** relating to pure beauty rather than to other considerations. **2b** artistic or relating to good taste: *an aesthetic consideration.* ◆ *n* **3** a principle of taste or style adopted by a particular person, group, or culture: *the Bauhaus aesthetic of functional modernity.* ► **aesˈthetically** *or U.S. (sometimes)* **esˈthetically** *adv*
aesthetician *or U.S. (sometimes)* **esthetician** (ˌiːsθɪˈtɪʃən, ˌɛs-) *n* a student of aesthetics.
aestheticism *or U.S. (sometimes)* **estheticism** (iːsˈθɛtɪˌsɪzəm, ɪs-) *n* **1** the doctrine that aesthetic principles are of supreme importance and that works of art should be judged accordingly. **2** sensitivity to beauty, esp. in art, music, literature, etc.
aesthetics *or U.S. (sometimes)* **esthetics** (iːsˈθɛtɪks, ɪs-) *n (functioning as sing)* **1** the branch of philosophy concerned with the study of such concepts as beauty, taste, etc. **2** the study of the rules and principles of art. [C18: from Greek *aisthētikos* perceptible by the senses, from *aisthesthai* to perceive]
aestival *or U.S.* **estival** (iːˈstaɪvᵊl, ˈɛstɪ-) *adj Rare.* of or occurring in summer. [C14: from French, from Late Latin *aestīvālis,* from Latin *aestās* summer]
aestivate *or U.S.* **estivate** (ˈiːstɪˌveɪt, ˈɛs-) *vb (intr)* **1** to pass the summer. **2** (of animals such as the lungfish) to pass the summer or dry season in a dormant condition. Compare **hibernate.** [C17: from Latin *aestīvātus,* from *aestīvāre* to stay during the summer, from *aestās* summer] ► **ˈaestiˌvator** *or U.S.* **ˈestiˌvator** *n*
aestivation *or U.S.* **estivation** (ˌiːstɪˈveɪʃən, ˌɛs-) *n* **1** the act or condition of aestivating. **2** the arrangement of the parts of a flower bud, esp. the sepals and petals.
aet. *or* **aetat.** *abbrev. for* aetatis. [Latin: at the age of]
Æthelbert (ˈæθəlˌbɜːt) *n* a variant spelling of **Ethelbert.**
Æthelred (ˈæθəlˌrɛd) *n* a variant spelling of **Ethelred.**
Æthelwulf (ˈæθəlˌwʊlf) *n* a variant spelling of **Ethelwulf.**
aether (ˈiːθə) *n* a variant spelling of **ether** (senses 3–5).
aethereal (ɪˈθɪərɪəl) *adj* a variant spelling of **ethereal** (senses 1, 2, 3). ► **aetherеality** (ɪˌθɪərɪˈælɪtɪ) *n* ► **aeˈthereally** *adv*
aetiological *or* **etiological** (ˌiːtɪəˈlɒdʒɪkᵊl) *adj* **1** of or relating to aetiology. **2** *Philosophy.* (of an explanation) in terms of causal precedents, as opposed, for instance, to the intentions of an agent. ► **ˌaetioˈlogically** *or* **ˌetioˈlogically** *adv*
aetiology *or* **etiology** (ˌiːtɪˈɒlədʒɪ) *n, pl* **-gies. 1** the philosophy or study of causation. **2** the study of the causes of diseases. **3** the cause of a disease. [C16: from Late Latin *aetologia,* from Greek *aitiologia,* from *aitia* cause] ► **ˌaetiˈologist** *or* **ˌetiˈologist** *n*
Aetna (ˈɛtnə) *n* the Latin name for Mount **Etna.**
Aetolia (iːˈtəʊlɪə) *n* a mountainous region forming (with the region of Acarnania) a department of W central Greece, north of the Gulf of Patras: a powerful federal state in the 3rd century B.C. Chief city: Missolonghi. Pop. (with Acarnania): 228 180 (1991). Area: 5461 sq. km (2108 sq. miles).
AEU (in Britain) *abbrev. for* Amalgamated Engineering Union.
AEW *abbrev. for* airborne early warning (aircraft).
AF *abbrev. for:* **1** Anglo-French. **2** automatic focus. **3** audio frequency.
Af. *abbrev. for* Africa(n).
a.f. *abbrev. for* audio frequency.
A/F (in auction catalogues, etc.) *abbrev. for* as found.
afar (əˈfɑː) *adv* **1** at, from, or to a great distance. ◆ *n* **2** a great distance (esp. in the phrase **from afar**). [C14 *a fer,* altered from earlier *on fer* and *of fer;* see A-[2], FAR]
Afars and the Issas (ˈɑːfɑːz; ˈiːsɑːs) *n* **Territory of the.** a former name (1967–77) of **Djibouti.**
AFB *abbrev. for* (U.S.) Air Force Base.
AFC *abbrev. for:* **1** Air Force Cross. **2** Association Football Club. **3** automatic flight control. **4** automatic frequency control.
afeard *or* **afeared** (əˈfɪəd) *adj (postpositive)* an archaic or dialect word for **afraid.** [Old English *āfǣred,* from *afǣran* to frighten, from *fǣran* to FEAR]
afebrile (æˈfiːbraɪl, eɪ-) *adj* without fever.
aff (æf) *Scot.* ◆ *adv* **1** off. ◆ *prep* **2** off. **3** from; out of. [Old English *of;* Old Norse *af*]
affable (ˈæfəbᵊl) *adj* **1** showing warmth and friendliness; kindly; mild; benign. **2** easy to converse with; approachable; amicable. [C16: from Latin *affābilis* easy to talk to, from *affārī* to talk to, from *ad-* to + *fārī* to speak; compare FABLE, FATE] ► **ˌaffaˈbility** *n* ► **ˈaffably** *adv*
affair (əˈfɛə) *n* **1** a thing to be done or attended to; matter; business: *this affair must be cleared up.* **2** an event or happening: *a strange affair.* **3** *(qualified by an adjective or descriptive phrase)* something previously specified, esp. a man-made object; thing: *our house is a tumbledown affair.* **4** a sexual relationship between two people who are not married to each other. ◆ See also **affairs.** [C13: from Old French, from *à faire* to do]
affaire *French.* (afɛr) *n* a love affair.
affaire d'amour *French.* (afɛr damur) *n, pl* ***affaires d'amour*** (afɛr damur). a love affair.
affaire de coeur *French.* (afɛr də kœr) *n, pl* ***affaires de coeur*** (afɛr də kœr). an affair of the heart; love affair.
affaire d'honneur *French.* (afɛr dɔnœr) *n, pl* ***affaires d'honneur*** (afɛr dɔnœr). a duel.
affairs (əˈfɛəz) *pl n* **1** personal or business interests: *his affairs were in disorder.* **2** matters of public interest: *current affairs.*
affect[1] *vb* (əˈfɛkt). *(tr)* **1** to act upon or influence, esp. in an adverse way: *damp affected the sparking plugs.* **2** to move or disturb emotionally or mentally: *her death affected him greatly.* **3** (of pain, disease, etc.) to attack. ◆ *n* (ˈæfɛkt, əˈfɛkt). **4** *Psychol.* the emotion associated with an idea or set of ideas. See also **affection.** [C17: from Latin *affectus,* past participle of *afficere* to act upon, from *ad-* to + *facere* to do]
affect[2] (əˈfɛkt) *vb (mainly tr)* **1** to put on an appearance or show of; make a pretence of: *to affect ignorance.* **2** to imitate or assume, esp. pretentiously: *to affect an accent.* **3** to have or use by preference: *she always affects funereal clothing.* **4** to adopt the character, manner, etc., of: *he was always affecting the politician.* **5** (of plants or animals) to live or grow in: *penguins affect an arctic climate.* **6** to incline naturally or habitually towards: *falling drops of liquid affect roundness.* [C15: from Latin *affectāre* to strive after, pretend to have; related to *afficere* to AFFECT[1]]
affectation (ˌæfɛkˈteɪʃən) *n* **1** an assumed manner of speech, dress, or behaviour, esp. one that is intended to impress others. **2** (often foll. by *of*) deliberate pretence or false display: *affectation of nobility.* [C16: from Latin *affectātiōn-* an aiming at, striving after, from *affectāre;* see AFFECT[2]]
affected[1] (əˈfɛktɪd) *adj (usually postpositive)* **1** deeply moved, esp. by sorrow or grief: *he was greatly affected by her departure.* **2** changed, esp. detrimentally. [C17: from AFFECT[1] + -ED[2]]
affected[2] (əˈfɛktɪd) *adj* **1** behaving, speaking, etc., in an artificial or assumed way, esp. in order to impress others. **2** feigned: *affected indifference.* **3** *Archaic.* inclined; disposed. [C16: from AFFECT[2] + -ED[2]] ► **afˈfectedly** *adv* ► **afˈfectedness** *n*
affecting (əˈfɛktɪŋ) *adj* evoking feelings of pity, sympathy, or pathos; moving. ► **afˈfectingly** *adv*
affection (əˈfɛkʃən) *n* **1** a feeling of fondness or tenderness for a person or thing; attachment. **2** *(often pl)* emotion, feeling, or sentiment: *to play on a person's affections.* **3** *Pathol.* any disease or pathological condition. **4** *Psychol.* any form of mental functioning that involves emotion. See also **affect**[1]. **5** the act of affecting or the state of being affected. **6** *Archaic.* inclination or disposition. [C13: from Latin *affectiōn-* disposition, from *afficere* to AFFECT[1]] ► **afˈfectional** *adj*
affectionate (əˈfɛkʃənɪt) *adj* having or displaying tender feelings, affection, or warmth: *an affectionate mother; an affectionate letter.* ► **afˈfectionately** *adv*
affective (əˈfɛktɪv) *adj* **1** *Psychol.* relating to affects. **2** concerned with or arousing the emotions or affection. ► **affectivity** (ˌæfɛkˈtɪvɪtɪ) *or* **afˈfectiveness** *n*
affective disorder *n* any mental disorder, such as depression or mania, that is characterized by abnormal disturbances of mood.
affective psychosis *n* a severe mental disorder characterized by extreme moods of either depression or mania.
affectless (əˈfɛktlɪs) *adj* **a** showing no emotion or concern for others. **b** not giving rise to any emotion or feeling: *an affectless novel.* [C20: from AFFECT[1] (sense 4) + -LESS]
affenpinscher (ˈæfənˌpɪnʃə) *n* a small wire-haired breed of dog of European origin, having tufts of hair on the muzzle. [German, literally: monkey-terrier, so called because its face resembles a monkey's]
afferent (ˈæfərənt) *adj* bringing or directing inwards to a part or an organ of the body, esp. towards the brain or spinal cord. Compare **efferent.** [C19: from Latin *afferre* to carry to, from *ad-* to + *ferre* to carry]
affettuoso (æˌfɛtjʊˈəʊsəʊ) *adj, adv Music.* with feeling. [C18: from Italian]
affiance (əˈfaɪəns) *vb* **1** *(tr)* to bind (a person or oneself) in a promise of marriage; betroth. ◆ *n* **2** *Archaic.* a solemn pledge, esp. a marriage contract. [C14: via Old French from Medieval Latin *affīdāre* to trust (oneself) to, from *fīdāre* to trust, from *fīdus* faithful]
affiant (əˈfaɪənt) *n U.S. law.* a person who makes an affidavit. [C19: Old French, from *affier* to trust to, from Medieval Latin *affīdāre;* see AFFIANCE]
affiche *French.* (afiʃ) *n* a poster or advertisement, esp. one drawn by an artist, as for the opening of an exhibition. [C18: from *afficher* to post]
affidavit (ˌæfɪˈdeɪvɪt) *n Law.* a declaration in writing made upon oath before a person authorized to administer oaths. [C17: from Medieval Latin, literally: he declares on oath, from *affīdāre* to trust (oneself) to; see AFFIANCE]
affiliate *vb* (əˈfɪlɪˌeɪt). **1** *(tr;* foll. by *to* or *with)* to receive into close connection or association (with a larger body, group, organization, etc.); adopt as a member, branch, etc. **2** (foll. by *with*) to associate (oneself) or be associated, esp. as a subordinate or subsidiary; bring or come into close connection: *he affiliated himself with the Union.* ◆ *n* (əˈfɪlɪɪt, -ˌeɪt). **3a** a person or organization that is affiliated with another. **3b** *(as modifier): an affiliate member.* [C18: from Medieval Latin *affīliātus* adopted as a son, from *affīliāre,* from Latin *filius* son] ► **afˌfiliˈation** *n*
affiliation order *n Law.* an order made by a magistrates' court that a man adjudged to be the father of an illegitimate child shall contribute a specified periodic sum towards the child's maintenance.
affiliation proceedings *pl n* legal proceedings, usually initiated by an unwed mother, claiming legal recognition that a particular man is the father of her child, often associated with a claim for financial support.
affine (ˈæfaɪn) *adj Maths.* of, characterizing, or involving transformations

which preserve collinearity, esp. in classical geometry, those of translation, rotation and reflection in an axis. [C16: via French from Latin *affinis* bordering on, related]

affined (əˈfaɪnd) *adj* closely related; connected.

affinity (əˈfɪnɪtɪ) *n, pl* **-ties.** **1** (foll. by *with* or *for*) a natural liking, taste, or inclination towards a person or thing. **2** the person or thing so liked. **3** a close similarity in appearance or quality; inherent likeness. **4** relationship by marriage or by ties other than of blood, as by adoption. Compare **consanguinity. 5** similarity in structure, form, etc., between different animals, plants, or languages. **6** *Chem.* **6a** the force holding atoms together in a molecule; chemical attraction. **6b** a measure of the tendency of a chemical reaction to take place expressed in terms of the free energy change. Symbol: *A* **7** *Immunol.* a measure of the degree of interaction between an antigen and an antibody. [C14: via Old French from Latin *affinitāt-* connected by marriage, from *affinis* bordering on, related] ▸ **afˈfinitive** *adj*

affinity card *n* **1** *Brit.* a credit card issued by a bank or credit-card company, which donates a small percentage of the money spent using the card to a specified charity. **2** *U.S.* a card entitling members of an affinity group (e.g. club, college) to a discount when used for purchases.

affirm (əˈfɜːm) *vb* (*mainly tr*) **1** (*may take a clause as object*) to declare to be true; assert positively. **2** to uphold, confirm, or ratify. **3** (*intr*) *Law.* to make an affirmation. [C14: via Old French from Latin *affirmāre* to present (something) as firm or fixed, assert, from *ad-* to + *firmāre* to make FIRM[1]] ▸ **afˈfirmer** *or* **afˈfirmant** *n*

affirmation (ˌæfəˈmeɪʃən) *n* **1** the act of affirming or the state of being affirmed. **2** a statement of the existence or truth of something; assertion. **3** *Law.* a solemn declaration permitted on grounds of conscientious objection to taking an oath.

affirmative (əˈfɜːmətɪv) *adj* **1** confirming or asserting something as true or valid: *an affirmative statement.* **2** indicating agreement or assent: *an affirmative answer.* **3** *Logic.* **3a** (of a categorial proposition) affirming the satisfaction by the subject of the predicate, as in *all birds have feathers; some men are married.* **3b** not containing negation. Compare **negative** (sense 12). ◆ *n* **4** a positive assertion. **5** a word or phrase stating agreement or assent, such as *yes* (esp. in the phrase **answer in the affirmative**). **6** *Logic.* an affirmative proposition. **7 the affirmative.** *Chiefly U.S. and Canadian.* the side in a debate that supports the proposition. ◆ *sentence substitute.* **8** *Military, etc.* a signal codeword used to express assent or confirmation. ▸ **afˈfirmatively** *adv*

affirmative action *n U.S.* a policy or programme designed to counter discrimination against minority groups and women in areas such as employment and education. Brit. equivalent: **positive discrimination.**

affix *vb* (əˈfɪks). (*tr;* usually foll. by *to* or *on*) **1** to attach, fasten, join, or stick: *to affix a poster to the wall.* **2** to add or append: *to affix a signature to a document.* **3** to attach or attribute (guilt, blame, etc.). ◆ *n* (ˈæfɪks). **4** a linguistic element added to a word or root to produce a derived or inflected form: *-ment* in *establishment* is a derivational affix; *-s* in *drowns* is an inflectional affix. See also **prefix, suffix, infix. 5** something fastened or attached; appendage. [C15: from Medieval Latin *affixāre,* from *ad-* to + *fixāre* to FIX] ▸ **affixation** (ˌæfɪkˈseɪʃən) *or* **affixture** (əˈfɪkstʃə) *n*

afflatus (əˈfleɪtəs) *n* an impulse of creative power or inspiration, esp. in poetry, considered to be of divine origin (esp. in the phrase **divine afflatus**). [C17: Latin, from *afflātus,* from *afflāre* to breathe or blow on, from *flāre* to blow]

afflict (əˈflɪkt) *vb* (*tr*) to cause suffering or unhappiness to; distress greatly. [C14: from Latin *afflictus,* past participle of *affligere* to knock against, from *fligere* to knock, to strike] ▸ **afˈflictive** *adj*

afflicting (əˈflɪktɪŋ) *adj* deeply distressing; painful.

affliction (əˈflɪkʃən) *n* **1** a condition of great distress, pain, or suffering. **2** something responsible for physical or mental suffering, such as a disease, grief, etc.

affluence (ˈæfluəns) *n* **1** an abundant supply of money, goods, or property; wealth. **2** *Rare.* abundance or profusion.

affluent (ˈæfluənt) *adj* **1** rich; wealthy. **2** abundant; copious. **3** flowing freely. ◆ *n* **4** a tributary stream. [C15: from Latin *affluent-,* present participle of *affluere* to flow towards, from *fluere* to flow]

affluent society *n* a society in which the material benefits of prosperity are widely available.

afflux (ˈæflʌks) *n* a flowing towards a point: *an afflux of blood to the head.* [C17: from Latin *affluxus,* from *fluxus* FLUX]

afford (əˈfɔːd) *vb* **1** (preceded by *can, could,* etc.) to be able to do or spare something, esp. without incurring financial difficulties or without risk of undesirable consequences: *we can afford to buy a small house; I can afford to give you one of my chess sets; we can't afford to miss this play.* **2** to give, yield, or supply: *the meeting afforded much useful information.* [Old English *geforthian* to further, promote, from *forth* FORTH; the Old English prefix *ge-* was later reduced to *a-,* and the modern spelling (C16) is influenced by words beginning *aff-*] ▸ **afˈfordable** *adj* ▸ **afˌfordaˈbility** *n*

afforest (əˈfɒrɪst) *vb* (*tr*) to plant trees on; convert into forested land. [C15: from Medieval Latin *afforestāre,* from *forestis* FOREST] ▸ **afˌforestˈation** *n*

affranchise (əˈfræntʃaɪz) *vb* (*tr*) to release from servitude or an obligation. [C15: from Old French *afranchiss-,* a stem of *afranchir,* from *franchir* to free; see FRANK] ▸ **afˈfranchisement** *n*

affray (əˈfreɪ) *n* **1** *Law.* a fight, noisy quarrel, or disturbance between two or more persons in a public place. ◆ *vb* **2** (*tr*) *Archaic.* to frighten. [C14: via Old French from Vulgar Latin *exfridāre* (unattested) to break the peace; compare German *Friede* peace]

affreightment (əˈfreɪtmənt) *n* a contract hiring a ship to carry goods. [C19: from French *affréter* to charter a ship, from *fret* FREIGHT]

affricate (ˈæfrɪkɪt) *n* a composite speech sound consisting of a stop and a fricative articulated at the same point, such as the sound written *ch,* as in *chair.* [C19: from Latin *affricāre* to rub against, from *fricāre* to rub; compare FRICTION]

affricative (əˈfrɪkətɪv, ˈæfrəˌkeɪ-) *n* **1** another word for **affricate.** ◆ *adj* **2** of, relating to, or denoting an affricate.

affright (əˈfraɪt) *Archaic or poetic.* ◆ *vb* **1** (*tr*) to frighten. ◆ *n* **2** a sudden terror. [Old English *āfyrhtan,* from *a-,* a prefix indicating the beginning or end of an action + *fyrhtan* to FRIGHT]

affront (əˈfrʌnt) *n* **1** a deliberate insult. ◆ *vb* (*tr*) **2** to insult, esp. openly. **3** to offend the pride or dignity of. **4** *Obsolete.* to confront defiantly. [C14: from Old French *afronter* to strike in the face, from Vulgar Latin *affrontāre* (unattested), from the Latin phrase *ad frontem* to the face]

affusion (əˈfjuːʒən) *n* the baptizing of a person by pouring water onto his head. Compare **aspersion** (sense 3), **immersion.** [C17: from Late Latin *affūsiōn-* a pouring upon, from *affundere,* from *fundere* to pour]

AFG *international car registration for* Afghanistan.

Afg. *or* **Afgh.** *abbrev. for* Afghanistan.

afghan (ˈæfgæn, -gən) *n* **1** a knitted or crocheted wool blanket or shawl, esp. one with a geometric pattern. **2** a sheepskin coat, often embroidered and having long fur trimming around the edges.

Afghan (ˈæfgæn, -gən) *or* **Afghani** (æfˈgænɪ, -ˈgɑː-) *n* **1** a native, citizen, or inhabitant of Afghanistan. **2** another name for **Pashto** (the language). **3** *History.* an Indian camel driver employed in the outback of Australia. ◆ *adj* **4** denoting or relating to Afghanistan, its people, or their language.

Afghan hound *n* a tall graceful breed of hound with a long silky coat.

afghani (æfˈgɑːnɪ) *n* the standard monetary unit of Afghanistan, divided into 100 puls.

Afghani (æfˈgɑːnɪ) *n* **Jamal ad-Din al-.** 1839–97, Iranian Muslim religious and political reformer; a proponent of Muslim unity, he resisted European interference in Muslim countries.

Afghanistan (æfˈgænɪˌstɑːn, -ˌstæn) *n* a republic in central Asia: became independent in 1919; occupied by Soviet troops, 1979–89; controlled by mujahed-din forces from 1992 until 1996 when Taliban forces seized power; generally arid and mountainous, with the Hindu Kush range rising over 7500 m (25 000 ft.) and fertile valleys of the Amu Darya, Helmand, and Kabul Rivers. Official languages: Pashto and Dari (Persian), Tajik also widely spoken. Religion: Muslim. Currency: afghani. Capital: Kabul. Pop.: 24 792 000 (1998 est.). Area: 657 500 sq. km (250 000 sq. miles).

aficionado (əˌfɪʃjəˈnɑːdəʊ; *Spanish* afiθjoˈnaðo) *n, pl* **-dos** (-dəʊz; *Spanish* -ðos). **1** an ardent supporter or devotee: *a jazz aficionado.* **2** a devotee of bullfighting [Spanish, from *aficionar* to arouse affection, from *afición* AFFECTION]

afield (əˈfiːld) *adv, adj* (*postpositive*) **1** away from one's usual surroundings or home (esp. in the phrase **far afield**). **2** off the subject; away from the point (esp. in the phrase **far afield**). **3** in or to the field, esp. the battlefield.

afire (əˈfaɪə) *adv, adj* (*postpositive*) **1** on fire; ablaze. **2** intensely interested or passionate: *he was afire with enthusiasm for the new plan.*

aflame (əˈfleɪm) *adv, adj* (*postpositive*) **1** in flames; ablaze. **2** deeply aroused, as with passion: *he was aflame with desire.* **3** (of the face) red or inflamed.

aflatoxin (ˌæfləˈtɒksɪn) *n* a toxin produced by the fungus *Aspergillus flavus* growing on peanuts, maize, etc., causing liver disease (esp. cancer) in man. [C20: from *A(spergillus) fla(vus)* + TOXIN]

AFL-CIO *abbrev. for* American Federation of Labor and Congress of Industrial Organizations; a federation of independent American trade unions formed by the union of these two groups in 1955.

afloat (əˈfləʊt) *adj* (*postpositive*), *adv* **1** floating. **2** aboard ship; at sea. **3** covered with water; flooded. **4** aimlessly drifting: *afloat in a sea of indecision.* **5** in circulation; afoot: *nasty rumours were afloat.* **6** free of debt; solvent.

aflutter (əˈflʌtə) *adj* (*postpositive*), *adv* in or into a nervous or excited state.

AFM *abbrev. for* Air Force Medal.

AFNOR *abbrev. for* Association Française de Normalisation: the standards organization of France.

afoot (əˈfʊt) *adj* (*postpositive*), *adv* **1** in circulation or operation; astir: *mischief was afoot.* **2** on or by foot.

afore (əˈfɔː) *adv, prep, conj* an archaic or dialect word for **before.**

aforementioned (əˈfɔːˌmɛnʃənd) *adj* (*usually prenominal*) (chiefly in legal documents) stated or mentioned before or already.

aforesaid (əˈfɔːˌsɛd) *adj* (*usually prenominal*) (chiefly in legal documents) spoken of or referred to previously.

aforethought (əˈfɔːˌθɔːt) *adj* (*immediately postpositive*) premeditated (esp. in the phrase **malice aforethought**).

aforetime (əˈfɔːˌtaɪm) *adv Archaic.* formerly.

a fortiori (eɪ ˌfɔːtɪˈɔːraɪ, -rɪ; ɑː) *adv* for similar but more convincing reasons: *if Britain cannot afford a space programme, then, a fortiori, neither can India.* [Latin]

afoul (əˈfaʊl) *adv, adj* (*postpositive*) **1** (usually foll. by *of*) in or into a state of difficulty, confusion, or conflict (with). **2** (often foll. by *of*) in or into an entanglement or collision (with) (often in the phrase **run afoul of**): *a yacht with its sails afoul; the boat ran afoul of a steamer.*

afp *abbrev. for* alpha-fetoprotein.

Afr. *abbrev. for* Africa(n).

AFRAeS (in Britain) *abbrev. for* Associate Fellow of the Royal Aeronautical Society.

afraid (əˈfreɪd) *adj* (*postpositive*) **1** (often foll. by *of*) feeling fear or apprehension; frightened: *he was afraid of cats.* **2** reluctant (to do something), as through fear or timidity: *he was afraid to let himself go.* **3** (often foll. by *that;* used to lessen the effect of an unpleasant statement) regretful: *I'm afraid that I shall have to tell you to go.* [C14 *affraied,* past participle of AFFRAY (to frighten)]

A-frame *adj* (of a house) constructed with an A-shaped elevation.

afreet *or* **afrit** ('æfri:t, ə'fri:t) *n Arabian myth.* a powerful evil demon or giant monster. [C19: from Arabic *'ifrīt*]

afresh (ə'freʃ) *adv* once more; once again; anew.

Africa ('æfrɪkə) *n* the second largest of the continents, on the Mediterranean in the north, the Atlantic in the west, and the Red Sea, Gulf of Aden, and Indian Ocean in the east. The Sahara desert divides the continent unequally into North Africa (an early centre of civilization, in close contact with Europe and W Asia, now inhabited chiefly by Arabs) and Africa south of the Sahara (relatively isolated from the rest of the world until the 19th century and inhabited chiefly by Negroid peoples). It was colonized mainly in the 18th and 19th centuries by Europeans and now comprises independent nations. The largest lake is Lake Victoria and the chief rivers are the Nile, Niger, Congo, and Zambezi. Pop.: 755 919 000 (1998 est.). Area: about 30 300 000 sq. km (11 700 000 sq. miles).

African ('æfrɪkən) *adj* **1** denoting or relating to Africa or any of its peoples, languages, nations, etc. ◆ *n* **2** a native, inhabitant, or citizen of any of the countries of Africa. **3** a member or descendant of any of the peoples of Africa, esp. a Black.

African-American *n* **1** an American of African descent. ◆ *adj* **2** of or relating to Americans of African descent.

Africanism ('æfrɪkə,nɪzəm) *n* something characteristic of Africa or Africans, esp. a characteristic feature of an African language when introduced into a non-African language.

Africanist ('æfrɪkənɪst) *n* a person specializing in the study of African affairs or culture.

Africanize *or* **Africanise** ('æfrɪkə,naɪz) *vb (tr)* to make African, esp. to give control of (policy, government, etc.) to Africans. ► **,Africani'zation** *or* **,Africani'sation** *n*

African lily *n* another name for **agapanthus.**

African mahogany *n* **1** any of several African trees of the meliaceous genus *Khaya,* esp. *K. ivorensis,* that have wood similar to that of true mahogany. **2** the wood of any of these trees, used for furniture, etc. **3** any of various other African woods that resemble true mahogany.

African National Congress *n* (in South Africa) a political party, founded in 1912 as an African nationalist movement and banned there from 1960 to 1990 because of its active opposition to apartheid: in 1994 won South Africa's first multiracial elections. Abbrev.: **ANC.**

African time *n S. African slang.* unpunctuality.

African violet *n* any of several tropical African plants of the genus *Saintpaulia,* esp. *S. ionantha,* cultivated as house plants, with violet, white, or pink flowers and hairy leaves: family *Gesneriaceae.*

Afrikaans (,æfrɪ'kɑ:ns, -'kɑ:nz) *n* one of the official languages of the Republic of South Africa, closely related to Dutch. Sometimes called: **South African Dutch.** [C20: from Dutch: African]

Afrikander *or* **Africander** (afri'kandə, ,æfrɪ'kændə) *n* **1** a breed of humpbacked beef cattle originally raised in southern Africa. **2** a southern African breed of fat-tailed sheep. **3** a former name for an **Afrikaner.** [C19: from South African Dutch, formed on the model of *Hollander*]

Afrikaner (afri'kɑ:nə, ,æfrɪ'kɑ:nə) *n* a White native of the Republic of South Africa whose mother tongue is Afrikaans. See also **Boer.**

Afrikanerdom (afri'kɑ:nədəm, ,æfrɪ'kɑ:nədəm) *n* (in South Africa) Afrikaner nationalism based on pride in the Afrikaans language and culture, conservative Calvinism, and a sense of heritage as pioneers.

afrit ('æfri:t, ə'fri:t) *n* a variant spelling of **afreet.**

Afro ('æfrəʊ) *n, pl* **-ros.** a hairstyle in which the hair is shaped into a wide frizzy bush. [C20: independent use of AFRO-]

Afro- *combining form.* indicating Africa or African: *Afro-Asiatic.*

Afro-American *n, adj* another word for **African-American.**

Afro-Asian *adj* of or relating to both Africa and Asia, esp. as part of the Third World.

Afro-Asiatic *n* **1** Also called: **Semito-Hamitic.** a family of languages of SW Asia and N Africa, consisting of the Semitic, ancient Egyptian, Berber, Cushitic, and Chadic subfamilies. ◆ *adj* **2** denoting, belonging to, or relating to this family of languages.

Afro-chain *n* (in the Caribbean) a large chain necklace with a central pendant: usually worn with a dashiki by men.

Afro-comb *n* a comb with a handle and long teeth used esp. on curly hair.

Afro-Cuban *adj* of or relating to a type of jazz influenced by Cuban variants of African rhythms. Compare **Cu-bop.**

afrormosia (,æfrɔ:'məʊzɪə) *n* a hard teaklike wood obtained from tropical African trees of the leguminous genus *Pericopsis.* [C20: from AFRO- + *Ormosia* (genus name)]

AFSLAET *abbrev. for* Associate Fellow of the Society of Licensed Aircraft Engineers and Technologists.

aft (ɑ:ft) *adv, adj Chiefly nautical.* towards or at the stern or rear: *the aft deck; aft of the engines.* [C17: perhaps a shortened form of earlier ABAFT]

after ('ɑ:ftə) *prep* **1** following in time; in succession to: *after dinner; time after time.* **2** following; behind: *they entered one after another.* **3** in pursuit or search of: *chasing after a thief; he's only after money.* **4** concerning: *to inquire after his health.* **5** considering: *after what you have done, you shouldn't complain.* **6** next in excellence or importance to: *he ranked Jonson after Shakespeare.* **7** in imitation of; in the manner of: *a statue after classical models.* **8** in accordance with or in conformity to: *a man after her own heart.* **9** with a name derived from: *Mary was named after her grandmother.* **10** *U.S.* past (the hour of): *twenty after three.* **11 after all. 11a** in spite of everything: *it's only a game, after all.* **11b** in spite of expectations, efforts, etc.: *he won the race after all!* **12 after you.** please go, enter, etc., before me. ◆ *adv* **13** at a later time; afterwards. **14** coming afterwards; in pursuit. **15** *Nautical.* further aft; sternwards. ◆ *conj* **16** *(subordinating)* at a time later than that at which: *he came after I had left.* ◆ *adj* **17** *Nautical.* further aft: *the after cabin.* [Old English *æfter;* related to Old Norse *aptr* back, *eptir* after, Old High German *aftar*]

afterbirth ('ɑ:ftə,bɜ:θ) *n* the placenta and fetal membranes expelled from the uterus after the birth of offspring.

afterbody ('ɑ:ftə,bɒdɪ) *n, pl* **-bodies.** any discarded part that continues to trail a satellite, rocket, etc., in orbit.

afterbrain ('ɑ:ftə,breɪn) *n* a nontechnical name for **myelencephalon.**

afterburner ('ɑ:ftə,bɜ:nə) *n* **1** a device in the exhaust system of an internal-combustion engine for removing or rendering harmless potentially dangerous components in the exhaust gases. **2** a system of fuel injection and combustion located behind the turbine of an aircraft jet engine to produce additional thrust.

afterburning ('ɑ:ftə,bɜ:nɪŋ) *n* **1** Also called: **reheat.** a process in which additional fuel is ignited in the exhaust gases of a jet engine to produce additional thrust. **2** irregular burning of fuel in a rocket motor after the main burning has ceased. **3** persistence of combustion in an internal-combustion engine, either in an incorrect part of the cycle or after the ignition has been switched off.

aftercare ('ɑ:ftə,keə) *n* **1** support services by a welfare agency for a person discharged from an institution, such as hospital, hostel, prison, or borstal. **2** *Med.* the care before discharge from hospital of a patient recovering from an illness or operation. **3** any system of maintenance or upkeep of an appliance or product: *contact lens aftercare.*

afterdamp ('ɑ:ftə,dæmp) *n* a poisonous gas, consisting mainly of carbon monoxide, formed after the explosion of firedamp in coal mines. See also **whitedamp.**

afterdeck ('ɑ:ftə,dek) *n Nautical.* the unprotected deck behind the bridge of a ship.

aftereffect ('ɑ:ftərɪ,fekt) *n* **1** any result occurring some time after its cause. **2** *Med.* any delayed response to a stimulus or agent. Compare **side effect. 3** *Psychol.* any illusory sensation caused by a stimulus that has ceased.

afterglow ('ɑ:ftə,gləʊ) *n* **1** the glow left after a light has disappeared, such as that sometimes seen after sunset. **2** the glow of an incandescent metal after the source of heat has been removed. **3** *Physics.* luminescence persisting on the screen of a cathode-ray tube or in a gas-discharge tube after the power supply has been disconnected. **4** a trace, impression, etc., of past emotion, brilliance, etc.

afterheat ('ɑ:ftə,hi:t) *n* the heat generated in a nuclear reactor after it has been shut down, produced by residual radioactivity in the fuel elements.

afterimage ('ɑ:ftər,ɪmɪdʒ) *n* a sustained or renewed sensation, esp. visual, after the original stimulus has ceased. Also called: **aftersensation, photogene.**

afterlife ('ɑ:ftə,laɪf) *n* life after death or at a later time in a person's lifetime.

aftermath ('ɑ:ftə,mɑ:θ, -,mæθ) *n* **1** signs or results of an event or occurrence considered collectively, esp. of a catastrophe or disaster: *the aftermath of war.* **2** *Agriculture.* a second mowing or crop of grass from land that has already yielded one crop earlier in the same year. [C16: AFTER + *math* a mowing, from Old English *mæth*]

aftermost ('ɑ:ftə,məʊst) *adj* closer or closest to the rear or (in a vessel) the stern; last.

afternoon (,ɑ:ftə'nu:n) *n* **1a** the period of the day between noon and evening. **1b** *(as modifier): afternoon tea.* **2** a middle or later part: *the afternoon of life.*

afternoons (,ɑ:ftə'nu:nz) *adv Informal.* during the afternoon, esp. regularly.

afterpains ('ɑ:ftə,peɪnz) *pl n* cramplike pains caused by contraction of the uterus after childbirth.

afterpeak ('ɑ:ftə,pi:k) *n Nautical.* the space behind the aftermost bulkhead, often used for storage.

afterpiece ('ɑ:ftə,pi:s) *n* a brief usually comic dramatic piece presented after a play.

after-ripening *n Botany.* the period of internal change that is necessary in some apparently mature seeds before germination can occur.

afters ('ɑ:ftəz) *n (functioning as sing or pl) Brit. informal.* dessert; sweet.

aftersensation ('ɑ:ftəsen,seɪʃən) *n* another word for **afterimage.**

aftershaft ('ɑ:ftə,ʃɑ:ft) *n Ornithol.* a secondary feather arising near the base of a contour feather.

aftershave lotion ('ɑ:ftə,ʃeɪv) *n* a lotion, usually styptic and perfumed, for application to the face after shaving. Often shortened to **aftershave.**

aftershock ('ɑ:ftə,ʃɒk) *n* one of a series of minor tremors occurring after the main shock of an earthquake. Compare **foreshock.**

aftertaste ('ɑ:ftə,teɪst) *n* **1** a taste that lingers on after eating or drinking. **2** a lingering impression or sensation.

afterthought ('ɑ:ftə,θɔ:t) *n* **1** a comment, reply, etc., that occurs to one after the opportunity to deliver it has passed. **2** an addition to something already completed.

afterwards ('ɑ:ftəwədz) *or* **afterward** *adv* after an earlier event or time; subsequently. [Old English *æfterweard, æfteweard,* from AFT + WARD]

afterword ('ɑ:ftə,wɜ:d) *n* an epilogue or postscript in a book, etc.

afterworld ('ɑ:ftə,wɜ:ld) *n* a world inhabited after death.

AFTN *abbrev. for* Aeronautical Fixed Telecommunications Network: a worldwide system of radio and cable links for transmitting and recording messages.

AFV *abbrev. for* armoured fighting vehicle.

Ag *the chemical symbol for* silver. [from Latin *argentum*]

AG *abbrev. for:* **1** Adjutant General. **2** Attorney General. **3** Aktiengesellschaft. [German: joint-stock company]

aga *or* **agha** ('ɑ:gə) *n* (in the Ottoman Empire) **1** a title of respect, often used with the title of a senior position. **2** a military commander. [C17: Turkish, literally: lord]

Agadir (,ægə'dɪə) *n* a port in SW Morocco, which became the centre of an international crisis (1911), when a gunboat arrived to protect German interests. Britain issued a strong warning to Germany but the French negotiated and war was averted. In 1960 the town was virtually destroyed by an earthquake, about 10 000 people being killed. Pop.: 155 244 (1994).

again (əˈgɛn, əˈgeɪn) *adv* **1** another or second time; once more; anew: *he had to start again.* **2** once more in a previously experienced or encountered place, state, or condition: *he is ill again; he came back again.* **3** in addition to the original amount, quantity, etc. (esp. in the phrases **as much again; half as much again**). **4** (*sentence modifier*) on the other hand: *he might come and then again he might not.* **5** besides; also: *she is beautiful and, again, intelligent.* **6** *Archaic.* in reply; back: *he answered again to the questioning voice.* **7** **again and again.** continuously; repeatedly. **8** (*used with a negative*) *Caribbean.* any more; any longer: *I don't eat pumpkin again.* ◆ *sentence connector.* **9** moreover; furthermore: *again, it could be said that he is not dead.* [Old English *ongegn* opposite to, from A-[2] + *gegn* straight]

against (əˈgɛnst, əˈgeɪnst) *prep* **1** opposed to; in conflict or disagreement with: *they fought against the legislation.* **2** standing or leaning beside or in front of: *a ladder against the wall.* **3** coming in contact with: *the branches of a tree brushed against the bus.* **4** in contrast to: *silhouettes are outlines against a light background.* **5** having an adverse or unfavourable effect on: *the economic system works against small independent companies.* **6** as a protection from or means of defence from the adverse effects of: *a safeguard against contaminated water.* **7** in exchange for or in return for. **8** *Now rare.* in preparation for: *he gave them warm clothing against their journey through the night.* **9** **as against.** as opposed to or as compared with: *he had two shots at him this time as against only one last time.* [C12 *ageines,* from *again, ageyn,* etc., AGAIN + *-es* genitive ending; the spelling with *-t* (C16) was probably due to confusion with superlatives ending in *-st*]

Aga Khan (ˈɑːgə ˈkɑːn) *n* the hereditary title of the head of the Ismaili sect of Muslims.

Aga Khan IV *n* Prince **Karim** (kəˈriːm). born 1936, spiritual leader of the Ismaili sect of Muslims from 1957.

agalactia (ˌægəˈlæktɪə) *n Pathol.* absence or failure of secretion of milk. [C19: New Latin, from A-[1] + Greek *galaktos* milk]

agalloch (əˈgælək) *n* another name for **eaglewood.** [C17: from Greek *agallokhon*]

agama (ˈægəmə, əˈgæmə) *n* **1** any small terrestrial lizard of the genus *Agama,* which inhabit warm regions of the Old World: family *Agamidae.* **2** Also called: **agamid** (ˈægəmɪd, əˈgæmɪd). any other lizard of the family *Agamidae,* which occur in the Old World and Australia and show a wide range of habits and diversity of structure. [C19: Carib]

Agamemnon (ˌægəˈmɛmnɒn) *n Greek myth.* a king of Mycenae who led the Greeks at the siege of Troy. On his return home he was murdered by his wife Clytemnestra and her lover Aegisthus. See also **Menelaus.**

agamete (əˈgæmiːt) *n* a reproductive cell, such as the merozoite of some protozoans, that develops into a new form without fertilization. [C19: from Greek *agametos* unmarried; see A-[1], GAMETE]

agamic (əˈgæmɪk) *adj* asexual; occurring or reproducing without fertilization. [C19: from Greek *agamos* unmarried, from A-[1] + *gamos* marriage] ► **aˈgamically** *adv*

agamogenesis (ˌægəməʊˈdʒɛnɪsɪs) *n* asexual reproduction, such as fission or parthenogenesis. [C19: AGAMIC + GENESIS] ► **agamogenetic** (ˌægəməʊdʒəˈnɛtɪk) *adj* ► **ˌagamogeˈnetically** *adv*

agamogony (ˌægəˈmɒgənɪ) *n* another name for **schizogony.**

agamont (ˈægəmɒnt) *n* another name for **schizont.**

agamospermy (ˈægəməʊˌspɜːmɪ) *n Botany.* formation of seeds in the absence of fertilization; a form of apomixis. [C19: AGAMIC + Greek *sperma* seed]

Agaña (əˈgɑːnjə) *n* the capital of the Pacific island of Guam, on its W coast. Pop.: 2000 (1995 est.).

agapanthus (ˌægəˈpænθəs) *n* a liliaceous plant, *Agapanthus africanus,* of southern Africa, having rounded clusters of blue or white funnel-shaped flowers. Also called: **African lily.** [C19: New Latin, from Greek *agapē* love + *anthos* flower]

agape (əˈgeɪp) *adj* (*postpositive*) **1** (esp. of the mouth) wide open. **2** very surprised, expectant, or eager, esp. as indicated by a wide open mouth. [C17: A-[2] + GAPE]

Agape (ˈægəpɪ) *n Christianity.* **1** Christian love, esp. as contrasted with erotic love; charity. **2** a communal meal in the early Church taken in commemoration of the Last Supper; love feast. [C17: Greek *agapē* love]

agar (ˈeɪgə) *n* a complex gelatinous carbohydrate obtained from seaweeds, esp. those of the genus *Gelidium,* used as a culture medium for bacteria, a laxative, in food such as ice cream as a thickening agent (**E406**), etc. Also called: **agar-agar.** [C19: Malay]

agaric (ˈægərɪk, əˈgærɪk) *n* **1** any saprotrophic basidiomycetous fungus of the family *Agaricaceae,* having gills on the underside of the cap. The group includes the edible mushrooms and poisonous forms such as the fly agaric. **2** the dried spore-producing bodies of certain fungi, esp. *Polyphorus officinalis* (or *Boletus laricis*), formerly used in medicine. [C16: via Latin *agaricum,* from Greek *agarikon,* perhaps named after *Agaria,* a town in Sarmatia] ► **agaricaceous** (əˌgærɪˈkeɪʃəs) *adj*

Agartala (ˈʌgətəˌlɑː) *n* a city in NE India, capital of the state of Tripura. Pop.: 157 636 (1991).

Agassi (ˈægəsɪ) *n* **Andre** (ˈɑːndreɪ). born 1970, U.S. tennis player: won the Wimbledon men's singles in 1992 and the U.S. Open in 1994 and 1999.

Agassiz (*French* agasi) *n* **Jean Louis Rodolphe** (ʒɑ̃ lwi rɔdɔlf). 1807–73, Swiss natural historian and geologist, settled in the U.S. after 1846.

agate (ˈægɪt) *n* **1** an impure microcrystalline form of quartz consisting of a variegated, usually banded chalcedony, used as a gemstone and in making pestles and mortars, burnishers, and polishers. Formula: SiO_2. **2** a playing marble of this quartz or resembling it. **3** *Printing.* the U.S. and Canadian name for **ruby** (sense 5). [C16: via French from Latin *achātēs,* from Greek *akhatēs*]

Agate (ˈægeɪt) *n* **James (Evershed).** 1877–1947, British theatre critic; drama critic for *The Sunday Times* (1923–47) and author of a nine-volume diary *Ego* (1935–49).

agateware (ˈægɪtˌwɛə) *n* ceramic ware made to resemble agate or marble.

agave (əˈgeɪvɪ, ˈægeɪv) *n* any plant of the genus *Agave* native to tropical America with tall flower stalks rising from thick fleshy leaves: family *Agavaceae.* Some species are the source of fibres such as sisal or of alcoholic beverages such as pulque and tequila. See also **century plant.** [C18: New Latin, from Greek *agauē,* feminine of *agauos* illustrious, probably alluding to the height of the plant]

AGC *abbrev. for* automatic gain control.

agcy *abbrev. for* agency.

age (eɪdʒ) *n* **1** the period of time that a person, animal, or plant has lived or is expected to live: *the age of a tree; what age was he when he died? the age of a horse is up to thirty years.* **2** the period of existence of an object, material, group, etc.: *the age of this table is 200 years.* **3a** a period or state of human life: *he should know better at his age; she had got beyond the giggly age.* **3b** (*as modifier*): *age group.* **4** the latter part of life. **5a** a period of history marked by some feature or characteristic; era. **5b** (*cap. when part of a name*): *the Middle Ages; the Space Age.* **6** generation: *the Edwardian age.* **7** *Geology, palaeontol.* **7a** a period of the earth's history distinguished by special characteristics: *the age of reptiles.* **7b** the period during which a stage of rock strata is formed; a subdivision of an epoch. **8** *Myth.* any of the successive periods in the legendary history of man, which were, according to Hesiod, the golden, silver, bronze, heroic, and iron ages. **9** (*often pl*) *Informal.* a relatively long time: *she was an age washing her hair; I've been waiting ages.* **10** *Psychol.* the level in years that a person has reached in any area of development, such as mental or emotional, compared with the normal level for his chronological age. See also **achievement age, mental age.** **11** **age before beauty.** (often said humorously when yielding precedence) older people take precedence over younger people. **12** **of age.** adult and legally responsible for one's actions (usually at 18 or, formerly, 21 years). ◆ *vb* **ages, ageing** *or* **aging, aged.** **13** to grow or make old or apparently old; become or cause to become old or aged. **14** to begin to seem older: *to have aged a lot in the past year.* **15** *Brewing.* to mature or cause to mature. [C13: via Old French from Vulgar Latin *aetatīcum* (unattested), from Latin *aetās,* ultimately from *aevum* lifetime; compare AEON]

-age *suffix forming nouns.* **1** indicating a collection, set, or group: *acreage; baggage.* **2** indicating a process or action or the result of an action: *haulage; passage; breakage.* **3** indicating a state, condition, or relationship: *bondage; parentage.* **4** indicating a house or place: *orphanage.* **5** indicating a charge or fee: *postage.* **6** indicating a rate: *dosage; mileage.* [from Old French, from Late Latin *-āticum,* noun suffix, neuter of *-āticus,* adjectival suffix, from *-ātus* -ATE[1] + *-icus* -IC]

age allowance *n* an income tax allowance given to taxpayers aged 65 or over.

aged (ˈeɪdʒɪd) *adj* **1a** advanced in years; old. **1b** (*as collective n;* preceded by *the*): *the aged.* **2** of, connected with, or characteristic of old age. **3** (eɪdʒd). (*postpositive*) having the age of: *a woman aged twenty.* **4** *Geography.* having reached an advanced stage of erosion.

agee *or* **ajee** (əˈdʒiː) *Scot. and English dialect.* ◆ *adj* **1** awry, crooked, or ajar. ◆ *adv* **2** awry; at an angle. [C19: A-[2] + GEE[1]]

Agee (ˈeɪdʒiː) *n* **James.** 1909–55, U.S. novelist, poet, and film critic. His works include the autobiographical novel *A Death in the Family* (1957).

age hardening *n* the hardening of metals by spontaneous structural changes over a period of time. See also **precipitation hardening.**

ageing *or* **aging** (ˈeɪdʒɪŋ) *n* **1** the process of growing old or developing the appearance and characteristics of old age. **2** the change of properties that occurs in some metals after heat treatment or cold working. ◆ *adj* **3** becoming or appearing older or elderly: *an ageing car.* **4** giving or creating the appearance of age or elderliness: *that dress is really ageing on her.*

ageism *or* **agism** (ˈeɪdʒɪzəm) *n* discrimination against people on the grounds of age; specifically, discrimination against the elderly. ► **ˈageist** *or* **ˈagist** *adj*

ageless (ˈeɪdʒlɪs) *adj* **1** apparently never growing old. **2** timeless; eternal: *an ageless quality.* ► **ˈagelessness** *n*

Agen (*French* aʒɛ̃) *n* a market town in SW France, on the Garonne river. Pop.: 32 220 (1990).

agency (ˈeɪdʒənsɪ) *n, pl* **-cies. 1** a business or other organization providing a specific service: *an employment agency.* **2** the place where an agent conducts business. **3** the business, duties, or functions of an agent. **4** action, power, or operation: *the agency of fate.* **5** intercession or mediation. **6** one of the administrative organizations of a government. [C17: from Medieval Latin *agentia,* from Latin *agere* to do]

agenda (əˈdʒɛndə) *n* **1** (*functioning as sing*) Also called: **agendum.** a schedule or list of items to be attended to. **2** (*functioning as pl*) Also called: **agendas, agendums.** matters to be attended to, as at a meeting of a committee. [C17: Latin, literally: things to be done, from *agere* to do]

agenesis (eɪˈdʒɛnɪsɪs) *n* **1** (of an animal or plant) imperfect development. **2** impotence or sterility. ► **agenetic** (ˌeɪdʒəˈnɛtɪk) *adj*

agent (ˈeɪdʒənt) *n* **1** a person who acts on behalf of another person, group, business, government, etc.; representative. **2** a person or thing that acts or has the power to act. **3** a phenomenon, substance, or organism that exerts some force or effect: *a chemical agent.* **4** the means by which something occurs or is achieved; instrument: *wind is an agent of plant pollination.* **5** a person representing a business concern, esp. a travelling salesman. **6** *Brit.* short for **estate agent.** **7** short for **secret agent.** [C15: from Latin *agent-,* noun use of the present participle of *agere* to do] ► **agential** (eɪˈdʒɛnʃəl) *adj*

agent-general *n, pl* **agents-general.** a representative in London of a Canadian province or an Australian state.

agentive ('eɪdʒəntɪv) *or* **agential** (eɪ'dʒɛnʃəl) *Grammar.* ◆ *adj* **1** (in some inflected languages) denoting a case of nouns, etc., indicating the agent described by the verb. **2** (of a speech element) indicating agency: *"-er" in "worker" is an agentive suffix.* ◆ *n* **3a** the agentive case. **3b** a word or element in the agentive case.

agent of production *n* another name for **factor of production.**

Agent Orange *n* a highly poisonous herbicide used as a spray for defoliation and crop destruction, esp. by U.S. forces during the Vietnam War. [C20: named after the identifying colour stripe on its container]

agent provocateur *French.* (aʒɑ̃ prɔvɔkatœr) *n, pl* ***agents provocateurs*** (aʒɑ̃ prɔvɔkatœr). a secret agent employed to provoke suspected persons to commit illegal acts and so be discredited or liable to punishment.

age of consent *n* **1** the age at which a person, esp. a female, is considered legally competent to consent to marriage or sexual intercourse. **2** the age at which a person can enter into a legally binding contract.

Age of Reason *n* (usually preceded by *the*) the 18th century in W Europe. See also **Enlightenment.**

age-old *or* **age-long** *adj* very old or of long duration; ancient.

ageratum (ˌædʒə'reɪtəm) *n* any tropical American plant of the genus *Ageratum,* such as *A. houstonianum* and *A. conyzoides,* which have thick clusters of purplish-blue flowers. [C16: New Latin, via Latin from Greek *agēraton* that which does not age, from A-[1] + *gērat-,* stem of *gēras* old age; the flowers of the plant remain vivid for a long time]

ageusia (eɪ'gjuːsɪə) *n Pathol.* lack or impairment of the sense of taste. [C20: from A-[1] + Greek *geusis* taste]

Aggadah (agə'da) *n, pl* **Aggadoth** (-'dɔːt, -'dəʊt). *Judaism.* **1a** a homiletic passage of the Talmud. **1b** collectively, the homiletic part of traditional Jewish literature, as contrasted with Halacha, consisting of elaborations on the biblical narratives or tales from the lives of the ancient Rabbis. **2** any traditional homiletic interpretation of scripture. ◆ Also called: **Aggadatah** (ə'gadəta), **Haggadah.** [from Hebrew]

agger ('ædʒə) *n* an earthwork or mound forming a rampart, esp. in a Roman military camp. [C14: from Latin *agger* a heap, from *ad-* to + *gerere* to carry, bring]

aggiornamento *Italian.* (addʒorna'mɛnto) *n, pl* **-ti** (-ti). *R.C. Church.* the process of bringing up to date methods, ideas, etc.

agglomerate *vb* (ə'glɒməˌreɪt). **1** to form or be formed into a mass or cluster; collect. ◆ *n* (ə'glɒmərɪt, -ˌreɪt). **2** a confused mass. **3** a volcanic rock consisting of angular fragments within a groundmass of lava. Compare **conglomerate** (sense 2). ◆ *adj* (ə'glɒmərɪt, -ˌreɪt). **4** formed into a mass. [C17: from Latin *agglomerāre,* from *glomerāre* to wind into a ball, from *glomus* ball, mass] ▸ **agˌglomer'ation** *n* ▸ **ag'glomerative** *adj*

agglutinate *vb* (ə'gluːtɪˌneɪt). **1** to adhere or cause to adhere, as with glue. **2** *Linguistics.* to combine or be combined by agglutination. **3** *(tr)* to cause (bacteria, red blood cells, etc.) to clump together. ◆ *adj* (ə'gluːtɪnɪt, -ˌneɪt). **4** united or stuck, as by glue. [C16: from Latin *agglūtināre* to glue to, from *gluten* glue] ▸ **agˌglutina'bility** *n* ▸ **ag'glutinable** *adj* ▸ **ag'glutinant** *adj*

agglutination (əˌgluːtɪ'neɪʃən) *n* **1** the act or process of agglutinating. **2** the condition of being agglutinated; adhesion. **3** a united mass or group of parts. **4** *Chemistry.* the formation of clumps of particles in a suspension. **5** *Immunol.* the formation of a mass of particles, such as erythrocytes, by the action of antibodies. **6** *Linguistics.* the building up of words from component morphemes in such a way that these undergo little or no change of form or meaning in the process of combination.

agglutinative (ə'gluːtɪnətɪv) *adj* **1** tending to join or capable of joining. **2** Also: **agglomerative.** *Linguistics.* denoting languages, such as Hungarian, whose morphology is characterized by agglutination. Compare **analytic** (sense 3), **synthetic** (sense 3), **polysynthetic.**

agglutinin (ə'gluːtɪnɪn) *n* an antibody that causes agglutination. [C19: AGGLUTINATE + -IN]

agglutinogen (ˌæglu'tɪnədʒən) *n* an antigen that reacts with or stimulates the formation of a specific agglutinin. [C20: from AGGLUTINATE + -GEN]

aggrade (ə'greɪd) *vb (tr)* to build up the level of (any land surface) by the deposition of sediment. Compare **degrade** (sense 4). ▸ **aggradation** (ˌægrə'deɪʃən) *n*

aggrandize *or* **aggrandise** ('ægrənˌdaɪz, ə'grænˌdaɪz) *vb (tr)* **1** to increase the power, wealth, prestige, scope, etc., of. **2** to cause (something) to seem greater; magnify; exaggerate. [C17: from Old French *aggrandiss-,* long stem of *aggrandir* to make bigger, from Latin *grandis* GRAND; the ending *-ize* is due to the influence of verbs ending in *-ise, -ize*] ▸ **aggrandizement** *or* **aggrandisement** (ə'grændɪzmənt) *n* ▸ **'aggranˌdizer** *or* **'aggranˌdiser** *n*

aggravate ('ægrəˌveɪt) *vb (tr)* **1** to make (a disease, situation, problem, etc.) worse or more severe. **2** *Informal.* to annoy; exasperate, esp. by deliberate and persistent goading. [C16: from Latin *aggravāre* to make heavier, from *gravis* heavy] ▸ **'aggraˌvating** *adj* ▸ **ˌaggra'vation** *n*

aggregate *adj* ('ægrɪgɪt, -ˌgeɪt). **1** formed of separate units collected into a whole; collective; corporate. **2** (of fruits and flowers) composed of a dense cluster of carpels or florets. ◆ *n* ('ægrɪgɪt, -ˌgeɪt). **3** a sum or assemblage of many separate units; sum total. **4** *Geology.* a rock, such as granite, consisting of a mixture of minerals. **5** the sand and stone mixed with cement and water to make concrete. **6 in the aggregate.** taken as a whole. ◆ *vb* ('ægrɪˌgeɪt). **7** to combine or be combined into a body, etc. **8** *(tr)* to amount to (a number). [C16: from Latin *aggregāre* to add to a flock or herd, attach (oneself) to, from *grex* flock] ▸ **'aggregately** *adv* ▸ **aggregative** ('ægrɪˌgeɪtɪv) *adj*

aggregation (ˌægrɪ'geɪʃən) *n* **1** the act or process of aggregating. **2** *Ecology.* dispersion in which the individuals of a species are closer together than if they were randomly dispersed.

aggress (ə'grɛs) *vb (intr)* to attack first or begin a quarrel. [C16: from Medieval Latin *aggressāre* to attack, from Latin *aggredī* to attack, approach]

aggression (ə'grɛʃən) *n* **1** an attack or harmful action, esp. an unprovoked attack by one country against another. **2** any offensive activity, practice, etc.: *an aggression against personal liberty.* **3** *Psychol.* a hostile or destructive mental attitude or behaviour. [C17: from Latin *aggression-,* from *aggrēdi* to attack] ▸ **aggressor** (ə'grɛsə) *n*

aggressive (ə'grɛsɪv) *adj* **1** quarrelsome or belligerent: *an aggressive remark.* **2** assertive; vigorous: *an aggressive business executive.* ▸ **ag'gressively** *adv* ▸ **ag'gressiveness** *n*

aggrieve (ə'griːv) *vb (tr)* **1** *(often impersonal or passive)* to grieve; distress; afflict: *it aggrieved her much that she could not go.* **2** to injure unjustly, esp. by infringing a person's legal rights. [C14 *agreven,* via Old French from Latin *aggravāre* to AGGRAVATE] ▸ **ag'grieved** *adj* ▸ **aggrievedly** (ə'griːvɪdlɪ) *adv*

aggro ('ægrəʊ) *n Brit. slang.* aggressive behaviour, esp. by youths in a gang. [C20: from AGGRAVATION]

agha ('ɑːgə) *n* a variant spelling of **aga.**

aghast (ə'gɑːst) *adj (postpositive)* overcome with amazement or horror. [C13 *agast,* from Old English *gæstan* to frighten. The spelling with *gh* is on the model of GHASTLY]

agile ('ædʒaɪl) *adj* **1** quick in movement; nimble. **2** mentally quick or acute. [C15: from Latin *agilis,* from *agere* to do, act] ▸ **'agilely** *adv* ▸ **agility** (ə'dʒɪlɪtɪ) *n*

agin (ə'gɪn) *prep* an informal, facetious, or dialect word for **against.** [C19: from obsolete *again* AGAINST]

Agincourt ('ædʒɪnˌkɔːt; *French* aʒɛ̃kur) *n* a battle fought in 1415 near the village of Azincourt, N France: a decisive victory for English longbowmen under Henry V over French forces vastly superior in number.

agio ('ædʒɪəʊ) *n, pl* **-ios. 1a** the difference between the nominal and actual values of a currency. **1b** the charge payable for conversion of the less valuable currency. **2** a percentage payable for the exchange of one currency into another. **3** an allowance granted to compensate for differences in currency values, as on foreign bills of exchange. **4** an informal word for **agiotage.** [C17: from Italian, literally: ease]

agiotage ('ædʒətɪdʒ) *n* **1** the business of exchanging currencies. **2** speculative dealing in stock exchange securities or foreign exchange. [C19: French, from AGIO]

agist (ə'dʒɪst) *vb (tr) Law.* **1** to care for and feed (cattle or horses) for payment. **2** to assess and charge (land or its owner) with a public burden, such as a tax. [C14: from Old French *agister,* from *gister* to lodge, ultimately from Latin *jacēre* to lie down]

agitate ('ædʒɪˌteɪt) *vb* **1** *(tr)* to excite, disturb, or trouble (a person, the mind or feelings); worry. **2** *(tr)* to cause to move vigorously; shake, stir, or disturb. **3** *(intr;* often foll. by *for* or *against)* to attempt to stir up public opinion for or against something. **4** *(tr)* to discuss or debate in order to draw attention to or gain support for (a cause, etc.): *to agitate a political cause.* [C16: from Latin *agitātus,* from *agitāre* to move to and fro, set into motion, from *agere* to act, do] ▸ **'agiˌtated** *adj* ▸ **'agiˌtatedly** *adv* ▸ **ˌagi'tation** *n* ▸ **ˌagi'tational** *adj*

agitated depression *n* severe depression accompanied by extreme anxiety and agitation. Also called: **agitated melancholia.**

agitato (ˌædʒɪ'tɑːtəʊ) *adj, adv Music.* (to be performed) in an agitated manner.

agitator ('ædʒɪˌteɪtə) *n* **1** a person who agitates for or against a cause, etc. **2** a device, machine, or part used for mixing, shaking, or vibrating a material.

agitpop ('ædʒɪtˌpɒp) *n* the use of pop music to promote political propaganda.

agitprop ('ædʒɪtˌprɒp) *n* **1** *(often cap.)* (formerly) a bureau of the Central Committee of the Communist Party of the Soviet Union, in charge of agitation and propaganda on behalf of Communism. **2a** any promotion, as in the arts, of political propaganda, esp. of a Communist nature. **2b** *(as modifier)*: *agitprop theatre.* [C20: short for Russian *Agitpropbyuro,* from *agit(atsiya)* agitation + *prop(aganda)* propaganda]

Aglaia (ə'glaɪə) *n Greek myth.* one of the three Graces. [Greek: splendour, from *aglaos* splendid]

agleam (ə'gliːm) *adj (postpositive)* glowing; gleaming.

aglet ('æglɪt) *or* **aiglet** *n* **1** a metal sheath or tag at the end of a shoelace, ribbon, etc. **2** a variant spelling of **aiguillette. 3** any ornamental pendant. [C15: from Old French *aiguillette* a small needle]

agley (ə'gleɪ, ə'glaɪ, ə'gliː) *or* **aglee** (ə'gliː) *adv, adj Scot.* awry; askew. [from *gley* squint]

aglimmer (ə'glɪmə) *adj (postpositive)* glimmering.

aglitter (ə'glɪtə) *adj (postpositive)* sparkling; glittering.

aglossia (ə'glɒsɪə) *n Pathol.* congenital absence of the tongue. [C19: from A-[1] + GLOSSA + -IA] ▸ **a'glossal** *adj* ▸ **a'glossate** *adj*

aglow (ə'gləʊ) *adj (postpositive)* glowing.

aglu *or* **agloo** ('ægluː) *n Canadian.* a breathing hole made in ice by a seal. [C19: from Eskimo]

AGM *abbrev. for* annual general meeting.

agma ('ægmə) *n Phonetics.* the symbol (ŋ), used to represent a velar nasal consonant, as in *long* (lɒŋ) or *tank* (tæŋk).

agminate ('ægmɪnɪt, -ˌneɪt) *adj* gathered or clustered together. [C19: from Latin *agmen* a moving throng]

agnail ('ægˌneɪl) *n* another name for **hangnail.**

agnate ('ægneɪt) *adj* **1** related by descent from a common male ancestor. **2** related in any way; cognate. ◆ *n* **3** a male or female descendant by male links from a common male ancestor. [C16: from Latin *agnātus* born in addition, added by birth, from *agnāsci,* from *ad-* in addition + *gnāsci* to be born] ▸ **ag'natic** (æg'nætɪk) *adj* ▸ **ag'nation** *n*

agnathan (æg'neɪθən) *n* **1** any jawless eel-like aquatic vertebrate of the superclass *Agnatha,* which includes the lampreys and hagfishes. ◆ *adj* **2** of, relating to, or belonging to the superclass *Agnatha.* See also **cyclostome.** [C19: from New Latin *agnatha,* from A-[1] + Greek *gnathos* jaw]

agnathous (æg'neɪθəs) *adj Zoology.* (esp. of lampreys and hagfishes) lacking jaws.

Agnes ('ægnɪs) *n* **Saint.** ?292–?304 A.D., Christian child martyr under Diocletian. Feast day: Jan. 21.

Agnesi (*Italian* aːn'jezi) *n* **Maria Gaetana.** 1718–99, Italian mathematician and philosopher, noted for her work on differential calculus. See **witch of Agnesi.**

Agnew ('ægnjuː) *n* **Spiro** ('spɪərəʊ) **Theodore.** 1918–96, U.S. Republican politician; vice president (1969–73).

Agni ('ʌgnɪ) *n Hinduism.* the god of fire, one of the three chief deities of the Vedas. [Sanskrit: fire]

agnomen (æg'nəʊmɛn) *n, pl* **-nomina** (-'nɒmɪnə). **1** the fourth name or second cognomen occasionally acquired by an ancient Roman. See also **cognomen, nomen, praenomen. 2** another word for **nickname.** [C18: from Late Latin, from *ad-* in addition to + *nōmen* name] ▸ **agnominal** (æg'nɒmɪn^əl) *adj*

Agnon ('ægnɒn) *n* **Shmuel Yosef,** real name *Samuel Josef Czaczkes.* 1888–1970, Israeli novelist, born in Austria-Hungary. His works, which treat contemporary Jewish themes, include *The Day Before Yesterday* (1945). Nobel prize for literature 1966.

agnosia (æg'nəʊzɪə) *n Psychol.* loss or diminution of the power to recognize familiar objects or people, usually as a result of brain damage. [C20: New Latin, from Greek *agnōsia,* from *a-* without + *gnōsis* knowledge] ▸ **ag'nosic** *adj*

agnostic (æg'nɒstɪk) *n* **1** a person who holds that knowledge of a Supreme Being, ultimate cause, etc., is impossible. Compare **atheist, theist. 2** a person who claims, with respect to any particular question, that the answer cannot be known with certainty. ◆ *adj* **3** of or relating to agnostics. [C19: coined 1869 by T. H. Huxley from A-[1] + GNOSTIC] ▸ **ag'nosticism** *n*

Agnus Dei ('ægnʊs 'deɪɪ) *n Christianity.* **1** the figure of a lamb bearing a cross or banner, emblematic of Christ. **2** a chant beginning with these words or a translation of them, forming part of the Roman Catholic Mass or sung as an anthem in the Anglican liturgy. **3** a wax medallion stamped with a lamb as emblem of Christ and blessed by the pope. [Latin: Lamb of God]

ago (ə'gəʊ) *adv* in the past: *five years ago; long ago.* [C14 *ago,* from Old English *āgān* to pass away]

USAGE The use of *ago* with *since* (*it's ten years ago since he wrote the novel*) is redundant and should be avoided: *it is ten years since he wrote the novel.*

agog (ə'gɒg) *adj* (*postpositive*) highly impatient, eager, or curious. [C15: perhaps from Old French *en gogues* in merriments, origin unknown]

à gogo (ə 'gəʊ,gəʊ) *adj, adv Informal.* as much as one likes; galore: *champagne à gogo.* [C20: from French]

-agogue *or esp. U.S.* **-agog** *n combining form.* **1** indicating a person or thing that leads or incites to action: *pedagogue; demagogue.* **2** denoting a substance that stimulates the secretion of something: *galactagogue.* [via Late Latin from Greek *agōgos* leading, from *agein* to lead] ▸ **-agogic** *adj combining form.* ▸ **-agogy** *n combining form.*

agon ('ægəʊn, -gɒn) *n, pl* **agones** (ə'gəʊniːz). (in ancient Greece) a festival at which competitors contended for prizes. Among the best known were the Olympic, Pythian, Nemean, and Isthmian Games. [C17: Greek: contest, from *agein* to lead]

agone (ə'gɒn) *adv* an archaic word for **ago.**

agonic (ə'gɒnɪk, eɪ'gɒnɪk) *adj* forming no angle. [C19: from Greek *agōnos,* from A-[1] + *gōnia* angle]

agonic line *n* an imaginary line on the surface of the earth connecting points of zero magnetic declination.

agonist ('ægənɪst) *n* **1** any muscle that is opposed in action by another muscle. Compare **antagonist** (sense 2). **2** a competitor, as in an agon. [C17: from Greek *agōn* AGON]

agonistic (,ægə'nɪstɪk) *adj* **1** striving for effect; strained. **2** eager to win in discussion or argument; competitive. [C17: via Late Latin from Greek *agōnistikos,* from *agōn* contest]

agonize *or* **agonise** ('ægə,naɪz) *vb* **1** to suffer or cause to suffer agony. **2** (*intr*) to make a desperate effort; struggle; strive. [C16: via Medieval Latin from Greek *agōnizesthai* to contend for a prize, from *agōn* AGON] ▸ **'ago,nizingly** *or* **'ago,nisingly** *adv*

agony ('ægənɪ) *n, pl* **-nies. 1** acute physical or mental pain; anguish. **2** the suffering or struggle preceding death. **3 pile, put,** *or* **turn on the agony.** *Brit. informal.* to exaggerate one's distress for sympathy or greater effect. **4** (*modifier*) relating to or advising on personal problems about which people have written to the media: *agony column; agony writer.* [C14: via Late Latin from Greek *agōnia* struggle, from *agōn* contest]

agony aunt *n* (*sometimes cap.*) a person who writes the replies to readers' letters in an **agony column** (sense 1).

agony column *n* **1** a magazine or newspaper feature in which advice is offered to readers who have sent in letters about their personal problems. **2** a part of a newspaper containing advertisements for lost relatives, personal messages, etc.

agora[1] ('ægərə) *n, pl* **-rae** (-riː, -raɪ) *or* **-ras.** (*often cap.*) **a** the marketplace in Athens, used for popular meetings, or any similar place of assembly in ancient Greece. **b** the meeting itself. [from Greek, from *agorein* to gather]

agora[2] (,ægə'rɑː) *n, pl* **-rot** (-'rɒt). an Israeli monetary unit worth one hundredth of a shekel. [Hebrew, from *āgōr* to collect]

agoraphobia (,ægərə'fəʊbɪə) *n* a pathological fear of being in public places, often resulting in the sufferer becoming housebound. ▸ **,agora'phobic** *adj, n*

Agostini (*Italian* agos'tiːni) *n* **Giacomo** ('dʒaːkomo). born 1944, Italian racing motorcyclist: world champion (500 cc. class) 1966–72, 1975; (350 cc. class) 1968–74.

Agostino di Duccio (*Italian* ago'stiːno dɪ 'duttʃo) *n* 1415–81, Italian sculptor, noted for his carved marble panels in the interior of the Tempio Malatestiano at Rimini.

agouti (ə'guːtɪ) *n, pl* **-tis** *or* **-ties. 1** any hystricomorph rodent of the genus *Dasyprocta,* of Central and South America and the Caribbean: family *Dasyproctidae.* Agoutis are agile and long-legged, with hooflike claws, and are valued for their meat. **2** a pattern of fur in certain rodents, characterized by irregular stripes. [C18: via French and Spanish from Guarani]

AGR *abbrev. for* advanced gas-cooled reactor.

agr. *or* **agric.** *abbrev. for:* **1** agricultural. **2** agriculture. **3** agricultur(al)ist.

Agra ('ɑːgrə) *n* a city in N India, in W Uttar Pradesh on the Jumna River: a capital of the Mogul empire until 1658; famous for its Mogul architecture, esp. the Taj Mahal. Pop.: 899 195 (1991).

agraffe *or U.S.* (*sometimes*) **agrafe** (ə'græf) *n* **1** a fastening consisting of a loop and hook, formerly used in armour and clothing. **2** a metal cramp used to connect stones. [C18: from French, from *grafe* a hook]

Agram ('aːgram) *n* the German name for **Zagreb.**

agranulocytosis (ə,grænjʊləʊsaɪ'təʊsɪs) *n* a serious and sometimes fatal illness characterized by a marked reduction of leucocytes, usually caused by hypersensitivity to certain drugs. [C20: New Latin; see A-[1], GRANULE, -CYTE, -OSIS]

agrapha ('ægrəfə) *pl n Christianity.* sayings of Jesus not recorded in the canonical Gospels. [Greek: things not written, from A-[1] + *graphein* to write]

agraphia (ə'græfɪə) *n* loss of the ability to write, resulting from a brain lesion. [C19: New Latin, from A-[1] + Greek *graphein* to write]

agrarian (ə'grɛərɪən) *adj* **1** of or relating to land or its cultivation or to systems of dividing landed property. **2** of or relating to rural or agricultural matters. **3** (of plants) growing wild. ◆ *n* **4** a person who favours the redistribution of landed property. [C16: from Latin *agrārius,* from *ager* field, land] ▸ **a'grarianism** *n*

agree (ə'griː) *vb* **agrees, agreeing, agreed.** (*mainly intr*) **1** (often foll. by *with*) to be of the same opinion; concur. **2** (*also tr;* when *intr,* often foll. by *to;* when *tr, takes a clause as object or an infinitive*) to give assent; consent: *she agreed to go home; I'll agree to that.* **3** (*also tr;* when *intr,* foll. by *on* or *about;* when *tr, may take a clause as object*) to come to terms (about); arrive at a settlement (on): *they agreed a price; they agreed on the main points.* **4** (foll. by *with*) to be similar or consistent; harmonize; correspond. **5** (foll. by *with*) to be agreeable or suitable (to one's health, temperament, etc.). **6** (*tr; takes a clause as object*) to concede or grant; admit: *they agreed that the price they were asking was too high.* **7** (*tr*) to make consistent with: *to agree the balance sheet with the records by making adjustments, writing off, etc.* **8** *Grammar.* to undergo agreement. [C14: from Old French *agreer,* from the phrase *a gre* at will or pleasure]

agreeable (ə'grɪəb^əl) *adj* **1** pleasing; pleasant. **2** prepared to consent. **3** (foll. by *to* or *with*) in keeping; consistent: *salaries agreeable with current trends.* **4** (foll. by *to*) to one's liking: *the terms were not agreeable to him.* ▸ **a'greeableness** *n* ▸ **a'greeably** *adv*

agreed (ə'griːd) *adj* **1** determined by common consent: *the agreed price.* ◆ *interj* **2** an expression of agreement or consent.

agreement (ə'griːmənt) *n* **1** the act of agreeing. **2** a settlement, esp. one that is legally enforceable; covenant; treaty. **3** a contract or document containing such a settlement. **4** the state of being of the same opinion; concord; harmony. **5** the state of being similar or consistent; correspondence; conformity. **6** *Grammar.* the determination of the inflectional form of one word by some grammatical feature, such as number or gender, of another word, esp. one in the same sentence. Also called: **concord. 7** See **collective agreement, national agreement.** [C14: from Old French]

agrestal (ə'grɛstəl) *adj* (of uncultivated plants such as weeds) growing on cultivated land.

agrestic (ə'grɛstɪk) *adj* **1** rural; rustic. **2** unpolished; uncouth. [C17: from Latin *agrestis,* from *ager* field]

agribusiness ('ægrɪ,bɪznɪs) *n* the various businesses collectively that process, distribute, and support farm products. [C20: from AGRI(CULTURE) + BUSINESS]

agric. *or* **agr.** *abbrev. for:* **1** agricultural. **2** agriculture. **3** agricultur(al)ist.

Agricola (ə'grɪkələ) *n* **Gnaeus Julius** ('niːəs 'dʒuːlɪəs) 40–93 A.D., Roman general; governor of Britain who advanced Roman rule north to the Firth of Forth.

agriculture ('ægrɪ,kʌltʃə) *n* the science or occupation of cultivating land and rearing crops and livestock; farming; husbandry. Related adj: **geoponic.** [C17: from Latin *agricultūra,* from *ager* field, land + *cultūra* CULTURE] ▸ **,agri'cultural** *adj* ▸ **,agri'culturally** *adv* ▸ **,agri'culturist** *or* **,agri'culturalist** *n*

Agrigento (*Italian* agri'dʒɛnto) *n* a town in Italy, in SW Sicily: site of six Greek temples. Pop.: 56 372 (1990). Former name (until 1927): **Girgenti** (gɜː'gɛntɪ).

agrimony ('ægrɪmənɪ) *n* **1** any of various temperate rosaceous plants of the genus *Agrimonia,* which have compound leaves, long spikes of small yellow flowers, and bristly burlike fruits. **2** any of several other plants, such as hemp agrimony. [C15: altered from *egrimonie* (C14), via Old French from Latin *agrimōnia,* variant of *argemōnia* from Greek *argemōnē* poppy]

Agrippa (ə'grɪpə) *n* **Marcus Vipsanius** ('mɑːkəs vɪp'seɪnɪəs). 63–12 B.C., Roman general: chief adviser and later son-in-law of Augustus.

Agrippina (,ægrɪ'piːnə) *n* **1** called *the Elder.* c. 14 B.C.–33 A.D., Roman matron: granddaughter of Augustus, wife of Germanicus, mother of Caligula and Agrippina the Younger. **2** called *the Younger.* 15–59 A.D., mother of Nero, who put her to death after he became emperor.

agro- *combining form.* denoting fields, soil, or agriculture: *agronomy.* [from Greek *agros* field]

agrobiology (ˌæɡrəʊbaɪˈɒlədʒɪ) *n* the science of plant growth and nutrition in relation to agriculture. ► **agrobiological** (ˌæɡrəʊˌbaɪəˈlɒdʒɪkᵊl) *adj* ► ˌ**agrobiˈologist** *n*

agrochemical (ˌæɡrəʊˈkɛmɪkᵊl) *n* a chemical, such as a pesticide, used for agricultural purposes.

agroforestry (ˌæɡrəʊˈfɒrɪstrɪ) *n* a method of farming integrating herbaceous and tree crops.

agrology (əˈɡrɒlədʒɪ) *n* the scientific study of soils and their potential productivity. ► **agrological** (ˌæɡrəˈlɒdʒɪkᵊl) *adj*

agron. *abbrev. for* agronomy.

agronomics (ˌæɡrəˈnɒmɪks) *n* (*functioning as sing*) the branch of economics dealing with the distribution, management, and productivity of land. ► ˌ**agroˈnomic** *or* ˌ**agroˈnomical** *adj*

agronomy (əˈɡrɒnəmɪ) *n* the science of cultivation of land, soil management, and crop production. ► **aˈgronomist** *n*

agrostemma (ˌæɡrəʊˈstɛmə) *n* **1** See **corncockle. 2** See **silene.** [New Latin, from Greek *agros* a field + *stemma* a garland]

agrostology (ˌæɡrəˈstɒlədʒɪ) *n* the branch of botany concerned with the study of grasses. [C19: from Greek *agrōstis* a type of grass + -LOGY]

aground (əˈɡraʊnd) *adv, adj* (*postpositive*) on or onto the ground or bottom, as in shallow water.

agrypnotic (ˌæɡrɪpˈnɒtɪk) *adj* **1** inducing, relating to, or characterized by insomnia. ◆ *n* **2** a drug or agent that induces insomnia. [C20: from Greek *agrupnos* wakeful, from *agrein* to pursue + *hupnos* sleep]

agt *abbrev. for:* **1** agent. **2** agreement.

agterskot (ˈaxtəˌskɒt) *n S. African.* the final payment to a farmer for crops. Compare **voorskot.** [C20: Afrikaans *agter* after + *skot* shot, payment]

aguardiente *Spanish.* (aɣwarˈðjente) *n* any inferior brandy or similar spirit, esp. from Spain, Portugal, or South America. [C19: Spanish: burning water]

Aguascalientes (*Spanish* ˌaɣwaskaˈljentes) *n* **1** a state in central Mexico. Pop.: 862 335 (1995 est.). Area: 5471 sq. km (2112 sq. miles). **2** a city in central Mexico, capital of Aguascalientes state, about 1900 m (6200 ft.) above sea level, with hot springs. Pop.: 440 425 (1990).

ague (ˈeɪɡjuː) *n* **1** malarial fever with successive stages of fever and chills. **2** a fit of shivering. [C14: from Old French (*fievre*) *ague* acute fever; see ACUTE] ► **ˈaguish** *adj*

agueweed (ˈeɪɡjuːˌwiːd) *n* **1** a North American gentianaceous plant, *Gentiana quinquefolia,* that has clusters of pale blue-violet or white flowers. **2** another name for **boneset.**

Agulhas (əˈɡʌləs) *n* **Cape.** a headland in South Africa, the southernmost point of the African continent.

ah (ɑː) *interj* an exclamation expressing pleasure, pain, sympathy, etc., according to the intonation of the speaker.

AH (indicating years in the Muslim system of dating, numbered from the Hegira (622 A.D.)) *abbrev. for* anno Hegirae. [Latin]

a.h. *abbrev. for* ampere-hour.

aha (ɑːˈhɑː) *interj* an exclamation expressing triumph, surprise, etc., according to the intonation of the speaker.

Ahab (ˈeɪhæb) *n Old Testament.* the king of Israel from approximately 869 to 850 B.C. and husband of Jezebel: rebuked by Elijah (I Kings 16:29–22:40).

Ahasuerus (əˌhæzjuːˈɪərəs) *n Old Testament.* a king of ancient Persia and husband of Esther, generally identified with Xerxes.

ahead (əˈhɛd) *adj* **1** (*postpositive*) in front; in advance. ◆ *adv* **2** at or in the front; in advance; before. **3** onwards; forwards: *go straight ahead.* **4 ahead of. 4a** in front of; at a further advanced position than. **4b** *Stock Exchange.* in anticipation of: *the share price rose ahead of the annual figures.* **5** *Informal.* **be ahead.** to have an advantage; be winning: *to be ahead on points.* **6 get ahead.** to advance or attain success.

ahem (əˈhɛm) *interj* a clearing of the throat, used to attract attention, express doubt, etc.

ahemeral (æˈhɛmərᵊl, eɪ-) *adj* not constituting a full 24-hour day. [C20: from Greek *a-* not + *hēmera* a day]

Ahern (əˈhɜːn) *n* **Bertie.** born 1951, Irish politician; leader of the Fianna Fáil party from 1994; prime minister of the Republic of Ireland from 1997.

ahimsa (ɑːˈhɪmsɑː) *n* (in Hindu, Buddhist, and Jainist philosophy) the law of reverence for, and nonviolence to, every form of life. [Sanskrit, from A-[1] + *himsā* injury]

ahistorical (ˌeɪhɪsˈtɒrɪkəl) *or* **ahistoric** *adj* not related to history; not historical.

Ahithophel (əˈhɪθəˌfɛl) *or* **Achitophel** *n Old Testament.* a member of David's council, who became one of Absalom's advisers in his rebellion and hanged himself when his advice was overruled (II Samuel 15:12–17:23).

Ahmadiyyah (ˌaməˈdiːjə) *or* **Ahmadiyah** *n* **1** a messianic Islamic sect founded in Qadian, India, in 1889 by Mirza Ghulam Ahmad; it split into two branches in 1914. **2** any of various Sufi sects.

Ahmedabad *or* **Ahmadabad** (ˈɑːmədəˌbɑːd) *n* a city in W India, in Gujarat: famous for its mosque. Pop.: 2 872 865 (1991).

Ahmednagar *or* **Ahmadnagar** (ˌɑːmədˈnʌɡə) *n* a city in W India, in Maharashtra: formerly one of the kingdoms of Deccan. Pop.: 181 015 (1991).

A horizon *n* the top layer of a soil profile, usually dark coloured and containing humus, from which the soluble salts have been leached. See **B horizon, C horizon.**

ahoy (əˈhɔɪ) *interj Nautical.* a hail used to call a ship or to attract attention.

AHQ *abbrev. for* Army Headquarters.

Ahriman (ˈɑːrɪmən) *n Zoroastrianism.* the supreme evil spirit and diabolical opponent of Ormazd.

Ahura Mazda (əˈhʊərə ˈmæzdə) *n Zoroastrianism.* another name for **Ormazd.**

Ahvenanmaa (ˈɑhvenɑnmɑː) *n* the Finnish name for the **Åland Islands.**

Ahwaz (ɑːˈwɑːz) *or* **Ahvaz** (ɑːˈvɑːz) *n* a town in SW Iran, on the Karun River. Pop.: 828 380 (1994 est.).

ai (ˈɑːɪ) *n, pl* **ais.** another name for **three-toed sloth** (see **sloth** (sense 1)). [C17: from Portuguese, from Tupi]

AI *abbrev. for:* **1** artificial insemination. **2** artificial intelligence.

AIA *abbrev. for* Associate of the Institute of Actuaries.

AICC *abbrev. for* All India Congress Committee: the national assembly of the Indian National Congress.

aid (eɪd) *vb* **1** to give support to (someone to do something); help or assist. **2** (*tr*) to assist financially. ◆ *n* **3** assistance; help; support. **4** a person, device, etc., that helps or assists: *a teaching aid.* **5** Also: **artificial aid.** *Mountaineering.* any of various devices such as piton or nut when used as a direct help in the ascent. **6** (in medieval Europe; in England after 1066) a feudal payment made to the king or any lord by his vassals, usually on certain occasions such as the marriage of a daughter or the knighting of an eldest son. **7 in aid of.** *Brit. informal.* in support of; for the purpose of. [C15: via Old French *aidier* from Latin *adjūtāre* to help, from *juvāre* to help] ► **ˈaider** *n*

Aid *or* **-aid** *n combining form.* denoting a charitable organization or function that raises money for a cause: *Band Aid; Ferryaid.*

AID *abbrev. for:* **1** acute infectious disease. **2** Agency for International Development. **3** artificial insemination (by) donor: former name for Donor Insemination (DI).

Aidan (ˈeɪdᵊn) *n* **Saint.** died 651 A.D., Irish missionary in Northumbria, who founded the monastery at Lindisfarne (635). Feast day: Aug. 31.

aid climbing *n Mountaineering.* climbing that employs mechanical devices (aids) to accomplish difficult manoeuvres (artificial moves). Also called: **peg climbing, pegging, artificial climbing.**

aide (eɪd) *n* **1** an assistant. **2** *Social welfare.* an unqualified assistant to a professional welfare worker. **3** short for **aide-de-camp.**

aide-de-camp *or* **aid-de-camp** (ˈeɪd də ˈkɒŋ) *n, pl* **aides-de-camp** *or* **aids-de-camp.** a military officer serving as personal assistant to a senior. Abbrev.: **ADC.** [C17: from French: camp assistant]

aide-mémoire *French.* (ɛdmemwar; *English* ˈeɪd mɛmˈwɑː) *n, pl* ***aides-mémoire*** (ɛdmemwar; *English* ˈeɪdz mɛmˈwɑː). a memorandum or summary of the items of an agreement, etc. [from *aider* to help + *mémoire* memory]

Aidin (ˈaɪdɪn) *n* a variant spelling of **Aydin.**

AIDS *or* **Aids** (eɪdz) *n acronym for* acquired immune (or immuno-) deficiency syndrome: a condition, caused by a virus, in which certain white blood cells (lymphocytes) are destroyed, resulting in loss of the body's ability to protect itself against disease. AIDS is transmitted by sexual intercourse, through infected blood and blood products, and through the placenta.

AIDS-related complex *n* See **ARC.**

AIF *History. abbrev. for* Australian Imperial Force.

aiglet (ˈeɪɡlɪt) *n* a variant of **aglet.**

aigrette *or* **aigret** (ˈeɪɡrɛt, eɪˈɡrɛt) *n* **1** a long plume worn on hats or as a headdress, esp. one of long egret feathers. **2** an ornament or piece of jewellery in imitation of a plume of feathers. [C19: French]

aiguille (eɪˈɡwiːl, ˈeɪɡwiːl) *n* **1** a rock mass or mountain peak shaped like a needle. **2** an instrument for boring holes in rocks or masonry. [C19: French, literally: needle]

aiguillette (ˌeɪɡwɪˈlɛt) *n* **1** an ornamentation worn by certain military officers, consisting of cords with metal tips. **2** a variant of **aglet.**

AIH *abbrev. for* artificial insemination (by) husband.

Aiken (ˈeɪkən) *n* **1 Conrad (Potter).** 1889–1973, U.S. poet, short-story writer, and critic. His works include *Collected Poems* (1953) and the novel *Blue Voyage* (1927). **2 Howard Hathaway.** 1900–73, U.S. mathematician; pioneered the construction of electronic computers.

aikido (ˈaɪkɪdəʊ) *n* a Japanese system of self-defence employing similar principles to judo, but including blows from the hands and feet. [from Japanese, from *ai* to join, receive + *ki* spirit, force + *do* way]

aikona (ˈaɪkɔːnə) *interj S. African.* an informal word expressing strong negation. [from Nguni]

ail (eɪl) *vb* **1** (*tr*) to trouble; afflict. **2** (*intr*) to feel unwell. [Old English *eglan* to trouble, from *egle* troublesome, painful, related to Gothic *agls* shameful]

ailanthus (eɪˈlænθəs) *n, pl.* **-thuses.** an E Asian simaroubaceous deciduous tree, *Ailanthus altissima,* planted in Europe and North America, having pinnate leaves, small greenish flowers, and winged fruits. Also called: **tree of heaven.** [C19: New Latin, from native name (in Amboina) *ai lanto* tree (of) the gods]

aileron (ˈeɪlərɒn) *n* a flap hinged to the trailing edge of an aircraft wing to provide lateral control, as in a bank or roll. [C20: from French, diminutive of *aile* wing]

ailing (ˈeɪlɪŋ) *adj* unwell or unsuccessful.

ailment (ˈeɪlmənt) *n* a slight but often persistent illness.

ailurophile (aɪˈlʊərəˌfaɪl) *n* a person who likes cats. [C20: facetious coinage from Greek *ailuros* cat + -PHILE] ► **ailurophilia** (aɪˌlʊərəˈfɪlɪə) *n*

ailurophobe (aɪˈlʊərəˌfəʊb) *n* a person who dislikes or is afraid of cats. [C20: from Greek *ailuros* cat + -PHOBE]

aim (eɪm) *vb* **1** to point (a weapon, missile, etc.) or direct (a blow) at a particular person or object; level. **2** (*tr*) to direct (satire, criticism, etc.) at a person, object, etc. **3** (*intr;* foll. by *at* or an infinitive) to propose or intend: *we aim to leave early.* **4** (*intr;* often foll. by *at* or *for*) to direct one's efforts or strive (towards): *to aim at better communications; to aim high.* ◆ *n* **5** the action of directing something at an object. **6** the direction in which something is pointed; line of sighting (esp. in the phrase **to take aim**). **7** the object at which something is aimed; target. **8** intention; purpose. [C14: via Old French *aesmer* from Latin *aestimāre* to ESTIMATE]

AIM *abbrev. for* Alternative Investment Market.

aimless ('eɪmlɪs) *adj* having no goal, purpose, or direction. ► **'aimlessly** *adv* ► **'aimlessness** *n*
ain[1] (eɪn) *determiner* a Scot. word for **own.**
ain[2] ('ɑːjɪn) *n* a variant of **ayin.**
Ain (*French* ɛ̃) *n* **1** a department in E central France, in Rhône-Alpes region. Capital: Bourg. Pop.: 500 400 (1995). Area: 5785 sq. km (2256 sq. miles). **2** a river in E France, rising in the Jura Mountains and flowing south to the Rhône. Length: 190 km (118 miles).
ain't (eɪnt) *Not standard. contraction of* am not, is not, are not, have not, *or* has not: *I ain't seen it.*
Aintab (aɪn'tɑːb) *n* the former name (until 1921) of **Gaziantep.**
Aintree ('eɪntrɪ) *n* a suburb of Liverpool, in Merseyside: site of the racecourse over which the Grand National steeplechase has been run since 1839.
Ainu ('aɪnuː) *n* **1** (*pl* **-nus** *or* **-nu**) a member of the aboriginal people of Japan, now mostly intermixed with Mongoloid immigrants whose skin colour is more yellowish. **2** the language of this people, sometimes tentatively associated with Altaic, still spoken in parts of Hokkaido and elsewhere. [Ainu: man]
aïoli (aɪ'əʊlɪ, eɪ-) *n* garlic mayonnaise. [from French *ail* garlic]
air (ɛə) *n* **1** the mixture of gases that forms the earth's atmosphere. At sea level dry air has a density of 1.226 kilograms per cubic metre and consists of 78.08 per cent nitrogen, 20.95 per cent oxygen, 0.93 per cent argon, 0.03 per cent carbon dioxide, with smaller quantities of ozone and inert gases; water vapour varies between 0 and 4 per cent and in industrial areas sulphur gases may be present as pollutants. **2** the space above and around the earth; sky. Related adj: **aerial. 3** breeze; slight wind. **4** public expression; utterance: *to give air to one's complaints.* **5** a distinctive quality: *an air of mystery.* **6** a person's distinctive appearance, manner, or bearing. **7** *Music.* **7a** a simple tune for either vocal or instrumental performance. **7b** another word for **aria. 8** transportation in aircraft (esp. in the phrase **by air**). **9** an archaic word for **breath** (senses 1–3). **10 clear the air.** to rid a situation of tension or discord by settling misunderstandings, etc. **11 give (someone) the air.** *Slang.* to reject or dismiss (someone). **12 in the air. 12a** in circulation; current. **12b** in the process of being decided; unsettled. **13 into thin air.** leaving no trace behind. **14 on** (*or* **off**) **the air.** (not) in the act of broadcasting or (not) being broadcast on radio or television. **15 out of** *or* **from thin air.** suddenly and unexpectedly. **16 take the air.** to go out of doors, as for a short walk or ride. **17 up in the air. 17a** uncertain. **17b** *Informal.* agitated or excited. **18 walk on air.** to feel elated or exhilarated. **19** (*modifier*) *Astrology.* of or relating to a group of three signs of the zodiac, Gemini, Libra, and Aquarius. Compare **earth** (sense 10), **fire** (sense 24), **water** (sense 12). ♦ *vb* **20** to expose or be exposed to the air so as to cool or freshen; ventilate: *to air a room.* **21** to expose or be exposed to warm or heated air so as to dry: *to air linen.* **22** (*tr*) to make known publicly; display; publicize: *to air one's opinions.* **23** (*intr*) (of a television or radio programme) to be broadcast. ♦ See also **airs.** [C13: via Old French and Latin from Greek *aēr* the lower atmosphere]
Aïr ('ɑːɪə) *n* a mountainous region of N central Niger, in the Sahara, rising to 1500 m (5000 ft.): a former native kingdom. Area: about 77 700 sq. km (30 000 sq. miles). Also called: **Asben, Azbine.**
AIR *abbrev. for* All India Radio.
air alert *n Military.* **1** the condition in which combat aircraft are airborne and ready for an operation. **2** a signal to prepare for this.
air bag *n* a safety device in a car, consisting of a bag that inflates automatically in an accident and prevents the passengers from being thrown forwards.
air base *n* a centre from which military aircraft operate. Also called: **air station.**
air bed *n* an inflatable mattress.
air bladder *n* **1** *Ichthyol.* an air-filled sac, lying above the alimentary canal in bony fishes, that regulates buoyancy at different depths by a variation in the pressure of the air. Also called: **swim bladder. 2** any air-filled sac, such as one of the bladders of seaweeds.
airboat ('ɛəˌbəʊt) *n* another name for **swamp boat.**
airborne ('ɛəˌbɔːn) *adj* **1** conveyed by or through the air. **2** (of aircraft) flying; in the air.
air brake *n* **1** a brake operated by compressed air, esp. in heavy vehicles and trains. **2** Also called: **dive brake.** an articulated flap or small parachute for reducing the speed of an aircraft. **3** a rotary fan or propeller connected to a shaft to reduce its speed.
airbrick ('ɛəˌbrɪk) *n Chiefly Brit.* a brick with holes in it, put into the wall of a building for ventilation.
air bridge *n Brit.* a link by air transport between two places, esp. two places separated by a stretch of sea.
airbrush ('ɛəˌbrʌʃ) *n* **1** an atomizer for spraying paint or varnish by means of compressed air. ♦ *vb* (*tr*) **2** to paint or varnish (something) by using an airbrush. **3** to improve the image of (a person or thing) by concealing defects beneath a bland exterior: *an airbrushed version of the government's record.*
airburst ('ɛəˌbɜːst) *n* the explosion of a bomb, shell, etc., in the air.
Airbus ('ɛəˌbʌs) *n Trademark.* a commercial aircraft manufactured and marketed by an international consortium of aerospace companies.
air chief marshal *n* a senior officer of the Royal Air Force and certain other air forces, of equivalent rank to admiral in the Royal Navy. Abbrev.: **ACM.**
air cleaner *n* a filter that prevents dust and other particles from entering the air-intake of an internal-combustion engine. Also called: **air filter.**
air commodore *n* a senior officer of the Royal Air Force and certain other air forces, of equivalent rank to brigadier in the Army.
air-condition *vb* (*tr*) to apply air conditioning to.
air conditioning *n* a system or process for controlling the temperature and sometimes the humidity and purity of the air in a house, etc. ► **air conditioner** *n*
air-cool *vb* (*tr*) to cool (an engine) by a flow of air. Compare **water-cool.**
air corridor *n* an air route along which aircraft are allowed to fly.
air cover *n* **a** the use of aircraft to provide aerial protection for ground forces against enemy air attack. **b** the aircraft used in this. ♦ Also called: **air support.**
aircraft ('ɛəˌkrɑːft) *n, pl* **-craft.** any machine capable of flying by means of buoyancy or aerodynamic forces, such as a glider, helicopter, or aeroplane.
aircraft carrier *n* a warship built with an extensive flat deck space for the launch and recovery of aircraft.
aircraft cloth *or* **fabric** *n* variants of **aeroplane cloth.**
aircraftman ('ɛəˌkrɑːftmən) *n, pl* **-men.** a serviceman of the most junior rank in the RAF. Also (not in official use): **aircraftsman.** ► **'aircraftˌwoman** *or* (not in official use) **'aircraftsˌwoman** *fem n*
aircrew ('ɛəˌkruː) *n* (*sometimes functioning as pl*) the crew of an aircraft.
air curtain *n* an air stream across a doorway to exclude draughts, etc.
air cushion *n* **1** an inflatable cushion, usually made of rubber or plastic. **2** the pocket of air that supports a hovercraft. **3** a form of pneumatic suspension consisting of an enclosed volume of air. See also **air spring.**
air cylinder *n* a cylinder containing air, esp. one fitted with a piston and used for damping purposes.
air dam *n* any device, such as a spoiler, that reduces air resistance and increases the stability of a car, aircraft, etc.
Airdrie ('ɛədrɪ; *Scot.* 'erdrɪ) *n* a town in W central Scotland, in North Lanarkshire, E of Glasgow: manufacturing and pharmaceutical industries. Pop.: 36 998 (1991).
airdrome ('ɛəˌdrəʊm) *n* the U.S. name for **aerodrome.**
airdrop ('ɛəˌdrɒp) *n* **1** a delivery of supplies, troops, etc., from an aircraft by parachute. ♦ *vb* **-drops, -dropping, -dropped. 2** (*tr*) to deliver (supplies, etc.) by an airdrop.
air-dry *vb* **-dries, -drying, -dried.** (*tr*) to dry by exposure to the air.
Aire (ɛə) *n* a river in N England rising in the Pennines and flowing southeast to the Ouse. Length: 112 km (70 miles).
Airedale ('ɛəˌdeɪl) *n* a large rough-haired tan-coloured breed of terrier characterized by a black saddle-shaped patch covering most of the back. Also called: **Airedale terrier.** [C19: name of a district in Yorkshire]
air embolism *n* another name for **aeroembolism.**
air engine *n* **1** an engine that uses the expansion of heated air to drive a piston. **2** a small engine that uses compressed air to drive a piston.
air-entrained concrete *n* a type of concrete throughout which small air bubbles are dispersed in order to increase its frost resistance: used for making roads.
airfield ('ɛəˌfiːld) *n* a landing and taking-off area for aircraft, usually with permanent buildings.
air filter *n* another name for **air cleaner.**
airflow ('ɛəˌfləʊ) *n* the flow of air in a wind tunnel or past a moving aircraft, car, train, etc.; airstream.
airfoil ('ɛəˌfɔɪl) *n* the U.S. and Canadian name for **aerofoil.**
air force *n* **1a** the branch of a nation's armed services primarily responsible for air warfare. **1b** (*as modifier*): *an air-force base.* **2** a formation in the U.S. and certain other air forces larger than an air division but smaller than an air command.
airframe ('ɛəˌfreɪm) *n* the body of an aircraft, excluding its engines.
air freight *n* **1** freight transported by aircraft. ♦ *vb* **air-freight. 2** (*tr*) to send (goods) to their destination by aircraft.
air frost *n* air whose temperature is at or below 0°C.
air gas *n* another name for **producer gas.**
airglow ('ɛəˌgləʊ) *n* the faint light from the upper atmosphere in the night sky, esp. in low latitudes.
air guitar *n* an imaginary guitar played while miming to rock music.
air gun *n* a gun discharged by means of compressed air.
air hardening *n* a process of hardening high-alloy steels by heating and cooling in a current of air. Compare **oil hardening.**
airhead[1] ('ɛəˌhɛd) *n Military.* an area secured in hostile territory, used as a base for the supply and evacuation of troops and equipment by air. [C20: modelled on BEACHHEAD]
airhead[2] ('ɛəˌhɛd) *n Slang.* a stupid or simple-minded person; idiot. [C20: from AIR + HEAD]
air hole *n* **1** a hole that allows the passage of air, esp. for ventilation. **2** a section of open water in a frozen surface. **3** a less common name for **air pocket** (sense 1).
air hostess *n* a stewardess on an airliner.
airily ('ɛərɪlɪ) *adv* **1** in a jaunty or high-spirited manner. **2** in a light or delicate manner.
airiness ('ɛərɪnɪs) *n* **1** the quality or condition of being fresh, light, or breezy. **2** lightness of heart; gaiety.
airing ('ɛərɪŋ) *n* **1a** exposure to air or warmth, as for drying or ventilation. **1b** (*as modifier*): *airing cupboard.* **2** an excursion in the open air. **3** exposure to public debate.
air-intake *n* **1a** an opening in an aircraft through which air is drawn, esp. for the engines. **1b** the amount of air drawn in. **2** the part of a carburettor or similar device through which air enters an internal-combustion engine. **3** any opening, etc., through which air enters.
air jacket *n* **1** an air-filled envelope or compartment surrounding a machine or part to reduce the rate at which heat is transferred to or from it. Compare **water jacket. 2** a less common name for **life jacket.**
airless ('ɛəlɪs) *adj* **1** lacking fresh air; stuffy or sultry. **2** devoid of air. ► **'airlessness** *n*
air letter *n* another name for **aerogram** (sense 1).
airlift ('ɛəˌlɪft) *n* **1** the transportation by air of passengers, troops, cargo, etc., esp. when other routes are blocked. ♦ *vb* **2** (*tr*) to transport by an airlift.

air-lift pump *n* a pump that pumps liquid by injecting air into the lower end of an open pipe immersed in the liquid: often used in boreholes.
airline ('ɛə,laɪn) *n* **1a** a system or organization that provides scheduled flights for passengers or cargo. **1b** (*as modifier*): *an airline pilot.* **2** a hose or tube carrying air under pressure. **3** *Chiefly U.S.* a beeline.
airliner ('ɛə,laɪnə) *n* a large passenger aircraft.
airlock ('ɛə,lɒk) *n* **1** a bubble in a pipe causing an obstruction or stoppage to the flow. **2** an airtight chamber with regulated air pressure used to gain access to a space that has air under pressure.
airmail ('ɛə,meɪl) *n* **1** the system of conveying mail by aircraft. **2** mail conveyed by aircraft. ◆ *adj* **3** of, used for, or concerned with airmail. ◆ *vb* **4** (*tr*) to send by airmail.
airman ('ɛəmən) *n, pl* **-men.** an aviator, esp. a man who serves in his country's air force. ▸ **'air,woman** *fem n*
air marshal *n* **1** a senior Royal Air Force officer of equivalent rank to a vice admiral in the Royal Navy. **2** a Royal Australian Air Force officer of the highest rank. **3** a Royal New Zealand Air Force officer of the highest rank when chief of defence forces.
air mass *n* a large body of air having characteristics of temperature, moisture, and pressure that are approximately uniform horizontally.
air mile *n* another name for **nautical mile** (sense 1).
Air Miles *pl n* points awarded by certain companies to purchasers of flight tickets and some other products that may be used to pay for other flights.
air-minded *adj* interested in or promoting aviation or aircraft. ▸ **'air-,mindedness** *n*
air miss *n* a situation in which two aircraft pass very close to one another in the air; near miss.
Air Officer *n* a term used to denote the appointment of any officer in the Royal Air Force above the rank of Air Commodore to a position of command.
airplane ('ɛə,pleɪn) *n* the U.S. and Canadian name for **aeroplane.**
air plant *n* a name given to some epiphytes grown as greenhouse or house plants, esp. orchids of the large Old World tropical genus *Aerides,* grown for their white scented flowers spotted with red, purple, or rose.
airplay ('ɛə,pleɪ) *n* (of recorded music) radio exposure.
air pocket *n* **1** a localized region of low air density or a descending air current, causing an aircraft to suffer an abrupt decrease in height. **2** any pocket of air that prevents the flow of a liquid or gas, as in a pipe.
airport ('ɛə,pɔːt) *n* a landing and taking-off area for civil aircraft, usually with surfaced runways and aircraft maintenance and passenger facilities.
air power *n* the strength of a nation's air force.
air pump *n* a device for pumping air in or out of something.
air raid *n* **a** an attack by hostile aircraft. **b** (*as modifier*): *an air-raid shelter.*
air-raid warden *n* a member of a civil defence organization responsible for enforcing regulations, etc., during an air attack.
air rifle *n* a rifle discharged by compressed air.
airs (ɛəz) *pl n* affected manners intended to impress others (esp. in the phrases **give oneself airs, put on airs**).
air sac *n* **1** any of the membranous air-filled extensions of the lungs of birds, which increase the efficiency of gaseous exchange in the lungs. **2** any of the thin-walled extensions of the tracheae of insects having a similar function.
air scoop *n* a device fitted to the surface of an aircraft to provide air pressure or ventilation from the airflow.
Air Scout *n* a scout belonging to a scout troop that specializes in flying, gliding, etc. See **Scout.**
airscrew ('ɛə,skruː) *n Brit.* an aircraft propeller.
air-sea rescue *n* an air rescue at sea.
air shaft *n* a shaft for ventilation, esp. in a mine or tunnel.
airship ('ɛə,ʃɪp) *n* a lighter-than-air self-propelled craft. Also called: **dirigible.**
air shot *n Golf.* a shot that misses the ball completely but counts as a stroke.
airshow ('ɛə,ʃəʊ) *n* an occasion when an air base is open to the public and a flying display and, usually, static exhibitions are held.
airsick ('ɛə,sɪk) *adj* sick or nauseated from travelling in an aircraft. ▸ **'air,sickness** *n*
airside ('ɛə,saɪd) *n* the part of an airport nearest the aircraft, the boundary of which is the security check, customs, passport control, etc. Compare **landside** (sense 1).
air sock *n* another name for **windsock.**
airspace ('ɛə,speɪs) *n* the atmosphere above the earth or part of the earth, esp. the atmosphere above a country deemed to be under its jurisdiction.
airspeed ('ɛə,spiːd) *n* the speed of an aircraft relative to the air in which it moves. Compare **groundspeed.**
air spray *n* another name for **aerosol** (sense 3).
air spring *n Mechanical engineering.* an enclosed pocket of air used to absorb shock or sudden fluctuations of load.
air station *n* an airfield, usually smaller than an airport but having facilities for the maintenance of aircraft.
airstream ('ɛə,striːm) *n* **1** a wind, esp. at a high altitude. **2** a current of moving air.
airstrip ('ɛə,strɪp) *n* a cleared area for the landing and taking off of aircraft; runway. Also called: **landing strip.**
airt (ɛət; *Scot.* ert) *or* **airth** (ɛəθ; *Scot.* erθ) *n Scot.* a direction or point of the compass, esp. the direction of the wind; quarter; region. **[C14:** from Scots Gaelic *aird* point of the compass, height**]**
air terminal *n Brit.* a building in a city from which air passengers are taken by road or rail to an airport.
airtight ('ɛə,taɪt) *adj* **1** not permitting the passage of air either in or out. **2** having no weak points; rigid or unassailable: *this categorization is hardly airtight.*
airtime ('ɛə,taɪm) *n* **1** the time allocated to a particular programme, item, topic, or type of material on radio or television. **2** the time of the start of a radio or television broadcast.
air-to-air *adj* operating between aircraft in flight.
air traffic *n* **1** the organized movement of aircraft within a given space. **2** the passengers, cargo, or mail carried by aircraft.
air-traffic control *n* an organization that determines the altitude, speed, and direction at which planes fly in a given area, giving instructions to pilots by radio. ▸ **air-traffic controller** *n*
air turbine *n* a small turbine driven by compressed air, esp. one used as a starter for engines.
air valve *n* **1** a device for controlling the flow of air in a pipe. **2** a valve for exhausting air from a fluid system, esp. from a central-heating installation. See also **bleed valve.**
air vesicle *or* **cavity** *n* **1** a large air-filled intercellular space in some aquatic plants. **2** a large intercellular space in a leaf into which a stoma opens.
air vice-marshal *n* **1** a senior Royal Air Force officer of equivalent rank to a rear admiral in the Royal Navy. **2** a Royal Australian Air Force officer of the second highest rank. **3** a Royal New Zealand Air Force officer of the highest rank. Abbrev.: **AVM.**
airwaves ('ɛə,weɪvz) *pl n Informal.* radio waves used in radio and television broadcasting.
airway ('ɛə,weɪ) *n* **1** an air route, esp. one that is fully equipped with emergency landing fields, navigational aids, etc. **2** a passage for ventilation, esp. in a mine. **3** the passage of air from the nose or mouth to the lungs. **4** *Med.* a tubelike device inserted via the throat to keep open the airway of an unconscious patient.
air waybill *n* a document made out by the consignor of goods by air freight giving details of the goods and the name of the consignee.
airworthy ('ɛə,wɜːðɪ) *adj* (of an aircraft) safe to fly.
airy ('ɛərɪ) *adj* **airier, airiest. 1** abounding in fresh air. **2** spacious or uncluttered. **3** nonchalant; superficial. **4** visionary; fanciful: *airy promises; airy plans.* **5** of or relating to air. **6** weightless and insubstantial: *an airy gossamer.* **7** light and graceful in movement. **8** having no material substance: *airy spirits.* **9** high up in the air; lofty. **10** performed in the air; aerial.
Airy ('ɛərɪ) *n* Sir **George Biddell.** 1801–92, British astronomer, noted for his estimate of the earth's density from gravity measurements in mines; astronomer royal (1835–81).
airy-fairy ('ɛərɪ'fɛərɪ) *adj* **1** *Informal.* fanciful and unrealistic: *an airy-fairy scheme.* **2** delicate to the point of being insubstantial; light. **[C19:** from Tennyson's poem *Lillian* (1830), where the central figure is described as "Airy, fairy Lillian"**]**
Aisha *or* **Ayesha** ('ɑːiː,ʃɑː) *n* ?613–678 A.D., the favourite wife of Mohammed; daughter of Abu Bekr.
aisle (aɪl) *n* **1** a passageway separating seating areas in a theatre, church, etc.; gangway. **2** a lateral division in a church flanking the nave or chancel. **3** (**rolling**) **in the aisles.** *Informal.* (of an audience) overcome with laughter. **[C14** *ele* (later *aile, aisle,* through confusion with *isle* (island)), via Old French from Latin *āla* wing**]** ▸ **aisled** *adj* ▸ **'aisleless** *adj*
Aisne (eɪn; *French* ɛn) *n* **1** a department of NE France, in Picardy region. Capital: Laon. Pop.: 539 500 (1995). Area: 7428 sq. km (2897 sq. miles). **2** a river in N France, rising in the Argonne Forest and flowing northwest and west to the River Oise: scene of a major Allied offensive in 1918 which turned the tide finally against Germany in World War I. Length: 282 km (175 miles).
ait (eɪt) *or* **eyot** *n Dialect.* an islet, esp. in a river. **[**Old English *ȳgett* small island, from *ieg* ISLAND**]**
aitch (eɪtʃ) *n* the letter *h* or the sound represented by it: *he drops his aitches.* **[C16:** a phonetic spelling**]**
aitchbone ('eɪtʃ,bəʊn) *n* **1** the rump bone or floor of the pelvis in cattle. **2** a cut of beef from or including the rump bone. **[C15** hach-boon, altered from earlier *nache-bone, nage-bone* (*a nache* mistaken for *an ache, an aitch;* compare ADDER[1]); *nache* buttock, via Old French from Late Latin *natica,* from Latin *natis* buttock**]**
Aitken ('eɪtkɪn) *n* **1 Robert Grant.** 1864–1951, U.S. astronomer who discovered over three thousand double stars. **2 William Maxwell.** See **Beaverbrook.**
Aix-en-Provence (*French* ɛksɑ̃prɔvɑ̃s) *n* a city and spa in SE France: the medieval capital of Provence. Pop.: 126 854 (1990). Also called: **Aix.**
Aix-la-Chapelle (*French* ɛkslaʃapɛl) *n* the French name for **Aachen.**
Aix-les-Bains (*French* ɛkslebɛ̃) *n* a town in E France: a resort with sulphurous springs. Pop.: 24 830 (1990).
Aíyina ('ejina) *n* transliteration of the Modern Greek name for **Aegina.**
AJA *abbrev. for* Australian Journalists' Association.
Ajaccio (ə'dʒætsɪ,əʊ, -'dʒeɪ-) *n* the capital of Corsica, a port on the W coast. Pop.: 55 279 (1990 est.).
ajar[1] (ə'dʒɑː) *adj* (*postpositive*), *adv* (esp. of a door or window) slightly open. **[C18:** altered form of obsolete *on char,* literally: on the turn; *char,* from Old English *cierran* to turn**]**
ajar[2] (ə'dʒɑː) *adj* (*postpositive*) not in harmony. **[C19:** altered form of *at jar* at discord. See JAR[2]**]**
Ajax ('eɪdʒæks) *n Greek myth.* **1** the son of Telamon; a Greek hero of the Trojan War who killed himself in vexation when Achilles' armour was given to Odysseus. **2** called *Ajax the Lesser,* a Locrian king, a swift-footed Greek hero of the Trojan War.
AJC *abbrev. for* Australian Jockey Club.
Ajmer (ʌdʒ'mɪə) *n* a city in NW India, in Rajasthan: textile centre. Pop.: 402 700 (1991).
AK *abbrev. for* Alaska.
AK-47 *n* a type of Kalashnikov.
a.k.a. *or* **AKA** *abbrev. for* also known as.
Akademi (ə'kɑːdəmɪ) *n* (in India) a learned society.

Akan ('ɑːkɑːn) *n* **1** (*pl* **-kan** *or* **-kans**) a member of a people of Ghana and the E Ivory Coast. **2** the language of this people, having two chief dialects, Fanti and Twi, and belonging to the Kwa branch of the Niger-Congo family.
akaryote (eɪ'kærɪəʊt) *n Biology.* a cell without a nucleus. [from A-[1] + KARYO- + *-ote* as in *zygote*] ▸ **a,kary'otic** *adj*
Akbar ('ækbɑː) *n* called *Akbar the Great.* 1542–1605, Mogul emperor of India (1556–1605), who extended the Mogul empire to include N India.
Akela (ɑː'keɪlə) *n Brit.* the adult leader of a pack of Cub Scouts. U.S. equivalent: **Den Mother.** [C20: after a character in Kipling's *The Jungle Book* (1894–95), who is the leader of a wolfpack]
akene (ə'kiːn) *n* a variant spelling of **achene.**
Akhaïa (a'xaːja) *n* transliteration of the modern Greek name for **Achaea.**
akhara (ə'kɑːrɑː) *n* (in India) a gymnasium.
Akhenaten *or* **Akhenaton** (,ækə'nɑːtᵊn) *n* original name *Amenhotep IV.* died ?1358 B.C., king of Egypt, of the 18th dynasty; he moved his capital from Thebes to Tell El Amarna and introduced the cult of Aten.
Akhmatova (*Russian* ax'matəvə) *n* **Anna** ('annə). pseudonym of *Anna Gorenko.* 1889–1966, Russian poet: noted for her concise and intensely personal lyrics.
Akihito (,ækɪ'hiːtəʊ) *n* born 1933, Emperor of Japan from 1989.
akimbo (ə'kɪmbəʊ) *adj, adv* (**with**) **arms akimbo.** with hands on hips and elbows projecting outwards. [C15 *in kenebowe,* literally: in keen bow, that is, in a sharp curve]
akin (ə'kɪn) *adj* (*postpositive*) **1** related by blood; of the same kin. **2** (often foll. by *to*) having similar characteristics, properties, etc.
Akkad *or* **Accad** ('ækæd) *n* **1** a city on the Euphrates in N Babylonia, the centre of a major empire and civilization (2360–2180 B.C.). Ancient name: **Agade** (ə'gɑːdɪ, ə'geɪdɪ). **2** an ancient region lying north of Babylon, from which the Akkadian language and culture is named.
Akkadian *or* **Accadian** (ə'kædɪən, ə'keɪ-) *n* **1** a member of an ancient Semitic people who lived in central Mesopotamia in the third millennium B.C. **2** the extinct language of this people, belonging to the E Semitic subfamily of the Afro-Asiatic family. ♦ *adj* **3** of or relating to this people or their language.
Akkerman (*Russian* akɪr'man) *n* the former name (until 1946) of **Byelgorod-Dnestrovski.**
Akmola *or* **Aqmola** (æk'məʊlə; *Kazakh* ɑkmɒ'lɑ) *n* the former name (1994–98) of **Astana.**
Akmolinsk (*Russian* ak'mɔlinsk) *n* the former name (until 1961) of **Akmola.**
akrasia (ə'kreɪzɪə) *n Philosophy.* weakness of will; acting in a way contrary to one's sincerely held moral values. [C20: from A-[2] + Greek *kratos* power] ▸ **a'kratic** *adj*
Akron ('ækrən) *n* a city in NE Ohio. Pop.: 216 882 (1996 est.).
Aksum *or* **Axum** ('ɑːksʊm) *n* an ancient town in N Ethiopia, in the Tigré region: capital of the Aksumite Empire (1st to 6th centuries A.D.). According to tradition, the Ark of the Covenant was brought here from Jerusalem.
Aktyubinsk (*Russian* ak'tjubinsk) *n* the former name (until 1991) of **Aqtöbe.**
Akubra (ə'kuːbrə) *n Trademark.* a brand of Australian hat.
Akure (ə'kuːre) *n* a city in SW Nigeria, capital of Ondo state: agricultural trade centre. Pop.: 162 300 (1996 est.).
akvavit ('ɑːkvɑː,viːt) *n* a variant spelling of **aquavit.**
Al *the chemical symbol for* aluminium.
AL *abbrev. for:* **1** Alabama. **2** Anglo-Latin. ♦ **3** *international car registration for* Albania.
al. *abbrev. for:* **1** alcohol. **2** alcoholic.
-al[1] *suffix forming adjectives.* of; related to; connected with: *functional; sectional; tonal.* [from Latin *-ālis*]
-al[2] *suffix forming nouns.* the act or process of doing what is indicated by the verb stem: *rebuttal; recital; renewal.* [via Old French *-aille, -ail,* from Latin *-ālia,* neuter plural used as substantive, from *-ālis* -AL[1]]
-al[3] *suffix forming nouns.* **1** indicating an aldehyde: *ethanal.* **2** indicating a pharmaceutical product: *phenobarbital.* [shortened from ALDEHYDE]
ala ('eɪlə) *n, pl* **alae** ('eɪliː). **1** *Zoology.* a wing or flat winglike process or structure, such as a part of some bones and cartilages. **2** *Botany.* a winglike part, such as one of the wings of a sycamore seed or one of the flat petals of a sweet pea flower. [C18: from Latin *āla* a wing]
à la (ɑː lɑː, æ lə; *French* a la) *prep* **1** in the manner or style of. **2** as prepared in (a particular place) or by or for (a particular person). [C17: from French, short for *à la mode de* in the style of]
Ala. *abbrev. for* Alabama.
Alabama (,ælə'bæmə) *n* **1** a state of the southeastern U.S., on the Gulf of Mexico: consists of coastal and W lowlands crossed by the Tombigbee, Black Warrior, and Alabama Rivers, with parts of the Tennessee Valley and Cumberland Plateau in the north; noted for producing cotton and white marble. Capital: Montgomery. Pop.: 4 319 154 (1997 est.). Area: 131 333 sq. km (50 708 sq. miles). Abbrevs.: **Ala.** or (with zip code) **AL** **2** a river in Alabama, flowing southwest to the Mobile and Tensaw Rivers. Length: 507 km (315 miles). ▸ **,Ala'bamian** *adj*
alabaster ('ælə,bɑːstə, -,bæstə) *n* **1** a fine-grained usually white, opaque, or translucent variety of gypsum used for statues, vases, etc. **2** a variety of hard semitranslucent calcite, often banded like marble. ♦ *adj* **3** of or resembling alabaster. [C14: from Old French *alabastre,* from Latin *alabaster,* from Greek *alabastros*] ▸ **,ala'bastrine** *adj*
à la carte (ɑː lɑː 'kɑːt, æ lə; *French* a la kart) *adj, adv* **1** (of a menu or a section of a menu) having dishes listed separately and individually priced. Compare **table d'hôte.** **2** (of a dish) offered on such a menu; not part of a set meal. [C19: from French, literally: according to the card]
alack (ə'læk) *or* **alackaday** (ə'lækə,deɪ) *interj* an archaic or poetic word for **alas.** [C15: from *a* ah! + *lack* loss, LACK]
alacrity (ə'lækrɪtɪ) *n* liveliness or briskness. [C15: from Latin *alacritās,* from *alacer* lively] ▸ **a'lacritous** *adj*
Ala Dağ *or* **Ala Dagh** (*Turkish* ɑ'lɑ dɑː) *n* **1** the E part of the Taurus Mountains, in SE Turkey, rising over 3600 m (12 000 ft.). **2** a mountain range in E Turkey, rising over 3300 m (11 000 ft.). **3** a mountain range in NE Turkey, rising over 3000 m (10 000 ft.).
Aladdin (ə'lædɪn) *n* (in *The Arabian Nights' Entertainments*) a poor youth who obtains a magic lamp and ring, with which he summons genies who grant his wishes.
Aladdin's cave *n* **1** a place containing fabulous riches. **2** a place where something is abundant: *an Aladdin's cave of presents for children.*
Alagez *or* **Alagöz** (ɑlɑ'gœz) *n* the Turkish name for (Mount) **Aragats.**
Alagoas (*Portuguese* ala'goːaʃ) *n* a state in NE Brazil, on the Atlantic coast. Capital: Maceió. Pop.: 2 685 400 (1995 est.). Area: 30 776 sq. km (11 031 sq. miles).
Alai (ɑː'laɪ) *n* a mountain range in central Asia, in SW Kyrgyzstan, running from the Tian Shan range in China into Tajikistan. Average height: 4800 m (16 000 ft.), rising over 5850 m (19 500 ft.).
Alain-Fournier (*French* alɛ̃furnje) *n* real name *Henri-Alban Fournier.* 1886–1914, French novelist; author of *Le Grand Meaulnes* (1913; translated as *The Lost Domain,* 1959).
à la king (ɑː lɑː 'kɪŋ, æ lə) *adj* (*usually postpositive*) cooked in a cream sauce with mushrooms and green peppers.
alalia (æ'leɪlɪə) *n* a complete inability to speak; mutism. [A-[1] + -LALIA]
alameda (,ælə'meɪdə) *n Chiefly southwestern U.S.* a public walk or promenade lined with trees, often poplars.
Alamein ('ælə,meɪn) *n* see **El Alamein.**
Alamo ('ælə,məʊ) *n* **the.** a mission in San Antonio, Texas, the site of a siege and massacre in 1836 by Mexican forces under Santa Anna of a handful of American rebels fighting for Texan independence from Mexico.
à la mode (ɑː lɑː 'məʊd, æ lə; *French* a la mɔd) *adj* **1** fashionable in style, design, etc. **2** (of meats) braised with vegetables in wine. **3** *Chiefly U.S. and Canadian.* (of desserts) served with ice cream. [C17: from French: according to the fashion]
alamode ('ælə,məʊd) *n* a soft light silk used for shawls and dresses, esp. in the 19th century. See also **surah.** [C17: from À LA MODE]
Alanbrooke ('ælən,brʊk) *n* **Alan Francis Brooke,** 1st Viscount. 1883–1963, British field marshal; chief of Imperial General Staff (1941–46).
Åland Islands ('ɑːlənd, 'ɔːlənd; *Swedish* 'oːland) *pl n* a group of over 6000 islands under Finnish administration, in the Gulf of Bothnia. Capital: Mariehamn. Pop.: 24 847 (1992). Finnish name: **Ahvenanmaa.**
Alania (ə'lænɪə) *n* another name for **North Ossetian Republic.**
alanine ('ælə,niːn, -,naɪn) *n* a nonessential aliphatic amino acid that occurs in many proteins. [C19: from German *Alanin,* from AL(DEHYDE) + *-an-* (euphonic infix) + *-in* -INE[2]]
alannah (ə'lænə) *interj Irish.* my child: used as a term of address or endearment. [from Irish Gaelic *a leanbh*]
Al-Anon ('ælə,nɒn) *n* an association for the families and friends of alcoholics to give mutual support.
Alaouite *or* **Alawite** ('ælə,wiːt) *n* **1** a member of a Shiite sect of Syrian Muslims. ♦ *adj* **2** of or relating to this sect. [via French from Arabic, from *'alaoui* upper, celestial, from *'ala* (vb) to excel, surpass]
alap (ə'lɑːp) *n* Indian vocal music without words.
al-Aqsa (æl 'æksə) *n* See **Dome of the Rock.**
alar ('eɪlə) *adj* relating to, resembling, or having wings or alae. [C19: from Latin *āla* a wing]
Alar ('eɪlɑː) *n* a chemical sprayed on cultivated apple trees in certain countries, to increase fruit set. Also called: **daminozide.**
Alarcón (*Spanish* alar'kon) *n* **Pedro Antonio de** ('peðro an'tonjo de). 1833–91, Spanish novelist and short-story writer, noted for his humorous sketches of rural life, esp. in *The Three-Cornered Hat* (1874).
Alaric ('ælərɪk) *n* ?370–410 A.D., king of the Visigoths, who served under the Roman emperor Theodosius I but later invaded Greece and Italy, capturing Rome in 410.
alarm (ə'lɑːm) *vb* (*tr*) **1** to fill with apprehension, anxiety, or fear. **2** to warn about danger; alert. **3** to fit or activate a burglar alarm on a house, car, etc. ♦ *n* **4** fear or terror aroused by awareness of danger; fright. **5** apprehension or uneasiness: *the idea of failing filled him with alarm.* **6** a noise, signal, etc., warning of danger. **7** any device that transmits such a warning: *a burglar alarm.* **8a** the device in an alarm clock that triggers off the bell or buzzer. **8b** short for **alarm clock.** **9** *Archaic.* a call to arms. **10** *Fencing.* a warning or challenge made by stamping the front foot. [C14: from Old French *alarme,* from Old Italian *all'arme* to arms; see ARM[2]] ▸ **a'larming** *adj* ▸ **a'larmingly** *adv*
alarm clock *n* a clock with a mechanism that sounds at a set time: used esp. for waking a person up.
alarmist (ə'lɑːmɪst) *n* **1** a person who alarms or attempts to alarm others needlessly or without due grounds. **2** a person who is easily alarmed. ♦ *adj* **3** characteristic of an alarmist. ▸ **a'larmism** *n*
alarum (ə'lærəm, -'lɑːr-, -'leər-) *n* **1** *Archaic.* an alarm, esp. a call to arms. **2** (used as a stage direction, esp. in Elizabethan drama) a loud disturbance or conflict (esp. in the phrase **alarums and excursions**). [C15: variant of ALARM]
alary ('eɪlərɪ, 'æ-) *adj* of, relating to, or shaped like wings. [C17: from Latin *ālārius,* from *āla* wing]
alas (ə'læs) *interj* an exclamation of grief, compassion, or alarm. [C13: from Old French *ha las!* oh wretched!; *las* from Latin *lassus* weary]
Alas. *abbrev. for* Alaska.
Alaska (ə'læskə) *n* **1** the largest state of the U.S., in the extreme northwest of North America: the aboriginal inhabitants are Eskimos; the earliest White set-

tlements were made by the Russians; it was purchased by the U.S. from Russia in 1867. It is mostly mountainous and volcanic, rising over 6000 m (20 000 ft.), with the Yukon basin in the central region; large areas are covered by tundra; it has important mineral resources (chiefly coal, oil, and natural gas). Capital: Juneau. Pop.: 609 311 (1997 est.). Area: 1 530 694 sq. km (591 004 sq. miles). Abbrevs.: **Alas.** or (with zip code) **AK** **2 Gulf of.** the N part of the Pacific, between the Alaska Peninsula and the Alexander Archipelago. ▸ **A'laskan** *adj, n*

Alaska Highway *n* a road extending from Dawson Creek, British Columbia, to Fairbanks, Alaska: built by the U.S. Army (1942). Length: 2452 km (1523 miles). Originally called: **Alcan Highway.**

Alaska Peninsula *n* an extension of the mainland of SW Alaska between the Pacific and the Bering Sea, ending in the Aleutian Islands. Length: about 644 km (400 miles).

Alaska Range *n* a mountain range in S central Alaska. Highest peak: Mount McKinley, 6194 m (20 320 ft.).

alate ('eɪleɪt) *adj* having wings or winglike extensions. **[C17:** from Latin *ālātus,* from *āla* wing**]**

alb (ælb) *n Christianity.* a long white linen vestment with sleeves worn by priests and others. **[**Old English *albe,* from Medieval Latin *alba (vestis)* white (clothing)**]**

Alb. *abbrev. for* Albania(n).

Alba (*Spanish* 'alβa) *n* See (Duke of) **Alva.**

Albacete (*Spanish* alβa'θete) *n* a city in SE Spain: metal goods manufacturing. Pop.: 143 779 (1995 est.).

albacore ('ælbəˌkɔː) *n* a tunny, *Thunnus alalunga,* occurring mainly in warm regions of the Atlantic and Pacific. It has very long pectoral fins and is a valued food fish. Also called: **long-fin tunny. [C16:** from Portuguese *albacor,* from Arabic *al-bakrah,* from *al* the + *bakr* young camel**]**

Alba Longa ('ælbə 'lɒŋgə) *n* a city of ancient Latium, southeast of modern Rome: the legendary birthplace of Romulus and Remus.

Alban ('ɔːlbən) *n* **Saint.** 3rd century A.D., the first English martyr. He was beheaded by the Romans on the site on which St Alban's Abbey now stands, for admitting his conversion to Christianity. Feast day: June 17.

Albania (æl'beɪnɪə) *n* a republic in SE Europe, on the Balkan Peninsula: became independent in 1912 after more than four centuries of Turkish rule; established as a republic (1946) under Communist rule; multiparty constitution adopted in 1991. It is generally mountainous, rising over 2700 m (9000 ft.), with extensive forests. Language: Albanian. Religion: Muslim majority. Currency: lek. Capital: Tirana. Pop.: 3 331 000 (1998 est.). Area: 28 749 sq. km (11 100 sq. miles).

Albanian (æl'beɪnɪən) *n* **1** the official language of Albania: of uncertain relationship within the Indo-European family, but thought to be related to ancient Illyrian. **2a** a native, citizen, or inhabitant of Albania. **2b** a native speaker of Albanian. ◆ *adj* **3** of or relating to Albania, its people, or their language.

Albany ('ɔːlbənɪ) *n* **1** a city in E New York State, on the Hudson River: the state capital. Pop.: 103 564 (1996 est.). **2** a river in central Canada, flowing east and northeast to James Bay. Length: 982 km (610 miles).

albata (æl'beɪtə) *n* a variety of German silver consisting of nickel, copper, and zinc. **[C19:** from Latin, literally: clothed in white, from *albus* white**]**

albatross ('ælbəˌtrɒs) *n* **1** any large oceanic bird of the genera *Diomedea* and *Phoebetria,* family *Diomedeidae,* of cool southern oceans: order *Procellariiformes* (petrels). They have long narrow wings and are noted for a powerful gliding flight. See also **wandering albatross. 2** a constant and inescapable burden or handicap: *an albatross of debt.* **3** *Golf.* a score of three strokes under par for a hole. **[C17:** from Portuguese *alcatraz* pelican, from Arabic *al-ghattās,* from *al* the + *ghattās* white-tailed sea eagle; influenced by Latin *albus* white: **C20** in sense 2, from S. T. COLERIDGE'S poem *The Rime of the Ancient Mariner* (1798)**]**

albedo (æl'biːdəʊ) *n* **1** the ratio of the intensity of light reflected from an object, such as a planet, to that of the light it receives from the sun. **2** *Physics.* the probability that a neutron passing through a surface will return through that surface. **[C19:** from Church Latin: whiteness, from Latin *albus* white**]**

Albee ('ɔːlbiː) *n* **Edward.** born 1928, U.S. dramatist. His plays include *Who's Afraid of Virginia Woolf?* (1962), *Seascape* (1975), *Marriage Play* (1986), *Three Tall Women* (1990), and *The Play About The Baby* (1998).

albeit (ɔːl'biːɪt) *conj* even though. **[C14** *al be it,* that is, although it be (that)**]**

Albemarle Sound ('ælbəˌmɑːl) *n* an inlet of the Atlantic in NE North Carolina. Length: about 96 km (60 miles).

Albéniz (*Spanish* al'βeniθ) *n* **Isaac** (isa'ak). 1860–1909, Spanish composer; noted for piano pieces inspired by folk music, such as the suite *Iberia.*

Alberich (*German* 'albərɪç) *n* (in medieval German legend) the king of the dwarfs and guardian of the treasures of the Nibelungs.

Albers ('ælbəz) *n* **Josef.** 1888–1976, U.S. painter, designer, and poet, born in Germany. His works include a series of abstract paintings entitled *Homage to the Square.*

albert ('ælbət) *n* **1** a kind of watch chain usually attached to a waistcoat. **2** *Brit.* a standard size of notepaper, 6 × 3⅞ inches. **[C19:** named after Prince ALBERT**]**

Albert[1] ('ælbət) *n* **Lake.** a lake in E Africa, between the Democratic Republic of the Congo (formerly Zaïre) and Uganda in the Great Rift Valley, 660 m (2200 ft.) above sea level: a source of the Nile, fed by the Victoria Nile, which leaves as the Albert Nile. Area: 5345 sq. km (2064 sq. miles). Former name: **Lake Mobutu.**

Albert[2] ('ælbət) *n* **Prince.** full name *Albert Francis Charles Augustus Emmanuel of Saxe-Coburg-Gotha.* 1819–61, Prince Consort of Queen Victoria of Great Britain and Ireland.

Albert I *n* **1** *c.* 1255–1308, king of Germany (1298–1308). **2** 1875–1934, king of the Belgians (1909–34). **3** called *Albert the Bear. c.* 1100–70. German military leader: first margrave of Brandenburg.

Albert II *n* full name *Albert Felix Humbert Theodore Christian Eugene Marie.* born 1934, king of Belgium from 1993.

Alberta (æl'bɜːtə) *n* a province of W Canada: mostly prairie, with the Rocky Mountains in the southwest. Capital: Edmonton. Pop.: 2 747 000 (1995 est.). Area: 661 188 sq. km (255 285 sq. miles). Abbrevs.: **Alta, AB** ▸ **Al'bertan** *adj, n*

Albert Edward *n* a mountain in SE New Guinea, in the Owen Stanley Range. Height: 3993 m (13 100 ft.).

Alberti (*Italian* al'berti) *n* **Leon Battista** (le'ɔn bat'tista). 1404–72, Italian Renaissance architect, painter, writer, and musician; among his architectural designs are the façades of Sta. Maria Novella at Florence and S. Francesco at Rimini.

albertite ('ælbəˌtaɪt) *n* a black solid variety of bitumen that has a conchoidal fracture and occurs in veins in oil-bearing strata. **[C19:** named after *Albert* county, New Brunswick, Canada, where it is mined**]**

Albertus Magnus (æl'bɜːtəs 'mægnəs) *n* **Saint.** original name *Albert, Count von Böllstadt.* ?1193–1280, German scholastic philosopher; teacher of Thomas Aquinas and commentator on Aristotle. Feast day: Nov. 15.

albescent (æl'besᵊnt) *adj* shading into, growing, or becoming white. **[C19:** from Latin *albēscere* to grow white, from *albus* white**]** ▸ **al'bescence** *n*

Albi (*French* albi) *n* a town in S France: connected with the Albigensian heresy and the crusade against it. Pop.: 48 700 (1990).

Albigenses (ˌælbɪ'dʒensiːz) *pl n* members of a Manichean sect that flourished in S France from the 11th to the 13th century. **[**from Medieval Latin: inhabitants of Albi, from *Albiga* ALBI**]** ▸ **ˌAlbi'gensian** *adj* ▸ **ˌAlbi'gensianism** *n*

albino (æl'biːnəʊ) *n, pl* **-nos. 1** a person with congenital absence of pigmentation in the skin, eyes, and hair. **2** any animal or plant that is deficient in pigment. **[C18:** via Portuguese from Spanish, from *albo* white, from Latin *albus***]** ▸ **albinic** (æl'bɪnɪk) *or* **ˌalbin'istic** *adj* ▸ **albinism** ('ælbɪˌnɪzəm) *n* ▸ **albinotic** (ˌælbɪ'nɒtɪk) *adj*

Albinoni (*Italian* albi'noːni) *n* **Tomaso** (to'maːzo). 1671–1750, Italian composer and violinist. He wrote concertos and over 50 operas.

Albinus (æl'biːnəs) *n* another name for **Alcuin.**

Albion ('ælbɪən) *n Archaic or poetic.* Britain or England. **[C13:** from Latin, of Celtic origin**]**

albite ('ælbaɪt) *n* a colourless, milky-white, yellow, pink, green, or black mineral of the feldspar group and plagioclase series, found in igneous sedimentary and metamorphic rocks. It is used in the manufacture of glass and ceramics. Composition: sodium aluminium silicate. Formula: $NaALSi_3O_8$. Crystal structure: triclinic. **[C19:** from Latin *albus* white**]** ▸ **albitic** (æl'bɪtɪk) *adj*

Alboin ('ælbɔɪn, -bəʊɪn) *n* died 573 A.D., king of the Lombards (565–73); conqueror of N Italy.

Ålborg (*Danish* 'ɔlbɔr) *n* a variant spelling of **Aalborg.**

album ('ælbəm) *n* **1** a book or binder consisting of blank pages, pockets, or envelopes for keeping photographs, stamps, autographs, drawings, poems, etc. **2** one or more CDs, cassettes, or long-playing records released as a single item. **3** a booklike holder containing sleeves for gramophone records. **4** *Chiefly Brit.* an anthology, usually large and illustrated. **[C17:** from Latin: blank tablet, from *albus* white**]**

albumblatt ('ælbəmˌblæt) *n Music.* a short occasional instrumental composition, usually light in character. **[C19:** German: album-leaf**]**

albumen ('ælbjʊmɪn, -mɛn) *n* **1** the white of an egg; the nutritive and protective gelatinous substance, mostly an albumin, that surrounds the yolk. **2** a rare name for **endosperm. 3** a variant spelling of **albumin. [C16:** from Latin: white of an egg, from *albus* white**]**

albumenize *or* **albumenise** (æl'bjuːmɪˌnaɪz) *vb (tr)* to coat with a solution containing albumen or albumin.

albumin *or* **albumen** ('ælbjʊmɪn) *n* any of a group of simple water-soluble proteins that are coagulated by heat and are found in blood plasma, egg white, etc. **[C19:** from ALBUMEN + -IN**]**

albuminate (æl'bjuːmɪˌneɪt) *n Now rare.* any of several substances formed from albumin by the action of acid or alkali.

albuminoid (æl'bjuːmɪˌnɔɪd) *adj* **1** resembling albumin. ◆ *n* **2** another name for **scleroprotein.**

albuminous (æl'bjuːmɪnəs) *adj* of or containing albumin.

albuminuria (ælˌbjuːmɪ'njʊərɪə) *n Pathol.* the presence of albumin in the urine. Also called: **proteinuria.**

albumose ('ælbjʊˌməʊs, -ˌməʊz) *n* the U.S. name for **proteose. [C19:** from ALBUMIN + -OSE[2]**]**

Albuquerque[1] ('ælbəˌkɜːkɪ) *n* a city in central New Mexico, on the Rio Grande. Pop.: 419 681 (1996 est.).

Albuquerque[2] ('ælbəˌkɜːkɪ; *Portuguese* ɑlbu'kɛrkə) *n* **Afonso de** (ə'fõsu də). 1453–1515, Portuguese navigator who established Portuguese colonies in the East by conquering Goa, Ceylon, Malacca, and Ormuz.

alburnum (æl'bɜːnəm) *n* a former name for **sapwood. [C17:** from Latin: sapwood, from *albus* white**]**

Albury-Wodonga ('ɔːbərɪ, -brɪ wə'dɒŋgə) *n* an urban growth centre in SE Australia, in S central New South Wales, on the Murray River: commercial centre of an agricultural region. Pop.: 63 610 (1991).

Alcaeus (æl'siːəs) *n* 7th century B.C., Greek lyric poet who wrote hymns, love songs, and political odes.

alcahest ('ælkəˌhɛst) *n* a variant spelling of **alkahest.**

Alcaic (æl'keɪɪk) *adj* **1** of or relating to a metre used by the poet Alcaeus, consisting of a strophe of four lines each with four feet. ◆ *n* **2** *(usually pl)* verse written in the Alcaic form. **[C17:** from Late Latin *Alcaicus* of ALCAEUS**]**

alcaide (æl'keɪd; *Spanish* al'kaiðe) *n* (in Spain and Spanish America) **1** the commander of a fortress or castle. **2** the governor of a prison. **[C16:** from Spanish, from Arabic *al-qā'id* the captain, commander, from *qād* to give orders**]**

alcalde (æl'kældɪ; *Spanish* al'kalde) *or* **alcade** (æl'keɪd) *n* (in Spain and Spanish America) the mayor or chief magistrate in a town. **[C17:** from Spanish, from Arabic *al-qādī* the judge, from *qadā* to judge**]**

Alcan Highway ('ælkæn) *n* original name of the **Alaska Highway.**

Alcántara (æl'kæntɑːrə) *n* a town in W Spain: a Roman bridge spans the River Tagus. Pop.: 2317 (1981).

Alcatraz ('ælkəˌtræz) *n* an island in W California, in San Francisco Bay: a federal prison until 1963.

alcazar (ˌælkə'zɑː; *Spanish* al'kaθar) *n* any of various palaces or fortresses built in Spain by the Moors. [C17: from Spanish, from Arabic *al-qasr* the castle]

Alcazar de San Juan ('ælkəˌzɑː; *Spanish* al'kaθar) *n* a town in S central Spain: associated with Cervantes and Don Quixote. Pop.: 25 679 (1991).

Alcestis (æl'sestɪs) *n Greek myth.* the wife of king Admetus of Thessaly. To save his life, she died in his place, but was rescued from Hades by Hercules.

alchemist ('ælkəmɪst) *n* a person who practises alchemy.

alchemize *or* **alchemise** ('ælkəˌmaɪz) *vb (tr)* to alter (an element, metal, etc.) by alchemy; transmute.

alchemy ('ælkəmɪ) *n, pl* **-mies. 1** the pseudoscientific predecessor of chemistry that sought a method of transmuting base metals into gold, an elixir to prolong life indefinitely, a panacea or universal remedy, and an alkahest or universal solvent. **2** a power like that of alchemy: *her beauty had a potent alchemy.* [C14 *alkamye,* via Old French from Medieval Latin *alchimia,* from Arabic *al-kīmiyā',* from *al* the + *kīmiyā'* transmutation, from Late Greek *khēmeia* the art of transmutation] ▸ **alchemic** (æl'kemɪk), **al'chemical,** *or* **ˌalchem'istic** *adj*

alcheringa (ˌæltʃə'rɪŋgə) *n* another name for **Dreamtime.** [from a native Australian language, literally: dream time]

Alchevsk (æl'tʃevsk) *n* a city in the E Ukraine. Pop.: 124 000 (1996 est.). Former name (until 1992): **Kommunarsk.**

Alcibiades (ˌælsɪ'baɪəˌdiːz) *n* 450–404 B.C., Athenian statesman and general in the Peloponnesian War: brilliant, courageous, and unstable, he defected to the Spartans in 415, but returned and led the Athenian victories at Abydos (411) and Cyzicus (410). ▸ **ˌAlciˌbia'dean** *adj*

Alcides (æl'saɪdiːz) *n* another name for **Hercules**[1] (sense 1).

alcidine ('ælsɪˌdaɪn) *adj* of, relating to, or belonging to the *Alcidae,* a family of sea birds including the auks, guillemots, puffins, and related forms. [C20: from New Latin *Alcidae,* from *Alca* type genus]

Alcinoüs (æl'sɪnəʊəs) *n* (in Homer's *Odyssey*) a Phaeacian king at whose court the shipwrecked Odysseus told of his wanderings. See also **Nausicaä.**

ALCM *abbrev. for* air-launched cruise missile: a type of cruise missile that can be launched from an aircraft.

Alcman ('ælkmən) *n* 7th century B.C., Greek lyric poet.

Alcmene (ælk'miːnɪ) *n Greek myth.* the mother of Hercules by Zeus who visited her in the guise of her husband, Amphitryon.

Alcock ('ɔːlkɒk) *n* Sir **John William.** 1892–1919, English aviator who with A.W. Brown made the first nonstop flight across the Atlantic (1919).

alcohol ('ælkəˌhɒl) *n* **1** a colourless flammable liquid, the active principle of intoxicating drinks, produced by the fermentation of sugars, esp. glucose, and used as a solvent and in the manufacture of organic chemicals. Formula: C_2H_5OH. Also called: **ethanol, ethyl alcohol. 2** a drink or drinks containing this substance. **3** *Chem.* any one of a class of organic compounds that contain one or more hydroxyl groups bound to carbon atoms that are not part of an aromatic ring. The simplest alcohols have the formula ROH, where R is an alkyl group. Compare **phenol** (sense 2). See also **diol, triol.** [C16: via New Latin from Medieval Latin, from Arabic *al-kuhl* powdered antimony; see KOHL]

alcohol-free *adj* **1** (of beer or wine) containing only a trace of alcohol. Compare **low-alcohol. 2** (of a period of time) during which no alcoholic drink is consumed: *there should be one or two alcohol-free days a week.*

alcoholic (ˌælkə'hɒlɪk) *n* **1** a person affected by alcoholism. ◆ *adj* **2** of, relating to, containing, or resulting from alcohol.

alcoholicity (ˌælkəhɒ'lɪsɪtɪ) *n* the strength of an alcoholic liquor.

Alcoholics Anonymous *n* an association of alcoholics who try, esp. by mutual assistance, to overcome alcoholism.

alcoholism ('ælkəhɒˌlɪzəm) *n* a condition in which dependence on alcohol harms a person's health, social functioning, or family life.

alcoholize *or* **alcoholise** ('ælkəhɒˌlaɪz) *vb (tr)* to turn into alcoholic drink, as by fermenting or mixing with alcohol. ▸ **ˌalcoˌholi'zation** *or* **ˌalcoˌholi'sation** *n*

alcoholometer (ˌælkəhɒ'lɒmɪtə) *n* an instrument, such as a specially calibrated hydrometer, for determining the percentage of alcohol in a liquid.

alcopop ('ælkəʊˌpɒp) *n Informal.* an alcoholic drink that tastes like a soft drink. [C20: from ALCO(HOL) + POP[1] (sense 11)]

Alcoran *or* **Alkoran** (ˌælkɒ'rɑːn) *n* another name for the **Koran.** ▸ **ˌAlco'ranic** *or* **ˌAlko'ranic** *adj*

Alcott ('ɔːlkət) *n* **Louisa May.** 1832–88, U.S. novelist, noted for her children's books, esp. *Little Women* (1869).

alcove ('ælkəʊv) *n* **1** a recess or niche in the wall of a room, as for a bed, books, etc. **2** any recessed usually vaulted area, as in a garden wall. **3** any covered or secluded spot, such as a summerhouse. [C17: from French *alcôve,* from Spanish *alcoba,* from Arabic *al-qubbah* the vault, arch]

Alcuin ('ælkwɪn) *or* **Albinus** *n* 735–804 A.D., English scholar and theologian; friend and adviser of Charlemagne.

Alcyone[1] (æl'saɪənɪ) *n Greek myth.* Also called: **Halcyone.** the daughter of Aeolus and wife of Ceyx, who drowned herself in grief for her husband's death. She was transformed into a kingfisher. See also **Ceyx.**

Alcyone[2] (æl'saɪənɪ) *n* the brightest star in the Pleiades, located in the constellation Taurus.

Ald. *or* **Aldm.** *abbrev. for* Alderman.

Aldabra (æl'dæbrə) *n* an island group in the Indian Ocean: part of the British Indian Ocean Territory (1965–76); now administratively part of the Seychelles.

Aldan (*Russian* al'dan) *n* a river in E Russia in the SE Sakha Republic, rising in the **Aldan Mountains** and flowing north and west to the Lena River. Length: about 2700 km (1700 miles).

Aldebaran (æl'debərən) *n* a binary star, one component of which is a red giant, the brightest star in the constellation Taurus. It is situated close to the star cluster Hyades. Visual magnitude: 1.06; spectral type: K5; distance: 55 light years. [C14: via Medieval Latin from Arabic *al-dabarān* the follower (of the Pleiades)]

Aldeburgh ('ɔːlbərə) *n* a small resort in SE England, in Suffolk: site of an annual music festival established in 1948 by Benjamin Britten. Pop.: 2654 (1991).

aldehyde ('ældɪˌhaɪd) *n* **1** any organic compound containing the group -CHO. Aldehydes are oxidized to carboxylic acids and take part in many addition reactions. **2** *(modifier)* consisting of, containing, or concerned with the group -CHO: *aldehyde group or radical.* [C19: from New Latin *al(cohol) dehyd(rogenātum)* dehydrogenated alcohol] ▸ **aldehydic** (ˌældə'hɪdɪk) *adj*

al dente *Italian.* (al 'dente) *adj* (of a pasta dish) cooked so as to be firm when eaten. [literally: to the tooth]

alder ('ɔːldə) *n* **1** any N temperate betulaceous shrub or tree of the genus *Alnus,* having toothed leaves and conelike fruits. The bark is used in dyeing and tanning and the wood for bridges, etc. because it resists underwater rot. **2** any of several similar trees or shrubs. [Old English *alor;* related to Old High German *elira,* Latin *alnus*]

alder buckthorn *n* a Eurasian rhamnaceous shrub, *Frangula alnus,* with small greenish flowers and black berry-like fruits.

alder fly *n* any of various neuropterous insects of the widely distributed group *Sialoidea,* such as *Sialis lutaria,* that have large broad-based hind wings, produce aquatic larvae, and occur near water.

alderman ('ɔːldəmən) *n, pl* **-men. 1** (in England and Wales until 1974) one of the senior members of a local council, elected by other councillors. **2** (in the U.S., Canada, Australia, etc.) a member of the governing body of a municipality. **3** *History.* a variant spelling of **ealdorman.** ◆ Abbrevs. (for senses 1, 2): **Ald., Aldm.** [Old English *aldormann,* from *ealdor* chief (comparative of *eald* OLD) + *mann* MAN] ▸ **aldermanic** (ˌɔːldə'mænɪk) *adj* ▸ **'aldermanry** *n* ▸ **'aldermanˌship** *n*

Aldermaston ('ɔːldəˌmɑːstən) *n* a village in S England, in Berkshire SW of Reading: site of the Atomic Weapons Research Establishment and starting point of the Aldermaston marches (1958–63), organized by the Campaign for Nuclear Disarmament. Pop.: 2157 (1987 est.).

Alderney ('ɔːldənɪ) *n* **1** one of the Channel Islands, in the English Channel: separated from the French coast by a dangerous tidal channel (the **Race of Alderney**). Pop.: 2375 (1994 est.). Area: 8 sq. km (3 sq. miles). French name: **Aurigny. 2** any of a breed of dairy cattle originating from the island of Alderney.

Aldershot ('ɔːldəˌʃɒt) *n* a town in S England, in Hampshire: site of a large military camp. Pop.: 51 356 (1991).

Aldine ('ɔːldaɪn, -diːn) *adj* **1** relating to Aldus Manutius or to his editions of the classics. ◆ *n* **2** a book printed by the Aldine press. **3** any of the several typefaces designed by Aldus Manutius.

Aldington ('ɔːldɪŋtən) *n* **Richard.** 1892–1962, English poet, novelist, and biographer. His novels include *Death of a Hero* (1929) and *The Colonel's Daughter* (1931), which reflect postwar disillusion following World War I.

Aldis lamp ('ɔːldɪs) *n* a portable lamp used to transmit Morse code. [C20: originally a trademark, after A. C. W. *Aldis,* its inventor]

Aldiss ('ɔːldɪs) *n* **Brian W(ilson).** born 1925, British novelist, best known for his science fiction. His works include *Non-Stop* (1958), *Enemies of the System* (1978), *The Helliconia Trilogy* (1983–86), *Forgotten Life* (1988), and *The Detached Retina* (1995).

aldohexose (ˌældəʊ'heksəʊs, -əʊz) *n* any aldose containing six carbon atoms, such as glucose or mannose.

aldol ('ældɒl) *n* **1** a colourless or yellowish oily liquid, miscible with water, used in the manufacture of rubber accelerators, as an organic solvent, in perfume, and as a hypnotic and sedative. Formula: $CH_3CHOHCH_2CHO$. **2** any organic compound containing the group $-CHOHCH_2CHO$. **3** *(modifier)* consisting of, containing, or concerned with the group $-CHOHCH_2CHO$: *aldol group or radical; aldol reaction.* [C19: from ALD(EHYDE) + -OL[1]]

aldose ('ældəʊs, -dəʊz) *n* a sugar that contains the aldehyde group or is a hemiacetal. [C20: from ALD(EHYDE) + -OSE[2]]

aldosterone (æl'dɒstəˌrəʊn) *n* the principal mineralocorticoid secreted by the adrenal cortex. A synthesized form is used in the treatment of Addison's disease. [C20: from ALD(EHYDE) + -O- + STER(OL) + -ONE]

aldoxime (æl'dɒksiːm) *n* an oxime formed by reaction between hydroxylamine and an aldehyde.

Aldridge-Brownhills ('ɔːldrɪdʒ'braʊnˌhɪlz) *n* a town in central England, in Walsall unitary authority, West Midlands: formed by the amalgamation of neighbouring towns in 1966. Pop.: 37 444 (1991).

aldrin ('ɔːldrɪn) *n* a brown to white poisonous crystalline solid, more than 95 per cent of which consists of the compound $C_{12}H_8Cl_6$, which is used as an insecticide. Melting pt.: 105°C. [C20: named after K. *Alder* (1902–58) German chemist]

Aldrin ('ɔːldrɪn) *n* **Edwin Eugene Jr.,** known as *Buzz.* born 1930, U.S. astronaut; the second man to set foot on the moon on July 20, 1969, during the Apollo 11 flight.

Aldus Manutius ('ɔːldəs mə'njuːʃɪəs) *n* 1450–1515, Italian printer, noted for his fine editions of the classics. He introduced italic type.

ale (eɪl) *n* **1** a beer fermented in an open vessel using yeasts that rise to the top of the brew. Compare **beer, lager**[1]. **2** (formerly) an alcoholic drink made by fermenting a cereal, esp. barley, but differing from beer by being unflavoured by hops. **3** *Chiefly Brit.* another word for **beer.** [Old English *alu, ealu;* related to Old Norse *öl,* Old Saxon *alofat*]

aleatory ('eɪlɪətərɪ, -trɪ) *or* **aleatoric** (ˌeɪlɪə'tɒrɪk) *adj* **1** dependent on chance.

2 (esp. of a musical composition) involving elements chosen at random by the performer. [C17: from Latin *āleātōrius*, from *āleātor* gambler, from *ālea* game of chance, dice, of uncertain origin]

alecithal (eɪ'lɛsɪθəl) *adj Zoology.* (of an ovum) having little or no yolk. [from A-[1] + Greek *lekithos* egg yolk]

ale conner *n English history.* a local official appointed to examine the measure and quality of ale, beer, and bread. [C14: from ALE + *conner*, from Old English *cunnere* one who tests]

alecost ('eɪl,kɒst) *n* another name for **costmary.**

Alecto (ə'lɛktəʊ) *n Greek myth.* one of the three Furies; the others are Megaera and Tisiphone.

alee (ə'liː) *adv, adj (postpositive) Nautical.* on or towards the lee: *with the helm alee.* Compare **aweather.**

alegar ('eɪlɪgə, 'æ-) *n* malt vinegar. [C14: from ALE + VINEGAR]

alehouse ('eɪl,haʊs) *n* **1** *Archaic.* a place where ale was sold; tavern. **2** *Informal.* another name for **pub.**

Aleichem (ɑː'leɪçəm) *n* **Sholom**, real name *Solomon Rabinowitz.* 1859–1916, U.S. Jewish writer, born in Russia. His works include *Tevye the Milkman*, which was adapted for the stage musical *Fiddler on the Roof.*

Alekhine ('ælɪ,kiːn; *Russian* a'ljɔxin) *n* **Alexander.** 1892–1946, Russian-born chess player who lived in France; world champion (1927–35, 1937–46).

Aleksandropol (*Russian* alɪksan'drɔpəlj) *n* the former name (from 1837 until after the Revolution) of **Leninakan.**

Aleksandrovsk (*Russian* alɪk'sandrəfsk) *n* the former name (until 1921) of **Zaporozhye.**

Alemán (*Spanish* ale'man) *n* **Mateo** (ma'teo). 1547–?1614, Spanish novelist, author of the picaresque novel *Guzmán de Alfarache* (1599).

Alemanni (,ælə'mɑːnɪ) *n* a West Germanic people who settled in the 4th century A.D. between the Rhine, the Main, and the Danube. [C18: from Latin, of Germanic origin; related to Gothic *alamans* a totality of people]

Alemannic (,ælə'mænɪk) *n* **1a** the group of High German dialects spoken in Alsace, Switzerland, and SW Germany. **1b** the language of the ancient Alemanni, from which these modern dialects have developed. See also **Old High German.** ◆ *adj* **2** of or relating to the Alemanni, their speech, or the High German dialects descended from it. [C18: from Late Latin *Alamannicus*, of Germanic origin]

Alembert, d' (*French* dalɑ̃bɛr) *n* **Jean Le Rond** (ʒɑ̃ lə rɔ̃). 1717–83, French mathematician, physicist, and rationalist philosopher, noted for his contribution to Newtonian physics in *Traité de dynamique* (1743) and for his collaboration with Diderot in editing the *Encyclopédie.*

alembic (ə'lɛmbɪk) *n* **1** an obsolete type of retort used for distillation. **2** anything that distils or purifies. [C14: from Medieval Latin *alembicum*, from Arabic *al-anbīq* the still, from Greek *ambix* cup]

alembicated (ə'lɛmbɪ,keɪtɪd) *adj* (of a literary style) excessively refined; precious. ▸ **a,lembi'cation** *n*

Alençon (*French* alɑ̃sɔ̃) *n* a town in NW France: early lace-manufacturing centre. Pop.: 31 140 (1990).

Alençon lace *n* an elaborate lace worked on a hexagonal mesh and used as a border, or a machine-made copy of this.

aleph ('ɑːlɪf; *Hebrew* 'alɛf) *n* the first letter in the Hebrew alphabet (א) articulated as a glottal stop and transliterated with a superior comma (ʼ). [Hebrew: ox]

aleph-bet ('ɑlef'bet) *or* **aleph-beis** ('ɑlef'beis) *n* the Hebrew alphabet. [from the first two letters]

aleph-null *or* **aleph-zero** *n* the smallest infinite cardinal number; the cardinal number of the set of positive integers. Symbol: $\aleph_0$.

Aleppo (ə'lɛpəʊ) *n* an ancient city in NW Syria: industrial and commercial centre. Pop.: 1 591 400 (1994 est.). French name: **Alep** (alɛp). Arabic name: **Haleb** ('halɛp).

Aleppo gall *n* a type of nutgall occurring in oaks in W Asia and E Europe.

alerce (ə'lɜːs, æ'lɜːsɪ) *n* **1** the wood of the sandarac tree. **2** a cupressus-like Chilean pine, *Fitzroya cupressoides*, cut for timber. [Spanish: larch, from Latin *larix*, influenced by Arabic *al-arz*]

alert (ə'lɜːt) *adj (usually postpositive)* **1** vigilantly attentive: *alert to the problems.* **2** brisk, nimble, or lively. ◆ *n* **3** an alarm or warning, esp. a siren warning of an air raid. **4** the period during which such a warning remains in effect. **5 on the alert. 5a** on guard against danger, attack, etc. **5b** watchful; ready: *on the alert for any errors.* ◆ *vb (tr)* **6** to warn or signal (troops, police, etc.) to prepare for action. **7** to warn of danger, an attack, etc. [C17: from Italian *all'erta* on the watch, from *erta* lookout post, from *ergere* to build up, from Latin *ērigere*; see ERECT] ▸ **a'lertly** *adv* ▸ **a'lertness** *n*

-ales *suffix forming plural proper nouns.* denoting plants belonging to an order: *Rosales; Filicales.* [New Latin, from Latin, plural of *-ālis* -AL[1]]

Alessandria (*Italian* ales'sandrja) *n* a town in NW Italy, in Piedmont. Pop.: 93 866 (1990).

Ålesund *or* **Aalesund** (*Norwegian* 'oːləsun) *n* a port and market town in W Norway, on an island between Bergen and Trondheim: fishing and sealing fleets. Pop.: 35 862 (1990).

alethic (ə'liːθɪk) *adj Logic.* **a** of or relating to such philosophical concepts as truth, necessity, possibility, contingency, etc. **b** designating the branch of modal logic that deals with the formalization of these concepts. [C20: from Greek *alētheia* truth]

aleurone (ə'lʊərən, -,rəʊn) *or* **aleuron** (ə'lʊərɒn, -rən) *n* an albuminoid protein that occurs in the form of storage granules in plant cells, esp. in seeds such as maize. [C19: from Greek *aleuron* flour]

Aleut (æ'luːt, 'æliː,ʊt) *n* **1** a member of a people inhabiting the Aleutian Islands and SW Alaska, related to the Eskimos. **2** the language of this people, related to Eskimo. [from Russian *aleút*, probably of Chukchi origin]

Aleutian (ə'luːʃən) *adj* **1** of, denoting, or relating to the Aleutian Islands, the Aleuts, or their language. ◆ *n* **2** another word for **Aleut.**

Aleutian Islands *n* a chain of over 150 volcanic islands, extending southwestwards from the Alaska Peninsula between the N Pacific and the Bering Sea.

A level *n* (in Britain) **1a** the advanced level of a subject taken for General Certificate of Education (**GCE**). **1b** (*as modifier*): *A level maths.* **2** a pass in a particular subject at A level: *she has three A levels.*

alevin ('ælɪvɪn) *n* a young fish, esp. a young salmon or trout. [C19: from French, from Old French *alever* to rear (young), from Latin *levāre* to raise]

alewife ('eɪl,waɪf) *n, pl* **-wives.** a North American fish, *Pomolobus pseudoharengus*, similar to the herring *Clupea harengus*: family *Clupeidae* (herrings). [C19: perhaps an alteration (through influence of *alewife*, that is, a large rotund woman, alluding to the fish's shape) of French *alose* shad]

Alexander (,ælɪg'zɑːndə) *n* **Harold** (**Rupert Leofric George**), Earl Alexander of Tunis. 1891–1969, British field marshal in World War II, who organized the retreat from Dunkirk and commanded in North Africa (1943) and Sicily and Italy (1944–45); governor general of Canada (1946–52); British minister of defence (1952–54).

Alexander I *n* **1** *c.* 1080–1124, king of Scotland (1107–24), son of Malcolm III. **2** 1777–1825, tsar of Russia (1801–25), who helped defeat Napoleon and formed the Holy Alliance (1815).

Alexander II *n* **1** 1198–1249, king of Scotland (1214–49), son of William (the Lion). **2** 1818–81, tsar of Russia (1855–81), son of Nicholas I, who emancipated the serfs (1861). He was assassinated by the Nihilists.

Alexander III *n* **1** 1241–86, king of Scotland (1249–86), son of Alexander II. **2** original name *Orlando Bandinelli.* died 1181, pope (1159–81), who excommunicated Barbarossa. **3** 1845–94, tsar of Russia (1881–94), son of Alexander II.

Alexander VI *n* original name *Rodrigo Borgia.* 1431–1503, pope (1492–1503): noted for his extravagance and immorality as well as for his patronage of the arts; father of Cesare and Lucrezia Borgia, with whom he is said to have committed incest.

Alexander Archipelago *n* a group of over 1000 islands along the coast of SE Alaska.

Alexander I Island *n* an island of Antarctica, west of Palmer Land, in the Bellingshausen Sea. Length: about 378 km (235 miles).

Alexander Nevski ('nɛvskɪ, 'nɛf-; *Russian* 'njɛfskij) *n* **Saint.** ?1220–63, Russian prince and military leader, who defeated the Swedes at the River Neva (1240) and the Teutonic knights at Lake Peipus (1242).

alexanders (,ælɪg'zɑːndəz) *n* **1** a biennial umbelliferous plant, *Smyrnium olusatrum*, native to S Europe, with dense umbels of yellow-green flowers and black fruits. **2 golden alexanders.** an umbelliferous plant, *Zizia aurea*, of North America, having yellow flowers in compound umbels. [Old English, from Medieval Latin *alexandrum*, probably (through association in folk etymology with *Alexander* the Great) changed from Latin *holus atrum* black vegetable]

Alexander technique *n* a technique for developing awareness of one's posture and movement in order to improve it. [C20: named after Frederick Matthias *Alexander* (died 1955), Australian actor who originated it]

Alexander the Great *n* 356–323 B.C., king of Macedon, who conquered Greece (336), Egypt (331), and the Persian Empire (328), and founded Alexandria.

Alexandra (,ælɪg'zɑːndrə) *n* **1** 1844–1925, queen consort of Edward VII of Great Britain and Ireland. **2** 1872–1918, the wife of Nicholas II of Russia; her misrule while Nicholas was supreme commander of the Russian forces during World War I precipitated the Russian Revolution.

Alexandretta (,ælɪgzɑːn'drɛtə) *n* the former name of **Iskenderun.**

Alexandria (,ælɪg'zændrɪə, -'zɑːn-) *n* the chief port of Egypt, on the Nile Delta: cultural centre of ancient times, founded by Alexander the Great (332 B.C.). Pop.: 3 700 000 (1996 est.). Arabic name: **El Iskandariyah.**

Alexandrian (,ælɪg'zændrɪən, -'zɑːn-) *adj* **1** of or relating to Alexandria in Egypt. **2** of or relating to Alexander the Great. **3** relating to the Hellenistic philosophical, literary, and scientific ideas that flourished in Alexandria in the last three centuries B.C. **4** (of writers, literary works, etc.) erudite and imitative rather than original or creative. ◆ *n* **5** a native or inhabitant of Alexandria.

Alexandrine (,ælɪg'zændraɪn, -drɪn, -'zɑːn-) *Prosody.* ◆ *n* **1** a line of verse having six iambic feet, usually with a caesura after the third foot. ◆ *adj* **2** of, characterized by, or written in Alexandrines. [C16: from French *alexandrin*, from *Alexandre*, title of 15th-century poem written in this metre]

alexandrite (,ælɪg'zændraɪt) *n* a green variety of chrysoberyl used as a gemstone. [C19: named after ALEXANDER I of Russia; see -ITE[1]]

Alexandroúpolis (*Greek* alɛksan'ðrupɔlis) *n* a port in NE Greece, in W Thrace. Pop.: 39 283 (1991 est.). Former name (until the end of World War I): **Dedéagach.**

alexia (ə'lɛksɪə) *n* a disorder of the central nervous system characterized by impaired ability to read. Nontechnical name: **word blindness.** Compare **aphasia.** [C19: from New Latin, from A-[1] + Greek *lexis* speech; influenced in meaning by Latin *legere* to read]

alexin (ə'lɛksɪn) *n Immunol.* a former word for **complement** (sense 9). [C19: from German, from Greek *alexein* to ward off] ▸ **alexinic** (,ælɪk'sɪnɪk) *adj*

alexipharmic (ə,lɛksɪ'fɑːmɪk) *Med.* ◆ *adj* **1** acting as an antidote. ◆ *n* **2** an antidote. [C17: from Greek *alexipharmakon* antidote, from *alexein* to avert + *pharmakon* drug]

Alexis Mikhailovich (ə'lɛksɪs mɪ'kaɪlə,vɪtʃ) *n* 1629–76, tsar of Russia (1645–76); father of Peter the Great.

Alexius I Comnenus (ə'lɛksɪəs; kɒm'niːnəs) *n* 1048–1118, ruler of the Byzantine Empire (1081–1118).

alf (ælf) *n Austral. slang.* an uncultivated Australian. [from shortening of the name *Alfred*]

ALF (in Britain) *abbrev. for* Animal Liberation Front.
Alfa ('ælfə) *n* a variant spelling of **Alpha** (sense 2).
alfalfa (æl'fælfə) *n* a papilionaceous plant, *Medicago sativa,* of Europe and Asia, having compound leaves with three leaflets and clusters of small purplish flowers. It is widely cultivated for forage and used as a commercial source of chlorophyll. Also called: **lucerne.** [C19: from Spanish, from Arabic *al-fasfasah,* from *al* the + *fasfasah* the best sort of fodder]
al-Farabi ('ælfə'rɑːbɪ) *n* **Mohammed ibn Tarkhan.** died 950, Muslim philosopher, physician, and mathematician, of central Asian origin.
Al Fatah (æl 'fætə) *n* See **Fatah.**
Alfieri (*Italian* al'fjɛri) *n* Count **Vittorio** (vit'tɔːrjo). 1749–1803, Italian dramatist and poet, noted for his classical tragedies and political satires.
alfilaria *or* **alfileria** (ˌælfɪ'lɛərɪə) *n* a geraniaceous plant, *Erodium cicutarium,* native to Europe, with finely divided leaves and small pink or purplish flowers. It is widely naturalized in North America and is used as fodder. Also called: **pin clover.** [via American Spanish from Spanish *alfilerillo,* from *alfiler* pin, from Arabic *al-khilāl* the thorn]
Alfonso VI (*Spanish* al'fonso) *n* died 1109, king of Léon (1065–1109) and of Castile (1072–1109). He appointed his vassal, the Spanish hero El Cid, ruler of Valencia.
Alfonso XIII (*Spanish* al'fonso) *n* 1886–1941, king of Spain (1886–1931), who was forced to abdicate on the establishment of the republic in 1931.
alforja (æl'fɔːdʒə) *n Southwestern U.S.* a saddlebag made of leather or canvas. [C17: from Spanish, from Arabic *al-khurj* the saddlebag]
Alfred the Great ('ælfrɪd) *n* 849–99, king of Wessex (871–99) and overlord of England, who defeated the Danes and encouraged learning and writing in English.
alfresco (æl'frɛskəʊ) *adj, adv* in the open air. [C18: from Italian: in the cool]
Alfvén (al'ven) *n* **Hannes Olaf Gösta** ('hannes'uːlaf 'jøsta). 1908–95, Swedish physicist, noted for his research on magnetohydrodynamics; shared the Nobel prize for physics in 1970.
Alfvén wave *n* a magnetohydrodynamic wave that is propagated in a plasma.
alg. *abbrev. for* algebra *or* algebraic.
Alg. *abbrev. for* Algeria(n).
algae ('ældʒiː) *pl n, sing* **alga** ('ælgə). unicellular or multicellular organisms formerly classified as plants, occurring in fresh or salt water or moist ground, that have chlorophyll and other pigments but lack true stems, roots, and leaves. Algae, which are now regarded as protoctists, include the seaweeds, diatoms, and spirogyra. [C16: from Latin, plural of *alga* seaweed, of uncertain origin] ▸ **algal** ('ælgəl) *adj*
algarroba *or* **algaroba** (ˌælgə'rəʊbə) *n* **1** another name for **mesquite** or **carob. 2** the edible pod of these trees. [C19: from Spanish, from Arabic *al* the + *kharrūbah* CAROB]
Algarve (æl'gɑːv) *n* **the.** an area in the south of Portugal, on the Atlantic; it approximately corresponds to the administrative district of Faro: fishing and tourism important.
algebra ('ældʒɪbrə) *n* **1** a branch of mathematics in which arithmetical operations and relationships are generalized by using alphabetic symbols to represent unknown numbers or members of specified sets of numbers. **2** any abstract calculus, a formal language in which functions and operations can be defined and their properties studied. Thus the **algebra of clauses** is another name for **set theory,** and the **algebra of logic** for **formal logic.** [C14: from Medieval Latin, from Arabic *al-jabr* the bone-setting, reunification, mathematical reduction] ▸ **algebraist** (ˌældʒɪ'breɪɪst) *n*
algebraic (ˌældʒɪ'breɪɪk) *or* **algebraical** *adj* **1** of or relating to algebra: *an algebraic expression.* **2** using or relating to finite numbers, operations, or relationships. ▸ ˌ**alge'braically** *adv*
algebraic function *n Maths.* any function which can be constructed in a finite number of steps from the elementary operations and the inverses of any function already constructed. Compare **transcendental function.**
algebraic notation *n Chess.* the standard method of denoting the squares on the chessboard, by allotting a letter, a, b, c, up to h, to each of the files running up the board from White's side, starting from the left, and a number to each of the ranks across the board, starting with White's first rank.
algebraic number *n* any number that is a root of a polynominal equation having rational coefficients such as $\sqrt{2}$ but not π. Compare **transcendental number.**
Algeciras (ˌældʒɪ'sɪrəs; *Spanish* alxe'θiras) *n* a port and resort in SW Spain, on the Strait of Gibraltar: scene of a conference of the Great Powers in 1906. Pop.: 104 216 (1995 est.).
Alger ('ældʒə) *n* **Horatio.** 1834–99, U.S. author of adventure stories for boys, including *Ragged Dick* (1867).
Algeria (æl'dʒɪərɪə) *n* a republic in NW Africa, on the Mediterranean: became independent in 1962, after more than a century of French rule; one-party constitution adopted in 1976; religious extremists began a campaign of violence in 1988; consists chiefly of the N Sahara, with the Atlas Mountains in the north, and contains rich deposits of oil and natural gas. Official language: Arabic; French also widely spoken, and Berber. Religion: Muslim. Currency: dinar. Capital: Algiers. Pop.: 30 045 000 (1998 est.). Area: about 2 382 800 sq. km (920 000 sq. miles). French name: **Algérie** (alʒeri). ▸ **Al'gerian** *or* **Algerine** ('ældʒəˌriːn) *adj, n*
algerine (ˌældʒə'riːn) *n* a soft striped woollen cloth. [C19: from French, from *algérien* Algerian: because the cloth was originally made in Algeria]
algesia (æl'dʒiːzɪə, -sɪə) *n Physiol.* the capacity to feel pain. [New Latin from Greek *algēsis* sense of pain] ▸ **al'gesic** *or* **al'getic** *adj*
-algia *n combining form.* denoting pain or a painful condition of the part specified: *neuralgia; odontalgia.* [from Greek *algos* pain] ▸ **-algic** *adj combining form.*
algicide ('ældʒɪˌsaɪd) *n* any substance that kills algae.
algid ('ældʒɪd) *adj Med.* chilly or cold. [C17: from Latin *algidus,* from *algēre* to be cold] ▸ **al'gidity** *n*
Algiers (æl'dʒɪəz) *n* the capital of Algeria, an ancient port on the Mediterranean; up to 1830 a centre of piracy. Pop.: 2 168 000 (1995 est.). Arabic name: **Al-Jezair** (ˌældʒɛ'zɑːɪə). French name: **Alger** (alʒe).
algin ('ældʒɪn) *n* alginic acid or one of its esters or salts, esp. the gelatinous solution obtained as a by-product in the extraction of iodine from seaweed, used in mucilages and for thickening jellies.
alginate ('ældʒɪˌneɪt) *n* a salt or ester of alginic acid.
alginic acid (æl'dʒɪnɪk) *n* a white or yellowish powdery polysaccharide having marked hydrophilic properties. Extracted from kelp, it is used mainly in the food and textile industries and in cosmetics and pharmaceuticals. Formula: $(C_6H_8O_6)_n$; molecular wt.: 32 000–250 000.
algo- *combining form.* denoting pain: *algometer; algophobia.* [from Greek *algos* pain]
algoid ('ælgɔɪd) *adj* resembling or relating to algae.
Algol[1] ('ælgɒl) *n* the second brightest star in Perseus, the first known eclipsing binary. Visual magnitude: 2.2–3.5; period: 68.8 hours; spectral type (brighter component): B8. [C14: from Arabic *al ghūl* the GHOUL]
Algol[2] ('ælgɒl) *n* a computer programming language designed for mathematical and scientific purposes; a high-level language. [C20 *alg(orithmic) o(riented) l(anguage)*]
algolagnia (ˌælgə'lægnɪə) *n* a perversion in which sexual pleasure is gained from the experience or infliction of pain. See also **sadism, masochism.** ▸ ˌ**algo'lagnic** *adj* ▸ ˌ**algo'lagnist** *n*
algology (æl'gɒlədʒɪ) *n* the branch of biology concerned with the study of algae. ▸ **algological** (ˌælgə'lɒdʒɪkᵊl) *adj* ▸ ˌ**algo'logically** *adv* ▸ **al'gologist** *n*
algometer (æl'gɒmɪtə) *n* an instrument for measuring sensitivity to pressure (**pressure algometer**) or to pain. ▸ **al'gometry** *n*
Algonkian (æl'gɒŋkɪən) *n, adj* **1** an obsolete term for **Proterozoic. 2** a variant of **Algonquian.**
Algonquian (æl'gɒŋkɪən, -kwɪ-) *or* **Algonkian** *n* **1** a family of North American Indian languages whose speakers ranged over an area stretching from the Atlantic between Newfoundland and Delaware to the Rocky Mountains, including Micmac, Mahican, Ojibwa, Fox, Blackfoot, Cheyenne, and Shawnee. Some linguists relate it to Muskogean in a Macro-Algonquian phylum. **2** (*pl* **-ans** *or* **-an**) a member of any of the North American Indian peoples that speak one of these languages. ◆ *adj* **3** denoting, belonging to, or relating to this linguistic family or its speakers.
Algonquin (æl'gɒŋkɪn, -kwɪn) *or* **Algonkin** (æl'gɒŋkɪn) *n* **1** (*pl* **-quins, -quin** *or* **-kins, -kin**) a member of a North American Indian people formerly living along the St Lawrence and Ottawa Rivers in Canada. **2** the language of this people, a dialect of Ojibwa. ◆ *n, adj* **3** a variant of **Algonquian.** [C17: from Canadian French, earlier written as *Algoumequin;* perhaps related to Micmac *algoomaking* at the fish-spearing place]
Algonquin Park *n* a provincial park in S Canada, in E Ontario, containing over 1200 lakes. Area: 7100 sq. km (2741 sq. miles).
algophobia (ˌælgə'fəʊbɪə) *n Psychiatry.* an acute fear of experiencing or witnessing bodily pain.
algor ('ælgɔː) *n Med.* chill. [C15: from Latin]
algorism ('ælgəˌrɪzəm) *n* **1** the Arabic or decimal system of counting. **2** the skill of computation using any system of numerals. **3** another name for **algorithm.** [C13: from Old French *algorisme,* from Medieval Latin *algorismus,* from Arabic *al-khuwārizmi,* from the name of abu-Ja'far Mohammed ibn-Mūsa *al-Khuwārizmi,* ninth-century Persian mathematician] ▸ ˌ**algo'rismic** *adj*
algorithm ('ælgəˌrɪðəm) *n* **1** a logical arithmetical or computational procedure that if correctly applied ensures the solution of a problem. Compare **heuristic. 2** *Logic, maths.* a recursive procedure whereby an infinite sequence of terms can be generated. ◆ Also called: **algorism.** [C17: changed from ALGORISM, through influence of Greek *arithmos* number] ▸ ˌ**algo'rithmic** *adj* ▸ ˌ**algo'rithmically** *adv*
Algren ('ɔːlgrən) *n* **Nelson.** 1909–81, U.S. novelist. His novels, mostly set in Chicago, include *Never Come Morning* (1942) and *The Man with the Golden Arm* (1949).
Alhambra (æl'hæmbrə) *n* a citadel and palace in Granada, Spain, built for the Moorish kings during the 13th and 14th centuries: noted for its rich ornamentation. ▸ **Alhambresque** (ˌælhæm'brɛsk) *adj*
Al Hijrah *or* **Al Hijra** (æl 'hɪdʒrə) *n* an annual Muslim festival marking the beginning of the Muslim year. It commemorates Mohammed's move from Mecca to Medina and involves the exchange of gifts and the telling of stories about Mohammed. See also **Hegira.** [from Arabic, *hijrah* emigration or flight]
Al Hufuf *or* **Al Hofuf** (æl hu'fuːf) *n* a town in E Saudi Arabia: a trading centre with nearby oilfields and oases. Pop.: 102 000 (latest est.).
Ali ('ɑːliː) *n* **1** ?600–661 A.D., fourth caliph of Islam (656–61 A.D.), considered the first caliph by the Shiites: cousin and son-in-law of Mohammed. **2 Mehemet.** See **Mehemet Ali. 3 Muhammad.** See **Muhammad Ali.**
alias ('eɪlɪəs) *adv* **1** at another time or place known as or named: *Dylan, alias Zimmerman.* ◆ *n, pl* **-ases. 2** an assumed name. [C16: from Latin *aliās* (adv) otherwise, at another time, from *alius* other]
aliasing ('eɪlɪəsɪŋ) *n Radio, television.* the error in a vision or sound signal arising from limitations in the system that generates or processes the signal.
Ali Baba ('ælɪ 'bɑːbə) *n* (in *The Arabian Nights' Entertainments*) a poor woodcutter who discovers that the magic words "open sesame" will open the doors of the cave containing the treasure of the Forty Thieves.
alibi ('ælɪˌbaɪ) *n, pl* **-bis. 1** *Law.* **1a** a defence by an accused person that he was elsewhere at the time the crime in question was committed. **1b** the evidence

given to prove this. **2** *Informal.* an excuse. ◆ *vb* **3** (*tr*) to provide with an alibi. [C18: from Latin *alibī* elsewhere, from *alius* other + *-bī* as in *ubī* where]

Alicante (ˌælɪ'kæntɪ) *n* a port in SE Spain: commercial centre. Pop.: 276 526 (1995 est.).

Alice ('ælɪs) *or* **the Alice** *n Austral. slang.* short for **Alice Springs.**

Alice band *n* an ornamental band worn across the front of the hair to hold it back from the face.

Alice-in-Wonderland *adj* fantastic; irrational. [C20: alluding to the absurdities of Wonderland in Lewis Carroll's book]

Alice Springs *n* a town in central Australia, in the Northern Territory, in the Macdonnell Ranges. Pop.: 24 852 (1994). Former name (until 1931): **Stuart.**

alicyclic (ˌælɪ'saɪklɪk, -'sɪk-) *adj* (of an organic compound) having aliphatic properties, in spite of the presence of a ring of carbon atoms. [C19: from German *alicyclisch,* from ALI(PHATIC) + CYCLIC]

alidade ('ælɪˌdeɪd) *or* **alidad** ('ælɪˌdæd) *n* **1** a surveying instrument used in plane-tabling for drawing lines of sight on a distant object and taking angular measurements. **2** the upper rotatable part of a theodolite, including the telescope and its attachments. [C15: from French, from Medieval Latin *allidada,* from Arabic *al-'idāda* the revolving radius of a circle]

alien ('eɪljən, 'eɪlɪən) *n* **1** a person owing allegiance to a country other than that in which he lives; foreigner. **2** any being or thing foreign to the environment in which it now exists. **3** (in science fiction) a being from another world, sometimes specifically an extraterrestrial. ◆ *adj* **4** unnaturalized; foreign. **5** having foreign allegiance: *alien territory.* **6** unfamiliar; strange: *an alien quality in a work of art.* **7** (*postpositive* and foll. by *to*) repugnant or opposed (to): *war is alien to his philosophy.* **8** (in science fiction) of or from another world. ◆ *vb* **9** (*tr*) *Rare.* to transfer (property, etc.) to another. [C14: from Latin *aliēnus* foreign, from *alius* other] ► **alienage** ('eɪljənɪdʒ, 'eɪlɪə-) *n*

alienable ('eɪljənəbəl, 'eɪlɪə-) *adj Law.* (of property) transferable to another owner. ► **ˌaliena'bility** *n*

alienate ('eɪljəˌneɪt, 'eɪlɪə-) *vb* (*tr*) **1** to cause (a friend, sympathizer, etc.) to become indifferent, unfriendly, or hostile; estrange. **2** to turn away; divert: *to alienate the affections of a person.* **3** *Law.* to transfer the ownership of (property, title, etc.) to another person. ► **'alienˌator** *n*

alienation (ˌeɪljə'neɪʃən, ˌeɪlɪə-) *n* **1** a turning away; estrangement. **2** the state of being an outsider or the feeling of being isolated, as from society. **3** *Psychiatry.* a state in which a person's feelings are inhibited so that eventually both the self and the external world seem unreal. **4** *Law.* **4a** the transfer of property, as by conveyance or will, into the ownership of another. **4b** the right of an owner to dispose of his property.

alienee (ˌeɪljə'niː, ˌeɪlɪə-) *n Law.* a person to whom a transfer of property is made.

alienism ('eɪljəˌnɪzəm, 'eɪlɪə-) *n Obsolete.* the study and treatment of mental illness.

alienist ('eɪljənɪst, 'eɪlɪə-) *n* **1** *U.S.* a psychiatrist who specializes in the legal aspects of mental illness. **2** *Obsolete.* a person who practises alienism.

alienor ('eɪljənə, 'eɪlɪə-) *n Law.* a person who transfers property to another.

aliform ('ælɪˌfɔːm, 'eɪlɪ-) *adj* wing-shaped; alar. [C19: from New Latin *āliformis,* from Latin *āla* a wing]

Aligarh (ˌɑːlɪ'gɜː, ˌælɪ-) *n* a city in N India, in W Uttar Pradesh, with a famous Muslim university (1920). Pop.: 480 520 (1991).

alight[1] (ə'laɪt) *vb* **alights, alighting, alighted** *or* **alit.** (*intr*) **1** (usually foll. by *from*) to step out (of) or get down (from): *to alight from a taxi.* **2** to come to rest; settle; land: *a thrush alighted on the wall.* [Old English *ālīhtan,* from A-[2] + *līhtan* to make less heavy, from *līht* LIGHT[2]]

alight[2] (ə'laɪt) *adj* (*postpositive*), *adv* **1** burning; on fire. **2** illuminated; lit up. [Old English *ālīht* lit up, from *ālīhtan* to light up; see LIGHT[1]]

alighting gear *n* another name for **undercarriage** (sense 1).

align (ə'laɪn) *vb* **1** to place or become placed in a line. **2** to bring (components or parts, such as the wheels of a car) into proper or desirable coordination or relation. **3** (*tr;* usually foll. by *with*) to bring (a person, country, etc.) into agreement or cooperation with the policy, etc. of another person or group. [C17: from Old French *aligner,* from *à ligne* into line]

alignment (ə'laɪnmənt) *n* **1** arrangement in a straight line. **2** the line or lines formed in this manner. **3** alliance or union with a party, cause, etc. **4** proper or desirable coordination or relation of components. **5** a ground plan of a railway, motor road, etc. **6** *Archaeol.* an arrangement of one or more ancient rows of standing stones, of uncertain significance.

alike (ə'laɪk) *adj* (*postpositive*) **1** possessing the same or similar characteristics: *they all look alike to me.* ◆ *adv* **2** in the same or a similar manner, way, or degree: *they walk alike.* [Old English *gelīc;* see LIKE[1]]

aliment *n* ('ælɪmənt). **1** something that nourishes or sustains the body or mind. **2** *Scots. Law.* another term for **alimony.** ◆ *vb* ('ælɪˌmɛnt). **3** (*tr*) *Obsolete.* to support or sustain. [C15: from Latin *alimentum* food, from *alere* to nourish] ► **ˌali'mental** *adj*

alimentary (ˌælɪ'mɛntərɪ, -trɪ) *adj* **1** of or relating to nutrition. **2** providing sustenance or nourishment. **3** *Scots. Law.* free from the claims of creditors: *an alimentary trust.*

alimentary canal *n* the tubular passage extending from the mouth to the anus, through which food is passed and digested.

alimentation (ˌælɪmɛn'teɪʃən) *n* **1** nourishment. **2** sustenance; support. ► **ˌali'mentative** *adj*

alimony ('ælɪmənɪ) *n Law.* (formerly) an allowance paid under a court order by one spouse to another when they are separated but not divorced. See also **maintenance.** [C17: from Latin *alimōnia* sustenance, from *alere* to nourish]

aline (ə'laɪn) *vb* a rare spelling of **align.** ► **a'linement** *n* ► **a'liner** *n*

A-line *adj* (of a garment, esp. a skirt or dress) flaring slightly from the waist or shoulders.

Ali Pasha ('ɑːliː 'pɑːʃə) *n* known as *the Lion of Janina.* 1741–1822, Turkish pasha and ruler of Albania (1787–1820), who was deposed and assassinated after intriguing against Turkey.

aliped ('ælɪˌpɛd) *adj* **1** (of bats and similar animals) having the digits connected by a winglike membrane. ◆ *n* **2** an aliped animal. [C19: from Latin *ālipēs* having winged feet, from *āla* wing + -PED]

aliphatic (ˌælɪ'fætɪk) *adj* (of an organic compound) not aromatic, esp. having an open chain structure, such as alkanes, alkenes, and alkynes. [C19: from Greek *aleiphat-, aleiphar* oil]

aliquant ('ælɪkwənt) *adj Maths.* of, signifying, or relating to a quantity or number that is not an exact divisor of a given quantity or number: *5 is an aliquant part of 12.* Compare **aliquot** (sense 1). [C17: from New Latin, from Latin *aliquantus* somewhat, a certain quantity of]

aliquot ('ælɪˌkwɒt) *adj* **1** *Maths.* of, signifying, or relating to an exact divisor of a quantity or number: *3 is an aliquot part of 12.* Compare **aliquant. 2** consisting of equal quantities: *the sample was divided into five aliquot parts.* ◆ *n* **3** an aliquot part. [C16: from Latin: several, a few]

alison ('ælɪsən) *n* **1** **sweet alison.** another name for **sweet alyssum. 2 small alison.** a rare compact cruciferous annual, *Alyssum alyssoides,* having small yellow flowers. [altered from ALYSSUM]

A list *n* **a** the most socially desirable category. **b** (*as modifier*): *an A-list event.* ◆ Compare **B list.**

alit (ə'lɪt) *vb* a rare past tense and past participle of **alight**[1].

aliterate (eɪ'lɪtərɪt) *n* **1** a person who is able to read but disinclined to do so. ◆ *adj* **2** of or relating to aliterates.

aliunde (ˌeɪlɪ'ʌndɪ) *adv, adj* from a source extrinsic to the matter, document, or instrument under consideration: *evidence aliunde.* [Latin: from elsewhere]

alive (ə'laɪv) *adj* (*postpositive*) **1** (of people, animals, plants, etc.) living; having life. **2** in existence; active: *they kept hope alive; the tradition was still alive.* **3** (*immediately postpositive and usually used with a superlative*) of those living; now living: *the happiest woman alive.* **4** full of life; lively: *she was wonderfully alive for her age.* **5** (usually foll. by *with*) animated: *a face alive with emotion.* **6** (foll. by *to*) aware (of); sensitive (to). **7** (foll. by *with*) teeming (with): *the mattress was alive with fleas.* **8** *Electronics.* another word for **live**[2] (sense 11). **9 alive and kicking.** (of a person) active and in good health. **10 look alive!** hurry up! get busy! [Old English *on līfe* in LIFE] ► **a'liveness** *n*

aliyah *n Judaism.* **1** (ali'ja). (*pl* **-yoth** (-'jɒt)) immigration to the Holy Land. **2** (ə'liːə). the honour of being called to read from the Torah. [from Hebrew, literally: act of going up, ascent]

alizarin (ə'lɪzərɪn) *n* a brownish-yellow powder or orange-red crystalline solid used as a dye and in the manufacture of other dyes. Formula: $C_6H_4(CO)_2C_6H_2(OH)_2$. [C19: probably from French *alizarine,* probably from Arabic *al-'asārah* the juice, from *'asara* to squeeze]

alk. *abbrev. for* alkali.

alkahest *or* **alcahest** ('ælkəˌhɛst) *n* the hypothetical universal solvent sought by alchemists. [C17: apparently coined by Paracelsus on the model of Arabic words]

alkali ('ælkəˌlaɪ) *n, pl* **-lis** *or* **-lies. 1** *Chemistry.* a soluble base or a solution of a base. **2** a soluble mineral salt that occurs in arid soils and some natural waters. [C14: from Medieval Latin, from Arabic *al-qili* the ashes (of the plant saltwort)]

alkalic (æl'kælɪk) *adj* **1** (of igneous rocks) containing large amounts of alkalis, esp. caustic soda and caustic potash. **2** another word for **alkaline.**

alkali flat *n* an arid plain encrusted with alkaline salts derived from the streams draining into it.

alkalify ('ælkəlɪˌfaɪ, æl'kæl-) *vb* **-fies, -fying, -fied.** to make or become alkaline.

alkali metal *n* any of the monovalent metals lithium, sodium, potassium, rubidium, caesium, and francium, belonging to group 1A of the periodic table. They are all very reactive and electropositive.

alkalimeter (ˌælkə'lɪmɪtə) *n* **1** an apparatus for determining the concentration of alkalis in solution. **2** an apparatus for determining the quantity of carbon dioxide in carbonates. ► **alkalimetric** (ˌælkəlɪ'mɛtrɪk) *adj*

alkalimetry (ˌælkə'lɪmɪtrɪ) *n* determination of the amount of alkali or base in a solution, measured by an alkalimeter or by volumetric analysis.

alkaline ('ælkəˌlaɪn) *adj* having the properties of or containing an alkali.

alkaline earth *n* **1** Also called: **alkaline earth metal** *or* **alkaline earth element.** any of the divalent electropositive metals beryllium, magnesium, calcium, strontium, barium, and radium, belonging to group 2A of the periodic table. **2** an oxide of one of the alkaline earth metals.

alkalinity (ˌælkə'lɪnɪtɪ) *n* **1** the quality or state of being alkaline. **2** the amount of alkali or base in a solution, often expressed in terms of pH.

alkali soil *n* a soil that gives a pH reaction of 8.5 or above, found esp. in dry areas where the soluble salts, esp. of sodium, have not been leached away but have accumulated in the B horizon of the soil profile.

alkalize *or* **alkalise** ('ælkəˌlaɪz) *vb* (*tr*) to make alkaline. ► **'alkaˌlizable** *or* **'alkaˌlisable** *adj*

alkaloid ('ælkəˌlɔɪd) *n* any of a group of nitrogenous basic compounds found in plants, typically insoluble in water and physiologically active. Common examples are morphine, strychnine, and quinine.

alkalosis (ˌælkə'ləʊsɪs) *n* an abnormal increase in alkalinity of the blood and extracellular fluids.

alkane ('ælkeɪn) *n* **a** any saturated aliphatic hydrocarbon with the general formula C_nH_{2n+2}. **b** (*as modifier*): *alkane series.* ◆ Also called: **paraffin.**

alkanet ('ælkəˌnɛt) *n* **1** a European boraginaceous plant, *Alkanna tinctoria,* the roots of which yield a red dye. **2** Also called: **anchusin, alkannin.** the dye obtained from this plant. **3** any of certain hairy blue-flowered Old World plants of the boraginaceous genus *Anchusa* (or *Pentaglottis*), such as *A. sempervirens* of Europe. See also **bugloss. 4** another name for **puccoon** (sense 1). [C14: from

Spanish *alcaneta,* diminutive of *alcana* henna, from Medieval Latin *alchanna,* from Arabic *al* the + *hinnā'* henna]

alkene ('ælkiːn) *n* **a** any unsaturated aliphatic hydrocarbon with the general formula C_nH_{2n}. **b** (*as modifier*): *alkene series.* ◆ Also called: **olefine.**

Alkmaar (*Dutch* 'alkmaːr) *n* a city in the W Netherlands, in North Holland. Pop.: 92 962 (1994).

Alkoran *or* **Alcoran** (ˌælkɒ'rɑːn) *n* a less common name for the **Koran.**

alky *or* **alkie** ('ælkɪ) *n, pl* **-kies.** *Slang.* a heavy drinker or alcoholic.

alkyd resin ('ælkɪd) *n* any synthetic resin made from a dicarboxylic acid, such as phthalic acid, and diols or triols: used in paints and adhesives.

alkyl ('ælkɪl) *n* **1** (*modifier*) of, consisting of, or containing the monovalent group C_nH_{2n+1}: *alkyl group or radical.* **2** an organometallic compound, such as tetraethyl lead, containing an alkyl group bound to a metal atom. [C19: from German, from *Alk(ohol)* ALCOHOL + -YL]

alkylating agent ('ælkɪˌleɪtɪŋ) *n* any cytotoxic drug containing alkyl groups that acts by damaging DNA; widely used in chemotherapy.

alkylation (ˌælkɪ'leɪʃən) *n* **1** the replacement of a hydrogen atom in an organic compound by an alkyl group. **2** the addition of an alkane hydrocarbon to an alkene in producing high-octane fuels.

alkyne ('ælkaɪn) *n* **a** any unsaturated aliphatic hydrocarbon that has a formula of the type C_nH_{2n-2}. **b** (*as modifier*): *alkyne series.* ◆ Also called: **acetylene.**

all (ɔːl) *determiner* **1a** the whole quantity or amount of; totality of; every one of a class: *all the rice; all men are mortal.* **1b** (*as pronoun; functioning as sing or pl*): *all of it is nice; all are welcome.* **1c** (*in combination with a noun used as a modifier*): *an all-ticket match; an all-amateur tournament; an all-night sitting.* **2** the greatest possible: *in all earnestness.* **3** any whatever: *to lose all hope of recovery; beyond all doubt.* **4 above all.** most of all; especially. **5 after all.** see **after** (sense 11). **6 all along.** all the time. **7 all but.** almost; nearly: *all but dead.* **8 all of.** no less or smaller than: *she's all of thirteen years.* **9 all over. 9a** finished; at an end: *the affair is all over between us.* **9b** over the whole area (of something); everywhere (in, on, etc.): *all over England.* **9c** Also (Irish): **all out.** typically; representatively (in the phrase **that's me (you, him, us, them,** *etc.*) **all over**). **9d** unduly effusive towards. **9e** *Sports.* in a dominant position over. **10** See **all in. 11 all in all. 11a** everything considered: *all in all, it was a great success.* **11b** the object of one's attention or interest: *you are my all in all.* **12 all that.** Also: **that.** (*usually used with a negative*) *Informal.* (intensifier): *she's not all that intelligent.* **13 all the.** (foll. by a comparative adjective or adverb) so much (more or less) than otherwise: *we must work all the faster now.* **14 all too.** definitely but regrettably: *it's all too true.* **15 and all.** *Brit. informal.* as well; too: *and you can take that smile off your face and all.* **16 and all that.** *Informal.* **16a** and similar or associated things; et cetera: *coffee, tea, and all that will be served in the garden.* **16b** used as a filler or to make what precedes more vague: in this sense, it often occurs with concessive force: *she was sweet and pretty and all that, but I still didn't like her.* **16c** See **that** (sense 4). **17 as all that.** as one might expect or hope: *she's not as pretty as all that, but she has personality.* **18 at all. 18a** (*used with a negative or in a question*) in any way whatsoever or to any extent or degree: *I didn't know that at all.* **18b** even so; anyway: *I'm surprised you came at all.* **19 be all for.** *Informal.* to be strongly in favour of. **20 for all. 20a** in so far as; to the extent that: *for all anyone knows, he was a baron.* **20b** notwithstanding: *for all my pushing, I still couldn't move it.* **21 for all that.** in spite of that: *he was a nice man for all that.* **22 in all.** altogether: *there were five of them in all.* ◆ *adv* **23** (in scores of games) apiece; each: *the score at half time was three all.* ◆ *n* **24** (preceded by *my, your, his,* etc.) (one's) complete effort or interest: *to give your all; you are my all.* **25** totality or whole. ◆ Related prefixes: **pan-, panto-.** [Old English *eall;* related to Old High German *al,* Old Norse *allr,* Gothic *alls* all]

all- *combining form.* a variant of **allo-** before a vowel.

alla breve ('ælə 'breɪvɪ; *Italian* 'alla 'breːve) *n* **1** a musical time signature indicating two or four minims to a bar. ◆ *adj, adv* **2** twice as fast as normal. Musical symbol: ¢ [C19: Italian, literally: (according) to the breve]

Allah ('ælə) *n Islam.* the Muslim name for God; the one Supreme Being. [C16: from Arabic, from *al* the + *Ilāh* god; compare Hebrew *elōah*]

Allahabad (ˌæləhə'bæd, -'bɑːd) *n* a city in N India, in SE Uttar Pradesh at the confluence of the Ganges and Jumna Rivers: Hindu pilgrimage centre. Pop.: 792 858 (1991).

Allahu Akbar ('æləˌhu 'akˌbaː) *interj Islam.* an exclamation used in the call to prayer and also used as a call to the defence of Muslims, an expression of approval, and a funeral litany. [from Arabic, literally: God is most great]

all-American *adj U.S.* **1** representative of the whole of the United States. **2** composed exclusively of American members. **3** (of a person) typically American: *the company looks for all-American clean-cut college students.*

Allan-a-Dale (ˌælənə'deɪl) *n* (in English balladry) a member of Robin Hood's band who saved his sweetheart from an enforced marriage and married her himself.

allanite ('æləˌnaɪt) *n* a rare black or brown mineral consisting of the hydrated silicate of calcium, aluminium, iron, cerium, lanthanum, and other rare earth minerals. It occurs in granites and other igneous rocks. Formula: $(Ca,Ce,La,Na)_2(Al,Fe,Be,Mn,Mg)_3(SiO_4)_3(OH)$. [C19: named after T. *Allan* (1777–1833), English mineralogist]

allantoid (ə'læntɔɪd) *adj* **1** relating to or resembling the allantois. **2** *Botany.* shaped like a sausage. ◆ *n* **3** another name for **allantois.** [C17: from Greek *allantoeidēs* sausage-shaped, from *allas* sausage + -OID] ▸ **allantoidal** (ˌælən'tɔɪdᵊl) *adj*

allantois (ˌælən'təʊɪs, ə'læntɔɪs) *n* a membranous sac growing out of the ventral surface of the hind gut of embryonic reptiles, birds, and mammals. It combines with the chorion to form the mammalian placenta. [C17: New Latin, irregularly from Greek *allantoeidēs* sausage-shaped, ALLANTOID] ▸ **allantoic** (ˌælən'təʊɪk) *adj*

alla prima ('ɑːlɑː 'priːmə) *adj* (of a painting) painted with a single layer of paint, in contrast to paintings built up layer by layer. [C19: from Italian: at once]

allargando (ˌɑːlɑː'gændəʊ). *adj, adv Music.* (to be performed) with increasing slowness. [Italian, from *allargare* to make slow or broad]

all-around *adj* (*prenominal*) the U.S. equivalent of **all-round.**

allay (ə'leɪ) *vb* **1** to relieve (pain, grief, etc.) or be relieved. **2** (*tr*) to reduce (fear, anger, etc.). [Old English *ālecgan* to put down, from *lecgan* to LAY¹]

All Blacks *pl n* **the.** the international Rugby Union football team of New Zealand. [so named because of the players' black playing strip]

all clear *n* **1** a signal, usually a siren, indicating that some danger, such as an air raid, is over. **2** an indication that obstacles are no longer present; permission to proceed: *he received the all clear on the plan.*

all-dayer (ˌɔːl'deɪə) *n* an entertainment, such as a pop concert or film screening, that lasts all day.

allegation (ˌælɪ'geɪʃən) *n* **1** the act of alleging. **2** an unproved statement or assertion, esp. one in an accusation.

allege (ə'lɛdʒ) *vb* (*tr; may take a clause as object*) **1** to declare in or as if in a court of law; state without or before proof: *he alleged malpractice.* **2** to put forward (an argument or plea) for or against an accusation, claim, etc. **3** *Archaic.* to cite or quote, as to confirm. [C14 *aleggen,* ultimately from Latin *allēgāre* to dispatch on a mission, from *lēx* law]

alleged (ə'lɛdʒd) *adj* (*prenominal*) **1** stated or described to be such; presumed: *the alleged murderer.* **2** dubious: *an alleged miracle.* ▸ **allegedly** (ə'lɛdʒɪdlɪ) *adv*

Allegheny Mountains (ˌælɪ'geɪnɪ) *or* **Alleghenies** *pl n* a mountain range in Pennsylvania, Maryland, Virginia, and West Virginia: part of the Appalachian system; rising from 600 m (2000 ft.) to over 1440 m (4800 ft.).

allegiance (ə'liːdʒəns) *n* **1** loyalty, as of a subject to his sovereign or of a citizen to his country. **2** (in feudal society) the obligations of a vassal to his liege lord. See also **fealty, homage** (sense 2). [C14: from Old French *ligeance,* from *lige* LIEGE]

allegorical (ˌælɪ'gɒrɪkᵊl) *or* **allegoric** *adj* used in, containing, or characteristic of allegory. ▸ ˌ**alle'gorically** *adv*

allegorize *or* **allegorise** ('ælɪgəˌraɪz) *vb* **1** to transform (a story, narrative, fable, etc.) into or compose in the form of allegory. **2** (*tr*) to interpret allegorically. ▸ ˌ**allegori'zation** *or* ˌ**allegori'sation** *n*

allegory ('ælɪgərɪ) *n, pl* **-ries. 1** a poem, play, picture, etc., in which the apparent meaning of the characters and events is used to symbolize a deeper moral or spiritual meaning. **2** the technique or genre that this represents. **3** use of such symbolism to illustrate truth or a moral. **4** anything used as a symbol or emblem. [C14: from Old French *allegorie,* from Latin *allēgoria,* from Greek, from *allēgorein* to speak figuratively, from *allos* other + *agoreuein* to make a speech in public, from *agora* a public gathering] ▸ **'allegorist** *n*

allegretto (ˌælɪ'grɛtəʊ) *Music.* ◆ *adj, adv* **1** (to be performed) fairly quickly or briskly. ◆ *n, pl* **-tos. 2** a piece or passage to be performed in this manner. [C19: diminutive of ALLEGRO]

Allegri (*Italian* al'legri) *n* **Gregorio.** 1582–1652, Italian composer and singer. His compositions include a *Miserere* for nine voices.

allegro (ə'leɪgrəʊ, -'lɛg-) *Music.* ◆ *adj, adv* **1** (to be performed) quickly, in a brisk lively manner. ◆ *n, pl* **-gros. 2** a piece or passage to be performed in this manner. [C17: from Italian: cheerful, from Latin *alacer* brisk, lively]

allele (ə'liːl) *n* any of two or more genes that have the same relative position on homologous chromosomes and are responsible for alternative characteristics, such as smooth or wrinkled seeds in peas. Also called: **allelomorph** (ə'liːləˌmɔːf). See also **multiple alleles.** [C20: from German *Allel,* shortened from *allelomorph,* from Greek *allēl-* one another + *morphē* form] ▸ **al'lelic** *adj* ▸ **al'lelism** *n*

allelopathy (ˌælɪ'lɒpəθɪ) *n* the effect of one living plant upon another, either harmful, as by exuding toxic substances, or beneficial, as by assisting the intake of nutrients. [from French *allélopathie,* from Greek *allēl-* one another + *pathos* suffering]

alleluia (ˌælɪ'luːjə) *interj* **1** praise the Lord! Used more commonly in liturgical contexts in place of *hallelujah.* ◆ *n* **2** a song of praise to God. [C14: via Medieval Latin from Hebrew *hallelūyāh*]

allemande ('ælɪmænd; *French* almɑ̃d) *n* **1** the first movement of the classical suite, composed in a moderate tempo in a time signature of four-four. **2** any of several German dances. **3** a figure in country dancing or square dancing by means of which couples change position in the set. [C17: from French *danse allemande* German dance]

Allen¹ ('ælən) *n* **1 Bog of.** a region of peat bogs in central Ireland, west of Dublin. Area: over 10 sq. km (3.75 sq. miles). **2 Lough.** a lake in Ireland, in county Leitrim.

Allen² ('ælən) *n* **1 Ethan.** 1738–89, American soldier during the War of Independence who led the Green Mountain Boys of Vermont. **2 Woody.** real name *Allen Stewart Konigsberg.* born 1935, U.S. film comedian, screenwriter, and director. His films as an actor and director include *Annie Hall* (1977), *Manhattan* (1979), *Hannah and Her Sisters* (1986), and *Celebrity* (1998).

Allenby ('ælənbɪ) *n* **Edmund Henry Hynman,** 1st Viscount. 1861–1936, British field marshal who captured Palestine and Syria from the Turks in 1918; high commissioner in Egypt (1919–25).

Allende (*Spanish* a'ʎende) *n* **1 Isabel.** born 1942, Chilean writer, born in Peru; her works include *Eva Luna* (1989). **2 Salvador** (salβa'ðor). 1908–73, Chilean Marxist politician; president of Chile from 1970 until 1973, when the army seized power and he was killed.

Allen key *n* an L-shaped tool consisting of a rod having a hexagonal cross section, used to turn a screw (**Allen screw**) with a hexagonal recess in the head. A different size of key is required for each size of screw.

Allentown ('ælən,taʊn) *n* a city in E Pennsylvania, on the Lehigh River. Pop.: 102 211 (1996 est.).
Alleppey ('ʌləpɪ) *n* a port in S India, in Kerala on the Malabar Coast. Pop.: 174 666 (1991).
allergen ('ælə,dʒɛn) *n* any substance, usually a protein, capable of inducing an allergy. ▸ **,aller'genic** *adj*
allergic (ə'lɜːdʒɪk) *adj* **1** of, relating to, having, or caused by an allergy. **2** (*postpositive;* foll. by *to*) *Informal.* having an aversion (to): *he's allergic to work.*
allergist ('ælədʒɪst) *n* a physician skilled in the diagnosis and treatment of diseases or conditions caused by allergy.
allergy ('ælədʒɪ) *n, pl* **-gies. 1** a hypersensitivity to a substance that causes the body to react to any contact with that substance. Hay fever is an allergic reaction to pollen. **2** *Informal.* aversion: *he has an allergy to studying.* [C20: from German *Allergie* (indicating a changed reaction), from Greek *allos* other + *ergon* activity]
allethrin (æ'leθrɪn) *n* a clear viscous amber-coloured liquid used as an insecticide and synergist. Formula: $C_{19}H_{26}O_3$; relative density: 1.005. [C20: from ALL(YL) + (PYR)ETHRIN]
alleviate (ə'liːvɪ,eɪt) *vb* (*tr*) to make (pain, sorrow, etc.) easier to bear; lessen; relieve. [C15: from Late Latin *alleviāre* to mitigate, from Latin *levis* light] ▸ **al,levi'ation** *n* ▸ **al'leviative** *adj* ▸ **al'levi,ator** *n*
USAGE See at **ameliorate.**
alley[1] ('ælɪ) *n* **1** a narrow lane or passage, esp. one between or behind buildings. **2** See **bowling alley. 3** *Tennis, chiefly U.S.* the space between the singles and doubles sidelines. **4** a walk in a park or garden, esp. one lined with trees or bushes. **5 up** (*or* **down**) **one's alley.** a variant of **up one's street** (see **street** (sense 8)). [C14: from Old French *alee,* from *aler* to go, ultimately from Latin *ambulāre* to walk]
alley[2] ('ælɪ) *n* a large playing marble. [C18: shortened and changed from ALABASTER]
alley cat *n* a homeless cat that roams in back streets.
alleyway ('ælɪ,weɪ) *n* a narrow passage; alley.
all-fired *Slang, chiefly U.S.* ◆ *adj* **1** (*prenominal*) excessive; extreme. ◆ *adv* **2** (intensifier): *don't be so all-fired sure of yourself!* [altered from *hell-fired*]
all-flying tail *n* a type of aircraft tailplane in which the whole of the tailplane is moved for control purposes.
All Fools' Day *n* another name for **April Fools' Day** (see **April fool**).
all fours *n* **1** both the arms and legs of a person or all the legs of a quadruped (esp. in the phrase **on all fours**). **2** another name for **seven-up.**
all hail *interj* an archaic greeting or salutation. [C14, literally: all health (to someone)]
Allhallows (,ɔːl'hæləʊz) *n* **1** a less common term for **All Saints' Day. 2 Allhallows Eve.** a less common name for **Halloween.**
Allhallowtide (,ɔːl'hæləʊ,taɪd) *n* the season of All Saints' Day (Allhallows).
allheal ('ɔːl,hiːl) *n* any of several plants reputed to have healing powers, such as selfheal and valerian.
alliaceous (,ælɪ'eɪʃəs) *adj* **1** of or relating to *Allium,* a genus of liliaceous plants that have a strong onion or garlic smell and often have bulbs. The genus occurs in the N hemisphere and includes onion, garlic, leek, chive, and shallot. **2** tasting or smelling like garlic or onions. [C18: from Latin *allium* garlic; see -ACEOUS]
alliance (ə'laɪəns) *n* **1** the act of allying or state of being allied; union; confederation. **2** a formal agreement or pact, esp. a military one, between two or more countries to achieve a particular aim. **3** the countries involved in such an agreement. **4** a union between families through marriage. **5** affinity or correspondence in qualities or characteristics. **6** *Botany.* a taxonomic category consisting of a group of related families; subclass. [C13: from Old French *aliance,* from *alier* to ALLY]
Alliance (ə'laɪəns) *n* (in Britain) **a the.** the Social Democratic Party and the Liberal Party acting or regarded as a political entity from 1981 to 1988. **b** (*as modifier*): *an Alliance candidate.*
allied (ə'laɪd, 'ælaɪd) *adj* **1** joined, as by treaty, agreement, or marriage; united. **2** of the same type or class; related.
Allied ('ælaɪd) *adj* of or relating to the Allies.
Allier (*French* alje) *n* **1** a department of central France, in Auvergne region. Capital: Moulins. Pop.: 352 500 (1995). Area: 7382 sq. km (2879 sq. miles). **2** a river in S central France, rising in the Cévennes and flowing north to the Loire. Length: over 403 km (250 miles).
allies ('ælaɪz) *n* the plural of **ally.**
Allies ('ælaɪz) *pl n* **1** (in World War I) the powers of the Triple Entente (France, Russia, and Britain) together with the nations allied with them. **2** (in World War II) the countries that fought against the Axis. The main Allied powers were Britain and the Commonwealth countries, the U.S., the Soviet Union, France, China, and Poland. See also **Axis.**
alligator ('ælɪ,geɪtə) *n* **1** a large crocodilian, *Alligator mississipiensis,* of the southern U.S., having powerful jaws and sharp teeth and differing from the crocodiles in having a shorter and broader snout: family *Alligatoridae* (alligators and caymans). **2** a similar but smaller species, *A. sinensis,* occurring in China near the Yangtse River. **3** any crocodilian belonging to the family *Alligatoridae.* **4** any of various tools or machines having adjustable toothed jaws, used for gripping, crushing, or compacting. [C17: from Spanish *el lagarto* the lizard, from Latin *lacerta*]
alligator pear *n* another name for **avocado.**
alligator pepper *n Chiefly W African.* **1** a tropical African zingiberaceous plant, *Amomum melegueta,* having red or orange spicy seed capsules. **2** the capsules or seeds of this plant, used as a spice.
all-important *adj* crucial; vital.
all in *adj* **1** (*postpositive*) *Informal.* completely exhausted; tired out. ◆ *adv, adj* (**all-in** *when prenominal*). **2a** with all expenses or costs included in the price: *the flat is one hundred pounds a week all in.* **2b** (*prenominal*): *the all-in price is thirty pounds.*
all-inclusive *adj* including everything; comprehensive.
Allingham ('ælɪŋəm) *n* **Margery.** 1904–66, British author of detective stories, featuring Albert Campion. Her works include *Tiger in the Smoke* (1952) and *The Mind Readers* (1965).
all-in wrestling *n* another name for **freestyle** (sense 2b).
alliterate (ə'lɪtə,reɪt) *vb* **1** to contain or cause to contain alliteration. **2** (*intr*) to speak or write using alliteration.
alliteration (ə,lɪtə'reɪʃən) *n* the use of the same consonant (**consonantal alliteration**) or of a vowel, not necessarily the same vowel (**vocalic alliteration**), at the beginning of each word or each stressed syllable in a line of verse, as in *around the rock the ragged rascal ran.* [C17: from Medieval Latin *alliterātiō* (from Latin *al-* (see AD-) + *litera* letter), on the model of *obliterātiō* OBLITERATION] ▸ **al'literative** *adj*
allium ('ælɪəm) *n* any liliaceous plant of the genus *Allium,* such as the onion, garlic, shallot, leek, and chive. [C19: from Latin: garlic]
all-nighter (,ɔːl'naɪtə) *n* an entertainment, such as a pop concert or film screening, that lasts all night.
allo- *or before a vowel* **all-** *combining form.* indicating difference, variation, or opposition: *allopathy; allomorph; allophone; allonym.* [from Greek *allos* other, different]
Alloa ('æləʊə) *n* a town in E central Scotland, the administrative centre of Clackmannanshire. Pop.: 18 842 (1991).
allocate ('ælə,keɪt) *vb* (*tr*) **1** to assign or allot for a particular purpose. **2** a less common word for **locate** (sense 2). [C17: from Medieval Latin *allocāre,* from Latin *locāre* to place, from *locus* a place] ▸ **'allo,catable** *adj*
allocation (,ælə'keɪʃən) *n* **1** the act of allocating or the state of being allocated. **2** a part that is allocated; share. **3** *Accounting, Brit.* a system of dividing overhead expenses between the various departments of a business. **4** *Social welfare.* (in a Social Services Department) the process of assigning **referrals** to individual workers, thus changing their status to **cases.**
allochthonous (ə'lɒkθənəs) *adj* (of rocks, deposits, etc.) found in a place other than where they or their constituents were formed. Compare **autochthonous** (sense 1). [C20: from Greek *allokhthon,* from ALLO- + *khthōn* (genitive *khthonos*) earth]
allocution (,ælə'kjuːʃən) *n Rhetoric.* a formal or authoritative speech or address, esp. one that advises, informs, or exhorts. [C17: from Late Latin *allocūtiō,* from Latin *alloquī* to address, from *loquī* to speak]
allodial (ə'ləʊdɪəl) *adj* **1** (of land) held as an allodium. **2** (of tenure) characterized by or relating to the system of holding land in absolute ownership: *the allodial system.* **3** (of people) holding an allodium.
allodium (ə'ləʊdɪəm) *or* **allod** ('ælɒd) *n, pl* **-lodia** (-'ləʊdɪə) *or* **-lods.** *History.* lands held in absolute ownership, free from such obligations as rent or services due to an overlord. Also: **alodium.** [C17: from Medieval Latin, from Old German *allōd* (unattested) entire property, from *al-* ALL + *-ōd* property; compare Old High German *ōt,* Old English *eād* property]
allogamy (ə'lɒgəmɪ) *n* cross-fertilization in flowering plants. ▸ **al'logamous** *adj*
allograft ('æləʊ,grɑːft) *n* a tissue graft from a donor genetically unrelated to the recipient.
allograph ('ælə,grɑːf) *n* **1** a document written by a person who is not a party to it. **2** a signature made by one person on behalf of another. Compare **autograph. 3** *Linguistics.* any of the written symbols that constitute a single grapheme: m *and* M *are allographs in the Roman alphabet.* ▸ **allographic** (,ælə'græfɪk) *adj*
allomerism (ə'lɒmə,rɪzəm) *n* similarity of crystalline structure in substances of different chemical composition. ▸ **allomeric** (,ælə'mɛrɪk) *or* **al'lomerous** *adj*
allometry (ə'lɒmɪtrɪ) *n* **1** the study of the growth of part of an organism in relation to the growth of the entire organism. **2** a change in proportion of any of the parts of an organism that occurs during growth. ▸ **allometric** (,ælə'mɛtrɪk) *adj*
allomone ('ælə,məʊn) *n* a chemical substance secreted externally by certain animals, such as insects, affecting the behaviour or physiology of another species. Compare **pheromone.**
allomorph ('ælə,mɔːf) *n* **1** *Linguistics.* any of the phonological representations of a single morpheme. For example, the final (s) and (z) sounds of *bets* and *beds* are allomorphs of the English noun-plural morpheme. **2** any of two or more different crystalline forms of a chemical compound, such as a mineral. ▸ **,allo'morphic** *adj*
allomorphism (,ælə'mɔːfɪzəm) *n* variation in the crystalline form of a chemical compound.
allonym ('ælənɪm) *n* a name, often one of historical significance or that of another person, assumed by a person, esp. an author.
allopath ('ælə,pæθ) *or* **allopathist** (ə'lɒpəθɪst) *n* a person who practises or is skilled in allopathy.
allopathy (ə'lɒpəθɪ) *n* the usual method of treating disease, by inducing a condition different from the cause of the disease. Compare **homeopathy.** ▸ **allopathic** (,ælə'pæθɪk) *adj* ▸ **,allo'pathically** *adv*
allopatric (,ælə'pætrɪk) *adj* (of biological speciation or species) taking place or existing in areas that are geographically isolated from one another. Compare **sympatric.** [C20: from ALLO- + *-patric,* from Greek *patris* native land] ▸ **,allo'patrically** *adv*
allophane ('ælə,feɪn) *n* a variously coloured amorphous mineral consisting of hydrated aluminium silicate and occurring in cracks in some sedimentary rocks. [C19: from Greek *allophanēs* appearing differently, from ALLO- + *phainesthai* to appear]

allophone ('ælə,fəʊn) *n* **1** any of several speech sounds that are regarded as contextual or environmental variants of the same phoneme. In English the aspirated initial (p) in *pot* and the unaspirated (p) in *spot* are allophones of the phoneme /p/. **2** *Canadian.* a Canadian whose native language is neither French nor English. ▶ **allophonic** (,ælə'fɒnɪk) *adj*
alloplasm ('ælə,plæzəm) *n Biology.* part of the cytoplasm that is specialized to form cilia, flagella, and similar structures. ▶ **,allo'plasmic** *adj*
allopolyploid (,ælə'pɒlɪ,plɔɪd) *adj* **1** (of cells, organisms, etc.) having more than two sets of haploid chromosomes inherited from different species. ◆ *n* **2** an interspecific hybrid of this type that is therefore fertile. ◆ See also **autopolyploid, polyploid.** ▶ **,allo'poly,ploidy** *n*
allopurinol (,æləʊ'pjʊərə,nɒl) *n* a synthetic drug that reduces blood levels of uric acid and is administered orally in the treatment of gout. Formula: $C_5H_4N_4O$. [C20: from ALLO- + PURINE + -OL[1]]
All-Ordinaries Index *n* an index of share prices on the Australian Stock Exchange giving a weighted arithmetic average of 245 ordinary shares.
allosaur ('ælə,sɔː) *or* **allosaurus** (,ælə'sɔːrəs) *n* any large carnivorous bipedal dinosaur of the genus *Antrodemus* (formerly *Allosaurus*), common in North America in late Jurassic times: suborder *Theropoda* (theropods). [C19: from ALLO- + -SAUR]
allosteric (,æləʊ'stɪərɪk) *adj Biochem.* of, relating to, or designating a function of an enzyme in which the structure and activity of the enzyme are modified by the binding of a metabolic molecule.
allot (ə'lɒt) *vb* **-lots, -lotting, -lotted.** (*tr*) **1** to assign or distribute (shares, etc.). **2** to designate for a particular purpose: *money was allotted to cover expenses.* **3** (foll. by *to*) apportion: *we allotted two hours to the case.* [C16: from Old French *aloter,* from *lot* portion, LOT]
allotment (ə'lɒtmənt) *n* **1** the act of allotting; apportionment. **2** a portion or amount allotted. **3** *Brit.* a small piece of usually public land rented by an individual for cultivation.
allotrope ('ælə,trəʊp) *n* any of two or more physical forms in which an element can exist: *diamond and graphite are allotropes of carbon.*
allotropous (ə'lɒtrəpəs) *adj* (of flowers) having the nectar accessible to any species of insect.
allotropy (ə'lɒtrəpɪ) *or* **allotropism** *n* the existence of an element in two or more physical forms. The most common elements having this property are carbon, sulphur, and phosphorus. ▶ **allotropic** (,ælə'trɒpɪk) *adj* ▶ **,allo'tropically** *adv*
all'ottava (ælə'tɑːvə) *adj, adv Music.* to be played an octave higher or lower than written. Symbol: 8va [Italian: at the octave]
allottee (əlɒt'iː) *n* a person to whom something is allotted.
allotype ('ælə,taɪp) *n Biology.* an additional type specimen selected because of differences from the original type specimen, such as opposite sex or morphological details.
all-out *Informal.* ◆ *adj* **1** using one's maximum powers: *an all-out effort.* ◆ *adv* **all out. 2** to one's maximum effort or capacity: *he went all out on the home stretch.*
all-over *adj* covering the entire surface.
allow (ə'laʊ) *vb* **1** (*tr*) to permit (to do something); let. **2** (*tr*) to set aside: *five hours were allowed to do the job.* **3** (*tr*) to let enter or stay: *they don't allow dogs.* **4** (*tr*) to acknowledge or concede (a point, claim, etc.). **5** (*tr*) to let have; grant: *he was allowed few visitors.* **6** (*intr;* foll. by *for*) to take into account: *allow for delays.* **7** (*intr;* often foll. by *of*) to permit; admit: *a question that allows of only one reply.* **8** (*tr; may take a clause as object*) *U.S. dialect.* to assert; maintain. **9** (*tr*) *Archaic.* to approve; accept. [C14: from Old French *alouer,* from Late Latin *allaudāre* to extol, influenced by Medieval Latin *allocāre* to assign, ALLOCATE]
allowable (ə'laʊəbᵊl) *adj* permissible; admissible. ▶ **al'lowably** *adv*
allowance (ə'laʊəns) *n* **1** an amount of something, esp. money or food, given or allotted usually at regular intervals. **2** a discount, as in consideration for something given in part exchange or to increase business; rebate. **3** (in Britain) an amount of a person's income that is not subject to income tax and is therefore deducted before his liability to taxation is assessed. **4** a portion set aside to compensate for something or to cover special expenses. **5** *Brit. Education.* a salary supplement given to a teacher who is appointed to undertake extra duties and responsibilities. **6** admission; concession. **7** the act of allowing; sanction; toleration. **8** something allowed. **9 make allowances** (*or* **allowance**). (usually foll. by *for*) **9a** to take mitigating circumstances into account in consideration (of). **9b** to allow (for). ◆ *vb* **10** (*tr*) to supply (something) in limited amounts.
Alloway ('ælə,weɪ) *n* a village in Scotland, in South Ayrshire, S of Ayr: birthplace of Robert Burns.
allowedly (ə'laʊɪdlɪ) *adv* (*sentence modifier*) by general admission or agreement; admittedly.
alloy *n* ('ælɔɪ, ə'lɔɪ). **1** a metallic material, such as steel, brass, or bronze, consisting of a mixture of two or more metals or of metallic elements with nonmetallic elements. Alloys often have physical properties markedly different from those of the pure metals. **2** something that impairs the quality or reduces the value of the thing to which it is added. ◆ *vb* (ə'lɔɪ). (*tr*) **3** to add (one metal or element to another metal or element) to obtain a substance with a desired property. **4** to debase (a pure substance) by mixing with an inferior element. **5** to diminish or impair. [C16: from Old French *aloi* a mixture, from *aloier* to combine, from Latin *alligāre,* from *ligāre* to bind]
alloyed junction *n* a semiconductor junction used in some junction transistors and formed by alloying metal contacts, functioning as emitter and collector regions, to a wafer of semiconductor that acts as the base region. Compare **diffused junction.**
allozyme ('æləʊ,zaɪm) *n* any one of a number of different structural forms of the same enzyme. [C20: from ALLO- + (EN)ZYME]
all-powerful *adj* possessing supreme power; omnipotent.
all right *adj* (*postpositive except in slang use*), *adv* **1** adequate; satisfactory. **2** unharmed; safe. **3 all-right.** *U.S. slang.* **3a** acceptable: *an all-right book.* **3b** reliable: *an all-right guy.* ◆ *sentence substitute.* **4** very well: used to express assent. ◆ *adv* **5** satisfactorily; adequately: *the car goes all right.* **6** without doubt: *he's a bad one, all right.* ◆ Also: **alright.**

USAGE See at **alright.**

all-round *adj* **1** efficient in all respects, esp. in sport; versatile: *an all-round player.* **2** comprehensive; many-sided; not narrow: *an all-round education.*
all-rounder *n* a versatile person, esp. in a sport.
All Saints' Day *n* a Christian festival celebrated on Nov. 1 to honour all the saints.
allseed ('ɔːl,siːd) *n* any of several plants that produce many seeds, such as knotgrass.
all-sorts *pl n* a mixture, esp. a mixture of liquorice sweets.
All Souls' Day *n R.C. Church.* a day of prayer (Nov. 2) for the dead in purgatory.
allspice ('ɔːl,spaɪs) *n* **1** a tropical American myrtaceous tree, *Pimenta officinalis,* having small white flowers and aromatic berries. **2** the whole or powdered seeds of this berry used as a spice, having a flavour said to resemble a mixture of cinnamon, cloves, and nutmeg. ◆ Also called: **pimento, Jamaica pepper.**
all square *adj* (*postpositive*) **1** mutually clear of all debts or obligations. **2** (of contestants or teams in sports) having equal scores.
all-star *adj* (*prenominal*) consisting of star performers.
Allston ('ɔːlstən) *n* **Washington.** 1779–1843, U.S. painter and author, regarded as the earliest U.S. Romantic painter. His paintings include *Elijah in the Desert* (1818) and *Moonlit Landscape* (1819).
all-time *adj* (*prenominal*) *Informal.* unsurpassed in some respect at a particular time: *an all-time record.*
all told *adv* (*sentence modifier*) taking every one into account; in all: *we were seven all told.*
allude (ə'luːd) *vb* (*intr;* foll. by *to*) **1** to refer indirectly, briefly, or implicitly. **2** (loosely) to mention. [C16: from Latin *allūdere,* from *lūdere* to sport, from *lūdus* a game]

USAGE Avoid confusion with **elude.**

allure (ə'ljʊə, ə'lʊə) *vb* **1** (*tr*) to entice or tempt (someone) to a person or place or to a course of action; attract. ◆ *n* **2** attractiveness; appeal: *the cottage's allure was its isolation.* [C15: from Old French *alurer,* from *lure* bait, LURE] ▶ **al'lurement** *n* ▶ **al'lurer** *n*
alluring (ə'ljʊərɪŋ, ə'lʊə-) *adj* enticing; fascinating; attractive. ▶ **al'luringly** *adv*
allusion (ə'luːʒən) *n* **1** the act of alluding. **2** a passing reference; oblique or obscure mention. [C16: from Late Latin *allūsiō,* from Latin *allūdere* to sport with, ALLUDE]
allusive (ə'luːsɪv) *adj* containing or full of allusions. ▶ **al'lusively** *adv* ▶ **al'lusiveness** *n*
alluvial (ə'luːvɪəl) *adj* **1** of or relating to alluvium. ◆ *n* **2** another name for **alluvium. 3** *Austral. and N.Z.* alluvium containing any heavy mineral, esp. gold.
alluvial fan *or* **cone** *n* a fan-shaped accumulation of silt, sand, gravel, and boulders deposited by fast-flowing mountain rivers when they reach flatter land.
alluvial mining *n* a method of extracting minerals by dredging alluvial deposits.
alluvion (ə'luːvɪən) *n* **1a** the wash of the sea or of a river. **1b** an overflow or flood. **1c** matter deposited as sediment; alluvium. **2** *Law.* the gradual formation of new land, as by the recession of the sea or deposit of sediment on a riverbed. [C16: from Latin *alluviō* an overflowing, from *luere* to wash]
alluvium (ə'luːvɪəm) *n, pl* **-viums** *or* **-via** (-vɪə). a fine-grained fertile soil consisting of mud, silt, and sand deposited by flowing water on flood plains, in river beds, and in estuaries. [C17: from Latin; see ALLUVION]
ally *vb* (ə'laɪ), **-lies, -lying, -lied.** (usually foll. by *to* or *with*) **1** to unite or be united, esp. formally, as by treaty, confederation, or marriage. **2** (*tr; usually passive*) to connect or be related, as through being similar or compatible. ◆ *n* ('ælaɪ, ə'laɪ), *pl* **-lies. 3** a country, person, or group allied with another. **4** a plant, animal, substance, etc., closely related to another in characteristics or form. [C14: from Old French *alier* to join, from Latin *alligāre* to bind to, from *ligāre* to bind]
allyl ('ælaɪl, 'ælɪl) *n* (*modifier*) of, consisting of, or containing the monovalent group CH_2:$CHCH_2^-$: *allyl group or radical; allyl resin.* [C19: from Latin *allium* garlic + -YL; first distinguished in a compound isolated from garlic]
allyl alcohol *n* a colourless pungent poisonous liquid used in the manufacture of resins, plasticizers, and other organic chemicals. Formula: CH_2:$CHCH_2OH$; relative density: 0.85; melting pt.: –129°C; boiling pt.: 96.9°C.
allyl resin *n* any of several thermosetting synthetic resins made by polymerizing esters of allyl alcohol with a dibasic acid. They are used as adhesives.
allyl sulphide *n* a colourless liquid that smells like garlic and is used as a flavouring. Formula: $(CH_2:CHCH_2)_2S$; relative density: 0.888; boiling pt.: 139°C.
allyou ('ɔːl,juː, 'ɔː,ju) *pron* (*used in addressing more than one person*) *Caribbean informal.* all of you.
Alma-Ata (*Russian* al'maa'ta) *n* the former name of **Almaty.**
Almada (*Portuguese* al'maːdə) *n* a town in S central Portugal, on the S bank of the Tagus estuary opposite Lisbon: statue of Christ 110 m (360 ft.) high, erected 1959. Pop.: 153 189 (1991).
Almadén (*Spanish* alma'θen) *n* a town in S Spain: rich cinnabar mines, worked since Roman times. Pop.: 7723 (1991).
Al Madinah (,æl mæ'diːnə) *n* the Arabic name for **Medina.**
Almagest ('ælmə,dʒest) *n* **1** a work on astronomy compiled by Ptolemy in the

2nd century A.D. containing a description of the geocentric system of the universe and a star catalogue. **2** (*sometimes not cap.*) any of various similar medieval treatises on astrology, astronomy, or alchemy. **[C14**: from Old French, from Arabic *al-majistī,* from *al* the + *majistī,* from Greek *megistē* greatest (treatise)**]**

alma mater ('ælmə 'mɑːtə, 'meɪtə) *n* (*often caps.*) one's school, college, or university. **[C17**: from Latin: bountiful mother**]**

almanac ('ɔːlmə,næk) *n* a yearly calendar giving statistical information on events and phenomena, such as the phases of the moon, times of sunrise and sunset, tides, anniversaries, etc. Also (archaic): **almanack. [C14**: from Medieval Latin *almanachus,* perhaps from Late Greek *almenikhiaka***]**

almandine ('ælməndɪn, -,daɪn) *n* a deep violet-red garnet that consists of iron aluminium silicate and is used as a gemstone. Formula: $Fe_3Al_2(SiO_4)_3$. **[C17**: from French, from Medieval Latin *alabandīna,* from *Alabanda,* ancient city of Asia Minor where these stones were cut**]**

Al Mansûrah (,æl mæn'sʊərə) *n* a variant of **El Mansûra.**

Al Marj (æl 'mɑːdʒ) *n* an ancient town in N Libya: founded in about 550 B.C. Pop.: 25 166 (latest est.). Italian name: **Barce.**

Alma-Tadema ('ælmə'tædɪmə) *n* Sir **Lawrence.** 1836–1912, Dutch-English painter of studies of Greek and Roman life.

Almaty (æl'mɑːtɪ) *n* a city in SE Kazakhstan; capital of Kazakhstan (1991–97): an important trading centre. Pop.: 1 150 500 (1995 est.). Former name (until 1927): **Verny.** Also called: **Alma-Ata.**

Almelo (*Dutch* 'ɑlməloː) *n* a city in the E Netherlands, in Overijssel province. Pop.: 64 589 (1994).

almemar (æl'miːmɑː) *n Judaism.* (in Ashkenazic usage) the raised platform in a synagogue on which the reading desk stands. Also called: **bema, bimah, bima. [**from Hebrew, from Arabic *al-minbar* the pulpit, platform**]**

Almería (*Spanish* alme'ria) *n* a port in S Spain. Pop.: 169 509 (1995 est.).

almighty (ɔːl'maɪtɪ) *adj* **1** all-powerful; omnipotent. **2** *Informal.* (intensifier): *an almighty row.* ◆ *adv* **3** *Informal.* (intensifier): *an almighty loud bang.* ▸ **al'mightily** *adv* ▸ **al'mightiness** *n*

Almighty (ɔːl'maɪtɪ) *n* **the.** another name for **God.**

Almohade ('ælmə,heɪd, -,heɪdiː) *or* **Almohad** ('ælmə,hæd) *n, pl* **-hades** *or* **-hads.** a member of a group of puritanical Muslims, originally Berbers, who arose in S Morocco in the 12th century as a reaction against the corrupt Almoravides and who ruled Spain and all Maghrib from about 1147 to after 1213. **[**from Arabic *al-muwaḥḥid***]**

almond ('ɑːmənd) *n* **1** a small widely cultivated rosaceous tree, *Prunus amygdalus,* that is native to W Asia and has pink flowers and a green fruit containing an edible nutlike seed. **2** the oval-shaped nutlike edible seed of this plant, which has a yellowish-brown shell. **3** (*modifier*) made of or containing almonds: *almond cake.* Related adjs.: **amygdaline, amygdaloid. 4a** a pale yellowish-brown colour. **4b** (*as adj*): *almond wallpaper.* **5** Also called: **almond green. 5a** a yellowish-green colour. **5b** (*as adj*): *an almond skirt.* **6** anything shaped like an almond nut. **[C13**: from Old French *almande,* from Medieval Latin *amandula,* from Latin *amygdala,* from Greek *amugdalē***]**

almond-eyed *adj* having narrow oval eyes.

almoner ('ɑːmənə) *n* **1** *Brit., obsolete.* a trained hospital social worker responsible for the welfare of patients. **2** (formerly) a person who distributes alms or charity on behalf of a household or institution. **[C13**: from Old French *almosnier,* from *almosne* alms, from Vulgar Latin *alemosina* (unattested), from Late Latin *eleēmosyna;* see ALMS**]**

almonry ('ɑːmənrɪ) *n, pl* **-ries.** *History.* the house of an almoner, usually the place where alms were given. **[C15**: from Old French *almosnerie;* see ALMONER, ALMS**]**

Almoravide (æl'mɔːrə,vaɪd) *or* **Almoravid** (æl'mɔːrəvɪd) *n* a member of a fanatical people of Berber origin and Islamic faith, who founded an empire in N Africa that spread over much of Spain in the 11th century A.D. **[**from Arabic *al-murābiṭūn* the holy ones**]**

almost ('ɔːlməʊst) *adv* little short of being; very nearly.

alms (ɑːmz) *pl n* charitable donations of money or goods to the poor or needy. **[**Old English *ælmysse,* from Late Latin *eleēmosyna,* from Greek *eleēmosunē* pity; see ELEEMOSYNARY**]**

almshouse ('ɑːmz,haʊs) *n* **1** *Brit. history.* a privately supported house offering accommodation to the aged or needy. **2** *Chiefly Brit.* another name for **poorhouse.**

almsman ('ɑːmzmən) *or* (*fem*) **almswoman** *n, pl* **-men** *or* **-women.** *Archaic.* a person who gives or receives alms.

almucantar *or* **almacantar** (,ælmə'kæntə) *n* **1** a circle on the celestial sphere parallel to the horizontal plane. **2** an instrument for measuring altitudes. **[C14**: from French, from Arabic *almukantarāt* sundial**]**

almuce ('ælmjuːs) *n* a fur-lined hood or cape formerly worn by members of certain religious orders, more recently by canons of France. **[C15**: from Old French *aumusse,* from Medieval Latin *almucia,* of unknown origin**]**

Alnico ('ælnɪ,kəʊ) *n Trademark.* an alloy of aluminium, nickel, cobalt, iron, and copper, used to make permanent magnets.

alodium (ə'ləʊdɪəm) *n, pl* **-dia** (-dɪə). a variant spelling of **allodium.** ▸ **a'lodial** *adj*

aloe ('æləʊ) *n, pl* **-oes. 1** any plant of the liliaceous genus *Aloe,* chiefly native to southern Africa, with fleshy spiny-toothed leaves and red or yellow flowers. **2 American aloe.** another name for **century plant. [C14**: from Latin *aloē,* from Greek**]** ▸ **aloetic** (,æləʊ'ɛtɪk) *adj*

aloes ('æləʊz) *n* (*functioning as sing*) **1** Also called: **aloes wood.** another name for **eaglewood. 2 bitter aloes.** a bitter purgative drug made from the leaves of several species of aloe.

aloe vera ('æləʊ 'vɪərə) *n* **1** a plant of the species *Aloe vera,* the leaves of which yield a juice used as an emollient. **2** the juice of this plant, used in skin and hair preparations.

aloft (ə'lɒft) *adv, adj* (*postpositive*) **1** in or into a high or higher place; up above. **2** *Nautical.* in or into the rigging of a vessel. **[C12**: from Old Norse *ā lopt* in the air; see LIFT[1], LOFT**]**

aloha (ə'ləʊə, ɑː'ləʊhɑː) *n, sentence substitute.* a Hawaiian word for **hello** or **goodbye.**

aloin ('æləʊɪn) *n* a bitter crystalline compound derived from various species of aloe and used as a laxative. **[C19**: from ALOE + -IN**]**

alone (ə'ləʊn) *adj* (*postpositive*), *adv* **1** apart from another or others; solitary. **2** without anyone or anything else: *one man alone could lift it.* **3** without equal; unique: *he stands alone in the field of microbiology.* **4** to the exclusion of others; only: *she alone believed him.* **5 leave** *or* **let alone** *or* **be.** to refrain from annoying or interfering with. **6 leave** *or* **let well (enough) alone.** to refrain from interfering with something that is satisfactory. **7 let alone.** much less; not to mention: *he can't afford beer, let alone whisky.* **[**Old English *al one,* literally: all (entirely) one**]**

along (ə'lɒŋ) *prep* **1** over or for the length of, esp. in a more or less horizontal plane: *along the road.* ◆ *adv* **2** continuing over the length of some specified thing. **3** in accompaniment; together with some specified person or people: *he says he'd like to come along.* **4** forward: *the horse trotted along at a steady pace.* **5** to a more advanced state: *he got the work moving along.* **6 along with.** accompanying; together with: *consider the advantages along with the disadvantages.* **[**Old English *andlang,* from *and-* against + *lang* LONG[1]; compare Old Frisian *andlinga,* Old Saxon *antlang***]**

USAGE See at **plus.**

alongshore (ə,lɒŋ'ʃɔː) *adv, adj* (*postpositive*) close to, by, or along a shore.

alongside (ə'lɒŋ,saɪd) *prep* **1** (often foll. by *of*) along the side of; along beside: *alongside the quay.* ◆ *adv* **2** along the side of some specified thing: *come alongside.*

aloof (ə'luːf) *adj* distant, unsympathetic, or supercilious in manner, attitude, or feeling. **[C16**: from A-[1] + *loof,* a variant of LUFF**]** ▸ **a'loofly** *adv* ▸ **a'loofness** *n*

alopecia (,ælə'piːʃɪə) *n* loss of hair, esp. on the head; baldness. **[C14**: from Latin, from Greek *alōpekia,* originally: mange in foxes, from *alōpēx* fox**]**

Alost (*French* alɔst) *n* a town in central Belgium, in East Flanders province. Pop.: 76 256 (1995 est.). Flemish name: **Aalst.**

aloud (ə'laʊd) *adv, adj* (*postpositive*) **1** in a normal voice; not in a whisper. **2** in a spoken voice; not silently. **3** *Archaic.* in a loud voice.

alow (ə'ləʊ) *adv, adj* (*postpositive*) *Nautical.* in or into the lower rigging of a vessel, near the deck.

Aloysius (,æləʊ'ɪʃəs) *n* **Saint.** full name *Aloysius Luigi Gonzaga.* 1568–91, Italian Jesuit who died nursing plague victims; the patron saint of youth. Feast day: June 21.

alp (ælp) *n* **1** (in Switzerland) a pasture on a mountain side. **2** a high mountain. ◆ See also **Alps, Australian Alps. [C14**: back formation from *Alps,* from French *Alpes* (pl), from Latin *Alpēs,* from Greek *Alpeis***]**

ALP *abbrev. for* Australian Labor Party.

alpaca[1] (æl'pækə) *n* **1** a domesticated cud-chewing artiodactyl mammal, *Lama pacos,* closely related to the llama and native to South America: family *Camelidae.* Its dark shaggy hair is a source of wool. **2** the cloth made from the wool of this animal. **3** a glossy fabric simulating this, used for linings, etc. **[C18**: via Spanish from Aymara *allpaca***]**

alpaca[2] *or* (*sometimes*) **alpacca** (æl'pækə) *n* a type of nickel silver used in jewellery. **[**of uncertain origin**]**

alpenglow ('ælpən,gləʊ) *n* a reddish light on the summits of snow-covered mountain peaks at sunset or sunrise. **[**partial translation of German *Alpenglühen,* from *Alpen* ALPS + *glühen* to GLOW**]**

alpenhorn ('ælpən,hɔːn) *n* another name for **alphorn.**

alpenstock ('ælpən,stɒk) *n* an early form of ice axe, consisting of a stout stick with an iron tip and sometimes having a pick and adze at the head, formerly used by mountain climbers. **[C19**: from German, from *Alpen* ALPS + *Stock* STICK[1]**]**

Alpes-de-Haute-Provence (*French* alpdəotprɔvɑ̃s) *n* a department of SE France in Provence-Alpes-Côte-d'Azur region. Capital: Digne. Pop.: 138 800 (1995). Area: 6988 sq. km (2725 sq. miles). Former name: **Basses-Alpes.**

Alpes Maritimes (*French* alp maritim) *n* a department of the SE corner of France in Provence-Alpes-Côte-d'Azur region. Capital: Nice. Pop.: 1 011 100 (1995). Area: 4298 sq. km (1676 sq. miles).

alpestrine (æl'pɛstrɪn) *adj* (of plants) growing at high altitudes; subalpine. **[C19**: from Medieval Latin *alpestris,* from Latin *Alpēs* the Alps**]**

alpha ('ælfə) *n* **1** the first letter in the Greek alphabet (Α, α), a vowel transliterated as *a.* **2** *Brit.* the highest grade or mark, as in an examination. **3** (*modifier*) **3a** involving or relating to helium nuclei: *an alpha particle.* **3b** relating to one of two or more allotropes or crystal structures of a solid: *alpha iron.* **3c** relating to one of two or more isomeric forms of a chemical compound, esp. one in which a group is attached to the carbon atom to which the principal group is attached. **4** (*modifier*) denoting the dominant person or animal in a group: *the alpha male.* **[**via Latin from Greek, of Phoenician origin; related to Hebrew *ālеph,* literally: ox**]**

Alpha ('ælfə) *n* **1** (*foll. by the genitive case of a specified constellation*) usually the brightest star in a constellation: *Alpha Centauri.* **2** *Communications.* a code word for the letter *a.*

alpha and omega *n* **1** the first and last, a phrase used in Revelation 1:8 to signify God's eternity. **2** the basic reason or meaning; most important part.

alphabet ('ælfə,bɛt) *n* **1** a set of letters or other signs used in a writing system, usually arranged in a fixed order, each letter or sign being used to represent one or sometimes more than one phoneme in the language being transcribed. **2** any set of symbols or characters, esp. one representing sounds of speech. **3** basic principles or rudiments, as of a subject. [C15: from Late Latin *alphabētum,* from Greek *alphabētos,* from the first two letters of the Greek alphabet; see ALPHA, BETA]

alphabetical (ˌælfəˈbɛtɪkᵊl) *or* **alphabetic** *adj* **1** in the conventional order of the letters or symbols of an alphabet. **2** of, characterized by, or expressed by an alphabet. ▸ **ˌalphaˈbetically** *adv*

alphabetize *or* **alphabetise** (ˈælfəbəˌtaɪz) *vb* (*tr*) **1** to arrange in conventional alphabetical order. **2** to express by an alphabet. ▸ **ˌalphabetiˈzation** *or* **ˌalphabetiˈsation** *n* ▸ **ˈalphabetˌizer** *or* **ˈalphabetˌiser** *n*

alpha-blocker *n* any of a class of drugs that prevent the stimulation of alpha receptors, a type of receptor in the sympathetic nervous system, by adrenaline and that therefore cause widening of blood vessels: used in the treatment of high blood pressure.

Alpha Centauri (sɛnˈtɔːrɪ) *n* a binary star that is the brightest in the constellation Centaurus and is the second nearest star to the sun. Visual magnitude: 0.0 (A), 1.4 (B); spectral type: G4 (A), K1 (B); distance from earth: 4.3 light years. Also called: **Rigil Kent.** See also **Proxima.**

alpha decay *n* the radioactive decay process resulting in emission of alpha particles.

alpha emitter *n* a radioactive isotope that emits alpha particles.

alpha-fetoprotein (ˌælfəˌfiːtəʊˈprəʊtiːn) *n* a protein that forms in the liver of the human fetus. Excessive quantities in the amniotic fluid and maternal blood may indicate spina bifida in the fetus; low levels may point to Down's syndrome. Abbrev.: **afp.**

alpha helix *n Biochem.* a helical conformation of a polypeptide chain, found abundantly in the structure of proteins.

alpha iron *n* a magnetic allotrope of iron that is stable below 910°C; ferrite.

alphanumeric (ˌælfənjuːˈmɛrɪk) *or* **alphameric** (ˌælfəˈmɛrɪk) *adj* (of a character set, code, or file of data) consisting of alphabetical and numerical symbols. ▸ **ˌalphanuˈmerically** *or* **ˌalphaˈmerically** *adv*

alpha particle *n* a helium nucleus, containing two neutrons and two protons, emitted during some radioactive transformations.

alpha privative *n* (in Greek grammar) the letter alpha (or *an-* before vowels) used as a negative or privative prefix. It appears in English words derived from Greek, as in *atheist, anaesthetic.*

alpha radiation *n* alpha particles emitted from a radioactive isotope.

alpha ray *n* ionizing radiation consisting of a stream of alpha particles.

alpha rhythm *or* **wave** *n Physiol.* the normal bursts of electrical activity from the cerebral cortex of a drowsy or inactive person, occurring at a frequency of 8 to 12 hertz and detectable with an electroencephalograph. See also **brain wave.**

alpha stock *n* any of the most active securities on the Stock Exchange of which there are between 100 and 200; at least ten market makers must continuously display the prices of an alpha stock and all transactions in them must be published immediately.

alpha-test *n* **1** an in-house test of a new or modified piece of computer software. ♦ *vb* (*tr*) **2** to test (software) in this way. Compare **beta-test.**

Alpheus (ælˈfiːəs) *n Greek myth.* a river god, lover of the nymph Arethusa. She changed into a spring to evade him, but he changed into a river and mingled with her.

Alphonsus (ælˈfɒnsəs) *n* a crater in the SE quadrant of the moon, about 112 kilometres in diameter, in which volcanic activity has been observed.

alphorn (ˈælpˌhɔːn) *or* **alpenhorn** *n Music.* a wind instrument used in the Swiss Alps, consisting of a very long tube of wood or bark with a cornet-like mouthpiece. [C19: from German *Alpenhorn* Alps horn]

alphosis (ælˈfəʊsɪs) *n Pathol.* absence of skin pigmentation, as in albinism. [C19: from New Latin, from Greek *alphos* leprosy]

alpine (ˈælpaɪn) *adj* **1** of or relating to high mountains. **2** (of plants) growing on mountains above the limit for tree growth. **3** connected with or used in mountaineering in medium-sized glaciated mountain areas such as the Alps. **4** *Skiing.* of or relating to racing events on steep prepared slopes, such as the slalom and downhill. Compare **nordic.** ♦ *n* **5** a plant that is native or suited to alpine conditions.

Alpine (ˈælpaɪn) *adj* **1** of or relating to the Alps or their inhabitants. **2** *Geology.* of or relating to an episode of mountain building in the Tertiary period during which the Alps were formed.

alpine-style *adj, adv Mountaineering.* of or in an ascent (esp. in high mountains like the Himalayas) in which the climbers carry all their equipment with them in a single ascent from base to summit.

alpinist (ˈælpɪnɪst) *n* a mountaineer who climbs in medium-sized glaciated mountain areas such as the Alps. ▸ **ˈalpinism** *n*

Alps (ælps) *pl n* **1** a mountain range in S central Europe, extending over 1000 km (650 miles) from the Mediterranean coast of France and NW Italy through Switzerland, N Italy, and Austria to Slovenia. Highest peak: Mont Blanc, 4807 m (15 771 ft.). **2** a range of mountains in the NW quadrant of the moon, which is cut in two by a straight fracture, the **Alpine Valley.**

already (ɔːlˈrɛdɪ) *adv* **1** by or before a stated or implied time: *he is already here.* **2** at a time earlier than expected: *is it ten o'clock already?*

alright (ɔːlˈraɪt) *adv, sentence substitute, adj* a variant spelling of **all right.**

USAGE The form *alright,* though very common, is still considered by many people to be wrong or less acceptable than *all right.*

ALS *abbrev. for* autograph letter signed.

Alsace (ælˈsæs; *French* alzas) *n* a region and former province of NE France, between the Vosges mountains and the Rhine: famous for its wines. Area: 8280 sq. km (3196 sq. miles). Ancient name: **Alsatia.** German name: **Elsass.**

Alsace-Lorraine *n* an area of NE France, comprising the modern regions of Alsace and Lorraine: under German rule 1871–1919 and 1940–44. Area: 14 522 sq. km (5607 sq. miles). German name: **Elsass-Lothringen.**

Alsatia (ælˈseɪʃə) *n* **1** the ancient name for **Alsace. 2** an area around Whitefriars, London, in the 17th century, which was a sanctuary for criminals and debtors.

Alsatian (ælˈseɪʃən) *n* **1** a large wolflike breed of dog often used as a guard or guide dog and by the police. Also called: **German shepherd, German shepherd dog. 2** a native or inhabitant of Alsace. **3** (in the 17th century) a criminal or debtor who took refuge in the Whitefriars area of London. ♦ *adj* **4** of or relating to Alsace or its inhabitants.

alsike (ˈælsaɪk, -sɪk, ˈɔːl-) *n* a clover, *Trifolium hybridum,* native to Europe and Asia but widely cultivated as a forage crop. It has trifoliate leaves and pink or whitish flowers. Also called: **alsike clover.** [C19: named after *Alsike,* Sweden]

Al Sirat (ˌæl sɪˈræt) *n Islam.* **1** the correct path of religion. **2** the razor-edged bridge by which all who enter paradise must pass. [from Arabic: the road, from Latin *via strāta* paved way]

also (ˈɔːlsəʊ) *adv* **1** (*sentence modifier*) in addition; as well; too. ♦ *sentence connector.* **2** besides; moreover. [Old English *alswā;* related to Old High German *alsō,* Old Frisian *alsa;* see ALL, SO[1]]

also-ran *n* **1** a contestant, horse, etc., failing to finish among the first three in a race. **2** an unsuccessful person; loser or nonentity.

alstroemeria (ˌælstrəˈmiːrɪə) *n* any plant of the tuberous perennial genus *Alstroemeria,* originally S American, grown for their brightly coloured orchid-like flowers: family *Amaryllidaceae.* Also called: **Peruvian lily.** [named by Linnaeus for his friend Baron Klas von *Alstroemer*]

alt (ælt) *Music.* ♦ *adj* **1** (esp. of vocal music) high in pitch. **2** of or relating to the octave commencing with the G above the top line of the treble staff. ♦ *n* **3 in alt.** in the octave directly above the treble staff. [C16: from Provençal, from Latin *altus* high, deep]

alt. *abbrev. for:* **1** alternate. **2** altitude. **3** alto.

Alta. *abbrev. for* Alberta.

Altaic (ælˈteɪɪk) *n* **1** a postulated family of languages of Asia and SE Europe, consisting of the Turkic, Mongolic, and Tungusic branches, and perhaps also Japanese, Korean, and Ainu. See also **Ural-Altaic.** ♦ *adj* **2** denoting, belonging to, or relating to this linguistic family or its speakers.

Altai Mountains (ɑːlˈtaɪ) *pl n* a mountain system of central Asia, in W Mongolia, W China, and S Russia. Highest peak: Belukha, 4506 m (14 783 ft.).

Altair (ˈæltɛə) *n* the brightest star in the constellation Aquila. Visual magnitude: 0.9; spectral type: A5; distance: 15.7 light years. [Arabic, from *al* the + *tā'ir* bird]

Altai Republic *n* another name for **Gorno-Altai Republic.**

Altamira (*Spanish* altaˈmira) *n* a cave in N Spain, SW of Santander, noted for Old Stone Age wall drawings.

altar (ˈɔːltə) *n* **1** a raised place or structure where sacrifices are offered and religious rites performed. **2** (in Christian churches) the communion table. **3** a step in the wall of a dry dock upon which structures supporting a vessel can stand. **4 lead to the altar.** *Informal.* to marry. [Old English, from Latin *altāria* (plural) altar, from *altus* high]

altar boy *n R.C. Church, Church of England.* a boy serving as an acolyte.

altar cloth *n Christianity.* the cloth used for covering an altar: often applied also to the frontal.

altarpiece (ˈɔːltəˌpiːs) *n* a work of art set above and behind an altar; a reredos.

altazimuth (ælˈtæzɪməθ) *n* an instrument for measuring the altitude and azimuth of a celestial body by the horizontal and vertical rotation of a telescope. [C19: from ALT(ITUDE) + AZIMUTH]

altazimuth mounting *n* a telescope mounting that allows motion of the telescope about a vertical axis (in altitude) and a horizontal axis (in azimuth).

Altdorf (*German* ˈaltdɔrf) *n* a town in central Switzerland, capital of Uri canton: setting of the William Tell legend. Pop.: 8150 (1990).

Altdorfer (*German* ˈaltdɔrfər) *n* **Albrecht** (ˈalbrɛçt). ?1480–?1538, German painter and engraver: one of the earliest landscape painters.

Alte Pinakothek (*German* ˈaltə pinakoˈteːk) *n* a museum in Munich housing a collection of paintings dating from the Middle Ages to the late 18th century.

alter (ˈɔːltə) *vb* **1** to make or become different in some respect; change. **2** (*tr*) *Informal, chiefly U.S.* a euphemistic word for **castrate** or **spay.** [C14: from Old French *alterer,* from Medieval Latin *alterāre* to change, from Latin *alter* other] ▸ **ˈalterable** *adj* ▸ **ˈalterably** *adv* ▸ **ˌalteraˈbility** *n*

alteration (ˌɔːltəˈreɪʃən) *n* **1** an adjustment, change, or modification. **2** the act of altering or state of being altered.

alterative (ˈɔːltərətɪv) *adj* **1** likely or able to produce alteration. **2** (of a drug) able to restore normal health. ♦ *n* **3** a drug that restores normal health.

altercate (ˈɔːltəˌkeɪt) *vb* (*intr*) to argue, esp. heatedly; dispute. [C16: from Latin *altercārī* to quarrel with another, from *alter* other]

altercation (ˌɔːltəˈkeɪʃən) *n* an angry or heated discussion or quarrel; argument.

altered chord *n Music.* a chord in which one or more notes are chromatically changed by the introduction of accidentals.

alter ego (ˈæltər ˈiːgəʊ, ˈɛgəʊ) *n* **1** a second self. **2** a very close and intimate friend. [Latin: other self]

alternant (ɔːlˈtɜːnənt) *adj* alternating. [C17: from French, from Latin *alternāre* to ALTERNATE]

alternate *vb* (ˈɔːltəˌneɪt). **1** (often foll. by *with*) to occur or cause to occur successively or by turns: *day and night alternate.* **2** (*intr;* often foll. by *between*) to swing repeatedly from one condition, action, etc., to another: *he alternates between success and failure.* **3** (*tr*) to interchange regularly or in succession. **4** (*intr*) (of an electric current, voltage, etc.) to reverse direction or sign at regular intervals, usually sinusoidally, the instantaneous value varying continuously. **5** (*intr;* often foll. by *for*) *Theatre.* to understudy another actor or actress. ♦ *adj* (ɔːlˈtɜːnɪt). **6** occurring by turns: *alternate feelings of love and hate.* **7** every other or second one of a series: *he came to work on alternate days.* **8** being a second or further choice; alternative: *alternate director.* **9** *Botany.* **9a** (of leaves, flowers, etc.) arranged singly at different heights on either side of the stem. **9b** (of parts of a flower) arranged opposite the spaces between other parts. Compare **opposite** (sense 4). ◆ *n* (ˈɔːltənɪt, ɔːlˈtɜːnɪt). **10** *U.S. and Canadian.* a person who substitutes for another in his absence; stand-in. **[C16:** from Latin *alternāre* to do one thing and then another, from *alternus* one after the other, from *alter* other**]**

alternate angles *pl n* two angles at opposite ends and on opposite sides of a transversal cutting two lines.

alternately (ɔːlˈtɜːnɪtlɪ) *adv* in an alternating sequence or position.

alternating current *n* a continuous electric current that periodically reverses direction, usually sinusoidally. Abbrev.: **AC.** Compare **direct current.**

alternating-gradient focusing *n Physics.* a method of focusing beams of charged particles in high-energy accelerators, in which a series of magnetic or electrostatic lenses alternately converge and diverge the beam, producing a net focusing effect and thus preventing the beam from spreading.

alternation (ˌɔːltəˈneɪʃən) *n* **1** successive change from one condition or action to another and back again repeatedly. **2** *Logic.* another name for **disjunction** (sense 3).

alternation of generations *n* the production within the life cycle of an organism of alternating asexual and sexual reproductive forms. It occurs in many plants and lower animals. Also called: **metagenesis, heterogenesis, digenesis, xenogenesis.**

alternative (ɔːlˈtɜːnətɪv) *n* **1** a possibility of choice, esp. between two things, courses of action, etc. **2** either of such choices: *we took the alternative of walking.* ◆ *adj* **3** presenting a choice, esp. between two possibilities only. **4** (of two things) mutually exclusive. **5** denoting a lifestyle, culture, art form, etc., regarded by its adherents as preferable to that of contemporary society because it is less conventional, materialistic, or institutionalized, and, often, more in harmony with nature. **6** *Logic.* another word for **disjunctive** (sense 3). ► **alˈternatively** *adv* ► **alˈternativeness** *n*

alternative curriculum *n Brit. Education.* any course of study offered as an alternative to the National Curriculum.

alternative energy *n* a form of energy derived from a natural source, such as the sun, wind, tides, or waves. Also called: **renewable energy.**

alternative hypothesis *n Statistics.* the hypothesis that given data do not conform with a given null hypothesis: accepted only if its probability exceeds a predetermined significance level. See **hypothesis testing.** Compare **null hypothesis.**

Alternative Investment Market *n* a market on the London Stock Exchange enabling small companies to raise capital and have their shares traded in a market without the expenses of a main-market listing. Abbrev.: **AIM.**

alternative medicine *n* the treatment, alleviation, or prevention of disease by techniques such as osteopathy and acupuncture, allied with attention to factors such as diet and emotional stability, which affect a person's general well-being. Also called: **complementary medicine.** See also **holism** (sense 2).

Alternative Vote *n* (*modifier*) of or relating to a system of voting in which voters list the candidates in order of preference. If no candidate obtains more than 50% of first-preference votes, the votes for the bottom candidate are redistributed according to the voters' next preference. See **proportional representation.**

alternator (ˈɔːltəˌneɪtə) *n* an electrical machine that generates an alternating current.

althaea *or U.S.* **althea** (ælˈθiːə) *n* **1** any Eurasian plant of the malvaceous genus *Althaea*, such as the hollyhock, having tall spikes of showy white, yellow, or red flowers. **2** another name for **rose of Sharon** (sense 2). **[C17:** from Latin *althaea*, from Greek *althaia* marsh mallow (literally: healing plant), from Greek *althein* to heal**]**

Althing (ˈælθɪŋ) *n* the bicameral parliament of Iceland.

althorn (ˈæltˌhɔːn) *n* a valved brass musical instrument belonging to the saxhorn or flügelhorn families.

Althorp House (ˈɑːlθɔːp, -θrʌp) *n* a mansion in Northamptonshire: seat of the Earls Spencer since 1508; originally a medieval house; altered (1787) to its present neoclassical style by Henry Holland. Diana, Princess of Wales is buried on Round Oval Island in the centre of the ornamental lake in Althorp Park.

although (ɔːlˈðəʊ) *conj* (*subordinating*) despite the fact that; even though: *although she was ill, she worked hard.*

Althusser (ˈɑːltuːsə; *French* altusɛr) *n* **Louis.** 1918–90, French Marxist philosopher, author of *For Marx* (1965) and *Reading Capital* (1965): committed to a mental hospital (1981) after killing his wife.

alti- *combining form.* indicating height or altitude: *altimeter.* **[**from Latin *altus* high**]**

altimeter (ælˈtɪmɪtə, ˈæltɪˌmiːtə) *n* an instrument that indicates height above sea level, esp. one based on an aneroid barometer and fitted to an aircraft.

altimetry (ælˈtɪmɪtrɪ) *n* the science of measuring altitudes, as with an altimeter. ► **altimetrical** (ˌæltɪˈmɛtrɪkᵊl) *adj* ► **ˌaltiˈmetrically** *adv*

Altiplano (*Spanish* altiˈplano) *n* a plateau of the Andes, covering two thirds of Bolivia and extending into S Peru: contains Lake Titicaca. Height: 3000 m (10 000 ft.) to 3900 m (13 000 ft.).

altissimo (ælˈtɪsɪˌməʊ) *adj* **1** (of music) very high in pitch. **2** of or relating to the octave commencing on the G lying an octave above the treble clef. ◆ *n* **3 in altissimo.** in the octave commencing an octave above the treble clef. **[**Italian, literally: highest**]**

altitude (ˈæltɪˌtjuːd) *n* **1** the vertical height of an object above some chosen level, esp. above sea level; elevation. **2** *Geometry.* the perpendicular distance from the vertex to the base of a geometrical figure or solid. **3** Also called: **elevation.** *Astronomy, navigation.* the angular distance of a celestial body from the horizon measured along the vertical circle passing through the body. Compare **azimuth** (sense 1). **4** *Surveying.* the angle of elevation of a point above the horizontal plane of the observer. **5** (*often pl*) a high place or region. **[C14:** from Latin *altitūdō*, from *altus* high, deep**]** ► **ˌaltiˈtudinal** *adj*

altitude sickness *n* another name for **mountain sickness.**

Altman (ˈɔːltmən) *n* **Robert.** U.S. film director; his films include *M*A*S*H* (1970) and *The Gingerbread Man* (1998).

alto (ˈæltəʊ) *n, pl* **-tos. 1** the highest adult male voice; countertenor. **2** (in choral singing) a shortened form of **contralto. 3** a singer with such a voice. **4** another name for **viola**[1] (sense 1). **5** a flute, saxophone, etc., that is the third or fourth highest instrument in its group. ◆ *adj* **6** denoting a flute, saxophone, etc., that is the third or fourth highest instrument in its group. **[C18:** from Italian: high, from Latin *altus***]**

alto- *combining form.* high: *altocumulus; altostratus.* **[**from Latin *altus* high**]**

alto clef *n* the clef that establishes middle C as being on the third line of the staff. Also called: **viola clef.** See also **C clef.**

altocumulus (ˌæltəʊˈkjuːmjʊləs) *n, pl* **-li** (-laɪ). a globular cloud at an intermediate height of about 2400 to 6000 metres (8000 to 20 000 feet).

altogether (ˌɔːltəˈgɛðə, ˈɔːltəˌgɛðə) *adv* **1** with everything included: *altogether he owed me sixty pounds.* **2** completely; utterly; totally: *he was altogether mad.* **3** on the whole: *altogether it was a very good party.* ◆ *n* **4 in the altogether.** *Informal.* naked.

alto horn *n* another term for **althorn.**

altoist (ˈæltəʊɪst) *n* a person who plays the alto saxophone.

Alton Towers (ˈɒltən) *n* a 19th-century Gothic Revival mansion with extensive gardens in NW central England, in Staffordshire: site of a large amusement park.

alto-relievo *or* **alto-rilievo** (ˌæltəʊrɪˈliːvəʊ) *n, pl* **-vos.** another name for **high relief. [C18:** from Italian**]**

altostratus (ˌæltəʊˈstreɪtəs, -ˈstrɑː-) *n, pl* **-ti** (-taɪ). a layer cloud at an intermediate height of about 2400 to 6000 metres (8000 to 20 000 feet).

altrices (ˈæltrɪsiːz) *pl n* altricial birds.

altricial (ælˈtrɪʃəl) *adj* **1** (of the young of some species of birds after hatching) naked, blind, and dependent on the parents for food. ◆ *n* **2** an altricial bird, such as a pigeon. ◆ Compare **precocial. [C19:** from New Latin *altriciālis*, from Latin *altrix* a nurse, from *alere* to nourish**]**

Altrincham (ˈɔːltrɪŋəm) *n* a residential town in NW England, in Trafford unitary authority, Greater Manchester. Pop.: 40 042 (1991).

altruism (ˈæltruːˌɪzəm) *n* **1** the principle or practice of unselfish concern for the welfare of others. **2** the philosophical doctrine that right action is that which produces the greatest benefit to others. ◆ Compare **egoism.** See also **utilitarianism. [C19:** from French *altruisme*, from Italian *altrui* others, from Latin *alterī*, plural of *alter* other**]** ► **ˈaltruist** *n* ► **ˌaltruˈistic** *adj* ► **ˌaltruˈistically** *adv*

ALU *Computing. abbrev. for* arithmetic and logic unit.

aludel (ˈæljʊˌdɛl) *n Chem.* a pear-shaped vessel, open at both ends, formerly used with similar vessels for collecting condensates, esp. of subliming mercury. **[C16:** via Old French from Spanish, from Arabic *al-uthāl* the vessel**]**

alula (ˈæljʊlə) *n, pl* **-lae** (-liː). another name for **bastard wing. [C18:** New Latin: a little wing, from Latin *āla* a wing**]** ► **ˈalular** *adj*

alum (ˈæləm) *n* **1** Also called: **potash alum.** a colourless soluble hydrated double sulphate of aluminium and potassium used in the manufacture of mordants and pigments, in dressing leather and sizing paper, and in medicine as a styptic and astringent. Formula: $K_2SO_4.Al_2(SO_4)_3.24H_2O$. **2** any of a group of isomorphic double sulphates of a monovalent metal or group and a trivalent metal. Formula: $X_2SO_4.Y_2(SO_4)_3.24H_2O$, where X is monovalent and Y is trivalent. **[C14:** from Old French, from Latin *alūmen***]**

alum. *abbrev. for* aluminium.

alumina (əˈluːmɪnə) *n* another name for **aluminium oxide. [C18:** from New Latin, plural of Latin *alūmen* ALUM**]**

aluminate (əˈluːmɪneɪt) *n* a salt of the ortho or meta acid forms of aluminium hydroxide containing the ions AlO_2^- or AlO_3^{3-}.

aluminiferous (əˌluːmɪˈnɪfərəs) *adj* containing or yielding aluminium or alumina.

aluminium (ˌæljʊˈmɪnɪəm) *or U.S. and Canadian* **aluminum** (əˈluːmɪnəm) *n* a light malleable ductile silvery-white metallic element that resists corrosion; the third most abundant element in the earth's crust (8.1 per cent), occurring only as a compound, principally in bauxite. It is used, esp. in the form of its alloys, in aircraft parts, kitchen utensils, etc. Symbol: Al; atomic no.: 13; atomic wt.: 26.9815; valency: 3; relative density: 2.699; melting pt.: 660.45°C; boiling pt.: 2520°C.

aluminium bronze *n* any of a range of copper alloys that contain between 5 and 10 per cent aluminium.

aluminium hydroxide *n* a white crystalline powder derived from bauxite and used in the manufacture of glass and ceramics, aluminium and its salts, and in dyeing. Formula: $Al(OH)_3$ or $Al_2O_3.3H_2O$.

aluminium oxide *n* a white or colourless insoluble powder occurring naturally as corundum and used in the production of aluminium and its compounds, abrasives, glass, and ceramics. Formula: Al_2O_3. Also called: **alumina.** See also **activated alumina.**

aluminium sulphate *n* a white crystalline salt used in the paper, textile, and dyeing industries and in the purification of water. Formula: $Al_2(SO_4)_3$.

aluminize *or* **aluminise** (əˈluːmɪˌnaɪz) *vb* (*tr*) to cover with aluminium or aluminium paint.

aluminosilicate (əˌluːmɪnəʊˈsɪlɪkɪt) *n* a silicate in which some of the silicon in the tetrahedral unit SiO_4 has been replaced by aluminium.

aluminothermy (əˌluːmɪnəʊˈθɜːmɪ) *n* a process for reducing metallic oxides using finely divided aluminium powder. The mixture of aluminium and oxide is ignited, causing the aluminium to be oxidized and the metal oxide to be reduced to the metal. Also called: **thermite process.**

aluminous (ə'lu:mɪnəs) *adj* **1** resembling aluminium. **2** another word for **aluminiferous.** ▸ **aluminosity** (ə,lu:mɪ'nɒsɪtɪ) *n*

aluminous cement *n* another term for **Ciment Fondu.**

alumnus (ə'lʌmnəs) *or (fem)* **alumna** (ə'lʌmnə) *n, pl* **-ni** (-naɪ) *or* **-nae** (-ni:). *Chiefly U.S. and Canadian.* a graduate of a school, college, etc. [C17: from Latin: nursling, pupil, foster son, from *alere* to nourish]

alumroot ('æləm,ru:t) *n* **1** any of several North American plants of the saxifragaceous genus *Heuchera,* having small white, reddish, or green bell-shaped flowers and astringent roots. **2** the root of such a plant.

Alundum (ə'lʌndəm) *n Trademark.* a hard material composed of fused alumina, used as an abrasive and a refractory.

alunite ('ælju,naɪt) *n* a white, grey, or reddish mineral consisting of hydrated aluminium sulphate. It occurs in volcanic igneous rocks and is a source of potassium and aluminium compounds. Formula: $KAl_3(SO_4)_2(OH)_6$. [C19: from French *alun* alum (from Latin *alūmen*) + -ITE[1]]

Alva *or* **Alba** ('ælvə; *Spanish* 'alβa) *n* **Duke of,** title of *Fernando Alvarez de Toledo.* 1508–82, Spanish general and statesman who suppressed the Protestant revolt in the Netherlands (1567–72) and conquered Portugal (1580).

Alvarez ('ælvərɛz) *n* **Luis Walter.** 1911–88, U.S. physicist. He made (with Felix Bloch) the first measurement of the neutron's magnetic moment (1939). Nobel prize for physics 1968.

alveolar (æl'vɪələ, ,ælvɪ'əʊlə) *adj* **1** *Anatomy.* of, relating to, or resembling an alveolus. **2** denoting the part of the jawbone containing the roots of the teeth. **3** (of a consonant) articulated with the tongue in contact with the projecting part of the jawbone immediately behind the upper teeth. ◆ *n* **4** an alveolar consonant, such as the speech sounds written *t, d,* and *s* in English.

alveolate (æl'vɪəlɪt, -,leɪt) *adj* **1** having many alveoli. **2** resembling the deep pits of a honeycomb. [C19: from Late Latin *alveolātus* forming a channel, hollowed, from Latin: ALVEOLUS] ▸ **,alveo'lation** *n*

alveolus (æl'vɪələs) *n, pl* **-li** (-,laɪ). **1** any small pit, cavity, or saclike dilation, such as a honeycomb cell. **2** any of the sockets in which the roots of the teeth are embedded. **3** any of the tiny air sacs in the lungs at the end of the bronchioles, through which oxygen is taken into the blood. [C18: from Latin: a little hollow, diminutive of *alveus*]

alvine ('ælvɪn, -vaɪn) *adj Obsolete.* of or relating to the intestines or belly. [C18: from Latin *alvus* belly]

always ('ɔ:lweɪz, -wɪz) *adv* **1** without exception; on every occasion; every time: *he always arrives on time.* **2** continually; repeatedly. **3** in any case: *you could always take a day off work.* **4 for always.** *Informal.* for ever; without end: *our marriage is for always.* ◆ Also (archaic): **alway.** [C13 *alles weiss,* from Old English *ealne weg,* literally: all the way; see ALL, WAY]

Alwyn ('ɔ:lwɪn) *n* **William.** 1905–85, British composer. His works include the oratorio *The Marriage of Heaven and Hell* (1936) and the *Suite of Scottish dances* (1946).

alyssum ('ælɪsəm) *n* any widely cultivated herbaceous garden plant of the genus *Alyssum,* having clusters of small yellow or white flowers: family *Cruciferae* (crucifers). See also **sweet alyssum, alison.** [C16: from New Latin, from Greek *alusson,* from *alussos* (adj) curing rabies, referring to the ancient belief in the plant's healing properties]

Alzheimer's disease ('ælts,haɪməz) *n* a disorder of the brain resulting in a progressive decline in intellectual and physical abilities and eventual dementia. Often shortened to **Alzheimer's.** [C20: named after A. *Alzheimer* (1864–1915), German physician who first identified it]

am[1] (æm; *unstressed* əm) *vb* (used with *I*) a form of the present tense (indicative mood) of **be.** [Old English *eam;* related to Old Norse *em,* Gothic *im,* Old High German *bim,* Latin *sum,* Greek *eimi,* Sanskrit *asmi*]

am[2] See **1 AM** (sense 4). **2 a.m.**

Am *the chemical symbol for* americium.

AM *abbrev. for:* **1** associate member. **2** Albert Medal. **3** *U.S.* Master of Arts. **4** Also: **am.** amplitude modulation. **5** See **a.m. 6** Member of the Order of Australia.

Am. *abbrev. for* America(n).

a.m., A.M., am, *or* **AM** (indicating the time period from midnight to midday) *abbrev. for* ante meridiem. Compare **p.m.** [Latin: before noon]

AMA *abbrev. for:* **1** American Medical Association. **2** Australian Medical Association.

amabokoboko (ama'bɒkɒbɒkɒ) *pl n S. African.* an African name for the **Springbok** rugby team. [C20: from Nguni *ama,* a plural prefix + *bokoboko,* from *bok* a diminutive of SPRINGBOK]

amadavat (,æmədə'væt) *n* another name for **avadavat.**

amadoda (ama'dəʊda) *pl n S. African.* grown men. [from Nguni *ama,* a plural prefix + *doda* men]

amadou ('æmə,du:) *n* a spongy substance made from certain fungi, such as *Polyporus* (or *Fomes*) *fomentarius* and related species, used as tinder to light fires, in medicine to stop bleeding, and, esp. formerly, by anglers to dry off dry flies between casts. [C18: from French, from Provençal: lover, from Latin *amātor,* from *amāre* to love; so called because it readily ignites]

Amagasaki (ə,mɑ:gə'sɑ:kɪ) *n* an industrial city in Japan, in W Honshu, on Osaka Bay. Pop.: 488 574 (1995).

amah ('ɑ:mə, 'æmə) *n* (in the East, esp. formerly) a nurse or maidservant, esp. one of Chinese origin. Compare **ayah.** [C19: from Portuguese *ama* nurse, wet nurse]

amain (ə'meɪn) *adv Archaic or poetic.* with great strength, speed, or haste. [C16: from A-[2] + MAIN[1]]

Amalekite (ə'mælə,kaɪt) *n Old Testament.* a member of a nomadic tribe descended from Esau (Genesis 36:12), dwelling in the desert between Sinai and Canaan and hostile to the Israelites: they were defeated by Saul and destroyed by David (I Samuel 15–30).

Amalfi (ə'mælfɪ) *n* a town in Italy: a major Mediterranean port from the 10th to the 18th century, now a resort.

amalgam (ə'mælgəm) *n* **1** an alloy of mercury with another metal, esp. with silver: *dental amalgam.* **2** a rare white metallic mineral that consists of silver and mercury and occurs in deposits of silver and cinnabar. **3** a blend or combination. [C15: from Medieval Latin *amalgama,* of obscure origin]

amalgamate (ə'mælgə,meɪt) *vb* **1** to combine or cause to combine; unite. **2** to alloy (a metal) with mercury.

amalgamation (ə,mælgə'meɪʃən) *n* **1** the action or process of amalgamating. **2** the state of being amalgamated. **3** a method of extracting precious metals from their ores by treatment with mercury to form an amalgam. **4** *Commerce.* another word for **merger** (sense 1).

Amalthea[1] (,æmæl'θi:ə) *n Greek myth.* **a** a nymph who brought up the infant Zeus on goat's milk. **b** the goat itself. ◆ Also: **Amaltheia.**

Amalthea[2] (,æmæl'θi:ə) *n* an inner satellite of Jupiter.

amandla (a'mɑ:ndla) *n S. African.* a political slogan calling for power to the Black population. [C20: Nguni, literally: power]

amanita (,æmə'naɪtə) *n* any of various saprotrophic agaricaceous fungi constituting the genus *Amanita,* having white gills and a broken membranous ring (volva) around the stalk. The genus includes several highly poisonous species, such as death cap, destroying angel, and fly agaric. [C19: from Greek *amanitai* (plural) a variety of fungus]

amanuensis (ə,mænju'ɛnsɪs) *n, pl* **-ses** (-si:z). a person employed to take dictation or to copy manuscripts. [C17: from Latin *āmanuensis,* from the phrase *servus ā manū* slave at hand (that is, handwriting)]

Amanullah Khan (,æmə'nʊlə kɑ:n) *n* 1892–1960, emir (1919–26) and king (1926–29) of Afghanistan; he obtained Afghan independence from Britain (1919).

Amapá (*Portuguese* ,amə'pɑ:) *n* a state of N Brazil, on the Amazon delta. Capital: Macapá. Pop.: 326 200 (1995 est.). Area: 143 716 sq. km (55 489 sq. miles).

amaranth ('æmə,rænθ) *n* **1** *Poetic.* an imaginary flower that never fades. **2** any of numerous tropical and temperate plants of the genus *Amaranthus,* having tassel-like heads of small green, red, or purple flowers: family *Amaranthaceae.* See also **love-lies-bleeding, tumbleweed, pigweed** (sense 1). **3** a synthetic red food colouring (**E123**), used in packet soups, cake mixes, etc. [C17: from Latin *amarantus,* from Greek *amarantos* unfading, from A-[1] + *marainein* to fade]

amaranthaceous (,æməræn'θeɪʃəs) *adj* of, relating to, or belonging to the *Amaranthaceae* (or *Amarantaceae*), a family of tropical and temperate herbaceous or shrubby flowering plants that includes the amaranths and cockscomb.

amaranthine (,æmə'rænθaɪn) *adj* **1** of a dark reddish-purple colour. **2** of or resembling the amaranth.

amarelle ('æmə,rɛl) *n* a variety of sour cherry that has pale red fruit and colourless juice. Compare **morello.** [C20: from German, from Medieval Latin *amārellum,* from Latin *amārus* bitter; compare MORELLO]

amaretto (æmə'rɛtəʊ) *n* an Italian liqueur with a flavour of almonds. [C20: from Italian *amaro* bitter]

Amarillo (,æmə'rɪləʊ) *n* an industrial city in NW Texas. Pop.: 165 036 (1994 est.).

amaryllidaceous (,æmə,rɪlɪ'deɪʃəs) *adj* of, relating to, or belonging to the *Amaryllidaceae,* a family of widely cultivated flowering plants having bulbs and including the amaryllis, snowdrop, narcissus, and daffodil.

amaryllis (,æmə'rɪlɪs) *n* **1** Also called: **belladonna lily.** an amaryllidaceous plant, *Amaryllis belladonna,* native to southern Africa and having large lily-like reddish or white flowers. **2** any of several related plants. [C18: from New Latin, from Latin: named after AMARYLLIS]

Amaryllis (,æmə'rɪlɪs) *n* (in pastoral poetry) a name for a shepherdess or country girl.

amass (ə'mæs) *vb* **1** (*tr*) to accumulate or collect (esp. riches, etc.). **2** to gather in a heap; bring together. [C15: from Old French *amasser,* from *masse* MASS] ▸ **a'masser** *n*

amateur ('æmətə, -tʃə, -,tjʊə; ,æmə'tɜ:) *n* **1** a person who engages in an activity, esp. a sport, as a pastime rather than professionally or for gain. **2** an athlete or sportsman. **3** a person unskilled in or having only a superficial knowledge of a subject or activity. **4** a person who is fond of or admires something. **5** (*modifier*) consisting of or for amateurs: *an amateur event.* ◆ *adj* **6** amateurish; not professional or expert: *an amateur approach.* [C18: from French, from Latin *amātor* lover, from *amāre* to love] ▸ **'amateurism** *n*

amateurish ('æmətərɪʃ, -tʃər-, -,tjʊər-; ,æmə'tɜ:rɪʃ) *adj* lacking professional skill or expertise. ▸ **'amateurishly** *adv* ▸ **'amateurishness** *n*

Amati *n* **1** (*Italian* a'ma:ti). a family of Italian violin makers, active in Cremona in the 16th and 17th centuries, esp. **Nicolò** (niko'lɔ), 1596–1684, who taught Guarneri and Stradivari. **2** (ə'mɑ:tɪ). (*pl* **Amatis**) a violin or other stringed instrument made by any member of this family.

amative ('æmətɪv) *adj* a rare word for **amorous.** [C17: from Medieval Latin *amātīvus,* from Latin *amāre* to love] ▸ **'amatively** *adv* ▸ **'amativeness** *n*

amatol ('æmə,tɒl) *n* an explosive mixture of ammonium nitrate and TNT, used in shells and bombs. [C20: from AM(MONIUM) + (TRINITRO)TOL(UENE)]

amatory ('æmətərɪ) *or* **amatorial** (,æmə'tɔ:rɪəl) *adj* of, relating to, or inciting sexual love or desire. [C16: from Latin *amātōrius,* from *amāre* to love]

amaurosis (,æmɔ:'rəʊsɪs) *n Pathol.* blindness, esp. when occurring without observable damage to the eye. [C17: via New Latin from Greek: darkening, from *amauroun* to dim, darken] ▸ **amaurotic** (,æmɔ:'rɒtɪk) *adj*

amaut *or* **amowt** (ə'maʊt) *n Canadian.* a hood on an Eskimo woman's parka for carrying a child. [from Eskimo]

amaze (əˈmeɪz) *vb* (*tr*) **1** to fill with incredulity or surprise; astonish. **2** an obsolete word for **bewilder.** ◆ *n* **3** an archaic word for **amazement.** [Old English *āmasian*]

amazement (əˈmeɪzmənt) *n* **1** incredulity or great astonishment; complete wonder or surprise. **2** *Obsolete.* bewilderment or consternation.

amazing (əˈmeɪzɪŋ) *adj* causing wonder or astonishment: *amazing feats.* ▸ **aˈmazingly** *adv*

amazon (ˈæməzᵊn) *n* any of various tropical American parrots of the genus *Amazona,* such as *A. farinosa* (green amazon), having a short tail and mainly green plumage.

Amazon[1] (ˈæməzᵊn) *n* **1** *Greek myth.* one of a race of women warriors of Scythia near the Black Sea. **2** one of a legendary tribe of female warriors of South America. **3** (*often not cap.*) any tall, strong, or aggressive woman. [C14: via Latin from Greek *Amazōn,* of uncertain origin] ▸ **Amazonian** (ˌæməˈzəʊnɪən) *adj*

Amazon[2] (ˈæməzᵊn) *n* a river in South America, rising in the Peruvian Andes and flowing east through N Brazil to the Atlantic: in volume, the largest river in the world; navigable for 3700 km (2300 miles). Length: over 6440 km (4000 miles). Area of basin: over 5 827 500 sq. km (2 250 000 sq. miles). ▸ **Amazonian** (ˌæməˈzəʊnɪən) *adj*

amazon ant *n* any of several small reddish ants of the genus *Polyergus,* esp. *P. rufescens,* that enslave the young of other ant species.

Amazonas (ˌæməˈzəʊnəs) *n* a state of W Brazil, consisting of the central Amazon basin: vast areas of unexplored tropical rainforest. Capital: Manaus. Pop.: 2 320 200 (1995 est.). Area: 1 542 277 sq. km (595 474 sq. miles).

Amazonia (æməˈzəʊnɪə) *n* the land around the Amazon river.

amazonite (ˈæməzəˌnaɪt) *n* a green variety of microcline used as a gemstone. Formula: $KAlSi_3O_8$. Also called: **Amazon stone.**

Ambala (əmˈbɑːlə) *n* a city in N India, in Haryana: site of archaeological remains of a prehistoric Indian civilization: grain, cotton, food processing. Pop.: 119 338 (1991).

Ambartsumian (*Russian* amˌbartsumˈjan) *n* **Viktor A(mazaspovich).** 1908–96, Armenian astrophysicist, renowned for his description of radio sources as explosions in the core of galaxies.

ambary *or* **ambari** (æmˈbɑːrɪ) *n, pl* **-ries** *or* **-ris. 1** a tropical Asian malvaceous plant, *Hibiscus cannabinus,* that yields a fibre similar to jute. **2** the fibre derived from this plant. ◆ Also called: **kenaf.** [C20: from Hindi *ambārī*]

ambassador (æmˈbæsədə) *n* **1** short for **ambassador extraordinary and plenipotentiary;** a diplomatic minister of the highest rank, accredited as permanent representative to another country or sovereign. **2 ambassador extraordinary.** a diplomatic minister of the highest rank sent on a special mission. **3 ambassador plenipotentiary.** a diplomatic minister of the first rank with treaty-signing powers. **4 ambassador-at-large.** *U.S.* an ambassador with special duties who may be sent to more than one government. **5** an authorized representative or messenger. [C14: from Old French *ambassadeur,* from Italian *ambasciator,* from Old Provençal *ambaisador,* from *ambaisa* (unattested) mission, errand; see EMBASSY] ▸ **amˈbassadress** *fem n* ▸ **ambassadorial** (æmˌbæsəˈdɔːrɪəl) *adj* ▸ **amˈbassadorˌship** *n*

ambatch *or* **ambach** (ˈæmˌbætʃ) *n* a tree or shrub of the Nile Valley, *Aeschynomene elaphroxylon,* valued for its light-coloured pithlike wood. [C19: probably from the Ethiopian name]

amber (ˈæmbə) *n* **1a** a yellow or yellowish-brown hard translucent fossil resin derived from extinct coniferous trees that occurs in Tertiary deposits and often contains trapped insects. It is used for jewellery, ornaments, etc. **1b** (*as modifier*): *an amber necklace.* Related adj: **succinic. 2 fly in amber.** a strange relic or reminder of the past. **3a** a medium to dark brownish-yellow colour, often somewhat orange, similar to that of the resin. **3b** (*as adj*): *an amber dress.* **4** an amber traffic light used as a warning between red and green. [C14: from Medieval Latin *ambar,* from Arabic *'anbar* ambergris]

amber fluid *n Austral. slang.* beer.

amber gambler *n Brit. informal.* a driver who races through traffic lights when they are at amber.

ambergris (ˈæmbəˌgriːs, -ˌgrɪs) *n* a waxy substance consisting mainly of cholesterol secreted by the intestinal tract of the sperm whale and often found floating in the sea: used in the manufacture of perfumes. [C15: from Old French *ambre gris* grey amber]

amberjack (ˈæmbəˌdʒæk) *n* any of several large carangid fishes of the genus *Seriola,* esp. *S. dumerili,* with golden markings when young, occurring in tropical and subtropical Atlantic waters. [C19: from AMBER + JACK[1]]

amberoid (ˈæmbəˌrɔɪd) *or* **ambroid** *n* a synthetic amber made by compressing pieces of amber and other resins together at a high temperature.

ambi- *combining form.* indicating both: *ambidextrous; ambivalence; ambiversion.* [from Latin: round, on both sides, both, from *ambo* both; compare AMPHI-]

ambidentate (ˌæmbɪˈdenteɪt) *adj Chem.* another word for **amphidentate.**

ambidextrous (ˌæmbɪˈdekstrəs) *adj* **1** equally expert with each hand. **2** *Informal.* highly skilled or adept. **3** underhanded; deceitful. ▸ **ambidexterity** (ˌæmbɪdekˈsterɪtɪ) *or* **ˌambiˈdextrousness** *n* ▸ **ˌambiˈdextrously** *adv*

ambience *or* **ambiance** (ˈæmbɪəns; *French* ɑ̃bjɑ̃s) *n* the atmosphere of a place. [C19: from French *ambiance,* from *ambiant* surrounding; see AMBIENT]

ambient (ˈæmbɪənt) *adj* **1** of or relating to the immediate surroundings: *the ambient temperature was 15°C.* **2** creating a relaxing atmosphere: *ambient music.* [C16: from Latin *ambiēns* going round, from *ambīre,* from AMBI- + *īre* to go]

ambient noise *n* the level of the total noise in an area.

ambiguity (ˌæmbɪˈgjuːɪtɪ) *n, pl* **-ties. 1** the possibility of interpreting an expression in two or more distinct ways. **2** an instance of this, as in the sentence *they are cooking apples.* **3** vagueness or uncertainty of meaning: *there are several ambiguities in the situation.*

ambiguous (æmˈbɪgjʊəs) *adj* **1** having more than one possible interpretation or meaning. **2** difficult to understand or classify; obscure. [C16: from Latin *ambiguus* going here and there, uncertain, from *ambigere* to go around, from AMBI- + *agere* to lead, act] ▸ **amˈbiguously** *adv* ▸ **amˈbiguousness** *n*

ambiophony (ˌæmbɪˈɒfənɪ) *n* the reproduction of sound to create an illusion to a listener of being in a spacious room, such as a concert hall.

ambipolar (ˌæmbɪˈpəʊlə) *adj Electronics.* (of plasmas and semiconductors) involving both positive and negative charge carriers.

ambisexual (ˌæmbɪˈseksjʊəl) *or* **ambosexual** *adj Biology.* relating to or affecting both the male and female sexes.

ambisonics (ˌæmbɪˈsɒnɪks) *n* (*functioning as sing*) the technique of reproducing and transmitting surround sound. See **surround sound.**

ambit (ˈæmbɪt) *n* **1** scope or extent. **2** limits, boundary, or circumference. [C16: from Latin *ambitus* a going round, from *ambīre* to go round, from AMBI- + *īre* to go]

ambition (æmˈbɪʃən) *n* **1** strong desire for success, achievement, or distinction. **2** something so desired; goal; aim. [C14: from Old French, from Latin *ambitiō* a going round (of candidates), a striving to please, from *ambīre* to go round; see AMBIT]

ambitious (æmˈbɪʃəs) *adj* **1** having a strong desire for success or achievement; wanting power, money, etc. **2** necessitating extraordinary effort or ability: *an ambitious project.* **3** (often foll. by *of*) having a great desire (for something or to do something). ▸ **amˈbitiously** *adv* ▸ **amˈbitiousness** *n*

ambivalence (æmˈbɪvələns) *or* **ambivalency** *n* the simultaneous existence of two opposed and conflicting attitudes, emotions, etc. ▸ **amˈbivalent** *adj*

ambivert (ˈæmbɪˌvɜːt) *n Psychol.* a person who is intermediate between an extrovert and an introvert. ▸ **ambiversion** (ˌæmbɪˈvɜːʃən) *n*

amble (ˈæmbᵊl) *vb* (*intr*) **1** to walk at a leisurely relaxed pace. **2** (of a horse) to move slowly, lifting both legs on one side together. **3** to ride a horse at an amble or leisurely pace. ◆ *n* **4** a leisurely motion in walking. **5** a leisurely walk. **6** the ambling gait of a horse. [C14: from Old French *ambler,* from Latin *ambulāre* to walk] ▸ **ˈambler** *n*

Ambler (ˈæmblə) *n* **Eric.** 1909–98, English novelist. His thrillers include *The Mask of Dimitrios* (1939), *Journey into Fear* (1940), *A Kind of Anger* (1964), and *Doctor Frigo* (1974).

Ambleside (ˈæmbᵊlˌsaɪd) *n* a town in NW England, in Cumbria: a tourist centre for the Lake District. Pop.: 2905 (1991).

amblygonite (æmˈblɪgəˌnaɪt) *n* a white or greyish mineral consisting of lithium aluminium fluophosphate in triclinic crystalline form. It is a source of lithium. Formula: $LiAl(PO_4)(F,OH)$. [C16: from Greek *amblugōnios,* from *amblus* blunt + *gōnia* angle; referring to the obtuse angles in its crystals]

amblyopia (ˌæmblɪˈəʊpɪə) *n* impaired vision with no discernible damage to the eye or optic nerve. [C18: New Latin, from Greek *ambluōpia,* from *amblus* dull, dim + *ōps* eye] ▸ **amblyopic** (ˌæmblɪˈɒpɪk) *adj*

ambo (ˈæmbəʊ) *n, pl* **ambos** *or* **ambones** (æmˈbəʊniːz). either of two raised pulpits from which the gospels and epistles were read in early Christian churches. [C17: from Medieval Latin, from Greek *ambōn* raised rim, pulpit]

amboceptor (ˈæmbəʊˌseptə) *n* an immune body formed in the blood during infection or immunization that serves to link the complement to the antigen. [C20: from Latin *ambō* both (see AMBI-) + (RE)CEPTOR]

Amboina (æmˈbɔɪnə) *n* **1** an island in Indonesia, in the Moluccas. Capital: Amboina. Area: 1000 sq. km (386 sq. miles). **2** Also called: **Ambon** (ˈɑːmbɔːn). a port in the Moluccas, the capital of Amboina island.

Amboise (*French* ɑ̃bwaz) *n* a town in NW central France, on the River Loire: famous castle, a former royal residence. Pop.: 11 415 (1982).

amboyna *or* **amboina** (æmˈbɔɪnə) *n* the mottled curly-grained wood of an Indonesian papilionaceous tree, *Pterocarpus indicus,* used in making furniture. [C19: from the island of AMBOINA]

ambroid (ˈæmbrɔɪd) *n* a variant of **amberoid.**

Ambrose (ˈæmbrəʊz) *n* **Saint.** ?340–397 A.D., bishop of Milan; built up the secular power of the early Christian Church; also wrote music and Latin hymns. Feast day: Dec. 7 or April 4. ▸ **Amˈbrosian** *adj*

ambrosia (æmˈbrəʊzɪə) *n* **1** *Classical myth.* the food of the gods, said to bestow immortality. Compare **nectar** (sense 2). **2** anything particularly delightful to taste or smell. **3** another name for **beebread. 4** any of various herbaceous plants constituting the genus *Ambrosia,* mostly native to America but widely naturalized: family *Compositae* (composites). The genus includes the ragweeds. [C16: via Latin from Greek: immortality, from *ambrotos,* from A-[1] + *brotos* mortal] ▸ **amˈbrosial** *or* **amˈbrosian** *adj* ▸ **amˈbrosially** *adv*

ambrosia beetle *n* any of various small beetles of the genera *Anisandrus, Xyleborus,* etc., that bore tunnels into solid wood, feeding on fungi growing in the tunnels: family *Scolytidae* (bark beetles).

ambrotype (ˈæmbrəʊˌtaɪp) *n Photog.* an early type of glass negative that could be made to appear as a positive by backing it with black varnish or paper. [C19: from Greek *ambrotos* immortal + -TYPE; see AMBROSIA]

ambry (ˈæmbrɪ) *or* **aumbry** (ˈɔːmbrɪ) *n, pl* **-bries. 1** a recessed cupboard in the wall of a church near the altar, used to store sacred vessels, etc. **2** *Obsolete.* a small cupboard or other storage space. [C14: from Old French *almarie,* from Medieval Latin *almārium,* from Latin *armārium* chest for storage, from *arma* arms]

ambsace *or* **amesace** (ˈeɪmzˌeɪs, ˈæmz-) *n* **1** double ace, the lowest throw at dice. **2** bad luck. [C13: from Old French *ambes as,* both aces; *as* from Latin: unit]

ambulacrum (ˌæmbjʊˈleɪkrəm) *n, pl* **-ra** (-rə). any of five radial bands on the ventral surface of echinoderms, such as the starfish and sea urchin, on which the tube feet are situated. [C19: from Latin: avenue, from *ambulāre* to walk] ▸ **ˌambuˈlacral** *adj*

ambulance (ˈæmbjʊləns) *n* a motor vehicle designed to carry sick or injured people. [C19: from French, based on *(hôpital) ambulant* mobile or field (hospital), from Latin *ambulāre* to walk]

ambulance chaser *n U.S. slang.* a lawyer who seeks to encourage and profit from the lawsuits of accident victims. ▸ **ambulance chasing** *n*

ambulance stocks *pl n* high performance stocks and shares recommended by a broker to a dissatisfied client to improve their relationship.

ambulant ('æmbjʊlənt) *adj* **1** moving about from place to place. **2** *Med.* another word for **ambulatory** (sense 3).

ambulate ('æmbjʊˌleɪt) *vb* (*intr*) to wander about or move from one place to another. [C17: from Latin *ambulāre* to walk, AMBLE] ▸ ˌ**ambu'lation** *n*

ambulatory ('æmbjʊlətərɪ) *adj* **1** of, relating to, or designed for walking. **2** changing position; not fixed. **3** Also: **ambulant.** able to walk. **4** *Law.* (esp. of a will) capable of being altered or revoked. ♦ *n, pl* **-ries. 5** *Architect.* **5a** an aisle running around the east end of a church, esp. one that passes behind the sanctuary. **5b** a place for walking, such as an aisle or a cloister.

ambuscade (ˌæmbə'skeɪd) *n* **1** an ambush. ♦ *vb* **2** to ambush or lie in ambush. [C16: from French *embuscade,* from Old Italian *imboscata,* probably of Germanic origin; compare AMBUSH]

ambush ('æmbʊʃ) *n* **1** the act of waiting in a concealed position in order to launch a surprise attack. **2** a surprise attack from such a position. **3** the concealed position from which such an attack is launched. **4** the person or persons waiting to launch such an attack. ♦ *vb* **5** to lie in wait (for). **6** (*tr*) to attack suddenly from a concealed position. [C14: from Old French *embuschier* to position in ambush, from *em-* IM- + *-buschier,* from *busche* piece of firewood, probably of Germanic origin; see BUSH[1]]

AMDG *abbrev. for* ad majorem Dei gloriam (the Jesuit motto). [Latin: to the greater glory of God]

ameba (ə'miːbə) *n, pl* **-bae** (-biː) *or* **-bas.** the usual U.S. spelling of **amoeba.** ▸ **a'mebic** *adj*

ameer (ə'mɪə) *n* **1** a variant spelling of **emir. 2** (formerly) the ruler of Afghanistan; amir.

ameiosis (ˌeɪmaɪ'əʊsɪs) *n Biology.* the nonpairing of chromosomes during meiosis.

amelia (ə'miːlɪə) *n Pathol.* the congenital absence of arms or legs. [from A-[1] + Greek *melos* limb + -IA]

ameliorate (ə'miːljəˌreɪt) *vb* to make or become better; improve. [C18: from MELIORATE, influenced by French *améliorer* to improve, from Old French *ameillorer* to make better, from *meillor* better, from Latin *melior*] ▸ **ameliorable** (ə'miːljərəb°l) *adj* ▸ **a'meliorant** *n* ▸ **a'meliorative** *adj* ▸ **a'melioˌrator** *n*

USAGE *Ameliorate* is often wrongly used where *alleviate* is meant. *Ameliorate* is properly used to mean 'improve', not 'make easier to bear', so one should talk about *alleviating* pain or hardship, not *ameliorating* it.

amelioration (əˌmiːljə'reɪʃən) *n* **1** the act or an instance of ameliorating or the state of being ameliorated. **2** something that ameliorates; an improvement. **3** Also called: **elevation.** *Linguistics.* (of the meaning of a word) a change from pejorative to neutral or positively pleasant. The word *nice* has achieved its modern meaning by amelioration from the earlier sense *foolish, silly.*

ameloblast (ə'miːləʊblæst, -blɑːst) *n* a type of cell involved in forming dental enamel. [C19: from (EN)AMEL + -O- + -BLAST]

amelogenesis (əˌmiːləʊ'dʒɛnɪsɪs) *n* the production of enamel by ameloblasts.

amen (ˌeɪ'mɛn, ˌɑː'mɛn) *interj* **1** so be it!: a term used at the end of a prayer or religious statement. ♦ *n* **2** the use of the word *amen,* as at the end of a prayer. **3 say amen to.** to express strong approval of or support for (an assertion, hope, etc.). [C13: via Late Latin via Greek from Hebrew *āmēn* certainly]

Amen, Amon, *or* **Amūn** ('ɑːmən) *n Egyptian myth.* a local Theban god, having a ram's head and symbolizing life and fertility, identified by the Egyptians with the national deity Amen-Ra.

amenable (ə'miːnəb°l) *adj* **1** open or susceptible to suggestion; likely to listen, cooperate, etc. **2** accountable for behaviour to some authority; answerable. **3** capable of being or liable to be tested, judged, etc. [C16: from Anglo-French, from Old French *amener* to lead up, from Latin *mināre* to drive (cattle), from *minārī* to threaten] ▸ **aˌmena'bility** *or* **a'menableness** *n* ▸ **a'menably** *adv*

amen corner *n* **the.** *U.S.* the part of a church, usually to one side of the pulpit, occupied by people who lead the responsive amens during the service.

amend (ə'mɛnd) *vb* (*tr*) **1** to improve; change for the better. **2** to remove faults from; correct. **3** to alter or revise (legislation, a constitution, etc.) by formal procedure. [C13: from Old French *amender,* from Latin *ēmendāre* to EMEND] ▸ **a'mendable** *adj* ▸ **a'mender** *n*

amendatory (ə'mɛndətərɪ, -trɪ) *adj U.S.* serving to amend; corrective.

amende honorable *French.* (amɑ̃d ɔnɔrablə) *n, pl* ***amendes honorables*** (amɑ̃dz ɔnɔrablə). a public apology and reparation made to satisfy the honour of the person wronged. Sometimes shortened to ***amende.*** [C18: literally: honourable compensation]

amendment (ə'mɛndmənt) *n* **1** the act of amending; correction. **2** an addition, alteration, or improvement to a motion, document, etc.

amends (ə'mɛndz) *n* (*functioning as sing*) recompense or compensation given or gained for some injury, insult, etc.: *to make amends.* [C13: from Old French *amendes* fines, from *amende* compensation, from *amender* to EMEND]

Amenhotep III (ˌæmɛn'həʊtɛp) *or* **Amenhotpe III** (ˌæmɛn'hɒtpɪ) *n* Greek name *Amenophis.* ?1411–?1375 B.C., Egyptian pharaoh who expanded Egypt's influence by peaceful diplomacy and erected many famous buildings.

Amenhotep IV *or* **Amenhotpe IV** *n* the original name of **Akhenaten.**

amenity (ə'miːnɪtɪ) *n, pl* **-ties. 1** (*often pl*) a useful or pleasant facility or service: *a swimming pool was just one of the amenities.* **2** the fact or condition of being pleasant or agreeable. **3** (*usually pl*) a social courtesy or pleasantry. [C14: from Latin *amoenitās* pleasantness, from *amoenus* agreeable]

amenity bed *n* (in Britain) a hospital bed whose occupant receives free treatment but pays for nonmedical advantages, such as privacy. Also called (informal): **pay bed.**

amenorrhoea *or esp. U.S.* **amenorrhea** (æˌmɛnə'rɪə, eɪ-) *n* abnormal absence of menstruation. [C19: from A-[1] + MENO- + -RRHOEA]

Amen-Ra (ˌɑːmən'rɑː) *n Egyptian myth.* the sun-god; the principal deity during the period of Theban hegemony.

a mensa et thoro (eɪ 'mɛnsə ɛt 'θɔːrəʊ) *adj Law.* denoting or relating to a form of divorce in which the parties remain married but do not cohabit: abolished in England in 1857. [Latin: from table and bed]

ament[1] ('æmənt, 'eɪmənt) *n* another name for **catkin.** Also called: **amentum** (ə'mɛntəm). [C18: from Latin *āmentum* strap, thong] ▸ ˌ**amen'taceous** *adj* ▸ ˌ**amen'tiferous** *adj*

ament[2] (æ'mɛnt, 'eɪmənt) *n Psychiatry.* a mentally deficient person. [C19: from Latin *āment-, āmens* without mind; see AMENTIA]

amentia (ə'mɛnʃə) *n* severe mental deficiency, usually congenital. Compare **dementia.** [C14: from Latin: insanity, from *āmēns* mad, from *mēns* mind]

Amer. *abbrev. for* America(n).

amerce (ə'mɜːs) *vb* (*tr*) *Obsolete.* **1** *Law.* to punish by a fine. **2** to punish with any arbitrary penalty. [C14: from Anglo-French *amercier,* from Old French *à merci* at the mercy (because the fine was arbitrarily fixed); see MERCY] ▸ **a'merceable** *adj* ▸ **a'mercement** *n* ▸ **a'mercer** *n*

America (ə'mɛrɪkə) *n* **1** short for the **United States of America. 2** Also called: **the Americas.** the American continent, including North, South, and Central America. [C16: from *Americus,* Latin form of *Amerigo;* see VESPUCCI]

American (ə'mɛrɪkən) *adj* **1** of or relating to the United States of America, its inhabitants, or their form of English. **2** of or relating to the American continent. ♦ *n* **3** a native or citizen of the U.S. **4** a native or inhabitant of any country of North, Central, or South America. **5** the English language as spoken or written in the United States.

Americana (əˌmɛrɪ'kɑːnə) *pl n* objects, such as books, documents, relics, etc., relating to America, esp. in the form of a collection.

American aloe *n* another name for **century plant.**

American chameleon *n* another name for **anole.**

American cheese *n* a type of smooth hard white or yellow cheese similar to a mild Cheddar.

American cloth *n* a glazed or waterproofed cotton cloth.

American Dream *n* **the.** the notion that the American social, economic, and political system makes success possible for every individual.

American eagle *n* another name for **bald eagle,** esp. when depicted as the national emblem of the U.S.

American Expeditionary Forces *pl n* the troops sent to Europe by the U.S. during World War I.

American Federation of Labor *n* the first permanent national labour movement in America, founded in 1886. It amalgamated with the Congress of Industrial Organizations in 1955. See also **AFL-CIO.**

American football *n* **1** a team game similar to rugby, with 11 players on each side. Forward passing is allowed and planned strategies and formations for play are decided during the course of the game. **2** the oval-shaped inflated ball used in this game.

American Indian *n* **1** Also called: **Indian, Red Indian, Amerindian, Native American.** a member of any of the indigenous peoples of North, Central, or South America, having Mongoloid affinities, notably straight black hair and a yellow to brown skin. ♦ *adj* **2** Also: **Amerindian.** of or relating to any of these peoples, their languages, or their cultures.

American Indian Movement *n* a militant movement or grouping of American Indians, organized in 1968 to combat discrimination, injustice, etc.

Americanism (ə'mɛrɪkəˌnɪzəm) *n* **1** a custom, linguistic usage, or other feature peculiar to or characteristic of the United States, its people, or their culture. **2** loyalty to the United States, its people, customs, etc.

Americanist (ə'mɛrɪkənɪst) *n* a person who studies some aspect of America, such as its history or languages.

Americanize *or* **Americanise** (ə'mɛrɪkəˌnaɪz) *vb* to make or become American in outlook, attitudes, etc. ▸ **Aˌmericani'zation** *or* **Aˌmericani'sation** *n* ▸ **A'mericanˌizer** *or* **A'mericanˌiser** *n*

American pit bull terrier *n* another name for **pit bull terrier.**

American plan *n U.S.* a hotel rate in which the charge includes meals. Compare **European plan.**

American Revolution *n* the usual U.S. term for **War of American Independence.**

American Samoa *n* the part of Samoa administered by the U.S. Capital: Pago Pago. Pop.: 62 100 (1998 est.). Area: 197 sq. km (76 sq. miles).

American sign language *n* See **Ameslan.**

American Standard Version *n* a revised version of the Authorized (King James) Version of the Bible, published by a committee of American scholars in 1901.

American trypanosomiasis *n Pathol.* another name for **Chagas' disease.**

American Wake *n Irish.* an all-night farewell party for a person about to emigrate to America.

America's Cup *n* an international yachting trophy, first won by the schooner *America* in 1851 and held as a challenge trophy by the New York Yacht Club until 1983.

americium (ˌæmə'rɪsɪəm) *n* a white metallic transuranic element artificially produced from plutonium. It is used as an alpha-particle source. Symbol: Am; atomic no.: 95; half-life of most stable isotope, ^{243}Am: 7.4 × 10^3 years; valency: 2,3,4,5, or 6; relative density: 13.67; melting pt.: 1176°C; boiling pt.: 2607°C (est.). [C20: from AMERICA (because it was discovered at Berkeley, California) + -IUM]

Amerigo Vespucci (*Italian* ame'riːgo ves'puttʃi) *n* See **Vespucci.**

Amerindian (ˌæməˈrɪndɪən) *n also* **Amerind** (ˈæmərɪnd), *adj* another word for **American Indian.** ▸ ˌ**Amerˈindic** *adj*

Amersfoort (*Dutch* ˈaːmərsfoːrt) *n* a town in the central Netherlands, in E Utrecht province. Pop.: 114 884 (1996 est.).

amesace (ˈeɪmzˌeɪs, ˈæmz-) *n* a variant spelling of **ambsace.**

Ameslan (ˈæməsˌlæn) *n* American sign language: a language in which meaning is conveyed by hand gestures and their position in relation to the upper part of the body. Abbrev.: **ASL.** [C20: from *Ame(rican) s(ign) lan(guage)*]

Ames test (eɪmz) *n* a method of preliminary screening for carcinogens, based on their ability to cause mutations in bacteria. [named after Bruce *Ames* (born 1928), U.S. biochemist who invented the test]

ametabolic (əˌmɛtəˈbɒlɪk) *adj* (of certain insects) having no obvious metamorphosis.

amethyst (ˈæmɪθɪst) *n* **1** a purple or violet transparent variety of quartz used as a gemstone. Formula: SiO_2. **2** a purple variety of sapphire; oriental amethyst. **3** the purple colour of amethyst. [C13: from Old French *amatiste,* from Latin *amethystus,* from Greek *amethustos,* literally: not drunken, from A-[1] + *methuein* to make drunk; referring to the belief that the stone could prevent intoxication] ▸ **amethystine** (ˌæmɪˈθɪstaɪn) *adj*

ametropia (ˌæmɪˈtrəʊpɪə) *n* loss of ability to focus images on the retina, caused by an imperfection in the refractive function of the eye. [C19: New Latin, from Greek *ametros* unmeasured (from A-[1] + *metron* measure) + *ōps* eye]

Amex (ˈæmɛks) *n acronym for* **1** *Trademark.* American Express. **2** American Stock Exchange.

AMF *abbrev. for* Australian Military Forces.

Amfortas (æmˈfɔːtəs) *n* (in medieval legend) the leader of the knights of the Holy Grail.

Amhara (æmˈhɑːrə) *n* **1** a region of NW Ethiopia: formerly a kingdom. **2** an inhabitant of the former kingdom of Amhara.

Amharic (æmˈhærɪk) *n* **1** the official language of Ethiopia, belonging to the SE Semitic subfamily of the Afro-Asiatic family. ◆ *adj* **2** denoting or relating to this language.

Amherst (ˈæmhɜːst) *n* **Jeffrey,** 1st Baron Amherst. 1717–97, British general who defeated the French in Canada (1758–60): governor general of British North America (1761–63).

ami *French.* (ami) *n* a male friend.

amiable (ˈeɪmɪəbᵊl) *adj* having or displaying a pleasant or agreeable nature; friendly. [C14: from Old French, from Late Latin *amīcābilis* AMICABLE] ▸ ˌ**amiaˈbility** *or* ˈ**amiableness** *n* ▸ ˈ**amiably** *adv*

amianthus (ˌæmɪˈænθəs) *n* any of the fine silky varieties of asbestos. [C17: from Latin *amiantus,* from Greek *amiantos* unsullied, from A-[1] + *miainein* to pollute] ▸ ˌ**amiˈanthine,** ˌ**amiˈanthoid,** *or* ˌ**amianˈthoidal** *adj*

amicable (ˈæmɪkəbᵊl) *adj* characterized by friendliness: *an amicable agreement.* [C15: from Late Latin *amīcābilis,* from Latin *amīcus* friend; related to *amāre* to love] ▸ ˌ**amicaˈbility** *or* ˈ**amicableness** *n* ▸ ˈ**amicably** *adv*

amice[1] (ˈæmɪs) *n Christianity.* a rectangular piece of white linen worn by priests around the neck and shoulders under the alb or, formerly, on the head. [C15: from Old French *amis,* plural of *amit,* or from Medieval Latin *amicia,* both from Latin *amictus* cloak, from *amicīre* to clothe, from *am-* AMBI- + *iacere* to throw]

amice[2] (ˈæmɪs) *n* another word for **almuce.**

AMICE *abbrev. for* Associate Member of the Institution of Civil Engineers.

AMIChemE *abbrev. for* Associate Member of the Institution of Chemical Engineers.

amicus curiae (æˈmiːkus ˈkjʊərɪˌiː) *n, pl* **amici curiae** (æˈmiːkaɪ) *Law.* a person not directly engaged in a case who advises the court. [Latin, literally: friend of the court]

amid (əˈmɪd) *or* **amidst** *prep* in the middle of; among. [Old English *on middan* in the middle; see MID[1]]

Amida (amidə) *n* the Japanese name for **Amitabha.**

Amidah (amiˈdaː, aˈmidə) *n Judaism.* the central prayer in each of the daily services, recited silently and standing. Also called: **Shemona Esrei.**

amide (ˈæmaɪd) *n* **1** any organic compound containing the group $-CONH_2$. **2** (*modifier*) consisting of, containing, or concerned with the group $-CONH_2$: *amide group or radical.* **3** an inorganic compound having the general formula $M(NH_2)_x$, where M is a metal atom. [C19: from AM(MONIA) + -IDE] ▸ **amidic** (əˈmɪdɪk) *adj*

amido- *combining form.* (in chemistry) indicating the presence of an amide group. [from AMIDE]

Amidol (ˈæmɪdɒl) *n Trademark.* a grey to colourless soluble crystalline solid that is used as a photographic developer; 2,4-diaminophenol dihydrochloride. Formula: $C_6H_3(NH_2)_2(OH).2HCl$.

amidships (əˈmɪdʃɪps) *adv, adj* (*postpositive*) *Nautical.* at, near, or towards the centre of a vessel.

amie *French.* (ami) *n* a female friend.

AMIEE (in Britain) *abbrev. for* Associate Member of the Institution of Electrical Engineers.

Amiens (ˈæmɪənz; *French* amjɛ̃) *n* a city in N France: its Gothic cathedral is the largest church in France. Pop.: 136 234 (1990).

amigo (æˈmiːgəʊ, ə-) *n, pl* **-gos.** a friend; comrade. [Spanish, from Latin *amicus*]

AMIMechE (in Britain) *abbrev. for* Associate Member of the Institution of Mechanical Engineers.

Amin[1] (æˈmiːn, ɑː-) *n* **Lake.** a former official name for (Lake) **Edward.**

Amin[2] (æˈmiːn, ɑː-) *n* **Idi** (ˈiːdiː). born 1925, Ugandan soldier; dictator and head of state (1971–79). Notorious for his brutality, he was overthrown and exiled.

amine (əˈmiːn, ˈæmɪn) *n* an organic base formed by replacing one or more of the hydrogen atoms of ammonia by organic groups. [C19: from AM(MONIUM) + -INE[2]]

-amine *n combining form.* indicating an amine: *histamine; methylamine.*

amino (əˈmaɪnəʊ, -ˈmiː-) *n* (*modifier*) of, consisting of, or containing the group of atoms $-NH_2$: *amino group or radical; amino acid.*

amino- *combining form.* indicating the presence of an amino group: *aminobenzoic acid.* [from AMINE]

amino acid *n* any of a group of organic compounds containing one or more amino groups, $-NH_2$, and one or more carboxyl groups, $-COOH$. The alpha-amino acids $RCH(NH_2)COOH$ (where R is either hydrogen or an organic group) are the component molecules of proteins; some can be synthesized in the body (**nonessential amino acids**) and others cannot and are thus essential components of the diet (**essential amino acids**).

amino acid sequence *n* the unique sequence of amino acids that characterizes a given protein.

aminobenzoic acid (əˌmaɪnəʊbɛnˈzəʊɪk, -ˌmiː-) *n* a derivative of benzoic acid existing in three isomeric forms, the *para-* form being used in the manufacture of dyes and sunburn preventatives. Formula: $NH_2C_6H_4COOH$.

aminophenol (əˌmaɪnəʊˈfiːnɒl, -ˌmiː-) *n Chem.* any of three isomeric forms that are white soluble crystalline solids, used as a dye intermediate (meta- and ortho-), in dyeing hair, fur, and textiles (ortho- and para-), and as a photographic developer (para-). Formula: $C_6H_4NH_2OH$.

aminophylline (æmɪˈnɒfɪliːn) *n* a derivative of theophylline that relaxes smooth muscle and is used mainly to dilate the airways in the treatment of asthma and emphysema. [C20: from AMINO- + PHYLLO- + -INE[2]]

aminopyrine (əˌmaɪnəʊˈpaɪriːn, -ˌmiː-) *n* a crystalline compound used to reduce pain and fever. Formula: $C_{13}H_{17}N_3O$.

amino resin *n* any thermosetting synthetic resin formed by copolymerization of amines with aldehydes. Amino resins are used as adhesives and as coatings for paper and textiles. See also **urea-formaldehyde resin, melamine.**

amir (əˈmɪə) *n* **1** a variant spelling of **emir. 2** (formerly) the ruler of Afghanistan; ameer. [C19: from Arabic, variant of EMIR] ▸ **aˈmirate** *n*

Amis (ˈeɪmɪs) *n* **1** Sir **Kingsley.** 1922–95, British novelist and poet, noted for his novels *Lucky Jim* (1954), *Jake's Thing* (1978), *Stanley and the Women* (1984), *The Old Devils* (1986), and *The Folks that Live on the Hill* (1990). **2** his son, **Martin.** born 1949, British novelist. His works include *The Rachel Papers* (1974), *London Fields* (1989), *The Information* (1994), and the short-story collection *Heavy Water* (1998).

Amish (ˈɑːmɪʃ, ˈæ-) *adj* **1** of or relating to a U.S. and Canadian Mennonite sect that traces its origin to Jakob Amman. ◆ *n* **2 the.** the Amish people. [C19: from German *Amisch,* after Jakob *Amman,* 17th-century Swiss Mennonite bishop]

amiss (əˈmɪs) *adv* **1** in an incorrect, inappropriate, or defective manner. **2 take (something) amiss.** to be annoyed or offended by (something). ◆ *adj* **3** (*postpositive*) wrong, incorrect, or faulty. [C13 *a mis,* from *mis* wrong; see MISS[1]]

Amitabha (ˌamɪˈtɑbə) *n Buddhism.* (in Pure Land sects) a Bodhisattva who presides over a Pure Land in the west of the universe. Japanese name: **Amida.** [Sanskrit, literally: immeasurable light, from *amita* infinite + *ābhā* light]

amitosis (ˌæmɪˈtəʊsɪs) *n* an unusual form of cell division in which the nucleus and cytoplasm divide by constriction without the formation of chromosomes; direct cell division. [C19: A-[1] + MITOSIS] ▸ **amitotic** (ˌæmɪˈtɒtɪk) *adj* ▸ ˌ**amiˈtotically** *adv*

amitriptyline (ˌæmɪˈtrɪptɪˌliːn, -lɪn) *n* a tricyclic antidepressant drug: a mild tranquillizer. Formula: $C_{20}H_{23}N$. [C20: from AMINO + TRYPTAMINE + METHYL + -INE[2]]

amity (ˈæmɪtɪ) *n, pl* **-ties.** friendship; cordiality. [C15: from Old French *amité,* from Medieval Latin *amīcitās* friendship, from Latin *amīcus* friend]

Amman (əˈmɑːn) *n* the capital of Jordan, northeast of the Dead Sea: ancient capital of the Ammonites, rebuilt by Ptolemy in the 3rd century B.C. Pop.: 963 490 (1994). Ancient names: **Rabbath Ammon, Philadelphia.**

ammeter (ˈæmˌmiːtə) *n* an instrument for measuring an electric current in amperes. [C19: AM(PERE) + -METER]

ammine (ˈæmiːn, əˈmiːn) *n* a compound that has molecules containing one or more ammonia molecules bound to another molecule, group, or atom by coordinate bonds. Also called: **ammoniate, ammonate.** [C19: from AMM(ONIA) + -INE[2]]

ammo (ˈæməʊ) *n Informal.* short for **ammunition.**

ammocoete (ˈæməˌsiːt) *n* the larva of primitive jawless vertebrates, such as the lamprey, that lives buried in mud and feeds on microorganisms. [C19: from New Latin *ammocoetēs,* literally: that lie in sand, from Greek *ammos* sand + *koitē* bed, from *keisthai* to lie]

Ammon[1] (ˈæmən) *n Old Testament.* the ancestor of the Ammonites.

Ammon[2] (ˈæmən) *n Myth.* the classical name of the Egyptian god Amen, identified by the Greeks with Zeus and by the Romans with Jupiter.

ammonal (ˈæmənᵊl) *n* an explosive made by mixing TNT, ammonium nitrate, and aluminium powder. [C20: from AMMON(IUM) + AL(UMINIUM)]

ammonate (ˈæməˌneɪt) *n* another name for **ammine.**

ammonia (əˈməʊnɪə, -njə) *n* **1** a colourless pungent highly soluble gas mainly used in the manufacture of fertilizers, nitric acid, and other nitrogenous compounds, and as a refrigerant and solvent. Formula: NH_3. **2** a solution of ammonia in water, containing the compound ammonium hydroxide. [C18: from New Latin, from Latin (*sal*) *ammōniacus* (sal) AMMONIAC[1]]

ammoniac[1] (əˈməʊnɪˌæk) *adj* a variant of **ammoniacal.**

ammoniac[2] (əˈməʊnɪˌæk) *n* a strong-smelling gum resin obtained from the stems of the N Asian umbelliferous plant *Dorema ammoniacum* and formerly used as an expectorant, stimulant, perfume, and in porcelain cement. Also called: **gum ammoniac.** [C14: from Latin *ammōniacum,* from Greek *ammōniakos* belonging to Ammon (apparently the gum resin was extracted from plants found in Libya near the temple of Ammon)]

ammoniacal (ˌæməˈnaɪəkᵊl) *adj* of, containing, using, or resembling ammonia. Also: **ammoniac.**

ammonia clock *n* an atomic clock based on the frequency of inversion of the ammonia molecule.

ammoniate (əˈməʊnɪˌeɪt) *vb* **1** to unite or treat with ammonia. ◆ *n* **2** another name for **ammine.** ▶ **amˌmoniˈation** *n*

ammonic (əˈmɒnɪk, əˈməʊnɪk) *adj* of or concerned with ammonia or ammonium compounds. ▶ **amˈmonical** *adj*

ammonify (əˈmɒnɪˌfaɪ, əˈməʊnɪ-) *vb* **-fies, -fying, -fied.** to treat or impregnate with ammonia or a compound of ammonia. ▶ **amˌmonifiˈcation** *n*

ammonite[1] (ˈæməˌnaɪt) *n* **1** any extinct marine cephalopod mollusc of the order *Ammonoidea,* which were common in Mesozoic times and had a coiled partitioned shell. Their closest modern relative is the pearly nautilus. **2** the shell of any of these animals, commonly occurring as a fossil. [C18: from New Latin *Ammōnītēs,* from Medieval Latin *cornū Ammōnis,* literally: horn of Ammon] ▶ **ammonitic** (ˌæməˈnɪtɪk) *adj*

ammonite[2] (ˈæməˌnaɪt) *n* **1** an explosive consisting mainly of ammonium nitrate with smaller amounts of other substances, such as TNT. **2** a nitrogenous fertilizer made from animal wastes. [C20: from AMMO(NIUM) + NI(TRA)TE]

Ammonites (ˈæməˌnaɪts) *pl n Old Testament.* a nomadic tribe living east of the Jordan: a persistent enemy of the Israelites.

ammonium (əˈməʊnɪəm, -njəm) *n* (*modifier*) of, consisting of, or containing the monovalent group NH_4– or the ion NH_4^+: *ammonium compounds.*

ammonium carbamate *n* a white soluble crystalline compound produced by reaction between dry ammonia and carbon dioxide and used as a nitrogen fertilizer. Formula: $(NH_4)CO_2NH_2$.

ammonium carbonate *n* **1** an unstable pungent soluble white powder that is a double salt of ammonium bicarbonate and ammonium carbamate: used in the manufacture of baking powder, smelling salts, and ammonium compounds. Formula: $(NH_4)HCO_3.(NH_4)CO_2NH_2$. **2** an unstable substance that is produced by treating this compound with ammonia. Formula: $(NH_4)_2CO_3$.

ammonium chloride *n* a white soluble crystalline solid used chiefly as an electrolyte in dry batteries and as a mordant and soldering flux. Formula: NH_4Cl. Also called: **sal ammoniac.**

ammonium hydroxide *n* a compound existing only in aqueous solution, formed when ammonia dissolves in water to form ammonium ions and hydroxide ions. Formula: NH_4OH.

ammonium ion *n* the ion NH_4^+, formed from ammonia and present in aqueous solutions of ammonia and in many salts.

ammonium nitrate *n* a colourless highly soluble crystalline solid used mainly as a fertilizer and in explosives and pyrotechnics. Formula: NH_4NO_3.

ammonium sulphate *n* a white soluble crystalline solid used mainly as a fertilizer and in water purification. Formula: $(NH_4)_2SO_4$.

ammonolysis (ˌæməˈnɒlɪsɪs) *n Chem.* solvolysis in liquid ammonia.

ammunition (ˌæmjʊˈnɪʃən) *n* **1** any projectiles, such as bullets, rockets, etc., that can be discharged from a weapon. **2** bombs, missiles, chemicals, biological agents, nuclear materials, etc., capable of use as weapons. **3** any means of defence or attack, as in an argument. [C17: from obsolete French *amunition,* by mistaken division from earlier *la munition;* see MUNITION]

amnesia (æmˈniːzjə, -ʒjə, -zɪə) *n* a defect in memory, esp. one resulting from pathological cause, such as brain damage or hysteria. [C19: via New Latin from Greek: forgetfulness, probably from *amnēstia* oblivion; see AMNESTY] ▶ **amnesiac** (æmˈniːzɪˌæk) *or* **amnesic** (æmˈniːsɪk, -zɪk) *adj, n*

amnesty (ˈæmnɪstɪ) *n, pl* **-ties. 1** a general pardon, esp. for offences against a government. **2** a period during which a law is suspended to allow offenders to admit their crime without fear of prosecution. **3** *Law.* a pardon granted by the Crown and effected by statute, effective for a limited period of time. ◆ *vb* **-ties, -tying, -tied. 4** (*tr*) to overlook or forget (an offence). [C16: from Latin *amnēstia,* from Greek: oblivion, from *amnēstos* forgetting, from A-[1] + *-mnēstos,* from *mnasthai* to remember]

Amnesty International *n* an international organization founded in Britain in 1961 that works to secure the release of people imprisoned for their beliefs, to ban the use of torture, and to abolish the death penalty. Abbrev.: **AI.**

amniocentesis (ˌæmnɪəʊsenˈtiːsɪs) *n, pl* **-ses** (-siːz). removal of some amniotic fluid by the insertion into the womb of a hollow needle, for therapeutic or diagnostic purposes. [C20: from AMNION + *centesis,* from Greek *kentēsis* a puncture, from *kentein* to prick]

amnion (ˈæmnɪən) *n, pl* **-nions** *or* **-nia** (-nɪə). the innermost of two membranes (see also **chorion**) enclosing an embryonic reptile, bird, or mammal. [C17: via New Latin from Greek: a little lamb, from *amnos* a lamb] ▶ **amniotic** (ˌæmnɪˈɒtɪk) *adj*

amniote (ˈæmnɪəʊt) *n* any vertebrate animal, such as a reptile, bird, or mammal, that possesses an amnion, chorion, and allantois during embryonic development. Compare **anamniote.**

amniotic fluid *n* the fluid surrounding the fetus in the womb.

amoeba *or U.S.* **ameba** (əˈmiːbə) *n, pl* **-bae** (-biː) *or* **-bas.** any protozoan of the phylum *Rhizopoda,* esp. any of the genus *Amoeba,* able to change shape because of the movements of cell processes (pseudopodia). They live in fresh water or soil or as parasites in man and animals. [C19: from New Latin, from Greek *amoibē* change, from *ameibein* to change, exchange] ▶ **aˈmoebic** *or U.S.* **aˈmebic** *adj*

amoebaean *or* **amoebean** (ˌæmɪˈbiːən) *adj Prosody.* of or relating to lines of verse dialogue that answer each other alternately.

amoebiasis (ˌæmɪˈbaɪəsɪs) *n, pl* **-ses** (-ˌsiːz). infection, esp. of the intestines, caused by the parasitic amoeba *Endamoeba histolytica.*

amoebic dysentery *n* inflammation of the intestines caused by the parasitic amoeba *Endamoeba histolytica.*

amoebocyte *or U.S.* **amebocyte** (əˈmiːbəˌsaɪt) *n* any amoeboid cell found in the blood and body fluids. Some kinds, such as the phagocytic white blood cell, can engulf foreign particles.

amoeboid *or U.S.* **ameboid** (əˈmiːbɔɪd) *adj* of, related to, or resembling amoebae.

amok (əˈmʌk, əˈmɒk) *or* **amuck** (əˈmʌk) *n* **1** a state of murderous frenzy, originally observed among Malays. ◆ *adv* **2 run amok.** to run about with or as if with a frenzied desire to kill. [C17: from Malay *amoq* furious assault]

Amon (ˈɑːmən) *n Egyptian myth.* a variant spelling of **Amen.**

among (əˈmʌŋ) *or* **amongst** *prep* **1** in the midst of: *he lived among the Indians.* **2** to each of: *divide the reward among yourselves.* **3** in the group, class, or number of: *ranked among the greatest writers.* **4** taken out of (a group): *he is only one among many.* **5** with one another within a group; by the joint action of: *a lot of gossip among the women employees; decide it among yourselves.* [Old English *amang,* contracted from *on gemang* in the group of, from ON + *gemang* crowd; see MINGLE, MONGREL]

USAGE See at **between.**

amontillado (əˌmɒntɪˈlɑːdəʊ) *n* a medium dry Spanish sherry, not as pale in colour as a fino. [C19: from Spanish *vino amontillado* wine of *Montilla,* town in Spain]

amoral (eɪˈmɒrəl) *adj* **1** having no moral quality; nonmoral. **2** without moral standards or principles. ▶ **amorality** (ˌeɪmɒˈrælɪtɪ) *n* ▶ **aˈmorally** *adv*

USAGE *Amoral* is often wrongly used where *immoral* is meant. *Immoral* is properly used to talk about the breaking of moral rules, *amoral* about people who have no moral code or about places or situations where moral considerations do not apply.

amoretto (ˌæməˈretəʊ) *or* **amorino** (ˌæmɔːˈriːnəʊ) *n, pl* **-retti** (-ˈretɪ) *or* **-rini** (-ˈriːnɪ). (esp. in painting) a small chubby naked boy representing a cupid. Also called: **putto.** [C16: from Italian, diminutive of *Amore* Cupid, from Latin *Amor* Love]

amorist (ˈæmərɪst) *n* a lover or a writer about love.

amoroso (ˌæməˈrəʊsəʊ) *adj, adv* **1** *Music.* (to be played) lovingly. ◆ *n* **2** a rich sweetened sherry of a dark colour. [from Italian and Spanish: AMOROUS]

amorous (ˈæmərəs) *adj* **1** inclined towards or displaying love or desire. **2** in love. **3** of or relating to love. [C14: from Old French, from Medieval Latin *amōrōsus,* from Latin *amor* love] ▶ **ˈamorously** *adv* ▶ **ˈamorousness** *n*

amor patriae *Latin.* (ˈæmɔː ˈpætrɪˌiː) *n* love of one's country; patriotism.

amorphous (əˈmɔːfəs) *adj* **1** lacking a definite shape; formless. **2** of no recognizable character or type. **3** (of chemicals, rocks, etc.) not having a crystalline structure. [C18: from New Latin, from Greek *amorphos* shapeless, from A-[1] + *morphē* shape] ▶ **aˈmorphism** *n* ▶ **aˈmorphously** *adv* ▶ **aˈmorphousness** *n*

amortization *or* **amortisation** (əˌmɔːtaɪˈzeɪʃən) *n* **1a** the process of amortizing a debt. **1b** the money devoted to amortizing a debt. **2** (in computing the redemption yield on a bond purchased at a premium) the amount that is subtracted from the annual yield. Compare **accumulation** (sense 3b). ▶ **amortizement** *or* **amortisement** (əˈmɔːtɪzmənt) *n*

amortize *or* **amortise** (əˈmɔːtaɪz) *vb* (*tr*) **1** *Finance.* to liquidate (a debt, mortgage, etc.) by instalment payments or by periodic transfers to a sinking fund. **2** to write off (a wasting asset) by annual transfers to a sinking fund. **3** *Property law.* (formerly) to transfer (lands, etc.) in mortmain. [C14: from Medieval Latin *admortizāre,* from Old French *amortir* to reduce to the point of death, ultimately from Latin *ad* to + *mors* death] ▶ **aˈmortizable** *or* **aˈmortisable** *adj*

Amos (ˈeɪmɒs) *n Old Testament.* **1** a Hebrew prophet of the 8th century B.C. **2** the book containing his oracles.

amount (əˈmaʊnt) *n* **1** extent; quantity; supply. **2** the total of two or more quantities; sum. **3** the full value, effect, or significance of something. **4** a principal sum plus the interest on it, as in a loan. ◆ *vb* **5** (*intr;* usually foll. by *to*) to be equal or add up in effect, meaning, or quantity. [C13: from Old French *amonter* to go up, from *amont* upwards, from *a* to + *mont* mountain (from Latin *mōns*)]

USAGE The use of a plural noun after *amount of (an amount of bananas; the amount of refugees)* should be avoided: *a quantity of bananas; the number of refugees.*

amount of substance *n* a measure of the number of entities (atoms, molecules, ions, electrons, etc.) present in a substance, expressed in moles.

amour (əˈmʊə) *n* a love affair, esp. a secret or illicit one. [C13: from Old French, from Latin *amor* love]

amour-propre *French.* (amurprɔprə) *n* self-respect.

amowt (əˈmaʊt) *n* a variant spelling of **amaut.**

Amoy (əˈmɔɪ) *n* **1** a port in SE China, in Fujian province on **Amoy Island,** at the mouth of the Jiu-long River opposite Taiwan: one of the first treaty ports opened to European trade (1842). Pop.: 368 786 (1990 est.). Modern Chinese name: **Xiamen. 2** the dialect of Chinese spoken in Amoy, Taiwan, and elsewhere: a Min dialect.

amp (æmp) *n* **1** an ampere. **2** *Informal.* an amplifier.

AMP *abbrev. for* **1** adenosine monophosphate. **2** Australian Mutual Provident Society.

amp. *abbrev. for:* **1** amperage. **2** ampere.

ampelopsis (ˌæmpɪˈlɒpsɪs) *n* any woody vine of the vitaceous genus *Ampelopsis,* of tropical and subtropical Asia and America. [C19: from New Latin, from Greek *ampelos* grapevine]

amperage (ˈæmpərɪdʒ) *n* the strength of an electric current measured in amperes, esp. the rated current of an electrical component or device.

ampere (ˈæmpeə) *n* **1** the basic SI unit of electric current; the constant current that, when maintained in two parallel conductors of infinite length and negligible cross section placed 1 metre apart in free space, produces a force of 2×10^{-7} newton per metre between them. 1 ampere is equivalent to 1 coulomb per second. **2** a former unit of electric current (**international ampere**); the current that, when passed through a solution of silver nitrate, deposits silver at the rate of 0.001118 gram per second. 1 international ampere equals 0.999835 ampere. ◆ Abbrev.: **amp.** Symbol: A **[C19:** named after A. M. AMPÈRE**]**

Ampère ('æmpɛə; *French* ɑ̃pɛr) *n* **André Marie** (ɑ̃dre mari). 1775–1836, French physicist and mathematician, who made major discoveries in the fields of magnetism and electricity.

ampere-hour *n* a practical unit of quantity of electricity; the quantity that flows in one hour through a conductor carrying a current of 1 ampere. 1 ampere-hour is equivalent to 3600 coulombs. Abbrev.: **a.h.**

ampere-turn *n* a unit of magnetomotive force; the magnetomotive force produced by a current of 1 ampere passing through one complete turn of a coil. 1 ampere-turn is equivalent to 4π/10 or 1.257 gilberts. Abbrevs.: **At, A.**

ampersand ('æmpəˌsænd) *n* the character (&), meaning *and: John Brown & Co.* **[C19:** shortened from *and per se and,* that is, the symbol & by itself (represents) *and***]**

amphetamine (æm'fɛtəˌmiːn, -mɪn) *n* a synthetic colourless volatile liquid used medicinally as the white crystalline sulphate, mainly for its stimulant action on the central nervous system, although it also stimulates the sympathetic nervous system. It can have unpleasant or dangerous side effects and drug dependence can occur; 1-phenyl-2-aminopropane. Formula: $C_6H_5CH_2CH(NH_2)CH_3$. **[C20:** from A(LPHA) + M(ETHYL) + PH(ENYL) + ET(HYL) + -AMINE**]**

amphi- *prefix* **1** on both sides; at both ends; of both kinds: *amphipod; amphitrichous; amphibious.* **2** around: *amphibole.* **[**from Greek**]**

amphiarthrosis (ˌæmfɪɑː'θrəʊsɪs) *n, pl* **-ses** (-siːz). *Anatomy.* a type of articulation permitting only slight movement, as between the vertebrae of the backbone. **[C19:** from AMPHI- + Greek *arthrōsis* articulation, from *arthron* a joint**]**

amphiaster ('æmfɪˌæstə) *n Cytology.* the structure that occurs in a cell undergoing mitosis, consisting of a spindle with an aster at each end. **[C19:** from AMPHI- + New Latin *aster;* see ASTER**]**

amphibian (æm'fɪbɪən) *n* **1** any cold-blooded vertebrate of the class *Amphibia,* typically living on land but breeding in water. Their aquatic larvae (tadpoles) undergo metamorphosis into the adult form. The class includes the newts and salamanders, frogs and toads, and caecilians. **2** a type of aircraft able to land and take off from both water and land. **3** any vehicle able to travel on both water and land. ◆ *adj* **4** another word for **amphibious. 5** of, relating to, or belonging to the class *Amphibia.*

amphibiotic (ˌæmfɪbaɪ'ɒtɪk) *adj* having an aquatic larval form and a terrestrial adult form, as amphibians.

amphibious (æm'fɪbɪəs) *adj* **1** able to live both on land and in the water, as frogs, toads, etc. **2** designed for operation on or from both water and land. **3** relating to military forces and equipment organized for operations launched from the sea against an enemy shore. **4** having a dual or mixed nature. **[C17:** from Greek *amphibios,* literally: having a double life, from AMPHI- + *bios* life**]** ▸ **am'phibiously** *adv* ▸ **am'phibiousness** *n*

amphiblastic (ˌæmfɪ'blæstɪk) *adj* (of animal ova) showing complete but unequal cleavage after fertilization.

amphiblastula (ˌæmfɪ'blæstjʊlə) *n* the free-swimming larva of certain sponges, which consists of a hollow spherical mass of cells some of which have flagella.

amphibole ('æmfɪˌbəʊl) *n* any of a large group of minerals consisting of the silicates of calcium, iron, magnesium, sodium, and aluminium, usually in the form of long slender dark-coloured crystals. Members of the group, including hornblende, actinolite, and tremolite, are common constituents of igneous rocks. **[C17:** from French, from Greek *amphibolos* uncertain; so called from the large number of varieties in the group**]**

amphibolite (æm'fɪbəˌlaɪt) *n* a metamorphic rock consisting mainly of amphibole and plagioclase.

amphibology (ˌæmfɪ'bɒlədʒɪ) *or* **amphiboly** (æm'fɪbəlɪ) *n, pl* **-gies** *or* **-lies.** ambiguity of expression, esp. when due to a grammatical construction, as in *save rags and waste paper.* **[C14:** from Late Latin *amphibologia,* ultimately from Greek *amphibolos* ambiguous; see AMPHIBOLE, -LOGY**]** ▸ **ˌamphi'bolic** *or* **amphibolous** (æm'fɪbələs) *adj* ▸ **amphibological** (æmˌfɪbə'lɒdʒɪkᵊl) *adj* ▸ **amˌphibo'logically** *adv*

amphibrach ('æmfɪˌbræk) *n Prosody.* a metrical foot consisting of a long syllable between two short syllables (⏑–⏑). Compare **cretic. [C16:** from Latin, from Greek *amphibrakhus,* literally: both ends being short, from AMPHI- + *brakhus* short**]** ▸ **ˌamphi'brachic** *adj*

amphichroic (ˌæmfɪ'krəʊɪk) *or* **amphichromatic** (ˌæmfɪkrəʊ'mætɪk) *adj* producing two colours, one on reacting with an acid, the other on reacting with a base.

amphicoelous (ˌæmfɪ'siːləs) *adj* (of the vertebrae of most fishes and some amphibians) concave at the anterior and posterior ends. **[C19:** from AMPHI- + Greek *koilos* hollow**]**

amphictyon (æm'fɪktɪən) *n* a delegate to an amphictyonic council. **[C16:** back formation from *amphictyons,* from Greek *amphiktiones* neighbours, from AMPHI- + *ktizein* to found**]**

amphictyony (æm'fɪktɪənɪ) *n, pl* **-nies.** (in ancient Greece) a religious association of states for the maintenance of temples and the cults connected with them. ▸ **amphictyonic** (æmˌfɪktɪ'ɒnɪk) *adj*

amphidentate (ˌæmfɪ'dɛnteɪt) *adj* (of a ligand) able to coordinate through either of two different atoms, as in CN^-. Also: **ambidentate.**

amphidiploid (ˌæmfɪ'dɪplɔɪd) *n* a hybrid plant in which the chromosome number is the sum of the chromosome numbers of both parental species.

amphigory ('æmfɪgərɪ) *or* **amphigouri** ('æmfɪˌgʊərɪ) *n, pl* **-ries** *or* **-ris.** a piece of nonsensical writing in verse or, less commonly, prose. **[C19:** from French *amphigouri,* of unknown origin**]** ▸ **amphigoric** (ˌæmfɪ'gɒrɪk) *adj*

amphimacer (æm'fɪməsə) *n Prosody.* another word for **cretic. [C16:** from Latin *amphimacrus,* from Greek *amphimakros* both ends being long, from AMPHI- + *makros* long**]**

amphimixis (ˌæmfɪ'mɪksɪs) *n, pl* **-mixes** (-'mɪksiːz). true sexual reproduction, esp. the fusion of gametes from two organisms. Compare **apomixis. [C19:** from AMPHI- + Greek *mixis* a blending, from *mignunai* to mingle**]** ▸ **amphimictic** (ˌæmfɪ'mɪktɪk) *adj*

amphioxus (ˌæmfɪ'ɒksəs) *n, pl* **-oxi** (-'ɒksaɪ) *or* **-oxuses.** another name for the **lancelet. [C19:** from New Latin: both ends being sharp, from AMPHI- + Greek *oxus* sharp**]**

amphipathic (ˌæmfɪ'pæθɪk) *or* **amphipath** ('æmfɪˌpæθ) *adj Chem., biochem.* of or relating to a molecule that possesses both hydrophobic and hydrophilic elements, such as are found in detergents, or phospholipids of biological membranes.

amphipod ('æmfɪˌpɒd) *n* **1** any marine or freshwater crustacean of the order *Amphipoda,* such as the sand hoppers, in which the body is laterally compressed: subclass *Malacostraca.* ◆ *adj* **2** of, relating to, or belonging to the *Amphipoda.*

amphipodous (æm'fɪpədəs) *adj* (of certain invertebrates, such as sand hoppers) having both swimming and jumping appendages.

amphiprostyle (æm'fɪprəˌstaɪl, ˌæmfɪ'prəʊstaɪl) *adj* **1** (esp. of a classical temple) having a set of columns at both ends but not at the sides. ◆ *n* **2** a temple of this kind. ▸ **amˌphipro'stylar** *adj*

amphiprotic (ˌæmfɪ'prəʊtɪk) *adj* another word for **amphoteric.**

amphisbaena (ˌæmfɪs'biːnə) *n, pl* **-nae** (-niː) *or* **-nas. 1** any worm lizard of the genus *Amphisbaena.* **2** *Classical myth.* a poisonous serpent having a head at each end and able to move forwards or backwards. **[C16:** via Latin from Greek *amphisbaina,* from *amphis* both ways + *bainein* to go**]** ▸ **ˌamphis'baenic** *adj*

amphistomatal (ˌæmfɪ'stəʊmətᵊl) *or* **amphistomatic** (ˌæmfɪstə'mætɪk) *adj* (of a leaf) having stomata on both surfaces.

amphistomous (ˌæmfɪ'stəʊməs) *adj* (of certain animals, such as leeches) having a sucker at either end of the body.

amphistylar (ˌæmfɪ'staɪlə) *adj* **1** (esp. of a classical temple) having a set of columns at both ends or at both sides. ◆ *n* **2** a temple of this kind.

amphitheatre *or U.S.* **amphitheater** ('æmfɪˌθɪətə) *n* **1** a building, usually circular or oval, in which tiers of seats rise from a central open arena, as in those of ancient Rome. **2** a place where contests are held; arena. **3** any level circular area of ground surrounded by higher ground. **4a** the first tier of seats in the gallery of a theatre. **4b** any similarly designated seating area in a theatre. **5** a lecture room in which seats are tiered away from a central area. ▸ **amphitheatric** (ˌæmfɪθɪ'ætrɪk) *or* **ˌamphithe'atrical** *adj* ▸ **ˌamphithe'atrically** *adv*

amphithecium (ˌæmfɪ'θiːsɪəm) *n, pl* **-cia** (-sɪə). the outer layer of cells of the embryo of mosses and liverworts that develops into the outer parts of the spore-bearing capsule. **[C19:** from New Latin, from AMPHI- + Greek *thēkion* a little case, from *thēkē* case**]**

amphitricha (æm'fɪtrɪkə) *pl n* bacteria that have flagella at both ends. **[C20:** from AMPHI- + *-tricha,* from Greek *thrix* hair**]** ▸ **am'phitrichous** *adj*

Amphitrite (ˌæmfɪ'traɪtɪ) *n Greek myth.* a sea goddess, wife of Poseidon and mother of Triton.

amphitropous (æm'fɪtrəpəs) *adj* (of a plant ovule) partially inverted so that the base and the micropyle at the apex are the same distance from the funicle.

Amphitryon (æm'fɪtrɪən) *n Greek myth.* the grandson of Perseus and husband of Alcmene.

amphora ('æmfərə) *n, pl* **-phorae** (-fəˌriː) *or* **-phoras.** an ancient Greek or Roman two-handled narrow-necked jar for oil, wine, etc. **[C17:** from Latin, from Greek *amphoreus,* from AMPHI- + *phoreus* bearer, from *pherein* to bear**]**

amphoric (æm'fɒrɪk) *adj* resembling the sound produced by blowing into a bottle. Amphoric breath sounds are heard through a stethoscope placed over a cavity in the lung.

amphoteric (ˌæmfə'tɛrɪk) *adj Chem.* able to function as either a base or an acid. Also: **amphiprotic. [C19:** from Greek *amphoteros* each of two (from *amphō* both) + -IC**]**

ampicillin (ˌæmpɪ'sɪlɪn) *n* a semisynthetic penicillin used to treat various infections.

ample ('æmpᵊl) *adj* **1** more than sufficient; abundant: *an ample helping.* **2** large in size, extent, or amount: *of ample proportions.* **[C15:** from Old French, from Latin *amplus* spacious**]** ▸ **'ampleness** *n*

amplexicaul (æm'plɛksɪˌkɔːl) *adj* (of some sessile leaves, stipules, etc.) having an enlarged base that encircles the stem. **[C18:** from New Latin *amplexicaulis,* from Latin *amplectī* to embrace + *caulis* stalk**]**

amplification (ˌæmplɪfɪ'keɪʃən) *n* **1** the act or result of amplifying. **2** material added to a statement, story, etc., in order to expand or clarify it. **3** a statement, story, etc., with such additional material. **4** *Electronics.* **4a** the increase in strength of an electrical signal by means of an amplifier. **4b** another word for **gain**[1] (sense 13). **5** *Genetics.* Also called: **gene amplification.** the production of multiple copies of a particular gene or DNA sequence. It can occur naturally or artificially, by genetic engineering techniques.

amplifier ('æmplɪˌfaɪə) *n* **1** an electronic device used to increase the strength of the current or voltage signal fed into it. **2** such a device used for the amplification of sound signals in a radio, record player, etc. **3** *Photog.* an additional lens for altering the focal length of a camera lens. **4** a person or thing that amplifies.

amplify ('æmplɪˌfaɪ) *vb* **-fies, -fying, -fied. 1** *(tr)* to increase in size, extent, effect, etc., as by the addition of extra material; augment; enlarge; expand. **2** *Electronics.* to produce amplification of (electrical signals); increase the amplitude of (signals). **3** *(tr) U.S.* to exaggerate. **4** *(intr)* to expand or enlarge a speech, narrative, etc. [C15: from Old French *amplifier,* ultimately from Latin *amplificāre* to enlarge, from *amplus* spacious + *facere* to make] ▸ **'ampli,fiable** *adj*

amplitude ('æmplɪ,tju:d) *n* **1** greatness of extent; magnitude. **2** abundance or copiousness. **3** breadth or scope, as of the mind. **4** *Astronomy.* the angular distance along the horizon measured from true east or west to the point of intersection of the vertical circle passing through a celestial body. **5** Also called: **argument.** *Maths.* (of a complex number) the angle that the vector representing the complex number makes with the positive real axis. If the point (x, y) has polar coordinates (r, θ), the amplitude of $x + iy$ is θ, that is, arctan Y/x. Compare **modulus** (sense 2). See also **Argand diagram. 6** *Physics.* the maximum displacement from the zero or mean position of a periodic motion or curve. [C16: from Latin *amplitūdō* breadth, from *amplus* spacious]

amplitude modulation *n* **1** one of the principal methods of transmitting audio, visual, or other types of information using radio waves, the relevant signal being superimposed onto a radio-frequency carrier wave. The frequency of the carrier wave remains unchanged but its amplitude is varied in accordance with the amplitude of the input signal. Abbrevs.: **AM, am.** Compare **frequency modulation. 2** a wave that has undergone this process.

amply ('æmplɪ) *adv* more than sufficiently; fully; generously: *he was amply rewarded.*

ampoule ('æmpu:l, -pju:l) *or esp. U.S.* **ampule** *n Med.* a small glass vessel in which liquids for injection are hermetically sealed.

ampulla (æm'pʊlə) *n, pl* **-pullae** (-'pʊli:). **1** *Anatomy.* the dilated end part of certain ducts or canals, such as the end of a uterine tube. **2** *Christianity.* **2a** a vessel for containing the wine and water used at the Eucharist. **2b** a small flask for containing consecrated oil. **3** a Roman two-handled bottle for oil, wine, or perfume. [C16: from Latin, diminutive of AMPHORA] ▸ **ampullaceous** (,æmpʊ'leɪʃəs) *or* **,ampul'laceal** *adj* ▸ **ampullar** (æm'pʊlə) *or* **ampullary** (æm'pʊlərɪ) *adj*

amputate ('æmpjʊ,teɪt) *vb Surgery.* to remove (all or part of a limb, esp. an arm or leg). [C17: from Latin *amputāre,* from *am-* around + *putāre* to trim, prune] ▸ **,ampu'tation** *n* ▸ **'ampu,tator** *n*

amputee (,æmpjʊ'ti:) *n* a person who has had a limb amputated.

Amravati (æm'rɑ:vətɪ) *n* a town in central India, in NE Maharashtra: cotton centre. Pop.: 421 576 (1991). Former name: **Amraoti** ('æm,rɑ:ətɪ, 'ʌm-).

amrit ('æmrɪt) *n Sikhism.* a sanctified solution of sugar and water used in the Amrit Ceremony. [from Punjabi: nectar]

amrita *or* **amreeta** (æm'ri:tə) *n Hindu myth.* **1** the ambrosia of the gods that bestows immortality. **2** the immortality it confers. [from Sanskrit *amrta* immortal, from *a-* without + *mrta* death]

Amrit Ceremony *n Sikhism.* the ceremony of initiation into the Khalsa, at which amrit is drunk by and sprinkled on the heads of candidates for initiation.

Amritsar (æm'rɪtsə) *n* a city in India, in NW Punjab: centre of the Sikh religion; site of a massacre in 1919 of unarmed supporters of Indian self-government by British troops; in 1984 the Golden Temple, fortified by Sikhs, was attacked by Indian troops with the loss of many Sikh lives. Pop.: 708 835 (1991).

Amsterdam (,æmstə'dæm; *Dutch* ɑmstər'dɑm) *n* the commercial capital of the Netherlands, a major industrial centre and port on the IJsselmeer, connected with the North Sea by canal: built on about 100 islands within a network of canals. Pop.: 718 119 (1996 est.).

amt *abbrev. for* amount.

amu *abbrev. for* atomic mass unit.

amuck (ə'mʌk) *n, adv* a variant of **amok.**

Amu Darya (*Russian* a'mu darj'ja) *n* a river in central Asia, rising in the Pamirs and flowing northwest through the Hindu Kush and across Turkmenistan and Uzbekistan to its delta in the Aral Sea: forms much of the N border of Afghanistan and is important for irrigation. Length: 2400 km (1500 miles). Ancient name: **Oxus.**

amulet ('æmjʊlɪt) *n* a trinket or piece of jewellery worn as a protection against evil; charm. [C17: from Latin *amulētum,* of unknown origin]

Amūn ('ɑ:mən) *n Egyptian myth.* a variant spelling of **Amen.**

Amundsen (*Norwegian* 'a:munsən) *n* **Roald** ('rɔald). 1872–1928, Norwegian explorer and navigator, who was the first man to reach the South Pole (1911).

Amundsen Sea ('ɑ:mʊndsən) *n* a part of the South Pacific Ocean, in Antarctica off Byrd Land.

Amur (ə'mʊə) *n* a river in NE Asia, rising in N Mongolia as the Argun and flowing southeast, then northeast to the Sea of Okhotsk: forms the boundary between Manchuria and Russia. Length: about 4350 km (2700 miles). Modern Chinese name: **Heilong Jiang.**

amuse (ə'mju:z) *vb (tr)* **1** to keep pleasantly occupied; entertain; divert. **2** to cause to laugh or smile. [C15: from Old French *amuser* to cause to be idle, from *muser* to MUSE[1]]

amusement (ə'mju:zmənt) *n* **1** something that amuses, such as a game or other pastime. **2** a mechanical device used for entertainment, as at a fair. **3** the act of amusing or the state or quality of being amused.

amusement arcade *n Brit.* a covered area having coin-operated game machines.

amusement park *n* an open-air entertainment area consisting of stalls, side shows, etc.

amusing (ə'mju:zɪŋ) *adj* mildly entertaining; pleasantly diverting; causing a smile or laugh. ▸ **a'musingly** *adv*

amygdala (ə'mɪgdələ) *n, pl* **-lae** (-,li:). *Anatomy.* an almond-shaped part, such as a tonsil or a lobe of the cerebellum. [C16: from Medieval Latin: ALMOND]

amygdalate (ə'mɪgdəlɪt, -,leɪt) *adj* relating to, having, or bearing almonds.

amygdale (ə'mɪgdeɪl) *n* an oval vesicle in a volcanic rock, formed from a bubble of escaping gas, that has become filled with a light-coloured mineral, such as quartz. Also called: **amygdule** (ə'mɪgdju:l). [C19: from Greek: ALMOND]

amygdalin (ə'mɪgdəlɪn) *n* a white soluble bitter-tasting crystalline glycoside extracted from bitter almonds and used as an expectorant. Formula: $C_6H_5CHCNOC_{12}H_{21}O_{10}$.

amygdaline (ə'mɪgdəlɪn, -,laɪn) *adj* **1** *Anatomy.* of or relating to a tonsil. **2** of or resembling almonds.

amygdaloid (ə'mɪgdə,lɔɪd) *n* **1** a volcanic igneous rock containing amygdales. ◆ *adj* **2** having the shape of an almond. **3** a less common form of **amygdaloidal** (sense 1).

amygdaloidal (ə,mɪgdə'lɔɪdᵊl) *adj* **1** (of a volcanic rock) containing amygdales. **2** a less common form of **amygdaloid** (sense 2).

amyl ('æmɪl) *n (modifier) (no longer in technical usage)* of, consisting of, or containing any of eight isomeric forms of the monovalent group C_5H_{11}-: *amyl group or radical.* See also **pentyl.** [C19: from Latin: AMYLUM]

amylaceous (,æmɪ'leɪʃəs) *adj* of or resembling starch.

amyl acetate *n* another name (no longer in technical usage) for **pentyl acetate.**

amyl alcohol *n* a colourless flammable liquid existing in eight isomeric forms that is used as a solvent and in the manufacture of organic compounds and pharmaceuticals. Formula: $C_5H_{11}OH$.

amylase ('æmɪ,leɪz) *n* any of several enzymes that hydrolyse starch and glycogen to simple sugars, such as glucose. They are present in saliva.

amylene ('æmɪ,li:n) *n* another name (no longer in technical usage) for **pentene.**

amyl nitrite *n* a yellowish unstable volatile fragrant liquid used in medicine as a vasodilator and in perfumes. Formula: $(CH_3)_2CHCH_2CH_2NO_2$.

amylo- *or before a vowel* **amyl-** *combining form.* indicating starch: *amylolysis; amylase.* [from Latin: AMYLUM]

amyloid ('æmɪ,lɔɪd) *n* **1** *Pathol.* a complex protein resembling starch, deposited in tissues in some degenerative diseases. **2** any substance resembling starch. ◆ *adj* **3** starchlike.

amyloidosis (,æmɪlɔɪ'dəʊsɪs) *n Pathol.* the deposition of amyloid in various tissues of the body, as occurs in certain chronic infections.

amylolysis (,æmɪ'lɒlɪsɪs) *n* the conversion of starch into sugar. ▸ **amylolytic** (ə,maɪləʊ'lɪtɪk) *adj*

amylopectin (,æmɪləʊ'pɛktɪn) *n* the major component of starch (about 80 per cent), consisting of branched chains of glucose units. It is insoluble and gives a red-brown colour with iodine. Compare **amylose.**

amylopsin (,æmɪ'lɒpsɪn) *n* an enzyme of the pancreatic juice that converts starch into sugar; pancreatic amylase. [C19: from AMYLO(LYSIS) + (PE)PSIN]

amylose ('æmɪ,ləʊz, -ləʊs) *n* the minor component (about 20 per cent) of starch, consisting of long unbranched chains of glucose units. It is soluble in water and gives an intense blue colour with iodine. Compare **amylopectin.**

amylum ('æmɪləm) *n* another name for **starch** (sense 2). [Latin, from Greek *amulon* fine meal, starch, from *amulos* not ground at the mill, from A-[1] + *mulē* mill]

amyotonia (,eɪmaɪə'təʊnɪə) *n* another name for **myotonia.**

amyotrophic lateral sclerosis (,æmɪəʊ'trəʊfɪk) *n* a form of motor neurone disease in which degeneration of motor tracts in the spinal cord causes progressive muscular paralysis starting in the limbs. Also called: **Lou Gehrig's disease.**

amyotrophy (,æmɪ'ɒtrəfɪ) *n Pathol.* wasting of muscles, caused by disease of the nerves supplying them.

Amytal ('æmɪ,tæl) *n Trademark.* a crystalline compound used as a sedative and hypnotic; sodium amytal.

an[1] (æn; *unstressed* ən) *determiner (indefinite article)* a form of **a**[1], used before an initial vowel sound: *an old car; an elf; an honour.* [Old English *ān* ONE]

USAGE *An* was formerly often used before words that begin with *h* and are unstressed on the first syllable: *an hotel; an historic meeting.* Sometimes the initial *h* was not pronounced. This usage is now becoming obsolete.

an[2] *or* **an'** (æn; *unstressed* ən) *conj (subordinating)* an obsolete or dialect word for **if.** See **and** (sense 9).

An[1] (ɑ:n) *n Myth.* the Sumerian sky god. Babylonian counterpart: **Anu.**

An[2] *the chemical symbol for* actinon.

AN *abbrev. for* Anglo-Norman.

an. *abbrev. for* anno. [Latin: in the year]

an- *or before a consonant* **a-** *prefix* not; without: *anaphrodisiac.* [from Greek]

-an, -ean, *or* **-ian** *suffix.* **1** *(forming adjectives and nouns)* belonging to or relating to; a person belonging to or coming from: *European.* **2** *(forming adjectives and nouns)* typical of or resembling; a person typical of: *Elizabethan.* **3** *(forming adjectives and nouns)* adhering to or following; an adherent of: *Christian.* **4** *(forming nouns)* a person who specializes or is expert in: *dietitian; phonetician.* [from Latin *-ānus,* suffix of adjectives]

ana[1] ('eɪnə, 'ɑ:nə) *adv Pharmacol.* (of ingredients in a prescription) in equal quantities. Abbrev.: **aa.** [C16: via Medieval Latin from Greek: of every one similarly]

ana[2] ('ɑ:nə) *n* **1** a collection of reminiscences, sketches, etc., of or about a person or place. **2** an item of or for such a collection. [C18: independent use of -ANA]

ANA *Commerce. abbrev. for* Article Number Association: (in Britain) an organization of manufacturers, retailers, and wholesalers that provides a system (**article numbering**) by which a product is identified by a unique machine-readable number (see **bar code**) compatible with article-numbering systems used in other countries.

ana- *or before a vowel* **an-** *prefix* **1** up; upwards: *anadromous.* **2** again: *anagram.* **3** back; backwards: *anatropous.* [from Greek *ana*]

-ana *or* **-iana** *suffix forming nouns.* denoting a collection of objects or information relating to a particular individual, subject, or place: *Shakespeareana; Victoriana; Americana.* [New Latin, from Latin *-āna,* literally: matters relating to, neuter plural of *-ānus;* see -AN]

anabaena (ˌænəˈbiːnə) *n, pl* **-nas.** any freshwater alga of the genus *Anabaena,* sometimes occurring in drinking water, giving it a fishy taste and smell. [New Latin, from Greek *anabainein* to shoot up, go up, from ANA- + *bainein* to go; so called because they rise to the surface at intervals]

anabantid (ˌænəˈbæntɪd) *n* **1** any of various spiny-finned fishes constituting the family *Anabantidae* and including the fighting fish, climbing perch, and gourami. See also **labyrinth fish.** ◆ *adj* **2** of, relating to, or belonging to the family *Anabantidae.*

Anabaptist (ˌænəˈbæptɪst) *n* **1** a member of any of various 16th-century Protestant movements that rejected infant baptism, insisted that adults be rebaptized, and sought to establish Christian communism. **2** a member of a later Protestant sect holding the same doctrines, esp. with regard to baptism. ◆ *adj* **3** of or relating to these movements or sects or their doctrines. [C16: from Ecclesiastical Latin *anabaptista,* from *anabaptīzāre* to baptize again, from Late Greek *anabaptizein;* see ANA-, BAPTIZE] ▸ ˌ**Anaˈbaptism** *n*

anabas (ˈænəˌbæs) *n* any of several labyrinth fishes of the genus *Anabas,* esp. the **climbing fish.** [C19: from New Latin, from Greek *anabainein* to go up; see ANABAENA]

anabasis (əˈnæbəsɪs) *n, pl* **-ses** (-ˌsiːz). **1** the march of Cyrus the Younger and his Greek mercenaries from Sardis to Cunaxa in Babylonia in 401 B.C., described by Xenophon in his *Anabasis.* Compare **katabasis. 2** any military expedition, esp. one from the coast to the interior. [C18: from Greek: a going up, ascent, from *anabainein* to go up; see ANABAENA]

anabatic (ˌænəˈbætɪk) *adj Meteorol.* (of air currents) rising upwards, esp. up slopes. Compare **katabatic.** [C19: from Greek *anabatikos* relating to ascents, from *anabainein* to go up; see ANABASIS]

anabiosis (ˌænəbaɪˈəʊsɪs) *n* the ability to return to life after apparent death; suspended animation. [C19: via New Latin from Greek, from *anabioein* to come back to life, from ANA- + *bios* life] ▸ **anabiotic** (ˌænəbaɪˈɒtɪk) *adj*

anableps (ˈænəˌbleps) *n, pl* **-bleps.** any of various cyprinodont fishes constituting the genus *Anableps,* which includes the four-eyed fishes. [New Latin, literally: one who looks up, from Greek, from *anablepein* to look up]

anabolic steroid (ˌænəˈbɒlɪk) *n* any of a group of synthetic steroid hormones (androgens) used to stimulate muscle and bone growth for athletic or therapeutic purposes.

anabolism (əˈnæbəˌlɪzəm) *n* a metabolic process in which complex molecules are synthesized from simpler ones with the storage of energy; constructive metabolism. Compare **catabolism.** [C19: from ANA- + (META)BOLISM] ▸ **anabolic** (ˌænəˈbɒlɪk) *adj*

anabolite (əˈnæbəˌlaɪt) *n* a product of anabolism. ▸ **anabolitic** (əˌnæbəˈlɪtɪk) *adj*

anabranch (ˈɑːnəˌbrɑːntʃ) *n* a stream that leaves a river and enters it again further downstream. [C19: from *ana(stomosing) branch*]

anacardiaceous (ˌænəˌkɑːdɪˈeɪʃəs) *adj* of, relating to, or belonging to the *Anacardiaceae,* a chiefly tropical family of trees and shrubs many of which have edible drupes. The family includes the cashew, mango, pistachio, and sumach. [C19: from New Latin *Anacardiāceae,* from ANA- + Greek *kardia* heart; so called from the shape of the top of the fruit stem]

anachorism (əˈnækəˌrɪzəm) *n* a geographical misplacement; something located in an incongruous position. Compare **anachronism.** [C19: from ANA- + *khōros* place]

anachronic (ˌænəˈkrɒnɪk) *or* **anachronical** *adj* out of chronological order or out of date. [C19: see ANACHRONISM] ▸ ˌ**anaˈchronically** *adv*

anachronism (əˈnækrəˌnɪzəm) *n* **1** the representation of an event, person, or thing in a historical context in which it could not have occurred or existed. **2** a person or thing that belongs or seems to belong to another time. [C17: from Latin *anachronismus,* from Greek *anakhronismos* a mistake in chronology, from *anakhronizein* to err in a time reference, from ANA- + *khronos* time] ▸ **aˌnachroˈnistic** *adj* ▸ **aˌnachroˈnistically** *adv*

anaclinal (ˌænəˈklaɪnᵊl) *adj* (of valleys and similar formations) progressing in a direction opposite to the dip of the surrounding rock strata. [C19: see ANA-, -CLINE]

anaclitic (ˌænəˈklɪtɪk) *adj Psychoanal.* of or relating to relationships that are characterized by the strong dependence of one person on others or another. [C20: from Greek *anaklitos* for leaning upon; see ANA-, -CLINE] ▸ **anaclisis** (ˌænəˈklaɪsɪs) *n*

anacoluthia (ˌænəkəˈluːθɪə) *n Rhetoric.* lack of grammatical sequence, esp. within a single sentence. ▸ ˌ**anacoˈluthic** *adj*

anacoluthon (ˌænəkəˈluːθɒn) *n, pl* **-tha** (-θə). *Rhetoric.* a construction that involves the change from one grammatical sequence to another within a single sentence; an example of anacoluthia. [C18: from Late Latin, from Greek *anakolouthon,* from *anakolouthos* not consistent, from AN- + *akolouthos* following]

anaconda (ˌænəˈkɒndə) *n* a very large nonvenomous arboreal and semiaquatic snake, *Eunectes murinus,* of tropical South America, which kills its prey by constriction: family *Boidae* (boas). [C18: probably changed from Sinhalese *henakandayā* whip snake, from *hena* lightning + *kanda* stem; originally referring to a snake of Sri Lanka]

anacoustic (ˌænəˈkuːstɪk) *adj* unable to support the propagation of sound; soundless.

Anacreon (əˈnækrɪˌɒn, -ən) *n* ?572–?488 B.C., Greek lyric poet, noted for his short songs celebrating love and wine.

Anacreontic (əˌnækrɪˈɒntɪk) *(sometimes not cap.)* ◆ *adj* **1** in the manner of Anacreon. **2** (of verse) in praise of love or wine; amatory or convivial. ◆ *n* **3** an Anacreontic poem. ▸ **Aˌnacreˈontically** *adv*

anacrusis (ˌænəˈkruːsɪs) *n, pl* **-ses** (-siːz). **1** *Prosody.* one or more unstressed syllables at the beginning of a line of verse. **2** *Music.* **2a** an unstressed note or group of notes immediately preceding the strong first beat of the first bar. **2b** another word for **upbeat.** [C19: from Greek *anakrousis* prelude, from *anakrouein* to strike up, from ANA- + *krouein* to strike] ▸ **anacrustic** (ˌænəˈkrʌstɪk) *adj*

anadem (ˈænəˌdem) *n Poetic.* a garland for the head. [C17: from Latin *anadēma* wreath, from Greek *anadēma,* from *anadein* to wreathe, from ANA- + *dein* to bind]

anadiplosis (ˌænədɪˈpləʊsɪs) *n Rhetoric.* repetition of the words or phrase at the end of one sentence, line, or clause at the beginning of the next. [C16: via Latin from Greek: repetition, from *anadiploun* to double back, from ANA- + *diploun* to double]

anadromous (əˈnædrəməs) *adj* (of fishes such as the salmon) migrating up rivers from the sea in order to breed. Compare **catadromous.** [C18: from Greek *anadromos* running upwards, from ANA- + *dromos* a running]

Anadyr (*Russian* aˈnadirj) *n* **1** a town in Russia, in NE Siberia at the mouth of the Anadyr River. Pop.: 6586 (1993 est.). **2** a mountain range in Russia, in NE Siberia, rising over 1500 m (5000 ft.). **3** a river in Russia, rising in mountains on the Arctic Circle, south of the Anadyr Range, and flowing east to the Gulf of Anadyr. Length: 725 km (450 miles). **4 Gulf of.** an inlet of the Bering Sea, off the coast of NE Russia.

anaemia *or U.S.* **anemia** (əˈniːmɪə) *n* **1** a deficiency in the number of red blood cells or in their haemoglobin content, resulting in pallor, shortness of breath, and lack of energy. **2** lack of vitality or vigour. **3** pallid complexion. [C19: from New Latin, from Greek *anaimia* lack of blood, from AN- + *haima* blood]

anaemic *or U.S.* **anemic** (əˈniːmɪk) *adj* **1** relating to or suffering from anaemia. **2** pale and sickly looking; lacking vitality.

anaerobe (æˈnɛərəʊb, ˈænərəʊb) *or* **anaerobium** (ˌænɛəˈrəʊbɪəm) *n, pl* **-obes** *or* **-obia** (-ˈəʊbɪə). an organism that does not require free oxygen or air for respiration. Compare **aerobe.**

anaerobic (ˌænɛəˈrəʊbɪk) *adj* **1** (of an organism or process) requiring the absence of or not dependent on the presence of free oxygen or air. **2** of or relating to anaerobes. ◆ Compare **aerobic.** ▸ ˌ**anaerˈobically** *adv*

anaerobiosis (ˌænɛərəʊbaɪˈəʊsɪs) *n* life in the absence of free oxygen.

anaesthesia *or U.S.* **anesthesia** (ˌænɪsˈθiːzɪə) *n* **1** local or general loss of bodily sensation, esp. of touch, as the result of nerve damage or other abnormality. **2** loss of sensation, esp. of pain, induced by drugs: called **general anaesthesia** when consciousness is lost and **local anaesthesia** when only a specific area of the body is involved. **3** a general dullness or lack of feeling. [C19: from New Latin, from Greek *anaisthēsia* absence of sensation, from AN- + *aisthēsis* feeling]

anaesthesiology *or U.S.* **anesthesiology** (ˌænɪsˌθiːzɪˈɒlədʒɪ) *n* the U.S. name for **anaesthetics.**

anaesthetic *or U.S.* **anesthetic** (ˌænɪsˈθetɪk) *n* **1** a substance that causes anaesthesia. ◆ *adj* **2** causing or characterized by anaesthesia.

anaesthetics (ˌænɪsˈθetɪks) *n (functioning as sing)* the science, study, and practice of anaesthesia and its application. U.S. name: **anesthesiology.**

anaesthetist (əˈniːsθətɪst) *n* **1** *Brit.* a qualified doctor specializing in the administration of anaesthetics. U.S. name: **anesthesiologist. 2** *U.S.* a person qualified to administer anaesthesia, often a nurse or someone other than a physician. Compare **anesthesiologist.**

anaesthetize, anaesthetise, *or U.S.* **anesthetize** (əˈniːsθəˌtaɪz) *vb (tr)* to render insensible to pain by administering an anaesthetic. ▸ **aˌnaesthetiˈzation, aˌnaesthetiˈsation,** *or U.S.* **aˌnesthetiˈzation** *n*

anaglyph (ˈænəˌglɪf) *n* **1** *Photog.* a stereoscopic picture consisting of two images of the same object, taken from slightly different angles, in two complementary colours, usually red and cyan (green-blue). When viewed through spectacles having one red and one cyan lens, the images merge to produce a stereoscopic sensation. **2** anything cut to stand in low relief, such as a cameo. [C17: from Greek *anagluphē* carved in low relief, from ANA- + *gluphē* carving, from *gluphein* to carve] ▸ ˌ**anaˈglyphic,** ˌ**anaˈglyphical** *or* **anaglyptic** (ˌænəˈglɪptɪk), ˌ**anaˈglyptical** *adj* ▸ **anaglyphy** (əˈnægləfɪ, ˈænəˌglɪfɪ) *n*

Anaglypta (ˌænəˈglɪptə) *n Trademark.* a type of thick embossed wallpaper. [C19: from Greek *anagluptos;* see ANAGLYPH]

anagnorisis (ˌænægˈnɒrɪsɪs) *n, pl* **-ses** (-ˌsiːz). (in Greek tragedy) the recognition or discovery by the protagonist of the identity of some character or the nature of his own predicament, which leads to the resolution of the plot; denouement. [from Greek: recognition]

anagoge *or* **anagogy** (ˈænəˌgɒdʒɪ) *n* **1** allegorical or spiritual interpretation, esp. of sacred works such as the Bible. **2** *Christianity.* allegorical interpretation of the Old Testament as typifying or foreshadowing subjects in the New Testament. [C18: via Late Latin from Greek *anagōgē* a lifting up, from *anagein,* from ANA- + *agein* to lead] ▸ **anagogic** (ˌænəˈgɒdʒɪk) *or* ˌ**anaˈgogical** *adj* ▸ ˌ**anaˈgogically** *adv*

anagram (ˈænəˌgræm) *n* a word or phrase the letters of which can be rearranged into another word or phrase. [C16: from New Latin *anagramma,* shortened from Greek *anagrammatismos,* from *anagrammatizein* to transpose letters, from ANA- + *gramma* a letter] ▸ **anagrammatic** (ˌænəgrəˈmætɪk) *or* ˌ**anagramˈmatical** *adj* ▸ ˌ**anagramˈmatically** *adv*

anagrammatize *or* **anagrammatise** (ˌænəˈgræməˌtaɪz) *vb* to arrange into an anagram. ▸ ˌ**anaˈgrammaˌtism** *n* ▸ ˌ**anaˈgrammatist** *n*

Anaheim (ˈænəˌhaɪm) *n* a city in SW California: site of Disneyland. Pop.: 288 945 (1996 est.).

anal (ˈeɪnᵊl) *adj* **1** of, relating to, or near the anus. **2** *Psychoanal.* **2a** relating to a stage of psychosexual development during which the child's interest is concentrated on the anal region and excremental functions. **2b** designating personality traits in the adult, such as orderliness, meanness, stubbornness, etc., due to fixation at the anal stage of development. Compare **oral** (sense 7). [C18: from New Latin *ānālis;* see ANUS] ▸ ˈ**anally** *adv*

anal. *abbrev. for:* **1** analogous. **2** analogy. **3** analysis. **4** analytic.

anal canal *n* the terminal part of the rectum forming the passage to the anus.

analcite (æ'nælsaɪt; 'æn[ə]l,saɪt, -sɪt) *or* **analcime** (æ'nælsɪm, -saɪm, -si:m) *n* a white, grey, or colourless zeolite mineral consisting of hydrated sodium aluminium silicate in cubic crystalline form. Formula: $NaAlSi_2O_6.H_2O$. **[C19:** from Greek *analkimos* weak (from AN- + *alkimos* strong, from *alkē* strength) + -ITE[1]**]**

analects ('ænə,lɛkts) *or* **analecta** (,ænə'lɛktə) *pl n* selected literary passages from one or more works. **[C17:** via Latin from Greek *analekta,* from *analegein* to collect up, from *legein* to gather**]** ▸ **,ana'lectic** *adj*

analemma (,ænə'lɛmə) *n, pl* **-mas** *or* **-mata** (-mətə). a graduated scale shaped like a figure eight that indicates the daily declination of the sun. **[C17:** from Latin: sundial, pedestal of sundial, from Greek *analēmma* pedestal, from *analambanein* to support**]** ▸ **analemmatic** (,ænəlɛ'mætɪk) *adj*

analeptic (,æn[ə]'lɛptɪk) *adj* **1** (of a drug, etc.) restorative or invigorating. ◆ *n* **2** a restorative remedy or drug. **[C17:** from New Latin *analēpticus,* from Greek *analēptikos* stimulating, from *analambanein* to take up; see ANALEMMA**]**

anal erotic *n* a person with anal personality traits.

anal fin *n* a median ventral unpaired fin, situated between the anus and the tail fin in fishes, that helps to maintain stable equilibrium.

analgesia (,æn[ə]l'dʒi:zɪə, -sɪə) *or* **analgia** (æn'ældʒɪə) *n* inability to feel pain. **[C18:** via New Latin from Greek: insensibility, from AN- + *algēsis* sense of pain**]**

analgesic (,æn[ə]l'dʒi:zɪk, -sɪk) *adj* **1** of or causing analgesia. ◆ *n* **2** a substance that produces analgesia.

anal intercourse *n* a form of sexual intercourse in which the penis is inserted into the anus.

analog ('ænə,lɒg) *n* a variant spelling of **analogue.**

USAGE The spelling *analog* is a U.S. variant of *analogue* in all its senses, and is also the generally preferred spelling in the computer industry.

analog computer *n* a mechanical, electrical, or electronic computer that performs arithmetical operations by using some variable physical quantity, such as mechanical movement or voltage, to represent numbers.

analogize *or* **analogise** (ə'nælə,dʒaɪz) *vb* **1** (*intr*) to make use of analogy, as in argument; draw comparisons. **2** (*tr*) to make analogous or reveal analogy in.

analogous (ə'næləgəs) *adj* **1** similar or corresponding in some respect. **2** *Biology.* (of organs and parts) having the same function but different evolutionary origin: *the paddle of a whale and the fin of a fish are analogous.* Compare **homologous** (sense 4). **3** *Linguistics.* formed by analogy: *an analogous plural.* **[C17:** from Latin *analogus,* from Greek *analogos* proportionate, from ANA- + *logos* speech, ratio**]** ▸ **a'nalogously** *adv* ▸ **a'nalogousness** *n*

USAGE The use of *with* after *analogous* should be avoided: *swimming has no event that is analogous to* (not *with*) *the 100 metres in athletics.*

analogue *or U.S. (sometimes)* **analog** ('ænə,lɒg) *n* **1a** a physical object or quantity, such as a pointer on a dial or a voltage, used to measure or represent another quantity. **1b** (*as modifier*): *analogue watch; analogue recording.* **2** something analogous to something else. **3** *Biology.* an analogous part or organ. **4** *Chem.* an organic chemical compound related to another by substitution of hydrogen atoms with alkyl groups: *toluene is an analogue of benzene.*

USAGE See at **analog.**

analogue clock *or* **watch** *n* a clock or watch in which the hours, minutes, and sometimes seconds are indicated by hands on a dial. Compare **digital clock.**

analogue-digital converter *n* a device converting an analogue electrical signal into its digital representation so that it can be processed by a digital system. Abbrev.: **ADC.**

analogue recording *n* a sound recording process in which an audio input is converted into an analogous electrical waveform.

analogy (ə'nælədʒɪ) *n, pl* **-gies. 1** agreement or similarity, esp. in a certain limited number of features or details. **2** a comparison made to show such a similarity: *to draw an analogy between an atom and the solar system.* **3** *Biology.* the relationship between analogous organs or parts. **4** *Logic, maths.* a form of reasoning in which a similarity between two or more things is inferred from a known similarity between them in other respects. **5** *Linguistics.* imitation of existing models or regular patterns in the formation of words, inflections, etc.: *a child may use "sheeps" as the plural of "sheep" by analogy with "dog," "dogs," "cat," "cats," etc.* **[C16:** from Greek *analogia* ratio, correspondence, from *analogos* ANALOGOUS**]** ▸ **analogical** (,ænə'lɒdʒɪk[ə]l) *or* **,ana'logic** *adj* ▸ **,ana'logically** *adv* ▸ **a'nalogist** *n*

analphabetic (,ænælfə'bɛtɪk, æn,æl-) *adj* **1** not in alphabetical order. ◆ *n, adj* **2** a less common word for **illiterate. [C20:** from Greek *analphabētos;* see AN-, ALPHABET**]** ▸ **,analpha'betically** *adv*

anal retentive *Psychoanal.* ◆ *n* **1** a person who exhibits anal personality traits. ◆ *adj* **anal-retentive. 2** exhibiting anal personality traits.

analysand (ə'nælɪ,sænd) *n* any person who is undergoing psychoanalysis. **[C20:** from ANALYSE + *-and,* on the model of *multiplicand***]**

analyse *or U.S.* **analyze** ('æn[ə],laɪz) *vb* (*tr*) **1** to examine in detail in order to discover meaning, essential features, etc. **2** to break down into components or essential features: *to analyse a financial structure.* **3** to make a mathematical, chemical, grammatical, etc., analysis of. **4** another word for **psychoanalyse. [C17:** back formation from ANALYSIS**]** ▸ **,ana'lysable** *or U.S.* **,ana'lyzable** *adj* ▸ **,analy'sation** *or U.S.* **,analy'zation** *n* ▸ **'ana,lyser** *or U.S.* **'ana,lyzer** *n*

analysis (ə'nælɪsɪs) *n, pl* **-ses** (-,si:z). **1** the division of a physical or abstract whole into its constituent parts to examine or determine their relationship or value. Compare **synthesis** (sense 1). **2** a statement of the results of this. **3** short for **psychoanalysis. 4** *Chem.* **4a** the decomposition of a substance into its elements, radicals, or other constituents in order to determine the kinds of constituents present (**qualitative analysis**) or the amount of each constituent (**quantitative analysis**). **4b** the result obtained by such a determination. **5** *Linguistics.* the use of word order together with word function to express syntactic relations in a language, as opposed to the use of inflections. Compare **synthesis** (sense 4). **6** *Maths.* the branch of mathematics principally concerned with the properties of functions, largely arising out of calculus. **7** *Philosophy.* (in the writings of Kant) the separation of a concept from another that contains it. Compare **synthesis** (sense 6a). **8 in the last, final,** *or* **ultimate analysis.** after everything has been given due consideration. **[C16:** from New Latin, from Greek *analusis,* literally: a dissolving, from *analuein,* from ANA- + *luein* to loosen**]**

analysis of variance *n Statistics.* any of a number of techniques for resolving the observed variance between sets of data into components, esp. to determine whether the difference between two samples is explicable as random sampling variation with the same underlying population.

analysis situs *n* a former name for **topology** (sense 2).

analyst ('ænəlɪst) *n* **1** a person who analyses or is skilled in analysis. **2** short for **psychoanalyst.**

analytic (,ænə'lɪtɪk) *or* **analytical** (,ænə'lɪtɪk[ə]l) *adj* **1** relating to analysis. **2** capable of or given to analysing: *an analytic mind.* **3** Also: **isolating.** *Linguistics.* denoting languages, such as Chinese, whose morphology is characterized by analysis. Compare **synthetic** (sense 3), **agglutinative** (sense 2), **polysynthetic. 4** *Logic.* (of a proposition) **4a** true by virtue of the meanings of the words alone without reference to the facts, as *all spinsters are unmarried.* **4b** true or false by virtue of meaning alone; so *all spinsters are married* is analytically false. ◆ Compare **synthetic** (sense 4), **a priori. 5** Also: **regular, holomorphic.** *Maths.* (of a function of a complex variable) having a derivative at each point of its domain. **[C16:** via Late Latin from Greek *analutikos* from *analuein* to dissolve, break down; see ANALYSIS**]** ▸ **,ana'lytically** *adv*

analytical geometry *n* the branch of geometry that uses algebraic notation and analysis to locate a geometric point in terms of a coordinate system; coordinate geometry.

analytical philosophy *n* a school of philosophy which flourished in the first half of the 20th century and which sought to resolve philosophical problems by analysing the language in which they are expressed, esp. in terms of formal logic as in Russell's theory of descriptions. Compare **linguistic philosophy.**

analytical psychology *n* a school of psychoanalysis founded by Jung as a result of disagreements with Freud. See also **archetype, collective unconscious.**

analytical reagent *n* a chemical compound of a known high standard of purity.

Anam (æ'næm, 'ænæm) *n* a variant spelling of **Annam.**

Anambra (ə'næmbrə) *n* a state of S Nigeria, formed in 1976 from part of East-Central State. Capital: Enugu. Pop.: 3 094 783 (1995 est.). Area: 4844 sq. km (1870 sq. miles).

anamnesis (,ænæm'ni:sɪs) *n, pl* **-ses** (-si:z). **1** the ability to recall past events; recollection. **2** the case history of a patient. **[C17:** via New Latin from Greek, from *anamimnēskein* to recall, from *mimnēskein* to call to mind**]**

anamnestic (,ænæm'nɛstɪk) *adj* **1** of or relating to anamnesis. **2** *Immunol.* denoting a response to antigenic stimulation characterized by the production of large amounts of antibody specific to a different antigen from that which elicited the response. ▸ **,anam'nestically** *adv*

anamniote (æn'æmnɪəʊt) *n* any vertebrate animal, such as a fish or amphibian, that lacks an amnion, chorion, and allantois during embryonic development. Compare **amniote.** ▸ **anamniotic** (æn,æmnɪ'ɒtɪk) *adj*

anamorphic (,ænə'mɔ:fɪk) *adj* of, relating to, or caused by anamorphosis or anamorphism.

anamorphic lens *n* a component in the optical system of a film projector for converting standard 35mm film images into wide-screen format.

anamorphism (,ænə'mɔ:,fɪzəm) *n* metamorphism of a rock in which complex minerals are formed from simpler ones.

anamorphoscope (,ænə'mɔ:fə,skəʊp) *n* an optical device, such as a cylindrical lens, for correcting an image that has been distorted by anamorphosis.

anamorphosis (,ænə'mɔ:fəsɪs, -mɔ:'fəʊsɪs) *n, pl* **-ses** (-,si:z). **1** *Optics.* **1a** an image or drawing distorted in such a way that it becomes recognizable only when viewed in a specified manner or through a special device. **1b** the process by which such images or drawings are produced. **2** the evolution of one type of organism from another by a series of gradual changes. **[C18:** from Greek, from *anamorphoun* to transform, from *morphē* form, shape**]**

ananas (ə'nænəs) *n* another name for the **pineapple,** or for a related tropical American bromeliaceous plant, the pinguin, that has an edible plum-shaped fruit. **[C17:** from the native name in Peru**]**

Ananda (ə'nændə) *n* 5th century B.C., the first cousin, favourite disciple, and personal attendant of the Buddha.

anandrous (æn'ændrəs) *adj* (of flowers) having no stamens. **[C19:** from Greek *anandros* lacking males, from AN- + *anēr* man**]**

Ananias (,ænə'naɪəs) *n* **1** *New Testament.* a Jewish Christian of Jerusalem who was struck dead for lying (Acts 5). **2** a liar.

Ananke (ə'næŋkɪ) *n* a small outer satellite of Jupiter.

ananthous (æn'ænθəs) *adj* (of higher plants) having no flowers. **[C19:** from Greek *ananthēs,* from AN- + *anthos* flower**]**

anapaest *or* **anapest** ('ænəpest, -pi:st) *n Prosody.* a metrical foot of three syllables, the first two short, the last long (◡◡–). **[C17:** via Latin from Greek *anapaistos* reversed (that is, a dactyl reversed), from *anapaiein,* from *ana-* back + *paiein* to strike**]** ▸ **,ana'paestic** *or* **,ana'pestic** *adj*

anaphase ('ænə,feɪz) *n* **1** the third stage of mitosis, during which the chromatids separate and migrate towards opposite ends of the spindle. See also **prophase, metaphase, telophase. 2** the corresponding stage of the first division of meiosis. **[C19:** from ANA- + PHASE**]**

anaphora (ə'næfərə) *n* **1** *Grammar.* the use of a word such as a pronoun that has the same reference as a word previously used in the same discourse. In the sentence *John wrote the essay in the library but Peter did it at home,* both *did* and *it* are examples of anaphora. Compare **cataphora, exophoric. 2** *Rhetoric.* the repetition of a word or phrase at the beginning of successive clauses. **[**C16: via Latin from Greek: repetition, from *anapherein,* from ANA- + *pherein* to bear**]** ► **anaphoric** (ˌænəˈfɒrɪk) *adj* ► ˌ**anaˈphorically** *adv*

anaphoresis (ˌænəfəˈriːsɪs) *n Chem.* the movement of suspended particles towards the anode in an electric field.

anaphrodisiac (ˌænæfrəˈdɪzɪˌæk) *adj* **1** tending to lessen sexual desire. ◆ *n* **2** an anaphrodisiac drug. ► ˌ**anaphroˈdisia** *n*

anaphylaxis (ˌænəfɪˈlæksɪs) *n* extreme sensitivity to an injected antigen, esp. a protein, following a previous injection. **[**C20: from ANA- + (PRO)PHYLAXIS**]** ► ˌ**anaphyˈlactic** *or* ˌ**anaphyˈlactoid** *adj* ► ˌ**anaphyˈlactically** *adv*

anaplasia (ˌænəˈpleɪsɪə) *n* reversion of plant or animal cells to a simpler less differentiated form.

anaplasmosis (ˌænəplæzˈməʊsɪs) *n* another name for **gallsickness.**

anaplastic (ˌænəˈplæstɪk) *adj* **1** of or relating to anaplasia. **2** relating to plastic surgery.

anaplasty (ˈænəˌplæstɪ) *n Surgery.* another name for **plastic surgery.**

anaptyxis (ˌænæpˈtɪksɪs) *n, pl* **-tyxes** (-ˈtɪksiːz). the insertion of a short vowel between consonants in order to make a word more easily pronounceable. **[**C19: via New Latin from Greek *anaptuxis,* from *anaptussein* to unfold, from ANA- + *ptussein* to fold**]** ► **anaptyctic** (ˌænæpˈtɪktɪk) *or* ˌ**anapˈtyctical** *adj*

Anapurna (ˌænəˈpʊənə) *n* a variant spelling of **Annapurna.**

anarch (ˈænɑːk) *n Archaic.* an instigator or personification of anarchy.

anarchism (ˈænəˌkɪzəm) *n* **1** *Political theory.* a doctrine advocating the abolition of government. **2** the principles or practice of anarchists.

anarchist (ˈænəkɪst) *n* **1** a person who advocates the abolition of government and a social system based on voluntary cooperation. **2** a person who causes disorder or upheaval. ► ˌ**anarˈchistic** *adj*

anarchy (ˈænəkɪ) *n* **1** general lawlessness and disorder, esp. when thought to result from an absence or failure of government. **2** the absence or lack of government. **3** the absence of any guiding or uniting principle; disorder; chaos. **4** the theory or practice of political anarchism. **[**C16: from Medieval Latin *anarchia,* from Greek *anarkhia,* from *anarkhos* without a ruler, from AN- + *arkh-* leader, from *arkhein* to rule**]** ► **anarchic** (ænˈɑːkɪk) *or* **anˈarchical** *adj* ► **anˈarchically** *adv*

anarthria (ænˈɑːθrɪə) *n Pathol.* loss of the ability to speak coherently. **[**C19: New Latin, from Greek *anarthros* lacking vigour, from AN- + *arthros* joint**]**

anarthrous (ænˈɑːθrəs) *adj* **1** (of a noun) used without an article. **2** having no joints or articulated limbs. **[**C19: from Greek *anarthros,* from AN- + *arthros* joint, definite article**]** ► **anˈarthrously** *adv* ► **anˈarthrousness** *n*

anasarca (ˌænəˈsɑːkə) *n Pathol.* a generalized accumulation of serous fluid within the subcutaneous connective tissue, resulting in oedema. **[**C14: from New Latin, from ANA- (puffed up) + Greek *sarx* flesh**]** ► ˌ**anaˈsarcous** *adj*

Anastasia (ˌænəˈstɑːzɪə, -ˈsteɪ-) *n* **Grand Duchess.** 1901–?18, daughter of Tsar Nicholas II, believed to have been executed by the Bolsheviks in 1918, although several women subsequently claimed to be her.

anastigmat (æˈnæstɪgˌmæt, ˌænəˈstɪgmæt) *n* a lens or system of lenses designed to be free of astigmatism.

anastigmatic (ˌænəstɪgˈmætɪk) *adj* (of a lens or optical device) not astigmatic. Also: **stigmatic.**

anastomose (əˈnæstəˌməʊz) *vb* to join (two parts of a blood vessel, etc.) by anastomosis.

anastomosis (əˌnæstəˈməʊsɪs) *n, pl* **-ses** (-siːz). **1** a natural connection between two tubular structures, such as blood vessels. **2** the surgical union of two hollow organs or parts that are normally separate. **3** a reticulate pattern, as in the veins of a leaf. **[**C16: via New Latin from Greek: opening, from *anastomoun* to equip with a mouth, from *stoma* mouth**]** ► **anastomotic** (əˌnæstəˈmɒtɪk) *adj*

anastrophe (əˈnæstrəfɪ) *n Rhetoric.* another term for **inversion** (sense 3). **[**C16: from Greek, from *anastrephein* to invert**]**

anat. *abbrev. for:* **1** anatomical. **2** anatomy.

anata (ˈænətə) *n* (in Theravada Buddhism) the belief that since all things are constantly changing, there can be no such thing as a permanent, unchanging self: one of the three basic characteristics of existence. Sanskrit word: **anatman.** Compare **anicca, dukkha.** [Pali, literally: no self]

anatase (ˈænəˌteɪz) *n* a rare blue or black mineral that consists of titanium oxide in tetragonal crystalline form and occurs in veins in igneous rocks. Formula: TiO_2. Also called: **octahedrite. [**C19: from French, from Greek *anatasis* an extending (referring to the length of the crystals), from *anateinein* to stretch out**]**

anathema (əˈnæθəmə) *n, pl* **-mas. 1** a detested person or thing: *he is anathema to me.* **2** a formal ecclesiastical curse of excommunication or a formal denunciation of a doctrine. **3** the person or thing so cursed. **4** a strong curse; imprecation. **[**C16: via Church Latin from Greek: something accursed, dedicated (to evil), from *anatithenai* to dedicate, from ANA- + *tithenai* to set**]**

anathematize *or* **anathematise** (əˈnæθɪməˌtaɪz) *vb* to pronounce an anathema (upon a person, etc.); curse. ► **aˌnathematiˈzation** *or* **aˌnathemaˈtiˈsation** *n*

Anatolia (ˌænəˈtəʊlɪə) *n* the Asian part of Turkey, occupying the peninsula between the Black Sea, the Mediterranean, and the Aegean: consists of a plateau, largely mountainous, with salt lakes in the interior. Historical name: **Asia Minor.**

Anatolian (ˌænəˈtəʊlɪən) *adj* **1** of or relating to Anatolia or its inhabitants. **2** denoting, belonging to, or relating to an ancient family of languages related to the Indo-European family and including Hittite. ◆ *n* **3** this family of languages, sometimes regarded as a branch of Indo-European. **4** a native or inhabitant of Anatolia.

anatomical (ˌænəˈtɒmɪkəl) *adj* of or relating to anatomy. ► ˌ**anaˈtomically** *adv*

anatomical snuffbox *n* the triangular depression on the back of the hand between the thumb and the index finger.

anatomist (əˈnætəmɪst) *n* an expert in anatomy.

anatomize *or* **anatomise** (əˈnætəˌmaɪz) *vb* (*tr*) **1** to dissect (an animal or plant). **2** to examine in minute detail. ► **aˌnatomiˈzation** *or* **aˌnatomiˈsation** *n* ► **aˈnatoˌmizer** *or* **aˈnatoˌmiser** *n*

anatomy (əˈnætəmɪ) *n, pl* **-mies. 1** the science concerned with the physical structure of animals and plants. **2** the physical structure of an animal or plant or any of its parts. **3** a book or treatise on this subject. **4** dissection of an animal or plant. **5** any detailed analysis: *the anatomy of a crime.* **6** *Informal.* the human body. **[**C14: from Latin *anatomia,* from Greek *anatomē,* from *anatemnein* to cut up, from ANA- + *temnein* to cut**]**

anatropous (əˈnætrəpəs) *adj* (of a plant ovule) inverted during development by a bending of the stalk (funicle) attaching it to the carpel wall. Compare **orthotropous. [**C19: from ANA- (inverted) + -TROPOUS**]**

anatto (əˈnætəʊ) *n, pl* **-tos.** a variant spelling of **annatto.**

Anaxagoras (ˌænækˈsægərəs) *n* ?500–428 B.C., Greek philosopher who maintained that all things were composed of minute particles arranged by an eternal intelligence.

anaxial (ænˈæksɪəl) *adj Biology.* asymmetrical.

Anaximander (əˌnæksɪˈmændə) *n* 611–547 B.C., Greek philosopher, astronomer, and mathematician who believed the first principle of the world to be the Infinite.

Anaximenes (ˌænækˈsɪməˌniːz) *n* 6th century B.C., Greek philosopher who believed air to be the primary substance.

anbury (ˈænbərɪ) *n, pl* **-buries. 1** a soft spongy tumour occurring in horses and oxen. **2** a disease of cruciferous plants, esp. root crops, in which the roots are clubbed. **[**C16: of uncertain origin**]**

ANC *abbrev. for* African National Congress.

-ance *or* **-ancy** *suffix forming nouns.* indicating an action, state or condition, or quality: *hindrance; tenancy; resemblance.* Compare **-ence. [**via Old French from Latin *-antia;* see -ANCY**]**

ancestor (ˈænsɛstə) *n* **1** (*often pl*) a person from whom another is directly descended, esp. someone more distant than a grandparent; forefather. **2** an early type of animal or plant from which a later, usually dissimilar, type has evolved. **3** a person or thing regarded as a forerunner of a later person or thing: *the ancestor of the modern camera.* **[**C13: from Old French *ancestre,* from Late Latin *antecēssor* one who goes before, from Latin *antecēdere;* see ANTECEDE**]** ► **ˈancestress** *fem n*

ancestral (ænˈsɛstrəl) *adj* **1** of, inherited from, or derived from ancestors. ◆ *n* **2** *Logic.* a relation that holds between *x* and *y* if there is a chain of instances of a given relation leading from *x* to *y.* Thus the ancestral of *parent of* is *ancestor of,* since *x* is the ancestor of *y* if and only if *x* is a parent of ... a parent of ... a parent of *y.* ► **anˈcestrally** *adv*

ancestry (ˈænsɛstrɪ) *n, pl* **-tries. 1** lineage or descent, esp. when ancient, noble, or distinguished. **2** ancestors collectively.

Anchises (ænˈkaɪsiːz) *n Classical myth.* a Trojan prince and father of Aeneas. In the *Aeneid,* he is rescued by his son at the fall of Troy and dies in Sicily.

anchor (ˈæŋkə) *n* **1** any of several devices, usually of steel, attached to a vessel by a cable and dropped overboard so as to grip the bottom and restrict the vessel's movement. **2** an object used to hold something else firmly in place: *the rock provided an anchor for the rope.* **3** a source of stability or security: *religion was his anchor.* **4a** a metal cramp, bolt, or similar fitting, esp. one used to make a connection to masonry. **4b** (*as modifier*): *anchor bolt; anchor plate.* **5a** the rear person in a tug-of-war team. **5b** short for **anchorman** or **anchorwoman. 6 at anchor.** (of a vessel) anchored. **7 cast, come to,** *or* **drop anchor.** to anchor a vessel. **8 drag anchor.** See **drag** (sense 13). **9 ride at anchor.** to be anchored. **10 weigh anchor.** to raise a vessel's anchor or (of a vessel) to have its anchor raised in preparation for departure. ◆ *vb* **11** to use an anchor to hold (a vessel) in one place. **12** to fasten or be fastened securely; fix or become fixed firmly. **13** (*tr*) *Radio, television.* to act as an anchorman on. ◆ See also **anchors. [**Old English *ancor,* from Latin *ancora,* from Greek *ankura;* related to Greek *ankos* bend; compare Latin *uncus* bent, hooked**]**

anchorage[1] (ˈæŋkərɪdʒ) *n* **1** the act of anchoring. **2** any place where a vessel is anchored. **3** a place designated for vessels to anchor. **4** a fee imposed for anchoring. **5** anything used as an anchor. **6** a source of security or strength. **7** something that supplies a secure hold for something else.

anchorage[2] (ˈæŋkərɪdʒ) *n* the cell or retreat of an anchorite.

Anchorage (ˈæŋkərɪdʒ) *n* the largest city in Alaska, a port in the south, at the head of Cook Inlet. Pop.: 253 649 (1994 est.).

anchorite (ˈæŋkəˌraɪt) *n* a person who lives in seclusion, esp. a religious recluse; hermit. **[**C15: from Medieval Latin *anchorīta,* from Late Latin *anachōrēta,* from Greek *anakhōrētēs,* from *anakhōrein* to retire, withdraw, from *khōra* a space**]** ► **ˈanchoress** *fem n*

anchorman (ˈæŋkəmæn) *n, pl* **-men. 1** *Sport.* the last person in a team to compete, esp. in a relay race. **2** (in broadcasting) a person in a central studio who links up and maintains contact with various outside camera units, reporters, etc. ► **ˈanchorˌwoman** *fem n*

anchor ring *n* a ring made from an iron bar of circular cross-section.

anchors (ˈæŋkəz) *pl n Slang.* the brakes of a motor vehicle: *he rammed on the anchors.*

anchoveta (ˌæntʃəˈvɛtə) *n* a small anchovy, *Cetengraulis mysticetus,* of the American Pacific, used as bait by tuna fishermen. **[**C20: Spanish, diminutive of *anchova* ANCHOVY**]**

anchovy ('æntʃəvɪ) *n, pl* **-vies** *or* **-vy.** any of various small marine food fishes of the genus *Engraulis* and related genera, esp. *E. encrasicolus* of S Europe: family *Clupeidae* (herrings). They have a salty taste and are often tinned or made into a paste or essence. [C16: from Spanish *anchova,* perhaps ultimately from Greek *aphuē* small fish]

anchovy pear *n* a West Indian tree, *Grias cauliflora,* bearing edible fruit that taste like the mango: family *Lecythidaceae.* [C18: so called from the use of the fruit as an hors d'oeuvre]

anchusa (æŋ'kjuːsə) *n* any Eurasian plant of the boraginaceous genus *Anchusa,* having rough hairy stems and leaves and blue flowers. See also **alkanet** (sense 3), **bugloss.** [C18: from Latin]

anchusin (æŋ'kjuːsɪn) *n* another name for **alkanet** (sense 2).

anchylose ('æŋkɪˌləʊz) *vb* a variant spelling of **ankylose.** ▸ **ˌanchy'losis** *n* ▸ **anchylotic** (ˌæŋkɪ'lɒtɪk) *adj*

anchylostomiasis (ˌæŋkɪˌlɒstə'maɪəsɪs) *n* a variant of **ancylostomiasis.**

ancien régime *French.* (ɑ̃sjɛ̃ reʒim) *n, pl* ***anciens régimes*** (ɑ̃sjɛ̃ reʒim). **1** the political and social system of France before the Revolution of 1789. **2** a former or outdated regime. [literally: old regime]

ancient[1] ('eɪnʃənt) *adj* **1** dating from very long ago: *ancient ruins.* **2** very old; aged. **3** of the far past, esp. before the collapse of the Western Roman Empire (476 A.D.). Compare **medieval, modern. 4** *Law.* having existed since before the time of legal memory. ◆ *n* **5** (*often pl*) a member of a civilized nation in the ancient world, esp. a Greek, Roman, or Hebrew. **6** (*often pl*) one of the classical authors of Greek or Roman antiquity. **7** *Archaic.* an old man. [C14: from Old French *ancien,* from Vulgar Latin *anteanus* (unattested), from Latin *ante* before] ▸ **'ancientness** *n*

ancient[2] ('eɪnʃənt) *n Archaic.* **1** a flag or other banner; standard. **2** a standard-bearer; ensign. [C16: changed from ENSIGN through the influence of ANCIENT[1]]

Ancient Greek *n* the Greek language from the earliest records to about 300 B.C., the chief dialect areas of which were Aeolic, Arcadic, Doric, and Ionic (including Attic). Compare **Koine, Late Greek, Medieval Greek.**

ancient history *n* **1** the history of the **ancient world,** from the earliest known civilizations to the collapse of the Western Roman Empire in 476 A.D.. **2** *Informal.* a recent event or fact sufficiently familiar to have lost its pertinence.

ancient lights *n* (*usually functioning as sing*) the legal right to receive, by a particular window or windows, adequate and unobstructed daylight.

anciently ('eɪnʃəntlɪ) *adv* in ancient times.

ancient monument *n Brit.* a historical building or the remains of one, usually dating from no later than the medieval period, that has been designated as worthy of preservation and is often in the care of a government department.

Ancient of Days *n* a name for God, originating in the Authorized Version of the Old Testament (Daniel 7:9).

ancillary (æn'sɪlərɪ) *adj* **1** subsidiary. **2** auxiliary; supplementary: *ancillary services.* ◆ *n, pl* **-laries. 3** a subsidiary or auxiliary thing or person: *the company has an ancillary abroad.* [C17: from Latin *ancillāris* concerning maid-servants, from *ancilla,* diminutive of *ancūla* female servant]

ancipital (æn'sɪpɪtᵊl) *or* **ancipitous** (æn'sɪpɪtəs) *adj Biology.* flattened and having two edges: *ancipital stems.* [C18: from Latin *anceps* two-headed]

Ancohuma (ˌæŋkəʊ'uːmə) *n* one of the two peaks of (Mount) **Sorata.**

ancon ('æŋkɒn) *or* **ancone** ('æŋkəʊn) *n, pl* **ancones** (æŋ'kəʊniːz). **1** *Architect.* a projecting bracket or console supporting a cornice. **2** a former technical name for **elbow.** [C18: from Greek *ankōn* a bend] ▸ **anconal** (æŋ'kəʊnᵊl) *or* **anconeal** (æŋ'kəʊnɪəl) *adj*

Ancona (*Italian* aŋ'koːna) *n* a port in central Italy, on the Adriatic, capital of the Marches: founded by Greeks from Syracuse in about 390 B.C. Pop.: 100 597 (1994 est.).

-ancy *suffix forming nouns.* a variant of **-ance,** indicating condition or quality: *expectancy; poignancy.*

ancylostomiasis (ˌænsɪˌlɒstə'maɪəsɪs), **ankylostomiasis,** *or* **anchylostomiasis** *n* infestation of the human intestine with blood-sucking hookworms, causing progressive anaemia. Also called: **hookworm disease.** [from New Latin, from *Ancylostoma* genus of hookworms, from Greek *ankulos* hooked, crooked + *stoma* mouth]

and (ænd; *unstressed* ənd, ən) *conj* (*coordinating*) **1** along with; in addition to: *boys and girls.* **2** as a consequence: *he fell down and cut his knee.* **3** afterwards: *we pay the man and go through that door.* **4** (preceded by *good* or *nice*) (intensifier): *the sauce is good and thick.* **5** plus: *two and two equals four.* **6** used to join identical words or phrases to give emphasis or indicate repetition or continuity: *better and better; we ran and ran; it rained and rained.* **7** used to join two identical words or phrases to express a contrast between instances of what is named: *there are jobs and jobs.* **8** *Informal.* used in place of *to* in infinitives after verbs such as *try, go,* and *come: try and see it my way.* **9** an obsolete word for **if:** *and it please you.* Informal spellings: **an, an', 'n.** ◆ *n* **10** (*usually pl*) an additional matter or problem: *ifs, ands, or buts.* [Old English *and;* related to Old Frisian *anda,* Old Saxon *ande,* Old High German *anti,* Sanskrit *atha*]

USAGE See at **to.**

AND *international car registration for* Andorra.

-and *or* **-end** *suffix forming nouns.* indicating a person or thing that is to be dealt with in a specified way: *analysand; dividend; multiplicand.* [from Latin gerundives ending in *-andus, -endus*]

Andalusia (ˌændə'luːzɪə) *n* a region of S Spain, on the Mediterranean and the Atlantic, with the Sierra Morena in the north, the Sierra Nevada in the southeast, and the Guadalquivir River flowing over fertile lands between them; a centre of Moorish civilization; it became an autonomous region in 1981. Area: about 87 280 sq. km (33 700 sq. miles). Spanish name: **Andalucía** (andalu'θia).

andalusite (ˌændə'luːsaɪt) *n* a grey, pink, or brown hard mineral consisting of aluminium silicate in orthorhombic crystalline form. It occurs in metamorphic rocks and is used as a refractory and as a gemstone. Formula: Al_2SiO_5.

Andaman and Nicobar Islands ('ændəmən; 'nɪkəʊˌbɑː) *pl n* a territory of India, in the E Bay of Bengal, consisting of two groups of over 200 islands. Capital: Port Blair. Pop.: 322 000 (1994 est.). Area: 8140 sq. km (3143 sq. miles).

Andaman Islands *pl n* a group of islands in the E Bay of Bengal, part of the Indian territory of the Andaman and Nicobar Islands. Area: 6408 sq. km (2474 sq. miles). Pop.: 240 089 (1991 est.).

Andaman Sea *n* part of the Bay of Bengal, between the Andaman and Nicobar Islands and the Malay Peninsula.

andante (æn'dæntɪ) *Music.* ◆ *adj, adv* **1** (to be performed) at a moderately slow tempo. ◆ *n* **2** a passage or piece to be performed in this manner. [C18: Italian: going, from *andare* to go, from Latin *ambulāre* to walk]

andantino (ˌændæn'tiːnəʊ) *Music.* ◆ *adj, adv* **1** (to be performed) slightly faster, or slightly more slowly, than andante. ◆ *n, pl* **-nos. 2** a passage or piece to be performed in this manner. [C19: diminutive of ANDANTE]

AND circuit *or* **gate** (ænd) *n Computing.* a logic circuit having two or more input wires and one output wire that has a high-voltage output signal if and only if all input signals are at a high voltage simultaneously: used extensively as a basic circuit in computers. Compare **NAND circuit, NOR circuit, OR circuit.** [C20: so named because the action performed on electrical signals is similar to the operation of the conjunction *and* in logical constructions]

Andean (æn'diːən, 'ændɪən) *adj* of, relating to, or resembling the Andes.

Anderlecht (*Flemish* 'ɑndərlɛxt) *n* a town in central Belgium, a suburb of Brussels. Pop.: 87 880 (1991).

Andersen ('ændəsᵊn) *n* **Hans Christian.** 1805–75, Danish author of fairy tales, including *The Ugly Duckling, The Tin Soldier,* and *The Snow Queen.*

Andersen Nexø ('anərsen) *n* See (Martin Andersen) **Nexø.**

Anderson[1] ('ændəsᵊn) *n* a river in N Canada, in the Northwest Territories, rising in lakes north of Great Bear Lake and flowing west and north to the Beaufort Sea. Length: about 580 km (360 miles).

Anderson[2] ('ændəsᵊn) *n* **1 Carl David.** 1905–91, U.S. physicist, who discovered the positron in cosmic rays (1932): Nobel prize for physics 1936. **2 Elizabeth Garrett.** 1836–1917, English physician and feminist: a campaigner for the admission of women to the professions. **3 John.** 1893–1962, Australian philosopher, born in Scotland, whose theories are expounded in *Studies in Empirical Philosophy* (1962). **4** Dame **Judith,** real name *Frances Margaret Anderson.* 1898–1992, Australian stage and film actress. **5 Lindsay** (**Gordon**). 1923–94, British film and theatre director: his films include *This Sporting Life* (1963), *If* (1968), and *O Lucky Man!* (1973). **6 Marian.** 1902–93, U.S. contralto, the first Black permanent member of the Metropolitan Opera Company, New York. **7 Philip Warren.** 1923–96, U.S. physicist, noted for his work on solid-state physics. Nobel prize for physics 1977. **8 Sherwood.** 1874–1941, U.S. novelist and short-story writer, best known for *Winesburg Ohio* (1919), a collection of short stories illustrating small-town life.

Anderson shelter *n Brit.* a small prefabricated air-raid shelter of World War II consisting of an arch of corrugated metal and designed to be partly buried in people's gardens and covered with earth for protection. [C20: so named because its use was adopted while Sir John *Anderson* was Home Secretary (1939–40)]

Anderssen ('ændəsᵊn) *n* **Adolf** ('aːdɔlf). 1818–79, German chess player: noted for the incisiveness of his combination play.

Andes ('ændiːz) *pl n* a major mountain system of South America, extending for about 7250 km (4500 miles) along the entire W coast, with several parallel ranges or cordilleras and many volcanic peaks: rich in minerals, including gold, silver, copper, iron ore, and nitrates. Average height: 3900 m (13 000 ft.). Highest peak: Aconcagua, 6960 m (22 835 ft.).

andesine ('ændɪˌziːn, -zɪn) *n* a rare feldspar mineral of the plagioclase series consisting of an aluminium silicate of sodium and calcium. Formula: $NaAlSi_3O_8.CaAl_2Si_2O_8$. [C19: from the ANDES (where it is found) + -INE[1]]

andesite ('ændɪˌzaɪt) *n* a fine-grained grey volcanic rock consisting of plagioclase feldspar, esp. andesine, amphibole, and pyroxene. [C19: from ANDES + -ITE[1]]

Andhra Pradesh ('ændrə prɑː'dɛʃ) *n* a state of SE India, on the Bay of Bengal: formed in 1953 from parts of Madras and Hyderabad states. Capital: Hyderabad. Pop.: 71 800 000 (1994 est.). Area: about 275 068 sq. km (106 204 sq. miles).

andiron ('ændˌaɪən) *n* either of a pair of decorative metal stands in a hearth for supporting logs. [C14: from Old French *andier,* of unknown origin; influenced by IRON]

Andizhan (*Russian* andi'ʒan) *n* a city in E Uzbekistan. Pop.: 303 000 (1993 est.).

Andong ('æn'dʊŋ) *n* a port in E China, in Liaoning province at the mouth of the Yalu River. Pop.: 188 452 (1995). Also called: **Tan-tung.**

and/or *conj* (*coordinating*) used to join terms when either one or the other or both is indicated: *passports and/or other means of identification.*

USAGE Many people think that *and/or* is only acceptable in legal and commercial contexts. In other contexts, it is better to use *or both: some alcoholics lose their jobs or their driving licences or both* (not *their jobs and/or their driving licences).*

Andorra (æn'dɔːrə) *n* a mountainous principality in SW Europe, between France and Spain: according to tradition, given independence by Charlemagne in the 9th century for helping to fight the Moors; placed under the joint sovereignty of the Comte de Foix and the Spanish bishop of Urgel in 1278; under the joint overlordship of the French head of state and the bishop of Urgel from the 16th century; adopted a constitution reducing the powers of the overlords in 1993. Languages: Catalan (official), French, and Spanish. Religion: Roman Catholic. Currency: French franc and Spanish peseta. Capital: Andorra la Vella. Pop.: 65 200 (1998 est.). Area: 464 sq. km (179 sq. miles). Official name: **Principat d'Andorra.** ▸ **An'dorran** *adj, n*

Andorra la Vella (*Spanish* an'dɔrra la 'beʎa) *n* the capital of Andorra, situated in the west of the principality. Pop.: 21 984 (1995 est.). French name: **Andorre la Vieille** (ɑ̃dɔr la vjɛj).

andradite ('ændrə,daɪt) *n* a yellow, green, or brownish-black garnet that consists of calcium iron silicate and is used as a gemstone. Formula: $Ca_3Fe_2(SiO_4)_3$ **[**C19: named after J. B. d'*Andrada* e Silva (1763–1838), Brazilian mineralogist; see -ITE[1]**]**

Andrássy (æn'dræsɪ; *Hungarian* 'ɔndra:ʃi) *n* Count **Gyula** ('djulɔ). 1823–90, Hungarian statesman; the first prime minister of Hungary under the Dual Monarchy of Austria-Hungary (1867).

André ('ɑ:ndreɪ, 'ændrɪ) *n* **John.** 1751–80, British major who was hanged as a spy for conspiring with Benedict Arnold during the War of American Independence.

Andrea del Sarto (*Italian* an'drea del 'sarto) *n* See **Sarto.**

Andreanof Islands (,ændrɪ'ɑ:nɒf) *pl n* a group of islands in the central Aleutian Islands, Alaska. Area: 3710 sq. km (1432 sq. miles).

Andretti (æn'dretɪ) *n* **Mario.** born 1940, U.S. racing driver: world champion (1978).

Andrew ('ændru:) *n New Testament.* **Saint.** one of the twelve apostles of Jesus; the brother of Peter; patron saint of Scotland. Feast day: Nov. 30.

Andrewes ('ændru:z) *n* **Lancelot.** 1555–1626, English bishop and theologian.

Andrews ('ændru:z) *n* **Thomas.** 1813–85, Irish physical chemist, noted for his work on the liquefaction of gases.

Andrić (*Serbo-Croat* 'andritʃ) *n* **Ivo** ('i:vɔ). 1892–1975, Serbian novelist; author of *The Bridge on the Drina* (1945): Nobel prize for literature 1961.

andro- *or before a vowel* **andr-** *combining form.* **1** male; masculine: *androsterone.* **2** (in botany) stamen or anther: *androecium.* **[**from Greek *anēr* (genitive *andros*) man**]**

androcentric (,ændrəʊ'sentrɪk) *adj* having or regarding man or the male sex as central or primary. ▸ **,andro'centrism** *n*

Androcles ('ændrə,kli:z) *or* **Androclus** ('ændrəkləs) *n* (in Roman legend) a slave whose life was spared in the arena by a lion from whose paw he had once extracted a thorn.

androclinium (,ændrə'klɪnɪəm) *n, pl* **-clinia** (-'klɪnɪə). another name for **clinandrium.** **[**C19: New Latin, from ANDRO- + *-clinium,* from Greek *klinē* slope; see CLINO-**]**

androdioecious (,ændrəʊdaɪ'i:ʃəs) *adj* (of a plant species) having hermaphrodite and male flowers on separate plants.

androecium (æn'dri:sɪəm) *n, pl* **-cia** (-sɪə). the stamens of a flowering plant collectively. **[**C19: from New Latin, from ANDRO- + Greek *oikion* a little house**]** ▸ **an'droecial** *adj*

androgen ('ændrədʒən) *n* any of several steroids, produced as hormones by the testes or made synthetically, that promote development of male sexual organs and male secondary sexual characteristics. ▸ **androgenic** (,ændrə'dʒenɪk) *adj*

androgenous (æn'drɒdʒɪnəs) *adj Biology.* producing only male offspring.

androgyne ('ændrə,dʒaɪn) *n* another word for **hermaphrodite.** **[**C17: from Old French, via Latin from Greek *androgunos,* from *anēr* man + *gunē* woman**]**

androgynophore (,ændrəʊ'gaɪnəʊfɔ:) *n* another name for **androphore.**

androgynous (æn'drɒdʒɪnəs) *adj* **1** *Botany.* having male and female flowers in the same inflorescence, as plantain. **2** having male and female characteristics; hermaphrodite. ▸ **an'drogyny** *n*

android ('ændrɔɪd) *n* **1** (in science fiction) a robot resembling a human being. ◆ *adj* **2** resembling a human being. **[**C18: from Late Greek *androeidēs* manlike; see ANDRO-, -OID**]**

andrology (æn'drɒlədʒɪ) *n* the branch of medicine concerned with diseases in men, esp. of the reproductive organs. **[**C20: from ANDRO- + -LOGY**]** ▸ **an'drologist** *n*

Andromache (æn'drɒməkɪ) *n Greek myth.* the wife of Hector.

Andromeda[1] (æn'drɒmɪdə) *n Greek myth.* the daughter of Cassiopeia and wife of Perseus, who saved her from a sea monster.

Andromeda[2] (æn'drɒmɪdə) *n, Latin genitive* **Andromedae** (æn'drɒmɪ,di:). a constellation in the N hemisphere lying between Cassiopeia and Pegasus, the three brightest stars being of the second magnitude. It contains the **Andromeda Galaxy,** a spiral galaxy 2.2 million light years away.

andromonoecious (,ændrəʊmɒ'ni:ʃəs) *adj* (of a plant species) having hermaphrodite and male flowers on the same plant.

androphore ('ændrəʊfɔ:) *n Botany.* an extension of the receptacle carrying the stamens. Also called: **androgynophore.**

Andropov[1] (æn'drɒpɒv; *Russian* ən'drɔ:pəf) *n* a former name (1984–91) for **Rybinsk.**

Andropov[2] (æn'drɒpɒv; *Russian* ən'drɔ:pəf) *n* **Yuri Vladimirovich.** 1914–84, Soviet statesman; president of the Soviet Union (1983–84).

Andros ('ændrəs) *n* **1** an island in the Aegean Sea, the northernmost of the Cyclades: long famous for wine. Capital: Andros. Pop.: 8155 (1990). Area: about 311 sq. km (120 sq. miles). **2** an island in the N Caribbean, the largest of the Bahamas. Pop.: 8177 (1990). Area: 4144 sq. km (1600 sq. miles).

androsphinx ('ændrə,sfɪŋks) *n, pl* **-sphinxes** *or* **-sphinges** (-,sfɪndʒi:z). a sphinx having the head of a man.

androsterone (æn'drɒstə,rəʊn) *n* an androgenic steroid hormone produced in the testes. Formula: $C_{19}H_{30}O_2$.

-androus *adj combining form.* (in botany) indicating number or type of stamens: *diandrous.* **[**from New Latin *-andrus,* from Greek *-andros,* from *anēr* man**]**

-andry *n combining form.* indicating number of husbands: *polyandry.* **[**from Greek *-andria,* from *anēr* man**]**

Andvari (æn'dwɑ:rɪ) *n Norse myth.* a dwarf who possessed a treasure hoard, which was robbed by Loki.

ane (eɪn) *determiner, pron, n* a Scot. word for **one.**

-ane *suffix forming nouns.* indicating an alkane hydrocarbon: *hexane.* **[**coined to replace *-ene, -ine,* and *-one***]**

anear (ə'nɪə) *Archaic.* ◆ *prep* **1** near. ◆ *adv* **2** nearly.

anecdotage ('ænɪk,dəʊtɪdʒ) *n* **1** anecdotes collectively. **2** *Humorous.* talkative or garrulous old age.

anecdotal (,ænek'dəʊtᵊl) *adj* containing or consisting exclusively of anecdotes rather than connected discourse or research conducted under controlled conditions.

anecdote ('ænɪk,dəʊt) *n* a short usually amusing account of an incident, esp. a personal or biographical one. **[**C17: from Medieval Latin *anecdota* unpublished items, from Greek *anekdotos* unpublished, from AN- + *ekdotos* published, from *ekdidonai,* from *ek-* out + *didonai* to give**]** ▸ **,anec'dotic** *adj* ▸ **,anec'dotalist** *or* **'anec,dotist** *n*

anecdysis (,ænek'daɪsɪs) *n* the period between moults in arthropods. **[**C20: New Latin, from Greek; see AN-, ECDYSIS**]**

anechoic (,ænɪ'kəʊɪk) *adj* having a low degree of reverberation of sound: *an anechoic recording studio.*

Aneirin (ə'naɪᵊrɪn) *n* 6th century A.D., Welsh poet. His *Y Gododdin,* preserved in *The Book of Aneirin* (?1250), is one of the earliest surviving Welsh poems.

anelace ('ænə,leɪs) *n* a variant spelling of **anlace.**

anele (ə'ni:l) *vb (tr) Archaic.* to anoint, esp. to give extreme unction to. **[**C14 *anelen,* from *an-* (from Old English *an-* ON) + *elen* to anoint (from *ele* oil, from Latin *oleum*)**]**

anemia (ə'ni:mɪə) *n* the usual U.S. spelling of **anaemia.** **[**C19: from New Latin, from Greek *anaimia* lack of blood**]**

anemic (ə'ni:mɪk) *adj* the usual U.S. spelling of **anaemic.**

anemo- *combining form.* indicating wind: *anemometer; anemophilous.* **[**from Greek *anemos* wind**]**

anemochore (ə'ni:məʊ,kɔ:) *n* a plant in which the fruits or seeds are dispersed by wind. ▸ **a,nemo'chorous** *adj*

anemograph (ə'neməʊ,grɑ:f) *n* a self-recording anemometer. ▸ **anemographic** (ə,neməʊ'græfɪk) *adj* ▸ **a,nemo'graphically** *adv*

anemography (,ænɪ'mɒgrəfɪ) *n Meteorol.* the technique of recording wind measurements.

anemology (,ænɪ'mɒlədʒɪ) *n* the study of winds.

anemometer (,ænɪ'mɒmɪtə) *n* **1** Also called: **wind gauge.** an instrument for recording the speed and often the direction of winds. **2** any instrument that measures the rate of movement of a fluid. ▸ **anemometric** (,ænɪməʊ'metrɪk) *or* **,anemo'metrical** *adj*

anemometry (,ænɪ'mɒmɪtrɪ) *n Meteorol.* the technique of measuring wind speed and direction.

anemone (ə'nemənɪ) *n* any ranunculaceous woodland plant of the genus *Anemone* of N temperate regions, such as the white-flowered *A. nemorosa* (**wood anemone** or **windflower**). Some cultivated anemones have lilac, pale blue, pink, purple, or red flowers. See also **pasqueflower.** Compare **sea anemone** (an animal). **[**C16: via Latin from Greek: windflower, from *anemos* wind**]**

anemone fish *n* any of various damselfishes of the genus *Amphiprion,* such as *A. percula* (clown anemone fish), that usually live closely associated with sea anemones.

anemophilous (,ænɪ'mɒfɪləs) *adj* (of flowering plants such as grasses) pollinated by the wind. Compare **entomophilous.** ▸ **,ane'mophily** *n*

anemoscope (ə'nemə,skəʊp) *n Meteorol.* any device that shows the presence and direction of a wind.

anencephalic (,ænensə'fælɪk) *adj* born with no or only a partial brain. **[**AN- + ENCEPHALIC**]** ▸ **anencephaly** (,ænen'sefəlɪ) *n*

anent (ə'nent) *prep Archaic or Scot.* **1** lying against; alongside. **2** concerning; about. **[**Old English *on efen,* literally: on even (ground)**]**

anergy ('ænədʒɪ) *n* **1** lack of energy. **2** *Immunol.* diminution or lack of immunity to an antigen. **[**from New Latin *anergia,* from AN- + Greek *ergon* work**]** ▸ **anergic** (æ'nɜ:dʒɪk) *adj*

aneroid ('ænə,rɔɪd) *adj* not containing a liquid. **[**C19: from French, from AN- + Greek *nēros* wet + -OID**]**

aneroid barometer *n* a device for measuring atmospheric pressure without the use of fluids. It consists of a partially evacuated metal chamber, the thin corrugated lid of which is displaced by variations in the external air pressure. This displacement is magnified by levers and made to operate a pointer.

anesthesia (,ænɪs'θi:zɪə) *n* the usual U.S. spelling of **anaesthesia.**

anesthesiologist *or* **anaesthesiologist** (,ænɪs,θi:zɪ'ɒlədʒɪst) *n* the U.S. name for an **anaesthetist;** in the U.S., a qualified doctor specializing in the administration of anaesthesia. Compare **anesthetist.**

anesthetic (,ænɪs'θetɪk) *n, adj* the usual U.S. spelling of **anaesthetic.**

anesthetist (ə'nesθətɪst) *n* (in the U.S.) a person qualified to administer anaesthesia, often a nurse or someone other than a physician. Compare **anesthesiologist.**

anestrus (æn'i:strəs) *n* a variant spelling (esp. U.S.) of **anoestrus.** ▸ **an'estrous** *adj*

anethole ('ænɪ,θəʊl) *n* a white water-soluble crystalline substance with a liquorice-like odour, used as a flavouring and a sensitizer in the processing of colour photographs. Formula: $CH_3CH{:}CHC_6H_4OCH_3$. **[**C19: from Latin *anēthum* dill, anise, from Greek *anēthon***]**

Aneto (*Spanish* a'neto) *n* **Pico de** ('piko de). a mountain in N Spain, near the French border: the highest in the Pyrenees. Height: 3404 m (11 168 ft.).

aneuploid ('ænju,plɔɪd) *adj* **1** (of polyploid cells or organisms) having a chromosome number that is not an exact multiple of the haploid number, caused by one chromosome set being incomplete. ◆ *n* **2** a cell or individual of this type. ◆ Compare **euploid.**

aneurin (əˈnjʊərɪn) *n* a less common name for **thiamine.** [C20: from A(NTI-) + (POLY)NEUR(ITIS) + (VITAM)IN]

aneurysm *or* **aneurism** (ˈænjəˌrɪzəm) *n* a sac formed by abnormal dilation of the weakened wall of a blood vessel. [C15: from Greek *aneurusma,* from *aneurunein* to dilate, from *eurunein* to widen] ▸ ˌ**aneuˈrysmal,** ˌ**aneuˈrismal,** ˌ**aneurysˈmatic,** *or* ˌ**aneurisˈmatic** *adj* ▸ ˌ**aneuˈrysmally,** ˌ**aneuˈrismally,** ˌ**aneurysˈmatically,** *or* ˌ**aneurisˈmatically** *adv*

anew (əˈnjuː) *adv* **1** over again; once more. **2** in a different way; afresh. [Old English *of nīwe;* see OF, NEW]

Anfinsen (ˈænfɪnsən) *n* **Christian Boehmer.** 1916–95, U.S. biochemist, noted for his research on the structure of enzymes. Nobel prize for chemistry 1972.

anfractuosity (ˌænfræktʃuˈɒsɪtɪ) *n* **1** the condition or quality of being anfractuous. **2** a winding, circuitous, or intricate passage, surface, process, etc.

anfractuous (ænˈfræktʃuəs) *adj* characterized by twists and turns; convoluted. [C17: from Late Latin *anfractuōsus,* from Latin *anfractus* a digression, literally: a bending]

Angara (*Russian* angaˈra) *n* a river in S Russia, in Siberia, flowing from Lake Baikal north and west to the Yenisei River: important for hydroelectric power. Length: 1840 km (1150 miles).

Angarsk (*Russian* anˈgarsk) *n* an industrial city in SE central Russia, northwest of Irkutsk. Pop.: 267 000 (1995 est.).

angary (ˈæŋgərɪ) *n International law.* the right of a belligerent state to use the property of a neutral state or to destroy it if necessary, subject to payment of full compensation to the owners. [C19: from French *angarie,* from Late Latin *angaria* enforced service, from Greek *angareia* office of a courier, from *angaros* courier, of Persian origin]

angashore (ˈæŋɪʃɔːr) *n Irish.* a miserable person given to complaining. [from Irish Gaelic *ainniseoir*]

angel (ˈeɪndʒəl) *n* **1** *Theol.* one of a class of spiritual beings attendant upon God. In medieval angelology they are divided by rank into nine orders: seraphim, cherubim, thrones, dominations (or dominions), virtues, powers, principalities (or princedoms), archangels, and angels. **2** a divine messenger from God. **3** a guardian spirit. **4** a conventional representation of any of these beings, depicted in human form with wings. **5** *Informal.* a person, esp. a woman, who is kind, pure, or beautiful. **6** *Informal.* an investor in a venture, esp. a backer of a theatrical production. **7** Also called: **angel-noble.** a former English gold coin with a representation of the archangel Michael on it, first minted in Edward IV's reign. **8** *Informal.* an unexplained signal on a radar screen. [Old English, from Late Latin *angelus,* from Greek *angelos* messenger]

angel cake *or esp. U.S.* **angel food cake** *n* a very light sponge cake made without egg yolks.

angel dust *n* a slang name for **PCP.**

Angeleno (ˌændʒəˈliːnəʊ) *n, pl* **-nos.** a native or inhabitant of Los Angeles.

Angel Falls *n* a waterfall in SE Venezuela, on the Caroní River. Height (probably the highest in the world): 979 m (3211 ft.).

angelfish (ˈeɪndʒəlˌfɪʃ) *n, pl* **-fish** *or* **-fishes. 1** any of various small tropical marine percoid fishes of the genus *Pomacanthus* and related genera, which have a deep flattened brightly coloured body and brushlike teeth: family *Chaetodontidae.* See also **butterfly fish. 2** Also called: **scalare.** a South American cichlid, *Pterophyllum scalare,* of the Amazon region, having a compressed body and large dorsal and anal fins: a popular aquarium fish. **3** another name for **angel shark.**

angelic (ænˈdʒelɪk) *adj* **1** of or relating to angels. **2** Also: **anˈgelical.** resembling an angel in beauty, purity, etc. ▸ **anˈgelically** *adv*

angelica (ænˈdʒelɪkə) *n* **1** Also called: **archangel.** any tall umbelliferous plant of the genus *Angelica,* having compound leaves and clusters of small white or greenish flowers, esp. *A. archangelica,* the aromatic seeds, leaves, and stems of which are used in medicine and cookery. **2** the candied stems of this plant, used for decorating and flavouring sweet dishes. [C16: from Medieval Latin (*herba*) *angelica* angelic (herb)]

Angelic Doctor *n* an epithet of Saint Thomas Aquinas.

Angelico (*Italian* anˈdʒɛːliko) *n* **Fra** (fra), original name *Guido di Pietro;* monastic name *Fra Giovanni da Fiesole.* ?1400–55, Italian fresco painter and Dominican friar.

Angell (ˈeɪndʒəl) *n* Sir **Norman,** real name *Ralph Norman Angell Lane.* 1874–1967, English writer, pacifist, and economist, noted for his work on the economic futility of war, *The Great Illusion* (1910): Nobel peace prize 1933.

angelology (ˌeɪndʒəˈlɒlədʒɪ) *n* a doctrine or theory treating of angels.

Angelou (ˈændʒəluː) *n* **Maya,** real name *Marguerite Johnson.* born 1928, U.S. Black novelist, poet, and dramatist. Her works include the autobiographical novel *I Know Why the Caged Bird Sings* (1970) and its sequels, the collection of poetry *I Shall Not be Moved* (1990), and *Phenomenal Woman* (1995).

angel shark *or* **angelfish** *n* any of several sharks constituting the family *Squatinidae,* such as *Squatina squatina,* that have very large flattened pectoral fins and occur in the Atlantic and Pacific Oceans. Also called: **monkfish.**

angels-on-horseback *n Brit.* a savoury of oysters wrapped in bacon slices and served on toast.

angel's tears *n* (*functioning as sing*) another name for **moonflower** (sense 2).

Angelus (ˈændʒɪləs) *n R.C. Church.* **1** a series of prayers recited in the morning, at midday, and in the evening, commemorating the Annunciation and Incarnation. **2** the bell (**Angelus bell**) signalling these prayers. [C17: Latin, from the phrase *Angelus domini nuntiavit Mariae* the angel of the Lord brought tidings to Mary]

anger (ˈæŋgə) *n* **1** a feeling of great annoyance or antagonism as the result of some real or supposed grievance; rage; wrath. ◆ *vb* (*tr*) **2** to make angry; enrage. [C12: from Old Norse *angr* grief; related to Old English *enge,* Old High German *engi* narrow, Latin *angere* to strangle]

Angers (*French* ɑ̃ʒe) *n* a city in W France, on the River Maine. Pop.: 146 163 (1990).

Angevin (ˈændʒɪvɪn) *n* **1** a native or inhabitant of Anjou. **2** *History.* a member of the Plantagenet royal line descended from Geoffrey, Count of Anjou, esp. one of the kings of England from Henry II to John (1154–1216). ◆ *adj* **3** of or relating to Anjou or its inhabitants. **4** of or relating to the Plantagenet kings of England between 1154 and 1216.

angina (ænˈdʒaɪnə) *n* **1** any disease marked by painful attacks of spasmodic choking, such as Vincent's angina and quinsy. **2** Also called: **angina pectoris** (ˈpektərɪs). a sudden intense pain in the chest, often accompanied by feelings of suffocation, caused by momentary lack of adequate blood supply to the heart muscle. [C16: from Latin: quinsy, from Greek *ankhonē* a strangling] ▸ **anˈginal** *adj* ▸ **anginose** (ænˈdʒaɪnəʊs, -nəʊz) *or* **anˈginous** *adj*

angio- *or before a vowel* **angi-** *combining form.* indicating a blood or lymph vessel; seed vessel: *angiology; angiosperm; angioma.* [from Greek *angeion* vessel]

angiogenesis (ˌændʒɪəˈgenɪsɪs) *n* the induction of blood-vessel growth, often in association with a particular organ or tissue, or with a tumour.

angiogram (ˈændʒɪəʊˌgræm) *n* an X-ray picture obtained by angiography.

angiography (ˌændʒɪˈɒgrəfɪ) *n* a method of obtaining an X-ray of blood vessels by injecting into them a substance, such as iodine, that shows up as opaque on an X-ray picture.

angiology (ˌændʒɪˈɒlədʒɪ) *n* the branch of medical science concerned with the blood vessels and the lymphatic system.

angioma (ˌændʒɪˈəʊmə) *n, pl* **-mas** *or* **-mata** (-mətə). a tumour consisting of a mass of blood vessels (**haemangioma**) or a mass of lymphatic vessels (**lymphangioma**). ▸ ˌ**angiˈomatous** *adj*

angioplasty (ˈændʒɪəˌplæstɪ) *n* a surgical technique for restoring normal blood flow through an artery narrowed or blocked by atherosclerosis, either by inserting a balloon into the narrowed section and inflating it or by using a laser beam.

angiosperm (ˈændʒɪəˌspɜːm) *n* any seed-bearing plant of the phylum *Angiospermophyta* (division *Angiospermae* in traditional systems), in which the ovules are enclosed in an ovary, which develops into the fruit after fertilization; any flowering plant. Compare **gymnosperm.** ▸ ˌ**angioˈspermous** *adj*

angiotensin (ˌændʒɪəˈtensɪn) *n* a peptide of physiological importance that is capable of causing constriction of blood vessels, which raises blood pressure. [from ANGIO- + TENSE[1] + -IN]

Angkor (ˈæŋkɔː) *n* a large area of ruins in NW Cambodia, containing **Angkor Thom** (tɔːm), the capital of the former Khmer Empire, and **Angkor Wat** (wɒt), a three-storey temple, which were overgrown with dense jungle from the 14th to 19th centuries.

Angl. *abbrev. for* Anglican.

angle[1] (ˈæŋgəl) *n* **1** the space between two straight lines that diverge from a common point or between two planes that extend from a common line. **2** the shape formed by two such lines or planes. **3** the extent to which one such line or plane diverges from another, measured in degrees or radians. **4** an angular projection or recess; corner. **5** standpoint; point of view: *look at the question from another angle; the angle of a newspaper article.* **6** *Informal.* a selfish or devious motive or purpose. **7** See **angle iron.** ◆ *vb* **8** to move in or bend into angles or an angle. **9** (*tr*) to produce (an article, statement, etc.) with a particular point of view. **10** (*tr*) to present, direct, or place at an angle. **11** (*intr*) to turn or bend in a different direction: *the path angled sharply to the left.* [C14: from French, from Old Latin *angulus* corner]

angle[2] (ˈæŋgl) *vb* (*intr*) **1** to fish with a hook and line. **2** (often foll. by *for*) to attempt to get: *he angled for a compliment.* ◆ *n* **3** *Obsolete.* any piece of fishing tackle, esp. a hook. [Old English *angul* fish-hook; related to Old High German *ango,* Latin *uncus,* Greek *onkos*]

Angle (ˈæŋgəl) *n* a member of a West Germanic people from N Germany who invaded and settled large parts of E and N England in the 5th and 6th centuries A.D. [from Latin *Anglus,* from Germanic (compare ENGLISH), an inhabitant of *Angul,* a district in Schleswig (now *Angeln*), a name identical with Old English *angul* hook, ANGLE[2], referring to its shape]

angle bracket *n* either of a pair of brackets having the shapes < and >.

angle iron *n* **1** Also called: **angle, angle bar.** an iron or a steel structural bar that has an L-shaped cross section. **2** any piece of iron or steel forming an angle, esp. a right angle.

angle of advance *n Engineering.* **1** the angle in excess of 90° that a steam-engine valve gear is in advance of the crank. **2** the angle between the point of ignition and bottom dead-centre in a spark-ignition engine.

angle of attack *n* the acute angle between the chord line of an aerofoil and the undisturbed relative airflow. Also called: **angle of incidence.**

angle of bank *n* the angle between the lateral axis of an aircraft in flight and the horizontal.

angle of deviation *n* the angle between the direction of the refracted ray and the direction of the incident ray when a ray of light passes from one medium to another.

angle of dip *n* the full name for **dip** (sense 27).

angle of friction *n Physics.* the angle of a plane to the horizontal when a body placed on the plane will just start to slide. The tangent of the angle of friction is the **coefficient of friction.**

angle of incidence *n* **1** the angle that a line or beam of radiation makes with a line perpendicular to the surface at the point of incidence. **2** another name for **angle of attack. 3** Also called: **rigging angle of incidence.** the angle between the chord line of an aircraft wing or tailplane and the aircraft's longitudinal axis.

angle of reflection *n* the angle that a beam of reflected radiation makes with the normal to a surface at the point of reflection.

angle of refraction *n* the angle that a refracted beam of radiation makes with the normal to the surface between two media at the point of refraction.

angle of repose *n* the maximum angle to the horizontal at which rocks, soil, etc., will remain without sliding.

angle plate *n* a steel structural plate, esp. one in the shape of a right-angled triangle, used to connect structural members and stiffen frameworks.

angler ('æŋglə) *n* **1** a person who fishes with a rod and line. **2** *Informal.* a person who schemes or uses devious methods to secure an advantage. **3** Also called: **angler fish.** any spiny-finned fish of the order *Pediculati* (or *Lophiiformes*). They live at the bottom of the sea and typically have a long spiny movable dorsal fin with which they lure their prey.

Anglesey ('æŋgᵊlsɪ) *n* an island and county of N Wales, formerly part of Gwynedd (1974–96), separated from the mainland by the Menai Strait. Administrative centre: Llangefni. Pop.: 68 400 (1994 est.). Area: 720 sq. km (278 sq. miles). Welsh name: **Ynys Môn.**

anglesite ('æŋgᵊlˌsaɪt) *n* a white or grey secondary mineral consisting of lead sulphate in orthorhombic crystalline form. It occurs in lead-ore deposits and is a source of lead. Formula: $PbSO_4$. **[C19:** from ANGLESEY, where it was first found**]**

angleworm ('æŋgᵊlˌwɜːm) *n* an earthworm used as bait by anglers.

Anglia ('æŋglɪə) *n* a Latin name for **England.**

Anglian ('æŋglɪən) *adj* **1** of or relating to the Angles or to the Anglian dialects of Old English. ◆ *n* **2** the group of Old and Middle English dialects spoken in the Midlands and the north of England, divided into Mercian and Northumbrian. See also **Kentish, West Saxon.** ◆ See also **East Anglia.**

Anglican ('æŋglɪkən) *adj* **1** denoting or relating to the Anglican communion. ◆ *n* **2** a member of the Church of England or one of the Churches in full communion with it. **[C17:** from Medieval Latin *Anglicānus,* from *Anglicus* English, from Latin *Anglī* the Angles**]**

Anglican Church *n* any Church of the Anglican Communion or the Anglican Communion itself.

Anglican Communion *n* a group of Christian Churches including the Church of England, the Church of Ireland, the Episcopal Church in Scotland, the Church in Wales, and the Episcopal Church in the U.S., all of which are in full communion with each other.

Anglicanism ('æŋglɪkəˌnɪzəm) *n* the doctrine and practice of the Church of England and other Anglican Churches.

Anglice ('æŋglɪsɪ) *adv* in English: *Roma, Anglice Rome.* **[**from Medieval Latin**]**

Anglicism ('æŋglɪˌsɪzəm) *n* **1** a word, phrase, or idiom peculiar to the English language, esp. as spoken in England. **2** an English attitude, custom, etc. **3** the fact or quality of being English.

Anglicist ('æŋglɪsɪst) *or* **Anglist** *n Rare.* an expert in or student of English literature or language.

anglicize, anglicise ('æŋglɪˌsaɪz), *or* **anglify** ('æŋglɪˌfaɪ) *vb* **-cizes, -cizing, -cized, -cises, -cising, -cised** *or* **-fies, -fying, -fied.** (*sometimes cap.*) to make or become English in outlook, attitude, form, etc. ▸ **ˌanglici'zation** *or* **ˌanglici'sation** *n*

angling ('æŋglɪŋ) *n* **a** the art or sport of catching fish with a rod and line and a baited hook or other lure, such as a fly; fishing. **b** (*as modifier*): *an angling contest.*

Anglo ('æŋgləʊ) *n, pl* **-glos. 1** *U.S.* a White inhabitant of the United States who is not of Latin extraction. **2** *Austral., derogatory.* an Australian of Anglo-Celtic descent.

Anglo- ('æŋgləʊ-) *combining form.* denoting English or England: *Anglo-Saxon.* **[**from Medieval Latin *Anglī***]**

Anglo-American *adj* **1** of or relating to relations between England and the United States or their peoples. ◆ *n* **2** *Chiefly U.S.* an inhabitant or citizen of the United States who was or whose ancestors were born in England.

Anglo-Catholic *adj* **1** of or relating to a group within the Church of England or the Anglican Communion that emphasizes the Catholic elements in its teaching and practice. ◆ *n* **2** a member of this group. ▸ **ˌAnglo-Ca'tholiˌcism** *n*

Anglo-Celtic *adj Austral.* of or relating to an inhabitant of Australia who was or whose ancestors were born in the British Isles.

Anglo-Egyptian Sudan *n* the former name (1899–1956) of the **Sudan.**

Anglo-French *adj* **1** of or relating to England and France. **2** of or relating to Anglo-French. ◆ *n* **3** the Norman-French language of medieval England.

Anglo-Indian *adj* **1** of or relating to England and India. **2** denoting or relating to Anglo-Indians. **3** (of a word) introduced into English from an Indian language. ◆ *n* **4** a person of mixed English and Indian descent. **5** an English person who lives or has lived for a long time in India.

Anglo-Irish *n* **1** (preceded by *the; functioning as pl*) the inhabitants of Ireland of English birth or descent. **2** the English language as spoken in Ireland. ◆ *adj* **3** of or relating to the Anglo-Irish. **4** of or relating to English and Irish. **5** of or relating to the English language as spoken in Ireland.

Anglomania (ˌæŋgləʊ'meɪnɪə) *n* excessive respect for English customs, etc. ▸ **ˌAnglo'maniˌac** *n*

Anglo-Norman *adj* **1** *History.* relating to the Norman conquerors of England, their society, or their language. ◆ *n* **2** *History.* a Norman inhabitant of England after 1066. **3** the Anglo-French language.

Anglophile ('æŋgləʊfɪl, -ˌfaɪl) *or* **Anglophil** *n* **1** a person having admiration for England or the English. ◆ *adj* **2** marked by or possessing such admiration. ▸ **Anglophilia** (ˌæŋgləʊ'fɪlɪə) *n* ▸ **Anglophiliac** (ˌæŋgləʊ'fɪlɪˌæk) *or* **Anglophilic** (ˌæŋgləʊ'fɪlɪk) *adj*

Anglophobe ('æŋgləʊˌfəʊb) *n* **1** a person who hates or fears England or its people. **2** *Canadian.* a person who hates or fears Canadian Anglophones. ▸ **ˌAnglo'phobia** *n*

Anglophone ('æŋgləˌfəʊn) (*often not cap.*) *n* **1** a person who speaks English, esp. a native speaker. ◆ *adj* **2** speaking English.

Anglo-Saxon *n* **1** a member of any of the West Germanic tribes (Angles, Saxons, and Jutes) that settled in Britain from the 5th century A.D. and were dominant until the Norman conquest. **2** the language of these tribes. See **Old English. 3** any White person whose native language is English and whose cultural affiliations are those common to Britain and the U.S. **4** *Informal.* plain blunt English, esp. English containing taboo words. ◆ *adj* **5** forming part of the Germanic element in Modern English: *"forget" is an Anglo-Saxon word.* **6** of or relating to the Anglo-Saxons or the Old English language. **7** of or relating to the White Protestant culture of Britain, Australia, and the U.S. **8** *Informal.* (of English speech or writing) plain and blunt. **9** of or relating to Britain and the U.S., esp. their common legal, political, and commercial cultures, as compared to continental Europe.

Angola (æŋ'gəʊlə) *n* a republic in SW Africa, on the Atlantic: includes the enclave of Cabinda, north of the River Congo; a Portuguese possession from 1575 until its independence in 1975; multiparty constitution adopted in 1991; factional violence. It consists of a narrow coastal plain with a large fertile plateau in the east. Currency: kwanza. Religion: Christian majority. Capital: Luanda. Pop.: 10 865 000 (1998 est.). Area: 1 246 693 sq. km (481 351 sq. miles). ▸ **An'golan** *adj, n*

angora (æŋ'gɔːrə) *n* (*sometimes cap.*) **a** the long soft hair of the outer coat of the Angora goat or the fur of the Angora rabbit. **b** yarn, cloth, or clothing made from this hair. **c** a material made to resemble this yarn or cloth. **d** (*as modifier*): *an angora sweater.* See also **mohair.**

Angora *n* **1** (æŋ'gɔːrə, 'æŋgərə). the former name (until 1930) of **Ankara. 2** (æŋ'gɔːrə). short for **Angora cat, Angora goat,** or **Angora rabbit.**

Angora cat *n* a former long-haired variety of cat, similar to the Persian.

Angora goat *n* a breed of domestic goat with long soft hair.

Angora rabbit *n* a breed of rabbit with long usually white silky hair.

Angostura (*Spanish* aŋgos'tura) *n* the former name (1764–1846) for **Ciudad Bolívar.**

angostura bark (ˌæŋgə'stjʊərə) *n* the bitter aromatic bark of certain South American rutaceous trees of the genus *Cusparia* or *Galipea,* formerly used medicinally to reduce fever.

angostura bitters *pl n* (*often cap.*) *Trademark.* a bitter aromatic tonic made from gentian and various spices and vegetable colourings, used as a flavouring in alcoholic drinks.

Angra do Heroísmo (*Portuguese* 'ɐ̃ŋgrə duː iru'iʃmu) *n* a port in the Azores, on Terceira Island. Pop.: 11 670 (1991).

angry ('æŋgrɪ) *adj* **-grier, -griest. 1** feeling or expressing annoyance, animosity, or resentment; enraged. **2** suggestive of anger: *angry clouds.* **3** severely inflamed: *an angry sore.* ▸ **'angrily** *adv*

USAGE It was formerly considered incorrect to talk about being *angry at* a person, but this use is now acceptable.

angry young man *n* **1** (*often caps.*) one of several British novelists and playwrights of the 1950s who shared a hostility towards the established traditions and ruling elements of their country. **2** any similarly rebellious person.

angst (æŋst; *German* aŋst) *n* **1** an acute but nonspecific sense of anxiety or remorse. **2** (in Existentialist philosophy) the dread caused by man's awareness that his future is not determined but must be freely chosen. **[**German**]**

angstrom ('æŋstrʌm, -strəm) *n* a unit of length equal to 10^{-10} metre, used principally to express the wavelengths of electromagnetic radiations. It is equivalent to 0.1 nanometre. Symbol: Å or A Also called: **angstrom unit. [C20:** named after Anders J. ÅNGSTRÖM**]**

Ångström ('æŋstrəm; *Swedish* 'ɔŋstrœm) *n* **Anders Jonas** ('andərs 'juːnas). 1814–74, Swedish physicist, noted for his work on spectroscopy and solar physics.

Anguilla (æŋ'gwɪlə) *n* an island in the Caribbean, in the Leeward Islands: part of the British associated state of St Kitts-Nevis-Anguilla from 1967 until 1980, when it reverted to the status of a British dependency and is now a UK Overseas Territory. Pop.: 8960 (1992). Area: 90 sq. km (35 sq. miles).

anguilliform (æŋ'gwɪlɪˌfɔːm) *adj* having the shape or form of an eel. **[C17:** from Latin *anguilla* eel, diminutive of *anguis* snake**]**

anguine ('æŋgwɪn) *adj* of, relating to, or similar to a snake. **[C17:** from Latin *anguīnus,* from *anguis* snake**]**

anguish ('æŋgwɪʃ) *n* **1** extreme pain or misery; mental or physical torture; agony. ◆ *vb* **2** to afflict or be afflicted with anguish. **[C13:** from Old French *angoisse* a strangling, from Latin *angustia* narrowness, from *angustus* narrow**]**

anguished ('æŋgwɪʃt) *adj* feeling or expressing anguish.

angular ('æŋgjʊlə) *adj* **1** lean or bony. **2** awkward or stiff in manner or movement. **3** having an angle or angles. **4** placed at an angle. **5** measured by an angle or by the rate at which an angle changes. **[C15:** from Latin *angulāris,* from *angulus* ANGLE[1]**]** ▸ **'angularly** *adv* ▸ **'angularness** *n*

angular acceleration *n* **1** the rate of change of angular velocity. **2** *Astronautics.* the acceleration of a space vehicle around an axis.

angular displacement *n Physics.* the angle through which a point, line, or body is rotated about a specific axis in a given direction.

angular frequency *n Physics.* the frequency of a periodic process, wave system, etc., expressed in radians per second.

angularity (ˌæŋgjʊ'lærɪtɪ) *n, pl* **-ties. 1** the condition of being angular. **2** an angular form or shape.

angular magnification *n Physics.* the ratio of the angle subtended at the eye by an image formed by an optical instrument to the angle subtended at the unaided eye by the object.

angular momentum *n* a measure of the momentum of a body caused by its circular motion around an axis of rotation, equal to the product of its mass and its angular velocity.

angular velocity *n* the velocity of a body rotating about a fixed point measured as the rate of change of the angle subtended at that fixed point by the path of the body. Symbol: ω

angulate *adj* ('æŋgjʊlɪt, -ˌleɪt). **1** having angles or an angular shape. ♦ *vb* ('æŋgjʊˌleɪt). **2** to make or become angular. [C18: from Late Latin *angulāre* to make angled, from Latin *angulus* ANGLE[1]] ► 'anguˌ**lated** *adj*

angulation (ˌæŋgjʊ'leɪʃən) *n* **1** an angular formation. **2** the precise measurement of angles.

Angus ('æŋgəs) *n* a council area of E Scotland on the North Sea: the historic county of Angus became part of Tayside region in 1975; reinstated as a unitary authority (excluding City of Dundee) in 1996. Administrative centre: Forfar. Pop.: 111 020 (1996 est.). Area: 2181 sq. km (842 sq. miles).

Angus Og (əʊg) *n Irish myth.* the god of love and beauty.

angwantibo (æŋ'gwæntɪˌbəʊ) *n, pl* **-bos**. a rare gold-coloured prosimian primate of tropical Africa, *Arctocebus calabarensis,* having digits that are specialized as a pair of pincers for climbing: family *Lorisidae* (lorises). Also called: **golden potto**. [C19: from Efik]

Anhalt (*German* 'anhalt) *n* a former duchy and state of central E Germany, now part of the state of Saxony-Anhalt: part of East Germany until 1990.

anharmonic (ˌænhɑː'mɒnɪk) *adj Physics.* of or concerned with an oscillation whose frequency is not an integral factor or multiple of the base frequency.

anhedral (æn'hiːdrəl) *n* the downward inclination of an aircraft wing in relation to the lateral axis. Compare **dihedral** (sense 4).

anhidrosis (ˌænhɪ'drəʊsɪs) *or* **anidrosis** *n Pathol.* the absence of sweating. [from AN- + Greek *hidrōs* sweat + -OSIS]

anhidrotic (ˌænhɪ'drɒtɪk) *Med.* ♦ *adj* **1** curbing the secretion of sweat. ♦ *n* **2** a substance that suppresses sweating.

anhinga (æn'hɪŋgə) *n* another name for **darter** (the bird). [C18: via Portuguese from Tupi]

Anhui *or* **Anhwei** ('æn'weɪ) *n* a province of E China, crossed by the Yangtze River. Capital: Hefei. Pop.: 60 130 000 (1996 est.). Area: 139 860 sq. km (54 000 sq. miles).

anhydride (æn'haɪdraɪd, -drɪd) *n* **1** a compound that has been formed from another compound by dehydration. **2** a compound that forms an acid or base when added to water. **3** Also called: **acid anhydride** or **acyl anhydride**. any organic compound containing the group -CO.O.CO- formed by removal of one water molecule from two carboxyl groups. [C19: from ANHYDR(OUS) + -IDE]

anhydrite (æn'haɪdraɪt) *n* a colourless or greyish-white mineral, found in sedimentary rocks. It is used in the manufacture of cement, fertilizers, and chemicals. Composition: anhydrous calcium sulphate. Formula: $CaSO_4$. Crystal structure: orthorhombic. [C19: from ANHYDR(OUS) + -ITE[1]]

anhydrous (æn'haɪdrəs) *adj* containing no water, esp. no water of crystallization. [C19: from Greek *anudros;* see AN-, HYDRO-]

ani ('ɑːnɪ) *n, pl* **anis**. any of several gregarious tropical American birds of the genus *Crotophaga:* family *Cuculidae* (cuckoos). They have a black plumage, long square-tipped tail, and heavily hooked bill. [Spanish *aní,* from Tupi]

Aniakchak (ˌænɪ'æktʃæk) *n* an active volcanic crater in SW Alaska, on the Alaska Peninsula: the largest explosion crater in the world. Height: 1347 m (4420 ft.). Diameter: 9 km (6 miles).

anicca ('ænɪkə) *n* (in Theravada Buddhism) the belief that all things, including the self, are impermanent and constantly changing: the first of the three basic characteristics of existence. Compare **anatta, dukkha**. [Pali, literally: impermanence]

aniconic (ˌænaɪ'kɒnɪk) *adj* (of images of deities, symbols, etc.) not portrayed in a human or animal form. [C19: from AN- + ICONIC]

anil ('ænɪl) *n* a leguminous West Indian shrub, *Indigofera suffruticosa:* a source of indigo. Also called: **indigo**. [C16: from Portuguese, from Arabic *an-nīl,* the indigo, from Sanskrit *nīla* dark blue]

anile ('ænaɪl, 'eɪnaɪl) *adj* of or like a feeble old woman. [C17: from Latin *anīlis,* from *anus* old woman] ► **anility** (ə'nɪlɪtɪ) *n*

aniline ('ænɪlɪn, -ˌliːn) *n* a colourless oily pungent poisonous liquid used in the manufacture of dyes, plastics, pharmaceuticals, and explosives. Formula: $C_6H_5NH_2$. Also called: **phenylamine**.

aniline dye *n* any synthetic dye originally made from raw materials, such as aniline, obtained from coal tar.

anilingus (ˌeɪnɪ'lɪŋgəs) *n* sexual stimulation involving oral contact with the anus. [C20: from *ani-* ANUS + *-lingus,* as in CUNNILINGUS]

anim. *abbrev. for* animato.

anima ('ænɪmə) *n* (in Jungian psychology) **a** the feminine principle as present in the male unconscious. **b** the inner personality, which is in communication with the unconscious. See also **animus**. [Latin: air, breath, spirit, feminine of ANIMUS]

animadversion (ˌænɪmæd'vɜːʃən) *n* **1** criticism or censure. **2** a carefully considered observation.

animadvert (ˌænɪmæd'vɜːt) *vb* (*intr*) **1** (usually foll. by *on* or *upon*) to comment with strong criticism (upon); make censorious remarks (about). **2** to make an observation or comment. [C16: from Latin *animadvertere* to notice, pay attention, from *animus* mind + *advertere* to turn to, from *vertere* to turn]

animal ('ænɪməl) *n* **1** *Zoology.* any living organism characterized by voluntary movement, the possession of cells with noncellulose cell walls and specialized sense organs enabling rapid response to stimuli, and the ingestion of complex organic substances such as plants and other animals. Related prefix: **zoo-**. **2** any mammal, esp. any mammal except man. **3** a brutish person. **4** *Facetious.* a person or thing (esp. in the phrase **no such animal**). ♦ *adj* **5** of, relating to, or derived from animals: *animal products; an animal characteristic.* **6** of or relating to the physical needs or desires; carnal; sensual. [C14: from Latin *animal* (n), from *animālis* (adj) living, breathing; see ANIMA]

animalcule (ˌænɪ'mælkjuːl) *or* **animalculum** (ˌænɪ'mælkjʊləm) *n, pl* **-cules** *or* **-cula** (-kjʊlə). a microscopic animal such as an amoeba or rotifer. [C16: from New Latin *animalculum* a small ANIMAL] ► ˌ**ani'malcular** *adj*

animal husbandry *n* the science of breeding, rearing, and caring for farm animals.

animalier ('ænɪməˌlɪə, ˌænɪ'mælɪeɪ) *n* **a** a painter or sculptor of animal subjects, esp. a member of a group of early 19th-century French sculptors who specialized in realistic figures of animals, usually in bronze. **b** (*as modifier*): *an animalier bronze.* [from French]

animalism ('ænɪməˌlɪzəm) *n* **1** satisfaction of or preoccupation with physical matters; sensuality. **2** the doctrine or belief that man lacks a spiritual nature. **3** a trait or mode of behaviour typical of animals. ► '**animalist** *n*

animality (ˌænɪ'mælɪtɪ) *n* **1** the animal side of man, as opposed to the intellectual or spiritual. **2** the fact of being or having the characteristics of an animal.

animalize *or* **animalise** ('ænɪməˌlaɪz) *vb* (*tr*) to rouse to brutality or sensuality or make brutal or sensual. ► ˌ**animali'zation** *or* ˌ**animali'sation** *n*

animal kingdom *n* a category of living organisms comprising all animals. Compare **plant kingdom, mineral kingdom**.

Animal Liberation Front *n* (in Britain) an animal-rights movement often using direct action. Abbrev.: **ALF**.

animal magnetism *n* **1** *Sometimes facetious.* the quality of being attractive, esp. to members of the opposite sex. **2** *Obsolete.* hypnotism.

animal rights *pl n* **a** the rights of animals to be protected from exploitation and abuse by humans. **b** (*as modifier*): *the animal-rights lobby.*

animal spirits *pl n* cheerful and exuberant boisterousness. [originally, referring to a vital force believed to be dispatched throughout the body by the brain]

animal starch *n* a less common name for **glycogen**.

animate *vb* ('ænɪˌmeɪt). (*tr*) **1** to give life to or cause to come alive. **2** to make lively; enliven. **3** to encourage or inspire. **4** to impart motion to; move to action or work. **5** to record on film or video tape so as to give movement to: *an animated cartoon.* ♦ *adj* ('ænɪmɪt). **6** being alive or having life. **7** gay, spirited, or lively. [C16: from Latin *animāre* to fill with breath, make alive, from *anima* breath, spirit]

animated ('ænɪˌmeɪtɪd) *adj* **1** full of vivacity and spirit; lively. **2** characterized by movement and activity: *an animated scene met her eye.* **3** possessing life; animate. **4** moving or appearing to move as if alive: *an animated display.* **5** pertaining to cinematographic animation. ► '**aniˌmatedly** *adv*

animated cartoon *n* a film produced by photographing a series of gradually changing drawings, etc., which give the illusion of movement when the series is projected rapidly.

animation (ˌænɪ'meɪʃən) *n* **1** liveliness; vivacity. **2** the condition of being alive. **3a** the techniques used in the production of animated cartoons. **3b** a variant of **animated cartoon**.

animatism ('ænɪməˌtɪzəm) *n* the belief that inanimate objects have consciousness.

animato (ˌænɪ'mɑːtəʊ) *adj, adv Music.* (to be performed) in a lively manner. [Italian]

animator *or* **animater** ('ænɪˌmeɪtə) *n* an artist who produces animated cartoons.

animatronic (ˌænɪmə'trɒnɪk) *adj* of, concerned with, or operated by animatronics: *animatronic dinosaurs.*

animatronics (ˌænɪmə'trɒnɪks) *n* (*functioning as sing*) a branch of film and theatre technology that combines traditional puppetry techniques with electronics to create lifelike animated effects. [C20: from ANIMA(TION) + (ELEC)TRONICS]

animé[1] ('ænɪˌmeɪ, -mɪ) *n* any of various resins, esp. that obtained from the tropical American leguminous tree *Hymenaea courbaril.* [French: of uncertain origin]

animé[2] ('ænɪˌmeɪ) *adj, adv Music.* the French word for **animato**.

animism ('ænɪˌmɪzəm) *n* **1** the belief that natural objects, phenomena, and the universe itself have desires and intentions. **2** (in the philosophies of Plato and Pythagoras) the hypothesis that there is an immaterial force that animates the universe. [C19: from Latin *anima* vital breath, spirit] ► '**animist** *n* ► **animistic** (ˌænɪ'mɪstɪk) *adj*

animosity (ˌænɪ'mɒsɪtɪ) *n, pl* **-ties**. a powerful and active dislike or hostility; enmity. [C15: from Late Latin *animōsitās,* from Latin *animōsus* spirited, from ANIMUS]

animus ('ænɪməs) *n* **1** intense dislike; hatred; animosity. **2** motive, intention, or purpose. **3** (in Jungian psychology) the masculine principle present in the female unconscious. See also **anima**. [C19: from Latin: mind, spirit]

anion ('ænˌaɪən) *n* a negatively charged ion; an ion that is attracted to the anode during electrolysis. Compare **cation**. [C19: from ANA- + ION] ► **anionic** (ˌænaɪ'ɒnɪk) *adj*

anise ('ænɪs) *n* a Mediterranean umbelliferous plant, *Pimpinella anisum,* having clusters of small yellowish-white flowers and liquorice-flavoured seeds (see **aniseed**). [C13: from Old French *anis,* via Latin from Greek *anison*]

aniseed ('ænɪˌsiːd) *n* the liquorice-flavoured aromatic seeds of the anise plant, used medicinally for expelling intestinal gas and in cookery as a flavouring, esp. in cakes. Also called: **anise**.

aniseikonia (ˌænaɪsaɪ'kəʊnɪə) *n* a condition caused by a defect in the lens of the eye in which the images produced in the two eyes differ in size or shape. [C20: New Latin, from ANISO- + Greek *eikon* image] ► ˌ**anisei'konic** *adj*

anisette (ˌænɪ'zɛt, -'sɛt) *n* a liquorice-flavoured liqueur made from aniseed. [C19: from French; see ANISE, -ETTE]

aniso- *or before a vowel* **anis-** *combining form.* not equal: *anisogamy.* [New Latin, from Greek *anisos;* see AN-, ISO-]

anisocercal (ænˌaɪsəʊ'sɜːkᵊl) *adj* (of fish) having unequal tail-fin lobes. [C19: from ANISO- + Greek *kerkos* tail]

anisodactyl (ænˌaɪsəʊ'dæktɪl, ˌænaɪ-) *adj also* **anisodactylous**. **1** (of the feet of passerine birds) having the first toe directed backwards and the other three toes directed forwards. ◆ *n* **2** a bird having this type of feet.

anisogamy (ˌænaɪˈsɒɡəmɪ) *n* a type of sexual reproduction in which the gametes are dissimilar, either in size alone or in size and form. ► **ˌaniˈsogamous** *adj*

anisole (ˈænɪˌsəʊl) *n* a colourless pleasant-smelling liquid used as a solvent and vermicide and in perfume and flavouring. Formula: $C_6H_5OCH_3$; relative density: 0.996; melting pt.: -37.5°C; boiling pt.: 155°C. [C19: from ANISE + -OLE[1]]

anisomeric (ænˌaɪsəʊˈmerɪk) *adj* (of a chemical compound) lacking isomers.

anisomerous (ˌænɪˈsɒmərəs) *adj* (of flowers) having floral whorls that differ in the number of their parts. Compare **isomerous** (sense 2).

anisometric (ænˌaɪsəʊˈmetrɪk) *adj* **1** not isometric; having unsymmetrical parts or unequal measurements. **2** (of a crystal) having unequal axes.

anisometropia (ænˌaɪsəʊməˈtrəʊpɪə, ˌænaɪ-) *n* an imbalance in the power of the two eyes to refract light.

anisomorphic (ænˌaɪsəʊˈmɔːfɪk) *adj Linguistics.* differing in the semantic scope of terms referring to the real world: for instance, English and Russian are anisomorphic with regard to colour terms, English treating light blue and navy blue as shades of one colour but Russian treating these two shades as unrelated.

anisophyllous (æˌnaɪsəʊˈfɪləs) *adj* another word for **heterophyllous.** ► **anˈisoˌphylly** *n*

anisotropic (ænˌaɪsəʊˈtrɒpɪk, ˌænaɪ-) *adj* **1** not isotropic; having different physical properties in different directions: *anisotropic crystals.* **2** (of a plant) responding unequally to an external stimulus in different parts of the plant. ► **anˌisoˈtropically** *adv* ► **anisotropy** (ˌænaɪˈsɒtrəpɪ) *n*

Anjou (*French* ɑ̃ʒu) *n* a former province of W France, in the Loire valley: a medieval countship from the 10th century, belonging to the English crown from 1154 until 1204; annexed by France in 1480. Related adj: **Angevin.**

Ankara (ˈæŋkərə) *n* the capital of Turkey: an ancient city in the Anatolian highlands: first a capital in the 3rd century B.C., in the Celtic kingdom of Galatia. Pop.: 2 837 937 (1995 est.). Ancient name: **Ancyra.** Former name (until 1930): **Angora.**

ankerite (ˈæŋkəˌraɪt) *n* a greyish to brown mineral that resembles dolomite and consists of a carbonate of calcium, magnesium, and iron. Formula: $(Ca,Mg,Fe)CO_3$. [C19: named after M. J. *Anker* (died 1843), Austrian mineralogist]

ankh (æŋk) *n* a tau cross with a loop on the top, symbolizing eternal life: often appearing in Egyptian personal names, such as Tutankhamen. Also called: **ansate cross, crux ansata.** [from Egyptian *ʿnh* life, soul]

Anking (ˈɑːnˈkɪŋ) *n* a variant transliteration of the Chinese name for **Anqing.**

ankle (ˈæŋkᵊl) *n* **1** the joint connecting the leg and the foot. See **talus**[1]. **2** the part of the leg just above the foot. [C14: from Old Norse; related to German, Dutch *enkel*, Latin *angulus* ANGLE[1]]

ankle biter *n Austral. slang.* a child.

anklebone (ˈæŋkᵊlˌbəʊn) *n* the nontechnical name for **talus**[1].

ankle sock *n* (*often pl*) *Brit.* a short sock coming up to the ankle. U.S. term: **anklet.**

anklet (ˈæŋklɪt) *n* **1** an ornamental chain worn around the ankle. **2** the U.S. word for **ankle sock.**

ankus (ˈæŋkəs) *n, pl* **-kus** *or* **-kuses.** a stick used, esp. in India, for goading elephants. [from Hindi]

ankylosaur (ˈæŋkɪləʊˌsɔː) *n* any of various quadrupedal herbivorous ornithischian dinosaurs constituting the suborder *Ankylosauria*, which were most abundant in upper Cretaceous times and had a very heavily armoured tanklike body. [C20: from New Latin, from Greek *ankulos* crooked + -SAUR]

ankylose *or* **anchylose** (ˈæŋkɪˌləʊs, -ˌləʊz) *vb* (of bones in a joint, etc.) to fuse or stiffen by ankylosis.

ankylosis *or* **anchylosis** (ˌæŋkɪˈləʊsɪs) *n* abnormal adhesion or immobility of the bones in a joint, as by a direct joining of the bones, a fibrous growth of tissues within the joint, or surgery. [C18: from New Latin, from Greek *ankuloun* to crook] ► **ankylotic** *or* **anchylotic** (ˌæŋkɪˈlɒtɪk) *adj*

ankylostomiasis (ˌæŋkɪˌlɒstəˈmaɪəsɪs) *n* a variant of **ancylostomiasis.**

anlace (ˈænlɪs) *or* **anelace** *n* a medieval short dagger with a broad tapering blade. [C13: of unknown origin]

anlage (ˈænˌlɑːɡə) *n, pl* **-gen** (-ɡən) *or* **-ges.** another word for **primordium.** [German: predisposition, layout]

An Lu Shan (æn luː ʃæn) *n* 703–57 A.D., Chinese military governor. He declared himself emperor (756) and seized the capital Chang An; murdered by a eunuch slave.

ann. *abbrev. for:* **1** annals (periodical publications). **2** annual. **3** annuity.

anna (ˈænə) *n* a former Indian copper coin, worth one sixteenth of a rupee. [C18: from Hindi *ānā*]

Annaba (ˈænəbə) *n* a port in NE Algeria: site of the Roman city of Hippo Regius. Pop.: 222 518 (1987). Former name: **Bône.**

annabergite (ˈænəˌbɜːɡaɪt) *n* a rare green secondary mineral consisting of hydrated nickel arsenate in monoclinic crystalline form. Formula: $Ni_3(AsO_4)_2.8H_2O$. Also called: **nickel bloom.** [C19: named after *Annaberg* in Saxony, where it was discovered; see -ITE[1]]

annal (ˈænᵊl) *n* the recorded events of one year. See also **annals.**

annals (ˈænᵊlz) *pl n* **1** yearly records of events, generally in chronological order. **2** history or records of history in general. **3** regular reports of the work of a society, learned body, etc. [C16: from Latin (*librī*) *annālēs* yearly (books), from *annus* year] ► **ˈannalist** *n* ► **ˌannalˈistic** *adj*

Annam *or* **Anam** (æˈnæm, ˈænæm) *n* a former kingdom (3rd century–1428), empire (1428–1884), and French protectorate (1884–1945) of E Indochina: now part of Vietnam.

Annamese (ˌænəˈmiːz) *adj* **1** of or relating to Annam. ◆ *adj, n* **2** a former word for **Vietnamese.**

Annan (ˈænæn) *n* **Kofi** (ˈkəʊfɪ). born 1938, Ghanaian international civil servant; secretary-general of the United Nations from 1997.

Annapolis (əˈnæpəlɪs) *n* the capital of Maryland, near the mouth of the Severn River on Chesapeake Bay: site of the U.S. Naval Academy. Pop.: 33 187 (1990).

Annapolis Royal *n* a town in SE Canada in W Nova Scotia on an arm of the Bay of Fundy: the first settlement in Canada (1605). Pop.: 633 (1991). Former name (until 1710): **Port Royal.**

Annapurna *or* **Anapurna** (ˌænəˈpʊənə) *n* a massif of the Himalayas, in Nepal. Highest peak: 8078 m (26 502 ft.).

Ann Arbor (æn ˈɑːbə) *n* a city in SE Michigan: seat of the University of Michigan. Pop.: 108 817 (1994 est.).

annates (ˈænerts, -əts) *pl n R.C. Church.* the first year's revenue of a see, an abbacy, or a minor benefice, paid to the pope. [C16: plural of French *annate*, from Medieval Latin *annāta*, from Latin *annus* year]

annatto *or* **anatto** (əˈnætəʊ) *n, pl* **-tos. 1** a small tropical American tree, *Bixa orellana*, having red or pinkish flowers and pulpy seeds that yield a dye: family *Bixaceae*. **2** the yellowish-red dye obtained from the pulpy outer layer of the coat of the seeds of this tree, used for colouring fabrics, butter, varnish, etc. [from Carib]

Anne (æn) *n* **1 Princess,** the Princess Royal. born 1950, daughter of Elizabeth II of Great Britain and Northern Ireland; a noted horsewoman and president of the Save the Children Fund. **2 Queen.** 1665–1714, queen of Great Britain and Ireland (1702–14), daughter of James II, and the last of the Stuart monarchs. **3 Saint.** (in Christian tradition) the mother of the Virgin Mary. Feast day: July 26 or 25.

anneal (əˈniːl) *vb* **1** to temper or toughen (something) by heat treatment. **2** to subject to or undergo some physical treatment, esp. heating, that removes internal stress, crystal defects, and dislocations. **3** (*tr*) to toughen or strengthen (the will, determination, etc.). **4** (often foll. by *out*) *Physics.* to disappear or cause to disappear by a rearrangement of atoms: *defects anneal out at different temperatures.* ◆ *n* **5** an act of annealing. [Old English *onǣlan*, from ON + *ǣlan* to burn, from *āl* fire] ► **anˈnealer** *n*

Anne Boleyn *n* See (Anne) **Boleyn.**

Annecy (*French* ansi) *n* **1** a city and resort in E France, on Lake Annecy. Pop.: 51 143 (1990). **2 Lake.** a lake in E France, in the Alps.

annelid (ˈænəlɪd) *n* **1** any worms of the phylum *Annelida*, in which the body is divided into segments both externally and internally. The group includes the earthworms, lugworm, ragworm, and leeches. ◆ *adj* **2** of, relating to, or belonging to the *Annelida*. [C19: from New Latin *Annelida*, from French *annelés*, literally: the ringed ones, from Old French *annel* ring, from Latin *ānellus*, from *ānulus* ring] ► **annelidan** (əˈnelɪdən) *n, adj*

Anne of Austria *n* 1601–66, wife of Louis XIII of France and daughter of Philip III of Spain: regent of France (1643–61) for her son Louis XIV.

Anne of Bohemia *n* 1366–94, queen consort of Richard II of England.

Anne of Cleves (kliːvz) *n* 1515–57, the fourth wife of Henry VIII of England: their marriage (1540) was annulled after six months.

Anne of Denmark *n* 1574–1619, wife (from 1589) of James I of England and VI of Scotland.

annex *vb* (æˈneks). (*tr*) **1** to join or add, esp. to something larger; attach. **2** to add (territory) by conquest or occupation. **3** to add or append as a condition, warranty, etc. **4** to appropriate without permission. ◆ *n* (ˈæneks). **5** a variant spelling (esp. U.S.) of **annexe.** [C14: from Medieval Latin *annexāre*, from Latin *annectere* to attach to, from *nectere* to join] ► **anˈnexable** *adj*

annexation (ˌænɪkˈseɪʃən, -ek-) *n* **1** the act of annexing, esp. territory, or the condition of being annexed. **2** something annexed. ► **ˌannexˈational** *adj* ► **ˌannexˈationism** *n* ► **ˌannexˈationist** *n*

annexe *or esp. U.S.* **annex** (ˈæneks) *n* **1a** an extension to a main building. **1b** a building used as an addition to a main building nearby. **2** something added or annexed, esp. a supplement to a document.

Annigoni (*Italian* anniˈɡoːni) *n* **Pietro** (ˈpjeːtro). 1910–88, Italian painter; noted esp. for his portraits of President Kennedy (1961) and Queen Elizabeth II (1955 and 1970).

annihilate (əˈnaɪəˌleɪt) *vb* **1** (*tr*) to destroy completely; extinguish. **2** (*tr*) *Informal.* to defeat totally, as in debate or argument. **3** (*intr*) *Physics.* to undergo annihilation. [C16: from Late Latin *annihilāre* to bring to nothing, from Latin *nihil* nothing] ► **annihilable** (əˈnaɪələbᵊl) *adj* ► **anˈnihilative** *adj* ► **anˈnihiˌlator** *n*

annihilation (əˌnaɪəˈleɪʃən) *n* **1** total destruction. **2** the act of annihilating. **3** *Physics.* the destruction of a particle and its antiparticle when they collide. The annihilation of an electron with a positron generates two or, very rarely, three photons of **annihilation radiation.** The annihilation of a nucleon with its antiparticle generates several pions.

anniversary (ˌænɪˈvɜːsərɪ) *n, pl* **-ries. 1** the date on which an event occurred in some previous year: *a wedding anniversary.* **2** the celebration of this. ◆ *adj* **3** of or relating to an anniversary. **4** recurring every year, esp. on the same date. [C13: from Latin *anniversārius* returning every year, from *annus* year + *vertere* to turn]

anniversary day *n N.Z.* a day for celebrating the foundation date of one of the former Provinces.

anno Domini (ˈænəʊ ˈdɒmɪˌnaɪ, -ˌniː) *adv* **1** the full form of **A.D.** or **AD.** ◆ *n* **2** *Informal.* advancing old age. [Latin: in the year of our Lord]

anno regni *Latin.* (ˈænəʊ ˈreɡnaɪ) in the year of the reign.

annotate (ˈænəʊˌteɪt, ˈænə-) *vb* to supply (a written work, such as an ancient text) with critical or explanatory notes. [C18: from Latin *annotāre*, from *nota* mark] ► **ˈannoˌtatable** *adj* ► **ˈannoˌtative** *adj* ► **ˈannoˌtator** *n*

annotation (ˌænəʊˈteɪʃən, ˌænə-) *n* **1** the act of annotating. **2** a note added in explanation, etc., esp. of some literary work.

announce (əˈnaʊns) *vb* **1** (*tr; may take a clause as object*) to make known publicly; proclaim. **2** (*tr*) to declare the arrival of: *to announce a guest.* **3** (*tr; may take a clause as object*) to reveal to the mind or senses; presage: *the dark clouds announced rain.* **4** (*intr*) to work as an announcer, as on radio or television. **5** *U.S.* to make known (one's intention to run as a candidate): *to announce for the presidency.* [C15: from Old French *anoncer,* from Latin *annuntiāre,* from *nuntius* messenger]

announcement (əˈnaunsmənt) *n* **1** a public statement. **2** a brief item or advertisement, as in a newspaper. **3** a formal printed or written invitation. **4** the act of announcing.

announcer (əˈnaunsə) *n* a person who announces, esp. one who reads the news, introduces programmes, etc., on radio or television.

anno urbis conditae *Latin.* (ˈænəu ˈɜːbɪs ˈkɒndɪˌtiː) the full form of **AUC** (sense b). [literally: in the year of the founding of the city]

annoy (əˈnɔɪ) *vb* **1** to irritate or displease. **2** to harass with repeated attacks. [C13: from Old French *anoier,* from Late Latin *inodiāre* to make hateful, from Latin *in odiō (esse)* (to be) hated, from *odium* hatred] ▸ **anˈnoyer** *n* ▸ **anˈnoying** *adj* ▸ **anˈnoyingly** *adv*

annoyance (əˈnɔɪəns) *n* **1** the feeling of being annoyed. **2** the act of annoying. **3** a person or thing that annoys.

annual (ˈænjuəl) *adj* **1** occurring, done, etc., once a year or every year; yearly: *an annual income.* **2** lasting for a year: *an annual subscription.* ◆ *n* **3** a plant that completes its life cycle in one year. Compare **perennial** (sense 3), **biennial** (sense 3). **4** a book, magazine, etc., published once every year. [C14: from Late Latin *annuālis,* from Latin *annuus* yearly, from *annus* year] ▸ **ˈannually** *adv*

annual general meeting *n Brit.* the statutory meeting of the directors and shareholders of a company or of the members of a society, held once every financial year, at which the annual report is presented. Abbrev.: **AGM.**

annualize *or* **annualise** (ˈænjuəˌlaɪz) *vb* (*tr*) to convert (a rate of interest) to an annual rate when it is quoted for a period of less than a year: *credit card companies are obliged to quote an annualized percentage rate to borrowers.*

annual parallax *n* See under **parallax** (sense 2).

annual percentage rate *n* the annual equivalent of a rate of interest when the rate is quoted more frequently than annually, usually monthly. Abbrev.: **APR.**

annual report *n* a report presented by the directors of a company to its shareholders each year, containing the profit-and-loss account, the balance sheet, and details of the past year's activity.

annual ring *n* a ring of wood indicating one year's growth, seen in the transverse section of stems and roots of woody plants growing in temperate climates. Also called: **tree ring.**

annuitant (əˈnjuːɪtənt) *n* a person in receipt of or entitled to an annuity.

annuity (əˈnjuːɪtɪ) *n, pl* **-ties. 1** a fixed sum payable at specified intervals, esp. annually, over a period, such as the recipient's life, or in perpetuity, in return for a premium paid either in instalments or in a single payment. **2** the right to receive or the duty to pay such a sum. [C15: from French *annuité,* from Medieval Latin *annuitās,* from Latin *annuus* ANNUAL]

annul (əˈnʌl) *vb* **-nuls, -nulling, -nulled.** (*tr*) to make (something, esp. a law or marriage) void; cancel the validity of; abolish. [C14: from Old French *annuller,* from Late Latin *annullāre* to bring to nothing, from Latin *nullus* not any; see NULL] ▸ **anˈnullable** *adj*

annular (ˈænjulə) *adj* ring-shaped; of or forming a ring. [C16: from Latin *annulāris,* from *annulus, ānulus* ring] ▸ **annularity** (ˌænjuˈlærɪtɪ) *n* ▸ **ˈannularly** *adv*

annular eclipse *n* an eclipse of the sun in which the moon does not cover the entire disc of the sun, so that a ring of sunlight surrounds the shadow of the moon. Compare **total eclipse, partial eclipse.**

annular ligament *n Anatomy.* any of various ligaments that encircle a part, such as the wrist, ankle, or trachea.

annulate (ˈænjulɪt, -ˌleɪt) *adj* having, composed of, or marked with rings. [C19: from Latin *ānulātus,* from *ānulus* a ring] ▸ **ˈannuˌlated** *adj*

annulation (ˌænjuˈleɪʃən) *n* **1** the formation of rings. **2** a ringlike formation or part.

annulet (ˈænjulɪt) *n* **1** *Architect.* a moulding in the form of a ring, as at the top of a column adjoining the capital. **2** *Heraldry.* a ring-shaped device on a shield; hollow roundel. **3** a little ring. [C16: from Latin *ānulus* ring + -ET]

annulment (əˈnʌlmənt) *n* **1** a formal invalidation, as of a marriage, judicial proceeding, etc. **2** the act of annulling.

annulose (ˈænjuˌləus, -ˌləuz) *adj* (of earthworms, crustaceans, and similar animals) having a body formed of a series of rings; segmented. [C19: from New Latin *annulōsus;* see ANNULUS]

annulus (ˈænjuləs) *n, pl* **-li** (-ˌlaɪ) *or* **-luses. 1** the area between two concentric circles. **2** a ring-shaped part, figure, or space. [C16: from Latin, variant of *ānulus* ring]

annunciate (əˈnʌnsɪˌeɪt, -ʃɪ-) *vb* (*tr*) a less common word for **announce.** [C16: from *annunciātus,* Medieval Latin misspelling of *annuntiātus,* past participle of Latin *annuntiāre;* see ANNOUNCE] ▸ **anˌnunciˈation** *n* ▸ **annunciative** (əˈnʌnsɪətɪv, -ʃətɪv) *or* **annunciatory** (əˈnʌnsɪətərɪ, -ʃə-) *adj*

Annunciation (əˌnʌnsɪˈeɪʃən) *n* **1 the.** *New Testament.* the announcement of the Incarnation by the angel Gabriel to the Virgin Mary (Luke 1:26–38). **2** Also called: **Annunciation Day.** the festival commemorating this, held on March 25 (Lady Day).

annunciator (əˈnʌnsɪˌeɪtə) *n* **1** a device that gives a visual indication as to which of a number of electric circuits has operated, such as an indicator in a hotel showing in which room a bell has been rung. **2** a device giving an audible signal indicating the position of a train. **3** a less common word for **announcer.**

annus horribilis (ˈænʊs hɒˈriːbɪlɪs) *n* a terrible year. [C20: from Latin, modelled on ANNUS MIRABILIS, first used by Elizabeth II of the year 1992]

annus mirabilis *Latin.* (ˈænʊs mɪˈræbɪlɪs) *n, pl* ***anni mirabiles*** (ˈænaɪ mɪˈræbɪliːz). a year of wonders, catastrophes, or other notable events.

anoa (əˈnəuə) *n* the smallest of the cattle tribe *Anoa depressicornis,* having small straight horns and inhabiting the island of Celebes in Indonesia. Compare **tamarau.** [from a native name in Celebes]

anobiid (əˈnəubɪɪd) *n* any coleopterous beetle of the family *Anobiidae,* in which the pronotum characteristically forms a hood that more or less covers the head. The family includes such notorious pests as the **furniture beetle** (*Anobium punctatum*) and the **deathwatch beetle,** the larvae of which attack furniture and beams. See also **deathwatch.**

anode (ˈænəud) *n* **1** the positive electrode in an electrolytic cell. **2** Also called (esp. U.S.): **plate.** the positively charged electrode in an electronic valve. **3** the negative terminal of a primary cell. Compare **cathode.** [C19: from Greek *anodos* a way up, from *hodos* a way; alluding to the movement of the current to or from the positive pole] ▸ **anodal** (eɪˈnəudᵊl) *or* **anodic** (əˈnɒdɪk) *adj*

anodize *or* **anodise** (ˈænəˌdaɪz) *vb* to coat (a metal, such as aluminium or magnesium) with a protective oxide film by electrolysis.

anodontia (ˌænəuˈdɒnʃɪə) *n* the congenital absence of teeth. [from AN- + Greek *odōn* tooth + -IA]

anodyne (ˈænəˌdaɪn) *n* **1** a drug that relieves pain; analgesic. **2** anything that alleviates mental distress. ◆ *adj* **3** capable of relieving pain or distress. [C16: from Latin *anōdynus,* from Greek *anōdunos* painless, from AN- + *odunē* pain]

anoestrus *or U.S.* **anestrus** (ænˈiːstrəs) *n* a period of sexual inactivity between two periods of oestrus in many mammals. [C20: New Latin; see AN-, OESTRUS] ▸ **anˈoestrous** *or U.S.* **anˈestrous** *adj*

anoint (əˈnɔɪnt) *vb* (*tr*) **1** to smear or rub over with oil or an oily liquid. **2** to apply oil to as a sign of consecration or sanctification in a sacred rite. [C14: from Old French *enoint,* from *enoindre,* from Latin *inunguere,* from IN-[2] + *unguere* to smear with oil] ▸ **aˈnointer** *n* ▸ **aˈnointment** *n*

anointing of the sick *n R.C. Church.* a sacrament in which a person who is seriously ill or dying is anointed by a priest with consecrated oil. Former name: **extreme unction.**

anole (əˈnəul) *n* any small arboreal tropical American insectivorous lizards of the genus *Anolis,* such as *A. carolinensis* (**green anole**): family *Iguanidae* (iguanas). They are able to change the colour of their skin. Also called: **American chameleon.** [C18 *annolis,* from French *anolis,* from Carib *anoli*]

anomalistic month *n* the interval between two successive passages of the moon through perigee; 27.55455 days.

anomalistic year *n* the interval between two successive passages of the earth through perihelion; 365.25964 mean solar days.

anomalous (əˈnɒmələs) *adj* deviating from the normal or usual order, type, etc.; irregular, abnormal, or incongruous. [C17: from Late Latin *anōmalus,* from Greek *anōmalos* uneven, inconsistent, from AN- + *homalos* even, from *homos* one and the same] ▸ **aˈnomalously** *adv* ▸ **aˈnomalousness** *n*

anomalous monism *n* the philosophical doctrine that although all mental states consist merely in states of the brain, there exist no regular correspondences between classes of mental and physical states, and so no psychophysical laws. See also **identity theory.**

anomaly (əˈnɒməlɪ) *n, pl* **-lies. 1** something anomalous. **2** deviation from the normal or usual order, type, etc.; irregularity. **3** *Astronomy.* the angle between a planet, the sun, and the previous perihelion of the planet. **4** *Geology.* **4a** Also called: **gravity anomaly.** a deviation from the normal value of gravity at the earth's surface, caused by density differences at depth, for example those caused by a buried mineral body. **4b** Also called: **magnetic anomaly.** a magnetic field, for example one produced by a buried mineral body, that deviates from an expected or standard value, usually that of the earth's magnetic field. ▸ **aˌnomaˈlistic** *adj* ▸ **aˌnomaˈlistically** *adv*

anomie *or* **anomy** (ˈænəumɪ) *n Sociol.* lack of social or moral standards in an individual or society. [from Greek *anomia* lawlessness, from A-[1] + *nomos* law] ▸ **anomic** (əˈnɒmɪk) *adj*

anon (əˈnɒn) *adv Archaic or literary.* **1** in a short time; soon. **2 ever and anon.** now and then. [Old English *on āne,* literally: in one, that is, immediately]

anon. *abbrev. for* anonymous.

anonym (ˈænənɪm) *n* **1** a less common word for **pseudonym. 2** an anonymous person or publication.

anonymize *or* **anonymise** (əˈnɒnɪˌmaɪz) *vb* (*tr*) to carry out or organize in such a way as to preserve anonymity: *anonymized AIDS screening.*

anonymous (əˈnɒnɪməs) *adj* **1** from or by a person, author, etc., whose name is unknown or withheld: *an anonymous letter.* **2** having no known name. **3** lacking individual characteristics; unexceptional. **4** (*often cap.*) denoting an organization which provides help to applicants who remain anonymous: *Alcoholics Anonymous.* [C17: via Late Latin from Greek *anōnumos,* from AN- + *onoma* name] ▸ **anonymity** (ˌænəˈnɪmɪtɪ) *n* ▸ **aˈnonymously** *adv* ▸ **aˈnonymousness** *n*

anopheles (əˈnɒfɪˌliːz) *n, pl* **-les.** any of various mosquitoes constituting the genus *Anopheles,* some species of which transmit the malaria parasite to man. [C19: via New Latin from Greek *anōphelēs* useless, from AN- + *ōphelein* to help, from *ophelos* help]

anorak (ˈænəˌræk) *n* **1** a warm waterproof hip-length jacket usually with a hood, originally worn in polar regions, but now worn for any outdoor activity. **2** *Informal.* a socially inept person with a hobby considered by most people to be boring. [from Eskimo *ánorâq*]

anorexia (ˌænɒˈrɛksɪə) *n* **1** loss of appetite. **2** Also called: **anorexia nervosa** (nɜːˈvəusə). a disorder characterized by fear of becoming fat and refusal of food, leading to debility and even death. [C17: via New Latin from Greek, from AN- + *orexis* appetite] ▸ **ˌanoˈrectic** *or* **ˌanoˈrexic** *adj, n*

anorthic (ænˈɔːθɪk) *adj* another word for **triclinic.** [C19: from AN- + ORTHO- + -IC]

anorthite (æn'ɔːθaɪt) *n* a white to greyish-white or reddish-white mineral of the feldspar group and plagioclase series, found chiefly in igneous rocks and more rarely in metamorphic rocks. It is used in the manufacture of glass and ceramics. Composition: calcium aluminium silicate. Formula: $CaAl_2Si_2O_8$. Crystal structure: triclinic. [C19: from AN- + ORTHO- + -ITE[1]] ► **anorthitic** (ˌænɔː'θɪtɪk) *adj*

anorthosite (æn'ɔːθəˌsaɪt) *n* a coarse-grained plutonic igneous rock consisting almost entirely of plagioclase feldspar. [C19: from French *anorthose* (see AN-, ORTHO-) + -ITE[1]]

anosmia (æn'ɒzmɪə, -'ɒs-) *n Pathol.* loss of the sense of smell, usually as the result of a lesion of the olfactory nerve, disease in another organ or part, or obstruction of the nasal passages. [C19: from New Latin, from AN- + Greek *osmē* smell, from *ozein* to smell] ► **anosmatic** (ˌænɒz'mætɪk) *or* **an'osmic** *adj*

another (ə'nʌðə) *determiner* **1a** one more; an added: *another chance.* **1b** (*as pronoun*): *help yourself to another.* **2a** a different; alternative: *another era from ours.* **2b** (*as pronoun*): *to try one path, then another.* **3a** a different example of the same sort: *another Beethoven.* **3b** (*as pronoun*): *we got rid of one loafer, but I think this new man's another.* **4 another place.** the other House of Parliament (used in the House of Commons to refer to the House of Lords and vice versa). [C14: originally *an other*]

A.N. Other *n Brit.* an unnamed person: used in team lists, etc., to indicate a place that remains to be filled.

Anouilh (*French* anuj) *n* **Jean** (ʒɑ̃). 1910–87, French dramatist, noted for his reinterpretations of Greek myths: his works include *Eurydice* (1942), *Antigone* (1944), and *Becket* (1959).

anoxaemia *or U.S.* **anoxemia** (ˌænɒk'siːmɪə) *n* a deficiency in the amount of oxygen in the arterial blood. [C19: from New Latin, from AN- + OX(YGEN) + -AEMIA] ► ˌ**anox'aemic** *or U.S.* ˌ**anox'emic** *adj*

anoxia (æn'ɒksɪə) *n* **1** lack or absence of oxygen. **2** a deficiency of oxygen in tissues and organs. Compare **hypoxia.** [C20: from AN- + OX(YGEN) + -IA] ► **an'oxic** *adj*

Anqing ('ɑːn'tʃɪŋ) *or* **Anking** *n* a city in E China, in SW Anhui province on the Yangtze River: famous seven-storeyed pagoda. Pop.: 250 718 (1990 est.).

ansate ('ænseɪt) *adj* having a handle or handle-like part. [C19: from Latin *ansātus*, from *ansa* handle]

Anschluss ('ænʃlʊs) *n* a political or economic union, esp. the annexation of Austria by Nazi Germany (1938). [German: from *anschliessen* to join]

Anselm ('ænsɛlm) *n* **Saint.** 1033–1109, Italian Benedictine monk; archbishop of Canterbury (1093–1109): one of the founders of scholasticism; author of *Cur Deus Homo?* (*Why did God become Man?*). Feast day: Aug. 21.

anserine ('ænsəˌraɪn, -rɪn) *or* **anserous** ('ænsərəs) *adj* **1** of or resembling a goose. **2** of, relating to, or belonging to the subfamily *Anserinae*, which includes geese, swans, and certain ducks: family *Anatidae*, order *Anseriformes.* **3** silly; foolish. [C19: from Latin *anserīnus*, from *anser* goose]

Ansermet (*French* ɑ̃sɛrmɛ) *n* **Ernest** (ɛrnest). 1883–1969, Swiss orchestral conductor; principal conductor of Diaghilev's Ballet Russe.

Anshan (ˌæn'ʃæn) *n* **1** a city in NE China, in Liaoning province. Pop.: 1 390 000 (1991 est.). **2** an ancient city and region in Persia, associated with Elam.

ANSI *abbrev. for* American National Standards Institution.

answer ('ɑːnsə) *n* **1** a reply, either spoken or written, as to a question, request, letter, or article. **2** a reaction or response in the form of an action: *drunkenness was his answer to disappointment.* **3** a solution, esp. of a mathematical problem. **4** *Law.* **4a** a party's written reply to his opponent's interrogatories. **4b** (in divorce law) the respondent's written reply to the petition. **5** a musical phrase that follows the subject of a fugue, reproducing it a fifth higher or a fourth lower. ◆ *vb* **6** (when *tr, may take a clause as object*) to reply or respond (to) by word or act: *to answer a question; he answered; to answer the door; he answered that he would come.* **7** (*tr*) to reply correctly to; solve or attempt to solve: *I could answer only three questions.* **8** (*intr*; usually foll. by *to*) to respond or react (to a stimulus, command, etc.): *the steering answers to the slightest touch.* **9** (*tr*) to pay off (a debt, obligation, etc.); discharge. **10** (when *intr*, often foll. by *for*) to meet the requirements (of); be satisfactory (for); serve the purpose (of): *this will answer his needs; this will answer for a chisel.* **11** (when *intr*, foll. by *to*) to match or correspond (esp. in the phrase **answer** (or **answer to**) **the description**). **12** (*tr*) to give a defence or refutation of (a charge) or in (an argument). [Old English *andswaru* an answer; related to Old Frisian *ondser*, Old Norse *andsvar*; see SWEAR]

answerable ('ɑːnsərəb[ə]l) *adj* **1** (*postpositive*; foll. by *for* or *to*) responsible or accountable: *answerable for someone's safety; answerable to one's boss.* **2** able to be answered. ► ˌ**answera'bility** *or* '**answerableness** *n* ► '**answerably** *adv*

answer back *vb* (*adv*) to reply rudely to (a person, esp. someone in authority) when one is expected to remain silent.

answer for *vb* (*intr, prep*) **1** to be liable or responsible for (a person's actions, behaviour, etc.). **2** to vouch for or speak on behalf of (a person). **3** to suffer or atone for (one's wrongdoing).

answering machine *n* a device by means of which a telephone call is answered automatically and the caller enabled to leave a recorded message. In full: **telephone answering machine.** Also called: **answerphone.**

ant (ænt) *n* **1** any small social insect of the widely distributed hymenopterous family *Formicidae*, typically living in highly organized colonies of winged males, wingless sterile females (workers), and fertile females (queens), which are winged until after mating. See also **army ant, fire ant, slave ant, wood ant.** Related adj: **formic. 2 white ant.** another name for a **termite. 3 have ants in one's pants.** *Slang.* to be restless or impatient. [Old English *ǣmette*; related to Old High German *āmeiza*, Old Norse *meita*; see EMMET]

ant. *abbrev. for* antonym.

an't *Chiefly Brit.* **1** (ɑːnt). a rare variant spelling of **aren't. 2** (eɪnt). *Dialect.* a variant spelling of **ain't.**

ant- *prefix* a variant of **anti-**: *antacid.*

-ant *suffix forming adjectives and nouns.* causing or performing an action or existing in a certain condition; the agent that performs an action: *pleasant; claimant; deodorant; protestant; servant.* [from Latin *-ant-*, ending of present participles of the first conjugation]

anta ('æntə) *n, pl* **antae** ('æntiː). *Architect.* a pilaster attached to the end of a side wall or sometimes to the side of a doorway.

Antabuse ('æntəˌbjuːs) *n Trademark.* a drug used in the treatment of alcoholism that acts by inducing nausea following ingestion of alcohol; tetraethylthiuram disulphide.

antacid (ænt'æsɪd) *n* **1** a substance used to treat acidity, esp. in the stomach. ◆ *adj* **2** having the properties of this substance.

Antaeus (æn'tiːəs) *n Greek myth.* an African giant who was invincible as long as he touched the ground, but was lifted into the air by Hercules and crushed to death.

antagonism (æn'tægəˌnɪzəm) *n* **1** openly expressed and usually mutual opposition. **2** the inhibiting or nullifying action of one substance or organism on another. **3** *Physiol.* the normal opposition between certain muscles. **4** *Biology.* the inhibition or interference of growth of one kind of organism by another.

antagonist (æn'tægənɪst) *n* **1** an opponent or adversary, as in a contest, drama, sporting event, etc. **2** any muscle that opposes the action of another. Compare **agonist** (sense 1). **3** a drug that neutralizes or counteracts the effects of another drug. Compare **synergist** (sense 1).

antagonistic (ænˌtægə'nɪstɪk) *adj* **1** in active opposition. **2** mutually opposed. ► **anˌtago'nistically** *adv*

antagonize *or* **antagonise** (æn'tægəˌnaɪz) *vb* (*tr*) **1** to make hostile; annoy or irritate. **2** to act in opposition to or counteract. [C17: from Greek *antagōnizesthai*, from ANTI- + *agōnizesthai* to strive, from *agōn* contest] ► **an'tagoˌnizable** *or* **an'tagoˌnisable** *adj* ► **anˌtagoni'zation** *or* **anˌtagoni'sation** *n*

Antakiya (ˌæntɑː'kiːjə) *n* the Arabic name for **Antioch.**

Antakya (ɑn'tɑkjɑ) *n* the Turkish name for **Antioch.**

antalkali (ænt'ælkəˌlaɪ) *n, pl* **-lis** *or* **-lies.** a substance that neutralizes alkalis, esp. one used to treat alkalosis. ► **antalkaline** (ænt'ælkəˌlaɪn, -lɪn) *adj, n*

Antalya (*Turkish* ɑn'tɑljɑ) *n* a port in SW Turkey, on the **Gulf of Antalya.** Pop.: 502 269 (1995 est.).

Antananarivo (ˌæntəˌnænə'riːvəʊ) *n* the capital of Madagascar, on the central plateau: founded in the 17th century by a Hova chief; university (1961). Pop.: 1 052 835 (1993). Former name: **Tananarive.**

Antarctic (ænt'ɑːktɪk) *n* **1 the.** Also called: **Antarctic Zone.** Antarctica and the surrounding waters. ◆ *adj* **2** of or relating to the south polar regions. [C14: via Latin from Greek *antarktikos*; see ANTI-, ARCTIC]

Antarctica (ænt'ɑːktɪkə) *n* a continent around the South Pole: consists of an ice-covered plateau, 1800–3000 m (6000 ft. to 10 000 ft.) above sea level, and mountain ranges rising to 4500 m (15 000 ft.) with some volcanic peaks; average temperatures all below freezing and human settlement is confined to research stations.

Antarctic Archipelago *n* the former name of the **Palmer Archipelago.**

Antarctic Circle *n* the imaginary circle around the earth, parallel to the equator, at latitude 66° 32′ S.

Antarctic Ocean *n* the sea surrounding Antarctica, consisting of the most southerly parts of the Pacific, Atlantic, and Indian Oceans. Also called: **Southern Ocean.**

Antarctic Peninsula *n* the largest peninsula of Antarctica, between the Weddell Sea and the Pacific: consists of Graham Land in the north and the Palmer Peninsula in the south. Former name (until 1964): **Palmer Peninsula.**

Antarctic prion *n* another name for **dove prion.**

Antares (æn'teəriːz) *n* the brightest star in the constellation Scorpius. It is a variable binary star whose main component, a red supergiant, is associated with a fainter green component. Visual magnitude: 1.2 (red), 6.8 (green); spectral type: MO (red); distance: 250 light years. [from Greek *Antarēs*, literally: simulating Mars (in colour), from ANTI- + *Arēs* Mars]

ant bear *n* another name for **aardvark.**

ant bird *n* any of various dull-coloured South American passerine birds of the family *Formicariidae*, such as *Hylophylax naevioides* (spotted ant bird), that typically feed on ants. Also called: **bush shrike, ant thrush.**

ant cow *n* an insect, esp. an aphid, that excretes a sweet honey-like substance that is collected and eaten by ants.

ante ('æntɪ) *n* **1** the gaming stake put up before the deal in poker by the players. **2** *Informal.* a sum of money representing a person's share, as in a syndicate. **3 up the ante.** *Informal.* to increase the costs, risks, or considerations involved in taking an action or reaching a conclusion: *whenever they reached their goal, they upped the ante by setting more complex challenges for themselves.* ◆ *vb* **-tes, -teing; -ted** *or* **-teed. 4** to place (one's stake) in poker. **5** (usually foll. by *up*) *Informal, chiefly U.S.* to pay.

ante- *prefix* before in time or position; previous to; in front of: *antedate; antechamber.* [from Latin]

anteater ('æntˌiːtə) *n* **1** any toothless edentate mammal of the family *Myrmecophagidae* of Central and South America, esp. *Myrmecophaga tridactyla* (or *jubata*) (**giant anteater**), having a long tubular snout used for eating termites. See also **tamandua. 2 scaly anteater.** another name for **pangolin. 3 spiny anteater.** another name for **echidna. 4 banded anteater.** another name for **numbat.**

antebellum (ˌæntɪ'bɛləm) *adj* of or during the period before a war, esp. the American Civil War: *the antebellum South.* [Latin *ante bellum*, literally: before the war]

antecede (ˌæntɪˈsiːd) *vb* (*tr*) to go before, as in time, order, etc.; precede. [C17: from Latin *antecēdere,* from *cēdere* to go]

antecedence (ˌæntɪˈsiːdᵊns) *n* **1** precedence; priority. **2** *Astronomy.* retrograde motion.

antecedent (ˌæntɪˈsiːdᵊnt) *n* **1** an event, circumstance, etc., that happens before another. **2** *Grammar.* a word or phrase to which a pronoun refers. In the sentence "People who live in glass houses shouldn't throw stones," *people* is the antecedent of *who.* **3** *Logic.* the hypothetical clause, usually introduced by "if", in a conditional statement: that which implies the other. **4** *Maths.* an obsolescent name for **numerator** (sense 1). **5 denying the antecedent.** *Logic.* the fallacy of inferring the falsehood of the consequent of a conditional statement, given the truth of the conditional and the falsehood of its antecedent, as *if there are five of them, there are more than four: there are not five, so there are not more than four.* ◆ *adj* **6** preceding in time or order; prior. ◆ See also **antecedents.**

antecedents (ˌæntɪˈsiːdᵊnts) *pl n* **1** ancestry. **2** a person's past history.

antechamber (ˈæntɪˌtʃeɪmbə) *n* another name for **anteroom.** [C17: from Old French, from Italian *anticamera;* see ANTE-, CHAMBER]

antechoir (ˈæntɪˌkwaɪə) *n* the part of a church in front of the choir, usually enclosed by screens, tombs, etc.

antedate *vb* (ˈæntɪˌdeɪt, ˌæntɪˈdeɪt). (*tr*) **1** to be or occur at an earlier date than. **2** to affix a date to (a document, etc.) that is earlier than the actual date. **3** to assign a date to (an event, etc.) that is earlier than its previously assigned date. **4** to cause to occur sooner. ◆ *n* (ˈæntɪˌdeɪt). **5** an earlier date.

antediluvian (ˌæntɪdɪˈluːvɪən, -daɪ-) *adj* **1** belonging to the ages before the biblical Flood (Genesis 7, 8). **2** old-fashioned or antiquated. ◆ *n* **3** an antediluvian person or thing. [C17: from ANTE- + Latin *dīluvium* flood]

antefix (ˈæntɪˌfɪks) *n, pl* **-fixes** *or* **-fixa** (-ˌfɪksə). a carved ornament at the eaves of a roof to hide the joint between the tiles. [C19: from Latin *antefixa* (things) fastened in front, from *fīgere* to FIX] ▸ **antefixal** (ˌæntɪˈfɪksəl) *adj*

antelope (ˈæntɪˌləʊp) *n, pl* **-lopes** *or* **-lope. 1** any bovid mammal of the subfamily *Antilopinae,* of Africa and Asia. They are typically graceful, having long legs and horns, and include the gazelles, springbok, impala, gerenuk, blackbuck, and dik-diks. **2** any of various similar bovids of Africa and Asia. **3 American antelope.** another name for **pronghorn.** [C15: from Old French *antelop,* from Medieval Latin *antalopus,* from Late Greek *antholops* a legendary beast]

antemeridian (ˌæntɪməˈrɪdɪən) *adj* before noon; in the morning. [C17: from Latin *antemerīdiānus;* see ANTE-, MERIDIAN]

ante meridiem (ˈæntɪ məˈrɪdɪəm) the full form of **a.m.** [Latin, from ANTE- + *merīdiēs* midday]

ante-mortem *adj, adv* (esp. in legal or medical contexts) before death. [Latin]

antenatal (ˌæntɪˈneɪtᵊl) *adj* **1** occurring or present before birth; during pregnancy. ◆ *n* **2** Also called: **prenatal.** *Informal.* an examination during pregnancy. ▸ **ˌanteˈnatally** *adv*

antenna (ænˈtenə) *n* **1** (*pl* **-nae** (-niː)) one of a pair of mobile appendages on the heads of insects, crustaceans, etc., that are often whiplike and respond to touch and taste but may be specialized for swimming or attachment. **2** (*pl* **-nas**) another name for **aerial** (sense 7). [C17: from Latin: sail yard, of obscure origin] ▸ **anˈtennal** *or* **anˈtennary** *adj*

antennule (ænˈtenjuːl) *n* one of a pair of small mobile appendages on the heads of crustaceans in front of the antennae, usually having a sensory function. [C19: from French, diminutive of ANTENNA]

antenuptial marriage contract *n S. African.* a contract made between a man and a woman before they marry, agreeing on the distribution of their assets in the event of divorce. Sometimes shortened to **antenuptial.**

antependium (ˌæntɪˈpendɪəm) *n, pl* **-dia** (-dɪə). a covering hung over the front of an altar. [C17: from Medieval Latin, from Latin ANTE- + *pendēre* to hang]

antepenult (ˌæntɪpɪˈnʌlt) *n* the third last syllable in a word. [C16: shortened from Latin (*syllaba*) *antepaenultima;* see ANTE-, PENULT]

antepenultimate (ˌæntɪpɪˈnʌltɪmɪt) *adj* **1** third from last. ◆ *n* **2** anything that is third from last.

anteposition (ˈæntɪpəˌzɪʃən) *n Botany.* the position opposite a given part of a plant.

anterior (ænˈtɪərɪə) *adj* **1** situated at or towards the front. **2** earlier in time. **3** *Zoology.* of or near the head end. **4** *Botany.* (of part of a flower or leaf) situated farthest away from the main stem. ◆ Compare **posterior.** [C17: from Latin, comparative of *ante* before] ▸ **anteriority** (ænˌtɪərɪˈɒrɪtɪ) *n*

anterograde amnesia (ˈæntərəʊˌgreɪd) *n* amnesia caused by brain damage in which the memory loss relates to events occurring after the damage. Compare **retrograde amnesia.** [from Latin *anterior* previous + -GRADE]

anteroom (ˈæntɪˌruːm, -ˌrʊm) *n* a room giving entrance to a larger room, often used as a waiting room.

antetype (ˈæntɪˌtaɪp) *n* an earlier form; prototype.

anteversion (ˌæntɪˈvɜːʃən) *n* abnormal forward tilting of a bodily organ, esp. the uterus.

antevert (ˌæntɪˈvɜːt) *vb* (*tr*) to displace (an organ or part) by tilting forward. [C17: from Latin *antevertere* to go in front, from *vertere* to turn]

Antheil (ˈæntaɪl) *n* **George.** 1900–59, U.S. composer. His best known work is the controversial *Le Ballet Méchanique* (1924) for motor horns, bells, and aeroplane propellers.

anthelion (æntˈhiːlɪən, ænˈθiː-) *n, pl* **-lia** (-lɪə). **1** a faint halo sometimes seen in polar or high altitude regions around the shadow of an object cast onto a thick cloud bank or fog. **2** a white spot occasionally appearing on the parhelic circle at the same height as and opposite to the sun. [C17: from Late Greek, from *anthēlios* opposite the sun, from ANTE- + *hēlios* sun]

anthelix (ænt'hiːlɪks, ænˈθiː-) *or* **antihelix** *n, pl* **-helices** (-ˈhiːlɪsiːz) *or* **-helixes.** *Anatomy.* a prominent curved fold of cartilage just inside the outer rim of the external ear.

anthelmintic (ˌænθelˈmɪntɪk) *or* **anthelminthic** (ˌænθelˈmɪnθɪk) *n Med.* another name for **vermifuge.**

anthem (ˈænθəm) *n* **1** a song of loyalty or devotion, as to a nation or college: *a national anthem.* **2** a musical composition for a choir, usually set to words from the Bible, sung as part of a church service. **3** a religious chant sung antiphonally. [Old English *antemne,* from Late Latin *antiphōna* ANTIPHON]

anthemion (ænˈθiːmɪən) *n, pl* **-mia** (-mɪə). a floral design, used esp. in ancient Greek and Roman architecture and decoration, usually consisting of honeysuckle, lotus, or palmette leaf motifs. [from Greek: a little flower, from *anthos* flower]

anther (ˈænθə) *n* the terminal part of a stamen consisting of two lobes each containing two sacs in which the pollen matures. [C18: from New Latin *anthēra,* from Latin: a remedy prepared from flowers, from Greek, from *anthēros* flowery, from *anthos* flower] ▸ **ˈantheral** *adj*

antheridium (ˌænθəˈrɪdɪəm) *n, pl* **-ia** (-ɪə). the male sex organ of algae, fungi, mosses, and ferns, which produces antherozoids. [C19: from New Latin, diminutive of *anthēra* ANTHER] ▸ **ˌantherˈidial** *adj*

antherozoid (ˌænθərəˈzəʊɪd, -ˈzɔɪd) *n* one of many small male gametes produced in an antheridium. [C19: see ANTHER, ZO(O)ID]

anthesis (ænˈθiːsɪs) *n* the process of flowering in plants. [C19: via New Latin from Greek: full bloom, from *anthein* to bloom, from *anthos* flower]

ant hill *n* **1** a mound of soil, leaves, etc., near the entrance of an ants' nest, carried and deposited there by the ants while constructing the nest. **2** a mound of earth, usually about 2 metres high, built up by termites in forming a nest.

antho- *combining form.* denoting a flower: *anthophore; anthotaxy; anthozoan.* [from Greek *anthos*]

anthocyanin (ˌænθəʊˈsaɪənɪn) *or* **anthocyan** (ˌænθəʊˈsaɪən) *n* any of a class of water-soluble glycosidic pigments, esp. those responsible for the red and blue colours in flowers. They are closely related to vitamins E and P. [C19: from ANTHO- + *-cyanin,* from Greek *kuanos* dark blue]

anthodium (ænˈθəʊdɪəm) *n, pl* **-dia** (-dɪə). *Botany.* another name for **capitulum** (sense 1). [C19: from New Latin, from Greek *anthōdēs* flower-like, from *anthos* flower + *-ōdēs* -OID]

anthologize *or* **anthologise** (ænˈθɒləˌdʒaɪz) *vb* to compile or put into an anthology.

anthology (ænˈθɒlədʒɪ) *n, pl* **-gies. 1** a collection of literary passages or works, esp. poems, by various authors. **2** any printed collection of literary pieces, songs, works of art, etc. [C17: from Medieval Latin *anthologia,* from Greek, literally: a flower gathering, from *anthos* flower + *legein* to collect] ▸ **anthological** (ˌænθəˈlɒdʒɪkᵊl) *adj* ▸ **anˈthologist** *n*

Anthony (ˈæntənɪ) *n* **Saint.** ?251–?356 A.D., Egyptian hermit, commonly regarded as the founder of Christian monasticism. Feast day: Jan. 17.

Anthony of Padua *n* **Saint.** 1195–1231, Franciscan friar, who preached in France and Italy. Feast day: June 13.

anthophilous (ænˈθɒfɪləs) *adj* **1** (esp. of insects) frequenting flowers. **2** feeding on flowers.

anthophore (ˈænθəʊˌfɔː, -θə-) *n* an elongation of the receptacle of a flower between the calyx and corolla.

anthotaxy (ˈænθəˌtæksɪ) *n* the arrangement of flowers on a stem or parts on a flower.

anthozoan (ˌænθəˈzəʊən) *n* **1** any of the solitary or colonial sessile marine coelenterates of the class *Anthozoa,* including the corals, sea anemones, and sea pens, in which the body is in the form of a polyp. ◆ *adj* **2** Also: **actinozoan.** of or relating to the class *Anthozoa.*

anthracene (ˈænθrəˌsiːn) *n* a colourless tricyclic crystalline solid having a slight blue fluorescence, used in the manufacture of chemicals, esp. diphenylamine and alizarin, and as crystals in scintillation counters. Formula: $C_6H_4(CH)_2C_6H_4$ [C19: from ANTHRAX + -ENE]

anthracite (ˈænθrəˌsaɪt) *n* a hard jet-black coal that burns slowly with a nonluminous flame giving out intense heat. Fixed carbon content: 86–98 per cent; calorific value: 3.14×10^7–3.63×10^7 J/kg. Also called: **hard coal.** [C19: from Latin *anthracītes* type of bloodstone, from Greek *anthrakitēs* coal-like, from *anthrax* coal, ANTHRAX] ▸ **anthracitic** (ˌænθrəˈsɪtɪk) *adj*

anthracnose (ænˈθræknəʊs) *n* any of several fungus diseases of plants and trees, such as vines and beans, characterized by oval dark depressed spots on the fruit and elsewhere. [C19: from French, from Greek *anthrax* coal, carbuncle + *nosos* disease]

anthracoid (ˈænθrəˌkɔɪd) *adj* **1** resembling anthrax. **2** resembling carbon, coal, or charcoal.

anthracosis (ˌænθrəˈkəʊsɪs) *n* a lung disease due to inhalation of coal dust. Informal name: **coal miner's lung.**

anthraquinone (ˌænθrəkwɪˈnəʊn, -ˈkwɪnəʊn) *n* a yellow crystalline solid used in the manufacture of dyes, esp. **anthraquinone dyes,** which have excellent colour properties. Formula: $C_6H_4(CO)_2C_6H_4$. [C19: ANTHRA(CENE) + QUINONE]

anthrax (ˈænθræks) *n, pl* **-thraces** (-θrəˌsiːz). **1** a highly infectious disease of animals, esp. cattle and sheep, characterized by fever, enlarged spleen and swelling of the throat. It is caused by the bacterium *Bacillus anthracis* and can be transmitted to man. **2** a pustule or other lesion caused by this disease. [C19: from Late Latin, from Greek: carbuncle]

anthrop. *abbrev. for:* **1** anthropological. **2** anthropology.

anthropic (ænˈθrɒpɪk) *adj* of or relating to human beings.

anthropic principle *n Astronomy.* the cosmological theory that the presence of life in the universe limits the ways in which the very early universe could have evolved.

anthropo- *combining form.* indicating man or human: *anthropology; anthropomorphism.* [from Greek *anthrōpos*]

anthropocentric (ˌænθrəpəʊˈsɛntrɪk) *adj* regarding man as the most important and central factor in the universe. ▸ **ˌanthropoˈcentrism** *n*

anthropogenesis (ˌænθrəpəʊˈdʒɛnɪsɪs) *or* **anthropogeny** (ˌænθrəˈpɒdʒɪnɪ) *n* the study of the origins of man. ▸ **ˌanthropogeˈnetic** *or* **ˌanthropoˈgenic** *adj*

anthropoid (ˈænθrəˌpɔɪd) *adj* **1** resembling man. **2** resembling an ape; apelike. **3** of or relating to the suborder *Anthropoidea.* ◆ *n* **4** any primate of the suborder *Anthropoidea,* including monkeys, apes, and man. Compare **prosimian.** ▸ **ˌanthroˈpoidal** *adj*

anthropoid ape *n* any primate of the family *Pongidae,* having no tail, elongated arms, and a highly developed brain. The group includes gibbons, orangutans, chimpanzees, and gorillas.

anthropol. *abbrev. for* anthropology.

anthropology (ˌænθrəˈpɒlədʒɪ) *n* the study of humans, their origins, physical characteristics, institutions, religious beliefs, social relationships, etc. See also **cultural anthropology, ethnology, physical anthropology, social anthropology.** ▸ **anthropological** (ˌænθrəpəˈlɒdʒɪkᵊl) *adj* ▸ **ˌanthropoˈlogically** *adv* ▸ **ˌanthroˈpologist** *n*

anthropometry (ˌænθrəˈpɒmɪtrɪ) *n* the comparative study of sizes and proportions of the human body. ▸ **anthropometric** (ˌænθrəpəˈmɛtrɪk) *or* **ˌanthropoˈmetrical** *adj* ▸ **ˌanthropoˈmetrically** *adv* ▸ **ˌanthroˈpometrist** *n*

anthropomorphic (ˌænθrəpəˈmɔːfɪk) *adj* **1** of or relating to anthropomorphism. **2** resembling the human form. ▸ **ˈanthropoˌmorph** *n* ▸ **ˌanthropoˈmorphically** *adv*

anthropomorphism (ˌænθrəpəˈmɔːfɪzəm) *n* the attribution of human form or behaviour to a deity, animal, etc. ▸ **ˌanthropoˈmorphist** *n*

anthropomorphize *or* **anthropomorphise** (ˌænθrəpəˈmɔːfaɪz) *vb* to attribute or ascribe human form or behaviour to (a god, animal, object, etc.).

anthropomorphosis (ˌænθrəpəˈmɔːfəsɪs) *n* transformation into human form.

anthropomorphous (ˌænθrəpəˈmɔːfəs) *adj* **1** shaped like a human being. **2** another word for **anthropomorphic.** ▸ **ˌanthropoˈmorphously** *adv*

anthropopathy (ˌænθrəˈpɒpəθɪ) *or* **anthropopathism** *n* the attribution of human passions, etc., to a deity, object, etc. ▸ **anthropopathic** (ˌænθrəpəˈpæθɪk) *adj*

anthropophagi (ˌænθrəˈpɒfəˌgaɪ) *pl n, sing* **-gus** (-gəs). cannibals. [C16: from Latin, from Greek *anthrōpophagos;* see ANTHROPO-, -PHAGY]

anthropophagite (ˌænθrəˈpɒfəˌgaɪt) *n* a rare word for **cannibal.** ▸ **anthropophagy** (ˌænθrəˈpɒfədʒɪ) *n* ▸ **anthropophagic** (ˌænθrəpəˈfædʒɪk) *adj* ▸ **ˌanthroˈpophagous** *adj*

anthropophyte (ænˈθrɒpəˌfaɪt) *n* a plant species accidentally introduced during the cultivation of another.

anthroposophy (ˌænθrəˈpɒsəfɪ) *n* the spiritual and mystical teachings of Rudolph Steiner, based on the belief that creative activities such as myth making, which formed a part of life in earlier times, are psychologically valuable, esp. for educational and therapeutic purposes. ▸ **anthroposophic** (ˌænθrəpəʊˈsɒfɪk) *adj* ▸ **ˌanthroˈposophist** *n*

anthurium (ænˈθjʊərɪəm) *n* any of various tropical American aroid plants constituting the genus *Anthurium,* many of which are cultivated as house plants for their showy foliage and their flowers, which have a long-stalked spike surrounded by a flaring heart-shaped white or red bract. [C19: New Latin, from ANTHO- + Greek *oura* a tail]

anti (ˈæntɪ) *Informal.* ◆ *adj* **1** opposed to a party, policy, attitude, etc.: *he won't join because he is rather anti.* ◆ *n* **2** an opponent of a party, policy, etc.

anti- *prefix* **1** against; opposing: *anticlerical; antisocial.* **2** opposite to: *anticlimax; antimere.* **3** rival; false: *antipope.* **4** counteracting, inhibiting, or neutralizing: *antifreeze; antihistamine.* [from Greek *anti*]

anti-aircraft (ˌæntɪˈɛəkrɑːft) *n* (*modifier*) of or relating to defence against aircraft attack: *anti-aircraft batteries.*

antiar (ˈæntɪˌɑː) *n* another name for **upas** (senses 1, 2). [from Javanese]

antibaryon (ˌæntɪˈbærɪɒn) *n Physics.* the antiparticle of any of the baryons.

Antibes (*French* ɑ̃tib) *n* a port and resort in SE France, on the Mediterranean: an important Roman town. Pop.: 60 000 (latest est.).

antibiosis (ˌæntɪbaɪˈəʊsɪs) *n* an association between two organisms, esp. microorganisms, that is harmful to one of them.

antibiotic (ˌæntɪbaɪˈɒtɪk) *n* **1** any of various chemical substances, such as penicillin, streptomycin, neomycin, and tetracycline, produced by various microorganisms, esp. fungi, or made synthetically and capable of destroying or inhibiting the growth of microorganisms, esp. bacteria. ◆ *adj* **2** of or relating to antibiotics.

antibody (ˈæntɪˌbɒdɪ) *n, pl* **-bodies.** any of various proteins produced in the blood in response to the presence of an antigen. By becoming attached to antigens on infectious organisms antibodies can render them harmless or cause them to be destroyed. See also **immunoglobulin.**

antic (ˈæntɪk) *n* **1** *Archaic.* an actor in a ludicrous or grotesque part; clown; buffoon. ◆ *adj* **2** *Archaic.* fantastic; grotesque. ◆ See also **antics.** [C16: from Italian *antico* something ancient, or grotesque (from its application to fantastic carvings found in ruins of ancient Rome); see ANTIQUE]

anticatalyst (ˌæntɪˈkætəlɪst) *n* **1** a substance that destroys or diminishes the activity of a catalyst. **2** another name for **inhibitor** (sense 2).

anticathode (ˌæntɪˈkæθəʊd) *n* the target electrode for the stream of electrons in a vacuum tube, esp. an X-ray tube.

antichlor (ˈæntɪˌklɔː) *n* a substance used to remove chlorine from a material after bleaching. [C19: from ANTI- + CHLOR(INE)] ▸ **ˌantichloˈristic** *adj*

anticholinergic (ˌæntɪˌkɒlɪˈnɜːdʒɪk) *adj* **1** *Physiol.* blocking nerve impulses through the parasympathetic nerves. ◆ *n* **2** *Med.* a drug or agent that blocks these nerve impulses, used esp. to control intestinal spasm.

anticholinesterase (ˌæntɪˌkɒləˈnɛstəˌreɪz) *n* any of a group of substances that inhibit the action of cholinesterase.

Antichrist (ˈæntɪˌkraɪst) *n* **1** *New Testament.* the antagonist of Christ, expected by early Christians to appear and reign over the world until overthrown at Christ's Second Coming. **2** (*sometimes not cap.*) an enemy of Christ or Christianity. ▸ **ˌAntiˈchristian** *adj*

anticipant (ænˈtɪsɪpənt) *adj* **1** operating in advance; expectant. ◆ *n* **2** a person who anticipates.

anticipate (ænˈtɪsɪˌpeɪt) *vb* (*mainly tr*) **1** (*may take a clause as object*) to foresee and act in advance of: *he anticipated the fall in value by selling early.* **2** to thwart by acting in advance of; forestall: *I anticipated his punch by moving out of reach.* **3** (*also intr*) to mention (something) before its proper time: *don't anticipate the climax of the story.* **4** (*may take a clause as object*) to regard as likely; expect; foresee: *he anticipated that it would happen.* **5** to make use of in advance of possession: *he anticipated his salary in buying a house.* **6** to pay (a bill, etc.) before it falls due. **7** to cause to happen sooner: *the spread of nationalism anticipated the decline of the Empire.* [C16: from Latin *anticipāre* to take before, realize beforehand, from *anti-* ANTE- + *capere* to take] ▸ **anˈticiˌpator** *n* ▸ **anˈticipatory** *or* **anˈticipative** *adj* ▸ **anˈticipatorily** *or* **anˈticipatively** *adv*

USAGE The use of *anticipate* to mean *expect* should be avoided.

anticipation (ænˌtɪsɪˈpeɪʃən) *n* **1** the act of anticipating; expectation, premonition, or foresight. **2** the act of taking or dealing with funds before they are legally available or due. **3** *Music.* an unstressed, usually short note introduced before a downbeat and harmonically related to the chord immediately following it. Compare **suspension** (sense 11).

anticlastic (ˌæntɪˈklæstɪk) *adj Maths.* (of a surface) having a curvature, at a given point and in a particular direction, that is of the opposite sign to the curvature at that point in a perpendicular direction. Compare **synclastic.**

anticlerical (ˌæntɪˈklɛrɪkᵊl) *adj* **1** opposed to the power and influence of the clergy, esp. in politics. ◆ *n* **2** a supporter of an anticlerical party. ▸ **ˌantiˈclericalism** *n*

anticlimax (ˌæntɪˈklaɪmæks) *n* **1** a disappointing or ineffective conclusion to a series of events, etc. **2** a sudden change from a serious subject to one that is disappointing or ludicrous. **3** *Rhetoric.* a descent in discourse from the significant or important to the trivial, inconsequential, etc. ▸ **anticlimactic** (ˌæntɪklaɪˈmæktɪk) *adj* ▸ **ˌanticliˈmactically** *adv*

anticlinal (ˌæntɪˈklaɪnᵊl) *adj* **1** of, relating to, or resembling an anticline. **2** *Botany.* of or relating to the plane at right angles to the surface of an organ.

anticline (ˈæntɪˌklaɪn) *n* a formation of stratified rock raised up, by folding, into a broad arch so that the strata slope down on both sides from a common crest. Compare **syncline.**

anticlinorium (ˌæntɪklaɪˈnɔːrɪəm) *n, pl* **-noria** (-ˈnɔːrɪə). a vast elongated anticline with its strata further folded into anticlines and synclines.

anticlockwise (ˌæntɪˈklɒkˌwaɪz) *adv, adj* in the opposite direction to the rotation of the hands of a clock. U.S. equivalent: **counterclockwise.**

anticoagulant (ˌæntɪkəʊˈægjʊlənt) *adj* **1** acting to prevent or retard coagulation, esp. of blood. ◆ *n* **2** an agent that prevents or retards coagulation.

anticoincidence (ˌæntɪkəʊˈɪnsɪdəns) *n* (*modifier*) of or relating to an electronic circuit that produces an output pulse if one but not both of its input terminals receives a pulse within a specified interval of time. Compare **coincidence** (sense 3).

anticonvulsant (ˌæntɪkənˈvʌlsənt) *n* **1** any of a class of drugs used to relieve convulsions. ◆ *adj* **2** of or relating to this class of drugs.

Anti-Corn Law League *n* an organization founded in 1839 by Richard Cobden and John Bright to oppose the Corn Laws, which were repealed in 1846.

Anticosti (ˌæntɪˈkɒstɪ) *n* an island of E Canada, in the Gulf of St Lawrence; part of Quebec. Area: 7881 sq. km (3043 sq. miles).

antics (ˈæntɪks) *pl n* absurd or grotesque acts or postures.

anticyclone (ˌæntɪˈsaɪkləʊn) *n Meteorol.* a body of moving air of higher pressure than the surrounding air, in which the pressure decreases away from the centre. Winds circulate around the centre in a clockwise direction in the N hemisphere and anticlockwise in the S hemisphere. Also called: **high.** ▸ **anticyclonic** (ˌæntɪsaɪˈklɒnɪk) *adj*

antidazzle mirror (ˈæntɪˌdæzᵊl) *n* a rear-view mirror for road vehicles that only partially reflects headlights behind.

ˌanti-aˈbortion *adj*	**ˌanti-aˈpartheid** *adj*	**ˌanti-ˈBritish** *adj*	**ˌantiˈcensorˌship** *adj, n*
ˌanti-aˈbortionist *n, adj*	**ˌantibacˈterial** *adj*	**ˌantiˈcapitalist** *n, adj*	**ˌanti-ˈCommunist** *n, adj*
ˌanti-ˈageing *adj*	**ˌantibalˈlistic** *adj*	**ˌanti-ˈCatholic** *adj, n*	**ˌantiˌconstiˈtutional** *adj*
ˌanti-Aˈmerican *adj*	**ˌanti-ˈBolshevik** *n, adj*	**ˌanti-Caˈtholiˌcism** *n*	

antidepressant (ˌæntɪdɪˈprɛsᵊnt) *n* **1** any of a class of drugs used to alleviate depression. ◆ *adj* **2** of or relating to this class of drugs.

antidiuretic hormone (ˌæntɪˌdaɪjʊˈrɛtɪk) *n* another name for **vasopressin.** Abbrev.: **ADH.**

antidote (ˈæntɪˌdəʊt) *n* **1** *Med.* a drug or agent that counteracts or neutralizes the effects of a poison. **2** anything that counteracts or relieves a harmful or unwanted condition; remedy. [C15: from Latin *antidotum,* from Greek *antidoton* something given as a countermeasure, from ANTI- + *didonai* to give] ▸ ˌantiˈ**dotal** *adj*

antidromic (ˌæntɪˈdrɒmɪk) *adj* **1** (of nerve fibres) conducting nerve impulses in a direction opposite to normal. **2** (of plants) showing twining to the left and right in members of the same species. [from ANTI- + Greek *dromos* course]

antidune (ˈæntɪˌdjuːn) *n* a sand hill or inclined bedding plane that forms a steep slope against the direction of a fast-flowing current.

antiemetic (ˌæntɪɪˈmɛtɪk) *adj* **1** preventing vomiting. ◆ *n* **2** any antiemetic drug, such as promethazine.

Antietam (ænˈtiːtəm) *n* a creek in NW Maryland, flowing into the Potomac: scene of a Civil War battle (1862), in which the Confederate forces of General Robert E. Lee were defeated.

antifebrile (ˌæntɪˈfiːbraɪl) *adj* **1** reducing fever; antipyretic. ◆ *n* **2** an antifebrile agent or drug.

Antifederalist (ˌæntɪˈfɛdərəlɪst, -ˈfɛdrə-) *n* **1** *U.S. history.* a person who opposed the ratification of the Constitution in 1789 and thereafter allied with Thomas Jefferson's Antifederal Party, which opposed extension of the powers of the federal Government. **2** (*often not cap.*) any person who opposes federalism.

antiferromagnetism (ˌæntɪˌfɛrəʊˈmægnɪˌtɪzəm) *n Physics.* the phenomenon exhibited by substances that resemble paramagnetic substances in the value of their relative permeability but that behave like ferromagnetic substances when their temperature is varied. See also **ferrimagnetism.**

antifouling (ˌæntɪˈfaʊlɪŋ) *adj* **1** (of a paint or other coating) inhibiting the growth of barnacles and other marine organisms on a ship's bottom. ◆ *n* **2** an antifouling paint or other coating.

antifreeze (ˈæntɪˌfriːz) *n* a liquid, usually ethylene glycol (ethanediol), added to cooling water to lower its freezing point, esp. for use in an internal-combustion engine.

antifriction metal (ˌæntɪˈfrɪkʃən) *n* another name for **white metal.**

antifungal (ˌæntɪˈfʌŋgᵊl) *adj* **1** inhibiting the growth of fungi. **2** (of a drug) possessing antifungal properties and therefore used to treat fungal infections. Also: **antimycotic.**

antigen (ˈæntɪdʒən, -ˌdʒɛn) *n* a substance that stimulates the production of antibodies. [C20: from ANTI(BODY) + -GEN] ▸ ˌantiˈ**genic** *adj* ▸ ˌantiˈ**genically** *adv*

antigenic determinant *n* the specific part of an antigen molecule to which an antibody becomes attached.

antiglobulin (ˌæntɪˈglɒbjʊlɪn) *n* a serum containing antibody specific to an immunoglobulin.

Antigone (ænˈtɪgənɪ) *n Greek myth.* daughter of Oedipus and Jocasta, who was condemned to death for cremating the body of her brother Polynices in defiance of an edict of her uncle, King Creon of Thebes.

Antigonus I (ænˈtɪgənəs) *n* known as *Cyclops.* 382–301 B.C., Macedonian general under Alexander the Great; king of Macedon (306–301).

anti-G suit *n* another name for **G-suit.**

Antigua (ænˈtiːgə) *n* an island in the Caribbean, one of the Leeward Islands: a British colony, with its dependency Barbuda, until 1967, when it became a British associated state; it became independent in 1981 as part of the state of Antigua and Barbuda. Area: 279 sq. km (108 sq. miles). ▸ **Anˈtiguan** *adj, n*

Antigua and Barbuda *n* a state in the Caribbean, comprising the islands of Antigua, Barbuda, and Redonda: gained independence in 1981: a member of the Commonwealth. Official language: English. Religion: Christian majority. Currency: East Caribbean dollar. Capital: St John's. Pop.: 69 100 (1998 est.). Area: 442 sq. km (171 sq. miles).

antihalation (ˌantɪhəˈleɪʃən) *n Photog.* **a** a process by which light, passing through the emulsion on a film or plate, is not reflected back into it but is absorbed by a layer of dye or pigment, usually on the back of the film, thus preventing halation. **b** (*as modifier*): *antihalation backing.*

antihelix (ˌæntɪˈhiːlɪks) *n, pl* **-helices** (-ˈhiːlɪsiːz) *or* **-helixes.** a variant spelling of **anthelix.**

antihero (ˈæntɪˌhɪərəʊ) *n, pl* **-roes.** a central character in a novel, play, etc., who lacks the traditional heroic virtues.

antihistamine (ˌæntɪˈhɪstəˌmiːn, -mɪn) *n* any drug that neutralizes the effects of histamine, used esp. in the treatment of allergies.

anti-icer *n* a device fitted to an aircraft to prevent the formation of ice. Compare **de-icer.**

anti-inflammatory *adj* **1** reducing inflammation. ◆ *n* **2** any anti-inflammatory drug, such as cortisone, aspirin, or ibuprofen.

antiknock (ˌæntɪˈnɒk) *n* a compound, such as lead tetraethyl, added to petrol to reduce knocking in the engine.

Anti-Lebanon *n* a mountain range running north and south between Syria and Lebanon, east of the Lebanon Mountains. Highest peak: Mount Hermon, 2814 m (9232 ft.).

antilepton (ˌæntɪˈlɛptɒn) *n Physics.* the antiparticle of any of the leptons.

Antilles (ænˈtɪliːz) *pl n* **the.** a group of islands in the Caribbean consisting of the **Greater Antilles** and the **Lesser Antilles.**

antilock brake (ˈæntɪˌlɒk) *n* a brake fitted to some road vehicles that prevents skidding and improves control by sensing and compensating for overbraking. Also called: **ABS brake.**

antilog (ˈæntɪˌlɒg) *n* short for **antilogarithm.**

antilogarithm (ˌæntɪˈlɒgəˌrɪðəm) *n* a number whose logarithm to a given base is a given number: *100 is the antilogarithm of 2 to base 10.* Often shortened to **antilog.** ▸ ˌantiˌlogaˈ**rithmic** *adj*

antilogy (ænˈtɪlədʒɪ) *n, pl* **-gies.** a contradiction in terms. [C17: from Greek *antilogia*]

antimacassar (ˌæntɪməˈkæsə) *n* a cloth covering the back and arms of chairs, etc., to prevent soiling or as decoration. [C19: from ANTI- + MACASSAR (OIL)]

antimagnetic (ˌæntɪmægˈnɛtɪk) *adj* of or constructed of a material that does not acquire permanent magnetism when exposed to a magnetic field: *an antimagnetic watch.*

antimalarial (ˌæntɪməˈlɛərɪəl) *adj* **1** effective in the treatment of malaria. ◆ *n* **2** an antimalarial drug or agent.

antimasque (ˈæntɪˌmɑːsk) *n* a comic or grotesque dance, presented between the acts of a masque.

antimatter (ˈæntɪˌmætə) *n* a form of matter composed of antiparticles, such as antihydrogen, consisting of antiprotons and positrons.

antimere (ˈæntɪˌmɪə) *n* a part or organ of a bilaterally or radially symmetrical organism that corresponds to a similar structure on the other side of the axis, such as the right or left limb of a four-legged animal. Also called: **actinomere.** ▸ **antimeric** (ˌæntɪˈmɛrɪk) *adj* ▸ **antimerism** (ænˈtɪməˌrɪzəm) *n*

antimetabolite (ˌæntɪmɪˈtæbəˌlaɪt) *n* any drug that acts by disrupting the normal growth of a cell. Antimetabolites are used in cancer treatment.

antimissile (ˌæntɪˈmɪsaɪl) *adj* **1** relating to defensive measures against missile attack: *an antimissile system.* ◆ *n* **2** Also called: **antimissile missile.** a defensive missile used to intercept and destroy attacking missiles.

antimonial (ˌæntɪˈməʊnɪəl) *adj* **1** of or containing antimony. ◆ *n* **2** a drug or agent containing antimony.

antimonic (ˌæntɪˈmɒnɪk) *adj* of or containing antimony in the pentavalent state.

antimonous (ˈæntɪmənəs) *adj* of or containing antimony in the trivalent state.

antimony (ˈæntɪmənɪ) *n* a toxic metallic element that exists in two allotropic forms and occurs principally in stibnite. The stable form is a brittle silvery-white crystalline metal that is added to alloys to increase their strength and hardness and is used in semiconductors. Symbol: Sb; atomic no.: 51; atomic wt.: 121.757; valency: 0, –3, +3, or +5; relative density: 6.691; melting pt.: 630.76°C; boiling pt.: 1587°C. [C15: from Medieval Latin *antimōnium,* of uncertain origin]

antimonyl (ˈæntɪmənɪl, ænˈtɪm-) *n* (*modifier*) of, consisting of, or containing the monovalent group SbO-: *an antimonyl group or radical.*

antimony potassium tartrate *n* a colourless odourless poisonous crystalline salt used as a mordant for textiles and leather, as an insecticide, and as an anthelmintic. Formula: $K(SbO)C_4H_4O_6$. Also called: **tartar emetic.**

antimuon (ˌæntɪˈmjuːɒn) *n* the antiparticle of a muon.

antimutagen (ˌæntɪˈmjuːtədʒən) *n* any substance that acts against a mutagen.

antimycotic (ˌæntɪmaɪˈkɒtɪk) *adj* another word for **antifungal.**

antineutrino (ˌæntɪnjuːˈtriːnəʊ) *n, pl* **-nos.** the antiparticle of a neutrino; a particle having the opposite spin to a neutrino.

antineutron (ˌæntɪˈnjuːtrɒn) *n* the antiparticle of a neutron; a particle having the same mass as the neutron but a magnetic moment of opposite sign.

anting (ˈæntɪŋ) *n* the placing or rubbing of ants by birds on their feathers. The body fluids of the ants are thought to repel parasites.

antinode (ˈæntɪˌnəʊd) *n Physics.* a point at which the amplitude of one of the two kinds of displacement in a standing wave has maximum value. Generally the other kind of displacement has its minimum value at this point. See also **standing wave.** Compare **node.** ▸ ˌantiˈ**nodal** *adj*

antinoise (ˈæntɪˌnɔɪz) *n* sound generated so that it is out of phase with a noise, such as that made by an engine, in order to reduce the noise level by interference.

antinomian (ˌæntɪˈnəʊmɪən) *adj* **1** relating to the doctrine that by faith and the dispensation of grace a Christian is released from the obligation of adhering to any moral law. ◆ *n* **2** a member of a Christian sect holding such a doctrine. ▸ ˌantiˈ**nomianism** *n*

antinomy (ænˈtɪnəmɪ) *n, pl* **-mies. 1** opposition of one law, principle, or rule to another; contradiction within a law. **2** *Philosophy.* contradiction existing between two apparently indubitable propositions; paradox. [C16: from Latin *antinomia,* from Greek: conflict between laws, from ANTI- + *nomos* law] ▸ **antinomic** (ˌæntɪˈnɒmɪk) *adj* ▸ ˌantiˈ**nomically** *adv*

antinovel (ˈæntɪˌnɒvᵊl) *n* a type of prose fiction in which conventional or traditional novelistic elements are rejected. Also called: **anti-roman, nouveau roman.**

antinuclear (ˌæntɪˈnjuːklɪə) *adj* opposed to nuclear weapons. ▸ ˌantiˈ**nuclearist** *n*

antinucleon (ˌæntɪˈnjuːklɪˌɒn) *n* an antiproton or an antineutron.

Antioch (ˈæntɪˌɒk) *n* a city in S Turkey, on the Orantes River: ancient commercial centre and capital of Syria (300–64 B.C.); early centre of Christianity. Pop.: 137 200 (1994 est.). Arabic name: **Antakiya.** Turkish name: **Antakya.**

ˌantiˌdemoˈ**cratic** *adj*	ˌantiˈ**fascist** *n, adj*	ˌantiˈ**labour** *adj*	ˌantiˈ**nationalist** *n, adj*
ˌantiˌdiuˈ**retic** *adj, n*	ˌ**anti-imˈperialˌism** *n*	ˌantimiˈ**crobial** *adj*	ˌ**anti-ˈNazi** *adj, n*
ˌ**anti-Esˈtablishment** *adj*	ˌ**anti-imˈperialist** *adj, n*	ˌantimoˈ**narchical** *adj*	ˌantiˈ**noise** *adj*
ˌ**anti-ˌEuroˈpeanism** *n*	ˌ**anti-inˈflationary** *adj*	ˌantiˈ**monarchist** *adj, n*	

Antiochus III (æn'taɪəkəs) *n* known as *Antiochus the Great*. 242–187 B.C., king of Syria (223–187), who greatly extended the Seleucid empire but was forced (190) to surrender most of Asia Minor to the Romans.

Antiochus IV *n* ?215–164 B.C., Seleucid king of Syria (175–164), who attacked the Jews and provoked the revolt of the Maccabees.

antioxidant (ˌæntɪ'ɒksɪdənt) *n* **1** any substance that retards deterioration by oxidation, esp. of fats, oils, foods, petroleum products, or rubber. **2** *Biol.* a substance, such as vitamin C, vitamin E, or beta carotene, that counteracts the damaging effects of oxidation in a living organism.

antiparallel (ˌæntɪ'pærəˌlɛl) *adj* **1** *Physics.* parallel but pointing or rotating in opposite directions. **2** *Maths.* (of two lines) cutting two given lines so that in the quadrilateral formed the interior opposite angles are supplementary. **3** *Maths.* (of vectors) parallel but having opposite directions.

antiparticle ('æntɪˌpɑːtɪkᵊl) *n* any of a group of elementary particles that have the same mass as their corresponding particle but have a charge, baryon number, strangeness, and isospin quantum number, I_3, of equal magnitude but opposite sign. When a particle collides with its antiparticle mutual annihilation occurs.

antipasto (ˌæntɪ'pɑːstəʊ, -'pæs-) *n, pl* **-tos.** a course of hors d'oeuvres in an Italian meal. **[**Italian: before food**]**

Antipater (æn'tɪpətə) *n* ?398–319 B.C., Macedonian general under Alexander the Great: regent of Macedon (334–323).

antipathetic (ænˌtɪpə'θɛtɪk, ˌæntɪpə-) *or* **antipathetical** *adj* (often foll. by *to*) having or arousing a strong aversion. ► **ˌantipa'thetically** *adv*

antipathy (æn'tɪpəθɪ) *n, pl* **-thies. 1** a feeling of intense aversion, dislike, or hostility. **2** the object of such a feeling. **[C17:** from Latin *antipathia,* from Greek *antipatheia,* from ANTI- + *patheia* feeling**]**

antiperiodic (ˌæntɪˌpɪərɪ'ɒdɪk) *Med.* ◆ *adj* **1** efficacious against recurring attacks of a disease. ◆ *n* **2** an antiperiodic drug or agent.

antiperistalsis (ˌæntɪˌpɛrɪ'stælsɪs) *n Physiol.* contractions of the intestine that force the contents in the opposite direction to the normal. ► **ˌantiˌperi'staltic** *adj*

antipersonnel (ˌæntɪˌpɜːsə'nɛl) *adj* (of weapons, etc.) designed to cause casualties to personnel rather than to destroy equipment or defences.

antiperspirant (ˌæntɪ'pɜːspərənt) *n* **1** an astringent substance applied to the skin to reduce or prevent perspiration. ◆ *adj* **2** reducing or preventing perspiration.

antiphlogistic (ˌæntɪflə'dʒɪstɪk) *adj* **1** of or relating to the prevention or alleviation of inflammation. ◆ *n* **2** an antiphlogistic agent or drug.

antiphon ('æntɪfən) *n* **1** a short passage, usually from the Bible, recited or sung as a response after certain parts of a liturgical service. **2** a psalm, hymn, etc., chanted or sung in alternate parts. **3** any response or answer. **[C15:** from Late Latin *antiphōna* sung responses, from Late Greek, plural of *antiphōnon* (something) responsive, from *antiphōnos,* from ANTI- + *phōnē* sound**]**

antiphonal (æn'tɪfənəl) *adj* **1** sung or recited in alternation. ◆ *n* **2** another word for **antiphonary.** ► **an'tiphonally** *adv*

antiphonary (æn'tɪfənərɪ) *n, pl* **-naries. 1** a bound collection of antiphons, esp. for use in the divine office. ◆ *adj* **2** of or relating to such a book.

antiphony (æn'tɪfənɪ) *n, pl* **-nies. 1** the antiphonal singing of a musical composition by two choirs. **2** any musical or other sound effect that answers or echoes another.

antiphrasis (æn'tɪfrəsɪs) *n Rhetoric.* the use of a word in a sense opposite to its normal one, esp. for ironic effect. **[C16:** via Late Latin from Greek, from ANTI- + *phrasis,* from *phrazein* to speak**]**

antipodal (æn'tɪpədᵊl) *adj* **1** of or relating to diametrically opposite points on the earth's surface. **2** exactly or diametrically opposite.

antipode ('æntɪpəʊd) *n* the exact or direct opposite.

antipodes (æn'tɪpəˌdiːz) *pl n* **1** either or both of two points, places, or regions that are situated diametrically opposite to one another on the earth's surface, esp. the country or region opposite one's own. **2** the people who live there. **3** (*often cap.*) **the.** Australia and New Zealand. **4** (*sometimes functioning as sing*) the exact or direct opposite. **[C16:** via Late Latin from Greek, plural of *antipous* having the feet opposite, from ANTI- + *pous* foot**]** ► **antipodean** (ænˌtɪpə'diːən) *adj*

Antipodes Islands *pl n* **the.** a group of small uninhabited islands in the South Pacific, southeast of and belonging to New Zealand. Area: 62 sq. km (24 sq. miles).

antipope ('æntɪˌpəʊp) *n* a rival pope elected in opposition to one who has been canonically chosen.

antiproton ('æntɪˌprəʊtɒn) *n* the antiparticle of the proton; a particle having the same mass as the proton but an equal and opposite charge.

antipsychiatry (ˌæntɪsaɪ'kaɪətrɪ) *n* an approach to mental disorders that makes use of concepts derived from existentialism, psychoanalysis, and sociological theory.

antipsychotic (ˌæntɪsaɪ'kɒtɪk) *adj* **1** preventing or treating psychosis. ◆ *n* **2** any antipsychotic drug, such as chlorpromazine: used to treat such conditions as schizophrenia.

antipyretic (ˌæntɪpaɪ'rɛtɪk) *adj* **1** preventing or alleviating fever. ◆ *n* **2** an antipyretic remedy or drug. ► **antipyresis** (ˌæntɪpaɪ'riːsɪs) *n*

antipyrine (ˌæntɪ'paɪrɪn, -riːn) *n* a white powder formerly used medicinally to reduce pain and fever. Formula: $C_{11}H_{12}N_2O$.

antiq. *abbrev. for:* **1** antiquarian. **2** antiquity.

antiquarian (ˌæntɪ'kwɛərɪən) *adj* **1** concerned with the study of antiquities or antiques. ◆ *n* **2** the largest size of handmade drawing paper, 53 × 31 inches. **3** a less common name for **antiquary.** ► **ˌanti'quarianism** *n*

antiquark ('æntɪkwɑːk) *n* the antiparticle of a quark.

antiquary ('æntɪkwərɪ) *n, pl* **-quaries.** a person who collects, deals in, or studies antiques, ancient works of art, or ancient times. Also called: **antiquarian.**

antiquate ('æntɪˌkweɪt) *vb* (*tr*) **1** to make obsolete or old-fashioned. **2** to give an old or antique appearance to. **[C15:** from Latin *antīquāre* to make old, from *antīquus* ancient**]**

antiquated ('æntɪˌkweɪtɪd) *adj* **1** outmoded; obsolete. **2** aged; ancient. ► **'antiˌquatedness** *n*

antique (æn'tiːk) *n* **1a** a decorative object, piece of furniture, or other work of art created in an earlier period, that is collected and valued for its beauty, workmanship, and age. **1b** (*as modifier*): *an antique shop.* **2** any object made in an earlier period. **3 the.** the style of ancient art, esp. Greek or Roman art, or an example of it. ◆ *adj* **4** made in or in the style of an earlier period. **5** of or belonging to the distant past, esp. of or in the style of ancient Greece or Rome. **6** *Informal.* old-fashioned; out-of-date. **7** *Archaic.* aged or venerable. **8** (of paper) not calendered or coated; having a rough surface. ◆ *vb* **9** (*tr*) to give an antique appearance to. **[C16:** from Latin *antīquus* ancient, from *ante* before**]**

antiquities (æn'tɪkwɪtɪz) *pl n* remains or relics, such as statues, buildings, or coins, that date from ancient times.

antiquity (æn'tɪkwɪtɪ) *n, pl* **-ties. 1** the quality of being ancient or very old: *a vase of great antiquity.* **2** the far distant past, esp. the time preceding the Middle Ages in Europe. **3** the people of ancient times collectively; the ancients.

antirachitic (ˌæntɪrə'kɪtɪk) *adj* **1** preventing or curing rickets. ◆ *n* **2** an antirachitic remedy or agent.

antiracism (ˌæntɪ'reɪsɪzəm) *n* the policy of challenging racism and promoting racial tolerance. ► **ˌanti'racist** *n, adj*

Antiremonstrant (ˌæntɪrɪ'mɒnstrənt) *n Dutch Reformed Church.* the party that opposed the Remonstrants.

anti-roll bar *n* a crosswise rubber-mounted bar in the suspension of a motor vehicle, which counteracts the movement downward on one side when cornering.

anti-roman *French.* (ɑ̃tirɔmɑ̃) *n, pl* ***anti-romans*** (ɑ̃tirɔmɑ̃) another term for **antinovel. [**literally: anti-novel**]**

antirrhinum (ˌæntɪ'raɪnəm) *n* any scrophulariaceous plant of the genus *Antirrhinum,* esp. the snapdragon, which have two-lipped flowers of various colours. **[C16:** via Latin from Greek *antirrhinon,* from ANTI- (imitating) + *rhis* nose; so called from a fancied likeness to an animal's snout**]**

Antisana (*Spanish* anti'sana) *n* a volcano in N central Ecuador, in the Andes. Height: 5756 m (18 885 ft.).

antiscorbutic (ˌæntɪskɔː'bjuːtɪk) *adj* **1** preventing or curing scurvy. ◆ *n* **2** an antiscorbutic remedy or agent.

anti-Semite *n* a person who persecutes or discriminates against Jews. ► **ˌanti-Se'mitic** *adj* ► **ˌanti-Se'mitically** *adv* ► **ˌanti-'Semitism** *n*

antisepsis (ˌæntɪ'sɛpsɪs) *n* **1** destruction of undesirable microorganisms, such as those that cause disease or putrefaction. Compare **asepsis. 2** the state or condition of being free from such microorganisms.

antiseptic (ˌæntɪ'sɛptɪk) *adj* **1** of, relating to, or effecting antisepsis. **2** entirely free from contamination. **3** *Informal.* lacking spirit or excitement; clinical. ◆ *n* **4** an antiseptic agent or substance. ► **ˌanti'septically** *adv*

antiserum (ˌæntɪ'sɪərəm) *n, pl* **-rums** *or* **-ra** (-rə). blood serum containing antibodies against a specific antigen, used to treat or provide immunity to a disease.

antislavery (ˌæntɪ'sleɪvərɪ) *adj* opposed to slavery, esp. slavery of Blacks.

antisocial (ˌæntɪ'səʊʃəl) *adj* **1** avoiding the company of other people; unsociable. **2** contrary or injurious to the interests of society in general. ► **ˌanti'socially** *adv*

antispasmodic (ˌæntɪspæz'mɒdɪk) *adj* **1** preventing or arresting spasms. ◆ *n* **2** an antispasmodic drug.

antistatic (ˌæntɪ'stætɪk) *adj* (of a substance, textile, etc.) retaining sufficient moisture to provide a conducting path, thus avoiding the effects of static electricity.

Antisthenes (æn'tɪsθəˌniːz) *n* ?445–365 B.C., Greek philosopher, founder of the Cynic school, who taught that the only good was virtue, won by self-control and independence from worldly needs.

antistrophe (æn'tɪstrəfɪ) *n* **1** (in ancient Greek drama) **1a** the second of two movements made by a chorus during the performance of a choral ode. **1b** the second part of a choral ode sung during this movement. **2** (in classical prosody) the second of two metrical systems used alternately within a poem. ◆ See **strophe. [C17:** via Late Latin from Greek *antistrophē* an answering turn, from ANTI- + *strophē* a turning**]** ► **antistrophic** (ˌæntɪ'strɒfɪk) *adj* ► **ˌanti'strophically** *adv*

antisymmetric (ˌæntɪsɪ'mɛtrɪk) *adj Logic.* (of a relation) never holding between a pair of arguments *x* and *y* when it holds between *y* and *x* except when *x* = *y,* as *"... is no younger than ...."* Compare **asymmetric, symmetric** (sense 1), **nonsymmetric.**

antitank (ˌæntɪ'tæŋk) *adj* designed to immobilize or destroy armoured vehicles: *antitank weapons.*

antithesis (æn'tɪθɪsɪs) *n, pl* **-ses** (-ˌsiːz). **1** the exact opposite. **2** contrast or op-

ˌantipo'litical *adj*
ˌantipol'lution *adj, n*
ˌanti-'Protestant *adj, n*
ˌantire'ligious *adj*
ˌantire'publican *adj, n*
ˌantiˌrevo'lutionary *adj, n, pl* **-aries.**
ˌanti'riot *adj*
ˌanti'rust *adj*
ˌantiˌscien'tific *adj*
ˌanti-'Soviet *adj, n*
ˌantiˌsubma'rine *adj*
ˌanti'terrorist *adj*

position. 3 *Rhetoric.* the juxtaposition of contrasting ideas, phrases, or words so as to produce an effect of balance, such as *my words fly up, my thoughts remain below.* 4 *Philosophy.* the second stage in the **Hegelian dialectic,** contradicting the **thesis** before resolution by the **synthesis.** [C15: via Latin from Greek: a setting against, from ANTI- + *tithenai* to place]

antithetical (ˌæntɪˈθɛtɪkᵊl) *or* **antithetic** *adj* 1 of the nature of antithesis. 2 directly contrasted.

antitoxin (ˌæntɪˈtɒksɪn) *n* 1 an antibody that neutralizes a toxin. 2 blood serum that contains a specific antibody. ▸ ˌantiˈtoxic *adj*

antitrades (ˈæntɪˌtreɪdz) *pl n* winds in the upper atmosphere blowing in the opposite direction from and above the trade winds.

antitragus (ænˈtɪtrəgəs) *n, pl* **-gi** (-ˌdʒaɪ). a cartilaginous projection of the external ear opposite the tragus. [C19: from New Latin, from Greek *antitragos;* see ANTI-, TRAGUS]

antitranspirant (ˌæntɪˈtrænspɪrənt) *n* any substance that decreases transpiration and, usually, photosynthesis.

antitrust (ˌæntɪˈtrʌst) *n* (*modifier*) *Chiefly U.S.* regulating or opposing trusts, monopolies, cartels, or similar organizations, esp. in order to prevent unfair competition.

antitussive (ˌæntɪˈtʌsɪv) *adj* 1 alleviating or suppressing coughing. ◆ *n* 2 an antitussive drug. [from ANTI- + Latin *tussis* a cough]

antitype (ˈæntɪˌtaɪp) *n* 1 a person or thing that is foreshadowed or represented by a type or symbol, esp. a character or event in the New Testament prefigured in the Old Testament. 2 an opposite type. ▸ **antitypic** (ˌæntɪˈtɪpɪk) *or* ˌ**antiˈtypical** *adj* ▸ ˌ**antiˈtypically** *adv*

antivenin (ˌæntɪˈvɛnɪn) *or* **antivenene** (ˌæntɪvɪˈniːn) *n* an antitoxin that counteracts a specific venom, esp. snake venom. [C19: from ANTI- + VEN(OM) + -IN]

antiviral (ˌæntɪˈvaɪrəl) *adj* 1 inhibiting the growth of viruses. ◆ *n* 2 any antiviral drug: used to treat diseases caused by viruses, such as herpes and AIDS.

antiworld (ˈæntɪˌwɜːld) *n* a hypothetical or supposed world or universe composed of antimatter.

antler (ˈæntlə) *n* one of a pair of bony outgrowths on the heads of male deer and some related species of either sex. The antlers are shed each year and grow more branches as the animal ages. [C14: from Old French *antoillier,* from Vulgar Latin *anteocularе* (unattested) (something) in front of the eye]

antler moth *n* a European noctuid moth, *Cerapteryx* (or *Charaeas*) *graminis,* that has white antler-like markings on the forewings and produces larvae that periodically cause great damage to pastures and grasslands.

Antlia (ˈæntlɪə) *n, Latin genitive* **Antliae** (ˈæntlɪˌiː). a faint constellation in the S hemisphere close to Hydra and Vela. [C19: from Latin, from Greek: bucket]

antlike (ˈæntˌlaɪk) *adj* 1 of or like an ant or ants. 2 characterized by scurrying activity or teeming restlessness.

antlion (ˈæntˌlaɪən) *n* 1 Also called: **antlion fly.** any of various neuropterous insects of the family *Myrmeleontidae,* which typically resemble dragonflies and are most common in tropical regions. 2 Also called (U.S.): **doodlebug.** the larva of this insect, which has very large jaws and buries itself in the sand to await its prey.

Antofagasta (ˌæntəfəˈgæstə; *Spanish* antofaˈɣasta) *n* a port in N Chile. Pop.: 236 730 (1995 est.).

Antoinette (*French* ɑ̃twanɛt) *n* See **Marie Antoinette.**

Antonello da Messina (ˌæntəˈnɛləʊ) *n* ?1430–?79, Italian painter, born in Sicily. His paintings include *St Jerome in His Study* and *Portrait of a Man.*

Antonescu (ˌæntɒˈneskjuː) *n* **Ion.** 1882–1946, Romanian general and statesman; appointed prime minister (1940) by King Carol II. He was executed for war crimes.

Antonine Wall (ˈæntənaɪn) *n* a Roman frontier defence work across S Scotland, extending between the River Clyde and the Firth of Forth. It was built in 142 A.D. on the orders of Antoninus Pius.

Antoninus (ˌæntəˈnaɪnəs) *n* See **Marcus Aurelius Antoninus.**

Antoninus Pius *n* 86–161 A.D., emperor of Rome (138–161); adopted son and successor of Hadrian.

Antonioni (ˌæntəʊnɪˈəʊnɪ) *n* **Michelangelo** (mikeˈlandʒelo). born 1912, Italian film director; his films include *L'Avventura* (1959), *La Notte* (1961), *Blow-Up* (1966), *Zabriskie Point* (1970), and *Beyond the Clouds* (1995).

Antonius (ænˈtəʊnɪəs) *n* **Marcus** (ˈmɑːkəs). Latin name of (Mark) **Antony.**

antonomasia (ˌæntənəˈmeɪzɪə) *n Rhetoric.* 1 the substitution of a title or epithet for a proper name, such as *his highness.* 2 the use of a proper name for an idea: *he is a Daniel come to judgment.* [C16: via Latin from Greek, from *antonomazein* to name differently, from *onoma* name] ▸ **antonomastic** (ˌæntənəˈmæstɪk) *adj* ▸ ˌ**antonoˈmastically** *adv*

Anton Piller order (ˈæntɒn ˈpɪlə) *n Law.* an injunction allowing a person to enter the premises of another to search for and take copies of evidence required for a court case, used esp. in cases of infringement of copyright. [C20: named after the plaintiff in a case (1976) in which such an order was made]

Antony (ˈæntənɪ) *n* **Mark.** Latin name *Marcus Antonius.* ?83–30 B.C., Roman general who served under Julius Caesar in the Gallic wars and became a member of the second triumvirate (43). He defeated Brutus and Cassius at Philippi (42) but having repudiated his wife for Cleopatra, queen of Egypt, he was defeated by his brother-in-law Octavian (Augustus) at Actium (31).

antonym (ˈæntənɪm) *n* a word that means the opposite of another word: *"empty" is an antonym of "full".* [C19: from Greek *antōnumia,* from ANTI- + *onoma* name] ▸ **antonymous** (ænˈtɒnɪməs) *adj*

antre (ˈæntə) *n Rare.* a cavern or cave. [C17: from French, from Latin *antrum,* from Greek *antron*]

Antrim (ˈæntrɪm) *n* 1 a historical county of NE Northern Ireland, famous for the Giant's Causeway on the N coast: in 1973 it was replaced for administrative purposes by the districts of Antrim, Ballymena, Ballymoney, Carrickfergus, Larne, Moyle, Newtownabbey, and parts of Belfast and Lisburn. Area: 3100 sq. km (1200 sq. miles). 2 a district of Northern Ireland, in Co. Antrim. Pop.: 44 516 (1991). Area: 415 sq. km (160 sq. miles).

antrorse (ænˈtrɔːs) *adj Biology.* directed or pointing upwards or forwards. [C19: from New Latin *antrorsus,* from *antero-* front + *-orsus,* as in Latin *introrsus;* see INTRORSE] ▸ **anˈtrorsely** *adv*

antrum (ˈæntrəm) *n, pl* **-tra** (-trə). *Anatomy.* a natural cavity, hollow, or sinus, esp. in a bone. [C14: from Latin: cave, from Greek *antron*] ▸ **ˈantral** *adj*

Antseranana (ˌæntsɪˈrænənə) *n* a port in N Madagascar: former French naval base. Pop.: 54 418 (1990). Former name: **Diégo-Suarez.**

Antung (ˈænˈtʊŋ) *n* a variant transliteration of the Chinese name for **Andong.**

Antwerp (ˈæntwɜːp) *n* 1 a province of N Belgium. Pop.: 1 631 243 (1996 est.). Area: 2859 sq. km (1104 sq. miles). 2 a port in N Belgium, capital of Antwerp province, on the River Scheldt: a major European port. Pop.: 455 852 (1996 est.). Flemish name: **Antwerpen** (ˈɑntwɛrpə). French name: **Anvers.**

Anu (ˈɑːnuː) *n Babylonian myth.* the sky god.

ANU *abbrev. for* Australian National University.

Anubis (əˈnjuːbɪs) *n Egyptian myth.* a deity, a son of Osiris, who conducted the dead to judgment. He is represented as having a jackal's head and was identified by the Greeks with Hermes.

Anuradhapura (əˈnʊərədəˌpʊərə, ˌʌnʊˈrɑːdə-) *n* a town in Sri Lanka: ancient capital of Ceylon; site of the sacred bo tree and place of pilgrimage for Buddhists. Pop.: 42 600 (1995 est.).

anuran (əˈnjʊərən) *n* 1 any of the vertebrates of the order *Anura* (or *Salientia*), characterized by absence of a tail and very long hind legs specialized for hopping: class *Amphibia* (amphibians). The group includes the frogs and toads. ◆ *adj* 2 of, relating to, or belonging to the order *Anura.* ◆ Also: **salientian.** [C20: from New Latin *Anura,* from AN- + Greek *oura* tail]

anuresis (ˌænjʊˈriːsɪs) *n Pathol.* inability to urinate even though urine is formed by the kidneys and retained in the urinary bladder. Compare **anuria.** [C20: New Latin, from AN- + Greek *ouresis* urination, from *ouron* urine]

anuria (əˈnjʊərɪə) *n Pathol.* complete suppression of urine formation, often as the result of a kidney disorder. Compare **anuresis, oliguria.** [C19: from New Latin, from AN- + Greek *ouron* urine]

anurous (æˈnjʊərəs) *adj Zoology.* lacking a tail; tailless; acaudate. [C19: from AN- + Greek *oura* tail]

anus (ˈeɪnəs) *n* the excretory opening at the end of the alimentary canal. Related adj: **anal.** [C16: from Latin]

Anvers (ɑ̃vɛr) *n* the French name for **Antwerp.**

anvil (ˈænvɪl) *n* 1 a heavy iron or steel block on which metals are hammered during forging. 2 any part having a similar shape or function, such as the lower part of a telegraph key. 3 the fixed jaw of a measurement device against which the piece to be measured is held. 4 *Anatomy.* the nontechnical name for **incus.** [Old English *anfealt;* related to Old High German *anafalz,* Middle Dutch *anvilte;* see ON, FELT[2]]

anxiety (æŋˈzaɪɪtɪ) *n, pl* **-ties.** 1 a state of uneasiness or tension caused by apprehension of possible future misfortune, danger, etc.; worry. 2 intense desire; eagerness. 3 *Psychol.* a state of intense apprehension or worry often accompanied by physical symptoms such as shaking, intense feelings in the gut, etc., common in mental illness or after a very distressing experience. See also **angst.** [C16: from Latin *anxietas;* see ANXIOUS]

anxiety disorder *n* any of various mental disorders characterized by extreme anxiety and including panic disorder, post-traumatic stress disorder, and **generalized anxiety disorder.**

anxiety neurosis *n* a relatively mild form of mental illness characterized by extreme distress and agitation, often occurring without any obvious cause.

anxiolytic (ˌæŋksɪəʊˈlɪtɪk) *n* 1 any of a class of drugs that reduce anxiety. ◆ *adj* 2 of or relating to this class of drugs.

anxious (ˈæŋkʃəs, ˈæŋʃəs) *adj* 1 worried and tense because of possible misfortune, danger, etc.; uneasy. 2 fraught with or causing anxiety; worrying; distressing: *an anxious time.* 3 intensely desirous; eager: *anxious for promotion.* [C17: from Latin *anxius;* related to Latin *angere* to torment; see ANGER, ANGUISH] ▸ **ˈanxiously** *adv* ▸ **ˈanxiousness** *n*

any (ˈɛnɪ) *determiner* **1a** one, some, or several, as specified, no matter how much or many, what kind or quality, etc.: *any cheese in the cupboard is yours; you may take any clothes you like.* **1b** (*as pronoun; functioning as sing or pl*): *take any you like.* 2 (*usually used with a negative*) **2a** even the smallest amount or even one: *I can't stand any noise.* **2b** (*as pronoun; functioning as sing or pl*): *don't give her any.* 3 whatever or whichever; no matter what or which: *any dictionary will do; any time of day.* 4 an indefinite or unlimited amount or number (esp. in the phrases **any amount** or **number**): *any number of friends.* ◆ *adv* 5 (*usually used with a negative*) **5a** (foll. by a comparative adj) to even the smallest extent: *it isn't any worse now.* **5b** *Not standard.* at all: *he doesn't care any.* [Old English *ǣnig;* related to Old Frisian *ēnig,* Old High German *einag,* Old Norse *einigr* anyone, Latin *ūnicus* unique; see AN[1], ONE]

Anyang (ˈɑːnˈjɑːŋ) *n* a town in E China, in Henan province: archaeological site and capital of the Shang dynasty. Pop.: 590 996 (1995).

anybody (ˈɛnɪˌbɒdɪ, -bədɪ) *pron* 1 any person; anyone. 2 (*usually used with a negative or a question*) a person of any importance: *he isn't anybody in this town.* ◆ *n, pl* **-bodies.** 3 (often preceded by *just*) any person at random; no matter who.

ˌ**antiˈtheft** *adj* ˌ**antiˌviviˈsection** *adj* ˌ**antiˈwar** *adj* ˌ**anti-ˈZionist** *n, adj*

anyhow ('ɛnɪ,haʊ) *adv* **1** in any case; at any rate. **2** in any manner or by any means whatever. **3** in a haphazard manner; carelessly.
any more *or esp. U.S.* **anymore** (,ɛnɪ'mɔː) *adv* any longer; still; now or from now on; nowadays: *he does not work here any more.*
anyone ('ɛnɪ,wʌn, -wən) *pron* **1** any person; anybody. **2** (*used with a negative or a question*) a person of any importance: *is he anyone in this town?* **3** (often preceded by *just*) any person at random; no matter who.
anyplace ('ɛnɪ,pleɪs) *adv U.S. and Canadian informal.* in, at, or to any unspecified place.
anyroad ('ɛnɪ,rəʊd) *adv* a northern English dialect word for **anyway**.
anything ('ɛnɪ,θɪŋ) *pron* **1** any object, event, action, etc., whatever: *anything might happen.* ◆ *n* **2** a thing of any kind: *have you anything to declare?* ◆ *adv* **3** in any way: *he wasn't anything like his father.* **4 anything but.** by no means; not in the least: *she was anything but happy.* **5 like anything.** (intensifier; usually euphemistic): *he ran like anything.*
anyway ('ɛnɪ,weɪ) *adv* **1** in any case; at any rate; nevertheless; anyhow. **2** in a careless or haphazard manner. **3** Usually **any way.** in any manner; by any means.
anyways ('ɛnɪ,weɪz) *adv U.S. and Canadian.* a nonstandard word for **anyway.**
anywhere ('ɛnɪ,wɛə) *adv* **1** in, at, or to any place. **2 get anywhere.** to be successful: *it took three years before he got anywhere.* **3 anywhere from.** any quantity, time, degree, etc., above a specified limit: *he could be anywhere from 40 to 50 years old.*
anywheres ('ɛnɪ,wɛəz) *adv U.S.* a nonstandard word for **anywhere.**
anywise ('ɛnɪ,waɪz) *adv Chiefly U.S.* in any way or manner; at all.
ANZAAS ('ænzəs, -zæs) *n acronym for* Australian and New Zealand Association for the Advancement of Science.
Anzac ('ænzæk) *n* **1** (in World War I) a soldier serving with the Australian and New Zealand Army Corps. **2** (now) any Australian or New Zealand soldier. **3** the Anzac landing at Gallipoli in 1915.
Anzac Day *n* 25 April, a public holiday in Australia and New Zealand commemorating the Anzac landing at Gallipoli in 1915.
Anzio ('ænzɪ,əʊ; *Italian* 'antsjo) *n* a port and resort on the W coast of Italy: site of Allied landings in World War II. Pop.: 32 383 (1991 est.).
ANZUS ('ænzəs) *n acronym for* Australia, New Zealand, and the United States, with reference to the security alliance between them.
AO *abbrev. for:* Officer of the Order of Australia.
A/O *or* **a/o** *Account., etc. abbrev. for* account of.
AOB *or* **a.o.b.** *abbrev. for* any other business.
AOC *abbrev. for* appellation d'origine contrôlée. See **AC** (sense 6).
AOCB *abbrev. for* any other competent business.
AOH *abbrev. for* Ancient Order of Hibernians: an Irish Catholic nationalist association founded in the 19th century; an important political force up to the founding of the Irish Free State (1922).
A-OK *or* **A-okay** *adj Informal, chiefly U.S.* in perfect working order; excellent. [C20: from *a(ll systems) OK*]
AONB (in England and Wales) *abbrev. for* area of outstanding natural beauty: an area designated by the Countryside Commission or the Countryside Council for Wales as requiring protection to conserve and enhance its natural beauty.
AOR *Music. abbrev. for:* **1** album-oriented rock. **2** adult-oriented rock. **3** *U.S.* album-oriented radio.
Aorangi-Mount Cook (,eɪəʊ'ræŋgɪ) *n* the official name for Mount **Cook.**
aorist ('eɪərɪst, 'ɛərɪst) *n Grammar.* a tense of the verb in classical Greek and in certain other inflected languages, indicating past action without reference to whether the action involved was momentary or continuous. Compare **perfect** (sense 8), **imperfect** (sense 4). [C16: from Greek *aoristos* not limited, from A-[1] + *horistos* restricted, from *horizein* to define] ► **,ao'ristic** *adj* ► **,ao'ristically** *adv*
aorta (eɪ'ɔːtə) *n, pl* **-tas** *or* **-tae** (-tiː). the main vessel in the arterial network, which conveys oxygen-rich blood from the heart to all parts of the body except the lungs. [C16: from New Latin, from Greek *aortē*, literally: something lifted, from *aeirein* to raise] ► **a'ortic** *or* **a'ortal** *adj*
aortitis (,eɪɔː'taɪtɪs) *n* inflammation of the aorta.
Aosta (*Italian* a'ɔsta) *n* a town in NW Italy, capital of Valle d'Aosta region: Roman remains. Pop.: 36 339 (1990).
Aotearoa ('æɒ,tɪə,rɔːə) *n* the Maori name for **New Zealand.** [from Maori *ao tea roa* Land of the Long White Cloud]
aoudad ('ɑːʊ,dæd) *n* a wild mountain sheep, *Ammotragus lervia*, of N Africa, having horns curved in a semicircle and long hair covering the neck and forelegs. Also called: **Barbary sheep.** [from French, from Berber *audad*]
Aouita (aʊ'iːtə) *n* **Saïd** (saɪ'iːd). born 1960, Moroccan middle-distance runner: winner of the 5000 metres in the 1984 Olympic Games.
ap (æp) son of: occurring as part of some surnames of Welsh origin: *ap Thomas* [from Welsh *mab* son]
AP *abbrev. for:* **1** Air Police. **2** Associated Press.
a.p. *abbrev. for:* **1** additional premium. **2** (in prescriptions, etc.) ante prandium. [Latin: before a meal]
ap- *prefix* a variant of **apo-**: *aphelion.*
apace (ə'peɪs) *adv* quickly; rapidly. [C14: probably from Old French *à pas*, at a (good) pace]
apache (ə'pɑːʃ, -'pæʃ; *French* apaʃ) *n* a Parisian gangster or ruffian. [from French: APACHE]
Apache (ə'pætʃɪ) *n* **1** (*pl* **Apaches** *or* **Apache**) a member of a North American Indian people, formerly nomadic and warlike, inhabiting the southwestern U.S. and N Mexico. **2** the language of this people, belonging to the Athapascan group of the Na-Dene phylum. [from Mexican Spanish, probably from Zuñi *Apachu*, literally: enemy]
apache dance *n* a fast violent dance in French vaudeville, supposedly between a Parisian gangster and his girl.
apanage ('æpənɪdʒ) *n* a variant spelling of **appanage.**
aparejo *Spanish.* (apa'rexo) *n, pl* **-jos** (-xos). *Southwestern U.S.* a kind of packsaddle made of stuffed leather cushions. [American Spanish: equipment, from *aparejar* to make ready; see APPAREL]
apart (ə'pɑːt) *adj* (*postpositive*), *adv* **1** to pieces or in pieces: *he had the television apart on the floor.* **2** placed or kept separately or to one side for a particular purpose, reason, etc.; aside (esp. in the phrases **set** *or* **put apart**). **3** separate in time, place, or position; at a distance: *he stood apart from the group; two points three feet apart.* **4** not being taken into account; aside: *these difficulties apart, the project ran smoothly.* **5** individual; distinct; separate: *a race apart.* **6** separately or independently in use, thought, or function: *considered apart, his reasoning was faulty.* **7 apart from.** (*prep*) besides; other than. ◆ See also **take apart, tell apart.** [C14: from Old French *a part* at (the) side]
apartheid (ə'pɑːthaɪt, -heɪt) *n* (in South Africa) the official government policy of racial segregation; officially renounced in 1992. [C20: Afrikaans, from *apart* APART + *-heid* -HOOD]
apartment (ə'pɑːtmənt) *n* **1** (*often pl*) any room in a building, usually one of several forming a suite, esp. one that is spacious and well furnished and used as living accommodation, offices, etc. **2a** another name (esp. U.S. and Canadian) for **flat**[2] (sense 1). **2b** (*as modifier*): *apartment building; apartment house.* [C17: from French *appartement*, from Italian *appartamento*, from *appartare* to set on one side, separate]
apatetic (,æpə'tɛtɪk) *adj* of or relating to coloration that disguises and protects an animal. [C19: from Greek *apatētikos* deceitful, from *apateuein* to deceive]
apathetic (,æpə'θɛtɪk) *adj* having or showing little or no emotion; indifferent. [C18: from APATHY + PATHETIC] ► **,apa'thetically** *adv*
apathy ('æpəθɪ) *n* **1** absence of interest in or enthusiasm for things generally considered interesting or moving. **2** absence of emotion. [C17: from Latin, from Greek *apatheia*, from *apathēs* without feeling, from A-[1] + *pathos* feeling]
apatite ('æpə,taɪt) *n* a pale green to purple mineral, found in igneous rocks and metamorphosed limestones. It is used in the manufacture of phosphorus, phosphates, and fertilizers. Composition: calcium fluorophosphate or calcium chlorophosphate. General formula: $Ca_5(PO_4,CO_3)_3(F,OH,Cl)$. Crystal structure: hexagonal. [C19: from German *Apatit*, from Greek *apatē* deceit; from its misleading similarity to other minerals]
APC *n* acetylsalicylic acid, phenacetin, and caffeine; the mixture formerly used in headache and cold tablets.
ape (eɪp) *n* **1** any of various primates, esp. those of the family *Pongidae* (see **anthropoid ape**), in which the tail is very short or absent. **2** (*not in technical use*) any monkey. **3** an imitator; mimic. **4** *U.S. informal.* a coarse, clumsy, or rude person. ◆ *vb* **5** (*tr*) to imitate. [Old English *apa*; related to Old Saxon *ape*, Old Norse *api*, Old High German *affo*] ► **'ape,like** *adj*
apeak (ə'piːk) *adv, adj Nautical.* in a vertical or almost vertical position: *with the oars apeak.*
Apeldoorn ('æpᵊl,dɔːn; *Dutch* 'aːpəldoːrn) *n* a town in the Netherlands, in central Gelderland province: nearby is the summer residence of the Dutch royal family. Pop.: 150 915 (1996 est.).
Apelles (ə'peliːz) *n* 4th century B.C., Greek painter of mythological subjects, none of whose work survives, his fame resting on the testimony of Pliny and other writers.
apeman ('eɪp,mæn) *n, pl* **-men.** any of various extinct apelike primates thought to have been the forerunners, or closely related to the forerunners, of modern man.
Apennines ('æpə,naɪnz) *pl n* **1** a mountain range in Italy, extending over 1250 km (800 miles) from the northwest to the southernmost tip of the peninsula. Highest peak: Monte Corno, 2912 m (9554 ft.). **2** a mountain range lying in the N quadrants of the moon, extending over 950 km along the SE border of the Mare Imbrium and rising to 6200 m.
aperçu *French.* (apersy) *n* **1** an outline; summary. **2** an insight. [from *apercevoir* to PERCEIVE]
aperient (ə'pɪərɪənt) *Med.* ◆ *adj* **1** laxative. ◆ *n* **2** a mild laxative. [C17: from Latin *aperīre* to open]
aperiodic (,eɪpɪərɪ'ɒdɪk) *adj* **1** not periodic; not occurring at regular intervals. **2** *Physics.* **2a** (of a system or instrument) being damped sufficiently to reach equilibrium without oscillation. **2b** (of an oscillation or vibration) not having a regular period. **2c** (of an electrical circuit) not having a measurable resonant frequency. ► **,aperi'odically** *adv* ► **aperiodicity** (,eɪpɪərɪə'dɪsɪtɪ) *n*
apéritif (ɑː,perɪ'tiːf, ə,per-) *n* an alcoholic drink, esp. a wine, drunk before a meal to whet the appetite. [C19: from French, from Medieval Latin *aperītīvus*, from Latin *aperīre* to open]
aperture ('æpətʃə) *n* **1** a hole, gap, crack, slit, or other opening. **2** *Physics.* **2a** a usually circular and often variable opening in an optical instrument or device that controls the quantity of radiation entering or leaving it. **2b** the diameter of such an opening. See also **relative aperture.** [C15: from Late Latin *apertūra* opening, from Latin *aperīre* to open]
aperture priority *n Photog.* an automatic exposure system in which the photographer selects the aperture and the camera then automatically sets the correct shutter speed. Compare **shutter priority.**
apery ('eɪpərɪ) *n, pl* **-eries.** imitative behaviour; mimicry.
apetalous (eɪ'pɛtələs) *adj* (of flowering plants such as the wood anemone) having no petals. [C18: from New Latin *apetalus*, see A-[1], PETAL] ► **a'petaly** *n*
apex ('eɪpɛks) *n, pl* **apexes** *or* **apices** ('æpɪ,siːz, 'eɪ-). **1** the highest point; vertex. **2** the pointed end or tip of something. **3** a pinnacle or high point, as of a career, etc. **4** Also called: **solar apex.** *Astronomy.* the point on the celestial sphere, lying in the constellation Hercules, towards which the sun appears to move at a

velocity of 7.5 kilometres per second relative to the nearest stars. [C17: from Latin: point]

APEX ('eɪpɛks) *n acronym for:* **1** Advance Purchase Excursion: a reduced airline or long-distance rail fare that must be paid a specified number of days in advance. **2** (in Britain) Association of Professional, Executive, Clerical, and Computer Staff.

Apex Club *n* (in Australia) an association of business and professional men founded to promote community welfare. ► **Apexian** (eɪ'pɛksɪən) *adj, n*

apgar score *or* **rating** ('æpgɑː) *n* a system for determining the condition of an infant at birth by allotting a maximum of 2 points to each of the following: heart rate, breathing effort, muscle tone, response to stimulation, and colour. [C20: named after V. *Apgar* (1909–74), U.S. anaesthetist]

aphaeresis *or* **apheresis** (ə'fɪərɪsɪs) *n* the omission of a letter or syllable at the beginning of a word. [C17: via Late Latin from Greek, from *aphairein* to remove] ► **aphaeretic** *or* **apheretic** (ˌæfə'rɛtɪk) *adj*

aphagia (ə'feɪdʒɪə) *n Pathol.* refusal or inability to swallow. [C20: from A-[1] + Greek *aphagein* to consume]

aphakia (ə'feɪkɪə) *n* absence of the lens of an eye, congenital or otherwise. [from A-[1] + Greek *phakos* lentil + -IA]

aphanite ('æfəˌnaɪt) *n* any fine-grained rock, such as a basalt, containing minerals that cannot be distinguished with the naked eye. [C19: from Greek *aphanēs* invisible]

aphasia (ə'feɪzɪə) *n* a disorder of the central nervous system characterized by partial or total loss of the ability to communicate, esp. in speech or writing. Compare **alexia.** [C19: via New Latin from Greek, from A-[1] + *-phasia,* from *phanai* to speak] ► **a'phasiˌac** *or* **a'phasic** *adj, n*

aphelandra (ˌæfə'lændrə) *n* any shrub of the evergreen genus *Aphelandra,* originally from tropical America, widely grown as a house plant for its variegated shiny leaves and brightly coloured flowers: family *Acanthaceae.* [from Greek *aphelēs* simple + *andros,* genitive of *anēr* man, male, because the anthers are single celled]

aphelion (æp'hiːlɪən, ə'fiː-) *n, pl* **-lia** (-lɪə). the point in its orbit when a planet or comet is at its greatest distance from the sun. Compare **perihelion.** [C17: from New Latin *aphēlium* (with pseudo-Greek ending *-ion*) from AP- + Greek *hēlios* sun] ► **ap'helian** *adj*

apheliotropic (æpˌhiːlɪə'trɒpɪk, əˌfiː-) *adj Biology.* growing in a direction away from the sunlight, as the roots of plants. [C19: see APO-, HELIOTROPIC] ► **apheliotropism** (æpˌhiːlɪ'ɒtrəˌpɪzəm) *n*

aphesis ('æfɪsɪs) *n* the gradual disappearance of an unstressed vowel at the beginning of a word, as in *squire* from *esquire.* [C19: from Greek, from *aphienai* to set free, send away] ► **aphetic** (ə'fɛtɪk) *adj* ► **a'phetically** *adv*

aphid ('eɪfɪd) *n* any of the small homopterous insects of the family *Aphididae,* which feed by sucking the juices from plants. Also called: **plant louse.** See also **greenfly, blackfly.** [C19: back formation from *aphides,* plural of APHIS] ► **aphidian** (ə'fɪdɪən) *adj, n* ► **a'phidious** *adj*

aphis ('eɪfɪs) *n, pl* **aphides** ('eɪfɪˌdiːz). **1** any of various aphids constituting the genus *Aphis,* such as the blackfly. **2** any other aphid. [C18: from New Latin (coined by Linnaeus for obscure reasons)]

aphonia (ə'fəʊnɪə) *or* **aphony** ('æfənɪ) *n* loss of the voice caused by damage to the vocal tract. [C18: via New Latin from Greek, from A-[1] + *phōnē* sound, voice]

aphonic (ə'fɒnɪk) *adj* **1** affected with aphonia. **2** *Phonetics.* **2a** not representing a spoken sound, as *k* in *know.* **2b** voiceless or devoiced.

aphorism ('æfəˌrɪzəm) *n* a short pithy saying expressing a general truth; maxim. [C16: from Late Latin *aphorismus,* from Greek *aphorismos* definition, from *aphorizein* to define, set limits to, from *horos* boundary] ► **'aphorist** *n*

aphoristic (ˌæfə'rɪstɪk) *adj* **1** of, relating to, or resembling an aphorism. **2** tending to write or speak in aphorisms.

aphorize *or* **aphorise** ('æfəˌraɪz) *vb (intr)* to write or speak in aphorisms.

aphotic (ə'fɒtɪk) *adj* **1** characterized by or growing in the absence of light: *an aphotic plant.* **2** of or relating to the zone of an ocean below about 90m (300 ft.), the lowest level at which photosynthesis can take place. [C20: from A-[1] + *-photic,* from Greek *phōs* light]

aphrodisiac (ˌæfrə'dɪzɪæk) *n* **1** a drug, food, etc., that excites sexual desire. ◆ *adj* **2** exciting or heightening sexual desire. [C18: from Greek *aphrodisiakos,* from *aphrodisios* belonging to APHRODITE]

Aphrodite (ˌæfrə'daɪtɪ) *n Greek myth.* the goddess of love and beauty, daughter of Zeus. Roman counterpart: **Venus.** Also called: **Cytherea.**

aphtha ('æfθə) *n, pl* **-thae** (-θiː). a small ulceration on a mucous membrane, as in thrush, caused by a fungal infection. [C17: via Latin from Greek: mouth-sore, thrush] ► **'aphthous** *adj*

aphyllous (ə'fɪləs) *adj* (of plants) having no leaves. [C19: from New Latin *aphyllus,* from Greek *aphullos,* from A-[1] + *phullon* leaf] ► **a'phylly** *n*

Apia (æ'pɪə, 'æpɪə) *n* the capital of (Western) Samoa: a port on the N coast of Upolu. Pop.: 33 000 (1995 est.).

apian ('eɪpɪən) *adj* of, relating to, or resembling bees. [C19: from Latin *apiānus,* from *apis* bee]

apiarian (ˌeɪpɪ'ɛərɪən) *adj* of or relating to the breeding and care of bees.

apiarist ('eɪpɪərɪst) *n* a person who studies or keeps bees.

apiary ('eɪpɪərɪ) *n, pl* **-aries.** a place where bees are kept, usually in beehives. [C17: from Latin *apiārium* from *apis* bee]

apical ('æpɪkəl, 'eɪ-) *adj* **1** of, at, or being the apex. **2** of or denoting a consonant articulated with the tip of the tongue, such as (t) or (d). [C19: from New Latin *apicālis,* from Latin: APEX] ► **'apically** *adv*

apices ('æpɪˌsiːz, 'eɪ-) *n* a plural of **apex.**

apiculate (ə'pɪkjʊlɪt, -ˌleɪt) *adj* (of leaves) ending in a short sharp point. [C19: from New Latin *apiculātus,* from *apiculus* a short point, from APEX]

apiculture ('eɪpɪˌkʌltʃə) *n* the breeding and care of bees. [C19: from Latin *apis* bee + CULTURE] ► **ˌapi'cultural** *adj* ► **ˌapi'culturist** *n*

apiece (ə'piːs) *adv (postpositive)* for, to, or from each one: *they were given two apples apiece.*

à pied *French.* (a pje) *adv, adj (postpositive)* on foot.

Apiezon (ˌæpɪ'eɪzɒn) *adj Trademark.* designating any of a number of hydrocarbon oils, greases, or waxes, characterized by a low vapour pressure and used in vacuum equipment.

API gravity scale *n* the American Petroleum Institute gravity scale: a universally accepted scale of the relative density of fluids that is used in fuel technology and is measured in degrees API. One degree API is equal to (141.5/*d*)–13.5, where *d* = relative density at 288.7K. See also **Baumé scale.**

Apis ('ɑːpɪs) *n* (in ancient Egypt) a sacred bull worshipped at Memphis.

apish ('eɪpɪʃ) *adj* **1** stupid; foolish. **2** resembling an ape. **3** slavishly imitative. ► **'apishly** *adv* ► **'apishness** *n*

apivorous (eɪ'pɪvərəs) *adj* eating bees: *apivorous birds.* [C19: from Latin *apis* bee + -VOROUS]

aplacental (ˌeɪplə'sɛntəl, ˌæplə-) *adj* (of monotremes and marsupials) having no placenta.

aplanatic (ˌæplə'nætɪk) *adj* (of a lens or mirror) free from spherical aberration. [C18: from Greek *aplanētos* prevented from wandering, from A-[1] + *planētos,* from *planaein* to wander] ► **ˌapla'natically** *adv*

aplanetic (ˌæplə'nɛtɪk) *adj* (esp. of some algal and fungal spores) nonmotile or lacking a motile stage. [variant of APLANATIC]

aplanospore (ə'pleɪnəʊˌspɔː) *n* a nonmotile asexual spore produced by certain algae and fungi. [C20: from A-[1] + Greek *planos* wandering + SPORE]

aplasia (ə'pleɪzɪə) *n Pathol.* congenital absence or abnormal development of an organ or part. [C19: New Latin, from A-[1] + *-plasia,* from Greek *plassein* to form]

aplastic (eɪ'plæstɪk) *adj* **1** relating to or characterized by aplasia. **2** failing to develop into new tissue; defective in the regeneration of tissue, as of blood cells: *aplastic anaemia.*

aplenty (ə'plɛntɪ) *adj (postpositive), adv* in plenty.

aplite ('æplaɪt) *or* **haplite** *n* a light-coloured fine-grained acid igneous rock with a sugary texture, consisting of quartz and feldspars. [C19: from German *Aplit,* from Greek *haploos* simple + -ITE[1]] ► **aplitic** (æp'lɪtɪk) *or* **hap'litic** *adj*

aplomb (ə'plɒm) *n* equanimity, self-confidence, or self-possession. [C18: from French: rectitude, uprightness, from *à plomb* according to the plumb line, vertically]

apneusis (æp'nuːsɪs) *n Pathol.* protracted gasping inhalation followed by short inefficient exhalation, which can cause asphyxia. [from A-[1] + Greek *pnein* to breathe]

apneustic (æp'nuːstɪk) *adj* **1** of or relating to apneusis. **2** (of certain animals) having no specialized organs for respiration.

apnoea *or U.S.* **apnea** (æp'nɪə) *n* a temporary inability to breathe. [C18: from New Latin, from Greek *apnoia,* from A-[1] + *pnein* to breathe]

Apo ('ɑːpəʊ) *n* the highest mountain in the Philippines, on SE Mindanao: active volcano with three peaks. Height: 2954 m (9690 ft.).

apo- *or* **ap-** *prefix* **1** away from; off: *apogee.* **2** indicating separation of: *apocarpous.* **3** indicating a lack or absence of: *apogamy.* **4** indicating derivation from or relationship to: *apomorphine.* [from Greek *apo* away, off]

Apoc. *abbrev. for:* **1** Apocalypse. **2** Apocrypha or Apocryphal.

apocalypse (ə'pɒkəlɪps) *n* **1** a prophetic disclosure or revelation. **2** an event of great importance, violence, etc., like the events described in the Apocalypse. [C13: from Late Latin *apocalypsis,* from Greek *apokalupsis,* from *apokaluptein* to disclose, from APO- + *kaluptein* to hide]

Apocalypse (ə'pɒkəlɪps) *n Bible.* (in the Vulgate and Douay versions of the Bible) the Book of Revelation.

apocalyptic (əˌpɒkə'lɪptɪk) *adj* **1** outstanding in revelation, prophecy, or significance. **2** of or like an apocalypse. ► **aˌpoca'lyptically** *adv*

apocarp ('æpəˌkɑːp) *n* an apocarpous gynoecium or fruit.

apocarpous (ˌæpə'kɑːpəs) *adj* (of the ovaries of flowering plants such as the buttercup) consisting of separate carpels. Compare **syncarpous.**

apochromat (ˌæpə'krəʊmæt) *or* **apochromatic lens** *n* a lens, consisting of three or more elements of different types of glass, that is designed to bring light of three colours to the same focal point, thus reducing its chromatic aberration. Compare **achromat.**

apochromatic (ˌæpəkrə'mætɪk) *adj* (of a lens) almost free from spherical and chromatic aberration. ► **apochromatism** (ˌæpə'krəʊməˌtɪzəm) *n*

apocopate (ə'pɒkəˌpeɪt) *vb (tr)* to omit the final sound or sounds of (a word). ► **aˌpoco'pation** *n*

apocope (ə'pɒkəpɪ) *n* omission of the final sound or sounds of a word. [C16: via Late Latin from Greek *apokopē,* from *apokoptein* to cut off]

Apocr. *abbrev. for* Apocrypha.

apocrine ('æpəkraɪn, -krɪn) *adj* denoting a type of glandular secretion in which part of the secreting cell is lost with the secretion, as in mammary glands. Compare **merocrine, holocrine.** [C20: from APO- + *-crine,* from Greek *krinein* to separate]

Apocrypha (ə'pɒkrɪfə) *n* **the.** *(functioning as sing or pl)* **1** the 14 books included as an appendix to the Old Testament in the Septuagint and the Vulgate but not included in the Hebrew canon. They are not printed in Protestant versions of the Bible. **2** *R.C. Church.* another name for the **Pseudepigrapha.** [C14: via Late Latin *apocrypha (scripta)* hidden (writings), from Greek, from *apokruptein* to hide away]

apocryphal (ə'pɒkrɪfəl) *adj* **1** of questionable authenticity. **2** *(sometimes cap.)* of or like the Apocrypha. **3** untrue; counterfeit. ► **a'pocryphally** *adv*

Apocryphal Gospels *pl n* accounts of Christ's life that are not recognized as part of the New Testament.

apocynaceous (ə,pɒsɪ'neɪʃəs) *adj* of, relating to, or belonging to the *Apocynaceae,* a family of mostly tropical flowering plants with latex in their stems, including the dogbane, periwinkle, oleander, and some lianas. [C19: from New Latin *Apocynum* type genus, from Latin: dogbane, from Greek *apokunon,* from *kuōn* dog]

apocynthion (,æpə'sɪnθɪən) *n* the point at which a spacecraft in lunar orbit is farthest from the moon. Compare **apolune, pericynthion.** [C20: from APO- (away) + *cynthion,* from Latin *Cynthia* goddess of the moon]

apodal ('æpədᵊl) *or* **apodous** *adj* (of snakes, eels, etc.) without feet; having no obvious hind limbs or pelvic fins. [C18: from Greek *apous* from A-[1] + *pous* foot]

apodeictic (,æpə'daɪktɪk) *or* **apodictic** (,æpə'dɪktɪk) *adj* **1** unquestionably true by virtue of demonstration. **2** *Logic, archaic.* **2a** necessarily true. **2b** asserting that a property holds necessarily. ◆ Compare **problematic** (sense 2), **assertoric.** [C17: from Latin *apodīcticus,* from Greek *apodeiktikos* clearly demonstrating, from *apodeiknunai* to demonstrate] ▸ **,apo'deictically** *or* **,apo'dictically** *adv*

apodosis (ə'pɒdəsɪs) *n, pl* **-ses** (-,si:z). *Logic, grammar.* the consequent of a conditional statement, as *the game will be cancelled* in *if it rains the game will be cancelled.* Compare **protasis.** [C17: via Late Latin from Greek: a returning or answering (clause), from *apodidonai* to give back]

apoenzyme (,æpəʊ'enzaɪm) *n* a protein component that together with a coenzyme forms an enzyme.

apogamy (ə'pɒgəmɪ) *n* a type of reproduction, occurring in some ferns, in which the sporophyte develops from the gametophyte without fusion of gametes. ▸ **apogamic** (,æpə'gæmɪk) *adj* ▸ **a'pogamous** *adj*

apogee ('æpə,dʒi:) *n* **1** the point in its orbit around the earth when the moon or an artificial satellite is at its greatest distance from the earth. Compare **perigee. 2** the highest point. [C17: from New Latin *apogaeum* (influenced by French *apogée*), from Greek *apogaion,* from *apogaios* away from the earth, from APO- + *gaia* earth] ▸ **,apo'gean** *adj*

apogeotropism (,æpədʒɪ'ɒtrə,pɪzəm) *n* negative geotropism, as shown by plant stems. [C19: from Greek *apogaios* away from the earth + *tropos* a turn] ▸ **apogeotropic** (,æpə,dʒɪə'trɒpɪk) *adj*

apolitical (,eɪpə'lɪtɪkᵊl) *adj* politically neutral; without political attitudes, content, or bias.

Apollinaire (*French* apɔlinɛr) *n* **Guillaume** (gijom), real name *Wilhelm Apollinaris de Kostrowitzki.* 1880–1918, French poet, novelist, and dramatist, regarded as a precursor of surrealism; author of *Alcoöls* (1913) and *Calligrammes* (1918).

Apollinaris (ə,pɒlɪ'neərɪs) *n* an effervescent mineral water. [C19: named after *Apollinarisburg,* near Bonn, Germany]

apollo[1] (ə'pɒləʊ) *n, pl* **-los.** a strikingly handsome youth.

apollo[2] (ə'pɒləʊ) *n, pl* **-los.** a handsome Eurasian mountain butterfly, *Parnassius apollo,* with palish wings and prominent red ocelli.

Apollo[1] (ə'pɒləʊ) *n Classical myth.* the god of light, poetry, music, healing, and prophecy: son of Zeus and Leto.

Apollo[2] (ə'pɒləʊ) *n* any of a series of manned U.S. spacecraft designed to explore the moon and surrounding space. **Apollo 11** made the first moon landing in July 1969.

Apollonian (,æpə'ləʊnɪən) *adj* **1** of or relating to Apollo or the cult of Apollo. **2** (*sometimes not cap.*) (in the philosophy of Nietzsche) denoting or relating to the set of static qualities that encompass form, reason, harmony, sobriety, etc. **3** (*often not cap.*) harmonious; serene; ordered. ◆ Compare **Dionysian.**

Apollonius of Perga (,æpə'ləʊnɪəs; 'pɜ:gə) *n* ?261–?190 B.C., Greek mathematician, remembered for his treatise on conic sections.

Apollonius of Rhodes (,æpə'ləʊnɪəs) *n* 3rd century B.C., Greek epic poet and head of the Library of Alexandria. His principal work is the four-volume *Argonautica.*

Apollyon (ə'pɒljən) *n New Testament.* the destroyer, a name given to the Devil (Revelation 9:11). [C14: via Late Latin from Greek, from *apollunai* to destroy totally]

apologetic (ə,pɒlə'dʒetɪk) *adj* **1** expressing or anxious to make apology; contrite. **2** protecting or defending in speech or writing. ▸ **a,polo'getically** *adv*

apologetics (ə,pɒlə'dʒetɪks) *n* (*functioning as sing*) **1** the branch of theology concerned with the defence and rational justification of Christianity. **2** a defensive method of argument.

apologia (,æpə'ləʊdʒɪə) *n* a formal written defence of a cause or one's beliefs or conduct.

apologist (ə'pɒlədʒɪst) *n* a person who offers a defence by argument.

apologize *or* **apologise** (ə'pɒlə,dʒaɪz) *vb* (*intr*) **1** to express or make an apology; acknowledge failings or faults. **2** to make a formal defence in speech or writing. ▸ **a'polo,gizer** *or* **a'polo,giser** *n*

apologue ('æpə,lɒg) *n* an allegory or moral fable. [C17: from Latin, from Greek *apologos*]

apology (ə'pɒlədʒɪ) *n, pl* **-gies. 1** a verbal or written expression of regret or contrition for a fault or failing. **2** a poor substitute or offering. **3** another word for **apologia.** [C16: from Old French *apologie,* from Late Latin *apologia,* from Greek: a verbal defence, from APO- + *logos* speech]

apolune ('æpə,lu:n) *n* the point in a lunar orbit when a spacecraft is at its greatest distance from the moon. Compare **apocynthion, perilune.** [C20: from APO- + *-lune,* from Latin *lūna* moon]

apomict ('æpə,mɪkt) *n* an organism, esp. a plant, produced by apomixis.

apomixis (,æpə'mɪksɪs) *n, pl* **-mixes** (-'mɪksi:z). any of several types of asexual reproduction, such as parthenogenesis and apogamy, in which fertilization does not take place. Compare **amphimixis.** [C20: New Latin, from Greek APO- + *mixis* a mixing] ▸ **,apo'mictic** *adj*

apomorphine (,æpə'mɔ:fi:n, -fɪn) *n* a white crystalline alkaloid, derived from morphine but less strong in action, that is used medicinally as an emetic, expectorant, and hypnotic. Formula: $C_{17}H_{17}NO_2$.

aponeurosis (,æpənjʊə'rəʊsɪs) *n, pl* **-ses** (-si:z). *Anatomy.* a white fibrous sheet of tissue by which certain muscles are attached to bones. [C17: via New Latin from Greek, from *aponeurousthai* to change into a tendon, from *neuron* tendon] ▸ **aponeurotic** (,æpənjʊə'rɒtɪk) *adj*

apophasis (ə'pɒfəsɪs) *n Rhetoric.* the device of mentioning a subject by stating that it will not be mentioned: *I shall not discuss his cowardice or his treachery.* [C17: via Latin from Greek: denial, from APO- + *phanai* to say]

apophthegm *or* **apothegm** ('æpə,θem) *n* a short cryptic remark containing some general or generally accepted truth; maxim. [C16: from Greek *apophthegma,* from *apophthengesthai* to speak one's opinion frankly, from *phthengesthai* to speak] ▸ **apophthegmatic** *or* **apothegmatic** (,æpəθeg'mætɪk) *adj*

apophyge (ə'pɒfɪdʒɪ) *n Architect.* the outward curve at each end of the shaft of a column, adjoining the base or capital. Also called: **hypophyge.** [C16: from Greek *apophugē,* literally: escape, from *apopheugein* to escape from]

apophyllite (ə'pɒfɪ,laɪt, ,æpə'fɪlaɪt) *n* a white, colourless, pink, or green mineral consisting of a hydrated silicate of calcium, potassium, and fluorine in tetragonal crystalline form. It occurs in cracks in volcanic rocks. Formula: $KCa_4FSi_4O_{10}.8H_2O$. [C19: from French, from APO- + Greek *phullon* leaf + -ITE[1]; referring to its tendency to exfoliate]

apophysis (ə'pɒfɪsɪs) *n, pl* **-ses** (-,si:z). **1** a process, outgrowth, or swelling from part of an animal or plant. **2** *Geology.* a tapering offshoot from a larger igneous intrusive mass. [C17: via New Latin from Greek *apophusis* a sideshoot, from APO- + *phusis* growth] ▸ **apophysate** (ə'pɒfɪsɪt, -seɪt) *adj* ▸ **apophysial** (,æpə'fɪzɪəl) *adj*

apoplast ('æpə,plæst) *n Botany.* the nonprotoplasmic component of a plant, including the cell walls and intercellular material.

apoplectic (,æpə'plektɪk) *adj* **1** of or relating to apoplexy. **2** *Informal.* furious. ◆ *n* **3** a person having apoplexy. ▸ **,apo'plectically** *adv*

apoplexy ('æpə,pleksɪ) *n* sudden loss of consciousness, often followed by paralysis, caused by rupture or occlusion of a blood vessel in the brain. [C14: from Old French *apoplexie,* from Late Latin *apoplēxia,* from Greek: from *apoplēssein* to cripple by a stroke, from *plēssein* to strike]

apoprotein ('æpə,prəʊti:n) *n Biochem.* any conjugated protein from which the prosthetic group has been removed, such as apohaemoglobin (the protein of haemoglobin without its haem group).

apoptosis (æpəp'təʊsɪs) *n Biology.* the controlled death of an organism's cells as part of its natural growth and development. [C20: from Greek: a falling away, from APO- + *ptōsis* a falling]

aporia (ə'pɔ:rɪə) *n* **1** *Rhetoric.* a doubt, real or professed, about what to do or say. **2** *Philosophy.* puzzlement occasioned by the raising of philosophical objections without any proffered solutions, esp. in the works of Socrates. [C16: from Greek, literally: a state of being at a loss] ▸ **aporetic** (,æpə'retɪk) *adj*

aport (ə'pɔ:t) *adv, adj* (*postpositive*) *Nautical.* on or towards the port side: *with the helm aport.*

aposematic (,æpəsɪ'mætɪk) *adj* (of the coloration of certain distasteful or poisonous animals) characterized by bright conspicuous markings, which predators recognize and learn to avoid; warning. [C19: from APO- + Greek *sēma* sign]

aposiopesis (,æpəʊ,saɪə'pi:sɪs) *n, pl* **-ses** (-si:z). *Rhetoric.* the device of suddenly breaking off in the middle of a sentence as if unwilling to continue. [C16: via Late Latin from Greek, from *aposiōpaein* to be totally silent, from *siōpaein* to be silent] ▸ **aposiopetic** (,æpəʊ,saɪə'petɪk) *adj*

apospory ('æpə,spɔ:rɪ) *n Botany.* development of the gametophyte from the sporophyte without the formation of spores. [C19: from APO- + SPORE + -Y[1]]

apostasy (ə'pɒstəsɪ) *n, pl* **-sies.** abandonment of one's religious faith, party, a cause, etc. [C14: from Church Latin *apostasia,* from Greek *apostasis* desertion, from *apostanai* to stand apart from, desert]

apostate (ə'pɒsteɪt, -tɪt) *n* **1** a person who abandons his religion, party, cause, etc. ◆ *adj* **2** guilty of apostasy. ▸ **apostatical** (,æpə'stætɪkᵊl) *adj*

apostatize *or* **apostatise** (ə'pɒstə,taɪz) *vb* (*intr*) to forsake or abandon one's belief, faith, or allegiance.

a posteriori (eɪ pɒs,terɪ'ɔ:raɪ, -rɪ; ɑ:) *adj Logic.* **1** relating to or involving inductive reasoning from particular facts or effects to a general principle. **2** derived from or requiring evidence for its validation or support; empirical; open to revision. **3** *Statistics.* See **posterior probability.** ◆ Compare **a priori, synthetic** (sense 4). [C18: from Latin, literally: from the latter (that is, from effect to cause)]

apostil (ə'pɒstɪl) *n* a marginal note. [C16: from French *apostille,* from Old French *apostiller* to make marginal notes, from Medieval Latin *postilla,* probably from Latin *post illa* (*verba*) after those (words)]

apostle (ə'pɒsᵊl) *n* **1** (*often cap.*) one of the 12 disciples chosen by Christ to preach his gospel. **2** any prominent Christian missionary, esp. one who first converts a nation or people. **3** an ardent early supporter of a cause, reform movement, etc. **4** *Mormon Church.* a member of a council of twelve officials appointed to administer and preside over the Church. [Old English *apostol,* from Church Latin *apostolus,* from Greek *apostolos* a messenger, from *apostellein* to send forth]

Apostles' Creed *n* a concise statement of Christian beliefs dating from about 500 A.D., traditionally ascribed to the Apostles.

apostle spoon *n* a silver spoon with a figure of one of the Apostles on the handle.

apostolate (ə'pɒstəlɪt, -,leɪt) *n* the office, authority, or mission of an apostle.

apostolic (,æpə'stɒlɪk) *adj* **1** of, relating to, deriving from, or contemporary with the Apostles. **2** of or relating to the teachings or practice of the Apostles. **3**

of or relating to the pope regarded as chief successor of the Apostles. ▸ ˌapos'tolical *adj* ▸ ˌapos'tolically *adv*

apostolic delegate *n R.C. Church.* a representative of the pope sent to countries that do not have full or regular diplomatic relations with the Holy See.

Apostolic Fathers *pl n* the Fathers of the early Church who immediately followed the Apostles.

Apostolic See *n* **1** *R.C. Church.* the see of the pope regarded as the successor to Saint Peter. **2** (*often not caps.*) a see established by one of the Apostles.

Apostolic succession *n* the doctrine that the authority of Christian bishops derives from the Apostles through an unbroken line of consecration.

apostrophe[1] (ə'pɒstrəfɪ) *n* the punctuation mark ' used to indicate the omission of a letter or number, such as *he's* for *he has* or *he is,* also used in English to form the possessive, as in *John's father* and *twenty pounds' worth.* [C17: from Late Latin, from Greek *apostrophos* mark of elision, from *apostrephein* to turn away]

apostrophe[2] (ə'pɒstrəfɪ) *n Rhetoric.* a digression from a discourse, esp. an address to an imaginary or absent person or a personification. [C16: from Latin *apostrophē,* from Greek: a turning away, digression] ▸ **apostrophic** (ˌæpə'strɒfɪk) *adj*

apostrophize *or* **apostrophise** (ə'pɒstrəˌfaɪz) *vb (tr) Rhetoric.* to address an apostrophe to.

apothecaries' measure *n* a system of liquid volume measure used in pharmacy in which 60 minims equal 1 fluid drachm, 8 fluid drachms equal 1 fluid ounce, and 20 fluid ounces equal 1 pint.

apothecaries' weight *n* a system of weights formerly used in pharmacy based on the Troy ounce, which contains 480 grains. 1 grain is equal to 0.065 gram.

apothecary (ə'pɒθɪkərɪ) *n, pl* **-caries. 1** an archaic word for **chemist. 2** *Law.* a chemist licensed by the Society of Apothecaries of London to prescribe, prepare, and sell drugs. [C14: from Old French *apotecaire,* from Late Latin *apothēcārius* warehouseman, from *apothēca,* from Greek *apothēkē* storehouse]

apothecium (ˌæpə'θiːsɪəm) *n, pl* **-cia** (-sɪə). *Botany.* a cup-shaped structure that contains the asci; a type of ascocarp. [C19: from New Latin, from APO- + Greek *thēkion* a little case] ▸ **apothecial** (ˌæpə'θiːsɪəl) *adj*

apothegm ('æpəˌθɛm) *n* a variant spelling of **apophthegm.**

apothem ('æpəˌθɛm) *n* the perpendicular line or distance from the centre of a regular polygon to any of its sides. [C20: from APO- + Greek *thema,* from *tithenai* to place]

apotheosis (əˌpɒθɪ'əʊsɪs) *n, pl* **-ses** (-siːz). **1** the elevation of a person to the rank of a god; deification. **2** glorification of a person or thing. **3** a glorified ideal. [C17: via Late Latin from Greek: deification, from *theos* god]

apotheosize *or* **apotheosise** (ə'pɒθɪəˌsaɪz) *vb (tr)* **1** to deify. **2** to glorify or idealize.

apotropaic (ˌæpəʊtrə'peɪɪk) *adj* preventing or intended to prevent evil. [C19: from Greek *apotropaios* turning away (evil), from *apotrepein;* see APO-, TROPE]

app. *abbrev. for:* **1** apparatus. **2** appendix (of a book). **3** applied. **4** appointed. **5** apprentice. **6** approved. **7** approximate.

appal *or U.S.* **appall** (ə'pɔːl) *vb* **-pals, -palling, -palled** *or U.S.* **-palls, -palling, -palled.** *(tr)* to fill with horror; shock or dismay. [C14: from Old French *appalir* to turn pale]

Appalachia (ˌæpə'leɪtʃɪə) *n* a highland region of the eastern U.S., containing the Appalachian Mountains, extending from Pennsylvania to Alabama.

Appalachian (ˌæpə'leɪtʃɪən) *adj* **1** of, from, or relating to the Appalachian Mountains. **2** *Geology.* of or relating to an episode of mountain building in the late Palaeozoic era during which the Appalachian Mountains were formed.

Appalachian Mountains *or* **Appalachians** *pl n* a mountain system of E North America, extending from Quebec province in Canada to central Alabama in the U.S.: contains rich deposits of anthracite, bitumen, and iron ore. Highest peak: Mount Mitchell, 2038 m (6684 ft.).

appalling (ə'pɔːlɪŋ) *adj* causing extreme dismay, horror, or revulsion. ▸ **ap'pallingly** *adv*

Appaloosa (ˌæpə'luːsə) *n* a breed of horse, originally from America, typically having a spotted rump. [C19: perhaps from *Palouse,* river in Idaho]

appanage *or* **apanage** ('æpənɪdʒ) *n* **1** land or other provision granted by a king for the support of a member of the royal family, esp. a younger son. **2** a natural or customary accompaniment or perquisite, as to a job or position. [C17: from Old French, from Medieval Latin *appānāgium,* from *appānāre* to provide for, from Latin *pānis* bread]

apparat (ˌæpə'rɑːt) *n* the Communist Party organization in the former Soviet Union and other states. [Russian, literally: APPARATUS]

apparatchik (ˌæpə'rɑːtʃɪk) *n* **1** a member of a Communist apparat. **2** an official or bureaucrat in any organization.

apparatus (ˌæpə'reɪtəs, -'rɑːtəs, 'æpəˌreɪtəs) *n, pl* **-ratus** *or* **-ratuses. 1** a collection of instruments, machines, tools, parts, or other equipment used for a particular purpose. **2** a machine having a specific function: *breathing apparatus.* **3** the means by which something operates; organization: *the apparatus of government.* **4** *Anatomy.* any group of organs having a specific function. [C17: from Latin, from *apparāre* to make ready]

apparatus criticus ('krɪtɪkəs) *n* textual notes, list of variant readings, etc., relating to a document, esp. in a scholarly edition of a text. [Latin: critical apparatus]

apparel (ə'pærəl) *n* **1** something that covers or adorns, esp. outer garments or clothing. **2** *Nautical.* a vessel's gear and equipment. ◆ *vb* **-els, -elling, -elled** *or U.S.* **-els, -eling, -eled. 3** *Archaic. (tr)* to clothe, adorn, etc. [C13: from Old French *apareillier* to make ready, from Vulgar Latin *appariculāre* (unattested), from Latin *apparāre,* from *parāre* to prepare]

apparent (ə'pærənt, ə'pɛər-) *adj* **1** readily seen or understood; evident; obvious. **2** (*usually prenominal*) seeming, as opposed to real: *his apparent innocence belied his complicity in the crime.* **3** *Physics.* as observed but ignoring such factors as the motion of the observer, changes in the environment, etc. Compare **true** (sense 9). [C14: from Latin *appārēns,* from *appārēre* to APPEAR] ▸ **ap'parently** *adv* ▸ **ap'parentness** *n*

apparent magnitude *n* another name for **magnitude** (sense 4).

apparent movement *n Psychol.* the sensation of seeing movement when nothing actually moves in the environment, as when two neighbouring lights are switched on and off in rapid succession.

apparition (ˌæpə'rɪʃən) *n* **1** an appearance, esp. of a ghost or ghostlike figure. **2** the figure so appearing; phantom; spectre. **3** the act of appearing or being visible. [C15: from Late Latin *appāritiō,* from Latin: attendance, from *appārēre* to APPEAR]

apparitor (ə'pærɪtə) *n* an officer who summons witnesses and executes the orders of an ecclesiastical and (formerly) a civil court. [C15: from Latin: public servant, from *appārēre* to APPEAR]

appassionato (əˌpæsjə'nɑːtəʊ) *adj, adv Music.* (to be performed) in an impassioned manner.

appeal (ə'piːl) *n* **1** a request for relief, aid, etc. **2** the power to attract, please, stimulate, or interest: *a dress with appeal.* **3** an application or resort to another person or authority, esp. a higher one, as for a decision or confirmation of a decision. **4** *Law.* **4a** the judicial review by a superior court of the decision of a lower tribunal. **4b** a request for such review. **4c** the right to such review. **5** *Cricket.* a verbal request to the umpire from one or more members of the fielding side to declare a batsman out. **6** *English law.* (formerly) a formal charge or accusation: *appeal of felony.* ◆ *vb* **7** *(intr)* to make an earnest request for relief, support, etc. **8** *(intr)* to attract, please, stimulate, or interest. **9** *Law.* to apply to a superior court to review (a case or particular issue decided by a lower tribunal). **10** *(intr)* to resort (to), as for a decision or confirmation of a decision. **11** *(intr) Cricket.* to ask the umpire to declare a batsman out. **12** *(intr)* to challenge the umpire's or referee's decision. [C14: from Old French *appeler,* from Latin *appellāre* to entreat (literally: to approach), from *pellere* to push, drive] ▸ **ap'pealable** *adj* ▸ **ap'pealer** *n*

appealing (ə'piːlɪŋ) *adj* attractive or pleasing. ▸ **ap'pealingly** *adv*

appear (ə'pɪə) *vb (intr)* **1** to come into sight or view. **2** (*copula; may take an infinitive*) to seem or look: *the evidence appears to support you.* **3** to be plain or clear, as after further evidence, etc.: *it appears you were correct after all.* **4** to develop or come into being; occur: *faults appeared during testing.* **5** to become publicly available; be published: *his biography appeared last month.* **6** to perform or act: *he has appeared in many London productions.* **7** to be present in court before a magistrate or judge: *he appeared on two charges of theft.* [C13: from Old French *aparoir,* from Latin *appārēre* to become visible, attend upon, from *pārēre* to appear]

appearance (ə'pɪərəns) *n* **1** the act or an instance of appearing, as to the eye, before the public, etc. **2** the outward or visible aspect of a person or thing: *her appearance was stunning; it has the appearance of powdered graphite.* **3** an outward show; pretence: *he gave an appearance of working hard.* **4** (*often pl*) one of the outward signs or indications by which a person or thing is assessed: *first appearances are deceptive.* **5** *Law.* **5a** the formal attendance in court of a party in an action. **5b** formal notice that a party or his legal representative intends to maintain or contest the issue: *to enter an appearance.* **6** *Philosophy.* **6a** the outward or phenomenal manifestation of things. **6b** the world as revealed by the senses, as opposed to its real nature. Compare **reality** (sense 4). **7** **keep up appearances.** to maintain the public impression of wellbeing or normality. **8** **put in** *or* **make an appearance.** to come or attend briefly, as out of politeness. **9** **to all appearances.** to the extent that can easily be judged; apparently.

appearance money *n* money paid by a promoter of an event to a particular celebrity in order to ensure that the celebrity takes part in the event.

appease (ə'piːz) *vb (tr)* **1** to calm, pacify, or soothe, esp. by acceding to the demands of. **2** to satisfy or quell (an appetite or thirst, etc.). [C16: from Old French *apaisier,* from *pais* peace, from Latin *pax*] ▸ **ap'peasable** *adj* ▸ **ap'peaser** *n*

appeasement (ə'piːzmənt) *n* **1** the policy of acceding to the demands of a potentially hostile nation in the hope of maintaining peace. **2** the act of appeasing.

appel (ə'pɛl; *French* apɛl) *n Fencing.* **1** a stamp of the foot, used to warn of one's intent to attack. **2** a sharp blow with the blade made to procure an opening. [from French: challenge]

Appel (*Dutch* 'ɑpəl) *n* **Karel** ('kaːrəl). born 1921, Dutch abstract expressionist painter.

appellant (ə'pɛlənt) *n* **1** a person who appeals. **2** *Law.* the party who appeals to a higher court from the decision of a lower tribunal. ◆ *adj* **3** *Law.* another word for **appellate.** [C14: from Old French; see APPEAL]

appellate (ə'pɛlɪt) *adj Law.* **1** of or relating to appeals. **2** (of a tribunal) having jurisdiction to review cases on appeal and to reverse decisions of inferior courts. [C18: from Latin *appellātus* summoned, from *appellāre* to APPEAL]

appellation (ˌæpɪ'leɪʃən) *n* **1** an identifying name or title. **2** the act of naming or giving a title to.

appellative (ə'pɛlətɪv) *n* **1** an identifying name or title; appellation. **2** *Grammar.* another word for **common noun.** ◆ *adj* **3** of or relating to a name or title. **4** (of a proper noun) used as a common noun. ▸ **ap'pellatively** *adv*

appellee (ˌæpɛ'liː) *n Law.* a person who is accused or appealed against. [C16: from Old French *apele* summoned; see APPEAL]

append (ə'pɛnd) *vb (tr)* **1** to add as a supplement: *to append a footnote.* **2** to attach; hang on. [C15: from Late Latin *appendere* to hang (something) from, from Latin *pendere* to hang]

appendage (ə'pɛndɪdʒ) *n* **1** an ancillary or secondary part attached to a main part; adjunct. 2 *Zoology.* any organ that projects from the trunk of animals such as arthropods. 3 *Botany.* any subsidiary part of a plant, such as a branch or leaf.

appendant (əˈpɛndənt) *adj* 1 attached, affixed, or added. 2 attendant or associated as an accompaniment or result. 3 a less common word for **pendent.** 4 *Law.* relating to another right. ◆ *n* 5 a person or thing attached or added. 6 *Property law.* a subordinate right or interest, esp. in or over land, attached to a greater interest and automatically passing with the sale of the latter.

appendicectomy (əˌpɛndɪˈsɛktəmɪ) *or esp. U.S. and Canadian* **appendectomy** (ˌæpənˈdɛktəmɪ) *n, pl* **-mies.** surgical removal of any appendage, esp. the vermiform appendix.

appendicitis (əˌpɛndɪˈsaɪtɪs) *n* inflammation of the vermiform appendix.

appendicle (əˈpɛndɪkᵊl) *n* a small appendage. [C17: from Latin *appendicula;* see APPENDIX]

appendicular (ˌæpənˈdɪkjʊlə) *adj* 1 relating to an appendage or appendicle. 2 *Anatomy.* of or relating to the vermiform appendix.

appendix (əˈpɛndɪks) *n, pl* **-dices** (-dɪˌsiːz). *or* **-dixes** 1 a body of separate additional material at the end of a book, magazine, etc., esp. one that is documentary or explanatory. 2 any part that is dependent or supplementary in nature or function; appendage. 3 *Anatomy.* See **vermiform appendix.** [C16: from Latin: an appendage, from *appendere* to APPEND]

Appenzell (*German* apənˈtsɛl, ˈapəntsɛl) *n* 1 a canton of NE Switzerland, divided in 1597 into the Protestant demicanton of **Appenzell Outer Rhodes** and the Catholic demicanton of **Appenzell Inner Rhodes.** Capitals: Herisau and Appenzell. Pop.: 54 104 and 14 750 (1996 est.) respectively. Areas: 243 sq. km (94 sq. miles) and 171 sq. km (66 sq. miles) respectively. 2 a town in NE Switzerland, capital of Appenzell Inner Rhodes demicanton. Pop.: 5157 (1990).

apperceive (ˌæpəˈsiːv) *vb (tr)* 1 to be aware of perceiving. 2 *Psychol.* to comprehend by assimilating (a perception) to ideas already in the mind. [C19: from Old French *aperceveir,* from Latin *percipere* to PERCEIVE]

apperception (ˌæpəˈsɛpʃən) *n Psychol.* 1 the attainment of full awareness of a sensation or idea. 2 the act or process of apperceiving. ▸ **ˌapperˈceptive** *adj*

appertain (ˌæpəˈteɪn) *vb (intr;* usually foll. by *to)* to belong (to) as a part, function, right, etc.; relate (to) or be connected (with). [C14: from Old French *apertenir* to belong, from Late Latin *appertinēre,* from Latin AD- + *pertinēre* to PERTAIN]

appestat (ˈæpɪstæt) *n* a neural control centre within the hypothalamus of the brain that regulates the sense of hunger and satiety. [C20: from APPE(TITE) + -STAT]

appetence (ˈæpɪtəns) *or* **appetency** *n, pl* **-tences** *or* **-tencies.** 1 a natural craving or desire. 2 a natural or instinctive inclination. 3 an attraction or affinity. [C17: from Latin *appetentia,* from *appetere* to crave]

appetite (ˈæpɪˌtaɪt) *n* 1 a desire for food or drink. 2 a desire to satisfy a bodily craving, as for sexual pleasure. 3 (usually foll. by *for)* a desire, liking, or willingness: *a great appetite for work.* [C14: from Old French *apetit,* from Latin *appetītus* a craving, from *appetere* to desire ardently] ▸ **appetitive** (əˈpɛtɪtɪv, ˈæpɪˌtaɪtɪv) *adj*

appetizer *or* **appetiser** (ˈæpɪˌtaɪzə) *n* 1 a small amount of food or drink taken to stimulate the appetite. 2 any stimulating foretaste.

appetizing *or* **appetising** (ˈæpɪˌtaɪzɪŋ) *adj* pleasing or stimulating to the appetite; delicious; tasty.

Appian Way (ˈæpɪən) *n* a Roman road in Italy, extending from Rome to Brindisi: begun in 312 B.C. by Appius Claudius Caecus. Length: about 560 km (350 miles).

applaud (əˈplɔːd) *vb* 1 to indicate approval of (a person, performance, etc.) by clapping the hands. 2 *(usually tr)* to offer or express approval or praise of (an action, person, or thing): *I applaud your decision.* [C15: from Latin *applaudere* to clap, from *plaudere* to beat, applaud] ▸ **apˈplauder** *n* ▸ **apˈplauding** *adj* ▸ **apˈplaudingly** *adv*

applause (əˈplɔːz) *n* appreciation or praise, esp. as shown by clapping the hands.

apple (ˈæpᵊl) *n* 1 a rosaceous tree, *Malus pumila* (or *Pyrus malus),* widely cultivated in temperate regions in many varieties, having pink or white fragrant flowers and firm rounded edible fruits. 2 the fruit of this tree, having red, yellow, or green skin and crisp whitish flesh. 3 the wood of this tree. 4 any of several unrelated trees that have fruit similar to the apple, such as the custard apple, sugar apple, and May apple. See also **love apple, oak apple, thorn apple.** 5 **apple of one's eye.** a person or thing that is very precious or much loved. 6 **bad** *or* **rotten apple.** a person with a corrupting influence. ◆ See also **apples.** [Old English *æppel;* related to Old Saxon *appel,* Old Norse *apall,* Old High German *apful*]

apple blight *n* an aphid, *Eriosoma lanigera,* that is covered with a powdery waxy secretion and infests apple trees. Also called: **American blight.**

apple box *n* an ornamental Australian tree, *Eucalyptus bridgesiana,* having heart-shaped juvenile leaves, large lanceolate adult leaves, and conical fruits. Also called: **apple gum.**

apple butter *n* a jam made from stewed spiced apples.

Appleby (ˈæpᵊlbɪ) *n* a town in NW England, in Cumbria: famous for its annual horse fair. Pop.: 2570 (1991).

applecart (ˈæpᵊlˌkɑːt) *n* 1 a cart or barrow from which apples and other fruit are sold in the street. 2 **upset the applecart.** to spoil plans or arrangements.

apple green *n* **a** a bright light green or moderate yellowish-green. **b** *(as adj): an apple-green carpet.*

Apple Isle *n* **the.** *Austral. informal.* Tasmania. ▸ **Apple Islander** *n*

applejack (ˈæpᵊlˌdʒæk) *n* a brandy made from apples; distilled cider. Also called: **applejack brandy, apple brandy.**

apple maggot *n* a fruit fly, *Rhagoletis pomonella,* the larvae of which bore into and feed on the fruit of apple trees: family *Trypetidae.*

apple of discord *n Greek myth.* a golden apple inscribed "For the fairest." It was claimed by Hera, Athena, and Aphrodite, to whom Paris awarded it, thus beginning a chain of events that led to the Trojan War.

apple-pie bed *n Brit.* a way of making a bed so as to prevent the person from entering it.

apple-pie order *n Informal.* perfect order or condition.

apple polisher *n Informal.* a sycophant; toady.

apples (ˈæpᵊlz) *pl n* 1 See **apples and pears.** 2 **she's apples.** *Austral. and N.Z. informal.* all is going well.

apples and pears *pl n Cockney rhyming slang.* stairs. Often shortened to **apples.**

apple sauce *n* 1 a purée of stewed apples often served with pork. 2 *U.S. and Canadian slang.* nonsense; rubbish.

applet (ˈæplɪt) *n Computing.* a computer program that runs within a page on the World Wide Web. [C20: from APP(LICATION PROGRAM) + -LET]

Appleton (ˈæpᵊltən) *n* Sir **Edward** (**Victor**). 1892–1965, English physicist, noted particularly for his research on the ionosphere: Nobel prize for physics 1947.

Appleton layer *n* another name for **F region** (of the ionosphere).

appliance (əˈplaɪəns) *n* 1 a machine or device, esp. an electrical one used domestically. 2 any piece of equipment having a specific function. 3 a device fitted to a machine or tool to adapt it for a specific purpose. 4 another name for a **fire engine.**

applicable (ˈæplɪkəbᵊl, əˈplɪkə-) *adj* being appropriate or relevant; able to be applied; fitting. ▸ **ˌapplicaˈbility** *or* **ˈapplicableness** *n* ▸ **ˈapplicably** *adv*

applicant (ˈæplɪkənt) *n* a person who applies, as for a job, grant, support, etc.; candidate. [C15: from Latin *applicāns,* from *applicāre* to APPLY]

application (ˌæplɪˈkeɪʃən) *n* 1 the act of applying to a particular purpose or use. 2 relevance or value: *the practical applications of space technology.* 3 the act of asking for something: *an application for leave.* 4 a verbal or written request, as for a job, etc.: *he filed his application.* 5 diligent effort or concentration: *a job requiring application.* 6 something, such as a healing agent or lotion, that is applied, esp. to the skin. 7 *Logic, maths.* the process of determining the value of a function for a given argument.

application program *n* a computer program that is written and designed for a specific need or purpose.

applications package *n Computing.* a specialized program or set of specialized programs and associated documentation designed to carry out a particular task.

applicative (əˈplɪkətɪv) *adj* relevant or applicable. ▸ **apˈplicatively** *adv*

applicator (ˈæplɪˌkeɪtə) *n* a device, such as a spatula or rod, for applying a medicine, glue, etc.

applicatory (ˈæplɪkətərɪ) *adj* suitable for application.

applied (əˈplaɪd) *adj* related to or put to practical use: *applied mathematics.* Compare **pure** (sense 5).

appliqué (æˈpliːkeɪ) *n* 1 a decoration or trimming of one material sewn or otherwise fixed onto another. 2 the practice of decorating in this way. ◆ *vb* **-qués, -quéing, -quéd.** 3 *(tr)* to sew or fix (a decoration) on as an appliqué. [C18: from French, literally: applied]

apply (əˈplaɪ) *vb* **-plies, -plying, -plied.** 1 *(tr)* to put to practical use; utilize; employ. 2 *(intr)* to be relevant, useful, or appropriate. 3 *(tr)* to cause to come into contact with; put onto. 4 *(intr;* often foll. by *for)* to put in an application or request. 5 *(tr;* often foll. by *to)* to devote (oneself, one's efforts) with diligence. 6 *(tr)* to bring into operation or use: *the police only applied the law to aliens.* 7 *(tr)* to refer (a word, epithet, etc.) to a person or thing. [C14: from Old French *aplier,* from Latin *applicāre* to attach to] ▸ **apˈplier** *n*

appoggiatura (əˌpɒdʒəˈtʊərə) *n, pl* **-ras** *or* **-re** (-rɛ). *Music.* an ornament consisting of a nonharmonic note (short or long) preceding a harmonic one either before or on the stress. See also **acciaccatura** (sense 2). [C18: from Italian, literally: a propping, from *appoggiare* to prop, support]

appoint (əˈpɔɪnt) *vb (mainly tr)* 1 *(also intr)* to assign officially, as for a position, responsibility, etc.: *he was appointed manager.* 2 to establish by agreement or decree; fix: *a time was appointed for the duel.* 3 to prescribe or ordain: *laws appointed by tribunal.* 4 *Property law.* to nominate (a person), under a power granted in a deed or will, to take an interest in property. 5 to equip with necessary or usual features; furnish: *a well-appointed hotel.* [C14: from Old French *apointer* to put into a good state, from *a point* in good condition, literally: to a POINT] ▸ **apˈpointer** *n*

appointee (əpɔɪnˈtiː, ˌæp-) *n* 1 a person who is appointed. 2 *Property law.* a person to whom property is granted under a power of appointment.

appointive (əˈpɔɪntɪv) *adj Chiefly U.S.* relating to or filled by appointment: *an appointive position.*

appointment (əˈpɔɪntmənt) *n* 1 an arrangement to meet a person or be at a place at a certain time. 2 the act of placing in a job or position. 3 the person who receives such a job or position. 4 the job or position to which such a person is appointed. 5 *(usually pl)* a fixture or fitting. 6 *Property law.* nomination to an interest in property under a deed or will.

appointor (əˈpɔɪntə, əpɔɪnˈtɔː) *n Property law.* a person to whom a power to nominate persons to take property is given by deed or will. See also **power of appointment.**

Appomattox (ˌæpəˈmætəks) *n* a village in central Virginia where the Confederate army under Robert E. Lee surrendered to Ulysses S. Grant's Union forces on April 9, 1865, effectively ending the American Civil War.

apport (əˈpɔːt) *n* 1a the production of objects by apparently supernatural means at a spiritualists' seance. 1b the objects produced. 2 *Obsolete.* bearing; demeanour. 3 *(pl) Obsolete.* things brought as offerings; revenues. [C15: from Old French *aport,* from *aporter* (vb), from Latin AD- + *portāre* to carry]

apportion (əˈpɔːʃən) *vb (tr)* to divide, distribute, or assign appropriate shares of; allot proportionally: *to apportion the blame.* ▸ **ap'portionable** *adj* ▸ **ap'portioner** *n*

apportionment (ə'pɔːʃənmənt) *n* **1** the act of apportioning. **2** *U.S. government.* the proportional distribution of the seats in a legislative body, esp. the House of Representatives, on the basis of population.

apposable (ə'pəʊzəbᵊl) *adj* **1** capable of being apposed or brought into apposition. **2** *Anatomy.* another word for **opposable** (sense 2).

appose (ə'pəʊz) *vb* (*tr*) **1** to place side by side or near to each other. **2** (usually foll. by *to*) to place (something) near or against another thing. [C16: from Old French *apposer,* from *poser* to put, from Latin *pōnere*]

apposite ('æpəzɪt) *adj* well suited for the purpose; appropriate; apt. [C17: from Latin *appositus* placed near, from *appōnere,* from *pōnere* to put, place] ▸ **'appositely** *adv* ▸ **'appositeness** *n*

apposition (ˌæpə'zɪʃən) *n* **1** a putting into juxtaposition. **2** a grammatical construction in which a word, esp. a noun phrase, is placed after another to modify its meaning. **3** *Biology.* growth in the thickness of a cell wall by the deposition of successive layers of material. Compare **intussusception** (sense 2). ▸ **ˌap-po'sitional** *adj*

appositive (ə'pɒzɪtɪv) *adj* **1** *Grammar.* **1a** standing in apposition. **1b** another word for **nonrestrictive.** **2** of or relating to apposition. ◆ *n* **3** an appositive word or phrase. ▸ **ap'positively** *adv*

appraisal (ə'preɪzᵊl) *or* **appraisement** *n* **1** an assessment or estimation of the worth, value, or quality of a person or thing. See also **performance appraisal.** **2** a valuation of property or goods.

appraisal drilling *n* (in the oil industry) drilling carried out once oil or gas has been discovered in order to assess the extent of the field, the reserves, the possible rate of production, and the properties of the oil or gas.

appraise (ə'preɪz) *vb* (*tr*) **1** to assess the worth, value, or quality of. **2** to make a valuation of, as for taxation purposes. [C15: from Old French *aprisier,* from *prisier* to PRIZE[2]] ▸ **ap'praisable** *adj* ▸ **ap'praiser** *n* ▸ **ap'praisingly** *adv* ▸ **ap'praisive** *adj* ▸ **ap'praisively** *adv*

USAGE *Appraise* is sometimes wrongly used where *apprise* is meant: *they had been apprised* (not *appraised*) *of my arrival.*

appreciable (ə'priːʃɪəbᵊl, -ʃəbᵊl) *adj* sufficient to be easily seen, measured, or noticed. ▸ **ap'preciably** *adv*

appreciate (ə'priːʃɪˌeɪt, -sɪ-) *vb* (*mainly tr*) **1** to feel thankful or grateful for: *to appreciate a favour.* **2** (*may take a clause as object*) to take full or sufficient account of: *to appreciate a problem.* **3** to value highly: *to appreciate Shakespeare.* **4** (*usually intr*) to raise or increase in value. [C17: from Medieval Latin *appretiāre* to value, prize, from Latin *pretium* PRICE] ▸ **ap'preciˌator** *n*

appreciation (əˌpriːʃɪ'eɪʃən, -sɪ-) *n* **1** thanks or gratitude. **2** assessment of the true worth or value of persons or things. **3** perceptive recognition of qualities, as in art. **4** an increase in value, as of goods or property. **5** a written review of a book, etc., esp. when favourable.

appreciative (ə'priːʃɪətɪv, -ʃə-) *or* **appreciatory** *adj* feeling, expressing, or capable of appreciation. ▸ **ap'preciatively** *or* **ap'preciatorily** *adv* ▸ **ap'preciativeness** *n*

apprehend (ˌæprɪ'hɛnd) *vb* **1** (*tr*) to arrest and escort into custody; seize. **2** to perceive or grasp mentally; understand. **3** (*tr*) to await with fear or anxiety; dread. [C14: from Latin *apprehendere* to lay hold of]

apprehensible (ˌæprɪ'hɛnsɪbᵊl) *adj* capable of being comprehended or grasped mentally. ▸ **ˌappreˌhensi'bility** *n* ▸ **ˌappre'hensibly** *adv*

apprehension (ˌæprɪ'hɛnʃən) *n* **1** fear or anxiety over what may happen. **2** the act of capturing or arresting. **3** the faculty of comprehending; understanding. **4** a notion or conception.

apprehensive (ˌæprɪ'hɛnsɪv) *adj* fearful or anxious. ▸ **ˌappre'hensively** *adv* ▸ **ˌappre'hensiveness** *n*

apprentice (ə'prɛntɪs) *n* **1** someone who works for a skilled or qualified person in order to learn a trade or profession, esp. for a recognized period. **2** any beginner or novice. ◆ *vb* **3** (*tr*) to take, place, or bind as an apprentice. [C14: from Old French *aprentis,* from Old French *aprendre* to learn, from Latin *apprehendere* to APPREHEND] ▸ **ap'prenticeˌship** *n*

appressed (ə'prɛst) *adj* pressed closely against, but not joined to, a surface: *leaves appressed to a stem.* [C18: from Latin *appressus,* from *apprimere,* from *premere* to press]

appressorium (ˌæprɛ'sɔːrɪəm) *n, pl* **-ria** (-rɪə). *Botany.* a flattened hypha of a parasitic fungus that penetrates the host tissues. [from New Latin, from Latin *appressus;* see APPRESSED]

apprise *or* **apprize** (ə'praɪz) *vb* (*tr;* often foll. by *of*) to make aware; inform. [C17: from French *appris,* from *apprendre* to teach; learn; see APPREHEND]

USAGE See at **appraise.**

appro ('æprəʊ) *n* an informal shortening of **approval:** *on appro.*

approach (ə'prəʊtʃ) *vb* **1** to come nearer in position, time, quality, character, etc., to (someone or something). **2** (*tr*) to make advances to, as with a proposal, suggestion, etc. **3** (*tr*) to begin to deal with: *to approach a problem.* **4** (*tr*) *Rare.* to cause to come near. ◆ *n* **5** the act of coming towards or drawing close or closer. **6** a close approximation. **7** the way or means of entering or leaving; access. **8** (*often pl*) an advance or overture to a person. **9** a means adopted in tackling a problem, job of work, etc. **10** Also called: **approach path.** the course followed by an aircraft preparing for landing. [C14: from Old French *aprochier,* from Late Latin *appropiāre* to draw near, from Latin *prope* near]

approachable (ə'prəʊtʃəbᵊl) *adj* **1** capable of being approached; accessible. **2** (of a person) friendly. ▸ **apˌproacha'bility** *or* **ap'proachableness** *n*

approach shot *n* **1** *Golf.* Also called: **approach.** a shot made to or towards the green after a tee shot. **2** *Tennis.* a deep drive, usually hit with slice to keep the ball low, designed to enable the player to make an approach to the net.

approbate ('æprəˌbeɪt) *vb* (*tr*) **1** *Scots Law.* to accept as valid. **2 approbate and reprobate.** *Scots Law.* to accept part of a document and reject those parts unfavourable to one's interests. **3** *Chiefly U.S.* to sanction officially. [C15: from Latin *approbāre* to approve, from *probāre* to test]

approbation (ˌæprə'beɪʃən) *n* **1** commendation; praise. **2** official recognition or approval. **3** an obsolete word for **proof.** ▸ **'approˌbative** *or* **'approˌbatory** *adj*

appropriacy (ə'prəʊprɪəsɪ) *n* the condition of delicate and precise fittingness of a word or expression to its context, even when it is chosen from a number of close synonyms.

appropriate *adj* (ə'prəʊprɪɪt). **1** right or suitable; fitting. **2** *Rare.* particular; own: *they had their appropriate methods.* ◆ *vb* (ə'prəʊprɪˌeɪt). (*tr*) **3** to take for one's own use, esp. illegally or without permission. **4** to put aside (funds, etc.) for a particular purpose or person. [C15: from Late Latin *appropriāre* to make one's own, from Latin *proprius* one's own; see PROPER] ▸ **ap'propriable** *adj* ▸ **ap'propriately** *adv* ▸ **ap'propriateness** *n* ▸ **ap'propriative** *adj* ▸ **ap'propriˌator** *n*

appropriation (əˌprəʊprɪ'eɪʃən) *n* **1** the act of setting apart or taking for one's own use. **2** a sum of money set apart for a specific purpose, esp. by a legislature.

approval (ə'pruːvᵊl) *n* **1** the act of approving. **2** formal agreement; sanction. **3** a favourable opinion; commendation. **4 on approval.** (of articles for sale) for examination with an option to buy or return.

approve[1] (ə'pruːv) *vb* **1** (when *intr,* often foll. by *of*) to consider fair, good, or right; commend (a person or thing). **2** (*tr*) to authorize or sanction. **3** (*tr*) *Obsolete.* to demonstrate or prove by trial. [C14: from Old French *aprover,* from Latin *approbāre* to approve, from *probāre* to test, PROVE] ▸ **ap'provingly** *adv*

approve[2] (ə'pruːv) *vb* (*tr*) *Law.* to improve or increase the value of (waste or common land), as by enclosure. [C15: from Old French *approuer* to turn to advantage, from *prou* advantage]

approved school *n* (in Britain) a former name for **community home.**

approved social worker *n Social welfare.* (in England) a qualified social worker specially trained in mental-health work, who is approved by his employing local authority to apply for a mentally disordered person to be admitted to hospital and detained there, or to apply for the person to be received into the guardianship of the local authority.

approx. *abbrev. for* approximate(ly).

approximal (ə'prɒksɪməl) *adj Anatomy.* situated side by side; close together: *approximal teeth or fillings.*

approximate *adj* (ə'prɒksɪmɪt). **1** almost accurate or exact. **2** inexact; rough; loose: *only an approximate fit.* **3** much alike; almost the same. **4** near; close together. ◆ *vb* (ə'prɒksɪˌmeɪt). **5** (usually foll. by *to*) to come or bring near or close; be almost the same (as). **6** *Maths.* to find an expression for (some quantity) accurate to a specified degree. See **accurate** (sense 4). [C15: from Late Latin *approximāre,* from Latin *proximus* nearest, from *prope* near] ▸ **ap'proximately** *adv* ▸ **ap'proximative** *adj*

approximation (əˌprɒksɪ'meɪʃən) *n* **1** the process or result of making a rough calculation, estimate, or guess: *he based his conclusion on his own approximation of the fuel consumption.* **2** an imprecise or unreliable record or version: *an approximation of what really happened.* **3** *Maths.* an inexact number, relationship, or theory that is sufficiently accurate for a specific purpose. **4** *Maths.* **4a** an estimate of the value of some quantity to a desired degree of accuracy. **4b** an expression in simpler terms than a given expression which approximates to it.

appulse (ə'pʌls) *n* a very close approach of two celestial bodies so that they are in conjunction but no eclipse or occultation occurs. [C17: from Latin *appulsus* brought near, from *appellere* to drive towards, from *pellere* to drive] ▸ **ap'pulsive** *adj* ▸ **ap'pulsively** *adv*

appurtenance (ə'pɜːtɪnəns) *n* **1** a secondary or less significant thing or part. **2** (*pl*) accessories or equipment. **3** *Property law.* a minor right, interest, or privilege which passes when the title to the principal property is transferred. [C14: from Anglo-French *apurtenance,* from Old French *apartenance,* from *apartenir* to APPERTAIN]

appurtenant (ə'pɜːtɪnənt) *adj* **1** relating, belonging, or accessory. ◆ *n* **2** another word for **appurtenance.**

APR *abbrev. for* annual percentage rate.

Apr. *abbrev. for* April.

apraxia (ə'præksɪə) *n* a disorder of the central nervous system caused by brain damage and characterized by impaired ability to carry out purposeful muscular movements. [C19: via New Latin from Greek: inactivity, from A-[1] + *praxis* action] ▸ **a'praxic** *or* **a'practic** *adj*

après-ski (ˌæpreɪ'skiː) *n* **a** social activity following a day's skiing. **b** (*as modifier*): *an après-ski outfit.* [French, literally: after ski]

apricot ('eɪprɪˌkɒt) *n* **1** a rosaceous tree, *Prunus armeniaca,* native to Africa and W Asia, but widely cultivated for its edible fruit. **2** the downy yellow juicy edible fruit of this tree, which resembles a small peach. [C16: earlier *apricock,* from Portuguese (*albricoque*) or Spanish, from Arabic *al-birqūq* the apricot, from Late Greek *praikokion,* from Latin *praecox* early-ripening; see PRECOCIOUS]

April ('eɪprəl) *n* the fourth month of the year, consisting of 30 days. [C14: from Latin *Aprīlis,* probably of Etruscan origin]

April fool *n* an unsuspecting victim of a practical joke or trick traditionally performed on the first of April (**April Fools' Day** *or* **All Fools' Day**).

a priori (eɪ praɪ'ɔːraɪ, ɑː prɪ'ɔːrɪ) *adj* **1** *Logic.* relating to or involving deductive reasoning from a general principle to the expected facts or effects. **2** *Logic.* known to be true independently of or in advance of experience of the subject matter; requiring no evidence for its validation or support. **3** *Statistics.* See **prior probability, mathematical probability.** ◆ Compare **a posteriori, analytic** (sense 4). [C18: from Latin, literally: from the previous (that is, from cause to effect)] ▸ **apriority** (ˌeɪpraɪ'ɒrɪtɪ) *n*

apriorism (eɪ'praɪəˌrɪzəm) *n* the philosophical doctrine that there may be genuine knowledge independent of experience. Compare **rationalism** (sense 2), **sensationalism** (sense 3).

apron ('eɪprən) *n* **1** a protective or sometimes decorative or ceremonial garment worn over the front of the body and tied around the waist. **2** the part of a stage extending in front of the curtain line; forestage. **3** a hard-surfaced area in front of or around an aircraft hangar, terminal building, etc., upon which aircraft can stand. **4** a continuous conveyor belt composed of metal slats linked together. **5** a protective plate screening the operator of a machine, artillery piece, etc. **6** a ground covering of concrete or other material used to protect the underlying earth from water erosion. **7** a panel or board between a window and a skirting in a room. **8** *Geology.* a sheet of sand, gravel, etc., deposited at the front of a moraine. **9** *Golf.* the part of the fairway leading onto the green. **10** *Machinery.* the housing for the lead screw gears of a lathe. **11** another name for **skirt** (sense 3). **12 tied to someone's apron strings.** dependent on or dominated by someone, esp. a mother or wife. ♦ *vb* **13** (*tr*) to protect or provide with an apron. [C16: mistaken division (as if *an apron*) of earlier *a napron,* from Old French *naperon* a little cloth, from *nape* cloth, from Latin *mappa* napkin]

apron stage *n* a stage that projects into the auditorium so that the audience sit on three sides of it.

apropos (ˌæprə'pəʊ) *adj* **1** appropriate; pertinent. ♦ *adv* **2** appropriately or pertinently. **3** by the way; incidentally. **4 apropos of.** (*prep*) with regard to; in respect of. [C17: from French *à propos* to the purpose]

aprotic (eɪ'prəʊtɪk) *adj Chem.* (of solvents) neither accepting nor donating hydrogen ions.

apse (æps) *n* **1** Also called: **apsis.** a domed or vaulted semicircular or polygonal recess, esp. at the east end of a church. **2** *Astronomy.* another name for **apsis** (sense 1). [C19: from Latin *apsis,* from Greek: a fitting together, arch, from *haptein* to fasten] ► **apsidal** (æp'saɪdᵊl, 'æpsɪdᵊl) *adj*

apsis ('æpsɪs) *n, pl* **apsides** (æp'saɪdiːz, 'æpsɪˌdiːz). **1** Also called: **apse.** either of two points lying at the extremities of an eccentric orbit of a planet, satellite, etc., such as the aphelion and perihelion of a planet or the apogee and perigee of the moon. The **line of apsides** connects two such points and is the principal axis of the orbit. **2** another name for **apse** (sense 1). [C17: via Latin from Greek; see APSE] ► **apsidal** (æp'saɪdᵊl, 'æpsɪdᵊl) *adj*

apt (æpt) *adj* **1** suitable for the circumstance or purpose; appropriate. **2** (*postpositive;* foll. by an infinitive) having a tendency (to behave as specified). **3** having the ability to learn and understand easily; clever (esp. in the phrase **an apt pupil**). [C14: from Latin *aptus* fitting, suitable, from *apere* to fasten] ► **'aptly** *adv* ► **'aptness** *n*

APT *abbrev. for* Advanced Passenger Train.

apt. *pl* **apts.** *abbrev. for* apartment.

apteral ('æptərəl) *adj* **1** (esp. of a classical temple) not having columns at the sides. **2** (of a church) having no aisles. [C19: from Greek *apteros* wingless; see APTEROUS]

apterous ('æptərəs) *adj* **1** (of insects) without wings, as silverfish and springtails. **2** without winglike expansions, as some plant stems, seeds, and fruits. [C18: from Greek *apteros* wingless, from A-[1] + *pteron* wing] ► **'apterˌism** *n*

apterygial (ˌæptə'rɪdʒɪəl) *adj* (of eels, certain insects, etc.) lacking such paired limbs as wings or fins. [C20: from New Latin *apteryx* wingless creature; see APTEROUS]

apteryx ('æptərɪks) *n* another name for **kiwi** (the bird). [C19: from New Latin: wingless creature; see APTEROUS]

aptitude ('æptɪˌtjuːd) *n* **1** inherent or acquired ability. **2** ease in learning or understanding; intelligence. **3** the condition or quality of being apt. [C15: via Old French from Late Latin *aptitūdō,* from Latin *aptus* APT]

aptitude test *n* a test designed to assess a person's ability to do a particular type of work.

APU (in Britain) *abbrev. for* Assessment of Performance Unit: a research unit founded by the Department of Education and Science in 1975 to monitor pupil performance and report upon findings in subject areas such as mathematics, English Language, and modern languages.

Apuleius (ˌæpjʊ'liːəs) *n* **Lucius** ('luːsɪəs). 2nd century A.D., Roman writer, noted for his romance *The Golden Ass.*

Apulia (ə'pjuːljə) *n* a region of SE Italy, on the Adriatic. Capital: Bari. Pop.: 4 082 953 (1996 est.). Area: 19 223 sq. km (7422 sq. miles). Italian name: **Puglia.**

Apure (*Spanish* a'pure) *n* a river in W Venezuela, rising in the Andes and flowing east to the Orinoco. Length: about 676 km (420 miles).

Apurimac (ˌæpuː'riːmæk) *n* a river in S Peru, rising in the Andes and flowing northwest into the Urubamba River. Length: about 885 km (550 miles).

Apus ('eɪpəs) *n, Latin genitive* **Apodis** ('æpədɪs). a constellation in the S hemisphere situated near Musca and Octans. [New Latin, from Greek *apous,* literally: footless, from A-[1] + *pous* foot]

apyrexia (ˌæpaɪ'rɛksɪə) *n* absence of fever. [C19: from A-[1] + Greek *puretos* fever] ► ˌ**apy'retic** *adj*

AQ *abbrev. for* achievement quotient.

aq. *or* **Aq.** *abbrev. for:* **1** aqua. [Latin: water] **2** aqueous.

Aqaba *or* **Akaba** ('ækəbə) *n* the only port in Jordan, in the southwest, on the **Gulf of Aqaba.** Pop.: 46 090 (1990 est.).

Aqmola (æk'məʊlə; *Kazakh* ɑkmɔ'lɑ) *n* a variant spelling of **Akmola.**

Aqtöbe (æk'tjuːbɪ; *Kazakh* aktø'be) *n* an industrial city in W Kazakhstan. Pop.: 258 900 (1995 est.). Former name (until 1991): **Aktyubinsk.**

aqua ('ækwə) *n, pl* **aquae** ('ækwiː) *or* **aquas. 1** water: used in compound names of certain liquid substances (as in **aqua regia**) or solutions of substances in water (as in **aqua ammoniae**), esp. in the names of pharmacological solutions. ♦ *adj* **2** short for **aquamarine** (sense 2). [Latin: water]

aquaculture ('ækwəˌkʌltʃə) *or* **aquiculture** *n* the cultivation of freshwater and marine resources, both plant and animal, for human consumption or use.

aquaerobics (ˌækwə'rəʊbɪks) *n* (*functioning as sing*) the practice of exercising to music in a swimming pool. [C20: from Latin *aqua* water + AEROBICS]

aqua fortis ('fɔːtɪs) *n* an obsolete name for **nitric acid.** [C17: from Latin, literally: strong water]

aqualung ('ækwəˌlʌŋ) *n* breathing apparatus used by divers, etc., consisting of a mouthpiece attached to air cylinders strapped to the back.

aquamarine (ˌækwəmə'riːn) *n* **1** a pale greenish-blue transparent variety of beryl used as a gemstone. **2a** a pale blue to greenish-blue colour. **2b** (*as adj*): *an aquamarine dress.* [C19: from New Latin *aqua marīna,* from Latin: sea water (referring to the gem's colour)]

aquanaut ('ækwəˌnɔːt) *n* **1** a person who lives and works underwater. **2** a person who swims or dives underwater. [C20: from AQUA + *-naut,* as in ASTRONAUT]

aquaphobia (ˌækwə'fəʊbɪə) *n* an abnormal fear of water, esp. because of the possibility of drowning. Compare **hydrophobia** (sense 2).

aquaplane ('ækwəˌpleɪn) *n* **1** a single board on which a person stands and is towed by a motorboat at high speed, as in water skiing. ♦ *vb* (*intr*) **2** to ride on an aquaplane. **3** (of a motor vehicle travelling at high speeds in wet road conditions) to rise up onto a thin film of water between the tyres and road surface so that actual contact with the road is lost.

aqua regia ('riːdʒɪə) *n* a yellow fuming corrosive mixture of one part nitric acid and three to four parts hydrochloric acid, used in metallurgy for dissolving metals, including gold. Also called: **nitrohydrochloric acid.** [C17: from New Latin: royal water; referring to its use in dissolving gold, the royal metal]

aquarelle (ˌækwə'rɛl) *n* **1** a method of watercolour painting in transparent washes. **2** a painting done in this way. [C19: from French] ► ˌ**aqua'rellist** *n*

aquarist ('ækwərɪst) *n* **1** the curator of an aquarium. **2** a person who studies aquatic life.

aquarium (ə'kwɛərɪəm) *n, pl* **-riums** *or* **-ria** (-rɪə). **1** a tank, bowl, or pool in which aquatic animals and plants are kept for pleasure, study, or exhibition. **2** a building housing a collection of aquatic life, as for exhibition. [C19: from Latin *aquārius* relating to water, on the model of VIVARIUM]

Aquarius (ə'kwɛərɪəs) *n, Latin genitive* **Aquarii** (ə'kwɛərɪˌaɪ). **1** *Astronomy.* a zodiacal constellation in the S hemisphere lying between Pisces and Capricorn on the ecliptic. **2** *Astrology.* **2a** Also called: the **Water Carrier.** the eleventh sign of the zodiac, symbol ♒, having a fixed air classification and ruled by the planets Saturn and Uranus. The sun is in this sign between about Jan. 20 and Feb. 18. **2b** a person born during a period when the sun is in this sign. ♦ *adj* **3** *Astrology.* born under or characteristic of Aquarius. ♦ Also (for senses 2b, 3): **Aquarian** (ə'kwɛərɪən). [Latin]

aquashow ('ækwəˌʃəʊ) *or U.S.* **aquacade** ('ækwəˌkeɪd) *n* an exhibition of swimming and diving, often accompanied by music.

aquatic (ə'kwætɪk, ə'kwɒt-) *adj* **1** growing, living, or found in water. **2** *Sport.* performed in or on water. ♦ *n* **3** a marine animal or plant. [C15: from Latin *aquāticus,* from *aqua* water]

aquatics (ə'kwætɪks, ə'kwɒt-) *pl n* sports or pastimes performed in or on the water.

aquatint ('ækwəˌtɪnt) *n* **1** a technique of etching copper with acid to produce an effect resembling the flat tones of wash or watercolour. The tone or tint is obtained by acid (aqua) biting through the pores of a ground that only partially protects the copper. **2** an etching made in this way. ♦ *vb* **3** (*tr*) to etch (a block, etc.) in aquatint. [C18: from Italian *acqua tinta:* dyed water]

aquavit ('ækwəˌvɪt) *n* a grain- or potato-based spirit from the Scandinavian countries, flavoured with aromatic seeds and spices, esp. caraway. Also called: **akvavit.** [from Scandinavian; see AQUA VITAE]

aqua vitae ('viːtaɪ, 'vaɪtiː) *n* an archaic name for **brandy.** [Medieval Latin: water of life]

aqueduct ('ækwɪˌdʌkt) *n* **1** a conduit used to convey water over a long distance. **2** a structure, often a bridge, that carries such a conduit or a canal across a valley or river. **3** a channel in an organ or part of the body, esp. one that conveys a natural body fluid. [C16: from Latin *aquaeductus,* from *aqua* water + *dūcere* to convey]

aqueous ('eɪkwɪəs, 'ækwɪ-) *adj* **1** of, like, or containing water. **2** dissolved in water: *aqueous ammonia.* **3** (of rocks, deposits, etc.) formed from material laid down in water. [C17: from Medieval Latin *aqueus,* from Latin *aqua* water]

aqueous humour *n Physiol.* the watery fluid within the eyeball between the cornea and the lens.

aquiculture ('eɪkwɪˌkʌltʃə, 'ækwɪ-) *n* **1** another name for **hydroponics. 2** a variant of **aquaculture.** ► **'aquiˌcultural** *adj* ► **'aquiˌculturist** *n*

aquifer ('ækwɪfə) *n* a deposit of rock, such as a sandstone, containing water that can be used to supply wells.

Aquila[1] ('ækwɪlə, ə'kwɪlə) *n, Latin genitive* **Aquilae** ('ækwɪˌliː). a constellation lying in the Milky Way close to Cygnus and situated on the celestial equator. The brightest star is Altair. [from Latin: eagle]

Aquila[2] ('ækwɪlə; *Italian* 'aːkwila) *or* **l'Aquila** *n* a city in central Italy, capital of Abruzzi region. Pop.: 67 820 (1990). Official name: **Aquila degli Abruzzi** ('deʎʎi a'bruttsi).

aquilegia (ˌækwɪ'liːdʒɪə) *n* another name for **columbine**[1]. [C19: from Medieval Latin, of uncertain origin]

Aquileia (ˌækwɪ'liːə) *n* a town in NE Italy, at the head of the Adriatic: important Roman centre, founded in 181 B.C. Pop.: 3451 (1990 est.).

aquiline ('ækwɪˌlaɪn) *adj* **1** (of a nose) having the curved or hooked shape of an eagle's beak. **2** of or resembling an eagle. [C17: from Latin *aquilīnus,* from *aquila* eagle]

Aquinas (ə'kwaɪnəs) *n* **Saint Thomas.** 1225–74, Italian theologian, scholastic philosopher, and Dominican friar, whose works include *Summa contra Gentiles* (1259–64) and *Summa Theologiae* (1267–73), the first attempt at a comprehensive theological system. Feast day: Jan. 28. See also **Thomism.**

Aquino (ə'ki:nəʊ) *n* **Corazón,** known as *Cory.* born 1933, Philippine stateswoman: president (1986–92).
Aquitaine (ˌækwɪ'teɪn; *French* akitɛn) *n* a region of SW France, on the Bay of Biscay: a former Roman province and medieval duchy. It is generally flat in the west, rising to the slopes of the Massif Central in the northeast and the Pyrenees in the south; mainly agricultural. Ancient name: **Aquitania** (ˌækwɪ'teɪnɪə).
Ar *the chemical symbol for* argon.
AR *abbrev. for:* **1** Arkansas. **2** Autonomous Region.
ar. *abbrev. for:* **1** arrival. **2** arrive(s).
Ar. *abbrev. for:* **1** Arabia(n). **2** Also: **Ar** Arabic. **3** Aramaic.
a.r. *abbrev. for* anno regni. [Latin: in the year of the reign]
-ar *suffix forming adjectives.* of; belonging to; like: *linear; polar; minuscular.* [via Old French *-er* from Latin *-āris,* replacing *-ālis* (-AL[1]) after stems ending in *l*]
Ara ('ɑːrə) *n, Latin genitive* **Arae** ('ɑːriː). a constellation in the S hemisphere near Scorpius. [from Latin: altar]
ARA *abbrev. for:* **1** (in Britain) Associate of the Royal Academy. **2** (in Britain) Aircraft Research Association. **3** (in New Zealand) Auckland Regional Authority.
Arab ('ærəb) *n* **1** a member of a Semitic people originally inhabiting Arabia, who spread throughout the Middle East, N Africa, and Spain during the seventh and eighth centuries A.D. **2** a small lively intelligent breed of horse, mainly used for riding. **3** (*modifier*) of or relating to the Arabs: *the Arab nations.* [C14: from Latin *Arabs,* from Greek *Araps,* from Arabic *'Arab*]
Arab. *abbrev. for:* **1** Arabia(n). **2** Arabic.
arabesque (ˌærə'bɛsk) *n* **1** *Ballet.* a classical position in which the dancer has one leg raised behind and both arms stretched out in one of several conventional poses. **2** *Music.* a piece or movement with a highly ornamented or decorated melody. **3** *Arts.* **3a** a type of curvilinear decoration in painting, metalwork, etc., with intricate intertwining leaf, flower, animal, or geometrical designs. **3b** a design of flowing lines. ◆ *adj* **4** designating, of, or decorated in this style. [C18: from French, from Italian *arabesco* in the Arabic style]
Arabia (ə'reɪbɪə) *n* a great peninsula of SW Asia, between the Red Sea and the Persian Gulf: consists chiefly of a desert plateau, with mountains rising over 3000 m (10 000 ft.) in the west and scattered oases; includes the present-day countries of Saudi Arabia, Yemen, Oman, Bahrain, Qatar, Kuwait, and the United Arab Emirates. Area: about 2 600 000 sq. km (1 000 000 sq. miles).
Arabian (ə'reɪbɪən) *adj* **1** of or relating to Arabia or the Arabs. ◆ *n* **2** another word for **Arab.**
Arabian camel *n* a domesticated camel, *Camelus dromedarius,* having one hump on its back and used as a beast of burden in the hot deserts of N Africa and SW Asia. See also **dromedary.** Compare **Bactrian camel.**
Arabian Desert *n* **1** a desert in E Egypt, between the Nile, the Gulf of Suez, and the Red Sea: mountainous parts rise over 1800 m (6000 ft.). Area: about 220 000 sq. km (85 000 sq. miles). **2** a desert, mainly in Saudi Arabia, forming the desert area of the Arabian Peninsula, esp. in the north. Area: about 2 330 000 sq. km (900 000 sq. miles).
Arabian Nights' Entertainments *n* **The.** a collection of oriental folk tales dating from the tenth century. Often shortened to **the Arabian Nights.** Also called: **the Thousand and One Nights.**
Arabian Sea *n* the NW part of the Indian Ocean, between Arabia and India.
Arabic ('ærəbɪk) *n* **1** the language of the Arabs, spoken in a variety of dialects; the official language of Algeria, Egypt, Iraq, Jordan, the Lebanon, Libya, Morocco, Saudi Arabia, the Sudan, Syria, Tunisia, and Yemen. It is estimated to be the native language of some 75 million people throughout the world. It belongs to the Semitic subfamily of the Afro-Asiatic family of languages and has its own alphabet, which has been borrowed by certain other languages such as Urdu. ◆ *adj* **2** denoting or relating to this language, any of the peoples that speak it, or the countries in which it is spoken.
arabica bean (ə'ræbɪkə) *n* a high-quality coffee bean, obtained from the tree *Coffea arabica.*
Arabic numeral *n* one of the numbers 0,1,2,3,4,5,6,7,8,9 (opposed to *Roman numerals*).
arabinose (ə'ræbɪˌnəʊz, -ˌnəʊs) *n* a pentose sugar in plant gums, esp. of cedars and pines. It is used as a culture medium in bacteriology. Formula: $C_5H_{10}O_5$. [C19: from *arabin* (from (GUM) ARAB(IC) + -IN) + -OSE[2]]
arabis ('ærəbɪs) *n* any plant of the annual or perennial genus *Arabis* that forms low-growing mats with downy grey foliage and white flowers: family *Cruciferae.* Also called: **rock cress.** [New Latin, from Greek *arabis* (fem) of Arabia]
Arabist ('ærəbɪst) *n* a student or expert in Arabic culture, language, history, etc.
arable ('ærəb°l) *adj* **1** (of land) being or capable of being tilled for the production of crops. **2** of, relating to, or using such land: *arable farming.* ◆ *n* **3** arable land or farming. [C15: from Latin *arābilis* that can be ploughed, from *arāre* to plough]
Arab League *n* the league of independent Arab states formed in 1945 to further cultural, economic, military, political, and social cooperation.
Araby ('ærəbɪ) *n* an archaic or poetic name for **Arabia.**
Aracajú (*Portuguese* arəkə'ʒu) *n* a port in E Brazil, capital of Sergipe state. Pop.: 401 676 (1991).
araceous (ə'reɪʃəs) *adj* another word for **aroid** (sense 1). [C19: from New Latin *Arāceae;* see ARUM]
arachidonic acid (ˌærəkə'dɒnɪk) *n* a fatty acid occurring in animal cells: the metabolic precursor of several groups of biologically active substances, including prostaglandins.
Arachne (ə'ræknɪ) *n Greek myth.* a maiden changed into a spider for having presumptuously challenged Athena to a weaving contest. [from Greek *arakhnē* spider]
arachnid (ə'ræknɪd) *n* any terrestrial chelicerate arthropod of the class *Arachnida,* characterized by simple eyes and four pairs of legs. The group includes the spiders, scorpions, ticks, mites, and harvestmen. [C19: from New Latin *Arachnida,* from Greek *arakhnē* spider] ▶ **a'rachnidan** *adj, n*
arachnoid (ə'ræknɔɪd) *n* **1** the middle of the three membranes (see **meninges**) that cover the brain and spinal cord. **2** another name for **arachnid.** ◆ *adj* **3** of or relating to the middle of the three meninges. **4** *Botany.* consisting of or covered with soft fine hairs or fibres. **5** of or relating to the arachnids.
arachnology (ˌæræk'nɒlədʒɪ) *n* the study of arachnids. ▶ ˌ**arach'nologist** *n*
arachnophobia (əˌræknə'fəʊbɪə) *n* an abnormal fear of spiders. [C20: from Greek *arakhnē* spider + -PHOBIA]
Arad ('æræd) *n* a city in W Romania, on the Mures River: became part of Romania after World War I, after belonging successively to Turkey, Austria, and Hungary. Pop.: 187 876 (1994 est.).
Arafat[1] ('ærəfæt) *n* a hill in W Saudi Arabia, near Mecca: a sacred site of Islam, visited by pilgrims performing the **hajj.** Also called: **Jabal ar Rahm.**
Arafat[2] *n* **Yasser** ('jæsə). born 1929, Palestinian leader; cofounder of Al Fatah (1956), leader from 1968 of the Palestine Liberation Organization, president of the Palestinian National Authority from 1996: signed a peace agreement with Israel (1993); Nobel peace prize 1994 with Shimon Peres and Yitzhak Rabin.
Arafura Sea (ˌærə'fʊərə) *n* a part of the W Pacific Ocean, between N Australia and SW New Guinea.
Aragats (*Russian* ˌara'gats) *n* **Mount.** a volcanic mountain in NW Armenia. Height: 4090 m (13 419 ft.). Turkish name: **Alagez.**
Aragon[1] ('ærəgən) *n* an autonomous region of NE Spain: independent kingdom from the 11th century until 1479, when it was united with Castile to form modern Spain. Pop.: 1 187 546 (1996 est.). Area: 47 609 sq. km (18 382 sq. miles). ▶ **Aragonese** (ˌærəgə'niːz) *n, adj*
Aragon[2] (*French* aragɔ̃) *n* **Louis** (lwi). 1897–1982, French poet, essayist, and novelist; an early surrealist, later a committed Communist. His works include the verse collections *Le Crève-Coeur* (1941) and *Les Yeux d'Elsa* (1942) and the series of novels *Le Monde réel* (1933–51).
aragonite (ə'rægəˌnaɪt) *n* a generally white or grey mineral, found in sedimentary rocks and as deposits from hot springs. Composition: calcium carbonate. Formula: $CaCO_3$. Crystal structure: orthorhombic. [C19: from ARAGON[1] + -ITE[1]]
Araguaia *or* **Araguaya** (ˌɑːrə'gwaɪə) *n* a river in central Brazil, rising in S central Mato Grosso state and flowing north to the Tocantins River. Length: over 1771 km (1100 miles).
arak ('ærək) *n* a variant spelling of **arrack.**
Arakan Yoma (ˌɑːrɑː'kɑːn 'jəʊmɑː) *n* a mountain range in Myanmar, between the Irrawaddy River and the W coast: forms a barrier between Myanmar and India; teak forests.
Araks (a'raks) *n* the Russian name for the **Aras.**
Araldite ('ærəlˌdaɪt) *n Trademark.* a strong epoxy resin best known as a glue.
aralia (ə'reɪlɪə) *n* any plant of the genus *Aralia* of trees, shrubs, and herbaceous plants. The greenhouse and house plant generally known as aralia is *Dizygotheca elegantissima* of a related genus, grown for its decorative evergreen crinkled foliage: family *Araliaceae.* [New Latin, of uncertain origin]
araliaceous (əˌreɪlɪ'eɪʃəs) *adj* of, relating to, or belonging to the *Araliaceae,* a chiefly tropical family of trees, shrubs, or woody climbers having small clusters of whitish or greenish flowers. The family includes the ivy and ginseng.
Aral Sea ('ærəl) *n* a lake in Kazakhstan and Uzbekistan, east of the Caspian Sea, formerly the fourth largest lake in the world: shallow and saline, now badly polluted; use of its source waters for irrigation led to a loss of 40% of its area between 1967 and 1987. Area: about 64 750 sq. km (25 000 sq. miles). Also called: **Lake Aral.**
Aram ('ɛəræm, -rəm) *n* the biblical name for ancient Syria. ▶ **Aramaean** *or* **Aramean** (ˌærə'miːən) *adj, n*
Aram. *abbrev. for* Aramaic.
Aramaic (ˌærə'meɪɪk) *n* **1** an ancient language of the Middle East, still spoken in parts of Syria and the Lebanon, belonging to the NW Semitic subfamily of the Afro-Asiatic family. Originally the speech of Aram, in the 5th century B.C. it spread to become the lingua franca of the Persian empire. See also **Biblical Aramaic.** ◆ *adj* **2** of, relating to, or using this language.
Aran ('ærən) *adj* **1** of or relating to the Aran Islands. **2** made of thick undyed wool with its natural oils retained: *an Aran sweater.*
Aranda ('ærəndə) *n* **1** an Aboriginal people of S central Australia. **2** the language of this people.
araneid (ə'reɪnɪɪd) *n* any of numerous arachnids constituting the order *Araneae* (or *Araneida*), which comprises the spiders. [C19: from New Latin *Araneida,* from Latin *arānea* spider]
Aran Islands *pl n* a group of three islands in the Atlantic, off the W coast of the Republic of Ireland: Aranmore or Inishmore (the largest), Inishmaan, and Inisheer. Pop.: 1000 (latest est.). Area: 46 sq. km (18 sq. miles).
Arany (*Hungarian* 'ɔrɔnj) *n* **János** ('jaːnoʃ). 1817–82, Hungarian epic poet, ballad writer, and scholar.
Arapaho (ə'ræpəˌhəʊ) *n* **1** (*pl* **-hos** *or* **-ho**) a member of a North American Indian people of the Plains, now living chiefly in Oklahoma and Wyoming. **2** the language of this people, belonging to the Algonquian family.
arapaima (ˌærə'paɪmə) *n* a very large primitive freshwater teleost fish, *Arapaima gigas,* that occurs in tropical South America and can attain a length of 4.5 m (15 ft.) and a weight of 200 kg (440 lbs): family *Osteoglossidae.* [via Portuguese from Tupi]
Ararat ('ærəˌræt) *n* an extinct volcanic mountain massif in E Turkey: two main peaks; **Great Ararat** 5155 m (16 916 ft.), said to be the resting place of Noah's Ark after the Flood (Genesis 8:4), and **Little Ararat** 3914 m (12 843 ft.).
araroba (ˌærə'rəʊbə) *n* **1** a Brazilian leguminous tree, *Andira araroba.* **2** Also called: **Goa powder.** a bitter yellow powder obtained from cavities in the wood of this tree, used in medicine to treat skin ailments. See also

chrysarobin. [from Portuguese, probably from Tupi, from *arara* parrot + *yba* tree]

Aras (æ'ræs) *n* a river rising in mountains in Turkish Armenia and flowing east to the Caspian Sea: forms part of the E border of Turkey and the N border of Iran. Length: about 1100 km (660 miles). Ancient name: **Araxes.** Russian name: **Araks.**

Araucania (ˌærɔː'keɪnɪə; *Spanish* arau'kanja) *n* a region of central Chile, inhabited by Araucanian Indians.

Araucanian (ˌærɔː'keɪnɪən) *n* **1** a South American Indian language; thought to be an isolated branch of the Penutian phylum, spoken in Chile and W Argentina. **2** a member of the people who speak this language. ◆ *adj* **3** of or relating to this people or their language.

araucaria (ˌærɔː'kɛərɪə) *n* any tree of the coniferous genus *Araucaria* of South America, Australia, and Polynesia, such as the monkey puzzle and bunya-bunya. [C19: from New Latin (*arbor*) *Araucaria* (tree) from *Arauco*, a province in Chile]

Arawakan (ˌærə'wækən) *n* **1** a family of American Indian languages found throughout NE South America. ◆ *adj* **2** of or relating to the peoples speaking these languages.

Araxes (ə'ræksiːz) *n* the ancient name for the **Aras.**

arbalest *or* **arbalist** ('ɑːbəlɪst) *n* a large medieval crossbow, usually cocked by mechanical means. [C11: from Old French *arbaleste*, from Late Latin *arcuballista*, from Latin *arcus* bow + BALLISTA]

Arbela (ɑː'biːlə) *n* an ancient city in Assyria, near which the **Battle of Arbela** took place (331 B.C.), in which Alexander the Great defeated the Persians. Modern name: **Erbil.**

Arber ('ɑːbə) *n* **Werner.** born 1929, Swiss microbiologist, noted for his work on restriction enzymes. Nobel prize for physiology or medicine 1978.

Arbil ('ɑːbɪl) *n* a variant spelling of **Erbil.**

arbiter ('ɑːbɪtə) *n* **1** a person empowered to judge in a dispute; referee; arbitrator. **2** a person having complete control of something. [C15: from Latin, of obscure origin] ▸ **'arbitress** *fem n*

arbitrage ('ɑːbɪˌtrɑːʒ, 'ɑːbɪtrɪdʒ) *n Finance.* **a** the purchase of currencies, securities, or commodities in one market for immediate resale in others in order to profit from unequal prices. **b** (*as modifier*): *arbitrage operations.* [C15: from French, from *arbitrer* to ARBITRATE] ▸ **arbitrageur** (ˌɑːbɪtræ'ʒɜː) *n*

arbitral ('ɑːbɪtrəl) *adj* of or relating to arbitration.

arbitrament (ɑː'bɪtrəmənt) *n* **1** the decision or award made by an arbitrator upon a disputed matter. **2** the power or authority to pronounce such a decision. **3** another word for **arbitration.**

arbitrary ('ɑːbɪtrərɪ) *adj* **1** founded on or subject to personal whims, prejudices, etc.; capricious. **2** having only relative application or relevance; not absolute. **3** (of a government, ruler, etc.) despotic or dictatorial. **4** *Maths.* not representing any specific value: *an arbitrary constant.* **5** *Law.* (esp. of a penalty or punishment) not laid down by statute; within the court's discretion. [C15: from Latin *arbitrārius* arranged through arbitration, uncertain] ▸ **'arbitrarily** *adv* ▸ **'arbitrariness** *n*

arbitrate ('ɑːbɪˌtreɪt) *vb* **1** to settle or decide (a dispute); achieve a settlement between parties. **2** to submit to or settle by arbitration. [C16: from Latin *arbitrārī* to give judgment; see ARBITER] ▸ **'arbitrable** *adj* ▸ **'arbiˌtrator** *n*

arbitration (ˌɑːbɪ'treɪʃən) *n* **1** *Law.* the hearing and determination of a dispute, esp. an industrial dispute, by an impartial referee selected or agreed upon by the parties concerned. **2** *International law.* the procedure laid down for the settlement of international disputes.

arbitress ('ɑːbɪtrɪs) *n* a female arbitrator.

Arblay, d' ('dɑːbleɪ; *French* darblɛ) *n* **Madame.** the married name of (Fanny) **Burney.**

arbor[1] ('ɑːbə) *n* the U.S. spelling of **arbour.**

arbor[2] ('ɑːbə) *n* **1** a rotating shaft in a machine or power tool on which a milling cutter or grinding wheel is fitted. **2** a rotating shaft or mandrel on which a workpiece is fitted for machining. **3** *Foundry.* a part, piece, or structure used to reinforce the core of a mould. [C17: from Latin: tree, mast]

arboraceous (ˌɑːbə'reɪʃəs) *adj Literary.* **1** resembling a tree. **2** wooded.

arboreal (ɑː'bɔːrɪəl) *adj* **1** of, relating to, or resembling a tree. **2** living in or among trees: *arboreal monkeys.*

arboreous (ɑː'bɔːrɪəs) *adj* **1** thickly wooded; having many trees. **2** another word for **arborescent.**

arborescent (ˌɑːbə'rɛsᵊnt) *adj* having the shape or characteristics of a tree. ▸ **ˌarbo'rescence** *n*

arboretum (ˌɑːbə'riːtəm) *n, pl* **-ta** (-tə) *or* **-tums.** a place where trees or shrubs are cultivated for their scientific or educational interest. [C19: from Latin, from *arbor* tree]

arboriculture ('ɑːbərɪˌkʌltʃə) *n* the cultivation of trees or shrubs, esp. for the production of timber. ▸ **ˌarbori'cultural** *adj* ▸ **ˌarbori'culturist** *n*

arborist ('ɑːbərɪst) *n* a specialist in the cultivation of trees.

arborization *or* **arborisation** (ˌɑːbəraɪ'zeɪʃən) *n* a branching treelike appearance in certain fossils and minerals.

arbor vitae ('ɑːbɔː 'viːtaɪ, 'vaɪtiː) *n* any of several Asian and North American evergreen coniferous trees of the genera *Thuja* and *Thujopsis*, esp. *Thuja occidentalis*, having tiny scalelike leaves and egglike cones. See also **red cedar.** [C17: from New Latin, literally: tree of life]

arbour ('ɑːbə) *n* **1** a leafy glade or bower shaded by trees, vines, shrubs, etc., esp. when trained about a trellis. **2** *Obsolete.* an orchard, garden, or lawn. [C14 *erber*, from Old French *herbier*, from Latin *herba* grass]

arbovirus ('ɑːbəʊˌvaɪrəs) *n* any one of a group of viruses that cause such diseases as encephalitis and dengue and are transmitted to humans by arthropods, esp. insects and ticks. [C20: from *ar*(*thropod-*)*bo*(*rne*) *virus*]

Arbroath (ɑː'brəʊθ) *n* a port and resort in E Scotland, in Angus: scene of the barons of Scotland's declaration of independence to Pope John XXII in 1320. Pop.: 23 474 (1991).

Arbus ('ɑːbəs) *n* **Diane,** original name *Diane Nemerov.* 1923–71, U.S. photographer, noted esp. for her portraits of vagrants, dwarfs, transvestites, etc.

Arbuthnot (ɑː'bʌθnɒt) *n* **John.** 1667–1735, Scottish physician and satirist: author of *The History of John Bull* (1712) and, with others, of the *Memoirs of Martinus Scriblerus* (1741).

arbutus (ɑː'bjuːtəs) *n, pl* **-tuses. 1** any of several temperate ericaceous shrubs of the genus *Arbutus*, esp. the strawberry tree of S Europe. They have clusters of white or pinkish flowers, broad evergreen leaves, and strawberry-like berries. **2** See **trailing arbutus.** [C16: from Latin; related to *arbor* tree]

arc (ɑːk) *n* **1** something curved in shape. **2** part of an unbroken curved line. **3** a luminous discharge that occurs when an electric current flows between two electrodes or any other two surfaces separated by a small gap and a high potential difference. **4** *Astronomy.* a circular section of the apparent path of a celestial body. **5** *Maths.* a section of a curve, graph, or geometric figure. ◆ *vb* **arcs, arcing, arced** *or* **arcs, arcking, arcked. 6** (*intr*) to form an arc. ◆ *prefix* **7** *Maths.* specifying an inverse trigonometric function: usually written **arcsin, arctanh, arcsec,** etc., or sometimes **sin**$^{-1}$**, tanh**$^{-1}$**, sec**$^{-1}$, etc. [C14: from Old French, from Latin *arcus* bow, arch]

ARC *abbrev. for* AIDS-related complex: an early condition in which a person infected with the AIDS virus may suffer from such mild symptoms as loss of weight, fever, etc.

arcade (ɑː'keɪd) *n* **1** a set of arches and their supporting columns. **2** a covered and sometimes arched passageway, usually with shops on one or both sides. **3** a building, or part of a building, with an arched roof. [C18: from French, from Italian *arcata*, from *arco*, from Latin *arcus* bow, arch]

Arcadia (ɑː'keɪdɪə) *n* **1** a department of Greece, in the central Peloponnese. Capital: Tripolis. Pop.: 105 309 (1991). Area: 4367 sq. km (1686 sq. miles). **2** Also called (poetic): **Arcady** ('ɑːkədɪ). the traditional idealized rural setting of Greek and Roman bucolic poetry and later in the literature of the Renaissance.

Arcadian (ɑː'keɪdɪən) *adj* **1** of or relating to Arcadia or its inhabitants, esp. the idealized Arcadia of pastoral poetry. **2** rustic or bucolic: *a life of Arcadian simplicity.* ◆ *n* **3** an inhabitant of Arcadia. **4** a person who leads or prefers a quiet simple rural life. ▸ **Ar'cadianism** *n*

Arcadic (ɑː'keɪdɪk) *adj* **1** of or relating to the Arcadians or to their dialect of Ancient Greek. ◆ *n* **2** one of four chief dialects of Ancient Greek; the dialect spoken by the Arcadians. See also **Attic** (sense 3). ◆ Compare **Aeolic, Doric, Ionic.**

arcana (ɑː'keɪnə, -'kɑː-) *n* either of the two divisions (the **minor arcana** and the **major arcana**) of a pack of tarot cards.

arcane (ɑː'keɪn) *adj* requiring secret knowledge to be understood; mysterious; esoteric. [C16: from Latin *arcānus* secret, hidden, from *arcēre* to shut up, keep safe] ▸ **ar'canely** *adv* ▸ **ar'caneness** *n*

arcanum (ɑː'keɪnəm) *n, pl* **-na** (-nə). **1** (*sometimes pl*) a profound secret or mystery known only to initiates. **2** a secret of nature sought by alchemists. [C16: from Latin; see ARCANE]

arcature ('ɑːkətʃə) *n* **1** a small-scale arcade. **2** a set of blind arches attached to the wall of a building as decoration.

arc-boutant *French.* (arkbutɑ̃) *n, pl* ***arcs-boutants*** (arkbutɑ̃). another name for **flying buttress.**

Arc de Triomphe ('ɑːk də 'triːəʊmf; *French* ark də trijɔ̃f) *n* the triumphal arch in Paris begun by Napoleon I to commemorate his victories of 1805-6 and completed in 1836.

arc furnace *n* a furnace in which the charge is heated by an electric arc.

arch[1] (ɑːtʃ) *n* **1** a curved structure, normally in the vertical plane, that spans an opening. **2** Also called: **archway.** a structure in the form of an arch that serves as a gateway. **3** something curved like an arch. **4a** any of various parts or structures of the body having a curved or archlike outline, such as the transverse portion of the aorta (**arch of the aorta**) or the raised bony vault formed by the tarsal and metatarsal bones (**arch of the foot**). **4b** one of the basic patterns of the human fingerprint, formed by several curved ridges one above the other. Compare **loop**[1] (sense 10a), **whorl** (sense 3). ◆ *vb* **5** (*tr*) to span (an opening) with an arch. **6** to form or cause to form an arch or a curve resembling that of an arch: *the cat arched its back.* **7** (*tr*) to span or extend over: *the bridge arched the flooded stream.* [C14: from Old French *arche*, from Vulgar Latin *arca* (unattested), from Latin *arcus* bow, ARC]

arch[2] (ɑːtʃ) *adj* **1** (*prenominal*) chief; principal; leading: *his arch rival.* **2** (*prenominal*) very experienced; expert: *an arch criminal.* **3** knowing or superior. **4** playfully or affectedly roguish or mischievous. [C16: independent use of ARCH-] ▸ **'archly** *adv* ▸ **'archness** *n*

arch. *abbrev. for:* **1** archaic. **2** archaism. **3** archery. **4** archipelago. **5** architect. **6** architectural. **7** architecture.

Arch. *abbrev. for* Archbishop.

arch- *or* **archi-** *combining form.* **1** chief; principal; of highest rank: *archangel; archbishop; archduke.* **2** eminent above all others of the same kind; extreme: *archenemy; archfiend; archfool.* [ultimately from Greek *arkhi-*, from *arkhein* to rule]

-arch *n combining form.* leader; ruler; chief: *patriarch; monarch; heresiarch.* [from Greek *-arkhēs*, from *arkhein* to rule; compare ARCH-]

Archaean *or esp. U.S.* **Archean** (ɑː'kiːən) *adj* of or relating to the highly metamorphosed rocks formed in the early Precambrian era.

archaebacteria (ˌɑːkɪbæk'tɪərɪə) *n* a subkingdom (*Archaea*) of bacteria capable of surviving in hostile environments, such as volcanic vents, and are probably direct descendants of the earliest living organisms. [from ARCHAEO- + BACTERIA]

archaeo- *or* **archeo-** *combining form.* **1** indicating ancient or primitive time or condition: *archaeology; archaeopteryx.* **2** of, involving, or denoting the study of remains from archaeological sites: *archaeozoology.* [from Greek *arkhaio-*, from *arkhaios*, from *arkhein* to begin]

archaeoastronomy *or* **archeoastronomy** (ˌɑːkɪəʊəˈstrɒnəmɪ) *n* the scientific study of the beliefs and practices concerning astronomy that existed in ancient and prehistoric civilizations. ▸ **ˌarchaeoasˈtronomer** *or* **ˌarcheoasˈtronomer** *n*

archaeobotany *or* **archeobotany** (ˌɑːkɪəʊˈbɒtənɪ) *n* the analysis and interpretation of plant remains found at archaeological sites. ▸ **ˌarchaeoˈbotanist** *or* **ˌarcheoˈbotanist** *n*

archaeol. *abbrev. for* archaeology.

archaeology *or* **archeology** (ˌɑːkɪˈɒlədʒɪ) *n* the study of man's past by scientific analysis of the material remains of his cultures. See also **prehistory, protohistory.** [C17: from Late Latin *archaeologia*, from Greek *arkhaiologia* study of what is ancient, from *arkhaios* ancient (from *arkhē* beginning)] ▸ **archaeological** *or* **archeological** (ˌɑːkɪəˈlɒdʒɪkᵊl) *adj* ▸ **ˌarchaeoˈlogically** *or* **ˌarcheoˈlogically** *adv* ▸ **ˌarchaeˈologist** *or* **ˌarcheˈologist** *n*

archaeomagnetism *or* **archeomagnetism** (ˌɑːkɪəʊˈmægnɪˌtɪzəm) *n* an archaeological technique for dating certain clay objects by measuring the extent to which they have been magnetized by the earth's magnetic field.

archaeopteryx (ˌɑːkɪˈɒptərɪks) *n* any of several extinct primitive birds constituting the genus *Archaeopteryx*, esp. *A. lithographica*, which occurred in Jurassic times and had teeth, a long tail, well-developed wings, and a body covering of feathers. [C19: from ARCHAEO- + Greek *pterux* winged creature]

archaeornis (ˌɑːkɪˈɔːnɪs) *n* an extinct primitive Jurassic bird, formerly placed in the genus *Archaeornis* but now thought to be a species of archaeopteryx. [C19: New Latin, from ARCHAEO- + Greek *ornis* bird]

Archaeozoic *or esp. U.S.* **Archeozoic** (ˌɑːkɪəˈzəʊɪk) *adj* **1** of or formed in the early Precambrian era. ◆ *n* **2** the earlier of two divisions of the Precambrian era, during which the earliest forms of life are assumed to have appeared. Compare **Proterozoic.**

archaeozoology *or* **archeozoology** (ˌɑːkɪəʊzəʊˈɒlədʒɪ, -zuː-) *n* the analysis and interpretation of animal remains found at archaeological sites. ▸ **ˌarchaeozoˈologist** *or* **ˌarcheozoˈologist** *n*

archaic (ɑːˈkeɪɪk) *adj* **1** belonging to or characteristic of a much earlier period; ancient. **2** out of date; antiquated: *an archaic prison system.* **3** (of idiom, vocabulary, etc.) characteristic of an earlier period of a language and not in ordinary use. [C19: from French *archaïque*, from Greek *arkhaïkos*, from *arkhaios* ancient, from *arkhē* beginning, from *arkhein* to begin] ▸ **arˈchaically** *adv*

archaism (ˈɑːkɪˌɪzəm, -keɪ-) *n* **1** the adoption or imitation of something archaic, such as a word or an artistic or literary style. **2** an archaic word, expression, style, etc. [C17: from New Latin *archaismus*, from Greek *arkhaïsmos*, from *arkhaizein* to model one's style upon that of ancient writers; see ARCHAIC] ▸ **ˈarchaist** *n* ▸ **ˌarchaˈistic** *adj*

archaize *or* **archaise** (ˈɑːkɪˌaɪz, -keɪ-) *vb* (*tr*) to give an archaic appearance or character to, as by the use of archaisms. ▸ **ˈarchaˌizer** *or* **ˈarchaˌiser** *n*

archangel (ˈɑːkˌeɪndʒəl) *n* **1** a principal angel, a member of the order ranking immediately above the angels in medieval angelology. **2** another name for **angelica** (sense 1). **3 yellow archangel.** a Eurasian herbaceous plant, *Galeobdolon luteum* (or *Lamium galeobdolon*), that has yellow helmet-shaped flowers: family *Labiatae* (labiates). **4** a bronze-coloured breed of domestic pigeon with black markings. ▸ **archangelic** (ˌɑːkænˈdʒɛlɪk) *adj*

Archangel (ˈɑːkˌeɪndʒəl) *n* a port in NW Russia, on the Dvina River: major centre for the timber trade and White Sea fisheries. Pop.: 374 000 (1995 est.). Russian name: **Arkhangelsk.**

archbishop (ˈɑːtʃˈbɪʃəp) *n* a bishop of the highest rank. Abbrevs.: **abp, Abp, Arch., Archbp.**

archbishopric (ˈɑːtʃˈbɪʃəprɪk) *n* **1** the rank, office, or jurisdiction of an archbishop. **2** the area governed by an archbishop.

Archbp *abbrev. for* archbishop.

Archd. *abbrev. for:* **1** archdeacon. **2** archduke.

archdeacon (ˈɑːtʃˈdiːkən) *n* **1** an Anglican clergyman ranking just below a bishop and having supervisory duties under the bishop. **2** a clergyman of similar rank in other Churches.

archdeaconry (ˈɑːtʃˈdiːkənrɪ) *n, pl* **-ries. 1** the office, rank, or duties of an archdeacon. **2** the residence of an archdeacon.

archdiocese (ˌɑːtʃˈdaɪəˌsiːs, -sɪs) *n* the diocese of an archbishop. ▸ **archdiocesan** (ˌɑːtʃdaɪˈɒsɪsᵊn) *adj*

archducal (ˈɑːtʃˈdjuːkᵊl) *adj* of or relating to an archduke, archduchess, or archduchy.

archduchess (ˈɑːtʃˈdʌtʃɪs) *n* **1** the wife or widow of an archduke. **2** (since 1453) a princess of the Austrian imperial family, esp. a daughter of the Austrian emperor.

archduchy (ˈɑːtʃˈdʌtʃɪ) *n, pl* **-duchies.** the territory ruled by an archduke or archduchess.

archduke (ˈɑːtʃˈdjuːk) *n* a chief duke, esp. (since 1453) a prince of the Austrian imperial dynasty.

Archean (ɑːˈkiːən) *adj* a variant spelling (esp. U.S.) of **Archaean.**

arched (ɑːtʃt) *adj* **1** provided with or spanned by an arch or arches. **2** shaped like an arch; curved.

archegonium (ˌɑːkɪˈgəʊnɪəm) *n, pl* **-nia** (-nɪə). a female sex organ, occurring in mosses, ferns, and evergreen trees, that produces a single egg cell in its swollen base. [C19: from New Latin, from Greek *arkhegonos* original parent, from *arkhe-* chief, first + *gonos* seed, race] ▸ **ˌarcheˈgoniate** *adj*

archenemy (ˈɑːtʃˈɛnɪmɪ) *n, pl* **-mies. 1** a chief enemy. **2** (*often cap.*; preceded by *the*) the devil.

archenteron (ɑːˈkɛntəˌrɒn) *n* the cavity within an embryo at the gastrula stage of development that eventually becomes the digestive cavity. [C19: from Greek *arkhē* beginning + *enteron* intestine] ▸ **archenteric** (ˌɑːkənˈtɛrɪk) *adj*

archeology (ˌɑːkɪˈɒlədʒɪ) *n* a variant spelling of **archaeology.**

Archeozoic (ˌɑːkɪəˈzəʊɪk) *adj* a variant spelling (esp. U.S.) of **Archaeozoic.**

archer (ˈɑːtʃə) *n* a person skilled in the use of a bow and arrow. [C13: from Old French *archier*, from Late Latin *arcārius*, from Latin *arcus* bow]

Archer[1] (ˈɑːtʃə) *n* **the.** the constellation Sagittarius, the ninth sign of the zodiac.

Archer[2] (ˈɑːtʃə) *n* **1 Frederick Scott.** 1813–57, British inventor and sculptor. He developed (1851) the wet collodion photographic process, enabling multiple copies of pictures to be made. **2 Jeffrey (Howard),** Baron Archer of Weston-Super-Mare. born 1940, British novelist and Conservative politician. He was an MP from 1969 until 1974. His novels include *Kane and Abel* (1979), *Honour Among Thieves* (1993), and *The Fourth Estate* (1996). **3 William.** 1856–1924, Scottish critic and dramatist: made the first English translations of Ibsen.

archerfish (ˈɑːtʃəˌfɪʃ) *n, pl* **-fish** *or* **-fishes.** any freshwater percoid fish of the family *Toxotidae* of S and SE Asia and Australia, esp. *Toxotes jaculatrix*, that catch insects by spitting water at them.

archery (ˈɑːtʃərɪ) *n* **1** the art or sport of shooting with bows and arrows. **2** archers or their weapons collectively.

Arches (ˈɑːtʃɪz) *pl n* **Court of.** *Church of England.* the court of appeal of the Province of Canterbury, formerly held under the arches of Bow Church.

archespore (ˈɑːkɪˌspɔː) *or* **archesporium** (ˌɑːkɪˈspɔːrɪəm) *n, pl* **-spores** *or* **-sporia** (-ˈspɔːrɪə). *Botany.* the cell or group of cells in a sporangium that gives rise to spores. ▸ **ˌarcheˈsporial** *adj*

archetype (ˈɑːkɪˌtaɪp) *n* **1** a perfect or typical specimen. **2** an original model or pattern; prototype. **3** *Psychoanal.* one of the inherited mental images postulated by Jung as the content of the collective unconscious. **4** a constantly recurring symbol or motif in literature, painting, etc. [C17: from Latin *archetypum* an original, from Greek *arkhetupon*, from *arkhetupos* first-moulded; see ARCH-, TYPE] ▸ **ˌarcheˈtypal** *or* **archetypical** (ˌɑːkɪˈtɪpɪkᵊl) *adj* ▸ **ˌarcheˈtypally** *or* **ˌarcheˈtypically** *adv*

archfiend (ˌɑːtʃˈfiːnd) *n* (*often cap.*) **the.** the chief of fiends or devils; Satan.

archi- *combining form.* a variant of **arch-.**

Archibald prize (ˈɑːtʃɪbɔːld) *n Austral.* an annual prize awarded by the Trustees of the Art Gallery of New South Wales since 1921, for outstanding contributions to art, letters, science, and politics. [named after Jules François *Archibald* (1856–1919), Australian journalist]

archicarp (ˈɑːkɪˌkɑːp) *n* a female reproductive structure in ascomycetous fungi that consists of a cell or hypha and develops into the ascogonium.

archidiaconal (ˌɑːkɪdaɪˈækənᵊl) *adj* of or relating to an archdeacon or his office.

archidiaconate (ˌɑːkɪdaɪˈækənɪt) *n* the office, term of office, or area of jurisdiction of an archdeacon.

archiepiscopal (ˌɑːkɪɪˈpɪskəpᵊl) *adj* of or associated with an archbishop.

archiepiscopate (ˌɑːkɪɪˈpɪskəpɪt, -ˌpeɪt) *or* **archiepiscopacy** (ˌɑːkɪɪˈpɪskəpəsɪ) *n* the rank, office, or term of office of an archbishop.

archil (ˈɑːtʃɪl) *n* a variant spelling of **orchil.**

Archilochian (ˌɑːkɪˈləʊkɪən) *adj* denoting or relating to Archilochus or his verse, esp. the iambic trimeters or trochaic tetrameters used by him.

Archilochus (ɑːˈkɪləkəs) *n* 7th century B.C., Greek poet of Paros, notable for using his own experience as subject matter.

archimage (ˈɑːkɪˌmeɪdʒ) *n* a great magician or wizard. [C16: from ARCHI- + *mage*, from Latin *magus* magician]

archimandrite (ˌɑːkɪˈmændraɪt) *n Greek Orthodox Church.* the head of a monastery or a group of monasteries. [C16: from Late Latin *archimandrīta*, from Late Greek *arkhimandritēs*, from ARCHI- + *mandra* monastery]

Archimedes[1] (ˌɑːkɪˈmiːdiːz) *n* ?287–212 B.C., Greek mathematician and physicist of Syracuse, noted for his work in geometry, hydrostatics, and mechanics. ▸ **Archimedean** (ˌɑːkɪˈmiːdɪən, -mɪˈdiːən) *adj*

Archimedes[2] (ˌɑːkɪˈmiːdiːz) *n* a walled plain in the NE quadrant of the moon, about 80 kilometres in diameter.

Archimedes' principle *n* a law of physics stating that the apparent loss in weight of a body immersed in a fluid is equal to the weight of the displaced fluid.

Archimedes' screw *or* **Archimedean screw** *n* an ancient type of water-lifting device making use of a spiral passage in an inclined cylinder. The water is raised when the spiral is rotated.

archine (ɑːˈʃiːn) *n* a Russian unit of length equal to about 71 cm. [from Russian *arshin*, of Turkic origin]

archipelago (ˌɑːkɪˈpɛlɪˌgəʊ) *n, pl* **-gos** *or* **-goes. 1** a group of islands. **2** a sea studded with islands. [C16 (meaning: the Aegean Sea): from Italian *arcipelago*, literally: the chief sea (perhaps originally a mistranslation of Greek *Aigaion pelagos* the Aegean Sea), from ARCHI- + *pelago* sea, from Latin *pelagus*, from Greek *pelagos*] ▸ **archipelagic** (ˌɑːkɪpəˈlædʒɪk) *or* **archipelagian** (ˌɑːkɪpəˈleɪdʒɪən) *adj*

Archipenko (*Russian* arˈxipɪnkə) *n* **Aleksandr Porfiryevich** (alɪkˈsandr parˈfirjɪvitʃ). 1887–1964, Russian sculptor and painter, in the U.S. after 1923, whose work is characterized by economy of form.

archiphoneme (ˈɑːkɪˌfəʊniːm, ˌɑːkɪˈfəʊniːm) *n Phonetics.* an abstract linguistic unit representing two or more phonemes when the distinction between these has been neutralized: conventionally shown by a capital letter within slashes, as /T/ for /t/ and /d/ in German *Rat* and *Rad.*

archiplasm (ˈɑːkɪˌplæzəm) *n* a variant spelling of **archoplasm.** ▸ **ˌarchiˈplasmic** *adj*

archit. *abbrev. for* architecture.

architect (ˈɑːkɪˌtɛkt) *n* **1** a person qualified to design buildings and to superintend their erection. **2** a person similarly qualified in another form of construction: *a naval architect.* **3** any planner or creator: *the architect of the expedition.* [C16: from French *architecte*, from Latin *architectus*, from Greek *arkhitektōn* director of works, from ARCHI- + *tektōn* workman; related to *tekhnē* art, skill]

architectonic (ˌɑːkɪtɛkˈtɒnɪk) *adj* **1** denoting, relating to, or having architectural qualities. **2** *Metaphysics.* of or relating to the systematic classification of knowledge. [C16: from Late Latin *architectonicus* concerning architecture; see ARCHITECT] ▸ ˌ**architecˈtonically** *adv*

architectonics (ˌɑːkɪtɛkˈtɒnɪks) *n* (*functioning as sing*) **1** the science of architecture. **2** *Metaphysics.* the scientific classification of knowledge.

architecture (ˈɑːkɪˌtɛktʃə) *n* **1** the art and science of designing and superintending the erection of buildings and similar structures. **2** a style of building or structure: *Gothic architecture.* **3** buildings or structures collectively. **4** the structure or design of anything: *the architecture of the universe.* **5** the internal organization of a computer's components with particular reference to the way in which data is transmitted. **6** the arrangement of the various devices in a complete computer system or network. ▸ ˌ**archiˈtectural** *adj* ▸ ˌ**archiˈtecturally** *adv*

architrave (ˈɑːkɪˌtreɪv) *n Architect.* **1** the lowest part of an entablature that bears on the columns. **2** a moulding around a doorway, window opening, etc. [C16: via French from Italian, from ARCHI- + *trave* beam, from Latin *trabs*]

archival storage *n* a method of retaining information outside of the internal memory of a computer.

archive (ˈɑːkaɪv) *n* (*often pl*) **1** a collection of records of or about an institution, family, etc. **2** a place where such records are kept. **3** *Computing.* data transferred to a tape or disk for long-term storage rather than frequent use. ◆ *vb* (*tr*) **4** to store (documents, data, etc.) in an archive or other repository. [C17: from Late Latin *archīvum,* from Greek *arkheion* repository of official records, from *arkhē* government] ▸ **arˈchival** *adj*

archivist (ˈɑːkɪvɪst) *n* a person in charge of archives, their collection, and cataloguing.

archivolt (ˈɑːkɪˌvəʊlt) *n Architect.* **1** a moulding around an arch, sometimes decorated. **2** the under surface of an arch. [C18: from Italian *archivolto;* see ARC, VAULT[1]]

archon (ˈɑːkɒn, -kən) *n* (in ancient Athens) one of the nine chief magistrates. [C17: from Greek *arkhōn* ruler, from *arkhein* to rule] ▸ **ˈarchonˌship** *n*

archoplasm (ˈɑːkəˌplæzəm) *or* **archiplasm** *n* the protoplasmic material surrounding the centrosome, formerly thought to be involved in the formation of the asters and spindle during mitosis. ▸ ˌ**archoˈplasmic** *adj*

archpriest (ˈɑːtʃˈpriːst) *n Christianity.* **1** (formerly) a chief assistant to a bishop, performing many of his sacerdotal functions during his absence. **2** a senior priest. ▸ **ˈarchˈpriestˌhood** *or* **ˈarchˈpriestˌship** *n*

archt *abbrev. for* architect.

archway (ˈɑːtʃˌweɪ) *n* a passageway or entrance under an arch or arches.

-archy *n combining form.* government; rule: *anarchy; monarchy.* [from Greek *-arkhia;* see -ARCH] ▸ **-archic** *adj combining form.* ▸ **-archist** *n combining form.*

Arcimboldo (*Italian* artʃimˈbɔldo) *n* **Giuseppe.** 1527–93, Italian painter, best remembered for painting grotesque figures composed of fruit, vegetables, and meat.

arc light *n* a light source in which an arc between two electrodes, usually carbon, produces intense white illumination. Also called: **arc lamp.**

ARCM *abbrev. for* Associate of the Royal College of Music.

arcograph (ˈɑːkəˌɡrɑːf, -ˌɡræf) *n Geometry.* an instrument used for drawing arcs without using a central point. Also called: **cyclograph.**

arcos (ˈɑːˌkɒs) *Maths. abbrev. for* arc-cosine: the function the value of which for a given argument between –1 and 1 is the angle in radians (between 0 and π), the cosine of which is that argument: the inverse of the cosine function.

ARCS *abbrev. for* Associate of the Royal College of Science.

arcsin (ˈɑːkˌsaɪn) *Maths. abbrev. for* arcsine: the function the value of which for a given argument between –1 and 1 is the angle in radians (between –π/2 and π/2), the sine of which is that argument: the inverse of the sine function.

arctan (ˈɑːkˌtæn) *Maths. abbrev. for* arctangent: the function the value of which for a given argument is the angle in radians (between –π and π) the tangent of which is that argument: the inverse of the tangent function.

arctic (ˈɑːktɪk) *adj* **1** of or relating to the Arctic: *arctic temperatures.* **2** *Informal.* cold; freezing: *the weather at Christmas was arctic.* ◆ *n* **3** *U.S.* a high waterproof overshoe with buckles. **4** (*modifier*) designed or suitable for conditions of extreme cold: *arctic clothing.* [C14: from Latin *arcticus,* from Greek *arktikos* northern, literally: pertaining to (the constellation of) the Bear, from *arktos* bear]

Arctic (ˈɑːktɪk) *n* **1 the.** Also called: **Arctic Zone.** the regions north of the Arctic Circle. ◆ *adj* **2** of or relating to the regions north of the Arctic Circle.

arctic char *n* a char, *Salvelinus alpinus,* that occurs in northern and arctic seas.

Arctic Circle *n* the imaginary circle round the earth, parallel to the equator, at latitude 66° 32′ N.

arctic fox *n* a fox, *Alopex lagopus,* of arctic regions, whose fur is dark grey in the summer and white in the winter. See also **blue fox.**

arctic hare *n* a large hare, *Lepus arcticus,* of the Canadian Arctic whose fur is white in winter.

Arctic Ocean *n* the ocean surrounding the North Pole, north of the Arctic Circle. Area: about 14 100 000 sq. km (5 440 000 sq. miles).

arctic tern *n* a black-capped tern, *Sterna paradisea,* that breeds in the Arctic and then migrates as far south as the Antarctic.

arctic willow *n* a low-growing shrub, *Salix arctica,* of the Canadian tundra.

arctiid (ˈɑːktɪɪd) *n* any moth of the family *Arctiidae,* which includes the footman, ermine, and tiger moths.

Arctogaea (ˌɑːktəˈdʒiːə) *n* a zoogeographical area comprising the Palaearctic, Nearctic, Oriental, and Ethiopian regions. Compare **Neogaea, Notogaea.** ▸ ˌ**Arctoˈgaean** *adj*

arctophile (ˈɑːktəʊˌfaɪl) *n* a person who collects teddy bears or is fond of them. [C20: from Greek *arktos* bear + -PHILE]

Arcturus (ɑːkˈtjʊərəs) *n* the brightest star in the constellation Boötes: a red giant. Visual magnitude: 0.24; spectral type: KO; distance: 36 light years. [C14: from Latin, from Greek *Arktouros,* from *arktos* bear + *ouros* guard, keeper] ▸ **Arcˈturian** *adj*

arcuate (ˈɑːkjuːɪt, -ˌeɪt) *adj* shaped or bent like an arc or bow: *arcuate leaves; arcuate fibres of the cerebrum.* Also: **arcuated.** [C17: from Latin *arcuāre,* from *arcus* ARC] ▸ **ˈarcuately** *adv*

arcuation (ˌɑːkjʊˈeɪʃən) *n* **1** the use of arches or vaults in buildings. **2** an arrangement of arches. [C17: from Late Latin *arcuātiō* arch, from Latin *arcuāre* to curve]

arcus senilis (ˈɑːkəs sɪˈnaɪlɪs) *n* an opaque circle around the cornea of the eye, often seen in elderly people. [Latin: senile bow]

arc welding *n* a technique in which metal is welded by heat generated by an electric arc struck between two electrodes or between one electrode and the metal workpiece. ▸ **arc welder** *n*

-ard *or* **-art** *suffix forming nouns.* indicating a person who does something, esp. to excess, or is characterized by a certain quality: *braggart; drunkard; dullard.* [via Old French from Germanic *-hard* (literally: hardy, bold), the final element in many Germanic masculine names, such as *Bernhard* Bernard, *Gerhart* Gerard, etc.]

ardeb (ˈɑːdɛb) *n* a unit of dry measure used in Egypt and other Middle Eastern countries. In Egypt it is approximately equal to 0.195 cubic metres. [C19: from Arabic *ardabb,* from Greek *artabē* a Persian measure]

Ardèche (*French* ardɛʃ) *n* a department of S France, in Rhône-Alpes region. Capital: Privas. Pop.: 282 900 (1995). Area: 5556 sq. km (2167 sq. miles).

Arden[1] (ˈɑːdᵊn) *n* **Forest of.** a region of N Warwickshire, part of a former forest: scene of Shakespeare's *As You Like It.*

Arden[2] (ˈɑːdᵊn) *n* **John.** born 1930, British dramatist, producer, and novelist. His plays include *Serjeant Musgrave's Dance* (1959), *The Workhouse Donkey* (1963), and *A Suburban Suicide* (1994): he often works in collaboration with Margaretta D'Arcy.

Ardennes (ɑːˈdɛn; *French* ardɛn) *n* **1** a department of NE France, in Champagne-Ardenne region. Capital: Mézières. Pop.: 292 000 (1995). Area: 5253 sq. km (2049 sq. miles). **2 the.** a wooded plateau in SE Belgium, Luxembourg, and NE France: scene of heavy fighting in both World Wars.

ardent (ˈɑːdᵊnt) *adj* **1** expressive of or characterized by intense desire or emotion; passionate: *ardent love.* **2** intensely enthusiastic; eager: *an ardent longing.* **3** glowing, flashing, or shining: *ardent eyes.* **4** *Rare.* burning: *an ardent fever.* [C14: from Latin *ārdēre* to burn] ▸ **ˈardency** *n* ▸ **ˈardently** *adv*

ardent spirits *pl n* spirits, such as rum, whisky, etc.

ardour *or U.S.* **ardor** (ˈɑːdə) *n* **1** feelings of great intensity and warmth; fervour. **2** eagerness; zeal. [C14: from Old French *ardour,* from Latin *ārdor,* from *ārdēre* to burn]

Ards (ɑːdz) *n* a district of Northern Ireland, in Co. Down. Pop.: 64 764 (1991). Area: 368 sq. km (142 sq. miles).

arduous (ˈɑːdjʊəs) *adj* **1** requiring great physical or mental effort; difficult to accomplish; strenuous. **2** hard to endure; harsh: *arduous conditions.* **3** hard to overcome or surmount; steep or difficult: *an arduous track.* [C16: from Latin *arduus* steep, difficult] ▸ **ˈarduously** *adv* ▸ **ˈarduousness** *n*

are[1] (ɑː; *unstressed* ə) *vb* the plural form of the present tense (indicative mood) of **be** and the singular form used with *you.* [Old English *aron,* second person plural of *bēon* to BE]

are[2] (ɑː) *n* a unit of area equal to 100 sq. metres or 119.599 sq. yards; one hundredth of a hectare. Symbol: a. [C19: from French, from Latin *ārea* piece of ground; see AREA]

area (ˈɛərɪə) *n* **1** any flat, curved, or irregular expanse of a surface. **2a** the extent of a two-dimensional surface enclosed within a specified boundary or geometric figure: *the area of Ireland; the area of a triangle.* **2b** the two-dimensional extent of the surface of a solid, or of some part thereof, esp. one bounded by a closed curve: *the area of a sphere.* **3** a section, portion, or part: *an area of the body; an area of the sky.* **4** region; district; locality: *a mountainous area.* **5a** a geographical division of administrative responsibility. **5b** (*as modifier*): *area manager.* **6** a part or section, as of a building, town, etc., having some specified function or characteristic: *reception area; commercial area; slum area.* **7** Also called: **areaway.** a sunken area, usually enclosed, giving light, air, and sometimes access to a cellar or basement. **8** the range, extent, or scope of anything. **9** a subject field or field of study. **10** any unoccupied or unused flat open piece of ground. **11** the ground on which a building stands, or the ground surrounding a building. **12** *Anatomy.* any of the various regions of the cerebral cortex. **13** *Computing.* any part of a computer memory assigned to store data of a specified type. [C16: from Latin: level ground, open space, threshing-floor; related to *ārēre* to be dry] ▸ **ˈareal** *adj*

area code *n* a number prefixed to an individual telephone number: used in making long-distance calls.

areaway (ˈɛərɪəˌweɪ) *n* **1** a passageway between parts of a building or between different buildings. **2** See **area** (sense 7).

areca (ˈærɪkə, əˈriːkə) *n* any of various tall palms of the genus *Areca,* which are native to SE Asia and have white flowers and orange or red egg-shaped nuts. [C16: from Portuguese, from Malayalam *adekka*]

areg (əˈrɛɡ) *n* a plural of **erg**[2].

arena (əˈriːnə) *n* **1a** an enclosure or platform, usually surrounded by seats on all sides, in which sports events, contests, entertainments, etc., take place: *a boxing arena.* **1b** (*as modifier*): *arena stage.* **2** the central area of an ancient Roman amphitheatre, in which gladiatorial contests and other spectacles were held. **3** a sphere or scene of conflict or intense activity: *the political arena.* [C17: from Latin *harēna* sand, place where sand was strewn for the combats]

arenaceous (ˌærɪˈneɪʃəs) *adj* **1** (of sedimentary rocks and deposits) composed of sand or sandstone. Compare **argillaceous** and **rudaceous.** **2** (of plants) growing best in a sandy soil. [C17: from Latin *harēnāceus* sandy, from *harēna* sand]

arena theatre *n* another term for **theatre-in-the-round.**

Arendt ('ɛərənt) *n* **Hannah.** 1906–75, U.S. political philosopher, born in Germany. Her publications include *The Origins of Totalitarianism* (1951) and *Eichmann in Jerusalem* (1961).

arene ('æriːn) *n* an aromatic hydrocarbon. [C20: from AR(OMATIC) + -ENE]

arenicolous (ˌærɪ'nɪkələs) *adj* growing or living in sand or sandy places: *arenicolous plants.* [C19: from Latin *harēna* sand + *colere* to inhabit]

arenite ('ærəˌnaɪt, ə'riː-) *n* any arenaceous rock; a sandstone. [C20: from Latin *harēna* sand + -ITE[1]] ▸ **arenitic** (ˌærə'nɪtɪk) *adj*

aren't (ɑːnt) **1** *contraction of* are not. **2** *Informal, chiefly Brit.* (used in interrogative sentences) *contraction of* am not.

areography (ˌɛərɪ'ɒgrəfɪ) *n* the description of the physical features, such as the surface, atmosphere, etc., of the planet Mars. [C19: from Greek *Areos* Mars + -GRAPHY]

areola (ə'rɪələ) *n, pl* **-lae** (-ˌliː) *or* **-las.** *Anatomy.* any small circular area, such as the pigmented ring around the human nipple or the inflamed area surrounding a pimple. [C17: from Latin: diminutive of AREA] ▸ **a'reolar** *or* **areolate** (ə'rɪəlɪt, -ˌleɪt) *adj* ▸ **areolation** (əˌrɪə'leɪʃən) *n*

areole ('ærɪəʊl) *n* **1** *Biology.* a space outlined on a surface, such as an area between veins on a leaf or on an insect's wing. **2** a sunken area on a cactus from which spines, hairs, etc., arise. ▸ **'areoˌlate** *adj*

Areopagus (ˌærɪ'ɒpəgəs) *n* **1a** the hill to the northwest of the Acropolis in Athens. **1b** (in ancient Athens) the judicial council whose members (Areopagites) met on this hill. **2** *Literary.* any high court. [via Latin from Greek *Areiopagus*, contracted from *Areios pagos,* hill of Ares] ▸ **Areopagite** (ˌærɪ'ɒpədʒaɪt) *n*

Arequipa (ˌærɪ'kiːpə; *Spanish* are'kipa) *n* a city in S Peru, at an altitude of 2250 m (7500 ft.): founded in 1540 on the site of an Inca city. Pop.: 725 838 (1995).

Ares ('ɛəriːz) *n Greek myth.* the god of war, born of Zeus and Hera. Roman counterpart: **Mars.**

arête (ə'reɪt, ə'rɛt) *n* a sharp ridge separating two cirques or glacial valleys in mountainous regions. [C19: from French: fishbone, backbone (of a fish), ridge, sharp edge, from Latin *arista* ear of corn, fishbone]

arethusa (ˌærɪ'θjuːzə) *n* a North American orchid, *Arethusa bulbosa,* having one long narrow leaf and one rose-purple flower fringed with yellow.

Arethusa (ˌærɪ'θjuːzə) *n Greek myth.* a nymph who was changed into a spring on the island of Ortygia to escape the amorous advances of the river god Alpheus.

Aretino (*Italian* are'tiːno) *n* **Pietro** ('pjɛːtro). 1492–1556, Italian satirist, poet, and dramatist, noted for his satirical attacks on leading political figures.

Arezzo (ə'rɛtsəʊ; *Italian* a'rettso) *n* a city in central Italy, in E Tuscany. Pop.: 91 527 (1990). Ancient Latin name: **Arretium.**

Arg. *abbrev. for* Argentina.

argal ('ɑːgəl) *n* another name for **argol.**

argali ('ɑːgəlɪ) *or* **argal** *n, pl* **-gali** *or* **-gals.** a wild sheep, *Ovis ammon,* inhabiting semidesert regions in central Asia: family *Bovidae,* order *Artiodactyla.* It is the largest of the sheep, having massive horns in the male, which may almost form a circle. [C18: from Mongolian]

Argand diagram ('ɑːgænd) *n Maths.* a diagram in which complex numbers are represented by the points in the plane the coordinates of which are respectively the real and imaginary parts of the number, so that the number $x + iy$ is represented by the point (x, y), or by the corresponding vector $\langle x, y\rangle$. If the polar coordinates of (x, y) are (r, θ), r is the modulus and θ the amplitude of $x + iy$. [C19: named after Jean-Robert *Argand* (1768–1822), French mathematician]

argent ('ɑːdʒənt) *n* **a** an archaic or poetic word for **silver. b** (*as adj; often postpositive, esp. in heraldry*): *a bend argent.* [C15: from Old French, from Latin]

Argenteuil (*French* arʒɑ̃tœj) *n* a suburb of Paris, France, with a convent (656) that became famous when Héloïse was abbess (12th century). Pop.: 93 096 (1990).

argentic (ɑː'dʒɛntɪk) *adj Chem.* of or containing silver in the divalent or trivalent state.

argentiferous (ˌɑːdʒən'tɪfərəs) *adj* containing or bearing silver.

Argentina (ˌɑːdʒən'tiːnə) *n* a republic in southern South America: colonized by the Spanish from 1516 onwards; gained independence in 1816 and became a republic in 1852; ruled by military dictatorships for much of the 20th century; civilian rule restored in 1983; consists chiefly of subtropical plains and forests (the Chaco) in the north, temperate plains (the pampas) in the central parts, the Andes in the west, and an infertile plain extending to Tierra del Fuego in the south (Patagonia); an important meat producer. Language: Spanish. Religion: Roman Catholic. Currency: peso. Capital: Buenos Aires. Pop.: 36 125 000 (1998 est.). Area: 2 776 653 sq. km (1 072 067 sq. miles). Also called: **the Argentine.**

argentine ('ɑːdʒənˌtaɪn) *adj* **1** of, relating to, or resembling silver. ◆ *n* **2** any of various small marine salmonoid fishes, such as *Argentina sphyraena,* that constitute the family *Argentinidae* and are characterized by a long silvery body.

Argentine ('ɑːdʒənˌtiːn, -ˌtaɪn) *n* **1 the.** another name for **Argentina. 2** a native or inhabitant of Argentina. ◆ *adj* **3** of or relating to Argentina. ◆ Also (for senses 2, 3): **Argentinian** (ˌɑːdʒən'tɪnɪən).

argentite ('ɑːdʒənˌtaɪt) *n* a dark grey mineral that consists of silver sulphide, usually in cubic crystalline forms, and occurs in veins, often with native silver. It is found esp. in Mexico, Nevada, and Saxony and is an important source of silver. Formula: Ag_2S.

argentous (ɑː'dʒɛntəs) *adj Chem.* of or containing silver in the monovalent state.

argentum (ɑː'dʒɛntəm) *n* an obsolete name for **silver.** [Latin]

argie-bargie ('ɑːdʒɪ'bɑːdʒɪ) *n* a variant spelling of **argy-bargy.**

argil ('ɑːdʒɪl) *n* clay, esp. potters' clay. [C16: from Latin *argilla* white clay, from Greek *argillos*]

argillaceous (ˌɑːdʒɪ'leɪʃəs) *adj* (of sedimentary rocks and deposits) composed of very fine-grained material, such as clay, shale, etc. Compare **arenaceous** (sense 1) and **rudaceous.**

argilliferous (ˌɑːdʒɪ'lɪfərəs) *adj* containing or yielding clay: *argilliferous rocks.*

argillite ('ɑːdʒɪˌlaɪt) *n* any argillaceous rock, esp. a hardened mudstone. [C18: from Latin *argilla* clay (from Greek *argillos*) + -ITE[1]] ▸ **argillitic** (ˌɑːdʒɪ'lɪtɪk) *adj*

arginine ('ɑːdʒɪˌnaɪn) *n* an essential amino acid of plant and animal proteins, necessary for nutrition and for the production of excretory urea. [C19: from German *Arginin,* of uncertain origin]

Argive ('ɑːdʒaɪv, -gaɪv) *adj* **1** (in Homer, Virgil, etc.) of or relating to the Greeks besieging Troy, esp. those from Argos. **2** of or relating to Argos or Argolis. **3** a literary word for **Greek.** ◆ *n* **4** an ancient Greek, esp. one from Argos or Argolis.

argle-bargle (ˌɑːgᵊl'bɑːgᵊl) *n* another word for **argy-bargy.**

Argo[1] ('ɑːgəʊ) *n Greek myth.* the ship in which Jason sailed in search of the Golden Fleece.

Argo[2] ('ɑːgəʊ) *n, Latin genitive* **Argus** ('ɑːgəs). an extensive constellation in the S hemisphere now subdivided into the smaller constellations of **Puppis, Vela, Carina,** and **Pyxis.** Also called: **Argo Navis** ('neɪvɪs).

argol ('ɑːgɒl) *or* **argal** *n* crude potassium hydrogentartrate, deposited as a crust on the sides of wine vats. [C14: from Anglo-French *argoil,* of unknown origin]

Argolis ('ɑːgəlɪs) *n* **1** a department and ancient region of Greece, in the NE Peloponnese. Capital: Nauplion. Pop.: 97 636 (1991). Area: 2261 sq. km (873 sq. miles). **2 Gulf of.** an inlet of the Aegean Sea, in the E Peloponnese.

argon ('ɑːgɒn) *n* an extremely unreactive colourless odourless element of the rare gas series that forms almost 1 per cent (by volume) of the atmosphere. It is used in electric lights. Symbol: Ar; atomic no.: 18; atomic wt.: 39.948; density: 1.7837 kg/m^3; freezing pt.: –189.3°C; boiling pt.: –185.9°C. [C19: from Greek, from *argos* idle, inactive, from A-[1] + *ergon* work]

Argonaut ('ɑːgəˌnɔːt) *n* **1** *Greek myth.* one of the heroes who sailed with Jason in quest of the Golden Fleece. **2** a person who took part in the Californian gold rush of 1849. **3** another name for the **paper nautilus.** [C16: from Greek *Argonautēs,* from *Argō* the name of Jason's ship + *nautēs* sailor] ▸ **ˌArgo'nautic** *adj*

Argonne ('ɑːgɒn; *French* argɔn) *n* **the.** a wooded region of NE France: scene of major battles in both World Wars.

argonon ('ɑːgəˌnɒn) *n* another name for **inert gas** (sense 1). [C20: from ARGON + -ON (indicating an inert gas)]

Argos ('ɑːgɒs, -gəs) *n* an ancient city in SE Greece, in the NE Peloponnese: one of the oldest Greek cities, it dominated the Peloponnese in the 7th century B.C. Pop.: 22 000 (1995 est.).

argosy ('ɑːgəsɪ) *n, pl* **-sies.** *Archaic or poetic.* a large abundantly laden merchant ship, or a fleet of such ships. [C16: from Italian *Ragusea* (*nave*) (ship) of Ragusa]

argot ('ɑːgəʊ) *n* slang or jargon peculiar to a particular group, esp. (formerly) a group of thieves. [C19: from French, of unknown origin] ▸ **argotic** (ɑː'gɒtɪk) *adj*

Argovie (argɔvi) *n* the French name for **Aargau.**

arguable ('ɑːgjʊəbᵊl) *adj* **1** capable of being disputed; doubtful. **2** capable of being supported by argument; plausible. ▸ **'arguably** *adv*

argue ('ɑːgjuː) *vb* **-gues, -guing, -gued. 1** (*intr*) to quarrel; wrangle: *they were always arguing until I arrived.* **2** (*intr;* often foll. by *for* or *against*) to present supporting or opposing reasons or cases in a dispute; reason. **3** (*tr; may take a clause as object*) to try to prove by presenting reasons; maintain. **4** (*tr; often passive*) to debate or discuss: *the case was fully argued before agreement was reached.* **5** (*tr*) to persuade: *he argued me into going.* **6** (*tr*) to give evidence of; suggest: *her looks argue despair.* [C14: from Old French *arguer* to assert, charge with, from Latin *arguere* to make clear, accuse; related to Latin *argūtus* clear, *argentum* silver] ▸ **'arguer** *n*

argufy ('ɑːgjʊˌfaɪ) *vb* **-fies, -fying, -fied.** *Facetious or dialect.* to argue or quarrel, esp. over something trivial.

argument ('ɑːgjʊmənt) *n* **1** a quarrel; altercation. **2** a discussion in which reasons are put forward in support of and against a proposition, proposal, or case; debate: *the argument on birth control will never be concluded.* **3** (*sometimes pl*) a point or series of reasons presented to support or oppose a proposition. **4** a summary of the plot or subject of a book, etc. **5** *Logic.* **5a** a process of deductive or inductive reasoning that purports to show its conclusion to be true. **5b** formally, a sequence of statements one of which is the conclusion and the remainder the premises. **6** *Logic.* an obsolete name for the middle term of a syllogism. **7** *Maths.* **7a** an element to which an operation, function, predicate, etc., applies, esp. the independent variable of a function. **7b** another name for **amplitude** (sense 5) of a complex number.

argumentation (ˌɑːgjʊmɛn'teɪʃən) *n* **1** the process of reasoning methodically. **2** a less common word for **argument** (senses 2, 3).

argumentative (ˌɑːgjʊ'mɛntətɪv) *adj* **1** given to arguing; contentious. **2** characterized by argument; controversial. ▸ **ˌargu'mentatively** *adv* ▸ **ˌargu'mentativeness** *n*

argument from design *n* another name for **teleological argument.**

argumentum ad hominem *Latin.* (ˌɑːgjʊ'mɛntʊm æd 'hɒmɪˌnɛm) *n Logic.* **1** fallacious argument that attacks not an opponent's beliefs but his motives or character. **2** argument that shows an opponent's statement to be inconsistent with his other beliefs. **3** an instance of either of these. [literally: argument to the person]

argus ('ɑːgəs) *n* any of various brown butterflies, esp. the **Scotch argus** (*Erebia aethiops*) found on moorland and in forests up to a height of 2000 m.

Argus ('ɑːgəs) *n* **1** *Greek myth.* a giant with a hundred eyes who was made guardian of the heifer Io. After he was killed by Hermes his eyes were transferred to the peacock's tail. **2** a vigilant person; guardian.

Argus-eyed *adj* keen-sighted; observant; vigilant.

argus pheasant *n* either of two pheasants, *Argusianus argus* (great argus) or *Rheinardia ocellata* (crested argus), occurring in SE Asia and Indonesia. The males have very long tails marked with eyelike spots.

argy-bargy *or* **argie-bargie** ('ɑːdʒɪ'bɑːdʒɪ) *n, pl* **-bargies.** *Brit. informal.* a wrangling argument or verbal dispute. Also called: **argle-bargle.** [C19: from Scottish, compound based on dialect *argle,* probably from ARGUE]

argyle (ɑː'gaɪl) *adj* **1** made of knitted or woven material with a diamond-shaped pattern of two or more colours. ◆ *n* **2** (*often pl*) a sock made of this. [C20: after Campbell of *Argyle* (Argyll), the pattern being an adaptation of the tartan of this clan]

Argyll and Bute (ɑː'gaɪl) *n* a council area in W Scotland on the Atlantic Ocean: in 1975 the historic counties of Argyllshire and Bute became part of Strathclyde region; in 1996 they were reinstated as a single unitary authority. Argyll and Bute is mountainous and includes the islands of Bute, Mull, Islay, and Jura. Administrative centre: Lochgilphead. Pop.: 90 550 (1996 est.). Area: 6930 sq. km (2676 sq. miles).

Argyllshire (ɑː'gaɪl,ʃɪə, -ʃə) *n* (until 1975) a county of W Scotland, part of Strathclyde region (1975–96), now part of Argyll and Bute.

Argyrol ('ɑːdʒɪ,rɒl, ɑː'dʒɪərɒl) *n Trademark.* a dark brown compound of silver and a protein, used medicinally as a local antiseptic.

arhat ('ɑːhət) *n* a Buddhist, esp. a monk who has achieved enlightenment and at death passes to nirvana. Compare **Bodhisattva.** [from Sanskrit: worthy of respect, from *arhati* he deserves]

Århus (*Danish* 'ɔrhuːs) *n* a variant spelling of **Aarhus.**

aria ('ɑːrɪə) *n* an elaborate accompanied song for solo voice from a cantata, opera, or oratorio. See also **da capo.** [C18: from Italian: tune, AIR]

Ariadne (,ærɪ'ædnɪ) *n Greek myth.* daughter of Minos and Pasiphaë: she gave Theseus the thread with which he found his way out of the Minotaur's labyrinth.

Arian ('ɛərɪən) *adj* **1** of, relating to, or characterizing Arius or Arianism. ◆ *n* **2** an adherent of Arianism. ◆ *adj, n* **3** a variant spelling of **Aryan.**

-arian *suffix forming nouns.* indicating a person or thing that advocates, believes, or is associated with something: *vegetarian; millenarian; librarian.* [from Latin *-ārius* -ARY + -AN]

Arianism ('ɛərɪə,nɪzəm) *n* the doctrine of Arius, pronounced heretical at the Council of Nicaea, which asserted that Christ was not of one substance with the Father, but a creature raised by the Father to the dignity of Son of God.

Arias Sánchez ('ærɪæs 'sæntʃɛz) *n* **Oscar.** born 1940, Costa Rican statesman; president (1986–90); Nobel peace prize 1987.

Arica (ə'riːkə; *Spanish* a'rika) *n* a port in extreme N Chile: awarded to Chile in 1929 after the lengthy Tacna-Arica dispute with Peru; outlet for Bolivian and Peruvian trade. Pop.: 173 336 (1995 est.). See also **Tacna-Arica.**

arid ('ærɪd) *adj* **1** having little or no rain; dry; parched with heat. **2** devoid of interest. [C17: from Latin *āridus,* from *ārēre* to be dry] ▸ **aridity** (ə'rɪdɪtɪ) *or* **'aridness** *n* ▸ **'aridly** *adv*

arid zone *n* either of the zones of latitude 15–30° N and S characterized by very low rainfall and desert or semidesert terrain.

Ariège (*French* arjɛʒ) *n* a department of SW France, in Midi-Pyrénées region. Capital: Foix. Pop.: 136 600 (1995). Area: 4903 sq. km (1912 sq. miles).

ariel ('ɛərɪəl) *n* an Arabian gazelle, *Gazella arabica* (or *dama*). [C19: from Arabic *aryal*]

Ariel ('ɛərɪəl) *n* the smallest of the four large satellites of Uranus.

Aries ('ɛəriːz) *n, Latin genitive* **Arietis** (ə'raɪɪtɪs). **1** *Astronomy.* a small zodiacal constellation in the N hemisphere lying between Taurus and Pisces on the ecliptic and having a second-magnitude star. **2** *Astrology.* **2a** Also called: the **Ram.** the first sign of the zodiac, symbol ♈, having a cardinal fire classification, ruled by the planet Mars. The sun is in this sign between about March 21 and April 19. **2b** a person born during the period when the sun is in this sign. ◆ *adj* **3** *Astrology.* born under or characteristic of Aries. ◆ Also (for senses 2b, 3): **Arien** ('ɛərɪən). [C14: from Latin: ram]

arietta (,ærɪ'ɛtə; *Italian* ari'etta) *or* **ariette** (,ærɪ'ɛt) *n, pl* **-ettas, -ette** (-'ette), *or* **-ettes.** a short relatively uncomplicated aria. [C18: from Italian, diminutive of ARIA]

aright (ə'raɪt) *adv* correctly; rightly; properly.

ariki ('ɑːrɪkɪ) *n, pl* **ariki.** *N.Z.* the first-born male or female in a notable family; chief. [Maori]

aril ('ærɪl) *n* an appendage on certain seeds, such as those of the yew and nutmeg, developed from or near the funicle of the ovule and often brightly coloured and fleshy. [C18: from New Latin *arillus,* from Medieval Latin *arilli* raisins, pips of grapes] ▸ **'aril,late** *adj*

arillode ('ærɪ,ləʊd) *n* a structure in certain seeds, such as the nutmeg, that resembles an aril but is developed from the micropyle of the ovule. [C19: from ARIL + -ODE[1]]

Arimathea *or* **Arimathaea** (,ærɪmə'θɪːə) *n* a town in ancient Palestine: location unknown.

Ariminum (ə'rɪmɪnəm) *n* the ancient name of **Rimini.**

arioso (,ɑːrɪ'əʊzəʊ, ,æ-) *n, pl* **-sos** *or* **-si** (-siː). *Music.* a recitative with the lyrical quality of an aria. [C18: from Italian, from ARIA]

Ariosto (*Italian* a'rjɔsto) *n* **Ludovico** (ludo'viːko). 1474–1533, Italian poet, famous for his romantic epic *Orlando Furioso* (1516).

arise (ə'raɪz) *vb* **arises, arising, arose, arisen.** (*intr*) **1** to come into being; originate. **2** (foll. by *from*) to spring or proceed as a consequence; result. **3** to get or stand up, as from a sitting, kneeling, or lying position. **4** to come into notice. **5** to move upwards; ascend. [Old English *ārīsan;* related to Old Saxon *arīsan,* Old High German *irrīsan;* see RISE]

arista (ə'rɪstə) *n, pl* **-tae** (-tiː). **1** a stiff bristle such as the awn of some grasses and cereals. **2** a bristle-like appendage on the antennae of some insects. [C17: from Latin: ear of corn, fishbone] ▸ **a'ristate** *adj*

Aristaeus (,ærɪ'stiːəs) *n Greek myth.* a son of Apollo and Cyrene: protector of herds and fields.

Aristarchus (,ærɪ'stɑːkəs) *n* a crater in the NE quadrant of the moon, having a diameter of about 37 kilometres, which is the brightest formation on the moon.

Aristarchus of Samos *n* 3rd century B.C., Greek astronomer who anticipated Copernicus in advancing the theory that the earth revolves around the sun.

Aristarchus of Samothrace *n* ?220–?150 B.C., Greek scholar: librarian at Alexandria, noted for his edition of Homer.

Aristides (,ærɪ'staɪdiːz) *n* known as *Aristides the Just.* ?530–?468 B.C., Athenian general and statesman, who played a prominent part in the Greek victories over the Persians at Marathon (490), Salamis (480), and Plataea (479).

Aristippus (,ærɪ'stɪpəs) *n* ?435–?356 B.C., Greek philosopher, who believed pleasure to be the highest good and founded the Cyrenaic school.

aristo ('ærɪstəʊ, ə'rɪstəʊ) *n, pl* **-tos.** *Informal.* short for **aristocrat.**

aristocracy (,ærɪ'stɒkrəsɪ) *n, pl* **-cies.** **1** a privileged class of people usually of high birth; the nobility. **2** such a class as the ruling body of a state. **3** government by such a class. **4** a state governed by such a class. **5** a class of people considered to be outstanding in a sphere of activity. [C16: from Late Latin *aristocratia,* from Greek *aristokratia* rule by the best-born, from *aristos* best; see -CRACY]

aristocrat ('ærɪstə,kræt) *n* **1** a member of the aristocracy; a noble. **2** a person who has the manners or qualities of a member of a privileged or superior class. **3** a person who advocates aristocracy as a form of government.

aristocratic (,ærɪstə'krætɪk) *adj* **1** relating to or characteristic of aristocracy or an aristocrat. **2** elegant or stylish in appearance and behaviour. ▸ **,aristo'cratically** *adv*

Aristophanes (,ærɪ'stɒfə,niːz) *n* ?448–?380 B.C., Greek comic dramatist, who satirized leading contemporary figures such as Socrates and Euripides. Eleven of his plays are extant, including *The Clouds, The Frogs, The Birds,* and *Lysistrata.*

Aristotelian (,ærɪstə'tiːlɪən) *adj* **1** of or relating to Aristotle or his philosophy. **2** (of a philosophical position) derived from that of Aristotle, or incorporating such of his major doctrines as the distinctions between matter and form, and substance and accident, or the primacy of individuals over universals. ◆ *n* **3** a follower of Aristotle.

Aristotelian logic *n* the logical theories of Aristotle as developed in the Middle Ages, concerned mainly with syllogistic reasoning: traditional as opposed to modern or symbolic logic.

Aristotle[1] ('ærɪ,stɒtᵊl) *n* 384–322 B.C., Greek philosopher; pupil of Plato, tutor of Alexander the Great, and founder of the Peripatetic school at Athens; author of works on logic, ethics, politics, poetics, rhetoric, biology, zoology, and metaphysics. His works influenced Muslim philosophy and science and medieval scholastic philosophy.

Aristotle[2] ('ærɪ,stɒtᵊl) *n* a prominent crater in the NW quadrant of the moon about 83 kilometres in diameter.

arithmetic (ə'rɪθmətɪk) *n* **1** the branch of mathematics concerned with numerical calculations, such as addition, subtraction, multiplication, and division. **2** one or more calculations involving numerical operations. **3** knowledge of or skill in using arithmetic: *his arithmetic is good.* ◆ *adj* (,ærɪθ'mɛtɪk), *also* **,arith'metical.** **4** of, relating to, or using arithmetic. [C13: from Latin *arithmētica,* from Greek *arithmētikē,* from *arithmein* to count, from *arithmos* number] ▸ **,arith'metically** *adv* ▸ **a,rithme'tician** *n*

arithmetic mean *n* the average value of a set of integers, terms, or quantities, expressed as their sum divided by their number: *the arithmetic mean of 3, 4, and 8 is 5.* Often shortened to **mean.** Also called: **average.** Compare **geometric mean.**

arithmetic progression *n* a sequence of numbers or quantities, each term of which differs from the succeeding term by a constant amount, such as 3,6,9,12. Compare **geometric progression.**

-arium *suffix forming nouns.* indicating a place for or associated with something: *aquarium; planetarium; solarium.* [from Latin *-ārium,* neuter of *-ārius* -ARY]

Arius ('ɛərɪəs) *n* ?250–336 A.D., Greek Christian theologian, originator of the doctrine of Arianism.

Ariz. *abbrev. for* Arizona.

Arizona (,ærɪ'zəʊnə) *n* a state of the southwestern U.S.: consists of the Colorado plateau in the northeast, including the Grand Canyon, divided from desert in the southwest by mountains rising over 3750 m (12 500 ft.). Capital: Phoenix. Pop.: 4 554 966 (1997 est.). Area: 293 750 sq. km (113 417 sq. miles). Abbrevs.: **Ariz.** or (with zip code) **AZ**

Arjuna ('ɑːdʒʊnə) *n Hindu myth.* the most important of the five princes in the *Mahabharata.* Krishna served as his charioteer in the battle with the Kauravas.

ark (ɑːk) *n* **1** the vessel that Noah built and in which he saved himself, his family, and a number of animals and birds during the Flood (Genesis 6–9). **2 out of the ark.** *Informal.* very old; out of date. **3** a place or thing offering shelter or protection. **4** *Dialect.* a chest, box, or coffer. [Old English *arc,* from Latin *arca* box, chest]

Ark (ɑːk) *n Judaism.* **1** Also called: **Holy Ark.** the cupboard at the front of a synagogue, usually in the eastern wall, in which the Torah scrolls are kept. **2** Also called: **Ark of the Covenant.** the most sacred symbol of God's presence among the Hebrew people, carried in their journey from Sinai to the Promised Land (Canaan) and eventually enshrined in the holy of holies of the Temple in Jerusalem.

Ark. *abbrev. for* Arkansas.

Arkansas *n* **1** ('ɑːkən,sɔː). a state of the southern U.S.: mountainous in the north and west, with the alluvial plain of the Mississippi in the east; has the only diamond mine in the U.S.; the chief U.S. producer of bauxite. Capital: Little Rock. Pop.: 2 522 819 (1997 est.). Area: 134 537 sq. km (51 945 sq. miles). Abbrevs.: **Ark.** or (with zip code) **AR** **2** (ɑː'kænzəs). a river in the S central U.S., rising in central Colorado and flowing east and southeast to join the Mississippi in Arkansas. Length: 2335 km (1450 miles). ► **Arkansan** (ɑː'kænzən) *n, adj*

Arkhangelsk (ar'xangɪljsk) *n* the Russian name for **Archangel.**

arkose ('ɑːkəʊs) *n* a sandstone consisting of grains of feldspar and quartz cemented by a mixture of quartz and clay minerals. [C19: from French]

Arkwright ('ɑːkraɪt) *n* Sir **Richard.** 1732–92, English cotton manufacturer: inventor of the spinning frame (1769) which produced cotton thread strong enough to be used as a warp.

Arlberg (*German* 'arl,bɛrk) *n* a mountain pass in W Austria: a winter sports region. Height: 1802 m (5910 ft.).

Arles (ɑːlz; *French* arl) *n* **1** a city in SE France, on the Rhône: Roman amphitheatre. Pop.: 52 590 (1990). **2 Kingdom of.** a kingdom in SE France which had dissolved by 1378: known as the Kingdom of Burgundy until about 1200.

Arlington ('ɑːlɪŋtən) *n* a county of N Virginia: site of **Arlington National Cemetery.**

Arlon (*French* arlɔ̃) *n* a town in SE Belgium, capital of Luxembourg province. Pop.: 17 000 (1991 est.).

arm[1] (ɑːm) *n* **1** (in man) either of the upper limbs from the shoulder to the wrist. Related adj: **brachial. 2** the part of either of the upper limbs from the elbow to the wrist; forearm. **3a** the corresponding limb of any other vertebrate. **3b** an armlike appendage of some invertebrates. **4** an object that covers or supports the human arm, esp. the sleeve of a garment or the side of a chair, sofa, etc. **5** anything considered to resemble an arm in appearance, position, or function, esp. something that branches out from a central support or larger mass: *an arm of the sea; the arm of a record player.* **6** an administrative subdivision of an organization: *an arm of the government.* **7** power; authority: *the arm of the law.* **8** any of the specialist combatant sections of a military force, such as cavalry, infantry, etc. **9** *Nautical.* See **yardarm. 10** *Sport, esp. ball games.* ability to throw or pitch: *he has a good arm.* **11 an arm and a leg.** *Informal.* a large amount of money. **12 arm in arm.** with arms linked. **13 at arm's length.** at a distance; away from familiarity with or subjection to another. **14 give one's right arm.** *Informal.* to be prepared to make any sacrifice. **15 in the arms of Morpheus.** sleeping. **16 with open arms.** with great warmth and hospitality: *to welcome someone with open arms.* ◆ *vb* **17** *(tr) Archaic.* to walk arm in arm with. [Old English; related to German *Arm,* Old Norse *armr* arm, Latin *armus* shoulder, Greek *harmos* joint] ► **'armless** *adj* ► **'arm,like** *adj*

arm[2] (ɑːm) *vb (tr)* **1** to equip with weapons as a preparation for war. **2** to provide (a person or thing) with something that strengthens, protects, or increases efficiency: *he armed himself against the cold.* **3a** to activate (a fuse) so that it will explode at the required time. **3b** to prepare (an explosive device) for use by introducing a fuse or detonator. **4** *Nautical.* to pack arming into (a sounding lead). ◆ *n* **5** *(usually pl)* a weapon, esp. a firearm. ◆ See also **arms.** [C14: (n) back formation from *arms,* from Old French *armes,* from Latin *arma;* (vb) from Old French *armer* to equip with arms, from Latin *armāre,* from *arma* arms, equipment]

Arm. *abbrev. for:* **1** Armenia(n). **2** Armoric *or* Armorican.

armada (ɑː'mɑːdə) *n* a large number of ships or aircraft. [C16: from Spanish, from Medieval Latin *armāta* fleet, armed forces, from Latin *armāre* to provide with arms]

Armada (ɑː'mɑːdə) *n* (usually preceded by *the*) See the **Spanish Armada.**

armadillo (,ɑːmə'dɪləʊ) *n, pl* **-los. 1** any edentate mammal of the family *Dasypodidae* of Central and South America and S North America, such as *Priodontes giganteus* (**giant armadillo**). They are burrowing animals, with peglike rootless teeth and a covering of strong horny plates over most of the body. **2 fairy armadillo.** another name for **pichiciego.** [C16: from Spanish, diminutive of *armado* armed (man), from Latin *armātus* armed; compare ARMADA]

Armageddon (,ɑːmə'gedᵊn) *n* **1** *New Testament.* the final battle at the end of the world between the forces of good and evil, God against the kings of the earth (Revelation 16:16). **2** a catastrophic and extremely destructive conflict, esp. World War I viewed as this. [C19: from Late Latin *Armagedōn,* from Greek, from Hebrew *har megiddōn,* mountain district of *Megiddo,* in N Palestine, site of various battles in the Old Testament]

Armagh (ɑː'mɑː) *n* **1** a historic county of S Northern Ireland: in 1973 it was replaced for administrative purposes by the districts of Armagh and Craigavon. Area: 1326 sq. km (512 sq. miles). **2** a district in Northern Ireland, in Co. Armagh. Pop.: 51 817 (1991). Area: 667 sq. km (258 sq. miles). **3** a town in S Northern Ireland, in Armagh district, Co. Armagh: seat of Roman Catholic and Protestant archbishops. Pop.: 14 640 (1991).

Armagnac ('ɑːmən,jæk) *n* a dry brown brandy distilled in the French district of Gers. [from *Armagnac,* the former name of this region]

Armalite ('ɑːməlaɪt) *n Trademark.* a lightweight high-velocity rifle of various calibres, capable of automatic and semiautomatic operation. [C20: from *Armalite* Division, Fairchild Engine and Airplane Company, manufacturers]

armament ('ɑːməmənt) *n* **1** *(often pl)* the weapon equipment of a military vehicle, ship, or aircraft. **2** a military force raised and armed ready for war. **3** preparation for war involving the production of equipment and arms. [C17: from Latin *armāmenta* utensils, from *armāre* to equip]

armamentarium (,ɑːməmen'tɛərɪəm) *n, pl* **-iums** *or* **-ia** (-ɪə). the items that comprise the material and equipment used by a physician in his professional practice.

Armani (ɑː'mɑːnɪ; *Italian* ar'maːni) *n* **Giorgio.** born 1936, Italian fashion designer, noted for his restrained classical style.

armature ('ɑːmətjʊə) *n* **1** a revolving structure in an electric motor or generator, wound with the coils that carry the current. **2** any part of an electric machine or device that moves under the influence of a magnetic field or within which an electromotive force is induced. **3** Also called: **keeper.** a soft iron or steel bar placed across the poles of a permanent magnet to close the magnetic circuit. **4** such a bar placed across the poles of an electromagnet to transmit mechanical force. **5** *Sculpture.* a framework to support the clay or other material used in modelling. **6** the protective outer covering of an animal or plant. **7** *Archaic.* armour. [C15: from Latin *armātūra* armour, equipment, from *armāre* to furnish with equipment; see ARM[2]]

armband ('ɑːm,bænd) *n* **1** a band of material worn round the arm, such as one bearing an identifying mark, etc., or a black one indicating mourning. **2** an inflatable buoyancy aid, worn on the upper arm of a person learning to swim. **3** an elasticated band worn round the upper arm to keep the shirtsleeve in place.

armchair ('ɑːm,tʃɛə) *n* **1** a chair, esp. an upholstered one, that has side supports for the arms or elbows. **2** *(modifier)* taking no active part; lacking practical experience; theoretical: *an armchair strategist.* **3** *(modifier)* participated in away from the place of action or in the home: *armchair theatre.*

Armco ('ɑːmkəʊ) *n Trademark.* a metal safety barrier erected at the side of motor-racing circuits, esp. on corners.

armed[1] (ɑːmd) *adj* **1** equipped with or supported by arms, armour, etc. **2** prepared for conflict or any difficulty. **3** (of an explosive device) prepared for use; having a fuse or detonator installed. **4** (of plants) having the protection of thorns, spines, etc.

armed[2] (ɑːmd) *adj* **a** having an arm or arms. **b** *(in combination): long-armed; one-armed.*

armed forces *pl n* the military forces of a nation or nations, including the army, navy, air force, marines, etc.

Armenia (ɑː'miːnɪə) *n* **1** a republic in NW Asia: originally part of the historic Armenian kingdom; acquired by Russia in 1828; became the Armenian Soviet Socialist Republic in 1936; gained independence in 1991. It is mountainous, rising over 4000 m (13 000 ft.). Language: Armenian. Religion: Christian (Armenian Apostolic) majority. Currency: dram. Capital: Yerevan. Pop.: 3 800 000 (1998 est.). Area: 29 800 sq. km (11 490 sq. miles). **2** a former kingdom in W Asia, between the Black Sea and the Caspian Sea, south of Georgia. **3** a town in central Colombia: centre of a coffee-growing district. Pop.: 283 842 (1997 est.).

Armenian (ɑː'miːnɪən) *n* **1** a native or inhabitant of Armenia or an Armenian-speaking person elsewhere. **2** the language of the Armenians: an Indo-European language probably belonging to the Thraco-Phrygian branch, but containing many non-Indo-European elements. **3** an adherent of the Armenian Church or its doctrines. ◆ *adj* **4** of or relating to Armenia, its inhabitants, their language, or the Armenian Church.

Armenian Church *n* the national Church of Armenia, founded in the early fourth century A.D., the dogmas and liturgy of which are similar to those of the Orthodox Church.

Armentières ('ɑːmən,tɪəz; *French* armɑ̃tjɛr) *n* a town in N France: site of battles in both World Wars. Pop.: 26 240 (1990).

armeria (ɑː'mɪːrɪə) *n* the generic name for **thrift** (sense 2). [New Latin, from *flos armeriae,* a species of dianthus]

armes parlantes (*French* arm parlɑ̃t) *pl n Heraldry.* arms using devices to illustrate the name of the bearers, such as a rose and a wall to illustrate the name *Rosewall.* [literally: speaking arms]

armet ('ɑːmet) *n* a close-fitting medieval visored helmet with a neck guard. [C16: from Old French, from Old Spanish *almete,* from Old French HELMET]

armful ('ɑːmfʊl) *n, pl* **-fuls.** the amount that can be held by one or both arms.

armhole ('ɑːm,həʊl) *n* the opening in an article of clothing through which the arm passes and to which a sleeve is often fitted.

Armidale ('ɑːmɪ,deɪl) *n* a town in Australia, in NE New South Wales: a centre for tourism. Pop.: 21 606 (1991 est.).

armiger ('ɑːmɪdʒə) *n* **1** a person entitled to bear heraldic arms, such as a sovereign or nobleman. **2** a squire carrying the armour of a medieval knight. [C16: from Medieval Latin: squire, from Latin: armour-bearer, from *arma* arms + *gerere* to carry, bear] ► **armigerous** (ɑː'mɪdʒərəs) *adj*

armillary ('ɑːmɪlərɪ, ɑː'mɪlərɪ) *adj* of or relating to bracelets. [C17: from New Latin *armillaris,* from Latin *armilla* bracelet]

armillary sphere *n* a model of the celestial sphere consisting of rings representing the relative positions of the celestial equator, ecliptic, etc., used by early astronomers for determining the positions of stars.

arming ('ɑːmɪŋ) *n* **1** the act of taking arms or providing with arms. **2** *Nautical.* a greasy substance, such as tallow, packed into the recess at the bottom of a sounding lead to pick up samples of sand, gravel, etc., from the bottom.

Arminian (ɑː'mɪnɪən) *adj* **1** denoting, relating to, or believing in the Christian Protestant doctrines of Jacobus Arminius, published in 1610, which rejected absolute predestination and insisted that the sovereignty of God is compatible with free will in man. These doctrines deeply influenced Wesleyan and Methodist theology. ◆ *n* **2** a follower of such doctrines. ► **Ar'minian,ism** *n*

Arminius (ɑː'mɪnɪəs) *n* **1** Also called: **Hermann.** ?17 B.C.–?21 A.D., Germanic chieftain: organized a revolt against the Romans in 9 A.D. **2 Jacobus** (dʒə'kəʊbəs), real name *Jacob Harmensen.* 1560–1609, Dutch Protestant theologian.

armipotent (ɑː'mɪpətənt) *adj Literary.* strong in arms or war. [C14: from Latin *armipotēns,* from *arma* arms + *potēns* powerful, from *posse* to be able] ► **ar'mipotence** *n*

armistice ('ɑːmɪstɪs) *n* an agreement between opposing armies to suspend hostilities in order to discuss peace terms; truce. [C18: from New Latin *armistitium,* from Latin *arma* arms + *sistere* to stop, stand still]

Armistice Day *n* the anniversary of the signing of the armistice that ended World War I, on Nov. 11, 1918, now kept on Remembrance Sunday. See also **Remembrance Sunday.** U.S. name: **Veterans Day.**

armlet ('ɑːmlɪt) *n* **1** a small arm, as of a lake, the sea, etc. **2** a band or bracelet worn round the arm for ornament, identification, etc. **3** a very short sleeve on a garment.

armoire (ɑːmˈwɑː) *n* a large cabinet, originally used for storing weapons. [C16: from French, from Old French *armaire,* from Latin *armārium* chest, closet; see AMBRY]

armor (ˈɑːmə) *n* the U.S. spelling of **armour.**

armorial (ɑːˈmɔːrɪəl) *adj* **1** of or relating to heraldry or heraldic arms. ◆ *n* **2** a book of coats of arms.

Armorica (ɑːˈmɒrɪkə) *n* an ancient name for Brittany. ▸ **Arˈmorican** *n, adj*

armour *or U.S.* **armor** (ˈɑːmə) *n* **1** any defensive covering, esp. that of metal, chain mail, etc., worn by medieval warriors to prevent injury to the body in battle. **2** the protective metal plates on a tank, warship, etc. **3** *Military.* armoured fighting vehicles in general; military units equipped with these. **4** any protective covering, such as the shell of certain animals. **5** *Nautical.* the watertight suit of a diver. **6** *Engineering.* permanent protection for an underwater structure. **7** heraldic insignia; arms. ◆ *vb* **8** (*tr*) to equip or cover with armour. [C13: from Old French *armure,* from Latin *armātūra* armour, equipment]

armour-bearer *n History.* a retainer who carried the arms or armour of a warrior.

armoured *or U.S.* **armored** (ˈɑːməd) *adj* **1** having a protective covering, such as armour or bone. **2** comprising units making use of armoured vehicles: *an armoured brigade.* **3** (of glass) toughened.

armoured car *n* **1** *Military.* a fast lightly armed and armoured vehicle, mainly used for reconnaissance. **2** any vehicle strengthened by armoured plate, esp. a security van for transporting cash and valuables.

armourer *or U.S.* **armorer** (ˈɑːmərə) *n* **1** a person who makes or mends arms and armour. **2** a person employed in the maintenance of small arms and weapons in a military unit.

armour plate *n* a tough heavy steel, usually containing chromium, nickel, and molybdenum and often hardened on the surface, used for protecting warships, tanks, etc.

armoury *or U.S.* **armory** (ˈɑːmərɪ) *n, pl* **-mouries** *or* **-mories. 1** a secure place for the storage of weapons. **2** armour generally. **3a** *U.S.* a building in which training in the use of arms and drill takes place; drill hall. **3b** (*pl*) *Canadian.* such a building used for training and as headquarters by a reserve unit of the armed forces. **4** resources, as of arguments or objections, on which to draw: *they thought they had proved him wrong, but he still had a few weapons in his armoury.* **5** *U.S.* a place where arms are made.

armpit (ˈɑːmˌpɪt) *n* **1** the small depression beneath the arm where it joins the shoulder. Technical name: **axilla.** Related adj: **axillary. 2** *Slang.* an extremely unpleasant place: *the armpit of the Mediterranean.*

armrest (ˈɑːmˌrɛst) *n* the part of a chair, sofa, etc., that supports the arm. Sometimes shortened to **arm.**

arms (ɑːmz) *pl n* **1** weapons collectively. See also **small arms. 2** military exploits: *prowess in arms.* **3** the official heraldic symbols of a family, state, etc., including a shield with distinctive devices, and often supports, a crest, or other insignia. **4 bear arms. 4a** to carry weapons. **4b** to serve in the armed forces. **4c** to have a coat of arms. **5 in** *or* **under arms.** armed and prepared for war. **6 lay down one's arms.** to stop fighting; surrender. **7 present arms.** *Military.* **7a** a position of salute in which the rifle is brought up to a position vertically in line with the body, muzzle uppermost and trigger guard to the fore. **7b** the command for this drill. **8 take (up) arms.** to prepare to fight. **9 to arms!** arm yourselves! **10 up in arms.** indignant; prepared to protest strongly. [C13: from Old French *armes,* from Latin *arma;* see ARM²]

arm's-length *adj* **1** lacking intimacy or friendliness, esp. when possessing some special connection, such as previous closeness: *we now have an arm's-length relationship.* **2** (of commercial transactions) in accordance with market values, disregarding any connection such as common ownership of the companies involved.

arms race *n* the continuing competitive attempt by two or more nations each to have available to it more and more powerful weapons than the other(s).

Armstrong (ˈɑːmˌstrɒŋ) *n* **1 Edwin Howard.** 1890–1954, U.S. electrical engineer; invented the superheterodyne radio receiver and the FM radio. **2 (Daniel) Louis,** known as *Satchmo.* 1900–71, U.S. jazz trumpeter, bandleader, and singer. **3 Gillian.** born 1950, Australian film director; her films include *My Brilliant Career* (1978). **4 Neil (Alden).** born 1930, U.S. astronaut; commanded Apollo 11 on the first manned lunar landing during which he became the first man to set foot on the moon on July 20, 1969.

armure (ˈɑːmjʊə) *n* a silk or wool fabric with a small cobbled pattern. [C19: from French: ARMOUR]

arm wrestling *n* a contest in which two people sit facing each other each with one elbow resting on a table, clasp hands, and each tries to force the other's arm flat onto the table while keeping his own elbow touching the table.

army (ˈɑːmɪ) *n, pl* **-mies. 1** the military land forces of a nation. **2** a military unit usually consisting of two or more corps with supporting arms and services. **3** (*modifier*) of, relating to, or characteristic of an army: *army rations.* **4** any large body of people united for some specific purpose. **5** a large number of people, animals, etc.; multitude. [C14: from Old French *armee,* from Medieval Latin *armāta* armed forces; see ARMADA]

army ant *n* any of various mainly tropical American predatory ants of the subfamily *Dorylinae,* which live in temporary nests and travel in vast hordes preying on other animals. Also called: **legionary ant.** See also **driver ant.**

Army List *n Brit.* an official list of all serving commissioned officers of the army and reserve officers liable for recall.

army worm *n* **1** the caterpillar of a widely distributed noctuid moth, *Leucania unipuncta,* which travels in vast hordes and is a serious pest of cereal crops in North America. **2** any of various similar caterpillars.

Arnaud (ˈɑːnəʊ; *French* arno) *n* **Yvonne.** 1892–1958, French actress, who was well-known on the London stage and in British films. A theatre in Guildford is named after her.

Arne (ɑːn) *n* **Thomas (Augustine).** 1710–78, English composer, noted for his setting of Shakespearean songs and for his song *Rule Britannia.*

Arnhem (ˈɑːnəm) *n* a city in the E Netherlands, capital of Gelderland province, on the Rhine: site of a World War II battle. Pop.: 135 026 (1996 est.).

Arnhem Land *n* a region of N Australia in the N Northern Territory, large areas of which are reserved for native Australians.

arnica (ˈɑːnɪkə) *n* **1** any N temperate or arctic plant of the genus *Arnica,* typically having yellow flowers: family *Compositae* (composites). **2** the tincture of the dried flower heads of any of these plants, esp. *A. montana,* used in treating bruises. [C18: from New Latin, of unknown origin]

Arnim (*German* ˈarnɪm) *n* **Achim von** (ˈaxɪm fɔn). 1781–1831, German romantic poet. He published, with Clemens Brentano, the collection of folk songs, *Des Knaben Wunderhorn* (1805–08).

Arno (ˈɑːnəʊ) *n* a river in central Italy, rising in the Apennines and flowing through Florence to the Ligurian Sea. Length: about 240 km (150 miles).

Arnold¹ (ˈɑːnᵊld) *n* a town in N central England, in S Nottinghamshire. Pop.: 37 646 (1991).

Arnold² (ˈɑːnᵊld) *n* **1** Sir **Malcolm.** born 1921, English composer, esp. of orchestral works in a traditional idiom. **2 Matthew.** 1822–88, English poet, essayist, and literary critic, noted particularly for his poems *Sohrab and Rustum* (1853) and *Dover Beach* (1867), and for his *Essays in Criticism* (1865) and *Culture and Anarchy* (1869). **3** his father, **Thomas.** 1795–1842, English historian and educationalist, headmaster of Rugby School, noted for his reforms in public-school education.

aroha (ˈɑːrɒhə) *n N.Z.* love, compassion, or affectionate regard. [Maori]

aroid (ˈærɔɪd, ˈɛər-) *adj* **1** Also: **araceous.** of, relating to, or belonging to the *Araceae,* a family of plants having small flowers massed on a spadix surrounded by a large petaloid spathe. The family includes arum, calla, and anthurium. ◆ *n* **2** any plant of the *Araceae.* [C19: from New Latin *Arum* type genus + -OID; see ARUM]

aroint thee *or* **ye** (əˈrɔɪnt) *sentence substitute. Archaic.* away! begone! [C17: of unknown origin]

aroma (əˈrəʊmə) *n* **1** a distinctive usually pleasant smell, esp. of spices, wines, and plants. **2** a subtle pervasive quality or atmosphere. [C18: via Latin from Greek: spice]

aromatherapy (əˌrəʊməˈθɛrəpɪ) *n* the use of fragrant essential oils extracted from plants as a treatment in alternative medicine to relieve tension and cure certain minor ailments. ▸ **aˌromaˈtherapist** *n*

aromatic (ˌærəˈmætɪk) *adj* **1** having a distinctive, usually fragrant smell. **2** (of an organic compound) having an unsaturated ring containing alternating double and single bonds, esp. containing a benzene ring; exhibiting aromaticity. Compare **aliphatic.** ◆ *n* **3** something, such as a plant or drug, giving off a fragrant smell. ▸ **ˌaroˈmatically** *adv*

aromaticity (əˌrəʊməˈtɪsɪtɪ) *n* **1** the property of certain planar cyclic conjugated molecules, esp. benzene, of behaving like unsaturated molecules and undergoing substitution reactions rather than addition. **2** the quality or state of having an aroma.

aromatize *or* **aromatise** (əˈrəʊməˌtaɪz) *vb* **1** (*tr*) to make aromatic. **2** to convert (an aliphatic compound) to an aromatic compound. ▸ **aˌromatiˈzation** *or* **aˌromatiˈsation** *n*

arose (əˈrəʊz) *vb* the past tense of **arise.**

around (əˈraʊnd) *prep* **1** situated at various points in: *a lot of shelves around the house.* **2** from place to place in: *driving around Ireland.* **3** somewhere in or near: *to stay around the house.* **4** approximately in: *it happened around 1957, I think.* ◆ *adv* **5** in all directions from a point of reference: *he owns the land for ten miles around.* **6** in the vicinity, esp. restlessly but idly: *to wait around; stand around.* **7** here and there; in no particular place or direction: *dotted around.* **8** *Informal.* (of people) active and prominent in a particular area or profession: *some pop stars are around for only a few years.* **9** *Informal.* present in some place (the exact location being inexact): *he's around here somewhere.* **10** *Informal.* in circulation; available: *that type of phone has been around for some years now.* **11** *Informal.* to many places, so as to have gained considerable experience, often of a worldly or social nature: *he gets around; I've been around.* [C17 (rare earlier): from A-² + ROUND]

USAGE In American English, *around* is usually used instead of *round* in adverbial and prepositional senses, except in a few fixed phrases such as *all year round.* The use of *around* in adverbial senses is less common in British English.

arouse (əˈraʊz) *vb* **1** (*tr*) to evoke or elicit (a reaction, emotion, or response); stimulate. **2** to awaken from sleep. ▸ **aˈrousal** *n* ▸ **aˈrouser** *n*

Arp (*French* arp) *n* **Jean** (ʒɑ̃) *or* **Hans** (hans). 1887–1966, Alsatian sculptor, painter, and poet, cofounder of the Dada movement in Zürich, noted particularly for his abstract organic sculptures based on natural forms.

Arpád (ˈɑːpɑːd) *n* died 907 A.D., Magyar chieftain who conquered Hungary in the late 9th century.

arpeggio (ɑːˈpɛdʒɪəʊ) *n, pl* **-gios. 1** a chord whose notes are played in rapid succession rather than simultaneously. **2** an ascending and descending figuration used in practising the piano, voice, etc. [C18: from Italian, from *arpeggiare* to perform on the harp, from *arpa* HARP]

arpent (ˈɑːpənt; *French* arpɑ̃) *n* **1** a former French unit of length equal to 190 feet (approximately 58 metres). **2** an old French unit of land area equal to about one acre: still used in Quebec and Louisiana. [C16: from Old French, probably from Late Latin *arepennis* half an acre, of Gaulish origin; related to Middle Irish *airchenn* unit of land measure]

arquebus (ˈɑːkwɪbəs) *or* **harquebus** *n* a portable long-barrelled gun dating from the 15th century: fired by a wheel-lock or matchlock. Also called: **hackbut, hagbut.** [C16: via Old French *harquebuse* from Middle Dutch *hake-*

busse, literally: hook gun, from the shape of the butt, from *hake* hook + *busse* box, gun, from Late Latin *busis* box]

arr. *abbrev. for:* **1** arranged (by). **2** arrival. **3** arrive(d).

arrack *or* **arak** ('ærək) *n* a coarse spirit distilled in various Eastern countries from grain, rice, sugar cane, etc. [C17: from Arabic *'araq* sweat, sweet juice, liquor]

arraign (ə'reɪn) *vb* **1** (*tr*) to bring (a prisoner) before a court to answer an indictment. **2** (*tr*) to call to account; complain about; accuse. [C14: from Old French *araisnier* to speak, accuse, from A-[2] + *raisnier,* from Vulgar Latin *ratiōnāre* (unattested) to talk, argue, from Latin *ratiō* a reasoning] ▸ **ar'raigner** *n* ▸ **ar'raignment** *n*

Arran ('ærən) *n* an island off the SW coast of Scotland, in the Firth of Clyde. Pop.: 4000 (latest est.). Area: 427 sq. km (165 sq. miles).

arrange (ə'reɪndʒ) *vb* **1** (*tr*) to put into a proper, systematic, or decorative order. **2** (*tr; may take a clause as object or an infinitive*) to arrive at an agreement or understanding about; settle. **3** (when *intr,* often foll. by *for;* when *tr, may take a clause as object or an infinitive*) to make plans or preparations in advance (for something): *we arranged for her to be met.* **4** (*tr*) to adapt (a musical composition) for performance in a different way, esp. on different instruments. **5** (*tr*) to adapt (a play, etc.) for broadcasting. **6** (*intr;* often foll. by *with*) to come to an agreement. [C14: from Old French *arangier,* from A-[2] + *rangier* to put in a row, RANGE] ▸ **ar'rangeable** *adj* ▸ **ar'ranger** *n*

arrangement (ə'reɪndʒmənt) *n* **1** the act of arranging or being arranged. **2** the form in which things are arranged: *he altered the arrangement of furniture in the room.* **3** a thing composed of various ordered parts; the result of arranging: *a flower arrangement.* **4** (*often pl*) a preparatory measure taken or plan made; preparation. **5** an agreement or settlement; understanding. **6** an adaptation of a piece of music for performance in a different way, esp. on different instruments from those for which it was originally composed. **7** an adaptation (of a play, etc.) for broadcasting.

arrant ('ærənt) *adj* utter; out-and-out: *an arrant fool.* [C14: a variant of ERRANT (wandering, vagabond); sense developed from its frequent use in phrases like *arrant thief* (hence: notorious)] ▸ **'arrantly** *adv*

arras ('ærəs) *n* a wall hanging, esp. of tapestry.

Arras ('ærəs; *French* arɑs) *n* a town in N France: formerly famous for tapestry; severely damaged in both World Wars. Pop.: 42 715 (1990).

Arrau (ə'raʊ) *n* **Claudio.** 1903–91, Chilean pianist.

array (ə'reɪ) *n* **1** an impressive display or collection. **2** an orderly or regular arrangement, esp. of troops in battle order. **3** *Poetic.* rich clothing; apparel. **4** *Maths.* a sequence of numbers or symbols in a specified order. **5** *Maths.* a set of numbers or symbols arranged in rows and columns, as in a determinant or matrix. **6** *Electronics.* an arrangement of aerials spaced to give desired directional characteristics, used esp. in radar. **7** *Law.* a panel of jurors. **8** the arming of military forces. **9** *Computing.* a regular data structure in which individual elements may be located by reference to one or more integer index variables, the number of such indices being the number of dimensions in the array. ◆ *vb* (*tr*) **10** to dress in rich attire; adorn. **11** to arrange in order (esp. troops for battle); marshal. **12** *Law.* to draw up (a panel of jurors). [C13: from Old French *aroi* arrangement, from *arayer* to arrange, of Germanic origin; compare Old English *arǣdan* to make ready] ▸ **ar'rayal** *n*

arrears (ə'rɪəz) *n* **1** (*sometimes sing*) Also called: **arrearage** (ə'rɪərɪdʒ). something outstanding or owed. **2 in arrears** *or* **arrear.** late in paying a debt or meeting an obligation. [C18: from obsolete *arrear* (adv) behindhand, from Old French *arere,* from Medieval Latin *adretrō,* from Latin *ad* to + *retrō* backwards]

arrest (ə'rest) *vb* (*tr*) **1** to deprive (a person) of liberty by taking him into custody, esp. under lawful authority. **2** to seize (a ship) under lawful authority. **3** to slow or stop the development or progress of (a disease, growth, etc.). **4** to catch and hold (one's attention, sight, etc.). **5 arrest judgment.** *Law.* to stay proceedings after a verdict, on the grounds of error or possible error. ◆ *n* **6** the act of taking a person into custody, esp. under lawful authority. **7** the act of seizing and holding a ship under lawful authority. **8** the state of being held, esp. under lawful authority: *under arrest.* **9** Also called: **arrestation** (ˌæres'teɪʃən). the slowing or stopping of the development or progress of something. **10** the stopping or sudden cessation of motion of something: *a cardiac arrest.* [C14: from Old French *arester,* from Vulgar Latin *arrestāre* (unattested), from Latin *ad* at, to + *restāre* to stand firm, stop]

arrestable (ə'restəbəl) *adj* **1** liable to be arrested. **2** (of an offence) such that an offender may be arrested without a warrant.

arrester (ə'restə) *n* **1** a person who arrests. **2** a thing that stops or checks motion, esp. a mechanism of wires for slowing aeroplanes as they land on an aircraft carrier.

arresting (ə'restɪŋ) *adj* attracting attention; striking. ▸ **ar'restingly** *adv*

arrestment (ə'restmənt) *n Scots Law.* the seizure of money or property to prevent a debtor paying one creditor in advance of another.

arrest of judgment *n Law.* a stay of proceedings after a verdict, on the grounds of error or possible error.

Arretine ware *n* another term for **Samian ware** (sense 2).

Arretium (ə'riːtɪəm, -'ret-) *n* the ancient Latin name of **Arezzo.** ▸ **Arretine** ('ærɪˌtaɪn) *adj*

Arrhenius (*Swedish* a'reːnius) *n* **Svante August** ('svantə 'august). 1859–1927, Swedish chemist and physicist, noted for his work on the theory of electrolytic dissociation: Nobel prize for chemistry 1903.

arrhythmia (ə'rɪðmɪə) *n* any variation from the normal rhythm in the heartbeat. [C19: New Latin, from Greek *arrhuthmia,* from A-[1] + *rhuthmos* RHYTHM]

arrière-ban *French.* (arjɛrbɑ̃) *n* **1** (in medieval France) a summons to the king's vassals to do military service. **2** the vassals so assembled for military service. [C16: changed from Old French *herban* call to arms, of Germanic origin; compare Old High German *heriban,* from *heri* army + *ban* summons, BAN[2]]

arrière-pensée *French.* (arjɛrpɑ̃se) *n* an unrevealed thought or intention. [C19: literally: behind thought]

Ar Rimal (ɑːr rɪ'mɑːl) *n* another name for **Rub' al Khali.**

arris ('ærɪs) *n, pl* **-ris** *or* **-rises.** a sharp edge at the meeting of two surfaces at an angle with one another, as at two adjacent sides of a stone block. [C17: apparently from Old French *areste* beard of grain, sharp ridge; see ARÊTE]

arrival (ə'raɪvəl) *n* **1** the act or time of arriving. **2** a person or thing that arrives or has arrived. **3** the reaching of a condition or objective.

arrive (ə'raɪv) *vb* (*intr*) **1** to come to a certain place during or after a journey; reach a destination. **2** (foll. by *at*) to agree upon; reach: *to arrive at a decision.* **3** to occur eventually: *the moment arrived when pretence was useless.* **4** *Informal.* (of a baby) to be born. **5** *Informal.* to attain success or gain recognition. [C13: from Old French *ariver,* from Vulgar Latin *arrīpāre* (unattested) to land, reach the bank, from Latin *ad* to + *rīpa* river bank] ▸ **ar'river** *n*

arrivederci *Italian.* (arrive'dertʃi) *sentence substitute.* goodbye.

arrivisme (ˌæriː'viːzmə; *French* arivism) *n* unscrupulous ambition.

arriviste (ˌæriː'viːst; *French* arivist) *n* a person who is unscrupulously ambitious. [French: see ARRIVE, -IST]

arroba (ə'rəʊbə) *n, pl* **-bas. 1** a unit of weight, approximately equal to 11 kilograms, used in some Spanish-speaking countries. **2** a unit of weight, approximately equal to 15 kilograms, used in some Portuguese-speaking countries. **3** a liquid measure used in some Spanish-speaking countries with different values, but in Spain used as a wine-measure, approximately equal to 16 litres. [C16: from Spanish, from Arabic *ar-rub'* the quarter (of a quintal)]

arrogant ('ærəgənt) *adj* having or showing an exaggerated opinion of one's own importance, merit, ability, etc.; conceited; overbearingly proud: *an arrogant teacher; an arrogant assumption.* [C14: from Latin *arrogāre* to claim as one's own; see ARROGATE] ▸ **'arrogance** *n* ▸ **'arrogantly** *adv*

arrogate ('ærəˌgeɪt) *vb* **1** (*tr*) to claim or appropriate for oneself presumptuously or without justification. **2** (*tr*) to attribute or assign to another without justification. [C16: from Latin *arrogāre,* from *rogāre* to ask] ▸ **ˌarro'gation** *n* ▸ **arrogative** (ə'rɒgətɪv) *adj* ▸ **'arroˌgator** *n*

arrondissement (*French* arɔ̃dismɑ̃) *n* (in France) **1** the largest administrative subdivision of a department. **2** a municipal district of certain cities, esp. Paris. [C19: from *arrondir* to make round, from AB-[1] + *-rondir* from *rond* ROUND]

arrow ('ærəʊ) *n* **1** a long slender pointed weapon, usually having feathers fastened at the end as a balance, that is shot from a bow. Related adj: **sagittal. 2** any of various things that resemble an arrow in shape, function, or speed, such as a sign indicating direction or position. ◆ See also **arrows.** [Old English *arwe;* related to Old Norse *ör,* Gothic *arhvazna,* Latin *arcus* bow, ARCH[1]]

arrowgrass ('ærəʊˌgrɑːs) *n* either of two species, **sea arrowgrass** (*Triglochin maritima*) or **marsh arrowgrass** (*T. palustris*), of monocotyledonous perennials having long thin fleshy leaves and spikes of inconspicuous flowers. [C18: named from the shape of the fruits when open]

arrowhead ('ærəʊˌhed) *n* **1** the pointed tip of an arrow, often removable from the shaft. **2** something that resembles the head of an arrow in shape, such as a triangular decoration on garments used to reinforce joins. **3** any aquatic herbaceous plant of the genus *Sagittaria,* esp. *S. sagittifolia,* having arrow-shaped aerial leaves and linear submerged leaves: family *Alismataceae.*

arrowroot ('ærəʊˌruːt) *n* **1** a white-flowered West Indian plant, *Maranta arundinacea,* whose rhizomes yield an easily digestible starch: family *Marantaceae.* **2** the starch obtained from this plant. **3** any of several other plants whose rhizomes or roots yield starch.

arrows ('ærəʊz) *n* (*functioning as sing*) *Brit.* an informal name for **darts.**

arrowwood ('ærəʊˌwʊd) *n* any of various trees or shrubs, esp. certain viburnums, having long straight tough stems formerly used by North American Indians to make arrows.

arrowworm ('ærəʊˌwɜːm) *n* any small marine invertebrate of the genus *Sagitta,* having an elongated transparent body with fins and prehensile oral bristles: phylum *Chaetognatha* (chaetognaths).

arroyo (ə'rɔɪəʊ) *n, pl* **-os.** *Chiefly southwestern U.S.* a steep-sided stream bed that is usually dry except after heavy rain. [C19: from Spanish]

Arru Islands ('ɑːruː) *pl n* a variant spelling of **Aru Islands.**

arse (ɑːs) *or U.S. and Canadian* **ass** *n Taboo.* **1** the buttocks. **2** the anus. **3** a stupid person; fool. **4** *Slang.* sexual intercourse. **5** *Austral. slang.* effrontery; cheek. ◆ Also called (for senses 2, 3): **arsehole** ('ɑːsˌhəʊl), (U.S., Canadian) **asshole.**

arse *or U.S. and Canadian* **ass about** *or* **around** *vb* (*intr, adv*) *Taboo slang.* to play the fool; act stupidly, esp. in an irritating manner.

arsed (ɑːst) *adj* **be arsed.** *Taboo slang.* to be willing, inclined, or prepared (esp. in the phrase **can't be arsed**).

arse *or U.S. and Canadian* **ass licker** *n Taboo slang.* a person who curries favour. ▸ **'arse-ˌlicking** *or U.S. and Canadian* **'ass-ˌlicking** *adj, n*

arsenal ('ɑːsənəl) *n* **1** a store for arms, ammunition, and other military items. **2** a workshop or factory that produces munitions. **3** a store of anything regarded as weapons: *an arsenal of destructive arguments.* [C16: from Italian *arsenale* dockyard, from the original Venetian *arsenal* dockyard and naval store, from Arabic *dār ṣināʻah,* from *dār* house + *ṣināʻah* manufacture]

arsenate ('ɑːsəˌneɪt, -nɪt) *n* a salt or ester of arsenic acid.

arsenic *n* ('ɑːsnɪk). **1** a toxic metalloid element, existing in several allotropic forms, that occurs principally in realgar and orpiment and as the free element. It is used in transistors, lead-based alloys, and high-temperature brasses. Symbol: As; atomic no.: 33; atomic wt.: 74.92159; valency: −3, 0, +3, or +5; relative density: 5.73 (grey); melting pt.: 817°C at a pressure of 3MN/m^2 (grey); sublimes at 613°C (grey). **2** a nontechnical name for **arsenic trioxide.** ◆ *adj* (ɑː'senɪk). **3** of or containing arsenic, esp. in the pentavalent state. [C14:

from Latin *arsenicum,* from Greek *arsenikon* yellow orpiment, from Syriac *zarnīg* (influenced in form by Greek *arsenikos* virile)]

arsenic acid *n* a white poisonous soluble crystalline solid used in the manufacture of arsenates and insecticides. Formula: H_3AsO_4.

arsenical (ɑːˈsɛnɪkᵊl) *adj* **1** of or containing arsenic. ♦ *n* **2** a drug or insecticide containing arsenic.

arsenic trioxide *n* a white poisonous powder used in the manufacture of glass and as an insecticide, rat poison, and weedkiller. Also called: **arsenic.** Formula: As_2O_3.

arsenide (ˈɑːsəˌnaɪd) *n* a compound in which arsenic is the most electronegative element.

arsenious (ɑːˈsiːnɪəs) *or* **arsenous** (ˈɑːsɪnəs) *adj* of or containing arsenic in the trivalent state.

arsenite (ˈɑːsɪˌnaɪt) *n* a salt or ester of arsenous acid.

arsenopyrite (ˌɑːsɪnəʊˈpaɪraɪt, ɑːˌsenə-) *n* a white or grey metallic mineral consisting of a sulphide of iron and arsenic that forms monoclinic crystals with an orthorhombic shape: an ore of arsenic. Formula: FeAsS. Also called: **mispickel.**

arsine (ˈɑːsiːn) *n* a colourless poisonous gas used in the manufacture of organic compounds, to dope transistors, and as a military poisonous gas. Formula: AsH_3.

arsis (ˈɑːsɪs) *n, pl* **-ses** (-siːz). (in classical prosody) the long syllable or part on which the ictus falls in a metrical foot. Compare **thesis** (sense 6). [C18: via Late Latin from Greek, from *airein* to raise]

ARSM (in Britain) *abbrev. for* Associate of the Royal School of Mines.

ars nova (ˈɑːz ˈnəʊvə) *n* a style of music of the 14th century, characterized by great freedom and variety of rhythm and melody contrasted with the strictness of the music of the 13th century. [Latin, literally: new art]

arson (ˈɑːsᵊn) *n Criminal law.* the act of intentionally or recklessly setting fire to another's property or to one's own property for some improper reason. [C17: from Old French, from Medieval Latin *ārsiō,* from Latin *ārdēre* to burn; see ARDENT] ▸ **ˈarsonist** *n*

arsphenamine (ɑːsˈfɛnəmɪn, -ˌmiːn) *n* a drug containing arsenic, formerly used in the treatment of syphilis and related infections.

ars poetica (ˈɑːz pəʊˈɛtɪkə) *n* the art of poetry.

arsy-versy (ˈɑːsɪˈvɜːsɪ) *adv Slang.* **1** backwards or upside down. **2** in reverse. [C16: from ARSE + Latin *versus* turned, modelled on compounds like *hurly-burly*]

art[1] (ɑːt) *n* **1a** the creation of works of beauty or other special significance. **1b** (*as modifier*)*: an art movement.* **2** the exercise of human skill (as distinguished from *nature*). **3** imaginative skill as applied to representations of the natural world or figments of the imagination. **4a** the products of man's creative activities; works of art collectively, esp. of the visual arts, sometimes also music, drama, dance, and literature. **4b** (*as modifier*)*: an art gallery.* See also **arts, fine art. 5** excellence or aesthetic merit of conception or execution as exemplified by such works. **6** any branch of the visual arts, esp. painting. **7** (*modifier*) intended to be artistic or decorative: *art needlework.* **8a** any field using the techniques of art to display artistic qualities: *advertising art.* **8b** (*as modifier*)*: an art film.* **9** *Journalism.* photographs or other illustrations in a newspaper, etc. **10** method, facility, or knack: *the art of threading a needle; the art of writing letters.* **11** the system of rules or principles governing a particular human activity: *the art of government.* **12** artfulness; cunning. **13 get something down to a fine art.** to become highly proficient at something through practice. ♦ See also **arts.** [C13: from Old French, from Latin *ars* craftsmanship]

art[2] (ɑːt) *vb Archaic.* (used with the pronoun *thou*) a singular form of the present tense (indicative mood) of **be.** [Old English *eart,* part of *bēon* to BE]

art. *abbrev. for:* **1** article. **2** artificial. **3** Also: **arty.** artillery.

-art *suffix forming nouns.* a variant of **-ard.**

artal (ˈɑːtɑːl) *n* a plural of **rotl.**

Artaud (*French* arto) *n* **Antonin** (ɑ̃tɔnɛ̃). 1896–1948, French stage director and dramatist, whose concept of the theatre of cruelty is expounded in *Manifeste du théâtre de la cruauté* (1932) and *Le Théâtre et son double* (1938).

Artaxerxes I (ˌɑːtəˈzɜːksiːz) *n* died 425 B.C., king of Persia (465–425): son of Xerxes I.

Artaxerxes II *n* died ?358 B.C., king of Persia (?404–?358). He defeated his brother Cyrus the Younger at Cunaxa (401).

Art Deco (ˈdɛkəʊ) *n* **a** a style of interior decoration, jewellery, architecture, etc., at its height in the 1930s and characterized by geometrical shapes, stylized natural forms, and symmetrical utilitarian designs adapted to mass production. **b** (*as modifier*)*: an Art-Deco carpet.* [C20: shortened from *art décoratif,* after the *Exposition des arts décoratifs* held in Paris in 1925]

art director *n* a person responsible for the sets and costumes in a film.

artefact *or* **artifact** (ˈɑːtɪˌfækt) *n* **1** something made or given shape by man, such as a tool or a work of art, esp. an object of archaeological interest. **2** anything man-made, such as a spurious experimental result. **3** *Cytology.* a structure seen in tissue after death, fixation, staining, etc., that is not normally present in the living tissue. [C19: from Latin phrase *arte factum,* from *ars* skill + *facere* to make]

artel (ɑːˈtɛl) *n* **1** (in the former Soviet Union) a cooperative union or organization, esp. of producers, such as peasants. **2** (in prerevolutionary Russia) a quasi-cooperative association of people engaged in the same activity. [from Russian *artel',* from Italian *artieri* artisans, from *arte* work, from Latin *ars* ART[1]]

Artemis (ˈɑːtɪmɪs) *n Greek myth.* the virgin goddess of the hunt and the moon: the twin sister of Apollo. Roman counterpart: **Diana.** Also called: **Cynthia.**

artemisia (ˌɑːtɪˈmiːzɪə) *n* any herbaceous perennial plant of the genus *Artemisia,* of the N hemisphere, such as mugwort, sagebrush, and wormwood: family *Compositae* (composites). [C14: via Latin from Greek, probably from *Artemis* ARTEMIS]

Arte Povera (*Italian* ˌarte poˈvera) *n* a style of minimal art originating in Italy in the late 1960s, making use of cheap and commonly available materials such as stones, newspapers etc. [C20: Italian, literally: poor art]

arterial (ɑːˈtɪərɪəl) *adj* **1** of, relating to, or affecting an artery or arteries: *arterial disease.* **2** denoting or relating to the usually bright red reoxygenated blood returning from the lungs or gills that circulates in the arteries. **3** being a major route, esp. one with many minor branches: *an arterial road.* ▸ **arˈterially** *adv*

arterialize *or* **arterialise** (ɑːˈtɪərɪəˌlaɪz) *vb* (*tr*) **1** to change (venous blood) into arterial blood by replenishing the depleted oxygen. **2** to vascularize (tissues). **3** to provide with arteries. ▸ **arˌterialiˈzation** *or* **arˌterialiˈsation** *n*

arterio- *combining form.* artery or arteries: *arteriosclerosis.* [from Greek; see ARTERY]

arteriography (ɑːˌtɪərɪˈɒgrəfɪ) *n* the X-ray examination of an artery or arterial system after injection of a contrast medium into the bloodstream.

arteriole (ɑːˈtɪərɪˌəʊl) *n Anat.* any of the small subdivisions of an artery that form thin-walled vessels ending in capillaries. [C19: from New Latin *arteriola,* from Latin *artēria* ARTERY]

arteriosclerosis (ɑːˌtɪərɪəʊsklɪəˈrəʊsɪs) *n, pl* **-ses** (-siːz). a pathological condition of the circulatory system characterized by thickening and loss of elasticity of the arterial walls. Nontechnical name: **hardening of the arteries.** ▸ **arteriosclerotic** (ɑːˌtɪərɪəʊsklɪəˈrɒtɪk) *adj*

arteriovenous (ɑːˌtɪərɪəʊˈviːnəs) *adj* of, relating to, or affecting an artery and a vein.

arteritis (ˌɑːtəˈraɪtɪs) *n Pathol.* inflammation of an artery.

artery (ˈɑːtərɪ) *n, pl* **-teries. 1** any of the tubular thick-walled muscular vessels that convey oxygenated blood from the heart to various parts of the body. Compare **pulmonary artery, vein. 2** a major road or means of communication in any complex system. [C14: from Latin *artēria,* related to Greek *aortē* the great artery, AORTA]

artesian well (ɑːˈtiːzɪən, -ʒən) *n* a well sunk through impermeable strata into strata receiving water from an area at a higher altitude than that of the well, so that there is sufficient pressure to force water to flow upwards. [C19: from French *artésien,* from Old French *Arteis* Artois, old province, where such wells were common]

Artex (ˈɑːtɛks) *n Trademark.* a brand of coating for walls and ceilings that gives a textured finish.

art form *n* **1** a conventionally established form of artistic composition, such as the symphony or the sonnet. **2** a genre or activity viewed or treated as an art form.

artful (ˈɑːtfʊl) *adj* **1** cunning or tricky. **2** skilful in achieving a desired end. **3** *Archaic.* characterized by skill or art. **4** *Archaic.* artificial. ▸ **ˈartfully** *adv* ▸ **ˈartfulness** *n*

art house *n* **1** a cinema which specializes in showing films which are not part of the commercial mainstream. ♦ *adj* **2a** of or relating to such films or a cinema which specializes in showing them. **2b** (*as modifier*)*: the surprise art-house hit of the season.*

arthralgia (ɑːˈθrældʒə) *n Pathol.* pain in a joint. ▸ **arˈthralgic** *adj*

arthrectomy (ɑːˈθrɛktəmɪ) *n, pl* **-mies.** surgical excision of a joint.

arthritis (ɑːˈθraɪtɪs) *n* inflammation of a joint or joints characterized by pain and stiffness of the affected parts, caused by gout, rheumatic fever, etc. See also **rheumatoid arthritis.** [C16: via Latin from Greek: see ARTHRO-, -ITIS] ▸ **arthritic** (ɑːˈθrɪtɪk) *adj, n*

arthro- *or before a vowel* **arthr-** *combining form.* indicating a joint: *arthritis; arthropod.* [from Greek *arthron*]

arthrodia (ɑːˈθrəʊdɪə) *n Anatomy, zoology.* a joint. ▸ **arˈthrodial** *adj*

arthrography (ɑːˈθrɒgrəfɪ) *n* the X-ray examination of a joint after injection of a contrast medium into the joint space.

arthromere (ˈɑːθrəˌmɪə) *n* any of the segments of the body of an arthropod. ▸ **arthromeric** (ˌɑːθrəˈmɛrɪk) *adj*

arthroplasty (ˈɑːθrəˌplæstɪ) *n* surgical repair of a diseased joint.

arthropod (ˈɑːθrəˌpɒd) *n* any invertebrate of the phylum *Arthropoda,* having jointed limbs, a segmented body, and an exoskeleton made of chitin. The group includes the crustaceans, insects, arachnids, and centipedes. ▸ **arthropodous** (ɑːˈθrɒpədəs) *or* **arˈthropodal** *adj*

arthroscope (ˈɑːθrəˌskəʊp) *n* a tubular instrument that is inserted into the capsule of a joint to examine the joint, extract tissue, etc. ▸ **ˌarthroˈscopic** *adj* ▸ **arthroscopy** (ɑːˈθrɒskəpɪ) *n*

arthrospore (ˈɑːθrəˌspɔː) *n* **1** a sporelike cell of ascomycetous fungi and some algae produced by a breaking of the hyphae. **2** a resting sporelike cell produced by some bacteria. ▸ **ˌarthroˈsporic** *or* **ˌarthroˈsporous** *adj*

Arthur (ˈɑːθə) *n* **1** a legendary king of the Britons in the sixth century A.D., who led Celtic resistance against the Saxons: possibly based on a historical figure; represented as leader of the Knights of the Round Table at Camelot. **2 Chester Alan.** 1830–86, 21st president of the U.S. (1881–85). **3 not know whether one is Arthur or Martha.** *Austral. and N.Z. informal.* to be in a state of confusion.

Arthurian (ɑːˈθjʊərɪən) *adj* of or relating to King Arthur and his Knights of the Round Table.

arti (ˈʌrtɪ) *n Hinduism.* a ritual performed in homes and temples in which incense and light is offered to a deity. [Hindi]

artic (ɑːˈtɪk) *n Informal.* short for **articulated lorry.**

artichoke (ˈɑːtɪˌtʃəʊk) *n* **1** Also called: **globe artichoke.** a thistle-like Eurasian plant, *Cynara scolymus,* cultivated for its large edible flower head containing many fleshy scalelike bracts: family *Compositae* (composites). **2** the unopened flower head of this plant, which can be cooked and eaten. **3** See **Jerusalem artichoke.** [C16: from Italian *articiocco,* from Old Spanish *alcarchofa,* from Arabic *al-kharshūf*]

article (ˈɑːtɪkᵊl) *n* **1** one of a class of objects; item: *an article of clothing.* **2** an unspecified or previously named thing, esp. a small object: *he put the article on the table.* **3** a distinct part of a subject or action. **4** a written composition on a subject, often being one of several found in a magazine, newspaper, etc. **5** *Grammar.* a kind of determiner, occurring in many languages including English, that lacks independent meaning but may serve to indicate the specificity of reference of the noun phrase with which it occurs. See also **definite article, indefinite article. 6** a clause or section in a written document such as a treaty, contract, statute, etc. **7 in articles.** undergoing training, according to the terms of a written contract, in the legal profession. **8** (*often cap.*) *Christianity.* See **article of faith, Thirty-nine Articles. 9** *Archaic.* a topic or subject. ◆ *vb* (*tr*) **10** *Archaic.* to accuse. [C13: from Old French, from Latin *articulus* small joint, from *artus* joint]

articled (ˈɑːtɪkəld) *adj* bound by a written contract, such as one that governs a period of training: *an articled clerk.*

article numbering *n Commerce.* See **ANA.**

article of faith *n* **1** *Christianity.* any of the clauses or propositions into which a creed or other statement of doctrine is divided. **2** a deeply held belief.

articles of association *pl n* **1** the constitution and regulations of a registered company as required by the British Companies Acts. **2** the document containing these.

Articles of Confederation *pl n* the agreement made by the original 13 states in 1777 establishing a confederacy to be known as the United States of America; replaced by the Constitution of 1788.

Articles of War *pl n* **1** the disciplinary and legal procedures by which the naval and military forces of Great Britain were bound before the 19th century. **2** the regulations of the U.S. army, navy, and air force until the Uniform Code of Military Justice replaced them in 1951.

articular (ɑːˈtɪkjʊlə) *adj* of or relating to joints or to the structural components in a joint. [C15: from Latin *articulāris* concerning the joints, from *articulus* small joint; see ARTICLE]

articulate *adj* (ɑːˈtɪkjʊlɪt). **1** able to express oneself fluently and coherently: *an articulate lecturer.* **2** having the power of speech. **3** distinct, clear, or definite; well-constructed: *an articulate voice; an articulate document.* **4** *Zoology.* (of arthropods and higher vertebrates) possessing joints or jointed segments. ◆ *vb* (ɑːˈtɪkjʊˌleɪt). **5** to speak or enunciate (words, syllables, etc.) clearly and distinctly. **6** (*tr*) to express coherently in words. **7** (*intr*) *Zoology.* to be jointed or form a joint. **8** (*tr*) to separate into jointed segments. [C16: from Latin *articulāre* to divide into joints; see ARTICLE] ▸ **arˈticulately** *adv* ▸ **arˈticulateness** *or* **arˈticulacy** *n*

articulated lorry *n* a large lorry made in two separate sections, a tractor and a trailer, connected by a pivoted bar.

articulation (ɑːˌtɪkjʊˈleɪʃən) *n* **1** the act or process of speaking or expressing in words. **2a** the process of articulating a speech sound. **2b** the sound so produced, esp. a consonant. **3** the act or the state of being jointed together. **4** the form or manner in which something is jointed. **5** *Zoology.* **5a** a joint such as that between bones or arthropod segments. **5b** the way in which jointed parts are connected. **6** *Botany.* the part of a plant at which natural separation occurs, such as the joint between leaf and stem. **7** a joint or jointing. ▸ **arˈticulatory** *adj*

articulator (ɑːˈtɪkjʊˌleɪtə) *n* **1** a person or thing that articulates. **2** *Phonetics.* any vocal organ that takes part in the production of a speech sound. Such organs are of two types: those that can move, such as the tongue, lips, etc. (**active articulators**), and those that remain fixed, such as the teeth, the hard palate, etc. (**passive articulators**).

articulatory loop *n Psychol.* a short-term memory system that enables a person to remember short strings of words by rehearsing them repeatedly in his head.

articulatory phonetics *n* (*functioning as sing*) the branch of phonetics concerned with the production of speech sounds. Compare **acoustic phonetics, auditory phonetics.**

artifact (ˈɑːtɪˌfækt) *n* a variant spelling of **artefact.**

artifice (ˈɑːtɪfɪs) *n* **1** a clever expedient; ingenious stratagem. **2** crafty or subtle deception. **3** skill; cleverness. **4** a skilfully contrived device. **5** *Obsolete.* craftsmanship. [C16: from Old French, from Latin *artificium* skill, from *artifex* one possessed of a specific skill, from *ars* skill + *-fex,* from *facere* to make]

artificer (ɑːˈtɪfɪsə) *n* **1** a skilled craftsman. **2** a clever or inventive designer. **3** a serviceman trained in mechanics.

artificial (ˌɑːtɪˈfɪʃəl) *adj* **1** produced by man; not occurring naturally: *artificial materials of great strength.* **2** made in imitation of a natural product, esp. as a substitute; not genuine: *artificial cream.* **3** pretended; assumed; insincere: *an artificial manner.* **4** lacking in spontaneity; affected: *an artificial laugh.* **5** *Biology.* relating to superficial characteristics not based on the interrelationships of organisms: *an artificial classification.* [C14: from Latin *artificiālis* belonging to art, from *artificium* skill, ARTIFICE] ▸ **artificiality** (ˌɑːtɪˌfɪʃɪˈælɪtɪ) *n* ▸ ˌ**artiˈficially** *adv*

artificial aid *n Mountaineering.* another name for **aid** (sense 5).

artificial climbing *n* another name for **aid climbing.**

artificial daylight *n Physics.* artificial light having approximately the same spectral characteristics as natural daylight.

artificial disintegration *n Physics.* radioactive transformation of a substance by bombardment with high-energy particles, such as alpha particles or neutrons.

artificial feel *n* a system, used in aircraft that have fully powered control surfaces, providing the pilot with simulated aerodynamic forces on the controls.

artificial horizon *n* **1** Also called: **gyro horizon.** an aircraft instrument, using a gyroscope, that indicates the aircraft's attitude in relation to the horizontal. **2** *Astronomy.* a level reflecting surface, such as one of mercury, that measures the altitude of a celestial body as half the angle between the body and its reflection.

artificial insemination *n* introduction of spermatozoa into the vagina or uterus by means other than sexual union. See **AI, AIH, DI.**

artificial intelligence *n* the study of the modelling of human mental functions by computer programs. Abbrev.: **AI.**

artificialize *or* **artificialise** (ˌɑːtɪˈfɪʃəˌlaɪz) *vb* (*tr*) to render artificial.

artificial kidney *n Med.* a mechanical apparatus for performing haemodialysis.

artificial language *n* an invented language, esp. one intended as an international medium of communication or for use with computers. Compare **natural language.**

artificial respiration *n* **1** any of various methods of restarting breathing after it has stopped, by manual rhythmic pressure on the chest, mouth-to-mouth breathing, etc. **2** any method of maintaining respiration artificially, as by use of an iron lung.

Artigas (ɑːˈtiːgɑːs) *n* **José Gervasio.** 1764–1850, the national hero of Uruguay. He fought for Uruguayan independence from Argentina, but was driven into exile in 1820.

artillery (ɑːˈtɪlərɪ) *n* **1** guns, cannon, howitzers, mortars, etc., of calibre greater than 20 mm. **2** troops or military units specializing in using such guns. **3** the science dealing with the use of guns. **4** devices for discharging heavy missiles, such as catapults or slings. [C14: from Old French *artillerie,* from *artillier* to equip with weapons, of uncertain origin]

artilleryman (ɑːˈtɪlərɪmən) *n, pl* **-men.** a serviceman who serves in an artillery unit.

artillery plant *n* any of various tropical urticaceous plants of the genus *Pilea,* such as *P. microphylla,* all having stamens that discharge their pollen explosively.

artiodactyl (ˌɑːtɪəʊˈdæktɪl) *n* **1** any placental mammal of the order *Artiodactyla,* having hooves with an even number of toes; an even-toed ungulate. The order includes pigs, hippopotamuses, camels, deer, cattle, and antelopes. ◆ *adj* **2** of, relating to, or belonging to the order *Artiodactyla.* [C19: from New Latin *artiodactylus,* from Greek *ártios* even + *daktulos* digit] ▸ ˌ**artioˈdactylous** *adj*

artisan (ˈɑːtɪˌzæn, ˌɑːtɪˈzæn) *n* **1** a skilled workman; craftsman. **2** *Obsolete.* an artist. [C16: from French, from Old Italian *artigiano,* from *arte* ART[1]] ▸ **artisanal** (ɑːˈtɪzənəl, ˈɑːtɪzənəl) *adj*

artist (ˈɑːtɪst) *n* **1** a person who practises or is skilled in an art, esp. painting, drawing, or sculpture. **2** a person who displays in his work qualities required in art, such as sensibility and imagination. **3** a person whose profession requires artistic expertise, esp. a designer: *a commercial artist.* **4** a person skilled in some task or occupation: *an artist at bricklaying.* **5** *Obsolete.* an artisan. **6** *Slang.* a person devoted to or proficient in something: *a booze artist; a con artist.*

artiste (ɑːˈtiːst; *French* artist) *n* **1** an entertainer, such as a singer or dancer. **2** a person who is highly skilled in some occupation: *a hair artiste.*

artistic (ɑːˈtɪstɪk) *adj* **1** of or characteristic of art or artists. **2** performed, made, or arranged decoratively and tastefully; aesthetically pleasing. **3** appreciative of and sensitive to beauty in art. **4** naturally gifted with creative skill. ▸ **arˈtistically** *adv*

artistry (ˈɑːtɪstrɪ) *n* **1** artistic workmanship, ability, or quality. **2** artistic pursuits. **3** great skill.

artless (ˈɑːtlɪs) *adj* **1** free from deceit, guile, or artfulness; ingenuous: *an artless remark.* **2** natural, without artifice; unpretentious: *artless elegance.* **3** without art or skill. ▸ **ˈartlessly** *adv* ▸ **ˈartlessness** *n*

art music *n* music written by a composer rather than passed on by oral tradition. Compare **folk music.**

Art Nouveau (ɑː nuːˈvəʊ; *French* ar nuvo) *n* **a** a style of art and architecture of the 1890s, characterized by swelling sinuous outlines and stylized natural forms, such as flowers and leaves. **b** (*as modifier*): *an Art-Nouveau mirror.* [French, literally: new art]

Artois (*French* artwa) *n* a former province of N France.

art paper *n* a high-quality type of paper having a smooth coating of china clay or similar substance on it.

arts (ɑːts) *pl n* **1a the.** imaginative, creative, and nonscientific branches of knowledge considered collectively, esp. as studied academically. **1b** (*as modifier*): *an arts degree.* **2** See **fine art. 3** cunning or crafty actions or plots; schemes.

Arts and Crafts *pl n* decorative handicraft and design, esp. that of the **Arts and Crafts movement,** in late nineteenth-century Britain, which sought to revive medieval craftsmanship.

art union *n Austral. and N.Z.* a lottery, often with prizes other than cash.

artwork (ˈɑːtˌwɜːk) *n* all the original nontextual matter in a publication, esp. the illustrations.

arty (ˈɑːtɪ) *adj* **artier, artiest.** *Informal.* having an ostentatious or affected interest in or desire to imitate artists or artistic standards. ▸ **ˈartiness** *n*

arty-crafty *adj Informal.* affectedly artistic, esp. in a homespun or rural style.

arty-farty *adj Informal.* artistic in a pretentious way.

Aruba (əˈruːbə; *Dutch* ɑˈryːbaː) *n* an island in the Caribbean, off the NW coast of Venezuela, a dependency of the Netherlands with special status; part of the Netherlands Antilles until 1986. Chief town: Oranjestad. Pop.: 88 600 (1998 est.). Area: about 181 sq. km (70 sq. miles).

Aru Islands *or* **Arru Islands** (ˈɑːruː) *pl n* a group of islands in Indonesia, in the SW Moluccas. Area: about 8500 sq. km (3300 sq. miles).

arum (ˈɛərəm) *n* **1** any plant of the aroid genus *Arum,* of Europe and the Mediterranean region, having arrow-shaped leaves and a typically white spathe. See also **cuckoopint. 2 arum lily.** another name for **calla** (sense 1). [C16: from Latin, a variant of *aros* wake-robin, from Greek *aron*]

Arunachal Pradesh (ˌɑːrəˈnɑːkəl prəˈdɛʃ) *n* a state in NE India, formed in 1986 from the former Union Territory. Capital: Itanagar. Pop.: 965 000 (1994 est.). Area: 83 743 sq. km (32 648 sq. miles). Former name (until 1972): **North East Frontier Agency.**

Arundel ('ærəndəl) *n* a town in S England, in West Sussex: 11th-century castle. Pop.: 3033 (1991).

arundinaceous (əˌrʌndɪ'neɪʃəs) *adj Botany.* resembling a reed. [C17: from Latin *harundinācеus,* from *harundō* a reed]

aruspex (ə'rʌspɛks) *n, pl* **-pices** (-pɪˌsiːz). a variant spelling of **haruspex.**

Aruwimi (ˌɑːruː'wiːmɪ) *n* a river in NE Democratic Republic of the Congo (formerly Zaïre), rising near Lake Albert as the Ituri and flowing west into the River Congo. Length: about 1288 km (800 miles).

arvo ('ɑːvəʊ) *n Austral. informal.* afternoon.

-ary *suffix.* **1** (*forming adjectives*) of; related to; belonging to: *cautionary; rudimentary.* **2** (*forming nouns*) **2a** a person connected with or engaged in: *missionary.* **2b** a thing relating to; a place for: *commentary; aviary.* [from Latin *-ārius, -āria, -ārium*]

Aryan *or* **Arian** ('ɛərɪən) *n* **1** (in Nazi ideology) a Caucasian of non-Jewish descent, esp. of the Nordic type. **2** a member of any of the peoples supposedly descended from the Indo-Europeans, esp. a speaker of an Iranian or Indic language in ancient times. ◆ *adj* **3** of, relating to, or characteristic of an Aryan or Aryans. ◆ *adj, n* **4** *Archaic.* Indo-European. [C19: from Sanskrit *ārya* of noble birth]

Aryanize *or* **Aryanise** ('ɛərɪəˌnaɪz) *vb (tr)* (in Nazi ideology) to purge (politics and society) of all non-Aryan elements or people; make characteristically Aryan.

aryl ('ærɪl) *n* **1** (*modifier*) *Chem.* of, consisting of, or containing an aromatic group: *aryl group or radical.* **2** an organometallic compound in which a metal atom is bound to an aryl or molecule. [C20: from AR(OMATIC) + -YL]

arytenoid *or* **arytaenoid** (ˌærɪ'tiːnɔɪd) *adj also* **arytenoidal. 1** denoting either of two small cartilages of the larynx that are attached to the vocal cords. **2** denoting any of three small muscles of the larynx that narrow the space between the vocal cords. ◆ *n* **3** an arytenoid cartilage or muscle. [C18: from New Latin *arytaenoīdes,* from Greek *arutainoeidēs* shaped like a ladle, from *arutaina* ladle]

as[1] (æz; *unstressed* əz) *conj* (*subordinating*) **1** (often preceded by *just*) while; when; at the time that: *he caught me as I was leaving.* **2** in the way that: *dancing as only she can.* **3** that which; what: *I did as I was told.* **4** (of) which fact, event, etc. (referring to the previous statement): *to become wise, as we all know, is not easy.* **5 as it were.** in a way; so to speak; as if it were really so. **6 as you were. 6a** a military command to return to the previous position. **6b** a statement to withdraw something just said. **7** since; seeing that: *as you're in charge here, you'd better tell me where to wait.* **8** in the same way that: *he died of cancer, as his father had done.* **9** in spite of the extent to which: *intelligent as you are, I suspect you will fail.* **10** for instance: *capital cities, as London.* ◆ *adv, conj* **11a** used correlatively before an adjective or adverb and before a noun phrase or a clause to indicate identity of extent, amount, etc.: *she is as heavy as her sister; she is as heavy now as she used to be.* **11b** used with this sense after a noun phrase introduced by *the same: the same height as her sister.* ◆ *prep* **12** in the role of; being: *as his friend, I am probably biased.* **13 as for** *or* **to.** with reference to: *as for my past, I'm not telling you anything.* **14 as from** *or* **of.** *Formal.* (in expressions of time) from: *fares will rise as from January 11.* **15 as if** *or* **though.** as it would be if: *he talked as if he knew all about it.* **16 as (it) is.** in the existing state of affairs: *as it is, I shall have difficulty finishing all this work, without any more.* **17 as per.** See **per** (sense 3). **18 as regards.** See **regard** (sense 6). **19 as such.** See **such** (sense 3). **20 such as.** See **such** (sense 5). **21 as was.** in a previous state. **22 as well.** See **well**[1] (sense 13). **23 as yet.** up to now; so far. [Old English *alswā* likewise; see ALSO]

USAGE See at **like.**

as[2] (æs) *n* **1** an ancient Roman unit of weight approximately equal to 1 pound troy (373 grams). **2** the standard monetary unit and copper coin of ancient Rome. [C17: from Latin *ās* unity, probably of Etruscan origin]

As *symbol for:* **1** *Chemistry.* arsenic. **2** altostratus.

AS *abbrev. for:* **1** Also: **A.S.** Anglo-Saxon. **2** antisubmarine.

As. *abbrev. for:* **1** Asia(n). **2** Asiatic.

ASA *abbrev. for:* **1** (in Britain) Amateur Swimming Association. **2** (in Britain) Advertising Standards Authority. **3** (in the U.S.) American Standards Association.

ASA/BS *abbrev.* an obsolete expression of the speed of a photographic film, replaced by the ISO rating. [C20: from *American Standards Association/British Standard*]

asafoetida *or* **asafetida** (ˌæsə'fɛtɪdə) *n* a bitter resin with an unpleasant onion-like smell, obtained from the roots of some umbelliferous plants of the genus *Ferula:* formerly used to treat flatulence, hysteria, etc. [C14: from Medieval Latin, from *asa* gum (compare Persian *azā* mastic) + Latin *foetidus* evil-smelling, FETID]

asana ('ɑːsənə) *n* any of various postures in yoga. See also **hatha yoga.** [Sanskrit]

Asantehene (æ'ʃæntɪˌhɛnɪ) *n* the ruler of the Ashanti people of Ghana.

a.s.a.p. *abbrev. for* as soon as possible.

asarabacca (ˌæsərə'bækə) *n* a perennial evergreen Eurasian plant, *Asarum europaeum,* having kidney-shaped leaves and a single brownish flower: family *Aristolochiaceae.*

asarum ('æsərəm) *n* the dried strong-scented root of the wild ginger plant: a flavouring agent and source of an aromatic oil used in perfumery, formerly used in medicine. [C19: via New Latin from Latin: hazelwort, from Greek *asaron*]

Asben (æs'bɛn) *n* another name for **Aïr** (region of the Sahara).

asbestos (æs'bɛstɒs, -təs) *n* **a** any of the fibrous amphibole and serpentine minerals, esp. chrysotile and tremolite, that are incombustible and resistant to chemicals. It was formerly widely used in the form of fabric or board as a heat-resistant structural material. **b** (*as modifier*): *asbestos matting.* [C14 (originally applied to a mythical stone the heat of which could not be extinguished): via Latin from Greek: from *asbestos* inextinguishable, from A-[1] + *sbennunai* to extinguish] ▸ **as'bestine** *adj*

asbestosis (ˌæsbɛs'təʊsɪs) *n* inflammation of the lungs resulting from chronic inhalation of asbestos particles.

ASBSBSW (in Britain) *abbrev. for* Amalgamated Society of Boilermakers, Shipwrights, Blacksmiths, and Structural Workers.

Asc. *Astrology. abbrev. for* Ascendant.

Ascanius (æ'skeɪnɪəs) *n Roman myth.* the son of Aeneas and Creusa; founder of Alba Longa, mother city of Rome. Also called: **Iulus.**

ASCAP ('æskæp) *n acronym for* American Society of Composers, Authors, and Publishers.

ascariasis (ˌæskə'raɪəsɪs) *n* infestation of the intestines with the roundworm *Ascaris lumbricoides,* causing abdominal pain, nausea and vomiting, weight loss, etc.

ascarid ('æskərɪd) *n* any parasitic nematode worm of the family *Ascaridae,* such as the common roundworm of man and pigs. [C14: from New Latin *ascaridae,* from Greek *askarides,* plural of *askaris*]

ascend (ə'sɛnd) *vb* **1** to go or move up (a ladder, hill, slope, etc.); mount; climb. **2** (*intr*) to slope or incline upwards. **3** (*intr*) to rise to a higher point, level, degree, etc. **4** to follow (a river) upstream towards its source. **5** to trace (a genealogy, etc.) back in time. **6** to sing or play (a scale, arpeggio, etc.) from the lower to higher notes. **7 ascend the throne.** to become king or queen. [C14: from Latin *ascendere,* from *scandere*]

ascendancy, ascendency (ə'sɛndənsɪ) *or* **ascendance, ascendence** *n* the condition of being dominant, esp. through superior economic or political power.

ascendant *or* **ascendent** (ə'sɛndənt) *adj* **1** proceeding upwards; rising. **2** dominant, superior, or influential. **3** *Botany.* another term for **ascending.** ◆ *n* **4** *Rare.* an ancestor. **5** a position or condition of dominance, superiority or control. **6** *Astrology.* (*sometimes cap.*) **6a** a point on the ecliptic that rises on the eastern horizon at a particular moment and changes as the earth rotates on its axis. **6b** the sign of the zodiac containing this point. **7 in the ascendant.** increasing in influence, prosperity, etc.

ascender (ə'sɛndə) *n* **1** *Printing.* **1a** the part of certain lower-case letters, such as *b* or *h,* that extends above the body of the letter. **1b** any letter having such a part. **2** a person or thing that ascends. **3** another word for **ascendeur.**

ascendeur (*French* asɑ̃dœr) *n Mountaineering.* a metal grip that is threaded on a rope and can be alternately tightened and slackened as an aid to climbing the rope: used attached to slings for the feet and waist. Also called: **ascender.** [C20]

ascending (ə'sɛndɪŋ) *adj* **1** moving upwards; rising. **2** *Botany.* sloping or curving upwards: *the ascending stem of a vine.*

ascension (ə'sɛnʃən) *n* **1** the act of ascending. **2** *Astronomy.* the rising of a star above the horizon. ▸ **as'censional** *adj*

Ascension[1] (ə'sɛnʃən) *n New Testament.* the passing of Jesus Christ from earth into heaven (Acts 1:9).

Ascension[2] (ə'sɛnʃən) *n* an island in the S Atlantic, northwest of St Helena: uninhabited until claimed by Britain in 1815. Pop.: 1117 (1993). Area: 88 sq. km (34 sq. miles).

Ascension Day *n Christianity.* the 40th day after Easter, when the Ascension of Christ into heaven is celebrated.

ascensionist (ə'sɛnʃənɪst) *n Mountaineering.* a person who has completed a mountain ascent, esp. a notable one.

Ascensiontide (ə'sɛnʃənˌtaɪd) *n* the ten days from Ascension Day to the day before Whit Sunday.

ascent (ə'sɛnt) *n* **1** the act of ascending; climb or upward movement: *the ascent of hot gases.* **2** an upward slope; incline or gradient. **3** movement back through time, as in tracing of earlier generations (esp. in the phrase **line of ascent**).

ascertain (ˌæsə'teɪn) *vb (tr)* **1** to determine or discover definitely. **2** *Archaic.* to make certain. [C15: from Old French *acertener* to make certain] ▸ **ˌascer'tainable** *adj* ▸ **ˌascer'tainably** *adv* ▸ **ˌascer'tainment** *n*

ascesis (ə'siːsɪs) *n, pl* **-ses** (-siːz). the exercise of self-discipline. [C19: from Greek, from *askein* to exercise]

ascetic (ə'sɛtɪk) *n* **1** a person who practises great self-denial and austerities and abstains from worldly comforts and pleasures, esp. for religious reasons. **2** (in the early Christian Church) a monk. ◆ *adj also* **as'cetical. 3** rigidly abstinent or abstemious; austere. **4** of or relating to ascetics or asceticism. **5** intensely rigorous in religious austerities. [C17: from Greek *askētikos,* from *askētēs,* from *askein* to exercise] ▸ **as'cetically** *adv*

asceticism (ə'sɛtɪˌsɪzəm) *n* **1** the behaviour, discipline, or outlook of an ascetic, esp. of a religious ascetic. **2** the principles of ascetic practices, esp. in the early Christian Church. **3** the theory and system of ascetic practices.

Asch (æʃ) *n* **Sholem** ('ʃəʊləm). 1880–1957, U.S. writer, born in Poland, who wrote in Yiddish. His works include biblical novels.

Aschaffenburg (*German* a'ʃafənbʊrk) *n* a city in Germany, on the River Main in Bavaria: seat of the Imperial Diet (1447); ceded to Bavaria in 1814. Pop.: 62 050 (1989 est.).

Ascham ('æskəm) *n* **Roger.** ?1515–68, English humanist writer and classical scholar: tutor to Queen Elizabeth I.

asci ('æsaɪ, 'æskaɪ) *n* the plural of **ascus.**

ascidian (ə'sɪdɪən) *n* **1** any minute marine invertebrate animal of the class *Ascidiacea,* such as the sea squirt, the adults of which are degenerate and sedentary: subphylum *Tunicata* (tunicates). **2 ascidian tadpole.** the free-swimming larva of an ascidian, having a tadpole-like tail containing the notochord and nerve cord. ◆ *adj* **3** of, relating to, or belonging to the *Ascidiacea.*

ascidium (ə'sɪdɪəm) *n, pl* **-cidia** (-'sɪdɪə). part of a plant that is shaped like a pitcher, such as the modified leaf of the pitcher plant. [C18: from New Latin, from Greek *askidion* a little bag, from *askos* bag]

ASCII ('æski:) *n acronym for* American standard code for information interchange: a computer code for representing alphanumeric characters.

ascites (ə'saɪti:z) *n, pl* **ascites.** *Pathol.* accumulation of serous fluid in the peritoneal cavity. [C14: from Latin: a kind of dropsy, from Greek *askitēs*, from *askos* wineskin] ▸ **ascitic** (ə'sɪtɪk) *adj*

asclepiadaceous (æˌskli:pɪə'deɪʃəs) *adj* of, relating to, or belonging to the *Asclepiadaceae*, a family of mostly tropical and subtropical flowering plants, including the milkweed and swallowwort, having pollen in the form of a waxy mass (pollinium). [C19: from New Latin *Asclēpias* genus name, from Latin, from Greek *asklēpias*, named after ASCLEPIUS]

Asclepiadean (æˌskli:pɪə'di:ən) *Prosody.* ◆ *adj* **1** of or relating to a type of classical verse line consisting of a spondee, two or three choriambs, and an iamb. ◆ *n* **2** Also called: **Asclepiad.** an Asclepiadean verse. [C17: via Latin from Greek *Asklēpiadēs* (about 270 B.C.), who invented the verse form]

asclepias (ə'skli:pɪəs) *n* any plant of the perennial mostly tuberous genus *Asclepias;* some are grown as garden or greenhouse plants for their showy orange-scarlet or purple flowers: family *Asclepiadaceae.* Sometimes called also: **milkweed.** [Greek *asklēpias* swallowwort]

Asclepius (ə'skli:pɪəs) *n Greek myth.* a god of healing; son of Apollo. Roman counterpart: **Aesculapius** (ˌi:skjʊ'leɪpɪəs).

asco- *combining form.* indicating a bladder or ascus: *ascomycete.* [from Greek *askos* bladder]

ascocarp ('æskəˌkɑ:p) *n* (in some ascomycetous fungi) a globular structure containing the asci. See **apothecium, perithecium.**

ascogonium (ˌæskə'gəʊnɪəm) *n, pl* **-nia** (-nɪə). a female reproductive body in some ascomycetous fungi in which, after fertilization, the asci develop.

Ascoli Piceno (*Italian* 'askoli pi'tʃɛ:no) *n* a town in E central Italy, in the Marches: capital of the Roman province of Picenum; site of the massacre of all its Roman citizens in the Social War in 90 B.C. Pop.: 52 667 (1990). Latin name: **Asculum Picenum** ('æskjʊləm paɪ'si:nəm).

ascomycete (ˌæskəmaɪ'si:t) *n* any fungus of the phylum *Ascomycota* (formerly class *Ascomycetes*) in which the spores (ascospores) are formed inside a club-shaped cell (ascus). The group includes yeast, penicillium, aspergillus, truffles, and certain mildews. ▸ ˌ**ascomy'cetous** *adj*

ascorbic acid (ə'skɔ:bɪk) *n* a white crystalline vitamin present in plants, esp. citrus fruits, tomatoes, and green vegetables. A deficiency in the diet of man leads to scurvy. Formula: $C_6H_8O_6$. Also called: **vitamin C.** [C20: *ascorbic* from A-[1] + SCORB(UT)IC]

ascospore ('æskəˌspɔ:) *n* one of the spores (usually eight in number) that are produced in an ascus.

ascot ('æskət) *n* a cravat with wide square ends, usually secured with an ornamental stud. [C20: named after ASCOT, where it was probably first worn]

Ascot ('æskət) *n* a town in S England, in Berkshire: noted for its horse race meetings, esp. **Royal Ascot**, a four-day meeting held in June. Pop.: 13 500 (latest est.).

ascribe (ə'skraɪb) *vb* (*tr*) **1** to credit or assign, as to a particular origin or period: *to ascribe parts of a play to Shakespeare.* **2** to attribute as a quality; consider as belonging to: *to ascribe beauty to youth.* [C15: from Latin *ascrībere* to enrol, from *ad* in addition + *scrībere* to write] ▸ **as'cribable** *adj*

USAGE *Ascribe* is sometimes wrongly used where *subscribe* is meant: *I do not subscribe* (not *ascribe*) *to this view.*

ascription (ə'skrɪpʃən) *or* **adscription** (əd'skrɪpʃən) *n* **1** the act of ascribing. **2** a statement ascribing something to someone, esp. praise to God. [C16: from Latin *ascrīptiō*, from *ascrībere* to ASCRIBE]

ascus ('æskəs) *n, pl* **asci** ('æsaɪ, 'æskaɪ). a saclike structure that produces (usually) eight ascospores during sexual reproduction in ascomycetous fungi such as yeasts and mildews. [C19: from New Latin, from Greek *askos* bag]

ASDE *abbrev. for* Airport Surface Detection Equipment: a radar system that is used by aircraft controllers to assist in the safe manoeuvring of aircraft on the ground.

asdic ('æzdɪk) *n* an early form of **sonar.** [C20: from *A(nti-)S(ubmarine) D(etection) I(nvestigation) C(ommittee)*]

-ase *suffix forming nouns.* indicating an enzyme: *oxidase.* [abstracted from DIASTASE]

ASEAN ('æsɪˌæn) *n acronym for* Association of Southeast Asian Nations.

aseismic (eɪ'saɪzmɪk) *adj* **1** denoting a region free of earthquakes. **2** (*not in technical use*) denoting a region free of all but a few small earthquakes. **3** (of buildings, etc.) designed to withstand earthquakes.

aseity (eɪ'si:ɪtɪ) *n Philosophy.* existence derived from itself, having no other source. [C17: from Medieval Latin *aseitas*, from Latin *ā* from + *sē* oneself]

asepalous (æ'sɛpələs) *adj* (of a plant or flower) having no sepals.

asepsis (ə'sɛpsɪs, eɪ-) *n* **1** the state of being free from living pathogenic organisms. **2** the methods of achieving a germ-free condition. ▸ **a'septic** *adj*

aseptate (eɪ'sɛpteɪt) *adj Biology.* not divided into cells or sections by septa.

asexual (eɪ'sɛksjʊəl, æ-) *adj* **1** having no apparent sex or sex organs. **2** (of reproduction) not involving the fusion of male and female gametes, as in vegetative reproduction, fission, and budding. ▸ ˌ**asexu'ality** *n* ▸ **a'sexually** *adv*

Asgard ('æsgɑ:d) *or* **Asgarth** ('æsgɑ:θ) *n Norse myth.* the dwelling place of the principal gods, the Aesir.

ash[1] (æʃ) *n* **1** the nonvolatile products and residue formed when matter is burnt. **2** any of certain compounds formed by burning. See **soda ash. 3** fine particles of lava thrown out by an erupting volcano. **4** a light silvery grey colour, often with a brownish tinge. ◆ See also **ashes.** Related adj: **cinereous.** [Old English *æsce;* related to Old Norse, Old High German *aska*, Gothic *azgō*, Latin *aridus* dry]

ash[2] (æʃ) *n* **1** any oleaceous tree of the genus *Fraxinus*, esp. *F. excelsior* of Europe and Asia, having compound leaves, clusters of small greenish flowers, and winged seeds. **2** the close-grained durable wood of any of these trees, used for tool handles, etc. **3** any of several trees resembling the ash, such as the mountain ash. [Old English *æsc;* related to Old Norse *askr*, Old Saxon, Old High German *ask*, Lithuanian *uosis*]

ash[3] (æʃ) *n* the digraph æ, as in Old English, representing a front vowel approximately like that of the *a* in Modern English *hat.* The character is also used to represent this sound in the International Phonetic Alphabet.

ASH (æʃ) *n* (in Britain) *acronym for* Action on Smoking and Health.

ashamed (ə'ʃeɪmd) *adj* (*usually postpositive*) **1** overcome with shame, guilt, or remorse. **2** (foll. by *of*) suffering from feelings of inferiority or shame in relation to (a person, thing, or deed). **3** (foll. by *to*) unwilling through fear of humiliation, shame, etc. [Old English *āscamod*, past participle of *āscamian* to shame, from *scamu* SHAME] ▸ **ashamedly** (ə'ʃeɪmɪdlɪ) *adv*

Ashanti (ə'ʃæntɪ) *n* **1** an administrative region of central Ghana: former native kingdom, suppressed by the British in 1900 after four wars. Capital: Kumasi. Pop.: 2 485 766 (1991 est.). Area: 24 390 sq. km (9417 sq. miles). **2** (*pl* **-ti** *or* **-tis**) a native or inhabitant of Ashanti.

A shares *pl n Brit.* those ordinary shares in a company which carry restricted voting rights or other restrictions.

ash blond *n* **1a** a very light blond colour. **1b** (*as adj*): *ash-blond hair.* **2** a person whose hair is this colour. ◆ Also: **ash blonde** *fem*

Ashby-de-la-Zouch (ˌæʃbɪˌdələ'zu:ʃ) *n* a town in central England, in Leicestershire: Mary, Queen of Scots, was imprisoned (1569) in the castle. Pop.: 10 595 (1991).

ash can *n* a U.S. word for **dustbin.** Also called: **garbage can, ash bin, trash can.**

Ash Can School *n* a group of U.S. painters including Robert Henri and later George Bellows, founded in 1907, noted for their depiction of the sordid aspects of city life.

Ashcroft ('æʃkrɒft) *n* Dame **Peggy.** 1907–91, English stage and film actress.

Ashdod ('æʃdɒd) *n* a town in central Israel, on the Mediterranean coast: an important city in the Philistine Empire, with its artificial harbour (1961) it is now a major port. Pop.: 128 400 (1996 est.).

Ashdown ('æʃdaʊn) *n* **Paddy,** real name *Jeremy John Durham Ashdown.* born 1941, British politician; leader of the Liberal Democrats (formerly the Social and Liberal Democrats) (1988–99).

Ashe (æʃ) *n* **Arthur (Robert).** 1943–93, U.S. tennis player: U.S. champion 1968; Wimbledon champion 1975.

ashen[1] ('æʃən) *adj* **1** drained of colour; pallid. **2** consisting of or resembling ashes. **3** of a pale greyish colour.

ashen[2] ('æʃən) *adj* of, relating to, or made from the ash tree or its timber.

Asher ('æʃə) *n* the son of Jacob and ancestor of one of the 12 tribes of Israel.

ashes ('æʃɪz) *pl n* **1** ruins or remains, as after destruction or burning: *the city was left in ashes.* **2** the remains of a human body after cremation.

Ashes ('æʃɪz) *pl n* **the.** a cremated cricket stump in a pottery urn now preserved at Lord's. Victory or defeat in test matches between England and Australia is referred to as winning, losing, or retaining the Ashes. [from the mock obituary of English cricket in *The Times* in 1882 after a great Australian victory at the Oval, in which it was said that the body would be cremated and the ashes taken to Australia]

ashet ('æʃɪt) *n Scot. and northern English dialect.* a shallow oval dish or large plate. [C16: from French *assiette*]

Ashford ('æʃfəd) *n* a market town in SE England, in central Kent. Pop.: 52 002 (1991).

Ashkenazi (ˌæʃkə'nɑ:zɪ) *n, pl* **-zim** (-zɪm). **1** (*modifier*) of or relating to the Jews of Germany and E Europe. **2** a Jew of German or E European descent. **3** the pronunciation of Hebrew used by these Jews. ◆ Compare **Sephardi.** [C19: Late Hebrew, from Hebrew *Ashkenaz*, the son of Gomer (Genesis 10:3; I Chronicles 1:6), a descendant of Noah through Japheth, and hence taken to be identified with the ancient Ascanians of Phrygia and, in the medieval period, the Germans]

Ashkenazy (ˌæʃkə'nɑ:zɪ) *n* **Vladimir.** born 1937, Soviet-born Icelandic pianist and conductor.

ashkey ('æʃki:) *n* the winged fruit of the ash.

Ashkhabad (*Russian* aʃxa'bat) *or* **Ashgabat** ('ɑ:ʃgəbæt; *Turkmen* ɑʃgɑ'bɑt) *n* the capital of Turkmenistan. Pop.: 536 000 (1995 est.).

ashlar *or* **ashler** ('æʃlə) *n* **1** a block of hewn stone with straight edges for use in building. **2** Also called: **ashlar veneer.** a thin dressed stone with straight edges, used to face a wall. **3** masonry made of ashlar. [C14: from Old French *aisselier* crossbeam, from *ais* board, from Latin *axis* axletree; see AXIS[1]]

ashlaring ('æʃlərɪŋ) *n* **1** ashlars collectively. **2** a number of short upright boards forming the wall of a garret, cutting off the acute angle between the rafters and the floor.

Ashley ('æʃlɪ) *n* **Laura.** 1925–85, British designer, who built up a successful chain of retail stores selling dresses and fabrics based on traditional English patterns.

Ashmolean Museum (æʃ'məʊlɪən, ˌæʃmə'lɪən) *n* a museum, attached to Oxford University and founded in 1683, noted for its paintings and archaeological collections. [C19: named after Elias *Ashmole* (1617–92), English antiquary who donated the first collection]

ashore (ə'ʃɔ:) *adv* **1** towards or onto land from the water: *we swam ashore.* ◆ *adj* (*postpositive*), *adv* **2** on land, having come from the water: *a day ashore before sailing.*

ashplant ('æʃˌplɑ:nt) *n* a walking stick made from an ash sapling.

ashram ('æʃrəm, 'ɑ:ʃ-) *n* **1** a religious retreat or community where a Hindu holy man lives. **2** a house that provides accommodation for destitute people. [from Sanskrit *āśrama*, from *ā-* near + *śrama* religious exertion]

Ashton ('æʃtən) *n* Sir **Frederick**. 1906–88, British ballet dancer and choreographer. His ballets include *Façade* (1931), to music by Walton, *La Fille mal gardée* (1960), *The Dream* (1964), and *A Month in the Country* (1976).

Ashton-under-Lyne (laın) *n* a town in NW England, in Tameside unitary authority, Greater Manchester. Pop.: 43 906 (1991).

Ashtoreth ('æʃtəˌreθ) *n Old Testament.* an ancient Semitic fertility goddess, identified with Astarte and Ishtar.

ashtray ('æʃˌtreı) *n* a receptacle for tobacco ash, cigarette butts, etc.

Ashur ('æʃʊə) *n* a variant spelling of **Assur**.

Ashurbanipal (ˌæʃʊə'bɑːnıˌpæl) *or* **Assurbanipal** *n* died ?626 B.C., king of Assyria (?668–?626): son of Esarhaddon. He built the magnificent palace and library at Nineveh. Greek name: **Sardanapalus.**

Ash Wednesday *n* the first day of Lent, named from the practice of Christians of placing ashes on their heads as a sign of penitence.

ashy ('æʃı) *adj* **ashier, ashiest. 1** of a pale greyish colour; ashen. **2** consisting of, covered with, or resembling ash.

'Asi ('æsı) *n* the Arabic name for the **Orontes.**

Asia ('eıʃə, 'eıʒə) *n* the largest of the continents, bordering on the Arctic Ocean, the Pacific Ocean, the Indian Ocean, and the Mediterranean and Red Seas in the west. It includes the large peninsulas of Asia Minor, India, Arabia, and Indochina and the island groups of Japan, Indonesia, the Philippines, and Ceylon (Sri Lanka); contains the mountain ranges of the Hindu Kush, Himalayas, Pamirs, Tian Shan, Urals, and Caucasus, the great plateaus of India, Iran, and Tibet, vast plains and deserts, and the valleys of many large rivers including the Mekong, Irrawaddy, Indus, Ganges, Tigris, and Euphrates. Pop.: 3 589 233 000 (1998 est.). Area: 44 391 162 sq. km (17 139 445 sq. miles).

Asia Minor *n* the historical name for **Anatolia.**

Asian ('eıʃən, 'eıʒən) *adj* **1** of or relating to Asia or to any of its peoples or languages. ◆ *n* **2** a native or inhabitant of Asia or a descendant of one.

USAGE The use of *Asian* or *Asiatic* as a noun can be offensive and should be avoided.

Asian flu *n* a type of influenza recurring in worldwide epidemics, caused by a virus (A2 strain or subsequent antigenic variants), which apparently originated in China in 1957.

Asian pear *n* **1** a tropical pear tree, esp. any of several varieties of Japanese pear *Pyrus serotina.* **2** Also called: **nashi.** the fruit of the Japanese pear, which resembles a large yellow apple, has crisp juicy flesh, and is cultivated in Japan, Korea, the U.S., and New Zealand.

Asiatic (ˌeıʃı'ætık, -zı-) *n, adj* another word for **Asian.**

USAGE See at **Asian.**

Asiatic beetle *n* a Japanese scarabaeid beetle, *Anomala orientalis,* introduced into Hawaii and the northeastern U.S.: a serious pest of sugar cane and cereal crops because it destroys the roots.

Asiatic cholera *n* another name for **cholera.**

aside (ə'saıd) *adv* **1** on or to one side: *they stood aside to let him pass.* **2** out of hearing; in or into seclusion: *he took her aside to tell her of his plan.* **3** away from oneself: *he threw the book aside.* **4** out of mind or consideration: *he put aside all fears.* **5** in or into reserve: *to put aside money for old age.* **6 aside from.** (*prep*) *Chiefly U.S. and Canadian.* **6a** besides: *he has money aside from his possessions.* **6b** except for: *he has nothing aside from the clothes he stands in.* Compare **apart** (sense 7). ◆ *n* **7** something spoken by an actor, intended to be heard by the audience, but not by the others on stage. **8** any confidential statement spoken in undertones. **9** a digression.

A-side *n* the side of a gramophone record regarded as the more important one.

Asimov ('æzımɒf) *n* **Isaac.** 1920–92, U.S. writer and biochemist, born in Russia. His science-fiction works include *Foundation Trilogy* (1951–53; sequel 1982) and the collection of stories *I, Robot* (1950).

asinine ('æsıˌnaın) *adj* **1** obstinate or stupid. **2** resembling an ass. [C16: from Latin *asinīnus,* from *asinus* ASS[1]] ▸ **'asiˌninely** *adv* ▸ **asininity** (ˌæsı'nınıtı) *n*

ASIO *abbrev. for* Australian Security Intelligence Organization.

Asir (æ'sıə) *n* a region of SW Saudi Arabia, in the Southern Province on the Red Sea: under Turkish rule until 1933. Area: 81 000 sq. km (31 000 sq. miles).

-asis *suffix forming nouns.* a variant of **-iasis.**

A sizes *or* **A series** *n* a series of paper sizes approved by the International Standards Organization, running from 2AO to A7, each size (defined in mm) being half as large as the one preceding it, as follows: **2AO,** 1189 × 1682; **AO,** 841 × 1189; **A1,** 594 × 841; **A2,** 420 × 594; **A3,** 297 × 420; **A4,** 210 × 297; **A5,** 148 × 210; **A6,** 105 × 148; **A7,** 74 × 105.

ask (ɑːsk) *vb* **1** (often foll. by *about*) to put a question (to); request an answer (from): *she asked (him) about God.* **2** (*tr*) to inquire about: *she asked him the time of the train; she asked the way.* **3** (*tr*) to direct or put (a question). **4** (*may take a clause as object or an infinitive;* often foll. by *for*) to make a request or demand: *she asked (him) for information; they asked for a deposit.* **5** (*tr*) to demand or expect (esp. in the phrases **ask a lot of, ask too much of**). **6** (*tr*) Also: **ask out, ask over.** to request (a person) politely to come or go to a place; invite: *he asked her to the party.* **7** (*tr*) to need; require: *the job asks both time and patience.* **8** (*tr*) *Archaic.* to proclaim (marriage banns). ◆ See also **ask after, ask for.** [Old English *āscian;* related to Old Frisian *āskia,* Old Saxon *ēscon,* Old High German *eiscōn*] ▸ **'asker** *n*

Ask (ɑːsk) *n Norse myth.* the first man, created by the gods from an ash tree.

ask after *or* (*Scot.*) **ask for** *vb* (*prep*) to make inquiries about the health of (someone): *he asked after her mother.*

askance (ə'skæns) *or* **askant** (ə'skænt) *adv* **1** with an oblique glance. **2** with doubt or mistrust. [C16: of unknown origin]

askari (as'kaːri) *n* (in East Africa) a soldier or policeman. [C19: from Arabic: soldier]

askew (ə'skjuː) *adv, adj* at an oblique angle; towards one side; awry.

Askey ('æskı) *n* **Arthur.** 1900–82, British comedian.

ask for *vb* (*prep*) **1** to try to obtain by requesting: *he asked for help.* **2** (*intr*) *Informal.* to behave in a provocative manner that is regarded as inviting (trouble): *she's asking for trouble; you're asking for it.* **3** *Scot.* to ask after.

asking price *n* the price suggested by a seller but usually considered to be subject to bargaining.

Askja ('ɑːskjə) *n* a volcano in E central Iceland: active in 1961; largest crater in Iceland. Height: 1510 m (4954 ft.). Area of crater: 88 sq. km (34 sq. miles).

ASL *abbrev. for* American Sign Language. See **Ameslan.**

aslant (ə'slɑːnt) *adv* **1** at a slant. ◆ *prep* **2** at a slant across or athwart.

asleep (ə'sliːp) *adj* (*postpositive*) **1** in or into a state of sleep. **2** in or into a dormant or inactive state. **3** (of limbs, esp. when the blood supply to them has been restricted) numb; lacking sensation. **4** *Euphemistic.* dead.

ASLEF ('æzlef) *n* (in Britain) *acronym for* Associated Society of Locomotive Engineers and Firemen.

AS level *n Brit.* **1a** an advanced level of a subject taken for the General Certificate of Education, with a smaller course content than an A level. **1b** (*as modifier*): *AS-level English.* **2** a pass in a subject at AS level: *I've got three AS levels.*

ASLIB ('æzlıb) *n acronym for* Association for Information Management.

aslope (ə'sləʊp) *adv, adj* (*postpositive*) sloping.

ASM *abbrev. for:* **1** air-to-surface missile. **2** *Theatre.* assistant stage manager.

Asmara (æs'mɑːrə) *n* the capital of Eritrea; cathedral (1922); Grand Mosque (1937); university (1958). Pop.: 431 000 (1995 est.).

Asmodeus (æs'məʊdıəs, ˌæsməʊ'diːəs) *n* (in Jewish demonology) prince of the demons. [via Latin *Asmodaeus,* from Avestan *Aēsma-daēva,* spirit of anger]

Asnières (*French* anjɛr) *n* a suburb of Paris, France, on the Seine. Pop.: 72 250 (1990).

Aso ('ɑːsəʊ) *n* a group of five volcanic cones in Japan on central Kyushu, one of which, Naka-dake, has the largest crater in the world, between 16 km (10 miles) and 24 km (15 miles) in diameter. Highest cone: 1592 m (5223 ft.). Also called: **Asosan** (ˌɑːsəʊ'sɑːn).

asocial (eı'səʊʃəl) *adj* **1** avoiding contact; not gregarious. **2** unconcerned about the welfare of others. **3** hostile to society or social practices.

Asoka (ə'səʊkə, ə'ʃəʊ-) *n* died 232 B.C., Indian emperor (?273–232 B.C.), who elevated Buddhism to the official state religion.

asp[1] (æsp) *n* **1** the venomous snake, probably *Naja haje* (Egyptian cobra), that caused the death of Cleopatra and was formerly used by the Pharaohs as a symbol of their power over life and death. See also **uraeus. 2** Also called: **asp viper.** a viper, *Vipera aspis,* that occurs in S Europe and is very similar to but smaller than the adder. **3 horned asp.** another name for **horned viper.** [C15: from Latin *aspis,* from Greek]

asp[2] (æsp) *n* an archaic name for the **aspen.** [Old English *æspe;* related to Old Norse *ösp,* Old High German *aspa*]

asparagine (ə'spærəˌdʒiːn, -dʒın) *n* a nonessential amino acid, a component of proteins. [C19: from French, from Latin *asparagus* ASPARAGUS + -INE[2]]

asparagus (ə'spærəgəs) *n* **1** any Eurasian liliaceous plant of the genus *Asparagus,* esp. the widely cultivated *A. officinalis,* having small scaly or needle-like leaves. **2** the succulent young shoots of *A. officinalis,* which may be cooked and eaten. **3 asparagus fern.** a fernlike species of asparagus, *A. plumosus,* native to southern Africa. [C15: from Latin, from Greek *asparagos,* of obscure origin]

aspartame (ə'spɑːˌteım) *n* an artificial sweetener produced from aspartic acid. Formula: $C_{14}H_{18}N_2O_5$. [C20: from ASPART(IC ACID) + *(phenyl)a(lanine) m(ethyl) e(ster)*]

aspartic acid (ə'spɑːtık) *n* a nonessential amino acid that is a component of proteins and acts as a neurotransmitter. [C19: from ASPAR(AGUS) + -IC]

Aspasia (ə'speızıə) *n* 5th century B.C., Greek courtesan; mistress of Pericles.

aspect ('æspekt) *n* **1** appearance to the eye; visual effect: *the physical aspect of the landscape.* **2** a distinct feature or element in a problem, situation, etc.; facet: *to consider every aspect of a problem.* **3** the way in which a problem, idea, etc., may be considered: *to consider a problem from every aspect.* **4** a facial expression; manner of appearing: *a severe aspect.* **5** a position facing a particular direction; outlook: *the southern aspect of a house.* **6** a view in a certain direction: *a good aspect of the village from the tower.* **7** a surface that faces in a given direction: *the ventral aspect of a fish.* **8** *Astrology.* any of several specific angular distances between two planets or a planet and the Ascendant or Midheaven measured, from the earth, in degrees along the ecliptic. **9** *Grammar.* a category of verbs or verbal inflections that expresses such features as the continuity, repetition, or completedness of the action described. Compare **perfective** (sense 2), **progressive** (senses 8, 10). **10** *Botany.* **10a** the extent to which a plant habitat is exposed to the sun, wind, etc. **10b** the effect of the seasons on the appearance of plants. **11** *Archaic.* glance or gaze. [C14: from Latin *aspectus* a sight, from *aspicere,* from *ad-* to, at + *specere* to look]

aspect ratio *n* **1** the ratio of width to height of a picture on a television or cinema screen. **2** *Aeronautics.* the ratio of the span of a wing to its mean chord.

aspectual (æ'spektjʊəl) *adj* of or relating to grammatical aspect.

aspen ('æspən) *n* **1** any of several trees of the salicaceous genus *Populus,* such as *P. tremula* of Europe, in which the leaves are attached to the stem by long flattened stalks so that they quiver in the wind. Archaic name: **asp.** ◆ *adj* **2** *Archaic, chiefly literary.* trembling. [Old English *æspe;* see ASP[2]]

asper ('æspə) *n* a former Turkish monetary unit, a silver coin, worth 1/120 of a piastre. [from Turkish, ultimately from Latin: rough, harsh]

asperate ('æspəˌreıt) *or* **asperous** ('æspərəs) *adj* (of plant parts) having a rough surface due to a covering of short stiff hairs.

Asperger's syndrome ('æspɜːgəz) *n* a form of autism in which the sufferer has limited but obsessive interests, and has difficulty relating to other people.

[C20: named after Hans *Asperger* (20th century), Austrian physician who first described it]

Asperges (æ'spɜːdʒiːz) *n R.C. Church.* **1** a short rite preceding Mass, in which the celebrant sprinkles those present with holy water to the accompaniment of the chant *Asperges me, Domine.* **2** the chant opening with these words. [C16: from Latin *Asperges (me hyssopo)* Thou shalt purge (me with hyssop)]

aspergillosis (æˌspɜːdʒɪ'ləʊsɪs) *n, pl* **-ses** (-siːz). a rare fungal infection, esp. of the mucous membranes or lungs, caused by various species of *Aspergillus.* [C19: from New Latin, from ASPERGILLUS]

aspergillum (ˌæspə'dʒɪləm) *or* **aspergill** ('æspədʒɪl) *n, pl* **-gilla** (-'dʒɪlə), **-gillums,** *or* **-gills.** another term for **aspersorium** (sense 2). [C17: from New Latin *aspergillum,* from Latin *aspergere,* from *spargere* to sprinkle]

aspergillus (ˌæspə'dʒɪləs) *n, pl* **-gilli** (-'dʒɪlaɪ). any ascomycetous fungus of the genus *Aspergillus,* having chains of spores attached like bristles to a club-shaped stalk: family *Aspergillaceae.* [C19: from New Latin: *aspergillum* (from its similar appearance)]

asperity (æ'spɛrɪtɪ) *n, pl* **-ties. 1** roughness or sharpness of temper. **2** roughness or harshness of a surface, sound, taste, etc. **3** a condition hard to endure; affliction. **4** *Physics.* the elastically compressed region of contact between two surfaces caused by the normal force. [C16: from Latin *asperitās,* from *asper* rough]

aspermia (ə'spɜːmɪə) *n Pathol.* the failure to form or emit semen.

asperse (ə'spɜːs) *vb (tr)* **1** to spread false rumours about; defame. **2** *Rare.* to sprinkle, as with water in baptism. [C15: from Latin *aspersus,* from *aspergere* to sprinkle] ▸ **as'perser** *n* ▸ **as'persive** *adj* ▸ **as'persively** *adv*

aspersion (ə'spɜːʃən) *n* **1** a disparaging or malicious remark; slanderous accusation (esp. in the phrase **cast aspersions (on)**). **2** the act of defaming. **3** *Rare.* the act of sprinkling, esp. of water in baptism.

aspersorium (ˌæspə'sɔːrɪəm) *n, pl* **-ria** (-rɪə) *or* **-riums.** *R.C. Church.* **1** a basin containing holy water with which worshippers sprinkle themselves. **2** Also called: **aspergillum.** a perforated instrument used to sprinkle holy water.

asphalt ('æsfælt, 'æʃ-, -fɔːlt) *n* **1** any of several black semisolid substances composed of bitumen and inert mineral matter. They occur naturally in parts of America and as a residue from petroleum distillation: used as a waterproofing material and in paints, dielectrics, and fungicides. **2** a mixture of this substance with gravel, used in road-surfacing and roofing materials. **3** *(modifier)* containing or surfaced with asphalt. ◆ *vb* **4** *(tr)* to cover with asphalt. [C14: from Late Latin *aspaltus,* from Greek *asphaltos,* probably from A-[1] + *sphallein* to cause to fall; referring to its use as a binding agent] ▸ **as'phaltic** *adj*

asphaltite (æs'fæltaɪt) *n* any of various naturally occurring hydrocarbons that resemble asphalt but have a higher melting point.

aspherical surface *n Photog.* a lens or mirror surface that does not form part of a sphere and is used to reduce aberrations.

asphodel ('æsfəˌdɛl) *n* **1** any of various S European liliaceous plants of the genera *Asphodelus* and *Asphodeline,* having clusters of white or yellow flowers. Compare **bog asphodel. 2** any of various other plants, such as the daffodil. **3** an unidentified flower of Greek legend, probably a narcissus, said to cover the Elysian fields. [C16: from Latin *asphodelus,* from Greek *asphodelos,* of obscure origin]

asphyxia (æs'fɪksɪə) *n* lack of oxygen in the blood due to restricted respiration; suffocation. If severe enough and prolonged, it causes death. [C18: from New Latin, from Greek *asphuxia* a stopping of the pulse, from A-[1] + *sphuxis* pulse, from *sphuzein* to throb] ▸ **as'phyxial** *adj*

asphyxiant (æs'fɪksɪənt) *adj* **1** causing asphyxia. ◆ *n* **2** anything that causes asphyxia: *carbon monoxide is an asphyxiant.*

asphyxiate (æs'fɪksɪˌeɪt) *vb* to cause asphyxia in or undergo asphyxia; smother; suffocate. ▸ **asˌphyxi'ation** *n* ▸ **as'phyxiˌator** *n*

aspic[1] ('æspɪk) *n* a savoury jelly based on meat or fish stock, used as a relish or as a mould for meat, vegetables, etc. [C18: from French: aspic (jelly), ASP[1]; variously explained as referring to its colour or coldness as compared to that of the snake]

aspic[2] ('æspɪk) *n* an archaic word for **asp**[1]. [C17: from French, from Old Provençal *espic* spike, from Latin *spīca,* head (of flower); compare SPIKENARD]

aspic[3] ('æspɪk) *n* either of two species of lavender, *Lavandula spica* or *L. latifolia,* that yield an oil used in perfumery: family *Labiatae* (labiates). [C16: from Old French, a variant of *aspe* ASP[2]]

aspidistra (ˌæspɪ'dɪstrə) *n* any Asian plant of the liliaceous genus *Aspidistra,* esp. *A. lurida,* a popular house plant with long tough evergreen leaves and small brownish flowers. [C19: from New Latin, from Greek *aspis* shield, on the model of *Tupistra* genus of liliaceous plants]

Aspinwall ('æspɪnˌwɔːl) *n* the former name of **Colón.**

aspirant ('æspɪrənt, ə'spaɪərənt) *n* **1** a person who aspires, as to a high position. ◆ *adj* **2** aspiring or striving.

aspirate *vb* ('æspɪˌreɪt). *(tr)* **1** *Phonetics.* **1a** to articulate (a stop) with some force, so that breath escapes with audible friction as the stop is released. **1b** to pronounce (a word or syllable) with an initial *h.* **2** to draw in or remove by inhalation or suction, esp. to suck (air or fluid) from a body cavity or to inhale (fluid) into the lungs after vomiting. **3** to supply air to (an internal-combustion engine). ◆ *n* ('æspɪrɪt). **4** *Phonetics.* **4a** a stop pronounced with an audible release of breath. **4b** the glottal fricative represented in English and several other languages as *h.* ◆ *adj* ('æspɪrɪt). **5** *Phonetics.* (of a stop) pronounced with a forceful and audible expulsion of breath.

aspiration (ˌæspɪ'reɪʃən) *n* **1** strong desire to achieve something, such as success. **2** the aim of such desire. **3a** the act of breathing. **3b** a breath. **4** *Phonetics.* **4a** the pronunciation of a stop with an audible and forceful release of breath. **4b** the friction of the released breath. **4c** an aspirated consonant. **5** removal of air or fluid from a body cavity by suction. **6** *Med.* **6a** the sucking of fluid or foreign matter into the air passages of the body. **6b** the removal of air or fluid from the body by suction. ▸ **aspiratory** (ə'spaɪrətərɪ, -trɪ; 'æspɪrətərɪ, -trɪ) *adj*

aspirator ('æspɪˌreɪtə) *n* a device employing suction, such as a jet pump or one for removing fluids from a body cavity.

aspire (ə'spaɪə) *vb (intr)* **1** (usually foll. by *to* or *after*) to yearn (for) or have a powerful or ambitious plan, desire, or hope (to do or be something): *to aspire to be a great leader.* **2** to rise to a great height. [C15: from Latin *aspīrāre* to breathe upon, from *spīrāre* to breathe] ▸ **as'pirer** *n* ▸ **as'piring** *adj*

aspirin ('æsprɪn) *n, pl* **-rin** *or* **-rins. 1** a white crystalline compound widely used in the form of tablets to relieve pain, fever, and colds and to reduce inflammation. Formula: $CH_3COOC_6H_4COOH$. Chemical name: **acetylsalicylic acid. 2** a tablet of aspirin. [C19: from German, from *A(cetyl)* + *Spir(säure)* spiraeic acid (modern salicylic acid) + -IN; see also SPIRAEA]

asplanchnic (eɪ'splæŋknɪk) *adj Zoology.* having no gut.

asplenium (æ'spliːnɪəm) *n* any fern of the very large genus *Asplenium,* of worldwide distribution. Some, esp. the bird's nest fern (*A. nidus*), are grown as greenhouse or house plants for their decorative deeply-cut evergreen fronds: family *Polypodiaceae.* See also **spleenwort.** [New Latin, from Latin *asplēnum,* from Greek *asplēnon* spleenwort, from *a-* not + *splēn* spleen (from its reputed medicinal properties)]

asquint (ə'skwɪnt) *adv, adj (postpositive)* with a glance from the corner of the eye, esp. a furtive one. [C13: perhaps from Dutch *schuinte* slant, of obscure origin]

Asquith ('æskwɪθ) *n* **Herbert Henry,** 1st Earl of Oxford and Asquith. 1852–1928, British statesman; prime minister (1908–16); leader of the Liberal Party (1908–26).

ass[1] (æs) *n* **1** either of two perissodactyl mammals of the horse family (*Equidae*), *Equus asinus* (**African wild ass**) or *E. hemionus* (**Asiatic wild ass**). They are hardy and sure-footed, having longer ears than the horse. Related adj: **asinine. 2** *(not in technical use)* the domesticated variety of the African wild ass; donkey. **3** a foolish or ridiculously pompous person. **4 not within an ass's roar of.** *Irish informal.* not close to obtaining, winning, etc.: *she wasn't within an ass's roar of it.* [Old English *assa,* probably from Old Irish *asan,* from Latin *asinus;* related to Greek *onos* ass]

ass[2] (æs) *n* **1** the usual U.S. and Canadian word for **arse. 2** *U.S. and Canadian slang, offensive, taboo.* sexual intercourse or a woman considered sexually (esp. in the phrase **piece of ass**). [Old English *ærs;* see ARSE]

Assad ('asat) *n* **Hafezal** ('hafɛzal). born 1928, Syrian statesman and general; president of Syria from 1971.

assagai ('æsəˌgaɪ) *n, pl* **-gais.** a variant spelling of **assegai.**

assai[1] (æ'saɪ) *adv Music.* (usually preceded by a musical direction) very: *allegro assai.* [Italian: enough]

assai[2] (æ'saɪ) *n* **1** any of several Brazilian palm trees of the genus *Euterpe,* esp. *E. edulis,* that have small dark purple fleshy edible fruit. **2** a beverage made from the fruit of this tree. [via Brazilian Portuguese from Tupi]

assail (ə'seɪl) *vb (tr)* **1** to attack violently; assault. **2** to criticize or ridicule vehemently, as in argument. **3** to beset or disturb: *his mind was assailed by doubts.* **4** to encounter with the intention of mastering: *to assail a problem; to assail a difficult mountain ridge.* [C13: from Old French *asalir,* from Vulgar Latin *assalīre* (unattested) to leap upon, from Latin *assilīre,* from *salīre* to leap] ▸ **as'sailable** *adj* ▸ **as'sailer** *n* ▸ **as'sailment** *n*

assailant (ə'seɪlənt) *n* a person who attacks another, either physically or verbally.

assam ('æsæm; *Malay* 'asam) *n* (in Malaysia) tamarind as used in cooking. **Assam ikan** is a dish of fish cooked with tamarind. [from Malay *asam* sour]

Assam (æ'sæm) *n* a state of NE India, situated in the central Brahmaputra valley: tropical forest, with the heaviest rainfall in the world; produces large quantities of tea. Capital: Dispur. Pop.: 24 200 000 (1994 est.). Area: 78 438 sq. km (30 673 sq. miles).

Assamese (ˌæsə'miːz) *n* **1** the state language of Assam, belonging to the Indic branch of the Indo-European family and closely related to Bengali. **2** *(pl* **-mese)** a native or inhabitant of Assam. ◆ *adj* **3** of or relating to Assam, its people, or their language.

assassin (ə'sæsɪn) *n* a murderer, esp. one who kills a prominent political figure. [C16: from Medieval Latin *assassīnus,* from Arabic *hashshāshīn,* plural of *hashshāsh* one who eats HASHISH]

Assassin (ə'sæsɪn) *n* a member of a secret sect of Muslim fanatics operating in Persia and Syria from about 1090 to 1256, murdering their victims, usually Crusaders.

assassinate (ə'sæsɪˌneɪt) *vb (tr)* **1** to murder (a person, esp. a public or political figure), usually by a surprise attack. **2** to ruin or harm (a person's reputation, etc.) by slander. ▸ **asˌsassi'nation** *n*

assassin bug *n* any long-legged predatory, often blood-sucking, insect of the heteropterous family *Reduviidae.*

assassin fly *n* another name for **robber fly.**

assault (ə'sɔːlt) *n* **1** a violent attack, either physical or verbal. **2** *Law.* an intentional or reckless act that causes another person to expect to be subjected to immediate and unlawful violence. Compare **battery** (sense 4), **assault and battery. 3a** the culmination of a military attack, in which fighting takes place at close quarters. **3b** *(as modifier): assault troops.* **4** rape or attempted rape. ◆ *vb (tr)* **5** to make an assault upon. **6** to rape or attempt to rape. [C13: from Old French *asaut,* from Vulgar Latin *assaltus* (unattested), from *assalīre* (unattested) to leap upon; see ASSAIL] ▸ **as'saulter** *n* ▸ **as'saultive** *adj*

assault and battery *n Criminal law.* a threat of attack to another person followed by actual attack, which need amount only to touching with hostile intent.

assault course *n* an obstacle course designed to give soldiers practice in negotiating hazards in making an assault.

assay *vb* (əˈseɪ). **1** to subject (a substance, such as silver or gold) to chemical analysis, as in the determination of the amount of impurity. **2** (*tr*) to attempt (something or to do something). **3** (*tr; may take a clause as object*) to test, analyse, or evaluate: *to assay the significance of early childhood experience.* ◆ *n* (əˈseɪ, ˈæseɪ). **4a** an analysis, esp. a determination of the amount of metal in an ore or the amounts of impurities in a precious metal. **4b** (*as modifier*): *an assay office.* **5** a substance undergoing an analysis. **6** a written report on the results of an analysis. **7** a test. **8** *Archaic.* an attempt. [C14: from Old Northern French *assai;* see ESSAY] ▸ **asˈsayable** *adj* ▸ **asˈsayer** *n*

assegai *or* **assagai** (ˈæsəˌgaɪ) *n, pl* **-gais. 1** a southern African cornaceous tree, *Curtisia faginea,* the wood of which is used for making spears. **2** a sharp light spear, esp. one made of this wood. [C17: from Portuguese *azagaia,* from Arabic *az zaghāyah,* from *al* the + *zaghāyah* assegai, from Berber]

assemblage (əˈsɛmblɪdʒ) *n* **1** a number of things or persons assembled together; collection; assembly. **2** a list of dishes served at a meal or the dishes themselves. **3** the act or process of assembling or the state of being assembled. **4** (ˌæsəmˈblɑːʒ). a three-dimensional work of art that combines various objects into an integrated whole.

assemble (əˈsɛmbᵊl) *vb* **1** to come or bring together; collect or congregate. **2** to fit or join together (the parts of something, such as a machine): *to assemble the parts of a kit.* **3** to run (a computer program) that converts a set of symbolic data, usually in the form of specific single-step instructions, into machine language. [C13: from Old French *assembler,* from Vulgar Latin *assimulāre* (unattested) to bring together, from Latin *simul* together]

assemblé *French.* (asɑ̃ble) *n Ballet.* a sideways leap in which the feet come together in the air in preparation for landing. [literally: brought together]

assembler (əˈsɛmblə) *n* **1** a type of computer program that converts a program written in assembly language into machine code. Compare **compiler** (sense 2). **2** another name for **assembly language.**

assembly (əˈsɛmblɪ) *n, pl* **-blies. 1** a number of people gathered together, esp. for a formal meeting held at regular intervals. **2** the act of assembling or the state of being assembled. **3** the process of putting together a number of parts to make a machine or other product. **4** *Machinery.* a group of mating components before or after fitting together. **5** *Military.* **5a** a signal for personnel to assemble, as by drum, bugle, etc. **5b** (*as modifier*): *an assembly area.*

Assembly (əˈsɛmblɪ) *n, pl* **-blies. 1** the lower chamber in various American state legislatures. See also **House of Assembly, legislative assembly, National Assembly. 2** *N.Z.* short for **General Assembly.**

assembly language *n Computing.* a low-level programming language that allows a programmer complete control of the machine code to be generated.

assembly line *n* a sequence of machines, tools, operations, workers, etc., in a factory, arranged so that at each stage a further process is carried out.

assemblyman (əˈsɛmblɪmən) *n, pl* **-men.** (*sometimes cap.*) a member of an assembly, esp. a legislature.

Assen (*Dutch* ˈɑsə) *n* a city in the N Netherlands, capital of Drenthe province. Pop.: 52 268 (1994).

assent (əˈsɛnt) *n* **1** agreement, as to a statement, proposal, etc.; acceptance. **2** hesitant agreement; compliance. **3** sanction. ◆ *vb* **4** (*intr;* usually foll. by *to*) to agree or express agreement. **5** *Archaic.* to concede. [C13: from Old French *assenter,* from Latin *assentīrī,* from *sentīre* to think]

assentation (ˌæsɛnˈteɪʃən) *n* servile or hypocritical agreement.

assentient (əˈsɛnʃɪənt) *adj* **1** approving or agreeing. ◆ *n* **2** a person who assents.

assentor (əˈsɛntə) *n Brit. government.* any of the eight voters legally required to endorse the nomination of a candidate in a parliamentary or local election in addition to the nominator and seconder.

assert (əˈsɜːt) *vb* (*tr*) **1** to insist upon (rights, claims, etc.). **2** (*may take a clause as object*) to state to be true; declare categorically. **3** to put (oneself) forward in an insistent manner. [C17: from Latin *asserere* to join to oneself, from *serere* to join] ▸ **asˈserter** *or* **asˈsertor** *n* ▸ **asˈsertible** *adj*

assertion (əˈsɜːʃən) *n* **1** a positive statement, usually made without an attempt at furnishing evidence. **2** the act of asserting.

assertive (əˈsɜːtɪv) *adj* **1** confident and direct in claiming one's rights or putting forward one's views. **2** given to making assertions or bold demands; dogmatic or aggressive. ▸ **asˈsertively** *adv* ▸ **asˈsertiveness** *n*

assertoric (ˌæsɜːˈtɒrɪk) *adj Logic.* **1** (of a statement) stating a fact, as opposed to expressing an evaluative judgment. **2** *Obsolete.* judging what is rather than what may or must be. ◆ Compare **apodeictic** (sense 2), **problematic** (sense 2).

assess (əˈsɛs) *vb* (*tr*) **1** to judge the worth, importance, etc., of; evaluate. **2** (foll. by *at*) to estimate the value of (income, property, etc.) for taxation purposes: *the estate was assessed at three thousand pounds.* **3** to determine the amount of (a fine, tax, damages, etc.). **4** to impose a tax, fine, etc., on (a person or property). [C15: from Old French *assesser,* from Latin *assidēre* to sit beside, from *sedēre* to sit] ▸ **asˈsessable** *adj*

assessment (əˈsɛsmənt) *n* **1** the act of assessing, esp. (in Britain) the evaluation of a student's achievement on a course. **2** an amount determined as payable. **3** a valuation set on taxable property, income, etc. **4** evaluation; estimation.

assessment arrangements *pl n Brit. Education.* nationally standardized plans for pupil assessment in different subjects based on attainment targets at the end of each key stage in the National Curriculum.

assessor (əˈsɛsə) *n* **1** a person who evaluates the merits, importance, etc., of something, esp. (in Britain) work prepared as part of a course of study. **2** a person who values property for taxation. **3** a person who estimates the value of damage to property for insurance purposes. **4** a person with technical expertise called in to advise a court on specialist matters. **5** a person who shares another's position or rank, esp. in an advisory capacity. ▸ **assessorial** (ˌæsɛˈsɔːrɪəl) *adj*

asset (ˈæset) *n* anything valuable or useful: *experience is their main asset.* See also **assets.** [C19: back formation from ASSETS]

asset-backed fund *n* a fund in which the money is invested in property, shares, etc., rather than being deposited with a bank or building society.

assets (ˈæsets) *pl n* **1** *Accounting.* the property and claims against debtors that a business enterprise may apply to discharge its liabilities. Assets may be fixed, current, liquid, or intangible and are shown balanced against liabilities. Compare **liabilities. 2** *Law.* the property available to an executor or administrator for settlement of the debts and payment of legacies of a deceased person's estate. **3** any property owned by a person or firm. [C16 (in the sense: enough to discharge one's liabilities): via Anglo-French from Old French *asez* enough, from Vulgar Latin *ad satis* (unattested), from Latin *ad* up to + *satis* enough]

asset-stripping *n Commerce.* the practice of taking over a failing company at a low price and then selling the assets piecemeal. ▸ **ˈasset-ˌstripper** *n*

asset value *n* the value of a share in a company calculated by dividing the difference between the total of its assets and its liabilities by the number of ordinary shares issued.

asseverate (əˈsɛvəˌreɪt) *vb* (*tr*) to assert or declare emphatically or solemnly. [C18: from Latin *assevērāre* to do (something) earnestly, from *sevērus* SEVERE] ▸ **asˌseverˈation** *n*

assez (ˈæseɪ) *adv Music.* (as part of a musical direction) fairly; rather. [C19: French: enough]

asshole (ˈæsˌhəʊl) *n Slang, derogatory.* the usual U.S. and Canadian word for **arsehole** (see **arse**).

Asshur (ˈæʃʊə) *n* a variant spelling of **Assur.**

assibilate (əˈsɪbɪˌleɪt) *vb Phonetics.* **1** (*intr*) (of a speech sound) to be changed into a sibilant. **2** (*tr*) to pronounce (a speech sound) with or as a sibilant. [C19: from Late Latin *assībilāre* to hiss at, from *sībilāre* to hiss; see SIBILANT] ▸ **asˌsibiˈlation** *n*

assiduity (ˌæsɪˈdjuːɪtɪ) *n, pl* **-ties. 1** constant and close application. **2** (*often pl*) devoted attention.

assiduous (əˈsɪdjʊəs) *adj* **1** hard-working; persevering: *an assiduous researcher.* **2** undertaken with perseverance and care: *assiduous editing.* [C16: from Latin *assiduus* sitting down to (something), from *assidēre* to sit beside, from *sedēre* to sit] ▸ **asˈsiduously** *adv* ▸ **asˈsiduousness** *n*

assign (əˈsaɪn) *vb* (*mainly tr*) **1** to select for and appoint to a post, etc.: *to assign an expert to the job.* **2** to give out or allot (a task, problem, etc.): *to assign advertising to an expert.* **3** to set apart (a place, person, time, etc.) for a particular function or event: *to assign a day for the meeting.* **4** to attribute to a specified cause, origin, or source; ascribe: *to assign a stone cross to the Vikings.* **5** to transfer (one's right, interest, or title to property) to someone else. **6** (*also intr*) *Law.* (formerly) to transfer (property) to trustees so that it may be used for the benefit of creditors. **7** *Military.* to allocate (men or materials) on a permanent basis. Compare **attach** (sense 6). **8** *Computing.* to place (a value corresponding to a variable) in a memory location. ◆ *n* **9** *Law.* a person to whom property is assigned; assignee. [C14: from Old French *assigner,* from Latin *assignāre,* from *signāre* to mark out] ▸ **asˈsignable** *adj* ▸ **asˌsignaˈbility** *n* ▸ **asˈsignably** *adv* ▸ **asˈsigner** *n*

assignat (ˈæsɪgˌnæt, ˌæsɪˈnjɑː; *French* asinja) *n French history.* the paper money issued by the Constituent Assembly in 1789, backed by the confiscated land of the Church and the émigrés. [C18: from French, from Latin *assignātum* something appointed; see ASSIGN]

assignation (ˌæsɪgˈneɪʃən) *n* **1** a secret or forbidden arrangement to meet, esp. one between lovers. **2** the act of assigning; assignment. **3** *Law, chiefly Scot.* another word for **assignment.** [C14: from Old French, from Latin *assignātiō* a marking out; see ASSIGN]

assignee (ˌæsaɪˈniː) *n* **1** *Law.* a person to whom some right, interest, or property is transferred. **2** *Austral. history.* a convict who had undergone assignment.

assignment (əˈsaɪnmənt) *n* **1** something that has been assigned, such as a mission or task. **2** a position or post to which a person is assigned. **3** the act of assigning or state of being assigned. **4** *Law.* **4a** the transfer to another of a right, interest, or title to property, esp. personal property: *assignment of a lease.* **4b** the document effecting such a transfer. **4c** the right, interest, or property transferred. **5** *Law.* (formerly) the transfer, esp. by an insolvent debtor, of property in trust for the benefit of his creditors. **6** *Logic.* a function that associates specific values with each variable in a formal expression. **7** *Austral. history.* a system (1789–1841) whereby a convict could become the unpaid servant of a freeman.

assignor (ˌæsɪˈnɔː) *n Law.* a person who transfers or assigns property.

assimilate (əˈsɪmɪˌleɪt) *vb* **1** (*tr*) to learn (information, a procedure, etc.) and understand it thoroughly. **2** (*tr*) to absorb (food) and incorporate it into the body tissues. **3** (*intr*) to become absorbed, incorporated, or learned and understood. **4** (usually foll. by *into* or *with*) to bring or come into harmony; adjust or become adjusted: *the new immigrants assimilated easily.* **5** (usually foll. by *to* or *with*) to become or cause to become similar. **6** (usually foll. by *to*) *Phonetics.* to change (a consonant) or (of a consonant) to be changed into another under the influence of one adjacent to it: (*n*) *often assimilates to* (ŋ) *before* (*k*), *as in "include".* [C15: from Latin *assimilāre* to make one thing like another, from *similis* like, SIMILAR] ▸ **asˈsimilable** *adj* ▸ **asˈsimilably** *adv* ▸ **asˌsimiˈlation** *n* ▸ **asˈsimilative** *or* **asˈsimilatory** *adj* ▸ **asˈsimiˌlator** *n* ▸ **asˈsimilatively** *adv*

Assiniboine[1] (əˈsɪnɪˌbɔɪn) *n* a river in W Canada, rising in E Saskatchewan and flowing southeast and east to the Red River at Winnipeg. Length: over 860 km (500 miles).

Assiniboine[2] (əˈsɪnəˌbɔɪn) *n* **1** (*pl* **-boine** *or* **-boines**) a member of a North American Indian people living in Alberta, Saskatchewan, and Montana; one of the Sioux peoples. **2** the language of this people, belonging to the Siouan family.

Assisi (*Italian* as'si:zi) *n* a town in central Italy, in Umbria: birthplace of St Francis, who founded the Franciscan religious order here in 1208. Pop.: 24 790 (1990).

assist (ə'sɪst) *vb* **1** to give help or support to (a person, cause, etc.); aid. **2** to work or act as an assistant or subordinate to (another). **3** *Ice hockey.* to help (a teammate) to score, as by passing the puck. **4** (*intr;* foll. by *at*) *Archaic.* to be present; attend. ◆ *n* **5** *U.S. and Canadian.* the act of helping; aid; assistance. **6** *Baseball.* the act of a player who throws or deflects a batted ball in such a way that a team is enabled to put out an opponent. **7** *Sport.* **7a** a pass or other action by a player which enables another player to score a goal. **7b** a credit given for such an action. [C15: from French *assister* to be present, from Latin *assistere* to stand by, from *sistere* to cause to stand, from *stāre* to stand] ▸ **as'sister** *n*

assistance (ə'sɪstəns) *n* **1** help; support. **2** the act of assisting. **3** *Brit. informal.* See **national assistance.**

assistant (ə'sɪstənt) *n* **1a** a person who assists, esp. in a subordinate position. **1b** (*as modifier*): *assistant manager.* **2** See **shop assistant.** ◆ *adj* **3** *Archaic.* helpful or useful as an aid.

assistant professor *n U.S. and Canadian.* a university teacher lower in rank than an associate professor.

assistant referee *n Soccer.* the official name for **linesman** (sense 1).

Assiut (æ'sju:t) *n* a variant spelling of **Asyut.**

assize (ə'saɪz) *n* **1** (in the U.S.) **1a** a sitting of a legislative assembly or administrative body. **1b** an enactment or order of such an assembly. **2** *English history.* a trial or judicial inquest, the writ instituting such inquest, or the verdict. **3** *Scots Law.* **3a** trial by jury. **3b** another name for **jury**[1]. [C13: from Old French *assise* session, from *asseoir* to seat, from Latin *assidēre* to sit beside; see ASSESS]

assizes (ə'saɪzɪz) *pl n* (formerly in England and Wales) the sessions, usually held four times a year, of the principal court in each county, exercising civil and criminal jurisdiction, attended by itinerant judges: replaced in 1971 by crown courts.

assn *abbrev. for* association.

assoc. *abbrev. for:* **1** associate(d). **2** association.

associate *vb* (ə'səʊʃɪ,eɪt, -sɪ-). (usually foll. by *with*) **1** (*tr*) to link or connect in the mind or imagination: *to associate Christmas with fun.* **2** (*intr*) to keep company; mix socially: *to associate with writers.* **3** (*intr*) to form or join an association, group, etc. **4** (*tr; usually passive*) to consider in conjunction; connect: *rainfall is associated with humidity.* **5** (*tr*) to bring (a person, esp. oneself) into friendship, partnership, etc. **6** (*tr; often passive*) to express agreement or allow oneself to be connected (with): *Bertrand Russell was associated with the peace movement.* ◆ *n* (ə'səʊʃɪɪt, -,eɪt, -sɪ-). **7** a person joined with another or others in an enterprise, business, etc.; partner; colleague. **8** a companion or friend. **9** something that usually accompanies another thing; concomitant: *hope is an associate to happiness.* **10** a person having a subordinate position in or admitted to only partial membership of an institution, association, etc. ◆ *adj* (ə'səʊʃɪɪt, -,eɪt, -sɪ-). (*prenominal*) **11** joined with another or others in an enterprise, business, etc.; having equal or nearly equal status: *an associate director.* **12** having partial rights and privileges or subordinate status: *an associate member.* **13** accompanying; concomitant. [C14: from Latin *associāre* to ally with, from *sociāre* to join, from *socius* an ally] ▸ **as'sociable** *adj* ▸ **as'soci,ator** *n* ▸ **as'sociatory** *adj* ▸ **as'sociate,ship** *n*

associated statehood *n* the semi-independent political status of various former British colonies in the Caribbean from 1967 until each became an independent state in the British Commonwealth, by which Britain retained responsibility for defence and some aspects of foreign affairs. The **associated states** were Anguilla, Antigua, Dominica, Grenada, St Kitts-Nevis, St Lucia, and St Vincent and the Grenadines.

associate professor *n* **1** (in the U.S. and Canada) a university teacher lower in rank than a full professor but higher than an assistant professor. **2** (in New Zealand) a senior lecturer holding the rank below professor.

association (ə,səʊsɪ'eɪʃən, -ʃɪ-) *n* **1** a group of people having a common purpose or interest; a society or club. **2** the act of associating or the state of being associated. **3** friendship or companionship: *their association will not last.* **4** a mental connection of ideas, feelings, or sensations: *association of revolution with bloodshed.* **5** *Psychol.* the mental process of linking ideas so that the recurrence of one idea automatically recalls the other. See also **free association.** **6** *Chem.* the formation of groups of molecules and ions, esp. in liquids, held together by weak chemical bonds. **7** *Ecology.* a group of similar plants that grow in a uniform environment and contain one or more dominant species.

association football *n* a more formal name for **soccer.**

associationism (ə,səʊsɪ'eɪʃə,nɪzəm) *n Psychol.* a theory that all mental activity is based on connections between basic mental events, such as sensations and feelings.

association law *n Psychol.* any law governing the association of ideas.

associative (ə'səʊʃɪətɪv) *adj* **1** of, relating to, or causing association or union. **2** *Maths, logic.* **2a** being independent of the grouping of numbers, symbols, or terms within a given set, as in conjunction or in an expression such as $(2 \times 3) \times 4 = 2 \times (3 \times 4)$. **2b** referring to this property: *the associative laws of arithmetic.*

associative cortex *n Anatomy.* the part of the cortex that does not have direct connections to the senses or motor system and is thought to be involved in higher mental processes.

associative storage *n Computing.* a storage device in which the information is identified by content rather than by an address. Also called: **content-addressable storage.**

assoil (ə'sɔɪl) *vb* (*tr*) *Archaic.* **1** to absolve; set free. **2** to atone for. [C13: from Old French *assoldre,* from Latin *absolvere* to ABSOLVE]

assonance ('æsənəns) *n* **1** the use of the same vowel sound with different consonants or the same consonant with different vowels in successive words or stressed syllables, as in a line of verse. Examples are *time* and *light* or *mystery* and *mastery.* **2** partial correspondence; rough similarity. [C18: from French, from Latin *assonāre* to sound, from *sonāre* to sound] ▸ **'assonant** *adj, n* ▸ **assonantal** (,æsə'nænt[ə]l) *adj*

assort (ə'sɔ:t) *vb* **1** (*tr*) to arrange or distribute into groups of the same type; classify. **2** (*intr;* usually foll. by *with*) to fit or fall into a class or group; match. **3** (*tr*) to supply with an assortment of merchandise. **4** (*tr*) to put in the same category as others; group. **5** (*intr;* usually foll. by *with*) *Rare.* to keep company; consort. [C15: from Old French *assorter,* from *sorte* SORT] ▸ **as'sortative** *or* **as'sortive** *adj* ▸ **as'sortatively** *adv* ▸ **as'sorter** *n*

assorted (ə'sɔ:tɪd) *adj* **1** consisting of various kinds mixed together; miscellaneous: *assorted sweets.* **2** arranged in sorts; classified: *assorted categories.* **3** matched; suited (esp. in the combinations **well-assorted, ill-assorted**).

assortment (ə'sɔ:tmənt) *n* **1** a collection or group of various things or sorts. **2** the act of assorting.

ASSR *abbrev. for* (formerly) Autonomous Soviet Socialist Republic.

asst *abbrev. for* assistant.

assuage (ə'sweɪdʒ) *vb* (*tr*) **1** to soothe, moderate, or relieve (grief, pain, etc.). **2** to give relief to (thirst, appetite, etc.); satisfy. **3** to pacify; calm. [C14: from Old French *assouagier,* from Vulgar Latin *assuāviāre* (unattested) to sweeten, from Latin *suāvis* pleasant; see SUAVE] ▸ **as'suagement** *n* ▸ **as'suager** *n* ▸ **assuasive** (ə'sweɪsɪv) *adj*

Assuan *or* **Assouan** (ɑ:s'wɑ:n) *n* variant spellings of **Aswan.**

assume (ə'sju:m) *vb* (*tr*) **1** (*may take a clause as object*) to take for granted; accept without proof; suppose: *to assume that someone is sane.* **2** to take upon oneself; undertake or take on or over (a position, responsibility, etc.): *to assume office.* **3** to pretend to; feign: *he assumed indifference, although the news affected him deeply.* **4** to take or put on; adopt: *the problem assumed gigantic proportions.* **5** to appropriate or usurp (power, control, etc.); arrogate: *the revolutionaries assumed control of the city.* **6** *Christianity.* (of God) to take up (the soul of a believer) into heaven. [C15: from Latin *assūmere* to take up, from *sūmere* to take up, from SUB- + *emere* to take] ▸ **as'sumable** *adj* ▸ **as'sumer** *n*

assumed (ə'sju:md) *adj* **1** false; fictitious: *an assumed name.* **2** taken for granted: *an assumed result.* **3** usurped; arrogated: *an assumed authority.*

assuming (ə'sju:mɪŋ) *adj* **1** expecting too much; presumptuous; arrogant. ◆ *conj* **2** (often foll. by *that*) if it is assumed or taken for granted (that): *even assuming he understands the problem, he will never take any action.*

assumpsit (ə'sʌmpsɪt) *n Law.* (before 1875) an action to recover damages for breach of an express or implied contract or agreement that was not under seal. [C17: from Latin, literally: he has undertaken, from *assūmere* to ASSUME]

assumption (ə'sʌmpʃən) *n* **1** the act of taking something for granted or something that is taken for granted. **2** an assuming of power or possession of something. **3** arrogance; presumption. **4** *Logic.* a statement that is used as the premise of a particular argument but may not be otherwise accepted. Compare **axiom** (sense 4). [C13: from Latin *assūmptiō* a taking up, from *assūmere* to ASSUME] ▸ **as'sumptive** *adj* ▸ **as'sumptively** *adv*

Assumption (ə'sʌmpʃən) *n Christianity.* **1** the taking up of the Virgin Mary (body and soul) into heaven when her earthly life was ended. **2** the feast commemorating this, celebrated by Roman Catholics on Aug. 15.

Assur, Asur ('æsə), **Asshur,** *or* **Ashur** ('æʃʊə) *n* **1** the supreme national god of the ancient Assyrians, chiefly a war god, whose symbol was an archer within a winged disc. **2** one of the chief cities of ancient Assyria, on the River Tigris about 100 km (60 miles) downstream from the present-day city of Mosul.

assurance (ə'ʃʊərəns) *n* **1** a statement, assertion, etc., intended to inspire confidence or give encouragement: *she was helped by his assurance that she would cope.* **2** a promise or pledge of support: *he gave an assurance of help when needed.* **3** freedom from doubt; certainty: *his assurance about his own superiority infuriated her.* **4** forwardness; impudence. **5** *Chiefly Brit.* insurance providing for certainties such as death as contrasted with fire or theft.

Assurbanipal (,æsʊə'bɑ:nɪ,pæl) *n* a variant spelling of **Ashurbanipal.**

assure (ə'ʃʊə) *vb* (*tr; may take a clause as object*) **1** to cause to feel sure or certain; convince: *to assure a person of one's love.* **2** to promise; guarantee: *he assured us that he would come.* **3** to state positively or with assurance. **4** to make (an event) certain; ensure. **5** *Chiefly Brit.* to insure against loss, esp. of life. **6** *Property law.* another word for **convey.** [C14: from Old French *aseürer* to assure, from Medieval Latin *assēcūrāre* to secure or make sure, from *sēcūrus* SECURE] ▸ **as'surable** *adj* ▸ **as'surer** *n*

assured (ə'ʃʊəd) *adj* **1** made certain; sure; guaranteed. **2** self-assured. **3** *Chiefly Brit.* insured, esp. by a life assurance policy. ◆ *n* **4** *Chiefly Brit.* **4a** the beneficiary under a life assurance policy. **4b** the person whose life is insured. ▸ **assuredly** (ə'ʃʊərɪdlɪ) *adv* ▸ **as'suredness** *n*

assured tenancy *n Brit.* an agreement between a government-approved body such as a housing association and a tenant for occupation of a newly-built house or flat at an agreed market rent, under which the tenant has security of tenure. Compare **regulated tenancy.**

assurgent (ə'sɜ:dʒənt) *adj* (of leaves, stems, etc.) curving or growing upwards; rising. [C16: from Latin *assurgere* to rise up, from *surgere* to rise] ▸ **as'surgency** *n*

Assyr. *abbrev. for* Assyrian.

Assyria (ə'sɪrɪə) *n* an ancient kingdom of N Mesopotamia: it established an empire that stretched from Egypt to the Persian Gulf, reaching its greatest extent between 721 and 633 B.C. Its chief cities were Assur and Nineveh.

Assyrian (ə'sɪrɪən) *n* **1** an inhabitant of ancient Assyria. **2** the extinct language of the Assyrians, belonging to the E Semitic subfamily of the Afro-Asiatic family and regarded as a dialect of Akkadian. ♦ *adj* **3** of, relating to, or characteristic of the ancient Assyrians, their language, or culture.

Assyriology (əˌsɪrɪˈɒlədʒɪ) *n* the study of the culture, history, and archaeological remains of ancient Assyria. ▸ **As,syri'ologist** *n*

AST *abbrev. for* Atlantic Standard Time.

astable (eɪˈsteɪbᵊl) *adj* **1** not stable. **2** *Electronics.* capable of oscillating between two states.

Astaire (əˈsteə) *n* **Fred**, real name *Frederick Austerlitz*. 1899–1987, U.S. dancer, singer, and actor, whose films include *Top Hat* (1935), *Swing Time* (1936), and *The Band Wagon* (1953).

Astana (æˈstænə) *n* the capital of Kazakhstan, in the N of the country; replaced Almaty as capital in 1997; an important railway junction. Pop.: 280 200 (1995 est.). Former names: **Akmolinsk** (until 1961), **Tselinograd** (1961–94), **Akmola** (1994–98).

Astarte (æˈstɑːtɪ) *n* a fertility goddess worshipped by the Phoenicians: identified with Ashtoreth of the Hebrews and Ishtar of the Babylonians and Assyrians.

astatic (æˈstætɪk, eɪ-) *adj* **1** not static; unstable. **2** *Physics.* **2a** having no tendency to assume any particular position or orientation. **2b** (of a galvanometer) having two mutually compensating magnets arranged so that the instrument is independent of the earth's magnetic field. **[C19**: from Greek *astatos* unsteady; see A-[1], STATIC**]** ▸ **a'statically** *adv* ▸ **a'stati,cism** *n*

astatide (ˈæstəˌtaɪd) *n Chem.* a binary compound of astatine with a more electropositive element.

astatine (ˈæstc2tiːn, -tɪn) *n* a radioactive element of the halogen series: a decay product of uranium and thorium that occurs naturally in minute amounts and is artificially produced by bombarding bismuth with alpha particles. Symbol: At; atomic no.: 85; half-life of most stable isotope, ^{210}At: 8.1 hours; probable valency: 1,3,5, or 7; melting pt.: 302°C; boiling pt.: 337°C (est.). **[C20**: from Greek *astatos* unstable (see ASTATIC) + -INE[2]**]**

Astbury (ˈæstbərɪ) *n* **John.** 1688–1743, English potter; earliest of the great Staffordshire potters.

aster (ˈæstə) *n* **1** any plant of the genus *Aster*, having white, blue, purple, or pink daisy-like flowers: family *Compositae* (composites). Compare **golden aster. 2 China aster.** a related Chinese plant, *Callistephus chinensis*, widely cultivated for its showy brightly coloured flowers. **3** *Cytology.* a group of radiating cytoplasmic threads that surrounds the centrosome before and during mitosis. **[C18**: from New Latin, from Latin *aster* star, from Greek**]**

-aster *suffix forming nouns.* a person or thing that is inferior or bears only a poor resemblance to what is specified: *poetaster.* **[**from Latin: suffix indicating imperfect resemblance**]**

astereognosis (əˌsterɪəʊgˈnəʊsɪs) *n* inability to recognize objects by touch. **[**A-[1] + STEREO- + -GNOSIS**]**

asteriated (æˈstɪərɪˌeɪtɪd) *adj* (of a crystal, esp. a gemstone) exhibiting a star-shaped figure in transmitted or reflected light.

asterisk (ˈæstərɪsk) *n* **1** a star-shaped character (*) used in printing or writing to indicate a cross-reference to a footnote, an omission, etc. **2a** (in historical linguistics) this sign used to indicate an unattested reconstructed form. **2b** (in descriptive linguistics) this sign used to indicate that an expression is ungrammatical or in some other way unacceptable. ♦ *vb* **3** (*tr*) to mark with an asterisk. **[C17**: from Late Latin *asteriscus* a small star, from Greek *asteriskos*, from *astēr* star**]**

asterism (ˈæstəˌrɪzəm) *n* **1** three asterisks arranged in a triangle (⁂ or ⁂), to draw attention to the text that follows. **2** a starlike effect seen in some minerals and gemstones when viewed by reflected or transmitted light. **3** a cluster of stars or a constellation. **[C16**: from Greek *asterismos* arrangement of constellations, from *astēr* star**]**

astern (əˈstɜːn) *adv, adj* (*postpositive*) *Nautical.* **1** at or towards the stern. **2** with the stern first: *full speed astern!* **3** aft of the stern of a vessel.

asternal (æˈstɜːnᵊl, eɪ-) *adj Anatomy.* **1** not connected or joined to the sternum. **2** lacking a sternum.

asteroid (ˈæstəˌrɔɪd) *n* **1** Also called: **minor planet, planetoid.** any of numerous small celestial bodies that move around the sun mainly between the orbits of Mars and Jupiter. Their diameters range from 930 kilometres (Ceres) to less than one kilometre. **2** Also called: **asteroidean** (ˌæstəˈrɔɪdɪən). any echinoderm of the class *Asteroidea*; a starfish. ♦ *adj also* **asteroidal** (ˌæstəˈrɔɪdᵊl). **3** of, relating to, or belonging to the class *Asteroidea*. **4** shaped like a star. **[C19**: from Greek *asteroeidēs* starlike, from *astēr* a star**]**

asthenia (æsˈθiːnɪə) *or* **astheny** (ˈæsθənɪ) *n Pathol.* an abnormal loss of strength; debility. **[C19**: via New Latin from Greek *astheneia* weakness, from A-[1] + *sthenos* strength**]**

asthenic (æsˈθenɪk) *adj* **1** of, relating to, or having asthenia; weak. **2** (in constitutional psychology) referring to a physique characterized by long limbs and a small trunk: claimed to be associated with a schizoid personality. See also **somatotype.** ♦ *n* **3** a person having long limbs and a small trunk.

asthenopia (ˌæsθɪˈnəʊpɪə) *n* a technical name for **eyestrain. [C19**: from New Latin, from Greek *asthenēs* weak (from A-[1] + *sthenos* strength) + *ōps* eye**]** ▸ **asthenopic** (ˌæsθɪˈnɒpɪk) *adj*

asthenosphere (əsˈθiːnəˌsfɪə, -ˈθen-) *n* a thin semifluid layer of the earth (100–200 km thick), below the outer rigid lithosphere, forming part of the mantle and thought to be able to flow vertically and horizontally, enabling sections of lithosphere to subside, rise, and undergo lateral movement. See also **isostasy. [C20**: from *astheno-*, from Greek *asthenēs* weak + SPHERE**]**

asthma (ˈæsmə) *n* a respiratory disorder, often of allergic origin, characterized by difficulty in breathing, wheezing, and a sense of constriction in the chest. **[C14**: from Greek: laborious breathing, from *azein* to breathe hard**]**

asthmatic (æsˈmætɪk) *adj* **1** of, relating to, or having asthma. ♦ *n* **2** a person who has asthma. ▸ **asth'matically** *adv*

Asti (ˈæstɪ) *n* a town in NW Italy: famous for its sparkling wine (**Asti spumante** (spuːˈmæntɪ)). Pop.: 74 649 (1990).

astigmatic (ˌæstɪgˈmætɪk) *adj* **1** relating to or affected with astigmatism. ♦ *n* **2** a person who has astigmatism. **[C19**: from A-[1] + Greek *stigmat-*, *stigma* spot, focus; see STIGMA**]** ▸ **,astig'matically** *adv*

astigmatism (əˈstɪgməˌtɪzəm) *or* **astigmia** (əˈstɪgmɪə) *n* **1** a defect of a lens resulting in the formation of distorted images; caused by the curvature of the lens being different in different planes. **2** faulty vision resulting from defective curvature of the cornea or lens of the eye.

astilbe (əˈstɪlbɪ) *n* any perennial saxifragaceous plant of the genus *Astilbe* of E Asia and North America: cultivated for their ornamental spikes or panicles of pink or white flowers. **[C19**: New Latin, from Greek: not glittering, from A-[1] + *stilbē*, from *stilbein* to glitter; referring to its inconspicuous individual flowers**]**

astir (əˈstɜː) *adj* (*postpositive*) **1** awake and out of bed. **2** in motion; on the move.

ASTM *abbrev. for* American Society for Testing Materials.

Astolat (ˈæstəʊˌlæt) *n* a town in Arthurian legend: location unknown.

astomatous (æˈstɒmətəs, -ˈstəʊ-) *adj* **1** (of animals) having no mouth. **2** (of plants) having no stomata.

Aston (ˈæstən) *n* **Francis William.** 1877–1945, English physicist and chemist, who developed the first mass spectrograph, using it to investigate the isotopic structures of elements: Nobel prize for chemistry 1922.

astonied (əˈstɒnɪd) *adj Archaic.* stunned; dazed. **[C14**: from *astonyen* to ASTONISH**]**

astonish (əˈstɒnɪʃ) *vb* (*tr*) to fill with amazement; surprise greatly. **[C15**: from earlier *astonyen* (see ASTONIED), from Old French *estoner*, from Vulgar Latin *extonāre* (unattested) to strike with thunder, from Latin *tonāre* to thunder**]** ▸ **a'stonishing** *adj* ▸ **a'stonishingly** *adv*

astonishment (əˈstɒnɪʃmənt) *n* **1** extreme surprise; amazement. **2** a cause of amazement.

Astor (ˈæstə) *n* **1 John Jacob**, 1st Baron Astor of Hever. 1886–1971, British proprietor of *The Times* (1922–66). **2 Nancy (Witcher)**, Viscountess, original name *Nancy Langhorne*. 1879–1964, British Conservative politician, born in the U.S.; the first woman to sit in the British House of Commons.

Astoria (əˈstɔːrɪə) *n* a port in NW Oregon, near the mouth of the Columbia River: founded as a fur-trading post in 1811 by John Jacob Astor. Pop.: 10 069 (1990).

astound (əˈstaʊnd) *vb* (*tr*) to overwhelm with amazement and wonder; bewilder. **[C17**: from *astoned* amazed, from Old French *estoné*, from *estoner* to ASTONISH**]** ▸ **a'stounding** *adj* ▸ **a'stoundingly** *adv*

astr. *or* **astron.** *abbrev. for:* **1** astronomer. **2** astronomical. **3** astronomy.

astraddle (əˈstrædᵊl) *adj* **1** (*postpositive*) with a leg on either side of something. ♦ *prep* **2** astride.

astragal (ˈæstrəgᵊl) *n* **1** *Architect.* **1a** Also called: **bead.** a small convex moulding, usually with a semicircular cross section. **1b** a moulding having the form of a string of beads. **2** *Furniture.* a glazing bar, esp. in a bookcase. **3** *Anatomy.* the ankle or anklebone. **[C17**: from Latin *astragalus*, from Greek *astragalos* anklebone, hence, small round moulding**]**

astragalus (æˈstrægələs) *n, pl* **-li** (-ˌlaɪ). *Anatomy.* another name for **talus**[1]. **[C16**: via New Latin from Latin: ASTRAGAL**]**

astrakhan (ˌæstrəˈkæn, -ˈkɑːn) *n* **1** a fur, usually black or grey, made of the closely curled wool of lambs from Astrakhan. **2** a cloth with curled pile resembling this. **3** (*modifier*) made of such fur or cloth: *an astrakhan collar.*

Astrakhan (ˌæstrəˈkæn, -ˈkɑːn; *Russian* ˈastrəxənj) *n* a city in SE Russia, on the delta of the Volga River, 21 m (70 ft.) below sea level. Pop.: 486 000 (1995 est.).

astral (ˈæstrəl) *adj* **1** relating to, proceeding from, consisting of, or resembling the stars: *an astral body.* **2** *Biology.* of or relating to the aster occurring in dividing cells. **3** *Theosophy.* denoting or relating to a supposed supersensible substance believed to form the material of a second body for each person, taking the form of an aura discernible to certain gifted individuals. **[C17**: from Late Latin *astrālis*, from Latin *astrum* star, from Greek *astron***]** ▸ **'astrally** *adv*

astraphobia *or* **astrophobia** (ˌæstrəˈfəʊbɪə) *n* a fear of thunder and lightning. **[C20**: see ASTRO-, -PHOBIA**]** ▸ **,astra'phobic** *or* **,astro'phobic** *adj*

astray (əˈstreɪ) *adj* (*postpositive*), *adv* **1** out of the correct path or direction. **2** out of the right, good, or expected way; into error. **[C13**: from Old French *estraie* roaming, from *estraier* to STRAY**]**

astrict (əˈstrɪkt) *vb* (*tr*) *Archaic.* to bind, confine, or constrict. **[C16**: from Latin *astrictus* drawn closely together, from *astringere* to tighten, from *stringere* to bind**]** ▸ **as'triction** *n* ▸ **as'trictive** *adj* ▸ **as'trictively** *adv*

astride (əˈstraɪd) *adj* (*postpositive*) **1** with a leg on either side. **2** with the legs far apart. ♦ *prep* **3** with a leg on either side of. **4** with a part on both sides of.

astringent (əˈstrɪndʒənt) *adj* **1** severe; harsh. **2** sharp or invigorating. **3** causing contraction of body tissues, checking blood flow, or restricting secretions of fluids; styptic. ♦ *n* **4** an astringent drug or lotion. **[C16**: from Latin *astringēns* drawing together; see ASTRICT**]** ▸ **as'tringency** *or* **as'tringence** *n* ▸ **as'tringently** *adv*

astro- *combining form.* **1** indicating a heavenly body, star, or star-shaped structure: *astrology; astrocyte.* **2** indicating outer space: *astronautics.* **[**from Greek, from *astron* star**]**

astrobiology (ˌæstrəʊbaɪˈɒlədʒɪ) *n* the branch of biology that investigates the possibility of life on other planets.

astrobleme (ˈæstrəˌbliːm) *n* a mark on the earth's surface, usually circular, formed by a large ancient meteorite impact. **[C20**: from ASTRO- + Greek *blēma* shot, wound**]**

astrobotany (ˌæstrəʊˈbɒtənɪ) *n* the branch of botany that investigates the possibility that plants grow on other planets.

astrochemistry (ˌæstrəʊˈkemɪstrɪ) *n* the study of the chemistry of celestial bodies and space, esp. by means of spectroscopy.

astrocompass (ˌæstrəʊˈkʌmpəs) *n* a navigational instrument for giving directional bearings from the centre of the earth to a particular star. It is carried in long-range aircraft, ships, spacecraft, etc.

astrocyte ('æstrəʊ,saɪt) *n* any of the star-shaped cells in the tissue supporting the brain and spinal cord (neuroglia).

astrodome ('æstrə,dəʊm) *n* a transparent dome on the top of an aircraft, through which observations can be made, esp. of the stars. Also called: **astrohatch.**

astrodynamics (,æstrəʊdaɪ'næmɪks) *n* (*functioning as sing*) the study of the motion of natural and artificial bodies in space.

astrogeology (,æstrəʊdʒɪ'ɒlədʒɪ) *n* the study of the structure, composition, and history of other planets and other bodies in the solar system.

astroid ('æstrɔɪd) *n Maths.* a hypocycloid having four cusps. **[C19:** from ASTRO- + -OID**]**

astrol. *abbrev. for:* **1** astrologer. **2** astrological. **3** astrology.

astrolabe ('æstrə,leɪb) *n* an instrument used by early astronomers to measure the altitude of stars and planets and also as a navigational aid. It consists of a graduated circular disc with a movable sighting device. Compare **sextant. [C13:** via Old French and Medieval Latin from Greek, from *astrolabos* (adj), literally: star-taking, from *astron* star + *lambanein* to take**]**

astrology (ə'strɒlədʒɪ) *n* **1** the study of the motions and relative positions of the planets, sun, and moon, interpreted in terms of human characteristics and activities. **2** the primitive study of celestial bodies, which formed the basis of astronomy. **[C14:** from Old French *astrologie,* from Latin *astrologia,* from Greek, from *astrologos* (originally: astronomer); see ASTRO-, -LOGY**]** ▸ **as'trologer** *or* **as'trologist** *n* ▸ **astrological** (,æstrə'lɒdʒɪkᵊl) *adj* ▸ **,astro'logically** *adv*

astrometry (ə'strɒmɪtrɪ) *n* the branch of astronomy concerned with the measurement of the position and motion of celestial bodies. ▸ **astrometric** (,æstrə'mɛtrɪk) *or* **,astro'metrical** *adj*

astronaut ('æstrə,nɔːt) *n* a person trained for travelling in space. See also **cosmonaut. [C20:** from ASTRO- + *-naut* from Greek *nautēs* sailor, on the model of *aeronaut***]**

astronautics (,æstrə'nɔːtɪks) *n* (*functioning as sing*) the science and technology of space flight. ▸ **,astro'nautic** *or* **,astro'nautical** *adj* ▸ **,astro'nautically** *adv*

astronavigation (,æstrəʊ,nævɪ'geɪʃən) *n* another term for **celestial navigation.** ▸ **,astro'navi,gator** *n*

astronomer (ə'strɒnəmə) *n* a scientist who studies astronomy.

Astronomer Royal *n* an honorary title awarded to an eminent British astronomer: until 1972, the Astronomer Royal was also director of the Royal Greenwich Observatory.

astronomical (,æstrə'nɒmɪkᵊl) *or* **astronomic** *adj* **1** enormously large; immense. **2** of or relating to astronomy. ▸ **,astro'nomically** *adv*

astronomical clock *n* **1** a complex clock showing astronomical phenomena, such as the phases of the moon. **2** any clock showing sidereal time used in observatories.

astronomical telescope *n* any telescope designed and mounted for use in astronomy. Such telescopes usually form inverted images. See **Cassegrain telescope, Newtonian telescope, equatorial mounting.**

astronomical unit *n* a unit of distance used in astronomy equal to the mean distance between the earth and the sun. 1 astronomical unit is equivalent to 1.495×10^{11} metres or about 9.3×10^{7} miles.

astronomical year *n* another name for **solar year.** See **year** (sense 4).

astronomy (ə'strɒnəmɪ) *n* the scientific study of the individual celestial bodies (excluding the earth) and of the universe as a whole. Its various branches include astrometry, astrodynamics, cosmology, and astrophysics. **[C13:** from Old French *astronomie,* from Latin *astronomia,* from Greek; see ASTRO-, -NOMY**]**

astrophotography (,æstrəʊfə'tɒgrəfɪ) *n* the photography of celestial bodies used in astronomy. ▸ **astrophotographic** (,æstrəʊ,fəʊtə'græfɪk) *adj*

astrophysics (,æstrəʊ'fɪzɪks) *n* (*functioning as sing*) the branch of physics concerned with the physical and chemical properties, origin, and evolution of the celestial bodies. ▸ **,astro'physical** *adj* ▸ **,astro'physicist** *n*

astrosphere ('æstrə,sfɪə) *n Cytology.* **1** another name for **centrosome. 2** Also called: **attraction sphere.** the part of the aster excluding the centrosome.

Asturias[1] (æ'stʊərɪ,æs) *n* a region and former kingdom of NW Spain, consisting of a coastal plain and the Cantabrian Mountains: a Christian stronghold against the Moors (8th to 13th centuries); rich mineral resources.

Asturias[2] (æ'stʊərɪ,æs) *n* **Miguel Ángel.** 1899–1974, Guatemalan novelist and poet. His novels include *El Señor Presidente* (1946). Nobel prize for literature 1967.

astute (ə'stjuːt) *adj* having insight or acumen; perceptive; shrewd. **[C17:** from Latin *astūtus* cunning, from *astus* (n) cleverness**]** ▸ **as'tutely** *adv* ▸ **as'tuteness** *n*

Astyanax (æ'staɪə,næks) *n Greek myth.* the young son of Hector and Andromache, who was hurled from the walls of Troy by the Greeks.

astylar (æ'staɪlə, eɪ-) *adj Architect.* without columns or pilasters. **[C19:** from A-[1] + Greek *stulos* pillar**]**

Asunción (*Spanish* asun'sjon) *n* the capital and chief port of Paraguay, on the Paraguay River, 1530 km (950 miles) from the Atlantic. Pop.: 502 426 (1992).

asunder (ə'sʌndə) *adv, adj* (*postpositive*) in or into parts or pieces; apart: *to tear asunder.* **[**Old English *on sundran* apart; see SUNDER**]**

Asur ('æsə) *n* a variant spelling of **Assur.**

ASW *abbrev. for* antisubmarine warfare.

Aswan, Assuan, *or* **Assouan** (ɑːs'wɑːn) *n* an ancient town in SE Egypt, on the Nile, just below the First Cataract. Pop.: 220 000 (1992 est.). Ancient name: **Syene.**

Aswan High Dam *n* a dam on the Nile forming a reservoir (Lake Nasser) extending 480 km (300 miles) from the First to the Third Cataracts: opened in 1971, it was built 6 km (4 miles) upstream from the old **Aswan Dam** (built in 1902 and twice raised). Height of dam: 109 m (365 ft.).

aswarm (ə'swɔːm) *adj* (*postpositive*) filled, esp. with moving things; swarming: *flower beds aswarm with bees.*

asyllabic (,æsɪ'læbɪk, ,eɪ-) *adj* not functioning in the manner of a syllable.

asylum (ə'saɪləm) *n* **1** a safe or inviolable place of refuge, esp. as formerly offered by the Christian Church to criminals, outlaws, etc.; sanctuary (often in the phrase **give asylum to**). **2** shelter; refuge. **3** *International law.* refuge afforded to a person whose extradition is sought by a foreign government: *political asylum.* **4** *Obsolescent.* an institution for the shelter, treatment, or confinement of individuals, esp. a mental hospital (formerly termed **lunatic asylum**). **[C15:** via Latin from Greek *asulon* refuge, from *asulos* that may not be seized, from A-[1] + *sulon* right of seizure**]**

asymmetric (,æsɪ'mɛtrɪk, ,eɪ-) *or* **asymmetrical** *adj* **1** not symmetrical; lacking symmetry; misproportioned. **2** *Chem.* **2a** (of a molecule) having its atoms and radicals arranged unsymmetrically. **2b** (of a carbon atom) attached to four different atoms or radicals so that stereoisomerism results. **2c** involving the isolation of an optically active compound from a racemic mixture: *asymmetric synthesis.* **3** *Electrical engineering.* (of conductors) having different conductivities depending on the direction of current flow, as of diodes. **4** *Aeronautics.* having unequal thrust, as caused by an inoperative engine in a twin-engined aircraft. **5** *Logic, maths.* (of a relation) never holding between a pair of values *x* and *y* when it holds between *y* and *x*, as "*... is the father of ...*". Compare **symmetric** (sense 1), **antisymmetric, nonsymmetric.** ▸ **,asym'metrically** *adv*

asymmetric bars *pl n Gymnastics.* **a** (*functioning as pl*) a pair of wooden or fibreglass bars placed parallel to each other but set at different heights, for various exercises. **b** (*functioning as sing*) an event in a gymnastic competition in which competitors exercise on such bars.

asymmetric time *n* musical time consisting of an odd number of beats in each bar divided into uneven combinations, such as 3 + 2, 4 + 3, 2 + 3 + 2, etc.

asymmetry (æ'sɪmɪtrɪ, eɪ-) *n* lack or absence of symmetry in spatial arrangements or in mathematical or logical relations.

asymptomatic (æ,sɪmptə'mætɪk, eɪ-) *adj* (of a disease or suspected disease) without symptoms; providing no subjective evidence of existence. ▸ **a,symp-to'matically** *adv*

asymptote ('æsɪm,təʊt) *n* a straight line that is closely approached by a plane curve so that the perpendicular distance between them decreases to zero as the distance from the origin increases to infinity. **[C17:** from Greek *asumptōtos* not falling together, from A-[1] + SYN- + *ptōtos* inclined to fall, from *piptein* to fall**]**

asymptotic (,æsɪm'tɒtɪk) *or* **asymptotical** *adj* **1** of or referring to an asymptote. **2** (of a function, series, formula, etc.) approaching a given value or condition, as a variable or an expression containing a variable approaches a limit, usually infinity. ▸ **,asymp'totically** *adv*

asynapsis (,eɪsɪn'æpsɪs) *n Biology.* failure of pairing of chromosomes at meiosis.

asynchronism (æ'sɪŋkrə,nɪzəm, eɪ-) *n* a lack of synchronism; occurrence at different times. ▸ **a'synchronous** *adj* ▸ **a'synchronously** *adv*

asyndetic (,æsɪn'dɛtɪk) *adj* **1** (of a catalogue or index) without cross references. **2** (of a linguistic construction) having no conjunction, as in *I came, I saw, I conquered.* ▸ **,asyn'detically** *adv*

asyndeton (æ'sɪndɪtən) *n, pl* **-deta** (-dɪtə). **1** the omission of a conjunction between the parts of a sentence. **2** an asyndetic construction. Compare **syndeton. [C16:** from New Latin, from Greek *asundeton,* from *asundetos* unconnected, from A-[1] + *sundein* to bind together**]**

asynergia (,æsɪ'nɜːdʒɪə) *or* **asynergy** (ə,sɪnədʒɪ) *n Pathol.* lack of coordination between muscles or parts, as occurs in cerebellar disease.

asystole (ə'sɪstəlɪ) *n Pathol.* the absence of heartbeat; cardiac arrest. ▸ **asystolic** (,æsɪs'tɒlɪk) *adj*

Asyut *or* **Assiut** (æ'sjuːt) *n* an ancient city in central Egypt, on the Nile. Pop.: 321 000 (1992 est.). Ancient Greek name: **Lycopolis.**

at[1] (æt) *prep* **1** used to indicate location or position: *are they at the table?; staying at a small hotel.* **2** towards; in the direction of: *looking at television; throwing stones at windows.* **3** used to indicate position in time: *come at three o'clock.* **4** engaged in; in a state of (being): *children at play; stand at ease; he is at his most charming today.* **5** (in expressions concerned with habitual activity) during the passing of (esp. in the phrase **at night**): *he used to work at night.* **6** for; in exchange for: *it's selling at four pounds.* **7** used to indicate the object of an emotion: *angry at the driver; shocked at his behaviour.* **8 where it's at.** *Slang.* the real place of action. **[**Old English *æt;* related to Old Norse *at* to, Latin *ad* to**]**

at[2] (ɑːt, æt) *n, pl* **at.** a Laotian monetary unit worth one hundredth of a kip. **[**from Thai**]**

At 1 *the chemical symbol for* astatine. **2** Also: **A** *symbol for* ampere-turn.

AT *abbrev. for* attainment target.

at. *abbrev. for:* **1** Also: **atm.** atmosphere (unit of pressure). **2** atomic.

Atabrine ('ætə,briːn, -brɪn) *n* See **Atebrin.**

Atacama Desert (*Spanish* ata'kama) *n* a desert region along the W coast of South America, mainly in N Chile: a major source of nitrates. Area: about 80 000 sq. km (31 000 sq. miles).

atactic (eɪ'tæktɪk) *adj* **1** *Chem.* (of a polymer) having random sequence of the stereochemical arrangement of groups on carbon atoms in the chain; not stereospecific. **2** *Pathol.* relating to or displaying ataxia.

ataghan ('ætə,gæn) *n* a variant of **yataghan.**

Atahualpa (,ætə'wɑːlpə) *or* **Atabalipa** (,ætə'bɑːlɪpə) *n* ?1500–33, the last Inca emperor of Peru (1525–33), who was put to death by the Spanish under Pizarro.

Atalanta (,ætə'læntə) *n Greek myth.* a maiden who agreed to marry any man who could defeat her in a running race. She lost to Hippomenes when she paused to pick up three golden apples that he had deliberately dropped.

ataman ('ætəmən) *n, pl* **-mans.** an elected leader of the Cossacks; hetman. [from Russian, from Polish *hetman,* from German *Hauptmann* (literally: head man)]

ataractic (ˌætə'ræktɪk) *or* **ataraxic** (ˌætə'ræksɪk) *adj* **1** able to calm or tranquillize. ◆ *n* **2** an ataractic drug.

ataraxia (ˌætə'ræksɪə) *or* **ataraxy** ('ætəˌræksɪ) *n* calmness or peace of mind; emotional tranquillity. [C17: from Greek: serenity, from *ataraktos* undisturbed, from A-[1] + *tarassein* to trouble]

Atatürk ('ætəˌtɜːk) *n* **Kemal** (kɛ'mɑːl), real name *Mustafa Kemal.* 1881–1938, Turkish general and statesman; founder of the Turkish republic and president of Turkey (1923–38), who westernized and secularized the country.

atavism ('ætəˌvɪzəm) *n* **1** the recurrence in a plant or animal of certain primitive characteristics that were present in an ancestor but have not occurred in intermediate generations. **2** reversion to a former or more primitive type. [C19: from French *atavisme,* from Latin *atavus* strictly: great-grandfather's grandfather, probably from *atta* daddy + *avus* grandfather] ▸ **'atavist** *n* ▸ **ˌata'vistic** *or* **atavic** (ə'tævɪk) *adj* ▸ **ˌata'vistically** *adv*

ataxia (ə'tæksɪə) *or* **ataxy** (ə'tæksɪ) *n Pathol.* lack of muscular coordination. [C17: via New Latin from Greek: lack of coordination, from A-[1] + *-taxia,* from *tassein* to put in order] ▸ **a'taxic** *or* **a'tactic** *adj*

Atbara ('ætbərə, æt'bɑː-) *n* **1** a town in NE Sudan. Pop.: 73 000 (latest est.). **2** a river in NE Africa, rising in N Ethiopia and flowing through E Sudan to the Nile at Atbara. Length: over 800 km (500 miles).

ATC *abbrev. for:* **1** air-traffic control. **2** (in Britain) Air Training Corps.

ate (ɛt, eɪt) *vb* the past tense of **eat.**

Ate ('eɪtɪ, 'ɑːtɪ) *n Greek myth.* a goddess who makes men blind so that they will blunder into guilty acts. [C16: via Latin from Greek *atē* a rash impulse]

-ate[1] *suffix.* **1** (*forming adjectives*) possessing; having the appearance or characteristics of: *fortunate; palmate; Latinate.* **2** (*forming nouns*) a chemical compound, esp. a salt or ester of an acid: *carbonate; stearate.* **3** (*forming nouns*) the product of a process: *condensate.* **4** forming verbs from nouns and adjectives: *hyphenate; rusticate.* [from Latin *-ātus,* past participial ending of verbs ending in *-āre*]

-ate[2] *suffix forming nouns.* denoting office, rank, or a group having a certain function: *episcopate; electorate.* [from Latin *-ātus,* suffix (fourth declension) of collective nouns]

Atebrin ('ætəbrɪn) *or U.S.* **Atabrine** ('ætəˌbriːn, -brɪn) *n Trademark.* proprietary names for **mepacrine.**

atelectasis (ˌætə'lɛktəsɪs) *n* **1** failure of the lungs to expand fully at birth. **2** collapse of the lung or a part of the lung, usually caused by bronchial obstruction. [C19: New Latin, from Greek *atelēs* imperfect + *ektasis* extension]

atelier ('ætəlˌjeɪ; *French* atəlje) *n* an artist's studio or workshop. [C17: from Old French *astelier* workshop, from *astele* chip of wood, from Latin *astula* splinter, from *assis* board]

a tempo (ɑː 'tɛmpəʊ) *Music.* ◆ *adj, adv* **1** to the original tempo. ◆ *n* **2** a passage thus marked. ◆ Also: **tempo primo.** [Italian: in (the original) time]

Aten *or* **Aton** ('ɑːtᵊn) *n* (in ancient Egypt) the solar disc worshipped as the sole god in the reign of Akhenaten.

Atget (*French* adʒɛ) *n* **(Jean) Eugène Auguste.** 1856–1927, French photographer, noted for his pictures of Parisian life.

Athabaska *or* **Athabasca** (ˌæθə'bæskə) *n* **1 Lake.** a lake in W Canada, in NW Saskatchewan and NE Alberta. Area: about 7770 sq. km (3000 sq. miles). **2** a river in W Canada, rising in the Rocky Mountains and flowing northeast to Lake Athabaska. Length: 1230 km (765 miles).

Athamas ('æθəˌmæs) *n Greek myth.* a king of Orchomenus in Boeotia; the father of Phrixus and Helle by his first wife Nephele, whom he deserted for Ino.

Athanasian Creed (ˌæθə'neɪʃən) *n Christianity.* a profession of faith widely used in the Western Church which, though formerly attributed to Athanasius, probably originated in Gaul between 381 and 428 A.D.

Athanasius (ˌæθə'neɪʃəs) *n* **Saint.** ?296–373 A.D., patriarch of Alexandria who championed Christian orthodoxy against Arianism. Feast day: May 2. ▸ **ˌAtha'nasian** *adj*

Athapascan, Athapaskan (ˌæθə'pæskən) *or* **Athabascan, Athabaskan** (ˌæθə'bæskən) *n* **1** a group of North American Indian languages belonging to the Na-Dene phylum, including Apache and Navaho. **2** a speaker of one of these languages. [from Cree *athapaskaaw* scattered grass or reeds]

Atharva-Veda (ə'tɑːvə'veɪdə) *n Hinduism.* the fourth and latest Veda, largely consisting of priestly spells and incantations.

atheism ('eɪθɪˌɪzəm) *n* rejection of belief in God or gods. [C16: from French *athéisme,* from Greek *atheos* godless, from A-[1] + *theos* god] ▸ **'atheist** *n, adj* ▸ **ˌathe'istic** *or* **ˌathe'istical** *adj* ▸ **ˌathe'istically** *adv*

atheling ('æθəlɪŋ) *n* (in Anglo-Saxon England) a prince of any of the royal dynasties. [Old English *ætheling,* from *æthelu* noble family + -ING[3]; related to Old High German *adaling,* Old Norse *öthlingr*]

Athelstan ('æθəlstən) *n* ?895–939 A.D., king of Wessex and Mercia (924–939 A.D.), who extended his kingdom to include most of England.

athematic (ˌæθɪ'mætɪk) *adj* **1** *Music.* not based on themes. **2** *Linguistics.* (of verbs) having a suffix attached immediately to the stem, without an intervening vowel.

Athena (ə'θiːnə) *or* **Athene** (ə'θiːnɪ) *n Greek myth.* a virgin goddess of wisdom, practical skills, and prudent warfare. She was born, fully armed, from the head of Zeus. Also called: **Pallas Athena, Pallas.** Roman counterpart: **Minerva.**

athenaeum *or U.S.* **atheneum** (ˌæθɪ'niːəm) *n* **1** an institution for the promotion of learning. **2** a building containing a reading room or library, esp. one used by such an institution. [C18: from Late Latin, from Greek *Athēnaion* temple of Athene, frequented by poets and teachers]

Athenaeum *or U.S.* (*sometimes*) **Atheneum** (ˌæθɪ'niːəm) *n* **1** (in ancient Greece) a building sacred to the goddess Athena, esp. the Athenian temple that served as a gathering place for the learned. **2** (in imperial Rome) the academy of learning established near the Forum in about 135 A.D. by Hadrian.

Athenian (ə'θiːnɪən) *n* **1** a native or inhabitant of Athens. ◆ *adj* **2** of or relating to Athens.

Athens ('æθɪnz) *n* the capital of Greece, in the southeast near the Saronic Gulf: became capital after independence in 1834; ancient city-state, most powerful in the 5th century B.C.; contains the hill citadel of the Acropolis. Pop.: 772 072 (1991). Greek name: **Athinai** (a'θinɛ).

athermancy (æ'θɜːmənsɪ) *n* an inability to transmit radiant heat or infrared radiation. Also called: **adiathermancy.** [C19: from Greek *athermantos* not heated, from A-[1] + *thermainein* to heat, from *thermē* heat; compare DIATHERMANCY]

athermanous (æ'θɜːmənəs) *adj* capable of stopping radiant heat or infrared radiation.

atherogenic (ˌæθərəʊ'dʒɛnɪk) *adj* causing atheroma. ▸ **ˌathero'genesis** *n*

atheroma (ˌæθə'rəʊmə) *n, pl* **-mas** *or* **-mata** (-mətə). *Pathol.* a fatty deposit on or within the inner lining of an artery, often causing an obstruction to the blood flow. [C18: via Latin from Greek *athērōma* tumour full of matter resembling gruel, from *athēra* gruel] ▸ **atheromatous** (ˌæθə'rɒmətəs, -'rəʊ-) *adj*

atherosclerosis (ˌæθərəʊsklɪə'rəʊsɪs) *n, pl* **-ses** (-siːz). a degenerative disease of the arteries characterized by patchy thickening of the inner lining of the arterial walls, caused by deposits of fatty material; a form of arteriosclerosis. See **atheroma.** [C20: from New Latin, from Greek *athēra* gruel (see ATHEROMA) + SCLEROSIS] ▸ **atherosclerotic** (ˌæθərəʊsklɪə'rɒtɪk) *adj*

Atherton ('æθətᵊn) *n* **Mike,** full name *Michael Andrew Atherton.* born 1968, English cricketer: plays for Lancashire (1987–) and England (1989–); captain of England (1993–98).

athetosis (ˌæθə'təʊsɪs) *n Pathol.* a condition characterized by uncontrolled rhythmic writhing movement, esp. of fingers, hands, head, and tongue, caused by cerebral lesion. [C19: from Greek *athetos* not in place, from A-[1] + *tithenai* to place] ▸ **'atheˌtoid** *adj*

athirst (ə'θɜːst) *adj* (*postpositive*) **1** (often foll. by *for*) having an eager desire; longing. **2** *Archaic.* thirsty.

athlete ('æθliːt) *n* **1** a person trained to compete in sports or exercises involving physical strength, speed, or endurance. **2** a person who has a natural aptitude for physical activities. **3** *Chiefly Brit.* a competitor in track and field events. [C18: from Latin via Greek *athlētēs,* from *athlein* to compete for a prize, from *athlos* a contest]

athlete's foot *n* a fungal infection of the skin of the foot, esp. between the toes and on the soles. Technical name: **tinea pedis.**

athletic (æθ'lɛtɪk) *adj* **1** physically fit or strong; muscular or active. **2** of, relating to, or suitable for an athlete or for athletics. **3** of or relating to a person with a muscular and well-proportioned body. See also **somatotype.** ▸ **ath'letically** *adv* ▸ **ath'leticism** *n*

athletics (æθ'lɛtɪks) *n* (*functioning as pl or sing*) **1a** track and field events. **1b** (*as modifier*): *an athletics meeting.* **2** sports or exercises engaged in by athletes. **3** the theory or practice of athletic activities and training.

athletic support *n* a more formal term for **jockstrap.**

athodyd ('æθəʊˌdaɪd) *n* another name for **ramjet.** [C20: from *a*(*ero*)-*th*(*erm*)*ody*(*namic*) *d*(*uct*)]

Atholl brose ('æθəl) *n Scot.* a mixture of whisky and honey left to ferment before consumption. [C19: after *Atholl,* a district of central Scotland]

at-home *n* **1** another name for **open day. 2** a social gathering in a person's home.

Athos ('æθɒs, 'eɪ-) *n* **Mount.** a mountain in NE Greece, in Macedonia Central region: site of the Monastic Republic of Mount Athos, autonomous since 1927 and inhabited by Greek Orthodox Basilian monks in 20 monasteries founded in the 10th century. Pop.: 1557 (1991).

athwart (ə'θwɔːt) *adv* **1** transversely; from one side to another. ◆ *prep* **2** across the path or line of (esp. a ship). **3** in opposition to; against. [C15: from A-[2] + THWART]

athwartships (ə'θwɔːtˌʃɪps) *adv Nautical.* from one side to the other of a vessel at right angles to the keel.

-atic *suffix forming adjectives.* of the nature of the thing specified: *problematic.* [from French *-atique,* from Greek *-atikos*]

atilt (ə'tɪlt) *adv, adj* (*postpositive*) **1** in a tilted or inclined position. **2** *Archaic.* in or as if in a joust.

-ation *suffix forming nouns.* indicating an action, process, state, condition, or result: *arbitration; cogitation; hibernation; moderation.* Compare **-ion, -tion.** [from Latin *-ātiōn-,* suffix of abstract nouns, from *-ātus* -ATE[1] + *-iōn* -ION]

-ative *suffix forming adjectives.* of, relating to, or tending to: *authoritative; decorative; informative.* [from Latin *-ātīvus,* from *ātus* -ATE[1] + *īvus* -IVE]

Atkinson ('ætkɪnsᵊn) *n* Sir **Harry Albert.** 1831–92, New Zealand statesman, born in England: prime minister of New Zealand (1876–77; 1883–84; 1887–91).

Atlanta (æt'læntə) *n* a city in N Georgia: the state capital. Pop.: 396 052 (1994 est.).

Atlantean (ˌætlæn'tiːən, æt'læntɪən) *adj* **1** *Literary.* of, relating to, or like Atlas; extremely strong. **2** of or connected with Atlantis.

atlantes (ət'læntiːz) *n* the plural of **atlas** (sense 4).

Atlantic (ət'læntɪk) *n* **1 the.** short for the **Atlantic Ocean.** ◆ *adj* **2** of or relating to or bordering the Atlantic Ocean. **3** of or relating to Atlas or the Atlas

Mountains. [C15: from Latin *Atlanticus,* from Greek (*pelagos*) *Atlantikos* (the sea) of Atlas (so called because it lay beyond the Atlas Mountains)]

Atlantic Charter *n* the joint declaration issued by F. D. Roosevelt and Winston Churchill on Aug. 14, 1941, consisting of eight principles to guide a postwar settlement.

Atlantic City *n* a resort in SE New Jersey on Absecon Beach, an island on the Atlantic coast. Pop.: 37 986 (1990).

Atlantic Intracoastal Waterway *n* a system of inland and coastal waterways along the Atlantic coast of the U.S. from Cape Cod to Florida Bay. Length: 2495 km (1550 miles).

Atlanticism (ət'læntɪˌsɪzəm) *n* advocacy of close cooperation in military, political, and economic matters between Western Europe, esp. the UK, and the U.S. ▸ **At'lanticist** *n*

Atlantic Ocean *n* the world's second largest ocean, bounded in the north by the Arctic, in the south by the Antarctic, in the west by North and South America, and in the east by Europe and Africa. Greatest depth: 9220 m (30 246 ft.). Area: about 81 585 000 sq. km (31 500 000 sq. miles).

Atlantic Provinces *pl n* **the.** certain of the Canadian provinces with coasts facing the Gulf of St Lawrence or the Atlantic: New Brunswick, Nova Scotia, Prince Edward Island, and Newfoundland.

Atlantic Standard Time *n* the local time used in eastern Canada, four hours behind Greenwich Mean Time. Abbrev.: **AST.**

Atlantis (ət'læntɪs) *n* (in ancient legend) a continent said to have sunk beneath the Atlantic Ocean west of the Straits of Gibraltar.

atlas ('ætləs) *n* **1** a collection of maps, usually in book form. **2** a book of charts, graphs, etc., illustrating aspects of a subject: *an anatomical atlas.* **3** *Anatomy.* the first cervical vertebra, attached to and supporting the skull in man. Compare **axis**[1] (sense 3). **4** (*pl* **atlantes**) *Architect.* another name for **telamon. 5** a standard size of drawing paper, 26 × 17 inches. [C16: via Latin from Greek; first applied to maps, from depictions of Atlas supporting the heavens in 16th-century collections of maps]

Atlas ('ætləs) *n* **1** *Greek myth.* a Titan compelled to support the sky on his shoulders as punishment for rebelling against Zeus. **2** a U.S. intercontinental ballistic missile, also used in launching spacecraft. **3** *Astronomy.* a small satellite of Jupiter, discovered in 1980.

Atlas Mountains *pl n* a mountain system of N Africa, between the Mediterranean and the Sahara. Highest peak: Mount Toubkal, 4165 m (13 664 ft.).

Atli ('ɑːtlɪ) *n Norse legend.* a king of the Huns who married Gudrun for her inheritance and was slain by her after he killed her brothers.

ATM *abbrev. for:* **1** automated teller machine. **2** asynchronous transfer mode: used in digital communications, etc.

atm. *abbrev. for:* **1** Also: **at.** atmosphere (unit of pressure). **2** atmospheric.

atman ('ɑːtmən) *n Hinduism.* **1** the personal soul or self; the thinking principle as manifested in consciousness. **2** Brahman considered as the Universal Soul, the great Self or Person that dwells in the entire created order. [from Sanskrit *ātman* breath; compare Old High German *ātum* breath]

atmo- *combining form.* air or vapour: *atmometer; atmosphere.* [via New Latin from Greek *atmos* vapour]

atmolysis (æt'mɒlɪsɪs) *n, pl* **-ses** (-ˌsiːz). a method of separating gases that depends on their differential rates of diffusion through a porous substance.

atmometer (æt'mɒmɪtə) *n* an instrument for measuring the rate of evaporation of water into the atmosphere. Also called: **evaporimeter, evaporometer.** ▸ **at'mometry** *n*

atmosphere ('ætməsˌfɪə) *n* **1** the gaseous envelope surrounding the earth or any other celestial body. See also **troposphere, stratosphere, mesosphere,** and **ionosphere. 2** the air or climate in a particular place: *the atmosphere was thick with smoke.* **3** a general pervasive feeling or mood: *an atmosphere of elation.* **4** the prevailing tone or mood of a novel, symphony, painting, or other work of art. **5** a special mood or character associated with a place. **6** any local gaseous environment or medium: *an inert atmosphere.* **7** Abbrevs.: **at., atm.** a unit of pressure; the pressure that will support a column of mercury 760 mm high at 0°C at sea level. 1 atmosphere is equivalent to 101 325 newtons per square metre or 14.72 pounds per square inch. ▸ **ˌatmos'pheric** *or* **ˌatmos'pherical** *adj* ▸ **ˌatmos'pherically** *adv*

atmospheric perspective *n* another term for **aerial perspective.**

atmospheric pressure *n* the pressure exerted by the atmosphere at the earth's surface. It has an average value of 1 atmosphere.

atmospherics (ˌætməs'fɛrɪks) *pl n* **1** electrical disturbances produced in the atmosphere by natural causes such as lightning. **2** radio interference, heard as crackling or hissing in receivers, caused by electrical disturbance.

ATN *abbrev. for:* **1** arc tangent. **2** augmented transition network.

at. no. *abbrev. for* atomic number.

A to J (in New Zealand) *abbrev. for* Appendices to Journals (of the House of Representatives or Parliament).

atoll ('ætɒl, ə'tɒl) *n* a circular coral reef or string of coral islands surrounding a lagoon. [C17: from *atollon,* native name in the Maldive Islands]

atom ('ætəm) *n* **1a** the smallest quantity of an element that can take part in a chemical reaction. **1b** this entity as a source of nuclear energy: *the power of the atom.* See also **atomic structure. 2** any entity regarded as the indivisible building block of a theory. **3** the hypothetical indivisible particle of matter postulated by certain ancient philosophers as the fundamental constituent of matter. See also **atomism. 4** a very small amount or quantity; minute fragment: *to smash something to atoms; there is not an atom of truth in his allegations.* [C16: via Old French and Latin, from Greek *atomos* (n), from *atomos* (adj) that cannot be divided, from A-[1] + *temnein* to cut]

atomic (ə'tɒmɪk) *adj* **1** of, using, or characterized by atomic bombs or atomic energy: *atomic warfare.* **2** of, related to, or comprising atoms: *atomic hydrogen.* **3** extremely small; minute. **4** *Logic.* (of a sentence, formula, etc.) having no internal structure at the appropriate level of analysis. In predicate calculus, *Fa* is an **atomic sentence** and *Fx* an **atomic predicate.** ▸ **a'tomically** *adv*

atomic age *n* **the.** the current historical period, initiated by the development of the first atomic bomb towards the end of World War II and now marked by a balance of power between nations possessing the hydrogen bomb and the use of nuclear power as a source of energy.

atomic bomb *or* **atom bomb** *n* a type of bomb in which the energy is provided by nuclear fission. Uranium-235 and plutonium-239 are the isotopes most commonly used in atomic bombs. Also called: **A-bomb, fission bomb.** Compare **fusion bomb.**

atomic clock *n* an extremely accurate clock in which an electrical oscillator is controlled by the natural vibrations of an atomic or molecular system such as caesium or ammonia.

atomic cocktail *n* an aqueous solution of radioactive substance, such as sodium iodide, administered orally as part of the treatment for cancer.

atomic energy *n* another name for **nuclear energy.**

Atomic Energy Authority *n* (in Britain) a government body established in 1954 to control research and development in atomic energy. Abbrev.: **AEA.**

Atomic Energy Commission *n* (in the U.S.) a federal board established in 1946 to administer and develop domestic atomic energy programmes. Abbrev.: **AEC.**

atomic heat *n* the product of an element's atomic weight and its specific heat (capacity).

atomicity (ˌætə'mɪsɪtɪ) *n* **1** the state of being made up of atoms. **2** the number of atoms in the molecules of an element. **3** a less common name for **valency.**

atomic mass *n Chem.* **1** the mass of an isotope of an element in atomic mass units. **2** short for **relative atomic mass;** see **atomic weight.**

atomic mass unit *n* a unit of mass used to express atomic and molecular weights that is equal to one twelfth of the mass of an atom of carbon-12. It is equivalent to 1.66×10^{-27} kg. Abbrev.: **amu.** Also called: **unified atomic mass unit, dalton.**

atomic number *n* the number of protons in the nucleus of an atom of an element. Abbrev.: **at. no.** Symbol: *Z* Also called: **proton number.**

atomic pile *n* the original name for a **nuclear reactor.**

atomic power *n* another name for **nuclear power.**

atomic structure *n* the concept of an atom as a central positively charged nucleus consisting of protons and neutrons surrounded by a number of electrons. The number of electrons is equal to the number of protons: the whole entity is thus electrically neutral.

atomic theory *n* **1** any theory in which matter is regarded as consisting of atoms, esp. that proposed by John Dalton postulating that elements are composed of atoms that can combine in definite proportions to form compounds. **2** the current concept of the atom as an entity with a definite structure. See **atomic structure.**

atomic volume *n* the atomic weight (relative atomic mass) of an element divided by its density.

atomic weight *n* the former name for **relative atomic mass.** Abbrev.: **at. wt.**

atomism ('ætəˌmɪzəm) *n* **1** an ancient philosophical theory that the ultimate constituents of the universe are atoms: see **atom** (sense 3). See also **Democritus, Lucretius. 2a** any of a number of theories that hold that some objects or phenomena can be explained as constructed out of a small number of distinct types of simple indivisible entities. **2b** any theory that holds that an understanding of the parts is logically prior to an understanding of the whole. Compare **holism** (sense 3). **3** *Psychol.* the theory that experiences and mental states are composed of elementary units. ▸ **'atomist** *n, adj* ▸ **ˌatom'istic** *or* **ˌatom'istical** *adj* ▸ **ˌatom'istically** *adv*

atomize *or* **atomise** ('ætəˌmaɪz) *vb* **1** to separate or be separated into free atoms. **2** to reduce (a liquid or solid) to fine particles or spray or (of a liquid or solid) to be reduced in this way. **3** (*tr*) to destroy by weapons, esp. nuclear weapons. ▸ **ˌatomi'zation** *or* **ˌatomi'sation** *n*

atomizer *or* **atomiser** ('ætəˌmaɪzə) *n* a device for reducing a liquid to a fine spray, such as the nozzle used to feed oil into a furnace or an enclosed bottle with a fine outlet used to spray perfumes or medicines.

atom smasher *n Physics.* the nontechnical name for **accelerator** (sense 2).

atomy[1] ('ætəmɪ) *n, pl* **-mies.** *Archaic.* **1** an atom or minute particle. **2** a minute creature. [C16: from Latin *atomī* atoms, but used as if singular; see ATOM]

atomy[2] ('ætəmɪ) *n, pl* **-mies.** an obsolete word for **skeleton.** [C16: from mistaken division of ANATOMY (as if *an atomy*)]

Aton ('ɑːtᵊn) *n* a variant spelling of **Aten.**

atonal (eɪ'təʊnᵊl, æ-) *adj Music.* having no established key. Compare **tonal** (sense 2). ▸ **a'tonalism** *n* ▸ **a'tonally** *adv*

atonality (ˌeɪtəʊ'nælɪtɪ, ˌæ-) *n* **1** absence of or disregard for an established musical key in a composition. **2** the principles of composition embodying this and providing a radical alternative to the diatonic system. ◆ Compare **tonality.**

atone (ə'təʊn) *vb* **1** (*intr;* foll. by *for*) to make amends or reparation (for a crime, sin, etc.). **2** (*tr*) to expiate: *to atone a guilt with repentance.* **3** *Obsolete.* to be in or bring into agreement. [C16: back formation from ATONEMENT] ▸ **a'tonable** *or* **a'toneable** *adj* ▸ **a'toner** *n*

atonement (ə'təʊnmənt) *n* **1** satisfaction, reparation, or expiation given for an injury or wrong. **2** (*often cap.*) *Christian theology.* **2a** the reconciliation of man with God through the life, sufferings, and sacrificial death of Christ. **2b** the sufferings and death of Christ. **3** *Christian Science.* the state in which the attributes of God are exemplified in man. **4** *Obsolete.* reconciliation or agreement. [C16: from Middle English phrase *at onement* in harmony]

atonic (eɪ'tɒnɪk, æ-) *adj* **1** (of a syllable, word, etc.) carrying no stress; unaccented. **2** *Pathol.* relating to or characterized by atony. ◆ *n* **3** an unaccented or unstressed syllable, word, etc., such as *for* in *food for thought.* [C18: from

Latin *atonicus,* from Greek *atonos* lacking tone; see ATONY] ▸ **atonicity** (ˌætəˈnɪsɪtɪ, ˌeɪtəʊ-) *n*

atony (ˈætənɪ) *n* **1** *Pathol.* lack of normal tone or tension, as in muscles; abnormal relaxation of a muscle. **2** *Phonetics.* lack of stress or accent on a syllable or word. [C17: from Latin *atonia,* from Greek: tonelessness, from *atonos* slack, from A-[1] + *tonos* TONE]

atop (əˈtɒp) *adv* **1** on top; at the top. ◆ *prep* **2** on top of; at the top of.

atopy (ˈætəʊpɪ) *n Immunol.* a hereditary tendency to be hypersensitive to certain allergens. ▸ **atopic** (əˈtɒpɪk) *adj*

-ator *suffix forming nouns.* a person or thing that performs a certain action: *agitator; escalator; radiator.* [from Latin *-ātor;* see -ATE[1], -OR[1]]

-atory *suffix forming adjectives.* of, relating to, characterized by, or serving to: *circulatory; exploratory; migratory; explanatory.* [from Latin *-ātōrius;* see -ATE[1], -ORY[2]]

ATP[1] *n* adenosine triphosphate; a nucleotide found in the mitochondria of all plant and animal cells. It is the major source of energy for cellular reactions, this energy being released during its conversion to ADP. Formula: $C_{10}H_{16}N_5O_{13}P_3$.

ATP[2] *abbrev. for:* **1** advanced turboprop. **2** Association of Tennis Professionals. **3** automatic train protection: a safety system which automatically prevents a train from passing through a stop signal.

ATPase (ˌeɪtiːˈpiːˌeɪz) *n* adenosine triphosphatase; an enzyme that converts ATP to ADP.

atrabilious (ˌætrəˈbɪljəs) *or* **atrabiliar** *adj Rare.* irritable. [C17: from Latin *ātra bīlis* black bile, from *āter* black + *bīlis* BILE[1]] ▸ ˌ**atraˈbiliousness** *n*

atrazine (ˈætrəziːn) *n* a white crystalline compound widely used as a weedkiller. Formula: $C_8H_{14}N_5Cl$. [C20: from A(MINO) TR(I)AZINE]

atresia (əˈtriːʒɪə, -ʒə) *n* absence of or unnatural narrowing of a body channel. [C19: New Latin, from Greek *atrētos* not perforated]

Atreus (ˈeɪtrɪˌuːs, ˈeɪtrɪəs) *n Greek myth.* a king of Mycenae, son of Pelops, father of Agamemnon and Menelaus, and member of the family known as the **Atreids** (ˈeɪtrɪɪdz).

atrioventricular (ˌeɪtrɪəʊvenˈtrɪkjʊlə) *adj Anatomy.* of, relating to, or affecting both the atria and the ventricles of the heart: *atrioventricular disease.* [C19: from *atrio-,* from New Latin *atrium* heart chamber (see ATRIUM) + VENTRICULAR]

atrip (əˈtrɪp) *adj* (*postpositive*) *Nautical.* (of an anchor) no longer caught on the bottom; tripped; aweigh.

atrium (ˈeɪtrɪəm, ˈɑː-) *n, pl* **atria** (ˈeɪtrɪə, ˈɑː-). **1** the open main court of a Roman house. **2** a central often glass-roofed hall that extends through several storeys in a building, such as a shopping centre or hotel. **3** a court in front of an early Christian or medieval church, esp. one flanked by colonnades. **4** *Anatomy.* a cavity or chamber in the body, esp. the upper chamber of each half of the heart. [C17: from Latin; related to *āter* black, perhaps originally referring to the part of the house that was blackened by smoke from the hearth] ▸ ˈ**atrial** *adj*

atrocious (əˈtrəʊʃəs) *adj* **1** extremely cruel or wicked; ruthless: *atrocious deeds.* **2** horrifying or shocking: *an atrocious road accident.* **3** *Informal.* very bad; detestable: *atrocious writing.* [C17: from Latin *ātrōx* dreadful, from *āter* black] ▸ **aˈtrociously** *adv* ▸ **aˈtrociousness** *n*

atrocity (əˈtrɒsɪtɪ) *n, pl* **-ties. 1** behaviour or an action that is wicked or ruthless. **2** the fact or quality of being atrocious. **3** (*usually pl*) acts of extreme cruelty, esp. against prisoners or civilians in wartime.

atrophy (ˈætrəfɪ) *n, pl* **-phies. 1** a wasting away of an organ or part, or a failure to grow to normal size as the result of disease, faulty nutrition, etc. **2** any degeneration or diminution, esp. through lack of use. ◆ *vb* **-phies, -phying, -phied. 3** to waste away or cause to waste away. [C17: from Late Latin *atrophia,* from Greek, from *atrophos* ill-fed, from A-[1] + *-trophos* from *trephein* to feed] ▸ **atrophic** (əˈtrɒfɪk) *adj*

atropine (ˈætrəˌpiːn, -pɪn) *or* **atropin** (ˈætrəpɪn) *n* a poisonous alkaloid obtained from deadly nightshade, having an inhibitory action on the autonomic nervous system. It is used medicinally in preanaesthetic medication, to treat peptic ulcers, biliary and renal colic, etc., and as an emergency first-aid counter to exposure to chemical warfare nerve agents. Formula: $C_{17}H_{23}NO_3$. [C19: from New Latin *atropa* deadly nightshade, from Greek *atropos* unchangeable, inflexible; see ATROPOS]

Atropos (ˈætrəˌpɒs) *n Greek myth.* the one of the three Fates who severs the thread of life. [Greek, from *atropos* that may not be turned, from A-[1] + *-tropos* from *trepein* to turn]

att. *abbrev. for:* **1** attached. **2** attorney.

attaboy (ˈætəˌbɔɪ) *sentence substitute. Slang, chiefly U.S.* an expression of approval or exhortation.

attach (əˈtætʃ) *vb* (*mainly tr*) **1** to join, fasten, or connect. **2** (*reflexive or passive*) to become associated with or join, as in a business or other venture: *he attached himself to the expedition.* **3** (*intr;* foll. by *to*) to be inherent (in) or connected (with): *responsibility attaches to the job.* **4** to attribute or ascribe: *to attach importance to an event.* **5** to include or append, esp. as a condition: *a proviso is attached to the contract.* **6** (*usually passive*) *Military.* to place on temporary duty with another unit. **7** (*usually passive*) to put (a member of an organization) to work in a different unit or agency, either with an expectation of reverting to, or while retaining some part of, the original working arrangement. **8** to appoint officially. **9** *Law.* to arrest or take (a person, property, etc.) with lawful authority. **10** *Obsolete.* to seize. [C14: from Old French *atachier* to fasten, changed from *estachier* to fasten with a stake, from *estache* STAKE[1]] ▸ **atˈtachable** *adj* ▸ **atˈtacher** *n*

attaché (əˈtæʃeɪ; *French* ataʃe) *n* **1** a specialist attached to a diplomatic mission: *military attaché.* **2** *Brit.* a junior member of the staff of an embassy or legation. [C19: from French: someone attached (to a mission), from *attacher* to ATTACH]

attaché case *n* a small flat rectangular briefcase used for carrying documents, papers, etc.

attached (əˈtætʃt) *adj* **1** (foll. by *to*) fond (of); full of regard (for): *he was very attached to the old lady.* **2** married, engaged, or associated in an exclusive sexual relationship: *it's no good dancing with her, she's already attached.*

attachment (əˈtætʃmənt) *n* **1** a means of securing; a fastening. **2** (often foll. by *to*) affection or regard (for); devotion (to): *attachment to a person or to a cause.* **3** an object to be attached, esp. a supplementary part: *an attachment for an electric drill.* **4** the act of attaching or the state of being attached. **5a** the arrest of a person for disobedience to a court order. **5b** the lawful seizure of property and placing of it under control of a court. **5c** a writ authorizing such arrest or seizure. **6** *Law.* the binding of a debt in the hands of a garnishee until its disposition has been decided by the court.

attachment of earnings *n* (in Britain) a court order requiring an employer to deduct amounts from an employee's wages to pay debts or honour financial obligations.

attack (əˈtæk) *vb* **1** to launch a physical assault (against) with or without weapons; begin hostilities (with). **2** (*intr*) to take the initiative in a game, sport, etc.: *after a few minutes, the team began to attack.* **3** (*tr*) to direct hostile words or writings at; criticize or abuse vehemently. **4** (*tr*) to turn one's mind or energies vigorously to (a job, problem, etc.). **5** (*tr*) to begin to injure or affect adversely; corrode, corrupt, or infect: *rust attacked the metal.* **6** (*tr*) to attempt to rape. ◆ *n* **7** the act or an instance of attacking. **8** strong criticism or abuse: *an unjustified attack on someone's reputation.* **9** an offensive move in a game, sport, etc. **10** commencement of a task, etc. **11** any sudden and usually severe manifestation of a disease or disorder: *a heart attack; an attack of indigestion.* **12 the attack.** *Ball games.* the players in a team whose main role is to attack the opponents' goal or territory. **13** *Music.* decisiveness in beginning a passage, movement, or piece. **14** *Music.* the speed with which a note reaches its maximum volume. **15** an attempted rape. [C16: from French *attaquer,* from Old Italian *attaccare* to attack, attach, from *estaccare* to attach, from *stacca* STAKE[1]; compare ATTACH] ▸ **atˈtackable** *adj* ▸ **atˈtacker** *n*

attain (əˈteɪn) *vb* **1** (*tr*) to achieve or accomplish (a task, goal, aim, etc.). **2** (*tr*) to reach or arrive at in space or time: *to attain old age.* **3** (*intr;* often foll. by *to*) to arrive (at) with effort or exertion: *to attain to glory.* [C14: from Old French *ateindre,* from Latin *attingere* to reach, from *tangere* to touch] ▸ **atˈtainable** *adj* ▸ **atˌtainaˈbility** *or* **atˈtainableness** *n*

attainder (əˈteɪndə) *n* **1** (formerly) the extinction of a person's civil rights resulting from a sentence of death or outlawry on conviction for treason or felony. See also **bill of attainder. 2** *Obsolete.* dishonour. ◆ Archaic equivalent: **attainture** (əˈteɪntʃə). [C15: from Anglo-French *attaindre* to convict, from Old French *ateindre* to ATTAIN]

attainment (əˈteɪnmənt) *n* an achievement or the act of achieving; accomplishment.

attainment target *n Brit. Education.* a general defined level of ability that a pupil is expected to achieve in every subject at each key stage in the National Curriculum. Abbrev.: **AT.**

attaint (əˈteɪnt) *vb* (*tr*) *Archaic.* **1** to pass judgment of death or outlawry upon (a person); condemn by bill of attainder. **2** to dishonour or disgrace. **3** to accuse or prove to be guilty. **4** (of sickness) to affect or strike (somebody). ◆ *n* **5** a less common word for **attainder. 6** a dishonour; taint. [C14: from Old French *ateint* convicted, from *ateindre* to ATTAIN]

attar (ˈætə), **otto** (ˈɒtəʊ), *or* **ottar** (ˈɒtə) *n* an essential oil from flowers, esp. the damask rose, used pure or as a base for perfume: *attar of roses.* [C18: from Persian *ʻatir* perfumed, from *ʻitr* perfume, from Arabic]

attemper (əˈtɛmpə) *vb* (*tr*) *Archaic.* **1** to modify by blending; temper. **2** to moderate or soothe. **3** to accommodate or bring into harmony. ▸ **atˈtemperment** *n*

attempt (əˈtɛmpt) *vb* (*tr*) **1** to make an effort (to do something) or to achieve (something); try. **2** to try to surmount (an obstacle). **3** to try to climb: *they will attempt the north wall of the Eiger.* **4** *Archaic.* to attack. **5** *Archaic.* to tempt. ◆ *n* **6** an endeavour to achieve something; effort. **7** a result of an attempt or endeavour. **8** an attack, esp. with the intention to kill: *an attempt on his life.* [C14: from Old French *attempter,* from Latin *attemptāre* to strive after, from *tentāre* to try] ▸ **atˈtemptable** *adj* ▸ **atˈtempter** *n*

USAGE *Attempt* should not be used in the passive when followed by an infinitive: *attempts were made to find a solution (*not *a solution was attempted to be found).*

Attenborough (ˈætᵊnbᵊrə) *n* **1** Sir **David.** born 1926, British naturalist and broadcaster; noted esp. for his TV series *Life on Earth* (1978), *The Living Planet* (1983), and *The Life of Birds* (1998). **2** his brother, **Richard,** Baron Attenborough. born 1923, British film actor, director, and producer; his films include *Gandhi* (1982), *Cry Freedom* (1987), and *Shadowlands* (1993).

attend (əˈtɛnd) *vb* **1** to be present at (an event, meeting, etc.). **2** (when *intr,* foll. by *to*) to give care; minister. **3** (when *intr,* foll. by *to*) to pay attention; listen. **4** (*tr; often passive*) to accompany or follow: *a high temperature attended by a severe cough.* **5** (*intr;* foll. by *on* or *upon*) to follow as a consequence (of). **6** (*intr;* foll. by *to*) to devote one's time; apply oneself: *to attend to the garden.* **7** (*tr*) to escort or accompany. **8** (*intr;* foll. by *on* or *upon*) to wait (on); serve; provide for the needs (of): *to attend on a guest.* **9** (*tr*) *Archaic.* to wait for; expect. **10** (*intr*) *Obsolete.* to delay. [C13: from Old French *atendre,* from Latin *attendere* to stretch towards, from *tendere* to extend] ▸ **atˈtender** *n*

attendance (əˈtɛndəns) *n* **1** the act or state of attending. **2** the number of persons present: *an attendance of 5000 at the festival.* **3** *Obsolete.* attendants collectively; retinue.

attendance allowance *n* (in Britain) a tax-free noncontributory welfare benefit for children over two years old and adults who are so severely disabled that they need frequent attention or continual supervision.

attendance centre *n* (in Britain) a place at which young offenders are required to attend regularly instead of going to prison.

attendant (ə'tɛndənt) *n* **1** a person who accompanies or waits upon another. **2** a person employed to assist, guide, or provide a service for others, esp. for the general public: *a lavatory attendant.* **3** a person who is present. **4** a logical consequence or natural accompaniment: *hatred is often an attendant of jealousy.* ◆ *adj* **5** being in attendance. **6** associated; accompanying; related: *attendant problems.*

attendee (əˌtɛn'diː) *n* a person who is present at a specified event.

attention (ə'tɛnʃən) *n* **1** concentrated direction of the mind, esp. to a problem or task. **2** consideration, notice, or observation: *a new matter has come to our attention.* **3** detailed care or special treatment: *to pay attention to one's appearance.* **4** (*usually pl*) an act of consideration, courtesy, or gallantry indicating affection or love: *attentions given to a lover.* **5** the motionless position of formal military alertness, esp. in drill when an upright position is assumed with legs and heels together, arms to the sides, head and eyes facing to the front. **6** *Psychol.* the act of concentrating on any one of a set of objects or thoughts. See also **selective attention.** ◆ *sentence substitute.* **7** the order to be alert or to adopt a position of formal military alertness. [C14: from Latin *attentiō,* from *attendere* to apply the mind to; see ATTEND]

attention deficit disorder *n* a disorder, particularly of children, characterized by excessive activity and inability to concentrate on one task for any length of time. Abbrev.: **ADD.**

attentive (ə'tɛntɪv) *adj* **1** paying attention; listening carefully; observant. **2** (*postpositive;* often foll. by *to*) careful to fulfil the needs or wants (of); considerate (about): *she was always attentive to his needs.* ▸ **at'tentively** *adv* ▸ **at'tentiveness** *n*

attenuant (ə'tɛnjuənt) *adj* **1** causing dilution or thinness, esp. of the blood. ◆ *n* **2** an attenuant drug or agent.

attenuate *vb* (ə'tɛnjuˌeɪt). **1** to weaken or become weak; reduce in size, strength, density, or value. **2** to make or become thin or fine; extend. **3** (*tr*) to make (a pathogenic bacterium, virus, etc.) less virulent, as by culture in special media or exposure to heat. ◆ *adj* (ə'tɛnjuɪt, -ˌeɪt). **4** diluted, weakened, slender, or reduced. **5** *Botany.* tapering gradually to a point. [C16: from Latin *attenuāre* to weaken, from *tenuis* thin]

attenuation (əˌtɛnju'eɪʃən) *n* **1** the act of attenuating or the state of being attenuated. **2** the loss of energy suffered by radiation as it passes through matter, esp. as a result of absorption or scattering.

attenuator (ə'tɛnjuˌeɪtə) *n* **1** *Physics.* any device designed to reduce the power of a wave or electrical signal without distorting it. **2** a person or thing that attenuates.

attest (ə'tɛst) *vb* **1** (*tr*) to affirm the correctness or truth of. **2** (when *intr,* usually foll. by *to*) to witness (an act, event, etc.) or bear witness to (an act, event, etc.) as by signature or oath. **3** (*tr*) to make evident; demonstrate: *his life of luxury attests his wealth.* **4** (*tr*) to provide evidence for: *the marks in the ground attested the presence of a fossil.* [C16: from Latin *attestārī* to prove, from *testārī* to bear witness, from *testis* a witness] ▸ **at'testable** *adj* ▸ **at'testant, at'tester** *or esp. in legal usage* **at'testor, at'testator** *n* ▸ **attestation** (ˌætɛ'steɪʃən) *n*

attested (ə'tɛstɪd) *adj Brit.* (of cattle, etc.) certified to be free from a disease, esp. from tuberculosis.

Att. Gen. *or* **Atty. Gen.** *abbrev. for* Attorney General.

attic ('ætɪk) *n* **1** a space or room within the roof of a house. **2** *Architect.* a storey or low wall above the cornice of a classical façade. [C18: special use of ATTIC, from the use of Attic-style pilasters to adorn the façade of the top storey]

Attic ('ætɪk) *adj* **1** of or relating to Attica, its inhabitants, or the dialect of Greek spoken there, esp. in classical times. **2** (*often not cap.*) classically elegant, simple, or pure: *an Attic style.* ◆ *n* **3** the dialect of Ancient Greek spoken and written in Athens: the chief literary dialect of classical Greek. See also **Aeolic, Arcadic, Doric, Ionic.**

Attica ('ætɪkə) *n* a region and department of E central Greece: in ancient times the territory of Athens. Capital: Athens. Pop.: 3 523 407 (1991). Area: 14 157 sq. km (5466 sq. miles).

Atticism ('ætɪˌsɪzəm) *n* **1** the idiom or character of the Attic dialect of Ancient Greek, esp. in the Hellenistic period. **2** an elegant, simple, and clear expression. ▸ **'Atticist** *n*

Attic order *n* a low pilaster of any order set into the cornice of a building.

Attic salt *or* **wit** *n* refined incisive wit.

Attila (ə'tɪlə) *n* ?406–453 A.D., king of the Huns, who devastated much of the Roman Empire, invaded Gaul in 451 A.D., but was defeated by the Romans and Visigoths at Châlons-sur-Marne.

attire (ə'taɪə) *vb* **1** (*tr*) to dress, esp. in fine elegant clothes; array. ◆ *n* **2** clothes or garments, esp. if fine or decorative. **3** the antlers of a mature male deer. [C13: from Old French *atirier* to put in order, from *tire* row; see TIER[1]]

Attis ('ætɪs) *n Classical myth.* a youth of Phrygia, loved by the goddess Cybele. In a jealous passion she caused him to go mad, whereupon he castrated himself and died.

attitude ('ætɪˌtjuːd) *n* **1** the way a person views something or tends to behave towards it, often in an evaluative way. **2** a theatrical pose created for effect (esp. in the phrase **strike an attitude**). **3** a position of the body indicating mood or emotion. **4** *Informal.* a hostile manner: *don't give me attitude, my girl.* **5** the orientation of an aircraft's axes in relation to some plane, esp. the horizontal. See also **axis**[1] (sense 1). **6** the orientation of a spacecraft in relation to its direction of motion. **7** *Ballet.* a classical position in which the body is upright and one leg raised and bent behind. [C17: from French, from Italian *attitudine* disposition, from Late Latin *aptitūdō* fitness, from Latin *aptus* APT] ▸ **ˌatti'tudinal** *adj*

attitudinize *or* **attitudinise** (ˌætɪ'tjuːdɪˌnaɪz) *vb* (*intr*) to adopt a pose or opinion for effect; strike an attitude. ▸ **ˌatti'tudiˌnizer** *or* **ˌatti'tudiˌniser** *n*

Attlee ('ætlɪ) *n* **Clement Richard,** 1st Earl Attlee. 1883–1967, British statesman; prime minister (1945–51); leader of the Labour party (1935–55). His government instituted the welfare state, with extensive nationalization.

attn *abbrev. for* attention.

atto- *prefix* denoting 10^{-18}: *attotesla.* Symbol: a [from Norwegian, Danish *atten* eighteen]

attorn (ə'tɜːn) *vb* **1** (*intr*) *Law.* to acknowledge a new owner of land as one's landlord. **2** (*intr*) *Feudal history.* to transfer allegiance or do homage to a new lord. [C15: from Old French *atourner* to direct to, from *tourner* to TURN] ▸ **at'tornment** *n*

attorney (ə'tɜːnɪ) *n* **1** a person legally appointed or empowered to act for another. **2** *U.S.* a lawyer qualified to represent clients in legal proceedings. [C14: from Old French *atourné,* from *atourner* to direct to; see ATTORN] ▸ **at'torneyˌship** *n*

attorney-at-law *n, pl* **attorneys-at-law.** *Law.* **1** *Now chiefly U.S.* a lawyer qualified to represent in court a party to a legal action. **2** *Brit. obsolete.* a solicitor.

attorney general *n, pl* **attorneys general** *or* **attorney generals. 1** a country's chief law officer and senior legal adviser to its government. **2** (in the U.S.) the chief law officer and legal adviser of a state government. **3** (in some states of the U.S.) a public prosecutor.

Attorney General *n* **1** (in the United Kingdom except Scotland) the senior law officer and chief legal counsel of the Crown: a member of the government and of the House of Commons. **2** (in the U.S.) the chief law officer and legal adviser to the Administration: head of the Department of Justice and member of the cabinet. **3** (in Australia and New Zealand) the chief government law officer: a member of Parliament and usually a cabinet minister.

attract (ə'trækt) *vb* (*mainly tr*) **1** to draw (notice, a crowd of observers, etc.) to oneself by conspicuous behaviour or appearance (esp. in the phrase **attract attention**). **2** (*also intr*) to exert a force on (a body) that tends to cause an approach or oppose a separation: *the gravitational pull of the earth attracts objects to it.* **3** to possess some property that pulls or draws (something) towards itself: *jam attracts wasps.* **4** (*also intr*) to exert a pleasing, alluring, or fascinating influence (upon); be attractive (to). [C15: from Latin *attrahere* to draw towards, from *trahere* to pull] ▸ **at'tractable** *adj* ▸ **at'tractor** *or* **at'tracter** *n*

attractant (ə'træktənt) *n* a substance that attracts, esp. a chemical (**sex attractant**) produced by an insect and attracting insects of the same species. See also **pheromone.**

attraction (ə'trækʃən) *n* **1** the act, power, or quality of attracting. **2** a person or thing that attracts or is intended to attract. **3** a force by which one object attracts another, such as the gravitational or magnetic force. **4** a change in the form of one linguistic element caused by the proximity of another element.

attraction sphere *n* another name for **astrosphere** (sense 2).

attractive (ə'træktɪv) *adj* **1** appealing to the senses or mind through beauty, form, character, etc. **2** arousing interest: *an attractive opportunity.* **3** possessing the ability to draw or pull: *an attractive force.* ▸ **at'tractively** *adv* ▸ **at'tractiveness** *n*

attrib. *abbrev. for:* **1** attribute. **2** attributive.

attribute *vb* (ə'trɪbjuːt). **1** (*tr;* usually foll. by *to*) to regard as belonging (to), produced (by), or resulting (from); ascribe (to): *to attribute a painting to Picasso.* ◆ *n* ('ætrɪˌbjuːt). **2** a property, quality, or feature belonging to or representative of a person or thing. **3** an object accepted as belonging to a particular office or position. **4** *Grammar.* **4a** an adjective or adjectival phrase. **4b** an attributive adjective. **5** *Logic.* the property, quality, or feature that is affirmed or denied concerning the subject of a proposition. [C15: from Latin *attribuere* to associate with, from *tribuere* to give] ▸ **at'tributable** *adj* ▸ **at'tributer** *or* **at'tributor** *n* ▸ **attribution** (ˌætrɪ'bjuːʃən) *n*

attribution theory *n Psychol.* the theory that tries to explain how people link actions and emotions to particular causes, both internal and external.

attributive (ə'trɪbjutɪv) *adj* **1** relating to an attribute. **2** *Grammar.* (of an adjective or adjectival phrase) modifying a noun and constituting part of the same noun phrase, in English normally preceding the noun, as *black* in *Fido is a black dog* (as opposed to *Fido is black*). Compare **predicative. 3** *Philosophy.* relative to an understood domain, as *small* in *that elephant is small.* ◆ *n* **4** an attributive adjective. ▸ **at'tributively** *adv* ▸ **at'tributiveness** *n*

attrit (ə'trɪt) *vb* (*tr*) **-trits, -tritting, -tritted.** *U.S. slang.* **1** to wear down or dispose of gradually. **2** to kill. [C18: back formation from ATTRITION]

attrition (ə'trɪʃən) *n* **1** the act of wearing away or the state of being worn away, as by friction. **2** constant wearing down to weaken or destroy (often in the phrase **war of attrition**). **3** Also called: **natural wastage.** a decrease in the size of the workforce of an organization achieved by not replacing employees who retire or resign. **4** *Geography.* the grinding down of rock particles by friction during transportation by water, wind, or ice. Compare **abrasion** (sense 3), **corrasion. 5** *Theol.* sorrow for sin arising from fear of damnation, esp. as contrasted with contrition, which arises purely from love of God. [C14: from Late Latin *attrītiō* a rubbing against something, from Latin *atterere* to weaken, from *terere* to rub] ▸ **at'tritional** *adj* ▸ **attritive** (ə'traɪtɪv) *adj*

Attu ('ætuː) *n* the westernmost of the Aleutian Islands, off the coast of SW Alaska: largest of the Near Islands.

attune (ə'tjuːn) *vb* (*tr*) **1** to adjust or accustom (a person or thing); acclimatize. **2** to tune (a musical instrument).

atty *abbrev. for* attorney.

atua ('ɑːtuːə) *n N.Z.* a spirit or demon. [Maori]

ATV *abbrev. for* all-terrain vehicle: a vehicle with treads or wheels designed to travel on rough uneven ground.

atween (ə'twiːn) *prep* an archaic or Scot. word for **between.**

Atwood (ˈætwʊd) *n* **Margaret** (**Eleanor**). born 1939, Canadian poet and novelist. Her novels include *Lady Oracle* (1976), *Life Before Man* (1979), *The Handmaid's Tale* (1986), and *Alias Grace* (1996).

at. wt. *abbrev. for* atomic weight.

atypical (eɪˈtɪpɪkᵊl) *adj* not typical; deviating from or not conforming to type. ▸ **aˈtypically** *adv*

Au *the chemical symbol for* gold. [from New Latin *aurum*]

AU *or* **a.u.** *abbrev. for:* **1** angstrom unit. **2** astronomical unit.

aubade (*French* obad) *n* **1** a song or poem appropriate to or greeting the dawn. **2** a romantic or idyllic prelude or overture. ◆ Compare **serenade.** [C19: from French, from Old Provençal *aubada* (unattested), from *auba* dawn, ultimately from Latin *albus* white]

Aube (*French* ob) *n* **1** a department of N central France, in Champagne-Ardenne region. Capital: Troyes. Pop.: 293 100 (1995). Area: 6026 sq. km (2350 sq. miles). **2** a river in N central France, flowing northwest to the Seine. Length: about 225 km (140 miles).

Auber (*French* obɛr) *n* **Daniel François Esprit** (danjɛl frɑ̃swa ɛspri). 1782–1871, French composer, who was prominent in development of opéra comique. His works include 48 operas.

auberge (*French* obɛrʒ) *n* an inn or tavern. [C17: from French, from Old Provençal *alberga,* of Germanic origin; compare Old Saxon *heriberga* army shelter]

aubergine (ˈəʊbəˌʒiːn) *n* **1** a tropical Old World solanaceous plant, *Solanum melongena,* widely cultivated for its egg-shaped typically dark purple fruit. U.S., Canadian, and Australian name: **eggplant. 2** the fruit of this plant, which is cooked and eaten as a vegetable. **3a** a dark purple colour. **3b** (*as adj*): *an aubergine dress.* [C18: from French, from Catalan *alberginia,* from Arabic *al-bādindjān,* ultimately from Sanskrit *vatin-ganah,* of obscure origin]

Aubervilliers (*French* obɛrvilje) *n* an industrial suburb of Paris, on the Seine. Pop.: 67 840 (1990). Former name: **Notre-Dame-des-Vertus** (*French* nɔtrədamdevɛrty).

Aubrey (ˈɔːbrɪ) *n* **John.** 1626–97, English antiquary and author, noted for his vivid biographies of his contemporaries, *Brief Lives* (edited 1898).

aubrietia, aubrieta, *or* **aubretia** (ɔːˈbriːʃə) *n* any trailing purple-flowered plant of the genus *Aubrietia,* native to European mountains but widely planted in rock gardens: family *Cruciferae* (crucifers). [C19: from New Latin, named after Claude *Aubriet,* 18th-century French painter of flowers and animals]

auburn (ˈɔːbᵊn) *n* **a** a moderate reddish-brown colour. **b** (*as adj*): *auburn hair.* [C15 (originally meaning: blond): from Old French *alborne* blond, from Medieval Latin *alburnus* whitish, from Latin *albus* white]

Aubusson (*French* obysɔ̃) *n* **1** a town in central France, in the Creuse department: a centre for flat-woven carpets and for tapestries since the 16th century. Pop.: 5000 (latest est.). ◆ *adj* **2** denoting or relating to these carpets or tapestries.

AUC *abbrev. for:* (indicating years numbered from the founding of Rome, taken as 753 B.C.) **a** ab urbe condita. **b** anno urbis conditae.

Auckland (ˈɔːklənd) *n* the chief port of New Zealand, in the northern part of North Island: former capital of New Zealand (1840–65). Pop. (urban area): 353 670 (1996).

Auckland Islands *pl n* a group of six uninhabited islands, south of New Zealand. Area: 611 sq. km (234 sq. miles).

au contraire *French.* (o kɔ̃trɛr) *adv* on the contrary.

au courant *French.* (o kurɑ̃) *adj* up-to-date, esp. in knowledge of current affairs. [literally: in the current]

auction (ˈɔːkʃən) *n* **1** a public sale of goods or property, esp. one in which prospective purchasers bid against each other until the highest price is reached. Compare **Dutch auction. 2** the competitive calls made in bridge and other games before play begins, undertaking to win a given number of tricks if a certain suit is trumps. **3** See **auction bridge.** ◆ *vb* **4** (*tr;* often foll. by *off*) to sell by auction. [C16: from Latin *auctiō* an increasing, from *augēre* to increase]

auction bridge *n* a variety of bridge, now generally superseded by contract bridge, in which all the tricks made score towards game.

auctioneer (ˌɔːkʃəˈnɪə) *n* **1** a person who conducts an auction by announcing the lots and controlling the bidding. ◆ *vb* **2** (*tr*) to sell by auction.

auctorial (ɔːkˈtɔːrɪəl) *adj* of or relating to an author. [C19: from Latin *auctor* AUTHOR]

aud. *abbrev. for:* **1** audit. **2** auditor.

audacious (ɔːˈdeɪʃəs) *adj* **1** recklessly bold or daring; fearless. **2** impudent or presumptuous. [C16: from Latin *audāx* bold, from *audēre* to dare] ▸ **auˈdaciously** *adv* ▸ **auˈdaciousness** *or* **audacity** (ɔːˈdæsɪtɪ) *n*

Aude (*French* od) *n* a department of S France on the Gulf of Lions, in Languedoc-Roussillon region. Capital: Carcassonne. Pop.: 305 300 (1995). Area: 6342 sq. km (2473 sq. miles).

Auden (ˈɔːdᵊn) *n* **W**(**ystan**) **H**(**ugh**). 1907–73, U.S. poet, dramatist, critic, and librettist, born in Britain; noted for his lyric and satirical poems and for plays written in collaboration with Christopher Isherwood.

audible (ˈɔːdɪbᵊl) *adj* **1** perceptible to the hearing; loud enough to be heard. ◆ *n* **2** *American football.* a change of playing tactics called by the quarterback when the offense is lined up at the line of scrimmage. [C16: from Late Latin *audibilis,* from Latin *audīre* to hear] ▸ **ˌaudiˈbility** *or* **ˈaudibleness** *n* ▸ **ˈaudibly** *adv*

audience (ˈɔːdɪəns) *n* **1** a group of spectators or listeners, esp. at a public event such as a concert or play. **2** the people reached by a book, film, or radio or television programme. **3** the devotees or followers of a public entertainer, lecturer, etc.; regular public. **4** an opportunity to put one's point of view, such as a formal interview with a monarch or head of state. [C14: from Old French, from Latin *audientia* a hearing, from *audīre* to hear]

audile (ˈɔːdɪl, ˈɔːdaɪl) *Psychol.* ◆ *n* **1** a person who possesses a faculty for auditory imagery that is more distinct than his visual or other imagery. ◆ *adj* **2** of or relating to such a person. [C19: from AUD(ITORY) + -ILE]

audio (ˈɔːdɪˌəʊ) *n* (*modifier*) **1** of or relating to sound or hearing: *audio frequency.* **2** relating to or employed in the transmission, reception, or reproduction of sound. **3** of, concerned with, or operating at audio frequencies. ◆ Compare **video.** [C20: independent use of AUDIO-]

audio- *combining form.* indicating hearing or sound: *audiometer; audiovisual.* [from Latin *audīre* to hear]

audio book *n* a reading of a book recorded on tape.

audio conference *n* a meeting that is conducted by the use of audio telecommunications.

audio frequency *n* a frequency in the range 20 hertz to 20 000 hertz. A sound wave of this frequency would be audible to the human ear.

audiogenic (ˌɔːdɪəʊˈdʒɛnɪk) *adj* caused or produced by sound or an audio frequency: *an audiogenic epileptic fit.*

audiogram (ˈɔːdɪəʊˌɡræm) *n* a graphic record of the acuity of hearing of a person obtained by means of an audiometer.

audiology (ˌɔːdɪˈɒlədʒɪ) *n* the scientific study of hearing, often including the treatment of persons with hearing defects. ▸ **audiological** (ˌɔːdɪəˈlɒdʒɪkᵊl) *adj* ▸ **ˌaudioˈlogically** *adv* ▸ **ˌaudiˈologist** *n*

audiometer (ˌɔːdɪˈɒmɪtə) *n* an instrument for testing the intensity and frequency range of sound that is capable of detection by the human ear. ▸ **audiometric** (ˌɔːdɪəʊˈmɛtrɪk) *adj* ▸ **ˌaudioˈmetrically** *adv* ▸ **ˌaudiˈometrist** *n* ▸ **ˌaudiˈometry** *n*

audiophile (ˈɔːdɪəʊˌfaɪl) *n* a person who has a great interest in high-fidelity sound reproduction.

audio response *n* a computer response that is audible rather than textual or graphical.

audiotypist (ˈɔːdɪəʊˌtaɪpɪst) *n* a typist trained to type from a dictating machine. ▸ **ˈaudioˌtyping** *n*

audiovisual (ˌɔːdɪəʊˈvɪzjʊəl, -ʒʊəl) *adj* (esp. of teaching aids) involving or directed at both hearing and sight: *the language class had new audiovisual equipment.* ▸ **ˌaudioˈvisually** *adv*

audiphone (ˈɔːdɪˌfəʊn) *n* a type of hearing aid consisting of a diaphragm that, when placed against the upper teeth, conveys sound vibrations to the inner ear.

audit (ˈɔːdɪt) *n* **1a** an inspection, correction, and verification of business accounts, conducted by an independent qualified accountant. **1b** (*as modifier*): *audit report.* **2** *U.S.* an audited account. **3** any thoroughgoing check or examination. **4** *Archaic.* a hearing. ◆ *vb* **5** to inspect, correct, and certify (accounts, etc.). **6** *U.S. and Canadian.* to attend (classes, etc.) as an auditor. [C15: from Latin *audītus* a hearing, from *audīre* to hear]

audition (ɔːˈdɪʃən) *n* **1** a test at which a performer or musician is asked to demonstrate his ability for a particular role, etc. **2** the act, sense, or power of hearing. ◆ *vb* **3** to judge by means of or be tested in an audition. [C16: from Latin *audītiō* a hearing, from *audīre* to hear]

auditor (ˈɔːdɪtə) *n* **1** a person qualified to audit accounts. **2** a person who hears or listens. **3** *U.S. and Canadian.* a registered student who attends a class that is not an official part of his course of study, without actively participating it. [C14: from Old French *auditeur,* from Latin *audītor* a hearer] ▸ **ˌaudiˈtorial** *adj*

auditorium (ˌɔːdɪˈtɔːrɪəm) *n, pl* **-toriums** *or* **-toria** (-ˈtɔːrɪə). **1** the area of a concert hall, theatre, school, etc., in which the audience sits. **2** *U.S. and Canadian.* a building for public gatherings or meetings. [C17: from Latin: a judicial examination, from *audītōrius* concerning a hearing; see AUDITORY]

auditory (ˈɔːdɪtərɪ, -trɪ) *adj also* **auditive** (ˈɔːdɪtɪv). **1** of or relating to hearing, the sense of hearing, or the organs of hearing. ◆ *n* **2** an archaic word for **audience** or **auditorium.** [C14: from Latin *audītōrius* relating to hearing, from *audīre* to hear]

auditory phonetics *n* (*functioning as sing*) the branch of phonetics concerned with the perception of speech sounds by humans. Compare **acoustic phonetics, articulatory phonetics.**

Audubon (ˈɔːdəˌbɒn) *n* **John James.** 1785–1851, U.S. naturalist and artist, noted particularly for his paintings of birds in *Birds of America* (1827–38).

Auer (*German* ˈauər) *n* **Karl** (karl), Baron von Welsbach. 1858–1929, Austrian chemist who discovered the cerium-iron alloy used for flints in cigarette lighters and invented the incandescent gas mantle.

Auerbach (ˈaʊəˌbɑːk) *n* **Frank** (**Helmuth**). born 1931, British painter, born in Germany, noted esp. for his use of impasto.

AUEW (in Britain) *abbrev. for* Amalgamated Union of Engineering Workers.

au fait *French.* (o fɛ; *English* əʊ ˈfeɪ) *adj* fully informed; in touch or expert. [C18: literally: to the point]

Aufklärung *German.* (ˈaufklɛːrʊŋ) *n* the Enlightenment, esp. in Germany.

au fond *French.* (o fɔ̃) *adv* fundamentally; essentially. [literally: at the bottom]

auf Wiedersehen *German.* (auf ˈviːdərzeːən) *sentence substitute.* goodbye, until we see each other again.

aug. *abbrev. for* augmentative.

Aug. *abbrev. for* August.

Augean (ɔːˈdʒiːən) *adj* extremely dirty or corrupt. [C16: after *Augeas;* see AUGEAN STABLES]

Augean stables *pl n Greek myth.* the stables, not cleaned for 30 years, where King Augeas kept 3000 oxen. Hercules diverted the River Alpheus through them and cleaned them in a day.

augend (ˈɔːdʒɛnd, ɔːˈdʒɛnd) *n* a number to which another number, the addend, is added. [from Latin *augendum* that is to be increased, from *augēre* to increase]

auger (ˈɔːɡə) *n* **1** a hand tool with a bit shaped like a corkscrew, for boring holes in wood. **2** a larger tool of the same kind for boring holes in the ground. [C15 *an augur,* resulting from mistaken division of earlier *a nauger,* from Old English *nafugār* nave (of a wheel) spear (that is, tool for boring hubs of wheels), from *nafu* NAVE[2] + *gār* spear; see GORE[2]]

Auger effect ('aʊgə) *n* the emission of an electron instead of a photon by an excited ion as a result of a vacancy being filled in an inner electron shell. [C20: named after Pierre *Auger* (1899–1993), French physicist]

aught[1] *or* **ought** (ɔːt) *(used with a negative or in conditional or interrogative sentences or clauses) Archaic or literary.* ◆ *pron* **1** anything at all; anything whatever (esp. in the phrase **for aught I know**). ◆ *adv* **2** *Dialect.* in any least part; to any degree. [Old English *āwiht,* from *ā* ever, AY[1] + *wiht* thing; see WIGHT[1]]

aught[2] *or* **ought** (ɔːt) *n* a less common word for **nought** (zero).

augite ('ɔːgaɪt) *n* a black or greenish-black mineral of the pyroxene group, found in igneous rocks. Composition: calcium magnesium iron aluminium silicate. General formula: $(Ca,Mg,Fe,Al)(Si,Al)_2O_6$. Crystal structure: monoclinic. [C19: from Latin *augītēs,* from Greek, from *augē* brightness] ► **augitic** (ɔː'gɪtɪk) *adj*

augment *vb* (ɔːg'mɛnt). **1** to make or become greater in number, amount, strength, etc.; increase. **2** *(tr) Music.* to increase (a major or perfect interval) by a semitone. Compare **diminish** (sense 3). **3** *(tr)* (in Greek and Sanskrit grammar) to prefix a vowel or diphthong to (a verb) to form a past tense. ◆ *n* ('ɔːgmɛnt). **4** (in Greek and Sanskrit grammar) a vowel or diphthong prefixed to a verb to form a past tense. [C15: from Late Latin *augmentāre* to increase, from *augmentum* growth, from Latin *augēre* to increase] ► **aug'mentable** *adj* ► **aug'mentor** *or* **aug'menter** *n*

augmentation (ˌɔːgmɛn'teɪʃən) *n* **1** the act of augmenting or the state of being augmented. **2** the amount by which something is increased. **3** *Music.* the presentation of a subject of a fugue, in which the note values are uniformly increased. Compare **diminution** (sense 2).

augmentative (ɔːg'mɛntətɪv) *adj* **1** tending or able to augment. **2** *Grammar.* **2a** denoting an affix that may be added to a word to convey the meaning *large* or *great;* for example, the suffix *-ote* in Spanish, where *hombre* means man and *hombrote* big man. **2b** denoting a word formed by the addition of an augmentative affix. ◆ *n* **3** *Grammar.* an augmentative word or affix. ◆ Compare (for senses 2, 3) **diminutive.** ► **aug'mentatively** *adv*

augmented (ɔːg'mɛntɪd) *adj* **1** *Music.* (of an interval) increased or expanded from the state of being perfect or major by the raising of the higher note or the dropping of the lower note by one semitone: *C to G is a perfect fifth, but C to G sharp is an augmented fifth.* Compare **diminished** (sense 2). **2** *Music.* **2a** denoting a chord based upon an augmented triad: *an augmented seventh chord.* **2b** denoting a triad consisting of the root plus a major third and an augmented fifth. **2c** *(postpositive)* (esp. in jazz) denoting a chord having as its root the note specified: *D augmented.* **3** having been increased, esp. in number: *an augmented orchestra.*

augmented transition network *n* (in certain schools of linguistics) a formalism, usually expressed as a diagram, having the power of a Turing machine, used as the basis of processes transforming sentences into their syntactic representations. Abbrev.: **ATN.**

au gratin *(French* o gratɛ̃) *adj* covered and cooked with browned breadcrumbs and sometimes cheese. [French, literally: with the grating]

Augsburg *(German* 'auksbʊrk) *n* a city in S Germany, in Bavaria: founded by the Romans in 14 B.C.; site of the diet that produced the **Peace of Augsburg** (1555), which ended the struggles between Lutherans and Catholics in the Holy Roman Empire and established the principle that each ruler should determine the form of worship in his lands. Pop.: 259 699 (1996 est.). Roman name: **Augusta Vindelicorum** (aʊ'guːstə vɪn'delɪˌkɔːrəm).

augur ('ɔːgə) *n* **1** Also called: **auspex.** (in ancient Rome) a religious official who observed and interpreted omens and signs to help guide the making of public decisions. **2** any prophet or soothsayer. ◆ *vb* **3** to predict (some future event), as from signs or omens. **4** *(tr; may take a clause as object)* to be an omen (of); presage. **5** *(intr)* to foreshadow future events to be as specified; bode: *this augurs well for us.* [C14: from Latin: a diviner, perhaps from *augēre* to increase] ► **augural** ('ɔːgjʊrəl) *adj* ► **'augurship** *n*

augury ('ɔːgjʊrɪ) *n, pl* **-ries. 1** the art of or a rite conducted by an augur. **2** a sign or portent; omen.

august (ɔː'gʌst) *adj* **1** dignified or imposing: *an august presence.* **2** of noble birth or high rank: *an august lineage.* [C17: from Latin *augustus;* related to *augēre* to increase] ► **au'gustly** *adv* ► **au'gustness** *n*

August ('ɔːgəst) *n* the eighth month of the year, consisting of 31 days. [Old English, from Latin, named after the emperor AUGUSTUS]

Augusta (ɔː'gʌstə) *n* **1** a town in the U.S., in Georgia. Pop.: 44 639 (1990). **2** a port in S Italy, in E Sicily. Pop.: 38 900 (latest est.). **3** a city in the U.S., in Maine: the state capital; founded (1628) as a trading post; timber industry. Pop.: 21 325 (1990).

Augustan (ɔː'gʌstən) *adj* **1** characteristic of, denoting, or relating to the Roman emperor Augustus Caesar, his period, or the poets, notably Virgil, Horace, and Ovid, writing during his reign. **2** of, relating to, or characteristic of any literary period noted for refinement and classicism, esp. the late 17th century in France (the period of the dramatists Corneille, Racine, and Molière) or the 18th century in England (the period of Swift, Pope, and Johnson, much influenced by Dryden). ◆ *n* **3** an author in an Augustan Age. **4** a student of or specialist in Augustan literature.

auguste *or* **august** (aʊ'guːst, 'aʊˌgʊst) *n (often cap.)* a type of circus clown who usually wears battered ordinary clothes and is habitually maladroit or unlucky. [C20: French, from German]

Augustine (ɔː'gʌstɪn) *n* **1 Saint.** 354–430 A.D., one of the Fathers of the Christian Church; bishop of Hippo in North Africa (396–430), who profoundly influenced both Catholic and Protestant theology. His most famous works are *Confessions,* a spiritual autobiography, and *De Civitate Dei,* a vindication of the Christian Church. Feast day: Aug. 28. **2 Saint.** died 604 A.D., Roman monk, sent to Britain (597 A.D.) to convert the Anglo-Saxons to Christianity and to establish the authority of the Roman See over the native Celtic Church; became the first archbishop of Canterbury (601–604). Feast day: May 26 or 27. **3** a member of an Augustinian order.

Augustinian (ˌɔːgə'stɪnɪən) *adj* **1** of or relating to Saint Augustine of Hippo, his doctrines, or any of the Christian religious orders that were founded on his doctrines. ◆ *n* **2** a member of any of several religious orders, such as the **Augustinian Canons, Augustinian Hermits,** and **Austin Friars,** which are governed by the rule of Saint Augustine. **3** a person who follows the doctrines of Saint Augustine.

Augustus (ɔː'gʌstəs) *n* original name *Gaius Octavianus;* after his adoption by Julius Caesar (44 B.C.) known as *Gaius Julius Caesar Octavianus.* 63 B.C.–14 A.D., Roman statesman, a member of the second triumvirate (43 B.C.). After defeating Mark Antony at Actium (31 B.C.), he became first emperor of Rome, adopting the title Augustus (27 B.C.).

au jus *(French* o ʒy) *adj* (of meat) served in its own gravy. [literally: with the juice]

auk (ɔːk) *n* **1** any of various diving birds of the family *Alcidae* of northern oceans having a heavy body, short tail, narrow wings, and a black-and-white plumage: order *Charadriiformes.* See also **great auk, razorbill. 2 little auk.** Also called: **dovekie.** a small short-billed auk, *Plautus alle,* abundant in Arctic regions. [C17: from Old Norse *ālka;* related to Swedish *alka,* Danish *alke*]

auklet ('ɔːklɪt) *n* any of various small auks of the genera *Aethia* and *Ptychoramphus.*

au lait (əʊ 'leɪ; *French* o lɛ) *adj* prepared or served with milk. [French, literally: with milk]

auld (ɔːld) *adj* a Scot. word for **old.** [Old English *āld*]

auld lang syne ('ɔːld læŋ 'saɪn, 'saɪn, 'zaɪn) *n* old times; times past, esp. those remembered with affection or nostalgia. [Scottish, literally: old long since]

Auld Reekie ('riːkɪ) *n Scot.* a nickname for **Edinburgh**[1]. [literally: Old Smoky]

aulic ('ɔːlɪk) *adj Rare.* relating to a royal court. [C18: from Latin *aulicus,* from Greek *aulikos* belonging to a prince's court, from *aulē* court]

Aulic Council *n* a council, founded in 1498, of the Holy Roman Emperor. It functioned mainly as a judicial body.

Aulis ('ɔːlɪs) *n* an ancient town in E central Greece, in Boeotia: traditionally the harbour from which the Greeks sailed at the beginning of the Trojan war.

Auliye-Ata ('aʊlijə æ'tə) *n* a city in S Kazakhstan: chemical manufacturing. Pop.: 310 600 (1995 est.). Former name (1938–91): **Dzhambul.**

aumbry ('ɔːmbrɪ) *n, pl* **-bries.** a variant of **ambry.**

au naturel *French.* (o natyrɛl) *adj, adv* **1** naked; nude. **2** uncooked or plainly cooked. [literally: in (a) natural (condition)]

Aung San Suu Kyi ('aʊŋ 'sæn 'suː 'kiː) *n* born 1945, Burmese politician; co-founder (1988) and general secretary (1988–91) and from 1995 of the National League for Democracy: Nobel peace prize 1991.

aunt (ɑːnt) *n (often cap., esp. as a term of address)* **1** a sister of one's father or mother. **2** the wife of one's uncle. **3** a term of address used by children for any woman, esp. for a friend of the parents. **4 my (sainted) aunt!** an exclamation of surprise or amazement. [C13: from Old French *ante,* from Latin *amita* a father's sister]

auntie *or* **aunty** ('ɑːntɪ) *n, pl* **-ies.** a familiar or diminutive word for **aunt.**

Auntie ('ɑːntɪ) *n Brit.* an informal name for the **BBC.**

auntie man *n Caribbean informal.* an effeminate or homosexual male.

Aunt Sally ('sælɪ) *n, pl* **-lies.** *Brit.* **1** a figure of an old woman's head, typically with a clay pipe, used in fairgrounds and fêtes as a target for balls or other objects. **2** any person who is a target for insults or criticism. **3** something set up as a target for disagreement or attack.

au pair (əʊ 'pɛə; *French* o pɛr) *n* **1a** a young foreigner, usually a girl, who undertakes housework in exchange for board and lodging, esp. in order to learn the language. **1b** *(as modifier): an au pair girl.* **2** a young person who lives temporarily with a family abroad in exchange for a reciprocal arrangement with his or her own family. ◆ *vb* **3** *(intr)* to work as an au pair. ◆ *adv* **4** as an au pair: *she worked au pair in Greece.* [C20: from French: on an equal footing]

aura ('ɔːrə) *n, pl* **auras** *or* **aurae** ('ɔːriː). **1** a distinctive air or quality considered to be characteristic of a person or thing. **2** any invisible emanation, such as a scent or odour. **3** *Pathol.* strange sensations, such as noises in the ears or flashes of light, that immediately precede an attack, esp. of epilepsy. **4** (in parapsychology) an invisible emanation produced by and surrounding a person or object: alleged to be discernible by individuals of supernormal sensibility. [C18: via Latin from Greek: breeze]

aural[1] ('ɔːrəl) *adj* of or relating to the sense or organs of hearing; auricular. [C19: from Latin *auris* ear] ► **'aurally** *adv*

aural[2] ('ɔːrəl) *adj* of or relating to an aura.

Aurangzeb *or* **Aurungzeb** ('ɔːrəŋˌzeb) *n* 1618–1707, Mogul emperor of Hindustan (1658–1707), whose reign marked both the height of Mogul prosperity and the decline of its power through the revolts of the Marathas.

aurar ('ɔːrɑː) *n* the plural of **eyrir.**

aureate ('ɔːrɪɪt, -ˌeɪt) *adj* **1** covered with gold; gilded. **2** of a golden colour. **3** (of a style of writing or speaking) excessively elaborate or ornate; florid. [C15: from Late Latin *aureātus* gilded, from Latin *aureus* golden, from *aurum* gold] ► **'aureately** *adv* ► **'aureateness** *n*

Aurelian (ɔː'riːlɪən) *n* Latin name *Lucius Domitius Aurelianus.* ?212–275 A.D., Roman emperor (270–275), who conquered Palmyra (273) and restored political unity to the Roman Empire.

Aurelius (ɔː'riːlɪəs) *n* See **Marcus Aurelius Antoninus.**

aureole ('ɔːrɪˌəʊl) *or* **aureola** (ɔː'riːələ) *n* **1** (esp. in paintings of Christian saints and the deity) a border of light or radiance enveloping the head or sometimes the whole of a figure represented as holy. **2** a less common word for **halo. 3** another name for **corona** (sense 2). [C13: from Old French *auréole,* from Medieval Latin (*corōna*) *aureola* golden (crown), from Latin *aureolus* golden, from *aurum* gold]

Aureomycin (ˌɔːrɪəʊˈmaɪsɪn) *n Trademark.* a brand of **chlortetracycline.**

aureus (ˈɔːrɪəs) *n, pl* **aurei** (ˈɔːrɪˌaɪ). a gold coin of the Roman Empire. [Latin: golden; see AUREATE]

au revoir *French.* (o rəvwar) *sentence substitute.* goodbye. [literally: to the seeing again]

auric (ˈɔːrɪk) *adj* of or containing gold in the trivalent state. [C19: from Latin *aurum* gold]

Auric (*French* ɔrik) *n* **Georges** (ʒɔrʒ). 1899–1983, French composer; one of *les Six.* His works include ballet and film music.

auricle (ˈɔːrɪkᵊl) *n* **1a** the upper chamber of the heart; atrium. **1b** a small sac in the atrium of the heart. **2** Also called: **pinna.** *Anat.* the external part of the ear. **3** Also called: **auricula.** *Biology.* an ear-shaped part or appendage, such as that occurring at the base of some leaves. [C17: from Latin *auricula* the external ear, from *auris* ear] ▸ **ˈauricled** *adj*

auricula (ɔːˈrɪkjʊlə) *n, pl* **-lae** (-ˌliː) *or* **-las. 1** Also called: **bear's-ear.** a widely cultivated alpine primrose, *Primula auricula,* with leaves shaped like a bear's ear. **2** another word for **auricle** (sense 3). [C17: from New Latin, from Latin: external ear; see AURICLE]

auricular (ɔːˈrɪkjʊlə) *adj* **1** of, relating to, or received by the sense or organs of hearing; aural. **2** shaped like an ear. **3** of or relating to an auricle of the heart. **4** (of feathers) occurring in tufts surrounding the ears of owls and similar birds. ◆ *n* **5** (*usually pl*) an auricular feather. ▸ **auˈricularly** *adv*

auriculate (ɔːˈrɪkjʊlɪt, -ˌleɪt) *or* **auriculated** *adj* **1** having ears. **2** *Botany.* having ear-shaped parts or appendages. **3** Also: **auriform** (ˈɔːrɪˌfɔːm). shaped like an ear; auricular. ▸ **auˈriculately** *adv*

auriferous (ɔːˈrɪfərəs) *adj* (of rock) containing gold; gold-bearing. [C18: from Latin *aurifer* gold-bearing, from *aurum* gold + *ferre* to bear]

Auriga (ɔːˈraɪgə) *n, Latin genitive* **Aurigae** (ɔːˈraɪdʒiː). a conspicuous constellation in the N hemisphere between the Great Bear and Orion, at the edge of the Milky Way. It contains the first magnitude star Capella and the binary star **Epsilon Aurigae,** which is the largest known star. [Latin: charioteer]

Aurignacian (ˌɔːrɪgˈneɪʃən) *adj* of, relating to, or produced during a flint culture of the Upper Palaeolithic type characterized by the use of bone and antler tools, pins, awls, etc., and also by cave art and evidence of the beginnings of religion. [C20: from French *Aurignacien,* after *Aurignac,* France, in the Pyrenees, near which is the cave where remains were discovered]

Auriol (*French* ɔrjɔl) *n* **Vincent** (vɛ̃sɑ̃). 1884–1966, French statesman; president of the Fourth Republic (1947–54).

aurist (ˈɔːrɪst) *n* an ear specialist.

aurochs (ˈɔːrɒks) *n, pl* **-rochs.** a recently extinct member of the cattle tribe, *Bos primigenius,* that inhabited forests in N Africa, Europe, and SW Asia. It had long horns and is thought to be one of the ancestors of modern cattle. Also called: **urus.** [C18: from German, from Old High German *ūrohso,* from *ūro* bison + *ohso* OX]

aurora (ɔːˈrɔːrə) *n, pl* **-ras** *or* **-rae** (-riː). **1** an atmospheric phenomenon consisting of bands, curtains, or streamers of light, usually green, red, or yellow, that move across the sky in polar regions. It is caused by collisions between air molecules and charged particles from the sun that are trapped in the earth's magnetic field. **2** *Poetic.* the dawn. [C14: from Latin: dawn; see EAST] ▸ **auˈroral** *adj* ▸ **auˈrorally** *adv*

Aurora[1] (ɔːˈrɔːrə) *n* **1** the Roman goddess of the dawn. Greek counterpart: **Eos. 2** the dawn or rise of something.

Aurora[2] (ɔːˈrɔːrə) *n* another name for **Maewo.**

aurora australis (ɒˈstreɪlɪs) *n* (*sometimes cap.*) the aurora seen around the South Pole. Also called: **southern lights.** [New Latin: southern aurora]

aurora borealis (ˌbɔːrɪˈeɪlɪs) *n* (*sometimes cap.*) the aurora seen around the North Pole. Also called: **northern lights.** [C17: New Latin: northern aurora]

aurous (ˈɔːrəs) *adj* of or containing gold, esp. in the monovalent state. [C19: apparently from French *aureux,* from Late Latin *aurōsus* gold-coloured, from Latin *aurum* gold]

aurum (ˈɔːrəm) *n Obsolete.* gold. [C16: Latin]

AUS 1 *international car registration for* Australia. **2** *abbrev. for* Australian Union of Students.

Aus. *abbrev. for:* **1** Australia(n). **2** Austria(n).

Auschwitz (*German* ˈauʃvɪts) *n* an industrial town in S Poland; site of a Nazi concentration camp during World War II. Pop.: 45 400 (1989 est.). Polish name: **Oświęcim.**

auscultate (ˈɔːskəlˌteɪt) *vb* to examine (a patient) by means of auscultation. ▸ **ˈauscultator** *n*

auscultation (ˌɔːskəlˈteɪʃən) *n* **1** the diagnostic technique in medicine of listening to the various internal sounds made by the body, usually with the aid of a stethoscope. **2** the act of listening. [C19: from Latin *auscultātiō* a listening, from *auscultāre* to listen attentively; related to Latin *auris* ear] ▸ **auscultatory** (ɔːˈskʌltətərɪ) *or* **auscultative** (ɔːˈskʌltətɪv, ˈɔːskəlˌteɪtɪv) *adj*

ausforming (ˈausˌfɔːmɪŋ) *n* a treatment to strengthen hard steels, prior to quenching, in which the specimen is plastically deformed while it is in the austenite temperature range. [C20: from AUS(TENITIC) + (DE)FORM]

Ausgleich *German.* (ˈausglaiç) *n* the agreement (1867) that established the Dual Monarchy of Austria-Hungary. [German: levelling out, from *aus* OUT + *gleichen* to be similar]

Auslese (ˈausˌleɪsə) *n* a white wine, usually sweet, produced in Germany from individually selected bunches of very ripe grapes. [C20: from German, literally: selection]

Ausonius (ɔːˈsəʊnɪəs) *n* **Decimus Magnus** (ˈdesɪməs ˈmægnəs). ?310–?395 A.D., Latin poet, born in Gaul.

auspex (ˈɔːspeks) *n, pl* **auspices** (ˈɔːspɪˌsiːz). *Roman history.* another word for **augur** (sense 1). [C16: from Latin: observer of birds, from *avis* bird + *specere* to look]

auspice (ˈɔːspɪs) *n, pl* **-pices** (-pɪsɪz). **1** (*usually pl*) patronage or guidance (esp. in the phrase **under the auspices of**). **2** (*often pl*) a sign or omen, esp. one that is favourable. [C16: from Latin *auspicium* augury from birds; see AUSPEX]

auspicious (ɔːˈspɪʃəs) *adj* **1** favourable or propitious. **2** *Archaic.* prosperous or fortunate. ▸ **ausˈpiciously** *adv* ▸ **ausˈpiciousness** *n*

USAGE The use of *auspicious* to mean 'very special' (as in *this auspicious occasion*) should be avoided.

Aussat (ˈɒsæt, ˈɒzæt) *n* the Australian-owned communications satellite launched in 1985.

Aussie (ˈɒzɪ) *adj, n* an informal word for **Australian** or (rare) **Australia.**

Aust. *abbrev. for:* **1** Australia(n). **2** Austria(n).

Austen (ˈɒstɪn, ˈɔː-) *n* **Jane.** 1775–1817, English novelist, noted particularly for the insight and delicate irony of her portrayal of middle-class families. Her completed novels are *Sense and Sensibility* (1811), *Pride and Prejudice* (1813), *Mansfield Park* (1814), *Emma* (1816), *Northanger Abbey* (1818), and *Persuasion* (1818).

austenite (ˈɔːstəˌnaɪt) *n* **1** a solid solution of carbon in face-centred-cubic gamma iron, usually existing above 723°C. **2** the gamma phase of iron, stabilized at low temperatures by the addition of such elements as nickel. [C20: named after Sir William C. Roberts-*Austen* (1843–1902), English metallurgist] ▸ **austenitic** (ˌɔːstəˈnɪtɪk) *adj*

austenitic stainless steel *n* an alloy of iron, usually containing at least 8 per cent of nickel and 18 per cent of chromium, used where corrosion resistance, heat resistance, creep resistance, or nonmagnetic properties are required.

Auster (ˈɔːstə) *n Poetic.* the south wind. [C14: Latin]

austere (ɒˈstɪə) *adj* **1** stern or severe in attitude or manner: *an austere schoolmaster.* **2** grave, sober, or serious: *an austere expression.* **3** self-disciplined, abstemious, or ascetic: *an austere life.* **4** severely simple or plain: *an austere design.* [C14: from Old French *austère,* from Latin *austērus* sour, from Greek *austēros* astringent; related to Greek *hauein* to dry] ▸ **ausˈterely** *adv* ▸ **ausˈtereness** *n*

austerity (ɒˈsterɪtɪ) *n, pl* **-ties. 1** the state or quality of being austere. **2** (*often pl*) an austere habit, practice, or act. **3a** reduced availability of luxuries and consumer goods, esp. when brought about by government policy. **3b** (*as modifier*): *an austerity budget.*

Austerlitz (ˈɔːstəlɪts) *n* a town in the Czech Republic, in Moravia: site of Napoleon's victory over the Russian and Austrian armies in 1805. Pop.: 4747 (latest est.). Czech name: **Slavkov.**

Austin[1] (ˈɒstɪn) *n* a city in central Texas, on the Colorado River: state capital since 1845. Pop.: 541 278 (1996 est.).

Austin[2] (ˈɒstɪn, ˈɔː-) *n* **1 Herbert,** 1st Baron. 1866–1941, British automobile engineer, who founded the Austin Motor Company. **2 John.** 1790–1859, British jurist, whose book *The Province of Jurisprudence Determined* (1832) greatly influenced legal theory and the English legal system. **3 J(ohn) L(angshaw)** (ˈlæŋʃɔː). 1911–60, English philosopher, whose lectures *Sense and Sensibilia* and *How to do Things with Words* were published posthumously in 1962.

Austin[3] (ˈɒstɪn) *adj, n* another word for **Augustinian.** [C14: shortened form of AUGUSTINE]

austral[1] (ˈɔːstrəl) *adj* of or coming from the south: *austral winds.* [C14: from Latin *austrālis,* from *auster* the south wind]

austral[2] (auˈstrɑːl) *n, pl* **-trales.** a former monetary unit of Argentina equal to 100 centavos, replaced by the peso. [from Spanish; see AUSTRAL[1]]

Austral. *abbrev. for:* **1** Australasia. **2** Australia(n).

Australasia (ˌɒstrəˈleɪzɪə) *n* **1** Australia, New Zealand, and neighbouring islands in the S Pacific Ocean. **2** (loosely) the whole of Oceania.

Australasian (ˌɒstrəˈleɪzɪən) *n* **1** a native or inhabitant of Australasia. ◆ *adj* **2** of or relating to Australia, New Zealand, and the neighbouring islands. **3** (of organizations) having members in Australia and New Zealand.

Australia (ɒˈstreɪlɪə) *n* a country and the smallest continent, situated between the Indian Ocean and the Pacific: a former British colony, now an independent member of the Commonwealth, constitutional links with Britain formally abolished in 1986; consists chiefly of a low plateau, mostly arid in the west, with the basin of the Murray River and the Great Dividing Range in the east and the Great Barrier Reef off the NE coast. Official language: English. Religion: Christian majority. Currency: dollar. Capital: Canberra. Pop.: 18 725 000 (1998 est.). Area: 7 682 300 sq. km (2 966 150 sq. miles).

Australia Day *n* a public holiday in Australia, commemorating the landing of the British in 1788: observed on the first Monday after January 26.

Australian (ɒˈstreɪlɪən) *n* **1** a native or inhabitant of Australia. **2** the form of English spoken in Australia. **3** a linguistic phylum consisting of the languages spoken by the native Australians. ◆ *adj* **4** of, relating to, or characteristic of Australia, the Australians, or their form of English. **5** of, relating to, or belonging to the phylum of languages spoken by the native Australians. **6** of or denoting a zoogeographical region consisting of Australia, New Zealand, Polynesia, New Guinea, and the Moluccas.

Australiana (ɒˌstreɪlɪˈɑːnə) *pl n* objects or documents relating to Australia and its history or culture esp. in the form of a collection.

Australian Alps *pl n* a mountain range in SE Australia, in E Victoria and SE New South Wales. Highest peak: Mount Kosciusko, 2195 m (7316 ft.).

Australian Antarctic Territory *n* the area of Antarctica, other than Adélie Land, that is administered by Australia, lying south of latitude 60°S and between longitudes 45°E and 160°E.

Australian Capital Territory *n* a territory of SE Australia, within New South

Wales: consists of two exclaves, one containing Canberra, the capital of Australia, and one at Jervis Bay. Pop.: 299 243 (1996). Area: 2432 sq. km (939 sq. miles). Former name: **Federal Capital Territory.**

Australianism (ɒ'streɪlɪə,nɪzəm) *n* **1** the Australian national character or spirit. **2** loyalty to Australia, its political independence, culture, etc. **3** a linguistic usage, custom, or other feature peculiar to or characteristic of Australia, its people, or their culture.

Australianize *or* **Australianise** (ɒ'streɪlɪə,naɪz) *vb* (esp. of a new immigrant) to adopt or cause to adopt Australian habits and attitudes; integrate into Australian society.

Australian Rules *n* (*functioning as sing*) a game resembling rugby football, played in Australia between teams of 18 men each on an oval pitch, with a ball resembling a large rugby ball. Players attempt to kick the ball between posts (without crossbars) at either end of the pitch, scoring six points for a goal (between the two main posts) and one point for a behind (between either of two outer posts and the main posts). They may punch or kick the ball and run with it provided that they bounce it every ten yards. Also called: **national code.**

Australian salmon *n* another name for **kahawai.**

Australian terrier *n* a small wire-haired breed of terrier similar to the cairn.

Austral Islands ('ɔːstrəl) *pl n* another name for the **Tubuai Islands.**

Australoid ('ɒstrə,lɔɪd) *adj* **1** denoting, relating to, or belonging to a racial group that includes the native Australians and certain other peoples of southern Asia and the Pacific islands, characterized by dark skin, flat retreating forehead, and medium stature. ◆ *n* **2** any member of this racial group.

australopithecine (,ɒstrələʊ'pɪθɪ,siːn) *n* **1** any of various extinct apelike primates of the genus *Australopithecus* and related genera, remains of which have been discovered in southern and E Africa. Some species are estimated to be over 4.5 million years old. See also **zinjanthropus.** ◆ *adj* **2** of or relating to any of these primates. [C20: from New Latin *Australopithecus,* from Latin *austrālis* southern, AUSTRAL[1] + Greek *pithēkos* ape]

Australorp ('ɒstrə,lɔːp) *n* a heavy black breed of domestic fowl. [shortened from *Austral(ian Black) Orp(ington)*]

Austrasia (ɒ'streɪʒə, -ʃə) *n* the eastern region of the kingdom of the Merovingian Franks that had its capital at Metz and lasted from 511 A.D. until 814 A.D. It covered the area now comprising NE France, Belgium, and western Germany.

Austria ('ɒstrɪə) *n* a republic in central Europe: ruled by the Hapsburgs from 1282 to 1918; formed a dual monarchy with Hungary in 1867 and became a republic in 1919; a member of the European Union; contains part of the Alps, the Danube basin in the east, and extensive forests. Official language: German. Religion: Roman Catholic majority. Currency: euro and schilling. Capital: Vienna. Pop.: 8 070 000 (1998 est.). Area: 83 849 sq. km (32 374 sq. miles). German name: **Österreich.** ► **'Austrian** *adj, n*

Austria-Hungary *n* the Dual Monarchy established in 1867, consisting of what are now Austria, Hungary, the Czech Republic, Slovakia, Slovenia, Croatia, and Bosnia-Herzegovina, and parts of Poland, Romania, Ukraine, and Italy. The empire was broken up after World War I. ► **,Austro-Hun'garian** *adj*

Austrian blind *n* a window blind consisting of rows of vertically gathered fabric that may be drawn up to form a series of ruches.

Austro-[1] ('ɒstrəʊ-) *combining form.* southern: *Austro-Asiatic.* [from Latin *auster* the south wind]

Austro-[2] ('ɒstrəʊ-) *combining form.* Austrian: *Austro-Hungarian.*

Austro-Asiatic *n* a hypothetical phylum or superfamily of languages consisting of Mon-Khmer and certain other languages of India and South-East Asia. Links with Malayo-Polynesian have also been suggested.

Austronesia (,ɒstrəʊ'niːʒə, -ʃə) *n* the islands of the central and S Pacific, including Indonesia, Melanesia, Micronesia, and Polynesia.

Austronesian (,ɒstrəʊ'niːʒən, -ʃən) *adj* **1** of or relating to Austronesia, its peoples, or their languages. ◆ *n* **2** another name for **Malayo-Polynesian.**

AUT *abbrev. for* Association of University Teachers.

aut- *combining form.* a variant of **auto-** before a vowel.

autacoid ('ɔːtə,kɔɪd) *n Physiol.* any natural internal secretion, esp. one that exerts an effect similar to a drug. [C20: from AUTO- + Greek *akos* cure + -OID]

autarchy[1] ('ɔːtɑːkɪ) *n, pl* **-chies. 1** unlimited rule; autocracy. **2** self-government; self-rule. [C17: from Greek *autarkhia,* from *autarkhos* autocratic; see AUTO-, -ARCHY] ► **au'tarchic** *or* **au'tarchical** *adj*

autarchy[2] ('ɔːtɑːkɪ) *n, pl* **-chies.** a variant spelling (now rare) of **autarky.**

autarky ('ɔːtɑːkɪ) *n, pl* **-kies. 1** (esp. of a political unit) a system or policy of economic self-sufficiency aimed at removing the need for imports. **2** an economically self-sufficient country. [C17: from Greek *autarkeia,* from *autarkēs* self-sufficient, from AUTO- + *arkein* to suffice] ► **au'tarkic** *adj* ► **'autarkist** *n*

autecious (ɔː'tiːʃəs) *adj* a variant spelling of **autoecious.**

autecology (,ɔːtɪ'kɒlədʒɪ) *n* the ecological study of an individual organism or species. Compare **synecology.** ► **,auteco'logical** *adj*

auteur (ɔː'tɜː) *n* a director whose creative influence on a film is so great as to be considered its author. [French: author] ► **au'teurism** *n* ► **au'teurist** *adj*

auth. *abbrev. for:* **1** author. **2** authority. **3** authorized.

authentic (ɔː'θɛntɪk) *adj* **1** of undisputed origin or authorship; genuine: *an authentic signature.* **2** accurate in representation of the facts; trustworthy; reliable: *an authentic account.* **3** (of a deed or other document) duly executed, any necessary legal formalities having been complied with. **4** *Music.* **4a** using period instruments and historically researched scores and playing techniques in an attempt to perform a piece as it would have been played at the time it was written. **4b** (*in combination*): *an authentic-instrument performance.* **5** *Music.* **5a** (of a mode as used in Gregorian chant) commencing on the final and ending an octave higher. **5b** (of a cadence) progressing from a dominant to a tonic chord. Compare **plagal.** [C14: from Late Latin *authenticus* coming from the author, from Greek *authentikos,* from *authentēs* one who acts independently, from AUTO- + *hentēs* a doer] ► **au'thentically** *adv* ► **authenticity** (,ɔːθɛn'tɪsɪtɪ) *n*

authenticate (ɔː'θɛntɪ,keɪt) *vb* (*tr*) **1** to establish as genuine or valid. **2** to give authority or legal validity to. ► **au,thenti'cation** *n* ► **au'thenti,cator** *n*

authigenic (,ɔːθɪ'dʒɛnɪk) *adj* (of minerals) having crystallized in a sediment during or after deposition. [C19: from German *authigene* from Greek *authigenēs* native + -IC]

author ('ɔːθə) *n* **1** a person who composes a book, article, or other written work. Related adj: **auctorial. 2** a person who writes books as a profession; writer. **3** the writings of such a person: *reviewing a postwar author.* **4** an originator or creator: *the author of this plan.* ◆ *vb* (*tr*) **5** to write or originate. [C14: from Old French *autor,* from Latin *auctor* author, from *augēre* to increase] ► **authorial** (ɔː'θɔːrɪəl) *adj*

authoress ('ɔːθə,rɛs) *n Now usually disparaging.* a female author.

authoritarian (ɔː,θɒrɪ'tɛərɪən) *adj* **1** favouring, denoting, or characterized by strict obedience to authority. **2** favouring, denoting, or relating to government by a small elite with wide powers. **3** despotic; dictatorial; domineering. ◆ *n* **4** a person who favours or practises authoritarian policies. ► **au,thori'tarianism** *n*

authoritative (ɔː'θɒrɪtətɪv) *adj* **1** recognized or accepted as being true or reliable: *an authoritative article on drugs.* **2** exercising or asserting authority; commanding: *an authoritative manner.* **3** possessing or supported by authority; official: *an authoritative communiqué.* ► **au'thoritatively** *adv* ► **au'thoritativeness** *n*

authority (ɔː'θɒrɪtɪ) *n, pl* **-ties. 1** the power or right to control, judge, or prohibit the actions of others. **2** (*often pl*) a person or group of people having this power, such as a government, police force, etc. **3** a position that commands such a power or right (often in the phrase **in authority**). **4** such a power or right delegated, esp. from one person to another; authorization: *she has his authority.* **5** the ability to influence or control others: *a man of authority.* **6** an expert or an authoritative written work in a particular field: *he is an authority on Ming china.* **7** evidence or testimony: *we have it on his authority that she is dead.* **8** confidence resulting from great expertise: *the violinist lacked authority in his cadenza.* **9** (*cap. when part of a name*) a public board or corporation exercising governmental authority in administering some enterprise: *Independent Broadcasting Authority.* **10** *Law.* **10a** a judicial decision, statute, or rule of law that establishes a principle; precedent. **10b** legal permission granted to a person to perform a specified act. [C14: from French *autorité,* from Latin *auctōritas,* from *auctor* AUTHOR]

authorize *or* **authorise** ('ɔːθə,raɪz) *vb* (*tr*) **1** to confer authority upon (someone to do something); empower. **2** to permit (someone to do or be something) with official sanction: *a dealer authorized by a manufacturer to retail his products.* ► **,authori'zation** *or* **,authori'sation** *n* ► **'author,izer** *or* **'author,iser** *n*

Authorized Version *n* **the.** an English translation of the Bible published in 1611 under James I. Also called: **King James Version, King James Bible.**

authorship ('ɔːθə,ʃɪp) *n* **1** the origin or originator of a written work, plan, etc.: *a book of unknown authorship.* **2** the profession of writing books.

Auth. Ver. *abbrev. for* Authorized Version (of the Bible).

autism ('ɔːtɪzəm) *n Psychiatry.* abnormal self-absorption, usually affecting children, characterized by lack of response to people and actions and limited ability to communicate: children suffering from autism often do not learn to speak. [C20: from Greek *autos* self + -ISM] ► **au'tistic** *adj, n*

auto ('ɔːtəʊ) *n, pl* **-tos.** *U.S. and Canadian informal.* **a** short for **automobile. b** (*as modifier*): *auto parts.*

auto. *abbrev. for:* **1** automatic. **2** automobile. **3** automotive.

auto- *or sometimes before a vowel* **aut-** *combining form.* **1** self; same; of or by the same one: *autobiography.* **2** acting from or occurring within; self-caused: *autohypnosis.* **3** self-propelling; automatic: *automobile.* [from Greek *autos* self]

autoallogamy (,ɔːtəʊə'lɒgəmɪ) *n* the ability of some plants of a species to cross-pollinate and others to self-pollinate.

autoantibody (,ɔːtəʊ'æntɪ,bɒdɪ) *n, pl* **-bodies.** an antibody reacting with an antigen that is a part of the organism in which the antibody is formed.

autobahn ('ɔːtə,bɑːn) *n* a motorway in German-speaking countries. [from German, from *Auto* car + *Bahn* road]

autobiographical (,ɔːtə,baɪə'græfɪkəl) *adj* **1** of or concerned with one's own life. **2** of or relating to an autobiography. ► **,auto,bio'graphically** *adv*

autobiography (,ɔːtəʊbaɪ'ɒgrəfɪ, ,ɔːtəbaɪ-) *n, pl* **-phies.** an account of a person's life written or otherwise recorded by that person. ► **,autobi'ographer** *n*

autocade ('ɔːtəʊ,keɪd) *n U.S.* another name for **motorcade.**

autocatalysis (,ɔːtəʊkə'tælɪsɪs) *n, pl* **-ses** (-,siːz). the catalysis of a reaction in which the catalyst is one of the products of the reaction.

autocephalous (,ɔːtəʊ'sɛfələs) *adj* **1** (of an Eastern Christian Church) governed by its own national synods and appointing its own patriarchs or prelates. **2** (of a bishop) independent of any higher governing body. ► **autocephalic** (,ɔːtəʊsɪ'fælɪk) *adj* ► **,auto'cephaly** *n*

autochanger ('ɔːtəʊ,tʃeɪndʒə) *n* **1** a device in a record player that enables a small stack of records to be dropped automatically onto the turntable one at a time and played separately. **2** a record player with such a device.

autochthon (ɔː'tɒkθən, -θɒn) *n, pl* **-thons** *or* **-thones** (-θə,niːz). **1** (*often pl*) one of the earliest known inhabitants of any country; aboriginal. **2** an animal or plant that is native to a particular region. [C17: from Greek *autokhthōn* from the earth itself, from AUTO- + *khthōn* the earth]

autochthonous (ɔː'tɒkθənəs), **autochthonic** (,ɔːtɒk'θɒnɪk), *or* **autochthonal** *adj* **1** (of rocks, deposits, etc.) found where they and their constituents were formed. Compare **allochthonous.** **2** inhabiting a place or region from earliest known times; aboriginal. **3** *Physiol.* (of some functions, such as heartbeat) originating within an organ rather than from external stimulation. ▸ **au'tochthonism** *or* **au'tochthony** *n* ▸ **au'tochthonously** *adv*

autocidal (ˌɔːtəʊ'saɪdᵊl) *adj* (of insect pest control) effected by the introduction of sterile or genetically altered individuals into the wild population.

autoclave ('ɔːtəˌkleɪv) *n* **1** a strong sealed vessel used for chemical reactions at high pressure. **2** an apparatus for sterilizing objects (esp. surgical instruments) or for cooking by means of steam under pressure. **3** *Civil engineering.* a vessel in which freshly cast concrete or sand-lime bricks are cured very rapidly in high-pressure steam. ◆ *vb* **4** (*tr*) to put in or subject to the action of an autoclave. [C19: from French AUTO- + *-clave,* from Latin *clāvis* key]

autocorrelation (ˌɔːtəʊˌkɒrɪ'leɪʃən) *n Statistics.* the condition occurring when successive items in a series are correlated so that their covariance is not zero and they are not independent. Also called: **serial correlation.**

autocracy (ɔː'tɒkrəsɪ) *n, pl* **-cies. 1** government by an individual with unrestricted authority. **2** the unrestricted authority of such an individual. **3** a country, society, etc., ruled by an autocrat.

autocrat ('ɔːtəˌkræt) *n* **1** a ruler who possesses absolute and unrestricted authority. **2** a domineering or dictatorial person. ▸ **ˌauto'cratic** *adj* ▸ **ˌauto'cratically** *adv*

autocross ('ɔːtəʊˌkrɒs) *n* a form of motor sport in which cars race over a half-mile circuit of rough grass. See also **motocross, rallycross.**

Autocue ('ɔːtəʊˌkjuː) *n Trademark.* an electronic television prompting device whereby a prepared script, unseen by the audience, is enlarged line by line for the speaker. U.S. and Canadian name (trademark): **Teleprompter.**

autocycle ('ɔːtəʊˌsaɪkᵊl) *n Obsolete.* a bicycle powered or assisted by a small engine.

auto-da-fé (ˌɔːtəʊdə'feɪ) *n, pl* **autos-da-fé. 1** *History.* a ceremony of the Spanish Inquisition including the pronouncement and execution of sentences passed on sinners or heretics. **2** the burning to death of people condemned as heretics by the Inquisition. [C18: from Portuguese, literally: act of the faith]

autodestruct (ˌɔːtəʊdɪ'strʌkt) *adj also* **autodestructive. 1** likely to or possessing the power to destroy or obliterate itself or its possessor: *autodestruct mechanism.* ◆ *vb* (*intr*) **2** (of a missile, machine, etc.) to destroy itself.

autodidact ('ɔːtəʊˌdaɪdækt) *n* a person who is self-taught. [C16: from Greek *autodidaktos* self-taught, from *autos* self + *didaskein* to teach] ▸ **ˌautodi'dactic** *adj*

autodyne ('ɔːtəʊˌdaɪn) *adj Electronics.* denoting or relating to an electrical circuit in which the same elements and valves are used as oscillator and detector.

autoecious *or U.S.* (*sometimes*) **autecious** (ɔː'tiːʃəs) *adj* (of parasites, esp. the rust fungi) completing the entire life cycle on a single species of host. Compare **heteroecious.** [C19: from AUTO- + *-oecious,* from Greek *oikia* house] ▸ **au'toecism** *or U.S.* (*sometimes*) **au'tecism** *n*

autoeroticism (ˌɔːtəʊɪ'rɒtɪˌsɪzəm) *or* **autoerotism** (ˌɔːtəʊ'ɛrəˌtɪzəm) *n Psychol.* the arousal and use of one's own body as a sexual object, as through masturbation. ▸ **ˌautoe'rotic** *adj*

autoexposure (ˌɔːtəɪk'spəʊʒə) *n* another name for **automatic exposure.**

autofocus ('ɔːtəʊˌfəʊkəs) *n* another name for **automatic focus.**

autogamy (ɔː'tɒgəmɪ) *n* **1** self-fertilization in flowering plants. **2** a type of sexual reproduction, occurring in some protozoans, in which the uniting gametes are derived from the same cell. ▸ **au'togamous** *or* **autogamic** (ˌɔːtə'gæmɪk) *adj*

autogenesis (ˌɔːtəʊ'dʒɛnɪsɪs) *or* **autogeny** (ɔː'tɒdʒɪnɪ) *n* another word for **abiogenesis.** ▸ **autogenetic** (ˌɔːtəʊdʒɪ'nɛtɪk) *adj*

autogenic training (ˌɔːtəʊ'dʒɛnɪk) *n* a technique for reducing stress through mental exercises to produce physical relaxation. Also called: **autogenics.**

autogenous (ɔː'tɒdʒɪnəs) *adj* **1a** originating within the body. Compare **heterogenous. 1b** denoting a vaccine made from bacteria obtained from the patient's own body. **2** self-generated; self-produced. **3** denoting a weld in which the filler metal and the parent metal are of similar composition. ▸ **au'togenously** *adv*

autogiro *or* **autogyro** (ˌɔːtəʊ'dʒaɪrəʊ) *n, pl* **-ros.** a self-propelled aircraft supported in flight mainly by unpowered rotating horizontal blades. Also called: **gyroplane.** Compare **helicopter.** [C20: originally a trademark]

autograft ('ɔːtəˌgrɑːft) *n Surgery.* a tissue graft obtained from one part of a patient's body for use on another part.

autograph ('ɔːtəˌgrɑːf, -ˌgræf) *n* **1a** a handwritten signature, esp. that of a famous person. **1b** (*as modifier*): *an autograph album.* **2** a person's handwriting. **3a** a book, document, etc., handwritten by its author; original manuscript; holograph. **3b** (*as modifier*): *an autograph letter.* ◆ *vb* (*tr*) **4** to write one's signature on or in; sign. **5** to write with one's own hand. [C17: from Late Latin, from Greek *autographos,* from *autos* self + *graphein* to write] ▸ **autographic** (ˌɔːtə'græfɪk) *or* **ˌauto'graphical** *adj* ▸ **ˌauto'graphically** *adv*

autography (ɔː'tɒgrəfɪ) *n* **1** the writing of something in one's own handwriting; something handwritten. **2** the precise reproduction of an illustration or of writing.

Autoharp ('ɔːtəʊˌhɑːp) *n Trademark.* a zither-like musical instrument used in country-and-western music, equipped with button-controlled dampers that can prevent selected strings from sounding, thus allowing chords to be played. It is plucked with the fingers or a plectrum.

autohypnosis (ˌɔːtəʊhɪp'nəʊsɪs) *n Psychol.* the process or result of self-induced hypnosis. ▸ **autohypnotic** (ˌɔːtəʊhɪp'nɒtɪk) *adj* ▸ **ˌautohyp'notically** *adv*

autoicous (ɔː'tɔɪkəs) *adj* (of plants, esp. mosses) having male and female reproductive organs on the same plant. [C19: from AUTO- + Greek *oikos* dwelling]

autoimmune (ˌɔːtəʊɪ'mjuːn) *adj* (of a disease) caused by the action of antibodies produced against substances normally present in the body. ▸ **ˌautoim'munity** *n*

autoinfection (ˌɔːtəʊɪn'fɛkʃən) *n* infection by a pathogenic agent already within the body or infection transferred from one part of the body to another.

autoinoculation (ˌɔːtəʊɪˌnɒkjʊ'leɪʃən) *n* the inoculation of microorganisms (esp. viruses) from one part of the body into another, usually in the form of a vaccine.

autointoxication (ˌɔːtəʊɪnˌtɒksɪ'keɪʃən) *n* self-poisoning caused by absorption of toxic products originating within the body. Also called: **autotoxaemia.**

autoionization *or* **autoionisation** (ˌɔːtəʊˌaɪənaɪ'zeɪʃən) *n Physics.* the process in which the decay of excited atoms or molecules results in emission of electrons, rather than photons.

autokinetic (ˌɔːtəʊkɪ'nɛtɪk, -kaɪ-) *adj* automatically self-moving.

autokinetic phenomenon *n Psychol.* the apparent movement of a fixed point of light when observed in a darkened room. The effect is produced by small eye movements for which the brain is unable to compensate, having no other reference points.

autoloading ('ɔːtəʊˌləʊdɪŋ) *adj* self-loading.

autologous (ɔː'tɒləgəs) *adj* (of a tissue graft, blood transfusion, etc.) originating from the recipient rather than from a donor.

Autolycus[1] (ɔː'tɒlɪkəs) *n* a crater in the NW quadrant of the moon about 38 kilometres in diameter and 3000 metres deep.

Autolycus[2] (ɔː'tɒlɪkəs) *n Greek myth.* a thief who stole cattle from his neighbour Sisyphus and prevented him from recognizing them by making them invisible.

autolyse *or U.S.* **autolyze** ('ɔːtəˌlaɪz) *vb Biochem.* to undergo or cause to undergo autolysis.

autolysin (ˌɔːtə'laɪsɪn, ɔː'tɒlɪ-) *n* any agent that produces autolysis.

autolysis (ɔː'tɒlɪsɪs) *n* the destruction of cells and tissues of an organism by enzymes produced by the cells themselves. [C20: via German from Greek *autos* self + *lusis* loosening, release] ▸ **autolytic** (ˌɔːtə'lɪtɪk) *adj*

automat ('ɔːtəˌmæt) *n* **1** Also called: **vending machine.** a machine that automatically dispenses goods, such as cigarettes, when money is inserted. **2** *Chiefly U.S.* an area or room, sometimes having restaurant facilities, where food and other goods are supplied from vending machines.

automata (ɔː'tɒmətə) *n* a plural of **automaton.**

automata theory *n* the formal study of the power of computation of abstract machines.

automate ('ɔːtəˌmeɪt) *vb* to make (a manufacturing process, factory, etc.) automatic, or (of a manufacturing process, etc.) to be made automatic.

automated teller machine *n* a computerized cash dispenser. Abbrev.: **ATM.**

automatic (ˌɔːtə'mætɪk) *adj* **1** performed from force of habit or without conscious thought; lacking spontaneity; mechanical: *an automatic smile.* **2a** (of a device, mechanism, etc.) able to activate, move, or regulate itself. **2b** (of an act or process) performed by such automatic equipment. **3** (of the action of a muscle, gland, etc.) involuntary or reflex. **4** occurring as a necessary consequence: *promotion is automatic after a year.* **5** (of a firearm) **5a** utilizing some of the force of each explosion to eject the empty shell, replace it with a new one, and fire continuously until release of the trigger. Compare **semiautomatic** (sense 2). **5b** short for **semiautomatic** (sense 2). ◆ See also **machine** (sense 5). ◆ *n* **6** an automatic firearm. **7** a motor vehicle having automatic transmission. **8** a machine that operates automatically. [C18: from Greek *automatos* acting independently] ▸ **ˌauto'matically** *adv* ▸ **automaticity** (ˌɔːtəʊmə'tɪsɪtɪ) *n*

automatic camera *n* a camera in which the lens aperture or the shutter speed or both are automatically adjusted to the prevailing conditions.

automatic door *n* a self-opening door.

automatic exposure *n* the automatic adjustment of the lens aperture and shutter speed of a camera by a control mechanism. Also called: **autoexposure.**

automatic focus *n* **a** a system in a camera which automatically adjusts the lens so that the object being photographed is in focus, often one using infrared light to estimate the distance of the object from the camera. **b** (*as modifier*): *automatic-focus lens. Abbrev.:* **AF.** Also called: **autofocus.**

automatic frequency control *n* a system in a radio or television receiver by which the tuning of an incoming signal is accurately maintained. Abbrev.: **AFC.**

automatic gain control *n* control of a radio receiver in which the gain varies inversely with the magnitude of the input, thus maintaining the output at an approximately constant level. Abbrev.: **AGC.**

automatic pilot *n* **1** Also called: **autopilot.** a device that automatically maintains an aircraft on a preset course. **2 on automatic pilot.** *Informal.* acting without conscious thought because of tiredness, shock, or familiarity with the task being performed.

automatic repeat *n* a key on the keyboard of a typewriter, computer, etc., which, when depressed continuously, produces the character repeatedly until the key is released.

automatic transmission *n* a transmission system in a motor vehicle, usually incorporating a fluid clutch, in which the gears change automatically.

automatic vending *n* selling goods by vending machines.

automation (ˌɔːtə'meɪʃən) *n* **1** the use of methods for controlling industrial processes automatically, esp. by electronically controlled systems, often reducing manpower. **2** the extent to which a process is so controlled.

automatism (ɔː'tɒməˌtɪzəm) *n* **1** the state or quality of being automatic; mechanical or involuntary action. **2** *Law, philosophy* the explanation of an action, or of action in general, as determined by the physiological states of the individual, admissible in law as a defence. **3** *Psychol.* the performance of actions, such as sleepwalking, without conscious knowledge or control. **4** the suspension of consciousness sought or achieved by certain artists and writers to allow free flow of uncensored thoughts. ▸ **au'tomatist** *n*

automatize *or* **automatise** (ɔː'tɒmə,taɪz) *vb* to make (a process, etc.) automatic or (of a process, etc.) to be made automatic. ▸ **au,tomati'zation** *or* **au,tomati'sation** *n*

automaton (ɔː'tɒmə,tɒn, -tᵊn) *n, pl* **-tons** *or* **-ta** (-tə). **1** a mechanical device operating under its own hidden power; robot. **2** a person who acts mechanically or leads a routine monotonous life. [C17: from Latin, from Greek, from *automatos* spontaneous, self-moving] ▸ **au'tomatous** *adj*

autometer ('ɔːtəʊ,miːtə) *n* a small device inserted in a photocopier to enable the process of copying to begin and to record the number of copies made.

automobile ('ɔːtəmə,biːl) *n* another word (esp. U.S.) for **car** (sense 1). ▸ **automobilist** (,ɔːtəmə'biːlɪst, -'məʊbɪlɪst) *n*

automobilia (,ɔːtəmə'biːlɪə) *pl n* items connected with cars and motoring of interest to the collector.

automotive (,ɔːtə'məʊtɪv) *adj* **1** relating to motor vehicles. **2** self-propelling.

autonomic (,ɔːtə'nɒmɪk) *adj* **1** occurring involuntarily or spontaneously. **2** of or relating to the autonomic nervous system. **3** Also: **autonomous.** (of plant movements) occurring as a result of internal stimuli. ▸ **,auto'nomically** *adv*

autonomic nervous system *n* the section of the nervous system of vertebrates that controls the involuntary actions of the smooth muscles, heart, and glands. Compare **somatic nervous system.**

autonomics (,ɔːtə'nɒmɪks) *n* (*functioning as sing*) *Electronics.* the study of self-regulating systems for process control.

autonomous (ɔː'tɒnəməs) *adj* **1** (of a community, country, etc.) possessing a large degree of self-government. **2** of or relating to an autonomous community. **3** independent of others. **4** *Philosophy.* **4a** acting or able to act in accordance with rules and principles of one's own choosing. **4b** (in the moral philosophy of Kant, of an individual's will) directed to duty rather than to some other end. Compare **heteronomous** (sense 3). See also **categorical imperative. 5** *Biol.* existing as an organism independent of other organisms or parts. **6** a variant spelling of **autonomic** (sense 3). [C19: from Greek *autonomos* living under one's own laws, from AUTO- + *nomos* law] ▸ **au'tonomously** *adv*

autonomy (ɔː'tɒnəmɪ) *n, pl* **-mies. 1** the right or state of self-government, esp. when limited. **2** a state, community, or individual possessing autonomy. **3** freedom to determine one's own actions, behaviour, etc. **4** *Philosophy.* **4a** the doctrine that the individual human will is or ought to be governed only by its own principles and laws. See also **categorical imperative. 4b** the state in which one's actions are autonomous. [C17: from Greek *autonomia* freedom to live by one's own laws; see AUTONOMOUS] ▸ **au'tonomist** *n*

autophyte ('ɔːtə,faɪt) *n* an autotrophic plant, such as any green plant. ▸ **autophytic** (,ɔːtə'fɪtɪk) *adj* ▸ **,auto'phytically** *adv*

autopilot (,ɔːtə'paɪlət, -təʊ-) *n* short for **automatic pilot.**

autopista (,ɔːtə'piːstə) *n* a Spanish motorway. [from Spanish: auto(mobile) track]

autoplasty ('ɔːtə,plæstɪ) *n* surgical repair of defects by grafting or transplanting tissue from the patient's own body. ▸ **,auto'plastic** *adj*

autopolyploid (,ɔːtəʊ'pɒlɪ,plɔɪd) *adj* **1** (of cells, organisms, etc.) having more than two sets of haploid chromosomes inherited from a single species. ◆ *n* **2** an organism or cell of this type. ◆ See also **allopolyploid, polyploid.** ▸ **,auto'poly,ploidy** *n*

autopsy ('ɔːtɒpsɪ, ɔː'tɒp-) *n, pl* **-sies. 1** Also called: **necropsy, postmortem examination.** dissection and examination of a dead body to determine the cause of death. **2** an eyewitness observation. **3** any critical analysis. [C17: from New Latin *autopsia,* from Greek: seeing with one's own eyes, from AUTO- + *opsis* sight]

autoput ('ɔːtəʊ,pʊt) *n* a Yugoslavian motorway. [from Serbo-Croat: auto(mobile) road]

autoradiograph (,ɔːtəʊ'reɪdɪə,grɑːf, -,græf) *n* a photograph showing the distribution of a radioactive substance in a specimen. The photographic plate is exposed by radiation from the specimen. Also called: **radioautograph.** ▸ **autoradiographic** (,ɔːtəʊ,reɪdɪə'græfɪk) *adj* ▸ **autoradiography** (,ɔːtəʊ,reɪdɪ'ɒgrəfɪ) *n*

autorickshaw ('ɔːtəʊ'rɪkʃɔː) *n* (in India) a light three-wheeled vehicle driven by a motorcycle engine.

autorotation (,ɔːtəʊrəʊ'teɪʃən) *n* the continuous rotation of a body in an airflow, such as that of the rotor blades of a helicopter in an unpowered descent.

autoroute ('ɔːtəʊ,ruːt) *n* a French motorway. [from French, from *auto* car + *route* road]

autosome ('ɔːtə,səʊm) *n* any chromosome that is not a sex chromosome. ▸ **,auto'somal** *adj*

autospore ('ɔːtəʊ,spɔː) *n* a nonmotile algal spore that develops adult characteristics before being released.

autostability (,ɔːtəʊstə'bɪlɪtɪ) *n* the property of being stable either as a result of inherent characteristics or of built-in devices.

autostrada ('ɔːtəʊ,strɑːdə) *n* an Italian motorway. [from Italian, from *auto* car + *strada* road]

autosuggestion (,ɔːtəʊsə'dʒɛstʃən) *n* a process of suggestion in which the person unconsciously supplies or consciously attempts to supply the means of influencing his own behaviour or beliefs. ▸ **,autosug'gestive** *adj*

autotimer ('ɔːtəʊ,taɪmə) *n* a device for turning an electric cooker on and off automatically at times predetermined by advance setting.

autotomize *or* **autotomise** (ɔː'tɒtə,maɪz) *vb* to cause (a part of the body) to undergo autotomy.

autotomy (ɔː'tɒtəmɪ) *n, pl* **-mies.** the casting off by an animal of a part of its body, to facilitate escape when attacked. ▸ **autotomic** (,ɔːtə'tɒmɪk) *adj*

autotoxaemia *or U.S.* **autotoxemia** (,ɔːtəʊtɒk'siːmɪə) *n* another name for **autointoxication.**

autotoxin (,ɔːtə'tɒksɪn) *n* any poison or toxin formed in the organism upon which it acts. See **autointoxication.** ▸ **,auto'toxic** *adj*

autotransformer (,ɔːtəʊtræns'fɔːmə) *n* a transformer in which part of the winding is common to both primary and secondary circuits.

autotrophic (,ɔːtə'trɒfɪk) *adj* (of organisms such as green plants) capable of manufacturing complex organic nutritive compounds from simple inorganic sources such as carbon dioxide, water, and nitrates. Compare **heterotrophic.** ▸ **autotroph** ('ɔːtətrəʊf) *n*

autotype ('ɔːtə,taɪp) *n* **1** a photographic process for producing prints in black and white, using a carbon pigment. **2** an exact copy of a manuscript, etc.; facsimile. ▸ **autotypic** (,ɔːtə'tɪpɪk) *adj* ▸ **'auto,typy** *n*

autowinder ('ɔːtəʊ,waɪndə) *n Photog.* a battery-operated device for advancing the film in a camera automatically after each exposure. Compare **motor drive.**

autoxidation (ɔː,tɒksɪ'deɪʃən) *n Chem.* **a** oxidation by exposure to atmospheric oxygen. **b** oxidation that will only occur when another oxidation reaction is taking place in the same system.

autumn ('ɔːtəm) *n* **1** (*sometimes cap.*) **1a** Also called (esp. U.S.): **fall.** the season of the year between summer and winter, astronomically from the September equinox to the December solstice in the N hemisphere and from the March equinox to the June solstice in the S hemisphere. **1b** (*as modifier*): *autumn leaves.* **2** a period of late maturity, esp. one followed by a decline. [C14: from Latin *autumnus,* perhaps of Etruscan origin]

autumnal (ɔː'tʌmnᵊl) *adj* of, occurring in, or characteristic of autumn. ▸ **au'tumnally** *adv*

autumnal equinox *n* **1** the time at which the sun crosses the plane of the equator away from the relevant hemisphere, making day and night of equal length. It occurs about Sept. 23 in the N hemisphere (March 21 in the S hemisphere). **2** *Astronomy.* the point on the celestial sphere, lying in the constellation of Virgo, at which the ecliptic intersects the celestial equator.

autumn crocus *n* a liliaceous plant, *Colchicum autumnale,* of Europe and N Africa having pink or purplish autumn flowers. Also called: **meadow saffron.** Compare **saffron.**

autunite ('ɔːtə,naɪt) *n* a yellowish fluorescent radioactive mineral consisting of a hydrated calcium uranium phosphate in tetragonal crystalline form. It is found in uranium ores. Formula: $Ca(UO_2)_2(PO_4)_2.10–12H_2O$. [C19: named after *Autun* in France, one of the places where it was found, + -ITE[1]]

Auvergne (əʊ'veən, əʊ'vɜːn; *French* ovɛrɲ) *n* a region of S central France: largely mountainous, rising over 1800 m (6000 ft.).

aux. *abbrev. for* auxiliary.

auxanometer (,ɔːksə'nɒmɪtə) *n* an instrument that measures the linear growth of plant shoots. [C19: from Greek *auxanein* to increase + -METER]

Aux Cayes (əʊ 'keɪ; *French* o kaj) *n* the former name of **Les Cayes.**

Auxerre (*French* ozɛr) *n* a town in central France, capital of the Yonne department; Gothic cathedral. Pop.: 40 600 (1990).

auxesis (ɔːg'ziːsɪs, ɔːk'siː-) *n* growth in animal or plant tissues resulting from an increase in cell size without cell division. [C16: via Latin from Greek: increase, from *auxein* to increase, grow]

auxiliaries (ɔːg'zɪljərɪz, -'zɪlə-) *pl n* foreign or allied troops serving another nation; mercenaries.

auxiliary (ɔːg'zɪljərɪ, -'zɪlə-) *adj* **1** secondary or supplementary. **2** supporting. **3** *Nautical.* (of a sailing vessel) having an engine: *an auxiliary sloop.* ◆ *n, pl* **-ries. 4** a person or thing that supports or supplements; subordinate or assistant. **5** *Nautical.* **5a** a sailing vessel with an engine. **5b** the engine of such a vessel. **6** *Navy.* a vessel such as a tug, hospital ship, etc., not used for combat. [C17: from Latin *auxiliārius* bringing aid, from *auxilium* help, from *augēre* to increase, enlarge, strengthen]

auxiliary note *n Music.* a nonharmonic note occurring between two harmonic notes.

auxiliary power unit *n* an additional engine fitted to an aircraft to operate when the main engines are not in use.

auxiliary rotor *n* the tail rotor of a helicopter, used for directional and rotary control.

auxiliary verb *n* a verb used to indicate the tense, voice, mood, etc., of another verb where this is not indicated by inflection, such as English *will* in *he will go, was* in *he was eating* and *he was eaten, do* in *I do like you,* etc.

auxin ('ɔːksɪn) *n* any of various plant hormones, such as indoleacetic acid, that promote growth and control fruit and flower development. Synthetic auxins are widely used in agriculture and horticulture. [C20: from Greek *auxein* to grow]

auxochrome ('ɔːksə,krəʊm) *n* a group of atoms that can be attached to a chromogen to convert it into a dye.

auxocyte ('ɔːksə,saɪt) *n* any cell undergoing meiosis, esp. an oocyte or spermatocyte.

auxospore ('ɔːksə,spɔː) *n* the protoplasm of a diatom before its cell wall is formed.

auxotonic (,ɔːksə'tɒnɪk) *adj* (of muscle contraction) occurring against increasing force.

auxotroph ('ɔːksətrəʊf) *n* a mutant strain of microorganism requiring growth factors not needed by the normal organism. ▸ **,auxo'trophic** *adj*

Av (æv) *or* **Ab** *n* (in the Jewish calendar) the fifth month of the year according to biblical reckoning and the eleventh month in the civil year, usually falling within July and August. [from Hebrew]

AV *abbrev. for* Authorized Version (of the Bible).

av. *abbrev. for:* **1** average. **2** avoirdupois.

Av. *or* **av.** *abbrev. for* avenue.

a.v. *or* **A/V** *abbrev. for* ad valorem.

a-v, A-V, *or* **AV** *abbrev. for* audiovisual.

ava (ə'vɔː) *adv Scot.* at all. [Scot. form of *of all*]

avadavat (ˌævədəˈvæt) *or* **amadavat** (ˌæmədəˈvæt) *n* either of two Asian weaverbirds of the genus *Estrilda*, esp. *E. amandava*, having a red plumage: often kept as cagebirds. [C18: from *Ahmadabad*, Indian city from which these birds were brought to Europe]

avail (əˈveɪl) *vb* **1** to be of use, advantage, profit, or assistance (to). **2 avail oneself of.** to make use of to one's advantage. ◆ *n* **3** use or advantage (esp. in the phrases **of no avail, to little avail**). [C13 *availen*, from *vailen*, from Old French *valoir*, from Latin *valēre* to be strong, prevail] ▸ **aˈvailingly** *adv*

available (əˈveɪləbᵊl) *adj* **1** obtainable or accessible; capable of being made use of; at hand. **2** *U.S. politics, derogatory.* suitable for public office, usually as a result of having an inoffensive character: *Smith was a particularly available candidate.* ▸ **aˌvailaˈbility** *or* **aˈvailableness** *n* ▸ **aˈvailably** *adv*

avalanche (ˈævəˌlɑːntʃ) *n* **1a** a fall of large masses of snow and ice down a mountain. **1b** a fall of rocks, sand, etc. **2** a sudden or overwhelming appearance of a large quantity of things: *an avalanche of letters.* **3** *Physics.* a group of ions produced by a single ion as a result of a collision with some other form of matter. ◆ *vb* **4** to come down overwhelmingly (upon). [C18: from French, by mistaken division from *la valanche*, from *valanche*, from (northwestern Alps) dialect *lavantse*; related to Old Provençal *lavanca*, of obscure origin]

Avalon (ˈævəˌlɒn) *n Celtic myth.* an island paradise in the western seas: in Arthurian legend it is where King Arthur was taken after he was mortally wounded. [from Medieval Latin *insula avallonis* island of Avalon, from Old Welsh *aballon* apple]

Avalon Peninsula *n* a large peninsula of Newfoundland, between Trinity and Placentia Bays. Area: about 10 000 sq. km (4000 sq. miles).

avant- *prefix* of or belonging to the avant-garde of a specified field.

avant-garde (ˌævɒŋˈgɑːd; *French* avɑ̃gard) *n* **1** those artists, writers, musicians, etc., whose techniques and ideas are markedly experimental or in advance of those generally accepted. ◆ *adj* **2** of such artists, etc., their ideas, or techniques. **3** radical; daring. [from French: VANGUARD] ▸ **ˌavant-ˈgardism** *n* ▸ **ˌavant-ˈgardist** *n*

avantist (æˈvɒntɪst) *n* short for **avant-gardist.**

Avar (ˈeɪvɑː, ˈævɑː) *n* **1** a member of a people of unknown origin in E Europe from the 6th to the early 9th century A.D.: crushed by Charlemagne around 800. **2** a member of a people of the Caucasas. **3** the language of this people, belonging to the North-East Caucasian family.

avarice (ˈævərɪs) *n* extreme greed for riches; cupidity. [C13: from Old French, from Latin *avaritia*, from *avārus* covetous, from *avēre* to crave] ▸ **ˌavaˈricious** *adj* ▸ **ˌavaˈriciously** *adv* ▸ **ˌavaˈriciousness** *n*

avascular (əˈvæskjʊlə) *adj* (of certain tissues, such as cartilage) lacking blood vessels.

avast (əˈvɑːst) *sentence substitute. Nautical.* stop! cease! [C17: perhaps from Dutch *hou'vast* hold fast]

avatar (ˈævəˌtɑː) *n* **1** *Hinduism.* the manifestation of a deity, notably Vishnu, in human, superhuman, or animal form. **2** a visible manifestation or embodiment of an abstract concept; archetype. [C18: from Sanskrit *avatāra* a going down, from *avatarati* he descends, from *ava* down + *tarati* he passes over]

avaunt (əˈvɔːnt) *sentence substitute. Archaic.* go away! depart! [C15: from Old French *avant!* forward!, from Late Latin *ab ante* forward, from Latin *ab* from + *ante* before]

avdp. *abbrev. for* avoirdupois.

ave (ˈɑːvɪ, ˈɑːveɪ) *sentence substitute.* welcome or farewell. [Latin]

Ave[1] (ˈɑːvɪ) *n R.C. Church.* **1** short for **Ave Maria:** see **Hail Mary. 2** the time for the Angelus to be recited, so called because of the threefold repetition of the Ave Maria in this devotion. **3** the beads of the rosary used to count the number of Ave Marias said. [C13: from Latin: hail!]

Ave[2] *or* **ave** *abbrev. for* avenue.

Avebury (ˈeɪvbərɪ) *n* a village in Wiltshire, site of an extensive neolithic stone circle.

Aveiro (*Portuguese* əˈveːiru) *n* a port in N central Portugal, on the **Aveiro lagoon:** ancient Roman town; linked by canal with the Atlantic Ocean. Pop.: 35 250 (1991). Ancient name: **Talabriga** (ˌtæləˈbriːgə).

avel (ˈavel) *n Judaism.* a variant of **ovel.**

Avellaneda (*Spanish* aβeʎaˈneða) *n* a city in E Argentina, an industrial suburb of Buenos Aires. Pop.: 346 620 (1991).

Ave Maria (məˈriːə) *n* another name for **Hail Mary.** [C14: from Medieval Latin: hail, Mary!]

avenge (əˈvɛndʒ) *vb* (*usually tr*) to inflict a punishment in retaliation for (harm, injury, etc.) done to (a person or persons); take revenge for or on behalf of: *to avenge a crime; to avenge a murdered friend.* [C14: from Old French *avengier*, from *vengier*, from Latin *vindicāre*; see VENGEANCE, VINDICATE] ▸ **aˈvenger** *n*

USAGE The use of *avenge* with a reflexive pronoun was formerly considered incorrect, but is now acceptable: *she avenged herself on the man who killed her daughter.*

avens (ˈævɪnz) *n, pl* **-ens.** (*functioning as sing*) **1** any of several temperate or arctic rosaceous plants of the genus *Geum*, such as *G. rivale* (**water avens**), which has a purple calyx and orange-pink flowers. See also **herb bennet. 2 mountain avens.** a trailing evergreen white-flowered rosaceous shrub, *Dryas octopetala*, that grows on mountains in N temperate regions. [C15: from Old French *avence*, from Medieval Latin *avencia* variety of clover]

Aventine (ˈævɪnˌtaɪn, -tɪn) *n* one of the seven hills on which Rome was built.

aventurine, aventurin (əˈvɛntjʊrɪn), *or* **avanturine** (əˈvæntjʊrɪn) *n* **1** a dark-coloured glass, usually green or brown, spangled with fine particles of gold, copper, or some other metal. **2** Also called: **sunstone.** a light-coloured translucent variety of orthoclase feldspar containing reddish-gold particles of iron compounds. **3** a variety of quartz containing red or greenish particles of iron oxide or mica: a gemstone. [C19: from French, from Italian *avventurina*, from *avventura* chance; so named because usually found by accident; see ADVENTURE]

avenue (ˈævɪˌnjuː) *n* **1a** a broad street, often lined with trees. **1b** (*cap. as part of a street name*) a road, esp. in a built-up area: *Shaftesbury Avenue.* **2** a main approach road, as to a country house. **3** a way bordered by two rows of trees: *an avenue of oaks.* **4** a line of approach: *explore every avenue.* [C17: from French, from *avenir* to come to, from Latin *advenīre*, from *venīre* to come]

aver (əˈvɜː) *vb* **avers, averring, averred.** (*tr*) **1** to state positively; assert. **2** *Law.* to allege as a fact or prove to be true. [C14: from Old French *averer*, from Medieval Latin *advērāre*, from Latin *vērus* true] ▸ **aˈverment** *n*

average (ˈævərɪdʒ, ˈævrɪdʒ) *n* **1** the typical or normal amount, quality, degree, etc.: *above average in intelligence.* **2** Also called: **arithmetic mean.** the result obtained by adding the numbers or quantities in a set and dividing the total by the number of members in the set: *the average of 3, 4, and 8 is 5.* **3** (of a continuously variable ratio, such as speed) the quotient of the differences between the initial and final values of the two quantities that make up the ratio: *his average over the journey was 30 miles per hour.* **4** *Maritime law.* **4a** a loss incurred or damage suffered by a ship or its cargo at sea. **4b** the equitable apportionment of such loss among the interested parties. **5** (*often pl*) *Stock exchange.* a simple or weighted average of the prices of a selected group of securities computed in order to facilitate market comparisons. **6 on (the** *or* **an) average.** usually; typically: *on average, he goes twice a week.* ◆ *adj* **7** usual or typical. **8** mediocre or inferior: *his performance was only average.* **9** constituting a numerical average: *the average age; an average speed.* **10** approximately typical of a range of values: *the average contents of a matchbox.* ◆ *vb* **11** (*tr*) to obtain or estimate a numerical average of. **12** (*tr*) to assess the general quality of. **13** (*tr*) to perform or receive a typical number of: *to average eight hours' work a day.* **14** (*tr*) to divide up proportionately: *they averaged the profits among the staff.* **15** (*tr*) to amount to or be on average: *the children averaged 15 years of age.* **16** (*intr*) *Stock Exchange.* to purchase additional securities in a holding whose price has fallen (**average down**) or risen (**average up**) in anticipation of a speculative profit after further increases in price. [C15 *averay* loss arising from damage to ships or cargoes (shared equitably among all concerned, hence the modern sense), from Old Italian *avaria*, ultimately from Arabic *awār* damage, blemish] ▸ **ˈaveragely** *adv*

average adjuster *n* a person who calculates average claims, esp. for marine insurance. See **average** (sense 4).

average deviation *n Statistics.* another name for **mean deviation.**

Averno (*Italian* aˈvɛrno) *n* a crater lake in Italy, near Naples: in ancient times regarded as an entrance to hell. Latin name: **Avernus** (əˈvɜːnəs). [from Latin, from Greek *aornos* without birds, from A-[1] + *ornis* bird; referring to the legend that the lake's sulphurous exhalations killed birds]

Averroës (əˈvɛrəʊˌiːz) *n* Arabic name *ibn-Rushd.* 1126–88, Arab philosopher and physician in Spain, noted particularly for his attempts to reconcile Aristotelian philosophy with Islamic religion, which profoundly influenced Christian scholasticism.

Averroism (ˌævəˈrəʊɪzəm, əˈvɛrəʊ-) *n* the teachings of Averroës. ▸ **ˌAverˈroist** *n* ▸ **ˌAverroˈistic** *adj*

averse (əˈvɜːs) *adj* **1** (*postpositive;* usually foll. by *to*) opposed, disinclined, or loath. **2** (of leaves, flowers, etc.) turned away from the main stem. Compare **adverse** (sense 4). [C16: from Latin *āversus*, from *āvertere* to turn from, from *vertere* to turn] ▸ **aˈversely** *adv* ▸ **aˈverseness** *n*

aversion (əˈvɜːʃən) *n* **1** (usually foll. by *to* or *for*) extreme dislike or disinclination; repugnance. **2** a person or thing that arouses this: *he is my pet aversion.*

aversion therapy *n Psychiatry.* a method of suppressing an undesirable habit, such as excessive smoking, by causing the subject to associate an unpleasant effect, such as an electric shock or nausea, with the habit.

aversive (əˈvɜːsɪv) *adj* tending to dissuade or repel. ▸ **aˈversively** *adv*

avert (əˈvɜːt) *vb* (*tr*) **1** to turn away or aside: *to avert one's gaze.* **2** to ward off; prevent from occurring: *to avert danger.* [C15: from Old French *avertir*, from Latin *āvertere;* see AVERSE] ▸ **aˈvertible** *or* **aˈvertable** *adj*

Aves (ˈeɪviːz) *pl n* the class of vertebrates comprising the birds. See **bird** (sense 1). [pl. of Latin *avis* bird]

Avesta (əˈvɛstə) *n* a collection of sacred writings of Zoroastrianism, including the Songs of Zoroaster.

Avestan (əˈvɛstən) *or* **Avestic** (əˈvɛstɪk) *n* **1** the oldest recorded language of the Iranian branch of the Indo-European family; the language of the Avesta. Formerly called: **Zend.** ◆ *adj* **2** of or relating to the Avesta or its language.

Aveyron (*French* avɛrɔ̃) *n* a department of S France in Midi-Pyrénées region. Capital: Rodez. Pop.: 266 700 (1995). Area: 8771 sq. km (3421 sq. miles).

avg. *abbrev. for* average.

avgolemono (ˌævgəˈlɛmənəʊ) *n* a Greek soup made with eggs, lemon juice, and rice. [C20: from Modern Greek]

avian (ˈeɪvɪən) *adj* of, relating to, or resembling a bird. [C19: from Latin *avis* bird]

aviarist (ˈeɪvjərɪst) *n* a person who keeps an aviary.

aviary (ˈeɪvjərɪ) *n, pl* **aviaries.** a large enclosure in which birds are kept. [C16: from Latin *aviārium*, from *aviārius* concerning birds, from *avis* bird]

aviate (ˈeɪvɪˌeɪt) *vb* to pilot or fly in an aircraft.

aviation (ˌeɪvɪˈeɪʃən) *n* **1a** the art or science of flying aircraft. **1b** the design, production, and maintenance of aircraft. **2** *U.S.* military aircraft collectively. [C19: from French, from Latin *avis* bird]

aviation medicine *n* the branch of medicine concerned with the effects on man of flight in the earth's atmosphere. Compare **space medicine.**

aviator (ˈeɪvɪˌeɪtə) *n Old-fashioned.* the pilot of an aeroplane or airship; flyer. ▸ **ˈaviˌatrix** *or* **ˈaviˌatress** *fem n*

Avicenna (ˌævɪˈsɛnə) *n* Arabic name *ibn-Sina.* 980–1037, Arab philosopher and physician whose philosophical writings, which combined Aristotelianism with neo-Platonist ideas, greatly influenced scholasticism, and whose medical work *Qanun* was the greatest single influence on medieval medicine.

aviculture ('eɪvɪˌkʌltʃə) *n* the keeping and rearing of birds. ▸ ˌ**avi'culturist** *n*

avid ('ævɪd) *adj* **1** very keen; enthusiastic: *an avid reader.* **2** (*postpositive;* often foll. by *for* or *of) eager (for); desirous (of); greedy (for): avid for revenge.* [C18: from Latin *avidus,* from *avēre* to long for] ▸ '**avidly** *adv*

avidin ('ævɪdɪn, ə'vɪdɪn) *n* a protein, found in egg-white, that combines with biotin to form a stable compound that cannot be absorbed, leading to a biotin deficiency in the consumer. [C20: from AVID + (BIOT)IN; from its characteristic avidity for biotin]

avidity (ə'vɪdɪtɪ) *n* **1** the quality or state of being avid. **2a** eagerness. **2b** greed; avarice. **3** *Chem.* **3a** the strength of an acid or base in proportion to its degree of dissociation. **3b** another term for **affinity** (sense 6b). **4** *Immunol.* a measure of antigen-to-antibody binding, based on the rate of formation of the complex.

Aviemore (ˌævɪ'mɔː) *n* a winter sports resort in Scotland, in Moray between the Monadhliath and Cairngorm Mountains. Pop.: 2214 (1991).

avifauna (ˌeɪvɪ'fɔːnə) *n* all the birds in a particular region. ▸ ˌ**avi'faunal** *adj*

Avignon (*French* aviɲɔ̃) *n* a city in SE France, on the Rhône: seat of the papacy (1309–77); famous 12th-century bridge, now partly destroyed. Pop.: 181 136 (1990).

Ávila (*Spanish* 'aβila) *n* a city in central Spain: 11th-century granite walls and Romanesque cathedral. Pop.: 45 092 (1988 est.).

avionics (ˌeɪvɪ'ɒnɪks) *n* **1** (*functioning as sing*) the science and technology of electronics applied to aeronautics and astronautics. **2** (*functioning as pl*) the electronic circuits and devices of an aerospace vehicle. [C20: from *avi(ation electr)onics*] ▸ ˌ**avi'onic** *adj*

avirulent (æ'vɪrʊlənt) *adj* (esp. of bacteria) not virulent.

avitaminosis (æˌvɪtəmɪn'əʊsɪs, ˌævɪˌtæmɪ'nəʊsɪs) *n, pl* **-ses** (-siːz). any disease caused by a vitamin deficiency in the diet.

avizandum (ˌævɪ'zændəm) *n Scots Law.* **a** a judge's or court's decision to consider a case privately before giving judgment. **b** a judge's or court's private consideration of a case before giving judgment. **c** the period during which judgment is delayed in these circumstances. A judge or court makes avizandum when time is needed to consider arguments or submissions made. ◆ Compare **CAV.** [from Medieval Latin, from *avizare* to consider; see ADVISE]

Avlona (æv'ləʊnə) *n* the ancient name for **Vlorë.**

AVM (in Britain) *abbrev. for* Air Vice-Marshal.

avn *abbrev. for* aviation.

avocado (ˌævə'kɑːdəʊ) *n, pl* **-dos. 1** a pear-shaped fruit having a leathery green or blackish skin, a large stony seed, and a greenish-yellow edible pulp. **2** the tropical American lauraceous tree, *Persea americana,* that bears this fruit. **3** a dull greenish colour resembling that of the fruit. ◆ Also called (for senses 1 & 2): **avocado pear, alligator pear.** [C17: from Spanish *aguacate,* from Nahuatl *ahuacatl* testicle, alluding to the shape of the fruit]

avocation (ˌævə'keɪʃən) *n* **1** *Formal.* a minor occupation undertaken as a diversion. **2** *Not standard.* a person's regular job or vocation. [C17: from Latin *āvocātiō* a calling away, diversion from, from *āvocāre* to distract, from *vocāre* to call]

avocet ('ævəˌsɛt) *n* any of several long-legged shore birds of the genus *Recurvirostra,* such as the European *R. avosetta,* having black-and-white plumage and a long upward-curving bill: family *Recurvirostridae,* order *Charadriiformes.* [C18: from French *avocette,* from Italian *avocetta,* of uncertain origin]

Avogadro (ˌævə'gɑːdrəʊ; *Italian* avo'gaːdro) *n* **Amedeo** (ame'dɛːo), *Conte di Quaregna.* 1776–1856, Italian physicist, noted for his work on gases.

Avogadro constant *or* **number** *n* the number of atoms or molecules in a mole of a substance, equal to $6.022\,52 \times 10^{23}$ per mole. Symbol: L or N_A

Avogadro's law *or* **hypothesis** *n* the principle that equal volumes of all gases contain the same number of molecules at the same temperature and pressure.

avoid (ə'vɔɪd) *vb* (*tr*) **1** to keep out of the way of. **2** to refrain from doing. **3** to prevent from happening: *to avoid damage to machinery.* **4** *Law.* to make (a plea, contract, etc.) void; invalidate; quash. **5** *Obsolete.* to expel. **6** *Obsolete.* to depart from. [C14: from Anglo-French *avoider,* from Old French *esvuidier,* from *vuidier* to empty, VOID] ▸ **a'voidable** *adj* ▸ **a'voidably** *adv* ▸ **a'voider** *n*

avoidance (ə'vɔɪdəns) *n* **1** the act of keeping away from or preventing from happening. **2** *Law.* **2a** the act of annulling or making void. **2b** the countering of an opponent's plea with fresh evidence. **3** *Ecclesiastical law.* the state of a benefice having no incumbent.

avoir. *abbrev. for* avoirdupois.

avoirdupois *or* **avoirdupois weight** (ˌævədə'pɔɪz,ˌævwɑːdjuː'pwɑː) *n* a system of weights used in many English-speaking countries. It is based on the pound, which contains 16 ounces or 7000 grains. 100 pounds (U.S.) or 112 pounds (Brit.) is equal to 1 hundredweight and 20 hundredweights equals 1 ton. Abbrevs.: **avdp., avoir.** [C14: from Old French *aver de peis* goods of weight]

Avon[1] ('eɪvᵊn) *n* **1** a former county of SW England, created in 1974 from areas of N Somerset and S Gloucestershire: replaced in 1996 by the unitary authorities of Bath and North East Somerset (Somerset), North Somerset (Somerset), South Gloucestershire (Gloucestershire), and Bristol. **2** a river in central England, rising in Northamptonshire and flowing southwest through Stratford-on-Avon to the River Severn at Tewkesbury. Length: 154 km (96 miles). **3** a river in SW England, rising in Gloucestershire and flowing south and west through Bristol to the Severn estuary at **Avonmouth.** Length: 120 km (75 miles). **4** a river in S England, rising in Wiltshire and flowing south to the English Channel. Length: about 96 km (60 miles).

Avon[2] ('eɪvᵊn) *n* **Earl of.** title of (Anthony) **Eden.**

avouch (ə'vaʊtʃ) *vb* (*tr*) *Archaic.* **1** to vouch for; guarantee. **2** to acknowledge. **3** to assert. [C16: from Old French *avochier* to summon, call on, from Latin *advocāre;* see ADVOCATE] ▸ **a'vouchment** *n*

avow (ə'vaʊ) *vb* (*tr*) **1** to state or affirm. **2** to admit openly. **3** *Law, rare.* to justify or maintain (some action taken). [C13: from Old French *avouer* to confess, from Latin *advocāre* to appeal to, call upon; see AVOUCH, ADVOCATE] ▸ **a'vowable** *adj* ▸ **a'vowal** *n* ▸ **avowed** (ə'vaʊd) *adj* ▸ **avowedly** (ə'vaʊɪdlɪ) *adv* ▸ **a'vower** *n*

avulsion (ə'vʌlʃən) *n* **1** a forcible tearing away or separation of a bodily structure or part, either as the result of injury or as an intentional surgical procedure. **2** *Law.* the sudden removal of soil from one person's land to that of another, as by flooding. [C17: from Latin *āvulsiō,* from *āvellere* to pluck away, from *vellere* to pull, pluck]

avuncular (ə'vʌŋkjʊlə) *adj* **1** of or concerned with an uncle. **2** resembling an uncle; friendly; helpful. [C19: from Latin *avunculus* (maternal) uncle, diminutive of *avus* grandfather]

avunculate (ə'vʌŋkjʊlɪt) *n* **1** the custom in some societies of assigning rights and duties to a maternal uncle concerning his sister's son. ◆ *adj* **2** of, relating to, or governed by this custom.

aw[1] (ɔː) *determiner Scot.* a variant spelling of **a'** (all).

aw[2] (ɔː) *interj Informal, chiefly U.S.* an expression of disapproval, commiseration, or appeal.

a.w. *abbrev. for* all water (shipping).

AWA *abbrev. for* Amalgamated Wireless (Australasia) Ltd.

awa' (ə'wɔː) *adv Scot.* away; departed; onward.

AWACS *or* **Awacs** ('eɪwæks) *n acronym for* airborne warning and control system.

await (ə'weɪt) *vb* **1** (*tr*) to wait for; expect. **2** (*tr*) to be in store for. **3** (*intr*) to wait, esp. with expectation. **4** (*tr*) *Obsolete.* to wait for in order to ambush.

awake (ə'weɪk) *vb* **awakes, awaking; awoke** *or* **awaked; awoken** *or* **awaked. 1** to emerge or rouse from sleep; wake. **2** to become or cause to become alert. **3** (usually foll. by *to*) to become or make aware (of): *to awake to reality.* **4** Also: **awaken.** (*tr*) to arouse (feelings, etc.) or cause to remember (memories, etc.). ◆ *adj* (*postpositive*) **5** not sleeping. **6** (sometimes foll. by *to*) lively or alert. [Old English *awacian, awacan;* see WAKE[1]]

USAGE See at **wake**[1].

awakening (ə'weɪkənɪŋ, ə'weɪknɪŋ) *n* the start of a feeling or awareness in a person: *a picture of an emotional awakening.*

award (ə'wɔːd) *vb* (*tr*) **1** to give (something due), esp. as a reward for merit: *to award prizes.* **2** *Law.* to declare to be entitled, as by decision of a court of law or an arbitrator. ◆ *n* **3** something awarded, such as a prize or medal: *an award for bravery.* **4** (in Australia and New Zealand) the amount of an award wage (esp. in the phrase **above award**). **5** *Law.* **5a** the decision of an arbitrator. **5b** a grant made by a court of law, esp. of damages in a civil action. [C14: from Anglo-Norman *awarder,* from Old Northern French *eswarder* to decide after investigation, from *es-* EX-[1] + *warder* to observe; see WARD] ▸ **a'wardable** *adj* ▸ **aˌward'ee** *n* ▸ **a'warder** *n*

award wage *n* (in Australia and New Zealand) statutory minimum pay for a particular group of workers. Sometimes shortened to **award.**

aware (ə'wɛə) *adj* **1** (*postpositive;* foll. by *of) having knowledge; cognizant: aware of his error.* **2** informed of current developments: *politically aware.* [Old English *gewær;* related to Old Saxon, Old High German *giwar* Latin *verērī* to be fearful; see BEWARE, WARY] ▸ **a'wareness** *n*

awash (ə'wɒʃ) *adv, adj* (*postpositive*) *Nautical.* **1** at a level even with the surface of the sea. **2** washed over by the waves.

away (ə'weɪ) *adv* **1** from a particular place; off: *to swim away.* **2** in or to another, usual, or proper place: *to put toys away.* **3** apart; at a distance: *to keep away from strangers.* **4** out of existence: *the music faded away.* **5** indicating motion, displacement, transfer, etc., from a normal or proper place, from a person's own possession, etc.: *to turn one's head away; to give away money.* **6** indicating activity that is wasteful or designed to get rid of something: *to sleep away the hours.* **7** continuously: *laughing away; fire away.* **8 away with.** a command for a person to go or be removed: *away with you; away with him to prison!* **9 far and away.** by a very great margin: *far and away the biggest meal he'd ever eaten.* **10 from away.** *Canadian.* from a part of Canada other than Newfoundland. ◆ *adj* (*usually postpositive*) **11** not present: *away from school.* **12** distant: *he is a good way away.* **13** having started; released: *he was away before sunrise; bombs away!* **14** (*also prenominal*) *Sport.* played on an opponent's ground: *an away game.* **15** *Golf.* (of a ball or player) farthest from the hole. **16** *Baseball.* (of a player) having been put out. **17** *Horse racing.* relating to the outward portion or first half of a race. ◆ *n* **18** *Sport.* a game played or won at an opponent's ground. ◆ *interj* **19** an expression of dismissal. [Old English *on weg* on way]

awe (ɔː) *n* **1** overwhelming wonder, admiration, respect, or dread. **2** *Archaic.* power to inspire fear or reverence. ◆ *vb* **3** (*tr*) to inspire with reverence or dread. [C13: from Old Norse *agi;* related to Gothic *agis* fear, Greek *akhesthai* to be grieved] ▸ '**aweless** *or U.S.* '**awless** *adj*

aweather (ə'wɛðə) *adv, adj* (*postpositive*) *Nautical.* towards the weather: *with the helm aweather.* Compare **alee.**

aweigh (ə'weɪ) *adj* (*postpositive*) *Nautical.* (of an anchor) no longer hooked into the bottom; hanging by its rode.

awe-inspiring *adj* causing or worthy of admiration or respect; amazing or magnificent.

awesome ('ɔːsəm) *adj* **1** inspiring or displaying awe. **2** *Slang.* excellent or outstanding. ▸ '**awesomely** *adv* ▸ '**awesomeness** *n*

awestruck ('ɔːˌstrʌk) *or* **awe-stricken** *adj* overcome or filled with awe.

awful ('ɔːfʊl) *adj* **1** nasty or ugly. **2** *Archaic.* inspiring reverence or dread. **3** *Archaic.* overcome with awe; reverential. ◆ *adv* **4** *Not standard.* (intensifier): *an awful cold day.* [C13: see AWE, -FUL] ▸ '**awfulness** *n*

awfully ('ɔːfəlɪ, 'ɔːflɪ) *adv* **1** in an unpleasant, bad, or reprehensible manner. **2** *Informal.* (intensifier): *I'm awfully keen to come.* **3** *Archaic.* so as to express or inspire awe.

awheel (əˈwiːl) *adv* on wheels.

awhile (əˈwaɪl) *adv* for a brief period.

awkward (ˈɔːkwəd) *adj* **1** lacking dexterity, proficiency, or skill; clumsy; inept: *the new recruits were awkward in their exercises.* **2** ungainly or inelegant in movements or posture. **3** unwieldy; difficult to use: *an awkward implement.* **4** embarrassing: *an awkward moment.* **5** embarrassed: *he felt awkward about leaving.* **6** difficult to deal with; requiring tact: *an awkward situation; an awkward customer.* **7** deliberately uncooperative or unhelpful. **8** dangerous or difficult: *an awkward ascent of the ridge.* **9** *Obsolete.* perverse. [C14 *awk,* from Old Norse *öfugr* turned the wrong way round + -WARD] ▸ **ˈawkwardly** *adv* ▸ **ˈawkwardness** *n*

awl (ɔːl) *n* a pointed hand tool with a fluted blade used for piercing wood, leather, etc. See also **bradawl.** [Old English *ǣl;* related to Old Norse *alr,* Old High German *āla,* Dutch *aal,* Sanskrit *ārā*]

awlwort (ˈɔːlˌwɜːt) *n* a small stemless aquatic plant, *Subularia aquatica,* of the N hemisphere, having slender sharp-pointed leaves and minute submerged white flowers: family *Cruciferae* (crucifers).

awn (ɔːn) *n* any of the bristles growing from the flowering parts of certain grasses and cereals. [Old English *agen* ear of grain; related to Old Norse *ögn* chaff, Gothic *ahana,* Old High German *agana,* Greek *akōn* javelin] ▸ **awned** *adj* ▸ **ˈawnless** *adj*

awning (ˈɔːnɪŋ) *n* a roof of canvas or other material supported by a frame to provide protection from the weather, esp. one placed over a doorway or part of a deck of a ship. [C17: of uncertain origin]

awoke (əˈwəʊk) *vb* a past tense or (now rare or dialectal) past participle of **awake.**

AWOL (ˈeɪwɒl) *or* **A.W.O.L.** *adj Military.* absent without leave; absent from one's post or duty without official permission but without intending to desert.

AWRE *abbrev. for* Atomic Weapons Research Establishment.

awry (əˈraɪ) *adv, adj* (*postpositive*) **1** with a slant or twist to one side; askew. **2** away from the appropriate or right course; amiss. [C14 *on wry;* see A-[2], WRY]

AWU *abbrev. for* Australian Workers' Union.

ax. *abbrev. for* axiom.

axe *or U.S.* **ax** (æks) *n, pl* **axes. 1** a hand tool with one side of its head forged and sharpened to a cutting edge, used for felling trees, splitting timber, etc. See also **hatchet. 2 an axe to grind. 2a** an ulterior motive. **2b** a grievance. **2c** a pet subject. **3 the axe.** *Informal.* **3a** dismissal, esp. from employment; the sack (esp. in the phrase **get the axe**). **3b** *Brit.* severe cutting down of expenditure, esp. the removal of unprofitable sections of a public service. **4** *U.S. slang.* any musical instrument, esp. a guitar or horn. ◆ *vb* (*tr*) **5** to chop or trim with an axe. **6** *Informal.* to dismiss (employees), restrict (expenditure or services), or terminate (a project). [Old English *æx;* related to Old Frisian *axa,* Old High German *acchus,* Old Norse *öx,* Latin *ascia,* Greek *axinē*]

axe-breaker *n Austral.* an Australian oleaceous tree, *Notelaea longifolia,* yielding very hard timber.

axel (ˈæksəl) *n Skating.* a jump in which the skater takes off from the forward outside edge of one skate, makes one and a half, two and a half, or three and a half turns in the air, and lands on the backward outside edge of the other skate. [C20: named after *Axel* Paulsen (died 1938), Norwegian skater]

Axelrod (ˈæksəlrɒd) *n* **Julius.** born 1912, U.S. neuropharmacologist, renowned for his work on catecholamines. Nobel prize for physiology or medicine (with von Euler and Bernard Katz) 1970.

axeman *or U.S.* **axman** (ˈæksmən) *n, pl* **-men. 1** a man who wields an axe, esp. to cut down trees. **2** a person who makes cuts in expenditure or services, esp. on behalf of another: *the chancellor's axeman.* **3** *U.S. slang.* a man who plays a musical instrument, esp. a guitar.

axenic (eɪˈziːnɪk) *adj* (of a biological culture or culture medium) free from undesirable microorganisms; uncontaminated. [C20: see A-[1], XENO-, -IC]

axes[1] (ˈæksiːz) *n* the plural of **axis**[1].

axes[2] (ˈæksɪz) *n* the plural of **axe.**

axial (ˈæksɪəl) *adj* **1** relating to, forming, or characteristic of an axis. **2** situated in, on, or along an axis. ▸ **ˌaxiˈality** *n* ▸ **ˈaxially** *adv*

axial-flow compressor *n* a device for compressing a gas by accelerating it tangentially by means of bladed rotors, to increase its kinetic energy, and then diffusing it through static vanes (stators), to increase its pressure.

axial skeleton *n* the bones that together comprise the skull and the vertebral column.

axial vector *n* another name for **pseudovector.**

axil (ˈæksɪl) *n* the angle between the upper surface of a branch or leafstalk and the stem from which it grows. [C18: from Latin *axilla* armpit]

axile (ˈæksɪl, -saɪl) *adj Botany.* of, relating to, or attached to the axis.

axilemma (ˌæksɪˈlɛmə) *n* a variant spelling of **axolemma.**

axilla (ækˈsɪlə) *n, pl* **-lae** (-liː). **1** the technical name for the **armpit. 2** the area on the undersurface of a bird's wing corresponding to the armpit. [C17: from Latin: armpit]

axillary (ækˈsɪlərɪ) *adj* **1** of, relating to, or near the armpit. **2** *Botany.* growing in or related to the axil: *an axillary bud.* ◆ *n, pl* **-laries. 3** (*usually pl*) Also called: **axillar** (ækˈsɪlə, ˈæksɪlə). one of the feathers growing from the axilla of a bird's wing.

axinite (ˈæksɪˌnaɪt) *n* a brilliant brown mineral with wedge-shaped triclinic crystals, a complex borosilicate of calcium and aluminium containing some iron and manganese. Formula: $H(Ca,Fe,Mn)_3Al_2B(SiO_4)_3$.

axiology (ˌæksɪˈɒlədʒɪ) *n Philosophy.* the theory of values, moral or aesthetic. [C20: from Greek *axios* worthy] ▸ **axiological** (ˌæksɪəˈlɒdʒɪkəl) *adj* ▸ **ˌaxioˈlogically** *adv* ▸ **ˌaxiˈologist** *n*

axiom (ˈæksɪəm) *n* **1** a generally accepted proposition or principle, sanctioned by experience; maxim. **2** a universally established principle or law that is not a necessary truth: *the axioms of politics.* **3** a self-evident statement. **4** *Logic, maths.* a statement or formula that is stipulated to be true for the purpose of a chain of reasoning: the foundation of a formal deductive system. Compare **assumption** (sense 4). [C15: from Latin *axiōma* a principle, from Greek, from *axioun* to consider worthy, from *axios* worthy]

axiomatic (ˌæksɪəˈmætɪk) *or* **axiomatical** *adj* **1** relating to or resembling an axiom; self-evident. **2** containing maxims; aphoristic. **3** (of a logical system) consisting of a set of axioms from which theorems are derived by **transformation rules.** Compare **natural deduction.** ▸ **ˌaxioˈmatically** *adv*

axion (ˈæksɪˌɒn) *n Physics.* a hypothetical neutral elementary particle postulated to account for certain conservation laws in the strong interaction. [C20: from AXI(OM) + -ON]

axis[1] (ˈæksɪs) *n, pl* **axes** (ˈæksiːz). **1** a real or imaginary line about which a body, such as an aircraft, can rotate or about which an object, form, composition, or geometrical construction is symmetrical. **2** one of two or three reference lines used in coordinate geometry to locate a point in a plane or in space. **3** *Anatomy.* the second cervical vertebra. Compare **atlas** (sense 3). **4** *Botany.* the main central part of a plant, typically consisting of the stem and root, from which secondary branches and other parts develop. **5** an alliance between a number of states to coordinate their foreign policy. **6** Also called: **principal axis.** *Optics.* the line of symmetry of an optical system, such as the line passing through the centre of a lens. **7** *Geology.* an imaginary line along the crest of an anticline or the trough of a syncline. **8** *Crystallog.* one of three lines passing through the centre of a crystal and used to characterize its symmetry. [C14: from Latin: axletree, earth's axis; related to Greek *axōn* axis]

axis[2] (ˈæksɪs) *n, pl* **axises.** any of several S Asian deer of the genus *Axis,* esp. *A. axis.* They typically have a reddish-brown white-spotted coat and slender antlers. [C18: from Latin: Indian wild animal, of uncertain identity]

Axis (ˈæksɪs) *n* **a the.** the alliance of Nazi Germany, Fascist Italy, and Japan, established in 1936 and lasting until their defeat in World War II. **b** (*as modifier*): *the Axis powers.*

axle (ˈæksəl) *n* a bar or shaft on which a wheel, pair of wheels, or other rotating member revolves. [C17: from Old Norse *öxull;* related to German *Achse;* see AXIS[1]]

axletree (ˈæksəlˌtriː) *n* a bar fixed across the underpart of a wagon or carriage that has rounded ends on which the wheels revolve.

Axminster carpet (ˈæksˌmɪnstə) *n* a type of patterned carpet with a cut pile. Often shortened to **Axminster.** [after *Axminster,* in Devon, where such carpets are made]

axolemma (ˌæksəˈlɛmə) *or* **axilemma** *n* the membrane that encloses the axon of a nerve cell.

axolotl (ˈæksəˌlɒtᵊl) *n* **1** any of several aquatic salamanders of the North American genus *Ambystoma,* esp. *A. mexicanum* (**Mexican axolotl**), in which the larval form (including external gills) is retained throughout life under natural conditions (see **neoteny**): family *Ambystomidae.* **2** any of various other North American salamanders in which neoteny occurs or is induced. [C18: from Nahuatl, from *atl* water + *xolotl* servant, doll]

axon (ˈæksɒn) *or* **axone** (ˈæksəʊn) *n* the long threadlike extension of a nerve cell that conducts nerve impulses from the cell body. Compare **dendrite.** [C19: via New Latin from Greek: axis, axle, vertebra] ▸ **ˈaxonal** *adj*

axonometric projection (ˌæksənəˈmɛtrɪk) *n* a geometric drawing of an object, such as a building, in three dimensions showing the verticals and horizontals projected to scale but with diagonals and curves distorted, so that the whole appears inclined.

axonometry (ˌæksəˈnɒmɪtrɪ) *n* the branch of crystallography concerned with measurement of the axes of crystals.

axseed (ˈæksˌsiːd) *n* another name for **crown vetch.**

Axum (ˈɑːksʊm) *n* a variant spelling of **Aksum.**

ay[1] (eɪ) *adv Archaic, poetic.* ever; always. [C12 *ai,* from Old Norse *ei;* related to Old English *ā* always, Latin *aevum* an age, Greek *aiōn*]

ay[2] *or* **aye** (eɪ) *interj Archaic, poetic.* an expression of misery or surprise. [C14 *ey:* from an involuntary cry of surprise]

ay[3] (aɪ) *sentence substitute, n* a variant spelling of **aye**[1].

Ayacucho (*Spanish* ajaˈkutʃo) *n* a city in SE Peru: nearby is the site of the battle (1824) that won independence for Peru. Pop.: 105 918 (1993).

ayah (ˈaɪə) *n* (in the East, Africa, and other parts of the former British Empire) a maidservant, nursemaid, or governess, esp. one of Indian or Malay origin. Compare **amah.** [C18: from Hindi *āyā,* from Portuguese *aia,* from Latin *avia* grandmother]

ayahuasca (ˌaɪəˈwɑːskə) *n* a Brazilian plant, *Banisteriopsis caapi,* that has winged fruits and yields a powerful hallucinogenic alkaloid sometimes used to treat certain disorders of the central nervous system: family *Malpighiaceae.* [C20: from Quechua]

ayatollah (ˌaɪəˈtɒlə) *n* one of a class of Iranian Shiite religious leaders. [via Persian from Arabic, from *aya* sign + *Allah* god]

Ayckbourn (ˈeɪkbɔːn) *n* Sir **Alan.** born 1939, English dramatist. His plays include *Absurd Person Singular* (1973), the trilogy *The Norman Conquests* (1974), *Man of the Moment* (1988), and *Haunting Julia* (1994).

Aycliffe (ˈeɪklɪf) *n* a town in Co. Durham: founded as a new town in 1947. Pop.: 40 000 (latest est.).

Aydin *or* **Aidin** (ˈaɪdɪn) *n* a town in SW Turkey: an ancient city of Lydia. Pop.: 123 163 (1995 est.). Ancient name: **Tralles.**

aye[1] *or* **ay** (aɪ) *sentence substitute.* **1** yes: archaic or dialectal except in voting by voice. **2 aye aye. 2a** an expression of compliance, esp. used by seamen. **2b** *Brit.* an expression of amused surprise, esp. at encountering something that confirms one's suspicions, expectations, etc. ◆ *n* **3a** a person who votes in the affirmative. **3b** an affirmative vote. ◆ Compare **nay.** [C16: probably from pronoun *I,* expressing assent]

aye[2] (aɪ) *adv Scot.* always; still. [Old Norse *ei* ever; Old English *ā;* compare Latin *aevum* an age, Greek *aion* aeon, *aiei* ever, always]

aye-aye ('aɪˌaɪ) *n* a rare nocturnal arboreal prosimian primate of Madagascar, *Daubentonia madagascariensis,* related to the lemurs: family *Daubentoniidae.* It has long bony fingers and rodent-like incisor teeth adapted for feeding on insect larvae and bamboo pith. [C18: from French, from Malagasy *aiay,* probably of imitative origin]

Ayer (ɛə) *n* Sir **Alfred Jules.** 1910–89, English positivist philosopher, noted particularly for his antimetaphysical work *Language, Truth, and Logic* (1936).

Ayers Rock (ɛəz) *n* the former name of **Uluru.**

Ayesha ('ɑːiːˌʃɑː) *n* a variant spelling of **Aisha.**

ayin ('ɑːjɪn; *Hebrew* 'ajiːn) *n* the 16th letter in the Hebrew alphabet (ע), originally a pharyngeal fricative, that is now silent and transliterated by a raised inverted comma ('). [Hebrew]

Aylesbury ('eɪlzbərɪ, -brɪ) *n* a town in SE central England, administrative centre of Buckinghamshire. Pop.: 58 058 (1991).

Aylward ('eɪlwəd) *n* **Gladys.** 1903–70, English missionary in China.

Aymara (ˌaɪmə'rɑː) *n* **1** (*pl* **-ras** *or* **-ra**) a member of a South American Indian people of Bolivia and Peru. **2** the language of this people, probably related to Quechua. [from Spanish *aimará,* of American Indian origin] ▸ **ˌAyma'ran** *adj*

Aymé (*French* ɛme) *n* **Marcel** (marsɛl). 1902–67, French writer: noted for his light and witty narratives.

Ayodha (aɪ'jəʊdjɑː) *n* an ancient town in N India, in Uttar Pradesh state: as the birthplace of Rama it is sacred to Hindus; also a Buddhist centre. Also called: **Awadh** (ə'wɒd), **Oudh** (aʊd).

ayont (ə'jɒnt) *adv, prep Scot.* beyond. [*a,* from Old English *an* on + *yont* YON]

Ayr (ɛə) *n* a port in SW Scotland, in South Ayrshire. Pop.: 47 962 (1991).

Ayrshire ('ɛəʃɪə, -ʃə) *n* **1** a historic county of SW Scotland, formerly part of Strathclyde region (1975–96), now divided into the council areas of North Ayrshire, South Ayrshire, and East Ayrshire. **2** any one of a hardy breed of brown and white dairy cattle.

Ayub Khan (aɪ'juːb 'kɑːn) *n* **Mohammed.** 1907–74, Pakistani field marshal; president of Pakistan (1958–69).

Ayurveda ('ɑːjuˌveɪdə, -ˌviːdə) *n Hinduism.* an ancient medical treatise on the art of healing and prolonging life, sometimes regarded as a fifth Veda. [from Sanskrit, from *āyur* life + *veda* knowledge] ▸ **ˌAyur'vedic** *adj*

Ayutthaya (ɑː'juːtəjə) *n* a city in S Thailand, on the Chao Phraya River: capital of the country until 1767; noted for its canals and ruins. Pop.: 61 185 (1990). Also called: **Ayudhya** (ɑː'juːdjə), **Ayuthia** (ɑː'juːθɪə).

AZ *abbrev. for* Arizona.

az. *abbrev. for* azimuth.

aza- *or before a vowel* **az-** *combining form.* denoting the presence of nitrogen, esp. a nitrogen atom in place of a -CH group or an -NH group in place of a $-CH_2$ group: *azathioprine.* [C20: from AZ(O)- + *-a-*]

azalea (ə'zeɪljə) *n* any ericaceous plant of the group *Azalea,* formerly a separate genus but now included in the genus *Rhododendron:* cultivated for their showy pink or purple flowers. [C18: via New Latin from Greek, from *azaleos* dry; from its supposed preference for a dry situation]

azan (ɑː'zɑːn) *n Islam.* the call to prayer five times a day, usually by a muezzin from a minaret. [from Arabic *adhān,* from *adhina* to proclaim, invite; see MUEZZIN]

Azaña (*Spanish* a'θaɲa) *n* **Manuel** (ma'nwel). 1880–1940, Spanish statesman; president of the Spanish Republic (1936–39) until overthrown by Franco.

Azania (ə'zɑːnɪə, ə'zɑːnjə) *n* another name (used esp. by many Black political activists) for **South Africa.** [perhaps from Arabic *Adzan* East Africa] ▸ **A'zanian** *n, adj*

AZAPO (a'zapəʊ) *n acronym for* Azanian People's Organization.

azathioprine (ˌæzə'θaɪəˌpriːn) *n* a synthetic drug that suppresses the normal immune responses of the body and is administered orally during and after organ transplantation and also in certain types of anaemia and rheumatoid arthritis. Formula: $C_9H_7N_7O_2S$. [C20: from AZA- + THIO- + P(U)RINE]

Azazel (ə'zeɪzᵊl, 'æzəˌzɛl) *n* **1** *Old Testament.* a desert demon to whom the scapegoat bearing the sins of Israel was sent out once a year on the Day of Atonement (Leviticus 16:1–28). **2** (in later Jewish and Gnostic writings and in Muslim tradition) a prince of demons.

Azbine (æz'biːn) *n* another name for **Aïr.**

azedarach (ə'zɛdəˌræk) *n* **1** the astringent bark of the chinaberry tree, formerly used as an emetic and cathartic. **2** another name for **chinaberry** (sense 1). [C18: from French *azédarac,* from Persian *āzād dirakht,* from *āzād* free, noble + *dirakht* tree]

azeotrope (ə'ziːəˌtrəʊp) *n* a mixture of liquids that boils at a constant temperature, at a given pressure, without change of composition. [C20: from A-[1] + *zeo-,* from Greek *zein* to boil + -TROPE] ▸ **azeotropic** (ˌeɪzɪə'trɒpɪk) *adj*

Azerbaijan (ˌæzəbaɪ'dʒɑːn) *n* **1** a republic in NW Asia: the region was acquired by Russia from Persia in the early 19th century; became the Azerbaijan Soviet Socialist Republic in 1936 and gained independence in 1991; consists of dry subtropical steppes around the Aras and Kura rivers, surrounded by the Caucasus; contains the extensive Baku oilfields. Language: Azerbaijani. Religion: Shiite Muslim. Currency: manat. Capital: Baku. Pop.: 7 650 200 (1998 est.). Area: 86 600 sq. km (33 430 sq. miles). **2** a mountainous region of NW Iran, separated from the republic of Azerbaijan by the Aras River: divided administratively into **Eastern Azerbaijan** and **Western Azerbaijan.** Capitals: Tabriz and Rezaiyeh. Pop.: 5 562 926 (1991).

Azerbaijani (ˌæzəbaɪ'dʒɑːnɪ) *n* **1** (*pl* **-ni** *or* **-nis**) a native or inhabitant of Azerbaijan. Sometimes shortened to **Azeri. 2** the language of this people, belonging to the Turkic branch of the Altaic family.

Azeri (ə'zɛərɪ) *n* short for **Azerbaijani** (sense 1).

azerty *or* **AZERTY keyboard** (ə'zɜːtɪ) *n* a common European version of typewriter keyboard layout with the characters a, z, e, r, t, and y positioned on the top row of alphabetic characters at the left side of the keyboard.

azide ('eɪzaɪd) *n* **1** any compound containing the monovalent group $-N_3$ or the monovalent ion N_3^-. **2** (*modifier*) consisting of, containing, or concerned with the group $-N_3$ or the ion N_3^-: *azide group or radical.*

Azikiwe (ˌɑːziː'kiːweɪ) *n* **Nnamdi** (ᵊn'næmdɪ). 1904–96, Nigerian statesman; first president of Nigeria (1963–66).

Azilian (ə'zɪlɪən) *n* **1** a Palaeolithic culture of Spain and SW France that can be dated to the 10th millennium B.C., characterized by flat bone harpoons and schematically painted pebbles. ◆ *adj* **2** of or relating to this culture. [C19: named after Mas d'*Azil,* France, where artefacts were found]

azimuth ('æzɪməθ) *n* **1** *Astronomy, navigation.* the angular distance usually measured clockwise from the south point of the horizon in astronomy or from the north point in navigation to the intersection with the horizon of the vertical circle passing through a celestial body. Compare **altitude** (sense 3). **2** *Surveying.* the horizontal angle of a bearing clockwise from a standard direction, such as north. [C14: from Old French *azimut,* from Arabic *as-sumūt,* plural of *as-samt* the path, from Latin *semita* path] ▸ **azimuthal** (ˌæzɪ'mʌθəl) *adj* ▸ **ˌazi'muthally** *adv*

azimuthal projection *n* another term for **zenithal projection.**

azine ('eɪziːn, -zɪn) *n* any organic compound having a six-membered ring containing at least one nitrogen atom. See also **diazine, triazine.**

azo ('eɪzəʊ, 'æ-) *adj* of, consisting of, or containing the divalent group -N:N-: *an azo group or radical.* See also **diazo.** [independent use of AZO-]

azo- *or before a vowel* **az-** *combining form.* indicating the presence of an azo group: *azobenzene.* [from French *azote* nitrogen, from Greek *azōos* lifeless, from A-[1] + *zōē* life]

azobenzene (ˌeɪzəʊ'bɛnziːn, -bɛn'ziːn) *n* **1** a yellow or orange crystalline solid used mainly in the manufacture of dyes. Formula: $C_6H_5N{:}NC_6H_5$. **2** any organic compound that is a substituted derivative of azobenzene.

azo dye *n* any of a class of artificial dyes that contain the azo group. They are usually red, brown, or yellow and are obtained from aromatic amines.

azoic (ə'zəʊɪk, eɪ-) *adj* without life; characteristic of the ages that have left no evidence of life in the form of organic remains. [C19: from Greek *azōos* lifeless; see AZO-]

azole ('eɪzəʊl, ə'zəʊl) *n* **1** an organic five-membered ring compound containing one or more atoms in the ring, the number usually being specified by a prefix: *diazole; triazole.* **2** a less common name for **pyrrole.** [from AZO- + -OLE[1], on the model of *diazole*]

azonal soil (eɪ'zəʊnᵊl) *n* soil that has a profile determined predominantly by factors other than local climate and vegetation. Azonal soils include some mountain, alluvial, marine, glacial, windblown, and volcanic soils. Compare **intrazonal soil, zonal soil.**

azoospermia (eɪˌzəʊə'spɜːmɪə) *n Pathol.* absence of spermatozoa in the semen. ▸ **aˌzoo'spermic** *adj*

Azores (ə'zɔːz) *pl n* **the.** three groups of volcanic islands in the N Atlantic, since 1976 an autonomous region of Portugal. Capital: Ponta Delgada (on São Miguel). Pop.: 237 800 (1993 est.). Area: 2335 sq. km (901 sq. miles). Portuguese name: **Açôres.**

Azorín (*Spanish* aθo'rin) *n* real name *José Martínez Ruiz.* 1874–1967, Spanish writer: noted for his stories of the Spanish countryside.

azotaemia *or esp. U.S.* **azotemia** (ˌæzə'tiːmɪə) *n Pathol.* a less common name for **uraemia.** [C20: see AZOTE, -AEMIA] ▸ **azotaemic** *or esp. U.S.* **azotemic** (ˌæzə'tiːmɪk) *adj*

azote ('eɪzəʊt, ə'zəʊt) *n* an obsolete name for **nitrogen.** [C18: from French, from Greek *azōtos* ungirded, intended for Greek *azōos* lifeless]

azoth ('æzɒθ) *n* **1** the alchemical name for **mercury,** regarded as the first principle of all metals. **2** the panacea postulated by Paracelsus. [from Arabic *az-zā'ūq* the mercury]

azotic (eɪ'zɒtɪk) *adj* of, containing, or concerned with nitrogen.

azotize *or* **azotise** ('eɪzəˌtaɪz) *vb* a less common word for **nitrogenize.**

azotobacter (ə'zəʊtəʊˌbæktə) *n* any bacterium of the family *Azotobacteriaceae,* important in nitrogen fixation in the soil. [New Latin; see AZOTE, BACTERIA]

Azov ('ɑːzɒv) *n* **Sea of.** a shallow arm of the Black Sea, to which it is connected by the Kerch Strait: almost entirely landlocked; fed chiefly by the River Don. Area: about 37 500 sq. km (14 500 sq. miles).

Azrael ('æzreɪl, -rɪəl) *n* (in Jewish and Islamic angelology) the angel who separates the soul from the body at death.

AZT *abbrev. for* azidothymidine: also called **zidovudine.**

Aztec ('æztɛk) *n* **1** a member of a Mexican Indian people who established a great empire, centred on the valley of Mexico, that was overthrown by Cortés and his followers in the early 16th century. **2** the language of the Aztecs. See also **Nahuatl.** ◆ *adj also* **Aztecan. 3** of, relating to, or characteristic of the Aztecs, their civilization, or their language. [C18: from Spanish *Azteca,* from Nahuatl *Aztecatl,* from *Aztlan,* their traditional place of origin, literally: near the cranes, from *azta* cranes + *tlan* near]

azure ('æʒə, -ʒʊə, 'eɪ-) *n* **1** a deep blue, occasionally somewhat purple, similar to the colour of a clear blue sky. **2** *Poetic.* a clear blue sky. ◆ *adj* **3** of the colour azure; serene. **4** (*usually postpositive*) *Heraldry.* of the colour blue. [C14: from Old French *azur,* from Old Spanish, from Arabic *lāzaward* lapis lazuli, from Persian *lāzhuward*]

azurite ('æʒʊˌraɪt) *n* an azure-blue mineral associated with copper deposits. It is a source of copper. Composition: copper carbonate. Formula: $Cu_3(CO_3)_2(OH)_2$. Crystal structure: monoclinic.

azygospore (ə'zaɪgəʊˌspɔː) *n* a thick-walled spore produced by parthenogenesis in certain algae and fungi. Also called: **parthenospore.**

azygous ('æzɪgəs) *adj Biology.* developing or occurring singly. [C17: via New Latin from Greek *azugos,* from A-[1] + *zugon* YOKE]

Bb

b or **B** (biː) *n, pl* **b's, B's,** *or* **Bs. 1** the second letter and first consonant of the modern English alphabet. **2** a speech sound represented by this letter, usually a voiced bilabial stop, as in *bell.* **3** Also: **beta.** the second in a series, esp. the second highest grade in an examination.

b *Chess.* See **algebraic notation.**

B *symbol for:* **1** *Music.* **1a** a note having a frequency of 493.88 hertz (**B above middle C**) or this value multiplied or divided by any power of 2; the seventh note of the scale of C major. **1b** a key, string, or pipe producing this note. **1c** the major or minor key having this note as its tonic. **2** the supporting or less important of two things: *the B side of a record.* **3** a human blood type of the ABO group, containing the B antigen. **4** (in Britain) a secondary road. **5** the number 11 in hexadecimal notation. **6** *Chem.* boron. **7** magnetic flux density. **8** *Chess.* bishop. **9** (on Brit. pencils, signifying degree of softness of lead) black: *B; 2B; 3B.* Compare **H** (sense 5). **10** Also: **b** *Physics.* bel. **11** *Physics.* baryon number. **12** balboa. **13** belga. **14** bolivar. **15** *Photog.* B-setting. **16a** a person whose job is in middle management, or who holds an intermediate administrative or professional position. **16b** (*as modifier*): *a B worker.* ◆ See also **occupation groupings.** ◆ **17** *international car registration for* Belgium.

b. *abbrev. for:* **1** born. **2** *Cricket.* bowled. **3** *Cricket.* bye.

b. *or* **B.** *abbrev. for:* **1** *Music.* bass *or* basso. **2** billion. **3** book. **4** breadth.

B. *abbrev. for:* **1** (on maps, etc.) bay. **2** Bible. **3** British.

B- (of U.S. military aircraft) *abbrev. for* bomber: *B-52.*

Ba[1] (bɑː) *n Egyptian myth.* the soul, represented as a bird with a human head.

Ba[2] *the chemical symbol for* barium.

BA *abbrev. for:* **1** Bachelor of Arts. **2** British Academy. **3** British Airways. **4** British Association (for the Advancement of Science). **5** British Association screw thread.

baa (bɑː) *vb* **baas, baaing, baaed. 1** (*intr*) to make the cry of a sheep; bleat. ◆ *n* **2** the cry made by sheep.

BAA *n* the main airports operator in the United Kingdom; until privatization in 1987, an abbreviation for British Airports Authority.

BAAB *abbrev. for* British Amateur Athletic Board.

Baader-Meinhof Gang (*German* ˈbaːdər ˈmainhoːf) *n* **the.** a group of West German guerrillas dedicated to the violent overthrow of capitalist society. Also called: **Red Army Faction.** [C20: named after its leading members, Andreas *Baader* (1943–77) and Ulrike *Meinhof* (1934–76)]

Baal (bɑːl) *n* **1** any of several ancient Semitic fertility gods. **2** *Phoenician myth.* the sun god and supreme national deity. **3** (*sometimes not cap.*) any false god or idol. [from Hebrew *báʿal* lord, master]

Baalbek (ˈbɑːlbɛk) *n* a town in E Lebanon: an important city in Phoenician and Roman times; extensive ruins. Pop.: 15 600 (1995 est.). Ancient name: **Heliopolis.**

baalebos (ˈbaləbɔs) *n, pl* **baalebatim.** *Yiddish.* **1** the master of the house. **2** the proprietor of a business, etc. **3** *Slang.* an officious person. [from Hebrew *baʿal La-bayis* master of the house]

Baal Shem Tov *or* **Baal Shem Tob** (bɑːl ˈʃɛm tɒv, ˈʃɑːm) *n* original name *Israel ben Eliezer.* ?1700–60, Jewish religious leader, teacher, and healer in Poland: founder of modern Hasidism.

baas (bɑːs) *n* a South African word for **boss**[1]: used by Africans and Coloureds in addressing European managers or overseers. [C17: from Afrikaans, from Middle Dutch *baes* master; see BOSS[1]]

baaskap *or* **baasskap** (ˈbɑːsˌkap) *n* (*sometimes cap.*) (in South Africa) control by Whites of non-Whites. [from Afrikaans, from BAAS + *-skap* -SHIP]

Ba'ath (bɑːˈɑːθ) *n* a variant of **Ba'th.**

Bab (bɑːb) *n* **the.** title of *Mirza Ali Mohammed.* 1819–50, Persian religious leader: founded Babism; executed as a heretic of Islam. [from Persian *bāb* gate, from Arabic]

baba (ˈbɑːbɑː; *French* baba) *n* a small cake of leavened dough, sometimes mixed with currants and usually soaked in rum (**rum baba**). [C19: from French, from Polish, literally: old woman]

babaco (ˈbæbəˌkəʊ, bəˈbɑːkəʊ) *n, pl* **-cos. 1** a subtropical parthenocarpic tree, *Carica pentagona,* originating in South America, cultivated for its fruit: family *Caricaceae.* **2** the greenish-yellow egg-shaped fruit of this tree, having a delicate fragrance and no pips.

babalas (ˈbabalas) *adj S. African.* drunk; hungover. [C20: Afrikaans, from Zulu *I-babalazi* drunk]

Babar (ˈbɑːbə) *n* a variant spelling of **Baber.**

babassu (ˌbɑːbəˈsuː) *n* a Brazilian palm tree, *Orbignya martiana* (or *O. speciosa*), having hard edible nuts that yield an oil used in making soap, margarine, etc. [from Portuguese *babaçú,* from a native Amerindian word]

Babbage (ˈbæbɪdʒ) *n* **Charles.** 1792–1871, English mathematician and inventor, who built a calculating machine that anticipated the modern electronic computer.

babbitt (ˈbæbɪt) *vb* (*tr*) to line (a bearing) or face (a surface) with Babbitt metal or a similar soft alloy.

Babbitt (ˈbæbɪt) *n U.S. derogatory.* a narrow-minded and complacent member of the middle class. [C20: after George *Babbitt,* central character in the novel *Babbitt* (1922) by Sinclair Lewis] ▸ ˈ**Babbittry** *n*

Babbitt metal *n* any of a number of alloys originally based on tin, antimony, and copper but now often including lead: used esp. in bearings. Sometimes shortened to **Babbitt.** [C19: named after Isaac *Babbitt* (1799–1862), American inventor]

babble (ˈbæbᵊl) *vb* **1** to utter (words, sounds, etc.) in an incoherent or indistinct jumble. **2** (*intr*) to talk foolishly, incessantly, or irrelevantly. **3** (*tr*) to disclose (secrets, confidences, etc.) carelessly or impulsively. **4** (*intr*) (of streams, birds, etc.) to make a low murmuring or bubbling sound. ◆ *n* **5** incoherent or foolish speech; chatter. **6** a murmuring or bubbling sound. [C13: compare Dutch *babbelen,* Swedish *babbla,* French *babiller* to prattle, Latin *babulus* fool; probably all of imitative origin] ▸ ˈ**babblement** *n* ▸ ˈ**babbling** *n, adj*

babbler (ˈbæblə) *n* **1** a person who babbles. **2** any of various insect-eating birds of the Old World tropics and subtropics that have a loud incessant song: family *Muscicapidae* (warblers, thrushes, etc.).

babe (beɪb) *n* **1** a baby. **2** *Informal.* a naive, gullible, or unsuspecting person (often in the phrase **a babe in arms**). **3** *Slang.* a girl or young woman, esp. an attractive one.

Babel[1] (ˈbeɪbᵊl) *n* **1** *Old Testament.* **1a** Also called: **Tower of Babel.** a tower presumptuously intended to reach from earth to heaven, the building of which was frustrated when Jehovah confused the language of the builders (Genesis 11:1–10). **1b** the city, probably Babylon, in which this tower was supposedly built. **2** (*often not cap.*) **2a** a confusion of noises or voices. **2b** a scene of noise and confusion. [from Hebrew *Bābhēl,* from Akkadian *Bāb-ilu,* literally: gate of God]

Babel[2] (*Russian* ˈbabɪl) *n* **Isaak Emmanuilovich** (iˈsak imənuˈiləvitʃ). 1894–1941, Russian short-story writer, whose works include *Stories from Odessa* (1924) and *Red Cavalry* (1926).

Bab el Mandeb (ˈbæb ɛl ˈmændɛb) *n* a strait between SW Arabia and E Africa, connecting the Red Sea with the Gulf of Aden.

Baber, Babar, *or* **Babur** (ˈbɑːbə) *n* original name *Zahir ud-Din Mohammed.* 1483–1530, founder of the Mogul Empire: conquered India in 1526.

Babeuf (*French* babœf) *n* **François Noël** (frɑ̃swa nɔɛl). 1760–97, French political agitator: plotted unsuccessfully to destroy the Directory and establish a communistic system.

Babi (ˈbɑːbɪ) *n* **1** a disciple of the Bab. **2** another word for **Babism.**

babiche (bɑːˈbiːʃ) *n Canadian.* thongs or lacings of rawhide. [C19: from Canadian French, of Algonquian origin]

babies'-breath *n* a variant of **baby's-breath.**

Babinet (*French* babinɛ) *n* **Jacques** (ʒɑk). 1794–1872, French physicist, noted for his work on the diffraction of light.

Babington (ˈbæbɪŋtən) *n* **Anthony.** 1561–86, English conspirator, executed for organizing an unsuccessful plot (1586) to assassinate Elizabeth I and place Mary, Queen of Scots, on the English throne.

Babinski effect (bəˈbɪnskɪ) *n Physiol.* the reflex curling upwards of the toes (instead of inwards) when the sole of the foot is stroked, normal in infants below the age of two but a pathological condition in adults. [after Joseph *Babinski* (1857–1932), French neuropathologist]

babirusa (ˌbɑːbɪˈruːsə) *n* a wild pig, *Babyrousa babyrussa,* inhabiting marshy forests in Indonesia. It has an almost hairless wrinkled skin and enormous curved canine teeth. [C17: from Malay, from *bābī* hog + *rūsa* deer]

Babism (ˈbɑːbɪzəm) *n* a pantheistic Persian religious sect, founded in 1844 by the Bab, forbidding polygamy, concubinage, begging, trading in slaves, and indulgence in alcohol and drugs. Compare **Baha'ism.**

baboon (bəˈbuːn) *n* any of several medium-sized omnivorous Old World monkeys of the genus *Papio* (or *Chaeropithecus*) and related genera, inhabiting open rocky ground or wooded regions of Africa. They have an elongated muzzle, large teeth, and a fairly long tail. See also **hamadryas, gelada.** [C14 *babewyn* gargoyle, later, baboon, from Old French *babouin,* from *baboue* grimace; related to Old French *babine* a thick lip]

Babo's law (ˈbæbəʊz) *n Chem.* the law stating that the vapour pressure of a solution is reduced in proportion to the amount of solute added. [C19: named after Lambert von *Babo* (1818–99), German chemist who formulated it]

babu (ˈbɑːbuː) *n* (in India) a title or form of address more or less equivalent to *Mr,* placed before a person's full name or after his first name. [Hindi, literally: father]

babul (bɑːˈbuːl, ˈbɑːbuːl) *n* any of several mimosaceous trees of the genus *Acacia,* esp. *A. arabica* of N Africa and India, which bear small yellow flowers and are a source of gum arabic, tannin, and hardwood. [from Persian *babūl;* related to Sanskrit *babbūla*]

Babur (ˈbɑːbə) *n* a variant spelling of **Baber.**

babushka (bəˈbuːʃkə) *n* **1** a headscarf tied under the chin, worn by Russian peasant women. **2** (in Russia) an old woman. [Russian: grandmother, from *baba* old woman]

baby (ˈbeɪbɪ) *n, pl* **-bies. 1a** a newborn or recently born child; infant. **1b** (*as modifier*): *baby food.* **2** the youngest or smallest of a family or group. **3a** a newborn or recently born animal. **3b** (*as modifier*): *baby rabbits.* **4** *Usually derogatory.* an immature person. **5** *Slang.* a young woman or sweetheart: often used as a term of address expressing affection. **6** a project of personal concern. **7 be left holding the baby.** to be left with the responsibility. **8 throw the baby out with the bath water.** to lose the essential element by indiscriminate rejection.

◆ *adj* 9 (*prenominal*) comparatively small of its type: *a baby car.* ◆ *vb* **-bies, -bying, -bied.** (*tr*) **10** to treat with love and attention. **11** to treat (someone) like a baby; pamper or overprotect. [C14: probably childish reduplication; compare MAMA, PAPA] ▸ **'babyhood** *n* ▸ **'babyish** *adj*

baby bonus *n Canadian informal.* family allowance.

baby boom *n* a sharp increase in the birth rate of a population, esp. the one that occurred after World War II. Also called (esp. Brit.): **the bulge.**

baby-boomer *n* a person born during a baby boom, esp. (in Britain and the U.S.) one born during the years 1945–55.

Baby-bouncer *n Trademark.* a seat on springs suspended from a door frame, etc., in which a baby may be placed for exercise.

baby buggy *n* **1** *Brit. Trademark.* a kind of child's light pushchair. **2** *U.S. and Canadian informal.* a small pram.

baby carriage *n* Also: **baby buggy.** the U.S. and Canadian name for **pram**[1].

baby-face *n* **1** a smooth round face like a baby's. **2** a person with such a face.

baby grand *n* a small grand piano, approximately 5 feet long. Compare **boudoir grand, concert grand.**

Babylon ('bæbɪlən) *n* **1** the chief city of ancient Mesopotamia: first settled around 3000 B.C. See also **Hanging Gardens of Babylon. 2** *Derogatory.* (in Protestant polemic) the Roman Catholic Church, regarded as the seat of luxury and corruption. **3** *Derogatory.* any society or group in a society considered as corrupt or as a place of exile by another society or group, esp. White Britain as viewed by some West Indians. [via Latin and Greek from Hebrew *Bābhel;* see BABEL[1]]

Babylonia (ˌbæbɪ'ləʊnɪə) *n* the southern kingdom of ancient Mesopotamia: a great empire from about 2200–538 B.C., when it was conquered by the Persians.

Babylonian (ˌbæbɪ'ləʊnɪən) *n* **1** an inhabitant of ancient Babylon or Babylonia. **2** the extinct language of Babylonia, belonging to the E Semitic subfamily of the Afro-Asiatic family: a dialect of Akkadian. ◆ *adj* **3** of, relating to, or characteristic of ancient Babylon or Babylonia, its people, or their language. **4** decadent or depraved.

Babylonian captivity *n* **1** the exile of the Jews in Babylonia from about 586 to about 538 B.C. **2** the exile of the seven popes in Avignon (1309–77).

baby-minder *n* a person who is paid to look after other people's babies or very young children. ▸ **'baby-ˌminding** *n*

baby's-breath *or* **babies'-breath** *n* **1** a tall Eurasian caryophyllaceous plant, *Gypsophila paniculata,* bearing small white or pink fragrant flowers. **2** any of several other plants, such as the grape hyacinth and certain bedstraws, that have small scented flowers.

baby-sit *vb* **-sits, -sitting, -sat.** (*intr*) to act or work as a baby-sitter. ▸ **'baby-ˌsitting** *n, adj*

baby-sitter *n* a person who takes care of a child or children while the parents are out.

baby snatcher *n Informal.* **1** a person who steals a baby from its pram. **2** another name for **cradle snatcher.**

baby talk *n* **1** the speech of very young children learning to talk. **2** an adult's imitation of this.

baby tooth *n* another term for **milk tooth.**

baby-walker *n* a light frame on casters or wheels to help a baby learn to walk. U.S. equivalent: **go-cart.**

baby wipe *n* a disposable moistened medicated paper towel, usually supplied in a plastic drum or packet, used for cleaning babies.

Bacău ('bækau) *n* a city in E Romania on the River Bistrila: oil refining, textiles, paper. Pop.: 207 730 (1994 est.).

Baccalauréat (ˌbækə'lɔːrɪˌɑː) *n* (esp. in France) a school-leaving examination that qualifies the successful candidates for entrance to university. [C20: from French, from Medieval Latin *baccalaureus* bachelor]

baccalaureate (ˌbækə'lɔːrɪɪt) *n* **1** the university degree of Bachelor or Arts, Bachelor of Science, etc. **2** an internationally recognized programme of study, comprising different subjects, offered as an alternative to a course of A levels in Britain. **3** *U.S.* a farewell sermon delivered at the commencement ceremonies in many colleges and universities. [C17: from Medieval Latin *baccalaureātus,* from *baccalaureus* advanced student, alteration of *baccalārius* BACHELOR; influenced in folk etymology by Latin *bāca* berry + *laureus* laurel]

baccarat ('bækəˌrɑː, ˌbækə'rɑː; *French* bakara) *n* a card game in which two or more punters gamble against the banker. [C19: from French *baccara,* of unknown origin]

baccate ('bækeɪt) *adj Botany.* **1** like a berry in form, texture, etc. **2** bearing berries. [C19: from Latin *bāca* berry]

Bacchae ('bækiː) *pl n* the priestesses or female devotees of Bacchus. [Latin, from Greek *Bakkhai,* plural of *Bakkhē* priestess of BACCHUS]

bacchanal ('bækənᵊl) *n* **1** a follower of Bacchus. **2** a drunken and riotous celebration. **3** a participant in such a celebration; reveller. ◆ *adj* **4** of or relating to Bacchus. [C16: from Latin *Bacchānālis;* see BACCHUS]

bacchanalia (ˌbækə'neɪlɪə) *pl n* **1** (*often cap.*) orgiastic rites associated with Bacchus. **2** any drunken revelry. ▸ **ˌbaccha'nalian** *adj, n*

bacchant ('bækənt) *or* (*fem*) **bacchante** (bə'kæntɪ) *n, pl* **bacchants, bacchantes** (bə'kæntɪz) *or* (*fem*) **bacchantes. 1** a priest, priestess, or votary of Bacchus. **2** a drunken reveller. [C17: from Latin *bacchāns,* from *bacchārī* to celebrate the BACCHANALIA]

Bacchic ('bækɪk) *adj* **1** of or relating to Bacchus. **2** (*often not cap.*) riotously drunk.

bacchius (bæ'kaɪəs) *n, pl* **-chii** (-'kaɪaɪ). *Prosody.* a metrical foot of one short syllable followed by two long ones (⏑ – –). Compare **dactyl.** [C16: from Latin, from Greek *Bakkheios* (*pous*) a Bacchic (foot)]

Bacchus ('bækəs) *n* (in ancient Greece and Rome) a god of wine and giver of ecstasy, identified with Dionysus. [C15: from Latin, from Greek *Bakkhos;* related to Latin *bāca* small round fruit, berry]

bacciferous (bæk'sɪfərəs) *adj* bearing berries. [C17: from Latin *bācifer,* from *bāca* berry + *ferre* to bear]

bacciform ('bæksɪˌfɔːm) *adj Botany.* shaped like a berry.

baccivorous (bæk'sɪvərəs) *adj* feeding on berries.

baccy ('bækɪ) *n Brit.* an informal name for **tobacco.**

bach[1] (bax, bɑːk) *n Welsh.* a term of friendly address: used esp. after a person's name. [Welsh, literally: little one]

bach[2] (bætʃ) *Chiefly N.Z.* ◆ *vb* **1** a variant spelling of **batch**[2]. ◆ *n* **2** a simple cottage, esp. at the seaside.

Bach (*German* bax) *n* **1 Johann Christian** (jo'han 'krɪstjan), 11th son of J. S. Bach. 1735–82, German composer, called *the English Bach,* resident in London from 1762. **2 Johann Christoph** ('krɪstɔf). 1642–1703, German composer: wrote oratorios, cantatas, and motets, some of which were falsely attributed to J. S. Bach, of whom he was a distant relative. **3 Johann Sebastian** (ze'bastjan). 1685–1750, German composer: church organist at Arnstadt (1703–07) and Mühlhausen (1707–08); court organist at Weimar (1708–17); musical director for Prince Leopold of Köthen (1717–28); musical director for the city of Leipzig (1728–50). His output was enormous and displays great vigour and invention within the northern European polyphonic tradition. His works include nearly 200 cantatas and oratorios, settings of the *Passion according to St John* (1723) and *St Matthew* (1729), the six *Brandenburg Concertos* (1720–21), the 48 preludes and fugues of the *Well-tempered Clavier* (completed 1744), and the *Mass in B Minor* (1733–38). **4 Karl** (*or* **Carl**) **Philipp Emanuel** (karl 'fiːlɪp e'maːnuɛl), 3rd son of J. S. Bach. 1714–88, German composer, chiefly of symphonies, keyboard sonatas, and church music. **5 Wilhelm Friedemann** ('vɪlhɛlm 'friːdəman), eldest son of J. S. Bach. 1710–84, German composer: wrote nine symphonies and much keyboard and religious music.

Bacharach ('bækəræk) *n* **Burt.** born 1928, U.S. composer of popular songs, usually with lyricist Hal David.

bachelor ('bætʃələ, 'bætʃlə) *n* **1a** an unmarried man. **1b** (*as modifier*): *a bachelor flat.* **2a** a person who holds the degree of Bachelor of Arts, Bachelor of Education, Bachelor of Science, etc. **2b** the degree itself. **3** Also called: **bachelor-at-arms.** (in the Middle Ages) a young knight serving a great noble. **4 bachelor seal.** a young male seal, esp. a fur seal, that has not yet mated. [C13: from Old French *bacheler* youth, squire, from Vulgar Latin *baccalāris* (unattested) farm worker, of Celtic origin; compare Irish Gaelic *bachlach* peasant] ▸ **'bachelorhood** *n*

bachelor girl *n* a young unmarried woman, esp. one who is self-supporting.

Bachelor of Arts *n* **1** a degree conferred on a person who has successfully completed his undergraduate studies, usually in a branch of the liberal arts or humanities. **2** a person who holds this degree.

Bachelor of Science *n* **1** a degree conferred on a person who has successfully completed his undergraduate studies in a branch of the sciences. **2** a person who holds this degree.

bachelor's-buttons *n* (*functioning as sing or pl*) any of various plants of the daisy family with button-like flower heads, esp. a double-flowered buttercup.

Bach flower remedy *n Trademark.* an alternative medicine consisting of a distillation from various flowers, designed to counteract negative states of mind and restore emotional balance. [C20: after Dr E. *Bach* (1886–1936), homeopath who developed this system]

Bach trumpet (bɑːx) *n* a modern small three-valved trumpet for playing clarino passages in Bach's music.

bacillaemia *or U.S.* **bacillemia** (ˌbæsɪ'liːmɪə) *n Pathol.* the presence of bacilli in the blood.

bacillary (bə'sɪlərɪ) *or* **bacillar** (bə'sɪlə) *adj* **1** of, relating to, or caused by bacilli. **2** Also: **bacilliform** (bə'sɪlɪˌfɔːm). shaped like a short rod.

bacilluria (ˌbæsɪ'ljʊərɪə) *n Pathol.* the presence of bacilli in the urine.

bacillus (bə'sɪləs) *n, pl* **-cilli** (-'sɪlaɪ). **1** any rod-shaped bacterium, such as a clostridium bacterium. Compare **coccus** (sense 1), **spirillum** (sense 1). **2** any of various rodlike spore-producing bacteria constituting the family *Bacillaceae,* esp. of the genus *Bacillus.* [C19: from Latin: a small staff, from *baculum* walking stick]

bacitracin (ˌbæsɪ'treɪsɪn) *n* an antibiotic used mainly in treating bacterial skin infections: obtained from the bacterium *Bacillus subtilis.* [C20: BACI(LLUS) + *-trac-* from Margaret *Tracy* (born 1936), American girl in whose blood *Bacillus subtilis* was found; see -IN]

back[1] (bæk) *n* **1** the posterior part of the human body, extending from the neck to the pelvis. Related adj: **dorsal. 2** the corresponding or upper part of an animal. **3** the spinal column. **4** the part or side of an object opposite the front. **5** the part or side of anything less often seen or used: *the back of a carpet; the back of a knife.* **6** the part or side of anything that is furthest from the front or from a spectator: *the back of the stage.* **7** the convex part of something: *the back of a hill; the back of a ship.* **8** something that supports, covers, or strengthens the rear of an object. **9** *Ball games.* **9a** a mainly defensive player behind a forward. **9b** the position of such a player. **10** the part of a book to which the pages are glued or that joins the covers. **11** *Mining.* **11a** the side of a passage or layer nearest the surface. **11b** the earth between that level and the next. **12** the upper surface of a joist, rafter, slate, tile, etc., when in position. Compare **bed** (sense 13). **13 at one's back.** behind, esp. in support or pursuit. **14 at the back of one's mind.** not in one's conscious thoughts. **15 behind one's back.** without one's knowledge; secretly or deceitfully. **16 break one's back.** to overwork or work very hard. **17 break the back of.** to complete the greatest or hardest part of (a task). **18** (**flat**) **on one's back.** incapacitated, esp. through illness. **19 get off someone's back.** *Informal.* to stop criticizing or pestering someone. **20 have on one's back.** to be burdened with. **21 on someone's back.** *Informal.* criticizing or pestering someone. **22 put one's back into.** to devote all one's strength to (a task). **23 put** (*or* **get**) **someone's back up.** to annoy someone. **24 see the back of.** to be rid of. **25 back of be-**

yond. 25a the. a very remote place. **25b** *Austral.* in such a place (esp. in the phrase **out back of beyond**). **26 turn one's back on. 26a** to turn away from in anger or contempt. **26b** to refuse to help; abandon. **27 with one's back to the wall.** in a difficult or desperate situation. ♦ *vb* (*mainly tr*) **28** (*also intr*) to move or cause to move backwards. **29** to provide support, money, or encouragement for (a person, enterprise, etc.). **30** to bet on the success of: *to back a horse.* **31** to provide with a back, backing, or lining. **32** to provide with a music accompaniment: *a soloist backed by an orchestra.* **33** to provide a background for; be at the back of: *mountains back the town.* **34** to countersign or endorse. **35** *Archaic.* to mount the back of. **36** (*intr*; foll. by *on* or *onto*) to have the back facing (towards): *the house backs onto a river.* **37** (*intr*) (of the wind) to change direction in an anticlockwise direction. Compare **veer**[1] (sense 3a). **38** *Nautical.* to position (a sail) so that the wind presses on its opposite side. **39 back and fill. 39a** *Nautical.* to manoeuvre the sails by alternately filling and emptying them of wind to navigate in a narrow place. **39b** to vacillate in one's opinion. ♦ *adj* (*prenominal*) **40** situated behind: *a back lane.* **41** of the past: *back issues of a magazine.* **42** owing from an earlier date: *back rent.* **43** *Chiefly U.S., Austral., and N.Z.* remote: *back country.* **44** (of a road) not direct. **45** moving in a backward direction: *back current.* **46** *Phonetics.* of, relating to, or denoting a vowel articulated with the tongue retracted towards the soft palate, as for the vowels in English *hard, fall, hot, full, fool.* ♦ *adv* **47** at, to, or towards the rear; away from something considered to be the front; backwards; behind. **48** in, to, or towards the original starting point, place, or condition: *to go back home; put the book back; my headache has come back.* **49** in or into the past: *to look back on one's childhood.* **50** in reply, repayment, or retaliation: *to hit someone back; pay back a debt; to answer back.* **51** in check: *the dam holds back the water.* **52** in concealment; in reserve: *to keep something back; to hold back information.* **53 back and forth.** to and fro. **54 back to front. 54a** in reverse. **54b** in disorder. ♦ See also **back down, back off, back out, back up.** [Old English *bæc*; related to Old Norse *bak*, Old Frisian *bek*, Old High German *bah*]

back[2] (bæk) *n* a large tub or vat, esp. one used by brewers. [C17: from Dutch *bak* tub, cistern, from Old French *bac*, from Vulgar Latin *bacca* (unattested) vessel for liquids]

backache (ˈbækˌeɪk) *n* an ache or pain in one's back.

backbeat (ˈbækˌbiːt) *n* the second and fourth beats in music written in even time or, in more complex time signatures, the last beat of the bar. Compare **downbeat** (sense 1).

backbencher (ˈbækˈbɛntʃə) *n Brit., Austral., and N.Z., etc.* a Member of Parliament who does not hold office in the government or opposition.

backbend (ˈbækˌbɛnd) *n* a gymnastic exercise in which the trunk is bent backwards until the hands touch the floor.

backbite (ˈbækˌbaɪt) *vb* **-bites, -biting, -bit; -bitten** *or* **-bit.** to talk spitefully about (an absent person). ▸ **ˈbackˌbiter** *n*

backblocks (ˈbækˌblɒks) *pl n Austral. and N.Z.* bush or remote farming area far distant from city amenities. ▸ **ˈbackˌblock** *adj* ▸ **ˈbackˌblocker** *n*

backboard (ˈbækˌbɔːd) *n* **1** a board that is placed behind something to form or support its back. **2** a board worn to straighten or support the back, as after surgery. **3** (in basketball) a flat upright surface supported on a high frame, under which the basket is attached.

back boiler *n* a tank or series of pipes at the back of a fireplace for heating water. U.S. name: **water back.**

backbone (ˈbækˌbəʊn) *n* **1** a nontechnical name for **spinal column. 2** something that resembles the spinal column in function, position, or appearance. **3** strength of character; courage. **4** the main or central mountain range of a country or region. **5** *Nautical.* the main longitudinal members of a vessel, giving structural strength. **6** *Computing.* (in computer networks) a large-capacity, high-speed central section by which other network segments are connected.

backbreaker (ˈbækˌbreɪkə) *n* **1** a wrestling hold in which a wrestler uses his knee or shoulder as a fulcrum to bend his opponent's body backwards. **2** *Informal.* an extremely arduous task.

backbreaking (ˈbækˌbreɪkɪŋ) *adj* demanding great effort; exhausting.

backburn (ˈbækˌbɜːn) *Austral. and N.Z.* ♦ *vb* (*tr*) **1** to clear (an area of scrub, bush, etc.) by creating a new fire that burns in the opposite direction to the line of advancing fire. ♦ *n* **2** the act or result of backburning.

back burner *n* **on the back burner.** put aside for the time being, as a subject that is not of immediate concern but that may be activated later; postponed.

backchat (ˈbækˌtʃæt) *n Informal.* the act of answering back, esp. impudently.

backcloth (ˈbækˌklɒθ) *n* a large painted curtain hanging at the back of a stage set. Also called: **backdrop.**

backcomb (ˈbækˌkəʊm) *vb* to comb the under layers of (the hair) towards the roots to give more bulk to a hairstyle. Also: **tease.**

back country *n Austral. and N.Z.* land remote from a town or settled area.

backcourt (ˈbækˌkɔːt) *n* **1** *Tennis, chiefly U.S.* the part of the court between the service line and the baseline. **2** (in various court games) the area nearest the back boundary line.

backcross (ˈbækˌkrɒs) *vb* **1** to mate (a hybrid of the first generation) with one of its parents. ♦ *n* **2** the offspring so produced. **3** the act or process of backcrossing.

backdate (ˌbækˈdeɪt) *vb* (*tr*) to make effective from an earlier date: *the pay rise was backdated to August.*

back door *n* **1** a door at the rear or side of a building. **2** a means of entry to a job, position, etc., that is secret, underhand, or obtained through influence.

back down *vb* **1** (*intr, adv*) to withdraw an earlier claim. **2** (*tr*) *Rowing.* to cause (a boat) to move backwards by pushing rather than pulling on the oars. ♦ *n* **backdown. 3** abandonment of an earlier claim.

backdrop (ˈbækˌdrɒp) *n* **1** another name for **backcloth. 2** the background to any scene or situation.

backed (bækt) *adj* **a** having a back or backing. **b** (*in combination*): *high-backed; black-backed.*

back emf *n Electrical engineering.* an electromagnetic force appearing in an inductive circuit in such a direction as to oppose any change of current in the circuit.

back emission *n Electronics.* the secondary emission of electrons from an anode.

back end 1 *n Northern English dialect.* autumn. ♦ *adj* **back-end. 2** (of money, costs, etc.) required or incurred after a project has been completed. [from the phrase *the back end of the year*]

back-end load *n* the final charges of commission and expenses made by an investment trust, insurance policy, etc., when the investor is paid out. ▸ **back-end loading** *n*

backer (ˈbækə) *n* **1** a person who gives financial or other support. **2** a person who bets on a competitor or contestant.

backfield (ˈbækˌfiːld) *n American football.* **1** (usually preceded by *the*) the quarterback and running backs in a team. **2** the area behind the line of scrimmage from which the backfield begin each play.

backfile (ˈbækˌfaɪl) *n* the archives of a newspaper or magazine.

backfill (ˈbækˌfɪl) *vb* **1** (*tr*) to refill an excavated trench, esp. (in archaeology) at the end of an investigation. ♦ *n* **2** the soil used to do this.

backfire (ˌbækˈfaɪə) *vb* (*intr*) **1** (of an internal-combustion engine) to emit a loud noise as a result of an explosion in the inlet manifold or exhaust system. **2** to fail to have the desired or expected effect: *his plans backfired on him.* **3** to start a controlled fire in order to halt an advancing forest or prairie fire by creating a barren area. ♦ *n* **4** (in an internal-combustion engine) **4a** an explosion of unburnt gases in the exhaust system. **4b** a premature explosion in a cylinder or inlet manifold. **5** a controlled fire started to create a barren area that will halt an advancing forest or prairie fire.

back formation *n* **1** the invention of a new word on the assumption that a familiar word is derived from it. The verbs *edit* and *burgle* in English were so created from *editor* and *burglar.* **2** a word formed by this process.

back four *n Soccer.* the defensive players in many modern team formations: usually two fullbacks and two centre backs.

backgammon (ˈbækˌgæmən, bækˈgæmən) *n* **1** a game for two people played on a board with pieces moved according to throws of the dice. **2** the most complete form of win in this game. [C17: BACK[1] + *gammon*, variant of GAME[1]]

back green *n Central Scot. urban dialect.* grass or a garden at the back of a house, esp. a tenement.

background (ˈbækˌgraʊnd) *n* **1** the part of a scene or view furthest from the viewer. **2a** an inconspicuous or unobtrusive position (esp. in the phrase **in the background**). **2b** (*as modifier*): *a background influence.* **3** *Art.* **3a** the plane or ground in a picture upon which all other planes or forms appear superimposed. **3b** the parts of a picture that appear most distant. Compare **foreground, middle-distance. 4** a person's social class, education, training, or experience. **5a** the social, historical, or technical circumstances that lead up to or help to explain something: *the background to the French Revolution.* **5b** (*as modifier*): *background information.* **6a** a low level of sound, lighting, etc., whose purpose is to be an unobtrusive or appropriate accompaniment to something else, such as a social activity, conversation, or the action of a film. **6b** (*as modifier*): *background music.* **7** Also called: **background radiation.** *Physics.* low-intensity radiation from small amounts of radioisotopes in soil, air, building materials, etc. **8** *Electronics.* **8a** unwanted effects, such as noise, occurring in a measuring instrument, electronic device, etc. **8b** (*as modifier*): *background interference.*

background processing *n Computing.* the ability of a system to handle two or more processes virtually simultaneously so that it appears to be printing one document while editing another document.

backhand (ˈbækˌhænd) *n* **1** *Tennis, squash, etc.* **1a** a stroke made across the body with the back of the hand facing the direction of the stroke. **1b** (*as modifier*): *a backhand return.* **2** the side on which backhand strokes are made. **3** handwriting slanting to the left. ♦ *adv* **4** with a backhand stroke. ♦ *vb* (*tr*) **5** *Sport.* to play (a shot) backhand.

backhanded (ˌbækˈhændɪd) *adj* **1** (of a blow, shot, stroke, etc.) performed with the arm moving across the body. **2** double-edged; equivocal: *a backhanded compliment.* **3** (of handwriting) slanting to the left. **4** (of a rope) twisted in the opposite way from the normal right-handed direction. ♦ *adv* **5** in a backhanded manner. ▸ **ˌbackˈhandedly** *adv* ▸ **ˌbackˈhandedness** *n*

backhander (ˈbækˌhændə) *n* **1** a backhanded stroke or blow. **2** *Informal.* an indirect attack. **3** *Slang.* a bribe.

backing (ˈbækɪŋ) *n* **1** support given to a person, cause, or enterprise. **2** a body of supporters. **3** something that forms, protects, supports, or strengthens the back of something. **4** *Theatre.* a scenic cloth or flat placed behind a window, door, etc., in a set to mask the offstage space. **5** musical accompaniment, esp. for a pop singer. **6** the support in gold or precious metals for a country's issue of money in notes. **7** *Meteorol.* an anticlockwise change in wind direction.

backing dog *n N.Z.* a dog that moves a flock of sheep by jumping on their backs.

backing store *n* a computer storage device, usually a disk, that provides additional storage space for information so that it can be accessed and referred to when required and may be copied into the processor if needed.

backlash (ˈbækˌlæʃ) *n* **1** a reaction or recoil between interacting worn or badly fitting parts in a mechanism. **2** the excessive play between such parts. **3** a sudden and adverse reaction, esp. to a political or social development: *the White backlash to the Black Power movement.*

backless (ˈbæklɪs) *adj* (of a dress) low-cut at the back.

back light *n* light falling on a photographic or television subject from the rear.

back list *n* a publisher's previously published books that are still available.

backlog ('bæk,lɒg) *n* **1** an accumulation of uncompleted work, unsold stock, etc., to be dealt with. **2** *Chiefly U.S. and Canadian.* a large log at the back of a fireplace.

backlot ('bæk,lɒt) *n* an area outside a film or television studio used for outdoor filming.

back marker *n* a competitor who is at the back of a field in a race.

back matter *n* the parts of a book, such as the index and appendices, that follow the main text. Also called: **end matter.**

backmost ('bæk,məʊst) *adj* furthest back.

back mutation *n Genetics.* the reversion of a mutant to the original phenotype.

back number *n* **1** an issue of a newspaper, magazine, etc., that appeared on a previous date. **2** *Informal.* a person or thing considered to be old-fashioned.

back o' Bourke (bɜːk) *adv Austral.* in a remote or backward place. [from *Bourke,* a town in New South Wales]

back off *vb* (*adv*) *Informal.* **1** (*intr*) to retreat. **2** (*tr*) to abandon (an intention, objective, etc.).

back out *vb* (*intr, adv;* often foll. by *of*) to withdraw (from an agreement, etc.).

backpack ('bæk,pæk) *n* **1** a rucksack or knapsack. **2** a pack carried on the back of an astronaut, containing oxygen cylinders, essential supplies, etc. ◆ *vb* **3** (*intr*) to travel about or go hiking with a backpack. **4** (*tr*) to transport (food or equipment) by backpack. ▸ **'back,packer** *n* ▸ **'back,packing** *n*

back passage *n* **1** the rectum. **2** an interior passageway towards the back of a building.

back pay *n* pay received by an employee from an increase awarded retrospectively.

back-pedal *vb* **-pedals, -pedalling, -pedalled** *or U.S.* **-pedals, -pedaling, -pedaled.** (*intr*) **1** to turn the pedals of a bicycle backwards. **2** to retract or modify a previous opinion, principle, etc. **3** *Boxing.* to take backward steps.

back pressure *n* **1** *Engineering.* the pressure that opposes the motion of a piston on its exhaust stroke in an internal-combustion engine. **2** *Med.* the local pressure that builds up when fluid flow is obstructed in the cardiovascular or urinary systems.

back projection *n* a method of projecting pictures onto a translucent screen so that they are viewed from the opposite side, used esp. in films to create the illusion that the actors in the foreground are moving. Also called: **background projection.**

back rest *n* a support for the back of something.

Back River *n* a river in N Canada, rising in the Northwest Territories and flowing northeast to the Arctic Ocean. Length: about 966 km (600 miles).

back room *n* **a** a place where research or planning is done, esp. secret research in wartime. **b** (*as modifier*): *back-room boys.*

Backs (bæks) *pl n* **the.** the grounds between the River Cam and certain Cambridge colleges.

back saw *n* a small handsaw stiffened along its upper edge by a metal section.

back scatter *n Physics.* **1** the scattering of radiation, such as X-rays or alpha-particles, by the atoms of the medium through which it passes, a proportion of this radiation emerging from the surface through which it entered. **2** the radiation so scattered. **3** a technique whereby very long-range radars locate targets hidden by the curvature of the earth. Radar beams are reflected off the underside of the troposphere onto the target and the return beams, similarly reflected, are measured.

backscratcher ('bæk,skrætʃə) *n* **1** an implement with a long handle, used for scratching one's own back. **2** *Informal.* a person who provides a service, corporate or public money etc., for another, in order to receive a similar service or reward in return. ▸ **'back,scratching** *n*

back seat *n* **1** a seat at the back, esp. of a vehicle. **2** *Informal.* a subordinate or inconspicuous position (esp. in the phrase **take a back seat**).

back-seat driver *n Informal.* **1** a passenger in a car who offers unwanted advice to the driver. **2** a person who offers advice on or tries to direct matters that are not his or her concern.

backsheesh ('bækʃiːʃ) *n* a variant spelling of **baksheesh.**

back shift *n Brit.* **1** a group of workers who work a shift from late afternoon to midnight in an industry or occupation where a day shift or a night shift is also worked. **2** the period worked. ◆ U.S. and Canadian name: **swing shift.**

backside (,bæk'saɪd) *n* **1** the back of something. **2** ('bæk,saɪd) *Informal.* the buttocks.

backsight ('bæk,saɪt) *n* **1** the sight of a rifle nearer the stock. **2** *Surveying.* a reading taken looking backwards to a previously occupied station. Compare **foresight** (sense 4).

back slang *n* a type of slang in which words are spelled and, as far as possible, pronounced backwards.

back-slapping *adj* energetically jovial; hearty.

back slash *n* a solidus which slopes to the left (\).

backslide ('bæk,slaɪd) *vb* **-slides, -sliding, -slid; -slid** *or* **-slidden.** (*intr*) to lapse into bad habits or vices from a state of virtue, religious faith, etc. ▸ **'back,slider** *n*

backspace ('bæk,speɪs) *vb* **1** to move a (typewriter carriage) backwards. ◆ *n* **2** a typewriter key that effects such a movements.

backspin ('bæk,spɪn) *n Sport.* a backward spinning motion imparted to a ball to reduce its speed at impact. Compare **topspin.**

backstage (,bæk'steɪdʒ) *adv* **1** behind the part of the theatre in view of the audience; in the dressing rooms, wings, etc. **2** towards the rear of the stage. ◆ *adj* **3** situated backstage. **4** *Informal.* away from public view.

backstairs ('bæk'stɛəz) *pl n* **1** a secondary staircase in a house, esp. one originally for the use of servants. ◆ *adj also* **backstair. 2** underhand: *backstairs gossip.*

backstay ('bæk,steɪ) *n* **1** *Nautical.* a stay leading aft from the upper part of a mast to the deck or stern. **2** *Machinery.* a supporting piece or arresting part. **3** anything that supports or strengthens the back of something, such as leather covering the back seam of a shoe.

backstitch ('bæk,stɪtʃ) *n* **1** a strong sewing stitch made by starting the next stitch at the middle or beginning of the preceding one. ◆ *vb* **2** to sew using this stitch.

backstop ('bæk,stɒp) *n* **1** *Sport.* a screen or fence to prevent balls leaving the playing area. **2** a block or catch to prevent excessive backward movement, such as one on the sliding seat of a rowing boat. ◆ *vb* **-stops, -stopping, -stopped.** (*tr*) **3** *U.S.* to provide with backing or support.

back straight *n* a straight part of a circuit, esp. of an athletics track, furthest from the finishing point.

backstreet ('bæk,striːt) *n* **1** a street in a town remote from the main roads. **2** (*modifier*) denoting illicit activities regarded as likely to take place in such a street: *a backstreet abortion.*

back stretch *n* a horse-racing term for **back straight.**

backstroke ('bæk,strəʊk) *n* **1** Also called: **back crawl.** *Swimming.* **1a** a stroke performed on the back, using backward circular strokes of each arm and flipper movements of the feet. **1b** (*as modifier*): *the backstroke champion.* **2** a return stroke or blow. **3** *Chiefly U.S.* a backhanded stroke. **4** *Bell-ringing.* the upward movement of the bell rope as the bell swings back and forth. Compare **handstroke.** ◆ *vb* **5** (*intr*) to swim the backstroke.

backswept ('bæk,swɛpt) *adj* **1** slanting backwards. **2** another word for **swept-back.**

backsword ('bæk,sɔːd) *n* **1** another name for **broadsword. 2** Also called: **'back,swordsman.** a person who uses the backsword. **3** a fencing stick with a basket-like protective hilt.

back-to-back *adj* (*usually postpositive*) **1** facing in opposite directions, often with the backs touching. **2** *Chiefly Brit.* (of urban houses) built so that their backs are joined or separated only by a narrow alley. **3** *Informal.* consecutive. **4** *Commerce.* **4a** denoting a credit arrangement in which a finance house acts as an intermediary to conceal the identity of the seller from the buyer. **4b** denoting a loan from one company to another in a different country using a finance house to provide the loan but not the funding. ◆ *n* **5** a house or terrace built in back-to-back style.

backtrack ('bæk,træk) *vb* (*intr*) **1** to return by the same route by which one has come. **2** to retract or reverse one's opinion, action, policy, etc. ▸ **'back,tracking** *n*

back up *vb* (*adv*) **1** (*tr*) to support or assist. **2** (*intr*) *Cricket.* (of a nonstriking batsman) to move down the wicket in readiness for a run as a ball is bowled. **3** (of water) to accumulate. **4** (of traffic) to become jammed behind an accident or other obstruction. **5** *Computing.* to make a copy of (a data file), esp. for storage in another place as a security copy. **6** *Printing.* to print the second side of (a sheet). **7** (*intr,* usually foll. by *on*) *Austral.* to repeat an action immediately. ◆ *n* **backup. 8** a support or reinforcement. **9a** a reserve or substitute. **9b** (*as modifier*): *backup troops.* **10** the overflow from a blocked drain or pipe.

back-up light *n* a U.S. and Canadian name for **reversing light.**

backward ('bækwəd) *adj* **1** (*usually prenominal*) directed towards the rear: *a backward glance.* **2** retarded in physical, material, or intellectual development: *backward countries; a backward child.* **3a** of or relating to the past; conservative or reactionary. **3b** (*in combination*): *backward-looking.* **4** reluctant or bashful: *a backward lover.* **5** *Chess.* (of a pawn) behind neighbouring pawns and unable to be supported by them. ◆ *adv* **6** a variant of **backwards.** ▸ **'backwardly** *adv* ▸ **'backwardness** *n*

backwardation (,bækwə'deɪʃən) *n Commerce.* **1** the difference between the spot price for a commodity, including rent and interest, and the forward price. **2** (formerly, on the Stock Exchange) postponement of delivery by a seller of securities until the next settlement period.

backwards ('bækwədz) *or* **backward** *adv* **1** towards the rear. **2** with the back foremost. **3** in the reverse of usual order or direction. **4** to or towards the past. **5** into a worse state: *the patient was slipping backwards.* **6** towards the point of origin. **7 bend, lean,** *or* **fall over backwards.** *Informal.* to make a special effort, esp. in order to please. **8 know backwards.** *Informal.* to understand completely.

backwash ('bæk,wɒʃ) *n* **1** a dashing movement of water, such as that of retreating waves. Compare **swash. 2** water washed backwards by the motion of oars or other propelling devices. **3** the backward flow of air set up by an aircraft's engines. **4** a condition resulting from a previous event; repercussion. ◆ *vb* **5** (*tr*) to remove oil from (combed wool).

backwater ('bæk,wɔːtə) *n* **1** a body of stagnant water connected to a river. **2** water held or driven back, as by a dam, flood, or tide. **3** an isolated, backward, or intellectually stagnant place or condition. ◆ *vb* **back water. 4** (*intr*) to reverse the direction of a boat, esp. to push the oars of a rowing boat.

backwoods ('bækwʊdz) *pl n* **1** *Chiefly U.S. and Canadian.* partially cleared, sparsely populated forests. **2** any remote sparsely populated place. **3** (*modifier*) of, from, or like the backwoods. **4** (*modifier*) uncouth; rustic.

backwoodsman ('bæk,wʊdzmən) *n, pl* **-men. 1** a person from the backwoods. **2** *U.S. informal.* an uncouth or rustic person. **3** *Brit. informal.* a peer who rarely attends the House of Lords.

backword ('bæk,wɜːd) *n Brit. dialect.* the act or an instance of failing to keep a promise or commitment (esp. in the phrase **give (someone) backword**).

back yard *n* **1** a yard at the back of a house, etc. **2 in one's own back yard. 2a** close at hand. **2b** involving or implicating one.

baclava ('bɑːklə,vɑː) *n* a variant spelling of **baklava.**

Bacolod (bə'kəʊləd) *n* a town in the Philippines, on the NW coast of Negros Island. Pop.: 343 048 (1994 est.).

bacon ('beɪkən) *n* **1** meat from the back and sides of a pig, dried, salted, and usually smoked. **2 bring home the bacon.** *Informal.* **2a** to achieve success.

2b to provide material support. 3 **save (someone's) bacon.** *Brit. informal.* to help (someone) to escape from danger. [C12: from Old French *bacon*, from Old High German *bahho;* related to Old Saxon *baco;* see BACK[1]]

Bacon ('beɪkən) *n* 1 **Francis,** Baron Verulam, Viscount St. Albans. 1561–1626, English philosopher, statesman, and essayist; described the inductive method of reasoning: his works include *Essays* (1625), *The Advancement of Learning* (1605), and *Novum Organum* (1620). 2 **Francis.** 1909–92, Irish painter, noted for his distorted, richly coloured human figures, dogs, and carcasses. 3 **Roger.** ?1214–92, English Franciscan monk, scholar, and scientist: stressed the importance of experiment, demonstrated that air is required for combustion, and first used lenses to correct vision. His *Opus Majus* (1266) is a compendium of all the sciences of his age.

bacon-and-eggs *n* another name for **bird's-foot trefoil.**

bacon beetle *n* See **dermestid.**

baconer ('beɪkənə) *n* a pig that weighs between 83 and 101 kg, from which bacon is cut.

Baconian (beɪ'kəʊnɪən) *adj* 1 of or relating to Francis Bacon, the philosopher, or his inductive method of reasoning. ◆ *n* 2 a follower of Bacon's philosophy. 3 one who believes that plays attributed to Shakespeare were written by Bacon.

BACS (bæks) *n acronym for* Bankers Automated Clearing System; a method of making payments direct to a creditor's bank without using a cheque.

bact. *abbrev. for* bacteria(l).

bacteraemia *or U.S.* **bacteremia** (ˌbæktə'riːmɪə) *n Pathol.* the presence of bacteria in the blood.

bacteria (bæk'tɪərɪə) *pl n, sing* **-rium** (-rɪəm). a large group of typically unicellular microorganisms that comprise the kingdom *Prokaryotae.* Most bacteria are parasites (many of which cause disease) or saprotrophs and reproduce by fission. See also **prokaryote.** [C19: plural of New Latin *bacterium*, from Greek *baktērion*, literally: a little stick, from *baktron* rod, staff] ▸ **bac'terial** *adj* ▸ **bac'terially** *adv*

bacteria bed *n* a layer of sand or gravel used to expose sewage effluent, in its final stages, to air and the action of microorganisms. Compare **filter bed** (sense 1).

bacterial plaque *n* another term for **dental plaque.**

bactericide (bæk'tɪərɪˌsaɪd) *n* a substance able to destroy bacteria. ▸ **bacˌteri'cidal** *adj*

bacterin ('bæktərɪn) *n* a vaccine prepared from bacteria.

bacterio-, bacteri-, *or sometimes before a vowel* **bacter-** *combining form.* indicating bacteria or an action or condition relating to bacteria: *bacteriology; bactericide; bacteroid.* [New Latin, from BACTERIA]

bacteriol. *abbrev. for:* 1 bacteriological. 2 bacteriology.

bacteriological warfare *n* another term for **germ warfare.**

bacteriology (bækˌtɪərɪ'ɒlədʒɪ) *n* the branch of science concerned with the study of bacteria. ▸ **bacteriological** (bækˌtɪərɪə'lɒdʒɪkᵊl) *adj* ▸ **bacˌterio'logically** *adv* ▸ **bacˌteri'ologist** *n*

bacteriolysis (bækˌtɪərɪ'ɒlɪsɪs) *n* the destruction of bacteria, esp. by antibodies. ▸ **bacteriolytic** (bækˌtɪərɪə'lɪtɪk) *adj*

bacteriophage (bæk'tɪərɪəˌfeɪdʒ) *n* a virus that is parasitic in a bacterium and multiplies within its host, which is destroyed when the new viruses are released. Often shortened to **phage.** ▸ **bacteriophagic** (bækˌtɪərɪə'fædʒɪk) *adj* ▸ **bacteriophagous** (bækˌtɪərɪ'ɒfəgəs) *adj*

bacteriostasis (bækˌtɪərɪəʊ'steɪsɪs, -'stæsɪs) *n, pl* **-stases** (-'steɪsiːz, -'stæsiːz). inhibition of the growth and reproduction of bacteria, esp. by the action of a chemical agent. ▸ **bacteriostatic** (bækˌtɪərɪəʊ'stætɪk) *adj* ▸ **bacˌterio'statically** *adv*

bacteriostat (bæk'tɪərɪəʊˌstæt) *n* any substance that arrests the growth or reproduction of bacteria but does not kill them.

bacteriotoxin (bækˌtɪərɪəʊ'tɒksɪn) *n* 1 any toxin that kills bacteria. 2 a toxin produced by a bacterium.

bacterium (bæk'tɪərɪəm) *n* the singular of **bacteria.**

bacteriuria (bækˌtɪərɪ'jʊərɪə) *or* **bacteruria** (ˌbæktə'rjʊərɪə) *n* the presence of bacteria in the urine.

bacteroid ('bæktəˌrɔɪd) *adj* 1 resembling a bacterium. ◆ *n* 2 any rodlike bacterium of the genus *Bacteroides*, occurring in the gut of man and animals.

Bactria ('bæktrɪə) *n* an ancient country of SW Asia, between the Hindu Kush mountains and the Oxus River: forms the present Balkh region in N Afghanistan. ▸ **'Bactrian** *adj, n*

Bactrian camel *n* a two-humped camel, *Camelus bactrianus*, used as a beast of burden in the cold deserts of central Asia. Compare **Arabian camel.**

baculiform (bə'kjuːlɪˌfɔːm, 'bækjuː-) *adj Biology.* shaped like a rod: *baculiform fungal spores.* [C19: from *baculi-*, from Latin *baculum* walking stick + -FORM]

baculum ('bækjʊləm) *n, pl* **-la** (-lə) *or* **-lums.** a bony support in the penis of certain mammals, esp. the carnivores. [C20: New Latin, from Latin: stick, staff]

bad[1] (bæd) *adj* **worse, worst.** 1 not good; of poor quality; inadequate; inferior: *bad workmanship; bad soil; bad light for reading.* 2 (often foll. by *at*) lacking skill or talent; incompetent: *a bad painter; bad at sports.* 3 (often foll. by *for*) harmful: *bad air; smoking is bad for you.* 4 immoral; evil: *a bad life.* 5 naughty; mischievous; disobedient: *a bad child.* 6 rotten; decayed; spoiled: *a bad egg.* 7 severe; intense: *a bad headache.* 8 incorrect; wrong; faulty: *bad pronunciation.* 9 ill or in pain (esp. in the phrase **feel bad**). 10 regretful, sorry, or upset (esp. in the phrase **feel bad about**). 11 unfavourable; distressing: *bad news; a bad business.* 12 offensive; unpleasant; disagreeable: *bad language; bad temper.* 13 not valid or sound; void: *a bad cheque.* 14 not recoverable: *a bad debt.* 15 (**badder, baddest**) *Slang.* good; excellent. 16 **go from bad to worse.** to deteriorate even more. 17 **go bad.** to putrefy; spoil. 18 **in a bad way.** *Informal.* 18a seriously ill, through sickness or injury. 18b in trouble of any kind. 19 **in someone's bad books.** See **book** (sense 21). 20 **make the best of a bad job.** to manage as well as possible in unfavourable circumstances. 21 **not bad** *or* **not so bad.** *Informal.* passable; fair; fairly good. 22 **not half bad.** *Informal.* very good. 23 **too bad.** *Informal.* (often used dismissively) regrettable. ◆ *n* 24 unfortunate or unpleasant events collectively (often in the phrase **take the bad with the good**). 25 an immoral or degenerate state (often in the phrase **go to the bad**). 26 the debit side of an account: *£200 to the bad.* ◆ *adv* 27 *Not standard.* badly: *to want something bad.* [C13: probably from *bæd-*, as the first element of Old English *bǣddel* hermaphrodite, *bǣdling* sodomite] ▸ **'baddish** *adj* ▸ **'badness** *n*

USAGE See at **good.**

bad[2] (bæd) *vb* a variant of **bade.**

Badajoz ('bædəˌhɒz; *Spanish* ba'ðaxoθ) *n* a city in SW Spain: strategically positioned near the frontier with Portugal. Pop.: 132 154 (1995 est.).

Badalona (*Spanish* baða'lona) *n* a port in NE Spain: an industrial suburb of Barcelona. Pop.: 217 983 (1995 est.).

bad blood *n* a feeling of intense hatred or hostility; enmity.

baddeleyite ('bædlɪˌaɪt) *n* a mineral consisting largely of zirconium dioxide: a source of zirconium. Formula: ZrO_2. [C19: named after J. *Baddeley*, British geologist]

badderlocks ('bædəˌlɒks) *n* a seaweed, *Alaria esculenta*, that has long brownish-green fronds and is eaten in parts of N Europe. [C18: of unknown origin]

baddie *or* **baddy** ('bædɪ) *n, pl* **-dies.** *Informal.* a bad character in a story, film, etc., esp. an opponent of the hero.

bade (bæd, beɪd) *or* **bad** *vb* past tense of **bid.**

Baden ('bɑːdən) *n* a former state of West Germany, now part of Baden-Württemberg.

Baden-Baden *n* a spa in SW Germany, in Baden-Württemberg. Pop.: 52 520 (1991).

Baden-Powell ('beɪdᵊn'pəʊəl, -'paʊəl) *n* **Robert Stephenson Smyth** (smɪθ, smaɪθ), 1st Baron Baden-Powell. 1857–1941, British general, noted for his defence of Mafeking (1899–1900) in the Boer War; founder of the Boy Scouts (1908) and (with his sister Agnes) the Girl Guides (1910).

Baden-Württemberg (*German* 'baːdən'vyrtəmbɛrk) *n* a state of SW Germany; formerly in West Germany. Capital: Stuttgart. Pop.: 10 319 400 (1996 est.). Area: 35 742 sq. km (13 800 sq. miles).

Bader ('bɑːdə) *n* Sir **Douglas.** 1910–82, British fighter pilot. Despite losing both legs after a flying accident (1931), he became a national hero as a pilot in World War II.

bad faith *n* 1 intention to deceive; treachery or dishonesty (esp. in the phrase **in bad faith**). 2 Also called: **mauvaise foi.** (in the philosophy of Sartre) self-deception, as when an agent regards his actions as conditioned by circumstances or conventions in order to evade his own responsibility for choosing them freely.

badge (bædʒ) *n* 1 a distinguishing emblem or mark worn to signify membership, employment, achievement, etc. 2 any revealing feature or mark. [C14: from Norman French *bage;* related to Anglo-Latin *bagia*]

badger ('bædʒə) *n* 1 any of various stocky omnivorous musteline mammals of the subfamily *Melinae*, such as *Meles meles* (**Eurasian badger**), occurring in Europe, Asia, and North America: order *Carnivora* (carnivores). They are typically large burrowing animals, with strong claws and a thick coat striped black and white on the head. Compare **ferret badger, hog badger.** 2 **honey badger.** another name for **ratel.** ◆ *vb* 3 (*tr*) to pester or harass. [C16: variant of *badgeard*, probably from BADGE (from the white mark on its forehead) + -ARD]

Bad Godesberg (*German* baːt 'goːdəsbɛrk) *n* the official name for **Godesberg.**

bad hair day *n Informal.* 1 a day on which one's hair is untidy and unmanageable. 2 a day of mishaps and general irritation.

badinage ('bædɪˌnɑːʒ) *n* playful or frivolous repartee or banter. [C17: from French, from *badiner* to jest, banter, from Old Provençal *badar* to gape]

badinerie (bəˌdɪnə'riː) *n Music.* a name given in the 18th century to a type of quick, light movement in a suite. [French: a pleasantry]

badlands ('bædˌlændz) *pl n* any deeply eroded barren area.

Bad Lands *pl n* a deeply eroded barren region of SW South Dakota and NW Nebraska.

badly ('bædlɪ) *adv* **worse, worst.** 1 poorly; defectively; inadequately: *the chair is badly made.* 2 unfavourably; unsuccessfully; unfortunately: *our scheme worked out badly.* 3 severely; gravely: *he was badly hurt.* 4 incorrectly or inaccurately: *to speak German badly.* 5 improperly; naughtily; wickedly: *to behave badly.* 6 without humanity; cruelly: *to treat badly.* 7 very much (esp. in the phrases **need badly, badly in need of, want badly**). 8 regretfully: *he felt badly about it.* 9 **badly off.** poor; impoverished. ◆ *adj* 10 (*postpositive*) *Northern English dialect.* ill; poorly.

badman ('bædˌmæn) *n, pl* **-men.** *Chiefly U.S.* a hired gunman, outlaw, or criminal.

badminton ('bædmɪntən) *n* 1 a game played with rackets and a shuttlecock, which is hit back and forth across a high net. 2 Also called: **badminton cup.** a long refreshing drink of claret with soda water and sugar. [C19: named after BADMINTON House, where the game was first played]

Badminton ('bædmɪntən) *n* a village in SW England, in South Gloucestershire unitary authority, Gloucestershire: site of Badminton House, seat of the Duke of Beaufort; annual horse trials.

bad-mouth *vb* (*tr*) *Slang.* to speak unfavourably about.

bad news *n Slang.* someone or something regarded as undesirable: *he's bad news around here.*

Badoglio (*Italian* ba'dɔʎʎo) *n* **Pietro** ('pjɛtro). 1871–1956, Italian marshal; premier (1943–44) following Mussolini's downfall: arranged an armistice with the Allies (1943).

bad-tempered *adj* angry, irritable, or ungracious.

BAe *abbrev. for* British Aerospace.

Baeck (*German* bɛk) *n* **Leo.** 1873–1956, German Jewish theologian: a leader of the German Jews during the Nazi period. His major work is *The Essence of Judaism* (1905).

Baeda ('bi:də) *n* the Latin name for (Saint) **Bede.**

Baedeker ('beɪdɪkə) *n* **1** any of a series of travel guidebooks issued by the German publisher Karl Baedeker (1801–59) or his firm. **2** any guidebook.

Baedeker raid *n Informal.* one of the German air raids in 1942 on places of cultural and historical importance in England.

bael ('beɪəl) *n* **1** a spiny Indian rutaceous tree, *Aegle marmelos.* **2** the edible thick-shelled fruit of this tree. [C17: from Hindi *bel*]

Baeyer (*German* 'baɪər) *n* **Johann Friedrich Wilhelm Adolf von** (jo'han 'fri:drɪç 'vɪlhɛlm 'a:dɔlf fɔn). 1835–1917, German chemist, noted for the synthesis of indigo: Nobel prize for chemistry 1905.

Baez ('baɪɛz) *n* **Joan.** born 1941, U.S. rock and folk singer and songwriter, noted for the pure quality of her voice and for her committed pacifist and protest songs.

BAF *abbrev. for* British Athletic Federation.

Bafana bafana (ba'fɑ:na) *pl n S. African.* an African name for the South African national soccer team. [C20: from Nguni *bafana* the boys]

Baffin Bay ('bæfɪn) *n* part of the Northwest Passage, situated between Baffin Island and Greenland. [named after William *Baffin*, 17th-century English navigator]

Baffin Island *n* the largest island of the Canadian Arctic, between Greenland and Hudson Bay. Area: 476 560 sq. km (184 000 sq. miles).

baffle ('bæfᵊl) *vb* (*tr*) **1** to perplex; bewilder; puzzle. **2** to frustrate (plans, efforts, etc.). **3** to check, restrain, or regulate (the flow of a fluid or the emission of sound or light). **4** to provide with a baffle. **5** *Obsolete.* to cheat or trick. ◆ *n* **6** Also called: **baffle board, baffle plate.** a plate or mechanical device designed to restrain or regulate the flow of a fluid, the emission of light or sound, or the distribution of sound, esp. in a loudspeaker or microphone. [C16: perhaps from Scottish dialect *bachlen* to condemn publicly; perhaps related to French *bafouer* to disgrace] ▸ **'bafflement** *n* ▸ **'baffler** *n* ▸ **'baffling** *adj* ▸ **'bafflingly** *adv*

BAFTA ('bæftə) *n acronym for* British Academy of Film and Television Arts.

bag (bæg) *n* **1** a flexible container with an opening at one end. **2** Also called: **bagful.** the contents of or amount contained in such a container. **3** any of various measures of quantity, such as a bag containing 1 hundredweight of coal. **4** a piece of portable luggage. **5** short for **handbag. 6** anything that hangs loosely, sags, or is shaped like a bag, such as a loose fold of skin under the eyes or the bulging part of a sail. **7** any pouch or sac forming part of the body of an animal, esp. the udder of a cow. **8** *Hunting.* the quantity of quarry taken in a single hunting trip or by a single hunter. **9** *Derogatory slang.* an ugly or bad-tempered woman or girl (often in the phrase **old bag**). **10** *Slang.* a measure of marijuana, heroin, etc., in folded paper. **11** *Slang.* a person's particular taste, field of skill, interest, activity, etc.: *blues is his bag.* **12 bag and baggage.** *Informal.* **12a** with all one's belongings. **12b** entirely. **13 a bag of bones.** a lean creature. **14 in the bag.** *Slang.* almost assured of succeeding or being obtained. **15 the (whole) bag of tricks.** *Informal.* every device; everything. ◆ *vb* **bags, bagging, bagged. 16** (*tr*) to put into a bag. **17** to bulge or cause to bulge; swell. **18** (*tr*) to capture or kill, as in hunting. **19** (*tr*) to catch, seize, or steal. **20** (*intr*) to hang loosely; sag. **21** (*tr*) to achieve or accomplish: *she bagged seven birdies.* **22** (*tr*) *Brit. informal.* to reserve or secure the right to do or to have something: *he bagged the best chair.* **23** (*tr*) *Austral. slang.* to criticize; disparage. ◆ See also **bags.** [C13: probably from Old Norse *baggi;* related to Old French *bague* bundle, pack, Medieval Latin *baga* chest, sack, Flemish *bagge*]

Baganda (bə'gændə, -'gɑ:n-) *n* (*functioning as pl*) a Negroid people of E Africa living chiefly in Uganda. See also **Ganda, Luganda.**

bagasse (bə'gæs) *n* **1** the pulp remaining after the extraction of juice from sugar cane or similar plants: used as fuel and for making paper, etc. **2** Also called: **megass, megasse.** a type of paper made from bagasse fibres. [C19: from French, from Spanish *bagazo* dregs, refuse, from *baga* husk, from Latin *bāca* berry]

bagassosis (,bægə'səʊsɪs) *n* an allergic response to the dust of bagasse, causing breathlessness and fever.

bagatelle (,bægə'tel) *n* **1** something of little value or significance; trifle. **2** a board game in which balls are struck into holes, with pins as obstacles; pinball. **3** another name for **bar billiards. 4** a short light piece of music, esp. for piano. [C17: from French, from Italian *bagattella,* from (dialect) *bagatta* a little possession, from *baga* a possession, probably from Latin *bāca* berry]

Bagdad (bæg'dæd) *n* a variant spelling of **Baghdad.**

Bagehot ('bædʒət) *n* **Walter.** 1826–77, English economist and journalist: editor of *The Economist;* author of *The English Constitution* (1867), *Physics and Politics* (1872), and *Lombard Street* (1873).

bagel *or* **beigel** ('beɪgᵊl) *n* a hard ring-shaped bread roll, characteristic of Jewish baking. [C20: from Yiddish *beygel,* ultimately from Old High German *boug* ring]

baggage ('bægɪdʒ) *n* **1a** suitcases, bags, etc., packed for a journey; luggage. **1b** *Chiefly U.S. and Canadian.* (*as modifier*): *baggage car.* **2** an army's portable equipment. **3** *Informal, old-fashioned.* **3a** a pert young woman. **3b** an immoral woman or prostitute. **4** *Irish informal.* a cantankerous old woman. **5** *Informal.* previous knowledge and experience that a person may use or be influenced by in new circumstances: *cultural baggage.* [C15: from Old French *bagage,* from *bague* a bundle, perhaps of Scandinavian origin; compare Old Norse *baggi* BAG]

bagging ('bægɪŋ) *n* coarse woven cloth; sacking.

baggy[1] ('bægɪ) *adj* **-gier, -giest.** (of clothes) hanging loosely; puffed out. ▸ **'baggily** *adv* ▸ **'bagginess** *n*

baggy[2] ('bægɪ) *n, pl* **-gies.** a variant spelling of **bagie.**

bagh (bɑ:g) *n* (in India and Pakistan) a garden. [Urdu]

Baghdad *or* **Bagdad** (bæg'dæd) *n* the capital of Iraq, on the River Tigris: capital of the Abbasid Caliphate (762–1258). Pop.: 4 478 000 (1995 est.).

bagie ('beɪgɪ) *or* **baggy** *n, pl* **-gies.** *Northumbrian dialect.* a turnip. [perhaps from RUTABAGA]

bag lady *n* a woman who is homeless and wanders city streets with all her possessions in shopping bags. Also called (in full): **shopping bag lady.**

bagman ('bægmən) *n, pl* **-men. 1** *Brit. informal.* a travelling salesman. **2** *Slang, chiefly U.S.* a person who collects or distributes money for racketeers. **3** *Informal, chiefly Canadian.* a person who solicits money or subscriptions for a political party. **4** *Austral. history.* a tramp or swagman, esp. one on horseback.

bag moth *n N.Z.* a moth, the larvae of which develop in bags or cases.

bagnette ('bægnet) *n* a variant of **baguette** (sense 3).

bagnio ('bɑ:njəʊ) *n, pl* **-ios. 1** a brothel. **2** *Obsolete.* an oriental prison for slaves. **3** *Obsolete.* an Italian or Turkish bathhouse. [C16: from Italian *bagno,* from Latin *balneum* bath, from Greek *balaneion*]

Bagnold ('bægnəʊld) *n* **Enid** (**Algerine**). 1889–1981, British novelist and playwright; her works include the novel *National Velvet* (1935) and the play *The Chalk Garden* (1955).

bagpipe ('bæg,paɪp) *n* (*modifier*) of or relating to the bagpipes: *a bagpipe maker.*

bagpipes ('bæg,paɪps) *pl n* any of a family of musical wind instruments in which sounds are produced in reed pipes supplied with air from a bag inflated either by the player's mouth, as in the **Irish bagpipes** or **Highland bagpipes** of Scotland, or by arm-operated bellows, as in the **Northumbrian bagpipes.**

bags (bægz) *pl n* **1** *Informal.* a lot; a great deal. **2** short for **Oxford bags. 3** *Brit. informal.* any pair of trousers. ◆ *interj* **4** Also: **bags I.** *Children's slang, Brit. and Austral.* an indication of the desire to do, be, or have something. **5 rough as bags** *or* **sacks.** *Austral. and N.Z.* uncouth.

baguette *or* **baguet** (bæ'get) *n* **1** a narrow French stick loaf. **2** a small gem cut as a long rectangle. **3** the shape of such a gem. **4** *Architect.* a small moulding having a semicircular cross section. [C18: from French, from Italian *bacchetta* a little stick, from *bacchio* rod, from Latin *baculum* walking stick]

Baguio ('bægɪ,əʊ) *n* a city in the N Philippines, on N Luzon: summer capital of the Republic. Pop.: 169 565 (1994 est.).

bagwash ('bæg,wɒʃ) *n Old-fashioned.* **1** a laundry that washes clothes without drying or pressing them. **2** the clothes so washed.

bagwig ('bæg,wɪg) *n* an 18th-century wig with hair pushed back into a bag.

bagworm ('bæg,wɜ:m) *n* **1** the larva of moths of the family *Psychidae,* which forms a protective case of silk covered with grass, leaves, etc. **2 bagworm moth.** any moth of the family *Psychidae.*

bah (bɑ:, bæ) *interj* an expression of contempt or disgust.

bahadur (bə'hɑ:də) *n* (*often in combination*) a title formerly conferred by the British on distinguished Indians. [C18: from Hindi *bahādur* hero, from Persian: valiant]

Baha'í (bə'hɑ:ɪ) *n* **1** an adherent of the Baha'í Faith ◆ *adj* **2** of or relating to the Baha'í Faith. [from Persian *bahā'ī,* literally: of glory, from *bahā' u'llāh* glory of God, from Arabic]

Baha'í Faith *or* **Baha'í** *n* a religious system founded in 1863 by Baha'ullah, based on Babism and emphasizing the value of all religions and the spiritual unity of all mankind. ▸ **Ba'ha'ist** *or* **Ba'ha'ite** *adj, n*

Baha'ism (bə'hɑ:,ɪzəm) *n* another name, not in Baha'í use, for the **Baha'í Faith.**

Bahamas (bə'hɑ:məz) *or* **Bahama Islands** *pl n* **the.** a group of over 700 coral islands (about 20 of which are inhabited) in the Caribbean: a British colony from 1783 until 1964; an independent nation within the Commonwealth from 1973. Language: English. Currency: Bahamian dollar. Capital: Nassau. Pop.: 293 000 (1998 est.). Area: 13 939 sq. km (5381 sq. miles). ▸ **Bahamian** (bə'heɪ- mɪən, -'hɑ:-) *adj, n*

Bahasa Indonesia (bɑ:'hɑ:sə) *n* the official language of Indonesia: developed from the form of Malay formerly widely used as a trade language in SE Asia.

Baha'ullah (,bɑ:hɑ:'ʊlə) *n* title of *Mirza Hosein Ali.* 1817–92, Persian religious leader: originally a Shiite Muslim, later a disciple of the Bab: founder of the Baha'í Faith.

Bahawalpur (,bæhə'wɒlpə) *n* an industrial city in Pakistan: cotton, soap. Pop.: 180 000 (latest est.).

Bahia (bə'hi:ə; *Portuguese* bə'i:ə) *n* **1** a state of E Brazil, on the Atlantic coast. Capital: Salvador. Pop.: 12 646 000 (1995 est.). Area: about 562 000 sq. km (217 000 sq. miles). **2** the former name of **San Salvador.**

Bahía Blanca (*Spanish* ba'ia 'blanka) *n* a port in E Argentina. Pop.: 260 096 (1991).

Bahia de los Cochinos (ba'ia de los ko'tʃinos) *n* the Spanish name for the **Bay of Pigs.**

Bahrain *or* **Bahrein** (bɑ:'reɪn) *n* an independent sheikhdom on the Persian Gulf, consisting of several islands: under British protection until the declaration of independence in 1971. It has large oil reserves. Language: Arabic. Religion: Muslim. Currency: dinar. Capital: Manama. Pop.: 633 000 (1998 est.). Area: 678 sq. km (262 sq. miles). ▸ **Bah'raini** *or* **Bah'reini** *adj, n*

baht (bɑ:t) *n, pl* **bahts** *or* **baht.** the standard monetary unit of Thailand, divided into 100 satangs. [from Thai *bāt*]

bahuvrihi (,bɑ:hu:'vri:hi:) *n Linguistics.* **1** a class of compound words consisting of two elements the first of which is a specific feature of the second. **2** a compound word of this type, such as *hunchback, bluebell, highbrow.* [C19: from Sanskrit *bahuvrīhi,* itself this type of compound, from *bahu* much + *vrīh* rice]

Baikal (baɪ'kɑ:l, -'kæl) *n* **Lake.** a lake in Russia, in SE Siberia: the largest freshwater lake in Eurasia and the deepest in the world. Greatest depth: over 1500 m (5000 ft.). Area: about 33 670 sq. km (13 000 sq. miles).

bail[1] (beɪl) *Law.* ◆ *n* **1** a sum of money by which a person is bound to take responsibility for the appearance in court of another person or himself, forfeited if the person fails to appear. **2** the person or persons so binding themselves; surety. **3** the system permitting release of a person from custody where such security has been taken: *he was released on bail.* **4 jump bail** *or* (*formal*) **forfeit bail.** to fail to appear in court to answer to a charge. **5 stand** *or* **go bail.** to act as surety (for someone). ◆ *vb* (*tr*) **6** (often foll. by *out*) to release or obtain the release of (a person) from custody, security having been made. ◆ See also **bail out.** [C14: from Old French: custody, from *baillier* to hand over, from Latin *bāiulāre* to carry burdens, from *bāiulus* carrier, of obscure origin]

bail[2] *or* **bale** (beɪl) *vb* (often foll. by *out*) to remove (water) from (a boat). [C13: from Old French *baille* bucket, from Latin *bāiulus* carrier] ► **'bailer** *or* **'baler** *n*

bail[3] (beɪl) *n* **1** *Cricket.* either of two small wooden bars placed across the tops of the stumps to form the wicket. **2** *Agriculture.* **2a** a partition between stalls in a stable or barn, for horses. **2b** a portable dairy house built on wheels or skids. **3** *Austral. and N.Z.* a framework in a cowshed used to secure the head of a cow during milking. ◆ *vb* **4** See **bail up.** [C18: from Old French *baile* stake, fortification, probably from Latin *baculum* stick]

bail[4] *or* **bale** (beɪl) *n* **1** the semicircular handle of a kettle, bucket, etc. **2** a semicircular support for a canopy. **3** a movable bar on a typewriter that holds the paper against the platen. [C15: probably of Scandinavian origin; compare Old Norse *beygja* to bend]

bailable ('beɪləbᵊl) *adj Law.* **1** eligible for release on bail. **2** admitting of bail: *a bailable offence.*

bail bond *n* a document in which a prisoner and one or more sureties guarantee that the prisoner will attend the court hearing of the charges against him if he is released on bail.

Baile Átha Cliath (blɑːˈklɪə) *n* the Irish Gaelic name for **Dublin.**

bailee (beɪˈliː) *n Contract law.* a person to whom goods are entrusted under a contract of bailment.

bailey ('beɪlɪ) *n* the outermost wall or court of a castle. [C13: from Old French *baille* enclosed court, from *bailler* to enclose; see BAIL[3]]

Bailey ('beɪlɪ) *n* **1 David.** born 1938, English photographer. **2 Nathan** *or* **Nathaniel.** died 1742, English lexicographer: compiler of *An Universal Etymological English Dictionary* (1721–27).

Bailey bridge *n* a temporary bridge made of prefabricated steel parts that can be rapidly assembled. [C20: named after Sir Donald Coleman *Bailey* (1901–85), its English designer]

bailie ('beɪlɪ) *n* **1** (in Scotland) a municipal magistrate. **2** an obsolete or dialect spelling of **bailiff.** [C13: from Old French *bailli,* from earlier *baillif* BAILIFF]

bailiff ('beɪlɪf) *n* **1** *Brit.* the agent or steward of a landlord or landowner. **2** a sheriff's officer who serves writs and summonses, makes arrests, and ensures that the sentences of the court are carried out. **3** *Chiefly Brit.* (formerly) a high official having judicial powers. **4** *Chiefly U.S.* an official having custody of prisoners appearing in court. [C13: from Old French *baillif,* from *bail* custody; see BAIL[1]]

bailiwick ('beɪlɪwɪk) *n* **1** *Law.* the area over which a bailiff has jurisdiction. **2** a person's special field of interest, authority, or skill. [C15: from BAILIE + WICK[2]]

Baillie ('beɪlɪ) *n* Dame **Isobel.** 1895–1983, British soprano.

bailment ('beɪlmənt) *n* **1** *Contract law.* a contractual delivery of goods in trust to a person for a specific purpose. **2** *Criminal law.* the act of granting bail.

bailor ('beɪlə, beɪˈlɔː) *n Contract law.* a person who delivers goods to another under a contract of bailment.

bail out *or* **bale out** *vb* (*adv*) **1** (*intr*) to make an emergency parachute jump from an aircraft. **2** (*tr*) *Informal.* to help (a person, organization, etc.) out of a predicament: *the government bailed the company out.* **3** (*intr*) *Informal.* to escape from a predicament.

bail up *vb* (*adv*) **1** *Austral and N.Z. informal.* to confine (a cow) or (of a cow) to be confined by the head in a bail. See **bail**[3]. **2** (*tr*) *Austral. history.* (of a bushranger) to hold under guard in order to rob. **3** (*intr*) *Austral.* to submit to robbery without offering resistance. **4** (*tr*) *Austral. informal.* to accost or detain, esp. in conversation; buttonhole.

Baily ('beɪlɪ) *n* one of the largest craters on the moon, about 293 kilometres in diameter, lying in the SE quadrant.

Baily's beads ('beɪlɪz) *pl n* the brilliant points of sunlight that appear briefly around the moon, just before and after a total eclipse. [C19: named after Francis *Baily* (died 1844), English astronomer who described them]

Bainbridge ('beɪn,brɪdʒ) *n* **Beryl.** born 1934, British novelist and playwright. Novels include *The Dressmaker* (1973), *Injury Time* (1977), and *Master Georgie* (1998); plays include *It's a Lovely Day Tomorrow* (1977).

báinín *or* **bawneen** ('bɑːniːn) *n Irish.* **1** a collarless revers-less unlined man's jacket made of white close-woven wool. **2** the material for such a jacket. **3 báinín skirt.** a skirt made of this material. **4 báinín wool.** white woollen thread. [C20: from Irish Gaelic *báinín,* diminutive of *bán* white]

bainite ('beɪnaɪt) *n* a mixture of iron and iron carbide found in incompletely hardened steels, produced when austenite is transformed at temperatures between the pearlite and martensite ranges. [C20: named after Edgar C. *Bain* (1891–1971), American physicist; see -ITE[1]]

bain-marie *French.* (bɛ̃mari) *n, pl* ***bains-marie*** (bɛ̃mari). a vessel for holding hot water, in which sauces and other dishes are gently cooked or kept warm. [C19: from French, from Medieval Latin *balneum Mariae,* literally: bath of Mary, inaccurate translation of Medieval Greek *kaminos Marios,* literally: furnace of *Miriam,* alleged author of a treatise on alchemy]

Bairam (baɪˈræm, 'baɪræm) *n* either of two Muslim festivals, one (**Lesser Bairam**) falling at the end of Ramadan, the other (**Greater Bairam**) 70 days later at the end of the Islamic year. [from Turkish *bayrām*]

Baird (bɛəd) *n* **John Logie** ('ləʊgɪ). 1888–1946, Scottish engineer: inventor of a 240-line mechanically scanned system of television, replaced in 1935 by a 405-line electrically scanned system.

bairn (bɛən; *Scot.* bern) *n Scot. and northern English.* a child. [Old English *bearn;* related to *bearm* lap, Old Norse, Old High German *barn* child]

Bairnsfather ('bɛənz,fɑːðə) *n* **Bruce.** 1888–1959, British cartoonist, born in India: best known for his cartoons of the war in the trenches during World War I.

Baisakhi (baɪˈsækiː) *n* an annual Sikh festival commemorating the founding (1699) of the Order of the Khalsa by Gobind Singh. [from Sanskrit, *Baisakh* (month of the year)]

bait[1] (beɪt) *n* **1** something edible, such as soft bread paste, worms, pieces of meat, etc., fixed to a hook or in a trap to attract fish or animals. **2** an enticement; temptation. **3** a variant spelling of **bate**[4]. **4** *Northern English dialect.* food, esp. a packed lunch. **5** *Archaic.* a short stop for refreshment during a journey. ◆ *vb* **6** (*tr*) to put a piece of food on or in (a hook or trap). **7** (*tr*) to persecute or tease. **8** (*tr*) to entice; tempt. **9** (*tr*) to set dogs upon (a bear, etc.). **10** (*tr*) *Archaic.* to feed (a horse), esp. during a break in a journey. **11** (*intr*) *Archaic.* to stop for rest and refreshment during a journey. [C13: from Old Norse *beita* to hunt, persecute; related to Old English *bǣtan* to restrain, hunt, Old High German *beizen*]

USAGE The phrase *with bated breath* is sometimes wrongly spelled *with baited breath.*

bait[2] (beɪt) *vb* a variant spelling of **bate**[2].

baize (beɪz) *n* **1** a woollen fabric resembling felt, usually green, used mainly for the tops of billiard tables. ◆ *vb* **2** (*tr*) to line or cover with such fabric. [C16: from Old French *baies,* plural of *baie* baize, from *bai* reddish brown, BAY[5], perhaps the original colour of the fabric]

Baja ('bæhə) **California Norte** ('nɔːteɪ) *n* **1** a state of NW Mexico, in the N part of the Lower California peninsula. Capital: Mexicali. Pop.: 2 108 118 (1995 est.). Area: about 71 500 sq. km (27 600 sq. miles). **2** the Spanish name for **Lower California.**

Baja California Sur *n* a state of NW Mexico, in the S part of the Lower California peninsula. Capital: La Paz. Pop.: 375 450 (1995 est.). Area: 73 475 sq. km (28 363 sq. miles).

Bajan ('beɪdʒən) *Caribbean informal.* ◆ *n* **1** a native of Barbados. ◆ *adj* **2** of or relating to Barbados or its inhabitants. [C20: variant of *Badian,* a shortened form of *Barbadian*]

bake (beɪk) *vb* **1** (*tr*) to cook by dry heat in or as if in an oven. **2** (*intr*) to cook bread, pastry, etc., in an oven. **3** to make or become hardened by heat. **4** (*intr*) *Informal.* to be extremely hot, as in the heat of the sun. ◆ *n* **5** *U.S.* a party at which the main dish is baked. **6** a batch of things baked at one time. **7** *Scot.* a kind of biscuit. **8** *Caribbean.* a small flat fried cake. [Old English *bacan;* related to Old Norse *baka,* Old High German *bahhan* to bake, Greek *phōgein* to parch, roast]

bakeapple ('beɪk,æpᵊl) *n Canadian.* the fruit of the cloudberry.

baked Alaska *n* a dessert consisting of cake and ice cream covered with meringue and cooked very quickly in a hot oven.

baked beans *pl n* haricot beans, baked and tinned in tomato sauce.

bakehouse ('beɪk,haʊs) *n* another word for **bakery.**

Bakelite ('beɪkə,laɪt) *n Trademark.* any one of a class of thermosetting resins used as electric insulators and for making plastic ware, telephone receivers, etc. [C20: named after L. H. *Baekeland* (1863–1944), Belgian-born U.S. inventor; see -ITE[1]]

baker ('beɪkə) *n* **1** a person whose business or employment is to make or sell bread, cakes, etc. **2** a portable oven. **3 on the baker's list.** *Irish informal.* in good health.

Baker ('beɪkə) *n* **1** Sir **Benjamin.** 1840–1907, British engineer who, with Sir John Fowler, designed and constructed much of the London underground railway, the Forth Railway Bridge, and the first Aswan Dam. **2** Dame **Janet.** born 1933, British mezzo-soprano. **3** Sir **Samuel White.** 1821–93, British explorer: discovered Lake Albert (1864).

baker's dozen *n* thirteen. [C16: from the bakers' former practice of giving thirteen rolls where twelve were requested, to protect themselves against accusations of giving light weight]

bakery ('beɪkərɪ) *n, pl* **-eries.** **1** Also called: **bakehouse.** a room or building equipped for baking. **2** a shop in which bread, cakes, etc., are sold.

Bakewell ('beɪkwel) *n* **Robert.** 1725–95, English agriculturist; radically improved livestock breeding, esp. of cattle and sheep.

Bakewell tart ('beɪkwel) *n Brit.* an open tart having a pastry base and a layer of jam and filled with almond-flavoured sponge cake. [C19: named after *Bakewell,* Derbyshire]

Bakhtaran (,bæktəˈrɑːn, -ˈræn) *n* a city in W Iran, in the valley of the Qareh Su: oil refinery. Pop.: 665 636 (1994 est.). Former name (until 1987): **Kermanshah.**

baking ('beɪkɪŋ) *n* **1a** the process of cooking bread, cakes, etc. **1b** (*as modifier*): *a baking dish.* **2** the bread, cakes, etc., cooked at one time. ◆ *adj* **3** (esp. of weather) very hot and dry.

baking powder *n* any of various powdered mixtures that contain sodium bicarbonate, starch (usually flour), and one or more slightly acidic compounds, such as cream of tartar: used in baking as a substitute for yeast.

bakkie ('bʌkiː) *n S. African.* a small truck with an open body and low sides. [C20: from Afrikaans *bak* container]

baklava *or* **baclava** ('bɑːklə,vɑː) *n* a rich cake of Middle Eastern origin consisting of thin layers of pastry filled with nuts and honey. [from Turkish]

bakra ('bækrə) *Caribbean.* ◆ *n, pl* **-ra** *or* **-ras.** **1** a White person, esp. one from Britain. ◆ *adj* **2** (of people) White, esp. British. [of African origin]

baksheesh *or* **backsheesh** ('bækʃiːʃ) (in some Eastern countries, esp. formerly) ◆ *n* **1** money given as a tip, a present, or alms. ◆ *vb* **2** to give such money to (a person). [C17: from Persian *bakhshīsh*, from *bakhshīdan* to give; related to Sanskrit *bhaksati* he enjoys]

Bakst (*Russian* bakst) *n* **Leon Nikolayevich** (lɪ'ɔn nika'lajɪvitʃ). 1866–1924, Russian painter and stage designer, noted particularly for his richly coloured sets for Diaghilev's *Ballet Russe* (1909–21).

Baku (*Russian* ba'ku) *n* the capital of Azerbaijan, a port on the Caspian Sea: important for its extensive oilfields. Pop.: 1 739 900 (1995 est.).

Bakunin (*Russian* ba'kunin) *n* **Mikhail** (mixa'il). 1814–76, Russian anarchist and writer: a prominent member of the First International, expelled from it after conflicts with Marx.

BAL *abbrev. for* British anti-lewisite. See **dimercaprol.**

bal. *Book-keeping. abbrev. for* balance.

Bala ('bælə) *n* **Lake.** a narrow lake in Gwynedd: the largest natural lake in Wales. Length: 6 km (4 miles).

Balaam ('beɪlæm) *n Old Testament.* a Mesopotamian diviner who, when summoned to curse the Israelites, prophesied future glories for them instead, after being reproached by his ass (Numbers 22–23).

Balaclava *or* **Balaclava helmet** (ˌbælə'klɑːvə) *n* (*often not caps.*) a close- fitting woollen hood that covers the ears and neck, as originally worn by soldiers in the Crimean War. [C19: named after BALAKLAVA]

Balaguer (ˌbælə'gweə) *n* **Joaquin** ('joːakɪn). born 1907, Dominican statesman; president of the Dominican Republic (1960–62, 1966–78, 1986–96).

Balakirev (*Russian* ba'lakirɪf) *n* **Mily Alexeyevich** ('milij alɪk'sjejɪvitʃ). 1837–1910, Russian composer, whose works include two symphonic poems, two symphonies, and many arrangements of Russian folk songs.

Balaklava *or* **Balaclava** (ˌbælə'klɑːvə; *Russian* bəla'klavə) *n* a small port in the Ukraine, in S Crimea: scene of an inconclusive battle (1854), which included the charge of the Light Brigade, during the Crimean War.

balalaika (ˌbælə'laɪkə) *n* a plucked musical instrument, usually having a triangular body and three strings: used chiefly for Russian folk music. [C18: from Russian]

balance ('bæləns) *n* **1** a weighing device, generally consisting of a horizontal beam pivoted at its centre, from the ends of which two pans are suspended. The substance to be weighed is placed in one pan and known weights are placed in the other until the beam returns to the horizontal. See also **microbalance. 2** an imagined device for events, actions, motives, etc., in relation to each other (esp. in the phrases **weigh in the balance, hang in the balance**). **3** a state of equilibrium. **4** something that brings about such a state. **5** equilibrium of the body; steadiness: *to lose one's balance.* **6** emotional stability; calmness of mind. **7** harmony in the parts of a whole: *balance in an artistic composition.* **8** the act of weighing factors, quantities, etc., against each other. **9** the power to influence or control: *he held the balance of power.* **10** something that remains or is left: *let me have the balance of what you owe me.* **11** *Accounting.* **11a** equality of debit and credit totals in an account. **11b** a difference between such totals. **12** *Chem.* the state of a chemical equation in which the number, kind, electrical charges, etc., of the atoms on opposite sides are equal. **13** a balancing movement. **14** short for **spring balance. 15 in the balance.** in an uncertain or undecided condition. **16 on balance.** after weighing up all the factors. **17 strike a balance.** to make a compromise. ♦ *vb* **18** (*tr*) to weigh in or as if in a balance. **19** (*intr*) to be or come into equilibrium. **20** (*tr*) to bring into or hold in equilibrium. **21** (*tr*) to assess or compare the relative weight, importance, etc., of. **22** (*tr*) to act so as to equalize; be equal to. **23** (*tr*) to compose or arrange so as to create a state of harmony. **24** (*tr*) to bring (a chemical or mathematical equation) into balance. **25** (*tr*) *Accounting.* **25a** to compute the credit and debit totals of (an account) in order to determine the difference. **25b** to equalize the credit and debit totals of (an account) by making certain entries. **25c** to settle or adjust (an account) by paying any money due. **26** (*intr*) (of a business account, balance sheet, etc.) to have the debit and credit totals equal. **27** to match or counter (one's dancing partner or his or her steps) by moving towards and away from him or her. [C13: from Old French, from Vulgar Latin *bilancia* (unattested), from Late Latin *bilanx* having two scalepans, from BI-[1] + *lanx* scale] ▸ '**balanceable** *adj*

Balance ('bæləns) *n* **the.** the constellation Libra, the seventh sign of the zodiac.

balance bridge *n* another name for **bascule bridge** (see **bascule** (sense 1)).

balanced ('bælənst) *adj* **1** having weight equally distributed. **2** (of a person) mentally and emotionally stable. **3** (of a discussion, programme, etc.) presenting opposing points of view fairly and without bias. **4** (of a diet) consisting of all essential nutrients in suitable form and amounts to maintain health. **5** (of a budget) having expenditure no greater than income. **6** *Electronics.* (of signals or circuitry) symmetrically disposed about earth or other reference potential. **7** (of a chemical equation) having the correct relative number of moles of reactants and products.

balance of nature *n* the stable state in which natural communities of animals and plants exist, maintained by adaptation, competition, and other interactions between members of the community and their nonliving environment.

balance of payments *n* the difference over a given time between total payments to foreign nations, arising from imports of goods and services and transfers abroad of capital, interest, grants, etc., and total receipts from foreign nations, arising from exports of goods and services and transfers from abroad of capital, interest, grants, etc.

balance of power *n* **1** the distribution of power among countries so that no one nation can seriously threaten the fundamental interests of another. **2** any similar distribution of power or influence.

balance of trade *n* the difference in value between total exports and total imports of goods. Also called: **visible balance.** Compare **invisible balance.**

balance pipe *n Engineering.* a pipe between two points used to equalize pressure.

balancer ('bælənsə) *n* **1** a person or thing that balances. **2** *Entomol.* another name for **haltere.**

balance sheet *n* a statement that shows the financial position of a business enterprise at a specified date by listing the asset balances and the claims on such assets.

balance weight *n Engineering.* a weight used in machines to counterbalance a part, as of a crankshaft. Also called: **bobweight.**

balance wheel *n* a wheel oscillating against the hairspring of a timepiece, thereby regulating its beat.

balancing act ('bælənsɪŋ) *n* **1** a circus act in which a performer displays his or her balancing ability. **2** a situation requiring careful balancing of opposing groups, views, or activities: *a delicate balancing act between Greek and Turkish interests.*

Balanchine ('bælənˌtʃiːn, ˌbælən'tʃiːn) *n* **George.** 1904–83, U.S. choreographer, born in Russia.

balanitis (ˌbælə'naɪtɪs) *n Med.* inflammation of the glans penis, usually due to infection. [from New Latin *balanus*, from Greek *balanos* acorn + -ITIS]

balas ('bæləs, 'beɪ-) *n* a red variety of spinel, used as a gemstone. Also called: **balas ruby.** [C15: from Old French *balais*, from Arabic *bālakhsh*, from *Badhakhshān*, region in Afghanistan where the gem is found]

balata ('bælətə) *n* **1** a tropical American sapotaceous tree, *Manilkara bidentata*, yielding a latex-like sap. **2** a rubber-like gum obtained from this sap: used as a substitute for gutta-percha. [from American Spanish, of Carib origin]

Balaton (*Hungarian* 'bɔlɔton) *n* **Lake.** a large shallow lake in W Hungary. Area: 689 sq. km (266 sq. miles).

Balbo (*Italian* 'balbo) *n* **Italo** ('italo). 1896–1940, Italian Fascist politician and airman: minister of aviation (1929–33).

balboa (bæl'bəʊə) *n* the standard currency unit of Panama, divided into 100 centesimos. [named after Vasco Núñez de BALBOA]

Balboa[1] (bæl'bəʊə; *Spanish* bal'βoa) *n* **Vasco Núñez de** ('basko 'nuɲeθ de). ?1475–1519, Spanish explorer, who discovered the Pacific Ocean in 1513.

Balboa[2] (bæl'bəʊə; *Spanish* bal'βoa) *n* a port in Panama at the Pacific end of the Panama Canal: the administrative centre of the former Canal Zone. Pop.: 2750 (1990).

balbriggan (bæl'brɪgən) *n* **1** a knitted unbleached cotton fabric. **2** (*often pl*) underwear made of this. [C19: from *Balbriggan*, Ireland, where it was originally made]

Balcon ('bɔːlkən) *n* Sir **Michael.** 1896–1977, British film producer; his films made at Ealing Studios include the comedies *Kind Hearts and Coronets* (1949) and *The Lavender Hill Mob* (1951).

balcony ('bælkənɪ) *n, pl* **-nies. 1** a platform projecting from the wall of a building with a balustrade or railing along its outer edge, often with access from a door or window. **2** a gallery in a theatre or auditorium, above the dress circle. **3** *U.S. and Canadian.* any circle or gallery in a theatre or auditorium including the dress circle. [C17: from Italian *balcone*, probably from Old High German *balko* beam; see BALK] ▸ '**balconied** *adj*

bald (bɔːld) *adj* **1** having no hair or fur, esp. (of a man) having no hair on all or most of the scalp. **2** lacking natural growth or covering. **3** plain or blunt: *a bald statement.* **4** bare or simple; unadorned. **5** Also: **baldfaced.** (of certain birds and other animals) having white markings on the head and face. **6** (of a tyre) having a worn tread. [C14 *ballede* (literally: having a white spot); related to Danish *bældet*, Greek *phalaros* having a white spot] ▸ '**baldish** *adj* ▸ '**baldly** *adv* ▸ '**baldness** *n*

baldachin, baldaquin ('bɔːldəkɪn), *or* **baldachino** (ˌbɔːldə'kiːnəʊ) *n* **1** a richly ornamented silk and gold brocade. **2** a canopy of fabric or stone over an altar, shrine, or throne in a Christian church or carried in Christian religious processions over an object of veneration. [Old English *baldekin*, from Italian *baldacchino*, literally: stuff from Baghdad, from *Baldacco* Baghdad, noted for its brocades]

bald cypress *n* another name for **swamp cypress.**

bald eagle *n* a large eagle, *Haliaeetus leucocephalus*, of North America, having a white head and tail, a yellow bill, and dark wings and body. It is the U.S. national bird (see also **American eagle**).

Balder ('bɔːldə) *n Norse myth.* a god, son of Odin and Frigg, noted for his beauty and sweet nature. He was killed by a bough of mistletoe thrown by the blind god Höd, misled by the malicious Loki.

balderdash ('bɔːldəˌdæʃ) *n* stupid or illogical talk; senseless rubbish. [C16: of unknown origin]

baldhead ('bɔːldˌhed) *n* a person with a bald head.

baldheaded (ˌbɔːld'hedɪd) *adj* having a bald head.

balding ('bɔːldɪŋ) *adj* somewhat bald or becoming bald.

baldmoney ('bɔːldˌmʌnɪ) *n* another name for **spignel.**

baldpate ('bɔːldˌpeɪt) *n* **1** a person with a bald head. **2** another name for the **American wigeon** (see **wigeon** (sense 2)).

baldric ('bɔːldrɪk) *n* a wide silk sash or leather belt worn over the right shoulder to the left hip for carrying a sword, etc. [C13: from Old French *baudrei*, of Frankish origin]

Baldwin ('bɔːldwɪn) *n* **1 James (Arthur).** 1924–87, U.S. Black writer, whose works include the novel *Go Tell it on the Mountain* (1954). **2 Stanley,** 1st Earl Baldwin of Bewdley. 1867–1947, British Conservative statesman: prime minister (1923–24, 1924–29, 1935–37).

Baldwin I *n* 1058–1118, crusader and first king of Jerusalem (1100–18), who captured Acre (1104), Beirut (1109), and Sidon (1110).

baldy ('bɔːldɪ) *Informal. adj* **1** bald. ♦ *n, pl* **baldies. 2** a bald person.

bale[1] (beɪl) *n* **1** a large bundle, esp. of a raw or partially processed material, bound by ropes, wires, etc., for storage or transportation: *bale of hay.* **2** a large package or carton of goods. **3** *U.S.* 500 pounds of cotton. **4** a group of turtles. **5** *Austral. and N.Z.* See **wool bale.** ♦ *vb* **6** to make (hay, etc.) into a bale or bales. **7** to put (goods) into packages or cartons. **8** *Austral. and N.Z.* to pack and compress (wool) into wool bales. ◆ See also **bail out**. [C14: probably from Old French *bale,* from Old High German *balla* BALL[1]]

bale[2] (beɪl) *n Archaic.* **1** evil; injury. **2** woe; suffering; pain. [Old English *bealu;* related to Old Norse *böl* evil, Gothic *balwa,* Old High German *balo*]

bale[3] (beɪl) *vb* a variant spelling of **bail**[2].

bale[4] (beɪl) *n* a variant spelling of **bail**[4].

Bâle (bɑl) *n* the French name for **Basel**.

Balearic Islands (ˌbælɪˈærɪk) *pl n* a group of islands in the W Mediterranean, consisting of Majorca, Minorca, Ibiza, Formentera, Cabrera, and 11 islets: a province of Spain. Capital: Palma, on Majorca. Pop.: 760 379 (1996 est.). Area: 5012 sq. km (1935 sq. miles). Spanish name: **Baleares** (baleˈares).

baleen (bəˈliːn) *n* whalebone. [C14: from Latin *bālaena* whale; related to Greek *phalaina* whale]

baleen whale *n* another name for **whalebone whale**.

balefire (ˈbeɪlˌfaɪə) *n Archaic.* **1** a bonfire. **2** a beacon fire. **3** a funeral pyre. [C14 *bale,* from Old English *bǣl* pyre; related to Old Norse *bāl* flame, pyre, Sanskrit *bhāla* brightness]

baleful (ˈbeɪlfʊl) *adj* **1** harmful, menacing, or vindictive. **2** *Archaic.* dejected. ▸ **ˈbalefully** *adv* ▸ **ˈbalefulness** *n*

Balenciaga (*Spanish* balenˈθjaɣa) *n* **Cristóbal** (krisˈtoβal). 1895–1972, Spanish couturier.

baler (ˈbeɪlə) *n* an agricultural machine for making bales of hay, etc. Also called: **baling machine**.

Balfour (ˈbælfɔː, -fə, -fʊə) *n* **Arthur James,** 1st Earl of Balfour. 1848–1930, British Conservative statesman: prime minister (1902–05); foreign secretary (1916–19).

Balfour Declaration *n* the statement made by Arthur Balfour in 1917 of British support for the setting up of a national home for the Jews in Palestine, provided that the rights of "existing non-Jewish communities" in Palestine could be safeguarded.

Bali (ˈbɑːlɪ) *n* an island in Indonesia, east of Java: mountainous, rising over 3000 m (10 000 ft.). Capital: Denpasar. Pop.: 2 902 200 (1995 est.). Area: 5558 sq. km (2146 sq. miles).

balibuntal (ˌbælɪˈbʌntᵊl) *n* **1** closely woven fine straw, used for making hats in the Philippines. **2** a hat of this straw. [C20: changed from *Baliuag buntal,* from *Baliuag* in the Philippines, where such hats were made]

Balikpapan (ˌbɑːlɪkˈpɑːpɑːn) *n* a city in Indonesia, on the SE coast of Borneo. Pop.: 416 200 (1995 est.).

Balinese (ˌbɑːlɪˈniːz) *adj* **1** of or relating to Bali, its people, or their language. ◆ *n* **2** (*pl* **-nese**) a native or inhabitant of Bali. **3** the language of the people of Bali, belonging to the Malayo-Polynesian family.

Baliol *or* **Balliol** (ˈbeɪlɪəl) *n* **1 Edward.** ?1283–1364, king of Scotland (1332, 1333–56). **2** his father, **John.** 1249–1315, king of Scotland (1292–96): defeated and imprisoned by Edward I of England (1296).

balk *or* **baulk** (bɔːk, bɔːlk) *vb* **1** (*intr;* usually foll. by *at*) to stop short, esp. suddenly or unexpectedly; jib: *the horse balked at the jump.* **2** (*intr;* foll. by *at*) to turn away abruptly; recoil: *he balked at the idea of murder.* **3** (*tr*) to thwart, check, disappoint, or foil: *he was balked in his plans.* **4** (*tr*) to avoid deliberately: *he balked the question.* **5** (*tr*) to miss unintentionally. ◆ *n* **6** a roughly squared heavy timber beam. **7** a timber tie beam of a roof. **8** an unploughed ridge to prevent soil erosion or mark a division on common land. **9** an obstacle; hindrance; disappointment. **10** *Baseball.* an illegal motion by a pitcher towards the plate or towards the base when there are runners on base, esp. without delivering the ball. ◆ See also **baulk**. [Old English *balca;* related to Old Norse *bálkr* partition, Old High German *balco* beam] ▸ **ˈbalker** *or* **ˈbaulker** *n*

Balkan (ˈbɔːlkən) *adj* of, denoting, or relating to the Balkan States or their inhabitants, the Balkan Peninsula, or the Balkan Mountains.

Balkanize *or* **Balkanise** (ˈbɔːlkəˌnaɪz) *vb* (*tr*) to divide (a territory) into small warring states. ▸ **ˌBalkaniˈzation** *or* **ˌBalkaniˈsation** *n*

Balkan Mountains *pl n* a mountain range extending across Bulgaria from the Black Sea to the eastern border. Highest peak: Mount Botev, 2376 m (7793 ft.).

Balkan Peninsula *n* a large peninsula in SE Europe, between the Adriatic and Aegean Seas.

Balkan States *pl n* the countries of the Balkan Peninsula: the former Yugoslavian Republics, Romania, Bulgaria, Albania, Greece, and the European part of Turkey. Also called: **the Balkans**.

Balkh (bɑːlk) *n* a region of N Afghanistan, corresponding to ancient Bactria. Chief town: Mazar-i-Sharif.

Balkhash (*Russian* balˈxaʃ) *n* **Lake.** a salt lake in SE Kazakhstan: fed by the Ili River. Area: about 18 000 sq. km (7000 sq. miles).

Balkis (ˈbælkɪs) *n* the name in the Koran of the queen of **Sheba**.

balky *or* **baulky** (ˈbɔːkɪ, ˈbɔːlkɪ) *adj* **balkier, balkiest** *or* **baulkier, baulkiest.** inclined to stop abruptly and unexpectedly: *a balky horse.* ▸ **ˈbalkily** *or* **ˈbaulkily** *adv* ▸ **ˈbalkiness** *or* **ˈbaulkiness** *n*

ball[1] (bɔːl) *n* **1** a spherical or nearly spherical body or mass: *a ball of wool.* **2** a round or roundish body, either solid or hollow, of a size and composition suitable for any of various games, such as football, golf, billiards, etc. **3** a ball propelled in a particular way in a sport: *a high ball.* **4** any of various rudimentary games with a ball: *to play ball.* **5** *Cricket.* a single delivery of the ball by the bowler to the batsman. **6** *Baseball.* a single delivery of the ball by a pitcher outside certain limits and not swung at by the batter. **7a** a solid nonexplosive projectile for a firearm. Compare **shell** (sense 6). **7b** such projectiles collectively. **8** any more or less rounded part or protuberance: *the ball of the foot.* **9** *Taboo slang.* a testicle. See **balls**. **10** *Vet. science.* another word for **bolus**. **11** *Horticulture.* the hard mass of roots and earth removed with the rest of the plant during transplanting. **12 ball of muscle.** *Austral.* a very strong, fit, or forceful person. **13 have the ball at one's feet.** to have the chance of doing something. **14 keep the ball rolling.** to maintain the progress of a project, plan, etc. **15 on the ball.** *Informal.* alert; informed. **16 play ball.** *Informal.* to cooperate. **17 set** *or* **start the ball rolling.** to open or initiate (an action, discussion, movement, etc.). **18 the ball is in your court.** you are obliged to make the next move. ◆ *vb* **19** (*tr*) to make, form, wind, etc., into a ball or balls: *to ball wool.* **20** (*intr*) to gather into a ball or balls. **21** *Taboo slang, chiefly U.S.* to copulate (with). [C13: from Old Norse *böllr;* related to Old High German *balla,* Italian *palla,* French *balle*]

ball[2] (bɔːl) *n* **1** a social function for dancing, esp. one that is lavish or formal. **2** *Informal.* a very enjoyable time (esp. in the phrase **have a ball**). [C17: from French *bal* (n), from Old French *baller* (vb), from Late Latin *ballāre* to dance, from Greek *ballizein*]

Ball (bɔːl) *n* **John.** died 1381, English priest: executed as one of the leaders of the Peasants' Revolt (1381).

ballad (ˈbæləd) *n* **1** a narrative song with a recurrent refrain. **2** a narrative poem in short stanzas of popular origin, originally sung to a repeated tune. **3** a slow sentimental song, esp. a pop song. [C15: from Old French *balade,* from Old Provençal *balada* song accompanying a dance, from *balar* to dance, from Late Latin *ballāre;* see BALL[2]]

ballade (bæˈlɑːd; *French* balad) *n* **1** *Prosody.* a verse form consisting of three stanzas and an envoy, all ending with the same line. The first three stanzas commonly have eight or ten lines each and the same rhyme scheme. **2** *Music.* an instrumental composition, esp. for piano, based on or intended to evoke a narrative.

balladeer (ˌbæləˈdɪə) *n* a singer of ballads.

ballad metre *n* the metre of a ballad stanza.

balladmonger (ˈbæləd,mʌŋgə) *n* **1** (formerly) a seller of ballads, esp. on broadsheets. **2** *Derogatory.* a writer of mediocre poetry.

ballad opera *n* an opera consisting of popular tunes to which appropriate words have been set, interspersed with spoken dialogue.

balladry (ˈbælədrɪ) *n* **1** ballad poetry or songs. **2** the art of writing, composing, or performing ballads.

ballad stanza *n* a four-line stanza, often used in ballads, in which the second and fourth lines rhyme and have three stresses each and the first and third lines are unrhymed and have four stresses each.

Ballance (ˈbæləns) *n* **John.** 1839–93, New Zealand statesman, born in Northern Ireland: prime minister of New Zealand (1891–93).

ball and chain *n* **1** (formerly) a heavy iron ball attached to a chain and fastened to a prisoner. **2** a heavy restraint. **3** *Slang.* one's wife.

ball-and-socket joint *n* **1** a coupling between two rods, tubes, etc., that consists of a spherical part fitting into a spherical socket, allowing free movement and rotation. **2** Also called: **multiaxial joint.** *Anatomy.* a bony joint, such as the hip joint, in which a rounded head fits into a rounded cavity, allowing a wide range of movement.

Ballantyne (ˈbælənˌtaɪn) *n* **R(obert) M(ichael).** 1825–94, British author, noted for such adventure stories as *The Coral Island* (1857).

Ballarat (ˈbæləˌræt, ˌbæləˈræt) *n* a town in SE Australia, in S central Victoria: originally the centre of a gold-mining region. Pop.: 64 980 (1991). See also **Eureka Stockade**.

Ballard (ˈbælɑːd) *n* **J(ames) G(raham).** born 1930, British novelist, born in China; his books include *Crash* (1973), *The Unlimited Dream Company* (1979), *Empire of the Sun* (1984), and *Cocaine Nights* (1996).

ballast (ˈbæləst) *n* **1** any dense heavy material, such as lead or iron pigs, used to stabilize a vessel, esp. one that is not carrying cargo. **2** crushed rock, broken stone, etc., used for the foundation of a road or railway track. **3** coarse aggregate of sandy gravel, used in making concrete. **4** anything that provides stability or weight. **5** *Electronics.* a device for maintaining the current in a circuit. ◆ *vb* (*tr*) **6** to give stability or weight to. [C16: probably from Low German; related to Old Danish, Old Swedish *barlast,* literally: bare load (without commercial value), from *bar* bare, mere + *last* load, burden]

ball bearing *n* **1** a bearing consisting of a number of hard steel balls rolling between a metal sleeve fitted over the rotating shaft and an outer sleeve held in the bearing housing, so reducing friction between moving parts. **2** a metal ball, esp. one used in such a bearing.

ball boy *n* (esp. in tennis) a person who retrieves balls that go out of play.

ballbreaker (ˈbɔːlˌbreɪkə) *n Slang.* a person, esp. a woman, whose character and behaviour may be regarded as threatening a man's sense of power. [C20: from BALL[1] (in the sense: testicle) + BREAKER[1]]

ball cock *n* a device for regulating the flow of a liquid into a tank, cistern, etc., consisting of a floating ball mounted at one end of an arm and a valve on the other end that opens and closes as the ball falls and rises.

ballerina (ˌbæləˈriːnə) *n* **1** a female ballet dancer. **2** *U.S.* the principal female dancer of a ballet company. [C18: from Italian, feminine of *ballerino* dancing master, from *ballare* to dance, from Late Latin *ballāre;* see BALL[2]]

Ballesteros (ˌbæləˈstɛrɒs; *Spanish* baʎesˈterɔs) *n* **Severiano** (seveˈrjano). born 1957, Spanish professional golfer: won the British Open Championship (1979; 1984; 1988).

ballet (ˈbæleɪ, bæˈleɪ) *n* **1a** a classical style of expressive dancing based on precise conventional steps with gestures and movements of grace and fluidity. **1b** (*as modifier*): *ballet dancer.* **2** a theatrical representation of a story or theme performed to music by ballet dancers. **3** a troupe of ballet dancers. **4** a piece of music written for a ballet. [C17: from French, from Italian *balletto,* literally: a little dance, from *ballare* to dance; see BALL[2]] ▸ **balletic** (bæˈlɛtɪk) *adj*

balletomania (ˌbælɪtəʊˈmeɪnɪə) *n* passionate enthusiasm for ballet. [C20: from BALLET + -O- + -MANIA] ▸ **balletomane** (ˈbælɪtəʊˌmeɪn) *n*

ballflower (ˈbɔːlˌflaʊə) *n Architect.* a carved ornament in the form of a ball enclosed by the three petals of a circular flower.

ball game *n* **1** any game played with a ball. **2** *U.S. and Canadian.* a game of baseball. **3** *Informal.* a situation; state of affairs (esp. in the phrase **a whole new ball game**).

Balliol ('beɪlɪəl) *n* See **Baliol.**

ballista (bə'lɪstə) *n, pl* **-tae** (-tiː). **1** an ancient catapult for hurling stones, etc. **2** an ancient form of large crossbow used to propel a spear. [C16: from Latin, ultimately from Greek *ballein* to throw]

ballistic (bə'lɪstɪk) *adj* **1** of or relating to ballistics. **2** denoting or relating to the flight of projectiles after power has been cut off, moving under their own momentum and the external forces of gravity and air resistance. **3** (of a measurement or measuring instrument) depending on a brief impulse or current that causes a movement related to the quantity to be measured: *a ballistic pendulum.* **4 go ballistic.** *Informal.* to become enraged or frenziedly violent. ▸ **bal'listically** *adv*

ballistic galvanometer *n Physics.* a type of galvanometer for measuring surges of current. After deflection the instrument returns slowly to its original reading.

ballistic missile *n* a missile that has no wings or fins and that follows a ballistic trajectory when its propulsive power is discontinued.

ballistics (bə'lɪstɪks) *n (functioning as sing)* the study of the flight dynamics of projectiles, either through the interaction of the forces of propulsion, the aerodynamics of the projectile, atmospheric resistance, and gravity (**exterior ballistics**), or through these forces along with the means of propulsion, and the design of the propelling weapon and projectile (**interior ballistics**).

ballistospore (bə'lɪstəˌspɔː) *n Botany.* a spore, esp. a fungal spore, that is forcefully ejected from its source.

ball lightning *n Meteorol.* a luminous ball occasionally seen during electrical storms.

ball mill *n Engineering.* a horizontal cylinder or cone in which a substance, such as a mineral, is ground by rotation with steel or ceramic balls.

ballocks ('bɒləks, 'bæl-) *pl n, interj, vb* a variant spelling of **bollocks.**

ball of fire *n Informal.* a very lively person.

ballon d'essai (bælõ dɛ'seɪ) *n, pl* **ballons d'essai** (bælõ dɛ'seɪ). a project or policy put forward experimentally to gauge reactions to it. Compare **trial balloon.** [C19: from French, literally: trial balloon]

ballonet (ˌbælə'nɛt) *n* an air or gas compartment in a balloon or nonrigid airship, used to control buoyancy and shape. [C20: from French *ballonnet* a little BALLOON]

balloon (bə'luːn) *n* **1** an inflatable rubber bag of various sizes, shapes, and colours: usually used as a plaything or party decoration. **2** a large impermeable bag inflated with a lighter-than-air gas, designed to rise and float in the atmosphere. It may have a basket or gondola for carrying passengers, etc. See also **barrage balloon, hot-air balloon. 3** a circular or elliptical figure containing the words or thoughts of a character in a cartoon. **4** *Brit.* **4a** a kick or stroke that propels a ball high into the air. **4b** *(as modifier): a balloon shot.* **5** *Chem.* a round-bottomed flask. **6** a large rounded brandy glass. **7** *Commerce.* **7a** a large sum paid as an irregular instalment of a loan repayment. **7b** *(as modifier): a balloon loan.* **8** *Surgery.* **8a** an inflatable plastic tube used for dilating obstructed blood vessels or parts of the alimentary canal. **8b** *(as modifier): balloon angioplasty.* **9 go down like a lead balloon.** *Informal.* to be completely unsuccessful or unpopular. **10 when the balloon goes up.** *Informal.* when the trouble or action begins. ◆ *vb* **11** *(intr)* to go up or fly in a balloon. **12** *(intr)* to increase or expand significantly and rapidly: *losses ballooned to £278 million.* **13** to inflate or be inflated; distend; swell: *the wind ballooned the sails.* **14** *(tr) Brit.* to propel (a ball) high into the air. [C16 (in the sense: ball, ball game): from Italian dialect *ballone,* from *balla,* of Germanic origin; compare Old High German *balla* BALL[1]] ▸ **bal'looning** *n* ▸ **bal'loonist** *n* ▸ **bal'loon-ˌlike** *adj*

balloon loan *n* a loan in respect of which interest and capital are paid off in instalments at irregular intervals.

balloon sail *n Nautical.* a large light bellying sail used in light winds. Compare **spinnaker.**

balloon sleeve *n* a sleeve fitting tightly from wrist to elbow and becoming fully rounded from elbow to shoulder.

balloon tyre *n* a pneumatic tyre containing air at a relatively low pressure and having a wide tread.

balloon vine *n* a tropical tendril-climbing sapindaceous plant, *Cardiospermum halicacabum,* cultivated for its ornamental balloon-like seed capsules.

ballot ('bælət) *n* **1** the democratic practice of selecting a representative, a course of action, or deciding some other choice by submitting the options to a vote of all qualified persons. **2** an instance of voting, usually in secret using ballot papers or a voting machine. **3** the paper on which a vote is recorded. **4** a list of candidates standing for office. **5** the number of votes cast in an election. **6** a random selection of successful applicants for something in which the demand exceeds the supply, esp. for shares in an oversubscribed new issue. **7** *N.Z.* the allocation by ballot of farming land among eligible candidates, such as ex-servicemen. **8** *N.Z.* a low-interest housing loan allocated by building societies by drawing lots among its eligible members. ◆ *vb* **-lots, -loting, -loted. 9** to vote or elicit a vote from: *we balloted the members on this issue.* **10** *(tr; usually foll. by for)* to select (officials, etc.) by lot or ballot or to select (successful applicants) at random. **11** *(tr; often foll. by for)* to vote or decide (on an issue, etc.). [C16: from Italian *ballotta,* literally: a little ball, from *balla* BALL[1]]

ballot box *n* a box into which ballot papers are dropped after voting.

ballotini (ˌbælə'tiːnɪ) *pl n* small glass beads used in reflective paints. [C20: from Italian *ballottini* small balls]

ballot paper *n* a paper used for voting in a ballot, esp. (in a parliamentary or local government election) one having the names of the candidates printed on it.

ballottement (bə'lɒtmənt) *n Med.* a technique of feeling for a movable object in the body, esp. confirmation of pregnancy by feeling the rebound of the fetus following a quick digital tap on the wall of the uterus. [C19: from French, literally: a tossing, shaking, from *ballotter* to toss, from *ballotte* a little ball, from Italian *ballotta;* see BALLOT]

ballpark ('bɔːlˌpɑːk) *n* **1** *U.S. and Canadian.* a stadium used for baseball games. **2** *Informal.* **2a** approximate range: *in the right ballpark.* **2b** *(as modifier): a ballpark figure.* **3** *Informal.* a situation; state of affairs: *its a whole new ballpark for him.*

ball-peen hammer *n* a hammer that has one end of its head shaped in a hemisphere for beating metal, etc.

ballplayer ('bɔːlˌpleɪə) *n* **1** a player, esp. in soccer, with outstanding ability to control the ball. **2** *U.S. and Canadian.* a baseball player, esp. a professional.

ballpoint, ballpoint pen ('bɔːlˌpɔɪnt), *or* **ball pen** *n* a pen having a small ball bearing as a writing point. Also called (Brit.): **Biro.**

ball race *n Engineering.* **1** a ball bearing. **2** one of the metal rings having a circular track within which the balls of the bearing roll.

ballroom ('bɔːlˌruːm, -ˌrʊm) *n* a large hall for dancing.

ballroom dancing *n* social dancing, popular since the beginning of the 20th century, to dances in conventional rhythms (**ballroom dances**) such as the foxtrot and the quickstep.

balls (bɔːlz) *Slang.* ◆ *pl n* **1** *Taboo.* the testicles. **2 by the balls.** *Taboo.* so as to be rendered powerless. **3** *Taboo.* nonsense; rubbish. **4** *Taboo.* courage; forcefulness. ◆ *interj* **5** *Taboo.* an exclamation of strong disagreement, contempt, annoyance, etc.

balls-up *or U.S.* **ballup** ('bɔːlʌp) *Taboo slang.* ◆ *n* **1** something botched or muddled. ◆ *vb* **balls up** *or U.S.* **ball up. 2** *(tr, adv)* to muddle or botch.

ball tearer *n Austral. slang.* something exceptional in its class, for good or bad qualities.

ball valve *n* a one-way valve consisting of a metal ball fitting into a concave seat over an opening.

bally ('bælɪ) *adj, adv* (intensifier) *Brit. slang.* a euphemistic word for **bloody** (sense 6).

ballyhoo (ˌbælɪ'huː) *n Informal.* **1** a noisy, confused, or nonsensical situation or uproar. **2** sensational or blatant advertising or publicity. ◆ *vb* **-hoos, -hooing, -hooed. 3** *(tr) Chiefly U.S.* to advertise or publicize by sensational or blatant methods. [C19: of uncertain origin]

Ballymena (ˌbælɪ'miːnə) *n* a district in central Northern Ireland, in Co. Antrim. Pop.: 56 641 (1991). Area: 634 sq. km (247 sq. miles).

Ballymoney (ˌbælɪ'mʌnɪ) *n* a district in N Northern Ireland, in Co. Antrim. Pop.: 24 198 (1991). Area: 417 sq. km (161 sq. miles).

ballyrag ('bælɪˌræg) *vb* **-rags, -ragging, -ragged.** a variant of **bullyrag.**

balm (bɑːm) *n* **1** any of various oily aromatic resinous substances obtained from certain tropical trees and used for healing and soothing. See also **balsam** (sense 1). **2** any plant yielding such a substance, esp. the balm of Gilead. **3** something comforting or soothing: *soft music is a balm.* **4** any aromatic or oily substance used for healing or soothing. **5** Also called: **lemon balm.** an aromatic Eurasian herbaceous plant, *Melissa officinalis,* having clusters of small fragrant white two-lipped flowers: family *Labiatae* (labiates). **6** a pleasant odour. [C13: from Old French *basme,* from Latin *balsamum* BALSAM] ▸ **'balmˌlike** *adj*

balmacaan (ˌbælmə'kɑːn) *n* a man's knee-length loose flaring overcoat with raglan sleeves. [C19: after *Balmacaan,* near Inverness, Scotland]

Balmain *(French* balmɛ̃) *n* **Pierre Alexandre** (pjɛr alɛksɑ̃drə). 1914–82, French couturier.

Balmer *(German* 'balmər) *n* **Johann Jakob.** 1825–98, Swiss mathematician; discovered (1885) a formula giving the wavelengths of a series of lines in the hydrogen spectrum (the **Balmer series**).

balm of Gilead *n* **1** any of several trees of the burseraceous genus *Commiphora,* esp. *C. opobalsamum* of Africa and W Asia, that yield a fragrant oily resin (see **balm** (sense 1)). Compare **myrrh** (sense 1). **2** the resin exuded by these trees. **3** a North American hybrid female poplar tree, *Populus gileadensis* (or *P. candicans*), with broad heart-shaped leaves. **4** a fragrant resin obtained from the balsam fir. See also **Canada balsam.**

Balmoral[1] (bæl'mɒrəl) *n (sometimes not cap.)* **1** a laced walking shoe. **2** a 19th-century woollen petticoat, worn showing below the skirt. **3** Also called: **bluebonnet.** a Scottish brimless hat traditionally of dark blue wool with a cockade and plume on one side. [C19: named after BALMORAL Castle]

Balmoral[2] (bæl'mɒrəl) *n* a castle in NE Scotland, in SW Aberdeenshire: a private residence of the British sovereign.

Balmung ('bælmʊŋ) *or* **Balmunc** ('bælmʊŋk) *n* (in the *Nibelungenlied*) Siegfried's sword.

balmy ('bɑːmɪ) *adj* **balmier, balmiest. 1** (of weather) mild and pleasant. **2** having the qualities of balm; fragrant or soothing. **3** a variant spelling of **barmy.** ▸ **'balmily** *adv* ▸ **'balminess** *n*

balneal ('bælnɪəl) *or* **balneary** ('bælnɪərɪ) *adj Rare.* of or relating to baths or bathing. [C17: from Latin *balneum* bath, from Greek *balaneion*]

balneology (ˌbælnɪ'ɒlədʒɪ) *n* the branch of medical science concerned with the therapeutic value of baths, esp. those taken with natural mineral waters. [C19: from Latin *balneum* bath] ▸ **balneological** (ˌbælnɪə'lɒdʒɪkᵊl) *adj* ▸ **ˌbalne'ologist** *n*

balneotherapy (ˌbælnɪə'θɛrəpɪ) *n* the treatment of disease by bathing, esp. to improve limb mobility in arthritic and neuromuscular disorders.

baloney *or* **boloney** (bə'ləʊnɪ) *n* **1** *Informal.* foolish talk; nonsense. **2** *Chiefly U.S.* another name for **bologna sausage.** [C20: changed from *Bologna* (sausage)]

BALPA ('bælpə) *n acronym for* British Airline Pilots' Association.

balsa ('bɔːlsə) *n* **1** a bombacaceous tree, *Ochroma lagopus,* of tropical America. **2** Also called: **balsawood.** the very light wood of this tree, used for making rafts, etc. **3** a light raft. [C18: from Spanish: raft]

balsam ('bɔːlsəm) *n* **1** any of various fragrant oleoresins, such as balm or tolu, obtained from any of several trees and shrubs and used as a base for medicines and perfumes. **2** any of various similar substances used as medicinal or ceremonial ointments. **3** any of certain aromatic resinous turpentines. See also **Canada balsam. 4** any plant yielding balsam. **5** Also called: **busy Lizzie.** any of several balsaminaceous plants of the genus *Impatiens,* esp. *I. balsamina,* cultivated for its brightly coloured flowers. **6** anything healing or soothing. [C15: from Latin *balsamum,* from Greek *balsamon,* from Hebrew *bāśām* spice] ▸ **balsamic** (bɔːl'sæmɪk) *adj* ▸ **'balsamy** *adj*

balsam apple *n* an ornamental cucurbitaceous vine, *Momordica balsamina,* of the Old World tropics, with yellow flowers and orange egg-shaped fruits.

balsam fir *n* a fir tree, *Abies balsamea,* of NE North America, that yields Canada balsam. Also called: **balsam, Canada balsam.** See also **balm of Gilead.**

balsamiferous (ˌbɔːlsə'mɪfərəs) *adj* yielding or producing balsam.

balsaminaceous (ˌbɔːlsəmɪ'neɪʃəs) *adj* of, relating to, or belonging to the *Balsaminaceae,* a family of flowering plants, including balsam and touch-me-not, that have irregular flowers and explosive capsules.

balsam of Peru *n* an aromatic balsam that is obtained from the tropical South American leguminous tree *Myroxylon pereirae* and is similar to balsam of Tolu. Also called: **Peru balsam.**

balsam of Tolu *n* the full name of **tolu.**

balsam poplar *n* a poplar tree, *Populus balsamifera,* of NE North America, having resinous buds and broad heart-shaped leaves. See also **tacamahac.**

balsam spruce *n* either of two North American coniferous trees of the genus *Picea, P. pungens* (the blue spruce) or *P. engelmanni.*

Balt (bɔːlt) *n* a member of any of the Baltic-speaking peoples of the Baltic States.

Balt. *abbrev. for* Baltic.

Balthazar[1] ('bælθəˌzɑː, bæl'θæzə) *n* a wine bottle holding the equivalent of sixteen normal bottles (approximately 12 litres). [C20: named after Balthazar (BELSHAZZAR) from his drinking wine at a great feast (Daniel 5:1)]

Balthazar[2] ('bælθəˌzɑː, bæl'θæzə) *n* one of the Magi, the others being Caspar and Melchior.

Balthus (*French* baltys) *n* real name *Balthasar Klossowski de Rola.* born 1908, French painter of Polish descent, noted esp. for his paintings of adolescent girls.

balti ('bɔːltɪ, 'bæltɪ) *n* **a** a spicy Indian dish, stewed until most of the liquid has evaporated, and served in a woklike pot. **b** (*as modifier*): *a balti house.* [C20: origin uncertain]

Baltic ('bɔːltɪk) *adj* **1** denoting or relating to the Baltic Sea or the Baltic States. **2** of, denoting, or characteristic of Baltic as a group of languages. ◆ *n* **3** a branch of the Indo-European family of languages consisting of Lithuanian, Latvian, and Old Prussian. **4** short for **Baltic Sea. 5** Also called: **Baltic Exchange.** a commodity and freight-chartering market in the City of London.

Baltics ('bɔːltɪks) *pl n* **the.** another name for the **Baltic States.**

Baltic Sea *n* a sea in N Europe, connected with the North Sea by the Skaggerak, Kattegat, and Öresund; shallow, with low salinity and small tides.

Baltic Shield *n* the wide area of ancient rock in Scandinavia. Also called: **Scandinavian Shield.** See **shield** (sense 7).

Baltic States *pl n* the republics of Estonia, Latvia, and Lithuania, which became constituent republics of the former Soviet Union in 1940, regaining their independence in 1991. Sometimes shortened to **the Baltics.**

Baltimore[1] ('bɔːltɪˌmɔː) *n* a port in N Maryland, on Chesapeake Bay. Pop.: 675 401 (1996 est.).

Baltimore[2] ('bɔːltɪˌmɔː) *n* **1 David.** born 1938, U.S. molecular biologist: shared the Nobel prize for physiology or medicine (1975) for his discovery of reverse transcriptase. **2 Lord.** See (Sir George) **Calvert.**

Baltimore oriole *n* a North American oriole, *Icterus galbula,* the male of which has orange and black plumage.

Balto-Slavonic *or* **Balto-Slavic** *n* a hypothetical subfamily of Indo-European languages consisting of Baltic and Slavonic. It is now generally believed that similarities between them result from geographical proximity rather than any special relationship.

Baluchi (bə'luːtʃɪ) *or* **Balochi** (bə'ləutʃɪ) *n* **1** (*pl* **-chis** *or* **-chi**) a member of a Muslim people living chiefly in coastal Pakistan and Iran. **2** the language of this people, belonging to the West Iranian branch of the Indo-European family. ◆ *adj* **3** of or relating to Baluchistan, its inhabitants, or their language.

Baluchistan (bə'luːtʃɪˌstɑːn, -ˌstæn) *or* **Balochistan** (bə'lɒtʃɪˌstɑːn, -ˌstæn) *n* **1** a mountainous region of SW Asia, in SW Pakistan and SE Iran. **2** a province of SW Pakistan: a former territory of British India (until 1947). Capital: Quetta. Pop.: 6 341 000 (1995 est.).

balun ('bælən) *n Electronics.* a device for coupling two electrical circuit elements, such as an aerial and its feeder cable, where one is balanced and the other is unbalanced. [C20: shortened from *bal(ance to) un(balance transformer)*]

baluster ('bæləstə) *n* **1** any of a set of posts supporting a rail or coping. ◆ *adj* **2** (of a shape) swelling at the base and rising in a concave curve to a narrow stem or neck: *a baluster goblet stem.* [C17: from French *balustre,* from Italian *balaustro* pillar resembling a pomegranate flower, ultimately from Greek *balaustion*]

balustrade ('bæləˌstreɪd) *n* an ornamental rail or coping with its supporting set of balusters. [C17: from French, from *balustre* BALUSTER]

Balzac ('bælzæk; *French* balzak) *n* **Honoré de** (ɔnɔre də). 1799–1850, French novelist: author of a collection of novels under the general title *La Comédie humaine,* including *Eugénie Grandet* (1833), *Le Père Goriot* (1834), and *La Cousine Bette* (1846).

Bamako (ˌbæmə'kəu) *n* the capital of Mali, in the south, on the River Niger. Pop.: 800 000 (1995 est.).

Bambara (bɑːm'bɑːrə) *n* **1** (*pl* **-ra** *or* **-ras**) a member of a Negroid people of W Africa living chiefly in Mali and by the headwaters of the River Niger in Guinea. **2** the language of this people, belonging to the Mande branch of the Niger-Congo family.

Bamberg ('bæmbɜːg; *German* 'bambɛrk) *n* a town in S Germany, in N Bavaria: seat of independent prince-bishops of the Holy Roman Empire (1007–1802). Pop.: 70 690 (1991).

bambino (bæm'biːnəu) *n, pl* **-nos** *or* **-ni** (-niː). **1** *Informal.* a young child, esp. an Italian one. **2** a representation of the infant Jesus. [C18: from Italian]

bamboo (bæm'buː) *n* **1** any tall treelike tropical or semitropical fast-growing grass of the genus *Bambusa,* having hollow woody-walled stems with ringed joints and edible young shoots (**bamboo shoots**). **2** the stem of any of these plants, used for building, poles, and furniture. **3** any of various bamboo-like grasses of the genera *Arundinaria, Phyllostachys,* or *Dendrocalamus.* **4** (*modifier*) made of bamboo: *a bamboo fence.* [C16: probably from Malay *bambu*]

bamboo curtain *n* (esp. in the 1950s and 1960s) the political and military barrier to communications around the People's Republic of China.

bamboozle (bæm'buːzᵊl) *vb* (*tr*) *Informal.* **1** to cheat; mislead. **2** to confuse. [C18: of unknown origin] ▸ **bam'boozler** *n* ▸ **bam'boozlement** *n*

ban[1] (bæn) *vb* **bans, banning, banned. 1** (*tr*) to prohibit, esp. officially, from action, display, entrance, sale, etc.; forbid: *to ban a book; to ban smoking.* **2** (*tr*) (in South Africa) to place (a person suspected of illegal political activity) under a government order restricting his movement and his contact with other people. **3** *Archaic.* to curse. ◆ *n* **4** an official prohibition or interdiction. **5** *Law.* an official proclamation or public notice, esp. of prohibition. **6** a public proclamation or edict, esp. of outlawry. **7** *Archaic.* public censure or condemnation. **8** *Archaic.* a curse; imprecation. [Old English *bannan* to proclaim; compare Old Norse *banna* to forbid, Old High German *bannan* to command]

ban[2] (bæn) *n* (in feudal England) the summoning of vassals to perform their military obligations. [C13: from Old French *ban,* of Germanic origin; related to Old High German *ban* command, Old Norse *bann* BAN[1]]

ban[3] (bæn) *n, pl* **bani** ('bɑːnɪ). a monetary unit of Romania and Moldova worth one hundredth of a leu. [from Romanian, from Serbo-Croat *bān* lord]

Banaba (bə'nɑːbə) *n* an island in the SW Pacific, in the Republic of Kiribati. Phosphates were mined by Britain (1900–79). Area: about 5 sq. km (2 sq. miles). Pop.: 284 (1990). Also called: **Ocean Island.** ▸ **Ba'naban** *adj, n*

banak ('bænək) *n* **1** a tree of the genus *Virola,* of Central America: family *Myristicaceae.* **2** the timber of this tree, used esp. in Honduras for turning and construction. [C20: Honduran name]

banal (bə'nɑːl) *adj* lacking force or originality; trite; commonplace. [C18: from Old French: relating to compulsory feudal service, hence common to all, commonplace, from *ban* BAN[2]] ▸ **banality** (bə'nælɪtɪ) *n* ▸ **ba'nally** *adv*

banana (bə'nɑːnə) *n* **1** any of several tropical and subtropical herbaceous treelike plants of the musaceous genus *Musa,* esp. *M. sapientum,* a widely cultivated species propagated from suckers and having hanging clusters of edible fruit. **2** the crescent-shaped fruit of any of these plants. ◆ Compare **plantain**[2]. [C16: from Spanish or Portuguese, of African origin]

banana belt *n Canadian informal.* a region with a warm climate, esp. one in Canada.

Banana bender *n Austral. slang, offensive.* a native or inhabitant of Queensland. Also called: **Bananalander** (bə'nɑːnəˌlændə).

banana oil *n* **1** a solution of cellulose nitrate in pentyl acetate or a similar solvent, which has a banana-like smell. **2** a nontechnical name for **pentyl acetate.**

banana plug *n Electrical engineering.* a small single-conductor electrical plug having a curved metal spring along its shank used to hold it in its socket.

banana republic *n Informal and derogatory.* a small country, esp. in Central America, that is politically unstable and has an economy dominated by foreign interest, usually dependent on one export, such as bananas.

bananas (bə'nɑːnəz) *adj Slang.* crazy (esp. in the phrase **go bananas**).

banana skin *n* **1** the soft outer covering of a banana. **2** *Informal.* something unforeseen that causes an obvious and embarrassing mistake. [sense 2 from the common slapstick joke of a person slipping after treading on a banana skin]

banana split *n* a dish of ice cream and banana cut in half lengthwise, usually topped with syrup, nuts, whipped cream, etc.

Banaras (bə'nɑːrəz) *n* a variant spelling of **Benares.**

Banat ('bænɪt, 'bɑːnɪt) *n* a fertile plain extending through Hungary, Romania, and Yugoslavia.

banausic (bə'nɔːsɪk) *adj* merely mechanical; materialistic; utilitarian. [C19: from Greek *banausikos* for mechanics, from *baunos* forge]

Banbridge ('bænbrɪdʒ) *n* a district in S Northern Ireland, in Co. Down. Pop.: 33 800 (1992). Area: 442 sq. km (170 sq. miles).

Banbury ('bænbərɪ) *n* a town in central England, in N Oxfordshire: telecommunications, financial services. Pop.: 39 906 (1991).

Banbury cake *n Brit.* a cake consisting of a pastry base filled with currants, raisins, candied peel, and sugar, with a criss-cross pattern on the top.

banc (bæŋk) *n* **in banc.** *Law.* sitting as a full court. [C18: from Anglo-French: bench]

banco ('bæŋkəu) *interj* a call in gambling games such as chemin de fer and baccarat by a player or bystander who wishes to bet against the entire bank. [C18: from French from Italian: bank]

band[1] (bænd) *n* **1** a company of people having a common purpose; group: *a band of outlaws.* **2** a group of musicians playing either brass and percussion instruments only (**brass band**) or brass, woodwind, and percussion instruments (**concert band** or **military band**). **3** a group of musicians who play popular music, jazz, etc., often for dancing. **4** a group of instrumentalists generally; orchestra. **5** *Canadian.* a formally recognized group of Indians on a reserve. **6** *Anthropol.* a division of a tribe; a family group or camp group. **7** *U.S. and Ca-*

nadian. a flock or herd. ◆ *vb* **8** (usually foll. by *together*) to unite; assemble. [C15: from French *bande,* probably from Old Provençal *banda,* of Germanic origin; compare Gothic *bandwa* sign, BANNER]

band[2] (bænd) *n* **1** a thin flat strip of some material, used esp. to encircle objects and hold them together: *a rubber band.* **2a** a strip of fabric or other material used as an ornament, distinguishing mark, or to reinforce clothing. **2b** (*in combination*): *waistband; hairband; hatband.* **3** a stripe of contrasting colour or texture. See also **chromosome band.** **4** a driving belt in machinery. **5** a range of values that are close or related in number, degree, or quality. **6a** *Physics.* a range of frequencies or wavelengths between two limits. **6b** *Radio.* such a range allocated to a particular broadcasting station or service. **7** short for **energy band.** **8** *Computing.* one or more tracks on a magnetic disk or drum. **9** *Anatomy.* any structure resembling a ribbon or cord that connects, encircles, or binds different parts. **10** the cords to which the folded sheets of a book are sewn. **11** a thin layer or seam of ore. **12** *Architect.* a strip of flat panelling, such as a fascia or plinth, usually attached to a wall. **13** a large white collar, sometimes edged with lace, worn in the 17th century. **14** either of a pair of hanging extensions of the collar, forming part of academic, legal, or (formerly) clerical dress. **15** a ring for the finger (esp. in phrases such as **wedding band, band of gold,** etc.). ◆ *vb* (*tr*) **16** to fasten or mark with a band. **17** *U.S. and Canadian.* to ring (birds). See **ring**[1] (sense 22). [C15: from Old French *bende,* of Germanic origin; compare Old High German *binda* fillet; see BAND[3]]

band[3] (bænd) *n* an archaic word for **bond** (senses 1, 3, 4). [C13: from Old Norse *band;* related to Old High German *bant* fetter; see BEND[1], BOND]

Banda (ˈbændə) *n* **Hastings Kamuzu** (kæˈmuːzuː). 1906–97, Malawi statesman. As first prime minister of Nyasaland (from 1963), he led his country to independence (1964) as Malawi: president (1966–94).

bandage (ˈbændɪdʒ) *n* **1** a piece of material used to dress a wound, bind a broken limb, etc. **2** a strip of any soft material used for binding, etc. ◆ *vb* **3** to cover or bind with a bandage. [C16: from French, from *bande* strip, BAND[2]]

bandanna *or* **bandana** (bænˈdænə) *n* a large silk or cotton handkerchief or neckerchief. [C18: from Hindi *bāndhnū* tie-dyeing, from *bāndhnā* to tie, from Sanskrit *bandhnāti* he ties]

Bandaranaike (ˌbændərəˈnaɪkə) *n* **1 Chandrika**. See Chandrika **Kumaratunga. 2** Mrs **Sirimavo** (ˌsɪrɪˈmɑːvəʊ). born 1916, prime minister of Sri Lanka, formerly Ceylon (1960–65; 1970–77; 1994–). **3** her husband, **Solomon.** 1899–1959, prime minister of Ceylon (1956–59); assassinated.

Bandar Seri Begawan (ˈbɑːndɑː ˈsɛrɪ bəˈgɑːwən) *n* the capital of Brunei. Pop.: 21 484 (1991). Former name: **Brunei.**

Banda Sea *n* a part of the Pacific in Indonesia, between Sulawesi and New Guinea.

B & B *abbrev. for* bed and breakfast.

bandbox (ˈbændˌbɒks) *n* a lightweight usually cylindrical box used for holding small articles, esp. hats.

bandeau (ˈbændəʊ) *n, pl* **-deaux** (-dəʊz). a narrow band of ribbon, velvet, etc., worn round the head. [C18: from French, from Old French *bandel* a little BAND[2]]

banderilla (ˌbændəˈriːə, -ˈriːljə) *n Bullfighting.* a decorated barbed dart, thrust into the bull's neck or shoulder. [Spanish, literally: a little banner, from *bandera* BANNER]

banderillero (ˌbændəriːˈɛərəʊ, -riːˈljɛərəʊ) *n, pl* **-ros.** a bullfighter's assistant who sticks banderillas into the bull.

banderole, banderol (ˈbændəˌrəʊl), *or* **bannerol** *n* **1** a long narrow flag, usually with forked ends, esp. one attached to the masthead of a ship; pennant. **2** a square flag draped over a tomb or carried at a funeral. **3** a ribbon-like scroll or sculptured band bearing an inscription, found esp. in Renaissance architecture. **4** a streamer on a knight's lance. [C16: from Old French, from Italian *banderuola,* literally: a little banner, from *bandiera* BANNER]

band-gala (ˈbʌndgəlɑː) *adj* (in India) (of a coat) closed at the neck. [from Hindi]

bandh *or* **bundh** (bʌnd) *n* (in India) a general strike. [Hindi, literally: a tying up]

bandicoot (ˈbændɪˌkuːt) *n* **1** any agile terrestrial marsupial of the family *Peramelidae* of Australia and New Guinea. They have a long pointed muzzle and a long tail and feed mainly on small invertebrates. **2 bandicoot rat.** Also called: **mole rat.** any of three burrowing rats of the genera *Bandicota* and *Nesokia,* of S and SE Asia: family *Muridae.* [C18: from Telugu *pandikokku,* from *pandi* pig + *kokku* bandicoot]

banding (ˈbændɪŋ) *n Brit.* the practice of grouping schoolchildren according to ability to ensure a balanced intake at different levels of ability to secondary school.

bandit (ˈbændɪt) *n, pl* **-dits** *or* **-ditti** (-ˈdɪtɪ). a robber, esp. a member of an armed gang; brigand. [C16: from Italian *bandito,* literally: banished man, from *bandire* to proscribe, from *bando* edict, BAN[1]] ▸ **ˈbanditry** *n*

Bandjarmasin *or* **Bandjermasin** (ˌbændʒəˈmɑːsɪn) *n* variant spellings of **Banjarmasin.**

bandmaster (ˈbændˌmɑːstə) *n* the conductor of a band.

bandobust *or* **bundobust** (ˈbʌndəʊbəst) *n* (in India and Pakistan) an arrangement. [Hindi *band-o-bast* tying and binding, from Persian]

Band of Hope *n* a society promoting lifelong abstention from alcohol among young people: founded in Britain in 1847.

bandolier *or* **bandoleer** (ˌbændəˈlɪə) *n* a soldier's broad shoulder belt having small pockets or loops for cartridges. [C16: from Old French *bandouliere,* from Old Spanish *bandolera, bandolero* guerrilla, from Catalan *bandoler,* from *bandol* band, from Spanish *bando;* see BAND[1]]

bandoline (ˈbændəˌliːn) *n* a glutinous hair dressing, used (esp. formerly) to keep the hair in place. [C19: *bando-,* from French BANDEAU + *-line,* from Latin *linere* to smear]

bandore (bænˈdɔː, ˈbændɔː) *n* a 16th-century plucked musical instrument resembling a lute but larger and fitted with seven pairs of metal strings. Also called: **pandore, pandora.** [C16: from Spanish *bandurria,* from Late Latin *pandūra* three-stringed instrument, from Greek *pandoura*]

band-pass filter *n* **1** *Electronics.* a filter that transmits only those currents having a frequency lying within specified limits. Compare **high-pass filter, low-pass filter. 2** an optical device, consisting of absorbing filters, for transmitting electromagnetic waves of predetermined wavelengths.

band saw *n* a power-operated saw consisting of an endless toothed metal band running over and driven by two wheels.

bandsman (ˈbændzmən) *n, pl* **-men.** a player in a musical band, esp. a brass or military band.

band spectrum *n* a spectrum consisting of a number of bands of closely spaced lines that are associated with emission or absorption of radiation by molecules.

bandspreading (ˈbændˌsprɛdɪŋ) *n* an additional tuning control in some radio receivers whereby a selected narrow band of frequencies can be spread over a wider frequency band, in order to give finer control of tuning.

bandstand (ˈbændˌstænd) *n* a platform for a band, usually out of doors and roofed.

band theory *n Physics.* a theory of the electrical properties of metals, semiconductors, and insulators based on energy bands.

Bandung (ˈbændʊŋ) *n* a city in Indonesia, in SW Java. Pop.: 2 026 893 (1990).

B & W *abbrev. for* black and white.

bandwagon (ˈbændˌwægən) *n* **1** *U.S.* a wagon, usually high and brightly coloured, for carrying the band in a parade. **2 jump, climb,** *or* **get on the bandwagon.** to join or give support to a party or movement that seems to be assured of success.

bandwidth (ˈbændˌwɪdθ) *n* **1** the range of frequencies within a given waveband used for a particular radio transmission. **2** the range of frequencies over which a receiver or amplifier should not differ appreciably from its maximum value. **3** the range of frequencies used in a specific telecommunications signal.

bandy (ˈbændɪ) *adj* **-dier, -diest. 1** Also: **bandy-legged.** having legs curved outwards at the knees. **2** (of legs) curved outwards at the knees. **3 knock (someone) bandy.** *Austral. informal.* to amaze or astound. ◆ *vb* **-dies, -dying, -died.** (*tr*) **4** to exchange (words) in a heated or hostile manner. **5** to give and receive (blows). **6** (often foll. by *about*) to circulate (a name, rumour, etc.). **7** to throw or strike to and fro; toss about. ◆ *n, pl* **-dies. 8** an early form of hockey, often played on ice. **9** a stick, curved at one end, used in the game of bandy. **10** an old form of tennis. [C16: probably from Old French *bander* to hit the ball back and forth at tennis]

bandy-bandy (ˈbændɪˈbændɪ) *n, pl* **-bandies.** a small Australian elapid snake, *Vermicella annulata,* ringed with black and yellow.

bandy legs *pl n* another term for **bow legs.**

bane[1] (beɪn) *n* **1** a person or thing that causes misery or distress (esp. in the phrase **bane of one's life**). **2** something that causes death or destruction. **3a** a fatal poison. **3b** (*in combination*): *ratsbane.* **4** *Archaic.* ruin or distress. [Old English *bana;* related to Old Norse *bani* death, Old High German *bano* destruction, death]

bane[2] (ben, beɪn) *n* a Scot. word for **bone.**

baneberry (ˈbeɪnbərɪ) *n, pl* **-ries. 1** Also called: **herb Christopher** (Brit.), **cohosh** (U.S.). any ranunculaceous plant of the genus *Actaea,* esp. *A. spicata,* which has small white flowers and red or white poisonous berries. **2** a berry of any of these plants.

baneful (ˈbeɪnfʊl) *adj Archaic.* destructive, poisonous, or fatal. ▸ **ˈbanefully** *adv* ▸ **ˈbanefulness** *n*

Banff (bæmf) *n* **1** a town in NE Scotland, in Aberdeenshire. Pop.: 6230 (1991). **2** a town in Canada, in SW Alberta, in the Rocky Mountains: surrounded by **Banff National Park.** Pop.: 5700 (1991).

Banffshire (ˈbæmfˌʃɪə, -ʃə) *n* (until 1975) a county of NE Scotland: formerly (1975–96) part of Grampian region, now part of Aberdeenshire.

bang[1] (bæŋ) *n* **1** a short loud explosive noise, as of the bursting of a balloon or the report of a gun. **2** a hard blow or knock, esp. a noisy one; thump: *he gave the ball a bang.* **3** *Informal.* a startling or sudden effect: *he realized with a bang that he was late.* **4** *Slang.* an injection of heroin or other narcotic. **5** *Taboo slang.* an act of sexual intercourse. **6 get a bang out of.** *U.S. and Canadian slang.* to experience a thrill or excitement from. **7 with a bang.** successfully: *the party went with a bang.* ◆ *vb* **8** to hit or knock, esp. with a loud noise; bump: *to bang one's head.* **9** to move noisily or clumsily: *to bang about the house.* **10** to close (a door, window, etc.) or (of a door, etc.) be closed noisily; slam. **11** (*tr*) to cause to move by hitting vigorously: *he banged the ball over the fence.* **12** to make or cause to make a loud noise, as of an explosion. **13** (*tr*) *Brit.* **13a** to cause (stock prices) to fall by rapid selling. **13b** to sell rapidly in (a stock market), thus causing prices to fall. **14** *Taboo slang.* to have sexual intercourse with. **15** (*intr*) *Slang.* to inject heroin, etc. **16 bang goes.** *Informal.* that is the end of: *bang goes my job in Wapping.* **17 bang one's head against a brick wall.** to try to achieve something impossible. ◆ *adv* **18** with a sudden impact or effect: *bang went his hopes of winning; the car drove bang into a lamp-post.* **19** precisely: *bang in the middle of the road.* **20 bang to rights.** *Slang.* caught red-handed. **21 go bang.** to burst, shut, etc., with a loud noise. ◆ See also **bang up.** [C16: from Old Norse *bang, banga* hammer; related to Low German *bangen* to beat; all of imitative origin]

bang[2] (bæŋ) *n* **1** a fringe or section of hair cut straight across the forehead. ◆ *vb* (*tr*) **2** to cut (the hair) in such a style. **3** to dock (the tail of a horse, etc.). [C19: probably short for *bangtail* short tail]

bang[3] (bæŋ) *n* a variant spelling of **bhang.**

Bangalore (ˌbæŋgəˈlɔː) *n* a city in S India, capital of Karnataka state: printing, textiles, pharmaceuticals. Pop.: 2 660 088 (1991).

bangalore torpedo *n* an explosive device in a long metal tube, used to blow gaps in barbed-wire barriers. [C20: named after BANGALORE, where it was used]

banger ('bæŋə) *n Brit.* **1** *Slang.* a sausage. **2** *Informal.* **2a** an old decrepit car. **2b** (*as modifier*): *banger racing.* **3** a type of firework that explodes loudly.

Bangka *or* **Banka** ('bæŋkə) *n* an island in Indonesia, separated from Sumatra by the **Bangka Strait.** Chief town: Pangkalpinang. Area: about 11 914 sq. km (4600 sq. miles).

Bangkok ('bæŋkɒk, bæŋ'kɒk) *n* the capital and chief port of Thailand, on the Chao Phraya River: became a royal city and the capital in 1782. Pop.: 5 584 228 (1993 est.). Thai name: **Krung Thep** ('krʊŋ 'teɪp).

Bangla ('bæŋlə) *n* another name for **Bengali** (sense 2).

Bangladesh (ˌbɑːŋglə'deʃ, ˌbæŋ-) *n* a republic in S Asia: formerly the Eastern Province of Pakistan; became independent in 1971 after civil war and the defeat of Pakistan by India; consists of the plains and vast deltas of the Ganges and Brahmaputra Rivers; prone to flooding: economy based on jute and jute products (over 80 per cent of world production); a member of the Commonwealth. Language: Bengali. Religion: Muslim. Currency: taka. Capital: Dhaka. Pop.: 127 567 000 (1998 est.). Area: 142 797 sq. km (55 126 sq. miles). ► ˌ**Bangla'deshi** *adj, n*

bangle ('bæŋgᵊl) *n* **1** a bracelet, usually without a clasp, often worn high up round the arm or sometimes round the ankle. **2** a disc or charm hanging from a bracelet, necklace, etc. [C19: from Hindi *bangrī*]

bang on *adj, adv Brit. informal.* **1** with absolute accuracy. **2** excellent or excellently. ◆ Also (U.S.): **bang up.**

Bangor ('bæŋgɔː, -gə) *n* **1** a university town in NW Wales, in Gwynedd, on the Menai Strait. Pop.: 12 330 (1991). **2** a town in SE Northern Ireland, in North Down district, Co. Down, on Belfast Lough. Pop.: 52 437 (1991).

bangtail ('bæŋˌteɪl) *n* **1** a horse's tail cut straight across but not through the bone. **2** a horse with a tail cut in this way. [C19: from *bangtail* short tail]

bangtail muster *n Austral. history.* a roundup of cattle to be counted, each one having the hairs on its tail docked as it is counted.

Bangui (*French* bɑ̃gi) *n* the capital of the Central African Republic, in the south part, on the Ubangi River. Pop.: 553 000 (1995 est.).

bang up *vb* (*tr, adv*) *Prison slang.* to lock up (a prisoner) in his cell, esp. for the night.

Bangweulu (ˌbæŋwɪ'uːluː) *n* **Lake.** a shallow lake in NE Zambia, discovered by David Livingstone, who died there in 1873. Area: about 9850 sq. km (3800 sq. miles), including swamps.

bani ('bɑːnɪ) *n* the plural of **ban**³.

banian ('bænjən) *n* a variant spelling of **banyan.**

banish ('bænɪʃ) *vb* (*tr*) **1** to expel from a place, esp. by an official decree as a punishment. **2** to drive away: *to banish gloom.* [C14: from Old French *banir,* of Germanic origin; compare Old High German *ban* BAN²] ► '**banishment** *n*

banisters *or* **bannisters** ('bænɪstəz) *pl n* the railing and supporting balusters on a staircase; balustrade. [C17: altered from BALUSTER]

Banja Luka (*Serbo-Croat* 'baːnja: ˌluːka) *n* a city in NW Bosnia-Herzegovina, on the Vrbas River: scene of battles between the Austrians and Turks in 1527, 1688, and 1737; besieged by Serb forces (1992–95). Pop.: 195 139 (1991).

Banjarmasin, Banjermasin, Bandjarmasin *or* **Bandjermasin** (ˌbændʒə'mɑːsɪn) *n* a port in Indonesia, in SW Borneo. Pop.: 534 600 (1995 est.).

banjo ('bændʒəʊ) *n, pl* **-jos** *or* **-joes. 1** a stringed musical instrument with a long neck (usually fretted) and a circular drumlike body overlaid with parchment, plucked with the fingers or a plectrum. **2** *Slang.* any banjo-shaped object, esp. a frying pan. **3** *Austral. and N.Z. slang.* a long-handled shovel with a wide blade. **4** (*modifier*) banjo-shaped: *a banjo clock.* [C18: variant (U.S. Southern pronunciation) of BANDORE] ► '**banjoist** *n*

Banjul (bæn'dʒuːl) *n* the capital of The Gambia, a port at the mouth of the Gambia River. Pop.: 42 407 (1993). Former name (until 1973): **Bathurst.**

bank¹ (bæŋk) *n* **1** an institution offering certain financial services, such as the safekeeping of money, conversion of domestic into and from foreign currencies, lending of money at interest, and acceptance of bills of exchange. **2** the building used by such an institution. **3** a small container used at home for keeping money. **4** the funds held by a gaming house or a banker or dealer in some gambling games. **5** (in various games) **5a** the stock, as of money, pieces, tokens, etc., on which players may draw. **5b** the player holding this stock. **6** any supply, store, or reserve, for future use: *a data bank; a blood bank.* ◆ *vb* **7** (*tr*) to deposit (cash, cheques, etc.) in a bank. **8** (*intr*) to transact business with a bank. **9** (*intr*) to engage in the business of banking. **10** (*intr*) to hold the bank in some gambling games. ◆ See also **bank on.** [C15: probably from Italian *banca* bench, moneychanger's table, of Germanic origin; compare Old High German *banc* BENCH]

bank² (bæŋk) *n* **1** a long raised mass, esp. of earth; mound; ridge. **2** a slope, as of a hill. **3** the sloping side of any hollow in the ground, esp. when bordering a river: *the left bank of a river is on a spectator's left looking downstream.* **4a** an elevated section, rising to near the surface, of the bed of a sea, lake, or river. **4b** (*in combination*): *sandbank; mudbank.* **5a** the area around the mouth of the shaft of a mine. **5b** the face of a body of ore. **6** the lateral inclination of an aircraft about its longitudinal axis during a turn. **7** Also called: **banking, camber, cant, superelevation.** a bend on a road or on a railway, athletics, cycling, or other track having the outside built higher than the inside in order to reduce the effects of centrifugal force on vehicles, runners, etc., rounding it at speed. **8** the cushion of a billiard table. ◆ *vb* **9** (when *tr,* often foll. by *up*) to form into a bank or mound. **10** (*tr*) to border or enclose (a road, etc.) with a bank. **11** (*tr; sometimes foll. by up*) to cover (a fire) with ashes, fresh fuel, etc., so that it will burn slowly. **12** to cause (an aircraft) to tip laterally about its longitudinal axis or (of an aircraft) to tip in this way, esp. while turning. **13** to travel round a bank, esp. at high speed. **14** (*tr*) *Billiards.* to drive (a ball) into the cushion. [C12: of Scandinavian origin; compare Old Icelandic *bakki* hill, Old Danish *banke,* Swedish *backe*]

bank³ (bæŋk) *n* **1** an arrangement of objects, esp. similar objects, in a row or in tiers: *a bank of dials.* **2a** a tier of oars in a galley. **2b** a bench for the rowers in a galley. **3** a grade of lightweight writing and printing paper used for airmail letters, etc. **4** *Telephony.* (in automatic switching) an assembly of fixed electrical contacts forming a rigid unit in a selector or similar device. ◆ *vb* **5** (*tr*) to arrange in a bank. [C17: from Old French *banc* bench, of Germanic origin; see BANK¹]

Banka ('bæŋkə) *n* a variant spelling of **Bangka.**

bankable ('bæŋkəbᵊl) *adj* **1** appropriate for receipt by a bank. **2** dependable or reliable: *a bankable promise.* **3** (esp. of a star) likely to ensure the financial success of a film. ► ˌ**banka'bility** *n*

bank acceptance *n* a bill of exchange or draft drawn on and endorsed by a bank. Also called: **banker's acceptance.**

bank account *n* **1** an account created by the deposit of money at a bank by a customer. **2** the amount of money credited to a depositor at a bank.

bank annuities *pl n* another term for **consols.**

bank bill *n* **1** Also called: **bank draft.** a bill of exchange drawn by one bank on another. **2** Also called: **banker's bill.** *U.S.* a banknote.

bankbook ('bæŋkˌbʊk) *n* a book held by depositors at certain banks, in which the bank enters a record of deposits, withdrawals, and earned interest. Also called: **passbook.**

bank clerk *n Brit.* an employee of a bank.

bank discount *n* interest on a loan deducted from the principal amount when the loan is made and based on the loan's face value.

bank draft *n* a cheque drawn by a bank on itself, which is bought by a person to pay a supplier unwilling to accept a normal cheque. Also called: **banker's cheque.**

banker¹ ('bæŋkə) *n* **1** a person who owns or is an executive in a bank. **2** an official or player in charge of the bank in any of various games, esp. gambling games. **3** a result that has been forecast identically in a series of entries on a football pool coupon.

banker² ('bæŋkə) *n* **1** a fishing vessel of Newfoundland. **2** a fisherman in such a vessel. **3** *Austral. and N.Z. informal.* a stream almost overflowing its banks (esp. in the phrase **run a banker**). **4** Also called: **bank engine.** *Brit.* a locomotive that is used to help a heavy train up a steep gradient.

banker³ ('bæŋkə) *n* **1** a craftsman's workbench. **2** a timber board used as a base for mixing building materials.

banker's order *n* another name for **standing order** (sense 1).

banket ('bæŋkɪt) *n* a gold-bearing conglomerate found in South Africa. [C19: from Dutch: a kind of almond hardbake, alluding to its appearance]

Bank Giro *n* a British giro system operated by clearing banks to enable customers to pay sums of money to others by credit transfer.

Bankhead ('bæŋkˌhɛd) *n* **Tallulah** (**Brockman**). 1902–68, U.S. stage and film actress; her successes included the plays *The Little Foxes* (1939) and *The Skin of Our Teeth* (1942).

bank holiday *n* (in Britain) any of several weekdays on which banks are closed by law and which are observed as national holidays.

banking¹ ('bæŋkɪŋ) *n* the business engaged in by a bank.

banking² ('bæŋkɪŋ) *n* **1** an embankment of a river. **2** another word for **bank**² (sense 7). **3** fishing on a sea bank, esp. off the coast of Newfoundland. **4** the manoeuvre causing an aircraft to bank.

bank manager *n* a person who directs the business of a local branch of a bank.

banknote ('bæŋkˌnəʊt) *n* a promissory note issued by a central bank, serving as money.

Bank of England *n* the central bank of the United Kingdom, which acts as banker to the government and the commercial banks. It is responsible for managing the government's debt and implementing its policy on other monetary matters: established in 1694, nationalized in 1946; in 1997 the government restored the authority to set interest rates to the Bank.

bank on *vb* (*intr, prep*) to expect or rely with confidence on: *you can bank on him always arriving on time.*

bankroll ('bæŋkˌrəʊl) *Chiefly U.S. and Canadian.* ◆ *n* **1** a roll of currency notes. **2** the financial resources of a person, organization, etc. ◆ *vb* **3** (*tr*) *Slang.* to provide the capital for; finance.

bankrupt ('bæŋkrʌpt, -rəpt) *n* **1** a person adjudged insolvent by a court, his property being transferred to a trustee and administered for the benefit of his creditors. **2** any person unable to discharge all his debts. **3** a person whose resources in a certain field are exhausted or nonexistent: *a spiritual bankrupt.* ◆ *adj* **4** adjudged insolvent. **5** financially ruined. **6** depleted in resources or having completely failed: *spiritually bankrupt.* **7** (foll. by *of*) *Brit.* lacking: *bankrupt of intelligence.* ◆ *vb* **8** (*tr*) to make bankrupt. [C16: from Old French *banqueroute,* from Old Italian *bancarotta,* from *banca* BANK¹ + *rotta* broken, from Latin *ruptus,* from *rumpere* to break]

bankruptcy ('bæŋkrʌptsɪ, -rəptsɪ) *n, pl* **-cies.** the state, condition, or quality of being or becoming bankrupt.

Banks (bæŋks) *n* Sir **Joseph.** 1743–1820, British botanist and explorer: circumnavigated the world with James Cook (1768–71).

banksia ('bæŋksɪə) *n* any shrub or tree of the Australian genus *Banksia,* having long leathery evergreen leaves and dense cylindrical heads of flowers that are often yellowish: family *Proteaceae.* See also **honeysuckle** (sense 3). [C19: New Latin, named after Sir Joseph BANKS]

Banks Island *n* **1** an island of N Canada, in the Northwest Territories: the westernmost island of the Arctic Archipelago. Area: about 67 340 sq. km (26 000 sq. miles). **2** an island of W Canada, off British Columbia. Length: about 72 km (45 miles).

banksman ('bæŋksmən) *n* a crane driver's helper, who signals instructions to the driver for the movement of the crane and its jib.
bank statement *n* a statement of transactions in a bank account, esp. one of a series sent at regular intervals to the depositor.
banlieue *French.* (bɑ̃ljø) *n* a suburb of a city.
banner ('bænə) *n* **1** a long strip of flexible material displaying a slogan, advertisement, etc., esp. one suspended between two points. **2** a placard or sign carried in a procession or demonstration. **3** something that represents a belief or principle: *a commitment to nationalization is the banner of British socialism.* **4** the flag of a nation, army, etc., used as a standard or ensign. **5** (formerly) the standard of an emperor, knight, etc. **6** Also called: **banner headline.** a large headline in a newspaper, etc., extending across the page, esp. the front page. **7** a square flag, often charged with the arms of its bearer. ◆ *adj* **8** *U.S.* outstandingly successful: *a banner year for orders.* [C13: from Old French *baniere,* of Germanic origin; compare Gothic *bandwa* sign; influenced by Medieval Latin *bannum* BAN[1], *bannīre* to BANISH] ▸ **'bannered** *adj*
banneret ('bænərɪt, -ə,rɛt) *n* (in the Middle Ages) **1** Also called: **knight banneret.** a knight who was entitled to command other knights and men-at-arms under his own banner. **2** a title of knighthood conferred by the king for valour on the battlefield. [C14: from Old French *banerete* a small BANNER]
bannerette *or* **banneret** (,bænə'rɛt) *n* a small banner. [C13: from Old French *baneret,* from *banere* BANNER]
bannerol ('bænə,rəʊl) *n* a variant of **banderole.**
Bannister ('bænɪstə) *n* Sir **Roger** (**Gilbert**). born 1929, British athlete and doctor: first man to run a mile in under four minutes (1954).
bannisters ('bænɪstəz) *pl n* a variant spelling of **banisters.**
bannock ('bænək) *n* a round flat unsweetened cake originating in Scotland, made from oatmeal or barley and baked on a griddle. [Old English *bannuc;* of Celtic origin; compare Gaelic *bannach,* Cornish *banna* a drop, bit; perhaps related to Latin *pānicium,* from *pānis* bread]
Bannockburn ('bænək,bɜːn) *n* a village in central Scotland, south of Stirling: nearby is the site of a victory (1314) of the Scots, led by Robert the Bruce, over the English. Pop.: 2675 (1991).
banns *or* **bans** (bænz) *pl n* **1** the public declaration of an intended marriage, usually formally announced on three successive Sundays in the parish churches of both the betrothed. **2 forbid the banns.** to raise an objection to a marriage announced in this way. [C14: plural of *bann* proclamation; see BAN[1]]
banquet ('bæŋkwɪt) *n* **1** a lavish and sumptuous meal; feast. **2** a ceremonial meal for many people, often followed by speeches. ◆ *vb* **-quets, -queting, -queted. 3** (*intr*) to hold or take part in a banquet. **4** (*tr*) to entertain or honour (a person) with a banquet. [C15: from Old French, from Italian *banchetto,* from *banco* a table, of Germanic origin; see BANK[1]] ▸ **'banqueter** *n*
banquette (bæŋ'kɛt) *n* **1** an upholstered bench. **2** (formerly) a raised part behind a parapet. **3** a footbridge. [C17: from French, from Provençal *banqueta,* literally: a little bench, from *banc* bench; see BANK[3]]
bans (bænz) *pl n* a variant spelling of **banns.**
bansela (ban'sɛlə) *n* a variant of **bonsela.**
banshee ('bænʃiː, bæn'ʃiː) *n* (in Irish folklore) a female spirit whose wailing warns of impending death. [C18: from Irish Gaelic *bean sídhe,* literally: woman of the fairy mound]
Banstead ('bæn,stɛd) *n* a town in S England, in NE Surrey: a dormitory town for London. Pop.: 37 245 (1991).
bant (bænt) *n Lancashire dialect.* string. [probably a dialect pronunciation of BAND[2]]
bantam ('bæntəm) *n* **1** any of various very small breeds of domestic fowl. **2** a small but aggressive person. **3** *Boxing.* short for **bantamweight.** [C18: after *Bantam,* village in Java, said to be the original home of this fowl]
bantamweight ('bæntəm,weɪt) *n* **1a** a professional boxer weighing 112–118 pounds (51–53.5 kg). **1b** an amateur boxer weighing 51–54 kg (112–119 pounds). **1c** (*as modifier*): *the bantamweight champion.* **2** a wrestler in a similar weight category (usually 115–126 pounds (52–57 kg)).
banter ('bæntə) *vb* **1** to speak to or tease lightly or jokingly. ◆ *n* **2** light, teasing, or joking language or repartee. [C17: of unknown origin] ▸ **'banterer** *n*
banting ('bæntɪŋ) *n Obsolete.* slimming by avoiding eating sugar, starch, and fat. [C19: named after William *Banting* (1797–1878), London undertaker who popularized this diet]
Banting ('bæntɪŋ) *n* Sir **Frederick Grant.** 1891–1941, Canadian physiologist: discovered the insulin treatment for diabetes with Best and Macleod (1922) and shared the Nobel prize for physiology or medicine with Macleod (1923).
bantling ('bæntlɪŋ) *n Archaic, disparaging.* a young child; brat. [C16: perhaps from German *Bänkling* illegitimate child, from *Bank* bench + -LING[1]]
Bantock ('bæntɒk) *n* Sir **Granville.** 1868–1946, British composer. His works include the *Hebridean Symphony* (1915), five ballets, and three operas.
Bantoid ('bɑːntɔɪd, 'bæn-) *adj* denoting or relating to languages, esp. in Cameroon and Nigeria, that possess certain Bantu characteristics. See also **Semi-Bantu.**
Bantu ('bɑːntʊ, 'bæntuː, bæn'tuː) *n* **1** a group of languages of Africa, including most of the principal languages spoken from the equator to the Cape of Good Hope, but excluding the Khoisan family: now generally regarded as part of the Benue-Congo branch of the Niger-Congo family. **2** (*pl* **-tu** *or* **-tus**) a member of any of the indigenous Negroid peoples who inhabit southern, eastern, and central Africa and speak any of these languages. ◆ *adj* **3** denoting, relating to, or belonging to this group of peoples or to any of their languages. [C19: from Bantu *Ba-ntu* people]
Bantu beer *n S. African.* a malted drink made from partly fermented and germinated millet.
Bantustan ('bɑːntʊ,stɑːn, ,bæntʊ'stɑːn) *n* (formerly, in South Africa) an area reserved for occupation by a Black African people, with limited self-government; abolished in 1993. Official name: **homeland.**
Banville (*French* bɑ̃vil) *n* **Théodore de** (teɔdɔr də). 1823–91, French poet, who anticipated the Parnassian school in his perfection of form and command of rhythm.
banyan *or* **banian** ('bænjən) *n* **1** a moraceous tree, *Ficus benghalensis,* of tropical India and the East Indies, having aerial roots that grow down into the soil forming additional trunks. **2** a member of the Hindu merchant caste of N and W India. **3** a loose-fitting shirt, jacket, or robe, worn originally in India. [C16: from Hindi *baniyā,* from Sanskrit *vānija* merchant]
banzai ('bɑːnzaɪ, bɑːn'zaɪ) *interj* a patriotic cheer, battle cry, or salutation. [Japanese: literally, (may you live for) ten thousand years]
banzai attack *n* a mass attack of troops, without concern for casualties, as practised by the Japanese in World War II.
baobab ('beɪəʊ,bæb) *n* a bombacaceous tree, *Adansonia digitata,* native to Africa and northern Australia that has a very thick trunk, large white flowers, and a gourdlike fruit with an edible pulp called monkey bread. Also called: **bottle tree, monkey bread tree.** [C17: probably from a native African word]
Baoding ('baʊ'dɪŋ), **Paoting,** *or* **Pao-ting** *n* a city in NE China, in N Hebei province. Pop.: 483 155 (1990 est.). Former name: **Tsingyuan** *or* **Ch'ing-yüan.**
BAOR *abbrev. for* British Army of the Rhine.
Baotou ('baʊ'tuː) *or* **Paotow** *n* an industrial city in N China, in the central Inner Mongolia AR on the Yellow River. Pop.: 1 200 000 (1991 est.).
bap (bæp) *n Brit.* a large soft bread roll. [C16: of unknown origin]
bapt. *abbrev. for:* **1** baptism. **2** baptized.
Bapt. *abbrev. for* Baptist.
baptism ('bæp,tɪzəm) *n* **1** a Christian religious rite consisting of immersion in or sprinkling with water as a sign that the subject is cleansed from sin and constituted as a member of the Church. **2** the act of baptizing or of undergoing baptism. **3** any similar experience of initiation, regeneration, or dedication. ▸ **bap'tismal** *adj* ▸ **bap'tismally** *adv*
baptism of fire *n* **1** a soldier's first experience of battle. **2** any initiating ordeal or experience. **3** *Christianity.* the penetration of the Holy Ghost into the human spirit to purify, consecrate, and strengthen it, as was believed to have occurred initially at Pentecost.
Baptist ('bæptɪst) *n* **1** a member of any of various Christian sects that affirm the necessity of baptism (usually of adults and by immersion) following a personal profession of the Christian faith. **2 the Baptist.** See **John the Baptist.** ◆ *adj* **3** denoting, relating to, or characteristic of any Christian sect that affirms the necessity of baptism following a personal profession of the Christian faith.
baptistry *or* **baptistery** ('bæptɪstrɪ) *n, pl* **-ries** *or* **-eries. 1** a part of a Christian church in which baptisms are carried out. **2** a tank in a Baptist church in which baptisms are carried out.
baptize *or* **baptise** (bæp'taɪz) *vb* **1** *Christianity.* to immerse (a person) in water or sprinkle water on (a person) as part of the rite of baptism. **2** (*tr*) to give a name to; christen. **3** (*tr*) to cleanse; purify. [C13: from Late Latin *baptīzāre,* from Greek *baptizein,* from *baptein* to bathe, dip]
bar[1] (bɑː) *n* **1** a rigid usually straight length of metal, wood, etc., that is longer than it is wide or thick, used esp. as a barrier or as a structural or mechanical part: *a bar of a gate.* **2** a solid usually rectangular block of any material: *a bar of soap.* **3** anything that obstructs or prevents. **4a** an offshore ridge of sand, mud, or shingle lying near the shore and parallel to it, across the mouth of a river, bay, or harbour, or linking an island to the mainland. **4b** *U.S. and Canadian.* an alluvial deposit in a stream, river, or lake. **5** a counter or room where alcoholic drinks are served. **6** a counter, room, or establishment where a particular range of goods, food, services, etc., are sold: *a coffee bar; a heel bar.* **7** a narrow band or stripe, as of colour or light. **8** a heating element in an electric fire. **9** (in England) the area in a court of law separating the part reserved for the bench and Queen's Counsel from the area occupied by junior barristers, solicitors, and the general public. See also **Bar. 10** the place in a court of law where the accused stands during his trial: *the prisoner at the bar.* **11** a particular court of law. **12** *Brit.* (in the House of Lords and House of Commons) the boundary where nonmembers wishing to address either House appear and where persons are arraigned. **13** a plea showing that a plaintiff has no cause of action, as when the case has already been adjudicated upon or the time allowed for bringing the action has passed. **14** anything referred to as an authority or tribunal: *the bar of decency.* **15** Also called: **measure.** *Music.* **15a** a group of beats that is repeated with a consistent rhythm throughout a piece or passage of music. The number of beats in the bar is indicated by the time signature. **15b** another word for **bar line. 16a** *Brit.* insignia added to a decoration indicating a second award. **16b** *U.S.* a strip of metal worn with uniform, esp. to signify rank or as an award for service. **17** a variant spelling of **barre. 18** *Football, etc.* See **crossbar. 19** *Gymnastics.* See **horizontal bar. 20a** part of the metal mouthpiece of a horse's bridle. **20b** the space between the horse's teeth in which such a part fits. **21** either of two horny extensions that project forwards and inwards from the rear of the outer layer of a horse's hoof. **22** See **crowbar** and **glazing-bar. 23** *Lacemaking, needlework.* another name for **bride**[2]. **24** *Heraldry.* an ordinary consisting of a horizontal line across a shield, typically narrower than a fesse, and usually appearing in twos or threes. **25** *Maths.* a superscript line ¯ placed over a letter symbol to indicate, for example, a mean value or the complex conjugate of a complex number. **26 behind bars.** in prison. **27 won't** (*or* **wouldn't**) **have a bar of.** *Austral. and N.Z. informal.* cannot tolerate; dislike. ◆ *vb* **bars, barring, barred.** (*tr*) **28** to fasten or secure with a bar: *to bar the door.* **29** to shut in or out with or as if with barriers: *to bar the entrances.* **30** to obstruct; hinder: *the fallen tree barred the road.* **31** (usually foll. by *from*) to prohibit; forbid: *to bar a couple from meeting.* **32** (usually foll. by *from*) to keep out; exclude: *to bar a person from membership.* **33** to mark with a bar or bars. **34** *Law.* to prevent or halt (an action) by showing that the plaintiff has no cause. **35** to mark off (music) into bars with bar lines. ◆ *prep* **36** except for: *the best recital bar*

last night's. **37 bar none.** without exception. [C12: from Old French *barre,* from Vulgar Latin *barra* (unattested) bar, rod, of unknown origin]

bar[2] (bɑː) *n* a cgs unit of pressure equal to 10^6 dynes per square centimetre. 1 bar is equivalent to 10^5 newtons per square metre. [C20: from Greek *baros* weight]

bar[3] (bɑː) *Southwest English dialect.* ◆ *n* **1** immunity from being caught or otherwise penalized in a game. ◆ *interj* **2** a cry for such immunity. [variant of BARLEY[2]]

Bar (bɑː) *n* **the. 1** (in England and elsewhere) barristers collectively. **2** *U.S.* the legal profession collectively. **3 be called to** *or* **go to the Bar.** *Brit.* to become a barrister. **4 be called within the Bar.** *Brit.* to be appointed as a Queen's Counsel.

BAR *abbrev. for* Browning Automatic Rifle.

bar. *abbrev. for:* **1** barometer. **2** barometric. **3** barrel (container or unit of measure). **4** barrister.

Bar- (bar, bɑː) *prefix* (before Jewish patronymic names) son of: *Bar-Kochba.*

Barabbas (bəˈræbəs) *n New Testament.* a condemned robber who was released at the Passover instead of Jesus (Matthew 27:16).

baraesthesia *or U.S.* **baresthesia** (ˌbærɪsˈθiːzɪə) *n Physiol.* the ability to sense pressure. [C20: from Greek *baros* weight + AESTHESIA]

Barak (ˈbærək) *n* **Ehud** (ɛˈhʊd). born 1942, Israeli politician, prime minister from 1999.

Baranof Island (ˈbærənɒf) *n* an island off SE Alaska, in the western part of the Alexander Archipelago. Area: 4162 sq. km (1607 sq. miles).

Bárány (*German* ˈbaːranɪ) *n* **Robert.** 1876–1936, Austrian physician; devised the **Bárány test,** which detects diseases of the semicircular canals of the inner ear: Nobel prize for physiology or medicine 1914.

barathea (ˌbærəˈθɪə) *n* a fabric made of silk and wool or cotton and rayon, used esp. for coats. [C19: of unknown origin]

baraza (baˈraza) *n E African.* **1** a place where public meetings are held. **2** a palaver or meeting. [C19: from Swahili]

barb[1] (bɑːb) *n* **1** a subsidiary point facing in the opposite direction to the main point of a fish-hook, harpoon, arrow, etc., intended to make extraction difficult. **2** any of various pointed parts, as on barbed wire. **3** a cutting remark; gibe. **4** any of the numerous hairlike filaments that form the vane of a feather. **5** a beardlike growth in certain animals. **6** a hooked hair or projection on certain fruits. **7** any small cyprinid fish of the genus *Barbus* (or *Puntius*) and related genera, such as *B. conchonius* (**rosy barb**). **8** (*usually pl*) any of the small fleshy protuberances beneath the tongue in horses and cattle. **9** a white linen cloth forming part of a headdress extending from the chin to the upper chest, originally worn by women in the Middle Ages, now worn by nuns of some orders. **10** *Obsolete.* a beard. ◆ *vb* **11** (*tr*) to provide with a barb or barbs. [C14: from Old French *barbe* beard, point, from Latin *barba* beard] ▸ **barbed** *adj*

barb[2] (bɑːb) *n* a breed of horse of North African origin, similar to the Arab but less spirited. [C17: from French *barbe,* from Italian *barbero* a Barbary (horse)]

barb[3] (bɑːb) *n Austral.* a black kelpie (see **kelpie**[1]). [C19: named after one that was named *Barb* after a winning racehorse]

BARB (bɑːb) *n* (in Britain) *acronym for* Broadcasters' Audience Research Board.

Barbados (bɑːˈbeɪdəʊs, -dəʊz, -dɒs) *n* an island in the Caribbean, in the E Lesser Antilles: a British colony from 1628 to 1966, now an independent state within the Commonwealth. Language: English. Currency: Barbados dollar. Capital: Bridgetown. Pop.: 265 000 (1998 est.). Area: 430 sq. km (166 sq. miles). ▸ **Barˈbadian** *adj, n*

Barbados earth *n* a diatomaceous marl found in Barbados.

barbarian (bɑːˈbeərɪən) *n* **1** a member of a primitive or uncivilized people. **2** a coarse, insensitive, or uncultured person. **3** a vicious person. ◆ *adj* **4** of an uncivilized culture. **5** insensitive, uncultured, or brutal. [C16: see BARBAROUS] ▸ **barˈbarianism** *n*

barbaric (bɑːˈbærɪk) *adj* **1** of or characteristic of barbarians. **2** primitive or unsophisticated; unrestrained. **3** brutal. [C15: from Latin *barbaricus* foreign, outlandish; see BARBAROUS] ▸ **barˈbarically** *adv*

barbarism (ˈbɑːbəˌrɪzəm) *n* **1** a brutal, coarse, or ignorant act. **2** the condition of being backward, coarse, or ignorant. **3** a substandard or erroneously constructed or derived word or expression; solecism. **4** any act or object that offends against accepted taste. [C16: from Latin *barbarismus* error of speech, from Greek *barbarismos,* from *barbaros* BARBAROUS]

barbarity (bɑːˈbærɪtɪ) *n, pl* **-ties. 1** the state or condition of being barbaric or barbarous. **2** a brutal or vicious act. **3** a crude or unsophisticated quality, style, expression, etc.

barbarize *or* **barbarise** (ˈbɑːbəˌraɪz) *vb* **1** to make or become barbarous. **2** to use barbarisms in (language). ▸ **ˌbarbariˈzation** *or* **ˌbarbariˈsation** *n*

Barbarossa (ˌbɑːbəˈrɒsə) *n* **1** the nickname of the Holy Roman Emperor **Frederick I.** See **Frederick Barbarossa. 2** real name *Khair ed-Din. c.* 1465–1546, Turkish pirate and admiral: conquered Tunis for the Ottomans (1534).

barbarous (ˈbɑːbərəs) *adj* **1** uncivilized; primitive. **2** brutal or cruel. **3** lacking refinement. [C15: via Latin from Greek *barbaros* barbarian, non-Greek, in origin imitative of incomprehensible speech; compare Sanskrit *barbara* stammering, non-Aryan] ▸ **ˈbarbarously** *adv* ▸ **ˈbarbarousness** *n*

Barbary (ˈbɑːbərɪ) *n* a region of N Africa, extending from W Egypt to the Atlantic and including the former **Barbary States** of Tripolitania, Tunisia, Algeria, and Morocco.

Barbary ape *n* a tailless macaque, *Macaca sylvana,* that inhabits rocky cliffs and forests in NW Africa and Gibraltar: family *Cercopithecidae,* order *Primates.*

Barbary Coast *n* **the.** the Mediterranean coast of North Africa: a centre of piracy against European shipping from the 16th to the 19th centuries.

barbastelle (ˌbɑːbəˈstɛl) *n* an insectivorous forest bat, *Barbastella barbastellus,* widely distributed across Eurasia, having a wrinkled face and prominent ears: roosts in trees or caves. [French: from Italian *barbastello,* from Latin *vespertilio* bat; see PIPISTRELLE]

barbate (ˈbɑːbeɪt) *adj Chiefly biology.* having tufts of long hairs; bearded. [C19: from Latin *barba* a beard]

barbecue (ˈbɑːbɪˌkjuː) *n* **1** a meal cooked out of doors over an open fire. **2** an outdoor party or picnic at which barbecued food is served. **3** a grill or fireplace used in barbecuing. **4** the food so cooked. ◆ *vb* **-cues, -cuing, -cued.** (*tr*) **5** to cook (meat, fish, etc.) on a grill, usually over charcoal and often with a highly seasoned sauce. **6** to cook (meat, fish, etc.) in a highly seasoned sauce. [C17: from American Spanish *barbacoa,* probably from Taino: frame made of sticks]

barbed wire *n* strong wire with sharply pointed barbs at close intervals. Also called (U.S.): **barbwire.**

barbed-wire grass *n Austral.* an aromatic grass, *Cymbopogon refractus,* with groups of seed heads resembling barbed wire.

barbel (ˈbɑːbᵊl) *n* **1** any of several slender tactile spines or bristles that hang from the jaws of certain fishes, such as the catfish and carp. **2** any of several European cyprinid fishes of the genus *Barbus,* esp. *B. barbus,* that resemble the carp but have a longer body and pointed snout. [C14: from Old French, from Latin *barbus,* from *barba* beard]

barbell (ˈbɑːˌbɛl) *n* a metal rod to which heavy discs are attached at each end for weightlifting exercises.

barbellate (ˈbɑːbɪˌleɪt; bɑːˈbɛlɪt, -eɪt) *adj* **1** (of plants or plant organs) covered with barbs, hooks, or bristles. **2** (of animals) possessing bristles or barbels. [C19: from New Latin *barbellātus,* from *barbella* short stiff hair, from Latin *barbula* a little beard, from *barba* beard]

barber (ˈbɑːbə) *n* **1** a person whose business is cutting men's hair and shaving or trimming beards. ◆ *vb* (*tr*) **2** to cut the hair of. **3** to shave or trim the beard of. [C13: from Old French *barbeor,* from *barbe* beard, from Latin *barba*]

Barber (ˈbɑːbə) *n* **Samuel.** 1910–81, U.S. composer: his works include an *Adagio for Strings,* adapted from the second movement of his string quartet No. 1 (1936) and the opera *Vanessa* (1958).

barberry (ˈbɑːbərɪ) *n, pl* **-ries. 1** any spiny Asian berberidaceous shrub of the genus *Berberis,* esp. *B. vulgaris,* having clusters of yellow flowers and orange or red berries: widely cultivated as hedge plants. **2** the fruit of any of these plants. [C15: from Old French *berberis,* from Arabic *barbāris*]

barbershop (ˈbɑːbəˌʃɒp) *n* **1** *Now chiefly U.S.* the premises of a barber. **2** (*modifier*) denoting or characterized by a type of close four-part harmony for male voices, popular in romantic and sentimental songs of the 1920s and 1930s: *a barbershop quartet.*

barber's itch *or* **rash** *n* any of various fungal infections of the bearded portion of the neck and face. Technical name: **tinea barbae.**

barber's pole *n* a sign outside a barber's shop consisting of a pole painted with red and white spiral stripes.

Barberton daisy (ˈbɑːbətən) *n* See **gerbera.** [from *Barberton,* a town in Mpumulanga Province, South Africa]

barbet (ˈbɑːbɪt) *n* any small tropical brightly coloured bird of the family *Capitonidae,* having short weak wings and a sharp stout bill with tuftlike feathers at its base: order *Piciformes* (woodpeckers, etc.). [C18: from French, ultimately from Latin *barbātus* bearded, BARBATE]

barbette (bɑːˈbɛt) *n* **1** (formerly) an earthen platform inside a parapet, from which heavy guns could fire over the top. **2** an armoured cylinder below a turret on a warship that protects the revolving structure and foundation of the turret. [C18: from French, diminutive of *barbe* a nun's BARB[1], from a fancied similarity between the earthwork around a cannon and this part of a nun's habit]

barbican (ˈbɑːbɪkən) *n* **1** a walled outwork or tower to protect a gate or drawbridge of a fortification. **2** a watchtower projecting from a fortification. [C13: from Old French *barbacane,* from Medieval Latin *barbacana,* of unknown origin]

Barbican (ˈbɑːbɪkən) *n* **the.** a building complex in the City of London: includes residential developments and the Barbican Arts Centre (completed 1982) housing concert and exhibition halls, theatres, cinemas, etc.

barbicel (ˈbɑːbɪˌsɛl) *n Ornithol.* any of the minute hooks on the barbules of feathers that interlock with those of adjacent barbules. [C19: from New Latin *barbicella,* literally: a small beard, from Latin *barba* beard]

barbie *or* **barby** (ˈbɑːbɪ) *n Informal, chiefly Austral.* short for **barbecue.**

Barbie doll *or* **Barbie** (ˈbɑːbɪ) *n* **1** *Trademark.* a teenage doll with numerous sets of clothes and accessories. **2** *Slang, usually derogatory.* a superficially attractive but insipid young woman.

bar billiards *n* (*functioning as sing*) *Brit.* a table game in pubs, etc., in which short cues are used to pocket balls into holes scoring various points and guarded by wooden pegs that incur penalties if they are knocked over.

Barbirolli (ˌbɑːbəˈrɒlɪ) *n* Sir **John.** 1899–1970, English conductor of the Hallé Orchestra (1943–68).

barbitone (ˈbɑːbɪˌtəʊn) *or U.S.* **barbital** (ˈbɑːbɪˌtæl) *n* a long-acting barbiturate used medicinally, usually in the form of the sodium salt, as a sedative or hypnotic. [C20: from BARBIT(URIC ACID) + -ONE]

barbiturate (bɑːˈbɪtjʊrɪt, -ˌreɪt) *n* a derivative of barbituric acid, such as barbitone or phenobarbitone, used in medicine as a sedative or hypnotic.

barbituric acid (ˌbɑːbɪˈtjʊərɪk) *n* a white crystalline solid used in the preparation of barbiturate drugs. Formula: $C_4H_4N_2O_3$. Also called: **malonylurea.** [C19: partial translation of German *Barbitursäure,* perhaps from the name *Barbara* + URIC + *Säure* acid]

Barbizon School (ˈbɑːbɪˌzɒn) *n* a group of French painters of landscapes of the 1840s, including Théodore Rousseau, Daubigny, Diaz, Corot, and Millet. [C19: from *Barbizon* a village near Paris and a favourite haunt of the painters]

Barbour (ˈbɑːbə) *n* **John.** *c.* 1320–95, Scottish poet: author of *The Bruce* (1376), a patriotic epic poem.

Barbour jacket *or* **Barbour** (ˈbɑːbə) *n Trademark.* a hard-wearing waterproof waxed jacket.

Barbuda (bɑːˈbuːdə) *n* a coral island in the E Caribbean, in the Leeward Islands:

part of the independent state of Antigua and Barbuda. Area: 160 sq. km (62 sq. miles).

barbule ('bɑːbjuːl) *n* **1** a very small barb. **2** *Ornithol.* any of the minute hairs that project from a barb and in some feathers interlock by hooks and grooves, forming a flat vane. **[C19:** from Latin *barbula* a little beard, from *barba* beard**]**

Barbusse (*French* barbys) *n* **Henri** (ɑ̃ri). 1873–1935, French novelist and poet. His novels include *L'Enfer* (1908) and *Le Feu* (1916), reflecting the horror of World War I.

Barca ('bɑːkə) *n* the surname of several noted Carthaginian generals, including Hamilcar, Hasdrubal, and Hannibal. ▸ **'Barcan** *adj*

barcarole *or* **barcarolle** ('bɑːkəˌrəʊl, -ˌrɒl; ˌbɑːkə'rəʊl) *n* **1** a Venetian boat song in a time of six or twelve quaver beats to the bar. **2** an instrumental composition resembling this. **[C18:** from French, from Italian *barcarola,* from *barcaruolo* boatman, from *barca* boat; see BARQUE**]**

Barce ('bartʃe) *or* **Barca** ('barka) *n* the Italian name for **Al Marj.**

Barcelona (ˌbɑːsɪ'ləʊnə) *n* the chief port of Spain, on the NE Mediterranean coast: seat of the Republican government during the Civil War (1936–39); the commercial capital of Spain. Pop.: 1 614 571 (1995 est.). Ancient name: **Barcino** (bɑː'siːnəʊ).

BArch *abbrev.* for Bachelor of Architecture.

barchan, barkhan, barchane, *or* **barkan** (bɑː'kɑːn) *n* a crescent-shaped shifting sand dune, convex on the windward side and steeper and concave on the leeward.

bar chart *n* another name for **bar graph.**

Barclay ('bɑːklɪ) *n* **Alexander.** *c.* 1475–1552, English poet. His works include *The Ship of Fools* (1509) and *Eclogues* (*c.* 1513–14).

Barclay de Tolly ('bɑːklɪ də 'tɒlɪ; *Russian* bar'klai də 'tɔlj) *n* Prince **Mikhail** (mixa'il). 1761–1818, Russian field marshal: commander in chief against Napoleon in 1812.

bar code *n Commerce.* a machine-readable arrangement of numbers and parallel lines of different widths printed on a package, which can be electronically scanned at a checkout to register the price of the goods and to activate computer stock-checking and reordering.

Barcoo River (bɑː'kuː) *n* a river in E central Australia, in SW Queensland: joins with the Thomson River to form Cooper Creek.

Barcoo salute *n Austral. informal.* a movement of the hand to brush flies away from the face.

bard[1] (bɑːd) *n* **1a** (formerly) one of an ancient Celtic order of poets who recited verses about the exploits, often legendary, of their tribes. **1b** (in modern times) a poet who wins a verse competition at a Welsh eisteddfod. **2** *Archaic or literary.* any poet, esp. one who writes lyric or heroic verse or is of national importance. **[C14:** from Scottish Gaelic; related to Welsh *bardd***]** ▸ **'bardic** *adj*

bard[2] *or* **barde** (bɑːd) *n* **1** a piece of larding bacon or pork fat placed on game or lean meat during roasting to prevent drying out. **2** an ornamental caparison for a horse. ◆ *vb (tr)* **3** to place a bard on. **[C15:** from Old French *barde,* from Old Italian *barda,* from Arabic *barda'ah* packsaddle**]**

Bard (bɑːd) *n* **the.** an epithet of (William) **Shakespeare.**

Bardeen (ˌbɑː'diːn) *n* **John.** 1908–91, U.S. physicist and electrical engineer; noted for his research on electrical conduction in solids; shared Nobel prize for physics 1956 for research on semiconductors leading to the invention of the transistor; shared Nobel prize for physics 1972 for contributions to the theory of superconductivity.

bar diagram *n* another name for **bar graph.**

bardie ('bɑːdiː) *n* **1** an edible white wood-boring grub of Australia. **2 starve the bardies!** *Austral. slang.* an exclamation of surprise or protest. **[**from a native Australian language**]**

bardolatry (bɑː'dɒlətrɪ) *n Facetious.* idolatry or excessive admiration of Shakespeare.

Bardolino (ˌbɑːdə'liːnəʊ) *n, pl* **-nos.** a light dry red wine produced around Verona in NE Italy.

Bardot (*French* bardo) *n* **Brigitte** (briʒit). born 1934, French film actress.

bare[1] (bɛə) *adj* **1** unclothed; exposed: used esp. of a part of the body. **2** without the natural, conventional, or usual covering or clothing: *a bare tree.* **3** lacking appropriate furnishings, etc.: *a bare room.* **4** unembellished; simple: *the bare facts.* **5** (*prenominal*) just sufficient; mere: *he earned the bare minimum.* **6 with one's bare hands.** without a weapon or tool. ◆ *vb* **7** *(tr)* to make bare; uncover; reveal. **[**Old English *bær;* compare Old Norse *berr,* Old High German *bar* naked, Old Slavonic *bosŭ* barefoot**]** ▸ **'bareness** *n*

bare[2] (bɛə) *vb Archaic.* a past tense of **bear**[1].

bareback ('bɛəˌbæk) *or* **barebacked** *adj, adv* (of horse-riding) without a saddle.

barefaced ('bɛəˌfeɪst) *adj* **1** unconcealed or shameless: *a barefaced lie.* **2** with the face uncovered or shaven. ▸ **barefacedly** ('bɛəˌfeɪsɪdlɪ) *adv* ▸ **'bareˌfacedness** *n*

barefoot ('bɛəˌfʊt) *or* **barefooted** *adj, adv* with the feet uncovered.

barefoot doctor *n* (esp. in developing countries) a worker trained as a medical auxiliary in a rural area who dispenses medicine, gives first aid, assists at childbirth, etc. **[C20:** translation of Chinese *chijiao yisheng,* officially translated as primary health worker**]**

barège *French.* (barɛʒ) *n* **1** a light silky gauze fabric made of wool. ◆ *adj* **2** made of such a fabric. **[C19:** named after *Barèges,* France, where it was originally made**]**

barehanded (ˌbɛə'hændɪd) *adv, adj* **1** without weapons, tools, etc. **2** with hands uncovered.

bareheaded (ˌbɛə'hɛdɪd) *adj, adv* with head uncovered.

Bareilly (bə'reɪlɪ) *n* a city in N India, in N central Uttar Pradesh. Pop.: 587 211 (1991).

bare-knuckle *adj* **1** without boxing gloves: *a bare-knuckle fight.* **2** aggressive and without reservations: *a bare-knuckle confrontation.*

barely ('bɛəlɪ) *adv* **1** only just; scarcely: *barely enough for their needs.* **2** *Informal.* not quite; nearly: *barely old enough.* **3** scantily; poorly: *barely furnished.* **4** *Archaic.* openly.

USAGE See at **hardly.**

Barenboim ('bærənˌbɔɪm) *n* **Daniel.** born 1942, Israeli concert pianist and conductor, born in Argentina.

Barents Sea ('bærənts) *n* a part of the Arctic Ocean, bounded by Norway, Russia, and the islands of Novaya Zemlya, Spitsbergen, and Franz Josef Land. **[**named after Willem *Barents* (1550–97) Dutch navigator and explorer**]**

baresark ('bɛəˌsɑːk) *n* another word for **berserk** (sense 2). **[C19:** literally: bare shirt**]**

barfly ('bɑːflaɪ) *n, pl* **-flies.** *Informal, chiefly U.S. and Canadian.* a person who frequents bars.

bargain ('bɑːgɪn) *n* **1** an agreement or contract establishing what each party will give, receive, or perform in a transaction between them. **2** something acquired or received in such an agreement. **3a** something bought or offered at a low price: *a bargain at an auction.* **3b** (*as modifier*): *a bargain price.* **4 into** *or* (*U.S.*) **in the bargain.** in excess of what has been stipulated; besides. **5 make** *or* **strike a bargain.** to agree on terms. ◆ *vb* **6** *(intr)* to negotiate the terms of an agreement, transaction, etc. **7** *(tr)* to exchange, as in a bargain. **8** to arrive at (an agreement or settlement). **[C14:** from Old French *bargaigne,* from *bargaignier* to trade, of Germanic origin; compare Medieval Latin *barcāniāre* to trade, Old English *borgian* to borrow**]** ▸ **'bargainer** *n* ▸ **'bargaining** *n, adj*

bargain away *vb (tr, adv)* to lose or renounce (freedom, rights, etc.) in return for something valueless or of little value.

bargain basement *n* part of a shop where goods are sold at reduced prices.

bargain for *vb (intr, prep)* to expect; anticipate (a style of behaviour, change in fortune, etc.): *he got more than he bargained for.*

bargaining agent *n* an organization, usually a trade union, that acts or bargains on behalf of a group of employees in collective bargaining.

bargaining level *n* the level within an organizational hierarchy, such as company level, national level, etc., at which collective bargaining takes place.

bargaining scope *n* the range of topics within the scope of a particular set of negotiations leading to a collective agreement.

bargaining unit *n* a specific group of employees who are covered by the same collective agreement or set of agreements and represented by the same bargaining agent or agents.

bargain on *vb (intr, prep)* to rely or depend on (something): *he bargained on her support.*

barge (bɑːdʒ) *n* **1** a vessel, usually flat-bottomed and with or without its own power, used for transporting freight, esp. on canals. **2** a vessel, often decorated, used in pageants, for state occasions, etc. **3** *Navy.* a boat allocated to a flag officer, used esp. for ceremonial occasions and often carried on board his flagship. **4** *Informal and derogatory.* any vessel, esp. an old or clumsy one. ◆ *vb* **5** *(intr;* foll. by *into) Informal.* to bump (into). **6** *Informal.* to push (someone or one's way) violently. **7** *(intr;* foll. by *into* or *in) Informal.* to interrupt rudely or clumsily: *to barge into a conversation.* **8** *Sailing.* to bear down on (another boat or boats) at the start of a race. **9** *(tr)* to transport by barge. **10** *(intr) Informal.* to move slowly or clumsily. **[C13:** from Old French, from Medieval Latin *barga,* probably from Late Latin *barca* a small boat; see BARQUE**]**

bargeboard ('bɑːdʒˌbɔːd) *n* a board, often decorated with carved ornaments, placed along the gable end of a roof. Also called: **vergeboard.**

barge couple *n* either of a pair of outside rafters along the gable end of a roof.

barge course *n* **1** the overhang of the gable end of a roof. **2** a course of bricks laid on edge to form the coping of a wall.

bargee (bɑː'dʒiː) *or U.S. and Canadian.* **bargeman** ('bɑːdʒmən) *n, pl* **bargees** *or* **bargemen.** a person employed on or in charge of a barge.

bargepole ('bɑːdʒˌpəʊl) *n* **1** a long pole used to propel a barge. **2 not touch with a bargepole.** *Informal.* to refuse to have anything to do with.

bar girl *n Chiefly U.S.* an attractive girl employed by the management of a bar to befriend male customers and encourage them to buy drinks.

bar graph *n* a graph consisting of vertical or horizontal bars whose lengths are proportional to amounts or quantities. Also called: **bar chart, bar diagram.**

Bari ('bɑːrɪ) *n* a port in SE Italy, capital of Apulia, on the Adriatic coast. Pop.: 336 560 (1996 est.).

baric[1] ('bɛərɪk, 'bærɪk) *adj* of or containing barium.

baric[2] ('bærɪk) *adj* of or concerned with weight, esp. that of the atmosphere as indicated by barometric pressure.

barilla (bə'rɪlə) *n* **1** an impure mixture of sodium carbonate and sodium sulphate obtained from the ashes of certain plants, such as the saltworts. **2** either of two chenopodiaceous plants, *Salsola kali* (or *soda*) or *Halogeton soda,* formerly burned to obtain a form of sodium carbonate. See also **saltwort. [C17:** from Spanish *barrilla,* literally: a little bar, from *barra* BAR[1]**]**

Baring ('bɛərɪŋ) *n* **Evelyn,** 1st Earl of Cromer. 1841–1917, English administrator. As consul general in Egypt with plenipotentiary powers, he controlled the Egyptian government from 1883 to 1907.

barit. *abbrev. for* baritone.

barite ('bɛəraɪt) *n* the usual U.S. and Canadian name for **barytes. [C18:** from BAR(IUM) + -ITE[1]**]**

baritone ('bærɪˌtəʊn) *n* **1** the second lowest adult male voice, having a range approximately from G an eleventh below middle C to F a fourth above it. **2** a singer with such a voice. **3** the second lowest instrument in the families of the saxophone, horn, oboe, etc. ◆ *adj* **4** relating to or denoting a baritone: *a baritone part.* **5** denoting the second lowest instrument in a family: *the baritone* *horn.* [C17: from Italian *baritono* a deep voice, from Greek *barutonos* deep-sounding, from *barus* heavy, low + *tonos* TONE]

barium ('bɛərɪəm) *n* a soft silvery-white metallic element of the alkaline earth group. It is used in bearing alloys and compounds are used as pigments. Symbol: Ba; atomic no.: 56; atomic wt.: 137.327; valency: 2; relative density: 3.5; melting pt.: 729°C; boiling pt.: 1805°C. [C19: from BAR(YTA) + -IUM]

barium enema *n* an injection into the rectum of a preparation of barium sulphate, which is opaque to X-rays, before X-raying the lower alimentary canal.

barium hydroxide *n* a white poisonous crystalline solid, used in the manufacture of organic compounds and in the preparation of beet sugar. Formula: $Ba(OH)_2$. Also called: **baryta.**

barium meal *n* a preparation of barium sulphate, which is opaque to X-rays, swallowed by a patient before X-ray examination of the upper part of his or her alimentary canal.

barium oxide *n* a white or yellowish-white poisonous heavy powder used esp. as a dehydrating agent. Formula: BaO. Also called: **baryta.**

barium sulphate *n* a white insoluble fine heavy powder, used as a pigment, as a filler for paper, rubber, etc., and in barium meals. Formula: $BaSO_4$. Also called: **blanc fixe.**

barium titanate *n* a crystalline ceramic used in capacitors and piezoelectric devices. Formula: $BaTiO_3$.

bark[1] (bɑːk) *n* **1** the loud abrupt usually harsh or gruff cry of a dog or any of certain other animals. **2** a similar sound, such as one made by a person, gun, etc. **3** **his bark is worse than his bite.** he is bad-tempered but harmless. ◆ *vb* **4** (*intr*) (of a dog or any of certain other animals) to make its typical loud abrupt cry. **5** (*intr*) (of a person, gun, etc.) to make a similar loud harsh sound. **6** to say or shout in a brusque, peremptory, or angry tone: *he barked an order.* **7** *U.S. informal.* to advertise (a show, merchandise, etc.) by loudly addressing passers-by. **8** **bark up the wrong tree.** *Informal.* to misdirect one's attention, efforts, etc.; be mistaken. [Old English *beorcan;* related to Lithuanian *burgěti* to quarrel, growl]

bark[2] (bɑːk) *n* **1** a protective layer of dead corky cells on the outside of the stems of woody plants. **2** any of several varieties of this substance that can be used in tanning, dyeing, or in medicine. **3** an informal name for **cinchona.** ◆ *vb* (*tr*) **4** to scrape or rub off skin, as in an injury. **5** to remove the bark or a circle of bark from (a tree or log). **6** to cover or enclose with bark. **7** to tan (leather), principally by the tannins in barks. [C13: from Old Norse *börkr;* related to Swedish, Danish *bark,* German *Borke;* compare Old Norse *björkr* BIRCH]

bark[3] (bɑːk) *n* a variant spelling (esp. U.S.) of **barque.**

bark beetle *n* any small beetle of the family *Scolytidae,* which bore tunnels in the bark and wood of trees, causing great damage. They are closely related to the weevils.

bark cloth *n* a papery fabric made from the fibrous inner bark of various trees, esp. of the moraceous genus *Ficus* and the leguminous genus *Brachystegia.*

barkeeper ('bɑːˌkiːpə) *n* another name (esp. U.S.) for **barman.**

barkentine *or* **barkantine** ('bɑːkənˌtiːn) *n* the usual U.S. and Canadian spellings of **barquentine.**

barker[1] ('bɑːkə) *n* **1** an animal or person that barks. **2** a person who stands at a show, fair booth, etc., and loudly addresses passers-by to attract customers.

barker[2] ('bɑːkə) *n* a person or machine that removes bark from trees or logs or prepares it for tanning.

Barker ('bɑːkə) *n* **1** **George** (**Granville**). 1913–91, British poet: author of *Calamiterror* (1937) and *The True Confession of George Barker* (1950). **2** **Howard.** born 1946, British playwright: his plays include *Claw* (1975), *The Castle* (1985), and *A Hard Heart* (1992). **3** **Ronnie**, full name *Ronald William George Barker.* born 1929, British comedian: known esp. for his partnership with Ronnie Corbett (born 1930) in the TV series *The Two Ronnies* (1971–85).

barkhan *or* **barkan** (bɑːˈkɑːn) *n* variant spellings of **barchan.**

Barkhausen (*German* 'barkhauzᵊn) *n* **Heinrich Georg.** 1881–1956, German physicist; discovered that ferromagnetic material in an increasing magnetic field becomes magnetized in discrete jumps (the **Barkhausen effect**).

barking ('bɑːkɪŋ) *Slang.* ◆ *adj* **1** mad; crazy.◆ *adv* **2** (intensifier): *barking mad.*

Barking and Dagenham ('bɑːkɪŋ) *n* a borough of E Greater London. Pop.: 143 180 (1991). Area: 34 sq. km (13 sq. miles).

barking deer *n* another name for **muntjac.**

Barkla ('bɑːklə) *n* **Charles Glover.** 1877–1944, British physicist, noted for his work on X-rays: Nobel prize for physics 1917.

Bar Kochba, Bar Kokhba, *or* **Bar Kosba** (bɑː 'kɒxbə, 'kɒs-) *n* **Simeon.** died 135 A.D. Jewish leader who led an unsuccessful revolt against the Romans in Palestine.

Barletta (*Italian* bar'letta) *n* a port in SE Italy, in Apulia. Pop.: 88 750 (1990).

barley[1] ('bɑːlɪ) *n* **1** any of various erect annual temperate grasses of the genus *Hordeum,* esp. *H. vulgare,* that have short leaves and dense bristly flower spikes and are widely cultivated for grain and forage. **2** the grain of any of these grasses, used in making beer and whisky and for soups, puddings, etc. See also **pearl barley.** [Old English *bærlīc* (adj); related to *bere* barley, Old Norse *barr* barley, Gothic *barizeins* of barley, Latin *farīna* flour]

barley[2] ('bɑːlɪ) *sentence substitute. Dialect.* a cry for truce or respite from the rules of a game. [C18: probably changed from PARLEY]

barleycorn ('bɑːlɪˌkɔːn) *n* **1** a grain of barley, or barley itself. **2** an obsolete unit of length equal to one third of an inch.

barley sugar *n* a brittle clear amber-coloured sweet made by boiling sugar, originally with a barley extract.

barley water *n* a drink made from an infusion of barley, usually flavoured with lemon or orange.

barley wine *n Brit.* an exceptionally strong beer.

bar line *or* **bar** *n Music.* the vertical line marking the boundary between one bar and the next.

barm (bɑːm) *n* **1** the yeasty froth on fermenting malt liquors. **2** an archaic or dialect word for **yeast.** [Old English *beorm;* related to *beran* to BEAR, Old Norse *barmr* barm, Gothic *barms,* Old High German *barm;* see FERMENT]

barmaid ('bɑːˌmeɪd) *n* a woman who serves in a pub.

barman ('bɑːmən) *n, pl* **-men.** a man who serves in a pub.

barmbrack ('bɑːmˌbræk) *n Irish.* a loaf of bread with currants in it. Also: **barnbrack.** Often shortened to **brack.** [from Irish Gaelic *bairín breac* speckled loaf]

barm cake *n Lancashire dialect.* a round flat soft bread roll.

Barmecide ('bɑːmɪˌsaɪd) *or* **Barmecidal** *adj* lavish or plentiful in imagination only; illusory; sham: *a Barmecide feast.* [C18: from the name of a prince in *The Arabian Nights* who served empty plates to beggars, alleging that they held sumptuous food]

Bar Mitzvah (bɑː 'mɪtsvə) (*sometimes not caps.*) *Judaism.* ◆ *adj* **1** (of a Jewish boy) having assumed full religious obligations, being at least thirteen years of age. ◆ *n* **2** the occasion, ceremony, or celebration of that event. **3** the boy himself on that day. [Hebrew: son of the law]

barmy ('bɑːmɪ) *adj* **-mier, -miest.** *Slang.* insane. Also: **balmy.** [C16: originally, full of BARM, hence frothing, excited, flighty, etc.]

barn[1] (bɑːn) *n* **1** a large farm outbuilding, used chiefly for storing hay, grain, etc., but also for housing livestock. **2** *U.S. and Canadian.* a large shed for sheltering railroad cars, trucks, etc. **3** any large building, esp. an unattractive one. **4** (*modifier*) relating to a system of poultry farming in which birds are allowed to move freely within a barn: *barn eggs.* [Old English *beren,* from *bere* barley + *ærn* room; see BARLEY[1]]

barn[2] (bɑːn) *n* a unit of nuclear cross section equal to 10^{-28} square metre. Symbol: b [C20: from BARN[1]; so called because of the relatively large cross section]

Barnabas ('bɑːnəbəs) *n* **Saint.** *New Testament.* original name: *Joseph.* a Cypriot Levite who supported Saint Paul in his apostolic work (Acts 4:36, 37). Feast day: June 11.

barnacle ('bɑːnəkᵊl) *n* **1** any of various marine crustaceans of the subclass *Cirripedia* that, as adults, live attached to rocks, ship bottoms, etc. They have feathery food-catching cirri protruding from a hard shell. See **acorn barnacle, goose barnacle. 2** a person or thing that is difficult to get rid of. [C16: related to Late Latin *bernicla,* of obscure origin] ▸ **'barnacled** *adj*

barnacle goose *n* **1** a N European goose, *Branta leucopsis,* that has a black-and-white head and body and grey wings. **2** a former name for **brent goose.** [C13 *bernekke,* related to Late Latin *bernaca,* from the belief that the goose developed from a shellfish; ultimate origin obscure]

Barnard ('bɑːnɑːd) *n* **1** **Christiaan** (**Neethling**). born 1923, South African surgeon, who performed the first human heart transplant (1967). **2** **Edward Emerson.** 1857–1923, U.S. astronomer: noted for his discovery of the fifth satellite of Jupiter and his discovery of comets, nebulae, and a red dwarf (1916).

Barnardo (bə'nɑːdəʊ, bɑː-) *n* Dr **Thomas John.** 1845–1905, British philanthropist, who founded homes for destitute children.

Barnard's star *n* a red dwarf star in the constellation Ophiuchus having the largest proper motion known. [C20: named after E. E. BARNARD]

Barnaul (*Russian* bərna'ul) *n* a city in S Russia, on the River Ob. Pop.: 596 000 (1995 est.).

Barnave (*French* barnav) *n* **Antoine Pierre.** 1761–93, French revolutionary. A prominent member of the National Assembly, he was executed for his royalist sympathies.

barn dance *n* **1** *Brit.* a progressive round country dance. **2** *U.S. and Canadian.* a party with hoedown music and square-dancing. **3** a party featuring country dancing. **4** a disco or party held in a barn.

barn door *n* **1** the door of a barn. **2** *Informal.* a target so large that it cannot be missed. **3** *Photog., television, etc.* an adjustable flap over the front of a studio or theatre lamp.

Barnes (bɑːnz) *n* **1** **Djuna.** 1892–1982, U.S. novelist, noted for *Nightwood* (1936). **2** **William.** 1801–86, British poet, best known for *Poems of Rural Life in the Dorset Dialect* (1879).

Barnet ('bɑːnɪt) *n* a borough of N Greater London: scene of a Yorkist victory (1471) in the Wars of the Roses. Pop.: 292 783 (1991). Area: 89 sq. km (34 sq. miles).

barney ('bɑːnɪ) *Informal.* ◆ *n* **1** a noisy argument. ◆ *vb* (*intr*) **2** *Chiefly Austral. and N.Z.* to argue or quarrel. [C19: of unknown origin]

barn owl *n* any owl of the genus *Tyto,* esp. *T. alba,* having a pale brown and white plumage, long slender legs, and a heart-shaped face: family *Tytonidae.*

Barnsley ('bɑːnzlɪ) *n* **1** an industrial town in N England, in Barnsley unitary authority, South Yorkshire. Pop.: 75 120 (1991). **2** a unitary authority in N England, in South Yorkshire. Pop.: 224 800 (1992 est.). Area: 329 sq. km (127 sq. miles).

Barnstaple ('bɑːnstəpᵊl) *n* a town in SW England, in Devon, on the estuary of the River Taw: tourism, agriculture. Pop.: 27 691 (1991).

barnstorm ('bɑːnˌstɔːm) *vb* (*intr*) **1** to tour rural districts putting on shows, esp. theatrical, athletic, or acrobatic shows. **2** *Chiefly U.S. and Canadian.* to tour rural districts making speeches in a political campaign. [C19: from BARN[1] + STORM (*vb*); from the performances often being in barns] ▸ **'barnˌstormer** *n* ▸ **'barnˌstorming** *n, adj*

barn swallow *n* the U.S. and Canadian name for the common swallow, *Hirundo rustica.* See **swallow**[2].

Barnum ('bɑːnəm) *n* **P(hineas) T(aylor).** 1810–91, U.S. showman, who created The Greatest Show on Earth (1871) and, with J. A. Bailey, founded the Barnum and Bailey Circus (1881).

barnyard ('bɑːnˌjɑːd) *n* **1** a yard adjoining a barn, in which farm animals are kept. **2** (*modifier*) belonging to or characteristic of a barnyard. **3** (*modifier*) crude or earthy: *barnyard humour.*

baro- *combining form.* indicating weight or pressure: *barometer.* [from Greek *baros* weight; related to Latin *gravis* heavy]

Barocchio (*Italian* ba'rɔkkjo) *n* **Giacomo** ('dʒakomo). See (Giacomo Barozzi da) **Vignola.**

Baroda (bə'rəudə) *n* **1** a former state of W India, part of Gujarat since 1960. **2** the former name (until 1976) of **Vadodara.**

barognosis (ˌbærəg'nəusɪs) *n Physiol.* the ability to judge weight. [C20: from Greek *baros* weight + *gnosis* knowledge]

barogram ('bærəˌgræm) *n Meteorol.* the record of atmospheric pressure traced by a barograph or similar instrument.

barograph ('bærəˌgrɑːf, -ˌgræf) *n Meteorol.* a self-recording aneroid barometer. ► **barographic** (ˌbærə'græfɪk) *adj*

Baroja (*Spanish* ba'roxa) *n* **Pio** ('pio). 1872–1956, Spanish Basque novelist, who wrote nearly 100 novels, including a series of twenty-two under the general title *Memorias de un Hombre de Acción* (1944–49).

Barolo (bə'rəuləu) *n* (*sometimes not cap.*) a dry red wine produced in the Piedmont region of Italy.

barometer (bə'rɒmɪtə) *n* **1** an instrument for measuring atmospheric pressure, usually to determine altitude or weather changes. **2** anything that shows change or impending change: *the barometer of social change.* ► **barometric** (ˌbærə'mɛtrɪk) *or* **ˌbaro'metrical** *adj* ► **ˌbaro'metrically** *adv* ► **ba'rometry** *n*

barometric pressure *n* atmospheric pressure as indicated by a barometer.

baron ('bærən) *n* **1** a member of a specific rank of nobility, esp. the lowest rank in the British Isles. **2** (in Europe from the Middle Ages) originally any tenant-in-chief of a king or other overlord, who held land from his superior by honourable service; a land-holding nobleman. **3** a powerful businessman or financier: *a press baron.* **4** *English law.* (formerly) the title held by judges of the Court of Exchequer. **5** short for **baron of beef.** [C12: from Old French, of Germanic origin; compare Old High German *baro* freeman, Old Norse *berjask* to fight]

baronage ('bærənɪdʒ) *n* **1** barons collectively. **2** the rank or dignity of a baron.

baroness ('bærənɪs) *n* **1** the wife or widow of a baron. **2** a woman holding the rank of baron in her own right.

baronet ('bærənɪt, -ˌnɛt) *n* (in Britain) a commoner who holds the lowest hereditary title of honour, ranking below a baron. Abbrevs.: **Bart.** or **Bt.** [C15: order instituted 1611, from BARON + -ET]

baronetage ('bærənɪtɪdʒ) *n* **1** the order of baronets; baronets collectively. **2** the rank of baronet; baronetcy.

baronetcy ('bærənɪtsɪ, -ˌnɛt-) *n, pl* **-cies.** the rank, position, or patent of a baronet.

barong (bæ'rɒŋ) *n* a broad-bladed cleaver-like knife used in the Philippines. [from Moro; see PARANG]

baronial (bə'rəunɪəl) *adj* of, relating to, or befitting a baron or barons.

baron of beef *n* a cut of beef consisting of a double sirloin joined at the backbone.

Barons' War *n* either of two civil wars in 13th-century England. The **First Barons' War** (1215–17) was precipitated by King John's failure to observe the terms of Magna Carta: many of the Barons' grievances were removed by his death (1216) and peace was concluded in 1217. The **Second Barons' War** (1264–67) was caused by Henry III's refusal to accept limitations on his authority: the rebel Barons (led (1264–65) by Simon de Montfort), initially successful, were defeated at the battle of Evesham (1265); sporadic resistance continued until 1267.

barony ('bærənɪ) *n, pl* **-nies. 1a** the domain of a baron. **1b** (in Ireland) a division of a county. **1c** (in Scotland) a large estate or manor. **2** the rank or dignity of a baron. **3** a sphere of influence dominated by an industrial magnate or other powerful individual.

barophilic (ˌbærə'fɪlɪk) *adj* (of bacteria) able to tolerate or growing best in conditions of high atmospheric pressure. ► **barophile** ('bærəˌfaɪl) *n*

barophoresis (ˌbærəfə'riːsɪs) *n Chem.* the diffusion of suspended particles at a rate dependent on external forces.

baroque (bə'rɒk, bə'rəuk) *n* (*often cap.*) **1** a style of architecture and decorative art that flourished throughout Europe from the late 16th to the early 18th century, characterized by extensive ornamentation. **2** a 17th-century style of music characterized by extensive use of the thorough bass and of ornamentation. **3** any ornate or heavily ornamented style. ◆ *adj* **4** denoting, being in, or relating to the baroque. **5** (of pearls) irregularly shaped. [C18: from French, from Portuguese *barroco* a rough or imperfectly shaped pearl]

baroreceptor ('bærəurɪˌsɛptə) *or* **baroceptor** *n* a collection of sensory nerve endings, principally in the carotid sinuses and the aortic arch, that monitor blood pressure changes in the body.

baroscope ('bærəˌskəup) *n* any instrument for measuring atmospheric pressure, esp. a manometer with one side open to the atmosphere. ► **baroscopic** (ˌbærə'skɒpɪk) *adj*

barostat ('bærəuˌstæt) *n* a device for maintaining constant pressure, such as one used in an aircraft cabin.

Barotse (bə'rɒtsɪ) *n* **1** (*pl* **-se** *or* **-ses**) a member of a Negroid people of central Africa living chiefly in SW Zambia. **2** the language spoken by this people; Lozi.

barouche (bə'ruːʃ) *n* a four-wheeled horse-drawn carriage, popular in the 19th century, having a retractable hood over the rear half, seats inside for two couples facing each other, and a driver's seat outside at the front. [C19: from German (dialect) *Barutsche,* from Italian *baroccio,* from Vulgar Latin *birotium* (unattested) vehicle with two wheels, from Late Latin *birotus* two-wheeled, from BI-[1] + *rota* wheel]

Barozzi (*Italian* ba'rɔttsi) *n* See (Giacomo Barozzi da) **Vignola.**

barperson ('bɑːˌpɜːsᵊn) *n, pl* **-persons.** a person who serves in a pub: used esp. in advertisements.

barque *or esp. U.S.* **bark** (bɑːk) *n* **1** a sailing ship of three or more masts having the foremasts rigged square and the aftermast rigged fore-and-aft. **2** *Poetic.* any boat, esp. a small sailing vessel. [C15: from Old French, from Old Provençal *barca,* from Late Latin, of unknown origin]

barquentine *or* **barquantine** ('bɑːkənˌtiːn) *n* a sailing ship of three or more masts rigged square on the foremast and fore-and-aft on the others. Usual U.S. and Canadian spelling: **barkentine.** [C17: from BARQUE + (BRIG)ANTINE]

Barquisimeto (*Spanish* barkisi'meto) *n* a city in NW Venezuela. Pop.: 625 450 (1990).

Barra ('bærə) *n* an island in NW Scotland, in the Outer Hebrides: fishing, crofting, tourism. Pop.: 1200 (latest est.).

barrack[1] ('bærək) *vb* to house (people, esp. soldiers) in barracks.

barrack[2] ('bærək) *vb Brit., Austral., and N.Z. informal.* **1** to criticize loudly or shout against (a player, team, speaker, etc.); jeer. **2** (*intr;* foll. by *for*) to shout support (for). [C19: from northern Irish: to boast] ► **'barracker** *n* ► **'barracking** *n, adj*

barrack-room lawyer *n* a person who freely offers opinions, esp. in legal matters, that he is unqualified to give.

barracks ('bærəks) *pl n* (*sometimes sing; when pl, sometimes functions as sing*) **1** a building or group of buildings used to accommodate military personnel. **2** any large building used for housing people, esp. temporarily. **3** a large and bleak building. [C17: from French *baraque,* from Old Catalan *barraca* hut, of uncertain origin]

barracoon (ˌbærə'kuːn) *n* (formerly) a temporary place of confinement for slaves or convicts, esp. those awaiting transportation. [C19: from Spanish *barracón,* from *barraca* hut, from Catalan]

barracouta (ˌbærə'kuːtə) *n* a large predatory Pacific fish, *Thyrsites atun,* with a protruding lower jaw and strong teeth: family *Gempylidae.* [C17: variant of BARRACUDA]

barracuda (ˌbærə'kjuːdə) *n, pl* **-da** *or* **-das.** any predatory marine teleost fish of the mostly tropical family *Sphyraenidae,* esp. *Sphyraena barracuda.* They have an elongated body, strong teeth, and a protruding lower jaw. [C17: from American Spanish, of unknown origin]

barrage ('bærɑːʒ) *n* **1** *Military.* the firing of artillery to saturate an area, either to protect against an attack or to support an advance. **2** an overwhelming and continuous delivery of something, as words, questions, or punches. **3** a construction across a watercourse, esp. one to increase the depth of water to assist navigation or irrigation. **4** *Fencing.* a heat or series of bouts in a competition. ◆ *vb* **5** (*tr*) to attack or confront with a barrage: *the speaker was barraged with abuse.* [C19: from French, from *barrer* to obstruct; see BAR[1]]

barrage balloon *n* one of a number of tethered balloons with cables or net suspended from them, used to deter low-flying air attack.

barramunda (ˌbærə'mʌndə) *n, pl* **-das,** *or* **-da.** the edible Australian lungfish, *Neoceratodus forsteri,* having paddle-like fins and a long body covered with large scales. [from a native Australian language]

barramundi (ˌbærə'mʌndɪ) *n, pl* **-dis, -dies,** *or* **-di.** any of several large edible Australian fishes, esp. the percoid species *Lates calcarifer* (family Centropomidae) of NE coastal waters or the freshwater species *Scleropages leichardti* (family Osteoglossidae) of Queensland.

barranca (bə'ræŋkə) *or* **barranco** (bə'ræŋkəu) *n, pl* **-cas** *or* **-cos.** *Southwestern U.S.* a ravine or precipice. [C19: from Spanish, of uncertain origin]

Barranquilla (*Spanish* barran'kiʎa) *n* a port in N Colombia, on the Magdalena River. Pop.: 1 157 826 (1997 est.).

Barras (*French* baras) *n* **Paul François Jean Nicolas,** Vicomte de Barras. 1755–1829, French revolutionary: member of the Directory (1795–99).

barrator ('bærətə) *n* a person guilty of barratry. [C14: from Old French *barateor,* from *barater* to BARTER]

barratry *or* **barretry** ('bærətrɪ) *n* **1** *Criminal law.* (formerly) the vexatious stirring up of quarrels or bringing of lawsuits. **2** *Maritime law.* a fraudulent practice committed by the master or crew of a ship to the prejudice of the owner or charterer. **3** *Scots Law.* the crime committed by a judge in accepting a bribe. **4** the purchase or sale of public or Church offices. [C15: from Old French *baraterie* deception, from *barater* to BARTER] ► **'barratrous** *or* **'barretrous** *adj* ► **'barratrously** *or* **'barretrously** *adv*

Barrault (*French* baro) *n* **Jean-Louis** (ʒɑ̃lwi). 1910–94, French actor and director, noted particularly as a mime.

barre *French.* (bar) *n* a rail at hip height used for ballet practice and leg exercises. [literally: bar]

barré ('bæreɪ) *n* **1** the act of laying the index finger over some or all of the strings of a guitar, lute, or similar instrument, so that the pitch of each stopped string is simultaneously raised. Compare **capo**[1]. **2** the playing of chords in this manner. ◆ *vb* **3** to execute (chords) in this manner. ◆ *adv* **4** by using the barré. [C19: from French, from *barrer* BAR[1]]

barrel ('bærəl) *n* **1** a cylindrical container usually bulging outwards in the middle and held together by metal hoops; cask. **2** Also called: **barrelful.** the amount that a barrel can hold. **3** a unit of capacity used in brewing, equal to 36 Imperial gallons. **4** a unit of capacity used in the oil and other industries, normally equal to 42 U.S. gallons or 35 Imperial gallons. **5** a thing or part shaped like a barrel, esp. a tubular part of a machine. **6** the tube through which the projectile of a firearm is discharged. **7** *Horology.* the cylindrical drum in a watch or clock that is rotated by the mainspring. **8** the trunk of a four-legged animal: *the barrel of a horse.* **9** the quill of a feather. **10** *Informal.* a large measure; a great deal (esp. in the phrases **barrel of fun, barrel of laughs**). **11 over a barrel.** *Informal.* powerless. **12 scrape the barrel.** *Informal.* to be forced to use one's last and weakest resource. ◆ *vb* **-rels, -relling, -relled** *or U.S.* **-rels, -reling, -reled. 13** (*tr*) to put into a barrel or barrels. **14** (*intr;* foll. by *along, in,* etc.) *Informal.* to travel or move very fast. [C14: from Old French *baril,* perhaps from *barre* BAR[1]]

barrel-chested *adj* having a large rounded chest.

barrel distortion *n Photog.* distortion of an image produced by an optical system that causes straight lines at image margins to bulge outwards.

barrelhouse ('bærəl,haus) *n* **1** *U.S.* a cheap and disreputable drinking establishment. **2a** a vigorous and unpolished style of jazz for piano, originating in the barrelhouses of New Orleans. **2b** (*as modifier*): *barrelhouse blues.*

barrel organ *n* **1** an instrument consisting of a cylinder turned by a handle and having pins on it that interrupt the air flow to certain pipes, thereby playing any of a number of tunes. See also **hurdy-gurdy. 2** a similar instrument in which the projections on a rotating barrel pluck a set of strings.

barrel roll *n* **1** a flight manoeuvre in which an aircraft rolls about its longitudinal axis while following a spiral course in line with the direction of flight. ◆ *vb* **barrel-roll. 2** (*intr*) (of an aircraft) to perform a barrel roll.

barrel vault *n Architect.* a vault in the form of a half cylinder. Also called: **wagon vault, tunnel vault.**

barren ('bærən) *adj* **1** incapable of producing offspring, seed, or fruit; sterile: *a barren tree.* **2** unable to support the growth of crops, etc.; unproductive; bare: *barren land.* **3** lacking in stimulation or ideas; dull: *a rather barren play.* **4** not producing worthwhile results; unprofitable: *a barren period in a writer's life.* **5** (foll. by *of*) totally lacking (in); devoid (of): *his speech was barren of wit.* **6** (of rock strata) having no fossils. [C13: from Old French *brahain,* of uncertain origin] ▸ **'barrenly** *adv* ▸ **'barrenness** *n*

Barren Lands *pl n* **the.** a region of tundra in N Canada, extending westwards from Hudson Bay: sparsely inhabited, chiefly by Inuit. Also called: **Barren Grounds.**

barrens ('bærənz) *pl n* (*sometimes sing*) (in North America) a stretch of usually level land that is sparsely vegetated or barren.

barrenwort ('bærən,wɜːt) *n* a herbaceous European berberidaceous plant, *Epimedium alpinum,* having red-and-yellow star-shaped flowers.

Barrès (*French* barɛs) *n* **Maurice** (mɔris). 1862–1923, French novelist, essayist, and politician: a fervent nationalist and individualist.

barret ('bærɪt) *n* a small flat cap resembling a biretta. [C19: from French *barrette,* from Italian *berretta* BIRETTA; compare BERET]

barrette (bə'ret) *n* a clasp or pin for holding women's hair in place. [C20: from French: a little bar, from *barre* BAR[1]]

barricade (,bærɪ'keɪd, 'bærɪ,keɪd) *n* **1** a barrier for defence, esp. one erected hastily, as during street fighting. ◆ *vb* (*tr*) **2** to erect a barricade across (an entrance, passageway, etc.) or at points of access to (a room, district of a town, etc.): *they barricaded the door.* **3** (*usually passive*) to obstruct; block: *his mind was barricaded against new ideas.* [C17: from Old French, from *barriquer* to barricade, from *barrique* a barrel, from Spanish *barrica,* from *barril* BARREL] ▸ **'barri,cader** *n*

Barrie ('bærɪ) *n* Sir **James Matthew.** 1860–1937, Scottish dramatist and novelist, noted particularly for his popular children's play *Peter Pan* (1904).

barrier ('bærɪə) *n* **1** anything serving to obstruct passage or to maintain separation, such as a fence or gate. **2** anything that prevents or obstructs passage, access, or progress: *a barrier of distrust.* **3** anything that separates or hinders union: *a language barrier.* **4a** an exposed offshore sand bar separated from the shore by a lagoon. **4b** (*as modifier*): *a barrier beach.* **5** (*sometimes cap.*) that part of the Antarctic icecap extending over the sea. [C14: from Old French *barriere,* from *barre* BAR[1]]

barrier cream *n* a cream used to protect the skin, esp. the hands, from dirt and from the action of oils or solvents.

barrier-nurse *vb* (*tr.*) to tend (infectious patients) in isolation, to prevent the spread of infection. ▸ **barrier nursing** *n*

barrier of ideas *n Philosophy.* the representations of objects which certain accounts of perception interpose between the objects themselves and our awareness of them, so that, as critics argue, we can never know whether there is in reality anything which resembles our perceptions. See **representationalism** (sense 1).

barrier reef *n* a long narrow coral reef near and lying parallel to the shore, separated from it by deep water. See **Great Barrier Reef.**

barring ('bɑːrɪŋ) *prep* unless (something) occurs; except for: *barring rain, the match will be held tomorrow.*

Barrington ('bærɪŋtən) *n* **Jonah.** born 1940, British squash player; winner of the Open Championship 1966–67, 1969–72.

barrio ('bærɪəu; *Spanish* 'barrjo) *n, pl* **-rios. 1** a Spanish-speaking quarter in a town or city, esp. in the U.S. **2** a Spanish-speaking community. [from Spanish, from Arabic *barrī* of open country, from *barr* open country]

barrister ('bærɪstə) *n* **1** Also called: **barrister-at-law.** (in England) a lawyer who has been called to the bar and is qualified to plead in the higher courts. Compare **solicitor.** See also **advocate, counsel. 2** (in Canada) a lawyer who pleads in court. **3** *U.S.* a less common word for **lawyer.** [C16: from BAR[1]]

barroom ('bɑː,ruːm, -,rum) *n U.S.* a room or building where alcoholic drinks are served over a counter.

Barros (*Portuguese* 'baːrruʃ) *n* **João de** (ʒuɐ̃u 'dəː). 1496–1570, Portuguese historian: noted for his history of the Portuguese in the East Indies, *Décadas da Ásia* (1552–1615).

barrow[1] ('bærəu) *n* **1** See **wheelbarrow, handbarrow. 2** Also called: **barrowful.** the amount contained in or on a barrow. **3** *Chiefly Brit.* a handcart, typically having two wheels and a canvas roof, used esp. by street vendors. **4** *Northern English dialect.* concern or business (esp. in the phrases **that's not my barrow, that's just my barrow**). **5 into one's barrow.** *Irish and Scot. dialect.* suited to one's interests or desires. [Old English *bearwe;* related to Old Norse *barar* BIER, Old High German *bāra*]

barrow[2] ('bærəu) *n* a heap of earth placed over one or more prehistoric tombs, often surrounded by ditches. **Long barrows** are elongated Neolithic mounds usually covering stone burial chambers; **round barrows** are Bronze Age, covering burials or cremations. [Old English *beorg;* related to Old Norse *bjarg,* Gothic *bairgahei* hill, Old High German *berg* mountain]

barrow[3] ('bærəu) *n* a castrated pig. [Old English *bearg;* related to Old Norse *börgr,* Old High German *barug*]

Barrow ('bærəu) *n* **1** a river in SE Ireland, rising in the Slieve Bloom Mountains and flowing south to Waterford Harbour. Length: about 193 km (120 miles). **2** See **Barrow-in-Furness** and **Barrow Point.**

barrow boy *n Brit.* a man who sells his wares from a barrow; street vendor.

Barrow-in-Furness *n* an industrial town in NW England, in S Cumbria. Pop.: 48 947 (1991).

Barrow Point *n* the northernmost tip of Alaska, on the Arctic Ocean.

Barry[1] ('bærɪ) *n* a port in SE Wales, in Vale of Glamorgan county borough on the Bristol Channel. Pop.: 49 887 (1991).

Barry[2] *n* **1** ('bærɪ). Sir **Charles.** 1795–1860, English architect: designer of the Houses of Parliament in London. **2** (*French* bari). **Comtesse du.** See **du Barry.**

Barrymore ('bærɪ,mɔː) *n* a U.S. family of actors, esp. **Ethel** (1879–1959), **John** (1882–1942), and **Lionel** (1878–1954).

Barsac ('bɑːsæk; *French* barsak) *n* a sweet French white wine produced around the town of Barsac in the Gironde.

bar sinister *n* **1** (not in heraldic usage) another name for **bend sinister. 2** the condition, implication, or stigma of being of illegitimate birth.

Bart (bɑːt) *n* **Lionel.** 1930–99, British composer and playwright. His musicals include *Oliver* (1960).

Bart. *abbrev. for* Baronet.

bartender ('bɑː,tendə) *n* another name (esp. U.S. and Canadian) for **barman.**

barter ('bɑːtə) *vb* **1** to trade (goods, services, etc.) in exchange for other goods, services, etc., rather than for money: *the refugees bartered for food.* **2** (*intr*) to haggle over the terms of such an exchange; bargain. ◆ *n* **3** trade by the exchange of goods. [C15: from Old French *barater* to cheat; perhaps related to Greek *prattein* to do] ▸ **'barterer** *n*

Barth *n* **1** (*German* bart). **Heinrich.** 1821–65, German explorer: author of *Travels and Discoveries in North and Central Africa* (1857–58). **2** (bɑːθ). **John (Simmons).** born 1930, U.S. novelist; his novels include *The Sot-Weed Factor* (1960), *Giles Goat-Boy* (1966), and *Once Upon a Time* (1994). **3** (*German* bart). **Karl.** 1886–1968, Swiss Protestant theologian. He stressed man's dependence on divine grace in such works as *Commentary on Romans* (1919).

Barthes (*French* bart) *n* **Roland.** 1915–80, French writer and critic, who applied structuralist theory to literature: his books include *Mythologies* (1957) and *Elements of Semiology* (1964).

Barthian ('bɑːtɪən, -θɪən) *adj* **1** of or relating to Karl Barth or his ideas. ◆ *n* **2** a person who supports or believes in the ideas of Karl Barth.

Bartholdi (*French* bartɔldɪ) *n* **Frédéric August.** 1834–1904, French sculptor and architect, who designed (1884) the Statue of Liberty.

Bartholin's glands ('bɑːθəlɪnz) *pl n Anatomy.* two small reddish-yellow glands, one on each side of the vaginal orifice, that secrete a mucous lubricating substance during sexual stimulation in females. Compare **Cowper's glands.** [named by Caspar *Bartholin* (1655–1738), Danish anatomist, in honour of his father, Thomas]

Bartholomew (bɑː'θɒlə,mjuː) *n New Testament.* **Saint.** one of the twelve apostles (Matthew 10:3). Feast day: Aug. 24 or June 11.

bartizan ('bɑːtɪzən, ,bɑːtɪ'zæn) *n* a small turret projecting from a wall, parapet, or tower. [C19: variant of *bertisene,* erroneously for *bretising,* from *bretasce* parapet; see BRATTICE] ▸ **bartizaned** ('bɑːtɪzənd, ,bɑːtɪ'zænd) *adj*

Bartlett *or* **Bartlett pear** ('bɑːtlɪt) *n* another name for **Williams pear:** used esp. in the U.S. and generally of tinned pears. [named after Enoch *Bartlett* (1779–1860), of Dorchester, Mass., who marketed it in the U.S.]

Bartók ('bɑːtɒk; *Hungarian* 'bɔrtoːk) *n* **Béla** ('beːlɔ). 1881–1945, Hungarian composer, pianist, and collector of folk songs, by which his music was deeply influenced. His works include six string quartets, three piano concertos, several piano pieces including *Mikrokosmos* (1926–37), ballets (including *The Miraculous Mandarin,* 1919), and the opera *Bluebeard's Castle* (produced 1918).

Bartolommeo (*Italian* bartolom'meo) *n* **Fra.** original name *Baccio della Porta.* 1472–1517, Italian painter of the Florentine school, noted for his austere religious works.

barton ('bɑːtᵊn) *n Archaic.* a farmyard. [Old English *beretūn,* from *bere* barley + *tūn* stockade; see TOWN]

Barton ('bɑːtᵊn) *n* **1** Sir **Derek** (**Harold Richard**). 1918–98, British organic chemist: shared the Nobel prize for chemistry (1969) for his work on conformational analysis. **2** Sir **Edmund.** 1849–1920, Australian statesman; first prime minister of Australia (1901–03). **3 Elizabeth,** known as the *Maid of Kent.* ?1506–34, English nun, who claimed the gift of prophecy. Her criticism of Henry VIII's attempt to annul his first marriage led to her execution. **4 John** (**Bernard Adie**). born 1928, British theatre director, noted esp. for his productions of Shakespeare.

bartsia ('bɑːtsɪə) *n* any of several species of semiparasitic scrophulariaceous perennials, including **red bartsia** (*Odontites verna*), a pink-flowered weed of cornfields. [C18: New Latin, named after Johann *Bartsch* (died 1738), German botanist]

Baruch ('beəruk, 'bɑː-) *n Bible.* **a** a disciple of Jeremiah (Jeremiah 32–36). **b** the book of the Apocrypha said to have been written by him.

barycentre ('bærɪ,sentə) *n* a centre of mass, esp. of the earth-moon system. [C20: from Greek *barus* heavy + CENTRE] ▸ **,bary'centric** *adj*

barye ('bærɪ) *n* a unit of pressure in the cgs system equal to one dyne per square centimetre. 1 barye is equivalent to 1 microbar. [C19: from French, from Greek *barus* heavy]

baryon ('bærɪ,ɒn) *n* any of a class of elementary particles that have a mass greater than or equal to that of the proton, participate in strong interactions, and have a spin of ½. Baryons are either nucleons or hyperons. The **baryon**

number is the number of baryons in a system minus the number of antibaryons. [C20: *bary-*, from Greek *barus* heavy + -ON] ▸ ˌ**bary'onic** *adj*

Baryshnikov (bəˈrɪʃnɪkɒf) *n* **Mikhail.** born 1948, Soviet-born ballet dancer, who defected (1974) to the West while on tour with the Kirov Ballet: director (1980–90) of the American Ballet Theatre.

barysphere (ˈbærɪˌsfɪə) *n* the central portion of the earth, thought to consist chiefly of iron and nickel. [C20: from Greek *barus* heavy + SPHERE]

baryta (bəˈraɪtə) *n* another name for **barium oxide** or **barium hydroxide.** [C19: New Latin, from Greek *barutēs* weight, from *barus* heavy] ▸ **barytic** (bəˈrɪtɪk) *adj*

barytes (bəˈraɪtiːz) *n* a colourless or white mineral consisting of barium sulphate in rhombic crystalline form, occurring in sedimentary rocks and with sulphide ores: a source of barium. Formula: $BaSO_4$. Also called: **barite** (esp. U.S. and Canadian), **heavy spar.** [C18: from Greek *barus* heavy + *-itēs* -ITE[1]]

baryton (ˈbærɪˌtəʊn) *n* a bass viol with sympathetic strings as well as its six main strings. [C18: from French: BARITONE]

barytone[1] (ˈbærɪˌtəʊn) *n* a less common spelling of **baritone.**

barytone[2] (ˈbærɪˌtəʊn) (in ancient Greek) ◆ *adj* **1** having the last syllable unaccented. ◆ *n* **2** a word in which the last syllable is unaccented. ◆ Compare **oxytone.** [C19: from Greek *barutonos* heavy-sounding, from *barus* heavy + *tonos* TONE]

basal (ˈbeɪsᵊl) *adj* **1** at, of, or constituting a base. **2** of or constituting a foundation or basis; fundamental; essential. ▸ ˈ**basally** *adv*

basal anaesthesia *n* preliminary and incomplete anaesthesia induced to prepare a surgical patient for total anaesthesia with another agent.

basal ganglia *pl n* the thalamus together with other closely related masses of grey matter, situated near the base of the brain.

basal metabolic rate *n* the rate at which heat is produced by the body at rest, 12 to 14 hours after eating, measured in kilocalories per square metre of body surface per hour. Abbrev.: **BMR.**

basal metabolism *n* the amount of energy required by an individual in the resting state, for such functions as breathing and circulation of the blood. See **basal metabolic rate.**

basalt (ˈbæsɔːlt) *n* **1** a fine-grained dark basic igneous rock consisting of plagioclase feldspar, a pyroxene, and olivine: the most common volcanic rock and usually extrusive. See **flood basalt. 2** a form of black unglazed pottery resembling basalt. [C18: from Late Latin *basaltēs*, variant of *basanītēs*, from Greek *basanitēs* touchstone, from *basanos*, of Egyptian origin] ▸ **baˈsaltic** *adj*

basaltware (ˈbæsɔːltˌwɛə, ˈbeɪsɔːlt-) *n* hard fine-grained black stoneware, made in Europe, esp. in England, in the late 18th century.

basanite (ˈbæsəˌnaɪt) *n* a black basaltic rock containing plagioclase, augite, olivine, and nepheline, leucite, or analcite, formerly used as a touchstone.

bas bleu *French.* (bɑ blø) *n, pl* ***bas bleus*** (bɑ blø). a bluestocking; intellectual woman. [C18: from French translation of English BLUESTOCKING]

bascinet (ˌbæsɪˈnɛt, ˈbæsɪˌnɛt) *n Armour.* a variant spelling of **basinet.**

bascule (ˈbæskjuːl) *n* **1** Also called: **balance bridge, counterpoise bridge.** a bridge with a movable section hinged about a horizontal axis and counterbalanced by a weight. Compare **drawbridge. 2** a movable roadway forming part of such a bridge: *Tower Bridge has two bascules.* [C17: from French: seesaw, from *bas* low + *cul* rump; see BASE[2], CULET]

base[1] (beɪs) *n* **1** the bottom or supporting part of anything. **2** the fundamental or underlying principle or part, as of an idea, system, or organization; basis. **3a** a centre of operations, organization, or supply: *the climbers made a base at 8000 feet.* **3b** (*as modifier*): *base camp.* **4** a centre from which military activities are coordinated. **5** anything from which a process, as of measurement, action, or thought, is or may be begun; starting point: *the new discovery became the base for further research.* **6** the main ingredient of a mixture: *to use rice as a base in cookery.* **7** a chemical compound that combines with an acid to form a salt and water. A solution of a base in water turns litmus paper blue, produces hydroxyl ions, and has a pH greater than 7. Bases are metal oxides or hydroxides or amines. See also **Lewis base. 8** a medium such as oil or water in which the pigment is dispersed in paints, inks, etc.; vehicle. **9** the inorganic material on which the dye is absorbed in lake pigments; carrier. **10** *Biology.* **10a** the part of an organ nearest to its point of attachment. **10b** the point of attachment of an organ or part. **11** the bottommost layer or part of anything. **12** *Architect.* **12a** the lowest division of a building or structure. **12b** the lower part of a column or pier. **13** another word for **baseline** (sense 2). **14** the lower side or face of a geometric construction. **15** *Maths.* **15a** the number of distinct single-digit numbers in a counting system, and so the number represented as *10* in a place-value system: *the binary system has two digits, 0 and 1, and 10 to base two represents 2.* See **place-value. 15b** (of a logarithm or exponential) the number whose powers are expressed: *since* $1000 = 10^3$, *the logarithm of 1000 to base 10 is 3.* **15c** (of a mathematical structure) a substructure from which the given system can be generated. **15d** the initial instance from which a generalization is proven by mathematical induction. **16** *Logic, maths.* Also called: **base clause.** the initial element of a recursive definition, that defines the first element of the infinite sequence generated thereby. **17** *Linguistics.* **17a** a root or stem. **17b** See **base component. 18** *Electronics.* the region in a transistor between the emitter and collector. **19** *Photog.* the glass, paper, or cellulose-ester film that supports the sensitized emulsion with which it is coated. **20** *Heraldry.* the lower part of the shield. **21** *Jewellery.* the quality factor used in pricing natural pearls. **22** a starting or finishing point in any of various games. **23** *Baseball.* any of the four corners of the diamond, which runners have to reach in order to score. **24 get to first base.** *U.S. and Canadian informal.* to accomplish the first stage in a project or a series of objectives. **25 off base.** *U.S. and Canadian informal.* wrong or badly mistaken. **26 touch base.** *Chiefly U.S. and Canadian.* to make contact. ◆ *vb* **27** (*tr;* foll. by *on* or *upon*) to use as a basis (for); found (on): *your criticisms are based on ignorance.* **28** (often foll. by *at* or *in*) to station, post, or place (a person or oneself). [C14: from Old French, from Latin *basis* pedestal; see BASIS]

base[2] (beɪs) *adj* **1** devoid of honour or morality; ignoble; contemptible. **2** of inferior quality or value. **3** debased; alloyed; counterfeit: *base currency.* **4** *English history.* **4a** (of land tenure) held by villein or other ignoble service. **4b** holding land by villein or other ignoble service. **5** *Archaic.* born of humble parents; plebeian. **6** *Archaic.* illegitimate. ◆ *adj, n* **7** *Music.* an obsolete spelling of **bass**[1]. [C14: from Old French *bas*, from Late Latin *bassus* of low height, perhaps from Greek *bassōn* deeper] ▸ ˈ**basely** *adv* ▸ ˈ**baseness** *n*

baseball (ˈbeɪsˌbɔːl) *n* **1** a team game with nine players on each side, played on a field with four bases connected to form a diamond. The object is to score runs by batting the ball and running round the bases. **2** the hard rawhide-covered ball used in this game.

baseball cap *n* a close-fitting thin cap with a deep peak.

baseband (ˈbeɪsˌbænd) *n* a transmission technique using a narrow range of frequencies that allows only one message to be telecommunicated at a time. See also **broadband.**

baseboard (ˈbeɪsˌbɔːd) *n* **1** a board functioning as the base of anything. **2** the usual U.S. and Canadian word for **skirting board.**

baseborn (ˈbeɪsˌbɔːn) *adj Archaic.* **1** born of humble parents. **2** illegitimate. **3** mean; contemptible.

baseburner (ˈbeɪsˌbɜːnə) *n U.S.* a stove into which coal is automatically fed from a hopper above the fire chamber.

base component *n* the system of rules in a transformational grammar that specify the deep structure of the language.

base hospital *n Austral.* a hospital serving a large rural area.

base jumping *n* a sport in which a participant parachutes from any of a variety of fixed objects such as high buildings, cliffs, etc. [C20: *b(uilding), a(ntennae), s(pan, and) e(arthbound object)*]

Basel (ˈbɑːzᵊl) *or* **Basle** (bɑːl) *n* **1** a canton of NW Switzerland, divided into the demicantons of **Basel-Landschaft** and **Basel-Stadt.** Pops.: 252 331 and 195 759 (1996 est.). Areas: 427 sq. km (165 sq. miles) and 36 sq. km (14 sq. miles) respectively. **2** a city in NW Switzerland, capital of Basel canton, on the Rhine: oldest university in Switzerland. Pop.: 174 007 (1996 est.). French name: **Bâle.**

baseless (ˈbeɪslɪs) *adj* not based on fact; unfounded: *a baseless supposition.* ▸ ˈ**baselessly** *adv* ▸ ˈ**baselessness** *n*

base level *n* the lowest level to which a land surface can be eroded by streams, which is, ultimately, sea level.

baseline (ˈbeɪsˌlaɪn) *n* **1** *Surveying.* a measured line through a survey area from which triangulations are made. **2** an imaginary line, standard of value, etc., by which things are measured or compared. **3** a line at each end of a tennis court that marks the limit of play.

base load *n* the more or less constant part of the total load on an electrical power-supply system. Compare **peak load.**

baseman (ˈbeɪsmən) *n, pl* **-men.** *Baseball.* a fielder positioned near a base.

basement (ˈbeɪsmənt) *n* **1a** a partly or wholly underground storey of a building, esp. the one immediately below the main floor. Compare **cellar. 1b** (*as modifier*): *a basement flat.* **2** the foundation or substructure of a wall or building. **3** *Geology.* a part of the earth's crust formed of hard igneous or metamorphic rock that lies beneath the cover of soft sedimentary rock, sediment, and soil.

base metal *n* any of certain common metals such as copper, lead, zinc, and tin, as distinct from the precious metals, gold, silver, and platinum.

basenji (bəˈsɛndʒɪ) *n* a small smooth-haired breed of dog of African origin having a tightly curled tail and an inability to bark. [C20: from a Bantu language]

base pairing *n Biochem.* the hydrogen bonding that occurs between complementary nitrogenous bases in the two polynucleotide chains of a DNA molecule.

base period *n Statistics.* a neutral period used as a standard for comparison in constructing an index to express a variable factor: 100 is usually taken as the index number for the variable in the base period.

base rate *n* **1** *Brit.* the rate of interest used by individual commercial banks as a basis for their lending rates. **2** *Brit. informal.* the rate at which the Bank of England lends to the discount houses, which effectively controls the interest rates charged throughout the banking system. **3** *Statistics.* the average number of times an event occurs divided by the average number of times on which it might occur.

base rate fallacy *n Statistics.* the tendency, when making judgments of the probability with which an event will occur, to ignore the base rate and to concentrate on other information.

bases[1] (ˈbeɪsiːz) *n* the plural of **basis.**

bases[2] (ˈbeɪsɪz) *n* the plural of **base**[1].

base station *n* a fixed transmitter that forms part of an otherwise mobile radio network.

base unit *n Physics.* any of the fundamental units in a system of measurement. The base SI units are the metre, kilogram, second, ampere, kelvin, candela, and mole.

bash (bæʃ) *Informal.* ◆ *vb* **1** (*tr*) to strike violently or crushingly. **2** (*tr;* often foll. by *in, down,* etc.) to smash, break, etc., with a crashing blow: *to bash a door down.* **3** (*intr;* foll. by *into*) to crash (into); collide (with): *to bash into a lamppost.* **4** to dent or be dented: *this tin is bashed; this cover won't bash easily.* ◆ *n* **5** a heavy blow, as from a fist. **6** a dent; indentation. **7** a party. **8 have a bash.** *Informal.* to make an attempt. ◆ See also **bash up.** [C17: of uncertain origin]

Bashan (ˈbeɪʃæn) *n Old Testament.* a region to the east of the Jordan, renowned for its rich pasture (Deuteronomy 32:14).

bashaw (bəˈʃɔː) *n* **1** a rare spelling of **pasha. 2** an important or pompous person. [C16: from Turkish *başa*, from *bas* head, chief]

bashful (ˈbæʃfʊl) *adj* **1** disposed to attempt to avoid notice through shyness or modesty; diffident; timid. **2** indicating or characterized by shyness or modesty. [C16: from *bash,* short for ABASH + -FUL] ▸ ˈ**bashfully** *adv* ▸ ˈ**bashfulness** *n*

bashibazouk (ˌbæʃɪbəˈzuːk) *n* (in the 19th century) one of a group of irregular Turkish soldiers notorious for their brutality. [C19: from Turkish *başibozuk* irregular soldier, from *bas* head + *bozuk* corrupt]

-bashing *n and adj combining form. Informal or slang.* **a** indicating a malicious attack on members of a particular group: *queer-bashing; union-bashing.* **b** indicating any of various other activities: *Bible-bashing; spud-bashing; square-bashing.* ▸ **-basher** *n combining form.*

Bashkir (bæʃˈkɪə) *n* **1** (*pl* **-kir** *or* **-kirs**) a member of a Mongoloid people of E central Russia, living chiefly in the Bashkir Republic. **2** the language of this people, belonging to the Turkic branch of the Altaic family.

Bashkir Republic *n* a constituent republic of E central Russia, in the S Urals: established as the first Soviet autonomous republic in 1919; rich mineral resources. Capital: Ufa. Pop.: 4 080 000 (1995 est.). Area: 143 600 sq. km (55 430 sq. miles). Also called: **Bashkiria** (bæʃˈkɪərɪə), **Bashkortostan** (bæʃˈkɔːtɔˌstɑːn; *Russian* baʃkɔrtɔˈstaːn).

Bashkirtseff *or* **Bashkirtsev** (bəʃˈkjirtsəf) *n* **Marie,** original name *Marya Konstantinovna Bashkirtseva.* 1858–84, Russian painter and diarist who wrote in French, noted esp. for her *Journal* (1887).

basho (ˈbæʃəʊ) *n, pl* **basho.** a grand tournament in sumo wrestling. [C20: from Japanese]

Basho (bɑːˈʃɔː) *n* full name **Matsuo Basho,** originally *Matsuo Munefusa.* 1644–94, Japanese poet and travel writer, noted esp. for his haiku.

bash up *vb* (*tr, adv*) *Brit. slang.* to thrash; beat violently.

basic (ˈbeɪsɪk) *adj* **1** of, relating to, or forming a base or basis; fundamental; underlying. **2** elementary or simple: *a few basic facts.* **3** excluding additions or extras: *basic pay.* **4** *Chem.* **4a** of, denoting, or containing a base; alkaline. **4b** (of a salt) containing hydroxyl or oxide groups not all of which have been replaced by an acid radical: *basic lead carbonate,* $2PbCO_3.Pb(OH)_2$. **5** *Metallurgy.* of, concerned with, or made by a process in which the furnace or converter is made of a basic material, such as magnesium oxide. **6** (of such igneous rocks as basalt) containing between 52 and 45 per cent silica. **7** *Military.* primary or initial: *basic training.* ◆ *n* **8** (*usually pl*) a fundamental principle, fact, etc. ▸ ˈ**basically** *adv*

BASIC *or* **Basic** (ˈbeɪsɪk) *n* a computer programming language that uses common English terms. [C20: acronym of *b(eginner's) a(ll-purpose) s(ymbolic) i(nstruction) c(ode)*]

Basic Curriculum *n Brit. Education.* the National Curriculum plus religious education.

basic education *n* (in India) education in which all teaching is correlated with the learning of a craft.

basic English *n* a simplified form of English, proposed by C. K. Ogden and I. A. Richards, containing a vocabulary of approximately 850 of the commonest English words, intended as an international language.

basic industry *n* an industry which is highly important in a nation's economy.

basicity (beɪˈsɪsɪtɪ) *n Chem.* **a** the state of being a base. **b** the extent to which a substance is basic.

basicranial (ˌbæsɪˈkreɪnɪəl) *adj Anatomy.* of or relating to the base of the skull.

basic rate *n* the standard or lowest level on a scale of money payable, esp. in taxation.

basic slag *n* a furnace slag produced in steel-making, containing large amounts of calcium phosphate: used as a fertilizer.

basidiocarp (bæˈsɪdɪəʊˌkɑːp) *n* the fruiting body of basidiomycetous fungi; the mushroom of agarics.

basidiomycete (bæˌsɪdɪəʊmaɪˈsiːt) *n* any fungus of the phylum Basidiomycota (formerly class *Basidiomycetes*), in which the spores are produced in basidia. The group includes puffballs, smuts, and rusts. [C19: from BASIDI(UM) + -MYCETE] ▸ **baˌsidiomyˈcetous** *adj*

basidiospore (bæˈsɪdɪəʊˌspɔː) *n* one of the spores, usually four in number, produced in a basidium. ▸ **baˌsidioˈsporous** *adj*

basidium (bæˈsɪdɪəm) *n, pl* **-ia** (-ɪə). the structure, produced by basidiomycetous fungi after sexual reproduction, in which spores are formed at the tips of projecting slender stalks. [C19: from New Latin, from Greek *basidion;* see BASIS, -IUM] ▸ **baˈsidial** *adj*

Basie (ˈbeɪsɪ) *n* **William,** known as *Count Basie.* 1904–84, U.S. jazz pianist, bandleader, and composer: associated particularly with the polished phrasing and style of big-band jazz.

basifixed (ˈbeɪsɪˌfɪkst) *adj Botany.* (of an anther) attached to the filament by its base.

basifugal (beɪˈsɪfjʊgəl) *adj Botany.* a less common word for **acropetal.**

basify (ˈbeɪsɪˌfaɪ) *vb* **-fies, -fying, -fied.** (*tr*) to make basic.

basil (ˈbæzəl) *n* **1** Also called: **sweet basil.** a Eurasian plant, *Ocimum basilicum,* having spikes of small white flowers and aromatic leaves used as herbs for seasoning: family *Labiatae* (labiates). **2** Also called: **wild basil.** a European plant, *Satureja vulgaris* (or *Clinopodium vulgare*), with dense clusters of small pink or whitish flowers: family *Labiatae.* **3 basil-thyme.** a European plant, *Acinos arvensis,* having clusters of small violet-and-white flowers: family *Labiatae.* [C15: from Old French *basile,* from Late Latin *basilicum,* from Greek *basilikon,* from *basilikos* royal, from *basileus* king]

Basil (ˈbæzəl) *n* **Saint,** called *the Great.* ?329–379 A.D., Greek patriarch: an opponent of Arianism and one of the founders of monasticism. Feast day: Jan. 2, June 14, or Jan. 1.

Basil I *n* known as *the Macedonian.* died 886 A.D., Byzantine emperor (876–86): founder of the Macedonian dynasty.

Basilan (bəˈsiːlɑːn, bæˈsiːlæn) *n* **1** a group of islands in the Philippines, SW of Mindanao. **2** the main island of this group, separated from Mindanao by the Basilan Strait. Area: 1282 sq. km (495 sq. miles). **3** a city on Basilan Island. Pop.: 201 407 (1980).

basilar (ˈbæsɪlə) *adj Chiefly anatomy.* of or situated at a base: *basilar artery* (at the base of the skull). Also: **basilary** (ˈbæsɪlərɪ, -sɪlrɪ). [C16: from New Latin *basilaris,* from Latin *basis* BASE[1]; compare Medieval Latin *bassile* pelvis]

Basildon (ˈbæzɪldən) *n* a town in SE England, in S Essex: designated a new town in 1955. Pop.: 100 924 (1991).

Basilian (bəˈzɪlɪən) *n* a monk of the Eastern Christian order of St. Basil, founded in Cappadocia in the 4th century A.D.

basilica (bəˈzɪlɪkə) *n* **1** a Roman building, used for public administration, having a large rectangular central nave with an aisle on each side and an apse at the end. **2** a rectangular early Christian or medieval church, usually having a nave with clerestories, two or four aisles, one or more vaulted apses, and a timber roof. **3** a Roman Catholic church having special ceremonial rights. [C16: from Latin, from Greek *basilikē* hall, from *basilikē oikia* the king's house, from *basileus* king; see BASIL] ▸ **baˈsilican** *or* **baˈsilic** *adj*

Basilicata (*Italian* baziliˈkata) *n* a region of S Italy, between the Tyrrhenian Sea and the Gulf of Taranto. Capital: Potenza. Pop.: 609 238 (1996 est.). Area: 9985 sq. km (3855 sq. miles).

basilic vein (bəˈzɪlɪk) *n* a large vein situated on the inner side of the arm. [C18: from Latin *basilicus* kingly; see BASIL]

basilisk (ˈbæzɪˌlɪsk) *n* **1** (in classical legend) a serpent that could kill by its breath or glance. **2** any small arboreal semiaquatic lizard of the genus *Basiliscus* of tropical America: family *Iguanidae* (iguanas). The males have an inflatable head crest, used in display. **3** a 16th-century medium cannon, usually made of brass. [C14: from Latin *basiliscus,* from Greek *basiliskos* royal child, from *basileus* king]

basin (ˈbeɪsən) *n* **1** a round container open and wide at the top with sides sloping inwards towards the bottom or base, esp. one in which liquids are mixed or stored. **2** Also called: **basinful.** the amount a basin will hold. **3** a washbasin or sink. **4** any partially enclosed or sheltered area where vessels may be moored or docked. **5** the catchment area of a particular river and its tributaries or of a lake or sea. **6** a depression in the earth's surface. **7** *Geology.* a part of the earth's surface consisting of rock strata that slope down to a common centre. [C13: from Old French *bacin,* from Late Latin *bacchīnon,* from Vulgar Latin *bacca* (unattested) container for water; related to Latin *bāca* berry]

basinet *or* **bascinet** (ˈbæsɪnɪt, -ˌnɛt) *n* a close-fitting medieval helmet of light steel usually with a visor. [C14: from Old French *bacinet,* a little basin, from *bacin* BASIN]

Basingstoke (ˈbeɪzɪŋˌstəʊk) *n* a town in S England, in N Hampshire. Pop.: 77 837 (1991).

basion (ˈbeɪsɪən) *n Anatomy.* the midpoint on the forward border of the foramen magnum. [C19: from New Latin, from Latin *basis* BASE[1]]

basipetal (beɪˈsɪpɪtəl) *adj* (of leaves and flowers) produced in order from the apex downwards so that the youngest are at the base. Compare **acropetal.**

basis (ˈbeɪsɪs) *n, pl* **-ses** (-siːz). **1** something that underlies, supports, or is essential to something else, esp. an abstract idea. **2** a principle on which something depends or from which something has issued. **3** *Maths.* (of a Euclidean space) a maximal set of mutually perpendicular vectors, in terms of which all the elements of the space are uniquely expressible, and the number of which is the dimension of the space: *the vectors* **x, y** *and* **z** *form a basis of the 3-dimensional space all members of which can be written as* a**x** + b**y** + c**z**. [C14: via Latin from Greek: step, from *bainein* to step, go]

bask (bɑːsk) *vb* (*intr;* usually foll. by *in*) **1** to lie in or be exposed to pleasant warmth, esp. that of the sun. **2** to flourish or feel secure under some benevolent influence or favourable condition. [C14: from Old Norse *bathask* to BATHE]

Baskerville (ˈbæskəˌvɪl) *n* a style of type. [C18: named after John *Baskerville* (1706–1775), English printer]

basket (ˈbɑːskɪt) *n* **1** a container made of interwoven strips of pliable materials, such as cane, straw, thin wood, or plastic, and often carried by means of a handle or handles. **2** Also called: **basketful.** the amount a basket will hold. **3** something resembling such a container in appearance or function, such as the structure suspended from a balloon. **4** *Basketball.* **4a** an open horizontal metal hoop fixed to the backboard, through which a player must throw the ball to score points. **4b** a point or points scored in this way. **5** a group or collection of similar of related things: *a basket of currencies.* **6** *Informal.* a euphemism for **bastard** (senses 1, 2). [C13: probably from Old Northern French *baskot* (unattested), from Latin *bascauda* basketwork holder, of Celtic origin]

basketball (ˈbɑːskɪtˌbɔːl) *n* **1** a game played by two opposing teams of five men (or six women) each, usually on an indoor court. Points are scored by throwing the ball through an elevated horizontal metal hoop. **2** the inflated ball used in this game.

basket case *n Slang.* **1** *Chiefly U.S. and Canadian.* a person who has had both arms and both legs amputated. **2** a person who is suffering from extreme nervous strain; nervous wreck. **3a** someone or something that is incapable of functioning normally. **3b** (*as modifier*): *a basket-case economy.*

basket chair *n* a chair made of wickerwork; a wicker chair.

basket clause *n* an all-inclusive or comprehensive clause in a contract.

basket hilt *n* a hilt fitted to a broadsword, with a generally padded basket-shaped guard to protect the hand. ▸ ˈ**basket-ˌhilted** *adj*

Basket Maker *n* a member of an early American Indian people of the south-western U.S., preceding the Pueblo people, known for skill in basket-making.

basketry (ˈbɑːskɪtrɪ) *n* **1** the art or practice of making baskets. **2** baskets collectively.

basket-star *n* any of several echinoderms of the genus *Gorgonocephalus,* in which long slender arms radiate from a central disc: order *Ophiuroidea* (brittle-stars).

basket weave *n* a weave of two or more yarns together, resembling that of a basket, esp. in wool or linen fabric.

basketwork ('bɑːskɪt,wɜːk) *n* another word for **wickerwork.**

basking shark *n* a very large plankton-eating shark, *Cetorhinus maximus,* often floating at the sea surface: family *Cetorhinidae.* Also called: **sailfish.**

Basle (bɑːl) *n* a variant spelling of **Basel.**

basmati rice (bəz'mætɪ) *n* a variety of long-grain rice with slender aromatic grains, used for savoury dishes. [from Hindi, literally: aromatic]

Bas Mitzvah (bɑːs 'mɪtsvə) *n* (*sometimes not caps.*) a variant of **Bat Mitzvah.**

basophil ('beɪsəfɪl) *or* **basophile** *adj also* **basophilic** (,beɪsə'fɪlɪk). **1** (of cells or cell contents) easily stained by basic dyes. ◆ *n* **2** a basophil cell, esp. a leucocyte. [C19: from Greek; see BASE[1] + -PHILE]

basophilia (,beɪsə'fɪlɪə) *n* **1** an abnormal increase of basophil leucocytes in the blood. **2** the affinity of a microscope specimen for basic dyes.

Basotho (bə'suːtuː, -'səʊtəʊ) *n, pl* **-tho** *or* **-thos.** a member of the subgroup of the Sotho people who chiefly inhabit Lesotho. Former name: **Basuto.**

Basotho-Qwaqwa (bə'suːtuː'kwɑːkwə, -'səʊtəʊ-) *n* (formerly) a Bantustan in South Africa, in the Orange Free State; the only Bantustan without exclaves: abolished in 1993. Also called: **Qwaqwa.** Former name (until 1972): **Basotho-Ba-Borwa.**

Basov (*Russian* 'basəf) *n* **Nikolai Gennediyevich** (nika'laj gji'nadjejivitj). born 1922, Russian physicist: shared the Nobel prize for physics (1964) for his pioneering work on the maser.

basque (bæsk, bɑːsk) *n* **1** a short extension below the waist to the bodice of a woman's jacket, etc. **2** a tight-fitting bodice for women. [C19: perhaps from BASQUE]

Basque (bæsk, bɑːsk) *n* **1** a member of a people of unknown origin living around the W Pyrenees in France and Spain. **2** the language of this people, of no known relationship with any other language. ◆ *adj* **3** relating to, denoting, or characteristic of this people or their language. [C19: from French, from Latin *Vascō* a Basque]

Basque Provinces *n* an autonomous region of N Spain, comprising the provinces of Álava, Guipúzcoa, and Viscaya: inhabited mainly by Basques, who retained virtual autonomy from the 9th to the 19th century. Pop.: 2 098 055 (1996 est.). Area: about 7250 sq. km (2800 sq. miles).

Basra, Basrah ('bæzrə), **Busra,** *or* **Busrah** ('bʌsrə) *n* a port in SE Iraq, on the Shatt-al-Arab. Pop.: 406 296 (1987).

bas-relief (,bɑːrɪ'liːf, ,bæs-; 'bɑːrɪ,liːf, 'bæs-) *n* sculpture in low relief, in which the forms project slightly from the background but no part is completely detached from it. Also called (Italian): **basso rilievo.** [C17: from French, from Italian *basso rilievo* low relief; see BASE[2], RELIEF]

Bas-Rhin (*French* barɛ̃) *n* a department of NE France in Alsace region. Capital: Strasbourg. Pop.: 994 100 (1995). Area: 4793 sq. km (1869 sq. miles).

bass[1] (beɪs) *n* **1** the lowest adult male voice usually having a range from E a 13th below middle C to D a tone above it. **2** a singer with such a voice. **3 the bass.** the lowest part in a piece of harmony. See also **thorough bass. 4** *Informal.* short for **bass guitar, double bass. 5a** the low-frequency component of an electrical audio signal, esp. in a record player or tape recorder. **5b** the knob controlling this on such an instrument. ◆ *adj* **6** relating to or denoting the bass: *bass pitch; the bass part.* **7** denoting the lowest and largest instrument in a family: *a bass trombone.* [C15 *bas* BASE[1]; modern spelling influenced by BASSO]

bass[2] (bæs) *n* **1** any of various sea perches, esp. *Morone labrax,* a popular game fish with one large spiny dorsal fin separate from a second smaller one. See also **sea bass, stone bass. 2** another name for the **European perch** (see **perch**[2] (sense 1)). **3** any of various predatory North American freshwater percoid fishes, such as *Micropterus salmoides* (**largemouth bass**): family *Centrarchidae* (sunfishes, etc.). See also **black bass, rock bass.** [C15: changed from BASE[2], influenced by Italian *basso* low]

bass[3] (bæs) *n* **1** another name for **bast. 2** short for **basswood. 3** Also called: **fish bass.** a bast fibre bag for holding an angler's catch. [C17: changed from BAST]

bass clef (beɪs) *n* the clef that establishes F a fifth below middle C on the fourth line of the staff. Symbol: 𝄢 Also called: **F clef.**

bass drum (beɪs) *n* a large shallow drum of low and indefinite pitch. Also called: **gran cassa.**

Bassein (bɑː'seɪn) *n* a city in Myanmar, on the Irrawaddy delta: a port on the **Bassein River** (the westernmost distributary of the Irrawaddy). Pop.: 150 000 (latest est.).

Basse-Normandie (*French* basnɔrmɑ̃di) *n* a region of NW France, on the English Channel: consists of the Cherbourg peninsula in the west rising to the Normandy hills in the east; mainly agricultural.

Bassenthwaite ('bæsᵊn,θweɪt) *n* a lake in NW England, in Cumbria near Keswick. Length: 6 km (4 miles).

Basses-Alpes (*French* basalp) *n* the former name for **Alpes-de-Haute-Provence.**

Basses-Pyrénées (*French* baspirene) *pl n* the former name for **Pyrénées (Atlantiques).**

basset[1] ('bæsɪt) *n* a long low smooth-haired breed of hound with short strong legs and long ears. Also called: **basset hound.** [C17: from French, from *basset* short, from *bas* low; see BASE[2]]

basset[2] ('bæsɪt) *vb* **-sets, -seting, -seted,** *n* a less common word for **outcrop.** [C17: perhaps from French: low stool, see BASSET[1]]

Basseterre (bæs'tɛə; *French* bastɛr) *n* a port in the Caribbean, on St Kitts in the Leeward Islands: the capital of St Kitts-Nevis. Pop.: 12 605 (1994 est.).

Basse-Terre ('bæs'tɛə; *French* bastɛr) *n* **1** a mountainous island in the Caribbean, in the Leeward Islands, comprising part of Guadeloupe. Area: 848 sq. km (327 sq. miles). **2** a port in W Guadeloupe, on Basse-Terre Island: the capital of the French Overseas Department of Guadeloupe. Pop.: 29 522 (1994 est.).

basset horn *n* an obsolete woodwind instrument of the clarinet family. [C19: probably from German *Bassetthorn,* from Italian *bassetto,* diminutive of BASSO + HORN]

bass guitar (beɪs) *n* a guitar that has the same pitch and tuning as a double bass, usually electrically amplified.

bassinet (,bæsɪ'nɛt) *n* a wickerwork or wooden cradle or pram, usually hooded. [C19: from French: little basin, from *bassin* BASIN; associated in folk etymology with French *barcelonnette* a little cradle, from *berceau* cradle]

bassist ('beɪsɪst) *n* a player of a double bass, esp. in a jazz band.

basso ('bæsəʊ) *n, pl* **-sos** *or* **-si** (-sɪ). (esp. in operatic or solo singing) a singer with a bass voice. [C19: from Italian, from Late Latin *bassus* low; see BASE[2]]

basso continuo *n* another term for **thorough bass.** Often shortened to **continuo.** [Italian, literally: continuous bass]

bassoon (bə'suːn) *n* **1** a woodwind instrument, the tenor of the oboe family. Range: about three and a half octaves upwards from the B flat below the bass staff. **2** an orchestral musician who plays the bassoon. [C18: from French *basson,* from Italian *bassone,* from *basso* deep; see BASE[2]] ▸ **bas'soonist** *n*

basso profundo (prəʊ'fʌndəʊ; *Italian* pro'fundo) *n, pl* **-dos.** (esp. in operatic solo singing) a singer with a very deep bass voice. [Italian, literally: deep bass]

basso rilievo (*Italian* 'basso ri'ljevo) *n, pl* **-vos.** Italian name for **bas-relief.**

bass response (beɪs) *n* the response of an audio reproduction system or component to low frequencies.

Bass Strait (bæs) *n* a channel between mainland Australia and Tasmania, linking the Indian Ocean and the Tasman Sea.

bass viol (beɪs) *n* **1** another name for **viola da gamba. 2** *U.S.* a less common name for **double bass** (sense 1).

basswood ('bæs,wʊd) *n* **1** any of several North American linden trees, esp. *Tilia americana.* Sometimes shortened to **bass. 2** the soft light-coloured wood of any of these trees, used for furniture. [C19: from BASS[3]; see BAST]

bast (bæst) *n* **1** *Botany.* another name for **phloem. 2** fibrous material obtained from the phloem of jute, hemp, flax, lime, etc., used for making rope, matting, etc. ◆ Also called: **bass.** [Old English *bæst;* related to Old Norse, Middle High German *bast*]

bastard ('bɑːstəd, 'bæs-) *n* **1** *Informal, offensive.* an obnoxious or despicable person. **2** *Informal, often humorous or affectionate.* a person, esp. a man: *lucky bastard.* **3** *Informal.* something extremely difficult or unpleasant: *that job is a real bastard.* **4** *Old-fashioned or offensive.* a person born of unmarried parents; an illegitimate baby, child, or adult. **5** something irregular, abnormal, or inferior. **6** a hybrid, esp. an accidental or inferior one. ◆ *adj* (*prenominal*) **7** *Old-fashioned or offensive.* illegitimate by birth. **8** irregular, abnormal, or inferior in shape, size, or appearance. **9** resembling a specified thing, but not actually being such: *a bastard cedar.* **10** counterfeit; spurious. [C13: from Old French *bastart,* perhaps from *bast* in the phrase *fils de bast* son of the packsaddle (that is, of an unlawful and not the marriage bed), from Medieval Latin *bastum* packsaddle, of uncertain origin] ▸ **'bastardly** *adj*

bastard cut *adj Mechanical engineering.* (of a file) having medium teeth; intermediate between a coarse cut and a fine cut.

bastardization *or* **bastardisation** (,bɑːstədaɪ'zeɪʃən, ,bæs-) *n* **1** the act of bastardizing. **2** *Austral.* **2a** an initiation ceremony in a school or military unit, esp. one involving brutality. **2b** brutality or bullying.

bastardize *or* **bastardise** ('bɑːstə,daɪz, 'bæs-) *vb* (*tr*) **1** to debase; corrupt. **2** *Archaic.* to declare illegitimate.

bastard measles *n Pathol.* an informal name for **rubella.**

bastardry ('bɑːstədrɪ, 'bæs-) *n Slang, chiefly Austral.* malicious or cruel behaviour.

bastard title *n* another name for **half-title** (of a book).

bastard wing *n* a tuft of feathers attached to the first digit of a bird, distinct from the wing feathers attached to the other digits and the ulna. Also called: **alula.**

bastardy ('bɑːstədɪ, 'bæs-) *n Archaic.* the condition of being a bastard; illegitimacy.

baste[1] (beɪst) *vb* (*tr*) to sew with loose temporary stitches. [C14: from Old French *bastir* to build, of Germanic origin; compare Old High German *besten* to sew with BAST]

baste[2] (beɪst) *vb* to moisten (meat) during cooking with hot fat and the juices produced. [C15: of uncertain origin]

baste[3] (beɪst) *vb* (*tr*) to beat thoroughly; thrash. [C16: probably from Old Norse *beysta*]

basti, bustee, *or* **busti** ('bʌstɪ) *n* (in India) a slum inhabited by poor people. [Urdu: settlement]

Bastia ('bɑːstjə) *n* a port in NE Corsica: the main commercial and industrial town of the island: capital of Haute-Corse department. Pop.: 38 728 (1990).

Bastille (bæ'stiːl; *French* bastij) *n* a fortress in Paris, built in the 14th century: a prison until its destruction in 1789, at the beginning of the French Revolution. [C14: from Old French *bastile* fortress, from Old Provençal *bastida,* from *bastir* to build, of Germanic origin; see BASTE[1]]

Bastille Day *n* (in France) an annual holiday on July 14, commemorating the fall of the Bastille.

bastinado (,bæstɪ'neɪdəʊ) *n, pl* **-does. 1** punishment or torture in which the soles of the feet are beaten with a stick. **2** a blow or beating with a stick. **3** a stick; cudgel. ◆ *vb* **-does, -doing, -doed.** (*tr*) **4** to beat (a person) on the soles of the feet. [C16: from Spanish *bastonada,* from *baston* stick, from Late Latin *bastum;* see BATON]

basting ('beɪstɪŋ) *n* **1** loose temporary stitches; tacking. **2** sewing with such stitches.

bastion ('bæstɪən) *n* **1** a projecting work in a fortification designed to permit fire to the flanks along the face of the wall. **2** any fortified place. **3** a thing or person regarded as upholding or defending an attitude, principle, etc.: *the last bastion of opposition.* [C16: from French, from earlier *bastillon* bastion, from *bastille* BASTILLE]

bastnaesite *or* **bastnasite** ('bæstnə,saɪt) *n* a rare yellow to reddish-brown mineral consisting of a carbonate of fluorine and several lanthanide metals. It occurs in association with zinc and is a source of the lanthanides. Formula: $LaFCO_3$. [C19: from Swedish *bastnäsit,* after *Bastnäs,* Sweden, where it was found]

Bastogne (bæ'stəʊn; *French* bastɔɲ) *n* a town in SE Belgium: of strategic importance to Allied defences during the Battle of the Bulge; besieged by the Germans during the winter of 1944–45. Pop.: 7000 (1991 est.).

Basuto (bə'suːtəʊ) *n, pl* **-tos** *or* **-to.** a former name for **Sotho** (senses 3, 4).

Basutoland (bə'suːtəʊ,lænd) *n* the former name (until 1966) of **Lesotho.**

BASW ('bæzwə) *n* (in Britain) *acronym for* British Association of Social Workers.

bat[1] (bæt) *n* **1** any of various types of club with a handle, used to hit the ball in certain sports, such as cricket, baseball, or table tennis. **2** a flat round club with a short handle, resembling a table-tennis bat, used by a man on the ground to guide the pilot of an aircraft when taxiing. **3** *Cricket.* short for **batsman. 4** any stout stick, esp. a wooden one. **5** *Informal.* a blow from such a stick. **6** *Austral.* a small board used for tossing the coins in the game of two-up. **7** *U.S. and Canadian slang.* a drinking spree; binge. **8** *Slang.* speed; rate; pace: *they went at a fair bat.* **9** another word for **batting** (sense 1). **10 carry one's bat.** *Cricket.* (of a batsman) to reach the end of an innings without being dismissed. **11 off one's own bat. 11a** of one's own accord; without being prompted by someone else. **11b** by one's own unaided efforts. **12 (right) off the bat.** *U.S. and Canadian informal.* immediately; without hesitation. ◆ *vb* **bats, batting, batted. 13** (*tr*) to strike with or as if with a bat. **14** (*intr*) *Cricket, etc.* (of a player or a team) to take a turn at batting. ◆ See also **bat around.** [Old English *batt* club, probably of Celtic origin; compare Gaelic *bat,* Russian *bat*]

bat[2] (bæt) *n* **1** any placental mammal of the order *Chiroptera,* being a nocturnal mouselike animal flying with a pair of membranous wings (patagia). The group is divided into the *Megachiroptera* (**fruit bats**) and *Microchiroptera* (**insectivorous bats**). Related adj: **chiropteran. 2** *Slang.* an irritating or eccentric woman (esp. in the phrase **old bat**). **3 blind as a bat.** having extremely poor eyesight. **4 have bats in the** (*or* **one's**) **belfry.** *Informal.* to be mad or eccentric; have strange ideas. **5 like a bat out of hell.** *Slang.* very quickly. [C14 *bakke,* probably of Scandinavian origin; compare Old Norse *ledhrblaka* leather-flapper, Swedish dialect *natt-batta* night bat] ▸ **'batlike** *adj*

bat[3] (bæt) *vb* **bats, batting, batted.** (*tr*) **1** to wink or flutter (one's eyelids). **2 not bat an eye** (*or* **eyelid**). *Informal.* to show no surprise or concern. [C17: probably a variant of BATE[2]]

Bataan (bə'tæn, -'tɑːn) *n* a peninsula in the Philippines, in W Luzon: scene of the surrender of U.S. and Philippine forces to the Japanese during World War II, later retaken by American forces.

Batangas (bə'tæŋgæs) *n* a port in the Philippines, in SW Luzon. Pop.: 190 627 (1994 est.).

Batan Islands (bə'tɑːn) *pl n* a group of islands in the Philippines, north of Luzon. Capital: Basco. Pop.: 12 091 (1980). Area: 197 sq. km (76 sq. miles).

bat around *vb* **1** (*tr, adv*) *U.S. and Canadian slang.* to discuss (an idea, proposition, etc.) informally. **2** (*intr*) Also: **bat along.** *Dialect, U.S. and Canadian slang.* to wander or move about.

batata (bə'tɑːtə) *n* another name for **sweet potato.** [C16: from Spanish, from Taino]

Batavia (bə'teɪvɪə) *n* **1** an ancient district of the Netherlands, on an island at the mouth of the Rhine. **2** an archaic or literary name for **Holland**[1]. **3** a former name for **Jakarta.** ▸ **Ba'tavian** *adj, n*

batch[1] (bætʃ) *n* **1** a group or set of usually similar objects or people, esp. if sent off, handled, or arriving at the same time. **2** the bread, cakes, etc., produced at one baking. **3** the amount of a material needed for an operation. **4** Also called: **batch loaf.** a tall loaf having a close texture and a thick crust on the top and bottom, baked as part of a batch: the sides of each loaf are greased so that they will pull apart after baking to have pale crumby sides; made esp. in Scotland and Ireland. Compare **pan loaf.** ◆ *vb* (*tr*) **5** to group (items) for efficient processing. **6** to handle by batch processing. [C15 *bache;* related to Old English *bacan* to BAKE; compare Old English *gebæc* batch, German *Gebäck*]

batch[2] *or* **bach** (bætʃ) *vb* (*intr*) *Austral. and N.Z. informal.* (of a man) to do his own cooking and housekeeping.

Bat Chayil (bɑːt 'xajil) *n* (*sometimes not caps.*) *Judaism.* **1** (in some congregations) a ceremony of confirmation for a girl of at least Bat Mitzvah age. **2** the girl herself. ◆ Also: **Bat Hayil.** [from Hebrew, literally: daughter of valour]

batch processing *n* **1** manufacturing products or treating materials in batches, by passing the output of one process to subsequent processes. Compare **continuous processing. 2** a system by which the computer programs of a number of individual users are submitted to the computer as a single batch. Compare **time sharing** (sense 2).

bate[1] (beɪt) *vb* **1** another word for **abate. 2 with bated breath.** holding one's breath in suspense or fear.

bate[2] (beɪt) *vb* (*intr*) (of hawks) to jump violently from a perch or the falconer's fist, often hanging from the leash while struggling to escape. [C13: from Old French *batre* to beat, from Latin *battuere;* related to BAT[1]]

bate[3] (beɪt) *vb* (*tr*) **1** to soak (skin or hides) in a special solution to soften them and remove chemicals used in previous treatments. ◆ *n* **2** the solution used. [Old English *bǣtan* to BAIT[1]]

bate[4] (beɪt) *n Brit. slang.* a bad temper or rage. [C19: from BAIT[1], alluding to the mood of a person who is being baited]

bateau (bæ'təʊ; *French* bato) *n, pl* **-teaux** (-təʊz; *French* -to). a light flat-bottomed boat used on rivers in Canada and the northern U.S. [C18: from French: boat, from Old French *batel,* from Old English *bāt;* see BOAT]

bateleur eagle ('bætəlɜː) *n* an African crested bird of prey, *Terathopius ecaudatus,* with a short tail and long wings: subfamily *Circaetinae,* family *Accipitridae* (hawks, etc.). [C19: from French *bateleur* juggler]

Bates (beɪts) *n* **1 Alan (Arthur).** born 1934, British film and stage actor. His films include *The Fixer* (1968) and *The Grotesque* (1996). **2 H(erbert) E(rnest).** 1905–74, English writer of short stories and novels, which include *The Darling Buds of May* (1958), *A Moment in Time* (1964), and *The Triple Echo* (1970).

Batesian mimicry ('beɪtsɪən) *n Zoology.* mimicry in which a harmless species is protected from predators by means of its resemblance to a harmful or inedible species. [C19: named after H. W. *Bates* (1825–92), British naturalist and explorer]

batfish ('bæt,fɪʃ) *n, pl* **-fish** *or* **-fishes.** any angler of the family *Ogcocephalidae,* having a flattened scaleless body and moving on the sea floor by means of fleshy pectoral and pelvic fins.

batfowl ('bæt,faʊl) *vb* (*intr*) to catch birds by temporarily blinding them with light. ▸ **'bat,fowler** *n*

bath[1] (bɑːθ) *n, pl* **baths** (bɑːðz). **1** a large container, esp. one made of enamelled iron or plastic, used for washing or medically treating the body. Related adj: **balneal. 2** the act or an instance of washing in such a container. **3** the amount of liquid contained in a bath. **4 run a bath.** to turn on the taps to fill a bath with water for bathing oneself. **5** (*usually pl*) a place that provides baths or a swimming pool for public use. **6a** a vessel in which something is immersed to maintain it at a constant temperature, to process it photographically, electrolytically, etc., or to lubricate it. **6b** the liquid used in such a vessel. ◆ *vb* **7** *Brit.* to wash in a bath. [Old English *bæth;* compare Old High German *bad,* Old Norse *bath;* related to Swedish *basa* to clean with warm water, Old High German *bāen* to warm]

bath[2] (bæθ) *n* an ancient Hebrew unit of liquid measure equal to about 8.3 Imperial gallons or 10 U.S. gallons. [Hebrew]

Bath (bɑːθ) *n* a city in SW England, in Bath and North East Somerset unitary authority, Somerset, on the River Avon: famous for its hot springs; a fashionable spa in the 18th century; Roman remains, notably the baths. Pop.: 85 202 (1991). Latin name: **Aquae Sulis** ('ækwiː'suːlɪs).

Ba'th (bɑːθ) *or* **Ba'ath** *n* an Arab Socialist party, esp. in Iraq and Syria, founded by Michel Aflaq in 1941. It attempts to combine Marxism with pan-Islamic nationalism. [C20: from Arabic: resurgence] ▸ **'Ba'thi** *adj* ▸ **'Ba'thism** *n* ▸ **'Ba'thist** *n*

Bath and North East Somerset ('sʌmət) *n* a unitary authority in SW England, in Somerset; formerly (1974–96) part of the county of Avon. Pop.: 158 692 (1996). Area: 351 sq. km (136 sq. miles).

Bat Hayil (bɑːt 'xajil) *n* a variant spelling of **Bat Chayil.**

bath bun *n Brit.* a sweet bun containing spices and dried fruit. [C19: from BATH, where it was originally made]

Bath chair *n* a wheelchair for invalids, often with a hood.

Bath chap *n* the lower part of the cheek of a pig, cooked and eaten, usually cold.

bath cube *n* a cube of soluble scented material for use in a bath.

bathe (beɪð) *vb* **1** (*intr*) to swim or paddle in a body of open water or a river, esp. for pleasure. **2** (*tr*) to apply liquid to (skin, a wound, etc.) in order to cleanse or soothe. **3** to immerse or be immersed in a liquid: *to bathe machine parts in oil.* **4** *Chiefly U.S. and Canadian.* to wash in a bath. **5** (*tr; often passive*) to suffuse: *her face was bathed with radiance.* **6** (*tr*) (of water, the sea, etc.) to lap; wash: *waves bathed the shore.* ◆ *n* **7** *Brit.* a swim or paddle in a body of open water or a river. [Old English *bathian;* related to Old Norse *batha,* Old High German *badōn*] ▸ **'bather** *n*

bathers ('beɪðəz) *pl n Austral.* a swimming costume.

bathetic (bə'θetɪk) *adj* containing or displaying bathos.

bathhouse ('bɑːθ,haʊs) *n* a building containing baths, esp. for public use.

bathing beauty ('beɪðɪŋ) *n* an attractive girl in a swimming costume. Also called (old-fashioned): **bathing belle.**

bathing cap ('beɪðɪŋ) *n* a tight rubber cap worn by a swimmer to keep the hair dry.

bathing costume ('beɪðɪŋ) *n* another name for **swimming costume.**

bathing machine ('beɪðɪŋ) *n* a small hut, on wheels so that it could be pulled to the sea, used in the 18th and 19th centuries for bathers to change their clothes.

bathing suit ('beɪðɪŋ) *n* **1** a garment worn for bathing, esp. an old-fashioned one that covers much of the body. **2** another name for **swimming costume.**

batho- *combining form.* a variant of **bathy-.**

bathochromic (,bæθə'krəʊmɪk) *adj Chem.* denoting or relating to a shift to a longer wavelength in the absorption spectrum of a compound. ▸ **'batho,chrome** *n*

batholith ('bæθəlɪθ) *or* **batholite** ('bæθə,laɪt) *n* a very large irregular-shaped mass of igneous rock, esp. granite, formed from an intrusion of magma at great depth, esp. one exposed after erosion of less resistant overlying rocks. ▸ **,batho'lithic** *or* **,batho'litic** *adj*

Bath Oliver *n Brit.* a kind of unsweetened biscuit. [C19: named after William *Oliver* (1695–1764), a physician at Bath]

bathometer (bə'θɒmɪtə) *n* an instrument for measuring the depth of water. ▸ **bathometric** (,bæθə'metrɪk) *adj* ▸ **,batho'metrically** *adv* ▸ **bathometry** (bə'θɒmɪtrɪ) *n*

Bathonian (bə'θəʊnɪən) *adj* **1** of or relating to Bath. **2** *Geology.* of or denoting a stage of the Jurassic system in NW Europe. ◆ *n* **3** a native or resident of Bath. **4** the Bathonian period or rock system.

bathophilous (bæ'θɒfɪləs) *adj* (of an organism) living in very deep water.

bathos ('beɪθɒs) *n* **1** a sudden ludicrous descent from exalted to ordinary matters or style in speech or writing. **2** insincere or excessive pathos. **3** triteness; flatness. **4** the lowest point; nadir. [C18: from Greek: depth, from *bathus* deep]

bathrobe ('bɑːθˌrəʊb) *n* **1** a loose-fitting garment of towelling, for wear before or after a bath or swimming. **2** *U.S. and Canadian.* a dressing gown.

bathroom ('bɑːθˌruːm, -ˌrʊm) *n* **1** a room containing a bath or shower and usually a washbasin and lavatory. **2** *U.S. and Canadian.* another name for **lavatory.**

bath salts *pl n* soluble scented salts for use in a bath.

Bathsheba (bæθ'ʃiːbə, 'bæθʃɪbə) *n Old Testament.* the wife of Uriah, who committed adultery with David and later married him and became the mother of his son Solomon (II Samuel 11–12).

Bath stone *n Brit.* a kind of limestone used as a building material, esp. at Bath in England.

bathtub ('bɑːθˌtʌb) *n* a bath, esp. one not permanently fixed.

Bathurst ('bæθəst) *n* **1** a city in SE Australia, in E New South Wales: scene of a gold rush in 1851. Pop.: 24 682 (1991). **2** a port in E Canada, in NE New Brunswick: rich mineral resources discovered in 1953. Pop.: 15 890 (1991). **3** the former name (until 1973) of **Banjul.**

Bathurst burr *n* an Australian plant, *Xanthium spinosum,* having numerous hooked burrs that became entangled in sheep's wool. [C19: from Bathurst region of New South Wales]

bathy- *or* **batho-** *combining form.* indicating depth: *bathysphere; bathometer.* [from Greek *bathus* deep]

bathyal ('bæθɪəl) *adj* denoting or relating to an ocean depth of between 200 and 2000 metres (about 100 and 1000 fathoms), corresponding to the continental slope.

bathylimnetic (ˌbæθɪlɪm'nɛtɪk) *adj* (of an organism) living in the depths of lakes and marshes.

bathymetry (bə'θɪmɪtrɪ) *n* measurement of the depth of an ocean or other large body of water. ▸ **bathymetric** (ˌbæθɪ'mɛtrɪk) *adj* ▸ **ˌbathy'metrically** *adv*

bathypelagic (ˌbæθɪpə'lædʒɪk) *adj* of, relating to, or inhabiting the lower depths of the ocean between approximately 1000 and 4000 metres.

bathyscaph ('bæθɪˌskæf), **bathyscaphe** ('bæθɪˌskeɪf, -ˌskæf), *or* **bathyscape** ('bæθɪˌskæp) *n* a submersible vessel having a flotation compartment with an observation capsule underneath, capable of reaching ocean depths of over 10 000 metres (about 5000 fathoms). [C20: from BATHY- + *-scaph,* from Greek *skaphē* light boat]

bathysphere ('bæθɪˌsfɪə) *n* a strong steel deep-sea diving sphere, lowered by cable.

batik *or* **battik** ('bætɪk) *n* **a** a process of printing fabric in which parts not to be dyed are covered by wax. **b** fabric printed in this way. **c** (*as modifier*): *a batik shirt.* [C19: via Malay from Javanese: painted]

Batista (*Spanish* ba'tista) *n* **Fulgencio** (ful'xenθjo), full name *Batista y Zaldívar.* 1901–73, Cuban military leader and dictator: president of Cuba (1940–44, 1952–59); overthrown by Fidel Castro.

batiste (bæ'tiːst) *n* a fine plain-weave cotton fabric: used esp. for shirts and dresses. [C17: from French, from Old French *toile de baptiste,* probably after *Baptiste* of Cambrai, 13th-century French weaver, its reputed inventor]

Batley ('bætlɪ) *n* a town in N England, in Kirklees unitary authority, West Yorkshire. Pop.: 48 030 (1991).

batman ('bætmən) *n, pl* **-men.** an officer's personal servant in any of the armed forces. [C18: from Old French *bat, bast,* from Medieval Latin *bastum* packsaddle]

Batman[1] ('bætˌmæn) *n* a character in an American comic strip and several films who secretly assumes a batlike costume in order to fight crime.

Batman[2] ('bætmən) *n* **John.** 1801–39, a pioneer who selected the site of the city of Melbourne.

Bat Mitzvah (bɑːt 'mɪtsvə) (*sometimes not caps.*) ◆ *adj* **1** (of a Jewish girl) having attained religious majority at the age of twelve. ◆ *n* **2** the date of, or, in some congregations, a ceremony marking, this event. **3** the girl herself on that day. ◆ Also called: **Bas Mitzvah.** [from Hebrew, literally: daughter of the commandment]

baton ('bætən, -tɒn) *n* **1** a thin stick used by the conductor of an orchestra, choir, etc., to indicate rhythm or expression. **2a** a short stick carried for use as a weapon, as by a policeman; truncheon. **2b** (*as modifier*): *a baton charge.* **3** *Athletics.* a short bar carried by a competitor in a relay race and transferred to the next runner at the end of each stage. **4** a long stick with a knob on one end, carried, twirled, and thrown up and down by a drum major or drum majorette, esp. at the head of a parade. **5** a staff or club carried by an official as a symbol of authority. **6** *Heraldry.* a single narrow diagonal line superimposed on all other charges, esp. one curtailed at each end, signifying a bastard line. [C16: from French *bâton,* from Late Latin *bastum* rod, probably ultimately from Greek *bastazein* to lift up, carry]

bâton de commandement *French.* (bɑtɔ̃ də kɔmɑ̃dmɑ̃) *n* an antler object found in Upper Palaeolithic sites from the Aurignacian period onwards, consisting of a rod, often ornately decorated, with a hole through the thicker end. [literally: baton of command, although the object was probably actually used in making shafts for arrows and spears]

Baton Rouge ('bætᵊn 'ruːʒ) *n* the capital of Louisiana, in the SE part on the Mississippi River. Pop.: 215 882 (1996 est.).

baton round *n* the official name for **plastic bullet.**

batrachian (bə'treɪkɪən) *n* **1** any amphibian, esp. a frog or toad. ◆ *adj* **2** of or relating to the frogs and toads. [C19: from New Latin *Batrachia,* from Greek *batrakhos* frog]

bats (bæts) *adj Informal.* crazy; very eccentric. [from BATS-IN-THE-BELFRY (sense 2)]

bats-in-the-belfry *n* (*functioning as sing*) **1** a hairy Eurasian campanulaceous plant, *Campanula trachelium,* with bell-shaped blue-purple flowers. ◆ *adj* **2** *Slang.* mad; demented.

batsman ('bætsmən) *n, pl* **-men. 1** *Cricket, etc.* **1a** a person who bats or whose turn it is to bat. **1b** a player who specializes in batting. **2** a person on the ground who uses bats to guide the pilot of an aircraft when taxiing. ▸ **'batsmanˌship** *n*

batt (bæt) *n* **1** *Textiles.* another word for **batting** (sense 1). **2** *Austral. and N.Z.* a slab-shaped piece of insulating material used in building houses.

battalion (bə'tæljən) *n* **1** a military unit comprised of three or more companies or formations of similar size. **2** (*usually pl*) any large array. [C16: from French *bataillon,* from Old Italian *battaglione,* from *battaglia* company of soldiers, BATTLE]

battels ('bætᵊlz) *pl n* (at some universities) the account of a member of a college for board, provisions, and other college expenses. [C16: perhaps from obsolete *battle* to feed, fatten, of uncertain origin]

battement (*French* batmɑ̃) *n Ballet.* extension of one leg forwards, sideways, or backwards, either once or repeatedly. [C19: French, literally: beating]

batten[1] ('bætᵊn) *n* **1** a sawn strip of wood used in building to cover joints, provide a fixing for tiles or slates, support lathing, etc. **2** a long narrow board used for flooring. **3** a narrow flat length of wood or plastic inserted in pockets of a sail to give it proper shape. **4** a lath used for holding a tarpaulin along the side of a raised hatch on a ship. **5** *Theatre.* **5a** a row of lights. **5b** the strip or bar supporting them. **6** Also called: **dropper.** *N.Z.* an upright part of a fence made of wood or other material, designed to keep wires at equal distances apart. ◆ *vb* **7** (*tr*) to furnish or strengthen with battens. **8 batten down the hatches. 8a** to use battens in nailing a tarpaulin over a hatch on a ship to make it secure. **8b** to prepare for action, a crisis, etc. [C15: from French *bâton* stick; see BATON] ▸ **'battening** *n*

batten[2] ('bætᵊn) *vb* (*intr*) (usually foll. by *on*) to thrive, esp. at the expense of someone else: *to batten on the needy.* [C16: probably from Old Norse *batna* to improve; related to Old Norse *betr* BETTER[1], Old High German *bazzen* to get better]

Batten ('bætᵊn) *n* **Jean.** 1909–82, New Zealand aviator: the first woman to fly single-handed from Australia to Britain (1935).

Battenburg ('bætᵊnˌbɜːg) *n* an oblong sponge cake divided longitudinally into four square sections, two coloured pink and two yellow, with an outer coating of marzipan. [perhaps named after *Battenberg,* a village in Prussia]

batten plate *n* (in structural design) a horizontal rectangular plate that is used to connect pairs of steel sections by being riveted or welded across them to form a composite section.

Batten's disease ('bætᵊnz) *n* a rare hereditary disease in which lipids accumulate in the nervous system, leading to mental deterioration, spasticity, and blindness that start in early childhood. [C20: named after F. E. *Batten* (1865–1918), British neurologist]

batter[1] ('bætə) *vb* **1** to hit (someone or something) repeatedly using heavy blows, as with a club or other heavy instrument; beat heavily. **2** (*tr; often passive*) to damage or injure, as by blows, heavy wear, etc. **3** (*tr*) *Social welfare.* to subject (a person, esp. a close relative living in the same house) to repeated physical violence. **4** (*tr*) to subject (a person, opinion, or theory) to harsh criticism; attack. [C14 *bateren,* probably from *batten* to BAT[1]]

batter[2] ('bætə) *n* a mixture of flour, eggs, and milk, used to make cakes, pancakes, etc., and to coat certain foods before frying. [C15 *bater,* probably from *bateren* to BATTER[1]]

batter[3] ('bætə) *n Baseball, etc.* a player who bats.

batter[4] ('bætə) *n* **1** the slope of the face of a wall that recedes gradually backwards and upwards. ◆ *vb* **2** (*intr*) to have such a slope. [C16 (vb: to incline): of uncertain origin]

batter[5] ('bætə) *n* a spree or debauch. [C19: of unknown origin]

battered ('bætəd) *adj* subjected to persistent physical violence, esp. by a close relative living in the same house: *a battered baby.*

batterer ('bætərə) *n* **a** a person who batters someone. **b** (*in combination*): *baby-batterer; wife-batterer.*

batterie de cuisine *French.* (batri də kɥizin) *n* cooking utensils collectively; pots and pans, etc. [C18: literally: battery of kitchen]

battering ('bætərɪŋ) *n* **a** the act or practice of battering someone. **b** (*in combination*): *baby-battering; granny-battering.*

battering ram *n* (esp. formerly) a large beam used to break down the walls or doors of fortifications.

Battersea ('bætəsɪ) *n* a district in London, in Wandsworth: noted for its dogs' home, power station (being developed into a leisure centre), and park.

battery ('bætərɪ) *n, pl* **-teries. 1a** two or more primary cells connected together, usually in series, to provide a source of electric current. **1b** short for **dry battery. 2** another name for **accumulator** (sense 1). **3** a number of similar things occurring together: *a battery of questions.* **4** *Criminal law.* unlawful beating or wounding of a person or mere touching in a hostile or offensive manner. See also **assault and battery. 5** a fortified structure on which artillery is mounted. **6** a group of guns, missile launchers, searchlights, or torpedo tubes of similar type or size operated as a single entity. **7** a small tactical unit of artillery usually consisting of two or more troops, each of two, three or four guns. **8** *Chiefly Brit.* **8a** a large group of cages for intensive rearing of poultry. **8b** (*as modifier*): *battery hens.* **9** *Psychol.* a series of tests. **10** *Chess.* two men of the same colour placed so that one can unmask an attack by the other by moving. **11** the percussion section in an orchestra. **12** *Baseball.* the pitcher and the catcher considered together. [C16: from Old French *batterie* beating, from *battre* to beat, from Latin *battuere*]

battik (ˈbætɪk) *n* a variant spelling of **batik**.

batting (ˈbætɪŋ) *n* **1** Also called: **batt.** cotton or woollen wadding used in quilts, mattresses, etc. **2** the action of a person or team that hits with a bat, esp. in cricket or baseball.

battle (ˈbætᵊl) *n* **1** a fight between large armed forces; military or naval engagement; combat. **2** conflict; contention; struggle: *his battle for recognition.* **3 do, give,** *or* **join battle.** to start fighting. ◆ *vb* **4** (when *intr*, often foll. by *against, for,* or *with*) to fight in or as if in military combat; contend (with): *she battled against cancer.* **5** to struggle in order to achieve something or arrive somewhere: *he battled through the crowd.* **6** (*intr*) *Austral.* to scrape a living, esp. by doing odd jobs. [C13: from Old French *bataile,* from Late Latin *battālia* exercises performed by soldiers, from *battuere* to beat] ▸ **ˈbattler** *n*

Battle[1] (ˈbætᵊl) *n* a town in SE England, in East Sussex: site of the Battle of Hastings (1066); medieval abbey. Pop.: 5234 (1991).

Battle[2] (ˈbætᵊl) *n* **Kathleen.** born 1948, U.S. opera singer: a coloratura soprano, she made her professional debut in 1972 and sang with New York City's Metropolitan Opera (1977–94).

battle-axe *n* **1** (formerly) a large broad-headed axe. **2** *Informal.* an argumentative domineering woman.

battle-axe block *n Austral.* a block of land behind another, with access from the street through a narrow drive.

battlebus (ˈbætᵊlˌbʌs) *n* the coach that transports politicians and their advisers round the country during an election campaign.

battle cruiser *n* a warship of battleship size but with lighter armour and fewer guns and capable of high speed.

battle cry *n* **1** a shout uttered by soldiers going into battle. **2** a slogan used to rally the supporters of a campaign, movement, etc.

battledore (ˈbætᵊlˌdɔː) *n* **1** Also called: **battledore and shuttlecock.** an ancient racket game. **2** a light racket, smaller than a tennis racket, used for striking the shuttlecock in this game. **3** (formerly) a wooden utensil used for beating clothes, in baking, etc. [C15 *batyldoure,* perhaps from Old Provençal *batedor* a beater, from Old French *battre* to beat, BATTER[1]]

battledress (ˈbætᵊlˌdrɛs) *n* the ordinary uniform of a soldier, consisting of tunic and trousers.

battle fatigue *n Psychol.* a type of mental disorder, characterized by anxiety, depression, and loss of motivation, caused by the stress of active warfare. Also called: **combat fatigue.** See also **shell shock.**

battlefield (ˈbætᵊlˌfiːld) *or* **battleground** (ˈbætᵊlˌgraʊnd) *n* the place where a battle is fought; an area of conflict.

battle line *n* **1** the line along which troops are positioned for battle. **2 the battle lines are drawn.** conflict or argument is about to occur between opposing people or groups.

battlement (ˈbætᵊlmənt) *n* a parapet or wall with indentations or embrasures, originally for shooting through. [C14: from Old French *batailles,* plural of *bataille* BATTLE] ▸ **ˈbattlemented** *adj*

Battle of Britain *n* **the.** from August to October 1940, the prolonged bombing of S England by the German Luftwaffe and the successful resistance by the RAF Fighter Command, which put an end to the German plan of invading Britain.

Battle of the Atlantic *n* the struggle for control of the sea routes around the United Kingdom during World War II, esp. 1940–43.

battlepiece (ˈbætᵊlˌpiːs) *n* a painting, relief, mosaic, etc., depicting a battle, usually commemorating an actual event.

battle royal *n* **1** a fight, esp. with fists or cudgels, involving more than two combatants; melee. **2** a long violent argument.

battleship (ˈbætᵊlˌʃɪp) *n* **1** a heavily armoured warship of the largest type having many large-calibre guns. **2** (formerly) a warship of sufficient size and armament to take her place in the line of battle; ship of the line.

battue (bæˈtuː, -ˈtjuː; *French* baty) *n* **1** the beating of woodland or cover to force game to flee in the direction of hunters. **2a** an organized shooting party using this method. **2b** the game disturbed or shot by this method. **3** indiscriminate slaughter, as of a defenceless crowd. [C19: from French, feminine of *battu* beaten, from *battre* to beat, from Latin *battuere*]

batty (ˈbætɪ) *adj* **-tier, -tiest.** *Slang.* **1** insane; crazy. **2** odd; eccentric. [C20: from BAT[2]; compare the phrase *have bats in the belfry*]

Batum (bɑːˈtuːm) *or* **Batumi** (bɑːˈtuːmɪ) *n* a city in Georgia: capital of the Adzhar Autonomous Republic; a major Black Sea port. Pop.: 137 100 (1994 est.).

batwing (ˈbætˌwɪŋ) *adj* shaped like the wings of a bat, as a black tie, collar, etc.

batwing sleeve *n* a sleeve of a garment with a deep armhole and a tight wrist.

batwoman (ˈbætwʊmən) *n, pl* **-women.** a female servant in any of the armed forces.

bauble (ˈbɔːbᵊl) *n* **1** a showy toy or trinket of little value; trifle. **2** (formerly) a mock staff of office carried by a court jester. [C14: from Old French *baubel* plaything, of obscure origin]

Bauchi (ˈbaʊtʃɪ) *n* **1** a state of N Nigeria: formed in 1976 from part of North-Eastern State; tin mining. Capital: Bauchi. Pop.: 4 801 569 (1995 est.). Area: 64 605 sq. km (24 944 sq. miles). **2** a town in N central Nigeria, capital of Bauchi state. Pop.: 76 070 (1991 est.).

bauchle (ˈbɒxᵊl) *n Scot.* **1** an old worn shoe. **2** a worthless or clumsy person. **3** a useless object. **4** a trout-fisher's term for a **perch**[2]. [C18: of unknown origin]

Baucis (ˈbɔːsɪs) *n Greek myth.* a poor peasant woman who, with her husband Philemon, was rewarded for hospitality to the disguised gods Zeus and Hermes.

baud (bɔːd) *n* a unit used to measure the speed of electronic code transmissions, equal to one unit interval per second. [C20: named after J. M. E. *Baudot* (1845–1903), French inventor]

Baudelaire (*French* bodlɛr) *n* **Charles Pierre** (ʃarl pjɛr). 1821–67, French poet, noted for his macabre imagery; author of *Les fleurs du mal* (1857).

Baudouin I (*French* bodwɛ̃) *n* 1930–93, king of Belgium (1951–93).

bauera (ˈbaʊərə) *n* any small evergreen Australian shrub of the genus *Bauera,* having pink or purple flowers. [C19: named after Franz (1758–1840) and Ferdinand (1760–1826) *Bauer,* Australian botanical artists]

Bauhaus (ˈbaʊˌhaʊs) *n* **a** a German school of architecture and applied arts founded in 1919 by Walter Gropius on experimental principles of functionalism and truth to materials. After being closed by the Nazis in 1933, its ideas were widely disseminated by its students and staff, including Kandinsky, Klee, Feininger, Moholy-Nagy, and Mies van der Rohe. **b** (*as modifier*): *Bauhaus wallpaper.* [C20: German, literally: building house]

bauhinia (bɔːˈhɪnɪə, bəʊ-) *n* any climbing leguminous plant of the genus *Bauhinia,* of tropical and warm regions, widely cultivated for ornament. [C18: New Latin, named after Jean and Gaspard *Bauhin,* 16th-century French herbalists]

baulk (bɔːk; *usually for sense 1* bɔːlk) *n* **1** Also (U.S.): **balk.** *Billiards.* **1a** (in billiards) the space, usually 29 inches deep, between the baulk line and the bottom cushion. **1b** (in baulk-line games) one of the spaces between the cushions and the baulk lines. **1c in baulk.** inside one of these spaces. **2** *Archaeol.* a strip of earth left between excavation trenches for the study of the complete stratigraphy of a site. **3** *Croquet.* either of two lines (**A baulk** and **B baulk**) at diagonally opposite ends of the court, from which the ball is struck into play. ◆ *vb, n* **4** a variant spelling of **balk.**

baulk line *or U.S.* **balk line** *n Billiards.* **1** Also called: **string line.** a straight line across a billiard table behind which the cue balls are placed at the start of a game. **2a** one of four lines parallel to the cushions dividing the table into a central panel and eight smaller ones (the baulks). **2b** a type of game using these lines as restrictions.

Baum (bɔːm, bɑːm) *n* **L(yman) Frank.** 1856–1919, U.S. novelist, author of *The Wonderful Wizard of Oz* (1900) and its sequels.

Baumé scale (bəʊˈmeɪ, ˈbəʊmeɪ) *n* a scale for calibrating hydrometers used for measuring the specific gravity of liquids. 1 degree Baumé is equal to 144.3($(s-1)/s$), where s is specific gravity. [C19: named after Antoine *Baumé* (1728–1804), French chemist]

Baumgarten (*German* ˈbaumgartən) *n* **Alexander Gottlieb.** 1714–62, German philosopher, noted for his pioneering work on aesthetics, a term that he originated.

Bautzen (ˈbaʊtsən) *n* a city in E Germany, in Saxony: site of an indecisive battle in 1813 between Napoleon's army and an allied army of Russians and Prussians. Pop.: 52 390 (1989 est.).

bauxite (ˈbɔːksaɪt) *n* a white, red, yellow, or brown amorphous claylike substance comprising aluminium oxides and hydroxides, often with such impurities as iron oxides. It is the chief ore of aluminium. General formula: $Al_2O_3.nH_2O$. [C19: from French, from (*Les*) *Baux* in southern France, where it was originally found]

Bav. *abbrev. for* Bavaria(n).

Bavaria (bəˈvɛərɪə) *n* a state of S Germany: a former duchy and kingdom; mainly wooded highland, with the Alps in the south. Capital: Munich. Pop.: 11 993 500 (1996 est.). Area: 70 531 sq. km (27 232 sq. miles). German name: **Bayern.** ▸ **Baˈvarian** *adj, n*

Bavarian cream *n* a cold dessert consisting of a rich custard set with gelatine and flavoured in various ways. Also called: **bavarois** (*French* bavarwa).

bawbee (bɔːˈbiː) *n* **1** a former Scottish silver coin. **2** *Scot.* an informal word for **halfpenny** (sense 2). [C16: named after Alexander Orok of *Sillebawby,* master of the mint]

bawcock (ˈbɔːˌkɒk) *n Archaic.* a fine fellow. [C16: from French *beau coq,* from *beau* handsome + *coq* COCK[1]]

bawd (bɔːd) *n Archaic.* **1** a person who runs a brothel, esp. a woman. **2** a prostitute. [C14: from Old French *baude,* feminine of *baud* merry, of Germanic origin; compare Old High German *bald* BOLD]

bawdry (ˈbɔːdrɪ) *n Archaic.* obscene talk or language.

bawdy (ˈbɔːdɪ) *adj* **bawdier, bawdiest.** **1** (of language, plays, etc.) containing references to sex, esp. to be humorous. ◆ *n* **2** obscenity or eroticism, esp. in writing or drama. ▸ **ˈbawdily** *adv* ▸ **ˈbawdiness** *n*

bawdyhouse (ˈbɔːdɪˌhaʊs) *n* an archaic word for **brothel.**

bawl (bɔːl) *vb* **1** (*intr*) to utter long loud cries, as from pain or frustration; wail. **2** to shout loudly, as in anger. ◆ *n* **3** a loud shout or cry. [C15: probably from Icelandic *baula* to low; related to Medieval Latin *baulāre* to bark, Swedish *böla* to low; all of imitative origin] ▸ **ˈbawler** *n* ▸ **ˈbawling** *n*

bawl out *vb* (*tr, adv*) *Informal.* to scold loudly.

bawneen (ˈbɑːniːn) *n Irish.* a variant spelling of **báinín.**

Bax (bæks) *n* Sir **Arnold** (**Edward Trevor**). 1883–1953, English composer of romantic works, often based on Celtic legends, including the tone poem *Tintagel* (1917).

Baxter (ˈbækstə) *n* **1 James** (**Keir**). 1926–72, New Zealand lyric poet. His works include *The Fallen House* (1953) and *In Fires of No Return* (1958). **2 Richard.** 1615–91, English Puritan divine and devotional writer: prominent in church affairs during the Restoration.

bay[1] (beɪ) *n* **1** a wide semicircular indentation of a shoreline, esp. between two headlands or peninsulas. **2** an extension of lowland into hills that partly surround it. **3** *U.S.* an extension of prairie into woodland. [C14: from Old French *baie,* perhaps from Old French *baer* to gape, from Medieval Latin *batāre* to yawn]

bay[2] (beɪ) *n* **1** an alcove or recess in a wall. **2** any partly enclosed compartment, as one in which hay is stored in a barn. **3** See **bay window.** **4** an area off a road in which vehicles may park or unload, esp. one adjacent to a shop, factory, etc. **5** a compartment in an aircraft, esp. one used for a specified purpose: *the bomb bay.* **6** *Nautical.* a compartment in the forward part of a ship between decks, often used as the ship's hospital. **7** *Brit.* a tracked recess in the platform of a railway station, esp. one forming the terminus of a branch line. [**C14**: from Old French *baee* gap or recess in a wall, from *baer* to gape; see BAY[1]]

bay[3] (beɪ) *n* **1** a deep howl or growl, esp. of a hound on the scent. **2 at bay. 2a** (of a person or animal) forced to turn and face attackers: *the dogs held the deer at bay.* **2b** at a distance: *to keep a disease at bay.* **3 bring to bay.** to force into a position from which retreat is impossible. ◆ *vb* **4** (*intr*) to howl (at) in deep prolonged tones. **5** (*tr*) to utter in a loud prolonged tone. **6** (*tr*) to drive to or hold at bay. [**C13**: from Old French *abaiier* to bark, of imitative origin]

bay[4] (beɪ) *n* **1** a Mediterranean laurel, *Laurus nobilis.* See **laurel** (sense 1). **2** any of several magnolias. See **sweet bay. 3** any of certain other trees or shrubs, esp. bayberry. **4** (*pl*) a wreath of bay leaves. See **laurel** (sense 6). [**C14**: from Old French *baie* laurel berry, from Latin *bāca* berry]

bay[5] (beɪ) *n* **1a** a moderate reddish-brown colour. **1b** (*as adj*): *a bay horse.* **2** an animal of this colour, esp. a horse. [**C14**: from Old French *bai,* from Latin *badius*]

bayadere (ˌbaɪəˈdɪə, -ˈdɛə) *n* **1** a dancing girl, esp. one serving in a Hindu temple. **2** a fabric or design with horizontal stripes, esp. of a bright colour. ◆ *adj* **3** (of fabric, etc.) having horizontal stripes. [**C18**: via French from Portuguese *bailadeira* dancing girl, from *bailar* to dance, from Latin *ballāre;* see BALL[2]]

Bayamón (*Spanish* bajaˈmon) *n* a city in NE central Puerto Rico, south of San Juan. Pop.: 231 334 (1995 est.).

Bayard[1] (ˈbeɪəd) *n* a legendary horse that figures prominently in medieval romance.

Bayard[2] (ˈbeɪəd; *French* bajar) *n* **Chevalier de** (ʃəvalje də), original name *Pierre de Terrail.* ?1473–1524, French soldier, known as *le chevalier sans peur et sans reproche* (the fearless and irreproachable knight).

Baybars I (baɪˈbɑːs) *n* 1223–77, sultan of Egypt and Syria (1260–77), of the Mameluke dynasty.

bayberry (ˈbeɪbərɪ) *or* **bay** *n, pl* **-ries. 1** any of several North American aromatic shrubs or small trees of the genus *Myrica,* that bear grey waxy berries: family *Myricaceae.* See also **wax myrtle. 2** Also called: **bay rum tree.** a tropical American myrtaceous tree, *Pimenta acris,* that yields an oil used in making bay rum. **3** the fruit of any of these plants.

Bayern (ˈbaiərn) *n* the German name for **Bavaria.**

Bayesian (ˈbeɪzɪən) *adj* (of a theory) presupposing known a priori probabilities which may be subjectively assessed and which can be revised in the light of experience in accordance with Bayes' theorem. A hypothesis is thus confirmed by an experimental observation which is likely given the hypothesis and unlikely without it. Compare **maximum likelihood.**

Bayes' theorem (beɪz) *n Statistics.* the fundamental result which expresses the conditional probability $P(E/A)$ of an event E given an event A as $P(A/E).P(E)/P(A)$; more generally, where E_n is one of a set of values E_i which partition the sample space, $P(E_n/A) = P(A/E_n)P(E_n)/\Sigma\, P(A/E_i)P(E_i)$. This enables prior estimates of probability to be continually revised in the light of observations. [**C20**: named after Thomas *Bayes* (1702–61), English mathematician and Presbyterian minister]

Bayeux (*French* bajø) *n* a town in NW France, on the River Aure: its museum houses the Bayeux tapestry and there is a 13th-century cathedral: dairy foods, plastic. Pop.: 14 704 (1990).

Bayeux tapestry *n* an 11th- or 12th-century tapestry in Bayeux, nearly 70.5 m (231 ft.) long by 50 cm (20 inches) high, depicting the Norman conquest of England.

Bayezid II (ˌbaɪjəˈziːd) *n* ?1447–1512, sultan of Turkey; he greatly extended Turkish dominions in Greece and the Balkans.

Bayle (*French* bɛl) *n* **Pierre** (pjɛr). 1647–1706, French philosopher and critic, noted for his *Dictionnaire historique et critique* (1697), which profoundly influenced Voltaire and the French Encyclopedists.

bay leaf *n* a leaf, usually dried, of the Mediterranean laurel, *Laurus nobilis,* used in cooking to flavour soups and stews.

Baylis (ˈbeɪlɪs) *n* **Lillian Mary.** 1874–1937, British theatre manager: founded the Old Vic (1912) and the Sadler's Wells company for opera and ballet (1931).

bay lynx *n* another name for **bobcat.**

Bay of Pigs *n* a bay on the SW coast of Cuba: scene of an unsuccessful invasion of Cuba by U.S.-backed troops (April 17, 1961). Spanish name: **Bahia de los Cochinos.**

bayonet (ˈbeɪənɪt) *n* **1** a blade for stabbing that can be attached to the muzzle of a firearm. **2** a type of fastening in which a cylindrical member is inserted into a socket against spring pressure and turned so that pins on its side engage in slots in the socket. ◆ *vb* **-nets, -neting, -neted,** *or* **-nets, -netting, -netted. 3** (*tr*) to stab or kill with a bayonet. [**C17**: from French *baïonnette,* from BAYONNE where it originated]

Bayonne (*French* bajɔn) *n* a port in SW France: a commercial centre for the Basque region. Pop.: 41 846 (1990).

bayou (ˈbaɪjuː) *n* (in the southern U.S.) a sluggish marshy tributary of a lake or river. [**C18**: from Louisiana French, from Choctaw *bayuk*]

Bayreuth (*German* baiˈrɔyt) *n* a city in E Germany, in NE Bavaria: home and burial place of Richard Wagner; annual festivals of his music. Pop.: 72 780 (1991).

bay rum *n* **1** an aromatic liquid, used in medicines and cosmetics, originally obtained by distilling the leaves of the bayberry tree (*Pimenta acris*) with rum: now also synthesized from alcohol, water, and various oils. **2 bay rum tree.** another name for **bayberry** (sense 2).

Bay Street *n* (in Canada) **1** the financial centre of Toronto, in which Canada's largest stock exchange is situated. **2** the financial interests and powers of Toronto.

bay tree *n* another name for **bay**[4] (sense 1).

bay window *n* a window projecting from the wall of a building and forming an alcove of a room. Sometimes shortened to **bay.** See also **bow window, oriel window.**

baywood (ˈbeɪˌwʊd) *n* the light soft wood of a tropical American mahogany tree, *Swietenia macrophylla,* of the bay region of SE Mexico.

bazaar *or* **bazar** (bəˈzɑː) *n* **1** (esp. in the Orient) a market area, esp. a street of small stalls. **2** a sale in aid of charity, esp. of miscellaneous secondhand or handmade articles. **3** a shop where a large variety of goods is sold. [**C16**: from Persian *bāzār,* from Old Persian *abēcharish*]

bazoo (bəˈzuː) *n* a U.S. slang word for **mouth.** [**C19**: of unknown origin]

bazooka (bəˈzuːkə) *n* a portable tubular rocket-launcher that fires a projectile capable of piercing armour: used by infantrymen as a short-range antitank weapon. [**C20**: named after a pipe instrument invented by Bob Burns (1896–1956), American comedian]

BB 1 *abbrev. for* Boys' Brigade. **2** (on Brit. pencils) *symbol for* double black: denoting a very soft lead.

BBBC *abbrev. for* British Boxing Board of Control.

BBC *abbrev. for* British Broadcasting Corporation.

BBFC *abbrev. for* British Board of Film Classification.

bbl. *abbrev. for* barrel (container or unit of measure).

B-boy (ˈbiːˌbɔɪ) *n* a male rap-music fan, who typically can be identified by his casual style of dress. [**C20**: from *Bronx boy*]

BBQ *abbrev. for* barbecue.

B bursary *n N.Z.* the lower of two bursaries available for students entering university, polytechnic, etc. Compare **A bursary.**

BC *abbrev. for* British Columbia.

B.C. *or* **BC** *abbrev. for* (indicating years numbered back from the supposed year of the birth of Christ) before Christ: *in 54* B.C. *Caesar came.* Compare **A.D.**

USAGE See at **A.D.**

BCA (in New Zealand) *abbrev. for* Bachelor of Commerce and Administration.

BCAR *abbrev. for* British Civil Airworthiness Requirements.

BCC *abbrev. for* British Coal Corporation (formerly the National Coal Board).

BCD *abbrev. for* binary-coded decimal.

BCE *abbrev. for* Before Common Era (used, esp. by non-Christians, in numbering years B.C.).

B-cell *n* another name for **B-lymphocyte.**

BCF *abbrev. for:* **1** British Chess Federation. **2** British Cycling Federation.

BCG *abbrev. for* bacille Calmette-Guérin (antituberculosis vaccine).

BCh *abbrev. for* Bachelor of Surgery. [from Latin *Baccalaureus Chirurgiae*]

BCL *abbrev. for* Bachelor of Civil Law.

BCNZ *abbrev. for* Broadcasting Corporation of New Zealand.

BCom *abbrev. for* Bachelor of Commerce.

B complex *n* short for **vitamin B complex.**

bd *abbrev. for:* **1** board. **2** *Insurance, finance, etc.* bond.

BD *abbrev. for:* **1** Bachelor of Divinity. **2** *Commerce.* bills discounted. **3** *international car registration for* Bangladesh.

B/D *abbrev. for:* **1** bank draft. **2** *Commerce.* bills discounted. **3** Also: **b/d** *Bookkeeping.* brought down.

BDA *abbrev. for* British Dental Association.

Bde *or* **bde** *abbrev. for* brigade.

bdellium (ˈdelɪəm) *n* **1** any of several African or W Asian trees of the burseraceous genus *Commiphora* that yield a gum resin. **2** the aromatic gum resin, similar to myrrh, produced by any of these trees. [**C16**: from Latin, from Greek *bdellion,* perhaps from Hebrew *bĕdhōlah*]

bd.ft. *abbrev. for* board foot.

bdl *abbrev. for* bundle.

bds *abbrev. for:* bundles.

BDS 1 *abbrev. for* Bachelor of Dental Surgery. **2** *international car registration for* Barbados.

be (biː; *unstressed* bɪ) *vb pres. sing 1st pers.* **am;** *2nd pers.* **are;** *3rd pers.* **is.** *pres. pl* **are.** *past sing 1st pers.* **was;** *2nd pers.* **were;** *3rd pers.* **was.** *past pl* **were.** *pres. part.* **being.** *past part.* **been.** (*intr*) **1** to have presence in the realm of perceived reality; exist; live: *I think, therefore I am; not all that is can be understood.* **2** (*used in the perfect or past perfect tenses only*) to pay a visit; go: *have you been to Spain?* **3** to take place; occur: *my birthday was last Thursday.* **4** (*copula*) used as a linking verb between the subject of a sentence and its noun or adjective complement or complementing phrase. In this case *be* expresses the relationship of either essential or incidental equivalence or identity (*John is a man; John is a musician*) or specifies an essential or incidental attribute (*honey is sweet; Susan is angry*). It is also used with an adverbial complement to indicate a relationship of location in space or time (*Bill is at the office; the dance is on Saturday*). **5** (*takes a present participle*) forms the progressive present tense: *the man is running.* **6** (*takes a past participle*) forms the passive voice of all transitive verbs and (archaically) certain intransitive ones: *a good film is being shown on television tonight; I am done.* **7** (*takes an infinitive*) expresses intention, expectation, supposition, or obligation: *the president is to arrive at 9.30; you are not to leave before I say so.* **8** (*takes a past participle*) forms the perfect or past perfect tense of certain intransitive verbs of motion, such as **go** or **come:** *the last train is gone.* **9 be that as it may.** the facts concerning (something) are of no importance. [Old English *bēon;* related to Old High German *bim* am, Latin *fui* I have been, Greek *phuein* to bring forth, Sanskrit *bhavati* he is]

Be *chemical symbol for* beryllium.

Bé *abbrev. for* Baumé.

BE *abbrev. for:* **1** bill of exchange. **2** (in the U.S.) Board of Education. **3** Bachelor of Education. **4** Bachelor of Engineering.

be- *prefix forming transitive verbs.* **1** (*from nouns*) to surround completely; cover on all sides: *befog.* **2** (*from nouns*) to affect completely or excessively: *bedazzle.* **3** (*from nouns*) to consider as or cause to be: *befool; befriend.* **4** (*from* *nouns*) to provide or cover with: *bejewel.* **5** (*from verbs*) at, for, against, on, or over: *bewail; berate.* [Old English *be-, bi-,* unstressed variant of *bī* BY]

B/E, BE, *or* **b.e.** *abbrev. for* bill of exchange.

BEA (formerly) *abbrev. for* British European Airways.

BEAB *abbrev. for* British Electrical Approvals Board.

beach (bi:tʃ) *n* **1** an extensive area of sand or shingle sloping down to a sea or lake, esp. the area between the high- and low-water marks on a seacoast. Related adj: **littoral.** ◆ *vb* **2** to run or haul (a boat) onto a beach. [C16: perhaps related to Old English *bæce* river, BECK[2]]

beach ball *n* a large light brightly coloured ball for playing with on a beach.

Beach Boys *pl n* **the.** U.S. pop group (formed 1961), noted for their complex vocal harmonies and advanced production: originally comprising Brian Wilson (born 1942), Dennis Wilson (1944–83), Carl Wilson (1946–98), Mike Love (born 1941), and Al Jardine (born 1942). Their recordings include the hit singles "Surfin' Safari" (1962), "California Girls" (1965), and "Good Vibrations" (1966), and the album *Pet Sounds* (1966). Most of their material was written and produced by Brian Wilson.

beach buggy *n* a low car, often open and with balloon tyres, for driving on sand. Also called: **dune buggy.**

beachcomber ('bi:tʃˌkəumə) *n* **1** a person who searches shore debris for anything of worth, esp. a vagrant living on a beach. **2** a long high wave rolling onto a beach. ▸ **'beach,combing** *n*

beach flea *n* another name for the **sand hopper.**

beachhead ('bi:tʃˌhɛd) *n Military.* **1** an area on a beach that has been captured from the enemy and on which troops and equipment are landed. **2** the object of an amphibious operation. [C20: modelled on BRIDGEHEAD]

Beach-la-Mar (ˌbi:tʃlə'mɑ:) *n* an English-based creole language spoken in Vanuatu and Fiji, and formerly much more widespread. Also called: **Biche-la-mar.** [C19: quasi-French, from BÊCHE-DE-MER (trepang, this being a major trading commodity in the SW Pacific; hence the name was applied to the trading language)]

beach plum *n* **1** a rosaceous shrub, *Prunus maritima,* of coastal regions of E North America. **2** its edible plumlike fruit.

Beachy Head ('bi:tʃɪ) *n* a headland in East Sussex, on the English Channel, consisting of chalk cliffs 171 m (570 ft.) high.

beacon ('bi:kən) *n* **1** a signal fire or light on a hill, tower, etc., esp. one used formerly as a warning of invasion. **2** a hill on which such fires were lit. **3** a lighthouse, signalling buoy, etc., used to warn or guide ships in dangerous waters. **4** short for **radio beacon. 5** a radio or other signal marking a flight course in air navigation. **6** short for **Belisha beacon. 7** a person or thing that serves as a guide, inspiration, or warning. ◆ *vb* **8** to guide or warn. **9** (*intr*) to shine. [Old English *beacen* sign; related to Old Frisian *bāken,* Old Saxon *bōcan,* Old High German *bouhhan*]

Beaconsfield[1] ('bɛkənzˌfi:ld, 'bi:k-) *n* a town in SE England, in Buckinghamshire: a residential centre for London. Pop.: 12 292 (1991).

Beaconsfield[2] ('bɛkənzˌfi:ld, 'bi:k-) *n* **1st Earl of.** title of (Benjamin) **Disraeli.**

bead (bi:d) *n* **1** a small usually spherical piece of glass, wood, plastic, etc., with a hole through it by means of which it may be strung with others to form a necklace, etc. **2** a small drop of moisture: *a bead of sweat.* **3** a small bubble in or on a liquid. **4** a small metallic knob acting as the sight of a firearm. **5 draw a bead on.** to aim a rifle or pistol at. **6** Also called: **astragal.** *Architect., furniture.* a small convex moulding having a semicircular cross section. **7** *Chem.* a small solid globule made by fusing a powdered sample with borax or a similar flux on a platinum wire. The colour of the globule serves as a test for the presence of certain metals (**bead test**). **8** *Metallurgy.* a deposit of welding metal on the surface of a metal workpiece, often used to examine the structure of the weld zone. **9** *R.C. Church.* one of the beads of a rosary. **10 count, say,** *or* **tell one's beads.** to pray with a rosary. ◆ *vb* **11** (*tr*) to decorate with beads. **12** to form into beads or drops. [Old English *bed* prayer; related to Old High German *gibet* prayer] ▸ **'beaded** *adj*

beadblast ('bi:dˌblɑ:st) *n* **1** a jet of small glass beads blown from a nozzle under air or steam pressure. ◆ *vb* **2** (*tr*) to clean or treat (a surface) with a beadblast. ▸ **'bead,blaster** *n*

beading ('bi:dɪŋ) *n* **1** another name for **bead** (sense 6). **2** Also called: **beadwork** ('bi:dˌwɜ:k). a narrow strip of some material used for edging or ornamentation.

beadle ('bi:d(ə)l) *n* **1** (formerly, in the Church of England) a minor parish official who acted as an usher and kept order. **2** (in Scotland) a church official attending on the minister. **3** *Judaism.* a synagogue attendant. See also **shammes. 4** an official in certain British universities and other institutions. [Old English *bydel;* related to Old High German *butil* bailiff] ▸ **'beadleship** *n*

Beadle ('bi:d(ə)l) *n* **George Wells.** 1903–89, U.S. biologist, who shared the Nobel prize for physiology or medicine in 1958 for his work in genetics.

beadledom ('bi:d(ə)ldəm) *n* petty officialdom.

beadroll ('bi:dˌrəul) *n Archaic.* a list of persons for whom prayers are to be offered.

bead-ruby *n, pl* **-bies.** a N temperate liliaceous plant, *Maianthemum canadense,* with small white bell-shaped flowers and small red berries.

beadsman *or* **bedesman** ('bi:dzmən) *n, pl* **-men.** *Archaic.* **1** a person who prays for another's soul, esp. one paid or fed for doing so. **2** a person kept in an almshouse.

beady ('bi:dɪ) *adj* **beadier, beadiest. 1** small, round, and glittering: used esp. of eyes. **2** resembling or covered with beads. ▸ **'beadily** *adv* ▸ **'beadiness** *n*

beady eye *n Informal.* keen watchfulness that may be somewhat hostile: *he's got his beady eye on you.* ▸ **ˌbeady-'eyed** *adj*

beagle ('bi:g(ə)l) *n* **1** a small sturdy breed of hound, having a smooth dense coat usually of white, tan, and black; often used (esp. formerly) for hunting hares. **2** *Archaic.* a person who spies on others. ◆ *vb* **3** (*intr*) to hunt with beagles, normally on foot. [C15: of uncertain origin]

Beaglehole ('bi:g(ə)lˌhəul) *n* **John.** 1901–71, New Zealand historian and author. His works include *Exploration of the Pacific* (1934) and *The Journals of James Cook* (1955).

beak[1] (bi:k) *n* **1** the projecting jaws of a bird, covered with a horny sheath; bill. **2** any beaklike mouthpart in other animals, such as turtles. **3** *Slang.* a person's nose, esp. one that is large, pointed, or hooked. **4** any projecting part, such as the pouring lip of a bucket. **5** *Architect.* the upper surface of a cornice, which slopes out to throw off water. **6** *Chem.* the part of a still or retort through which vapour passes to the condenser. **7** *Nautical.* another word for **ram** (sense 5). [C13: from Old French *bec,* from Latin *beccus,* of Gaulish origin] ▸ **beaked** (bi:kt) *adj* ▸ **'beakless** *adj* ▸ **'beak,like** *adj* ▸ **'beaky** *adj*

beak[2] (bi:k) *n* a Brit. slang word for **judge, magistrate, headmaster,** or **schoolmaster.** [C19: originally thieves' jargon]

beaker ('bi:kə) *n* **1** a cup usually having a wide mouth: *a plastic beaker.* **2** a cylindrical flat-bottomed container used in laboratories, usually made of glass and having a pouring lip. **3** the amount a beaker holds. [C14: from Old Norse *bikarr;* related to Old High German *behhāri,* Middle Dutch *bēker* beaker, Greek *bikos* earthenware jug]

Beaker folk *n* a prehistoric people thought to have originated in the Iberian peninsula and spread to central Europe and Britain during the second millennium B.C. [C20: named after the beakers found among their remains]

Beale (bi:l) *n* **Dorothea.** 1831–1906, British schoolmistress, a champion of women's education and suffrage. As principal of Cheltenham Ladies' College (1858–1906) she introduced important reforms.

be-all and end-all *n Informal.* **1** the ultimate aim or justification: *to provide help for others is the be-all and end-all of this group.* **2** *Often humorous.* a person or thing considered to be beyond improvement.

beam (bi:m) *n* **1** a long thick straight-sided piece of wood, metal, concrete, etc., esp. one used as a horizontal structural member. **2** any rigid member or structure that is loaded transversely. **3** the breadth of a ship or boat taken at its widest part, usually amidships. **4** a ray or column of light, as from a beacon. **5** a broad smile. **6** one of the two cylindrical rollers on a loom, one of which holds the warp threads before weaving, the other the finished work. **7** the main stem of a deer's antler from which the smaller branches grow. **8** the central shaft of a plough to which all the main parts are attached. **9** a narrow unidirectional flow of electromagnetic radiation or particles: *a beam of light; an electron beam.* **10** the horizontal centrally pivoted bar in a balance. **11** *Informal.* the width of the hips (esp. in the phrase **broad in the beam**). **12 a beam in one's eye.** a fault or grave error greater in oneself than in another person. **13 off (the) beam. 13a** not following a radio beam to maintain a course. **13b** *Informal.* wrong, mistaken, or irrelevant. **14 on the beam. 14a** following a radio beam to maintain a course. **14b** *Nautical.* opposite the beam of a vessel; abeam. **14c** *Informal.* correct, relevant, or appropriate. ◆ *vb* **15** to send out or radiate (rays of light). **16** (*tr*) to divert or aim (a radio signal or broadcast, light, etc.) in a certain direction: *to beam a programme to Tokyo.* **17** (*intr*) to smile broadly with pleasure or satisfaction. [Old English *beam;* related to Gothic *bagms* tree, Old High German *boum* tree] ▸ **beamed** *adj* ▸ **'beaming** *adj, n* ▸ **'beamless** *adj* ▸ **'beam,like** *adj* ▸ **'beamy** *adj*

beam aerial *n* an aerial system, such as a Yagi aerial, having directional properties. Also called (esp. U.S.): **beam antenna.**

beam compass *n* an instrument for drawing large circles or arcs, consisting of a horizontal beam along which two vertical legs slide. Also called: **trammel.**

beam-ends *pl n* **1** the ends of a vessel's beams. **2 on her beam-ends.** (of a vessel) heeled over through an angle of 90°. **3 on one's beam-ends. 3a** out of resources; destitute. **3b** desperate.

beam engine *n* an early type of steam engine, in which a pivoted beam is vibrated by a vertical steam cylinder at one end, so that it transmits motion to the workload, such as a pump, at the other end.

beamer ('bi:mə) *n Cricket.* a full-pitched ball bowled at the batsman's head.

beam hole *n* a hole in the shield of a nuclear reactor through which a beam of radiation, esp. of neutrons, is allowed to escape for experimental purposes.

beam riding *n* a method of missile guidance in which the missile steers itself along the axis of a conically scanned microwave beam. ▸ **beam rider** *n*

beam splitter *n* a system that divides a beam of light, electrons, etc., into two or more paths.

bean (bi:n) *n* **1** any of various papilionaceous plants of the widely cultivated genus *Phaseolus* producing edible seeds in pods. See **French bean, lima bean, scarlet runner, string bean. 2** any of several other papilionaceous plants that bear edible pods or seeds, such as the broad bean and soya bean. **3** any of various other plants whose seeds are produced in pods or podlike fruits. **4** the seed or pod of any of these plants. **5** any of various beanlike seeds, such as coffee. **6** *U.S. and Canadian slang* another word for **head. 7 not have a bean.** *Slang.* to be without money: *I haven't got a bean.* **8 full of beans.** *Informal.* **8a** full of energy and vitality. **8b** *U.S.* mistaken; erroneous. **9 spill the beans.** *Informal.* to disclose something confidential. ◆ *vb* **10** *Chiefly U.S. and Canadian slang.* (*tr*) to hit (a person) on the head. [Old English *bēan;* related to Old Norse *baun,* Old Frisian *bāne,* Old High German *bōna* bean]

beanbag ('bi:nˌbæg) *n* **1** a small cloth bag filled with dried beans and thrown in games. **2** a very large cushion loosely filled with foam rubber or polystyrene granules so that it moulds into a comfortable shape: used as an informal low seat.

bean caper *n* a shrub, *Zygophyllum fabago,* of E Mediterranean regions, whose flower buds are eaten as a substitute for capers: family *Zygophyllaceae.*

bean-counter *n Informal.* an accountant.

bean curd *n* another name for **tofu.**

beanery ('bi:nərɪ) *n, pl* **-eries.** *U.S. informal.* a cheap restaurant.

beanfeast ('bi:n,fi:st) *n Brit. informal.* **1** an annual dinner given by employers to employees. **2** any festive or merry occasion.
beanie *or* **beany** ('bi:nɪ) *n, pl* **beanies.** a round close-fitting hat resembling a skullcap.
beano ('bi:nəʊ) *n, pl* **beanos.** *Brit. slang.* a celebration, party, or other enjoyable time.
beanpole ('bi:n,pəʊl) *n* **1** a tall stick or pole used to support bean plants. **2** *Slang.* a tall thin person.
bean sprout *n* the sprout of a newly germinated mung bean, eaten as a vegetable, esp. in Chinese dishes.
beanstalk ('bi:n,stɔ:k) *n* the stem of a bean plant.
bean tree *n* any of various trees having beanlike pods, such as the catalpa and carob.
bear[1] (bɛə) *vb* **bears, bearing, bore, borne.** (*mainly tr*) **1** to support or hold up; sustain. **2** to bring or convey: *to bear gifts.* **3** to take, accept, or assume the responsibility of: *to bear an expense.* **4** (*past participle* **born** in passive use except when foll. by *by*) to give birth to: *to bear children.* **5** (*also intr*) to produce by or as if by natural growth: *to bear fruit.* **6** to tolerate or endure: *she couldn't bear him.* **7** to admit of; sustain: *his story does not bear scrutiny.* **8** to hold in the conscious mind or in one's feelings: *to bear a grudge; I'll bear that idea in mind.* **9** to show or be marked with: *he still bears the scars.* **10** to transmit or spread: *to bear gossip.* **11** to render or supply (esp. in the phrase **bear witness**). **12** to conduct or manage (oneself, the body, etc.): *she bore her head high.* **13** to have, be, or stand in (relation or comparison): *his account bears no relation to the facts.* **14** (*intr*) to move, be located, or lie in a specified direction: *the way bears east.* **15** to have by right; be entitled to (esp. in the phrase **bear title**). **16 bear a hand.** to give assistance. **17 bring to bear.** to bring into operation or effect: *he brought his knowledge to bear on the situation.* ◆ See also **bear down, bear off, bear on, bear out, bear up, bear with, born.** [Old English *beran;* related to Old Norse *bera,* Old High German *beran* to carry, Latin *ferre,* Greek *pherein* to bear, Sanskrit *bharati* he carries]
bear[2] (bɛə) *n, pl* **bears** *or* **bear. 1** any plantigrade mammal of the family *Ursidae:* order *Carnivora* (carnivores). Bears are typically massive omnivorous animals with a large head, a long shaggy coat, and strong claws. See also **black bear, brown bear, polar bear.** Related adj: **ursine. 2** any of various bearlike animals, such as the koala and the ant bear. **3** a clumsy, churlish, or ill-mannered person. **4** a teddy bear. **5** *Stock Exchange.* **5a** a speculator who sells in anticipation of falling prices to make a profit on repurchase. **5b** (*as modifier*): *a bear market.* Compare **bull**[1] (sense 5). ◆ *vb* **bears, bearing, beared. 6** (*tr*) to lower or attempt to lower the price or prices of (a stock market or a security) by speculative selling. [Old English *bera;* related to Old Norse *bjorn,* Old High German *bero*]
Bear (bɛə) *n* **the. 1** the English name for either **Ursa Major (Great Bear)** or **Ursa Minor (Little Bear). 2** an informal name for **Russia.**
bearable ('bɛərəbᵊl) *adj* endurable; tolerable. ▸ **'bearably** *adv*
bear-baiting *n* (formerly) an entertainment in which dogs attacked and enraged a chained bear.
bearberry ('bɛəbərɪ) *n, pl* **-ries. 1** a trailing evergreen ericaceous shrub, *Arctostaphylos uva-ursi,* with small pinkish-white flowers, red berries, and astringent leaves. **2 alpine** or **black bearberry.** a related species, *A. alpina* of European mountains, having black berries.
bearcat ('bɛə,kæt) *n* another name for **lesser panda** (see **panda** (sense 2)).
beard (bɪəd) *n* **1** the hair growing on the lower parts of a man's face. **2** any similar growth in animals. **3** a tuft of long hairs in plants such as barley and wheat; awn. **4** the gills of an oyster. **5** a barb, as on an arrow or fish-hook. **6** *Printing.* the part of a piece of type that connects the face with the shoulder. ◆ *vb* (*tr*) **7** to oppose boldly or impertinently. **8** to pull or grasp the beard of. [Old English *beard;* related to Old Norse *barth,* Old High German *bart,* Latin *barba*] ▸ **'bearded** *adj*
bearded collie *n* a medium-sized breed of dog having a profuse long straight coat, usually grey or fawn and often with white on the head, legs, and chest, a long tail, and a distinctive beard.
bearded lizard *or* **dragon** *n* another name for **jew lizard.**
bearded tit *n* another name for **reedling.**
bearded vulture *n* another name for **lammergeier.**
beardless ('bɪədlɪs) *adj* **1** without a beard. **2** too young to grow a beard; immature. ▸ **'beardlessness** *n*
bear down *vb* (*intr, adv;* often foll. by *on* or *upon*) **1** to press or weigh down. **2** to approach in a determined or threatening manner. **3** (of a vessel) to make an approach (to another vessel, obstacle, etc.) from windward. **4** (of a woman during childbirth) to exert a voluntary muscular pressure to assist delivery.
Beardsley ('bɪədzlɪ) *n* **Aubrey (Vincent).** 1872–98, English illustrator: noted for his stylized black-and-white illustrations, esp. those for Oscar Wilde's *Salome* and Pope's *Rape of the Lock.*
bearer ('bɛərə) *n* **1** a person or thing that bears, presents, or upholds. **2** a person who presents a note or bill for payment. **3** (in Africa, India, etc., formerly) **3a** a native carrier, esp. on an expedition. **3b** a native servant. **4** See **pallbearer. 5** the holder of a rank, position, office, etc. **6** (*modifier*) *Finance.* payable to the person in possession: *bearer bonds.*
bear garden *n* **1** (formerly) a place where bears were exhibited and where bear-baiting took place. **2** a place or scene of tumult and disorder.
bear hug *n* **1** a wrestling hold in which the arms are locked tightly round an opponent's chest and arms. **2** any similar tight embrace. **3** *Commerce.* an approach to the board of one company by another to indicate that an offer is to be made for their shares.
bearing ('bɛərɪŋ) *n* **1** a support, guide, or locating piece for a rotating or reciprocating mechanical part. **2** (foll. by *on* or *upon*) relevance (to): *it has no bearing on this problem.* **3** a person's general social conduct, esp. in manners, dress, and behaviour. **4a** the act, period, or capability of producing fruit or young. **4b** an amount produced; yield. **5** the part of a beam or lintel that rests on a support. **6** anything that carries weight or acts as a support. **7** the angular direction of a line, point, or course measured from true north or south (**true bearing**), magnetic north or south (**magnetic bearing**), or one's own position. **8** (*usually pl*) the position or direction, as of a ship, fixed with reference to two or more known points. **9** (*usually pl*) a sense of one's relative position or situation; orientation (esp. in the phrases **lose, get,** *or* **take one's bearings**). **10** *Heraldry.* **10a** a device or emblem on a heraldic shield; charge. **10b** another name for **coat of arms.**
bearing pedestal *n* an independent support for a bearing, usually incorporating a bearing housing.
bearing pile *n* a foundation pile that supports weight vertically. Compare **sheet pile.**
bearing rein *n Chiefly Brit.* a rein from the bit to the saddle, designed to keep the horse's head in the desired position. Usual U.S. word: **checkrein.**
bearish ('bɛərɪʃ) *adj* **1** like a bear; rough; clumsy; churlish. **2** *Stock Exchange.* causing, expecting, or characterized by a fall in prices: *a bearish market.* ▸ **'bearishly** *adv* ▸ **'bearishness** *n*
Béarnaise (,beɪə'neɪz) *n* a rich sauce made from egg yolks, lemon juice or wine vinegar, butter, shallots, herbs, and seasoning. [C19: French, from *Béarn* in SW France]
bear off *vb* (*adv*) *Nautical.* (of a vessel) to avoid hitting an obstacle, another vessel, etc., by swerving onto a different course.
bear on *vb* (*intr, prep*) **1** to be relevant to; relate to. **2** to be burdensome to or afflict: *his misdeeds bore heavily on his conscience.*
bear out *vb* (*tr, adv*) to show to be true or truthful; confirm: *the witness will bear me out.*
bear raid *n* an attempt to force down the price of a security or commodity by sustained selling.
bear's-breech *or* **bear's-breeches** *n* a widely cultivated S European acanthus plant, *Acanthus mollis,* having whitish purple-veined flowers.
bear's-ear *n* another name for **auricula** (sense 1).
bear's-foot *n* either of two Eurasian hellebore plants, *Helleborus foetidus* or *H. viridis,* having leaves shaped like the foot and claws of a bear.
bearskin ('bɛə,skɪn) *n* **1** the pelt of a bear, esp. when used as a rug. **2** a tall helmet of black fur worn by certain regiments in the British Army. **3** a rough shaggy woollen cloth, used for overcoats.
bear up *vb* (*intr, adv*) to endure cheerfully.
bear with *vb* (*intr, prep*) to be patient with: *bear with me while I tell you my story.*
bearwood ('bɛə,wʊd) *n* another name for **cascara** (sense 2).
beast (bi:st) *n* **1** any animal other than man, esp. a large wild quadruped. **2** savage nature or characteristics: *the beast in man.* **3** a brutal, uncivilized, or filthy person. [C13: from Old French *beste,* from Latin *bestia,* of obscure origin]
beastie ('bi:stɪ) *n* **1** *Scot.* a small animal. **2** *Informal.* an insect.
beastings ('bi:stɪŋz) *n* a U.S. spelling of **beestings.**
beastly ('bi:stlɪ) *adj* **-lier, -liest. 1** *Informal.* unpleasant; disagreeable; nasty: *beastly weather.* **2** *Obsolete.* of or like a beast; bestial. ◆ *adv* **3** *Informal.* (intensifier): *the weather is so beastly hot.* ▸ **'beastliness** *n*
beast of burden *n* an animal, such as a donkey or ox, used for carrying loads.
beast of prey *n* any animal that hunts other animals for food.
beat (bi:t) *vb* **beats, beating, beat; beaten** *or* **beat. 1** (when *intr,* often foll. by *against, on,* etc.) to strike with or as if with a series of violent blows; dash or pound repeatedly (against). **2** (*tr*) to punish by striking; flog. **3** to move or cause to move up and down; flap: *the bird beat its wings heavily.* **4** (*intr*) to throb rhythmically; pulsate: *her heart beat fast.* **5** (*tr*) to make (one's way) by or as if by blows: *she beat her way out of the crowd.* **6** (*tr;* sometimes foll. by *up*) *Cookery.* to stir or whisk (an ingredient or mixture) vigorously. **7** (*tr;* sometimes foll. by *out*) to shape, make thin, or flatten (a piece of metal) by repeated blows. **8** (*tr*) *Music.* to indicate (time) by the motion of one's hand, baton, etc., or by the action of a metronome. **9** (when *tr,* sometimes foll. by *out*) to produce (a sound or signal) by or as if by striking a drum. **10** to sound or cause to sound, by or as if by beating: *beat the drums!* **11** to overcome (an opponent) in a contest, battle, etc. **12** (*tr;* often foll. by *back, down, off,* etc.) to drive, push, or thrust. **13** (*tr*) to arrive or finish before (someone or something); anticipate or forestall: *they set off early to beat the rush hour.* **14** (*tr*) to form (a path or track) by repeatedly walking or riding over it. **15** to scour (woodlands, coverts, or undergrowth) so as to rouse game for shooting. **16** (*tr*) *Slang.* to puzzle or baffle: *it beats me how he can do that.* **17** (*intr*) *Physics.* (of sounds or electrical signals) to combine and produce a pulsating sound or signal. **18** (*intr*) *Nautical.* to steer a sailing vessel as close as possible to the direction from which the wind is blowing. **19** (*tr*) *Slang, chiefly U.S.* to cheat or defraud: *he beat his brother out of the inheritance.* **20 beat about the bush.** to avoid the point at issue; prevaricate. **21 beat a retreat.** to withdraw or depart in haste. **22 beat it.** *Slang.* (*often imperative*) to go away. **23 beat one's breast.** See **breast** (sense 10). **24 beat someone's brains out.** *Slang.* to kill by knocking severely about the head. **25 beat someone to it.** *Informal.* to reach a place or achieve an objective before someone else. **26 beat the bounds.** *Brit.* (formerly) to define the boundaries of a parish by making a procession around them and hitting the ground with rods. **27 can you beat it** *or* **that?** *Slang.* an expression of utter amazement or surprise. ◆ *n* **28** a stroke or blow. **29** the sound made by a stroke or blow. **30** a regular sound or stroke; throb. **31a** an assigned or habitual round or route, as of a policeman or sentry. **31b** (*as modifier*): *beat police officers.* **32** the basic rhythmic unit in a piece of music, usually grouped in twos, threes, or fours. **33a** pop or rock music characterized by a heavy rhythmic beat. **33b** (*as modifier*): *a beat group.* **34** *Physics.* one of the regular pulses produced by combining two sounds or electrical signals that have similar frequencies. **35** *Horology.* the im-

pulse given to the balance wheel by the action of the escapement. **36** *Prosody.* the accent, stress, or ictus in a metrical foot. **37** *Nautical.* a course that steers a sailing vessel as close as possible to the direction from which the wind is blowing. **38a** the act of scouring for game by beating. **38b** the organized scouring of a particular woodland so as to rouse the game in it. **38c** the woodland where game is so roused. **39** short for **beatnik. 40** *Fencing.* a sharp tap with one's blade on an opponent's blade to deflect it. **41** (*modifier*) (*often cap.*) of, characterized by, or relating to the Beat Generation: *a beat poet; beat philosophy.* ◆ *adj* **42** (*postpositive*) *Slang.* totally exhausted. ◆ See also **beat down, beat up.** [Old English *bēatan;* related to Old Norse *bauta,* Old High German *bōzan*] ► **'beatable** *adj*

beatbox ('biːtˌbɒks) *n Informal.* a drum machine.

beat down *vb* (*adv*) **1** (*tr*) *Informal.* to force or persuade (a seller) to accept a lower price: *I beat him down three pounds.* **2** (*intr*) (of the sun) to shine intensely; be very hot.

beaten ('biːtᵊn) *adj* **1** defeated or baffled. **2** shaped or made thin by hammering: *a bowl of beaten gold.* **3** much travelled; well trodden (esp. in the phrase **the beaten track**). **4 off the beaten track. 4a** in or into unfamiliar territory. **4b** out of the ordinary; unusual. **5** (of food) mixed by beating; whipped. **6** tired out; exhausted. **7** *Hunting.* (of woods, undergrowth, etc.) scoured so as to rouse game.

beater ('biːtə) *n* **1** a person who beats or hammers: *a panel beater.* **2** an instrument or device used for beating: *a carpet beater.* **3** a person who rouses wild game from woodland, undergrowth, etc.

Beat Generation *n* (*functioning as sing or pl*) **1** members of the generation that came to maturity in the 1950s, whose rejection of the social and political systems of the West was expressed through contempt for regular work, possessions, traditional dress, etc., and espousal of anarchism, communal living, drugs, etc. **2** a group of U.S. writers, notably Jack Kerouac, Allen Ginsberg, and William Burroughs, who emerged in the 1950s.

beatific (ˌbiːə'tɪfɪk) *adj* **1** displaying great happiness, calmness, etc.: *a beatific smile.* **2** of, conferring, or relating to a state of celestial happiness. [C17: from Late Latin *beātificus,* from Latin *beātus,* from *beāre* to bless + *facere* to make] ► **ˌbea'tifically** *adv*

beatify (bɪ'ætɪˌfaɪ) *vb* **-fies, -fying, -fied. 1** (*tr*) *R.C. Church.* (of the pope) to declare formally that (a deceased person) showed a heroic degree of holiness in his or her life and therefore is worthy of public veneration: the first step towards canonization. **2** (*tr*) to make extremely happy. [C16: from Old French *beatifier,* from Late Latin *beātificāre* to make blessed; see BEATIFIC] ► **beatification** (bɪˌætɪfɪ'keɪʃən) *n*

beating ('biːtɪŋ) *n* **1** a whipping or thrashing, as in punishment. **2** a defeat or setback. **3 take some** *or* **a lot of beating.** to be difficult to improve upon.

beatitude (bɪ'ætɪˌtjuːd) *n* **1** supreme blessedness or happiness. **2** an honorific title of the Eastern Christian Church, applied to those of patriarchal rank. [C15: from Latin *beātitūdō,* from *beātus* blessed; see BEATIFIC]

Beatitude (bɪ'ætɪˌtjuːd) *n New Testament.* any of eight distinctive sayings of Jesus in the Sermon on the Mount (Matthew 5:3–11) in which he declares that the poor, the meek, those that mourn, the merciful, the peacemakers, the pure of heart, those that thirst for justice, and those that are persecuted will, in various ways, receive the blessings of heaven.

Beatles ('biːtᵊlz) *pl n* **the.** English rock group (1961–70): comprised John Lennon (guitar, vocals), Paul McCartney (bass guitar, vocals), George Harrison (guitar, vocals), and Ringo Starr (drums, vocals). Their recordings include the hit singles "Please Please me" (1963), "She Loves you" (1963), "Can't Buy me Love" (1964), "All you Need is Love" (1967), and "Hey Jude" (1968), and the albums *A Hard Day's Night* (film soundtrack, 1964), *Help!* (film soundtrack, 1965), *Revolver* (1966), *Sgt. Pepper's Lonely Hearts Club Band* (1967), and *Abbey Road* (1969). Most of their material was written by Lennon and McCartney. See also (George) **Harrison,** (John Winston Ono) **Lennon,** (Paul) **McCartney,** (Ringo) **Starr.**

beatnik ('biːtnɪk) *n* **1** a member of the Beat Generation (sense 1). **2** *Informal.* any person with long hair and shabby clothes. [C20: from BEAT (n) + -NIK, by analogy with SPUTNIK]

Beaton ('biːtᵊn) *n* Sir **Cecil** (**Walter Hardy**). 1904–80, British photographer, noted esp. for his society portraits.

Beatrix ('biːətrɪks) *n* full name *Beatrix Wilhelmina Armgard.* born 1938, queen of the Netherlands from 1980.

Beatty ('biːtɪ) *n* **David,** 1st Earl Beatty. 1871–1936, British admiral of the fleet in World War I.

beat up *Informal.* ◆ *vb* **1** (*tr, adv*) to strike or kick (a person), usually repeatedly, so as to inflict severe physical damage. ◆ *adj* **beat-up. 2** worn-out; dilapidated.

beau (bəʊ) *n, pl* **beaux** (bəʊ, bəʊz) *or* **beaus** (bəʊz). **1** a lover, sweetheart, or escort of a girl or woman. **2** a man who is greatly concerned with his clothes and appearance; dandy. [C17: from French, from Old French *biau,* from Latin *bellus* handsome, charming]

Beaufort ('bəʊfət) *n* **1 Henry.** ?1374–1447, English cardinal, half-brother of Henry IV; chancellor (1403–04, 1413–17, 1424–26). **2** Lady **Margaret,** Countess of Richmond and Derby. ?1443–1509, mother of Henry VII. She helped to found two Cambridge colleges and was a patron of Caxton.

Beaufort scale *n Meteorol.* an international scale of wind velocities ranging for practical purposes from 0 (calm) to 12 (hurricane force). In the U.S. an extension of the scale, from 13 to 17 for winds over 64 knots, is used. [C19: after Sir Francis *Beaufort* (1774–1857), British admiral and hydrographer who devised it]

Beaufort Sea *n* part of the Arctic Ocean off the N coast of North America.

beau geste *French.* (bo ʒɛst) *n, pl* ***beaux gestes*** (bo ʒɛst). a noble or gracious gesture or act, esp. one that is meaningless. [literally: beautiful gesture]

Beauharnais (*French* boarnɛ) *n* **1 Alexandre** (alɛksɑ̃dr), Vicomte de. 1760–94, French general, who served in the War of American Independence and the French Revolutionary wars; first husband of Empress Joséphine: guillotined. **2** his son, **Eugène de** (øʒɛn də). 1781–1824, viceroy of Italy (1805–14) for his stepfather Napoleon I. **3** (**Eugénie**) (øʒeni) **Hortense de** (ɔrtɑ̃s də). 1783–1837, queen of Holland (1806–10) as wife of Louis Bonaparte; daughter of Alexandre Beauharnais and sister of Eugène: mother of Napoleon III. **4 Joséphine de** (ʒozefin də). See (Empress) **Josephine.**

beau idéal *French.* (bo ideal) *n, pl* ***beaux idéals*** (boz ideal). perfect beauty or excellence. [literally: ideal beauty]

beaujolais ('bəʊʒəˌleɪ) *n* (*sometimes cap.*) a popular fresh-tasting red or white wine from southern Burgundy in France.

Beaulieu ('bjuːlɪ) *n* a village in S England, in Hampshire: site of Palace House, seat of Lord Montagu and once the gatehouse of the ruined 13th-century abbey; the National Motor Museum is in its grounds. Pop.: 1200 (latest est.).

Beaumarchais (*French* bomarʃɛ) *n* **Pierre Augustin Caron de** (pjɛr ogystɛ̃ karɔ̃ də). 1732–99, French dramatist, noted for his comedies *The Barber of Seville* (1775) and *The Marriage of Figaro* (1784).

Beaumaris (bəʊ'mærɪs) *n* a resort in N Wales, on the island of Anglesey: 13th-century castle. Pop.: 1561 (1991).

beau monde ('bəʊ 'mɒnd; *French* bo mɔ̃d) *n* the world of fashion and society. [C18: French, literally: fine world]

Beaumont[1] ('bəʊmɒnt) *n* a city in SE Texas. Pop.: 111 224 (1996 est.).

Beaumont[2] *n* ('bəʊmɒnt). **Francis.** 1584–1616, English dramatist, who collaborated with John Fletcher on plays including *The Knights of the Burning Pestle* (1607) and *The Maid's Tragedy* (1611).

Beaune (bəʊn) *n* **1** a city in E France, near Dijon: an important trading centre for Burgundy wines. Pop.: 22 170 (1990). **2** a wine produced in this district.

beaut (bjuːt) *Slang, chiefly Austral. and N.Z.* ◆ *n* **1** a person or thing that is outstanding or distinctive. ◆ *adj, interj* **2** good or excellent: an expression of approval.

beauteous ('bjuːtɪəs) *adj* a poetic word for **beautiful.** ► **'beauteously** *adv* ► **'beauteousness** *n*

beautician (bjuː'tɪʃən) *n* a person who works in or manages a beauty salon.

beautiful ('bjuːtɪfʊl) *adj* **1** possessing beauty; aesthetically pleasing. **2** highly enjoyable; very pleasant: *the party was beautiful.* ► **'beautifulness** *n*

beautifully ('bjuːtɪflɪ) *adv* **1** in a beautiful manner. **2** *Informal.* (intensifier): *you did beautifully well in the race.*

beautiful people *pl n* (*sometimes caps.;* preceded by *the*) rich, fashionable people in international high society.

beautify ('bjuːtɪˌfaɪ) *vb* **-fies, -fying, -fied.** to make or become beautiful. ► **beautification** (ˌbjuːtɪfɪ'keɪʃən) *n* ► **'beautiˌfier** *n*

beauty ('bjuːtɪ) *n, pl* **-ties. 1** the combination of all the qualities of a person or thing that delight the senses and please the mind. **2** a very attractive and well-formed girl or woman. **3** *Informal.* an outstanding example of its kind: *the horse is a beauty.* **4** *Informal.* an advantageous feature: *one beauty of the job is the short hours.* **5** *Informal, old-fashioned.* a light-hearted and affectionate term of address: *hello, my old beauty!* ◆ *interj* **6** (*N.Z.* 'bjuːdɪ) *Austral. and N.Z. slang.* an expression of approval or agreement. Also (Scot., Austral., and N.Z.): **you beauty.** [C13: from Old French *biauté,* from *biau* beautiful; see BEAU]

beauty contest *n* **1** a competition in which the participants, usually women, are judged on their attractiveness, with a prize, and often a title, awarded to the winner. **2** *Informal.* any contest decided on the basis of superficial attractiveness, popularity, etc.: *the referendum might turn into a party political beauty contest.*

beauty queen *n* an attractive young woman, esp. one who has won a beauty contest.

beauty salon *or* **parlour** *n* an establishment providing women with services to improve their beauty, such as hairdressing, manicuring, facial treatment, and massage.

beauty sleep *n Informal.* sleep, esp. sleep before midnight.

beauty spot *n* **1** a place of outstanding beauty. **2** a small dark-coloured patch or spot worn on a lady's face as an adornment or as a foil to her complexion. **3** a mole or other similar natural mark on the skin.

Beauvais (*French* bovɛ) *n* a market town in N France, 64 km (40 miles) north-west of Paris. Pop.: 56 280 (1990).

Beauvoir (*French* bovwar) *n* **Simone de** (simɔn də). 1908–86, French existentialist novelist and feminist, whose works include *Le sang des autres* (1944), *Le deuxième sexe* (1949), and *Les mandarins* (1954).

beaux (bəʊ, bəʊz) *n* a plural of **beau.**

beaux-arts (bəʊ'zɑː) *pl n* **1** another word for **fine art. 2** (*modifier*) relating to the classical decorative style, esp. that of the École des Beaux-Arts in Paris: *beaux-arts influences.* [C19: French, literally: fine arts]

beaver[1] ('biːvə) *n* **1** a large amphibious rodent, *Castor fiber,* of Europe, Asia, and North America: family *Castoridae.* It has soft brown fur, a broad flat hairless tail, and webbed hind feet, and constructs complex dams and houses (lodges) in rivers. **2** the fur of this animal. **3 mountain beaver.** a burrowing rodent, *Aplodontia rufa,* of W North America: family *Aplodontidae.* **4** a tall hat of beaver fur or a fabric resembling it, worn, esp. by men, during the 19th century. **5** a woollen napped cloth resembling beaver fur, formerly much used for overcoats, etc. **6** a greyish- or yellowish-brown. **7** *Obsolete.* a full beard. **8** a bearded man. **9** (*modifier*) having the colour of beaver or made of beaver fur or some similar material: *a beaver lamb coat; a beaver stole.* ◆ *vb* **10** (*intr;* usually foll. by *away*) to work industriously or steadily. [Old English *beofor;* compare Old Norse *biōrr,* Old High German *bibar,* Latin *fiber,* Sanskrit *babhrú* red-brown]

beaver[2] ('bi:və) *n* a movable piece on a medieval helmet used to protect the lower part of the face. [C15: from Old French *baviere*, from *baver* to dribble]

Beaver ('bi:və) *n* a member of a **Beaver Colony,** the youngest group of boys (aged 6–8 years) in the Scout Association.

beaverboard ('bi:və,bɔ:d) *n* a stiff light board of compressed wood fibre, used esp. to surface partitions.

Beaverbrook ('bi:və,brʊk) *n* **1st Baron,** title of *William Maxwell Aitken.* 1879–1964, British newspaper proprietor and Conservative politician, born in Canada, whose newspapers included the *Daily Express;* minister of information (1918); minister of aircraft production (1940–41).

bebeerine (bə'bɪəri:n, -rɪn) *n* an alkaloid, resembling quinine, obtained from the bark of the greenheart and other plants. [C19: from German *Bebeerin;* see BEBEERU, -INE[2]]

bebeeru (bə'bɪəru:) *n* another name for **greenheart** (sense 1). [C19: from Spanish *bibirú,* of Carib origin]

Bebel (*German* 'be:bəl) *n* **August** ('august). 1840–1913, German socialist leader: one of the founders of the Social Democratic Party (1869).

Bebington ('bɛbɪŋtən) *n* a town in NW England, in Wirral unitary authority, Merseyside: docks and chemical works. Pop.: 60 148 (1991).

bebop ('bi:bɒp) *n* the full name for **bop**[1] (sense 1). [C20: imitative of the rhythm of the music] ▸ **'bebopper** *n*

becalmed (bɪ'kɑ:md) *adj* (of a sailing boat or ship) motionless through lack of wind.

became (bɪ'keɪm) *vb* the past tense of **become.**

because (bɪ'kɒz, -'kəz) *conj* **1** (*subordinating*) on account of the fact that; on account of being; since: *because it's so cold we'll go home.* **2 because of.** (*prep*) on account of: *I lost my job because of her.* [C14 *bi cause,* from *bi* BY + CAUSE]

USAGE See at **reason.**

beccafico (,bɛkə'fi:kəʊ) *n, pl* **-cos.** any of various European songbirds, esp. warblers of the genus *Sylvia,* eaten as a delicacy in Italy and other countries. [C17: from Italian, from *beccare* to peck + *fico* fig, from Latin *fīcus*]

Beccaria (*Italian* bekaˈria) *n* **Cesare Bonesana** ('tʃezare bone'zɑ:na), Marchese de. 1738–94, Italian legal theorist and political economist; author of the influential treatise *Crimes and Punishments* (1764), which attacked corruption, torture, and capital punishment.

béchamel sauce (,beɪʃə'mɛl) *n* a thick white sauce flavoured with onion and seasonings. [C18: named after the Marquis of *Béchamel,* steward of Louis XIV of France and its inventor]

bechance (bɪ'tʃɑ:ns) *vb* (*intr*) *Archaic.* to happen (to).

Béchar (*French* beʃar) *n* a city in NW Algeria: an oasis. Pop.: 107 311 (1987). Former name: **Colomb-Béchar.**

bêche-de-mer (,beʃdə'mɛə) *n, pl* **bêches-de-mer** (,beʃdə'mɛə) *or* **bêche-de-mer. 1** another name for **trepang. 2** See **Beach-la-Mar.** [C19: quasi-French, from earlier English *biche de mer,* from Portuguese *bicho do mar* worm of the sea]

Bechet ('beʃeɪ) *n* **Sidney (Joseph).** 1897–1959, U.S. jazz soprano saxophonist and clarinettist.

Bechstein (*German* 'bɛçʃtaɪn) *n* **Karl.** 1826–1900, German piano maker; founder (1853) of the Bechstein company of piano manufacturers in Berlin.

Bechuana (be'tʃwɑ:nə; ,betʃu'ɑ:nə, ,bɛkju-) *n, pl* **-na** *or* **-nas. 1** a former name for **Tswana. 2** a former name for a member of the Bantu people of Botswana.

Bechuanaland (be'tʃwɑ:nə,lænd; ,betʃu'ɑ:nə,lænd, ,bɛkju-) *n* the former name (until 1966) of **Botswana.**

beck[1] (bɛk) *n* **1** a nod, wave, or other gesture or signal. **2 at (someone's) beck and call.** ready to obey (someone's) orders instantly; subject to (someone's) slightest whim. [C14: short for *becnen* to BECKON]

beck[2] (bɛk) *n* (in N England) a stream, esp. a swiftly flowing one. [Old English *becc,* from Old Norse *bekkr;* related to Old English *bece,* Old Saxon *beki,* Old High German *bah* brook, Sanskrit *bhanga* wave]

Beckenbauer ('bɛkən,baʊə) *n* **Franz.** born 1945, German footballer: team captain when West Germany won the World Cup (1974): manager of West Germany (1984–90), coaching the team to success in the 1990 World Cup.

Becker ('bɛkə) *n* **Boris** ('bɒrɪs). born 1967, German tennis player: Wimbledon champion 1985, 1986, and 1989: the youngest man ever to win Wimbledon.

becket ('bɛkɪt) *n Nautical.* **1** a clevis forming part of one end of a sheave, used for securing standing lines by means of a thimble. **2** a short line with a grommet or eye at one end and a knot at the other, used for securing spars or other gear in place. [C18: of unknown origin]

Becket ('bɛkɪt) *n* **Saint Thomas à.** 1118–70, English prelate; chancellor (1155–62) to Henry II; archbishop of Canterbury (1162–70): murdered following his opposition to Henry's attempts to control the clergy. Feast day: Dec. 29 or July 7.

becket bend *n* another name for **sheet bend.**

Beckett ('bɛkɪt) *n* **1 Margaret Mary.** born 1943, British Labour politician; president of the board of trade and secretary of state for trade and industry from 1997. **2 Samuel (Barclay).** 1906–89, Irish dramatist and novelist writing in French and English, whose works portray the human condition as insignificant or absurd in a bleak universe. They include the plays *En attendant Godot* (*Waiting for Godot,* 1952), *Fin de partie* (*Endgame,* 1957), and *Not I* (1973) and the novel *Malone meurt* (*Malone Dies,* 1951): Nobel prize for literature 1969.

Beckford ('bɛkfəd) *n* **William.** 1759–1844, English writer and dilettante; author of the oriental romance *Vathek* (1787).

Beckmann (*German* 'bɛkman) *n* **1 Ernst Otto** (ɛrnst'ɔ:to). 1853–1923, German chemist: devised the **Beckmann thermometer,** used for measuring small temperature changes in liquids. **2 Max** (maks). 1884–1950, German expressionist painter.

beckon ('bɛkən) *vb* **1** to summon with a gesture of the hand or head. **2** to entice or lure. ◆ *n* **3** a summoning gesture. [Old English *bīecnan,* from *bēacen* sign; related to Old Saxon *bōknian;* see BEACON] ▸ **'beckoner** *n* ▸ **'beckoning** *adj, n*

becloud (bɪ'klaʊd) *vb* (*tr*) **1** to cover or obscure with a cloud. **2** to confuse or muddle: *to becloud the issues.*

become (bɪ'kʌm) *vb* **-comes, -coming, -came, -come.** (*mainly intr*) **1** (*copula*) to come to be; develop or grow into: *he became a monster.* **2** (foll. by *of; usually used in a question*) to fall to or be the lot (of); happen (to): *what became of him?* **3** (*tr*) (of clothes, etc.) to enhance the appearance of (someone); suit: *that dress becomes you.* **4** (*tr*) to be appropriate; befit: *it ill becomes you to complain.* [Old English *becuman* to happen; related to Old High German *biqueman* to come to, Gothic *biquiman* to appear suddenly]

becoming (bɪ'kʌmɪŋ) *adj* **1** suitable; appropriate. ◆ *n* **2** any process of change. **3** (in the philosophy of Aristotle) any change from the lower level of potentiality to the higher level of actuality. ▸ **be'comingly** *adv* ▸ **be'comingness** *n*

becquerel (,bɛkə'rɛl) *n* the derived SI unit of radioactivity equal to one disintegration per second. Symbol: **Bq** [C20: named after A. H. BECQUEREL]

Becquerel (*French* bɛkrɛl) *n* **Antoine Henri** (ɑ̃twan ɑ̃ri). 1852–1908, French physicist, who discovered the photographic action of the rays emitted by uranium salts and so instigated the study of radioactivity: Nobel prize for physics 1903.

bed (bɛd) *n* **1** a piece of furniture on which to sleep. **2** the mattress and bedclothes on such a piece of furniture: *an unmade bed.* **3** sleep or rest: *time for bed.* **4** any place in which a person or animal sleeps or rests. **5** *Med.* a unit of potential occupancy in a hospital or residential institution. **6** *Informal.* a place for sexual intercourse. **7** *Informal.* sexual intercourse. **8** a plot of ground in which plants are grown, esp. when considered together with the plants in it: *a flower bed.* **9** the bottom of a river, lake, or sea. **10** a part of this used for cultivation of a plant or animal: *oyster beds.* **11** a layer of crushed rock, gravel, etc., used as a foundation for a road, railway, etc. **12** a layer of mortar in a masonry wall. **13** the underside of a brick, tile, slate, etc., when in position. Compare **back**[1] (sense 12). **14** any underlying structure or part. **15** a layer of rock, esp. sedimentary rock. **16** the flat part of a letterpress printing press onto or against which the type forme is placed. **17** a layer of solid particles of an absorbent, catalyst, or reagent through which a fluid is passed during the course of a chemical reaction or other process. **18** a machine base on which a moving part carrying a tool or workpiece slides: *lathe bed.* **19 a bed of roses.** a situation of comfort or ease. **20 be brought to bed (of).** *Archaic.* to give birth (to). **21 bed of nails. 21a** a situation or position of extreme difficulty. **21b** a bed studded with nails on which a fakir lies. **22 get out of bed on the wrong side.** *Informal.* to be ill-tempered from the start of the day. **23 go to bed. 23a** (often foll. by *with*) to have sexual intercourse (with). **23b** *Journalism, printing.* (of a newspaper, magazine, etc.) to go to press; start printing. **24 put to bed. 24a** *Journalism.* to finalize work on (a newspaper, magazine, etc.) so that it is ready to go to press. **24b** *Letterpress printing.* to lock up the type forme of (a publication) in the press before printing. **25 take to one's bed.** to remain in bed, esp. because of illness. ◆ *vb* **beds, bedding, bedded. 26** (usually foll. by *down*) to go to or put into a place to sleep or rest. **27** (*tr*) to have sexual intercourse with. **28** (*tr*) to place, fix, or sink firmly into position; embed. **29** *Geology.* to form or be arranged in a distinct layer; stratify. **30** (*tr;* often foll. by *out*) to plant in a bed of soil. ◆ See also **bed in.** [Old English *bedd;* related to Old Norse *bethr,* Old High German *betti,* Gothic *badi*]

BEd *abbrev. for* Bachelor of Education.

bed and board *n* **1** sleeping accommodation and meals. **2 divorce from bed and board.** *U.S. law.* a form of divorce whereby the parties are prohibited from living together but the marriage is not dissolved.

bed and breakfast *Chiefly Brit.* ◆ *n* **1** (in a hotel, boarding house, etc.) overnight accommodation and breakfast. ◆ *adj* **2** (of a stock-exchange transaction) establishing a loss for tax purposes, shares being sold after hours one evening and bought back the next morning when the market opens.

bed and PEP *adj Brit.* (of a stock-exchange transaction) complying with regulations for self-select PEPs, a shareholding being sold in the evening and bought back the next morning for the shareholder's own PEP.

bedaub (bɪ'dɔ:b) *vb* (*tr*) **1** to smear all over with something thick, sticky, or dirty. **2** to ornament in a gaudy or vulgar fashion.

bedazzle (bɪ'dæzəl) *vb* (*tr*) to dazzle or confuse, as with brilliance. ▸ **be'dazzlement** *n*

bed bath *n* another name for **blanket bath.**

bedbug ('bɛd,bʌg) *n* any of several bloodsucking insects of the heteropterous genus *Cimex,* esp. *C. lectularius* of temperate regions, having an oval flattened wingless body and infesting dirty houses: family *Cimicidae.*

bedchamber ('bɛd,tʃeɪmbə) *n* an archaic word for **bedroom.**

bedclothes ('bɛd,kləʊðz) *pl n* sheets, blankets, and other coverings of a bed.

beddable ('bɛdəbəl) *adj* sexually attractive.

bedder ('bɛdə) *n* **1** *Brit.* (at some universities) a college servant employed to keep students' rooms in order. **2** a plant that may be grown in a garden bed.

bedding ('bɛdɪŋ) *n* **1** bedclothes, sometimes considered together with a mattress. **2** litter, such as straw, for animals. **3** something acting as a foundation, such as mortar under a brick. **4** the arrangement of a mass of rocks into distinct layers; stratification.

bedding plant *n* a plant that may be grown in a garden bed.

Beddoes ('bɛdəʊz) *n* **Thomas Lovell.** 1803–49, British poet, noted for his macabre imagery, esp. in *Death's Jest-Book* (1850).

Bede (bi:d) *n* **Saint,** known as *the Venerable Bede.* ?673–735 A.D., English monk, scholar, historian, and theologian, noted for his Latin *Ecclesiastical History of the English People* (731). Feast day: May 27 or 25. Latin name: **Baeda.**

bedeck (bɪˈdɛk) *vb* (*tr*) to cover with decorations; adorn.
bedel *or* **bedell** (ˈbiːdᵊl) *n* archaic spellings of **beadle** (sense 4).
bedesman (ˈbiːdzmən) *n, pl* **-men.** a variant spelling of **beadsman.**
bedevil (bɪˈdevᵊl) *vb* **-ils, -illing, -illed** *or U.S.* **-ils, -iling, -iled.** (*tr*) **1** to harass or torment. **2** to throw into confusion. **3** to possess, as with a devil. ▸ **beˈdevilment** *n*
bedew (bɪˈdjuː) *vb* (*tr*) to wet or cover with or as if with drops of dew.
bedfast (ˈbɛd,fɑːst) *adj* an archaic word for **bedridden.**
bedfellow (ˈbɛd,fɛləʊ) *n* **1** a person with whom one shares a bed. **2** a temporary ally or associate.
Bedford[1] (ˈbɛdfəd) *n* **1** a town in SE central England, administrative centre of Bedfordshire, on the River Ouse. Pop.: 73 917 (1991). **2** short for **Bedfordshire.**
Bedford[2] (ˈbɛdfəd) *n* **1 David.** born 1937, British composer, influenced by rock music. **2 Duke of,** title of *John of Lancaster.* 1389–1435, son of Henry IV of England: protector of England and regent of France (1422–35).
Bedford cord *n* a heavy corded cloth, similar to corduroy. [C19: named after BEDFORD[1]]
Bedfordshire (ˈbɛdfəd,ʃɪə, -ʃə) *n* a county of S central England: mainly low-lying, with the Chiltern Hills in the south: the geographical county includes Luton, which became a separate unitary authority in 1997. Administrative centre: Bedford. Pop. (including Luton): 543 100 (1994 est.). Area (including Luton): 1235 sq. km (477 sq. miles). Abbrev.: **Beds.**
bedight (bɪˈdaɪt) *Archaic.* ◆ *vb* **-dights, -dighting, -dight** *or* **-dighted. 1** (*tr*) to array or adorn. ◆ *adj* **2** (*past participle of the verb*) adorned or bedecked. [C14: from DIGHT]
bedim (bɪˈdɪm) *vb* **-dims, -dimming, -dimmed.** (*tr*) to make dim or obscure.
bed in *vb* (*prep*) *Engineering.* to fit (parts) together accurately or (of parts) to be fitted together, either through machining or use, as in fitting a bearing to its shaft.
Bedivere (ˈbɛdɪ,vɪə) *n* **Sir.** (in Arthurian legend) a knight who took the dying King Arthur to the barge in which he was carried to Avalon.
bedizen (bɪˈdaɪzᵊn, -ˈdɪzᵊn) *vb* (*tr*) *Archaic.* to dress or decorate gaudily or tastelessly. [C17: from BE- + obsolete *dizen* to dress up, of uncertain origin] ▸ **beˈdizenment** *n*
bed jacket *n* a woman's short upper garment worn over a nightgown when sitting up in bed.
bedlam (ˈbɛdləm) *n* **1** a noisy confused place or situation; state of uproar: *his speech caused bedlam.* **2** *Archaic.* a lunatic asylum; madhouse. [C13 *bedlem, bethlem,* after the Hospital of St Mary of *Bethlehem* in London]
bedlamite (ˈbɛdlə,maɪt) *n Archaic.* a lunatic; insane person.
bed linen *n* sheets and pillowcases for a bed.
Bedlington terrier (ˈbɛdlɪŋtən) *n* a lithe, graceful breed of terrier having a long tapering head with no stop and a thick fleecy coat. Often shortened to **Bedlington.** [C19: named after the town *Bedlington* in Northumberland, where they were first bred]
Bedloe's Island (ˈbɛdləʊz) *or* **Bedloe Island** *n* the former name (until 1956) of **Liberty Island.**
bed moulding *n Architect.* **1** a moulding in an entablature between the corona and the frieze. **2** any moulding below a projection.
Bedouin *or* **Beduin** (ˈbɛdʊɪn) *n* **1** (*pl* **-ins** *or* **-in**) a member of any of the nomadic tribes of Arabs inhabiting the deserts of Arabia, Jordan, and Syria, as well as parts of the Sahara. **2** a wanderer or rover. ◆ *adj* **3** of or relating to the Bedouins. **4** wandering or roving. [C14: from Old French *beduin,* from Arabic *badāwi,* plural of *badwi,* from *badw* desert]
bedpan (ˈbɛd,pæn) *n* **1** a shallow vessel placed under a bedridden patient to collect faeces and urine. **2** another name for **warming pan.**
bedplate (ˈbɛd,pleɪt) *n* a heavy metal platform or frame to which an engine or machine is attached.
bedpost (ˈbɛd,pəʊst) *n* **1** any of the four vertical supports at the corners of a bedstead. **2 between you and me and the bedpost.** *Informal.* confidentially; in secret.
bedraggle (bɪˈdrægᵊl) *vb* (*tr*) to make (hair, clothing, etc.) limp, untidy, or dirty, as with rain or mud. ▸ **beˈdraggled** *adj*
bedrail (ˈbɛd,reɪl) *n* a rail or board along the side of a bed that connects the headboard with the footboard.
bedridden (ˈbɛd,rɪdᵊn) *adj* confined to bed because of illness, esp. for a long or indefinite period. [Old English *bedreda,* from *bedd* BED + *-rida* rider, from *rīdan* to RIDE]
bedrock (ˈbɛd,rɒk) *n* **1** the solid unweathered rock that lies beneath the loose surface deposits of soil, alluvium, etc. **2** basic principles or facts (esp. in the phrase **get down to bedrock**). **3** the lowest point, level, or layer.
bedroll (ˈbɛd,rəʊl) *n* a portable roll of bedding, such as a sleeping bag, used esp. for sleeping in the open.
bedroom (ˈbɛd,ruːm, -,rʊm) *n* **1** a room furnished with beds or used for sleeping. **2** (*modifier*) containing references to sex: *a bedroom comedy.*
Beds *abbrev. for* Bedfordshire.
bedside (ˈbɛd,saɪd) *n* **a** the space by the side of a bed, esp. of a sick person. **b** (*as modifier*): *a bedside lamp; a doctor's bedside manner.*
bedsit (ˈbɛd,sɪt) *n* a furnished sitting room containing sleeping accommodation and sometimes cooking and washing facilities. Also called: **,bedˈsitter, ,bedˈsitting room.**
bedsore (ˈbɛd,sɔː) *n* the nontechnical name for **decubitus ulcer.**
bedspread (ˈbɛd,sprɛd) *n* a top cover on a bed over other bedclothes.
bedstead (ˈbɛd,stɛd) *n* the framework of a bed, usually including a headboard and springs but excluding the mattress and other coverings.
bedstraw (ˈbɛd,strɔː) *n* any of numerous rubiaceous plants of the genus *Galium,* which have small white or yellow flowers and prickly or hairy fruits: formerly used as straw for beds. See also **lady's bedstraw.**
bed tea *n* (in some Asian countries) tea served to a guest in bed in the morning.
bedtime (ˈbɛd,taɪm) *n* **a** the time when one usually goes to bed. **b** (*as modifier*): *a bedtime story.*
bedwarmer (ˈbɛd,wɔːmə) *n* a metal pan containing hot coals, formerly used to warm a bed.
bed-wetting *n* the act or habit of involuntarily urinating in bed. Technical term: **enuresis.** ▸ **ˈbed-,wetter** *n*
Bedworth (ˈbɛdwəθ) *n* a town in central England, in N Warwickshire. Pop.: 31 932 (1991).
bee[1] (biː) *n* **1** any hymenopterous insect of the superfamily *Apoidea,* which includes social forms such as the honeybee and solitary forms such as the carpenter bee. See also **bumblebee, mason bee.** Related adj: **apian. 2 busy bee.** a person who is industrious or has many things to do. **3 have a bee in one's bonnet.** to be preoccupied or obsessed with an idea. [Old English *bīo;* related to Old Norse *bȳ,* Old High German *bīa,* Dutch *bij,* Swedish *bi*]
bee[2] (biː) *n* **1** a social gathering for a specific purpose, as to carry out a communal task or hold competitions: *quilting bee.* **2** See **spelling bee.** [C18: perhaps from dialect *bean* neighbourly help, from Old English *bēn* boon]
bee[3] (biː) *n Nautical.* a small sheave with one cheek removed and the pulley and other cheek fastened flat to a boom or another spar, used for reeving outhauls or stays. [Old English *bēag;* related to Old High German *boug* ring, Old Norse *bogi* a bow]
Beeb (biːb) *n* **the.** an informal name for the **BBC.**
bee beetle *n* a European beetle, *Trichodes apiarius,* that is often parasitic in beehives: family *Cleridae.*
beebread (ˈbiː,brɛd) *n* a mixture of pollen and nectar prepared by worker bees and fed to the larvae. Also called: **ambrosia.**
beech (biːtʃ) *n* **1** any N temperate tree of the genus *Fagus,* esp. *F. sylvatica* of Europe, having smooth greyish bark: family *Fagaceae.* **2** any tree of the related genus *Nothofagus,* of temperate Australasia and South America. **3** the hard wood of any of these trees, used in making furniture, etc. **4** See **copper beech.** [Old English *bēce;* related to Old Norse *bōk,* Old High German *buohha,* Middle Dutch *boeke,* Latin *fāgus* beech, Greek *phēgos* edible oak] ▸ **ˈbeechen** *or* **ˈbeechy** *adj*
Beecham (ˈbiːtʃəm) *n* Sir **Thomas.** 1879–1961, English conductor who did much to promote the works of Delius, Sibelius, and Richard Strauss.
Beecher (ˈbiːtʃə) *n* **Henry Ward.** 1813–87, U.S. clergyman: a leader in the movement for the abolition of slavery.
Beecher Stowe *n* See (Harriet Elizabeth Beecher) **Stowe.**
beech fern *n* a fern, *Thelypteris phegopteris,* that grows in damp N temperate woods: family *Polypodiaceae.*
beech marten *n* another name for **stone marten.**
beechnut (ˈbiːtʃ,nʌt) *n* the small brown triangular edible nut of the beech tree. Collectively, the nuts are often termed **beech mast,** esp. when lying on the ground.
bee-eater *n* any insectivorous bird of the family *Meropidae* of tropical and subtropical regions of the Old World, having a long downward-curving bill and long pointed wings and tail: order *Coraciiformes* (kingfishers, etc.).
beef (biːf) *n* **1** the flesh of various bovine animals, esp. the cow, when killed for eating. **2** (*pl* **beeves** (biːvz)) an adult ox, bull, cow, etc., reared for its meat. **3** *Informal.* human flesh, esp. when muscular. **4** (*pl* **beefs**) *Slang.* a complaint. ◆ *vb* **5** (*intr*) *Slang.* to complain, esp. repeatedly: *he was beefing about his tax.* **6** (*tr;* often foll. by *up*) *Informal.* to strengthen; reinforce. [C13: from Old French *boef,* from Latin *bōs* ox; see COW[1]]
beefburger (ˈbiːf,bɜːgə) *n* a flat fried cake of minced beef; hamburger.
beefcake (ˈbiːf,keɪk) *n Slang.* men displayed for their muscular bodies, esp. in photographs. Compare **cheesecake** (sense 2).
beefeater (ˈbiːf,iːtə) *n* a nickname often applied to the Yeomen of the Guard and the Yeomen Warders at the Tower of London.
bee fly *n* any hairy beelike nectar-eating dipterous fly of the family *Bombyliidae,* whose larvae are parasitic on those of bees and related insects.
beef road *n Austral.* a road used for transporting cattle.
beefsteak (ˈbiːf,steɪk) *n* a piece of beef that can be grilled, fried, etc., cut from any lean part of the animal.
beefsteak fungus *n* an edible reddish bracket fungus, *Fistulina hepatica,* that grows esp. on oak trees and oozes a bloodlike juice.
beef stroganoff *n* a dish of thin strips of beef cooked with onions, mushrooms, and seasonings, served in a sour-cream sauce. [C19: named after Count Paul *Stroganoff,* 19th-century Russian diplomat]
beef tea *n* a drink made by boiling pieces of lean beef: often given to invalids to stimulate the appetite.
beef tomato *n* a very large fleshy variety of tomato. Also called: **beefsteak tomato.**
beefwood (ˈbiːf,wʊd) *n* **1** any of various trees that produce very hard wood, esp. the Australian tree *Casuarina equisetifolia* (see **casuarina**), widely planted in warm regions. **2** the wood of any of these trees. [from the red colour and grain]
beefy (ˈbiːfɪ) *adj* **beefier, beefiest. 1** like beef. **2** *Informal.* muscular; brawny. **3** *Informal.* fleshy; obese. ▸ **ˈbeefily** *adv* ▸ **ˈbeefiness** *n*
bee glue *n* another name for **propolis.**
beehive (ˈbiː,haɪv) *n* **1** a man-made receptacle used to house a swarm of bees. **2** a dome-shaped hair style in which the hair is piled high on the head. **3** a place where busy people are assembled.
Beehive (ˈbiː,haɪv) *n* **the.** *Informal.* **1** the dome-shaped building that houses sections of Parliament in Wellington, New Zealand. **2** the New Zealand government.

beehive house *n* a prehistoric circular building found in various parts of Europe, usually of stone and having a dome-shaped roof.
beekeeper ('biː,kiːpə) *n* a person who keeps bees for their honey; apiarist. ▸ **'bee,keeping** *n*
bee killer *n* another name for **robber fly.**
beeline ('biː,laɪn) *n* the most direct route between two places (esp. in the phrase **make a beeline for**).
Beelzebub (bɪ'ɛlzɪ,bʌb) *n* **1** *Old Testament.* a god of the Philistines (2 Kings 1:2). **2** Satan or any devil or demon. [Old English *Belzebub,* ultimately from Hebrew *bá'al zebūb,* literally: lord of flies]
bee moth *n* any of various pyralid moths, such as the wax moth, whose larvae live in the nests of bees or wasps, feeding on nest materials and host larvae.
been (biːn, bɪn) *vb* the past participle of **be.**
beento ('biːntuː, 'bɪntʊ) *W African informal.* ◆ *n, pl* **-tos. 1** a person who has resided in Britain, esp. during part of his education. ◆ *adj* **2** of, relating to, or characteristic of such a person. [C20: from BEEN + TO]
bee orchid *n* a European orchid, *Ophrys apifera,* whose flower resembles a bumble bee in shape and colour.
beep (biːp) *n* **1** a short high-pitched sound, esp. one made by the horn of a car, bicycle, etc., or by electronic apparatus. ◆ *vb* **2** to make or cause to make such a noise. [C20: of imitative origin] ▸ **'beeper** *n*
bee plant *n* any of various plants much visited by bees for nectar and pollen.
beer (bɪə) *n* **1** an alcoholic drink brewed from malt, sugar, hops, and water and fermented with yeast. Compare **ale. 2** a slightly fermented drink made from the roots or leaves of certain plants: *ginger beer; nettle beer.* **3** (*modifier*) relating to or used in the drinking of beer: *beer glass; beer mat.* **4** (*modifier*) in which beer is drunk, esp. (of licensed premises) having a licence to sell beer: *beer house; beer cellar; beer garden.* [Old English *beor;* related to Old Norse *bjōrr,* Old Frisian *biār,* Old High German *bior*]
beer and skittles *n* (*functioning as sing*) *Informal.* enjoyment or pleasure.
beer belly *n Informal.* a protruding belly caused by excessive beer drinking. Also called: **beer gut.**
Beerbohm ('bɪəbəʊm) *n* Sir (**Henry**) **Max(imilian).** 1872–1956, English critic, wit, and caricaturist, whose works include *Zuleika Dobson* (1911), a satire on Oxford undergraduates.
Beersheba (bɪə'ʃiːbə) *n* a town in S Israel: commercial centre of the Negev. In biblical times it marked the southern limit of Palestine. Pop.: 156 500 (1997 est.).
beer-up *n Austral. dated slang.* a drinking bout.
beery ('bɪərɪ) *adj* **beerier, beeriest. 1** smelling or tasting of beer. **2** given to drinking beer. ▸ **'beerily** *adv* ▸ **'beeriness** *n*
bee's knees *n* the (*functioning as sing*) *Informal.* an excellent or ideally suitable person or thing.
beestings, biestings *or U.S.* **beastings** ('biːstɪŋz) *n* (*functioning as sing*) the first milk secreted by the mammary glands of a cow or similar animal immediately after giving birth; colostrum. [Old English *bȳsting,* from *bēost* beestings; related to Middle Dutch *biest*]
bee-stung *adj* (of the lips) pouting and sensuous.
beeswax ('biːz,wæks) *n* **1a** a yellowish or dark brown wax secreted by honeybees for constructing honeycombs. **1b** this wax after refining, purifying, etc., used in polishes, ointments, and for modelling. ◆ *vb* **2** (*tr*) to polish with such wax.
beeswing ('biːz,wɪŋ) *n* **1** a light filmy crust of tartar that forms in port and some other wines after long keeping in the bottle. **2** a port or other wine containing beeswing.
beet (biːt) *n* **1** any chenopodiaceous plant of the genus *Beta,* esp. the Eurasian species *B. vulgaris,* widely cultivated in such varieties as the sugar beet, mangel-wurzel, beetroot, and spinach beet. See also **chard. 2** the leaves of any of several varieties of this plant, which are cooked and eaten as a vegetable. **3 red beet.** the U.S. name for **beetroot.** [Old English *bēte,* from Latin *bēta*]
beetfly ('biːt,flaɪ) *n, pl* **-flies.** a muscid fly, *Pegomyia hyoscyami:* a common pest of beets and mangel-wurzels. Also called: **mangold fly.**
Beethoven ('beɪt,həʊvᵊn) *n* **Ludwig van** ('luːtvɪç fan). 1770–1827, German composer, who greatly extended the form and scope of symphonic and chamber music, bridging the classical and romantic traditions. His works include nine symphonies, 32 piano sonatas, 16 string quartets, five piano concertos, a violin concerto, two masses, the opera *Fidelio* (1805), and choral music.
beetle[1] ('biːtᵊl) *n* **1** any insect of the order *Coleoptera,* having biting mouthparts and forewings modified to form shell-like protective elytra. Related adj: **coleopteran. 2** a game played with dice in which the players draw or assemble a beetle-shaped form. ◆ *vb* (*intr;* foll. by *along, off,* etc.) **3** *Informal.* to scuttle or scurry; hurry. [Old English *bitela;* related to *bitol* teeth, BIT, *bītan* to BITE]
beetle[2] ('biːtᵊl) *n* **1** a heavy hand tool, usually made of wood, used for ramming, pounding, or beating. **2** a machine used to finish cloth by stamping it with wooden hammers. ◆ *vb* (*tr*) **3** to beat or pound with a beetle. **4** to finish (cloth) by means of a beetle. [Old English *bīetel,* from *bēatan* to BEAT; related to Middle Low German *bētel* chisel, Old Norse *beytill* penis]
beetle[3] ('biːtᵊl) *vb* **1** (*intr*) to overhang; jut. ◆ *adj* **2** overhanging; prominent. [C14: perhaps related to BEETLE[1]] ▸ **'beetling** *adj*
beetle-browed *adj* **1** having bushy or overhanging eyebrows. **2** sullen in appearance; scowling.
beetle drive *n* a social occasion at which a progressive series of games of beetle is played. See **beetle**[1] (sense 2).
Beeton ('biːtᵊn) *n* **Isabella Mary,** known as *Mrs Beeton.* 1836–65, British cookery writer, author of *The Book of Household Management* (1861).
beetroot ('biːt,ruːt) *n* **1** a variety of the beet plant, *Beta vulgaris,* that has a bulbous dark red root that may be eaten as a vegetable, in salads, or pickled. **2** the root of this plant. ◆ U.S. name: **red beet.**
beet sugar *n* the sucrose obtained from sugar beet, identical in composition to cane sugar.
beeves (biːvz) *n* the plural of **beef** (sense 2).
beezer ('biːzə) *Slang.* ◆ *n* **1** *Brit., old fashioned.* a person or chap. **2** *Brit., old fashioned.* the nose. **3** *Scot.* an extreme example of its kind. ◆ *adj* **4** *Brit., old fashioned.* excellent; most attractive. [C20: of uncertain origin]
BEF *abbrev. for* British Expeditionary Force, the British army that served in France 1939–40.
befall (bɪ'fɔːl) *vb* **-falls, -falling, -fell, -fallen.** *Archaic or literary.* **1** (*intr*) to take place; come to pass. **2** (*tr*) to happen to. **3** (*intr;* usually foll. by *to*) to be due, as by right. [Old English *befeallan;* related to Old High German *bifallan,* Dutch *bevallen;* see BE-, FALL]
befit (bɪ'fɪt) *vb* **-fits, -fitting, -fitted.** (*tr*) to be appropriate to or suitable for. [C15: from BE- + FIT[1]] ▸ **be'fitting** *adj* ▸ **be'fittingly** *adv*
befog (bɪ'fɒg) *vb* **-fogs, -fogging, -fogged.** (*tr*) **1** to surround with fog. **2** to make confused, vague, or less clear.
befool (bɪ'fuːl) *vb* (*tr*) to make a fool of.
before (bɪ'fɔː) *conj* (*subordinating*) **1** earlier than the time when. **2** rather than: *he'll resign before he agrees to it.* ◆ *prep* **3** preceding in space or time; in front of; ahead of: *standing before the altar.* **4** when confronted by: *to withdraw before one's enemies.* **5** in the presence of: *to be brought before a judge.* **6** in preference to: *to put friendship before money.* ◆ *adv* **7** at an earlier time; previously; beforehand; in front. [Old English *beforan;* related to Old Frisian *befara,* Old High German *bifora*]
beforehand (bɪ'fɔː,hænd) *adj* (*postpositive*), *adv* early; in advance; in anticipation: *she came an hour beforehand.*
beforetime (bɪ'fɔː,taɪm) *adv Archaic.* formerly.
befoul (bɪ'faʊl) *vb* (*tr*) to make dirty or foul; soil; defile. ▸ **be'fouler** *n* ▸ **be'foulment** *n*
befriend (bɪ'frɛnd) *vb* (*tr*) to be a friend to; assist; favour.
befuddle (bɪ'fʌdᵊl) *vb* (*tr*) **1** to confuse, muddle, or perplex. **2** to make stupid with drink. ▸ **be'fuddlement** *n*
beg[1] (bɛg) *vb* **begs, begging, begged. 1** (when *intr,* often foll. by *for*) to solicit (for money, food, etc.), esp. in the street. **2** to ask (someone) for (something or leave to do something) formally, humbly, or earnestly: *I beg forgiveness; I beg to differ.* **3** (*intr*) (of a dog) to sit up with forepaws raised expectantly. **4** to leave unanswered or unresolved: *to beg a point.* **5 beg the question. 5a** to evade the issue. **5b** to assume the thing under examination as proved. **5c** to suggest that a question needs to be asked: *the firm's success begs the question: why aren't more companies doing the same?* **6 go (a-)begging.** to be unwanted or unused. ◆ See also **beg off.** [C13: probably from Old English *bedecian;* related to Gothic *bidagwa* BEGGAR]
USAGE The use of *beg the question* to mean that a question needs to be asked is considered by some people to be incorrect.
beg[2] (bɛg) *n* a variant of **bey.**
begad (bɪ'gæd) *interj Archaic slang.* an emphatic exclamation. [C18: euphemistic alteration of *by God!*]
began (bɪ'gæn) *vb* the past tense of **begin.**
begat (bɪ'gæt) *vb Archaic.* a past tense of **beget.**
beget (bɪ'gɛt) *vb* **-gets, -getting, -got** *or* **-gat; -gotten** *or* **-got.** (*tr*) **1** to father. **2** to cause or create. [Old English *begietan;* related to Old Saxon *bigetan,* Old High German *pigezzan,* Gothic *bigitan* to find; see BE-, GET] ▸ **be'getter** *n*
beggar ('bɛgə) *n* **1** a person who begs, esp. one who lives by begging. **2** a person who has no money or resources; pauper. **3** *Ironic or jocular, chiefly Brit.* fellow: *lucky beggar!* ◆ *vb* (*tr*) **4** to be beyond the resources of (esp. in the phrase **to beggar description**). **5** to impoverish; reduce to begging. ▸ **'beggar,hood** *or* **'beggardom** *n*
beggarly ('bɛgəlɪ) *adj* meanly inadequate; very poor: *beggarly living conditions.* ▸ **'beggarliness** *n*
beggar-my-neighbour *n* **1** a card game in which one player tries to win all the cards of the other player. **2** (*modifier*) relating to or denoting an advantage gained by one side at the expense of the other: *beggar-my-neighbour policies.*
beggar's-lice *n* (*functioning as sing*) **1** any of several plants, esp. the stickseed, having small prickly fruits that adhere to clothing, fur, etc. **2** the seed or fruit of any of these plants.
beggar-ticks *or* **beggar's-ticks** *n* (*functioning as sing*) **1** any of various plants, such as the bur marigold and tick trefoil, having fruits or seeds that cling to clothing, fur, etc. **2** the seed or fruit of any of these plants.
beggarweed ('bɛgə,wiːd) *n* any of various leguminous plants of the genus *Desmodium,* esp. *D. purpureum* of the Caribbean, grown in the southern U.S. as forage plants and to improve the soil. See also **tick trefoil.**
beggary ('bɛgərɪ) *n* **1** extreme poverty or need. **2** the condition of being a beggar.
begging bowl *n* a bowl carried by a beggar, esp. a Franciscan or other friar or a Buddhist monk, to receive food or alms.
begging letter *n* a letter asking for money sent esp. by a stranger to someone known to be rich.
Beghard ('bɛgəd, bɪ'gɑːd) *n* a member of a Christian brotherhood that was founded in Flanders in the 13th century and followed a life based on that of the Beguines. Also called: **Beguin.** [C17: from Medieval Latin *beghardus,* from BEG(UINE) + -ARD; compare Old French *bégard,* Middle Dutch *beggaert,* Middle High German *beghart*]
begin (bɪ'gɪn) *vb* **-gins, -ginning, -gan, -gun. 1** to start or cause to start (something or to do something). **2** to bring or come into being for the first time; arise or originate. **3** to start to say or speak. **4** (*used with a negative*) to have the least capacity (to do something): *he couldn't begin to compete with her.* **5 to begin with.** in the first place. [Old English *beginnan;* related to Old High German *biginnan,* Gothic *duginnan*]

Begin ('bɛgɪn) *n* **Menachem** (mə'nɑːkɪm). 1913–92, Israeli statesman, born in Poland. In Palestine after 1942, he became a leader of the militant Zionists; prime minister of Israel (1977–83); Nobel peace prize jointly with Sadat 1978. In 1979 he concluded the Camp David treaty with Anwar Sadat of Egypt.

beginner (bɪ'gɪnə) *n* a person who has just started to do or learn something; novice.

beginning (bɪ'gɪnɪŋ) *n* **1** a start; commencement. **2** (*often pl*) a first or early part or stage. **3** the place or time when something starts. **4** an origin; source.

begird (bɪ'gɜːd) *vb* **-girds, -girding, -girt** *or* **-girded.** (*tr*) *Poetic.* **1** to surround; gird around. **2** to bind. [Old English *begierdan;* see BE-, GIRD[1]]

beg off *vb* (*intr, adv*) to ask to be released from an engagement, obligation, etc.

begone (bɪ'gɒn) *sentence substitute* go away! [C14: from BE (imperative) + GONE]

begonia (bɪ'gəʊnjə) *n* any plant of the genus *Begonia,* of warm and tropical regions, widely cultivated for their ornamental leaves and waxy flowers: family *Begoniaceae.* [C18: New Latin, named after Michel *Bégon* (1638–1710), French patron of science]

begorra (bɪ'gɒrə) *interj* an emphatic exclamation, regarded as a characteristic utterance of Irishmen. [C19: euphemistic alteration of *by God!*]

begot (bɪ'gɒt) *vb* a past tense and past participle of **beget.**

begotten (bɪ'gɒtᵊn) *vb* a past participle of **beget.**

begrime (bɪ'graɪm) *vb* (*tr*) to make dirty; soil.

begrudge (bɪ'grʌdʒ) *vb* (*tr*) **1** to give, admit, or allow unwillingly or with a bad grace. **2** to envy (someone) the possession of (something). ▸ **be'grudgingly** *adv*

beguile (bɪ'gaɪl) *vb* **-guiles, -guiling, -guiled.** (*tr*) **1** to charm; fascinate. **2** to delude; influence by slyness. **3** (often foll. by *of* or *out of*) to deprive (someone) of something by trickery; cheat (someone) of. **4** to pass pleasantly; while away. ▸ **be'guilement** *n* ▸ **be'guiler** *n* ▸ **be'guiling** *adj* ▸ **be'guilingly** *adv*

Beguin ('bɛgɪn; *French* begẽ) *n* another word for **Beghard.**

beguine (bɪ'giːn) *n* **1** a dance of South American origin in bolero rhythm. **2** a piece of music in the rhythm of this dance. **3** a variant of **biggin**[1]. [C20: from Louisiana French, from French *béguin* flirtation]

Beguine ('begiːn) *n* a member of a Christian sisterhood that was founded in Liège in the 12th century, and, though not taking religious vows, followed an austere life. [C15: from Old French, perhaps after *Lambert le Bègue* (the Stammerer), 12th-century priest of Liège, who founded the sisterhood]

begum ('beɪgəm) *n* (in Pakistan and certain other Muslim countries) a woman of high rank, esp. the widow of a prince. [C18: from Urdu *begam,* from Turkish *begim;* see BEY]

begun (bɪ'gʌn) *vb* the past participle of **begin.**

behalf (bɪ'hɑːf) *n* interest, part, benefit, or respect (only in the phrases **on (someone's) behalf, on** *or U.S. and Canadian* **in behalf of, in this** (*or* **that**) **behalf**). [Old English *be halfe* from *be* by + *halfe* side; compare Old Norse *af halfu*]

Behan ('biːən) *n* **Brendan.** 1923–64, Irish writer, noted esp. for his plays *The Quare Fellow* (1954) and *The Hostage* (1958) and for an account of his detention as a member of the Irish Republican Army, *Borstal Boy* (1958).

behave (bɪ'heɪv) *vb* **1** (*intr*) to act or function in a specified or usual way. **2** to conduct (oneself) in a specified way: *he behaved badly towards her.* **3** to conduct (oneself) properly or as desired: *the child behaved himself all day.* [C15: see BE-, HAVE]

behaviour *or U.S.* **behavior** (bɪ'heɪvjə) *n* **1** manner of behaving or conducting oneself. **2 on one's best behaviour.** behaving with careful good manners. **3** *Psychol.* **3a** the aggregate of all the responses made by an organism in any situation. **3b** a specific response of a certain organism to a specific stimulus or group of stimuli. **4** the action, reaction, or functioning of a system, under normal or specified circumstances. [C15: from BEHAVE; influenced in form by Middle English *havior,* from Old French *havoir,* from Latin *habēre* to have] ▸ **be'havioural** *or U.S.* **be'havioral** *adj*

behavioural contagion *n* the spread of a particular type of behaviour, such as crying, through a crowd or group of people.

behavioural science *n* the application of scientific methods to the study of the behaviour of organisms.

behavioural sink *n Psychol.* a small area in which people or animals live in overcrowded conditions.

behaviourism *or U.S.* **behaviorism** (bɪ'heɪvjəˌrɪzəm) *n* **1** a school of psychology that regards the objective observation of the behaviour of organisms (usually by means of automatic recording devices) as the only proper subject for study and that often refuses to postulate any intervening mechanisms between the stimulus and the response. **2** the doctrine that the mind has no separate existence but that statements about the mind and mental states can be analysed into statements about actual and potential behaviour. Compare **materialism** (sense 2). See also **mind-body problem.** ▸ **be'haviourist** *or U.S.* **be'haviorist** *adj, n* ▸ **beˌhaviour'istic** *or U.S.* **beˌhavior'istic** *adj*

behaviour therapy *n* any of various means of treating psychological disorders, such as desensitization, aversion therapy, and instrumental conditioning, that depend on the patient systematically learning new modes of behaviour.

behead (bɪ'hɛd) *vb* (*tr*) to remove the head from; decapitate. [Old English *behēafdian,* from BE- + *heafod* HEAD; related to Middle High German *behoubeten*]

beheld (bɪ'hɛld) *vb* the past tense and past participle of **behold.**

behemoth (bɪ'hiːmɒθ) *n* **1** *Old Testament.* a gigantic beast, probably a hippopotamus, described in Job 40:15. **2** a huge or monstrous person or thing. [C14: from Hebrew *bĕhēmōth,* plural of *bĕhēmāh* beast]

behest (bɪ'hɛst) *n* an authoritative order or earnest request. [Old English *behǣs,* from *behātan;* see BE-, HEST]

behind (bɪ'haɪnd) *prep* **1** in or to a position further back than; at the rear of; at the back of. **2** in the past in relation to: *I've got the exams behind me now.* **3** late according to; not keeping up with: *running behind schedule.* **4** concerning the circumstances surrounding: *the reasons behind his departure.* **5** backing or supporting: *I'm right behind you in your application.* ◆ *adv* **6** in or to a position further back; following. **7** remaining after someone's departure: *he left it behind.* **8** in debt; in arrears: *to fall behind with payments.* ◆ *adj* **9** (*postpositive*) in a position further back; retarded: *the man behind prodded me.* ◆ *n* **10** *Informal.* the buttocks. **11** *Australian Rules football.* a score of one point made by kicking the ball over the **behind line** between a goalpost and one of the smaller outer posts (**behind posts**). [Old English *behindan*]

behindhand (bɪ'haɪndˌhænd) *adj* (*postpositive*), *adv* **1** remiss in fulfilling an obligation. **2** in debt; in arrears. **3** delayed in development; backward. **4** late; behind time.

Behistun (ˌbeɪhɪ'stuːn), **Bisitun,** *or* **Bisutun** *n* a village in W Iran by the ancient road from Ecbatana to Babylon. On a nearby cliff is an inscription by Darius in Old Persian, Elamite, and Babylonian describing his enthronement.

Behn (bɛn) *n* **Aphra** ('æfrə). 1640–89, English dramatist and novelist, best known for her play *The Rover* (1678) and her novel *Oroonoko* (1688).

behold (bɪ'həʊld) *vb* **-holds, -holding, -held.** (often used in the imperative to draw attention to something) *Archaic or literary.* to look (at); observe. [Old English *bihealdan;* related to Old High German *bihaltan,* Dutch *behouden;* see BE-, HOLD] ▸ **be'holder** *n*

beholden (bɪ'həʊldᵊn) *adj* indebted; obliged; under a moral obligation. [Old English *behealden,* past participle of *behealdan* to BEHOLD]

behoof (bɪ'huːf) *n, pl* **-hooves.** *Rare.* advantage or profit. [Old English *behōf;* related to Middle High German *behuof* something useful; see BEHOVE]

behove (bɪ'həʊv) *or U.S.* **behoove** (bɪ'huːv) *vb* (*tr; impersonal*) *Archaic.* to be necessary or fitting for: *it behoves me to arrest you.* [Old English *behōfian;* related to Middle Low German *behōven*]

Behrens ('bɛərənz; *German* 'beːrəns) *n* **Peter.** 1868–1940, German architect.

Behring *n* **1** (*German* 'beːrɪŋ), **Emil** (**Adolf**) **von** ('eːmiːl fɔn). 1854–1917, German bacteriologist, who discovered diphtheria and tetanus antitoxins: Nobel prize for physiology or medicine 1901. **2** ('bɛrɪŋ, 'bɛər-). See (Vitus) **Bering.**

Beiderbecke ('baɪdəˌbɛk) *n* **Leon Bismarcke,** known as *Bix.* 1903–31, U.S. jazz cornettist, composer, and pianist.

beige (beɪʒ) *n* **1a** a very light brown, sometimes with a yellowish tinge, similar to the colour of undyed wool. **1b** (*as adj*): *beige gloves.* **2** a fabric made of undyed or unbleached wool. [C19: from Old French, of obscure origin]

beigel ('beɪgᵊl) *n* a variant spelling of **bagel.**

Beijing ('beɪ'dʒɪŋ) *n* the capital of the People's Republic of China, in the northeast in central Hebei province: dates back to the 12th century B.C.; consists of two central walled cities, the Outer City (containing the commercial quarter) and the Inner City, which contains the Imperial City, within which is the Purple or Forbidden City; three universities. Pop.: 7 000 000 (1991 est.). Former English name: **Peking.**

being ('biːɪŋ) *n* **1** the state or fact of existing; existence. **2** essential nature; self: *she put her whole being into the part.* **3** something that exists or is thought to exist, esp. something that cannot be assigned to any category: *a being from outer space.* **4** a person; human being. **5** (in the philosophy of Aristotle) actuality. Compare **becoming** (sense 3).

Beira ('baɪərə) *n* a port in E Mozambique: terminus of a transcontinental railway from Lobito, Angola, through the Democratic Republic of the Congo (formerly Zaïre), Zambia, and Zimbabwe. Pop.: 298 847 (1991 est.).

Beirut *or* **Beyrouth** (ˌbeɪ'ruːt) *n* the capital of Lebanon, a port on the Mediterranean: part of the Ottoman Empire from the 16th century until 1918; four universities (Lebanese, American, French, and Arab). Pop.: 1 100 000 (1991 est.).

Beit Knesset *or* **Beth Knesseth** (bet 'knɛset) *n* a synagogue: often used in the names of congregations. [from Hebrew, literally: house of assembly]

Béjart (*French* beʒar) *n* **Maurice** (mɔris). born 1927, French dancer and choreographer. His choreography is characterized by a combination of classic and modern dance and acrobatics.

bejesus (bɪ'dʒeɪzəz) *Informal.* ◆ *interj* **1** an exclamation of surprise, emphasis, etc., regarded as a characteristic utterance of Irish people. ◆ *n* **2 the bejesus.** (intensifier): used in such phrases as **beat the bejesus out of, scare the bejesus out of,** etc. [C20: alteration of *by Jesus!*]

bejewel (bɪ'dʒuːəl) *vb* **-els, -elling, -elled** *or U.S.* **-els, -eling, -eled.** (*tr*) to decorate with or as if with jewels. ▸ **be'jewelled** *or U.S.* **be'jeweled** *adj*

Bekaa *or* **Beqaa** (bɪ'kɑː) *n* a broad valley in central Lebanon, between the Lebanon and Anti-Lebanon Mountains. Ancient name: **Coelesyria** (ˌsiːliː'sɪrɪə).

Békésy (*Hungarian* 'beːkeʃɪ) *n* **Georg von** ('geːɔrk fɔn). 1899–1972, U.S. physicist, born in Hungary; noted for his work on the mechanism of hearing: Nobel prize for physiology or medicine 1961.

bel (bɛl) *n* a unit for comparing two power levels, equal to the logarithm to the base ten of the ratio of the two powers. Symbols: **B, b** See also **decibel.** [C20: named after A. G. BELL]

Bel (beɪl) *n* (in Babylonian and Assyrian mythology) the god of the earth.

belabour *or U.S.* **belabor** (bɪ'leɪbə) *vb* (*tr*) **1** to beat severely; thrash. **2** to attack verbally; criticize harshly. **3** an obsolete word for **labour.**

belah *or* **belar** ('biːlɑː) *n* an Australian casuarina tree, *Casuarina glauca,* yielding a useful timber.

Belarus ('bɛləˌrʌs, -ˌrʊs) *or* **Byelorussia** *or* **Belorussia** (ˌbjɛləʊ'rʌʃə, ˌbɛl-) *n* a republic in E Europe; part of the medieval Lithuanian and Polish empires before occupied by Russia; a Soviet republic (1919–91); in 1997 formed a close political and economic union with Russia: mainly low-lying and forested. Languages: Belarussian; Russian. Religion: believers are mostly Christian. Currency: rouble. Capital: Minsk. Pop.: 10 235 000 (1998 est.). Area: 207 600 sq. km (80 134 sq. miles). Also called: **Byelorussian Republic, Bielorussia, White Russia.**

Belarussian *or* **Belarusian** *or* **Byelorussian** *or* **Belorussian** (ˌbeləʊ'rʌʃən, ˌbjɛl-) *adj* **1** of, relating to, or characteristic of Belarus, its people, or their language. ◆ *n* **2** the official language of Belarus: an East Slavonic language closely related to Russian. **3** a native or inhabitant of Belarus. ◆ Also called: **White Russian.**

belated (bɪ'leɪtɪd) *adj* late or too late: *belated greetings.* ► **be'latedly** *adv* ► **be'latedness** *n*

Belau (bə'laʊ) *n* **Republic of.** a republic comprising a group of islands in the W Pacific, in the W Caroline Islands; administratively part of the U.N. Trust Territory of the Pacific Islands 1947–87; entered into an agreement of free association with the U.S. (1980); became fully independent in 1994. Chief island: Babelthuap. Capital: Koror. Pop.: 18 100 (1998 est.). Area: 476 sq. km (184 sq. miles). Former names: **Pelew Islands,** (until 1981) **Palau Islands.**

belay (bɪ'leɪ) *vb* **-lays, -laying, -layed. 1** *Nautical.* to make fast (a line) by securing to a pin, cleat, or bitt. **2** (*usually imperative*) *Nautical.* to stop; cease. **3** ('biːˌleɪ). *Mountaineering.* to secure (a climber) to a mountain by tying the rope off round a rock spike, piton, nut, etc. ◆ *n* **4** ('biːˌleɪ). *Mountaineering.* the attachment (of a climber) to a mountain by tying the rope off round a rock spike, piton, nut, etc., to safeguard the party in the event of a fall. See also **running belay.** [Old English *belecgan;* related to Old High German *bileggen,* Dutch *beleggen*]

belaying pin *n Nautical.* a cylindrical, sometimes tapered pin, usually of metal or wood, that fits into a hole in a pin or fife rail: used for belaying.

bel canto ('bɛl 'kæntəʊ) *n Music.* **a** a style of singing characterized by beauty of tone rather than dramatic power. **b** (*as modifier*): *a bel canto aria.* [C19: Italian, literally: beautiful singing]

belch (bɛltʃ) *vb* **1** (*usually intr*) to expel wind from the stomach noisily through the mouth; eructate. **2** to expel or be expelled forcefully from inside: *smoke belching from factory chimneys.* **3** to say (curses, insults, etc.) violently or bitterly. ◆ *n* **4** an act of belching; eructation. [Old English *bialcan;* related to Middle Low German *belken* to shout, Dutch *balken* to bray]

beldam *or* **beldame** ('bɛldəm) *n* **1** *Archaic.* an old woman, esp. an ugly or malicious one; hag. **2** an obsolete word for **grandmother.** [C15: from *bel-*grand (as in *grandmother*), from Old French *bel* beautiful, from Latin *bellus* + *dam* mother, variant of DAME]

beleaguer (bɪ'liːgə) *vb* (*tr*) **1** to trouble persistently; harass. **2** to lay siege to. [C16: from BE- + LEAGUER[1]]

Belém (*Portuguese* bə'lẽi) *n* a port in N Brazil, the capital of Pará state, on the Pará River: major trading centre for the Amazon basin. Pop.: 765 476 (1991).

belemnite ('bɛləmˌnaɪt) *n* **1** any extinct marine cephalopod mollusc of the order *Belemnoidea,* related to the cuttlefish. **2** the long pointed conical internal shell of any of these animals: a common Mesozoic fossil. [C17: from Greek *belemnon* dart]

belemnoid ('bɛləmˌnɔɪd) *adj Anatomy, zoology.* shaped like a dart.

bel esprit *French.* (bɛl ɛspri) *n, pl* ***beaux esprits*** (boz ɛspri). a witty or clever person. [literally: fine wit]

Belfast ('bɛlfɑːst, bɛl'fɑːst) *n* **1** the capital of Northern Ireland, a port on Belfast Lough in Belfast district, Co. Antrim and Co. Down: became the centre of Irish Protestantism and of the linen industry in the 17th century. Pop.: 279 237 (1991). **2** a district of W Northern Ireland, in Co. Antrim and Co. Down. Pop.: 296 237 (1992 est.). Area: 115 sq. km (44 sq. miles).

Belfort (*French* bɛlfɔr) *n* **1 Territoire de** (tɛritwar də). a department of E France, now in Franche-Comté region: the only part of Alsace remaining to France after 1871. Capital: Belfort. Pop.: 137 100 (1995). Area: 608 sq. km (237 sq. miles). **2** a fortress town in E France: strategically situated in the **Belfort Gap** between the Vosges and the Jura mountains. Pop.: 50 125 (1990).

belfry ('bɛlfrɪ) *n, pl* **-fries. 1** the part of a tower or steeple in which bells are hung. **2** a tower or steeple. Compare **campanile. 3** the timber framework inside a tower or steeple on which bells are hung. **4** (formerly) a movable tower for attacking fortifications. [C13: from Old French *berfrei,* of Germanic origin; compare Middle High German *bercfrit* fortified tower, Medieval Latin *berfredus* tower]

Belg. *or* **Bel.** *abbrev. for:* **1** Belgian. **2** Belgium.

belga ('bɛlgə) *n* a former Belgian monetary unit worth five francs.

Belgae ('bɛldʒiː, 'bɛlgaɪ) *n* an ancient Celtic people who in Roman times inhabited present-day Belgium and N France. ► **'Belgic** *adj*

Belgaum (bɛl'gaʊm) *n* a city in India, in Karnataka: cotton, furniture, leather. Pop.: 326 399 (1991).

Belgian ('bɛldʒən) *n* **1** a native, citizen, or inhabitant of Belgium. See also **Fleming[1], Walloon.** ◆ *adj* **2** of, relating to, or characteristic of Belgium or the Belgians. **3** of or relating to the Walloon French or the Flemish languages.

Belgian Congo *n* a former name (1908–60) of (the Democratic Republic of the) **Congo** (sense 2).

Belgian hare *n* a large red breed of domestic rabbit.

Belgium ('bɛldʒəm) *n* a federal kingdom in NW Europe: at various times under the rulers of Burgundy, Spain, Austria, France, and the Netherlands before becoming an independent kingdom in 1830. It formed the Benelux customs union with the Netherlands and Luxembourg in 1947 and was a founder member of the EEC (now the EU). It consists chiefly of a low-lying region of sand, woods, and heath (the Campine) in the north and west, and a fertile undulating central plain rising to the Ardennes Mountains in the southeast. Languages: French, Flemish (Dutch), German. Religion: Roman Catholic majority. Currency: euro and Belgian franc. Capital: Brussels. Pop.: 10 208 000 (1998 est.). Area: 30 513 sq. km (11 778 sq. miles).

Belgorod-Dnestrovski *or* **Byelgorod-Dnestrovski** (*Russian* 'bjɛlgərət-dnjɪ'strɔfskij) *n* a port in the SW Ukraine, on the Dniester estuary: belonged to Romania from 1918 until 1940; under Soviet rule (1944–91). Pop.: 56 800 (1991 est.). Romanian name: **Cetatea Albă.** Former name (until 1946): **Akkerman.**

Belgrade (bɛl'greɪd, 'bɛlgreɪd) *n* the capital of Yugoslavia and of Serbia, in the E part at the confluence of the Danube and Sava Rivers: became the capital of Serbia in 1878 and of Yugoslavia in 1929. Pop.: 1 168 454 (1991). Serbo-Croat name: **Beograd.**

Belgravia (bɛl'greɪvɪə) *n* a fashionable residential district of W central London, around Belgrave Square.

Belial ('biːlɪəl) *n* **1** a demon mentioned frequently in apocalyptic literature: identified in the Christian tradition with the devil or Satan. **2** (in the Old Testament and rabbinical literature) worthlessness or wickedness. [C13: from Hebrew *bəlīyya'al,* from *bəlī* without + *ya'al* worth]

belie (bɪ'laɪ) *vb* **-lies, -lying, -lied.** (*tr*) **1** to show to be untrue; contradict. **2** to misrepresent; disguise the nature of: *the report belied the real extent of the damage.* **3** to fail to justify; disappoint. [Old English *belēogan;* related to Old Frisian *biliuga,* Old High German *biliugan;* see BE-, LIE[1]] ► **be'lier** *n*

belief (bɪ'liːf) *n* **1** a principle, proposition, idea, etc., accepted as true. **2** opinion; conviction. **3** religious faith. **4** trust or confidence, as in a person or a person's abilities, probity, etc.

believe (bɪ'liːv) *vb* **1** (*tr; may take a clause as object*) to accept (a statement, supposition, or opinion) as true: *I believe God exists.* **2** (*tr*) to accept the statement or opinion of (a person) as true. **3** (*intr;* foll. by *in*) to be convinced of the truth or existence (of): *to believe in fairies.* **4** (*intr*) to have religious faith. **5** (*when tr, takes a clause as object*) to think, assume, or suppose: *I believe that he has left already.* **6** (*tr;* foll. by *of; used with can, could, would, etc.*) to think that someone is able to do (a particular action): *I wouldn't have believed it of him.* [Old English *beliefan*] ► **be'lievaˌbility** *n* ► **be'lievable** *adj* ► **be'lievably** *adv* ► **be'liever** *n* ► **be'lieving** *n, adj*

belike (bɪ'laɪk) *adv Archaic or dialect.* perhaps; maybe.

Belisarius (ˌbɛlɪ'sɑːrɪəs) *n* ?505–565 A.D., Byzantine general under Justinian I. He recovered North Africa from the Vandals and Italy from the Ostrogoths and led forces against the Persians.

Belisha beacon (bə'liːʃə) *n* a flashing light in an orange globe mounted on a post, indicating a pedestrian crossing on a road. [C20: named after Leslie Hore-*Belisha* (1893–1957), British politician]

belittle (bɪ'lɪtᵊl) *vb* (*tr*) **1** to consider or speak of (something) as less valuable or important than it really is; disparage. **2** to cause to make small; dwarf. ► **be'littlement** *n* ► **be'littler** *n* ► **be'littlingly** *adv*

Belitung (bɪ'liːtʊŋ) *n* another name for **Billiton.**

Belize (bə'liːz) *n* a state in Central America, on the Caribbean Sea: site of a Mayan civilization until the 9th century A.D.; colonized by the British from 1638; granted internal self-government in 1964; became an independent state within the Commonwealth in 1981. Official language: English; Carib and Spanish are also spoken. Currency: Belize dollar. Capital: Belmopan. Pop.: 235 000 (1998 est.). Area: 22 965 sq. km (8867 sq. miles). Former name (until 1973): **British Honduras.** ► **Be'lizean** *adj, n*

Belize City *n* a port and the largest city in Belize, on the Caribbean coast: capital until 1973, when it was abandoned as hurricane-prone. Pop.: 48 655 (1994).

bell[1] (bɛl) *n* **1** a hollow, usually metal, cup-shaped instrument that emits a musical ringing sound when struck, often by a clapper hanging inside it. **2** the sound made by such an instrument or device, as for showing the hours or marking the beginning or end of a period of time. **3** an electrical device that rings or buzzes as a signal. **4** the bowl-shaped termination of the tube of certain musical wind instruments, such as the trumpet or oboe. **5** any musical percussion instrument emitting a ringing tone, such as a glockenspiel, one of a set of hand bells, etc. Compare **chime[1]** (sense 3). **6** *Nautical.* a signal rung on a ship's bell to count the number of half-hour intervals during each of six four-hour watches reckoned from midnight. Thus, one bell may signify 12.30, 4.30, or 8.30 a.m. or p.m. **7** See **diving bell. 8** *Biology.* a structure resembling a bell in shape, such as the corolla of certain flowers or the body of a jellyfish. **9** *Brit. slang.* a telephone call (esp. in the phrase **give someone a bell**). **10 bell, book, and candle. 10a** instruments used formerly in excommunications and other ecclesiastical acts. **10b** *Informal.* the solemn ritual ratification of such acts. **11 ring a bell.** to sound familiar; recall to the mind something previously experienced, esp. indistinctly. **12 sound as a bell.** in perfect condition. **13 the bells.** the ringing of bells, in a church or other public building, at midnight on December 31st, symbolizing the beginning of a new year. ◆ *vb* **14** to be or cause to be shaped like a bell. **15** (*tr*) to attach a bell or bells to. **16 bell the cat.** to undertake a dangerous mission. [Old English *belle;* related to Old Norse *bjalla,* Middle Low German *bell;* see BELL[2]]

bell[2] (bɛl) *n* **1** a bellowing or baying cry, esp. that of a hound or a male deer in rut. ◆ *vb* **2** to utter (such a cry). [Old English *bellan;* related to Old Norse *belja* to bellow, Old High German *bellan* to roar, Sanskrit *bhāsate* he talks; see BELLOW]

Bell (bɛl) *n* **1 Acton, Currer** ('kʌrə), and **Ellis.** pen names of the sisters Anne, Charlotte, and Emily **Brontë. 2 Alexander Graham.** 1847–1922, U.S. scientist, born in Scotland, who invented the telephone (1876). **3** Sir **Francis Henry Dillon.** 1851–1936, New Zealand statesman; prime minister of New Zealand (1925). **4 Gertrude (Margaret Lowthian).** 1868–1926, British traveller, writer, and diplomat; secretary to the British High Commissioner in Baghdad (1917–26). **5 (Susan) Jocelyn,** married name *Jocelyn Burnell,* born 1943, British radio astronomer, who discovered the first pulsar. **6 Vanessa,** original name *Vanessa Stephen.* 1879–1961, British painter; a member of the Bloomsbury group, sister of Virginia Woolf and wife of the art critic Clive Bell (1881–1964).

belladonna (ˌbɛlə'dɒnə) *n* **1** either of two alkaloid drugs, atropine or hyoscyamine, obtained from the leaves and roots of the deadly nightshade. **2** another

name for **deadly nightshade.** [C16: from Italian, literally: beautiful lady; supposed to refer to its use by women as a cosmetic]
belladonna lily *n* another name for **amaryllis.**
Bellamy ('bɛləmɪ) *n* **David (James).** born 1933, British botanist, writer, and broadcaster.
bellarmine ('bɛlɑːˌmiːn) *n* a large stoneware or earthenware jug for ale or spirits, bearing a bearded mask. [C18: named after Robert BELLARMINE, whom these jugs were intended to caricature]
Bellarmine ('bɛlɑːˌmiːn) *n* **Saint Robert.** 1542–1621, Italian Jesuit theologian and cardinal; an important influence during the Counter-Reformation.
Bellatrix ('bɛlətrɪks) *n* the third brightest star in the constellation Orion.
Bellay (*French* bɛlɛ) *n* **Joachim du** (ʒɔaʃɛ̃ dy). 1522–60, French poet, a member of the Pléiade.
bellbird ('bɛlˌbɜːd) *n* **1** any of several tropical American passerine birds of the genus *Procnias* having a bell-like call: family *Cotingidae* (cotingas). **2** either of two other birds with a bell-like call: an Australian flycatcher, *Oreoica gutturalis* (**crested bellbird**), or a New Zealand honeyeater, *Anthornis melanura.*
bell-bottoms *pl n* trousers that flare from the knee and have wide bottoms. ▸ **'bell-ˌbottomed** *adj*
bellboy ('bɛlˌbɔɪ) *n* a man or boy employed in a hotel, club, etc., to carry luggage and answer calls for service; page; porter. Also called (U.S. and Canadian): **bellhop.**
bell bronze *n* an alloy of copper and tin that contains a high proportion (at least 20 per cent) of tin: used for bell founding.
bell buoy *n* a navigational buoy fitted with a bell, the clapper of which strikes when the waves move the buoy.
bell captain *n U.S. and Canadian.* another name for **captain** (sense 9).
bell crank *n Engineering.* a lever with two arms having a common fulcrum at their junction.
belle (bɛl) *n* **1** a beautiful girl or woman. **2** the most attractive or admired girl or woman at a place, function, etc. (esp. in the phrase **the belle of the ball**). [C17: from French, feminine of BEAU]
Belleau Wood ('bɛləʊ; *French* bɛlo) *n* a forest in N France: site of a battle (1918) in which the U.S. Marines halted a German advance on Paris.
Belleek (bə'liːk) *n Trademark.* **a** a kind of thin fragile porcelain with a lustrous glaze. **b** (*as modifier*): *a Belleek vase.* [named after *Belleek*, a town in Northern Ireland where such porcelain is made]
belle époque *French.* (bɛl epɔk) *n* the period of comfortable well-established life before World War I. [literally: fine period]
Belle Isle *n* an island in the Atlantic, at the N entrance to the **Strait of Belle Isle,** between Labrador and Newfoundland. Area: about 39 sq. km (15 sq. miles).
Bellerophon (bə'lɛrəˌfɒn) *n Greek myth.* a hero of Corinth who performed many deeds with the help of the winged horse Pegasus, notably the killing of the monster Chimera.
belles-lettres (*French* bɛllɛtrə) *n* (*functioning as sing*) literary works, esp. essays and poetry, valued for their aesthetic rather than their informative or moral content. [C17: from French: fine letters]
belletrist (bɛl'lɛtrɪst) *n* a writer of belles-lettres. ▸ **bel'letrism** *n* ▸ **belletristic** (ˌbɛlɪ'trɪstɪk) *adj*
bellflower ('bɛlˌflaʊə) *n* another name for **campanula.**
bellfounder ('bɛlˌfaʊndə) *n* a foundry worker who casts bells. ▸ **'bellˌfoundry** *n*
bell glass *n* another name for **bell jar.**
bell heather *n* an ericaceous shrub, *Erica cinerea.* See **heath** (sense 2).
bellhop ('bɛlˌhɒp) *n U.S. and Canadian.* another name for **bellboy.**
bellicose ('bɛlɪˌkəʊs, -ˌkəʊz) *adj* warlike; aggressive; ready to fight. [C15: from Latin *bellicōsus,* from *bellum* war] ▸ **'belliˌcosely** *adv* ▸ **bellicosity** (ˌbɛlɪ'kɒsɪtɪ) *n*
belligerence (bɪ'lɪdʒərəns) *n* the act or quality of being belligerent or warlike; aggressiveness.
belligerency (bɪ'lɪdʒərənsɪ) *n* the state of being at war.
belligerent (bɪ'lɪdʒərənt) *adj* **1** marked by readiness to fight or argue; aggressive: *a belligerent tone.* **2** relating to or engaged in a legally recognized war or warfare. ◆ *n* **3** a person or country engaged in fighting or war. [C16: from Latin *belliger,* from *bellum* war + *gerere* to wage]
Bellingshausen Sea ('bɛlɪŋzˌhaʊzᵊn) *n* an area of the S Pacific Ocean off the coast of Antarctica. [named after Fabian Gottlieb *Bellingshausen* (1778–1852), Russian explorer]
Bellini (*Italian* bel'lini) *n* **1 Giovanni** (dʒo'vanni). ?1430–1516, Italian painter of the Venetian school, noted for his altarpieces, landscapes, and Madonnas. His father **Jacopo** (?1400–70) and his brother **Gentile** (?1429–1507) were also painters. **2 Vincenzo** (vin'tʃɛntso). 1801–35, Italian composer of operas, esp. *La Sonnambula* (1831) and *Norma* (1831).
Bellinzona (*Italian* bellin'tsona) *n* a town in SE central Switzerland, capital of Ticino canton. Pop.: 35 860 (1990).
bell jar *n* a bell-shaped glass cover used to protect flower arrangements or fragile ornaments or to cover apparatus in experiments, esp. to prevent gases escaping.
bell magpie *n* another name for **currawong.**
bellman ('bɛlmən) *n, pl* **-men.** a man who rings a bell, esp. (formerly) a town crier.
bell metal *n* an alloy of copper and tin, with some zinc and lead, used in casting bells.
bell moth *n* any moth of the family *Tortricidae,* which when at rest resemble the shape of a bell.
Belloc ('bɛlɒk) *n* **Hilaire** ('hɪlɛə, hɪ'lɛə). 1870–1953, British poet, essayist, and historian, born in France, noted particularly for his verse for children in *The Bad Child's Book of Beasts* (1896) and *Cautionary Tales* (1907).
Bellona (bə'ləʊnə) *n* the Roman goddess of war.
bellow ('bɛləʊ) *vb* **1** (*intr*) to make a loud deep raucous cry like that of a bull; roar. **2** to shout (something) unrestrainedly, as in anger or pain; bawl. ◆ *n* **3** the characteristic noise of a bull. **4** a loud deep sound, as of pain or anger. [C14: probably from Old English *bylgan;* related to *bellan* to BELL[2]] ▸ **'bellower** *n*
Bellow ('bɛləʊ) *n* **Saul.** born 1915, U.S. novelist, born in Canada. His works include *Dangling Man* (1944), *Herzog* (1964), *Humboldt's Gift* (1975), *Him with his Foot in his Mouth* (1986), and *The Actual* (1997): Nobel prize for literature 1976.
bellows ('bɛləʊz) *n* (*functioning as sing or pl*) **1** Also called: **pair of bellows.** an instrument consisting of an air chamber with flexible sides, a means of compressing it, an inlet valve, and a constricted outlet that is used to create a stream of air, as for producing a draught for a fire or for sounding organ pipes. **2** *Photog.* a telescopic light-tight sleeve, connecting the lens system of some cameras to the body of the instrument. **3** a flexible corrugated element used as an expansion joint, pump, or means of transmitting axial motion. [C16: from plural of Old English *belig* BELLY]
bellows fish *n* another name for **snipefish.**
bell pull *n* a handle, rope, or cord pulled to operate a doorbell or servant's bell.
bell punch *n* a machine that issues or stamps a ticket, etc., ringing a bell as it does so.
bell push *n* a button pressed to operate an electric bell.
bell-ringer *n* **1** a person who rings church bells. **2** a person who plays musical handbells. ▸ **'bell-ˌringing** *n*
bells and whistles *pl n* **1** additional features or accessories which are nonessential but very attractive: *my car has all the latest bells and whistles.* **2** additions, such as options or warranties, made to a financial product to increase its market appeal. [C20: from the bells and whistles which used to decorate fairground organs]
bell sheep *n Austral.* a sheep that a shearer is just starting to shear (and which he is allowed to finish) as the bell rings for the end of a work period.
bells of Ireland *n* (*functioning as sing*) an annual garden plant, *Moluccella laevis,* whose flowers have a green cup-shaped calyx: family *Labiatae* (labiates).
Bell's palsy *n* a usually temporary paralysis of the muscles of the face, normally on one side. [C19: named after Sir Charles *Bell* (1774–1842), British anatomist]
bell tent *n* a cone-shaped tent having a single central supporting pole.
bell-topper *n N.Z. obsolete, informal.* a tall silk hat.
bellwether ('bɛlˌwɛðə) *n* **1** a sheep that leads the herd, often bearing a bell. **2** a leader, esp. one followed blindly.
bellwort ('bɛlˌwɜːt) *n U.S.* **1** any plant of the North American liliaceous genus *Uvularia,* having slender bell-shaped yellow flowers. **2** another name for **campanula.**
belly ('bɛlɪ) *n, pl* **-lies. 1** the lower or front part of the body of a vertebrate, containing the intestines and other abdominal organs; abdomen. Related adj: **ventral. 2** the stomach, esp. when regarded as the seat of gluttony. **3** a part, line, or structure that bulges deeply: *the belly of a sail.* **4** the inside or interior cavity of something: *the belly of a ship.* **5** the front or inner part or underside of something. **6** the surface of a stringed musical instrument over which the strings are stretched. **7** the thick central part of certain muscles. **8** *Austral. and N.Z.* the wool from a sheep's belly. **9** *Tanning.* the portion of a hide or skin on the underpart of an animal. **10** *Archery.* the surface of the bow next to the bowstring. **11** *Archaic.* the womb. **12 go belly up.** *Informal.* to die, fail, or come to an end. ◆ *vb* **-lies, -lying, -lied. 13** to swell out or cause to swell out; bulge. [Old English *belig;* related to Old High German *balg,* Old Irish *bolg* sack, Sanskrit *barhi* chaff]
bellyache ('bɛlɪˌeɪk) *n* **1** an informal term for **stomachache.** ◆ *vb* **2** (*intr*) *Slang.* to complain repeatedly. ▸ **'bellyˌacher** *n*
bellyband ('bɛlɪˌbænd) *n* a strap around the belly of a draught animal, holding the shafts of a vehicle.
bellybutton ('bɛlɪˌbʌtᵊn) *n* an informal name for the **navel.**
belly dance *n* **1** a sensuous and provocative dance of Middle Eastern origin, performed by women, with undulating movements of the hips and abdomen. ◆ *vb* **belly-dance. 2** (*intr*) to perform such a dance. ▸ **belly dancer** *n*
belly flop *n* **1** a dive into water in which the body lands horizontally. **2** another name for **belly landing.** ◆ *vb* **belly-flop, -flops, -flopping, -flopped. 3** (*intr*) to perform a belly flop.
bellyful ('bɛlɪˌfʊl) *n* **1** as much as one wants or can eat. **2** *Slang.* more than one can tolerate.
belly landing *n* the landing of an aircraft on its fuselage without use of its landing gear.
belly laugh *n* a loud deep hearty laugh.
Belmondo (bɛl'mɒndəʊ; *French* bɛlmɔ̃do) *n* **Jean-Paul** (ʒɑ̃pol). born 1933, French film actor.
Belmopan (ˌbɛlmə'pæn) *n* (since 1973) the capital of Belize, about 50 miles inland: founded in 1970. Pop.: 6490 (1996 est.).
Belo Horizonte (*Portuguese* 'bɛːlori'zɔ̃ːntə) *n* a city in SE Brazil, the capital of Minas Gerais state. Pop.: 1 529 566 (1991).
belong (bɪ'lɒŋ) *vb* (*intr*) **1** (foll. by *to*) to be the property or possession (of). **2** (foll. by *to*) to be bound to (a person, place, or club) by ties of affection, dependence, allegiance, or membership. **3** (foll. by *to, under, with,* etc.) to be classified (with): *this plant belongs to the daisy family.* **4** (foll. by *to*) to be a part or adjunct (of): *this top belongs to the smaller box.* **5** to have a proper or usual place: *that plate belongs in the cupboard.* **6** *Informal.* to be suitable or acceptable, esp. socially: *although they were rich, they just didn't belong.* [C14 *belongen,* from BE- (intensive) + *longen;* related to Old High German *bilangēn* to reach; see LONG[3]]

belonging (bɪˈlɒŋɪŋ) *n* secure relationship; affinity (esp. in the phrase **a sense of belonging**).

belongings (bɪˈlɒŋɪŋz) *pl n* (*sometimes sing*) the things that a person owns or has with him; possessions; effects.

Belorussia (ˌbjɛləʊˈrʌʃə, ˌbɛl-) *n* a variant spelling of **Belarus.** ▸ **Belorussian** *n, adj*

Belostok (bjɪlaˈstɔk) *n* transliteration of the Russian name for **Białystok.**

beloved (bɪˈlʌvɪd, -ˈlʌvd) *adj* **1** dearly loved. ◆ *n* **2** a person who is dearly loved, such as a wife or husband.

Belovo (*Russian* ˈbjɛləvə) *n* a variant spelling of **Byelovo.**

below (bɪˈləʊ) *prep* **1** at or to a position lower than; under. **2** less than in quantity or degree. **3** south of. **4** downstream of. **5** unworthy of; beneath. ◆ *adv* **6** at or to a lower position or place. **7** at a later place (in something written): *see below.* **8** *Archaic.* beneath heaven; on earth or in hell. [C14: *bilooghe,* from *bi* BY + *looghe* LOW[1]]

below stairs *adv* (formerly) at or in the basement of a large house, considered as the place where the servants live and work.

Bel Paese (ˈbɛl pɑːˈeɪzɪ) *n* a mild creamy Italian cheese. [C20: from Italian, literally: beautiful country]

Belsen (ˈbɛlsᵊn; *German* ˈbɛlzən) *n* a village in NE Germany: with Bergen, the site of a Nazi concentration camp (1943–45).

Belshazzar (bɛlˈʃæzə) *n* 6th century B.C., the son of Nabonidus, coregent of Babylon with his father for eight years: referred to as king and son of Nebuchadnezzar in the Old Testament (Daniel 5:1, 17; 8:1); described as having received a divine message of doom written on a wall at a banquet (**Belshazzar's Feast**).

belt (bɛlt) *n* **1** a band of cloth, leather, etc., worn, usually around the waist, to support clothing, carry tools, weapons, or ammunition, or as decoration. **2** a narrow band, circle, or stripe, as of colour. **3** an area, esp. an elongated one, where a specific thing or specific conditions are found; zone: *the town belt; a belt of high pressure.* **4** a belt worn as a symbol of rank (as by a knight or an earl), or awarded as a prize (as in boxing or wrestling), or to mark particular expertise (as in judo or karate). **5** See **seat belt. 6** a band of flexible material between rotating shafts or pulleys to transfer motion or transmit goods: *a fan belt; a conveyer belt.* **7** short for **beltcourse** (see **cordon** (sense 4)). **8** *Informal.* a sharp blow, as with a bat or the fist. **9 below the belt. 9a** *Boxing.* below the waist, esp. in the groin. **9b** *Informal.* in an unscrupulous or cowardly way. **10 tighten one's belt.** to take measures to reduce expenditure. **11 under one's belt. 11a** (of food or drink) in one's stomach. **11b** in one's possession. **11c** as part of one's experience: *he had a linguistics degree under his belt.* ◆ *vb* **12** (*tr*) to fasten or attach with or as if with a belt. **13** (*tr*) to hit with a belt. **14** (*tr*) *Slang.* to give a sharp blow; punch. **15** (*intr;* often foll. by *along*) *Slang.* to move very fast, esp. in a car: *belting down the motorway.* **16** (*tr*) *Rare.* to mark with belts, as of colour. **17** (*tr*) *Rare.* to encircle; surround. ◆ See also **belt out, belt up.** [Old English, from Latin *balteus*]

Beltane (ˈbɛlteɪn, -tən) *n* an ancient Celtic festival with a sacrificial bonfire on May Day. [C15: from Scottish Gaelic *bealltainn*]

beltcourse (ˈbɛltˌkɔːs) *n* another name for **cordon** (sense 4).

belt drive *n Engineering.* a transmission system using a flexible belt to transfer power.

belter (ˈbɛltə) *n Slang.* **1** an event, person, quality, etc., that is admirable, outstanding, or thrilling: *a real belter of a match.* **2a** a rousing or spirited popular song that is sung loudly and enthusiastically. **2b** a person who sings popular songs in a loud and spirited manner.

belting (ˈbɛltɪŋ) *n* **1** the material used to make a belt or belts. **2** belts collectively. **3** *Informal.* a beating.

belt man *n Austral. and N.Z.* (formerly) the member of a beach life-saving team who swam out with a line attached to his belt.

belt out *vb* (*tr, adv*) *Informal.* to sing loudly or emit (sound, esp. pop music) loudly: *a jukebox belting out the latest hits.*

belt up *vb* (*adv*) **1** *Slang.* to become or cause to become silent; stop talking: often used in the imperative. **2** to fasten with or by a belt, esp. a seat belt.

beltway (ˈbɛltˌweɪ) *n* the usual U.S. name for a **ring road.**

beluga (bɪˈluːɡə) *n* **1** a large white sturgeon, *Acipenser* (or *Huso*) *huso,* of the Black and Caspian Seas: a source of caviar and isinglass. **2** another name for **white whale.** [C18: from Russian *byeluga,* from *byely* white]

belvedere (ˈbɛlvɪˌdɪə, ˌbɛlvɪˈdɪə) *n* a building, such as a summerhouse or roofed gallery, sited to command a fine view. See also **gazebo.** [C16: from Italian: beautiful sight]

Belvoir Castle (ˈbiːvə) *n* a castle in Leicestershire, near Grantham (in Lincolnshire): seat of the Dukes of Rutland; rebuilt by James Wyatt in 1816.

Belyi *or* **Bely** (ˈbjɛlɪ) *n* **Andrei** (ʌnˈdreɪ), real name *Boris Nikolayevich Bugaev.* 1880–1934, Russian poet, novelist, and critic: a leading exponent of symbolism. His novels include *Petersburg* (1913).

BEM *abbrev. for* British Empire Medal.

bema, bimah, *or* **bima** (ˈbiːmə) *n* **1** the speaker's platform in the assembly in ancient Athens. **2** *Christian Orthodox Church.* a raised area surrounding the altar in a church; the sanctuary. **3** *Judaism.* another word for **almemar.** [C17: via Late Latin, from Greek *bēma,* from *bainein* to go]

Bemba (ˈbɛmbə) *n* **1** (*pl* **-ba** *or* **-bas**) a member of a Negroid people of Africa, living chiefly in Zambia on a high infertile plateau. **2** the language of this people, belonging to the Bantu group of the Niger-Congo family.

Bembo[1] (*Italian* ˈbɛmbo) *n* **Pietro** (ˈpjɛːtro). 1470–1547, Italian scholar, poet, and cardinal (1539). His treatise *Prose della volgar lingua* (1525) helped to establish a standard form of literary Italian.

Bembo[2] (ˈbɛmbəʊ) *n* a style of type. [C20: named after Pietro BEMBO, because the design of the typeface was based on one used for an edition of his tract *De ætna* by the printer Aldus Manutius]

bemean (bɪˈmiːn) *vb* a less common word for **demean**[1].

bemire (bɪˈmaɪə) *vb* (*tr*) **1** to soil with or as if with mire. **2** (*usually passive*) to stick fast in mud or mire.

bemoan (bɪˈməʊn) *vb* to grieve over (a loss, etc.); mourn; lament (esp. in the phrase **bemoan one's fate**). [Old English *bemǣnan;* see BE-, MOAN]

bemuse (bɪˈmjuːz) *vb* (*tr*) to confuse; bewilder. ▸ **beˈmusement** *n* ▸ **beˈmusing** *adj*

bemused (bɪˈmjuːzd) *adj* preoccupied; lost in thought. ▸ **bemusedly** (bɪˈmjuːzɪdlɪ) *adv*

ben[1] (bɛn) *Scot.* ◆ *n* **1** an inner room in a house or cottage. ◆ *prep, adv* **2** in; within; inside; into the inner part (of a house). ◆ *adj* **3** inner. Compare **but**[2]. [Old English *binnan,* from BE- + *innan* inside]

ben[2] (bɛn) *n* **1** any of several Asiatic trees of the genus *Moringa,* esp. *M. oleifera* of Arabia and India, whose seeds yield **oil of ben,** used in manufacturing perfumes and cosmetics, lubricating delicate machinery, etc.: family *Moringaceae.* **2** the seed of such a tree. [C15: from Arabic *bān*]

ben[3] (bɛn) *n Scot., Irish.* a mountain peak (esp. in place names): *Ben Lomond.* [C18: from Gaelic *beinn,* from *beann*]

Benacerraf (ˌbɛnəˈsɛrɑːf) *n* **Baruj.** U.S. immunologist: shared the Nobel prize for physiology or medicine (1980) for his work on histocompatibility antigens.

Benadryl (ˈbɛnədrɪl) *n Trademark.* an antihistamine drug used in sleeping pills; diphenhydramine. Formula: $C_{17}H_{21}NO$.

bename (bɪˈneɪm) *vb* **-names, -naming, -named; -named** *or* **-nempt.** an archaic word for **name** (sense 12). [Old English *benemnan;* see BE-, NAME]

Benares (bɪˈnɑːrɪz) *or* **Banaras** *n* the former name of **Varanasi.**

Benavente y Martínez (*Spanish* benaˈvente i marˈtineθ) *n* **Jacinto.** 1866–1954, Spanish dramatist and critic, who wrote over 150 plays. Nobel prize for literature 1922.

Ben Bella (bɛn ˈbɛlə) *n* **Mohammed Ahmed** (ˈɑːmɪd). born 1916, Algerian statesman: first prime minister (1962–65) and president (1963–65) of independent Algeria: overthrown and imprisoned (1965–80).

Benbow (ˈbɛnbəʊ) *n* **John.** 1653–1702, English admiral, noted esp. for his heroic death during the War of the Spanish Succession.

bench (bɛntʃ) *n* **1** a long seat for more than one person, usually lacking a back or arms. **2** a plain stout worktable. **3 the bench.** (*sometimes cap.*) **3a** a judge or magistrate sitting in court in a judicial capacity. **3b** judges or magistrates collectively. **4** *Sport.* the seat on which reserve players and officials sit during a game. **5** *Geology.* a flat narrow platform of land, esp. one marking a former shoreline. **6** a ledge in a mine or quarry from which work is carried out. **7** a platform on which dogs or other domestic animals are exhibited at shows. **8** *N.Z.* a hollow on a hillside formed by sheep. ◆ *vb* (*tr*) **9** to provide with benches. **10** to exhibit (a dog, etc.) at a show. **11** *N.Z.* to form (a track) up a hill by excavating a flattened area. **12** *U.S. and Canadian, Sports.* to take or keep (a player) out of a game, often for disciplinary reasons. [Old English *benc;* related to Old Norse *bekkr,* Old High German *bank,* Danish, Swedish *bänk;* see BANK[3]]

bencher (ˈbɛntʃə) *n* (*often pl*) *Brit.* **1** a member of the governing body of one of the Inns of Court, usually a judge or a Queen's Counsel. **2** See **backbencher.**

benchmark (ˈbɛntʃˌmɑːk) *n* **1** a mark on a stone post or other permanent feature, at a point whose exact elevation and position is known: used as a reference point in surveying. Abbrev.: **BM. 2a** a criterion by which to measure something; standard; reference point. **2b** (*as modifier*): *a benchmark test.*

benchmark position *n N.Z.* a public service job used for comparison with a similar position, such as a position in commerce, for wage settlements.

bench press *n* a weight-training exercise in which a person lies on a bench and pushes a barbell upwards with both hands from chest level until the arms are straight, then lowers it again.

bench test *n* the critical evaluation of a new or repaired component, device, apparatus, etc., prior to installation to ensure that it is in perfect condition.

bench warrant *n* a warrant issued by a judge or court directing that an offender be apprehended.

benchy (ˈbɛntʃɪ) *adj N.Z.* (of a hillside) hollowed out in benches.

bend[1] (bɛnd) *vb* **bends, bending, bent. 1** to form or cause to form a curve, as by pushing or pulling. **2** to turn or cause to turn from a particular direction: *the road bends left past the church.* **3** (*intr;* often foll. by *down,* etc.) to incline the body; stoop; bow. **4** to submit or cause to submit: *to bend before superior force.* **5** (*tr*) to turn or direct (one's eyes, steps, attention, etc.). **6** (*tr*) to concentrate (the mind); apply oneself closely. **7** (*tr*) *Nautical.* to attach or fasten, as a sail to a boom or a line to a cleat. **8 bend over backwards.** *Informal.* to make a special effort, esp. in order to please: *he bends over backwards to accommodate his customers.* **9 bend (someone's) ear.** *Informal.* to speak at length to an unwilling listener, esp. to voice one's troubles. **10 bend the rules.** *Informal.* to ignore rules or change them to suit one's own convenience. ◆ *n* **11** a curved part, as in a road or river. **12** *Nautical.* a knot or eye in a line for joining it to another or to an object. **13** the act or state of bending. **14 round the bend.** *Brit. slang.* mad; crazy; eccentric. ◆ See also **bends.** [Old English *bendan;* related to Old Norse *benda,* Middle High German *benden;* see BIND, BAND[3]]

bend[2] (bɛnd) *n Heraldry.* an ordinary consisting of a diagonal line traversing a shield. [Old English *bend* BAND[2]; see BEND[1]]

Benda (*French* bɛ̃da). *n* **Julien** (ʒyljɛ̃). 1867–1956, French philosopher and novelist, who defended reason and intellect and attacked the influence of Bergson: author of *La Trahison des clercs* (1927).

Ben Day process *n Printing.* a method of adding texture, shading, or detail to line drawings by overlaying a transparent sheet of dots or any other pattern during platemaking. [C20: named after *Benjamin Day* (1838–1916), American printer]

bender (ˈbɛndə) *n Informal.* **1** a drinking bout. **2** a makeshift shelter constructed by placing tarpaulin or plastic sheeting over bent saplings or woven branches.

Bendigo ('bendɪ,gəu) *n* a city in SE Australia, in central Victoria: founded in 1851 after the discovery of gold. Pop.: 57 427 (1991).

bends (bendz) *pl n* **the.** (*functioning as sing or pl*) a nontechnical name for **decompression sickness.**

bend sinister *n Heraldry.* a diagonal line bisecting a shield from the top right to the bottom left, typically indicating a bastard line.

bendy[1] ('bendɪ) *adj* **bendier, bendiest. 1** flexible or pliable. **2** having many bends: *a bendy road.*

bendy[2] *or* **bendee** ('bendɪ) *adj* (*usually postpositive*) *Heraldry.* striped diagonally.

beneath (bɪ'ni:θ) *prep* **1** below, esp. if covered, protected, or obscured by. **2** not as great or good as would be demanded by: *beneath his dignity.* ◆ *adv* **3** below; underneath. [Old English *beneothan,* from BE- + *neothan* low; see NETHER]

benedicite (,benɪ'daɪsɪtɪ) *n* **1** (esp. in Christian religious orders) a blessing or grace. ◆ *interj* **2** *Obsolete.* an expression of surprise. [C13: from Latin, from *benedīcere,* from *bene* well + *dīcere* to speak]

Benedicite (,benɪ'daɪsɪtɪ) *n Christianity.* a canticle that originated as part of the *Song of the Three Holy Children* in the secondary addition to the Book of Daniel, beginning *Benedicite omnia opera Domini Domino* in Latin, and *O all ye Works of the Lord* in English.

Benedict ('benɪ,dɪkt) *n* **Saint.** ?480–?547 A.D., Italian monk: founded the Benedictine order at Monte Cassino in Italy in about 540 A.D. His *Regula Monachorum* became the basis of the rule of all Western Christian monastic orders. Feast day: July 11 or March 14.

Benedict XV *n* original name *Giacomo della Chiesa.* 1854–1922, pope (1914–22); noted for his repeated attempts to end World War I and for his organization of war relief.

Benedictine *n* **1** (,benɪ'dɪktɪn, -taɪn). a monk or nun who is a member of a Christian religious community founded by or following the rule of Saint Benedict. **2** (,benɪ'dɪkti:n). a greenish-yellow liqueur made from a secret formula developed at the Benedictine monastery at Fécamp in France in about 1510. ◆ *adj* **3** (,benɪ'dɪktɪn, -taɪn). of or relating to Saint Benedict, his order, or his rule.

benediction (,benɪ'dɪkʃən) *n* **1** an invocation of divine blessing, esp. at the end of a Christian religious ceremony. **2** a Roman Catholic service in which the congregation is blessed with the sacrament. **3** the state of being blessed. [C15: from Latin *benedictio,* from *benedīcere* to bless; see BENEDICITE] ▸ **,bene'dictory** *adj*

Benedict's solution *or* **reagent** *n* a chemical solution used to detect the presence of glucose and other reducing sugars. Medically, it is used to test the urine of diabetics. [named after S. R. *Benedict* (1884–1936), U.S. chemist]

Benedictus (,benɪ'dɪktəs) *n* (*sometimes not cap.*) *Christianity.* **1** a short canticle beginning *Benedictus qui venit in nomine Domini* in Latin and *Blessed is he that cometh in the name of the Lord* in English. **2** a canticle beginning *Benedictus Dominus Deus Israel* in Latin and *Blessed be the Lord God of Israel* in English.

benefaction (,benɪ'fækʃən) *n* **1** the act of doing good, esp. by giving a donation to charity. **2** the donation or help given. [C17: from Late Latin *benefactiō,* from Latin *bene* well + *facere* to do]

benefactor ('benɪ,fæktə, ,benɪ'fæk-) *n* a person who supports or helps a person, institution, etc., esp. by giving money; patron. ▸ **'bene,factress** *fem n*

benefic (bɪ'nefɪk) *adj* a rare word for **beneficent.**

benefice ('benɪfɪs) *n* **1** *Christianity.* an endowed Church office yielding an income to its holder; a Church living. **2** the property or revenue attached to such an office. **3** (in feudal society) a tenement (piece of land) held by a vassal from a landowner on easy terms or free, esp. in return for military support. See also **vassalage.** ◆ *vb* **4** (*tr*) to provide with a benefice. [C14: from Old French, from Latin *beneficium* benefit, from *beneficus,* from *bene* well + *facere* to do]

beneficence (bɪ'nefɪsəns) *n* **1** the act of doing good; kindness. **2** a charitable act or gift.

beneficent (bɪ'nefɪsənt) *adj* charitable; generous. [C17: from Latin *beneficent-,* from *beneficus;* see BENEFICE] ▸ **be'neficently** *adv*

beneficial (,benɪ'fɪʃəl) *adj* **1** (sometimes foll. by *to*) causing a good result; advantageous. **2** *Law.* entitling a person to receive the profits or proceeds of property: *a beneficial interest in land.* [C15: from Late Latin *beneficiālis,* from Latin *beneficium* kindness] ▸ **,bene'ficially** *adv*

beneficiary (,benɪ'fɪʃərɪ) *n, pl* **-ciaries. 1** a person who gains or benefits in some way from something. **2** *Law.* a person entitled to receive funds or other property under a trust, will, or insurance policy. **3** the holder of an ecclesiastical or other benefice. **4** *N.Z.* a person who receives government assistance: *social security beneficiary.* ◆ *adj* **5** of or relating to a benefice or the holder of a benefice.

benefit ('benɪfɪt) *n* **1** something that improves or promotes. **2** advantage or sake: *this is for your benefit.* **3a** *Brit.* an allowance paid by the government as for sickness, unemployment, etc., to which a person is entitled under social security or the national insurance scheme. **3b** any similar allowance in various other countries. **4** (*sometimes pl*) a payment or series of payments made by an institution, such as an insurance company or trade union, to a person who is ill, unemployed, etc. **5** a theatrical performance, sports event, etc., to raise money for a charity. ◆ *vb* **-fits, -fiting, -fited** *or esp. U.S.* **-fits, -fitting, -fitted. 6** to do or receive good; profit. [C14: from Anglo-French *benfet,* from Latin *benefactum,* from *bene facere* to do well]

benefit in kind *n* a nonpecuniary benefit, such as a company car or medical insurance, given to an employee.

benefit of clergy *n Christianity.* **1** sanction by the church: *marriage without benefit of clergy.* **2** (in the Middle Ages) a privilege that placed the clergy outside the jurisdiction of secular courts and entitled them to trial in ecclesiastical courts.

benefit society *n* a U.S. term for **friendly society.**

Benelux ('benɪ,lʌks) *n* **1** the customs union formed by Belgium, the Netherlands, and Luxembourg in 1948; became an economic union in 1960. **2** these countries collectively.

benempt (bɪ'nempt) *vb Archaic.* a past participle of **bename.**

Beneš (*Czech* 'beneʃ) *n* **Eduard** ('e:duart). 1884–1948, Czech statesman; president of Czechoslovakia (1935–38; 1946–48) and of its government in exile (1939–45).

Benét (bə'neɪ) *n* **Stephen Vincent.** 1898–1943, U.S. poet and novelist, best known for his poem on the American Civil War *John Brown's Body* (1928).

Benevento (,benə'ventəu) *n* a city in S Italy, in N Campania: at various times under Samnite, Roman, Lombard, Saracen, Norman, and papal rule. Pop.: 64 690 (1990). Ancient name: **Beneventum** (,benə'ventum).

benevolence (bɪ'nevələns) *n* **1** inclination or tendency to help or do good to others; charity. **2** an act of kindness. **3** (in the Middle Ages) a forced loan or contribution exacted by English kings from their nobility and subjects.

benevolent (bɪ'nevələnt) *adj* **1** intending or showing goodwill; kindly; friendly: *a benevolent smile; a benevolent old man.* **2** doing good or giving aid to others, rather than making profit; charitable: *a benevolent organization.* [C15: from Latin *benevolēns,* from *bene* well + *velle* to wish] ▸ **be'nevolently** *adv*

Benfleet ('ben,fli:t) *n* a town in SE England, in S Essex on an inlet of the Thames estuary. Pop.: 49 701 (1991).

BEng *abbrev. for* Bachelor of Engineering.

Beng. *abbrev. for* Bengal(i).

Bengal (beŋ'gɔ:l, beŋ-) *n* **1** a former province of NE India, in the great deltas of the Ganges and Brahmaputra Rivers: in 1947 divided into West Bengal (belonging to India) and East Bengal (Bangladesh). **2 Bay of.** a wide arm of the Indian Ocean, between India and Myanmar.

Bengali (beŋ'gɔ:lɪ, beŋ-) *n* **1** a member of a people living chiefly in Bangladesh and in West Bengal. The West Bengalis are mainly Hindus; the East Bengalis of Bangladesh are mainly Muslims. **2** the language of this people: the official language of Bangladesh and the chief language of West Bengal; it belongs to the Indic branch of the Indo-European family. Also called: **Bangla.** ◆ *adj* **3** of or relating to Bengal, the Bengalis, or their language.

bengaline ('beŋgə,li:n, ,beŋgə'li:n) *n* a heavy corded fabric, esp. silk with woollen or cotton cord. [C19: from French; see BENGAL, -INE[1]; first produced in Bengal]

Bengal light *n* a firework or flare that burns with a steady bright blue light, formerly used as a signal.

Bengbu ('beŋ'bu:), **Pengpu** *or* **Pang-fou** *n* a city in E China, in Anhui province. Pop.: 449 245 (1990 est.).

Benghazi *or* **Bengasi** (ben'gɑ:zɪ) *n* a port in N Libya, on the Gulf of Sidra: centre of Italian colonization (1911–42); scene of much fighting in World War II. Pop.: 446 250 (1988 est.). Ancient names: **Hesperides, Berenice** (berə'naɪsɪ).

Benguela (beŋ'gwelə) *n* a port in W Angola: founded in 1617; a terminus (with Lobito) of the railway that runs from Beira in Mozambique through the Copper Belt of Zambia and Zimbabwe. Pop.: 41 000 (latest est.).

Ben-Gurion (ben'guərɪən) *n* **David,** original name *David Gruen.* 1886–1973, Israeli socialist statesman, born in Poland; first prime minister of Israel (1948–53, 1955–63).

Beni (*Spanish* 'beni) *n* a river in N Bolivia, rising in the E Cordillera of the Andes and flowing north to the Marmoré River. Length: over 1600 km (1000 miles).

benighted (bɪ'naɪtɪd) *adj* **1** lacking cultural, moral, or intellectual enlightenment; ignorant. **2** *Archaic.* overtaken by night. ▸ **be'nightedly** *adv* ▸ **be'nightedness** *n*

benign (bɪ'naɪn) *adj* **1** showing kindliness; genial. **2** (of soil, climate, etc.) mild; gentle. **3** favourable; propitious. **4** *Pathol.* (of a tumour, etc.) not threatening to life or health; not malignant. [C14: from Old French *benigne,* from Latin *benignus,* from *bene* well + *gignere* to produce] ▸ **be'nignly** *adv*

benignant (bɪ'nɪgnənt) *adj* **1** kind; gracious, as a king to his subjects. **2** a less common word for **benign** (senses 3, 4). ▸ **be'nignancy** *n* ▸ **be'nignantly** *adv*

benignity (bɪ'nɪgnɪtɪ) *n, pl* **-ties. 1** the quality of being benign; favourable attitude. **2** a kind or gracious act.

Beni Hasan ('benɪ hæ'sɑ:n) *n* a village in central Egypt, on the Nile, with cliff-cut tombs dating from 2000 B.C.

Benin (be'ni:n) *n* **1** a republic in W Africa, on the **Bight of Benin,** a section of the Gulf of Guinea: in the early 19th century a powerful kingdom, famed for its women warriors; became a French colony in 1893, gaining independence in 1960. It consists chiefly of coastal lagoons and swamps in the south, a fertile plain and marshes in the centre, and the Atakora Mountains in the northwest. Official language: French. Religion: animist majority. Currency: franc. Capital: Porto Novo (the government is based in Cotonou). Pop.: 6 101 000 (1998 est.). Area: 112 622 sq. km (43 474 sq. miles). Former name (until 1975): **Dahomey. 2** a former kingdom of W Africa, powerful from the 14th to the 17th centuries: now a province of S Nigeria: noted for its bronzes. ▸ **Be,ni'nese** *adj, n* ▸ **Beninois** (,beni:'nwɑ:) *adj, n*

Benin City *n* a city in S Nigeria, capital of Edo state: former capital of the kingdom of Benin. Pop.: 229 400 (1996 est.).

Benioff zone ('benɪəf) *n* a long narrow region, usually adjacent to a continent, along which earthquake foci lie on a plane which dips downwards at about 45° and along which the oceanic lithosphere is thought to be descending into the earth's interior. Also called: **subduction zone.** [C20: named after Hugo *Benioff* (1899–1968), American seismologist, who first discovered the phenomenon]

benison ('benɪzᵊn, -sᵊn) *n Archaic.* a blessing, esp. a spoken one. [C13: from Old French *beneison,* from Latin *benedictiō* BENEDICTION]

benjamin ('bendʒəmɪn) *n* **1** another name for **benzoin** (sense 1). **2 benjamin bush.** another name for **spicebush.** **[C16:** variant of *benzoin;* influenced in form by the name *Benjamin***]**

Benjamin[1] ('bendʒəmɪn) *n* **1** *Old Testament.* **1a** the youngest and best-loved son of Jacob and Rachel (Genesis 35:16–18; 42:4). **1b** the tribe descended from this patriarch. **1c** the territory of this tribe, northwest of the Dead Sea. **2** *Archaic.* a youngest and favourite son.

Benjamin[2] ('bendʒəmɪn) *n* **1 Arthur.** 1893–1960, Australian composer. In addition to *Jamaican Rumba* (1938), he wrote five operas and a harmonica concerto (1953). **2** (*German* 'benɪamin). **Walter** ('valtər). 1892–1940, German critic and cultural theorist.

Ben Lomond (ben 'ləumənd) *n* **1** a mountain in W central Scotland, on the E side of Loch Lomond. Height: 973 m (3192 ft.). **2** a mountain in NE Tasmania. Height: 1527 m (5010 ft.). **3** a mountain in SE Australia, in NE New South Wales. Height: 1520 m (4986 ft.).

Benn (ben) *n* **Antony (Neil) Wedgwood,** known as *Tony Benn.* born 1925, British Labour politician, a leading figure on the party's left wing. He renounced (1963) the title of Viscount Stansgate.

benne ('benɪ) *n* **1** another name for **sesame. 2 benne oil.** the edible oil obtained from sesame seeds. **[C18:** from Malay *bene;* compare Bambara *bene***]**

bennet ('benɪt) *n* short for **herb bennet.**

Bennett ('benɪt) *n* **1 Alan.** born 1934, British actor playwright. His plays include *Forty Years On* (1968), *The Old Country* (1977), *The Madness of George III* (1991), and many television productions. **2 (Enoch) Arnold.** 1867–1931, British novelist, noted for *The Old Wives' Tale* (1908), *Clayhanger* (1910), and other works set in the Staffordshire Potteries. **3 James Gordon.** 1837–1931, U.S. newspaper editor, born in Scotland. He founded (1835) the *New York Herald* and introduced techniques of modern news reporting. **4 Jill.** 1931–90, British actress. **5 Richard Bedford,** 1st Viscount. 1870–1947, Canadian Conservative statesman; prime minister (1930–35). **6** Sir **Richard Rodney.** born 1936, British composer, noted for his operas *The Mines of Sulphur* (1965) and *Victory* (1970).

Ben Nevis (ben 'nevɪs) *n* a mountain in W Scotland, in the Grampian mountains: highest peak in Great Britain. Height: 1343 m (4406 ft.).

Bennington ('benɪŋtən) *n* a town in SW Vermont: the site of a British defeat (1777) in the War of American Independence. Pop.: 16 451 (1990).

benny[1] ('benɪ) *n, pl* **-nies.** *Dated slang.* an amphetamine tablet, esp. benzedrine: a stimulant. **[C20:** shortened from BENZEDRINE**]**

benny[2] ('benɪ) *n, pl* **-nies.** *U.S. slang.* a man's overcoat. **[C19:** from *Benjamin,* perhaps from a tailor's name**]**

Benny ('benɪ) *n* **Jack,** real name *Benjamin Kubelsky.* 1894–1974, U.S. comedian.

Benoît de Sainte-Maure (*French* bənwa də sɛ̃t mɔr) *n* 12th-century French trouvère: author of the *Roman de Troie,* which contains the episode of Troilus and Cressida.

Benoni (bɪ'nəunɪ) *n* a city in NE South Africa: gold mines. Pop.: 113 501 (1991).

Benson ('bensən) *n* **E(dward) F(rederic).** 1867–1940, British writer, noted esp. for a series of comic novels featuring the characters Mapp and Lucia.

bent[1] (bent) *adj* **1** not straight; curved. **2** (foll. by *on*) fixed (on a course of action); resolved (to); determined (to). **3** *Slang.* **3a** dishonest; corrupt. **3b** (of goods) stolen. **3c** crazy; mad. **3d** sexually deviant, esp. homosexual. ◆ *n* **4** personal inclination, propensity, or aptitude. **5** capacity of endurance (esp. in the phrase **to the top of one's bent**). **6** *Civil engineering.* a framework placed across a structure to stiffen it.

bent[2] (bent) *n* **1** short for **bent grass. 2** a stalk of bent grass. **3** *Archaic.* any stiff grass or sedge. **4** *Archaic or Scot. and northern English dialect.* heath or moorland. **[**Old English *bionot;* related to Old Saxon *binet,* Old High German *binuz* rush**]**

bent grass *n* any perennial grass of the genus *Agrostis,* esp. *A. tenuis,* which has a spreading panicle of tiny flowers. Some species are planted for hay or in lawns. Sometimes shortened to **bent.**

Bentham ('benθəm) *n* **Jeremy.** 1748–1832, British philosopher and jurist: a founder of utilitarianism. His works include *A Fragment on Government* (1776) and *Introduction to the Principles of Morals and Legislation* (1789).

Benthamism ('benθə,mɪzəm) *n* the philosophy of utilitarianism as first expounded by Jeremy Bentham in terms of an action being good that has a greater tendency to augment the happiness of the community than to diminish it. ▸ **'Bentha,mite** *n, adj*

benthos ('benθɒs) *or* **benthon** *n* **1** the animals and plants living at the bottom of a sea or lake. **2** the bottom of a sea or lake. **[C19:** from Greek: depth; related to *bathus* deep**]** ▸ **'benthic, 'benthal,** *or* **ben'thonic** *adj*

Bentinck ('bentɪŋk) *n* Lord **William Cavendish.** 1774–1839, British statesman, governor general of Bengal (1828–35).

Bentley ('bentlɪ) *n* **Edmund Clerihew.** 1875–1956, English journalist, noted for his invention of the clerihew.

Benton ('bentən) *n* **Thomas Hart.** 1889–1975, U.S. painter of rural life; a leader of the American Regionalist painters in the 1930s.

bentonite ('bentə,naɪt) *n* a valuable clay, formed by the decomposition of volcanic ash, that swells as it absorbs water: used as a filler in the building, paper, and pharmaceutical industries. **[C19:** from Fort *Benton,* Montana, U.S.A., where found, + -ITE[1]**]**

bentwood ('bent,wud) *n* **a** wood bent in moulds after being heated by steaming, used mainly for furniture. **b** (*as modifier*): *a bentwood chair.*

Benue ('benu,eɪ) *n* **1** a state of SE Nigeria, formed in 1976 from part of Benue-Plateau state. Capital: Makurdi. Pop.: 3 108 754 (1995 est.). Area: 34 059 sq. km (13 150 sq. miles). **2** a river in W Africa, rising in N Cameroon and flowing west across Nigeria: chief tributary of the River Niger. Length: 1400 km (870 miles).

Benue-Congo *n* **1** a branch of the Niger-Congo family of African languages, consisting of the Bantu languages together with certain other languages of W Africa. ◆ *adj* **2** relating or belonging to this group of languages.

benumb (bɪ'nʌm) *vb* (*tr*) **1** to make numb or powerless; deaden physical feeling in, as by cold. **2** (*usually passive*) to make inactive; stupefy (the mind, senses, will, etc.). ▸ **be'numbingly** *adv*

Benxi ('ben'ʃi:), **Penchi,** *or* **Penki** *n* an industrial city in SE China, in S Liaoning province. Pop.: 768 778 (1990 est.).

Benz (benz; *German* bents) *n* **Karl (Friedrich)** (karl). 1844–1929, German engineer; designed and built the first car to be driven by an internal-combustion engine (1885).

benzaldehyde (ben'zældɪ,haɪd) *n* a yellowish fragrant volatile oil occurring in almond kernels and used in the manufacture of dyes, perfumes, and flavourings and as a solvent for oils and resins. Formula: C_6H_5CHO. Systematic name: **benzenecarbaldehyde.**

Benzedrine ('benzɪ,dri:n, -drɪn) *n* a trademark for **amphetamine.**

benzene ('benzi:n, ben'zi:n) *n* a colourless flammable poisonous aromatic liquid used in the manufacture of styrene, phenol, etc., as a solvent for fats, resins, etc., and as an insecticide. Formula: C_6H_6. See also **benzene ring.**

benzenecarbaldehyde (,benzi:nkɑ:'bældɪ,haɪd) *n* the systematic name for **benzaldehyde.**

benzenecarbonyl (,benzi:n'kɑ:bɒnaɪl) *n* (*modifier*) the systematic name for **benzoyl.**

benzenecarboxylate (,benzi:nkɑ:'bɒksɪ,leɪt) *n* the systematic name for **benzoate.**

benzenecarboxylic acid (,benzi:n,kɑ:bɒk'sɪlɪk) *n* the systematic name for **benzoic acid.**

benzene hexachloride *n* another name for **hexachlorocyclohexane.**

benzene ring *n* the hexagonal ring of bonded carbon atoms in the benzene molecule or its derivatives. Also called: **benzene nucleus.** See also **Kekulé formula.**

benzidine ('benzɪ,di:n, -dɪn) *n* a grey or reddish poisonous crystalline powder that is used mainly in the manufacture of dyes, esp. Congo red. Formula: $NH_2(C_6H_4)_2NH_2$.

benzine ('benzi:n, ben'zi:n) *or* **benzin** ('benzɪn) *n* a volatile mixture of the lighter aliphatic hydrocarbon constituents of petroleum. See **ligroin, petroleum ether.**

benzo- *or sometimes before a vowel* **benz-** *combining form.* **1** indicating a benzene ring fused to another ring in a polycyclic compound: *benzofuran.* **2** indicating derivation from benzene or benzoic acid or the presence of phenyl groups: *benzophenone.* **[**from BENZOIN**]**

benzoate ('benzəu,eɪt, -ɪt) *n* any salt or ester of benzoic acid, containing the group C_6H_5COO– or the ion $C_6H_5COO^-$. Systematic name: **benzenecarboxylate.**

benzoate of soda *n* another name for **sodium benzoate.**

benzocaine ('benzəu,keɪn) *n* a white crystalline ester used as a local anaesthetic; ethyl *para*-aminobenzoate. Formula: $C_9H_{11}NO_2$.

benzodiazepine (,benzəudaɪ'eɪzə,pi:n) *n* any of a group of chemical compounds that are used as minor tranquillizers, such as diazepam (Valium) and chlordiazepoxide (Librium). **[C20:** from BENZO- + DI-[1] + AZA- + EP- + -INE[2]**]**

benzofuran (,benzəu'fjuəræn) *n* a colourless insoluble aromatic liquid obtained from coal tar and used in the manufacture of synthetic resins. Formula: C_8H_6O. Also called: **coumarone, cumarone.**

benzoic (ben'zəuɪk) *adj* of, containing, or derived from benzoic acid or benzoin.

benzoic acid *n* a white crystalline solid occurring in many natural resins, used in the manufacture of benzoates, plasticizers, and dyes and as a food preservative (**E210**). Formula: C_6H_5COOH. Systematic name: **benzenecarboxylic acid.**

benzoin ('benzɔɪn, -zəuɪn; ben'zəuɪn) *n* **1** Also called: **benjamin.** a gum resin containing benzoic acid, obtained from various trees of the genus *Styrax,* esp. *S. benzoin* of Java and Sumatra, and used in ointments, perfume, etc. **2** a white or yellowish crystalline compound with a camphor-like odour used as an antiseptic and flavouring; 2-hydroxy-2-phenylacetophenone. Formula: $C_6H_5CHOHCOC_6H_5$. **3** any lauraceous aromatic shrub or tree of the genus *Lindera,* esp. *L. benzoin* (spicebush). **[C16:** from French *benjoin,* from Old Catalan *benjui,* from Arabic *lubān jāwī,* literally: frankincense of Java**]**

benzol *or* **benzole** ('benzɒl) *n* **1** a crude form of benzene, containing toluene, xylene, and other hydrocarbons, obtained from coal tar or coal gas and used as a fuel. **2** an obsolete name for **benzene.**

benzophenone (,benzəufɪ'nəun) *n* a white sweet-smelling crystalline solid used mainly in the manufacture of organic compounds and in perfume. Formula: $C_6H_5COC_6H_5$.

benzoquinone (,benzəukwɪ'nəun, -'kwɪnəun) *n* a yellow crystalline water-soluble unsaturated ketone manufactured from aniline and used in the production of dyestuffs. Formula: $C_6H_4O_2$. Also called: **quinone.** Systematic name: **cyclohexadiene-1,4-quinone.**

benzoyl ('benzəuɪl) *n* (*modifier*) of, consisting of, or containing the monovalent group C_6H_5CO-: *benzoyl group or radical.* Systematic name: **benzenecarbonyl.**

Ben-Zvi (ben'zvi:; *Hebrew* ben'tsvi:) *n* **Itzhak** ('jɪtsxak). 1884–1963, Israeli statesman; president (1952–63).

benzyl ('benzaɪl) *n* (*modifier*) of, consisting of, or containing the monovalent group $C_6H_5CH_2$–: *benzyl alcohol.* Systematic name: **phenylmethyl.**

Beograd (be'ɔgrad) *n* the Serbo-Croat name for **Belgrade.**

Beowulf ('beɪə,wulf) *n* an anonymous Old English epic poem in alliterative verse, believed to have been composed in the 8th century A.D.

bequeath (bɪ'kwi:ð, -'kwi:θ) *vb* (*tr*) **1** *Law.* to dispose of (property, esp. personal property) by will. Compare **devise** (sense 2). **2** to hand down; pass on, as to following generations. [Old English *becwethan;* related to Old Norse *kvetha* to speak, Gothic *qithan,* Old High German *quethan*] ▸ **be'queather** *n*

bequest (bɪ'kwɛst) *n* **1a** the act of bequeathing. **1b** something that is bequeathed. **2** *Law.* a gift of property by will, esp. personal property. Compare **devise** (senses 4, 5). [C14: BE- + Old English *-cwiss* degree; see BEQUEATH]

Béranger (*French* berɑ̃ʒe) *n* **Pierre Jean de** (pjɛr ʒɑ̃ də). 1780–1857, French lyric and satirical poet.

Berar (bɛ'rɑː) *n* a region of W central India: part of Madhya Pradesh state since 1950; important for cotton growing.

berate (bɪ'reɪt) *vb (tr)* to scold harshly.

Berber ('bɜːbə) *n* **1** a member of a Caucasoid Muslim people of N Africa. **2** the language of this people, forming a subfamily of the Afro-Asiatic family of languages. There are extensive differences between dialects. ◆ *adj* **3** of or relating to this people or their language.

Berbera ('bɜːbərə) *n* a port in N Somalia, on the Gulf of Aden. Pop.: 70 000 (latest est.).

berberidaceous (ˌbɜːbərɪ'deɪʃəs) *adj* of, relating to, or belonging to the *Berberidaceae,* a mainly N temperate family of flowering plants (mostly shrubs), including barberry and barrenwort. [C19: from Medieval Latin *berberis,* from Arabic *barbārīs* BARBERRY]

berberine ('bɜːbəˌriːn) *n* a yellow bitter-tasting alkaloid obtained from barberry and other plants and used medicinally, esp. in tonics. Formula: $C_{20}H_{19}NO_5$. [C19: from German *Berberin,* from New Latin *berberis* BARBERRY]

berberis ('bɜːbərɪs) *n* any shrub of the berberidaceous genus *Berberis.* See **barberry.** [C19: from Medieval Latin, of unknown origin]

berbice chair ('bɜːbiːs) *n* a large armchair with long arms that can be folded inwards to act as leg rests. [C20: named after *Berbice,* a river and former county in Guyana]

berceuse (*French* bɛrsøz) *n* **1** a cradlesong or lullaby. **2** an instrumental piece suggestive of this, in six-eight time. [C19: from French: lullaby, from *bercer* to rock]

Berchtesgaden (*German* 'bɛrçtəsgaːdən) *n* a town in Germany, in SE Bavaria: site of the fortified mountain retreat of Adolf Hitler. Pop.: 7865 (1992 est.).

Berdyayev (*Russian* bɪr'djajɪf) *n* **Nikolai Aleksandrovich** (nikaˈlaj alɪk'sandrəvitʃ). 1874–1948, Russian philosopher. Although he was a Marxist, his Christian views led him to criticize Soviet communism and he was forced into exile (1922).

bereave (bɪ'riːv) *vb (tr)* **1** (usually foll. by *of*) to deprive (of) something or someone valued, esp. through death. **2** *Obsolete.* to remove by force. ◆ See also **bereft.** [Old English *bereafian;* see REAVE[1]] ▸ **be'reaved** *adj* ▸ **be'reavement** *n*

bereft (bɪ'rɛft) *adj* (usually foll. by *of*) deprived; parted (from): *bereft of hope.*

Berenson ('bɛrənsən) *n* **Bernard.** 1865–1959, U.S. art historian, born in Lithuania: an authority on art of the Italian Renaissance.

beret ('bɛreɪ) *n* a round close-fitting brimless cap of soft wool material or felt. [C19: from French *béret,* from Old Provençal *berret,* from Medieval Latin *birrettum* cap; see BIRETTA]

Berezina (*Russian* bɪrɪzi'na) *n* a river in Belarus, rising in the north and flowing south to the River Dnieper: linked with the River Dvina and the Baltic Sea by the **Berezina Canal.** Length: 563 km (350 miles).

Berezniki (*Russian* bɪrɪzni'ki) *n* a city in E Russia: chemical industries. Pop.: 184 000 (1995 est.).

berg[1] (bɜːg) *n* short for **iceberg.**

berg[2] (bɜːg) *n* a South African word for **mountain.**

Berg (bɜːg; *German* bɛrk) *n* **1 Alban** (**Maria Johannes**) ('albaːn). 1885–1935, Austrian composer: a pupil of Schoenberg. His works include the operas *Wozzeck* (1921) and *Lulu* (1935), a violin concerto (1935), chamber works, and songs. **2 Paul.** born 1926, U.S. molecular biologist, the first to identify transfer RNA (1956). Nobel prize for chemistry 1980.

Bergamo (*Italian* 'bergamo) *n* a walled city in N Italy, in Lombardy. Pop.: 116 990 (1996 est.).

bergamot ('bɜːgəˌmɒt) *n* **1** Also called: **bergamot orange.** a small Asian spiny rutaceous tree, *Citrus bergamia,* having sour pear-shaped fruit. **2 essence of bergamot.** a fragrant essential oil from the fruit rind of this plant, used in perfumery. **3** a Mediterranean mint, *Mentha citrata,* that yields an oil similar to essence of bergamot. **4a wild bergamot.** a North American plant, *Monarda fistulosa,* with clusters of purple flowers: family *Labiatae* (labiates). **4b** a garden plant of the same genus, usually *M. didyma* (bee balm), grown for its scarlet or pink flowers. **5** a variety of pear. [C17: from French *bergamote,* from Italian *bergamotta,* of Turkic origin; related to Turkish *bey-armudu* prince's pear; see BEY]

Bergdama (ˌbɜːg'dɑːmə) *n* another name for a **Damara.**

bergen ('bɜːgən) *n* a large rucksack with a capacity of over 50 litres.

Bergen *n* **1** (*Norwegian* 'bærgən) a port in SW Norway: chief city in medieval times. Pop.: 224 130 (1997 est.). **2** ('bɛrxən). the Flemish name for **Mons.**

Bergerac (*French* bɛrʒərak) *n* See **Cyrano de Bergerac.**

bergère (bɜː'ʒɛə) *n* **1** a type of French armchair made from about 1725 having a wide deep seat and upholstered sides and back. In later examples, woven cane is often used instead of upholstery. **2** a sofa of a similar design. [French, literally: shepherdess]

Bergie ('bɜːgɪ) *n S. African informal.* a vagabond, esp. one living on the slopes of Table Mountain in the Western Cape province of South Africa. [from Afrikaans *berg* mountain]

Bergius (*German* 'bɛrgjʊs) *n* **Friedrich** (**Karl Rudolph**) ('friːdrɪç). 1884–1949, German chemist, who invented a process for producing oil by high-pressure hydrogenation of coal: Nobel prize for chemistry 1931.

Bergman ('bɜːgmən) *n* **1** (**Ernst**) **Ingmar** ('iŋmar). born 1918, Swedish film and stage director, whose films include *The Seventh Seal* (1956), *Wild Strawberries* (1957), *Persona* (1966), *Scenes from a Marriage* (1974), *Autumn Sonata* (1978), and *Fanny and Alexander* (1982). **2 Ingrid.** 1915–82, Swedish film and stage actress, working in Hollywood 1938–48; noted for her leading roles in many films, including *Casablanca* (1942), *For Whom the Bell Tolls* (1943), *Anastasia* (1956), and *The Inn of the Sixth Happiness* (1958).

bergschrund ('bɛrkʃrʊnt, 'bɜːgʃruːnd) *n* a crevasse at the head of a glacier. Also called: **rimaye.** [C19: German: mountain crack]

Bergson ('bɜːgsᵊn; *French* bɛrksɔn) *n* **Henri Louis** (ɑ̃ri lwi). 1859–1941, French philosopher, who sought to bridge the gap between metaphysics and science. His main works are *Memory and Matter* (1896, trans. 1911) and *Creative Evolution* (1907, trans. 1911): Nobel prize for literature 1927. ▸ **Bergsonian** (bɜːg'səʊnɪən) *adj, n*

Bergsonism ('bɜːgsəˌnɪzəm) *n* the philosophy of Bergson, which emphasizes duration as the basic element of experience and asserts the existence of a life-giving force that permeates the entire natural order. Compare **élan vital.**

Bergström (*Swedish* 'bærjstrøm) *n* **Sune.** born 1916, Swedish biochemist; shared the Nobel prize for medicine and physiology (1982) for work on prostaglandin.

berg wind *n* a hot dry wind in South Africa blowing from the plateau down to the coast.

Beria ('bɛrɪə; *Russian* 'bjerijə) *n* **Lavrenti Pavlovich** (la'vrjentij 'pavləvitʃ). 1899–1953, Soviet chief of secret police; killed by his associates shortly after Stalin's death.

beriberi (ˌbɛrɪ'bɛrɪ) *n* a disease, endemic in E and S Asia, caused by dietary deficiency of thiamine (vitamin B_1). It affects the nerves to the limbs, producing pain, paralysis, and swelling. [C19: from Sinhalese, by reduplication from *beri* weakness]

Bering *or* **Behring** ('bɛrɪŋ, 'bɛər-; *Danish* 'beːreŋ) *n* **Vitus** ('viːtus). 1681–1741, Danish navigator, who explored the N Pacific for the Russians and discovered Bering Island and the Bering Strait.

Bering Sea *n* a part of the N Pacific Ocean, between NE Siberia and Alaska. Area: about 2 275 000 sq. km (878 000 sq. miles).

Bering Strait *n* a strait between Alaska and Russia, connecting the Bering Sea and the Arctic Ocean.

Berio (*Italian* 'berjo) *n* **Luciano** (lu'tʃano). 1925–98, Italian composer, living in the U.S., noted esp. for works that exploit instrumental and vocal timbre and technique.

Beriosova (bɛrɪ'əʊsəvə) *n* **Svetlana** (svɪt'lanə). 1932–98, British ballet dancer, born in Lithuania.

berk *or* **burk** (bɜːk) *n Brit. slang.* a stupid person; fool. [C20: shortened from *Berkeley* or *Berkshire Hunt,* rhyming slang for *cunt*]

Berkeleian (bɑː'klɪən) *adj* **1** denoting or relating to the philosophy of George Berkeley. ◆ *n* **2** a follower of his teachings.

Berkeleianism (bɑː'klɪəˌnɪzəm) *n* the philosophical system of George Berkeley, holding that objects exist only when perceived, that God's perception sustains the universe, and that there is no independent substratum or substance in which these perceptions inhere.

Berkeley[1] ('bɜːklɪ) *n* a city in W California, on San Francisco Bay: seat of the University of California. Pop.: 103 243 (1996 est.).

Berkeley[2] *n* **1** ('bɜːklɪ). **Busby.** real name *William Berkeley Enos.* 1895–1976, U.S. dance director, noted esp. for his elaborate choreography in film musicals. **2** ('bɑːklɪ). **George.** 1685–1753, Irish philosopher and Anglican bishop, whose system of subjective idealism was expounded in his works *A Treatise concerning the Principles of Human Knowledge* (1710) and *Three Dialogues between Hylas and Philonous* (1713). He also wrote *Essay towards a New Theory of Vision* (1709). **3** ('bɑːklɪ). Sir **Lennox** (**Randal Francis**). 1903–89, British composer; his works include four symphonies, four operas, and the *Serenade for Strings* (1939).

Berkeley Castle ('bɑːklɪ) *n* a castle in Gloucestershire: scene of the murder of Edward II in 1327.

berkelium (bɜː'kiːlɪəm, 'bɜːklɪəm) *n* a metallic transuranic element produced by bombardment of americium. Symbol: Bk; atomic no.: 97; half-life of most stable isotope, ^{247}Bk: 1400 years; valency: 3 or 4; relative density: 14 (est.). [C20: named after BERKELEY[1], where it was discovered]

Berks (bɑːks) *abbrev. for* Berkshire.

Berkshire ('bɑːkʃɪə, -ʃə) *n* **1** a historic county of S England: the River Thames marks the N boundary and the **Berkshire Downs** occupy central parts; the county council was replaced by six unitary authorities in 1998. Area: 1259 sq. km (486 sq. miles). Abbrev.: **Berks. 2** a breed of pork and bacon pig having a black body and white points.

berley *or* **burley** ('bɜlɪ) *Austral.* ◆ *n* **1** bait scattered on water to attract fish. **2** *Slang.* rubbish; nonsense. ◆ *vb (tr)* **3** to scatter (bait) on water. **4** to hurry (someone); urge on. [origin unknown]

Berlichingen (*German* 'bɛrlɪçɪŋən) *n* **Götz von** (gœts fɔn), called *the Iron Hand.* 1480–1562, German warrior knight, who robbed merchants and kidnapped nobles for ransom.

berlin (bə'lɪn, 'bɜːlɪn) *n* **1** (*sometimes cap.*) Also called: **berlin wool.** a fine wool yarn used for tapestry work, etc. **2** a four-wheeled two-seated covered carriage, popular in the 18th century. **3** a limousine with a glass partition between the front and rear seats. ◆ Also called (for senses 2, 3): **berline** (bə'liːn,'bɜːliːn). [C18: named after BERLIN[1]]

Berlin[1] (bɜː'lɪn; *German* bɛr'liːn) *n* the capital of Germany (1871–1945 and from 1990), formerly divided (1945–90) into the eastern sector, capital of East Germany, and the western sectors, which formed an exclave in East German territory closely affiliated with West Germany: a wall dividing the sectors was built in 1961 by the East German authorities to stop the flow of refugees from east to west; demolition of the wall began in 1989 and the city was formally reunited in 1990: formerly (1618–1871) the capital of Brandenburg and Prussia. Pop.: 3 471 418 (1996 est.). ▸ **Ber'liner** *n*

Berlin[2] (bɜː'lɪn) *n* **1 Irving.** original name *Israel Baline,* 1888–1989, U.S. composer and writer of lyrics, born in Russia. His musical comedies include *Annie Get Your Gun* (1946); his most popular song is *White Christmas.* **2** Sir **Isaiah.** 1909–97, British philosopher, born in Latvia, historian, and diplomat. His books include *Historical Inevitability* (1954) and *The Magus of the North* (1993).

Berlioz ('bεəlɪˌəʊz; *French* bεrljoz) *n* **Hector (Louis)** (εktɔr). 1803–69, French composer, regarded as a pioneer of modern orchestration. His works include the cantata *La Damnation de Faust* (1846), the operas *Les Troyens* (1856–59) and *Béatrice et Bénédict* (1860–62), the *Symphonie fantastique* (1830), and the oratorio *L'Enfance du Christ* (1854).

berm *or* **berme** (bɜːm) *n* **1** a narrow path or ledge at the edge of a slope, road, or canal. **2** *N.Z.* the grass verge of a suburban street, usually kept mown. **3** *Fortifications.* a narrow path or ledge between a moat and a rampart. **4** *Military.* a man-made ridge of sand, designed as an obstacle to tanks, which, in crossing it, have to expose their vulnerable underparts. [C18: from French *berme,* from Dutch *berm,* probably from Old Norse *barmr* BRIM]

Bermejo (*Spanish* ber'mexo) *n* a river in Argentina, rising in the northwest and flowing southeast to the Paraguay River. Length: about 1600 km (1000 miles).

Bermuda (bə'mjuːdə) *n* a UK Overseas Territory consisting of a group of over 150 coral islands (**the Bermudas**) in the NW Atlantic: discovered in about 1503, colonized by the British by 1612, although not acquired by the British crown until 1684. Capital: Hamilton. Pop.: 62 100 (1998 est.). Area: 53 sq. km (20 sq. miles). ▸ **Ber'mudian** *n, adj*

Bermuda grass *n* a widely distributed grass, *Cynodon dactylon,* with wiry creeping rootstocks and several purplish spikes of flowers arising from a single point: used for lawns, pasturage, binding sand dunes, etc. Also called: **scutch grass, wire grass.**

Bermuda rig *n* a fore-and-aft sailing boat rig characterized by a tall mainsail (**Bermudian mainsail**) that tapers to a point. ▸ **Ber'muda-'rigged** *adj*

Bermuda shorts *pl n* close-fitting shorts that come down to the knees. Also called: **Ber'mudas.**

Bermuda Triangle *n* an area in the Atlantic Ocean bounded by Bermuda, Puerto Rico, and Florida where ships and aeroplanes are alleged to have disappeared mysteriously.

Bern (bɜːn; *German* bεrn) *n* **1** the capital of Switzerland, in the W part, on the Aar River: entered the Swiss confederation in 1353 and became the capital in 1848. Pop.: 127 469 (1996 est.). **2** a canton of Switzerland, between the French frontier and the Bernese Alps. Capital: Bern. Pop.: 941 952 (1996 est.). Area: 6884 sq. km (2658 sq. miles). French name: **Berne** (bεrn).

Bernadette of Lourdes (ˌbɜːnə'dεt) *n* **Saint.** original name *Marie Bernarde Soubirous.* 1844–79, French peasant girl born in Lourdes, whose visions of the Virgin Mary led to the establishment of Lourdes as a centre of pilgrimage, esp. for the sick or crippled. Feast day: Feb. 18.

Bernadotte *n* **1** (*Swedish* 'bεrnadɔt). **Folke** ('fɔlke), Count. 1895–1948, Swedish diplomat, noted for his work with the Red Cross during World War II and as United Nations mediator in Palestine (1948). He was assassinated by Jewish terrorists. **2** ('bɜːnəˌdɒt; *French* bεrnadɔt). **Jean Baptiste Jules** (ʒɑ̃ batist ʒyl). 1764–1844, French marshal under Napoleon; king of Norway and Sweden (1818–44) as Charles XIV.

Bernanos (*French* bεrnanos) *n* **Georges** (ʒɔrʒ). 1888–1948, French novelist and Roman Catholic pamphleteer, best known for *The Diary of a Country Priest* (1936).

Bernard *n* **1** (*French* bεrnar). **Claude** (klod). 1813–78, French physiologist, noted for his research on the action of secretions of the alimentary canal and the glycogenic function of the liver. **2** ('bɜːnəd). **Saint,** known as *Bernard of Menthon* and the *Apostle of the Alps.* 923–1008, French monk who founded hospices in the Alpine passes. Feast day: Aug. 20.

Bernardine ('bɜːnədɪn, -ˌdiːn) *n* **1** a monk of one of the reformed and stricter branches of the Cistercian order. ◆ *adj* **2a** of or relating to this branch of the Cistercians. **2b** of or relating to Saint Bernard of Clairvaux.

Bernard of Clairvaux *n* **Saint.** ?1090–1153, French abbot and theologian, who founded the stricter branch of the Cistercians in 1115.

Berners-Lee ('bɜːnəz 'liː) *n* **Tim.** born 1955, British computer scientist who created the World Wide Web.

Bernese Alps *or* **Oberland** ('bɜːniːz) *n* a mountain range in SW Switzerland, the N central part of the Alps. Highest peak: Finsteraarhorn, 4274 m (14 022 ft.).

Bernhardt ('bɜːnhɑːt; *French* bεrnar) *n* **Sarah.** original name *Rosine Bernard.* 1844–1923, French actress, regarded as one of the greatest tragic actresses of all time.

bernicle goose ('bɜːnɪkᵊl) *n* a former name for the **brent goose** or **barnacle goose.**

Bernina (bə'niːnə; *Italian* ber'nina) *n* **Piz.** a mountain in SE Switzerland, the highest peak of the **Bernina Alps,** in the S Rhaetian Alps. Height: 4049 m (13 284 ft.).

Bernina Pass *n* a pass in the Alps between SE Switzerland and N Italy, east of Piz Bernina. Height: 2323 m (7622 ft.).

Bernini (*Italian* ber'nini) *n* **Gian Lorenzo** (dʒan lo'rεntso). 1598–1680, Italian painter, architect, and sculptor: the greatest exponent of the Italian baroque.

Bernoulli *or* **Bernouilli** (*French* bεrnuji; *German* bεr'nʊli) *n* **1 Daniel** (danjεl), son of Jean Bernoulli. 1700–82, Swiss mathematician and physicist, who developed an early form of the kinetic theory of gases and stated the principle of conservation of energy in fluid dynamics. **2 Jacques** (ʒɑk) *or* **Jakob** ('jaːkɔp). 1654–1705, Swiss mathematician, noted for his work on calculus and the theory of probability. **3** his brother, **Jean** (ʒɑ̃) *or* **Johann** (jo'han). 1667–1748, Swiss mathematician who developed the calculus of variations.

Bernoulli's principle *or* **law** *n Physics.* the principle that in a liquid flowing through a pipe the pressure difference that accelerates the flow when the bore changes is equal to the product of half the density times the change of the square of the speed, provided friction is negligible. [C19: named after Daniel BERNOULLI]

Bernoulli trial *n Statistics.* one of a sequence of independent experiments each of which has the same probability of success, such as successive throws of a die, the outcome of which is described by a binomial distribution. See also **binomial experiment.** [named after Jacques BERNOULLI]

Bernstein ('bɜːnstaɪn, -stiːn) *n* **Leonard.** 1918–90, U.S. conductor and composer, whose works include *The Age of Anxiety* (1949), the score of the musical *West Side Story* (1957), and *Mass* (1971).

berretta (bɪ'rεtə) *n* a variant spelling of **biretta.**

berry ('bεrɪ) *n, pl* **-ries. 1** any of various small edible fruits such as the blackberry and strawberry. **2** *Botany.* an indehiscent fruit with two or more seeds and a fleshy pericarp, such as the grape or gooseberry. **3** any of various seeds or dried kernels, such as a coffee bean. **4** the egg of a lobster, crayfish, or similar animal. ◆ *vb* **-ries, -rying, -ried.** (*intr*) **5** to bear or produce berries. **6** to gather or look for berries. [Old English *berie;* related to Old High German *beri,* Dutch *bezie*] ▸ **'berried** *adj*

Berry *n* **1** ('bεrɪ). **Chuck,** full name *Charles Edward Berry.* born 1926, U.S. rock-and-roll guitarist, singer, and songwriter. His frequently covered songs include "Maybellene" (1955), "Roll over Beethoven" (1956), "Johnny B. Goode" (1958), "Memphis, Tennessee" (1959), and "Promised Land" (1964). **2** (*French* bεri). **Jean de France** (ʒɑ̃ də frɑ̃s), Duc de. 1340–1416, French prince, son of King John II; coregent (1380–88) for Charles VI and a famous patron of the arts.

Berryman ('bεrɪmən) *n* **John.** 1914–72, U.S. poet and critic, author of *Homage to Mistress Bradstreet* (1956) and *Dream Songs* (1964–68).

bersagliere (ˌbεəsɑː'ljεərɪ) *n, pl* **-ri** (-riː). a member of a rifle regiment in the Italian Army. [C19: from Italian, from *bersaglio* target, from Old French *bersail,* from *berser* to fire at]

berseem (bɜː'siːm) *n* a Mediterranean clover, *Trifolium alexandrinum,* grown as a forage crop and to improve the soil in the southwestern U.S. and the Nile valley. Also called: **Egyptian clover.** [C20: from Arabic *barsīm,* from Coptic *bersīm*]

berserk (bə'zɜːk, -'sɜːk) *adj* **1** frenziedly violent or destructive (esp. in the phrase **go berserk**). ◆ *n* **2** Also called: **berserker.** a member of a class of ancient Norse warriors who worked themselves into a frenzy before battle and fought with insane fury and courage. [C19: Icelandic *berserkr,* from *björn* bear + *serkr* shirt]

berth (bɜːθ) *n* **1** a bed or bunk in a vessel or train, usually narrow and fixed to a wall. **2** *Nautical.* a place assigned to a ship at a mooring. **3** *Nautical.* sufficient distance from the shore or from other ships or objects for a ship to manoeuvre. **4 give a wide berth to.** to keep clear of; avoid. **5** *Nautical.* accommodation on a ship. **6** *Informal.* a job, esp. as a member of a ship's crew. ◆ *vb* **7** (*tr*) *Nautical.* to assign a berth to (a vessel). **8** *Nautical.* to dock (a vessel). **9** (*tr*) to provide with a sleeping place, as on a vessel or train. **10** (*intr*) *Nautical.* to pick up a mooring in an anchorage. [C17: probably from BEAR[1] + -TH[1]]

bertha ('bɜːθə) *n* a wide deep capelike collar, often of lace, usually to cover up a low neckline. [C19: from French *berthe,* from *Berthe,* 8th-century Frankish queen, mother of Charlemagne]

Bertillon system ('bɜːtɪˌlɒn; *French* bεrtijɔ̃) *n* a system formerly in use for identifying persons, esp. criminals, by means of a detailed record of physical characteristics. [C19: named after Alphonse *Bertillon* (1853–1914), French criminal investigator]

Bertolucci (*Italian* berto'luttʃi) *n* **Bernardo** (ber'nardo). born 1940, Italian film director: his films include *The Spider's Stratagem* (1970), *The Conformist* (1970), *1900* (1976), *The Last Emperor* (1987), *The Sheltering Sky* (1990), and *Besieged* (1999).

Berwick ('bεrɪk) *n* **James Fitzjames,** Duke of Berwick. 1670–1734, marshal of France and illegitimate son of James II of England. He led French forces during the War of the Spanish Succession (1701–14).

Berwickshire ('bεrɪkˌʃɪə, -ʃə) *n* (until 1975) a county of SE Scotland: part of the Borders region from 1975 to 1996, now part of Scottish Borders council area.

Berwick-upon-Tweed (twiːd) *n* a town in N England, in N Northumberland at the mouth of the Tweed: much involved in border disputes between England and Scotland between the 12th and 16th centuries; neutral territory 1551–1885. Pop.: 13 544 (1991). Also called: **Berwick.**

beryl ('bεrɪl) *n* a white, blue, yellow, green, or pink mineral, found in coarse granites and igneous rocks. It is a source of beryllium and used as a gemstone; the green variety is emerald, the blue is aquamarine. Composition: beryllium aluminium silicate. Formula: $Be_3Al_2Si_6O_{18}$. Crystal structure: hexagonal. [C13: from Old French, from Latin *bēryllus,* from Greek *bērullos,* of Indic origin] ▸ **'beryline** *adj*

beryllium (bε'rɪlɪəm) *n* a corrosion-resistant toxic silvery-white metallic element that occurs chiefly in beryl and is used mainly in X-ray windows and in the manufacture of alloys. Symbol: Be; atomic no.: 4; atomic wt.: 9.012; valency: 2; relative density: 1.848; melting pt.: 1289°C; boiling pt.: 2472°C. Former names: **glucinum, glucinium.** [C19: from Latin *bēryllus,* from Greek *bērullos*]

Berzelius (bə'ziːlɪəs; *Swedish* bær'seːlius) *n* Baron **Jöns Jakob** ('jœns 'jɑːkɔp). 1779–1848, Swedish chemist, who invented the present system of chemical symbols and formulas, discovered several elements, and determined the atomic and molecular weight of many substances.

Bes (bɛs) *n* an ancient Egyptian god represented as a grotesque hairy dwarf: the patron of music and pleasure.

Besançon (*French* bəzɑ̃sɔ̃) *n* a city in E France, on the Doubs River: university (1422). Pop.: 119 194 (1990).

Besant ('bɛzᵊnt, bɪ'zænt) *n* **Annie,** *née* **Wood.** 1847–1933, British theosophist, writer, and political reformer in England and India.

beseech (bɪ'si:tʃ) *vb* **-seeches, -seeching, -sought** *or* **-seeched.** (*tr*) to ask (someone) earnestly (to do something *or* for something); beg. [C12: see BE-, SEEK; related to Old Frisian *besēka*] ▸ **be'seecher** *n* ▸ **be'seeching** *adj* ▸ **be'seechingly** *adv*

beseem (bɪ'si:m) *vb Archaic.* to be suitable for; befit.

beset (bɪ'sɛt) *vb* **-sets, -setting, -set.** (*tr*) **1** (esp. of dangers, temptations, or difficulties) to trouble or harass constantly. **2** to surround or attack from all sides. **3** *Archaic.* to cover with, esp. with jewels. ▸ **be'setter** *n*

besetting (bɪ'sɛtɪŋ) *adj* tempting, harassing, or assailing (esp. in the phrase **besetting sin**).

beshrew (bɪ'ʃru:) *vb* (*tr*) *Archaic.* to wish evil on; curse (used in mild oaths such as **beshrew me**). [C14: see BE-, SHREW]

beside (bɪ'saɪd) *prep* **1** next to; at, by, or to the side of. **2** as compared with. **3** away from; wide of: *beside the point.* **4** *Archaic.* besides. **5 beside oneself.** (*postpositive;* often foll. by *with*) overwhelmed; overwrought: *beside oneself with grief.* ◆ *adv* **6** at, by, to, or along the side of something or someone. [Old English *be sīdan;* see BY, SIDE]

besides (bɪ'saɪdz) *prep* **1** apart from; even considering: *besides costing too much, the scheme is impractical.* ◆ *sentence connector.* **2** anyway; moreover. ◆ *adv* **3** as well.

besiege (bɪ'si:dʒ) *vb* (*tr*) **1** to surround (a fortified area, esp. a city) with military forces to bring about its surrender. **2** to crowd round; hem in. **3** to overwhelm, as with requests or queries. ▸ **be'sieger** *n*

besmear (bɪ'smɪə) *vb* (*tr*) **1** to smear over; daub. **2** to sully; defile (often in the phrase **besmear (a person's) reputation**).

besmirch (bɪ'smɜ:tʃ) *vb* (*tr*) **1** to make dirty; soil. **2** to reduce the brightness or lustre of. **3** to sully (often in the phrase **besmirch (a person's) name**).

besom[1] ('bi:zəm) *n* **1** a broom, esp. one made of a bundle of twigs tied to a handle. **2** *Curling.* a broom or brush used to sweep the ice in front of the stone to make it slide farther. ◆ *vb* (*tr*) **3** to sweep with a besom. [Old English *besma;* related to Old High German *besmo* broom]

besom[2] ('bɪzəm, 'bizəm) *n Scot. and northern English dialect.* a derogatory term for a **woman.** [perhaps from Old English *bysen* example; related to Old Norse *bysn* wonder]

besotted (bɪ'sɒtɪd) *adj* **1** stupefied with drink; intoxicated. **2** infatuated; doting. **3** foolish; muddled.

besought (bɪ'sɔ:t) *vb* the past tense and past participle of **beseech.**

bespangle (bɪ'spæŋgᵊl) *vb* (*tr*) to cover or adorn with or as if with spangles.

bespatter (bɪ'spætə) *vb* (*tr*) **1** to splash all over, as with dirty water. **2** to defile; slander; besmirch.

bespeak (bɪ'spi:k) *vb* **-speaks, -speaking, -spoke; -spoken** *or* **-spoke.** (*tr*) **1** to engage, request, or ask for in advance. **2** to indicate or suggest: *this act bespeaks kindness.* **3** *Poetic.* to speak to; address. **4** *Archaic.* to foretell.

bespectacled (bɪ'spɛktəkᵊld) *adj* wearing spectacles.

bespoke (bɪ'spəʊk) *adj Chiefly Brit.* **1** (esp. of a suit, jacket, etc.) made to the customer's specifications. **2** making or selling such suits, jackets, etc.: *a bespoke tailor.*

bespread (bɪ'sprɛd) *vb* **-spreads, -spreading, -spread.** (*tr*) to cover (a surface) with something.

besprent (bɪ'sprɛnt) *adj Poetic.* sprinkled over. [C14: past participle of Old English *besprengan* to BESPRINKLE]

besprinkle (bɪ'sprɪŋkᵊl) *vb* (*tr*) to sprinkle all over with liquid, powder, etc.

Bessarabia (ˌbɛsə'reɪbɪə) *n* a region in E Europe, mostly in Moldova and the Ukraine: long disputed by the Turks and Russians; a province of Romania from 1918 until 1940. Area: about 44 300 sq. km (17 100 sq. miles).

Bessel ('bɛsᵊl) *n* **Friedrich Wilhelm** ('fri:drɪç'vɪlhɛlm). 1784–1846, German astronomer and mathematician. He made the first authenticated measurement of a star's distance (1841) and systematized a series of mathematical functions used in physics.

Bessemer converter ('bɛsɪmə) *n* a refractory-lined furnace used to convert pig iron into steel by the Bessemer process.

Bessemer process *n* **1** (formerly) a process for producing steel by blowing air through molten pig iron at about 1250°C in a Bessemer converter: silicon, manganese, and phosphorus impurities are removed and the carbon content is controlled. **2** a similar process for removing sulphur and iron from copper matte. [C19: named after Sir Henry *Bessemer* (1813–98), English engineer]

best (bɛst) *adj* **1** the superlative of **good. 2** most excellent of a particular group, category, etc. **3** most suitable, advantageous, desirable, attractive, etc. **4 the best part of.** most of: *the best part of an hour.* **5 put one's best foot forward. 5a** to do one's utmost to make progress. **5b** to hurry. ◆ *adv* **6** the superlative of **well. 7** in a manner surpassing all others; most excellently, advantageously, attractively, etc. **8** (*in combination*) in or to the greatest degree or extent; most: *the best-loved hero.* **9 as best one can** *or* **may.** as effectively as possible within one's limitations. **10 had best.** would be wise, sensible, etc., to: *you had best go now.* ◆ *n* **11 the best.** the most outstanding or excellent person, thing, or group in a category. **12** (often preceded by *at*) the most excellent, pleasing, or skilled quality or condition: *journalism at its best.* **13** the most effective effort of which a person or group is capable: *even their best was inadequate.* **14** a winning majority: *the best of three games.* **15** Also: **all the best.** best wishes: *she sent him her best.* **16** a person's smartest outfit of clothing. **17 at best. 17a** in the most favourable interpretation. **17b** under the most favourable conditions. **18 for the best. 18a** for an ultimately good outcome. **18b** with good intentions: *he meant it for the best.* **19 get** *or* **have the best of.** to surpass, defeat, or outwit; better. **20 give (someone) the best.** to concede (someone's) superiority. **21 make the best of.** to cope as well as possible in the unfavourable circumstances of (often in the phrases **make the best of a bad job, make the best of it**). **22 six of the best.** *Informal.* six strokes with a cane on the buttocks or hand. ◆ *vb* **23** (*tr*) to gain the advantage over or defeat. [Old English *betst;* related to Gothic *batista,* Old High German *bezzist*]

Best (bɛst) *n* **1 Charles Herbert.** 1899–1978, Canadian physiologist: associated with Banting and Macleod in their discovery of insulin in 1922. **2 George.** born 1946, Northern Ireland footballer.

best-ball *adj Golf.* of, relating to, or denoting a match in which one player competes against the best individual totals of two or more other players at each hole.

best boy *n Chiefly U.S.* the assistant to the senior electrician or to the key grip in a film crew.

best end *n* the end of the neck of lamb, pork, etc., nearest to the ribs.

best girl *n Archaic.* one's sweetheart.

bestial ('bɛstɪəl) *adj* **1** brutal or savage. **2** sexually depraved; carnal. **3** lacking in refinement; brutish. **4** of or relating to a beast. [C14: from Late Latin *bestiālis,* from Latin *bestia* BEAST] ▸ **'bestially** *adv*

bestiality (ˌbɛstɪ'ælɪtɪ) *n, pl* **-ties. 1** bestial behaviour, character, or action. **2** sexual activity between a person and an animal.

bestialize *or* **bestialise** ('bɛstɪəˌlaɪz) *vb* (*tr*) to make bestial or brutal.

bestiary ('bɛstɪərɪ) *n, pl* **-aries.** a moralizing medieval collection of descriptions of real and/or mythical animals.

bestir (bɪ'stɜ:) *vb* **-stirs, -stirring, -stirred.** (*tr*) to cause (oneself, or, rarely, another person) to become active; rouse.

best man *n* the (male) attendant of the bridegroom at a wedding.

bestow (bɪ'stəʊ) *vb* (*tr*) **1** to present (a gift) or confer (an award or honour). **2** *Archaic.* to apply (energy, resources, etc.). **3** *Archaic.* to house (a person) or store (goods). ▸ **be'stowal** *or* **be'stowment** *n* ▸ **be'stower** *n*

bestrew (bɪ'stru:) *vb* **-strews, -strewing, -strewed; -strewn** *or* **-strewed.** (*tr*) to scatter or lie scattered over (a surface).

bestride (bɪ'straɪd) *vb* **-strides, -striding, -strode** *or* (*Archaic*) **-strid; -stridden** *or* (*Archaic*) **-strid.** (*tr*) **1** to have or put a leg on either side of. **2** to extend across; span. **3** to stride over or across.

bestseller (ˌbɛst'sɛlə) *n* **1** a book, record, CD, or other product that has sold in great numbers, esp. over a short period. **2** the author of one or more such books, etc. ▸ **ˌbest'selling** *adj*

bet (bɛt) *n* **1** an agreement between two parties that a sum of money or other stake will be paid by the loser to the party who correctly predicts the outcome of an event. **2** the money or stake risked. **3** the predicted result in such an agreement: *his bet was that the horse would win.* **4** a person, event, etc., considered as likely to succeed or occur: *it's a good bet that they will succeed.* **5** a course of action (esp. in the phrase **one's best bet**). **6** *Informal.* an opinion; view: *my bet is that you've been up to no good.* ◆ *vb* **bets, betting, bet** *or* **betted. 7** (when *intr* foll. by *on* or *against*) to make or place a bet with (a person or persons). **8** (*tr*) to stake (money, etc.) in a bet. **9** (*tr; may take a clause as object*) *Informal.* to predict (a certain outcome): *I bet she fails.* **10 you bet.** *Informal.* of course; naturally. [C16: probably short for ABET]

bet. *abbrev. for* between.

beta ('bi:tə) *n* **1** the second letter in the Greek alphabet (Β or β), a consonant, transliterated as *b.* **2** the second highest grade or mark, as in an examination. **3** (*modifier*) **3a** involving or relating to electrons: *beta emitter.* **3b** relating to one of two or more allotropes or crystal structures of a solid: *beta iron.* **3c** relating to one of two or more isomeric forms of a chemical compound. [from Greek *bēta,* from Hebrew; see BETH]

Beta ('bi:tə) *n* (*foll. by the genitive case of a specified constellation*) a star in a constellation, usually the second brightest: *Beta Persei.*

beta-blocker *n* any of a class of drugs, such as propranolol, that inhibit the activity of the nerves that stimulate secretions of adrenaline and that therefore decrease the activity of the heart: used in the treatment of high blood pressure and angina pectoris.

betacarotene (ˌbi:tə'kærəˌti:n) *n* the most important form of the plant pigment carotene, which occurs in milk, vegetables, and other foods and, when eaten by man and animals, is converted in the body to vitamin A.

betacyanin (ˌbi:tə'saɪənɪn) *n* any one of a group of red nitrogenous pigments found in certain plants, such as beetroot.

beta decay *n* the radioactive transformation of an atomic nucleus accompanying the emission of an electron. It involves unit change of atomic number but none in mass number. Also called: **beta transformation** *or* **process.**

beta globulin *n* another name for **transferrin.**

betaine ('bi:təˌi:n, -ɪn, bɪ'teɪi:n, -ɪn) *n* **1** a sweet-tasting alkaloid that occurs in the sugar beet and other plants and in animals. Formula: $C_5H_{11}NO_2$. **2** (*pl*) a group of chemical compounds that resemble betaine and are slightly basic zwitterions. [C19: from New Latin *Bēta* beet + -INE[2]]

beta iron *n* a nonmagnetic allotrope of pure iron stable between 770°C and 910°C.

betake (bɪ'teɪk) *vb* **-takes, -taking, -took, -taken.** (*tr*) **1 betake oneself.** to go; move. **2** *Archaic.* to apply (oneself) to.

beta particle *n* a high-speed electron or positron emitted by a nucleus during radioactive decay or nuclear fission.

beta ray *n* a stream of beta particles.

beta rhythm *or* **wave** *n Physiol.* the normal electrical activity of the cerebral cortex, occurring at a frequency of 13 to 30 hertz and detectable with an electroencephalograph. See also **brain wave.**

beta stock *n* any of the second rank of active securities on the Stock Exchange, of which there are about 500. Continuous display of prices by market makers is required but not immediate publication of transactions.

beta-test *n* **1** a test of a new or modified piece of computer software by customers who volunteer to do so. ◆ *vb (tr)* **2** to test (software) in this way. Compare **alpha-test.**

betatopic (ˌbiːtəˈtɒpɪk) *adj* (of atoms) differing in proton number by one, theoretically as a result of emission of a beta particle.

betatron (ˈbiːtəˌtrɒn) *n* a type of particle accelerator for producing high-energy beams of electrons, having an alternating magnetic field to keep the electrons in a circular orbit of fixed radius and accelerate them by magnetic induction. It produces energies of up to about 300 MeV.

betel (ˈbiːtᵊl) *n* an Asian piperaceous climbing plant, *Piper betle,* the leaves of which are chewed, with the betel nut, by the peoples of SE Asia. [C16: from Portuguese, from Malayalam *vettila*]

Betelgeuse *or* **Betelgeux** (ˌbiːtᵊlˈdʒɜːz, ˈbiːtᵊlˌdʒɜːz) *n* a very remote luminous red supergiant, Alpha Orionis: the second brightest star in the constellation Orion. It is a variable star. [C18: from French, from Arabic *bīt al-jauzā',* literally: shoulder of the giant, that is, of Orion]

betel nut *n* the seed of the betel palm, chewed with betel leaves and lime by people in S and SE Asia as a digestive stimulant and narcotic.

betel palm *n* a tropical Asian feather palm, *Areca catechu,* with scarlet or orange fruits. See **betel nut.**

bête noire *French.* (bɛt nwar) *n, pl* ***bêtes noires*** (bɛt nwar) a person or thing that one particularly dislikes or dreads. [literally: black beast]

beth (bɛt) *n* the second letter of the Hebrew alphabet (ב) transliterated as *b.* [from Hebrew *bēth-, bayith* house]

Bethany (ˈbɛθənɪ) *n* a village in the West Bank, near Jerusalem at the foot of the Mount of Olives: in the New Testament, the home of Lazarus and the lodging place of Jesus during Holy Week.

Beth Din *or* **Bet Din** (bɛθ dɪn; *Hebrew* bet din) *n Judaism.* a rabbinical court, consisting of at least three dayanim, and having authority over such matters as divorce and conversion and other communal ecclesiastical matters such as Kashruth. It may also try civil disputes with the consent of both parties. [from Hebrew, literally: house of judgment]

Bethe (ˈbeɪtə) *n* **Hans Albrecht** (hans ˈalbrɛçt). born 1906, U.S. physicist, born in Germany; noted for his research on astrophysics and nuclear physics: Nobel prize for physics 1967.

Bethel (ˈbɛθəl) *n* **1** an ancient town in the West Bank, near Jerusalem: in the Old Testament, the place where the dream of Jacob occurred (Genesis 28:19). **2** a chapel of any of certain Nonconformist Christian sects. **3** a seamen's chapel. [C17: from Hebrew *bēth 'Ēl* house of God]

Bethesda (bəˈθɛzdə) *n* **1** *New Testament.* a pool in Jerusalem reputed to have healing powers, where a paralytic was healed by Jesus (John 5:2). **2** a chapel of any of certain Nonconformist Christian sects.

bethink (bɪˈθɪŋk) *vb* **-thinks, -thinking, -thought.** *Archaic or dialect.* **1** to cause (oneself) to consider or meditate. **2** *(tr; often foll. by of)* to remind (oneself).

Bethlehem (ˈbɛθlɪˌhɛm, -lɪəm) *n* a town in the West Bank, near Jerusalem: birthplace of Jesus and early home of King David.

Bethmann Hollweg (*German* ˈbeːtman ˈhɔlveːk) *n* **Theobald von** (ˈteːobalt fɔn). 1856–1921, chancellor of Germany (1909–17).

bethought (bɪˈθɔːt) *vb* the past tense and past participle of **bethink.**

Bethsaida (bɛθˈseɪdə) *n* a ruined town in N Israel, near the N shore of the Sea of Galilee.

betide (bɪˈtaɪd) *vb* to happen or happen to; befall (often in the phrase **woe betide (someone)**). [C13: see BE-, TIDE[2]]

betimes (bɪˈtaɪmz) *adv Archaic.* **1** in good time; early. **2** in a short time; soon. [C14 *bitimes;* see BY, TIME]

bêtise (bɛˈtiːz) *n Rare.* folly or lack of perception. [French, from *bête* foolish, from *bête* (n) stupid person, BEAST]

Betjeman (ˈbɛtʃəmən) *n* Sir **John.** 1906–84, English poet, noted for his nostalgic and humorous verse and essays and for his concern for the preservation of historic buildings, esp. of the Victorian era. Poet laureate (1972–84).

betoken (bɪˈtəʊkən) *vb (tr)* **1** to indicate; signify: *black clothes betoken mourning.* **2** to portend; augur.

betony (ˈbɛtənɪ) *n, pl* **-nies. 1** a Eurasian plant, *Betonica* (or *Stachys*) *officinalis,* with a spike of reddish-purple flowers, formerly used in medicine and dyeing: family *Labiatae* (labiates). **2** any of several related plants of the genus *Stachys.* **3 wood betony.** a North American scrophulariaceous plant, *Pedicularis canadensis.* See also **lousewort.** [C14: from Old French *betoine,* from Latin *betonica,* variant of *vettonica,* probably named after the *Vettones,* an ancient Iberian tribe]

betook (bɪˈtʊk) *vb* the past tense of **betake.**

betray (bɪˈtreɪ) *vb (tr)* **1** to aid an enemy of (one's nation, friend, etc.); be a traitor to: *to betray one's country.* **2** to hand over or expose (one's nation, friend, etc.) treacherously to an enemy. **3** to disclose (a secret, confidence, etc.) treacherously. **4** to break (a promise) or be disloyal to (a person's trust). **5** to disappoint the expectations of; fail: *his tired legs betrayed him.* **6** to show signs of; indicate: *if one taps china, the sound betrays any faults.* **7** to reveal unintentionally: *his grin betrayed his satisfaction.* **8 betray oneself.** to reveal one's true character, intentions, etc. **9** to lead astray; deceive. **10** *Euphemistic.* to seduce and then forsake (a woman). [C13: from BE- + *trayen,* from Old French *trair,* from Latin *trādere*] ▸ **be'trayal** *n* ▸ **be'trayer** *n*

betroth (bɪˈtrəʊð) *vb (tr) Archaic.* to promise to marry or to give in marriage. [C14 *betreuthen,* from BE- + *treuthe* TROTH, TRUTH]

betrothal (bɪˈtrəʊðəl) *n* **1** engagement to be married. **2** a mutual promise to marry.

betrothed (bɪˈtrəʊðd) *adj* **1** engaged to be married: *he was betrothed to her.* ◆ *n* **2** the person to whom one is engaged; fiancé or fiancée.

betta (ˈbɛtə) *n* another name for **fighting fish.** [C19: from New Latin, of unknown origin]

better[1] (ˈbɛtə) *adj* **1** the comparative of **good. 2** more excellent than other members of a particular group, category, etc. **3** more suitable, advantageous, attractive, etc. **4** improved in health. **5** fully recovered in health. **6 better off.** in more favourable circumstances, esp. financially. **7 the better part of.** a large part of: *the better part of a day.* ◆ *adv* **8** the comparative of **well. 9** in a more excellent manner; more advantageously, attractively, etc. **10** in or to a greater degree or extent; more: *she is better loved than her sister.* **11 go one better.** *(Brit. intr; U.S. tr)* to outdo (a person) or improve upon (someone else's effort). **12 had better.** would be wise, sensible, etc. to: *I had better be off.* **13 know better than to.** not to be so stupid as to. **14 think better of. 14a** to change one's course of action after reconsideration. **14b** to rate (a person) more highly. ◆ *n* **15 the better.** something that is the more excellent, useful, etc., of two such things. **16** *(usually pl)* a person who is superior, esp. in social standing or ability. **17 all the better for.** improved as a result of. **18 all the better to.** more suitable to. **19 for better for worse.** whatever the subsequent events or changes may be. **20 for the better.** by way of improvement: *a change for the better.* **21 get the better of.** to defeat, outwit, or surpass. **22 the better of.** *Irish.* having recovered from: *I'm not the better of it yet.* ◆ *vb* **23** to make or become better. **24** *(tr)* to improve upon; surpass. [Old English *betera;* related to Old Norse *betri,* Gothic *batiza,* Old High German *beziro*]

better[2] *or esp. U.S.* **bettor** (ˈbɛtə) *n* a person who bets.

better half *n Humorous.* one's spouse.

betterment (ˈbɛtəmənt) *n* **1** a change for the better; improvement. **2** *Property law.* an improvement effected on real property that enhances the value of the property.

Betti (*Italian* ˈbetti) *n* **Ugo** (ˈugo). 1892–1953, Italian writer, noted esp. for his plays, including *La Padrona* (1927), *Corruzione al palazzo di giustizia* (1949), and *La Regina e gli insorte* (1951).

betting shop *n* (in Britain) a licensed bookmaker's premises not on a racecourse.

bettong (bɛˈtɒŋ) *n* a species of rat kangaroo of Australia having a short nose. [C19: from a native Australian language]

betulaceous (ˌbɛtjʊˈleɪʃəs) *adj* of, relating to, or belonging to the *Betulaceae,* a family of mostly N temperate catkin-bearing trees and shrubs such as birch and alder, some species of which reach the northern limits of tree growth. [C19: from Latin *betula* birch]

between (bɪˈtwiːn) *prep* **1** at a point or in a region intermediate to two other points in space, times, degrees, etc. **2** in combination; together: *between them, they saved enough money to buy a car.* **3** confined or restricted to: *between you and me.* **4** indicating a reciprocal relation or comparison: *an argument between a man and his wife.* **5** indicating two or more alternatives: *a choice between going now and staying all night.* ◆ *adv also* **in between. 6** between one specified thing and another: *two houses with a garage between.* [Old English *betwēonum;* related to Gothic *tweihnai* two together; see TWO, TWAIN]

USAGE After *distribute* and words with a similar meaning, *among* should be used rather than *between: this enterprise issued shares which were distributed among its workers.*

between-subjects design *n (modifier) Statistics.* (of an experiment) concerned with measuring the value of the dependent variable for distinct and unrelated groups subjected to each of the experimental conditions. Compare **within-subjects design, matched-pairs design.**

betweentimes (bɪˈtwiːnˌtaɪmz) *or* **betweenwhiles** (bɪˈtwiːnˌwaɪlz) *adv* between other activities; during intervals.

betwixt (bɪˈtwɪkst) *prep, adv* **1** *Archaic.* another word for **between. 2 betwixt and between.** in an intermediate, indecisive, or middle position. [Old English *betwix;* related to Old High German *zwiski* two each]

Betws-y-Coed (ˌbɛtsɪˈkɔɪd) *n* a village in N Wales, in Conwy county borough, on the River Conwy: noted for its scenery. Pop.: 2860 (1991).

Beulah (ˈbjuːlə) *n Old Testament.* the land of Israel (Isaiah 62:4). [Hebrew, literally: married woman]

Beuthen (ˈbɔytən) *n* the German name for **Bytom.**

Beuys (*German* bɔis) *n* **Joseph** (ˈjoːzɛf). 1921–86, German artist, a celebrated figure of the avant-garde, noted esp. for his sculptures made of felt and animal fat.

BeV (in the U.S.) *abbrev. for* gigaelectronvolts (GeV). [C20: from *b(illion) e(lectron) v(olts)*]

Bevan (ˈbɛvən) *n* **Aneurin** (əˈnaɪᵊrɪn), known as *Nye.* 1897–1960, British Labour statesman, born in Wales: noted for his oratory. As minister of health (1945–51) he introduced the National Health Service (1948). ▸ **'Bevan,ite** *n, adj*

bevatron (ˈbɛvəˌtrɒn) *n* a proton synchrotron at the University of California. [C20: from BEV + -TRON]

bevel (ˈbɛvᵊl) *n* **1a** Also called: **cant.** a surface that meets another at an angle other than a right angle. Compare **chamfer** (sense 1). **1b** *(as modifier): a bevel edge; bevel square.* ◆ *vb* **-els, -elling, -elled** *or U.S.* **-els, -eling, -eled. 2** *(intr)* to be inclined; slope. **3** *(tr)* to cut a bevel on (a piece of timber, etc.). [C16: from Old French *bevel* (unattested), from *baïf,* from *baer* to gape; see BAY[1]] ▸ **'bevelled** *or U.S.* **'beveled** *adj* ▸ **'beveller** *or U.S.* **'beveler** *n*

bevel gear *n* a gear having teeth cut into a conical surface known as the pitch zone. Two such gears mesh together to transmit power between two shafts at an angle to each other.

bevel square *n* a woodworker's square with an adjustable arm that can be set to mark out an angle or to check the slope of a surface.

beverage ('bevərɪdʒ, 'bevrɪdʒ) *n* any drink, usually other than water. [C13: from Old French *bevrage,* from *beivre* to drink, from Latin *bibere*]

Beveridge ('bevərɪdʒ) *n* **William Henry,** 1st Baron Beveridge. 1879–1963, British economist, whose *Report on Social Insurance and Allied Services* (1942) formed the basis of social-security legislation in Britain.

Beverley ('bevəlɪ) *n* a market town in NE England, the administrative centre of the East Riding of Yorkshire. Pop.: 23 632 (1991).

Beverly Hills ('bevəlɪ) *n* a city in SW California, near Los Angeles: famous as the home of film stars. Pop.: 31 970 (1990).

Bevin ('bevɪn) *n* **Ernest.** 1881–1951, British Labour statesman and trade unionist, who was largely responsible for the creation of the Transport and General Workers' Union (1922): minister of labour (1940–45); foreign secretary (1945–51).

Bevin boy *n* (in Britain during World War II) a young man selected by ballot to work in a coal mine instead of doing conventional military service. [C20: named after Ernest BEVIN, who originated the scheme]

bevvy ('bevɪ) *Dialect.* ◆ *n, pl* **-vies. 1** a drink, esp. an alcoholic one: *we had a few bevvies last night.* **2** a session of drinking. ◆ *vb* **-vies, -vying, -vied.** (*intr*) **3** to drink alcohol. [probably from Old French *bevee, buvee* drinking] ▸ **'bevvied** *adj*

bevy ('bevɪ) *n, pl* **bevies. 1** a flock of quails. **2** a group, esp. of girls. **3** a group of roedeer. [C15: of uncertain origin]

bewail (bɪ'weɪl) *vb* to express great sorrow over (a person or thing); lament. ▸ **be'wailed** *adj* ▸ **be'wailer** *n* ▸ **be'wailing** *n, adj* ▸ **be'wailingly** *adv*

beware (bɪ'weə) *vb* (*usually used in the imperative or infinitive,* often foll. by *of*) to be cautious or wary (of); be on one's guard (against). [C13 *be war,* from BE (imperative) + *war* WARY]

bewhiskered (bɪ'wɪskəd) *adj* having whiskers on the cheeks.

Bewick ('bju:ɪk) *n* **Thomas.** 1753–1828, English wood engraver; his best-known works are *Chillingham Bull* (1789), a large woodcut, *Aesop's Fables* (1818), and his *History of British Birds* (1797–1804).

Bewick's swan *n* a white Old World swan, *Cygnus bewickii,* having a black bill with a small yellow base. [named after Thomas BEWICK]

bewilder (bɪ'wɪldə) *vb* (*tr*) **1** to confuse utterly; puzzle. **2** *Archaic.* to cause to become lost. [C17: see BE-, WILDER] ▸ **be'wildering** *adj* ▸ **be'wilderingly** *adv* ▸ **be'wilderment** *n*

bewitch (bɪ'wɪtʃ) *vb* (*tr*) **1** to attract and fascinate; enchant. **2** to cast a spell over. [C13 *bewicchen;* see BE-, WITCH] ▸ **be'witching** *adj* ▸ **be'witchingly** *adv*

bewray (bɪ'reɪ) *vb* (*tr*) an obsolete word for **betray.** [C13: from BE- + Old English *wrēgan* to accuse; related to Gothic *wrōhjan*] ▸ **be'wrayer** *n*

Bexhill(-on-Sea) (ˌbeks'hɪl) *n* a resort in S England, in East Sussex on the English Channel. Pop.: 38 905 (1991).

Bexley ('bekslɪ) *n* a borough of SE Greater London. Pop.: 210 257 (1991). Area: 61 sq. km (23 sq. miles).

bey (beɪ) *n* **1** (in the Ottoman Empire) a title given to senior officers, provincial governors, certain other officials or nobles, and (sometimes) Europeans. **2** (in modern Turkey) a title of address, corresponding to *Mr.* ◆ Also called: **beg.** [C16: Turkish: lord]

Beyoğlu ('beɪɔ:lu:) *n* a district of Istanbul, north of the Golden Horn: the European quarter. Former name: **Pera.**

beyond (bɪ'jɒnd) *prep* **1** at or to a point on the other side of; at or to the further side of: *beyond those hills there is a river.* **2** outside the limits or scope of: *beyond this country's jurisdiction.* ◆ *adv* **3** at or to the other or far side of something. **4** outside the limits of something. ◆ *n* **5 the beyond.** the unknown; the world outside the range of man's perception, esp. life after death in certain religious beliefs. [Old English *begeondan;* see BY, YONDER]

Beyrouth (beɪ'ru:t, 'beɪru:t) *n* a variant spelling of **Beirut.**

Beza (*French* bəza) *or* **de Bèze** (*French* də bɛz) *n* **Théodore** (teodɔr). 1519–1605, French Calvinist theologian and scholar, who lived in Switzerland. He succeeded Calvin as leader of the Swiss Protestants.

bezant, bezzant ('bezᵊnt, bɪ'zænt), *or* **byzant** *n* **1** a medieval Byzantine gold coin. **2** *Architect.* an ornament in the form of a flat disc. **3** *Heraldry.* a small gold circle. [C13: from Old French *besant,* from Medieval Latin *Bӯzantius* Byzantine (coin)]

bezel ('bezᵊl) *n* **1** the sloping face adjacent to the working edge of a cutting tool. **2** the upper oblique faces of a cut gem. **3** a grooved ring or part holding a gem, watch crystal, etc. **4** a retaining outer rim used in vehicle instruments, e.g. in tachometers and speedometers. **5** a small indicator light used in vehicle instrument panels. [C17: probably from French *biseau,* perhaps from Latin *bis* twice]

Béziers (*French* bezje) *n* a city in S France: scene of a massacre (1209) during the Albigensian Crusade. It is a centre of the wine trade. Pop.: 70 996 (1990).

bezique (bɪ'zi:k) *n* **1** a card game for two or more players with tricks similar to whist but with additional points scored for honours and sequences: played with two packs with nothing below a seven. **2** (in this game) the queen of spades and jack of diamonds declared together. [C19: from French *bésigue,* of unknown origin]

bezoar ('bi:zɔ:) *n* a hard mass, such as a stone or hairball, in the stomach and intestines of animals, esp. ruminants, and man: formerly thought to be an antidote to poisons. [C15: from Old French *bézoard,* from Arabic *bāzahr,* from Persian *bādzahr,* from *bād* against + *zahr* poison]

bezonian (bɪ'zəʊnɪən) *n Archaic.* a knave or rascal. [C16: from Italian *bisogno* ill-equipped raw recruit; literally, need]

Bezwada ('beɪzˌwɑ:də) *n* the former name of **Vijayawada.**

B/F *or* **b/f** *Book-keeping. abbrev. for* brought forward.

BFI *abbrev. for* British Film Institute.

BFPO *abbrev. for* British Forces Post Office.

BG *international car registration for* Bulgaria.

BH *international car registration for* Belize.

Bhagalpur ('bɑ:gəlˌpʊə) *n* a city in India, in Bihar: agriculture, textiles, university (1960). Pop.: 253 225 (1991).

Bhagavad-Gita ('bʌgəvəd'gi:tə) *n* a sacred Hindu text composed about 200 B.C. and incorporated into the *Mahabharata,* a Sanskrit epic. [from Sanskrit: song of the Blessed One, from *bhaga* blessing + *gītā* a song]

Bhai (baɪ) *n* a title or form of address prefixed to the names of distinguished Sikhs. [from Hindi *bhāī,* from Sanskrit *bhrātr* BROTHER]

bhajan ('bʌdʒən) *n Hinduism, Sikhism.* the singing of devotional songs and hymns. [from Sanskrit, literally: adoration, worship]

bhaji ('bɑ:dʒɪ) *n* an Indian savoury made of chopped vegetables mixed in a spiced batter and deep-fried. [C19: from Hindi *bhājī* fried vegetables]

bhakti ('bʌktɪ) *n Hinduism.* loving devotion to God leading to nirvana. [from Sanskrit: portion, from *bhajati* he allocates]

bhang *or* **bang** (bæŋ) *n* a preparation of the leaves and flower tops of Indian hemp, which has psychoactive properties: much used in India. See also **cannabis.** [C16: from Hindi *bhāng*]

bhangra ('bæŋgrə) *n* a type of Asian pop music that combines elements of traditional Punjabi music with Western pop. [C20: from Hindi]

bharal *or* **burhel** ('bʌrəl) *n* a wild Himalayan sheep, *Pseudois nayaur,* with a bluish-grey coat and round backward-curving horns. [Hindi]

Bharat ('bʌrʌt) *n* transliteration of the Hindi name for **India.**

Bharatiya ('bɑ:rəˌti:jə) *adj* of or relating to India; Indian.

Bharat Natyam ('bʌrət 'nɑ:tjəm) *n* a form of Indian classical ballet. [from Sanskrit *bharatanātya* Bharata's dancing, from *Bharata* the sage supposed to have written of dramatic art and dancing + *nātya* dancing]

Bhatpara (bɑ:t'pɑ:rə) *n* a city in NE India, in West Bengal on the Hooghly River: jute and cotton mills. Pop.: 304 952 (1991).

bhavan ('bʌvən) *or* **bhawan** *n* (in India) a large house or building.

Bhavnagar ('bɑ:vnəgə) *n* a port in W India, in S Gujarat. Pop.: 402 338 (1991).

bhikhu ('bi:ˌku) *n* a fully ordained Buddhist monk. [Pali, literally: beggar]

bhikkhuni ('bi:kuˌni) *n* a fully ordained Buddhist nun. [Pali, literally: beggar]

bhindi ('bɪndɪ) *n* the okra as used in Indian cooking: its green pods are eaten as vegetables. Also called: **lady's finger.** [Hindi]

bhishti *or* **bheesty** ('bi:stɪ) *n, pl* **-ties.** (formerly in India) a water-carrier. [C18: from Hindi *bhīstī,* from Persian *bihishtī* heavenly one, from *bihisht* paradise]

Bhopal (bəʊ'pɑ:l) *n* a city in central India, the capital of Madhya Pradesh state and of the former state of Bhopal: site of a poisonous gas leak from a US-owned factory, which killed over 2000 people in 1984. Pop.: 1 062 771 (1991).

B horizon *n* the layer of a soil profile immediately below the A horizon, containing deposits of leached material.

bhp *abbrev. for* brake horsepower.

BHP (in Australia) *abbrev. for* Broken Hill Proprietary.

Bhubaneswar (ˌbubə'neɪʃwə) *n* an ancient city in E India, the capital of Orissa state: many temples built between the 7th and 16th centuries. Pop.: 411 542 (1991).

Bhutan (bu:'tɑ:n) *n* a kingdom in central Asia: disputed by Tibet, China, India, and Britain since the 18th century, the conflict now being chiefly between China and India (which is responsible for Bhutan's external affairs); contains inaccessible stretches of the E Himalayas in the north. Official language: Dzongka; Nepali is also spoken. Official religion: Mahayana Buddhist. Currencies: ngultrum and Indian rupee. Capital: Thimbu. Pop.: 633 000 (1998 est.). Area: about 46 600 sq. km (18 000 sq. miles). ▸ **ˌBhutan'ese** *n, adj*

Bhutto ('bu:təʊ) *n* **1 Benazir** ('benəzɪə). born 1953, Pakistani stateswoman; prime minister of Pakistan (1988–90; 1993–96); deposed and subsequently defeated in elections in 1997. **2** her father, **Zulfikar Ali** ('zʊlfɪkɑ: 'ɑ:lɪ). 1928–79, Pakistani statesman; president (1971–73) and prime minister (1973–77) of Pakistan: executed for the murder of a political rival.

bi (baɪ) *adj, n Slang.* short for **bisexual** (senses 1, 6).

Bi *the chemical symbol for* bismuth.

bi-[1] *or sometimes before a vowel* **bin-** *combining form.* **1** two; having two: *bifocal.* **2** occurring every two; lasting for two: *biennial.* **3** on both sides, surfaces, directions, etc.: *bilateral.* **4** occurring twice during: *biweekly.* **5a** denoting an organic compound containing two identical cyclic hydrocarbon systems: *biphenyl.* **5b** (rare in technical usage) indicating an acid salt of a dibasic acid: *sodium bicarbonate.* **5c** (not in technical usage) equivalent of **di-**[1] (sense 2a). [from Latin, from *bis* TWICE]

bi-[2] *combining form.* a variant of **bio-.**

Biafra (bɪ'æfrə) *n* **1** a region of E Nigeria, formerly a local government region: seceded as an independent republic (1967–70) during the Civil War, but defeated by Nigerian government forces. **2 Bight of.** former name (until 1975) of (the Bight of) **Bonny.** ▸ **Bi'afran** *adj, n*

Biak (bi:'jɑ:k) *n* an island in Indonesia, north of West Irian: the largest of the Schouten Islands. Area: 2455 sq. km (948 sq. miles).

Bialik ('bjɑ:lɪk) *n* **Hayyim Nahman** ('haɪm 'nɑxman) *or* **Chaim Nachman.** 1873–1934, Russian Jewish poet and writer. His long poems *The Talmud Student* (1894) and *In the City of Slaughter* (1903) established him as the major Hebrew poet of modern times.

Białystok (*Polish* bja'wɪstɔk) *n* a city in E Poland: belonged to Prussia (1795–1807) and to Russia (1807–1919). Pop.: 277 800 (1996 est.). Russian name: **Belostock.**

biannual (baɪ'ænjʊəl) *adj* occurring twice a year. Compare **biennial.** ▸ **bi'annually** *adv*

biannulate (baɪ'ænjʊlɪt, -ˌleɪt) *adj Zoology.* having two bands, esp. of colour.

Biarritz ('bɪərɪts, bɪə'rɪts; *French* bjarits) *n* a town in SW France, on the Bay of

Biscay: famous resort, patronized by Napoleon III and by Queen Victoria and Edward VII of Great Britain and Ireland. Pop.: 28 890 (1990).

bias ('baɪəs) *n* **1** mental tendency or inclination, esp. an irrational preference or prejudice. **2** a diagonal line or cut across the weave of a fabric. **3** *Electronics.* the voltage applied to an electrode of a transistor or valve to establish suitable working conditions. **4** *Bowls.* **4a** a bulge or weight inside one side of a bowl. **4b** the curved course of such a bowl on the green. **5** *Statistics.* **5a** an extraneous latent influence on, unrecognized conflated variable in, or selectivity in a sample which influences its distribution and so renders it unable to reflect the desired population parameters. **5b** if T is an estimator of the parameter θ, the estimated value of (T-θ). **6** an inaudible high-frequency signal used to improve the quality of a tape recording. ◆ *adj* **7** slanting obliquely; diagonal: *a bias fold.* ◆ *adv* **8** obliquely; diagonally. ◆ *vb* **-ases, -asing, -ased** *or* **-asses, -assing, -assed.** (*tr*) **9** (*usually passive*) to cause to have a bias; prejudice; influence. [C16: from Old French *biais,* from Old Provençal, perhaps ultimately from Greek *epikarsios* oblique] ▸ **'biased** *or* **'biassed** *adj*

bias binding *n* a strip of material cut on the bias for extra stretch and often doubled, used for binding hems, interfacings, etc., or for decoration.

biathlon (baɪ'æθlən, -lɒn) *n Sport.* a contest in which skiers with rifles shoot at four targets along a 20-kilometre (12.5-mile) cross-country course.

biauriculate (,baɪɔː'rɪkjʊlɪt, -,leɪt) *or* **biauricular** *adj* having two auricles or earlike parts.

biaxial (baɪ'æksɪəl) *adj* (esp. of a crystal) having two axes.

bib (bɪb) *n* **1** a piece of cloth or plastic worn, esp. by babies, to protect their clothes while eating. **2** the upper part of some aprons, dungarees, etc., that covers the upper front part of the body. **3** Also called: **pout, whiting pout.** a light-brown European marine gadoid food fish, *Gadus* (or *Trisopterus*) *luscus,* with a barbel on its lower jaw. **4** short for **bibcock. 5 stick one's bib in.** *Austral. informal.* to interfere. ◆ *vb* **bibs, bibbing, bibbed.** **6** *Archaic.* to drink (something); tipple. [C14 *bibben* to drink, probably from Latin *bibere*]

Bib. *abbrev. for:* **1** Bible. **2** Biblical.

bib and brace *n* a work garment consisting of trousers and an upper front part supported by straps over the shoulders.

bib and tucker *n Informal.* an outfit of clothes (esp. in the phrase **best bib and tucker**).

bibb (bɪb) *n Nautical.* a wooden support on a mast for the trestletrees. [C18: variant of BIB]

bibber ('bɪbə) *n* a drinker; tippler (esp. in the expression **wine-bibber**).

bibcock ('bɪb,kɒk) *or* **bib** *n* a tap having a nozzle bent downwards and supplied from a horizontal pipe.

bibelot ('bɪbləʊ; *French* biblo) *n* **1** an attractive or curious trinket. **2** a miniature book. [C19: from French, from Old French *beubelet,* perhaps from a reduplication of *bel* beautiful]

bibl. *abbrev. for:* **1** bibliographical. **2** bibliography.

Bibl. *abbrev. for* Biblical.

Bible ('baɪbᵊl) *n* **1a the.** the sacred writings of the Christian religion, comprising the Old and New Testaments and, in the Roman Catholic Church, the Apocrypha. **1b** (*as modifier*): *a Bible reading.* **2** (*often not cap.*) any book containing the sacred writings of a religion. **3** (*usually not cap.*) a book regarded as authoritative: *the angler's bible.* [C13: from Old French, from Medieval Latin *biblia* books, from Greek, plural of *biblion* book, diminutive of *biblos* papyrus, from *Bublos* Phoenician port from which Greece obtained Egyptian papyrus]

Bible Belt *n* **the.** those states of the S U.S. where Protestant fundamentalism is dominant.

Bible paper *n* **1** a thin tough opaque paper used for Bibles, prayer books, and reference books. **2** (not in technical usage) another name for **India paper.**

Bible-thumper *n Slang.* an enthusiastic or aggressive exponent of the Bible. Also called: **Bible-basher, Bible-pounder, Bible-puncher.** ▸ **'Bible-,thumping** *n, adj*

biblical ('bɪblɪkᵊl) *adj* **1** of, occurring in, or referring to the Bible. **2** resembling the Bible in written style. ▸ **'biblically** *adv*

Biblical Aramaic *n* the form of Aramaic that was the common language of Palestine in New Testament times. It was widespread throughout the Persian Empire from the 5th century and is found in the later books of the Old Testament (esp. Daniel 2:4–7:28).

Biblical Latin *n* the form of Latin used in versions of the Bible, esp. the form used in the Vulgate. See also **Late Latin.**

Biblicist ('bɪblɪsɪst) *or* **Biblist** *n* **1** a biblical scholar. **2** a person who takes the Bible literally.

biblio- *combining form.* indicating book or books: *bibliography; bibliomania.* [from Greek *biblion* book]

bibliog. *abbrev. for:* **1** bibliographer. **2** bibliography.

bibliography (,bɪblɪ'ɒgrəfɪ) *n, pl* **-phies. 1** a list of books or other material on a subject. **2** a list of sources used in the preparation of a book, thesis, etc. **3** a list of the works of a particular author or publisher. **4a** the study of the history, classification, etc., of literary material. **4b** a work on this subject. ▸ **,bibli'ographer** *n* ▸ **bibliographic** (,bɪblɪəʊ'græfɪk) *or* **,biblio'graphical** *adj* ▸ **,biblio'graphically** *adv*

bibliolatry (,bɪblɪ'ɒlətrɪ) *n* **1** excessive devotion to or reliance on the Bible. **2** extreme fondness for books.

bibliomancy ('bɪblɪəʊ,mænsɪ) *n* prediction of the future by interpreting a passage chosen at random from a book, esp. the Bible.

bibliomania (,bɪblɪəʊ'meɪnɪə) *n* extreme fondness for books. ▸ **,biblio'mani,ac** *n, adj*

bibliophile ('bɪblɪə,faɪl) *or* **bibliophil** ('bɪblɪəfɪl) *n* a person who collects or is fond of books. ▸ **bibliophilism** (,bɪblɪ'ɒfə,lɪzəm) *n* ▸ **,bibli,ophi'listic** *adj*

bibliopole ('bɪblɪəʊ,pəʊl) *or* **bibliopolist** (,bɪblɪ'ɒpəlɪst) *n* a dealer in books, esp. rare or decorative ones. [C18: from Latin *bibliopōla,* from Greek *bibliopōlēs* bookseller, from BIBLIO- + *pōlein* to sell] ▸ **,bibli'opoly** *n*

bibliotheca (,bɪblɪəʊ'θiːkə) *n, pl* **-cas** *or* **-cae** (-kiː). **1** a library or collection of books. **2** a printed catalogue compiled by a bibliographer. [Latin: library, from Greek *bibliothēkē,* from BIBLIO- + *thēkē* receptacle]

bibulous ('bɪbjʊləs) *adj* addicted to alcohol. [C17: from Latin *bibulus,* from *bibere* to drink] ▸ **'bibulously** *adv* ▸ **'bibulousness** *n*

bicameral (baɪ'kæmərəl) *adj* (of a legislature) consisting of two chambers. [C19: from BI-[1] + Latin *camera* CHAMBER] ▸ **bi'cameral,ism** *n* ▸ **bi'cameralist** *n*

bicapsular (baɪ'kæpsjʊlə) *adj* (of plants) having two capsules or one capsule with two chambers.

bicarb ('baɪkɑːb) *n* short for **bicarbonate of soda.** See **sodium bicarbonate.**

bicarbonate (baɪ'kɑːbənɪt, -,neɪt) *n* **1** a salt of carbonic acid containing the ion HCO_3^-; an acid carbonate. **2** (*modifier*) consisting of, containing, or concerned with the ion HCO_3^-: *a bicarbonate compound.* Systematic name: **hydrogen carbonate. 3** short for **bicarbonate of soda.**

bicarbonate of soda *n* sodium bicarbonate, esp. when used as a medicine or as a raising agent in baking.

bicarpellary (,baɪkɑː'pelərɪ) *adj Botany.* (of an ovary) having two carpels.

bice (baɪs) *n* **1** Also called: **bice blue.** a medium blue colour; azurite. **2** Also called: **bice green.** a yellowish-green colour; malachite. [C14: from Old French *bis* dark grey, of uncertain origin]

bicentenary (,baɪsen'tiːnərɪ) *or U.S.* **bicentennial** (,baɪsen'tenɪəl) *adj* **1** marking a 200th anniversary. **2** occurring every 200 years. **3** lasting 200 years. ◆ *n, pl* **-naries. 4** a 200th anniversary.

bicephalous (baɪ'sefələs) *adj* **1** *Biology.* having two heads. **2** crescent-shaped.

biceps ('baɪseps) *n, pl* **-ceps.** *Anatomy.* any muscle having two heads or origins, esp. the muscle that flexes the forearm. Related adj: **bicipital.** [C17: from Latin: having two heads, from BI-[1] + *caput* head]

Biche-la-mar (,biːtʃlə'mɑː) *n* another name for **Beach-la-Mar.**

bichloride (baɪ'klɔːraɪd) *n* another name for **dichloride.**

bichloride of mercury *n* another name for **mercuric chloride.**

bichon frise ('biːʃɒn 'friːzeɪ) *n, pl* **bichon frises.** a small white poodle-like dog with a silky, loosely curling coat. [C20: French, literally: curly toy dog]

bichromate (baɪ'krəʊ,meɪt, -mɪt) *n* another name for **dichromate.**

bicipital (baɪ'sɪpɪtᵊl) *adj* **1** having two heads. **2** of or relating to a biceps muscle. [C17: see BICEPS, -AL[1]]

bicker ('bɪkə) *vb* (*intr*) **1** to argue over petty matters; squabble. **2** *Poetic.* **2a** (esp. of a stream) to run quickly. **2b** to flicker; glitter. ◆ *n* **3** a petty squabble. [C13: of unknown origin] ▸ **'bickerer** *n* ▸ **'bickering** *n, adj*

bickie ('bɪkɪ) *n Informal.* **1** short for **biscuit** (sense 1). **2 big bickies.** *Austral. slang.* a large sum of money.

bicoastal (baɪ'kəʊstᵊl) *adj* relating to both the east and west coasts of the U.S.: *she had a bicoastal upbringing.*

bicollateral (,baɪkɒ'lætərəl) *adj Botany.* (of a vascular bundle) having two phloem groups to the inside and outside, respectively, of the xylem.

bicolour ('baɪ,kʌlə), **bicoloured** *or U.S.* **bicolor, bicolored** *adj* two-coloured.

biconcave (baɪ'kɒnkeɪv, ,baɪkɒn'keɪv) *adj* (of a lens) having concave faces on both sides; concavo-concave. ▸ **biconcavity** (,baɪkɒn'kævɪtɪ) *n*

biconditional (,baɪkən'dɪʃənᵊl) *n* another name for **equivalence** (sense 2).

biconvex (baɪ'kɒnveks, ,baɪkɒn'veks) *adj* (of a lens) having convex faces on both sides; convexo-convex.

bicorn ('baɪkɔːn), **bicornate** (baɪ'kɔːnɪt, -,neɪt), *or* **bicornuate** (baɪ'kɔːnjʊɪt, -,eɪt) *adj* having two horns or hornlike parts. [C19: from Latin *bicornis,* from BI-[1] + *cornu* horn]

bicuspid (baɪ'kʌspɪd) *or* **bicuspidate** (baɪ'kʌspɪ,deɪt) *adj* **1** having or terminating in two cusps or points. ◆ *n* **2** a bicuspid tooth; premolar.

bicuspid valve *n* another name for **mitral valve.**

bicycle ('baɪsɪkᵊl) *n* **1** a vehicle with a tubular metal frame mounted on two spoked wheels, one behind the other. The rider sits on a saddle, propels the vehicle by means of pedals that drive the rear wheel through a chain, and steers with handlebars on the front wheel. Often shortened to **bike** (informal), **cycle.** ◆ *vb* **2** (*intr*) to ride a bicycle; cycle. [C19: from BI-[1] + Late Latin *cyclus,* from Greek *kuklos* wheel] ▸ **'bicyclist** *or* **'bicycler** *n*

bicycle chain *n* a chain that transmits power from the pedals to the rear wheel of a bicycle.

bicycle clip *n* one of a pair of clips worn around the ankles by cyclists to keep the trousers tight and out of the chain.

bicycle pump *n* a hand pump for pumping air into the tyres of a bicycle.

bicyclic (baɪ'saɪklɪk, -'sɪklɪk) *or* **bicyclical** *adj* **1** of, forming, or formed by two circles, cycles, etc. **2** (of stamens, petals, etc.) arranged in two whorls. **3** (of a chemical compound) having atoms arranged in two rings fused together with at least two atoms common to each ring: *naphthalene is bicyclic.*

bid (bɪd) *vb* **bids; bidding; bad, bade,** *or* (esp. for senses 1, 2, 5, 7) **bid; bidden** *or* (esp. for senses 1, 2, 5, 7) **bid. 1** (often foll. by *for* or *against*) to offer (an amount) in attempting to buy something, esp. in competition with others as at an auction. **2** *Commerce.* to respond to an offer by a seller by stating (the more favourable terms) on which one is willing to make a purchase. **3** (*tr*) to say (a greeting, blessing, etc.): *to bid farewell.* **4** to order; command: *do as you are bid!* **5** (*intr;* usually foll. by *for*) to attempt to attain power, etc. **6** (*tr*) to invite; ask kindly: *she bade him sit down.* **7** *Bridge, etc.* to declare in the auction before play how many tricks one expects to make. **8 bid defiance.** to resist boldly. **9 bid fair.** to seem probable. ◆ *n* **10a** an offer of a specified amount, as at an auction. **10b** the price offered. **11** *Commerce.* **11a** a statement by a buyer, in response to an offer by a seller, of the more favourable terms that would be acceptable. **11b** the price or other terms so stated. **12** an attempt, esp.

an attempt to attain power. **13** *Bridge, etc.* **13a** the number of tricks a player undertakes to make. **13b** a player's turn to make a bid. **14** short for **bid price.** ◆ See also **bid in, bid up.** [Old English *biddan;* related to German *bitten*] ▸ **'bidder** *n*

b.i.d. (in prescriptions) *abbrev. for* bis in die. [Latin: twice a day]

Bida ('baɪdɑː) *or* **El Beda** (ɛl 'beɪdɑː) *n* the former name of **Doha.**

bidarka (baɪ'dɑːkə) *or* **bidarkee** (baɪ'dɑːkiː) *n* a canoe covered in animal skins, esp. sealskin, used by the Eskimos of Alaska. [C19: from Russian *baidarka,* diminutive of *baidara* umiak]

Bidault (*French* bido) *n* **Georges** (ʒɔːrʒ). 1899–1983, French statesman; prime minister (1946, 1949–50). His opposition to Algerian independence led him to support the OAS: he was charged with treason (1963) and fled abroad.

biddable ('bɪdəbᵊl) *adj* **1** having sufficient value to be bid on, as a hand or suit at bridge. **2** docile; obedient. ▸ **'biddableness** *n* ▸ **'biddably** *adv*

bidden ('bɪdᵊn) *vb* a past participle of **bid.**

bidding ('bɪdɪŋ) *n* **1** an order; command (often in the phrases **do** *or* **follow the bidding of, at someone's bidding**). **2** an invitation; summons. **3** the act of making bids, as at an auction or in bridge. **4** *Bridge, etc.* a group of bids considered collectively, esp. those made on a particular deal.

Biddle ('bɪdᵊl) *n* **John.** 1615–62, English theologian; founder of Unitarianism in England.

biddy[1] ('bɪdɪ) *n, pl* **-dies.** a dialect word for **chicken** or **hen.** [C17: perhaps imitative of calling chickens]

biddy[2] ('bɪdɪ) *n, pl* **-dies.** *Informal.* a woman, esp. an old gossipy or interfering one. [C18: from pet form of *Bridget*]

biddy-biddy *or* **biddi-biddi** ('bɪdɪ,bɪdɪ) *n, pl* **-biddies. 1** a low-growing rosaceous plant, *Acaena viridior,* of New Zealand, having prickly burs. **2** the burs of this plant. ◆ Also: (N.Z.) **biddy-bid,** (Austral.) **bidgee-widgee** ('bɪdʒɪ,wɪdʒɪ). [from Maori *piri piri*]

bide (baɪd) *vb* **bides, biding, bided** *or* **bode, bided. 1** (*intr*) *Archaic or dialect.* to continue in a certain place or state; stay. **2** (*intr*) *Archaic or dialect.* to live; dwell. **3** (*tr*) *Archaic or dialect.* to tolerate; endure. **4 bide a wee.** *Scot.* to stay a little. **5 bide by.** *Scot.* to abide by. **6 bide one's time.** to wait patiently for an opportunity. ◆ Also (Scot.) **byde.** [Old English *bīdan;* related to Old Norse *bītha* to wait, Gothic *beidan,* Old High German *bītan*]

bidentate (baɪ'dɛn,teɪt) *adj* **1** having two teeth or toothlike parts or processes. **2** *Chem.* (of a ligand) having two atoms from which electrons can be donated to the central coordinated atom.

bidet ('biːdeɪ) *n* a small low basin for washing the genitals and anal area. [C17: from French: small horse, probably from Old French *bider* to trot]

bidie-in (,baɪdɪ'ɪn) *n Scot.* a live-in sexual partner.

bid in *vb* (*adv*) (in an auction) to outbid all previous offers for (one's own property) to retain ownership or increase the final selling price.

bidirectional (,baɪdɪ'rɛkʃənᵊl) *adj Computing.* (of a printhead) capable of printing from left to right and from right to left.

bid price *n Stock Exchange.* the price at which a stockjobber is prepared to purchase a specific security. Compare **offer price.**

bid up *vb* (*adv*) to increase the market price of (a commodity) by making artificial bids.

Biedermeier ('biːdə,maɪə) *adj* **1** of or relating to a decorative and furnishing style in mid-19th-century Germany, characterized by solidity and conventionality. **2** boringly conventional in outlook; bourgeois. [C19: after Gottlieb *Biedermeier,* a fictitious character portrayed as a conventional unimaginative bourgeois and the author of poems actually written by several satirical poets]

Biel (biːl) *n* **1** a town in NW Switzerland, on Lake Biel. Pop.: 52 197 (1994). French name: **Bienne. 2 Lake.** a lake in NW Switzerland: remains of lake dwellings were discovered here in the 19th century. Area: 39 sq. km (15 sq. miles). German name: **Bielersee** ('biːləzeː).

bield (biːld) *Scot. and northern English dialect.* ◆ *n* **1** a shelter; house. ◆ *vb* **2** to shelter or take shelter. [Old English *bieldo, byldo* boldness (hence: refuge); related to Gothic *balthei,* Old English *beald* BOLD]

Bielefeld (*German* 'biːləfɛlt) *n* a city in Germany, in NE North Rhine-Westphalia: food, textiles. Pop.: 324 066 (1996 est.).

Bielsko-Biała (*Polish* 'bjɛlskɔ'bjawa) *n* a town in S Poland: created in 1951 by the union of Bielsko and Biala Krakowska; a leading textile centre since the 16th century. Pop.: 180 700 (1996 est.).

Bien Hoa ('bjɛn 'həʊə) *n* a town in S Vietnam: a former capital of Cambodia. Pop.: 273 879 (1989).

Bienne (bjɛn) *n* the French name for **Biel.**

biennial (baɪ'ɛnɪəl) *adj* **1** occurring every two years. **2** lasting two years. Compare **biannual.** ◆ *n* **3** a plant, such as the carrot, that completes its life cycle in two years, developing vegetative storage parts during the first year. Compare **annual** (sense 3), **perennial** (sense 3). **4** an event that takes place every two years. ▸ **bi'ennially** *adv*

bien-pensant (bjɛ̃pɑ̃sɑ̃) *adj* **1** right-thinking; orthodox. ◆ *n* ***bien pensant,*** *pl* ***bien pensants*** (bjɛ̃pɑ̃sɑ̃). **2** a right-thinking person. [French: well-thinking]

bier (bɪə) *n* a platform or stand on which a corpse or a coffin containing a corpse rests before burial. [Old English *bǣr;* related to *beran* to BEAR[1], Old High German *bāra* bier, Sanskrit *bhārá* a burden]

Bierce (bɪəs) *n* **Ambrose** (**Gwinett**). 1842–?1914, U.S. journalist and author of humorous sketches, horror stories, and tales of the supernatural: he disappeared during a mission in Mexico (1913).

bierkeller ('bɪə,kɛlə) *n Brit.* a public house decorated in German style, selling German beers. [C20: German, literally: beer cellar]

biestings ('biːstɪŋz) *n* a variant spelling of **beestings.**

bifacial (baɪ'feɪʃəl) *adj* **1** having two faces or surfaces. **2** *Botany.* (of leaves, etc.) having upper and lower surfaces differing from each other. **3** *Archaeol.* (of flints) flaked by percussion from two sides along the chopping edge.

bifarious (baɪ'fɛərɪəs) *adj Botany.* having parts arranged in two rows on either side of a central axis. [C17: from Latin *bifārius* double] ▸ **bi'fariously** *adv*

biff (bɪf) *Slang.* ◆ *n* **1** a blow with the fist. **2** *Irish school slang.* a blow to the palm of the hand with a strap or cane as a punishment. ◆ *vb* **3** (*tr*) to give (someone) such a blow. [C20: probably of imitative origin]

biffin ('bɪfɪn) *n Brit.* a variety of red cooking apple. [C18: from *beefin* ox for slaughter, from BEEF; referring to the apple's colour]

bifid ('baɪfɪd) *adj* divided into two lobes by a median cleft: *bifid leaves.* [C17: from Latin *bifidus* from BI-[1] + *-fidus,* from *findere* to split] ▸ **bi'fidity** *n* ▸ **'bifidly** *adv*

bifilar (baɪ'faɪlə) *adj* **1** having two parallel threads, as in the suspension of certain measuring instruments. **2** of or relating to a resistor in which the wire is wound in a loop around a coil, the two leads being parallel, to reduce the inductance. ▸ **bi'filarly** *adv*

biflagellate (baɪ'flædʒɪ,leɪt, -lɪt) *adj Biology.* having two flagella: *biflagellate protozoans.*

bifocal (baɪ'fəʊkᵊl) *adj* **1** *Optics.* having two different focuses. **2** relating to a compound lens permitting near and distant vision.

bifocals (baɪ'fəʊkᵊlz) *pl n* a pair of spectacles with bifocal lenses.

bifoliate (baɪ'fəʊlɪ,eɪt, -ɪt) *adj* having two leaves or leaflets.

bifoliolate (baɪ'fəʊlɪəʊ,leɪt, -lɪt) *adj* (of compound leaves) consisting of two leaflets.

biforate ('baɪfə,reɪt) *adj Biology.* having two openings, pores, or perforations. [C19: from New Latin *biforātus,* from BI-[1] + *forāre* to pierce]

biform ('baɪ,fɔːm) *or* **biformed** *adj* having or combining the characteristics of two forms, as a centaur.

Bifrost ('bɪvrɒst, 'biːfrɒst) *n Norse myth.* the rainbow bridge of the gods from their realm Asgard to earth. [from Icelandic, from *bifa* to shake + *rost* path]

bifurcate *vb* ('baɪfə,keɪt). **1** to fork or divide into two parts or branches. ◆ *adj* ('baɪfə,keɪt, -kɪt). **2** forked or divided into two sections or branches. [C17: from Medieval Latin *bifurcātus,* from Latin *bifurcus,* from BI-[1] + *furca* fork] ▸ **,bifur'cation** *n*

big[1] (bɪg) *adj* **bigger, biggest. 1** of great or considerable size, height, weight, number, power, or capacity. **2** having great significance; important: *a big decision.* **3** important through having power, influence, wealth, authority, etc.: *the big four banks.* **4** (intensifier usually qualifying something undesirable): *a big dope.* **5** *Informal.* considerable in extent or intensity (esp. in the phrase **in a big way**). **6a** elder: *my big brother.* **6b** grown-up: *when you're big, you can stay up later.* **7a** generous; magnanimous: *that's very big of you.* **7b** (in combination): *big-hearted.* **8** (often foll. by *with*) brimming; full: *my heart is big with sadness.* **9** extravagant; boastful: *he's full of big talk.* **10 too big for one's boots** *or* **breeches.** conceited; unduly self-confident. **11** in an advanced stage of pregnancy (esp. in the phrase **big with child**). **12 big on.** *Informal, chiefly U.S.* enthusiastic about: *that company is big on research.* ◆ *adv Informal.* **13** boastfully; pretentiously (esp. in the phrase **talk big**). **14** in an exceptional way; well: *his talk went over big with the audience.* **15** on a grand scale (esp. in the phrase **think big**). ◆ See also **big up.** [C13: perhaps of Scandinavian origin; compare Norwegian dialect *bugge* big man] ▸ **'biggish** *adj* ▸ **'bigness** *n*

big[2] (bɪg) *vb* **bigs, bigging, bigged** *or* **bug** (bʌg). *Scot.* **1** to build. **2** to excavate (earth) into a pile. [from Old Norse *byggja;* related to Old English *būian* to inhabit]

bigamy ('bɪgəmɪ) *n, pl* **-mies.** the crime of marrying a person while one is still legally married to someone else. [C13: via French from Medieval Latin *bigamus;* see BI-[1], -GAMY] ▸ **'bigamist** *n* ▸ **'bigamous** *adj* ▸ **'bigamously** *adv*

Big Apple *n* **the.** *Informal.* New York City. [C20: probably from U.S. jazzmen's earlier use to mean any big, esp. northern, city; of obscure origin]

bigarreau ('bɪgə,rəʊ, ,bɪgə'rəʊ) *n* any of several heart-shaped varieties of sweet cherry that have firm flesh. [C17: from French, from *bigarré* mottled]

big band *n* a large jazz or dance band, popular esp. in the 1930s to the 1950s.

big bang *n* **1** any sudden forceful beginning or radical change. **2** (*modifier*) of or relating to the big-bang theory. **3** (*sometimes caps.*) the major modernization that took place on the London Stock Exchange on Oct. 27 1986, after which the distinction between jobbers and brokers was abolished and operations became fully computerized.

big-bang theory *n* a cosmological theory postulating that approximately 15 000 million years ago all the matter of the universe, packed into a small superdense mass, was hurled in all directions by a cataclysmic explosion. As the fragments slowed down, the galaxies and stars evolved but the universe is still expanding. Compare **steady-state theory.**

Big Ben *n* **1** the bell in the clock tower of the Houses of Parliament, London. **2** the clock in this tower. **3** the tower. [C19: named after Sir *Benjamin* Hall, Chief Commissioner of Works in 1856 when it was cast]

Big Bertha *n* any of three large German guns of World War I used to bombard Paris. [C20: approximate translation of German *dicke Bertha:* fat Bertha; named after *Bertha* Krupp, at whose works in Essen a very effective 42 cm mortar was made]

Big Board *n U.S. informal.* **1** the quotation board in the New York Stock Exchange. **2** the New York Stock Exchange.

Big Brother *n* a person, organization, etc., that exercises total dictatorial control. [C20: after a character in George Orwell's novel *1984* (1949)]

big bucks *pl n Informal, chiefly U.S.* **1** large quantities of money. **2** the power and influence of people or organizations that control large quantities of money.

big bud *n* a serious disease of plants, esp. of blackcurrants, in which the buds swell up as a result of attack by the gall mite *Cecidophyopsis ribis.*

big business *n* large commercial organizations collectively, esp. when considered as exploitative or socially harmful.

big cheese *n Slang.* an important person.
big Chief *or* **big Daddy** *n Informal.* other terms for **big White Chief.**
big deal *interj Slang.* an exclamation of scorn, derision, etc., used esp. to belittle a claim or offer.
big dipper *n* (in amusement parks) a narrow railway with open carriages that run swiftly over a route of sharp curves and steep inclines. Also called: **roller coaster.**
Big Dipper *n* the U.S. and Canadian name for the **Plough** (constellation).
big end *n Brit.* **1** Also called (in vertical engines): **bottom end.** the larger end of a connecting rod in an internal-combustion engine. Compare **little end. 2** the bearing surface between the larger end of a connecting rod and the crankpin of the crankshaft.
bigener ('baɪdʒɪnə) *n Biology.* a hybrid between individuals of different genera. [C20: back formation from *bigeneric;* see BI-[1], GENUS]
bigeneric (ˌbaɪdʒə'nɛrɪk) *adj* (of a hybrid plant) derived from parents of two different genera.
bigeye ('bɪgˌaɪ) *n, pl* **-eye** *or* **-eyes.** any tropical or subtropical red marine percoid fish of the family *Priacanthidae,* having very large eyes and rough scales.
big fish *n Informal.* **1** an important or powerful person. **2 a big fish in a small pond.** the most important or powerful person in a small group.
Big Five *n* **the. 1** the five countries considered to be the major world powers. In the period immediately following World War II, the U.S., Britain, the Soviet Union, China, and France were regarded as the Big Five. **2** a small powerful group, as of banks, companies, etc. Also: **Big Four, Big Three.**
big game *n* **1** large animals that are hunted or fished for sport. **2** *Informal.* the objective of an important or dangerous undertaking.
biggin[1] *or* **biggon** ('bɪgɪn) *n* a plain close-fitting cap, often tying under the chin, worn in the Middle Ages and by children in the 17th century. [C16: from French *béguin;* see BEGUINE]
biggin[2] ('bɪgən) *n Scot.* a construction, esp. a house or cottage. [see BIG[2]]
big gun *n Informal.* an important or influential person.
bighead ('bɪgˌhɛd) *n* **1** *Informal.* a conceited person. **2** *U.S. and Canadian informal.* conceit; egotism. **3** *Vet. science.* **3a** an abnormal bulging or increase in the size of an animal's skull, as from osteomalacia. **3b** any of various diseases of sheep characterized by swelling of the head, esp. any caused by infection with *Clostridium* bacteria. ► **ˌbig'headed** *adj* ► **ˌbig'headedly** *adv* ► **ˌbig'headedness** *n*
big-hearted *adj* warmly generous. ► **ˌbig-'heartedness** *n*
bighorn ('bɪgˌhɔːn) *n, pl* **-horns** *or* **-horn.** a large wild sheep, *Ovis canadensis,* inhabiting mountainous regions in North America and NE Asia: family *Bovidae,* order *Artiodactyla.* The male has massive curved horns, and the species is well adapted for climbing and leaping.
bight (baɪt) *n* **1** a wide indentation of a shoreline, or the body of water bounded by such a curve. **2** the slack middle part of an extended rope. **3** a curve or loop in a rope. ◆ *vb* **4** *(tr)* to fasten or bind with a bight. [Old English *byht;* see BOW[2]]
Bight *n* **the.** *Austral. informal.* the major indentation of the S coast of Australia, from Cape Pasley in W Australia to the Eyre Peninsula in S Australia. In full: **the Great Australian Bight.**
big money *n* large sums of money: *there's big money in professional golf.*
bigmouth ('bɪgˌmaʊθ) *n Slang.* a noisy, indiscreet, or boastful person. ► **'big-ˌmouthed** *adj*
big name *n Informal.* **a** a famous person. **b** *(as modifier): a big-name performer.*
big noise *n Informal.* an important person.
bignonia (bɪg'nəʊnɪə) *n* any tropical American bignoniaceous climbing shrub of the genus *Bignonia* (or *Doxantha*), cultivated for their trumpet-shaped yellow or reddish flowers. See also **cross vine.** [C19: from New Latin, named after the Abbé Jean-Paul *Bignon* (1662–1743)]
bignoniaceous (bɪgˌnəʊnɪ'eɪʃəs) *adj* of, relating to, or belonging to the *Bignoniaceae,* a chiefly tropical family of trees, shrubs, and lianas, including jacaranda, bignonia, and catalpa.
big-note *vb Austral. informal.* to boast about (oneself).
bigot ('bɪgət) *n* a person who is intolerant of any ideas other than his or her own, esp. on religion, politics, or race. [C16: from Old French: name applied contemptuously to the Normans by the French, of obscure origin] ► **'bigoted** *adj*
bigotry ('bɪgətrɪ) *n, pl* **-ries.** the attitudes, behaviour, or way of thinking of a bigot; prejudice; intolerance.
big science *n* scientific research that requires a large investment of capital.
big screen *n* an informal name for the **cinema.**
big shot *n Informal.* an important or influential person.
Big Smoke *n* **the.** *Informal.* a large city, esp. London.
big stick *n Informal.* force or the threat of using force.
big time *n Informal.* **a the.** the highest or most profitable level of an occupation or profession, esp. the entertainment business. **b** *(as modifier): a big-time comedian.* ► **'big-'timer** *n*
big top *n Informal.* **1** the main tent of a circus. **2** the circus itself.
big tree *n* a giant Californian coniferous tree, *Sequoiadendron giganteum,* with a wide tapering trunk and thick spongy bark: family *Taxodiaceae.* It often reaches a height of 90 metres. Also called: **giant sequoia.** See also **sequoia.**
biguanide (baɪ'gwɑːnaɪd) *n* any of a class of compounds some of which are used in the treatment of certain forms of diabetes. See also **phenformin.** [C19: from BI-[1] + GUANIDINE + -IDE]
big up *vb* **bigs, bigging, bigged.** *(tr, adv) Slang, chiefly Caribbean.* to make important, prominent, or famous: *we'll do our best to big you up.*
big wheel *n* **1** another name for a **Ferris wheel. 2** *Informal.* an important person.
big White Chief *n Informal.* an important person, boss, or leader. Also called: **big Chief, big Daddy.**
bigwig ('bɪgˌwɪg) *n Informal.* an important person.
Bihar (bɪ'hɑː) *n* a state of NE India: hilly in the south, with the Ganges plain in the north; important for rice and mineral resources, esp. coal. Capital: Patna. Pop.: 93 080 000 (1994 est.). Area: 174 038 sq. km (67 875 sq. miles).
Bihari (bɪ'hɑːrɪ) *n* **1** *(pl* **Bihari** *or* **Biharis)** a member of an Indian people living chiefly in Bihar but also in Bangladesh and Pakistan. **2** the language of this people, comprising a number of highly differentiated dialects, belonging to the Indic branch of the Indo-European family. ◆ *adj* **3** of or relating to this people, their language, or Bihar.
Biisk (*Russian* bijsk) *n* a variant spelling of **Biysk.**
Bijapur (bɪ'dʒɑːpʊə) *n* an ancient city in W India, in N Mysore: capital of a former kingdom, which fell at the end of the 17th century: cotton. Pop.: 186 939 (1991).
bijection (baɪ'dʒɛkʃən) *n* a mathematical function or mapping that is both an injection and a surjection and therefore has an inverse. See also **injection** (sense 5), **surjection.**
bijective (baɪ'dʒɛktɪv) *adj Maths.* (of a function, relation, etc.) associating two sets in such a way that every member of each set is uniquely paired with a member of the other: *the mapping from the set of married men to the set of married women is bijective in a monogamous society.*
bijou ('biːʒuː) *n, pl* **-joux** (-ʒuːz). **1** something small and delicately worked, such as a trinket. **2** *(modifier) Often ironic.* small but elegant and tasteful: *a bijou residence.* [C19: from French, from Breton *bizou* finger ring, from *biz* finger; compare Welsh *bys* finger, Cornish *bis*]
bijouterie (biː'ʒuːtərɪ) *n* **1** jewellery esteemed for the delicacy of the work rather than the value of the materials. **2** a collection of such jewellery.
bijugate ('baɪdʒʊˌgeɪt, baɪ'dʒuːgeɪt) *or* **bijugous** *adj* (of compound leaves) having two pairs of leaflets.
Bikaner ('biːkəˌnɪə) *n* a walled city in NW India, in Rajasthan: capital of the former state of Bikaner, on the edge of the Thar Desert. Pop.: 416 289 (1991).
bike[1] (baɪk) *n, vb* **1** *Informal.* short for **bicycle** or **motorcycle. 2 on your bike.** *Brit. slang.* away you go. **3 get off one's bike.** *Austral. and N.Z. slang.* to lose one's self-control. ◆ *n* **4** *Slang.* a promiscuous woman: *the town bike.*
bike[2] *or* **byke** (bəɪk, baɪk) *Scot.* ◆ *n* **1** a wasps' or bees' nest. ◆ *vb (intr)* **2** to swarm. [C14: of uncertain origin]
biker ('baɪkə) *n Informal.* a member of a motorcyle gang.
biker jacket *n* a short, close-fitting leather jacket with zips and studs, often worn by motorcyclists.
bikie ('baɪkɪ) *n Austral. and N.Z. slang.* a member of a motorcycle gang.
Bikila (bɪ'kiːlə) *n* **Abebe** (ə'beɪbeɪ). 1932–73, Ethiopian long-distance runner: winner of the Marathon at the Olympic Games in Rome (1960) and Tokyo (1964).
bikini (bɪ'kiːnɪ) *n, pl* **-nis.** a woman's very brief two-piece swimming costume. [C20: after Bikini atoll, from a comparison between the devastating effect of the atomic-bomb test and the effect caused by women wearing bikinis]
Bikini (bɪ'kiːnɪ) *n* an atoll in the N Pacific; one of the Marshall Islands: site of a U.S. atomic-bomb test in 1946.
Biko ('biːkəʊ) *n* **Steven Bantu,** known as *Steve.* 1946–77, Black South African civil rights leader: founder of the South African Students Organization. His death in police custody caused worldwide concern.
bilabial (baɪ'leɪbɪəl) *adj* **1** of, relating to, or denoting a speech sound articulated using both lips: *(p) is a bilabial stop, (w) a bilabial semivowel.* ◆ *n* **2** a bilabial speech sound.
bilabiate (baɪ'leɪbɪˌeɪt, -ɪt) *adj Botany.* divided into two lips: *the snapdragon has a bilabiate corolla.*
bilander ('bɪləndə) *n* a small two-masted cargo ship. [C17: from Dutch, literally: by-lander, because used on canals]
bilateral (baɪ'lætərəl) *adj* **1** having or involving two sides. **2** affecting or undertaken by two parties; mutual: *a bilateral treaty.* **3** denoting or relating to bilateral symmetry. **4** having identical sides or parts on each side of an axis; symmetrical. **5** *Sociol.* relating to descent through both maternal and paternal lineage. Compare **unilateral** (sense 5). **6** *Brit.* relating to an education that combines academic and technical courses. ► **bi'laterally** *adv*
bilateral symmetry *n* the property of an organism or part of an organism such that, if cut in only one plane, the two cut halves are mirror images of each other. See also **radial symmetry.**
bilateral trade *n* a system of trading between two countries in which each country attempts to balance its trade with that of the other.
Bilbao (bɪl'bɑːəʊ; *Spanish* bil'βau) *n* a port in N Spain, on the Bay of Biscay: famous since medieval times for the production of iron and steel goods, esp. swords; still contains the country's largest iron and steel works and exports iron ore. Pop.: 370 997 (1995 est.).
bilberry ('bɪlbərɪ) *n, pl* **-ries. 1** any of several ericaceous shrubs of the genus *Vaccinium,* such as the whortleberry, having edible blue or blackish berries. See also **blueberry. 2a** the fruit of any of these plants. **2b** *(as modifier): bilberry pie.* [C16: probably of Scandinavian origin; compare Danish *böllebær,* from *bölle* bilberry + *bær* BERRY]
bilbo ('bɪlbəʊ) *n, pl* **-bos** *or* **-boes.** (formerly) a sword with a marked temper and elasticity. [C16: from *Bilboa,* variant (in English) of *Bilbao,* Spain, noted for its blades]
bilboes ('bɪlbəʊz) *pl n* a long iron bar with two sliding shackles, formerly used to confine the ankles of a prisoner. [C16: perhaps changed from BILBAO]
bilby ('bɪlbɪ) *n, pl* **-bies.** a burrowing marsupial of the genus *Macrotis* of Australia having long pointed ears and grey fur. Also called: **rabbit bandicoot, dalgyte.**

Bildungsroman *German.* ('bɪldʊŋsroma:n) *n* a novel concerned with a person's formative years and development. [literally: education novel]

bile[1] (baɪl) *n* **1** a bitter greenish to golden brown alkaline fluid secreted by the liver and stored in the gall bladder. It is discharged during digestion into the duodenum, where it aids the emulsification and absorption of fats. **2** irritability or peevishness. **3** *Archaic.* either of two bodily humours, one of which (**black bile**) was thought to cause melancholy and the other (**yellow bile**) anger. [C17: from French, from Latin *bīlis,* probably of Celtic origin; compare Welsh *bustl* bile]

bile[2] (baɪl) *vb* a Scot. word for **boil**[1].

bilection (baɪ'lɛkʃən) *n* another word for **bolection.**

bilestone ('baɪl,stəʊn) *n* another name for **gallstone.**

bilge (bɪldʒ) *n* **1** *Nautical.* the parts of a vessel's hull where the vertical sides curve inwards to form the bottom. **2** (*often pl*) the parts of a vessel between the lowermost floorboards and the bottom. **3** Also called: **bilge water.** the dirty water that collects in a vessel's bilge. **4** *Informal.* silly rubbish; nonsense. **5** the widest part of the belly of a barrel or cask. ◆ *vb* **6** (*intr*) *Nautical.* (of a vessel) to take in water at the bilge. **7** (*tr*) *Nautical.* to damage (a vessel) in the bilge, causing it to leak. [C16: probably a variant of BULGE] ▶ **'bilgy** *adj*

bilge keel *n* one of two keel-like projections along the bilges of some vessels to improve sideways stability.

bilharzia (bɪl'hɑ:tsɪə) *n* **1** another name for a **schistosome. 2** another name for **schistosomiasis.** [C19: New Latin, named after Theodor *Bilharz* (1825–62), German parasitologist who discovered schistosomes]

bilharziasis (,bɪlhɑ:'tsaɪəsɪs) *or* **bilharziosis** (bɪl,hɑ:tsɪ'əʊsɪs) *n* another name for **schistosomiasis.**

biliary ('bɪlɪərɪ) *adj* of or relating to bile, to the ducts that convey bile, or to the gall bladder.

bilinear (baɪ'lɪnɪə) *adj* **1** of or referring to two lines. **2** of or relating to a function of two variables that is linear in each independently, as f(x, y) = xy.

bilingual (baɪ'lɪŋgwəl) *adj* **1** able to speak two languages, esp. with fluency. **2** written or expressed in two languages. ◆ *n* **3** a bilingual person. ▶ **bi'lingual,ism** *n* ▶ **bi'lingually** *adv*

bilious ('bɪlɪəs) *adj* **1** of or relating to bile. **2** affected with or denoting any disorder related to excess secretion of bile. **3** *Informal.* (esp. of colours) extremely distasteful; nauseating: *a bilious green.* **4** *Informal.* bad-tempered; irritable. [C16: from Latin *bīliōsus* full of BILE[1]] ▶ **'biliousness** *n*

bilirubin (,bɪlɪ'ru:bɪn, ,baɪ-) *n* an orange-yellow pigment in the bile formed as a breakdown product of haemoglobin. Excess amounts in the blood produce the yellow appearance associated with jaundice. Formula: $C_{32}H_{36}O_6N_4$. [C19: from BILE[1] + Latin *ruber* red + -IN]

biliverdin (,bɪlɪ'vɜ:dɪn) *n* a dark green pigment in the bile formed by the oxidation of bilirubin. Formula: $C_{33}H_{34}O_6N_4$. [C19: coined in Swedish, from Latin *bīlis* bile + Old French *verd* green + -IN]

bilk (bɪlk) *vb* (*tr*) **1** to balk; thwart. **2** (often foll. by *of*) to cheat or deceive, esp. to avoid making payment to. **3** to escape from; elude. **4** *Cribbage.* to play a card that hinders (one's opponent) from scoring in his crib. ◆ *n* **5** a swindle or cheat. **6** a person who swindles or cheats. [C17: perhaps variant of BALK] ▶ **'bilker** *n*

bill[1] (bɪl) *n* **1** money owed for goods or services supplied: *an electricity bill.* **2** a written or printed account or statement of money owed. **3** *Chiefly Brit.* such an account for food and drink in a restaurant, hotel, etc. Usual U.S. and Canadian word: **check. 4** any printed or written list of items, events, etc., such as a theatre programme: *who's on the bill tonight?* **5 fit** *or* **fill the bill.** *Informal.* to serve or perform adequately. **6** a statute in draft, before it becomes law. **7** a printed notice or advertisement; poster. **8** *U.S. and Canadian.* a piece of paper money; note. **9** an obsolete name for **promissory note. 10** *Law.* See **bill of indictment. 11** See **bill of exchange. 12** See **bill of fare. 13** *Archaic.* any document. ◆ *vb* (*tr*) **14** to send or present an account for payment to (a person). **15** to enter (items, goods, etc.) on an account or statement. **16** to advertise by posters. **17** to schedule as a future programme: *the play is billed for next week.* [C14: from Anglo-Latin *billa,* alteration of Late Latin *bulla* document, BULL[3]]

bill[2] (bɪl) *n* **1** the mouthpart of a bird, consisting of projecting jaws covered with a horny sheath; beak. It varies in shape and size according to the type of food eaten and may also be used as a weapon. **2** any beaklike mouthpart in other animals. **3** a narrow promontory: *Portland Bill.* **4** *Nautical.* the pointed tip of the fluke of an anchor. ◆ *vb* (*intr*) (esp. in the phrase **bill and coo**). **5** (of birds, esp. doves) to touch bills together. **6** (of lovers) to kiss and whisper amorously. [Old English *bile;* related to *bill* BILL[3]]

bill[3] (bɪl) *n* **1** a pike or halberd with a narrow hooked blade. **2** short for **billhook.** [Old English *bill* sword, related to Old Norse *bīldr* instrument used in blood-letting, Old High German *bil* pickaxe]

bill[4] (bɪl) *n Ornithol.* another word for **boom**[1] (sense 4). [C18: from dialect *beel* BELL[2] (vb)]

billabong ('bɪlə,bɒŋ) *n Austral.* **1** a backwater channel that forms a lagoon or pool. **2** a branch of a river running to a dead end. [C19: from a native Australian language, from *billa* river + *bong* dead]

billboard[1] ('bɪl,bɔ:d) *n* another name for **hoarding.** [C19: from BILL[1] + BOARD]

billboard[2] ('bɪl,bɔ:d) *n* a fitting at the bow of a vessel for securing an anchor. [C19: from BILL[2] + BOARD]

bill broker *n* a person whose business is the purchase and sale of bills of exchange.

billet[1] ('bɪlɪt) *n* **1** accommodation, esp. for a soldier, in civilian lodgings. **2** the official requisition for such lodgings. **3** a space or berth allocated, esp. for slinging a hammock, in a ship. **4** *Informal.* a job. **5** *Archaic.* a brief letter or document. ◆ *vb* **-lets, -leting, -leted. 6** (*tr*) to assign a lodging to (a soldier). **7** (*tr*) *Informal.* to assign to a post or job. **8** to lodge or be lodged. [C15: from Old French *billette,* from *bulle* a document; see BULL[3]] ▶ **,billet'ee** *n* ▶ **'billeter** *n*

billet[2] ('bɪlɪt) *n* **1** a chunk of wood, esp. for fuel. **2** *Metallurgy.* **2a** a metal bar of square or circular cross section. **2b** an ingot cast into the shape of a prism. **3** *Architect.* a carved ornament in a moulding, with short cylinders or blocks evenly spaced. [C15: from Old French *billette* a little log, from *bille* log, probably of Celtic origin]

billet-doux (,bɪlɪ'du:; *French* bijɛdu) *n, pl* **billets-doux** (,bɪlɪ'du:z; *French* bijɛdu). *Old-fashioned or jocular.* a love letter. [C17: from French, literally: a sweet letter, from *billet* (see BILLET[1]) + *doux* sweet, from Latin *dulcis*]

billfish ('bɪl,fɪʃ) *n, pl* **-fish** *or* **-fishes.** *U.S.* any of various fishes having elongated jaws, esp. any fish of the family *Istiophoridae,* such as the spearfish and marlin.

billfold ('bɪl,fəʊld) *n* a U.S. and Canadian word for **wallet.**

billhook ('bɪl,hʊk) *n* a cutting tool with a wooden handle and a curved blade terminating in a hook at its tip, used for pruning, chopping, etc. Also called: **bill.**

billiard ('bɪljəd) *n* (*modifier*) of or relating to billiards: *a billiard table; a billiard cue; a billiard ball.*

billiards ('bɪljədz) *n* (*functioning as sing*) **1** any of various games in which long cues are used to drive balls now made of composition or plastic. It is played on a rectangular table covered with a smooth tight-fitting cloth and having raised cushioned edges. **2** a version of this, played on a rectangular table having six pockets let into the corners and the two longer sides. Points are scored by striking one of three balls with the cue to contact the other two or one of the two. Compare **pool**[2] (sense 5), **snooker.** [C16: from Old French *billard* curved stick, from Old French *bille* log; see BILLET[2]]

billing ('bɪlɪŋ) *n* **1** *Theatre.* the relative importance of a performer or act as reflected in the prominence given in programmes, advertisements, etc. **2** *Chiefly U.S. and Canadian.* public notice or advertising (esp. in the phrase **advance billing**).

billingsgate ('bɪlɪŋz,geɪt) *n* obscene or abusive language. [C17: after BILLINGSGATE, which was notorious for such language]

Billingsgate ('bɪlɪŋgz,geɪt) *n* the largest fish market in London, on the N bank of the River Thames; moved to new site on the Isle of Dogs in 1982.

Billings method *n* a natural method of birth control that involves examining the colour and viscosity of the cervical mucus to discover when ovulation is occurring. Also called: **ovulation method, mucus method.** [C20: devised by Drs John and Evelyn *Billings* in the 1960s]

billion ('bɪljən) *n, pl* **-lions** *or* **-lion. 1** one thousand million: it is written as 1 000 000 000 or 10^9. **2** (formerly, in Britain) one million million: it is written as 1 000 000 000 000 or 10^{12}. **3** (*often pl*) any exceptionally large number. ◆ *determiner* **4** (preceded by *a* or a cardinal number) **4a** amounting to a billion: *it seems like a billion years ago.* **4b** (*as pronoun*): *we have a billion here.* [C17: from French, from BI-[1] + *-llion* as in *million*] ▶ **'billionth** *adj, n*

billionaire (,bɪljə'nɛə) *n* a person whose assets are worth over a billion of the monetary units of his country.

Billiton ('bɪlɪtɒn, bɪ'li:tɒn) *n* an island of Indonesia, in the Java Sea between Borneo and Sumatra. Chief town: Tandjungpandan. Area: 4833 sq. km (1866 sq. miles). Also called: **Belitung.**

bill of adventure *n* a certificate made out by a merchant to show that goods handled by him and his agents are the property of another party at whose risk the dealing is done.

bill of attainder *n* (formerly) a legislative act finding a person guilty without trial of treason or felony and declaring him attainted. See also **attainder** (sense 1).

bill of exchange *n* (now chiefly in foreign transactions) a document, usually negotiable, containing an instruction to a third party to pay a stated sum of money at a designated future date or on demand.

bill of fare *n* another name for **menu.**

bill of health *n* **1** a certificate, issued by a port officer, that attests to the health of a ship's company. **2 clean bill of health.** *Informal.* **2a** a good report of one's physical condition. **2b** a favourable account of a person's or a company's financial position.

bill of indictment *n Criminal Law.* a formal document accusing a person or persons of crime, formerly presented to a grand jury for certification as a true bill but now signed by a court official.

bill of lading *n* (in foreign trade) a document containing full particulars of goods shipped or for shipment. Usual U.S. and Canadian name: **waybill.**

bill of quantities *n* a document drawn up by a quantity surveyor providing details of the prices, dimensions, etc., of the materials required to build a large structure, such as a factory.

Bill of Rights *n* **1** an English statute of 1689 guaranteeing the rights and liberty of the individual subject. **2** the first ten amendments to the U.S. Constitution, added in 1791, which guarantee the liberty of the individual. **3** (in Canada) a statement of basic human rights and freedoms enacted by Parliament in 1960. **4** (*usually not caps.*) any charter or summary of basic human rights.

bill of sale *n Law.* a deed transferring personal property, either outright or as security for a loan or debt.

billon ('bɪlən) *n* **1** an alloy consisting of gold or silver and a base metal, usually copper, used esp. for coinage. **2** any coin made of such an alloy. [C18: from Old French: ingot, from *bille* log; see BILLET[2]]

billow ('bɪləʊ) *n* **1** a large sea wave. **2** a swelling or surging mass, as of smoke or sound. **3** (*pl*) *Poetic.* the sea itself. ◆ *vb* **4** to rise up, swell out, or cause to rise up or swell out. [C16: from Old Norse *bylgja;* related to Swedish *bölja,* Danish *bölg,* Middle High German *bulge;* see BELLOW, BELLY] ▶ **'billowing** *adj, n*

billowy ('bɪləʊɪ) *adj* full of or forming billows: *a billowy sea.* ▶ **'billowiness** *n*

billposter ('bɪlˌpəʊstə) *or* **billsticker** *n* a person who is employed to stick advertising posters to walls, fences, etc. ▶ **'bill,posting** *or* **'bill,sticking** *n*

billy[1] ('bɪlɪ) *n, pl* **-lies**. *U.S. and Canadian.* a wooden club esp. a policeman's truncheon. [C19: special use of the name *Billy*, pet form of *William*]

billy[2] ('bɪlɪ) *or* **billycan** ('bɪlɪˌkæn) *n, pl* **-lies** *or* **-lycans**. **1** a metal can or pot for boiling water, etc., over a campfire. **2** *Austral. and N.Z.* (*as modifier*): *billy-tea.* **3 boil the billy.** *Austral. and N.Z. informal.* to make tea. [C19: from Scot. *billypot* cooking vessel]

billy-bread *n N.Z.* bread baked in a billy over a camp fire.

billycock ('bɪlɪkɒk) *n Rare, chiefly Brit.* any of several round-crowned brimmed hats of felt, such as the bowler. [C19: named after *William Coke*, Englishman for whom it was first made]

billy goat *n* a male goat. Compare **nanny goat**.

billyo *or* **billyoh** ('bɪlɪˌəʊ) *n* **like billyo**. *Informal.* (intensifier): *snowing like billyo.* [C19: of unknown origin]

Billy the Kid *n* nickname of *William H. Bonney*. 1859–81, U.S. outlaw.

bilobate (baɪ'ləʊˌbeɪt) *or* **bilobed** ('baɪˌləʊbd) *adj* divided into or having two lobes: *a bilobate leaf.*

bilocular (baɪ'lɒkjʊlə) *or* **biloculate** *adj Biology.* divided into two chambers or cavities: *some flowering plants have bilocular ovaries.*

biltong ('bɪlˌtɒŋ) *n S. African.* strips of meat dried and cured in the sun. [C19: Afrikaans, from Dutch *bil* buttock + *tong* TONGUE]

Bim (bɪm) *n Informal.* a native or inhabitant of Barbados. [C19: of unknown origin]

BIM *abbrev. for* British Institute of Management.

bimah *or* **bima** ('biːmə) *n* variant spellings of **bema**.

bimanous ('bɪmənəs, baɪ'meɪ-) *adj* (of man and the higher primates) having two hands distinct in form and function from the feet. [C19: from New Latin *bimana* two handed, from BI-[1] + Latin *manus* hand]

bimanual (baɪ'mænjʊəl) *adj* using or requiring both hands. ▶ **bi'manually** *adv*

bimbo ('bɪmbəʊ) *n, pl* **-bos** *or* **-boes**. *Slang, usually derogatory.* **1** an attractive but empty-headed young woman. **2** a fellow; person esp. a foolish one. [C20: from Italian: little child, perhaps via Polari]

bimestrial (baɪ'mɛstrɪəl) *adj* **1** lasting for two months. **2** a less common word for **bimonthly** (sense 1). [C19: from Latin *bimēstris*, from BI-[1] + *mēnsis* month] ▶ **bi'mestrially** *adv*

bimetallic (ˌbaɪmɪ'tælɪk) *adj* **1** consisting of two metals. **2** of, relating to, or based on bimetallism.

bimetallic strip *n* a strip consisting of two metals of different coefficients of expansion welded together so that it buckles on heating: used in thermostats, etc.

bimetallism (baɪ'mɛtəˌlɪzəm) *n* **1** the use of two metals, esp. gold and silver, in fixed relative values as the standard of value and currency. **2** the economic policies or doctrine supporting a bimetallic standard. ▶ **bi'metallist** *n*

bimillenary (ˌbaɪmɪ'liːnərɪ, baɪ'mɪlɪnərɪ) *adj* **1** marking a two-thousandth anniversary. ◆ *n pl,* **-naries**. **2** a two-thousandth anniversary.

bimodal distribution (baɪ'məʊdᵊl) *n Statistics.* a frequency distribution with two modes.

bimolecular (ˌbaɪmə'lɛkjʊlə) *adj* (of a chemical complex, collision, etc.) having or involving two molecules.

bimonthly (baɪ'mʌnθlɪ) *adj, adv* **1** every two months. **2** (often avoided because of confusion with sense 1) twice a month; semimonthly. See **bi-**[1]. ◆ *n, pl* **-lies**. **3** a periodical published every two months.

bimorph ('baɪmɔːf) *or* **bimorph cell** *n Electronics.* an assembly of two piezoelectric crystals cemented together so that an applied voltage causes one to expand and the other to contract, converting electrical signals into mechanical energy. Conversely, bending can generate a voltage: used in loudspeakers, gramophone pick-ups, etc.

bin (bɪn) *n* **1** a large container or enclosed space for storing something in bulk, such as coal, grain, or wool. **2** Also called: **bread bin**. a small container for bread. **3** Also called: **dustbin, rubbish bin**. a container for litter, rubbish, etc. **4** *Brit.* **4a** a storage place for bottled wine. **4b** one particular bottling of wine. ◆ *vb* **bins, binning, binned**. **5** (*tr*) to store in a bin. **6** (*tr*) to put in a wastepaper bin. [Old English *binne* basket, probably of Celtic origin; related to *bindan* to BIND]

bin- *prefix* a variant, esp. before a vowel, of **bi-**[1]: *binocular.*

binal ('baɪnᵊl) *adj* twofold; double. [C17: from New Latin *bīnālis*; see BIN-]

binary ('baɪnərɪ) *adj* **1** composed of, relating to, or involving two; dual. **2** *Maths, computing.* of, relating to, or expressed in binary notation or binary code. **3** (of a compound or molecule) containing atoms of two different elements. **4** *Metallurgy.* (of an alloy) consisting of two components or phases. **5** (of an educational system) consisting of two parallel forms of education such as the grammar school and the secondary modern in Britain. **6** *Maths, logic.* (of a relation, expression, or operation) applying to two elements of its domain; having two argument places; dyadic. ◆ *n, pl* **-ries**. **7** something composed of two parts or things. **8** *Astronomy.* See **binary star**. **9** short for **binary weapon**. [C16: from Late Latin *bīnārius*; see BIN-]

binary code *n Computing.* the representation of each one of a set of numbers, letters, etc., as a unique sequence of bits, as in ASCII.

binary-coded decimal *n* a number in binary code written in groups of four bits, each group representing one digit of the corresponding decimal number. Abbrev.: **BCD**.

binary digit *n* either of the two digits 0 or 1, used in binary notation. See also: **bit**[4].

binary fission *n* asexual reproduction in unicellular organisms by division into two similar daughter cells.

binary form *n Music.* a structure consisting of two sections, each being played twice.

binary notation *or* **system** *n* a number system having a base of two, numbers being represented by sequences of the digits 0 and 1: used in computing, as 0 and 1 can be represented electrically as *off* and *on.*

binary number *n* a number expressed in binary notation, as $1101.101 = 1 \times 2^3 + 1 \times 2^2 + 0 \times 2^1 + 1 \times 2^0 + 1 \times 2^{-1} + 0 \times 2^{-2} + 1 \times 2^{-3} = 13\frac{5}{8}$.

binary star *n* a double star system containing two associated stars revolving around a common centre of gravity in different orbits. A **visual binary** can be seen through a telescope. A **spectroscopic binary** can only be observed by the spectroscopic Doppler shift as each star moves towards or away from the earth. Sometimes shortened to **binary**. See also **optical double star, eclipsing binary**.

binary weapon *n* a chemical weapon consisting of a projectile containing two substances separately that mix to produce a lethal agent when the projectile is fired.

binate ('baɪˌneɪt) *adj Botany.* occurring in two parts or in pairs: *binate leaves.* [C19: from New Latin *bīnātus*, probably from Latin *combīnātus* united] ▶ **'bi,nately** *adv*

binaural (baɪ'nɔːrəl, bɪn-) *adj* **1** relating to, having, or hearing with both ears. **2** employing two separate channels for recording or transmitting sound; so creating an impression of depth: *a binaural recording.* ▶ **bin'aurally** *adv*

bind (baɪnd) *vb* **binds, binding, bound**. **1** to make or become fast or secure with or as if with a tie or band. **2** (*tr;* often foll. by *up*) to encircle or enclose with a band: *to bind the hair.* **3** (*tr*) to place (someone) under obligation; oblige. **4** (*tr*) to impose legal obligations or duties upon (a person or party to an agreement). **5** (*tr*) to make (a bargain, agreement, etc.) irrevocable; seal. **6** (*tr*) to restrain or confine with or as if with ties, as of responsibility or loyalty. **7** (*tr*) to place under certain constraints; govern. **8** (*tr;* often foll. by *up*) to bandage or swathe: *to bind a wound.* **9** to cohere or stick or cause to cohere or stick: *egg binds fat and flour.* **10** to make or become compact, stiff, or hard: *frost binds the earth.* **11a** (*tr*) to enclose and fasten (the pages of a book) between covers. **11b** (*intr*) (of a book) to undergo this process. **12** (*tr*) to provide (a garment, hem, etc.) with a border or edging, as for decoration or to prevent fraying. **13** (*tr;* sometimes foll. by *out* or *over*) to employ as an apprentice; indenture. **14** (*intr*) *Slang.* to complain. **15** (*tr*) *Logic.* to bring (a variable) into the scope of an appropriate quantifier. See also **bound**[1] (sense 9). ◆ *n* **16** something that binds. **17** the act of binding or state of being bound. **18** *Informal.* a difficult or annoying situation. **19** another word for **bine**. **20** *Music.* another word for **tie** (sense 17). **21** *Mining.* clay between layers of coal. **22** *Fencing.* a pushing movement with the blade made to force one's opponent's sword from one line into another. **23** *Chess.* a position in which one player's pawns have a hold on the centre that makes it difficult for the opponent to advance there. ◆ See also **bind over**. [Old English *bindan*; related to Old Norse *binda*, Old High German *bintan*, Latin *offendix* BAND[2], Sanskrit *badhnāti* he binds]

binder ('baɪndə) *n* **1** a firm cover or folder with rings or clasps for holding loose sheets of paper together. **2** a material used to bind separate particles together, give an appropriate consistency, or facilitate adhesion to a surface. **3a** a person who binds books; bookbinder. **3b** a machine that is used to bind books. **4** something used to fasten or tie, such as rope or twine. **5** *N.Z. informal.* a square meal. **6** Also called: **reaper binder**. *Obsolete.* a machine for cutting grain and binding it into bundles or sheaves. Compare **combine harvester**. **7** an informal agreement giving insurance coverage pending formal issue of a policy. **8** a tie, beam, or girder, used to support floor joists. **9** a stone for binding masonry; bondstone. **10** the nonvolatile component of the organic media in which pigments are dispersed in paint. **11** (in systemic grammar) a word that introduces a bound clause; a subordinating conjunction or a relative pronoun. Compare **linker** (sense 2).

bindery ('baɪndərɪ) *n, pl* **-eries**. a place in which books are bound.

bindi-eye ('bɪndɪˌaɪ) *n Austral.* **1** any of various small weedy Australian herbaceous plants of the genus *Calotis*, with burlike fruits: family *Compositae* (composites). **2** any bur or prickle. [C20: perhaps from a native Australian language]

binding ('baɪndɪŋ) *n* **1** anything that binds or fastens. **2** the covering within which the pages of a book are bound. **3** the material or tape used for binding hems, etc. ◆ *adj* **4** imposing an obligation or duty: *a binding promise.* **5** causing hindrance; restrictive.

binding energy *n Physics.* **1** the energy that must be supplied to a stable nucleus before it can undergo fission. It is equal to the mass defect. **2** the energy required to remove a particle from a system, esp. an electron from an atom.

bind over *vb* (*tr, adv*) to place (a person) under a legal obligation, such as one to keep the peace.

bindweed ('baɪndˌwiːd) *n* **1** any convolvulaceous plant of the genera *Convolvulus* and *Calystegia* that twines around a support. See also **convolvulus**. **2** any of various other trailing or twining plants, such as black bindweed.

bine (baɪn) *n* **1** the climbing or twining stem of any of various plants, such as the woodbine or bindweed. **2** any plant with such a stem. [C19: variant of BIND]

Binet-Simon scale ('biːneɪ'saɪmən) *n Psychol.* a test comprising questions and tasks, used to determine the mental age of subjects, usually children. Also called: **Binet scale** *or* **test**. See also **Stanford-Binet test**. [C20: named after Alfred *Binet* (1857–1911) + Théodore *Simon* (1873–1961), French psychologists]

bing (bɪŋ) *n Dialect.* a heap or pile, esp. of spoil from a mine. [C16: from Old Norse *bingr* heap]

binge (bɪndʒ) *n Informal.* **1** a bout of excessive eating or drinking. **2** excessive indulgence in anything: *a shopping binge.* ◆ *vb* **binges, bingeing** *or* **binging, binged**. (*intr*) **3** to indulge in a binge (esp. of eating or drinking). [C19: probably Lincolnshire dialect *binge* to soak]

Bingen ('bɪŋən) *n* a town in W Germany on the Rhine: wine trade and tourist centre. Pop.: 23 141 (1989 est.).

bingle ('bɪŋgᵊl) *n Austral. old-fashioned informal.* a minor crash or upset, as in a car or on a surfboard. [C20: of uncertain origin]

bingo ('bɪŋgəʊ) *n, pl* **-gos. 1** a gambling game, usually played with several people, in which numbers selected at random are called out and the players cover the numbers on their individual cards. The first to cover a given arrangement of numbers is the winner. Compare **lotto.** ◆ *sentence substitute.* **2** a cry by the winner of a game of bingo. **3** an expression of surprise at a sudden occurrence or the successful completion of something: *and bingo! the lights went out.* [C19: perhaps from *bing,* imitative of a bell ringing to mark the win]

Bini *or* **Beni** (bə'niː) *n, pl* **-ni** *or* **-nis.** other names for **Edo.**

binman ('bɪn,mæn, 'bɪnmən) *n, pl* **-men.** *Informal.* another name for **dustman.**

binnacle ('bɪnəkᵊl) *n* a housing for a ship's compass. [C17: changed from C15 *bitakle,* from Portuguese *bitácula,* from Late Latin *habitāculum* dwelling-place, from Latin *habitāre* to inhabit; spelling influenced by BIN]

Binnig (*German* 'binig) *n* **Gerd** (**Karl**). born 1947, German physicist: shared the Nobel prize for physics (1986) for work on the superconductivity of semiconductors and development of the scanning tunnelling microscope.

binocular (bɪ'nɒkjʊlə, baɪ-) *adj* involving, relating to, seeing with or intended for both eyes: *binocular vision.* [C18: from BI-[1] + Latin *oculus* eye]

binocular disparity *n Physiol.* the small differences in the positions of the parts of the images falling on each eye as a result of each eye viewing the scene from a slightly different position; these differences make stereoscopic vision possible.

binocular rivalry *n Psychol.* the inability to see simultaneously different images presented one to each eye; usually in some areas of the eye the image presented to the left eye is seen, in others that presented to the right eye. Also called: **retinal rivalry.**

binoculars (bɪ'nɒkjʊləz, baɪ-) *pl n* an optical instrument for use with both eyes, consisting of two small telescopes joined together. Also called: **field glasses.**

binomial (baɪ'nəʊmɪəl) *n* **1** a mathematical expression consisting of two terms, such as $3x + 2y$. **2** a two-part taxonomic name for an animal or plant. See **binomial nomenclature.** ◆ *adj* **3** referring to two names or terms. [C16: from Medieval Latin *binōmius* from BI-[1] + Latin *nōmen* NAME] ▸ **bi'nomially** *adv*

binomial coefficient *n Maths.* any of the numerical factors which multiply the successive terms in a binomial expansion; any term of the form $n!/(n-k)!k!$: written $\binom{n}{k}$, ${}^{n}C_{k}$, or C^{n}_{k}. See also **combination** (sense 6).

binomial distribution *n* a statistical distribution giving the probability of obtaining a specified number of successes in a specified number of independent trials of an experiment with a constant probability of success in each. Symbol: *Bi* (*n, p*), where *n* is the number of trials and *p* the probability of success in each.

binomial experiment *n Statistics.* an experiment consisting of a fixed number of independent trials each with two possible outcomes, success and failure, and the same probability of success. The probability of a given number of successes is described by a binominal distribution. See also **Bernoulli trial.**

binomial *or* **binominal nomenclature** *n* a system for naming plants and animals by means of two Latin names: the first indicating the genus and the second the species to which the organism belongs, as in *Panthera leo* (the lion).

binomial theorem *n* a mathematical theorem that gives the expansion of any binomial raised to a positive integral power, *n*. It contains $n + 1$ terms: $(x + a)^n = x^n + nx^{n-1} a + [n(n-1)/2] \quad x^{n-2}a^2 + \ldots + \binom{n}{k} \quad x^{n-k}a^k + \ldots + a^n$, where $\binom{n}{k} = n!/(n-k)!k!$, the number of combinations of *k* items selected from *n*.

binominal (baɪ'nɒmɪnᵊl) *Biology.* ◆ *adj* **1** of or denoting the binomial nomenclature. ◆ *n* **2** a two-part taxonomic name; binomial.

binovular (bɪ'nɒvjʊlə) *adj Physiol.* relating to or derived from two different ova: *binovular fertilization; binovular twins.*

bint (bɪnt) *n Slang.* a derogatory term for **girl** or **woman.** [C19: from Arabic, literally: daughter]

binturong ('bɪntjʊ,rɒŋ, bɪn'tjʊərɒŋ) *n* an arboreal SE Asian viverrine mammal, *Arctictis binturong,* closely related to the palm civets but larger and having long shaggy black hair. [from Malay]

binucleate (baɪ'njuːklɪ,eɪt, -ɪt) *adj Biology.* having two nuclei: *a binucleate cell.* Also: **bi'nuclear, bi'nucle,ated.**

Binyon ('bɪnjən) *n* (**Robert**) **Laurence.** 1869–1943, British poet and art historian, best known for his elegiac war poems "For the Fallen" (1914) and "The Burning of the Leaves" (1944).

bio ('baɪəʊ) *n, pl* **bios.** *Informal.* short for **biography.**

bio- *or before a vowel* **bi-** *combining form.* **1** indicating or involving life or living organisms: *biogenesis; biolysis.* **2** indicating a human life or career: *biography; biopic.* [from Greek *bios* life]

bioaeration (,baɪəʊεə'reɪʃən) *n* the oxidative treatment of raw sewage by aeration.

bioaeronautics (,baɪəʊ,εərə'nɔːtɪks) *n* (*functioning as sing*) the use of aircraft in the discovery, development, and protection of natural and biological resources.

bioassay *n* (,baɪəʊə'seɪ, -'æseɪ). **1** a method of determining the concentration, activity, or effect of a drug, hormone, or vitamin by testing its effect on a living organism and comparing this with the activity of an agreed standard. ◆ *vb* (,baɪəʊə'seɪ). **2** (*tr*) to subject to a bioassay.

bioastronautics (,baɪəʊ,æstrə'nɔːtɪks) *n* (*functioning as sing*) the study of the effects of space flight on living organisms. See **space medicine.**

bioavailability (,baɪəʊə,veɪlə'bɪlɪtɪ) *n* the extent to which a drug or other substance is taken up by a specific tissue or organ after administration. ▸ **,bioa'vailable** *adj*

Bío-Bío (*Spanish* 'biːo'biːo) *n* a river in central Chile, rising in the Andes and flowing northwest to the Pacific. Length: about 390 km (240 miles).

biocatalyst (,baɪəʊ'kætəlɪst) *n* a chemical, esp. an enzyme, that initiates or modifies the rate of a biochemical reaction. ▸ **biocatalytic** (,baɪəʊ,kætə'lɪtɪk) *adj*

biocellate (baɪ'ɒsɪ,leɪt, ,baɪəʊ'sεlɪt) *adj* (of animals and plants) marked with two eyelike spots or ocelli. [C19: from BI-[1] + *ocellate,* from Latin *ocellus,* diminutive of *oculus* eye]

biochemical oxygen demand *n* a measure of the organic pollution of water: the amount of oxygen, in mg per litre of water, absorbed by a sample kept at 20°C for five days. Abbrev.: **BOD.**

biochemistry (,baɪəʊ'kεmɪstrɪ) *n* the study of the chemical compounds, reactions, etc., occurring in living organisms. ▸ **biochemical** (,baɪəʊ'kεmɪkᵊl) *adj* ▸ **,bio'chemically** *adv* ▸ **,bio'chemist** *n*

biocide ('baɪə,saɪd) *n* a chemical, such as a pesticide, capable of killing living organisms. ▸ **,bio'cidal** *adj*

bioclastic (,baɪəʊ'klæstɪk) *adj* (of deposits, esp. limestones) derived from shell fragments or similar organic remains.

bioclimatology (,baɪəʊ,klaɪmə'tɒlədʒɪ) *n* the study of the effects of climatic conditions on living organisms. ▸ **,bio,clima'tologist** *n*

biocoenology *or* **biocenology** (,baɪəʊsɪ'nɒlədʒɪ) *n* the branch of ecology concerned with the relationships and interactions between the members of a natural community. [C20: from BIO- + *ceno-,* from Greek *koinos* common + -LOGY]

biocoenosis *or* **biocenosis** (,baɪəʊsɪ'nəʊsɪs) *n* a diverse community inhabiting a single biotope. ▸ **,biocoe'notic** *or* **,bioce'notic** *adj*

bioconversion (,baɪəʊkən'vɜːʃən) *n* the use of biological processes or materials to change organic substances into a new form, such as the conversion of waste into methane by fermentation.

biocycle ('baɪəʊ,saɪkᵊl) *n Ecology.* any of the major regions of the biosphere, such as the land or sea, which are capable of supporting life.

biodegradable (,baɪəʊdɪ'greɪdəbᵊl) *adj* (of sewage constituents, packaging material, etc.) capable of being decomposed by bacteria or other biological means. ▸ **biodegradation** (,baɪəʊ,dεgrə'deɪʃən) *n* ▸ **biodegradability** (,baɪəʊ,dεgreɪdɪ'bɪlɪtɪ) *n*

biodiversity (,baɪəʊdaɪ'vɜːsɪtɪ) *n* the existence of a wide variety of plant and animal species in their natural environments, which is the aim of conservationists concerned about the indiscriminate destruction of rainforests and other habitats.

biodot ('baɪəʊ,dɒt) *n* a temperature-sensitive device stuck to the skin in order to monitor stress levels.

biodynamics (,baɪəʊdaɪ'næmɪks, -dɪ-) *n* (*functioning as sing*) the branch of biology that deals with the energy production and activities of organisms. ▸ **,biody'namic** *or* **,biody'namical** *adj*

bioecology (,baɪəʊɪ'kɒlədʒɪ) *n* another word for **ecology** (sense 1). ▸ **bioecological** (,baɪəʊ,iːkə'lɒdʒɪkᵊl) *adj* ▸ **,bio,eco'logically** *adv* ▸ **,bioe'cologist** *n*

bioelectricity (,baɪəʊ,ɪlεk'trɪsɪtɪ) *n* electricity generated by a living organism. ▸ **,bioe'lectric** *adj*

bioenergetics (,baɪəʊ,εnə'dʒεtɪks) *n* (*functioning as sing*) the study of energy relationships in living organisms. ▸ **,bio,ener'getic** *adj*

bioengineering (,baɪəʊ,εndʒɪ'nɪərɪŋ) *n* **1** the design and manufacture of aids, such as artificial limbs, to rectify defective body functions. **2** the design, manufacture, and maintenance of engineering equipment used in biosynthetic processes, such as fermentation. ▸ **,bio,engi'neer** *n*

bioethics (,baɪəʊ'εθɪks) *n* (*functioning as sing*) the study of ethical problems arising from biological research and its applications in such fields as organ transplantation, genetic engineering, or artificial insemination. ▸ **,bio'ethical** *adj* ▸ **bioethicist** (,baɪəʊ'εθɪsɪst) *n*

biofeedback (,baɪəʊ'fiːd,bæk) *n Physiol., psychol.* a technique for teaching the control of autonomic functions, such as the rate of heartbeat or breathing, by recording the activity and presenting it (usually visually) so that the person can know the state of the autonomic function he is learning to control.

bioflavonoid (,baɪəʊ'fleɪvə,nɔɪd) *n* another name for **vitamin P.**

biofuel ('baɪəʊ,fjʊəl) *n* a gaseous, liquid, or solid substance of biological origin that is used as a fuel.

biog. *abbrev. for:* **1** biographical. **2** biography.

biogas ('baɪəʊ,gæs) *n* a gas that is produced by the action of bacteria on organic waste matter: used as a fuel.

biogen ('baɪədʒən) *n* a hypothetical protein assumed to be the basis of the formation and functioning of body cells and tissues.

biogenic (,baɪəʊ'dʒεnɪk) *adj* produced or originating from a living organism.

biogenesis (,baɪəʊ'dʒεnɪsɪs) *n* the principle that a living organism must originate from a parent organism similar to itself. Compare **abiogenesis.** ▸ **,bioge'netic, ,bioge'netical,** *or* **biogenous** (baɪ'ɒdʒənəs) *adj* ▸ **,bioge'netically** *adv*

biogeography (,baɪəʊdʒɪ'ɒgrəfɪ) *n* the branch of biology concerned with the geographical distribution of plants and animals. ▸ **biogeographical** (,baɪəʊ,dʒɪə'græfɪkᵊl) *adj* ▸ **,bio,geo'graphically** *adv*

biography (baɪ'ɒgrəfɪ) *n, pl* **-phies. 1** an account of a person's life by another. **2** such accounts collectively. ▸ **bi'ographer** *n* ▸ **biographical** (,baɪə'græfɪkᵊl) *or* (*archaic*) **,bio'graphic** *adj* ▸ **,bio'graphically** *adv*

biohazard (,baɪəʊ'hæzəd) *n* the risk of contracting a disease or contaminating the environment in the course of biological research. ▸ **,bio'hazardous** *adj*

bioherm ('baɪəʊ,hɜːm) *n* a mass of organic material, esp. a coral reef, surrounded by rocks of different origin. [C20: from BIO- + Greek *herma* submerged rock]

Bioko (baɪ'əʊkəʊ) *n* an island in the Gulf of Guinea, off the coast of Cameroon:

part of Equatorial Guinea. Capital: Malabo. Area: 2017 sq. km (786 sq. miles). Former names: **Fernando Po** (until 1973), **Macías Nguema** (1973–79).

biol. *abbrev. for:* **1** biological. **2** biology.

biological (ˌbaɪəˈlɒdʒɪkᵊl) *or (archaic)* **biologic** *adj* **1** of or relating to biology. ◆ *n* **2** (of a detergent) containing enzymes said to be capable of removing stains of organic origin from items to be washed. **3** (*usually pl*) a drug, such as a vaccine, that is derived from a living organism. ▸ **ˌbioˈlogically** *adv*

biological clock *n* **1** an inherent periodicity in the physiological processes of living organisms that is not dependent on the periodicity of external factors. **2** the hypothetical mechanism responsible for this periodicity. ◆ See also **circadian.**

biological control *n* the control of destructive organisms by nonchemical means, such as introducing a natural predator of the pest.

biological shield *n* a protective shield impervious to radiation, esp. the thick concrete wall surrounding the core of a nuclear reactor.

biological warfare *n* the use of living organisms or their toxic products to induce death or incapacity in humans and animals and damage to plant crops, etc. Abbrev.: **BW.**

biology (baɪˈɒlədʒɪ) *n* **1** the study of living organisms, including their structure, functioning, evolution, distribution, and interrelationships. **2** the structure, functioning, etc., of a particular organism or group of organisms. **3** the animal and plant life of a particular region. ▸ **biˈologist** *n*

bioluminescence (ˌbaɪəʊˌluːmɪˈnɛsəns) *n* the production of light by living organisms as a result of the oxidation of a light-producing substance (luciferin) by the enzyme luciferase: occurs in many marine organisms, insects such as the firefly, etc. ▸ **ˌbioˌlumiˈnescent** *adj*

biolysis (baɪˈɒlɪsɪs) *n* **1** the death and dissolution of a living organism. **2** the disintegration of organic matter by the action of bacteria etc. ▸ **biolytic** (ˌbaɪəˈlɪtɪk) *adj*

biomass (ˈbaɪəʊˌmæs) *n* **1** the total number of living organisms in a given area, expressed in terms of living or dry weight per unit area. **2** vegetable matter used as a source of energy.

biomathematics (ˌbaɪəʊˌmæθəˈmætɪks, -ˌmæθˈmæt-) *n* (*functioning as sing*) the study of the application of mathematics to biology.

biome (ˈbaɪˌəʊm) *n* a major ecological community, extending over a large area and usually characterized by a dominant vegetation. See **formation** (sense 6). [C20: from BIO- + -OME]

biomechanics (ˌbaɪəʊmɪˈkænɪks) *n* (*functioning as sing*) the study of the mechanics of the movement of living organisms.

biomedicine (ˌbaɪəʊˈmɛdɪsɪn, -ˈmɛdsɪn) *n* **1** the medical study of the effects of unusual environmental stress on human beings, esp. in connection with space travel. **2** the study of herbal remedies. ▸ **ˌbioˈmedical** *adj*

biometeorology (ˌbaɪəʊˌmiːtɪəˈrɒlədʒɪ) *n* the study of the effect of weather conditions on living organisms.

biometry (baɪˈɒmɪtrɪ) *or* **biometrics** (ˌbaɪəˈmɛtrɪks) *n* (*functioning as sing*) **1** the study of biological data by means of statistical analysis. **2** the statistical calculation of the probable duration of human life. ▸ **biometric** (ˌbaɪəˈmɛtrɪk) *adj* ▸ **ˌbioˈmetrically** *adv*

bionic (baɪˈɒnɪk) *adj* **1** of or relating to bionics. **2** (in science fiction) having certain physiological functions augmented or replaced by electronic equipment: *the bionic man.*

bionics (baɪˈɒnɪks) *n* (*functioning as sing*) **1** the study of certain biological functions, esp. those relating to the brain, that are applicable to the development of electronic equipment, such as computer hardware, designed to operate in a similar manner. **2** the technique of replacing a limb or body part by an artificial limb or part that is electronically or mechanically powered. [C20: from BIO- + (ELECTR)ONICS]

bionomics (ˌbaɪəˈnɒmɪks) *n* (*functioning as sing*) a less common name for **ecology** (senses 1, 2). [C19: from BIO- + *nomics* on pattern of ECONOMICS] ▸ **ˌbioˈnomic** *adj* ▸ **ˌbioˈnomically** *adv* ▸ **bionomist** (baɪˈɒnəmɪst) *n*

biophysics (ˌbaɪəʊˈfɪzɪks) *n* (*functioning as sing*) the physics of biological processes and the application of methods used in physics to biology. ▸ **ˌbioˈphysical** *adj* ▸ **ˌbioˈphysically** *adv* ▸ **biophysicist** (ˌbaɪəʊˈfɪzɪsɪst) *n*

biopic (ˈbaɪəʊˌpɪk) *n Informal.* a film based on the life of a famous person, esp. one giving a popular treatment. [C20: from *bio(graphical)* + *pic(ture)*]

bioplasm (ˈbaɪəʊˌplæzəm) *n* living matter; protoplasm. ▸ **ˌbioˈplasmic** *adj*

biopoiesis (ˌbaɪəʊpɔɪˈiːsɪs) *n* the synthesis of living matter from nonliving matter, esp. considered as an evolutionary process.

biopsy (ˈbaɪɒpsɪ) *n, pl* **-sies.** examination, esp. under a microscope, of tissue from a living body to determine the cause or extent of a disease. [C20: from BIO- + Greek *opsis* sight] ▸ **bioptic** (baɪˈɒptɪk) *adj*

biorhythm (ˈbaɪəʊˌrɪðəm) *n* a cyclically recurring pattern of physiological states in an organism or organ, such as alpha rhythm or circadian rhythm; believed by some to affect physical and mental states and behaviour. ▸ **ˌbioˈrhythmic** *adj* ▸ **ˌbioˈrhythmically** *adv*

biorhythmics (ˌbaɪəʊˈrɪðmɪks) *n* (*functioning as sing*) the study of biorhythms.

bioscience (ˈbaɪəʊˌsaɪəns) *n* the science of biology. ▸ **ˌbioscienˈtific** *adj* ▸ **ˌbioˈscientist** *n*

bioscope (ˈbaɪəˌskəʊp) *n* **1** a kind of early film projector. **2** a South African word for **cinema.**

bioscopy (baɪˈɒskəpɪ) *n, pl* **-pies.** examination of a body to determine whether it is alive.

-biosis *n combining form.* indicating a specified mode of life: *symbiosis.* [New Latin, from Greek *biōsis*; see BIO-, -OSIS] ▸ **-biotic** *adj combining form.*

biosphere (ˈbaɪəˌsfɪə) *n* the part of the earth's surface and atmosphere inhabited by living things.

biostatics (ˌbaɪəʊˈstætɪks) *n* (*functioning as sing*) the branch of biology that deals with the structure of organisms in relation to their function. ▸ **ˌbioˈstatic** *adj* ▸ **ˌbioˈstatically** *adv*

biostrome (ˈbaɪəˌstrəʊm) *n* a thin rocky layer consisting of a deposit of organic material, such as fossils. [C20: from BIO- + Greek *strōma* covering]

biosynthesis (ˌbaɪəʊˈsɪnθɪsɪs) *n* the formation of complex compounds from simple substances by living organisms. ▸ **biosynthetic** (ˌbaɪəʊsɪnˈθɛtɪk) *adj* ▸ **ˌbiosynˈthetically** *adv*

biosystematics (ˌbaɪəʊˌsɪstɪˈmætɪks) *n* (*functioning as sing*) the study of the variation and evolution of a population of organisms in relation to their taxonomic classification.

biota (baɪˈəʊtə) *n* the plant and animal life of a particular region or period. [C20: from New Latin, from Greek *biotē* way of life, from *bios* life]

biotechnology (ˌbaɪəʊtɛkˈnɒlədʒɪ) *n* **1** (in industry) the technique of using microorganisms, such as bacteria, to perform chemical processing, such as waste recycling, or to produce other materials, such as beer and wine, cheese, antibiotics, and (using genetic engineering) hormones, vaccines, etc. **2** another name for **ergonomics.** ▸ **biotechnological** (ˌbaɪəʊˌtɛknəˈlɒdʒɪkᵊl) *adj* ▸ **ˌbioˌtechnoˈlogically** *adv* ▸ **ˌbiotechˈnologist** *n*

biotelemetry (ˌbaɪəʊtɪˈlɛmɪtrɪ) *n* the monitoring of biological functions in humans or animals by means of a miniature transmitter that sends data to a distant point to be read by electronic instruments. ▸ **biotelemetric** (ˌbaɪəʊtɛlɪˈmɛtrɪk) *adj*

biotic (baɪˈɒtɪk) *adj* **1** of or relating to living organisms. **2** (of a factor in an ecosystem) produced by the action of living organisms. Compare **edaphic.** [C17: from Greek *biotikos*, from *bios* life]

biotin (ˈbaɪətɪn) *n* a vitamin of the B complex, abundant in egg yolk and liver, deficiency of which causes dermatitis and loss of hair. Formula: $C_{10}H_{16}N_2O_3S$. See also **avidin.** [C20: *biot-* from Greek *biotē* life, way of life + -IN]

biotite (ˈbaɪəˌtaɪt) *n* a black or dark green mineral of the mica group, found in igneous and metamorphic rocks. Composition: hydrous magnesium iron potassium aluminium silicate. General formula: $K(Mg,Fe)_3(Al,Fe)Si_3O_{10}(OH)_2$. Crystal structure: monoclinic. ▸ **biotitic** (ˌbaɪəˈtɪtɪk) *adj*

biotope (ˈbaɪəˌtəʊp) *n Ecology.* a small area, such as the bark of a tree, that supports its own distinctive community. [C20: from BIO- + Greek *topos* place]

biotroph (ˈbaɪəʊˌtrəʊf) *n* a parasitic organism, esp. a fungus.

biotype (ˈbaɪəˌtaɪp) *n* a group of plants or animals within a species that resemble, but differ physiologically from, other members of the species. ▸ **biotypic** (ˌbaɪəˈtɪpɪk) *adj*

biparietal (ˌbaɪpəˈraɪɪtᵊl) *adj Anatomy.* relating to or connected to both parietal bones.

biparous (ˈbɪpərəs) *adj* **1** *Zoology.* producing offspring in pairs. **2** *Botany.* (esp. of an inflorescence) producing two branches from one stem.

bipartisan (ˌbaɪpɑːtɪˈzæn, baɪˈpɑːtɪˌzæn) *adj* consisting of or supported by two political parties. ▸ **ˌbipartiˈsanship** *n*

bipartite (baɪˈpɑːtaɪt) *adj* **1** consisting of or having two parts. **2** affecting or made by two parties; bilateral: *a bipartite agreement.* **3** *Botany.* (esp. of some leaves) divided into two parts almost to the base. ▸ **biˈpartitely** *adv* ▸ **bipartition** (ˌbaɪpɑːˈtɪʃən) *n*

biped (ˈbaɪpɛd) *n* **1** any animal with two feet. ◆ *adj also* **bipedal** (baɪˈpiːdᵊl, -ˈpɛdᵊl). **2** having two feet.

bipetalous (baɪˈpɛtələs) *adj* having two petals.

biphasic (baɪˈfeɪzɪk) *adj* **1** having two phases. **2** See **two-phase.**

biphenyl (baɪˈfɛnᵊl, -ˈfiː-) *n* **1** a white or colourless crystalline solid used as a heat-transfer agent, as a fungicide, as an antifungal food preservative (**E230**) on the skins of citrus fruit, and in the manufacture of dyes, etc. Formula: $C_6H_5C_6H_5$. **2** any substituted derivative of biphenyl. ◆ Also called: **diphenyl.**

bipinnate (baɪˈpɪnˌeɪt) *adj* (of compound leaves) having both the leaflets and the stems bearing them arranged pinnately. ▸ **biˈpinˌnately** *adv*

biplane (ˈbaɪˌpleɪn) *n* an early type of aeroplane having two sets of wings, one above the other. Compare **monoplane.**

bipod (ˈbaɪpɒd) *n* a two-legged support or stand.

bipolar (baɪˈpəʊlə) *adj* **1** having two poles: *a bipolar dynamo; a bipolar neuron.* **2** relating to or found at the North and South Poles. **3** having or characterized by two opposed opinions, natures, etc. **4** (of a transistor) utilizing both majority and minority charge carriers. ▸ **bipoˈlarity** *n*

bipolar manic-depressive disorder *or* **bipolar syndrome** *n* See **manic-depressive.**

biprism (ˈbaɪˌprɪzəm) *n* a prism having a highly obtuse angle to facilitate beam splitting.

bipropellant (ˌbaɪprəˈpɛlənt) *n* a rocket propellant consisting of two substances, usually a fuel and an oxidizer. Also called: **dipropellant.** Compare **monopropellant.**

bipyramid (ˌbaɪˈpɪrəmɪd) *n* a geometrical form consisting of two pyramids with a common polygonal base.

biquadrate (baɪˈkwɒdreɪt, -rɪt) *n Maths.* the fourth power.

biquadratic (ˌbaɪkwɒˈdrætɪk) *Maths.* ◆ *adj also* **quartic. 1** of or relating to the fourth power. ◆ *n* **2** a biquadratic equation, such as $x^4 + x + 6 = 0$.

biquarterly (baɪˈkwɔːtəlɪ) *adj* occurring twice every three months.

biracial (baɪˈreɪʃəl) *adj* for, representing, or including members of two races, esp. White and Black. ▸ **biˈracialism** *n* ▸ **biˈracially** *adv*

biradial (baɪˈreɪdɪəl) *adj* showing both bilateral and radial symmetry, as certain sea anemones.

biramous (ˈbɪrəməs) *adj* divided into two parts, as the appendages of crustaceans.

birch (bɜːtʃ) *n* **1** any betulaceous tree or shrub of the genus *Betula*, having thin peeling bark. See also **silver birch. 2** the hard close-grained wood of any of these trees. **3 the birch.** a bundle of birch twigs or a birch rod used, esp. formerly, for flogging offenders. ◆ *adj* **4** of, relating to, or belonging to the birch.

5 consisting or made of birch. ◆ *vb* 6 (*tr*) to flog with a birch. [Old English *bierce;* related to Old High German *birihha,* Sanskrit *bhūrja*] ▸ **'birchen** *adj*

Bircher ('bɜːtʃə), **Birchist,** *or* **Birchite** *n* a member or supporter of the John Birch Society. ▸ **'Birch,ism** *n*

bird (bɜːd) *n* **1** any warm-blooded egg-laying vertebrate of the class *Aves,* characterized by a body covering of feathers and forelimbs modified as wings. Birds vary in size between the ostrich and the humming bird. Related adjs: **avian, ornithic. 2** *Informal.* a person (usually preceded by a qualifying adjective, as in the phrases **rare bird, odd bird, clever bird**). **3** *Slang, chiefly Brit.* a girl or young woman, esp. one's girlfriend. **4** *Slang.* prison or a term in prison (esp. in the phrase **do bird;** shortened from *birdlime,* rhyming slang for *time*). **5 a bird in the hand.** something definite or certain. **6 the bird has flown.** *Informal.* the person in question has fled or escaped. **7 the birds and the bees.** *Euphemistic or jocular.* sex and sexual reproduction. **8 birds of a feather.** people with the same characteristics, ideas, interests, etc. **9 get the bird.** *Informal.* **9a** to be fired or dismissed. **9b** (esp. of a public performer) to be hissed at, booed, or derided. **10 give (someone) the bird.** *Informal.* to tell (someone) rudely to depart; scoff at; hiss. **11 kill two birds with one stone.** to accomplish two things with one action. **12 like a bird.** without resistance or difficulty. **13 a little bird.** a (supposedly) unknown informant: *a little bird told me it was your birthday.* **14 (strictly) for the birds.** *Informal.* deserving of disdain or contempt; not important. [Old English *bridd,* of unknown origin] ▸ **'birdlike** *adj*

Bird (bɜːd) *n* nickname of (Charlie) **Parker.**

birdbath ('bɜːd,bɑːθ) *n* a small basin or trough for birds to bathe in, usually in a garden.

bird-brained *adj Informal.* silly; stupid.

birdcage ('bɜːd,keɪdʒ) *n* **1** a wire or wicker cage in which captive birds are kept. **2** any object of a similar shape, construction, or purpose. **3** *Austral. and N.Z.* an area on a racecourse where horses parade before a race.

bird call *n* **1** the characteristic call or song of a bird. **2** an imitation of this. **3** an instrument imitating the call of a bird, used esp. by hunters or bird-catchers.

bird cherry *n* a small Eurasian rosaceous tree, *Prunus padus,* with clusters of white flowers and small black fruits. See also **cherry** (sense 1).

bird dog *U.S. and Canadian.* ◆ *n* **1** *Hunting.* a dog used or trained to retrieve game birds after they are shot. ◆ *vb* **bird-dog, -dogs, -dogging, -dogged. 2** *Informal.* to control closely with unceasing vigilance.

birder ('bɜːdə) *n* an informal name for a **bird-watcher.** ▸ **'birding** *n*

birdhouse ('bɜːd,haʊs) *n U.S.* **1** a small shelter or box for birds to nest in. **2** an enclosure or large cage for captive birds; aviary.

birdie ('bɜːdɪ) *n* **1** *Golf.* a score of one stroke under par for a hole. **2** *Informal.* a bird, esp. a small bird. ◆ *vb* **3** *(tr) Golf.* to play (a hole) in one stroke under par.

birdlime ('bɜːd,laɪm) *n* **1** a sticky substance, prepared from holly, mistletoe, or other plants, smeared on twigs to catch small birds. ◆ *vb* **2** (*tr*) to smear (twigs) with birdlime to catch (small birds).

birdman ('bɜːd,mæn, -mən) *n, pl* **-men. 1** a man concerned with birds, such as a fowler or ornithologist. **2** a man who attempts to fly using his own muscle power. **3** an obsolete informal name for **airman.**

bird-nesting *or* **birds'-nesting** *n* searching for birds' nests as a hobby, often to steal the eggs.

bird of paradise *n* **1** any songbird of the family *Paradisaeidae* of New Guinea and neighbouring regions, the males of which have brilliantly coloured ornate plumage. **2 bird-of-paradise flower.** any of various musaceous plants of the genus *Strelitzia,* esp. *S. reginae,* that are native to tropical southern Africa and South America and have purple bracts and large orange or yellow flowers resembling birds' heads.

bird of passage *n* **1** a bird that migrates seasonally. **2** a transient person or one who roams about.

bird of peace *n* a figurative name for **dove**[1] (sense 1).

bird of prey *n* a bird, such as a hawk, eagle, or owl, that hunts and kills other animals, esp. vertebrates, for food. It has strong talons and a sharp hooked bill. Related adj: **raptorial.**

bird pepper *n* **1** a tropical solanaceous plant, *Capsicum frutescens,* thought to be the ancestor of the sweet pepper and many hot peppers. **2** the narrow podlike hot-tasting fruit of this plant.

birdseed ('bɜːd,siːd) *n* a mixture of various kinds of seeds for feeding cagebirds. Also called: **canary seed.**

bird's-eye *adj* **1a** seen or photographed from high above. **1b** summarizing the main points of a topic; summary (esp. in the phrase **bird's-eye view**). **2** having markings resembling birds' eyes. ◆ *n* **3 bird's-eye primrose.** a Eurasian primrose, *Primula farinosa,* having clusters of purplish flowers with yellow centres. **4 bird's-eye speedwell.** the usual U.S. name for **germander speedwell. 5** any of several other plants having flowers of two contrasting colours. **6** a pattern in linen and cotton fabrics, made up of small diamond shapes with a dot in the centre of each. **7** a linen or cotton fabric with such a pattern.

bird's-foot *or* **bird-foot** *n, pl* **-foots. 1** a European papilionaceous plant, *Ornithopus perpusillus,* with small red-veined white flowers and curved pods resembling a bird's claws. **2** any of various other plants whose flowers, leaves, or pods resemble a bird's foot or claw.

bird's-foot trefoil *n* a creeping papilionaceous Eurasian plant, *Lotus corniculatus,* with red-tipped yellow flowers and seed pods resembling the claws of a bird. Also called: **bacon-and-eggs.**

birdshot ('bɜːd,ʃɒt) *n* small pellets designed for shooting birds.

bird's-nest *vb* (*intr*) to search for the nests of birds in order to collect the eggs.

bird's-nest fungus *n* any fungus of the family *Nidulariaceae,* having a nestlike spore-producing body containing egglike spore-filled structures.

bird's-nest orchid *n* a brown parasitic Eurasian orchid, *Neottia nidus-avis,* whose thick fleshy roots resemble a bird's nest and contain a fungus on which the orchid feeds.

bird's-nest soup *n* a rich spicy Chinese soup made from the outer part of the nests of SE Asian swifts of the genus *Collocalia.*

birdsong ('bɜːd,sɒŋ) *n* the musical call of a bird or birds.

bird spider *n* any large hairy predatory bird-eating spider of the family *Aviculariidae,* of tropical America.

bird strike *n* a collision of an aircraft with a bird.

bird table *n* a table or platform in the open on which food for birds may be placed.

bird-watcher *n* a person who studies wild birds in their natural surroundings. ▸ **'bird-,watching** *n*

birefringence (,baɪrɪ'frɪndʒəns) *n* another name for **double refraction.** ▸ **,bire'fringent** *adj*

bireme ('baɪriːm) *n* an ancient galley having two banks of oars. [C17: from Latin *birēmus,* from BI-[1] + *-rēmus* oar]

Birendra Bir Bikram Shah Dev (bɪ'rendrɑː bɪə 'bɪkræm ʃɑː dev) *n* born 1945, king of Nepal from 1972.

biretta *or* **berretta** (bɪ'retə) *n R.C. Church.* a stiff clerical cap having either three or four upright pieces projecting outwards from the centre to the edge: coloured black for priests, purple for bishops, red for cardinals, and white for certain members of religious orders. [C16: from Italian *berretta,* from Old Provençal *berret,* from Late Latin *birrus* hooded cape]

Birgitta (bɪə'gɪtə) *n* **Saint.** See (Saint) **Bridget** (sense 2).

biriani (,bɪrɪ'ɑːnɪ) *n* a variant spelling of **biryani.**

birk (bɪrk, bɜːk) *Chiefly Scot.* ◆ *n* **1** a birch tree. **2** (*pl*) a birch wood. ◆ *adj* **3** consisting or made of birch. [C14: from Old Norse; compare BIRCH]

Birkbeck ('bɜːk,bek) *n* **George.** 1776–1841, British educationalist, who helped to establish vocational training for working men: founder and first president of the London Mechanics Institute (1824), which later became Birkbeck College.

Birkenhead[1] (,bɜːkən'hed) *n* a port in NW England, in Wirral unitary authority, Merseyside: former shipbuilding centre. Pop.: 93 087 (1991).

Birkenhead[2] ('bɜːkən,hed) *n* **Frederick Edwin Smith,** 1st Earl of, known as *F. E. Smith.* 1872–1930, British Conservative statesman, lawyer, and orator.

birkie ('bɪrkɪ) *n Scot.* **1** a spirited or lively person. **2** a foolish posturer. [C18: perhaps related to Old English *beorcan* to bark; compare Old Norse *berkia*]

birl[1] (bɜːl; *Scot.* bɪrl) *vb* **1** *Scot.* to spin; twirl. **2** *U.S. and Canadian.* to cause (a floating log) to spin using the feet while standing on it, esp. as a sport among lumberjacks. ◆ *n* **3** a variant spelling of **burl**[2]. [C18: probably imitative and influenced by WHIRL and HURL]

birl[2] (bɜːl; *Scot.* bɪrl) *vb Archaic, Scot.* to ply (one's guests, etc.) with drink. [Old English *byrelian;* related to *byrele* cup-bearer]

Birmingham ('bɜːmɪŋəm) *n* **1** an industrial city in central England, in Birmingham unitary authority, in the West Midlands: the second largest city in Great Britain; two cathedrals; three universities. Pop.: 965 928 (1994 est.). Related adj: **Brummie. 2** a unitary authority in central England, in the West Midlands. Pop.: 1 008 400 (1994 est.). Area: 283 sq. km (109 sq. miles). **3** ('bɜːmɪŋ,hæm) an industrial city in N central Alabama: rich local deposits of coal, iron ore, and other minerals. Pop.: 258 543 (1996 est.).

Biro ('baɪrəʊ) *n, pl* **-ros.** *Trademark, Brit.* a kind of ballpoint. [C20: named after Laszlo *Bíró* (1900–85), Hungarian inventor]

Birobidzhan *or* **Birobijan** (*Russian* birəbid'ʒan) *n* **1** a city in SE Russia: capital of the Jewish Autonomous Region. Pop.: 82 000 (1994). **2** another name for the **Jewish Autonomous Region.**

birr[1] (bɜː) *Chiefly U.S. and Scot.* ◆ *vb* **1** to make or cause to make a whirring sound. ◆ *n* **2** a whirring sound. **3** force, as of wind. **4** vigour; energy. [Old English *byre* storm, related to Old Norse *byrr* favourable wind]

birr[2] (bɜː) *n* the standard monetary unit of Ethiopia, divided into 100 cents. [C20: from Amharic]

birth (bɜːθ) *n* **1** the process of bearing young; parturition; childbirth. Related adj: **natal. 2** the act or fact of being born; nativity. **3** the coming into existence of something; origin. **4** ancestry; lineage: *of high birth.* **5** noble ancestry: *a man of birth.* **6** natural or inherited talent: *an artist by birth.* **7** *Archaic.* the offspring or young born at a particular time or of a particular mother. **8 give birth (to). 8a** to bear (offspring). **8b** to produce, originate, or create (an idea, plan, etc.). ◆ *vb* (*tr*) *Rare.* **9** to bear or bring forth (a child). [C12: from Old Norse *byrth;* related to Gothic *gabaurths,* Old Swedish *byrdh,* Old High German *berd* child; see BEAR[1], BAIRN]

birth certificate *n* an official form giving details of the time and place of a person's birth, and his or her name, sex, mother's name and (usually) father's name.

birth control *n* limitation of child-bearing by means of contraception. See also **family planning.**

birthday ('bɜːθ,deɪ) *n* **1a** an anniversary of the day of one's birth. **1b** (*as modifier*): *birthday present.* **2** the day on which a person was born. **3** any anniversary.

Birthday honours *pl n* (in Britain) honorary titles conferred on the official birthday of the sovereign.

birthday suit *n Informal, humorous.* a state of total nakedness, as at birth.

birthing centre ('bɜːθɪŋ) *n N.Z.* a private maternity hospital.

birthing chair *n* a chair constructed to allow a woman in labour to give birth in a sitting position.

birthmark ('bɜːθ,mɑːk) *n* a blemish or new growth on skin formed before birth, usually brown or dark red; naevus.

birth mother *n* the woman who gives birth to a child, regardless of whether she is the genetic mother or subsequently brings up the child.

birthplace ('bɜːθ,pleɪs) *n* the place where someone was born or where something originated.

birth rate *n* the ratio of live births in a specified area, group, etc., to the population of that area, etc., usually expressed per 1000 population per year.

birthright ('bɜːθ,raɪt) *n* **1** privileges or possessions that a person has or is believed to be entitled to as soon as he is born. **2** the privileges or possessions of a first-born son. **3** inheritance; patrimony.

birthroot ('bɜːθ,ruːt) *n* any of several North American plants of the genus *Trillium,* esp. *T. erectum,* whose tuber-like roots were formerly used by the American Indians as an aid in childbirth: family *Trilliaceae.*

birthstone ('bɜːθ,stəʊn) *n* a precious or semiprecious stone associated with a month or sign of the zodiac and thought to bring luck if worn by a person born in that month or under that sign.

birthwort ('bɜːθ,wɜːt) *n* any of several climbing plants of the genus *Aristolochia,* esp. *A. clematitis* of Europe, once believed to ease childbirth: family *Aristolochiaceae.*

Birtwistle ('bɜːt,wɪsəl) *n* Sir **Harrison.** born 1934, English composer, whose works include the operas *Punch and Judy* (1967), *The Mask of Orpheus* (1984), *Gawain* (1991), and *Exody* (1998).

biryani *or* **biriani** (,bɪrɪ'ɑːnɪ) *n* any of a variety of Indian dishes made with rice, highly flavoured and coloured with saffron or turmeric, mixed with meat or fish. **[**from Urdu**]**

bis (bɪs) *adv* **1** twice; for a second time (used in musical scores to indicate a part to be repeated). ◆ *sentence substitute* **2** encore! again! **[C19:** via Italian from Latin, from Old Latin *duis***]**

BIS *abbrev. for* Bank for International Settlements: an institution, based in Basel, Switzerland, that accepts deposits, makes loans for national central banks, and assists in offsetting speculative movements of funds between the major currencies; set up in 1930.

Bisayan (bɪ'sɑːjən) *n* a variant of **Visayan.**

Bisayas (bi'sajas) *pl n.* the Spanish name for the **Visayan Islands.**

Biscay ('bɪskeɪ, -kɪ) *n* **Bay of.** a large bay of the Atlantic Ocean between W France and N Spain: notorious for storms.

biscuit ('bɪskɪt) *n* **1** *Brit.* a small flat dry sweet or plain cake of many varieties, baked from a dough. U.S. and Canadian word: **cookie. 2** *U.S. and Canadian.* a kind of small roll similar to a muffin. **3a** a pale brown or yellowish-grey colour. **3b** *(as adj): biscuit gloves.* **4** Also called: **bisque.** earthenware or porcelain that has been fired but not glazed. **5 take the biscuit.** *Slang.* to be regarded (by the speaker) as the most surprising thing that could have occurred. **[C14:** from Old French, from *(pain) bescuit* twice-cooked (bread), from *bes* BIS + *cuire* to cook, from Latin *coquere***]**

bise (biːz) *n* a cold dry northerly wind in Switzerland and the neighbouring parts of France and Italy, usually in the spring. **[C14:** from Old French, of Germanic origin; compare Old Swedish *bīsa* whirlwind**]**

bisect (baɪ'sɛkt) *vb* **1** *(tr) Maths.* to divide into two equal parts. **2** to cut or split into two. **[C17:** BI-[1] + *-sect* from Latin *secāre* to cut**]** ▸ **bisection** (baɪ'sɛkʃən) *n*

bisector (baɪ'sɛktə) *n Maths.* **1** a straight line or plane that bisects an angle. **2** a line or plane that bisects another line.

bisectrix (baɪ'sɛktrɪks) *n, pl* **bisectrices** (baɪ'sɛktrɪ,siːz). **1** another name for **bisector. 2** the bisector of the angle between the optic axes of a crystal.

biseriate (,baɪ'sɪərɪɪt) *adj* (of plant parts, such as petals) arranged in two whorls, cycles, rows, or series.

biserrate (baɪ'sɛreɪt, -ɪt) *adj* **1** *Botany.* (of leaf margins, etc.) having serrations that are themselves serrated. **2** *Zoology.* serrated on both sides, as the antennae of some insects.

bisexual (baɪ'sɛksjʊəl) *adj* **1** sexually attracted by both men and women. **2** showing characteristics of both sexes: *a bisexual personality.* **3** (of some plants and animals) having both male and female reproductive organs. **4** of or relating to both sexes. ◆ *n* **5** a bisexual organism; a hermaphrodite. **6** a bisexual person. ▸ **bisexuality** (baɪ,sɛksjʊ'ælɪtɪ) *or esp. U.S.* **bi'sexualism** *n* ▸ **bi'sexually** *adv*

bish (bɪʃ) *n Brit. slang.* a mistake. **[C20:** of unknown origin**]**

Bishkek (bɪʃ'kɛk) *n* the capital of Kyrgyzstan. Pop.: 589 800 (1996 est.). Also called: **Pishpek.** Former name (1926–91): **Frunze.**

bishop ('bɪʃəp) *n* **1** (in the Roman Catholic, Anglican, and Greek Orthodox Churches) a clergyman having spiritual and administrative powers over a diocese or province of the Church. See also **suffragan.** Related adj: **episcopal. 2** (in some Protestant Churches) a spiritual overseer of a local church or a number of churches. **3** a chesspiece, capable of moving diagonally over any number of unoccupied squares of the same colour. **4** mulled wine, usually port, spiced with oranges, cloves, etc. **[**Old English *biscop,* from Late Latin *episcopus,* from Greek *episkopos,* from EPI- + *skopos* watcher**]**

Bishop ('bɪʃəp) *n* **Elizabeth.** 1911–79, U.S. poet, who lived in Brazil. Her poetry reflects her travelling experience, esp. in the tropics.

Bishop Auckland *n* a town in N England, in central Durham: seat of the bishops of Durham since the 12th century: light industries. Pop.: 23 154 (1991).

bishopbird ('bɪʃəp,bɜːd) *n* any African weaverbird of the genus *Euplectes* (or *Pyromelana*), the males of which have black plumage marked with red or yellow.

bishopric ('bɪʃəprɪk) *n* the see, diocese, or office of a bishop.

bishop's-cap *n* another name for **mitrewort.**

bishop sleeve *n* a full sleeve gathered at the wrist.

bishop's mitre *n* a European heteropterous bug, *Aelia acuminata,* whose larvae are a pest of cereal grasses: family *Pentatomidae.*

bishop's weed *n* another name for **goutweed.**

Bisitun (,biːsɪ'tuːn) *n* another name for **Behistun.**

bisk (bɪsk) *n* a less common spelling of **bisque**[1].

Bisk (*Russian* bijsk) *n* a variant spelling of **Biysk.**

Biskra ('bɪskrɑː) *n* a town and oasis in NE Algeria, in the Sahara. Pop.: 128 280 (1987).

Bisley ('bɪzlɪ) *n* a village in SE England, in Surrey: annual meetings of the National Rifle Association.

Bismarck[1] ('bɪzmɑːk) *n* a city in North Dakota, on the Missouri River: the state capital. Pop.: 49 256 (1990).

Bismarck[2] (*German* 'bɪsmark) *n* Prince **Otto** (**Eduard Leopold**) **von** ('ɔto fɔn), called *the Iron Chancellor.* 1815–98, German statesman; prime minister of Prussia (1862–90). Under his leadership Prussia defeated Austria and France, and Germany was united. In 1871 he became the first chancellor of the German Reich.

Bismarck Archipelago *n* a group of over 200 islands in the SW Pacific, northeast of New Guinea: part of Papua New Guinea. Main islands: New Britain, New Ireland, Lavongai, and the Admiralty Islands. Chief town: Rabaul, on New Britain. Pop.: 424 000 (1995 est.). Area: 49 658 sq. km (19 173 sq. miles).

Bismarck herring *n* marinaded herring, served cold.

Bismillah (,bɪsmɪ'lɑː) *interj* the words which preface all except one of the surahs of the Koran, used by Muslims as a blessing before eating or some other action. **[**shortened from *Bismillah-ir-Rahman-ir-Rahim,* from Arabic, literally: in the name of God, the merciful and compassionate**]**

bismuth ('bɪzməθ) *n* a brittle pinkish-white crystalline metallic element having low thermal and electrical conductivity, which expands on cooling. It is widely used in alloys, esp. low-melting alloys in fire safety devices; its compounds are used in medicines. Symbol: Bi; atomic no.: 83; atomic wt.: 208.98037; valency: 3 or 5; relative density: 9.747; melting pt.: 271.4°C; boiling pt.: 1564±5°C. **[C17:** from New Latin *bisemūtum,* from German *Wismut,* of unknown origin**]** ▸ **bismuthal** ('bɪzməθəl) *adj*

bismuthic (bɪz'mjuːθɪk, -'mʌθɪk) *adj* of or containing bismuth in the pentavalent state.

bismuthinite (bɪz'mʌθɪ,naɪt) *or* **bismuth glance** *n* a grey mineral consisting of bismuth sulphide in orthorhombic crystalline form. It occurs in veins associated with tin, copper, silver, lead, etc., and is a source of bismuth. Formula: Bi_2S_3.

bismuthous ('bɪzməθəs) *adj* of or containing bismuth in the trivalent state.

bison ('baɪsᵊn) *n, pl* **-son. 1** Also called: **American bison, buffalo.** a member of the cattle tribe, *Bison bison,* formerly widely distributed over the prairies of W North America but now confined to reserves and parks, with a massive head, shaggy forequarters, and a humped back. **2** Also called: **wisent, European bison.** a closely related and similar animal, *Bison bonasus,* formerly widespread in Europe. **[C14:** from Latin *bisōn,* of Germanic origin; related to Old English *wesand,* Old Norse *vīsundr***]**

bisque[1] (bɪsk) *n* a thick rich soup made from shellfish. **[C17:** from French**]**

bisque[2] (bɪsk) *n* **1a** a pink to yellowish tan colour. **1b** *(as adj): a bisque tablecloth.* **2** *Ceramics.* another name for **biscuit** (sense 4). **[C20:** shortened from BISCUIT**]**

bisque[3] (bɪsk) *n Tennis, golf, croquet.* an extra point, stroke, or turn allowed to an inferior player, usually taken when desired. **[C17:** from French, of obscure origin**]**

Bissau (bɪ'saʊ) *or* **Bissão** (*Portuguese* bi'sɐ̃u) *n* the capital of Guinea-Bissau, a port on the Atlantic: until 1974 the capital of Portuguese Guinea. Pop.: 233 000 (1995 est.).

bissextile (bɪ'sɛkstaɪl) *adj* **1** (of a month or year) containing the extra day of a leap year. ◆ *n* **2** a rare name for **leap year. [C16:** from Late Latin *bissextilis annus* leap year, from Latin *bissextus,* from BI-[1] + *sextus* sixth; referring to February 24, the 6th day before the Calends of March**]**

bist (bɪst) *vb Archaic or dialect.* a form of the second person singular of **be.**

bistable (baɪ'steɪbᵊl) *adj* **1** having two stable states: *bistable circuit.* ◆ *n* **2** *Computing.* another name for **flip-flop** (sense 2).

Bisto ('bɪstəʊ) *n Trademark.* a preparation for thickening, flavouring, and browning gravy.

bistort ('bɪstɔːt) *n* **1** Also called: **snakeroot, snakeweed, Easter-ledges.** a Eurasian polygonaceous plant, *Polygonum bistorta,* having leaf stipules fused to form a tube around the stem and a spike of small pink flowers. **2** Also called: **snakeroot.** a related plant, *Polygonum bistortoides,* of W North America, with oval clusters of pink or white flowers. **3** any of several other plants of the genus *Polygonum.* **[C16:** from French *bistorte,* from Latin *bis* twice + *tortus* from *torquēre* to twist**]**

bistoury ('bɪstərɪ) *n, pl* **-ries.** a long surgical knife with a narrow blade. **[C15:** from Old French *bistorie* dagger, of unknown origin**]**

bistre *or U.S.* **bister** ('bɪstə) *n* **1** a transparent water-soluble brownish-yellow pigment made by boiling the soot of wood, used for pen and wash drawings. **2a** a yellowish-brown to dark brown colour. **2b** *(as adj): bistre paint.* **[C18:** from French, of unknown origin**]**

bistro ('biːstrəʊ) *n, pl* **-tros.** a small restaurant. **[**French: of obscure origin; perhaps from Russian *bistro* fast**]**

bisulcate (baɪ'sʌl,keɪt) *adj* **1** marked by two grooves. **2** *Zoology.* **2a** cleft or cloven, as a hoof. **2b** having cloven hoofs.

bisulphate (baɪ'sʌl,feɪt) *n* **1** a salt or ester of sulphuric acid containing the monovalent group $-HSO_4$ or the ion HSO_4^-. **2** *(modifier)* consisting of, containing, or concerned with the group $-HSO_4$ or the ion HSO_4^-: *bisulphate ion.* ◆ Systematic name: **hydrogen sulphate.**

bisulphide (baɪ'sʌlfaɪd) *n* another name for **disulphide.**

bisulphite (baɪ'sʌlfaɪt) *n* **1** a salt or ester of sulphurous acid containing the monovalent group $-HSO_3$ or the ion HSO_3^-. **2** *(modifier)* consisting of or containing the group $-HSO_3$ or the ion HSO_3^-: *bisulphite ion.* ◆ Systematic name: **hydrogen sulphite.**

Bisutun (,biːsʊ'tuːn) *n* another name for **Behistun.**

bisymmetric (,baɪsɪ'mɛtrɪk) *or* **bisymmetrical** *adj* **1** *Botany.* showing symmetry in two planes at right angles to each other. **2** (of plants and animals) showing bilateral symmetry. ► ˌ**bisym'metrically** *adv* ► **bisymmetry** (baɪ'sɪmɪtrɪ) *n*

bit[1] (bɪt) *n* **1** a small piece, portion, or quantity. **2** a short time or distance. **3** *U.S. and Canadian informal.* the value of an eighth of a dollar: spoken of only in units of two: *two bits.* **4** any small coin. **5** short for **bit part. 6** *Informal.* way of behaving, esp. one intended to create a particular impression: *she's doing the prima donna bit.* **7 a bit.** rather; somewhat: *a bit dreary.* **8 a bit of. 8a** rather: *a bit of a dope.* **8b** a considerable amount: *that must take quite a bit of courage.* **9 a bit of all right, bit of crumpet, bit of skirt, bit of stuff,** *or* **bit of tail.** *Brit. slang.* a sexually attractive woman. **10 bit by bit.** gradually. **11 bit on the side.** *Informal.* an extramarital affair. **12 do one's bit.** to make one's expected contribution. **13 every bit.** (foll. by *as*) to the same degree: *she was every bit as clever as her brother.* **14 not a bit (of it).** not in the slightest; not at all. **15 to bits.** completely apart: *to fall to bits.* [Old English *bite* action of biting; see BITE]

bit[2] (bɪt) *n* **1** a metal mouthpiece, for controlling a horse on a bridle. **2** anything that restrains or curbs. **3 take** *or* **have the bit in** *or* **between one's teeth. 3a** to undertake a task with determination. **3b** to rebel against control. **4** a cutting or drilling tool, part, or head in a brace, drill, etc. **5** the blade of a plane. **6** the part of a pair of pincers designed to grasp an object. **7** the copper end of a soldering iron. **8** the part of a key that engages the levers of a lock. ♦ *vb* **bits, bitting, bitted.** (*tr*) **9** to put a bit in the mouth of (a horse). **10** to restrain; curb. [Old English *bita;* related to Old English *bītan* to BITE]

bit[3] (bɪt) *vb* the past tense and (archaic) past participle of **bite.**

bit[4] (bɪt) *n Maths., computing.* **1** a single digit of binary notation, represented either by 0 or by 1. **2** the smallest unit of information, indicating the presence or absence of a single feature. **3** a unit of capacity of a computer, consisting of an element of its physical structure capable of being in either of two states, such as a switch with *on* and *off* positions, or a microscopic magnet capable of alignment in two directions. [C20: from abbreviation of BINARY DIGIT]

bitartrate (baɪ'tɑːˌtreɪt) *n* (not in technical usage) a salt or ester of tartaric acid containing the monovalent group $-HC_4H_4O_6$ or the ion $HC_4H_4O_6^-$. Also called: **hydrogen tartrate.**

bitch (bɪtʃ) *n* **1** a female dog or other female canine animal, such as a wolf. **2** *Slang, derogatory.* a malicious, spiteful, or coarse woman. **3** *Informal.* a complaint. **4** *Informal.* a difficult situation or problem. ♦ *vb Informal.* **5** (*intr*) to complain; grumble. **6** to behave (towards) in a spiteful or malicious manner. **7** (*tr,* often foll. by *up*) to botch; bungle. [Old English *bicce*]

bitchin' ('bɪtʃɪn) *or* **bitching** ('bɪtʃɪŋ) *U.S. slang.* ♦ *adj* **1** wonderful or excellent. ♦ *adv* **2** extremely: *bitchin' good.*

bitchy ('bɪtʃɪ) *adj* **bitchier, bitchiest.** *Informal.* characteristic of or behaving like a bitch; malicious; snide. ► '**bitchily** *adv* ► '**bitchiness** *n*

bite (baɪt) *vb* **bites, biting, bit, bitten. 1** to grip, cut off, or tear with or as if with the teeth or jaws. **2** (of animals, insects, etc.) to injure by puncturing or tearing (the skin or flesh) with the teeth, fangs, etc., esp. as a natural characteristic. **3** (*tr*) to cut or penetrate, as with a knife. **4** (of corrosive material such as acid) to eat away or into. **5** to smart or cause to smart; sting: *mustard bites the tongue.* **6** (*intr*) *Angling.* (of a fish) to take or attempt to take the bait or lure. **7** to take firm hold of or act effectively upon. **8** to grip or hold (a workpiece) with a tool or chuck. **9** (of a screw, thread, etc.) to cut into or grip (an object, material, etc.). **10** (*tr*) *Informal.* to annoy or worry: *what's biting her?* **11** (*often passive*) *Slang.* to cheat. **12** (*tr;* often foll. by *for*) *Austral. and N.Z. slang.* to ask (for); scrounge from. **13 bite off more than one can chew.** *Informal.* to attempt a task beyond one's capability. **14 bite the bullet.** to face up to (pain, trouble, etc.) with fortitude; be stoical. **15 bite someone's head off.** to respond harshly and rudely (to). **16 bite the dust.** See **dust** (sense 11). **17 bite the hand that feeds one.** to repay kindness with injury or ingratitude. **18 once bitten, twice shy.** after an unpleasant experience one is cautious in similar situations. **19 put the bite on (someone).** *Austral. slang.* to ask (someone) for money. ♦ *n* **20** the act of biting. **21** a thing or amount bitten off. **22** a wound, bruise, or sting inflicted by biting. **23** *Angling.* an attempt by a fish to take the bait or lure. **24** *Informal.* an incisive or penetrating effect or quality: *that's a question with a bite.* **25** a light meal; snack. **26** a cutting, stinging, or smarting sensation. **27** the depth of cut of a machine tool. **28** the grip or hold applied by a tool or chuck to a workpiece. **29** *Dentistry.* the angle or manner of contact between the upper and lower teeth when the mouth is closed naturally. **30** the surface of a file or rasp with cutting teeth. **31** the corrosive action of acid, as on a metal etching plate. [Old English *bītan;* related to Latin *findere* to split, Sanskrit *bhedati* he splits] ► '**biter** *n*

bite back *vb* (*tr, adv*) to restrain (a hurtful, embarrassing, or indiscreet remark); avoid saying.

Bithynia (bɪ'θɪnɪə) *n* an ancient country on the Black Sea in NW Asia Minor.

biting ('baɪtɪŋ) *adj* **1** piercing; keen: *a biting wind.* **2** sarcastic; incisive: *a biting comment.* ► '**bitingly** *adv*

biting *or* **bird louse** *n* See **louse** (sense 2).

biting midge *n* any small fragile dipterous fly of the family *Ceratopogonidae,* most of which suck the blood of mammals, birds, or other insects.

bitmap ('bɪtˌmæp) *n Computing.* **1** a picture created on a visual display unit where each pixel corresponds to one or more bits in memory, the number of bits per pixel determining the number of available colours. ♦ *vb* **-maps, -mapping, -mapped. 2** (*tr*) to create a bitmap of.

Bitolj (*Serbo-Croat* 'bitolj) *or* **Bitola** ('biːtəʊlə) *n* a city in SW Macedonia: under Turkish rule from 1382 until 1913 when it was taken by the Serbs. Pop.: 75 386 (1994).

bit part *n* a very small acting role with few lines to speak.

bit rate *n Computing.* the rate of flow of binary digits in a digital data-processing system.

bitser ('bɪtsə) *n Austral. informal.* a mongrel dog. [C20: from *bits o'* bits of, as in *his dog is bits o' this and bits o' that*]

bit slice *adj Computing.* (of central processing units) able to be built up in sections to form complete central processing units with various word lengths.

bitstock ('bɪtˌstɒk) *n* the handle or stock of a tool into which a drilling bit is fixed.

bitt (bɪt) *Nautical.* ♦ *n* **1** one of a pair of strong posts on the deck of a ship for securing mooring and other lines. **2** another word for **bollard** (sense 1). ♦ *vb* **3** (*tr*) to secure (a line) by means of a bitt. [C14: probably of Scandinavian origin; compare Old Norse *biti* cross beam, Middle High German *bizze* wooden peg]

bitten ('bɪtᵊn) *vb* the past participle of **bite.**

bitter ('bɪtə) *adj* **1** having or denoting an unpalatable harsh taste, as the peel of an orange or coffee dregs. Compare **sour** (sense 1). **2** showing or caused by strong unrelenting hostility or resentment: *he was still bitter about the divorce.* **3** difficult or unpleasant to accept or admit: *a bitter blow.* **4** cutting; sarcastic: *bitter words.* **5** bitingly cold: *a bitter night.* ♦ *adv* **6** very; extremely (esp. in the phrase **bitter cold**). ♦ *n* **7** a thing that is bitter. **8** *Brit.* beer with a high hop content, with a slightly bitter taste. ♦ *vb* **9** to make or become bitter. ♦ See also **bitters.** [Old English *biter;* related to *bītan* to BITE] ► '**bitterly** *adv* ► '**bitterness** *n*

bitter apple *n* another name for **colocynth.**

bittercress ('bɪtəˌkres) *n* one of several perennial or annual cruciferous plants of the genus *Cardamine,* that are related to lady's-smock, including **hairy bittercress** (*C. hirsuta*), a common weed resembling shepherd's purse, with which it is often confused.

bitter end *n* **1** *Nautical.* the end of a line, chain, or cable, esp. the end secured in the chain locker of a vessel. **2 to the bitter end. 2a** until the finish of a task, job, or undertaking, however unpleasant or difficult. **2b** until final defeat or death. [C19: in both senses perhaps from BITT]

Bitter Lakes *pl n* two lakes, the **Great Bitter Lake** and **Little Bitter Lake,** in NE Egypt: part of the Suez Canal.

bitterling ('bɪtəlɪŋ) *n* a small brightly coloured European freshwater cyprinid fish, *Rhodeus sericeus:* a popular aquarium fish. [C19: from German; see BITTER + -LING[1]]

bittern[1] ('bɪtən) *n* any wading bird of the genera *Ixobrychus* and *Botaurus,* related and similar to the herons but with shorter legs and neck, a stouter body, and a booming call: family *Ardeidae,* order *Ciconiiformes.* [C14: from Old French *butor,* perhaps from Latin *būtiō* bittern + *taurus* bull; referring to its cry]

bittern[2] ('bɪtən) *n* the bitter liquid remaining after common salt has been crystallized out of sea water: a source of magnesium, bromine, and iodine compounds. [C17: variant of *bittering;* see BITTER]

bitternut ('bɪtəˌnʌt) *n* **1** an E North American hickory tree, *Carya cordiformis,* with thin-shelled nuts and bitter kernels. **2** the nut of this plant.

bitter orange *n* another name for **Seville orange.**

bitter principle *n* any of various bitter-tasting substances, such as aloin, usually extracted from plants.

bitters ('bɪtəz) *pl n* **1** bitter-tasting spirits of varying alcoholic content flavoured with plant extracts. **2** a similar liquid containing a bitter-tasting substance, used as a tonic to stimulate the appetite or improve digestion.

bittersweet ('bɪtəˌswiːt) *n* **1** any of several North American woody climbing plants of the genus *Celastrus,* esp. *C. scandens,* having orange capsules that open to expose scarlet-coated seeds: family *Celastraceae.* **2** another name for **woody nightshade.** ♦ *adj* **3** tasting of or being a mixture of bitterness and sweetness. **4** pleasant but tinged with sadness.

bitterweed ('bɪtəˌwiːd) *n* any of various plants that contain a bitter-tasting substance.

bitterwood ('bɪtəˌwʊd) *n* any of several simaroubaceous trees of the genus *Picrasma* of S and SE Asia and the Caribbean, whose bitter bark and wood are used in medicine as a substitute for quassia.

bitty ('bɪtɪ) *adj* **-tier, -tiest. 1** lacking unity; disjointed. **2** containing bits, sediment, etc. ► '**bittiness** *n*

bitumen ('bɪtjʊmɪn) *n* **1** any of various viscous or solid impure mixtures of hydrocarbons that occur naturally in asphalt, tar, mineral waxes, etc.: used as a road surfacing and roofing material. **2** the constituents of coal that can be extracted by an organic solvent. **3 the bitumen. 3a** *Austral. and N.Z. informal.* any road with a bitumen surface. **3b** (*cap.*) *Austral. informal.* the road in the Northern Territory between Darwin and Alice Springs. **4** a transparent brown pigment or glaze made from asphalt. [C15: from Latin *bitūmen,* perhaps of Celtic origin] ► **bituminous** (bɪ'tjuːmɪnəs) *adj*

bituminize *or* **bituminise** (bɪ'tjuːmɪˌnaɪz) *vb* (*tr*) to treat with or convert into bitumen. ► **biˌtumini'zation** *or* **biˌtumini'sation** *n*

bituminous coal *n* a soft black coal, rich in volatile hydrocarbons, that burns with a smoky yellow flame. Fixed carbon content: 46–86 per cent; calorific value: $1.93 \times 10^7 - 3.63 \times 10^7$ J/kg. Also called: **soft coal.**

bivalence (baɪ'veɪləns, 'bɪvə-) *n Logic, philosophy.* the semantic principle that there are exactly two truth values, so that every meaningful statement is either true of false. Compare **many-valued logic.**

bivalent (baɪ'veɪlənt, 'bɪvə-) *adj* **1** *Chem.* another word for **divalent. 2** (of homologous chromosomes) associated together in pairs. ♦ *n* **3** a structure formed during meiosis consisting of two homologous chromosomes associated together. ► **bi'valency** *n*

bivalve ('baɪˌvælv) *n* **1** Also called: **pelecypod, lamellibranch.** any marine or freshwater mollusc of the class *Pelecypoda* (formerly *Bivalvia* or *Lamellibranchia*), having a laterally compressed body, a shell consisting of two hinged valves, and gills for respiration. The group includes clams, cockles, oysters, and mussels. ♦ *adj* **2** Also: **pelecypod, lamellibranch.** of, relating to, or belonging to the *Pelecypoda.* 3 Also: **bivalvate** (baɪˈvælveɪt). *Biology.* having or consisting of two valves or similar parts: *a bivalve seed capsule.* ▸ **biˈvalvular** *adj*

bivariate (baɪˈvɛərɪɪt) *adj Statistics.* (of a distribution) involving two random variables, not necessarily independent of one another.

bivouac (ˈbɪvʊˌæk, ˈbɪvwæk) *n* **1** a temporary encampment with few facilities, as used by soldiers, mountaineers, etc. ◆ *vb* **-acs, -acking, -acked.** **2** (*intr*) to make such an encampment. [C18: from French *bivuac,* probably from Swiss German *Beiwacht,* literally: BY + WATCH]

bivvy (ˈbɪvɪ) *n, pl* **-vies.** *Slang.* a small tent or shelter. [C20: shortened from BIVOUAC]

biweekly (baɪˈwiːklɪ) *adj, adv* **1** every two weeks. **2** (often avoided because of confusion with sense 1) twice a week; semiweekly. See **bi-**[1]. ◆ *n, pl* **-lies.** **3** a periodical published every two weeks.

biyearly (baɪˈjɪəlɪ) *adj, adv* **1** every two years; biennial or biennially. **2** (often avoided because of confusion with sense 1) twice a year; biannual or biannually. See **bi-**[1].

Biysk, Biisk, *or* **Bisk** (*Russian* bijsk) *n* a city in SW Russia, at the foot of the Altai Mountains. Pop: 228 000 (1995 est.).

biz (bɪz) *n Informal.* short for **business.**

bizarre (bɪˈzɑː) *adj* odd or unusual, esp. in an interesting or amusing way. [C17: from French: from Italian *bizzarro* capricious, of uncertain origin] ▸ **biˈzarrely** *adv* ▸ **biˈzarreness** *n*

bizarrerie (bɪˈzɑːrərɪ) *n* **1** the quality of being bizarre. **2** a bizarre act.

Bizerte (bɪˈzɜːtə; *French* bizɛrt) *or* **Bizerta** *n* a port in N Tunisia, on the Mediterranean at the canalized outlet of **Lake Bizerte.** Pop.: 98 900 (1994).

Bizet (ˈbiːzeɪ; *French* bizɛ) *n* **Georges** (ʒɔrʒ). 1838–75, French composer, whose works include the opera *Carmen* (1875) and incidental music to Daudet's *L'Arlésienne* (1872).

bizzy (ˈbɪzɪ) *n, pl* **-zies.** *Brit. slang, chiefly Liverpudlian.* a policeman. [C20: from BUSY]

Björneborg (bjœrnəˈbɔrj) *n* the Swedish name for **Pori.**

Bjørnson (ˈbjɜːnsən; *Norwegian* ˈbjørnsᵊn) *n* **Bjørnstjerne** (ˈbjɜːnstjeənə; *Norwegian* ˈbjørnstjernə). 1832–1910, Norwegian poet, dramatist, novelist, theatre director, and newspaper editor; mainly remembered for social dramas, such as *The Bankrupt* (1875): Nobel prize for literature 1903.

bk *abbrev. for:* **1** bank. **2** book.

Bk *the chemical symbol for* berkelium.

bkcy *abbrev. for* bankruptcy.

bkg *abbrev. for* banking.

bkpt *abbrev. for* bankrupt.

bks *abbrev. for:* **1** barracks. **2** books.

bl *abbrev. for* barrel.

BL *abbrev. for:* **1** Bachelor of Law. **2** Bachelor of Letters. **3** Barrister-at-Law. **4** British Leyland. **5** British Library.

bl. *abbrev. for:* **1** bale. **2** black. **3** blue.

B/L, b/l, *or* **b.l.** *pl* **Bs/L, bs/l,** *or* **bs.l.** *abbrev. for* bill of lading.

blab (blæb) *vb* **blabs, blabbing, blabbed.** **1** to divulge (secrets) indiscreetly. **2** (*intr*) to chatter thoughtlessly; prattle. ◆ *n* **3** a less common word for **blabber** (senses 1, 2). [C14: of Germanic origin; compare Old High German *blabbizōn,* Icelandic *blabbra*] ▸ **ˈblabbing** *n, adj*

blabber (ˈblæbə) *n* **1** a person who blabs. **2** idle chatter. ◆ *vb* **3** (*intr*) to talk without thinking; chatter. [C15 *blabberen,* probably of imitative origin]

blabbermouth (ˈblæbəˌmaʊθ) *n Informal.* a person who talks too much or indiscreetly.

black (blæk) *adj* **1** of the colour of jet or carbon black, having no hue due to the absorption of all or nearly all incident light. Compare **white** (sense 1). **2** without light; completely dark. **3** without hope or alleviation; gloomy: *the future looked black.* **4** very dirty or soiled: *black factory chimneys.* **5** angry or resentful: *she gave him black looks.* **6** (of a play or other work) dealing with the unpleasant realities of life, esp. in a pessimistic or macabre manner: *black comedy.* **7** (of coffee or tea) without milk or cream. **8** causing, resulting from, or showing great misfortune: *black areas of unemployment.* **9a** wicked or harmful: *a black lie.* **9b** (*in combination*): *black-hearted.* **10** causing or deserving dishonour or censure: *a black crime.* **11** (of the face) purple, as from suffocation. **12** *Brit.* (of goods, jobs, works, etc.) being subject to boycott by trade unionists, esp. in support of industrial action elsewhere. ◆ *n* **13** a black colour. **14** a dye or pigment of or producing this colour. **15** black clothing, worn esp. as a sign of mourning. **16** *Chess, draughts.* **16a** a black or dark-coloured piece or square. **16b** (*usually cap.*) the player playing with such pieces. **17** complete darkness: *the black of the night.* **18** a black ball in snooker, etc. **19** (in roulette and other gambling games) one of two colours on which players may place even bets, the other being red. **20 in the black.** in credit or without debt. **21** *Archery.* a black ring on a target, between the outer and the blue, scoring three points. ◆ *vb* **22** another word for **blacken.** **23** (*tr*) to polish (shoes, etc.) with blacking. **24** (*tr*) to bruise so as to make black: *he blacked her eye.* **25** (*tr*) *Brit., Austral., and N.Z.* (of trade unionists) to organize a boycott of (specified goods, jobs, work, etc.), esp. in support of industrial action elsewhere. ◆ See also **blackout.** [Old English *blæc;* related to Old Saxon *blak* ink, Old High German *blakra* to blink] ▸ **ˈblackish** *adj* ▸ **ˈblackishly** *adv* ▸ **ˈblackly** *adv* ▸ **ˈblackness** *n*

Black[1] (blæk) *n* **1** *Sometimes derogatory.* a member of a dark-skinned race, esp. someone of Negroid or Australoid origin. ◆ *adj* **2** of or relating to a Black or Blacks: *a Black neighbourhood.*

Black[2] (blæk) *n* **1** Sir **James** (**Whyte**). born 1924, British biochemist. He discovered beta-blockers and drugs for peptic ulcers: Nobel prize for physiology or medicine 1988. **2 Joseph.** 1728–99, Scottish physician and chemist, noted for his pioneering work on carbon dioxide and heat.

blackamoor (ˈblækəˌmʊə, -ˌmɔː) *n Archaic.* a Black or other person with dark skin. [C16: see BLACK, MOOR]

black-and-blue *adj* **1** (of the skin) discoloured, as from a bruise. **2** feeling pain or soreness, as from a beating.

black and tan *n* a mixture of stout or porter and ale.

Black and Tans *pl n* **the.** a specially recruited armed auxiliary police force sent to Ireland in 1921 by the British Government to combat Sinn Féin. [name suggested by the colour of their uniforms and the *Black and Tans* hunt in Munster]

black-and-tan terrier *n* a less common name for **Manchester terrier.**

black-and-white *n* **1a** a photograph, picture, sketch, etc., in black, white, and shades of grey rather than in colour. **1b** (*as modifier*): *black-and-white film.* **2** the neutral tones of black, white, and intermediate shades of grey. Compare **colour** (sense 2). **3 in black and white. 3a** in print or writing. **3b** in extremes: *he always saw things in black and white.*

black art *n* **the.** another name for **black magic.**

black-backed gull *n* either of two common black-and-white European coastal gulls, *Larus fuscus* (**lesser black-backed gull**) and *L. marinus* (**great black-backed gull**).

blackball (ˈblækˌbɔːl) *n* **1** a negative vote or veto. **2** a black wooden ball used to indicate disapproval or to veto in a vote. ◆ *vb* (*tr*) **3** to vote against in a ballot. **4** to exclude (someone) from a group, profession, etc.; ostracize. [C18: see sense 2]

black bass (bæs) *n* any of several predatory North American percoid freshwater game fishes of the genus *Micropterus:* family *Centrarchidae* (sunfishes, etc.).

black bean *n* an Australian leguminous tree, *Castanospermum australe,* having thin smooth bark and yellow or reddish flowers: used in furniture manufacture. Also called: **Moreton Bay chestnut.**

black bear *n* **1 American black bear.** a bear, *Euarctos* (or *Ursus*) *americanus,* inhabiting forests of North America. It is smaller and less ferocious than the brown bear. **2 Asiatic black bear.** a bear, *Selenarctos thibetanus,* of central and E Asia, whose coat is black with a pale V-shaped mark on the chest.

Blackbeard (ˈblækˌbɪəd) *n* nickname of (Edward) **Teach.**

black beetle *n* another name for the **oriental cockroach** (see **cockroach**).

black belt *n* **1** *Judo, karate, etc.* **1a** a black belt worn by an instructor or expert competitor in the dan grades, usually from first to fifth dan. **1b** a person entitled to wear this. **2 the.** a region of the southern U.S. extending from Georgia across central Alabama and Mississippi, in which the population contains a large number of Blacks: also noted for its fertile black soil.

blackberry (ˈblækbərɪ) *n, pl* **-ries.** **1** Also called: **bramble.** any of several woody plants of the rosaceous genus *Rubus,* esp. *R. fruticosus,* that have thorny stems and black or purple glossy edible berry-like fruits (drupelets). **2a** the fruit of any of these plants. **2b** (*as modifier*): *blackberry jam.* **3 blackberry lily.** an ornamental Chinese iridaceous plant, *Belamcanda chinensis,* that has red-spotted orange flowers and clusters of black seeds that resemble blackberries. ◆ *vb* **-ries, -rying, -ried.** **4** (*intr*) to gather blackberries.

black bile *n Archaic.* one of the four bodily humours; melancholy. See **humour** (sense 8).

black bindweed *n* a twining polygonaceous European plant, *Polygonum convolvulus,* with heart-shaped leaves and triangular black seed pods.

blackbird (ˈblækˌbɜːd) *n* **1** a common European thrush, *Turdus merula,* in which the male has a black plumage and yellow bill and the female is brown. **2** any of various American orioles having a dark plumage, esp. any of the genus *Agelaius.* **3** *History.* a person, esp. a South Sea Islander, who was kidnapped and sold as a slave, esp. in Australia. ◆ *vb* **4** (*tr*) (formerly) to kidnap and sell into slavery.

blackboard (ˈblækˌbɔːd) *n* a hard or rigid surface made of a smooth usually dark substance, used for writing or drawing on with chalk, esp. in teaching.

black body *n Physics.* a hypothetical body that would be capable of absorbing all the electromagnetic radiation falling on it. Also called: **full radiator.**

black book *n* **1** a book containing the names of people to be punished, blacklisted, etc. **2 in someone's black books.** *Informal.* out of favour with someone.

black bottom *n* a dance of the late 1920s that originated in America, involving a sinuous rotation of the hips.

black box *n* **1** a self-contained unit in an electronic or computer system whose circuitry need not be known to understand its function. **2** an informal name for **flight recorder.**

blackboy (ˈblækˌbɔɪ) *n* another name for **grass tree** (sense 1).

black bread *n* a kind of very dark coarse rye bread.

black bryony *n* a climbing herbaceous Eurasian plant, *Tamus communis,* having small greenish flowers and poisonous red berries: family *Dioscoreaceae.*

blackbuck (ˈblækˌbʌk) *n* an Indian antelope, *Antilope cervicapra,* the male of which has spiral horns, a dark back, and a white belly.

black bun *n Scot.* a very rich dark fruitcake, usually in a pastry case. Also called **currant bun.**

Blackburn (ˈblækbɜːn) *n* **1** a city in NW England, in central Lancashire: textile industries. Pop: 105 994 (1991). **2 Mount.** a mountain in SE Alaska, the highest peak in the Wrangell Mountains. Height: 5037 m (16 523 ft.).

Blackburn with Darwen (ˈdɑːwen) *n* a unitary authority in NW England, in Lancashire. Pop.: 140 300 (1995 est.). Area: 137 sq. km (53 sq. miles).

blackbutt (ˈblækˌbʌt) *n* any of various Australian eucalyptus trees having rough fibrous bark and hard wood used as timber.

blackcap (ˈblækˌkæp) *n* **1** a brownish-grey Old World warbler, *Sylvia atricapilla,* the male of which has a black crown. **2** any of various similar birds, such as the black-capped chickadee (*Parus atricapillus*). **3** *U.S.* a popular name for **raspberry** (sense 3). **4** *Brit.* (formerly) the cap worn by a judge when passing a death sentence.

black-coated *adj Brit.* (esp. formerly) (of a worker) clerical or professional, as distinguished from commercial or industrial.

blackcock ('blæk,kɒk) *n* the male of the black grouse. Also called: **heath cock.** Compare **greyhen.**
Black Country *n* **the.** the formerly heavily industrialized region of central England, northwest of Birmingham.
blackcurrant (,blæk'kʌrənt) *n* **1** a N temperate shrub, *Ribes nigrum,* having red or white flowers and small edible black berries: family *Grossulariaceae.* **2a** the fruit of this shrub. **2b** (*as modifier*): *blackcurrant jelly.*
blackdamp ('blæk,dæmp) *n* air that is low in oxygen content and high in carbon dioxide as a result of an explosion in a mine. Also called: **chokedamp.**
Black Death *n* **the.** a form of bubonic plague pandemic in Europe and Asia during the 14th century, when it killed over 50 million people. See **bubonic plague.**
black diamond *n* **1** another name for **carbonado**[2]. **2** (*usually pl*) a figurative expression for **coal.**
black disc *n* a conventional black vinyl gramophone record as opposed to a compact disc.
black dog *n Informal.* depression or melancholy.
black earth *n* another name for **chernozem.**
black economy *n* that portion of the income of a nation that remains illegally undeclared either as a result of payment in kind or as a means of tax avoidance.
blacken ('blækən) *vb* **1** to make or become black or dirty. **2** (*tr*) to defame; slander (esp. in the phrase **blacken someone's name**).
Blackett ('blækɪt) *n* **Patrick Maynard Stuart,** Baron. 1897–1974, English physicist, noted for his work on cosmic radiation and his discovery of the positron. Nobel prize for physics 1948.
black eye *n* bruising round the eye.
black-eyed pea *n* another name for **cowpea** (sense 2).
black-eyed Susan *n* **1** any of several North American plants of the genus *Rudbeckia,* esp. *R. hirta,* having flower heads of orange-yellow rays and brown-black centres: family *Compositae* (composites). **2** a tropical African climbing plant, *Thunbergia alata,* having yellow flowers with purple centres, grown as a greenhouse annual.
blackface ('blæk,feɪs) *n* **1a** a performer made up to imitate a Black person. **1b** the make-up used by such a performer, usually consisting of burnt cork. **2** a breed of sheep having a dark face.
blackfish ('blæk,fɪʃ) *n, pl* **-fish** *or* **-fishes. 1** a minnow-like Alaskan freshwater fish, *Dallia pectoralis,* related to the pikes and thought to be able to survive prolonged freezing. **2** a female salmon that has recently spawned. Compare **redfish** (sense 1). **3** any of various other dark fishes, esp. a common edible Australian estuary fish. **4** another name for **pilot whale.**
black flag *n* another name for the **Jolly Roger.**
blackfly ('blæk,flaɪ) *n, pl* **-flies.** a black aphid, *Aphis fabae,* that infests beans, sugar beet, and other plants. Also called: **bean aphid.**
black fly *n* any small blackish stout-bodied dipterous fly of the family *Simuliidae,* which sucks the blood of man, mammals, and birds. See also **buffalo gnat.**
Blackfoot ('blæk,fʊt) *n* **1** (*pl* **-feet** *or* **-foot**) a member of a warlike group of North American Indian peoples formerly living in the northwestern Plains. **2** any of the languages of these peoples, belonging to the Algonquian family. [C19: translation of Blackfoot *Siksika*]
Black Forest *n* **the.** a hilly wooded region of SW Germany, in Baden-Württemberg: a popular resort area. German name: **Schwarzwald.**
Black Friar *n* a Dominican friar.
black frost *n* a frost without snow or rime that is severe enough to blacken vegetation.
black game *n* another name for **black grouse** (sense 1).
black grouse *n* **1** Also called: **black game.** a large N European grouse, *Lyrurus tetrix,* the male of which has a bluish-black plumage and lyre-shaped tail. **2** a related and similar species, *Lyrurus mlokosiewiczi,* of W Asia.
blackguard ('blægɑːd, -gəd) *n* **1a** an unprincipled contemptible person; scoundrel. **1b** (*as modifier*): *blackguard language.* ◆ *vb* **2** (*tr*) to ridicule or denounce with abusive language. **3** (*intr*) to behave like a blackguard. [C16: originally a collective noun referring to the lowest menials in court, camp followers, vagabonds; see BLACK, GUARD] ▸ **'blackguardism** *n* ▸ **'blackguardly** *adj*
black guillemot *n* a common guillemot, *Cepphus grylle:* its summer plumage is black with white wing patches and its winter plumage white with greyish wings.
Black Hand *n* **1** a group of Sicilian blackmailers and terrorists formed in the 1870s and operating in the U.S. in the early 20th century. **2** (in 19th-century Spain) an organization of anarchists.
blackhead ('blæk,hɛd) *n* **1** a black-tipped plug of fatty matter clogging a pore of the skin, esp. the duct of a sebaceous gland. Technical name: **comedo. 2** an infectious and often fatal disease of turkeys and some other fowl caused by parasitic protozoa. Technical name: **infectious enterohepatitis. 3** any of various birds, esp. gulls or ducks, with black plumage on the head.
blackheart ('blæk,hɑːt) *n* **1** an abnormal darkening of the woody stems of some plants, thought to be caused by extreme cold. **2** any of various diseases of plants, such as the potato, in which the central tissues are blackened. **3** a variety of cherry that has large sweet fruit with purplish flesh and an almost black skin.
black heat *n* heat emitted by an electric element made from low-resistance thick wire that does not glow red.
Blackheath ('blækhiːθ) *n* a residential district in London, mainly in the borough of Lewisham and Greenwich: a large heath formerly notorious for highwaymen.
Black Hills *pl n* a group of mountains in W South Dakota and NE Wyoming: famous for the gigantic sculptures of U.S. presidents on the side of Mount Rushmore. Highest peak: Harney Peak, 2207 m (7242 ft.).
black hole *Astronomy n* **1a** a hypothetical region of space resulting from the gravitational collapse of a star following the exhaustion of its nuclear fuel. The gravitational field around the region would be so high that neither matter nor radiation could escape from it. **1b** a similar but much more massive region of space at the centre of a galaxy. **2** any place regarded as resembling a black hole in that items or information entering it cannot be retrieved.
Black Hole of Calcutta *n* **1** a small dungeon in which in 1756 the Nawab of Bengal reputedly confined 146 English prisoners, of whom only 23 survived. **2** *Informal, chiefly Brit.* any uncomfortable or overcrowded place.
black horehound *n* a hairy unpleasant-smelling chiefly Mediterranean plant, *Ballota nigra,* having clusters of purple flowers: family *Labiatae* (labiates).
black ice *n* a thin transparent layer of new ice on a road or similar surface.
blacking ('blækɪŋ) *n* any preparation, esp. one containing lampblack, for giving a black finish to shoes, metals, etc.
Black Isle *n* **the.** a peninsula in NE Scotland, in Highland council area, between the Cromarty and Moray Firths. [so called because until the late 18th century much of it was uncultivated black moor]
blackjack[1] ('blæk,dʒæk) *Chiefly U.S. and Canadian.* ◆ *n* **1** a truncheon of leather-covered lead with a flexible shaft. ◆ *vb* **2** (*tr*) to hit with or as if with a blackjack. **3** (*tr*) to compel (a person) by threats. [C19: from BLACK + JACK[1] (implement)]
blackjack[2] ('blæk,dʒæk) *n Cards.* **1** pontoon or any of various similar card games. **2** the ace of spades. [C20: from BLACK + JACK[1] (the knave)]
blackjack[3] ('blæk,dʒæk) *n* a dark iron-rich variety of the mineral sphalerite. [C18: from BLACK + JACK[1] (originally a miner's name for this useless ore)]
blackjack[4] ('blæk,dʒæk) *n* a small oak tree, *Quercus marilandica,* of the southeastern U.S., with blackish bark and fan-shaped leaves. Also called: **blackjack oak.** [C19: from BLACK + JACK[1] (from the proper name, popularly used in many plant names)]
blackjack[5] ('blæk,dʒæk) *n* a tarred leather tankard or jug. [C16: from BLACK + JACK[3]]
black japan *n* a black bituminous varnish.
black knight *n Commerce.* a person or firm that makes an unwelcome takeover bid for a company. Compare **grey knight, white knight.**
black knot *n* a fungal disease of plums and cherries caused by *Dibotryon morbosum,* characterized by rough black knotlike swellings on the twigs and branches.
black lead (lɛd) *n* another name for **graphite.**
blackleg ('blækleg) *n* **1** Also called: **scab.** *Brit.* **1a** a person who acts against the interests of a trade union, as by continuing to work during a strike or taking over a striker's job. **1b** (*as modifier*): *blackleg labour.* **2** an acute infectious disease of cattle, sheep, and pigs, characterized by gas-filled swellings, esp. on the legs, caused by *Clostridium* bacteria. **3** *Plant pathol.* **3a** a fungal disease of cabbages and related plants caused by *Phoma lingam,* characterized by blackening and decay of the lower stems. **3b** a similar disease of potatoes, caused by bacteria. **4** a person who cheats in gambling, esp. at cards or in racing. ◆ *vb* **-legs, -legging, -legged. 5** *Brit.* to act against the interests of a trade union, esp. by refusing to join a strike.
black letter *n Printing.* another name for **Gothic** (sense 10).
black light *n* the invisible electromagnetic radiation in the ultraviolet and infrared regions of the spectrum.
blacklist ('blæk,lɪst) *n* **1** a list of persons or organizations under suspicion, or considered untrustworthy, disloyal, etc., esp. one compiled by a government or an organization. ◆ *vb* **2** (*tr*) to put on a blacklist. ▸ **'black,listing** *n*
black lung *n* another name for **pneumoconiosis.**
black magic *n* magic used for evil purposes by invoking the power of the devil.
blackmail ('blæk,meɪl) *n* **1** the act of attempting to obtain money by intimidation, as by threats to disclose discreditable information. **2** the exertion of pressure or threats, esp. unfairly, in an attempt to influence someone's actions. ◆ *vb* (*tr*) **3** to exact or attempt to exact (money or anything of value) from (a person) by threats or intimidation; extort. **4** to attempt to influence the actions of (a person), esp. by unfair pressure or threats. [C16: see BLACK, MAIL[3]] ▸ **'blackmailer** *n*
Black Maria (mə'raɪə) *n* a police van for transporting prisoners.
black mark *n* an indication of disapproval, failure, etc.
black market *n* **1a** any system in which goods or currencies are sold and bought illegally, esp. in violation of controls or rationing. **1b** (*as modifier*): *black market lamb.* **2** the place where such a system operates. ◆ *vb* **black-market. 3** to sell (goods) on the black market. ▸ **black marketeer** *n*
black mass *n* (*sometimes caps.*) a blasphemous travesty of the Christian Mass, performed by practitioners of black magic.
black measles *pl n* (*often functioning as sing*) a severe form of measles characterized by dark eruptions caused by bleeding under the skin.
black medick *n* a small European papilionaceous plant, *Medicago lupulina,* with trifoliate leaves, small yellow flowers, and black pods. Also called: **nonesuch.**
black money *n* **1** that part of a nation's income that relates to its black economy. **2** any money that a person or organization acquires illegally, as by a means that involves tax evasion. **3** *U.S.* money to fund a government project that is concealed in the cost of some other project.
Black Monk *n* a Benedictine monk.
Blackmore ('blæk,mɔː) *n* **R(ichard) D(oddridge).** 1825–1900, English novelist; author of *Lorna Doone* (1869).
black mould *n* another name for **bread mould.**
Black Mountain *n* **the.** a mountain range in S Wales, in E Carmarthenshire and W Powys. Highest peak: Carmarthen Van, 802 m (2632 ft.).
Black Mountains *pl n* a mountain range running from N Monmouthshire and SE Powys (Wales) to SW Hereford and Worcester (England). Highest peak: Waun Fach, 811 m (2660 ft.).

Black Muslim *n* (esp. in the U.S.) a member of a political and religious movement of Black people who adopt the religious practices of Islam and seek to establish a new Black nation. Official name: **Nation of Islam.**

black mustard *n* a Eurasian cruciferous plant, *Brassica* (or *Sinapsis*) *nigra,* with clusters of yellow flowers and pungent seeds from which the condiment mustard is made.

black nightshade *n* a poisonous solanaceous plant, *Solanum nigrum,* a common weed in cultivated land, having small white flowers with backward-curved petals and black berry-like fruits.

black opal *n* any opal of a dark coloration, not necessarily black.

blackout ('blækaʊt) *n* **1** the extinguishing or hiding of all artificial light, esp. in a city visible to an enemy attack from the air. **2** a momentary loss of consciousness, vision, or memory. **3** a temporary electrical power failure or cut. **4** *Electronics.* a temporary loss of sensitivity in a valve following a short strong pulse. **5** a temporary loss of radio communications between a spacecraft and earth, esp. on re-entry into the earth's atmosphere. **6** the suspension of radio or television broadcasting, as by a strike or for political reasons. ◆ *vb* **black out.** (*adv*) **7** (*tr*) to obliterate or extinguish (lights). **8** (*tr*) to create a blackout in (a city etc.). **9** (*intr*) to lose vision, consciousness, or memory temporarily. **10** (*tr, adv*) to stop (news, a television programme) from being released or broadcast.

Black Panther *n* (in the U.S.) a member of a militant Black political party founded in 1965 to end the political dominance of Whites.

black pepper *n* a pungent condiment made by grinding the dried unripe berries, together with their black husks, of the pepper plant *Piper nigrum.*

black pine *n* See **matai.**

blackpoll ('blæk,pəʊl) *n* a North American warbler, *Dendroica striata,* the male of which has a black-and-white head.

Blackpool ('blæk,pu:l) *n* a town and resort in NW England, in Lancashire on the Irish Sea: famous for its tower, 158 m (518 ft.) high, and its illuminations. Pop.: 146 262 (1991).

black powder *n* another name for **gunpowder.**

Black Power *n* a social, economic, and political movement of Black people, esp. in the U.S., to obtain equality with Whites.

Black Prince *n* **the.** See **Edward** (Prince of Wales).

black pudding *n* a kind of black sausage made from minced pork fat, pig's blood, and other ingredients. Also called: **blood pudding.** Usual U.S. and Canadian name: **blood sausage.**

black rat *n* a common rat, *Rattus rattus:* a household pest that has spread from its native Asia to all countries.

Black Rod *n* **1** (in Britain) an officer of the House of Lords and of the Order of the Garter, whose main duty is summoning the Commons at the opening and proroguing of Parliament. **2** a similar officer in any of certain other legislatures.

black rot *n* any of various plant diseases of fruits and vegetables, producing blackening, rotting, and shrivelling and caused by bacteria (including *Xanthomonas campestris*) and fungi (such as *Physalospora malorum*).

black run *n Skiing.* an extremely difficult run, suitable for expert skiers.

black rust *n* a stage in any of several diseases of cereals and grasses caused by rust fungi in which black masses of spores appear on the stems or leaves.

Black Sash *n* (formerly, in South Africa) an organization of women opposed to apartheid.

Black Sea *n* an inland sea between SE Europe and Asia: connected to the Aegean Sea by the Bosporus, the Sea of Marmara, and the Dardanelles, and to the Sea of Azov by the Kerch Strait. Area: about 415 000 sq. km (160 000 sq. miles). Also called: **Euxine Sea.** Ancient name: **Pontus Euxinus.**

black section *n* (in Britain) an unofficial group within the Labour Party in any constituency that represents the interests of local Black people.

black sheep *n* a person who is regarded as a disgrace or failure by his family or peer group.

Blackshirt ('blæk,ʃɜ:t) *n* (in Europe) a member of a fascist organization, esp. a member of the Italian Fascist party before and during World War II.

blacksmith ('blæk,smɪθ) *n* an artisan who works iron with a furnace, anvil, hammer, etc. [C14: see BLACK, SMITH]

blacksnake ('blæk,sneɪk) *n* **1** any of several Old World black venomous elapid snakes, esp. *Pseudechis porphyriacus* (**Australian blacksnake**). **2** any of various dark nonvenomous snakes, such as *Coluber constrictor* (black racer). **3** *U.S. and Canadian.* a long heavy pliant whip of braided leather or rawhide.

black spot *n* **1** a place on a road where accidents frequently occur. **2** any dangerous or difficult place. **3** a disease of roses, *Diplocarpon rosae,* that causes circular black blotches on the leaves.

black spruce *n* a coniferous tree, *Picea mariana,* of the northern regions of North America, growing mostly in cold bogs and having dark green needles. Also called: **spruce pine.**

Blackstone ('blæk,stəʊn, -stən) *n* Sir **William.** 1723–80, English jurist noted particularly for his *Commentaries on the Laws of England* (1765–69), which had a profound influence on jurisprudence in the U.S.

blackstrap molasses ('blæk,stræp) *pl n* (*functioning as sing*) the molasses remaining after the maximum quantity of sugar has been extracted from the raw material.

black stump *n* **1 the.** *Austral.* an imaginary marker of the extent of civilization (esp. in the phrase **beyond the black stump**). **2** *N.Z.* a long way off.

black swan *n* a large Australian swan, *Cygnus atratus,* that has a black plumage and red bill.

blacktail ('blæk,teɪl) *n* a variety of mule deer having a black tail.

blackthorn ('blæk,θɔ:n) *n* **1** Also called: **sloe.** a thorny Eurasian rosaceous shrub, *Prunus spinosa,* with black twigs, white flowers, and small sour plumlike fruits. **2** a walking stick made from its wood.

black tie *n* **1** a black bow tie worn with a dinner jacket. **2** (*modifier*) denoting an occasion when a dinner jacket should be worn. ◆ Compare **white tie.**

blacktop ('blæk,tɒp) *n Chiefly U.S. and Canadian.* **1** a bituminous mixture used for paving. **2** a road paved with this mixture.

black tracker *n Austral.* an Aboriginal tracker working for the police.

black treacle *n Brit.* another term for **treacle** (sense 1).

black velvet *n* **1** a mixture of stout and champagne in equal proportions. **2** *Austral. slang.* Aboriginal women as sexual partners.

Black Volta *n* a river in W Africa, rising in SW Burkina-Faso and flowing northeast, then south into Lake Volta: forms part of the border of Ghana with Burkina-Faso and with the Ivory Coast. Length: about 800 km (500 miles).

black vomit *n* **1** vomit containing blood, often a manifestation of disease, such as yellow fever. **2** *Informal.* yellow fever.

Blackwall hitch ('blæk,wɔ:l) *n* a knot for hooking tackle to the end of a rope, holding fast when pulled but otherwise loose. [C19: named after *Blackwall,* former docks in London]

black walnut *n* **1** a North American walnut tree, *Juglans nigra,* with hard dark wood and edible oily nuts. **2** the valuable wood of this tree, used for cabinet work. **3** the nut of this tree. ◆ Compare **butternut** (senses 1–4).

Black Watch *n* **the.** the Royal Highland Regiment in the British army. [so called for their dark tartan]

blackwater fever ('blæk,wɔ:tə) *n* a rare and serious complication of chronic malaria caused by *Plasmodium falciparum,* characterized by massive destruction of red blood cells, producing dark red or blackish urine.

black whale *n* another name for **pilot whale.**

black widow *n* an American spider, *Latrodectus mactans,* the female of which is black with red markings, highly venomous, and commonly eats its mate.

blackwood ('blæk,wʊd) *n* a tall Australian acacia tree, *A. melanoxylon,* having small clusters of flowers and curved pods and yielding highly valued black timber. Also called: **Sally Wattle.**

Blackwood[1] ('blæk,wʊd) *n Bridge.* a conventional bidding sequence of four and five no-trumps, which are requests to the partner to show aces and kings respectively. [C20: named after Easeley F. *Blackwood,* its American inventor]

Blackwood[2] ('blæk,wʊd) *n* **Algernon** (**Henry**). 1869–1951, British novelist and short-story writer; noted for his supernatural tales.

bladder ('blædə) *n* **1** *Anatomy.* a distensible membranous sac, usually containing liquid or gas, esp. the urinary bladder. Related adj: **vesical. 2** an inflatable part of something. **3** a blister, cyst, vesicle, etc., usually filled with fluid. **4** a hollow vesicular or saclike part or organ in certain plants, such as the bladderwrack. [Old English *blǣdre*] ▸ **'bladdery** *adj*

bladder campion *n* a European caryophyllaceous plant, *Silene vulgaris,* having white flowers with an inflated calyx.

bladder fern *n* a small fern, *Cystoperis fragilis,* with graceful lanceolate leaves, typically growing on limestone rocks and walls. [C19: named from the bladder-shaped indusium]

bladder ketmia ('ketmɪə) *n* another name for **flower-of-an-hour.**

bladdernose ('blædə,nəʊz) *n* another name for **hooded seal.**

bladdernut ('blædə,nʌt) *n* **1** any temperate shrub or small tree of the genus *Staphylea,* esp. *S. pinnata* of S Europe, that has bladder-like seed pods: family *Staphyleaceae.* **2** the pod of any such tree.

bladder senna *n* a Eurasian papilionaceous plant, *Colutea arborescens,* with yellow and red flowers and membranous inflated pods.

bladder worm *n* an encysted saclike larva of the tapeworm. The main types are cysticercus, hydatid and coenurus.

bladderwort ('blædə,wɜ:t) *n* any aquatic plant of the genus *Utricularia,* some of whose leaves are modified as small bladders to trap minute aquatic animals: family *Lentibulariaceae.*

bladderwrack ('blædə,ræk) *n* any of several seaweeds of the genera *Fucus* and *Ascophyllum,* esp. *F. vesiculosus,* that grow in the intertidal regions of rocky shores and have branched brown fronds with air bladders.

blade (bleɪd) *n* **1** the part of a sharp weapon, tool, etc., that forms the cutting edge. **2** (*pl*) *Austral. and N.Z.* hand shears used for shearing sheep. **3** the thin flattish part of various tools, implements, etc., as of a propeller, turbine, etc. **4** the flattened expanded part of a leaf, sepal, or petal. **5** the long narrow leaf of a grass or related plant. **6** the striking surface of a bat, club, stick, or oar. **7** the metal runner on an ice skate. **8** *Archaeol.* a long thin flake of flint, possibly used as a tool. **9** the upper part of the tongue lying directly behind the tip. **10** *Archaic.* a dashing or swaggering young man. **11** short for **shoulder blade. 12** a poetic word for a **sword** or **swordsman.** [Old English *blæd;* related to Old Norse *blath* leaf, Old High German *blat,* Latin *folium* leaf] ▸ **'bladed** *adj*

blade grader *n* another name for **grader** (sense 2).

blade-shearing *n N.Z.* the shearing of sheep using hand shears. ▸ **'blade-,shearer** *n*

blade slap *n* the regular noise beat generated by the rotor blades of a helicopter.

blae (ble, bleɪ) *adj Scot.* bluish-grey; slate-coloured. [from Old Norse *blár*]

blaeberry ('bleɪbərɪ) *n, pl* **-ries.** *Brit.* another name for **whortleberry** (senses 1, 2). [C15: from BLAE + BERRY]

Blaenau Gwent ('blaɪ,naʊ 'gwent) *n* a county borough of SE Wales, created in 1996 from NW Gwent. Administrative centre: Ebbw Vale. Pop.: 74 700 (1991 est.). Area: 109 sq. km (42 sq. miles).

blaes (blez, bleɪz) *n Scot.* **a** hardened clay or shale, esp. when crushed and used to form the top layer of a sports pitch: bluish-grey or reddish in colour. **b** (*as modifier*): *a blaes pitch.* [C18: from BLAE]

blag (blæg) *Slang.* ◆ *n* **1** a robbery, esp. with violence. ◆ *vb* **blags, blagging, blagged.** (*tr*) **2** to obtain by wheedling or cadging: *she blagged free tickets from her mate.* **3** to snatch (wages, someone's handbag, etc.); steal. **4** to rob (esp. a bank or post office). [C19: of unknown origin] ▸ **'blagger** *n*

Blagoveshchensk (*Russian* bləga'vjeʃtʃɪnsk) *n* a city and port in E Russia, in Siberia on the Amur River. Pop.: 214 000 (1995 est.).

blague (blɑːg) *n* pretentious but empty talk; nonsense. [C19: from French] ▸ **'blaguer** *n*

blah *or* **blah blah** (blɑː) *Slang.* ◆ *n* **1** worthless or silly talk; claptrap. ◆ *adj* **2** uninteresting; insipid. ◆ *vb* **3** (*intr*) to talk nonsense or boringly.

blain (bleɪn) *n* a blister, blotch, or sore on the skin. [Old English *blegen;* related to Middle Low German *bleine*]

Blair (bleə) *n* **Tony,** full name *Anthony Charles Lynton Blair.* born 1953, British politician; leader of the Labour Party from 1994; prime minister from 1997.

Blairite ('bleəraɪt) *adj* **1** of or relating to the modernizing policies of Tony Blair. ◆ *n* **2** a supporter of the modernizing policies of Tony Blair.

Blake (bleɪk) *n* **1 Peter.** born 1932, British painter, a leading exponent of pop art in the 1960s: co-founder of the Brotherhood of Ruralists (1969). **2 Robert.** 1599–1657, English admiral, who commanded Cromwell's fleet against the Royalists, the Dutch, and the Spanish. **3 William.** 1757–1827, English poet, painter, engraver, and mystic. His literary works include *Songs of Innocence* (1789) and *Songs of Experience* (1794), *The Marriage of Heaven and Hell* (1793), and *Jerusalem* (1820). His chief works in the visual arts include engravings of a visionary nature, such as the illustrations for *The Book of Job* (1826), for Dante's poems, and for his own *Prophetic Books* (1783–1804).

Blakey ('bleɪkɪ) *n* **Art,** full name *Arthur Blakey.* (1919–90), U.S. Black jazz drummer and leader of the Jazz Messengers band.

blame (bleɪm) *n* **1** responsibility for something that is wrong or deserving censure; culpability. **2** an expression of condemnation; reproof. **3 be to blame.** to be at fault or culpable. ◆ *vb* (*tr*) **4** (usually foll. by *for*) to attribute responsibility to; accuse: *I blame him for the failure.* **5** (usually foll. by *on*) to ascribe responsibility for (something) to: *I blame the failure on him.* **6** to find fault with. [C12: from Old French *blasmer,* ultimately from Late Latin *blasphēmāre* to BLASPHEME] ▸ **'blamable** *or* **'blameable** *adj* ▸ **'blamably** *or* **'blameably** *adv*

blamed (bleɪmd) *adj, adv Chiefly U.S.* a euphemistic word for **damned** (senses 2, 3).

blameful ('bleɪmfʊl) *adj* deserving blame; guilty. ▸ **'blamefully** *adv* ▸ **'blamefulness** *n*

blameless ('bleɪmlɪs) *adj* free from blame; innocent. ▸ **'blamelessly** *adv* ▸ **'blamelessness** *n*

blameworthy ('bleɪm,wɜːðɪ) *adj* deserving disapproval or censure. ▸ **'blame,worthiness** *n*

Blanc[1] (*French* blɑ̃) *n* **1 Mont.** See **Mont Blanc. 2 Cape.** a headland in N Tunisia: the northernmost point of Africa. **3 Cape.** Also called: **Cape Blanco** ('blæŋkəʊ). a peninsula in Mauritania, on the Atlantic coast.

Blanc[2] (*French* blɑ̃) *n* (**Jean Joseph Charles**) **Louis** (lwi). 1811–82, French socialist and historian: author of *L'Organisation du travail* (1840), in which he advocated the establishment of cooperative workshops subsidized by the state.

blanc fixe *French.* (blɑ̃ fiks) *n* another name for **barium sulphate.** [literally: fixed white]

blanch (blɑːntʃ) *vb* (*mainly tr*) **1** (*also intr*) to remove colour from, or (of colour) to be removed; whiten; fade: *the sun blanched the carpet; over the years the painting blanched.* **2** (*usually intr*) to become or cause to become pale, as with sickness or fear. **3** to plunge tomatoes, nuts, etc., into boiling water to loosen the skin. **4** to plunge (meat, green vegetables, etc.) in boiling water or bring to the boil in water in order to whiten, preserve the natural colour, or reduce or remove a bitter or salty taste. **5** to cause (celery, chicory, etc.) to grow free of chlorophyll by the exclusion of sunlight. **6** *Metallurgy.* to whiten (a metal), usually by treating it with an acid or by coating it with tin. **7** (*tr,* usually foll. by *over*) to attempt to conceal something. [C14: from Old French *blanchir* from *blanc* white; see BLANK]

Blanche of Castile (blaːntʃ) *n* ?1188–1252, queen consort (1223–26) of Louis VIII of France, born in Spain. The mother of Louis IX, she acted as regent during his minority (1226–36) and his absence on a crusade (1248–52).

blancmange (blə'mɒnʒ) *n* a jelly-like dessert, stiffened usually with cornflour and set in a mould. [C14: from Old French *blanc manger,* literally: white food]

bland (blænd) *adj* **1** devoid of any distinctive or stimulating characteristics; uninteresting; dull: *bland food.* **2** gentle and agreeable; suave. **3** (of the weather) mild and soothing. **4** unemotional or unmoved: *a bland account of atrocities.* [C15: from Latin *blandus* flattering] ▸ **'blandly** *adv* ▸ **'blandness** *n*

blandish ('blændɪʃ) *vb* (*tr*) to seek to persuade or influence by mild flattery; coax. [C14: from Old French *blandir* from Latin *blandīrī*]

blandishments ('blændɪʃmənts) *pl n* (*rarely sing*) flattery intended to coax or cajole.

blank (blæŋk) *adj* **1** (of a writing surface) bearing no marks; not written on. **2** (of a form, etc.) with spaces left for details to be filled in. **3** without ornament or break; unrelieved: *a blank wall.* **4** not filled in; empty; void: *a blank space.* **5** exhibiting no interest or expression: *a blank look.* **6** lacking understanding; confused: *he looked blank even after the explanations.* **7** absolute; complete: *blank rejection.* **8** devoid of ideas or inspiration: *his mind went blank in the exam.* **9** unproductive; barren. ◆ *n* **10** an emptiness; void; blank space. **11** an empty space for writing in, as on a printed form. **12** a printed form containing such empty spaces. **13** something characterized by incomprehension or mental confusion: *my mind went a complete blank.* **14** a mark, often a dash, in place of a word, esp. a taboo word. **15** short for **blank cartridge. 16** a plate or plug used to seal an aperture. **17** a piece of material prepared for stamping, punching, forging, etc. **18** *Archery.* the white spot in the centre of a target. **19 draw a blank. 19a** to choose a lottery ticket that fails to win. **19b** to get no results from something. ◆ *vb* (*tr*) **20** (usually foll. by *out*) to cross out, blot, or obscure. **21** *Slang.* to ignore or be unresponsive towards (someone): *the crowd blanked her for the first four numbers.* **22** to forge, stamp, punch, or cut (a piece of material) in preparation for forging, die-stamping, or drawing operations. **23** (often foll. by *off*) to seal (an aperture) with a plate or plug. **24** *U.S. and Canadian informal.* to prevent (an opponent) from scoring in a game. [C15: from Old French *blanc* white, of Germanic origin; related to Old English *blanca* a white horse] ▸ **'blankly** *adv* ▸ **'blankness** *n*

blank cartridge *n* a cartridge containing powder but no bullet: used in battle practice or as a signal.

blank cheque *n* **1** a signed cheque on which the amount payable has not been specified. **2** complete freedom of action.

blank endorsement *n* an endorsement on a bill of exchange, cheque, etc., naming no payee and thus making the endorsed sum payable to the bearer. Also called: **endorsement in blank.**

blanket ('blæŋkɪt) *n* **1** a large piece of thick cloth for use as a bed covering, animal covering, etc., enabling a person or animal to retain much of his natural body heat. **2** a concealing cover or layer, as of smoke, leaves, or snow. **3** a rubber or plastic sheet wrapped round a cylinder, used in offset printing to transfer the image from the plate, stone, or forme to the paper. **4** *Physics.* a layer of a fertile substance placed round the core of a nuclear reactor as a reflector and often to breed new fissionable fuel. **5** (*modifier*) applying to or covering a wide group or variety of people, conditions, situations, etc.: *blanket insurance against loss, injury, and theft.* **6** (**born**) **on the wrong side of the blanket.** *Informal.* illegitimate. ◆ *vb* (*tr*) **7** to cover with or as if with a blanket; overlie. **8** to cover a very wide area, as in a publicity campaign; give blanket coverage. **9** (usually foll. by *out*) to obscure or suppress: *the storm blanketed out the TV picture.* **10** *Nautical.* to prevent wind from reaching the sails of (another sailing vessel) by passing to windward of it. [C13: from Old French *blancquete,* from *blanc;* see BLANK]

blanket bath *n* an all-over wash given to a person confined to bed.

blanket bog *n* a very acid peat bog, low in nutrients, extending widely over a flat terrain, found in cold wet climates.

blanket finish *n Athletics, horse racing.* a finish so close that a blanket would cover all the contestants involved.

blanket stitch *n* a strong reinforcing stitch for the edges of blankets and other thick material.

blankety ('blæŋkɪtɪ) *adj, adv* a euphemism for any taboo word. [C20: from BLANK]

blank verse *n Prosody.* unrhymed verse, esp. in iambic pentameters.

blanquette de veau (blæŋ'ket də 'vəʊ) *n* a ragout or stew of veal in a white sauce. [French]

Blanqui (*French* blɑ̃ki) *n* **Louis Auguste** (*French* lwi ogyst). 1805–81, French revolutionary, who organized secret socialist societies and preached violent insurrection; he spent over 30 years in prison.

Blantyre-Limbe (blæn'taɪə'lɪmbeɪ) *n* a city in S Malawi: largest city in the country; formed in 1956 from the adjoining towns of Blantyre and Limbe. Pop.: 446 800 (1994 est.).

blare (bleə) *vb* **1** to sound loudly and harshly. **2** to proclaim loudly and sensationally. ◆ *n* **3** a loud and usually harsh or grating noise. [C14: from Middle Dutch *bleren;* of imitative origin]

blarney ('blɑːnɪ) *n* **1** flattering talk. ◆ *vb* **2** to cajole with flattery; wheedle. [C19: after the BLARNEY STONE]

Blarney Stone *n* a stone in **Blarney Castle,** in the SW Republic of Ireland, said to endow whoever kisses it with skill in flattery.

Blasco Ibáñez (*Spanish* 'blasko i'βaɲeθ) *n* **Vicente** (bi'θente). 1867–1928, Spanish novelist, whose books include *Blood and Sand* (1909) and *The Four Horsemen of the Apocalypse* (1916).

blasé ('blɑːzeɪ) *adj* **1** indifferent to something because of familiarity or surfeit. **2** lacking enthusiasm; bored. [C19: from French, past participle of *blaser* to cloy]

blaspheme (blæs'fiːm) *vb* **1** (*tr*) to show contempt or disrespect for (God, a divine being, or sacred things), esp. in speech. **2** (*intr*) to utter profanities, curses, or impious expressions. [C14: from Late Latin *blasphēmāre,* from Greek *blasphēmein* from *blasphēmos* BLASPHEMOUS] ▸ **blas'phemer** *n*

blasphemous ('blæsfɪməs) *adj* expressing or involving impiousness or gross irreverence towards God, a divine being, or something sacred. [C15: via Late Latin, from Greek *blasphēmos* evil-speaking, from *blapsis* evil + *phēmē* speech] ▸ **'blasphemously** *adv*

blasphemy ('blæsfɪmɪ) *n, pl* **-mies. 1** blasphemous behaviour or language. **2** Also called: **blasphemous libel.** *Law.* the crime committed if a person insults, offends, or vilifies the deity, Christ, or the Christian religion.

blast (blɑːst) *n* **1** an explosion, as of dynamite. **2a** the rapid movement of air away from the centre of an explosion, combustion of rocket fuel, etc. **2b** a wave of overpressure caused by an explosion; shock wave. **3** the charge of explosive used in a single explosion. **4** a sudden strong gust of wind or air. **5** a sudden loud sound, as of a trumpet. **6** a violent verbal outburst, as of criticism. **7** a forcible jet or stream of air, esp. one used to intensify the heating effect of a furnace, increase the draught in a steam engine, or break up coal at a coalface. **8** any of several diseases of plants and animals, esp. one producing withering in plants. **9** *U.S. slang.* a very enjoyable or thrilling experience: *the party was a blast.* **10** (**at**) **full blast.** at maximum speed, volume etc. ◆ *interj* **11** *Slang.* an exclamation of annoyance (esp. in phrases such as **blast it! blast him!**). ◆ *vb* **12** to destroy or blow up with explosives, shells, etc. **13** to make or cause to make a loud harsh noise. **14** (*tr*) to remove, open, etc., by an explosion: *to blast a hole in a wall.* **15** (*tr*) to ruin; shatter: *the rain blasted our plans for a picnic.* **16** to wither or cause to wither; blight or be blighted. **17** to criticize severely. **18** to shoot or shoot at: *he blasted the hat off her head; he blasted away at the trees.* ◆ See also **blastoff.** [Old English *blǣst,* related to Old Norse *blāstr*] ▸ **'blaster** *n*

-blast *n combining form.* (in biology) indicating an embryonic cell or formative layer: *mesoblast.* [from Greek *blastos* bud]

blasted ('blɑːstɪd) *adj* 1 blighted or withered. ◆ *adj (prenominal), adv* 2 *Slang.* (intensifier): *a blasted idiot.*

blastema (blæ'stiːmə) *n, pl* **-mas** *or* **-mata** (-mətə). a mass of undifferentiated animal cells that will develop into an organ or tissue: present at the site of regeneration of a lost part. [C19: from New Latin, from Greek: offspring, from *blastos* bud] ▸ **blastemic** (blæ'stiːmɪk, -'stem-) *adj*

blast furnace *n* a vertical cylindrical furnace for smelting iron, copper, lead, and tin ores. The ore, scrap, solid fuel, and slag-forming materials are fed through the top and a blast of preheated air is forced through the charge from the bottom. Metal and slag are run off from the base.

blast-furnace cement *n* a type of cement made from a blend of ordinary Portland cement and crushed slag from a blast furnace. It has lower setting properties than ordinary Portland cement.

blasting ('blɑːstɪŋ) *n* a distortion of sound caused by overloading certain components of a radio system.

blast injection *n* the injection of liquid fuel directly into the cylinder of an internal-combustion engine using a blast of high-pressure air to atomize the spray of fuel. Compare **solid injection.**

blasto- *combining form.* (in biology) indicating an embryo or bud or the process of budding: *blastoderm.* [from Greek *blastos.* See -BLAST]

blastochyle ('blæstəʊˌkaɪl) *n Embryol.* the fluid in a blastocoel.

blastocoel *or* **blastocoele** ('blæstəʊˌsiːl) *n Embryol.* the cavity within a blastula. Also called: **segmentation cavity.**

blastocyst ('blæstəʊˌsɪst) *n Embryol.* 1 Also called: **blastosphere.** the blastula of mammals: a sphere of cells (trophoblast) enclosing an inner mass of cells and a fluid-filled cavity (blastocoel). 2 another name for **germinal vesicle.**

blastoderm ('blæstəʊˌdɜːm) *n Embryol.* 1 a flat disc of cells formed after cleavage in a heavily yolked egg, such as a bird's egg. 2 a layer of cells on the inside of the blastula surrounding the blastocoel. ▸ ˌ**blasto'dermic** *adj*

blastoff ('blɑːstˌɒf) *n* 1 the launching of a rocket under its own power. 2 the time at which this occurs. ◆ *vb* **blast off.** 3 (*adv; when tr, usually passive*) (of a rocket, spacemen, etc.) to be launched.

blastogenesis (ˌblæstəʊ'dʒenɪsɪs) *n* 1 the theory that inherited characteristics are transmitted only by germ plasm. See also **pangenesis.** 2 asexual reproduction, esp. budding. ▸ ˌ**blasto'genic** *or* ˌ**blastoge'netic** *adj*

blastoma (ˌblæs'təʊmə) *n, pl* **-mata** *or* **-mas.** *Pathol.* **a** a tumour composed of embryonic tissue that has not yet developed a specialized function. **b** (*in combination*): *neuroblastoma.* [C20: New Latin, from BLASTO- + -OMA]

blastomere ('blæstəʊˌmɪə) *n Embryol.* any of the cells formed by cleavage of a fertilized egg. ▸ **blastomeric** (ˌblæstəʊ'merɪk) *adj*

blastopore ('blæstəʊˌpɔː) *n Embryol.* the opening of the archenteron in the gastrula that develops into the anus of some animals. ▸ ˌ**blasto'poric** *or* ˌ**blasto'poral** *adj*

blastosphere ('blæstəʊˌsfɪə) *n* 1 another name for **blastula.** 2 another name for **blastocyst** (sense 1).

blastospore ('blæstəʊˌspɔː) *n Botany.* a spore formed by budding, as in certain fungi.

blastula ('blæstjʊlə) *n, pl* **-las** *or* **-lae** (-liː). an early form of an animal embryo that develops from a morula, consisting of a sphere of cells with a central cavity. Also called: **blastosphere.** [C19: New Latin; see BLASTO-] ▸ '**blastular** *adj*

blastulation (ˌblæstjʊ'leɪʃən) *n Embryol.* the process of blastula formation.

blat (blæt) *vb* **blats, blatting, blatted.** *U.S. and Canadian.* 1 (*intr*) to cry out or bleat like a sheep. 2 (*tr*) to utter indiscreetly in a loud voice. [C19: of imitative origin]

blatant ('bleɪtᵊnt) *adj* 1 glaringly conspicuous or obvious: *a blatant lie.* 2 offensively noticeable: *blatant disregard for a person's feelings.* 3 offensively noisy. [C16: coined by Edmund Spenser; probably influenced by Latin *blatīre* to babble; compare Middle Low German *pladderen*] ▸ '**blatancy** *n* ▸ '**blatantly** *adv*

blather ('blæðə) *or Scot.* **blether** *vb* 1 (*intr*) to speak foolishly. ◆ *n* 2 foolish talk; nonsense. 3 a person who blathers. [C15: from Old Norse *blathra,* from *blathr* nonsense]

blatherskite ('blæðəˌskaɪt) *n* 1 a talkative silly person. 2 foolish talk; nonsense. [C17: see BLATHER, SKATE[3]]

Blaue Reiter (*German* 'blauə 'raitər) *n* **der.** a group of German expressionist painters formed in Munich in 1911, including Kandinsky and Klee, who sought to express the spiritual side of man and nature, which they felt had been neglected by impressionism. [C20: literally: blue rider, name adopted by Kandinsky and Marc because they liked the colour blue, horses, and riders]

Blavatsky (blə'vætskɪ) *n* **Elena Petrovna** (jɪ'ljenə pɪ'trɒvnə), called *Madame Blavatsky.* 1831–91, Russian theosophist; author of *Isis Unveiled* (1877).

blaxsploitation (ˌblæksplɔɪ'teɪʃən) *n* a genre of films featuring Black stereotypes. [C20: from BLA(CK) + (E)XPLOITATION]

Blaydon ('bleɪdᵊn) *n* an industrial town in NE England, in Gateshead unitary authority, Tyne and Wear. Pop: 15 510 (1991).

blaze[1] (bleɪz) *n* 1 a strong fire or flame. 2 a very bright light or glare. 3 an outburst (of passion, acclaim, patriotism, etc.). 4 brilliance; brightness. ◆ *vb (intr)* 5 to burn fiercely. 6 to shine brightly. 7 (often foll. by *up*) to become stirred, as with anger or excitement. 8 (usually foll. by *away*) to shoot continuously. ◆ See also **blazes.** [Old English *blæse*]

blaze[2] (bleɪz) *n* 1 a mark, usually indicating a path, made on a tree, esp. by chipping off the bark. 2 a light-coloured marking on the face of a domestic animal, esp. a horse. ◆ *vb* (*tr*) 3 to indicate or mark (a tree, path, etc.) with a blaze. 4 **blaze a trail.** to explore new territories, areas of knowledge, etc., in such a way that others can follow. [C17: probably from Middle Low German *bles* white marking; compare BLEMISH]

blaze[3] (bleɪz) *vb* (*tr;* often foll. by *abroad*) to make widely known; proclaim. [C14: from Middle Dutch *blāsen,* from Old High German *blāsan;* related to Old Norse *blāsa*]

blazer ('bleɪzə) *n* a fairly lightweight jacket, often striped or in the colours of a sports club, school, etc.

blazes ('bleɪzɪz) *pl n* 1 *Slang.* a euphemistic word for **hell** (esp. in the phrase **go to blazes**). 2 *Informal.* (intensifier): *to run like blazes; what the blazes are you doing?*

blazing star *n U.S.* 1 a North American plant, *Chamaelirium luteum,* with a long spike of small white flowers: family *Compositae* (composites). 2 any plant of the related North American genus *Liatris,* having clusters of small red or purple flowers.

blazon ('bleɪzᵊn) *vb* (*tr*) 1 (often foll. by *abroad*) to proclaim loudly and publicly. 2 *Heraldry.* to describe (heraldic arms) in proper terms. 3 to draw and colour (heraldic arms) conventionally. ◆ *n* 4 *Heraldry.* a conventional description or depiction of heraldic arms. 5 any description or recording, esp. of good qualities. [C13: from Old French *blason* coat of arms] ▸ '**blazoner** *n*

blazonry ('bleɪzənrɪ) *n, pl* **-ries.** 1 the art or process of describing heraldic arms in proper form. 2 heraldic arms collectively. 3 colourful or ostentatious display.

bldg *abbrev. for* building.

bleach (bliːtʃ) *vb* 1 to make or become white or colourless, as by exposure to sunlight, by the action of chemical agents, etc. ◆ *n* 2 a bleaching agent. 3 the degree of whiteness resulting from bleaching. 4 the act of bleaching. [Old English *blǣcan;* related to Old Norse *bleikja,* Old High German *bleih* pale] ▸ '**bleachable** *adj* ▸ '**bleacher** *n*

bleachers ('bliːtʃəz) *pl n* 1 (*sometimes sing*) a tier of seats in a sports stadium, etc., that are unroofed and inexpensive. 2 the people occupying such seats.

bleaching powder *n* a white powder with the odour of chlorine, consisting of chlorinated calcium hydroxide with an approximate formula $CaCl(OCl).4H_2O$. It is used in solution as a bleaching agent and disinfectant. Also called: **chloride of lime, chlorinated lime.**

bleak[1] (bliːk) *adj* 1 exposed and barren; desolate. 2 cold and raw. 3 offering little hope or excitement; dismal: *a bleak future.* [Old English *blāc* bright, pale; related to Old Norse *bleikr* white, Old High German *bleih* pale] ▸ '**bleakly** *adv* ▸ '**bleakness** *n*

bleak[2] (bliːk) *n* any slender silvery European cyprinid fish of the genus *Alburnus,* esp. *A. lucidus,* occurring in slow-flowing rivers. [C15: probably from Old Norse *bleikja* white colour; related to Old High German *bleiche* BLEACH]

blear (blɪə) *Archaic.* ◆ *vb* 1 (*tr*) to make (eyes or sight) dim with or as if with tears; blur. ◆ *adj* 2 a less common word for **bleary.** [C13: *blere* to make dim; related to Middle High German *blerre* blurred vision]

bleary ('blɪərɪ) *adj* **blearier, bleariest.** 1 (of eyes or vision) dimmed or blurred, as by tears or tiredness. 2 indistinct or unclear. 3 exhausted; tired. ▸ '**blearily** *adv* ▸ '**bleariness** *n*

bleary-eyed *or* **blear-eyed** *adj* 1 with eyes blurred, as with old age or after waking. 2 physically or mentally unperceptive.

bleat (bliːt) *vb* 1 (*intr*) (of a sheep, goat, or calf) to utter its characteristic plaintive cry. 2 (*intr*) to speak with any similar sound. 3 to whine; whimper. ◆ *n* 4 the characteristic cry of sheep, goats, and young calves. 5 any sound similar to this. 6 a weak complaint or whine. [Old English *blǣtan;* related to Old High German *blāzen,* Dutch *blaten,* Latin *flēre* to weep; see BLARE] ▸ '**bleater** *n* ▸ '**bleating** *n, adj*

bleb (bleb) *n* 1 a fluid-filled blister on the skin. 2 a small air bubble. [C17: variant of BLOB] ▸ '**blebby** *adj*

bleed (bliːd) *vb* **bleeds, bleeding, bled.** 1 (*intr*) to lose or emit blood. 2 (*tr*) to remove or draw blood from (a person or animal). 3 (*intr*) to be injured or die, as for a cause or one's country. 4 (of plants) to exude (sap or resin), esp. from a cut. 5 (*tr*) *Informal.* to obtain relatively large amounts of money, goods, etc., esp. by extortion. 6 (*tr*) to draw liquid or gas from (a container or enclosed system): *to bleed the hydraulic brakes.* 7 (*intr*) (of dye or paint) to run or become mixed, as when wet. 8 to print or be printed so that text, illustrations, etc., run off the trimmed page. 9 (*tr*) to trim (the edges of a printed sheet) so closely as to cut off some of the printed matter. 10 (*intr*) *Civil engineering, building trades.* (of a mixture) to exude (a liquid) during compaction, such as water from cement. 11 **bleed (someone or something) dry.** to extort gradually all the resources of (a person or thing). 12 **one's heart bleeds.** used to express sympathetic grief, but often used ironically. ◆ *n* 13 *Printing.* 13a an illustration or sheet trimmed so that some matter is bled. 13b (*as modifier*): *a bleed page.* 14 *Printing.* the trimmings of a sheet that has been bled. [Old English *blēdan;* see BLOOD]

bleeder ('bliːdə) *n* 1 *Slang.* 1a *Derogatory.* a despicable person: *a rotten bleeder.* 1b any person; fellow: *where's the bleeder gone?* 2 *Pathol.* a nontechnical name for a **haemophiliac.**

bleeder resistor *n* a resistor connected across the output terminals of a power supply in order to improve voltage regulation and to discharge filter capacitors.

bleeder's disease *n* a nontechnical name for **haemophilia.**

bleeding ('bliːdɪŋ) *adj, adv Brit. slang.* (intensifier): *a bleeding fool; it's bleeding beautiful.*

bleeding heart *n* 1 any of several plants of the genus *Dicentra,* esp. the widely cultivated Japanese species *D. spectabilis,* which has finely divided leaves and heart-shaped nodding pink flowers: family *Fumariaceae.* 2 *Informal.* 2a a person who is excessively softhearted. 2b (*as modifier*): *a bleeding-heart liberal.*

bleed valve *n* a valve for running off a liquid from a tank, tube, etc., or for allowing accumulations of gas in a liquid to blow off. Also called: **bleed nipple.**

bleep (bliːp) *n* 1 a single short high-pitched signal made by an electronic apparatus; beep. 2 another word for **bleeper.** ◆ *vb* 3 (*intr*) to make such a noise. 4 (*tr*) to call (someone) by triggering the bleeper he or she is wearing. [C20: of imitative origin]

bleeper ('bliːpə) *n* a small portable radio receiver, carried esp. by doctors, that sounds a coded bleeping signal to call the carrier. Also called: **bleep.**

blemish ('blɛmɪʃ) *n* **1** a defect; flaw; stain. ◆ *vb* **2** (*tr*) to flaw the perfection of; spoil; tarnish. [C14: from Old French *blemir* to make pale, probably of Germanic origin.]

blench[1] (blɛntʃ) *vb* (*intr*) to shy away, as in fear; quail. [Old English *blencan* to deceive.]

blench[2] (blɛntʃ) *vb* to make or become pale or white. [C19: variant of BLANCH]

blend (blɛnd) *vb* **1** to mix or mingle (components) together thoroughly. **2** (*tr*) to mix (different grades or varieties of tea, whisky, tobacco, etc.) to produce a particular flavour, consistency, etc. **3** (*intr*) to look good together; harmonize. **4** (*intr*) (esp. of colours) to shade imperceptibly into each other. ◆ *n* **5** a mixture or type produced by blending. **6** the act of blending. **7** Also called: **portmanteau word.** a word formed by joining together the beginning and the end of two other words: *"brunch" is a blend of "breakfast" and "lunch."* [Old English *blandan;* related to *blendan* to deceive, Old Norse *blanda,* Old High German *blantan*]

blende (blɛnd) *n* **1** another name for **sphalerite. 2** any of several sulphide ores, such as antimony sulphide. [C17: German *Blende,* from *blenden* to deceive, BLIND; so called because it is easily mistaken for galena]

blender ('blɛndə) *n* **1** a person or thing that blends. **2** Also called: **liquidizer.** a kitchen appliance with blades used for puréeing vegetables, blending liquids, etc.

Blenheim[1] ('blɛnɪm) *n* a village in SW Germany, site of a victory of Anglo-Austrian forces under the Duke of Marlborough and Prince Eugène of Savoy that saved Vienna from the French and Bavarians (1704) during the War of the Spanish Succession. Modern name: **Blindheim.**

Blenheim[2] ('blɛnɪm) *n* **1** a type of King Charles spaniel having red-and-white markings. **2** Also called: **Blenheim orange. 2a** a type of apple tree bearing gold-coloured apples. **2b** the fruit of this tree. [C19: named after BLENHEIM PALACE]

Blenheim Palace *n* a palace in Woodstock in Oxfordshire: built (1705–22) by Sir John Vanbrugh for the 1st Duke of Marlborough as a reward from the nation for his victory at Blenheim; gardens laid out by Henry Wise and Capability Brown; birthplace of Sir Winston Churchill (1874).

blennioid ('blɛnɪˌɔɪd) *adj* **1** of, relating to, or belonging to the *Blennioidea,* a large suborder of small mainly marine spiny-finned fishes having an elongated body with reduced pelvic fins. The group includes the blennies, butterfish, and gunnel. ◆ *n* **2** any fish belonging to the *Blennioidea.*

blennorrhoea *or U.S.* **blennorrhea** (ˌblɛnəˈrɪə) *n Pathol.* an excessive discharge of watery mucus, esp. from the urethra or the vagina.

blenny ('blɛnɪ) *n, pl* **-nies. 1** any blennioid fish of the family *Blenniidae* of coastal waters, esp. of the genus *Blennius,* having a tapering scaleless body, a long dorsal fin, and long raylike pelvic fins. **2** any of various related fishes. [C18: from Latin *blennius,* from Greek *blennos* slime; from the mucus that coats its body]

blent (blɛnt) *vb Archaic or literary.* a past participle of **blend.**

blepharism ('blɛfərɪzəm) *n* spasm of the eyelids, causing rapid involuntary blinking.

blepharitis (ˌblɛfəˈraɪtɪs) *n* inflammation of the eyelids. [C19: from Greek *blephar(on)* eyelid + -ITIS] ► **blepharitic** (ˌblɛfəˈrɪtɪk) *adj*

blepharospasm ('blɛfərəʊˌspæzəm) *n* spasm of the muscle of the eyelids, causing the eyes to shut tightly, either as a response to painful stimuli or occurring as a form of dystonia. [C19: from Greek *blepharo(n)* eyelid + SPASM]

Blériot (*French* blerjo) *n* **Louis** (lwi). 1872–1936, French aviator and aeronautical engineer: made the first flight across the English Channel (1909).

blesbok *or* **blesbuck** ('blɛsˌbʌk) *n, pl* **-boks, -bok** *or* **-bucks, -buck.** an antelope, *Damaliscus dorcas* (or *albifrons*), of southern Africa. The coat is a deep reddish-brown with a white blaze between the eyes; the horns are lyre-shaped. [C19: Afrikaans, from Dutch *bles* BLAZE[2] + *bok* goat, BUCK[1]]

bless (blɛs) *vb* **blesses, blessing, blessed** *or* **blest.** (*tr*) **1** to consecrate or render holy, beneficial, or prosperous by means of a religious rite. **2** to give honour or glory to (a person or thing) as divine or holy. **3** to call upon God to protect; give a benediction to. **4** to worship or adore (God); call or hold holy. **5** (*often passive*) to grant happiness, health, or prosperity to: *they were blessed with perfect peace.* **6** (*usually passive*) to endow with a talent, beauty, etc.: *she was blessed with an even temper.* **7** *Rare.* to protect against evil or harm. **8 bless you!** (*interj*) **8a** a traditional phrase said to a person who has just sneezed. **8b** an exclamation of well-wishing or surprise. **9 bless me!** *or* **(God) bless my soul!** (*interj*) an exclamation of surprise. **10 not have a penny to bless oneself with.** to be desperately poor. [Old English *blǣdsian* to sprinkle with sacrificial blood; related to *blōd* BLOOD]

blessed ('blɛsɪd, blɛst) *adj* **1** made holy by religious ceremony; consecrated. **2** worthy of deep reverence or respect. **3** *R.C. Church.* (of a person) beatified by the pope. **4** characterized by happiness or good fortune: *a blessed time.* **5** bringing great happiness or good fortune. **6** a euphemistic word for **damned,** used in mild oaths: *I'm blessed if I know.* ◆ *n* **7 the blessed.** *Christianity.* the dead who are already enjoying heavenly bliss. ► **'blessedly** *adv* ► **'blessedness** *n*

Blessed Sacrament *n Chiefly R.C. Church.* the consecrated elements of the Eucharist.

Blessed Virgin *n Chiefly R.C. Church.* another name for **Mary** (sense 1a).

blessing ('blɛsɪŋ) *n* **1** the act of invoking divine protection or aid. **2** the words or ceremony used for this. **3** a short prayer of thanksgiving before or after a meal; grace. **4** *Judaism.* Also called: **brachah, brocho. 4a** a short prayer prescribed for a specific occasion and beginning "Blessed art thou, O Lord ...". **4b** a section of the liturgy including a similar formula. **5** approval; good wishes: *her father gave his blessing to the marriage.* **6** the bestowal of a divine gift or favour. **7** a happy event or state of affairs: *a blessing in disguise.*

blest (blɛst) *vb* a past tense and past participle of **bless.**

blet (blɛt) *n* a state of softness or decay in certain fruits, such as the medlar, brought about by overripening. [C19: from French *blettir* to become overripe]

blether ('blɛðə) *vb, n Scot.* a variant spelling of **blather.** [C16: from Old Norse *blathra,* from *blathr* nonsense]

blew (bluː) *vb* the past tense of **blow**[1].

blewits ('bluːɪts) *n* (*functioning as sing*) an edible saprotroph agaricaceous fungus, *Tricholoma saevum,* having a pale brown cap and bluish stalk. [C19: probably based on BLUE]

Blida ('bliːdə) *n* a city in N Algeria, on the edge of the Mitidja Plain. Pop.: 127 284 (1987).

Bligh (blaɪ) *n* **William.** 1754–1817, British admiral; Governor of New South Wales (1806–9), deposed by the New South Wales Corps: as a captain, commander of *H.M.S. Bounty* when the crew mutinied in 1789.

blight (blaɪt) *n* **1** any plant disease characterized by withering and shrivelling without rotting. **2** any factor, such as bacterial attack or air pollution, that causes the symptoms of blight in plants. **3** a person or thing that mars or prevents growth, improvement, or prosperity. **4** an ugly urban district. **5** the state or condition of being blighted or spoilt. ◆ *vb* **6** to cause or suffer a blight. **7** (*tr*) to frustrate or disappoint. **8** (*tr*) to spoil; destroy. [C17: perhaps related to Old English *blǣce* rash; compare BLEACH]

blighter ('blaɪtə) *n Brit. informal.* **1** a fellow: *where's the blighter gone?* **2** a despicable or irritating person or thing.

blighty *or* **blighty bird** ('blaɪtɪ) *n N.Z.* another name for **white-eye.**

Blighty ('blaɪtɪ) *n* (*sometimes not cap.*) *Brit. slang.* (used esp. by troops serving abroad) **1** England; home. **2** (esp. in World War I) **2a** Also called: **a blighty one.** a slight wound that causes the recipient to be sent home to England. **2b** leave in England. [C20: from Hindi *bilāyatī* foreign land, England, from Arabic *wilāyat* country, from *waliya* he rules]

blimey ('blaɪmɪ) *interj Brit. slang.* an exclamation of surprise or annoyance. [C19: short for *gorblimey* God blind me]

blimp[1] (blɪmp) *n* **1** a small nonrigid airship, esp. one used for observation or as a barrage balloon. **2** *Films.* a soundproof cover fixed over a camera during shooting. [C20: probably from (*type*) *B-limp*]

blimp[2] (blɪmp) *n* (*often cap.*) *Chiefly Brit.* a person, esp. a military officer, who is stupidly complacent and reactionary. Also called: **Colonel Blimp.** [C20: after a character created by David Low]

blin (blɪn) *adj* a Scot. word for **blind.**

blind (blaɪnd) *adj* **1a** unable to see; sightless. **1b** (*as collective n; preceded by the*): *the blind.* **2** (usually foll. by *to*) unable or unwilling to understand or discern. **3** not based on evidence or determined by reason: *blind hatred.* **4** acting or performed without control or preparation. **5** done without being able to see, relying on instruments for information. **6** hidden from sight: *a blind corner; a blind stitch.* **7** closed at one end: *a blind alley.* **8** completely lacking awareness or consciousness: *a blind stupor.* **9** *Informal.* very drunk. **10** having no openings or outlets: *a blind wall.* **11** without having been seen beforehand: *a blind purchase.* **12** (of cultivated plants) having failed to produce flowers or fruits. **13** (intensifier): *not a blind bit of notice.* **14 turn a blind eye (to).** to disregard deliberately or pretend not to notice (something, esp. an action of which one disapproves). ◆ *adv* **15** without being able to see ahead or using only instruments: *to drive blind; flying blind.* **16** without adequate knowledge or information; carelessly: *to buy a house blind.* **17** (intensifier) (in the phrase **blind drunk**). **18 bake blind.** to bake (the empty crust of a pie, pastry, etc.) by half filling with dried peas, crusts of bread, etc., to keep it in shape. ◆ *vb* (*mainly tr*) **19** to deprive of sight permanently or temporarily. **20** to deprive of good sense, reason, or judgment. **21** to darken; conceal. **22** (foll. by *with*) to overwhelm by showing detailed knowledge: *to blind somebody with science.* **23** (*intr*) *Brit. slang.* to drive very fast. **24** (*intr*) *Brit. slang.* to curse (esp. in the phrase **effing and blinding**). ◆ *n* **25** (*modifier*) for or intended to help the blind: *a blind school.* **26** a shade for a window, usually on a roller. **27** any obstruction or hindrance to sight, light, or air. **28** a person, action, or thing that serves to deceive or conceal the truth. **29** a person who acts on behalf of someone who does not wish his identity or actions to be known. **30** *Brit. slang.* Also called: **blinder.** a drunken orgy; binge. **31** *Poker.* a stake put up by a player before he examines his cards. **32** *Hunting, chiefly U.S. and Canadian.* a screen of brush or undergrowth, in which hunters hide to shoot their quarry. Brit. name: **hide. 33** *Military.* a round or demolition charge that fails to explode. [Old English *blind;* related to Old Norse *blindr,* Old High German *blint;* Lettish *blendu* to see dimly; see BLUNDER] ► **'blindly** *adv* ► **'blindness** *n*

USAGE See at **disabled.**

blindage ('blaɪndɪdʒ) *n Military.* (esp. formerly) a protective screen or structure, as over a trench.

blind alley *n* **1** an alley open at one end only; cul-de-sac. **2** *Informal.* a situation in which no further progress can be made.

blind blocking *n Bookbinding.* another name for **blind stamping.**

blind date *n Informal.* **1** a social meeting between a man and a woman who have not met before. **2** either of the persons involved.

blinder ('blaɪndə) *n* **1** an outstanding performance in sport. **2** *Brit. slang.* another name for **blind** (sense 30).

blinders ('blaɪndəz) *pl n* the usual U.S. and Canadian word for **blinkers.**

blindfish ('blaɪndˌfɪʃ) *n, pl* **-fish** *or* **-fishes.** any of various small fishes, esp. the cavefish, that have rudimentary or functionless eyes and occur in subterranean streams.

blindfold ('blaɪndˌfəʊld) *vb* (*tr*) **1** to prevent (a person or animal) from seeing by covering (the eyes). **2** to prevent from perceiving or understanding. ◆ *n* **3** a piece of cloth, bandage, etc., used to cover the eyes. **4** any interference to sight. ◆ *adj, adv* **5** having the eyes covered with a cloth or bandage. **6** *Chess.* not seeing the board and pieces. **7** rash; inconsiderate. [changed (C16) through association with FOLD[1] from Old English *blindfellian* to strike blind; see BLIND, FELL[2]]

Blind Freddie *n Austral. informal.* an imaginary person representing the highest degree of incompetence (esp. in the phrase **Blind Freddie could see that!**).

blind gut *n Informal.* another name for the **caecum.**

Blindheim ('blɪnt,haɪm) *n* the German name for **Blenheim**[1].

blinding ('blaɪndɪŋ) *n* **1** sand or grit spread over a road surface to fill up cracks. **2** the process of laying blinding. **3** Also called: **mattress.** a layer of concrete made with little cement spread over soft ground to seal it so that reinforcement can be laid on it. ◆ *adj* **4** making one blind or as if blind: *blinding snow.* **5** most noticeable; brilliant or dazzling: *a blinding display of skill.* ▸ **'blindingly** *adv*

blind man's buff *n* a game in which a blindfolded person tries to catch and identify the other players. [C16: *buff,* perhaps from Old French *buffe* a blow; see BUFFET[2]]

blind register *n* (in the UK) a list of those who are blind and are therefore entitled to financial and other benefits.

blindsight ('blaɪnd,saɪt) *n* the ability to respond to visual stimuli without having any conscious visual experience; it can occur after some forms of brain damage.

blind snake *n* any burrowing snake of the family *Typhlopidae* and related families of warm and tropical regions, having very small or vestigial eyes.

blind spot *n* **1** a small oval-shaped area of the retina in which vision is not experienced. It marks the nonphotosensitive site of entrance into the eyeball of the optic nerve. See **optic disc. 2** a place or area, as in an auditorium or part of a road, where vision is completely or partially obscured or hearing is difficult or impossible. **3** a subject about which a person is ignorant or prejudiced, or an occupation in which he is inefficient. **4** a location within the normal range of a radio transmitter with weak reception.

blind staggers *n* (*functioning as sing*) *Vet. science.* another name for **staggers.**

blind stamping *n Bookbinding.* an impression on a book cover without using colour or gold leaf. Also called: **blind blocking.**

blindstorey *or* **blindstory** ('blaɪnd,stɔːrɪ) *n, pl* **-reys** *or* **-ries.** a storey without windows, such as a gallery in a Gothic church. Compare **clerestory.**

blindworm ('blaɪnd,wɜːm) *n* another name for **slowworm.**

blini ('blɪnɪ), **bliny,** *or* **blinis** ('blɪnɪz) *pl n* Russian pancakes made of buckwheat flour and yeast. [C19: from Russian: plural of *blin,* from Old Russian *mlinŭ,* related to Russian *molot'* to grind]

blink (blɪŋk) *vb* **1** to close and immediately reopen (the eyes or an eye), usually involuntarily. **2** (*intr*) to look with the eyes partially closed, as in strong sunlight. **3** to shine intermittently, as in signalling, or unsteadily. **4** (*tr;* foll. by *away, from,* etc.) to clear the eyes of (dust, tears, etc.). **5** (when *tr,* usually foll. by *at*) to be surprised or amazed: *he blinked at the splendour of the ceremony.* **6** (when *intr,* foll. by *at*) to pretend not to know or see (a fault, injustice, etc.). ◆ *n* **7** the act or an instance of blinking. **8** a glance; glimpse. **9** short for **iceblink** (sense 1). **10 on the blink.** *Slang.* not working properly. [C14: variant of BLENCH[1]; related to Middle Dutch *blinken* to glitter, Danish *blinke* to wink, Swedish *blinka*]

blinker ('blɪŋkə) *n* **1** a flashing light for sending messages, as a warning device, etc., such as a direction indicator on a road vehicle. **2** (*often pl*) a slang word for **eye**[1]. ◆ *vb* (*tr*) **3** to provide (a horse) with blinkers. **4** to obscure with or as if with blinkers.

blinkered ('blɪŋkəd) *adj* **1** considering only a narrow point of view. **2** (of a horse) wearing blinkers.

blinkers ('blɪŋkəz) *pl n* **1** (*sometimes sing*) *Chiefly Brit.* leather sidepieces attached to a horse's bridle to prevent sideways vision. Usual U.S. and Canadian word: **blinders. 2** a slang word for **goggle** (sense 4).

blinking ('blɪŋkɪŋ) *adj, adv Informal.* (intensifier): *a blinking fool; a blinking good film.*

blinks (blɪŋks) *n* (*functioning as sing*) a small temperate portulacaceous plant, *Montia fontana* with small white flowers. [C19: from BLINK, because the flowers do not fully open and thus seem to blink at the light]

blintz *or* **blintze** (blɪnts) *n* a thin pancake folded over a filling usually of apple, cream cheese, or meat. [C20: from Yiddish *blintse,* from Russian *blinyets* little pancakes; see BLINI]

blip (blɪp) *n* **1** a repetitive sound, such as that produced by an electronic device, by dripping water, etc. **2** Also called: **pip.** the spot of light or a sharply peaked pulse on a radar screen indicating the position of an object. **3** a temporary irregularity recorded in performance of something. ◆ *vb* **blips, blipping, blipped. 4** (*intr*) to produce such a noise. [C20: of imitative origin]

bliss (blɪs) *n* **1** perfect happiness; serene joy. **2** the ecstatic joy of heaven. [Old English *blīths;* related to *blīthe* BLITHE, Old Saxon *blīdsea* bliss] ▸ **'blissless** *adj*

Bliss (blɪs) *n* Sir **Arthur.** 1891–1975, British composer; Master of the Queen's Musick (1953–75). His works include the *Colour Symphony* (1922), film and ballet music, and a cello concerto (1970).

blissful ('blɪsful) *adj* **1** serenely joyful or glad. **2 blissful ignorance.** unawareness or inexperience of something unpleasant. ▸ **'blissfully** *adv* ▸ **'blissfulness** *n*

B list *n* **a** a category considered to be slightly below the most socially desirable. **b** (*as modifier*): *B-list celebrities.* ◆ Compare **A list.**

blister ('blɪstə) *n* **1** a small bubble-like elevation of the skin filled with serum, produced as a reaction to a burn, mechanical irritation, etc. **2** a swelling containing air or liquid, as on a painted surface. **3** a transparent dome or any bulge on the fuselage of an aircraft, such as one used for observation. **4** *Slang.* an irritating person. **5** *N.Z. slang.* a rebuke. ◆ *vb* **6** to have or cause to have blisters. **7** (*tr*) to attack verbally with great scorn or sarcasm. [C13: from Old French *blestre,* probably from Middle Dutch *bluyster* blister; see BLAST] ▸ **'blistered** *adj* ▸ **'blistery** *adj*

blister beetle *n* any beetle of the family *Meloidae,* many of which produce a secretion that blisters the skin. See also **Spanish fly.**

blister copper *n* an impure form of copper having a blister-like surface due to the release of gas during cooling.

blistering ('blɪstərɪŋ, -trɪŋ) *adj* **1** (of weather) extremely hot. **2** (of criticism) extremely harsh. ▸ **'blisteringly** *adv*

blister pack *n* a type of packet in which small items are displayed and sold, consisting of a transparent dome of plastic or similar material mounted on a firm backing such as cardboard. Also called: **bubble pack.**

blister rust *n* a disease of certain pines caused by rust fungi of the genus *Cronartium,* causing swellings on the bark from which orange masses of spores are released.

BLit *abbrev. for* Bachelor of Literature.

blithe (blaɪð) *adj* **1** very happy or cheerful. **2** heedless; casual and indifferent. [Old English *blīthe*] ▸ **'blithely** *adv* ▸ **'blitheness** *n*

blithering ('blɪðərɪŋ) *adj* **1** talking foolishly; jabbering. **2** *Informal.* stupid; foolish: *you blithering idiot.* [C19: variant of BLATHER + -ING[2]]

blithesome ('blaɪðsəm) *adj Literary.* cheery; merry. ▸ **'blithesomely** *adv* ▸ **'blithesomeness** *n*

BLitt *abbrev. for* Bachelor of Letters. [Latin *Baccalaureus Litterarum*]

blitz (blɪts) *n* **1** a violent and sustained attack, esp. with intensive aerial bombardment. **2** any sudden intensive attack or concerted effort. **3** *American football.* a defensive charge on the quarterback. ◆ *vb* **4** (*tr*) to attack suddenly and intensively. [C20: shortened from German *Blitzkrieg* lightning war]

Blitz (blɪts) *n* **the.** the systematic night-time bombing of the British in 1940–41 by the German Luftwaffe.

blitzkrieg ('blɪts,kriːg) *n* a swift intensive military attack designed to defeat the opposition quickly. [C20: from German: lightning war]

Blixen ('blɪksən) *n* **Karen.** See (Isak) **Dinesen.**

blizzard ('blɪzəd) *n* a strong bitterly cold wind accompanied by a widespread heavy snowfall. [C19: of uncertain origin]

blk *abbrev. for:* **1** black. **2** block. **3** bulk.

BLL *abbrev. for* Bachelor of Laws.

BL Lac object *n* an extremely compact violently variable form of active galaxy. [C20: named after BL Lacertae, first identified example found in the constellation Lacerta and originally thought to be a variable star]

bloat (bləut) *vb* **1** to swell or cause to swell, as with a liquid, air, or wind. **2** to become or cause to be puffed up, as with conceit. **3** (*tr*) to cure (fish, esp. herring) by half-drying in smoke. ◆ *n* **4** *Vet. science.* an abnormal distention of the abdomen in cattle, sheep, etc., caused by accumulation of gas in the stomach. [C17: probably related to Old Norse *blautr* soaked, Old English *blāt* pale] ▸ **'bloated** *adj*

bloater ('bləutə) *n* a herring, or sometimes a mackerel, that has been salted in brine, smoked, and cured.

blob (blɒb) *n* **1** a soft mass or drop, as of some viscous liquid. **2** a spot, dab, or blotch of colour, ink, etc. **3** an indistinct or shapeless form or object. ◆ *vb* **blobs, blobbing, blobbed. 4** (*tr*) to put blobs, as of ink or paint, on. [C15: perhaps of imitative origin; compare BUBBLE] ▸ **'blobby** *adj*

bloc (blɒk) *n* a group of people or countries combined by a common interest or aim: *the Soviet bloc.* [C20: from French: BLOCK]

Bloch (blɒk) *n* **1 Ernest.** 1880–1959, U.S. composer, born in Switzerland, who found inspiration in Jewish liturgical and folk music: his works include the symphonies *Israel* (1916) and *America* (1926). **2 Felix.** 1905–83, U.S. physicist, born in Switzerland: Nobel prize for physics (1952) for his work on the magnetic moments of atomic particles. **3 Konrad Emil.** born 1912, U.S. biochemist, born in Germany: shared the Nobel prize for physiology or medicine in 1964 for his work on fatty-acid metabolism. **4** (*French* blɔk). **Marc.** 1886–1944, French historian and Resistance fighter; author of *Feudal Society* (1935) and *Strange Defeat* (1940), an essay on the fall of France: killed by the Nazis.

block (blɒk) *n* **1** a large solid piece of wood, stone, or other material with flat rectangular sides, as for use in building. **2** any large solid piece of wood, stone, etc., usually having at least one face fairly flat. **3** such a piece on which particular tasks may be done, as chopping, cutting, or beheading. **4** Also called: **building block.** one of a set of wooden or plastic cubes as a child's toy. **5** a form on which things are shaped or displayed: *a wig block.* **6** *Slang.* a person's head (esp. in the phrase **knock someone's block off**). **7 do one's block.** *Austral. and N.Z. slang.* to become angry. **8** a dull, unemotional, or hardhearted person. **9** a large building of offices, flats, etc. **10a** a group of buildings in a city bounded by intersecting streets on each side. **10b** the area or distance between such intersecting streets. **11** *Austral. and N.Z.* an area of land for a house, farm, etc. **12** *Austral. and N.Z.* a log, usually a willow, fastened to a timber base and used in a wood-chopping competition. **13** an area of land, esp. one to be divided for building or settling. **14** See **cylinder block. 15a** a piece of wood, metal, or other material having an engraved, cast, or carved design in relief, used either for printing or for stamping book covers, etc. **15b** *Brit.* a letterpress printing plate, esp. one mounted type-high on wood or metal. **16** a casing housing one or more freely rotating pulleys. See also **block and tackle. 17 on the block.** *Chiefly U.S. and Canadian.* up for auction. **18** the act of obstructing or condition of being obstructed, as in sports. **19** an obstruction or hindrance. **20** *Pathol.* **20a** interference in the normal physiological functioning of an organ or part. **20b** See **heart block. 20c** See **nerve block. 21** *Psychol.* a short interruption of perceptual or thought processes. **22** obstruction of an opponent in a sport. **23a** a section or quantity, as of tickets or shares, handled or considered as a single unit. **23b** (*as modifier*): *a block booking; block voting.* **24a** a stretch of railway in which only one train may travel at a time. **24b** (*as *modifier): a block signal.* **25** an unseparated group of four or more postage stamps. Compare **strip**[2] (sense 3). **26** a pad of paper. **27** *Computing.* a group of words on magnetic tape treated as a unit of data. **28** *Athletics.* short for **starting block. 29** *Cricket.* a mark made near the popping crease by a batsman to indicate his position in relation to the wicket. **30 a chip off the old block.** *Informal.* a person who resembles one of his or her parents in behaviour. ♦ *vb (mainly tr)* **31** to shape or form (something) into a block. **32** to fit with or mount on a block. **33** to shape by use of a block: *to block a hat.* **34** (often foll. by *up*) to obstruct (a passage, channel, etc.) or prevent or impede the motion or flow of (something or someone) by introducing an obstacle: *to block the traffic; to block up a pipe.* **35** to impede, retard, or prevent (an action, procedure, etc.). **36** to stamp (a title, design, etc.) on (a book cover, etc.) by means of a block (see sense 15a.), esp. using gold leaf or other foil. **37** (esp. of a government or central bank) to limit the use or conversion of assets or currency. **38** (*also intr*) *Sport.* to obstruct or impede movement by (an opponent). **39** (*intr*) to suffer a psychological block. **40** to interrupt a physiological function, as by use of an anaesthetic. **41** (*also intr*) *Cricket.* to play (a ball) defensively. ♦ See also **block in, block out.** [C14: from Old French *bloc,* from Dutch *blok;* related to Old High German *bloh*] ▸ **'blocker** *n*

blockade (blɒ'keɪd) *n* **1** *Military.* the interdiction of a nation's sea lines of communications, esp. of an individual port by the use of sea power. **2** something that prevents access or progress. **3** *Med.* the inhibition of the effect of a hormone or the action of a nerve by a drug. ♦ *vb (tr)* **4** to impose a blockade on. **5** to obstruct the way to. [C17: from BLOCK + *-ade,* as in AMBUSCADE] ▸ **block'ader** *n*

blockage ('blɒkɪdʒ) *n* **1** the act of blocking or state of being blocked. **2** an object causing an obstruction.

block and tackle *n* a hoisting device in which a rope or chain is passed around a pair of blocks containing one or more pulleys. The upper block is secured overhead and the lower block supports the load, the effort being applied to the free end of the rope or chain.

blockboard ('blɒk,bɔːd) *n* a type of plywood in which soft wood strips are bonded together and sandwiched between two layers of veneer.

blockbuster ('blɒk,bʌstə) *n Informal.* **1** a large bomb used to demolish extensive areas or strengthened targets. **2** a very successful, effective, or forceful person, thing, etc.

blockbusting ('blɒk,bʌstɪŋ) *n U.S. informal.* the act or practice of inducing the sale of property cheaply by exploiting the owners' fears of lower prices if racial minorities live in the area.

block capital *n* another term for **block letter.**

block diagram *n* **1** a diagram showing the interconnections between the parts of an industrial process. **2** a three-dimensional drawing representing a block of the earth's crust, showing geological structure. **3** *Computing.* a diagram showing the interconnections between electronic components or parts of a program.

blocked (blɒkt) *adj Slang.* functionally impeded by amphetamine.

blocked shoe *n* a dancing shoe with a stiffened toe that enables a ballet dancer to dance on the tips of the toes.

block grant *n* (in Britain) an annual grant made by the government to a local authority to help to pay for the public services it provides, such as health, education, and housing.

blockhead ('blɒk,hɛd) *n Derogatory.* a stupid person. ▸ **'block,headed** *adj* ▸ **'block,headedly** *adv* ▸ **'block,headedness** *n*

blockhouse ('blɒk,haʊs) *n* **1** (formerly) a wooden fortification with ports or loopholes for defensive fire, observation, etc. **2** a concrete structure strengthened to give protection against enemy fire, with apertures to allow defensive gunfire. **3** a building constructed of logs or squared timber. **4** a reinforced concrete building close to a rocket-launching site for protecting personnel and equipment during launching.

block in *vb (tr, adv)* to sketch in outline, with little detail.

blocking ('blɒkɪŋ) *n Electronics.* the interruption of anode current in a valve because of the application of a high negative voltage to the grid.

blockish ('blɒkɪʃ) *adj* lacking vivacity or imagination; stupid. ▸ **'blockishly** *adv* ▸ **'blockishness** *n*

block lava *n* volcanic lava occurring as rough-surfaced jagged blocks.

block letter *n* Also called: **block capital.** a plain capital letter.

block out *vb (tr, adv)* **1** to plan or describe (something) in a general fashion. **2** to prevent the entry or consideration of (something). **3** *Photography, printing.* to mask part of (a negative), in order that light may not pass through it.

block plane *n* a carpenter's small plane used to cut across the end grain of wood.

block printing *n* printing from hand engraved or carved blocks of wood or linoleum.

block release *n Brit.* the release of industrial trainees from work for study at a college for several weeks.

block sampling *n* the selection of a corpus for statistical literary analysis by random selection of a starting point and consideration of the continuous passage following it. Compare **spread sampling.**

block tin *n* pure tin, esp. when cast into ingots.

block vote *n Brit.* (at a conference, esp. of trade unionists) the system whereby each delegate's vote has a value in proportion to the number of people he represents.

Bloemfontein ('bluːmfɒn,teɪn) *n* a city in central South Africa: capital of Free State province and judicial capital of the country. Pop.: 126 867 (1991).

Blois (*French* blwa) *n* a city in N central France, on the Loire: 13th-century castle. Pop.: 51 550 (1990).

Blok (blɒk) *n* **Aleksandr Aleksandrovich** (alɪk'sandr alɪk'sandrəvitʃ). 1880–1921, Russian poet whose poems, which include *Verses about the Beautiful Lady* (1901–2) and *Rasput'ya* (1902–4), contain a mixture of symbolism, romanticism, tragedy, and irony.

bloke (bləʊk) *n Brit. and Austral.* an informal word for **man.** [C19: from Shelta]

blokeish *or* **blokish** ('bləʊkɪʃ) *adj Informal, sometimes derogatory.* denoting or exhibiting the characteristics believed typical of an ordinary man. Also: **blokey** ('bləʊkɪ). ▸ **'blokeishness** *or* **'blokishness** *n*

blonde *or* (*masc*) **blond** (blɒnd) *adj* **1** (of hair) of a light colour; fair. **2** (of a person, people or a race) having fair hair, a light complexion, and, typically, blue or grey eyes. **3** (of soft furnishings, wood, etc.) light in colour. ♦ *n* **4** a person having light-coloured hair and skin. **5** Also called: **blonde lace.** a French pillow lace, originally of unbleached cream-coloured Chinese silk, later of bleached or black-dyed silk. [C15: from Old French *blond* (fem *blonde*), probably of Germanic origin; related to Late Latin *blundus* yellow, Italian *biondo,* Spanish *blondo*] ▸ **'blondeness** *or* **'blondness** *n*

Blondin (*French* blɔ̃dɛ̃) *n* **Charles,** real name *Jean-François Gravelet.* 1824–97, French acrobat and tightrope walker; best known for walking a tightrope across Niagara Falls (1859).

blood (blʌd) *n* **1** a reddish fluid in vertebrates that is pumped by the heart through the arteries and veins, supplies tissues with nutrients, oxygen, etc., and removes waste products. It consists of a fluid (see **blood plasma**) containing cells (erythrocytes and leucocytes) and platelets. Related adjs.: **haemal, haematic, sanguineous. 2** a similar fluid in such invertebrates as annelids and arthropods. **3** bloodshed, esp. when resulting in murder. **4** the guilt or responsibility for killing or injuring (esp. in the phrase **to have blood on one's hands** *or* **head**). **5** life itself; lifeblood. **6** relationship through being of the same family, race, or kind; kinship. **7 blood, sweat, and tears.** *Informal.* hard work and concentrated effort. **8 flesh and blood. 8a** near kindred or kinship, esp. that between a parent and child. **8b** human nature (esp. in the phrase **it's more than flesh and blood can stand**). **9** ethnic or national descent: *of Spanish blood.* **10 in one's blood.** as a natural or inherited characteristic or talent. **11 the blood.** royal or noble descent: *a prince of the blood.* **12** temperament; disposition; temper. **13a** good or pure breeding; pedigree. **13b** (*as modifier*): *blood horses.* **14** people viewed as members of a group, esp. as an invigorating force (in the phrases **new blood, young blood**). **15** *Chiefly Brit., rare.* a dashing young man; dandy; rake. **16** the sensual or carnal nature of man. **17** *Obsolete.* one of the four bodily humours. See **humour** (sense 8). **18 bad blood.** hatred; ill feeling. **19 blood is thicker than water.** family duties and loyalty outweigh other ties. **20 have** *or* **get one's blood up.** to be or cause to be angry or inflamed. **21 in cold blood.** showing no passion; deliberately; ruthlessly. **22 make one's blood boil.** to cause to be angry or indignant. **23 make one's blood run cold.** to fill with horror. ♦ *vb (tr)* **24** *Hunting.* to cause (young hounds) to taste the blood of a freshly killed quarry and so become keen to hunt. **25** *Hunting.* to smear the cheeks or forehead of (a person) with the blood of the kill as an initiation in hunting. **26** to initiate (a person) to war. [Old English *blōd;* related to Old Norse *blōth,* Old High German *bluot*]

Blood (blʌd) *n* **Thomas,** known as *Colonel Blood.* ?1618–80, Irish adventurer, who tried to steal the crown jewels (1671).

blood-and-thunder *adj* denoting or relating to a melodramatic adventure story.

blood bank *n* a place where whole blood or blood plasma is stored until required in transfusion.

blood bath *n* indiscriminate slaughter; a massacre.

blood brother *n* **1** a brother by birth. **2** a man or boy who has sworn to treat another as his brother, often in a ceremony in which their blood is mingled.

blood cell *n* any of the cells that circulate in the blood. See **erythrocyte, leucocyte.**

blood count *n* determination of the number of red and white blood corpuscles in a specific sample of blood. See **haemocytometer.**

bloodcurdling ('blʌd,kɜːdlɪŋ) *adj* terrifying; horrifying. ▸ **'blood,curdlingly** *adv*

blood donor *n* a person who gives his blood to be used for transfusion.

blood doping *n* the illegal practice of removing a quantity of blood from an athlete long before a race and reinjecting it shortly before a race, so boosting oxygenation of the blood.

blood-drop emlets ('ɛmlɪts) *n (functioning as sing)* a Chilean scrophulariaceous plant, *Mimulus luteus,* naturalized in central Europe, having red-spotted yellow flowers. See also **monkey flower, musk** (sense 3).

blooded ('blʌdɪd) *adj* **1** (of horses, cattle, etc.) of good breeding. **2** (*in combination*) having blood or temperament as specified: *hot-blooded, cold-blooded, warm-blooded, red-blooded, blue-blooded.*

blood feud *n* a feud in which the members of hostile families or clans murder each other.

bloodfin ('blʌd,fɪn) *n* a silvery red-finned South American freshwater fish, *Aphyocharax rubripinnis:* a popular aquarium fish: family *Characidae* (characins).

blood fluke *n* any parasitic flatworm, such as a schistosome, that lives in the blood vessels of man and other vertebrates: class *Digenea.* See also **trematode.**

blood group *n* any one of the various groups into which human blood is classified on the basis of its agglutinogens. Also called: **blood type.**

blood guilt *n* guilt of murder or shedding blood. ▸ **'blood-,guilty** *adj* ▸ **'blood-,guiltiness** *n*

blood heat *n* the normal temperature of the human body, 98.4°F or 37°C.

bloodhound ('blʌd,haʊnd) *n* **1** a large breed of hound having a smooth glossy coat of red, tan, or black and loose wrinkled skin on its head: formerly much used in tracking and police work. **2** *Informal.* a detective.

bloodless ('blʌdlɪs) *adj* **1** without blood. **2** conducted without violence (esp. in the phrase **bloodless revolution**). **3** anaemic-looking; pale. **4** lacking vitality;

lifeless. **5** lacking in emotion; cold; unfeeling. ▸ **'bloodlessly** *adv* ▸ **'bloodlessness** *n*

Bloodless Revolution *n* **the.** another name for the **Glorious Revolution.**

blood-letting ('blʌd,letɪŋ) *n* **1** the therapeutic removal of blood, as in relieving congestive heart failure. See also **phlebotomy. 2** bloodshed, esp. in a blood feud.

bloodline ('blʌd,laɪn) *n* all the members of a family group over generations, esp. regarding characteristics common to that group; pedigree.

bloodmobile ('blʌdmə,bi:l) *n U.S.* a motor vehicle equipped for collecting blood from donors.

blood money *n* **1** compensation paid to the relatives of a murdered person. **2** money paid to a hired murderer. **3** a reward for information about a criminal, esp. a murderer.

blood orange *n* a variety of orange all or part of the pulp of which is dark red when ripe.

blood plasma *n* **1** the pale yellow fluid portion of the blood; blood from which blood cells and platelets have been removed. **2** a sterilized preparation of this fluid for use in transfusions.

blood poisoning *n* a nontechnical term for **septicaemia.**

blood pressure *n* the pressure exerted by the blood on the inner walls of the arteries, being relative to the elasticity and diameter of the vessels and the force of the heartbeat.

blood pudding *n* another name for **black pudding.**

blood red *n* **a** a deep red colour. **b** (*as adj*): *blood-red roses.*

blood relation *or* **relative** *n* a person related to another by birth, as distinct from one related by marriage.

bloodroot ('blʌd,ru:t) *n* **1** Also called: **red puccoon.** a North American papaveraceous plant, *Sanguinaria canadensis,* having a single whitish flower and a fleshy red root that yields a red dye. **2** another name for **tormentil.**

blood sausage *n* another term (esp. U.S. and Canadian) for **black pudding.**

blood serum *n* blood plasma from which the clotting factors have been removed.

bloodshed ('blʌd,ʃed) *n* slaughter; killing.

bloodshot ('blʌd,ʃɒt) *adj* (of an eye) inflamed.

blood sport *n* any sport involving the killing of an animal, esp. hunting.

bloodstain ('blʌd,steɪn) *n* a dark discoloration caused by blood, esp. dried blood. ▸ **'blood,stained** *adj*

bloodstock ('blʌd,stɒk) *n* thoroughbred horses, esp. those bred for racing.

bloodstock industry *n* the breeding and training of racehorses.

bloodstone ('blʌd,stəʊn) *n* a dark-green variety of chalcedony with red spots: used as a gemstone. Also called: **heliotrope.**

bloodstream ('blʌd,stri:m) *n* the flow of blood through the vessels of a living body.

blood substitute *n* a mixture of plasma, albumin, and dextran used to replace lost blood or increase the blood volume.

bloodsucker ('blʌd,sʌkə) *n* **1** an animal that sucks blood, esp. a leech or mosquito. **2** a person or thing that preys upon another person, esp. by extorting money.

blood sugar *n Med.* the glucose circulating in the blood: the normal fasting level is between 3.9 and 5.6 mmol/l.

blood test *n* analysis of a blood sample to determine blood group, alcohol level, etc.

bloodthirsty ('blʌd,θɜ:stɪ) *adj* **-thirstier, -thirstiest. 1** murderous; cruel. **2** taking pleasure in bloodshed or violence. **3** describing or depicting killing and violence; gruesome: *a bloodthirsty film.* ▸ **'blood,thirstily** *adv* ▸ **'blood,thirstiness** *n*

blood type *n* another name for **blood group.**

blood vessel *n* an artery, capillary, or vein.

blood volume *n Med.* the total quantity of blood in the body.

bloodwood ('blʌd,wʊd) *n* any of several species of Australian eucalyptus that exude a red sap.

bloodworm ('blʌd,wɜ:m) *n* **1** the red wormlike aquatic larva of the midge, *Chironomus plumosus,* which lives at the bottom of stagnant pools and ditches. **2** a freshwater oligochaete tubifex worm. **3** any of several small reddish worms used as angling bait.

bloody ('blʌdɪ) *adj* **bloodier, bloodiest. 1** covered or stained with blood. **2** resembling or composed of blood. **3** marked by much killing and bloodshed: *a bloody war.* **4** cruel or murderous: *a bloody tyrant.* **5** of a deep red colour; blood-red. ◆ *adv, adj* **6** *Slang, chiefly Brit.* (intensifier): *a bloody fool; bloody fine food.* ◆ *vb* **bloodies, bloodying, bloodied. 7** (*tr*) to stain with blood. ▸ **'bloodily** *adv* ▸ **'bloodiness** *n*

Bloody Mary *n* a drink consisting of tomato juice and vodka.

bloody-minded *adj Brit. informal.* deliberately obstructive and unhelpful.

bloody-nosed beetle *n* a beetle, *Timarcha tenebricosa,* that exudes bright red blood when alarmed: family *Chrysomelidae.*

bloom[1] (blu:m) *n* **1** a blossom on a flowering plant; a flower. **2** the state, time, or period when flowers open (esp. in the phrases **in bloom, in full bloom**). **3** open flowers collectively: *a tree covered with bloom.* **4** a healthy, vigorous, or flourishing condition; prime (esp. in the phrase **the bloom of youth**). **5** youthful or healthy rosiness in the cheeks or face; glow. **6** a fine whitish coating on the surface of fruits, leaves, etc., consisting of minute grains of a waxy substance. **7** any coating similar in appearance, such as that on new coins. **8** *Ecology.* a visible increase in the algal constituent of plankton, which may be seasonal or due to excessive organic pollution. **9** Also called: **chill.** a dull area formed on the surface of gloss paint, lacquer, or varnish. ◆ *vb* (*mainly intr*) **10** (of flowers) to open; come into flower. **11** to bear flowers; blossom. **12** to flourish or grow. **13** to be in a healthy, glowing, or flourishing condition. **14** (*tr*) *Physics.* to coat (a lens) with a thin layer of a substance, often magnesium fluoride, to eliminate surface reflection. [C13: of Germanic origin; compare Old Norse *blōm* flower, Old High German *bluomo,* Middle Dutch *bloeme;* see BLOW[3]] ▸ **'bloomy** *adj*

bloom[2] (blu:m) *n* **1** a rectangular mass of metal obtained by rolling or forging a cast ingot. See also **billet**[2] (sense 2). ◆ *vb* **2** (*tr*) to convert (an ingot) into a bloom by rolling or forging. [Old English *blōma* lump of metal]

bloomed (blu:md) *adj Photog., optics.* (of a lens) coated with a thin film of magnesium fluoride or some other substance to reduce the amount of light lost by reflection. Also: **coated.**

bloomer[1] ('blu:mə) *n* a plant that flowers, esp. in a specified way: *a night bloomer.*

bloomer[2] ('blu:mə) *n Brit. informal.* a stupid mistake; blunder. [C20: from BLOOMING]

bloomer[3] ('blu:mə) *n Brit.* a medium-sized loaf, baked on the sole of the oven, glazed and notched on top. [C20: of uncertain origin]

bloomers ('blu:məz) *pl n* **1** *Informal.* women's or girls' baggy knickers. **2** (formerly) loose trousers gathered at the knee worn by women for cycling and athletics. **3** *History.* Also called: **rational dress.** long loose trousers gathered at the ankle and worn under a shorter skirt. [from *bloomer,* a garment introduced in about 1850 and publicized by Mrs A. *Bloomer* (1818–94), U.S. social reformer]

bloomery ('blu:mərɪ) *n, pl* **-eries.** a place in which malleable iron is produced directly from iron ore.

Bloomfield ('blu:m,fi:ld) *n* **Leonard.** 1887–1949, U.S. linguist, influential for his strictly scientific and descriptive approach to comparative linguistics; author of *Language* (1933).

blooming ('blu:mɪŋ) *adv, adj Brit. informal.* (intensifier): *a blooming genius; blooming painful.* [C19: euphemistic for BLOODY]

Bloomington ('blu:mɪŋtən) *n* a city in central Indiana: seat of the University of Indiana (1820). Pop.: 60 633 (1990).

Bloomsbury ('blu:mzbərɪ, -brɪ) *n* **1** a district of central London in the borough of Camden: contains the British Museum, part of the University of London, and many publishers' offices. ◆ *adj* **2** relating to or characteristic of the Bloomsbury Group.

Bloomsbury Group *n* a group of writers, artists, and intellectuals living and working in and around Bloomsbury in London from about 1907 to 1930. Influenced by the philosophy of G. E. Moore, they included Leonard and Virginia Woolf, Clive and Vanessa Bell, Roger Fry, E. M. Forster, Lytton Strachey, Duncan Grant, and John Maynard Keynes.

blooper ('blu:pə) *n Informal, chiefly U.S. and Canadian.* a blunder; bloomer; stupid mistake. [C20: from *bloop* (imitative of an embarrassing sound) + -ER[1]]

Bloc Quebecois (blɒk keɪbe'kwɑ:) *n* (in Canada) a political party that advocates autonomy for Quebec.

blossom ('blɒsəm) *n* **1** the flower or flowers of a plant, esp. conspicuous flowers producing edible fruit. **2** the time or period of flowering (esp. in the phrases **in blossom, in full blossom**). ◆ *vb* (*intr*) **3** (of plants) to come into flower. **4** to develop or come to a promising stage: *youth had blossomed into maturity.* [Old English *blōstm;* related to Middle Low German *blōsem,* Latin *flōs* flower] ▸ **'blossoming** *n, adj* ▸ **'blossomless** *adj* ▸ **'blossomy** *adj*

blot[1] (blɒt) *n* **1** a stain or spot of ink, paint, dirt, etc. **2** something that spoils or detracts from the beauty or worth of something. **3** a blemish or stain on one's character or reputation. ◆ *vb* **blots, blotting, blotted. 4** (of ink, dye, etc.) to form spots or blobs on (a material) or (of a person) to cause such spots or blobs to form on (a material). **5 blot one's copybook.** *Informal.* to spoil one's reputation by making a mistake, offending against social customs, etc. **6** (*intr*) to stain or become stained or spotted. **7** (*tr*) to cause a blemish in or on; disgrace. **8** to soak up (excess ink, etc.) by using blotting paper or some other absorbent material. **9** (of blotting paper or some other absorbent material) to absorb (excess ink, etc.). **10** (*tr;* often foll. by *out*) **10a** to darken or hide completely; obscure; obliterate. **10b** to destroy; annihilate. [C14: probably of Germanic origin; compare Middle Dutch *bluyster* BLISTER]

blot[2] (blɒt) *n* **1** *Backgammon.* a man exposed by being placed alone on a point and therefore able to be taken by the other player. **2** *Archaic.* a weak spot. [C16: perhaps from Middle Dutch *bloot* poor]

blot analysis *n Biochem.* a technique for analysing biological molecules, such as proteins (**Western blot analysis**), DNA (**Southern blot analysis**), and RNA (**Northern blot analysis**), involving their separation by gel electrophoresis, transfer to a nitrocellulose sheet, and subsequent analysis by autoradiography. Also called: **blotting.**

blotch (blɒtʃ) *n* **1** an irregular spot or discoloration, esp. a dark and relatively large one such as an ink stain. ◆ *vb* **2** to become or cause to become marked by such discoloration. **3** (*intr*) (of a pen or ink) to write or flow unevenly in blotches. [C17: probably from BOTCH, influenced by BLOT[1]] ▸ **'blotchy** *adj* ▸ **'blotchily** *adv* ▸ **'blotchiness** *n*

blotter ('blɒtə) *n* **1** something used to absorb excess ink or other liquid, esp. a sheet of blotting paper with a firm backing. **2** *U.S.* a daily record of events, such as arrests, in a police station (esp. in the phrase **police blotter**).

blotting paper *n* a soft absorbent unsized paper, used esp. for soaking up surplus ink.

blotto ('blɒtəʊ) *adj Slang.* unconscious, esp. through drunkenness. [C20: from BLOT[1] (vb); compare *blot out*]

blouse (blaʊz) *n* **1** a woman's shirtlike garment made of cotton, nylon, etc. **2** a loose-fitting smocklike garment, often knee length and belted, worn esp. by E European peasants. **3** a loose-fitting waist-length belted jacket worn by soldiers. ◆ *vb* **4** to hang or make so as to hang in full loose folds. [C19: from French, of unknown origin]

blouson ('blu:zɒn) *n* a short jacket or top having the shape of a blouse. [C20: French]

blow[1] (bləʊ) *vb* **blows, blowing, blew, blown. 1** (of a current of air, the wind, etc.) to be or cause to be in motion. **2** (*intr*) to move or be carried by or as if by wind or air: *a feather blew in through the window.* **3** to expel (air, cigarette smoke, etc.) through the mouth or nose. **4** to force or cause (air, dust, etc.) to move (into, in, over, etc.) by using an instrument or by expelling breath. **5** (*intr*) to breathe hard; pant. **6** (sometimes foll. by *up*) to inflate with air or the breath. **7** (*intr*) (of wind, a storm, etc.) to make a roaring or whistling sound. **8** to cause (a whistle, siren, etc.) to sound by forcing air into it, as a signal, or (of a whistle, etc.) to sound thus. **9** (*tr*) to force air from the lungs through (the nose) to clear out mucus or obstructing matter. **10** (often foll. by *up, down, in,* etc.) to explode, break, or disintegrate completely: *the bridge blew down in the gale.* **11** *Electronics.* to burn out (a fuse, valve, etc.) because of excessive current or (of a fuse, valve, etc.) to burn out. **12 blow a fuse.** *Slang.* to lose one's temper. **13** (*intr*) (of a whale) to spout water or air from the lungs. **14** (*tr*) to wind (a horse) by making it run excessively. **15** to cause (a wind instrument) to sound by forcing one's breath into the mouthpiece, or (of such an instrument) to sound in this way. **16** (*intr*) *Jazz slang.* to play in a jam session. **17** (*intr*) (of flies) to lay eggs (in). **18** to shape (glass, ornaments, etc.) by forcing air or gas through the material when molten. **19** (*intr*) *Chiefly Scot., Austral., and N.Z.* to boast or brag. **20** (*tr*) *Slang.* **20a** to spend (money) freely. **20b** *U.S.* to treat or entertain. **21** (*tr*) *Slang.* to use (an opportunity) ineffectively. **22** *Slang.* to go suddenly away (from). **23** (*tr*) *Slang.* to expose or betray (a person or thing meant to be kept secret). **24** (*tr*) *U.S. slang.* to inhale (a drug). **25** (*intr*) *Slang.* to masturbate. **26** (past participle: **blowed**). *Informal.* another word for **damn** (esp. in the phrases **I'll be blowed, blow it! blow me down!**). **27** *Draughts.* another word for **huff** (sense 4). **28 blow hot and cold.** to vacillate. **29 blow a kiss** *or* **kisses.** to kiss one's hand, then blow across it as if to carry the kiss through the air to another person. **30 blow one's own trumpet.** to boast of one's own skills or good qualities. **31 blow someone's mind.** *Slang.* **31a** (of a drug, esp. LSD) to alter someone's mental state. **31b** to astound or surprise someone. **32 blow one's top** *or* (esp. U.S. and Canadian) **lid** *or* **stack.** *Informal.* to lose one's temper. ◆ *n* **33** the act or an instance of blowing. **34** the sound produced by blowing. **35** a blast of air or wind. **36** *Metallurgy.* **36a** a stage in the Bessemer process in which air is blasted upwards through molten pig iron. **36b** the quantity of metal treated in a Bessemer converter. **37** *Mining.* **37a** a rush of air into a mine. **37b** the collapse of a mine roof. **38** *Jazz slang.* a jam session. **39a** *Brit.* a slang name for **cannabis** (sense 2). **39b** *U.S.* a slang name for **cocaine.** ◆ See also **blow away, blow in, blow into, blow off, blow on, blow out, blow over, blow through, blow up.** [Old English *blāwan,* related to Old Norse *blǣr* gust of wind, Old High German *blāen,* Latin *flāre*]

blow[2] (bləʊ) *n* **1** a powerful or heavy stroke with the fist, a weapon, etc. **2 at one** *or* **a blow.** by or with only one action; all at one time. **3** a sudden setback; unfortunate event: *to come as a blow.* **4 come to blows. 4a** to fight. **4b** to result in a fight. **5** an attacking action: *a blow for freedom.* **6** *Austral. and N.Z.* a stroke of the shears in sheep-shearing. [C15: probably of Germanic origin; compare Old High German *bliuwan* to beat]

blow[3] (bləʊ) *vb* **blows, blowing, blew, blown. 1** (*intr*) (of a plant or flower) to blossom or open out. **2** (*tr*) to produce (flowers). ◆ *n* **3** a mass of blossoms. **4** the state or period of blossoming (esp. in the phrase **in full blow**). [Old English *blōwan;* related to Old Frisian *blōia* to bloom, Old High German *bluoen,* Latin *flōs* flower; see BLOOM[1]]

blow away *vb* (*tr, adv*) *Slang, chiefly U.S.* **1** to kill (someone) by shooting. **2** to defeat decisively.

blowback ('bləʊ,bæk) *n* **1** the escape to the rear of gases formed during the firing of a weapon or in a boiler, internal-combustion engine, etc. **2** the action of a light automatic weapon in which the expanding gases of the propellant force back the bolt, thus reloading the weapon.

blow-by-blow *adj* (*prenominal*) explained in great detail: *a blow-by-blow account of the argument.*

blowdown ('bləʊ,daʊn) *n* an accident in a nuclear reactor in which a cooling pipe bursts causing the loss of essential coolant.

blow-dry *vb* **-dries, -drying, -dried.** (*tr*) **1** to style (one's own or somebody else's hair) while drying it with a hand-held hairdryer. ◆ *n* **2** this method of styling the hair.

blower ('bləʊə) *n* **1** a mechanical device, such as a fan, that blows. **2** a low-pressure compressor, esp. in a furnace or internal-combustion engine. See also **supercharger. 3** an informal name for **telephone. 4** an informal name for **speaking tube. 5** an informal name for a **whale. 6** *Mining.* a discharge of firedamp from a crevice.

blowfish ('bləʊ,fɪʃ) *n, pl* **-fish** *or* **-fishes.** a popular name for **puffer** (sense 2).

blowfly ('bləʊ,flaɪ) *n, pl* **-flies.** any of various dipterous flies of the genus *Calliphora* and related genera that lay their eggs in rotting meat, dung, carrion, and open wounds: family *Calliphoridae.* Also called: **bluebottle.**

blowgun ('bləʊ,gʌn) *n* the U.S. word for **blowpipe** (sense 1).

blowhard ('bləʊ,hɑːd) *Informal.* ◆ *n* **1** a boastful person. ◆ *adj* **2** blustering or boastful.

blowhole ('bləʊ,həʊl) *n* **1** the nostril, paired or single, of whales, situated far back on the skull. **2** a hole in ice through which whales, seals, etc., breathe. **3a** a vent for air or gas, esp. to release fumes from a tunnel, passage, etc. **3b** *N.Z.* a hole emitting gas or steam in a volcanic region. **4** a bubble-like defect in an ingot resulting from gas being trapped during solidification. **5** *Geology.* a hole in a cliff top leading to a sea cave through which air is forced by the action of the sea.

blowie ('bləʊɪ) *n Austral. informal.* a blowfly.

blow in *vb* (*intr, adv*) *Informal.* to arrive or enter suddenly.

blow-in *n Austral. informal.* an unwelcome newcomer or stranger.

blow into *vb* (*intr, prep*) *Informal.* to arrive in or enter (a room, etc.) suddenly.

blow job *n Taboo.* a slang term for **fellatio.**

blowlamp ('bləʊ,læmp) *n* another name for **blowtorch.**

blow moulding *n* a process for moulding single-piece plastic objects in which a thermoplastic is extruded into a split mould and blown against its sides.

blown (bləʊn) *vb* the past participle of **blow**[1] and **blow**[3].

blow off *vb* (*adv*) **1** to permit (a gas under pressure, esp. steam) to be released. **2** (*intr*) *Brit. slang.* to emit wind noisily from the anus. **3 blow off steam.** See **steam** (sense 6). ◆ *n* **blow-off. 4** a discharge of a surplus fluid, such as steam, under pressure. **5** a device through which such a discharge is made.

blow on *vb* (*intr, prep*) to defame or discredit (a person).

blow out *vb* (*adv*) **1** to extinguish (a flame, candle, etc.) or (of a flame, candle, etc.) to become extinguished. **2** (*intr*) (of a tyre) to puncture suddenly, esp. at high speed. **3** (*intr*) (of a fuse) to melt suddenly. **4** (*tr; often reflexive*) to diminish or use up the energy of: *the storm blew itself out.* **5** (*intr*) (of an oil or gas well) to lose oil or gas in an uncontrolled manner. **6** (*tr*) *Slang.* to cancel: *the band had to blow out the gig.* **7 blow one's brains out.** to kill oneself by shooting oneself in the head. ◆ *n* **blowout. 8** the sudden melting of an electrical fuse. **9** a sudden burst in a tyre. **10** the uncontrolled escape of oil or gas from an oil or gas well. **11** the failure of a jet engine, esp. when in flight. **12** *Slang.* a large filling meal or lavish entertainment.

blow over *vb* (*intr, adv*) **1** to cease or be finished: *the storm blew over.* **2** to be forgotten: *the scandal will blow over.*

blowpipe ('bləʊ,paɪp) *n* **1** a long tube from which pellets, poisoned darts, etc., are shot by blowing. U.S. word: **blowgun. 2** Also called: **blow tube.** a tube for blowing air or oxygen into a flame to intensify its heat and direct it onto a small area. **3** a long narrow iron pipe used to gather molten glass and blow it into shape.

blowsy *or* **blowzy** ('blaʊzɪ) *adj* **blowsier, blowsiest** *or* **blowzier, blowziest. 1** (esp. of a woman) untidy in appearance; slovenly or sluttish. **2** (of a woman) ruddy in complexion; red-faced. [C18: from dialect *blowze* beggar girl, of unknown origin] ▸ **'blowsily** *or* **'blowzily** *adv* ▸ **'blowsiness** *or* **'blowziness** *n*

blow through *vb* (*intr, adv*) *Austral. informal.* to leave; make off.

blowtorch ('bləʊ,tɔːtʃ) *n* a small burner that produces a very hot flame, used to remove old paint, melt soft metal, etc.

blow up *vb* (*adv*) **1** to explode or cause to explode. **2** (*tr*) to increase the importance of (something): *they blew the whole affair up.* **3** (*intr*) to come into consideration: *we lived well enough before this thing blew up.* **4** (*intr*) to come into existence with sudden force: *a storm had blown up.* **5** *Informal.* to lose one's temper (with a person). **6** (*tr*) *Informal.* to reprimand (someone). **7** (*tr*) *Informal.* to enlarge the size or detail of (a photograph). ◆ *n* **blow-up. 8** an explosion. **9** *Informal.* an enlarged photograph or part of a photograph. **10** *Informal.* a fit of temper or argument. **11** Also called: **blowing up.** *Informal.* a reprimand.

blowy ('bləʊɪ) *adj* **blowier, blowiest.** another word for **windy** (sense 1).

blub (blʌb) *vb* **blubs, blubbing, blubbed.** *Brit.* a slang word for **blubber** (senses 1-3).

blubber ('blʌbə) *vb* **1** to sob without restraint. **2** to utter while sobbing. **3** (*tr*) to make (the face) wet and swollen or disfigured by crying. ◆ *n* **4** a thick insulating layer of fatty tissue below the skin of aquatic mammals such as the whale: used by man as a source of oil. **5** *Informal.* excessive and flabby body fat. **6** the act or an instance of weeping without restraint. ◆ *adj* **7** (*often in combination*) swollen or fleshy: *blubber-faced; blubber-lips.* [C12: perhaps from Low German *blubbern* to BUBBLE, of imitative origin] ▸ **'blubberer** *n* ▸ **'blubbery** *adj*

blucher ('bluːkə, -tʃə) *n Obsolete.* a high shoe with laces over the tongue. [C19: named after Field Marshal BLÜCHER]

Blücher (*German* 'blyçər) *n* **Gebhard Leberecht von** ('gephart 'leːbərεçt fɔn). 1742–1819, Prussian field marshal, who commanded the Prussian army against Napoleon at Waterloo (1815).

bludge (blʌdʒ) *Austral. and N.Z. informal.* ◆ *vb* **1** (when *intr*, often foll. by *on*) to scrounge from (someone). **2** (*intr*) to evade work. ◆ *n* **3** a very easy task; undemanding employment. [C19: back formation from slang *bludger* pimp, from BLUDGEON]

bludgeon ('blʌdʒən) *n* **1** a stout heavy club, typically thicker at one end. **2** a person, line of argument, etc., that is effective but unsubtle. ◆ *vb* (*tr*) **3** to hit or knock down with or as with a bludgeon. **4** (often foll. by *into*) to force; bully; coerce: *they bludgeoned him into accepting the job.* [C18: of uncertain origin] ▸ **'bludgeoner** *n*

bludger ('blʌdʒə) *n Austral. and N.Z. informal.* **1** a person who scrounges. **2** a person who avoids work. **3** a person in authority regarded as ineffectual by those working under him.

blue (bluː) *n* **1** any of a group of colours, such as that of a clear unclouded sky, that have wavelengths in the range 490–445 nanometres. Blue is the complementary colour of yellow and with red and green forms a set of primary colours. Related adj: **cyanic. 2** a dye or pigment of any of these colours. **3** blue cloth or clothing: *dressed in blue.* **4a** a sportsman who represents or has represented Oxford or Cambridge University and has the right to wear the university colour (dark blue for Oxford, light blue for Cambridge): *an Oxford blue.* **4b** the honour of so representing one's university. **5** *Brit.* an informal name for **Tory. 6** any of numerous small blue-winged butterflies of the genera *Lampides, Polyommatus,* etc.: family *Lycaenidae.* **7** *Archaic.* short for **bluestocking. 8** *Slang.* a policeman. **9** *Archery.* a blue ring on a target, between the red and the black, scoring five points. **10** a blue ball in snooker, etc. **11** another name for **blueing. 12** *Austral. and N.Z. slang.* an argument or fight: *he had a blue with a taxi driver.* **13** Also: **bluey.** *Austral. and N.Z. slang.* a court summons, esp. for a traffic offence. **14** *Austral. and N.Z. informal.* a mistake; error. **15 out of the blue.** apparently from nowhere; unexpectedly: *the opportunity came out of the blue.* **16 into the blue.** into the unknown or the far distance. ◆ *adj* **blu-**

er, bluest. 17 of the colour blue. **18** (of the flesh) having a purple tinge, as from cold or contusion. **19** depressed, moody, or unhappy. **20** dismal or depressing: *a blue day.* **21** indecent, titillating, or pornographic: *blue films.* **22** bluish in colour or having parts or marks that are bluish: *a blue fox; a blue whale.* **23** *Rare.* aristocratic; noble; patrician: *a blue family.* See **blue blood.** ◆ *vb* **blues, blueing** *or* **bluing, blued. 24** to make, dye, or become blue. **25** (*tr*) to treat (laundry) with blueing. **26** (*tr*) *Slang.* to spend extravagantly or wastefully; squander. ◆ See also **blues.** [C13: from Old French *bleu,* of Germanic origin; compare Old Norse *blār,* Old High German *blāo,* Middle Dutch *blā;* related to Latin *flāvus* yellow] ▸ **'bluely** *adv* ▸ **'blueness** *n*

Blue (bluː) *or* **Bluey** *n Austral. informal.* a person with red hair.

blue baby *n* a baby born with a bluish tinge to the skin because of lack of oxygen in the blood, esp. caused by a congenital defect of the heart.

blue bag *n* (in Britain) **1** a fabric bag for a barrister's robes. **2** a small bag containing blueing for laundering.

Bluebeard ('bluːˌbɪəd) *n* **1** a villain in European folk tales who marries several wives and murders them in turn. In many versions the seventh and last wife escapes the fate of the others. **2** a man who has had several wives.

bluebeat ('bluːˌbiːt) *n* a type of West Indian pop music of the 1960s; a precursor of reggae.

bluebell ('bluːˌbɛl) *n* **1** Also called: **wild** or **wood hyacinth.** a European liliaceous woodland plant, *Endymion* (or *Scilla*) *non-scriptus,* having a one-sided cluster of blue bell-shaped flowers. **2** a Scot. name for **harebell. 3** any of various other plants with blue bell-shaped flowers.

blue beret *n* an informal name for a soldier of a United Nations peacekeeping force.

blueberry ('bluːbərɪ, -brɪ) *n, pl* **-ries. 1** Also called: **huckleberry.** any of several North American ericaceous shrubs of the genus *Vaccinium,* such as *V. pennsylvanicum,* that have blue-black edible berries with tiny seeds. See also **bilberry. 2a** the fruit of any of these plants. **2b** (*as modifier*): *blueberry pie.*

bluebill ('bluːˌbɪl) *n U.S.* another name for **scaup.**

blue billy *n N.Z.* an informal name for **dove prion.** [probably from the name *Billy*]

bluebird ('bluːˌbɜːd) *n* **1** any North American songbird of the genus *Sialia,* having a blue or partly blue plumage: subfamily *Turdinae* (thrushes). **2 fairy bluebird.** any songbird of the genus *Irena,* of S and SE Asia, having a blue-and-black plumage: family *Irenidae.* **3** any of various other birds having a blue plumage.

blue blood *n* royal or aristocratic descent. [C19: translation of Spanish *sangre azul*] ▸ **'blue-'blooded** *adj*

bluebonnet ('bluːˌbɒnɪt) *or* **bluecap** ('bluːˌkæp) *n* other names for **Balmoral**[1] (sense 3).

bluebook ('bluːˌbʊk) *n* **1** (in Britain) a government publication bound in a stiff blue paper cover: usually the report of a royal commission or a committee. **2** *Informal, chiefly U.S.* a register of well-known people. **3** (in Canada) an annual statement of government accounts.

bluebottle ('bluːˌbɒtᵊl) *n* **1** another name for the **blowfly. 2** any of various blue-flowered plants, esp. the cornflower. **3** *Brit.* an informal word for a **policeman. 4** *Austral. and N.Z.* an informal name for **Portuguese man-of-war.**

blue buck *n* another name for the **blaubok.**

blue cheese *n* cheese containing a blue mould, esp. Stilton, Roquefort, or Danish blue. Also called (Austral., N.Z.): **blue vein.**

blue chip *n* **1** a gambling chip with the highest value. **2** *Finance.* **2a** a stock considered reliable with respect to both dividend income and capital value. **2b** (*as modifier*): *a blue-chip company.* **3** (*modifier*) denoting something considered to be a valuable asset.

blue cod *n* a common marine spiny-finned food fish, *Parapercis colias,* of the sub-Antarctic waters of New Zealand, esp. at the Chatham Islands, which is greenish blue with brown marbling and inhabits rocky bottoms. Its smoked flesh is considered a delicacy. Also called: **rock cod, pakirikiri, patutuki.**

blue-collar *adj* of, relating to, or designating manual industrial workers: *a blue-collar union.* Compare **white-collar, pink-collar.**

blue devils *pl n* **1** a fit of depression or melancholy. **2** an attack of delirium tremens.

blue duck *n* a mountain duck, *Hymenolaimus malacorhynchos,* of New Zealand having a mostly lead-blue plumage.

Blue Ensign *n* an ensign having the Union Jack on a blue background at the upper corner of the vertical edge alongside the hoist: flown by Royal Navy auxiliary vessels, and, with some extra distinguishing mark or insignia, by certain yacht clubs. Compare **Red Ensign, White Ensign.**

blue-eyed boy *n Informal, chiefly Brit.* the favourite or darling of a person or group. Usual U.S. equivalent: **fair-haired boy.**

blue-eyed grass *n* any of various mainly North American iridaceous marsh plants of the genus *Sisyrinchium* that have grasslike leaves and small flat starlike blue flowers.

blue-eyed Mary *n* a blue-flowered boraginaceous plant, *Omphalodes verna,* native to S Europe and cultivated in Britain.

blue-eyed soul *n Informal.* soul music written and performed by White singers in a style derived from the blues.

bluefish ('bluːˌfɪʃ) *n, pl* **-fish** *or* **-fishes. 1** Also called: **snapper.** a bluish marine percoid food and game fish, *Pomatomus saltatrix,* related to the horse mackerel: family *Pomatomidae.* **2** any of various other bluish fishes.

Blue Flag *n* an award given to a seaside resort that meets EU standards of cleanliness of beaches and purity of water in bathing areas.

blue fox *n* **1** a variety of the arctic fox that has a pale grey winter coat and is bred for its fur. **2** the fur of this animal.

blue funk *n Slang.* a state of great terror or loss of nerve.

bluegill ('bluːˌgɪl) *n* a common North American freshwater sunfish, *Lepomis macrochirus:* an important food and game fish.

blue goose *n* a variety of the snow goose that has a bluish-grey body and white head and neck.

bluegrass ('bluːˌgrɑːs) *n* **1** any of several North American bluish-green grasses of the genus *Poa,* esp. *P. pratensis* (**Kentucky bluegrass**), grown for forage. **2** a type of folk music originating in Kentucky, characterized by a simple harmonized accompaniment.

blue-green algae *pl n* the former name for **cyanobacteria.**

blue ground *n Mineralogy.* another name for **kimberlite.**

blue grouse *n* a grouse, *Dendragapus obscurus,* of W North America, having a bluish-grey plumage with a black tail.

blue gum *n* **1** a tall fast-growing widely cultivated Australian myrtaceous tree, *Eucalyptus globulus,* having aromatic leaves containing a medicinal oil, bark that peels off in shreds, and hard timber. The juvenile leaves are bluish in colour. **2** any of several other eucalyptus trees. ◆ See also **red gum** (sense 1).

blue heeler *n Austral. and N.Z.* a cattle dog that controls cattle by biting their heels. Also called: **heeler.**

blueing *or* **bluing** ('bluːɪŋ) *n* **1** a blue material, such as indigo, used in laundering to counteract yellowing. **2** the formation of a film of blue oxide on a steel surface.

bluejacket ('bluːˌdʒækɪt) *n* a sailor in the Navy.

blue jay *n* a common North American jay, *Cyanocitta cristata,* having bright blue plumage with greyish-white underparts.

blue john *n* a blue or purple fibrous variety of fluorspar occurring only in Derbyshire: used for vases, etc.

blue laws *pl n U.S. history.* a number of repressive puritanical laws of the colonial period, forbidding any secular activity on Sundays.

blue lias *n* a type of rock composed of alternating layers of bluish shale or clay and grey argillaceous limestone. See also **Lias.**

Blue Mantle *n* one of the four pursuivants of the British College of Arms.

blue merle *n* See **merle**[2].

blue moon *n* **once in a blue moon.** *Informal.* very rarely; almost never.

blue mould *n* **1** Also called: **green mould.** any fungus of the genus *Penicillium* that forms a bluish mass on decaying food, leather, etc. **2** any fungal disease of fruit trees characterized by necrosis and a bluish growth on the affected tissue: mostly caused by *Penicillium* species.

Blue Mountains *pl n* **1** a mountain range in the U.S., in NE Oregon and SE Washington. Highest peak: Rock Creek Butte, 2773 m (9097 ft.). **2** a mountain range in the Caribbean, in E Jamaica: Blue Mountain coffee is grown on its slopes. Highest peak: Blue Mountain Peak, 2256 m (7402 ft.). **3** a plateau in SE Australia, in E New South Wales: part of the Great Dividing Range. Highest part: about 1134 m (3871 ft.).

blue murder *n Informal.* a great outcry, noise; horrible din (esp. in such phrases as **cry, howl, scream,** etc., **blue murder**).

Blue Nile *n* a river in E Africa, rising in central Ethiopia as the Abbai and flowing southeast, then northwest to join the White Nile. Length: about 1530 km (950 miles).

bluenose ('bluːˌnəʊz) *n* **1** *U.S. slang.* a puritanical or prudish person. **2** (*often cap.*) *Informal.* a native or inhabitant of Nova Scotia.

blue note *n Jazz.* a flattened third or seventh, used frequently in the blues.

blue pencil *n* **1** deletion, alteration, or censorship of the contents of a book or other work. ◆ *vb* **blue-pencil, -cils, -cilling, -cilled** *or U.S.* **-cils, -ciling, -ciled. 2** (*tr*) to alter or delete parts of (a book, film, etc.), esp. to censor.

blue peter *n* a signal flag of blue with a white square at the centre, displayed by a vessel about to leave port. [C19: from the name *Peter*]

blue pointer *n* a large shark, *Isuropsis mako,* of Australian coastal waters, having a blue back and pointed snout.

blueprint ('bluːˌprɪnt) *n* **1** Also called: **cyanotype.** a photographic print of plans, technical drawings, etc., consisting of white lines on a blue background. **2** an original plan or prototype that influences subsequent design or practice: *the Montessori method was the blueprint for education in the 1940s.* ◆ *vb* **3** (*tr*) to make a blueprint of (a plan).

blue racer *n* a long slender blackish-blue fast-moving colubrid snake, *Coluber constrictor flaviventris,* of the U.S.

blue riband *or* **ribband** *n* **1** (*sometimes caps.*) Also called (esp. U.S.) **blue ribbon.** the record for the fastest sea journey between two places, esp. (in the 1920s and 30s) for a passenger liner between New York and Southampton. **2a** the most distinguished achievement in any field. **2b** (*as modifier*): *the blue-riband event of the meeting.*

blue ribbon *n* **1** (in Britain) a badge of blue silk worn by members of the Order of the Garter. **2** a badge awarded as the first prize in a competition. **3** *U.S.* a badge worn by a member of a temperance society.

blue-ribbon jury *n* a U.S. name for a **special jury.**

Blue Ridge Mountains *pl n* a mountain range in the eastern U.S., extending from West Virginia into Georgia: part of the Appalachian mountains. Highest peak: Mount Mitchell, 2038 m (6684 ft.).

blue rinse *n* **1** a rinse for tinting grey hair a silvery-blue colour. ◆ *adj* **blue-rinse. 2** denoting or typifying an elderly, well-groomed, socially active, and comparatively wealthy woman.

Blue Rod *n Brit.* officer of the Order of St Michael and St George. Full title: **Gentleman Usher of the Blue Rod.**

blue run *n Skiing.* an easy run, suitable for beginners.

blues (bluːz) *pl n* (*sometimes functioning as sing*) **the. 1** a feeling of depression or deep unhappiness. **2** a type of folk song devised by Black Americans at the beginning of the 20th century, usually employing a basic 12-bar chorus, the tonic, subdominant, and dominant chords, frequent minor intervals, and blue notes. ▸ **'bluesy** *adj*

Blues (bluːz) *pl n* **the.** *Brit.* the Royal Horse Guards.

blue schist *n* a metamorphic rock formed under conditions of high pressure and relatively low temperature.

blue shift *n* a shift in the spectral lines of a stellar spectrum towards the blue end of the visible region relative to the wavelengths of these lines in the terrestrial spectrum: thought to be a result of the **Doppler effect** caused by stars approaching the solar system. Compare **red shift.**

blue-sky *n* (*modifier*) of or denoting theoretical research without regard to any future application of its result: *a blue-sky project.*

blue-sky law *n U.S.* a state law regulating the trading of securities: intended to protect investors from fraud.

blue spruce *n* a spruce tree, *Picea pungens glauca,* native to the Rocky Mountains of North America, having blue-green needle-like leaves. Also called: **balsam spruce.**

blue stain *n Forestry.* a bluish discoloration of sapwood caused by growth of fungi.

bluestocking ('bluːˌstɒkɪŋ) *n Usually disparaging.* a scholarly or intellectual woman. [from the blue worsted stockings worn by members of a C18 literary society]

bluestone ('bluːˌstəʊn) *n* **1** a blue-grey sandstone containing much clay, used for building and paving. **2** the blue crystalline form of copper sulphate. **3** a blue variety of basalt found in Australia and used as a building stone.

bluet ('bluːɪt) *n* a North American rubiaceous plant, *Houstonia caerulea,* with small four-petalled blue flowers.

bluethroat ('bluːˌθrəʊt) *n* a small brownish European songbird, *Cyanosylvia svecica,* related to the thrushes, the male of which has a blue throat: family *Muscicapidae.*

bluetit ('bluːˌtɪt) *n* a common European tit, *Parus caeruleus,* having a blue crown, wings, and tail, yellow underparts, and a black and grey head.

bluetongue ('bluːˌtʌŋ) *n* an Australian lizard, *Tiliqua scincoides,* having a cobalt-blue tongue.

blue vein *n Austral. and N.Z.* another name for **blue cheese.**

blue vitriol *n* the fully hydrated blue crystalline form of copper sulphate.

blueweed ('bluːˌwiːd) *n U.S.* another name for **viper's bugloss.**

blue whale *n* the largest mammal: a widely distributed bluish-grey whalebone whale, *Sibbaldus* (or *Balaenoptera*) *musculus,* closely related and similar to the rorquals: family *Balaenopteridae.* Also called: **sulphur-bottom.**

bluey ('bluːɪ) *n Austral. informal.* **1** a blanket. **2** a swagman's bundle. **3 hump (one's) bluey.** to carry one's bundle; tramp. **4** *Slang.* a variant of **blue** (sense 13). **5** a cattle dog. [(for senses 1, 2, 5) C19: from BLUE (on account of their colour) + -Y[2]]

Bluey ('bluːɪ) *n* a variant of **Blue.**

bluff[1] (blʌf) *vb* **1** to pretend to be confident about an uncertain issue or to have undisclosed resources, in order to influence or deter (someone). ◆ *n* **2** deliberate deception intended to create the impression of a stronger position or greater resources than one actually has. **3 call someone's bluff.** to challenge someone to give proof of his claims. [C19: originally U.S. poker-playing term, from Dutch *bluffen* to boast] ▸ **'bluffer** *n*

bluff[2] (blʌf) *n* **1** a steep promontory, bank, or cliff, esp. one formed by river erosion on the outside bend of a meander. **2** *Canadian.* a clump of trees on the prairie; copse. ◆ *adj* **3** good-naturedly frank and hearty. **4** (of a bank, cliff, etc.) presenting a steep broad face. [C17 (in the sense: nearly perpendicular): perhaps from Middle Dutch *blaf* broad] ▸ **'bluffly** *adv* ▸ **'bluffness** *n*

bluish *or* **blueish** ('bluːɪʃ) *adj* somewhat blue. ▸ **'bluishness** *or* **'blueishness** *n*

Blum (bluːm) *n* **Léon** (leɔ̃). 1872–1950, French socialist statesman; premier of France (1936–37; 1938; 1946–47).

Blumberg ('blʊmbɜːg) *n* **Baruch Samuel.** born 1925, U.S. physician, noted for work on antigens: shared the Nobel prize for physiology or medicine 1976.

Blunden ('blʌndən) *n* **Edmund** (**Charles**). 1896–1974, British poet and scholar, noted esp. for *Undertones of War* (1928), a memoir of World War I in verse and prose.

blunder ('blʌndə) *n* **1** a stupid or clumsy mistake. **2** a foolish tactless remark. ◆ *vb* (*mainly intr*) **3** to make stupid or clumsy mistakes. **4** to make foolish tactless remarks. **5** (often foll. by *about, into,* etc.) to act clumsily; stumble: *he blundered into a situation he knew nothing about.* **6** (*tr*) to mismanage; botch. [C14: of Scandinavian origin; compare Old Norse *blunda* to close one's eyes, Norwegian dialect *blundra;* see BLIND] ▸ **'blunderer** *n* ▸ **'blundering** *n, adj* ▸ **'blunderingly** *adv*

blunderbuss ('blʌndəˌbʌs) *n* **1** an obsolete short musket with large bore and flared muzzle, used to scatter shot at short range. **2** *Informal.* a clumsy unsubtle person. [C17: changed (through the influence of BLUNDER) from Dutch *donderbus;* from *donder* THUNDER + obsolete *bus* gun]

blunge (blʌndʒ) *vb* (*tr*) to mix (clay or a similar substance) with water in order to form a suspension for use in ceramics. [C19: probably from BLEND + PLUNGE]

blunger ('blʌndʒə) *n* a large vat in which the contents, esp. clay and water, are mixed by rotating arms.

Blunkett ('blʌnkɪt) *n* **David.** born 1947, British Labour politician; secretary of state for education and employment from 1997.

blunt (blʌnt) *adj* **1** (esp. of a knife or blade) lacking sharpness or keenness; dull. **2** not having a sharp edge or point: *a blunt instrument.* **3** (of people, manner of speaking, etc.) lacking refinement or subtlety; straightforward and uncomplicated. **4** outspoken; direct and to the point: *a blunt Yorkshireman.* ◆ *vb* (*tr*) **5** to make less sharp. **6** to diminish the sensitivity or perception of; make dull. [C12: probably of Scandinavian origin; compare Old Norse *blundr* dozing, *blunda* to close one's eyes; see BLUNDER, BLIND] ▸ **'bluntly** *adv* ▸ **'bluntness** *n*

Blunt (blʌnt) *n* **1 Anthony.** 1907–83, British art historian and Soviet spy. **2 Wilfred Scawen.** 1840–1922, British poet, traveller, and anti-imperialist.

blur (blɜː) *vb* **blurs, blurring, blurred. 1** to make or become vague or less distinct: *heat haze blurs the hills; education blurs class distinctions.* **2** to smear or smudge. **3** (*tr*) to make (the judgment, memory, or perception) less clear; dim. ◆ *n* **4** something vague, hazy, or indistinct. **5** a smear or smudge. [C16: perhaps variant of BLEAR] ▸ **blurred** (blɜːd) *adj* ▸ **blurredly** ('blɜːrɪdlɪ, 'blɜːd-) *adv* ▸ **'blurredness** *n* ▸ **'blurriness** *n* ▸ **'blurry** *adj*

blurb (blɜːb) *n* a promotional description, as found on the jackets of books. [C20: coined by Gelett Burgess (1866–1951), U.S. humorist and illustrator]

blurt (blɜːt) *vb* (*tr;* often foll. by *out*) to utter suddenly and involuntarily. [C16: probably of imitative origin]

blush (blʌʃ) *vb* **1** (*intr*) to become suddenly red in the face from embarrassment, shame, modesty, or guilt; redden. **2** to make or become reddish or rosy. ◆ *n* **3** a sudden reddening of the face from embarrassment, shame, modesty, or guilt. **4** a rosy glow: *the blush of a peach.* **5** a reddish or pinkish tinge. **6** a cloudy area on the surface of freshly applied gloss paint. **7 at first blush.** when first seen; as a first impression. [Old English *blȳscan;* related to *blȳsian* to burn, Middle Low German *blüsen* to light a fire] ▸ **'blushful** *adj* ▸ **'blushing** *n, adj* ▸ **'blushingly** *adv*

blusher ('blʌʃə) *n* a cosmetic applied to the face to give a rosy colour.

bluster ('blʌstə) *vb* **1** to speak or say loudly or boastfully. **2** to act in a bullying way. **3** (*tr,* foll. by *into*) to force or attempt to force (a person) into doing something by behaving thus. **4** (*intr*) (of the wind) to be noisy or gusty. ◆ *n* **5** boisterous talk or action; swagger. **6** empty threats or protests. **7** a strong wind; gale. [C15: probably from Middle Low German *blüsteren* to storm, blow violently] ▸ **'blusterer** *n* ▸ **'blustering** *n, adj* ▸ **'blusteringly** *or* **'blusterously** *adv* ▸ **'blustery** *or* **'blusterous** *adj*

Blvd *abbrev. for* Boulevard.

B-lymphocyte *n* a type of lymphocyte, originating in bone marrow, that produces antibodies. Also called: **B-cell.** See also **T-lymphocyte.**

Blyth[1] (blaɪð) *n* a port in N England, in SE Northumberland, on the North Sea. Pop.: 35 327 (1991).

Blyth[2] (blaɪð) *n* Sir **Chay** (tʃeɪ). born 1940, British yachtsman. He sailed round the world alone (1970–71) and has won many races.

Blyton ('blaɪtᵊn) *n* **Enid** (**Mary**). 1897–1968, British writer of children's books; creator of Noddy and the *Famous Five* series of adventure stories.

bm *abbrev. for:* **1** board measure. **2** bowel movement.

BM *abbrev. for:* **1** Bachelor of Medicine. **2** *Surveying.* benchmark. **3** British Museum.

BMA *abbrev. for* British Medical Association.

BMI *abbrev. for* Broadcast Music Incorporated.

BMJ *abbrev. for* British Medical Journal.

B-movie *n* a film originally made (esp. in Hollywood in the 1940s and 50s) as a supporting film, now often considered as a genre in its own right.

BMR *abbrev. for* basal metabolic rate.

BMus *abbrev. for* Bachelor of Music.

BMX *abbrev. for:* **1** bicycle motocross; stunt riding on rough ground or over an obstacle course on a bicycle. **2** a bicycle designed for bicycle motocross.

bn *abbrev. for* billion.

Bn *abbrev. for:* **1** Baron. **2** Also: **bn** Battalion.

B'nai B'rith (bə'neɪ bə'riːθ; brɪθ) *n* a Jewish fraternal organization founded in New York in 1843, having moral, philanthropic, social, educational, and political aims. [from Hebrew *benē brīth* sons of the covenant]

BNFL *abbrev. for* British Nuclear Fuels Limited.

bo *or* **boh** (bəʊ) *interj* an exclamation uttered to startle or surprise someone, esp. a child in a game.

BO *abbrev. for:* **1** *Informal.* body odour. **2** box office.

b.o. *abbrev. for:* **1** back order. **2** branch office. **3** broker's order. **4** buyer's option.

B/O *abbrev. for:* **1** *Book-keeping.* brought over. **2** buyer's option.

boa ('bəʊə) *n* **1** any large nonvenomous snake of the family *Boidae*, most of which occur in Central and South America and the Caribbean. They have vestigial hind limbs and kill their prey by constriction. **2** a woman's long thin scarf, usually of feathers or fur. [C19: from New Latin, from Latin: a large Italian snake, water snake]

boab ('bəʊæb) *n Austral.* short for **baobab.**

Boabdil (*Spanish* boaβ'ðil) *n* original name *Abu-Abdullah,* called *El Chico,* ruled as *Mohammed XI.* died ?1538, last Moorish king of Granada (1482–83; 1486–92).

BOAC (formerly) *abbrev. for* British Overseas Airways Corporation.

boa constrictor *n* a very large snake, *Constrictor constrictor,* of tropical America and the Caribbean, that kills its prey by constriction: family *Boidae* (boas).

Boadicea (ˌbəʊədɪ'siːə) *n* another name for **Boudicca.**

boak (bok, bəʊk) *vb, n* a variant spelling of **boke.**

Boanerges (ˌbəʊə'nɜːdʒiːz) *n* **1** *New Testament.* a nickname applied by Jesus to James and John in Mark 3:17. **2** a fiery preacher, esp. one with a powerful voice. [C17: from Hebrew *benē reghesh* sons of thunder]

boar (bɔː) *n* **1** an uncastrated male pig. **2** See **wild boar.** [Old English *bār;* related to Old High German *bēr*]

board (bɔːd) *n* **1** a long wide flat relatively thin piece of sawn timber. **2a** a smaller flat piece of rigid material for a specific purpose: *ironing board.* **2b** (*in combination*)*: breadboard; cheeseboard.* **3** a person's food or meals, provided regularly for money or sometimes as payment for work done (esp. in the phrases **full board, board and lodging**). **4** *Archaic.* a table, esp. one used for eating at, and esp. when laden with food. **5a** (*sometimes functioning as pl*) a group of people who officially administer a company, trust, etc.: *a board of directors.* **5b** (*as modifier*)*: a board meeting.* **6** any other committee or council: *a board of interviewers.* **7 the boards.** (*pl*) the acting profession; the stage. **8** short for **blackboard, chessboard, notice board, printed circuit board** (see printed circuit), **springboard,** or **surfboard. 9** stiff cardboard or similar material covered with paper, cloth, etc., used for the outside covers of a book. **10** a flat thin rectangular sheet of composite material, such as plasterboard or chipboard. **11** *Chiefly U.S.* **11a** a list on which stock-exchange securities and their prices are posted. **11b** *Informal.* the stock exchange itself. **12** *Nautical.* **12a** the side of a ship. **12b** the leg that a sailing vessel makes on a beat to windward. **13** *Austral. and N.Z.* the part of the floor of a sheep-shearing shed, esp. a raised part, where the shearers work. **14** *N.Z.* the killing floor of an abattoir or freezing works. **15a** any of various portable surfaces specially designed for indoor games such as chess, backgammon, etc. **15b** (*as modifier*): *board games.* **16a** a set of hands in duplicate bridge. **16b** a wooden or metal board containing four slots, or often nowadays, a plastic wallet, in which the four hands are placed so that the deal may be replayed with identical hands. **17** the hull of a sailboard, usually made of plastic, to which the mast is jointed and on which a windsurfer stands. **18** See **above board. 19 go by the board.** to be in disuse, neglected, or lost: *in these days courtesy goes by the board.* **20 on board.** on or in a ship, boat, aeroplane, or other vehicle. **21 sweep the board. 21a** (in gambling) to win all the cards or money. **21b** to win every event or prize in a contest. **22 take on board.** to accept (new ideas, situations, theories, etc.). ◆ *vb* **23** to go aboard (a vessel, train, aircraft, or other vehicle). **24** *Nautical.* to come alongside (a vessel) before attacking or going aboard. **25** to attack (a ship) by forcing one's way aboard. **26** (*tr;* often foll. by *up, in,* etc.) to cover or shut with boards. **27** (*intr*) to give or receive meals or meals and lodging in return for money or work. **28** (sometimes foll. by *out*) to receive or arrange for (someone, esp. a child) to receive food and lodging away from home, usually in return for payment. [Old English *bord;* related to Old Norse *borth* ship's side, table, Old High German *bort* ship's side, Sanskrit *bardhaka* a cutting off] ▸ **'boardable** *adj*

board-and-shingle *n Caribbean.* a small peasant dwelling with wooden walls and a shingle roof.

board bridge *n* another name for **duplicate bridge.**

boarder ('bɔːdə) *n* **1** *Brit.* a pupil who lives at school during term time. **2** *U.S.* a child who lives away from its parents and is cared for by a person or organization receiving payment. **3** another word for **lodger. 4** a person who boards a ship, esp. one who forces his way aboard in an attack: *stand by to repel boarders.*

board foot *n* a unit of board measure: the cubic content of a piece of wood one foot square and one inch thick.

boarding ('bɔːdɪŋ) *n* **1** a structure of boards, such as a floor or fence. **2** timber boards collectively. **3a** the act of embarking on an aircraft, train, ship, etc. **3b** (*as modifier*): *a boarding pass.* **4** a process used in tanning to accentuate the natural grain of hides, in which the surface of a softened leather is lightly creased by folding grain to grain and the fold is worked to and fro across the leather.

boarding house *n* **1** a private house in which accommodation and meals are provided for paying guests. **2** *Austral.* a house for boarders at a school. See also **house** (sense 10).

boarding out *n Social welfare, Brit.* **a** the local-authority practice of placing a client in a foster family or voluntary establishment and paying for it. **b** (*as modifier*): *boarding-out allowances.*

boarding school *n* a school providing living accommodation for some or all of its pupils.

board measure *n* a system of units for measuring wood based on the board foot. 1980 board feet equal one standard.

board of trade *n U.S. and Canadian.* another name for a **chamber of commerce.**

Board of Trade *n* (in the United Kingdom) a ministry within the Department of Trade: responsible for the supervision of commerce and the promotion of export trade.

Board of Trade Unit *n* a unit of electrical energy equal to 1 kilowatt-hour. Abbrev.: **BTU.**

boardroom ('bɔːd,ruːm, -,rʊm) *n* **a** a room where the board of directors of a company meets. **b** (*as modifier*): *a boardroom power struggle.*

board rule *n* a measuring device for estimating the number of board feet in a quantity of wood.

boardsailing ('bɔːd,seɪlɪŋ) *n* another name for **windsurfing.** ▸ **'board,sailor** *n*

board school *n Brit.* (formerly) a school managed by a board elected by local ratepayers.

boardwalk ('bɔːd,wɔːk) *n U.S. and Canadian.* a promenade, esp. along a beach, usually made of planks.

boarfish ('bɔː,fɪʃ) *n, pl* **-fish** *or* **-fishes.** any of various spiny-finned marine teleost fishes of the genera *Capros, Antigonia,* etc., related to the dories, having a deep compressed body, a long snout, and large eyes.

boarish ('bɔːrɪʃ) *adj* coarse, cruel, or sensual. ▸ **'boarishly** *adv* ▸ **'boarishness** *n*

boart (bɔːt) *n* a variant spelling of **bort.**

Boas ('bəuæz; *German* 'boːas) *n* **Franz** (frants). 1858–1942, U.S. anthropologist, born in Germany. He made major contributions to cultural and linguistic anthropology in studies of North American Indians, including *The Mind of Primitive Man* (1911; 1938).

boast[1] (bəust) *vb* **1** (*intr;* sometimes foll. by *of* or *about*) to speak in exaggerated or excessively proud terms of one's possessions, skills, or superior qualities; brag. **2** (*tr*) to possess (something to be proud of): *the city boasts a fine cathedral.* ◆ *n* **3** a bragging statement. **4** a possession, attribute, attainment, etc., that is or may be bragged about. [C13: of uncertain origin] ▸ **'boaster** *n* ▸ **'boasting** *n, adj* ▸ **'boastingly** *adv*

boast[2] (bəust) *vb* (*tr*) to shape or dress (stone) roughly with a broad chisel. [C19: of unknown origin]

boast[3] (bəust) *Squash.* ◆ *n* **1** a stroke in which the ball is hit on to one of the side walls before hitting the front wall. ◆ *vb* **2** to hit (the ball) in this way or make such a stroke. [C19: perhaps from French *bosse* the place where the ball hits the wall] ▸ **'boasted** *adj*

boastful ('bəustfʊl) *adj* tending to boast; characterized by boasting. ▸ **'boastfully** *adv* ▸ **'boastfulness** *n*

boat (bəut) *n* **1** a small vessel propelled by oars, paddle, sails, or motor for travelling, transporting goods, etc., esp. one that can be carried aboard a larger vessel. **2** (not in technical use) another word for **ship. 3** *Navy.* a submarine. **4** a container for gravy, sauce, etc. **5** a small boat-shaped container for incense, used in some Christian churches. **6 in the same boat.** sharing the same problems. **7 burn one's boats.** See **burn**[1] (sense 19). **8 miss the boat.** to lose an opportunity. **9 push the boat out.** *Brit. informal.* to celebrate, esp. lavishly and expensively. **10 rock the boat.** *Informal.* to cause a disturbance in the existing situation. ◆ *vb* **11** (*intr*) to travel or go in a boat, esp. as a form of recreation. **12** (*tr*) to transport or carry in a boat. [Old English *bāt;* related to Old Norse *beit* boat]

boatbill ('bəut,bɪl) *or* **boat-billed heron** *n* a nocturnal tropical American wading bird, *Cochlearius cochlearius,* similar to the night herons but with a broad flattened bill: family *Ardeidae,* order *Ciconiiformes.*

boat deck *n* the deck of a ship on which the lifeboats are kept.

boat drill *n* practice in launching the lifeboats and taking off the passengers and crew of a ship.

boatel *or* **botel** (bəu'tɛl) *n* **1** a waterside hotel catering for boating people. **2** a ship that functions as a hotel. [C20: from BOAT + (HOT)EL]

boater ('bəutə) *n* a stiff straw hat with a straight brim and flat crown.

boathook ('bəut,hʊk) *n* a pole with a hook at one end, used aboard a vessel for fending off other vessels or obstacles or for catching a line or mooring buoy.

boathouse ('bəut,haus) *n* a shelter by the edge of a river, lake, etc., for housing boats.

boatie ('bəutɪ) *n Austral. and N.Z. informal.* a boating enthusiast.

boating ('bəutɪŋ) *n* the practice of rowing, sailing, or cruising in boats as a form of recreation.

boatload ('bəut,ləud) *n* the amount of cargo or number of people held by a boat or ship.

boatman ('bəutmən) *n, pl* **-men. 1** a man who works on, hires out, repairs, or operates a boat or boats. **2** short for **water boatman.**

boat neck *n* a high slitlike neckline of a garment that extends onto the shoulders. Also called: **bateau neckline.**

boat people *pl n* refugees, esp. from Vietnam in the late 1970s, who leave by boat hoping to be picked up by ships of another country.

boat race *n* **the.** *Brit.* a rowing event held annually in the spring, in which an eight representing Oxford University rows against one representing Cambridge University on the Thames between Putney and Mortlake.

boatswain, bosun, *or* **bo's'n** ('bəusᵊn) *n* a petty officer on a merchant ship or a warrant officer on a warship who is responsible for the maintenance of the ship and its equipment. [Old English *bātswegen;* see BOAT, SWAIN]

boatswain's chair *n Nautical.* a seat consisting of a short flat board slung from ropes, used to support a person working on the side of a vessel or in its rigging.

boat train *n* a train scheduled to take passengers to or from a particular ship.

Boa Vista (*Portuguese* 'boːə 'viʃtə) *n* a town in N Brazil, capital of the federal territory of Roraima, on the Rio Branco. Pop.: 118 928 (1991).

Boaz ('bəuæz) *n Old Testament.* a kinsman of Naomi, who married her daughter-in-law Ruth (Ruth 2–4); one of David's ancestors.

bob[1] (bɒb) *vb* **bobs, bobbing, bobbed. 1** to move or cause to move up and down repeatedly, as while floating in water. **2** to move or cause to move with a short abrupt movement, as of the head. **3** to make (a bow or curtsy): *the little girl bobbed before the visitor.* **4** (*intr;* usually foll. by *up*) to appear or emerge suddenly. **5** (*intr;* foll. by *under, below,* etc.) to disappear suddenly, as beneath a surface. **6** (*intr;* usually foll. by *for*) to attempt to get hold (of a floating or hanging object, esp. an apple) in the teeth as a game. ◆ *n* **7** a short abrupt movement, as of the head. **8** a quick curtsy or bow. **9** *Changeringing.* a particular set of changes. **10** *Angling.* **10a** short for **bobfloat. 10b** the topmost fly on a cast of three, often fished bobbing at the surface. **10c** this position on a wet-fly cast. [C14: of uncertain origin]

bob[2] (bɒb) *n* **1** a hairstyle for women and children in which the hair is cut short evenly all round the head. **2** a dangling or hanging object, such as the weight on a pendulum or on a plumb line. **3** a polishing disc on a rotating spindle. It is usually made of felt, leather, etc., impregnated with an abrasive material. **4** short for **bob skate** or **bobsleigh. 5** a runner or pair of runners on a bobsled. **6** *Angling.* a small knot of worms, maggots, etc., used as bait. **7** a very short line of verse at the end of a stanza or preceding a rhyming quatrain (the wheel) at the end of a stanza. **8** a refrain or burden with such a short line or lines. **9** a docked tail, esp. of a horse. **10** *Brit. dialect.* a hanging cluster, as of flowers or ribbons. ◆ *vb* **bobs, bobbing, bobbed. 11** (*tr*) to cut (the hair) in a bob. **12** (*tr*) to cut short (something, esp. the tail of an animal); dock or crop. **13** (*intr*) to ride on a bobsled. [C14 *bobbe* bunch of flowers, perhaps of Celtic origin]

bob[3] (bɒb) *vb* **bobs, bobbing, bobbed. 1** to tap or cause to tap or knock lightly (against). ◆ *n* **2** a light knock; tap. [C13 *bobben* to rap, beat; see BOP[2]]

bob[4] (bɒb) *n, pl* **bob.** *Brit.* (formerly) an informal word for a **shilling.** [C19: of unknown origin]

Bob (bɒb) *n* **Bob's your uncle.** *Slang.* everything is or will turn out all right. [C19: perhaps from pet form of *Robert*]

bobbejaan ('bɒbə,jɑːn) *n S. African.* **1** a baboon. **2** a large black spider. **3** a monkey wrench. [Afrikaans]

bobbery ('bɒbərɪ) *n, pl* **-beries. 1** Also called: **bobbery pack.** a mixed pack of hunting dogs, often not belonging to any of the hound breeds. **2** *Informal.* a noisy commotion. ◆ *adj* **3** *Informal.* noisy or excitable. [C19: from Hindi *bāp re,* literally: oh father!]

bobbin ('bɒbɪn) *n* **1** a spool or reel on which thread or yarn is wound, being unwound as required; spool; reel. **2** narrow braid or cord used as binding or for trimming. **3** a device consisting of a short bar and a length of string, used to control a wooden door latch. **4a** a spool on which insulated wire is wound to form the coil of a small electromagnetic device, such as a bell or buzzer. **4b** the coil of such a spool. [C16: from Old French *bobine,* of unknown origin]

bobbinet (ˌbɒbɪ'nɛt) *n* a netted fabric of hexagonal mesh, made on a lace machine. [C19: see BOBBIN, NET[1]]

bobbin lace *n* lace made with bobbins rather than with needle and thread (needlepoint lace); pillow lace.

bobble ('bɒbᵊl) *n* **1** a short jerky motion, as of a cork floating on disturbed water; bobbing movement. **2** a tufted ball, usually for ornament, as on a knitted hat. **3** any small dangling ball or bundle. ◆ *vb* **4** (*intr*) *Sport.* (of a ball) to bounce with a rapid erratic motion due to an uneven playing surface. **5** *U.S. informal.* to handle (something) ineptly; muff; bungle: *he bobbled the ball and lost the game.* [C19: from BOB[1] (vb)]

bobby ('bɒbɪ) *n, pl* **-bies.** *Informal.* a British policeman. [C19: from *Bobby,* after *Robert* PEEL, who, as Home Secretary, set up the Metropolitan Police Force in 1828]

bobby calf *n* an unweaned calf culled for slaughter.

bobby-dazzler *n Dialect.* anything outstanding, striking, or showy, esp. an attractive girl. [C19: expanded form of *dazzler* something striking or attractive]

bobby pin *n U.S., Canadian, Austral., and N.Z.* a metal hairpin bent in order to hold the hair in place. Brit. terms: **hairgrip, kirby grip.**

bobby socks *pl n* ankle-length socks worn by teenage girls, esp. in the U.S. in the 1940s.

bobbysoxer ('bɒbɪˌsɒksə) *n Informal, chiefly U.S.* an adolescent girl wearing bobby socks, esp. in the 1940s.

bobcat ('bɒbˌkæt) *n* a North American feline mammal, *Lynx rufus,* closely related to but smaller than the lynx, having reddish-brown fur with dark spots or stripes, tufted ears, and a short tail. Also called: **bay lynx.** [C19: from BOB[2] (referring to its short tail) + CAT[1]]

bobfloat ('bɒbˌfləʊt) *n Angling.* a small buoyant float, usually consisting of a quill stuck through a piece of cork.

boblet ('bɒblɪt) *n* a two-man bobsleigh. [C20: from BOB[2] + -LET]

Bobo-Dioulasso ('bəʊbəʊdjuː'læsəʊ) *n* a city in W Burkina-Faso. Pop.: 300 000 (1993 est.).

bobol ('bʌbɔːl) *E Caribbean.* ◆ *n* **1** a fraud carried out by one or more persons with access to public funds in collusion with someone in a position of authority. ◆ *vb* **2** (*intr*) to commit a bobol. [C20: of uncertain origin]

bobolink ('bɒbəˌlɪŋk) *n* an American songbird, *Dolichonyx oryzivorus,* the male of which has a white back and black underparts in the breeding season: family *Icteridae* (American orioles). Also called (U.S.): **reedbird, ricebird.** [C18: of imitative origin]

bobotie (bʊ'bʊtɪ) *n* a South African dish consisting of curried mincemeat with a topping of beaten egg baked to a crust. [C19: from Afrikaans, probably from Malay]

bobowler ('bɒbˌaʊlə) *n Midland English dialect.* a large moth. [of uncertain origin]

Bobruisk *or* **Bobruysk** (bɔ'bruːɪsk) *n* a port in Belarus, on the River Berezina: engineering, timber, tyre manufacturing. Pop.: 227 100 (1996 est.).

bob skate *n Chiefly U.S. and Canadian.* an ice skate with two parallel blades. [C20: from *bob(sled)* + SKATE[1]]

bobsleigh ('bɒbˌsleɪ) *n* **1** a racing sledge for two or more people, with a steering mechanism enabling the driver to direct it down a steeply banked ice-covered run. **2** (esp. formerly) **2a** a sleigh made of two short sledges joined one behind the other. **2b** one of these two short sledges. ◆ *vb* **3** (*intr*) to ride on a bobsleigh. ◆ Also called (esp. U.S. and Canadian): **bobsled** ('bɒbˌslɛd). [C19: BOB[2] + SLEIGH]

bobstay ('bɒbˌsteɪ) *n* a strong stay between a bowsprit and the stem of a vessel for holding down the bowsprit. [C18: perhaps from BOB[1] + STAY[3]]

bobsy-die ('bɒbzɪˌdaɪ) *n N.Z. informal.* fuss; confusion; pandemonium (esp. in the phrases **kick up bobsy-die, play bobsy-die**). [from C19 *bob's a-dying*]

bobtail ('bɒbˌteɪl) *n* **1** a docked or diminutive tail. **2** an animal with such a tail. ◆ *adj also* **bobtailed. 3** having the tail cut short. ◆ *vb* (*tr*) **4** to dock the tail of. **5** to cut short; curtail. [C16: from BOB[2] + TAIL[1]]

bobweight ('bɒbˌweɪt) *n* another name for **balance weight.**

bobwhite ('bɒbˌwaɪt) *n* a brown North American quail, *Colinus virginianus,* the male of which has white markings on the head: a popular game bird. [C19: of imitative origin]

bocage (bɒ'kɑːʒ) *n* **1** the wooded countryside characteristic of northern France, with small irregular-shaped fields and many hedges and copses. **2** woodland scenery represented in ceramics. [C17: from French, from Old French *bosc;* see BOSCAGE]

Boccaccio (*Italian* bok'kattʃo) *n* **Giovanni** (dʒo'vani). 1313–75, Italian poet and writer, noted particularly for his *Decameron* (1353), a collection of 100 short stories. His other works include *Filostrato* (?1338) and *Teseida* (1341).

Boccherini (*Italian* bokke'rini) *n* **Luigi** (lu'idʒi). 1743–1805, Italian composer and cellist.

boccie, bocci, bocce ('bɒtʃiː), *or* **boccia** ('bɒtʃə) *n* an Italian version of bowls played on a lawn smaller than a bowling green. [from Italian *bocce* bowls, plural of *boccia* ball; see BOSS[2]]

Boccioni (*Italian* bot'tʃoni) *n* **Umberto** (um'berto). 1882–1916, Italian painter and sculptor: principal theorist of the futurist movement.

Boche (bɒʃ) *n Derogatory slang.* (esp. in World Wars I and II) **1** a German, esp. a German soldier. **2 the.** (*usually functioning as pl*) Germans collectively, esp. German soldiers regarded as the enemy. [C20: from French, probably shortened from *alboche* German, from *allemand* German + *caboche* pate]

Bochum (*German* 'boːxum) *n* an industrial city in NW Germany, in W North Rhine-Westphalia: university (1965). Pop.: 400 395 (1996 est.).

bock (bɒk, bəʊk) *vb, n* a variant spelling of **boke.**

bock beer *or* **bock** (bɒk) *n* **1** *U.S. and Canadian.* heavy dark strong beer. **2** (in France) a light beer. [C19: from German *Bock bier,* literally: buck beer, name given through folk etymology to beer brewed in *Einbeck,* near Hanover]

bockedy ('bɒkədɪ) *adj Irish.* (of a structure, piece of furniture, etc.) unsteady. [from Irish Gaelic *bacaideach* limping]

bod (bɒd) *n Informal.* **1** a fellow; chap: *he's a queer bod.* **2** another word for **body** (sense 1). [C18: short for BODY]

BOD *abbrev. for* biochemical oxygen demand.

bodacious (bəʊ'deɪʃəs) *adj Slang, chiefly U.S.* impressive or remarkable; excellent. [C19: from English dialect; blend of BOLD + AUDACIOUS]

bode[1] (bəʊd) *vb* **1** to be an omen of (good or ill, esp. of ill); portend; presage. **2** (*tr*) *Archaic.* to predict; foretell. [Old English *bodian;* related to Old Norse *botha* to proclaim, Old Frisian *bodia* to invite] ▸ **'boding** *n, adj* ▸ **'bodement** *n*

bode[2] (bəʊd) *vb* the past tense of **bide.**

bodega (bəʊ'diːgə; *Spanish* bo'ðeɣa) *n* a shop selling wine and sometimes groceries, esp. in a Spanish-speaking country. [C19: from Spanish, ultimately from Greek *apothēkē* storehouse, from *apotithenai* to store, put away]

Bodensee ('boːdənzeː) *n* the German name for (Lake) **Constance.**

Bode's law (bəʊdz) *n Astronomy.* an empirical rule relating the distances of the planets from the sun, based on the numerical sequence 0, 3, 6, 12, 24, ... Adding 4 to each number and dividing by 10 gives the sequence 0.4, 0.7, 1, 1.6, 2.8, ..., which is a reasonable representation of distances in astronomical units for most planets if the minor planets are counted as a single entity at 2.8. [named after Johann Elert *Bode* (1747–1826), who in 1772 published the law, formulated by Johann Titius in 1766]

bodge (bɒdʒ) *vb Informal.* to make a mess of; botch. [C16: changed from BOTCH]

bodger ('bɒdʒə) *adj Austral. informal.* worthless or second-rate. [C20: from BODGE]

bodgie ('bɒdʒɪ) *n Austral. and N.Z.* an unruly or uncouth young man, esp. in the 1950s; teddy boy. [C20: from BODGER]

Bodh Gaya ('bɒd gə'jɑː) *n* a variant spelling of **Buddh Gaya.**

Bodhidharma (ˌbəʊdɪ'dɑːmə, ˌbɒd-) *n* 6th century A.D., Indian Buddhist monk, who taught in China (from 520): considered to be the founder of Zen Buddhism.

Bodhisattva (ˌbəʊdɪ'sætvə, -wə, ˌbɒd-; ˌbəʊdiː'sʌtvə) *n* (in Mahayana Buddhism) a divine being worthy of nirvana who remains on the human plane to help men to salvation. Compare **arhat.** [Sanskrit, literally: one whose essence is enlightenment, from *bodhi* enlightenment + *sattva* essence]

Bodhi Tree (ˌbəʊdɪ) *n* the sacred peepul at Buddh Gaya under which Gautama Siddhartha attained enlightenment and became the Buddha. [Sanskrit *bodhi* enlightenment]

bodhrán (baʊ'rɑːn, 'bɔːrɑːn) *n* a shallow one-sided drum popular in Irish and Scottish folk music. [Irish Gaelic]

bodice ('bɒdɪs) *n* **1** the upper part of a woman's dress, from the shoulder to the waist. **2** a tight-fitting corset worn laced over a blouse, as in certain national costumes, or (formerly) as a woman's undergarment. [C16: originally Scottish *bodies,* plural of BODY]

bodice ripper *n Informal.* a romantic novel, usually on a historical theme, that involves some sex and violence.

Bo Diddley beat (ˌbəʊ 'dɪdlɪ 'biːt) *n* a type of syncopated Black rhythm, frequently used in rock music. [C20: named after *Bo Diddley* (born 1929), U.S. rhythm-and-blues performer and songwriter]

-bodied *adj* (*in combination*) having a body or bodies as specified: *able-bodied; long-bodied; many-bodied.*

bodiless ('bɒdɪlɪs) *adj* having no body or substance; incorporeal or insubstantial.

bodily ('bɒdɪlɪ) *adj* **1** relating to or being a part of the human body. ◆ *adv* **2** by taking hold of the body: *he threw him bodily from the platform.* **3** in person; in the flesh.

bodkin ('bɒdkɪn) *n* **1** a blunt large-eyed needle used esp. for drawing tape through openwork. **2** *Archaic.* a dagger. **3** *Printing.* a pointed steel tool used for extracting characters when correcting metal type. **4** *Archaic.* a long ornamental hairpin. [C14: probably of Celtic origin; compare Gaelic *biodag* dagger]

Bodleian (bɒd'liːən, 'bɒdlɪ-) *n* the principal library of Oxford University: a copyright deposit library. [C17: named after Sir Thomas *Bodley* (1545–1613), English scholar who founded it in 1602]

Bodmin ('bɒdmɪn) *n* a market town in SW England, in Cornwall, near **Bodmin Moor,** a granite upland rising to 420 m (1375 ft.). Pop.: 12 553 (1991).

Bodoni (bə'dəʊnɪ) *n* a style of type designed by the Italian printer Giambattista **Bodoni** (1740–1813).

body ('bɒdɪ) *n, pl* **bodies. 1a** the entire physical structure of an animal or human being. Related adjs.: **corporeal, physical. 1b** (*as modifier*): *body odour.* **2** the flesh, as opposed to the spirit: *while we are still in the body.* **3** the trunk or torso, not including the limbs, head, or tail. **4** a dead human or animal; corpse. **5** the largest or main part of anything: *the body of a vehicle; the body of a plant.* **6** a separate or distinct mass of water or land. **7** the main part; majority: *the body of public opinion.* **8** the central part of a written work: *the body of a thesis as opposed to the footnotes.* **9** a number of individuals regarded as a single entity; group: *the student body; they marched in a body.* **10** *Maths.*

a three-dimensional region with an interior. **11** *Physics.* an object or substance that has three dimensions, a mass, and is distinguishable from surrounding objects. **12** fullness in the appearance of the hair. **13** the characteristic full quality of certain wines, determined by the density and the content of alcohol or tannin: *a Burgundy has a heavy body.* **14** substance or firmness, esp. of cloth. **15** the sound box of a guitar, violin, or similar stringed instrument. **16** a woman's close-fitting one-piece garment for the torso. **17** the part of a dress covering the body from the shoulders to the waist. **18** another name for **shank** (sense 11). **19a** the pigment contained in or added to paint, dye, etc. **19b** the opacity of a paint in covering a surface. **19c** the apparent viscosity of a paint. **20** (in watercolour painting) **20a** a white filler mixed with pigments to make them opaque. **20b** (*as modifier*): *body colour.* See also **gouache. 21** *Printing.* the measurement from top to bottom of a piece of type, usually ascender to descender. **22** an informal or dialect word for a **person. 23 keep body and soul together.** to manage to keep alive; survive. **24** (*modifier*) of or relating to the main reading matter of a book as distinct from headings, illustrations, appendices, etc.: *the body text.* ◆ *vb* **bodies, bodying, bodied.** (*tr*) **25** (usually foll. by *forth*) to give a body or shape to. [Old English *bodig;* related to Old Norse *buthkr* box, Old High German *botah* body]

body bag *n Military.* a large heavy plastic bag used to contain and transport human remains, esp. those of battle casualties.

body blow *n* **1** *Boxing.* Also called: **body punch.** a blow to the body of an opponent. **2** a severe disappointment or setback: *unavailability of funds was a body blow to the project.*

body building *n* the practice of performing regular exercises designed to make the muscles of the body conspicuous.

body cavity *n* the internal cavity of any multicellular animal that contains the digestive tract, heart, kidneys, etc. In vertebrates it develops from the coelom.

body-centred *adj* (of a crystal) having a lattice point at the centre of each unit cell as well as at the corners. Compare **face-centred.**

bodycheck ('bɒdɪˌtʃɛk) *n* **1** *Ice hockey, etc.* obstruction of another player. **2** *Wrestling.* the act of blocking a charging opponent with the body. ◆ *vb* **3** (*tr*) to deliver a bodycheck to (an opponent).

body corporate *n Law.* a group of persons incorporated to carry out a specific enterprise. See **corporation** (sense 1).

body double *n Films.* a person who substitutes for a star for the filming of a scene that involves shots of the body rather than the face.

bodyguard ('bɒdɪˌgɑːd) *n* a person or group of people who escort and protect someone, esp. a political figure.

body horror *n* a horror film genre in which the main feature is the graphically depicted destruction or degeneration of a human body or bodies.

body image *n Psychol.* an individual's concept of his own body.

body language *n* the nonverbal imparting of information by means of conscious or subconscious bodily gestures, posture, etc.

body-line *adj Cricket.* denoting or relating to fast bowling aimed at the batsman's body.

Body of Christ *n* the Christian Church.

body politic *n* **the.** the people of a nation or the nation itself considered as a political entity; the state.

body search *n* **1** a form of search by police, customs officials, etc., that involves examination of a prisoner's or suspect's bodily orifices. ◆ *vb* **body-search. 2** (*tr*) to search (a prisoner or suspect) in this manner.

body shop *n* a place where the bodywork of motor vehicles is built or repaired.

body snatcher *n* (formerly) a person who robbed graves and sold the corpses for dissection. ▸ **body snatching** *n*

body stocking *n* a one-piece undergarment for women, usually of nylon, covering the torso.

bodysuit ('bɒdɪˌsuːt, -ˌsjuːt) *n* **1** another name for **body** (sense 16). **2** a one-piece undergarment for a baby.

body-surf *vb* (*intr*) to ride a wave by lying on it without a surfboard. ▸ **'body-ˌsurfer** *n* ▸ **'body-ˌsurfing** *n*

body swerve *n* **1** *Sport.* (esp. in football games) the act or an instance of swerving past an opponent. **2** *Scot.* the act or an instance of avoiding (a situation considered unpleasant): *I think I'll give the meeting a body swerve.* ◆ *vb* **body-swerve. 3** *Sport.* (esp. in football games) to pass (an opponent) using a body swerve. **4** *Scot.* to avoid (a situation or person considered unpleasant).

body warmer *n* a sleeveless type of jerkin, usually quilted, worn as an outer garment for extra warmth.

bodywork ('bɒdɪˌwɜːk) *n* the external shell of a motor vehicle.

Boehmite ('bɜːmaɪt) *n* a grey, red, or brown mineral that consists of alumina in rhombic crystalline form and occurs in bauxite. Formula: AlO(OH). [C20: from German *Böhmit,* after J. *Böhm,* 20th-century German scientist]

Boeotia (bɪ'əʊʃɪə) *n* **1** a region of ancient Greece, northwest of Athens. It consisted of ten city-states, which formed the Boeotian League, led by Thebes: at its height in the 4th century B.C. **2** transliteration of the Modern Greek name for **Voiotia.** ▸ **Boe'otian** *n, adj*

boere- (bʊə, 'bəʊə, bɔː) *combining form. S. African.* rustic or country-style: *boeremusiek.* [Afrikaans]

Boer (bʊə, 'bəʊə, bɔː) *n, adj* **a** a descendant of any of the Dutch or Huguenot colonists who settled in South Africa, mainly in Cape Colony, the Orange Free State, and the Transvaal. **b** (*as modifier*): *a Boer farm.* [C19: from Dutch *Boer;* see BOOR]

boerbul ('bʊəˌbʊl) *n S. African.* a crossbred mastiff used esp. as a watchdog. [from Afrikaans *boerboel* a breed of mastiff]

boeremusiek ('bʊərəˌmjuːzɪk) *n S. African.* a special variety of light music associated with the culture of the Afrikaners. [Afrikaans]

boerewors ('bʊərəˌvɔs) *n S. African.* a highly seasoned traditional sausage made from minced or pounded meat. [Afrikaans]

Boer War *n* either of two conflicts between Britain and the South African Boers, the first (1880–1881) when the Boers sought to regain the independence given up for British aid against the Zulus, the second (1899–1902) when the Orange Free State and Transvaal declared war on Britain.

boet (bʊt) *n S. African.* brother; mate, chum. [Afrikaans]

Boethius (bəʊ'iːθɪəs) *n* **Anicius Manlius Severinus** (ə'nɪsɪəs 'mænlɪəs ˌsɛvə'raɪnəs). ?480–?524 A.D., Roman philosopher and statesman, noted particularly for his work *De Consolatione Philosophiae.* He was accused of treason and executed by Theodoric.

boeuf bourguignon (*French* bœf burgiɲɔ̃) *n* a casserole of beef, vegetables, herbs, etc., cooked in red wine. Also called: **boeuf à la bourguignonne.** [French: Burgundy beef]

boffin ('bɒfɪn) *n Brit. informal.* a scientist, esp. one carrying out military research. [C20: of uncertain origin]

boffo ('bɒfəʊ) *adj Slang.* very good; highly successful. [C20: of uncertain origin]

Bofors gun ('bəʊfəz) *n* an automatic single- or double-barrelled anti-aircraft gun with 40 millimetre bore. [C20: named after *Bofors,* Sweden, where it was first made]

bog (bɒg) *n* **1** wet spongy ground consisting of decomposing vegetation, which ultimately forms peat. **2** an area of such ground. **3** a place or thing that prevents or slows progress or improvement. **4** a slang word for **lavatory** (sense 1). **5** *Austral. slang.* the act or an instance of defecating. ◆ See also **bog down, bog in.** [C13: from Gaelic *bogach* swamp, from *bog* soft] ▸ **'boggy** *adj* ▸ **'bogginess** *n*

bogan ('bəʊgən) *n Canadian.* (esp. in the Maritime Provinces) a sluggish side stream. Also called: **logan, pokelogan.** [of Algonquian origin]

Bogarde ('bəʊgɑːd) *n* Sir **Dirk,** real name *Derek Jules Gaspard Ulric Niven van den Bogaerde.* 1920–99, British film actor and writer: his films include *The Servant* (1963) and *Death in Venice* (1970). His writings include the autobiographical *A Postillion Struck by Lightning* (1977), and the novels *Jericho* (1992) and *A Period of Adjustment* (1994).

Bogart ('bəʊgɑːt) *n* **Humphrey (DeForest).** nicknamed *Bogie.* 1899–1957, U.S. film actor: his films include *High Sierra* (1941), *Casablanca* (1942), *The Big Sleep* (1946), *The African Queen* (1951), and *The Caine Mutiny* (1954).

bog asphodel *n* either of two liliaceous plants, *Narthecium ossifragum* of Europe or *N. americanum* of North America, that grow in boggy places and have small yellow flowers and grasslike leaves.

Boğazköy (*Turkish* bɔː'ɑzkœi) *n* a village in central Asia Minor: site of the ancient Hittite capital.

bogbean ('bɒgˌbiːn) *n* another name for **buckbean.**

bog cotton *n* another name for **cotton grass.**

bog deal *n* pine wood found preserved in peat bogs.

bog down *vb* **bogs, bogging, bogged.** (*adv;* when *tr, often passive*) to impede or be impeded physically or mentally.

bogey[1] *or* **bogy** ('bəʊgɪ) *n* **1** an evil or mischievous spirit. **2** something that worries or annoys. **3** *Golf.* **3a** a score of one stroke over par on a hole. Compare **par** (sense 5). **3b** *Obsolete.* a standard score for a hole or course, regarded as one that a good player should make. **4** *Slang.* a piece of dried mucus discharged from the nose. **5** *Air Force slang.* an unidentified or hostile aircraft. **6** *Slang.* a detective; policeman. ◆ *vb* **7** (*tr*) *Golf.* to play (a hole) in one stroke over par. [C19: probably related to BUG[2] and BOGLE[1]; compare BUGABOO]

bogey[2] *or* **bogie** ('bəʊgɪ) *Austral.* ◆ *vb* **1** to bathe or swim. ◆ *n* **2** a bathe or swim. [C19: from a native Australian language]

bogey hole *n Austral.* a natural pool used for swimming.

bogeyman ('bəʊgɪˌmæn) *n, pl* **-men.** a person, real or imaginary, used as a threat, esp. to children.

boggart ('bɒgət) *n Northern English dialect.* a ghost or poltergeist. [perhaps from *bog,* variant of BUG[2] + -ARD]

boggle ('bɒg°l) *vb* (*intr;* often foll. by *at*) **1** to be surprised, confused, or alarmed (esp. in the phrase **the mind boggles**). **2** to hesitate or be evasive when confronted with a problem. [C16: probably variant of BOGLE[1]]

bogie[1] *or* **bogy** ('bəʊgɪ) *n* **1** an assembly of four or six wheels forming a pivoted support at either end of a railway coach. It provides flexibility on curves. **2** *Chiefly Brit.* a small railway truck of short wheelbase, used for conveying coal, ores, etc. **3** a Scottish word for **soapbox** (sense 3). [C19: of unknown origin]

bogie[2] ('bəʊgɪ) *n* a variant spelling of **bogey**[2].

bog in *vb* **bogs, bogging, bogged.** (*intr, adv*) *Austral. and N.Z. informal.* **1** to start energetically on a task. **2** to start eating; tuck in. ◆ Also (prep): **bog into.**

bogle[1] ('bəʊg°l, 'bɒg-) *n* **1** a dialect or archaic word for **bogey**[1] (sense 1). **2** *Scot.* a scarecrow. [C16: from Scottish *bogill,* perhaps from Gaelic; compare Welsh *bygel;* see BUG[2]]

bogle[2] ('bəʊg°l) *n* **1** a rhythmic dance, originating in the early 1990s, performed to ragga music. ◆ *vb* **2** (*intr*) to perform such a dance.

bogman ('bɒgˌmæn) *n, pl* **-men.** *Archaeol.* the body of a person found preserved in a peat bog.

bog moss *n* another name for **peat moss.**

bog myrtle *n* another name for **sweet gale.**

Bognor Regis ('bɒgnə 'riːdʒɪs) *n* a resort in S England, in West Sussex on the English Channel: electronics industries. *Regis* was added to the name after King George V's convalescence there in 1929. Pop.: 56 744 (1991).

bog oak *n* oak or other wood found preserved in peat bogs; bogwood.

bogong ('bəʊˌgɒŋ) *or* **bugong** ('buːˌgɒŋ) *n* an edible dark-coloured Australian noctuid moth, *Agrotis infusa.*

Bogor ('bəʊgɔː) *n* a city in Indonesia, in W Java: botanical gardens and research institutions. Pop.: 271 711 (1990). Former name: **Buitenzorg.**

bog orchid *n* an orchid, *Hammarbya* (or *Malaxis*) *paludosa,* growing in sphagnum bogs in the N hemisphere. It has greenish-yellow flowers and its leaves bear a fringe of tiny bulbils.

Bogotá (ˌbəʊgəˈtɑː; *Spanish* boɣoˈta) *n* the capital of Colombia, on a central plateau of the E Andes: originally the centre of Chibcha civilization; founded as a city in 1538 by the Spaniards. Pop.: 6 004 782 (1997 est.).

bog rush *n* a blackish tufted cyperaceous plant, *Schoenus nigricans,* growing on boggy ground.

bogtrotter (ˈbɒgˌtrɒtə) *n* a derogatory term for an Irishman, esp. an Irish peasant.

bogus (ˈbəʊgəs) *adj* spurious or counterfeit; not genuine: *a bogus note.* [C19: from *bogus* apparatus for making counterfeit money; perhaps related to BOGEY[1]] ► ˈ**bogusly** *adv* ► ˈ**bogusness** *n*

bogwood (ˈbɒgˌwʊd) *n* another name for **bog oak.**

bogy (ˈbəʊgɪ) *n, pl* **-gies.** a variant spelling of **bogey**[1] or **bogie**[1].

boh (bəʊ) *interj* a variant spelling of **bo.**

Bohai (ˈbɔːˈhaɪ) *or* **Pohai** *n* a large inlet of the Yellow Sea on the coast of NE China. Also called: (Gulf of) **Chihli.**

bohea (bəʊˈhiː) *n* a black Chinese tea, once regarded as the choicest, but now as an inferior grade. [C18: from Chinese (Fukien dialect) *bu-i,* from Mandarin Chinese *Wu-i Shan* range of hills on which this tea was grown]

Bohemia (bəʊˈhiːmɪə) *n* **1** a former kingdom of central Europe, surrounded by mountains: independent from the 9th to the 13th century; belonged to the Hapsburgs from 1526 until 1918. **2** an area of the W Czech Republic, formerly a province of Czechoslovakia (1918–49). From 1939 until 1945 it formed part of the German protectorate of **Bohemia-Moravia.** Czech name: **Čechy.** German name: **Böhmen** (ˈbøːmən). **3** a district frequented by unconventional people, esp. artists or writers.

Bohemian (bəʊˈhiːmɪən) *n* **1** a native or inhabitant of Bohemia, esp. of the old kingdom of Bohemia; a Czech. **2** (*often not cap.*) a person, esp. an artist or writer, who lives an unconventional life. **3** the Czech language. ◆ *adj* **4** of, relating to, or characteristic of Bohemia, its people, or their language. **5** unconventional in appearance, behaviour, etc.

Bohemian Brethren *pl n* a Protestant Christian sect formed in the 15th century from various Hussite groups, which rejected oaths and military service and advocated a pure and disciplined spiritual life. It was reorganized in 1722 as the Moravian Church. Also called: **Unitas Fratrem** (ˈjuːnɪtæs ˈfrætrem).

Bohemian Forest *n* a mountain range between the SW Czech Republic and SE Germany. Highest peak: Arber, 1457 m (4780 ft.). Czech name: **Český Les** (ˈtʃeskiː ˈles). German name: **Böhmerwald** (ˈbøːmərˌvalt).

Bohemianism (bəʊˈhiːmɪəˌnɪzəm) *n* unconventional behaviour or appearance, esp. of an artist.

Bohemond I (ˈbəʊəmənd) *n* ?1056–?1111, prince of Antioch (1099–1111); a leader of the first crusade, he helped to capture Antioch (1098).

Böhm (*German* bøːm) *n* **Karl** (karl). 1894–1981, Austrian orchestral conductor.

Böhme, Boehme (*German* ˈbøːmə), *or* **Böhm** *n* **Jakob** (ˈjaːkɔp). 1575–1624, German mystic.

Böhm flute *n* a type of flute in which the holes are covered with keys; the standard type of modern flute. [C19: named after Theobald *Böhm* (1793–1881), German flautist who invented it]

Bohol (bəʊˈhɔːl) *n* an island of the central Philippines. Chief town: Tagbilaran. Pop.: 948 000 (1990). Area: about 3900 sq. km (1500 sq. miles).

Bohr (bɔː; *Danish* boːr) *n* **1 Aage Niels** (ˈɔgə neːls). born 1922, Danish physicist, noted for his work on nuclear structure. He shared the Nobel prize for physics 1975. **2** his father, **Niels** (**Henrik David**). 1885–1962, Danish physicist, who applied the quantum theory to Rutherford's model of the atom to explain spectral lines: Nobel prize for physics 1922.

bohrium (ˈbɔːrɪəm) *n* a transuranic element artificially produced in minute quantities by bombarding ^{204}Bi atoms with ^{54}Cr nuclei. Symbol: Bh; atomic no. 107. Former names: **element 107, unnilheptium.** [C20: after N. BOHR]

Bohr theory *n* a theory of atomic structure that explains the spectrum of hydrogen atoms. It assumes that the electron orbiting around the nucleus can exist only in certain energy states, a jump from one state to another being accompanied by the emission or absorption of a quantum of radiation. [C20: after N. BOHR]

bohunk (ˈbəʊˌhʌŋk) *n U.S. and Canadian, derogatory slang.* a labourer from east or central Europe. [C20: blend of *Bo(hemian)* + *Hung(arian),* with alteration of *g* to *k*]

Boiardo (*Italian* boˈjardo) *n* **Matteo Maria** (matˈteːo maˈria), conte de Scandiano. 1434–94, Italian poet; author of the historical epic *Orlando Innamorato* (1487).

boil[1] (bɔɪl) *vb* **1** to change or cause to change from a liquid to a vapour so rapidly that bubbles of vapour are formed copiously in the liquid. Compare **evaporate. 2** to reach or cause to reach boiling point. **3** to cook or be cooked by the process of boiling. **4** (*intr*) to bubble and be agitated like something boiling; seethe: *the ocean was boiling.* **5** (*intr*) to be extremely angry or indignant (esp. in the phrase **make one's blood boil**): *she was boiling at his dishonesty.* **6** (*intr*) to contain a boiling liquid: *the pot is boiling.* ◆ *n* **7** the state or action of boiling (esp. in the phrases **on the boil, off the boil**). ◆ See also **boil away, boil down, boil off, boil over, boil up.** [C13: from Old French *boillir,* from Latin *bullīre* to bubble, from *bulla* a bubble] ► ˈ**boilable** *adj*

boil[2] (bɔɪl) *n* a red painful swelling with a hard pus-filled core caused by bacterial infection of the skin and subcutaneous tissues, esp. at a hair follicle. Technical name: **furuncle.** [Old English *bȳle;* related to Old Norse *beyla* swelling, Old High German *būlla* bladder, Gothic *ufbauljan* to inflate]

boil away *vb* (*adv*) to cause (liquid) to evaporate completely by boiling or (of liquid) to evaporate completely.

boil down *vb* (*adv*) **1** to reduce or be reduced in quantity and usually altered in consistency by boiling: *to boil a liquid down to a thick glue.* **2 boil down to. 2a** (*intr*) to be the essential element in something. **2b** (*tr*) to summarize; reduce to essentials.

Boileau (*French* bwalo) *n* **Nicolas** (nikɔla). full name *Nicolas Boileau-Despréaux.* 1636–1711, French poet and critic; author of satires, epistles, and *L'Art poétique* (1674), in which he laid down the basic principles of French classical literature.

boiled shirt *n Informal.* a dress shirt with a stiff front.

boiled sweet *n Brit.* a hard sticky sweet of boiled sugar with any of various flavourings.

boiler (ˈbɔɪlə) *n* **1** a closed vessel or arrangement of enclosed tubes in which water is heated to supply steam to drive an engine or turbine or provide heat. **2** a domestic device burning solid fuel, gas, or oil, to provide hot water, esp. for central heating. **3** a large tub for boiling laundry. **4** a tough old chicken for cooking by boiling.

boilermaker (ˈbɔɪləˌmeɪkə) *n* **1** a person who works with metal in heavy industry; plater or welder. **2** *Brit. slang.* a beer drink consisting half of draught mild and half of bottled brown ale. **3** *U.S. slang.* a drink of whisky followed by a beer chaser.

boilerplate (ˈbɔɪləˌpleɪt) *n* **1** a form of mild-steel plate used in the production of boiler shells. **2** a copy made with the intention of making other copies from it. **3** a set of instructions incorporated in several places in a computer program or a standard form of words used repeatedly in drafting contracts, guarantees, etc. **4** a draft contract that can easily be modified to cover various types of transaction.

boiler suit *n Brit.* a one-piece work garment consisting of overalls and a shirt top usually worn over ordinary clothes to protect them.

boiling (ˈbɔɪlɪŋ) *adj, adv* **1** very warm: *a boiling hot day.* ◆ *n* **2 the whole boiling.** *Slang.* the whole lot.

boiling point *n* **1** the temperature at which a liquid boils at a given pressure, usually atmospheric pressure at sea level; the temperature at which the vapour pressure of a liquid equals the external pressure. **2** *Informal.* the condition of being angered or highly excited.

boiling-water reactor *n* a nuclear reactor using water as coolant and moderator, steam being produced in the reactor itself: enriched uranium oxide cased in zirconium is the fuel. Abbrev.: **BWR.**

boil off *vb* to remove or be removed (from) by boiling: *to boil off impurities.*

boilover (ˈbɔɪlˌəʊvə) *n Austral.* a surprising result in a sporting event, esp. in a horse race.

boil over *vb* (*adv*) **1** to overflow or cause to overflow while boiling. **2** (*intr*) to burst out in anger or excitement: *she boiled over at the mention of his name.*

boil up *vb* (*intr, adv*) *Austral. and N.Z.* to make tea.

bois-brûlé (ˌbwɑːbruːˈleɪ) *n* (*sometimes cap.*) *Canadian archaic.* a mixed-race person of Indian and White (usually French Canadian) ancestry; Métis. Also called: **Brule.** [French, literally: burnt wood]

Bois de Boulogne (*French* bwa də bulɔɲ) *n* a large park in W Paris, formerly a forest: includes the racecourses of Auteuil and Longchamp.

Boise *or* **Boise City** (ˈbɔɪzɪ, -sɪ) *n* a city in SW Idaho: the state capital. Pop.: 152 737 (1996 est.).

Bois-le-Duc (bwa lə dyk) *n* the French name for **'s Hertogenbosch.**

boisterous (ˈbɔɪstərəs, -strəs) *adj* **1** noisy and lively; unrestrained or unruly. **2** (of the wind, sea, etc.) turbulent or stormy. [C13 *boistuous,* of unknown origin] ► ˈ**boisterously** *adv* ► ˈ**boisterousness** *n*

Boito (*Italian* ˈbɔːito) *n* **Arrigo** (arˈrigo). 1842–1918, Italian operatic composer and librettist, whose works include the opera *Mefistofele* (1868) and the librettos for Verdi's *Otello* and *Falstaff.*

Bokassa I (bəˈkæsə) *n* original name *Jean Bedel Bokassa.* 1921–96, president of the Central African Republic (1972–76); emperor of the renamed Central African Empire from 1976 until overthrown in 1979.

boke, boak, *or* **bock** (bok, bəʊk) *Scot.* ◆ *vb* **1** to retch or vomit. ◆ *n* **2** a retch; vomiting fit. [Middle English *bolken;* related to BELCH, German *bölken* to roar]

Bokhara (bʊˈxɑːrə) *n* a variant spelling of **Bukhara.**

bokmakierie (ˌbɒkməˈkɪərɪ) *n S. African.* a large yellow shrike, *Telephorus zeylonus,* of southern Africa, known for its melodious song. [C19: from Afrikaans, imitative of its call]

Bokmål (*Norwegian* ˈbuːkmoːl) *n* one of the two official forms of written Norwegian, closely related to Danish. Also called: **Dano-Norwegian.** Formerly called: **Riksmål.** Compare **Nynorsk.** [Norwegian, literally: book language]

Bol. *abbrev. for* Bolivia(n).

bola (ˈbəʊlə) *or* **bolas** (ˈbəʊləs) *n, pl* **-las** *or* **-lases.** a missile used by gauchos and Indians of South America, consisting of two or more heavy balls on a cord. It is hurled at a running quarry, such as an ox or emu, so as to entangle its legs. [Spanish: ball, from Latin *bulla* knob]

Boland (ˈbʊəlant) *n* an area of high altitude in S South Africa.

Bolan Pass (bəʊˈlɑːn) *n* a mountain pass in W central Pakistan through the Brahui Range, between Sibi and Quetta, rising to 1800 m (5900 ft.).

bold (bəʊld) *adj* **1** courageous, confident, and fearless; ready to take risks. **2** showing or requiring courage: *a bold plan.* **3** immodest or impudent: *she gave him a bold look.* **4** standing out distinctly; conspicuous: *a figure carved in bold relief.* **5** very steep: *the bold face of the cliff.* **6** imaginative in thought or expression: *the novel's bold plot.* **7** *Printing.* set in bold face. ◆ *n* **8** *Printing.* short for **bold face.** [Old English *beald;* related to Old Norse *ballr* dangerous, terrible, *baldinn* defiant, Old High German *bald* bold] ► ˈ**boldly** *adv* ► ˈ**boldness** *n*

Bolden (ˈbəʊldən) *n* **Buddy,** real name *Charles Bolden.* 1868–1931, U.S. Black jazz cornet player; a pioneer of the New Orleans style and a celebrated improviser.

bold face *n* **1** *Printing.* a weight of type characterized by thick heavy lines, as the entry words in this dictionary. Compare **light face.** ◆ *adj* **boldface. 2** (of type) having this weight.

Boldrewood ('bəʊldəˌwʊd) *n* **Rolf,** real name *Thomas Alexander Browne.* 1826–1915, Australian writer, born in the UK, noted for his novels of the Australian outback, esp. *Robbery Under Arms* (1882–3).

bole[1] (bəʊl) *n* the trunk of a tree. [C14: from Old Norse *bolr;* related to Middle High German *bole* plank]

bole[2] (bəʊl) *or* **bolus** *n* **1** a reddish soft variety of clay used as a pigment. **2** a moderate reddish-brown colour. [C13: from Late Latin *bōlus* lump, from Greek *bōlos*]

bolection (bəʊ'lɛkʃən) *n Architect.* a stepped moulding covering and projecting beyond the joint between two members having surfaces at different levels. Also called: **bilection.** [C18: of unknown origin]

bolero (bə'lɛərəʊ) *n, pl* **-ros. 1** a Spanish dance, often accompanied by the guitar and castanets, usually in triple time. **2** a piece of music composed for or in the rhythm of this dance. **3** (*also* 'bɒlərəʊ) a kind of short jacket not reaching the waist, with or without sleeves and open at the front: worn by men in Spain and by women elsewhere. [C18: from Spanish; perhaps related to *bola* ball]

boletus (bəʊ'liːtəs) *n, pl* **-tuses** *or* **-ti** (-ˌtaɪ). any saprotroph basidiomycetous fungus of the genus *Boletus,* having a brownish umbrella-shaped cap with spore-bearing tubes in the underside: family *Boletineae.* Many species are edible. [C17: from Latin: variety of mushroom, from Greek *bōlitēs;* perhaps related to Greek *bōlos* lump]

Boleyn (bʊ'lɪn, 'bʊlɪn) *n* **Anne.** 1507–36, second wife of Henry VIII of England; mother of Elizabeth I. She was executed on a charge of adultery.

Bolger ('bəʊldʒə) *n* **James.** born 1935, New Zealand politician; prime minister (1990–97).

bolide ('bəʊlaɪd, -lɪd) *n* a large exceptionally bright meteor that often explodes. Also called: **fireball.** [C19: from French, from *bolis* missile; see BALLISTA]

Bolingbroke ('bɒlɪŋˌbrʊk) *n* **1** the surname of **Henry IV** of England. **2 Henry St John,** 1st Viscount Bolingbroke. 1678–1751, English politician; fled to France in 1714 and acted as secretary of state to the Old Pretender; returned to England in 1723. His writings include *A Dissertation on Parties* (1733–34) and *Idea of a Patriot King* (1738).

bolívar ('bɒlɪˌvɑː; *Spanish* bo'liβar) *n, pl* **-vars** *or* **-vares** (-βares). the standard monetary unit of Venezuela, equal to 100 céntimos. [named after Simon BOLIVAR]

Bolivar ('bɒlɪˌvɑː; *Spanish* bo'liβar) *n* **Simon** (si'mon). 1783–1830, South American soldier and liberator. He drove the Spaniards from Venezuela, Colombia, Ecuador, and Peru and hoped to set up a republican confederation, but was prevented by separatist movements in Venezuela and Colombia (1829–30). Upper Peru became a separate state and was called Bolivia in his honour.

Bolivia (bə'lɪvɪə) *n* an inland republic in central S America: original Aymará Indian population conquered by the Incas in the 13th century; colonized by Spain from 1538; became a republic in 1825; consists of low plains in the east, with ranges of the Andes rising to over 6400 m (21 000 ft.) and the Altiplano, a plateau averaging 3900 m (13 000 ft.) in the west; contains some of the world's highest inhabited regions; important producer of tin and other minerals. Official languages: Spanish, Quechua, and Aymara. Religion: Roman Catholic. Currency: boliviano. Capital: La Paz (administrative); Sucre (judicial). Pop.: 7 957 000 (1998 est.). Area: 1 098 580 sq. km (424 260 sq. miles). ▸ **Bo'livian** *adj, n*

boliviano (bəˌlɪvɪ'ɑːnəʊ; *Spanish* boli'vjano) *n, pl* **-nos** (-nəʊz; *Spanish* -nos). (until 1963 and from 1987) the standard monetary unit of Bolivia, equal to 100 centavos.

boll (bəʊl) *n* the fruit of such plants as flax and cotton, consisting of a rounded capsule containing the seeds. [C13: from Dutch *bolle;* related to Old English *bolla* BOWL[1]]

Böll (*German* bœl) *n* **Heinrich** ('haɪnrɪç) **(Theodor).** 1917–85, German novelist and short-story writer; his novels include *Group Portrait with Lady* (1971): Nobel prize for literature 1972.

bollard ('bɒlɑːd, 'bɒləd) *n* **1** a strong wooden or metal post mounted on a wharf, quay, etc., used for securing mooring lines. **2** *Brit.* a small post or marker placed on a kerb or traffic island to make it conspicuous to motorists. **3** *Mountaineering.* an outcrop of rock or pillar of ice that may be used to belay a rope. [C14: perhaps from BOLE[1] + -ARD]

bollocking ('bɒləkɪŋ) *n Slang.* a severe telling-off; dressing-down. [from *bollock* (vb) in the sense "to reprimand"]

bollocks ('bɒləks), **ballocks,** *or U.S.* **bollix** ('bɒlɪks) *Taboo slang.* ◆ *pl n* **1** another word for **testicles. 2** nonsense; rubbish. ◆ *interj* **3** an exclamation of annoyance, disbelief, etc. ◆ *vb* (usually foll. by *up*) **4** to muddle or botch. [Old English *beallucas,* diminutive (pl) of *beallu* (unattested); see BALL[1]]

boll weevil *n* a greyish weevil, *Anthonomus grandis,* of the southern U.S. and Mexico, whose larvae live in and destroy cotton bolls. See also **weevil** (sense 1).

bollworm ('bəʊlˌwɜːm) *n* any of various moth caterpillars, such as *Pectinophora* (or *Platyedra*) *gossypiella* (**pink bollworm**), that feed on and destroy cotton bolls.

Bollywood ('bɒlɪˌwʊd) *n Informal.* **a** the Indian film industry. **b** (*as modifier*): *a Bollywood star.* [C20: from BO(MBAY) + (HO)LLYWOOD]

bolo ('bəʊləʊ) *n, pl* **-los.** a large single-edged knife, originating in the Philippines. [Philippine Spanish, probably from a native word]

Bologna[1] (bə'ləʊnjə; *Italian* bo'loɲɲa) *n* a city in N Italy, at the foot of the Apennines: became a free city in the Middle Ages; university (1088). Pop.: 386 491 (1996 est.). Ancient name: **Bononia** (bə'nəʊnɪə). ▸ **Bolognese** (ˌbɒlə'niːz, -'neɪz) *adj, n*

Bologna[2] (bə'ləʊnjə; *Italian* bo'loɲɲa) *n* **Giovanni da.** See **Giambologna.**

bologna sausage *n Chiefly U.S. and Canadian.* a large smoked sausage made of seasoned mixed meats. Also called: **baloney, boloney,** (esp. Brit.) **polony.**

bolometer (bəʊ'lɒmɪtə) *n* a sensitive instrument for measuring radiant energy by the increase in the resistance of an electrical conductor. [C19: from *bol-,* from Greek *bolē* ray of light, stroke, from *ballein* to throw + -METER] ▸ **bolometric** (ˌbəʊlə'metrɪk) *adj* ▸ ˌ**bolo'metrically** *adv* ▸ **bo'lometry** *n*

boloney (bə'ləʊnɪ) *n* **1** a variant spelling of **baloney. 2** *Chiefly U.S.* another name for **bologna sausage.**

Bolshevik ('bɒlʃɪvɪk) *n, pl* **-viks** *or* **-viki** (-'viːkɪ). **1** (formerly) a Russian Communist. Compare **Menshevik. 2** any Communist. **3** (*often not cap.*) *Informal and derogatory.* any political radical, esp. a revolutionary. [C20: from Russian *Bol'shevik* majority, from *bol'shoi* great; from the fact that this group formed a majority of the Russian Social Democratic Party in 1903] ▸ **'Bolsheˌvism** *n* ▸ **'Bolshevist** *adj, n* ▸ ˌ**Bolshe'vistic** *adj*

bolshie *or* **bolshy** ('bɒlʃɪ) (*sometimes cap.*) *Brit. informal.* ◆ *adj* **1** difficult to manage; rebellious. **2** politically radical or left-wing. ◆ *n, pl* **-shies. 3** *Derogatory.* any political radical. [C20: shortened from BOLSHEVIK]

bolson (bəʊl'səʊn) *n Southwestern U.S.* a desert valley surrounded by mountains, with a shallow lake at the centre. [C19: from American Spanish *bolsón,* from Spanish *bolsa* purse, from Late Latin *bursa* bag; see PURSE]

bolster ('bəʊlstə) *vb* (*tr*). **1** (often foll. by *up*) to support or reinforce; strengthen: *to bolster morale.* **2** to prop up with a pillow or cushion. **3** to add padding to: *to bolster a dress.* ◆ *n* **4** a long narrow pillow or cushion. **5** any pad or padded support. **6** *Architect.* a short horizontal length of timber fixed to the top of a post to increase the bearing area and reduce the span of the supported beam. **7** a cold chisel having a broad blade splayed towards the cutting edge, used for cutting stone slabs, etc. [Old English *bolster;* related to Old Norse *bolstr,* Old High German *bolstar,* Dutch *bulster*] ▸ **'bolsterer** *n* ▸ **'bolstering** *n, adj*

bolt[1] (bəʊlt) *n* **1** a bar that can be slid into a socket to lock a door, gate, etc. **2** a bar or rod that forms part of a locking mechanism and is moved by a key or a knob. **3** a metal rod or pin that has a head at one end and a screw thread at the other to take a nut. **4** a sliding bar in a breech-loading firearm that ejects the empty cartridge, replaces it with a new one, and closes the breech. **5** a flash of lightning. **6** a sudden start or movement, esp. in order to escape: *they made a bolt for the door.* **7** *U.S.* a sudden desertion, esp. from a political party. **8** a roll of something, such as cloth, wallpaper, etc. **9** an arrow, esp. for a crossbow. **10** *Printing.* a folded edge on a sheet of paper that is removed when cutting to size. **11** *Mountaineering.* short for **expansion bolt. 12 a bolt from the blue.** a sudden, unexpected, and usually unwelcome event. **13 shoot one's bolt.** to exhaust one's efforts: *the runner had shot his bolt.* ◆ *vb* **14** (*tr*) to secure or lock with or as with a bolt or bolts: *bolt your doors.* **15** (*tr*) to eat hurriedly: *don't bolt your food.* **16** (*intr;* usually foll. by *from* or *out*) to move or jump suddenly: *he bolted from the chair.* **17** (*intr*) (esp. of a horse) to start hurriedly and run away without warning. **18** (*tr*) to roll or make (cloth, wallpaper, etc.) into bolts. **19** *U.S.* to desert (a political party, etc.). **20** (*intr*) (of cultivated plants) to produce flowers and seeds prematurely. **21** (*tr*) to cause (a wild animal) to leave its lair; start: *terriers were used for bolting rats.* ◆ *adv* **22** stiffly, firmly, or rigidly (archaic except in the phrase **bolt upright**). [Old English *bolt* arrow; related to Old High German *bolz* bolt for a crossbow]

bolt[2] *or* **boult** (bəʊlt) *vb* (*tr*) **1** to pass (flour, a powder, etc.) through a sieve. **2** to examine and separate. [C13: from Old French *bulter,* probably of Germanic origin; compare Old High German *būtil* bag] ▸ **'bolter** *or* **'boulter** *n*

Bolt (bəʊlt) *n* **Robert (Oxton).** 1924–95, British playwright. His plays include *A Man for All Seasons* (1960) and he also wrote a number of screenplays.

bolter ('bəʊltə) *n Austral. informal.* **1** an outsider in a contest or race. **2** *History.* an escaped convict; bushranger.

bolt hole *n* a place of escape from danger.

Bolton ('bəʊltən) *n* **1** a town in NW England, in Bolton unitary authority, Greater Manchester: centre of the woollen trade since the 14th century; later important for cotton. Pop.: 139 020 (1991). **2** a unitary authority in NW England, in Greater Manchester. Pop.: 258 584 (1991 est.). Area: 140 sq. km (54 sq. miles).

bolt-on *adj* supplementary or additional: *a bolt-on prologue.*

boltonia (bəʊl'təʊnɪə) *n* any North American plant of the genus *Boltonia,* having daisy-like flowers with white, violet, or pinkish rays: family *Compositae* (composites). [C18: New Latin, named after James *Bolton,* C18 English botanist]

boltrope ('bəʊltˌrəʊp) *n Nautical.* a rope sewn to the foot or luff of a sail to strengthen it. [C17: from BOLT[1] + ROPE]

Boltzmann (*German* 'bɔltsman) *n* **Ludwig** ('luːtvɪç). 1844–1906, Austrian physicist. He established the principle of the equipartition of energy and developed the kinetic theory of gases with J. C. Maxwell.

Boltzmann constant *n Physics.* the ratio of the gas constant to the Avogadro constant, equal to $1.380\ 622 \times 10^{-23}$ joule per kelvin. Symbol: k

bolus ('bəʊləs) *n, pl* **-luses. 1** a small round soft mass, esp. of chewed food. **2** a large pill or tablet used in veterinary and clinical medicine. **3** another word for **bole**[2]. [C17: from New Latin, from Greek *bōlos* clod, lump]

Bolzano (*Italian* bol'tsano) *n* a city in NE Italy, in Trentino-Alto Adige: belonged to Austria until 1919. Pop.: 100 380 (1990). German name: **Bozen.**

boma ('boːma) *n* (in central and E Africa) **1** an enclosure, esp. a palisade or fence of thorn bush, set up to protect a camp, herd of animals, etc. **2a** a police post. **2b** a magistrate's office. [C19: from Swahili]

Boma ('bəʊmə) *n* a port in the Democratic Republic of the Congo (formerly Zaïre), on the Congo River, capital of the Belgian Congo until 1926: forest products. Pop.: 135 284 (1994 est.).

bomb (bɒm) *n* **1a** a hollow projectile containing explosive, incendiary, or other destructive substance, esp. one carried by aircraft. **1b** (*as modifier*): *bomb dis-*

posal; a bomb bay. **1c** (*in combination*): *a bombload; bombproof.* **2** any container filled with explosive: *a car bomb; a letter bomb.* **3 the bomb.** a hydrogen or atomic bomb considered as the ultimate destructive weapon. **4** a round or pear-shaped mass of volcanic rock, solidified from molten lava that has been thrown into the air. **5** *Med.* a container for radioactive material, applied therapeutically to any part of the body: *a cobalt bomb.* **6** *Brit. slang.* a large sum of money (esp. in the phrase **make a bomb**). **7** *U.S. and Canadian slang.* a disastrous failure: *the new play was a total bomb.* **8** *Austral. and N.Z. slang.* an old or dilapidated motorcar. **9** *American football.* a very long high pass. **10 like a bomb.** *Brit. and N.Z. informal.* with great speed or success; very well (esp. in the phrase **go like a bomb**). ◆ *vb* **11** to attack with or as if with a bomb or bombs; drop bombs (on). **12** (*intr; often foll. by off, along, etc.*) *Informal.* to move or drive very quickly. **13** (*intr*) *Slang, chiefly U.S. and Canadian.* to fail disastrously; be a flop: *the new play bombed.* ◆ See also **bomb out.** [C17: from French *bombe,* from Italian *bomba,* probably from Latin *bombus* a booming sound, from Greek *bombos,* of imitative origin; compare Old Norse *bumba* drum]

bombacaceous (ˌbɒmbəˈkeɪʃəs) *adj* of, relating to, or belonging to the *Bombacaceae,* a family of tropical trees, including the kapok tree and baobab, that have very thick stems, often with water-storing tissue. [C19: from New Latin *Bombācāceae,* from Medieval Latin *bombāx* cotton, from Latin *bombyx* silkworm, silk, from Greek *bombux*]

bombard *vb* (bɒmˈbɑːd). (*tr*) **1** to attack with concentrated artillery fire or bombs. **2** to attack with vigour and persistence: *the boxer bombarded his opponent with blows to the body.* **3** to attack verbally, esp. with questions: *the journalists bombarded her with questions.* **4** *Physics.* to direct high-energy particles or photons against (atoms, nuclei, etc.), esp. to produce ions or nuclear transformations. ◆ *n* (ˈbɒmbɑːd). **5** an ancient type of cannon that threw stone balls. [C15: from Old French *bombarder* to pelt, from *bombarde* stone-throwing cannon, probably from Latin *bombus* booming sound; see BOMB] ▸ **bomˈbardment** *n*

bombardier (ˌbɒmbəˈdɪə) *n* **1** the member of a bomber aircrew responsible for aiming and releasing the bombs. **2** *Brit.* a noncommissioned rank below the rank of sergeant in the Royal Artillery. **3** Also called: **bombardier beetle.** any of various small carabid beetles of the genus *Brachinus,* esp. *B. crepitans* of Europe, which defend themselves by ejecting a jet of volatile fluid. [C16: from Old French: one directing a bombard; see BOMBARD]

Bombardier (ˌbɒmbəˈdɪə) *n Canadian trademark.* a snow tractor, typically having caterpillar tracks at the rear and skis at the front. [C20: named after J. A. *Bombardier,* Canadian inventor and manufacturer]

bombardon (ˈbɒmbədən, bɒmˈbɑːdᵊn) *n* **1** a brass instrument of the tuba type, similar to a sousaphone. **2** a 16-foot bass reed stop on an organ. [C19: from Italian *bombardone;* see BOMBARD]

bombast (ˈbɒmbæst) *n* **1** pompous and grandiloquent language. **2** *Obsolete.* material used for padding. [C16: from Old French *bombace,* from Medieval Latin *bombāx* cotton; see BOMBACACEOUS] ▸ **bomˈbastic** *adj* ▸ **bomˈbastically** *adv*

Bombay (bɒmˈbeɪ) *n* a port in W India, capital of Maharashtra state, on the Arabian Sea: ceded by Portugal to England in 1661 and of major importance in British India; commercial and industrial centre, esp. for cotton. Pop.: 9 925 891 (1991). Official and Hindi name: **Mumbai.**

Bombay duck *n* a teleost fish, *Harpodon nehereus,* that resembles and is related to the lizard fishes: family *Harpodontidae.* It is eaten dried with curry dishes as a savoury. Also called: **bummalo.** [C19: changed from *bombil* (see BUMMALO) through association with Bombay, from which it was exported]

bombazine *or* **bombasine** (ˌbɒmbəˈziːn, ˈbɒmbəˌziːn) *n* a twilled fabric, esp. one with a silk warp and worsted weft, formerly worn dyed black for mourning. [C16: from Old French *bombasin,* from Latin *bombȳcinus* silken, from *bombyx* silkworm, silk; see BOMBACACEOUS]

bomb calorimeter *n Chem.* a device for determining heats of combustion by igniting a sample in a high pressure of oxygen in a sealed vessel and measuring the resulting rise in temperature: used for measuring the calorific value of foods.

bombe (bɒmb) *n* **1** Also called: **bombe glacée.** a dessert of ice cream lined or filled with custard, cake crumbs, etc. **2** a mould shaped like a bomb in which this dessert is made. [C19: from French, literally: BOMB; from its rounded shape]

bombé (bɒmˈbeɪ; *French* bɔ̃be) *adj* (of furniture) having a projecting swollen shape. [French, literally: bomb-shaped, from *bombe* BOMB]

bombed (bɒmd) *adj Slang.* under the influence of alcohol or drugs (esp. in the phrase **bombed out of one's mind** *or* **skull**).

bomber (ˈbɒmə) *n* **1** a military aircraft designed to carry out bombing missions. **2** a person who plants bombs. **3** *Navy slang.* a Polaris submarine.

Bomberg (ˈbɒmbɜːg) *n* **David.** 1890–1957, British painter, noted esp. for his landscapes.

bomber jacket *n* a short jacket finishing at the waist with an elasticated band, usually having a zip front and cuffed sleeves.

bombinate (ˈbɒmbɪˌneɪt) *vb* (*intr*) *Literary.* to make a buzzing noise. Also (rare): **bombilate.** [C19: from Latin *bombināre,* variant of *bombilāre* to buzz] ▸ ˌ**bombiˈnation** *n*

bombing run *n* an approach by a bomber to a target.

bombora (bɒmˈbɔːrə) *n Austral.* **1** a submerged reef. **2** a turbulent area of sea over such a reef. [from a native Australian language]

bomb out *vb* (*adv; tr, usually passive*) to make homeless by bombing: *24 families in this street have been bombed out.*

bombshell (ˈbɒmˌʃel) *n* **1** (esp. formerly) a bomb or artillery shell. **2** a shocking or unwelcome surprise: *the news of his death was a bombshell.* **3** *Informal.* an attractive girl or woman (esp. in the phrase **blonde bombshell**).

bombsight (ˈbɒmˌsaɪt) *n* a mechanical or electronic device in an aircraft for aiming bombs.

bomb site *n* an area where the buildings have been destroyed by bombs.

bombycid (ˈbɒmbɪsɪd) *n* **1** any moth, including the silkworm moth, of the family *Bombycidae,* most of which occur in Africa and SE Asia. ◆ *adj* **2** of, relating to, or belonging to the *Bombycidae.* [C19: from Latin *bombyx* silkworm]

Bomu (ˈbəʊmuː) *or* **Mbomu** (ᵊmˈbəʊmuː) *n* a river in central Africa, rising in the SE Central African Republic and flowing west into the Uele River, forming the Ubangi River. Length: about 800 km (500 miles).

Bon[1] (bɔːn) *n* **1** Also called: **Feast** (*or* **Festival**) **of Lanterns.** an annual festival celebrated by Japanese Buddhists. **2a** the pre-Buddhist priests of Tibet or one such priest. **2b** their religion. [from Japanese *bon,* originally *Urabon,* from Sanskrit *ullambana* hanging upside down]

Bon[2] (bɒn) *n* **Cape.** a peninsula of NE Tunisia.

Bona (ˈbəʊnə) *n* **Mount.** a mountain in S Alaska, in the Wrangell Mountains. Height: 5005 m (16 420 ft.).

bona fide *adj* (ˈbəʊnə ˈfaɪdɪ). **1** real or genuine: *a bona fide manuscript.* **2** undertaken in good faith: *a bona fide agreement.* ◆ *n* (ˈbɔːnə faɪd). **3** *Irish informal.* a public house licensed to remain open after normal hours to serve bona fide travellers. [C16: from Latin]

bona fides (ˈbəʊnə ˈfaɪdiːz) *n Law.* good faith; honest intention. [Latin]

Bonaire (bɒnˈɛə) *n* an island in the S Caribbean, in the E Netherlands Antilles: one of the Leeward Islands. Chief town: Kralendijk. Pop.: 12 533 (1994 est.). Area: about 288 sq. km (111 sq. miles).

bonanza (bəˈnænzə) *n* **1** a source, usually sudden and unexpected, of luck or wealth. **2** *U.S. and Canadian.* a mine or vein rich in ore. [C19: from Spanish, literally: calm sea, hence, good luck, from Medieval Latin *bonacia,* from Latin *bonus* good + *malacia* dead calm, from Greek *malakia* softness]

Bonaparte (ˈbəʊnəˌpɑːt; *French* bɔnapart) *n* **1** See **Napoleon I. 2 Jérôme** (ʒerom), brother of Napoleon I. 1784–1860, king of Westphalia (1807–13). **3 Joseph** (ʒozɛf), brother of Napoleon I. 1768–1844, king of Naples (1806–08) and of Spain (1808–13). **4 Louis** (lwi), brother of Napoleon I. 1778–1846, king of Holland (1806–10). **5 Lucien** (lysjɛ̃), brother of Napoleon I. 1775–1840, prince of Canino.

Bonapartism (ˈbəʊnəpɑːˌtɪzəm) *n* **1** a political system resembling the rules of the Bonapartes, esp. Napoleon I and Napoleon III: centralized government by a military dictator, who enjoys popular support given expression in plebiscites. **2** (esp. in France) support for the government or dynasty of Napoleon Bonaparte. ▸ **ˈBonaˌpartist** *n*

Bonar Law (ˈbɒnə lɔː) *n* **Andrew.** See (Andrew Bonar) **Law.**

bona vacantia (ˈbəʊnə vəˈkæntɪə) *pl n Law.* unclaimed goods.

Bonaventura (ˌbɒnəvenˈtjʊərə) *or* **Bonaventure** (ˈbɒnəˌventʃə) *n* **Saint,** called *the Seraphic Doctor.* 1221–74, Italian Franciscan monk, mystic, theologian, and philosopher; author of a *Life of St Francis* and *Journey of the Soul to God.* Feast day: July 14.

bonbon (ˈbɒnbɒn) *n* a sweet. [C19: from French, originally a children's word from *bon* good]

bonce (bɒns) *n Brit. slang.* the head. [C19 (originally: a type of large playing marble): of unknown origin]

bond (bɒnd) *n* **1** something that binds, fastens, or holds together, such as a chain or rope. **2** (*often pl*) something that brings or holds people together; tie: *a bond of friendship.* **3** (*pl*) something that restrains or imprisons; captivity or imprisonment. **4** something that governs behaviour; obligation; duty. **5** a written or spoken agreement, esp. a promise: *marriage bond.* **6** adhesive quality or strength. **7** *Finance.* a certificate of debt issued in order to raise funds. It carries a fixed rate of interest and is repayable with or without security at a specified future date. **8** *Law.* a written acknowledgment of an obligation to pay a sum or to perform a contract. **9** *Insurance, U.S. and Canadian.* a policy guaranteeing payment of a stated sum to an employer in compensation for financial losses incurred through illegal or unauthorized acts of an employee. **10** any of various arrangements of bricks or stones in a wall in which they overlap so as to provide strength. **11** See **chemical bond. 12** See **bond paper. 13 in bond.** *Commerce.* deposited in a bonded warehouse. ◆ *vb* (*mainly tr*) **14** (*also intr*) to hold or be held together, as by a rope or an adhesive; bind; connect. **15** *Aeronautics.* to join (metallic parts of an aircraft) together such that they are electrically interconnected. **16** to put or hold (goods) in bond. **17** *Law.* to place under bond. **18** *Finance.* to issue bonds on; mortgage. **19** to arrange (bricks, etc.) in a bond. [C13: from Old Norse *band;* see BAND[2]]

Bond (bɒnd) *n* **Edward.** born 1934, British dramatist: his plays, including *Saved* (1965), *Lear* (1971), *Restoration* (1981), and *In the Company of Men* (1990), are noted for their violent imagery and socialist commitment.

bondage (ˈbɒndɪdʒ) *n* **1** slavery or serfdom; servitude. **2** Also called: **villeinage.** (in medieval Europe) the condition and status of unfree peasants who provided labour and other services for their lord in return for holdings of land. **3** a sexual practice in which one partner is physically bound.

bonded (ˈbɒndɪd) *adj* **1** *Finance.* consisting of, secured by, or operating under a bond or bonds. **2** *Commerce.* deposited in a bonded warehouse; placed or stored in bond.

bonded warehouse *n* a warehouse in which dutiable goods are deposited until duty is paid or the goods are cleared for export.

bondholder (ˈbɒndˌhəʊldə) *n* an owner of one or more bonds issued by a company or other institution.

Bondi (ˈbɒndɪ) *n* Sir **Hermann.** born 1919, British mathematician and cosmologist, born in Austria; joint originator (with Sir Fred Hoyle and Thomas Gold) of the steady-state theory of the universe.

Bondi Beach (ˈbɒndaɪ) *n* a beach in Sydney, Australia, popular with surfers.

bonding (ˈbɒndɪŋ) *n* the process by which individuals become emotionally attached to one another. See also **pair bond.**

bondmaid ('bɒnd,meɪd) *n* an unmarried female serf or slave.

bond paper *n* a superior quality of strong white paper, used esp. for writing and typing.

bondservant ('bɒnd,sɜːvənt) *n* a serf or slave.

bondsman ('bɒndzmən) *n, pl* **-men. 1** *Law.* a person bound by bond to act as surety for another. **2** another word for **bondservant.**

bondstone ('bɒnd,stəʊn) *n* a long stone or brick laid in a wall as a header. Also called: **bonder.**

bond washing *n* a series of illegal deals in bonds made with the intention of avoiding taxation.

bone (bəʊn) *n* **1** any of the various structures that make up the skeleton in most vertebrates. **2** the porous rigid tissue of which these parts are made, consisting of a matrix of collagen and inorganic salts, esp. calcium phosphate, interspersed with canals and small holes. Related adjs.: **osseous, osteal. 3** something consisting of bone or a bonelike substance. **4** (*pl*) the human skeleton or body: *they laid his bones to rest; come and rest your bones.* **5** a thin strip of whalebone, light metal, plastic, etc., used to stiffen corsets and brassieres. **6** (*pl*) the essentials (esp. in the phrase **the bare bones**): *to explain the bones of a situation.* **7** (*pl*) dice. **8** (*pl*) an informal nickname for a **doctor. 9 close to** *or* **near the bone. 9a** risqué or indecent: *his jokes are rather close to the bone.* **9b** in poverty; destitute. **10 feel in one's bones.** to have an intuition of. **11 have a bone to pick.** to have grounds for a quarrel. **12 make no bones about. 12a** to be direct and candid about. **12b** to have no scruples about. **13 point the bone.** (often foll. by *at*) *Austral.* **13a** to wish bad luck (on). **13b** to threaten to bring about the downfall (of). ◆ *vb* (*mainly tr*) **14** to remove the bones from (meat for cooking, etc.). **15** to stiffen (a corset, etc.) by inserting bones. **16** to fertilize with bone meal. **17** *Brit.* a slang word for **steal.** ◆ See also **bone up.** [Old English *bān;* related to Old Norse *bein,* Old Frisian *bēn,* Old High German *bein*] ► **'boneless** *adj*

Bône (*French* bon) *n* a former name of **Annaba.**

bone ash *n* the residue obtained when bones are burned in air, consisting mainly of calcium phosphate. It is used as a fertilizer and in the manufacture of bone china.

bone bed *n Geology.* a sediment containing large quantities of fossilized animal remains, such as bones, teeth, scales, etc.

boneblack ('bəʊn,blæk) *n* a black residue from the destructive distillation of bones, containing about 10 per cent carbon and 80 per cent calcium phosphate, used as a decolorizing agent and pigment.

bone china *n* porcelain containing bone ash.

bone-dry *adj Informal.* **a** completely dry: *a bone-dry well.* **b** (*postpositive*): *the well was bone dry.*

bonefish ('bəʊn,fɪʃ) *n, pl* **-fish** *or* **-fishes. 1** a silvery marine clupeoid game fish, *Albula vulpes,* occurring in warm shallow waters: family *Albulidae.* **2** a similar related fish, *Dixonina nemoptera,* of the Pacific Ocean.

bonehead ('bəʊn,hɛd) *n Slang.* a stupid or obstinate person. ► **,bone'headed** *adj*

bone idle *adj* very idle; extremely lazy.

bone marrow *n* See **marrow**[1] (sense 1).

bone meal *n* the product of dried and ground animal bones, used as a fertilizer or in stock feeds.

bone of contention *n* the grounds or subject of a dispute.

bone oil *n* a dark brown pungent oil, containing pyridine and hydrocarbons, obtained by the destructive distillation of bones.

boner ('bəʊnə) *n* **1** *Slang.* a blunder. **2** *N.Z.* a low-grade slaughtered animal suitable for use in pies, sausages, etc.

boneset ('bəʊn,sɛt) *n* any of various North American plants of the genus *Eupatorium,* esp. *E. perfoliatum,* which has flat clusters of small white flowers: family *Compositae* (composites). Also called: **agueweed, feverwort, thoroughwort.**

bonesetter ('bəʊn,sɛtə) *n* a person who sets broken or dislocated bones, esp. one who has no formal medical qualifications.

boneshaker ('bəʊn,ʃeɪkə) *n* **1** an early type of bicycle having solid tyres and no springs. **2** *Slang.* any decrepit or rickety vehicle.

bone turquoise *n* fossilized bone or tooth stained blue with iron phosphate and used as a gemstone. Also called: **odontolite.**

bone up *vb* (*adv;* when *intr,* usually foll. by *on*) *Informal.* to study intensively.

boneyard ('bəʊn,jɑːd) *n* an informal name for a **cemetery.**

bonfire ('bɒn,faɪə) *n* a large outdoor fire. [C15: alteration (through influence of French *bon* good) of *bone-fire;* from the use of bones as fuel]

bong[1] (bɒŋ) *n* **1** a deep reverberating sound, as of a large bell. ◆ *vb* (*intr*) **2** to make a deep reverberating sound. [C20: of imitative origin]

bong[2] (bɒŋ) *n* a type of water pipe for smoking marijuana, crack, etc. [C20: of unknown origin]

bongo[1] ('bɒŋgəʊ) *n, pl* **-go** *or* **-gos.** a rare spiral-horned antelope, *Boocercus* (or *Taurotragus*) *eurycerus,* inhabiting forests of central Africa. The coat is bright red-brown with narrow cream stripes. [of African origin]

bongo[2] ('bɒŋgəʊ) *n, pl* **-gos** *or* **-goes.** a small bucket-shaped drum, usually one of a pair, played by beating with the fingers. [American Spanish, probably of imitative origin]

Bongo ('bɒŋgəʊ) *n* **Omar.** original name *Albert Bernard Bongo.* born 1935, Gabonese statesman; president of Gabon from 1967.

bonham ('bɒnəv) *n Irish.* a piglet. [C19: from Irish Gaelic *banbh*]

Bonheur (*French* bɔnœr) *n* **Rosa** (roza). 1822–99, French painter of animals.

Bonhoeffer (*German* 'boːnhœfər) *n* **Dietrich** ('diːtrɪç). 1906–45, German Lutheran theologian: executed by the Nazis.

bonhomie ('bɒnəmiː; *French* bɔnɔmi) *n* exuberant friendliness. [C18: from French, from *bonhomme* good-humoured fellow, from *bon* good + *homme* man]

bonhomous ('bɒnəməs) *adj* exhibiting bonhomie.

Boniface ('bɒnɪ,feɪs) *n* **Saint.** original name *Wynfrith.* ?680–?755 A.D. Anglo-Saxon missionary: archbishop of Mainz (746–755). Feast day: June 5.

Boniface VIII *n* original name *Benedict Caetano.* ?1234–1303, pope (1294–1303).

Bonington ('bɒnɪŋtən) *n* **1** Sir **Chris(tian John Storey).** born 1934, British mountaineer and writer; led 1970 Annapurna I and 1975 Everest expeditions; reached Everest summit in 1985. **2 Richard Parkes.** 1801–28, British painter of landscapes and historical scenes.

Bonin Islands ('bəʊnɪn) *pl n* a group of 27 volcanic islands in the W Pacific: occupied by the U.S. after World War II; returned to Japan in 1968. Largest island: Chichijima. Area: 103 sq. km (40 sq. miles). Japanese name: **Ogasawara Gunto.**

bonism ('bəʊ,nɪzəm) *n* the doctrine that the world is good, although not the best of all possible worlds. [C19: from Latin *bonus* good + -ISM] ► **'bonist** *n, adj*

bonito (bə'niːtəʊ) *n, pl* **-tos. 1** any of various small tunny-like marine food fishes of the genus *Sarda,* of warm Atlantic and Pacific waters: family *Scombridae* (tunnies and mackerels). **2** any of various similar or related fishes, such as *Katsuwonus pelamis* (**oceanic bonito**), the flesh of which is dried and flaked and used in Japanese cookery. [C16: from Spanish *bonito,* from Latin *bonus* good]

bonk (bɒŋk) *vb Informal.* **1** (*tr*) to hit. **2** to have sexual intercourse (with). [C20: probably of imitative origin] ► **'bonking** *n*

bonkbuster ('bɒŋk,bʌstə) *Informal.* a novel characterized by graphic descriptions of the heroine's frequent sexual encounters. [C20: from BONK (sense 2) + (BLOCK)BUSTER]

bonkers ('bɒŋkəz) *adj Slang, chiefly Brit.* mad; crazy. [C20 (originally in the sense: slightly drunk, tipsy): of unknown origin]

bon mot (*French* bɔ̃ mo) *n, pl* **bons mots** (bɔ̃ mo). a clever and fitting remark. [French, literally: good word]

Bonn (bɒn; *German* bɔn) *n* a city in W Germany, in North Rhine-Westphalia on the Rhine: the former capital (1949–90) of West Germany; university (1786). Pop.: 291 431 (1996 est.).

Bonnard (*French* bɔnar) *n* **Pierre** (pjɛr). 1867–1947, French painter and lithographer, noted for the effects of light and colour in his landscapes and sunlit interiors.

bonne *French.* (bɔn) *n* a housemaid or female servant. [C18: from feminine of *bon* good]

bonne bouche *French.* (bɔn buʃ) *n, pl* ***bonnes bouches*** (bɔn buʃ). a tasty titbit or morsel. [literally: good mouth(ful)]

bonnet ('bɒnɪt) *n* **1** any of various hats worn, esp. formerly, by women and girls, usually framing the face and tied with ribbons under the chin. **2** (in Scotland) Also called: **bunnet** ('bʌnɪt). **2a** a soft cloth cap. **2b** formerly, a flat brimless cap worn by men. **3** the hinged metal part of a motor vehicle body that provides access to the engine, or to the luggage space in a rear-engined vehicle. **4** a cowl on a chimney. **5** *Nautical.* a piece of sail laced to the foot of a foresail to give it greater area in light winds. **6** (in the U.S. and Canada) a headdress of feathers worn by some tribes of American Indians, esp. formerly as a sign of war. [C14: from Old French *bonet,* from Medieval Latin *abonnis,* of unknown origin]

bonnet monkey *n* an Indian macaque, *Macaca radiata,* with a bonnet-like tuft of hair.

bonnet rouge *French.* (bɔnɛ ruʒ) *n* **1** a red cap worn by ardent supporters of the French Revolution. **2** an extremist or revolutionary. [literally: red cap]

Bonnie Prince Charlie ('bɒnɪ) *n* See (Charles Edward) **Stuart.**

bonny ('bɒnɪ) *adj* **-nier, -niest. 1** *Scot. and northern English dialect.* beautiful or handsome: *a bonny lass.* **2** merry or lively: *a bonny family.* **3** good or fine: *a bonny house.* **4** (esp. of babies) plump. **5** *Scot. and northern English dialect.* considerable; to be reckoned with: *cost a bonny penny.* ◆ *adv* **6** *Informal.* agreeably or well: *to speak bonny.* [C15: of uncertain origin; perhaps from Old French *bon* good, from Latin *bonus*] ► **'bonnily** *adv*

Bonny ('bɒnɪ) *n* **Bight of.** a wide bay at the E end of the Gulf of Guinea off the coasts of Nigeria and Cameroon. Former name (until 1975): **Bight of Biafra.**

Bonporti (*Italian* bon'pɔrti) *n* **Francesco Antonio.** 1672–1749, Italian composer and violinist, noted esp. for his *Invenzioni* (1712), a series of short instrumental suites.

bonsai ('bɒnsaɪ) *n, pl* **-sai. 1** the art of growing dwarfed ornamental varieties of trees or shrubs in small shallow pots or trays by selective pruning, etc. **2** a tree or shrub grown by this method. [C20: Japanese: plant grown in a pot, from *bon* basin, bowl + *sai* to plant]

bonsela (bɒn'sɛlə) *n S. African. informal.* a present or gratuity. Also called: **bansela, pasela** (pə'sɛlə). [from Zulu *Ibanselo* a gift]

bonspiel ('bɒn,spiːl, -spəl) *n* a curling match. [C16: probably from Low German; compare Flemish *bonespel* children's game; see SPIEL]

bontebok ('bɒntɪ,bʌk) *n, pl* **-boks** *or* **-bok.** an antelope, *Damaliscus pygargus* (or *dorcas*), of southern Africa, having a deep reddish-brown coat with a white blaze, tail, and rump patch. [C18: Afrikaans, from *bont* pied + *bok* BUCK[1]]

Bontempelli (*Italian* bontem'pɛlli) *n* **Massimo.** 1878–1960, Italian dramatist, poet, novelist, and critic. His works include the play *Nostra Dea* (1925) and the novel *The Faithful Lover* (1953).

bon ton *French.* (bɔ̃ tɔ̃) *n Literary.* **1** sophisticated manners or breeding. **2** fashionable society. [literally: good tone]

bonus ('bəʊnəs) *n* **1** something given, paid, or received above what is due or expected: *a Christmas bonus for all employees.* **2** *Chiefly Brit.* an extra dividend allotted to shareholders out of profits. **3** *Insurance, Brit.* a dividend, esp. a percentage of net profits, distributed to policyholders either annually or when the policy matures. 4 *Brit.* a slang word for a **bribe.** [C18: from Latin *bonus* (adj) good]

bonus issue *n Brit.* an issue of shares made by a company without charge and distributed pro rata among existing shareholders. Also called: **scrip issue.**

bon vivant *French.* (bɔ̃ vivɑ̃) *n, pl* ***bons vivants*** (bɔ̃ vivɑ̃). a person who enjoys luxuries, esp. good food and drink. Also called (but not in French): **bon viveur** (ˌbɒn viːˈvɜː). [literally: good living (man)]

bon voyage (*French* bɔ̃ vwajaʒ) *sentence substitute.* a phrase used to wish a traveller a pleasant journey. [French, literally: good journey]

bonxie (ˈbɒŋksɪ) *n* a name, originally Shetland, for the **great skua** (see **skua**). [C19: probably of Scandinavian origin: compare Norwegian *bunke* heap, something dumpy]

bony (ˈbəʊnɪ) *adj* **bonier, boniest. 1** resembling or consisting of bone or bones. **2** having many bones. **3** having prominent bones: *bony cheeks.* **4** thin or emaciated: *a bony old woman.* ▸ **ˈboniness** *n*

bony fish *n* any fish of the class *Osteichthyes,* including most of the extant species, having a skeleton of bone rather than cartilage.

Bonynge (ˈbɒnɪŋ) *n* **Richard.** born 1930, Australian conductor, esp. of opera; married to the soprano Joan Sutherland.

bonze (bɒnz) *n* a Chinese or Japanese Buddhist priest or monk. [C16: from French, from Portuguese *bonzo,* from Japanese *bonsō,* from Sanskrit *bon* + *sō* priest or monk]

bonzer (ˈbɒnzə) *adj Austral. and N.Z. slang, archaic.* excellent; very good. [C20: of uncertain origin; perhaps from BONANZA]

boo (buː) *interj* **1** an exclamation uttered to startle or surprise someone, esp. a child. **2** a shout uttered to express disgust, dissatisfaction, or contempt, esp. at a theatrical production, political meeting, etc. **3 would not say boo to a goose.** is extremely timid or diffident. ◆ *vb* **boos, booing, booed. 4** to shout "boo" at (someone or something), esp. as an expression of disgust, dissatisfaction, or disapproval: *to boo the actors.*

boob (buːb) *Slang.* ◆ *n* **1** an ignorant or foolish person; booby. **2** *Brit.* an embarrassing mistake; blunder. **3** a female breast. ◆ *vb* **4** (*intr*) *Brit.* to make a blunder. [C20: back formation from BOOBY]

boobialla (ˌbuːbɪˈælə) *n Austral.* **1** another name for **golden wattle** (sense 2). **2** any of various trees or shrubs of the genus *Myoporum,* esp. *M. insulare.* [from a native Australian language]

boo-boo *n, pl* **-boos.** *Informal.* an embarrassing mistake; blunder. [C20: perhaps from nursery talk; compare BOOHOO]

boobook (ˈbuːbʊk) *n* a small spotted brown Australian owl, *Ninox boobook.*

boob tube *n Slang.* **1** a close-fitting strapless top, worn by women. **2** *Austral.* a strapless, boneless, shapeless brassiere made of a stretch fabric. **3** *Chiefly U.S. and Canadian.* a television receiver.

booby (ˈbuːbɪ) *n, pl* **-bies. 1** an ignorant or foolish person. **2** *Brit.* the losing player in a game. **3** any of several tropical marine birds of the genus *Sula:* family *Sulidae,* order *Pelecaniformes* (pelicans, cormorants, etc.). They have a straight stout bill and the plumage is white with darker markings. Compare **gannet.** [C17: from Spanish *bobo,* from Latin *balbus* stammering]

booby hatch *n* **1** a hoodlike covering for a hatchway on a ship. **2** *U.S. slang.* a mental hospital.

booby prize *n* a mock prize given to the person having the lowest score or giving the worst performance in a competition.

booby trap *n* **1** a hidden explosive device primed in such a way as to be set off by an unsuspecting victim. **2** a trap for an unsuspecting person, esp. one intended as a practical joke, such as an object balanced above a door to fall on the person who opens it. ◆ *vb* **booby-trap, -traps, -trapping, -trapped. 3** (*tr*) to set a booby trap in or on (a building or object) or for (a person).

boodle (ˈbuːdᵊl) *Slang.* ◆ *n* **1** money or valuables, esp. when stolen, counterfeit, or used as a bribe. **2** *Chiefly U.S.* another word for **caboodle.** ◆ *vb* **3** to give or receive money corruptly or illegally. [C19: from Dutch *boedel* all one's possessions, from Old Frisian *bōdel* movable goods, inheritance; see CABOODLE]

boofhead (ˈbʊfhɛd) *n Slang, chiefly Austral.* **1** a stupid person. **2** a person or animal with a large head.

boogie (ˈbuːgɪ) *Slang.* ◆ *vb* **-gies, -gieing, -gied.** (*intr*) **1** to dance to pop music. **2** to make love. ◆ *n* **3** a session of dancing to pop music. [C20: originally African-American slang, perhaps from Kongo *mbugi* devilishly good]

boogie-woogie (ˈbʊgɪˈwʊgɪ, ˈbuːgɪˈwuːgɪ) *n* a style of piano jazz using a dotted bass pattern, usually with eight notes in a bar and the harmonies of the 12-bar blues.

boohai (buːˈhaɪ) *n* **up the boohai.** *N.Z. informal.* thoroughly lost. [from the remote township of *puhoi*]

boohoo (ˌbuːˈhuː) *vb* **-hoos, -hooing, -hooed. 1** to sob or pretend to sob noisily. ◆ *n, pl* **-hoos. 2** (*sometimes pl*) distressed or pretended sobbing. [C20: nursery talk]

boo-hurrah theory *n Philosophy.* an informal term for **emotivism.**

book (bʊk) *n* **1** a number of printed or written pages bound together along one edge and usually protected by thick paper or stiff pasteboard covers. See also **hardback, paperback. 2a** a written work or composition, such as a novel, technical manual, or dictionary. **2b** (*as modifier*): *the book trade; book reviews.* **2c** (*in combination*): *bookseller; bookshop; bookshelf; bookrack.* **3** a number of blank or ruled sheets of paper bound together, used to record lessons, keep accounts, etc. **4** (*pl*) a record of the transactions of a business or society. **5** the script of a play or the libretto of an opera, musical, etc. **6** a major division of a written composition, as of a long novel or of the Bible. **7** a number of tickets, sheets, stamps, etc., fastened together along one edge. **8** *Bookmaking.* a record of the bets made on a horse race or other event. **9** (in card games) the number of tricks that must be taken by a side or player before any trick has a scoring value: *in bridge, six of the 13 tricks form the book.* **10** strict or rigid regulations, rules, or standards (esp. in the phrases **according to the book, by the book**). **11** a source of knowledge or authority: *the book of life.* **12** a telephone directory (in the phrase **in the book**). **13 the book.** (*sometimes cap.*) the Bible. **14 an open book.** a person or subject that is thoroughly understood. **15 a closed book.** a person or subject that is unknown or beyond comprehension: *chemistry is a closed book to him.* **16 bring to book.** to reprimand or require (someone) to give an explanation of his conduct. **17 close the book on.** to bring to a definite end: *we have closed the book on apartheid.* **18 close the books.** *Book-keeping.* to balance accounts in order to prepare a statement or report. **19 cook the books.** *Informal.* to make fraudulent alterations to business or other accounts. **20 in my book.** according to my view of things. **21 in someone's good** (*or* **bad**) **books.** regarded by someone with favour (or disfavour). **22 keep the books.** to keep written records of the finances of a business or other enterprise. **23 on the books. 23a** enrolled as a member. **23b** registered or recorded. **24 read (someone) like a book.** to understand (a person, his motives, character, etc.) thoroughly and clearly. **25 throw the book at. 25a** to charge with every relevant offence. **25b** to inflict the most severe punishment on. ◆ *vb* **26** to reserve (a place, passage, etc.) or engage the services of (a performer, driver, etc.) in advance: *to book a flight; to book a band.* **27** (*tr*) to take the name and address of (a person guilty of a minor offence) with a view to bringing a prosecution: *he was booked for ignoring a traffic signal.* **28** (*tr*) (of a football referee) to take the name of (a player) who grossly infringes the rules while playing, two such acts resulting in the player's dismissal from the field. **29** (*tr*) *Archaic.* to record in a book. ◆ See also **book in, book into, book out, book up.** [Old English *bōc;* related to Old Norse *bōk,* Old High German *buoh* book, Gothic *bōka* letter; see BEECH (the bark of which was used as a writing surface)]

bookbinder (ˈbʊkˌbaɪndə) *n* a person whose business or craft is binding books. ▸ **ˈbookˌbinding** *n*

bookbindery (ˈbʊkˌbaɪndərɪ) *n, pl* **-eries.** a place in which books are bound. Often shortened to **bindery.**

bookcase (ˈbʊkˌkeɪs) *n* a piece of furniture containing shelves for books, often fitted with glass doors.

book club *n* a club that sells books at low prices to members, usually by mail order, esp. on condition that they buy a minimum number.

booked up *adj* unable to offer any appointments or accept any reservations, etc.; fully booked; full up.

book end *n* one of a pair of usually ornamental supports for holding a row of books upright.

Booker Prize (ˈbʊkə) *n* an annual prize for a work of British, Commonwealth, or Irish fiction of £20,000, awarded since 1969 by the Booker McConnell engineering company.

bookie (ˈbʊkɪ) *n Informal.* short for **bookmaker.**

book in *vb* (*adv*) **1** to reserve a room for (oneself or someone else) at a hotel. **2** *Chiefly Brit.* to record something in a book or register, esp. one's arrival at a hotel.

booking (ˈbʊkɪŋ) *n* **1** *Chiefly Brit.* **1a** a reservation, as of a table or room in a hotel, seat in a theatre, or seat on a train, aircraft, etc. **1b** (*as modifier*): *the booking office at a railway station.* **2** *Theatre.* an engagement for the services of an actor or acting company.

book into *vb* (*prep*) to reserve a room for (oneself or someone else) at (a hotel).

bookish (ˈbʊkɪʃ) *adj* **1** fond of reading; studious. **2** consisting of or forming opinions or attitudes through reading rather than direct personal experience; academic: *a bookish view of life.* **3** of or relating to books: *a bookish career in publishing.* ▸ **ˈbookishly** *adv* ▸ **ˈbookishness** *n*

book-keeping *n* the skill or occupation of systematically recording business transactions. ▸ **ˈbook-ˌkeeper** *n*

book-learning *n* **1** knowledge gained from books rather than from direct personal experience. **2** formal education.

booklet (ˈbʊklɪt) *n* a thin book, esp. one having paper covers; pamphlet.

booklouse (ˈbʊkˌlaʊs) *n, pl* **-lice.** any small insect of the order *Psocoptera,* esp. *Trogium pulsatorium* (**common booklouse**), a wingless species that feeds on bookbinding paste, etc.

bookmaker (ˈbʊkˌmeɪkə) *n* a person who as an occupation accepts bets, esp. on horseraces, and pays out to winning betters. ▸ **ˈbookˌmaking** *n*

bookmark (ˈbʊkˌmɑːk) *n* **1** Also called: **bookmarker.** a strip or band of some material, such as leather or ribbon, put between the pages of a book to mark a place. **2** *Computing.* an identifier put on a website that enables the user to return to it quickly and easily. ◆ *vb* **3** (*tr*) *Computing.* to identify and store (a website) so that one can return to it quickly and easily.

bookmobile (ˈbʊkməˌbiːl) *n* the U.S. and Canadian word for **mobile library.**

book of account *n* another name for **journal** (sense 4a).

Book of Changes *n* another name for the **I Ching.**

Book of Common Prayer *n* the official book of church services of the Church of England, until 1980, when the Alternative Service Book was sanctioned.

book of hours *n* (*often caps.*) a book used esp. in monasteries during the Middle Ages that contained the prayers and offices of the canonical hours.

Book of Kells *n* See **Kells.**

Book of Mormon *n* a sacred book of the Mormon Church, believed by Mormons to be a history of certain ancient peoples in America, written on golden tablets (now lost) and revealed by the prophet Mormon to Joseph Smith.

book of original entry *n* another name for **journal** (sense 4a).

book out *vb* (*usually intr, adv*) to leave or cause to leave a hotel.

bookplate (ˈbʊkˌpleɪt) *n* a label bearing the owner's name and an individual design or coat of arms, pasted into a book.

book scorpion *n* any of various small arachnids of the order *Pseudoscorpionida* (false scorpions), esp. *Chelifer cancroides,* which are sometimes found in old books, etc.

bookstall ('bʊk,stɔːl) *n* a stall or stand where periodicals, newspapers, or books are sold. U.S. word: **newsstand.**

booksy ('bʊksɪ) *adj* inclined to be bookish or literary.

book token *n Brit.* a gift token to be exchanged for books.

book up *vb (adv)* **1** to make a reservation (for); book. **2** See **booked up.**

book value *n* **1** the value of an asset of a business according to its books. **2a** the net capital value of an enterprise as shown by the excess of book assets over book liabilities. **2b** the value of a share computed by dividing the net capital value of an enterprise by its issued shares. Compare **par value, market value.**

bookworm ('bʊk,wɜːm) *n* **1** a person excessively devoted to studying. **2** any of various small insects that feed on the binding paste of books, esp. the book louse.

bool (bʊl) *Scot.* ◆ *n* **1** a bowling bowl. **2** a playing marble. **3** *(pl)* the game of bowls or marbles. ◆ *vb (intr)* **4** to play bowls. [Scot. variant of BOWL[2]]

Boole (buːl) *n* **George.** 1815–64, English mathematician. In *Mathematical Analysis of Logic* (1847) and *An Investigation of the Laws of Thought* (1854), he applied mathematical formulae to logic, creating Boolean algebra.

Boolean algebra ('buːlɪən) *n* a system of symbolic logic devised by George Boole to codify nonmathematical logical operations. It is used in computers.

boom[1] (buːm) *vb* **1** to make a deep prolonged resonant sound, as of thunder or artillery fire. **2** to prosper or cause to prosper vigorously and rapidly: *business boomed.* ◆ *n* **3** a deep prolonged resonant sound: *the boom of the sea.* **4** the cry of certain animals, esp. the bittern. **5** a period of high economic growth characterized by rising wages, profits, and prices, full employment, and high levels of investment, trade, and other economic activity. Compare **depression** (sense 5). [C15: perhaps from Dutch *bommen,* of imitative origin]

boom[2] (buːm) *n* **1** *Nautical.* a spar to which a sail is fastened to control its position relative to the wind. **2** a beam or spar pivoting at the foot of the mast of a derrick, controlling the distance from the mast at which a load is lifted or lowered. **3** a pole, usually extensible, carrying an overhead microphone and projected over a film or television set. **4a** a barrier across a waterway, usually consisting of a chain of connected floating logs, to confine free-floating logs, protect a harbour from attack, etc. **4b** the area so barred off. [C16: from Dutch *boom* tree, BEAM]

boomer ('buːmə) *n* **1** *Austral.* a large male kangaroo. **2** *Austral. and N.Z. informal.* anything exceptionally large. [from English dialect]

boomerang ('buːmə,ræŋ) *n* **1** a curved flat wooden missile of native Australians, which can be made to return to the thrower. **2** an action or statement that recoils on its originator. ◆ *vb* **3** *(intr)* to recoil or return unexpectedly, causing harm to its originator; backfire. [C19: from a native Australian language]

boomkin ('buːmkɪn) *n Nautical.* a short boom projecting from the deck of a ship, used to secure the main-brace blocks or to extend the lower edge of the foresail. [C17: from Dutch *boomken,* from *boom* tree; see BEAM, -KIN]

boomslang ('buːm,slæŋ) *n* a large greenish venomous arboreal colubrid snake, *Dispholidus typus,* of southern Africa. [C18: from Afrikaans, from *boom* tree + *slang* snake]

boom town *n* a town that is enjoying sudden prosperity or has grown rapidly.

boon[1] (buːn) *n* **1** something extremely useful, helpful, or beneficial; a blessing or benefit: *the car was a boon to him.* **2** *Archaic.* a favour; request: *he asked a boon of the king.* [C12: from Old Norse *bōn* request; related to Old English *bēn* prayer]

boon[2] (buːn) *adj* **1** close, special, or intimate (in the phrase **boon companion**). **2** *Archaic.* jolly or convivial. [C14: from Old French *bon,* from Latin *bonus* good]

boondocks ('buːn,dɒks) *pl n* **the.** *U.S. and Canadian slang.* **1** wild, desolate, or uninhabitable country. **2** a remote rural or provincial area. ◆ Sometimes shortened to **the Boonies.** [C20: from Tagalog *bundok* mountain]

boondoggle ('buːn,dɒgᵊl) *Informal, chiefly U.S. and Canadian.* ◆ *vb* **1** *(intr)* to do futile and unnecessary work. ◆ *n* **2** a futile and unnecessary project or work. [C20: said to have been coined by R. H. Link, American scoutmaster] ► **'boon,doggler** *n*

Boone (buːn) *n* **Daniel.** 1734–1820, American pioneer, explorer, and guide, esp. in Kentucky.

boong (buːŋ) *n Austral. offensive.* a Black person. [C20: perhaps of native Australian origin]

boongary ('buːŋgærɪ) *n* a tree kangaroo, *Dendrolagus lumholtzi,* of northeastern Queensland. [from a native Australian language]

boor (bʊə) *n* an ill-mannered, clumsy, or insensitive person. [Old English *gebūr;* related to Old High German *gibūr* farmer, dweller, Albanian *būr* man; see NEIGHBOUR] ► **'boorish** *adj* ► **'boorishly** *adv* ► **'boorishness** *n*

boost (buːst) *n* **1** encouragement, improvement, or help: *a boost to morale.* **2** an upward thrust or push: *he gave him a boost over the wall.* **3** an increase or rise: *a boost in salary.* **4** a publicity campaign; promotion. **5** the amount by which the induction pressure of a supercharged internal-combustion engine exceeds that of the ambient pressure. ◆ *vb (tr)* **6** to encourage, assist, or improve: *to boost morale.* **7** to lift by giving a push from below or behind. **8** to increase or raise: *to boost the voltage in an electrical circuit.* **9** to cause to rise; increase: *to boost sales.* **10** to advertise on a big scale. **11** to increase the induction pressure of (an internal-combustion engine) above that of the ambient pressure; supercharge. [C19: of unknown origin]

booster ('buːstə) *n* **1** a person or thing that supports, assists, or increases power or effectiveness. **2** Also called: **launch vehicle.** the first stage of a multistage rocket. **3** *Radio, television.* **3a** a radio-frequency amplifier connected between an aerial and a receiver to amplify weak incoming signals. **3b** a radio-frequency amplifier that amplifies incoming signals, retransmitting them at higher power. **4** another name for **supercharger. 5** short for **booster shot. 6** *Slang, chiefly U.S.* a shoplifter.

booster shot *n* a supplementary injection of a vaccine given to maintain the immunization provided by an earlier dose.

boot[1] (buːt) *n* **1** a strong outer covering for the foot; shoe that extends above the ankle, often to the knee. See also **chukka boot, top boot, Wellington boot, surgical boot. 2** *Brit.* an enclosed compartment of a car for holding luggage, etc., usually at the rear. U.S. and Canadian name: **trunk. 3** a protective covering over a mechanical device, such as a rubber sheath protecting a coupling joining two shafts. **4** *U.S. and Canadian.* a rubber patch used to repair a puncture in a tyre. **5** an instrument of torture used to crush the foot and lower leg. **6** a protective covering for the lower leg of a horse. **7** a kick: *he gave the door a boot.* **8** *Brit. slang.* an ugly person (esp. in the phrase **old boot**). **9** *U.S. slang.* a navy or marine recruit, esp. one in training. **10** *Computing.* short for **bootstrap** (sense 4a). **11 bet one's boots.** to be certain: *you can bet your boots he'll come.* **12** See **boots and all. 13 die with one's boots on. 13a** to die while still active. **13b** to die in battle. **14 lick the boots of.** to be servile, obsequious, or flattering towards. **15 put the boot in.** *Slang.* **15a** to kick a person, esp. when he is already down. **15b** to harass someone or aggravate a problem. **15c** to finish off (something) with unnecessary brutality. **16 the boot.** *Slang.* dismissal from employment; the sack. **17 the boot is on the other foot** *or* **leg.** the situation is or has now reversed. **18 too big for one's boots.** self-important or conceited. ◆ *vb (tr)* **19** (esp. in football) to kick. **20** to equip with boots. **21** *Informal.* **21a** (often foll. by *out*) to eject forcibly. **21b** to dismiss from employment. ◆ See also **boots.** [C14 *bote,* from Old French, of uncertain origin]

boot[2] (buːt) *vb (usually impersonal)* **1** *Archaic.* to be of advantage or use to (a person): *what boots it to complain?* ◆ *n* **2** *Obsolete.* an advantage. **3** *Dialect.* something given in addition, esp. to equalize an exchange: *a ten pound boot to settle the bargain.* **4 to boot.** as well; in addition: *it's cold and musty, and damp to boot.* [Old English *bōt* compensation; related to Old Norse *bōt* remedy, Gothic *bōta,* Old High German *buoza* improvement]

bootblack ('buːt,blæk) *n Chiefly U.S.* another word for **shoeblack.**

boot boy *n* a member of a gang of hooligans who usually wear heavy boots.

boot camp *n* **1** *U.S. slang.* a basic training camp for new recruits to the U.S. Navy or Marine Corps. **2** a centre for juvenile offenders, with a strict disciplinary regime, hard physical exercise, and community labour programmes.

booted ('buːtɪd) *adj* **1** wearing boots. **2** *Ornithol.* **2a** (of birds) having an undivided tarsus covered with a horny sheath. **2b** (of poultry) having a feathered tarsus.

bootee ('buːtiː, buː'tiː) *n* **1** a soft shoe for a baby, esp. a knitted one. **2** a boot for women and children, esp. an ankle-length one.

Boötes (bəʊ'əutiːz) *n, Latin genitive* **Boötis** (bəʊ'əutɪs). a constellation in the N hemisphere lying near Ursa Major and containing the first magnitude star Arcturus. [C17: via Latin from Greek: ploughman, from *boōtein* to plough, from *bous* ox]

booth (buːð, buːθ) *n, pl* **booths** (buːðz). **1** a stall for the display or sale of goods, esp. a temporary one at a fair or market. **2** a small enclosed or partially enclosed room or cubicle, such as one containing a telephone (**telephone booth**) or one in which a person casts his vote at an election (**polling booth**). **3** two long high-backed benches with a long table between, used esp. in bars and inexpensive restaurants. **4** (formerly) a temporary structure for shelter, dwelling, storage, etc. [C12: of Scandinavian origin; compare Old Norse *buth,* Swedish, Danish *bod* shop, stall; see BOWER[1]]

Booth (buːð) *n* **1 Edwin Thomas,** son of Junius Brutus Booth. 1833–93, U.S. actor. **2 John Wilkes,** son of Junius Brutus Booth. 1838–65, U.S. actor; assassin of Abraham Lincoln. **3 Junius Brutus** ('dʒuːnɪəs 'bruːtəs). 1796–1852, U.S. actor, born in England. **4 William.** 1829–1912, British religious leader; founder and first general of the Salvation Army (1878).

Boothia Peninsula ('buːθɪə) *n* a peninsula of N Canada: the northernmost part of the mainland of North America, lying west of the **Gulf of Boothia,** an arm of the Arctic Ocean.

Boothroyd ('buːθrɔɪd) *n* **Betty.** born 1929, British politician; speaker of the House of Commons from 1992.

bootie ('buːtɪ) *n Brit. slang.* a Royal Marine. [C20: from *bootneck,* so called from the leather tab used to close their tunic collars]

bootjack ('buːt,dʒæk) *n* a device that grips the heel of a boot to enable the foot to be withdrawn easily.

bootlace ('buːt,leɪs) *n* a strong lace for fastening a boot.

bootlace fungus *n* another name for **honey fungus.**

bootlace worm *n* a nemertean worm, *Linens longissimus,* that inhabits shingly shores and attains lengths of over 6 m (20 ft.).

Bootle ('buːtᵊl) *n* a port in NW England, in Sefton unitary authority, Merseyside; on the River Mersey adjoining Liverpool. Pop.: 65 454 (1991).

bootleg ('buːt,lɛg) *vb* **-legs, -legging, -legged. 1** to make, carry, or sell (illicit goods, esp. alcohol). ◆ *n* **2** something made or sold illicitly, such as alcohol during Prohibition in the U.S. **3** an illegally made copy of a CD, tape, etc. ◆ *adj* **4** produced, distributed, or sold illicitly: *bootleg whisky; bootleg tapes.* [C17: see BOOT[1], LEG; from the practice of smugglers of carrying bottles of liquor concealed in their boots] ► **'boot,legger** *n*

bootless ('buːtlɪs) *adj* of little or no use; vain; fruitless: *a bootless search.* [Old English *bōtlēas,* from *bōt* compensation; Old Norse *bótalauss*] ► **'bootlessly** *adv*

bootlick ('buːt,lɪk) *vb Informal.* to seek favour by servile or ingratiating behaviour towards (someone, esp. someone in authority); toady. ► **'boot,licker** *n*

bootloader ('buːt,ləudə) *n Computing.* short for **bootstrap loader:** see **bootstrap** (sense 4).

boot money *n Informal.* unofficial bonuses in the form of illegal cash payments made by a professional sports club to its players.

boots (bu:ts) *n, pl* **boots.** *Brit.* (formerly) a shoeblack who cleans the guests' shoes in a hotel.

boots and all *Austral. and N.Z. informal.* ◆ *adv* **1** making every effort; with no holds barred. ◆ *adj* (**boots-and-all** *when prenominal*) **2** behaving or conducted in such a manner.

boots and saddles *n* a bugle call formerly used in the U.S. Cavalry to summon soldiers to mount.

bootstrap ('bu:t,stræp) *n* **1** a leather or fabric loop on the back or side of a boot for pulling it on. **2 by one's (own) bootstraps.** by one's own efforts; unaided. **3** (*modifier*) self-acting or self-sufficient, as an electronic amplifier that uses its output voltage to bias its input or a self-consistent theory of nuclear interactions. **4a** a technique for loading the first few program instructions into a computer main store to enable the rest of the program to be introduced from an input device. **4b** (*as modifier*): *a bootstrap loader.* **5** *Commerce.* an offer to purchase a controlling interest in a company, esp. with the intention of purchasing the remainder of the equity at a lower price.

boot topping *n Nautical.* **1** the part of a ship's hull that is between the load line and the water line when the ship is not loaded. **2** a coating applied to this part of a ship to remove marine growth.

boot tree *n* **1** a shoetree for a boot, often having supports to stretch the leg of the boot. **2** a last for making boots.

booty ('bu:tɪ) *n, pl* **-ties.** any valuable article or articles, esp. when obtained as plunder. [C15: from Old French *butin,* from Middle Low German *buite* exchange; related to Old Norse *býta* to exchange, *býti* barter]

boo-word ('bu:,wɜ:d) *n* any word that seems to cause irrational fear: *"communism" became a boo-word in the McCarthy era.*

booze (bu:z) *Informal.* ◆ *n* **1** alcoholic drink. **2** a drinking bout or party. ◆ *vb* **3** (*usually intr*) to drink (alcohol), esp. in excess. [C13: from Middle Dutch *būsen*] ▸ **boozed** *adj* ▸ **'boozing** *n*

boozer ('bu:zə) *n Informal.* **1** a person who is fond of drinking. **2** *Brit., Austral., and N.Z.* a bar or pub.

booze-up *n Brit., Austral., and N.Z. slang.* a drinking spree.

boozy ('bu:zɪ) *adj* **boozier, booziest.** *Informal.* inclined to or involving excessive drinking of alcohol; drunken: *a boozy lecturer; a boozy party.* ▸ **'booziness** *n*

bop[1] (bɒp) *n* **1** a form of jazz originating in the 1940s, characterized by rhythmic and harmonic complexity and instrumental virtuosity. Originally called: **bebop. 2** *Informal.* a session of dancing to pop music. ◆ *vb* **bops, bopping, bopped. 3** (*intr*) *Informal.* to dance to pop music. [C20: shortened from BEBOP] ▸ **'bopper** *n*

bop[2] (bɒp) *Informal.* ◆ *vb* **bops, bopping, bopped. 1** (*tr*) to strike; hit. ◆ *n* **2** a blow. [C19: of imitative origin]

bo-peep (,bəʊ'pi:p) *n* **1** a game for very young children, in which one hides (esp. hiding one's face in one's hands) and reappears suddenly. **2** *Austral. and N.Z. informal.* a look (esp. in the phrase **have a bo-peep**).

Bophuthatswana (,bəupu:tɑ:t'swɑ:nə) *n* (formerly) a Bantu homeland in N South Africa: consists of six separate areas; granted independence by South Africa in 1977 although this was not internationally recognized; abolished in 1993. Capital: Mmabatho.

bor. *abbrev. for* borough.

bora[1] ('bɔ:rə) *n* (*sometimes cap.*) a violent cold north wind blowing from the mountains to the E coast of the Adriatic, usually in winter. [C19: from Italian (Venetian dialect), from Latin *borēas* the north wind]

bora[2] ('bɔ:rə) *n* an initiation ceremony of native Australians, introducing youths to manhood. [from a native Australian language]

Bora Bora ('bɔ:rə 'bɔ:rə) *n* an island in the S Pacific, in French Polynesia, in the Society Islands: one of the Leeward Islands. Area: 39 sq. km (15 sq. miles).

boracic (bə'ræsɪk) *adj* another word for **boric.**

boracite ('bɔ:rə,saɪt) *n* a white mineral that forms salt deposits of magnesium borate and chloride in cubic crystalline form. Formula: $Mg_6Cl_2B_{14}O_{26}$.

borage ('bɒrɪdʒ, 'bʌrɪdʒ) *n* **1** a Mediterranean boraginaceous plant, *Borago officinalis,* with star-shaped blue flowers. The young leaves have a cucumber-like flavour and are sometimes used in salads or as seasoning. **2** any of several related plants. [C13: from Old French *bourage,* perhaps from Arabic *abū ʿāraq* literally: father of sweat, from its use as a diaphoretic]

boraginaceous (bə,rædʒɪ'neɪʃəs) *adj* of, relating to, or belonging to the *Boraginaceae,* a family of temperate and tropical typically hairy-leaved flowering plants that includes forget-me-not, lungwort, borage, comfrey, and heliotrope. [C19: from New Latin *Borāginācēae,* from *Borāgō* genus name; see BORAGE]

borak ('bɔ:rək) *or* **borax** ('bɔ:ræks) *n Austral. and N.Z. slang, archaic.* **1** rubbish; nonsense. **2 poke borak at (someone).** to jeer at (someone). [from a native Australian language]

borane ('bɔ:reɪn) *n* any compound of boron and hydrogen, used in the synthesis of other boron compounds and as high-energy fuels. [C20: from BOR(ON) + -ANE]

Borås (*Swedish* bu'ro:s) *n* a city in SW Sweden, chiefly producing textiles. Pop.: 96 123 (1994).

borate *n* ('bɔ:reɪt, -ɪt). **1** a salt or ester of boric acid. Salts of boric acid consist of BO_3 and BO_4 units linked together. ◆ *vb* ('bɔ:reɪt). **2** (*tr*) to treat with borax, boric acid, or borate.

borax ('bɔ:ræks) *n, pl* **-raxes** *or* **-races** (-rə,si:z). **1** Also called: **tincal.** a soluble readily fusible white mineral consisting of impure hydrated disodium tetraborate in monoclinic crystalline form, occurring in alkaline soils and salt deposits. Formula: $Na_2B_4O_7.10H_2O$. **2** pure disodium tetraborate. [C14: from Old French *boras,* from Medieval Latin *borax,* from Arabic *būraq,* from Persian *būrah*]

borazon ('bɔ:rə,zɒn, -zən) *n* an extremely hard form of boron nitride. [C20: from BOR(ON) + AZO- + -ON]

borborygmus (,bɔ:bə'rɪgməs) *n, pl* **-mi** (-maɪ). rumbling of the stomach. [C18: from Greek] ▸ **,borbo'rygmal** *or* **,borbo'rygmic** *adj*

Bordeaux (bɔ:'dəʊ; *French* bɔrdo) *n* **1** a port in SW France, on the River Garonne: a major centre of the wine trade. Pop.: 213 274 (1990). **2** any of several red, white, or rosé wines produced around Bordeaux. Related adj: **Bordelais.**

Bordeaux mixture *n Horticulture.* a fungicide consisting of a solution of equal quantities of copper sulphate and quicklime. [C19: loose translation of French *bouillie bordelaise,* from *bouillir* to boil + *bordelais* of BORDEAUX]

Bordelaise (,bɔ:də'leɪz; *French* bɔrdəlɛz) *adj Cookery.* denoting a brown sauce flavoured with red wine and sometimes mushrooms. [French: of BORDEAUX]

bordello (bɔ:'deləʊ) *n, pl* **-los.** a brothel. Also called (archaic): **bordel** ('bɔ:dᵊl). [C16: from Italian, from Old French *borde* hut, cabin]

border ('bɔ:də) *n* **1** a band or margin around or along the edge of something. **2** the dividing line or frontier between political or geographic regions. **3a** a region straddling such a boundary. **3b** (*as modifier*): *border country.* **4a** a design or ornamental strip around the edge or rim of something, such as a printed page or dinner plate. **4b** (*as modifier*): *a border illustration.* **5** a long narrow strip of ground planted with flowers, shrubs, trees, etc., that skirts a path or wall or surrounds a lawn or other area: *a herbaceous border.* ◆ *vb* **6** (*tr*) to decorate or provide with a border. **7** (when *intr,* foll. by *on* or *upon*) **7a** to be adjacent (to); lie along the boundary (of): *his land borders on mine.* **7b** to be nearly the same (as); verge (on): *his stupidity borders on madness.* [C14: from Old French *bordure,* from *border* to border, from *bort* side of a ship, of Germanic origin; see BOARD]

Border[1] ('bɔ:də) *n* **the. 1** (*often pl*) the area straddling the border between England and Scotland. **2** the area straddling the border between Northern Ireland and the Republic of Ireland. **3** the region in S South Africa around East London.

Border[2] ('bɔ:də) *n* **Allan (Robert).** born 1955, Australian cricketer; captain of Australia (1985–94).

Border collie *n* a medium-sized breed of collie with a silky usually black-and-white coat: used mainly as sheepdogs.

bordereau (,bɔ:də'rəʊ; *French* bɔrdəro) *n, pl* **-reaux** (-'rəʊ, -'rəʊz; *French* -ro). a memorandum or invoice prepared for a company by an underwriter, containing a list of reinsured risks. [C20: from French]

borderer ('bɔ:dərə) *n* a person who lives in a border area, esp. the border between England and Scotland.

borderland ('bɔ:də,lænd) *n* **1** land located on or near a frontier or boundary. **2** an indeterminate region: *the borderland between intellect and intelligence.*

Border Leicester *n* a breed of sheep originally developed in the border country between Scotland and England by crossing English Leicesters with Cheviots: large numbers in Scotland, Australia, and New Zealand. It has a long white fleece with no wool on the head.

borderline ('bɔ:də,laɪn) *n* **1** a border; dividing line; line of demarcation. **2** an indeterminate position between two conditions or qualities: *the borderline between friendship and love.* ◆ *adj* **3** on the edge of one category and verging on another: *a borderline failure in the exam.*

Borders Region *n* a former local government region in S Scotland, formed in 1975 from Berwick, Peebles, Roxburgh, Selkirk, and part of Midlothian; replaced in 1996 by Scottish Borders council area.

border terrier *n* a small rough-coated breed of terrier.

Bordet (*French* bɔrdɛ) *n* **Jules (Jean Baptiste Vincent)** (ʒyl). 1870–1961, Belgian bacteriologist and immunologist, who discovered complement. Nobel prize for physiology or medicine 1919.

bordure ('bɔ:djʊə) *n Heraldry.* the outer edge of a shield, esp. when decorated distinctively. [C15: from Old French; see BORDER]

bore[1] (bɔ:) *vb* **1** to produce (a hole) in (a material) by use of a drill, auger, or rotary cutting tool. **2** to increase the diameter of (a hole), as by an internal turning operation on a lathe or similar machine. **3** (*tr*) to produce (a hole in the ground, tunnel, mine shaft, etc.) by digging, drilling, cutting, etc. **4** (*intr*) *Informal.* (of a horse or athlete in a race) to push other competitors, esp. in order to try to get them out of the way. ◆ *n* **5** a hole or tunnel in the ground, esp. one drilled in search of minerals, oil, etc. **6a** a circular hole in a material produced by drilling or turning. **6b** the diameter of such a hole. **7a** the hollow part of a tube or cylinder, esp. of a gun barrel. **7b** the diameter of such a hollow part; calibre. **8** *Austral.* an artesian well. [Old English *borian;* related to Old Norse *bora,* Old High German *borōn* to bore, Latin *forāre* to pierce, Greek *pharos* ploughing, *phárunx* PHARYNX]

bore[2] (bɔ:) *vb* **1** (*tr*) to tire or make weary by being dull, repetitious, or uninteresting. ◆ *n* **2** a dull, repetitious, or uninteresting person, activity, or state. [C18: of unknown origin] ▸ **bored** *adj*

bore[3] (bɔ:) *n* a high steep-fronted wave moving up a narrow estuary, caused by the tide. [C17: from Old Norse *bāra* wave, billow]

bore[4] (bɔ:) *vb* the past tense of **bear**[1].

boreal ('bɔ:rɪəl) *adj* of or relating to the north or the north wind. [C15: from Latin *boreās* the north wind]

Boreal ('bɔ:rɪəl) *adj* **1** of or denoting the coniferous forests in the north of the N hemisphere. **2** designating a climatic zone having snowy winters and short summers. **3** designating a dry climatic period from about 7500 to 5500 B.C., characterized by cold winters, warm summers, and a flora dominated by pines and hazels.

Boreas ('bɔ:rɪəs) *n Greek myth.* the god personifying the north wind. [C14: via Latin from Greek]

borecole ('bɔ:kəʊl) *n* another name for **kale.**

boredom ('bɔ:dəm) *n* the state of being bored; tedium.

boree ('bɔ:ri:) *n Austral.* another name for **myall.** [from a native Australian language]

boreen ('bɔːriːn) *n Irish.* a country lane or narrow road. [C19: from Irish Gaelic *bóithrín,* diminutive of *bóthar* road]
borehole ('bɔːˌhəʊl) *n* a hole driven into the ground to obtain geological information, release water, etc.
borer ('bɔːrə) *n* **1** a machine or hand tool for boring holes. **2** any of various insects, insect larvae, molluscs, or crustaceans that bore into rock or plant material, esp. wood. See also **woodborer, corn borer, marine borer, rock borer.**
borer bomb *n N.Z.* a device that emits pesticide fumes.
Borg (bɔːg; *Swedish* bɔrj) *n* **Björn** (bjœrn). born 1956, Swedish tennis player: Wimbledon champion 1976–80.
Borgerhout (*Flemish* bɔrxər'hɔut) *n* a city in N Belgium, near Antwerp. Pop.: 44 000 (latest est.).
Borges (*Spanish* 'borxes) *n* **Jorge Luis** ('xorxe lwis). 1899–1986, Argentinian poet, short-story writer, and literary scholar. The short stories collected in *Ficciones* (1944) he described as "games with infinity".
Borghese (*Italian* bor'geze) *n* a noble Italian family whose members were influential in Italian art and politics from the 16th to the 19th century.
Borgia (*Italian* 'bordʒa) *n* **1 Cesare** ('tʃezare), son of Rodrigo Borgia (Pope Alexander VI). 1475–1507, Italian cardinal, politician, and military leader; model for Machiavelli's *The Prince.* **2** his sister, **Lucrezia** (lu'krɛttsja), daughter of Rodrigo Borgia. 1480–1519, Italian noblewoman. After her third marriage (1501), to the Duke of Ferrara, she became a patron of the arts and science. **3 Rodrigo** (rod'rigo). See **Alexander VI.**
Borglum ('bɔːgləm) *n* **(John) Gutzon** ('gʌtsən). 1867–1941, U.S. sculptor, noted for his monumental busts of U.S. presidents carved in the mountainside of Mount Rushmore.
boric ('bɔːrɪk) *adj* of or containing boron. Also: **boracic.**
boric acid *n* **1** Also called: **orthoboric acid.** Systematic name: **trioxoboric(III) acid.** a white soluble weakly acid crystalline solid used in the manufacture of heat-resistant glass and porcelain enamels, as a fireproofing material, and as a mild antiseptic. Formula: H_3BO_3. **2** any other acid containing boron.
boride ('bɔːraɪd) *n* a compound in which boron is the most electronegative element. [C19: from BOR(ON) + -IDE]
boring[1] ('bɔːrɪŋ) *n* **1a** the act or process of making or enlarging a hole. **1b** the hole made in this way. **2** (*often pl*) a fragment, particle, chip, etc., produced during boring.
boring[2] ('bɔːrɪŋ) *adj* dull; repetitious; uninteresting. ▸ **'boringly** *adv*
boring mill *n Engineering.* a large vertical lathe having a rotating table on which work is secured. Tools are held on a fixed post and the work is rotated around it. Also called (informal): **roundabout.**
Boris I (bɒrɪs) *n* known as *Boris of Bulgaria.* died 907 A.D., khan of Bulgaria. His reign saw the conversion of Bulgaria to Christianity and the birth of a national literature.
Borlaug ('bɔːlɔːg) *n* **Norman (Ernest).** born 1914, U.S. agronomist, who bred new strains of high-yielding cereal crops for use in developing countries. Nobel peace prize 1970.
borlotti bean (bɔː'lɒtɪ) *n* a variety of kidney bean with a pinkish-brown speckled skin that turns brown when cooked: grown in southern Europe, East Africa, and Taiwan. [from Italian, plural of *borlotto* kidney bean]
Bormann (*German* 'bɔrman) *n* **Martin.** 1900–45, German Nazi politician; Hitler's adviser and private secretary (1942–45): committed suicide.
born (bɔːn) *vb* **1** the past participle (in most passive uses) of **bear**[1] (sense 4). **2 was not born yesterday.** is not gullible or foolish. ♦ *adj* **3** possessing or appearing to have possessed certain qualities from birth: *a born musician.* **4a** being at birth in a particular social status or other condition as specified: *ignobly born.* **4b** (*in combination*): *lowborn.* **5 in all one's born days.** *Informal.* so far in one's life.

USAGE Care should be taken not to use *born* where *borne* is intended: *he had borne (*not *born) his ordeal with great courage; the following points should be borne in mind.*

Born (bɔːn) *n* **Max.** 1882–1970, British nuclear physicist, born in Germany, noted for his fundamental contribution to quantum mechanics: Nobel prize for physics 1954.
born-again ('bɔːnəˌgen) *adj* **1** having experienced conversion, esp. to evangelical Christianity. **2** showing the enthusiasm of one newly converted to any cause: *a born-again monetarist.* ♦ *n* **3** a person who shows fervent enthusiasm for a new-found cause, belief, etc.
borne (bɔːn) *vb* **1** the past participle of **bear**[1] (for all active uses of the verb; also for all passive uses except sense 4 unless foll. by *by*). **2 be borne in on** *or* **upon.** (of a fact) to be realized by (someone): *it was borne in on us how close we had been to disaster.*
Borneo ('bɔːnɪˌəʊ) *n* an island in the W Pacific, between the Sulu and Java Seas, part of the Malay Archipelago: divided into Kalimantan (**Indonesian Borneo**), the Malaysian states of Sarawak and Sabah, and the British-protected sultanate of Brunei; mountainous and densely forested. Area: about 750 000 sq. km (290 000 sq. miles). ▸ **'Bornean** *adj, n*
borneol ('bɔːnɪˌɒl) *n* a white solid terpene alcohol extracted from the Malaysian tree *Dryobalanops aromatica,* used in perfume and in the manufacture of organic esters. Formula: $C_{10}H_{17}OH$. [C19: from BORNE(O) + -OL[1]]
Bornholm (*Danish* bɔrn'hɔlm) *n* an island in the Baltic Sea, south of Sweden: administratively part of Denmark. Chief town: Rønne. Pop.: 46 100 (1990). Area: 588 sq. km (227 sq. miles).
Bornholm disease ('bɔːnˌhɒlm) *n* an epidemic virus infection characterized by pain round the base of the chest. [C20: named after BORNHOLM, where it was first described]
bornite ('bɔːnaɪt) *n* a mineral consisting of a sulphide of copper and iron that tarnishes to purple or dark red. It occurs in copper deposits. Formula: Cu_5FeS_4. Also called: **peacock ore.** [C19: named after I. von *Born* (1742–91), Austrian mineralogist; see -ITE[1]]
Borno ('bɔːnəʊ) *n* a state of NE Nigeria, on Lake Chad: the second largest state, formed in 1976 from part of North-Eastern State. Capital: Maiduguri. Pop.: 2 903 238 (1995 est.). Area: 70 898 sq. km (27 374 sq. miles).
Borodin ('bɒrədɪn; *Russian* bəra'din) *n* **Aleksandr Porfirevich** (alɪk'sandr pərfi'rjevitʃ). 1834–87, Russian composer, whose works include the unfinished opera *Prince Igor,* symphonies, songs, and chamber music.
Borodino (ˌbɒrə'diːnəʊ; *Russian* bərədi'nɔ) *n* a village in E central Russia, about 110 km (70 miles) west of Moscow: scene of a battle (1812) in which Napoleon defeated the Russians but irreparably weakened his army.
boron ('bɔːrɒn) *n* a very hard almost colourless crystalline metalloid element that in impure form exists as a brown amorphous powder. It occurs principally in borax and is used in hardening steel. The naturally occurring isotope **boron-10** is used in nuclear control rods and neutron detection instruments. Symbol: B; atomic no.: 5; atomic wt.: 10.81; valency: 3; relative density: 2.34 (crystalline), 2.37 (amorphous); melting pt.: 2092°C; boiling pt.: 4002°C. [C19: from BOR(AX) + (CARB)ON]
boron carbide *n* a black extremely hard inert substance having a high capture cross section for thermal neutrons. It is used as an abrasive and refractory and in control rods in nuclear reactors. Formula: B_4C.
boronia (bə'rəʊnɪə) *n* any aromatic rutaceous shrub of the Australian genus *Boronia.*
boron nitride *n* a white inert crystalline solid existing both in a graphite-like form and in an extremely hard diamond-like form (borazon). It is used as a refractory, high temperature lubricant and insulator, and heat shield. Formula BN.
borosilicate (ˌbɔːrəʊ'sɪlɪkɪt, -ˌkeɪt) *n* a salt of boric and silicic acids.
borosilicate glass *n* any of a range of heat- and chemical-resistant glasses, such as Pyrex, prepared by fusing together boron(III) oxide, silicon dioxide, and, usually, a metal oxide.
Borotra (bɔrɔtra) *n* **Jean (Robert)** (ʒɑ̃). 1898–1994, French tennis player: secretary general of physical education under the Vichy government (1940).
borough ('bʌrə) *n* **1** a town, esp. (in Britain) one that forms the constituency of an MP or that was originally incorporated by royal charter. See also **burgh. 2** any of the 32 constituent divisions that together with the City of London make up Greater London. **3** any of the five constituent divisions of New York City. **4** (in the U.S.) a self-governing incorporated municipality. **5** (in medieval England) a fortified town or village or a fort. **6** (in New Zealand) a small municipality with a governing body. [Old English *burg;* related to *beorgan* to shelter, Old Norse *borg* wall, Gothic *baurgs* city, Old High German *burg* fortified castle]
borough-English *n English law.* (until 1925) a custom in certain English boroughs whereby the youngest son inherited land to the exclusion of his older brothers. Compare **primogeniture, gavelkind.** [C14: from Anglo-French *tenure en burgh Engloys* tenure in an English borough; so called because the custom was unknown in France]
Borromini (*Italian* borro'miːni) *n* **Francesco,** original name *Francesco Castelli.* 1599–1667, Italian baroque architect, working in Rome: his buildings include the churches of San Carlo (1641) and Sant' Ivo (1660).
borrow ('bɒrəʊ) *vb* **1** to obtain or receive (something, such as money) on loan for temporary use, intending to give it, or something equivalent or identical, back to the lender. **2** to adopt (ideas, words, etc.) from another source; appropriate. **3** *Not standard.* to lend. **4** *Golf.* to putt the ball uphill of the direct path to the hole. **5** (*intr*) *Golf.* (of a ball) to deviate from a straight path because of the slope of the ground. ♦ *n* **6** *Golf.* a deviation of a ball from a straight path because of the slope of the ground: *a left borrow.* **7** material dug from a borrow pit to provide fill at another. **8 living on borrowed time. 8a** living an unexpected extension of life. **8b** close to death. [Old English *borgian;* related to Old High German *borgēn* to take heed, give security] ▸ **'borrower** *n*

USAGE The use of *off* after *borrow* was formerly considered incorrect, but is now acceptable in informal contexts.

Borrow ('bɒrəʊ) *n* **George (Henry).** 1803–81, English traveller and writer. His best-known works are the semiautobiographical novels of Gypsy life and language, *Lavengro* (1851) and its sequel *The Romany Rye* (1857).
borrow pit *n Civil engineering.* an excavation dug to provide fill to make up ground elsewhere.
Bors (bɔːs) *n* **Sir.** (in Arthurian legend) **1** one the knights of the Round Table, nephew of Lancelot. **2** an illegitimate son of King Arthur.
borscht (bɔːʃt), **borsch** (bɔːʃ), *or* **borshch** (bɔːʃtʃ) *n* a Russian and Polish soup based on beetroot. [C19: from Russian *borshch*]
borsic ('bɔːsɪk) *n Aeronautics.* a strong light composite material of boron fibre and silicon carbide used in aviation.
borstal ('bɔːstəl) *n* **1** (formerly in Britain) an informal name for an establishment in which offenders aged 15 to 21 could be detained for corrective training. Since the Criminal Justice Act 1982, they have been replaced by **youth custody centres** (now known as **young offender institutions**). **2** (formerly) a similar establishment in Australia and New Zealand. [C20: named after *Borstal,* village in Kent where the first institution was founded]
bort, boart (bɔːt), *or* **bortz** (bɔːts) *n* an inferior grade of diamond used for cutting and drilling or, in powdered form, as an industrial abrasive. [Old English *gebrot* fragment; related to Old Norse *brot* piece, Old High German *broz* bud] ▸ **'borty** *adj*
borzoi ('bɔːzɔɪ) *n, pl* **-zois.** a tall graceful fast-moving breed of dog with a long silky coat, originally used in Russia for hunting wolves. Also called: **Russian wolfhound.** [C19: from Russian *borzoi,* literally: swift; related to Old Slavonic *brŭzŭ* swift]
bosberaad ('bɒsbəˌrɑːd) *n S. African.* a meeting in an isolated venue to break a political deadlock. [C20: Afrikaans, from *bos* bush + *beraad* council]

boscage *or* **boskage** (ˈbɒskɪdʒ) *n Literary.* a mass of trees and shrubs; thicket. [C14: from Old French *bosc,* probably of Germanic origin; see BUSH[1], -AGE]

Bosch (bɒʃ) *n* **1 Carl.** 1874–1940, German chemist, who adapted the Haber process to produce ammonia for industrial use. He shared the Nobel prize for chemistry 1931. **2 Hieronymus** (hɪˈrɒnɪməs), original name probably *Jerome van Aken* (or *Aeken*). ?1450–1516, Dutch painter, noted for his macabre allegorical representations of biblical subjects in brilliant transparent colours, esp. the triptych *The Garden of Earthly Delights*.

Bosch process *n* an industrial process for manufacturing hydrogen by the catalytic reduction of steam with carbon monoxide. [C20: named after Carl BOSCH]

boschvark (ˈbɒʃˌvɑːk) *n S. African.* another name for **bushpig.** [Afrikaans]

Bose (bəʊs) *n* **1** Sir **Jagadis Chandra** (dʒəgəˈdiːsˈtʃʌndrə). 1858–1937, Indian physicist and plant physiologist. **2 Satyendra Nath** (səˈtjendrə ˈnɑːθ). 1894–1974, Indian physicist, who collaborated with Einstein in devising Bose-Einstein statistics. **3 Subhas Chandra** (sʊbˈhɑːʃ ˈtʃʌndrə), known as *Netaji*. 1897–1945, Indian nationalist leader; president of the Indian National Congress (1938–39); organized the Indian National Army, with Japanese support, in Singapore to free India from British Rule.

Bose-Einstein statistics *pl n* (*functioning as sing*) *Physics.* the branch of quantum statistics applied to systems of particles that do not obey the exclusion principle. Compare **Fermi-Dirac statistics.**

bosh[1] (bɒʃ) *n Informal.* empty or meaningless talk or opinions; nonsense. [C19: from Turkish *boş* empty]

bosh[2] (bɒʃ) *n* **1** the lower tapering portion of a blast furnace, situated immediately above the air-inlet tuyères. **2** the deposit of siliceous material that occurs on the surfaces of vessels in which copper is refined. **3** a water tank for cooling glass-making tools, etc. **4** *South Wales dialect.* a kitchen sink or wash basin. [C17: probably from German; compare *böschen* to slope, *Böschung* slope]

bosk (bɒsk) *n Literary.* a small wood of bushes and small trees. [C13: variant of *busk* BUSH[1]]

bosket *or* **bosquet** (ˈbɒskɪt) *n* a clump of small trees or bushes; thicket. [C18: from French *bosquet,* from Italian *boschetto,* from *bosco* wood, forest; see BUSH[1]]

Boskop (ˈbɒskɒp) *n* **a** a prehistoric race of the late Pleistocene period in sub-Saharan Africa. **b** (*as modifier*): *Boskop man.* [C20: named after *Boskop,* in the Transvaal, where remains of this race were first discovered]

bosky (ˈbɒskɪ) *adj* **boskier, boskiest.** *Literary.* containing or consisting of bushes or thickets: *a bosky wood.*

Bosman ruling (ˈbɒzmən) *n Soccer.* an EU ruling that allows out-of-contract footballers to leave their clubs without the clubs receiving a transfer fee. [C20: named after Jean-Marc *Bosman* (born 1964), Belgian footballer whose court case brought about the ruling]

bo's'n (ˈbəʊsᵊn) *n Nautical.* a variant spelling of **boatswain.**

Bosnia (ˈbɒznɪə) *n* a region of central Bosnia-Herzegovina: belonged to Turkey (1463–1878), to Austria-Hungary (1879–1918), then to Yugoslavia (1918–91). ▸ **ˈBosnian** *adj*

Bosnia-Herzegovina *or esp. U.S.* **Bosnia and Herzegovina** *n* a country in SW Europe; a constituent republic of Yugoslavia until 1991; in a state of civil war (1992–95); Serbian and Croatian forces were also involved: mostly barren and mountainous, with forests in the east. Language: Serbo-Croatian. Religion: Muslim, Serbian Orthodox, and Roman Catholic. Currency: marka (temporary currency). Capital: Sarajevo. Pop.: 3 366 000 (1998 est.). Area: 51 129 sq. km (19 737 sq. miles).

bosom (ˈbʊzəm) *n* **1** the chest or breast of a person, esp. the female breasts. **2** the part of a woman's dress, coat, etc., that covers the chest. **3** a protective centre or part: *the bosom of the family.* **4** the breast considered as the seat of emotions. **5** (*modifier*) very dear; intimate: *a bosom friend.* ◆ *vb* (*tr*) **6** to embrace. **7** to conceal or carry in the bosom. [Old English *bōsm;* related to Old High German *buosam*]

bosomy (ˈbʊzəmɪ) *adj* (of a woman) having large breasts.

boson (ˈbəʊzɒn) *n* any of a group of elementary particles, such as a photon or pion, that has zero or integral spin and obeys the rules of Bose-Einstein statistics. Compare **fermion.** [C20: named after Satyendra Nath BOSE; see -ON]

Bosporus (ˈbɒspərəs) *or* **Bosphorus** (ˈbɒsfərəs) *n* **the.** a strait between European and Asian Turkey, linking the Black Sea and the Sea of Marmara.

bosquet (ˈbɒskɪt) *n* a variant spelling of **bosket.**

boss[1] (bɒs) *Informal.* ◆ *n* **1** a person in charge of or employing others. **2** *Chiefly U.S.* a professional politician who controls a party machine or political organization, often using devious or illegal methods. ◆ *vb* **3** to employ, supervise, or be in charge of. **4** (usually foll. by *around* or *about*) to be domineering or overbearing towards (others). ◆ *adj* **5** *Slang.* excellent; fine: *a boss hand at carpentry; that's boss!* [C19: from Dutch *baas* master; probably related to Old High German *basa* aunt, Frisian *baes* master]

boss[2] (bɒs) *n* **1** a knob, stud, or other circular rounded protuberance, esp. an ornamental one on a vault, a ceiling, or a shield. **2** *Biology.* any of various protuberances or swellings in plants and animals. **3a** an area of increased thickness, usually cylindrical, that strengthens or provides room for a locating device on a shaft, hub of a wheel, etc. **3b** a similar projection around a hole in a casting or fabricated component. **4** a rounded mass of igneous rock, esp. the uppermost part of an underlying batholith. ◆ *vb* (*tr*) **5** to ornament with bosses; emboss. [C13: from Old French *boce,* from Vulgar Latin *bottia* (unattested); related to Italian *bozza* metal knob, swelling]

boss[3] (bɒs) *or* **bossy** *n, pl* **bosses** *or* **bossies.** *U.S.* a calf or cow. [C19: from dialect *buss* calf, perhaps ultimately from Latin *bōs* cow, ox]

BOSS (bɒs) *n* (formerly) *acronym for* Bureau of State Security; a branch of the South African security police.

bossa nova (ˈbɒsə ˈnəʊvə) *n* **1** a dance similar to the samba, originating in Brazil. **2** a piece of music composed for or in the rhythm of this dance. [C20: Portuguese, literally: new voice]

bossboy (ˈbɒsˌbɔɪ) *n S. African.* a Black African foreman of a gang of workers.

boss cocky *n Austral. informal.* a boss or person in power.

bosset (ˈbɒsɪt) *n* either of the rudimentary antlers found in young deer. [C19: from French *bossette* a small protuberance, from *bosse* BOSS[2]]

boss-eyed *adj Informal.* having a squint. [C19: from *boss* to miss or bungle a shot at a target (dialect)]

bossing (ˈbɒsɪŋ) *n Civil engineering.* the act of shaping malleable metal, such as lead cladding, with mallets to fit a surface.

bossism (ˈbɒsˌɪzəm) *n U.S.* the domination or the system of domination of political organizations by bosses.

Bossuet (*French* bɔsɥɛ) *n* **Jacques Bénigne** (ʒɑk beniɲ). 1627–1704, French bishop: noted for his funeral orations.

bossy[1] (ˈbɒsɪ) *adj* **bossier, bossiest.** *Informal.* domineering, overbearing, or authoritarian. ▸ **ˈbossily** *adv* ▸ **ˈbossiness** *n*

bossy[2] (ˈbɒsɪ) *adj* (of furniture) ornamented with bosses.

bosthoon (ˈbɒsduːn) *n Irish.* a boor. [C19: from Irish Gaelic *bastún,* from Old French *baston* penis]

boston (ˈbɒstən) *n* **1** a card game for four, played with two packs. **2** *Chiefly U.S.* a slow gliding dance, a variation of the waltz.

Boston (ˈbɒstən) *n* **1** a port in E Massachusetts, the state capital. Pop.: 558 394 (1996 est.). **2** a port in E England, in SE Lincolnshire. Pop.: 34 606 (1991).

Boston crab *n* a wrestling hold in which a wrestler seizes both or one of his opponent's legs, turns him face downwards, and exerts pressure over his back.

Boston ivy *n* the U.S. name for **Virginia creeper** (sense 2).

Boston matrix *n* a two-dimensional matrix, used in planning the business strategy of a large organization, that identifies those business units in the organization that generate cash and those that use it. [C20: from the Boston Consultancy Group, a leading firm of strategic consultants, who developed it]

Boston Tea Party *n American history.* a raid in 1773 made by citizens of Boston (disguised as Indians) on three British ships in the harbour as a protest against taxes on tea and the monopoly given to the East India Company. The contents of several hundred chests of tea were dumped into the harbour.

Boston terrier *or* **bull terrier** *n* a short stocky smooth-haired breed of terrier with a short nose, originally developed by crossing the French and English bulldogs with the English bull terrier.

bosun (ˈbəʊsᵊn) *n Nautical.* a variant spelling of **boatswain.**

Boswell (ˈbɒzwəl) *n* **James.** 1740–95, Scottish author and lawyer, noted particularly for his *Life of Samuel Johnson* (1791). ▸ **Boswellian** (bɒzˈwelɪən) *adj*

Bosworth Field (ˈbɒzwɜːθ, -wəθ) *n English history.* the site, two miles south of Market Bosworth in Leicestershire, of the battle that ended the Wars of the Roses (August, 1485). Richard III was killed and Henry Tudor was crowned king as Henry VII.

bot[1] *or* **bott** (bɒt) *n* **1** the larva of a botfly, which typically develops inside the body of a horse, sheep, or man. **2** any similar larva. ◆ See also **bots.** [C15: probably from Low German; related to Dutch *bot,* of obscure origin]

bot[2] (bɒt) *Austral. informal.* ◆ *vb* **1** to scrounge or borrow. **2** (*intr;* often foll. by *on*) to scrounge (from); impose (on). ◆ *n* **3** a scrounger. **4 on the bot** (**for**). wanting to scrounge: *he's on the bot for a cigarette.* [C20: perhaps from BOT-FLY, alluding to the creature's bite; see BITE (sense 12)]

BOT *abbrev. for* Board of Trade.

bot. *abbrev. for:* **1** botanical. **2** botany. **3** bottle.

botanical (bəˈtænɪkᵊl) *or* **botanic** *adj* **1** of or relating to botany or plants. ◆ *n* **2** any drug or pesticide that is made from parts of a plant. [C17: from Medieval Latin *botanicus,* from Greek *botanikos* relating to plants, from *botanē* plant, pasture, from *boskein* to feed; perhaps related to Latin *bōs* ox, cow] ▸ **boˈtanically** *adv*

botanic garden *n* a place in which plants are grown, studied, and exhibited.

botanize *or* **botanise** (ˈbɒtəˌnaɪz) *vb* **1** (*intr*) to collect or study plants. **2** (*tr*) to explore and study the plants in (an area or region).

botany (ˈbɒtənɪ) *n, pl* **-nies. 1** the study of plants, including their classification, structure, physiology, ecology, and economic importance. **2** the plant life of a particular region or time. **3** the biological characteristics of a particular group of plants. [C17: from BOTANICAL; compare ASTRONOMY, ASTRONOMICAL] ▸ **ˈbotanist** *n*

Botany Bay *n* **1** an inlet of the Tasman Sea, on the SE coast of Australia: surrounded by the suburbs of Sydney. **2** (in the 19th century) a British penal settlement that was in fact at Port Jackson, New South Wales.

Botany wool *n* a fine wool from the merino sheep. [C19: from BOTANY BAY, where the wool came from originally]

botargo (bəˈtɑːgəʊ) *n, pl* **-gos** *or* **-goes.** a relish consisting of the roe of mullet or tunny, salted and pressed into rolls. [C15: from obsolete Italian, from Arabic *butarkhah*]

BOTB *abbrev. for* British Overseas Trade Board.

botch (bɒtʃ) *vb* (*tr;* often foll. by *up*) **1** to spoil through clumsiness or ineptitude. **2** to repair badly or clumsily. ◆ *n* **3** Also called: **botch-up.** a badly done piece of work or repair (esp. in the phrase **make a botch of** (**something**)). [C14: of unknown origin] ▸ **ˈbotcher** *n*

botchy (ˈbɒtʃɪ) *adj* **botchier, botchiest.** clumsily done or made. ▸ **ˈbotchily** *adv* ▸ **ˈbotchiness** *n*

botel (bəʊˈtel) *n* a variant spelling of **boatel.**

botfly (ˈbɒtˌflaɪ) *n, pl* **-flies.** any of various stout-bodied hairy dipterous flies of the families *Oestridae* and *Gasterophilidae,* the larvae of which are parasites of man, sheep, and horses.

both (bəʊθ) *determiner* **1a** the two; two considered together: *both dogs were dirty.* **1b** (*as pronoun*): *both are to blame.* ◆ *conj* **2** (*coordinating*) used preceding words, phrases, or clauses joined by *and,* used to emphasize that not just one, but also the other of the joined elements is included: *both Ellen and Keith enjoyed the play; both new and exciting.* [C12: from Old Norse *bāthir;* related to Old High German *bēde,* Latin *ambō,* Greek *amphō*]

Botha ('bəʊtə) *n* **1 Louis.** 1862–1919, South African statesman and general; first prime minister of the Union of South Africa (1910–19). **2 P(ieter) W(illem)** born 1916, South African politician; defence minister (1965–78); prime minister (1978–84); state president (1984–89).

Botham ('bəʊθəm) *n* **Ian (Terence).** born 1955, English cricketer: played for Somerset (1973–86), Worcestershire (1987–91), and Durham (1991–93); captained England (1980–81).

Bothe (*German* 'boːte) *n* **Walther (Wilhelm Georg Franz)** ('valtər). 1891–1957, German physicist, who developed new methods of detecting subatomic particles. He shared the Nobel prize for physics 1954.

bother ('bɒðə) *vb* **1** (*tr*) to give annoyance, pain, or trouble to; irritate: *his bad leg is bothering him again.* **2** (*tr*) to trouble (a person) by repeatedly disturbing; pester: *stop bothering your father!* **3** (*intr*) to take the time or trouble; concern oneself: *don't bother to come with me.* **4** (*tr*) to make (a person) alarmed or confused: *the thought of her husband's return clearly bothered her.* ◆ *n* **5** a state of worry, trouble, or confusion. **6** a person or thing that causes fuss, trouble, or annoyance. **7** *Informal.* a disturbance or fight; trouble (esp. in the phrase **a spot of bother**). ◆ *interj* **8** *Chiefly Brit.* an exclamation of slight annoyance. [C18: perhaps from Irish Gaelic *bodhar* deaf, vexed; compare Irish Gaelic *buairim* I vex]

botheration (ˌbɒðəˈreɪʃən) *n, interj Informal.* another word for **bother** (senses 5, 8).

bothersome ('bɒðəsəm) *adj* causing bother; troublesome.

Bothnia ('bɒθnɪə) *n* **Gulf of.** an arm of the Baltic Sea, extending north between Sweden and Finland.

both ways *adj, adv* **1** another term for **each way. 2 have it both ways.** (*usually with a negative*) to try to get the best of a situation, argument, etc., by chopping and changing between alternatives or opposites.

Bothwell ('bɒθwəl, 'bɒð-) *n* **Earl of,** title of *James Hepburn.* 1535–78, Scottish nobleman; third husband of Mary Queen of Scots. He is generally considered to have instigated the murder of Darnley (1567).

bothy ('bɒθɪ) *n, pl* **bothies.** *Chiefly Scot.* **1** a cottage or hut. **2** (esp. in NE Scotland) a farmworker's summer quarters. **3** a mountain shelter. [C18: perhaps related to BOOTH]

bothy ballad *n Scot.* a folk song, esp. one from the farming community of NE Scotland.

bo tree (bəʊ) *n* another name for the **peepul.** [C19: from Sinhalese, from Pali *bodhitaru* tree of wisdom, from Sanskrit *bodhi* wisdom, awakening; see BODHISATTVA]

botryoidal (ˌbɒtrɪˈɔɪdᵊl) *or* **botryose** ('bɒtrɪˌəʊs, -ˌəʊz) *adj* (of minerals, parts of plants, etc.) shaped like a bunch of grapes. [C18: from Greek *botruoeidēs,* from *botrus* cluster of grapes; see -OID]

botrytis (bɒˈtraɪtɪs) *n* **1** any of a group of fungi of the genus *Botrytis,* several of which cause plant diseases. **2** *Winemaking.* a fungus of this genus, *Botrytis cinerea,* which causes noble rot.

bots (bɒts) *n* (*functioning as sing*) a digestive disease of horses and some other animals caused by the presence of botfly larvae in the stomach.

Botswana (bʊˈtʃwɑːnə; bʊtˈswɑːnə, bɒt-) *n* a republic in southern Africa: established as the British protectorate of Bechuanaland in 1885 as a defence against the Boers; became an independent state within the Commonwealth in 1966; consists mostly of a plateau averaging 1000 m (3300 ft.), with the extensive Okavango swamps in the northwest and the Kalahari Desert in the southwest. Languages: English and Tswana. Religion: animist majority. Currency: pula. Capital: Gaborone. Pop.: 1 448 000 (1998 est.). Area: about 570 000 sq. km (220 000 sq. miles).

bott (bɒt) *n* a variant spelling of **bot**[1].

botte *French.* (bɔt) *n Fencing.* a thrust or hit.

Botticelli (*Italian* bottiˈtʃɛlli) *n* **Sandro** ('sandro), original name *Alessandro di Mariano Filipepi.* 1444–1510, Italian (Florentine) painter, illustrator, and engraver, noted for the graceful outlines and delicate details of his mythological and religious paintings.

bottine (bɒˈtiːn) *n* a light boot for women or children; half-boot. [C19: from French: little boot, from *botte* boot]

bottle[1] ('bɒtᵊl) *n* **1a** a vessel, often of glass and typically cylindrical with a narrow neck that can be closed with a cap or cork, for containing liquids. **1b** (*as modifier*): *a bottle rack.* **2** Also called: **bottleful.** the amount such a vessel will hold. **3a** a container equipped with a teat that holds a baby's milk or other liquid; nursing bottle. **3b** the contents of such a container: *the baby drank his bottle.* **4** short for **magnetic bottle. 5** *Brit. slang.* nerve; courage (esp. in the phrase **lose one's bottle**). **6** *Brit. slang.* money collected by street entertainers or buskers. **7 full bottle.** *Austral. slang.* well-informed and enthusiastic about something. **8 the bottle.** *Informal.* drinking of alcohol, esp. to excess. ◆ *vb* (*tr*) **9** to put or place (wine, beer, jam, etc.) in a bottle or bottles. **10** to store (gas) in a portable container under pressure. **11** *Slang.* to injure by thrusting a broken bottle into (a person). **12** *Brit. slang.* (of a busker) to collect money from the bystanders. ◆ See also **bottle out, bottle up.** [C14: from Old French *botaille,* from Medieval Latin *butticula,* literally: a little cask, from Late Latin *buttis* cask, BUTT[4]]

bottle[2] ('bɒtᵊl) *n Dialect.* a bundle, esp. of hay. [C14: from Old French *botel,* from *botte* bundle, of Germanic origin]

bottle bank *n* a large container into which the public may throw glass bottles for recycling.

bottlebrush ('bɒtᵊlˌbrʌʃ) *n* **1** a cylindrical brush on a thin shaft, used for cleaning bottles. **2** Also called: **callistemon.** any of various Australian myrtaceous shrubs or trees of the genera *Callistemon* and *Melaleuca,* having dense spikes of large red flowers with protruding brushlike stamens. **3** any of various similar trees or shrubs.

bottled *or* **bottle gas** *n* butane or propane gas liquefied under pressure in portable containers and used in camping stoves, blowtorches, etc.

bottle-feed *vb* **-feeds, -feeding, -fed.** to feed (a baby) with milk from a bottle instead of breast-feeding.

bottle glass *n* glass used for making bottles, consisting of a silicate of sodium, calcium, and aluminium.

bottle gourd *n* **1** an Old World cucurbitaceous climbing plant, *Lagenaria siceraria,* having large hard-shelled gourds as fruits. **2** the fruit of this plant. ◆ Also called: **calabash.**

bottle green *n, adj* **a** a dark green colour. **b** (*as adj*): *a bottle-green car.*

bottle-jack *n N.Z.* a large jack used for heavy lifts.

bottleneck ('bɒtᵊlˌnɛk) *n* **1a** a narrow stretch of road or a junction at which traffic is or may be held up. **1b** the hold up. **2** something that holds up progress, esp. of a manufacturing process. **3** *Music.* **3a** the broken-off neck of a bottle placed over a finger and used to produce a buzzing effect in a style of guitar-playing originally part of the American blues tradition. **3b** the style of guitar playing using a bottleneck. ◆ *vb* **4** (*tr*) *U.S.* to be or cause an obstruction in.

bottlenose dolphin ('bɒtᵊlˌnəʊz) *n* any dolphin of the genus *Tursiops,* esp. *T. truncatus,* some of which have been kept in captivity and trained to perform tricks.

bottle-o *or* **bottle-oh** *n Austral. and N.Z. history, informal.* a dealer in empty bottles.

bottle out *vb* (*intr, adv*) *Brit. slang.* to lose one's nerve.

bottle party *n* a party to which guests bring drink.

bottler ('bɒtᵊlə) *n Austral. and N.Z. informal.* an excellent or outstanding person or thing.

bottle shop *n Austral. and N.Z.* a shop or part of a hotel where alcohol is sold in unopened containers for consumption elsewhere. Also called: **bottle store.**

bottle tree *n* any of several Australian sterculiaceous trees of the genus *Sterculia* (or *Brachychiton*) that have a bottle-shaped swollen trunk.

bottle up *vb* (*tr, adv*) **1** to restrain (powerful emotion). **2** to keep (an army or other force) contained or trapped: *the French fleet was bottled up in Le Havre.*

bottle-washer *n Informal.* a menial or factotum.

bottom ('bɒtəm) *n* **1** the lowest, deepest, or farthest removed part of a thing: *the bottom of a hill.* **2** the least important or successful position: *the bottom of a class.* **3** the ground underneath a sea, lake, or river. **4 touch bottom.** to run aground. **5** the inner depths of a person's true feelings (esp. in the phrase **from the bottom of one's heart**). **6** the underneath part of a thing. **7** *Nautical.* the parts of a vessel's hull that are under water. **8** (in literary or commercial contexts) a boat or ship. **9** *Billiards, etc.* a strike in the centre of the cue ball. **10** a dry valley or hollow. **11** (*often pl*) *U.S. and Canadian.* the low land bordering a river. **12** the lowest level worked in a mine. **13** (esp. of horses) staying power; stamina. **14** importance, seriousness, or influence: *his views all have weight and bottom.* **15** *Informal.* the buttocks. **16 at bottom.** in reality; basically or despite appearances to the contrary: *he's a kind man at bottom.* **17 be at the bottom of.** to be the ultimate cause of. **18 get to the bottom of.** to discover the real truth about. **19 knock the bottom out of.** to destroy or eliminate. ◆ *adj* (*prenominal*) **20** lowest or last: *the bottom price.* **21 bet** (*or* **put**) **one's bottom dollar on.** to be absolutely sure of (one's opinion, a person, project, etc.). **22** of, relating to, or situated at the bottom or a bottom: *the bottom shelf.* **23** fundamental; basic. ◆ *vb* **24** (*tr*) to provide (a chair, etc.) with a bottom or seat. **25** (*tr*) to discover the full facts or truth of; fathom. **26** (usually foll. by *on* or *upon*) to base or be founded (on an idea, etc.). **27** (*intr*) *Nautical.* to strike the ground beneath the water with a vessel's bottom. **28** *Austral. mining.* **28a** to mine (a hole, claim, etc.) deep enough to reach any gold there is. **28b** (*intr;* foll. by *on*) to reach (gold, mud, etc.) on bottoming. **29** *Electronics.* to saturate a transistor so that further increase of input produces no change in output. ◆ See also **bottom out.** [Old English *botm;* related to Old Norse *botn,* Old High German *bodam,* Latin *fundus,* Greek *puthmēn*]

bottom dead centre *n Engineering.* the position of the crank of a reciprocating engine when the piston is at its nearest point to the crankshaft. Also called: **outer dead centre.**

bottom drawer *n Brit.* a young woman's collection of clothes, linen, cutlery, etc., in anticipation of marriage. U.S., Canadian, and N.Z. equivalent: **hope chest.**

bottom end *n* (in vertical engines) another name for **big end** (sense 1).

bottom house *n Caribbean.* **1** the open space beneath a house built upon high pillars. **2** such a space partially enclosed and floored for use as servants' quarters.

bottoming ('bɒtəmɪŋ) *n* the lowest level of foundation material for a road or other structure.

bottomless ('bɒtəmlɪs) *adj* **1** having no bottom. **2** unlimited; inexhaustible. **3** very deep.

bottom line *n* **1** the last line of a financial statement that shows the net profit or loss of a company or organization. **2** the final outcome of a process, discussion, etc. **3** the most important or fundamental aspect of a situation.

bottommost ('bɒtəmˌməʊst) *adj* lowest or most fundamental.

bottom out *vb* (*intr, adv*) to reach the lowest point and level out: *the recession shows no sign of bottoming out.*

bottomry ('bɒtəmrɪ) *n, pl* **-ries.** *Maritime law.* a contract whereby the owner of a ship borrows money to enable the vessel to complete the voyage and pledges the ship as security for the loan. [C16: from Dutch *bodemerij,* from *bodem* BOTTOM (hull of a ship) + *-erij* -RY]

bottomset bed ('bɒtəmˌsɛt) *n* the fine sediment deposited at the front of a growing delta.

bottoms up *interj* an informal drinking toast.
bottom-up processing *n* a processing technique, either in the brain or in a computer, in which incoming information is analysed in successive steps and later-stage processing does not affect processing in earlier stages.
Bottrop (*German* 'bɔtrɔp) *n* an industrial city in W Germany, in North Rhine-Westphalia in the Ruhr. Pop.: 120 642 (1996 est.).
botulin ('bɒtjʊlɪn) *n* a potent toxin produced by the bacterium *Clostridium botulinum* in imperfectly preserved food, etc., causing botulism. [C19: from BOTULINUS]
botulinum toxin (ˌbɒtjʊ'laɪnəm) *n* a pharmaceutical preparation of botulin used in minute doses to treat various forms of muscle spasm.
botulinus (ˌbɒtjʊ'laɪnəs) *n, pl* **-nuses.** an anaerobic bacterium, *Clostridium botulinum,* whose toxins (botulins) cause botulism: family *Bacillaceae.* [C19: from New Latin, from Latin *botulus* sausage]
botulism ('bɒtjʊˌlɪzəm) *n* severe poisoning from ingestion of botulin, which affects the central nervous system producing difficulty in swallowing, visual disturbances, and respiratory paralysis: often fatal. [C19: first formed as German *Botulismus* literally: sausage poisoning, from Latin *botulus* sausage]
Botvinnik ('bɒtvɪnɪk) *n* **Mikhail Moiseivich** (mixa'il məi'sjejɪvitʃ). 1911–95, Soviet chess player; world champion (1948–57, 1958–60, 1961–63).
Bouaké (*French* bwake) *n* a market town in S central Côte d'Ivoire. Pop.: 330 000 (1995 est.).
boubou *or* **bubu** ('bu:bu:) *n* a long flowing garment worn by men and women in Mali, Nigeria, Senegal, and some other parts of Africa. [a native name in Mali]
bouchée (bu:'ʃeɪ) *n* a small pastry case filled with a savoury mixture, served hot with cocktails or as an hors d'oeuvre. [C19: from French: mouthful]
Boucher (*French* buʃe) *n* **François** (frɑ̃swa). 1703–70, French rococo artist, noted for his delicate ornamental paintings of pastoral scenes and mythological subjects.
Bouches-du-Rhône (*French* buʃdyron) *n* a department of S central France, in Provence-Alpes-Côte d'Azur region. Capital: Marseille. Pop.: 1 797 000 (1995). Area: 5284 sq. km (2047 sq. miles).
Boucicault ('bu:sɪˌkəʊ) *n* **Dion** ('daɪɒn). real name *Dionysius Lardner Boursiquot.* 1822–90, Irish dramatist and actor. His plays include *London Assurance* (1841), *The Octoroon* (1859), and *The Shaughran* (1874).
bouclé ('bu:kleɪ) *n* **1** a curled or looped yarn or fabric giving a thick knobbly effect. ◆ *adj* **2** of or designating such a yarn or fabric: *a bouclé wool coat.* [C19: from French *bouclé* curly, from *boucle* a curl, BUCKLE]
bouclée ('bu:kleɪ) *n* a support for a cue in billiards formed by doubling the first finger so that its tip is aligned with the thumb at its second joint, to form a loop through which the cue may slide. [from French, literally: curled]
Boudicca (bəʊ'dɪkə) *n* died 62 A.D., a queen of the Iceni, who led a revolt against Roman rule in Britain; after being defeated she poisoned herself. Also called: **Boadicea.**
Boudin (*French* budɛ̃) *n* **Eugène** (øʒɛn). 1824–98, French painter: one of the first French landscape painters to paint in the open air; a forerunner of impressionism.
boudoir ('bu:dwɑ:, -dwɔ:) *n* a woman's bedroom or private sitting room. [C18: from French, literally: room for sulking in, from *bouder* to sulk]
boudoir grand *n* a domestic grand piano between 5 and 6 feet in length. Compare **baby grand, concert grand.**
bouffant ('bu:fɒŋ) *adj* **1** (of a hair style) having extra height and width through back-combing; puffed out. **2** (of sleeves, skirts, etc.) puffed out. ◆ *n* **3** a bouffant hair style. [C20: from French, from *bouffer* to puff up]
bouffe (bu:f) *n* See **opéra bouffe.**
Bougainville[1] ('bu:gənˌvɪl) *n* an island in the W Pacific, in Papua New Guinea: the largest of the Solomon Islands: unilaterally declared independence in 1990; occupied by government troops in 1992. Chief town: Kieta. Area: 10 049 sq. km (3880 sq. miles).
Bougainville[2] (*French* bugɛ̃vil) *n* **Louis Antoine de** (lwi ɑ̃twan də). 1729–1811, French navigator.
bougainvillea *or* **bougainvillaea** (ˌbu:gən'vɪlɪə) *n* any tropical woody nyctaginaceous widely cultivated climbing plant of the genus *Bougainvillea,* having inconspicuous flowers surrounded by showy red or purple bracts. [C19: New Latin, named after L. A. de BOUGAINVILLE]
bough (baʊ) *n* any of the main branches of a tree. [Old English *bōg* arm, twig; related to Old Norse *bōgr* shoulder, ship's bow, Old High German *buog* shoulder, Greek *pēkhus* forearm, Sanskrit *bāhu;* see BOW[3], ELBOW]
bought (bɔ:t) *vb* **1** the past tense and past participle of **buy.** ◆ *adj* **2** purchased from a shop; not homemade.
boughten ('bɔ:tᵊn) *adj* a dialect word for **bought** (sense 2).
bougie ('bu:ʒi:, bu:'ʒi:) *n Med.* a long slender semiflexible cylindrical instrument for inserting into body passages such as the rectum or urethra to dilate structures, introduce medication, etc. [C18: from French, originally a wax candle from *Bougie* (Bujiya), Algeria]
bouillabaisse (ˌbu:jə'bɛs) *n* a rich stew or soup of fish and vegetables flavoured with spices, esp. saffron. [C19: from French, from Provençal *bouiabaisso,* literally: boil down]
bouillon ('bu:jɒn) *n* a plain unclarified broth or stock. [C18: from French, from *bouillir* to BOIL[1]]
Boulanger (*French* bulɑ̃ʒe) *n* **1 Georges** (ʒɔrʒ). 1837–91, French general and minister of war (1886–87). Accused of attempting a coup d'état, he fled to Belgium, where he committed suicide. **2 Nadia** (**Juliette**) (nadja). 1887–1979, French teacher of musical composition: her pupils included Elliott Carter, Aaron Copland, Darius Milhaud, and Virgil Thomson. She is noted also for her work in reviving the works of Monteverdi.
boulder ('bəʊldə) *n* **1** a smooth rounded mass of rock that has been shaped by erosion and transported by ice or water from its original position. **2** *Geology.* a rock fragment with a diameter greater than 256 mm and thus bigger than a cobble. [C13: probably of Scandinavian origin; compare Swedish dialect *bullersten,* from Old Swedish *bulder* rumbling + *sten* STONE] ▸ **'bouldery** *adj*
boulder clay *n* an unstratified glacial deposit consisting of fine clay, boulders, and pebbles. See also **till**[4].
Boulder Dam *n* the former name (1933–47) of **Hoover Dam.**
bouldering ('bəʊldərɪŋ) *n* rock climbing on large boulders or small outcrops either as practice or as a sport in its own right.
boule[1] ('bu:li:) *n* **1** the parliament in modern Greece. **2** the senate of an ancient Greek city-state. [C19: from Greek *boulē* senate]
boule[2] (bu:l) *n* a pear-shaped imitation ruby, sapphire, etc., made from synthetic corundum. [C19: from French: ball]
boules *French.* (bul) *pl n* (*functioning as sing*) a game, popular in France, in which metal bowls are thrown to land as near as possible to a target ball. It is played on rough surfaces. [plural of *boule* BALL[1]; see BOWL[2]]
boulevard ('bu:lvɑ:, -vɑ:d) *n* **1a** a wide usually tree-lined road in a city, often used as a promenade. **1b** (*cap. as part of a street name*): *Sunset Boulevard.* **2** *Chiefly Canadian.* **2a** a grass strip between the pavement and road. **2b** the strip of ground between the edge of a private property and the road. **2c** the centre strip of a road dividing traffic travelling in different directions. [C18: from French, from Middle Dutch *bolwerc* BULWARK; so called because originally often built on the ruins of an old rampart]
boulevardier (bu:l'vɑ:dɪˌeɪ) *n* (originally in Paris) a fashionable man, esp. one who frequents public places.
Boulez ('bu:lɛz; *French* bulɛ) *n* **Pierre** (pjɛr). born 1925, French composer and conductor, whose works employ total serialization.
boulle, boule, *or* **buhl** (bu:l) *adj* **1** denoting or relating to a type of marquetry of patterned inlays of brass and tortoiseshell, occasionally with other metals such as pewter, much used on French furniture from the 17th century. ◆ *n* **2** Also called: **'boullework.** something ornamented with such marquetry. [C18: named after André Charles *Boulle* (1642–1732), French cabinet-maker]
Boulogne (bʊ'lɔɪn; *French* bulɔɲ) *n* a port in N France, on the English Channel. Pop.: 44 244 (1990). Official name: **Boulogne-sur-Mer** (*French* bulɔɲsyrmer).
Boulogne-Billancourt (*French* bulɔɲbijɑ̃kur) *n* an industrial suburb of SW Paris. Pop.: 101 971 (1990). Also called: **Boulogne-sur-Seine** (*French* bulɔɲsyrsɛn).
boult (bəʊlt) *vb* a variant spelling of **bolt**[2].
Boult (bəʊlt) *n* Sir **Adrian** (**Cedric**). 1889–1983, English conductor.
Boulton ('bəʊltən) *n* **Matthew.** 1728–1809, British engineer and manufacturer, who financed Watt's steam engine and applied it to various industrial purposes.
Boumédienne (bu:ˌmeɪdɪ'ɛn) *n* **Houari** ('haʊərɪ). 1927–78, Algerian statesman and soldier: president of Algeria (1965–78) after overthrowing Ben Bella in a coup.
bounce (baʊns) *vb* **1** (*intr*) (of an elastic object, such as a ball) to rebound from an impact. **2** (*tr*) to cause (such an object) to hit a solid surface and spring back. **3** to rebound or cause to rebound repeatedly. **4** to move or cause to move suddenly, excitedly, or violently; spring: *she bounced up from her chair.* **5** *Slang.* (of a bank) to send (a cheque) back or (of a cheque) to be sent back unredeemed because of lack of funds in the drawer's account. **6** (*tr*) *Slang.* to force (a person) to leave (a place or job); throw out; eject. **7** (*tr*) *Brit.* to hustle (a person) into believing or doing something. ◆ *n* **8** the action of rebounding from an impact. **9** a leap; jump; bound. **10** the quality of being able to rebound; springiness. **11** *Informal.* vitality; vigour; resilience. **12** *Brit.* swagger or impudence. **13 the bounce.** *Australian Rules.* the start of play at the beginning of each quarter or after a goal. **14 get** *or* **give the bounce.** *U.S. informal.* to dismiss from or be dismissed from a job. [C13: probably of imitative origin; compare Low German *bunsen* to beat, Dutch *bonken* to thump]
bounce back *vb* (*intr, adv*) to recover one's health, good spirits, confidence, etc., easily after a setback.
bouncer ('baʊnsə) *n* **1** *Slang.* a man employed at a club, pub, disco, etc., to throw out drunks or troublemakers and stop those considered undesirable from entering. **2** *Slang.* a dishonoured cheque. **3** *Cricket.* another word for **bumper**[1]. **4** a person or thing that bounces.
bouncing ('baʊnsɪŋ) *adj* (when *postpositive,* foll. by *with*) vigorous and robust (esp. in the phrase **a bouncing baby**).
bouncing Bet (bɛt) *n* another name for **soapwort.**
bouncy ('baʊnsɪ) *adj* **bouncier, bounciest. 1** lively, exuberant, or self-confident. **2** having the capability or quality of bouncing: *a bouncy ball.* **3** responsive to bouncing; springy: *a bouncy bed.* ▸ **'bouncily** *adv* ▸ **'bounciness** *n*
bouncy castle *n Trademark.* a very large inflatable model, usually of a castle, on which children may bounce at fairs, etc.
bound[1] (baʊnd) *vb* **1** the past tense and past participle of **bind.** ◆ *adj* **2** in bonds or chains; tied with or as if with a rope: *a bound prisoner.* **3** (*in combination*) restricted; confined: *housebound; fogbound.* **4** (*postpositive,* foll. by an infinitive) destined; sure; certain: *it's bound to happen.* **5** (*postpositive,* often foll. by *by*) compelled or obliged to act, behave, or think in a particular way, as by duty, circumstance, or convention. **6** (of a book) secured within a cover or binding: *to deliver bound books.* See also **half-bound. 7** (*postpositive,* foll. by *on*) *U.S.* resolved; determined: *bound on winning.* **8** *Linguistics.* **8a** denoting a morpheme, such as the prefix *non-,* that occurs only as part of another word and not as a separate word in itself. Compare **free** (sense 21). **8b** (in systemic grammar) denoting a clause that has a nonfinite predicator or that is introduced by a binder, and that occurs only together with a freestanding clause. **9** *Logic.* (of a variable) occurring within the scope of a quantifier that indicates

the degree of generality of the open sentence in which the variable occurs: in (*x*) (*Fx* → *bxy*), *x* is bound and *y* is free. Compare **free** (sense 22). **10 bound up with.** closely or inextricably linked with: *his irritability is bound up with his work.* **11 I'll be bound.** I am sure (something) is true.

bound[2] (baʊnd) *vb* **1** to move forwards or make (one's way) by leaps or jumps. **2** to bounce; spring away from an impact. ◆ *n* **3** a jump upwards or forwards. **4 by leaps and bounds.** with unexpectedly rapid progess: *her condition improved by leaps and bounds.* **5** a sudden pronounced sense of excitement: *his heart gave a sudden bound when he saw her.* **6** a bounce, as of a ball. **[C16:** from Old French *bond* a leap, from *bondir* to jump, resound, from Vulgar Latin *bombitīre* (unattested) to buzz, hum, from Latin *bombus* booming sound**]**

bound[3] (baʊnd) *vb* **1** (*tr*) to place restrictions on; limit. **2** (when *intr*, foll. by *on*) to form a boundary of (an area of land or sea, political or administrative region, etc.). ◆ *n* **3** *Maths.* **3a** a number which is greater than all the members of a set of numbers (an **upper bound**), or less than all its members (a **lower bound**). See also **bounded** (sense 1). **3b** more generally, an element of an ordered set that has the same ordering relation to all the members of a given subset. **3c** whence, an estimate of the extent of some set. **4** See **bounds. [C13:** from Old French *bonde,* from Medieval Latin *bodina,* of Gaulish origin**]**

bound[4] (baʊnd) *adj* **a** (*postpositive,* often foll. by *for*) going or intending to go towards; on the way to: *a ship bound for Jamaica; homeward bound.* **b** (*in combination*): *northbound traffic.* **[C13:** from Old Norse *buinn,* past participle of *būa* to prepare**]**

boundary ('baʊndərɪ, -drɪ) *n, pl* **-ries. 1** something that indicates the farthest limit, as of an area; border. **2** *Cricket.* **2a** the marked limit of the playing area. **2b** a stroke that hits the ball beyond this limit. **2c** the four runs scored with such a stroke, or the six runs if the ball crosses the boundary without touching the ground.

Boundary Commission *n* (in Britain) a body established by statute to undertake periodic reviews of the boundaries of parliamentary constituencies and to recommend changes to take account of population shifts.

boundary layer *n* the layer of fluid closest to the surface of a solid past which the fluid flows: it has a lower rate of flow than the bulk of the fluid because of its adhesion to the solid.

boundary rider *n Austral.* an employee on a sheep or cattle station whose job is to maintain fences in good repair and to prevent stock from straying.

bounded ('baʊndɪd) *adj Maths.* **1** (of a set) having a bound, esp. where a measure is defined in terms of which all the elements of the set, or the differences between all pairs of members, are less than some value, or else all its members lie within some other well-defined set. **2** (of an operator, function, etc.) having a bounded set of values.

bounden ('baʊndən) *adj* morally obligatory (archaic except in the phrase **bounden duty**).

bounder ('baʊndə) *n* **1** *Old-fashioned Brit. slang.* a morally reprehensible person; cad. **2** a person or animal that bounds.

boundless ('baʊndlɪs) *adj* unlimited; vast: *boundless energy.* ▸ **'boundlessly** *adv* ▸ **'boundlessness** *n*

bounds (baʊndz) *pl n* **1** (*sometimes sing*) a limit; boundary (esp. in the phrase **know no bounds**). **2** something that restrains or confines, esp. the standards of a society: *within the bounds of modesty.* **3 beat the bounds.** See **beat** (sense 26). ◆ See also **out of bounds.**

bounteous ('baʊntɪəs) *adj Literary.* **1** giving freely; generous: *the bounteous goodness of God.* **2** plentiful; abundant. ▸ **'bounteously** *adv* ▸ **'bounteousness** *n*

bountiful ('baʊntɪfʊl) *adj* **1** plentiful; ample (esp. in the phrase **a bountiful supply**). **2** giving freely; generous. ▸ **'bountifully** *adv* ▸ **'bountifulness** *n*

bounty ('baʊntɪ) *n, pl* **-ties. 1** generosity in giving to others; liberality. **2** a generous gift; something freely provided. **3** a payment made by a government, as, formerly, to a sailor on enlisting or to a soldier after a campaign. **4** any reward or premium: *a bounty of 20p for every rat killed.* **[C13** (in the sense: goodness): from Old French *bontet,* from Latin *bonitās* goodness, from *bonus* good**]**

Bounty ('baʊntɪ) *n* a British naval ship commanded by Captain William Bligh, which was on a scientific voyage in 1789 between Tahiti and the West Indies when her crew mutinied.

bouquet *n* **1** (bəʊ'keɪ, buː-). a bunch of flowers, esp. a large carefully arranged one. **2** (buː'keɪ). Also called: **nose.** the characteristic aroma or fragrance of a wine or liqueur. **3** a compliment or expression of praise. **[C18:** from French: thicket, from Old French *bosc* forest, wood, probably of Germanic origin; see BUSH[1]**]**

bouquet garni ('buːkeɪ gɑː'niː) *n, pl* **bouquets garnis** ('buːkeɪz gɑː'niː). a bunch of herbs tied together and used for flavouring soups, stews, etc. **[C19:** from French, literally: garnished bouquet**]**

Bourbaki ('bɔːbəkɪ) *n* **Nicholas.** the pseudonym of a group of mainly French mathematicians that, since 1939, has been producing a monumental work on advanced mathematics, *Eléments de Mathématique.*

bourbon ('bɜːbᵊn) *n* a whiskey distilled, chiefly in the U.S., from maize, esp. one containing at least 51 per cent maize (the rest being malt and rye) and aged in charred white-oak barrels. **[C19:** named after *Bourbon* county, Kentucky, where it was first made**]**

Bourbon ('bʊəbᵊn; *French* burbɔ̃) *n* **a** a member of the European royal line that ruled in France from 1589 to 1793 (when Louis XVI was executed by the revolutionaries) and was restored in 1815, continuing to rule in its Orleans branch from 1830 until 1848. Bourbon dynasties also ruled in Spain (1700–1808; 1813–1931) and Naples and Sicily (1734–1806; 1815–1860). **b** (*as modifier*): *the Bourbon kings.*

Bourbon biscuit *n* a rich chocolate-flavoured biscuit with a chocolate-cream filling.

Bourbonism ('bʊəbəˌnɪzəm) *n* **1** support for Bourbon rule. **2** *U.S.* extreme political and social conservatism.

bourdon ('bʊədᵊn, 'bɔːdᵊn) *n* **1** a 16-foot organ stop of the stopped diapason type. **2** the drone of a bagpipe. **3** a drone or pedal point in the bass of a harmonized melody. **[C14:** from Old French: drone (of a musical instrument), of imitative origin**]**

Bourdon gauge *n* a type of pressure gauge consisting of a flattened curved tube attached to a pointer that moves around a dial. As the pressure in the tube increases the tube tends to straighten and the pointer indicates the applied pressure. **[C19:** named after Eugène *Bourdon* (1808–84), French hydraulic engineer, who invented it**]**

bourg (bʊəg; *French* bur) *n* a French market town, esp. one beside a castle. **[C15:** French, from Old French *borc,* from Late Latin *burgus* castle, of Germanic origin; see BOROUGH**]**

bourgeois[1] ('bʊəʒwɑː, bʊə'ʒwɑː) *Often disparaging.* ◆ *n, pl* **-geois. 1** a member of the middle class, esp. one regarded as being conservative and materialistic or (in Marxist thought) a capitalist exploiting the working class. **2** a mediocre, unimaginative, or materialistic person. ◆ *adj* **3** characteristic of, relating to, or comprising the middle class. **4** conservative or materialistic in outlook: *a bourgeois mentality.* **5** (in Marxist thought) dominated by capitalists or capitalist interests. **[C16:** from Old French *borjois, burgeis* burgher, citizen, from *bourg* town; see BURGESS**]** ▸ **bourgeoise** ('bʊəʒwɑːz, bʊə'ʒwɑːz) *fem n*

bourgeois[2] (bə'dʒɔɪs) *n* (formerly) a size of printer's type approximately equal to 9 point. **[C19:** perhaps from its size, midway between long primer and brevier**]**

Bourgeois (*French* burʒwa) *n* **Léon Victor Auguste** (leɔ̃ viktɔr ogyst). 1851–1925, French statesman; first chairman of the League of Nations: Nobel peace prize 1920.

bourgeoisie (ˌbʊəʒwɑː'ziː) *n* **the. 1** the middle classes. **2** (in Marxist thought) the ruling class of the two basic classes of capitalist society, consisting of capitalists, manufacturers, bankers, and other employers. The bourgeoisie owns the most important of the means of production, through which it exploits the working class.

bourgeon ('bɜːdʒən) *n, vb* a variant spelling of **burgeon.**

Bourges (*French* burʒ) *n* a city in central France. Pop.: 75 609 (1990).

Bourgogne (burgɔɲ) *n* the French name for **Burgundy.**

Bourguiba (bʊə'giːbə) *n* **Habib ben Ali** (hæ'bɪb bɛn 'ɑːlɪ). born 1903, Tunisian statesman: president of Tunisia (1957–87); a moderate and an advocate of gradual social change. He was deposed and put under house arrest in a bloodless coup.

Bourke-White (ˌbɜːk'waɪt) *n* **Margaret.** 1906–71, U.S. photographer, a pioneer of modern photojournalism: noted esp. for her coverage of World War II.

bourn[1] *or* **bourne** (bɔːn) *n Archaic.* **1** a destination; goal. **2** a boundary. **[C16:** from Old French *borne;* see BOUND[3]**]**

bourn[2] (bɔːn) *n Chiefly southern Brit.* a stream, esp. an intermittent one in chalk areas. Compare **burn**[2]. **[C16:** from Old French *bodne* limit; see BOUND[3]**]**

Bournemouth ('bɔːnməθ) *n* **1** a resort in S England, in Bournemouth unitary authority, Dorset, on the English Channel. Pop.: 155 488 (1991). **2** a unitary authority in SE Dorset. Pop.: 160 900 (1995). Area: 46 sq. km (17 sq. miles).

bourrée ('bʊəreɪ) *n* **1** a traditional French dance in fast duple time, resembling a gavotte. **2** a piece of music composed in the rhythm of this dance. **[C18:** from French *bourrée* a bundle of faggots (it was originally danced round a fire of faggots)**]**

Bourse (bʊəs) *n* a stock exchange of continental Europe, esp. Paris. **[C19:** from French, literally: purse, from Medieval Latin *bursa,* ultimately from Greek: leather**]**

bouse *or* **bowse** (baʊz) *vb* (*tr*) *Nautical.* to raise or haul with a tackle. **[C16:** of unknown origin**]**

boustrophedon (ˌbuːstrə'fiːdᵊn, ˌbaʊ-) *adj* having alternate lines written from right to left and from left to right. **[C17:** from Greek, literally: turning as in ploughing with oxen, from *bous* ox + *-strophēdon* from *strephein* to turn; see STROPHE**]**

bout (baʊt) *n* **1a** a period of time spent doing something, such as drinking. **1b** a period of illness. **2** a contest or fight, esp. a boxing or wrestling match. **[C16:** variant of obsolete *bought* turn; related to German *Bucht* BIGHT; see ABOUT**]**

boutade (buː'tɑːd) *n* an outburst; sally. **[C17:** from French, from *bouter* to thrust**]**

boutique (buː'tiːk) *n* **1** a shop, esp. a small one selling fashionable clothes and other items. **2** (*modifier*) of or denoting a small specialized producer or business: *a boutique operation; a boutique winery.* **[C18:** from French, probably from Old Provençal *botica,* ultimately from Greek *apothēkē* storehouse; see APOTHECARY**]**

boutonniere (ˌbuːtɒnɪ'ɛə) *n* another name for **buttonhole** (sense 2). **[C19:** from French: buttonhole, from *bouton* BUTTON**]**

bouvier ('buːvɪeɪ) *n* a large powerful dog of a Belgian breed, having a rough shaggy coat: used esp. for cattle herding and guarding. **[C20:** from French, literally: cowherd**]**

bouzouki (buː'zuːkɪ) *n* a Greek long-necked stringed musical instrument related to the mandolin. **[C20:** from Modern Greek *mpouzouki,* perhaps from Turkish *büjük* large**]**

Bovet (*French* bɔvɛ) *n* **Daniel.** 1907–92, Italian pharmacologist, born in Switzerland, noted for his pioneering work on antihistamine drugs. Nobel prize for physiology or medicine 1957.

bovid ('bəʊvɪd) *adj* **1** of, relating to, or belonging to the *Bovidae,* a family of ruminant artiodactyl hollow-horned mammals including sheep, goats, cattle, antelopes, and buffalo. ◆ *n* **2** any bovid animal. **[C19:** from New Latin *Bovidae,* from Latin *bōs* ox**]**

bovine ('bəʊvaɪn) *adj* **1** of, relating to, or belonging to the *Bovini* (cattle), a bovid tribe including domestic cattle. 2 (of people) dull; sluggish; stolid. ◆ *n* 3 any animal belonging to the *Bovini.* [C19: from Late Latin *bovīnus* concerning oxen or cows, from Latin *bōs* ox, cow] ▸ **'bovinely** *adv*

bovine somatotrophin *n* the full name for **BST** (sense 1).

bovine spongiform encephalopathy *n* the full name for **BSE.**

Bovril ('bɒvrɪl) *n Trademark.* a concentrated beef extract, used for flavouring, as a stock, etc.

bovver ('bɒvə) *n Brit. slang.* **a** rowdiness, esp. caused by gangs of teenage youths. **b** (*as modifier*): *a bovver boy.* [C20: slang pronunciation of BOTHER]

bovver boots *pl n Brit. slang.* heavy boots worn by some teenage youths in Britain, used in gang fights.

bow[1] (baʊ) *vb* **1** to lower (one's head) or bend (one's knee or body) as a sign of respect, greeting, assent, or shame. **2** to bend or cause to bend; incline downwards. **3** (*intr; usually foll. by to or before*) to comply or accept: *bow to the inevitable.* **4** (*tr;* foll. by *in, out, to,* etc.) to usher (someone) into or out of a place with bows and deference: *the manager bowed us to our car.* **5** (*tr;* usually foll. by *down*) to bring (a person, nation, etc.) to a state of submission. **6 bow and scrape.** to behave in an excessively deferential or obsequious way. ◆ *n* **7** a lowering or inclination of the head or body as a mark of respect, greeting, or assent. **8 take a bow.** to acknowledge or receive applause or praise. ◆ See also **bow out.** [Old English *būgan,* related to Old Norse *bjūgr* bent, Old High German *biogan* to bend, Dutch *buigen*]

bow[2] (bəʊ) *n* **1** a weapon for shooting arrows, consisting of an arch of flexible wood, plastic, metal, etc. bent by a string (**bowstring**) fastened at each end. See also **crossbow. 2a** a long slightly curved stick across which are stretched strands of horsehair, used for playing the strings of a violin, viola, cello, or related instrument. **2b** a stroke with such a stick. **3a** a decorative interlacing of ribbon or other fabrics, usually having two loops and two loose ends. **3b** the knot forming such an interlacing; bowknot. **4a** something that is curved, bent, or arched. **4b** (*in combination*): *rainbow; oxbow; saddlebow.* **5** a person who uses a bow and arrow; archer. **6** *U.S.* **6a** a frame of a pair of spectacles. **6b** a sidepiece of the frame of a pair of spectacles that curls round behind the ear. **7** a metal ring forming the handle of a pair of scissors or of a large old-fashioned key. **8** *Architect.* part of a building curved in the form of a bow. See also **bow window.** ◆ *vb* **9** to form or cause to form a curve or curves. **10** to make strokes of a bow across (violin strings). [Old English *boga* arch, bow; related to Old Norse *bogi* a bow, Old High German *bogo,* Old Irish *bocc,* and BOW[1]]

bow[3] (baʊ) *n* **1** *Chiefly Nautical.* **1a** (*often pl*) the forward end or part of a vessel. **1b** (*as modifier*): *the bow mooring line.* **2** *Rowing.* short for **bowman**[2]. **3 on the port** (*or* **starboard**) **bow.** *Nautical.* within 45 degrees to the port (or starboard) of straight ahead. **4 a shot across someone's bows.** *Informal.* a warning. [C15: probably from Low German *boog;* related to Dutch *boeg,* Danish *bov* ship's bow, shoulder; see BOUGH]

Bow (bəʊ) *n* **Clara,** known as the *It Girl.* 1905–65, U.S. film actress, noted for her vivacity and sex appeal.

bow collector (bəʊ) *n* a sliding current collector, consisting of a bow-shaped strip mounted on a hinged framework, used on trains, etc., to collect current from an overhead-wire. Compare **skate**[1] (sense 4).

bow compass (bəʊ) *n Geometry.* a compass in which the legs are joined by a flexible metal bow-shaped spring rather than a hinge, the angle being adjusted by a screw. Also called: **bow-spring compass.**

bowdlerize *or* **bowdlerise** ('baʊdləˌraɪz) *vb* (*tr*) to remove passages or words regarded as indecent from (a play, novel, etc.); expurgate. [C19: after Thomas *Bowdler* (1754–1825), English editor who published an expurgated edition of Shakespeare] ▸ **ˌbowdleri'zation** *or* **ˌbowdleri'sation** *n* ▸ **'bowdlerˌizer** *or* **'bowdlerˌiser** *n* ▸ **'bowdlerism** *n*

bowed (baʊd) *adj* **1** lowered; bent forward; curved: *bowed head; bowed back.* **2 bowed down.** (foll. by *by* or *with*) weighed down; troubled: *bowed down by grief.*

bowel ('baʊəl) *n* **1** an intestine, esp. the large intestine in man. **2** (*pl*) innards; entrails. **3** (*pl*) the deep or innermost part (esp. in the phrase **the bowels of the earth**). **4** (*pl*) *Archaic.* the emotions, esp. of pity or sympathy. [C13: from Old French *bouel,* from Latin *botellus* a little sausage, from *botulus* sausage]

bowel movement *n* **1** the discharge of faeces; defecation. **2** the waste matter discharged; faeces.

Bowen ('bəʊən) *n* **Elizabeth** (**Dorothea Cole**). 1899–1973, British novelist and short-story writer, born in Ireland. Her novels include *The Death of the Heart* (1938) and *The Heat of the Day* (1949).

bower[1] ('baʊə) *n* **1** a shady leafy shelter or recess, as in a wood or garden; arbour. **2** *Literary.* a lady's bedroom or apartments, esp. in a medieval castle; boudoir. **3** *Literary.* a country cottage, esp. one regarded as charming or picturesque. [Old English *būr* dwelling; related to Old Norse *būr* pantry, Old High German *būr* dwelling] ▸ **'bowery** *adj*

bower[2] ('baʊə) *n Nautical.* a vessel's bow anchor. [C18: from BOW[3] + -ER[1]]

bower[3] ('baʊə) *n* a jack in euchre and similar card games. [C19: from German *Bauer* peasant, jack (in cards)]

bowerbird ('baʊəˌbɜːd) *n* **1** any of various songbirds of the family *Ptilonorhynchidae,* of Australia and New Guinea. The males build bower-like display grounds in the breeding season to attract the females. **2** *Informal, chiefly Austral.* a person who collects miscellaneous objects.

Bowery ('baʊərɪ) *n* **the.** a street in New York City noted for its cheap hotels and bars, frequented by vagrants and drunks. [C17: from Dutch *bouwerij,* from *bouwen* to farm + *-erij* -ERY; see BOOR, BOER]

bowfin ('bəʊˌfɪn) *n* a primitive North American freshwater bony fish, *Amia calva,* with an elongated body and a very long dorsal fin: family *Amiidae.*

bowhead ('bəʊˌhɛd) *n* a large-mouthed arctic whale, *Balaena mysticetus,* that has become rare through overfishing but is now a protected species.

Bowie *n* **1** ('baʊɪ, 'bəʊɪ). **David,** real name *David Jones.* born 1947, British rock singer, songwriter, and film actor. His recordings include "Space Oddity" (1969), *The Rise and Fall of Ziggy Stardust and the Spiders from Mars* (1972), *Heroes* (1977), *Let's Dance* (1983), and *Earthling* (1997). **2** ('bəʊɪ). **James,** known as *Jim Bowie.* 1796–1836, U.S. frontiersman. A hero of the Texas Revolution against Mexico (1835–36), he died at the Battle of the Alamo.

bowie knife ('bəʊɪ) *n* a stout hunting knife with a short hilt and a guard for the hand. [C19: named after Jim BOWIE, who popularized it]

bowing ('bəʊɪŋ) *n* the technique of using the bow in playing a violin, viola, cello, or related instrument.

bowknot ('bəʊˌnɒt) *n* a decorative knot usually having two loops and two loose ends; bow.

bowl[1] (bəʊl) *n* **1** a round container open at the top, used for holding liquid, keeping fruit, serving food, etc. **2** Also: **bowlful.** the amount a bowl will hold. **3** the rounded or hollow part of an object, esp. of a spoon or tobacco pipe. **4** any container shaped like a bowl, such as a sink or lavatory. **5** *Chiefly U.S.* a bowl-shaped building or other structure, such as a football stadium or amphitheatre. **6** a bowl-shaped depression of the land surface. See also **dust bowl. 7** *Literary.* **6a** a drinking cup. **6b** intoxicating drink. [Old English *bolla;* related to Old Norse *bolli,* Old Saxon *bollo*]

bowl[2] (bəʊl) *n* **1** a wooden ball used in the game of bowls, having flattened sides, one side usually being flatter than the other in order to make it run on a curved course. **2** a large heavy ball with holes for gripping with the fingers and thumb, used in tenpin bowling. ◆ *vb* **3** to roll smoothly or cause to roll smoothly, esp. by throwing underarm along the ground. **4** (*intr;* usually foll. by *along*) to move easily and rapidly, as in a car. **5** *Cricket.* **5a** to send (a ball) down the pitch from one's hand towards the batsman, keeping the arm straight while doing so. **5b** Also: **bowl out.** to dismiss (a batsman) by delivering a ball that breaks his wicket. **6** (*intr*) to play bowls or tenpin bowling. **7** (*tr*) (in tenpin bowling) to score (a specified amount): *he bowled 120.* ◆ See also **bowl over, bowls.** [C15: from French *boule,* ultimately from Latin *bulla* bubble]

bow legs (bəʊ) *pl n* a condition in which the legs curve outwards like a bow between the ankle and the thigh. Also called: **bandy legs.** ▸ **bow-legged** (bəʊ'legɪd, bəʊ'legd) *adj*

bowler[1] ('bəʊlə) *n* **1** one who bowls in cricket. **2** a player at the game of bowls.

bowler[2] ('bəʊlə) *n* a stiff felt hat with a rounded crown and narrow curved brim. U.S. and Canadian name: **derby.** [C19: named after John *Bowler,* 19th-century London hatter]

bowler[3] ('bəʊlə) *n Dublin dialect.* a dog. [perhaps from B(OW-WOW) + (H)OWLER]

Bowles (bəʊlz) *n* **Paul.** born 1910, U.S. novelist, short-story writer, and composer, living in Tangiers. His novels include *The Sheltering Sky* (1949) and *The Spider's House* (1955).

bowline ('bəʊlɪn) *n Nautical.* **1** a line for controlling the weather leech of a square sail when a vessel is close-hauled. **2 on a bowline.** beating close to the wind. **3** a knot used for securing a loop that will not slip at the end of a piece of rope. [C14: probably from Middle Low German *bōlīne,* equivalent to BOW[3] + LINE[1]]

bowling ('bəʊlɪŋ) *n* **1** any of various games in which a heavy ball is rolled down a special alley, usually made of wood, at a group of wooden pins, esp. the games of tenpin bowling (tenpins) and skittles (ninepins). **2** the game of bowls. **3** *Cricket.* the act of delivering the ball to the batsman. **4** (*modifier*) of or relating to bowls or bowling: *a bowling team.*

bowling alley *n* **1a** a long narrow wooden lane down which the ball is rolled in tenpin bowling. **1b** a similar lane or alley, usually with raised sides, for playing skittles (ninepins). **2** a building having several lanes for tenpin bowling.

bowling crease *n Cricket.* a line marked at the wicket, over which a bowler must not advance fully before delivering the ball.

bowling green *n* an area of closely mown turf on which the game of bowls is played.

bowl over *vb* (*tr, adv*) **1** *Informal.* to surprise (a person) greatly, esp. in a pleasant way; astound; amaze: *he was bowled over by our gift.* **2** to knock (a person or thing) down; cause to fall over.

bowls (bəʊlz) *n* (*functioning as sing*) **1a** a game played on a bowling green in which a small bowl (the jack) is pitched from a mark and two opponents or opposing teams take turns to roll biased wooden bowls towards it, the object being to finish as near the jack as possible. **1b** (*as modifier*): *a bowls tournament.* **2** skittles or tenpin bowling.

bowman[1] ('bəʊmən) *n, pl* **-men.** *Archaic.* an archer.

bowman[2] ('baʊmən) *n, pl* **-men.** *Nautical.* an oarsman at the bow of a boat. Also called: **bow oar.**

bow out (baʊ) *vb* (*adv; usually tr*) often foll. by *of*) to retire or withdraw gracefully.

bowsaw ('bəʊˌsɔː) *n* a saw with a thin blade in a bow-shaped frame.

bowse (bauz) *vb* a variant spelling of **bouse.**

bowser ('bauzə) *n* **1** a tanker containing fuel for aircraft, military vehicles, etc. **2** *Austral. and N.Z. obsolete.* a petrol pump at a filling station. [originally a U.S. proprietary name, from S. F. *Bowser,* U.S. inventor, who made the first one in 1885]

bowshot ('bəʊˌʃɒt) *n* the distance an arrow travels from the bow.

bowsie ('bauzi:) *n Irish.* a low-class mean or obstreperous person. [of unknown origin]

bowsprit ('bəʊsprɪt) *n Nautical.* a spar projecting from the bow of a vessel, esp. a sailing vessel, used to carry the headstay as far forward as possible. [C13: from Middle Low German *bōchsprēt,* from *bōch* BOW[3] + *sprēt* pole]

Bow Street runner (bəʊ) *n* (in Britain from 1749 to 1829) an officer at Bow Street magistrates' court, London, whose duty was to pursue and arrest criminals.

bowstring ('bəʊˌstrɪŋ) *n* the string of an archer's bow, usually consisting of three strands of hemp.

bowstring hemp *n* a hemplike fibre obtained from the sansevieria.

bow tie (bəʊ) *n* a man's tie tied in a bow, now chiefly in plain black for formal evening wear.

bow weight (bəʊ) *n Archery.* the poundage required to draw a bow to the full length of the arrow.

bow window (bəʊ) *n* a bay window in the shape of a curve.

bow-wow ('baʊˌwaʊ, -'waʊ) *n* **1** a child's word for **dog.** **2** an imitation of the bark of a dog. ◆ *vb* **3** (*intr*) to bark or imitate a dog's bark.

bowyangs ('bəʊjæŋz) *pl n Austral. and N.Z. history.* a pair of strings or straps secured round each trouser leg below the knee, worn esp. by sheep-shearers and other labourers. **[C19:** from English dialect *bowy-yanks* leggings**]**

bowyer ('bəʊjə) *n* a person who makes or sells archery bows.

box[1] (bɒks) *n* **1** a receptacle or container made of wood, cardboard, etc., usually rectangular and having a removable or hinged lid. **2** Also called: **boxful.** the contents of such a receptacle or the amount it can contain: *he ate a whole box of chocolates.* **3** any of various containers for a specific purpose: *a money box; letter box.* **4** (*often in combination*) any of various small cubicles, kiosks, or shelters: *a telephone box or callbox; a sentry box; a signal box on a railway.* **5** a separate compartment in a public place for a small group of people, as in a theatre or certain restaurants. **6** an enclosure within a courtroom. See **jury box, witness box.** **7** a compartment for a horse in a stable or a vehicle. See **loosebox, horsebox.** **8** *Brit.* a small country house occupied by sportsmen when following a field sport, esp. shooting. **9a** a protective housing for machinery or mechanical parts. **9b** the contents of such a box. **9c** (*in combination*): *a gearbox.* **10** a shaped device of light tough material worn by sportsmen to protect the genitals, esp. in cricket. **11** a section of printed matter on a page, enclosed by lines, a border, or white space. **12** a central agency to which mail is addressed and from which it is collected or redistributed: *a post-office box; to reply to a box number in a newspaper advertisement.* **13** short for **penalty box.** **14** *Baseball.* either of the designated areas for the batter or the pitcher. **15** the raised seat on which the driver sits in a horse-drawn coach. **16** *N.Z.* a wheeled container for transporting coal in a mine. **17** *Austral. and N.Z.* an accidental mixing of herds or flocks. **18** a hole cut into the base of a tree to collect the sap. **19** short for **Christmas box.** **20** a device for dividing water into two or more ditches in an irrigation system. **21** an informal name for a **coffin.** **22** *Austral. taboo slang.* the female genitals. **23 be a box of birds.** *N.Z.* to be very well indeed. **24 the box.** *Brit. informal.* television. **25 out of the box.** *Austral. informal.* outstanding or excellent: *a day out of the box.* ◆ *vb* **26** (*tr*) to put into a box. **27** (*tr; usually foll. by in or up*) to prevent from moving freely; confine. **28** (*tr; foll. by in*) *Printing.* to enclose (text) within a ruled frame. **29** (*tr*) to make a cut in the base of (a tree) in order to collect the sap. **30** (*tr*) *Austral. and N.Z.* to mix (flocks or herds) accidentally. **31** (*tr; sometimes foll. by up*) *N.Z.* to confuse: *I am all boxed up.* **32** *Nautical.* short for **boxhaul.** **33 box the compass.** *Nautical.* to name the compass points in order. **[**Old English *box,* from Latin *buxus, from Greek puxos* BOX[3]**]** ▸ **'box,like** *adj*

box[2] (bɒks) *vb* **1** (*tr*) to fight (an opponent) in a boxing match. **2** (*intr*) to engage in boxing. **3** (*tr*) to hit (a person) with the fist; punch or cuff. **4 box clever.** to behave in a careful and cunning way. ◆ *n* **5** a punch with the fist, esp. on the ear. **[C14:** of uncertain origin; perhaps related to Dutch *boken* to shunt, push into position**]**

box[3] (bɒks) *n* **1** a dense slow-growing evergreen tree or shrub of the genus *Buxus,* esp. *B. sempervirens,* which has small shiny leaves and is used for hedges, borders, and garden mazes: family *Buxaceae.* **2** the wood of this tree. See **boxwood** (sense 1). **3** any of several trees the timber or foliage of which resembles this tree, esp. various species of *Eucalyptus* with rough bark. **[**Old English, from Latin *buxus***]**

box beam *n* another name for **box girder.**

boxberry ('bɒksbərɪ) *n, pl* **-ries. 1** the fruit of the partridgeberry or wintergreen. **2** another name for **partridgeberry** and **wintergreen** (sense 1).

boxboard ('bɒksˌbɔːd) *n* a tough paperboard made from wood and wastepaper pulp: used for making boxes, etc.

box calf *n* black calfskin leather, tanned with chromium salts, having a pattern of fine creases formed by boarding. **[C20:** named after Joseph *Box,* London shoemaker**]**

box camera *n* a simple box-shaped camera having an elementary lens, shutter, and viewfinder.

box canyon *n Western U.S.* a canyon with vertical or almost vertical walls.

boxcar ('bɒksˌkɑː) *n U.S. and Canadian.* a closed railway freight van.

box chronometer *n Nautical.* a ship's chronometer, supported on gimbals in a wooden box.

box coat *n* **1** a plain short coat that hangs loosely from the shoulders. **2** a heavy overcoat, worn formerly by coachmen.

box elder *n* a medium-sized fast-growing widely cultivated North American maple, *Acer negundo,* which has compound leaves with lobed leaflets. Also called: **ash-leaved maple.**

boxer ('bɒksə) *n* **1** a man who boxes, either professionally or as a hobby; pugilist. **2** a medium-sized smooth-haired breed of dog with a short nose and a docked tail.

Boxer ('bɒksə) *n* **a** a member of a nationalistic Chinese secret society that led an unsuccessful rebellion in 1900 against foreign interests in China. **b** (*as modifier*): *the Boxer Rebellion.* **[C18:** rough translation of Chinese *I Ho Ch'üan,* literally: virtuous harmonious fist, altered from *I Ho T'uan* virtuous harmonious society**]**

boxer shorts *pl n* men's underpants shaped like shorts but having a front opening. Also called: **boxers.**

boxfish ('bɒksˌfɪʃ) *n, pl* **-fish** *or* **-fishes.** another name for **trunkfish.**

box girder *n* **a** a girder that is hollow and square or rectangular in shape. **b** (*as modifier*): *a box-girder bridge.* ◆ Also called: **box beam.**

boxhaul ('bɒksˌhɔːl) *vb Nautical.* to bring (a square-rigger) onto a new tack by backwinding the foresails and steering hard round.

boxing ('bɒksɪŋ) *n* **a** the act, art, or profession of fighting with the fists, esp. the modern sport practised under Queensberry rules. **b** (*as modifier*): *a boxing enthusiast.*

Boxing Day *n Brit.* the first day (traditionally and strictly, the first weekday) after Christmas, observed as a holiday. **[C19:** from the custom of giving Christmas boxes to tradesmen and staff on this day**]**

boxing glove *n* one of a pair of thickly padded mittens worn for boxing.

box jellyfish *n* any of various highly venomous jellyfishes of the order *Cubomedusae,* esp. *Chironex fleckeri,* of Australian tropical waters, having a cuboidal body with tentacles hanging from each of the lower corners. Also called (Austral.): **sea wasp.**

box junction *n* (in Britain) a road junction having yellow cross-hatching painted on the road surface. Vehicles may only enter the hatched area when their exit is clear.

box kite *n* a kite with a boxlike frame open at both ends.

box number *n* **1** the number of an individual pigeonhole at a newspaper to which replies to an advertisement may be addressed. **2** the number of an individual pigeonhole at a post office from which mail may be collected.

box office *n* **1** an office at a theatre, cinema, etc., where tickets are sold. **2** the receipts from a play, film, etc. **3a** the public appeal of an actor or production: *the musical was bad box office.* **3b** (*as modifier*): *a box-office success.*

box pleat *n* a flat double pleat made by folding under the fabric on either side of it.

boxroom ('bɒksˌruːm, -ˌrʊm) *n* a small room or large cupboard in which boxes, cases, etc., may be stored.

box seat *n* **1** a seat in a theatre box. **2 in the box seat.** *Brit., Austral., and N.Z.* in the best position.

box spanner *n* a spanner consisting of a steel cylinder with a hexagonal end that fits over a nut: used esp. to turn nuts in positions that are recessed or difficult of access.

box spring *n* a coiled spring contained in a boxlike frame, used as base for mattresses, chairs, etc.

boxthorn ('bɒksˌθɔːn) *n* another name for **matrimony vine.**

boxwood ('bɒksˌwʊd) *n* **1** the hard close-grained yellow wood of the box tree, used to make tool handles, small turned or carved articles, etc. **2** the box tree.

boxy ('bɒksɪ) *adj* squarish or chunky in style or appearance: *a boxy square-cut jacket.*

boy (bɔɪ) *n* **1** a male child; lad; youth. **2** a man regarded as immature or inexperienced: *he's just a boy when it comes to dealing with women.* **3** See **old boy.** **4 the boys.** *Informal.* a group of men, esp. a group of friends. **5** *Usually derogatory.* (esp. in former colonial territories) a Black or native male servant of any age. **6** *Austral.* a jockey or apprentice. **7** short for **boyfriend.** **8 boys will be boys.** youthful indiscretion or exuberance must be expected and tolerated. **9 jobs for the boys.** *Informal.* appointment of one's supporters to posts, without reference to their qualifications or ability. **10 the boy.** *Irish informal.* the right tool for a particular task: *that's the boy to cut it.* ◆ *interj* **11** an exclamation of surprise, pleasure, contempt, etc. **[C13** (in the sense: male servant; C14: young male): of uncertain origin; perhaps from Anglo-French *abuié* fettered (unattested), from Latin *boia* fetter**]**

boyar ('bəʊjɑː, 'bɔɪə) *n* a member of an old order of Russian nobility, ranking immediately below the princes: abolished by Peter the Great. **[C16:** from Old Russian *boyarin,* from Old Slavic *boljarinŭ,* probably from Old Turkic *boila* a title**]**

Boyce (bɔɪs) *n* **William.** ?1710–79, English composer, noted esp. for his church music and symphonies.

boycott ('bɔɪkɒt) *vb* **1** (*tr*) to refuse to have dealings with (a person, organization, etc.) or refuse to buy (a product) as a protest or means of coercion: *to boycott foreign produce.* ◆ *n* **2** an instance or the use of boycotting. **[C19:** after Captain C. C. *Boycott* (1832–97), Irish land agent for the Earl of Erne, County Mayo, Ireland, who was a victim of such practices for refusing to reduce rents**]**

Boycott ('bɔɪkɒt) *n* **Geoff(rey).** born 1940, English cricketer: captained Yorkshire (1970–78); played for England (1964–74, 1977–82).

Boyd (bɔɪd) *n* **1 Arthur.** 1920–99, Australian painter and sculptor, noted for his large ceramic sculptures and his series of engravings. **2 Martin (A'Beckett).** 1893–1972, Australian novelist, author of *Lucinda Brayford* (1946) and of the Langton tetralogy *The Cardboard Crown* (1952), *A Difficult Young Man* (1955), *Outbreak of Love* (1957), and *When Blackbirds Sing* (1962).

Boyd Orr (ɔː) *n* **John,** 1st Baron Boyd Orr of Brechin Mearns. 1880–1971, Scottish biologist; director general of the United Nations Food and Agriculture Organization: Nobel peace prize 1949.

Boyer (*French* bwaje) *n* **Charles** (ʃarl), known as *the Great Lover.* 1899–1978, French film actor.

boyfriend ('bɔɪˌfrɛnd) *n* a male friend with whom a person is romantically or sexually involved; sweetheart or lover.

boyhood ('bɔɪhʊd) *n* the state or time of being a boy: *his boyhood was happy.*

boyish ('bɔɪɪʃ) *adj* of or like a boy in looks, behaviour, or character, esp. when regarded as attractive or endearing: *a boyish smile.* ▸ **'boyishly** *adv* ▸ **'boyishness** *n*

Boyle (bɔɪl) *n* **Robert.** 1627–91, Irish scientist who helped to dissociate chemistry from alchemy. He established that air has weight and studied the behaviour of gases; author of *The Sceptical Chymist* (1661).

Boyle's law *n* the principle that the pressure of a gas varies inversely with its volume at constant temperature. **[C18:** named after Robert BOYLE**]**

boy-meets-girl *adj* conventionally or trivially romantic: *a boy-meets-girl story.*
Boyne (bɔɪn) *n* a river in the E Republic of Ireland, rising in the Bog of Allen and flowing northeast to the Irish Sea: William III of England defeated the deposed James II in a battle (**Battle of the Boyne**) on its banks in 1690, completing the overthrow of the Stuart cause in Ireland. Length: about 112 km (70 miles).
boyo (ˈbɔɪəʊ) *n Brit. informal.* a boy or young man: often used in direct address. [from Irish and Welsh]
Boyoma Falls (bɔɪˈəʊmə) *pl n* a series of seven cataracts in the NE Democratic Republic of the Congo (formerly Zaïre), on the upper River Congo: forms an unnavigable stretch of 90 km (56 miles), which falls 60 m (200 ft.). Former name: **Stanley Falls.**
Boys' Brigade *n* (in Britain) an organization for boys, founded in 1883, with the aim of promoting discipline and self-respect.
boy scout *n* See **Scout.**
boysenberry (ˈbɔɪzᵊnbərɪ) *n, pl* **-ries. 1** a type of bramble: a hybrid of the loganberry and various blackberries and raspberries. **2** the large red edible fruit of this plant. [C20: named after Rudolph *Boysen,* American botanist who developed it]
Boz (bɒz) *n* pen name of (Charles) **Dickens.**
Bozcaada (ˌbɔzdʒaaˈda) *n* the Turkish name for **Tenedos.**
Bozen (ˈboːtsən) *n* the German name for **Bolzano.**
bozo (ˈbəʊzəʊ) *n, pl* **-zos.** *U.S. slang.* a man, esp. a stupid one. [C20: of uncertain origin; perhaps based on BEAU]
bp *abbrev. for:* **1** (of alcoholic density) below proof. **2** boiling point. **3** bishop. **4** Also: **B/P.** bills payable.
BP *abbrev. for:* **1** blood pressure. **2** British Pharmacopoeia.
bp. *abbrev. for:* **1** baptized. **2** birthplace.
B/P *or* **bp** *abbrev. for* bills payable.
BPC *abbrev. for* British Pharmaceutical Codex.
BPharm *abbrev. for* Bachelor of Pharmacy.
BPhil *abbrev. for* Bachelor of Philosophy.
bpi *abbrev. for* bits per inch (used of a computer tape).
BPR *abbrev. for* business process re-engineering.
bps *Computing. abbrev. for* bits per second.
b.pt. *abbrev. for* boiling point.
Bq *symbol for* becquerel(s).
br *abbrev. for:* **1** brother. **2** Also: **B/R.** bills receivable.
Br 1 *abbrev. for* (in a religious order) Brother. **2** *the chemical symbol for* bromine.
BR 1 (formerly) *abbrev. for* British Rail. **2** *international car registration for* Brazil.
br. *abbrev. for:* **1** branch. **2** bronze.
Br. *abbrev. for:* **1** Breton. **2** Britain. **3** British.
B/R *or* **br** *abbrev. for* bills receivable.
bra (brɑː) *n* short for **brassiere.**
braai (braɪ) *S. African.* ◆ *vb* **1** to grill or roast (meat) over open coals. ◆ *n* **2** short for **braaivleis.** [Afrikaans]
braaivleis (ˈbraɪˌfleɪs) *n S. African.* **1** a picnic at which meat is cooked over an open fire; a barbecue. **2** the meat cooked at such a barbecue. [from Afrikaans *braai* roast + *vleis* meat]
braata (ˈbrɑːtə) *or* **braatas** (ˈbrɑːtəs) *n Caribbean.* a small portion added to a purchase of food by a market vendor, to encourage the customer to return. Also called: **broughta, broughtas.** [perhaps from Spanish *barata* a bargain]
Brabant (brəˈbænt) *n* **1** a former duchy of W Europe: divided when Belgium became independent (1830), the south forming the Belgian provinces of Antwerp and Brabant and the north forming the province of North Brabant in the Netherlands. **2** a former province of central Belgium; replaced in 1995 by the provinces of **Flemish Brabant** and **Walloon Brabant.**
brabble (ˈbræbᵊl) *vb, n* a rare word for **squabble.** [C16: from Middle Dutch *brabbelen* to jabber] ► **ˈbrabbler** *n*
Brabham (ˈbræbəm) *n* Sir **John Arthur,** known as *Jack.* born 1926, Australian motor-racing driver: world champion 1959, 1960, and 1966.
braccate (ˈbrækeɪt) *adj* (of birds) having feathered legs. [from Latin *braccātus,* from *brăccae* breeches + -ATE[1]]
brace (breɪs) *n* **1** in full: **hand brace.** a hand tool for drilling holes, with a socket to hold the drill at one end and a cranked handle by which the tool can be turned. See also **brace and bit. 2** something that steadies, binds, or holds up another thing. **3** a structural member, such as a beam or prop, used to stiffen a framework. **4** a sliding loop, usually of leather, attached to the cords of a drum: used to change its tension. **5** a pair; two, esp. of game birds: *a brace of partridges.* **6** either of a pair of characters, { }, used for connecting lines of printing or writing or as a third sign of aggregation in complex mathematical or logical expressions that already contain parentheses and square brackets. **7** Also called: **accolade.** a line or bracket connecting two or more staves of music. **8** (*often pl*) an appliance of metal bands and wires that can be tightened to maintain steady pressure on the teeth for correcting uneven alignment. **9** *Med.* any of various appliances for supporting the trunk or a limb. **10** another word for **bracer**[2]. **11** (in square-rigged sailing ships) a rope that controls the movement of a yard and thus the position of a sail. **12** See **braces.** ◆ *vb* (*mainly tr*) **13** to provide, strengthen, or fit with a brace. **14** to steady or prepare (oneself or something) as before an impact. **15** (*also intr*) to stimulate; freshen; invigorate: *sea air is bracing.* **16** to control the horizontal movement of (the yards of a square-rigged sailing ship). [C14: from Old French: the two arms, from Latin *bracchia* arms]
brace and bit *n* a hand tool for boring holes, consisting of a cranked handle into which a drilling bit is inserted.
bracelet (ˈbreɪslɪt) *n* **1** an ornamental chain worn around the arm or wrist. **2** an expanding metal band for a wristwatch. Related adj: **armillary.** [C15: from Old French, from *bracel,* literally: a little arm, from Latin *bracchium* arm; see BRACE]
bracelets (ˈbreɪslɪts) *pl n* a slang name for **handcuffs.**
bracer[1] (ˈbreɪsə) *n* **1** a person or thing that braces. **2** *Informal.* a tonic, esp. an alcoholic drink taken as a tonic.
bracer[2] (ˈbreɪsə) *n Archery, fencing.* a leather guard worn to protect the arm. [C14: from Old French *braciere,* from *braz* arm, from Latin *bracchium* arm]
braces (ˈbreɪsɪz) *pl n Brit.* a pair of straps worn over the shoulders by men for holding up the trousers. U.S. and Canadian word: **suspenders.**
brach (brætʃ) *or* **brachet** (ˈbrætʃɪt) *n Archaic.* a bitch hound. [C14: back formation from *brachez* hunting dogs, from Old French, plural of *brachet,* of Germanic origin; compare Old High German *braccho* hound]
brachah (braˈxa) *or* **brocho** *n Judaism.* Hebrew terms usually translated as "blessing". See **blessing** (sense 4).
brachial (ˈbreɪkɪəl, ˈbræk-) *adj* of or relating to the arm or to an armlike part or structure.
brachiate *adj* (ˈbreɪkɪɪt, -ˌeɪt, ˈbræk-). **1** *Botany.* having widely divergent paired branches. ◆ *vb* (ˈbreɪkɪˌeɪt, ˈbræk-). **2** (*intr*) (of some arboreal apes and monkeys) to swing by the arms from one hold to the next. [C19: from Latin *bracchiātus* with armlike branches] ► ˌ**brachiˈation** *n*
brachio- *or before a vowel* **brachi-** *combining form.* indicating a brachium: *brachiopod.*
brachiocephalic (ˌbreɪkɪəsɪˈfælɪk) *adj* of, relating to, or supplying the arm and head: *brachiocephalic artery.*
brachiopod (ˈbreɪkɪəˌpɒd, ˈbræk-) *n* any marine invertebrate animal of the phylum *Brachiopoda,* having a ciliated feeding organ (lophophore) and a shell consisting of dorsal and ventral valves. Also called: **lamp shell.** See also **bryozoan.** [C19: from New Latin *Brachiopoda;* see BRACHIUM, -POD]
brachiosaurus (ˌbreɪkɪəˈsɔːrəs, ˌbræk-) *n* a dinosaur of the genus *Brachiosaurus,* up to 30 metres long: the largest land animal ever known. See also **sauropod.**
brachistochrone (brəˈkɪstəˌkrəʊn) *n Maths.* the curve between two points through which a body moves under the force of gravity in a shorter time than for any other curve; the path of quickest descent. [C18: from Greek *brakhistos,* superlative of *brakhus* short + *chronos* time]
brachium (ˈbreɪkɪəm, ˈbræk-) *n, pl* **-chia** (-kɪə). **1** *Anatomy.* the arm, esp. the upper part. **2** a corresponding part, such as a wing, in an animal. **3** *Biology.* a branching or armlike part. [C18: New Latin, from Latin *bracchium* arm, from Greek *brakhiōn*]
brachy- *combining form.* indicating something short: *brachycephalic.* [from Greek *brakhus* short]
brachycephalic (ˌbrækɪsɪˈfælɪk) *adj also* **brachycephalous** (ˌbrækɪˈsefələs). **1** having a head nearly as broad from side to side as from front to back, esp. one with a cephalic index over 80. ◆ *n* **2** an individual with such a head. ◆ Compare **dolichocephalic, mesocephalic.** ► ˌ**brachyˈcephaly** *or* ˌ**brachyˈcephalism** *n*
brachycerous (bræˈkɪsərəs) *adj* (of insects) having short antennae.
brachydactylic (ˌbrækɪdækˈtɪlɪk) *or* **brachydactylous** (ˌbrækɪˈdæktɪləs) *adj* having abnormally short fingers or toes. ► ˌ**brachyˈdactyly** *or* ˌ**brachyˈdactylˌism** *n*
brachylogy (bræˈkɪlədʒɪ) *n, pl* **-gies. 1** a concise style in speech or writing. **2** a colloquial shortened form of expression that is not the result of a regular grammatical process: *the omission of "good" in the expression "Afternoon" is a brachylogy.* ► **braˈchylogous** *adj*
brachyodont (ˈbrækɪəˌdɒnt) *adj* (of mammals, such as humans) having teeth with short crowns.
brachypterous (bræˈkɪptərəs) *adj* having very short or incompletely developed wings: *brachypterous insects.* ► **braˈchypterism** *n*
brachyuran (ˌbrækɪˈjʊərən) *n* **1** any decapod crustacean of the group (formerly suborder) *Brachyura,* which includes the crabs. ◆ *adj* **2** of, relating to, or belonging to the *Brachyura.* [C19: from New Latin *Brachyura* (literally: short-tailed creatures), from BRACHY- + Greek *oura* tail]
bracing (ˈbreɪsɪŋ) *adj* **1** refreshing; stimulating; invigorating: *the air here is bracing.* ◆ *n* **2** a system of braces used to strengthen or support: *the bracing supporting the building is perfectly adequate.* ► **ˈbracingly** *adv*
bracken (ˈbrækən) *n* **1** Also called: **brake.** any of various large coarse ferns, esp. *Pteridium aquilinum,* having large fronds with spore cases along the undersides and extensive underground stems. **2** a clump of any of these ferns. [C14: of Scandinavian origin; compare Swedish *bräken,* Danish *bregne*]
bracket (ˈbrækɪt) *n* **1** an L-shaped or other support fixed to a wall to hold a shelf, etc. **2** one or more wall shelves carried on brackets. **3** *Architect.* a support projecting from the side of a wall or other structure. See also **corbel, ancon, console**[2]. **4** Also called: **square bracket.** either of a pair of characters, [ ], used to enclose a section of writing or printing to separate it from the main text. **5** a general name for **parenthesis, square bracket,** and **brace** (sense 6). **6** a group or category falling within or between certain defined limits: *the lower income bracket.* **7** the distance between two preliminary shots of artillery fire in range-finding. **8** a skating figure consisting of two arcs meeting at a point, tracing the shape ⋎. ◆ *vb* (*tr*) **-kets, -keting, -keted. 9** to fix or support by means of a bracket or brackets. **10** to put (written or printed matter) in brackets, esp. as being irrelevant, spurious, or bearing a separate relationship of some kind to the rest of the text. **11** to couple or join (two lines of text, etc.) with a brace. **12** (often foll. by *with*) to group or class together: *to bracket Marx with the philosophers.* **13** to adjust (artillery fire) until the target is hit. [C16: from Old French *braguette* codpiece, diminutive of *bragues* breeches, from Old Provençal *braga,* from Latin *brāca* breeches]
bracket fungus *n* any saprotroph or parasitic fungus of the basidiomycetous

family *Polyporaceae,* growing as a shelflike mass (bracket) from tree trunks and producing spores in vertical tubes in the bracket.

bracketing ('brækɪtɪŋ) *n* **1** a set of brackets. **2** *Photog.* a technique in which a series of test pictures are taken at different exposure levels in order to obtain the optimum exposure.

brackish ('brækɪʃ) *adj* (of water) slightly briny or salty. [C16: from Middle Dutch *brac* salty; see -ISH] ▸ **'brackishness** *n*

Bracknell ('bræknəl) *n* a town in SE England, in E Berkshire, designated a new town in 1949. Pop.: 60 895 (1991).

bract (brækt) *n* a specialized leaf with a single flower or inflorescence growing in its axil. [C18: from New Latin *bractea,* Latin: thin metal plate, gold leaf, variant of *brattea,* of obscure origin] ▸ **'bracteal** *adj* ▸ **'bractless** *adj*

bracteate ('bræktɪɪt, -ˌeɪt) *adj* **1** (of a plant) having bracts. ◆ *n* **2** *Archaeol.* a fine decorated dish or plate of precious metal. [C19: from Latin *bracteātus* gold-plated; see BRACT]

bracteole ('bræktɪˌəʊl) *n* a secondary or small bract. Also called: **'bractlet.** [C19: from New Latin *bracteola,* from *bractea* thin metal plate; see BRACT] ▸ **bracteolate** ('bræktɪəlɪt, -ˌleɪt) *adj*

brad (bræd) *n* a small tapered nail having a small head that is either symmetrical or formed on one side only. [Old English *brord* point, prick; related to Old Norse *broddr* spike, sting, Old High German *brort* edge]

bradawl ('brædˌɔːl) *n* an awl used to pierce wood, leather, or other materials for the insertion of brads, screws, etc.

Bradbury ('brædbrɪ) *n* **1 Malcolm (Stanley).** born 1932, British novelist and critic. His novels include *The History Man* (1975), *Rates of Exchange* (1983), *Cuts* (1988), and *Doctor Criminale* (1992). **2 Ray.** born 1920, U.S. science-fiction writer. His novels include *Fahrenheit 451* (1953), *Death is a Lonely Business* (1986), and *A Graveyard for Lunatics* (1990).

Bradford ('brædfəd) *n* **1** an industrial city in N England, in Bradford unitary authority, West Yorkshire: a centre of the woollen industry from the 14th century and of the worsted trade from the 18th century. Pop.: 289 376 (1991). **2** a unitary authority in West Yorkshire. Pop.: 481 700 (1994 est.). Area: 370 sq. km (143 sq. miles).

Bradlaugh ('brædlɔː) *n* **Charles.** 1833–91, British radical and freethinker: barred from taking his seat in parliament (1880–86) for refusing to take the parliamentary oath.

Bradley ('brædlɪ) *n* **1 A(ndrew) C(ecil).** 1851–1935, English critic; author of *Shakespearian Tragedy* (1904). **2 F(rancis) H(erbert).** 1846–1924, English idealist philosopher and metaphysical thinker; author of *Ethical Studies* (1876), *Principles of Logic* (1883), and *Appearance and Reality* (1893). **3 Henry.** 1845–1923, English lexicographer; one of the editors of the *Oxford English Dictionary.* **4 James.** 1693–1762, English astronomer, who discovered the aberration of light and the nutation of the earth's axis.

Bradman ('brædmən) *n* (Sir) **Don(ald George).** born 1908, Australian cricketer: an outstanding batsman.

Bradshaw ('brædˌʃɔː) *n* a British railway timetable, published annually from 1839 to 1961. [C19: named after its original publisher, George *Bradshaw* (1801–53)]

Bradstreet ('brædˌstriːt) *n* **Anne (Dudley).** ?1612–72, U.S. poet, born in England: regarded as the first significant U.S. poet.

brady- *combining form.* indicating slowness: *bradycardia.* [from Greek *bradus* slow]

bradycardia (ˌbrædɪ'kɑːdɪə) *n Pathol.* an abnormally low rate of heartbeat. Compare **tachycardia.** ▸ **bradycardiac** (ˌbrædɪ'kɑːdɪˌæk) *adj*

bradykinesia (ˌbrædɪkɪ'niːzɪə) *n Physiol.* abnormal slowness of physical movement, esp. as a symptom of Parkinson's disease. [C20: from BRADY- + Greek *kinēsis* motion]

bradykinin (ˌbrædɪ'kaɪnɪn, ˌbreɪdɪ-) *n* a peptide in blood plasma that dilates blood vessels and causes contraction of smooth muscles. Formula: $C_{50}H_{73}N_{15}O_{11}$. [C20: from BRADY- + Greek *kin(ēsis)* motion + -IN]

brae (breɪ; *Scot.* bre) *n Scot.* **1** a hill or hillside; slope. **2** (*pl*) an upland area: *the Gleniffer braes.* [C14 *bra;* related to Old Norse *brā* eyelash, Old High German *brāwa* eyelid, eyebrow; compare BROW]

braeheid (bre'hiːd) *n Scot.* the summit of a hill or slope.

Braemar (ˌbreɪ'mɑː) *n* a village in NE Scotland, in Aberdeenshire; Balmoral castle is nearby: site of the Royal Braemar Gathering, an annual Highland Games meeting.

brag (bræg) *vb* **brags, bragging, bragged. 1** to speak of (one's own achievements, possessions, etc.) arrogantly and boastfully. ◆ *n* **2** boastful talk or behaviour, or an instance of this. **3** something boasted of: *his brag was his new car.* **4** a braggart; boaster. **5** a card game: an old form of poker. [C13: of unknown origin] ▸ **'bragger** *n* ▸ **'bragging** *n, adj* ▸ **'braggingly** *adv*

Braga (*Portuguese* 'brɑːgə) *n* a city in N Portugal: capital of the Roman province of Lusitania; 12th-century cathedral, seat of the Primate of Portugal. Pop.: 90 535 (1991). Ancient name: **Bracara Augusta.**

Bragg (bræg) *n* Sir **William Henry,** 1862–1942, and his son, Sir (**William**) **Lawrence,** 1890–1971, British physicists, who shared a Nobel prize for physics (1915) for their study of crystal structures by means of X-rays.

braggadocio (ˌbrægə'dəʊtʃɪˌəʊ) *n, pl* **-os. 1** vain empty boasting. **2** a person who boasts; braggart. [C16: from *Braggadocchio,* name of a boastful character in Spenser's *Faerie Queene;* probably from BRAGGART + Italian *-occhio* (augmentative suffix)]

braggart ('brægət) *n* **1** a person who boasts loudly or exaggeratedly; bragger. ◆ *adj* **2** boastful. [C16: see BRAG]

Bragg's law *n* the principle that when a beam of X-rays of wavelength λ enters a crystal, the maximum intensity of the reflected ray occurs when $\sin \theta = n\lambda/2d$, where θ is the complement of the angle of incidence, n is a whole number, and d is the distance between layers of atoms. [C20: named after father and son. See BRAGG]

Bragi ('brɑːgɪ) *or* **Brage** ('brɑːgə) *n Norse myth.* the god of poetry and music, son of Odin.

Brahe (brɑː, 'brɑːhɪ; *Danish* 'braːə) *n* **Tycho** ('tyːço). 1546–1601, Danish astronomer, who designed and constructed instruments that he used to plot accurately the positions of the planets, sun, moon, and stars.

Brahma[1] ('brɑːmə) *n* **1** a Hindu god: in later Hindu tradition, the Creator who, with Vishnu, the Preserver, and Shiva, the Destroyer, constitutes the triad known as the Trimurti. **2** another name for **Brahman** (sense 2). [from Sanskrit, from *brahman* praise]

Brahma[2] ('brɑːmə, 'breɪ-) *n* a heavy breed of domestic fowl with profusely feathered legs and feet. [C19: shortened from *Brahmaputra* (river); from its having been imported originally from Lakhimpur, a town on the Brahmaputra]

Brahman ('brɑːmən) *n, pl* **-mans. 1** (*sometimes not cap.*) Also called (esp. formerly): **Brahmin.** a member of the highest or priestly caste in the Hindu caste system. **2** *Hinduism.* the ultimate and impersonal divine reality of the universe, from which all being originates and to which it returns. **3** another name for **Brahma**[1]. [C14: from Sanskrit *brāhmana,* from *brahman* prayer] ▸ **Brahmanic** (brɑː'mænɪk) *or* **Brah'manical** *adj*

Brahmana ('brɑːmənə) *n Hinduism.* any of a number of sacred treatises added to each of the Vedas.

Brahmani ('brɑːmənɪ) *n, pl* **-nis.** (*sometimes not cap.*) a woman of the Brahman caste.

Brahmanism ('brɑːməˌnɪzəm) *or* **Brahminism** *n* (*sometimes not cap.*) **1** the religious and social system of orthodox Hinduism, characterized by diversified pantheism, the caste system, and the sacrifices and family ceremonies of Hindu tradition. **2** the form of Hinduism prescribed in the Vedas, Brahmanas, and Upanishads. ▸ **'Brahmanist** *or* **'Brahminist** *n*

Brahmaputra (ˌbrɑːmə'puːtrə) *n* a river in S Asia, rising in SW Tibet as the Tsangpo and flowing through the Himalayas and NE India to join the Ganges at its delta in Bangladesh. Length: about 2900 km (1800 miles).

Brahmin ('brɑːmɪn) *n, pl* **-min** *or* **-mins. 1** the older spelling of **Brahman** (a Hindu priest). **2** (in the U.S.) a highly intelligent or socially exclusive person, esp. a member of one of the older New England families. **3** an intellectual or social snob. ▸ **Brah'minic** *or* **Brah'minical** *adj*

Brahms (brɑːmz) *n* **Johannes** (jo'hanəs). 1833–97, German composer, whose music, though classical in form, exhibits a strong lyrical romanticism. His works include four symphonies, four concertos, chamber music, and *A German Requiem* (1868).

Brahui (brɑː'huːɪ) *n* **1** a language spoken in Pakistan, forming an isolated branch of the Dravidian family. **2** (*pl* **-hui** *or* **-huis**) a member of the people that speaks this language.

braid[1] (breɪd) *vb* (*tr*) **1** to interweave several strands of (hair, thread, etc.); plait. **2** to make by such weaving: *to braid a rope.* **3** to dress or bind (the hair) with a ribbon, etc. **4** to decorate with an ornamental trim or border: *to braid a skirt.* ◆ *n* **5** a length of hair, fabric, etc., that has been braided; plait. **6** narrow ornamental tape of woven silk, wool, etc. [Old English *bregdan* to move suddenly, weave together; compare Old Norse *bregtha,* Old High German *brettan* to draw a sword] ▸ **'braider** *n*

braid[2] (bred, breɪd) *Scot.* ◆ *adj* **1** broad. ◆ *adv* **2** broadly; frankly. [Scot. variant of BROAD]

braided ('breɪdɪd) *adj* (of a river or stream) flowing in several shallow interconnected channels separated by banks of deposited material.

braiding ('breɪdɪŋ) *n* **1** braids collectively. **2** work done in braid. **3** a piece of braid.

brail (breɪl) *Nautical.* ◆ *n* **1** one of several lines fastened to the leech of a fore-and-aft sail to aid in furling it. ◆ *vb* **2** (*tr;* sometimes foll. by *up*) to furl (a fore-and-aft sail) using brails. [C15: from Old French *braiel,* from Medieval Latin *brācāle* belt for breeches, from Latin *brāca* breeches]

Brăila (*Romanian* brə'ila) *n* a port in E Romania: belonged to Turkey (1544–1828). Pop.: 235 763 (1994 est.).

Braille[1] (breɪl) *n* **1** a system of writing for the blind consisting of raised dots that can be interpreted by touch, each dot or group of dots representing a letter, numeral, or punctuation mark. **2** any writing produced by this method. Compare **Moon**[1]. ◆ *vb* **3** (*tr*) to print or write using this method.

Braille[2] (*French* braj) *n* **Louis** (lwi). 1809–52, French inventor, musician, and teacher of the blind, who himself was blind from the age of three and who devised the Braille system of raised writing.

brain (breɪn) *n* **1** the soft convoluted mass of nervous tissue within the skull of vertebrates that is the controlling and coordinating centre of the nervous system and the seat of thought, memory, and emotion. It includes the cerebrum, brainstem, and cerebellum. Technical name: **encephalon.** Related adjs.: **cerebral, encephalic. 2** the main neural bundle or ganglion of certain invertebrates. **3** (*often pl*) *Informal.* intellectual ability: *he's got brains.* **4** *Informal.* shrewdness or cunning. **5** *Informal.* an intellectual or intelligent person. **6** (*usually pl; functioning as sing*) *Informal.* a person who plans and organizes an undertaking or is in overall control of an organization, etc. **7** an electronic device, such as a computer, that performs apparently similar functions to the human brain. **8 on the brain.** constantly in mind: *I had that song on the brain.* **9 pick someone's brains.** to obtain information or ideas from someone. ◆ *vb* (*tr*) **10** to smash the skull of. **11** *Slang.* to hit hard on the head. [Old English *brægen;* related to Old Frisian *brein,* Middle Low German *bregen,* Greek *brekhmos* forehead]

brainbox ('breɪnˌbɒks) *n Slang.* **1** the skull. **2** a clever person.

brainchild ('breɪnˌtʃaɪld) *n, pl* **-children.** *Informal.* an idea or plan produced by creative thought; invention.

brain coral *n* a stony coral of the genus *Meandrina,* in which the polyps lie in troughlike thecae resembling the convoluted surface of a human brain.

braindead ('breɪn,dɛd) *adj* **1** having suffered brain death. **2** *Informal.* not using or showing intelligence; stupid.

brain death *n* irreversible cessation of respiration due to irreparable brain damage, even though the heart may continue beating with the aid of a mechanical ventilator: widely considered as the criterion of death.

brain drain *n Informal.* the emigration of scientists, technologists, academics, etc., for better pay, equipment, or conditions.

Braine (breɪn) *n* **John (Gerard).** 1922–86, English novelist, whose works include *Room at the Top* (1957) and *Life at the Top* (1962).

brain fever *n* inflammation of the brain or its covering membranes.

brain-fever bird *n* an Indian cuckoo, *Cuculus varius,* that utters a repetitive call.

brainless ('breɪnlɪs) *adj* stupid or foolish. ▸ **'brainlessly** *adv* ▸ **'brainlessness** *n*

brainpan ('breɪn,pæn) *n Informal.* the skull.

brainpower ('breɪn,paʊə) *n* intelligence; mental ability.

brainsick ('breɪn,sɪk) *adj* relating to or caused by insanity; crazy; mad. ▸ **'brain,sickly** *adv* ▸ **'brain,sickness** *n*

brainstem ('breɪn,stɛm) *n* the stalklike part of the brain consisting of the medulla oblongata, the midbrain, and the pons Varolii.

brainstorm ('breɪn,stɔːm) *n* **1** a severe outburst of excitement, often as the result of a transitory disturbance of cerebral activity. **2** *Brit. informal.* a sudden mental aberration. **3** *Informal.* another word for **brainwave.**

brainstorming ('breɪn,stɔːmɪŋ) *n* intensive discussion to solve problems or generate ideas.

brains trust *n* **1** a group of knowledgeable people who discuss topics in public or on radio or television. **2** Also called: **brain trust.** *U.S.* a group of experts who advise the government.

brain-teaser *or* **brain-twister** *n Informal.* a difficult problem.

brainwash ('breɪn,wɒʃ) *vb* (*tr*) to effect a radical change in the ideas and beliefs of (a person), esp. by methods based on isolation, sleeplessness, hunger, extreme discomfort, pain, and the alternation of kindness and cruelty. ▸ **'brain,washer** *n* ▸ **'brain,washing** *n*

brainwave ('breɪn,weɪv) *n Informal.* a sudden inspiration or idea. Also: **brainstorm.**

brain wave *n* any of the fluctuations of electrical potential in the brain as represented on an electroencephalogram. They vary in frequency from 1 to 30 hertz. See also **alpha rhythm, beta rhythm, delta rhythm.**

brainy ('breɪnɪ) *adj* **brainier, brainiest.** *Informal.* clever; intelligent. ▸ **'brainily** *adv* ▸ **'braininess** *n*

braise (breɪz) *vb* to cook (meat, vegetables, etc.) by lightly browning in fat and then cooking slowly in a closed pan with a small amount of liquid. [C18: from French *braiser,* from Old French *brese* live coals, probably of Germanic origin; compare Old English *brǣdan,* Old High German *brātan* to roast]

brak (brak) *adj S. African.* (of water) brackish or salty. [C19: Afrikaans]

brake[1] (breɪk) *n* **1a** (*often pl*) a device for slowing or stopping a vehicle, wheel, shaft, etc., or for keeping it stationary, esp. by means of friction. See also **drum brake, disc brake, hydraulic brake, air brake, handbrake. 1b** (*as modifier*): *the brake pedal.* **2** a machine or tool for crushing or breaking flax or hemp to separate the fibres. **3** Also called: **brake harrow.** a heavy harrow for breaking up clods. **4** short for **brake van. 5** short for **shooting brake. 6** Also spelt: **break.** an open four-wheeled horse-drawn carriage. **7** an obsolete word for the **rack** (an instrument of torture). ♦ *vb* **8** to slow down or cause to slow down, by or as if by using a brake. **9** (*tr*) to crush or break up using a brake. [C18: from Middle Dutch *braeke;* related to *breken* to BREAK] ▸ **'brakeless** *adj*

brake[2] (breɪk) *n* an area of dense undergrowth, shrubs, brushwood, etc.; thicket. [Old English *bracu;* related to Middle Low German *brake,* Old French *bracon* branch]

brake[3] (breɪk) *n* another name for **bracken** (sense 1). See also **rock brake.**

brake[4] (breɪk) *vb Archaic, chiefly biblical.* a past tense of **break.**

brake band *n* a strip of fabric, leather, or metal tightened around a pulley or shaft to act as a brake.

brake drum *n* the cast-iron drum attached to the hub of a wheel of a motor vehicle fitted with drum brakes. See also **brake shoe.**

brake-fade *n* the decrease in efficiency of braking of a motor vehicle due to overheating of the brakes.

brake fluid *n* an oily liquid used to transmit pressure in a hydraulic brake or clutch system.

brake horsepower *n* the rate at which an engine does work, expressed in horsepower. It is measured by the resistance of an applied brake. Abbrev.: **bhp.**

brake light *n* a red light attached to the rear of a motor vehicle that lights up when the brakes are applied, serving as a warning to following drivers. Also called: **stoplight.**

brake lining *n* a curved thin strip of an asbestos composition riveted to a brake shoe to provide it with a renewable surface.

brakeman ('breɪkmən) *n, pl* **-men. 1** *U.S. and Canadian.* a crew member of a goods or passenger train. His duties include controlling auxiliary braking power and inspecting the train. **2** the man at the back of a two- or four-man bobsleigh, who operates the brake.

brake pad *n* the flat metal casting, together with the bound friction material, in a disc brake.

brake parachute *n* a parachute attached to the rear of a vehicle and opened to assist braking. Also called: **brake chute, parachute brake, parabrake.**

brake shoe *n* **1** the curved metal casting to which the brake lining is riveted in a drum brake. **2** the curved metal casting together with the attached brake lining. Sometimes shortened (for both senses) to **shoe.**

brakesman ('breɪksmən) *n, pl* **-men.** a pithead winch operator.

brake van *n Railways, Brit.* the coach or vehicle from which the guard applies the brakes; guard's van.

Brakpan ('bræk,pæn) *n* a city in E South Africa: gold-mining centre. Pop.: 46 416 (1985).

Bramante (*Italian* bra'mante) *n* **Donato** (do'nato). ?1444–1514, Italian architect and artist of the High Renaissance. He modelled his designs for domed centrally planned churches on classical Roman architecture.

bramble ('bræmb^əl) *n* **1** any of various prickly herbaceous plants or shrubs of the rosaceous genus *Rubus,* esp. the blackberry. See also **stone bramble. 2** *Scot.* **2a** a blackberry. **2b** (*as modifier*): *bramble jelly.* **3** any of several similar and related shrubs, such as the dog rose. ♦ *vb* (*intr*) **4** to gather blackberries. [Old English *brǣmbel;* related to Old Saxon *brāmal,* Old High German *brāmo*] ▸ **'brambly** *adj*

brambling ('bræmblɪŋ) *n* a Eurasian finch, *Fringilla montifringilla,* with a speckled head and back and, in the male, a reddish brown breast and darker wings and tail.

Bramley ('bræmlɪ) *or* **Bramley's seedling** *n* a variety of cooking apple having juicy firm flesh. [C19: named after Matthew *Bramley,* 19th-century English butcher, said to have first grown it]

bran (bræn) *n* **1** husks of cereal grain separated from the flour by sifting. **2** food prepared from these husks. Related adj: **furfuraceous.** [C13: from Old French, probably of Gaulish origin]

Branagh ('brænə) *n* **Kenneth.** born 1961, British actor and director, born in Northern Ireland. He founded the Renaissance Theatre Company in 1986. His films include *Henry V* (1989), *Peter's Friends* (1992), and *Wild Wild West* (1999).

branch (brɑːntʃ) *n* **1** a secondary woody stem arising from the trunk or bough of a tree or the main stem of a shrub. **2** a subdivision of the stem or root of any other plant. **3** an offshoot or secondary part: *a branch of a deer's antlers.* **4a** a subdivision or subsidiary section of something larger or more complex: *branches of learning; branch of the family.* **4b** (*as modifier*): *a branch office.* **5** *U.S.* any small stream. **6** *Maths.* a section of a curve separated from the rest of the curve by discontinuities or special points. **7** Also called: **jump.** *Computing.* a departure from the normal sequence of programmed instructions into a separate program area. **8** an alternative route in a radioactive decay series. ♦ *vb* **9** (*intr*) (of a tree or other plant) to produce or possess branches. **10** (*intr;* usually foll. by *from*) (of stems, roots, etc.) to grow and diverge (from another part). **11** to divide or be divided into subsidiaries or offshoots. **12** (*intr;* often foll. by *off*) to diverge from the main way, road, topic, etc. ♦ See also **branch out.** [C13: from Old French *branche,* from Late Latin *branca* paw, foot] ▸ **'branchless** *adj* ▸ **'branch,like** *adj* ▸ **'branchy** *adj*

-branch *adj and n combining form.* (in zoology) indicating gills: *lamellibranch.* [from Latin: BRANCHIA]

branched chain *n Chem.* an open chain of atoms with one or more side chains attached to it. Compare **straight chain.**

branchia ('bræŋkɪə) *n, pl* **-chiae** (-kɪ,iː). a gill in aquatic animals. ▸ **'branchi,ate** *adj*

branchial ('bræŋkɪəl) *adj* **1** of or relating to the gills of an aquatic animal, esp. a fish. **2** of or relating to homologous structures in higher vertebrates: *branchial cyst.*

branching ('brɑːntʃɪŋ) *n Physics.* the occurrence of several decay processes (**branches**) in the disintegration of a particular nuclide. The **branching fraction** is the proportion of the disintegrating nuclei that follow a particular branch to the total number of disintegrating nuclides.

branch instruction *n Computing.* a machine-language or assembly-language instruction that causes the computer to branch to another instruction.

branchiopod ('bræŋkɪə,pɒd) *n* any crustacean of the mainly freshwater subclass *Branchiopoda,* having flattened limblike appendages for swimming, feeding, and respiration. The group includes the water fleas.

branchiostegal (,bræŋkɪ'stiːg^əl) *adj Zoology.* of or relating to the operculum covering the gill slits of fish: *branchiostegal membrane; branchiostegal rays.* [from BRANCHIA + Greek *stegos* roof]

branch line *n Railways.* a secondary route to a place or places not served by a main line.

branch officer *n* (in the British navy since 1949) any officer who holds warrant.

branch out *vb* (*intr, adv;* often foll. by *into*) to expand or extend one's interests: *our business has branched out into computers now.*

Brancusi (bræŋ'kuːzɪ; *Romanian* briŋ'kuʃj) *n* **Constantin** (konstan'tin). 1876–1957, Romanian sculptor, noted for his streamlined abstractions of animal forms.

brand (brænd) *n* **1** a particular product or a characteristic that serves to identify a particular product. **2** a trade name or trademark. **3** a particular kind or variety: *he had his own brand of humour.* **4** an identifying mark made, usually by burning, on the skin of animals or (formerly) slaves or criminals, esp. as a proof of ownership. **5** an iron heated and used for branding animals, etc. **6** a mark of disgrace or infamy; stigma: *he bore the brand of a coward.* **7** a burning or burnt piece of wood, as in a fire. **8** *Archaic or poetic.* **8a** a flaming torch. **8b** a sword. **9** a fungal disease of garden plants characterized by brown spots on the leaves, caused by the rust fungus *Puccinia arenariae.* ♦ *vb* (*tr*) **10** to label, burn, or mark with or as with a brand. **11** to place indelibly in the memory: *the scene of slaughter was branded in their minds.* **12** to denounce; stigmatize: *they branded him a traitor.* [Old English *brand-,* related to Old Norse *brandr,* Old High German *brant;* see BURN[1]] ▸ **'brander** *n*

branded ('brændɪd) *adj* identifiable as being the product of a particular manufacturer or marketing company.

Brandenburg ('brændən,bɜːg; *German* 'brandənburk) *n* **1** a state in NE Germany, part of East Germany until 1990. A former electorate, it expanded under the Hohenzollerns to become the kingdom of Prussia (1701). The district east of the Oder River became Polish in 1945. Capital: Potsdam. Pop.: 2 542 000 (1996 est.). Area: 29 481 sq. km (11 219 sq. miles). **2** a city in NE Germany: former capital of the Prussian province of Brandenburg. Pop.: 93 660 (1989 est.).

brand image *n* the attributes of a brand as perceived by potential and actual customers.

brandish ('brændɪʃ) *vb (tr).* **1** to wave or flourish (a weapon) in a triumphant, threatening, or ostentatious way. ◆ *n* **2** a threatening or defiant flourish. [C14: from Old French *brandir,* from *brand* sword, of Germanic origin; compare Old High German *brant* weapon] ▸ **'brandisher** *n*

brand leader *n Marketing.* a product with the highest number of total sales within its category.

brandling ('brændlɪŋ) *n* a small red earthworm, *Eisenia foetida* (or *Helodrilus foetidus*), found in manure and used as bait by anglers. [C17: from BRAND + -LING[1]]

brand name *n* another name for **brand** (sense 2).

brand-new *adj* absolutely new. [C16: from BRAND (n) + NEW, likened to newly forged iron]

Brando ('brændəʊ) *n* **Marlon.** born 1924, U.S. actor; his films include *On the Waterfront* (1954) and *The Godfather* (1972), for both of which he won Oscars, *Last Tango in Paris* (1972), *Apocalypse Now* (1979), and *The Island of Doctor Moreau* (1996).

Brandt (brænt) *n* **1 Bill,** full name *William Brandt.* 1905–83, British photographer. His photographic books include *The English at Home* (1936) and *Perspectives of Nudes* (1961). **2 Georg** ('geɪɔːg). 1694–1768, Swedish chemist, who isolated cobalt (1742) and exposed fraudulent alchemists. **3** (*German* brant). **Willy** ('vɪli). 1913–92, German statesman; socialist chancellor of West Germany (1969–74); chairman of the Social Democratic party (1964–87). His policy of détente and reconciliation with E Europe brought him international acclaim. Nobel peace prize 1971.

brandy ('brændɪ) *n, pl* **-dies. 1** an alcoholic drink consisting of spirit distilled from grape wine. **2** a distillation of wines made from other fruits: *plum brandy.* [C17: from earlier *brandewine,* from Dutch *brandewijn* burnt wine, from *bernen* to burn or distil + *wijn* WINE; compare German *Branntwein*]

brandy bottle *n* another name for a **yellow water lily.**

brandy butter *n* butter and sugar creamed together with brandy and served with Christmas pudding, etc.

brandy snap *n* a crisp sweet biscuit, rolled into a cylinder after baking and often filled with whipped cream.

branks (bræŋks) *pl n* (formerly) an iron bridle used to restrain scolding women. [C16: of unknown origin]

branle ('bræn°l) *n* an old French country dance performed in a linked circle. [C17: from Old French *branler* to shake, variant of *brandir* to BRANDISH]

Branson ('brænsən) *n* **Richard.** born 1950, British entrepreneur. In 1969 he founded the Virgin record company, adding other interests later, including the Virgin airline (1984), Virgin Radio (1993), and Virgin Cola (1994): made the fastest crossing of the Atlantic by boat (1986) and the first by hot-air balloon (1987).

brant (brænt) *n, pl* **brants** *or* **brant.** another name (esp. U.S. and Canadian) for **brent goose.**

Brantford ('bræntfəd) *n* a city in central Canada, in SW Ontario. Pop.: 81 997 (1991).

Branting (*Swedish* 'brantiŋ) *n* **Karl Hjalmar** (jalmar). 1860–1925, Swedish politician; prime minister (1920; 1921–23; 1924–25). He founded Sweden's welfare state and shared the Nobel peace prize 1921.

bran tub *n* (in Britain) a tub containing bran in which small wrapped gifts are hidden, used at parties, fairs, etc.

Braque (*French* brak) *n* **Georges** (ʒɔrʒ). 1882–1963, French painter who developed cubism (1908–14) with Picasso.

brash[1] (bræʃ) *adj* **1** tastelessly or offensively loud, showy, or bold. **2** hasty; rash. **3** impudent. [C19: perhaps influenced by RASH[1]] ▸ **'brashly** *adv* ▸ **'brashness** *n*

brash[2] (bræʃ) *n* loose rubbish, such as broken rock, hedge clippings, etc.; debris. [C18: of unknown origin]

brash[3] (bræʃ) *n Pathol.* another name for **heartburn.** [C16: perhaps of imitative origin]

brashy ('bræʃɪ) *adj* **brashier, brashiest. 1** loosely fragmented; rubbishy. **2** (of timber) brittle. ▸ **'brashiness** *n*

brasier ('breɪzɪə) *n* a less common spelling of **brazier.**

brasil (brə'zɪl) *n* a variant spelling of **brazil.**

Brasil (brə'ziːl) *n* the Portuguese spelling of **Brazil.**

brasilein (brə'zɪlɪɪn) *n* a variant spelling of **brazilein.**

Brasília (brə'zɪljə; *Portuguese* brəzi'liːa) *n* the capital of Brazil (since 1960), on the central plateau: the former capital was Rio de Janeiro. Pop.: 1 778 000 (1995).

brasilin ('bræzɪlɪn) *n* a variant spelling of **brazilin.**

Braşov (*Romanian* bra'ʃov) *n* an industrial city in central Romania: formerly a centre for expatriate Germans; ceded by Hungary to Romania in 1920. Pop.: 324 210 (1994 est.). Former name (1950–61): **Stalin.** German name: **Kronstadt.** Hungarian name: **Brassó.**

brass (brɑːs) *n* **1** an alloy of copper and zinc containing more than 50 per cent of copper. **Alpha brass** (containing less than 35 per cent of zinc) is used for most engineering materials requiring forging, pressing, etc. **Alpha-beta brass** (35–45 per cent zinc) is used for hot working and extrusion. **Beta brass** (45–50 per cent zinc) is used for castings. Small amounts of other metals, such as lead or tin, may be added. Compare **bronze** (sense 1). **2** an object, ornament, or utensil made of brass. **3a** the large family of wind instruments including the trumpet, trombone, French horn, etc., each consisting of a brass tube blown directly by means of a cup- or funnel-shaped mouthpiece. **3b** (*sometimes functioning as pl*) instruments of this family forming a section in an orchestra. **3c** (*as modifier*): *a brass ensemble.* **4** a renewable sleeve or bored semicylindrical shell made of brass or bronze, used as a liner for a bearing. **5** (*functioning as pl*) *Informal.* important or high-ranking officials, esp. military officers: *the top brass.* See also **brass hat. 6** *Northern English dialect.* money: *where there's muck, there's brass!* **7** *Brit.* an engraved brass memorial tablet or plaque, set in the wall or floor of a church. **8** *Informal.* bold self-confidence; cheek; nerve: *he had the brass to ask for more time.* **9** *Slang.* a prostitute. **10** (*modifier*) of, consisting of, or relating to brass or brass instruments: *a brass ornament; a brass band.* Related adj: **brazen.** [Old English *bræs;* related to Old Frisian *bres* copper, Middle Low German *bras* metal]

Brassaï (*French* brasai) *n* real name *Gyula Halész.* 1899–1984, French photographer, artist, and writer, born in Hungary: noted for his photographs of Paris by night.

brassard ('bræsɑːd) *or* **brassart** ('bræsət) *n* **1** an identifying armband or badge. **2** a piece of armour for the upper arm. [C19: from French, from *bras* arm, from Latin BRACHIUM]

brass band *n* See **band**[1] (sense 2).

brassbound ('brɑːs,baʊnd) *adj* inflexibly entrenched: *brassbound traditions.*

brassed off *adj Brit. slang.* fed up; disgruntled.

brasserie ('bræsərɪ) *n* **1** a bar in which drinks and often food are served. **2** a small and usually cheap restaurant. [C19: from French, from *brasser* to stir, brew]

brass farthing *n Brit. informal.* something of little or no value: *his opinion isn't worth a brass farthing.* [C18: probably coined when farthings were first minted in bronze rather than silver]

brass hat *n Brit. informal.* a top-ranking official, esp. a military officer. [C20: from the gold leaf decoration on the peaks of caps worn by officers of high rank]

brassica ('bræsɪkə) *n* any cruciferous plant of the genus *Brassica,* such as cabbage, rape, turnip, and mustard. [C19: from Latin: cabbage] ▸ **brassicaceous** (,bræsɪ'keɪʃəs) *adj*

brassie *or* **brassy** ('bræsɪ, 'brɑː-) *n, pl* **brassies.** *Golf.* a former name for a club, a No. 2 wood, originally having a brass-plated sole and with a shallower face than a driver to give more loft.

brassiere ('bræsɪə, 'bræz-) *n* a woman's undergarment for covering and supporting the breasts. Often shortened to **bra.** [C20: from C17 French: bodice, from Old French *braciere* a protector for the arm, from *braz* arm]

brass neck *n Brit. informal.* effrontery; nerve.

Brassó ('brɔʃʃoː) *n* the Hungarian name for **Braşov.**

brass rubbing *n* **1** the taking of an impression of an engraved brass tablet or plaque by placing a piece of paper over it and rubbing the paper with graphite, heelball, or chalk. **2** an impression made in this way.

brass tacks *pl n Informal.* basic realities; hard facts (esp. in the phrase **get down to brass tacks**).

brassy ('brɑːsɪ) *adj* **brassier, brassiest. 1** insolent; brazen. **2** flashy; showy. **3** (of sound) harsh, strident, or resembling the sound of a brass instrument. **4** like brass, esp. in colour. **5** decorated with or made of brass. ▸ **'brassily** *adv* ▸ **'brassiness** *n*

brat[1] (bræt) *n* a child, esp. one who is ill-mannered or unruly: used contemptuously or playfully. [C16: perhaps special use of earlier *brat* rag, from Old English *bratt* cloak, of Celtic origin; related to Old Irish *bratt* cloth, BRAT[2]]

brat[2] (bræt) *n Northern English dialect.* an apron or overall. [from Old English *bratt* cloak; related to Old Irish *bratt* cloth used to cover the body]

Bratislava (,brætɪ'slɑːvə) *n* the capital of Slovakia since 1918, a port on the River Danube; capital of Hungary (1541–1784) and seat of the Hungarian parliament until 1848. Pop.: 452 053 (1996 est.). German name: **Pressburg.** Hungarian name: **Pozsony.**

bratpack ('bræt,pæk) *n* **1** a group of precocious and successful young actors, writers, etc. **2** a group of ill-mannered young people. ▸ **'brat,packer** *n*

Brattain ('bræt°n) *n* **Walter Houser.** 1902–87, U.S. physicist, who shared the Nobel prize for physics (1956) with W. B. Shockley and John Bardeen for their invention of the transistor.

brattice ('brætɪs) *n* **1** a partition of wood or treated cloth used to control ventilation in a mine. **2** *Medieval fortifications.* a fixed wooden tower or parapet. ◆ *vb* **3** (*tr*) *Mining.* to fit with a brattice. [C13: from Old French *bretesche* wooden tower, from Medieval Latin *breteschia,* probably from Latin *Britō* a Briton]

brattishing ('brætɪʃɪŋ) *n Architect.* decorative work along the coping or on the cornice of a building. [C16: variant of *bratticing;* see BRATTICE]

bratwurst ('brɑːt,wɜːst; *German* 'braːtvurst) *n* a type of small pork sausage. [C20: German, from Old High German, from *brāto* meat + *wurst* sausage; related to Old Saxon *brādo* ham]

Braun (*German* braun) *n* **1 Eva** ('eːfa). 1910–45, Adolf Hitler's mistress, whom he married shortly before their suicides in 1945. **2 Karl Ferdinand.** 1850–1918, German physicist, who invented crystal diodes (leading to the development of crystal radio) and the oscilloscope. He shared the Nobel prize for physics (1909) with Marconi. **3** See (Wernher) **von Braun.**

braunite ('braʊnaɪt) *n* a brown or black mineral that consists of manganese oxide and silicate and is a source of manganese. Formula: Mn_7SiO_{12}. [C19: named after A. E. *Braun* (1809–56), German official in the treasury at Gotha]

Braunschweig ('braunʃvaik) *n* the German name for **Brunswick.**

bravado (brə'vɑːdəʊ) *n, pl* **-does** *or* **-dos.** vaunted display of courage or self-confidence; swagger. [C16: from Spanish *bravada* (modern *bravata*), from Old Italian *bravare* to challenge, provoke, from *bravo* wild, BRAVE]

Bravais lattice ('brævei, brə'vei) *n Crystallog.* any of 14 possible space lattices found in crystals. [named after Auguste *Bravais,* 19th-century French physicist]

brave (breɪv) *adj* **1a** having or displaying courage, resolution, or daring; not cowardly or timid. **1b** (*as collective n* preceded by *the*): *the brave.* **2** fine; splendid: *a brave sight; a brave attempt.* **3** *Archaic.* excellent or admirable. ◆ *n* **4** a warrior of a North American Indian tribe. **5** an obsolete word for **bully**[1]. ◆ *vb* (*tr*) **6** to dare or defy: *to brave the odds.* **7** to confront with resolution or courage: *to brave the storm.* **8** *Obsolete.* to make splendid, esp. in dress. [C15: from French, from Italian *bravo* courageous, wild, perhaps ultimately from Latin *barbarus* BARBAROUS] ▸ **'bravely** *adv* ▸ **'braveness** *n* ▸ **'bravery** *n*

bravissimo (brɑː'vɪsɪˌməʊ) *interj* very well done! excellent! [C18: from Italian, superlative of BRAVO]

bravo *interj* **1** (brɑː'vəʊ). well done! ◆ *n* **2** (brɑː'vəʊ), *pl* **-vos.** a cry of "bravo." **3** ('brɑːvəʊ), *pl* **-voes** *or* **-vos.** a hired killer or assassin. [C18: from Italian: splendid!; see BRAVE]

Bravo ('brɑːvəʊ) *n Communications.* a code word for the letter *b.*

bravura (brə'vjʊərə, -'vʊərə) *n* **1** a display of boldness or daring. **2** *Music.* **2a** brilliance of execution. **2b** (*as modifier*): *a bravura passage.* [C18: from Italian: spirit, courage, from *bravare* to show off, see BRAVADO]

braw (brɔː, brɑː) *Chiefly Scot.* ◆ *adj* **1** fine or excellent, esp. in appearance or dress. ◆ *pl n* **2** best clothes. [C16: Scottish variant of BRAVE] ▸ **'brawly** *adv*

brawl[1] (brɔːl) *n* **1** a loud disagreement or fight. **2** *U.S. slang.* an uproarious party. ◆ *vb* (*intr*) **3** to quarrel or fight noisily; squabble. **4** (esp. of water) to flow noisily. [C14: probably related to Dutch *brallen* to boast, behave aggressively] ▸ **'brawler** *n* ▸ **'brawling** *n, adj*

brawl[2] (brɔːl) *n* a dance: the English version of the branle.

brawn (brɔːn) *n* **1** strong well-developed muscles. **2** physical strength, esp. as opposed to intelligence. **3** *Brit.* a seasoned jellied loaf made from the head and sometimes the feet of a pig or calf. [C14: from Old French *braon* slice of meat, of Germanic origin; compare Old High German *brāto,* Old English *brǣd* flesh]

brawny ('brɔːnɪ) *adj* **brawnier, brawniest.** muscular and strong. ▸ **'brawnily** *adv* ▸ **'brawniness** *n*

braxy ('bræksɪ) *n* an acute and usually fatal bacterial disease of sheep characterized by high fever, coma, and inflammation of the fourth stomach, caused by infection with *Clostridium septicum.* [C18: of unknown origin]

bray[1] (breɪ) *vb* **1** (*intr*) (of a donkey) to utter its characteristic loud harsh sound; heehaw. **2** (*intr*) to make a similar sound, as in laughing: *he brayed at the joke.* **3** (*tr*) to utter with a loud harsh sound. ◆ *n* **4** the loud harsh sound uttered by a donkey. **5** a similar loud cry or uproar: *a bray of protest.* [C13: from Old French *braire,* probably of Celtic origin] ▸ **'brayer** *n*

bray[2] (breɪ) *vb* **1** (*tr*) to distribute (ink) over printing type or plates. **2** (*tr*) to pound into a powder, as in a mortar. **3** *Northern English dialect.* to hit or beat (someone or something) hard; bang. [C14: from Old French *breier,* of Germanic origin; see BREAK] ▸ **'brayer** *n*

Braz. *abbrev. for* Brazil(ian).

braze[1] (breɪz) *vb* (*tr*) **1** to decorate with or make of brass. **2** to make like brass, as in hardness. [Old English *bræsen,* from *bræs* BRASS]

braze[2] (breɪz) *vb* (*tr*) to make a joint between (two metal surfaces) by fusing a layer of brass or high-melting solder between them. [C16: from Old French: to burn, of Germanic origin; see BRAISE] ▸ **'brazer** *n*

brazen ('breɪzᵊn) *adj* **1** shameless and bold. **2** made of or resembling brass. **3** having a ringing metallic sound like that of a brass trumpet. ◆ *vb* (*tr*) **4** (usually foll. by *out* or *through*) to face and overcome boldly or shamelessly: *the witness brazened out the prosecutor's questions.* **5** to make (oneself, etc.) bold or brash. [Old English *bræsen,* from *bræs* BRASS] ▸ **'brazenly** *adv* ▸ **'brazenness** *n*

brazen-faced *adj* shameless or impudent.

brazier[1] *or* **brasier** ('breɪzɪə) *n* a person engaged in brass-working or brass-founding. [C14: from Old English *bræsian* to work in brass + -ER[1]] ▸ **'braziery** *n*

brazier[2] *or* **brasier** ('breɪzɪə) *n* a portable metal receptacle for burning charcoal or coal, used for cooking, heating, etc. [C17: from French *brasier,* from *braise* live coals; see BRAISE]

brazil *or* **brasil** (brə'zɪl) *n* **1** Also called: **brazil wood.** the red wood obtained from various caesalpiniaceous tropical trees of the genus *Caesalpinia,* such as *C. echinata* of America: used for cabinetwork. **2** the red or purple dye extracted from any of these woods. See also **brazilin. 3** short for **brazil nut.** [C14: from Old Spanish *brasil,* from *brasa* glowing coals, of Germanic origin; referring to the redness of the wood; see BRAISE]

Brazil (brə'zɪl) *n* a republic in South America, comprising about half the area and half the population of South America: colonized by the Portuguese from 1500 onwards; became independent in 1822 and a republic in 1889; consists chiefly of the tropical Amazon basin in the north, semiarid scrub in the northeast, and a vast central tableland; an important producer of coffee and minerals, esp. iron ore. Official language: Portuguese. Religion: Roman Catholic majority. Currency: real. Capital: Brasília. Pop.: 161 766 000 (1998 est.). Area: 8 511 957 sq. km (3 286 470 sq. miles). ▸ **Bra'zilian** *adj, n*

brazilein *or* **brasilein** (brə'zɪlɪɪn) *n* a red crystalline solid obtained by the oxidation of brazilin and used as a dye. Formula: $C_{16}H_{12}O_5$. [C19: from German *Brasilein,* from BRAZILIN]

brazilin *or* **brasilin** ('bræzɪlɪn) *n* a pale yellow soluble crystalline solid, turning red in alkaline solution, extracted from brazil wood and sappanwood and used in dyeing and as an indicator. Formula: $C_{16}H_{14}O_5$. [C19: from French *brésiline,* from *brésil* brazil wood]

brazil nut *n* **1** a tropical South American tree, *Bertholletia excelsa,* producing large globular capsules, each containing several closely packed triangular nuts: family *Lecythidaceae.* **2** the nut of this tree, having an edible oily kernel and a woody shell. ◆ Often shortened to **brazil.**

Brazzaville (*French* brazavil) *n* the capital of the Congo Republic, in the south on the River Congo. Pop.: 937 579 (1995 est.). [C19: named after Pierre de *Brazza* (1852–1905), French explorer]

BRCS *abbrev. for* British Red Cross Society.

BRE (in Britain) *abbrev. for* Building Research Establishment.

breach (briːtʃ) *n* **1** a crack, break, or rupture. **2** a breaking, infringement, or violation of a promise, obligation, etc. **3** any severance or separation: *there was a breach between the two factions of the party.* **4** the act of a whale in breaking clear of the water. **5** the breaking of sea waves on a shore or rock. **6** an obsolete word for **wound**[1]. ◆ *vb* **7** (*tr*) to break through or make an opening, hole, or incursion in. **8** (*tr*) to break a promise, law, etc. **9** (*intr*) (of a whale) to break clear of the water. [Old English *bræc;* influenced by Old French *brèche,* from Old High German *brecha,* from *brechan* to BREAK]

breach of promise *n Law.* (formerly) failure to carry out one's promise to marry.

breach of the peace *n Law.* an offence against public order causing an unnecessary disturbance of the peace.

breach of trust *n Law.* a violation of duty by a trustee or any other person in a fiduciary position.

bread (brɛd) *n* **1** a food made from a dough of flour or meal mixed with water or milk, usually raised with yeast or baking powder and then baked. **2** necessary food; nourishment: *give us our daily bread.* **3** a slang word for **money. 4** *Christianity.* a small loaf, piece of bread, or wafer of unleavened bread used in the Eucharist. **5 bread and circuses.** something offered as a means of distracting attention from a problem or grievance. **6 break bread.** See **break** (sense 46). **7 cast one's bread upon the waters.** to do good without expectation of advantage or return. **8 know which side one's bread is buttered.** to know what to do in order to keep one's advantages. **9 take the bread out of (someone's) mouth.** to deprive (someone) of a livelihood. ◆ *vb* **10** (*tr*) to cover with breadcrumbs before cooking: *breaded veal.* [Old English *brēad;* related to Old Norse *braud,* Old Frisian *brād,* Old High German *brōt*]

bread and butter *Informal.* ◆ *n* **1** a means of support or subsistence; livelihood: *the inheritance was their bread and butter.* ◆ *modifier.* **2** (**bread-and-butter**) **2a** providing a basic means of subsistence: *a bread-and-butter job.* **2b** solid, reliable, or practical: *a bread-and-butter player.* **2c** expressing gratitude, as for hospitality (esp. in the phrase **bread-and-butter letter**).

breadbasket ('brɛdˌbɑːskɪt) *n* **1** a basket for carrying bread or rolls. **2** a slang word for **stomach.**

breadboard ('brɛdˌbɔːd) *n* **1** a wooden board on which dough is kneaded or bread is sliced. **2** an experimental arrangement of electronic circuits giving access to components so that modifications can be carried out easily.

breadcrumb ('brɛdˌkrʌm) *n* **1** the soft inner part of bread. **2** (*pl*) bread crumbled into small fragments, as for use in cooking. ◆ *vb* (*tr*) **3** to coat (food) with breadcrumbs: *egg and breadcrumb the escalopes.*

breadfruit ('brɛdˌfruːt) *n, pl* **-fruits** *or* **-fruit. 1** a moraceous tree, *Artocarpus communis* (or *A. altilis*), of the Pacific Islands, having edible round, usually seedless, fruit. **2** the fruit of this tree, which is eaten baked or roasted and has a texture like bread.

breadline ('brɛdˌlaɪn) *n* **1** a queue of people waiting for free food given out by a government agency or a charity organization. **2 on the breadline.** impoverished; living at subsistence level.

bread mould *or* **black mould** *n* a black saprotrophic zygomycete fungus, *Rhizopus nigricans,* occurring on decaying bread and vegetable matter.

breadnut ('brɛdˌnʌt) *n* **1** a moraceous tree, *Brosimum alicastrum,* of Central America and the Caribbean. **2** the nutlike fruit of this tree, ground to produce a substitute for wheat flour, esp. in the West Indies.

breadroot ('brɛdˌruːt) *n* a papilionaceous plant, *Psoralea esculenta,* of central North America, having an edible starchy root. Also called: **prairie turnip.**

bread sauce *n* a milk sauce thickened with breadcrumbs and served with roast poultry, esp. chicken.

breadth (brɛdθ, brɛtθ) *n* **1** the linear extent or measurement of something from side to side; width. **2** a piece of fabric having a standard or definite width. **3** distance, extent, size, or dimension. **4** openness and lack of restriction, esp. of viewpoint or interest; liberality. [C16: from obsolete *brēde* (from Old English *brǣdu,* from *brād* BROAD) + -TH[1]; related to Gothic *braidei,* Old High German *breitī*]

breadthways ('brɛdθˌweɪz, 'brɛtθ-) *or esp. U.S.* **breadthwise** ('brɛdθˌwaɪz, 'brɛtθ-) *adv* from side to side.

breadwinner ('brɛdˌwɪnə) *n* a person supporting a family with his or her earnings. ▸ **'breadˌwinning** *n, adj*

break (breɪk) *vb* **breaks, breaking, broke, broken. 1** to separate or become separated into two or more pieces: *this cup is broken.* **2** to damage or become damaged so as to be inoperative: *my radio is broken.* **3** to crack or become cracked without separating. **4** to burst or cut the surface of (skin, etc.). **5** to discontinue or become discontinued: *they broke for lunch; to break a journey.* **6** to disperse or become dispersed: *the clouds broke.* **7** (*tr*) to fail to observe (an agreement, promise, law, etc.): *to break one's word.* **8** (foll. by *with*) to discontinue an association (with). **9** to disclose or be disclosed: *he broke the news gently.* **10** (*tr*) to fracture (a bone) in (a limb, etc.). **11** (*tr*) to divide (something complete or perfect): *to break a set of books.* **12** to bring or come to an end: *the summer weather broke at last.* **13** (*tr*) to bring to an end by or as if by force: *to break a strike.* **14** (when *intr,* often foll. by *out*) to escape (from): *he broke jail; he broke out of jail.* **15** to weaken or overwhelm or be weakened or overwhelmed, as in spirit. **16** (*tr*) to cut through or penetrate: *a cry broke the silence.* **17** (*tr*) to improve on or surpass: *to break a record.* **18** (*tr;* often foll. by *in*) to accustom (a horse) to the bridle and saddle, to being ridden, etc. **19** (*tr;* often foll. by *of*) to cause (a person) to give up (a habit): *this cure will break you of smoking.* **20** (*tr*) to weaken the impact or force of: *this net will break his fall.* **21** (*tr*) to decipher: *to break a code.* **22** (*tr*) to lose the order of: *to break ranks.*

23 (*tr*) to reduce to poverty or the state of bankruptcy. **24** (when *intr,* foll. by *into*) to obtain, give, or receive smaller units in exchange for; change: *to break a pound note.* **25** (*tr*) *Chiefly military.* to demote to a lower rank. **26** (*intr;* often foll. by *from* or *out of*) to proceed suddenly. **27** (*intr*) to come into being: *light broke over the mountains.* **28** (*intr;* foll. by *into* or *out into*) to burst into song, laughter, etc. **29** (*tr*) to open with explosives: *to break a safe.* **30** (*intr*) (of waves) **30a** (often foll. by *against*) to strike violently. **30b** to collapse into foam or surf. **31** (*intr*) (esp. of fish) to appear above the surface of the water. **32** (*intr*). (of the amniotic fluid surrounding an unborn baby) to be released when the amniotic sac ruptures in the first stage of labour: *her waters have broken.* **33** (*intr*) *Informal, chiefly U.S.* to turn out in a specified manner: *things are breaking well.* **34** (*intr*) (of prices, esp. stock exchange quotations) to fall sharply. **35** (*intr*) to make a sudden effort, as in running, horse racing, etc. **36** (*intr*) *Cricket.* (of a ball) to change direction on bouncing. **37** (*tr*) *Cricket.* (of a player) to knock down at least one bail from (a wicket). **38** (*intr*) *Billiards, snooker.* to scatter the balls at the start of a game. **39** (*intr*) *Horse racing.* to commence running in a race: *they broke even.* **40** (*intr*) *Boxing, wrestling.* (of two fighters) to separate from a clinch. **41** (*intr*) *Music.* **41a** (of the male voice) to undergo a change in register, quality, and range at puberty. **41b** (of the voice or some instruments) to undergo a change in tone, quality, etc., when changing registers. **42** (*intr*) *Phonetics.* (of a vowel) to turn into a diphthong, esp. as a development in the language. **43** (*tr*) to open the breech of (certain firearms) by snapping the barrel away from the butt on its hinge. **44** (*tr*) to interrupt the flow of current in (an electrical circuit). Compare **make**[1] (sense 27). **45** (*intr*) *Informal, chiefly U.S.* to become successful; make a breakthrough. **46 break bread. 46a** to eat a meal, esp. with others. **46b** *Christianity.* to administer or participate in Holy Communion. **47 break camp.** to pack up equipment and leave a camp. **48 break (new) ground.** to do something that has not been done before. **49 break one's back** *or* (*Taboo*) **balls.** to overwork or work very hard. **50 break the back of.** to complete the greatest or hardest part of (a task). **51 break the bank.** to ruin financially or deplete the resources of a bank (as in gambling). **52 break the ice. 52a** to relieve shyness or reserve, esp. between strangers. **52b** to be the first of a group to do something. **53 break the mould.** to make a change that breaks an established habit, pattern, etc. **54 break service.** *Tennis.* to win a game in which an opponent is serving. **55 break wind.** to emit wind from the anus. ♦ *n* **56** the act or result of breaking; fracture. **57** a crack formed as the result of breaking. **58** a brief respite or interval between two actions: *a break from one's toil.* **59** a sudden rush, esp. to escape: *to make a break for freedom.* **60** a breach in a relationship: *she has made a break from her family.* **61** any sudden interruption in a continuous action. **62** *Brit.* a short period between classes at school. U.S. and Canadian equivalent: **recess. 63** *Informal.* a fortunate opportunity, esp. to prove oneself. **64** *Informal.* a piece of (good or bad) luck. **65** (esp. in a stock exchange) a sudden and substantial decline in prices. **66** *Prosody.* a pause in a line of verse; caesura. **67** *Billiards, snooker.* **67a** a series of successful shots during one turn. **67b** the points scored in such a series. **68** *Billiards, snooker.* **68a** the opening shot with the cue ball that scatters the placed balls. **68b** the right to take this first shot. **69** Also called: **service break, break of serve.** *Tennis.* the act or instance of breaking an opponent's service. **70** one of the intervals in a sporting contest. **71** *Horse racing.* the start of a race: *an even break.* **72** (in tenpin bowling) failure to knock down all the pins after the second attempt. **73a** *Jazz.* a short usually improvised solo passage. **73b** an instrumental passage in a pop song. **74** a discontinuity in an electrical circuit. **75** access to a radio channel by a citizen's band operator. **76** a variant spelling of **brake**[1] (sense 6). ♦ *interj* **77** *Boxing, wrestling.* a command by a referee for two opponents to separate. ♦ See also **breakaway, break down, break even, break in, break into, break off, break out, break through, break up, break with.** [Old English *brecan;* related to Old Frisian *breka,* Gothic *brikan,* Old High German *brehhan,* Latin *frangere,* Sanskrit *bhráj* bursting forth]

breakable ('breɪkəbᵊl) *adj* **1** capable of being broken. ♦ *n* **2** (*usually pl*) a fragile easily broken article.

breakage ('breɪkɪdʒ) *n* **1** the act or result of breaking. **2** the quantity or amount broken: *the total breakage was enormous.* **3** compensation or allowance for goods damaged while in use, transit, etc.

breakaway ('breɪkəˌweɪ) *n* **1a** loss or withdrawal of a group of members from an association, club, etc. **1b** (*as modifier*): *a breakaway faction.* **2** *Sport.* **2a** a sudden attack, esp. from a defensive position, in football, hockey, etc. **2b** an attempt to get away from the rest of the field in a race. **3** *Austral.* a stampede of cattle, esp. at the smell of water. ♦ *vb* **break away.** (*intr, adv*) **4** (often foll. by *from*) to leave hastily or escape. **5** to withdraw or secede. **6** *Sport.* to make a breakaway. **7** *Horse racing.* to start prematurely.

breakbone fever ('breɪkˌbəʊn) *n* another name for **dengue.**

break dance *n* **1** an acrobatic dance style of the 1980s. ♦ *vb* **break-dance. 2** (*intr*) to perform a break dance. ▸ **break dancer** *n* ▸ **break dancing** *n*

break down *vb* (*adv*) **1** (*intr*) to cease to function; become ineffective: *communications had broken down.* **2** to yield or cause to yield, esp. to strong emotion or tears: *she broke down in anguish.* **3** (*tr*) to crush or destroy. **4** (*intr*) to have a nervous breakdown. **5** to analyse or be subjected to analysis. **6** to separate or cause to separate into simpler chemical elements; decompose. **7** (*tr*) *N.Z.* to saw (a large log) into planks. **8 break it down.** *Austral. and N.Z. informal.* **8a** stop it. **8b** don't expect me to believe that; come off it. ♦ *n* **breakdown. 9** an act or instance of breaking down; collapse. **10** short for **nervous breakdown. 11** an analysis or classification of something into its component parts: *he prepared a breakdown of the report.* **12** the sudden electrical discharge through an insulator or between two electrodes in a vacuum or gas discharge tube. **13** *Electrical engineering.* the sudden transition, dependent on the bias magnitude, from a high to a low dynamic resistance in a semiconductor device. **14** a lively American country dance.

breakdown van *or* **truck** *n* a motor vehicle equipped for towing away wrecked or disabled cars. U.S. and Canadian names: **wrecker, tow truck.**

breaker[1] ('breɪkə) *n* **1** a person or thing that breaks something, such as a person or firm that breaks up old cars, etc. **2** a large wave with a white crest on the open sea or one that breaks into foam on the shore. **3** *Electronics.* short for **circuit breaker. 4** a machine or plant for crushing rocks or coal. **5** Also called: **breaking plough.** a plough with a long shallow mouldboard for turning virgin land or sod land. **6** *Textiles.* a machine for extracting fibre preparatory to carding. **7** an operator on citizen's band radio.

breaker[2] ('breɪkə) *n* a small water cask for use in a boat. [C19: anglicized variant of Spanish *barrica,* from French (Gascon dialect) *barrique*]

break even *vb* **1** (*intr, adv*) to attain a level of activity, as in commerce, or a point of operation, as in gambling, at which there is neither profit nor loss. ♦ *n* **breakeven. 2** *Accounting.* **2a** the level of commercial activity at which the total cost and total revenue of a business enterprise are equal. **2b** (*as modifier*): *breakeven prices.*

breakeven chart ('breɪkˌiːvᵊn) *n Accounting.* a graph measuring the value of an enterprise's revenue and costs against some index of its activity, such as percentage capacity. The intersection of the total revenue and total cost curves gives the breakeven point.

breakfast ('brɛkfəst) *n* **1a** the first meal of the day. **1b** (*as modifier*): *breakfast cereal; a breakfast room.* **2** the food at this meal. **3** (in the Caribbean) a midday meal. ♦ *vb* **4** to eat or supply with breakfast. [C15: from BREAK + FAST[2]] ▸ **'breakfaster** *n*

break feeding *n N.Z.* the feeding of animals on paddocks where feeding space is controlled by the frequent movement of an electric fence.

breakfront ('breɪkˌfrʌnt) *adj* (*prenominal*) (of a bookcase, bureau, etc.) having a slightly projecting central section.

break in *vb* (*adv*) **1** (sometimes foll. by *on*) to interrupt. **2** (*intr*) to enter a house, etc., illegally, esp. by force. **3** (*tr*) to accustom (a person or animal) to normal duties or practice. **4** (*tr*) to use or wear (shoes, new equipment, etc.) until comfortable or running smoothly. **5** (*tr*) *Austral. and N.Z.* to bring (new land) under cultivation. ♦ *n* **break-in. 6a** the illegal entering of a building, esp. by thieves. **6b** (*as modifier*): *the break-in plans.*

breaking ('breɪkɪŋ) *n Linguistics.* (in Old English, Old Norse, etc.) the change of a vowel into a diphthong. [C19: translation of German *Brechung*]

breaking and entering *n* (formerly) the gaining of unauthorized access to a building with intent to commit a crime or, having committed the crime, the breaking out of the building.

breaking point *n* **1** the point at which something or someone gives way under strain. **2** the moment of crisis in a situation.

break into *vb* (*intr, prep*) **1** to enter (a house, etc.) illegally, esp. by force. **2** to change abruptly from a slower to a faster speed: *the horse broke into a gallop.* **3** to consume (supplies held in reserve): *at the end of the exercise the soldiers had to break into their iron rations.*

breakneck ('breɪkˌnɛk) *adj* (*prenominal*) (of speed, pace, etc.) excessive and dangerous.

break of day *n* another term for **dawn** (sense 1).

break off *vb* **1** to sever or detach or be severed or detached: *it broke off in my hands; he broke a piece off the bar of chocolate.* **2** (*adv*) to end (a relationship, association, etc.) or (of a relationship, etc.) to be ended. **3** (*intr, adv*) to stop abruptly; halt: *he broke off in the middle of his speech.* ♦ *n* **breakoff. 4** the act or an instance of breaking off or stopping.

break out *vb* (*intr, adv*) **1** to begin or arise suddenly: *panic broke out.* **2** to make an escape, esp. from prison or confinement. **3** (foll. by *in*) (of the skin) to erupt (in a rash, pimples, etc.). ♦ *n* **break-out. 4** an escape, esp. from prison or confinement.

breakpoint ('breɪkˌpɔɪnt) *n Computing.* **a** an instruction inserted by a debug program causing a return to the debug program. **b** the point in a program at which such an instruction operates.

break point *n Tennis.* a point which allows the receiving player to break the service of the server.

break through *vb* **1** (*intr*) to penetrate. **2** (*intr, adv*) to achieve success, make a discovery, etc., esp. after lengthy efforts. ♦ *n* **breakthrough. 3** a significant development or discovery, esp. in science. **4** the penetration of an enemy's defensive position or line in depth and strength.

break up *vb* (*adv*) **1** to separate or cause to separate. **2** to put an end to (a relationship) or (of a relationship) to come to an end. **3** to dissolve or cause to dissolve; disrupt or be disrupted: *the meeting broke up at noon.* **4** (*intr*) *Brit.* (of a school) to close for the holidays. **5** *Informal.* to lose or cause to lose control of the emotions: *the news of his death broke her up.* **6** *Slang.* to be or cause to be overcome with laughter. ♦ *n* **break-up. 7** a separation or disintegration.

break-up value *n Commerce.* **1** the value of an organization assuming that it will not continue to trade. **2** the value of a share in a company based only on the value of its assets.

breakwater ('breɪkˌwɔːtə) *n* **1** Also called: **mole.** a massive wall built out into the sea to protect a shore or harbour from the force of waves. **2** another name for **groyne.**

break with *vb* (*intr, prep*) to end a relationship or association with (someone or an organization or social group).

bream[1] (briːm; *Austral.* brɪm) *or Austral.* **brim** (brɪm) *n, pl* **bream** *or* **brim. 1** any of several Eurasian freshwater cyprinid fishes of the genus *Abramis,* esp. *A. brama,* having a deep compressed body covered with silvery scales. **2 white** *or* **silver bream.** a similar cyprinid, *Blicca bjoerkna.* **3** short for **sea bream.** [C14: from Old French *bresme,* of Germanic origin; compare Old High German *brahsema;* perhaps related to *brehan* to glitter]

bream[2] (briːm) *vb Nautical.* (formerly) to clean debris from (the bottom of a vessel) by heating to soften the pitch. [C15: probably from Middle Dutch *bremme* broom; from using burning broom as a source of heat]

Bream (briːm) *n* **Julian (Alexander).** born 1933, English guitarist and lutenist.

breast (brɛst) *n* **1** the front part of the body from the neck to the abdomen; chest. **2** either of the two soft fleshy milk-secreting glands on the chest in sexually mature human females. Related adj: **mammary.** **3** a similar organ in certain other mammals. **4** anything that resembles a breast in shape or position: *the breast of the hill.* **5** a source of nourishment: *the city took the victims to its breast.* **6** the source of human emotions. **7** the part of a garment that covers the breast. **8** a projection from the side of a wall, esp. that formed by a chimney. **9** *Mining.* the face being worked at the end of a tunnel. **10 beat one's breast.** to display guilt and remorse publicly or ostentatiously. **11 make a clean breast of.** to make a confession of. ◆ *vb* (*tr*) **12** to confront boldly; face: *breast the storm.* **13** to oppose with the breast or meet at breast level: *breasting the waves.* **14** to come alongside of: *breast the ship.* **15** to reach the summit of: *breasting the mountain top.* [Old English *brēost;* related to Old Norse *brjōst,* Old High German *brust,* Dutch *borst,* Swedish *bräss,* Old Irish *brū* belly, body]

breastbone (ˈbrɛst,bəʊn) *n* the nontechnical name for **sternum.**

breast-feed *vb* **-feeds, -feeding, -fed.** to feed (a baby) with milk from the breast; suckle. ▸ **ˈbreast-ˌfed** *adj* ▸ **ˈbreast-ˌfeeding** *n*

breastpin (ˈbrɛst,pɪn) *n* a brooch worn on the breast, esp. to close a garment.

breastplate (ˈbrɛst,pleɪt) *n* **1** a piece of armour covering the chest. **2** the strap of a harness covering a horse's breast. **3** *Judaism.* an ornamental silver plate hung on the scrolls of the Torah. **4** *Old Testament.* a square vestment ornamented with 12 precious stones, representing the 12 tribes of Israel, worn by the high priest when praying before the holy of holies. **5** *Zoology.* a nontechnical name for **plastron.**

breaststroke (ˈbrɛst,strəʊk) *n* a swimming stroke in which the arms are extended in front of the head and swept back on either side while the legs are drawn up beneath the body and thrust back together.

breastwork (ˈbrɛst,wɜːk) *n Fortifications.* a temporary defensive work, usually breast-high. Also called: **parapet.**

breath (brɛθ) *n* **1** the intake and expulsion of air during respiration. **2** the air inhaled or exhaled during respiration. **3** a single respiration or inhalation of air, etc. **4** the vapour, heat, or odour of exhaled air: *his breath on the window melted the frost.* **5** a slight gust of air. **6** a short pause or rest: *take a breath for five minutes.* **7** a brief time: *it was done in a breath.* **8** a suggestion or slight evidence; suspicion: *a breath of scandal.* **9** a whisper or soft sound. **10** life, energy, or vitality: *the breath of new industry.* **11** *Phonetics.* the passage of air through the completely open glottis without vibration of the vocal cords, as in exhaling or pronouncing fricatives such as (f) or (h) or stops such as (p) or (k). Compare **voice** (sense 11). **12 a breath of fresh air.** a refreshing change from what one is used to. **13 catch one's breath.** to rest until breathing is normal, esp. after exertion. **14 hold one's breath.** to wait expectantly or anxiously. **15 in the same breath.** done or said at the same time. **16 out of breath.** gasping for air after exertion. **17 save one's breath.** to refrain from useless talk. **18 take one's breath away.** to overwhelm with surprise, etc. **19 under** *or* **below one's breath.** in a quiet voice or whisper. [Old English *brǣth;* related to *brǣdan* to burn, Old High German *brādam* heat, breath]

breathable (ˈbriːðəbᵊl) *adj* **1** (of air) fit to be breathed. **2** (of a material) allowing air to pass through so that perspiration can evaporate.

breathalyse *or U.S.* **breathalyze** (ˈbrɛθə,laɪz) *vb* (*tr*) to apply a Breathalyser test to (someone).

Breathalyser *or* **Breathalyzer** (ˈbrɛθə,laɪzə) *n Trademark.* a device for estimating the amount of alcohol in the breath: used in testing people suspected of driving under the influence of alcohol. [C20: BREATH + (AN)ALYSER]

breathe (briːð) *vb* **1** to take in oxygen from (the surrounding medium, esp. air) and give out carbon dioxide; respire. **2** (*intr*) to exist; be alive: *every animal that breathes on earth.* **3** (*intr*) to rest to regain breath, composure, etc.: *stop your questions, and give me a chance to breathe.* **4** (*intr*) (esp. of air) to blow lightly: *the wind breathed through the trees.* **5** (*intr*) *Machinery.* **5a** to take in air, esp. for combustion: *the engine breathes through this air filter.* **5b** to equalize the pressure within a container, chamber, etc., with atmospheric pressure: *the crankcase breathes through this duct.* **6** (*tr*) *Phonetics.* to articulate (a speech sound) without vibration of the vocal cords. Compare **voice** (sense 19). **7** to exhale or emit: *the dragon breathed fire.* **8** (*tr*) to impart; instil: *to breathe confidence into the actors.* **9** (*tr*) to speak softly; whisper: *to breathe words of love.* **10** (*tr*) to permit to rest: *to breathe a horse.* **11** (*intr*) (of a material) to allow air to pass through so that perspiration can evaporate. **12 breathe again, freely,** *or* **easily.** to feel relief: *I could breathe again after passing the exam.* **13 breathe down (someone's) neck.** to stay close to (someone), esp. to oversee what they are doing. **14 breathe one's last.** to die or be finished or defeated. [C13: from BREATH]

breathed (brɛθt, briːðd) *adj Phonetics.* relating to or denoting a speech sound for whose articulation the vocal cords are not made to vibrate. Compare **voiced.**

breather (ˈbriːðə) *n* **1** *Informal.* a short pause for rest. **2** a person who breathes in a specified way: *a deep breather.* **3** a vent in a container to equalize internal and external pressure, such as the pipe in the crankcase of an internal-combustion engine. **4** a small opening in a room, container, cover, etc., supplying air for ventilation.

breathing (ˈbriːðɪŋ) *n* **1** the passage of air into and out of the lungs to supply the body with oxygen. **2** a single breath: *a breathing between words.* **3** an utterance: *a breathing of hate.* **4** a soft movement, esp. of air. **5** a rest or pause. **6** *Phonetics.* **6a** expulsion of breath (**rough breathing**) or absence of such expulsion (**smooth breathing**) preceding the pronunciation of an initial vowel or rho in ancient Greek. **6b** either of two symbols indicating this.

breathing space *n* **1** enough area to permit freedom of movement: *the country gives us some breathing space.* **2** a pause for rest, etc.: *a coffee break was their only breathing space.*

breathless (ˈbrɛθlɪs) *adj* **1** out of breath; gasping, etc. **2** holding one's breath or having it taken away by excitement, etc.: *a breathless confrontation.* **3** (esp. of the atmosphere) motionless and stifling. **4** *Rare.* lifeless; dead. ▸ **ˈbreathlessly** *adv* ▸ **ˈbreathlessness** *n*

breathtaking (ˈbrɛθ,teɪkɪŋ) *adj* causing awe or excitement: *a breathtaking view.* ▸ **ˈbreath,takingly** *adv*

breath test *n Brit.* a chemical test of a driver's breath to determine the amount of alcohol he has consumed.

breathy (ˈbrɛθɪ) *adj* **breathier, breathiest. 1** (of the speaking voice) accompanied by an audible emission of breath. **2** (of the singing voice) lacking resonance. ▸ **ˈbreathily** *adv* ▸ **ˈbreathiness** *n*

breccia (ˈbrɛtʃɪə) *n* a rock consisting of angular fragments embedded in a finer matrix, formed by erosion, volcanic activity, etc. [C18: from Italian, from Old High German *brecha* a fragment; see BREACH] ▸ **ˈbrecci,ated** *adj*

Brecht (*German* brɛçt) *n* **Bertolt** (ˈbɛrtɔlt). 1898–1956, German dramatist, theatrical producer, and poet, who developed a new style of "epic" theatre and a new theory of theatrical alienation, notable also for his wit and compassion. His early works include *The Threepenny Opera* (1928) and *Rise and Fall of the City of Mahagonny* (1930) (both with music by Kurt Weill). His later plays are concerned with moral and political dilemmas and include *Mother Courage and her Children* (1941), *The Good Woman of Setzuan* (1943), and *The Caucasian Chalk Circle* (1955). ▸ **ˈBrechtian** *adj, n*

Brecon (ˈbrɛkən) *or* **Brecknock** (ˈbrɛknɒk) *n* **1** a town in SE Wales, in Powys: textile and leather industries. Pop.: 7523 (1991). **2** short for **Breconshire.**

Breconshire (ˈbrɛkən,ʃɪə, -ʃə) *or* **Brecknockshire** (ˈbrɛknɒk,ʃɪə, -ʃə) *n* (until 1974) a county of SE Wales, now mainly in Powys: over half its area forms the **Brecon Beacons National Park.**

bred (brɛd) *vb* the past tense and past participle of **breed.**

Breda (ˈbriːdə; *Dutch* breˈdaː) *n* a city in the S Netherlands, in North Brabant province: residence of Charles II of England during his exile. Pop.: 130 033 (1996 est.).

brede (briːd) *n, vb* an archaic spelling of **braid**[1].

bredie (ˈbriːdɪ) *n S. African.* a meat and vegetable stew. [C19: from Portuguese *bredo* ragout]

bree[1] *or* **brie** (briː) *n Scot.* broth, stock, or juice. [Old English *brīg,* variant of *brīw* pottage; related to Old High German *brīo* soup, Old English *brīwan* to cook, Middle Irish *brēo* flame]

bree[2] (briː) *n* a Scottish word for **brunt.** [C19: perhaps from earlier *bree* brow]

breech *n* (briːtʃ). **1** the lower dorsal part of the human trunk; buttocks; rump. **2** the lower part or bottom of something: *the breech of the bridge.* **3** the lower portion of a pulley block, esp. the part to which the rope or chain is secured. **4** the part of a firearm behind the barrel or bore. **5** *Obstetrics.* short for **breech delivery.** ◆ *vb* (briːtʃ, brɪtʃ). (*tr*) **6** to fit (a gun) with a breech. **7** *Archaic.* to clothe in breeches or any other clothing. ◆ See also **breeches.** [Old English *brēc,* plural of *brōc* leg covering; related to Old Norse *brōk,* Old High German *bruoh*]

USAGE *Breech* is sometimes wrongly used as a verb where *breach* is meant: *the barrier/agreement was breached (*not *breeched).*

breechblock (ˈbriːtʃ,blɒk) *n* a metal block in breech-loading firearms that is withdrawn to insert the cartridge and replaced to close the breech before firing.

breechcloth (ˈbriːtʃ,klɒθ) *or* **breechclout** (ˈbriːtʃ,klaʊt) *n* other names for **loincloth.**

breech delivery *n* birth of a baby with the feet or buttocks appearing first.

breeches (ˈbrɪtʃɪz, ˈbriː-) *pl n* **1** trousers extending to the knee or just below, worn for riding, mountaineering, etc. **2** *Informal or dialect.* any trousers. **3 too big for one's breeches.** conceited; unduly self-confident.

breeches buoy *n* a ring-shaped life buoy with a support in the form of a pair of short breeches, in which a person is suspended for safe transfer from a ship.

breeching (ˈbrɪtʃɪŋ, ˈbriː-) *n* **1** the strap of a harness that passes behind a horse's haunches. **2** *Naval.* (formerly) the rope used to check the recoil run of a ship's guns or to secure them against rough weather. **3** the parts comprising the breech of a gun.

breech-loader (ˈbriːtʃ,ləʊdə) *n* a firearm that is loaded at the breech. ▸ **ˈbreech-ˌloading** *adj*

breed (briːd) *vb* **breeds, breeding, bred. 1** to bear (offspring). **2** (*tr*) to bring up; raise. **3** to produce or cause to produce by mating; propagate. **4** to produce and maintain new or improved strains of (domestic animals and plants). **5** to produce or be produced; generate: *to breed trouble; violence breeds in densely populated areas.* ◆ *n* **6** a group of organisms within a species, esp. a group of domestic animals, originated and maintained by man and having a clearly defined set of characteristics. **7** a lineage or race: *a breed of Europeans.* **8** a kind, sort, or group: *a special breed of hatred.* [Old English *brēdan,* of Germanic origin; related to BROOD]

breeder (ˈbriːdə) *n* **1** a person who breeds plants or animals. **2** something that reproduces, esp. to excess: *rabbits are persistent breeders.* **3** an animal kept for breeding purposes. **4** a source or cause: *a breeder of discontent.* **5** short for **breeder reactor.**

breeder reactor *n* a type of nuclear reactor that produces more fissionable material than it consumes. Compare **converter reactor.** See also **fast-breeder reactor.**

breeding (ˈbriːdɪŋ) *n* **1** the process of bearing offspring; reproduction. **2** the process of producing plants or animals by hybridization, inbreeding, or other methods of reproduction. **3** the result of good training, esp. the knowledge of correct social behaviour; refinement: *a man of breeding.* **4** a person's line of descent: *his breeding was suspect.* **5** *Physics.* a process occurring in a nuclear reactor as a result of which more fissionable material is produced than is used up.

Breed's Hill (bri:dz) *n* a hill in E Massachusetts, adjoining Bunker Hill: site of the Battle of Bunker Hill (1775).

breeks (bri:ks) *pl n Scot.* trousers. [Scot. variant of BREECHES]

breenge *or* **breinge** (bri:ndʒ) *Scot.* ◆ *vb* (*intr*) **1** to lunge forward; move violently or dash. ◆ *n* **2** a violent movement. [of unknown origin]

breeze[1] (bri:z) *n* **1** a gentle or light wind. **2** *Meteorol.* a wind of force two to six inclusive on the Beaufort scale. **3** *Informal.* an easy task or state of ease: *being happy here is a breeze.* **4** *Informal, chiefly Brit.* a disturbance, esp. a lively quarrel. **5 shoot the breeze.** *Informal.* to chat. ◆ *vb* (*intr*) **6** to move quickly or casually: *he breezed into the room.* **7** (of wind) to blow: *the south wind breezed over the fields.* [C16: probably from Old Spanish *briza* northeast wind]

breeze[2] (bri:z) *n* an archaic or dialect name for the **gadfly.** [Old English *briosa,* of unknown origin]

breeze[3] (bri:z) *n* ashes of coal, coke, or charcoal used to make breeze blocks. [C18: from French *braise* live coals; see BRAISE]

breeze block *n* a light building brick made from the ashes of coal, coke, etc., bonded together by cement and used esp. for walls that bear relatively small loads. Usual U.S. names: **cinder block, clinker block.**

breezeway ('bri:z,weɪ) *n* a roofed passageway connecting two buildings, sometimes with the sides enclosed.

breezy ('bri:zɪ) *adj* **breezier, breeziest. 1** fresh; windy: *a breezy afternoon.* **2** casual or carefree; lively; light-hearted: *her breezy nature.* **3** lacking substance; light: *a breezy conversation.* ► **'breezily** *adv* ► **'breeziness** *n*

Bregenz (*German* bre:'gɛnts) *n* a resort in W Austria, the capital of Vorarlberg province. Pop.: 26 730 (1989).

bregma ('brɛgmə) *n, pl* **-mata** (-mətə). the point on the top of the skull where the coronal and sagittal sutures meet: in infants this corresponds to the anterior fontanelle. [C16: New Latin from Greek: front part of the head]

brei (breɪ) *vb* **breis, breiing, breid.** (*intr*) *S. African informal.* to speak with a uvular *r*, esp. in Afrikaans. Also: **brey.** Compare **burr**[2]. [C20: from Afrikaans; compare BRAY[1]]

breid (bri:d) *n* a Scot. word for **bread.**

breist *or* **breest** (bri:st) *n* a Scot. word for **breast.**

brekky ('brɛkɪ) *n* a slang word for **breakfast.**

Brel (brɛl) *n* **Jacques** (ʒak). 1929–78, Belgian-born composer and singer, based in Paris. His songs include "Ne me quitte pas" ("If you Go away").

Bremen ('breɪmən) *n* **1** a state of NW Germany, centred on the city of Bremen and its outport Bremerhaven; formerly in West Germany. Pop.: 679 800 (1996 est.). Area: 404 sq. km (156 sq. miles). **2** an industrial city and port in NW Germany, on the Weser estuary. Pop.: 549 357 (1996 est.).

Bremerhaven (*German* bre:mər'ha:fən) *n* a port in NW Germany: an outport for Bremen. Pop.: 130 400 (1996 est.). Former name (until 1947): **Wesermünde.**

bremsstrahlung ('bremz,ʃtrɑ:ləŋ) *n* the x-radiation produced when an electrically charged particle, such as an electron, is slowed down by the electric field of an atomic nucleus. [C20: German: braking radiation]

Brendel (*German* 'brɛndəl) *n* **Alfred.** born 1931, Austrian pianist and poet.

Bren gun (brɛn) *n* an air-cooled gas-operated light machine gun taking .303 calibre ammunition: used by British and Commonwealth forces in World War II. [C20: after *Br(no),* now in the Czech Republic, where it was first made and *En(field),* England, where manufacture was continued]

Brennan ('brɛnən) *n* **Christopher John.** 1870–1932, Australian poet and classical scholar, disciple of Mallarmé and exponent of French symbolism in Australian verse.

Brenner Pass ('brɛnə) *n* a pass over the E Alps, between Austria and Italy. Highest point: 1372 m (4501 ft.).

Brent (brɛnt) *n* a borough of NW Greater London. Pop.: 244 500 (1994 est.). Area: 44 sq. km (17 sq. miles).

Brentano (*German* brɛn'ta:no) *n* **Clemens (Maria)** ('kle:mənz). 1778–1842, German romantic poet and compiler of fairy stories and folk songs esp. (with Achim von Arnim) the collection *Des Knaben Wunderhorn* (1805–08).

brent goose (brɛnt) *n* a small goose, *Branta bernicla,* that has a dark grey plumage and short neck and occurs in most northern coastal regions. Also called: **brent,** (esp. U.S. and Canadian) **brant.** [C16: perhaps of Scandinavian origin; compare Old Norse *brandgās* sheldrake]

Brenton ('brɛnt[ə]n) *n* **Howard.** born 1942, British dramatist, author of such controversial plays as *The Romans in Britain* (1980), (with David Hare) *Pravda* (1985), and (with Tariq Ali) *Ugly Rumours* (1998).

Brentwood ('brɛnt,wʊd) *n* a residential town in SE England, in SW Essex near London. Pop.: 49 463 (1991).

br'er (brɜ:, breə) *n Southern African-American dialect.* brother: usually prefixed to a name: *Br'er Jones.*

Brescia (*Italian* 'breʃʃa) *n* a city in N Italy, in Lombardy: at its height in the 16th century. Pop.: 191 875 (1994 est.). Ancient name: **Brixia** ('brɪksɪə).

Breslau ('brezlau) *n* the German name for **Wrocław.**

Bresson (*French* brɛsɔ̃) *n* **Robert** (rɔbɛr). born 1901, French film director: his films include *Le Journal d'un curé de campagne* (1951), *Une Femme douce* (1970), and *L'Argent* (1983).

Brest (brɛst) *n* **1** a port in NW France, in Brittany: chief naval station of the country, planned by Richelieu in 1631 and fortified by Vauban. Pop.: 153 099 (1990). **2** a city in SW Belarus: Polish until 1795 and from 1921 to 1945. Pop.: 293 000 (1996 est.). Former name (until 1921): **Brest Litovsk** (brɛst li'tɔfsk). Polish name: **Brześć nad Bugiem.**

Bretagne (brətaɲ) *n* the French name for **Brittany.**

brethren ('brɛðrɪn) *pl n Archaic except when referring to fellow members of a religion, sect, society, etc.* a plural of **brother.**

Breton[1] ('brɛt[ə]n; *French* brətɔ̃) *adj* **1** of, relating to, or characteristic of Brittany, its people, or their language. ◆ *n* **2** a native or inhabitant of Brittany, esp. one who speaks the Breton language. **3** the indigenous language of Brittany, belonging to the Brythonic subgroup of the Celtic family of languages.

Breton[2] (*French* brətɔ̃) *n* **André** (ɑ̃dre). 1896–1966, French poet and art critic: founder and chief theorist of surrealism, publishing the first surrealist manifesto in 1924.

Bretton Woods Conference ('brɛt[ə]n) *n* an international monetary conference held in 1944 at Bretton Woods in New Hampshire, which resulted in the establishment of the World Bank and the International Monetary Fund.

Breuer ('brɔɪə) *n* **1 Josef** ('jo:zɛf). 1842–1925, Austrian physician: treated the mentally ill by hypnosis. **2 Marcel Lajos** (mɑ:'sel 'lɔjoʃ). 1902–81, U.S. architect and furniture designer, born in Hungary. He developed bent plywood and tubular metal furniture and designed the UNESCO building in Paris (1953–58).

Breughel ('brɔɪg[ə]l) *n* a variant spelling of **Brueghel.**

breunnerite ('brɔɪnə,raɪt) *n* an iron-containing type of magnesite used in the manufacture of refractory bricks. [C19: named after Count *Breunner,* Austrian nobleman, + -ITE[1]]

breve (bri:v) *n* **1** an accent (˘) placed over a vowel to indicate that it is of short duration or is pronounced in a specified way. **2** *Music.* a note, now rarely used, equivalent in time value to two semibreves. **3** *R.C. Church.* a less common word for **brief** (papal letter). [C13: from Medieval Latin *breve,* from Latin *brevis* short; see BRIEF]

brevet ('brɛvɪt) *n* **1** a document entitling a commissioned officer to hold temporarily a higher military rank without the appropriate pay and allowances. ◆ *vb* **-vets, -vetting, -vetted** *or* **-vets, -veting, -veted. 2** (*tr*) to promote by brevet. [C14: from Old French *brievet* a little letter, from *brief* letter; see BRIEF] ► **'brevetcy** *n*

breviary ('bri:vjərɪ) *n, pl* **-ries. 1** *R.C. Church.* a book of psalms, hymns, prayers, etc., to be recited daily by clerics in major orders and certain members of religious orders as part of the divine office. **2** a similar book in the Orthodox Church. [C16: from Latin *breviārium* an abridged version, from *breviāre* to shorten, from *brevis* short]

brevier (brə'vɪə) *n* (formerly) a size of printer's type approximately equal to 8 point. [C16: probably from Dutch, literally: BREVIARY; so called because this type size was used for breviaries]

brevity ('brɛvɪtɪ) *n, pl* **-ties. 1** conciseness of expression; lack of verbosity. **2** a short duration; brief time. [C16: from Latin *brevitās* shortness, from *brevis* BRIEF]

brew (bru:) *vb* **1** to make (beer, ale, etc.) from malt and other ingredients by steeping, boiling, and fermentation. **2** to prepare (a drink, such as tea) by boiling or infusing. **3** (*tr*) to devise or plan: *to brew a plot.* **4** (*intr*) to be in the process of being brewed: *the tea was brewing in the pot.* **5** (*intr*) to be impending or forming: *there's a storm brewing.* ◆ *n* **6** a beverage produced by brewing, esp. tea or beer: *a strong brew.* **7** an instance or time of brewing: *last year's brew.* **8** a mixture: *an eclectic brew of mysticism and political discontent.* ◆ See also **brew up.** [Old English *brēowan;* related to Old Norse *brugga,* Old Saxon *breuwan,* Old High German *briuwan*] ► **'brewer** *n*

brewage ('bru:ɪdʒ) *n* **1** a product of brewing; brew. **2** the process of brewing.

brewer's yeast *n* **1** a yeast, *Saccharomyces cerevisiae,* used in brewing. See **yeast** (sense 2). **2** yeast obtained as a by-product of brewing.

brewery ('brʊərɪ) *n, pl* **-eries.** a place where beer, ale, etc., is brewed.

brewing ('bru:ɪŋ) *n* a quantity of a beverage brewed at one time.

brewis ('bru:ɪs) *or* **brevis** ('brɛvɪs) *n Dialect, chiefly northern English, Canadian, or U.S.* **1** bread soaked in broth, gravy, etc. **2** thickened broth. **3** (bru:z). *Canadian.* a Newfoundland stew of cod or pork, hardtack, and potatoes. [C16: from Old French *broez,* from *broet,* diminutive of *breu* BROTH]

Brewster ('bru:stə) *n* Sir **David.** 1781–1868, Scottish physicist, noted for his studies of the polarization of light.

brew up *Brit. and N.Z. informal.* ◆ *vb* (*intr, adv*) **1** to make tea, esp. out of doors or in informal circumstances. ◆ *n* **brew-up. 2** a making of tea.

brey (breɪ) *vb* (*intr*) *S. African informal.* a variant spelling of **brei.**

Brezhnev ('brɛʒnɛf; *Russian* 'brjɛʒnɪf) *n* **Leonid Ilyich** (lɪa'nit 'ilitʃ). 1906–82, Soviet statesman; president of the Soviet Union (1977–82); general secretary of the Soviet Communist Party (1964–82).

Brian ('braɪən) *n* **Havergal** ('hævəgəl). 1876–1972, English composer, who wrote 32 symphonies, including the large-scale *Gothic Symphony* (1919–27).

Brian Boru (bə'ru:) *n* ?941–1014, king of Ireland (1002–14): killed during the defeat of the Danes at the battle of Clontarf.

Briand (*French* briɑ̃) *n* **Aristide** (aristid). 1862–1932, French socialist statesman: prime minister of France 11 times. He was responsible for the separation of Church and State (1905) and he advocated a United States of Europe. Nobel peace prize 1926.

briar[1] *or* **brier** ('braɪə) *n* **1** Also called: **tree heath.** an ericaceous shrub, *Erica arborea,* of S Europe, having a hard woody root (briarroot). **2** a tobacco pipe made from the root of this plant. [C19: from French *bruyère* heath, from Late Latin *brūcus,* of Gaulish origin] ► **'briary** *or* **'briery** *adj*

briar[2] ('braɪə) *n* a variant spelling of **brier**[1].

briard (bri:'ɑ:d, bri:'ɑ:) *n* a medium-sized dog of an ancient French sheep-herding breed having a long rough coat of a single colour. [French, literally: of *Brie* (region in N France)]

Briareus (braɪ'eərɪəs) *n Greek myth.* a giant with a hundred arms and fifty heads who aided Zeus and the Olympians against the Titans. ► **Bri'arean** *adj*

briarroot *or* **brierroot** ('braɪə,ru:t) *n* **1** the hard woody root of the briar, used for making tobacco pipes. **2** any of several other woods used to make tobacco pipes. ◆ Also called: **'briar,wood, 'brier,wood.**

bribe (braɪb) *vb* **1** to promise, offer, or give something, usually money, to (a person) to procure services or gain influence, esp. illegally. ◆ *n* **2** a reward, such as money or favour, given or offered for this purpose. **3** any persuasion or lure. **4** a length of flawed or damaged cloth removed from the main piece. [C14: from Old French *briber* to beg, of obscure origin] ▶ 'bribable *or* 'bribeable *adj* ▶ 'briber *n*

bribery ('braɪbərɪ) *n, pl* **-eries.** the process of giving or taking bribes.

bric-a-brac ('brɪkəˌbræk) *n* miscellaneous small objects, esp. furniture and curios, kept because they are ornamental or rare. [C19: from French; phrase based on *bric* piece]

Brice (braɪs) *n* **Fanny,** real name *Fannie Borach.* 1891–1951, U.S. actress and singer. The film *Funny Girl* was based on her life.

bricht (brɪxt) *adj* a Scot. word for **bright.**

brick (brɪk) *n* **1a** a rectangular block of clay mixed with sand and fired in a kiln or baked by the sun, used in building construction. **1b** (*as modifier*): *a brick house.* **2** the material used to make such blocks. **3** any rectangular block: *a brick of ice.* **4** bricks collectively. **5** *Informal.* a reliable, trustworthy, or helpful person. **6** *Brit.* a child's building block. **7** short for **brick red. 8 drop a brick.** *Brit. informal.* to make a tactless or indiscreet remark. **9 like a ton of bricks.** *Informal.* (used esp. of the manner of punishing or reprimanding someone) with great force; severely: *when he spotted my mistake he came down on me like a ton of bricks.* ◆ *vb* **10** (*tr;* usually foll. by *in, up,* or *over*) to construct, line, pave, fill, or wall up with bricks: *to brick up a window; brick over a patio.* [C15: from Old French *brique,* from Middle Dutch *bricke;* related to Middle Low German *brike,* Old English *brecan* to BREAK] ▶ 'bricky *adj*

brickbat ('brɪkˌbæt) *n* **1** a piece of brick or similar material, esp. one used as a weapon. **2** blunt criticism: *the critic threw several brickbats at the singer.*

brickearth ('brɪkˌɜːθ) *n* a clayey alluvium suitable for the making of bricks: specifically, such a deposit in southern England, yielding a fertile soil.

brickie ('brɪkɪ) *n Brit. informal.* a bricklayer.

bricklayer ('brɪkˌleɪə) *n* a person trained or skilled in laying bricks.

bricklaying ('brɪkˌleɪɪŋ) *n* the technique or practice of laying bricks.

brick red *n, adj* **a** a reddish-brown colour. **b** (*as adj*): *a brick-red carpet.*

brick veneer *n* (in Australia) a timber-framed house with a brick exterior.

brickwork ('brɪkˌwɜːk) *n* **1** a structure, such as a wall, built of bricks. **2** construction using bricks.

brickyard ('brɪkˌjɑːd) *n* a place in which bricks are made, stored, or sold.

bricolage ('brɪkəˌlɑːʒ; *French* brɪkɔlaʒ) *n Architecture.* **1** the jumbled effect produced by the close proximity of buildings from different periods and in different architectural styles. **2** the deliberate creation of such an effect in certain modern developments: *the post-modernist bricolage of the new shopping centre.*

bricole (brɪ'kəʊl, 'brɪkᵊl) *n* **1** *Billiards.* a shot in which the cue ball touches a cushion after striking the object ball and before touching another ball. **2** (in ancient and medieval times) a military catapult for throwing stones, etc. **3** (esp. formerly) a harness worn by soldiers for dragging guns. **4** an indirect or unexpected action. [C16: from Old French: catapult, from Medieval Latin *bricola,* of uncertain origin]

bridal ('braɪdᵊl) *adj* **1** of or relating to a bride or a wedding; nuptial. ◆ *n* **2** *Obsolete.* a wedding or wedding feast. [Old English *brȳdealu,* literally: "bride ale", that is, wedding feast]

bridal wreath *n* any of several N temperate rosaceous shrubs of the genus *Spiraea,* esp. *S. prunifolia,* cultivated for their sprays of small white flowers.

bride[1] (braɪd) *n* a woman who has just been or is about to be married. [Old English *brȳd;* related to Old Norse *brūthr,* Gothic *brūths* daughter-in-law, Old High German *brūt*]

bride[2] (braɪd) *n Lacemaking, needlework.* a thread or loop that joins parts of a pattern. Also called: **bar.** [C19: from French, literally: BRIDLE, probably of Germanic origin]

Bride (braɪd) *n* See (Saint) **Bridget.**

bridegroom ('braɪdˌgruːm, -ˌgrʊm) *n* a man who has just been or is about to be married. [C14: changed (through influence of GROOM) from Old English *brȳdguma,* from *brȳd* BRIDE[1] + *guma* man; related to Old Norse *brūthgumi,* Old High German *brūtigomo*]

bride price *or* **wealth** *n* (in some societies) money, property, or services given by a bridegroom to the kinsmen of his bride in order to establish his rights over the woman.

bridesmaid ('braɪdzˌmeɪd) *n* a girl or young unmarried woman who attends a bride at her wedding. Compare **matron of honour, maid of honour.**

bridewell ('braɪdˌwel, -wəl) *n* a house of correction; jail, esp. for minor offences. [C16: after *Bridewell* (originally, *St Bride's Well*), a house of correction in London]

bridge[1] (brɪdʒ) *n* **1** a structure that spans and provides a passage over a road, railway, river, or some other obstacle. **2** something that resembles this in shape or function: *his letters provided a bridge across the centuries.* **3a** the hard ridge at the upper part of the nose, formed by the underlying nasal bones. **3b** any anatomical ridge or connecting structure. Compare **pons. 4** the part of a pair of glasses that rests on the nose. **5** Also called: **bridgework.** a dental plate containing one or more artificial teeth that is secured to the surrounding natural teeth. **6** a platform athwartships and above the rail, from which a ship is piloted and navigated. **7** a piece of wood, usually fixed, supporting the strings of a violin, guitar, etc., and transmitting their vibrations to the sounding board. **8** Also called: **bridge passage.** a passage in a musical, literary, or dramatic work linking two or more important sections. **9** Also called: **bridge circuit.** *Electronics.* any of several networks, such as a Wheatstone bridge, consisting of two branches across which a measuring device is connected. The resistance, capacitance, etc., of one component can be determined from the known values of the others when the voltage in each branch is balanced. **10** *Billiards, snooker.* **10a** a support for a cue made by placing the fingers on the table and raising the thumb. **10b** a cue rest with a notched end for shots beyond normal reach. **11** *Theatre.* **11a** a platform of adjustable height above or beside the stage for the use of stagehands, light operators, etc. **11b** *Chiefly Brit.* a part of the stage floor that can be raised or lowered. **12** a partition in a furnace or boiler to keep the fuel in place. **13 build bridges.** to promote reconciliation or cooperation between hostile groups or people. **14 burn one's bridges.** See **burn**[1] (sense 19). **15 cross a bridge when (one) comes to it.** to deal with a problem only when it arises; not to anticipate difficulties. ◆ *vb* (*tr*) **16** to build or provide a bridge over something; span: *to bridge a river.* **17** to connect or reduce the distance between: *let us bridge our differences.* [Old English *brycg;* related to Old Norse *bryggja* gangway, Old Frisian *bregge,* Old High German *brucka,* Danish, Swedish *bro*] ▶ 'bridgeable *adj* ▶ 'bridgeless *adj*

bridge[2] (brɪdʒ) *n* a card game for four players, based on whist, in which one hand (the dummy) is exposed and the trump suit decided by bidding between the players. See also **contract bridge, duplicate bridge, rubber bridge, auction bridge.** [C19: of uncertain origin, but compare Turkish *bir-üç* (unattested phrase) one-three (said perhaps to refer to the one exposed hand and the three players' hands]

Bridge (brɪdʒ) *n* **Frank.** 1879–1941, English composer, esp. of chamber music. He taught Benjamin Britten.

bridgeboard ('brɪdʒˌbɔːd) *n* a board on both sides of a staircase that is cut to support the treads and risers. Also called: **cut string.**

bridgehead ('brɪdʒˌhɛd) *n Military.* **1** an area of ground secured or to be taken on the enemy's side of an obstacle. **2** a fortified or defensive position at the end of a bridge nearest to the enemy. **3** an advantageous position gained for future expansion.

Bridgend (ˌbrɪdʒ'ɛnd) *n* a county borough in S Wales, created in 1996 from S Mid Glamorgan. Administrative centre: Bridgend. Pop.: 130 874 (1996 est.). Area: 264 sq. km (102 sq. miles).

Bridge of Sighs *n* a covered 16th-century bridge in Venice, between the Doge's Palace and the prisons, through which prisoners were formerly led to trial or execution.

bridge passage *n* See **bridge** (sense 8).

Bridgeport ('brɪdʒˌpɔːt) *n* a port in SW Connecticut, on Long Island Sound. Pop.: 137 990 (1996 est.).

bridge rectifier *n Electrical engineering.* a full-wave rectifier consisting of a bridge with a rectifier in each of the four arms.

bridge roll *n Brit.* a soft bread roll in a long thin shape. [C20: from BRIDGE[2] or perhaps BRIDGE[1]]

Bridges ('brɪdʒɪz) *n* **Robert (Seymour).** 1844–1930, English poet: poet laureate (1913–30).

Bridget ('brɪdʒɪt) *n* **Saint. 1** Also called: **Bride, Brigid.** 453–523 A.D., Irish abbess; a patron saint of Ireland. Feast day: Feb. 1. **2** Also called: **Birgitta.** ?1303-73, Swedish nun and visionary; patron saint of Sweden. Feast day: July 23.

Bridgetown ('brɪdʒˌtaʊn) *n* the capital of Barbados, a port on the SW coast. Pop.: 6070 (1990).

bridgework ('brɪdʒˌwɜːk) *n* **1a** a partial denture attached to the surrounding teeth. See **bridge**[1] (sense 5). **1b** the technique of making such appliances. **2** the process or occupation of constructing bridges.

bridging ('brɪdʒɪŋ) *n* **1** one or more timber struts fixed between floor or roof joists to stiffen the construction and distribute the loads. **2** *Mountaineering.* a technique for climbing a wide chimney by pressing left hand and foot against one side of it and right hand and foot against the other side.

bridging loan *n* a loan made to cover the period between two transactions, such as the buying of another house before the sale of the first is completed.

Bridgman ('brɪdʒmən) *n* **Percy Williams.** 1882–1961, U.S. physicist: Nobel prize for physics (1946) for his work on high-pressure physics and thermodynamics.

Bridgwater ('brɪdʒˌwɔːtə) *n* a town in SW England, in central Somerset. Pop.: 34 610 (1991).

bridie ('braɪdɪ; *Scot.* 'brəɪdɪ) *n Scot.* a semicircular pie containing meat and onions. [of unknown origin]

Bridie ('braɪdɪ) *n* **James,** real name *Osborne Henry Mavor.* 1888–1951, Scottish physician and dramatist, who founded the Glasgow Citizens' Theatre. His plays include *The Anatomist* (1930).

bridle ('braɪdᵊl) *n* **1** a headgear for a horse, etc., consisting of a series of buckled straps and a metal mouthpiece (bit) by which the animal is controlled through the reins. **2** something that curbs or restrains; check. **3** a Y-shaped cable, rope, or chain, used for holding, towing, etc. **4** *Machinery.* a device by which the motion of a component is limited, often in the form of a linkage or flange. ◆ *vb* **5** (*tr*) to put a bridle on (a horse, mule, etc.). **6** (*intr*) (of a horse) to respond correctly to the pull of the reins. **7** (*tr*) to restrain; curb: *he bridled his rage.* **8** (*intr;* often foll. by *at*) to show anger, scorn, or indignation. [Old English *brigdels;* related to *bregdan* to BRAID[1], Old High German *brittil,* Middle Low German *breidel*] ▶ 'bridler *n*

bridle path *n* a path suitable for riding or leading horses. Also called (N.Z.): **bridle track.**

bridlewise ('braɪdᵊlˌwaɪz) *adj U.S.* (of a horse) obedient to the pressure of the reins on the neck rather than to the bit.

bridoon (brɪ'duːn) *n* a horse's bit: a small snaffle used in double bridles. [C18: from French *bridon,* from *bride* bridle; compare Middle English *bride*]

brie (briː) *n* a variant spelling of **bree**[1].

Brie (briː) *n* **1** a soft creamy white cheese, similar to Camembert but milder. **2** a mainly agricultural area in N France, between the Rivers Marne and Seine: noted esp. for its cheese.

brief (briːf) *adj* **1** short in duration: *a brief holiday.* **2** short in length or extent; scanty: *a brief bikini.* **3** abrupt in manner; brusque: *the professor was brief with me this morning.* **4** terse or concise; containing few words: *he made a brief statement.* ◆ *n* **5** a condensed or short statement or written synopsis; abstract.

6 *Law.* a document containing all the facts and points of law of a case by which a solicitor instructs a barrister to represent a client. **7** *R.C. Church.* a letter issuing from the Roman court written in modern characters, as contrasted with a papal bull; papal brief. **8** short for **briefing. 9** a paper outlining the arguments and information on one side of a debate. **10** *Brit. slang.* a lawyer, esp. a barrister. **11 hold a brief for.** to argue for; champion. **12 in brief.** in short; to sum up. ♦ *vb (tr)* **13** to prepare or instruct by giving a summary of relevant facts. **14** to make a summary or synopsis of. **15** *English law.* **15a** to instruct (a barrister) by brief. **15b** to retain (a barrister) as counsel. ♦ See also **briefs.** [C14: from Old French *bref,* from Latin *brevis;* related to Greek *brakhus*] ▸ **'briefly** *adv* ▸ **'briefness** *n*

briefcase ('bri:fˌkeɪs) *n* a flat portable case, often of leather, for carrying papers, books, etc.

briefing ('bri:fɪŋ) *n* **1** a meeting at which detailed information or instructions are given, as for military operations, etc. **2** the facts presented during such a meeting.

briefless ('bri:flɪs) *adj* (said of a barrister) without clients.

briefs (bri:fs) *pl n* men's underpants or women's pants without legs.

brier[1] *or* **briar** ('braɪə) *n* any of various thorny shrubs or other plants, such as the sweetbrier and greenbrier. [Old English *brēr, brǣr,* of obscure origin] ▸ **'briery** *or* **'briary** *adj*

brier[2] ('braɪə) *n* a variant spelling of **briar**[1].

brierroot ('braɪəˌru:t) *n* a variant spelling of **briarroot.** Also called: **'brierˌwood.**

brig[1] (brɪg) *n* **1** *Nautical.* a two-masted square-rigger. **2** *Chiefly U.S.* a prison, esp. in a navy ship. [C18: shortened from BRIGANTINE]

brig[2] (brɪg) *n* a Scot. and northern English word for a **bridge**[1].

Brig. *abbrev. for* Brigadier.

brigade (brɪ'geɪd) *n* **1** a formation of fighting units, together with support arms and services, smaller than a division and usually commanded by a brigadier. **2** a group of people organized for a certain task: *a rescue brigade.* ♦ *vb (tr)* **3** to organize into a brigade. **4** to put or group together. [C17: from Old French, from Old Italian, from *brigare* to fight, perhaps of Celtic origin; see BRIGAND]

brigadier (ˌbrɪgə'dɪə) *n* **1** an officer of the British Army or Royal Marines who holds a rank junior to a major general but senior to a colonel, usually commanding a brigade. **2** an equivalent rank in other armed forces. **3** *U.S. Army.* short for **brigadier general. 4** *History.* a noncommissioned rank in the armies of Napoleon I. [C17: from French, from BRIGADE]

brigadier general *n, pl* **brigadier generals. 1** an officer of the U.S. Army, Air Force, or Marine Corps who holds a rank junior to a major general but senior to a colonel, usually commanding a brigade. **2** the former name for a **brigadier** (sense 1).

brigalow ('brɪgələʊ) *n Austral.* **a** any of various acacia trees. **b** *(as modifier): brigalow country.* [C19: from a native Australian language]

brigand ('brɪgənd) *n* a bandit or plunderer, esp. a member of a gang operating in mountainous areas. [C14: from Old French, from Old Italian *brigante* fighter, from *brigare* to fight, from *briga* strife, of Celtic origin] ▸ **'brigandage** *or* **'brigandry** *n*

brigandine ('brɪgənˌdi:n, -ˌdaɪn) *n* a coat of mail, invented in the Middle Ages to increase mobility, consisting of metal rings or sheets sewn on to cloth or leather. [C15: from Old French, from BRIGAND + -INE[1]]

brigantine ('brɪgənˌti:n, -ˌtaɪn) *n* a two-masted sailing ship, rigged square on the foremast and fore-and-aft with square topsails on the mainmast. [C16: from Old Italian *brigantino* pirate ship, from *brigante* BRIGAND]

Brig. Gen. *abbrev. for* brigadier general.

Briggs (brɪgz) *n* **Henry.** 1561–1631, English mathematician: introduced common logarithms.

Brighouse[1] ('brɪgˌhaʊs) *n* a town in N England, in Calderdale unitary authority, West Yorkshire: machine tools, textiles, engineering. Pop.: 32 198 (1991).

Brighouse[2] ('brɪgˌhaʊs) *n* **Harold.** 1882–1958, British novelist and dramatist, best known for his play *Hobson's Choice* (1915).

bright (braɪt) *adj* **1** emitting or reflecting much light; shining. **2** (of colours) intense or vivid. **3** full of promise: *a bright future.* **4** full of animation; cheerful: *a bright face.* **5** *Informal.* quick witted or clever: *a bright child.* **6** magnificent; glorious: *a bright victory.* **7** polished; glistening: *a bright finish.* **8** (of the voice) distinct and clear. **9** (of a liquid) translucent and clear: *a circle of bright water.* **10 bright and early.** very early in the morning. ♦ *n* **11** a thin flat paintbrush with a straight sharp edge used for highlighting in oil painting. **12** *Poetic.* brightness or splendour: *the bright of his armour.* ♦ *adv* **13** brightly: *the fire was burning bright.* ♦ See also **brights.** [Old English *beorht;* related to Old Norse *bjartr,* Gothic *bairhts* clear, Old High German *beraht,* Norwegian *bjerk,* Swedish *brokig* pied] ▸ **'brightly** *adv*

Bright (braɪt) *n* **John.** 1811–89, British liberal statesman, economist, and advocate of free trade: with Richard Cobden he led the Anti-Corn-Law League (1838–46).

brighten ('braɪt^ən) *vb* **1** to make or become bright or brighter. **2** to make or become cheerful. ▸ **'brightener** *n*

brightening agent *n* a compound applied to a textile to increase its brightness by the conversion of ultraviolet radiation to visible (blue) light, used in detergents.

bright-eyed *adj* **1** eager; fresh and enthusiastic. **2 bright-eyed and bushy-tailed.** *Informal.* keen, confident, and alert.

bright lights *pl n* **the.** places of entertainment in a city.

brightness ('braɪtnɪs) *n* **1** the condition of being bright. **2** *Physics.* a former name for **luminosity** (sense 4). **3** *Psychol.* the experienced intensity of light.

Brighton ('braɪt^ən) *n* a coastal resort in S England, in Brighton and Hove unitary authority, East Sussex: patronized by the Prince Regent, who had the Royal Pavilion built (1782); seat of the University of Sussex and the University of Brighton. Pop.: 124 851 (1991).

Brighton and Hove (həʊv) *n* a unitary authority in S England, in East Sussex; created in 1997. Pop.: 246 200 (1994 est.). Area: 72 sq. km (28 sq. miles).

brights (braɪts) *pl n U.S.* the high beam of the headlights of a motor vehicle.

Bright's disease (braɪts) *n* chronic inflammation of the kidneys; chronic nephritis. [C19: named after Richard *Bright* (1789–1858), British physician]

brightwork ('braɪtˌwɜ:k) *n* **1** shiny metal trimmings or fittings on ships, cars, etc. **2** varnished or plain woodwork on a vessel.

Brigid ('brɪdʒɪd) *n* See (Saint) **Bridget.**

brill (brɪl) *n, pl* **brill** *or* **brills.** a European food fish, *Scophthalmus rhombus,* a flatfish similar to the turbot but lacking tubercles on the body: family *Bothidae.* [C15: probably from Cornish *brȳthel* mackerel, from Old Cornish *brȳth* speckled; related to Welsh *brith* spotted]

Brillat-Savarin (*French* brijasavarɛ̃) *n* **Anthelme** (ɑ̃tɛlm). 1755–1826, French politician and gourmet; author of *Physiologie du Goût* (1825).

brilliance ('brɪljəns) *or* **brilliancy** *n* **1** great brightness; radiance. **2** excellence or distinction in physical or mental ability; exceptional talent. **3** splendour; magnificence: *the brilliance of the royal court.* **4** *Physics.* a former term for **luminance.**

brilliant ('brɪljənt) *adj* **1** shining with light; sparkling. **2** (of a colour) having a high saturation and reflecting a considerable amount of light; vivid. **3** outstanding; exceptional: *a brilliant success.* **4** splendid; magnificent: *a brilliant show.* **5** of outstanding intelligence or intellect: *a brilliant mind; a brilliant idea.* **6** *Music.* **6a** (of the tone of an instrument) having a large proportion of high harmonics above the fundamental. **6b** Also: **brilliant** (*French* brijɑ̃), **brilliante** (*French* brijɑ̃t). with spirit; lively. ♦ *n* **7** Also called: **brilliant cut. 7a** a popular circular cut for diamonds and other gemstones in the form of two many-faceted pyramids (the top one truncated) joined at their bases. **7b** a diamond of this cut. **8** (formerly) a size of a printer's type approximately equal to 4 point. [C17: from French *brillant* shining, from *briller* to shine, from Italian *brillare,* from *brillo* BERYL] ▸ **'brilliantly** *adv*

brilliantine ('brɪljənˌti:n) *n* **1** a perfumed oil used to make the hair smooth and shiny. **2** *Chiefly U.S.* a glossy fabric made of mohair and cotton. [C19: from French, from *brillant* shining]

brim (brɪm) *n* **1** the upper rim of a vessel: *the brim of a cup.* **2** a projecting rim or edge: *the brim of a hat.* **3** the brink or edge of something. ♦ *vb* **brims, brimming, brimmed. 4** to fill or be full to the brim: *eyes brimming with tears.* [C13: from Middle High German *brem,* probably from Old Norse *barmr;* see BERM] ▸ **'brimless** *adj*

brimful *or* **brimfull** (ˌbrɪm'fʊl) *adj (postpositive,* foll. by *of)* filled up to the brim (with).

brimmer ('brɪmə) *n* a vessel, such as a glass or bowl, filled to the brim.

brimstone ('brɪmˌstəʊn) *n* **1** an obsolete name for **sulphur. 2** a common yellow butterfly, *Gonepteryx rhamni,* of N temperate regions of the Old World: family *Pieridae.* **3** *Archaic.* a scolding nagging woman; virago. [Old English *brynstān;* related to Old Norse *brennistein;* see BURN[1], STONE]

Brindisi (*Italian* 'brindizi) *n* a port in SE Italy, in SE Apulia: important naval base in Roman times and a centre of the Crusades in the Middle Ages. Pop.: 93 290 (1991). Ancient name: **Brundisium.**

brindle ('brɪnd^əl) *n* **1** a brindled animal. **2** a brindled colouring. [C17: back formation from BRINDLED]

brindled ('brɪnd^əld) *adj* brown or grey streaked or patched with a darker colour: *a brindled dog.* [C17: changed from C15 *brended,* literally: branded, probably of Scandinavian origin; compare Old Norse *bröndottr;* see BRAND]

Brindley ('brɪndlɪ) *n* **James.** 1716–72, British canal builder, who constructed (1759–61) the Bridgewater Canal, the first in England.

brine (braɪn) *n* **1** a strong solution of salt and water, used for salting and pickling meats, etc. **2** the sea or its water. **3** *Chem.* any solution of a salt in water: *a potassium chloride brine.* ♦ *vb* **4** *(tr)* to soak in or treat with brine. [Old English *brīne;* related to Middle Dutch *brīne,* Old Slavonic *bridŭ* bitter, Sanskrit *bibhrāya* burnt] ▸ **'brinish** *adj*

brinelling ('brɪnəlɪŋ) *n* a localized surface corrosion; a cause of damage to bearings.

Brinell number (brɪ'nɛl) *n* a measure of the hardness of a material obtained by pressing a hard steel ball into its surface; it is expressed as the ratio of the load on the ball in kilograms to the area of the depression made by the ball in square millimetres. [C19: named after Johann A. *Brinell* (1849–1925), Swedish engineer]

bring (brɪŋ) *vb* **brings, bringing, brought.** *(tr)* **1** to carry, convey, or take (something or someone) to a designated place or person: *bring that book to me; will you bring Jessica to Tom's party?* **2** to cause to happen or occur to (oneself or another): *to bring disrespect on oneself.* **3** to cause to happen as a consequence: *responsibility brings maturity.* **4** to cause to come to mind: *it brought back memories.* **5** to cause to be in a certain state, position, etc.: *the punch brought him to his knees.* **6** to force, persuade, or make (oneself): *I couldn't bring myself to do it.* **7** to sell for; fetch: *the painting brought 20 pounds.* **8** *Law.* **8a** to institute (proceedings, charges, etc.). **8b** to put (evidence, etc.) before a tribunal. **9 bring forth.** to give birth to. **10 bring home to. 10a** to convince of: *his account brought home to us the gravity of the situation.* **10b** to place the blame on. **11 bring to bear.** See **bear**[1] (sense 17). ♦ See also **bring about, bring down, bring forward, bring in, bring off, bring on, bring out, bring over, bring round, bring to, bring up.** [Old English *bringan;* related to Gothic *briggan,* Old High German *bringan*] ▸ **'bringer** *n*

bring about *vb (tr, adv)* **1** to cause to happen: *to bring about a change in the law.* **2** to turn (a ship) around.

bring-and-buy sale *n Brit. and N.Z.* an informal sale, often conducted for charity, to which people bring items for sale and buy those that others have brought.

bring down *vb (tr, adv)* **1** to cause to fall: *the fighter aircraft brought the enemy down; the ministers agreed to bring down the price of oil.* **2** *(usually passive) Slang.* to cause to be elated and then suddenly depressed, as from using drugs.

bring forward *vb (tr, adv)* **1** to present or introduce (a subject) for discussion. **2** *Book-keeping.* to transfer (a figure representing the sum of the figures on a page or in a column) to the top of the next page or column.

bring in *vb (tr, adv)* **1** to yield (income, profit, or cash): *his investments brought him in £100.* **2** to produce or return (a verdict). **3** to put forward or introduce (a legislative bill, etc.).

bringing-up *n* another term for **upbringing.**

bring off *vb (tr, adv)* **1** to succeed in achieving (something), esp. with difficulty or contrary to expectations: *he managed to bring off the deal.* **2** *Taboo.* to cause to have an orgasm.

bring on *vb (tr, adv)* **1** to induce or cause: *these pills will bring on labour.* **2** *Taboo.* to cause sexual excitement in; stimulate.

bring out *vb (tr, adv)* **1** to produce or publish or have published: *when are you bringing out a new dictionary?* **2** to expose, reveal, or cause to be seen: *she brought out the best in me.* **3** to encourage (a shy person) to be less reserved (often in the phrase **bring (someone) out of himself** *or* **herself**). **4** *Brit.* (of a trade union, provocative action by management, misunderstanding, etc.) to cause (workers) to strike. **5** (foll. by *in*) to cause (a person) to become covered (with spots, a rash, etc.). **6** *Brit.* to introduce (a girl) formally into society as a debutante.

bring over *vb (tr, adv)* to cause (a person) to change allegiances.

bring round *or* **around** *vb (tr, adv)* **1** to restore (a person) to consciousness, esp. after a faint. **2** to convince (another person, usually an opponent) of an opinion or point of view.

bring to *vb (tr)* **1** *(adv)* to restore (a person) to consciousness. **2** *(adv)* to cause (a ship) to turn into the wind and reduce her headway. **3** *(prep)* to make (something) equal to (an amount of money): *that brings your bill to £17.*

bring up *vb (tr, adv)* **1** to care for and train (a child); rear: *we had been brought up to go to church.* **2** to raise (a subject) for discussion; mention. **3** to vomit (food). **4** (foll. by *against*) to cause (a person) to face or confront. **5** (foll. by *to*) to cause (something) to be of a required standard.

brinjal ('brɪndʒəl) *n* (in India and Africa) another name for the **aubergine.** [C17: from Portuguese *berinjela,* from Arabic; see AUBERGINE]

brink (brɪŋk) *n* **1** the edge, border, or verge of a steep place: *the brink of the precipice.* **2** the highest point; top: *the sun fell below the brink of the hill.* **3** the land at the edge of a body of water. **4** the verge of an event or state: *the brink of disaster.* [C13: from Middle Dutch *brinc,* of Germanic origin; compare Old Norse *brekka* slope, Middle Low German *brink* edge of a field]

brinkmanship ('brɪŋkmən,ʃɪp) *n* the art or practice of pressing a dangerous situation, esp. in international affairs, to the limit of safety and peace in order to win an advantage from a threatening or tenacious foe.

brinny ('brɪnɪ) *n, pl* **-nies.** *Austral. children's slang, old-fashioned.* a stone, esp. when thrown.

briny ('braɪnɪ) *adj* **brinier, briniest. 1** of or resembling brine; salty. ◆ *n* **2** (preceded by *the*) an informal name for the **sea.** ▸ **'brininess** *n*

brio ('bri:əʊ) *n* liveliness or vigour; spirit. See also **con brio.** [C19: from Italian, of Celtic origin]

brioche ('bri:əʊʃ, -ɒʃ; *French* briɔʃ) *n* a soft roll or loaf made from a very light yeast dough, sometimes mixed with currants. [C19: from Norman dialect, from *brier* to knead, of Germanic origin; compare French *broyer* to pound, BREAK]

briolette (,bri:əʊ'lɛt) *n* a pear-shaped gem cut with long triangular facets. [C19: from French, alteration of *brillolette,* from *brignolette* little dried plum, after *Brignoles,* France, where these plums are produced]

briony ('braɪənɪ) *n, pl* **-nies.** a variant spelling of **bryony.**

briquette *or* **briquet** (brɪ'kɛt) *n* **1** a small brick made of compressed coal dust, sawdust, charcoal, etc., used for fuel. **2** a small brick of any substance: *an ice-cream briquette.* ◆ *vb* **3** *(tr)* to make into the form of a brick or bricks: *to briquette clay.* [C19: from French: a little brick, from *brique* BRICK]

bris (brɪs) *or* **brith** *n Judaism.* ritual circumcision of male babies, usually at eight days old, regarded as the formal entry of the child to the Jewish community. [from Hebrew, literally: covenant]

brisance ('bri:zəns; *French* brizɑ̃s) *n* the shattering effect or power of an explosion or explosive. [C20: from French, from *briser* to break, ultimately of Celtic origin; compare Old Irish *brissim* I break] ▸ **'brisant** *adj*

Brisbane ('brɪzbən) *n* a port in E Australia, the capital of Queensland: founded in 1824 as a penal settlement; vast agricultural hinterland. Pop.: 1 489 100 (1995 est.).

brise-soleil (,bri:zsəʊ'leɪ) *n* a structure used in hot climates to protect a window from the sun, usually consisting of horizontal or vertical strips of wood, concrete, etc. [C20: French: break-sun, from *briser* to break + *soleil* sun]

brisk (brɪsk) *adj* **1** lively and quick; vigorous: *a brisk walk; trade was brisk.* **2** invigorating or sharp: *brisk weather.* ◆ *vb* **3** (often foll. by *up*) to enliven; make or become brisk. [C16: probably variant of BRUSQUE] ▸ **'briskly** *adv* ▸ **'briskness** *n*

brisken ('brɪskən) *vb* to make or become more lively or brisk.

brisket ('brɪskɪt) *n* **1** the breast of a four-legged animal. **2** the meat from this part, esp. of beef. [C14: probably of Scandinavian origin; related to Old Norse *brjōsk* gristle, Norwegian and Danish *brusk*]

brisling ('brɪslɪŋ) *n* another name for a **sprat,** esp. a Norwegian sprat seasoned, smoked, and canned in oil. [C20: from Norwegian; related to obsolete Danish *bretling,* German *Breitling*]

Brissot (*French* briso) *n* **Jacques-Pierre** (ʒakpjɛr). 1754–93, French journalist and revolutionary; leader of the Girondists: executed by the Jacobins.

bristle ('brɪs^{ə}l) *n* **1** any short stiff hair of an animal or plant, such as any of the hairs on a pig's back. **2** something resembling these hairs: *toothbrush bristle.* ◆ *vb* **3** (when *intr,* often foll. by *up*) to stand up or cause to stand up like bristles: *the angry cat's fur bristled.* **4** *(intr;* sometimes foll. by *up)* to show anger, indignation, etc.: *she bristled at the suggestion.* **5** *(intr)* to be thickly covered or set: *the target bristled with arrows.* **6** *(intr)* to be in a state of agitation or movement: *the office was bristling with activity.* **7** *(tr)* to provide with a bristle or bristles. [C13 *bristil, brustel,* from earlier *brust,* from Old English *byrst;* related to Old Norse *burst,* Old High German *borst*] ▸ **'bristly** *adj*

bristlecone pine ('brɪs^{ə}l,kəʊn) *n* a coniferous tree, *Pinus aristata,* of the western U.S., bearing cones with bristle-like prickles: the longest-lived known tree, useful in radiocarbon dating.

bristle-grass *n* any of various grasses of the genus *Setaria,* such as *S. viridis,* having a bristly inflorescence.

bristletail ('brɪs^{ə}l,teɪl) *n* any primitive wingless insect of the orders *Thysanura* and *Diplura,* such as the silverfish and firebrat, having a flattened body and long tail appendages.

bristle worm *n* a popular name for a **polychaete.**

Bristol ('brɪst^{ə}l) *n* **1** a port and industrial city in SW England, mainly in Bristol unitary authority, on the River Avon seven miles from its mouth on the Bristol Channel: a major port, trading with America, in the 17th and 18th centuries; the modern port consists chiefly of docks at Avonmouth and Portishead; noted for the **Clifton Suspension Bridge** (designed by I. K. Brunel, 1834) over the Avon gorge; Bristol university (1909) and University of the West of England. Pop.: 407 992 (1991). **2** a unitary authority in SW England, created in 1996 from part of Avon county. Pop.: 374 300 (1996 est.). Area: 110 sq. km (42 sq. miles).

Bristol board *n* a heavy smooth cardboard of fine quality, used for printing and drawing.

Bristol Channel *n* an inlet of the Atlantic, between S Wales and SW England, merging into the Severn estuary. Length: about 137 km (85 miles).

Bristol fashion *adv, adj (postpositive)* **1** *Nautical.* clean and neat, with newly painted and scrubbed surfaces, brass polished, etc. **2 shipshape and Bristol fashion.** in good order; efficiently arranged.

bristols ('brɪst^{ə}lz) *pl n Brit. slang.* a woman's breasts. [C20: short for *Bristol Cities,* rhyming slang for *titties*]

Bristow ('brɪstəʊ) *n* **Eric.** born 1957, British darts player.

brit (brɪt) *n (functioning as sing or pl)* **1** the young of a herring, sprat, or similar fish. **2** minute marine crustaceans, esp. copepods, forming food for many fishes and whales. [C17: perhaps from Cornish *brȳthel* mackerel; see BRILL]

Brit (brɪt) *n Informal.* a British person.

Brit. *abbrev. for:* **1** Britain. **2** British.

Britain ('brɪt^{ə}n) *n* another name for **Great Britain** or the **United Kingdom.**

Britannia (brɪ'tænɪə) *n* **1** a female warrior carrying a trident and wearing a helmet, personifying Great Britain or the British Empire. **2** (in the ancient Roman Empire) the S part of Great Britain. **3** short for **Britannia coin.**

Britannia coin *n* any of four British gold coins introduced in 1987 for investment purposes; their denominations are £100, £50, £25, and £10.

Britannia metal *n* an alloy of low melting point consisting of tin with 5–10 per cent antimony, 1–3 per cent copper, and sometimes small quantities of zinc, lead, or bismuth: used for decorative purposes and for bearings.

Britannic (brɪ'tænɪk) *adj* of Britain; British (esp. in the phrases **His** *or* **Her Britannic Majesty**).

britches ('brɪtʃɪz) *pl n* a variant spelling of **breeches.**

brith (brit) *n* a variant of **bris.**

Briticism ('brɪtɪ,sɪzəm) *n* a custom, linguistic usage, or other feature peculiar to Britain or its people.

British ('brɪtɪʃ) *adj* **1** relating to, denoting, or characteristic of Britain or any of the natives, citizens, or inhabitants of the United Kingdom. **2** relating to or denoting the English language as spoken and written in Britain, esp. the S dialect generally regarded as standard. See also **Southern British English, Received Pronunciation. 3** relating to or denoting the ancient Britons. ◆ *n* **4 the British.** *(functioning as pl)* the natives or inhabitants of Britain. **5** the extinct Celtic language of the ancient Britons. See also **Brythonic.** ▸ **'Britishness** *n*

British Antarctic Territory *n* a UK Overseas Territory in the S Atlantic: created in 1962 and consisting of the South Shetland Islands, the South Orkney Islands, and Graham Land; formerly part of the Falkland Islands Dependencies.

British Association screw thread *n Engineering.* a system of screw sizes designated from 0 to 25. Now superseded by standard metric sizes. Abbrev.: **BA.**

British Cameroons *pl n* a former British trust territory of West Africa. See **Cameroon.**

British Civil Airworthiness Requirements *pl n* (in Britain) documents specifying aerodynamic, engineering design, construction, and performance requirements, which must be met before an aircraft is given permission to fly.

British Columbia *n* a province of W Canada, on the Pacific coast: largely mountainous with extensive forests, rich mineral resources, and important fisheries. Capital: Victoria. Pop.: 3 933 300 (1997 est.). Area: 930 532 sq. km (359 279 sq. miles). Abbrev.: **BC.** ▸ **British Columbian** *n, adj*

British Commonwealth of Nations *n* the former name of the **Commonwealth.**

British Council *n* an organization founded (1934) to extend the influence of British culture and education throughout the world.

British disease *n* (usually preceded by *the*) the pattern of strikes and industrial unrest in the 1970s and early 1980s supposed by many during this time to be endemic in Britain and to weaken the British economy.

British East Africa *n* the former British possessions of Uganda, Kenya, Tanganyika, and Zanzibar, before their independence in the 1960s.

British Empire *n* (formerly) the United Kingdom and the territories under its control, which reached its greatest extent at the end of World War I when it embraced over a quarter of the world's population and more than a quarter of the world's land surface.

Britisher ('brɪtɪʃə) *n* (not used by the British) **1** a native or inhabitant of Great Britain. **2** any British subject.

British Guiana *n* the former name (until 1966) of **Guyana.**

British Honduras *n* the former name of **Belize.**

British India *n* the 17 provinces of India formerly governed by the British under the British sovereign: ceased to exist in 1947 when the independent states of India and Pakistan were created.

British Indian Ocean Territory *n* a UK Overseas Territory in the Indian Ocean: consists of the Chagos Archipelago (formerly a dependency of Mauritius) and formerly included (until 1976) Aldabra, Farquhar, and Des Roches, now administratively part of the Seychelles. Diego Garcia is an important naval base.

British Isles *pl n* a group of islands in W Europe, consisting of Great Britain, Ireland, the Isle of Man, Orkney, the Shetland Islands, the Channel Islands belonging to Great Britain, and the islands adjacent to these.

Britishism ('brɪtɪˌʃɪzəm) *n* a variant of **Briticism.**

British Israelite *n* a member of a religious movement claiming that the British people are descended from the lost tribes of Israel.

British Legion *n Brit.* an organization founded in 1921 to provide services and assistance for former members of the armed forces.

British Library *n* the British national library, formed in 1973 from the British Museum library and other national collections: housed mainly in the British Museum until 1997 when a purpose-built library in St Pancras, London, was completed.

British List *n* a list, maintained by the British Ornithologists' Union, of birds accepted as occurring at least once in the British Isles.

British Museum *n* a museum in London, founded in 1753: contains one of the world's richest collections of antiquities and (until 1997) most of the British Library.

British National Party *n* (in the U.K.) a neo-Nazi political party. Abbrev.: **BNP.**

British North America *n* (formerly) Canada or its constituent regions or provinces that formed part of the British Empire.

British Somaliland *n* a former British protectorate (1884–1960) in E Africa, on the Gulf of Aden: united with Italian Somaliland in 1960 to form the Somali Republic.

British Standard brass thread *n Engineering.* a Whitworth screw thread having 26 threads per inch, used for thin-walled tubing and designated by the diameter of the tubing. Abbrev.: **BSB.**

British Standard fine thread *n Engineering.* a screw thread having a Whitworth profile but a finer pitch for a given diameter. Abbrev.: **BSF.**

British Standard pipe thread *n Engineering.* a screw thread of Whitworth profile used for piping and designated by the bore of the pipe. Abbrev.: **BSP.**

British Standards Institution *n* an association, founded in London in 1901, that establishes and maintains standards for units of measurements, clothes sizes, technical terminology, etc., as used in Britain. Abbrev.: **BSI.** Compare **National Bureau of Standards, International Standards Organization.**

British Standard Time *n* the standard time used in Britain all the year round from 1968 to 1971, set one hour ahead of Greenwich Mean Time and equalling Central European Time.

British Standard Whitworth thread *n* See **Whitworth screw thread.** Abbrev.: **BSW.**

British Summer Time *n* time set one hour ahead of Greenwich Mean Time: used in Britain from the end of March to the end of October, providing an extra hour of daylight in the evening. Abbrev.: **BST.** Compare **daylight-saving time.**

British Technology Group *n* a government-appointed organization formed in 1981 by the merger of the National Enterprise Board and the National Research and Development Corporation to encourage and finance technological innovation. Abbrev.: **BTG.**

British thermal unit *n* a unit of heat in the fps system equal to the quantity of heat required to raise the temperature of 1 pound of water by 1°F. 1 British thermal unit is equivalent to 1055.06 joules or 251.997 calories. Abbrevs.: **btu, BThU.**

British Union of Fascists *n* the British fascist party founded by Sir Oswald Mosley (1932), which advocated a strong corporate state and promoted anti-Semitism.

British Virgin Islands *pl n* a UK Overseas Territory in the Caribbean, consisting of 36 islands in the E Virgin Islands: formerly part of the Federation of the Leeward Islands (1871–1956). Capital: Road Town, on Tortola. Pop.: 17 000 (1993 est.). Area: 153 sq. km (59 sq. miles).

British warm *n* an army officer's short thick overcoat.

British West Africa *n* the former British possessions of Nigeria, The Gambia, Sierra Leone, and the Gold Coast, and the former trust territories of Togoland and Cameroons.

British West Indies *pl n* the states in the Caribbean that are members of the Commonwealth: the Bahamas, Barbados, Jamaica, Trinidad and Tobago, Antigua and Barbuda, Saint Kitts-Nevis, Dominica, Grenada, Saint Lucia, and Saint Vincent and the Grenadines.

brit milah ('brit mi'lɑː, 'milɑ) *n Judaism.* a Hebrew term usually translated as **circumcision.**

Briton ('brɪtᵊn) *n* **1** a native or inhabitant of Britain. **2** a citizen of the United Kingdom. **3** *History.* any of the early Celtic inhabitants of S Britain who were largely dispossessed by the Anglo-Saxon invaders after the 5th century A.D. **[C13:** from Old French *Breton,* from Latin *Britto,* of Celtic origin**]**

Britpop ('brɪtˌpɒp) *n* the characteristic pop music performed by some British bands of the mid 1990s.

Brittany ('brɪtənɪ) *n* a region of NW France, the peninsula between the English Channel and the Bay of Biscay: settled by Celtic refugees from Wales and Cornwall during the Anglo-Saxon invasions; disputed between England and France until 1364. Breton name: **Breiz** (braɪz). French name: **Bretagne.** Related adj: **Breton.**

Britten ('brɪtᵊn) *n* **(Edward) Benjamin,** Baron Britten. 1913–76, English composer, pianist, and conductor. His works include the operas *Peter Grimes* (1945) and *Billy Budd* (1951), the choral works *Hymn to St Cecilia* (1942) and *A War Requiem* (1962), and numerous orchestral pieces.

brittle ('brɪtᵊl) *adj* **1** easily cracked, snapped, or broken; fragile. **2** curt or irritable: *a brittle reply.* **3** hard or sharp in quality. ◆ *n* **4** a crunchy sweet made with treacle and nuts: *peanut brittle.* **[C14:** from Old English *brytel* (unattested); related to *brytsen* fragment, *brēotan* to break**]** ▸ **'brittlely** *or* **'brittly** *adv*

brittle bone disease *n* the nontechnical name for *osteogenesis imperfecta.*

brittleness ('brɪtᵊlnɪs) *n* **1** the quality of being brittle. **2** *Metallurgy.* the tendency of a metal to break without being significantly distorted or exposed to a high level of stress. Compare **toughness** (sense 2), **softness** (sense 2).

brittle-star *n* any echinoderm of the class *Ophiuroidea,* occurring on the sea bottom and having five long slender arms radiating from a small central disc. See also **basket-star.**

Brittonic (brɪ'tɒnɪk) *n, adj* another word for **Brythonic.**

britzka *or* **britska** ('brɪtskə) *n* a long horse-drawn carriage with a folding top over the rear seat and a rear-facing front seat. **[C19:** from German, variant of *Britschka,* from Polish *bryczka* a little cart, from *bryka* cart**]**

Brix scale (brɪks) *n* a scale for calibrating hydrometers used for measuring the concentration and density of sugar solutions at a given temperature. **[C19:** named after A. F. W. *Brix,* 19th-century German inventor**]**

BRN *international car registration for* Bahrain.

Brno ('bɜːnəʊ; *Czech* 'brnɔ) *n* a city in the Czech Republic; formerly the capital of Moravia: the country's second largest city. Pop.: 388 899 (1996 est.). German name: **Brünn.**

bro. (brəʊ) *abbrev. for* brother.

broach[1] (brəʊtʃ) *vb* **1** *(tr)* to initiate (a topic) for discussion: *to broach a dangerous subject.* **2** *(tr)* to tap or pierce (a container) to draw off (a liquid): *to broach a cask; to broach wine.* **3** *(tr)* to open in order to begin to use: *to broach a shipment.* **4** *(intr)* to break the surface of the water: *the trout broached after being hooked.* **5** *(tr) Machinery.* to enlarge and finish (a hole) by reaming. ◆ *n* **6** a long tapered toothed cutting tool for enlarging holes. **7** a spit for roasting meat, etc. **8** a roof covering the corner triangle on the top of a square tower having an octagonal spire. **9** a pin, forming part of some types of lock, that registers in the hollow bore of a key. **10** a tool used for tapping casks. **11** a less common spelling of **brooch. [C14:** from Old French *broche,* from Vulgar Latin *brocca* (unattested), from Latin *brochus* projecting**]** ▸ **'broacher** *n*

broach[2] (brəʊtʃ) *vb Nautical.* (usually foll. by *to*) to cause (a sailing vessel) to swerve sharply and dangerously or (of a sailing vessel) to swerve sharply and dangerously in a following sea, so as to be broadside to the waves. **[C18:** perhaps from BROACH[1] in obsolete sense of turn on a spit**]**

broad (brɔːd) *adj* **1** having relatively great breadth or width. **2** of vast extent; spacious: *a broad plain.* **3** *(postpositive)* from one side to the other: *four miles broad.* **4** of great scope or potential: *that invention had broad applications.* **5** not detailed; general: *broad plans.* **6** clear and open; full (esp. in the phrase **broad daylight**). **7** obvious or plain: *broad hints.* **8** liberal; tolerant: *a broad political stance.* **9** widely spread; extensive: *broad support.* **10** outspoken or bold: *a broad manner.* **11** vulgar; coarse; indecent: *a broad joke.* **12** unrestrained; free: *broad laughter.* **13** (of a dialect or pronunciation) consisting of a large number of speech sounds characteristic of a particular geographical area: *a broad Yorkshire accent.* **14** *Finance.* denoting an assessment of liquidity as including notes and coin in circulation with the public, banks' till money and balances, most private-sector bank deposits, and sterling bank-deposit certificates: *broad money.* Compare **narrow** (sense 7). **15** *Phonetics.* **15a** of or relating to a type of pronunciation transcription in which symbols correspond approximately to phonemes without taking account of allophonic variations. **15b broad a** the long vowel in English words such as *father, half,* as represented in the received pronunciation of Southern British English. **16 as broad as it is long.** amounting to the same thing; without advantage either way. ◆ *n* **17** the broad part of something. **18** *Slang, chiefly U.S. and Canadian.* **18a** a girl or woman. **18b** a prostitute. **19** *Brit. dialect.* a river spreading over a lowland. See also **Broads. 20** *East Anglia dialect.* a shallow lake. **21** a wood-turning tool used for shaping the insides and bottoms of cylinders. ◆ *adv* **22** widely or fully: *broad awake.* **[**Old English *brād;* related to Old Norse *breithr,* Old Frisian *brēd,* Old High German *breit,* Gothic *braiths***]** ▸ **'broadly** *adv* ▸ **'broadness** *n*

B-road *n* (in Britain) a secondary road.

broad arrow *n* **1** a mark shaped like a broad arrowhead designating British government property and formerly used on prison clothing. **2** an arrow with a broad head.

broadband ('brɔːdˌbænd) *n* a transmission technique using a wide range of frequencies that enables messages to be telecommunicated simultaneously. See also **baseband.**

broad bean *n* **1** an erect annual Eurasian bean plant, *Vicia faba,* cultivated for its large edible flattened seeds, used as a vegetable. **2** the seed of this plant. ◆ Also called: **horse bean.**

broadbill ('brɔːdˌbɪl) *n* **1** any passerine bird of the family *Eurylaimidae,* of tropical Africa and Asia, having bright plumage and a short wide bill. **2** *U.S.* any of various wide-billed birds, such as the scaup and shoveler. **3** *U.S.* another name for **swordfish.**

broadbrim ('brɔːdˌbrɪm) *n* a broad-brimmed hat, esp. one worn by the Quakers in the 17th century.

broadbrush ('brɔːdˌbrʌʃ) *adj* lacking full detail or information; incomplete or rough: *anything other than a broadbrush strategy for the industry will be overloaded with detail.*

broadcast ('brɔːdˌkɑːst) *vb* **-casts, -casting, -cast** *or* **-casted. 1** to transmit (announcements or programmes) on radio or television. **2** (*intr*) to take part in a radio or television programme. **3** (*tr*) to make widely known throughout an area: *to broadcast news.* **4** (*tr*) to scatter (seed, etc.) over an area, esp. by hand. ◆ *n* **5a** a transmission or programme on radio or television. **5b** (*as modifier*): *a broadcast signal.* **6a** the act of scattering seeds. **6b** (*as modifier*): *the broadcast method of sowing.* ◆ *adj* **7** dispersed over a wide area: *broadcast seeds.* ◆ *adv* **8** far and wide: *seeds to be sown broadcast.* ▸ **'broadˌcaster** *n* ▸ **'broadˌcasting** *n*

Broad Church *n* **1** a party within the Church of England which favours a broad and liberal interpretation of Anglican formularies and rubrics and objects to positive definition in theology. Compare **High Church, Low Church. 2** (*usually not caps.*) a group or movement which embraces a wide and varied number of views, approaches, and opinions. ◆ *adj* **Broad-Church. 3** of or relating to this party in the Church of England.

broadcloth ('brɔːdˌklɒθ) *n* **1** fabric woven on a wide loom. **2** a closely woven fabric of wool, worsted, cotton, or rayon with lustrous finish, used for clothing.

broaden ('brɔːdᵊn) *vb* to make or become broad or broader; widen.

broad gauge *n* **1** a railway track with a greater distance between the lines than the standard gauge of 56½ inches (about 1.44 metres) used now by most mainline railway systems. ◆ *adj* **broad-gauge. 2** of, relating to, or denoting a railway having this track.

broad jump *n* a U.S. and Canadian term for **long jump.**

Broadlands ('brɔːdləndz) *n* a Palladian mansion near Romsey in Hampshire: formerly the home of Lord Palmerston and Lord Mountbatten.

broadleaf ('brɔːdˌliːf) *n, pl* **-leaves.** any tobacco plant having broad leaves, used esp. in making cigars.

broad-leaved *adj* denoting trees other than conifers; having broad rather than needleshaped leaves.

broadloom ('brɔːdˌluːm) *n* (*modifier*) of or designating carpets or carpeting woven on a wide loom to obviate the need for seams.

broad-minded *adj* **1** tolerant of opposing viewpoints; not prejudiced; liberal. **2** not easily shocked by permissive sexual habits, pornography, etc. ▸ ˌ**broad-'mindedly** *adv* ▸ ˌ**broad-'mindedness** *n*

Broadmoor ('brɔːdˌmɔː) *n* an institution in Berkshire, England, for housing and treating mentally ill criminals.

Broads (brɔːdz) *pl n* **the. 1** a group of shallow navigable lakes, connected by a network of rivers, in E England, in Norfolk and Suffolk. **2** the region around these lakes: a tourist centre; several bird sanctuaries.

broad seal *n* the official seal of a nation and its government.

broadsheet ('brɔːdˌʃiːt) *n* **1** a newspaper having a large format, approximately 15 by 24 inches (38 by 61 centimetres). Compare **tabloid. 2** another word for **broadside** (sense 4).

broadside ('brɔːdˌsaɪd) *n* **1** *Nautical.* the entire side of a vessel, from stem to stern and from waterline to rail. **2** *Naval.* **2a** all the armament fired from one side of a warship. **2b** the simultaneous discharge of such armament. **3** a strong or abusive verbal or written attack. **4** Also called: **broadside ballad.** a ballad or popular song printed on one side of a sheet of paper and sold by hawkers, esp. in 16th-century England. **5** any standard size of paper before cutting or folding: *demy broadside.* **6** another name for **broadsheet** (sense 1). **7** a large flat surface: *the broadside of the barn.* ◆ *adv* **8** with a broader side facing an object; sideways: *the train hit the lorry broadside.*

broad-spectrum *n* (*modifier*) effective against a wide variety of diseases or microorganisms: *a broad-spectrum antibiotic.*

broadsword ('brɔːdˌsɔːd) *n* a broad-bladed sword used for cutting rather than stabbing. Also called: **backsword.**

broadtail ('brɔːdˌteɪl) *n* **1** the highly valued black wavy fur obtained from the skins of newly born karakul lambs; caracul. **2** another name for **karakul.**

Broadway ('brɔːdˌweɪ) *n* **1** a thoroughfare in New York City, famous for its theatres: the centre of the commercial theatre in the U.S. ◆ *adj* **2** of or relating to or suitable for the commercial theatre, esp. on Broadway.

Brobdingnagian (ˌbrɒbdɪŋ'nægɪən) *adj* gigantic; huge; immense. [C18: from *Brobdingnag,* an imaginary country of giants in Swift's *Gulliver's Travels* (1726)]

Broca (*French* brɔka) *n* **Paul** (pɔl). 1824–80, French surgeon and anthropologist who discovered the motor speech centre of the brain and did pioneering work in brain surgery.

brocade (brəʊ'keɪd) *n* **1a** a rich fabric woven with a raised design, often using gold or silver threads. **1b** (*as modifier*): *brocade curtains.* ◆ *vb* **2** (*tr*) to weave with such a design. [C17: from Spanish *brocado,* from Italian *broccato* embossed fabric, from *brocco* spike, from Latin *brochus* projecting; see BROACH[1]]

Broca's area *or* **centre** ('brɒkəz) *n* the region of the cerebral cortex of the brain concerned with speech; the speech centre. [C19: named after Paul BROCA]

brocatelle *or U.S.* **brocatel** (ˌbrɒkə'tel) *n* **1** a heavy brocade with the design in deep relief, used chiefly in upholstery. **2** a type of variegated marble from France and Italy. [C17: from French, from Italian *broccatello,* diminutive of *broccato* BROCADE]

broccoli ('brɒkəlɪ) *n* **1** a cultivated variety of cabbage, *Brassica oleracea italica,* having branched greenish flower heads. **2** the flower head of this plant, eaten as a vegetable before the buds have opened. **3** a variety of this plant that does not form a head, whose stalks are eaten as a vegetable. [C17: from Italian, plural of *broccolo* a little sprout, from *brocco* sprout, spike; see BROCADE]

broch (brɒk, brɒx) *n* (in Scotland) a circular dry-stone tower large enough to serve as a fortified home; they date from the Iron Age and are found esp. in the north and the islands. [C17: from Old Norse *borg;* related to Old English *burh* settlement, burgh]

broché (brəʊ'ʃeɪ; *French* brɔʃe) *adj* woven with a raised design, as brocade. [C19: from French *brocher* to brocade, stitch; see BROACH[1]]

brochette (brɒ'ʃet; *French* brɔʃɛt) *n* a skewer or small spit, used for holding pieces of meat, etc., while roasting or grilling. [C19: from Old French *brochete* small pointed tool; see BROACH[1]]

brocho ('brɒxəʊ) *n* a variant of **brachah.**

brochure ('brəʊʃjʊə, -ʃə) *n* a pamphlet or booklet, esp. one containing summarized or introductory information or advertising. [C18: from French, from *brocher* to stitch (a book)]

brock (brɒk) *n* a Brit. name for **badger** (sense 1): used esp. as a form of address in stories, etc. [Old English *broc,* of Celtic origin; compare Welsh *broch*]

Brocken (*German* 'brɔkən) *n* a mountain in central Germany, formerly in East Germany: the highest peak of the Harz Mountains; important in German folklore. Height: 1142 m (3747 ft.). The **Brocken Bow** or **Brocken Spectre** is an atmospheric phenomenon in which an observer, when the sun is low, may see his enlarged shadow against the clouds, often surrounded by coloured lights.

brocket ('brɒkɪt) *n* any small deer of the genus *Mazama,* of tropical America, having small unbranched antlers. [C15: from Anglo-French *broquet,* from *broque* horn, from Vulgar Latin *brocca* (unattested); see BROACH[1]]

broddle ('brɒdᵊl) *vb* (*tr*) *Yorkshire dialect.* to poke or pierce (something). [perhaps from BRADAWL]

broderie anglaise (ˌbrəʊdəriː ɑːŋ'gleɪz) *n* open embroidery on white cotton, fine linen, etc. [C19: French: English embroidery]

Brodsky ('brɒdskɪ) *n* **Joseph,** original name *Iosif Aleksandrovich Brodsky.* 1940–96, U.S. poet, born in the Soviet Union. His collections include *The End of a Beautiful Era* (1977). Nobel prize for literature 1987.

Broederbond ('brʊdəˌbɔːnt, 'bruːdəˌbɒnt) *n* (in South Africa) a secret society of Afrikaner Nationalists committed to securing and maintaining Afrikaner control over important areas of government. [Afrikaans: band of brothers]

broekies ('brʊkiːz) *pl n S. African informal.* underpants. [C19: Afrikaans]

brog (brɒg, brɔːg, brog) *n Scot.* a bradawl. [C19: of uncertain origin]

brogan ('brəʊgən) *n* a heavy laced usually ankle-high work boot. [C19: from Gaelic *brōgan* a little shoe, from *brōg* shoe; see BROGUE[2]]

Broglie (brɔj) *n* **1** Prince **Louis Victor de** (lwi viktɔr də). 1892–1987, French physicist, noted for his research in quantum mechanics and his development of wave mechanics: Nobel prize for physics 1929. **2** his brother, **Maurice** (mɔris), Duc de Broglie. 1875–1960, French physicist, noted for his research into X-ray spectra.

brogue[1] (brəʊg) *n* a broad gentle-sounding dialectal accent, esp. that used by the Irish in speaking English. [C18: probably from BROGUE[2], alluding to the footwear of the peasantry]

brogue[2] (brəʊg) *n* **1** a sturdy walking shoe, often with ornamental perforations. **2** an untanned shoe worn formerly in Ireland and Scotland. [C16: from Irish Gaelic *bróg* boot, shoe, probably from Old Norse *brōk* leg covering]

broider ('brɔɪdə) *vb* (*tr*) an archaic word for **embroider.** [C15: from Old French *brosder,* of Germanic origin; see EMBROIDER]

broil[1] (brɔɪl) *vb* **1** the usual U.S. and Canadian word for **grill**[1] (sense 1). **2** to become or cause to become extremely hot. **3** (*intr*) to be furious. ◆ *n* **4** the process of broiling. **5** something broiled. [C14: from Old French *bruillir* to burn, of uncertain origin]

broil[2] (brɔɪl) *Archaic.* ◆ *n* **1** a loud quarrel or disturbance; brawl. ◆ *vb* **2** (*intr*) to brawl; quarrel. [C16: from Old French *brouiller* to mix, from *breu* broth; see BREWIS, BROSE]

broiler ('brɔɪlə) *n* **1** a young tender chicken suitable for roasting. **2** *Chiefly U.S.* a pan, grate, etc. for broiling food. **3** a very hot day.

broiler house *n* a building in which broiler chickens are reared in confined conditions.

broke (brəʊk) *vb* **1** the past tense of **break.** ◆ *adj* **2** *Informal.* having no money; bankrupt. **3 go for broke.** *Slang.* to risk everything in a gambling or other venture.

broken ('brəʊkən) *vb* **1** the past participle of **break.** ◆ *adj* **2** fractured, smashed, or splintered: *a broken vase.* **3** imperfect or incomplete; fragmentary: *a broken set of books.* **4** interrupted; disturbed; disconnected: *broken sleep.* **5** intermittent or discontinuous: *broken sunshine.* **6** varying in direction or intensity, as of pitch: *a broken note; a broken run.* **7** not functioning: *a broken radio.* **8** spoilt or ruined by divorce (esp. in the phrases **broken home, broken marriage**). **9** (of a trust, promise, contract, etc.) violated; infringed. **10** overcome with grief or disappointment: *a broken heart.* **11** (of the speech of a foreigner) imperfect in grammar, vocabulary, and pronunciation: *broken English.* **12** Also: **broken-in.** made tame or disciplined by training: *a broken horse; a broken recruit.* **13** exhausted or weakened as through ill-health or misfortune. **14** confused or disorganized: *broken ranks of soldiers.* **15** breached or opened: *broken defensive lines.* **16** irregular or rough; uneven: *broken ground.* **17** bankrupt or out of money: *a broken industry.* **18** (of colour) having a multicoloured decorative effect, as by stippling paint onto a surface. ▸ **'brokenly** *adv*

broken chord *n Music.* a chord played as an arpeggio.

broken consort *n* See **consort** (sense 4).

broken-down *adj* **1** worn out, as by age or long use; dilapidated: *a broken-down fence.* **2** not in working order: *a broken-down tractor.* **3** physically or mentally ill.

brokenhearted (ˌbrəʊkənˈhɑːtɪd) *adj* overwhelmed by grief or disappointment. ▸ ˌ**broken'heartedly** *adv* ▸ ˌ**broken'heartedness** *n*

Broken Hill *n* a city in SE Australia, in W New South Wales: mining centre for lead, silver, and zinc. Pop.: 24 500 (1988 est.).

broken wind (wɪnd) *n Vet. science.* another name for **heaves** (sense 1).

broker (ˈbrəʊkə) *n* **1** an agent who, acting on behalf of a principal, buys or sells goods, securities, etc., in return for a commission: *insurance broker.* **2** short for **stockbroker. 3** a dealer in second-hand goods. ◆ *vb* **4** to act as a broker (in). [C14: from Anglo-French *brocour* broacher (of casks, hence, one who sells, agent), from Old Northern French *broquier* to tap a cask, from *broque* tap of a cask; see BROACH[1]]

brokerage (ˈbrəʊkərɪdʒ) *n* **1** commission charged by a broker to his principals. **2** a broker's business or office.

broking (ˈbrəʊkɪŋ) *adj* **1** acting as a broker. ◆ *n* **2** the business of a broker. [C16: from obsolete verb *broke;* see BROKER]

brolga (ˈbrɒlgə) *n* a large grey Australian crane, *Grus rubicunda,* having a red-and-green head and a trumpeting call. Also called: **Australian crane, native companion.** [C19: from a native Australian language]

brolly (ˈbrɒlɪ) *n, pl* **-lies.** an informal Brit. name for **umbrella** (sense 1).

bromal (ˈbrəʊməl) *n* a yellowish oily synthetic liquid used medicinally as a sedative and hypnotic; tribromoacetaldehyde. Formula: Br_3CCHO. [C19: from BROM(INE) + AL(COHOL)]

bromate (ˈbrəʊmeɪt) *n* **1** any salt or ester of bromic acid, containing the monovalent group $-BrO_3$ or ion BrO_3^-. ◆ *vb* **2** another word for **brominate.** [C19: probably from German *Bromat;* see BROMO-, -ATE[1]]

Bromberg (ˈbrɔmbɛrk) *n* the German name for **Bydgoszcz.**

brome grass *or* **brome** (brəʊm) *n* any of various grasses of the genus *Bromus,* having small flower spikes in loose drooping clusters. Some species are used for hay. [C18: via Latin from Greek *bromos* oats, of obscure origin]

bromeliad (brəʊˈmiːlɪˌæd) *n* any plant of the tropical American family *Bromeliaceae,* typically epiphytes with a rosette of fleshy leaves. The family includes the pineapple and Spanish moss. [C19: from New Latin *Bromelia* type genus, after Olaf *Bromelius* (1639–1705), Swedish botanist] ▸ **broˌmeli'aceous** *adj*

bromeosin (brəʊˈmiːəsɪn) *n Chem.* another name for **eosin.** [C20: from BROMO- + EOSIN]

bromic (ˈbrəʊmɪk) *adj* of or containing bromine in the trivalent or pentavalent state.

bromic acid *n* a colourless unstable water-soluble liquid used as an oxidizing agent in the manufacture of dyes and pharmaceuticals. Formula: $HBrO_3$.

bromide (ˈbrəʊmaɪd) *n* **1** any salt of hydrobromic acid, containing the monovalent ion Br^- (**bromide ion**). **2** any compound containing a bromine atom, such as methyl bromide. **3** a dose of sodium or potassium bromide given as a sedative. **4a** a trite saying; platitude. **4b** a dull or boring person. [C19, C20 (cliché): from BROM(INE) + -IDE]

bromide paper *n* a type of photographic paper coated with an emulsion of silver bromide usually containing a small quantity of silver iodide.

bromidic (brəʊˈmɪdɪk) *adj* ordinary; dull.

brominate (ˈbrəʊmɪˌneɪt) *vb* to treat or react with bromine. Also: **bromate.** ▸ ˌ**bromin'ation** *n*

bromine (ˈbrəʊmiːn, -mɪn) *n* a pungent dark red volatile liquid element of the halogen series that occurs in brine and is used in the production of chemicals, esp. ethylene dibromide. Symbol: Br; atomic no.: 35; atomic wt.: 79.904; valency: 1, 3, 5, or 7; relative density 3.12; density (gas): 7.59 kg/m^3; melting pt.: −7.2°C; boiling pt.: 58.78°C. [C19: from French *brome* bromine, from Greek *brōmos* bad smell + -INE[2], of uncertain origin]

bromism (ˈbrəʊˌmɪzəm) *or U.S.* **brominism** *n* poisoning caused by the excessive intake of bromine or compounds containing bromine.

Bromley (ˈbrɒmlɪ) *n* a borough of SE Greater London. Pop.: 293 000 (1994 est.). Area: 153 sq. km (59 sq. miles).

bromo- *or before a vowel* **brom-** *combining form.* indicating the presence of bromine: *bromoform.*

bromoform (ˈbrəʊməˌfɔːm) *n* a heavy colourless liquid substance with a sweetish taste and an odour resembling that of chloroform. Systematic name: **tribromomethane.** Formula: $CHBr_3$.

Bromsgrove (ˈbrɒmzˌgrəʊv) *n* a town in W central England, in N Worcestershire. Pop.: 26 366 (1991).

bronchi (ˈbrɒŋkaɪ) *n* the plural of **bronchus.**

bronchia (ˈbrɒŋkɪə) *pl n* another name for **bronchial tubes.** [C17: from Late Latin, from Greek *bronkhia,* plural of *bronkhion,* diminutive of *bronkhus* windpipe, throat]

bronchial (ˈbrɒŋkɪəl) *adj* of or relating to the bronchi or the bronchial tubes. ▸ **'bronchially** *adv*

bronchial tubes *pl n* the bronchi or their smaller divisions.

bronchiectasis (ˌbrɒŋkɪˈɛktəsɪs) *n* chronic dilation of the bronchi or bronchial tubes, which often become infected. [C19: from BRONCHO- + Greek *ektasis* a stretching]

bronchiole (ˈbrɒŋkɪˌəʊl) *n* any of the smallest bronchial tubes, usually ending in alveoli. [C19: from New Latin *bronchiolum,* diminutive of Late Latin *bronchium,* singular of BRONCHIA] ▸ **bronchiolar** (ˌbrɒŋkɪˈəʊlə) *adj*

bronchitis (brɒŋˈkaɪtɪs) *n* inflammation of the bronchial tubes, characterized by coughing, difficulty in breathing, etc., caused by infection or irritation of the respiratory tract. ▸ **bronchitic** (brɒŋˈkɪtɪk) *adj, n*

broncho- *or before a vowel* **bronch-** *combining form.* indicating or relating to the bronchi: *bronchitis.* [from Greek: BRONCHUS]

bronchodilator (ˈbrɒŋkəʊdaɪˌleɪtə) *n* any drug or other agent that causes dilation of the bronchial tubes by relaxing bronchial muscle: used, esp. in the form of aerosol sprays, for the relief of asthma and chronic bronchitis.

bronchography (brɒŋˈkɒgrəfɪ) *n* radiography of the bronchial tubes after the introduction of a radiopaque medium into the bronchi.

bronchopneumonia (ˌbrɒŋkəʊnjuːˈməʊnɪə) *n* inflammation of the lungs, originating in the bronchioles.

bronchoscope (ˈbrɒŋkəˌskəʊp) *n* an instrument for examining and providing access to the interior of the bronchial tubes. ▸ **bronchoscopic** (ˌbrɒŋkəˈskɒpɪk) *adj* ▸ **bronchoscopist** (brɒŋˈkɒskəpɪst) *n* ▸ **bron'choscopy** *n*

bronchus (ˈbrɒŋkəs) *n, pl* **-chi** (-kaɪ). either of the two main branches of the trachea, which contain cartilage within their walls. [C18: from New Latin, from Greek *bronkhos* windpipe]

bronco *or* **broncho** (ˈbrɒŋkəʊ) *n, pl* **-cos** *or* **-chos.** (in the U.S. and Canada) a wild or partially tamed pony or mustang of the western plains. [C19: from Mexican Spanish, short for Spanish *potro bronco* unbroken colt, probably from Latin *broccus* projecting (as knots on wood), hence, rough, wild]

broncobuster (ˈbrɒŋkəʊˌbʌstə) *n* (in the western U.S. and Canada) a cowboy who breaks in broncos or wild horses.

Brontë (ˈbrɒntɪ) *n* **1 Anne,** pen name *Acton Bell.* 1820–49, English novelist; author of *The Tenant of Wildfell Hall* (1847). **2** her sister, **Charlotte,** pen name *Currer Bell.* 1816–55, English novelist, author of *Jane Eyre* (1847), *Villette* (1853), and *The Professor* (1857). **3** her sister, **Emily (Jane),** pen name *Ellis Bell.* 1818–48, English novelist and poet; author of *Wuthering Heights* (1847).

brontosaurus (ˌbrɒntəˈsɔːrəs) *or* **brontosaur** (ˈbrɒntəˌsɔː) *n* any very large herbivorous quadrupedal dinosaur of the genus *Apatosaurus,* common in North America during Jurassic times, having a long neck and long tail: suborder *Sauropoda* (sauropods). [C19: from New Latin, from Greek *brontē* thunder + *sauros* lizard]

Bronx (brɒŋks) *n* **the.** a borough of New York City, on the mainland, separated from Manhattan by the Harlem River. Pop.: 1 203 789 (1990).

Bronx cheer *n Chiefly U.S.* a loud noise, imitating a fart, made with the lips and tongue and expressing derision or contempt; raspberry.

bronze (brɒnz) *n* **1a** any hard water-resistant alloy consisting of copper and smaller proportions of tin and sometimes zinc and lead. **1b** any similar copper alloy containing other elements in place of tin, such as aluminium bronze, beryllium bronze, etc. See also **phosphor bronze, gunmetal.** Compare **brass** (sense 1). **2** a yellowish-brown colour or pigment. **3** a statue, medal, or other object made of bronze. **4** short for **bronze medal.** ◆ *adj* **5** made of or resembling bronze. **6** of a yellowish-brown colour: *a bronze skin.* ◆ *vb* **7** (esp. of the skin) to make or become brown; tan. **8** (*tr*) to give the appearance of bronze to. [C18: from French, from Italian *bronzo,* perhaps ultimately from Latin *Brundisium* Brindisi, famed for its bronze] ▸ **'bronzy** *adj*

bronze age *n Classical myth.* a period of man's existence marked by war and violence, following the golden and silver ages and preceding the iron age.

Bronze Age *n Archaeol.* **a** a technological stage between the Stone and Iron Ages, beginning in the Middle East about 4500 B.C. and lasting in Britain from about 2000 to 500 B.C., during which weapons and tools were made of bronze and there was intensive trading. **b** (*as modifier*): *a Bronze-Age tool.*

bronze medal *n* a medal of bronze, awarded to a competitor who comes third in a contest or race. Compare **gold medal, silver medal.**

bronzing (ˈbrɒnzɪŋ) *n Building trades.* **1** blue pigment producing a metallic lustre when ground into paint media at fairly high concentrations. **2** the application of a mixture of powdered metal or pigments of a metallic lustre, and a binding medium, such as gold size, to a surface.

Bronzino, Il (bronˈdziːno) *n* real name *Agnolo di Cosimo.* 1503–72, Florentine mannerist painter.

bronzite (ˈbrɒnzaɪt) *n* a type of orthopyroxene often having a metallic sheen.

brooch (brəʊtʃ) *n* an ornament with a hinged pin and catch, worn fastened to clothing. [C13: from Old French *broche;* see BROACH[1]]

brood (bruːd) *n* **1** a number of young animals, esp. birds, produced at one hatching. **2** all the offspring in one family: often used jokingly or contemptuously. **3** a group of a particular kind; breed. **4** (*as modifier*) kept for breeding: *a brood mare.* ◆ *vb* **5** (of a bird) **5a** to sit on or hatch (eggs). **5b** (*tr*) to cover (young birds) protectively with the wings. **6** (when *intr,* often foll. by *on, over,* or *upon*) to ponder morbidly or persistently. [Old English *brōd;* related to Middle High German *bruot,* Dutch *broed;* see BREED] ▸ **'brooding** *n, adj* ▸ **'broodingly** *adv*

brooder (ˈbruːdə) *n* **1** an enclosure or other structure, usually heated, used for rearing young chickens or other fowl. **2** a person or thing that broods.

brood pouch *n* **1** a pouch or cavity in certain animals, such as frogs and fishes, in which their eggs develop and hatch. **2** another name for **marsupium.**

broody (ˈbruːdɪ) *adj* **broodier, broodiest. 1** moody; meditative; introspective. **2** (of poultry) wishing to sit on or hatch eggs. **3** *Informal.* (of a woman) wishing to have a baby of her own. ▸ **'broodiness** *n*

brook[1] (brʊk) *n* a natural freshwater stream smaller than a river. [Old English *brōc;* related to Old High German *bruoh* swamp, Dutch *broek*]

brook[2] (brʊk) *vb* (*tr*) (*usually used with a negative*) to bear; tolerate. [Old English *brūcan;* related to Gothic *brūkjan* to use, Old High German *brūhhan,* Latin *fruī* to enjoy] ▸ **'brookable** *adj*

Brook (brʊk) *n* **Peter (Paul Stephen).** born 1925, British stage and film director, noted esp. for his experimental work in the theatre.

Brooke (brʊk) *n* **1 Alan Francis.** See (1st Viscount) **Alanbrooke. 2** Sir **James.** 1803–68, British soldier; first rajah of Sarawak (1841–63). **3 Rupert (Chawner).** 1887–1915, British lyric poet, noted for his idealistic war poetry, which made him a national hero.

Brook Farm *n* an experimental communist community established by writers and scholars in West Roxbury, Massachusetts, from 1841 to 1847.

brookite (ˈbrʊkaɪt) *n* a reddish-brown to black mineral consisting of titanium oxide in orthorhombic crystalline form: occurs in silica veins. Formula: TiO_2. [C19: named after Henry J. *Brooke* (died 1857), English mineralogist]

brooklet ('brʊklɪt) *n* a small brook.

brooklime ('brʊk,laɪm) *n* either of two blue-flowered scrophulariaceous trailing plants, *Veronica americana* of North America or *V. beccabunga* of Europe and Asia, growing in moist places. See also **speedwell.** [C16: variant of C15 *brokelemk* speedwell, from BROOK[1] + *-lemk,* from Old English *hleomoce;* influenced by *lime*]

Brooklyn ('brʊklɪn) *n* a borough of New York City, on the SW end of Long Island. Pop.: 2 291 664 (1990).

Brookner ('brʊknə) *n* **Anita.** born 1928, British writer and art historian. Her novels include *Hotel du Lac* (1984), which won the Booker Prize, *Latecomers* (1988), *Brief Lives* (1990), and *Visitors* (1997).

Brooks (brʊks) *n* **Mel,** real name *Melvyn Kaminsky.* born 1926, U.S. comedy writer, actor, and film director. His films include *The Producers* (1968), *Blazing Saddles* (1974), *High Anxiety* (1977), and *Dracula: Dead and Loving It* (1996).

Brooks Range (brʊks) *n* a mountain range in N Alaska. Highest peak: Mount Isto, 2761 m (9058 ft.).

brook trout *n* a North American freshwater trout, *Salvelinus fontinalis,* introduced in Europe and valued as a food and game fish. Also called: **speckled trout.**

brookweed ('brʊk,wiːd) *n* either of two white-flowered primulaceous plants, *Samolus valerandi* of Europe or *S. floribundus* of North America, growing in moist places. Also called: **water pimpernel.** See also **pimpernel.**

broom (bruːm, brʊm) *n* **1** an implement for sweeping consisting of a long handle to which is attached either a brush of straw, bristles, or twigs, bound together, or a solid head into which are set tufts of bristles or fibres. **2** any of various yellow-flowered Eurasian papilionaceous shrubs of the genera *Cytisus* and *Sarothamnus,* esp. *S. scoparius.* **3** any of various similar Eurasian plants of the related genera *Genista* and *Spartium.* **4 new broom.** a newly appointed official, etc., eager to make changes. ◆ *vb* **5** (*tr*) to sweep with a broom. [Old English *brōm;* related to Old High German *brāmo,* Middle Dutch *bremme*]

broomcorn ('bruːm,kɔːn, 'brʊm-) *n* a variety of sorghum, *Sorghum vulgare technicum,* the long stiff flower stalks of which have been used for making brooms.

broomrape ('bruːm,reɪp, 'brʊm-) *n* any orobanchaceous plant of the genus *Orobanche:* brownish small-flowered leafless parasites on the roots of other plants, esp. on broom. [C16: adaptation and partial translation of Medieval Latin *rāpum genistae* tuber (hence: root nodule) of Genista (a type of broom plant); compare PLANTAGENET]

broomstick ('bruːm,stɪk, 'brʊm-) *n* the long handle of a broom.

Broonzy ('bruːnzɪ) *n* **William Lee Conley,** called *Big Bill.* 1893–1958, U.S. blues singer and guitarist.

bros. *or* **Bros.** *abbrev. for* brothers.

brose (brəʊz) *n Scot.* oatmeal or pease porridge, sometimes with butter or fat added. See also **Atholl brose.** [C13 *broys,* from Old French *broez,* from *breu* broth, of Germanic origin]

broth (brɒθ) *n* **1** a soup made by boiling meat, fish, vegetables, etc., in water. **2** another name for **stock** (sense 19). [Old English *broth;* related to Old Norse *broth,* Old High German *brod,* German *brodeln* to boil; see BREW]

brothel ('brɒθəl) *n* **1** a house or other place where men pay to have sexual intercourse with prostitutes. **2** *Austral. informal.* any untidy or messy place. [C16: short for *brothel-house,* from C14 *brothel* useless person, from Old English *brēothan* to deteriorate; related to *briethel* worthless]

brother ('brʌðə) *n, pl* **brothers** *or* (*Archaic except when referring to fellow members of a religion, sect, society, etc.*) **brethren. 1** a male person having the same parents as another person. **2** short for **half-brother** or **stepbrother. 3a** a male person belonging to the same group, profession, nationality, trade union, etc., as another or others; fellow member. **3b** (*as modifier*): *brother workers.* **4** comrade; friend: used as a form of address. **5** *Christianity.* **5a** a member of a male religious order who undertakes work for the order without actually being in holy orders. **5b** a lay member of a male religious order. ◆ Related adj: **fraternal.** ◆ *interj* **6** *Slang.* an exclamation of amazement, disgust, surprise, disappointment, etc. [Old English *brōthor;* related to Old Norse *brōthir,* Old High German *bruoder,* Latin *frāter,* Greek *phratēr,* Sanskrit *bhrātar*]

brotherhood ('brʌðə,hʊd) *n* **1** the state of being related as a brother or brothers. **2** an association or fellowship, such as a trade union. **3** all persons engaged in a particular profession, trade, etc. **4** the belief, feeling, or hope that all men should regard and treat one another as brothers.

brother-in-law *n, pl* **brothers-in-law. 1** the brother of one's wife or husband. **2** the husband of one's sister.

brotherly ('brʌðəlɪ) *adj* **1** of, resembling, or suitable to a brother, esp. in showing loyalty and affection; fraternal. ◆ *adv* **2** in a brotherly way; fraternally. ▸ **'brotherliness** *n*

brougham ('bruːəm, bruːm) *n* **1** a four-wheeled horse-drawn closed carriage having a raised open driver's seat in front. **2** *Obsolete.* a large car with an open compartment at the front for the driver. **3** *Obsolete.* an early electric car. [C19: named after Henry Peter, Lord *Brougham* (1778–1868)]

brought (brɔːt) *vb* the past tense and past participle of **bring.**

broughta ('brɔːtə) *or* **broughtas** ('brɔːtəs) *n* variants of **braata.**

brouhaha ('bruːhɑːhɑː) *n* a loud confused noise; commotion; uproar. [French, of imitative origin]

brow (braʊ) *n* **1** the part of the face from the eyes to the hairline; forehead. **2** short for **eyebrow. 3** the expression of the face; countenance: *a troubled brow.* **4** the top of a mine shaft; pithead. **5** the jutting top of a hill, etc. **6** *Northern English dialect.* a steep slope on a road. [Old English *brū;* related to Old Norse *brūn* eyebrow, Lithuanian *bruvis,* Greek *ophrus,* Sanskrit *bhrūs*]

browband ('braʊ,bænd) *n* the strap of a horse's bridle that goes across the forehead.

browbeat ('braʊ,biːt) *vb* **-beats, -beating, -beat, -beaten.** (*tr*) to discourage or frighten with threats or a domineering manner; intimidate. ▸ **'brow,beater** *n*

-browed *adj* (*in combination*) having a brow or brows as specified: *dark-browed.*

brown (braʊn) *n* **1** any of various colours, such as those of wood or earth, produced by low intensity light in the wavelength range 620–585 nanometres. **2** a dye or pigment producing these colours. **3** brown cloth or clothing: *dressed in brown.* **4** any of numerous mostly reddish-brown butterflies of the genera *Maniola, Lasiommata,* etc., such as *M. jurtina* (**meadow brown**): family *Satyridae.* ◆ *adj* **5** of the colour brown. **6** (of bread) made from a flour that has not been bleached or bolted, such as wheatmeal or wholemeal flour. **7** deeply tanned or sunburnt. ◆ *vb* **8** to make (esp. food as a result of cooking) brown or (esp. of food) to become brown. [Old English *brūn;* related to Old Norse *brūnn,* Old High German *brūn,* Greek *phrunos* toad, Sanskrit *babhru* reddish-brown] ▸ **'brownish** *or* **'browny** *adj* ▸ **'brownness** *n*

Brown (braʊn) *n* **1** Sir **Arthur Whitten** ('wɪtᵊn). 1886–1948, British aviator who with J. W. Alcock made the first flight across the Atlantic (1919). **2 Ford Madox.** 1821–93, British painter, associated with the Pre-Raphaelite Brotherhood. His paintings include *The Last of England* (1865) and *Work* (1865). **3 George** (**Alfred**), Lord George-Brown. 1914–85, British Labour politician; vice-chairman and deputy leader of the Labour party (1960–70); foreign secretary 1966–68. **4 George Mackay.** 1921–96, Scottish poet, novelist, and short-story writer. His works, which include the novels *Greenvoe* (1972) and *Magnus* (1973), reflect the history and culture of Orkney. **5** (**James**) **Gordon.** born 1951, British Labour politician; Chancellor of the Exchequer from 1997. **6 Herbert Charles.** born 1912, U.S. chemist, who worked on the compounds of boron. Nobel prize for chemistry 1979. **7 James.** born 1928, U.S. soul singer and songwriter, noted for his dynamic stage performances and for his commitment to Black rights. **8 John.** 1800–59, U.S. abolitionist leader, hanged after leading an unsuccessful rebellion of slaves at Harper's Ferry, Virginia. **9 Lancelot,** called *Capability Brown.* 1716–83, British landscape gardener. **10 Michael** (**Stuart**). born 1941, U.S. physician: shared the Nobel prize for physiology or medicine (1985) for work on cholesterol. **11 Robert.** 1773–1858, Scottish botanist who was the first to observe the Brownian movement in fluids.

brown algae *pl n* any algae of the phylum *Phaeophyta,* such as the wracks and kelps, which contain a brown pigment in addition to chlorophyll.

brown bear *n* a large ferocious brownish bear, *Ursus arctos,* inhabiting temperate forests of North America, Europe, and Asia. See also **grizzly bear, Kodiak bear.**

brown coal *n* another name for **lignite.**

brown creeper *n* a small bush bird, *Finschia novaeseelandiae,* of South Island, New Zealand. Also called: **bush canary.**

brown dwarf *n* a type of celestial body midway in size between a large planet and a small star, thought to be one possible explanation of dark matter in the universe.

Browne (braʊn) *n* **1 Coral** (**Edith**). 1913–91, Australian actress: married to Vincent Price. **2 Hablot Knight.** See **Phiz. 3** Sir **Thomas.** 1605–82, English physician and author, noted for his magniloquent prose style. His works include *Religio Medici* (1642) and *Hydriotaphia or Urn Burial* (1658).

brown earth *n* an intrazonal soil of temperate humid regions typically developed under deciduous forest into a dark rich layer (mull): characteristic of much of southern and central England.

browned-off *adj Informal.* thoroughly discouraged or disheartened; fed up.

brown fat *n* tissue composed of a type of fat cell that dissipates as heat most of the energy released when food is oxidized; brown adipose tissue. It is present in hibernating animals and human babies and is thought to be important in adult weight control.

brownfield ('braʊn,fiːld) *n* (*modifier*) denoting or located in an urban area that has previously been built on: *Hampshire has many brownfield developments.*

brown goods *pl n Marketing.* consumer goods such as televisions, radios, or videos. Compare **white goods** (sense 1).

Brownian movement ('braʊnɪən) *n* random movement of microscopic particles suspended in a fluid, caused by bombardment of the particles by molecules of the fluid. First observed in 1827, it provided strong evidence in support of the kinetic theory of molecules. [C19: named after Robert BROWN]

brownie ('braʊnɪ) *n* **1** (in folklore) an elf said to do helpful work at night, esp. household chores. **2** a small square nutty chocolate cake. **3** *Austral. history.* a bread made with currants. [C16: diminutive of BROWN (that is, a small brown man)]

Brownie ('braʊnɪ) *n* **1** another name for **Brownie Guide. 2** *Trademark.* (formerly) a popular make of simple box camera.

Brownie Guide *or* **Brownie** ('braʊnɪ) *n* a member of the junior branch of the Guides.

Brownie Guider *n* the adult leader of a pack of Brownie Guides. Former name: **Brown Owl.**

Brownie point *n* a notional mark to one's credit earned for being seen to do the right thing. [C20: from the mistaken notion that Brownie Guides earn points for good deeds]

browning ('braʊnɪŋ) *n Brit.* a substance used to darken soups, gravies, etc.

Browning[1] ('braʊnɪŋ) *n* **1 Elizabeth Barrett.** 1806–61, English poet and critic; author of the *Sonnets from the Portuguese* (1850). **2** her husband, **Robert.** 1812–89, English poet, noted for his dramatic monologues and *The Ring and the Book* (1868–69).

Browning[2] ('braʊnɪŋ) *n* **1** Also called: **Browning automatic rifle.** a portable gas-operated air-cooled automatic rifle using .30 calibre ammunition and capable of firing between 200 and 350 rounds per minute. Abbrev.: **BAR. 2** Also called: **Browning machine gun.** a water-cooled automatic machine gun using .30 or .50 calibre ammunition and capable of firing over 500 rounds per minute. **[C20**: named after John M. *Browning* (1855–1926), American designer of firearms**]**

Brownist ('braʊnɪst) *n* a person who supported the principles of church government advocated by Robert Browne and adopted in modified form by the Independents or Congregationalists. **[C16**: named after Robert *Browne* (?1550–1633), English Puritan**]** ▸ **'Brownism** *n*

brown lung disease *n* another name for **byssinosis.**

brown-nose ('braʊn,nəʊz) *Taboo slang.* ◆ *vb* **1** to be abjectly subservient (to); curry favour (with). ◆ *n* **2** an abjectly subservient person; sycophant. **[C20**: from the notion that a subservient person kisses the backside of the person with whom he is currying favour**]**

brownout ('braʊn,aʊt) *n Chiefly U.S.* **1** a dimming or reduction in the use of electric lights in a city, esp. to conserve electric power or as a defensive precaution in wartime. **2** a temporary reduction in electrical power. Compare **blackout** (sense 3).

brown owl *n* another name for **tawny owl.**

Brown Owl *n* a name (no longer in official use) for **Brownie Guider.**

brown paper *n* a coarse unbleached paper used for wrapping.

brown rat *n* a common brownish rat, *Rattus norvegicus:* a serious pest in all parts of the world. Also called: **Norway rat.**

brown rice *n* unpolished rice, in which the grains retain the outer yellowish-brown layer (bran).

brown rot *n* **1** a disease of apples, peaches, etc., caused by fungi of the genus *Sclerotinia* and characterized by yellowish-brown masses of spores on the plant surface. **2** decay of timber caused by the action of fungi on the cellulose.

brown seaweed *n* another term for **brown algae.**

Brown Shirt *n* **1** (in Nazi Germany) a storm trooper. **2** a member of any fascist party or group.

brown snake *n Austral.* any of various common venomous snakes of the genus *Pseudonaja.*

brown-state *adj* (of linen and lace fabrics) undyed.

brownstone ('braʊn,stəʊn) *n U.S.* **1** a reddish-brown iron-rich sandstone used for building. **2** a house built of or faced with this stone.

brown study *n* a mood of deep absorption or thoughtfulness; reverie.

brown sugar *n* sugar that is unrefined or only partially refined.

brown-tail moth *n* a small brown-and-white European moth, *Euproctis phaeorrhoea,* naturalized in the eastern U.S. where it causes damage to shade trees: family *Lymantriidae* (or *Liparidae*). See also **tussock moth.**

brown trout *n* a common brownish variety of the trout *Salmo trutta* that occurs in the rivers of N Europe and has been successfully introduced in North America. Compare **sea trout** (sense 1).

browse (braʊz) *vb* **1** to look through (a book, articles for sale in a shop, etc.) in a casual leisurely manner. **2** *Computing.* to search for and read hypertext, esp. on the World Wide Web. **3** (of deer, goats, etc.) to feed upon (vegetation) by continual nibbling. ◆ *n* **4** the act or an instance of browsing. **5** the young twigs, shoots, leaves, etc., on which certain animals feed. **[C15**: from French *broust, brost* (modern French *brout*) bud, of Germanic origin; compare Old Saxon *brustian* to bud**]**

browser ('braʊzə) *n* **1** a person or animal that browses. **2** *Computing.* a software package that enables a user to find and read hypertext files, esp. on the World Wide Web.

Broz (*Serbo-Croat* brɔːz) *n* **Josip** ('jɔsip). original name of (Marshal) **Tito.**

BRS *abbrev. for* British Road Services.

BRU *international car registration for* Brunei.

Brubeck ('bruːbɛk) *n* **Dave.** born 1920, U.S. modern jazz pianist and composer; formed his own quartet in 1951.

Bruce[1] (bruːs) *n* **1 James.** 1730–94, British explorer, who discovered the source of the Blue Nile (1770). **2 Lenny.** 1925–66, U.S. comedian, whose satirical sketches, esp. of the sexual attitudes of his contemporaries, brought him prosecutions for obscenity, but are now regarded as full of insight as well as wit. **3 Robert the.** See **Robert I. 4 Stanley Melbourne,** 1st Viscount Bruce of Melbourne. 1883–1967, Australian statesman; prime minister, in coalition with Sir Earle Page's Country Party, of Australia (1923–29).

Bruce[2] (bruːs) *n Brit.* a jocular name for an Australian man.

brucellosis (,bruːsɪ'ləʊsɪs) *n* an infectious disease of cattle, goats, and pigs, caused by bacteria of the genus *Brucella* and transmittable to man (e.g. by drinking contaminated milk): symptoms include fever, chills, and severe headache. Also called: **undulant fever. [C20**: from New Latin *Brucella,* named after Sir David *Bruce* (1855–1931), Australian bacteriologist and physician**]**

Bruch (*German* brʊx) *n* **Max** (maks). 1838–1920, German composer, noted chiefly for his three violin concertos.

brucine ('bruːsiːn, -sɪn) *n.* a bitter poisonous alkaloid resembling strychnine and obtained from the tree *Strychnos nuxvomica:* used mainly in the denaturation of alcohol. Formula: $C_{23}H_{26}N_2O_4$. **[C19**: named after James *Bruce* (1730–94), Scottish explorer of Africa**]**

Brücke (*German* 'brykə) *n* **die** (diː). a group of German Expressionist painters (1905–13), including Karl Schmidt-Rottluff, Fritz Bleyl, Erich Heckel, and Ernst Ludwig Kirchner. In 1912 they exhibited with *der Blaue Reiter.* **[**German: literally, the bridge**]**

Bruckner (*German* 'brʊknər) *n* **Anton** ('antoːn). 1824–96, Austrian composer and organist in the Romantic tradition. His works include nine symphonies, four masses, and a Te Deum.

Brudenell ('bruːdənɛl) *n* **James Thomas.** See (7th Earl of) **Cardigan.**

Brueghel, Bruegel, *or* **Breughel** ('brɔɪgᵊl; *Flemish* 'brøːxəl) *n* **1 Jan** (jɑn). 1568–1625, Flemish painter, noted for his detailed still lifes and landscapes. **2** his father, **Pieter** ('piːtər), called *the Elder.* ?1525–69, Flemish painter, noted for his landscapes, his satirical paintings of peasant life, and his allegorical biblical scenes. **3** his son, **Pieter,** called *the Younger.* ?1564–1637, Flemish painter, noted for his gruesome pictures of hell.

Bruges (bruːʒ; *French* bryʒ) *n* a city in NW Belgium, capital of West Flanders province: centre of the medieval European wool and cloth trade. Pop.: 116 273 (1995 est.). Flemish name: **Brugge** ('bryxə).

bruin ('bruːɪn) *n* a name for a bear, used in children's tales, fables, etc. **[C17**: from Dutch *bruin* brown, the name of the bear in the epic *Reynard the Fox***]**

bruise (bruːz) *vb* (*mainly tr*) **1** (*also intr*) to injure (tissues) without breaking the skin, usually with discoloration, or (of tissues) to be injured in this way. **2** to offend or injure (someone's feelings) by an insult, unkindness, etc. **3** to damage the surface of (something), as by a blow. **4** to crush (food, etc.) by pounding or pressing. ◆ *n* **5** a bodily injury without a break in the skin, usually with discoloration; contusion. **[**Old English *brȳsan,* of Celtic origin; compare Irish *brūigim* I bruise**]** ▸ **'bruising** *n, adj*

bruiser ('bruːzə) *n* a strong tough person, esp. a boxer or a bully.

bruit (bruːt) *vb* **1** (*tr; often passive;* usually foll. by *about*) to report; rumour: *it was bruited about that the king was dead.* ◆ *n* **2** *Med.* an abnormal sound heard within the body during auscultation, esp. a heart murmur. **3** *Archaic.* **3a** a rumour. **3b** a loud outcry; clamour. **[C15**: via French from Medieval Latin *brūgītus,* probably from Vulgar Latin *bragere* (unattested) to yell + Latin *rugīre* to roar**]**

Brule *or* **Brûlé** (bruː'leɪ) *n* (*sometimes not cap.*) short for **bois-brûlé.**

Brumaire *French.* (brymɛr) *n* the month of mist: the second month of the French revolutionary calendar, extending from Oct. 23 to Nov. 21. **[C19**: from *brume* mist, from Latin *brūma* winter; see BRUME**]**

brumal ('bruːməl) *adj* of, characteristic of, or relating to winter; wintry.

brumby ('brʌmbɪ) *n, pl* **-bies.** *Austral.* **1** a wild horse, esp. one descended from runaway stock. **2** *Informal.* a wild or unruly person. **[C19**: of unknown origin**]**

brume (bruːm) *n Poetic.* heavy mist or fog. **[C19**: from French: mist, winter, from Latin *brūma,* contracted from *brevissima diēs* the shortest day**]** ▸ **'brumous** *adj*

Brummagem ('brʌmədʒəm) *n* **1** an informal name for **Birmingham.** Often shortened to **Brum. 2** (*sometimes not cap.*) something that is cheap and flashy, esp. imitation jewellery. ◆ *adj* **3** (*sometimes not cap.*) cheap and gaudy; tawdry. **[C17**: from earlier *Bromecham,* local variant of BIRMINGHAM**]**

Brummell ('brʌməl) *n* **George Bryan,** called *Beau Brummell.* 1778–1840, English dandy: leader of fashion in the Regency period.

Brummie ('brʌmɪ) *n Informal.* a native or inhabitant of Birmingham. **[C20**: from BRUMMAGEM**]**

brunch (brʌntʃ) *n* a meal eaten late in the morning, combining breakfast with lunch. **[C20**: from BR(EAKFAST) + (L)UNCH**]**

Brundisium (brʌn'dɪzɪəm) *n* the ancient name for **Brindisi.**

Brunei (bruː'naɪ, 'bruːnaɪ) *n* **1** a sultanate in NW Borneo, consisting of two separate areas on the South China Sea, otherwise bounded by Sarawak: controlled all of Borneo and parts of the Philippines and the Sulu Islands in the 16th century; under British protection since 1888; internally self-governing since 1971; became independent in 1984 as a member of the Commonwealth. The economy depends chiefly on oil and natural gas. Official language: Malay; English is also widely spoken. Religion: Muslim. Currency: Brunei dollar. Capital: Bandar Seri Begawan. Pop.: 315 000 (1998 est.). Area: 5765 sq. km (2226 sq. miles). **2** the former name of **Bandar Seri Begawan.**

Brunel (bruː'nɛl) *n* **1 Isambard Kingdom** ('ɪzəm,bɑːd). 1806–59, English engineer: designer of the Clifton Suspension Bridge (1828), many railway lines, tunnels, bridges, etc., and the steamships *Great Western* (1838), *Great Britain* (1845), and *Great Eastern* (1858). **2** his father, Sir **Marc Isambard.** 1769–1849, French engineer in England.

Brunelleschi (*Italian* brunel'leski) *n* **Filippo** (fi'lippo). 1377–1446, Italian architect, whose works in Florence include the dome of the cathedral, the Pazzi chapel of Santa Croce, and the church of San Lorenzo.

brunette (bruː'nɛt) *n* **1** a girl or woman with dark brown hair. ◆ *adj also* **brunet. 2** dark brown: *brunette hair.* **[C17**: from French, feminine of *brunet* dark, brownish, from *brun* brown, of Germanic origin; see BROWN**]**

Brunhild ('brʊnhɪld, -hɪlt) *or* **Brünnhilde** (*German* bryn'hɪldə) *n* (in the *Nibelungenlied*) a legendary queen won for King Gunther by the magic of Siegfried: corresponds to Brynhild in Norse mythology.

Brüning (*German* 'bryːnɪŋ) *n* **Heinrich** ('hainrɪç). 1885–1970, German statesman; chancellor (1930–32). He was forced to resign in 1932, making way for the Nazis.

Brünn (bryn) *n* the German name for **Brno.**

Bruno ('bruːnəʊ) *n* **1 Franklin Roy,** known as *Frank.* born 1961, British heavyweight boxer. **2** (*Italian* 'bruno) **Giordano** (dʒor'dano). 1548–1600, Italian philosopher, who developed a pantheistic monistic philosophy: he was burnt at the stake for heresy.

Brunswick ('brʌnzwɪk) *n* **1** a former duchy (1635–1918) and state (1918–46) of central Germany, now part of the state of Lower Saxony; formerly (1949–90) part of West Germany. **2** a city in central Germany: formerly capital of the duchy and state of Brunswick. Pop.: 252 544 (1996 est.). German name: **Braunschweig.**

brunt (brʌnt) *n* the main force or shock of a blow, attack, etc. (esp. in the phrase **bear the brunt of**). **[C14**: of unknown origin**]**

Brusa (*Turkish* 'bruːsɑː) *n* the former name of **Bursa.**

bruschetta (bru'ʃɛtə) *n* an Italian open sandwich of toasted bread topped with olive oil and tomatoes, olives, etc. [C20: from Italian *bruscare,* from *abbrustolire* to toast]

brush[1] (brʌʃ) *n* **1** a device made of bristles, hairs, wires, etc., set into a firm back or handle: used to apply paint, clean or polish surfaces, groom the hair, etc. **2** the act or an instance of brushing. **3** a light stroke made in passing; graze. **4** a brief encounter or contact, esp. an unfriendly one; skirmish. **5** the bushy tail of a fox, often kept as a trophy after a hunt, or of certain breeds of dog. **6** an electric conductor, esp. one made of carbon, that conveys current between stationary and rotating parts of a generator, motor, etc. **7** a dark brush-shaped region observed when a biaxial crystal is viewed through a microscope, caused by interference between beams of polarized light. ◆ *vb* **8** (*tr*) to clean, polish, scrub, paint, etc., with a brush. **9** (*tr*) to apply or remove with a brush or brushing movement: *brush the crumbs off the table.* **10** (*tr*) to touch lightly and briefly. **11** (*intr*) to move so as to graze or touch something lightly. ◆ See also **brush aside, brush off, brush up.** [C14: from Old French *broisse,* perhaps from *broce* BRUSH[2]] ▸ **ˈbrusher** *n* ▸ **ˈbrushˌlike** *or* **ˈbrushy** *adj*

brush[2] (brʌʃ) *n* **1** a thick growth of shrubs and small trees; scrub. **2** land covered with scrub. **3** broken or cut branches or twigs; brushwood. **4** wooded sparsely populated country; backwoods. [C16 (dense undergrowth), C14 (cuttings of trees): from Old French *broce,* from Vulgar Latin *bruscia* (unattested) brushwood] ▸ **ˈbrushy** *adj*

brush aside *or* **away** *vb* (*tr, adv*) to dismiss without consideration; disregard.

brush border *n Physiol.* a layer of tightly packed minute finger-like protuberances on cells that line absorptive surfaces, such as those of the intestine and kidney. See also: **microvillus.**

brush discharge *n* a slightly luminous electrical discharge between points of high charge density when the charge density is insufficient to cause a spark or around sharp points on a highly charged conductor because of ionization of air molecules in their vicinity.

brushed (brʌʃt) *adj Textiles.* treated with a brushing process to raise the nap and give a softer, warmer finish: *brushed nylon.*

brush fire *n* **1** a fire in bushes and scrub. **2** a minor local war.

brushmark (ˈbrʌʃˌmɑːk) *n* the indented lines sometimes left by the bristles of a brush on a painted surface.

brush off *Slang.* ◆ *vb* (*tr, adv*) **1** to dismiss and ignore (a person), esp. curtly. ◆ *n* **brushoff. 2** an abrupt dismissal or rejection.

brush-tailed phalanger *n Austral.* another name for **tuan**[2].

brush turkey *n* any of several gallinaceous birds, esp. *Alectura lathami,* of New Guinea and Australia, having a black plumage: family *Megapodidae* (megapodes).

brush up *vb* (*adv*). **1** (*tr;* often foll. by *on*) to refresh one's knowledge, skill, or memory of (a subject). **2** to make (a person or oneself) tidy, clean, or neat as after a journey. ◆ *n* **brush-up. 3** *Brit.* the act or an instance of tidying one's appearance (esp. in the phrase **wash and brush-up**).

brushwood (ˈbrʌʃˌwʊd) *n* **1** cut or broken-off tree branches, twigs, etc. **2** another word for **brush**[2] (sense 1).

brushwork (ˈbrʌʃˌwɜːk) *n* **1** a characteristic manner of applying paint with a brush: *that is not Rembrandt's brushwork.* **2** work done with a brush.

brusque (bruːsk, brʊsk) *adj* blunt or curt in manner or speech. [C17: from French, from Italian *brusco* sour, rough, from Medieval Latin *bruscus* butcher's broom] ▸ **ˈbrusquely** *adv* ▸ **ˈbrusqueness** *or* (*less commonly*) **brusquerie** (ˈbruːskərɪ) *n*

Brussels (ˈbrʌsəlz) *n* the capital of Belgium, in the central part: became capital of Belgium in 1830; seat of the European Commission. Pop.: 948 122 (1996 est.). Flemish name: **Brussel** (ˈbrysəl). French name: **Bruxelles.**

Brussels carpet *n* a worsted carpet with a heavy pile formed by uncut loops of wool on a linen warp.

Brussels lace *n* a fine lace with a raised or appliqué design.

Brussels sprout *n* **1** a variety of cabbage, *Brassica oleracea gemmifera,* having a stout stem studded with budlike heads of tightly folded leaves, resembling tiny cabbages. **2** the head of this plant, eaten as a vegetable.

brut (bruːt; *French* bryt) *adj* (of champagne) not sweet; dry. [C19: from French raw, rough, from Latin *brūtus* heavy; see BRUTE]

brutal (ˈbruːtəl) *adj* **1** cruel; vicious; savage. **2** extremely honest or coarse in speech or manner. **3** harsh; severe; extreme: *brutal cold.* ▸ **bruˈtality** *n* ▸ **ˈbrutally** *adv*

brutalism (ˈbruːtəˌlɪzəm) *n* an austere style of architecture characterized by emphasis on such structural materials as undressed concrete and unconcealed service pipes. Also called: **new brutalism.** ▸ **ˈbrutalist** *n, adj*

brutalize *or* **brutalise** (ˈbruːtəˌlaɪz) *vb* **1** to make or become brutal. **2** (*tr*) to treat brutally. ▸ **ˌbrutaliˈzation** *or* **ˌbrutaliˈsation** *n*

brute (bruːt) *n* **1a** any animal except man; beast; lower animal. **1b** (*as modifier*): *brute nature.* **2** a brutal person. ◆ *adj* (*prenominal*) **3** wholly instinctive or physical (esp. in the phrases **brute strength, brute force**). **4** without reason or intelligence. **5** coarse and grossly sensual. [C15: from Latin *brūtus* heavy, irrational; related to *gravis* heavy]

brutify (ˈbruːtɪˌfaɪ) *vb* **-fies, -fying, -fied.** a less common word for **brutalize** (sense 1).

brutish (ˈbruːtɪʃ) *adj* **1** of, relating to, or resembling a brute or brutes; animal. **2** coarse; cruel; stupid. ▸ **ˈbrutishly** *adv* ▸ **ˈbrutishness** *n*

Bruton (ˈbruːtən) **John Gerard.** born 1947, Irish politician: leader of the Fine Gael party from 1990; prime minister of the Republic of Ireland (1994–97).

Brutus (ˈbruːtəs) *n* **1 Lucius Junius** (ˈluːʃəs ˈdʒuːnɪəs). late 6th century B.C., Roman statesman who ousted the tyrant Tarquin (509) and helped found the Roman republic. **2 Marcus Junius** (ˈmɑːkəs ˈdʒuːnɪəs) ?85–42 B.C., Roman statesman who, with Cassius, led the conspiracy to assassinate Caesar (44): committed suicide after being defeated by Antony and Octavian (Augustus) at Philippi (42).

Bruxelles (brysɛl) *n* the French name for **Brussels.**

bruxism (ˈbrʌksɪzəm) *n* the habit of grinding the teeth, esp. unconsciously. [irregularly formed from Greek *brykein* to gnash the teeth + -ISM]

Bryansk (brɪˈænsk; *Russian* brjansk) *n* a city in W Russia. Pop.: 462 000 (1995 est.).

Bryant (ˈbraɪənt) *n* **David.** born 1931, British bowler; many times world champion.

Brynhild (ˈbrɪnhɪld) *n Norse myth.* a Valkyrie won as the wife of Gunnar by Sigurd who wakes her from an enchanted sleep: corresponds to Brunhild in the *Nibelungenlied.*

bryology (braɪˈɒlədʒɪ) *n* the branch of botany concerned with the study of bryophytes. ▸ **bryological** (ˌbraɪəˈlɒdʒɪkəl) *adj* ▸ **bryˈologist** *n*

bryony *or* **briony** (ˈbraɪənɪ) *n, pl* **-nies.** any of several herbaceous climbing plants of the cucurbitaceous genus *Bryonia,* of Europe and N Africa. See also **black bryony, white bryony.** [Old English *bryōnia,* from Latin, from Greek *bruōnia*]

bryophyte (ˈbraɪəˌfaɪt) *n* any plant of the phylum *Bryophyta,* having stems and leaves but lacking true vascular tissue and roots and reproducing by spores: includes the mosses and liverworts. [C19: New Latin, from Greek *bruon* moss + -PHYTE] ▸ **bryophytic** (ˌbraɪəˈfɪtɪk) *adj*

bryozoan (ˌbraɪəˈzəʊən) *n* **1** any aquatic invertebrate animal of the phylum *Bryozoa,* forming colonies of polyps each having a ciliated feeding organ (lophophore). Popular name: **sea mat.** ◆ *adj* **2** of, relating to, or belonging to the *Bryozoa.* ◆ Also: **polyzoan, ectoproct.** [C19: from Greek *bruon* moss + *zōion* animal]

Brython (ˈbrɪθən) *n* a Celt who speaks a Brythonic language. Compare **Goidel.** [C19: from Welsh; see BRITON]

Brythonic (brɪˈθɒnɪk) *n* **1** the S group of Celtic languages, consisting of Welsh, Cornish, and Breton. ◆ *adj* **2** of, relating to, or characteristic of this group of languages. ◆ Also called: **Brittonic.**

Brześć nad Bugiem (bʒɛʃtʃ nad ˈbugjɛm) *n* the Polish name for **Brest** (sense 2).

bs *abbrev. for:* **1** balance sheet. **2** bill of sale.

BS *abbrev. for:* **1** Bachelor of Surgery. **2** British Standard(s) (indicating the catalogue or publication number of the British Standards Institution). ◆ **3** *international car registration for* Bahamas.

B/S *or* **b/s** *abbrev. for:* **1** bags. **2** bales. **3** bill of sale.

BSB *abbrev. for:* **1** British Sky Broadcasting (formerly for British Satellite Broadcasting). **2** British Standard brass thread.

BSc *abbrev. for* Bachelor of Science.

BSC *abbrev. for:* **1** British Steel Corporation. **2** British Sugar Corporation. **3** (in Britain) Broadcasting Standards Commission.

BSE *abbrev. for* bovine spongiform encephalopathy: a fatal slow-developing virus disease of cattle, affecting the nervous system. Informal name: **mad cow disease.**

B-setting *n Photog.* a shutter setting in which the shutter remains open until the shutter control is released.

BSF *abbrev. for* British Standard fine thread.

BSI *abbrev. for* British Standards Institution.

B-side *n* the less important side of a gramophone record. Also called: **flip side.**

BSL *abbrev. for* British Sign Language.

Bs/L *abbrev. for* bills of lading.

BSP *abbrev. for* British Standard pipe thread.

B Special *n* a member of a part-time largely Protestant police force formerly functioning in Northern Ireland.

BSS *abbrev. for* British Standards Specification.

BSSc *or* **BSocSc** *abbrev. for* Bachelor of Social Science

BST *abbrev. for:* **1** bovine somatotrophin: a growth hormone that can be used to increase milk production in dairy cattle. **2** British Summer Time.

BSW *abbrev. for* British Standard Whitworth thread.

Bt *abbrev. for* Baronet.

BT *abbrev. for* British Telecom. [C20: shortened from TELECOMMUNICATIONS]

BTEC (ˈbiːtɛk) *n acronym for* Business and Technician Education Council.

BTG *abbrev. for* British Technology Group.

btl. *abbrev. for* bottle.

btu *or* **BThU** *abbrev. for* British thermal unit. U.S. abbrev.: **BTU.**

BTU *abbrev. for* Board of Trade Unit.

bty *or* **btry.** *Military. abbrev. for* battery.

bu. *abbrev. for* bushel.

bub (bʌb) *n* **1** *U.S. informal.* fellow; youngster: used as a form of address. **2** *Austral. and N.Z. slang.* **2a** a baby. **2b bubs grade.** the first grade of schooling; nursery school. [C20: perhaps from German *Bube* boy]

bubal (ˈbjuːbəl) *or* **bubalis** (ˈbjuːbəlɪs) *n* any of various antelopes, esp. an extinct N African variety of hartebeest. [C15: from Latin *būbalus* African gazelle, from Greek *boubalos,* from Greek *bous* ox]

bubaline (ˈbjuːbəˌlaɪn, -lɪn) *adj* **1** (of antelopes) related to or resembling the bubal. **2** resembling or relating to the buffalo. [C19: from New Latin, from Latin *būbalus;* see BUBAL]

bubble (ˈbʌbəl) *n* **1** a thin film of liquid forming a hollow globule around air or a gas: *a soap bubble.* **2** a small globule of air or a gas in a liquid or a solid, as in carbonated drinks, glass, etc. **3** the sound made by a bubbling liquid. **4** something lacking substance, stability, or seriousness. **5** an unreliable scheme or enterprise. **6** a dome, esp. a transparent glass or plastic one. ◆ *vb* **7** to form or cause to form bubbles. **8** (*intr*) to move or flow with a gurgling sound. **9** (*intr;* often foll. by *over*) to overflow (with excitement, anger, etc.). **10** (*intr*) *Scot.* to snivel; blubber. [C14: probably of Scandinavian origin; compare Swedish *bubbla,* Danish *boble,* Dutch *bobbel,* all of imitative origin]

bubble and squeak *n* (in Britain and Australia) a dish of leftover boiled cabbage, potatoes, and sometimes cooked meat fried together. [C18: so called from the sounds of this dish cooking]

bubble bath *n* **1** a powder, liquid, or crystals used to scent, soften, and foam in bath water. **2** a bath to which such a substance has been added.

bubble car *n* (in Britain, formerly) a small car, often having three wheels, with a transparent bubble-shaped top.

bubble chamber *n* a device that enables the tracks of ionizing particles to be photographed as a row of bubbles in a superheated liquid. Immediately before the particles enter the chamber the pressure is reduced so that the ionized particles act as centres for small vapour bubbles.

bubble float *n Angling.* a hollow spherical float that can be weighted with water to aid casting.

bubble gum *n* **1** a type of chewing gum that can be blown into large bubbles. **2** *Slang.* **2a** crassly commercial pop music aimed at the very young. **2b** (*as modifier*): *a bubble-gum hit.*

bubble memory *n Computing.* a method of storing high volumes of data by the use of minute pockets of magnetism (bubbles) in a semiconducting material: the bubbles may be caused to migrate past a read head or to a buffer area for storage.

bubble pack *n* another term for **blister pack.**

bubble point *n Chem.* the temperature at which bubbles just start to appear in a heated liquid mixture.

bubbler ('bʌblə) *n* **1** a drinking fountain in which the water is forced in a stream from a small vertical nozzle. **2** *Chem.* any device for bubbling gas through a liquid.

bubble wrap *n* a type of polythene wrapping containing many small air pockets, used as a protective covering when transporting breakable goods.

bubbly ('bʌblɪ) *adj* **-blier, -bliest. 1** full of or resembling bubbles. **2** lively; animated; excited: *a bubbly personality.* ◆ *n* **3** an informal name for **champagne.**

Buber ('bu:bə) *n* **Martin.** 1878–1965, Jewish theologian, existentialist philosopher, and scholar of Hasidism, born in Austria, whose works include *I and Thou* (1923), *Between Man and Man* (1946), and *Eclipse of God* (1952).

bubo ('bju:bəʊ) *n, pl* **-boes.** *Pathol.* inflammation and swelling of a lymph node, often with the formation of pus, esp. in the region of the armpit or groin. [C14: from Medieval Latin *bubō* swelling, from Greek *boubōn* groin, glandular swelling] ► **bubonic** (bju:'bɒnɪk) *adj*

bubonic plague *n* an acute infectious febrile disease characterized by chills, prostration, delirium, and formation of buboes: caused by the bite of a rat flea infected with the bacterium *Yersinia pestis.* See also **plague.**

bubonocele (bju:'bɒnəˌsi:l) *n* an incomplete hernia in the groin; partial inguinal hernia. [C17: from Greek *boubōn* groin + *kēlē* tumour]

bubu ('bu:bu:) *n* a variant spelling of **boubou.**

Bucaramanga (*Spanish* bukara'manga) *n* a city in N central Colombia, in the Cordillera Oriental: centre of a district growing coffee, tobacco, and cotton. Pop.: 508 240 (1997 est.).

buccal ('bʌkᵊl) *adj* **1** of or relating to the cheek. **2** of or relating to the mouth; oral: *buccal lesion.* [C19: from Latin *bucca* cheek]

buccaneer (ˌbʌkə'nɪə) *n* **1** a pirate, esp. one who preyed on the Spanish colonies and shipping in America and the Caribbean in the 17th and 18th centuries. ◆ *vb* (*intr*) **2** to be or act like a buccaneer. [C17: from French *boucanier,* from *boucaner* to smoke meat, from Old French *boucan* frame for smoking meat, of Tupian origin; originally applied to French and English hunters of wild oxen in the Caribbean]

buccinator ('bʌksɪˌneɪtə) *n* a thin muscle that compresses the cheeks and holds them against the teeth during chewing, etc. [C17: from Latin, from *buccināre* to sound the trumpet, from *buccina* trumpet]

bucentaur (bju:'sɛntɔ:) *n* the state barge of Venice from which the doge and other officials dropped a ring into the sea on Ascension Day to symbolize the ceremonial marriage of the state with the Adriatic. [C17: from Italian *bucentoro,* of uncertain origin]

Bucephalus (bju:'sɛfələs) *n* the favourite horse of Alexander the Great. [C17: from Latin, from Greek *Boukephalos,* from *bous* ox + *kephalē* head]

Buchan ('bʌkən) *n* **John,** 1st Baron Tweedsmuir. 1875–1940, Scottish statesman, historian, and writer of adventure stories, esp. *The Thirty-Nine Steps* (1915) and *Greenmantle* (1916); governor general of Canada (1935–40).

Buchanan (bju:'kænən) *n* **1 George.** 1506–82, Scottish historian, who was tutor to Mary, Queen of Scots and James VI; author of *History of Scotland* (1582). **2 James.** 1791–1868, 15th president of the U.S. (1857–61).

Bucharest (ˌbu:kə'rɛst, ˌbju:-) *n* the capital of Romania, in the southeast. Pop.: 2 060 551 (1994 est.). Romanian name: **Bucureşti.**

Buchenwald (*German* 'bu:xənvalt) *n* a village in E central Germany, near Weimar; site of a Nazi concentration camp (1937–45).

Buchmanism ('bʊkməˌnɪzəm) *n* another name for **Moral Rearmament.** [C20: named after Frank *Buchman* (1878–1961), U.S. evangelist who founded it] ► **'Buchmanˌite** *n, adj*

Buchner (*German* 'bu:xnər) *n* **Eduard** ('e:duart). 1860–1917, German chemist who demonstrated that alcoholic fermentation is due to enzymes in the yeast: Nobel prize for chemistry 1907.

Büchner (*German* 'by:çnər) *n* **Georg** ('ge:ɔrk). 1813–37, German dramatist; regarded as a forerunner of the Expressionists: author of *Danton's Death* (1835) and *Woyzeck* (1837).

Buchner funnel ('bʌknə) *n* a laboratory filter funnel used under reduced pressure. It consists of a shallow porcelain cylinder with a flat perforated base. [named after its inventor, E. BUCHNER]

buchu ('bu:ku:) *n* any of several S. African rutaceous shrubs of the genus *Barosma,* esp. *B. betulina,* whose leaves are used as an antiseptic and diuretic. [C18: from a South African Bantu name]

buck[1] (bʌk) *n* **1a** the male of various animals including the goat, hare, kangaroo, rabbit, and reindeer. **1b** (*as modifier*): *a buck antelope.* **2** *S. African.* an antelope or deer of either sex. **3** *U.S. informal.* a young man. **4** *Archaic.* a robust spirited young man. **5** *Archaic.* a dandy; fop. **6** the act of bucking. ◆ *vb* **7** (*intr*) (of a horse or other animal) to jump vertically, with legs stiff and back arched. **8** (*tr*) (of a horse, etc.) to throw (its rider) by bucking. **9** (when *intr,* often foll. by *against*) *Informal, chiefly U.S. and Canadian.* to resist or oppose obstinately: *to buck against change; to buck change.* **10** (*tr; usually passive*) *Informal.* to cheer or encourage: *I was very bucked at passing the exam.* **11** *U.S. and Canadian informal.* (esp. of a car) to move forward jerkily; jolt. **12** *U.S. and Canadian.* to charge against (something) with the head down; butt. ◆ See also **buck up.** [Old English *bucca* he-goat; related to Old Norse *bukkr,* Old High German *bock,* Old Irish *bocc*] ► **'bucker** *n*

buck[2] (bʌk) *n* **1** *U.S., Canadian, and Austral. informal.* a dollar. **2 a fast buck.** easily gained money. [C19: of obscure origin]

buck[3] (bʌk) *n* **1** *Gymnastics.* a type of vaulting horse. **2** a U.S. and Canadian word for **sawhorse.** ◆ *vb* **3** (*tr*) *U.S. and Canadian.* to cut (a felled or fallen tree) into lengths. [C19: short for SAWBUCK]

buck[4] (bʌk) *n* **1** *Poker.* a marker in the jackpot to remind the winner of some obligation when his turn comes to deal. **2 pass the buck.** *Informal.* to shift blame or responsibility onto another. **3** *Informal.* the ultimate responsibility lies here. [C19: probably from *buckhorn knife,* placed before a player in poker to indicate that he was the next dealer]

Buck (bʌk) *n* **Pearl S(ydenstricker).** 1892–1973, U.S. novelist, noted particularly for her novel of Chinese life *The Good Earth* (1931): Nobel prize for literature 1938.

buck and wing *n U.S.* a boisterous tap dance, derived from Black and Irish clog dances.

buckaroo ('bʌkəˌru:, ˌbʌkə'ru:) *n, pl* **-roos.** *Southwestern U.S.* a cowboy. [C19: variant of Spanish *vaquero,* from *vaca* cow, from Latin *vacca*]

buckbean ('bʌkˌbi:n) *n* a marsh plant, *Menyanthes trifoliata,* with white or pink flowers: family *Menyanthaceae.* Also called: **bogbean.**

buckboard ('bʌkˌbɔ:d) *n U.S. and Canadian.* an open four-wheeled horse-drawn carriage with the seat attached to a flexible board between the front and rear axles.

buckeen (bʌ'ki:n) *n* (in Ireland) a poor young man who aspires to the habits and dress of the wealthy. [C18: from Irish Gaelic *boicín,* diminutive of *boc* an important person]

bucket ('bʌkɪt) *n* **1** an open-topped roughly cylindrical container; pail. **2** Also called: **bucketful.** the amount a bucket will hold. **3** any of various bucket-like parts of a machine, such as the scoop on a mechanical shovel. **4** a cupped blade or bucket-like compartment on the outer circumference of a water wheel, paddle wheel, etc. **5** *Computing.* a unit of storage on a direct-access device from which data can be retrieved. **6** *Chiefly U.S.* a turbine rotor blade. **7** *Austral. and N.Z.* an ice cream container. **8 kick the bucket.** *Slang.* to die. ◆ *vb* **-kets, -keting, -keted. 9** (*tr*) to carry in or put into a bucket. **10** (*intr*) (often foll. by *down*) (of rain) to fall very heavily: *it bucketed all day.* **11** (*intr;* often foll. by *along*) *Chiefly Brit.* to travel or drive fast. **12** (*tr*) *Chiefly Brit.* to ride (a horse) hard without consideration. **13** (*tr*) *Austral. slang.* to criticize severely. [C13: from Anglo-French *buket,* from Old English *būc;* compare Old High German *būh* belly, German *Bauch* belly]

bucket about *vb* (*intr*) *Brit.* (esp. of a boat in a storm) to toss or shake violently.

bucket ladder *n* **a** a series of buckets that move in a continuous chain, used to dredge riverbeds, etc., or to excavate land. **b** (*as modifier*): *a bucket-ladder dredger.*

bucket out *vb* (*tr*) to empty out with or as if with a bucket.

bucket seat *n* a seat in a car, aircraft, etc., having curved sides that partially enclose and support the body.

bucket shop *n* **1** an unregistered firm of stockbrokers that engages in speculation with clients' funds. **2** *Chiefly Brit.* any small business that cannot be relied upon, esp. one selling cheap airline tickets.

buckeye ('bʌkˌaɪ) *n* any of several North American trees of the genus *Aesculus,* esp. *A. glabra* (Ohio buckeye), having erect clusters of white or red flowers and prickly fruits: family *Hippocastanaceae.* See also **horse chestnut.**

buck fever *n* nervous excitement felt by inexperienced hunters at the approach of game.

buckhorn ('bʌkˌhɔ:n) *n* **1a** horn from a buck, used for knife handles, etc. **1b** (*as modifier*): *a buckhorn knife.* **2** Also called: **buck's horn plantain.** a Eurasian plant, *Plantago coronopus,* having leaves resembling a buck's horn: family *Plantaginaceae.*

buckhound ('bʌkˌhaʊnd) *n* a hound, smaller than a staghound, used for hunting the smaller breeds of deer, esp. fallow deer.

buckie ('bʌkɪ) *n Scot.* **1** a whelk or its shell. **2** a lively or boisterous person, esp. a youngster. [related to Latin *buc(c)inum* whelk, from *buc(c)ina* trumpet, horn]

Buckingham[1] ('bʌkɪŋəm) *n* a town in S central England, in Buckinghamshire; university (1975). Pop.: 2786 (1991).

Buckingham[2] ('bʌkɪŋəm) *n* **1 George Villiers, 1st Duke of.** 1592–1628, English courtier and statesman; favourite of James I and Charles I: his arrogance, military incompetence, and greed increased the tensions between the King and Parliament that eventually led to the Civil War. **2** his son, **George Villiers, 2nd Duke of.** 1628–87, English courtier and writer; chief minister of Charles II and member of the Cabal (1667–73).

Buckingham Palace *n* the London residence of the British sovereign: built in 1703, rebuilt by John Nash in 1821–36 and partially redesigned in the early 20th century.

Buckinghamshire ('bʌkɪŋəmˌʃɪə, -ʃə) *n* a county in SE central England, containing the Vale of Aylesbury and parts of the Chiltern Hills: the geographic and ceremonial county includes Milton Keynes, which became an independent unitary authority in 1997. Administrative centre: Aylesbury. Pop. (including Milton Keynes): 658 400 (1994 est.). Area (including Milton Keynes): 1883 sq. km (727 sq. miles). Abbrev.: **Bucks.**

buckjumper ('bʌk,dʒʌmpə) *n Austral.* an untamed horse.

buckjumping ('bʌk,dʒʌmpɪŋ) *n Austral.* a competitive event for buckjumpers in a rodeo.

Buckland ('bʌklənd) *n* **William.** 1784–1856, English geologist; he became a proponent of the idea of catastrophic ice ages.

buckle ('bʌkəl) *n* **1** a clasp for fastening together two loose ends, esp. of a belt or strap, usually consisting of a frame with an attached movable prong. **2** an ornamental representation of a buckle, as on a shoe. **3** a kink, bulge, or other distortion: *a buckle in a railway track.* ◆ *vb* **4** to fasten or be fastened with a buckle. **5** to bend or cause to bend out of shape, esp. as a result of pressure or heat. [C14: from Old French *bocle,* from Latin *buccula* a little cheek, hence, cheek strap of a helmet, from *bucca* cheek]

buckle down *vb (intr, adv) Informal.* to apply oneself with determination: *to buckle down to a job.*

buckler ('bʌklə) *n* **1** a small round shield worn on the forearm or held by a short handle. **2** a means of protection; defence. ◆ *vb* **3** *(tr) Archaic.* to defend. [C13: from Old French *bocler,* from *bocle* shield boss; see BUCKLE, BOSS[2]]

buckler fern *n* any of various ferns of the genus *Dryopteris,* such as *D. dilatata* (broad buckler fern): family *Polypodiaceae.*

Buckley's chance ('bʌklɪz) *n Austral. and N.Z. slang.* no chance at all. Often shortened to **Buckley's.** [C19: of obscure origin]

buckling ('bʌklɪŋ) *n* another name for a **bloater.** [C20: from German *Bückling*]

buckminsterfullerene (,bʌkmɪnstə'fʊlə,riːn) *n* a form of carbon that contains molecules having 60 carbon atoms arranged at the vertices of a polyhedron with hexagonal and pentagonal faces. It is produced in carbon arcs and occurs naturally in small amounts in certain minerals. Also called: **fullerene.** [C20: named after Buckminster FULLER, from the resemblance of the molecular structure to that of Fuller's geodesic dome]

bucko ('bʌkəʊ) *n, pl* **-oes.** *Irish.* a lively young fellow: often a term of address.

buckra ('bʌkrə) *n* (used contemptuously by Black people, esp. in the U.S.) a White man. [C18: probably from Efik *mba-ka-ra* master]

buck rabbit *or* **rarebit** *n Brit.* Welsh rabbit with either an egg or a piece of toast on top.

buckram ('bʌkrəm) *n* **1a** cotton or linen cloth stiffened with size, etc., used in lining or stiffening clothes, bookbinding, etc. **1b** *(as modifier): a buckram cover.* **2** *Archaic.* stiffness of manner. ◆ *vb* **-rams, -raming, -ramed. 3** *(tr)* to stiffen with buckram. [C14: from Old French *boquerant,* from Old Provençal *bocaran,* ultimately from BUKHARA, once an important source of textiles]

Bucks (bʌks) *abbrev. for* Buckinghamshire.

bucksaw ('bʌk,sɔː) *n* a woodcutting saw having its blade set in a frame and tensioned by a turnbuckle across the back of the frame.

buck's fizz *n* a cocktail made of champagne and orange juice.

buckshee (,bʌk'ʃiː) *adj Brit. slang.* without charge; free. [C20: from BAKSHEESH]

buckshot ('bʌk,ʃɒt) *n* lead shot of large size used in shotgun shells, esp. for hunting game. [C15 (original sense: the distance at which a buck can be shot)]

buckskin ('bʌk,skɪn) *n* **1** the skin of a male deer. **2a** a strong greyish-yellow suede leather, originally made from deerskin but now usually made from sheepskin. **2b** *(as modifier): buckskin boots.* **3** *U.S. (sometimes cap.)* a person wearing buckskin clothes, esp. an American soldier of the Civil War. **4** a stiffly starched cotton cloth. **5** a strong satin-woven woollen fabric. ◆ *adj* **6** greyish-yellow.

buckskins ('bʌk,skɪnz) *pl n* (in the U.S. and Canada) breeches, shoes, or a suit of buckskin.

buck's party *or* **night** *n* the Australian name for a **stag party.**

buckthorn ('bʌk,θɔːn) *n* any of several thorny small-flowered shrubs of the genus *Rhamnus,* esp. the Eurasian species *R. cathartica,* whose berries were formerly used as a purgative: family *Rhamnaceae.* See also **sea buckthorn.** [C16: from BUCK[1] (from the spiny branches, imagined as resembling antlers) + THORN]

bucktooth ('bʌk,tuːθ) *n, pl* **-teeth.** *Derogatory.* a projecting upper front tooth. [C18: from BUCK[1] (deer) + TOOTH] ▸ **'buck-toothed** *adj*

buck up *vb (adv) Informal.* **1** to make or cause to make haste. **2** to make or become more cheerful, confident, etc.

buckwheat ('bʌk,wiːt) *n* **1** any of several polygonaceous plants of the genus *Fagopyrum,* esp. *F. esculentum,* which has fragrant white flowers and is cultivated, esp. in the U.S., for its seeds. **2** the edible seeds of this plant, ground into flour or used as animal fodder. **3** the flour obtained from these seeds. [C16: from Middle Dutch *boecweite,* from *boeke* BEECH + *weite* WHEAT, from the resemblance of their seeds to beechnuts]

buckyball ('bʌkɪ,bɔːl) *n Informal.* a ball-like polyhedral carbon molecule of the type found in buckminsterfullerene and other fullerenes. [C20: from BUCK(MINSTERFULLERENE) + -Y[2] + BALL[1]]

buckytube ('bʌkɪ,tjuːb) *n Informal.* a tube of carbon atoms structurally similar to buckminsterfullerene.

bucolic (bjuː'kɒlɪk) *adj also* **bucolical. 1** of or characteristic of the countryside or country life; rustic. **2** of or relating to shepherds; pastoral. ◆ *n* **3** *(sometimes pl)* a pastoral poem, often in the form of a dialogue. **4** a rustic; farmer or shepherd. [C16: from Latin *būcolicus,* from Greek *boukolikos,* from *boukolos* cowherd, from *bous* ox] ▸ **bu'colically** *adv*

Bucovina (,buːkə'viːnə) *n* a variant spelling of **Bukovina.**

Bucureşti (buku'reʃtj) *n* the Romanian name for **Bucharest.**

bud[1] (bʌd) *n* **1** a swelling on a plant stem consisting of overlapping immature leaves or petals. **2a** a partially opened flower. **2b** *(in combination): rosebud.* **3** any small budlike outgrowth: *taste buds.* **4** something small or immature. **5** an asexually produced outgrowth in simple organisms, such as yeasts, and the hydra that develops into a new individual. **6 in bud.** at the stage of producing buds. **7 nip in the bud.** to put an end to (an idea, movement, etc.) in its initial stages. ◆ *vb* **buds, budding, budded. 8** *(intr)* (of plants and some animals) to produce buds. **9** *(intr)* to begin to develop or grow. **10** *(tr) Horticulture.* to graft (a bud) from one plant onto another, usually by insertion under the bark. [C14 *budde,* of Germanic origin; compare Icelandic *budda* purse, Dutch *buide*]

bud[2] (bʌd) *n Informal, chiefly U.S.* short for **buddy**: used as a term of address.

Budapest (,bjuːdə'pest; *Hungarian* 'budɔpeʃt) *n* the capital of Hungary, on the River Danube: formed in 1873 from the towns of Buda and Pest. Traditionally Buda, the old Magyar capital, was the administrative and Pest the trade centre: suffered severely in the Russian siege of 1945 and in the unsuccessful revolt against the Communist regime (1956). Pop.: 1 885 000 (1997 est.).

buddha ('budə) *n* **1** *Buddhism. (often cap.)* a person who has achieved a state of perfect enlightenment. **2** an image or picture of the Buddha. [C17: from Sanskrit: awakened, enlightened, from *budh* to awake, know]

Buddha ('budə) *n* **the.** ?563–483 B.C., a title applied to Gautama Siddhartha, a nobleman and religious teacher of N India, regarded by his followers as the most recent rediscoverer of the path to enlightenment: the founder of Buddhism.

Buddh Gaya ('bud gə'jɑː), **Buddha Gaya,** *or* **Bodh Gaya** *n* a village in NE India, in central Bihar: site of the sacred bo tree under which Gautama Siddhartha attained enlightenment and became the Buddha; pilgrimage centre. Pop.: 21 686 (1991 est.).

Buddhism ('budɪzəm) *n* a religious teaching propagated by the Buddha and his followers, which declares that by destroying greed, hatred, and delusion, which are the causes of all suffering, man can attain perfect enlightenment. See **nirvana.** ▸ **'Buddhist** *n, adj*

budding ('bʌdɪŋ) *adj* at an early stage of development but showing promise or potential: *a budding genius.*

buddle ('bʌdəl) *n* **1** a sloping trough in which ore is washed. ◆ *vb* **2** *(tr)* to wash (ore) in a buddle. [C16: of unknown origin]

buddleia ('bʌdlɪə) *n* any ornamental shrub of the genus *Buddleia,* esp. *B. davidii,* which has long spikes of mauve flowers and is frequently visited by butterflies: family *Buddleiaceae.* Also called: **butterfly bush.** [C19: named after A. *Buddle* (died 1715), British botanist]

buddy ('bʌdɪ) *n, pl* **-dies. 1** *Chiefly U.S. and Canadian.* an informal word for **friend.** Also called (as a term of address): **bud. 2** a volunteer who visits and gives help and support to a person suffering from AIDS. ◆ *vb* **-dying, -died. 3** *(intr)* to act as a buddy to a person suffering from AIDS. [C19: probably a baby-talk variant (U.S.) of BROTHER]

buddy movie *or* **film** *n* a genre of film dealing with the relationship and adventures of two friends.

budge[1] (bʌdʒ) *vb (usually used with a negative)* **1** to move, however slightly: *the car won't budge.* **2** to change or cause to change opinions, etc. [C16: from Old French *bouger,* from Vulgar Latin *bullicāre* (unattested) to bubble, from Latin *bullīre* to boil, from *bulla* bubble]

budge[2] (bʌdʒ) *n* a lambskin dressed for the fur to be worn on the outer side. [C14: from Anglo-French *bogee,* of obscure origin]

Budge (bʌdʒ) *n* **Don(ald).** born 1915, U.S. tennis player, the first man to win the Grand Slam of singles championships (Australia, France, Wimbledon, and the U.S.) in one year (1938).

budgerigar ('bʌdʒərɪ,gɑː) *n* a small green Australian parrot, *Melopsittacus undulatus:* a popular cagebird that is bred in many different coloured varieties. Often shortened (informal) to **budgie.** [C19: from a native Australian language]

budget ('bʌdʒɪt) *n* **1** an itemized summary of expected income and expenditure of a country, company, etc., over a specified period, usually a financial year. **2** an estimate of income and a plan for domestic expenditure of an individual or a family, often over a short period, such as a month or a week. **3** a restriction on expenditure (esp. in the phrase **on a budget**). **4** *(modifier)* economical; inexpensive: *budget meals for a family.* **5** the total amount of money allocated for a specific purpose during a specified period. **6** *Archaic.* a stock, quantity, or supply. ◆ *vb* **-gets, -geting, -geted. 7** *(tr)* to enter or provide for in a budget. **8** to plan the expenditure of (money, time, etc.). **9** *(intr)* to make a budget. [C15 (meaning: leather pouch, wallet): from Old French *bougette,* diminutive of *bouge,* from Latin *bulga,* of Gaulish origin; compare Old English *bælg* bag] ▸ **'budgetary** *adj*

Budget ('bʌdʒɪt) *n* **the.** an estimate of British government expenditures and revenues and the financial plans for the ensuing fiscal year presented annually to the House of Commons by the Chancellor of the Exchequer.

budget account *n* **1** an account with a department store, etc., enabling a customer to make monthly payments to cover his past and future purchases. **2** a bank account for paying household bills, being credited with regular or equal monthly payments from the customer's current account.

budgetary control *n* a system of managing a business by applying a financial value to each forecast activity. Actual performance is subsequently compared with the estimates.

budget deficit *n* the amount by which government expenditure exceeds income from taxation, customs duties, etc., in any one fiscal year.

budget for *vb (tr, prep)* to allocate, save, or set aside money for (a particular purpose, period, etc.): *we need to budget for a fuel increase this winter.*

budgie ('bʌdʒɪ) *n Informal.* short for **budgerigar.**

bud scale *n* one of the hard protective sometimes hairy or resinous specialized leaves surrounding the buds of certain plants, such as the rhododendron.

bud sport *n Horticulture.* a shoot, inflorescence, etc., that differs from another such structure on a plant and is caused by a mutation; the differences can be retained by vegetative propagation.

Budweis ('bʊtvaɪs) *n* the German name for **České Budějovice.**

Buenaventura (*Spanish* bwenaβen'tura) *n* a major port in W Colombia, on the Pacific coast. Pop.: 266 988 (1995 est.).

Buena Vista (*Spanish* 'bwena 'vista) *n* a village in NE Mexico, near Saltillo: site of the defeat of the Mexicans by U.S. forces (1847).

Buenos Aires ('bweɪnɒs 'aɪrɪz; *Spanish* 'bwenos 'aires) *n* the capital of Argentina, a major port and industrial city on the Río de la Plata estuary: became capital in 1880; university (1821). Pop.: 2 988 006 (1995 est.).

BUF *abbrev. for* British Union of Fascists.

buff[1] (bʌf) *n* **1a** a soft thick flexible undyed leather made chiefly from the skins of buffalo, oxen, and elk. **1b** (*as modifier*): *a buff coat.* **2a** a dull yellow or yellowish-brown colour. **2b** (*as adj*): *buff paint.* **3** Also called: **buffer. 3a** a cloth or pad of material used for polishing an object. **3b** a flexible disc or wheel impregnated with a fine abrasive for polishing metals, etc., with a power tool. **4** *Informal.* one's bare skin (esp. in the phrase **in the buff**). ◆ *vb* **5** to clean or polish (a metal, floor, shoes, etc.) with a buff. **6** to remove the grain surface of (a leather). **[C16:** from Old French *buffle,* from Old Italian *bufalo,* from Late Latin *būfalus* BUFFALO**]**

buff[2] (bʌf) *vb* **1** (*tr*) to deaden the force of. ◆ *n* **2** *Archaic.* a blow or buffet (now only in the phrase **blind man's buff**). **[C15:** back formation from BUFFET[1]**]**

buff[3] (bʌf) *n Informal.* an expert on or devotee of a given subject: *a cheese buff.* **[C20:** originally U.S.: an enthusiastic fire watcher, from the buff-coloured uniforms worn by volunteer firemen in New York City**]**

buffalo ('bʌfə,ləʊ) *n, pl* **-loes** *or* **-lo. 1** Also called: **Cape buffalo.** a member of the cattle tribe, *Syncerus caffer,* mostly found in game reserves in southern and eastern Africa and having upward-curving horns. **2** short for **water buffalo. 3** a U.S. and Canadian name for **bison** (sense 1). Related adj: **bubaline.** ◆ *vb* (*tr*) *U.S. and Canadian informal.* **4** (*often passive*) to confuse. **5** to intimidate. **[C16:** from Italian *bufalo,* from Late Latin *būfalus,* alteration of Latin *būbalus;* see BUBAL**]**

Buffalo ('bʌfə,ləʊ) *n* a port in W New York State, at the E end of Lake Erie. Pop.: 310 548 (1996 est.).

Buffalo Bill *n* nickname of *William Frederick Cody.* 1846–1917, U.S. showman who toured Europe and the U.S. with his famous *Wild West Show.*

buffalo fish *n* any of several freshwater North American hump-backed cyprinoid fishes of the genus *Ictiobus:* family *Catostomidae* (suckers).

buffalo gnat *n* any of various small North American blood-sucking dipterous insects of the genus *Simulium* and related genera: family *Simuliidae.* Also called: **black fly.**

buffalo grass *n* **1** a short grass, *Buchloë dactyloides,* growing on the dry plains of the central U.S. **2** *Austral.* a grass, *Stenotaphrum americanum,* introduced from North America.

buffer[1] ('bʌfə) *n* **1** one of a pair of spring-loaded steel pads attached at both ends of railway vehicles and at the end of a railway track to reduce shock due to contact. **2** a person or thing that lessens shock or protects from damaging impact, circumstances, etc. **3** *Chem.* **3a** an ionic compound, usually a salt of a weak acid or base, added to a solution to resist changes in its acidity or alkalinity and thus stabilize its pH. **3b** Also called: **buffer solution.** a solution containing such a compound. **4** *Computing.* a memory device for temporarily storing data. **5** *Electronics.* an isolating circuit used to minimize the reaction between a driving and a driven circuit. **6** short for **buffer state.** ◆ *vb* (*tr*) **7** to insulate against or protect from shock; cushion. **8** *Chem.* to add a buffer to (a solution). **[C19:** from BUFF[2]**]**

buffer[2] ('bʌfə) *n* **1** any device used to shine, polish, etc.; buff. **2** a person who uses such a device.

buffer[3] ('bʌfə) *n Brit. informal.* a stupid or bumbling man (esp. in the phrase **old buffer**). **[C18:** perhaps from Middle English *buffer* stammerer**]**

buffer state *n* a small neutral state between two rival powers.

buffer stock *n Commerce.* a stock of a commodity built up by a government or trade organization with the object of using it to stabilize prices.

buffet[1] *n* **1** ('bʊfeɪ). a counter where light refreshments are served. **2** ('bʊfeɪ). **2a** a meal at which guests help themselves from a number of dishes and often eat standing up. **2b** (*as modifier*): *a buffet lunch.* **3** ('bʌfɪt, 'bʊfeɪ). a piece of furniture used from medieval times to the 18th century for displaying plate, etc. and typically comprising one or more cupboards and some open shelves. **4** ('bʌfɪ). *Scot. and northern English dialect.* a kind of low stool, pouffe, or hassock. **[C18:** from French, of unknown origin**]**

buffet[2] ('bʌfɪt) *vb* **-fets, -feting, -feted. 1** (*tr*) to knock against or about; batter: *the wind buffeted the boat.* **2** (*tr*) to hit, esp. with the fist; cuff. **3** to force (one's way), as through a crowd. **4** (*intr*) to struggle; battle. ◆ *n* **5** a blow, esp. with a fist or hand. **6** aerodynamic excitation of an aircraft structure by separated flows. **[C13:** from Old French *buffeter,* from *buffet* a light blow, from *buffe,* of imitative origin**]** ▸ **'buffeter** *n*

Buffet (*French* byfɛ) *n* **Bernard** (bɛrnar). born 1928, French painter and engraver. His works are characterized by sombre tones and thin angular forms.

buffet car ('bʊfeɪ) *n Brit.* a railway coach where light refreshments are served.

buffeting ('bʌfɪtɪŋ) *n* response of an aircraft structure to buffet, esp. an irregular oscillation of the tail.

buffing wheel *n* a wheel covered with a soft material, such as lamb's wool or leather, used for shining and polishing. Also called: **buff wheel.**

bufflehead ('bʌfᵊl,hɛd) *n* a small North American diving duck, *Bucephala* (or *Glaucionetta*) *albeola:* the male has black-and-white plumage and a fluffy head. Also called: **butterball. [C17** *buffle* from obsolete *buffle* wild ox (see BUFF[1]), referring to the duck's head**]**

buffo ('bʊfəʊ; *Italian* 'buffo) *n, pl* **-fi** (-fɪ) *or* **-fos. 1** (in Italian opera of the 18th century) a comic part, esp. one for a bass. **2** Also called: **buffo bass, basso buffo** (*Italian* 'basso 'buffo). a bass singer who performs such a part. **[C18:** from Italian (adj): comic, from *buffo* (n) BUFFOON**]**

Buffon (*French* byfɔ̃) *n* **Georges Louis Leclerc** (ʒɔrʒ lwi ləklɛr), **Comte de.** 1707–88, French encyclopedist of natural history; principal author of *Histoire naturelle* (36 vols., 1749–89), containing the *Époques de la nature* (1777), which foreshadowed later theories of evolution.

buffoon (bə'fuːn) *n* **1** a person who amuses others by ridiculous or odd behaviour, jokes, etc. **2** a foolish person. **[C16:** from French *bouffon,* from Italian *buffone,* from Medieval Latin *būfō,* from Latin: toad**]** ▸ **buf'foonery** *n*

Buffs (bʌfs) *pl n* **the.** the Third Regiment of Foot, esp. the Royal East Kent Regiment. **[C19:** from their buff-coloured facings**]**

buff-tip moth *n* a large European moth, *Phalera bucephala,* having violet-brown buff-tipped forewings held at rest around the body so that it resembles a snapped-off twig.

bug[1] (bʌg) *n* **1** any insect of the order *Hemiptera,* esp. any of the suborder *Heteroptera,* having piercing and sucking mouthparts specialized as a beak (rostrum). See also **assassin bug, bedbug, chinch bug. 2** *Chiefly U.S. and Canadian.* any insect, such as the June bug or the Croton bug. **3** *Informal.* **3a** a microorganism, esp. a bacterium, that produces disease. **3b** a disease, esp. a stomach infection, caused by a microorganism. **4** *Informal.* an obsessive idea, hobby, etc.; craze. **5** *Informal.* a person having such a craze; enthusiast. **6** (*often pl*) *Informal.* an error or fault, as in a machine or system, esp. in a computer or computer program. **7** *Informal.* a concealed microphone used for recording conversations, as in spying. **8** *U.S.* (in poker) a joker used as an ace or wild card to complete a straight or flush. ◆ *vb* **bugs, bugging, bugged.** *Informal.* **9** (*tr*) to irritate; bother. **10** (*tr*) to conceal a microphone in (a room, etc.). **11** (*intr*) *U.S.* (of eyes) to protrude. ◆ See also **bug out. [C16:** of uncertain origin; perhaps related to Old English *budda* beetle**]**

bug[2] (bʌg) *n Obsolete.* an evil spirit or spectre; hobgoblin. **[C14** *bugge,* perhaps from Middle Welsh *bwg* ghost. See also BUGBEAR, BUGABOO**]**

bug[3] (bʌg) *vb* a past tense and past participle of **big**[2].

Bug (*Russian* buk) *n* **1** Also called: **Southern Bug.** a river in E Europe, rising in the W Ukraine and flowing southeast to the Dnieper estuary and the Black Sea. Length: 853 km (530 miles). **2** Also called: **Western Bug.** a river in E Europe, rising in the SW Ukraine and flowing northwest to the River Vistula in Poland, forming part of the border between Poland and the Ukraine. Length: 724 km (450 miles).

bugaboo ('bʌgə,buː) *n, pl* **-boos.** an imaginary source of fear; bugbear; bogey. **[C18:** probably of Celtic origin; compare Cornish *buccaboo* the devil**]**

Buganda (bʊ'gændə) *n* a region of Uganda: a powerful Bantu kingdom from the 17th century.

Bugatti (*Italian* bu'gattɪ) *n* **Ettore** (**Arco Isidoro**) ('ɛttore). 1881–1947, Italian car manufacturer; founder of the Bugatti car factory at Molsheim (1909).

bugbane ('bʌg,beɪn) *n* any of several ranunculaceous plants of the genus *Cimicifuga,* esp. *C. foetida* of Europe, whose flowers are reputed to repel insects.

bugbear ('bʌg,bɛə) *n* **1** a thing that causes obsessive fear or anxiety. **2** (in English folklore) a goblin said to eat naughty children and thought to be in the form of a bear. **[C16:** from BUG[2] + BEAR[2]; compare BUGABOO**]**

bugger ('bʌgə) *n* **1** a person who practises buggery. **2** *Taboo slang.* a person or thing considered to be contemptible, unpleasant, or difficult. **3** *Slang.* a humorous or affectionate term for a man or child: *a silly old bugger; a friendly little bugger.* **4 bugger all.** *Slang.* nothing. ◆ *vb* **5** to practise buggery (with). **6** (*tr*) *Slang, chiefly Brit.* to ruin, complicate, or frustrate. **7** *Slang.* to tire; weary: *he was absolutely buggered.* ◆ *interj* **8** *Taboo slang.* an exclamation of annoyance or disappointment. **[C16:** from Old French *bougre,* from Medieval Latin *Bulgarus* Bulgarian; from the condemnation of the Eastern Orthodox Bulgarians as heretics**]**

bugger about *or* **around** *vb* (*adv*) *Brit. slang.* **1** (*intr*) to fool about and waste time. **2** (*tr*) to create difficulties or complications for (a person).

bugger off *vb* (*intr, adv*) *Brit. taboo slang.* to go away; depart.

buggery ('bʌgərɪ) *n* anal intercourse between a man and another man, a woman, or an animal. Compare **sodomy.**

Buggins' turn ('bʌgɪnz) *or* **Buggins's turn** *n Brit. slang.* the principle of awarding an appointment to members of a group in turn, rather than according to merit. **[C20:** origin unknown**]**

buggy[1] ('bʌgɪ) *n, pl* **-gies. 1** a light horse-drawn carriage having either four wheels (esp. in the U.S. and Canada) or two wheels (esp. in Britain and India). **2** short for **beach buggy. 3** short for **baby buggy. 4** a small motorized vehicle designed for a particular purpose: *golf buggy, moon buggy.* **[C18:** of unknown origin**]**

buggy[2] ('bʌgɪ) *adj* **-gier, -giest. 1** infested with bugs. **2** *U.S. slang.* insane. ▸ **'bugginess** *n*

bughouse ('bʌg,haʊs) *Offensive slang, chiefly U.S.* ◆ *n* **1** a mental hospital or asylum. ◆ *adj* **2** insane; crazy. **[C20:** from BUG[1] + (MAD)HOUSE**]**

bugle[1] ('bjuːgᵊl) *n* **1** *Music.* a brass instrument similar to the cornet but usually without valves: used for military fanfares, signal calls, etc. ◆ *vb* **2** (*intr*) to play or sound (on) a bugle. **[C14:** short for *bugle horn* ox horn (musical instrument), from Old French *bugle,* from Latin *būculus* young bullock, from *bōs* ox**]** ▸ **'bugler** *n*

bugle[2] ('bjuːgᵊl) *n* any of several Eurasian plants of the genus *Ajuga,* esp. *A. reptans,* having small blue or white flowers: family *Labiatae* (labiates). Also called: **bugleweed.** See also **ground pine. [C13:** from Late Latin *bugula,* of uncertain origin**]**

bugle[3] ('bju:gᵊl) *n* a tubular glass or plastic bead sewn onto clothes for decoration. [C16: of unknown origin]

bugleweed ('bju:gᵊl,wi:d) *n* **1** Also called: **water horehound.** *U.S.* any aromatic plant of the genus *Lycopus,* having small whitish or pale blue flowers: family *Labiatae* (labiates). See also **gipsywort. 2** another name for **bugle**[2].

bugloss ('bju:glɒs) *n* any of various hairy Eurasian boraginaceous plants of the genera *Anchusa, Lycopsis,* and *Echium,* esp. *L. arvensis,* having clusters of blue flowers. See also **viper's bugloss.** [C15: from Latin *būglōssa,* from Greek *bouglōssos* ox-tongued, from *bōs* ox + *glōssa* tongue]

bugong ('bu:gɒŋ) *n* another name for **bogong.**

bug out *vb (intr, adv) Slang, chiefly U.S.* to depart hurriedly; run away; retreat.

buhl (bu:l) *adj, n* the usual U.S. spelling of **boulle.**

buhrstone, burstone, *or* **burrstone** ('bɜ:,stəʊn) *n* **1** a hard tough rock containing silica, fossils, and cavities, formerly used as a grindstone. **2** a grindstone or millstone made of this rock. [C18 *burr,* perhaps identical to BURR[1] (alluding to roughness)]

buibui ('buɪ'buɪ) *n* a piece of black cloth worn as a shawl by Muslim women, esp. on the E African coast. [from Swahili]

build (bɪld) *vb* **builds, building, built. 1** to make, construct, or form by joining parts or materials: *to build a house.* **2** *(intr)* to be a builder by profession. **3** *(tr)* to order the building of: *the government builds most of our hospitals.* **4** (foll. by *on* or *upon*) to base; found: *his theory was not built on facts.* **5** *(tr)* to establish and develop: *it took ten years to build a business.* **6** *(tr)* to make in a particular way or for a particular purpose: *the car was not built for speed.* **7** *(intr;* often foll. by *up)* to increase in intensity: *the wind was building.* **8** *Card games.* **8a** to add cards to each other to form (a sequence or set). **8b** *(intr)* to add to the layout of cards on the table from one's hand. ◆ *n* **9** physical form, figure, or proportions: *a man with an athletic build.* ◆ See also **build in, build into, build up.** [Old English *byldan;* related to *bylda* farmer, *bold* building, Old Norse *bōl* farm, dwelling; see BOWER[1]]

builder ('bɪldə) *n* **1** a person who builds, esp. one who contracts for and supervises the construction or repair of buildings. **2** a substance added to a soap or detergent as a filler or abrasive.

build in *vb (tr, adv)* to incorporate or construct as an integral part: *to build in safety features.*

building ('bɪldɪŋ) *n* **1** something built with a roof and walls, such as a house or factory. **2** the act, business, occupation, or art of building houses, boats, etc.

building and loan association *n* a U.S. name for **building society.**

building block *n* **1** a block of stone or other material, larger than a brick, used in building. **2** a component that fits with others to form a whole: *standardized software building blocks.* **3** another name for **block** (sense 4) (the child's toy).

building line *n* the boundary line along a street beyond which buildings must not project.

building paper *n* any of various types of heavy-duty paper that usually consist of bitumen reinforced with fibre sandwiched between two sheets of kraft paper: used in damp-proofing or as insulation between the soil and a road surface.

building society *n* a cooperative organization that accepts deposits of money from savers and uses them to make loans, secured by mortgages, to house buyers. Since 1986 they have been empowered to offer banking services.

build into *vb (tr, prep)* to make (something) a definite part of (a contract, agreement, etc.).

build up *vb (adv)* **1** *(tr)* to construct gradually, systematically, and in stages. **2** to increase, accumulate, or strengthen, esp. by degrees: *the murmur built up to a roar.* **3** *(intr)* to prepare for or gradually approach a climax. **4** *(tr)* to improve the health or physique of (a person). **5** *(tr, usually passive)* to cover (an area) with buildings. **6** *(tr)* to cause (a person, enterprise, etc.) to become better known; publicize: *they built several actresses up into stars.* ◆ *n* **build-up. 7** progressive increase in number, size, etc.: *the build-up of industry.* **8** a gradual approach to a climax or critical point. **9** extravagant publicity or praise, esp. in the form of a campaign. **10** *Military.* the process of attaining the required strength of forces and equipment, esp. prior to an operation.

built (bɪlt) *vb* the past tense and past participle of **build.**

built cane *n Angling.* another name for **split cane.**

built-in *adj* **1** made or incorporated as an integral part: *a built-in cupboard; a built-in escape clause.* **2** essential; inherent. ◆ *n* **3** *Austral.* a built-in cupboard or wardrobe.

built-in obsolescence *n* See **planned obsolescence.**

built-up *adj* **1** having many buildings (esp. in the phrase **built-up area**). **2** increased by the addition of parts: *built-up heels.*

Buitenzorg *(Dutch* 'bœitənzɔrx) *n* the former name of **Bogor.**

Bujumbura (,bu:dʒəm'bʊərə) *n* the capital of Burundi, a port at the NE end of Lake Tanganyika. Pop.: 300 000 (1994 est.). Former name: **Usumbura.**

Bukavu (bu:'kɑ:vu:) *n* a port in E Democratic Republic of the Congo (formerly Zaïre), on Lake Kivu: commercial and industrial centre. Pop.: 201 569 (1994 est.). Former name (until 1966): **Costermansville.**

Bukhara *or* **Bokhara** (bʊ'xɑ:rə) *n* **1** a city in S Uzbekistan. Pop.: 236 000 (1993 est.). **2** a former emirate of central Asia: a powerful kingdom and centre of Islam; became a territory of the Soviet Union (1920) and was divided between the former Uzbek, Tajik, and Turkmen Soviet Socialist Republics.

Bukhara rug *or* **Bokhara rug** *n* a kind of rug, typically having a black-and-white geometrical pattern on a reddish ground.

Bukharin *(Russian* bu'xarin) *n* **Nikolai Ivanovich** (nika'laj i'vanəvitʃ). 1888–1938, Soviet Bolshevik leader: executed in one of Stalin's purges.

Bukovina *or* **Bucovina** (,bu:kə'vi:nə) *n* a region of E central Europe, part of the NE Carpathians: the north was seized by the Soviet Union (1940) and later became part of the Ukraine; the south remained Romanian.

Bul (bu:l) *n* the eighth month of the Old Hebrew calendar, corresponding to Heshvan of the Babylonian or post-exilic Jewish calendar: a period from mid-October to mid-November. [from Hebrew *būl,* of Canaanite origin]

bul. *abbrev. for* bulletin.

Bulawayo (,bulə'weɪəʊ) *n* a city in SW Zimbabwe founded (1893) on the site of the kraal of Lobengula, the last Matabele king; the country's main industrial centre. Pop.: 620 936 (1992).

bulb (bʌlb) *n* **1** a rounded organ of vegetative reproduction in plants such as the tulip and onion: a flattened stem bearing a central shoot surrounded by fleshy nutritive inner leaves and thin brown outer leaves. Compare **corm. 2** a plant, such as a hyacinth or daffodil, that grows from a bulb. **3** See **light bulb. 4** a rounded part of an instrument such as a syringe or thermometer. **5** *Anatomy.* a rounded expansion of a cylindrical organ or part, such as the medulla oblongata. **6** Also called: **bulbous bow.** a bulbous protuberance at the forefoot of a ship to reduce turbulence. [C16: from Latin *bulbus,* from Greek *bolbos* onion]

bulbar ('bʌlbə) *adj Chiefly anatomy.* of or relating to a bulb, esp. the medulla oblongata.

bulb fly *n* a hoverfly the larvae of which live in bulbs and can become serious pests, esp. the yellow and black **narcissus bulb fly** *(Meridon equestris).*

bulbiferous (bʌl'bɪfərəs) *adj* (of plants) producing bulbs.

bulbil ('bʌlbɪl) *or* **bulbel** ('bʌlbᵊl) *n* **1** a small bulblike organ of vegetative reproduction growing in leaf axils or on flower stalks of plants such as the onion and tiger lily. **2** any small bulb of a plant. **3** any small bulblike structure in an animal. [C19: from New Latin *bulbillus,* from Latin *bulbus* BULB]

bulb mite *n* a widespread mite, *Rhizaglophus eclinops,* that tunnels in the bulbs of lilies and other plants.

bulbous ('bʌlbəs) *adj* **1** shaped like a bulb; swollen; bulging. **2** growing from or bearing bulbs. ► **'bulbously** *adv*

bulbul ('bʊlbʊl) *n* **1** any songbird of the family *Pycnonotidae* of tropical Africa and Asia, having brown plumage and, in many species, a distinct crest. **2** a songbird, taken to be the nightingale, often mentioned in Persian poetry. [C18: via Persian from Arabic]

Bulg. *abbrev. for* Bulgaria(n).

Bulgakov *(Russian* bul'gakəf) *n* **Mikhail Afanaseyev** (ʌfʌ'nasjef). 1891–1940, Soviet novelist, dramatist, and short-story writer; his novels include *The Master and Margerita* (1966–67).

Bulganin *(Russian* bul'ganin) *n* **Nikolai Aleksandrovich** (nika'laj alɪk'sandrəvitʃ). 1895–1975, Soviet statesman and military leader; chairman of the council of ministers (1955–58).

Bulgar ('bʌlgɑ:, 'bʊl-) *n* **1** a member of a group of non-Indo-European peoples that settled in SE Europe in the late 7th century A.D. and adopted the language and culture of their Slavonic subjects. **2** a rare name for a **Bulgarian.**

Bulgaria (bʌl'gɛərɪə, bʊl-) *n* a republic in SE Europe, on the Balkan Peninsula on the Black Sea: under Turkish rule from 1395 until 1878; became an independent kingdom in 1908 and a republic in 1946; consists chiefly of the Danube valley in the north, the Balkan Mountains in the central part, separated from the Rhodope Mountains of the south by the valley of the Maritsa River. Language: Bulgarian. Religion: Christian (Bulgarian Orthodox) majority. Currency: lev. Capital: Sofia. Pop.: 8 273 000 (1998 est.). Area: 110 911 sq. km (42 823 sq. miles).

Bulgarian (bʌl'gɛərɪən, bʊl-) *adj* **1** of, relating to, or characteristic of Bulgaria, its people, or their language. ◆ *n* **2** the official language of Bulgaria, belonging to the S Slavonic branch of the Indo-European family. **3** a native, inhabitant, or citizen of Bulgaria.

bulge (bʌldʒ) *n* **1** a swelling or an outward curve. **2** a sudden increase in number or volume, esp. of population. **3 the bulge.** *Brit.* another name for **baby boom. 4** *Brit.* the projecting part of an army's front line; salient. ◆ *vb* **5** to swell outwards. [C13: from Old French *bouge,* from Latin *bulga* bag, probably of Gaulish origin] ► **'bulging** *adj* ► **'bulgingly** *adv* ► **'bulgy** *adj* ► **'bulginess** *n*

Bulge (bʌldʒ) *n* **Battle of the.** (in World War II) the final major German counteroffensive in 1944 when the Allied forces were pushed back into NE Belgium: the Germans were repulsed by Jan. 1945.

bulgur ('bʌlgə) *n* a kind of dried cracked wheat. [C20: from Turkish, from Arabic *burghul,* from Persian]

bulimia (bju:'lɪmɪə) *n* **1** pathologically insatiable hunger, esp. when caused by a brain lesion. **2** Also called: **bulimia nervosa.** a disorder characterized by compulsive overeating followed by vomiting: sometimes associated with anxiety about gaining weight. [C17: from New Latin, from Greek *boulimia,* from *bous* ox + *limos* hunger] ► **bu'limic** *n, adj*

bulk (bʌlk) *n* **1** volume, size, or magnitude, esp. when great. **2** the main part: *the bulk of the work is repetitious.* **3** a large body, esp. of a person: *he eased his bulk out of the chair.* **4** unpackaged cargo or goods. **5** a ship's cargo or hold. **6** *Printing.* **6a** the thickness of a number of sheets of paper or cardboard. **6b** the thickness of a book excluding its covers. **7 in bulk. 7a** in large quantities. **7b** (of a cargo, etc.) unpackaged. ◆ *vb* **8** to cohere or cause to cohere in a mass. **9** to place, hold, or transport (several cargoes of goods) in bulk. **10 bulk large.** to be or seem important or prominent: *the problem bulked large in his mind.* [C15: from Old Norse *bulki* cargo]

USAGE The use of a plural noun after *bulk* was formerly considered incorrect, but is now acceptable.

bulk buying *n* **1** the purchase at one time, and often at a reduced price, of a large quantity of a particular commodity. **2** the purchase of the whole or greater part of the output of a commodity of a country or state by a single buyer, usually another country or state; state trading.

bulk carrier *n* a ship that carries unpackaged cargo, usually consisting of a single dry commodity, such as coal or grain. Also called: **'bulker.**

bulkhead ('bʌlk,hɛd) *n* **1** any upright wall-like partition in a ship, aircraft, vehicle, etc. **2** a wall or partition built to hold back earth, fire, water, etc. [C15: probably from *bulk* projecting framework, from Old Norse *bálkr* partition + HEAD]

bulking ('bʌlkɪŋ) *n* the expansion of excavated material to a volume greater than that of the excavation from which it came.

bulk modulus *n* a coefficient of elasticity of a substance equal to minus the ratio of the applied stress (*p*) to the resulting fractional change in volume (d*V*/*V*) in a specified reference state (d*V*/*V* is the **bulk strain**). Symbol: *K*

bulk up *vb* (*adv*) to increase or cause to increase in size or importance.

bulky ('bʌlkɪ) *adj* **bulkier, bulkiest.** very large and massive, esp. so as to be unwieldy. ▸ **'bulkily** *adv* ▸ **'bulkiness** *n*

bull[1] (bʊl) *n* **1** any male bovine animal, esp. one that is sexually mature. Related adj: **taurine. 2** the uncastrated adult male of any breed of domestic cattle. **3** the male of various other animals including the elephant and whale. **4** a very large, strong, or aggressive person. **5** *Stock Exchange.* **5a** a speculator who buys in anticipation of rising prices in order to make a profit on resale. **5b** (*as modifier*): *a bull market.* Compare **bear**[2] (sense 5). **6** *Chiefly Brit.* short for **bull's-eye** (senses 1, 2). **7** *Slang.* short for **bullshit. 8** short for **bulldog, bull terrier. 9 a bull in a china shop.** a clumsy person. **10 shoot the bull.** *U.S. and Canadian slang.* **10a** to pass time talking lightly. **10b** to boast or exaggerate. **11 take the bull by the horns.** to face and tackle a difficulty without shirking. ◆ *adj* **12** male; masculine: *a bull elephant.* **13** large; strong. ◆ *vb* **14** (*tr*) to raise or attempt to raise the price or prices of (a stock market or a security) by speculative buying. **15** (*intr*) (of a cow) to be on heat. **16** (*intr*) *U.S. slang.* to talk lightly or foolishly. [Old English *bula,* from Old Norse *boli;* related to Middle Low German *bulle,* Middle Dutch *bolle*]

bull[2] (bʊl) *n* a ludicrously self-contradictory or inconsistent statement. Also called: **Irish bull.** [C17: of uncertain origin]

bull[3] (bʊl) *n* a formal document issued by the pope, written in antiquated characters and often sealed with a leaden bulla. [C13: from Medieval Latin *bulla* seal attached to a bull, from Latin: round object]

Bull[1] (bʊl) *n* **the.** the constellation Taurus, the second sign of the zodiac.

Bull[2] (bʊl) *n* **1 John.** 1563–1628, English composer and organist. **2** See **John Bull.**

bull. *abbrev. for* bulletin.

bulla ('bʊlə, 'bʌlə) *n, pl* **-lae** (-liː). **1** a leaden seal affixed to a papal bull, having a representation of Saints Peter and Paul on one side and the name of the reigning pope on the other. **2** an ancient Roman rounded metal or leather box containing an amulet, worn around the neck. **3** *Pathol.* another word for **blister** (sense 1). **4** *Anatomy.* a rounded bony projection. [C19: from Latin: round object, bubble]

bullace ('bʊlɪs) *n* a small Eurasian rosaceous tree, *Prunus domestica insititia* (or *P. insititia*), of which the damson is the cultivated form. See also **plum**[1] (sense 1). [C14: from Old French *beloce,* from Medieval Latin *bolluca,* perhaps of Gaulish origin]

Bullamakanka (ˌbuːləmə'kæŋkə) *n Austral. slang.* an imaginary very remote and backward place.

bullate ('bʌleɪt, -ɪt, 'bʊl-) *adj Botany, anatomy, etc.* puckered or blistered in appearance: *the bullate leaves of the primrose.* [C19: from Medieval Latin *bullātus* inflated, from Latin *bulla* bubble]

bull bars *pl n* a large protective metal grille on the front of some vehicles, esp. four-wheel-drive vehicles.

bullbat ('bʊlˌbæt) *n* another name for **nighthawk** (sense 1).

bulldog ('bʊlˌdɒg) *n* **1** a sturdy thickset breed of dog with an undershot jaw, broad head, and a muscular body. **2** (at Oxford University) an official who accompanies the proctors on ceremonial occasions. **3** *Commerce.* a fixed-interest bond issued in Britain by a foreign borrower.

bulldog ant *n* any large Australian ant of the genus *Myrmecia,* having a powerful stinging bite: subfamily *Ponerinae.* Sometimes shortened to **bull ant.**

bulldog clip *n* a clip for holding papers together, consisting of two T-shaped metal clamps held in place by a cylindrical spring.

bulldoze ('bʊlˌdəʊz) *vb* (*tr*) **1** to move, demolish, flatten, etc., with a bulldozer. **2** *Informal.* to force; push: *he bulldozed his way through the crowd.* **3** *Informal.* to intimidate or coerce. [C19: probably from BULL[1] + DOSE]

bulldozer ('bʊlˌdəʊzə) *n* **1** a powerful tractor fitted with caterpillar tracks and a blade at the front, used for moving earth, rocks, etc. **2** *Informal.* a person who bulldozes.

bull dust *n Austral.* **1** fine dust. **2** *Slang.* nonsense.

bull dyke *n Slang.* a lesbian who is markedly masculine.

bullet ('bʊlɪt) *n* **1a** a small metallic missile enclosed in a cartridge, used as the projectile of a gun, rifle, etc. **1b** the entire cartridge. **2** something resembling a bullet, esp. in shape or effect. **3** *Stock Exchange.* a fixed interest security with a single maturity date. **4** *Commerce.* a security that offers a fixed interest and matures on a fixed date. **5** *Commerce.* **5a** the final repayment of a loan that repays the whole of the sum borrowed, as interim payments have been for interest only. **5b** (*as modifier*): *a bullet loan.* **6** *Brit. slang.* dismissal, sometimes without notice (esp. in the phrases **get** *or* **give the bullet**). **7** *Printing.* see **centred dot. 8 bite the bullet.** See **bite** (sense 14). [C16: from French *boulette,* diminutive of *boule* ball; see BOWL[2]] ▸ **'bullet-ˌlike** *adj*

bulletin ('bʊlɪtɪn) *n* **1** an official statement on a matter of public interest, such as the illness of a public figure. **2** a broadcast summary of the news. **3** a periodical publication of an association, etc. ◆ *vb* **4** (*tr*) to make known by bulletin. [C17: from French, from Italian *bullettino,* from *bulletta,* diminutive of *bulla* papal edict, BULL[3]]

bulletin board *n* **1** the U.S. and Canadian name for **notice board. 2** *Computing.* a facility on a computer network allowing any user to leave messages that can be read by any other user, and to download software and information to the user's own computer.

bulletproof ('bʊlɪtˌpruːf) *adj* **1** not penetrable by bullets: *bulletproof glass.* ◆ *vb* **2** (*tr*) to make bulletproof.

bulletwood ('bʊlɪtˌwʊd) *n* the wood of a tropical American sapotaceous tree, *Manilkara bidentata,* widely used for construction due to its durability and toughness.

bullfight ('bʊlˌfaɪt) *n* a traditional Spanish, Portuguese, and Latin American spectacle in which a matador, assisted by banderilleros and mounted picadors, baits and usually kills a bull in an arena. ▸ **'bullˌfighter** *n* ▸ **'bullˌfighting** *n*

bullfinch[1] ('bʊlˌfɪntʃ) *n* **1** a common European finch, *Pyrrhula pyrrhula:* the male has a bright red throat and breast, black crown, wings, and tail, and a grey-and-white back. **2** any of various similar finches. [C14: see BULL[1], FINCH; probably so called from its stocky shape and thick neck]

bullfinch[2] ('bʊlˌfɪntʃ) *n Brit.* a high thick hedge too difficult for a horse and rider to jump. [C19: perhaps changed from the phrase *bull fence*]

bullfrog ('bʊlˌfrɒg) *n* any of various large frogs, such as *Rana catesbeiana* (**American bullfrog**), having a loud deep croak.

bullhead ('bʊlˌhɛd) *n* **1** any of various small northern mainly marine scorpaenoid fishes of the family *Cottidae* that have a large head covered with bony plates and spines. **2** any freshwater North American catfish of the genus *Ameiurus* (or *Ictalurus*), having a large head bearing several long barbels. **3** a scorpion fish, *Scorpaena guttata,* of North American Pacific coastal waters. **4** *Informal.* a stupidly stubborn or unintelligent person.

bull-headed *adj* blindly obstinate; stubborn, headstrong, or stupid. ▸ **ˌbull-'headedly** *adv* ▸ **ˌbull-'headedness** *n*

bullhead rail *n Railways.* a rail having a cross section with a bulbous top and bottom, the top being larger. Now largely superseded by **flat-bottomed rail.**

bullhorn ('bʊlˌhɔːn) *n* the U.S. and Canadian name for **loud-hailer.**

bullion ('bʊljən) *n* **1** gold or silver in mass. **2** gold or silver in the form of bars and ingots, suitable for further processing. **3** Also called: **bullion fringe.** a thick gold or silver wire or fringed cord used as a trimming, as on military uniforms. [C14 (in the sense: melted gold or silver): from Anglo-French: mint, probably from Old French *bouillir* to boil, from Latin *bullīre*]

bullish ('bʊlɪʃ) *adj* **1** like a bull. **2** *Stock Exchange.* causing, expecting, or characterized by a rise in prices: *a bullish market.* **3** *Informal.* cheerful and optimistic: *the prime minister was in a bullish mood.* ▸ **'bullishness** *n*

bull kelp *n* any of various large brown seaweeds of Pacific and Antarctic waters.

bull mastiff *n* a large powerful breed of dog with a short usually fawn or brindle coat, developed by crossing the bulldog with the mastiff.

bull-necked *adj* having a short thick neck.

bull nose *n* **1** a disease of pigs caused by infection with the bacterium *Actinomyces necrophorus,* characterized by swelling of the snout. **2** a rounded edge of a brick, step, etc. **3** a rounded exterior angle, as where two walls meet.

bull-nosed *adj* having a rounded end.

bullock ('bʊlək) *n* **1** a gelded bull; steer. **2** *Archaic.* a bull calf. ◆ *vb* **3** (*intr*) *Austral. and N.Z. informal.* to work hard and long. [Old English *bulluc;* see BULL[1], -OCK]

bullock's heart *n* another name for **custard apple** (senses 1, 2).

bullocky ('bʊləkɪ) *n, pl* **-ockies.** *Austral. and N.Z. informal.* the driver of a team of bullocks.

bullpen ('bʊlˌpɛn) *n* **1** *U.S. informal.* a large cell where prisoners are confined together temporarily. **2** *Baseball.* a part of a baseball field where relief pitchers warm up.

bullring ('bʊlˌrɪŋ) *n* an arena for bullfighting.

bullroarer ('bʊlˌrɔːrə) *n* a wooden slat attached to a thong that makes a roaring sound when the thong is whirled: used esp. by native Australians in religious rites.

Bull Run *n* **Battles of.** two battles fought at Manassas Junction near a stream named Bull Run, during the American Civil War (July, 1861 and August, 1862), in both of which the Federal army was routed by the Confederates. Also called: **First and Second Manassas.** See also **Manassas.**

bull session *n Informal, chiefly U.S. and Canadian.* an informal discussion, often among men. [C20: from BULL[2]]

bull's-eye *n* **1** the small central disc of a target, usually the highest valued area. **2** a shot hitting this. **3** *Informal.* something that exactly achieves its aim. **4** a small circular or oval window or opening. **5** a thick disc of glass set into a ship's deck, etc., to admit light. **6** the glass boss at the centre of a sheet of blown glass. **7a** a small thick plano-convex lens used as a condenser. **7b** a lamp or lantern containing such a lens. **8** a peppermint-flavoured, usually striped, boiled sweet. **9** *Nautical.* a circular or oval wooden block with a groove around it for the strop of a shroud and a hole at its centre for a line. Compare **deadeye. 10** *Meteorol.* the eye or centre of a cyclone.

bullshit ('bʊlʃɪt) *Taboo slang.* ◆ *n* **1** exaggerated or foolish talk; nonsense. **2** (in the British Army) exaggerated zeal, esp. for ceremonial drill, cleaning, polishing, etc. Usually shortened to **bull.** ◆ *vb* **-shits, -shitting, -shitted. 3** (*intr*) to talk in an exaggerated or foolish manner. ▸ **'bullshitter** *n*

bull snake *n* any burrowing North American nonvenomous colubrid snake of the genus *Pituophis,* typically having yellow and brown markings. Also called: **gopher snake.**

bull's wool *n Austral. and N.Z. informal.* nonsense.

bull terrier *n* a breed of terrier having a muscular body and thick neck, with a short smooth often white coat: developed by crossing the bulldog with various terriers. See also **pit bull terrier, Staffordshire bull terrier.**

bull tongue *n Chiefly U.S.* **1** a heavy plough used in growing cotton, having an almost vertical mouldboard. **2** a plough or cultivator with a single shovel.

bull trout *n* any large trout, esp. the salmon trout.

bullwhip ('bʊlˌwɪp) *n* **1** a long tapering heavy whip, esp. one of plaited rawhide. ◆ *vb* **-whips, -whipping, -whipped. 2** (*tr*) to whip with a bullwhip.

bully[1] ('bʊlɪ) *n, pl* **-lies. 1** a person who hurts, persecutes, or intimidates weaker people. **2** *Archaic.* a hired ruffian. **3** *Obsolete.* a procurer; pimp. **4** *Obsolete.* a fine fellow or friend. **5** *Obsolete.* a sweetheart; darling. ◆ *vb* **-lies, -lying, -lied. 6** (when *tr*, often foll. by *into*) to hurt, intimidate, or persecute (a weaker or smaller person), esp. to make him do something. ◆ *adj* **7** dashing; jolly: *my bully boy.* **8** *Informal.* very good; fine. ◆ *interj* **9** Also: **bully for you, him,** etc. *Informal.* well done! bravo! [C16 (in the sense: sweetheart, hence fine fellow, hence swaggering coward): probably from Middle Dutch *boele* lover, from Middle High German *buole,* perhaps childish variant of *bruoder* BROTHER]

bully[2] ('bʊlɪ) *n* any of various small freshwater fishes of the genera *Gobiomorphus* and *Philynodon* of New Zealand. Also called (N.Z.): **pakoko, titarakura, toitoi.** [C20: short for COCKABULLY]

bully beef *n* tinned corned beef. Often shortened to **bully.** [C19 *bully,* anglicized version of French *bouilli,* from *boeuf bouilli* boiled beef]

bullyboy ('bʊlɪˌbɔɪ) *n* **a** a ruffian or tough, esp. a hired one. **b** (*as modifier*): *bullyboy tactics.*

bully-off *Hockey.* ◆ *n* **1** a method by which a game is restarted after a stoppage. Two opposing players stand with the ball between them and alternately strike their sticks together and against the ground three times before trying to hit the ball. ◆ *vb* **bully off. 2** (*intr, adv*) to restart play after a stoppage with a bully-off. ◆ Often shortened to **bully.** Compare **face-off.** [C19: perhaps from *bully* scrum in Eton football; of unknown origin]

bullyrag ('bʊlɪˌræg) *vb* **-rags, -ragging, -ragged.** (*tr*) to bully, esp. by means of cruel practical jokes. Also: **ballyrag.** [C18: of unknown origin]

bulnbuln ('bʊln'bʊln) *n Austral.* another name for **lyrebird.** [C19: from a native Australian language]

Bülow (*German* 'bylo) *n* Prince **Bernhard von** ('bɛrnhart fɔn). 1849–1929, chancellor of Germany (1900–09).

bulrush ('bʊlˌrʌʃ) *n* **1** a grasslike cyperaceous marsh plant, *Scirpus lacustris,* used for making mats, chair seats, etc. **2** a popular name for **reed mace** (sense 1): the name derived from Alma-Tadema's painting of the finding of the infant Moses in the "bulrushes" —actually reed mace. **3** a biblical word for **papyrus** (the plant). [C15 *bulrish, bul-* perhaps from BULL[1] + *rish* RUSH[2], referring to the largeness of the plant]

Bultmann (*German* 'bʊltman) *n* **Rudolf Karl.** 1884–1976, German theologian, noted for his demythologizing approach to the New Testament.

bulwark ('bʊlwək) *n* **1** a wall or similar structure used as a fortification; rampart. **2** a person or thing acting as a defence against injury, annoyance, etc. **3** (*often pl*) *Nautical.* a solid vertical fencelike structure along the outward sides of a deck. **4** a breakwater or mole. ◆ *vb* **5** (*tr*) to defend or fortify with or as if with a bulwark. [C15: via Dutch from Middle High German *bolwerk,* from *bol* plank, BOLE[1] + *werk* WORK]

Bulwer-Lytton ('bʊlwə'lɪtᵊn) *n* See (1st Baron) **Lytton.**

bum[1] (bʌm) *n Brit. slang.* the buttocks or anus. [C14: of uncertain origin]

bum[2] (bʌm) *Informal.* ◆ *n* **1** a disreputable loafer or idler. **2** a tramp; hobo. **3** an irresponsible, unpleasant, or mean person. **4** a person who spends a great deal of time on a specified sport: *baseball bum.* **5 on the bum. 5a** living as a loafer or vagrant. **5b** out of repair; broken. ◆ *vb* **bums, bumming, bummed. 6** (*tr*) to get by begging; cadge: *to bum a lift.* **7** (*intr;* often foll. by *around*) to live by begging or as a vagrant or loafer. **8** (*intr;* usually foll. by *around*) to spend time to no good purpose; loaf; idle. **9 bum (someone) off.** *U.S. and Canadian slang.* to disappoint, annoy, or upset (someone). ◆ *adj* **10** (*prenominal*) of poor quality; useless. **11** wrong or inappropriate: *a bum note.* [C19: probably shortened from earlier *bummer* a loafer, probably from German *bummeln* to loaf]

bumbailiff (ˌbʌm'beɪlɪf) *n Brit. derogatory.* (formerly) an officer employed to collect debts and arrest debtors for nonpayment. [C17: from BUM[1] + bailiff, so called because he follows hard behind debtors]

bumble[1] ('bʌmbᵊl) *vb* **1** to speak or do in a clumsy, muddled, or inefficient way: *he bumbled his way through his speech.* **2** (*intr*) to proceed unsteadily; stumble. ◆ *n* **3** a blunder or botch. [C16: perhaps a blend of BUNGLE + STUMBLE] ► **'bumbler** *n* ► **'bumbling** *n, adj*

bumble[2] ('bʌmbᵊl) *vb* (*intr*) to make a humming sound. [C14 *bomblen* to buzz, boom, of imitative origin]

bumblebee ('bʌmbᵊlˌbiː) *or* **humblebee** *n* any large hairy social bee of the genus *Bombus* and related genera, of temperate regions: family *Apidae.* [C16: from BUMBLE[2] + BEE[1]]

bumbledom ('bʌmbəldəm) *n* self-importance in a minor office. [C19: after *Bumble,* name of the beadle in Dickens' *Oliver Twist* (1837–38)]

bumble-puppy *n* **1** a game in which a ball, attached by string to a post, is hit so that the string winds round the post. **2** (*modifier*) (of whist or bridge) played unskilfully.

bumboat ('bʌmˌbəʊt) *n* any small boat used for ferrying supplies or goods for sale to a ship at anchor or at a mooring. [C17 (in the sense: scavenger's boat): *bum,* from Dutch *boomschip* canoe (from *bom* tree) + BOAT]

Bumbry ('bʌmbrɪ) *n* **Grace.** born 1937, U.S. soprano and mezzo-soprano.

bumf *or* **bumph** (bʌmf) *n Brit.* **1** *Informal, derogatory.* official documents, forms, etc. **2** *Slang.* toilet paper. [C19: short for earlier *bumfodder;* see BUM[1]]

bumfreezer ('bʌmˌfriːzə) *n* **1** a slang name for an **Eton jacket. 2** *Slang.* any of various similar styles of short jacket worn by men.

bumkin ('bʌmkɪn) *n* a variant spelling of **boomkin.**

bummalo ('bʌməˌləʊ) *n, pl* **-lo.** another name for **Bombay duck.** [C17: from Marathi *bombīla*]

bummaree (ˌbʌmə'riː) *n Brit.* (formerly) **1** a dealer at Billingsgate fish market. **2** a porter at Smithfield meat market. [C18: of unknown origin]

bummer ('bʌmə) *n Slang.* **1** an unpleasant or disappointing experience. **2** *Chiefly U.S.* a vagrant or idler. **3** an adverse reaction to a drug, characterized by panic or fear.

bump (bʌmp) *vb* **1** (when *intr,* usually foll. by *against* or *into*) to knock or strike with a jolt. **2** (*intr;* often foll. by *along*) to travel or proceed in jerks and jolts. **3** (*tr*) to hurt by knocking: *he bumped his head on the ceiling.* **4** (*tr*) to knock out of place; dislodge: *the crash bumped him from his chair.* **5** (*tr*) *Brit.* to throw (a child) into the air, one other child holding each limb, and let him down again to touch the ground. **6** (in rowing races, esp. at Oxford and Cambridge) to catch up with and touch (another boat that started a fixed distance ahead). **7** *Cricket.* to bowl (a ball) so that it bounces high on pitching or (of a ball) to bounce high when bowled. **8** (*intr*) *Chiefly U.S. and Canadian.* to dance erotically by thrusting the pelvis forward (esp. in the phrase **bump and grind**). **9** (*tr*) *Poker.* to raise (someone). **10** (*tr*) *Informal.* to exclude a ticket-holding passenger from a flight as a result of overbooking. ◆ *n* **11** an impact; knock; jolt; collision. **12** a dull thud or other noise from an impact or collision. **13** the shock of a blow or collision. **14** a lump on the body caused by a blow. **15** a protuberance, as on a road surface. **16** any of the natural protuberances of the human skull, said by phrenologists to indicate underlying faculties and character. **17** a rising current of air that gives an aircraft a severe upward jolt. **18** (*pl*) the act of bumping a child. See sense 5. **19** *Rowing.* the act of bumping. See **bumping race. 20 bump ball.** *Cricket.* a ball that bounces into the air after being hit directly into the ground by the batsman. ◆ See also **bump into, bump off, bump up.** [C16: probably of imitative origin]

bumper[1] ('bʌmpə) *n* **1** a horizontal metal bar attached to the front or rear end of a car, lorry, etc., to protect against damage from impact. **2** a person or machine that bumps. **3** *Cricket.* a ball bowled so that it bounces high on pitching; bouncer.

bumper[2] ('bʌmpə) *n* **1** a glass, tankard, etc., filled to the brim, esp. as a toast. **2** an unusually large or fine example of something. ◆ *adj* **3** unusually large, fine, or abundant: *a bumper crop.* ◆ *vb* **4** (*tr*) to toast with a bumper. **5** (*tr*) to fill to the brim. **6** (*intr*) to drink bumpers. [C17 (in the sense: a brimming glass): probably from *bump* (obsolete vb) to bulge; see BUMP]

bumper[3] ('bʌmpə) *n Austral. old-fashioned informal.* a cigarette end. [C19: perhaps from a blend of BUTT[1] and STUMP]

bumper car *n* a low-powered electrically propelled vehicle driven and bumped against similar cars in a special rink at a funfair. Also called: **Dodgem.**

bumper sticker *n* a label affixed to the rear windscreen or bumper of a motor vehicle displaying an advertisement or slogan.

bumph (bʌmf) *n* a variant spelling of **bumf.**

bumping race *n* (esp. at Oxford and Cambridge) a race in which rowing eights start an equal distance one behind the other and each tries to bump the boat in front.

bump into *vb* (*intr, prep*) *Informal.* to meet by chance; encounter unexpectedly.

bumpkin[1] ('bʌmpkɪn) *n* an awkward simple rustic person (esp. in the phrase **country bumpkin**). [C16 (perhaps originally applied to Dutchmen): perhaps from Dutch *boomken* small tree, or from Middle Dutch *boomekijn* small barrel, alluding to a short or squat person]

bumpkin[2] ('bʌmpkɪn) *or* **bumkin** *n* variant spellings of **boomkin.**

bump off *vb* (*tr, adv*) *Slang.* to murder; kill.

bump start *Brit.* ◆ *n* **1** a method of starting a motor vehicle by engaging a low gear with the clutch depressed and pushing it or allowing it to run down a hill until sufficient momentum has been acquired to turn the engine by releasing the clutch. ◆ *vb* **bump-start. 2** (*tr*) to start (a motor vehicle) using this method.

bumptious ('bʌmpʃəs) *adj* offensively self-assertive or conceited. [C19: perhaps a blend of BUMP + FRACTIOUS] ► **'bumptiously** *adv* ► **'bumptiousness** *n*

bump up *vb* (*tr, adv*) *Informal.* to raise or increase: *prices are being bumped up daily.*

bumpy ('bʌmpɪ) *adj* **bumpier, bumpiest. 1** having an uneven surface: *a bumpy road.* **2** full of jolts; rough: *a bumpy flight.* ► **'bumpily** *adv* ► **'bumpiness** *n*

bum rap *n U.S. slang.* **1** a trumped-up or false charge. **2** an unjust punishment.

bum's rush *n Slang.* **1** forcible ejection, as from a gathering. **2** rapid dismissal, as of an idea.

bum steer *n Slang, chiefly U.S.* false or misleading information or advice.

bumsucking ('bʌmˌsʌkɪŋ) *n Brit. taboo slang.* obsequious behaviour; toadying. ► **'bumˌsucker** *n*

bun (bʌn) *n* **1** a small roll, similar to bread but usually containing sweetening, currants, spices, etc. **2** any of various types of small round sweet cakes. **3** a hairstyle in which long hair is gathered into a bun shape at the back of the head. **4 have a bun in the oven.** *Slang.* to be pregnant. [C14: of unknown origin]

Buna ('buːnə, 'bjuː-) *n Trademark.* a synthetic rubber formed by polymerizing butadiene or by copolymerizing it with such compounds as acrylonitride or styrene.

bunch (bʌntʃ) *n* **1** a number of things growing, fastened, or grouped together: a *bunch of grapes; a bunch of keys.* **2** a collection; group: *a bunch of queries.* **3** *Informal.* a group or company: *a bunch of boys.* **4** *Archaic.* a protuberance. ◆ *vb* **5** (sometimes foll. by *up*) to group or be grouped into a bunch. ◆ See also **bunches.** [C14: of obscure origin]

Bunche (bʌntʃ) *n* **Ralph Johnson.** 1904–71, U.S. diplomat and United Nations official: awarded the Nobel peace prize in 1950 for his work as UN mediator in Palestine (1948–49); UN undersecretary (1954–71).

bunches ('bʌntʃɪz) *pl n Brit.* a hairstyle in which hair is tied into two sections on either side of the head at the back.

bunchy ('bʌntʃɪ) *adj* **bunchier, bunchiest. 1** composed of or resembling bunches. **2** bulging. ► **'bunchiness** *n*

bunco *or* **bunko** ('bʌŋkəʊ) *U.S. informal.* ◆ *n, pl* **-cos** *or* **-kos. 1** a swindle, esp. one by confidence tricksters. ◆ *vb* **-cos, -coing, -coed** *or* **-kos, -koing,**

-koed. 2 (*tr*) to swindle; cheat. [C19: perhaps from Spanish *banca* bank (in gambling), from Italian *banca* BANK[1]]

buncombe ('bʌŋkəm) *n* a variant spelling (esp. U.S.) of **bunkum.**

bund (bʌnd) *n* (in India and the Far East) **1** an embankment; dyke. **2** an embanked road or quay. [C19: from Hindi *band,* from Persian; related to Sanskrit *bandha* BAND[1]]

Bund (bund; *German* bunt) *n, pl* **Bunds** *or* **Bünde** (*German* 'byndə). **1** (*sometimes not cap.*) a federation or league. **2** short for **German American Bund,** an organization of U.S. Nazis and Nazi sympathizers in the 1930s and 1940s. **3** an organization of socialist Jewish workers in Russia founded in 1897. **4** the confederation of N German states, which existed from 1867-71. [C19: German; related to BAND[2], BIND]

Bundaberg ('bʌndəˌbɜːg) *n* a city in E Australia, near the E coast of Queensland: centre of a sugar-growing area, with a nearby deep-water port. Pop.: 52 267 (1993).

Bundelkhand (ˌbʌndəl'kʌnd, -'xʌnd) *n* a region of central India: formerly native states, now mainly part of Madhya Pradesh.

Bundesrat ('bundəsˌrɑːt) *n* **1** (in Germany and formerly in West Germany) the council of state ministers with certain legislative and administrative powers, representing the state governments at federal level. **2** (in Austria) an assembly with some legislative power that represents state interests at the federal level. **3** (in Switzerland) the executive council of the confederation. **4** (in the German empire from 1871–1918) the council representing the governments of the constituent states, with administrative, judicial, and legislative powers. [C19: German, from *Bund* federation + *Rat* council]

Bundestag ('bundəsˌtɑːg) *n* (in Germany and formerly in West Germany) the legislative assembly, which is elected by universal adult suffrage and elects the federal chancellor. [C19: German, from *Bund* federation + *-tag,* from *tagen* to meet]

bundh (bʌnd) *n* a variant spelling of **bandh.**

bundle ('bʌndəl) *n* **1** a number of things or a quantity of material gathered or loosely bound together: *a bundle of sticks.* Related adj: **fascicular. 2** something wrapped or tied for carrying; package. **3** *Slang.* a large sum of money. **4 go a bundle on.** *Slang.* to be extremely fond of. **5** *Biology.* a collection of strands of specialized tissue such as nerve fibres. **6** *Botany.* short for **vascular bundle. 7** *Textiles.* a measure of yarn or cloth; 60 000 yards of linen yarn; 5 or 10 pounds of cotton hanks. **8 drop one's bundle.** *Austral. and N.Z. slang.* to panic or give up hope. ◆ *vb* **9** (*tr;* often foll. by *up*) to make into a bundle. **10** (foll. by *out, off, into,* etc.) to go or cause to go, esp. roughly or unceremoniously: *we bundled him out of the house.* **11** (*tr;* usually foll. by *into*) to push or throw, esp. quickly and untidily: *to bundle shirts into a drawer.* **12** (*tr*) to sell (computer hardware and software) as one indivisible package. **13** (*tr*) to give away (a relatively cheap product) when selling an expensive one to attract business: *several free cassettes are often bundled with music centres.* **14** (*intr*) to sleep or lie in one's clothes on the same bed as one's betrothed: formerly a custom in New England, Wales, and elsewhere. [C14: probably from Middle Dutch *bundel;* related to Old English *bindele* bandage; see BIND, BOND] ► **'bundler** *n*

bundle up *vb* (*adv*) **1** to dress (somebody) warmly and snugly. **2** (*tr*) to make (something) into a bundle or bundles, esp. by tying.

bundobust ('bʌndəbʌst) *n* a variant spelling of **bandobust.**

bundu ('bundu) *n S. African and Zimbabwean slang.* **a** a largely uninhabited wild region far from towns. **b** (*as modifier*): *a bundu hat.* [C20: from a Bantu language]

bundwall ('bʌndˌwɔːl) *n* a concrete or earth wall surrounding a storage tank containing crude oil or its refined product, designed to hold the contents of the tank in the event of a rupture or leak. [C20: from BUND + WALL]

bundy ('bʌndɪ) *n, pl* **-dies.** *Austral.* **1** a time clock. ◆ *vb* **2** (*intr;* foll. by *on* or *off*) to arrive or depart from work, esp. when it involves registering the time of arrival or departure on a card. [from a trademark]

bun fight *n Brit. slang.* **1** a tea party. **2** *Ironic.* an official function.

bung[1] (bʌŋ) *n* **1** a stopper, esp. of cork or rubber, for a cask, piece of laboratory glassware, etc. **2** short for **bunghole.** ◆ *vb* (*tr*) **3** (often foll. by *up*) to close or seal with or as with a bung: *the car's exhaust was bunged up with mud.* **4** *Brit. slang.* to throw; sling. [C15: from Middle Dutch *bonghe,* from Late Latin *puncta* PUNCTURE]

bung[2] (bʌŋ) *Brit. slang.* ◆ *n* **1** a gratuity; tip. **2** a bribe. ◆ *vb* **3** (*tr*) to give (someone) a tip or bribe. [C16 (originally in the sense: a purse): perhaps from Old English *pung,* changed through the influence of BUNG[1]]

bung[3] (bʌŋ) *adj Austral. and N.Z. informal.* **1** useless. **2 go bung.** to fail or collapse. [C19: from a native Australian language]

bungalow ('bʌŋgəˌləʊ) *n* **1** a one-storey house, sometimes with an attic. **2** (in India) a one-storey house, usually surrounded by a veranda. [C17: from Hindi *banglā* (house) of the Bengal type]

bungee jumping *or* **bungy jumping** ('bʌndʒɪ) *n* a sport in which a participant jumps from a high bridge, building, etc., secured only by a rubber cord attached to the ankles. [C20: from *bungie,* slang for India rubber, of unknown origin]

bunger ('bʌŋə) *n Austral. slang.* a firework.

bunghole ('bʌŋˌhəʊl) *n* a hole in a cask, barrel, etc., through which liquid can be poured or drained.

bungle ('bʌŋgəl) *vb* **1** (*tr*) to spoil (an operation) through clumsiness, incompetence, etc.; botch. ◆ *n* **2** a clumsy or unsuccessful performance or piece of work; mistake; botch. [C16: perhaps of Scandinavian origin; compare dialect Swedish *bangla* to work without results] ► **'bungler** *n* ► **'bungling** *adj, n*

Bunin (*Russian* 'bunin) *n* **Ivan Alekseyevich** (i'van alɪk'sjejɪvitʃ). 1870–1953, Russian novelist and poet; author of *The Gentleman from San Francisco* (1922).

bunion ('bʌnjən) *n* swelling of the first joint of the big toe, which is displaced to one side. An inflamed bursa forms over the joint. [C18: perhaps from obsolete *bunny* a swelling, of uncertain origin]

bunk[1] (bʌŋk) *n* **1** a narrow shelflike bed fixed along a wall. **2** short for **bunk bed. 3** *Informal.* any place where one sleeps. ◆ *vb* **4** (*intr;* often foll. by *down*) to prepare to sleep: *he bunked down on the floor.* **5** (*intr*) to occupy a bunk or bed. **6** (*tr*) to provide with a bunk or bed. [C19: probably short for BUNKER]

bunk[2] (bʌŋk) *n Informal.* short for **bunkum** (sense 1).

bunk[3] (bʌŋk) *Brit. slang.* ◆ *n* **1** a hurried departure, usually under suspicious circumstances (esp. in the phrase **do a bunk**). ◆ *vb* **2** (usually foll. by *off*) to play truant from (school, work, etc.). [C19: perhaps from BUNK[1] (in the sense: to occupy a bunk, hence a hurried departure, as on a ship)]

bunk bed *n* one of a pair of beds constructed one above the other.

bunker ('bʌŋkə) *n* **1** a large storage container or tank, as for coal. **2** Also called (esp. U.S. and Canadian): **sand trap.** an obstacle on a golf course, usually a sand-filled hollow bordered by a ridge. **3** an underground shelter, often of reinforced concrete and with a bank and embrasures for guns above ground. ◆ *vb* **4** (*tr*) *Golf.* **4a** to drive (the ball) into a bunker. **4b** (*passive*) to have one's ball trapped in a bunker. **5** (*tr*) *Nautical.* **5a** to fuel (a ship). **5b** to transfer (cargo) from a ship to a storehouse. [C16 (in the sense: chest, box): from Scottish *bonkar,* of unknown origin]

Bunker Hill *n* the first battle of the American Revolution, actually fought on Breed's Hill, next to Bunker Hill, near Boston, on June 17, 1775. Though defeated, the colonists proved that they could stand against British regular soldiers.

bunkhouse ('bʌŋkˌhaʊs) *n* (in the U.S. and Canada) a building containing the sleeping quarters of workers on a ranch.

bunko ('bʌŋkəʊ) *n, pl* **-kos,** *vb* **-kos, -koing, -koed.** a variant spelling of **bunco.**

bunkum *or* **buncombe** ('bʌŋkəm) *n* **1** empty talk; nonsense. **2** *Chiefly U.S.* empty or insincere speechmaking by a politician to please voters or gain publicity. [C19: after *Buncombe,* a county in North Carolina, alluded to in an inane speech by its Congressional representative Felix Walker (about 1820)]

bunny ('bʌnɪ) *n, pl* **-nies. 1** Also called: **bunny rabbit.** a child's word for **rabbit** (sense 1). **2** Also called: **bunny girl.** a night-club hostess whose costume includes rabbit-like tail and ears. **3** *Austral. informal.* a mug; dupe. [C17: from Scottish Gaelic *bun* scut of a rabbit]

bunny hug *n* **1** a ballroom dance with syncopated rhythm, popular in America in the early 20th century. **2** a piece of music in the rhythm of this dance.

bunodont ('bjuːnəˌdɒnt) *adj* (of the teeth of certain mammals) having cusps that are separate and rounded. [from Greek *bounos* hill + -ODONT]

bunraku (bun'rɑːkuː) *n* a Japanese form of puppet theatre in which the puppets are usually about four feet high, with moving features as well as limbs and each puppet is manipulated by up to three puppeteers who remain onstage. [C20: Japanese]

buns (bʌnz) *pl n Informal, chiefly U.S.* the buttocks.

Bunsen ('bʌnsən; *German* 'bunzən) *n* **Robert Wilhelm** ('roːbert 'vɪlhelm). 1811–99, German chemist who with Kirchhoff developed spectrum analysis and discovered the elements caesium and rubidium. He invented the Bunsen burner and the ice calorimeter.

Bunsen burner *n* a gas burner, widely used in scientific laboratories, consisting of a metal tube with an adjustable air valve at the base. [C19: named after R. W. BUNSEN]

bunt[1] (bʌnt) *vb* **1** (of an animal) to butt (something) with the head or horns. **2** to cause (an aircraft) to fly in part of an inverted loop or (of an aircraft) to fly in such a loop. **3** *U.S. and Canadian.* (in baseball) to hit (a pitched ball) very gently. ◆ *n* **4** the act or an instance of bunting. [C19: perhaps nasalized variant of BUTT[3]]

bunt[2] (bʌnt) *n Nautical.* the baggy centre of a fishing net or other piece of fabric, such as a square sail. [C16: perhaps from Middle Low German *bunt* BUNDLE]

bunt[3] (bʌnt) *n* a disease of cereal plants caused by smut fungi (genus *Tilletia*). [C17: of unknown origin]

buntal ('bʌntəl) *n* straw obtained from leaves of the talipot palm. [C20: from Tagalog]

bunting[1] ('bʌntɪŋ) *n* **1** a coarse, loosely woven cotton fabric used for flags, etc. **2** decorative flags, pennants, and streamers. **3** flags collectively, esp. those of a boat. [C18: of unknown origin]

bunting[2] ('bʌntɪŋ) *n* any of numerous seed-eating songbirds of the families *Fringillidae* (finches, etc.) or *Emberizidae,* esp. those of the genera *Emberiza* of the Old World and *Passerina* of North America. They all have short stout bills. [C13: of unknown origin]

Bunting ('bʌntɪŋ) *n* **Basil.** 1900–85, British poet, author of *Briggflatts* (1966).

buntline ('bʌntlɪn, -ˌlaɪn) *n Nautical.* one of several lines fastened to the foot of a square sail for hauling it up to the yard when furling. [C17: from BUNT[2] + LINE[1]]

Buñuel (*Spanish* bu'ɲwel) *n* **Luis** (lwis). 1900–83, Spanish film director. He collaborated with Salvador Dali on the first surrealist films, *Un Chien andalou* (1929) and *L'Age d'or* (1930). His later films include *Viridiana* (1961), *Belle de jour* (1966), and *The Discreet Charm of the Bourgeoisie* (1972).

bunya ('bʌnjə) *n* a tall dome-shaped Australian coniferous tree, *Araucaria bidwillii,* having edible cones (**bunya nuts**) and thickish flattened needles. Also called: **bunya-bunya.** [C19: from a native Australian language]

Bunyan ('bʌnjən) *n* **John.** 1628–88, English preacher and writer, noted particularly for his allegory *The Pilgrim's Progress* (1678).

bunyip ('bʌnjɪp) *n Austral.* a legendary monster said to inhabit swamps and lagoons of the Australian interior. [C19: from a native Australian language]

Buonaparte (bwona'parte) *n* the Italian spelling of **Bonaparte.**

Buonarroti (*Italian* bwonar'roti) *n* See **Michelangelo.**

buoy (bɔɪ; *U.S.* 'buːɪ) *n* **1** a distinctively shaped and coloured float, anchored to the bottom, for designating moorings, navigable channels, or obstructions in a body of water. See also **life buoy.** ♦ *vb* **2** (*tr;* usually foll. by *up*) to prevent from sinking: *the belt buoyed him up.* **3** (*tr;* usually foll. by *up*) to raise the spirits of; hearten. **4** (*tr*) *Nautical.* to mark (a channel or obstruction) with a buoy or buoys. **5** (*intr*) to rise to the surface. [C13: probably of Germanic origin; compare Middle Dutch *boeie, boeye;* see BEACON]

buoyage ('bɔɪɪdʒ) *n* **1** a system of buoys. **2** the buoys used in such a system. **3** the providing of buoys.

buoyancy ('bɔɪənsɪ) *n* **1** the ability to float in a liquid or to rise in a fluid. **2** the tendency of a fluid to exert a lifting effect on a body that is wholly or partly submerged in it. **3** the ability to recover quickly after setbacks; resilience. **4** cheerfulness.

buoyancy bags *pl n* another term for **flotation bags.**

buoyant ('bɔɪənt) *adj* **1** able to float in or rise to the surface of a liquid. **2** (of a liquid or gas) able to keep a body afloat or cause it to rise. **3** cheerful or resilient. [C16: probably from Spanish *boyante,* from *boyar* to float, from *boya* buoy, ultimately of Germanic origin]

BUPA ('buːpə) *n acronym for* The British United Provident Association Limited: a company which provides private medical insurance.

bupivacaine (bjuː'pɪvəkeɪn) *n* a local anaesthetic of long duration, used for nerve blocks. [C20: perhaps from BU(TYL) + *pi(pecoloxylidide),* the drug's chemical components + *-vacaine,* from (NO)VOCAINE]

buprenorphine (bjuː'prenɔːfiːn) *n* an opiate used medicinally as a powerful analgesic.

buprestid (bjuː'prestɪd) *n* **1** any beetle of the mainly tropical family *Buprestidae,* the adults of which are brilliantly coloured and the larvae of which bore into and cause damage to trees, roots, etc. ♦ *adj* **2** of, relating to, or belonging to the family *Buprestidae.* [C19: from Latin *buprestis* poisonous beetle, causing the cattle who eat it to swell up, from Greek, from *bous* ox + *prēthein* to swell up]

bur (bɜː) *n* **1** a seed vessel or flower head, as of burdock, having hooks or prickles. **2** any plant that produces burs. **3** a person or thing that clings like a bur. **4** a small surgical or dental drill. **5** a variant spelling of **burr**[3], **burr**[4]. ♦ *vb* **burs, burring, burred. 6** (*tr*) to remove burs from. ♦ Also (for senses 1–4, 6): **burr.** [C14: probably of Scandinavian origin; compare Danish *burre* bur, Swedish *kardborre* burdock]

BUR *international car registration for* Myanmar (Burma).

Bur. *abbrev. for* Burma (now called Myanmar).

buran (buː'rɑːn) *or* **bura** (buː'rɑː) *n* (in central Asia) **1** a blizzard, with the wind blowing from the north and reaching gale force. **2** a summer wind from the north, causing dust storms. [C19: from Russian, of Turkic origin; related to Kazan Tatar *buran*]

Buraydah *or* **Buraida** (bu'raɪdə) *n* a town and oasis in central Saudi Arabia. Pop.: 69 940 (latest est.).

Burbage ('bɜːbɪdʒ) *n* **1 James.** ?1530–97, English actor and theatre manager, who built (1576) the first theatre in England. **2** his son, **Richard.** ?1567–1619, English actor, associated with Shakespeare.

Burberry ('bɜːbərɪ) *n, pl* **-ries.** *Trademark.* a light good-quality raincoat, esp. of gabardine.

burble ('bɜːbᵊl) *vb* **1** to make or utter with a bubbling sound; gurgle. **2** (*intr;* often foll. by *away* or *on*) to talk quickly and excitedly. **3** (*intr*) (of the airflow around a body) to become turbulent. ♦ *n* **4** a bubbling or gurgling sound. **5** a flow of excited speech. **6** turbulence in the airflow around a body. [C14: probably of imitative origin; compare Spanish *borbollar* to bubble, gush, Italian *borbugliare*] ▸ **'burbler** *n*

burbot ('bɜːbət) *n, pl* **-bots** *or* **-bot.** a freshwater gadoid food fish, *Lota lota,* that has barbels around its mouth and occurs in Europe, Asia, and North America. [C14: from Old French *bourbotte,* from *bourbeter* to wallow in mud, from *bourbe* mud, probably of Celtic origin]

Burckhardt (*German* 'burkhart) *n* **Jacob Christoph.** 1818–97, Swiss art and cultural historian; author of *The Civilisation of the Renaissance in Italy* (1860).

burden[1] ('bɜːdᵊn) *n* **1** something that is carried; load. **2** something that is exacting, oppressive, or difficult to bear: *the burden of responsibility.* Related adj: **onerous. 3** *Nautical.* **3a** the cargo capacity of a ship. **3b** the weight of a ship's cargo. ♦ *vb* (*tr*) **4** (sometimes foll. by *up*) to put or impose a burden on; load. **5** to weigh down; oppress: *the old woman was burdened with cares.* [Old English *byrthen;* related to *beran* to BEAR[1], Old Frisian *berthene* burden, Old High German *burdin*]

burden[2] ('bɜːdᵊn) *n* **1** a line of words recurring at the end of each verse of a ballad or similar song; chorus or refrain. **2** the principal or recurrent theme of a speech, book, etc. **3** another word for **bourdon.** [C16: from Old French *bourdon* bass horn, droning sound, of imitative origin]

burden of proof *n Law.* the obligation, in criminal cases resting initially on the prosecution, to provide evidence that will convince the court or jury of the truth of one's contention.

burdensome ('bɜːdᵊnsəm) *adj* hard to bear; onerous.

burdock ('bɜːˌdɒk) *n* a coarse weedy Eurasian plant of the genus *Arctium,* having large heart-shaped leaves, tiny purple flowers surrounded by hooked bristles, and burlike fruits: family *Compositae* (composites). [C16: from BUR + DOCK[4]]

bureau ('bjʊərəʊ) *n, pl* **-reaus** *or* **-reaux** (-rəʊz). **1** *Chiefly Brit.* a writing desk with pigeonholes, drawers, etc., against which the writing surface can be closed when not in use. **2** *U.S.* a chest of drawers. **3** an office or agency, esp. one providing services for the public. **4a** a government department. **4b** a branch of a government department. [C17: from French: desk, office, originally: type of cloth used for covering desks and tables, from Old French *burel,* from Late Latin *burra* shaggy cloth]

bureaucracy (bjʊə'rɒkrəsɪ) *n, pl* **-cies. 1** a system of administration based upon organization into bureaus, division of labour, a hierarchy of authority, etc.: designed to dispose of a large body of work in a routine manner. **2** government by such a system. **3** government or other officials collectively. **4** any administration in which action is impeded by unnecessary official procedures and red tape.

bureaucrat ('bjʊərəˌkræt) *n* **1** an official in a bureaucracy. **2** an official who adheres to bureaucracy, esp. rigidly. ▸ **ˌbureau'cratic** *adj* ▸ **ˌbureau'cratically** *adv* ▸ **bureaucratism** (bjʊə'rɒkrəˌtɪzəm) *n*

bureaucratize *or* **bureaucratise** (bjʊə'rɒkrəˌtaɪz) *vb* (*tr*) to administer by or transform into a bureaucracy. ▸ **buˌreaucrati'zation** *or* **buˌreaucrati'sation** *n*

burette *or U.S.* **buret** (bjʊ'ret) *n* a graduated glass tube with a stopcock on one end for dispensing and transferring known volumes of fluids, esp. liquids. [C15: from French: cruet, oil can, from Old French *buire* ewer, of Germanic origin; compare Old English *būc* pitcher, belly]

burg (bɜːg) *n* **1** *History.* a fortified town. **2** *U.S. informal.* a town or city. [C18 (in the sense: fortress): from Old High German *burg* fortified town; see BOROUGH]

burgage ('bɜːgɪdʒ) *n History.* **1** (in England) tenure of land or tenement in a town or city, which originally involved a fixed money rent. **2** (in Scotland) the tenure of land direct from the crown in Scottish royal burghs in return for watching and warding. [C14: from Medieval Latin *burgāgium,* from *burgus,* from Old English *burg;* see BOROUGH]

Burgas (*Bulgarian* bur'gas) *n* a port in SE Bulgaria on an inlet of the Black Sea. Pop.: 199 470 (1996 est.).

burgee ('bɜːdʒiː) *n Nautical.* a triangular or swallow-tailed flag flown from the mast of a merchant ship for identification and from the mast of a yacht to indicate its owner's membership of a particular yacht club. [C18: perhaps from French (Jersey dialect) *bourgeais* shipowner, from Old French *borgeis;* see BOURGEOIS[1], BURGESS]

Burgenland (*German* 'burgənˌlant) *n* a state of E Austria. Capital: Eisenstadt. Pop.: 274 000 (1995 est.). Area: 3965 sq. km (1531 sq. miles).

burgeon *or* **bourgeon** ('bɜːdʒən) *vb* **1** (often foll. by *forth* or *out*) (of a plant) to sprout (buds). **2** (*intr;* often foll. by *forth* or *out*) to develop or grow rapidly; flourish. ♦ *n* **3** a bud of a plant. [C13: from Old French *burjon,* perhaps ultimately from Late Latin *burra* shaggy cloth; from the downiness of certain buds]

burger ('bɜːgə) *n Informal.* **a** a short for **hamburger. b** (*in combination*): *a cheeseburger.*

Bürger (*German* 'byrgər) *n* **Gottfried August** ('gɔtfriːt 'august). 1747–94, German lyric poet, noted particularly for his ballad *Lenore* (1773).

burgess ('bɜːdʒɪs) *n* **1** (in England) **1a** a citizen or freeman of a borough. **1b** any inhabitant of a borough. **2** *English history.* a Member of Parliament from a borough, corporate town, or university. **3** a member of the colonial assembly of Maryland or Virginia. [C13: from Old French *burgeis,* from *borc* town, from Late Latin *burgus,* of Germanic origin; see BOROUGH]

Burgess ('bɜːdʒɪs) *n* **1 Anthony,** real name *John Burgess Wilson.* 1917–93, English novelist and critic: his novels include *A Clockwork Orange* (1962), *Tremor of Intent* (1966), *Earthly Powers* (1980), and *Any Old Iron* (1989). **2 Guy.** 1911–63, British spy, who fled to the Soviet Union (with Donald Maclean) in 1951.

burgh ('bʌrə) *n* **1** (in Scotland) a town, esp. one incorporated by charter, that enjoyed a degree of self-government until the local-government reorganization of 1975. **2** an archaic form of **borough** (sense 1). [C14: Scottish form of BOROUGH] ▸ **burghal** ('bɜːgᵊl) *adj*

burgher ('bɜːgə) *n* **1** a member of the trading or mercantile class of a medieval city. **2** a respectable citizen; bourgeois. **3** *Archaic.* a citizen or inhabitant of a corporate town, esp. on the Continent. **4** *S. African history.* **4a** a citizen of the Cape Colony or of one of the Transvaal and Free State republics. **4b** (*as modifier*): *burgher troops.* [C16: from German *Bürger,* or Dutch *burger* freeman of a BOROUGH]

Burghley *or* **Burleigh** ('bɜːlɪ) *n* **William Cecil,** 1st Baron Burghley. 1520–98, English statesman: chief adviser to Elizabeth I; secretary of state (1558–72) and Lord High Treasurer (1572–98).

Burghley House *n* an Elizabethan mansion near Stamford in Lincolnshire: seat of the Cecil family; site of the annual Burghley Horse Trials.

burglar ('bɜːglə) *n* a person who commits burglary; housebreaker. [C15: from Anglo-French *burgler,* from Medieval Latin *burglātor,* probably from *burgāre* to thieve, from Latin *burgus* castle, fortress, of Germanic origin]

burglarize *or* **burglarise** ('bɜːgləˌraɪz) *vb* (*tr*) *U.S. and Canadian.* to break into (a place) and steal from (someone); burgle.

burglary ('bɜːglərɪ) *n, pl* **-ries.** *English criminal law.* the crime of either entering a building as a trespasser with the intention of committing theft, rape, grievous bodily harm, or damage, or, having entered as a trespasser, of committing one or more of these offences. ▸ **burglarious** (bɜː'glɛərɪəs) *adj*

burgle ('bɜːgᵊl) *vb* to commit burglary upon (a house, etc.).

burgomaster ('bɜːgəˌmɑːstə) *n* **1** the chief magistrate of a town in Austria, Belgium, Germany, or the Netherlands; mayor. **2** a popular name for the **glaucous gull.** [C16: partial translation of Dutch *burgemeester;* see BOROUGH, MASTER]

burgonet ('bɜːgəˌnet) *n* a light 16th-century helmet, usually made of steel, with hinged cheekpieces. [C16: from French *bourguignotte,* from *bourguignot* of Burgundy, from *Bourgogne* Burgundy]

burgoo ('bɜːguː, bɜː'guː) *n, pl* **-goos. 1** *Nautical slang.* porridge. **2** *Southern U.S.* **2a** a thick highly seasoned soup or stew of meat and vegetables. **2b** a picnic or gathering at which such soup is served. [C18: perhaps from Arabic *burghul* crushed grain]

Burgos ('bɜːgɒs) *n* a city in N Spain, in Old Castile: cathedral. Pop.: 166 732 (1995 est.).

Burgoyne (bɜː'gɔɪn) *n* **John.** 1722–92, British general in the War of American Independence who was forced to surrender at Saratoga (1777).

burgrave ('bɜːgreɪv) *n* **1** the military governor of a German town or castle, esp. in the 12th and 13th centuries. **2** a nobleman ruling a German town or castle by hereditary right. [C16: from German *Burggraf,* from Old High German *burg* BOROUGH + *grāve* count]

Burgundy ('bɜːgəndɪ) *n, pl* **-dies. 1** a region of E France famous for its wines, lying west of the Saône: formerly a semi-independent duchy; annexed to France in 1482. French name: **Bourgogne. 2 Free County of.** another name for **Franche-Comté. 3** a monarchy (1384–1477) of medieval Europe, at its height including the Low Countries, the duchy of Burgundy, and Franche-Comté. **4 Kingdom of.** a kingdom in E France, established in the early 6th century A.D., eventually including the later duchy of Burgundy, Franche-Comté, and the Kingdom of Provence: known as the Kingdom of Arles from the 13th century. **5a** any red or white wine produced in the region of Burgundy, around Dijon. **5b** any heavy red table wine. **6** (*often not cap.*) a blackish-purple to purplish-red colour. ▸ **Burgundian** (bɜː'gʌndɪən) *adj, n*

burhel ('bʌrəl) *n* a variant spelling of **bharal.**

burial ('bɛrɪəl) *n* the act of burying, esp. the interment of a dead body. [Old English *byrgels* burial place, tomb; see BURY, -AL[2]]

burial ground *n* a graveyard or cemetery.

Buridan's ass ('bjʊərɪdænz) *n Philosophy.* an example intended to show the deficiency of reason. An ass standing equidistant from two identical heaps of oats starves to death because reason provides no grounds for choosing to eat one rather than the other. [named after Jean *Buridan,* 14th-century French philosopher, to whom it was incorrectly attributed]

burier ('bɛrɪə) *n* a person or thing that buries.

burin ('bjʊərɪn) *n* **1** a chisel of tempered steel with a sharp lozenge-shaped point, used for engraving furrows in metal, wood, or marble. **2** an engraver's individual style. **3** *Archaeol.* a prehistoric flint tool with a very small transverse edge. [C17: from French, perhaps from Italian *burino,* of Germanic origin: compare Old High German *boro* auger; see BORE[1]]

burk (bɜːk) *n Brit. slang.* a variant spelling of **berk.**

burka ('bɜːkə) *n* a long enveloping garment worn by Muslim women in public. [C19: from Arabic]

burke (bɜːk) *vb (tr)* **1** to murder in such a way as to leave no marks on the body, usually by suffocation. **2** to get rid of, silence, or suppress. [C19: named after William BURKE, executed in Edinburgh for a murder of this type]

Burke (bɜːk) *n* **1 Edmund.** 1729–97, British Whig statesman, conservative political theorist, and orator, born in Ireland: defended parliamentary government and campaigned for a more liberal treatment of the American colonies; denounced the French Revolution. **2 Robert O'Hara.** 1820–61, Irish explorer, who led the first expedition (1860–61) across Australia from south to north. He was accompanied by W. J. Wills, George Grey, and John King; King alone survived the return journey. **3 William.** 1792–1829, Irish murderer and body snatcher; associate of William Hare.

Burkina-Faso (bɜː'kiːnə'fæsəʊ) *n* an inland republic in W Africa: dominated by Mossi kingdoms (10th–19th centuries); French protectorate established in 1896; became an independent republic in 1960; consists mainly of a flat savanna plateau. Official language: French; Mossi and other African languages also widely spoken. Religion: mostly animist, with a large Muslim minority. Currency: franc. Capital: Ouagadougou. Pop.: 11 266 000 (1998 est.). Area: 273 200 sq. km (105 900 sq. miles). Former name (until 1984): **Upper Volta.** ▸ **Burkinabé** (ˌbɜːkɪnə'beɪ) *adj, n*

Burkitt lymphoma ('bɜːkɪt) *or* **Burkitt's lymphoma** ('bɜːkɪts) *n* a rare type of tumour of the white blood cells, occurring mainly in Africa and associated with infection by Epstein-Barr virus. [named after Dennis *Burkitt* (1911–93), British surgeon who first described the tumour]

burl[1] (bɜːl) *n* **1** a small knot or lump in wool. **2** a roundish warty outgrowth from the trunk, roots, or branches of certain trees. ♦ *vb* **3** *(tr)* to remove the burls from (cloth). [C15: from Old French *burle* tuft of wool, probably ultimately from Late Latin *burra* shaggy cloth] ▸ **'burler** *n*

burl[2] *or* **birl** (bɜːl) *n Informal.* **1** *Scot., Austral., and N.Z.* an attempt; try (esp. in the phrase **give it a burl**). **2** *Austral. and N.Z.* a ride in a car. [C20: perhaps from BIRL[1] in the Scot. sense: a twist or turn]

burlap ('bɜːlæp) *n* a coarse fabric woven from jute, hemp, or the like. [C17: from *borel* coarse cloth, from Old French *burel* (see BUREAU) + LAP[1]]

Burleigh ('bɜːlɪ) *n* a variant spelling of **Burghley.**

burlesque (bɜː'lɛsk) *n* **1** an artistic work, esp. literary or dramatic, satirizing a subject by caricaturing it. **2** a ludicrous imitation or caricature. **3** a play of the 17th–19th centuries that parodied some contemporary dramatic fashion or event. **4** Also: **burlesk.** *U.S. and Canadian theatre.* a bawdy comedy show of the late 19th and early 20th centuries: the striptease eventually became one of its chief elements. Slang name: **burleycue.** ♦ *adj* **5** of, relating to, or characteristic of a burlesque. ♦ *vb* **-lesques, -lesquing, -lesqued. 6** to represent or imitate (a person or thing) in a ludicrous way; caricature. [C17: from French, from Italian *burlesco,* from *burla* a jest, piece of nonsense] ▸ **bur'lesquer** *n*

burley[1] ('bɜːlɪ) *n, vb* a variant spelling of **berley.**

burley[2] ('bɜːlɪ) *n* a light thin-leaved tobacco, grown esp. in Kentucky. [C19: probably from the name *Burley*]

Burlington ('bɜːlɪŋtən) *n* **1** a city in S Canada on Lake Ontario, northeast of Hamilton. Pop.: 129 575 (1991). **2** a city in NW Vermont on Lake Champlain: largest city in the state; University of Vermont (1791). Pop.: 39 127 (1990).

burly ('bɜːlɪ) *adj,* **-lier, -liest.** large and thick of build; sturdy; stout. [C13: of Germanic origin; compare Old High German *burlīh* lofty] ▸ **'burliness** *n*

Burma ('bɜːmə) *n* the former name (until 1989) of **Myanmar.**

bur marigold *n* any plant of the genus *Bidens* that has yellow flowers and pointed fruits that cling to fur and clothing: family *Compositae* (composites). Also called: **beggar-ticks, sticktight.**

Burma Road *n* the route extending from Lashio in Burma (now Myanmar) to Chongqing in China, which was used by the Allies during World War II to supply military equipment to Chiang Kai-shek's forces in China.

Burmese (bɜː'miːz) *adj also* **Burman. 1** of, relating to, or characteristic of Burma (Myanmar), its people, or their language. ♦ *n, pl* **-mese. 2** a native or inhabitant of Burma (Myanmar). **3** the official language of Burma (Myanmar), belonging to the Sino-Tibetan family.

Burmese cat *n* a breed of cat similar in shape to the Siamese but typically having a dark brown or blue-grey coat.

burn[1] (bɜːn) *vb* **burns, burning, burnt** *or* **burned. 1** to undergo or cause to undergo combustion. **2** to destroy or be destroyed by fire. **3** *(tr)* to damage, injure, or mark by heat: *he burnt his hand; she was burnt by the sun.* **4** to die or put to death by fire: *to burn at the stake.* **5** *(intr)* to be or feel hot: *my forehead burns.* **6** to smart or cause to smart: *brandy burns one's throat.* **7** *(intr)* to feel strong emotion, esp. anger or passion. **8** *(tr)* to use for the purposes of light, heat, or power: *to burn coal.* **9** *(tr)* to form by or as if by fire: *to burn a hole.* **10** to char or become charred: *the potatoes are burning in the saucepan.* **11** *(tr)* to brand or cauterize. **12** *(tr)* to cut (metal) with an oxygen-rich flame. **13** to produce by or subject to heat as part of a process: *to burn charcoal.* **14** *Astronomy.* to convert (a lighter element) to a heavier one by nuclear fusion in a star: *to burn hydrogen.* **15** *Card games, chiefly Brit.* to discard or exchange (one or more useless cards). **16** *(tr; usually passive) Informal.* to cheat, esp. financially. **17** *Slang, chiefly U.S.* to electrocute or be electrocuted. **18** *(tr) Austral. slang.* to drive fast (esp. in the phrase **go for a burn**). **19 burn one's bridges** *or* **boats.** to commit oneself to a particular course of action with no possibility of turning back. **20 burn the candle at both ends.** See **candle** (sense 3). **21 burn one's fingers.** to suffer from having meddled or been rash. ♦ *n* **22** an injury caused by exposure to heat, electrical, chemical, or radioactive agents. Burns are classified according to the depth of tissue affected: **first-degree burn:** skin surface painful and red; **second-degree burn:** blisters appear on the skin; **third-degree burn:** destruction of both epidermis and dermis. **23** a mark, e.g. on wood, caused by burning. **24** a controlled use of rocket propellant, esp. for a course correction. **25** a hot painful sensation in a muscle, experienced during vigorous exercise: *go for the burn!* **26** *Austral. and N.Z.* a controlled fire to clear an area of scrub. **27** *Slang.* tobacco or a cigarette. ♦ See also **burn in, burn off, burn out.** [Old English *beornan* (intr), *bærnan* (tr); related to Old Norse *brenna* (tr or intr), Gothic *brinnan* (intr), Latin *fervēre* to boil, seethe]

burn[2] (bɜːn; *Scot.* bʌrn) *n Scot. and northern English.* a small stream; brook. [Old English *burna;* related to Old Norse *brunnr* spring, Old High German *brunno,* Lithuanian *briáutis* to burst forth]

burned (bɜːnd) *adj Slang.* having been cheated in a sale of drugs.

Burne-Jones (bɜːndʒəʊnz) *n* Sir **Edward.** 1833–98, English Pre-Raphaelite painter and designer of stained-glass windows and tapestries.

burner ('bɜːnə) *n* **1** the part of a stove, lamp, etc., that produces flame or heat. **2** an apparatus for burning something, as fuel or refuse: *an oil burner.*

burnet ('bɜːnɪt) *n* **1** a plant of the rosaceous genus *Sanguisorba* (or *Poterium*), such as *S. minor* (or *P. sanguisorba*) (**salad burnet**), which has purple-tinged green flowers and leaves that are sometimes used for salads. **2 burnet rose.** Also called: **Scotch rose.** a very prickly Eurasian rose, *Rosa pimpinellifolia,* with white flowers and purplish-black fruits. **3 burnet saxifrage.** a Eurasian umbelliferous plant of the genus *Pimpinella,* having umbrella-like clusters of white or pink flowers. **4** a moth of the genus *Zygaena,* having red-spotted dark green wings and antennae with enlarged tips: family *Zygaenidae.* [C14: from Old French *burnete,* variant of *brunete* dark brown (see BRUNETTE); so called from the colour of the flowers of some of the plants]

Burnet (bə'nɛt, 'bɜːnɪt) *n* **1 Gilbert.** 1643–1715, Scottish bishop and historian, who played a prominent role in the Glorious Revolution (1688–89); author of *The History of My Own Times* (2 vols: 1724 and 1734). **2** Sir (**Frank**) **Macfarlane** (mək'fɑːlən). 1899–1985, Australian physician and virologist, who shared a Nobel prize for physiology or medicine in 1960 with P. B. Medawar for their work in immunology. **3 Thomas.** 1635–1715, English theologian who tried to reconcile science and religion in his *Sacred theory of the Earth* (1680–89).

Burnett (bɜː'nɛt) *n* **Frances Hodgson** ('hɒdʒsən). 1849–1924, U.S. novelist, born in England; author of *Little Lord Fauntleroy* (1886) and *The Secret Garden* (1911).

Burney ('bɜːnɪ) *n* **1 Charles.** 1726–1814, English composer and music historian, whose books include *A General History of Music* (1776–89). **2** his daughter, **Frances.** known as *Fanny;* married name *Madame D'Arblay.* 1752–1840, English novelist and diarist: author of *Evelina* (1778). Her *Diaries and Letters* (1768–1840) are of historical interest.

Burnham scale ('bɜːnəm) *n* the salary scale for teachers in English state schools, which is revised periodically. [C20: named after Lord *Burnham* (1862–1933), chairman of the committee that originally set it up]

burn in *vb (tr, adv)* to darken (areas on a photographic print) by exposing them to light while masking other regions.

burning ('bɜːnɪŋ) *adj* **1** intense; passionate. **2** urgent; crucial: *a burning problem.* ♦ *n* **3** a form of heat treatment used to harden and finish ceramic materials or to prepare certain ores for further treatment by calcination. **4** overheating of an alloy during heat treatment in which local fusion or excessive oxide formation and penetration occur, weakening the alloy. **5** the heat treatment of particular kinds of gemstones to change their colour. ▸ **'burningly** *adv*

burning bush *n* **1** any of several shrubs or trees, esp. the wahoo, that have bright red fruits or seeds. **2** another name for **gas plant. 3** any of several plants, esp. kochia, with a bright red autumn foliage. **4** *Old Testament.* the bush that burned without being consumed, from which God spoke to Moses (Exodus 3:2–4).

burning glass *n* a convex lens for concentrating the sun's rays into a small area to produce heat or fire.

burnish ('bɜːnɪʃ) *vb* **1** to make or become shiny or smooth by friction; polish. ♦ *n* **2** a shiny finish; lustre. [C14 *burnischen,* from Old French *brunir* to make brown, from *brun* BROWN] ► '**burnishable** *adj* ► '**burnisher** *n*

Burnley ('bɜːnlɪ) *n* an industrial town in NW England, in E Lancashire. Pop.: 74 661 (1991).

burn off *vb* (*tr, adv*) **1** to clear (land) of vegetation by burning. **2** to get rid of (unwanted gas at an oil well, etc.) by burning. ♦ *n* **burn-off. 3** an act or the process of burning off.

burnous, burnouse, *or U.S.* **burnoose** (bɜː'nuːs, -'nuːz) *n* a long circular cloak with a hood attached, worn esp. by Arabs. [C17: via French *burnous* from Arabic *burnus,* from Greek *birros* cloak] ► **bur'noused** *or U.S.* **bur'noosed** *adj*

burn out *vb* (*adv*) **1** to become or cause to become worn out or inoperative as a result of heat or friction: *the clutch burnt out.* **2** (*intr*) (of a rocket, jet engine, etc.) to cease functioning as a result of exhaustion of the fuel supply. **3** (*tr; usually passive*) to destroy by fire. **4** to become or cause to become exhausted through overwork or dissipation. ♦ *n* **burnout. 5** the failure of a mechanical device from excessive heating. **6** a total loss of energy and interest and an inability to function effectively, experienced as a result of excessive demands upon one's resources or chronic overwork.

Burns (bɜːnz) *n* **Robert.** 1759–96, Scottish lyric poet. His verse, written mostly in dialect, includes love songs, nature poetry, and satires. *Auld Lang Syne* and *Tam o' Shanter* are among his best known poems.

burnsides ('bɜːnˌsaɪdz) *pl n U.S.* thick side whiskers worn with a moustache and clean-shaven chin. [C19: named after General A. E. *Burnside* (1824–81), Union general in the U.S. Civil War]

burnt (bɜːnt) *vb* **1** a past tense and past participle of **burn**[1]. ♦ *adj* **2** affected by or as if by burning; charred. **3** (of various pigments, such as ochre and orange) calcined, with a resultant darkening of colour.

burnt almond *n* a sweet consisting of an almond enclosed in burnt sugar.

burnt offering *n* a sacrificial offering burnt, usually on an altar, to honour, propitiate, or supplicate a deity.

burnt shale *n* carbonaceous shale formed by destructive distillation of oil shale or by spontaneous combustion of shale after it has been some years in a tip: sometimes used in road making.

burnt sienna *n* **1** a reddish-brown dye or pigment obtained by roasting raw sienna in a furnace. **2** a dark reddish-orange to reddish-brown colour.

burnt-tip orchid *n* a small orchid, *Orchis ustulata,* resembling the lady orchid, having dark reddish-brown hoods that give a burnt look to the tip of the flower spike.

burnt umber *n* **1** a brown pigment obtained by heating umber. **2** a dark brown colour.

burn-up *n Slang.* a period of fast driving.

bur oak *n* an E North American oak, *Quercus macrocarpa,* having fringed acorn cups and durable timber.

buroo (bə'ruː, bruː) *n, pl* **-roos.** *Scot. and Irish dialect.* **1** the government office from which unemployment benefit is distributed. **2** the unemployment benefit itself (esp. in the phrase **on the buroo**). [C20: from BUREAU]

burp (bɜːp) *n* **1** *Informal.* a belch. ♦ *vb* **2** (*intr*) *Informal.* to belch. **3** (*tr*) to cause (a baby) to burp to relieve flatulence after feeding. [C20: of imitative origin]

burp gun *n U.S. slang.* an automatic pistol or submachine gun.

burr[1] (bɜː) *n* **1** a small power-driven hand-operated rotary file, esp. for removing burrs or for machining recesses. **2** a rough edge left on a workpiece after cutting, drilling, etc. **3** a rough or irregular protuberance, such as a burl on a tree. **4** *Brit.* a burl on the trunk or root of a tree, sliced across for use as decorative veneer. ♦ *n, vb* **5** a variant spelling of **bur.** ♦ *vb* (*tr*) **6** to form a rough edge on (a workpiece). **7** to remove burrs from (a workpiece) by grinding, filing, etc.; deburr. [C14: variant of BUR]

burr[2] (bɜː) *n* **1** *Phonetics.* an articulation of (r) characteristic of certain English dialects, esp. the uvular fricative trill of Northumberland or the retroflex *r* of the West of England. **2** a whirring sound. ♦ *vb* **3** to pronounce (words) with a burr. **4** to make a whirring sound. [C18: either special use of BUR (in the sense: rough sound) or of imitative origin]

burr[3] *or* **bur** (bɜː) *n* **1** a washer fitting around the end of a rivet. **2** a blank punched out of sheet metal. [C16 (in the sense: broad ring on a spear): variant of *burrow* (in obsolete sense: BOROUGH)]

burr[4]**, buhr,** *or* **bur** (bɜː) *n* **1** short for **buhrstone. 2** a mass of hard siliceous rock surrounded by softer rock. [C18: probably from BUR, from its qualities of roughness]

Burr (bɜː) *n* **Aaron.** 1756–1836, U.S. vice-president (1800–04), who fled after killing a political rival in a duel and plotted to create an independent empire in the western U.S.; acquitted (1807) of treason.

Burra (bʌrə) *n* **Edward (John).** 1905–76, British painter, noted esp. for his depiction of squalid and grotesque subjects.

burramys ('bʌrəmɪs) *n* the very rare mountain pigmy possum, *Burramys parvus,* of Australia. It is about the size of a rat and restricted in habitat to very high altitudes, mainly Mt Hotham, Victoria. Until 1966 it was known only as a fossil.

burrawang ('bʌrəwæŋ) *n* any of several Australian cycads of the genus *Macrozamia,* having an edible nut. [C19: from Mount *Budawang,* New South Wales]

bur reed *n* a marsh plant of the genus *Sparganium,* having narrow leaves, round clusters of small green flowers, and round prickly fruit: family *Sparganiaceae.*

Burrell Collection ('bʌrəl) *n* a gallery in Glasgow, noted for its collection of paintings, textiles, furniture, ceramics, etc. [C20: named after Sir William *Burrell* (1861–1958), Scottish shipping magnate, and his wife Constance, who founded the collection]

Burren ('bʌrən) *n* **the.** a limestone area on the North Clare coast in the Irish Republic, famous for its wild flowers, caves, and dolmens.

burrito (bə'riːtəʊ) *n, pl* **-tos.** *Mexican cookery.* a tortilla folded over a filling of minced beef, chicken, cheese, or beans. [C20: from Mexican Spanish, from Spanish: literally, a young donkey]

burro ('bʊrəʊ) *n, pl* **-ros.** a donkey, esp. one used as a pack animal. [C19: Spanish, from Portuguese, from *burrico* donkey, ultimately from Latin *burrīcus* small horse]

Burroughs ('bʌrəʊz) *n* **1 Edgar Rice.** 1875–1950, U.S. novelist, author of the *Tarzan* stories. **2 William S(eward).** 1914–97, U.S. novelist, noted for his experimental works exploring themes of drug addiction, violence, and homosexuality. His novels include *Junkie* (1953), *The Naked Lunch* (1959), and *Interzone* (1989).

burrow ('bʌrəʊ) *n* **1** a hole or tunnel dug in the ground by a rabbit, fox, or other small animal, for habitation or shelter. **2** a small snug place affording shelter or retreat. ♦ *vb* **3** to dig (a burrow) in, through, or under (ground). **4** (*intr;* often foll. by *through*) to move through by or as by digging: *to burrow through the forest.* **5** (*intr*) to hide or live in a burrow. **6** (*intr*) to delve deeply: *he burrowed into his pockets.* **7** to hide (oneself). [C13: probably a variant of BOROUGH] ► '**burrower** *n*

burrstone ('bɜːˌstəʊn) *n* a variant spelling of **buhrstone.**

burry ('bɜːrɪ) *adj* **-rier, -riest. 1** full of or covered in burs. **2** resembling burs; prickly.

bursa ('bɜːsə) *n, pl* **-sae** (-siː) *or* **-sas. 1** a small fluid-filled sac that reduces friction between movable parts of the body, esp. at joints. **2** *Zoology.* any saclike cavity or structure. [C19: from Medieval Latin: bag, pouch, from Greek: skin, hide; see PURSE] ► '**bursal** *adj*

Bursa ('bɜːsə) *n* a city in NW Turkey: founded in the 2nd century B.C.; seat of Bithynian kings. Pop.: 1 016 760 (1995 est.). Former name: **Brusa.**

bursar ('bɜːsə) *n* **1** an official in charge of the financial management of a school, college, or university. **2** *Chiefly Scot. and N.Z.* a student holding a bursary. [C13: from Medieval Latin *bursārius* keeper of the purse, from *bursa* purse]

bursarial (bɜː'sɛərɪəl) *adj* of, relating to, or paid by a bursar or bursary.

bursary ('bɜːsərɪ) *n, pl* **-ries. 1** Also called: '**bursarˌship.** a scholarship or grant awarded esp. in Scottish and New Zealand schools, universities etc. **2** *Brit.* **2a** the treasury of a college, etc. **2b** the bursar's room in a college.

Burschenschaft *German.* ('bʊrʃənʃaft) *n* a students' fraternity, originally one concerned with Christian ideals, patriotism, etc. [literally: youth association]

burse (bɜːs) *n* **1** *Chiefly R.C. Church.* a flat case used at Mass as a container for the corporal. **2** *Scot.* **2a** a fund providing allowances for students. **2b** the allowance provided. [C19: from Medieval Latin *bursa* purse]

burseraceous (ˌbɜːsə'reɪʃəs) *adj* of, relating to, or belonging to the *Burseraceae,* a tropical family of trees and shrubs having compound leaves and resin or balsam in their stems. The family includes bdellium and some balsams. [C19: from New Latin *Bursera* type genus, named after J. *Burser* (1593–1649), German botanist]

bursicon ('bɜːsɪkɒn) *n* a hormone, produced by the insect brain, that regulates processes associated with ecdysis, such as darkening of the cuticle.

bursiform ('bɜːsɪˌfɔːm) *adj* shaped like a pouch or sac. [C19: from Latin *bursa* bag + -FORM]

bursitis (bɜː'saɪtɪs) *n* inflammation of a bursa, esp. one in the shoulder joint.

burst (bɜːst) *vb* **bursts, bursting, burst. 1** to break or cause to break open or apart suddenly and noisily, esp. from internal pressure; explode. **2** (*intr*) to come, go, etc., suddenly and forcibly: *he burst into the room.* **3** (*intr*) to be full to the point of breaking open. **4** (*intr*) to give vent (to) suddenly or loudly: *to burst into song.* **5** to cause or suffer the rupture of: *to burst a blood vessel.* ♦ *n* **6** a sudden breaking open or apart; explosion. **7** a break; breach; rupture. **8** a sudden display or increase of effort or action; spurt: *a burst of speed.* **9** a sudden and violent emission, occurrence, or outbreak: *a burst of heavy rain; a burst of applause.* **10** a volley of fire from a weapon or weapons. ♦ *adj* **11** broken apart; ruptured: *a burst pipe.* [Old English *berstan;* related to Old Norse *bresta,* Old Frisian *bersta,* Old High German *brestan;* compare BREAK] ► '**burster** *n*

burstone ('bɜːˌstəʊn) *n* a variant spelling of **buhrstone.**

burthen ('bɜːðən) *n, vb* an archaic word for **burden**[1]. ► '**burthensome** *adj*

burton ('bɜːtᵊn) *n* **1** *Nautical.* a kind of light hoisting tackle. **2 go for a burton.** *Brit. slang.* **2a** to be broken, useless, or lost. **2b** to die. [C15: of uncertain origin]

Burton ('bɜːtᵊn) *n* **1** Sir **Richard Francis.** 1821–90, English explorer, Orientalist, and writer who discovered Lake Tanganyika with John Speke (1858); produced the first unabridged translation of *The Thousand Nights and a Night* (1885–88). **2 Richard,** real name *Richard Jenkins.* 1925–84, Welsh stage and film actor: films include *Becket* (1964), *Who's Afraid of Virginia Woolf?* (1966), and *Equus* (1977). **3 Robert,** pen name *Democritus Junior.* 1577–1640, English clergyman, scholar, and writer, noted for his *Anatomy of Melancholy* (1621).

Burton-upon-Trent *n* a town in W central England, in E Staffordshire: famous for brewing. Pop.: 60 525 (1991).

Burundi (bə'rʊndɪ) *n* a republic in E central Africa: inhabited chiefly by the Hutu, Tutsi, and Twa (Pygmy); made part of German East Africa in 1899; part of the Belgian territory of Ruanda-Urundi from 1923 until it became independent in 1962; ethnic violence has continued since independence; consists mainly of high plateaus along the main Nile-Congo dividing range, dropping rapidly to the Great Rift Valley in the west. Official languages: Kirundi and French. Religion: Christian majority. Currency: Burundi franc. Capital: Bujumbura. Pop.: 5 537 000 (1998 est.). Area: 27 731 sq. km (10 707 sq. miles). Former name (until 1962): **Urundi.** ► **Bu'rundian** *adj, n*

burweed ('bɜːˌwiːd) *n* any of various plants that bear burs, such as the burdock.

bury ('bɛrɪ) *vb* **buries, burying, buried.** (*tr*) **1** to place (a corpse) in a grave, usually with funeral rites; inter. **2** to place in the earth and cover with soil. **3** to lose through death. **4** to cover from sight; hide. **5** to embed; sink: *to bury a nail in plaster.* **6** to occupy (oneself) with deep concentration; engross: *to be buried in a book.* **7** to dismiss from the mind; abandon: *to bury old hatreds.* **8 bury the hatchet.** to cease hostilities and become reconciled. **9 bury one's head in the sand.** to refuse to face a problem. [Old English *byrgan* to bury, hide; related to Old Norse *bjarga* to save, preserve, Old English *beorgan* to defend]

Bury ('bɛrɪ) *n* **1** a town in NW England, in Bury unitary authority, Greater Manchester: an early textile centre. Pop.: 62 633 (1991). **2** a unitary authority in NW England, in Greater Manchester. Pop.: 182 200 (1994 est.). Area: 99 sq. km (38 sq. miles).

Buryat *or* **Buriat** (bʊə'jɑːt, bʊərɪ'ɑːt) *n* **1** a member of a Mongoloid people living chiefly in the Buryat Republic. **2** the language of this people, belonging to the Mongolic branch of the Altaic family.

Buryat Republic *or* **Buryatia** (bʊə'jɑːtɪə; *Russian* bu'rjaːtija) *n* a constituent republic of SE central Russia, on Lake Baikal: mountainous, with forests covering over half the total area. Capital: Ulan-Ude. Pop.: 1 053 000 (1995 est.). Area: 351 300 sq. km (135 608 sq. miles).

burying beetle *n* a beetle of the genus *Necrophorous,* which buries the dead bodies of small animals by excavating beneath them, using the corpses as food for themselves and their larvae: family *Silphidae.* Also called: **sexton.**

Bury St Edmunds ('bɛrɪ sənt 'ɛdməndz) *n.* a market town in E England, in Suffolk. Pop.: 31 237 (1991).

bus (bʌs) *n, pl* **buses** *or* **busses. 1** a large motor vehicle designed to carry passengers between stopping places along a regular route. More formal name: **omnibus.** Sometimes called: **motorbus. 2** short for **trolleybus. 3** (*modifier*) of or relating to a bus or buses: *a bus driver; a bus station.* **4** *Informal.* a car or aircraft, esp. one that is old and shaky. **5** *Electronics, computing.* short for **busbar. 6** the part of a MIRV missile payload containing the re-entry vehicles and guidance and thrust devices. **7** *Astronautics.* a platform in a space vehicle used for various experiments and processes. **8 miss the bus.** to miss an opportunity; be too late. ♦ *vb* **buses, busing, bused** *or* **busses, bussing, bussed. 9** to travel or transport by bus. **10** *Chiefly U.S. and Canadian.* to transport (children) by bus from one area to a school in another in order to create racially integrated classes. [C19: short for OMNIBUS]

bus. *abbrev. for* business.

busbar ('bʌzˌbɑː) *n* **1** an electrical conductor, maintained at a specific voltage and capable of carrying a high current, usually used to make a common connection between several circuits in a system. **2** a group of such electrical conductors at a low voltage, used for carrying data in binary form between the various parts of a computer or its peripherals. ♦ Sometimes shortened to **bus.**

bus boy *n U.S. and Canadian.* a waiter's assistant.

busby ('bʌzbɪ) *n, pl* **-bies. 1** a tall fur helmet with a bag hanging from the top to the right side, worn by certain soldiers, usually hussars, as in the British Army. **2** (not in official usage) another name for **bearskin** (the hat). [C18 (in the sense: large bushy wig): perhaps from a proper name]

Busby ('bʌzbɪ) *n* Sir **Matthew,** known as *Matt.* 1909–94, British footballer. He managed Manchester United (1946–69).

busera (bu'sɛrə) *n* **1** a Ugandan alcoholic drink made from millet: sometimes mixed with honey. **2** a porridge made out of millet. [from Rukiga, a language of SW Uganda]

bush[1] (bʊʃ) *n* **1** a dense woody plant, smaller than a tree, with many branches arising from the lower part of the stem; shrub. **2** a dense cluster of such shrubs; thicket. **3** something resembling a bush, esp. in density: *a bush of hair.* **4a** (often preceded by *the*) an uncultivated or sparsely settled area, esp. in Africa, Australia, New Zealand, or Canada: usually covered with trees or shrubs, varying from open shrubby country to dense rainforest. **4b** (*as modifier*): *bush flies.* **5** *Canadian.* an area of land on a farm on which timber is grown and cut. Also called: **bush lot, woodlot. 6** a forested area; woodland. **7** (often preceded by *the*) *Informal.* the countryside, as opposed to the city: *out in the bush.* **8** a fox's tail; brush. **9** *Obsolete.* **9a** a bunch of ivy hung as a vintner's sign in front of a tavern. **9b** any tavern sign. **10 beat about the bush.** to avoid the point at issue; prevaricate. ♦ *adj* **11** *West African informal.* ignorant or stupid, esp. as considered typical of unwesternized rustic life. **12** *U.S. and Canadian informal.* unprofessional, unpolished, or second-rate. **13 go bush.** *Informal, Austral. and N.Z.* **13a** to abandon city amenities and live rough. **13b** to run wild. ♦ *vb* **14** (*intr*) to grow thick and bushy. **15** (*tr*) to cover, decorate, support, etc., with bushes. [C13: of Germanic origin; compare Old Norse *buski,* Old High German *busc,* Middle Dutch *bosch;* related to Old French *bosc* wood, Italian *bosco*]

bush[2] (bʊʃ) *n* **1** Also called (esp. U.S. and Canadian): **bushing.** a thin metal sleeve or tubular lining serving as a bearing or guide. ♦ *vb* **2** to fit a bush to (a casing, bearing, etc.). [C15: from Middle Dutch *busse* box, bush; related to German *Büchse* tin, Swedish *hjulbössa* wheel-box, Late Latin *buxis* BOX[1]]

Bush (bʊʃ) *n* **George.** born 1924, U.S. Republican politician; vice president of the U.S. (1981–89): 41st president of the U.S. (1989–93).

bushbaby ('bʊʃˌbeɪbɪ) *n, pl* **-babies.** any agile nocturnal arboreal prosimian primate of the genera *Galago* and *Euoticus,* occurring in Africa south of the Sahara: family *Lorisidae* (lorises). They have large eyes and ears and a long tail. Also called: **galago.**

bush ballad *n* an old Australian bush poem in a ballad metre dealing with aspects of life and characters in the bush.

bushbashing ('bʊʃˌbæʃɪŋ) *n Austral. and N.Z. slang.* the process of forcing a path through the bush.

bushbuck ('bʊʃˌbʌk) *or* **boschbok** *n, pl* **-bucks, -buck** *or* **-boks, -bok.** a small nocturnal spiral-horned antelope, *Tragelaphus scriptus,* of the bush and tropical forest of Africa. Its coat is reddish-brown with a few white markings.

bush canary *n N.Z.* another name for **brown creeper.**

bush carpenter *n Austral. and N.Z. slang.* a rough-and-ready unskilled workman.

bushcraft ('bʊʃˌkrɑːft) *n Austral. and N.Z.* ability and experience in matters concerned with living in the bush.

bushed (bʊʃt) *adj Informal.* **1** (*postpositive*) extremely tired; exhausted. **2** *Canadian.* mentally disturbed from living in isolation, esp. in the north. **3** *Austral. and N.Z.* lost or bewildered, as in the bush.

bushel[1] ('bʊʃəl) *n* **1** a Brit. unit of dry or liquid measure equal to 8 Imperial gallons. 1 Imperial bushel is equivalent to 0.036 37 cubic metres. **2** a U.S. unit of dry measure equal to 64 U.S. pints. 1 U.S. bushel is equivalent to 0.035 24 cubic metres. **3** a container with a capacity equal to either of these quantities. **4** *U.S. informal.* a large amount; great deal. **5 hide one's light under a bushel.** to conceal one's abilities or good qualities. [C14: from Old French *boissel,* from *boisse* one sixth of a bushel, of Gaulish origin]

bushel[2] ('bʊʃəl) *vb* **-els, -elling, -elled** *or* **-els, -eling, -eled.** (*tr*) *U.S.* to alter or mend (a garment). [C19: probably from German *bosseln* to do inferior work, patch, from Middle High German *bōzeln* to beat, from Old High German *bōzan*] ► **'busheller, 'busheler,** *or* **'bushelman** *n*

bushfire ('bʊʃˌfaɪə) *n* an uncontrolled fire in the bush; a scrub or forest fire.

bushfly ('bʊʃˌflaɪ) *n, pl* **-flies.** any of various small black dipterous flies of Australia, esp. *Musca vetustissima,* that breed in faeces and dung: family *Calliphoridae.*

bush grass *n* a coarse reedlike grass, *Calamagrostis epigejos,* 1–1½ metres (3–4½ ft.) high that grows on damp clay soils in Europe and temperate parts of Asia.

bushhammer ('bʊʃˌhæmə) *n* a hammer with small pyramids projecting from its working face, used for dressing stone. [C19: from German *Bosshammer,* from *bossen* to beat + HAMMER]

bush house *n Chiefly Austral.* a shed or hut in the bush or a garden.

Bushido (ˌbuːʃɪ'dəʊ) *n* (*sometimes not cap.*) the feudal code of the Japanese samurai, stressing self-discipline, courage and loyalty. [C19: from Japanese *bushi* warrior (from Chinese *wushih*) + *dō* way (from Chinese *tao*)]

bushie ('bʊʃɪ) *n* a variant spelling of **bushy**[2].

bushing ('bʊʃɪŋ) *n* **1** another word for **bush**[2] (sense 1). **2** an adaptor having ends of unequal diameters, often with internal screw threads, used to connect pipes of different sizes. **3** a layer of electrical insulation enabling a live conductor to pass through an earthed wall, etc.

Bushire (bjuː'ʃaɪə) *n* a port in SW Iran, on the Persian Gulf. Pop.: 140 615 (1994 est.). Persian name: **Bushehr** (bu'ʃehr).

bush jacket *or* **shirt** *n* a casual jacket or shirt having four patch pockets and a belt.

bush lawyer *n Austral. and N.Z.* **1** any of several prickly trailing plants of the genus *Rubus cissoides.* **2** *Informal.* a person who gives opinions but is not qualified to do so.

bush-line *n N.Z.* the contour at which the growth of the bush ceases.

bush lot *n Canadian.* another name for **bush**[1] (sense 5).

bushman ('bʊʃmən) *n, pl* **-men.** *Austral. and N.Z.* a person who lives or travels in the bush, esp. one versed in bush lore.

Bushman ('bʊʃmən) *n, pl* **-man** *or* **-men. 1** a member of a hunting and gathering people of southern Africa, esp. the Kalahari region, typically having leathery yellowish skin, short stature, and prominent buttocks. **2** any language of this people, belonging to the Khoisan family. [C18: from Afrikaans *boschjesman*]

bushman's singlet *n N.Z.* a sleeveless heavy black woollen singlet, used as working clothing by timber fellers.

bushmaster ('bʊʃˌmɑːstə) *n* a large greyish-brown highly venomous snake, *Lachesis muta,* inhabiting wooded regions of tropical America: family *Crotalidae* (pit vipers).

bush oyster *n Austral., euphemistic.* a bull's testicle when cooked and eaten.

bushpig ('bʊʃˌpɪg) *n* a wild pig, *Potamochoerus porcus,* inhabiting forests in tropical Africa and Madagascar. It is brown or black, with pale markings on the face. Also called: **boschvark.**

bushranger ('bʊʃˌreɪndʒə) *n* **1** *Austral. history.* an escaped convict or robber living in the bush. **2** *U.S.* a person who lives away from civilization; backwoodsman.

bush shrike *n* **1** any shrike of the African subfamily *Malaconotinae,* such as *Chlorophoneus nigrifrons* (**black-fronted bush shrike**). **2** another name for **ant bird.**

bush sickness *n N.Z.* an animal disease caused by mineral deficiency in old bush country. ► **'bush-ˌsick** *adj*

bush tea *n* **1** a leguminous shrub of the genus *Cyclopia,* of southern Africa. **2** a beverage prepared from the dried leaves of any of these plants.

bush telegraph *n* **1** a means of communication between primitive peoples over large areas, as by drum beats. **2** a means of spreading rumour, gossip, etc.

bushtit ('bʊʃˌtɪt) *n* any small grey active North American songbird of the genus *Psaltriparus,* such as *P. minimus* (**common bushtit**): family *Paridae* (titmice).

bush tram *n N.Z.* a railway line in the bush to facilitate the entry of workers and the removal of timber.

bushveld ('bʊʃˌfɛlt, -ˌvɛlt) *n* **the.** an area of low altitude in N South Africa, having scrub vegetation. Also called: **lowveld.**

bushwalking ('bʊʃˌwɔːkɪŋ) *n Austral.* an expedition on foot in the bush.

bushwhack ('bʊʃˌwæk) *vb* **1** (*tr*) *U.S., Canadian, and Austral.* to ambush. **2** (*intr*) *U.S., Canadian, and Austral.* to cut or beat one's way through thick woods. **3** (*intr*) *U.S., Canadian, and Austral.* to range or move around in woods or the bush. **4** (*intr*) *U.S. and Canadian.* to fight as a guerrilla in wild or uncivilized regions. **5** (*intr*) *N.Z.* to work in the bush, esp. at timber felling.

bushwhacker ('bʊʃˌwækə) *n* **1** *U.S., Canadian, and Austral.* a person who travels around or lives in thinly populated woodlands. **2** *Austral. informal.* an unsophisticated person; boor. **3** a Confederate guerrilla during the American Civil War. **4** *U.S.* any guerrilla. **5** *N.Z.* a person who works in the bush, esp. at timber felling.

bush wren *n* a wren, *Xenicus longipes,* occurring in New Zealand: family *Xenicidae.* See also **rifleman** (sense 2).

bushy[1] ('bʊʃɪ) *adj* **bushier, bushiest. 1** covered or overgrown with bushes. **2** thick and shaggy: *bushy eyebrows.* ► **'bushily** *adv* ► **'bushiness** *n*

bushy[2] *or* **bushie** ('bʊʃɪ) *n, pl* **bushies.** *Austral. informal.* **1** a person who lives in the bush. **2** an unsophisticated uncouth person.

busily ('bɪzɪlɪ) *adv* in a busy manner; industriously.

business ('bɪznɪs) *n* **1** a trade or profession. **2** an industrial, commercial, or professional operation; purchase and sale of goods and services: *the tailoring business.* **3** a commercial or industrial establishment, such as a firm or factory. **4** commercial activity; dealings (esp. in the phrase **do business**). **5** volume or quantity of commercial activity: *business is poor today.* **6** commercial policy or procedure: *overcharging is bad business.* **7** proper or rightful concern or responsibility (often in the phrase **mind one's own business**). **8** a special task; assignment. **9** a matter or matters to be attended to: *the business of the meeting.* **10** an affair; matter: *a queer business; I'm tired of the whole business.* **11** serious work or activity: *get down to business.* **12** a complicated affair; rigmarole. **13** *Informal.* a vaguely defined collection or area: *jets, fast cars, and all that business.* **14** Also called: **stage business.** *Theatre.* an incidental action, such as lighting a pipe, performed by an actor for dramatic effect. **15 like nobody's business.** *Informal.* extremely well or fast. **16 mean business.** to be in earnest. **17** a euphemistic word for **defecation** (esp. in the phrase **do one's business**). **18** a slang word for **prostitution.** [Old English *bisignis* solicitude, attentiveness, from *bisig* BUSY + *-nis* -NESS]

business college *n* a college providing courses in secretarial studies, business management, accounting, commerce, etc.

business cycle *n* another name (esp. U.S. and Canadian) for **trade cycle.**

business end *n Informal.* the part of a tool or weapon that does the work, as contrasted with the handle.

businesslike ('bɪznɪsˌlaɪk) *adj* **1** efficient and methodical. **2** earnest or severe.

businessman ('bɪznɪsˌmæn, -mən) *or (fem)* **businesswoman** *n, pl* **-men** *or* **-women.** a person engaged in commercial or industrial business, esp. as an owner or executive.

business park *n* an area specially designated and landscaped to accommodate business offices, warehouses, light industry, etc.

business plan *n* a detailed plan setting out the objectives of a business, the strategy and tactics planned to achieve them, and the expected profits, usually over a period of three to ten years.

business process re-engineering *n* restructuring an organization by means of a radical reassessment of its core processes and predominant competencies. Abbrev.: **BPR.**

busk[1] (bʌsk) *n* **1** a strip of whalebone, wood, steel, etc., inserted into the front of a corset to stiffen it. **2** *Archaic or dialect.* the corset itself. [C16: from Old French *busc,* probably from Old Italian *busco* splinter, stick, of Germanic origin]

busk[2] (bʌsk) *vb (intr) Brit.* to make money by singing, dancing, acting, etc., in public places, as in front of theatre queues. [C20: perhaps from Spanish *buscar* to look for] ► **'busker** *n* ► **'busking** *n*

busk[3] (bʌsk) *vb (tr) Scot. and archaic.* **1** to make ready; prepare. **2** to dress or adorn. [C14: from Old Norse *būask,* from *būa* to make ready, dwell; see BOWER[1]]

buskin ('bʌskɪn) *n* **1** (formerly) a sandal-like covering for the foot and leg, reaching the calf and usually laced. **2** Also called: **cothurnus.** a thick-soled laced half boot resembling this, worn esp. by actors of ancient Greece. **3** (usually preceded by *the*) *Chiefly literary.* tragic drama. [C16: perhaps from Spanish *borzeguí;* related to Old French *bouzequin,* Italian *borzacchino,* of obscure origin]

bus lane *n* one track of a road marked for use by buses only.

busman's holiday ('bʌsmənz) *n Informal.* a holiday spent doing the same sort of thing as one does at work. [C20: alluding to a bus driver having a driving holiday]

Busra *or* **Busrah** ('bʌsrə) *n* variant spellings of **Basra.**

buss (bʌs) *n, vb* an archaic or dialect word for **kiss.** [C16: probably of imitative origin; compare French *baiser,* German dialect *Bussi* little kiss]

Buss (bʌs) *n* **Frances Mary.** 1827–94, British educationalist; a pioneer of secondary education for girls, who campaigned for women's admission to university.

bus shelter *n* a covered structure at a bus stop providing protection against the weather for people waiting for a bus.

bus stop *n* a place on a bus route, usually marked by a sign, at which buses stop for passengers to alight and board.

bust[1] (bʌst) *n* **1** the chest of a human being, esp. a woman's bosom. **2** a sculpture of the head, shoulders, and upper chest of a person. [C17: from French *buste,* from Italian *busto* a sculpture, of unknown origin]

bust[2] (bʌst) *Informal.* ◆ *vb* **busts, busting, busted** *or* **bust. 1** to burst or break. **2** to make or become bankrupt. **3** *(tr)* (of the police) to raid, search, or arrest: *the girl was busted for drugs.* **4** *(tr) U.S. and Canadian.* to demote, esp. in military rank. **5** *(tr) U.S. and Canadian.* to break or tame (a horse, etc.). **6** *(tr) Chiefly U.S.* to punch; hit. ◆ *n* **7** a raid, search, or arrest by the police. **8** *Chiefly U.S.* a punch; hit. **9** *U.S. and Canadian.* a failure, esp. a financial one; bankruptcy. **10** a drunken party. ◆ *adj* **11** broken. **12** bankrupt. **13 go bust.** to become bankrupt. [C19: from a dialect pronunciation of BURST]

bustard ('bʌstəd) *n* any terrestrial bird of the family *Otididae,* inhabiting open regions of the Old World: order *Gruiformes* (cranes, rails, etc.). They have long strong legs, a heavy body, a long neck, and speckled plumage. [C15: from Old French *bistarde,* influenced by Old French *oustarde,* both from Latin *avis tarda* slow bird]

bustee *or* **busti** ('bʌstiː) *n* variant spellings of **basti.**

buster ('bʌstə) *n Slang.* **1** (in combination) a person or thing destroying something as specified: *dambuster.* **2** *U.S. and Canadian.* a term of address for a boy or man. **3** *U.S. and Canadian.* a person who breaks horses. **4** *Chiefly U.S. and Canadian.* a spree, esp. a drinking bout.

bustier ('buːstɪeɪ) *n* a type of close-fitting usually strapless top worn by women.

bustle[1] ('bʌsᵊl) *vb* **1** (when *intr,* often foll. by *about*) to hurry or cause to hurry with a great show of energy or activity. ◆ *n* **2** energetic and noisy activity. [C16: probably from obsolete *buskle* to make energetic preparation, from dialect *busk,* from Old Norse *būask* to prepare] ► **'bustler** *n* ► **'bustling** *adj*

bustle[2] ('bʌsᵊl) *n* a cushion or a metal or whalebone framework worn by women in the late 19th century at the back below the waist in order to expand the skirt. [C18: of unknown origin]

bust-up *Informal.* ◆ *n* **1** a quarrel, esp. a serious one ending a friendship, etc. **2** *Brit.* a disturbance or brawl. ◆ *vb* **bust up** *(adv).* **3** *(intr)* to quarrel and part. **4** *(tr)* to disrupt (a meeting), esp. violently.

busty ('bʌstɪ) *adj* **bustier, bustiest.** (of a woman) having a prominent bust.

busuuti (buː'suːtɪ) *n* a long garment with short sleeves and a square neckline, worn by Ugandan women, esp. in S Uganda. [C20: from Luganda]

busy ('bɪzɪ) *adj* **busier, busiest. 1** actively or fully engaged; occupied. **2** crowded with or characterized by activity: *a busy day.* **3** *Chiefly U.S. and Canadian.* (of a room, telephone line, etc.) in use; engaged. **4** overcrowded with detail: *a busy painting.* **5** meddlesome; inquisitive; prying. ◆ *vb* **busies, busying, busied. 6** *(tr)* to make or keep (someone, esp. oneself) busy; occupy. [Old English *bisig;* related to Middle Dutch *besich,* perhaps to Latin *festīnāre* to hurry] ► **'busyness** *n*

busybody ('bɪzɪˌbɒdɪ) *n, pl* **-bodies.** a meddlesome, prying, or officious person. ► **'busyˌbodying** *n*

busy Lizzie ('lɪzɪ) *n* a balsaminaceous plant, *Impatiens balsamina,* that has pink, red, or white flowers and is often grown as a pot plant.

busy signal *n* U.S. and Canadian equivalent of **engaged tone.**

but[1] (bʌt; *unstressed* bət) *conj (coordinating)* **1** contrary to expectation: *he cut his knee but didn't cry.* **2** in contrast; on the contrary: *I like opera but my husband doesn't.* **3** *(usually used after a negative)* other than: *we can't do anything but wait.* **4** only: *I can but try.* ◆ *conj (subordinating).* **5** *(usually used after a negative)* without it happening or being the case that: *we never go out but it rains.* **6** (foll. by *that*) except that: *nothing is impossible but that we live forever.* **7** *Archaic.* if not; unless. ◆ *sentence connector.* **8** *Informal.* used to introduce an exclamation: *my, but you're nice.* ◆ *prep* **9** except; save: *they saved all but one of the pigs.* **10 but for.** were it not for: *but for you, we couldn't have managed.* ◆ *adv* **11** just; merely: *he was but a child.* **12** *Dialect and Austral.* though; however: *it's a rainy day; warm, but.* **13 all but.** almost; practically: *he was all but dead when we found him.* ◆ *n* **14** an objection (esp. in the phrase **ifs and buts**). [Old English *būtan* without, outside, except, from *be* BY + *ūtan* OUT; related to Old Saxon *biūtan,* Old High German *biūzan*]

but[2] (bʌt) *Scot.* ◆ *n* **1** the outer room of a two-roomed cottage: usually the kitchen. ◆ *prep, adv* **2** in or into the outer part (of a house). Compare **ben**[1]. [C18: from *but* (adv) outside, hence, outer room; see BUT[1]]

butadiene (ˌbjuːtə'daɪiːn) *n* a colourless easily liquefiable flammable gas that polymerizes readily and is used mainly in the manufacture of synthetic rubbers. Formula: CH_2:CHCH:CH_2. Systematic name: **buta-1,3-diene.** [C20: from BUTA(NE) + DI-[1] + -ENE]

but and ben *n Scot.* a two-roomed cottage consisting of an outer room or kitchen (**but**) and an inner room (**ben**).

butane ('bjuːteɪn, bjuː'teɪn) *n* a colourless flammable gaseous alkane that exists in two isomeric forms, both of which occur in natural gas. The stable isomer, *n*-butane, is used mainly in the manufacture of rubber and fuels (such as Calor Gas). Formula: C_4H_{10}. [C19: from BUT(YL) + -ANE]

butanol ('bjuːtəˌnɒl) *n* a colourless substance existing in four isomeric forms. The three liquid isomers are used as solvents for resins, lacquers, etc., and in the manufacture of organic compounds. Formula: C_4H_9OH. Also called: **butyl alcohol.** [C19: from BUTAN(E) + -OL[1]]

butanone ('bjuːtəˌnəʊn) *n* a colourless soluble flammable liquid used mainly as a solvent for resins, as a paint remover, and in lacquers, cements, and adhesives. Formula: $CH_3COC_2H_5$. Also called: **methyl ethyl ketone.** [C20: from BUTAN(E) + -ONE]

butch (bʊtʃ) *Slang.* ◆ *adj* **1** (of a woman or man) markedly or aggressively masculine. ◆ *n* **2** a lesbian who is noticeably masculine. **3** a strong rugged man. [C18: back formation from BUTCHER]

butcher ('bʊtʃə) *n* **1** a retailer of meat. **2** a person who slaughters or dresses meat for market. **3** an indiscriminate or brutal murderer. **4** a person who destroys, ruins, or bungles something. ◆ *vb (tr)* **5** to slaughter or dress (animals) for meat. **6** to kill indiscriminately or brutally. **7** to make a mess of; botch; ruin. [C13: from Old French *bouchier,* from *bouc* he-goat, probably of Celtic origin; see BUCK[1]; compare Welsh *bwch* he-goat]

butcherbird ('bʊtʃəˌbɜːd) *n* **1** a shrike, esp. one of the genus *Lanius.* **2** any of several Australian magpies of the genus *Cracticus* that impale their prey on thorns.

butcher's ('bʊtʃəz) *or* **butcher's hook** *n Brit. slang.* a look. [C19: rhyming slang]

butcher's-broom *n* a liliaceous evergreen shrub, *Ruscus aculeatus,* that has stiff prickle-tipped flattened green stems, which resemble and function as true leaves. The plant was formerly used for making brooms.

butchery ('bʊtʃərɪ) *n, pl* **-eries. 1** the business or work of a butcher. **2** wanton and indiscriminate slaughter; carnage. **3** a less common word for **slaughterhouse.**

Bute[1] (bju:t) *n* an island off the coast of SW Scotland, in Argyll and Bute council area: situated in the Firth of Clyde, separated from the Cowal peninsula by the **Kyles of Bute.** Chief town: Rothesay. Pop.: 8000 (latest est.). Area: 121 sq. km (47 sq. miles).

Bute[2] (bju:t) *n* **John Stuart,** 3rd Earl of Bute. 1713–92, British Tory statesman; prime minister (1762–63).

Butenandt (*German* 'butənant) *n* **Adolf Frederick Johann.** 1903–95, German organic chemist. He shared the Nobel prize for chemistry (1939) for his pioneering work on sex hormones.

butene ('bju:ti:n) *n* a pungent colourless gas existing in four isomeric forms, all of which are used in the manufacture of organic compounds. Formula: C_4H_8. Also called: **butylene.** [C20: from BUT(YL) + -ENE]

butenedioic acid (ˌbju:ti:ndaɪ'əʊɪk) *n* either of two geometrical isomers with the formula HOOCCH:CHCOOH. See **fumaric acid, maleic acid.**

Buteshire ('bju:tˌʃɪə, -ʃə) *n* (until 1975) a county of SW Scotland, consisting of islands in the Firth of Clyde and Kilbrannan Sound: formerly part of Strathclyde region (1975–96), now part of Argyll and Bute council area.

Buthelezi (ˌbutə'leɪzɪ) *n* **Mangosouthu Gatsha** (ˌmæŋgəʊ'su:tu: 'gætʃə), known as *Chief Buthelezi.* born 1928, Zulu leader, chief minister of the KwaZulu territory of South Africa from 1970 until its abolition in 1994; founder of the Inkatha movement and advocate of Zulu autonomy; minister of home affairs from 1994.

butler ('bʌtlə) *n* the male servant of a household in charge of the wines, table, etc.: usually the head servant. [C13: from Old French *bouteillier,* from *bouteille* BOTTLE[1]]

Butler ('bʌtlə) *n* **1 Joseph.** 1692–1752, English bishop and theologian, author of *Analogy of Religion* (1736). **2 Josephine (Elizabeth).** 1828–1906, British social reformer, noted esp. for her campaigns against state regulation of prostitution. **3 Reg,** full name *Reginald Cotterell Butler.* 1913–81, British metal sculptor; his works include *The Unknown Political Prisoner* (1953). **4 R(ichard) A(usten),** Baron Butler of Saffron Walden, known as *Rab Butler.* 1902–82, British Conservative politician: Chancellor of the Exchequer (1951–55); Home Secretary (1957–62); Foreign Secretary (1963–64). **5 Samuel.** 1612–80, English poet and satirist; author of *Hudibras* (1663–78). **6 Samuel.** 1835–1902, British novelist, noted for his satirical work *Erewhon* (1872) and his autobiographical novel *The Way of All Flesh* (1903).

butlery ('bʌtlərɪ) *n, pl* **-leries. 1** a butler's room. **2** another name for **buttery**[2] (sense 1).

butt[1] (bʌt) *n* **1** the thicker or blunt end of something, such as the end of the stock of a rifle. **2** the unused end of something, esp. of a cigarette; stub. **3** *Tanning.* the portion of a hide covering the lower backside of the animal. **4** *U.S. and Canadian informal.* the buttocks. **5** *U.S.* a slang word for **cigarette. 6** *Building.* short for **butt joint** or **butt hinge.** [C15 (in the sense: thick end of something, buttock): related to Old English *buttuc* end, ridge, Middle Dutch *bot* stumpy]

butt[2] (bʌt) *n* **1** a person or thing that is the target of ridicule, wit, etc. **2** *Shooting, archery.* **2a** a mound of earth behind the target on a target range that stops bullets or wide shots. **2b** the target itself. **2c** (*pl*) the target range. **3** a low barrier, usually of sods or peat, behind which sportsmen shoot game birds, esp. grouse. **4** *Archaic.* goal; aim. ◆ *vb* **5** (usually foll. by *on* or *against*) to lie or be placed end on to; abut: *to butt a beam against a wall.* [C14 (in the sense: mark for archery practice): from Old French *but;* related to French *butte* knoll, target]

butt[3] (bʌt) *vb* **1** to strike or push (something) with the head or horns. **2** (*intr*) to project; jut. **3** (*intr;* foll. by *in* or *into*) to intrude, esp. into a conversation; interfere; meddle. **4 butt out.** *Informal, chiefly U.S. and Canadian.* to stop interfering or meddling. ◆ *n* **5** a blow with the head or horns. [C12: from Old French *boter,* of Germanic origin; compare Middle Dutch *botten* to strike; see BEAT, BUTTON] ▸ **'butter** *n*

butt[4] (bʌt) *n* **1** a large cask, esp. one with a capacity of two hogsheads, for storing wine or beer. **2** a U.S. unit of liquid measure equal to 126 U.S. gallons. [C14: from Old French *botte,* from Old Provençal *bota,* from Late Latin *buttis* cask, perhaps from Greek *butinē* chamber pot]

Butt (bʌt) *n* Dame **Clara.** 1872–1936, English contralto.

butte (bju:t) *n Western U.S. and Canadian.* an isolated steep-sided flat-topped hill. [C19: from French, from Old French *bute* mound behind a target, from *but* target; see BUTT[2]]

butter ('bʌtə) *n* **1a** an edible fatty whitish-yellow solid made from cream by churning, for cooking and table use. **1b** (*as modifier*): *butter icing.* Related adj: **butyraceous. 2** any substance with a butter-like consistency, such as peanut butter or vegetable butter. **3 look as if butter wouldn't melt in one's mouth.** to look innocent, although probably not so. ◆ *vb* (*tr*) **4** to put butter on or in. **5** to flatter. ◆ See also **butter up.** [Old English *butere,* from Latin *būtyrum,* from Greek *bouturon,* from *bous* cow + *turos* cheese]

butter-and-eggs *n* (*functioning as sing*) any of various plants, such as toadflax, the flowers of which are of two shades of yellow.

butterball ('bʌtəˌbɔ:l) *n U.S.* **1** another name for **bufflehead. 2** *Informal.* a chubby or fat person.

butter bean *n* a variety of lima bean that has large pale flat edible seeds and is grown in the southern U.S.

butterbur ('bʌtəˌbɜ:) *n* a plant of the Eurasian genus *Petasites* with fragrant whitish or purple flowers, woolly stems, and leaves formerly used to wrap butter: family *Compositae* (composites).

buttercup ('bʌtəˌkʌp) *n* any of various yellow-flowered ranunculaceous plants of the genus *Ranunculus,* such as *R. acris* (meadow buttercup), which is native to Europe but common throughout North America. See also **crowfoot, goldilocks** (sense 2), **spearwort, lesser celandine.**

butterfat ('bʌtəˌfæt) *n* the fatty substance of milk from which butter is made, consisting of a mixture of glycerides, mainly butyrin, olein, and palmitin.

butterfat cheque *n* **the.** *N.Z.* the total annual cash return for operations on a dairy farm.

Butterfield ('bʌtəˌfi:ld) *n* **William.** 1814–1900, British architect of the Gothic Revival; his buildings include Keble College, Oxford (1870) and All Saints, Margaret Street, London (1849–59).

butterfingers ('bʌtəˌfɪŋgəz) *n* (*functioning as sing*) *Informal.* a person who drops things inadvertently or fails to catch things. ▸ **'butterˌfingered** *adj*

butterfish ('bʌtəˌfɪʃ) *n, pl* **-fish** *or* **-fishes. 1** an eel-like blennioid food fish, *Pholis gunnellus,* occurring in North Atlantic coastal regions: family *Pholidae* (gunnels). It has a slippery scaleless golden brown skin with a row of black spots along the base of the long dorsal fin. **2** Also called: **greenbone,** (Maori) **marari.** an edible reef fish, *Coridodax pullus,* of esp. S New Zealand. It has a slippery purplish-grey to olive-green skin and is often found browsing on kelp.

butterflies ('bʌtəˌflaɪz) *pl n Informal.* tremors in the stomach region due to nervousness.

butterfly ('bʌtəˌflaɪ) *n, pl* **-flies. 1** any diurnal insect of the order *Lepidoptera* that has a slender body with clubbed antennae and typically rests with the wings (which are often brightly coloured) closed over the back. Compare **moth.** Related adj: **lepidopteran. 2** a person who never settles with one group, interest, or occupation for long. **3** a swimming stroke in which the arms are plunged forward together in large circular movements. **4** *Commerce.* the simultaneous purchase and sale of traded call options, at different exercise prices or with different expiry dates, on a stock exchange or commodity market. [Old English *buttorflēoge;* the name perhaps is based on a belief that butterflies stole milk and butter]

butterfly bush *n* another name for **buddleia.**

butterfly collar *n* the Irish name for **wing collar.**

butterfly diagram *n Astronomy.* a graphical butterfly-shaped representation of the sunspot density in the 11-year sunspot cycle.

butterfly effect *n* the idea, used in chaos theory, that a very small difference in the initial state of a physical system can make a significant difference to the state at some later time. [C20: from the theory that a butterfly flapping its wings in one part of the world might ultimately cause a hurricane in another part of the world]

butterfly fish *n* any small tropical marine percoid fish of the genera *Chaetodon, Chelmon,* etc., that has a deep flattened brightly coloured body and brushlike teeth: family *Chaetodontidae.* See also **angelfish** (sense 1).

butterfly nut *n* another name for **wing nut.**

butterfly valve *n* **1** a disc that acts as a valve by turning about a diameter, esp. one used as the throttle valve in a carburettor. **2** a non-return valve consisting of two semicircular plates hinged about a common central spindle.

butterfly weed *n* a North American asclepiadaceous plant, *Asclepias tuberosa* (or *A. decumbens*), having flat-topped clusters of bright orange flowers. Also called: **orange milkweed, pleurisy root.**

butterine ('bʌtəˌri:n, -rɪn) *n* an artificial butter made partly from milk.

Buttermere ('bʌtəˌmɪə) *n* a lake in NW England, in Cumbria, in the Lake District, southwest of Keswick. Length: 2 km (1.25 miles).

buttermilk ('bʌtəˌmɪlk) *n* the sourish liquid remaining after the butter has been separated from milk, often used for making scones and soda bread.

butter muslin *n* a fine loosely woven cotton material originally used for wrapping butter.

butternut ('bʌtəˌnʌt) *n* **1** a walnut tree, *Juglans cinerea* of E North America. Compare **black walnut. 2** the oily edible egg-shaped nut of this tree. **3** the hard brownish-grey wood of this tree. **4** the bark of this tree or an extract from it, formerly used as a laxative. **5** a brownish colour or dye. **6** *N.Z.* short for **butternut pumpkin.** ◆ Also called (for senses 1–4): **white walnut.**

butternut pumpkin *n Austral.* a variety of pumpkin, eaten as vegetable. Also called (N.Z.): **butternut.**

butterscotch ('bʌtəˌskɒtʃ) *n* **1** a kind of hard brittle toffee made with butter, brown sugar, etc. **2a** a flavouring made from these ingredients. **2b** (*as modifier*): *butterscotch icing.* [C19: perhaps first made in Scotland]

butter up *vb* (*tr, adv*) to flatter.

butterwort ('bʌtəˌwɜ:t) *n* a plant of the genus *Pinguicula,* esp. *P. vulgaris,* that grows in wet places and has violet-blue spurred flowers and fleshy greasy glandular leaves on which insects are trapped and digested: family *Lentibulariaceae.*

Butterworth ('bʌtəwəθ) *n* **George.** 1885–1916, British composer, noted for his interest in folk song and his settings of Housman's poems.

buttery[1] ('bʌtərɪ) *adj* **1** containing, like, or coated with butter. **2** *Informal.* grossly or insincerely flattering; obsequious. ▸ **'butteriness** *n*

buttery[2] ('bʌtərɪ) *n, pl* **-teries. 1** a room for storing foods or wines. **2** *Brit.* (in some universities) a room in which food is supplied or sold to students. [C14: from Anglo-French *boterie,* from Anglo-Latin *buteria,* probably from *butta* cask, BUTT[4]]

butt hinge *n* a hinge made of two matching leaves, one recessed into a door and the other into the jamb so that they are in contact when the door is shut. Sometimes shortened to **butt.**

butt joint *n* a joint between two plates, planks, bars, sections, etc., when the components are butted together and do not overlap or interlock. The joint may be strapped with jointing plates laid across it or welded (**butt weld**). Sometimes shortened to **butt.**

buttock ('bʌtək) *n* **1** either of the two large fleshy masses of thick muscular tissue that form the human rump. See also **gluteus.** Related adjs.: **gluteal, natal. 2** the analogous part in some mammals. [C13: perhaps from Old English *buttuc* round slope, diminutive of *butt* (unattested) strip of land; see BUTT[1], -OCK]

button ('bʌtᵊn) *n* **1** a disc or knob of plastic, wood, etc., attached to a garment, etc., usually for fastening two surfaces together by passing it through a buttonhole or loop. **2** a small round object, such as any of various sweets, decorations, or badges. **3** a small disc that completes an electric circuit when pushed, as one that operates a doorbell or machine. **4** *Biology.* any rounded knoblike part or organ, such as an unripe mushroom. **5** *Fencing.* the protective knob fixed to the point of a foil. **6** a small amount of metal, usually lead, with which gold or silver is fused, thus concentrating it during assaying. **7** the piece of a weld that pulls out during the destructive testing of spot welds. **8** *Rowing.* a projection around the loom of an oar that prevents it slipping through the rowlock. **9** *Brit.* an object of no value (esp. in the phrase **not worth a button**). **10** *Slang.* intellect; mental capacity (in such phrases as **a button short, to have all one's buttons,** etc.). **11 on the button.** *Informal.* exactly; precisely. ◆ *vb* **12** to fasten with a button or buttons. **13** (*tr*) to provide with buttons. **14** (*tr*) *Fencing.* to hit (an opponent) with the button of one's foil. **15 button (up) one's lip** *or* **mouth.** *Slang.* to stop talking: often imperative. ◆ See also **buttons, button up.** [C14: from Old French *boton,* from *boter* to thrust, butt, of Germanic origin; see BUTT[3]] ▸ **'buttoner** *n* ▸ **'buttonless** *adj* ▸ **'buttony** *adj*

buttonball ('bʌtᵊnˌbɔːl) *n U.S. and Canadian.* a North American plane tree, *Platanus occidentalis.* See **plane tree.**

buttonhole ('bʌtᵊnˌhəʊl) *n* **1** a slit in a garment, etc., through which a button is passed to fasten two surfaces together. **2** a flower or small bunch of flowers worn pinned to the lapel or in the buttonhole, esp. at weddings, formal dances, etc. U.S. name: **boutonniere.** ◆ *vb* (*tr*) **3** to detain (a person) in conversation. **4** to make buttonholes in. **5** to sew with buttonhole stitch.

buttonhole stitch *n* a reinforcing looped stitch for the edge of material, such as around a buttonhole.

buttonhook ('bʌtᵊnˌhʊk) *n* a thin tapering hooked instrument formerly used for pulling buttons through the buttonholes of gloves, shoes, etc.

buttonmould ('bʌtᵊnˌməʊld) *n* the small core of plastic, wood, or metal that is the base for buttons covered with fabric, leather, etc.

button quail *n* any small quail-like terrestrial bird of the genus *Turnix,* such as *T. sylvatica* (striped button quail), occurring in tropical and subtropical regions of the Old World: family *Turnicidae,* order *Gruiformes* (cranes, rails, etc.). Also called: **hemipode.**

buttons ('bʌtᵊnz) *n* (*functioning as sing*) *Brit. informal.* a page boy.

button-through *adj* (of a dress or skirt) fastened with buttons from top to hem.

button tow *n* a kind of ski lift for one person consisting of a pole that has a circular plate at the bottom and is attached to a moving cable. The person places the pole between his legs so that the plate takes his weight.

button up *vb* (*tr, adv*) **1** to fasten (a garment) with a button or buttons. **2** *Informal.* to conclude (business) satisfactorily. **3 buttoned up.** *Slang.* taciturn; silent and somewhat tense.

buttonwood ('bʌtᵊnˌwʊd) *or* **button tree** *n* **1** Also called: **buttonball.** a North American plane tree, *Platanus occidentalis.* See **plane tree. 2** a small West Indian tree, *Conocarpus erectus,* with button-like fruits and heavy hard compact wood: family *Combretaceae.*

butt plate *n* a plate made usually of metal and attached to the butt end of a gunstock.

buttress ('bʌtrɪs) *n* **1** Also called: **pier.** a construction, usually of brick or stone, built to support a wall. See also **flying buttress. 2** any support or prop. **3** something shaped like a buttress, such as a projection from a mountainside. **4** either of the two pointed rear parts of a horse's hoof. ◆ *vb* (*tr*) **5** to support (a wall) with a buttress. **6** to support or sustain. [C13: from Old French *bouterez,* short for *ars bouterez* thrusting arch, from *bouter* to thrust, BUTT[3]]

buttress root *n* a root that supports the trunk of a tree, usually growing from the stem, as in the mangrove.

buttress thread *n* a screw thread having one flank that is vertical while the other is inclined, and a flat top and bottom: used in machine tools and designed to withstand heavy thrust in one direction.

butt shaft *n* a blunt-headed unbarbed arrow.

butt weld *n* See **butt joint.**

butty[1] ('bʌtɪ) *n, pl* **-ties.** *Chiefly northern English dialect.* a sandwich: *a jam butty.* [C19: from *buttered* (*bread*)]

butty[2] ('bʌtɪ) *n, pl* **-ties.** *English dialect.* (esp. in mining parlance) a friend or workmate. [C19: perhaps from obsolete *booty* sharing, from BOOT[2], later applied to a middleman in a mine]

Butung ('buːtʊŋ) *n* an island of Indonesia, southeast of Sulawesi: hilly and forested. Chief town: Baubau. Pop.: 317 124 (1980). Area: 4555 sq. km (1759 sq. miles).

butut (bʊ'tuːt) *n* a Gambian monetary unit worth one hundredth of a dalasi.

butyl ('bjuːˌtaɪl, -tɪl) *n* (*modifier*) of, consisting of, or containing any of four isomeric forms of the group C_4H_9–: *butyl rubber.* [C19: from BUT(YRIC ACID) + -YL]

butyl acetate *n* a colourless liquid with a fruity odour, existing in four isomeric forms. Three of the isomers are important solvents for cellulose lacquers. Formula: $CH_3COOC_4H_9$.

butyl alcohol *n* another name for **butanol.**

butylene ('bjuːtɪˌliːn) *n* another name for **butene.**

butyl rubber *n* a copolymer of isobutene and isoprene, used in tyres and as a waterproofing material.

butyraceous (ˌbjuːtɪ'reɪʃəs) *adj* of, containing, or resembling butter. [C17 *butyr-,* from Latin *būtyrum* BUTTER + -ACEOUS]

butyraldehyde (ˌbjuːtɪ'rældɪˌhaɪd) *n* a colourless flammable pungent liquid used in the manufacture of resins. Formula: $CH_3(CH_2)_2CHO$. [C20: from BUTYR(IC ACID) + ALDEHYDE]

butyrate ('bjuːtɪˌreɪt) *n* any salt or ester of butyric acid, containing the monovalent group C_3H_7COO- or ion $C_3H_7COO^-$.

butyric acid (bjuː'tɪrɪk) *n* a carboxylic acid existing in two isomeric forms, one of which produces the smell in rancid butter. Its esters are used in flavouring. Formula: $CH_3(CH_2)_2COOH$. [C19 *butyric,* from Latin *būtyrum* BUTTER]

butyrin ('bjuːtɪrɪn) *n* a colourless liquid ester or oil found in butter. It is formed from butyric acid and glycerine. [C20: from BUTYR(IC ACID + GLYCER)IN(E)]

buxom ('bʌksəm) *adj* **1** (esp. of a woman) healthily plump, attractive, and vigorous. **2** (of a woman) full-bosomed. [C12: *buhsum* compliant, pliant, from Old English *būgan* to bend, BOW[1]; related to Middle Dutch *būchsam* pliant, German *biegsam*] ▸ **'buxomly** *adv* ▸ **'buxomness** *n*

Buxtehude (*German* bʊkstə'huːdə) *n* **Dietrich** ('diːtrɪç). 1637–1707, Danish composer and organist, resident in Germany from 1668, who influenced Bach and Handel.

Buxton ('bʌkstən) *n* a town in N England, in NW Derbyshire in the Peak District: thermal springs. Pop.: 19 854 (1991).

buy (baɪ) *vb* **buys, buying, bought.** (*mainly tr*) **1** to acquire by paying or promising to pay a sum of money or the equivalent; purchase. **2** to be capable of purchasing: *money can't buy love.* **3** to acquire by any exchange or sacrifice: *to buy time by equivocation.* **4** (*intr*) to act as a buyer. **5** to bribe or corrupt; hire by or as by bribery. **6** *Slang.* to accept as true, practical, etc. **7** (*intr; foll. by into*) to purchase shares of (a company): *we bought into General Motors.* **8** (*tr*) *Theol.* (esp. of Christ) to ransom or redeem (a Christian or the soul of a Christian). **9 have bought it.** *Slang.* to be killed. ◆ *n* **10** a purchase (often in the phrases **good** or **bad buy**). ◆ See also **buy in, buy into, buy off, buy out, buy up.** [Old English *bycgan;* related to Old Norse *byggja* to let out, lend, Gothic *bugjan* to buy]

USAGE The use of *off* after *buy* as in *I bought this off my neighbour* was formerly considered incorrect, but is now acceptable in informal contexts.

buy-back ('baɪˌbæk) *n Commerce.* the repurchase by a company of some or all of its shares from an investor, who acquired them by putting venture capital into the company when it was formed.

buyer ('baɪə) *n* **1** a person who buys; purchaser; customer. **2** a person employed to buy merchandise, materials, etc., as for a shop or factory.

buyers' market *n* a market in which supply exceeds demand and buyers can influence prices.

buy in *vb* (*adv*) **1** (*tr*) to buy back for the owner (an item in an auction) at or below the reserve price. **2** (*intr*) to purchase shares in a company. **3** (*intr*) to buy goods or securities on the open market against a defaulting seller, charging this seller with any market differences. **4** (*tr*) Also: **buy into.** *U.S. informal.* to pay money to secure a position or place for (someone, esp. oneself) in some organization, esp. a business or club. **5** to purchase (goods, etc.) in large quantities: *to buy in for the winter.* ◆ *n* **buy-in. 6** the purchase of a company by a manager or group who does not work for that company.

buy into *vb* (*intr, prep*) **1** to agree with or accept as valid (an argument, theory, etc.). **2** *Austral. and N.Z. informal.* to get involved in (an argument, fight, etc.).

buy off *vb* (*tr, adv*) to pay (a person or group) to drop a charge, end opposition, relinquish a claim, etc.

buy out *vb* (*tr, adv*) **1** to purchase the ownership, controlling interest, shares, etc., of (a company, etc.). **2** to gain the release of (a person) from the armed forces by payment of money. **3** to pay (a person) once and for all to give up (property, interest, etc.). ◆ *n* **buyout. 4** the purchase of a company, esp. by its former management or staff. See also **leveraged buyout, management buyout.**

Buys Ballot's Law (baɪs bə'lɒts, bɔɪs) *n* a law stating that if an observer stands with his back to the wind in the N hemisphere, atmospheric pressure is lower on his left, and vice versa in the S hemisphere. [named after C. H. D. *Buys Ballot* (1817–90), Dutch meteorologist]

buy up *vb* (*tr, adv*) **1** to purchase all, or all that is available, of (something). **2** *Commerce.* to purchase a controlling interest in (a company, etc.), as by the acquisition of shares.

buzz (bʌz) *n* **1** a rapidly vibrating humming sound, as that of a prolonged *z* or of a bee in flight. **2** a low sound, as of many voices in conversation. **3** a rumour; report; gossip. **4** *Informal.* a telephone call: *I'll give you a buzz.* **5** *Slang.* **5a** a pleasant sensation, as from a drug such as cannabis. **5b** a sense of excitement; kick. ◆ *vb* **6** (*intr*) to make a vibrating sound like that of a prolonged *z.* **7** (*intr*) to talk or gossip with an air of excitement or urgency: *the town buzzed with the news.* **8** (*tr*) to utter or spread (a rumour). **9** (*intr;* often foll. by *about*) to move around quickly and busily; bustle. **10** (*tr*) to signal or summon with a buzzer. **11** (*tr*) *Informal.* to call by telephone. **12** (*tr*) *Informal.* **12a** to fly an aircraft very low over (an object): *to buzz a ship.* **12b** to fly an aircraft very close to or across the path of (another aircraft), esp. to warn or intimidate. **13** (*tr*) (esp. of insects) to make a buzzing sound with (wings, etc.). [C16: of imitative origin] ▸ **'buzzing** *n, adj*

buzzard ('bʌzəd) *n* **1** any diurnal bird of prey of the genus *Buteo,* typically having broad wings and tail and a soaring flight: family *Accipitridae* (hawks, etc.). See **honey buzzard.** Compare **turkey buzzard. 2** a mean or cantankerous person. [C13: from Old French *buisard,* variant of *buison* buzzard, from Latin *būteō* hawk, falcon]

buzz bomb *n* another name for the **V-1.**

buzzer ('bʌzə) *n* **1** a person or thing that buzzes. **2** a device that produces a buzzing sound, esp. one similar to an electric bell without a hammer or gong. **3** *N.Z.* a wood planing machine.

buzz off *vb* (*intr, adv; often imperative*) *Informal, chiefly Brit.* to go away; leave; depart.

buzz saw *n U.S. and Canadian.* a power-operated circular saw.

buzz word *n Informal.* a word, often originating in a particular jargon, that becomes a vogue word in the community as a whole or among a particular group.

BV *abbrev. for:* **1** Beata Virgo. [Latin: Blessed Virgin] **2** bene vale. [Latin: farewell]

BVM *abbrev. for* Beata Virgo Maria. [Latin: Blessed Virgin Mary]

BW *abbrev. for* biological warfare.

B/W *Photog. abbrev. for* black and white.

bwana ('bwɑːnə) *n* (in E Africa) a master, often used as a respectful form of address corresponding to *sir*. [Swahili, from Arabic *abūna* our father]
BWG *abbrev. for* Birmingham Wire Gauge: a notation for the diameters of metal rods, ranging from 0 (0.340 inch) to 36 (0.004 inch).
BWR *abbrev. for* boiling-water reactor.
BWV (*preceding a number*) *Music. abbrev. for* Bach Werke-Verzeichnis: indicating the serial number in the catalogue of the works of J. S. Bach made by Wolfgang Schmieder (born 1901), published in 1950.
bx *abbrev. for* box.
by (baɪ) *prep* **1** used to indicate the agent after a passive verb: *seeds eaten by the birds.* **2** used to indicate the person responsible for a creative work: *this song is by Schubert.* **3** via; through: *enter by the back door.* **4** foll. by a gerund to indicate a means used: *he frightened her by hiding behind the door.* **5** beside; next to; near: *a tree by the house.* **6** passing the position of; past: *he drove by the old cottage.* **7** not later than; before: *return the books by Tuesday.* **8** used to indicate extent, after a comparative: *it is hotter by five degrees than it was yesterday.* **9** (esp. in oaths) invoking the name of: *I swear by all the gods.* **10** multiplied by: *four by three equals twelve.* **11** (*in habitual sentences*) during the passing of (esp. in the phrases **by day, by night**). **12** placed between measurements of the various dimensions of something: *a plank fourteen inches by seven.* ◆ *adv* **13** near: *the house is close by.* **14** away; aside: *he put some money by each week for savings.* **15** passing a point near something; past: *he drove by.* **16** *Scot.* past; over and done with: *that's a' by now.* **17** *Scot.* aside; behind one: *you must put that by you.* ◆ *n, pl* **byes. 18** a variant spelling of **bye.** [Old English *bī*; related to Gothic *bi*, Old High German *bī*, Sanskrit *abhi* to, towards]
by- *or* **bye-** *prefix* **1** near: *bystander.* **2** secondary or incidental: *by-effect; by-election; by-path; by-product.* [from BY]
Byam Shaw ('baɪəm ʃɔː) *n* **Glen Alexander.** 1904–81, British actor and theatre director; director of the Shakespeare Memorial Theatre (1953–59).
by and by *adv* **1** presently or eventually. ◆ *n* **by-and-by. 2** *U.S. and Canadian.* a future time or occasion.
by and large *adv* in general; on the whole. [C17: originally nautical (meaning: to the wind and off it)]
Byatt ('baɪət) *n* Dame **A(ntonia) S(usan).** born 1936, British novelist; her books include *Possession* (1990).
by-bidder *n* a bidder at an auction who bids up the price of an item for the benefit of a seller.
by-blow *n* **1** a passing or incidental blow. **2** an archaic word for a **bastard.**
byde (bəɪd) *vb Scot.* a variant spelling of **bide.**
Bydgoszcz (*Polish* 'bidgɔʃtʃ) *n* an industrial city and port in N Poland: under Prussian rule from 1772 to 1919. Pop.: 386 100 (1996 est.). German name: **Bromberg.**
bye[1] (baɪ) *n* **1** *Sport.* the situation in which a player or team in an eliminatory contest wins a preliminary round by virtue of having no opponent. **2** *Golf.* one or more holes of a stipulated course that are left unplayed after the match has been decided. **3** *Cricket.* a run scored off a ball not struck by the batsman: allotted to the team as an extra and not to the individual batsman. See also **leg bye. 4** something incidental or secondary. **5 by the bye.** incidentally; by the way: used as a sentence connector. [C16: a variant of BY]
bye[2] *or* **bye-bye** *sentence substitute. Brit informal.* goodbye.
bye-byes *n* (*functioning as sing*) an informal word for **sleep,** used esp. in addressing children (as in the phrase **go to bye-byes**).
by-election *or* **bye-election** *n* **1** (in the United Kingdom and other countries of the Commonwealth) an election held during the life of a parliament to fill a vacant seat in the lower chamber. **2** (in the U.S.) a special election to fill a vacant elective position with an unexpired term.
Byelgorod-Dnestrovski *n* a variant spelling of **Belgorod-Dnestrovski.**
Byelorussia *n* a variant spelling of **Belarus.**
Byelorussian *adj, n* a variant spelling of **Belarussian.**
Byelostok (bjɪla'stɔk) *n* a Russian name for **Białystok.**
Byelovo *or* **Belovo** (*Russian* 'bjeləvə) *n* a city in W central Russia. Pop.: 118 000 (1989).
by-form *n* a subsidiary or variant form.
bygone ('baɪˌgɒn) *adj* **1** (*usually prenominal*) past; former. ◆ *n* **2** (*often pl*) a past occurrence. **3** (*often pl*) an artefact, implement, etc., of former domestic or industrial use, now often collected for interest. **4 let bygones be bygones.** to agree to forget past quarrels.
byke (bəɪk, baɪk) *n Scot.* a variant spelling of **bike**[2].
bylane ('baɪˌleɪn) *n* a side lane or alley off a road.
bylaw *or* **bye-law** ('baɪˌlɔː) *n* **1** a rule made by a local authority for the regulation of its affairs or management of the area it governs. **2** a regulation of a company, society, etc. **3** a subsidiary law. [C13: probably of Scandinavian origin; compare Old Norse *bȳr* dwelling, town; see BOWER[1], LAW[1]]
by-line *n* **1** *Journalism.* a line under the title of a newspaper or magazine article giving the author's name. **2** *Soccer.* another word for **touchline.**
Byng (bɪŋ) *n* **1 George,** Viscount Torrington. 1663–1733, British admiral: defeated fleet of James Edward Stuart, the Old Pretender, off Scotland (1708); defeated Spanish fleet off Messina (1717). **2** his son **John.** 1704–57, English admiral: executed after failing to relieve Minorca. **3 Julian Hedworth George,** 1st Viscount Byng of Vimy. 1862–1935, British general in World War I; governor general of Canada (1921–26).
BYO *n Austral. and N.Z.* an unlicensed restaurant at which diners may drink their own wine, etc. [C20: from the phrase *bring your own*]
BYOB *abbrev. for:* **1** bring your own beer. **2** bring your own booze. **3** bring your own bottle.
bypass ('baɪˌpɑːs) *n* **1** a main road built to avoid a city or other congested area. **2** a means of redirecting the flow of a substance around an appliance through which it would otherwise pass. **3** *Surgery.* **3a** the redirection of blood flow, either to avoid a diseased blood vessel or in order to perform heart surgery. See **coronary bypass. 3b** (*as modifier*): *bypass surgery.* **4** *Electronics.* **4a** an electrical circuit, esp. one containing a capacitor, connected in parallel around one or more components, providing an alternative path for certain frequencies. **4b** (*as modifier*): *a bypass capacitor.* ◆ *vb* **-passes, -passing, -passed** *or* **-past.** (*tr*) **5** to go around or avoid (a city, obstruction, problem, etc.). **6** to cause (traffic, fluid, etc.) to go through a bypass. **7** to proceed without reference to (regulations, a superior, etc.); get round; avoid.
bypass engine *n* a gas turbine in which a part of the compressor delivery bypasses the combustion zone, flowing directly into or around the main exhaust gas flow to provide additional thrust. Compare **turbofan.**
bypass ratio *n Aeronautics.* the ratio of the amount of air that bypasses the combustion chambers of an aircraft gas turbine to that passing through them.
bypath ('baɪˌpɑːθ) *n* a little-used path or track, esp. in the country.
by-play *n* secondary action or talking carried on apart while the main action proceeds, esp. in a play.
by-product *n* **1** a secondary or incidental product of a manufacturing process. **2** a side effect.
Byrd (bɜːd) *n* **1 Richard Evelyn.** 1888–1957, U.S. rear admiral, aviator, and polar explorer. **2 William.** 1543–1623, English composer and organist, noted for his madrigals, masses, and music for virginals.
Byrd Land *n* a part of Antarctica, east of the Ross Ice Shelf and the Ross Sea: claimed for the U.S. by Richard E. Byrd in 1929. Former name: **Marie Byrd Land.**
Byrds (bɜːdz) *pl n* **the** U.S. folk-rock and country-rock group (1964–73), noted for their vocal harmonies and 12-string guitar sound. Their albums include *Mr. Tambourine Man* (1965), *Younger Than Yesterday* (1967), and *Sweetheart of the Rodeo* (1968).
byre (baɪə) *n Brit.* a shelter for cows. [Old English *bȳre*; related to *būr* hut, cottage; see BOWER[1]]
byrnie ('bɜːnɪ) *n* an archaic word for **coat of mail.** [Old English *byrne*; related to Old Norse *brynja*, Gothic *brunjō*, Old High German *brunnia* coat of mail, Old Irish *bruinne* breast]
byroad ('baɪˌrəʊd) *n* a secondary or side road.
Byron ('baɪərən) *n* **George Gordon,** 6th Baron. 1788–1824, British Romantic poet, noted also for his passionate and disastrous love affairs. His major works include *Childe Harold's Pilgrimage* (1812–18), and *Don Juan* (1819–24). He spent much of his life abroad and died while fighting for Greek independence. ▸ **Byronic** (baɪ'rɒnɪk) *adj* ▸ **By'ronically** *adv* ▸ **'Byron,ism** *n*
byssinosis (ˌbɪsɪ'nəʊsɪs) *n* a lung disease caused by prolonged inhalation of fibre dust in textile factories. [C19: from New Latin, from Greek *bussinos* of linen (see BYSSUS) + -OSIS]
byssus ('bɪsəs) *n, pl* **byssuses** *or* **byssi** ('bɪsaɪ). a mass of strong threads secreted by a sea mussel or similar mollusc that attaches the animal to a hard fixed surface. [C17: from Latin, from Greek *bussos* linen, flax, ultimately of Egyptian origin]
bystander ('baɪˌstændə) *n* a person present but not involved; onlooker; spectator.
bystreet ('baɪˌstriːt) *n* an obscure or secondary street.
byte (baɪt) *n Computing.* **1** a group of bits, usually eight, processed as a single unit of data. **2** the storage space in a memory or other storage device that is allocated to such a group of bits. **3** a subdivision of a word. [C20: probably a blend of BIT[4] + BITE]
Bytom (*Polish* 'bitɔm) *n* an industrial city in SW Poland, in Upper Silesia: under Prussian and German rule from 1742 to 1945. Pop.: 227 600 (1996 est.). German name: **Beuthen.**
byway ('baɪˌweɪ) *n* **1** a secondary or side road, esp. in the country. **2** an area, field of study, etc., that is very obscure or of secondary importance.
byword ('baɪˌwɜːd) *n* **1** a person, place, or thing regarded as a perfect or proverbial example of something: *their name is a byword for good service.* **2** an object of scorn or derision. **3** a common saying; proverb. [Old English *bīwyrde*; see BY, WORD; compare Old High German *pīwurti*, from Latin *prōverbium* proverb]
by-your-leave *n* a request for permission (esp. in the phrase **without so much as a by-your-leave**).
Byz. *abbrev. for* Byzantine.
Byzantine (bɪ'zænˌtaɪn, -ˌtiːn, baɪ-; 'bɪzənˌtiːn, -ˌtaɪn) *adj* **1** of, characteristic of, or relating to Byzantium or the Byzantine Empire. **2** of, relating to, or characterizing the Orthodox Church or its rites and liturgy. **3** of or relating to the highly coloured stylized form of religious art developed in the Byzantine Empire. **4** of or relating to the style of architecture developed in the Byzantine Empire, characterized by massive domes with square bases, rounded arches, spires and minarets, and the extensive use of mosaics. **5** denoting the Medieval Greek spoken in the Byzantine Empire. **6** (of attitudes, etc.) inflexible or complicated. ◆ *n* **7** an inhabitant of Byzantium. ▸ **Byzantinism** (bɪ'zæntaɪˌnɪzəm, -tiː, baɪ-; 'bɪzəntiːˌnɪzəm, -taɪ-) *n*
Byzantine Church *n* another name for the **Orthodox Church.**
Byzantine Empire *n* the continuation of the Roman Empire in the East, esp. after the deposition of the last emperor in Rome (476 A.D.). It was finally extinguished by the fall of Constantinople, its capital, in 1453. See also **Eastern Roman Empire.**
Byzantium (bɪ'zæntɪəm, baɪ-) *n* an ancient Greek city on the Bosphorus: founded about 660 B.C.; rebuilt by Constantine I in 330 A.D. and called Constantinople; present-day Istanbul.
Bz *or* **bz.** *abbrev. for* benzene.

Cc

c *or* **C** (siː) *n, pl* **c's, C's,** *or* **Cs. 1** the third letter and second consonant of the modern English alphabet. **2** a speech sound represented by this letter, in English usually either a voiceless alveolar fricative, as in *cigar*, or a voiceless velar stop, as in *case*. **3** the third in a series, esp. the third highest grade in an examination. **4a** something shaped like a C. **4b** (*in combination*): *a C-spring*.

c *symbol for:* **1** centi-. **2** cubic. **3** cycle. **4** *Maths.* constant. **5** specific heat capacity. **6** the speed of light and other types of electromagnetic radiation in a free space. **7** *Chess.* See **algebraic notation.**

C *symbol for:* **1** *Music.* **1a** a note having a frequency of 261.63 hertz (**middle C**) or this value multiplied or divided by any power of 2; the first degree of a major scale containing no sharps or flats (**C major**). **1b** a key, string, or pipe producing this note. **1c** the major or minor key having this note as its tonic. **1d** a time signature denoting four crotchet beats to the bar. See also **alla breve** (sense 2), **common time. 2** *Chem.* carbon. **3** *Biochem.* cytosine. **4** capacitance. **5** heat capacity. **6** cold (water). **7** *Physics.* compliance. **8** Celsius. **9** centigrade. **10** century: *C20.* **11** coulomb. ◆ **12** *the Roman numeral for* 100. See **Roman numerals.** ◆ **13** *international car registration for* Cuba. ◆ *n* **14** a computer programming language combining the advantages of a high-level language with the ability to address the computer at a level comparable with that of an assembly language.

c. *abbrev. for:* **1** carat. **2** carbon (paper). **3** *Cricket.* caught. **4** cent(s). **5** century or centuries. **6** (*pl* **cc.**) chapter. **7** (used esp. preceding a date) circa: *c. 1800.* [Latin: about] **8** colt. **9** contralto. **10** copyright.

C. *abbrev. for:* **1** (on maps as part of name) Cape. **2** Catholic. **3** Celtic. **4** Conservative. **5** Corps.

c/- *Austral.* (in addresses) *abbrev. for* care of.

C- (of U.S. military aircraft) *abbrev. for* cargo transport: *C-5.*

© *symbol for* copyright.

C1 (ˈsiːˈwʌn) *n* **a** a person whose job is supervisory or clerical, or who works in junior management. **b** (*as adj*): *C1 worker.* ◆ See also **occupation groupings.**

C2 (ˈsiːˈtuː) *n* **a** a skilled manual worker, or a manual worker with responsibility for other people. **b** (*as adj*): *C2 worker.* ◆ See also **occupation groupings.**

C3 *or* **C-3** (ˈsiːˈθriː) *adj* **1** in poor health or having a poor physique. **2** *Informal.* inferior; worthless. Compare **A1.**

Ca *the chemical symbol for* calcium.

CA *abbrev. for:* **1** California. **2** Central America. **3** chartered accountant. **4** chief accountant. **5** consular agent. **6** (in Britain) Consumers' Association.

ca. *abbrev. for* circa. [Latin: about]

C/A *abbrev. for:* **1** capital account. **2** credit account. **3** current account.

caa[1] *or* **ca'**[1] (kɔː) *vb, n* a Scot. word for **call.**

caa[2] *or* **ca'**[2] (kɔː) *vb Scot.* **1** to drive or propel. **2** to knock. **3 caa** *or* **ca' canny.** to proceed cautiously; go slow. **4 caa** *or* **ca' the feet frae.** to send (a person) sprawling. [see CAA[1]]

CAA (in Britain) *abbrev. for* Civil Aviation Authority.

Caaba (ˈkɑːbə) *n* a variant spelling of **Kaaba.**

cab[1] (kæb) *n* **1a** a taxi. **1b** (*as modifier*): *a cab rank.* **2** the enclosed compartment of a lorry, locomotive, crane, etc., from which it is driven or operated. **3** (formerly) a light horse-drawn vehicle used for public hire. **4 first cab off the rank.** *Austral. informal.* the first person, etc., to do or take advantage of something. [C19: shortened from CABRIOLET]

cab[2] *or* **kab** (kæb) *n* an ancient Hebrew measure equal to about 2.3 litres (4 pints). [C16: from Hebrew *qabh* container, something hollowed out]

CAB *abbrev. for:* **1** (in Britain) Citizens' Advice Bureau. **2** (in the U.S.) Civil Aeronautics Board.

cabal (kəˈbæl) *n* **1** a small group of intriguers, esp. one formed for political purposes. **2** a secret plot, esp. a political one; conspiracy; intrigue. **3** a secret or exclusive set of people; clique. ◆ *vb* **-bals, -balling, -balled.** (*intr*) **4** to form a cabal; conspire; plot. [C17: from French *cabale*, from Medieval Latin *cabala*; see CABBALA]

Cabal (kəˈbæl) *n* **the.** *English history.* a group of ministers of Charles II that governed from 1667–73: consisting of Clifford, Ashley, Buckingham, Arlington, and Lauderdale. [see CABBALA; by a coincidence, the initials of Charles II's ministers can be arranged to form this word]

cabala (kəˈbɑːlə) *n* a variant spelling of **cabbala.** ▸ **cabalism** (ˈkæbəˌlɪzəm) *n* ▸ **ˈcabalist** *n* ▸ **ˌcabaˈlistic** *adj*

Caballé (*Spanish* kaβaˈʎe) *n* **Montserrat** (monserˈrat). born 1933, Spanish operatic soprano.

caballero (ˌkæbəˈljeərəʊ; *Spanish* kaβaˈʎero) *n, pl* **-ros** (-rəʊz; *Spanish* -ros). **1** a Spanish gentleman. **2** a southwestern U.S. word for **horseman.** [C19: from Spanish: gentleman, horseman, from Late Latin *caballārius* rider, groom, from *caballus* horse; compare CAVALIER]

cabana (kəˈbɑːnə) *n Chiefly U.S.* a tent used as a dressing room by the sea. [from Spanish *cabaña*: CABIN]

cabaret (ˈkæbəˌreɪ) *n* **1** a floor show of dancing, singing, or other light entertainment at a nightclub or restaurant. **2** *Chiefly U.S.* a nightclub or restaurant providing such entertainment. [C17: from Norman French: tavern, probably from Late Latin *camera* an arched roof, CHAMBER]

cabbage[1] (ˈkæbɪdʒ) *n* **1** Also called: **cole.** any of various cultivated varieties of the cruciferous plant *Brassica oleracea capitata*, typically having a short thick stalk and a large head of green or reddish edible leaves. See also **brassica, savoy.** Compare **skunk cabbage, Chinese cabbage. 2 wild cabbage.** a Mediterranean cruciferous plant, *Brassica oleracea*, with broad leaves and a long spike of yellow flowers: the plant from which the cabbages, cauliflower, broccoli, and Brussels sprout have been bred. **3a** the head of a cabbage. **3b** the edible leaf bud of the cabbage palm. **4** *Informal.* a dull or unimaginative person. **5** *Informal.* a person who has no mental faculties and is dependent on others for his subsistence. [C14: from Norman French *caboche* head; perhaps related to Old French *boce* hump, bump, Latin *caput* head]

cabbage[2] (ˈkæbɪdʒ) *Brit. slang.* ◆ *n* **1** snippets of cloth appropriated by a tailor from a customer's material. ◆ *vb* **2** to steal; pilfer. [C17: of uncertain origin; perhaps related to Old French *cabas* theft]

cabbage bug *n* another name for the **harlequin bug.**

cabbage lettuce *n* any of several varieties of lettuce that have roundish flattened heads resembling cabbages.

cabbage moth *n* a common brownish noctuid moth, *Mamestra brassicae*, the larva of which is destructive of cabbages and other plants.

cabbage palm *or* **tree** *n* **1** a West Indian palm, *Roystonea* (or *Oreodoxa*) *oleracea*, whose leaf buds are eaten like cabbage. **2** a similar Brazilian palm, *Euterpe oleracea.* **3** an Australian palm tree, *Livistona australis.*

cabbage palmetto *n* a tropical American fan palm, *Sabal palmetto*, with edible leaf buds and leaves used in thatching.

cabbage root fly *n* a dipterous fly, *Erioischia brassicae*, whose larvae feed on the roots and stems of cabbages and other brassicas: family *Muscidae* (houseflies, etc.).

cabbage rose *n* a rose, *Rosa centifolia*, with a round compact full-petalled head.

cabbagetown (ˈkæbɪdʒˌtaʊn) *n Canadian.* a city slum. [C20: from *Cabbagetown*, a depressed area of Toronto, where the Anglo-Saxon population was thought to exist on cabbage]

cabbage tree *n* a tree, *Cordyline australis*, of New Zealand having a tall branchless trunk and a palmlike top. Also called: **ti.**

cabbage white *n* any large white butterfly of the genus *Pieris*, esp. the Eurasian species *P. brassicae*, the larvae of which feed on the leaves of cabbages and related vegetables: family *Pieridae.*

cabbageworm (ˈkæbɪdʒˌwɜːm) *n U.S.* any caterpillar that feeds on cabbages, esp. that of the cabbage white.

cabbala, cabala, kabbala, *or* **kabala** (kəˈbɑːlə) *n* **1** an ancient Jewish mystical tradition based on an esoteric interpretation of the Old Testament. **2** any secret or occult doctrine or science. [C16: from Medieval Latin, from Hebrew *qabbālāh* tradition, what is received, from *qābal* to receive] ▸ **cabbalism, cabalism, kabbalism,** *or* **kabalism** (ˈkæbəˌlɪzəm) *n* ▸ **ˈcabbalist, ˈcabalist, ˈkabbalist,** *or* **ˈkabalist** *n* ▸ **ˌcabbaˈlistic, ˌcabaˈlistic, ˌkabbaˈlistic,** *or* **ˌkabaˈlistic** *adj*

cabbie *or* **cabby** (ˈkæbɪ) *n, pl* **-bies.** *Informal.* a cab driver.

caber (ˈkeɪbə; *Scot.* ˈkebər) *n Scot.* a heavy section of trimmed tree trunk thrown in competition at Highland games (**tossing the caber**). [C16: from Gaelic *cabar* pole]

Cabernet Sauvignon (ˈkæbəneɪ ˈsəʊvɪnjɒn; *French* kabɛrnɛ soviɲõ) *n* (*sometimes not caps.*) **1** a black grape grown in the Bordeaux area of France, Australia, California, Bulgaria, and elsewhere, used for making wine. **2** any of various red wines made from this grape. [French]

cabezon (ˈkæbɪzɒn) *or* **cabezone** (ˈkæbɪˌzəʊn) *n* a large food fish, *Scorpaenichthys marmoratus*, of North American Pacific coastal waters, having greenish flesh: family *Cottidae* (bullheads and sea scorpions). [Spanish, from *cabeza* head, ultimately from Latin *caput*]

Cabimas (*Spanish* kaˈβimas) *n* a town in NW Venezuela, on the NE shore of Lake Maracaibo. Pop.: 165 755 (1994 est.).

cabin (ˈkæbɪn) *n* **1** a small simple dwelling; hut. **2** a simple house providing accommodation for travellers or holiday-makers at a motel or holiday camp. **3** a room used as an office or living quarters in a ship. **4** a covered compartment used for shelter or living quarters in a small boat. **5** (in a warship) the compartment or room reserved for the commanding officer. **6** *Brit.* another name for **signal box. 7a** the enclosed part of a light aircraft in which the pilot and passengers sit. **7b** the part of an airliner in which the passengers are carried. **7c** the section of an aircraft used for cargo. ◆ *vb* **8** to confine in a small space. [C14: from Old French *cabane*, from Old Provençal *cabana*, from Late Latin *capanna* hut]

cabin boy *n* a boy who waits on the officers and passengers of a ship.

cabin class *n* a class of accommodation on a passenger ship between first class and tourist class.

cabin cruiser *n* a power boat fitted with a cabin and comforts for pleasure cruising or racing.

Cabinda (kəˈbiːndə) *n* an exclave of Angola, separated from the rest of the country by part of the Democratic Republic of the Congo (formerly Zaïre). Pop.: 174 000 (1993 est.). Area: 7270 sq. km (2807 sq. miles).

cabinet (ˈkæbɪnɪt) *n* **1a** a piece of furniture containing shelves, cupboards, or drawers for storage or display. **1b** (*as modifier*): *cabinet teak.* **2** the outer case of a television, radio, etc. **3a** (*often cap.*) the executive and policy-making body of a country, consisting of all government ministers or just the senior ministers. **3b** (*sometimes cap.*) an advisory council to a president, sovereign, governor, etc. **3c** (*as modifier*): *a cabinet reshuffle; a cabinet minister.* **4a** a standard size of paper, 6 × 4 inches (15 × 10 cm) or 6½ × 4¼ inches (16.5 × 10.5 cm), for mounted photographs. **4b** (*as modifier*): *a cabinet photograph.* **5** *Printing.* an enclosed rack for holding cases of type, etc. **6** *Archaic.* a private room. **7** (*modifier*) suitable in size, value, decoration, etc., for a display cabinet: *a cabinet edition of Shakespeare.* **8** (*modifier*) (of a drawing or projection of a three-dimensional object) constructed with true horizontal and vertical representation of scale but with oblique distances reduced to about half scale to avoid the appearance of distortion. **9** (*modifier*) (of a wine) specially selected and usually rare. [C16: from Old French, diminutive of *cabine,* of uncertain origin]

cabinet beetle *n* See **dermestid.**

cabinet-maker *n* a craftsman specializing in the making of fine furniture. ▸ **'cabinet-,making** *n*

cabinet pudding *n* a steamed suet pudding containing dried fruit.

cabinetwork ('kæbɪnɪt,wɜːk) *n* **1** the making of furniture, esp. of fine quality. **2** an article made by a cabinet-maker.

cabin fever *n Canadian.* acute depression resulting from being isolated or sharing cramped quarters in the wilderness, esp. during the long northern winter.

cable ('keɪbᵊl) *n* **1** a strong thick rope, usually of twisted hemp or steel wire. **2** *Nautical.* an anchor chain or rope. **3a** a unit of distance in navigation, equal to one tenth of a sea mile (about 600 feet). **3b** Also called: **cable length, cable's length.** a unit of length in nautical use that has various values, including 100 fathoms (600 feet). **4** a wire or bundle of wires that conducts electricity: *a submarine cable.* See also **coaxial cable. 5** Also called: **overseas** *or* **international telegram, cablegram.** a telegram sent abroad by submarine cable, radio, communications satellite, or by telephone line. **6** See **cable stitch.** ◆ *vb* **7** to send (a message) to (someone) by cable. **8** (*tr*) to fasten or provide with a cable or cables. **9** (*tr*) to supply (a place) with or link (a place) to cable television. [C13: from Old Norman French, from Late Latin *capulum* halter]

cable car *n* **1** a cabin suspended from and moved by an overhead cable in a mountain area. **2** a cableway. **3** a passenger car on a cable railway.

cablegram ('keɪbᵊl,græm) *n* a more formal name for **cable** (sense 5).

cable-laid *adj* (of a rope) made of three plain-laid ropes twisted together in a left-handed direction.

cable railway *n* a railway on which individual cars are drawn along by a strong cable or metal chain operated by a stationary motor.

cable release *n* a short length of flexible cable, used to operate the shutter of a camera without shaking it.

cable-stayed bridge *n* a type of suspension bridge in which the supporting cables are connected directly to the bridge deck without the use of suspenders.

cable stitch *n* **a** a pattern or series of knitting stitches producing a design like a twisted rope. **b** (*as modifier*): *a cable-stitch sweater.* Sometimes shortened to **cable.**

cablet ('keɪblɪt) *n* a small cable, esp. a cable-laid rope that has a circumference of less than 25 centimetres (ten inches).

cable television *n* a television service in which programmes are distributed to subscribers' televisions by cable rather than by broadcast transmission.

cableway ('keɪbᵊl,weɪ) *n* a system for moving people or bulk materials in which suspended cars, buckets, etc., run on cables that extend between terminal towers.

cabman ('kæbmən) *n, pl* **-men.** the driver of a cab.

cabob (kə'bɒb) *n* a variant of **kebab.**

cabochon ('kæbə,ʃɒn; *French* kabɔʃɔ̃) *n* a smooth domed gem, polished but unfaceted. [C16: from Old French, from Old Norman French *caboche* head; see CABBAGE[1]]

caboodle (kə'buːdᵊl) *n Informal.* a lot, bunch, or group (esp. in the phrases **the whole caboodle, the whole kit and caboodle**). [C19: probably contraction of KIT[1] and BOODLE]

caboose (kə'buːs) *n* **1** *U.S. informal.* short for **calaboose. 2** *Railways. U.S. and Canadian.* a guard's van, esp. one with sleeping and eating facilities for the train crew. **3** *Nautical.* **3a** a deckhouse for a galley aboard ship or formerly in Canada, on a lumber raft. **3b** *Chiefly Brit.* the galley itself. **4** *Canadian.* **4a** a mobile bunkhouse used by lumbermen, etc. **4b** an insulated cabin on runners, equipped with a stove. [C18: from Dutch *cabūse,* of unknown origin]

Cabora Bassa (kə'bɔːrə 'bæsə) *n* the site on the Zambezi River in N Mozambique of the largest dam in southern Africa.

Cabot ('kæbət) *n* **1 John,** Italian name *Giovanni Caboto.* 1450–98, Italian explorer, who landed in North America in 1497, under patent from Henry VII of England, and explored the coast from Nova Scotia to Newfoundland. **2** his son, **Sebastian.** ?1476–1557, Italian navigator and cartographer, who served the English and Spanish crowns: explored the La Plata region of Brazil (1526–30).

cabotage ('kæbə,tɑːʒ) *n* **1** *Nautical.* coastal navigation or shipping, esp. within the borders of one country. **2** reservation to a country's carriers of its internal traffic, esp. air traffic. [C19: from French, from *caboter* to sail near the coast, apparently from Spanish *cabo* CAPE[2]]

Cabral (*Portuguese* kə'brɑl) *n* **Pedro Álvarez** ('peːdru 'ɑlvərəʃ). ?1460–?1526, Portuguese navigator: discovered and took possession of Brazil for Portugal in 1500.

cabretta (kə'brɛtə) *n Chiefly U.S.* a soft leather obtained from the skins of certain South American or African sheep. [from Spanish *cabra* she-goat]

cabrilla (kə'brɪlə) *n* any of various serranid food fishes, esp. *Epinephelus analogus,* occurring in warm seas around Florida and the Caribbean. [Spanish, literally: little goat]

cabriole ('kæbrɪ,əʊl) *n* **1** Also called: **cabriole leg.** a type of furniture leg, popular in the first half of the 18th century, in which an upper convex curve descends tapering to a concave curve. **2** *Ballet.* a leap in the air with one leg outstretched and the other beating against it. [C18: from French, from *cabrioler* to caper; from its being based on the leg of a capering animal; see CABRIOLET]

cabriolet (,kæbrɪəʊ'leɪ) *n* **1** a small two-wheeled horse-drawn carriage with two seats and a folding hood. **2** a former name for a **drophead coupé.** [C18: from French, literally: a little skip, from *cabriole,* from Latin *capreolus* wild goat, from *caper* goat; referring to the lightness of movement]

ca'canny (,kɔː'kænɪ) *n Scot.* **1** moderation or wariness. **2a** a policy of restricting the output of work; a go-slow. **2b** (*as modifier*): *a ca'canny policy.* See also **caa**[2]. [C19: literally, *call canny* to drive gently]

cacao (kə'kɑːəʊ, -'keɪəʊ) *n* **1** a small tropical American evergreen tree, *Theobroma cacao,* having yellowish flowers and reddish-brown seed pods from which cocoa and chocolate are prepared: family *Sterculiaceae.* **2 cacao bean.** another name for **cocoa bean. 3 cacao butter.** another name for **cocoa butter.** [C16: from Spanish, from Nahuatl *cacauatl* cacao beans]

cacciatore (,kɑːtʃə'tɔːrɪ, ,kætʃ-) *or* **cacciatora** *adj* (*immediately postpositive*) prepared with tomatoes, mushrooms, herbs, and other seasonings. [Italian, literally: hunter]

Cáceres (*Spanish* 'kaθeres) *n* a city in W Spain: held by the Moors (1142–1229). Pop.: 71 745 (1991).

cachalot ('kæʃə,lɒt) *n* another name for **sperm whale.** [C18: from French, from Portuguese, *cachalote,* of unknown origin]

cache (kæʃ) *n* **1** a hidden store of provisions, weapons, treasure, etc. **2** the place where such a store is hidden. **3** *Computing.* a small high-speed memory that improves computer performance. ◆ *vb* **4** (*tr*) to store in a cache. [C19: from French, from *cacher* to hide]

cache memory *n Computing.* a small area of memory in a computer that can be accessed very quickly.

cachepot ('kæʃ,pɒt, ,kæʃ'pəʊ) *n* an ornamental container for a flowerpot. [French: pot-hider]

cachet ('kæʃeɪ) *n* **1** an official seal on a document, letter, etc. **2** a distinguishing mark; stamp. **3** prestige; distinction. **4** *Philately.* **4a** a mark stamped by hand on mail for commemorative purposes. **4b** a small mark made by dealers and experts on the back of postage stamps. Compare **overprint** (sense 3), **surcharge** (sense 5). **5** a hollow wafer, formerly used for enclosing an unpleasant-tasting medicine. [C17: from Old French, from *cacher* to hide]

cachexia (kə'kɛksɪə) *or* **cachexy** *n* a generally weakened condition of body or mind resulting from any debilitating chronic disease. [C16: from Late Latin from Greek *kakhexia,* from *kakos* bad + *hexis* condition, habit] ▸ **cachectic** (kə'kɛktɪk) *adj*

cachinnate ('kækɪ,neɪt) *vb* (*intr*) to laugh loudly. [C19: from Latin *cacchināre,* probably of imitative origin] ▸ **,cachin'natory** *adj*

cachinnation (,kækɪ'neɪʃən) *n* **1** raucous laughter. **2** *Psychiatry.* inappropriate laughter, sometimes found in schizophrenia.

cachou ('kæʃuː, kæ'ʃuː) *n* **1** a lozenge eaten to sweeten the breath. **2** another name for **catechu.** [C18: via French from Portuguese, from Malay *kāchu*]

cachucha (kə'tʃuːtʃə) *n* **1** a graceful Spanish solo dance in triple time. **2** music composed for this dance. [C19: from Spanish]

cacique (kə'siːk) *or* **cazique** (kə'ziːk) *n* **1** an American Indian chief in a Spanish-speaking region. **2** (esp. in Spanish America) a local political boss. **3** any of various tropical American songbirds of the genus *Cacicus* and related genera: family *Icteridae* (American orioles). [C16: from Spanish, of Arawak origin; compare Taino *cacique* chief]

caciquism (kə'siːk,ɪzəm) *n* (esp. in Spanish America) government by local political bosses.

cack-handed (,kæk'hændɪd) *adj Informal.* **1** left-handed. **2** clumsy. [from dialect *cack* excrement, from the fact that clumsy people usually make a mess; via Middle Low German or Middle Dutch from Latin *cacāre* to defecate]

cackle ('kækᵊl) *vb* **1** (*intr*) (esp. of a hen) to squawk with shrill notes. **2** (*intr*) to laugh or chatter raucously. **3** (*tr*) to utter in a cackling manner. ◆ *n* **4** the noise or act of cackling. **5** noisy chatter. **6 cut the cackle.** *Informal.* to stop chattering; be quiet. [C13: probably from Middle Low German *kākelen,* of imitative origin] ▸ **'cackler** *n*

caco- *combining form.* bad, unpleasant, or incorrect: *cacophony.* [from Greek *kakos* bad]

cacodemon *or* **cacodaemon** (,kækə'diːmən) *n* an evil spirit or devil. [C16: from Greek *kakodaimōn* evil genius]

cacodyl ('kækədaɪl) *n* an oily poisonous liquid with a strong garlic smell; tetramethyldiarsine. [C19: from Greek *kakōdēs* evil-smelling (from *kakos* CACO- + *ozein* to smell) + -YL] ▸ **cacodylic** (,kækə'dɪlɪk) *adj*

cacoepy (kə'kəʊɪpɪ) *n* bad or mistaken pronunciation. [C19: from Greek *kakoepeia*] ▸ **cacoepistic** (kə,kəʊɪ'pɪstɪk) *adj*

cacoethes (,kækəʊ'iːθiːz) *n* an uncontrollable urge or desire, esp. for something harmful; mania: *a cacoethes for smoking.* [C16: from Latin *cacoēthes* malignant disease, from Greek *kakoēthēs* of an evil disposition, from *kakos* CACO- + *ēthos* character] ▸ **cacoethic** (,kækəʊ'ɛθɪk) *adj*

cacogenics (,kækəʊ'dʒɛnɪks) *n* another name for **dysgenics.** [C20: from CACO- + EUGENICS] ▸ **,caco'genic** *adj*

cacography (kæ'kɒgrəfɪ) *n* **1** bad handwriting. Compare **calligraphy. 2** incorrect spelling. Compare **orthography.** ▸ **ca'cographer** *n* ▸ **cacographic** (,kækə'græfɪk) *or* **,caco'graphical** *adj*

cacology (kə'kɒlədʒɪ) *n* a bad choice of words; faulty speech. [C17 (in the sense: ill report): from Greek *kakologia*]

cacomistle ('kækə,mɪsᵊl) *or* **cacomixle** ('kækə,mɪksᵊl) *n* **1** a catlike omnivorous mammal, *Bassariscus astutus,* of S North America, related to but smaller than the raccoons: family *Procyonidae,* order *Carnivora* (carnivores). It has yellowish-grey fur and a long bushy tail banded in black and white. **2** a related smaller animal, *Jentinkia* (or *Bassariscus*) *sumichrasti,* of Central America.

[C19: from Mexican Spanish, from Nahuatl *tlacomiztli,* from *tlaco* half + *miztli* cougar]

cacophonous (kəˈkɒfənəs) *or* **cacophonic** (ˌkækəˈfɒnɪk) *adj* jarring in sound; discordant; harsh. ► **caˈcophonously** *or* **ˌcacoˈphonically** *adv*

cacophony (kəˈkɒfənɪ) *n, pl* **-nies. 1** harsh discordant sound; dissonance. **2** the use of unharmonious or dissonant speech sounds in language. Compare **euphony.**

cactus (ˈkæktəs) *n, pl* **-tuses** *or* **-ti** (-taɪ). **1** any spiny succulent plant of the family *Cactaceae* of the arid regions of America. Cactuses have swollen tough stems, leaves reduced to spines or scales, and large brightly coloured flowers. **2 cactus dahlia.** a double-flowered variety of dahlia. [C17: from Latin: prickly plant, from Greek *kaktos* cardoon] ► **cactaceous** (kækˈteɪʃəs) *adj*

cacuminal (kæˈkjuːmɪnᵊl) *Phonetics.* ◆ *adj* **1** Also called: **cerebral.** relating to or denoting a consonant articulated with the tip of the tongue turned back towards the hard palate. ◆ *n* **2** a consonant articulated in this manner. [C19: from Latin *cacūmen* point, top]

cad (kæd) *n Brit. informal; old-fashioned.* a man who does not behave in a gentlemanly manner towards others. [C18: shortened from CADDIE] ► **ˈcaddish** *adj*

CAD *acronym for* computer-aided design.

cadaster *or* **cadastre** (kəˈdæstə) *n* an official register showing details of ownership, boundaries, and value of real property in a district, made for taxation purposes. [C19: from French, from Provençal *cadastro,* from Italian *catastro,* from Late Greek *katastikhon* register, from *kata stikhon* line by line, from *kata* (see CATA-) + *stikhos* line, STICH] ► **caˈdastral** *adj*

cadaver (kəˈdeɪvə, -ˈdɑːv-) *n Med.* a corpse. [C16: from Latin, from *cadere* to fall] ► **caˈdaveric** *adj*

cadaverine (kəˈdævəˌriːn) *n* a toxic diamine with an unpleasant smell, produced by protein hydrolysis during putrefaction of animal tissue. Formula: $NH_2(CH_2)_5NH_2$.

cadaverous (kəˈdævərəs) *adj* **1** of or like a corpse, esp. in being deathly pale; ghastly. **2** thin and haggard; gaunt. ► **caˈdaverously** *adv* ► **caˈdaverousness** *n*

Cadbury (ˈkædbərɪ) *n* **George.** 1839–1922, British Quaker industrialist and philanthropist. He established, with his brother **Richard Cadbury** (1835–99), the chocolate-making company Cadbury Brothers and the garden village Bournville, near Birmingham, for their workers.

CADCAM (ˈkædˌkæm) *n acronym for* computer-aided design and manufacture.

caddie *or* **caddy** (ˈkædɪ) *n, pl* **-dies. 1** *Golf.* an attendant who carries clubs, etc., for a player. ◆ *vb* **-dies, -dying, -died. 2** (*intr*) to act as a caddie. [C17 (originally: a gentleman learning the military profession by serving in the army without a commission, hence C18 (Scottish): a person looking for employment, an errand-boy): from French CADET]

caddie car *or* **caddie cart** *n Golf.* a small light two-wheeled trolley for carrying clubs.

caddis *or* **caddice** (ˈkædɪs) *n* a type of coarse woollen yarn, braid, or fabric.

caddis fly *n* any small mothlike insect of the order *Trichoptera,* having two pairs of hairy wings and aquatic larvae (caddis worms). [C17: of unknown origin]

caddis worm *or* **caddis** *n* the aquatic larva of a caddis fly, which constructs a protective case around itself made of silk, sand, stones, etc. Also called: **caseworm, strawworm.**

Caddoan (ˈkædəʊən) *n* a family of North American Indian languages, including Pawnee, formerly spoken in a wide area of the Midwest, and probably distantly related to Siouan.

caddy[1] (ˈkædɪ) *n, pl* **-dies.** *Chiefly Brit.* a small container, esp. for tea. [C18: from Malay *kati;* see CATTY[2]]

caddy[2] (ˈkædɪ) *n, pl* **-dies,** *vb* **-dies, -dying, -died.** a variant spelling of **caddie.**

cade[1] (keɪd) *n* a juniper tree, *Juniperus oxycedrus* of the Mediterranean region, the wood of which yields an oily brown liquid (**oil of cade**) used to treat skin ailments. [C16: via Old French from Old Provençal, from Medieval Latin *catanus*]

cade[2] (keɪd) *adj* (of a young animal) left by its mother and reared by humans, usually as a pet. [C15: of unknown origin]

Cade (keɪd) *n* **Jack.** died 1450, English leader of the Kentish rebellion against the misgovernment of Henry VI (1450).

-cade *n combining form.* indicating a procession of a specified kind: *motorcade.* [abstracted from CAVALCADE]

cadelle (kəˈdɛl) *n* a widely distributed beetle, *Tenebroides mauritanicus,* that feeds on flour, grain, and other stored foods: family *Trogositidae.* [French, from Provençal *cadello,* from Latin *catellus* a little dog]

cadence (ˈkeɪdᵊns) *or* **cadency** *n, pl* **-dences** *or* **-dencies. 1** the beat or measure of something rhythmic. **2** a fall in the pitch of the voice, as at the end of a sentence. **3** modulation of the voice; intonation. **4** a rhythm or rhythmic construction in verse or prose; measure. **5** the close of a musical phrase or section. [C14: from Old French, from Old Italian *cadenza,* literally: a falling, from Latin *cadere* to fall]

cadency (ˈkeɪdᵊnsɪ) *n, pl* **-cies. 1** *Heraldry.* the line of descent from a younger member of a family. **2** another word for **cadence.**

cadent (ˈkeɪdᵊnt) *adj* **1** having cadence; rhythmic. **2** *Archaic.* falling; descending. [C16: from Latin *cadēns* falling, from *cadere* to fall]

cadenza (kəˈdɛnzə) *n* **1** a virtuoso solo passage occurring near the end of a piece of music, formerly improvised by the soloist but now usually specially composed. **2** *S. African. informal.* a fit or convulsion. [C19: from Italian; see CADENCE]

cadet (kəˈdɛt) *n* **1** a young person undergoing preliminary training, usually before full entry to the uniformed services, police, etc., esp. for officer status. **2** a school pupil receiving elementary military training in a school corps. **3** (in England and in France before 1789) a gentleman, usually a younger son, who entered the army to prepare for a commission. **4** a younger son or brother. **5 cadet branch.** the family or family branch of a younger son. **6** (in New Zealand) a person learning sheep farming on a sheep station. [C17: from French, from dialect (Gascon) *capdet* captain, ultimately from Latin *caput* head] ► **caˈdetship** *n*

cadge (kædʒ) *vb* **1** to get (food, money, etc.) by sponging or begging. ◆ *n* **2** *Brit.* a person who cadges. **3 on the cadge.** *Brit. informal.* engaged in cadging. [C17: of unknown origin]

cadger *n* **1** (ˈkædʒə). *Brit.* a person who cadges. **2** (ˈkædʒər). *Scot.* a pedlar or carrier.

cadi *or* **kadi** (ˈkɑːdɪ, ˈkeɪdɪ) *n, pl* **-dis.** a judge in a Muslim community. [C16: from Arabic *qādī* judge]

Cádiz (kəˈdɪz; *Spanish* ˈkaðiθ) *n* a port in SW Spain, on a narrow peninsula that forms the **Bay of Cádiz** at the E end of the **Gulf of Cádiz:** founded about 1100 B.C. as a Phoenician trading colony; centre of trade with America from the 16th to 18th centuries. Pop.: 154 511 (1995 est.).

Cadmean victory (ˈkædmɪən) *n* another name for **Pyrrhic victory.**

cadmium (ˈkædmɪəm) *n* a malleable ductile toxic bluish-white metallic element that occurs in association with zinc ores. It is used in electroplating, alloys, and as a neutron absorber in the control of nuclear fission. Symbol: Cd; atomic no.: 48; atomic wt.: 112.411; valency: 2; relative density: 8.65; melting pt.: 321.1°C; boiling pt.: 767°C. [C19: from New Latin, from Latin *cadmīa* zinc ore, CALAMINE, referring to the fact that both calamine and cadmium are found in the ore]

cadmium cell *n* **1** a photocell with a cadmium electrode that is especially sensitive to ultraviolet radiation. **2** a former name for **Weston standard cell.**

cadmium sulphide *n* an orange or yellow insoluble solid used as a pigment in paints, etc. (**cadmium yellow**). Formula: CdS.

Cadmus (ˈkædməs) *n Greek myth.* a Phoenician prince who killed a dragon and planted its teeth, from which sprang a multitude of warriors who fought among themselves until only five remained, who joined Cadmus to found Thebes. ► **ˈCadmean** *adj*

cadre (ˈkɑːdə) *n* **1** the nucleus of trained professional servicemen forming the basis for the training of new units or other military expansion. **2** a basic unit or structure, esp. of personnel; nucleus; core. **3** a member of a cadre. [C19: from French, from Italian *quadro,* from Latin *quadrum* square]

caduceus (kəˈdjuːsɪəs) *n, pl* **-cei** (-sɪˌaɪ). **1** *Classical myth.* a staff entwined with two serpents and bearing a pair of wings at the top, carried by Hermes (Mercury) as messenger of the gods. **2** an insignia resembling this staff used as an emblem of the medical profession. Compare **staff of Aesculapius.** [C16: from Latin, from Doric Greek *karukeion,* from *karux* herald]

caducibranchiate (kəˌdjuːsɪˈbræŋkɪˌeɪt) *adj* (of many amphibians, such as frogs) having gills during one stage of the life cycle only. [from Latin *cadūcus* CADUCOUS + BRANCHIA]

caducity (kəˈdjuːsɪtɪ) *n* **1** perishableness. **2** senility. [C18: from French, from Latin *cadūcus* CADUCOUS]

caducous (kəˈdjuːkəs) *adj Biology.* (of parts of a plant or animal) shed during the life of the organism. [C17: from Latin *cadūcus* falling, from *cadere* to fall]

Cadwalader (kædˈwɒlədə) *n* 7th century A.D., legendary king of the Britons, probably a confusion of several historical figures.

CAE *abbrev. for:* computer-aided engineering.

caecilian (siːˈsɪlɪən) *n* any tropical limbless cylindrical amphibian of the order *Apoda* (or *Gymnophiona*), resembling earthworms and inhabiting moist soil. [C19: from Latin *caecilia* a kind of lizard, from *caecus* blind]

caecum *or U.S.* **cecum** (ˈsiːkəm) *n, pl* **-ca** (-kə). *Anatomy.* any structure or part that ends in a blind sac or pouch, esp. the pouch that marks the beginning of the large intestine. [C18: short for Latin *intestinum caecum* blind intestine, translation of Greek *tuphlon enteron*] ► **ˈcaecal** *or U.S.* **ˈcecal** *adj*

Cædmon (ˈkædmən) *n* 7th century A.D., Anglo-Saxon poet and monk, the earliest English poet whose name survives.

Caelian (ˈsiːlɪən) *n* the southeasternmost of the Seven Hills of Rome.

Caelum (ˈsiːləm) *n, Latin genitive* **Caeli** (ˈsiːlaɪ). a small faint constellation in the S hemisphere close to Eridanus. [Latin: the sky, heaven]

Caen (kɒŋ; *French* kɑ̃) *n* an industrial city in NW France. Pop.: 115 624 (1990).

caenogenesis (ˌsiːnəʊˈdʒɛnɪsɪs), **cainogenesis, kainogenesis** *or U.S.* **cenogenesis, kenogenesis** *n* the development of structures and organs in an embryo or larva that are adaptations to its way of life and are not retained in the adult form. Compare **recapitulation** (sense 2). ► **caenogenetic** (ˌsiːnəʊdʒəˈnɛtɪk), **ˌcainogeˈnetic, ˌkainogeˈnetic** *or U.S.* **ˌcenogeˈnetic, ˌkenogeˈnetic** *adj* ► **ˌcaenogeˈnetically, ˌcainogeˈnetically, ˌkainogeˈnetically** *or U.S.* **ˌcenogeˈnetically, ˌkenogeˈnetically** *adv*

Caenozoic (ˌsiːnəˈzəʊɪk) *adj* a variant spelling of **Cenozoic.**

caeoma (siːˈəʊmə) *n* an aecium in some rust fungi that has no surrounding membrane. [New Latin, from Greek *kaiein* to burn; referring to its glowing colour]

Caerleon (kɑːˈlɪən) *n* a town in SE Wales, in Newport county borough on the River Usk: traditionally the seat of King Arthur's court. Pop.: 8931 (1991).

Caernarfon, Caernarvon, *or* **Carnarvon** (kɑːˈnɑːvᵊn) *n* a port and resort in NW Wales, in Gwynedd on the Menai Strait: 13th-century castle. Pop.: 9695 (1991).

Caernarvonshire (kɑːˈnɑːvᵊnˌʃɪə, -ʃə) *n* (until 1974) a county of NW Wales, now part of Gwynedd.

Caerphilly (kɛəˈfɪlɪ) *n* **1** a market town in SE Wales, in Caerphilly county borough: site of the largest castle in Wales (13th–14th centuries). Pop.: 28 481 (1991). **2** a county borough in SE Wales, created in 1996 from parts of Mid Glamorgan and Gwent. Pop.: 170 000 (1996 est.). Area: 275 sq. km (106 sq. miles). **3** a creamy white mild-flavoured cheese.

caesalpiniaceous (ˌsɛzælˌpɪnɪˈeɪʃəs) *adj* of, relating to, or belonging to the *Caesalpiniaceae,* a mainly tropical family of leguminous plants that have irregular flowers: includes carob, senna, brazil, cassia, and poinciana. **[**from New Latin *Caesalpinia* type genus, named after Andrea *Cesalpino* (1519–1603), Italian botanist**]**

Caesar (ˈsiːzə) *n* **1 Gaius Julius** (ˈgaɪəs ˈdʒuːlɪəs). 100–44 B.C., Roman general, statesman, and historian. He formed the first triumvirate with Pompey and Crassus (60), conquered Gaul (58–50), invaded Britain (55–54), mastered Italy (49), and defeated Pompey (46). As dictator of the Roman Empire (49–44) he destroyed the power of the corrupt Roman nobility. He also introduced the Julian calendar and planned further reforms, but fear of his sovereign power led to his assassination (44) by conspirators led by Marcus Brutus and Cassius Longinus. **2** any Roman emperor. **3** (*sometimes not cap.*) any emperor, autocrat, dictator, or other powerful ruler. **4** a title of the Roman emperors from Augustus to Hadrian. **5** (in the Roman Empire) **5a** a title borne by the imperial heir from the reign of Hadrian. **5b** the heir, deputy, and subordinate ruler to either of the two emperors under Diocletian's system of government.

Caesaraugusta (ˌsiːzərɔːˈgʌstə) *n* the Latin name for **Zaragoza.**

Caesarea (ˌsiːzəˈrɪə) *n* an ancient port in NW Israel, capital of Roman Palestine: founded by Herod the Great.

Caesarea Mazaca (ˈmæzəkə) *n* the ancient name of **Kayseri.**

Caesarean, Caesarian, *or U.S.* **Cesarean, Cesarian** (sɪˈzɛərɪən) *adj* **1** of or relating to any of the Caesars, esp. Julius Caesar. ◆ *n* **2** (*sometimes not cap.*) *Surgery.* **2a** short for **Caesarean section. 2b** (*as modifier*): *Caesarean birth; Caesarean operation.*

Caesarean section *n* surgical incision through the abdominal and uterine walls in order to deliver a baby. **[C17:** from the belief that Julius Caesar was so delivered, the name allegedly being derived from *caesus,* past participle of *caedere* to cut**]**

Caesarism (ˈsiːzəˌrɪzəm) *n* an autocratic system of government. See also **Bonapartism.** ▸ **ˈCaesarist** *n* ▸ **ˌCaesarˈistic** *adj*

caesious *or U.S.* **cesious** (ˈsiːzɪəs) *adj Botany.* having a waxy bluish-grey coating. **[C19:** from Latin *caesius* bluish grey**]**

caesium *or U.S.* **cesium** (ˈsiːzɪəm) *n* a ductile silvery-white element of the alkali metal group that is the most electropositive metal. It occurs in pollucite and lepidolite and is used in photocells. The radioisotope **caesium-137,** with a half-life of 30.2 years, is used in radiotherapy. Symbol: Cs; atomic no.: 55; atomic wt.: 132.90543; valency: 1; relative density: 1.873; melting pt.: 28.39±0.01°C; boiling pt.: 671°C.

caesium clock *n* a type of atomic clock that uses the frequency of radiation absorbed in changing the spin of electrons in caesium atoms. See also **second**[2].

caespitose *or U.S.* **cespitose** (ˈsɛspɪˌtəʊs) *adj Botany.* growing in dense tufts. **[C19:** from New Latin *caespitōsus,* from *caespitem* turf**]** ▸ **ˈcaespiˌtosely** *or U.S.* **ˈcespiˌtosely** *adv*

caesura (sɪˈzjʊərə) *n, pl* **-ras** *or* **-rae** (-riː). **1** (in modern prosody) a pause, esp. for sense, usually near the middle of a verse line. Usual symbol: ‖ **2** (in classical prosody) a break between words within a metrical foot, usually in the third or fourth foot of the line. **[C16:** from Latin, literally: a cutting, from *caedere* to cut**]** ▸ **caeˈsural** *adj*

Caetano (kaɪˈtɑːnəʊ; *Portuguese* kɑiˈtɐnu) *n* **Marcello** (marˈsɛlu). 1906–80, prime minister of Portugal from 1968 until he was replaced by an army coup in 1974.

CAF *abbrev. for* cost and freight.

cafard (*French* kafar) *n* a feeling of severe depression. **[C20:** from French, literally: cockroach, hypocrite**]**

café (ˈkæfeɪ, ˈkæfɪ) *n* **1** a small or inexpensive restaurant or coffee bar, serving light meals and refreshments. **2** *S. African.* a corner shop or grocer. **[C19:** from French: COFFEE**]**

café au lait *French.* (kafe o lɛ) *n* **1** coffee with milk. **2** a light brown colour.

café noir *French.* (kafe nwar) *n* black coffee.

cafeteria (ˌkæfɪˈtɪərɪə) *n* a self-service restaurant. **[C20:** from American Spanish: coffee shop**]**

cafetiere (ˌkæfəˈtjɛə, ˌkæfəˈtɪə) *n* a kind of coffeepot in which boiling water is poured onto ground coffee and a plunger fitted with a metal filter is pressed down, forcing the grounds to the bottom. **[C20:** from French *cafetière* coffeepot**]**

caff (kæf) *n* a slang word for **café.**

caffeine *or* **caffein** (ˈkæfiːn, ˈkæfɪˌiːn) *n* a white crystalline bitter alkaloid responsible for the stimulant action of tea, coffee, and cocoa: a constituent of many tonics and analgesics. Formula: $C_8H_{10}N_4O_2$. See also **xanthine** (sense 2). **[C19:** from German *Kaffein,* from *Kaffee* COFFEE**]**

caftan (ˈkæfˌtæn, -ˌtɑːn) *n* a variant spelling of **kaftan.**

cag (kæg) *n Mountaineering.* short for **cagoule.**

cage (keɪdʒ) *n* **1a** an enclosure, usually made with bars or wire, for keeping birds, monkeys, mice, etc. **1b** (*as modifier*): *cagebird.* **2** a thing or place that confines or imprisons. **3** something resembling a cage in function or structure: *the rib cage.* **4** the enclosed platform of a lift, esp. as used in a mine. **5** *Engineering.* a skeleton ring device that ensures that the correct amount of space is maintained between the individual rollers or balls in a rolling bearing. **6** *Informal.* the basket used in basketball. **7** *Informal.* the goal in ice hockey. **8** *U.S.* a steel framework on which guns are supported. **9 rattle someone's cage.** *Informal.* to upset or anger someone. ◆ *vb* **10** (*tr*) to confine in or as in a cage. **[C13:** from Old French, from Latin *cavea* enclosure, from *cavus* hollow**]**

Cage (keɪdʒ) *n* **John.** 1912–92, U.S. composer of experimental music for a variety of conventional, modified, or invented instruments. He evolved a type of music apparently undetermined by the composer, such as in *Imaginary Landscape* (1951) for 12 radio sets. Other works include *Reunion* (1968), *Apartment Building 1776* (1976), and *Europeras 3 and 4* (1990).

cageling (ˈkeɪdʒlɪŋ) *n* a bird kept in a cage.

cagey *or* **cagy** (ˈkeɪdʒɪ) *adj* **-ier, -iest.** *Informal.* not open or frank; cautious; wary. **[C20:** of unknown origin**]** ▸ **ˈcagily** *adv* ▸ **ˈcaginess** *n*

cag-handed (ˌkægˈhændɪd) *adj Dialect.* a variant of **cack-handed.**

Cagliari[1] (kælˈjɑːrɪ; *Italian* kaʎˈʎari) *n* a port in Italy, the capital of Sardinia, on the S coast. Pop.: 174 543 (1996 est.).

Cagliari[2] (*Italian* kaʎˈʎari) *n* **Paolo** (ˈpaːolo), original name of (Paolo) **Veronese.**

Cagliostro (*Italian* kaʎˈʎostro) *n* Count **Alessandro di** (alesˈsandro di), original name *Giuseppe Balsamo.* 1743–95, Italian adventurer and magician, who was imprisoned for life by the Inquisition for his association with freemasonry.

cagmag (ˈkægˌmæg) *Midland English dialect.* ◆ *adj* **1** done shoddily; left incomplete. ◆ *vb* **-mags, -magging, -magged.** (*intr*) **2** to chat idly; gossip. **[C18:** of uncertain origin**]**

Cagney (ˈkægnɪ) *n* **James.** 1899–1986, U.S. film actor, esp. in gangster roles; his films include *The Public Enemy* (1931), *Angels with Dirty Faces* (1938), *The Roaring Twenties* (1939), and *Yankee Doodle Dandy* (1942) for which he won an Oscar.

cagoule (kəˈguːl) *n* a lightweight usually knee-length type of anorak. Also spelt: **kaˈgoul, kaˈgoule.** Sometimes shortened to **cag. [C20:** from French**]**

cahier *French.* (kaje) *n* **1** a notebook. **2** a written or printed report, esp. of the proceedings of a meeting.

Cahokia Mounds (kəˈhəʊkɪə) *pl n* the largest group of prehistoric Indian earthworks in the U.S., located northeast of East St Louis.

cahoots (kəˈhuːts) *pl n* (*sometimes sing*) *Informal.* **1** *U.S.* partnership; league (esp. in the phrases **go in cahoots with, go cahoot**). **2 in cahoots.** in collusion. **[C19:** of uncertain origin**]**

CAI *abbrev. for* computer-aided instruction.

Caiaphas (ˈkaɪəˌfæs) *n New Testament.* the high priest at the beginning of John the Baptist's preaching and during the trial of Jesus (Luke 3:2; Matthew 26).

Caicos Islands (ˈkeɪkəs) *pl n* a group of islands in the Caribbean: part of the British dependency of the **Turks and Caicos Islands.**

cailleach (ˈkæljəx) *n Scot.* an old woman. **[**Gaelic**]**

caiman (ˈkeɪmən) *n, pl* **-mans.** a variant spelling of **cayman.**

cain *or* **kain** (keɪn) *n History.* (in Scotland and Ireland) payment in kind, usually farm produce paid as rent. **[C12:** from Scottish Gaelic *cāin* rent, perhaps ultimately from Late Latin *canōn* tribute (see CANON); compare Middle Irish *cāin* law**]**

Cain (keɪn) *n* **1** the first son of Adam and Eve, who killed his brother Abel (Genesis 4:1–16). **2 raise Cain. 2a** to cause a commotion. **2b** to react or protest heatedly.

Caine (keɪn) *n* **Michael.** real name *Maurice Micklewhite.* born 1933, British film actor. His films include *The Ipcress File* (1965), *Educating Rita* (1983), *Hannah and Her Sisters* (1986), and *Little Voice* (1999).

cainogenesis (ˌkaɪnəʊˈdʒɛnɪsɪs) *n* a variant spelling of **caenogenesis.** ▸ **cainogenetic** (ˌkaɪnəʊdʒəˈnɛtɪk) *adj* ▸ **ˌcainogeˈnetically** *adv*

Cainozoic (ˌkaɪnəʊˈzəʊɪk, ˌkeɪ-) *adj* a variant of **Cenozoic.**

caïque (kaɪˈiːk) *n* **1** a long narrow light rowing skiff used on the Bosporus. **2** a sailing vessel of the E Mediterranean with a sprit mainsail, square topsail, and two or more jibs or other sails. **[C17:** from French, from Italian *caicco,* from Turkish *kayik***]**

caird (kɛəd; *Scot.* kerd) *n Scot. obsolete.* a travelling tinker; vagrant. **[C17:** from Scottish Gaelic; related to Welsh *cerdd* craft**]**

Caird Coast (kɛəd) *n* a region of Antarctica: a part of Coats Land on the SE coast of the Weddell Sea; now included in the British Antarctic Territory.

cairn (kɛən) *n* **1** a mound of stones erected as a memorial or marker. **2** Also called: **cairn terrier.** a small rough-haired breed of terrier originally from Scotland. **[C15:** from Gaelic *carn***]**

cairngorm (ˈkɛənˌgɔːm, ˌkernˈgɔrm) *n* a smoky yellow, grey, or brown variety of quartz, used as a gemstone. Also called: **smoky quartz. [C18:** from *Cairn Gorm* (literally: blue cairn), mountain in Scotland where it is found**]**

Cairngorm Mountains *pl n* a mountain range of NE Scotland: part of the Grampians. Highest peak: Ben Macdhui, 1309 m (4296 ft.). Also called: **the Cairngorms.**

Cairns (kænz, kɛənz) *n* a port in NE Australia, in Queensland. Pop.: 100 900 (1995 est.).

Cairo (ˈkaɪrəʊ) *n* the capital of Egypt, on the Nile: the largest city in Africa and in the Middle East; industrial centre; site of the university and mosque of Al Azhar (founded in 972). Pop.: 6 849 000 (1994 est.). Arabic name: **El Qahira** (ɛl ˈkahiːrə). ▸ **ˈCairene** *n, adj*

caisson (kəˈsuːn, ˈkeɪsᵊn) *n* **1** a watertight chamber open at the bottom and containing air under pressure, used to carry out construction work under water. **2** a watertight float filled with air, used to raise sunken ships. See also **camel** (sense 2). **3** a watertight structure placed across the entrance of a basin, dry dock, etc., to exclude water from it. **4a** a box containing explosives formerly used as a mine. **4b** an ammunition chest. **4c** a two-wheeled vehicle containing an ammunition chest. **5** another name for **coffer** (sense 3). **[C18:** from French, assimilated to *caisse* CASE[2]**]**

caisson disease *n* another name for **decompression sickness.**

Caithness (keɪθˈnɛs, ˈkeɪθnɛs) *n* (until 1975) a county of NE Scotland, now part of Highland.

caitiff (ˈkeɪtɪf) *Archaic or poetic.* ◆ *n* **1** a cowardly or base person. ◆ *adj* **2** cowardly; base. **[C13:** from Old French *caitif* prisoner, from Latin *captīvus* CAPTIVE**]**

Caius (ˈkaɪəs) *n* a variant of **Gaius.**

Cajal (*Spanish* kaˈxal) *n* **Santiago Ramon y.** 1852–1934, Spanish histologist, a pioneer of modern neurophysiology: shared the Nobel prize for medicine 1906.

cajeput (ˈkædʒəˌpʊt) *n* a variant spelling of **cajuput.**

cajole (kə'dʒəʊl) *vb* to persuade (someone) by flattery or pleasing talk to do what one wants; wheedle; coax. [C17: from French *cajoler* to coax, of uncertain origin] ▸ **ca'jolement** *n* ▸ **ca'joler** *n* ▸ **ca'jolery** *n* ▸ **ca'jolingly** *adv*

Cajun ('keɪdʒən) *n* **1** a native of Louisiana descended from 18th-century Acadian immigrants. **2** the dialect of French spoken by such people. **3** the music of this ethnic group, combining blues and European folk music. ◆ *adj* **4** denoting or relating to such people, their language, or their music. [C19: alteration of ACADIAN; compare *Injun* for *Indian*]

cajuput *or* **cajeput** ('kædʒə,pʊt) *n* **1** a small myrtaceous tree or shrub, *Melaleuca leucadendron,* native to the East Indies and Australia, with whitish flowers and leaves. **2** a green aromatic oil derived from this tree, used to treat skin diseases. **3** a lauraceous tree, *Umbellularia californica,* whose aromatic leaves are used in medicine. [C18: from Malay *kayu puteh,* from *kayu* wood + *puteh* white]

cake (keɪk) *n* **1** a baked food, usually in loaf or layer form, typically made from a mixture of flour, sugar, and eggs. **2** a flat thin mass of bread, esp. unleavened bread. **3** a shaped mass of dough or other food of similar consistency: *a fish cake.* **4** a mass, slab, or crust of a solidified or compressed substance, as of soap or ice. **5 have one's cake and eat it.** to enjoy both of two desirable but incompatible alternatives. **6 go** *or* **sell like hot cakes.** *Informal.* to be sold very quickly or in large quantities. **7 piece of cake.** *Informal.* something that is easily achieved or obtained. **8 take the cake.** *Informal.* to surpass all others, esp. in stupidity, folly, etc. **9** *Informal.* the whole or total of something that is to be shared or divided: *the miners are demanding a larger slice of the cake; that is a fair method of sharing the cake.* ◆ *vb* **10** (*tr*) to cover with a hard layer; encrust: *the hull was caked with salt.* **11** to form or be formed into a hardened mass. [C13: from Old Norse *kaka;* related to Danish *kage,* German *Kuchen*] ▸ **'cakey** *or* **'caky** *adj*

cakewalk ('keɪk,wɔːk) *n* **1** a dance based on a march with intricate steps, originally performed by African-Americans with the prize of a cake for the best performers. **2** a piece of music composed for this dance. **3** *Informal.* an easily accomplished task. ◆ *vb* **4** (*intr*) to perform the cakewalk. ▸ **'cake,walker** *n*

CAL *abbrev. for* computer-aided (or -assisted) learning.

cal. *abbrev. for:* **1** calibre. **2** calorie (small).

Cal. *abbrev. for:* **1** Calorie (large). **2** California.

Calabar ('kælə,bɑː) *n* a port in SE Nigeria, capital of Cross River state. Pop.: 174 400 (1996 est.).

Calabar bean (,kælə'bɑː, 'kælə,bɑː) *n* the dark brown very poisonous seed of a leguminous woody climbing plant, *Physostigma venenosum* of tropical Africa, used as a source of the drug physostigmine.

calabash ('kælə,bæʃ) *n* **1** Also called: **calabash tree.** a tropical American evergreen tree, *Crescentia cujete,* that produces large round gourds: family *Bignoniaceae.* **2** another name for the **bottle gourd. 3** the gourd of either of these plants. **4** the dried hollow shell of a gourd used as the bowl of a tobacco pipe, a bottle, rattle, etc. **5 calabash nutmeg.** a tropical African shrub, *Monodora myristica,* whose oily aromatic seeds can be used as nutmegs: family *Annonaceae.* [C17: from obsolete French *calabasse,* from Spanish *calabaza,* perhaps from Arabic *qar'ah yābisah* dry gourd, from *qar'ah* gourd + *yābisah* dry]

calaboose ('kælə,buːs) *n U.S. informal.* a prison; jail. [C18: from Creole French, from Spanish *calabozo* dungeon, of unknown origin]

calabrese (,kælə'breɪzɪ) *n* a variety of green sprouting broccoli. [C20: from Italian: Calabrian]

Calabria (kə'læbrɪə) *n* **1** a region of SW Italy: mostly mountainous and subject to earthquakes. Chief town: Reggio di Calabria. Pop.: 2 075 842 (1996 est.). Area: 15 080 sq. km (5822 sq. miles). **2** an ancient region of extreme SE Italy (3rd century B.C. to about 668 A.D.); now part of Apulia. ▸ **Ca'labrian** *adj, n*

caladium (kə'leɪdɪəm) *n* any of various tropical plants of the aroid genus *Caladium,* which are widely cultivated as potted plants for their colourful variegated foliage. [C19: from New Latin, from Malay *kĕladi* araceous plant]

Calais ('kæleɪ, 'kælɪ; *French* kalɛ) *n* a port in N France, on the Strait of Dover: the nearest French port to England; belonged to England 1347–1558. Pop.: 75 309 (1990).

calalu *or* **calaloo** ('kælәluː) *n Caribbean.* the edible leaves of various plants, used as greens or in making thick soups. [probably of African origin]

calamanco (,kælə'mæŋkəʊ) *n* a glossy woollen fabric woven with a checked design that shows on one side only. [C16: of unknown origin]

calamander ('kælə,mændə) *n* the hard black-and-brown striped wood of several trees of the genus *Diospyros,* esp. *D. quaesita* of India and Sri Lanka, used in making furniture: family *Ebenaceae.* See also **ebony** (sense 2). [C19: metathetic variant of *coromandel* in COROMANDEL COAST]

calamine ('kælə,maɪn) *n* **1** a pink powder consisting of zinc oxide and ferric oxide, (iron(III) oxide), used medicinally in the form of soothing lotions or ointments. **2** *U.S.* another name for **smithsonite.** [C17: from Old French, from Medieval Latin *calamīna,* from Latin *cadmīa;* see CADMIUM]

calamint ('kæləmɪnt) *n* any aromatic Eurasian plant of the genus *Satureja* (or *Calamintha*), having clusters of purple or pink flowers: family *Labiatae* (labiates). [C14: from Old French *calament* (but influenced by English MINT[1]), from Medieval Latin *calamentum,* from Greek *kalaminthē*]

calamite ('kælə,maɪt) *n* any extinct treelike plant of the genus *Calamites,* of Carboniferous times, related to the horsetails. [C19: from New Latin *Calamītes* type genus, from Greek *kalamitēs* reedlike, from *kalamos* reed]

calamitous (kə'læmɪtəs) *adj* causing, involving, or resulting in a calamity; disastrous. ▸ **ca'lamitously** *adv* ▸ **ca'lamitousness** *n*

calamity (kə'læmɪtɪ) *n, pl* **-ties. 1** a disaster or misfortune, esp. one causing extreme havoc, distress, or misery. **2** a state or feeling of deep distress or misery. [C15: from French *calamité,* from Latin *calamitās;* related to Latin *incolumis* uninjured]

Calamity Jane *n* real name *Martha Canary.* ?1852–1903, U.S. frontierswoman, noted for her skill at shooting and riding.

calamondin ('kælə,mʌndɪn) *or* **calamondin orange** *n* **1** a small citrus tree, *Citrus mitis,* of the Philippines. **2** the acid-tasting fruit of this tree, resembling a small orange. [from Tagalog *kalamunding*]

calamus ('kæləməs) *n, pl* **-mi** (-,maɪ). **1** any tropical Asian palm of the genus *Calamus,* some species of which are a source of rattan and canes. **2** another name for **sweet flag. 3** the aromatic root of the sweet flag. **4** *Ornithol.* the basal hollow shaft of a feather; quill. [C14: from Latin, from Greek *kalamos* reed, cane, stem]

calando (kə'lændəʊ) *adj, adv Music.* (to be performed) with gradually decreasing tone and speed. [Italian: dropping, from *calare* to lower, to drop]

calandria (kə'lændrɪə) *n* a cylindrical vessel through which vertical tubes pass, esp. one forming part of an evaporator, heat exchanger, or nuclear reactor. [C20: arbitrarily named, from Spanish, literally: lark]

calash (kə'læʃ) *or* **calèche** *n* **1** a horse-drawn carriage with low wheels and a folding top. **2** the folding top of such a carriage. **3** a woman's folding hooped hood worn in the 18th century. [C17: from French *calèche,* from German *Kalesche,* from Czech *kolesa* wheels]

calathea (,kælə'θɪə) *n* any plant of the S. American perennial genus *Calathea,* many species of which are grown as greenhouse or house plants for their decorative variegated leaves, esp. the zebra plant (*C. zebrina*), the leaves of which are purplish below and dark green with lighter stripes above: family *Marantaceae.* [New Latin, from Greek *kalathos* a basket]

calathus ('kæləθəs) *n, pl* **-thi** (-,θaɪ). a vase-shaped basket represented in ancient Greek art, used as a symbol of fruitfulness. [C18: from Latin, from Greek *kalathos*]

calaverite (kə'lævə,raɪt) *n* a metallic pale yellow mineral consisting of a telluride of gold in the form of elongated striated crystals. It is a source of gold in Australia and North America. Formula: $AuTe_2$. [C19: named after *Calaveras,* county in California where it was discovered]

calc- *combining form.* a variant of **calci-** before a vowel.

calcaneus (kæl'keɪnɪəs) *or* **calcaneum** *n, pl* **-nei** (-nɪaɪ) *or* **-nea** (-nɪə). **1** the largest tarsal bone, forming the heel in man. Nontechnical name: **heel bone. 2** the corresponding bone in other vertebrates. [C19: from Late Latin: heel, from Latin *calx* heel] ▸ **cal'caneal** *or* **cal'canean** *adj*

calcar ('kæl,kɑː) *n, pl* **calcaria** (kæl'kɛərɪə). a spur or spurlike process, as on the leg of a bird or the corolla of a flower. [C19: from Latin, from *calx* heel]

calcareous (kæl'kɛərɪəs) *adj* of, containing, or resembling calcium carbonate; chalky. [C17: from Latin *calcārius,* from *calx* lime]

calcariferous (,kælkə'rɪfərəs) *adj Biology.* having a spur or spurs.

calceiform ('kælsɪɪ,fɔːm, kæl'siː-) *or* **calceolate** ('kælsɪə,leɪt) *adj Botany.* shaped like a shoe or slipper. [C19: from Latin *calceus* shoe]

calceolaria (,kælsɪə'lɛərɪə) *n* any tropical American scrophulariaceous plant of the genus *Calceolaria:* cultivated for its speckled slipper-shaped flowers. Also called: **slipperwort.** [C18: from Latin *calceolus* small shoe, from *calceus*]

calces ('kælsiːz) *n* a plural of **calx.**

Calchas ('kælkæs) *n Greek myth.* a soothsayer who assisted the Greeks in the Trojan War.

calci- *or before a vowel* **calc-** *combining form.* indicating lime or calcium: *calcify.* [from Latin *calx, calc-* limestone]

calcic ('kælsɪk) *adj* of, containing, or concerned with lime or calcium. [C19: from Latin *calx* lime]

calcicole ('kælsɪ,kəʊl) *n* any plant that thrives in lime-rich soils. [C20: from CALCI- + *-cole,* from Latin *colere* to dwell] ▸ **calcicolous** (kæl'sɪkələs) *adj*

calciferol (kæl'sɪfərɒl) *n* a fat-soluble steroid, found esp. in fish-liver oils, produced by the action of ultraviolet radiation on ergosterol. It increases the absorption of calcium from the intestine and is used in the treatment of rickets. Formula: $C_{28}H_{43}OH$. Also called: **vitamin** D_2. [C20: from CALCIF(EROUS + ERGOST)EROL]

calciferous (kæl'sɪfərəs) *adj* forming or producing salts of calcium, esp. calcium carbonate.

calcific (kæl'sɪfɪk) *adj* forming or causing to form lime or chalk.

calcification (,kælsɪfɪ'keɪʃən) *n* **1** the process of calcifying or becoming calcified. **2** *Pathol.* a tissue hardened by deposition of lime salts. **3** any calcified object or formation.

calcifuge ('kælsɪ,fjuːdʒ) *n* any plant that thrives in acid soils. ▸ **calcifugal** (,kælsɪ'fjuːgᵊl) *adj* ▸ **calcifugous** (kæl'sɪfjəgəs) *adj*

calcify ('kælsɪ,faɪ) *vb* **-fies, -fying, -fied. 1** to convert or be converted into lime. **2** to harden or become hardened by impregnation with calcium salts.

calcimine ('kælsɪ,maɪn, -mɪn) *or* **kalsomine** *n* **1** a white or pale tinted wash for walls. ◆ *vb* **2** (*tr*) to cover with calcimine. [C19: changed from *Kalsomine,* a trademark]

calcine ('kælsaɪn, -sɪn) *vb* **1** (*tr*) to heat (a substance) so that it is oxidized, reduced, or loses water. **2** (*intr*) to oxidize as a result of heating. [C14: from Medieval Latin *calcināre* to heat, from Latin *calx* lime] ▸ **calcination** (,kælsɪ'neɪʃən) *n*

calcinosis (,kælsɪ'nəʊsɪs) *n* the abnormal deposition of calcium salts in the tissues of the body.

calcite ('kælsaɪt) *n* a colourless or white mineral (occasionally tinged with impurities), found in sedimentary and metamorphic rocks, in veins, in limestone, and in stalagmites and stalactites. It is used in the manufacture of cement, plaster, paint, glass, and fertilizer. Composition: calcium carbonate. Formula: $CaCO_3$. Crystal structure: hexagonal (rhombohedral). ▸ **calcitic** (kæl'sɪtɪk) *adj*

calcitonin (,kælsɪ'təʊnɪn) *n* a hormone secreted by the thyroid that inhibits the release of calcium from the skeleton and prevents a build-up of calcium in the blood. Also called: **thyrocalcitonin.** Compare **parathyroid hormone.** [C20: from CALCI- + TON(IC) + -IN]

calcium ('kælsɪəm) *n* a malleable silvery-white metallic element of the alkaline earth group; the fifth most abundant element in the earth's crust (3.6 per cent), occurring esp. as forms of calcium carbonate. It is an essential constituent of bones and teeth and is used as a deoxidizer in steel. Symbol: Ca; atomic no.: 20; atomic wt.: 40.078; valency: 2; relative density: 1.55; melting pt.: 842±2°C; boiling pt.: 1494°C. [C19: from New Latin, from Latin *calx* lime]

calcium antagonist *or* **blocker** *n* any drug that prevents the influx of calcium ions into cardiac and smooth muscle: used to treat high blood pressure and angina.

calcium carbide *n* a grey salt of calcium used in the production of acetylene (by its reaction with water) and calcium cyanamide. Formula: CaC_2. Sometimes shortened to **carbide.**

calcium carbonate *n* a white crystalline salt occurring in limestone, chalk, marble, calcite, coral, and pearl: used in the production of lime and cement. Formula: $CaCO_3$.

calcium chloride *n* a white deliquescent salt occurring naturally in seawater and used in the de-icing of roads and as a drying agent. Formula: $CaCl_2$.

calcium cyanamide *n* a white crystalline compound formed by heating calcium carbide with nitrogen. It is important in the fixation of nitrogen and can be hydrolysed to ammonia or used as a fertilizer. Formula: $CaCN_2$.

calcium hydroxide *n* a white crystalline slightly soluble alkali with many uses, esp. in cement, water softening, and the neutralization of acid soils. Formula: $Ca(OH)_2$. Also called: **lime, slaked lime, hydrated lime, calcium hydrate, caustic lime, lime hydrate.**

calcium light *n* another name for **limelight.**

calcium oxide *n* a white crystalline base used in the production of calcium hydroxide and bleaching powder and in the manufacture of glass, paper, and steel. Formula: CaO. Also called: **lime, quicklime, calx, burnt lime, calcined lime, fluxing lime.**

calcium phosphate *n* **1** the insoluble nonacid calcium salt of orthophosphoric acid (phosphoric(V) acid): it occurs in bones and is the main constituent of bone ash. Formula: $Ca_3(PO_4)_2$. **2** any calcium salt of a phosphoric acid. Calcium phosphates are found in many rocks and used esp. in fertilizers.

calcsinter ('kælk,sɪntə) *n* another name for **travertine.** [C19: from German *Kalksinter,* from *Kalk* lime + *sinter* dross; see CHALK, SINTER]

calcspar ('kælk,spɑː) *n* another name for **calcite.** [C19: partial translation of Swedish *kalkspat,* from *kalk* lime (ultimately from Latin *calx*) + *spat* SPAR[3]]

calc-tufa ('kælk,tuːfə) *or* **calc-tuff** ('kælk,tʌf) *n* another name for **tufa.**

calculable ('kælkjʊləbᵊl) *adj* **1** that may be computed or estimated. **2** predictable; dependable. ► ,**calcula'bility** *n* ► '**calculably** *adv*

calculate ('kælkjʊ,leɪt) *vb* **1** to solve (one or more problems) by a mathematical procedure; compute. **2** (*tr; may take a clause as object*) to determine beforehand by judgment, reasoning, etc.; estimate. **3** (*tr; usually passive*) to design specifically; aim: *the car was calculated to appeal to women.* **4** (*intr;* foll. by *on* or *upon*) to depend; rely. **5** (*tr; may take a clause as object*) *U.S. dialect.* **5a** to suppose; think. **5b** to intend (to do something). [C16: from Late Latin *calculāre,* from *calculus* pebble used as a counter; see CALCULUS] ► **calculative** ('kælkjʊlətɪv) *adj*

calculated ('kælkjʊ,leɪtɪd) *adj* (*usually prenominal*) **1** undertaken after considering the likelihood of success or failure: *a calculated risk.* **2** deliberately planned; premeditated: *a calculated insult.*

calculating ('kælkjʊ,leɪtɪŋ) *adj* **1** selfishly scheming. **2** shrewd; cautious. ► '**calcu,latingly** *adv*

calculation (,kælkjʊ'leɪʃən) *n* **1** the act, process, or result of calculating. **2** an estimation of probability; forecast. **3** careful planning or forethought, esp. for selfish motives.

calculator ('kælkjʊ,leɪtə) *n* **1** a device for performing mathematical calculations, esp. an electronic device that can be held in the hand. **2** a person or thing that calculates. **3** a set of tables used as an aid to calculations.

calculous ('kælkjʊləs) *adj Pathol.* of or suffering from a calculus.

calculus ('kælkjʊləs) *n, pl* **-luses. 1** a branch of mathematics, developed independently by Newton and Leibnitz. Both **differential calculus** and **integral calculus** are concerned with the effect on a function of an infinitesimal change in the independent variable as it tends to zero. **2** any mathematical system of calculation involving the use of symbols. **3** *Logic.* an uninterpreted formal system. Compare **formal language** (sense 2). **4** *pl* **-li** (-,laɪ). *Pathol.* a stonelike concretion of minerals and salts found in ducts or hollow organs of the body. [C17: from Latin: pebble, stone used in reckoning, from *calx* small stone, counter]

calculus of variations *n* a branch of calculus concerned with maxima and minima of definite integrals.

Calcutta (kæl'kʌtə) *n* a port in E India, capital of West Bengal state, on the Hooghly River: former capital of the country (1833–1912); major commercial and industrial centre; three universities. Pop.: 4 399 819 (1991). Official name: **Kolkata.**

caldarium (kæl'dɛərɪəm) *n, pl* **-daria** (-'dɛərɪə). (in ancient Rome) a room for taking hot baths. [C18: from Latin, from *calidus* warm, from *calēre* to be warm]

Calder ('kɔːldə) *n* **Alexander.** 1898–1976, U.S. sculptor, who originated mobiles and stabiles (moving or static abstract sculptures, generally suspended from wire).

caldera (kæl'dɛərə, 'kɔːldərə) *n* a large basin-shaped crater at the top of a volcano, formed by the collapse or explosion of the cone but not by glacial erosion. See **cirque.** [C19: from Spanish *Caldera* (literally: CAULDRON), name of a crater in the Canary Islands]

Calderdale ('kɔːldə,deɪl) *n* a unitary authority in N England, in West Yorkshire. Pop.: 193 600 (1994). Area: 364 sq. km (140 sq. miles).

Calderón de la Barca (*Spanish* kalde'ron de la 'barka) *n* **Pedro** ('peðro). 1600–81, Spanish dramatist, whose best-known work is *La Vida es Sueño.* He also wrote *autos sacramentales,* outdoor plays for the feast of Corpus Christi, 76 of which survive.

caldron ('kɔːldrən) *n* a variant spelling of **cauldron.**

Caldwell ('kɔːldwɛl, -wəl) *n* **Erskine** ('ɜːskɪn). 1903–87, U.S. novelist whose works include *Tobacco Road* (1933).

calèche (*French* kalɛʃ) *n* a variant of **calash.**

Caledonia (,kælɪ'dəʊnɪə) *n* the Roman name for **Scotland:** used poetically in later times.

Caledonian (,kælɪ'dəʊnɪən) *adj* **1** of or relating to Scotland. **2** of or denoting a period of mountain building in NW Europe in the Palaeozoic era. ♦ *n* **3** *Literary.* a native or inhabitant of Scotland.

Caledonian Canal *n* a canal in N Scotland, linking the Atlantic with the North Sea through the Great Glen: built 1803–47; now little used.

calefacient (,kælɪ'feɪʃənt) *adj* **1** causing warmth. ♦ *n* **2** *Med.* an agent that warms, such as a mustard plaster. [C17: from Latin *calefaciēns,* from *calefacere* to heat] ► **calefaction** (,kælɪ'fækʃən) *n*

calefactory (,kælɪ'fæktərɪ, -trɪ) *adj* **1** giving warmth. ♦ *n, pl* **-ries. 2** a heated sitting room in a monastery. [C16: from Latin *calefactōrius,* from *calefactus* made warm; see CALEFACIENT]

calendar ('kælɪndə) *n* **1** a system for determining the beginning, length, and order of years and their divisions. See also **Gregorian calendar, Jewish calendar, Julian calendar, Revolutionary calendar, Roman calendar. 2** a table showing any such arrangement, esp. as applied to one or more successive years. **3** a list, register, or schedule of social events, pending court cases, appointments, etc. ♦ *vb* **4** (*tr*) to enter in a calendar; schedule; register. [C13: via Norman French from Medieval Latin *kalendārium* account book, from *Kalendae* the CALENDS, when interest on debts became due] ► **calendrical** (kæ'lɛndrɪkᵊl) *or* **ca'lendric** *adj*

calendar day *n* See **day** (sense 1).

calendar month *n* See **month** (sense 1).

calendar year *n* See **year** (sense 1).

calender[1] ('kælɪndə) *n* **1** a machine in which paper or cloth is glazed or smoothed by passing between rollers. ♦ *vb* **2** (*tr*) to subject (material) to such a process. [C17: from French *calandre,* of unknown origin]

calender[2] ('kælɪndə) *n* a member of a mendicant order of dervishes in Turkey, Iran, and India. [from Persian *kalandar*]

calends *or* **kalends** ('kælɪndz) *pl n* the first day of each month in the ancient Roman calendar. [C14 from Latin *kalendae;* related to Latin *calāre* to proclaim]

calendula (kæ'lɛndjʊlə) *n* **1** any Eurasian plant of the genus *Calendula,* esp. the pot marigold, having orange-and-yellow rayed flowers: family *Compositae* (composites). **2** the dried flowers of the pot marigold, formerly used medicinally and for seasoning. [C19: from Medieval Latin, from Latin *kalendae* CALENDS; perhaps from its supposed efficacy in curing menstrual disorders]

calenture ('kælən,tjʊə) *n* a mild fever of tropical climates, similar in its symptoms to sunstroke. [C16: from Spanish *calentura* fever, ultimately from Latin *calēre* to be warm]

calf[1] (kɑːf) *n, pl* **calves. 1** the young of cattle, esp. domestic cattle. Related adj: **vituline. 2** the young of certain other mammals, such as the buffalo, elephant, giraffe, and whale. **3** a large piece of ice detached from an iceberg, etc. **4 kill the fatted calf.** to celebrate lavishly, esp. as a welcome. **5** another name for **calfskin.** [Old English *cealf;* related to Old Norse *kālfr,* Gothic *kalbō,* Old High German *kalba*]

calf[2] (kɑːf) *n, pl* **calves.** the thick fleshy part of the back of the leg between the ankle and the knee. Related adj: **sural.** [C14: from Old Norse *kalfi*]

calf love *n* temporary infatuation or love of an adolescent for a member of the opposite sex. Also called: **puppy love.**

calf's-foot jelly *n* a jelly made from the stock of boiled calves' feet and flavourings, formerly often served to invalids.

calfskin ('kɑːf,skɪn) *n* **1** the skin or hide of a calf. **2** Also called: **calf. 2a** fine leather made from this skin. **2b** (*as modifier*): *calfskin boots.*

Calgary ('kælgərɪ) *n* a city in Canada, in S Alberta: centre of a large agricultural region; oilfields. Pop.: 710 677 (1991).

Calgon ('kælgɒn) *n Trademark.* a chemical compound, sodium hexametaphosphate, with water-softening properties, used in detergents.

Cali (*Spanish* 'kali) *n* a city in SW Colombia: commercial centre in a rich agricultural region. Pop.: 1 718 871 (1995 est.).

Caliban ('kælɪ,bæn) *n* a brutish or brutalized man. [C19: after a character in Shakespeare's *The Tempest* (1611)]

calibrate ('kælɪ,breɪt) *vb* (*tr*) **1** to measure the calibre of (a gun, mortar, etc.). **2** to mark (the scale of a measuring instrument) so that readings can be made in appropriate units. **3** to determine the accuracy of (a measuring instrument, etc.). **4** to determine or check the range and accuracy of (a piece of artillery). ► ,**cali'bration** *n* ► '**cali,brator** *or* '**cali,brater** *n*

calibre *or U.S.* **caliber** ('kælɪbə) *n* **1** the diameter of a cylindrical body, esp. the internal diameter of a tube or the bore of a firearm. **2** the diameter of a shell or bullet. **3** ability; distinction: *a musician of high calibre.* **4** personal character: *a man of high calibre.* [C16: from Old French, from Italian *calibro,* from Arabic *qālib* shoemaker's last, mould] ► '**calibred** *or U.S.* '**calibered** *adj*

calices ('kælɪ,siːz) *n* the plural of **calix.**

caliche (kæ'liːtʃɪ) *n* **1** a bed of sand or clay in arid regions that contains Chile saltpetre, sodium chloride, and other soluble minerals. **2** a surface layer of soil encrusted with calcium carbonate, occurring in arid regions. [C20: from American Spanish, from Latin *calx* lime]

calicle ('kælɪkᵊl) *n* a variant spelling of **calycle.** ► **calicular** (kə'lɪkjʊlə) *adj*

calico ('kælɪ,kəʊ) *n, pl* **-coes** *or* **-cos. 1** a white or unbleached cotton fabric with no printed design. **2** *Chiefly U.S.* a coarse printed cotton fabric. **3** (*modifier*) made of calico. [**C16**: based on *Calicut*, town in India]

calico bush *n* another name for **mountain laurel.**

Calicut ('kælɪˌkʌt) *n* the former name for **Kozhikode.**

calif ('keɪlɪf, 'kæl-) *n* a variant spelling of **caliph.**

Calif. *abbrev. for* California.

califate ('keɪlɪˌfeɪt, -fɪt, 'kæl-) *n* a variant spelling of **caliphate.**

califont ('kæləfɒnt) *n N.Z.* a gas water heater. [from a trade name]

California (ˌkælɪ'fɔːnɪə) *n* **1** a state on the W coast of the U.S.: the third largest state in area and the largest in population; consists of a narrow, warm coastal plain rising to the Coast Range, deserts in the south, the fertile central valleys of the Sacramento and San Joaquin Rivers, and the mountains of the Sierra Nevada in the east; major industries include the growing of citrus fruits and grapes, fishing, oil production, electronics, information technology, and films. Capital: Sacramento. Pop.: 32 268 301 (1997 est.). Area: 411 015 sq. km (158 693 sq. miles). Abbrevs.: **Cal., Calif.** or (with zip code) **CA** **2 Gulf of.** an arm of the Pacific Ocean, between Sonora and Lower California. ▸ **ˌCali'fornian** *adj, n*

California poppy *n* a papaveraceous plant, *Eschscholtzia californica,* of the Pacific coast of North America, having yellow or orange flowers and finely divided bluish-green leaves.

californium (ˌkælɪ'fɔːnɪəm) *n* a metallic transuranic element artificially produced from curium. Symbol: Cf; atomic no.: 98; half-life of most stable isotope, ^{251}Cf: 800 years (approx.). [**C20**: New Latin; discovered at the University of *California*]

caliginous (kə'lɪdʒɪnəs) *adj Archaic.* dark; dim. [**C16**: from Latin *cālīginōsus,* from *cālīgō* darkness] ▸ **caliginosity** (kəˌlɪdʒɪ'nɒsɪtɪ) *n*

Caligula (kə'lɪgjʊlə) *n* original name *Gaius Caesar,* son of Germanicus. 12–41 A.D., Roman emperor (37–41), noted for his cruelty and tyranny; assassinated.

Calimere ('kælɪmɪə) *n* **Point.** a cape on the SE coast of India, on the Palk Strait.

calipash *or* **callipash** ('kælɪˌpæʃ) *n* the greenish glutinous edible part of the turtle found next to the upper shell, considered a delicacy. [**C17**: perhaps changed from Spanish *carapacho* CARAPACE]

calipee ('kælɪˌpiː) *n* the yellow glutinous edible part of the turtle found next to the lower shell, considered a delicacy. [**C17**: perhaps a variant of CALIPASH]

caliper ('kælɪpə) *n* the usual U.S. spelling of **calliper.**

caliph, calif, kalif, *or* **khalif** ('keɪlɪf, 'kæl-) *n Islam.* the title of the successors of Mohammed as rulers of the Islamic world, later assumed by the Sultans of Turkey. [**C14**: from Old French, from Arabic *khalīfa* successor]

caliphate, califate, *or* **kalifate** ('keɪlɪˌfeɪt, -fɪt, 'kæl-) *n* the office, jurisdiction, or reign of a caliph.

calisaya (ˌkælɪ'seɪə) *n* the bark of any of several tropical trees of the rubiaceous genus *Cinchona,* esp. *C. calisaya,* from which quinine is extracted. Also called: **calisaya bark, yellowbark, cinchona.** [**C19**: from Spanish, from the name of a Bolivian Indian who taught the uses of quinine to the Spanish]

calisthenics (ˌkælɪs'θenɪks) *n* a variant spelling (esp. U.S.) of **callisthenics.** ▸ **ˌcalis'thenic** *adj*

calix ('keɪlɪks, 'kæ-) *n, pl* **calices** ('kælɪˌsiːz). a cup; chalice. [**C18**: from Latin: CHALICE]

calk[1] (kɔːk) *vb* a variant spelling of **caulk.**

calk[2] (kɔːk) *or* **calkin** ('kɔːkɪn, 'kæl-) *n* **1** a metal projection on a horse's shoe to prevent slipping. **2** *Chiefly U.S. and Canadian.* a set of spikes or a spiked plate attached to the sole of a boot, esp. by loggers, to prevent slipping. ◆ *vb (tr)* **3** to provide with calks. **4** to wound with a calk. [**C17**: from Latin *calx* heel]

calk[3] (kɔːk) *vb (tr)* to transfer (a design) by tracing it with a blunt point from one sheet backed with loosely fixed colouring matter onto another placed underneath. [**C17**: from French *calquer* to trace; see CALQUE]

call (kɔːl) *vb* **1** (often foll. by *out*) to speak or utter (words, sounds, etc.) loudly so as to attract attention: *he called out her name.* **2** (*tr*) to ask or order to come: *to call a policeman.* **3** (*intr;* sometimes foll. by *on*) to make a visit (to): *she called on him.* **4** (often foll. by *up*) to telephone (a person): *he called back at nine.* **5** (*tr*) to summon to a specific office, profession, etc.: *he was called to the ministry.* **6** (of animals or birds) to utter (a characteristic sound or cry). **7** (*tr*) to summon (a bird or animal) by imitating its cry. **8** (*tr*) to name or style: *they called the dog Rover.* **9** (*tr*) to designate: *they called him a coward.* **10** (*tr*) *Brit. dialect.* to speak ill of or scold. **11** (*tr*) to regard in a specific way: *I call it a foolish waste of time.* **12** (*tr*) to attract (attention). **13** (*tr*) to read (a list, register, etc.) aloud to check for omissions or absentees. **14** (when *tr,* usually foll. by *for*) to give an order (for): *to call a strike.* **15** (*intr*) to try to predict the result of tossing a coin. **16** (*tr*) to awaken: *I was called early this morning.* **17** (*tr*) to cause to assemble: *to call a meeting.* **18** (*tr*) *Sport.* (of an umpire, referee, etc.) to pass judgment upon (a shot, player, etc.) with a call. **19** (*tr*) *Austral. and N.Z.* to broadcast a commentary on (a horse race or other sporting event). **20** (*tr*) to demand repayment of (a loan, redeemable bond, security, etc.). **21** (*tr;* often foll. by *up*) *Company accounting.* to demand payment of (a portion of a share issue not yet paid by subscribers). **22** (*tr*) *Brit.* to award (a student at an Inn of Court) the degree of barrister (esp. in the phrase **call to the bar**). **23** (*tr*) *Computing.* to transfer control to (a named subprogram). **24** (*tr*) *Poker.* to demand that (a player) expose his hand, after equalling his bet. **25** (*intr*) *Bridge.* to make a bid. **26** (in square-dancing) to call out (instructions) to the dancers. **27** *Billiards.* to ask (a player) to say what kind of shot he will play or (of a player) to name his shot. **28** (*intr;* foll. by *for*) **28a** to require: *this problem calls for study.* **28b** to come or go (for) in order to fetch: *I will call for my book later.* **29** (*intr;* foll. by *on* or *upon*) to make an appeal or request (to): *they called upon him to reply.* **30 call into being.** to create. **31 call into play.** to begin to operate. **32 call in** *or* **into question.** See **question** (sense 12). **33 call it a day.** to stop work or other activity. **34 call to mind.** to remember or cause to be remembered. ◆ *n* **35** a cry or shout. **36** the characteristic cry of a bird or animal. **37** a device, such as a whistle, intended to imitate the cry of a bird or animal. **38** a summons or invitation. **39** a summons or signal sounded on a horn, bugle, etc. **40** *Hunting.* any of several notes or patterns of notes, blown on a hunting horn as a signal **41** *Hunting.* **41a** an imitation of the characteristic cry of a wild animal or bird to lure it to the hunter. **41b** an instrument for producing such an imitation. **42** a short visit: *the doctor made six calls this morning.* **43** an inner urge to some task or profession; vocation. **44** allure or fascination, esp. of a place: *the call of the forest.* **45** *Brit.* the summons to the bar of a student member of an Inn of Court. **46** need, demand, or occasion: *there is no call to shout; we don't get much call for stockings these days.* **47** demand or claim (esp. in the phrase **the call of duty**). **48** *Theatre.* a notice to actors informing them of times of rehearsals. **49** (in square dancing) an instruction to execute new figures. **50** a conversation or a request for a connection by telephone. **51** *Commerce.* **51a** a demand for repayment of a loan. **51b** (*as modifier*): *call money.* **52** *Finance.* **52a** a demand for redeemable bonds or shares to be presented for repayment. **52b** a demand for an instalment payment on the issue price of bonds or shares. **53** *Billiards.* a demand to an opponent to say what kind of shot he will play. **54** *Poker.* a demand for a hand or hands to be exposed. **55** *Bridge.* a bid, or a player's turn to bid. **56** *Sport.* a decision of an umpire or referee regarding a shot, pitch, etc. **57** *Austral.* a broadcast commentary on a horse race or other sporting event. **58** Also called: **call option.** *Stock Exchange.* an option to buy a stated amount of securities at a specified price during a specified period. Compare **put** (sense 20). **59** See **roll call. 60 call for margin.** *Stock Exchange.* a demand made by a stockbroker for partial payment of a client's debt due to decreasing value of the collateral. **61 call of nature.** See **nature** (sense 16). **62 on call. 62a** (of a loan, etc.) repayable on demand. **62b** available to be called for work outside normal working hours. **63 within call.** within range; accessible. ◆ See also **call down, call forth, call in, call off, call out, call up.** [Old English *ceallian;* related to Old Norse *kalla,* Old High German *kallōn,* Old Slavonic *glasŭ* voice]

calla ('kælə) *n* **1** Also called: **calla lily, arum lily.** any southern African plant of the aroid genus *Zantedeschia,* esp. *Z. aethiopica,* which has a white funnel-shaped spathe enclosing a yellow spadix. **2** an aroid plant, *Calla palustris,* that grows in wet places and has a white spathe enclosing a greenish spadix, and red berries. [**C19**: from New Latin, probably from Greek *kalleia* wattles on a cock, probably from *kallos* beauty]

callable ('kɔːləbᵊl) *adj* **1** (of a security) subject to redemption before maturity. **2** (of money loaned) repayable on demand.

Callaghan ('kæləˌhæn) *n* (**Leonard**) **James,** Baron Callaghan of Cardiff. born 1912, British Labour statesman; prime minister (1976–79).

callais (kə'leɪɪs) *n* a green stone found as beads and ornaments in the late Neolithic and early Bronze Age of W Europe. [**C19**: from Greek *kallais*]

call alarm *n* **a** an electronic device that sends an alarm signal, usually to a distant monitoring centre, when activated by a person in distress, often a handicapped or frail old person living alone. **b** (*as modifier*): *a call-alarm system.*

Callanetics (ˌkælə'netɪks) *n* (*functioning as sing*) *Trademark.* a system of exercise involving frequent repetition of small muscular movements and squeezes, designed to improve muscle tone. [**C20**: named after *Callan* Pinckney (born 1939), its U.S. inventor]

callant ('kælənt) *or* **callan** ('kælən) *n Scot.* a youth; lad. [**C16**: from Dutch or Flemish *kalant* customer, fellow]

Callao (*Spanish* ka'ʎao) *n* a port in W Peru, near Lima, on **Callao Bay:** chief import centre of Peru. Pop.: 684 135 (1995).

Callas ('kæləs) *n* **Maria,** real name *Maria Anna Cecilia Kalageropoulos.* 1923–77, Greek operatic soprano, born in the U.S.

call box *n* a soundproof enclosure for a public telephone. Also called: **telephone box, telephone kiosk.**

callboy ('kɔːlˌbɔɪ) *n* a person who notifies actors when it is time to go on stage.

call down *vb (tr, adv)* to request or invoke: *to call down God's anger.*

caller[1] ('kɔːlə) *n* a person or thing that calls, esp. a person who makes a brief visit.

caller[2] ('kælə; *Scot.* 'kælər, 'kɒlər) *adj Scot.* **1** (of food, esp. fish) fresh. **2** cool: *a caller breeze.* [**C14**: perhaps a Scottish variant of *calver* to prepare fresh salmon or trout in a certain way; perhaps from Old English *calwer* curds, from a fancied resemblance with the flaked flesh of the fish]

call forth *vb (tr, adv)* to cause (something) to come into action or existence: *she called forth all her courage.*

call girl *n* a prostitute with whom appointments are made by telephone.

calli- *combining form.* beautiful: *calligraphy.* [from Greek *kalli-,* from *kallos* beauty]

Callicrates (kə'lɪkrəˌtiːz) *n* 5th century B.C., Greek architect: with Ictinus, designed the Parthenon.

calligraphy (kə'lɪgrəfɪ) *n* handwriting, esp. beautiful handwriting considered as an art. Also called: **chirography.** ▸ **cal'ligrapher** *or* **cal'ligraphist** *n* ▸ **calligraphic** (ˌkælɪ'græfɪk) *adj* ▸ **ˌcalli'graphically** *adv*

Callimachus (kə'lɪməkəs) *n* **1** late 5th century B.C., Greek sculptor, reputed to have invented the Corinthian capital. **2** ?305–?240 B.C., Greek poet of the Alexandrian School; author of hymns and epigrams.

call in *vb (adv)* **1** (*intr;* often foll. by *on*) to pay a visit, esp. a brief or informal one: *call in if you are in the neighbourhood.* **2** (*tr*) to demand payment of: *to call in a loan.* **3** (*tr*) to take (something) out of circulation, because it is defective or no longer useful. **4** (*tr*) to summon to one's assistance: *they had to call in a specialist.*

calling ('kɔːlɪŋ) *n* **1** a strong inner urge to follow an occupation, etc.; vocation. **2** an occupation, profession, or trade.

calling card *n* a small card bearing the name and usually the address of a person, esp. for giving to business or social acquaintances. Also called **visiting card.**

calliope (kəˈlaɪəpɪ) *n U.S. and Canadian.* a steam organ. [C19: after CALLIOPE (literally: beautiful-voiced)]

Calliope (kəˈlaɪəpɪ) *n Greek myth.* the Muse of epic poetry.

calliopsis (ˌkælɪˈɒpsɪs) *n* another name for **coreopsis.**

callipash (ˈkælɪˌpæʃ) *n* a variant spelling of **calipash.**

calliper *or U.S.* **caliper** (ˈkælɪpə) *n* **1** *(often pl)* Also called: **calliper compasses.** an instrument for measuring internal or external dimensions, consisting of two steel legs hinged together. **2** Also called: **calliper splint.** *Med.* a splint consisting of two metal rods with straps attached, for supporting or exerting tension on the leg. ◆ *vb* **3** *(tr)* to measure the dimensions of (an object) with callipers. [C16: variant of CALIBRE]

calliper rule *n* a measuring instrument having two parallel jaws, one fixed at right angles to the end of a calibrated scale and the other sliding along it.

callipygian (ˌkælɪˈpɪdʒɪən) *or* **callipygous** (ˌkælɪˈpaɪgəs) *adj* having beautifully shaped buttocks. [C19: from Greek *kallipugos,* epithet of a statue of Aphrodite, from CALLI- + *pugē* buttocks]

callistemon (kəˈlɪstəmən) *n* another name for **bottlebrush** (sense 2).

callisthenics *or* **calisthenics** (ˌkælɪsˈθɛnɪks) *n* **1** *(functioning as pl)* light exercises designed to promote general fitness, develop muscle tone, etc. **2** *(functioning as sing)* the practice of callisthenic exercises. [C19: from CALLI- + Greek *sthenos* strength] ▸ ˌ**callisˈthenic** *or* ˌ**calisˈthenic** *adj*

Callisto[1] (kəˈlɪstəʊ) *n Greek myth.* a nymph who attracted the love of Zeus and was changed into a bear by Hera. Zeus then set her in the sky as the constellation Ursa Major.

Callisto[2] (kəˈlɪstəʊ) *n* the second largest of the four Galilean satellites of Jupiter, discovered in 1610 by Galileo. Approximate diameter: 4800 km; orbital radius: 1 883 000 km. See also **Galilean satellite.**

call letters *pl n* the call sign of an American or Canadian radio station, esp. that of a commercial broadcasting station.

call loan *n* a loan that is repayable on demand. Also called: **demand loan.** Compare **time loan.**

call money *n* money loaned by banks and recallable on demand.

call number *n* the number given to a book in a library, indicating its shelf location. Also called: **call mark.**

call off *vb (tr, adv)* **1** to cancel or abandon: *the game was called off because of rain.* **2** to order (an animal or person) to desist or summon away: *the man called off his dog.* **3** to stop (something) or give the order to stop.

callop (ˈkæləp) *n* an edible freshwater fish, *Plectroplites ambiguus,* of Australia, often golden or pale yellow in colour. [from a native Australian language]

callose (ˈkæləʊz) *n* a carbohydrate, a polymer of glucose, found in plants, esp. in the sieve tubes.

callosity (kəˈlɒsɪtɪ) *n, pl* **-ties. 1** hardheartedness. **2** another name for **callus** (sense 1).

callous (ˈkæləs) *adj* **1** unfeeling; insensitive. **2** (of skin) hardened and thickened. ◆ *vb* **3** *Pathol.* to make or become callous. [C16: from Latin *callōsus;* see CALLUS] ▸ ˈ**callously** *adv* ▸ ˈ**callousness** *n*

call out *vb (adv)* **1** to utter aloud, esp. loudly. **2** *(tr)* to summon. **3** *(tr)* to order (workers) to strike. **4** *(tr)* to summon (an employee) to work at a time outside his normal working hours, usually in an emergency.

callow (ˈkæləʊ) *adj* **1** lacking experience of life; immature. **2** *Rare.* (of a young bird) unfledged and usually lacking feathers. [Old English *calu;* related to Old High German *kalo,* Old Slavonic *golú* bare, naked, Lithuanian *galva* head, Latin *calvus* bald] ▸ ˈ**callowness** *n*

Callow (ˈkæləʊ) *n* **Simon.** born 1949, British actor and theatre director.

call rate *n* the interest rate on a call loan.

call sign *n* a group of letters and numbers identifying a radio transmitting station, esp. an amateur radio station. Compare **call letters.**

call slip *n* a form for requesting a library book by title and call number. Also called: **call card, requisition form.**

call up *vb (adv)* **1** to summon to report for active military service, as in time of war. **2** *(tr)* to recall (something); evoke: *his words called up old memories.* **3** *(tr)* to bring or summon (people, etc.) into action: *to call up reinforcements.* ◆ *n* **call-up. 4a** a general order to report for military service. **4b** the number of men so summoned.

callus (ˈkæləs) *n, pl* **-luses. 1** Also called: **callosity.** an area of skin that is hard or thick, esp. on the palm of the hand or sole of the foot, as from continual friction or pressure. **2** an area of bony tissue formed during the healing of a fractured bone. **3** *Botany.* **3a** a mass of hard protective tissue produced in woody plants at the site of an injury. **3b** an accumulation of callose in the sieve tubes. ◆ *vb* **4** to produce or cause to produce a callus. [C16: from Latin, variant of *callum* hardened skin]

calm (kɑːm) *adj* **1** almost without motion; still: *a calm sea.* **2** *Meteorol.* of force 0 on the Beaufort scale; without wind. **3** not disturbed, agitated, or excited; under control: *he stayed calm throughout the confusion.* **4** tranquil; serene: *a calm voice.* ◆ *n* **5** an absence of disturbance or rough motion; stillness. **6** absence of wind. **7** tranquillity. ◆ *vb* **8** (often foll. by *down*) to make or become calm. [C14: from Old French *calme,* from Old Italian *calma,* from Late Latin *cauma* heat, hence a rest during the heat of the day, from Greek *kauma* heat, from *kaiein* to burn] ▸ ˈ**calmly** *adv* ▸ ˈ**calmness** *n*

calmative (ˈkælmətɪv, ˈkɑːmə-) *adj* **1** (of a remedy or agent) sedative. ◆ *n* **2** a sedative remedy or drug.

calmodulin (kælˈmɒdjʊlɪn) *n Biochem.* a protein found in most living cells; it regulates many enzymic processes that are dependent on calcium. [from CAL(CIUM) + MODUL(ATE) + -IN]

calomel (ˈkæləˌmɛl, -məl) *n* a colourless tasteless powder consisting chiefly of mercurous chloride, used medicinally, esp. as a cathartic. Formula: Hg_2Cl_2. [C17: perhaps from New Latin *calomelas* (unattested), literally: beautiful black (perhaps so named because it was originally sublimed from a black mixture of mercury and mercuric chloride), from Greek *kalos* beautiful + *melas* black]

calorescence (ˌkæləˈrɛsəns) *n Physics.* the absorption of radiation by a body, subsequently re-emitted at a higher frequency (lower wavelength). ▸ ˌ**caloˈrescent** *adj*

Calor Gas (ˈkælə) *n Trademark.* butane gas liquefied under pressure in portable containers for domestic use.

caloric (kəˈlɒrɪk, ˈkælərɪk) *adj* **1** of or concerned with heat or calories. ◆ *n* **2** *Obsolete.* a hypothetical elastic fluid formerly postulated as the embodiment of heat. ▸ **caloricity** (ˌkæləˈrɪsɪtɪ) *n*

calorie *or* **calory** (ˈkælərɪ) *n, pl* **-ries.** a unit of heat, equal to 4.1868 joules (**International Table calorie**): formerly defined as the quantity of heat required to raise the temperature of 1 gram of water by 1°C under standard conditions. It has now largely been replaced by the joule for scientific purposes. Abbrev.: **cal.** Also called: **gram calorie, small calorie.** Compare **Calorie.** [C19: from French, from Latin *calor* heat]

Calorie (ˈkælərɪ) *n* **1** Also called: **kilogram calorie, kilocalorie, large calorie.** a unit of heat, equal to one thousand calories, often used to express the heat output of an organism or the energy value of food. Abbrev.: **Cal. 2** the amount of a specific food capable of producing one thousand calories of energy.

calorific (ˌkæləˈrɪfɪk) *adj* of, concerning, or generating heat. ▸ ˌ**caloˈrifically** *adv*

calorific value *n* the quantity of heat produced by the complete combustion of a given mass of a fuel, usually expressed in joules per kilogram.

calorimeter (ˌkæləˈrɪmɪtə) *n* an apparatus for measuring amounts of heat, esp. to find specific heat capacities, calorific values, etc. ▸ **calorimetric** (ˌkælərɪˈmɛtrɪk) *or* ˌ**caloriˈmetrical** *adj* ▸ ˌ**caloriˈmetrically** *adv* ▸ ˌ**caloˈrimetry** *n*

calorize (ˈkæləˌraɪz) *vb (tr)* to coat (a ferrous metal) by spraying with aluminium powder and then heating.

calotte (kəˈlɒt) *n* **1** a skullcap worn by Roman Catholic clergy. **2** *Architect.* a concavity in the form of a niche or cup, serving to reduce the apparent height of an alcove or chapel. [C17: from French, from Provençal *calota,* perhaps from Greek *kaluptra* hood]

calotype (ˈkæləʊˌtaɪp) *n* **1** an early photographic process invented by W. H. Fox Talbot, in which the image was produced on paper treated with silver iodide and developed by sodium thiosulphite. **2** a photograph made by this process. [C19: from Greek *kalos* beautiful + -TYPE]

caloyer (ˈkælɔɪə) *n* a monk of the Greek Orthodox Church, esp. of the Basilian Order. [C17: from French, from Medieval Greek *kalogēros* venerable, from Greek *kalos* beautiful + *gēras* old age]

calpac, calpack, *or* **kalpak** (ˈkælpæk) *n* a large black brimless hat made of sheepskin or felt, worn by men in parts of the Near East. [C16: from Turkish *kalpāk*]

Calpe (ˈkælpɪ) *n* the ancient name for (the Rock of) **Gibraltar.**

calque (kælk) *n* **1** another word for **loan translation.** ◆ *vb* **calques, calquing, calqued. 2** *(tr)* another word for **calk**[3]. [C20: from French: a tracing, from *calquer,* from Latin *calcāre* to tread]

Caltanissetta (*Italian* kaltanisˈsɛtta) *n* a city in central Sicily: sulphur mines. Pop.: 60 000 (latest est.).

Caltech (ˈkælˈtɛk) *n* the California Institute of Technology.

caltrop, caltrap (ˈkæltrəp), *or* **calthrop** (ˈkælθrəp) *n* **1** any tropical or subtropical plant of the zygophyllaceous genera *Tribulus* and *Kallstroemia* that have spiny burs or bracts. **2 water caltrop.** another name for **water chestnut** (sense 1). **3** another name for the **star thistle. 4** *Military.* a four-spiked iron ball or four joined spikes laid upon the ground as a device to lame cavalry horses, puncture tyres, etc. [Old English *calcatrippe* (the plant), from Medieval Latin *calcatrippa,* probably from Latin *calx* heel + *trippa* TRAP[1]]

calumet (ˈkæljʊˌmɛt) *n* a less common name for **peace pipe.** [C18: from Canadian French, from French (Normandy dialect): straw, from Late Latin *calamellus* a little reed, from Latin: CALAMUS]

calumniate (kəˈlʌmnɪˌeɪt) *vb (tr)* to slander. ▸ **caˈlumniable** *adj* ▸ **caˌlumniˈation** *n* ▸ **caˈlumniˌator** *n*

calumnious (kəˈlʌmnɪəs) *or* **calumniatory** (kəˈlʌmnɪətərɪ, -trɪ) *adj* **1** of or using calumny. **2** (of a person) given to calumny.

calumny (ˈkæləmnɪ) *n, pl* **-nies. 1** the malicious utterance of false charges or misrepresentation; slander; defamation. **2** such a false charge or misrepresentation. [C15: from Latin *calumnia* deception, slander]

calutron (ˈkæljʊˌtrɒn) *n* a large mass spectrometer used for the separation of isotopes. [C20: from Cal(ifornia) U(niversity) + -TRON]

Calvados (ˈkælvəˌdɒs) *n* **1** a department of N France in the Basse-Normandie region. Capital: Caen. Pop.: 633 800 (1995). Area: 5693 sq. km (2198 sq. miles). **2** an apple brandy distilled from cider in this region.

calvaria (kælˈvɛərɪə) *n* the top part of the skull of vertebrates. Nontechnical name: **skullcap.** [C14: from Late Latin: (human) skull, from Latin *calvus* bald]

calvary (ˈkælvərɪ) *n, pl* **-ries. 1** *(often cap.)* a representation of Christ's crucifixion, usually sculptured and in the open air. **2** any experience involving great suffering.

Calvary (ˈkælvərɪ) *n* the place just outside the walls of Jerusalem where Jesus was crucified. Also called: **Golgotha.** [from Late Latin *Calvāria,* translation of Greek *kranion* skull, translation of Aramaic *gulgulta* Golgotha]

Calvary cross *n* a Latin cross with a representation of three steps beneath it.

calve (kɑːv) *vb* **1** to give birth to (a calf). **2** (of a glacier or iceberg) to release (masses of ice) in breaking up.

Calvert (ˈkælvət) *n* **1** Sir **George,** 1st Baron Baltimore. ?1580–1632, English statesman; founder of the colony of Maryland. **2** his son, **Leonard.** 1606–47, English statesman; first colonial governor of Maryland (1634–47).

calves (kɑːvz) *n* the plural of **calf**[1] and **calf**[2].
Calvin ('kælvɪn) *n* **1 John**, original name *Jean Cauvin, Caulvin,* or *Chauvin.* 1509–64, French theologian: a leader of the Protestant Reformation in France and Switzerland, establishing the first presbyterian government in Geneva. His theological system is described in his *Institutes of the Christian Religion* (1536). **2 Melvin.** 1911–97, U.S. chemist, noted particularly for his research on photosynthesis: Nobel prize for chemistry 1961.
Calvin cycle *n Botany.* a series of reactions, occurring during photosynthesis, in which glucose is synthesized from carbon dioxide. [C20: named after M. CALVIN, who elucidated it]
Calvinism ('kælvɪˌnɪzəm) *n* the theological system of John Calvin and his followers, characterized by emphasis on the doctrines of predestination, the irresistibility of grace, and justification by faith. ▸ **'Calvinist** *n, adj* ▸ **ˌCalvin'istic** *or* **ˌCalvin'istical** *adj*
Calvino (kæl'viːnəʊ) *n* **Italo.** 1923–85, Italian novelist and short-story writer. His works include *Our Ancestors* (1960) and *Invisible Cities* (1972).
calvities (kæl'vɪʃɪˌiːz) *n* baldness. [C17: from Late Latin, from Latin *calvus* bald]
calx (kælks) *n, pl* **calxes** *or* **calces** ('kælsiːz). **1** the powdery metallic oxide formed when an ore or mineral is roasted. **2** another name for **calcium oxide. 3** *Anatomy.* the heel. [C15: from Latin: lime, from Greek *khalix* pebble]
calyces ('kælɪˌsiːz, 'keɪlɪ-) *n* a plural of **calyx.**
calycine ('kælɪˌsaɪn) *or* **calycinal** (kə'lɪsɪnᵊl) *adj* relating to, belonging to, or resembling a calyx.
calycle, calicle ('kælɪkᵊl) *or* **calyculus** (kə'lɪkjʊləs) *n* **1** *Zoology.* a cup-shaped structure, as in the coral skeleton. **2** *Botany.* another name for **epicalyx.** [C18: from Latin, diminutive of CALYX] ▸ **calycular** (kə'lɪkjʊlə) *adj*
Calydonian boar (ˌkælɪ'dəʊnɪən) *n Greek myth.* a savage boar sent by Artemis to destroy Calydon, a city in Aetolia, because its king had neglected to sacrifice to her. It was killed by Meleager, the king's son.
calypso[1] (kə'lɪpsəʊ) *n, pl* **-sos. 1** a popular type of satirical, usually topical, West Indian ballad, esp. from Trinidad, usually extemporized to a percussive syncopated accompaniment. **2** a dance done to the rhythm of this song. [C20: probably from CALYPSO]
calypso[2] (kə'lɪpsəʊ) *n, pl* **-sos.** a rare N temperate orchid, *Calypso* (or *Cytherea*) *bulbosa,* whose flower is pink or white with purple and yellow markings. [C19: named after CALYPSO]
Calypso (kə'lɪpsəʊ) *n Greek myth.* (in Homer's *Odyssey*) a sea nymph who detained Odysseus on the island of Ogygia for seven years.
calyptra (kə'lɪptrə) *n Botany.* **1** a membranous hood covering the spore-bearing capsule of mosses and liverworts. **2** any hoodlike structure, such as a root cap. [C18: from New Latin, from Greek *kaluptra* hood, from *kaluptein* to cover] ▸ **calyptrate** (kə'lɪpˌtreɪt) *adj*
calyptrogen (kə'lɪptrədʒən) *n* a layer of rapidly dividing cells at the tip of a plant root, from which the root cap is formed. It occurs in grasses and many other plants. [C19: from CALYPTRA + -GEN]
calyx ('keɪlɪks, 'kælɪks) *n, pl* **calyxes** *or* **calyces** ('kælɪˌsiːz, 'keɪlɪ-). **1** the sepals of a flower collectively, forming the outer floral envelope that protects the developing flower bud. Compare **corolla. 2** any cup-shaped cavity or structure, esp. any of the divisions of the human kidney (**renal calyx**) that form the renal pelvis. [C17: from Latin, from Greek *kalux* shell, from *kaluptein* to cover, hide] ▸ **calycate** ('kælɪˌkeɪt) *adj*
calzone (kæl'tsəʊnɪ) *n* a dish of Italian origin consisting of pizza dough folded over a filling of cheese and tomatoes, herbs, ham, etc. [C20: Italian, literally: trouser leg, from *calzoni* trousers]
cam (kæm) *n* a slider or roller attached to a moving shaft to give a particular type of motion to a part in contact with its profile. [C18: from Dutch *kam* comb]
Cam (kæm) *n* a river in E England, in Cambridgeshire, flowing through Cambridge to the River Ouse. Length: about 64 km (40 miles).
CAM *abbrev. for:* **1** computer-aided manufacture. **2** *Botany.* **2a** crassulacean acid metabolism: a form of photosynthesis, first described in crassulaceous plants, in which carbon dioxide is taken up only at night. **2b** (*as modifier*): *a CAM plant.*
Camagüey ('kæməˌgweɪ; *Spanish* kama'ɣwej) *n* a city in E central Cuba. Pop.: 293 961 (1994 est.).
camail ('kæmeɪl) *n Armour.* a neck and shoulders covering of mail worn with and laced to the basinet.
caman ('kæmən) *n Shinty.* the wooden stick used to hit the ball. [C19: from Gaelic]
camaraderie (ˌkæmə'rɑːdərɪ) *n* a spirit of familiarity and trust existing between friends. [C19: from French, from COMRADE]
Camargue (kæ'mɑːg) *n* **la** (la). a delta region in S France, between the channels of the Grand and Petit Rhône: cattle, esp. bulls for the Spanish bullrings, and horses are reared.
camarilla (ˌkæmə'rɪlə; *Spanish* kama'riʎa) *n* a group of confidential advisers, esp. formerly, to the Spanish kings; cabal. [C19: from Spanish: literally: a little room]
camass *or* **camas** ('kæmæs) *n* **1** Also called: **quamash.** any of several North American plants of the liliaceous genus *Camassia,* esp. *C. quamash,* which has a cluster of blue or white flowers and a sweet edible bulb. **2 death camass.** any liliaceous plant of the genus *Zygadenus* (or *Zigadenus*), of the western U.S., that is poisonous to livestock, esp. sheep. [C19: from Chinook Jargon *kamass,* from Nootka *chamas* sweet]
Camb. *abbrev. for* Cambridge.
Cambay (kæm'beɪ) *n* **Gulf of.** an inlet of the Arabian Sea on the W coast of India, southeast of the Kathiawar Peninsula.
camber ('kæmbə) *n* **1** a slight upward curve to the centre of the surface of a road, ship's deck, etc. **2** another name for **bank**[2] (sense 7). **3** an outward inclination of the front wheels of a road vehicle so that they are slightly closer together at the bottom than at the top. **4** Also called: **hog.** a small arching curve of a beam or girder provided to lessen deflection and improve appearance. **5** aerofoil curvature expressed by the ratio of the maximum height of the aerofoil mean line to its chord. ◆ *vb* **6** to form or be formed with a surface that curves upwards to its centre. [C17: from Old French (northern dialect) *cambre* curved, from Latin *camurus;* related to *camera* CHAMBER]
Camberwell beauty ('kæmbəˌwɛl, -wəl) *n* a nymphalid butterfly, *Nymphalis antiopa,* of temperate regions, having dark purple wings with cream-yellow borders. U.S. name: **mourning cloak.** [C19: named after *Camberwell,* a district of S London]
cambist ('kæmbɪst) *n Finance.* **1** a dealer or expert in foreign exchange. **2** a manual of currency exchange rates and similar equivalents of weights and measures. [C19: from French *cambiste,* from Italian *cambista,* from *cambio* (money) exchange] ▸ **'cambistry** *n*
cambium ('kæmbɪəm) *n, pl* **-biums** *or* **-bia** (-bɪə). *Botany.* a meristem that increases the girth of stems and roots by producing additional xylem and phloem. See also **cork cambium.** [C17: from Medieval Latin: exchange, from Late Latin *cambiāre* to exchange, barter] ▸ **'cambial** *adj*
Cambodia (kæm'bəʊdɪə) *n* a country in SE Asia: became part of French Indochina in 1887; achieved self-government in 1949 and independence in 1953; civil war (1970–74) ended in victory for the Khmer Rouge, who renamed the country Kampuchea (1975); Vietnamese forces ousted the Khmer Rouge in 1979 and set up a pro-Vietnamese government who reverted (1981) to the name Cambodia; in 1982 exiled factions formed the Coalition Government of Democratic Kampuchea (CGDK), which is recognized by the UN; after the Vietnamese withdrawal in 1989 CGDK guerrillas continued to engage government forces; a peace settlement was followed in 1993 by elections and the adoption of a democratic monarchist constitution restoring Sihanouk to the throne: contains the central plains of the Mekong River and the Cardamom Mountains in the SW. Official language: Khmer; French is also widely spoken. Currency: riel. Capital: Phnom Penh. Pop.: 10 751 000 (1998 est.). Area: 181 000 sq. km (69 895 sq. miles). ▸ **Cam'bodian** *adj, n*
cambogia (kæm'bəʊdʒɪə) *n* another name for **gamboge** (senses 1, 2).
camboose (kæm'buːs) *n* (formerly in Canada) **1** a cabin built as living quarters for a gang of lumbermen. **2** an open fireplace in such a cabin. [C19: from Canadian French, from French *cambuse* hut, store, from Dutch *kambuis*]
Camborne-Redruth ('kæmbɔːn'rɛdˌruːθ) *n* a former (until 1974) urban district in SW England, in Cornwall: formed in 1934 by the amalgamation of the neighbouring towns of Camborne and Redruth. Pop.: 35 915 (1991).
Cambrai (*French* kɑ̃brɛ) *n* a town in NE France: textile industry: scene of a battle in which massed tanks were first used and broke through the German line (November, 1917). Pop.: 34 210 (1990).
cambrel ('kæmbrəl) *n* a variant of **gambrel.**
Cambria ('kæmbrɪə) *n* the Medieval Latin name for **Wales.**
Cambrian ('kæmbrɪən) *adj* **1** of, denoting, or formed in the first 100 million years of the Palaeozoic era, during which marine invertebrates, esp. trilobites, flourished. **2** of or relating to Wales. ◆ *n* **3 the.** the Cambrian period or rock system. **4** a Welshman.
Cambrian Mountains *pl n* a mountain range in Wales, extending from Carmarthenshire in the S to Denbighshire in the N. Highest peak: Aran Fawddwy, 891 m (2970 ft.).
cambric ('keɪmbrɪk) *n* a fine white linen or cotton fabric. [C16: from Flemish *Kamerijk* CAMBRAI]
Cambridge ('keɪmbrɪdʒ) *n* **1** a city in E England, administrative centre of Cambridgeshire, on the River Cam: centred around the university, founded in the 12th century. Pop.: 113 800 (1994 est.). Medieval Latin name: **Cantabrigia. 2** short for **Cambridgeshire. 3** a city in the U.S., in E Massachusetts: educational centre, with Harvard University (1636) and the Massachusetts Institute of Technology. Pop.: 93 707 (1996 est.). Related adj: **Cantabrigian.**
Cambridge blue *n* **1a** a lightish blue colour. **1b** (*as adj*): *a Cambridge-blue scarf.* **2** a person who has been awarded a blue from Cambridge University.
Cambridgeshire ('keɪmbrɪdʒˌʃɪə, -ʃə) *n* a county of E England, in East Anglia: includes the former counties of the Isle of Ely and Huntingdon and lies largely in the Fens. Administrative centre: Cambridge. Pop.: 686 900 (1994 est.). Area: 3409 sq. km (1350 sq. miles).
Cambs *abbrev. for* Cambridgeshire.
Cambyses (kæm'baɪsiːz) *n* died ?522 B.C., king of Persia (529–522 B.C.), who conquered Egypt (525); son of Cyrus the Great.
camcorder ('kæmˌkɔːdə) *n* a video camera and recorder combined in a portable unit.
Camden[1] ('kæmdən) *n* a borough of N Greater London. Pop.: 182 500 (1994 est.). Area: 21 sq. km (8 sq. miles).
Camden[2] ('kæmdən) *n* **William.** 1551–1623, English antiquary and historian; author of *Britannia* (1586).
came[1] (keɪm) *vb* the past tense of **come.**
came[2] (keɪm) *n* a grooved strip of lead used to join pieces of glass in a stained-glass window or a leaded light. [C17: of unknown origin]
camel ('kæməl) *n* **1** either of two cud-chewing artiodactyl mammals of the genus *Camelus* (see **Arabian camel, Bactrian camel**): family *Camelidae.* They are adapted for surviving long periods without food or water in desert regions, esp. by using humps on the back for storing fat. **2** a float attached to a vessel to increase its buoyancy. See also **caisson** (sense 2). **3** a raft or float used as a fender between a vessel and a wharf. **4a** a fawn colour. **4b** (*as adj*): *a camel dress.* [Old English, from Latin *camēlus,* from Greek *kamēlos,* of Semitic origin; related to Arabic *jamal*]
cameleer (ˌkæmɪ'lɪə) *n* a camel-driver.
camel hair *or* **camel's hair** *n* **1** the hair of the camel or dromedary, used in

clothing, rugs, etc. **2a** soft cloth made of or containing this hair or a substitute, usually tan in colour. **2b** (*as modifier*): *a camelhair coat.* **3a** the hair of the squirrel's tail, used for paintbrushes. **3b** (*as modifier*): *a camelhair brush.*

camellia (kə'mi:lɪə) *n* any ornamental shrub of the Asian genus *Camellia,* esp. *C. japonica,* having glossy evergreen leaves and showy roselike flowers, usually white, pink or red in colour: family *Theaceae.* Also called: **japonica.** [**C18**: New Latin, named after Georg Josef *Kamel* (1661–1706), Moravian Jesuit missionary, who introduced it to Europe]

camelopard ('kæmɪlə,pɑ:d, kə'mɛl-) *n* an obsolete word for **giraffe.** [**C14**: from Medieval Latin *camēlopardus,* from Greek *kamēlopardalis,* from *kamēlos* CAMEL + *pardalis* LEOPARD, because the giraffe was thought to have a head like a camel's and spots like a leopard's]

Camelopardus (kə,mɛlə'pɑ:dəs) *or* **Camelopardalis** (kə,mɛlə'pɑ:dəlɪs) *n, Latin genitive* **Camelopardi** (kə,mɛlə'pɑ:daɪ) or **Camelopardalis** (kə,mɛlə'pɑ:dəlɪs). a faint extensive constellation in the N hemisphere close to Ursa Major and Cassiopeia.

Camelot ('kæmɪ,lɒt) *n* **1** (in Arthurian legend) the English town where King Arthur's palace and court were situated. **2** (in the U.S.) the supposedly golden age of the presidency of John F. Kennedy, 1961–63.

camel's hair *n* See **camel hair.**

Camembert ('kæməm,bɛə; *French* kamɑ̃bɛr) *n* a rich soft creamy cheese. [French, from *Camembert,* a village in Normandy where it originated]

Camenae (kə'mi:ni:) *pl n Roman myth.* a group of nymphs originally associated with a sacred spring in Rome, later identified with the Greek Muses.

cameo ('kæmɪ,əʊ) *n, pl* **cameos. 1a** a medallion, as on a brooch or ring, with a profile head carved in relief. **1b** (*as modifier*): *a cameo necklace.* **2** an engraving upon a gem or other stone of at least two differently coloured layers, such as sardonyx, so carved that the background is of a different colour from the raised design. **3** a stone with such an engraving. **4a** a single and often brief dramatic scene played by a well-known actor or actress in a film or television play. **4b** (*as modifier*): *a cameo role.* **5a** a short literary work or dramatic sketch. **5b** (*as modifier*): *a cameo sketch.* [**C15**: from Italian *cammeo,* of uncertain origin]

cameo ware *n* jasper ware with applied decoration of classical motifs, resembling a cameo.

camera ('kæmərə, 'kæmrə) *n* **1** an optical device consisting of a lens system set in a light-proof construction inside which a light-sensitive film or plate can be positioned. See also **cine camera. 2** *Television.* the equipment used to convert the optical image of a scene being televised into the corresponding electrical signals. **3** See **camera obscura. 4** *pl* **-erae** (-ə,ri:). a judge's private room. **5 in camera. 5a** *Law.* relating to a hearing from which members of the public are excluded. **5b** in private. **6 off camera.** not within an area being filmed. **7 on camera.** (esp. of an actor) being filmed. [**C18**: from Latin: vault, from Greek *kamara*]

cameral ('kæmərəl) *adj* of or relating to a judicial or legislative chamber. [**C18**: from Medieval Latin *camerālis;* see CAMERA]

camera lucida ('lu:sɪdə) *n* an instrument attached to a microscope, etc. to enable an observer to view simultaneously the image and a drawing surface to facilitate the sketching of the image. [New Latin: light chamber]

cameraman ('kæmərə,mæn, 'kæmrə-) *n, pl* **-men.** a person who operates a film or television camera.

camera obscura (ɒb'skjʊərə) *n* a darkened chamber or small building in which images of outside objects are projected onto a flat surface by a convex lens in an aperture. Sometimes shortened to **camera.** [New Latin: dark chamber]

camera-ready copy *n Printing.* type matter ready to be photographed for plate-making without further alteration. Also called: **mechanical.**

camera-shy *adj* having an aversion to being photographed or filmed.

caméra stylo (*French* kamera stilo) *n Films.* the use of the camera as a means of personal expression, especially as practised by some directors of the New Wave. [French, literally: camera stylograph]

camera tube *n* the part of a television camera that converts an optical image into electrical signals of video frequency. See also **image orthicon, vidicon, Plumbicon, iconoscope.**

camerlengo (,kæmə'lɛŋgəʊ) *or* **camerlingo** (,kæmə'lɪŋgəʊ) *n, pl* **-gos.** *R.C. Church.* a cardinal who acts as the pope's financial secretary and the papal treasurer. [**C17**: from Italian *camerlingo,* of Germanic origin; compare CHAMBERLAIN]

Cameron ('kæmərən) *n* **1** (**Mark**) **James** (**Walter**). 1911–85, British journalist, author, and broadcaster. His books include *Witness in Vietnam* (1966) and *Point of Departure* (1967). **2 James.** born 1954, Canadian film director; his films include *Aliens* (1986) and *Titanic* (1997). **3 Julia Margaret.** 1815–79, British photographer, born in India, renowned for her portrait photographs.

Cameroon (,kæmə'ru:n, 'kæmə,ru:n) *n* **1** a republic in West Africa, on the Gulf of Guinea: became a German colony in 1884; divided in 1919 into the **Cameroons** (administered by Britain) and **Cameroun** (administered by France); Cameroun and the S part of the Cameroons formed a republic in 1961 (the N part joined Nigeria); became a member of the Commonwealth in 1995. Official languages: French and English. Religions: Christian, Muslim, and animist. Currency: franc. Capital: Yaoundé. Pop.: 15 029 000 (1998 est.). Area: 475 500 sq. km (183 591 sq. miles). French name: **Cameroun.** German name: **Kamerun. 2** an active volcano in W Cameroon: the highest peak on the West African coast. Height: 4070 m (13 352 ft.).

Cameroun (kamrun) *n* the French name for **Cameroon.**

cam follower *n Engineering.* the slider or roller in contact with the cam that transmits the movement dictated by the cam profile.

camiknickers ('kæmɪ,nɪkəz) *pl n* women's knickers attached to a camisole top. Often shortened to **'cami,knicks.**

camion ('kæmɪən; *French* kamjɔ̃) *n* a lorry, or, esp. formerly, a large dray. [**C19**: from French, of obscure origin]

camisado (,kæmɪ'sɑ:dəʊ) *or* **camisade** (,kæmɪ'seɪd) *n, pl* **-sados** *or* **-sades.** (formerly) an attack made under cover of darkness. [**C16**: from obsolete Spanish *camisada,* literally: an attack in one's shirt (worn over the armour as identification), from *camisa* shirt]

camise (kə'mi:z) *n* a loose light shirt, smock, or tunic originally worn in the Middle Ages. [**C19**: from Arabic *qamīs,* from Late Latin *camīsia*]

camisole ('kæmɪ,səʊl) *n* **1** a woman's underbodice with shoulder straps, originally designed as a cover for a corset. **2** a woman's dressing jacket or short negligée. **3** (*modifier*) resembling a camisole (the underbodice), as in fitting snugly around the bust and having a straight neckline: *a camisole slip; a camisole top.* [**C19**: from French, from Provençal *camisola,* from *camisa* shirt, from Late Latin *camīsia*]

camlet ('kæmlɪt) *n* **1** a tough waterproof cloth. **2** a garment or garments made from such cloth. **3** a soft woollen fabric used in medieval Asia. [**C14**: from Old French *camelot,* perhaps from Arabic *hamlat* plush fabric]

Camoëns ('kæməʊ,ɛns) *or* **Camões** (*Portuguese* ka'mõiʃ) *n* **Luis Vaz de** (lwiʃ vaʃ 'də:). 1524–80, Portuguese epic poet; author of *The Lusiads* (1572).

camogie (ka'mo:gi:) *n Irish.* a form of hurling played by women. [from Irish Gaelic *camógaíocht,* from *camóg* crooked stick]

camomile *or* **chamomile** ('kæmə,maɪl) *n* **1** any aromatic plant of the Eurasian genus *Anthemis,* esp. *A. nobilis,* whose finely dissected leaves and daisy-like flowers are used medicinally: family *Compositae* (composites). **2** any plant of the related genus *Matricaria,* esp. *M. chamomilla* (**German** or **wild camomile**). **3 camomile tea.** a medicinal beverage made from the fragrant leaves and flowers of any of these plants. [**C14**: from Old French *camomille,* from Medieval Latin *chamomilla,* from Greek *khamaimēlon,* literally, earth-apple (referring to the apple-like scent of the flowers)]

camoodi (kæ'mu:dɪ) *n* a Caribbean name for **anaconda.** [**C19**: from an American Indian language of Guyana]

Camorra (kə'mɒrə) *n* **1** a secret society organized in about 1820 in Naples, which thrives on blackmail and extortion. **2** any similar clandestine group. [**C19**: from Italian, probably from Spanish: quarrel]

camouflage ('kæmə,flɑ:ʒ) *n* **1** the exploitation of natural surroundings or artificial aids to conceal or disguise the presence of military units, equipment, etc. **2** (*modifier*) (of fabric or clothing) having a design of irregular patches of dull colours (such as browns and greens), as used in military camouflage. **3** the means by which animals escape the notice of predators, usually because of a resemblance to their surroundings: includes cryptic and apatetic coloration. **4** a device or expedient designed to conceal or deceive. ◆ *vb* **5** (*tr*) to conceal by camouflage. [**C20**: from French, from *camoufler,* from Italian *camuffare* to disguise, deceive, of uncertain origin]

camp[1] (kæmp) *n* **1** a place where tents, cabins, or other temporary structures are erected for the use of military troops, for training soldiers, etc. **2** the military life. **3** tents, cabins, etc., used as temporary lodgings by a group of travellers, holiday-makers, Scouts, Gypsies, etc. **4** the group of people living in such lodgings. **5** *S. African.* a field or paddock fenced off as pasture. **6** a group supporting a given doctrine or theory: *the socialist camp.* **7** (*modifier*) suitable for use in temporary quarters, on holiday, etc., esp. by being portable and easy to set up: *a camp bed; a camp chair.* ◆ *vb* **8** (*intr;* often foll. by *down*) to establish or set up a camp. **9** (*intr;* often foll. by *out*) to live temporarily in or as if in a tent. **10** (*tr*) to put in a camp. [**C16**: from Old French, ultimately from Latin *campus* field] ▸ **'camping** *n*

camp[2] (kæmp) *Informal.* ◆ *adj* **1** effeminate; affected in mannerisms, dress, etc. **2** homosexual. **3** consciously artificial, exaggerated, vulgar, or mannered; self-parodying, esp. when in dubious taste. ◆ *vb* **4** (*tr*) to perform or invest with a camp quality. **5 camp it up. 5a** to seek to focus attention on oneself by making an ostentatious display, overacting, etc. **5b** to flaunt one's homosexuality. ◆ *n* **6** a camp quality, style, etc. [**C20**: of uncertain origin] ▸ **'campy** *adj*

Camp (kæmp) *n* **Walter** (**Chauncey**). 1859–1925, U.S. sportsman and administrator; he introduced new rules to American football, which distinguished it from rugby.

campagna (kæm'pɑ:njə) *n* another word for **champaign** (sense 1).

Campagna (kæm'pɑ:njə) *n* a low-lying plain surrounding Rome, Italy: once fertile, it deteriorated to malarial marshes; recently reclaimed. Area: about 2000 sq. km (800 sq. miles). Also called: **Campagna di Roma** (dɪ 'rəʊmə).

campaign (kæm'peɪn) *n* **1** a series of coordinated activities, such as public speaking and demonstrating, designed to achieve a social, political, or commercial goal: *a presidential campaign; an advertising campaign.* **2** *Military.* a number of complementary operations aimed at achieving a single objective, usually constrained by time or geographic area. ◆ *vb* **3** (*intr;* often foll. by *for*) to conduct, serve in, or go on a campaign. [**C17**: from French *campagne* open country, from Italian *campagna,* from Late Latin *campānia,* from Latin *campus* field] ▸ **cam'paigner** *n*

Campanella (*Italian* kampa'nɛlla) *n* **Tommaso.** 1568–1639, Italian philosopher and Dominican friar. During his imprisonment by the Spaniards (1599–1626) he wrote his celebrated utopian fantasy, *La città del sole.*

Campania (kæm'peɪnɪə; *Italian* kam'paɲɲa) *n* a region of SW Italy: includes the islands of Capri and Ischia. Chief town: Naples. Pop.: 5 762 518 (1996 est.). Area: 13 595 sq. km (5248 sq. miles).

campanile (,kæmpə'ni:lɪ) *n* (esp. in Italy) a bell tower, not usually attached to another building. Compare **belfry.** [**C17**: from Italian, from *campana* bell]

campanology (,kæmpə'nɒlədʒɪ) *n* the art or skill of ringing bells musically. [**C19**: from New Latin *campānologia,* from Late Latin *campāna* bell] ▸ **campanological** (,kæmpənə'lɒdʒɪkəl) *adj* ▸ **,campa'nologist** *or* **,campa'nologer** *n*

campanula (kæm'pænjʊlə) *n* any N temperate plant of the campanulaceous genus *Campanula,* typically having blue or white bell-shaped flowers. Also called: **bellflower.** See also **Canterbury bell, harebell.** [C17: from New Latin: a little bell, from Late Latin *campāna* bell; see CAMPANILE]

campanulaceous (kəm,pænjʊ'leɪʃəs) *adj* of, relating to, or belonging to the *Campanulaceae,* a family of temperate and subtropical plants, including the campanulas, having bell-shaped nodding flowers.

campanulate (kæm'pænjʊlɪt, -,leɪt) *adj* (esp. of flower corollas) shaped like a bell. [C17: from New Latin *campanulātus;* see CAMPANULA]

Campbell ('kæmbᵊl) *n* **1** Sir **Colin,** Baron Clyde. 1792–1863, British field marshal who relieved Lucknow for the second time (1857) and commanded in Oudh, suppressing the Indian Mutiny. **2 Donald.** 1921–67, English water speed record-holder. **3** Sir **Malcolm,** father of Donald Campbell. 1885–1948, English racing driver and land speed record-holder. **4** Mrs **Patrick,** original name *Beatrice Stella Tanner.* 1865–1940, English actress. **5 Roy.** 1901–57, South African poet. His poetry is often satirical and includes *The Flaming Terrapin* (1924). **6 Thomas.** 1777–1844, Scottish poet and critic, noted particularly for his war poems *Hohenlinden* and *Ye Mariners of England.*

Campbell-Bannerman ('kæmbᵊl'bænəmən) *n* Sir **Henry.** 1836–1908, British statesman and leader of the Liberal Party (1899–1908); prime minister (1905–08), who granted self-government to the Transvaal and the Orange River Colony.

Campbell-Stokes recorder *n* an instrument for recording hours of sunshine per day, consisting of a solid glass sphere that focuses rays of sunlight onto a light-sensitive card on which a line is traced.

Camp David *n* the U.S. president's retreat in the Appalachian Mountains, Maryland: scene of the **Camp David Agreement** (Sept., 1978) between Anwar Sadat of Egypt and Menachem Begin of Israel, mediated by Jimmy Carter, which outlined a framework for establishing peace in the Middle East. This agreement was the basis of the peace treaty between Israel and Egypt signed in Washington (March, 1979).

camp-drafting *n Austral.* a competitive test, esp. at an agricultural show, of horsemen's skill in drafting cattle.

Campeche (*Spanish* kam'petʃe) *n* **1** a state of SE Mexico, on the SW of the Yucatán peninsula: forestry and fishing. Capital: Campeche. Pop.: 642 082 (1995 est.). Area: 56 114 sq. km (21 666 sq. miles). **2** a port in SE Mexico, capital of Campeche state. Pop.: 150 518 (1990). **3 Bay of.** Also called: **Gulf of Campeche.** the SW part of the Gulf of Mexico.

camper ('kæmpə) *n* **1** a person who lives or temporarily stays in a tent, cabin, etc. **2** a vehicle equipped for camping out.

camper van *n* a motor caravan.

Campese (kæm'peɪzɪ) *n* **David.** born 1962, Australian rugby union player.

campestral (kæm'pestrəl) *adj* of or relating to open fields or country. [C18: from Latin *campester,* from *campus* field]

campfire ('kæmp,faɪə) *n* an outdoor fire in a camp, esp. one used for cooking or as a focal point for community events.

camp follower *n* **1** any civilian, esp. a prostitute, who unofficially provides services to military personnel. **2** a nonmember who is sympathetic to a particular group, theory, etc.

camphene ('kæmfiːn) *n* a colourless crystalline insoluble optically active terpene derived from pinene and present in many essential oils. Formula: $C_{10}H_{16}$. [C19: from CAMPH(OR) + -ENE]

camphire ('kæmfaɪə) *n* an archaic name for **henna** (senses 1, 2).

camphor ('kæmfə) *n* a whitish crystalline aromatic terpene ketone obtained from the wood of the camphor tree or made from pinene: used in the manufacture of celluloid and in medicine as a liniment and treatment for colds. Formula: $C_{10}H_{16}O$. [C15: from Old French *camphre,* from Medieval Latin *camphora,* from Arabic *kāfūr,* from Malay *kāpūr* chalk; related to Khmer *kāpōr* camphor] ▸ **camphoric** (kæm'fɒrɪk) *adj*

camphorate ('kæmfə,reɪt) *vb* (*tr*) to apply, treat with, or impregnate with camphor.

camphorated oil *n* a liniment consisting of camphor and peanut oil, used as a counterirritant.

camphor ball *n* another name for **mothball** (sense 1).

camphor ice *n* an ointment consisting of camphor, white wax, spermaceti, and castor oil, used to treat skin ailments, esp. chapped skin.

camphor tree *n* **1** a lauraceous evergreen E Asian tree, *Cinnamomum camphora,* whose aromatic wood yields camphor. **2** any similar tree, such as the dipterocarpaceous tree *Dryobalanops aromatica* of Borneo.

campimetry (kæm'pɪmɪtrɪ) *n* a technique for assessing the central part of the visual field. [C20: from New Latin, from Latin *campus* field + *-metry;* see -METER]

Campin ('kæmpɪn) *n* **Robert.** 1379–1444, Flemish painter, noted esp. for his altarpieces: usually identified with the so-called Master of Flémalle.

Campina Grande (*Portuguese* kəm'piːnə 'grəːndə) *n* a city in NE Brazil, in E Paraíba state. Pop.: 298 331 (1991).

Campinas (kæm'piːnəs; *Portuguese* kəm'piːnəʃ) *n* a city in SE Brazil, in São Paulo state: centre of a rich agricultural region, producing esp. coffee. Pop.: 748 076 (1991).

camping ground *n* another word for **camp site.**

campion ('kæmpɪən) *n* any of various caryophyllaceous plants of the genera *Silene* and *Lychnis,* having red, pink, or white flowers. See also **bladder campion.** [C16: probably from *campion,* obsolete variant of CHAMPION, perhaps so called because originally applied to *Lychnis coronaria,* the leaves of which were used to crown athletic champions]

Campion ('kæmpɪən) *n* **1 Saint Edmund.** 1540–81, English Jesuit martyr. He joined the Jesuits in 1573 and returned to England (1580) as a missionary. He was charged with treason and hanged. **2 Thomas.** 1567–1620, English poet and musician, noted particularly for his songs for the lute.

CAM plant (kæm) *n* any plant that undergoes a form of photosynthesis known as crassulacean acid metabolism, in which carbon dioxide is taken up only at night. [*C*(*rassulacean*) *A*(*cid*) *M*(*etabolism*) *plant*]

camp meeting *n Chiefly U.S.* a religious meeting held in a large tent or outdoors, often lasting several days.

campo ('kæmpəʊ) *n, pl* **-pos.** (*often pl*) level or undulating savanna country, esp. in the uplands of Brazil. [American Spanish, from Latin *campus*]

Campobello (,kæmpə'beləʊ) *n* an island in the Bay of Fundy, off the coast of SE Canada: part of New Brunswick province. Area: about 52 sq. km (20 sq. miles). Pop.: 1317 (1991).

Campo Formio (*Italian* 'kampo 'fɔrmjo) *n* a village in NE Italy, in Friuli-Venezia Giulia: scene of the signing of a treaty in 1797 that ended the war between revolutionary France and Austria. Modern name: **Campoformido** (kampo'fɔrmido).

Campo Grande (*Portuguese* 'kəːmpu 'grəːndə) *n* a city in SW Brazil, capital of Mato Grosso do Sul state on the São Paulo–Corumbá railway: market centre. Pop.: 516 403 (1991).

camporee (,kæmpə'riː) *n* a local meeting or assembly of Scouts. [C20: from CAMP[1] + (JAMB)OREE]

Campos (*Portuguese* 'kəːmpuʃ) *n* a city in E Brazil, in E Rio de Janeiro state on the Paraíba River. Pop.: 275 508 (1991).

camp oven *n Austral. and N.Z.* a metal pot or box with a heavy lid, used for baking over an open fire.

camp pie *n Austral. history.* tinned meat.

camp site *n* an area on which holiday-makers may pitch a tent, etc. Also called: **camping site.**

campus ('kæmpəs) *n, pl* **-puses. 1** the grounds and buildings of a university. **2** *Chiefly U.S.* the outside area of a college, university, etc. [C18: from Latin: field]

campus university *n Brit.* a university in which the buildings, often including shops and cafés, are all on one site. Compare **redbrick.**

campylobacter (,kæmpɪləʊ'bæktə) *n* a rod-shaped bacterium that causes infections in cattle and man. Unpasteurized milk infected with campylobacter is a common cause of gastroenteritis. [from Greek *kampulos* bent + BACTER(IUM)]

CAMRA ('kæmrə) *n acronym for* Campaign for Real Ale.

Cam Ranh ('kæm 'ræn) *n* a port in SE Vietnam: large natural harbour, in recent years used as a naval base by French, Japanese, U.S., and Russian forces successively. Pop.: 114 041 (1989).

camshaft ('kæm,ʃɑːft) *n* a shaft having one or more cams attached to it, esp. one used to operate the valves of an internal-combustion engine.

Camus (*French* kamy) *n* **Albert** (albɛr). 1913–60, French novelist, dramatist, and essayist, noted for his pessimistic portrayal of man's condition of isolation in an absurd world: author of the novels *L'Étranger* (1942) and *La Peste* (1947), the plays *Le Malentendu* (1945) and *Caligula* (1946), and the essays *Le Mythe de Sisyphe* (1942) and *L'Homme révolté* (1951): Nobel prize for literature 1957.

camwood ('kæm,wʊd) *n* **1** a W African leguminous tree, *Baphia nitida,* whose hard wood was formerly used in making a red dye. **2** the wood of this tree. [C20: perhaps from Temne]

can[1] (kæn; *unstressed* kən) *vb past* **could.** (takes an infinitive without *to* or an implied infinitive) used as an auxiliary: **1** to indicate ability, skill, or fitness to perform a task: *I can run a mile in under four minutes.* **2** to indicate permission or the right to something: *can I have a drink?* **3** to indicate knowledge of how to do something: *he can speak three languages fluently.* **4** to indicate the possibility, opportunity, or likelihood: *my trainer says I can win the race if I really work hard.* [Old English *cunnan;* related to Old Norse *kunna,* Old High German *kunnan,* Latin *cognōscere* to know, Sanskrit *jānāti* he knows; see KEN, UNCOUTH]

USAGE See at **may.**

can[2] (kæn) *n* **1** a container, esp. for liquids, usually of thin sheet metal: *a petrol can; beer can.* **2** another name (esp. U.S.) for **tin** (metal container). **3** Also called: **'canful.** the contents of a can or the amount a can will hold. **4** a slang word for **prison. 5** *U.S. and Canadian.* a slang word for **toilet** or **buttocks. 6** *U.S. Navy.* a slang word for **destroyer. 7** *Naval slang.* a depth charge. **8** a shallow cylindrical metal container of varying size used for storing and handling film. **9 can of worms.** *Informal.* a complicated problem. **10 in the can. 10a** (of a film, piece of music, etc.) having been recorded, processed, edited, etc. **10b** *Informal.* arranged or agreed: *the contract is almost in the can.* **11 carry the can.** See **carry** (sense 37). ◆ *vb* **cans, canning, canned. 12** to put (food, etc.) into a can or cans; preserve in a can. **13** (*tr*) *U.S. slang.* to dismiss from a job. **14** (*tr*) *U.S. informal.* to stop (doing something annoying or making an annoying noise) (esp. in the phrase **can it!**). [Old English *canne;* related to Old Norse, Old High German *kanna,* Irish *gann,* Swedish *kana* sled]

can. *abbrev. for:* **1** *Music.* canon. **2** canto.

Can. *abbrev. for:* **1** Canada. **2** Canadian.

Cana ('keɪnə) *n New Testament.* the town in Galilee, north of Nazareth, where Jesus performed his first miracle by changing water into wine (John 2:1, 11).

Canaan ('keɪnən) *n* an ancient region between the River Jordan and the Mediterranean, corresponding roughly to Israel: the Promised Land of the Israelites.

Canaanite ('keɪnə,naɪt) *n* **1** a member of an ancient Semitic people who occupied the land of Canaan before the Israelite conquest. **2** the extinct language of this people, belonging to the Canaanitic branch of the Semitic subfamily of the Afro-Asiatic family. **3** (in later books of the Old Testament) a merchant or trader (Job 40:30; Proverbs 31:24).

Canaanitic (,keɪnə'nɪtɪk) *n* **1** a group of ancient languages belonging to the Semitic subfamily of the Afro-Asiatic family and including Canaanite, Phoenician, Ugaritic, and Hebrew. ◆ *adj* **2** denoting, relating to, or belonging to this group of languages.

Canad. *abbrev. for* Canadian.

Canada ('kænədə) *n* a country in North America: the second largest country in the world; first permanent settlements made by the French from 1605; ceded to Britain in 1763 after a series of colonial wars; established as the Dominion of Canada in 1867; a member of the Commonwealth. It consists generally of sparsely inhabited tundra regions, rich in natural resources, in the north, the Rocky Mountains in the west, the Canadian Shield in the east, and vast central prairies; the bulk of the population is concentrated along the U.S. border and the Great Lakes in the south. Languages: English and French. Religion: Christian majority. Currency: Canadian dollar. Capital: Ottawa. Pop.: 30 677 000 (1998 est.). Area: 9 976 185 sq. km (3 851 809 sq. miles).

Canada balsam *n* **1** a yellow transparent resin obtained from the balsam fir. Because its refractive index is similar to that of glass, it is used as an adhesive in optical devices and as a mounting medium for microscope specimens. **2** another name for **balsam fir.**

Canada Day *n* (in Canada) July 1, the anniversary of the day in 1867 when Canada became the first British colony to receive dominion status: a bank holiday. Former name: **Dominion Day.**

Canada goose *n* a large common greyish-brown North American goose, *Branta canadensis,* with a black neck and head and a white throat patch.

Canada jay *n* a large common jay of North America, *Perisoreus canadensis,* with a grey body, and a white-and-black crestless head.

Canada lily *n* a lily, *Lilium canadense,* of NE North America, with small orange funnel-shaped nodding flowers. Also called: **meadow lily.**

Canada thistle *n* the U.S. and Canadian name for **creeping thistle.**

Canadian (kə'neɪdɪən) *adj* **1** of or relating to Canada or its people. ◆ *n* **2** a native, citizen, or inhabitant of Canada.

Canadian football *n* a game resembling American football, played on a grass pitch between two teams of 12 players.

Canadian French *n* **1** the French language as spoken in Canada, esp. in Quebec. ◆ *adj* **2** denoting this language or a French-speaking Canadian.

Canadianism (kə'neɪdɪəˌnɪzəm) *n* **1** the Canadian national character or spirit. **2** loyalty to Canada, its political independence, culture, etc. **3** a linguistic usage, custom, or other feature peculiar to or characteristic of Canada, its people, or their culture.

Canadian pondweed *n* a North American aquatic plant, *Elodea* (or *Anacharis*) *canadensis,* naturalized in Europe, having crowded dark green leaves: family *Hydrocharitaceae.* It is used in aquariums.

Canadian River *n* a river in the southern U.S., rising in NE New Mexico and flowing east to the Arkansas River in E Oklahoma. Length: 1458 km (906 miles).

Canadian Shield *n* (in Canada) the wide area of Precambrian rock extending west from the Labrador coast to the basin of the Mackenzie and north from the Great Lakes to Hudson Bay and the Arctic: rich in minerals. Also called: **Laurentian Shield, Laurentian Plateau.** See **shield** (sense 7).

canaigre (kə'naɪgə) *n* a dock, *Rumex hymenosepalus,* of the southern U.S., the root of which yields a substance used in tanning. **[C19:** from Mexican Spanish**]**

canaille *French.* (kanɑj) *n* the masses; mob; rabble. **[C17:** from French, from Italian *canaglia* pack of dogs**]**

canakin ('kænɪkɪn) *n* a variant spelling of **cannikin.**

canal (kə'næl) *n* **1** an artificial waterway constructed for navigation, irrigation, water power, etc. **2** any of various tubular passages or ducts: *the alimentary canal.* **3** any of various elongated intercellular spaces in plants. **4** *Astronomy.* any of the indistinct surface features of Mars originally thought to be a network of channels but not seen on close-range photographs. They are caused by an optical illusion in which faint geological features appear to have a geometric structure. ◆ *vb* **-nals, -nalling, -nalled** *or U.S.* **-nals, -naling, -naled.** (*tr*) **5** to dig a canal through. **6** to provide with a canal or canals. **[C15** (in the sense: pipe, tube): from Latin *canālis* channel, water pipe, from *canna* reed, CANE[1]**]**

canal boat *n* a long narrow boat used on canals, esp. for carrying freight.

Canaletto (*Italian* kana'lɛtto) *n* original name *Giovanni Antonio Canale.* 1697–1768, Italian painter and etcher, noted particularly for his highly detailed paintings of cities, esp. Venice, which are marked by strong contrasts of light and shade.

canaliculus (ˌkænə'lɪkjʊləs) *n, pl* **-li** (-ˌlaɪ). a small channel, furrow, or groove, as in some bones and parts of plants. **[C16:** from Latin: a little channel, from *canālis* CANAL**]** ▸ **ˌcana'licular, canaliculate** (ˌkænə'lɪkjʊlɪt, -ˌleɪt), *or* **ˌcana'licuˌlated** *adj*

canalize *or* **canalise** ('kænəˌlaɪz) *vb* (*tr*) **1** to provide with or convert into a canal or canals. **2** to give a particular direction to or provide an outlet for; channel. ▸ **ˌcanali'zation** *or* **ˌcanali'sation** *n*

canal ray *n Physics.* a stream of positive ions produced in a discharge tube by allowing them to pass through holes in the cathode.

Canal Zone *n* a former administrative region of the U.S., on the Isthmus of Panama around the Panama Canal: bordered on each side by the Republic of Panama, into which it was incorporated in 1979. Also called: **Panama Canal Zone.**

canapé ('kænəpɪ, -ˌpeɪ; *French* kanape) *n* **1** a small piece of bread, toast, etc., spread with a savoury topping. **2** (in French cabinetwork) a sofa. **[C19:** from French: sofa**]**

Canara (kə'nɑːrə) *n* a variant spelling of **Kanara.**

canard (kæ'nɑːd; *French* kanar) *n* **1** a false report; rumour or hoax. **2** an aircraft in which the tailplane is mounted in front of the wing. **[C19:** from French: a duck, hoax, from Old French *caner* to quack, of imitative origin**]**

Canarese (ˌkænə'riːz) *n, pl* **-rese,** *adj* a variant spelling of **Kanarese.**

canary (kə'nɛərɪ) *n, pl* **-naries. 1** a small finch, *Serinus canaria,* of the Canary Islands and Azores: a popular cagebird noted for its singing. Wild canaries are streaked yellow and brown, but most domestic breeds are pure yellow. **2** See **canary yellow. 3** *Austral. history.* a convict. **4** *Archaic.* a sweet wine from the Canary Islands similar to Madeira. **[C16:** from Old Spanish *canario* of or from the Canary Islands**]**

canary creeper *n* a climbing plant, *Tropaeolum peregrinum,* similar to the nasturtium but with smaller yellow flowers and lobed leaves.

canary grass *n* **1** any of various grasses of the genus *Phalaris,* esp. *P. canariensis,* that is native to Europe and N Africa and has straw-coloured seeds used as birdseed. **2 reed canary grass.** a related plant, *Phalaris arundinacea,* used as fodder throughout the N hemisphere.

Canary Islands *or* **Canaries** *pl n* a group of mountainous islands in the Atlantic off the NW coast of Africa, forming an Autonomous Community of Spain. Pop.: 1 606 534 (1996 est.).

canary seed *n* another name for **birdseed.**

canary yellow *n* **a** a moderate yellow colour, sometimes with a greenish tinge. **b** (*as adj*): *a canary-yellow car.* Sometimes shortened to **canary.**

canasta (kə'næstə) *n* **1** a card game for two to six players who seek to amass points by declaring sets of cards. **2** Also called: **meld.** a declared set in this game, containing seven or more like cards, worth 500 points if the canasta is pure or 300 if wild (containing up to three jokers). **[C20:** from Spanish: basket (because two packs, or a basketful, of cards are required), variant of *canastro,* from Latin *canistrum;* see CANISTER**]**

canaster ('kænəstə) *n* coarsely broken dried tobacco leaves. **[C19:** (meaning: rush basket in which tobacco was packed): from Spanish *canastro;* see CANISTER**]**

Canaveral (kə'nævərəl) *n* **Cape.** a cape on the E coast of Florida: site of the U.S. Air Force Missile Test Centre, from which the majority of U.S. space missions have been launched. Former name (1963–73): Cape **Kennedy.**

Canberra ('kænbərə, -brə) *n* the capital of Australia, in Australian Capital Territory: founded in 1913 as a planned capital. Pop.: 303 700 (1995 est.).

can buoy *n Nautical.* a buoy with a flat-topped cylindrical shape above water, marking the left side of a channel leading into a harbour: red in British waters but green (occasionally black) in U.S. waters. Compare **nun buoy.**

canc. *abbrev. for:* **1** cancelled. **2** cancellation.

cancan ('kænˌkæn) *n* a high-kicking dance performed by a female chorus, originating in the music halls of 19th-century Paris. **[C19:** from French, of uncertain origin**]**

cancel ('kæns^{ə}l) *vb* **-cels, -celling, -celled** *or U.S.* **-cels, -celing, -celed.** (*mainly tr*) **1** to order (something already arranged, such as a meeting or event) to be postponed indefinitely; call off. **2** to revoke or annul: *the order for the new television set was cancelled.* **3** to delete (writing, numbers, etc.); cross out: *he cancelled his name and substituted hers.* **4** to mark (a cheque, postage stamp, ticket, etc.) with an official stamp or by a perforation to prevent further use. **5** (*also intr;* usually foll. by *out*) to counterbalance; make up for (a deficiency, etc.): *his generosity cancelled out his past unkindness.* **6a** to close (an account) by discharging any outstanding debts. **6b** (sometimes foll. by *out*) *Accounting.* to eliminate (a debit or credit) by making an offsetting entry on the opposite side of the account. **7** *Maths.* **7a** to eliminate (numbers, quantities, or terms) as common factors from both the numerator and denominator of a fraction or as equal terms from opposite sides of an equation. **7b** (*intr*) to be able to be eliminated in this way. ◆ *n* **8** a new leaf or section of a book replacing a defective one, one containing errors, or one that has been omitted. **9** a less common word for **cancellation. 10** *Music.* a U.S. word for **natural** (sense 19a). **[C14:** from Old French *canceller,* from Medieval Latin *cancellāre,* from Late Latin: to strike out, make like a lattice, from Latin *cancellī* lattice, grating**]** ▸ **'canceller** *or U.S.* **'canceler** *n*

cancellate ('kænsɪˌleɪt), **cancellous** ('kænsɪləs), *or* **cancellated** *adj* **1** *Anatomy.* having a spongy or porous internal structure: *cancellate bones.* **2** *Botany.* forming a network; reticulate: *a cancellate venation.* **[C17:** from Latin *cancellāre* to make like a lattice; see CANCEL**]**

cancellation (ˌkænsɪ'leɪʃən) *n* **1** the fact or an instance of cancelling. **2** something that has been cancelled, such as a theatre ticket, esp. when it is available for another person to take: *we have a cancellation in the stalls.* **3** the marks or perforation made by cancelling.

cancer ('kænsə) *n* **1** any type of malignant growth or tumour, caused by abnormal and uncontrolled cell division: it may spread through the lymphatic system or blood stream to other parts of the body. **2** the condition resulting from this. **3** an evil influence that spreads dangerously. ◆ Related prefix: **carcino-. [C14:** from Latin: crab, a creeping tumour; related to Greek *karkinos* crab, Sanskrit *karkata***]** ▸ **'cancerous** *adj* ▸ **'cancerously** *adv*

Cancer ('kænsə) *n, Latin genitive* **Cancri** ('kæŋkriː). **1** *Astronomy.* a small faint zodiacal constellation in the N hemisphere, lying between Gemini and Leo on the ecliptic and containing the star cluster Praesepe. **2** *Astrology.* **2a** Also called: the **Crab.** the fourth sign of the zodiac, symbol ♋, having a cardinal water classification and ruled by the moon. The sun is in this sign between about June 21 and July 22. **2b** a person born during a period when the sun is in this sign. **3 tropic of Cancer.** See **tropic** (sense 1). ◆ *adj* **4** *Astrology.* born under or characteristic of Cancer. ◆ Also (for senses 2b, 4): **Cancerian** (kæn'sɪərɪən).

cancerophobia (ˌkænsərəʊ'fəʊbɪə) *n* a morbid dread of being afflicted by cancer.

cancer stick *n* a slang name for **cigarette.**

cancrizans ('kænkrɪˌzæns, 'kæŋ-) *adj* See **crab canon. [**Medieval Latin: moving backwards, from *cancrizāre* to move crabwise**]**

cancroid ('kæŋkrɔɪd) *adj* **1** resembling a cancerous growth. **2** resembling a crab. ◆ *n* **3** a skin cancer, esp. one of only moderate malignancy.

c & b *Cricket. abbrev. for* caught and bowled (by).

candela (kæn'diːlə, -'deɪlə) *n* the basic SI unit of luminous intensity; the luminous intensity in a given direction of a source that emits monochromatic radiation of frequency 540×10^{12} hertz and that has a radiant intensity in that direction of (1/683) watt per steradian. Symbol: cd Also called: **candle, standard candle.** [C20: from Latin: CANDLE]

Candela (kæn'diːlə) *n* **Felix.** born 1910, Mexican architect, noted for his naturalistic modern style and thin prestressed concrete roofs.

candelabrum (ˌkændɪ'lɑːbrəm) *or* **candelabra** *n, pl* **-bra** (-brə), **-brums,** *or* **-bras.** a large branched candleholder or holder for overhead lights. [C19: from Latin, from *candēla* CANDLE]

candent ('kændənt) *adj* an archaic word for **incandescent.** [C16: from Latin *candēre* to shine]

candescent (kæn'dɛsᵊnt) *adj Rare.* glowing or starting to glow with heat. [C19: from Latin *candescere,* from *candēre* to be white, shine] ▸ **can'descence** *n* ▸ **can'descently** *adv*

c & f *abbrev. for* cost and freight.

C & G *abbrev. for* City and Guilds.

Candia ('kandja) *n* the Italian name for **Iráklion.**

candid ('kændɪd) *adj* **1** frank and outspoken: *he was candid about his dislike of our friends.* **2** without partiality; unbiased. **3** unposed or informal: *a candid photograph.* **4** *Obsolete.* **4a** white. **4b** clear or pure. [C17: from Latin *candidus* white, from *candēre* to be white] ▸ **'candidly** *adv* ▸ **'candidness** *n*

candida ('kændɪdə) *n* any yeastlike parasitic fungus of the genus *Candida,* esp. *C. albicans,* which causes thrush (**candidiasis**). [New Latin, feminine of *candidus* white]

candidate ('kændɪˌdeɪt, -dɪt) *n* **1** a person seeking or nominated for election to a position of authority or honour or selection for a job, promotion, etc. **2** a person taking an examination or test. **3** a person or thing regarded as suitable or likely for a particular fate or position: *this wine is a candidate for his cellar.* [C17: from Latin *candidātus* clothed in white (because the candidate wore a white toga), from *candidus* white] ▸ **candidacy** ('kændɪdəsɪ) *or* **candidature** ('kændɪdətʃə) *n*

candid camera *n* **a** a small camera that may be used to take informal photographs of people, usually without their knowledge. **b** (*as modifier*): *a candid-camera photograph.*

candied ('kændɪd) *adj* **1** impregnated or encrusted with or as if with sugar or syrup: *candied peel.* **2** (of sugar, honey, etc.) crystallized.

Candiot ('kændɪˌɒt) *or* **Candiote** ('kændɪˌəʊt) *adj* **1** of or relating to Candia (Iráklion) or Crete; Cretan. ◆ *n* **2** a native or inhabitant of Crete; a Cretan.

candle ('kændᵊl) *n* **1** a cylindrical piece of wax, tallow, or other fatty substance surrounding a wick, which is burned to produce light. **2** *Physics.* **2a** see **international candle. 2b** another name for **candela. 3 burn the candle at both ends.** to exhaust oneself, esp. by being up late and getting up early to work. **4 not hold a candle to.** *Informal.* to be inferior or contemptible in comparison with: *your dog doesn't hold a candle to mine.* **5 not worth the candle.** *Informal.* not worth the price or trouble entailed (esp. in the phrase **the game's not worth the candle**). ◆ *vb* **6** (*tr*) to examine (eggs) for freshness or the likelihood of being hatched by viewing them against a bright light. [Old English *candel,* from Latin *candēla,* from *candēre* to be white, glitter] ▸ **'candler** *n*

candleberry ('kændᵊlbərɪ) *n, pl* **-ries.** another name for **wax myrtle.**

candlefish ('kændᵊlˌfɪʃ) *n, pl* **-fish** *or* **-fishes.** a salmonoid food fish, *Thaleichthys pacificus,* that occurs in the N Pacific and has oily flesh. Also called: **eulachon.**

candlelight ('kændᵊlˌlaɪt) *n* **1a** the light from a candle or candles: *they ate by candlelight.* **1b** (*as modifier*): *a candlelight dinner.* **2** dusk; evening.

Candlemas ('kændᵊlməs) *n Christianity.* Feb. 2, the Feast of the Purification of the Virgin Mary and the presentation of Christ in the Temple: the day on which the church candles are blessed. In Scotland it is one of the four quarter days.

candlenut ('kændᵊlˌnʌt) *n* **1** a euphorbiaceous tree, *Aleurites mollucana,* of tropical Asia and Polynesia. **2** the nut of this tree, which yields an oil used in paints and varnishes. In their native regions the nuts are strung together and burned as candles.

candlepin ('kændᵊlˌpɪn) *n* a bowling pin, as used in skittles, tenpin bowling, candlepins, etc.

candlepins ('kændᵊlˌpɪnz) *n* (*functioning as sing*) a type of bowling game, employing a smaller ball than tenpins, in which three balls are allowed to a frame and fallen pins are not removed from the alley.

candlepower ('kændᵊlˌpaʊə) *n* the luminous intensity of a source of light in a given direction: now expressed in candelas but formerly in terms of the international candle.

candlestick ('kændᵊlˌstɪk) *or* **candleholder** ('kændᵊlˌhəʊldə) *n* a holder, usually ornamental, with a spike or socket for a candle.

candle-tree *n* another name for **wax myrtle.**

candlewick ('kændᵊlˌwɪk) *n* **1** unbleached cotton or muslin into which loops of yarn are hooked and then cut to give a tufted pattern. It is used for bedspreads, dressing gowns, etc. **2** the wick of a candle. **3** (*modifier*) being or made of candlewick fabric.

candlewood ('kændᵊlˌwʊd) *n* **1** the resinous wood of any of several trees, used for torches and candle substitutes. **2** any tree or shrub, such as ocotillo, that produces this wood.

C & M *abbrev. for* care and maintenance.

Candolle (*French* kɑ̃dɔl) *n* **Augustin Pyrame de.** 1778–1841, Swiss botanist; his *Théorie élémentaire de la botanique* (1813) introduced a new system of plant classification.

candour *or U.S.* **candor** ('kændə) *n* **1** the quality of being open and honest; frankness. **2** fairness; impartiality. **3** *Obsolete.* purity or brightness. [C17: from Latin *candor,* from *candēre* to be white, shine]

C & W *abbrev. for* country and western.

candy ('kændɪ) *n, pl* **-dies. 1** *Chiefly U.S. and Canadian.* confectionery in general; sweets, chocolate, etc. **2 like taking candy from a baby.** *Informal.* very easy to accomplish. ◆ *vb* **-dies, -dying, -died. 3** to cause (sugar, etc.) to become crystalline, esp. by boiling or (of sugar) to become crystalline through boiling. **4** to preserve (fruit peel, ginger, etc.) by boiling in sugar. **5** to cover with any crystalline substance, such as ice or sugar. [C18: from Old French *sucre candi* candied sugar, from Arabic *qandi* candied, from *qand* cane sugar, of Dravidian origin]

candyfloss ('kændɪˌflɒs) *n Brit.* a very light fluffy confection made from coloured spun sugar, usually held on a stick. U.S. and Canadian name: **cotton candy.** Austral. name: **fairyfloss.**

candy store *n* a U.S. and Canadian term for **sweet shop.**

candy-striped *adj* (esp. of clothing fabric) having narrow coloured stripes on a white background. ▸ **candy stripe** *n*

candytuft ('kændɪˌtʌft) *n* either of two species of *Iberis* grown as annual garden plants for their umbels ("tufts") of white, red, or purplish flowers. See **iberis.** [C17: from *Candy,* obsolete variant of CANDIA (Crete) + TUFT]

cane[1] (keɪn) *n* **1a** the long jointed pithy or hollow flexible stem of the bamboo, rattan, or any similar plant. **1b** any plant having such a stem. **2a** strips of such stems, woven or interlaced to make wickerwork, the seats and backs of chairs, etc. **2b** (*as modifier*): *a cane chair.* **3** the woody stem of a reed, young grapevine, blackberry, raspberry, or loganberry. **4** any of several grasses with long stiff stems, esp. *Arundinaria gigantea* of the southeastern U.S. **5** a flexible rod with which to administer a beating as a punishment, as to schoolboys. **6** a slender rod, usually wooden and often ornamental, used for support when walking; walking stick. **7** see **sugar cane. 8** a slender rod or cylinder, as of glass. ◆ *vb* (*tr*) **9** to whip or beat with or as if with a cane. **10** to make or repair with cane. **11** *Informal.* to defeat: *we got well caned in the match.* [C14: from Old French, from Latin *canna,* from Greek *kanna,* of Semitic origin; related to Arabic *qanāh* reed] ▸ **'caner** *n*

cane[2] (keɪn) *n Dialect.* a female weasel. [C18: of unknown origin]

Canea (kæ'nɪə) *or* **Chania** ('hɑːnɪə) *n* the capital and chief port of Crete, on the NW coast. Pop.: 50 000 (latest est.). Greek name: **Khaniá.**

canebrake ('keɪnˌbreɪk) *n U.S.* a thicket of canes.

cane grass *n Austral.* any of several tall perennial hard-stemmed grasses, esp. *Eragrostis australasica,* of inland swamps.

canella (kə'nɛlə) *n* the fragrant cinnamon-like inner bark of a West Indian tree, *Canella winterana* (family *Canellaceae*) used as a spice and in medicine. [C17: from Medieval Latin: cinnamon, from Latin *canna* cane, reed]

cane piece *n* (in the Caribbean) a field of sugar cane, esp. a peasant's isolated field.

cane rat *n* **1** Also called (in W Africa): **cutting grass.** a tropical African cavy-like hystricomorph rodent, *Thryonomys swinderianus,* that lives in swampy regions: family *Thryonomyidae.* **2** a similar but smaller species, *T. gregorianus.*

canescent (kə'nɛsᵊnt) *adj* **1** *Biology.* white or greyish due to the presence of numerous short white hairs. **2** becoming hoary, white, or greyish. [C19: from Latin *cānescere* to grow white, become hoary, from *cānēre* to be white] ▸ **ca'nescence** *n*

cane sugar *n* **1** the sucrose obtained from sugar cane, which is identical to that obtained from sugar beet. See also **beet sugar. 2** another name for **sucrose.**

Canes Venatici ('kɑːniːz vɪ'nætɪˌsaɪ) *n, Latin genitive* **Canum Venaticorum** ('kɑːnəm vɪˌnætɪ'kɔːrəm). a small faint constellation in the N hemisphere near Ursa Major that contains the globular cluster M3 and the spiral galaxy M51. [Latin: hunting dogs]

cane toad *n* a large toad, *Bufo marinus,* native to Central and South America but introduced into many countries to control insects and other pests of sugar-cane plantations. Also called: **giant toad, marine toad.**

Canetti (kə'nɛtɪ) *n* **Elias.** 1905–94, British novelist and writer, born in Bulgaria, who usually wrote in German. His works include the novel *Auto da Fé* (1935). Nobel prize for literature 1981.

canfield ('kænˌfiːld) *n Cards.* a gambling game adapted from a type of patience. [C20: named after R. A. *Canfield* (1855–1914), U.S. gambler]

cangue *or* **cang** (kæŋ) *n* (formerly in China) a large wooden collar worn by petty criminals as a punishment. [C18: from French, from Portuguese *canga* yoke]

Canicula (kə'nɪkjʊlə) *n* another name for **Sirius.** [Latin, literally: little dog, from *canis* dog]

canicular (kə'nɪkjʊlə) *adj* of or relating to the star Sirius or its rising.

canikin ('kænɪkɪn) *n* a variant spelling of **cannikin.**

canine ('keɪnaɪn, 'kæn-) *adj* **1** of or resembling a dog; doglike. **2** of, relating to, or belonging to the *Canidae,* a family of mammals, including dogs, jackals, wolves, and foxes, typically having a bushy tail, erect ears, and a long muzzle: order *Carnivora* (carnivores). **3** of or relating to any of the four teeth, two in each jaw, situated between the incisors and the premolars. ◆ *n also* **canid** ('kænɪd). **4** any animal of the family *Canidae.* **5** a canine tooth. [C17: from Latin *canīnus,* from *canis* dog]

canine distemper *n* See **distemper**[1].

caning ('keɪnɪŋ) *n* **1** a beating with a cane as a punishment. **2** *Informal.* a severe defeat.

Canis Major ('keɪnɪs) *n, Latin genitive* **Canis Majoris** (mə'dʒɔːrɪs). a constellation in the S hemisphere close to Orion, containing Sirius, the brightest star in the sky. Also called: the **Great Dog.** [Latin: the greater dog]

Canis Minor *n, Latin genitive* **Canis Minoris** (maɪ'nɔːrɪs). a small constellation in the N hemisphere close to Orion, containing the first magnitude star Procyon. Also called: the **Little Dog.** [Latin: the lesser dog]

canister ('kænɪstə) *n* **1** a container, usually made of metal, in which dry food, such as tea or coffee, is stored. **2** (formerly) **2a** a type of shrapnel shell for firing from a cannon. **2b** Also called: **canister shot, case shot.** the shot or shrapnel packed inside this. [C17: from Latin *canistrum* basket woven from reeds, from Greek *kanastron,* from *kanna* reed, CANE[1]]

canker ('kæŋkə) *n* **1** an ulceration, esp. of the lips or lining of the oral cavity. **2**

Vet. science. **2a** a disease of horses in which the horn of the hoofs becomes soft and spongy. **2b** an ulcerative disease of the lining of the external ear, esp. in dogs and cats. **2c** ulceration or abscess of the mouth, eyelids, ears, or cloaca of birds. **3** an open wound in the stem of a tree or shrub, caused by injury or parasites. **4** something evil that spreads and corrupts. ♦ *vb* **5** to infect or become infected with or as if with canker. **[**Old English *cancer,* from Latin *cancer* crab, cancerous sore**]**

cankerous ('kæŋkərəs) *adj* **1** having cankers. **2** infectious; corrupting.

cankerworm ('kæŋkəˌwɜːm) *n* the larva of either of two geometrid moths, *Paleacrita vernata* or *Alsophila pometaria,* which feed on and destroy fruit and shade trees in North America.

canna ('kænə) *n* any of various tropical plants constituting the genus *Canna,* having broad leaves and red or yellow showy flowers for which they are cultivated: family *Cannaceae.* **[C17:** from New Latin CANE[1]**]**

cannabin ('kænəbɪn) *n* a greenish-black poisonous resin obtained from the hemp plant and thought to be the active narcotic principle. Also called: **cannabis resin.**

cannabis ('kænəbɪs) *n* **1** another name for **hemp** (the plant), esp. Indian hemp (*Cannabis indica*). **2** the drug obtained from the dried leaves and flowers of the hemp plant, which is smoked or chewed for its psychoactive properties. It produces euphoria and relaxation; repeated use may lead to psychological dependence. See also **cannabin, hashish, marijuana, bhang. [C18:** from Latin, from Greek *kannabis;* see HEMP**]** ▸ **'cannabic** *adj*

Cannae ('kæniː) *n* an ancient city in SE Italy: scene of a victory by Hannibal over the Romans (216 B.C.).

canned (kænd) *adj* **1** preserved and stored in airtight cans or tins: *canned meat.* **2** *Informal.* prepared or recorded in advance; artificial; not spontaneous: *canned music.* **3** a slang word for **drunk** (sense 1).

cannel coal *or* **cannel** ('kænᵊl) *n* a dull coal having a high volatile content and burning with a smoky luminous flame. **[C16:** from northern English dialect *cannel* candle: so called from its bright flame**]**

cannelloni *or* **canneloni** (ˌkænɪ'ləʊnɪ) *pl n* tubular pieces of pasta filled with meat or cheese. **[**Italian, plural of *cannellone,* from *cannello* stalk, from *canna* CANE[1]**]**

cannelure ('kænəˌlʊə) *n* a groove or fluting, esp. one around the cylindrical part of a bullet. **[C18:** from French, ultimately from Latin *canālis* CANAL**]**

canner ('kænə) *n* a person or organization whose job is to can foods.

cannery ('kænərɪ) *n, pl* **-neries.** a place where foods are canned.

Cannes (kæn, kænz; *French* kan) *n* a port and resort in SE France: developed in the 19th century from a fishing village; annual film festival. Pop.: 335 647 (1990).

cannibal ('kænɪbᵊl) *n* **1a** a person who eats the flesh of other human beings. **1b** (*as modifier*): *cannibal tribes.* **2** an animal that feeds on the flesh of others of its kind. **[C16:** from Spanish *Canibales,* name used by Columbus to designate the Caribs of Cuba and Haiti, from Arawak *caniba,* variant of CARIB**]**

cannibalism ('kænɪbəˌlɪzəm) *n* **1** the act of eating human flesh or the flesh of one's own kind. **2** savage and inhuman cruelty. ▸ **ˌcannibal'istic** *adj* ▸ **ˌcannibal'istically** *adv*

cannibalize *or* **cannibalise** ('kænɪbəˌlaɪz) *vb* (*tr*) to use (serviceable parts from one machine or vehicle) to repair another, esp. as an alternative to using new parts. ▸ **ˌcannibali'zation** *or* **ˌcannibali'sation** *n*

cannikin, canakin, *or* **canikin** ('kænɪkɪn) *n* a small can, esp. one used as a drinking vessel. **[C16:** from Middle Dutch *kanneken;* see CAN[2], -KIN**]**

canning ('kænɪŋ) *n* the process or business of sealing food in cans or tins to preserve it.

Canning ('kænɪŋ) *n* **1 Charles John,** 1st Earl Canning. 1812–62, British statesman; governor general of India (1856–58) and first viceroy (1858–62). **2** his father, **George.** 1770–1827, British Tory statesman; foreign secretary (1822–27) and prime minister (1827).

Canning Basin *n* an arid basin in NW Western Australia, largely unexplored. Area: 400 000 sq. km (150 000 sq. miles).

Cannock ('kænək) *n* a town in W central England, in S Staffordshire: **Cannock Chase** (a public area of heathland, once a royal preserve) is just to the east. Pop.: 60 106 (1991).

cannon ('kænən) *n, pl* **-nons** *or* **-non. 1** an automatic aircraft gun of large calibre. **2** *History.* a heavy artillery piece consisting of a metal tube mounted on a carriage. **3** a heavy tube or drum, esp. one that can rotate freely on the shaft by which it is supported. **4** the metal loop at the top of a bell, from which it is suspended. **5** See **cannon bone. 6** *Billiards.* **6a** a shot in which the cue ball is caused to contact one object ball after another. **6b** the points scored by this. Usual U.S. and Canadian word: **carom. 7** a rebound or bouncing back, as of a ball off a wall. **8** either of the two parts of a vambrace. ♦ *vb* **9** (*intr;* often foll. by *into*) to collide (with). **10** short for **cannonade. 11** (*intr*) *Billiards.* to make a cannon. **[C16:** from Old French *canon,* from Italian *cannone* cannon, large tube, from *canna* tube, CANE[1]**]**

cannonade (ˌkænə'neɪd) *n* **1** an intense and continuous artillery bombardment. ♦ *vb* **2** to attack (a target) with cannon.

cannonball ('kænənˌbɔːl) *n* **1** a projectile fired from a cannon: usually a solid round metal shot. **2** *Tennis.* **2a** a very fast low serve. **2b** (*as modifier*): *a cannonball serve.* **3** a jump into water by a person who has his arms tucked into the body to form a ball. ♦ *vb* (*intr*) **4** (often foll. by *along,* etc.) to rush along, like a cannonball. **5** to execute a cannonball jump. ♦ *adj* **6** very fast or powerful.

cannon bone *n* a bone in the legs of horses and other hoofed animals consisting of greatly elongated fused metatarsals or metacarpals.

cannoneer (ˌkænə'nɪə) *n* (formerly) a soldier who served and fired a cannon; artilleryman.

cannon fodder *n* men regarded as expendable because they are part of a huge army.

cannonry ('kænənrɪ) *n, pl* **-ries.** *Rare.* **1** a volley of artillery fire. **2** artillery in general.

cannot ('kænɒt, kæ'nɒt) *vb* an auxiliary verb expressing incapacity, inability, withholding permission, etc.; can not.

cannula *or* **canula** ('kænjʊlə) *n, pl* **-las** *or* **-lae** (-ˌliː). *Surgery.* a narrow tube for insertion into a bodily cavity, as for draining off fluid, introducing medication, etc. **[C17:** from Latin: a small reed, from *canna* a reed**]**

cannulate *or* **canulate** *vb* ('kænjʊˌleɪt). **1** to insert a cannula into. ♦ *adj* ('kænjʊˌleɪt, -ˌlɪt), *also* **cannular** *or* **canular. 2** shaped like a cannula. ▸ **ˌcannu'lation** *or* **ˌcanu'lation** *n*

canny ('kænɪ) *adj* **-nier, -niest. 1** shrewd, esp. in business; astute or wary; knowing. **2** *Scot. and northeast English dialect.* good or nice: used as a general term of approval. **3** *Scot.* lucky or fortunate. ♦ *adv* **4** *Scot. and northeast English dialect.* quite; rather: *a canny long while.* **[C16:** from CAN[1] (in the sense: to know how) + -Y[1]**]** ▸ **'cannily** *adv* ▸ **'canniness** *n*

canoe (kə'nuː) *n* **1** a light narrow open boat, propelled by one or more paddles. **2** *N.Z.* another word for **waka** (sense 1). **3 in the same canoe.** *N.Z.* of the same tribe. ♦ *vb* **-noes, -noeing, -noed. 4** to go in a canoe or transport by canoe. **[C16:** from Spanish *canoa,* of Carib origin**]** ▸ **ca'noeing** *n* ▸ **ca'noeist** *n*

canoewood (kə'nuːˌwʊd) *n* another name for the **tulip tree.**

canon[1] ('kænən) *n* **1** *Christianity.* a Church decree enacted to regulate morals or religious practices. **2** (*often pl*) a general rule or standard, as of judgment, morals, etc. **3** (*often pl*) a principle or accepted criterion applied in a branch of learning or art. **4** *R.C. Church.* the complete list of the canonized saints. **5** *R.C. Church.* the prayer in the Mass in which the Host is consecrated. **6** a list of writings, esp. sacred writings, officially recognized as genuine. **7** a piece of music in which an extended melody in one part is imitated successively in one or more other parts. See also **round** (sense 31), **catch** (sense 33). **8** a list of the works of an author that are accepted as authentic. **9** (formerly) a size of printer's type equal to 48 point. **[**Old English, from Latin, from Greek *kanōn* rule, rod for measuring, standard; related to *kanna* reed, CANE[1]**]**

canon[2] ('kænən) *n* **1** one of several priests on the permanent staff of a cathedral, who are responsible for organizing services, maintaining the fabric, etc. **2** *R.C. Church.* Also called: **canon regular.** a member of either of two religious orders, the Augustinian or Premonstratensian Canons, living communally as monks but performing clerical duties. **[C13:** from Anglo-French *canunie,* from Late Latin *canonicus* one living under a rule, from CANON[1]**]**

cañon ('kænjən) *n* a variant spelling of **canyon.**

canoness ('kænənɪs) *n R.C. Church.* a woman belonging to any one of several religious orders and living under a rule but not under a vow.

canonical (kə'nɒnɪkᵊl) *or* **canonic** *adj* **1** belonging to or included in a canon of sacred or other officially recognized writings. **2** belonging to or in conformity with canon law. **3** according to recognized law; accepted. **4** *Music.* in the form of a canon. **5** of or relating to a cathedral chapter. **6** of or relating to a canon (clergyman). ▸ **ca'nonically** *adv*

canonical hour *n* **1** *R.C. Church.* **1a** one of the seven prayer times appointed for each day by canon law. **1b** the services prescribed for these times, namely matins, prime, terce, sext, nones, vespers, and compline. **2** *Church of England.* any time between 8:00 a.m. and 6:00 p.m. at which marriages may lawfully be celebrated.

canonicals (kə'nɒnɪkᵊlz) *pl n* the vestments worn by clergy when officiating.

canonicate (kə'nɒnɪˌkeɪt, -kɪt) *n* the office or rank of a canon; canonry.

canonicity (ˌkænə'nɪsɪtɪ) *n* the fact or quality of being canonical.

canonist ('kænənɪst) *n* a specialist in canon law.

canonize *or* **canonise** ('kænəˌnaɪz) *vb* (*tr*) **1** *R.C. Church.* to declare (a person) to be a saint and thus admit to the canon of saints. **2** to regard as holy or as a saint. **3** to sanction by canon law; pronounce valid. ▸ **ˌcanoni'zation** *or* **ˌcanoni'sation** *n*

canon law *n* the law governing the affairs of a Christian Church, esp. the law created or recognized by papal authority in the Roman Catholic Church. See **Corpus Juris Canonici, Codex Juris Canonici.**

canonry ('kænənrɪ) *n, pl* **-ries. 1** the office, benefice, or status of a canon. **2** canons collectively. **[C15:** from CANON[2] + -RY**]**

canoodle (kə'nuːdᵊl) *vb* (*intr;* often foll. by *with*) *Slang.* to kiss and cuddle; pet; fondle. **[C19:** of unknown origin**]** ▸ **ca'noodler** *n*

can-opener *n* another name for **tin-opener.**

Canopic jar, urn, *or* **vase** (kə'nəʊpɪk) *n* (in ancient Egypt) one of four containers with tops in the form of animal heads of the gods, for holding the entrails of a mummy.

Canopus[1] (kə'nəʊpəs) *n* the brightest star in the constellation Carina and the second brightest star in the sky. Visual magnitude: -0.7; spectral type: F0; distance: 110 light years.

Canopus[2] (kə'nəʊpəs) *n* a port in ancient Egypt east of Alexandria where granite monuments have been found inscribed with the name of Rameses II and written in languages similar to those of the Rosetta stone. ▸ **Ca'nopic** *adj*

canopy ('kænəpɪ) *n, pl* **-pies. 1** an ornamental awning above a throne or bed or held over a person of importance on ceremonial occasions. **2** a rooflike covering over an altar, niche, etc. **3** a roofed structure serving as a sheltered passageway or area. **4** a large or wide covering, esp. one high above: *the sky was a grey canopy.* **5** the nylon or silk hemisphere that forms the supporting surface of a parachute. **6** the transparent cover of an aircraft cockpit. **7** the highest level of branches and foliage in a forest, formed by the crowns of the trees. ♦ *vb* **-pies, -pying, -pied. 8** (*tr*) to cover with or as if with a canopy. **[C14:** from Medieval Latin *canōpeum* mosquito net, from Latin *cōnōpeum* gauze net, from Greek *kōnōpeion* bed with protective net, from *kōnōps* mosquito**]**

canorous (kə'nɔːrəs) *adj Rare.* tuneful; melodious. **[C17:** from Latin *canōrus,* from *canere* to sing**]** ▸ **ca'norously** *adv* ▸ **ca'norousness** *n*

Canossa (kəˈnɒsə; *Italian* kaˈnɔssa) *n* a ruined castle in N Italy, in Emilia near Reggio nell'Emilia: scene of the penance done by the Holy Roman Emperor Henry IV before Pope Gregory VII.

Canova (*Italian* kaˈnɔːva) *n* **Antonio** (anˈtɔːnjo). 1757–1822, Italian neoclassical sculptor.

cans (kænz) *pl n* an informal name for **headphones.**

Canso (ˈkænsəʊ) *n* **1 Cape.** a cape in Canada, at the NE tip of Nova Scotia. **2 Strait of.** Also called: **Gut of Canso.** a channel in Canada, between the Nova Scotia mainland and S Cape Breton Island.

canst (kænst) *vb Archaic.* the form of **can**[1] used with the pronoun *thou* or its relative form.

cant[1] (kænt) *n* **1** insincere talk, esp. concerning religion or morals; pious platitudes. **2** stock phrases that have become meaningless through repetition. **3** specialized vocabulary of a particular group, such as thieves, journalists, or lawyers; jargon. **4** singsong whining speech, as used by beggars. ◆ *vb* **5** (*intr*) to speak in or use cant. [C16: probably via Norman French *canter* to sing, from Latin *cantāre;* used disparagingly, from the 12th century, of chanting in religious services] ▸ **ˈcanter** *n* ▸ **ˈcantingly** *adv*

cant[2] (kænt) *n* **1** inclination from a vertical or horizontal plane; slope; slant. **2** a sudden movement that tilts or turns something. **3** the angle or tilt thus caused. **4** a corner or outer angle, esp. of a building. **5** an oblique or slanting surface, edge, or line. ◆ *vb* (*tr*) **6** to tip, tilt, or overturn, esp. with a sudden jerk. **7** to set in an oblique position. **8** another word for **bevel** (sense 1). ◆ *adj* **9** oblique; slanting. **10** having flat surfaces and without curves. [C14 (in the sense: edge, corner): perhaps from Latin *canthus* iron hoop round a wheel, of obscure origin] ▸ **ˈcantic** *adj*

cant[3] (kɑːnt) *adj Scot. and northern English dialect.* lusty; merry; hearty. [C14: related to Low German *kant* bold, merry]

Cant. *abbrev. for:* **1** Canterbury. **2** *Bible.* Canticles.

can't (kɑːnt) *vb contraction of* cannot.

Cantab. (kænˈtæb) *abbrev. for* Cantabrigiensis. [Latin: of Cambridge]

cantabile (kænˈtɑːbɪlɪ) *Music.* ◆ *adj, adv* **1** (to be performed) in a singing style, i.e. flowingly and melodiously. ◆ *n* **2** a piece or passage performed in this way. [Italian, from Late Latin *cantābilis,* from Latin *cantāre* to sing]

Cantabrian Mountains (kænˈteɪbrɪən) *pl n* a mountain chain along the N coast of Spain, consisting of a series of high ridges that rise over 2400 m (8000 ft.): rich in minerals (esp. coal and iron).

Cantabrigian (ˌkæntəˈbrɪdʒɪən) *adj* **1** of, relating to, or characteristic of Cambridge or Cambridge University, or of Cambridge, Massachusetts, or Harvard University. ◆ *n* **2** a member or graduate of Cambridge University or Harvard University. **3** an inhabitant or native of Cambridge. [C17: from Medieval Latin *Cantabrigia*]

Cantal (*French* kɑ̃tal) *n* **1** a department of S central France, in the Auvergne region. Capital: Aurillac. Pop.: 155 200 (1995). Area: 5779 sq. km (2254 sq. miles). **2** a hard strong cheese made in this area.

cantala (kænˈtɑːlə) *n* **1** a tropical American plant, *Agave cantala,* similar to the century plant: family *Agavaceae* (agaves). **2** the coarse tough fibre of this plant, used in making twine. [of unknown origin]

cantaloupe *or* **cantaloup** (ˈkæntəˌluːp) *n* **1** a cultivated variety of muskmelon, *Cucumis melo cantalupensis,* with ribbed warty rind and orange flesh. **2** any of several other muskmelons. [C18: from French, from *Cantaluppi,* former papal villa near Rome, where it was first cultivated in Europe]

cantankerous (kænˈtæŋkərəs) *adj* quarrelsome; irascible. [C18: perhaps from C14 (obsolete) *conteckour* a contentious person, from *conteck* strife, from Anglo-French *contek,* of obscure origin] ▸ **canˈtankerously** *adv* ▸ **canˈtankerousness** *n*

cantata (kænˈtɑːtə) *n* a musical setting of a text, esp. a religious text, consisting of arias, duets, and choruses interspersed with recitatives. [C18: from Italian, from *cantare* to sing, from Latin]

cantatrice (*French* kɑ̃tatris) *n* a female singer, esp. a professional soloist.

canteen (kænˈtiːn) *n* **1** a restaurant attached to a factory, school, etc., providing meals for large numbers of people. **2a** a small shop that provides a limited range of items, such as toilet requisites, to a military unit. **2b** a recreation centre for military personnel. **3** a soldier's eating and drinking utensils. **4** a temporary or mobile stand at which food is provided. **5a** a box in which a set of cutlery is laid out. **5b** the cutlery itself. **6** a flask or canister for carrying water or other liquids, as used by soldiers or travellers. [C18: from French *cantine,* from Italian *cantina* wine cellar, from *canto* corner, from Latin *canthus* iron hoop encircling chariot wheel; see CANT[2]]

canteen culture *n* the alleged clannishness of the police force, whereby the prevalent attitudes inhibit officers from reporting or speaking out against malpractice, racism, etc.

Canteloube (ˈkæntəˌluːb; *French* kɑ̃tlub) *n* (**Marie**) **Joseph** (*French* ʒozɛf). 1879–1957, French composer, best known for his *Chants d'Auvergne* (1923–30).

canter (ˈkæntə) *n* **1** an easy three-beat gait of horses, etc., between a trot and a gallop in speed. **2 at a canter.** easily; without effort: *he won at a canter.* ◆ *vb* **3** to move or cause to move at a canter. [C18: short for *Canterbury trot,* the supposed pace at which pilgrims rode to Canterbury]

canterbury (ˈkæntəbərɪ, -brɪ) *n Antiques.* **1** a late 18th-century low wooden stand with partitions for holding cutlery and plates: often mounted on casters. **2** a similar 19th-century stand used for holding sheet music, music books, or magazines.

Canterbury (ˈkæntəbərɪ, -brɪ) *n* **1** a city in SE England, in E Kent: starting point for St Augustine's mission to England (597 A.D.); cathedral where St Thomas à Becket was martyred (1170); seat of the archbishop and primate of England; seat of the University of Kent. Pop.: 36 464 (1991). Latin name: **Durovernum** (ˌduːrəʊˈvɜːnəm, ˌdjʊə-). **2** a regional council area of New Zealand, on E central South Island on **Canterbury Bight:** mountainous with coastal lowlands; agricultural. Chief town: Christchurch. Pop.: 477 667 (1996). Area: 43 371 sq. km (16 742 sq. miles).

Canterbury bell *n* a campanulaceous biennial European plant, *Campanula medium,* widely cultivated for its blue, violet, or white flowers.

Canterbury lamb *n* New Zealand lamb exported chilled or frozen to the United Kingdom.

Canterbury Pilgrims *pl n* **1** the pilgrims whose stories are told in Chaucer's *Canterbury Tales.* **2** *N.Z.* the early settlers in Christchurch, Canterbury region.

cantharid (ˈkænθərɪd) *n* any beetle of the family *Cantharidae,* having a soft elongated body; though found frequenting flowers, they are carnivorous.

cantharides (kænˈθærɪˌdiːz) *pl n, sing* **cantharis** (ˈkænθərɪs). a diuretic and urogenital stimulant or irritant prepared from the dried bodies of Spanish fly (family *Meloidae,* not *Cantharidae*), once thought to be an aphrodisiac. Also called: **Spanish fly.** [C15: from Latin, plural of *cantharis,* from Greek *kantharis* Spanish fly]

Can Tho (ˈkʌn ˈtəʊ, ˈkæn) *n* a town in S Vietnam, on the River Mekong. Pop.: 215 587 (1992 est.).

cant hook *or* **dog** *n Forestry.* a wooden pole with a blunt steel tip and an adjustable hook at one end, used for handling logs.

canthus (ˈkænθəs) *n, pl* **-thi** (-ˌθaɪ). the inner or outer corner or angle of the eye, formed by the natural junction of the eyelids. [C17: from New Latin, from Latin: iron tyre] ▸ **ˈcanthal** *adj*

canticle (ˈkæntɪkᵊl) *n* **1** a nonmetrical hymn, derived from the Bible and used in the liturgy of certain Christian churches. **2** a song, poem, or hymn, esp. one that is religious in character. [C13: from Latin *canticulum,* diminutive of *canticus* a song, from *canere* to sing]

Canticle of Canticles *n* another name for the **Song of Solomon,** used in the Douay Bible.

cantilena (ˌkæntɪˈleɪnə) *n* a smooth flowing style in the writing of vocal music. [C18: Italian, from Latin *cantilēna* a song]

cantilever (ˈkæntɪˌliːvə) *n* **1a** a beam, girder, or structural framework that is fixed at one end only. **1b** (*as modifier*): *a cantilever wing.* **2** a wing or tailplane of an aircraft that has no external bracing or support. **3** a part of a beam or a structure projecting outwards beyond its support. ◆ *vb* **4** (*tr*) to construct (a building member, beam, etc.) so that it is fixed at one end only. **5** (*intr*) to project like a cantilever. [C17: perhaps from CANT[2] + LEVER]

cantilever bridge *n* a bridge having spans that are constructed as cantilevers and often a suspended span or spans, each end of which rests on one end of a cantilever span.

cantillate (ˈkæntɪˌleɪt) *vb* **1** to chant (passages of the Hebrew Scriptures) according to the traditional Jewish melody. **2** to intone or chant. [C19: from Late Latin *cantillāre* to sing softly, from Latin *cantāre* to sing]

cantillation (ˌkæntɪˈleɪʃən) *n* **1** the traditional notation representing the various traditional Jewish melodies to which scriptural passages are chanted. **2** chanting or intonation.

cantina (kænˈtiːnə) *n* a bar or wine shop, esp. in a Spanish-speaking country. [from Spanish]

canting arms *pl n Heraldry.* a coat of arms making visual reference to the surname of its owner.

cantle (ˈkæntᵊl) *n* **1** the back part of a saddle that slopes upwards. **2** a slice; a broken-off piece. [C14: from Old Northern French *cantel,* from *cant* corner; see CANT[2]]

canto (ˈkæntəʊ) *n, pl* **-tos. 1** *Music.* another word for **cantus** (sense 2). **2** a main division of a long poem. [C16: from Italian: song, from Latin *cantus,* from *canere* to sing]

canto fermo (ˈkæntəʊ ˈfɜːməʊ) *or* **cantus firmus** (ˈkæntəs ˈfɜːməs) *n* **1** a melody that is the basis to which other parts are added in polyphonic music. **2** the traditional plainchant as prescribed by use and regulation in the Christian Church. [Italian, from Medieval Latin, literally: fixed song]

canton *n* (ˈkæntɒn, kænˈtɒn). **1** any of the 23 political divisions of Switzerland. **2** a subdivision of a French arrondissement. **3** (ˈkæntən). *Heraldry.* a small square or oblong charge on a shield, usually in the top left corner. ◆ *vb* **4** (kænˈtɒn). (*tr*) to divide into cantons. **5** (kənˈtuːn). (esp. formerly) to allocate accommodation to (military personnel). [C16: from Old French: corner, division, from Italian *cantone,* from *canto* corner, from Latin *canthus* iron rim; see CANT[2]] ▸ **ˈcantonal** *adj*

Canton *n* **1** (kænˈtɒn). a port in SE China, capital of Guangdong province, on the Zhu Jiang (Pearl River): the first Chinese port open to European trade. Pop.: 3 580 000 (1991 est.). Chinese names: **Guangzhou, Kwangchow. 2** (ˈkæntən). a city in the U.S., in NE Ohio. Pop.: 81 079 (1996 est.).

Canton crepe (ˈkæntɒn, -tən) *n* a fine crinkled silk or rayon crepe fabric, slightly heavier than crepe de Chine. [C19: named after *Canton,* China, where it was originally made]

Cantonese (ˌkæntəˈniːz) *n* **1** the Chinese language spoken in the city of Canton, Guangdong and Guanxi provinces, Hong Kong, and elsewhere outside China. **2** (*pl* **-ese**) a native or inhabitant of the city of Canton or Guangdong province. ◆ *adj* **3** of or relating to the city of Canton, Guangdong province, or the Chinese language spoken there.

Canton flannel (ˈkæntɒn, -tən) *n* another name for **cotton flannel.** [C19: named after *Canton,* China]

cantonment (kənˈtuːnmənt) *n Military.* (esp. formerly) **1** a large training camp. **2** living accommodation, esp. the winter quarters of a campaigning army. **3** *History.* a permanent military camp in British India.

Canton River (kænˈtɒn) *n* another name for the **Zhu Jiang.**

cantor (ˈkæntɔː) *n* **1** *Judaism.* Also called: **chazan.** a man employed to lead synagogue services, esp. to traditional modes and melodies. **2** *Christianity.* the leader of the singing in a church choir. **[C16**: from Latin: singer, from *canere* to sing**]**

cantorial (kæn'tɔːrɪəl) *adj* **1** of or relating to a precentor. **2** (of part of a choir) on the same side of a cathedral, etc., as the precentor; on the N side of the choir. Compare **decanal**.

cantoris (kæn'tɔːrɪs) *adj* (in antiphonal music) to be sung by the cantorial side of a choir. Compare **decani**. **[**Latin: genitive of *cantor* precentor**]**

Cantor's paradox ('kæntɔːz) *n Logic.* the paradox derived from the supposition of an all-inclusive universal set, since every set has more subsets than members while every subset of such a universal set would be a member of it. **[**named after Georg *Cantor* (1845–1918), German mathematician, born in Russia**]**

cantrip ('kæntrɪp) *Scot.* ◆ *n* **1** a magic spell. **2** (*often pl*) a mischievous trick. ◆ *adj* **3** (of an effect) produced by black magic. **[C18**: Scottish, of unknown origin**]**

Cantuar. ('kæntjʊˌɑː) *abbrev. for* Cantuariensis. **[**Latin: (Archbishop) of Canterbury**]**

cantus ('kæntəs) *n, pl* **-tus. 1** a medieval form of church singing; chant. **2** Also called: **canto.** the highest part in a piece of choral music. **3** (in 15th- or 16th-century music) a piece of choral music, usually secular, in polyphonic style. **[**Latin: song, from *canere* to sing**]**

canty ('kæntɪ, 'kɑːn-) *adj* **cantier, cantiest.** *Scot. and northern English dialect.* lively; brisk; in good spirits. **[C18**: see CANT[3]**]** ▸ **'cantily** *adv* ▸ **'cantiness** *n*

Canuck (kə'nʌk) *n U.S. and Canadian informal.* **a** a Canadian. **b** (formerly) esp. a French Canadian. **[C19**: of uncertain origin**]**

canula ('kænjʊlə) *n, pl* **-las** *or* **-lae** (-ˌliː). *Surgery.* a variant spelling of **cannula.**

Canute, Cnut, *or* **Knut** (kə'njuːt) *n* died 1035, Danish king of England (1016–35), Denmark (1018–35), and Norway (1028–35). He defeated Edmund II of England (1016), but divided the kingdom with him until Edmund's death. An able ruler, he invaded Scotland (1027) and drove Olaf II from Norway (1028).

canvas ('kænvəs) *n* **1a** a heavy durable cloth made of cotton, hemp, or jute, used for sails, tents, etc. **1b** (*as modifier*): *a canvas bag.* **2a** a piece of canvas or a similar material on which a painting is done, usually in oils. **2b** a painting on this material, esp. in oils. **3** a tent or tents collectively. **4** *Nautical.* any cloth of which sails are made. **5** *Nautical.* the sails of a vessel collectively. **6** any coarse loosely woven cloth on which embroidery, tapestry, etc., is done. **7** (preceded by *the*) the floor of a boxing or wrestling ring. **8** *Rowing.* the tapering covered part at either end of a racing boat, sometimes referred to as a unit of length: *to win by a canvas.* **9 under canvas. 9a** in tents. **9b** *Nautical.* with sails unfurled. **[C14**: from Norman French *canevas,* ultimately from Latin *cannabis* hemp**]**

canvasback ('kænvəsˌbæk) *n, pl* **-backs** *or* **-back.** a North American diving duck, *Aythya valisineria,* the male of which has a white body and reddish-brown head.

canvass ('kænvəs) *vb* **1** to solicit votes, orders, advertising, etc., from. **2** to determine the feelings and opinions of (voters before an election, etc.), esp. by conducting a survey. **3** to investigate (something) thoroughly, esp. by discussion or debate. **4** *Chiefly U.S.* to inspect (votes) officially to determine their validity. ◆ *n* **5** a solicitation of opinions, votes, sales orders, etc. **6** close inspection; scrutiny. **[C16**: probably from obsolete sense of CANVAS (to toss someone in a canvas sheet, hence, to harass, criticize); the development of current senses is unexplained**]** ▸ **'canvasser** *n* ▸ **'canvassing** *n*

canyon *or* **cañon** ('kænjən) *n* a gorge or ravine, esp. in North America, usually formed by the down-cutting of a river in a dry area where there is insufficient rainfall to erode the sides of the valley. **[C19**: from Spanish *cañon,* from *caña* tube, from Latin *canna* cane**]**

canzona (kæn'zəʊnə) *n* a type of 16th- or 17th-century contrapuntal music, usually for keyboard, lute, or instrumental ensemble. **[C19**: from Italian, from Latin *cantiō* song, from *canere* to sing**]**

canzone (kæn'zəʊnɪ) *n, pl* **-ni** (-nɪ). **1** a Provençal or Italian lyric, often in praise of love or beauty. **2a** a song, usually of a lyrical nature. **2b** (in 16th-century choral music) a polyphonic song from which the madrigal developed. **[C16**: from Italian: song, from Latin *cantiō,* from *canere* to sing**]**

canzonetta (ˌkænzə'nɛtə) *or* **canzonet** (ˌkænzə'nɛt) *n* a short cheerful or lively song, typically of the 16th to 18th centuries. **[C16**: Italian *canzonetta,* diminutive of CANZONE**]**

caoutchouc ('kaʊtʃuːk, -tʃʊk; kaʊ'tʃuːk, -'tʃʊk) *n* another name for **rubber**[1] (sense 1). **[C18**: from French, from obsolete Spanish *cauchuc,* from Quechua**]**

cap (kæp) *n* **1** a covering for the head, esp. a small close-fitting one made of cloth or knitted. **2** such a covering serving to identify the wearer's rank, occupation, etc.: *a nurse's cap.* **3** something that protects or covers, esp. a small lid or cover: *lens cap.* **4** an uppermost surface or part: *the cap of a wave.* **5a** See **percussion cap. 5b** a small amount of explosive enclosed in paper and used in a toy gun. **6** *Sport, chiefly Brit.* **6a** an emblematic hat or beret given to someone chosen for a representative team: *he has won three England caps.* **6b** a player chosen for such a team. **7** the upper part of a pedestal in a classical order. **8** the roof of a windmill, sometimes in the form of a dome. **9** *Botany.* the pileus of a mushroom or toadstool. **10** *Hunting.* **10a** money contributed to the funds of a hunt by a follower who is neither a subscriber nor a farmer, in return for a day's hunting. **10b** a collection taken at a meet of hounds, esp. for a charity. **11** *Anatomy.* **11a** the natural enamel covering a tooth. **11b** an artificial protective covering for a tooth. **12** See **Dutch cap** (sense 2). **13** an upper financial limit. **14** a mortarboard when worn with a gown at an academic ceremony (esp. in the phrase **cap and gown**). **15** *Meteorol.* **15a** the cloud covering the peak of a mountain. **15b** the transient top of detached clouds above an increasing cumulus. **16 set one's cap for** *or* **at.** (of a woman) to be determined to win as a husband or lover. **17 cap in hand.** humbly, as when asking a favour. **18 if the cap fits.** *Brit.* the allusion or criticism seems to be appropriate to a particular person. ◆ *vb* **caps, capping, capped.** (*tr*) **19** to cover, as with a cap: *snow capped the mountain tops.* **20** *Informal.* to outdo; excel: *your story caps them all; to cap an anecdote.* **21 cap it all.** to provide the finishing touch: *we had sun, surf, cheap wine, and to cap it all a free car.* **22** *Sport, Brit.* to select (a player) for a representative team: *he was capped 30 times by Scotland.* **23** to seal off (an oil or gas well). **24** to impose an upper limit on the level of increase of (a tax, such as the council tax): *rate-capping.* **25** *Hunting.* to ask (hunt followers) for a cap. **26** *Chiefly Scot. and N.Z.* to award a degree to. **[**Old English *cæppe,* from Late Latin *cappa* hood, perhaps from Latin *caput* head**]** ▸ **'capper** *n*

CAP *abbrev. for* Common Agricultural Policy: (in the EU) the system for supporting farm incomes by maintaining agricultural prices at agreed levels.

cap. *abbrev. for:* **1** capacity. **2** capital. **3** capitalize. **4** capital letter. **5** caput. **[**Latin: chapter**]**

Capa ('kæpə) *n* **Robert,** real name *André Friedmann.* 1913–54, Hungarian photographer, who established his reputation as a photojournalist during the Spanish Civil War.

capability (ˌkeɪpə'bɪlɪtɪ) *n, pl* **-ties. 1** the quality of being capable; ability. **2** the quality of being susceptible to the use or treatment indicated: *the capability of a metal to be fused.* **3** (*usually pl*) a characteristic that may be developed; potential aptitude.

Capablanca (*Spanish* kapa'βlaŋka) *n* **José Raúl** (xo'se ra'ul), called *Capa* or *the Chess Machine.* 1888–1942, Cuban chess player; world champion 1921–27.

capable ('keɪpəb[ə]l) *adj* **1** having ability, esp. in many different fields; competent. **2** (*postpositive;* foll. by *of*) able or having the skill (to do something): *she is capable of hard work.* **3** (*postpositive;* foll. by *of*) having the temperament or inclination (to do something): *he seemed capable of murder.* **[C16**: from French, from Late Latin *capābilis* able to take in, from Latin *capere* to take**]** ▸ **'capableness** *n* ▸ **'capably** *adv*

capacious (kə'peɪʃəs) *adj* capable of holding much; roomy; spacious. **[C17**: from Latin *capāx,* from Latin *capere* to take**]** ▸ **ca'paciously** *adv* ▸ **ca'paciousness** *n*

capacitance (kə'pæsɪtəns) *n* **1** the property of a system that enables it to store electric charge. **2** a measure of this, equal to the charge that must be added to such a system to raise its electrical potential by one unit. Symbol: *C* Former name: **capacity. [C20**: from CAPACIT(Y) + -ANCE**]** ▸ **ca'pacitive** *adj* ▸ **ca'pacitively** *adv*

capacitate (kə'pæsɪˌteɪt) *vb* (*tr*) **1** to make legally competent. **2** *Rare.* to make capable. ▸ **caˌpaci'tation** *n*

capacitor (kə'pæsɪtə) *n* a device for accumulating electric charge, usually consisting of two conducting surfaces separated by a dielectric. Former name: **condenser.**

capacity (kə'pæsɪtɪ) *n, pl* **-ties. 1** the ability or power to contain, absorb, or hold. **2** the amount that can be contained; volume: *a capacity of six gallons.* **3a** the maximum amount something can contain or absorb (esp. in the phrase **filled to capacity**). **3b** (*as modifier*): *a capacity crowd.* **4** the ability to understand or learn; aptitude; capability: *he has a great capacity for Greek.* **5** the ability to do or produce (often in the phrase **at capacity**): *the factory's output was not at capacity.* **6** a specified position or function: *he was employed in the capacity of manager.* **7** a measure of the electrical output of a piece of apparatus such as a motor, generator, or accumulator. **8** *Electronics.* a former name for **capacitance. 9** *Computing.* **9a** the number of words or characters that can be stored in a particular storage device. **9b** the range of numbers that can be processed in a register. **10** legal competence: *the capacity to make a will.* **[C15**: from Old French *capacite,* from Latin *capācitās,* from *capāx* spacious, from *capere* to take**]**

cap and bells *n* the traditional garb of a court jester, including a cap with bells attached to it.

cap-a-pie (ˌkæpə'piː) *adv* (dressed, armed, etc.) from head to foot. **[C16**: from Old French**]**

caparison (kə'pærɪs[ə]n) *n* **1** a decorated covering for a horse or other animal, esp. (formerly) for a warhorse. **2** rich or elaborate clothing and ornaments. ◆ *vb* **3** (*tr*) to put a caparison on. **[C16**: via obsolete French from Old Spanish *caparazón* saddlecloth, probably from *capa* CAPE[1]**]**

cape[1] (keɪp) *n* **1** a sleeveless garment like a cloak but usually shorter. **2** a strip of material attached to a coat or other garment so as to fall freely, usually from the shoulders. **[C16**: from French, from Provençal *capa,* from Late Latin *cappa;* see CAP**]**

cape[2] (keɪp) *n* a headland or promontory. **[C14**: from Old French *cap,* from Old Provençal, from Latin *caput* head**]**

Cape (keɪp) *n* **the. 1** the SW region of South Africa, in Western Cape province. **2** See **Cape of Good Hope.**

Cape Breton Island *n* an island off SE Canada, in NE Nova Scotia, separated from the mainland by the Strait of Canso: its easternmost point is **Cape Breton.** Pop.: 120 098 (1991). Area: 10 280 sq. km (3970 sq. miles).

Cape buffalo *n* another name for **buffalo** (sense 1).

Cape cart *n S. African.* a two-wheeled horse-drawn vehicle sometimes with a canvas hood.

Cape Cod *n* **1** a long sandy peninsula in SE Massachusetts, between **Cape Cod Bay** and the Atlantic. **2** Also called: **Cape Cod cottage.** a one-storey cottage of timber construction with a simple gable roof and a large central chimney: originated on Cape Cod in the 18th century.

Cape Colony *n* the name from 1652 until 1910 of the former **Cape Province** of South Africa.

Cape Coloured *n* (in South Africa) another name for a **Coloured** (sense 2).

Cape doctor *n S. African informal.* a strong fresh SE wind blowing in the vicinity of Cape Town, esp. in the summer.

Cape Dutch *n* **1** an obsolete name for **Afrikaans. 2** (in South Africa) a distinctive style of furniture or architecture.

Cape Flats *pl n* the strip of low-lying land in South Africa joining the Cape Peninsula proper to the African mainland.

cape gooseberry *n* another name for **strawberry tomato.**

Cape Horn *n* a rocky headland on an island at the extreme S tip of South America, belonging to Chile. It is notorious for gales and heavy seas; until the building of the Panama Canal it lay on the only sea route between the Atlantic and the Pacific. Also called: **the Horn.**

Cape jasmine *n* a widely cultivated gardenia shrub, *Gardenia jasminoides.* See **gardenia.**

Čapek (*Czech* 'tʃapɛk) *n* **Karel** ('karel). 1890–1938, Czech dramatist and novelist; author of *R.U.R.* (1921), which introduced the word "robot", and (with his brother **Josef**) *The Insect Play* (1921).

capelin ('kæpəlɪn) *or* **caplin** *n* a small marine food fish, *Mallotus villosus,* occurring in northern and Arctic seas: family *Osmeridae* (smelts). **[C17:** from French *capelan,* from Old Provençal, literally: CHAPLAIN**]**

Capella (kə'pɛlə) *n* the brightest star in the constellation Auriga; it is a yellow giant and a spectroscopic binary. Visual magnitude: 0.1; spectral type: G8; distance: 40 light years. **[C17:** New Latin, from Latin, diminutive of *capra* she-goat, from *caper* goat**]**

capellmeister *or* **kapellmeister** (kæ'pɛl,maɪstə) *n* a person in charge of an orchestra, esp. in an 18th-century princely household. See also **maestro di cappella. [**from German, from *Kapelle* chapel + *Meister* MASTER**]**

Cape of Good Hope *n* a cape in SW South Africa south of Cape Town.

Cape Peninsula *n* (in South Africa) the peninsula and the part of the mainland on which Cape Town and most of its suburbs are located.

Cape pigeon *n* a species of seagoing petrel, *Daption capensis,* with characteristic white wing patches: a common winter visitor off the coasts of southern Africa: family *Diomedeidae.* Also called: **pintado petrel.**

Cape primrose *n* See **streptocarpus.**

Cape Province *n* a former province of S South Africa; replaced in 1994 by the new provinces of Northern Cape, Western Cape, Eastern Cape and part of North-West. Capital: Cape Town. Official name: **Cape of Good Hope Province.** Former name (1652–1910): **Cape Colony.**

caper[1] ('keɪpə) *n* **1** a playful skip or leap. **2** a high-spirited escapade. **3 cut a caper** *or* **capers. 3a** to skip or jump playfully. **3b** to act or behave playfully; frolic. **4** *Slang.* a crime, esp. an organized robbery. ◆ *vb* **5** (*intr*) to leap or dance about in a light-hearted manner. **[C16:** probably from CAPRIOLE**]** ► **'caperer** *n* ► **'caperingly** *adv*

caper[2] ('keɪpə) *n* **1** a spiny trailing Mediterranean capparidaceous shrub, *Capparis spinosa,* with edible flower buds. **2** any of various similar plants or their edible parts. See also **bean caper, capers. [C15:** from earlier *capers, capres* (assumed to be plural), from Latin *capparis,* from Greek *kapparis***]**

capercaillie (,kæpə'keɪljɪ) *or* **capercailzie** (,kæpə'keɪljɪ, -'keɪlzɪ) *n* a large European woodland grouse, *Tetrao urogallus,* having a black plumage and fan-shaped tail in the male. **[C16:** from Scottish Gaelic *capull coille* horse of the woods**]**

Capernaum (kə'pɜːnɪəm) *n* a ruined town in N Israel, on the NW shore of the Sea of Galilee: closely associated with Jesus Christ during his ministry.

capers ('keɪpəz) *pl n* the flower buds of the caper plant, which are pickled and used as a condiment.

capeskin ('keɪp,skɪn) *n* **1** a soft leather obtained from the skins of a type of lamb or sheep having hairlike wool. ◆ *adj* **2** made of this leather. **[C19:** named after the *Cape of Good Hope***]**

Cape sparrow *n* a sparrow, *Passer melanurus,* very common in southern Africa: family *Ploceidae.* Also called (esp. S. African): **mossie.**

Capet ('kæpɪt, kæ'pet; *French* kapɛ) *n* **Hugh** *or* **Hugues** (yg). ?938–996 A.D., king of France (987–96); founder of the Capetian dynasty.

Capetian (kə'piːʃən) *n* **1** a member of the dynasty founded by Hugh Capet, which ruled France from 987–1328 A.D. ◆ *adj* **2** of, or relating to, the Capetian kings or their rule.

Cape Town *n* the legislative capital of South Africa and capital of Western Cape province, situated in the southwest on Table Bay: founded in 1652, the first White settlement in southern Africa; important port. Pop.: 854 616 (1991).

Cape Verde (vɜːd) *n* a republic in the Atlantic off the coast of West Africa, consisting of a group of ten islands and five islets: an overseas territory of Portugal until 1975, when the islands became independent. Official language: Portuguese. Religion: Christian (Roman Catholic) majority; animist minority. Currency: Cape Verdean escudo. Capital: Praia. Pop.: 400 000 (1998 est.). Area: 4033 sq. km (1557 sq. miles). ► **Cape Verdean** ('vɜːdɪən) *adj, n*

Cape York *n* the northernmost point of the Australian mainland, in N Queensland on the Torres Strait at the tip of **Cape York Peninsula** (a peninsula between the Coral Sea and the Gulf of Carpentaria).

Cap-Haitien (*French* kapaisjɛ̃, -tjɛ̃) *n* a port in N Haiti: capital during the French colonial period. Pop.: 100 638 (1995 est.). Also called: **le Cap** (lə kap).

capias ('keɪpɪ,æs, 'kæp-) *n Law.* a writ directing a sheriff or other officer to arrest a named person. **[C15:** from Latin, literally: you must take, from *capere***]**

capillaceous (,kæpɪ'leɪʃəs) *adj* **1** having numerous filaments resembling hairs or threads. **2** resembling a hair; capillary. **[C18:** from Latin *capillāceus* hairy, from *capillus* hair**]**

capillarity (,kæpɪ'lærɪtɪ) *n* a phenomenon caused by surface tension and resulting in the distortion, elevation, or depression of the surface of a liquid in contact with a solid. Also called: **capillary action.**

capillary (kə'pɪlərɪ) *adj* **1** resembling a hair; slender. **2** (of tubes) having a fine bore. **3** *Anatomy.* of or relating to any of the delicate thin-walled blood vessels that form an interconnecting network between the arterioles and the venules. **4** *Physics.* of or relating to capillarity. ◆ *n, pl* **-laries. 5** *Anatomy.* any of the capillary blood vessels. **6** a fine hole or narrow passage in any substance. **[C17:** from Latin *capillāris,* from *capillus* hair**]**

capillary tube *n* a glass tube with a fine bore and thick walls, used in thermometers, etc.

capita ('kæpɪtə) *n* **1** See **per capita. 2** *Anatomy.* the plural of **caput.**

capital[1] ('kæpɪtᵊl) *n* **1a** the seat of government of a country or other political unit. **1b** (*as modifier*)*: a capital city.* **2** material wealth owned by an individual or business enterprise. **3** wealth available for or capable of use in the production of further wealth, as by industrial investment. **4 make capital** (**out**) **of.** to get advantage from. **5** (*sometimes cap.*) the capitalist class or their interests: *capital versus labour.* **6** *Accounting.* **6a** the ownership interests of a business as represented by the excess of assets over liabilities. **6b** the nominal value of the authorized or issued shares. **6c** (*as modifier*)*: capital issues.* **7** any assets or resources, esp. when used to gain profit or advantage. **8a** a capital letter. Abbrev.: **cap** *or* **cap. 8b** (*as modifier*)*: capital B.* **9 with a capital A, B,** etc. (used to give emphasis to a statement): *he is mean with a capital M.* ◆ *adj* **10** (*prenominal*) *Law.* involving or punishable by death: *a capital offence.* **11** very serious; fatal: *a capital error.* **12** primary, chief, or principal: *our capital concern is that everyone be fed.* **13** of, relating to, or designating the large modern majuscule letter used chiefly as the initial letter in personal names and place names and other uniquely specificatory nouns, and often for abbreviations and acronyms. Compare **small** (sense 9). See also **upper case. 14** *Chiefly Brit.* excellent; first-rate: *a capital idea.* **[C13:** from Latin *capitālis* (adj) concerning the head, chief, from *caput* head; compare Medieval Latin *capitāle* (n) wealth, from *capitālis* (adj)**]**

capital[2] ('kæpɪtᵊl) *n* the upper part of a column or pier that supports the entablature. Also called: **chapiter, cap. [C14:** from Old French *capitel,* from Late Latin *capitellum,* diminutive of *caput* head**]**

capital account *n* **1** *Economics.* that part of a balance of payments composed of movements of capital and international loans and grants. Compare **current account** (sense 2). **2** *Accounting.* a financial statement showing the net value of a company at a specified date. It is defined as total assets minus total liabilities and represents ownership interests. **3** *U.S.* an account of fixed assets.

capital allowance *n* the allowing of a certain amount of money spent by a company on fixed assets to be taken off the profits of the company before tax is imposed.

capital assets *pl n* another name for **fixed assets.**

capital expenditure *n* expenditure on acquisitions of or improvements to fixed assets.

capital gain *n* the amount by which the selling price of a financial asset exceeds its cost.

capital gains tax *n* a tax on the profit made from the sale of an asset. Abbrev.: **CGT.**

capital goods *pl n Economics.* goods that are themselves utilized in the production of other goods rather than being sold to consumers. Also called: **producer goods.** Compare **consumer goods.**

capitalism ('kæpɪtə,lɪzəm) *n* an economic system based on the private ownership of the means of production, distribution, and exchange, characterized by the freedom of capitalists to operate or manage their property for profit in competitive conditions. Also called: **free enterprise, private enterprise.** Compare **socialism** (sense 1).

capitalist ('kæpɪtəlɪst) *n* **1** a person who owns capital, esp. capital invested in a business. **2** *Politics.* a supporter of capitalism. **3** *Informal, usually derogatory.* a rich person. ◆ *adj* **4** of or relating to capital, capitalists, or capitalism. ► **,capital'istic** *adj*

capitalization *or* **capitalisation** (,kæpɪtəlaɪ'zeɪʃən) *n* **1a** the act of capitalizing. **1b** the sum so derived. **2** *Accounting.* the par value of the total share capital issued by a company, including the loan capital and sometimes reserves. **3** the act of estimating the present value of future payments, earnings, etc. **4** the act of writing or printing in capital letters.

capitalization issue *n* another name for **rights issue.**

capitalize *or* **capitalise** ('kæpɪtə,laɪz) *vb* (*mainly tr*) **1** (*intr;* foll. by *on*) to take advantage (of); profit (by). **2** to write or print (text) in capital letters or with the first letter of (a word or words) in capital letters. **3** to convert (debt or retained earnings) into capital stock. **4** to authorize (a business enterprise) to issue a specified amount of capital stock. **5** to provide with capital. **6** *Accounting.* to treat (expenditures) as assets. **7a** to estimate the present value of (a periodical income). **7b** to compute the present value of (a business) from actual or potential earnings.

capital levy *n* a tax on capital or property as contrasted with a tax on income.

capitally ('kæpɪtəlɪ) *adv Chiefly Brit.* in an excellent manner; admirably.

capital market *n* the financial institutions collectively that deal with medium-term and long-term capital and loans. Compare **money market.**

capital punishment *n* the punishment of death for a crime; death penalty.

capital ship *n* one of the largest and most heavily armed ships in a naval fleet.

capital stock *n* **1** the par value of the total share capital that a company is authorized to issue. **2** the total physical capital existing in an economy at any moment of time.

capital surplus *n* another name (esp. U.S.) for **share premium.**

capital transfer tax *n* (in Britain) a tax payable from 1974 to 1986 at progressive rates on the cumulative total of gifts of money or property made during the donor's lifetime or after his death. It was replaced by inheritance tax.

capitate ('kæpɪ,teɪt) *adj* **1** *Botany.* shaped like a head, as certain flowers or inflorescences. **2** *Zoology.* having an enlarged headlike end: *a capitate bone.* **[C17:** from Latin *capitātus* having a (large) head, from *caput* head**]**

capitation (,kæpɪ'teɪʃən) *n* **1** a tax levied on the basis of a fixed amount per head. **2 capitation grant.** a grant of money given to every person who qualifies under certain conditions. **3** the process of assessing or numbering by counting heads. [C17: from Late Latin *capitātiō,* from Latin *caput* head] ▸ **'capitative** *adj*

capitellum (ˌkæpɪ'tɛləm) *n, pl* **-la** (-lə). Anatomy. an enlarged knoblike structure at the end of a bone that forms an articulation with another bone; capitulum. [C19: from Latin, diminutive of CAPITULUM]

Capitol ('kæpɪtᵊl) *n* **1a** another name for the **Capitoline. 1b** the temple on the Capitoline. **2 the.** the main building of the U.S. Congress. **3** (*sometimes not cap.*) Also called: **statehouse.** (in the U.S.) the building housing any state legislature. [C14: from Latin *Capitōlium,* from *caput* head]

Capitoline ('kæpɪtᵊˌlaɪn, kə'pɪtəʊ-) *n* **1 the.** the most important of the Seven Hills of Rome. The temple of Jupiter was on the southern summit and the ancient citadel on the northern summit. ◆ *adj* **2** of or relating to the Capitoline or the temple of Jupiter.

capitular (kə'pɪtjʊlə) *adj* **1** of or associated with a cathedral chapter. **2** of or relating to a capitulum. [C17: from Medieval Latin *capitulāris,* from *capitulum* CHAPTER] ▸ **ca'pitularly** *adv*

capitulary (kə'pɪtjʊlərɪ) *n, pl* **-laries.** any of the collections of ordinances promulgated by the Frankish kings (8th–10th centuries A.D.). [C17: from Medieval Latin *capitulāris;* see CAPITULAR]

capitulate (kə'pɪtjʊˌleɪt) *vb* (*intr*) to surrender, esp. under agreed conditions. [C16 (meaning: to arrange under heads, draw up in order; hence, to make terms of surrender): from Medieval Latin *capitulare* to draw up under heads, from *capitulum* CHAPTER] ▸ **ca'pituˌlator** *n*

capitulation (kəˌpɪtjʊ'leɪʃən) *n* **1** the act of capitulating. **2** a document containing terms of surrender. **3** a statement summarizing the main divisions of a subject. ▸ **ca'pitulatory** *adj*

capitulum (kə'pɪtjʊləm) *n, pl* **-la** (-lə). **1** a racemose inflorescence in the form of a disc of sessile flowers, the youngest at the centre. It occurs in the daisy and related plants. **2** *Anatomy, zoology.* a headlike part, esp. the enlarged knoblike terminal part of a long bone, antenna, etc. [C18: from Latin, literally: a little head, from *caput* head]

capiz ('kæpɪz) *n* the bivalve shell of a mollusc (*Placuna placenta*) found esp. in the Philippines and having a smooth translucent shiny interior: used in jewellery, ornaments, lampshades, etc. Also called: **jingle shell, window shell.** [from the native name in the Philippines]

caplin ('kæplɪn) *n* a variant of **capelin.**

capo[1] ('keɪpəʊ, 'kæpəʊ) *n, pl* **-pos.** a device fitted across all the strings of a guitar, lute, etc., so as to raise the pitch of each string simultaneously. Compare **barré.** Also called: **capo tasto** ('kæpəʊ 'tæstəʊ). [from Italian *capo tasto* head stop]

capo[2] ('kæpəʊ; *Italian* 'kapo) *n, pl* **-pos.** the presumed title of a leader in the Mafia. [Italian: head]

cap of maintenance *n* a ceremonial cap or hat worn or carried as a symbol of office, rank, etc.

capon ('keɪpən) *n* a castrated cock fowl fattened for eating. [Old English *capun,* from Latin *cāpō* capon; related to Greek *koptein* to cut off]

Capone (kə'pəʊn) *n* **Alphonse,** called *Al.* 1899–1947, U.S. gangster in Chicago during Prohibition.

caponize *or* **caponise** ('keɪpəˌnaɪz) *vb* (*tr*) to make (a cock) into a capon.

caporal (ˌkæpə'rɑːl) *n* a strong coarse dark tobacco. [C19: from French *tabac du caporal* corporal's tobacco, denoting its superiority to *tabac du soldat* soldier's tobacco]

Caporetto (kapo'retto) *n* the Italian name for **Kobarid.**

capot (kə'pɒt) *n Piquet.* the winning of all the tricks by one player. [C17: from French]

capote (kə'pəʊt; *French* kapɔt) *n* a long cloak or soldier's coat, usually with a hood. [C19: from French: cloak, from *cape;* see CAPE[1]]

Capote (kə'pəʊtɪ) *n* **Truman.** 1924–84, U.S. writer; his novels include *Other Voices, Other Rooms* (1948) and *In Cold Blood* (1964), based on an actual multiple murder.

Capp (kæp) *n* **Al,** full name *Alfred Caplin.* 1909–79, U.S. cartoonist, famous for his comic strip *Li'l Abner.*

Cappadocia (ˌkæpə'dəʊsɪə) *n* an ancient region of E Asia Minor famous for its horses. ▸ **ˌCappa'docian** *adj, n*

capparidaceous (ˌkæpærɪ'deɪʃəs) *adj* of, relating to, or belonging to the *Capparidaceae,* a family of plants, mostly shrubs including the caper, of warm and tropical regions. [C19: from New Latin *Capparidaceae,* from Latin *capparis* caper]

cappuccino (ˌkæpʊ'tʃiːnəʊ) *n, pl* **-nos.** coffee with steamed milk, sometimes served with whipped cream or sprinkled with powdered chocolate. [Italian: CAPUCHIN]

Capra ('kæprə) *n* **Frank.** 1896–1992, U.S. film director born in Italy. His films include *It Happened One Night* (1934), *It's a Wonderful Life* (1946), and several propaganda films during World War II.

capreolate ('kæprɪəˌleɪt, kə'priː-) *adj Biology.* possessing or resembling tendrils. [C18: from Latin *capreolus* tendril]

Capri (kə'priː; *Italian* 'kapri) *n* an island off W Italy, in the Bay of Naples: resort since Roman times. Pop.: 8000 (latest est.). Area: about 13 sq. km (5 sq. miles).

capric acid ('kæprɪk) *n* another name for **decanoic acid.** [C19: from Latin *caper* goat, so named from its smell]

capriccio (kə'prɪtʃɪˌəʊ) *or* **caprice** *n, pl* **-priccios, -pricci** (-'priːtʃɪ), *or* **-prices.** *Music.* a lively piece composed freely and without adhering to the rules for any specific musical form. [C17: from Italian: CAPRICE]

capriccioso (kəˌprɪtʃɪ'əʊzəʊ) *adv Music.* to be played in a free and lively style. [Italian: from *capriccio* CAPRICE]

caprice (kə'priːs) *n* **1** a sudden or unpredictable change of attitude, behaviour, etc.; whim. **2** a tendency to such changes. **3** another word for **capriccio.** [C17: from French, from Italian *capriccio* a shiver, caprice, from *capo* head + *riccio* hedgehog, suggesting a convulsive shudder in which the hair stood on end like a hedgehog's spines; meaning also influenced by Italian *capra* goat, by folk etymology]

capricious (kə'prɪʃəs) *adj* characterized by or liable to sudden unpredictable changes in attitude or behaviour; impulsive; fickle. ▸ **ca'priciously** *adv* ▸ **ca'priciousness** *n*

Capricorn ('kæprɪˌkɔːn) *n* **1** *Astrology.* **1a** Also called: the **Goat, Capricornus.** the tenth sign of the zodiac, symbol ♑, having a cardinal earth classification and ruled by the planet Saturn. The sun is in this sign between about Dec. 22 and Jan. 19. **1b** a person born during the period when the sun is in this sign. **2** *Astronomy.* another name for **Capricornus. 3 tropic of Capricorn.** See **tropic** (sense 1). ◆ *adj* **4** *Astrology.* born under or characteristic of Capricorn. ◆ Also (for senses 1b, 4): **Capricornean** (ˌkæprɪ'kɔːnɪən). [C14: from Latin *Capricornus* (translating Greek *aigokerōs* goat-horned), from *caper* goat + *cornū* horn]

Capricornia (ˌkæprɪ'kɔːnɪə) *n* the regions of Australia in the tropic of Capricorn.

Capricornus (ˌkæprɪ'kɔːnəs) *n, Latin genitive* **-ni** (-naɪ). a faint zodiacal constellation in the S hemisphere, lying between Sagittarius and Aquarius.

caprification (ˌkæprɪfɪ'keɪʃən) *n* a method of pollinating the edible fig by hanging branches of caprifig flowers in edible fig trees. Parasitic wasps in the caprifig flowers transfer pollen to the edible fig flowers. [C17: from Latin *caprificātiō,* from *caprificāre* to pollinate figs by this method, from *caprificus* CAPRIFIG]

caprifig ('kæprɪˌfɪg) *n* a wild variety of fig, *Ficus carica sylvestris,* of S Europe and SW Asia, used in the caprification of the edible fig. [C15: from Latin *caprificus* literally: goat fig, from *caper* goat + *fīcus* FIG[1]]

caprifoliaceous (ˌkæprɪˌfəʊlɪ'eɪʃəs) *adj* of, relating to, or belonging to the *Caprifoliaceae,* a family of N temperate shrubs or small trees including honeysuckle, elder, and guelder-rose. [C19: from New Latin *caprifoliāceae,* from *caprifolium* type genus, from Medieval Latin: honeysuckle, from Latin *caper* goat + *folium* leaf]

caprine ('kæpraɪn) *adj* of or resembling a goat. [C17: from Latin *caprīnus,* from *caper* goat]

capriole ('kæprɪˌəʊl) *n* **1** *Dressage.* a high upward but not forward leap made by a horse with all four feet off the ground. **2** *Dancing.* a leap from bent knees. ◆ *vb* **3** (*intr*) to perform a capriole. [C16: from French, from Old Italian *capriola,* from *capriolo* roebuck, from Latin *capreolus, caper* goat]

Capri pants *or* **Capris** *pl n* women's tight-fitting trousers.

cap rock *n* **1** a layer of rock that overlies a salt dome and consists of limestone, gypsum, etc. **2** a layer of relatively impervious rock overlying an oil- or gas-bearing rock.

caproic acid (kə'prəʊɪk) *n* another name for **hexanoic acid.** [C19: *caproic,* from Latin *caper* goat, alluding to its smell]

caprolactam (ˌkæprəʊ'læktæm) *n* a white crystalline cyclic imine used in the manufacture of nylon. Formula: $C_5H_{10}NHCO$. [C20: from CAPRO(IC ACID) + LACTAM]

caps. *abbrev. for:* **1** capital letters. **2** capsule.

capsaicin (kæp'seɪɪsɪn) *n* a colourless crystalline bitter alkaloid found in capsicums and used as a flavouring in vinegar and pickles. Formula: $C_{18}H_{27}O_3N$. [C19 *capsicine,* from CAPSICUM + -INE[2]; modern form refashioned from Latin *capsa* box, case + -IN]

cap screw *n* a screwed bolt with a cylindrical head having a hexagonal recess. The bolt is turned using a wrench of hexagonal cross section.

Capsian ('kæpsɪən) *n* **1** a late Palaeolithic culture, dating from about 12 000 B.C., found mainly around the salt lakes of Tunisia. The culture is characterized by the presence of microliths, backed blades, and engraved limestone slabs. ◆ *adj* **2** of or relating to this culture. [C20: from French *capsien,* from *Capsa,* Latinized form of *Gafsa,* Tunisia]

capsicum ('kæpsɪkəm) *n* **1** any tropical American plant of the solanaceous genus *Capsicum,* such as *C. frutescens,* having mild or pungent seeds enclosed in a pod-shaped or bell-shaped fruit. **2** the fruit of any of these plants, used as a vegetable or ground to produce a condiment. ◆ See also **pepper** (sense 4). [C18: from New Latin, from Latin *capsa* box, CASE[2]]

capsid[1] ('kæpsɪd) *n* any heteropterous bug of the family *Miridae* (formerly *Capsidae*), most of which feed on plant tissues, causing damage to crops. [C19: from New Latin *Capsus* (genus)]

capsid[2] ('kæpsɪd) *n* the outer protein coat of a mature virus. [C20: from French *capside,* from Latin *capsa* box]

capsize (kæp'saɪz) *vb* to overturn accidentally; upset. [C18: of uncertain origin] ▸ **cap'sizal** *n*

capsomere ('kæpsəˌmɪə) *n* any of the protein units that together form the capsid of a virus.

capstan ('kæpstən) *n* **1** a machine with a drum that rotates round a vertical spindle and is turned by a motor or lever, used for hauling in heavy ropes, etc. **2** any similar device, such as the rotating shaft in a tape recorder that pulls the tape past the head. [C14: from Old Provençal *cabestan,* from Latin *capistrum* a halter, from *capere* to seize]

capstan bar *n* a lever, often wooden, for turning a capstan.

capstan lathe *n* a lathe for repetitive work, having a rotatable turret resembling a capstan to hold tools for successive operations. Also called: **turret lathe.**

capstone ('kæpˌstəʊn) *or* **copestone** ('kəʊpˌstəʊn) *n* **1** one of a set of slabs on the top of a wall, building, etc. **2** *Mountaineering.* a chockstone occurring at the top of a gully or chimney. **3** a crowning achievement; peak.

capsulate ('kæpsjʊˌleɪt, -lɪt) *or* **capsulated** *adj* within or formed into a capsule. ▸ **ˌcapsu'lation** *n*

capsule ('kæpsjuːl) *n* **1** a soluble case of gelatine enclosing a dose of medicine. **2**

a thin metal cap, seal, or cover, such as the foil covering the cork of a wine bottle. **3** *Botany.* **3a** a dry fruit that liberates its seeds by splitting, as in the violet, or through pores, as in the poppy. **3b** the spore-producing organ of mosses and liverworts. **4** *Bacteriol.* a gelatinous layer of polysaccharide or protein surrounding the cell wall of some bacteria: thought to be responsible for the virulence in pathogens. **5** *Anatomy.* **5a** a cartilaginous, fibrous, or membranous envelope surrounding any of certain organs or parts. **5b** a broad band of white fibres (**internal capsule**) near the thalamus in each cerebral hemisphere. **6** See **space capsule. 7** an aeroplane cockpit that can be ejected in a flight emergency, complete with crew, instruments, etc. **8** (*modifier*) in a highly concise form: *a capsule summary.* **9** (*modifier*) (in the fashion industry) consisting of a few important representative items: *a capsule collection.* [C17: from French, from Latin *capsula,* diminutive of *capsa* box]

capsulize *or* **capsulise** ('kæpsjʊˌlaɪz) *vb* (*tr*) **1** to state (information) in a highly condensed form. **2** to enclose in a capsule.

Capt. *abbrev. for* Captain.

captain ('kæptɪn) *n* **1** the person in charge of and responsible for a vessel. **2** an officer of the navy who holds a rank junior to a rear admiral but senior to a commander. **3** an officer of the army, certain air forces, and the marine corps who holds a rank junior to a major but senior to a lieutenant. **4** the officer in command of a civil aircraft, usually the senior pilot. **5** the leader of a team in games. **6** a person in command over a group, organization, etc.; leader: *a captain of industry.* **7** *U.S.* a policeman in charge of a precinct. **8** *U.S. and Canadian.* (formerly) a head waiter. **9** Also called: **bell captain.** *U.S. and Canadian.* a supervisor of bellboys in a hotel. ◆ *vb* **10** (*tr*) to be captain of. [C14: from Old French *capitaine,* from Late Latin *capitāneus* chief, from Latin *caput* head] ▸ **'captaincy** *or* **'captainˌship** *n*

Captain Cooker ('kʊkə) *n N.Z.* a wild pig. [from Captain James COOK, who first released pigs in the New Zealand bush]

captain's biscuit *n* a type of hard fancy biscuit.

caption ('kæpʃən) *n* **1** a title, brief explanation, or comment accompanying an illustration; legend. **2** a heading, title, or headline of a chapter, article, etc. **3** graphic material, usually containing lettering, used in television presentation. **4** another name for **subtitle** (sense 2). **5** the formal heading of a legal document stating when, where, and on what authority it was taken or made. ◆ *vb* **6** to provide with a caption or captions. [C14 (meaning: seizure, an arrest; later, heading of a legal document): from Latin *captiō* a seizing, from *capere* to take]

captious ('kæpʃəs) *adj* apt to make trivial criticisms; fault-finding; carping. [C14 (meaning: catching in error): from Latin *captiōsus,* from *captiō* a seizing; see CAPTION] ▸ **'captiously** *adv* ▸ **'captiousness** *n*

captivate ('kæptɪˌveɪt) *vb* (*tr*) **1** to hold the attention of by fascinating; enchant. **2** an obsolete word for **capture.** [C16: from Late Latin *captivāre,* from *captīvus* CAPTIVE] ▸ **'captiˌvatingly** *adv* ▸ **ˌcapti'vation** *n* ▸ **'captiˌvator** *n*

captive ('kæptɪv) *n* **1** a person or animal that is confined or restrained, esp. a prisoner of war. **2** a person whose behaviour is dominated by some emotion: *a captive of love.* ◆ *adj* **3** held as prisoner. **4** held under restriction or control; confined: *captive water held behind a dam.* **5** captivated; enraptured. **6** unable by circumstances to avoid speeches, advertisements, etc. (esp. in the phrase **captive audience**). [C14: from Latin *captīvus,* from *capere* to take]

captive market *n* a group of consumers who are obliged through lack of choice to buy a particular product, thus giving the supplier a monopoly.

captivity (kæp'tɪvɪtɪ) *n, pl* **-ties. 1** the condition of being captive; imprisonment. **2** the period of imprisonment.

captopril ('kæptəprɪl) *n* an ACE inhibitor used to treat high blood pressure and congestive heart failure.

captor ('kæptə) *n* a person or animal that holds another captive. [C17: from Latin, from *capere* to take]

capture ('kæptʃə) *vb* (*tr*) **1** to take prisoner or gain control over: *to capture an enemy; to capture a town.* **2** (in a game or contest) to win control or possession of: *to capture a pawn in chess.* **3** to succeed in representing or describing (something elusive): *the artist captured her likeness.* **4** *Physics.* (of an atom, molecule, ion, or nucleus) to acquire (an additional particle). **5** to insert or transfer (data) into a computer. ◆ *n* **6** the act of taking by force; seizure. **7** the person or thing captured; booty. **8** *Physics.* a process by which an atom, molecule, ion, or nucleus acquires an additional particle. **9** Also called: **piracy.** *Geography.* the process by which the headwaters of one river are diverted into another through erosion caused by the second river's tributaries. **10** the act or process of inserting or transferring data into a computer. [C16: from Latin *captūra* a catching, that which is caught, from *capere* to take] ▸ **'capturer** *n*

Capua ('kæpjʊə; *Italian* 'kapua) *n* a town in S Italy, in NW Campania: strategically important in ancient times, situated on the Appian Way. Pop.: 19 520 (1990).

Capuana (*Italian* ka'pwa:na) *n* **Luigi.** 1839–1915, Italian realist novelist, dramatist, and critic. His works include the novel *Giacinta* (1879) and the play *Malia* (1895).

capuche *or* **capouch** (kə'pu:ʃ) *n* a large hood or cowl, esp. that worn by Capuchin friars. [C17: from French, from Italian *cappuccio* hood, from Late Latin *cappa* cloak]

capuchin ('kæpjʊtʃɪn, -ʃɪn) *n* **1** any agile intelligent New World monkey of the genus *Cebus,* inhabiting forests in South America, typically having a cowl of thick hair on the top of the head. **2** a woman's hooded cloak. **3** (*sometimes cap.*) a rare variety of domestic fancy pigeon. [C16: from French, from Italian *cappuccino,* from *cappuccio* hood; see CAPUCHE]

Capuchin ('kæpjʊtʃɪn, 'kæpjʊʃɪn) *n* **a** a friar belonging to a strict and autonomous branch of the Franciscan order founded in 1525. **b** (*as modifier*): *a Capuchin friar.* [C16: from French; see CAPUCHE]

caput ('keɪpət, 'kæp-) *n, pl* **capita** ('kæpɪtə). **1** *Anatomy.* a technical name for the **head. 2** the main or most prominent part of an organ or structure. [C18: from Latin]

capybara (ˌkæpɪ'bɑ:rə) *n* the largest rodent: a pig-sized amphibious hystricomorph, *Hydrochoerus hydrochaeris,* resembling a guinea pig and inhabiting river banks in Central and South America: family *Hydrochoeridae.* [C18: from Portuguese *capibara,* from Tupi]

Caquetá (*Spanish* kake'ta) *n* the Japurá River from its source in Colombia to the border with Brazil.

car (kɑ:) *n* **1a** Also called: **motorcar, automobile.** a self-propelled road vehicle designed to carry passengers, esp. one with four wheels that is powered by an internal-combustion engine. **1b** (*as modifier*): *car coat.* **2** a conveyance for passengers, freight, etc., such as a cable car or the carrier of an airship or balloon. **3** *Brit.* a railway vehicle for passengers only, such as a sleeping car or buffet car. **4** *Chiefly U.S. and Canadian.* a railway carriage or van. **5** *Chiefly U.S.* the enclosed platform of a lift. **6** a poetic word for **chariot.** [C14: from Anglo-French *carre,* ultimately related to Latin *carra, carrum* two-wheeled wagon, probably of Celtic origin; compare Old Irish *carr*]

CAR *abbrev. for* compound annual return.

carabao (ˌkærə'beɪəʊ) *n, pl* **-os.** another name for **water buffalo.** [from Visayan *karabáw;* compare Malay *karbaw*]

carabid ('kærəbɪd) *n* **1** any typically dark-coloured beetle of the family *Carabidae,* including the bombardier and other ground beetles. ◆ *adj* **2** of, relating to, or belonging to the *Carabidae.* [C19: from New Latin, from Latin *cārabus* a kind of crab (name applied to these beetles)]

carabin ('kærəbɪn) *or* **carabine** ('kærəˌbaɪn) *n* variants of **carbine** (sense 2).

carabineer *or* **carabinier** (ˌkærəbɪ'nɪə) *n* variants of **carbineer.**

carabiner (ˌkærə'bi:nə) *n* a variant spelling of **karabiner.**

carabiniere *Italian.* (karabi'njɛ:re) *n, pl* ***-ri*** (-ri). an Italian national policeman.

caracal ('kærəˌkæl) *n* **1** Also called: **desert lynx.** a lynxlike feline mammal, *Lynx caracal,* inhabiting deserts of N Africa and S Asia, having long legs, a smooth coat of reddish fur, and black-tufted ears. **2** the fur of this animal. [C18: from French, from Turkish *kara kūlāk,* literally: black ear]

Caracalla (ˌkærə'kælə) *n* real name *Marcus Aurelius Antoninus,* original name *Bassianus.* 188–217 A.D., Roman emperor (211–17): ruled with cruelty and extravagance; assassinated.

caracara (ˌkɑ:rə'kɑ:rə) *n* any of various large carrion-eating diurnal birds of prey of the genera *Caracara, Polyborus,* etc., of S North, Central, and South America, having long legs and naked faces: family *Falconidae* (falcons). [C19: from Spanish or Portuguese, from Tupi; of imitative origin]

Caracas (kə'rækəs, -'rɑ:-; *Spanish* ka'rakas) *n* the capital of Venezuela, in the north: founded in 1567; major industrial and commercial centre, notably for oil companies. Pop.: 1 822 465 (1990).

caracole ('kærəˌkəʊl) *or* **caracol** ('kærəˌkɒl) *n* **1** *Dressage.* a half turn to the right or left. **2** a spiral staircase. ◆ *vb* (*intr*) **3** *Dressage.* to execute a half turn to the right or left. [C17: from French, from Spanish *caracol* snail, spiral staircase, turn]

Caractacus (kə'ræktəkəs) *n* a variant of **Caratacus.**

caracul ('kærəˌkʌl) *n* **1** Also called: **Persian lamb.** the black loosely curled fur obtained from the skins of newly born lambs of the karakul sheep. **2** a variant spelling of **karakul.**

carafe (kə'ræf, -'rɑ:f) *n* **a** an open-topped glass container for serving water or wine at table. **b** (*as modifier*): *a carafe wine.* [C18: from French, from Italian *caraffa,* from Spanish *garrafa,* from Arabic *gharrāfah* vessel]

carageen ('kærəˌgi:n) *n* a variant spelling of **carrageen.**

carambola (ˌkærəm'bəʊlə) *n* **1** a tree, *Averrhoa carambola,* probably native to Brazil but cultivated in the tropics, esp. SE Asia, for its edible fruit. **2** Also called: **star fruit.** the smooth-skinned yellow fruit of this tree, which is star-shaped on cross section. [C18: Spanish *carambola* a sour greenish fruit, from Portuguese, from Marathi *karambal*]

caramel ('kærəməl, -ˌmɛl) *n* **1** burnt sugar, used for colouring and flavouring food. **2** a chewy sweet made from sugar, butter, milk, etc. ◆ See also **crème caramel.** [C18: from French, from Spanish *caramelo,* of uncertain origin]

caramelize *or* **caramelise** ('kærəməˌlaɪz) *vb* to convert or be converted into caramel.

carangid (kə'rændʒɪd, -'ræŋgɪd) *or* **carangoid** (kə'ræŋgɔɪd) *n* **1** any marine percoid fish of the family *Carangidae,* having a compressed body and deeply forked tail. The group includes the jacks, horse mackerel, pompano, and pilot fish. ◆ *adj* **2** of, relating to, or belonging to the *Carangidae.* [C19: from New Latin *Carangidae,* from *Caranx* type genus, from French *carangue* shad, from Spanish *caranga,* of obscure origin]

carapace ('kærəˌpeɪs) *n* the thick hard shield, made of chitin or bone, that covers part of the body of crabs, lobsters, tortoises, etc. [C19: from French, from Spanish *carapacho,* of unknown origin]

carat ('kærət) *n* **1** a measure of the weight of precious stones, esp. diamonds. It was formerly defined as 3.17 grains, but the international carat is now standardized as 0.20 grams. **2** Usual U.S. spelling: **karat.** a measure of the proportion of gold in an alloy, expressed as the number of parts of gold in 24 parts of the alloy. [C16: from Old French, from Medieval Latin *carratus,* from Arabic *qīrāt* weight of four grains, carat, from Greek *keration* a little horn, from *keras* horn]

Caratacus (kə'rætəkəs), **Caractacus,** *or* **Caradoc** (kə'rædək) *n* died ?54 A.D., British chieftain: led an unsuccessful resistance against the Romans (43–50).

Caravaggio (*Italian* kara'vaddʒo) *n* **Michelangelo Merisi da** (mike'landʒelo me'ri:zi da). 1571–1610, Italian painter, noted for his realistic depiction of religious subjects and for his dramatic use of chiaroscuro.

caravan ('kærəˌvæn) *n* **1a** a large enclosed vehicle capable of being pulled by a car or lorry and equipped to be lived in. U.S. and Canadian name: **trailer. 1b** (*as modifier*): *a caravan site.* **2** (esp. in some parts of Asia and Africa) a company of traders or other travellers journeying together, often with a train of camels, through the desert. **3** a group of wagons, pack mules, camels, etc., esp. travelling in single file. **4** a large covered vehicle, esp. a gaily coloured one used by Gypsies, circuses, etc. ◆ *vb* **-vans, -vanning, -vanned. 5** (*intr*) *Brit.* to travel or have a holiday in a caravan. [C16: from Italian *caravana,* from Persian *kārwān*] ▸ **'cara,vanning** *n*

caravanserai (,kærə'vænsə,raɪ, -,reɪ) *or* **caravansary** (,kærə'vænsərɪ) *n, pl* **-rais** *or* **-ries.** (in some Eastern countries, esp. formerly) a large inn enclosing a courtyard, providing accommodation for caravans. [C16: from Persian *kārwānsarāī* caravan inn]

caravel ('kærə,vɛl) *or* **carvel** *n* a two- or three-masted sailing ship, esp. one with a broad beam, high poop deck, and lateen rig that was used by the Spanish and Portuguese in the 15th and 16th centuries. [C16: from Portuguese *caravela,* diminutive of *caravo* ship, ultimately from Greek *karabos* crab, horned beetle]

caraway ('kærə,weɪ) *n* **1** an umbelliferous Eurasian plant, *Carum carvi,* having finely divided leaves and clusters of small whitish flowers. **2 caraway seed.** the pungent aromatic one-seeded fruit of this plant, used in cooking and in medicine. [C14: probably from Medieval Latin *carvi,* from Arabic *karawyā,* from Greek *karon*]

carbamate ('kɑːbə,meɪt) *n* a salt or ester of carbamic acid. The salts contain the monovalent ion NH_2COO^-, and the esters contain the group $NH_2COO–$.

carbamazepine (,kɑːbə'mæzə,piːn) *n* an anticonvulsant drug used in the management of epilepsy.

carbamic acid (kɑː'bæmɪk) *n* a hypothetical compound known only in the form of carbamate salts and esters. Formula: NH_2COOH.

carbamide ('kɑːbə,maɪd) *n* another name for **urea.**

carbamidine (kɑː'bæmɪ,daɪn) *n* another name for **guanidine.**

carbanion (kɑː'bænaɪən) *n Chem.* a negatively charged organic ion, such as H_3C^-, derived from a free radical by addition of one electron. Compare **carbonium ion.**

carbaryl ('kɑːbərɪl) *n* an organic compound of the carbamate group: used as an insecticide, esp. to treat head lice.

carbazole ('kɑːbə,zəʊl) *n* a colourless insoluble solid obtained from coal tar and used in the production of some dyes. Formula: $C_{12}H_9N$. Also called: **diphenylenimine** (daɪ,fiːnaɪ'lenɪmiːn).

carbene ('kɑːbiːn) *n Chem.* a neutral divalent free radical, such as methylene: CH_2.

carbide ('kɑːbaɪd) *n* **1** a binary compound of carbon with a metal. See also **acetylide. 2** See **calcium carbide.**

carbimazole (kɑː'bɪmə,zəʊl) *n* a drug that inhibits the synthesis of the hormone thyroxine, used in the management of hyperthyroidism.

carbine ('kɑːbaɪn) *n* **1** a light automatic or semiautomatic rifle of limited range. **2** Also called: **carabin, carabine.** a light short-barrelled shoulder rifle formerly used by cavalry. [C17: from French *carabine,* from Old French *carabin* carabineer, perhaps variant of *escarrabin* one who prepares corpses for burial, from *scarabée,* from Latin *scarabaeus* SCARAB]

carbineer (,kɑːbɪ'nɪə), **carabineer,** *or* **carabinier** (,kærəbɪ'nɪə) *n* (formerly) a soldier equipped with a carbine.

carbo- *or before a vowel* **carb-** *combining form.* carbon: *carbohydrate; carbonate.*

carbocyclic (,kɑːbəʊ'saɪklɪk) *adj* (of a chemical compound) containing a closed ring of carbon atoms.

carbohydrate (,kɑːbəʊ'haɪdreɪt) *n* any of a large group of organic compounds, including sugars, such as sucrose, and polysaccharides, such as cellulose, glycogen, and starch, that contain carbon, hydrogen, and oxygen, with the general formula $C_m(H_2O)_n$: an important source of food and energy for animals.

carbolated ('kɑːbə,leɪtɪd) *adj* containing carbolic acid.

carbolic acid (kɑː'bɒlɪk) *n* another name for **phenol,** esp. when it is used as an antiseptic or disinfectant. [C19: *carbolic,* from CARBO- + -OL[1] + -IC]

carbolize *or* **carbolise** ('kɑːbə,laɪz) *vb* (*tr*) another word for **phenolate.**

carbon ('kɑːbᵊn) *n* **1a** a nonmetallic element existing in the three crystalline forms: graphite, diamond, and buckminsterfullerene: occurring in carbon dioxide, coal, oil, and all organic compounds. The isotope **carbon-12** has been adopted as the standard for atomic wt.; **carbon-14,** a radioisotope with a half-life of 5700 years, is used in radiocarbon dating and as a tracer. Symbol: C; atomic no.: 6; atomic wt.: 12.011; valency: 2, 3, or 4; relative density: 1.8–2.1 (amorphous), 1.9–2.3 (graphite), 3.15–3.53 (diamond); sublimes at 3367±25°C; boiling pt.: 4827°C. **1b** (*as modifier*): *a carbon compound.* **2** short for **carbon paper** or **carbon copy. 3** a carbon electrode used in a carbon-arc light or in carbon-arc welding. **4** a rod or plate, made of carbon, used in some types of battery. [C18: from French *carbone,* from Latin *carbō* charcoal, dead or glowing coal] ▸ **'carbonous** *adj*

carbonaceous (,kɑːbə'neɪʃəs) *adj* of, resembling, or containing carbon.

carbonade (,kɑːbə'neɪd, -'nɑːd) *n* a stew of beef and onions cooked in beer. [C20: from French]

carbonado[1] (,kɑːbə'neɪdəʊ, -'nɑːdəʊ) *n, pl* **-does** *or* **-dos. 1** a piece of meat, fish, etc., scored and grilled. ◆ *vb* **-dos, -doing, -doed.** (*tr*) **2** to score and grill (meat, fish, etc.). **3** *Archaic.* to hack or slash. [C16: from Spanish *carbonada,* from *carbón* charcoal; see CARBON]

carbonado[2] (,kɑːbə'neɪdəʊ, -'nɑːdəʊ) *n, pl* **-dos** *or* **-does.** an inferior dark massive variety of diamond used in industry for polishing and drilling. Also called: **black diamond.** [Portuguese, literally: carbonated]

carbon arc *n* **1a** an electric arc produced between two carbon electrodes, formerly used as a light source. **1b** (*as modifier*): *carbon-arc light.* **2a** an electric arc produced between a carbon electrode and material to be welded. **2b** (*as modifier*): *carbon-arc welding.*

Carbonari (,kɑːbə'nɑːrɪ) *pl n, sing* **-naro** (-'nɑːrəʊ). members of a secret political society with liberal republican aims, originating in S Italy about 1811 and particularly engaged in the struggle for Italian unification. [C19: from Italian, plural of *carbonaro* seller or burner of charcoal, name adopted by the society]

carbonate *n* ('kɑːbə,neɪt, -nɪt). **1** a salt or ester of carbonic acid. Carbonate salts contain the divalent ion CO_3^{2-}. ◆ *vb* ('kɑːbə,neɪt). **2** to form or turn into a carbonate. **3** (*tr*) to treat with carbon dioxide or carbonic acid, as in the manufacture of soft drinks. [C18: from French, from *carbone* CARBON]

carbonation (,kɑːbə'neɪʃən) *n* **1** absorption of or reaction with carbon dioxide. **2** another word for **carbonization.**

carbon bisulphide *n* (not in technical usage) another name for **carbon disulphide.**

carbon black *n* a black finely divided form of amorphous carbon produced by incomplete combustion of natural gas or petroleum: used to reinforce rubber and in the manufacture of pigments and ink.

carbon brush *n* a small block of carbon used to convey current between the stationary and moving parts of an electric generator, motor, etc.

carbon copy *n* **1** a duplicate copy of writing, typewriting, or drawing obtained by using carbon paper. Often shortened to **carbon. 2** *Informal.* a person or thing that is identical or very similar to another.

carbon cycle *n* **1** the circulation of carbon between living organisms and their surroundings. Carbon dioxide from the atmosphere is synthesized by plants into plant tissue, which is ingested and metabolized by animals and reduced to carbon dioxide again during respiration and decay. **2** four thermonuclear reactions believed to be the source of energy in many stars. Carbon nuclei function as catalysts in the fusion of protons to form helium nuclei.

carbon dating *n* short for **radiocarbon dating.**

carbon dioxide *n* a colourless odourless incombustible gas present in the atmosphere and formed during respiration, the decomposition and combustion of organic compounds, and in the reaction of acids with carbonates: used in carbonated drinks, fire extinguishers, and as dry ice for refrigeration. Formula: CO_2. Also called: **carbonic-acid gas.**

carbon dioxide snow *n* solid carbon dioxide, used as a refrigerant.

carbon disulphide *n* a colourless slightly soluble volatile flammable poisonous liquid commonly having a disagreeable odour due to the presence of impurities: used as an organic solvent and in the manufacture of rayon and carbon tetrachloride. Formula: CS_2. Also called (not in technical usage): **carbon bisulphide.**

carbonette (,kɑːbə'nɛt) *n N.Z.* a ball of compressed coal dust used as fuel.

carbon fibre *n* a black silky thread of pure carbon made by heating and stretching textile fibres and used because of its lightness and strength at high temperatures for reinforcing resins, ceramics, and metals, esp. in turbine blades and for fishing rods.

carbon fixation *n* the process by which plants assimilate carbon from carbon dioxide in the atmosphere to form metabolically active compounds.

carbon-14 dating *n* another name for **radiocarbon dating.**

carbonic (kɑː'bɒnɪk) *adj* (of a compound) containing carbon, esp. tetravalent carbon.

carbonic acid *n* a weak acid formed when carbon dioxide combines with water: obtained only in aqueous solutions, never in the pure state. Formula: H_2CO_3.

carbonic-acid gas *n* another name for **carbon dioxide.**

carbonic anhydrase *n* an enzyme in blood cells that catalyses the decomposition of carbonic acid into carbon dioxide and water, facilitating the transport of carbon dioxide from the tissues to the lungs.

carboniferous (,kɑːbə'nɪfərəs) *adj* yielding coal or carbon.

Carboniferous (,kɑːbə'nɪfərəs) *adj* **1** of, denoting, or formed in the fifth period of the Palaeozoic era, between the Devonian and Permian periods, lasting for nearly 80 million years during which coal measures were formed. ◆ *n* **2 the.** the Carboniferous period or rock system.

carbonium ion (kɑː'bəʊnɪəm) *n Chem.* a positively charged organic ion, such as H_3C^+, derived from a free radical by removal of one electron. Compare **carbanion.**

carbonize *or* **carbonise** ('kɑːbə,naɪz) *vb* **1** to turn or be turned into carbon as a result of heating, fossilization, chemical treatment, etc. **2** (*tr*) to enrich or coat (a substance) with carbon. **3** (*intr*) to react or unite with carbon. ◆ Also (for senses 2, 3): **carburize.** ▸ **,carboni'zation** *or* **,carboni'sation** *n* ▸ **'carbon,izer** *or* **'carbon,iser** *n*

carbonless paper *n* a sheet of paper impregnated with dye which transfers writing or typing onto the copying surface below without the necessity for carbon pigment. See **carbon paper.**

carbon microphone *n* a microphone in which a diaphragm, vibrated by sound waves, applies a varying pressure to a container packed with carbon granules, altering the resistance of the carbon. A current flowing through the carbon is thus modulated at the frequency of the sound waves.

carbon monoxide *n* a colourless odourless poisonous flammable gas formed when carbon compounds burn in insufficient air and produced by the action of steam on hot carbon: used as a reducing agent in metallurgy and as a fuel. Formula: CO.

carbon paper *n* **1** a thin sheet of paper coated on one side with a dark waxy pigment, often containing carbon, that is transferred by the pressure of writing or of typewriter keys onto the copying surface below. Often shortened to **carbon. 2** another name for **carbon tissue.**

carbon process *or* **printing** *n* a photographic process for producing positive prints by exposing sensitized carbon tissue to light passing through a negative. Washing removes the unexposed gelatine leaving the pigmented image in the exposed insoluble gelatine.

carbon steel *n* steel whose characteristics are determined by the amount of carbon it contains.

carbon tetrachloride *n* a colourless volatile nonflammable sparingly soluble liquid made from chlorine and carbon disulphide; tetrachloromethane. It is used as a solvent, cleaning fluid, and insecticide. Formula: CCl_4.
carbon tissue *n* a sheet of paper coated with pigmented gelatine, used in the carbon process. Also called: **carbon paper.**
carbon value *n Chem.* an empirical measurement of the tendency of a lubricant to form carbon when in use.
carbonyl ('kɑːbəˌnaɪl, -nɪl) *n Chem.* **1** (*modifier*) of, consisting of, or containing the divalent group =CO: *a carbonyl group or radical.* **2** any one of a class of inorganic complexes in which carbonyl groups are bound directly to metal atoms. ▸ **carbonylic** (ˌkɑːbəˈnɪlɪk) *adj*
carbonyl chloride *n* (not in technical usage) another name for **phosgene.**
car-boot sale *n* a sale of goods from car boots in a site hired for the occasion.
Carborundum (ˌkɑːbəˈrʌndəm) *n Trademark.* **a** any of various abrasive materials, esp. one consisting of silicon carbide. **b** (*as modifier*): *a Carborundum wheel.*
carboxyhaemoglobin *or U.S.* **carboxyhemoglobin** (kɑːˌbɒksɪˌhiːməʊˈɡləʊbɪn, -ˌhɛm-) *n* haemoglobin coordinated with carbon monoxide, formed as a result of carbon monoxide poisoning. As carbon monoxide is bound in preference to oxygen, tissues are deprived of oxygen.
carboxylase (kɑːˈbɒksɪˌleɪz) *n* any enzyme that catalyses the release of carbon dioxide from certain acids.
carboxylate (kɑːˈbɒksɪˌleɪt) *n* any salt or ester of a carboxylic acid having a formula of the type $M(RCOO)_x$, where M is a metal and R an organic group, or R_1COOR_2, where R_1 and R_2 are organic groups.
carboxyl group *or* **radical** (kɑːˈbɒksaɪl, -sɪl) *n* the monovalent group –COOH, consisting of a carbonyl group bound to a hydroxyl group: the functional group in organic acids. **[C19** *carboxyl,* from CARBO- + OXY-[2] + -YL**]**
carboxylic acid (ˌkɑːbɒkˈsɪlɪk) *n* any of a class of organic acids containing the carboxyl group. See also **fatty acid.**
carboy (ˈkɑːˌbɔɪ) *n* a large glass or plastic bottle, usually protected by a basket or box, used for containing corrosive liquids such as acids. **[C18:** from Persian *qarāba***]**
carbuncle (ˈkɑːˌbʌŋkᵊl) *n* **1** an extensive skin eruption, similar to but larger than a boil, with several openings: caused by staphylococcal infection. **2** a rounded gemstone, esp. a garnet cut without facets. **3** a dark reddish-greyish-brown colour. **[C13:** from Latin *carbunculus* diminutive of *carbō* coal**]** ▸ **ˈcarˌbuncled** *adj* ▸ **carbuncular** (kɑːˈbʌŋkjʊlə) *adj*
carburation (ˌkɑːbjʊˈreɪʃən) *n* the process of mixing a hydrocarbon fuel with a correct amount of air to make an explosive mixture for an internal-combustion engine.
carburet (ˈkɑːbjʊˌrɛt, ˌkɑːbjʊˈrɛt, -bə-) *vb* **-rets, -retting, -retted** *or U.S.* **-rets, -reting, -reted.** (*tr*) to combine or mix (a gas) with carbon or carbon compounds. **[C18:** from CARB(ON) + -URET**]**
carburettor, carburetter (ˌkɑːbjʊˈrɛtə, ˈkɑːbjʊˌrɛtə, -bə-) *or U.S.* **carburetor** (ˈkɑːbjʊˌreɪtə, -bə-) *n* a device used in petrol engines for atomizing the petrol, controlling its mixture with air, and regulating the intake of the air-petrol mixture into the engine. Compare **fuel injection.**
carburize *or* **carburise** (ˈkɑːbjʊˌraɪz, -bə-) *vb* **1** another word for **carbonize** (senses 2, 3). **2** (*tr*) to increase the carbon content of (the surface of a low-carbon steel) so that the surface can be hardened by heat treatment. ▸ **ˌcarburiˈzation** *or* **ˌcarburiˈsation** *n*
carby (ˈkɑːbɪ) *n, pl* **-bies.** *Austral. informal.* short for **carburettor.**
carbylamine (ˌkɑːbɪləˈmiːn, -ˈæmɪn) *n* another name for **isocyanide.**
carcajou (ˈkɑːkəˌdʒuː, -ˌʒuː) *n* a North American name for **wolverine. [C18:** from Canadian French, from Algonquian *karkajou***]**
carcanet (ˈkɑːkəˌnɛt, -nɪt) *n Archaic.* a jewelled collar or necklace. **[C16:** from French *carcan,* of Germanic origin; compare Old Norse *kverkband* chin strap**]**
carcass *or* **carcase** (ˈkɑːkəs) *n* **1** the dead body of an animal, esp. one that has been slaughtered for food, with the head, limbs, and entrails removed. **2** *Informal, usually facetious or derogatory.* a person's body. **3** the skeleton or framework of a structure: *the carcass of an old tyre.* **4** the remains of anything when its life or vitality is gone; shell. **[C14:** from Old French *carcasse,* of obscure origin**]**
Carcassonne (*French* karkasɔn) *n* a city in SW France: extensive remains of medieval fortifications. Pop.: 44 990 (1990).
Carchemish (ˈkɑːkəmɪʃ, kɑːˈkiː-) *n* an ancient city in Syria on the Euphrates, lying on major trade routes; site of a victory of the Babylonians over the Egyptians (605 B.C.).
carcinogen (kɑːˈsɪnədʒən, ˈkɑːsɪnəˌdʒɛn) *n Pathol.* any substance that produces cancer. **[C20:** from Greek *karkinos* CANCER + -GEN**]** ▸ **ˌcarcinoˈgenic** *adj* ▸ **ˌcarcinogenˈicity** *n*
carcinogenesis (ˌkɑːsɪnəʊˈdʒɛnɪsɪs) *n Pathol.* the development of cancerous cells from normal ones.
carcinoma (ˌkɑːsɪˈnəʊmə) *n, pl* **-mas** *or* **-mata** (-mətə). *Pathol.* **1** any malignant tumour derived from epithelial tissue. **2** another name for **cancer** (sense 1). **[C18:** from Latin, from Greek *karkinōma,* from *karkinos* CANCER**]** ▸ **ˌcarciˈnomaˌtoid** *or* **ˌcarciˈnomatous** *adj*
carcinomatosis (ˌkɑːsɪˌnəʊməˈtəʊsɪs) *n Pathol.* a condition characterized by widespread dissemination of carcinomas or by a carcinoma that affects a large area. Also called: **carcinosis** (ˌkɑːsɪˈnəʊsɪs).
card[1] (kɑːd) *n* **1** a piece of stiff paper or thin cardboard, usually rectangular, with varied uses, as for filing information in an index, bearing a written notice for display, entering scores in a game, etc. **2** such a card used for identification, reference, proof of membership, etc.: *library card; identity card; visiting card.* **3** such a card used for sending greetings, messages, or invitations, often bearing an illustration, printed greetings, etc.: *Christmas card; birthday card.* **4** one of a set of small pieces of cardboard, variously marked with significant figures, symbols, etc., used for playing games or for fortune-telling. **5a** short for **playing card. 5b** (*as modifier*): *a card game.* **5c** (*in combination*): *cardsharp.* **6** *Informal.* a witty, entertaining, or eccentric person. **7** short for **cheque card** or **credit card. 8** See **compass card. 9** Also called: **race card.** *Horse racing.* a daily programme of all the races at a meeting, listing the runners, riders, weights to be carried, distances to be run, and conditions of each race. **10** a thing or action used in order to gain an advantage, esp. one that is concealed and kept in reserve until needed (esp. in the phrase **a card up one's sleeve**). **11** short for **printed circuit card.** See **printed circuit.** ◆ **See also cards. [C15:** from Old French *carte,* from Latin *charta* leaf of papyrus, from Greek *khartēs,* probably of Egyptian origin**]**
card[2] (kɑːd) *vb* **1** (*tr*) to comb out and clean fibres of wool or cotton before spinning. ◆ *n* **2** (formerly) a machine or comblike tool for carding fabrics or for raising the nap on cloth. **[C15:** from Old French *carde* card, teasel, from Latin *carduus* thistle**]** ▸ **ˈcarding** *n* ▸ **ˈcarder** *n*
Card. *abbrev. for* Cardinal.
cardamom, cardamum (ˈkɑːdəməm), *or* **cardamon** *n* **1** a tropical Asian zingiberaceous plant, *Elettaria cardamomum,* that has large hairy leaves. **2** the seeds of this plant, used esp. as a spice or condiment. **3** a related East Indian plant, *Amomum cardamomum,* whose seeds are used as a substitute for cardamom seeds. **[C15:** from Latin *cardamōmum,* from Greek *kardamōmon,* from *kardamon* cress + *amōmon* an Indian spice**]**
cardan joint (ˈkɑːdæn) *n Engineering.* a type of universal joint in a shaft that enables it to rotate when out of alignment. **[C20:** named after Geronimo *Cardan* (1501–76), Italian mathematician**]**
cardboard (ˈkɑːdˌbɔːd) *n* **1a** a thin stiff board made from paper pulp and used esp. for making cartons. **1b** (*as modifier*): *cardboard boxes.* ◆ *adj* **2** (*prenominal*) without substance: *a cardboard smile; a cardboard general.*
cardboard city *n Informal.* an area of a city in which homeless people sleep rough, often in cardboard boxes.
card-carrying *adj* being an official member of a specified organization: *a card-carrying union member; a card-carrying Communist.*
card catalogue *n* a catalogue of books, papers, etc., filed on cards.
Cardenal (*Spanish* karðeˈnal) *n* **Ernesto** (ɜːˈnɛstəʊ). born 1925, Nicaraguan poet, revolutionary, and Roman Catholic priest; an influential figure in the Sandinista movement.
Cárdenas (*Spanish* ˈkarðenas) *n* **Lázaro** (ˈlaθaro). 1895–1970, Mexican statesman and general; president of Mexico (1934–40).
card file *n* another term for **card index.**
cardiac (ˈkɑːdɪˌæk) *adj* **1** of or relating to the heart. **2** of or relating to the portion of the stomach connected to the oesophagus. ◆ *n* **3** a person with a heart disorder. **4** a drug that stimulates the heart muscle. **[C17:** from Latin *cardiacus,* from Greek, from *kardia* heart**]**
cardiac arrest *n* failure of the pumping action of the heart, resulting in loss of consciousness and absence of pulse and breathing: a medical emergency requiring immediate resuscitative treatment.
cardialgia (ˌkɑːdɪˈældʒɪə, -dʒə) *n* **1** pain in or near the heart. **2** a technical name for **heartburn.** ▸ **ˌcardiˈalgic** *adj*
cardie *or* **cardy** (ˈkɑːdɪ) *n Informal.* short for **cardigan.**
Cardiff (ˈkɑːdɪf) *n* **1** the capital of Wales, situated in the southeast, in Cardiff county borough: formerly an important port. Pop.: 272 129 (1991). **2** a county borough in SE Wales, created in 1996 from part of South Glamorgan. Pop.: 306 500 (1996 est.). Area: 139 sq. km (54 sq. miles).
cardigan (ˈkɑːdɪɡən) *n* a knitted jacket or sweater with buttons up the front. **[C19:** named after the 7th Earl of CARDIGAN**]**
Cardigan[1] (ˈkɑːdɪɡən) *n* the larger variety of corgi, having a long tail.
Cardigan[2] (ˈkɑːdɪɡən) *n* **7th Earl of,** title of *James Thomas Brudenell.* 1797–1868, British cavalry officer. He led the charge of the Light Brigade at Balaklava (1854) during the Crimean War.
Cardigan Bay *n* an inlet of St George's Channel, on the W coast of Wales.
Cardiganshire (ˈkɑːdɪɡənˌʃɪə, -ʃə) *n* a former county of W Wales: became part of Dyfed in 1974; reinstated as **Ceredigion** in 1996.
Cardin (*French* kardɛ̃) *n* **Pierre** (pjɛr). born 1922, French couturier, noted esp. for his collections for men.
cardinal (ˈkɑːdɪnᵊl) *n* **1** *R.C. Church.* any of the members of the Sacred College, ranking next after the pope, who elect the pope and act as his chief counsellors. **2** Also called: **cardinal red.** a deep vivid red colour. **3** See **cardinal number. 4** Also called: **cardinal grosbeak,** (U.S.) **redbird.** a crested North American bunting, *Richmondena* (or *Pyrrhuloxia*) *cardinalis,* the male of which has a bright red plumage and the female a brown one. **5** a fritillary butterfly, *Pandoriana pandora,* found in meadows of southern Europe. **6** a woman's hooded shoulder cape worn in the 17th and 18th centuries. ◆ *adj* **7** (*usually prenominal*) fundamentally important; principal. **8** of a deep vivid red colour. **9** *Astrology.* of or relating to the signs Aries, Cancer, Libra, and Capricorn. Compare **mutable** (sense 2), **fixed** (sense 10). **[C13:** from Latin *cardinālis,* literally: relating to a hinge, hence, that on which something depends, principal, from *cardō* hinge**]** ▸ **ˈcardinally** *adv*
cardinalate (ˈkɑːdɪnᵊˌleɪt) *or* **cardinalship** *n* **1** the rank, office, or term of office of a cardinal. **2** the cardinals collectively.
cardinal beetle *n* any of various large N temperate beetles of the family *Pyrochroidae,* such as *Pyrochroa serraticornis,* typically scarlet or partly scarlet in colour.
cardinal flower *n* a campanulaceous plant, *Lobelia cardinalis* of E North America, that has brilliant scarlet, pink, or white flowers.
cardinality (ˌkɑːdɪˈnælɪtɪ) *n* **1** *Maths.* the property of possessing a cardinal number. **2** *Maths, logic.* (of a class) the cardinal number associated with the given class. Two classes have the same cardinality if they can be put in one-to-one correspondence.

cardinal number *or* **numeral** *n* **1** a number denoting quantity but not order in a group. Sometimes shortened to **cardinal. 2** *Maths, logic.* **2a** a measure of the size of a set that does not take account of the order of its members. Compare **natural number. 2b** a particular number having this function. ◆ Compare **ordinal number.**
cardinal points *pl n* the four main points of the compass: north, south, east, and west.
cardinal spider *n* a large house spider, *Tegenaria parietina.*
cardinal virtues *pl n* the most important moral qualities, traditionally justice, prudence, temperance, and fortitude.
cardinal vowels *pl n* a set of theoretical vowel sounds, based on the shape of the mouth needed to articulate them, that can be used to classify the vowel sounds of any speaker in any language.
card index *or* **file** *n* **1** an index in which each item is separately listed on systematically arranged cards. ◆ *vb* **card-index.** (*tr*) **2** to make such an index of (a book).
carding (ˈkɑːdɪŋ) *n* the process of preparing the fibres of cotton, wool, etc., for spinning.
cardio- *or before a vowel* **cardi-** *combining form.* heart: *cardiogram.* [from Greek *kardia* heart]
cardiocentesis (ˌkɑːdɪəʊsɛnˈtiːsɪs) *n Med.* surgical puncture of the heart.
cardiogram (ˈkɑːdɪəʊˌɡræm) *n* short for **electrocardiogram.**
cardiograph (ˈkɑːdɪəʊˌɡrɑːf, -ˌɡræf) *n* **1** an instrument for recording the mechanical force and form of heart movements. **2** short for **electrocardiograph.** ▸ **cardiographer** (ˌkɑːdɪˈɒɡrəfə) *n* ▸ **cardiographic** (ˌkɑːdɪəʊˈɡræfɪk) *or* **ˌcardioˈgraphical** *adj* ▸ **ˌcardioˈgraphically** *adv* ▸ **ˌcardiˈography** *n*
cardioid (ˈkɑːdɪˌɔɪd) *n* a heart-shaped curve generated by a fixed point on a circle as it rolls around another fixed circle of equal radius, *a*. Equation: $r = a(1 - \cos \phi)$, where *r* is the radius vector and ϕ is the polar angle.
cardiology (ˌkɑːdɪˈɒlədʒɪ) *n* the branch of medical science concerned with the heart and its diseases. ▸ **cardiological** (ˌkɑːdɪəˈlɒdʒɪkᵊl) *adj* ▸ **ˌcardiˈologist** *n*
cardiomegaly (ˌkɑːdɪəʊˈmɛɡəlɪ) *n Pathol.* another name for **megalocardia.**
cardiomyopathy (ˌkɑːdɪəʊmaɪˈɒpəθɪ) *n Pathol.* a disease of the heart muscle usually caused by a biochemical defect or a toxin such as alcohol.
cardioplegia (ˌkɑːdɪəʊˈpliːdʒɪə) *n Med.* deliberate arrest of the action of the heart, as by hypothermia or the injection of chemicals, to enable complex heart surgery to be carried out.
cardiopulmonary (ˌkɑːdɪəʊˈpʌlmənərɪ, -mənrɪ, -ˈpʊl-) *adj* of, relating to, or affecting the heart and lungs.
cardiopulmonary resuscitation *n* an emergency measure to revive a patient whose heart has stopped beating, in which compressions applied with the hands to the patient's chest are alternated with mouth-to-mouth respiration. Abbrev.: **CPR.**
cardiovascular (ˌkɑːdɪəʊˈvæskjʊlə) *adj* of or relating to the heart and the blood vessels.
carditis (kɑːˈdaɪtɪs) *n* inflammation of the heart.
cardoon (kɑːˈduːn) *n* a thistle-like S European plant, *Cynara cardunculus,* closely related to the artichoke, with spiny leaves, purple flowers, and a leafstalk that may be blanched and eaten: family *Compositae* (composites). [C17: from French *cardon,* ultimately from Latin *carduus* thistle, artichoke]
cardphone (ˈkɑːdfəʊn) *n* a public telephone operated by the insertion of a phonecard instead of coins.
card punch *n* **1** a device, no longer widely used, controlled by a computer, for transferring information from the central processing unit onto punched cards. Compare **card reader. 2** another name for **key punch.**
card reader *n* a device, no longer widely used, for reading information on a punched card and transferring it to a computer. Compare **card punch.**
cards (kɑːdz) *n* **1** (*usually functioning as sing*) **1a** any game or games played with cards, esp. playing cards. **1b** the playing of such a game. **2** an employee's national insurance and other documents held by the employer. **3 get one's cards.** to be told to leave one's employment. **4 on the cards.** possible or likely. U.S. equivalent: **in the cards. 5 play one's cards.** to carry out one's plans; take action (esp. in the phrase **play one's cards right**). **6 put** *or* **lay one's cards on the table.** Also: **show one's cards.** to declare one's intentions, resources, etc.
cardsharp (ˈkɑːdˌʃɑːp) *or* **cardsharper** *n* a professional card player who cheats. ▸ **ˈcardˌsharping** *n*
carduaceous (ˌkɑːdjʊˈeɪʃəs) *adj* of, relating to, or belonging to the *Carduaceae,* a subfamily of composite plants that includes the thistle. [C19: from New Latin *Carduāceae,* from *Carduus* type genus, from Latin: thistle]
Carducci (*Italian* karˈduttʃi) *n* **Giosuè** (dʒozuˈɛ). 1835–1907, Italian poet: Nobel prize for literature 1906.
Cardus (ˈkɑːdəs) *n* Sir **Neville.** 1889–1975, British music critic and cricket writer.
card vote *n Brit.* a vote by delegates, esp. at a trade-union conference, in which each delegate's vote counts as a vote by all his constituents.
cardy (ˈkɑːdɪ) *n, pl* **-dies.** *Informal.* a variant spelling of **cardie.**
care (kɛə) *vb* **1** (when *tr, may take a clause as object*) to be troubled or concerned; be affected emotionally: *he is dying, and she doesn't care.* **2** (*intr;* foll. by *for* or *about*) to have regard, affection, or consideration (for): *he cares more for his hobby than his job.* **3** (*intr;* foll. by *for*) to have a desire or taste (for): *would you care for some tea?* **4** (*intr;* foll. by *for*) to provide physical needs, help, or comfort (for): *the nurse cared for her patients.* **5** (*tr*) to agree or like (to do something): *would you care to sit down, please?* **6 for all I care** *or* **I couldn't care less.** I am completely indifferent. ◆ *n* **7** careful or serious attention: *under her care the plant flourished; he does his work with care.* **8** protective or supervisory control: *in the care of a doctor.* **9** (*often pl*) trouble; anxiety; worry. **10** an object of or cause for concern: *the baby's illness was her only care.* **11** caution: *handle with care.* **12 care of.** at the address of: written on envelopes. Usual abbrev.: **c/o. 13 in** (*or* **into**) **care.** *Social welfare.* made the legal responsibility of a local authority by order of a court. [Old English *cearu* (n), *cearian* (vb), of Germanic origin; compare Old High German *chara* lament, Latin *garrīre* to gossip]
CARE (kɛə) *n acronym for* **1** Cooperative for American Relief Everywhere, Inc.; a federation of U.S. charities, giving financial and technical assistance to many regions of the world. **2** communicated authenticity, regard, empathy: the three qualities believed to be essential in the therapist practising client-centred therapy.
care and maintenance *n Commerce.* the state of a building, ship, machinery, etc., that is not in current use although it is kept in good condition to enable it to be quickly brought into service if there is demand for it. Abbrev.: **C & M.**
care attendant *n Social welfare.* (in Britain) a person who is paid to look after one or more severely handicapped people by visiting them frequently and staying when needed, but who does not live in.
careen (kəˈriːn) *vb* **1** to sway or cause to sway dangerously over to one side. **2** (*tr*) *Nautical.* to cause (a vessel) to keel over to one side, esp. in order to clean or repair its bottom. **3** (*intr*) *Nautical.* (of a vessel) to keel over to one side. [C17: from French *carène* keel, from Italian *carena,* from Latin *carīna* keel] ▸ **caˈreenage** *n* ▸ **caˈreener** *n*
career (kəˈrɪə) *n* **1** a path or progress through life or history. **2** a profession or occupation chosen as one's life's work. **3** (*modifier*) having or following a career as specified: *a career diplomat.* **4** a course or path, esp. a swift or headlong one. ◆ *vb* **5** (*intr*) to move swiftly along; rush in an uncontrolled way. [C16: from French *carrière,* from Late Latin *carrāria* carriage road, from Latin *carrus* two-wheeled wagon, CAR]
career girl *or* **woman** *n* a girl or woman, often unmarried, who follows a career or profession.
careerist (kəˈrɪərɪst) *n* a person who values success in his career above all else and seeks to advance it by any possible means. ▸ **caˈreerism** *n*
careers master *or* (*fem*) **careers mistress** *n* a teacher who gives advice and information about careers to his or her pupils.
Careers Officer *n* a person trained in giving vocational advice, esp. to school leavers.
carefree (ˈkɛəˌfriː) *adj* without worry or responsibility. ▸ **ˈcareˌfreeness** *n*
careful (ˈkɛəfʊl) *adj* **1** cautious in attitude or action; prudent. **2** painstaking in one's work; thorough: *he wrote very careful script.* **3** (*usually postpositive;* foll. by *of, in,* or *about*) solicitous; protective: *careful of one's reputation.* **4** *Archaic.* full of care; anxious. **5** *Brit.* mean or miserly. ▸ **ˈcarefully** *adv* ▸ **ˈcarefulness** *n*
caregiver (ˈkɛəˌɡɪvə) *n* the usual U.S. and Canadian term for **carer.**
careless (ˈkɛəlɪs) *adj* **1** done with or acting with insufficient attention; negligent. **2** (often foll. by *in, of,* or *about*) unconcerned in attitude or action; heedless; indifferent (to): *she's very careless about her clothes.* **3** (*usually prenominal*) carefree. **4** (*usually prenominal*) unstudied; artless: *an impression of careless elegance.* ▸ **ˈcarelessly** *adv* ▸ **ˈcarelessness** *n*
Carême (karɛm) *n* **Marie Antonin.** 1784–1833, French chef, regarded as the founder of *haute cuisine.*
carer (ˈkɛərə) *n Social welfare.* a person who has accepted responsibility for looking after a vulnerable neighbour or relative. See also **caretaker** (sense 3). Usual U.S. and Canadian term: **caregiver.**
caress (kəˈrɛs) *n* **1** a gentle touch or embrace, esp. one given to show affection. ◆ *vb* **2** (*tr*) to touch or stroke gently with affection or as with affection: *the wind caressed her face.* [C17: from French *caresse,* from Italian *carezza,* from Latin *cārus* dear] ▸ **caˈresser** *n* ▸ **caˈressingly** *adv*
caret (ˈkærɪt) *n* a symbol (‸) used to indicate the place in written or printed matter at which something is to be inserted. [C17: from Latin, literally: there is missing, from *carēre* to lack]
caretaker (ˈkɛəˌteɪkə) *n* **1** a person who is in charge of a place or thing, esp. in the owner's absence: *the caretaker of a school.* **2** (*modifier*) holding office temporarily; interim: *a caretaker government.* **3** *Social welfare.* a person who takes care of a vulnerable person, often a close relative. See also **carer.** ▸ **ˈcareˌtaking** *n*
Carew (kəˈruː) *n* **Thomas.** ?1595–?1639, English Cavalier poet.
careworn (ˈkɛəˌwɔːn) *adj* showing signs of care, stress, worry, etc.
Carey (ˈkɛərɪ) *n* **1 George (Leonard).** born 1935, Archbishop of Canterbury from 1991. **2 William.** 1761–1834, British orientalist and pioneer Baptist missionary in India.
Carey Street *n* **1** (formerly) the street in which the London bankruptcy court was situated. **2** the state of bankruptcy.
carfare (ˈkɑːˌfɛə) *n U.S. and Canadian.* the fare that a passenger is charged for a ride on a bus, etc.
carfax (ˈkɑːfæks) *n* a place where principal roads or streets intersect, esp. a place in a town where four roads meet. [C14: from Anglo-French *carfuks,* from Old French *carrefures,* from Latin *quadrifurcus* four-forked]
carfuffle (kəˈfʌfᵊl) *n Informal, chiefly Brit.* a variant spelling of **kerfuffle.** [C20: of unknown origin]
cargo (ˈkɑːɡəʊ) *n, pl* **-goes** *or esp. U.S.* **-gos. 1a** goods carried by a ship, aircraft, or other vehicle; freight. **1b** (*as modifier*): *a cargo vessel.* **2** any load: *the train pulled in with its cargo of new arrivals.* [C17: from Spanish: from *cargar* to load, from Late Latin *carricāre* to load a vehicle, from *carrus* CAR]
cargo cult *n* a religious movement of the SW Pacific, characterized by expectation of the return of spirits in ships or aircraft carrying goods that will provide for the needs of the followers.

carhop ('kɑːˌhɒp) *n U.S. and Canadian informal.* a waiter or waitress at a drive-in restaurant.

Caria ('kɛərɪə) *n* an ancient region of SW Asia Minor, on the Aegean Sea: chief cities were Halicarnassus and Cnidus: corresponds to the present-day Turkish districts of S Aydin and W Muğla.

Carib ('kærɪb) *n* **1** (*pl* **-ibs** *or* **-ib**) a member of a group of American Indian peoples of NE South America and the Lesser Antilles. **2** the family of languages spoken by these peoples. [C16: from Spanish *Caribe,* from Arawak] ► **'Cariban** *adj*

Caribbean (ˌkærɪ'biːən; *U.S.* kə'rɪbɪən) *adj* **1** of, or relating to, the Caribbean Sea and its islands. **2** of, or relating to, the Carib or any of their languages. ◆ *n* **3 the.** the states and islands of the Caribbean Sea, including the West Indies, when considered as a geopolitical region. **4** short for the **Caribbean Sea. 5** a member of any of the peoples inhabiting the islands of the Caribbean Sea, such as a West Indian or a Carib.

Caribbean Sea *n* an almost landlocked sea, part of the Atlantic Ocean, bounded by the Caribbean islands, Central America, and the N coast of South America. Area: 2 718 200 sq. km (1 049 500 sq. miles).

Caribbee bark ('kærɪˌbiː) *n* the bark of any of various tropical American and Caribbean rubiaceous trees of the genus *Exostema,* used as a substitute for cinchona bark.

Caribbees ('kærɪˌbiːz) *pl n* **the.** another name for the **Lesser Antilles.**

Cariboo ('kærɪˌbuː) *n* **the.** *Canad.* a region in the W foothills of the Cariboo Mountains, scene of a gold rush beginning in 1860.

Cariboo Mountains *pl n* a mountain range in SW Canada, in SE British Columbia. Highest peak: Mount Sir Wilfrid Laurier, 3582 m (11 750 ft.).

caribou ('kærɪˌbuː) *n, pl* **-bou** *or* **-bous.** a large deer, *Rangifer tarandus,* of Arctic regions of North America, having large branched antlers in the male and female: also occurs in Europe and Asia, where it is called a reindeer. Also called (Canadian): **tuktu.** [C18: from Canadian French, of Algonquian origin; compare Micmac *khalibu* literally: scratcher]

Caribou Eskimo *n* a member of any of the Inuit peoples who inhabit the Barren Lands of N Canada.

caricature ('kærɪkəˌtjʊə) *n* **1** a pictorial, written, or acted representation of a person, which exaggerates his characteristic traits for comic effect. **2** a ludicrously inadequate or inaccurate imitation: *he is a caricature of a statesman.* ◆ *vb* **3** (*tr*) to represent in caricature or produce a caricature of. [C18: from Italian *caricatura* a distortion, exaggeration, from *caricare* to load, exaggerate; see CARGO] ► **'caricaˌtural** *adj* ► **'caricaˌturist** *n*

CARICOM ('kærɪˌkɒm) *n acronym for* Caribbean Community and Common Market.

caries ('kɛəriːz) *n, pl* **-ies.** progressive decay of a bone or a tooth. [C17: from Latin: decay; related to Greek *kēr* death]

CARIFTA (kæ'rɪftə) *n acronym for* Caribbean Free Trade Area.

carillon (kə'rɪljən) *n Music.* **1** a set of bells usually hung in a tower and played either by keys and pedals or mechanically. **2** a tune played on such bells. **3** an organ stop giving the effect of a bell. **4** a form of celesta or keyboard glockenspiel. ◆ *vb* **-lons, -lonning, -lonned. 5** (*intr*) to play a carillon. [C18: from French: set of bells, from Old French *quarregnon,* ultimately from Latin *quattuor* four]

carillonneur (kəˌrɪljə'nɜː) *n* a person who plays a carillon.

carina (kə'riːnə, -'raɪ-) *n, pl* **-nae** (-niː) *or* **-nas.** a keel-like part or ridge, as in the breastbone of birds or the fused lower petals of a leguminous flower. [C18: from Latin: keel]

Carina (kə'riːnə, -'raɪ-) *n, Latin genitive* **Carinae** (kə'riːniː, -'raɪ-). a large conspicuous constellation in the S hemisphere close to the Southern Cross that contains Canopus, the second brightest star in the sky. It was originally considered part of Argo.

carinate ('kærɪˌneɪt) *or* **carinated** *adj Biology.* having a keel or ridge; shaped like a keel. [C17: from Latin *carīnāre* to furnish with a keel or shell, from *carīna* keel]

caring ('kɛərɪŋ) *adj* **1** feeling or showing care and compassion: *a caring attitude.* **2** of or relating to professional social or medical care: *nursing is a caring job.* ◆ *n* **3** the practice or profession of providing social or medical care.

Carinthia (kə'rɪnθɪə) *n* a state of S Austria: an independent duchy from 976 to 1276; mainly mountainous, with many lakes and resorts. Capital: Klagenfurt. Pop.: 561 000 (1995 est.). Area: 9533 sq. km (3681 sq. miles). German name: **Kärnten.**

carioca (ˌkærɪ'əʊkə) *n* **1** a Brazilian dance similar to the samba. **2** a piece of music composed for this dance. [C19: from Brazilian Portuguese]

Cariocan (ˌkærɪ'əʊkən) *or* **Carioca** *n* a native of Rio de Janeiro, Brazil.

cariogenic (ˌkɛərɪəʊ'dʒɛnɪk) *adj* (of a substance) producing caries, esp. in the teeth.

cariole *or* **carriole** ('kærɪˌəʊl) *n* **1** a small open two-wheeled horse-drawn vehicle. **2** a covered cart. [C19: from French *carriole,* ultimately from Latin *carrus;* see CAR]

carious ('kɛərɪəs) *or* **cariose** ('kɛərɪˌəʊz) *adj* (of teeth or bone) affected with caries; decayed. ► **cariosity** (ˌkærɪ'ɒsɪtɪ, ˌkɛərɪ-) *or* **'cariousness** *n*

Carisbrooke Castle ('kærɪzˌbrʊk) *n* a castle near Newport on the Isle of Wight: Charles I was held prisoner here from 1647 until his execution in 1649.

carjack ('kɑːˌdʒæk) *vb* (*tr*) to attack (a driver in a car) in order to rob the driver or to steal the car for another crime. [C20: CAR + (HI)JACK] ► **'carˌjacker** *n*

cark[1] (kɑːk) *n, vb* an archaic word for **worry** (senses 1, 2, 11, 13). [C13 *carken* to burden, from Old Northern French *carquier,* from Late Latin *carricāre* to load]

cark[2] (kɑːk) *vb* (*intr*) *Austral. slang.* to break down; die. [perhaps from the cry of the crow, as a carrion feeding bird]

carl *or* **carle** (kɑːl) *n Archaic or Scot.* another word for **churl.** [Old English, from Old Norse *karl*]

Carl XVI Gustaf (*Swedish* kaːrl 'gʉstav) *n* born 1946, king of Sweden from 1973.

carlin ('kɑːlɪn) *n* another name for **pug**[1]. [C18: named after a French actor who played Harlequin, because of the resemblance of the dog's face to the black mask of the Harlequin]

carline[1] ('kɑːlɪn) *n* a Eurasian thistle-like plant, *Carlina vulgaris,* having spiny leaves and flower heads surrounded by raylike whitish bracts: family *Compositae* (composites). Also called: **carline thistle.** [C16: from French, probably from Latin *cardō* thistle]

carline[2] *or* **carlin** ('kɑːlɪn) *n* **1** *Chiefly Scot.* an old woman, hag, or witch. **2** a variant of **carling.** [C14: from Old Norse *kerling* old woman, diminutive of *karl* man, CHURL]

carling ('kɑːlɪŋ) *or* **carline** *n* a fore-and-aft beam in a vessel, used for supporting the deck, esp. around a hatchway or other opening. [C14: from Old Norse *kerling* old woman, CARLINE[2]]

Carlisle (kɑː'laɪl, 'kɑːlaɪl) *n* a city in NW England, administrative centre of Cumbria: railway and industrial centre. Pop.: 72 439 (1991). Latin name: **Luguvallum** (ˌluːguː'væləm).

Carlist ('kɑːlɪst) *n* **1** (in Spain) a supporter of Don Carlos or his descendants as the rightful kings of Spain. **2** (in France) a supporter of Charles X or his descendants. ► **'Carlism** *n*

Carlos ('kɑːlɒs) *n* **Don.** full name *Carlos María Isidro de Borbón.* 1788–1855, second son of Charles IV: pretender to the Spanish throne and leader of the Carlists.

Carlota (*Spanish* kar'lota) *n* original name *Marie Charlotte Amélie Augustine Victoire Clémentine Léopoldine.* 1840–1927, wife of Maximilian; empress of Mexico (1864–67).

Carlovingian (ˌkɑːləʊ'vɪndʒɪən) *adj, n History.* a variant of **Carolingian.**

Carlow ('kɑːləʊ) *n* **1** a county of SE Republic of Ireland, in Leinster: mostly flat, with barren mountains in the southeast. County town: Carlow. Pop.: 42 000 (1996). Area: 896 sq. km (346 sq. miles). **2** a town in SE Republic of Ireland, county town of Co. Carlow. Pop.: 11 275 (1991).

Carlsbad ('karlsbaːt) *n* a variant spelling of the German name for **Karlovy Vary.**

Carlton ('kɑːltən) *n* a town in N central England, in S Nottinghamshire. Pop.: 47 302 (1991).

Carlyle (kɑː'laɪl) *n* **1 Robert.** born 1962, Scottish TV and film actor. **2 Thomas.** 1795–1881, Scottish essayist and historian. His works include *Sartor Resartus* (1833–34), a spiritual autobiography, *The French Revolution* (1837), lectures *On Heroes, Hero-Worship, and the Heroic in History* (1841), and the *History of Frederick the Great* (1858–65).

carmagnole (ˌkɑːmən'jəʊl; *French* karmaɲɔl) *n* **1** a dance and song popular during the French Revolution. **2** the costume worn by many French Revolutionaries, consisting of a short jacket with wide lapels, black trousers, a red liberty cap, and a tricoloured sash. [C18: from French, probably named after *Carmagnola,* Italy, taken by French Revolutionaries in 1792]

carman ('kɑːmən) *n, pl* **-men. 1** a man who drives a car or cart; carter. **2** a man whose business is the transport of goods; haulier. **3** *U.S. and Canadian.* a tram driver.

Carmarthen (kə'mɑːðən) *n* a market town in S Wales, the administrative centre of Carmarthenshire: Norman castle. Pop.: 13 524 (1991).

Carmarthenshire (kə'mɑːðənˌʃɪə, -ʃə) *n* a county of S Wales, formerly part of Dyfed (1974–96): on Carmarthen Bay, with the Cambrian Mountains in the N: generally agricultural (esp. dairying). Administrative centre: Carmarthen. Pop.: 169 000 (1996 est.). Area: 2398 sq. km (926 sq. miles).

Carme[1] ('kɑːmɪ) *n Greek myth.* a nymph who was one of Diana's attendants and mother of Britomaris by Jupiter.

Carme[2] ('kɑːmɪ) *n* a small outer satellite of the planet Jupiter.

Carmel ('kɑːməl) *n* **Mount.** a mountain ridge in NW Israel, extending from the Samarian Hills to the Mediterranean. Highest point: about 540 m (1800 ft.).

Carmelite ('kɑːməˌlaɪt) *n R.C. Church.* **1** a member of an order of mendicant friars founded about 1154; a White Friar. **2** a member of a corresponding order of nuns founded in 1452, noted for its austere rule. **3** (*modifier*) of or relating to the Carmelite friars or nuns. [C14: from French; named after Mount CARMEL, where the order was founded]

Carmichael (kɑː'maɪk[ə]l) *n* **Hoaglund Howard** ('həʊglənd), known as *Hoagy.* 1899–1981, U.S. pianist, singer, and composer of such standards as "Star Dust" (1929).

carminative ('kɑːmɪnətɪv) *adj* **1** able to relieve flatulence. ◆ *n* **2** a carminative drug. [C15: from French *carminatif,* from Latin *carmināre* to card wool, remove impurities, from *cārere* to card]

carmine ('kɑːmaɪn) *n* **1a** a vivid red colour, sometimes with a purplish tinge. **1b** (*as adj*): *carmine paint.* **2** a pigment of this colour obtained from cochineal. [C18: from Medieval Latin *carmīnus,* from Arabic *qirmiz* KERMES]

Carnac ('kɑːnæk) *n* a village in NW France: noted for its many megalithic monuments, including alignments of stone menhirs.

carnage ('kɑːnɪdʒ) *n* extensive slaughter, esp. of human beings in battle. [C16: from French, from Italian *carnaggio,* from Medieval Latin *carnāticum,* from Latin *carō* flesh]

carnal ('kɑːn[ə]l) *adj* relating to the appetites and passions of the body; sensual; fleshly. [C15: from Late Latin: relating to flesh, from Latin *carō* flesh] ► **'carnalist** *n* ► **car'nality** *n* ► **'carnally** *adv*

carnal knowledge *n Chiefly law.* **1** sexual intercourse. **2 have carnal knowledge of.** to have sexual intercourse with.

carnallite ('kɑːnəˌlaɪt) *n* a white or sometimes coloured mineral consisting of a hydrated chloride of potassium and magnesium in rhombic crystalline form: a source of potassium and also used as a fertilizer. Formula: $KCl.MgCl_2.6H_2O$.

[C19: named after Rudolf von *Carnall* (1804–74), German mining engineer; see -ITE[1]]

Carnap ('kɑːnæp) *n* **Rudolf.** 1891–1970, U.S. logical positivist philosopher, born in Germany: attempted to construct a formal language for the empirical sciences that would eliminate ambiguity.

Carnarvon (kɑː'nɑːvᵊn) *n* a variant spelling of **Caernarfon.**

carnassial (kɑː'næsɪəl) *adj* **1** *Zoology.* of, relating to, or designating the last upper premolar and first lower molar teeth of carnivores, which have sharp edges for tearing flesh. ♦ *n* **2** a carnassial tooth. [C19: from French *carnassier* meat-eating, from Provençal, from *carnasso* abundance of meat, from *carn* meat, flesh, from Latin *carō*]

Carnatic (kɑː'nætɪk) *n* a region of S India, between the Eastern Ghats and the Coromandel Coast: originally the country of the Kanarese; historically important as a rich and powerful trading centre; now part of Madras state.

carnation (kɑː'neɪʃən) *n* **1** Also called: **clove pink.** a Eurasian caryophyllaceous plant, *Dianthus caryophyllus,* cultivated in many varieties for its white, pink, or red flowers, which have a fragrant scent of cloves. **2** the flower of this plant. **3a** a pink or reddish-pink colour. **3b** (*as adj*): *a carnation dress.* **4** (*often pl*) a flesh tint in painting. [C16: from French: flesh colour, from Late Latin *carnātiō* fleshiness, from Latin *carō* flesh]

carnauba (kɑː'naʊbə) *n* **1** Also called: **wax palm.** a Brazilian fan palm, *Copernicia cerifera.* **2** Also called: **carnauba wax.** the wax obtained from the young leaves of this tree, used esp. as a polish. [from Brazilian Portuguese, probably of Tupi origin]

Carné (karne) *n* **Marcel** (marsel). 1906–96, French film director. His films include *Le Jour se lève* (1939), *Les Portes de la nuit* (1946), and *La Bible* (1976).

Carnegie ('kɑːnəgɪ, kɑː'neɪ-) *n* **Andrew.** 1835–1919, U.S. steel manufacturer and philanthropist, born in Scotland: endowed public libraries, education, and research trusts.

Carnegie Hall ('kɑːnəgɪ) *n* a famous concert hall in New York (opened 1891); endowed by Andrew Carnegie.

carnelian (kɑː'niːljən) *n* a red or reddish-yellow translucent variety of chalcedony, used as a gemstone. [C17: variant of *cornelian,* from Old French *corneline,* of uncertain origin; *car-* spelling influenced by Latin *carneus* flesh-coloured]

carnet ('kɑːneɪ) *n* **1a** a customs licence authorizing the temporary importation of a motor vehicle. **1b** an official document permitting motorists to cross certain frontiers. **2** a book of tickets, travel coupons, etc. [French: notebook, from Old French *quernet,* ultimately from Latin *quaternī* four at a time; see QUIRE[1]]

carnify ('kɑːnɪˌfaɪ) *vb* **-fies, -fying, -fied.** (*intr*) *Pathol.* (esp. of lung tissue, as the result of pneumonia) to be altered so as to resemble skeletal muscle. [C17: from Latin *carō* flesh + *facere* to make] ► **carnification** (ˌkɑːnɪfɪ'keɪʃən) *n*

Carniola (ˌkɑːnɪ'əʊlə) *n* a region of N Slovenia: a former duchy and crownland of Austria (1335–1919); divided between Yugoslavia and Italy in 1919; part of Yugoslavia (1947–92). German name: **Krain** (krain). Slovene name: **Kranj.**

carnival ('kɑːnɪvᵊl) *n* **1a** a festive occasion or period marked by merrymaking, processions, etc.: esp. in some Roman Catholic countries, the period just before Lent. **1b** (*as modifier*): *a carnival atmosphere.* **2** a travelling fair having merry-go-rounds, etc. **3** a show or display arranged as an amusement. **4** *Austral.* a sports meeting. [C16: from Italian *carnevale,* from Old Italian *carnelevare* a removing of meat (referring to the Lenten fast)]

carnivore ('kɑːnɪˌvɔː) *n* **1** any placental mammal of the order *Carnivora,* typically having large pointed canine teeth and sharp molars and premolars, specialized for eating flesh. The order includes cats, dogs, bears, raccoons, hyenas, civets, and weasels. **2** any other animal or any plant that feeds on animals. **3** *Informal.* an aggressively ambitious person. [C19: probably back formation from CARNIVOROUS]

carnivorous (kɑː'nɪvərəs) *adj* **1** (esp. of animals) feeding on flesh. **2** (of plants such as the pitcher plant and sundew) able to trap and digest insects and other small animals. **3** of or relating to the *Carnivora.* **4** *Informal.* aggressively ambitious or reactionary. [C17: from Latin *carnivorus,* from *carō* flesh + *vorāre* to consume] ► **car'nivorously** *adv* ► **car'nivorousness** *n*

Carnot ('kɑːnəʊ; *French* karno) *n* **1 Lazare (Nicolas Marguerite)** (lazar), known as *the Organizer of Victory.* 1753–1823, French military engineer and administrator: organized the French Revolutionary army (1793–95). **2 Nicolas Léonard Sadi** (nikɔla leɔnar sadi). 1796–1832, French physicist, whose work formed the basis for the second law of thermodynamics, enunciated in 1850; author of *Réflexions sur la puissance motrice du feu* (1824).

Carnot cycle *n* an idealized reversible heat-engine cycle giving maximum efficiency and consisting of an isothermal expansion, an adiabatic expansion, an isothermal compression, and an adiabatic compression back to the initial state.

carnotite ('kɑːnəˌtaɪt) *n* a radioactive yellow mineral consisting of hydrated uranium potassium vanadate: occurs in sedimentary rocks and is a source of uranium, radium, and vanadium. Formula: $K_2(UO_2)_2(V_2O_4)_2.3H_2O$. [C20: named after A. *Carnot* (died 1920), French inspector general of mines]

Carnot principle *n* the principle that the efficiency of a reversible heat engine depends on the maximum and minimum temperatures of the working fluid during the operating cycle and not on the properties of the fluid.

carny[1] *or* **carney** ('kɑːnɪ) *vb* **-nies, -nying, -nied** *or* **-neys, -neying, -neyed.** *Brit. informal.* to coax or cajole or act in a wheedling manner. [C19: of unknown origin]

carny[2], **carney,** *or* **carnie** ('kɑːnɪ) *n, pl* **-nies.** *U.S. and Canadian slang.* **1** short for **carnival. 2** a person who works in a carnival.

Caro *n* **1** ('kærəʊ). Sir **Antony.** born 1924, British sculptor, best known for his abstract steel sculptures. **2** ('kɑːrəʊ). **Joseph (ben Ephraim).** 1488–1575, Jewish legal scholar and mystic, born in Spain; compiler of the *Shulhan Arukh* (1564–65), the most authoritative Jewish legal code.

carob ('kærəb) *n* **1** Also called: **algarroba.** an evergreen caesalpiniaceous Mediterranean tree, *Ceratonia siliqua,* with compound leaves and edible pods. **2** Also called: **algarroba, Saint John's bread.** the long blackish sugary pod of this tree, used as a substitute for chocolate and for animal fodder. [C16: from Old French *carobe,* from Medieval Latin *carrūbium,* from Arabic *al kharrūbah*]

caroche (kə'rɒʃ) *n* a stately ceremonial carriage used in the 16th and 17th centuries. [C16: from French, ultimately from Latin *carrus* CAR]

carol ('kærəl) *n* **1** a joyful hymn or religious song, esp. one (a **Christmas carol**) celebrating the birth of Christ. **2** *Archaic.* an old English circular dance. ♦ *vb* **-ols, -olling, -olled** *or U.S.* **-ols, -oling, -oled. 3** (*intr*) to sing carols at Christmas. **4** to sing (something) in a joyful manner. [C13: from Old French, of uncertain origin] ► **'caroler** *or* **'caroller** *n* ► **'caroling** *or* **'carolling** *n*

Carol II ('kærəl) *n* 1893–1953, king of Romania (1930–40), who was deposed by the Iron Guard.

Carolina (ˌkærə'laɪnə) *n* a former English colony on the E coast of North America, first established in 1663: divided in 1729 into North and South Carolina, which are often referred to as **the Carolinas.**

Caroline ('kærəˌlaɪn) *or* **Carolean** (ˌkærə'liːən) *adj* **1** Also called: **Carolinian.** characteristic of or relating to Charles I or Charles II, kings of England, Scotland, and Ireland, the society over which they ruled, or their government. **2** of or relating to any other king called Charles.

Caroline Islands *pl n* an archipelago of over 500 islands and islets in the W Pacific Ocean east of the Philippines, all are now part of the Federated States of Micronesia, except for the Belau group: formerly part of the U.S. Trust Territory of the Pacific Islands; centre of a typhoon zone. Area: (land) 1183 sq. km (457 sq. miles).

Caroline of Ansbach ('ænzbæk) *n* 1683–1737, wife of George II of Great Britain.

Caroline of Brunswick *n* 1768–1821, wife of George IV of the United Kingdom: tried for adultery (1820).

Carolingian (ˌkærə'lɪndʒɪən) *adj* **1** of or relating to the Frankish dynasty founded by Pepin the Short, son of Charles Martel, which ruled in France from 751–987 A.D. and in Germany until 911 A.D. ♦ *n* **2** a member of the dynasty of the Carolingian Franks. ♦ Also: **Carlovingian, Carolinian.**

Carolinian[1] (ˌkærə'lɪnɪən) *adj, n* a variant of **Caroline** or **Carolingian.**

Carolinian[2] (ˌkærə'lɪnɪən) *adj* **1** of or relating to North or South Carolina. ♦ *n* **2** a native or inhabitant of North or South Carolina.

carolus ('kærələs) *n, pl* **-luses** *or* **-li** (-ˌlaɪ). any of several coins struck in the reign of a king called Charles, esp. an English gold coin from the reign of Charles I.

carom ('kærəm) *n Billiards.* another word (esp. U.S. and Canadian) for **cannon** (sense 6). [C18: from earlier *carambole* (taken as *carom ball*), from Spanish CARAMBOLA]

Caro's acid ('kærəʊz, 'kɑː-) *n* another name for **peroxysulphuric acid.** [C19: named after Heinrich *Caro* (died 1910), German chemist]

carotene ('kærəˌtiːn) *or* **carotin** ('kærətɪn) *n* any of four orange-red isomers of an unsaturated hydrocarbon present in many plants (β-carotene is the orange pigment of carrots) and converted to vitamin A in the liver. Formula: $C_{40}H_{56}$. [C19: *carotin,* from Latin *carōta* CARROT; see -ENE]

carotenoid *or* **carotinoid** (kə'rɒtɪˌnɔɪd) *n* **1** any of a group of red or yellow pigments, including carotenes, found in plants and certain animal tissues. ♦ *adj* **2** of or resembling carotene or a carotenoid.

carotid (kə'rɒtɪd) *n* **1** either one of the two principal arteries that supply blood to the head and neck. ♦ *adj* **2** of or relating to either of these arteries. [C17: from French, from Greek *karōtides,* from *karoun* to stupefy; so named by Galen, because pressure on them produced unconsciousness] ► **ca'rotidal** *adj*

carousal (kə'raʊzᵊl) *n* a merry drinking party.

carouse (kə'raʊz) *vb* **1** (*intr*) to have a merry drinking spree; drink freely. ♦ *n* **2** another word for **carousal.** [C16: via French *carrousser* from German (*trinken*) *gar aus* (to drink) right out] ► **ca'rouser** *n*

carousel (ˌkærə'sel, -'zel) *n* **1** a circular magazine in which slides for a projector are held: it moves round as each slide is shown. **2** a rotating conveyor belt for luggage, as at an airport. **3** the usual U.S. and Canadian name for **merry-go-round. 4** *History.* a tournament in which horsemen took part in races and various manoeuvres in formation. [C17: from French *carrousel,* from Italian *carosello,* of uncertain origin]

carp[1] (kɑːp) *n, pl* **carp** *or* **carps. 1** a freshwater teleost food fish, *Cyprinus carpio,* having a body covered with cycloid scales, a naked head, one long dorsal fin, and two barbels on each side of the mouth: family *Cyprinidae.* **2** any other fish of the family *Cyprinidae;* a cyprinid. Related adjs.: **cyprinid, cyprinoid.** [C14: from Old French *carpe,* of Germanic origin; compare Old High German *karpfo,* Old Norse *karfi*]

carp[2] (kɑːp) *vb* (*intr;* often foll. by *at*) to complain or find fault; nag pettily. [C13: from Old Norse *karpa* to boast; related to Latin *carpere* to pluck] ► **'carper** *n*

-carp *n combining form.* (in botany) fruit or a reproductive structure that develops into a particular part of the fruit: *epicarp.* [from New Latin *-carpium,* from Greek *-karpion,* from *karpos* fruit]

Carpaccio (ˌkɑː'pætʃɪəʊ, -tʃəʊ; *Italian* kar'pattʃo) *n* **Vittore** (vit'toːre). ?1460–?1525, Italian painter of the Venetian school.

carpal ('kɑːpᵊl) *n* **a** any bone of the wrist. **b** (*as modifier*): *carpal bones.* ♦ Also: **carpale** (kɑː'peɪlɪ). [C18: from New Latin *carpālis,* from Greek *karpos* wrist]

carpal tunnel syndrome *n* a condition characterized by pain and tingling in the fingers, caused by pressure on a nerve as it passes under the ligament situated across the front of the wrist.

car park *n* an area or building reserved for parking cars. Usual U.S. and Canadian term: **parking lot.**

Carpathian Mountains (kɑːˈpeɪθɪən) *or* **Carpathians** *pl n* a mountain system of central and E Europe, extending from Slovakia to central Romania: mainly forested, with rich iron ore resources. Highest peak: Gerlachovka, 2663 m (8788 ft.).

Carpatho-Ukraine (kɑːˈpeɪθəʊjuːˈkreɪn) *n* another name for **Ruthenia.**

carpe diem *Latin.* (ˈkɑːpɪ ˈdiːɛm) *sentence substitute.* enjoy the pleasures of the moment, without concern for the future. [literally: seize the day!]

carpel (ˈkɑːpəl) *n* the female reproductive organ of flowering plants, consisting of an ovary, style, and stigma. The carpels are separate or fused to form a single pistil. [C19: from New Latin *carpellum,* from Greek *karpos* fruit] ▸ **ˈcarpellary** *adj* ▸ **carpellate** (ˈkɑːpɪˌleɪt) *adj*

Carpentaria (ˌkɑːpənˈtɛərɪə) *n* **Gulf of.** a shallow inlet of the Arafura Sea, in N Australia between Arnhem Land and Cape York Peninsula.

carpenter (ˈkɑːpɪntə) *n* **1** a person skilled in woodwork, esp. in buildings, ships, etc. ◆ *vb* **2** (*intr*) to do the work of a carpenter. **3** (*tr*) to make or fit together by or as if by carpentry. [C14: from Anglo-French, from Latin *carpentārius* wagon-maker, from *carpentum* wagon; of Celtic origin]

Carpenter (ˈkɑːpɪntə) *n* **John Alden.** 1876–1951, U.S. composer, who used jazz rhythms in orchestral music: his works include the ballet *Skyscrapers* (1926) and the orchestral suite *Adventures in a Perambulator* (1915).

carpenter bee *n* any large solitary bee of the genus *Xylocopa* and related genera that lays its eggs in tunnels bored into wood or in plant stems: family *Apidae.*

carpenter moth *n* any of various large moths of the family *Cossidae,* the larvae of which bore beneath and cause damage to tree bark.

Carpentier (*French* karpɑ̃tje) *n* **Georges** (ʒɔrʒ), known as *Gorgeous Georges.* 1894–1975, French boxer: world light-heavyweight champion (1920–22).

carpentry (ˈkɑːpɪntrɪ) *n* **1** the art or technique of working wood. **2** the work produced by a carpenter; woodwork.

carpet (ˈkɑːpɪt) *n* **1a** a heavy fabric for covering floors. **1b** (*as modifier*): *a carpet sale.* **2** a covering like a carpet: *a carpet of leaves.* **3 on the carpet.** *Informal.* **3a** before authority to be reproved for misconduct or error. **3b** under consideration. ◆ *vb* (*tr*) **-pets, -peting, -peted. 4** to cover with or as if with a carpet. **5** *Informal.* to reprimand. [C14: from Old French *carpite,* from Old Italian *carpita,* from Late Latin *carpeta,* literally: (wool) that has been carded, from Latin *carpere* to pluck, card]

carpetbag (ˈkɑːpɪtˌbæg) *n* a travelling bag originally made of carpeting.

carpetbagger (ˈkɑːpɪtˌbægə) *n* **1** a politician who seeks public office in a locality where he has no real connections. **2** *Brit.* a person who makes a short-term investment in a mutual savings or life-assurance organization in order to benefit from free shares issued following the organization's conversion to a public limited company. **3** *U.S.* a Northern White who went to the South after the Civil War to profit from Reconstruction.

carpet beetle *or U.S.* **carpet bug** *n* any of various beetles of the genus *Anthrenus,* the larvae of which feed on carpets, furnishing fabrics, etc.: family *Dermestidae.*

carpet bombing *n* systematic intensive bombing of an area.

carpet bowling *n* a form of bowls played indoors on a strip of carpet, at the centre of which lies an obstacle round which the bowl has to pass.

carpeting (ˈkɑːpɪtɪŋ) *n* carpet material or carpets in general.

carpet knight *n Disparaging.* a soldier who spends his life away from battle; idler.

carpet moth *n* any of several geometrid moths with black- (or brown-)and-white mottled wings. [C19: so named from the patterns on their wings]

carpet plot *n Maths.* the graphed values of a function of more than one variable, read from an ordinate at points located by the intersection of curves of constant values of each of the variables. [C20: from the shape of the graph, thought to resemble a flying carpet]

carpet shark *n* any of various sharks of the family *Orectolobidae,* having two dorsal fins and a patterned back, typically marked with white and brown.

carpet slipper *n* one of a pair of slippers, originally one made with woollen uppers resembling carpeting.

carpet snake *or* **python** *n* a large nonvenomous Australian snake, *Morelia variegata,* having a carpetlike pattern on its back.

carpet-sweeper *n* a household device with a revolving brush for sweeping carpets.

carpet tiles *pl n* small pieces of carpeting laid as tiles to cover a floor.

car phone *n* a telephone that operates by cellular radio for use in a car.

carpi (ˈkɑːpaɪ) *n* the plural of **carpus.**

-carpic *adj combining form.* a variant of **-carpous.**

carping (ˈkɑːpɪŋ) *adj* tending to make petty complaints; fault-finding. ▸ **ˈcarpingly** *adv*

carpo-[1] *combining form.* (in botany) indicating fruit or a reproductive structure that develops into part of the fruit: *carpophore; carpogonium.* [from Greek *karpos* fruit]

carpo-[2] *combining form.* carpus or carpal bones: *carpometacarpus.*

carpogonium (ˌkɑːpəˈgəʊnɪəm) *n, pl* **-nia** (-nɪə). the female sex organ of red algae, consisting of a swollen base containing the ovum and a long neck down which the male gametes pass. ▸ **ˌcarpoˈgonial** *adj*

carpology (kɑːˈpɒlədʒɪ) *n* the branch of botany concerned with the study of fruits and seeds. ▸ **carpological** (ˌkɑːpəˈlɒdʒɪkəl) *adj* ▸ **carˈpologist** *n*

carpometacarpus (ˌkɑːpəʊˌmɛtəˈkɑːpəs) *n* a bone in the wing of a bird that consists of the metacarpal bones and some of the carpal bones fused together.

carpophagous (kɑːˈpɒfəgəs) *adj Zoology.* feeding on fruit: *carpophagous bats.*

carpophore (ˈkɑːpəˌfɔː) *n* **1** an elongated part of the receptacle in flowers such as the geranium that bears the carpels and stamens. **2** a spore-bearing structure in some of the higher fungi.

carport (ˈkɑːˌpɔːt) *n* a shelter for a car usually consisting of a roof built out from the side of a building and supported by posts.

carpospore (ˈkɑːpəʊˌspɔː) *n* a sexual spore produced by red algae after fertilization of the carpogonium.

-carpous *or* **-carpic** *adj combining form.* (in botany) indicating a certain kind or number of fruit: *apocarpous.* [from New Latin *-carpus,* from Greek *karpos* fruit]

carpus (ˈkɑːpəs) *n, pl* **-pi** (-paɪ). **1** the technical name for **wrist. 2** the eight small bones of the human wrist that form the joint between the arm and the hand. **3** the corresponding joint in other tetrapod vertebrates. [C17: New Latin, from Greek *karpos*]

carr (kɑː) *n Brit.* an area of bog or fen in which scrub, esp. willow, has become established. [C15: from Old Norse]

Carracci (kəˈrɑːtʃɪ; *Italian* karˈrattʃi) *n* a family of Italian painters, born in Bologna: **Agostino** (agosˈtiːno) (1557–1602); his brother, **Annibale** (anˈniːbale) (1560–1609), noted for his frescoes, esp. in the Palazzo Farnese, Rome; and their cousin, **Ludovico** (ludoˈviːko) (1555–1619). They were influential in reviving the classical tradition of the Renaissance and founded a teaching academy (1582) in Bologna.

carrack (ˈkærək) *n* a galleon sailed in the Mediterranean as a merchantman in the 15th and 16th centuries. [C14: from Old French *caraque,* from Old Spanish *carraca,* from Arabic *qarāqīr* merchant ships]

carrageen, carragheen, *or* **carageen** (ˈkærəˌgiːn) *n* an edible red seaweed, *Chondrus crispus,* of North America and N Europe. Also called: **Irish moss.** [C19: from *Carragheen,* near Waterford, Ireland, where it is plentiful]

carrageenan, carragheenan, *or* **carageenan** (ˌkærəˈgiːnən) *n* a carbohydrate extracted from carrageen, used to make a beverage, medicine, and jelly, and as an emulsifying and gelling agent (**E407**) in various processed desserts and drinks.

Carrantuohill *or* **Carrauntoohill** (ˌkærənˈtuːl) *n* a mountain in SW Republic of Ireland, in Macgillicuddy's Reeks in Kerry: the highest peak in Ireland. Height: 1041 m (3414 ft.).

Carrara (kəˈrɑːrə; *Italian* karˈraːra) *n* a town in NW Italy, in NW Tuscany: famous for its marble. Pop.: 68 480 (1990).

carrefour (ˈkærəˌfʊə) *n* **1** a rare word for **crossroads. 2** a public square, esp. one at the intersection of several roads. [C15: from Old French *quarrefour,* ultimately from Latin *quadrifurcus* having four forks]

carrel *or* **carrell** (ˈkærəl) *n* a small individual study room or private desk, often in a library, where a student or researcher can work undisturbed. [C16: a variant of CAROL]

Carrel (kəˈrɛl, ˈkærəl; *French* karɛl) *n* **Alexis** (əˈlɛksɪs; *French* alɛksi). 1873–1944, French surgeon and biologist, active in the U.S. (1905–39): developed a method of suturing blood vessels, making the transplantation of arteries and organs possible: Nobel prize for physiology or medicine 1912.

Carreras (kəˈrɛərəs) *n* **José** (həʊsˈzeɪ). born 1947, Spanish tenor.

carriage (ˈkærɪdʒ) *n* **1** *Brit.* a railway coach for passengers. **2** the manner in which a person holds and moves his head and body; bearing. **3** a four-wheeled horse-drawn vehicle for persons. **4** the moving part of a machine that bears another part: *a typewriter carriage; a lathe carriage.* **5** (ˈkærɪdʒ, ˈkærɪɪdʒ). **5a** the act of conveying; carrying. **5b** the charge made for conveying (esp. in the phrases **carriage forward,** when the charge is to be paid by the receiver, and **carriage paid**). [C14: from Old Northern French *cariage,* from *carier* to CARRY]

carriage bolt *n Chiefly U.S. and Canadian.* another name for **coach bolt.**

carriage clock *n* a portable clock, usually in a rectangular case with a handle on the top, of a type originally used by travellers.

carriage dog *n* a former name for **Dalmatian.**

carriage line *n* another term for **coach line.**

carriage trade *n* trade from the wealthy part of society.

carriageway (ˈkærɪdʒˌweɪ) *n Brit.* the part of a road along which traffic passes in a single line moving in one direction only: *a dual carriageway.*

carrick bend (ˈkærɪk) *n* a knot used for joining two ropes or cables together. [C19: perhaps variant of CARRACK]

carrick bitt *n Nautical.* either of a pair of strong posts used for supporting a windlass.

Carrickfergus (ˌkærɪkˈfɜːgəs) *n* **1** a town in E Northern Ireland, in Carrickfergus district, Co. Antrim; historic settlement of Scottish Protestants on Belfast Lough; Norman castle. Pop.: 22 885 (1991). **2** a district of E Northern Ireland, in Co. Antrim. Pop.: 32 750 (1991). Area: 83 sq. km (32 sq. miles).

carrier (ˈkærɪə) *n* **1** a person, thing, or organization employed to carry goods, passengers, etc. **2** a mechanism by which something is carried or moved, such as a device for transmitting rotation from the faceplate of a lathe to the workpiece. **3** *Pathol.* another name for **vector** (sense 3). **4** *Pathol.* a person or animal that, without having any symptoms of a disease, is capable of transmitting it to others. **5** Also called: **charge carrier.** *Physics.* an electron or hole that carries the charge in a conductor or semiconductor. **6** short for **carrier wave. 7** *Chem.* **7a** the inert solid on which a dyestuff is adsorbed in forming a lake. **7b** a substance, such as kieselguhr or asbestos, used to support a catalyst. **7c** an inactive substance containing a radioisotope used in radioactive tracing. **7d** an inert gas used to transport the sample through a gas-chromatography column. **7e** a catalyst that effects the transfer of an atom or group from one molecule to another. **8** See **aircraft carrier. 9** a breed of domestic fancy pigeon having a large walnut-shaped wattle over the beak; a distinct variety of pigeon from the homing or carrier pigeon. See also **carrier pigeon. 10** a U.S. name for **roof rack.**

carrier bag *n Brit.* a large paper or plastic bag for carrying shopping.

carrier pigeon *n* any homing pigeon, esp. one used for carrying messages.

carrier wave *n Radio.* a wave of fixed amplitude and frequency that is modulated in amplitude, frequency, or phase in order to carry a signal in radio transmission, etc. See **amplitude modulation, frequency modulation.**

Carrington ('kærɪŋtən) *n* **1 Dora**, known as *Carrington.* 1893–1932, British painter, engraver, and letter writer; a member of the Bloomsbury Group. **2 Peter (Alexander Rupert)**, 6th Baron. born 1919, British Conservative politician: secretary of state for defence (1970–74); foreign secretary (1979–82); secretary general of NATO (1984–88).

carriole ('kærɪˌəʊl) *n* a variant spelling of **cariole.**

carrion ('kærɪən) *n* **1** dead and rotting flesh. **2** (*modifier*) eating carrion: *carrion beetles.* **3** something rotten or repulsive. [C13: from Anglo-French *caroine,* ultimately from Latin *carō* flesh]

carrion beetle *n* any beetle of the family *Silphidae* that track carrion by a keen sense of smell: best known are the **burying** or **sexton beetles.**

carrion crow *n* a common predatory and scavenging European crow, *Corvus corone,* similar to the rook but having a pure black bill. See also **hooded crow.**

carrion flower *n* **1** a liliaceous climbing plant, *Smilax herbacea* of E North America, whose small green flowers smell like decaying flesh. **2** any of several other plants, esp. any of the genus *Stapelia,* whose flowers have an unpleasant odour.

Carroll ('kærəl) *n* **Lewis.** real name *the Reverend Charles Lutwidge Dodgson.* 1832–98, English writer; an Oxford mathematics don who wrote *Alice's Adventures in Wonderland* (1865) and *Through the Looking-Glass* (1872) and the nonsense poem *The Hunting of the Snark* (1876).

carronade (ˌkærə'neɪd) *n* an obsolete naval gun of short barrel and large bore. [C18: named after *Carron,* Scotland, where it was first cast; see -ADE]

carron oil ('kærən) *n* an ointment of limewater and linseed oil, formerly used to treat burns. [C19: named after *Carron,* Scotland, where it was used among the ironworkers]

carrot ('kærət) *n* **1** an umbelliferous plant, *Daucus carota sativa,* with finely divided leaves and flat clusters of small white flowers. See also **wild carrot. 2** the long tapering orange root of this plant, eaten as a vegetable. **3a** something offered as a lure or incentive. **3b carrot and stick.** reward and punishment as methods of persuasion. [C16: from Old French *carotte,* from Late Latin *carōta,* from Greek *karōton;* perhaps related to Greek *karē* head]

carrot fly *n* a dipterous insect, *Psila rosae,* that is a serious pest of carrots. The larvae tunnel into the root to feed.

carroty ('kærətɪ) *adj* **1** of a reddish or yellowish-orange colour. **2** having red hair.

carrousel (ˌkærə'sɛl, -'zɛl) *n* a variant spelling of **carousel.**

carry ('kærɪ) *vb* **-ries, -rying, -ried.** (*mainly tr*) **1** (*also intr*) to take or bear (something) from one place to another: *to carry a baby in one's arms.* **2** to transfer for consideration; take: *he carried his complaints to her superior.* **3** to have on one's person: *he always carries a watch.* **4** (*also intr*) to be transmitted or serve as a medium for transmitting: *sound carries best over water.* **5** to contain or be capable of containing: *the jug carries water.* **6** to bear or be able to bear the weight, pressure, or responsibility of: *her efforts carry the whole production.* **7** to have as an attribute or result: *this crime carries a heavy penalty.* **8** to bring or communicate: *to carry news.* **9** (*also intr*) to be pregnant with (young): *she is carrying her third child.* **10** to bear (the head, body, etc.) in a specified manner: *she carried her head high.* **11** to conduct or bear (oneself) in a specified manner: *she carried herself well in a difficult situation.* **12** to continue or extend: *the war was carried into enemy territory.* **13** to cause to move or go: *desire for riches carried him to the city.* **14** to influence, esp. by emotional appeal: *his words carried the crowd.* **15** to secure the passage of (a bill, motion, etc.). **16** to win (an election). **17** to obtain victory for (a candidate or measure) in an election. **18** *Chiefly U.S.* to win a plurality or majority of votes in (a district, legislative body, etc.): *the candidate carried 40 states.* **19** to capture: *our troops carried the town.* **20** (of communications media) to include as the content: *this newspaper carries no book reviews.* **21** Also (esp. U.S.): **carry over.** *Book-keeping.* to transfer (an item) to another account, esp. to transfer to the following year's account instead of writing off against profit and loss: *to carry a loss.* **22** *Maths.* to transfer (a number) from one column of figures to the next, as from units to tens in multiplication and addition. **23** (of a shop, trader, etc.) to keep in stock: *to carry confectionery.* **24** to support (a musical part or melody) against the other parts. **25** to sustain (livestock): *this land will carry twelve ewes to the acre.* **26** to maintain (livestock) in good health but without increasing their weight or obtaining any products from them. **27** (*intr*) (of a ball, projectile, etc.) to travel through the air or reach a specified point: *his first drive carried to the green.* **28** *Sport, esp. golf.* (of a ball) to travel beyond: *the drive carried the trees.* **29** (*intr*) (of a gun) to have a range as specified: *this rifle carries for 1200 yards.* **30** to retain contact with and pursue (a line of scent). **31** (*intr*) (of ground) to be in such a condition that scent lies well upon it. **32** *Ice hockey.* to move (the puck) forwards, keeping it against the blade of the stick. **33** *Informal.* to imbibe (alcoholic drink) without showing ill effects. **34** (*intr*) *Slang.* to have drugs on one's person. **35 carry all before (one).** to win unanimous support or approval for (oneself). **36 carry a tune.** to be able to sing in tune. **37 carry the can (for).** *Informal.* to take the responsibility for some misdemeanour, etc. (on behalf of). **38 carry the day.** to win a contest or competition; succeed. ◆ *n, pl* **-ries. 39** the act of carrying. **40** *U.S. and Canadian.* a portion of land over which a boat must be portaged. **41** the range of a firearm or its projectile. **42** the distance travelled by a ball, etc., esp. (in golf) the distance from where the ball is struck to where it first touches the ground. [C14 *carien,* from Old Northern French *carier* to move by vehicle, from *car,* from Latin *carrum* transport wagon; see CAR]

carryall[1] ('kærɪˌɔːl) *n* a light four-wheeled horse-drawn carriage usually designed to carry four passengers.

carryall[2] ('kærɪˌɔːl) *n* the usual U.S. and Canadian name for a **holdall.**

carry away *vb* (*tr, adv*) **1** to remove forcefully. **2** (usually passive) to cause (a person) to lose self-control. **3** (usually passive) to delight or enrapture: *he was carried away by the music.*

carry back *Tax accounting.* ◆ *vb* **1** (*tr, adv*) to apply (a legally permitted credit, esp. an operating loss) to the taxable income of previous years in order to ease the overall tax burden. ◆ *n* **carry-back. 2** an amount carried back.

carrycot ('kærɪˌkɒt) *n* a light cot with handles, similar to but smaller than the body of a pram and often attachable to an unsprung wheeled frame.

carry forward *vb* (*tr, adv*) **1** *Book-keeping.* to transfer (a balance) to the next page, column, etc. **2** *Tax accounting.* to apply (a legally permitted credit, esp. an operating loss) to the taxable income of following years to ease the overall tax burden. ◆ Also: **carry over.** ◆ *n* **carry-forward. 3** Also called: **carry-over.** *Tax accounting.* an amount carried forward.

carrying capacity *n Ecology.* the maximum number of individuals that an area of land can support, usually determined by their food requirements.

carrying charge *n* the opportunity cost of unproductive assets, such as goods stored in a warehouse.

carrying-on *n, pl* **carryings-on.** *Informal.* **1** unconventional or questionable behaviour. **2** excited or flirtatious behaviour, esp. when regarded as foolish.

carrying place *n Canadian.* another name for **portage.**

carry off *vb* (*tr, adv*) **1** to remove forcefully. **2** to win: *he carried off all the prizes.* **3** to manage or handle (a situation) successfully: *he carried off the introductions well.* **4** to cause to die: *he was carried off by pneumonia.*

carry on *vb* (*adv*) **1** (*intr*) to continue or persevere: *we must carry on in spite of our difficulties.* **2** (*tr*) to manage or conduct: *to carry on a business.* **3** (*intr; often foll. by with*) *Informal.* to have an affair. **4** (*intr*) *Informal.* to cause a fuss or commotion. ◆ *n* **carry-on. 5** *Informal, chiefly Brit.* a fuss or commotion.

carry out *vb* (*tr, adv*) **1** to perform or cause to be implemented: *I wish he could afford to carry out his plan.* **2** to bring to completion; accomplish. ◆ *n* **carry-out.** *Chiefly Scot.* **3** alcohol bought at a pub or off-licence for consumption elsewhere. **4a** hot cooked food bought at a shop or restaurant for consumption elsewhere. **4b** a shop or restaurant that sells such food: *we'll get something from the Chinese carry-out.* **4c** (*as modifier*): *a carry-out shop.*

carry over *vb* (*tr, adv*) **1** to postpone or defer. **2** *Book-keeping, tax accounting.* another term for **carry forward. 3** (on the London Stock Exchange) to postpone (payment or settlement) until the next account day. ◆ *n* **carry-over. 4** something left over for future use, esp. goods to be sold. **5** *Book-keeping.* a sum or balance carried forward. **6** another name for **contango. 7** *Tax accounting.* another name for **carry-forward.**

carry through *vb* (*tr, adv*) **1** to bring to completion. **2** to enable to endure (hardship, trouble, etc.); support.

carse (kɑːs; *Scot.* kærs) *n Scot.* a riverside area of flat fertile alluvium. [C14: of uncertain origin; perhaps from a plural form of CARR]

carsick ('kɑːˌsɪk) *adj* nauseated from riding in a car or other vehicle. ▸ **'carˌsickness** *n*

Carson ('kɑːsᵊn) *n* **1 Christopher,** known as *Kit Carson.* 1809–68, U.S. frontiersman, trapper, scout, and Indian agent. **2 Edward Henry,** Baron. 1854–1935, Irish politician and lawyer; led northern Irish resistance to the British government's home rule for Ireland. **3 Rachel (Louise).** 1907–64, U.S. marine biologist and science writer; author of *Silent Spring* (1962). **4 Willie,** full name *William Hunter Fisher Carson.* born 1942, Scottish jockey; retired in 1997.

Carson City *n* a city in W Nevada, capital of the state. Pop.: 46 770 (1995 est.).

Carstensz ('kɑːstənz) *n* **Mount.** a former name of (Mount) **Jaya.**

cart[1] (kɑːt) *n* **1** a heavy open vehicle, usually having two wheels and drawn by horses, used in farming and to transport goods. **2** a light open horse-drawn vehicle having two wheels and springs, for business or pleasure. **3** any small vehicle drawn or pushed by hand, such as a trolley. **4 put the cart before the horse.** to reverse the usual or natural order of things. ◆ *vb* **5** (*usually tr*) to use or draw a cart to convey (goods, etc.): *to cart groceries.* **6** (*tr*) to carry with effort; haul: *to cart wood home.* [C13: from Old Norse *kartr;* related to Old English *cræt* carriage, Old French *carete;* see CAR] ▸ **'cartable** *adj* ▸ **'carter** *n*

cart[2] (kɑːt) *n Radio, television.* short for **cartridge** (sense 4).

cartage ('kɑːtɪdʒ) *n* the process or cost of carting.

Cartagena (ˌkɑːtə'dʒiːnə; *Spanish* karta'xena) *n* **1** a port in NW Colombia, on the Caribbean: centre for the Inquisition and the slave trade in the 16th century; chief oil port of Colombia. Pop.: 812 595 (1997 est.). **2** a port in SE Spain, on the Mediterranean: important since Carthaginian and Roman times for its minerals. Pop.: 179 659 (1994 est.).

carte (kɑːt) *n* a variant spelling of **quarte** (in fencing).

Carte (kɑːt) *n* See (Richard) **D'Oyly Carte.**

carte blanche ('kɑːt 'blɑːntʃ; *French* kart blɑ̃ʃ) *n, pl* **cartes blanches** ('kɑːts 'blɑːntʃ; *French* kart blɑ̃ʃ). **1** complete discretion or authority: *the government gave their negotiator carte blanche.* **2** *Cards.* a piquet hand containing no court cards: scoring ten points. [C18: from French: blank paper]

carte du jour ('kɑːt də 'ʒʊə, duː; *French* kart dy ʒur) *n, pl* **cartes du jour** ('kɑːts də 'ʒʊə, duː; *French* kart dy ʒur). a menu listing dishes available on a particular day. [French, literally: card of the day]

cartel (kɑː'tɛl) *n* **1** Also called: **trust.** a collusive international association of independent enterprises formed to monopolize production and distribution of a product or service, control prices, etc. **2** *Politics.* an alliance of parties or interests to further common aims. [C20: from German *Kartell,* from French, from Italian *cartello* a written challenge, public notice, diminutive of *carta* CARD[1]]

cartelize *or* **cartelise** ('kɑːtəlaɪz) *vb* to form or be formed into a cartel. ▸ **ˌcarteli'zation** *or* **ˌcarteli'sation** *n*

Carter ('kɑːtə) *n* **1 Angela.** 1940–92, British novelist and writer; her novels include *The Magic Toyshop* (1967) and *Nights at the Circus* (1984). **2 Elliot (Cook).** born 1908, U.S. composer. His works include the *Piano Sonata*

(1945–46), four string quartets, and other orchestral pieces: Pulitzer Prize 1960, 1973. **3 Howard.** 1873–1939, English Egyptologist: excavated the tomb of the Pharaoh Tutankhamen. **4 James Earl,** known as *Jimmy.* born 1924, U.S. Democratic statesman; 39th president of the U.S. (1977–81).

Carteret ('kɑːtərɪt) *n* **John,** 1st Earl Granville. 1690–1763, British statesman, diplomat, and orator who led the opposition to Walpole (1730–42), after whose fall he became a leading minister as secretary of state (1742–44).

Cartesian (kɑː'tiːzɪən, -ʒjən) *adj* **1** of or relating to the works of Descartes. **2** of, relating to, or used in Descartes' mathematical system: *Cartesian coordinates.* **3** of, relating to, or derived from Descartes' philosophy, esp. his contentions that personal identity consists in the continued existence of a unique mind and that the mind and body are connected causally. See also **dualism** (sense 2). ◆ *n* **4** a follower of the teachings and methods of Descartes. ▸ **Car'tesian,ism** *n*

Cartesian coordinates *pl n* a system of representing points in space in terms of their distance from a given origin measured along a set of mutually perpendicular axes. Written *(x,y,z)* with reference to three axes.

Cartesian product *n Maths, logic.* the set of all ordered pairs of members of two given sets. The product $A \times B$ is the set of all pairs $< a, b >$ where a is a member of A and b is a member of B. Also called: **cross product.**

cartful ('kɑːt,fʊl) *n* the amount a cart can hold.

Carthage ('kɑːθɪdʒ) *n* an ancient city state, on the N African coast near present-day Tunis. Founded about 800 B.C. by Phoenician traders, it grew into an empire dominating N Africa and the Mediterranean. Destroyed and then rebuilt by Rome, it was finally razed by the Arabs in 697 A.D. See also **Punic Wars.** ▸ **Carthaginian** (,kɑːθə'dʒɪnɪən) *adj, n*

carthorse ('kɑːt,hɔːs) *n* a large heavily built horse kept for pulling carts or carriages.

Carthusian (kɑː'θjuːzɪən) *n R.C. Church.* **a** a member of an austere monastic order founded by Saint Bruno in 1084 near Grenoble, France. **b** (*as modifier*): *a Carthusian monastery.* [C14: from Medieval Latin *Carthusianus,* from Latin *Carthusia* Chartreuse, near Grenoble]

Cartier (*French* kartje) *n* **Jacques** (ʒɑk). 1491–1557, French navigator and explorer in Canada, who discovered the St Lawrence River (1535).

Cartier-Bresson (*French* kartjebrɛsɔ̃) *n* **Henri** (ɑ̃ri). born 1908, French photographer.

cartilage ('kɑːtɪlɪdʒ, 'kɑːtlɪdʒ) *n* a tough elastic tissue composing most of the embryonic skeleton of vertebrates. In the adults of higher vertebrates it is mostly converted into bone, remaining only on the articulating ends of bones, in the thorax, trachea, nose, and ears. Nontechnical name: **gristle.** [C16: from Latin *cartilāgō*] ▸ **cartilaginous** (,kɑːtɪ'lædʒɪnəs) *adj*

cartilage bone *n* any bone that develops within cartilage rather than in a fibrous tissue membrane. Compare **membrane bone.**

cartilaginous fish *n* any fish of the class *Chondrichthyes,* including the sharks, skates, and rays, having a skeleton composed entirely of cartilage.

Cartland ('kɑːtlənd) *n* Dame **Barbara** (**Hamilton**). born 1901, British novelist, noted for her prolific output of popular romantic fiction.

cartload ('kɑːt,ləʊd) *n* **1** the amount a cart can hold. **2** a quantity of rubble, ballast, etc., of between one quarter and one half of a cubic yard.

cart off, away, *or* **out** *vb (tr, adv) Informal.* to carry or remove brusquely or by force.

cartogram ('kɑːtə,græm) *n* a map showing statistical information in diagrammatic form. [C20: from French *cartogramme,* from *carte* map, CHART; see -GRAM]

cartography *or* **chartography** (kɑː'tɒgrəfɪ) *n* the art, technique, or practice of compiling or drawing maps or charts. [C19: from French *cartographie,* from *carte* map, CHART] ▸ **car'tographer** *or* **char'tographer** *n* ▸ **cartographic** (,kɑːtə'græfɪk), **,carto'graphical** *or* **,charto'graphic, ,charto'graphical** *adj* ▸ **,carto'graphically** *or* **,charto'graphically** *adv*

cartomancy ('kɑːtə,mænsɪ) *n* the telling of fortunes with playing cards. [C19: from French *carte* card + -MANCY]

carton ('kɑːtᵊn) *n* **1** a cardboard box for containing goods. **2** a container of waxed paper or plastic in which liquids, such as milk, are sold. **3** *Shooting.* **3a** a white disc at the centre of a target. **3b** a shot that hits this disc. ◆ *vb (tr)* **4** to enclose (goods) in a carton. [C19: from French, from Italian *cartone* pasteboard, from *carta* CARD[1]]

cartoon (kɑː'tuːn) *n* **1** a humorous or satirical drawing, esp. one in a newspaper or magazine, concerning a topical event. **2** Also called: **comic strip. 3** a sequence of drawings in a newspaper, magazine, etc., relating a comic or adventurous situation. See **animated cartoon. 4** a full-size preparatory sketch for a fresco, tapestry, mosaic, etc., from which the final work is traced or copied. [C17: from Italian *cartone* pasteboard, sketch on stiff paper; see CARTON] ▸ **car'toonist** *n*

cartophily (kɑː'tɒfɪlɪ) *n* the hobby of collecting cigarette cards. [C20: from French *carte* card + -O- + *-phily* from Greek *philos* loving] ▸ **car'tophilist** *n*

cartouche *or* **cartouch** (kɑː'tuːʃ) *n* **1** a carved or cast ornamental tablet or panel in the form of a scroll, sometimes having an inscription. **2** an oblong figure enclosing characters expressing royal or divine names in Egyptian hieroglyphics. **3** the paper case holding combustible materials in certain fireworks. **4** *Now rare.* a cartridge or a box for cartridges. [C17: from French: scroll, cartridge, from Italian *cartoccio,* from *carta* paper; see CARD[1]]

cartridge ('kɑːtrɪdʒ) *n* **1** a cylindrical, usually metal casing containing an explosive charge and often a bullet, for a rifle or other small arms. **2** a case for an explosive, such as a blasting charge. **3** an electromechanical transducer in the pick-up of a record player, usually either containing a piezoelectric crystal (**crystal cartridge**) or an electromagnet (**magnetic cartridge**). **4** a container for magnetic tape that is inserted into a tape deck. It is about four times the size of a cassette. **5** Also called: **cassette, magazine.** *Photog.* a light-tight film container that enables a camera to be loaded and unloaded in normal light. **6** *Computing.* a removable unit in a computer, such as an integrated circuit, containing software. [C16: from earlier *cartage,* variant of CARTOUCHE (cartridge)]

cartridge belt *n* a belt with pockets for cartridge clips or loops for cartridges.

cartridge clip *n* a metallic container holding cartridges for an automatic firearm.

cartridge paper *n* **1** an uncoated type of drawing or printing paper, usually made from bleached sulphate wood pulp with an addition of esparto grass. **2** a heavy paper used in making cartridges or as drawing or printing paper.

cartridge pen *n* a pen having a removable ink reservoir that is replaced when empty.

cart track *n* a rough track or road in a rural area. Also called: **cart road.**

cartulary ('kɑːtjʊlərɪ) *or* **chartulary** ('tʃɑːtjʊlərɪ) *n, pl* **-laries.** *Law.* **a** a collection of charters or records, esp. relating to the title to an estate or monastery. **b** any place where records are kept. [C16: from Medieval Latin *cartulārium,* from Latin *chartula* a little paper, from *charta* paper; see CARD[1]]

cartwheel ('kɑːt,wiːl) *n* **1** the wheel of a cart, usually having wooden spokes and metal tyres. **2** an acrobatic movement in which the body makes a sideways revolution supported on the hands with arms and legs outstretched. **3** *U.S. slang.* a large coin, esp. the silver dollar.

cartwheel flower *n* another name for **giant hogweed.**

cartwright ('kɑːt,raɪt) *n* a person who makes carts.

Cartwright ('kɑːt,raɪt) *n* **Edmund.** 1743–1823, British clergyman, who invented the power loom.

caruncle ('kærəŋkᵊl, kə'rʌŋ-) *n* **1** a fleshy outgrowth on the heads of certain birds, such as a cock's comb. **2** an outgrowth near the hilum on the seeds of some plants. **3** any small fleshy mass in or on the body, either natural or abnormal. [C17: from obsolete French *caruncule,* from Latin *caruncula* a small piece of flesh, from *carō* flesh] ▸ **caruncular** (kə'rʌŋkjʊlə) *or* **ca'runculous** *adj* ▸ **caruncular** (kə'rʌŋkjʊlɪt, -,leɪt) *or* **ca'runcu,lated** *adj*

Caruso (*Italian* ka'ruːso) *n* **Enrico** (en'riːko). 1873–1921, an outstanding Italian operatic tenor; one of the first to make gramophone records.

carve (kɑːv) *vb* **1** *(tr)* to cut or chip in order to form something: *to carve wood.* **2** to decorate or form (something) by cutting or chipping: *to carve statues.* **3** to slice (meat) into pieces: *to carve a turkey.* [Old English *ceorfan;* related to Old Frisian *kerva,* Middle High German *kerben* to notch]

carvel ('kɑːvᵊl) *n* another word for **caravel.**

carvel-built *adj* (of a vessel) having a hull with planks made flush at the seams. Compare **clinker-built.**

carven ('kɑːvᵊn) *vb* an archaic or literary past participle of **carve.**

carve out *vb (tr, adv)* to make or create (a career): *he carved out his own future.*

carver ('kɑːvə) *n* **1** a carving knife. **2** *(pl)* a large matched knife and fork for carving meat. **3** *Brit.* a chair having arms that forms part of a set of dining chairs.

Carver ('kɑːvə) *n* **George Washington.** ?1864–1943, U.S. agricultural chemist and botanist.

carvery ('kɑːvərɪ) *n, pl* **-veries.** an eating establishment at which customers pay a set price and may then have unrestricted helpings of food from a variety of meats, salads, and other vegetables.

carve up *vb (tr, adv)* **1** to cut (something) into pieces. **2** to divide or dismember (a country, land, etc.). ◆ *n* **carve-up. 3** *Informal.* an act or instance of dishonestly prearranging the result of a competition. **4** *Slang.* the distribution of something, as of booty.

carving ('kɑːvɪŋ) *n* a figure or design produced by carving stone, wood, etc. Related adj: **glyptic.**

carving knife *n* a long-bladed knife for carving cooked meat for serving.

Cary ('keərɪ, 'kærɪ) *n* (**Arthur**) **Joyce** (**Lunel**). 1888–1957, British novelist; author of *Mister Johnson* (1939), *A House of Children* (1941), and *The Horse's Mouth* (1944).

caryatid (,kærɪ'ætɪd) *n, pl* **-ids** *or* **-ides** (-ɪ,diːz). a column, used to support an entablature, in the form of a draped female figure. Compare **telamon.** [C16: from Latin *Caryātides,* from Greek *Karuatides* priestesses of Artemis at *Karuai* (Caryae), village in Laconia] ▸ **,cary'atidal, ,cary,ati'dean, ,cary'atic,** *or* **caryatidic** (,kærɪə'tɪdɪk) *adj*

caryo- *combining form.* a variant of **karyo-.**

caryophyllaceous (,kærɪəʊfɪ'leɪʃəs) *adj* of, relating to, or belonging to the *Caryophyllaceae,* a family of flowering plants including the pink, carnation, sweet william, and chickweed. [C19: from New Latin *Caryophyllāceae,* from *Caryophyllus* former type genus, from Greek *karuophullon* clove tree, from *karuon* nut + *phullon* leaf]

caryopsis (,kærɪ'ɒpsɪs) *n, pl* **-ses** (-siːz) *or* **-sides** (-sɪ,diːz). a dry seedlike fruit having the pericarp fused to the seed coat of the single seed: produced by the grasses. [C19: New Latin; see KARYO-, -OPSIS]

casaba *or* **cassaba** (kə'sɑːbə) *n* a kind of winter muskmelon having a yellow rind and sweet juicy flesh. [from *Kassaba,* former name of Turgutlu, Turkey]

Casablanca (,kæsə'blæŋkə) *n* a port in NW Morocco, on the Atlantic: largest city in the country; industrial centre. Pop.: 523 279 (1994).

Casals (*Spanish* ka'sals) *n* **Pablo** ('paβlo). 1876–1973, Spanish cellist and composer, noted for his interpretation of J. S. Bach's cello suites.

Casanova (,kæsə'nəʊvə) *n* **1 Giovanni Jacopo** (dʒo'vanni 'jaːkopo). 1725–98, Italian adventurer noted for his *Mémoires,* a vivid account of his sexual adventures and of contemporary society. **2** any man noted for his amorous adventures; a rake.

Casaubon (kə'sɔːbᵊn; *French* kazobɔ̃) *n* **Isaac** (izaak). 1559–1614, French Protestant theologian and classical scholar.

casbah ('kæzbɑː) *n* (*sometimes cap.*) a variant spelling of **kasbah.**

cascabel ('kæskə,bɛl) *n* **1** a knoblike protrusion on the rear part of the breech of an obsolete muzzle-loading cannon. **2** the rear part itself. [C17: from Spanish: small bell, rattle, of uncertain origin]

cascade (kæs'keɪd) *n* **1** a waterfall or series of waterfalls over rocks. **2** something resembling this, such as folds of lace. **3a** a consecutive sequence of chemical or physical processes. **3b** (*as modifier*): *cascade liquefaction.* **4a** a series of stages in the processing chain of an electrical signal where each operates the next in turn. **4b** (*as modifier*): *a cascade amplifier.* **5** the cumulative process responsible for the formation of an electrical discharge, cosmic-ray shower, or Geiger counter avalanche in a gas. ◆ *vb* **6** (*intr*) to flow or fall in or like a cascade. [C17: from French, from Italian *cascata,* from *cascare* to fall, ultimately from Latin *cadere* to fall]

Cascade Range *n* a chain of mountains in the U.S. and Canada: a continuation of the Sierra Nevada range from N California through Oregon and Washington to British Columbia. Highest peak: Mount Rainier, 4392 m (14 408 ft.).

cascara (kæs'kɑːrə) *n* **1** See **cascara sagrada. 2** Also called: **cascara buckthorn, bearwood.** a shrub or small tree, *Rhamnus purshiana* of NW North America, whose bark is a source of cascara sagrada: family *Rhamnaceae.* [C19: from Spanish: bark, from *cascar* to break, from Vulgar Latin *quassicāre* (unattested) to shake violently, shatter, from Latin *quassāre* to dash to pieces]

cascara sagrada (sə'grɑːdə) *n* the dried bark of the cascara buckthorn, used as a laxative and stimulant. Often shortened to **cascara.** [Spanish, literally: sacred bark]

cascarilla (ˌkæskə'rɪlə) *n* **1** a West Indian euphorbiaceous shrub, *Croton eluteria,* whose bitter aromatic bark is used as a tonic. **2** the bark of this shrub. [C17: from Spanish, diminutive of *cáscara* bark; see CASCARA]

case[1] (keɪs) *n* **1** a single instance, occurrence, or example of something. **2** an instance of disease, injury, hardship, etc. **3** a question or matter for discussion: *the case before the committee.* **4** a specific condition or state of affairs; situation. **5** a set of arguments supporting a particular action, cause, etc. **6a** a person attended or served by a doctor, social worker, solicitor, etc.; patient or client. **6b** (*as modifier*): *a case study.* **7a** an action or suit at law or something that forms sufficient grounds for bringing an action: *he has a good case.* **7b** the evidence offered in court to support a claim. **8** *Grammar.* **8a** a set of grammatical categories of nouns, pronouns, and adjectives, marked by inflection in some languages, indicating the relation of the noun, adjective, or pronoun to other words in the sentence. **8b** any one of these categories: *the nominative case.* **9** *Informal.* a person in or regarded as being in a specified condition: *the accident victim was a hospital case; he's a mental case.* **10** *Informal.* a person of a specified character (esp. in the phrase **a hard case**). **11** *Informal.* an odd person; eccentric. **12** *U.S. informal.* love or infatuation. **13** short for **case shot.** See **canister** (sense 2b). **14 as the case may be.** according to the circumstances. **15 in any case.** (*adv*) no matter what; anyhow: *we will go in any case.* **16 in case.** (*adv*) **16a** in order to allow for eventualities. **16b** (*as conj*) in order to allow for the possibility that: *take your coat in case it rains.* **16c** *U.S.* if. **17 in case of.** (*prep*) in the event of. **18 in no case.** (*adv*) under no circumstances: *in no case should you fight back.* [Old English *casus* (grammatical) case, associated also with Old French *cas* a happening; both from Latin *cāsus,* a befalling, occurrence, from *cadere* to fall]

case[2] (keɪs) *n* **1a** a container, such as a box or chest. **1b** (*in combination*): *suitcase; briefcase.* **2** an outer cover or sheath, esp. for a watch. **3** a receptacle and its contents: *a case of ammunition.* **4** a pair or brace, esp. of pistols. **5** *Architect.* another word for **casing** (sense 3). **6** a completed cover ready to be fastened to a book to form its binding. **7** *Printing.* a tray divided into many compartments in which a compositor keeps individual metal types of a particular size and style. Cases were originally used in pairs, one (the **upper case**) for capitals, the other (the **lower case**) for small letters. **8** *Metallurgy.* the surface of a piece of steel that has been case-hardened. ◆ *vb* (*tr*) **9** to put into or cover with a case: *to case the machinery.* **10** *Slang.* to inspect carefully (esp. a place to be robbed). [C13: from Old French *casse,* from Latin *capsa,* from *capere* to take, hold]

casease ('keɪsɪˌeɪz) *n* a proteolytic enzyme formed by certain bacteria that activates the solution of albumin and casein in milk and cheese. [C20: from CASE(IN) + -ASE]

caseate ('keɪsɪˌeɪt) *vb* (*intr*) *Pathol.* to undergo caseation. [C19: from Latin *cāseus* CHEESE[1]]

caseation (ˌkeɪsɪ'eɪʃən) *n* **1** the formation of cheese from casein during the coagulation of milk. **2** *Pathol.* the degeneration of dead tissue into a soft cheeselike mass.

casebook ('keɪsˌbʊk) *n* a book in which records of legal or medical cases are kept.

casebound ('keɪsˌbaʊnd) *adj* another word for **hardback.**

casefy ('keɪsɪˌfaɪ) *vb* **-fies, -fying, -fied.** to make or become similar to cheese. [C20: from Latin *cāseus* CHEESE[1] + -FY]

case grammar *n Linguistics.* a system of grammatical description based on the functional relations that noun groups have to the main verb of a sentence. Compare **systemic grammar, transformational grammar.**

case-harden *vb* (*tr*) **1** *Metallurgy.* to form a hard surface layer of high carbon content on (a steel component) by heating in a carburizing environment with subsequent quenching or heat treatment. **2** to harden the spirit or disposition of; make callous: *experience had case-hardened the judge.*

case history *n* a record of a person's background, medical history, etc., esp. one used for determining medical treatment.

casein ('keɪsɪɪn, -siːn) *n* a phosphoprotein, precipitated from milk by the action of rennin, forming the basis of cheese: used in the manufacture of plastics and adhesives. Also called (U.S.): **paracasein.** [C19: from Latin *cāseus* cheese + -IN]

caseinogen (ˌkeɪsɪ'ɪnədʒən, keɪ'siːnə-) *n* the principal protein of milk, converted to casein by rennin. Sometimes called (U.S.) **casein.**

case knife *n* another name for **sheath knife.**

case law *n* law established by following judicial decisions given in earlier cases. Compare **statute law.** See also **precedent** (sense 1).

caseload ('keɪsləʊd) *n* the number of cases constituting the work of a doctor, solicitor, social worker, etc. over a specified period.

casemate ('keɪsˌmeɪt) *n* an armoured compartment in a ship or fortification in which guns are mounted. [C16: from French, from Italian *casamatta,* perhaps from Greek *khasmata* apertures, plural of *khasma* CHASM] ▶ **'caseˌmated** *adj*

casement ('keɪsmənt) *n* **1** a window frame that is hinged on one side. **2** a window containing frames hinged at the side or at the top or bottom. **3** a poetic word for **window.** [C15: probably from Old Northern French *encassement* frame, from *encasser* to frame, encase, from *casse* framework, crate, CASE[2]]

Casement ('keɪsmənt) *n* Sir **Roger** (**David**). 1864–1916, British diplomat and Irish nationalist: hanged by the British for treason in attempting to gain German support for Irish independence.

caseose ('keɪsɪˌəʊz, -ˌəʊs) *n* a peptide produced by the peptic digestion of casein. [C20: from Latin *cāseus* cheese + -OSE[2]]

caseous ('keɪsɪəs) *adj* of or like cheese. [C17: from Latin *cāseus* CHEESE[1]]

casern *or* **caserne** (kə'zɜːn) *n* (formerly) a billet or accommodation for soldiers in a town. [C17: from French *caserne,* from Old Provençal *cazerna* group of four men, ultimately from Latin *quattuor* four]

Caserta (*Italian* ka'zɛrta) *n* a town in S Italy, in Campania: centre of Garibaldi's campaigns for the unification of Italy (1860); Allied headquarters in World War II. Pop.: 69 350 (1990).

case shot *n* another name for **canister** (sense 2b).

case stated *n Law.* a statement of the facts of a case prepared by one court for the opinion or judgment of another court. Also called: **stated case.**

case study *n* the act or an instance of analysing one or more particular cases or case histories with a view to making generalizations.

casework ('keɪsˌwɜːk) *n* social work based on close study of the personal histories and circumstances of individuals and families. ▶ **'caseˌworker** *n*

caseworm ('keɪsˌwɜːm) *n* another name for a **caddis worm.**

cash[1] (kæʃ) *n* **1** banknotes and coins, esp. in hand or readily available; money or ready money. **2** immediate payment, in full or part, for goods or services (esp. in the phrase **cash down**). **3** (*modifier*) of, for, or paid by cash: *a cash transaction.* ◆ *vb* **4** (*tr*) to obtain or pay ready money for: *to cash a cheque.* ◆ See also **cash in, cash up.** [C16: from Old Italian *cassa* money box, from Latin *capsa* CASE[2]] ▶ **'cashable** *adj*

cash[2] (kæʃ) *n, pl* **cash.** any of various Chinese, Indonesian, or Indian coins of low value. [C16: from Portuguese *caixa,* from Tamil *kāsu,* from Sanskrit *karsa* weight of gold or silver]

Cash (kæʃ) *n* **Johnny.** born 1932, U.S. country-and-western singer, guitarist, and songwriter. His hits include "I Walk the Line" (1956), "Ring of Fire" (1963), and "A Boy named Sue" (1969).

cash-and-carry *adj, adv* **1** sold or operated on a basis of cash payment for merchandise that is not delivered but removed by the purchaser. ◆ *n* **2** a wholesale store, esp. for groceries, that operates on this basis. **3** an operation on a commodities futures market in which spot goods are purchased and sold at a profit on a futures contract.

cashback ('kæʃˌbæk) *n* **1a** a discount offered in return for immediate payment. **1b** (*as modifier*): *cashback price £519.99 — save £30!* **2a** a service provided by some supermarkets in which customers paying by debit card can draw cash. **2b** the cash so drawn.

cash-book *n Book-keeping.* a journal in which all cash or cheque receipts and disbursements are recorded.

cash card *n* an embossed plastic card bearing the name and account details of a bank or building-society customer, used with a personal identification number to obtain money from a cash dispenser. Also called: **cash-point card.**

cash cow *n* a product, acquisition, etc., that produces a steady flow of cash, esp. one with a well-known brand name commanding a high market share.

cash crop *n* a crop grown for sale rather than for subsistence.

cash desk *n* a counter or till in a shop where purchases are paid for.

cash discount *n* a discount granted to a purchaser who pays before a stipulated date.

cash dispenser *n* a computerized device outside a bank that supplies cash or account information when the user inserts his cash card and keys in his identification number. Also called: **automated teller machine.**

cashed up *adj Austral. informal.* having plenty of money.

cashew ('kæʃuː, kæ'ʃuː) *n* **1** a tropical American anacardiaceous evergreen tree, *Anacardium occidentale,* bearing kidney-shaped nuts that protrude from a fleshy receptacle. **2** Also called: **cashew nut.** the edible nut of this tree. [C18: from Portuguese *cajú,* from Tupi *acajú*]

cash flow *n* **1** the movement of money into and out of a business. **2** a prediction of such movement over a given period.

cashier[1] (kæ'ʃɪə) *n* **1** a person responsible for receiving payments for goods, services, etc., as in a shop. **2** Also called: **teller.** an employee of a bank responsible for receiving deposits, cashing cheques, and other financial transactions; bank clerk. **3** any person responsible for handling cash or maintaining records of its receipt and disbursement. [C16: from Dutch *cassier* or French *caissier,* from *casse* money chest; see CASE[2]]

cashier[2] (kæ'ʃɪə) *vb* (*tr*) **1** to dismiss with dishonour, esp. from the armed forces. **2** *Rare.* to put away or discard; reject. [C16: from Middle Dutch *kasseren,* from Old French *casser* to QUASH, from Latin *quassāre* to QUASH]

cash in *vb* (*adv*) **1** (*tr*) to give (something) in exchange, esp. for money. **2** (*intr;* often foll. by *on*) *Informal.* **2a** to profit (from). **2b** to take advantage (of). **3** (*intr*) a slang expression for **die**[1].

cashless ('kæʃlɪs) *adj* functioning, operated, or performed without using coins or banknotes for money transactions but instead using credit cards or electronic transfer of funds: *cashless shopping.*

cash limit *n* (*often pl*) a limit imposed as a method of curtailing overall expenditure without specifying the precise means of budgetary control.

cashmere *or* **kashmir** ('kæʃmɪə) *n* **1** a fine soft wool from goats of the Kashmir area. **2a** cloth or knitted material made from this or similar wool. **2b** (*as modifier*): *a cashmere sweater.*

Cashmere (kæʃ'mɪə) *n* a variant spelling of **Kashmir.**

cash on delivery *n* a service entailing cash payment to the carrier on delivery of merchandise. Abbrev: **COD.**

cashpoint *n* a cash dispenser.

cash ratio *n* the ratio of cash on hand to total deposits that by law or custom commercial banks must maintain.

cash register *n* a till with a keyboard that operates a mechanism for displaying and adding the amounts of cash received in individual sales.

cash up *vb* (*intr, adv*) *Brit.* (of cashiers, shopkeepers, etc.) to add up the money taken, esp. at the end of a working day.

casimere ('kæsɪˌmɪə) *n* a variant spelling of **cassimere.**

Casimir III ('kæzɪmɪə) *n* known as *the Great.* 1310–70, king of Poland (1333–70).

Casimir IV *n* 1427–92, grand duke of Lithuania (1440–92) and king of Poland (1447–92).

casing ('keɪsɪŋ) *n* **1** a protective case or cover. **2** material for a case or cover. **3** Also called: **case.** a frame containing a door, window, or staircase. **4** the intestines of cattle, pigs, etc., or a synthetic substitute, used as a container for sausage meat. **5** the outer cover of a pneumatic tyre. **6** a pipe or tube used to line a hole or shaft. **7** the outer shell of a steam or gas turbine.

casino (kə'siːnəʊ) *n, pl* **-nos. 1** a public building or room in which gaming takes place, esp. roulette and card games such as baccarat and chemin de fer. **2** a variant spelling of **cassino.** [C18: from Italian, diminutive of *casa* house, from Latin]

cask (kɑːsk) *n* **1** a strong wooden barrel used mainly to hold alcoholic drink: *a wine cask.* **2** any barrel. **3** the quantity contained in a cask. **4** *Austral.* a lightweight cardboard container with plastic lining and a small tap, used to hold and serve wine. **5** *Engineering.* another name for **flask** (sense 6). [C15: from Spanish *casco* helmet, perhaps from *cascar* to break]

casket ('kɑːskɪt) *n* **1** a small box or chest for valuables, esp. jewels. **2** *Chiefly U.S.* another name for **coffin** (sense 1). [C15: probably from Old French *cassette* little box; see CASE[2]]

Caslon ('kæzlən) *n* a style of type designed by William Caslon, English type founder (1692–1766).

Caspar ('kæspə, 'kæspɑː) *or* **Gaspar** *n* (in Christian tradition) one of the Magi, the other two being Melchior and Balthazar.

Casparian strip (kæ'speərɪən) *n Botany.* a band of suberized material around the radial walls of endodermal cells: impervious to gases and liquids. [C20: named after Robert *Caspary,* 19th-century German botanist]

Caspian Sea ('kæspɪən) *n* a salt lake between SE Europe and Asia: the largest inland sea in the world; fed mainly by the River Volga. Area: 394 299 sq. km (152 239 sq. miles).

casque (kæsk) *n Zoology.* a helmet or a helmet-like process or structure, as on the bill of most hornbills. [C17: from French, from Spanish *casco;* see CASK] ▸ **casqued** *adj*

cassaba (kə'sɑːbə) *n* a variant spelling of **casaba.**

Cassandra (kə'sændrə) *n* **1** *Greek myth.* a daughter of Priam and Hecuba, endowed with the gift of prophecy but fated never to be believed. **2** anyone whose prophecies of doom are unheeded.

cassareep ('kæsəˌriːp) *n* the juice of the bitter cassava root, boiled down to a syrup and used as a flavouring, esp. in West Indian cookery. [C19: of Carib origin]

cassata (kə'sɑːtə) *n* an ice cream, originating in Italy, usually containing nuts and candied fruit. [from Italian]

cassation (kæ'seɪʃən) *n Chiefly law.* (esp. in France) annulment, as of a judicial decision by a higher court. [C15: from Old French, from Medieval Latin *cassātiō,* from Late Latin *cassāre* to cancel, from Latin *quassāre* to QUASH]

Cassatt (kə'sæt) *n* **Mary.** 1845–1926, U.S. impressionist painter, who lived in France.

cassava (kə'sɑːvə) *n* **1** Also called: **manioc.** any tropical euphorbiaceous plant of the genus *Manihot,* esp. the widely cultivated American species *M. esculenta* (or *utilissima*) (**bitter cassava**) and *M. dulcis* (**sweet cassava**). **2** a starch derived from the root of this plant: an important food in the tropics and a source of tapioca. [C16: from Spanish *cazabe* cassava bread, from Taino *caçábi*]

Cassegrain telescope ('kæsɪˌgreɪn) *n* an astronomical reflecting telescope in which incident light is reflected from a large concave mirror onto a smaller convex mirror and then back through a hole in the concave mirror to form the image. [C19: named after N. *Cassegrain,* 17th-century French scientist who invented it]

Cassel (*German* 'kasəl) *n* a variant spelling of **Kassel.**

casserole ('kæsəˌrəʊl) *n* **1** a covered dish of earthenware, glass, etc., in which food is cooked and served. **2** any food cooked and served in such a dish: *chicken casserole.* ◆ *vb* **3** to cook or be cooked in a casserole. [C18: from French, from Old French *casse* ladle, pan for dripping, from Old Provençal *cassa,* from Late Latin *cattia* dipper, from Greek *kuathion,* diminutive of *kuathos* cup]

cassette (kæ'set) *n* **1a** a plastic container for magnetic tape, inserted into a tape deck to be played or used. **1b** (*as modifier*): *a cassette recorder.* **2** *Photog.* another term for **cartridge** (sense 5). **3** *Films.* a container for film used to facilitate the loading of a camera or projector, esp. when the film is used in the form of a loop. **4** the injection of genes from one species into the fertilized egg of another species. [C18: from French: little box; see CASE[2]]

cassia ('kæsɪə) *n* **1** any plant of the mainly tropical caesalpiniaceous genus *Cassia,* esp. *C. fistula,* whose pods yield **cassia pulp,** a mild laxative. See also **senna. 2** a lauraceous tree, *Cinnamomum cassia,* of tropical Asia. **3 cassia bark.** the cinnamon-like bark of this tree, used as a spice. [Old English, from Latin *casia,* from Greek *kasia,* of Semitic origin; related to Hebrew *qesīʿāh* cassia]

cassimere *or* **casimere** ('kæsɪˌmɪə) *n* a woollen suiting cloth of plain or twill weave. [C18: variant of *cashmere,* from KASHMIR]

Cassini (kæ'siːnɪ) *n* **Giovanni Domenico.** 1625–1712, French astronomer, born in Italy. He discovered (1675) **Cassini's division,** the gap that divides Saturn's rings into two parts, and four of Saturn's moons.

cassino *or* **casino** (kə'siːnəʊ) *n* a card game for two to four players in which players pair cards from their hands with others exposed on the table.

Cassino (*Italian* kas'siːno) *n* a town in central Italy, in Latium at the foot of Monte Cassino: an ancient Volscian (and later Roman) town and citadel. Pop.: 34 590 (1990). Latin name: **Casinum.**

Cassiodorus (ˌkæsɪəʊ'dɔːrəs) *n* **Flavius Magnus Aurelius** ('fleɪvɪəs 'mægnəs ɔː'riːlɪəs). ?490–?585 A.D., Roman statesman, writer, and monk; author of *Variae,* a collection of official documents written for the Ostrogoths.

Cassiopeia[1] (ˌkæsɪə'piːə) *n Greek myth.* the wife of Cepheus and mother of Andromeda.

Cassiopeia[2] (ˌkæsɪə'piːə) *n, Latin genitive* **Cassiopeiae** (ˌkæsɪə'piːiː). a very conspicuous W-shaped constellation near the Pole Star. **Cassiopeia A** is a very strong radio and X-ray source, identified as faint nebulous filaments that are the remains of the supernova observed in 1572. ▸ **ˌCassio'peian** *adj*

Cassirer (*German* ka'siːrər) *n* **Ernst** (ɛrnst). 1874–1945, German neo-Kantian philosopher. *The Philosophy of Symbolic Forms* (1923–29) analyses the symbols that underlie all manifestations, including myths and language, of human culture.

cassis (kɑː'siːs) *n* a blackcurrant cordial. [C19: from French]

cassiterite (kə'sɪtəˌraɪt) *n* a black or brown mineral, found in igneous rocks and hydrothermal veins. It is a source of tin. Composition: tin oxide. Formula: SnO_2. Crystal structure: tetragonal. Also called: **tinstone.** [C19: from Greek *kassiteros* tin]

Cassius Longinus ('kæsɪəs lɒn'dʒaɪnəs) *n* **Gaius** ('gaɪəs). died 42 B.C., Roman general: led the conspiracy against Julius Caesar (44); defeated at Philippi by Antony (42).

Cassivelaunus (ˌkæsɪvə'lɔːnəs) *n* 1st century B.C., British chieftain, king of the Catuvellauni tribe, who organized resistance to Caesar's invasion of Britain (54 B.C.).

cassock ('kæsək) *n Christianity.* an ankle-length garment, usually black, worn by priests and choristers. [C16: from Old French *casaque,* from Italian *casacca* a long coat, of uncertain origin] ▸ **'cassocked** *adj*

Casson ('kæsᵊn) *n* Sir **Hugh** (**Maxwell**). 1910–99, British architect; president of the Royal Academy of Arts (1976–84).

cassoulet (ˌkæsə'leɪ) *n* a stew originating from France, made from haricot beans and goose, duck, pork, etc. [French, related to *casse* saucepan, bowl]

cassowary ('kæsəˌwɛərɪ) *n, pl* **-waries.** any large flightless bird of the genus *Casuarius,* inhabiting forests in NE Australia, New Guinea, and adjacent islands, having a horny head crest, black plumage, and brightly coloured neck and wattles: order *Casuariiformes* (see **ratite**). [C17: from Malay *kĕsuari*]

casspir ('kæspɜː) *n S. African.* an armoured military vehicle. [C20: coined from an anagram of *CSIR* (Council for Scientific and Industrial Research) and *SAP* (South African Police)]

cast (kɑːst) *vb* **casts, casting, cast.** (*mainly tr*) **1** to throw or expel with violence or force. **2** to throw off or away: *she cast her clothes to the ground.* **3** to reject or dismiss: *he cast the idea from his mind.* **4** to shed or drop: *the snake cast its skin; the horse cast a shoe; the ship cast anchor.* **5 be cast.** *N.Z.* (of a sheep) to have fallen and been unable to rise. **6** to cause to appear: *to cast a shadow.* **7** to express (doubts, suspicions, etc.) or cause (them) to be felt. **8** to direct (a glance, attention, etc.): *cast your eye over this.* **9** to place, esp. in a violent manner: *he was cast into prison.* **10** (*also intr*) *Angling.* to throw (a line) into the water. **11** to draw or choose (lots). **12** to give or deposit (a vote). **13** to select (actors) to play parts in (a play, film, etc.). **14a** to shape (molten metal, glass, etc.) by pouring or pressing it into a mould. **14b** to make (an object) by such a process. **15** (*also intr; often foll. by up*) to compute (figures or a total). **16** to predict: *the old woman cast my fortune.* **17** *Astrology.* to draw on (a horoscope) details concerning the positions of the planets in the signs of the zodiac at a particular time for interpretation in terms of human characteristics, behaviour, etc. **18** to contrive (esp. in the phrase **cast a spell**). **19** to formulate: *he cast his work in the form of a chart.* **20** (*also intr*) to twist or cause to twist. **21** (*also intr*) *Nautical.* to turn the head of (a sailing vessel) or (of a sailing vessel) to be turned away from the wind in getting under way. **22** *Hunting.* to direct (a pack of hounds) over (ground) where their quarry may recently have passed. **23** (*intr*) (of birds of prey) to eject from the crop and bill a pellet consisting of the indigestible parts of birds or animals previously eaten. **24** *Falconry.* to hold the body of a hawk between the hands so as to perform some operation upon it. **25** *Printing.* to stereotype or electrotype. **26 cast** *or* **throw in one's lot with.** to share in the activities or fortunes of (someone else). ◆ *n* **27** the act of casting or throwing. **28a** Also called: **casting.** something that is shed, dropped, or egested, such as the coil of earth left by an earthworm. **28b** another name for **pellet** (sense 4). **29** an object that is thrown. **30** the distance an object is or may be thrown. **31a** a throw at dice. **31b** the resulting number shown. **32** *Angling.* **32a** a trace with a fly or flies attached. **32b** the act or an instance of casting. **33** the wide sweep made by a sheepdog to get behind a flock of sheep or by a hunting dog in search of a scent. **34a** the actors in a play collectively. **34b** (*as modifier*): *a cast list.* **35a** an object made of metal, glass, etc., that has been shaped in a molten state by being poured or pressed into a mould. **35b** the mould used to shape such an object. **36** form or appearance. **37** sort, kind, or style. **38** a fixed twist or defect, esp. in the eye. **39** a distortion of shape. **40** *Surgery.* a rigid encircling casing, often made of plaster of Paris, for immobilizing broken bones while they heal. **41** *Pathol.* a mass of fatty, waxy, cellular, or other material formed in a diseased body cavity, passage, etc. **42** the act of casting a pack of hounds. **43** *Falconry.* a pair of falcons working in combination to pursue the same quarry. **44** *Archery.* the speed imparted to an arrow by a particular bow. **45** a slight tinge or trace, as of colour. **46** a computation or calculation. **47** a forecast or conjecture. **48** fortune or a stroke of fate. **49** *Palaeontol.* a mineral representation of an organic object, esp. a lump of mineral that indicates the shape and internal structure of a shell. ◆ See also **cast about, castaway, cast back, cast down, cast-off, cast on, cast out, cast up.** [C13: from Old Norse *kasta*]

cast about *or* **around** *vb (intr, adv)* to make a mental or visual search: *to cast about for an idea for a book.*

Castalia (kæ'steɪlɪə) *n* a spring on Mount Parnassus: in ancient Greece sacred to Apollo and the Muses and believed to be a source of inspiration. ▸ **Cas'talian** *adj*

castanets (ˌkæstə'nɛts) *pl n* curved pieces of hollow wood, usually held between the fingers and thumb and made to click together: used esp. by Spanish dancers. [C17 *castanet,* from Spanish *castañeta,* diminutive of *castaña* CHESTNUT]

castaway ('kɑːstəˌweɪ) *n* **1** a person who has been shipwrecked. **2** something thrown off or away; castoff. ◆ *adj (prenominal)* **3** shipwrecked or put adrift. **4** thrown away or rejected. ◆ *vb* **cast away. 5** *(tr, adv; often passive)* to cause (a ship, person, etc.) to be shipwrecked or abandoned.

cast back *vb (adv)* to turn (the mind) to the past.

cast down *vb (tr, adv)* to make (a person) discouraged or dejected.

caste (kɑːst) *n* **1a** any of the four major hereditary classes, namely the **Brahman, Kshatriya, Vaisya,** and **Sudra,** into which Hindu society is divided. **1b** Also called: **caste system.** the system or basis of such classes. **1c** the social position or rank conferred by this system. **2** any social class or system based on such distinctions as heredity, rank, wealth, profession, etc. **3** the position conferred by such a system. **4** *Entomol.* any of various types of specialized individual, such as the worker, in social insects (hive bees, ants, etc.). [C16: from Portuguese *casta* race, breed, ancestry, from *casto* pure, chaste, from Latin *castus*]

Castellammare di Stabia (*Italian* kastellam'maːre di 'stabja) *n* a port and resort in SW Italy, in Campania on the Bay of Naples: site of the Roman resort of Stabiae, which was destroyed by the eruption of Vesuvius in 79 A.D. Pop.: 67 974 (1993 est.).

castellan ('kæstɪlən) *n Rare.* a keeper or governor of a castle. Also called: **chatelain.** [C14: from Latin *castellānus,* from *castellum* CASTLE]

castellated ('kæstɪˌleɪtɪd) *adj* **1** having turrets and battlements, like a castle. **2** having indentations similar to battlements: *a castellated nut; a castellated filament.* [C17: from Medieval Latin *castellātus,* from *castellāre* to fortify as a CASTLE] ▸ ˌ**castel'lation** *n*

Castellón de la Plana (*Spanish* kaste'ʎon de la'plana) *n* a port in E Spain. Pop.: 139 889 (1995 est.).

caster ('kɑːstə) *n* **1** a person or thing that casts. **2** Also: **castor.** a bottle with a perforated top for sprinkling sugar, etc., or a stand containing such bottles. **3** Also: **castor.** a small wheel mounted on a swivel so that the wheel tends to turn into its plane of rotation.

caster action *n* the tendency, caused by the design of the mounting, of a wheel to turn into its plane of rotation.

caster sugar ('kɑːstə) *n* finely ground white sugar.

castigate ('kæstɪˌgeɪt) *vb (tr)* to rebuke or criticize in a severe manner; chastise. [C17: from Latin *castīgāre* to correct, punish, from *castum* pure + *agere* to compel (to be)] ▸ ˌ**casti'gation** *n* ▸ **'castiˌgator** *n* ▸ ˌ**casti'gatory** *adj*

Castiglione (ˌkæstɪl'jəʊnɪ, *Italian* kasti'ʎoːne) *n* Count **Baldassare** (baldas'saːre). 1478–1529, Italian diplomat and writer, noted particularly for his dialogue on ideal courtly life, *Il Libro del Cortegiano* (The Courtier) (1528).

Castile (kæ'stiːl) *or* **Castilla** (*Spanish* kas'tiʎa) *n* a former kingdom comprising most of modern Spain: originally part of León, it became an independent kingdom in the 10th century and united with Aragon (1469), the first step in the formation of the Spanish state.

Castile soap *n* a hard soap made from olive oil and sodium hydroxide.

Castilian (kæ'stɪljən) *n* **1** the Spanish dialect of Castile; the standard form of European Spanish. **2** a native or inhabitant of Castile. ◆ *adj* **3** denoting, relating to, or characteristic of Castile, its inhabitants, or the standard form of European Spanish.

Castilla la Vieja (kas'tiʎa la 'bjexa) *n* the Spanish name for **Old Castile.**

casting ('kɑːstɪŋ) *n* **1** an object or figure that has been cast, esp. in metal from a mould. **2** the process of transferring molten steel to a mould. **3** the choosing of actors for a production. **4** *Hunting.* the act of directing a pack of hounds over ground where their quarry may recently have passed so that they can quest for, discover, or recapture its scent. **5** *Zoology.* another word for **cast** (sense 28) or **pellet** (sense 4).

casting couch *n Informal.* a couch on which a casting director is said to seduce girls seeking a part in a film or play.

casting vote *n* the deciding vote used by the presiding officer of an assembly when votes cast on both sides are equal in number.

cast iron *n* **1** iron containing so much carbon (1.7 to 4.5 per cent) that it cannot be wrought and must be cast into shape. ◆ *adj* **cast-iron. 2** made of cast iron. **3** rigid, strong, or unyielding: *a cast-iron decision.*

castle ('kɑːsᵊl) *n* **1** a fortified building or set of buildings, usually permanently garrisoned, as in medieval Europe. **2** any fortified place or structure. **3** a large magnificent house, esp. when the present or former home of a nobleman or prince. **4** the citadel and strongest part of the fortifications of a medieval town. **5** *Chess.* another name for **rook**[2]. ◆ *vb* **6** *Chess.* to move (the king) two squares laterally on the first rank and place the nearest rook on the square passed over by the king, either towards the king's side (**castling short**) or the queen's side (**castling long**). [C11: from Latin *castellum,* diminutive of *castrum* fort]

Castlebar (ˌkɑːsᵊl'bɑː) *n* the county town of Co. Mayo, Republic of Ireland; site of the battle (1798) between the French and British known as Castlebar Races. Pop.: 6070 (1991).

castled ('kɑːsᵊld) *adj* **1** like a castle in construction; castellated: *a castled mansion.* **2** (of an area) having many castles.

Castleford ('kɑːsᵊlfəd) *n* a town in N England, in Wakefield unitary authority, West Yorkshire on the River Aire. Pop.: 38 536 (1991).

Castle Howard *n* a mansion near York in Yorkshire: designed in 1700 by Sir John Vanbrugh and Nicholas Hawksmoor; the grounds include the Temple of the Four Winds and a mausoleum.

castle in the air *or* **in Spain** *n* a hope or desire unlikely to be realized; daydream.

castle nut *n* a hexagonal nut with six slots in the head, two of which take a locking pin to hold it firmly in position.

Castlereagh[1] ('kɑːsᵊlˌreɪ) *n* a district of E Northern Ireland, in Co. Down. Pop.: 60 799 (1991). Area.: 85 sq. km (33 sq. miles).

Castlereagh[2] ('kɑːsᵊlˌreɪ) *n* **Viscount.** title of *Robert Stewart,* Marquis of Londonderry. 1769–1822, British statesman: as foreign secretary (1812–22) led the Grand Alliance against Napoleon and attended the Congress of Vienna (1815).

Castner ('kæstnə) *n* **Hamilton Young.** 1858–98, U.S. chemist, who devised the **Castner process** for extracting sodium from sodium hydroxide.

cast-off *adj* **1** *(prenominal)* thrown away; abandoned: *cast-off shoes.* ◆ *n* **'castoff. 2** a person or thing that has been discarded or abandoned. **3** *Printing.* an estimate of the amount of space that a piece of copy will occupy when printed in a particular size and style of type. ◆ *vb* **cast off.** *(adv)* **4** to remove (mooring lines) that hold (a vessel) to a dock. **5** to knot (a row of stitches, esp. the final row) in finishing off knitted or woven material. **6** *Printing.* to estimate the amount of space that will be taken up by (a book, piece of copy, etc.) when it is printed in a particular size and style of type. **7** *(intr)* (in Scottish country dancing) to perform a progressive movement during which each partner of a couple dances separately behind one line of the set and then reunites with the other in their original position in the set or in a new position.

cast on *vb (adv)* to form (the first row of stitches) in knitting and weaving.

castor[1] ('kɑːstə) *n* **1** the brownish aromatic secretion of the anal glands of a beaver, used in perfumery and medicine. **2** the fur of the beaver. **3** a hat made of beaver or similar fur. **4** a less common name for **beaver**[1] (sense 1). [C14: from Latin, from Greek *kastōr* beaver]

castor[2] ('kɑːstə) *n* a variant spelling of **caster** (senses 2, 3).

Castor ('kɑːstə) *n* **1** the second brightest star, Alpha Geminorum, in the constellation Gemini: a multiple star consisting of six components lying close to the star Pollux. Distance: 46 light years. **2** *Classical myth.* See **Castor and Pollux.**

Castor and Pollux *n Classical myth.* the twin sons of Leda: Pollux was fathered by Zeus, Castor by the mortal Tyndareus. After Castor's death, Pollux spent half his days with his half-brother in Hades and half with the gods in Olympus.

castor bean *n U.S. and Canadian.* **1** another name for **castor-oil plant. 2** the seed of this plant.

castor oil *n* a colourless or yellow glutinous oil obtained from the seeds of the castor-oil plant and used as a fine lubricant and as a cathartic.

castor-oil plant *n* a tall euphorbiaceous Indian plant, *Ricinus communis,* cultivated in tropical regions for ornament and for its poisonous seeds, from which castor oil is extracted. Also called (U.S. and Canadian): **castor bean.**

cast out *vb (intr, adv) Scot.* to quarrel; be no longer friends.

castrate (kæ'streɪt) *vb (tr)* **1** to remove the testicles of; emasculate; geld. **2** to deprive of vigour, masculinity, etc. **3** to remove the ovaries of; spay. **4** to expurgate or censor (a book, play, etc.). [C17: from Latin *castrāre* to emasculate, geld] ▸ **cas'tration** *n* ▸ **cas'trator** *n*

castration complex *n Psychoanal.* an unconscious fear of having one's genitals removed, as a punishment for wishing to have sex with a parent.

castrato (kæ'strɑːtəʊ) *n, pl* **-ti** (-tɪ) *or* **-tos.** (in 17th- and 18th-century opera) a male singer whose testicles were removed before puberty, allowing the retention of a soprano or alto voice. [C18: from Italian, from Latin *castrātus* castrated]

Castries (kæs'triːs) *n* the capital and chief port of St Lucia. Pop.: 13 615 (1992 est.).

Castro ('kæstrəʊ; *Spanish* 'kastro) *n* **Fidel** (fɪ'dɛl; *Spanish* fi'ðel). full name *Fidel Castro Ruz.* born 1927, Cuban statesman: prime minister from 1959, when he led the Communist overthrow of Batista and president from 1976.

Castrop-Rauxel *or* **Kastrop-Rauxel** (*German* 'kastrɔp-'rauksəl) *n* an industrial city in W Germany, in North Rhine-Westphalia. Pop.: 80 000 (1989 est.).

cast steel *n* steel containing varying amounts of carbon, manganese, phosphorus, silicon, and sulphur that is cast into shape rather than wrought.

cast stone *n Building trades.* a building component, such as a block or lintel, made from cast concrete with a facing that resembles natural stone.

cast up *vb (tr, adv)* **1** (of the sea) to cast ashore. **2** to compute (figures or a total). **3** to bring up as a reproach against a person.

casual ('kæʒjʊəl) *adj* **1** happening by accident or chance: *a casual meeting.* **2** offhand; not premeditated: *a casual remark.* **3** shallow or superficial: *a casual affair.* **4** being or seeming unconcerned or apathetic: *he assumed a casual attitude.* **5** (esp. of dress) for informal wear: *a casual coat.* **6** occasional or irregular: *casual visits; a casual labourer.* **7** *Biology.* another term for **adventive.** ◆ *n* **8** *(usually pl)* an informal article of clothing or footwear. **9** an occasional worker. **10** *Biology.* another term for an **adventive. 11** *(usually pl)* a young man dressed in expensive casual clothes who goes to football matches in order to start fights. [C14: from Late Latin *cāsuālis* happening by chance, from Latin *cāsus* event, from *cadere* to fall; see CASE[1]] ▸ **'casually** *adv* ▸ **'casualness** *n*

casualization *or* **casualisation** (ˌkæʒjuəlaɪˈzeɪʃən) *n* the altering of working practices so that regular workers are re-employed on a casual or short-term basis.

casualty (ˈkæʒjuəltɪ) *n, pl* **-ties. 1** a serviceman who is killed, wounded, captured, or missing as a result of enemy action. **2** a person who is injured or killed in an accident. **3** a hospital department where victims of accidents, violence, etc., are treated. **4** anything that is lost, damaged, or destroyed as the result of an accident, etc.

casuarina (ˌkæsjuəˈriːnə) *n* any tree of the genus *Casuarina*, of Australia and the East Indies, having jointed leafless branchlets: family *Casuarinaceae*. See also **beefwood, she-oak.** [C19: from New Latin, from Malay *kĕsuari* CASSOWARY, referring to the resemblance of the branches to the feathers of the cassowary]

casuist (ˈkæzjuɪst) *n* **1** a person, esp. a theologian, who attempts to resolve moral dilemmas by the application of general rules and the careful distinction of special cases. **2** a person who is oversubtle in his analysis of fine distinctions; sophist. [C17: from French *casuiste*, from Spanish *casuista*, from Latin *cāsus* CASE[1]] ▸ ˌ**casuˈistic** *or* ˌ**casuˈistical** *adj* ▸ ˌ**casuˈistically** *adv*

casuistry (ˈkæzjuɪstrɪ) *n, pl* **-ries. 1** *Philosophy.* the resolution of particular moral dilemmas, esp. those arising from conflicting general moral rules, by careful distinction of the cases to which these rules apply. **2** reasoning that is specious, misleading, or oversubtle.

casus belli *Latin.* (ˈkɑːsʊs ˈbeliː) *n, pl* ***casus belli*** (ˈkɑːsʊs ˈbeliː). **1** an event or act used to justify a war. **2** the immediate cause of a quarrel. [literally: occasion of war]

cat[1] (kæt) *n* **1** Also called: **domestic cat.** a small domesticated feline mammal, *Felis catus* (or *domesticus*), having thick soft fur and occurring in many breeds in which the colour of the fur varies greatly: kept as a pet or to catch rats and mice. **2** Also called: **big cat.** any of the larger felines, such as a lion or tiger. **3** any wild feline mammal of the genus *Felis*, such as the lynx or serval, resembling the domestic cat. ◆ Related adj: **feline. 4** *Informal.* a woman who gossips maliciously. **5** *Slang.* a man; guy. **6** *Nautical.* a heavy tackle for hoisting an anchor to the cathead. **7** a short sharp-ended piece of wood used in the game of tipcat. **8** short for **catboat. 9** *Informal.* short for **caterpillar** (the vehicle). **10** short for **cat-o'-nine-tails. 11 a bag of cats.** *Irish informal.* a bad-tempered person: *she's a real bag of cats this morning.* **12 fight like Kilkenny cats.** to fight until both parties are destroyed. **13 let the cat out of the bag.** to disclose a secret, often by mistake. **14 like a cat on a hot tin roof** *or* **on hot bricks.** in an uneasy or agitated state. **15 like cat and dog.** quarrelling savagely. **16 look like something the cat brought in.** to appear dishevelled or bedraggled. **17 not a cat in hell's chance.** no chance at all. **18 not have room to swing a cat.** to have very little space. **19 put, set,** etc., **the cat among the pigeons.** to introduce some violently disturbing new element. **20 play cat and mouse.** to play with a person or animal in a cruel or teasing way, esp. before a final act of cruelty or unkindness. **21 rain cats and dogs.** to rain very heavily. ◆ *vb* **cats, catting, catted. 22** (*tr*) to flog with a cat-o'-nine-tails. **23** (*tr*) *Nautical.* to hoist (an anchor) to the cathead. **24** (*intr*) a slang word for **vomit.** [Old English *catte*, from Latin *cattus*; related to Old Norse *köttr*, Old High German *kazza*, Old French *chat*, Russian *kot*] ▸ ˈ**catˌlike** *adj* ▸ ˈ**cattish** *adj*

cat[2] (kæt) *n Informal.* short for **catamaran** (sense 1).

cat[3] (kæt) *n* **1a** short for **catalytic converter. 1b** (*as modifier*): *a cat car.* ◆ *adj* **2** short for **catalytic**: *a cat cracker.*

CAT (in Britain) *abbrev. for:* **1** College of Advanced Technology. **2** computer-aided teaching. **3** computer-assisted trading.

cat. *abbrev. for:* **1** catalogue. **2** catamaran. **3** *Christianity.* catechism.

cata-, kata-, *before an aspirate* **cath-,** *or before a vowel* **cat-** *prefix* **1** down; downwards; lower in position: *catadromous; cataphyll.* **2** indicating reversal, opposition, degeneration, etc.: *cataplasia; catatonia.* [from Greek *kata-*, from *kata.* In compound words borrowed from Greek, *kata-* means: down (*catabolism*), away, off (*catalectic*), against (*category*), according to (*catholic*), and thoroughly (*catalogue*)]

catabasis (kəˈtæbəsɪs) *n, pl* **-ses** (-ˌsiːz). **1** a descent or downward movement. **2** the decline of a disease. ▸ **catabatic** (ˌkætəˈbætɪk) *adj*

catabolism *or* **katabolism** (kəˈtæbəˌlɪzəm) *n* a metabolic process in which complex molecules are broken down into simple ones with the release of energy; destructive metabolism. Compare **anabolism.** [C19 *katabolism*, from Greek *katabolē* a throwing down, from *kataballein*, from *kata-* down + *ballein* to throw] ▸ **catabolic** *or* **katabolic** (ˌkætəˈbɒlɪk) *adj* ▸ ˌ**cataˈbolically** *or* ˌ**kataˈbolically** *adv*

catabolite (kəˈtæbəˌlaɪt) *n* a substance produced as a result of catabolism.

catacaustic (ˌkætəˈkɔːstɪk, -ˈkɒs-) *Physics.* ◆ *adj* **1** (of a caustic curve or surface) formed by reflected light rays. Compare **diacaustic.** ◆ *n* **2** a catacaustic curve or surface.

catachresis (ˌkætəˈkriːsɪs) *n* the incorrect use of words, as *luxuriant* for *luxurious.* [C16: from Latin, from Greek *katakhrēsis* a misusing, from *katakhrēsthai*, from *khrēsthai* to use] ▸ **catachrestic** (ˌkætəˈkrɛstɪk) *or* ˌ**cataˈchrestical** *adj* ▸ ˌ**cataˈchrestically** *adv*

cataclasis (ˌkætəˈkleɪsɪs) *n, pl* **-ses** (-siːz). *Geology.* the deformation of rocks by crushing and shearing. [C19: New Latin, from Greek, from CATA- + *klasis* a breaking] ▸ **cataclastic** (ˌkætəˈklæstɪk) *adj*

cataclinal (ˌkætəˈklaɪnᵊl) *adj* (of streams, valleys, etc.) running in the direction of the dip of the surrounding rock strata.

cataclysm (ˈkætəˌklɪzəm) *n* **1** a violent upheaval, esp. of a political, military, or social nature. **2** a disastrous flood; deluge. **3** *Geology.* another name for **catastrophe** (sense 4). [C17: via French from Latin, from Greek *kataklusmos* deluge, from *katakluzein* to flood, from *kluzein* to wash] ▸ ˌ**cataˈclysmic** *or* ˌ**cataˈclysmal** *adj* ▸ ˌ**cataˈclysmically** *adv*

catacomb (ˈkætəˌkəʊm, -ˌkuːm) *n* **1** (*usually pl*) an underground burial place, esp. the galleries at Rome, consisting of tunnels with vaults or niches leading off them for tombs. **2** a series of underground tunnels or caves. [Old English *catacumbe*, from Late Latin *catacumbas* (singular), name of the cemetery under the Basilica of St Sebastian, near Rome; origin unknown]

catadioptric (ˌkætədaɪˈɒptrɪk) *adj* involving a combination of reflecting and refracting components: *a catadioptric telescope.* [C18: from CATA- + DIOPTRIC]

catadromous (kəˈtædrəməs) *adj* (of fishes such as the eel) migrating down rivers to the sea in order to breed. Compare **anadromous.** [C19: from Greek *katadromos*, from *kata-* down + *dromos*, from *dremein* to run]

catafalque (ˈkætəˌfælk) *n* a temporary raised platform on which a body lies in state before or during a funeral. [C17: from French, from Italian *catafalco*, of uncertain origin; compare SCAFFOLD]

Catalan (ˈkætəˌlæn, -lən) *n* **1** a language of Catalonia, quite closely related to Spanish and Provençal, belonging to the Romance group of the Indo-European family. **2** a native or inhabitant of Catalonia. ◆ *adj* **3** denoting, relating to, or characteristic of Catalonia, its inhabitants, or their language.

catalase (ˈkætəˌleɪs) *n* an enzyme that catalyses the decomposition of hydrogen peroxide.

catalectic (ˌkætəˈlɛktɪk) *adj Prosody.* (of a line of verse) having an incomplete final foot. [C16: via Late Latin from Greek *katalēktikos* incomplete, from *katalēgein*, from *kata-* off + *lēgein* to stop]

catalepsy (ˈkætəˌlɛpsɪ) *n* a state of prolonged rigid posture, occurring for example in schizophrenia or in hypnotic trances. [C16: from Medieval Latin *catalēpsia*, variant of Late Latin *catalēpsis*, from Greek *katalēpsis*, literally: a seizing, from *katalambanein* to hold down, from *kata-* down + *lambanein* to grasp] ▸ ˌ**cataˈleptic** *adj*

Catalina Island (ˌkætəˈliːnə) *n* another name for **Santa Catalina.**

catalo (ˈkætəˌləʊ) *n, pl* **-loes** *or* **-los.** a variant spelling of **cattalo.**

catalogue *or U.S.* **catalog** (ˈkætəˌlɒg) *n* **1** a complete, usually alphabetical list of items, often with notes giving details. **2** a book, usually illustrated, containing details of items for sale, esp. as used by mail-order companies. **3** a list of all the books or resources of a library. **4** *U.S. and Canadian.* a publication issued by a university, college, etc., listing courses offered, regulations, services, etc. **5** *N.Z.* a list of wool lots prepared for auction. ◆ *vb* **-logues, -loguing, -logued** *or U.S.* **-logs, -loging, -loged. 6** to compile a catalogue of (a library). **7** to add (books, items, etc.) to an existing catalogue. [C15: from Late Latin *catalogus*, from Greek *katalogos*, from *katalegein* to list, from *kata-* completely + *legein* to collect] ▸ ˈ**cataˌloguer** *or* ˈ**cataˌloguist** *n*

catalogue raisonné (*French* katalɔg rɛzɔne) *n* a descriptive catalogue, esp. one covering works of art in an exhibition or collection.

Catalonia (ˌkætəˈləʊnɪə) *n* a region of NE Spain, with a strong separatist tradition: became an autonomous region with its own parliament in 1979; an important agricultural and industrial region, with many resorts. Pop.: 6 090 040 (1996 est.). Area: 31 929 sq. km (12 328 sq. miles). Catalan name: **Catalunya** (ˌkatəˈluːnɪə). Spanish name: **Cataluña** (kataˈluɲa).

catalpa (kəˈtælpə) *n* any bignoniaceous tree of the genus *Catalpa* of North America and Asia, having large leaves, bell-shaped whitish flowers, and long slender pods. [C18: New Latin, from Carolina Creek *kutuhlpa*, literally: winged head, referring to the appearance of the flowers]

catalyse *or U.S.* **catalyze** (ˈkætəˌlaɪz) *vb* (*tr*) to influence (a chemical reaction) by catalysis. ▸ ˈ**cataˌlyser** *or U.S.* ˈ**cataˌlyzer** *n*

catalysis (kəˈtælɪsɪs) *n, pl* **-ses** (-ˌsiːz). acceleration of a chemical reaction by the action of a catalyst. [C17: from New Latin, from Greek *katalusis*, from *kataluein* to dissolve] ▸ **catalytic** (ˌkætəˈlɪtɪk) *adj* ▸ ˌ**cataˈlytically** *adv*

catalyst (ˈkætəlɪst) *n* **1** a substance that increases the rate of a chemical reaction without itself suffering any permanent chemical change. Compare **inhibitor** (sense 2). **2** a person or thing that causes a change.

catalytic converter *n* a device using three-way catalysts to reduce the obnoxious and poisonous components of the products of combustion (mainly oxides of nitrogen, carbon monoxide, and unburnt hydrocarbons) from the exhausts of motor vehicles.

catalytic cracker *n* a unit in an oil refinery in which mineral oils with high boiling points are converted to fuels with lower boiling points by a catalytic process. Often shortened to **cat cracker.**

catamaran (ˌkætəməˈræn) *n* **1** a sailing, or sometimes motored, vessel with twin hulls held parallel by a rigid framework. **2** a primitive raft made of logs lashed together. **3** *Informal.* a quarrelsome woman. [C17: from Tamil *kattumaram* tied timber]

catamenia (ˌkætəˈmiːnɪə) *pl n Physiol.* another word for **menses.** [C18: from New Latin, from Greek *katamēnia* menses] ▸ ˌ**cataˈmenial** *adj*

catamite (ˈkætəˌmaɪt) *n* a boy kept for homosexual purposes. [C16: from Latin *Catamītus*, variant of *Ganymēdēs* GANYMEDE[1]]

catamount (ˈkætəˌmaunt) *or* **catamountain** *n* any of various medium-sized felines, such as the puma or lynx. [C17: short for *cat of the mountain*]

catananche (ˌkætəˈnæŋkɪ) *n* any of the hardy perennial genus *Catananche*, from S Europe; some, esp. *C. caerulea*, are grown for their blue-and-white flowers that can be dried as winter decoration: family *Compositae*. Also called **cupid's dart.** [from Greek *katanangkē* a spell (from their use in love potions)]

Catania (*Italian* kaˈtaːnja) *n* a port in E Sicily, near Mount Etna. Pop.: 341 623 (1996 est.).

Catanzaro (*Italian* katanˈdzaːro) *n* a city in S Italy, in Calabria. Pop.: 103 800 (1990).

cataphora (kəˈtæfərə) *n Grammar.* the use of a word such as a pronoun that has the same reference as a word used subsequently in the same discourse. Compare **anaphora.** [from CATA- + Greek *pherein* to bear] ▸ **cataphoric** (ˌkætəˈfɒrɪk) *adj*

cataphoresis (ˌkætəfəˈriːsɪs) *n* another name for **electrophoresis**. ▸ **cataphoretic** (ˌkætəfəˈrɛtɪk) *adj* ▸ ˌ**cataphoˈretically** *adv*

cataphyll (ˈkætəˌfɪl) *n* a simplified form of plant leaf, such as a scale leaf or cotyledon.

cataplasia (ˌkætəˈpleɪzɪə) *n* the degeneration of cells and tissues to a less highly developed form. ▸ **cataplastic** (ˌkætəˈplæstɪk) *adj*

cataplasm (ˈkætəˌplæzəm) *n Med.* another name for **poultice**. [C16: from Latin *cataplasma*, from Greek, from *kataplassein* to cover with a plaster, from *plassein* to shape]

cataplexy (ˈkætəˌplɛksɪ) *n* **1** sudden temporary paralysis, brought on by severe shock. **2** a state of complete absence of movement assumed by animals while shamming death. [C19: from Greek *kataplēxis* amazement, from *kataplēssein* to strike down (with amazement), confound, from *kata-* down + *plēssein* to strike] ▸ ˌ**cataˈplectic** *adj*

catapult (ˈkætəˌpʌlt) *n* **1** a Y-shaped implement with a loop of elastic fastened to the ends of the two prongs, used mainly by children for shooting small stones, etc. U.S. and Canadian name: **slingshot. 2** a heavy war engine used formerly for hurling stones, etc. **3** a device installed in warships to launch aircraft. ◆ *vb* **4** (*tr*) to shoot forth from or as if from a catapult. **5** (foll. by *over, into,* etc.) to move precipitately: *she was catapulted to stardom overnight.* [C16: from Latin *catapulta*, from Greek *katapeltēs*, from *kata-* down + *pallein* to hurl]

cataract (ˈkætəˌrækt) *n* **1** a large waterfall or rapids. **2** a deluge; downpour. **3** *Pathol.* **3a** partial or total opacity of the crystalline lens of the eye. **3b** the opaque area. [C15: from Latin *catarracta*, from Greek *katarrhaktēs*, from *katarassein* to dash down, from *arassein* to strike]

catarrh (kəˈtɑː) *n* inflammation of a mucous membrane with increased production of mucus, esp. affecting the nose and throat in the common cold. [C16: via French from Late Latin *catarrhus*, from Greek *katarrous*, from *katarrhein* to flow down, from *kata-* down + *rhein* to flow] ▸ **caˈtarrhal** *or* **caˈtarrhous** *adj*

catarrhine (ˈkætəˌraɪn) *adj* **1** (of apes and Old World monkeys) having the nostrils set close together and opening to the front of the face. **2** Also: **leptorrhine**. (of humans) having a thin or narrow nose. ◆ *n* **3** an animal or person with this characteristic. ◆ Compare **platyrrhine**. [C19: from New Latin *Catarrhina* (for sense 1), all ultimately from Greek *katarrhin* having a hooked nose, from *kata-* down + *rhis* nose]

catastrophe (kəˈtæstrəfɪ) *n* **1** a sudden, extensive, or notable disaster or misfortune. **2** the denouement of a play, esp. a classical tragedy. **3** a final decisive event, usually causing a disastrous end. **4** Also called: **cataclysm**. any sudden and violent change in the earth's surface caused by flooding, earthquake, or some other process. [C16: from Greek *katastrophē*, from *katastrephein* to overturn, from *strephein* to turn] ▸ **catastrophic** (ˌkætəˈstrɒfɪk) *adj* ▸ ˌ**cataˈstrophically** *adv*

catastrophe theory *n* **a** the mathematical theory that classifies surfaces according to their form. **b** the popular application of this theory to the explanation of abruptly changing phenomena, as by the discontinuity of a line on the topmost fold of a folded surface.

catastrophism (kəˈtæstrəˌfɪzəm) *n* **1** an old doctrine, now discarded, that the earth was created and has subsequently been shaped by sudden divine acts which have no logical connection with each other rather than by gradual evolutionary processes. **2** Also called: **neo-catastrophism**. a modern doctrine that the gradual evolutionary processes shaping the earth have been supplemented in the past by the effects of huge natural catastrophes. See **uniformitarianism**. Compare **gradualism** (sense 2). ▸ **caˈtastrophist** *n*

catatonia (ˌkætəˈtəʊnɪə) *n* a state of muscular rigidity and stupor, sometimes found in schizophrenia. [C20: New Latin, from German *Katatonie*, from CATA- + *-tonia*, from Greek *tonos* tension] ▸ **catatonic** (ˌkætəˈtɒnɪk) *adj, n*

Catawba (kəˈtɔːbə) *n* **1** (*pl* **-ba** *or* **-bas**) a member of a North American Indian people, formerly of South Carolina, now almost extinct. **2** their language, belonging to the Siouan family. **3** a cultivated variety of red North American grape, widely grown in the eastern U.S. **4** the wine made from these grapes.

catbird (ˈkætˌbɜːd) *n* **1** any of several North American songbirds of the family *Mimidae* (mockingbirds), esp. *Dumetella carolinensis*, whose call resembles the mewing of a cat. **2** any of several Australian bowerbirds of the genera *Ailuroedus* and *Scenopoeetes*, having a catlike call.

catboat (ˈkætˌbəʊt) *n* a sailing vessel with a single mast, set well forward and often unstayed, and a large sail, usually rigged with a gaff. Shortened form: **cat**.

cat brier *n* another name for **greenbrier**.

cat burglar *n* a burglar who enters buildings by climbing through upper windows, skylights, etc.

catcall (ˈkætˌkɔːl) *n* **1** a shrill whistle or cry expressing disapproval, as at a public meeting, etc. ◆ *vb* **2** to utter such a call (at); deride with catcalls. ▸ ˈ**catˌcaller** *n*

catch (kætʃ) *vb* **catches, catching, caught. 1** (*tr*) to take hold of so as to retain or restrain: *he caught the ball.* **2** (*tr*) to take, seize, or capture, esp. after pursuit. **3** (*tr*) to ensnare or deceive, as by trickery. **4** (*tr*) to surprise or detect in an act: *he caught the dog rifling the larder.* **5** (*tr*) to reach with a blow: *the stone caught him on the side of the head.* **6** (*tr*) to overtake or reach in time to board: *if we hurry we should catch the next bus.* **7** (*tr*) to see or hear; attend: *I didn't catch the Ibsen play.* **8** (*tr*) to be infected with: *to catch a cold.* **9** to hook or entangle or become hooked or entangled: *her dress caught on a nail.* **10** to fasten or be fastened with or as if with a latch or other device. **11** (*tr*) to attract or arrest: *she tried to catch his eye.* **12** (*tr*) to comprehend: *I didn't catch his meaning.* **13** (*tr*) to hear accurately: *I didn't catch what you said.* **14** (*tr*) to captivate or charm. **15** (*tr*) to perceive and reproduce accurately: *the painter managed to catch his model's beauty.* **16** (*tr*) to hold back or restrain: *he caught his breath in surprise.* **17** (*intr*) to become alight: *the fire won't catch.* **18** (*tr*) *Cricket.* to dismiss (a batsman) by intercepting and holding a ball struck by him before it touches the ground. **19** (*intr;* often foll. by *at*) **19a** to grasp or attempt to grasp. **19b** to take advantage (of), esp. eagerly: *he caught at the chance.* **20** (*intr; used passively*) *Informal.* to make pregnant. **21 catch it.** *Informal.* to be scolded or reprimanded. **22 catch oneself on.** *Slang.* to realize that one's actions are mistaken. ◆ *n* **23** the act of catching or grasping. **24** a device that catches and fastens, such as a latch. **25** anything that is caught, esp. something worth catching. **26** the amount or number caught. **27** *Informal.* a person regarded as an eligible matrimonial prospect. **28** a check or break in the voice. **29** a break in a mechanism. **30** *Informal.* **30a** a concealed, unexpected, or unforeseen drawback or handicap. **30b** (*as modifier*): *a catch question.* **31** a game in which a ball is thrown from one player to another. **32** *Cricket.* the catching of a ball struck by a batsman before it touches the ground, resulting in him being out. **33** *Music.* a type of round popular in the 17th, 18th, and 19th centuries, having a humorous text that is often indecent or bawdy and hard to articulate. See **round** (sense 31), **canon**[1] (sense 7). ◆ See also **catch on, catch out, catch up.** [C13 *cacchen* to pursue, from Old Northern French *cachier*, from Latin *captāre* to snatch, from *capere* to seize] ▸ ˈ**catchable** *adj*

catch-all *n* **a** something designed to cover a variety of situations or possibilities. **b** (*as modifier*): *a catch-all clause.*

catch-as-catch-can *n* **1** a style of wrestling in which trips, holds below the waist, etc., are allowed. ◆ *adj, adv* **2** *Chiefly U.S. and Canadian.* using any method or opportunity that comes to hand.

catch basin *n* the U.S. and Canadian name for **catch pit**.

catch crop *n* a quick-growing crop planted between two regular crops grown in consecutive seasons, or between two rows of regular crops in the same season.

catcher (ˈkætʃə) *n* **1** a person or thing that catches, esp. in a game or sport. **2** *Baseball.* a fielder who stands behind home plate and catches pitched balls not hit by the batter.

catchfly (ˈkætʃˌflaɪ) *n, pl* **-flies**. any of several caryophyllaceous plants of the genus *Silene* that have sticky calyxes and stems on which insects are sometimes trapped.

catching (ˈkætʃɪŋ) *adj* **1** infectious. **2** attractive; captivating.

catching pen *n Austral. and N.Z.* a pen adjacent to a shearer's stand containing the sheep ready for shearing.

catchment (ˈkætʃmənt) *n* **1** the act of catching or collecting water. **2** a structure in which water is collected. **3** the water so collected. **4** *Brit.* the intake of a school from one catchment area.

catchment area *n* **1** the area of land bounded by watersheds draining into a river, basin, or reservoir. Also called: **catchment basin, drainage area, drainage basin. 2** the area from which people are allocated to a particular school, hospital, etc.

Catchment board *n N.Z.* a public body concerned with the conservation and organization of water supply from a catchment area.

catch on *vb* (*intr, adv*) *Informal.* **1** to become popular or fashionable. **2** to grasp mentally; understand.

catch out *vb* (*tr, adv*) *Informal, chiefly Brit.* to trap (a person), esp. in an error or doing something reprehensible.

catchpenny (ˈkætʃˌpɛnɪ) *adj* **1** (*prenominal*) designed to have instant appeal, esp. in order to sell quickly and easily without regard for quality: *catchpenny ornaments.* ◆ *n, pl* **-nies**. **2** an item or commodity that is cheap and showy.

catch phrase *n* a well-known frequently used phrase, esp. one associated with a particular group, etc.

catch pit *n* a pit in a drainage system in which matter is collected that might otherwise block a sewer. U.S. and Canadian name: **catch basin**.

catch points *pl n* railway points designed to derail a train running back in the wrong direction to prevent collision with a following train.

catchpole *or* **catchpoll** (ˈkætʃˌpəʊl) *n* (in medieval England) a sheriff's officer who arrested debtors. [Old English *cæcepol*, from Medieval Latin *cacepollus* tax-gatherer, literally: chicken-chaser, from *cace-* CATCH + *pollus* (from Latin *pullus* chick)]

catch-22 *n* **1** a situation in which a person is frustrated by a paradoxical rule or set of circumstances that preclude any attempt to escape from them. **2** a situation in which any move that a person can make will lead to trouble. [C20: from the title of a novel (1961) by J. Heller]

catchup (ˈkætʃəp, ˈkɛtʃ-) *n* a variant spelling (esp. U.S.) of **ketchup**.

catch up *vb* (*adv*) **1** (*tr*) to seize and take up (something) quickly. **2** (when *intr,* often foll. by *with*) to reach or pass (someone or something), after following: *he soon caught him up.* **3** (*intr;* usually foll. by *on* or *with*) to make up for lost ground or deal with a backlog (in some specified task or activity). **4** (*tr; often passive*) to absorb or involve: *she was caught up in her reading.* **5** (*tr*) to raise by or as if by fastening: *the hem of her dress was caught up with ribbons.*

catchwater drain (ˈkætʃˌwɔːtə) *n* a channel cut along the edge of high ground to catch surface water from it and divert it away from low-lying ground.

catchweight (ˈkætʃˌweɪt) *adj Wrestling.* of or relating to a contest in which normal weight categories have been waived by agreement.

catchword (ˈkætʃˌwɜːd) *n* **1** a word or phrase made temporarily popular, esp. by a political campaign; slogan. **2** a word printed as a running head in a reference book. **3** *Theatre.* an actor's cue to speak or enter. **4** the first word of a printed or typewritten page repeated at the bottom of the page preceding.

catchy (ˈkætʃɪ) *adj* **catchier, catchiest. 1** (of a tune, etc.) pleasant and easily remembered or imitated. **2** tricky or deceptive: *a catchy question.* **3** irregular: *a catchy breeze.* ▸ ˈ**catchiness** *n*

cat cracker *n* an informal name for **catalytic cracker**.

cat door *n* a small door or flap in a larger door through which a cat can pass.

catechetical (ˌkætɪˈkɛtɪkᵊl) *or* **catechetic** *adj* of or relating to teaching by question and answer. ▸ ˌ**cateˈchetically** *adv*

catechin (ˈkætəkɪn) *n* a soluble yellow solid substance found in catechu and mahogany wood and used in tanning and dyeing. Formula: $C_{15}H_{14}O_6$. [C19: from CATECHU + -IN]

catechism ('kætɪˌkɪzəm) *n* **1** instruction by a series of questions and answers, esp. a book containing such instruction on the religious doctrine of a Christian Church. **2** rigorous and persistent questioning, as in a test or interview. [C16: from Late Latin *catēchismus,* ultimately from Greek *katēkhizein* to CATECHIZE] ► **ˌcate'chismal** *adj*

catechize *or* **catechise** ('kætɪˌkaɪz) *vb* (*tr*) **1** to teach or examine by means of questions and answers. **2** to give oral instruction in Christianity, esp. by using a catechism. **3** to put questions to (someone). [C15: from Late Latin *catēchizāre,* from Greek *katēkhizein,* from *katēkhein* to instruct orally, literally: to shout down, from *kata-* down + *ēkhein* to sound] ► **'catechist, 'cateˌchizer** *or* **'cateˌchiser** *n* ► **ˌcate'chistic** *or* **ˌcate'chistical** *adj* ► **ˌcate'chistically** *adv* ► **ˌcatechi'zation** *or* **ˌcatechi'sation** *n*

catechol ('kætɪˌtʃɒl, -ˌkɒl) *n* a colourless crystalline phenol found in resins and lignins; 1,2-dihydroxybenzene. It is used as a photographic developer. Formula: $C_6H_4(OH)_2$. Also called: **pyrocatechol.** [C20: from CATECHU + -OL[1]]

catecholamine (ˌkætə'kɒləˌmiːn) *n* any of a group of hormones that are catechol derivatives, esp. adrenaline and noradrenaline. [C20: from CATECHU + -OL[1] + AMINE]

catechu ('kætɪˌtʃuː), **cachou,** *or* **cutch** *n* a water-soluble astringent resinous substance obtained from any of certain tropical plants, esp. the leguminous tree *Acacia catechu* of S Asia, and used in medicine, tanning, and dyeing. See also **gambier.** [C17: probably from Malay *kachu,* of Dravidian origin]

catechumen (ˌkætɪ'kjuːmɛn) *n Christianity.* a person, esp. in the early Church, undergoing instruction prior to baptism. [C15: via Old French, from Late Latin, from Greek *katēkhoumenos* one being instructed verbally, from *katēkhein;* see CATECHIZE] ► **ˌcate'chumenal** *or* **catechumenical** (ˌkætəkju'mɛnɪkᵊl) *adj* ► **ˌcate'chumenate** *n* ► **ˌcate'chumenism** *n*

categorial (ˌkætɪ'gɔːrɪəl) *adj* **1** of or relating to a category. **2** *Logic.* (of a statement) consisting of a subject, S, and a predicate, P, each of which denotes a class, and having one of the following forms: *all S are P* (universal affirmative); *some S are P* (particular affirmative); *some S are not P* (particular negative); *no S are P* (universal negative). See **syllogism.**

categorial grammar *n* a theory that characterizes syntactic categories in terms of functions between classes of expressions. The basic classes are names (*N*) and sentences (*S*). Intransitive verbs are symbols for functions which take a name and yield a sentence (written: *S/N*), adverbs form compound verbs from verbs (for example, *run fast*) and so are (*S/N*)/(*S/N*), etc.

categorical (ˌkætɪ'gɒrɪkᵊl) *or* **categoric** *adj* **1** unqualified; positive; unconditional: *a categorical statement.* **2** relating to or included in a category. **3** *Logic.* another word for **categorial.** ► **ˌcate'gorically** *adv* ► **ˌcate'goricalness** *n*

categorical imperative *n* (in the ethics of Kant) the unconditional moral principle that one's behaviour should accord with universalizable maxims which respect persons as ends in themselves; the obligation to do one's duty for its own sake and not in pursuit of further ends. Compare **hypothetical imperative.**

categorize *or* **categorise** ('kætɪgəˌraɪz) *vb* (*tr*) to place in a category; classify. ► **ˌcategori'zation** *or* **ˌcategori'sation** *n*

category ('kætɪgərɪ) *n, pl* **-ries. 1** a class or group of things, people, etc., possessing some quality or qualities in common; a division in a system of classification. **2** *Metaphysics.* any one of the most basic classes into which objects and concepts can be analysed. **3a** (in the philosophy of Aristotle) any one of ten most fundamental modes of being, such as quantity, quality, and substance. **3b** (in the philosophy of Kant) one of twelve concepts required by human beings to interpret the empirical world. **3c** any set of objects, concepts, or expressions distinguished from others within some logical or linguistic theory by the intelligibility of a specific set of statements concerning them. See also **category mistake.** [C15: from Late Latin *catēgoria,* from Greek *katēgoria,* from *katēgorein* to accuse, assert]

Category A *adj* **1** (of a prisoner) regarded as highly dangerous and therefore requiring constant observation and maximum security. **2** (of a prison or prison unit) designed for such prisoners.

category management *n Marketing.* the management of a range of related products in a way designed to increase sales of all of the products.

category mistake *n Philosophy, logic.* a sentence that says of something in one category what can only intelligibly be said of something in another, as when speaking of the mind located in space.

catena (kə'tiːnə) *n, pl* **-nae** (-niː). a connected series, esp. of patristic comments on the Bible. [C17: from Latin: chain]

catenaccio (*Italian* kate'nattʃo) *n Football.* an extremely defensive style of play. [C20: from Latin *catena* chain]

catenane ('kætɪˌneɪn) *n* a type of chemical compound in which the molecules have two or more rings that are interlocked like the links of a chain. [C20: from Latin *catena* chain + -ANE]

catenary (kə'tiːnərɪ) *n, pl* **-ries. 1** the curve assumed by a heavy uniform flexible cord hanging freely from two points. When symmetrical about the *y*-axis and intersecting it at $y = a$, the equation is $y = a \cosh x/a$. **2** the hanging cable between pylons along a railway track, from which the trolley wire is suspended. ◆ *adj also* **catenarian** (ˌkætɪ'nɛərɪən). **3** of, resembling, relating to, or constructed using a catenary or suspended chain. [C18: from Latin *catēnārius* relating to a chain]

catenate ('kætɪˌneɪt) *vb* **1** *Biology.* to arrange or be arranged in a series of chains or rings. ◆ *adj* **2** another word for **catenulate.** [C17: from Latin *catēnāre* to bind with chains] ► **ˌcate'nation** *n*

catenoid ('kætəˌnɔɪd) *n* the geometrical surface generated by rotating a catenary about its axis.

catenulate (kə'tɛnjʊˌleɪt, -lɪt) *adj* (of certain spores) formed in a row or chain. [C19: from Latin *catēnula,* diminutive of *catēna* chain]

cater ('keɪtə) *vb* **1** (*intr;* foll. by *for* or *to*) to provide what is required or desired (for): *to cater for a need; cater to your tastes.* **2** (when *intr,* foll. by *for*) to provide food, services, etc. (for): *we cater for parties; to cater a banquet.* [C16: from earlier *catour* purchaser, variant of *acatour,* from Anglo-Norman *acater* to buy, ultimately related to Latin *acceptāre* to ACCEPT]

cateran ('kætərən) *n* (formerly) a member of a band of brigands and marauders in the Scottish highlands. [C14: probably from Scottish Gaelic *ceathairneach* robber, plunderer]

cater-cornered ('kætəˌkɔːnəd) *adj, adv U.S. and Canadian informal.* diagonally placed; diagonal. Also: **catty-cornered, kitty-cornered.** [C16 *cater,* from dialect *cater* (adv) diagonally, from obsolete *cater* (n) four-spot of dice, from Old French *quatre* four, from Latin *quattuor*]

cater-cousin ('keɪtəˌkʌzᵊn) *n Archaic.* a close friend. [C16: perhaps from obsolete *cater* caterer; for sense, compare FOSTER, as in *foster brother,* etc.]

caterer ('keɪtərə) *n* a person who caters, esp. one who as a profession provides food for large social events, etc.

catering ('keɪtərɪŋ) *n* **1** the trade of a professional caterer. **2** the food, etc., provided at a function by a caterer.

caterpillar ('kætəˌpɪlə) *n* **1** the wormlike larva of butterflies and moths, having numerous pairs of legs and powerful biting jaws. It may be brightly coloured, hairy, or spiny. **2** *Trademark.* an endless track, driven by sprockets or wheels, used to propel a heavy vehicle and enable it to cross soft or uneven ground. **3** *Trademark.* a vehicle, such as a tractor, tank, bulldozer, etc., driven by such tracks. [C15 *catyrpel,* probably from Old Northern French *catepelose,* literally: hairy cat]

caterpillar hunter *n* any of various carabid beetles of the genus *Calosoma,* of Europe and North America, which prey on the larvae of moths and butterflies.

caterwaul ('kætəˌwɔːl) *vb* (*intr*) **1** to make a yowling noise, as a cat on heat. ◆ *n* **2** a shriek or yell made by or sounding like a cat on heat. [C14: of imitative origin] ► **'caterˌwauler** *n*

cates (keɪts) *pl n* (*sometimes sing*) *Archaic.* choice dainty food; delicacies. [C15: variant of *acates* purchases, from Old Northern French *acater* to buy, from Vulgar Latin *accaptāre* (unattested); ultimately related to Latin *acceptāre* to ACCEPT]

Catesby ('keɪtzbɪ) *n* **Robert.** 1573–1605, English conspirator, leader of the Gunpowder Plot (1605): killed while resisting arrest.

catfall ('kætˌfɔːl) *n Nautical.* the line used in a cat.

catfish ('kætˌfɪʃ) *n, pl* **-fish** *or* **-fishes. 1** any of numerous mainly freshwater teleost fishes having whisker-like barbels around the mouth, esp. the silurids of Europe and Asia and the horned pouts of North America. **2** another name for **wolffish.**

catgut ('kætˌgʌt) *n* a strong cord made from the dried intestines of sheep and other animals that is used for stringing certain musical instruments and sports rackets, and, when sterilized, as surgical ligatures. Often shortened to **gut.**

Cath. *abbrev. for:* **1** Cathedral. **2** Catholic.

cath- *prefix* a variant of **cata-** before an aspirate: *cathode.*

Cathar ('kæθə) *or* **Catharist** ('kæθərɪst) *n, pl* **-ars, -ari** (-ərɪ), *or* **-arists.** a member of a Christian sect in Provence in the 12th and 13th centuries who believed the material world was evil and only the spiritual was good. [from Medieval Latin *Cathari,* from Greek *katharoi* the pure] ► **'Catharˌism** *n*

catharsis (kə'θɑːsɪs) *n, pl* **-ses. 1** (in Aristotelian literary criticism) the purging or purification of the emotions through the evocation of pity and fear, as in tragedy. **2** *Psychoanal.* the bringing of repressed ideas or experiences into consciousness, thus relieving tensions. See also **abreaction. 3** purgation, esp. of the bowels. [C19: New Latin, from Greek *katharsis,* from *kathairein* to purge, purify]

cathartic (kə'θɑːtɪk) *adj* **1** purgative. **2** effecting catharsis. ◆ *n* **3** a purgative drug or agent. ► **ca'thartically** *adv*

Cathay (kæ'θeɪ) *n* a literary or archaic name for **China.** [C14: from Medieval Latin *Cataya,* of Turkic origin]

cathead ('kætˌhɛd) *n* a fitting at the bow of a vessel for securing the anchor when raised.

cathectic (kə'θɛktɪk) *adj* of or relating to cathexis.

cathedra (kə'θiːdrə) *n* **1** a bishop's throne. **2** the office or rank of a bishop. **3** See **ex cathedra.** [from Latin: chair]

cathedral (kə'θiːdrəl) *n* **a** the principal church of a diocese, containing the bishop's official throne. **b** (*as modifier*): *a cathedral city; cathedral clergy.* [C13: from Late Latin (*ecclesia*) *cathedrālis* cathedral (church), from *cathedra* bishop's throne, from Greek *kathedra* seat]

cathepsin (kə'θɛpsɪn) *n* a proteolytic enzyme responsible for the autolysis of cells after death. [C20: from Greek *kathepsein* to boil down, soften]

Cather ('kæðə) *n* **Willa (Sibert).** 1873–1947, U.S. novelist, whose works include *O Pioneers!* (1913) and *My Ántonia* (1918).

Catherine ('kæθrɪn) *n* **Saint.** died 307 A.D., legendary Christian martyr of Alexandria, who was tortured on a spiked wheel and beheaded.

Catherine I *n* ?1684–1727, second wife of Peter the Great, whom she succeeded as empress of Russia (1725–27).

Catherine II *n* known as *Catherine the Great.* 1729–96, empress of Russia (1762–96), during whose reign Russia extended her boundaries at the expense of Turkey, Sweden, and Poland: she was a patron of literature and the arts.

Catherine de' Medici *or* **de Médicis** *n* 1519–89, queen of Henry II of France; mother of Francis II, Charles IX, and Henry III of France; regent of France (1560–74). She was largely responsible for the massacre of Protestants on Saint Bartholomew's Day (1572).

Catherine of Aragon *n* 1485–1536, first wife of Henry VIII of England and mother of Mary I. The annulment of Henry's marriage to her (1533) against papal authority marked an initial stage in the English Reformation.

Catherine of Braganza *n* 1638–1705, wife of Charles II of England, daughter of John IV of Portugal.

Catherine of Siena *n* **Saint.** 1347–80, Italian mystic and ascetic; patron saint of the Dominican order. Feast day: April 29.

Catherine wheel *n* **1** Also called: **pinwheel.** a type of firework consisting of a powder-filled spiral tube, mounted with a pin through its centre. When lit it rotates quickly, producing a display of sparks and coloured flame. **2** a circular window having ribs radiating from the centre. [C16: named after St CATHERINE of Alexandria]

catheter ('kæθɪtə) *n Med.* a long slender flexible tube for inserting into a natural bodily cavity or passage for introducing or withdrawing fluid. [C17: from Late Latin, from Greek *kathetēr,* from *kathienai* to send down, insert]

catheterize *or* **catheterise** ('kæθɪtəˌraɪz) *vb* (*tr*) to insert a catheter into. ▶ **ˌcatheteri'zation** *or* **ˌcatheteri'sation** *n*

cathexis (kə'θɛksɪs) *n, pl* **-thexes** (-'θɛksiːz). *Psychoanal.* concentration of psychic energy on a single goal. [C20: from New Latin, from Greek *kathexis,* from *katekhein* to hold fast, intended to render German *Besetzung* a taking possession of]

cathode ('kæθəʊd) *n* **1** the negative electrode in an electrolytic cell; the electrode by which electrons enter a device from an external circuit. **2** the negatively charged electron source in an electronic valve. **3** the positive terminal of a primary cell. ◆ Compare **anode.** [C19: from Greek *kathodos* a descent, from *kata-* down + *hodos* way] ▶ **cathodal** (kæ'θəʊdᵊl), **cathodic** (kæ'θɒdɪk, -'θəʊ-), *or* **ca'thodical** *adj*

cathode rays *pl n* a stream of electrons emitted from the surface of a cathode in a valve.

cathode-ray tube *n* a valve in which a beam of high-energy electrons is focused onto a fluorescent screen to give a visible spot of light. The device, with appropriate deflection equipment, is used in television receivers, visual display units, oscilloscopes, etc. Abbrev.: **CRT.**

cathodic protection *n Metallurgy.* a technique for protecting metal structures, such as steel ships and pipelines, from electrolytic corrosion by making the structure the cathode in a cell, either by applying an electromotive force directly or by putting it into contact with a more electropositive metal. See also **sacrificial anode.**

cathodoluminescence (ˌkæθədəʊˌluːmɪ'nɛsəns) *n Physics.* luminescence caused by irradiation with electrons (cathode rays).

cat hole *n* one of a pair of holes in the after part of a ship through which hawsers are passed for steadying the ship or heaving astern.

catholic ('kæθəlɪk, 'kæθlɪk) *adj* **1** universal; relating to all men; all-inclusive. **2** comprehensive in interests, tastes, etc.; broad-minded; liberal. [C14: from Latin *catholicus,* from Greek *katholikos* universal, from *katholou* in general, from *kata-* according to + *holos* whole] ▶ **catholically** *or* **catholicly** (kə'θɒlɪklɪ) *adv*

Catholic ('kæθəlɪk, 'kæθlɪk) *adj Christianity.* **1** denoting or relating to the entire body of Christians, esp. to the Church before separation into the Greek or Eastern and Latin or Western Churches. **2** denoting or relating to the Latin or Western Church after this separation. **3** denoting or relating to the Roman Catholic Church. **4** denoting or relating to any church, belief, etc., that claims continuity with or originates in the ancient undivided Church. ◆ *n* **5** a member of any of the Churches regarded as Catholic, esp. the Roman Catholic Church.

Catholic Church *n* **1** short for **Roman Catholic Church. 2** any of several Churches claiming to have maintained continuity with the ancient and undivided Church.

Catholic Epistles *pl n New Testament.* the epistles of James, I and II Peter, I John, and Jude, which were addressed to the universal Church rather than to an individual or a particular church.

Catholicism (kə'θɒlɪˌsɪzəm) *n* **1** short for **Roman Catholicism. 2** the beliefs, practices, etc., of any Catholic Church.

catholicity (ˌkæθə'lɪsɪtɪ) *n* **1** a wide range of interests, tastes, etc.; liberality. **2** universality; comprehensiveness.

Catholicity (ˌkæθə'lɪsɪtɪ) *n* the beliefs, etc., of the Catholic Church.

catholicize *or* **catholicise** (kə'θɒlɪˌsaɪz) *vb* **1** to make or become catholic. **2** (*often cap.*) to convert to or become converted to Catholicism. ▶ **caˌtholici'zation** *or* **caˌtholici'sation** *n*

catholicon (kə'θɒlɪkən) *n* a remedy for all ills; panacea. [C15: from Medieval Latin; see CATHOLIC]

cathouse ('kætˌhaʊs) *n U.S. and Canadian.* a slang word for **brothel.**

Catiline ('kætɪˌlaɪn) *n* Latin name *Lucius Sergius Catilina.* ?108–62 B.C., Roman politician: organized an unsuccessful conspiracy against Cicero (63–62). ▶ **Catilinarian** (ˌkætɪlɪ'nɛərɪən) *adj*

cation ('kætaɪən) *n* a positively charged ion; an ion that is attracted to the cathode during electrolysis. Compare **anion.** [C19: from CATA- + ION] ▶ **cationic** (ˌkætaɪ'ɒnɪk) *adj*

cationic detergent *n* a type of detergent in which the active part of the molecule is a positive ion (cation). Cationic detergents are usually quaternary ammonium salts and often also have bactericidal properties.

catkin ('kætkɪn) *n* an inflorescence consisting of a hanging spike of much reduced flowers of either sex: occurs in birch, hazel, etc. Also called: **ament.** [C16: from obsolete Dutch *katteken* kitten, identical in meaning with French *chaton,* German *Kätzchen*]

catling ('kætlɪŋ) *n* **1** a long double-edged surgical knife for amputations. **2** *Rare.* catgut or a string made from it. **3** an archaic word for **kitten.** [C17: from CAT[1] + -LING[1]]

cat litter *n* absorbent material, often in a granular form, that is used to line a receptacle in which a domestic cat can urinate and defecate indoors.

catmint ('kætˌmɪnt) *n* a Eurasian plant, *Nepeta cataria,* having spikes of purple-spotted white flowers and scented leaves of which cats are fond: family *Labiatae* (labiates). Also called: **catnip.**

catnap ('kætˌnæp) *n* **1** a short sleep or doze. ◆ *vb* **-naps, -napping, -napped. 2** (*intr*) to sleep or doze for a short time or intermittently.

catnip ('kætˌnɪp) *n* another name for **catmint.**

Cato ('keɪtəʊ) *n* **1 Marcus Porcius** ('mɑːkəs'pɔːʃɪəs), known as *Cato the Elder* or *the Censor.* 234–149 B.C., Roman statesman and writer, noted for his relentless opposition to Carthage. **2** his great-grandson, **Marcus Porcius,** known as *Cato the Younger* or *Uticensis.* 95–46 B.C., Roman statesman, general, and Stoic philosopher; opponent of Catiline and Caesar.

catolyte ('kætəʊˌlaɪt) *or* **catholyte** ('kæθəʊˌlaɪt) *n Electronics.* the part of the electrolyte that surrounds the cathode in an electrolytic cell.

cat-o'-mountain *n* another name for **catamount.**

cat-o'-nine-tails *n, pl* **-tails.** a rope whip consisting of nine knotted thongs, used formerly to flog prisoners. Often shortened to **cat.**

catoptrics (kə'tɒptrɪks) *n* (*functioning as sing*) the branch of optics concerned with reflection, esp. the formation of images by mirrors. [C18: from Greek *katoptrikos,* from *katoptron* mirror] ▶ **ca'toptric** *or* **ca'toptrical** *adj*

cat rig *n* the rig of a catboat. ▶ **'catˌrigged** *adj*

CATS (kæts) *acronym for* credit accumulation transfer scheme: a scheme enabling school-leavers and others to acquire transferable certificates for relevant work experience and study towards a recognized qualification.

CAT scanner (kæt) *n* former name for **CT scanner.** [C20: *(C)omputerized (A)xial (T)omography*]

cat's cradle *n* a game played by making intricate patterns with a loop of string between the fingers.

cat's-ear *n* any of various European plants of the genus *Hypochoeris,* esp. *H. radicata,* having dandelion-like heads of yellow flowers: family *Compositae* (composites).

cat's-eye *n* any of a group of gemstones, esp. a greenish-yellow variety of chrysoberyl, that reflect a streak of light when cut in a rounded unfaceted shape.

Catseye ('kætsˌaɪ) *n Trademark, Brit.* a glass reflector set into a small fixture, placed at intervals along roads to indicate traffic lanes at night.

cat's-foot *n, pl* **-feet.** a European plant, *Antennaria dioica,* with whitish woolly leaves and heads of typically white flowers: family *Compositae* (composites). Also called: **mountain everlasting.**

Catskill Mountains ('kætskɪl) *pl n* a mountain range in SE New York State: resort. Highest peak: Slide Mountain, 1261 m (4204 ft.). Also called: **Catskills.**

cat's-paw *n* **1** a person used by another as a tool; dupe. **2** *Nautical.* a hitch in the form of two loops, or eyes, in the bight of a line, used for attaching it to a hook. **3** a pattern of ripples on the surface of water caused by a light wind. [(sense 1) C18: so called from the tale of the monkey who used a cat's paw to draw chestnuts out of a fire]

cat's-tail *n* **1** another name for **reed mace** (sense 1). **2** another name for **catkin.**

catsuit ('kætˌsuːt) *n* a one-piece usually close-fitting trouser suit.

catsup ('kætsəp) *n* a variant (esp. U.S.) of **ketchup.**

cat's whisker *n* **1** a pointed wire formerly used to make contact with the crystal in a crystal radio receiver. **2** any wire used to make contact with a semiconductor.

cat's whiskers *or* **cat's pyjamas** *n* **the.** *Slang.* a person or thing that is excellent or superior.

cattalo *or* **catalo** ('kætəˌləʊ) *n, pl* **-loes** *or* **-los.** a hardy breed of cattle developed by crossing the American bison with domestic cattle. [C20: from CATT(LE + BUFF)ALO]

Cattegat ('kætɪˌgæt) *n* a variant spelling of **Kattegat.**

Catterick ('kætərɪk) *n* a village in N England, in North Yorkshire on the River Swale: site of an important army garrison and a racecourse.

cattery ('kætərɪ) *n, pl* **-teries.** a place where cats are bred or looked after.

cattle ('kætᵊl) *n* (*functioning as pl*) **1** bovid mammals of the tribe *Bovini* (bovines), esp. those of the genus *Bos.* **2** Also called: **domestic cattle.** any domesticated bovine mammals, esp. those of the species *Bos taurus* (domestic ox). ◆ Related adj: **bovine.** [C13: from Old Northern French *catel,* Old French *chatel* CHATTEL]

cattle-cake *n* concentrated food for cattle in the form of cakes.

cattle-grid *n* a grid of metal bars covering a hollow or hole dug in a roadway, intended to prevent the passage of livestock while allowing vehicles, etc., to pass unhindered.

cattleman ('kætᵊlmən) *n, pl* **-men. 1** a person who breeds, rears, or tends cattle. **2** *Chiefly U.S. and Canadian.* a person who owns or rears cattle on a large scale, usually for beef, esp. the owner of a cattle ranch.

cattle market *n Brit. slang.* a situation or place, such as a beauty contest or nightclub, in which women are felt to be, or feel themselves to be, on display and judged solely by their appearance.

cattle plague *n* another name for **rinderpest.**

cattle prod *n* a hand-held electrified rod with low voltage used to control cattle.

cattle-stop *n* the N.Z. name for **cattle-grid.**

cattle truck *n* a railway wagon designed for carrying livestock. U.S. and Canadian equivalent: **stock car.**

cattleya ('kætlɪə) *n* any tropical American orchid of the genus *Cattleya,* cultivated for their purplish-pink or white showy flowers. [C19: New Latin, named after William *Cattley* (died 1832), English botanist]

cat-train *or* **cat-swing** *n Canadian.* a train of sleds, cabooses, etc., pulled by a caterpillar tractor, used chiefly in the north during winter to transport freight.

catty[1] ('kætɪ) *or* **cattish** *adj* **-tier, -tiest. 1** *Informal.* spiteful: *a catty remark.* **2**

of or resembling a cat. ▸ 'cattily *or* 'cattishly *adv* ▸ 'cattiness *or* 'cattishness *n*

catty[2] *or* **cattie** ('kætɪ) *n, pl* **-ties.** a unit of weight, used esp. in China, equal to about one and a half pounds or about 0.67 kilogram. [C16: from Malay *kati*]

catty-cornered *adj* a variant of **cater-cornered.**

Catullus (kə'tʌləs) *n* **Gaius Valerius** ('gaɪəs və'lɪərɪəs). ?84–?54 B.C., Roman lyric poet, noted particularly for his love poems. ▸ **Catullan** (kə'tʌlən) *adj*

CATV *abbrev. for* community antenna television.

catwalk ('kæt,wɔːk) *n* **1** a narrow ramp extending from the stage into the audience in a theatre, nightclub, etc., esp. as used by models in a fashion show. **2** a narrow pathway over the stage of a theatre, along a bridge, etc.

catworm ('kæt,wɜːm) *n* an active carnivorous polychaete worm, *Nephthys hombergi,* that is about 10cm (4in) long, having a pearly sheen to its body: often dug for bait. Also called: **white worm, white cat.**

Cauca (*Spanish* 'kauka) *n* a river in W Colombia, rising in the northwest and flowing north to the Magdalena River. Length: about 1350 km (840 miles).

Caucasia (kɔː'keɪzɪə, -ʒə) *n* a region in SW Russia, Georgia, Armenia, and Azerbaijan, between the Caspian Sea and the Black Sea: contains the Caucasus Mountains, dividing it into Ciscaucasia in the north and Transcaucasia in the south; one of the most complex ethnic areas in the world, with over 50 different peoples. Also called: the **Caucasus.**

Caucasian (kɔː'keɪzɪən, -ʒən) *or* **Caucasic** (kɔː'keɪzɪk) *adj* **1** another word for **Caucasoid. 2** of or relating to the Caucasus. ◆ *n* **3** a member of the Caucasoid race; a white man. **4** a native or inhabitant of Caucasia. **5** any of three possibly related families of languages spoken in the Caucasus: **North-West Caucasian,** including Circassian and Abkhaz, **North-East Caucasian,** including Avar, and **South Caucasian,** including Georgian.

Caucasoid ('kɔːkə,zɔɪd) *adj* **1** denoting, relating to, or belonging to the light-complexioned racial group of mankind, which includes the peoples indigenous to Europe, N Africa, SW Asia, and the Indian subcontinent and their descendants in other parts of the world. ◆ *n* **2** a member of this racial group.

Caucasus ('kɔːkəsəs) *n* **the. 1** a mountain range in SW Russia, running along the N borders of Georgia and Azerbaijan, between the Black Sea and the Caspian Sea: mostly over 2700 m (9000 ft.). Highest peak: Mount Elbrus, 5642 m (18 510 ft.). Also called: **Caucasus Mountains. 2** another name for **Caucasia.**

Cauchy ('kauʃɪ; *French* koʃi) *n* **Augustin Louis** (ogystɛ̃ lwi), Baron Cauchy. 1789–1857, French mathematician, noted for his work on the theory of functions and the wave theory of light.

caucus ('kɔːkəs) *n, pl* **-cuses. 1** *Chiefly U.S. and Canadian.* **1a** a closed meeting of the members of one party in a legislative chamber, etc., to coordinate policy, choose candidates, etc. **1b** such a bloc of politicians: *the Democratic caucus in Congress.* **2** *Chiefly U.S.* **2a** a group of leading politicians of one party. **2b** a meeting of such a group. **3** *Chiefly U.S.* a local meeting of party members. **4** *Brit.* a group or faction within a larger group, esp. a political party, who discuss tactics, choose candidates, etc. **5** *Austral.* a meeting of the members of the Federal parliamentary Labor Party. **6** *N.Z.* a formal meeting of all Members of Parliament belonging to one political party. ◆ *vb* **7** (*intr*) to hold a caucus. [C18: probably of Algonquian origin; related to *caucauasu* adviser]

cauda ('kɔːdə) *n* **1** *Zoology.* the area behind the anus of an animal; tail. **2** *Anatomy.* **2a** any tail-like structure. **2b** the posterior part of an organ. [Latin: tail]

caudad ('kɔːdæd) *adv Anatomy.* towards the tail or posterior part. Compare **cephalad.** [C19: from CAUDA + -AD[2]]

caudal ('kɔːdᵊl) *adj* **1** *Anatomy.* of or towards the posterior part of the body. **2** *Zoology.* relating to, resembling, or in the position of the tail. [C17: from New Latin *caudālis,* from CAUDA] ▸ **'caudally** *adv*

caudal fin *n* the tail fin of fishes and some other aquatic vertebrates, used for propulsion during locomotion.

caudate ('kɔːdeɪt) *or* **caudated** *adj* having a tail or a tail-like appendage. [C17: from New Latin *caudātus,* from CAUDA] ▸ **cau'dation** *n*

caudex ('kɔːdeks) *n, pl* **-dices** (-dɪ,siːz) *or* **-dexes. 1** the thickened persistent stem base of some herbaceous perennial plants. **2** the woody stem of palms and tree ferns. [C19: from Latin]

caudillo (kɔː'diːljəʊ; *Spanish* kau'ðiʎo) *n, pl* **-los** (-jəuz; *Spanish* -ʎos). (in Spanish-speaking countries) a military or political leader. [Spanish, from Late Latin *capitellum,* diminutive of Latin *caput* head]

Caudine Forks ('kɔːdaɪn) *pl n* a narrow pass in the Apennines, in S Italy, between Capua and Benevento: scene of the defeat of the Romans by the Samnites (321 B.C.).

caudle ('kɔːdᵊl) *n* a hot spiced wine drink made with gruel, formerly used medicinally. [C13: from Old Northern French *caudel,* from Medieval Latin *caldellum,* from Latin *calidus* warm]

caught (kɔːt) *vb* the past tense and past participle of **catch.**

caul (kɔːl) *n Anatomy.* **1** a portion of the amniotic sac sometimes covering a child's head at birth. **2** a large fold of peritoneum hanging from the stomach across the intestines; the large omentum. [C13: from Old French *cale,* back formation from *calotte* close-fitting cap, of Germanic origin]

cauld (kɔːld) *adj, n* a Scot. word for **cold.**

cauldrife ('kɔːldrɪf) *adj Scot.* **1** susceptible to cold; chilly. **2** lifeless. [C18: from CAULD + RIFE]

cauldron *or* **caldron** ('kɔːldrən) *n* a large pot used for boiling, esp. one with handles. [C13: from earlier *cauderon,* from Anglo-French, from Latin *caldārium* hot bath, from *calidus* warm]

caulescent (kɔː'lesᵊnt) *adj* having a stem clearly visible above the ground. [C18: from Latin *caulis* stalk]

caulicle ('kɔːlɪkᵊl) *n Botany.* a small stalk or stem. [C17: from Latin *cauliculus,* from *caulis* stem]

cauliflory ('kɔːlɪ,flɔːrɪ) *n Botany.* the production of flowers on the trunk, branches, etc., of a woody plant, as opposed to the ends of the twigs. [C20: from Latin *caulis* stem + *-flory,* from *flōs* flower] ▸ **,cauli'florous** *adj*

cauliflower ('kɒlɪ,flauə) *n* **1** a variety of cabbage, *Brassica oleracea botrytis,* having a large edible head of crowded white flowers on a very short thick stem. **2** the flower head of this plant, used as a vegetable. [C16: from Italian *caoli fiori,* literally: cabbage flowers, from *cavolo* cabbage (from Latin *caulis*) + *fiore* flower (from Latin *flōs*)]

cauliflower cheese *n* a dish of cauliflower with a cheese sauce, eaten hot.

cauliflower ear *n* permanent swelling and distortion of the external ear as the result of ruptures of the blood vessels: usually caused by blows received in boxing. Also called: **boxer's ear.** Technical name: **aural haematoma.**

cauline ('kɔːlɪn, -laɪn) *adj* relating to or growing from a plant stem. [C18: from New Latin *caulīnus,* from Latin *caulis* stem]

caulis ('kɔːlɪs) *n, pl* **-les** (-liːz). *Rare.* the main stem of a plant. [C16: from Latin]

caulk *or* **calk** (kɔːk) *vb* **1** to stop up (cracks, crevices, etc.) with a filler. **2** *Nautical.* to pack (the seams) between the planks of the bottom of (a vessel) with waterproof material to prevent leakage. [C15: from Old Northern French *cauquer* to press down, from Latin *calcāre* to trample, from *calx* heel] ▸ **'caulker** *or* **'calker** *n*

caus. *abbrev. for* causative.

causal ('kɔːzᵊl) *adj* **1** acting as or being a cause. **2** stating, involving, or implying a cause: *the causal part of the argument.* **3** *Philosophy.* (of a theory) explaining a phenomenon or analysing a concept in terms of some causal relation. ▸ **'causally** *adv*

causalgia (kɔː'zældʒɪə) *n Pathol.* a burning sensation along the course of a peripheral nerve together with local changes in the appearance of the skin. [C19: from New Latin, from Greek *kausos* fever + -ALGIA]

causality (kɔː'zælɪtɪ) *n, pl* **-ties. 1a** the relationship of cause and effect. **1b** the principle that nothing can happen without being caused. **2** causal agency or quality.

causation (kɔː'zeɪʃən) *n* **1** the act or fact of causing; the production of an effect by a cause. **2** the relationship of cause and effect. ▸ **cau'sational** *adj*

causative ('kɔːzətɪv) *adj* **1** *Grammar.* relating to a form or class of verbs, such as *persuade,* that express causation. **2** (*often postpositive* and foll. by *of*) producing an effect. ◆ *n* **3** the causative form or class of verbs. ▸ **'causatively** *adv* ▸ **'causativeness** *n*

cause (kɔːz) *n* **1** a person, thing, event, state, or action that produces an effect. **2** grounds for action; motive; justification: *she had good cause to shout like that.* **3** the ideals, etc., of a group or movement: *the Communist cause.* **4** the welfare or interests of a person or group in a dispute: *they fought for the miners' cause.* **5** a matter of widespread concern or importance: *the cause of public health.* **6a** a ground for legal action; matter giving rise to a lawsuit. **6b** the lawsuit itself. **7** (in the philosophy of Aristotle) any of four requirements for a thing's coming to be, namely material (material cause), its nature (formal cause), an agent (efficient cause), and a purpose (final cause). **8 make common cause with.** to join with (a person, group, etc.) for a common objective. ◆ *vb* **9** (*tr*) to be the cause of; bring about; precipitate; be the reason for. [C13: from Latin *causa* cause, reason, motive] ▸ **'causable** *adj* ▸ **,causa'bility** *n* ▸ **'causeless** *adj* ▸ **'causer** *n*

cause célèbre ('kɔːz sə'lebrə, -'leb; *French* koz selɛbrə) *n, pl* **causes célèbres** ('kɔːz sə'lebrəz, -'leb; 'kɔːzɪz sə'lebrə, -'lebz; *French* koz selɛbrə). a famous lawsuit, trial, or controversy. [C19: from French: famous case]

cause list *n Brit.* a list of cases awaiting trial.

causerie ('kəuzərɪ; *French* kozri) *n* an informal talk or conversational piece of writing. [C19: from French, from *causer* to chat]

causeway ('kɔːz,weɪ) *n* **1** a raised path or road crossing water, marshland, sand, etc. **2** a paved footpath. [C15 *cauciwey* (from *cauci* + WAY); *cauci* paved road, from Medieval Latin (*via*) *calciāta, calciātus* paved with limestone, from Latin *calx* limestone]

causey ('kɔːzɪ) *n* **1** an archaic or dialect word for **causeway. 2** *Scot.* a cobbled street. **3** *Scot.* a cobblestone.

caustic ('kɔːstɪk) *adj* **1** capable of burning or corroding by chemical action: *caustic soda.* **2** sarcastic; cutting: *a caustic reply.* **3** of, relating to, or denoting light that is reflected or refracted by a curved surface. ◆ *n* **4** Also called: **caustic surface.** a surface that envelopes the light rays reflected or refracted by a curved surface. **5** Also called: **caustic curve.** a curve formed by the intersection of a caustic surface with a plane. **6** *Chem.* a caustic substance, esp. an alkali. [C14: from Latin *causticus,* from Greek *kaustikos,* from *kaiein* to burn] ▸ **'caustical** *adj* ▸ **'caustically** *adv* ▸ **'causticness** *or* **causticity** (kɔː'stɪsɪtɪ) *n*

caustic potash *n* another name for **potassium hydroxide.**

caustic soda *n* another name for **sodium hydroxide.**

cauterant ('kɔːtərənt) *adj* **1** caustic; cauterizing. ◆ *n* **2** another name for **cautery** (sense 2).

cauterize *or* **cauterise** ('kɔːtə,raɪz) *vb* (*tr*) (esp. in the treatment of a wound) to burn or sear (body tissue) with a hot iron or caustic agent. [C14: from Old French *cauteriser,* from Late Latin *cautērizāre,* from *cautērium* branding iron, from Greek *kautērion,* from *kaiein* to burn] ▸ **,cauteri'zation** *or* **,cauteri'sation** *n*

cautery ('kɔːtərɪ) *n, pl* **-teries. 1** the coagulation of blood or destruction of body tissue by cauterizing. **2** Also called: **cauterant.** an instrument or chemical agent for cauterizing. [C14: from Old French *cautère,* from Latin *cautērium;* see CAUTERIZE]

caution ('kɔːʃən) *n* **1** care, forethought, or prudence, esp. in the face of danger; wariness. **2** something intended or serving as a warning; admonition. **3** *Law, chiefly Brit.* a formal warning given to a person suspected or accused of an offence that his words will be taken down and may be used in evidence. **4** a notice entered on the register of title to land that prevents a proprietor from disposing of his land without a notice to the person who entered the caution. **5** *Informal.* an amusing or surprising person or thing: *she's a real caution.* ◆ *vb* **6** (*tr*) to urge or warn (a person) to be careful. **7** (*tr*) *Law, chiefly Brit.* to give a caution to (a person). **8** (*intr*) to warn, urge, or advise: *he cautioned against optimism.* [C13: from Old French, from Latin *cautiō,* from *cavēre* to beware] ▸ **'cautioner** *n*

cautionary ('kɔːʃənərɪ) *adj* serving as a warning; intended to warn: *a cautionary tale.*

caution money *n Chiefly Brit.* a sum of money deposited as security for good conduct, against possible debts, etc.

cautious ('kɔːʃəs) *adj* showing or having caution; wary; prudent. ▸ **'cautiously** *adv* ▸ **'cautiousness** *n*

Cauvery *or* **Kaveri** ('kɔːvərɪ) *n* a river in S India, rising in the Western Ghats and flowing southeast to the Bay of Bengal. Length: 765 km (475 miles).

CAV *or* **Cur. adv vult** *Law. abbrev. for* Curia advisari vult: used in English law to indicate that a court has decided to consider a case privately before giving judgment, as when time is needed to consider arguments or submissions made to it. Compare **avizandum.** [Medieval Latin: the court wishes to consider]

Cav. *or* **cav.** *abbrev. for* cavalry.

Cavaco Silva ('kavaku 'silvə) *n* **Aníbal** (a'nibal). born 1939, Portuguese statesman; prime minister of Portugal (1985–95).

Cavafy (kə'vɑːfɪ) *n* **Constantine.** Greek name *Kavafis.* 1863–1933, Greek poet of Alexandria in Egypt.

cavalcade (ˌkævəl'keɪd) *n* **1** a procession of people on horseback, in cars, etc. **2** any procession: *a cavalcade of guests.* [C16: from French, from Italian *cavalcata,* from *cavalcare* to ride on horseback, from Late Latin *caballicāre,* from *caballus* horse]

Cavalcanti (*Italian* kaval'kanti) *n* **Guido** ('gwiːdo). ?1255–1300, Italian poet, noted for his love poems.

cavalier (ˌkævə'lɪə) *adj* **1** showing haughty disregard; offhand. ◆ *n* **2** a gallant or courtly gentleman, esp. one acting as a lady's escort. **3** *Archaic.* a horseman, esp. one who is armed. [C16: from Italian *cavaliere,* from Old Provençal *cavalier,* from Late Latin *caballārius* rider, from *caballus* horse, of obscure origin] ▸ **ˌcava'lierly** *adv*

Cavalier (ˌkævə'lɪə) *n* a supporter of Charles I during the English Civil War. Compare **Roundhead.**

cavalier King Charles spaniel *n* See **King Charles spaniel.**

Cavalier poets *pl n* a group of mid-17th century English lyric poets, mostly courtiers of Charles I. Chief among them were Robert Herrick, Thomas Carew, Sir John Suckling, and Richard Lovelace.

cavalla (kə'vælə) *or* **cavally** *n, pl* **-la, -las,** *or* **-lies.** any of various tropical carangid fishes, such as *Gnathanodon speciosus* (golden cavalla). [C19: from Spanish *caballa,* from Late Latin, feminine of *caballus* horse]

Cavallini (*Italian* kaval'liːni) *n* **Pietro** ('pjɛːtro). ?1250–?1330, Italian fresco painter and mosaicist. His works include the mosaics of the *Life of the Virgin* in Santa Maria, Trastevere, Rome.

cavalry ('kævəlrɪ) *n, pl* **-ries. 1** (esp. formerly) the part of an army composed of mounted troops. **2** the armoured element of a modern army. ◆ **3** (*as modifier*): *a cavalry unit; a cavalry charge.* [C16: from French *cavallerie,* from Italian *cavalleria,* from *cavaliere* horseman; see CAVALIER] ▸ **'cavalryman** *n*

cavalry twill *n* a strong woollen twill fabric used for trousers, etc.

Cavan ('kævᵊn) *n* **1** a county of N Republic of Ireland: hilly, with many small lakes and bogs. County town: Cavan. Pop.: 53 000 (1996). Area: 1890 sq. km (730 sq. miles). **2** a market town in N Republic of Ireland, county town of Co. Cavan. Pop.: 4500 (latest est.).

cavatina (ˌkævə'tiːnə) *n, pl* **-ne** (-nɪ). **1** a solo song resembling a simple aria. **2** an instrumental composition reminiscent of this. [C19: from Italian]

cave[1] (keɪv) *n* **1** an underground hollow with access from the ground surface or from the sea, often found in limestone areas and on rocky coastlines. **2** *Brit. history.* a secession or a group seceding from a political party on some issue. See **Adullamite. 3** (*modifier*) living in caves. ◆ *vb* **4** (*tr*) to hollow out. ◆ See also **cave in, caving.** [C13: from Old French, from Latin *cava,* plural of *cavum* cavity, from *cavus* hollow]

cave[2] ('keɪvɪ) *Brit. school slang.* ◆ *n* **1** guard or lookout (esp. in the phrase **keep cave**). ◆ *sentence substitute.* **2** watch out! [from Latin *cavē!* beware!]

caveat ('keɪvɪˌæt, 'kæv-) *n* **1** *Law.* a formal notice requesting the court or officer to refrain from taking some specified action without giving prior notice to the person lodging the caveat. **2** a warning; caution. [C16: from Latin, literally: let him beware]

caveat emptor ('ɛmptɔː) *n* the principle that the buyer must bear the risk for the quality of goods purchased unless they are covered by the seller's warranty. [Latin: let the buyer beware]

caveator ('keɪvɪˌeɪtə, 'kæv-) *n Law.* a person who enters a caveat.

cavefish ('keɪvˌfɪʃ) *n, pl* **-fish** *or* **-fishes.** any of various small freshwater cyprinodont fishes of the genera *Amblyopsis, Chologaster,* etc., living in subterranean and other waters in S North America. See also **blindfish.**

cave in *vb* (*intr, adv*) **1** to collapse; subside. **2** *Informal.* to yield completely, esp. under pressure. ◆ *n* **cave-in. 3** the sudden collapse of a roof, piece of ground, etc., into a hollow beneath it; subsidence. **4** the site of such a collapse, as at a mine or tunnel.

cavel ('keɪvᵊl) *n N.Z.* a drawing of lots among miners for an easy and profitable place at the coalface. [C19: from English dialect *cavel* to cast lots, apportion]

Cavell ('kævᵊl) *n* **Edith Louisa.** 1865–1915, English nurse: executed by the Germans in World War I for helping Allied prisoners to escape.

caveman ('keɪvˌmæn) *n, pl* **-men. 1** a man of the Palaeolithic age; cave dweller. **2** *Informal and facetious.* a man who is primitive or brutal in behaviour, etc.

cavendish ('kævəndɪʃ) *n* tobacco that has been sweetened and pressed into moulds to form bars. [C19: perhaps from the name of the first maker]

Cavendish ('kævəndɪʃ) *n* **Henry.** 1731–1810, British physicist and chemist: recognized hydrogen, determined the composition of water, and calculated the density of the earth by an experiment named after him.

cavern ('kævᵊn) *n* **1** a cave, esp. when large and formed by underground water, or a large chamber in a cave. ◆ *vb* (*tr*) **2** to shut in or as if in a cavern. **3** to hollow out. [C14: from Old French *caverne,* from Latin *caverna,* from *cavus* hollow; see CAVE[1]]

cavernous ('kævənəs) *adj* **1** suggestive of a cavern in vastness, darkness, etc.: *cavernous hungry eyes.* **2** filled with small cavities; porous. **3** (of rocks) containing caverns or cavities. ▸ **'cavernously** *adv*

cavesson ('kævɪsən) *n* a kind of hard noseband, used (esp. formerly) in breaking a horse in. [C16: via French from Italian *cavezzone,* from *cavezza* halter, ultimately related to Latin *caput* head]

cavetto (kə'vɛtəʊ; *Italian* ka'vetto) *n, pl* **-ti** (-tɪ; *Italian* -ti). *Architect.* a concave moulding, shaped to a quarter circle in cross section. [C17: from Italian, from *cavo* hollow, from Latin *cavus*]

caviar *or* **caviare** ('kævɪˌɑː, ˌkævɪ'ɑː) *n* the salted roe of sturgeon, esp. the beluga, usually served as an hors d'oeuvre. [C16: from earlier *cavery,* from Old Italian *caviari,* plural of *caviaro* caviar, from Turkish *havyār*]

CAVIAR ('kævɪˌɑː) *n acronym for* Cinema and Video Industry Audience Research.

cavicorn ('kævɪˌkɔːn) *adj* (of sheep, goats, etc.) having hollow horns as distinct from the solid antlers of deer. [C19: from Latin *cavus* hollow + *cornū* horn]

cavie ('keɪvɪ) *n Scot.* a hen coop. [C18: via Dutch or Flemish *kavie,* from Latin *cavea* cavity]

cavil ('kævɪl) *vb* **-ils, -illing, -illed** *or U.S.* **-ils, -iling, -iled. 1** (*intr;* foll. by *at* or *about*) to raise annoying petty objections; quibble; carp. ◆ *n* **2** a captious trifling objection. [C16: from Old French *caviller,* from Latin *cavillārī* to jeer, from *cavilla* raillery] ▸ **'caviller** *n* ▸ **'cavilling** *adj*

caving ('keɪvɪŋ) *n* the sport of climbing in and exploring caves. ▸ **'caver** *n*

cavitation (ˌkævɪ'teɪʃən) *n* **1** the formation of vapour- or gas-filled cavities in a flowing liquid when tensile stress is superimposed on the ambient pressure. **2** the formation of cavities in a structure.

Cavite (kə'viːtɪ, -teɪ) *n* a port in the N Philippines, in S Luzon on Manila Bay: U.S. naval base. Pop.: 103 422 (1994 est.).

cavity ('kævɪtɪ) *n, pl* **-ties. 1** a hollow space; hole. **2** *Dentistry.* a soft decayed area on a tooth. See **caries. 3** any empty or hollow space within the body: *the oral cavity.* **4** *Electronics.* See **cavity resonator.** [C16: from French *cavité,* from Late Latin *cavitās,* from Latin *cavus* hollow]

cavity block *n* a precast concrete block that contains a cavity or cavities.

cavity resonator *n Electronics.* a conducting surface enclosing a space in which an oscillating electromagnetic field can be maintained, the dimensions of the cavity determining the resonant frequency of the oscillations. It is used in microwave devices, such as the klystron, for frequencies exceeding 300 megahertz. Also called: **resonant cavity, rhumbatron.**

cavity wall *n* a wall that consists of two separate walls, joined by wall-ties, with an airspace between them.

cavo-relievo *or* **cavo-rilievo** (ˌkɑːvəʊrɪ'liːvəʊ, ˌkeɪ-) *n, pl* **-vos** *or* **-vi** (-vɪ). a relief sculpture in which the highest point in the carving is below the level of the original surface. [Italian, literally: hollow relief]

cavort (kə'vɔːt) *vb* (*intr*) to prance; caper. [C19: perhaps from CURVET] ▸ **ca'vorter** *n*

Cavour (*Italian* ka'vur) *n* Conte **Camillo Benso di** (ka'millo 'bɛnzo di). 1810–61, Italian statesman and premier of Piedmont-Sardinia (1852–59; 1860–61): a leader of the movement for the unification of Italy.

cavy ('keɪvɪ) *n, pl* **-vies.** any small South American hystricomorph rodent of the family *Caviidae,* esp. any of the genus *Cavia,* having a thickset body and very small tail. See also **guinea pig.** [C18: from New Latin *Cavia,* from Galibi *cabiai*]

caw (kɔː) *n* **1** the cry of a crow, rook, or raven. ◆ *vb* **2** (*intr*) to make this cry. [C16: of imitative origin]

Cawdrey ('kɔːdrɪ) *n* **Robert.** 16th–17th-century English schoolmaster and lexicographer: compiled the first English dictionary (*A Table Alphabeticall*) in 1604.

Cawley ('kɔːlɪ) *n* **Evonne** (née *Goolagong*). born 1951, Australian tennis player: Wimbledon champion 1971 and 1980; Australian champion 1974–76.

Cawnpore (ˌkɔːn'pɔː) *or* **Cawnpur** (ˌkɔːn'pʊə) *n* the former name of **Kanpur.**

CAWU *abbrev. for* Clerical and Administrative Workers' Union.

Caxton[1] ('kækstən) *n* **1** a book printed by William Caxton. **2** a style of type, imitating the Gothic, that Caxton used in his books.

Caxton[2] ('kækstən) *n* **William.** ?1422–91, English printer and translator: published, in Bruges, the first book printed in English (1475) and established the first printing press in England (1477).

cay (keɪ, kiː) *n* a small low island or bank composed of sand and coral fragments, esp. in the Caribbean area. Also called: **key.** [C18: from Spanish *cayo,* probably from Old French *quai* QUAY]

Cayenne (keɪ'ɛn) *n* the capital of French Guiana, on an island at the mouth of the Cayenne River: French penal settlement from 1854 to 1938. Pop.: 41 659 (1990).

cayenne pepper (keɪ'ɛn) *n* a very hot condiment, bright red in colour, made from the dried seeds and pods of various capsicums. Often shortened to **cayenne.** Also called: **red pepper.** [C18: ultimately from Tupi *quiynha*]

Cayes (keɪ; *French* kaj) *n* short for **Les Cayes.**

Cayley ('keɪlɪ) *n* **1 Arthur.** 1821–93, British mathematician, who invented matrices. **2** Sir **George.** 1773–1857, British engineer and pioneer of aerial navigation. He constructed the first man-carrying glider (1853) and invented the caterpillar tractor.

cayman *or* **caiman** ('keɪmən) *n, pl* **-mans.** any tropical American crocodilian of the genus *Caiman* and related genera, similar to alligators but with a more heavily armoured belly: family *Alligatoridae* (alligators, etc.). **[C16:** from Spanish *caimán,* from Carib *cayman,* probably of African origin**]**

Cayman Islands ('keɪmən) *pl n* three coral islands in the Caribbean Sea northwest of Jamaica: a dependency of Jamaica until 1962, now a UK Overseas Territory. Capital: Georgetown. Pop.: 31 930 (1994). Area: about 260 sq. km (100 sq. miles).

Cayuga (keɪ'juːgə, kaɪ-) *n* **1** (*pl* **-gas** *or* **-ga**) a member of a North American Indian people (one of the Iroquois peoples) formerly living around Cayuga Lake. **2** the language of this people, belonging to the Iroquoian family.

cayuse ('kaɪuːs) *n Western U.S. and Canadian.* a small American Indian pony used by cowboys. **[C19:** from a Chinookan language**]**

cb *abbrev. for* centre of buoyancy (of a boat, etc.).

Cb *the chemical symbol for* columbium.

CB *abbrev. for:* **1** Citizens' Band. **2** Companion of the (Order of the) Bath (an English title). **3** County Borough.

CBC *abbrev. for* Canadian Broadcasting Corporation.

CBD *or* **cbd** *abbrev. for:* **1** cash before delivery. **2** central business district.

CBE *abbrev. for* Commander of the (Order of the) British Empire.

CBI *abbrev. for* Confederation of British Industry.

CBR (of weapons or warfare) *abbrev. for* chemical, bacteriological, and radiation.

CBS *abbrev. for* Columbia Broadcasting System.

CBSO *abbrev. for* City of Birmingham Symphony Orchestra.

CBT *abbrev. for* computer-based training.

cc *or* **c.c.** *abbrev. for:* **1** carbon copy *or* copies. **2** cubic centimetre(s).

CC *abbrev. for:* **1** City Council. **2** County Council. **3** Cricket Club.

cc. *abbrev. for* chapters.

c.c.c. *abbrev. for* cwmni cyfyngedig cyhoeddus; a public limited company in Wales.

CCD *Electronics. abbrev. for* charge-coupled device.

CCF (in Britain) *abbrev. for* Combined Cadet Force.

C clef *n Music.* a symbol (𝄡), placed at the beginning of the staff, establishing middle C as being on its centre line. See **alto clef, soprano clef, tenor clef.**

CCTV *abbrev. for* closed-circuit television.

CCW *abbrev. for* Curriculum Council for Wales.

cd 1 *abbrev. for* cash discount. ◆ **2** *symbol for* candela.

Cd 1 (in Britain) *abbrev. for* command (paper). ◆ **2** *the chemical symbol for* cadmium.

CD *abbrev. for:* **1** Civil Defence (Corps). **2** compact disc. **3** Corps Diplomatique (Diplomatic Corps). **4** Conference on Disarmament: a United Nations standing conference, held in Geneva, to negotiate a global ban on chemical weapons.

c/d *Book-keeping. abbrev. for* carried down.

CDE *abbrev. for* compact disc erasable: a compact disc that can be used to record and rerecord. Compare **CDR.**

cdf *Statistics. abbrev. for* cumulative distribution function.

Cdn *abbrev. for* Canadian.

CDN *international car registration for* Canada.

cDNA *abbrev. for* complementary DNA.

CD player *n* a device for playing compact discs. In full: **compact-disc player.**

Cdr *Military. abbrev. for* Commander.

CDR *abbrev. for* compact disc recordable: a compact disc that can be used to record only once. Compare **CDE.**

Cdre *abbrev. for* Commodore.

CD-ROM (-rɒm) *abbrev. for* compact disc read-only memory; a compact disc used with a computer system as a read-only optical disk.

CDT *abbrev. for:* **1** *U.S. and Canadian.* Central Daylight Time. **2** Craft, Design, and Technology: a subject on the GCSE syllabus, related to the National Curriculum.

CDU *abbrev. for* Christlich-Demokratische Union: a German (until 1990 West German) political party. **[**German: Christian Democratic Union**]**

CDV *abbrev. for:* **1** CD-video. **2** compact video disc.

CD-video *n* a compact-disc player that, when connected to a television and hi-fi, produces high-quality stereo sound and synchronized pictures from a disc resembling a compact audio disc. In full: **compact-disc video.**

Ce *the chemical symbol for* cerium.

CE *abbrev. for:* **1** chief engineer. **2** Church of England. **3** civil engineer. **4** Common Entrance. **5** Common Era.

ceanothus (ˌsiːə'nəʊθəs) *n* any shrub of the North American rhamnaceous genus *Ceanothus:* grown for their ornamental, often blue, flower clusters. **[C19:** New Latin, from Greek *keanōthos* a kind of thistle**]**

Ceará (*Portuguese* sia'ra) *n* **1** a state of NE Brazil: sandy coastal plain, rising to a high plateau. Capital: Fortaleza. Pop.: 6 714 200 (1995 est.). Area: 150 630 sq. km (58 746 sq. miles). **2** another name for **Fortaleza.**

cease (siːs) *vb* **1** (when *tr,* may take a gerund or an infinitive as object) to bring or come to an end; desist from; stop. ◆ *n* **2 without cease.** without stopping; incessantly. **[C14:** from Old French *cesser,* from Latin *cessāre,* frequentative of *cēdere* to yield, CEDE**]**

cease-fire *Chiefly military.* ◆ *n* **1** a period of truce, esp. one that is temporary and a preliminary step to establishing a more permanent peace on agreed terms. ◆ *interj, n* **2** the order to stop firing.

ceaseless ('siːslɪs) *adj* without stop or pause; incessant. ▸ **'ceaselessly** *adv*

Ceauşescu (tʃaʊ'ʃeskuː) *n* **Nicolae** (ˌnɪkɒ'laɪ). 1918–89, Romanian statesman; chairman of the state council (1967–89) and president of Romania (1974–89): deposed and executed.

Cebú (sɪ'buː) *n* **1** an island in the central Philippines. Pop.: 2 091 602 (1980). Area: 4422 sq. km (1707 sq. miles). **2** a port in the Philippines, on E Cebú island. Pop.: 688 196 (1994 est.).

Čechy ('tʃexi) *n* the Czech name for **Bohemia.**

Cecil ('sɛsᵊl, 'sɪs-) *n* **1** Lord **David.** 1902–86, English literary critic and biographer. **2 Robert.** See (3rd Marquess of) **Salisbury. 3 William.** See (William Cecil) **Burghley.**

Cecilia (sɪ'siːljə) *n* **Saint.** died ?230 A.D., Roman martyr; patron saint of music. Feast day: Nov. 22.

cecity ('siːsɪtɪ) *n* a rare word for **blindness. [C16:** from Latin *caecitās,* from *caecus* blind**]**

cecropia moth (sɪ'krəʊpɪə) *n* a large North American saturniid moth, *Hyalophora* (or *Samia*) *cecropia,* with brightly coloured wings and feathery antennae. **[C19:** New Latin, from Latin *Cecropius* belonging to CECROPS**]**

Cecrops ('siːkrɒps) *n* (in ancient Greek tradition) the first king of Attica, represented as half-human, half-dragon.

cecum ('siːkəm) *n, pl* **-ca** (-kə). *U.S.* a variant spelling of **caecum.** ▸ **'cecal** *adj*

cedar ('siːdə) *n* **1** any Old World coniferous tree of the genus *Cedrus,* having spreading branches, needle-like evergreen leaves, and erect barrel-shaped cones: family *Pinaceae.* See also **cedar of Lebanon, deodar. 2** any of various other conifers, such as the red cedars and white cedars. **3** the wood of any of these trees. **4** any of certain other plants, such as the Spanish cedar. ◆ *adj* **5** made of the wood of a cedar tree. **[C13:** from Old French *cedre,* from Latin *cedrus,* from Greek *kedros***]**

cedar of Lebanon *n* a cedar, *Cedrus libani,* of SW Asia with level spreading branches and fragrant wood.

Cedar Rapids *n* a city in the U.S., in E Iowa. Pop.: 113 482 (1996 est.).

cede (siːd) *vb* **1** (when *intr,* often foll. by *to*) to transfer, make over, or surrender (something, esp. territory or legal rights): *the lands were ceded by treaty.* **2** (*tr*) to allow or concede (a point in an argument, etc.). **[C17:** from Latin *cēdere* to yield, give way**]** ▸ **'ceder** *n*

cedi ('seɪdɪ) *n, pl* **-di.** the standard monetary unit of Ghana, divided into 100 pesewas.

cedilla (sɪ'dɪlə) *n* a character (¸) placed underneath a *c* before *a, o,* or *u,* esp. in French, Portuguese, or Catalan, denoting that it is to be pronounced (s), not (k). The same character is used in the scripts of other languages, as in Turkish under *s.* **[C16:** from Spanish: little *z,* from *ceda* zed, from Late Latin *zeta;* a small *z* was originally written after *c* in Spanish, to indicate a sibilant**]**

Ceefax ('siːˌfæks) *n Trademark.* the BBC Teletext service. See **Teletext.**

CEGB *Brit. abbrev. for* Central Electricity Generating Board.

ceiba ('seɪbə) *n* **1** any bombacaceous tropical tree of the genus *Ceiba,* such as the silk-cotton tree. **2** silk cotton; kapok. **[C19:** from New Latin, from Spanish, of Arawak origin**]**

ceil (siːl) *vb* **1** (*tr*) to line (a ceiling) with plaster, boarding, etc. **2** (*tr*) to provide with a ceiling. **[C15** *celen,* perhaps back formation from CEILING**]**

ceilidh ('keɪlɪ) *n* (esp. in Scotland and Ireland) an informal social gathering with folk music, singing, dancing, and storytelling. **[C19:** from Gaelic**]**

ceiling ('siːlɪŋ) *n* **1** the inner upper surface of a room. **2a** an upper limit, such as one set by regulation on prices or wages. **2b** (*as modifier*): *ceiling prices.* **3** the upper altitude to which an aircraft can climb measured under specified conditions. See also **service ceiling, absolute ceiling. 4** *Meteorol.* the highest level in the atmosphere from which the earth's surface is visible at a particular time, usually the base of a cloud layer. **5** a wooden or metal surface fixed to the interior frames of a vessel for rigidity. **[C14:** of uncertain origin**]**

ceilometer (siː'lɒmɪtə) *n* a device for determining the cloud ceiling, esp. by means of a reflected light beam. **[C20:** from CEILING + -METER**]**

cel *or* **cell** (sɛl) *n* short for **celluloid** (senses 2b, c).

Cela (*Spanish* 'θela) *n* **Camilo José** (ka'milo xo'se). born 1916, Spanish novelist and essayist. His works include *The Family of Pascual Duarte* (1942), *La Colmena* (1951), and *La Cruz de San Andres* (1994). Nobel prize for literature 1989.

celadon ('sɛləˌdɒn) *n* **1** a type of porcelain having a greyish-green glaze: mainly Chinese. **2** a pale greyish-green colour, sometimes somewhat yellow. **[C18:** from French, from the name of the shepherd hero of *L'Astrée* (1610), a romance by Honoré d'Urfé**]**

Celaeno (se'liːnəʊ) *n Greek myth.* one of the Pleiades.

Celan ('sɛlæn) *n* **Paul,** real name *Paul Antschel.* 1920–70, Romanian Jewish poet, writing in German, whose work reflects the experience of Nazi persecution.

celandine ('sɛlənˌdaɪn) *n* either of two unrelated plants, *Chelidonium majus* (see **greater celandine**) or *Ranunculus ficaria* (see **lesser celandine**). **[C13:** earlier *celydon,* from Latin *chelīdonia* (the plant), from *chelīdonius* of the swallow, from Greek *khelidōn* swallow; the plant's season was believed to parallel the migration of swallows**]**

Celaya (*Spanish* θe'laja) *n* a city in central Mexico, in Guanajuato state: market town, famous for its sweetmeats; textile-manufacturing. Pop.: 214 856 (1990).

-cele *n combining form.* tumour or hernia: *hydrocele.* **[**from Greek *kēlē* tumour**]**

celeb (sɪ'lɛb) *n Informal.* a celebrity.

Celebes ('sɛlɪbiːz, se'liːbɪz) *n* the English name for **Sulawesi.**

Celebes Sea *n* the part of the Pacific Ocean between Sulawesi, Borneo, and Mindanao.

celebrant ('sɛlɪbrənt) *n* **1** a person participating in a religious ceremony. **2** *Christianity.* an officiating priest, esp. at the Eucharist.

celebrate ('sɛlɪˌbreɪt) *vb* **1** to rejoice in or have special festivities to mark (a happy day, event, etc.). **2** (*tr*) to observe (a birthday, anniversary, etc.): *she celebrates her ninetieth birthday next month.* **3** (*tr*) to perform (a solemn or religious ceremony), esp. to officiate at (Mass). **4** (*tr*) to praise publicly; proclaim. **[C15:** from Latin *celebrāre,* from *celeber* numerous, thronged, renowned**]**

► ˌceleˈbration *n* ► ˈcelebrative *adj* ► ˈceleˌbrator *n* ► ˈceleˌbratory *adj*

celebrated (ˈsɛlɪˌbreɪtɪd) *adj (usually prenominal)* famous: *a celebrated pianist; a celebrated trial.*

celebrity (sɪˈlɛbrɪtɪ) *n, pl* **-ties.** **1** a famous person: *a show-business celebrity.* **2** fame or notoriety.

celeriac (sɪˈlɛrɪˌæk) *n* a variety of celery, *Apium graveolens rapaceum,* with a large turnip-like root, used as a vegetable. **[C18:** from CELERY + *-ac,* of unexplained origin**]**

celerity (sɪˈlɛrɪtɪ) *n* rapidity; swiftness; speed. **[C15:** from Old French *celerite,* from Latin *celeritās,* from *celer* swift**]**

celery (ˈsɛlərɪ) *n* **1** an umbelliferous Eurasian plant, *Apium graveolens dulce,* whose blanched leafstalks are used in salads or cooked as a vegetable. See also **celeriac. 2 wild celery.** a related and similar plant, *Apium graveolens.* **[C17:** from French *céleri,* from Italian (Lombardy) dialect *selleri* (plural), from Greek *selinon* parsley**]**

celery pine *n* a New Zealand gymnosperm tree, *Phyllocladus trichomanoides,* with celerylike shoots and useful wood: family *Phyllocladaceae.*

celesta (sɪˈlɛstə) *or* **celeste** (sɪˈlɛst) *n Music.* a keyboard percussion instrument consisting of a set of steel plates of graduated length that are struck with key-operated hammers. The tone is an ethereal tinkling sound. Range: four octaves upwards from middle C. **[C19:** from French, Latinized variant of *céleste* heavenly**]**

celestial (sɪˈlɛstɪəl) *adj* **1** heavenly; divine; spiritual: *celestial peace.* **2** of or relating to the sky: *celestial bodies.* **[C14:** from Medieval Latin *cēlestiālis,* from Latin *caelestis,* from *caelum* heaven**]** ► ceˈlestially *adv*

Celestial Empire *n* an archaic or literary name for the **Chinese Empire.**

celestial equator *n* the great circle lying on the celestial sphere the plane of which is perpendicular to the line joining the north and south celestial poles. Also called: **equinoctial, equinoctial circle.**

celestial globe *n* a spherical model of the celestial sphere showing the relative positions of stars, constellations, etc.

celestial guidance *n* the guidance of a spacecraft or missile by reference to the position of one or more celestial bodies.

celestial horizon *n* See **horizon** (sense 2b).

celestial latitude *n* the angular distance of a celestial body north or south from the ecliptic. Sometimes shortened to **latitude.**

celestial longitude *n* the angular distance measured eastwards from the vernal equinox to the intersection of the ecliptic with the great circle passing through a celestial body and the poles of the ecliptic. Sometimes shortened to **longitude.**

celestial mechanics *n* the study of the motion of celestial bodies under the influence of gravitational fields.

celestial navigation *n* navigation by observation of the positions of the stars. Also called: **astronavigation.**

celestial pole *n* either of the two points at which the earth's axis, extended to infinity, would intersect the celestial sphere. Sometimes shortened to **pole.**

celestial sphere *n* an imaginary sphere of infinitely large radius enclosing the universe so that all celestial bodies appear to be projected onto its surface.

celestite (ˈsɛlɪˌstaɪt) *or* **celestine** (ˈsɛlɪstɪn, -ˌstaɪn) *n* a white, red, or blue mineral consisting of strontium sulphate in orthorhombic crystalline form: a source of strontium compounds. Formula: $SrSO_4$. **[C19:** from German *Zölestin,* from Latin *caelestis* CELESTIAL (referring to the blue colour) + -ITE[1]**]**

celiac (ˈsiːlɪˌæk) *adj Anatomy.* the usual U.S. spelling of **coeliac.**

celibate (ˈsɛlɪbɪt) *n* **1** a person who is unmarried, esp. one who has taken a religious vow of chastity. ◆ *adj* **2** unmarried, esp. by vow. **3** abstaining from sexual intercourse. **[C17:** from Latin *caelibātus,* from *caelebs* unmarried, of obscure origin**]** ► ˈcelibacy *n*

Céline (serˈliːn) *n* **Louis-Ferdinand** (lwiferdinɑ̃), real name *Louis-Ferdinand Destouches.* 1894–1961, French novelist and physician; became famous with his controversial first novel *Journey to the End of the Night* (1932).

cell[1] (sɛl) *n* **1** a small simple room, as in a prison, convent, monastery, or asylum; cubicle. **2** any small compartment: *the cells of a honeycomb.* **3** *Biology.* the smallest unit of an organism that is able to function independently. It consists of a nucleus, containing the genetic material, surrounded by the cytoplasm in which are mitochondria, lysosomes, ribosomes, and other organelles. All cells are bounded by a cell membrane; plant cells have an outer cell wall in addition. **4** *Biology.* any small cavity or area, such as the cavity containing pollen in an anther. **5** a device for converting chemical energy into electrical energy, usually consisting of a container with two electrodes immersed in an electrolyte. See also **primary cell, secondary cell, dry cell, wet cell, fuel cell. 6** short for **electrolytic cell. 7** a small religious house dependent upon a larger one. **8** a small group of persons operating as a nucleus of a larger political, religious, or other organization: *Communist cell.* **9** *Maths.* a small unit of volume in a mathematical coordinate system. **10** *Zoology.* one of the areas on an insect wing bounded by veins. **11** the geographical area served by an individual transmitter in a cellular radio network. **[C12:** from Medieval Latin *cella* monk's cell, from Latin: room, storeroom; related to Latin *cēlāre* to hide**]** ► ˈcell-ˌlike *adj*

cell[2] (sɛl) *n* a variant spelling of **cel.**

cella (ˈsɛlə) *n, pl* **-lae** (-liː). the inner room of a classical temple, esp. the room housing the statue of a deity. Also called: **naos. [C17:** from Latin: room, shrine; see CELL[1]**]**

cellar (ˈsɛlə) *n* **1** an underground room, rooms, or storey of a building, usually used for storage. Compare **basement. 2** a place where wine is stored. **3** a stock of bottled wines. ◆ *vb* **4** *(tr)* to store in a cellar. **[C13:** from Anglo-French, from Latin *cellārium* food store, from *cella* CELLA**]**

cellarage (ˈsɛlərɪdʒ) *n* **1** an area of a cellar. **2** a charge for storing goods in a cellar, etc.

cellarer (ˈsɛlərə) *n* a monastic official responsible for food, drink, etc.

cellaret (ˌsɛləˈrɛt) *n* a case, cabinet, or sideboard with compartments for holding wine bottles.

cell cycle *n* the growth cycle of eukaryotic cells. It is divided into five stages, known as G_0, in which the cell is quiescent, G_1 and G_2, in which it increases in size, S, in which it duplicates its DNA, and M, in which it undergoes mitosis and divides.

cell division *n Cytology.* the division of a cell into two new cells during growth or reproduction. See **amitosis, meiosis, mitosis.**

Celle (*German* ˈtsɛlə) *n* a city in N Germany, on the Aller River in Lower Saxony: from 1378 to 1705 the residence of the Dukes of Brunswick-Lüneburg. Pop.: 71 050 (1989 est.).

Cellini (tʃɪˈliːnɪ; *Italian* tʃelˈliːni) *n* **Benvenuto** (benveˈnuːto). 1500–71, Italian sculptor, goldsmith, and engraver, noted also for his autobiography.

cell line *n Biology.* a cell culture derived from a single cell and thus of invariable genetic make-up.

cell lineage *n Biology.* the developmental history of a tissue from the time its constituent cells are initially produced to their full differentiation in the mature tissue.

cell membrane *n* a very thin membrane, composed of lipids and protein, that surrounds the cytoplasm of a cell and controls the passage of substances into and out of the cell. Also called: **plasmalemma, plasma membrane.**

Cellnet (ˈsɛlˌnɛt) *n Trademark.* a British Telecom mobile phone.

cello (ˈtʃɛləʊ) *n, pl* **-los.** *Music.* a bowed stringed instrument of the violin family. Range: more than four octaves upwards from C below the bass staff. It has four strings, is held between the knees, and has an extendible metal spike at the lower end, which acts as a support. Full name: **violoncello.** ► ˈcellist *n*

cellobiose (ˌsɛləʊˈbaɪəʊz) *or* **cellose** (ˈsɛləʊz) *n* a disaccharide obtained by the hydrolysis of cellulose by cellulase. Formula: $C_{12}H_{22}O_{11}$. **[C20:** from CELLULOSE + BI-[1] + -OSE[2]**]**

celloidin (səˈlɔɪdɪn) *n* a nitrocellulose compound derived from pyroxylin, used in a solution of alcohol and ether for embedding specimens before cutting sections for microscopy. **[C20:** from CELLULOSE + -OID + -IN**]**

Cellophane (ˈsɛləˌfeɪn) *n Trademark.* a flexible thin transparent sheeting made from wood pulp and used as a moisture-proof wrapping. **[C20:** from CELLULOSE + -PHANE**]**

Cellosolve (ˈsɛləʊˌsɒlv) *n Trademark.* an organic compound used as a solvent in the plastics industry; 2-ethoxyethan-1-ol. Formula: $C_2H_5OCH_2CH_2OH$.

cellphone (ˈsɛlˌfəʊn) *n* a portable telephone operated by cellular radio. In full: **cellular telephone.**

cellular (ˈsɛljʊlə) *adj* **1** of, relating to, resembling, or composed of a cell or cells. **2** having cells or small cavities; porous. **3** divided into a network of cells. **4** *Textiles.* woven with an open texture: *a cellular blanket.* **5** designed for or involving cellular radio. ► **cellularity** (ˌsɛljʊˈlærɪtɪ) *n*

cellular radio *n* radio communication based on a network of transmitters each serving a small area known as a cell: used in personal communications systems in which the mobile receiver switches frequencies automatically as it passes from one cell to another.

cellulase (ˈsɛljʊˌleɪz) *n* any enzyme that converts cellulose to the disaccharide cellobiose. **[C20:** from CELLULOSE + -ASE**]**

cellule (ˈsɛljuːl) *n* a very small cell. **[C17:** from Latin *cellula,* diminutive of *cella* CELL[1]**]**

cellulite (ˈsɛljʊˌlaɪt) *n* a name sometimes given to subcutaneous fat alleged to resist dieting. **[C20:** from French, from *cellule* cell**]**

cellulitis (ˌsɛljʊˈlaɪtɪs) *n* inflammation of any of the tissues of the body, characterized by fever, pain, swelling, and redness of the affected area. **[C19:** from Latin *cellula* CELLULE + -ITIS**]**

celluloid (ˈsɛljʊˌlɔɪd) *n* **1** a flammable thermoplastic material consisting of cellulose nitrate mixed with a plasticizer, usually camphor: used in sheets, rods, and tubes for making a wide range of articles. **2a** a cellulose derivative used for coating film. **2b** one of the transparent sheets on which the constituent drawings of an animated film are prepared. **2c** a transparent sheet used as an overlay in artwork. **2d** cinema film.

cellulose (ˈsɛljʊˌləʊz, -ˌləʊs) *n* a polysaccharide consisting of long unbranched chains of linked glucose units: the main constituent of plant cell walls and used in making paper, rayon, and film. **[C18:** from French *cellule* cell (see CELLULE) + -OSE[2]**]** ► ˌcelluˈlosic *adj, n*

cellulose acetate *n* nonflammable material made by acetylating cellulose: used in the manufacture of film, dopes, lacquers, and artificial fibres.

cellulose nitrate *n* a compound made by treating cellulose with nitric and sulphuric acids, used in plastics, lacquers, and explosives: a nitrogen-containing ester of cellulose. Also called (not in chemical usage): **nitrocellulose.** See also **guncotton.**

cell wall *n* the outer layer of a cell, esp. the structure in plant cells that consists of cellulose, lignin, etc., and gives mechanical support to the cell.

celom (ˈsiːləm) *n* a less frequent U.S. spelling of **coelom.**

celosia (səˈləʊsɪə) *n* See **cockscomb** (sense 2). **[**New Latin, from Greek *kēlos* dry, burnt (from the appearance of the flowers of some species)**]**

Celsius (ˈsɛlsɪəs) *adj* denoting a measurement on the Celsius scale. Symbol: C **[C18:** named after Anders *Celsius* (1701–44), Swedish astronomer who invented it**]**

Celsius scale *n* a scale of temperature in which 0° represents the melting point of ice and 100° represents the boiling point of water. See also **centigrade.** Compare **Fahrenheit scale.**

celt (sɛlt) *n Archaeol.* a stone or metal axelike instrument with a bevelled edge. **[C18:** from Late Latin *celtes* chisel, of obscure origin**]**

Celt (kɛlt, sɛlt) *or* **Kelt** *n* **1** a person who speaks a Celtic language. **2** a member of an Indo-European people who in pre-Roman times inhabited Britain, Gaul, Spain, and other parts of W and central Europe.

Celt. *abbrev. for* Celtic.

Celtiberian (ˌkɛltɪˈbɪərɪən, -taɪ-, ˌsɛl-) *n* **1** a member of a Celtic people (**Celtiberi**) who inhabited the Iberian peninsula during classical times. **2** the extinct language of this people, possibly belonging to the Celtic branch of the Indo-European family, recorded in a number of inscriptions.

Celtic (ˈkɛltɪk, ˈsɛl-) *or* **Keltic** *n* **1** a branch of the Indo-European family of languages that includes Gaelic, Welsh, and Breton, still spoken in parts of Scotland, Ireland, Wales, and Brittany. Modern Celtic is divided into the Brythonic (southern) and Goidelic (northern) groups. ◆ *adj* **2** of, relating to, or characteristic of the Celts or the Celtic languages. ▸ **ˈCeltically** *or* **ˈKeltically** *adv* ▸ **Celticism** (ˈkɛltɪˌsɪzəm, ˈsɛl-) *or* **ˈKeltiˌcism** *n* ▸ **ˈCelticist, ˈCeltist** *or* **ˈKelticist, ˈKeltist** *n*

Celtic cross *n* a Latin cross with a broad ring surrounding the point of intersection.

cembalo (ˈtʃɛmbələʊ) *n, pl* **-li** (-lɪ) *or* **-los.** another word for **harpsichord.** [C19: shortened from CLAVICEMBALO] ▸ **ˈcembalist** *n*

cement (sɪˈmɛnt) *n* **1** a fine grey powder made of a mixture of calcined limestone and clay, used with water and sand to make mortar, or with water, sand, and aggregate, to make concrete. **2** a binder, glue, or adhesive. **3** something that unites or joins; bond. **4** *Dentistry.* any of various materials used in filling teeth. **5** mineral matter, such as silica and calcite, that binds together particles of rock, bones, etc., to form a solid mass of sedimentary rock. **6** another word for **cementum.** ◆ *vb* (*tr*) **7** to reinforce or consolidate: *once a friendship is cemented it will last for life.* **8** to join, bind, or glue together with or as if with cement. **9** to coat or cover with cement. [C13: from Old French *ciment,* from Latin *caementum* stone from the quarry, from *caedere* to hew] ▸ **ceˈmenter** *n*

cementation (ˌsiːmɛnˈteɪʃən) *n* **1** the process of heating a solid with a powdered material to modify the properties of the solid, esp. the heating of wrought iron, surrounded with charcoal, to 750–900°C to produce steel. **2** the process of cementing or being cemented. **3** *Civil engineering.* the injection of cement grout into fissured rocks to make them watertight.

cementite (sɪˈmɛntaɪt) *n* the hard brittle compound of iron and carbon that forms in carbon steels and some cast irons. Formula: Fe_3C.

cementum (sɪˈmɛntəm) *n* a thin bonelike tissue that covers the dentine in the root of a tooth. [C19: New Latin, from Latin: CEMENT]

cemetery (ˈsɛmɪtrɪ) *n, pl* **-teries.** a place where the dead are buried, esp. one not attached to a church. [C14: from Late Latin *coemētērium,* from Greek *koimētērion* room for sleeping, from *koiman* to put to sleep]

cen. *abbrev. for* central.

cenacle *or* **coenacle** (ˈsɛnək^əl) *n* **1** a supper room, esp. one on an upper floor. **2** (*cap.*) the room in which the Last Supper took place. [C14: from Old French, from Late Latin *cēnāculum,* from *cēna* supper]

-cene *n and adj combining form.* denoting a recent geological period: *Miocene.* [from Greek *kainos* new]

CENELEC (ˈsɛnəˌlɛk) *n acronym for* Commission Européenne de Normalisation Électrique: the EU standards organization for electrical goods. Also called: **CEN.**

cenesthesia (ˌsiːnɪsˈθiːzɪə) *n Psychol.* a variant spelling (esp. U.S.) of **coenaesthesia.**

CEng *abbrev. for* chartered engineer.

Cenis (*French* səni) *n* **Mont.** a pass over the Graian Alps in SE France, between Lanslebourg (France) and Susa (Italy): nearby tunnel, opened in 1871. Highest point: 2082 m (6831 ft.). Italian name: **Monte Cenisio** (ˈmonte tʃeˈniːzjo).

cenobite (ˈsiːnəʊˌbaɪt) *n* a variant spelling of **coenobite.**

cenogenesis (ˌsiːnəʊˈdʒɛnɪsɪs) *n* a U.S. spelling of **caenogenesis.**

cenospecies (ˈsiːnəˌspiːʃiːz) *n, pl* **-species.** a species related to another by the ability to interbreed: *dogs and wolves are cenospecies.* [C20: from Greek *koinos* common + SPECIES]

cenotaph (ˈsɛnəˌtɑːf) *n* a monument honouring a dead person or persons buried elsewhere. [C17: from Latin *cenotaphium,* from Greek *kenotaphion,* from *kenos* empty + *taphos* tomb] ▸ **ˌcenoˈtaphic** *adj*

Cenotaph (ˈsɛnəˌtɑːf) *n* **the.** the monument in Whitehall, London, honouring the dead of both World Wars: designed by Sir Edwin Lutyens: erected in 1920.

cenote (sɪˈnəʊteɪ) *n* (esp. in the Yucatán peninsula) a natural well formed by the collapse of an overlying limestone crust: often used as a sacrificial site by the Mayas. [C19: via Mexican Spanish from Maya *conot*]

Cenozoic, Caenozoic (ˌsiːnəʊˈzəʊɪk), *or* **Cainozoic** *adj* **1** of, denoting, or relating to the most recent geological era, which began 70 000 000 years ago: characterized by the development and increase of the mammals. ◆ *n* **2 the.** the Cenozoic era. [C19: from Greek *kainos* new, recent + *zōikos,* from *zōion* animal]

cense (sɛns) *vb* (*tr*) to burn incense near or before (an altar, shrine, etc.). [C14: from Old French *encenser;* see INCENSE[1]]

censer (ˈsɛnsə) *n* a container for burning incense, esp. one swung at religious ceremonies. Also called: **thurible.**

censor (ˈsɛnsə) *n* **1** a person authorized to examine publications, theatrical presentations, films, letters, etc., in order to suppress in whole or part those considered obscene, politically unacceptable, etc. **2** any person who controls or suppresses the behaviour of others, usually on moral grounds. **3** (in republican Rome) either of two senior magistrates elected to keep the list of citizens up to date, control aspects of public finance, and supervise public morals. **4** *Psychoanal.* the postulated factor responsible for regulating the translation of ideas and desires from the unconscious to the conscious mind. See also **superego.** ◆ *vb* (*tr*) **5** to ban or cut portions of (a publication, film, letter, etc.). **6** to act as a censor of (behaviour, etc.). [C16: from Latin, from *cēnsēre* to consider, assess] ▸ **ˈcensorable** *adj* ▸ **censorial** (sɛnˈsɔːrɪəl) *adj*

censorious (sɛnˈsɔːrɪəs) *adj* harshly critical; fault-finding. ▸ **cenˈsoriously** *adv* ▸ **cenˈsoriousness** *n*

censorship (ˈsɛnsəˌʃɪp) *n* **1** a policy or programme of censoring. **2** the act or system of censoring. **3** *Psychoanal.* the activity of the mind in regulating impulses, etc., from the unconscious so that they are modified before reaching the conscious mind.

censurable (ˈsɛnʃərəb^əl) *adj* deserving censure, condemnation, or blame. ▸ **ˈcensurableness** *or* **ˌcensuraˈbility** *n* ▸ **ˈcensurably** *adv*

censure (ˈsɛnʃə) *n* **1** severe disapproval; harsh criticism. ◆ *vb* **2** to criticize (someone or something) severely; condemn. [C14: from Latin *cēnsūra,* from *cēnsēre* to consider, assess] ▸ **ˈcensurer** *n*

census (ˈsɛnsəs) *n, pl* **-suses. 1** an official periodic count of a population including such information as sex, age, occupation, etc. **2** any offical count: *a traffic census.* **3** (in ancient Rome) a registration of the population and a property evaluation for purposes of taxation. [C17: from Latin, from *cēnsēre* to assess] ▸ **ˈcensual** *adj*

cent (sɛnt) *n* **1** a monetary unit of Antigua and Barbuda, Australia, the Bahamas, Barbados, Belize, Brunei, Canada, Cyprus, Dominica, Estonia, Ethiopia, the countries of the European Union who have adopted European Monetary Union, Fiji, Grenada, Guyana, Jamaica, Kenya, Kiribati, Liberia, Malaysia, Malta, the Marshall Islands, Mauritius, Micronesia, Namibia, Nauru, the Netherlands, New Zealand, Saint Kitts and Nevis, Saint Lucia, Saint Vincent and the Grenadines, the Seychelles, Sierra Leone, Singapore, the Solomon Islands, Somalia, South Africa, Sri Lanka, Surinam, Swaziland, Taiwan, Tanzania, Trinidad and Tobago, Tuvalu, Uganda, the United States, and Zimbabwe. It is worth one hundredth of their respective standard units. **2** an interval of pitch between two frequencies f_2 and f_1 equal to 3986.31 log (f_2/f_1); one twelve-hundredth of the interval between two frequencies having the ratio 1:2 (an octave). [C16: from Latin *centēsimus* hundredth, from *centum* hundred]

cent. *abbrev. for:* **1** centigrade. **2** central. **3** century.

cental (ˈsɛnt^əl) *n* a unit of weight equal to 100 pounds (45.3 kilograms). [C19: from Latin *centum* hundred]

centas (ˈtsæntæs) *n, pl* **centai** (ˈtsæntaɪ). a monetary unit of Lithuania, worth one hundredth of a litas.

centaur (ˈsɛntɔː) *n Greek myth.* one of a race of creatures with the head, arms, and torso of a man, and the lower body and legs of a horse. [C14: from Latin, from Greek *kentauros,* of unknown origin]

centaurea (ˌsɛntɔːˈrɪə, sɛnˈtɔːrɪə) *n* any plant of the genus *Centaurea,* which includes the cornflower and knapweed. [C19: ultimately from Greek *Kentauros* the Centaur; see CENTAURY]

Centaurus (sɛnˈtɔːrəs) *n, Latin genitive* **Centauri** (sɛnˈtɔːraɪ). a conspicuous extensive constellation in the S hemisphere, close to the Southern Cross, that contains two first magnitude stars, Alpha Centauri and Beta Centauri, and the globular cluster Omega Centauri. Also called: **The Centaur.**

centaury (ˈsɛntɔːrɪ) *n, pl* **-ries. 1** any Eurasian plant of the genus *Centaurium,* esp. *C. erythraea,* having purplish-pink flowers and formerly believed to have medicinal properties: family *Gentianaceae.* **2** any plant of the genus *Centaurea,* which includes the cornflower and knapweed: family *Compositae* (composites). [C14: ultimately from Greek *Kentauros* the Centaur; from the legend that Chiron the Centaur divulged its healing properties]

centavo (sɛnˈtɑːvəʊ) *n, pl* **-vos.** a monetary unit of Argentina, Bolivia, Brazil, Cape Verde, Chile, Colombia, Cuba, the Dominican Republic, Ecuador, El Salvador, Guatemala, Guinea-Bissau, Honduras, Mexico, Mozambique, Nicaragua, the Philippines, Portugal, and São Tomé e Principe. It is worth one hundredth of their respective standard units. [Spanish: one hundredth part]

centenarian (ˌsɛntɪˈnɛərɪən) *n* **1** a person who is at least 100 years old. ◆ *adj* **2** being at least 100 years old. **3** of or relating to a centenarian.

centenary (sɛnˈtiːnərɪ) *adj* **1** of or relating to a period of 100 years. **2** occurring once every 100 years: *centenary celebrations.* ◆ *n, pl* **-naries. 3** a 100th anniversary or its celebration. [C17: from Latin *centēnārius* of a hundred, from *centēnī* a hundred each, from *centum* hundred]

centennial (sɛnˈtɛnɪəl) *adj* **1** relating to, lasting for, or completing a period of 100 years. **2** occurring every 100 years. ◆ *n* **3** *Chiefly U.S. and Canadian.* another name for **centenary.** [C18: from Latin *centum* hundred, on the model of BIENNIAL] ▸ **cenˈtennially** *adv*

center (ˈsɛntə) *n, vb* the U.S. spelling of **centre.**

centering (ˈsɛntərɪŋ) *n* a U.S. spelling of **centring.**

centesimal (sɛnˈtɛsɪməl) *n* **1** hundredth. ◆ *adj* **2** relating to division into hundredths. [C17: from Latin *centēsimus,* from *centum* hundred] ▸ **cenˈtesimally** *adv*

centesimo (sɛnˈtɛsɪˌməʊ) *n, pl* **-mos** *or* **-mi.** a monetary unit of Panama and Uruguay. It is worth one hundredth of their respective standard units. It is also a monetary unit of Italy, San Marino, and the Vatican City but is virtually valueless, being worth one hundredth of a lira. [C19: from Spanish and Italian, from Latin *centēsimus* hundredth, from *centum* hundred]

centi- *or before a vowel* **cent-** *prefix* **1** denoting one hundredth: *centimetre.* Symbol: c **2** *Rare.* denoting a hundred: *centipede.* [from French, from Latin *centum* hundred]

centiare (ˈsɛntɪˌɛə; *French* sɑ̃tjar) *or* **centare** (ˈsɛntɛə; *French* sɑ̃tar) *n* a unit of area equal to one square metre. [French, from CENTI- + *are* from Latin *ārea;* see ARE[2], AREA]

centigrade (ˈsɛntɪˌgreɪd) *adj* **1** a former name for **Celsius.** ◆ *n* **2** a unit of angle equal to one hundredth of a grade.

USAGE Although still used in meteorology, *centigrade,* when indicating the Celsius scale of temperature, is now usually avoided because of its possible confusion with the hundredth part of a grade.

centigram *or* **centigramme** ('sɛntɪˌgræm) *n* one hundredth of a gram.
centile ('sɛntaɪl) *n* another word for **percentile.**
centilitre *or U.S.* **centiliter** ('sɛntɪˌliːtə) *n* one hundredth of a litre.
centillion (sɛn'tɪljən) *n, pl* **-lions** *or* **-lion. 1** (in Britain and Germany) the number represented as one followed by 600 zeros (10^{600}). **2** (in the U.S., Canada, and France) the number represented as one followed by 303 zeros (10^{303}).
centime ('sɒnˌtiːm; *French* sɑ̃tim) *n* a monetary unit of Algeria, Belgium, Benin, Burkina-Faso, Burundi, Cameroon, the Central African Republic, Chad, the Comoros, Congo, Democratic Republic of the Congo, Côte d'Ivoire, Djibouti, Equatorial Guinea, France, Gabon, Guinea, Haiti, Liechtenstein, Luxembourg, Madagascar, Mali, Monaco, Morocco, Niger, Rwanda, Senegal, Switzerland, and Togo. It is worth one hundredth of their respective standard units. **[C18:** from French, from Old French *centiesme* from Latin *centēsimus* hundredth, from *centum* hundred**]**
centimetre *or U.S.* **centimeter** ('sɛntɪˌmiːtə) *n* one hundredth of a metre.
centimetre-gram-second *n* See **cgs units.**
céntimo ('sɛntɪˌməʊ) *n, pl* **-mos.** a monetary unit of Costa Rica, Paraguay, Peru, Spain, and Venezuela. It is worth one hundredth of their respective standard currency units. **[**from Spanish; see CENTIME**]**
centimorgan ('sɛntɪˌmɔːgən) *n Genetics.* a unit of chromosome length, used in genetic mapping, equal to the length of chromosome over which crossing over occurs with 1 per cent frequency. **[C20:** named after Thomas Hunt MORGAN**]**
centipede ('sɛntɪˌpiːd) *n* any carnivorous arthropod of the genera *Lithobius, Scutigera,* etc., having a body of between 15 and 190 segments, each bearing one pair of legs: class *Chilopoda.* See also **myriapod.**
centipoise ('sɛntɪˌpɔɪz) *n* one hundredth of a poise. 1 centipoise is equal to 0.001 newton second per square metre.
centner ('sɛntnə) *n* **1** Also called (esp. U.S.): **short hundredweight.** a unit of weight equivalent to 100 pounds (45.3 kilograms). **2** (in some European countries) a unit of weight equivalent to 50 kilograms (110.23 pounds). **3** a unit of weight equivalent to 100 kilograms. **[C17:** from German *Zentner,* ultimately from Latin *centēnārius* of a hundred; see CENTENARY**]**
cento ('sɛntəʊ) *n, pl* **-tos.** a piece of writing, esp. a poem, composed of quotations from other authors. **[C17:** from Latin, literally: patchwork garment**]**
CENTO ('sɛntəʊ) *n acronym for* Central Treaty Organization; an organization for military and economic cooperation formed in 1959 by the UK, Iran, Pakistan, and Turkey as a successor to the Baghdad Pact: disbanded 1979.
centra ('sɛntrə) *n* a plural of **centrum.**
central ('sɛntrəl) *adj* **1** in, at, of, from, containing, or forming the centre of something: *the central street in a city; the central material of a golf ball.* **2** main, principal, or chief; most important: *the central cause of a problem.* **3a** of or relating to the central nervous system. **3b** of or relating to the centrum of a vertebra. **4** of, relating to, or denoting a vowel articulated with the tongue held in an intermediate position halfway between the positions for back and front vowels, as for the *a* of English *soda.* **5** (of a force) directed from or towards a point. ► **'centrally** *adv*
Central African Federation *n* another name for the **Federation of Rhodesia and Nyasaland.**
Central African Republic *n* a landlocked country of central Africa: joined with Chad as a territory of French Equatorial Africa in 1910; became an independent republic in 1960; a parliamentary monarchy (1976–79); consists of a huge plateau, mostly savanna, with dense forests in the south; drained chiefly by the Shari and Ubangi Rivers. Official language: French; Sango is the national language. Religion: Christian and animist. Currency: franc. Capital: Bangui. Pop.: 3 376 000 (1998 est.). Area: 622 577 sq. km (240 376 sq. miles). Former names: (until 1958) **Ubangi-Shari;** (1976-79) **Central African Empire.** French name: **République Centrafricaine** (repyblik sɑ̃trafrikɛn).
Central America *n* an isthmus joining the continents of North and South America, extending from the S border of Mexico to the NW border of Colombia and consisting of Belize, Guatemala, Honduras, El Salvador, Nicaragua, Costa Rica, and Panama. Area: about 518 000 sq. km (200 000 sq. miles). ► **Central American** *adj*
central angle *n* an angle whose vertex is at the centre of a circle.
central bank *n* a national bank that does business mainly with a government and with other banks: it regulates the volume and cost of credit.
Central Committee *n* (in Communist parties) the body responsible for party policy between meetings of the party congress: in practice, it is in charge of day-to-day operations of the party bureaucracy.
Central European Time *n* the standard time adopted by Western European countries one hour ahead of Greenwich Mean Time, corresponding to British Summer Time. Abbrev.: **CET.**
central heating *n* a system for heating the rooms of a building by means of radiators or air vents connected by pipes or ducts to a central source of heat.
Central India Agency *n* a former group of 89 states in India, under the supervision of a British political agent until 1947: most important were Indore, Bhopal, and Rewa.
Central Intelligence Agency *n* See **CIA.**
centralism ('sɛntrəˌlɪzəm) *n* the principle or act of bringing something under central control; centralization. ► **'centralist** *n, adj* ► **ˌcentral'istic** *adj*
centrality (sɛn'trælɪtɪ) *n, pl* **-ties.** the state or condition of being central.
centralize *or* **centralise** ('sɛntrəˌlaɪz) *vb* **1** to draw or move (something) to or towards a centre. **2** to bring or come under central control, esp. governmental control. ► **ˌcentrali'zation** *or* **ˌcentrali'sation** *n* ► **'centralˌizer** *or* **'centralˌiser** *n*
Central Karoo (kə'ruː) *n* an arid plateau of S central South Africa, in Cape Province, separated from the Little Karoo to the southwest by the Swartberg range. Average height: 750 m (2500 ft.).
central limit theorem *n Statistics.* the fundamental result that the sum (or mean) of independent identically distributed random variables with finite variance approaches a normally distributed random variable as their number increases, whence in particular if enough samples are repeatedly drawn from any population, the sum of the sample values can be thought of, approximately, as an outcome from a normally distributed random variable.
central locking *n* a system by which all the doors of a motor vehicle can be locked simultaneously when the driver's door is locked.
central nervous system *n* the mass of nerve tissue that controls and coordinates the activities of an animal. In vertebrates it consists of the brain and spinal cord. Abbrev.: **CNS.** Compare **autonomic nervous system.**
Central Powers *pl n European history* **a** (before World War I) Germany, Italy, and Austria-Hungary after they were linked by the Triple Alliance in 1882. **b** (during World War I) Germany and Austria-Hungary, together with their allies Turkey and Bulgaria.
central processing unit *n* the part of a computer that performs logical and arithmetical operations on the data as specified in the instructions. Abbrev.: **CPU.**
Central Provinces and Berar (be'rɑː) *n* a former province of central India: reorganized and renamed Madhya Pradesh in 1950.
Central Region *n* a former local government region in central Scotland, formed in 1975 from Clackmannanshire, most of Stirlingshire, and parts of Perthshire, West Lothian, Fife, and Kinross-shire; in 1996 it was replaced by the council areas of Stirling, Clackmannanshire, and Falkirk.
central reserve *or* **reservation** *n Brit.* the strip, often covered with grass, that separates the two sides of a motorway or dual carriageway. U.S. and Austral. name: **median strip.** Canadian name: **median.**
Central Standard Time *n* one of the standard times used in North America, based on the local time of the 90° meridian, six hours behind Greenwich Mean Time. Abbrev.: **CST.**
central sulcus *n* a deep cleft in each hemisphere of the brain separating the frontal lobe from the parietal lobe.
central tendency *n Statistics.* the tendency of the values of a random variable to cluster around the mean, median, and mode.
centre *or U.S.* **center** ('sɛntə) *n* **1** *Geom.* **1a** the midpoint of any line or figure, esp. the point within a circle or sphere that is equidistant from any point on the circumference or surface. **1b** the point within a body through which a specified force may be considered to act, such as the centre of gravity. **2** the point, axis, or pivot about which a body rotates. **3** a point, area, or part that is approximately in the middle of a larger area or volume. **4** a place at which some specified activity is concentrated: *a shopping centre.* **5** a person or thing that is a focus of interest. **6** a place of activity or influence: *a centre of power.* **7** a person, group, policy, or thing in the middle. **8** (*usually cap.*) *Politics.* **8a** a political party or group favouring moderation, esp. the moderate members of a legislative assembly. **8b** (*as modifier*): *a Centre-Left alliance.* **9** *Physiol.* any part of the central nervous system that regulates a specific function: *respiratory centre.* **10** a bar with a conical point upon which a workpiece or part may be turned or ground. **11** a punch mark or small conical hole in a part to be drilled, which enables the point of the drill to be located accurately. **12** *Football, hockey, etc.* **12a** a player who plays in the middle of the forward line. **12b** the act or an instance of passing the ball from a wing to the middle of the field, court, etc. **13** *Basketball.* **13a** the position of a player who jumps for the ball at the start of play. **13b** the player in this position. **14** *Archery.* **14a** the ring around the bull's eye. **14b** a shot that hits this ring. ◆ *vb* **15** to move towards, mark, put, or be at a centre. **16** (*tr*) to focus or bring together: *to centre one's thoughts.* **17** (*intr;* often foll. by *on*) to have as a main point of view or theme: *the novel centred on crime.* **18** (*tr*) to adjust or locate (a workpiece or part) using a centre. **19** (*intr;* foll. by *on* or *round*) to have as a centre. **20** (*tr*) *Football, hockey, etc.* to pass (the ball) into the middle of the field or court. **[C14:** from Latin *centrum* the stationary point of a compass, from Greek *kentron* needle, from *kentein* to prick**]**
Centre *n* **1** ('sɛntə). **the.** the sparsely inhabited central region of Australia. **2** (*French* sɑ̃trə) a region of central France: generally low-lying; drained chiefly by the Rivers Loire, Loir, and Cher.
centre bit *n* a drilling bit with a central projecting point and two side cutters.
centreboard ('sɛntəˌbɔːd) *n* a supplementary keel for a sailing vessel, which may be adjusted by raising and lowering. Compare **daggerboard.**
centred dot *n Printing.* **1** Also called (esp. U.S. and Canadian): **bullet.** a heavy dot (•) used to draw attention to a particular paragraph. **2** a dot placed at a central level in a line of type or writing.
centre-fire *adj* **1** (of a cartridge) having the primer in the centre of the base. **2** (of a firearm) adapted for such cartridges. ◆ Compare **rim-fire.**
centrefold *or U.S.* **centerfold** ('sɛntəˌfəʊld) *n* **1** a large coloured illustration folded so that it forms the central spread of a magazine. **2** a photograph of a nude or nearly nude woman (or man) in a magazine on such a spread.
centre forward *n Soccer, hockey, etc.* the central forward in the attack.
centre half *or* **centre back** *n Soccer.* a defender who plays in the middle of the defence.
centre of curvature *n* the centre of a circle whose radius, the **radius of curvature,** is normal to the concave side of a curve at a given point.
centre of gravity *n* the point through which the resultant of the gravitational forces on a body always acts.
centre of mass *n* the point at which the mass of a system could be concentrated without affecting the behaviour of the system under the action of external linear forces.
centre of pressure *n* **1** *Physics.* the point in a body at which the resultant pressure acts when the body is immersed in a fluid. **2** *Aeronautics.* the point at which the resultant aerodynamic forces intersect the chord line of the aerofoil.

centre pass *n Hockey.* a push or hit made in any direction to start the game or to restart the game after a goal has been scored.
centrepiece ('sɛntə,pi:s) *n* an object used as the centre of something, esp. for decoration.
centre punch *n* a small steel tool with a conical tip used to punch a small indentation at the location of the centre of a hole to be drilled.
centre spread *n* **1** the pair of two facing pages in the middle of a magazine, newspaper, etc., often illustrated. **2** a photograph of a nude or nearly nude woman (or man) in a magazine on such pages.
centre stage *n* **1** the centre point on a stage. **2** the main focus of attention.
centre three-quarter *n Rugby.* either of two middle players on the three-quarter line.
centrex ('sɛntrɛks) *n* a telephone switching system that enables telephone calls to bypass the switchboard.
centri- *combining form.* a variant of **centro-**.
centric ('sɛntrɪk) *or* **centrical** *adj* **1** being central or having a centre. **2** relating to or originating at a nerve centre. **3** *Botany.* **3a** Also: **concentric.** (of vascular bundles) having one type of tissue completely surrounding the other. **3b** (of leaves, such as those of the onion) cylindrical. ▸ **'centrically** *adv* ▸ **centricity** (sɛn'trɪsɪtɪ) *n*
-centric *suffix forming adjectives.* having a centre as specified: *heliocentric.* [abstracted from ECCENTRIC, CONCENTRIC, etc.]
centrifugal (sɛn'trɪfjʊgᵊl, 'sɛntrɪ,fju:gᵊl) *adj* **1** acting, moving, or tending to move away from a centre. Compare **centripetal. 2** of, concerned with, or operated by centrifugal force: *centrifugal pump.* **3** *Botany.* (esp. of certain inflorescences) developing outwards from a centre. **4** *Physiol.* another word for **efferent.** ◆ *n* **5** any device that uses centrifugal force for its action. **6** the rotating perforated drum in a centrifuge. [C18: from New Latin *centrifugus,* from CENTRI- + Latin *fugere* to flee] ▸ **cen'trifugally** *adv*
centrifugal brake *n* a safety mechanism on a hoist, crane, etc., that consists of revolving brake shoes that are driven outwards by centrifugal force into contact with a fixed brake drum when the rope drum revolves at excessive speed.
centrifugal clutch *n Engineering.* an automatic clutch in which the friction surfaces are engaged by weighted levers acting under centrifugal force at a certain speed of rotation.
centrifugal force *n* a fictitious force that can be thought of as acting outwards on any body that rotates or moves along a curved path.
centrifugal pump *n* a pump having a high-speed rotating impeller whose blades throw the water outwards.
centrifuge ('sɛntrɪ,fju:dʒ) *n* **1** any of various rotating machines that separate liquids from solids or dispersions of one liquid in another, by the action of centrifugal force. **2** any of various rotating devices for subjecting human beings or animals to varying accelerations for experimental purposes. ◆ *vb* **3** (*tr*) to subject to the action of a centrifuge. ▸ **centrifugation** (,sɛntrɪfju'geɪʃən) *n*
centring ('sɛntrɪŋ) *or U.S.* **centering** *n* a temporary structure, esp. one made of timber, used to support an arch during construction.
centriole ('sɛntrɪ,əʊl) *n* either of two rodlike bodies in most animal cells that form the poles of the spindle during mitosis. [C19: from New Latin *centriolum,* diminutive of Latin *centrum* CENTRE]
centripetal (sɛn'trɪpɪtᵊl, 'sɛntrɪ,pi:tᵊl) *adj* **1** acting, moving, or tending to move towards a centre. Compare **centrifugal. 2** of, concerned with, or operated by centripetal force. **3** *Botany.* (esp. of certain inflorescences) developing from the outside towards the centre. **4** *Physiol.* another word for **afferent.** [C17: from New Latin *centripetus* seeking the centre; see CENTRI-, -PETAL] ▸ **cen'tripetally** *adv*
centripetal force *n* a force that acts inwards on any body that rotates or moves along a curved path and is directed towards the centre of curvature of the path or the axis of rotation. Compare **centrifugal force.**
centrist ('sɛntrɪst) *n* a person holding moderate political views. ▸ **'centrism** *n*
centro-, centri-, *or before a vowel* **centr-** *combining form.* denoting a centre: *centroclinal; centromere; centrosome; centrosphere; centrist.* [from Greek *kentron* CENTRE]
centrobaric (,sɛntrəʊ'bærɪk) *adj* of or concerned with a centre of gravity. [C18: from Late Greek *kentrobarikos,* from Greek *kentron bareos* centre of gravity]
centroclinal (,sɛntrəʊ'klaɪnᵊl) *adj Geology.* of, relating to, or designating a rock formation in which the strata slope down and in towards a central point or area.
centroid ('sɛntrɔɪd) *n* **a** the centre of mass of an object of uniform density, esp. of a geometric figure. **b** the point in a set whose coordinates are the mean values of the coordinates of the other points in the set.
centrolecithal (,sɛntrəʊ'lɛsɪθəl) *adj Zoology.* (of animal eggs) having a centrally located yolk.
centromere ('sɛntrə,mɪə) *n* the dense nonstaining region of a chromosome that attaches it to the spindle during mitosis. ▸ **centromeric** (,sɛntrə'mɛrɪk, -'mɪərɪk) *adj*
centrosome ('sɛntrə,səʊm) *n* a small protoplasmic body that surrounds the centriole. Also called: **centrosphere, astrosphere.** ▸ **centrosomic** (,sɛntrə'sɒmɪk) *adj*
centrosphere ('sɛntrə,sfɪə) *n* **1** the central part of the earth, below the crust. **2** another name for **centrosome.**
centrum ('sɛntrəm) *n, pl* **-trums** *or* **-tra** (-trə). the main part or body of a vertebra. [C19: from Latin: CENTRE]
centum ('sɛntəm) *adj* denoting or belonging to the Indo-European languages in which original velar stops (*k*) were not palatalized, namely languages of the Hellenic, Italic, Celtic, Germanic, Anatolian, and Tocharian branches. Compare **satem.** [Latin: HUNDRED, chosen because the *c* represents the Indo-European *k*]
centuplicate *vb* (sɛn'tju:plɪ,keɪt). **1** (*tr*) to increase 100 times. ◆ *adj* (sɛn'tju:plɪkɪt, -,keɪt). **2** increased a hundredfold. ◆ *n* (sɛn'tju:plɪkɪt, -,keɪt). **3** one hundredfold. ◆ Also **centuple** ('sɛntjʊpᵊl). [C17: from Late Latin *centuplicāre,* from *centuplex* hundredfold, from Latin *centum* hundred + *-plex* -fold] ▸ **cen,tupli'cation** *n*
centurial (sɛn'tjʊərɪəl) *adj* **1** of or relating to a Roman century. **2** *Rare.* involving a period of 100 years.
centurion (sɛn'tjʊərɪən) *n* the officer commanding a Roman century. [C14: from Latin *centuriō,* from *centuria* CENTURY]
century ('sɛntʃərɪ) *n, pl* **-ries. 1** a period of 100 years. **2** one of the successive periods of 100 years dated before or after an epoch or event, esp. the birth of Christ. **3a** a score or grouping of 100: *to score a century in cricket.* **3b** *Chiefly U.S. (as modifier): the basketball team passed the century mark in their last game.* **4** (in ancient Rome) a unit of foot soldiers, originally 100 strong, later consisting of 60 to 80 men. See also **maniple. 5** (in ancient Rome) a division of the people for purposes of voting. **6** (*often cap.*) a style of type. [C16: from Latin *centuria,* from *centum* hundred]
century plant *n* a tropical American agave, *Agave americana,* having large greyish leaves and greenish flowers on a tall fleshy stalk. It blooms only once in 10 to 30 years and was formerly thought to flower once in a century. Also called: **American aloe.**
ceorl (tʃeəl) *n* a freeman of the lowest class in Anglo-Saxon England. [Old English; see CHURL] ▸ **'ceorlish** *adj*
cep (sɛp) *n* another name for **porcino.** [C19: from French *cèpe,* from Gascon dialect *cep,* from Latin *cippus* stake]
cepaceous (sɪ'peɪʃəs) *adj Botany.* having an onion-like smell or taste. [from Latin *caepa* onion + -ACEOUS]
cephalad ('sɛfə,læd) *adv Anatomy.* towards the head or anterior part. Compare **caudad.**
cephalalgia (,sɛfə'lældʒɪə, -dʒə) *n* a technical name for **headache.**
cephalic (sɪ'fælɪk) *adj* **1** of or relating to the head. **2** situated in, on, or near the head.
-cephalic *or* **-cephalous** *adj combining form.* indicating skull or head; -headed: *brachycephalic.* [from Greek *-kephalos*] ▸ **-cephaly** *or* **-cephalism** *n combining form*
cephalic index *n* the ratio of the greatest width of the human head to its greatest length, multiplied by 100.
cephalin ('sɛfəlɪn, 'kɛf-) *or* **kephalin** ('kɛfəlɪn) *n* a phospholipid, similar to lecithin, that occurs in the nerve tissue and brain. Systematic name: **phosphatidylethanolamine.**
cephalization *or* **cephalisation** (,sɛfəlaɪ'zeɪʃən) *n* (in the evolution of animals) development of a head by the concentration of feeding and sensory organs and nervous tissue at the anterior end.
cephalo- *or before a vowel* **cephal-** *combining form.* indicating the head: *cephalopod.* [via Latin from Greek *kephalo-,* from *kephale* head]
cephalochordate (,sɛfələʊ'kɔ:deɪt) *n* **1** any chordate animal of the subphylum *Cephalochordata,* having a fishlike body and no vertebral column; a lancelet. ◆ *adj* **2** of, relating to, or belonging to the *Cephalochordata.*
cephalometer (,sɛfə'lɒmɪtə) *n* an instrument for positioning the human head for X-ray examination in cephalometry.
cephalometry (,sɛfə'lɒmɪtrɪ) *n* **1** measurement of the dimensions of the human head by radiography: used mainly in orthodontics. **2** measurement of the dimensions of the fetal head by radiography or ultrasound. ▸ **cephalometric** (,sɛfələʊ'mɛtrɪk) *adj*
Cephalonia (,sɛfə'ləʊnɪə) *n* a mountainous island in the Ionian Sea, the largest of the Ionian Islands, off the W coast of Greece. Pop.: 32 474 (1991). Area: 935 sq. km (365 sq. miles). Modern Greek name: **Kephallinía.**
cephalopod ('sɛfələ,pɒd) *n* **1** any marine mollusc of the class *Cephalopoda,* characterized by well-developed head and eyes and a ring of sucker-bearing tentacles. The group includes the octopuses, squids, cuttlefish, and pearly nautilus. ◆ *adj also* **cephalopodic** *or* **cephalopodous** (,sɛfə'lɒpədəs). **2** of, relating to, or belonging to the *Cephalopoda.* ▸ **,cepha'lopodan** *adj, n*
cephalosporin (,sɛfələʊ'spɔ:rɪn) *n* any of a group of broad-spectrum antibiotics obtained from fungi of the genus *Cephalosporium.*
cephalothorax (,sɛfələʊ'θɔ:ræks) *n, pl* **-raxes** *or* **-races** (-rə,si:z). the anterior part of many crustaceans and some other arthropods consisting of a united head and thorax. ▸ **cephalothoracic** (,sɛfələʊθə'ræsɪk) *adj*
-cephalus *n combining form.* denoting a cephalic abnormality: *hydrocephalus.* [New Latin *-cephalus;* see -CEPHALIC]
Cepheid variable ('si:fɪɪd) *n Astronomy.* any of a class of variable stars with regular cycles of variations in luminosity (most ranging from three to fifty days). There is a relationship between the periods of variation and the absolute magnitudes, which is used for measuring the distance of such stars.
Cepheus[1] ('si:fju:s) *n, Latin genitive* **Cephei** ('si:fɪ,aɪ). a faint constellation in the N hemisphere near Cassiopeia and the Pole Star. See also **Cepheid variable.** [from Latin *Cēpheus* named after the mythical king]
Cepheus[2] ('si:fju:s) *n Greek myth.* a king of Ethiopia, father of Andromeda and husband of Cassiopeia.
ceraceous (sɪ'reɪʃəs) *adj* waxlike or waxy. [C18: from Latin *cēra* wax]
Ceram (sɪ'ræm) *n* a variant spelling of **Seram.**
ceramal (sə'reɪməl) *n* another name for **cermet.** [C20: from CERAM(IC) + AL(LOY)]
ceramic (sɪ'ræmɪk) *n* **1** a hard brittle material made by firing clay and similar substances. **2** an object made from such a material. ◆ *adj* **3** of, relating to, or made from a ceramic: *this vase is ceramic.* **4** of or relating to ceramics: *ceramic arts and crafts.* [C19: from Greek *keramikos,* from *keramos* potter's clay, pottery]
ceramic hob *n* (on an electric cooker) a flat ceramic cooking surface having

heating elements fitted on the underside, usually patterned to show the areas where heat is produced.

ceramic oxide *n* a compound of oxygen with nonorganic material: recently discovered to act as a high-temperature superconductor.

ceramics (sɪ'ræmɪks) *n* (*functioning as sing*) the art and techniques of producing articles of clay, porcelain, etc. ▸ **ceramist** ('sɛrəmɪst) *or* **ce'ramicist** *n*

cerargyrite (sɪ'rɑːdʒɪ,raɪt) *n* a greyish-yellow or colourless soft secondary mineral consisting of silver chloride in cubic crystalline form: a source of silver. Formula: AgCl. Also called: **horn silver.** [C19: from Greek *keras* horn + *arguros* silver + -ITE[1]]

cerastes (sə'ræstiːz) *n, pl* **-tes.** any venomous snake of the genus *Cerastes,* esp. the horned viper. [C16: from Latin: horned serpent, from Greek *kerastēs* horned, from *keras* horn]

cerate ('sɪərɪt, -reɪt) *n* a hard ointment or medicated paste consisting of lard or oil mixed with wax or resin. [C16: from Latin *cērātum,* from *cēra* wax]

cerated ('sɪəreɪtɪd) *adj* (of certain birds, such as the falcon) having a cere.

cerato- *or before a vowel* **cerat-** *combining form.* **1** denoting horn or a hornlike part: *ceratodus.* **2** *Anatomy.* denoting the cornea. ◆ Also: **kerato-.** [from Greek *kerat-, keras* horn]

ceratodus (sɪ'rætədəs, ,sɛrə'təʊdəs) *n, pl* **-duses.** any of various extinct lungfish constituting the genus *Ceratodus,* common in Cretaceous and Triassic times. Compare **barramunda.** [C19: New Latin, from CERATO- + Greek *odous* tooth]

ceratoid ('sɛrə,tɔɪd) *adj* having the shape or texture of animal horn.

Cerberus ('sɜːbərəs) *n* **1** *Greek myth.* a dog, usually represented as having three heads, that guarded the entrance to Hades. **2 a sop to Cerberus.** a bribe or something given to propitiate a potential source of danger or problems. ▸ **Cerberean** (sə'bɪərɪən) *adj*

cercal ('sɜːkᵊl) *adj Zoology.* **1** of or relating to a tail. **2** of or relating to the cerci.

cercaria (sə'kɛərɪə) *n, pl* **-iae** (-ɪ,iː). one of the larval forms of trematode worms. It has a short forked tail and resembles an immature adult. [C19: New Latin, literally: tailed creature, from Greek *kerkos* tail] ▸ **cer'carial** *adj* ▸ **cer'carian** *adj, n*

cercis ('sɜːsɪs) *n* any tree or shrub of the leguminous genus *Cercis,* which includes the redbud and Judas tree. [C19: New Latin, from Greek *kerkis* weaver's shuttle, Judas tree]

cercopithecoid (,sɜːkəʊpɪ'θiːkɔɪd) *adj* **1** of, relating to, or belonging to the primate superfamily *Cercopithecoidea* (Old World monkeys). ◆ *n also* **cercopithecid** (,sɜːkəʊpɪ'θiːsɪd) **2** an Old World monkey. [C19: from Latin *cercopithēcus* monkey with a tail (from Greek *kerkopithēkos,* from *kerkos* tail + *pithēkos* ape) + -OID]

cercus ('sɜːkəs) *n, pl* **-ci** (-siː). one of a pair of sensory appendages at the tip of the abdomen of some insects and other arthropods. [C19: from New Latin, from Greek *kerkos* tail]

cere[1] (sɪə) *n* a soft waxy swelling, containing the nostrils, at the base of the upper beak in such birds as the parrot. [C15: from Old French *cire* wax, from Latin *cēra*]

cere[2] (sɪə) *vb* (*tr*) to wrap (a corpse) in a cerecloth. [C15: from Latin *cērāre,* from *cēra* wax]

cereal ('sɪərɪəl) *n* **1** any grass that produces an edible grain, such as oat, rye, wheat, rice, maize, sorghum, and millet. **2** the grain produced by such a plant. **3** any food made from this grain, esp. breakfast food. **4** (*modifier*) of or relating to any of these plants or their products: *cereal farming.* [C19: from Latin *cereālis* concerning agriculture, of CERES[1]]

cerebellar syndrome *n* a disease of the cerebellum characterized by unsteady movements and mispronunciation of words. Also called: **Nonne's syndrome.**

cerebellum (,sɛrɪ'bɛləm) *n, pl* **-lums** *or* **-la** (-lə). one of the major divisions of the vertebrate brain, situated in man above the medulla oblongata and beneath the cerebrum, whose function is coordination of voluntary movements and maintenance of bodily equilibrium. [C16: from Latin, diminutive of CEREBRUM] ▸ ,**cere'bellar** *adj*

cerebral ('sɛrɪbrəl; *U.S. also* sə'riːbrəl) *adj* **1** of or relating to the cerebrum or to the entire brain. **2** involving intelligence rather than emotions or instinct. **3** *Phonetics.* another word for **cacuminal.** ◆ *n* **4** *Phonetics.* a consonant articulated in the manner of a cacuminal consonant. ▸ **'cerebrally** *adv*

cerebral dominance *n* the normal tendency for one half of the brain, usually the left cerebral hemisphere in right-handed people, to exercise more control over certain functions (e.g. handedness and language) than the other.

cerebral haemorrhage *n* bleeding from an artery in the brain, which in severe cases causes a stroke.

cerebral hemisphere *n* either half of the cerebrum.

cerebral palsy *n* a nonprogressive impairment of muscular function and weakness of the limbs, caused by lack of oxygen to the brain immediately after birth, brain injury during birth, or viral infection.

cerebrate ('sɛrɪ,breɪt) *vb* (*intr*) *Usually facetious.* to use the mind; think; ponder; consider.

cerebration (,sɛrɪ'breɪʃən) *n* the act of thinking; consideration; thought. [C19: from Latin *cerebrum* brain]

cerebro- *or before a vowel* **cerebr-** *combining form.* indicating the brain: *cerebrospinal.* [from CEREBRUM]

cerebroside ('sɛrɪbrəʊ,saɪd) *n Biochem.* any glycolipid in which *N*-acyl sphingosine is combined with glucose or galactose: occurs in the myelin sheaths of nerves.

cerebrospinal (,sɛrɪbrəʊ'spaɪnᵊl) *adj* of or relating to the brain and spinal cord.

cerebrospinal fluid *n* the clear colourless fluid in the spaces inside and around the spinal cord and brain. Abbrev.: **CSF.**

cerebrospinal meningitis *or* **fever** *n* an acute infectious form of meningitis caused by the bacterium *Neisseria meningitidis,* characterized by high fever, skin rash, delirium, stupor, and sometimes coma. Also called: **epidemic meningitis.**

cerebrotonia (,sɛrɪbrəʊ'təʊnɪə) *n* a personality type characterized by restraint, alertness, and an intellectual approach to life: said to be correlated with an ectomorph body type. Compare **somatotonia, viscerotonia.**

cerebrovascular (,sɛrɪbrəʊ'væskjʊlə) *adj* of or relating to the blood vessels and the blood supply of the brain.

cerebrovascular accident *or* **cerebral vascular accident** *n* a sudden interruption of the blood supply to the brain caused by rupture of an artery in the brain (**cerebral haemorrhage**) or the blocking of a blood vessel, as by a clot of blood (**cerebral occlusion**). See **apoplexy, stroke** (sense 4).

cerebrum ('sɛrɪbrəm) *n, pl* **-brums** *or* **-bra** (-brə). **1** the anterior portion of the brain of vertebrates, consisting of two lateral hemispheres joined by a thick band of fibres: the dominant part of the brain in man, associated with intellectual function, emotion, and personality. See **telencephalon. 2** the brain considered as a whole. **3** the main neural bundle or ganglion of certain invertebrates. [C17: from Latin: the brain] ▸ **'cere,broid** *adj* ▸ **cerebric** ('sɛrɪbrɪk) *adj*

cerecloth ('sɪə,klɒθ) *n* waxed waterproof cloth of a kind formerly used as a shroud. [C15: from earlier *cered cloth,* from Latin *cērāre* to wax; see CERE[2]]

Ceredigion (,kɛrə'dɪgjᵊn) *n* a county of W Wales, on Cardigan Bay: created in 1996 from part of Dyfed; corresponds to the former Cardiganshire (abolished 1974): mainly agricultural, with the Cambrian Mountains in the E and N. Administrative centre: Aberaeron. Pop.: 63 700 (1996 est.). Area: 1793 sq. km (692 sq. miles).

cerement ('sɪəmənt) *n* **1** another name for **cerecloth. 2** any burial clothes. [C17: from French *cirement,* from *cirer* to wax; see CERE[2]]

ceremonial (,sɛrɪ'məʊnɪəl) *adj* **1** involving or relating to ceremony or ritual. ◆ *n* **2** the observance of formality, esp. in etiquette. **3** a plan for formal observances on a particular occasion; ritual. **4** *Christianity.* **4a** the prescribed order of rites and ceremonies. **4b** a book containing this. ▸ ,**cere'monialism** *n* ▸ ,**cere'monialist** *n* ▸ ,**cere'monially** *adv*

ceremonious (,sɛrɪ'məʊnɪəs) *adj* **1** especially or excessively polite or formal. **2** observing ceremony; involving formalities. ▸ ,**cere'moniously** *adv* ▸ ,**cere'moniousness** *n*

ceremony ('sɛrɪmənɪ) *n, pl* **-nies. 1** a formal act or ritual, often set by custom or tradition, performed in observation of an event or anniversary: *a ceremony commemorating Shakespeare's birth.* **2** a religious rite or series of rites. **3** a courteous gesture or act: *the ceremony of toasting the Queen.* **4** ceremonial observances or gestures collectively: *the ceremony of a monarchy.* **5 stand on ceremony.** to insist on or act with excessive formality. **6 without ceremony.** in a casual or informal manner. [C14: from Medieval Latin *cērēmōnia,* from Latin *caerimōnia* what is sacred, a religious rite]

Cerenkov (*Russian* tʃɪ'rjɛnkəf) *n* See (Pavel Alekseyevich) **Cherenkov.**

Ceres[1] ('sɪəriːz) *n* the Roman goddess of agriculture. Greek counterpart: **Demeter.**

Ceres[2] ('sɪəriːz) *n* the largest asteroid and the first to be discovered. It has a diameter of 930 kilometres.

ceresin ('sɛrɪsɪn) *n* a white wax extracted from ozocerite. [C19: irregularly from Latin *cēra* wax]

cereus ('sɪərɪəs) *n* **1** any tropical American cactus of the genus *Cereus,* esp. *C. jamacaru* of N Brazil, which grows to a height of 13 metres (40 feet). **2** any of several similar and related cacti, such as the night-blooming cereus. [C18: from New Latin, from Latin *cēreus* a wax taper, from *cēra* wax]

ceria ('sɪərɪə) *n* another name (not in technical usage) for **ceric oxide.** [New Latin, from CERIUM]

ceric ('sɪərɪk) *adj* of or containing cerium in the tetravalent state.

ceric oxide *n* a white or yellow solid used in ceramics, enamels, and radiation shields. Formula: CeO_2. Also called: **cerium dioxide, ceria.**

ceriferous (sɪ'rɪfərəs) *adj Biology.* producing or bearing wax.

cerise (sə'riːz, -'riːs) *n* **a** a moderate to dark red colour. **b** (*as adj*): *a cerise scarf.* [C19: from French: CHERRY]

cerium ('sɪərɪəm) *n* a malleable ductile steel-grey element of the lanthanide series of metals, used in lighter flints and as a reducing agent in metallurgy. Symbol: Ce; atomic no.: 58; atomic wt.: 140.115; valency: 3 or 4; relative density: 6.770; melting pt.: 798°C; boiling pt.: 3443°C. [C19: New Latin, from CERES (the asteroid) + -IUM]

cerium metals *pl n* the metals lanthanum, cerium, praseodymium, neodymium, promethium, and samarium, forming a sub-group of the lanthanides.

cermet ('sɜːmɪt) *n* any of several materials consisting of a metal matrix with ceramic particles disseminated through it. They are hard and resistant to high temperatures. Also called: **ceramal.** [C20: from CER(AMIC) + MET(AL)]

CERN (sɜːn) *n acronym for* Conseil Européen pour la Recherche Nucléaire; an organization of European states with a centre in Geneva for research in high-energy particle physics, now called the European Laboratory for Particle Physics.

Cernăuţi (tʃernə'utsj) *n* the Romanian name for **Chernovtsy.**

Cernuda (*Spanish* θer'nuða) *n* **Luis** (lwiʃ). 1902–63, Spanish poet. His major work is the autobiographical *Reality and Desire* (1936–64).

cernuous ('sɜːnjʊəs) *adj Botany.* (of some flowers or buds) drooping. [C17: from Latin *cernuus* leaning forwards, of obscure origin]

cero ('sɪərəʊ, 'sɪrəʊ) *n, pl* **-ro** *or* **-ros. 1** a large spiny-finned food fish, *Scomberomorus regalis,* of warm American coastal regions of the Atlantic: family *Scombridae* (mackerels, tunnies, etc.). **2** any similar or related fish. [C19: from Spanish: saw, sawfish, altered spelling of SIERRA]

cero- *combining form.* indicating the use of wax: *ceroplastic.* [from Greek *kēros* wax]

cerography (sɪəˈrɒgrəfɪ) *n* the art of engraving on a waxed plate on which a printing surface is created by electrotyping. ▸ **cerographic** (ˌsɪərəʊˈgræfɪk) *or* **ˌceroˈgraphical** *adj* ▸ **ceˈrographist** *n*

ceroplastic (ˌsɪərəʊˈplæstɪk) *adj* **1** relating to wax modelling. **2** modelled in wax.

ceroplastics (ˌsɪərəʊˈplæstɪks) *n* (*functioning as sing*) the art of wax modelling.

cerotic acid (sɪˈrɒtɪk) *n* another name (not in technical usage) for **hexacosanoic acid.**

cerotype (ˈsɪərəˌtaɪp) *n* a process for preparing a printing plate by engraving a wax-coated copper plate and then using this as a mould for an electrotype.

cerous (ˈsɪərəs) *adj* of or containing cerium in the trivalent state. [C19: from CERIUM + -OUS]

Cerro de Pasco (*Spanish* ˈθɛrrɔ ðe ˈpasko) *n* a town in central Peru, in the Andes: one of the highest towns in the world, 4400 m (14 436 ft.) above sea level; mining centre. Pop.: 62 749 (1993).

Cerro Gordo (*Spanish* ˈθɛrrɔ ˈgorðo) *n* a mountain pass in E Mexico, between Veracruz and Jalapa: site of a battle in the Mexican War (1847) in which American forces under General Scott decisively defeated the Mexicans.

cert (sɜːt) *n Informal.* something that is a certainty, esp. a horse that is certain to win a race (esp. in the phrase **a dead cert**).

cert. *abbrev. for:* **1** certificate. **2** certification. **3** certified.

certain (ˈsɜːtᵊn) *adj* **1** (*postpositive*) positive and confident about the truth of something; convinced: *I am certain that he wrote a book.* **2** (*usually postpositive*) definitely known: *it is certain that they were on the bus.* **3** (*usually postpositive*) sure; bound; destined: *he was certain to fail.* **4** decided or settled upon; fixed: *the date is already certain for the invasion.* **5** unfailing; reliable: *his judgment is certain.* **6** moderate or minimum: *to a certain extent.* **7 make certain of.** to ensure (that one will get something); confirm. ◆ *adv* **8 for certain.** definitely; without a doubt: *he will win for certain.* ◆ *determiner* **9a** known but not specified or named: *certain people may doubt this.* **9b** (*as pronoun; functioning as pl*): *certain of the members have not paid their subscriptions.* **10** named but not known: *he had written to a certain Mrs Smith.* [C13: from Old French, from Latin *certus* sure, fixed, from *cernere* to discern, decide]

certainly (ˈsɜːtᵊnlɪ) *adv* **1** with certainty; without doubt: *he certainly rides very well.* ◆ *sentence substitute.* **2** by all means; definitely: used in answer to questions.

certainty (ˈsɜːtᵊntɪ) *n, pl* **-ties. 1** the condition of being certain. **2** something established as certain or inevitable. **3 for a certainty.** without doubt.

CertEd (in Britain) *abbrev. for* Certificate in Education.

certes (ˈsɜːtɪz) *adv Archaic.* with certainty; truly. [C13: from Old French, ultimately from Latin *certus* CERTAIN]

certifiable (ˈsɜːtɪˌfaɪəbᵊl) *adj* **1** capable of being certified. **2** fit to be certified as insane. ▸ **ˈcertiˌfiably** *adv*

certificate *n* (səˈtɪfɪkɪt). **1** an official document attesting the truth of the facts stated, as of birth, marital status, death, health, completion of an academic course, ability to practise a profession, etc. **2** short for **share certificate.** ◆ *vb* (səˈtɪfɪˌkeɪt). **3** (*tr*) to authorize by or present with an official document. [C15: from Old French *certificat,* from *certifier* CERTIFY] ▸ **cerˈtificatory** *adj*

certificate of deposit *n* a negotiable certificate issued by a bank in return for a deposit of money for a term of up to five years. Abbrev.: **CD.**

certificate of incorporation *n Company law.* a signed statement that a company is duly incorporated.

certificate of origin *n* a document stating the name of the country that produced a specified shipment of goods: often required before importation of goods.

Certificate of Secondary Education *n* See **CSE.**

certificate of unruliness *n* (in Britain) the decision of a juvenile court that a young person on remand is too unmanageable for local-authority care and should be taken into custody.

certification (ˌsɜːtɪfɪˈkeɪʃən) *n* **1** the act of certifying or state of being certified. **2** *Law.* a document attesting the truth of a fact or statement.

certified (ˈsɜːtɪˌfaɪd) *adj* **1** holding or guaranteed by a certificate. **2** endorsed or guaranteed: *a certified cheque.* **3** (of a person) declared legally insane.

certified accountant *n* (in Britain) a member of the Chartered Association of Certified Accountants, who is authorized to audit company accounts. Compare **chartered accountant, certified public accountant.**

certified public accountant *n* (in the U.S.) a public accountant certified to have met state legal requirements. Compare **certified accountant.**

certify (ˈsɜːtɪˌfaɪ) *vb* **-fies, -fying, -fied. 1** to confirm or attest (to), usually in writing: *the letter certified her age.* **2** (*tr*) to endorse or guarantee (that certain required standards have been met). **3** to give reliable information or assurances: *he certified that it was Walter's handwriting.* **4** (*tr*) to declare legally insane. **5** (*tr*) *U.S. and Canadian.* (of a bank) to state in writing on (a cheque) that payment is guaranteed. [C14: from Old French *certifier,* from Medieval Latin *certificāre* to make certain, from Latin *certus* CERTAIN + *facere* to make] ▸ **ˈcertiˌfier** *n*

certiorari (ˌsɜːtɪɔːˈrɛəraɪ) *n Law.* an order of a superior court directing that a record of proceedings in a lower court be sent up for review. See also **mandamus, prohibition.** [C15: from legal Latin: to be informed]

certitude (ˈsɜːtɪˌtjuːd) *n* confidence; certainty. [C15: from Church Latin *certitūdō,* from Latin *certus* CERTAIN]

cerulean (sɪˈruːlɪən) *n* **a** a deep blue colour; azure. **b** (*as adj*): *a cerulean sea.* [C17: from Latin *caeruleus,* probably from *caelum* sky]

cerumen (sɪˈruːmɛn) *n* the soft brownish-yellow wax secreted by glands in the auditory canal of the external ear. Nontechnical name: **earwax.** [C18: from New Latin, from Latin *cēra* wax + ALBUMEN] ▸ **ceˈruminous** *adj*

ceruse (səˈruːs) *n* another name for **white lead** (sense 1). [C14: from Old French *céruse,* from Latin *cērussa,* perhaps ultimately from Greek *kēros* wax]

cerussite *or* **cerusite** (ˈsɪərəˌsaɪt) *n* a usually white mineral, found in veins. It is a source of lead. Composition: lead carbonate. Formula: $PbCO_3$. Crystal structure: orthorhombic. Also called: **white lead ore.** [C19: from Latin *cērussa* (see CERUSE) + -ITE[1]]

Cervantes (səˈvæntiːz; *Spanish* θɛrˈβantes) *n* **Miguel de** (miˈɣel ðe), full surname *Cervantes Saavedra.* 1547–1616, Spanish dramatist, poet, and prose writer, most famous for *Don Quixote* (1605), which satirizes the chivalric romances and greatly influenced the development of the novel.

cervelat (ˈsɜːvəˌlæt, -ˌlɑː) *n* a smoked sausage made from pork and beef. [C17: via obsolete French from Italian *cervellata*]

cervical (ˈsɜːvɪkᵊl, səˈvaɪ-) *adj* of or relating to the neck or cervix. [C17: from New Latin *cervīcālis,* from Latin *cervīx* neck]

cervical smear *n Med.* a smear of cellular material taken from the neck (cervix) of the uterus for detection of cancer. Also called: **Pap test** *or* **smear.**

cervicitis (ˌsɜːvɪˈsaɪtɪs) *n* inflammation of the neck of the uterus.

cervicography (ˌsɜːvɪˈkɒgrəfɪ) *n Med.* a method of cervical screening in which the neck of the uterus is photographed to facilitate the early detection of cancer.

cervicum (ˈsɜːvɪkəm, səˈvaɪ-) *n Zoology.* the flexible region between the prothorax and head in insects.

cervid (ˈsɜːvɪd) *n* **1** any ruminant mammal of the family *Cervidae,* including the deer, characterized by the presence of antlers. ◆ *adj* **2** of, relating to, or belonging to the *Cervidae.* [C19: from New Latin *Cervidae,* from Latin *cervus* deer]

Cervin (sɛrvɛ̃) *n* **Mont.** the French name for the **Matterhorn.**

cervine (ˈsɜːvaɪn) *adj* **1** resembling or relating to a deer. **2** of a dark yellowish-brown colour. [C19: from Latin *cervīnus,* from *cervus* a deer]

cervix (ˈsɜːvɪks) *n, pl* **cervixes** *or* **cervices** (səˈvaɪsiːz). **1** the technical name for **neck. 2** any necklike part of an organ, esp. the lower part of the uterus that extends into the vagina. [C18: from Latin]

Cesarean *or* **Cesarian** (sɪˈzɛərɪən) *adj U.S.* variant spellings of **Caesarean.**

Cesena (*Italian* tʃeˈzɛːna) *n* a city in N Italy, in Emilia-Romagna. Pop.: 89 500 (1990).

cesium (ˈsiːzɪəm) *n* the usual U.S. spelling of **caesium.**

České Budějovice (*Czech* ˈtʃɛskɛː ˈbudjɛjɔvitsɛ) *n* a city in the S Czech Republic, on the Vltava (Moldau) River. Pop.: 175 000 (1993). German name: **Budweis.**

Československo (ˈtʃɛskɔslɔvɛnskɔ) *n* the Czech name for **Czechoslovakia.**

cespitose (ˈsɛspɪˌtəʊs) *adj* a variant spelling (esp. U.S.) of **caespitose.** ▸ **ˈcespiˌtosely** *adv*

cess[1] (sɛs) *n* **1** *Brit.* any of several special taxes, such as a land tax in Scotland. **2** (formerly in Ireland) **2a** the obligation to provide the soldiers and household of the lord deputy with supplies at fixed prices. **2b** any military exaction. ◆ *vb* **3** (*tr*) *Brit.* to tax or assess for taxation. **4** (*tr*) (formerly in Ireland) to impose (soldiers) upon a population, to be supported by them. [C16: short for ASSESSMENT]

cess[2] (sɛs) *n* an Irish slang word for **luck** (esp. in the phrase **bad cess to you!**). [C19: probably from CESS[1] (sense 2)]

cess[3] (sɛs) *n* short for **cesspool.**

cessation (sɛˈseɪʃən) *n* a ceasing or stopping; discontinuance; pause: *temporary cessation of hostilities.* [C14: from Latin *cessātiō* a delaying, inactivity, from *cessāre* to be idle, desist from, from *cēdere* to yield, CEDE]

cesser (ˈsɛsə) *n Law.* the coming to an end of a term interest or annuity.

cession (ˈsɛʃən) *n* **1** the act of ceding, esp. of ceding rights, property, or territory. **2** something that is ceded, esp. land or territory. [C14: from Latin *cessiō,* from *cēdere* to yield]

cessionary (ˈsɛʃənərɪ) *n, pl* **-aries.** *Law.* a person to whom something is transferred; assignee; grantee.

cesspool (ˈsɛsˌpuːl) *or* **cesspit** (ˈsɛsˌpɪt) *n* **1** Also called: **sink, sump.** a covered cistern, etc., for collecting and storing sewage or waste water. **2** a filthy or corrupt place: *a cesspool of iniquity.* [C17: changed (through influence of POOL[1]) from earlier *cesperalle,* from Old French *souspirail* vent, air, from *soupirer* to sigh; see SUSPIRE]

c'est la vie *French.* (sɛ la vi) that's life.

cestode (ˈsɛstəʊd) *n* any parasitic flatworm of the class *Cestoda,* which includes the tapeworms. [C19: from New Latin *Cestoidea* ribbon-shaped creatures, from Latin *cestus* belt, girdle; see CESTUS[1]]

cestoid (ˈsɛstɔɪd) *adj* (esp. of tapeworms and similar animals) ribbon-like in form.

cestus[1] (ˈsɛstəs) *or* **cestos** (ˈsɛstɒs) *n Classical myth.* the girdle of Aphrodite (Venus) decorated to cause amorousness. [C16: from Latin, from Greek *kestos* belt, from *kentein* to stitch]

cestus[2] *or* **caestus** (ˈsɛstəs) *n, pl* **-tus** *or* **-tuses.** (in classical Roman boxing) a pugilist's gauntlet of bull's hide loaded or studded with metal. [C18: from Latin *caestus,* probably from *caedere* to strike, slay]

cesura (sɪˈzjʊərə) *n, pl* **-ras** *or* **-rae** (-riː). *Prosody.* a variant spelling of **caesura.** ▸ **ceˈsural** *adj*

CET *abbrev. for:* **1** Central European Time. **2** Common External Tariff.

cetacean (sɪˈteɪʃən) *adj also* **cetaceous. 1** of, relating to, or belonging to the *Cetacea,* an order of aquatic placental mammals having no hind limbs and a blowhole for breathing: includes toothed whales (dolphins, porpoises, etc.) and whalebone whales (rorquals, right whales, etc.). ◆ *n* **2** a whale. [C19: from New Latin *Cētācea,* ultimately from Latin *cētus* whale, from Greek *kētos*]

cetane (ˈsiːteɪn) *n* a colourless insoluble liquid alkane hydrocarbon used in the determination of the cetane number of diesel fuel. Formula: $C_{16}H_{34}$. Also called: **hexadecane.** [C19: from Latin *cētus* whale + -ANE, so called because related compounds are found in sperm whale oil]

cetane number *n* a measure of the quality of a diesel fuel expressed as the percentage of cetane in a mixture of cetane and 1-methylnapthalene of the same quality as the given fuel. Also called: **cetane rating.** Compare **octane number.**

Cetatea Albă (tʃe'tatea 'albə) *n* the Romanian name for **Byelgorod-Dnestrovski.**

cete (siːt) *n* a group of badgers. [C15: perhaps from Latin *coetus* assembly, from *coīre* to come together]

ceteris paribus ('ketərɪs 'pɑːrɪbʊs) other things being equal. [C17: Latin]

Cetinje (*Serbo-Croat* 'tsetinjɛ) *n* a city in S Yugoslavia, in SW Montenegro: former capital of Montenegro (until 1945); palace and fortified monastery, residences of Montenegrin prince-bishops. Pop.: 15 924 (1991).

Cetnik ('tʃetnɪk, tʃet'niːk) *n* a variant spelling of **Chetnik.**

cetology (siː'tɒlədʒɪ) *n* the branch of zoology concerned with the study of whales (cetaceans). [C19: from Latin *cētus* whale] ► **cetological** (ˌsiːtə'lɒdʒɪkᵊl) *adj* ► **ce'tologist** *n*

cetrimide ('setrɪˌmaɪd) *n* a quaternary ammonium compound used as a detergent and, having powerful antiseptic properties, for sterilizing surgical instruments, cleaning wounds, etc.

Cetshwayo *or* **Cetewayo** (*Zulu* ke'tʃwɑːjɒ) *n* ?1826–84, king of the Zulus (1873–79): defeated the British at Isandhlwana (1879) but was overwhelmed by them at Ulundi (1879); captured, he stated his case in London, and was reinstated as ruler of part of Zululand (1883).

Cetus ('siːtəs) *n, Latin genitive* **Ceti** ('siːtaɪ) a large constellation on the celestial equator near Pisces and Aquarius. It contains the variable star Mira Ceti. [Latin: whale]

Ceuta (*Spanish* 'θeuta) *n* an enclave in Morocco on the Strait of Gibraltar, consisting of a port and military station: held by Spain since 1580. Pop.: 68 796 (1996 est.).

Cévennes (*French* sevɛn) *n* a mountain range in S central France, on the SE edge of the Massif Central. Highest peak: 1754 m (5755 ft.).

Ceylon (sɪ'lɒn) *n* **1** the former name (until 1972) of **Sri Lanka. 2** an island in the Indian Ocean, off the SE coast of India: consists politically of the republic of Sri Lanka. Area: 64 644 sq. km (24 959 sq. miles). ► **Ceylonese** (ˌselə'niːz, ˌsiːlə-) *adj*

Ceylon moss *n* a red East Indian seaweed, *Gracilaria lichenoides,* from which agar is made.

Ceyx ('siːɪks) *n Greek myth.* a king of Trachis in Thessaly and the husband of Alcyone. He died in a shipwreck and his wife drowned herself in grief. Compare **Alcyone**[1] (sense 1).

Cézanne (*French* sezan) *n* **Paul** (pɔl). 1839–1906, French postimpressionist painter, who was a major influence on modern art, esp. cubism, in stressing the structural elements latent in nature, such as the sphere and the cone.

cf *or* **CF** *abbrev. for* cost and freight. Also: **c & f.**

Cf *the chemical symbol for* californium.

CF *Chiefly Brit. abbrev. for* Chaplain to the Forces.

cf. *abbrev. for* confer. [Latin: compare]

c/f *Book-keeping. abbrev. for* carried forward.

CFC *abbrev. for* chlorofluorocarbon.

CFD *abbrev. for* computational fluid dynamics.

CFE *abbrev. for:* **1** College of Further Education. **2** Conventional Forces in Europe: negotiations between NATO and the Warsaw Pact to reduce conventional forces located between the Atlantic and the Urals.

cfi *or* **CFI** *abbrev. for* cost, freight, and insurance (included in the price quoted). Also: **c.i.f.**

CFS *abbrev. for* chronic fatigue syndrome.

cg 1 *abbrev. for* centre of gravity. ◆ **2** *symbol for* centigram.

CG *abbrev. for:* **1** captain general. **2** coastguard. **3** Coldstream Guards. **4** consul general.

CGBR *abbrev. for* Central Government Borrowing Requirement.

CGM *Chiefly Brit. abbrev. for* Conspicuous Gallantry Medal.

CGS (in Britain) *abbrev. for* Chief of General Staff.

cgs units *pl n* a metric system of units based on the centimetre, gram, and second. For scientific and technical purposes these units have been replaced by SI units.

CGT *abbrev. for* capital gains tax.

ch *abbrev. for* custom house.

CH 1 *abbrev. for* Companion of Honour (a Brit. title). ◆ **2** *international car registration for* Switzerland. [from French *Confédération Helvétique*]

ch. *abbrev. for:* **1** chain (unit of measure). **2** chapter. **3** *Chess.* check. **4** chief. **5** church.

chabazite ('kæbəˌzaɪt) *n* a pink, white, or colourless zeolite mineral consisting of a hydrated silicate of calcium, sodium, potassium, and aluminium in hexagonal crystalline form. Formula: $(Ca,Na,K)Al_2Si_4O_{12}.6H_2O$. [C19: from French *chabazie* from Late Greek *khabazios,* erroneous for *khalazios* stone similar to a hailstone, from Greek *khalazios* of hail, from *khalaza* hailstone + -ITE[1]]

Chablis ('ʃæblɪ; *French* ʃabli) *n* (*sometimes not caps.*) a dry white burgundy wine made around Chablis, in central France.

Chabrier ('ʃæbrɪeɪ; *French* ʃabrie) *n* (**Alexis**) **Emmanuel** (emanɥel). 1841–94, French composer; noted esp. for the orchestral rhapsody *España* (1883).

Chabrol (*French* ʃabrɔl) *n* **Claude** (klod). born 1930, French film director, whose films, such as *Les Biches* (1968), *Le Boucher* (1969), and *Au couleur du mensonge* (1999), show a penchant for the bizarre.

cha-cha-cha (ˌtʃɑːtʃɑː'tʃɑː) *or* **cha-cha** *n* **1** a Latin-American ballroom dance with small steps and swaying hip movements. **2** a piece of music composed for this dance. ◆ *vb* (*intr*) **3** to perform this dance. [C20: from American (Cuban) Spanish]

chacma ('tʃækmə) *n* a baboon, *Papio* (or *Chaeropithecus*) *ursinus,* having coarse greyish hair and occurring in southern and eastern Africa. [C19: from Khoikhoi]

Chaco (*Spanish* 'tʃako) *n* See **Gran Chaco.**

chaconne (ʃə'kɒn; *French* ʃakɔn) *n* **1** a musical form consisting of a set of continuous variations upon a ground bass. See also **passacaglia. 2** *Archaic.* a dance in slow triple time probably originating in Spain. [C17: from French, from Spanish *chacona,* probably imitative of the castanet accompaniment]

chacun à son goût *French.* (ʃakœ̃n a sɔ̃ gu) each to his own taste.

chad (tʃæd) *n* the small pieces of cardboard or paper removed during the punching of holes in computer printer paper, paper tape, etc. [C20: perhaps based on CHAFF[1]]

Chad (tʃæd) *n* **1** a republic in N central Africa: made a territory of French Equatorial Africa in 1910; became independent in 1960; contains much desert and the Tibesti Mountains, with Lake Chad in the west; produces chiefly cotton and livestock; has suffered intermittent civil war from 1963 and prolonged drought. Official languages: Arabic; French. Religion: Muslim majority, also Christian and animist. Currency: franc. Capital: Ndjamena. Pop.: 7 360 000 (1998 est.). Area: 1 284 000 sq. km (495 750 sq. miles). French name: **Tchad. 2 Lake.** a lake in N central Africa: fed chiefly by the Shari River, it has no apparent outlet. Area: 10 000 to 26 000 sq. km (4000 to 10 000 sq. miles), varying seasonally.

Chadderton ('tʃædətᵊn) *n* a town in NW England, in Oldham unitary authority, in Greater Manchester. Pop.: 34 026 (1991).

Chadic ('tʃædɪk) *n* **1** a subfamily of the Afro-Asiatic family of languages, spoken in an area west and south of Lake Chad, the chief member of which is Hausa. ◆ *adj* **2** denoting, relating to, or belonging to this group of languages.

chador ('tʃʌdə) *n* a variant spelling of **chuddar.**

Chadwick ('tʃædwɪk) *n* **1** Sir **Edwin.** 1800–90, British social reformer, known for his *Report on the Sanitary Condition of the Labouring Population of Great Britain* (1842). **2** Sir **James.** 1891–1974, British physicist: discovered the neutron (1932): Nobel prize for physics 1935. **3 Lynn** (**Russell**). born 1914, British sculptor in metal.

Chaeronea (ˌkerə'niːə) *n* an ancient Greek town in W Boeotia: site of the victory of Philip of Macedon over the Athenians and Thebans (338 B.C.) and of Sulla over Mithridates (86 B.C.).

chaeta ('kiːtə) *n, pl* **-tae** (-tiː). any of the chitinous bristles on the body of such annelids as the earthworm and the lugworm: used in locomotion; a seta. [C19: New Latin, from Greek *khaitē* long hair]

chaetiferous (kiː'tɪfərəs) *adj Zoology.* having bristles.

chaetognath ('kiːtɒgˌnæθ) *n* any small wormlike marine invertebrate of the phylum *Chaetognatha,* including the arrowworms, having a coelom and a ring of bristles around the mouth. [C19: New Latin *Chaetognatha,* literally: hair-jaw, from CHAETA + Greek *gnathos* jaw]

chaetopod ('kiːtəˌpɒd) *n* any annelid worm of the classes *Oligochaeta* or *Polychaeta.* See **oligochaete, polychaete.** [C19: from New Latin *Chaetopoda;* see CHAETA, -POD]

chafe (tʃeɪf) *vb* **1** to make or become sore or worn by rubbing. **2** (*tr*) to warm (the hands, etc.) by rubbing. **3** to irritate or be irritated or impatient: *he was chafed because he was not allowed out.* **4** (*intr;* often foll. by *on, against,* etc.) to cause friction; rub. **5 chafe at the bit.** See **champ**[1] (sense 3). ◆ *n* **6** a soreness or irritation caused by friction. [C14: from Old French *chaufer* to warm, ultimately from Latin *calefacere,* from *calēre* to be warm + *facere* to make]

chafer ('tʃeɪfə) *n* any of various scarabaeid beetles, such as the cockchafer and rose chafer. [Old English *ceafor;* related to Old Saxon *kevera,* Old High German *chevar*]

chaff[1] (tʃɑːf) *n* **1** the mass of husks, etc., separated from the seeds during threshing. **2** finely cut straw and hay used to feed cattle. **3** something of little worth; rubbish (esp. in the phrase **separate the wheat from the chaff**). **4** the dry membranous bracts enclosing the flowers of certain composite plants. **5** thin strips of metallic foil released into the earth's atmosphere to deflect radar signals and prevent detection. [Old English *ceaf;* related to Old High German *keva* husk] ► **'chaffy** *adj*

chaff[2] (tʃɑːf) *n* **1** light-hearted teasing or joking; banter. ◆ *vb* **2** to tease good-naturedly; banter. [C19: probably slang variant of CHAFE, perhaps influenced by CHAFF[1]] ► **'chaffer** *n*

chaffer ('tʃæfə) *vb* **1** (*intr*) to haggle or bargain. **2** to chatter, talk, or say idly; bandy (words). **3** (*tr*) *Obsolete.* to deal in; barter. ◆ *n* **4** haggling or bargaining. [C13 *chaffare,* from *chep* bargain + *fare* journey; see CHEAP, FARE] ► **'chafferer** *n*

chaffinch ('tʃæfɪntʃ) *n* a common European finch, *Fringilla coelebs,* with black and white wings and, in the male, a reddish body and blue-grey head. [Old English *ceaffinc,* from *ceaf* CHAFF[1] + *finc* FINCH]

chafing dish ('tʃeɪfɪŋ) *n* a vessel with a heating apparatus beneath it, for cooking or keeping food warm at the table.

Chagall (*French* ʃagal) *n* **Marc** (mark). 1887–1985, French painter and illustrator, born in Russia, noted for his richly coloured pictures of men, animals, and objects in fantastic combinations and often suspended in space: his work includes 12 stained glass windows for a synagogue in Jerusalem (1961) and the decorations for the ceiling of the Paris Opera House (1964).

Chagas' disease ('ʃɑːgəs) *n* a form of trypanosomiasis found in South America, caused by the protozoan *Trypanosoma cruzi,* characterized by fever and, often, inflammation of the heart muscles. Also called: (**South**) **American trypanosomiasis.** Compare **sleeping sickness.** [C20: named after Carlos *Chagas* (1879–1934), Brazilian physician who first described it]

Chagres (*Spanish* 'tʃaɣres) *n* a river in Panama, flowing southwest through Gatún Lake, then northwest to the Caribbean Sea.

chagrin ('ʃægrɪn) *n* **1** a feeling of annoyance or mortification. ◆ *vb* (*tr*) **2** to embarrass and annoy; mortify. [C17: from French *chagrin, chagriner,* of unknown origin] ▸ 'chagrined *adj*

chain (tʃeɪn) *n* **1** a flexible length of metal links, used for confining, connecting, pulling, etc., or in jewellery. **2** (*usually pl*) anything that confines, fetters, or restrains: *the chains of poverty.* **3** (*usually pl*) Also called: **snow chains.** a set of metal links that fit over the tyre of a motor vehicle to increase traction and reduce skidding on an icy surface. **4a** a number of establishments such as hotels, shops, etc., having the same owner or management. **4b** (*as modifier*): *a chain store.* **5** a series of related or connected facts, events, etc. **6** (of reasoning) a sequence of arguments each of which takes the conclusion of the preceding as a premise. See (as an example) **sorites. 7** Also called: **Gunter's chain.** a unit of length equal to 22 yards. **8** Also called: **engineer's chain.** a unit of length equal to 100 feet. **9** *Chem.* two or more atoms or groups bonded together so that the configuration of the resulting molecule, ion, or radical resembles a chain. See also **open chain, ring**[1] (sense 18). **10** *Geography.* a series of natural features, esp. approximately parallel mountain ranges. **11 off the chain.** *Austral. and N.Z. informal.* free from responsibility. ◆ *vb* **12** *Surveying.* to measure with a chain or tape. **13** (*tr;* often foll. by *up*) to confine, tie, or make fast with or as if with a chain. **14** short for **chain-stitch.** [C13: from Old French *chaine,* ultimately from Latin; see CATENA]

Chain (tʃeɪn) *n* Sir **Ernst Boris.** 1906–79, British biochemist, born in Germany: purified and adapted penicillin for clinical use; with Fleming and Florey shared the Nobel prize for physiology or medicine 1945.

chain drive *n Engineering.* a chain of links passing over sprockets that transmits rotation from one shaft to another.

chain gang *n U.S.* a group of convicted prisoners chained together, usually while doing hard labour.

chain grate *n* a type of mechanical stoker for a furnace, in which the grate consists of an endless chain that draws the solid fuel into the furnace as it rotates.

chain letter *n* a letter, often with a request for and promise of money, that is sent to many people who add to or recopy it and send it on to others: illegal in many countries.

chain lightning *n* another name for **forked lightning.**

chain mail *n* another term for **mail**[2] (sense 1).

chainman ('tʃeɪnmən) *n, pl* **-men.** *Surveying.* a person who does the chaining in a survey.

chainplate ('tʃeɪn,pleɪt) *n* a metal plate on the side of a vessel, to which the shrouds are attached.

chain printer *n* a line printer in which the type is on a continuous chain, used to print computer output.

chain-react *vb* (*intr*) to undergo a chain reaction.

chain reaction *n* **1** a process in which a neutron colliding with an atomic nucleus causes fission and the ejection of one or more other neutrons, which induce other nuclei to split. **2** a chemical reaction in which the product of one step is a reactant in the following step. **3** a series of rapidly occurring events, each of which precipitates the next.

chain rule *n Maths.* a theorem that may be used in the differentiation of the function of a function. It states that $du/dx = (du/dy)(dy/dx)$, where y is a function of x and u a function of y.

chain saw *n* a motor-driven saw, usually portable, in which the cutting teeth form links in a continuous chain.

chain shot *n* cannon shot comprising two balls or half balls joined by a chain, much used formerly, esp. in naval warfare to destroy rigging.

chain-smoke *vb* to smoke (cigarettes, etc.) continually, esp. lighting one from the preceding one. ▸ **chain smoker** *n*

chain stitch *n* **1** an ornamental looped embroidery stitch resembling the links of a chain. ◆ *vb* **chain-stitch. 2** to sew (something) with this stitch.

chain store *n* one of several retail enterprises under the same ownership and management. Also called: **multiple store.**

chain wheel *n Engineering.* a toothed wheel that meshes with a roller chain to transmit motion.

chair (tʃeə) *n* **1** a seat with a back on which one person sits, typically having four legs and often having arms. **2** an official position of authority: *a chair on the board of directors.* **3** the chairman of a debate or meeting: *the speaker addressed the chair.* **4** a professorship: *the chair of German.* **5** *Railways.* an iron or steel cradle bolted to a sleeper in which the rail sits and is locked in position. **6** short for **sedan chair. 7 in the chair.** chairing a debate or meeting. **8 take the chair.** to preside as chairman for a meeting, etc. **9 the chair.** an informal name for **electric chair.** ◆ *vb* (*tr*) **10** to preside over (a meeting). **11** *Brit.* to carry aloft in a sitting position after a triumph or great achievement. **12** to provide with a chair of office. **13** to install in a chair. [C13: from Old French *chaiere,* from Latin *cathedra,* from Greek *kathedra,* from *kata-* down + *hedra* seat; compare CATHEDRAL]

chairborne ('tʃeə,bɔːn) *adj Informal.* having an administrative or desk job rather than a more active one.

chairbound ('tʃeə,baʊnd) *adj Social welfare.* unable to walk; dependent on a wheelchair for mobility.

chairlift ('tʃeə,lɪft) *n* a series of chairs suspended from a power-driven cable for conveying people, esp. skiers, up a mountain.

chairman ('tʃeəmən) *n, pl* **-men. 1** Also called: **chairperson;** (*fem*) **chairwoman.** a person who presides over a company's board of directors, a committee, a debate, an administrative department, etc. **2** *Hist.* someone who carries a sedan chair. ▸ **'chairman,ship** *n*

USAGE *Chairman* can seem inappropriate when applied to a woman, while *chairwoman* can be offensive. *Chair* and *chairperson* can be applied to either a man or a woman; *chair* is generally preferred to *chairperson.*

chairperson ('tʃeə,pɜːsᵊn) *n* another word for **chairman** (sense 1).

USAGE See at **chairman.**

chaise (ʃeɪz) *n* **1** a light open horse-drawn carriage, esp. one with two wheels designed for two passengers. **2** short for **post chaise** and **chaise longue. 3** a gold coin first issued in France in the 14th century, depicting the king seated on a throne. [C18: from French, variant of Old French *chaiere* CHAIR]

chaise longue ('ʃeɪz 'lɒŋ; *French* ʃɛz lɔ̃g) *n, pl* **chaise longues** *or* **chaises longues** ('ʃeɪz 'lɒŋ; *French* ʃɛz lɔ̃g) a long low chair for reclining, with a back and single armrest. [C19: from French: long chair]

Chaka ('ʃaka) *n* a variant spelling of **Shaka.**

chakra ('tʃækrə, 'tʃʌkrə) *n* (in yoga) any of the seven major energy centres in the body. [C19: from Sanskrit *cakra* wheel, circle]

chalaza (kə'leɪzə) *n, pl* **-zas** *or* **-zae** (-ziː). **1** one of a pair of spiral threads of albumen holding the yolk of a bird's egg in position. **2** the basal part of a plant ovule, where the integuments and nucellus are joined. [C18: New Latin, from Greek: hailstone] ▸ **cha'lazal** *adj*

chalazion (kə'leɪzɪən) *n* a small cyst on the eyelid resulting from chronic inflammation of a meibomian gland. Also called: **meibomian cyst.** [C18: from Greek: a small CHALAZA]

chalcanthite (kæl'kænθaɪt) *n* a blue secondary mineral consisting of hydrated copper sulphate in triclinic crystalline form. Formula: $CuSO_4.5H_2O$. [C19: via German from Latin *chalcanthum* copper sulphate solution, from Greek *khalkanthon,* from *khalkos* copper + *anthos* flower; see -ITE[1]]

chalcedony (kæl'sɛdənɪ) *n, pl* **-nies.** a microcrystalline often greyish form of quartz with crystals arranged in parallel fibres: a gemstone. Formula: SiO_2. [C15: from Late Latin *chalcēdōnius,* from Greek *khalkēdōn* a precious stone (Revelation 21:19), perhaps named after *Khalkēdōn* Chalcedon, town in Asia Minor] ▸ **chalcedonic** (,kælsɪ'dɒnɪk) *adj*

chalcid *or* **chalcid fly** ('kælsɪd) *n* any tiny hymenopterous insect of the family *Chalcididae* and related families, whose larvae are parasites of other insects. [C19: from New Latin *Chalcis* type genus, from Greek *khalkos* copper, referring to its metallic sheen]

Chalcidice (kæl'sɪdɪsɪ) *n* a peninsula of N central Greece, in Macedonia Central, ending in the three promontories of Kassandra, Sithonia, and Akti. Area: 2945 sq. km (1149 sq. miles). Modern Greek name: **Khalkidíki.**

Chalcis ('kælsɪs) *n* a city in SE Greece, at the narrowest point of the Euripus strait: important since the 7th century B.C., founding many colonies in ancient times. Pop.: 47 600 (1995 est.). Modern Greek name: **Khalkís.** Medieval English name: **Negropont.**

chalco- *or before a vowel* **chalc-** *combining form.* indicating copper or a copper alloy: *chalcopyrite; chalcolithic.* [from Greek *khalkos* copper]

chalcocite ('kælkə,saɪt) *n* a lead-grey or black mineral, found as a copper ore or in veins. It is a source of copper. Composition: copper sulphide. Formula: Cu_2S. Crystal structure: orthorhombic. [C19: changed from earlier *chalcosine,* from Greek *khalkos* copper + -ITE[1]]

chalcogen ('kælkə,dʒɛn) *n* any of the elements oxygen, sulphur, selenium, tellurium, or polonium, of group 6A of the periodic table. [C20: from CHALCO(PYRITE) + -GEN]

chalcography (kæl'kɒgrəfɪ) *n* the art of engraving on copper or brass. ▸ **chal'cographer** *or* **chal'cographist** *n* ▸ **chalcographic** (,kælkə'græfɪk) *or* **,chalco'graphical** *adj*

chalcolithic (,kælkə'lɪθɪk) *adj Archaeol.* of or relating to a period characterized by the use of both stone and bronze implements.

chalcopyrite (,kælkə'paɪraɪt, -'paɪə-) *n* a widely distributed yellow mineral consisting of a sulphide of copper and iron in tetragonal crystalline form: the principal ore of copper. Formula: $CuFeS_2$. Also called: **copper pyrites.**

Chaldea *or* **Chaldaea** (kæl'diːə) *n* **1** an ancient region of Babylonia; the land lying between the Euphrates delta, the Persian Gulf, and the Arabian desert. **2** another name for **Babylonia.**

Chaldean *or* **Chaldaean** (kæl'diːən) *n* **1** a member of an ancient Semitic people who controlled S Babylonia from the late 8th to the late 7th century B.C. **2** the dialect of Babylonian spoken by this people. ◆ *adj* **3** of or relating to the ancient Chaldeans or their language.

Chaldee (kæl'diː) *n* **1** a nontechnical term for **Biblical Aramaic,** once believed to be the language of the ancient Chaldeans. **2** the actual language of the ancient Chaldeans. See also **Chaldean** (sense 2). **3** an inhabitant of ancient Chaldea; a Chaldean. ◆ Also (for senses 1, 2): **Chaldaic** (kæl'deɪɪk).

chaldron ('tʃɔːldrən) *n* a unit of capacity equal to 36 bushels. Formerly used in the U.S. for the measurement of solids, being equivalent to 1.268 cubic metres. Used in Britain for both solids and liquids, it is equivalent to 1.309 cubic metres. [C17: from Old French *chauderon* CAULDRON]

chalet ('ʃæleɪ; *French* ʃalɛ) *n* **1** a type of wooden house of Swiss origin, typically low, with wide projecting eaves. **2** a similar house used esp. as a ski lodge, garden house, etc. [C19: from French (Swiss dialect)]

Chaliapin (*Russian* ʃa'ljapin) *n* **Fyodor Ivanovich** ('fjɔdər i'vanəvitʃ). 1873–1938, Russian operatic bass singer.

chalice ('tʃælɪs) *n* **1** *Poetic.* a drinking cup; goblet. **2** *Christianity.* a gold or silver cup containing the wine at Mass. **3** a cup-shaped flower. [C13: from Old French, from Latin *calix* cup; related to Greek *kalux* calyx]

chaliced ('tʃælɪst) *adj* (of plants) having cup-shaped flowers.

chalicothere ('kælɪkəʊ,θɪə) *n* any of various very large extinct Tertiary horse-like perissodactyl mammals that had clawed feet but otherwise resembled titanotheres. [C19: from New Latin *Chalicotherium* type genus, from Greek *khalix* gravel + Greek *thērion* a little beast, from *thēr* wild animal]

chalk (tʃɔːk) *n* **1** a soft fine-grained white sedimentary rock consisting of nearly pure calcium carbonate, containing minute fossil fragments of marine organisms, usually without a cementing material. **2** a piece of chalk or a substance like chalk, often coloured, used for writing and drawing on a blackboard. **3** a line, mark, etc. made with chalk. **4** *Billiards, etc.* a small cube of prepared chalk or similar substance for rubbing the tip of a cue. **5** *Brit.* a score, tally, or record.

6 as alike (*or* **different**) **as chalk and cheese.** *Informal.* totally different in essentials. **7 by a long chalk.** *Brit. informal.* by far. **8 can't tell** (*or* **doesn't know**) **chalk from cheese.** to be unable to judge or appreciate important differences. **9 not by a long chalk.** *Brit. informal.* by no means; not possibly. **10** (*modifier*) made of chalk. ♦ *vb* **11** to draw or mark (something) with chalk. **12** (*tr*) to mark, rub, or whiten with or as if with chalk. **13** (*intr*) (of paint) to become chalky; powder. **14** (*tr*) to spread chalk on (land) as a fertilizer. ♦ See also **chalk out, chalk up.** [Old English *cealc,* from Latin *calx* limestone, from Greek *khalix* pebble] ▸ **'chalk,like** *adj* ▸ **'chalky** *adj* ▸ **'chalkiness** *n*

chalk and talk *n Sometimes derogatory.* a formal method of teaching, in which the focal points are the blackboard and the teacher's voice, as contrasted with more informal child-centred activities.

chalkboard ('tʃɔːk,bɔːd) *n* a U.S. and Canadian word for **blackboard.**

chalkface ('tʃɔːk,feɪs) *n Brit. informal.* **a** the work or art of teaching in a school, esp. classroom teaching as distinct from organizational responsibilities (esp. in the phrase **at the chalkface**). **b** (*as modifier*): *chalkface experience.*

chalk out *vb (tr, adv)* to outline (a plan, scheme, etc.); sketch.

chalkpit ('tʃɔːk,pɪt) *n* a quarry for chalk.

chalkstone ('tʃɔːk,stəʊn) *n Pathol.* another name for **tophus.**

chalk talk *n U.S. and Canadian.* an informal lecture with pertinent points, explanatory diagrams, etc., shown on a blackboard.

chalk up *vb (tr, adv) Informal.* **1** to score or register (something): *we chalked up 100 in the game.* **2** to credit (money) to an account etc. (esp. in the phrase **chalk it up**).

challah *or* **hallah** ('hɑːlə; *Hebrew* xa'la) *n, pl* **-lahs** *or* **-loth** (*Hebrew* -'lɔt). bread, usually in the form of a plaited loaf, traditionally eaten by Jews to celebrate the Sabbath. [from Hebrew *hallāh*]

challenge ('tʃælɪndʒ) *vb (mainly tr)* **1** to invite or summon (someone to do something, esp. to take part in a contest). **2** (*also intr*) to call (something) into question; dispute. **3** to make demands on; stimulate: *the job challenges his ingenuity.* **4** to order (a person) to halt and be identified or to give a password. **5** *Law.* to make formal objection to (a juror or jury). **6** to lay claim to (attention, etc.). **7** (*intr*) *Hunting.* (of a hound) to cry out on first encountering the scent of a quarry. **8** to inject (an experimental animal immunized with a test substance) with disease microorganisms to test for immunity to the disease. ♦ *n* **9** a call to engage in a fight, argument, or contest. **10** a questioning of a statement or fact; a demand for justification or explanation. **11** a demanding or stimulating situation, career, object, etc. **12** a demand by a sentry, watchman, etc., for identification or a password. **13** *U.S.* an assertion that a person is not entitled to vote or that a vote is invalid. **14** *Law.* a formal objection to a person selected to serve on a jury (**challenge to the polls**) or to the whole body of jurors (**challenge to the array**). [C13: from Old French *chalenge,* from Latin *calumnia* CALUMNY] ▸ **'challengeable** *adj* ▸ **'challenger** *n*

challenging ('tʃælɪndʒɪŋ) *adj* demanding or stimulating: *a challenging new job.*

challis ('ʃælɪ, -lɪs) *or* **challie** ('ʃælɪ) *n* a lightweight plain-weave fabric of wool, cotton, etc., usually with a printed design. [C19: probably from a surname]

chalone ('kæləʊn) *n* any internal secretion that inhibits a physiological process or function. [C20: from Greek *khalōn,* from *khalan* to slacken]

Châlons-sur-Marne (*French* ʃalɔ̃syrmarn) *n* a city in NE France, on the River Marne: scene of Attila's defeat by the Romans (451 A.D.). Pop.: 51 530 (1990). Shortened form: **Châlons.**

Chalon-sur-Saône (*French* ʃalɔ̃syrson) *n* an industrial city in E central France, on the Saône River. Pop.: 54 575 (1990). Shortened form: **Chalon.**

chalutz *or* ***halutz*** *Hebrew.* (xa'lʊts; *English* hɑː'lʊts) *n, pl* **-lutzim** (-luː'tsiːm; *English* -'luːtsɪm). a member of an organization of immigrants to Israeli agricultural settlements. [literally: pioneer, fighter]

chalybeate (kə'lɪbɪɪt) *adj* **1** containing or impregnated with iron salts. ♦ *n* **2** any drug containing or tasting of iron. [C17: from New Latin *chalybēātus,* ultimately from *khalups* iron]

chalybite ('kælɪ,baɪt) *n* another name for **siderite** (sense 1).

cham (kæm) *n* an archaic word for **khan**[1] (sense 1). [C16: from French, from Persian *khān;* see KHAN[1]]

Cham (tʃæm) *n* **1** (*pl* **Cham** *or* **Chams**) a member of a people of Indonesian stock living in Cambodia and central Vietnam. **2** the language of this people, belonging to the Malayo-Polynesian family.

chamade (ʃə'mɑːd) *n Military.* (formerly) a signal by drum or trumpet inviting an enemy to a parley. [C17: from French, from Portuguese *chamada,* from *chamar* to call, from Latin *clamāre*]

Chamaeleon (kə'miːlɪən) *n, Latin genitive* **Chamaeleontis** (kə,miːlɪ'ɒntɪs). a faint constellation lying between Volans and the South celestial pole.

chamaephyte ('kæmə,faɪt) *n* a plant whose buds are close to the ground. [C20: from Greek *khamai* on the ground + -PHYTE]

chamber ('tʃeɪmbə) *n* **1** a meeting hall, esp. one used for a legislative or judicial assembly. **2** a reception room or audience room in an official residence, palace, etc. **3** *Archaic or poetic.* a room in a private house, esp. a bedroom. **4a** a legislative, deliberative, judicial, or administrative assembly. **4b** any of the houses of a legislature. **5** an enclosed space; compartment; cavity: *the smallest chamber in the caves.* **6** the space between two gates of the locks of a canal, dry dock, etc. **7** an enclosure for a cartridge in the cylinder of a revolver or for a shell in the breech of a cannon. **8** *Obsolete.* a place where the money of a government, corporation, etc., was stored; treasury. **9** short for **chamber pot. 10** *N.Z.* the freezing room in an abattoir. **11** (*modifier*) of, relating to, or suitable for chamber music: *a chamber concert.* ♦ *vb* **12** (*tr*) to put in or provide with a chamber. ♦ See also **chambers.** [C13: from Old French *chambre,* from Late Latin *camera* room, Latin: vault, from Greek *kamara*]

chamber counsel *or* **counsellor** *n* a counsel who advises in private and does not plead in court.

chambered nautilus *n* another name for the **pearly nautilus.**

chamberhand ('tʃeɪmbə,hænd) *n N.Z.* a worker in the cold storage area of a slaughterhouse.

chamberlain ('tʃeɪmbəlɪn) *n* **1** an officer who manages the household of a king. **2** the steward of a nobleman or landowner. **3** the treasurer of a municipal corporation. [C13: from Old French *chamberlayn,* of Frankish origin; related to Old High German *chamarling* chamberlain, Latin *camera* CHAMBER] ▸ **'chamberlain,ship** *n*

Chamberlain ('tʃeɪmbəlɪn) *n* **1** Sir (**Joseph**) **Austen.** 1863–1937, British Conservative statesman; foreign secretary (1924–29); awarded a Nobel peace prize for his negotiation of the Locarno Pact (1925). **2** his father, **Joseph.** 1836–1914, British statesman; originally a Liberal, he resigned in 1886 over Home Rule for Ireland and became leader of the Liberal Unionists; a leading advocate of preferential trading agreements with members of the British Empire. **3** his son, (**Arthur**) **Neville.** 1869–1940, British Conservative statesman; prime minister (1937–40): pursued a policy of appeasement towards Germany; following the German invasion of Poland, he declared war on Germany on Sept. 3, 1939. **4 Owen.** born 1920, U.S. physicist, who discovered the antiproton. Nobel prize for physics jointly with Emilio Segré 1959.

chambermaid ('tʃeɪmbə,meɪd) *n* a woman or girl employed to clean and tidy bedrooms, now chiefly in hotels.

chamber music *n* music for performance by a small group of instrumentalists.

chamber of commerce *n* (*sometimes caps.*) an organization composed mainly of local businessmen to promote, regulate, and protect their interests.

chamber of trade *n* (*sometimes caps.*) a national organization representing local chambers of commerce.

chamber orchestra *n* a small orchestra of about 25 players, used for the authentic performance of baroque and early classical music as well as modern music written specifically for a small orchestra.

chamber organ *n Music.* a small compact organ used esp. for the authentic performance of preclassical music.

chamber pot *n* a vessel for urine, used in bedrooms.

chambers ('tʃeɪmbəz) *pl n* **1** a judge's room for hearing private cases not taken in open court. **2** (in England) the set of rooms occupied by barristers where clients are interviewed (in London, mostly in the Inns of Court). **3** *Brit. archaic.* a suite of rooms; apartments. **4** (in the U.S.) the private office of a judge.

Chambertin (*French* ʃɑ̃bɛrtɛ̃) *n* a dry red burgundy wine produced in Gevrey-Chambertin in E France.

Chambéry (*French* ʃɑ̃beri) *n* a city in SE France, in the Alps: skiing centre; former capital of the duchy of Savoy. Pop.: 54 120 (1990).

Chambord (*French* ʃɑ̃bɔr) *n* a village in N central France: site of a famous Renaissance chateau.

chambray ('ʃæmbreɪ) *n* a smooth light fabric of cotton, linen, etc., with white weft and a coloured warp. [C19: after *Cambrai;* see CAMBRIC]

chambré ('ʃɑ̃breɪ) *adj* (of wine) at room temperature. [from French, from *chambrer* to bring (wine) to room temperature, from *chambre* room]

chameleon (kə'miːlɪən) *n* **1** any lizard of the family *Chamaeleontidae* of Africa and Madagascar, having long slender legs, a prehensile tail and tongue, and the ability to change colour. **2** a changeable or fickle person. [C14: from Latin *chamaeleon,* from Greek *khamaileōn,* from *khamai* on the ground + *leōn* LION] ▸ **chameleonic** (kə,miːlɪ'ɒnɪk) *adj* ▸ **cha'meleon-,like** *adj*

chametz *or* ***chometz*** *Hebrew.* (*Hebrew* xa'mɛtʒ; *Yiddish* 'xɔmətʒ) *n Judaism.* leavened food which may not be eaten during Passover.

chamfer ('tʃæmfə) *n* **1** a narrow flat surface at the corner of a beam, post, etc., esp. one at an angle of 45°. Compare **bevel** (sense 1). ♦ *vb (tr)* **2** to cut such a surface on (a beam, etc.). **3** another word for **chase**[2] (sense 4). [C16: back formation from *chamfering,* from Old French *chamfrein,* from *chant* edge (see CANT[2]) + *fraindre* to break, from Latin *frangere*] ▸ **'chamferer** *n*

chamfron, chamfrain ('tʃæmfrən), *or* **chanfron** *n* a piece of armour for a horse's head. [C14: from Old French *chanfrein,* from *chafresner* to harness, from *chief* head + *frener* to bridle]

chamois ('ʃæmɪ; *French* ʃamwa) *n, pl* **-ois. 1** ('ʃæmwɑː). a sure-footed goat antelope, *Rupicapra rupicapra,* inhabiting mountains of Europe and SW Asia, having vertical horns with backward-pointing tips. **2** a soft suede leather formerly made from the hide of this animal, now obtained from the skins of sheep and goats. **3** Also called: **chamois leather, shammy** (**leather**), **chammy** (**leather**) ('ʃæmɪ). a piece of such leather or similar material used for polishing, etc. **4** ('ʃæmwɑː). a yellow to greyish-yellow colour. ♦ *vb (tr)* **5** to dress (leather or skin) like chamois. **6** to polish with a chamois. [C16: from Old French, from Late Latin *camox* of uncertain origin]

chamomile ('kæmə,maɪl) *n* a variant spelling of **camomile.**

Chamonix ('ʃæmənɪ; *French* ʃamɔni) *n* a town in SE France, in the Alps at the foot of Mont Blanc: skiing and tourist centre. Pop.: 9255 (latest est.).

champ[1] (tʃæmp) *vb* **1** to munch (food) noisily like a horse. **2** (when *intr,* often foll. by *on, at,* etc.) to bite (something) nervously or impatiently; gnaw. **3 champ** (*or* **chafe**) **at the bit.** *Informal.* to be impatient to start work, a journey, etc. ♦ *n* **4** the act or noise of champing. **5** *Ulster dialect.* a dish of mashed potatoes and spring onions or leeks. [C16: probably of imitative origin] ▸ **'champer** *n*

champ[2] (tʃæmp) *n Informal.* short for **champion** (sense 1).

champac *or* **champak** ('tʃæmpæk, 'tʃʌmpʌk) *n* a magnoliaceous tree, *Michelia champaca,* of India and the East Indies. Its fragrant yellow flowers yield an oil used in perfumes and its wood is used for furniture. [C18: from Hindi *campak,* from Sanskrit *campaka,* of Dravidian origin]

champagne (ʃæm'peɪn) *n* **1** (*sometimes cap.*) a white sparkling wine produced around Reims and Epernay, France. **2** (loosely) any effervescent white wine. **3a** a colour varying from a pale orange-yellow to a greyish-yellow. **3b** (*as adj*): *a* *champagne carpet.* **4** (*modifier*) denoting a luxurious lifestyle: *a champagne capitalist.*

Champagne-Ardenne (ʃæm'peɪnɑː'dɛn; *French* ʃɑ̃paɲ- ardɛn) *n* a region of NE France: a countship and commercial centre in medieval times; it consists of a great plain, with sheep and dairy farms and many vineyards.

champagne socialist *n* a professed socialist who enjoys an extravagant lifestyle.

champaign (ʃæm'peɪn) *n* **1** Also called: **campagna.** an expanse of open level or gently undulating country. **2** an obsolete word for **battlefield.** [C14: from Old French *champaigne,* from Late Latin *campānia;* see CAMPAIGN]

Champaigne (ʃæm'peɪn; *French* ʃɑ̃pɛɲ) *n* **Philippe de** (filip də). 1602–74, French painter, born in Brussels: noted particularly for his portraits and historical and religious scenes.

champers ('ʃæmpəz) *n* a slang name for **champagne.**

champerty ('tʃæmpətɪ) *n, pl* **-ties.** *Law.* (formerly) an illegal bargain between a party to litigation and an outsider whereby the latter agrees to pay for the action and thereby share in any proceeds recovered. See also **maintenance.** [C14: from Anglo-French *champartie,* from Old French *champart* share of produce, from *champ* field + *part* share (a feudal lord's)] ► **'champertous** *adj*

champignon (tʃæm'pɪnjən) *n* any of various agaricaceous edible mushrooms, esp. *Marasmius oreades* (**fairy ring champignon**) and the meadow mushroom. [C16: from French, perhaps from Vulgar Latin *campīnus* (unattested) of the field, from Latin *campus* plain, field]

Champigny-sur-Marne (*French* ʃɑ̃piɲisyrmarn) *n* a suburb of Paris, on the River Marne. Pop.: 80 290 (latest est.).

champion ('tʃæmpɪən) *n* **1a** a person who has defeated all others in a competition: *a chess champion.* **1b** (*as modifier*): *a champion team.* **2a** a plant or animal that wins first place in a show, etc. **2b** (*as modifier*): *a champion marrow.* **3** a person who defends a person or cause: *champion of the underprivileged.* **4** (formerly) a warrior or knight who did battle for another, esp. a king or queen, to defend their rights or honour. ◆ *adj* **5** *Northern English dialect.* first rate; excellent. ◆ *adv* **6** *Northern English dialect.* very well; excellently. ◆ *vb* (*tr*) **7** to support; defend: *we champion the cause of liberty.* [C13: from Old French, from Late Latin *campiō,* from Latin *campus* field, battlefield]

championship ('tʃæmpɪən,ʃɪp) *n* **1** (*sometimes pl*) any of various contests held to determine a champion. **2** the title or status of being a champion. **3** support for or defence of a cause, person, etc.

Champlain[1] (ʃæm'pleɪn) *n* **Lake.** a lake in the northeastern U.S., between the Green Mountains and the Adirondack Mountains: linked by the **Champlain Canal** to the Hudson River and by the Richelieu River to the St Lawrence; a major communications route in colonial times.

Champlain[2] (ʃæm'pleɪn; *French* ʃɑ̃plɛ̃) *n* **Samuel de** (samyel də). ?1567–1635, French explorer; founder of Quebec (1608) and governor of New France (1633–35).

champlevé *French.* (ʃɑ̃lve; *English* ,ʃæmplə'veɪ) *adj* **1** of or relating to a process of enamelling by which grooves are cut into a metal base and filled with enamel colours. ◆ *n* **2** an object enamelled by this process. [C19: from *champ* field (level surface) + *levé* raised]

Champollion (*French* ʃɑ̃pɔljɔ̃) *n* **Jean François** (ʒɑ̃ frɑ̃swa). 1790–1832, French Egyptologist, who deciphered the hieroglyphics on the Rosetta stone.

Champs Elysées (ʃɒnz eɪ'liːzeɪ; *French* ʃɑ̃z elize) *n* a major boulevard in Paris, leading from the Arc de Triomphe: site of the Elysées Palace and government offices.

Chanc. *abbrev. for:* **1** Chancellor. **2** Chancery.

chance (tʃɑːns) *n* **1a** the unknown and unpredictable element that causes an event to result in a certain way rather than another, spoken of as a real force. **1b** (*as modifier*): *a chance meeting.* Related adj: **fortuitous. 2** fortune; luck; fate. **3** an opportunity or occasion. **4** a risk; gamble: *you take a chance with his driving.* **5** the extent to which an event is likely to occur; probability. **6** an unpredicted event, esp. a fortunate one: *that was quite a chance, finding him here.* **7** *Archaic.* an unlucky event; mishap. **8 by chance. 8a** accidentally: *he slipped by chance.* **8b** perhaps: *do you by chance have a room?* **9** (**the**) **chances are …** it is likely (that) …. **10 on the chance.** acting on the possibility; in case. **11 the main chance.** the opportunity for personal gain (esp. in the phrase **an eye to the main chance**). ◆ *vb* **12** (*tr*) to risk; hazard: *I'll chance the worst happening.* **13** to happen by chance; be the case by chance: *I chanced to catch sight of her as she passed.* **14 chance on** (*or* **upon**). to come upon by accident: *he chanced on the solution to his problem.* **15 chance one's arm.** to attempt to do something although the chance of success may be slight. [C13: from Old French *cheance,* from *cheoir* to fall, occur, from Latin *cadere*] ► **'chanceful** *adj* ► **'chanceless** *adj*

chancel ('tʃɑːnsəl) *n* the part of a church containing the altar, sanctuary, and choir, usually separated from the nave and transepts by a screen. [C14: from Old French, from Latin *cancellī* (plural) lattice]

chancellery *or* **chancellory** ('tʃɑːnsələrɪ, -slərɪ) *n, pl* **-leries** *or* **-lories. 1** the building or room occupied by a chancellor's office. **2** the position, rank, or office of a chancellor. **3** *U.S.* **3a** the residence or office of an embassy or legation. **3b** the office of a consulate. **4** *Brit.* another name for a diplomatic **chancery.** [C14: from Anglo-French *chancellerie,* from Old French *chancelier* CHANCELLOR]

chancellor ('tʃɑːnsələ, -slə) *n* **1** the head of the government in several European countries. **2** *U.S.* the president of a university or, in some colleges, the chief administrative officer. **3** *Brit. and Canadian.* the honorary head of a university. Compare **vice chancellor** (sense 1). **4** *U.S.* (in some states) the presiding judge of a court of chancery or equity. **5** *Brit.* the chief secretary of an embassy. **6** *Christianity.* a clergyman acting as the law officer of a bishop. **7** *Archaic.* the chief secretary of a prince, nobleman, etc. [C11: from Anglo-French *chanceler,* from Late Latin *cancellārius* porter, secretary, from Latin *cancellī* lattice; see CHANCEL] ► **'chancellor,ship** *n*

Chancellor of the Duchy of Lancaster *n Brit.* a minister of the crown, nominally appointed as representative of the Queen (who is the Duke, not Duchess, of Lancaster), but in practice chiefly employed on parliamentary work determined by the prime minister.

Chancellor of the Exchequer *n Brit.* the cabinet minister responsible for finance.

chance-medley *n Law.* a sudden quarrel in which one party kills another; unintentional but not blameless killing. [C15: from Anglo-French *chance medlee* mixed chance]

chancer ('tʃɑːnsə) *n Slang.* an unscrupulous or dishonest opportunist who is prepared to try any dubious scheme for making money or furthering his own ends. [C19: from CHANCE + -ER[1]]

chancery ('tʃɑːnsərɪ) *n, pl* **-ceries. 1** Also called: **Chancery Division.** (in England) the Lord Chancellor's court, now a division of the High Court of Justice. **2** Also called: **court of chancery.** (in the U.S.) a court of equity. **3** *Brit.* the political section or offices of an embassy or legation. **4** another name for **chancellery. 5** a court of public records; archives. **6** *Christianity.* a diocesan office under the supervision of a bishop's chancellor, having custody of archives, issuing official enactments, etc. **7 in chancery. 7a** *Law.* (of a suit) pending in a court of equity. **7b** *Wrestling, boxing.* (of a competitor's head) locked under an opponent's arm. **7c** in an awkward or helpless situation. [C14: shortened from CHANCELLERY]

chancre ('ʃæŋkə) *n Pathol.* a small hard nodular growth, which is the first diagnostic sign of acquired syphilis. [C16: from French, from Latin: CANCER] ► **'chancrous** *adj*

chancroid ('ʃæŋkrɔɪd) *n* **1** a soft venereal ulcer, esp. of the male genitals, caused by infection with the bacillus *Haemophilus ducreyi.* ◆ *adj* **2** relating to or resembling a chancroid or chancre. ► **chan'croidal** *adj*

chancy *or* **chancey** ('tʃɑːnsɪ) *adj* **chancier, chanciest.** *Informal.* of uncertain outcome or temperament; risky. ► **'chancily** *adv* ► **'chanciness** *n*

chandelier (,ʃændɪ'lɪə) *n* an ornamental hanging light with branches and holders for several candles or bulbs. [C17: from French: candleholder, from Latin CANDELABRUM]

chandelle (ʃæn'del; *French* ʃɑ̃dɛl) *n* **1** *Aeronautics.* an abrupt climbing turn almost to the point of stalling, in which an aircraft's momentum is used to increase its rate of climb. ◆ *vb* **2** (*intr*) to carry out a chandelle. [French, literally: CANDLE]

Chandernagore (,tʃʌndənə'gɔː) *n* a port in E India, in S West Bengal on the Hooghly River: a former French settlement (1686–1950). Pop.: 120 378 (1991).

Chandigarh (,tʃʌndɪ'gɑː) *n* a city and Union Territory of N India, joint capital of the Punjab and Haryana: modern city planned in the 1950s by Le Corbusier. Pop.: 504 094 (1991), of city; 642 015 (1991), of union territory. Area (of union territory): 114 sq. km (44 sq. miles).

chandler ('tʃɑːndlə) *n* **1** a dealer in a specified trade or merchandise: *corn chandler; ship's chandler.* **2** a person who makes or sells candles. **3** *Brit. obsolete.* a retailer of grocery provisions; shopkeeper. [C14: from Old French *chandelier* one who makes or deals in candles, from *chandelle* CANDLE]

Chandler ('tʃɑːndlə) *n* **Raymond** (**Thornton**). 1888–1959, U.S. thriller writer: created Philip Marlowe, one of the first detective heroes in fiction.

chandlery ('tʃɑːndlərɪ) *n, pl* **-dleries. 1** the business, warehouse, or merchandise of a chandler. **2** a place where candles are kept.

Chandragupta (,tʃʌndrə'guptə) *n* Greek name *Sandracottos.* died ?297 B.C., ruler of N India, who founded the Maurya dynasty (325) and defeated Seleucus (?305).

Chandrasekhar (,tʃændrə'siːkə) *n* **Subrahmanyan** (,subrə'mænjən). 1910–95, U.S. astronomer born in Lahore, India (now Pakistan). His work on stellar evolution led to an understanding of white dwarfs: shared the Nobel prize for physics 1983.

Chandrasekhar limit *n Astronomy.* the upper limit to the mass of a white dwarf, equal to 1.44 solar masses. A star having a mass above this limit will continue to collapse to form a neutron star. [C20: named after S. CHANDRASEKHAR, who calculated it]

Chanel (*French* ʃanɛl) *n* **Gabrielle** (gabriɛl), known as *Coco Chanel.* 1883–1971, French couturière and perfumer, who created "the little black dress" and the perfume Chanel No. 5.

Chang (tʃæŋ) *n* another name for the **Yangtze.**

Changan ('tʃæŋ'ɑːn) *n* a former name of **Xi An.**

Changchiakow *or* **Changchiak'ou** ('tʃæŋ'tʃjɑː'kəʊ) *n* a variant transliteration of the Chinese name for **Zhangjiakou.**

Changchow *or* **Ch'ang-chou** ('tʃæŋ'tʃaʊ) *n* a variant transliteration of the Chinese name for **Zhangzhou.**

Changchun *or* **Ch'ang Ch'un** ('tʃæŋ'tʃʊn) *n* a city in NE China, capital of Jilin province: as **Hsinking,** capital of the Japanese state of Manchukuo (1932–45). Pop.: 2 110 000 (1991 est.).

Changde ('tʃæŋ'deɪ), **Changteh,** *or* **Ch'ang-te** *n* a port in SE central China, in N Hunan province, near the mouth of the Yuan River: severely damaged by the Japanese in World War II. Pop.: 301 276 (1990 est.).

change (tʃeɪndʒ) *vb* **1** to make or become different; alter. **2** (*tr*) to replace with or exchange for another: *to change one's name.* **3** (sometimes foll. by *to* or *into*) to transform or convert or be transformed or converted. **4** to give and receive (something) in return; interchange: *to change places with someone.* **5** (*tr*) to give or receive (money) in exchange for the equivalent sum in a smaller denomination or different currency. **6** (*tr*) to remove or replace the coverings of: *to change a baby.* **7** (when *intr,* may be foll. by *into* or *out of*) to put on other clothes. **8** (*intr*) (of the moon) to pass from one phase to the following one. **9** to operate (the gear lever of a motor vehicle) in order to change the gear ratio: *to* *change gear.* **10** to alight from (one bus, train, etc.) and board another. **11 change face.** to rotate the telescope of a surveying instrument through 180° horizontally and vertically, taking a second sighting of the same object in order to reduce error. **12 change feet.** *Informal.* to put on different shoes, boots, etc. **13 change front.** **13a** *Military.* to redeploy (a force in the field) so that its main weight of weapons points in another direction. **13b** to alter one's attitude, opinion, etc. **14 change hands.** to pass from one owner to another. **15 change one's mind.** to alter one's decision or opinion. **16 change one's tune.** to alter one's attitude or tone of speech. ◆ *n* **17** the act or fact of changing or being changed. **18** a variation, deviation, or modification. **19** the substitution of one thing for another; exchange. **20** anything that is or may be substituted for something else. **21** variety or novelty (esp. in the phrase **for a change**): *I want to go to France for a change.* **22** a different or fresh set, esp. of clothes. **23** money given or received in return for its equivalent in a larger denomination or in a different currency. **24** the balance of money given or received when the amount tendered is larger than the amount due. **25** coins of a small denomination regarded collectively. **26** (*often cap.*) *Archaic.* a place where merchants meet to transact business; an exchange. **27** the act of passing from one state or phase to another. **28** the transition from one phase of the moon to the next. **29** the order in which a peal of bells may be rung. **30** *Sport.* short for **changeover** (sense 3b). **31** *Slang.* desirable or useful information. **32** *Obsolete.* fickleness or caprice. **33 change of heart.** a profound change of outlook, opinion, etc. **34 get no change out of (someone).** *Slang.* not to be successful in attempts to exploit or extract information from (someone). **35 ring the changes.** to vary the manner or performance of an action that is often repeated. ◆ See also **change down, changeover, change round, change up.** [C13: from Old French *changier,* from Latin *cambīre* to exchange, barter] ▸ **'changeless** *adj* ▸ **'changelessly** *adv* ▸ **'changelessness** *n* ▸ **'changer** *n*

changeable ('tʃeɪndʒəbəl) *adj* **1** able to change or be changed; fickle: *changeable weather.* **2** varying in colour when viewed from different angles or in different lights. ▸ ˌ**changea'bility** *or* **'changeableness** *n* ▸ **'changeably** *adv*

change down *vb* (*intr, adv*) to select a lower gear when driving.

changeful ('tʃeɪndʒfʊl) *adj* often changing; inconstant; variable. ▸ **'changefully** *adv* ▸ **'changefulness** *n*

changeling ('tʃeɪndʒlɪŋ) *n* **1** a child believed to have been exchanged by fairies for the parents' true child. **2** *Archaic.* **2a** an idiot. **2b** a fickle or changeable person.

change of life *n* a nontechnical name for **menopause.**

change of venue *n Law.* the removal of a trial out of one jurisdiction into another.

changeover ('tʃeɪndʒˌəʊvə) *n* **1** an alteration or complete reversal from one method, system, or product to another: *a changeover to decimal currency.* **2** a reversal of a situation, attitude, etc. **3** *Sport.* **3a** the act of transferring to or being relieved by a team-mate in a relay race, as by handing over a baton, etc. **3b** Also called: **change, takeover.** the point in a relay race at which the transfer is made. **4** *Sport, chiefly Brit.* the exchange of ends by two teams, esp. at half time. ◆ *vb* **change over.** (*adv*) **5** to adopt (a completely different position or attitude): *the driver and navigator changed over after four hours.* **6** (*intr*) *Sport, chiefly Brit.* (of two teams) to exchange ends of a playing field, etc., as after half time.

change point *n Surveying.* a point to which a foresight and backsight are taken in levelling; turning point.

change-ringing *n* **1** the art of bell-ringing in which a set of bells is rung in an established order which is then changed. **2** variations on a topic or theme.

change round *vb* (*adv*) **1** to place in or adopt a different or opposite position. ◆ *n* **changeround. 2** the act of changing to a different position.

change up *vb* (*intr, adv*) to select a higher gear when driving.

Changsha *or* **Ch'ang-sha** ('tʃæŋ'ʃɑː) *n* a port in SE China, capital of Hunan province, on the Xiang River. Pop.: 1 330 000 (1991 est.).

Changteh *or* **Ch'ang-te** ('tʃæŋ'teɪ) *n* a variant transliteration of the Chinese name for **Changde.**

Chania ('hɑːnɪə) *n* a variant spelling of **Canea.**

channel[1] ('tʃænəl) *n* **1** a broad strait connecting two areas of sea. **2** the bed or course of a river, stream, or canal. **3** a navigable course through a body of water. **4** (*often pl*) a means or agency of access, communication, etc.: *to go through official channels.* **5** a course into which something can be directed or moved: *a new channel of thought.* **6** *Electronics.* **6a** a band of radio frequencies assigned for a particular purpose, esp. the broadcasting of a television signal. **6b** a path for an electrical signal: *a stereo set has two channels.* **6c** a thin semiconductor layer between the source and drain of a field-effect transistor, the conductance of which is controlled by the gate voltage. **7** a tubular or trough-shaped passage for fluids. **8** a groove or flute, as in the shaft of a column. **9** *Computing.* **9a** a path along which data can be transmitted between a central processing unit and one or more peripheral devices. **9b** one of the lines along the length of a paper tape on which information can be stored in the form of punched holes. **10** short for **channel iron.** ◆ *vb* **-nels, -nelling, -nelled** *or U.S.* **-nels, -neling, -neled. 11** to provide or be provided with a channel or channels; make or cut channels in (something). **12** (*tr*) to guide into or convey through a channel or channels: *information was channelled through to them.* **13** to serve as a medium through whom the spirit of (a person of a former age) allegedly communicates with the living. **14** (*tr*) to form a groove or flute in (a column, etc.). [C13: from Old French *chanel,* from Latin *canālis* pipe, groove, conduit; see CANAL] ▸ **'channeller** *n*

channel[2] ('tʃænəl) *n Nautical.* a flat timber or metal ledge projecting from the hull of a vessel above the chainplates to increase the angle of the shrouds. [C18: variant of earlier *chainwale;* see CHAIN, WALE[1] (planking)]

Channel ('tʃænəl) *n* **the.** short for **English Channel.**

channel captain *n Marketing.* the most powerful member, and often the one that decides specifications, in a channel for distributing goods (which usually consists of a manufacturer, wholesaler, and retailer). The channel captain is sometimes the manufacturer but in the case of a chain store it may be the retailer.

Channel Country *n* **the.** an area of E central Australia, in SW Queensland: crossed by intermittent rivers and subject to both flooding and long periods of drought.

channel-hop *vb* **-hops, -hopping, -hopped.** (*intr*) to change television channels repeatedly using a remote control device.

channel iron *or* **bar** *n* a rolled-steel bar with a U-shaped cross section. Sometimes shortened to **channel.**

Channel Islands *pl n* a group of islands in the English Channel, off the NW coast of France, consisting of Jersey, Guernsey, Alderney, Brechou, Great Sark, Little Sark, Herm, Jethou, and Lihou (British crown dependencies), and the Roches Douvres and the Îles Chausey (which belong to France): the only part of the duchy of Normandy remaining to Britain. Pop.: 142 949 (1991). Area: 194 sq. km (75 sq. miles).

channelize *or* **channelise** ('tʃænəlaɪz) *vb* (*tr*) to guide through or as if through a channel; provide a channel for.

Channel Tunnel *n* the Anglo-French railway tunnel that runs beneath the English Channel, between Folkestone and Coquelles, near Calais; opened in 1994. Also called: **Chunnel, Eurotunnel.**

chanson de geste *French.* (ʃɑ̃sɔ̃ də ʒɛst) *n* one of a genre of Old French epic poems celebrating heroic deeds, the most famous of which is the *Chanson de Roland.* [literally: song of exploits]

chant (tʃɑːnt) *n* **1** a simple song or melody. **2** a short simple melody in which several words or syllables are assigned to one note, as in the recitation of psalms. **3** a psalm or canticle performed by using such a melody. **4** a rhythmic or repetitious slogan, usually spoken or sung, as by sports supporters, etc. **5** monotonous or singsong intonation in speech. ◆ *vb* **6** to sing or recite (a psalm, prayer, etc.) as a chant. **7** to intone (a slogan) rhythmically or repetitiously. **8** to speak or say monotonously as if intoning a chant. [C14: from Old French *chanter* to sing, from Latin *cantāre,* frequentative of *canere* to sing] ▸ **'chantingly** *adv*

chanter ('tʃɑːntə) *n* **1** a person who chants. **2** the pipe on a set of bagpipes that is provided with finger holes and on which the melody is played.

chanterelle (ˌtʃæntə'rɛl) *n* any saprotrophic basidiomycetous fungus of the genus *Cantharellus,* esp. *C. cibarius,* having an edible yellow funnel-shaped mushroom: family *Cantharellaceae.* [C18: from French, from New Latin *cantharella,* diminutive of Latin *cantharus* drinking vessel, from Greek *kantharos*]

chanteuse (*French* ʃɑ̃tøz) *n* a female singer, esp. in a nightclub or cabaret. [French: singer]

chantey ('ʃæntɪ, 'tʃæn-) *n, pl* **-teys.** the usual U.S. spelling of **shanty**[2].

chanticleer (ˌtʃæntɪ'klɪə) *or* **chantecler** (ˌtʃæntɪ'klɛə) *n* a name for a cock, used esp. in fables. [C13: from Old French *Chantecler,* from *chanter cler* to sing clearly]

Chantilly (ʃæn'tɪlɪ; *French* ʃɑ̃tiji) *n* **1** a town in N France, near the **Forest of Chantilly:** formerly famous for lace and porcelain. Pop.: 11 341 (1990). ◆ *adj* **2** (of cream) lightly sweetened and whipped.

Chantilly lace *n* (*sometimes not cap.*) a delicate ornamental lace.

chantry ('tʃɑːntrɪ) *n, pl* **-tries.** *Christianity.* **1** an endowment for the singing of Masses for the soul of the founder or others designated by him. **2** a chapel or altar so endowed. **3** (*as modifier*): *a chantry priest.* [C14: from Old French *chanterie,* from *chanter* to sing; see CHANT]

chanty ('ʃæntɪ, 'tʃæn-) *n, pl* **-ties.** a variant of **shanty**[2].

Chanukah ('hɑːnəkə, -nʊˌkɑː; *Hebrew* xanu'ka) *n* a variant spelling of **Hanukkah.**

chanukiah *n* a variant spelling of **hanukiah.**

Chaoan ('tʃaʊ'ɑːn) *n* a city in SE China, in E Guangdong province, on the Han River: river port. Pop.: 313 469 (1990). Also called: **Chaochow.**

Chaochow ('tʃaʊ'tʃəʊ) *n* another name for **Chaoan.**

chaology (keɪ'ɒlədʒɪ) *n* the study of chaos theory. ▸ **cha'ologist** *n*

Chao Phraya ('tʃaʊ prə'jɑː) *n* a river in N Thailand, rising in the N highlands and flowing south to the Gulf of Siam. Length: (including the headstreams Nan and Ping) 1200 km (750 miles). Also called: **Menam.**

chaos ('keɪɒs) *n* **1** complete disorder; utter confusion. **2** (*usually cap.*) the disordered formless matter supposed to have existed before the ordered universe. **3** an obsolete word for **abyss.** [C15: from Latin, from Greek *khaos;* compare CHASM, YAWN] ▸ **chaotic** (keɪ'ɒtɪk) *adj* ▸ **cha'otically** *adv*

chaos theory *n* a theory, applied in various branches of science, that apparently random phenomena have underlying order.

chap[1] (tʃæp) *vb* **chaps, chapping, chapped. 1** (of the skin) to make or become raw and cracked, esp. by exposure to cold. **2** *Scot.* (of a clock) to strike (the hour). **3** *Scot.* to knock (at a door, window, etc.). ◆ *n* **4** (*usually pl*) a cracked or sore patch on the skin caused by chapping. **5** *Scot.* a knock. [C14: probably of Germanic origin; compare Middle Dutch, German *kappen* to chop off]

chap[2] (tʃæp) *n Informal.* a man or boy; fellow. [C16 (in the sense: buyer): shortened from CHAPMAN]

chap[3] (tʃɒp, tʃæp) *n* a less common word for **chop**[3].

chap. *abbrev. for:* **1** chaplain. **2** chapter.

chaparejos (ˌʃæpə'reɪəʊs; *Spanish* tʃapa'rexos) *or* **chaparajos** (ˌʃæpə'reɪəʊs; *Spanish* tʃapa'raxos) *pl n* another name for **chaps.** [from Mexican Spanish]

chaparral (ˌtʃæpə'ræl, ˌʃæp-) *n* (in the southwestern U.S.) a dense growth of shrubs and trees, esp. evergreen oaks. [C19: from Spanish, from *chaparra* evergreen oak]

chaparral cock *n* another name for **roadrunner.**

chaparral pea *n* a thorny leguminous Californian shrub, *Pickeringia montana,* with reddish-purple showy flowers.

chapati *or* **chapatti** (tʃəˈpætɪ, -ˈpʌtɪ, -ˈpɑːtɪ) *n, pl* **-ti, -tis,** *or* **-ties.** (in Indian cookery) a flat coarse unleavened bread resembling a pancake. [from Hindi]

chapbook (ˈtʃæpˌbʊk) *n* a book of popular ballads, stories, etc., formerly sold by chapmen or pedlars.

chape (tʃeɪp) *n* **1** a metal tip or trimming for a scabbard. **2** the metal tongue of a buckle. [C14: from Old French: hood, metal cover, from Late Latin *cappa* CAP] ▸ **ˈchapeless** *adj*

chapeau (ˈʃæpəʊ; *French* ʃapo) *n, pl* **-peaux** (-pəʊ, -pəʊz; *French* -po) *or* **-peaus.** a hat. [C16: from French, from Late Latin *cappellus* hood, from *cappa* CAP]

chapel (ˈtʃæpᵊl) *n* **1** a place of Christian worship in a larger building, esp. a place set apart, with a separate altar, in a church or cathedral. **2** a similar place of worship in or attached to a large house or institution, such as a college, hospital or prison. **3** a church subordinate to a parish church. **4** (in Britain) **4a** a Nonconformist place of worship. **4b** Nonconformist religious practices or doctrine. **4c** (*as adj*): *he is chapel, but his wife is church.* Compare **church** (sense 8). **5** (in Scotland) a Roman Catholic church. **6** the members of a trade union in a particular newspaper office, printing house, etc. **7** a printing office. [C13: from Old French *chapele,* from Late Latin *cappella,* diminutive of *cappa* cloak (see CAP); originally denoting the sanctuary where the cloak of St Martin of Tours was kept as a relic]

chapel of ease *n* a church built to accommodate those living at a distance from the parish church.

chaperon *or* **chaperone** (ˈʃæpəˌrəʊn) *n* **1** (esp. formerly) an older or married woman who accompanies or supervises a young unmarried woman on social occasions. **2** someone who accompanies and supervises a group, esp. of young people, usually when in public places. ◆ *vb* **3** to act as a chaperon to. [C14: from Old French, from *chape* hood, protective covering; see CAP] ▸ **chaperonage** (ˈʃæpərənɪdʒ) *n*

chapess (tʃæpˈɛs) *n Brit. informal.* a woman.

chapfallen (ˈtʃæpˌfɔːlən) *or* **chopfallen** *adj* dejected; downhearted; crestfallen. [C16: from CHOPS + FALLEN]

chapiter (ˈtʃæpɪtə) *n Architect.* another name for **capital**[2]. [C15: from Old French *chapitre,* from Latin *capitellum* CAPITAL[2]]

chaplain (ˈtʃæplɪn) *n* a Christian clergyman attached to a private chapel of a prominent person or institution or ministering to a military body, professional group, etc: *a military chaplain; a prison chaplain.* [C12: from Old French *chapelain,* from Late Latin *cappellānus,* from *cappella* CHAPEL] ▸ **ˈchaplaincy, ˈchaplainˌship,** *or* **ˈchaplainry** *n*

chaplet (ˈtʃæplɪt) *n* **1** an ornamental wreath of flowers, beads, etc., worn on the head. **2** a string of beads or something similar. **3** *R.C. Church.* **3a** a string of prayer beads constituting one third of the rosary. **3b** the prayers counted on this string. **4** a narrow convex moulding in the form of a string of beads; astragal. **5** a metal support for the core in a casting mould, esp. for the core of a cylindrical pipe. [C14: from Old French *chapelet* garland of roses, from *chapel* hat; see CHAPEAU] ▸ **ˈchapleted** *adj*

Chaplin (ˈtʃæplɪn) *n* Sir **Charles Spencer,** known as *Charlie Chaplin.* 1889–1977, English comedian, film actor, and director. He is renowned for his portrayal of a downtrodden little man with baggy trousers, bowler hat, and cane. His films, most of which were made in Hollywood, include *The Gold Rush* (1924), *Modern Times* (1936), and *The Great Dictator* (1940). ▸ **ˌChaplinˈesque** *adj*

chapman (ˈtʃæpmən) *n, pl* **-men.** *Archaic.* a trader, esp. an itinerant pedlar. [Old English *cēapman,* from *cēap* buying and selling (see CHEAP)] ▸ **ˈchapmanˌship** *n*

Chapman (ˈtʃæpmən) *n* **George.** 1559–1634, English dramatist and poet, noted for his translation of Homer.

chappal (ˈtʃʌpᵊl) *n* one of a pair of sandals, usually of leather, worn in India. [from Hindi]

Chappell (ˈtʃæpᵊl) *n* **Greg(ory Stephen).** born 1948, Australian cricketer: first Australian to score over 7000 test runs.

chappie (ˈtʃæpɪ) *n Informal.* another word for **chap**[2].

chaps (tʃæps, ʃæps) *pl n* leather overalls without a seat, worn by cowboys. Also called: **chaparejos, chaparajos.** [C19: shortened from CHAPAREJOS]

chapstick (ˈtʃæpˌstɪk) *n Chiefly U.S. and Canadian.* a cylinder of a substance for preventing or soothing chapped lips. [C20: from a trademark]

chaptalize *or* **chaptalise** (ˈtʃæptəˌlaɪz) *vb* (*tr*) to add sugar to (a fermenting wine) to increase the alcohol content. [C19: after J. A. *Chaptal* (1756–1832), French chemist who originated the process] ▸ **ˌchaptaliˈzation** *or* **ˌchaptaliˈsation** *n*

chapter (ˈtʃæptə) *n* **1** a division of a written work, esp. a narrative, usually titled or numbered. **2** a sequence of events having a common attribute: *a chapter of disasters.* **3 chapter of accidents. 3a** a series of misfortunes. **3b** the unforeseeable course of events. **4** an episode or period in a life, history, etc. **5** a numbered reference to that part of a Parliamentary session which relates to a specified Act of Parliament. **6** a branch of some societies, clubs, etc., esp. of a secret society. **7** the collective body or a meeting of the canons of a cathedral or collegiate church or of the members of a monastic or knightly order. Related adj: **capitular. 8** a general assembly of some organization. **9 chapter and verse.** exact authority for an action or statement. ◆ *vb* **10** (*tr*) to divide into chapters. [C13: from Old French *chapitre,* from Latin *capitulum,* literally: little head, hence, section of writing, from *caput* head; in Medieval Latin: chapter of scripture or of a religious rule, a gathering for the reading of this, hence, assemblage of clergy]

chapter 7 *n U.S.* the statute regarding liquidation proceedings that empowers a court to appoint a trustee to operate a failing business to prevent further loss. [C20: from *chapter 7* of the Bankruptcy Reform Act (1978)]

chapter 11 *n U.S.* the statute regarding the reorganization of a failing business empowering a court to allow the debtors to remain in control of the business to attempt to save it: *they are in chapter 11.* [C20: from *chapter 11* of the Bankruptcy Reform Act (1978)]

chapterhouse (ˈtʃæptəˌhaʊs) *n* **1** the building attached to a cathedral, collegiate church, or religious house in which the chapter meets. **2** *U.S.* the meeting place of a college fraternity or sorority.

char[1] (tʃɑː) *vb* **chars, charring, charred. 1** to burn or be burned partially, esp. so as to blacken the surface; scorch. **2** (*tr*) to reduce (wood) to charcoal by partial combustion. [C17: short for CHARCOAL]

char[2] *or* **charr** (tʃɑː) *n, pl* **char, chars** *or* **charr, charrs.** any of various troutlike fishes of the genus *Salvelinus,* esp. *S. alpinus,* occurring in cold lakes and northern seas: family *Salmonidae* (salmon). [C17: of unknown origin]

char[3] (tʃɑː) *n* **1** *Informal.* short for **charwoman.** ◆ *vb* **chars, charring, charred. 2** *Brit. informal.* to do housework, cleaning, etc., as a job. [C18: from Old English *cerr*]

char[4] (tʃɑː) *n Brit.* a slang word for **tea.** [from Chinese *ch'a*]

charabanc (ˈʃærəˌbæŋ; *French* ʃarabɑ̃) *n Brit.* a motor coach, esp. one used for sightseeing tours. [C19: from French *char-à-bancs,* wagon with seats]

characin (ˈkærəsɪn) *or* **characid** *n* any small carnivorous freshwater cyprinoid fish of the family *Characidae,* of Central and South America and Africa. They are similar to the carps but more brightly coloured. [C19: from New Latin *Characinidae,* from *characinus,* from Greek *kharax* a fish, probably the sea bream]

character (ˈkærɪktə) *n* **1** the combination of traits and qualities distinguishing the individual nature of a person or thing. **2** one such distinguishing quality; characteristic. **3** moral force; integrity: *a man of character.* **4a** reputation, esp. a good reputation. **4b** (*as modifier*): *character assassination.* **5** a summary or account of a person's qualities and achievements; testimonial: *my last employer gave me a good character.* **6** capacity, position, or status: *he spoke in the character of a friend rather than a father.* **7** a person represented in a play, film, story, etc.; role. **8** an outstanding person: *one of the great characters of the century.* **9** *Informal.* an odd, eccentric, or unusual person: *he's quite a character.* **10** an informal word for **person:** *a shady character.* **11** a symbol used in a writing system, such as a letter of the alphabet. **12** Also called: **sort.** *Printing.* any single letter, numeral, punctuation mark, or symbol cast as a type. **13** *Computing.* any letter, numeral, etc., which is a unit of information and can be represented uniquely by a binary pattern. **14** a style of writing or printing. **15** *Genetics.* any structure, function, attribute, etc., in an organism that is determined by a gene or group of genes. **16** a short prose sketch of a distinctive type of person, usually representing a vice or virtue. **17 in** (*or* **out of**) **character.** typical (or not typical) of the apparent character of a person or thing. ◆ *vb* (*tr*) **18** to write, print, inscribe, or engrave. **19** *Rare.* to portray or represent. [C14: from Latin: distinguishing mark, from Greek *kharaktēr* engraver's tool, from *kharassein* to engrave, stamp] ▸ **ˈcharacterful** *adj* ▸ **ˈcharacterless** *adj*

character actor *n* an actor who specializes in playing odd or eccentric characters.

character armour *n Psychol.* the defence an individual exhibits to others and to himself to disguise his underlying weaknesses: a term coined by William Reich.

character assassination *n* the act of deliberately attempting to destroy a person's reputation by defamatory remarks.

character code *n Computing.* a machine-readable code that identifies a specified character or a set of such codes.

characteristic (ˌkærɪktəˈrɪstɪk) *n* **1** a distinguishing quality, attribute, or trait. **2** *Maths.* **2a** the integral part of a common logarithm, indicating the order of magnitude of the associated number: *the characteristic of 2.4771 is 2.* Compare **mantissa. 2b** another name for **exponent** (sense 4), esp. in number representation in computing. ◆ *adj* **3** indicative of a distinctive quality, etc.; typical. ▸ **ˌcharacterˈistically** *adv*

characteristic curve *n Photog.* a graph of the density of a particular photographic material plotted against the logarithm of the exposure producing this density.

characteristic function *n* **1** *Maths.* a function that assigns the value 1 to the members of a given set and the value 0 to its nonmembers. **2** *Statistics.* a function derived from the probability distribution function that enables the distribution of the sum of given random variables to be analysed.

characterization *or* **characterisation** (ˌkærɪktəraɪˈzeɪʃən) *n* **1** description of character, traits, etc. **2** the act of characterizing.

characterize *or* **characterise** (ˈkærɪktəˌraɪz) *vb* (*tr*) **1** to be a characteristic of: *loneliness characterized the place.* **2** to distinguish or mark as a characteristic. **3** to describe or portray the character of. ▸ **ˈcharacterˌizable** *or* **ˈcharacterˌisable** *adj* ▸ **ˈcharacterˌizer** *or* **ˈcharacterˌiser** *n*

character recognition *n Computing.* a magnetic or optical process used to detect the shape of individual characters printed or written on paper.

character sketch *n* a brief description or portrayal of a person's character, qualities, etc.

character type *n Psychol.* a cluster of personality traits commonly occurring together in an individual.

charactery (ˈkærɪktərɪ, -trɪ) *n, pl* **-teries.** *Archaic.* **1** the use of symbols to express thoughts. **2** the group of symbols so used.

charade (ʃəˈrɑːd) *n* **1** an episode or act in the game of charades. **2** *Chiefly Brit.* an absurd act; travesty.

charades (ʃəˈrɑːdz) *n* (*functioning as sing*) a parlour game in which one team acts out each syllable of a word, the other team having to guess the word.

[C18: from French *charade* entertainment, from Provençal *charrado* chat, from *charra* chatter, of imitative origin]

charas ('tʃɑːrəs) *n* another name for **hashish.** [C19: from Hindi]

charcoal ('tʃɑːˌkəʊl) *n* **1** a black amorphous form of carbon made by heating wood or other organic matter in the absence of air: used as a fuel, in smelting metal ores, in explosives, and as an absorbent. See **activated carbon. 2** a stick or pencil of this for drawing. **3** a drawing done in charcoal. **4** short for **charcoal grey.** ◆ *vb* **5** (*tr*) to write, draw, or blacken with charcoal. [C14: from *char* (origin obscure) + COAL]

charcoal-burner *n* (formerly) a person whose work was making charcoal by burning wood.

charcoal grey *n* **a** a very dark grey colour. **b** (*as adj*): *charcoal-grey trousers.*

Charcot (*French* ʃarko) *n* **Jean Martin** (ʒɑ̃ martɛ̃). 1825–93, French neurologist, noted for his attempt using hypnotism to find an organic cause for hysteria, which influenced Freud.

charcuterie (ʃɑːˈkuːtəriː) *n* **1** cooked cold meats. **2** a shop selling cooked cold meats. [French]

chard (tʃɑːd) *n* a variety of beet, *Beta vulgaris cicla,* with large succulent leaves and thick stalks, used as a vegetable. Also called: **Swiss chard, leaf beet, seakale beet.** [C17: probably from French *carde* edible leafstalk of the artichoke, but associated also with French *chardon* thistle, both ultimately from Latin *carduus* thistle; see CARDOON]

Chardin (*French* ʃardɛ̃) *n* **Jean-Baptiste Siméon** (ʒɑ̃batist simeɔ̃). 1699–1779, French still-life and genre painter, noted for his subtle use of scumbled colour.

Chardonnay ('ʃɑːdəˌneɪ) *n* (*sometimes not cap.*) **1** a white grape grown in the Burgundy region of France, Australia, California, New Zealand and elsewhere, used for making wine. **2** any of various white wines made from this grape. [French]

Chardonnet (*French* ʃardɔnɛ) *n* (**Louis Marie**) **Hilaire Bernigaud** (ilɛr bɛrnigo), Comte de. 1839–1924, French chemist and industrialist who produced rayon, the first artificial fibre.

Charente (*French* ʃarɑ̃t) *n* **1** a department of W central France, in Poitou-Charentes region. Capital: Angoulême. Pop.: 341 200 (1995). Area: 5972 sq. km (2329 sq. miles). **2** a river in W France, flowing west to the Bay of Biscay. Length: 362 km (225 miles).

Charente-Maritime (*French* ʃarɑ̃tmaritim) *n* a department of W France, in Poitou-Charentes region. Capital: La Rochelle. Pop.: 540 700 (1995). Area: 7232 sq. km (2820 sq. miles).

Chargaff ('ʃɑːgæf) *n* **Erwin.** born 1905, U.S. biochemist, born in Austria, noted esp. for his work on DNA.

charge (tʃɑːdʒ) *vb* **1** to set or demand (a price): *he charges too much for his services.* **2** (*tr*) to hold financially liable; enter a debit against. **3** (*tr*) to enter or record as an obligation against a person or his account. **4** (*tr*) to accuse or impute a fault to (a person, etc.), as formally in a court of law. **5** (*tr*) to command; place a burden upon or assign responsibility to: *I was charged to take the message to headquarters.* **6** to make a rush at or sudden attack upon (a person or thing). **7** (*tr*) to fill (a receptacle) with the proper or appropriate quantity. **8** (often foll. by *up*) to cause (an accumulator, capacitor, etc.) to take or store electricity or (of an accumulator) to have electricity fed into it. **9** to fill or suffuse or to be filled or suffused with matter by dispersion, solution, or absorption: *to charge water with carbon dioxide.* **10** (*tr*) to fill or suffuse with feeling, emotion, etc.: *the atmosphere was charged with excitement.* **11** (*tr*) *Law.* (of a judge) to address (a jury) authoritatively. **12** (*tr*) to load (a firearm). **13** (*tr*) to aim (a weapon) in position ready for use. **14** (*tr*) *Heraldry.* to paint (a shield, banner, etc.) with a charge. **15** (*intr*) (of hunting dogs) to lie down at command. ◆ *n* **16** a price charged for some article or service; cost. **17** a financial liability, such as a tax. **18** a debt or a book entry recording it. **19** an accusation or allegation, such as a formal accusation of a crime in law. **20a** an onrush, attack, or assault. **20b** the call to such an attack in battle. **21** custody or guardianship. **22** a person or thing committed to someone's care. **23a** a cartridge or shell. **23b** the explosive required to discharge a firearm or other weapon. **23c** an amount of explosive material to be detonated at any one time. **24** the quantity of anything that a receptacle is intended to hold. **25** *Physics.* **25a** the attribute of matter responsible for all electrical phenomena, existing in two forms to which the signs negative and positive are arbitrarily assigned. **25b** a similar property of a body or system determined by the extent to which it contains an excess or deficiency of electrons. **25c** a quantity of electricity determined by the product of an electric current and the time for which it flows, measured in coulombs. **25d** the total amount of electricity stored in a capacitor. **25e** the total amount of electricity held in an accumulator, usually measured in ampere-hours. Symbol: q or Q **26** a load or burden. **27** a duty or responsibility; control. **28** a command, injunction, or order. **29** *Slang.* a thrill. **30** *Law.* the address made by a judge to the jury at the conclusion of the evidence. **31** *Heraldry.* a design, device, or image depicted on heraldic arms: *a charge of three lions.* **32** the solid propellant used in rockets, sometimes including the inhibitor. **33 in charge.** in command. **34 in charge of. 34a** having responsibility for. **34b** *U.S.* under the care of. [C13: from Old French *chargier* to load, from Late Latin *carricāre;* see CARRY]

chargeable ('tʃɑːdʒəbᵊl) *adj* **1** charged or liable to be charged. **2** liable to result in a legal charge. ▸ **'chargeableness** *or* **ˌchargea'bility** *n* ▸ **'chargeably** *adv*

chargeable asset *n* any asset that can give rise to assessment for capital gains tax on its disposal. Exempt assets include principal private residences, cars, investments held in a personal equity plan, and government securities.

chargeable transfer *n* a transfer of value made as a gift during a person's lifetime that is not covered by a specific exemption and therefore gives rise to liability under inheritance tax.

charge account *n* another term for **credit account.**

charge-cap ('tʃɑːdʒˌkæp) *vb* (*tr*) **-caps, -capping, -capped.** (in Britain) to impose on (a local authority) an upper limit on the community charge it may levy. ▸ **'charge-ˌcapping** *n*

charge card *n* a card issued by a chain store, shop, or organization, that enables customers to obtain goods and services for which they pay at a later date.

charge carrier *n* an electron, hole, or ion that transports the electric charge in an electric current.

charge-coupled device *n Computing.* an electronic device, used in imaging and signal processing, in which information is represented as packets of electric charge that are stored in an array of tiny closely spaced capacitors and can be moved from one capacitor to another in a controlled way. Abbrev.: **CCD.**

chargé d'affaires ('ʃɑːʒeɪ dæ'fɛə; *French* ʃarʒe dafɛr) *n, pl* **chargés d'affaires** ('ʃɑːʒeɪ, -ʒeɪz; *French* ʃarʒe). **1** the temporary head of a diplomatic mission in the absence of the ambassador or minister. **2** the head of a diplomatic mission of the lowest level. [C18: from French: (one) charged with affairs]

charge density *n* the electric charge per unit volume of a medium or body or per unit area of a surface.

charge hand *n Brit.* a workman whose grade of responsibility is just below that of a foreman.

charge nurse *n Brit.* a nurse in charge of a ward in a hospital: the male equivalent of **sister.**

charge of quarters *n U.S.* a member of the armed forces who handles administration in his unit, esp. after duty hours.

charger[1] ('tʃɑːdʒə) *n* **1** a person or thing that charges. **2** a large strong horse formerly ridden into battle. **3** a device for charging or recharging an accumulator.

charger[2] ('tʃɑːdʒə) *n Antiques.* a large dish for serving at table or for display. [C14 *chargeour* something to bear a load, from *chargen* to CHARGE]

charge sheet *n Brit.* a document on which a police officer enters details of the charge against a prisoner and the court in which he will appear.

char-grilled *adj* (of food) grilled over charcoal.

Chari ('tʃɑːrɪ) *or* **Shari** *n* a river in N central Africa, rising in the N Central African Republic and flowing north to Lake Chad. Length: about 2250 km (1400 miles).

charily ('tʃɛərɪlɪ) *adv* **1** cautiously; carefully. **2** sparingly.

chariness ('tʃɛərɪnɪs) *n* the state of being chary.

Charing Cross ('tʃærɪŋ) *n* a district of London, in the city of Westminster: the modern cross (1863) in front of Charing Cross railway station replaces the one erected by Edward I (1290), the last of twelve marking the route of the funeral procession of his queen, Eleanor.

Chari-Nile ('tʃɑːrɪ'naɪl) *n* **1** a group of languages of E Africa, now generally regarded as a branch of the Nilo-Saharan family, spoken in parts of the Sudan, the Democratic Republic of the Congo (formerly Zaïre), Uganda, Kenya, Tanzania, and adjacent countries. ◆ *adj* **2** relating to or belonging to this group of languages.

chariot ('tʃærɪət) *n* **1** a two-wheeled horse-drawn vehicle used in ancient Egypt, Greece, Rome, etc., in war, races, and processions. **2** a light four-wheeled horse-drawn ceremonial carriage. **3** *Poetic.* any stately vehicle. [C14: from Old French, augmentative of *char* CAR]

charioteer (ˌtʃærɪə'tɪə) *n* the driver of a chariot.

charisma (kə'rɪzmə) *or* **charism** ('kærɪzəm) *n* **1** a special personal quality or power of an individual making him capable of influencing or inspiring large numbers of people. **2** a quality inherent in a thing which inspires great enthusiasm and devotion. **3** *Christianity.* a divinely bestowed power or talent. [C17: from Church Latin, from Greek *kharisma,* from *kharis* grace, favour] ▸ **charismatic** (ˌkærɪz'mætɪk) *adj*

charismatic movement *n Christianity.* any of various groups, within existing denominations, that emphasize communal prayer and the charismatic gifts of speaking in tongues, healing, etc.

charitable ('tʃærɪtəbᵊl) *adj* **1** generous in giving to the needy. **2** kind or lenient in one's attitude towards others. **3** concerned with or involving charity. ▸ **'charitableness** *n* ▸ **'charitably** *adv*

charitable trust *n* a trust set up for the benefit of a charity that complies with the regulations of the Charity Commissioners to enable it to be exempt from paying income tax.

charity ('tʃærɪtɪ) *n, pl* **-ties. 1a** the giving of help, money, food, etc., to those in need. **1b** (*as modifier*): *a charity show.* **2a** an institution or organization set up to provide help, money, etc., to those in need. **2b** (*as modifier*): *charity funds.* **3** the help, money, etc., given to the needy; alms. **4** a kindly and lenient attitude towards people. **5** love of one's fellow men. [C13: from Old French *charite,* from Latin *cāritās* affection, love, from *cārus* dear]

Charity Commissioners *pl n* (in Britain) members of a commission constituted to keep a register of charities and control charitable trusts.

charivari (ˌʃɑːrɪ'vɑːrɪ), **shivaree,** *or esp. U.S.* **chivaree** *n* **1** a discordant mock serenade to newlyweds, made with pans, kettles, etc. **2** a confused noise; din. [C17: from French, from Late Latin *caribaria* headache, from Greek *karēbaria,* from *karē* head + *barus* heavy]

charkha *or* **charka** ('tʃɑːkə) *n* (in India) a spinning wheel, esp. for cotton. [from Hindi]

charlady ('tʃɑːˌleɪdɪ) *n, pl* **-dies.** another name for **charwoman.**

charlatan ('ʃɑːlətᵊn) *n* someone who professes knowledge or expertise, esp. in medicine, that he does not have; quack. [C17: from French, from Italian *ciarlatano,* from *ciarlare* to chatter] ▸ **'charlatanˌism** *or* **'charlatanry** *n* ▸ **ˌcharlatan'istic** *adj*

Charlemagne ('ʃɑːləˌmeɪn) *n* ?742–814 A.D., king of the Franks (768–814) and, as Charles I, Holy Roman Emperor (800–814). He conquered the Lombards (774), the Saxons (772–804), and the Avars (791–799). He instituted many judicial and ecclesiastical reforms, and promoted commerce and agriculture throughout his empire, which extended from the Ebro to the Elbe. Under Alcuin his court at Aachen became the centre of a revival of learning.

Charleroi (*French* ʃarlərwa) *n* a town in SW Belgium, in Hainaut province: centre of an industrial region. Pop.: 205 591 (1996 est.).

Charles (tʃɑːlz) *n* **1** *Prince of Wales.* born 1948, son of Elizabeth II; heir apparent to the throne of Great Britain and Northern Ireland. He married (1981) Lady Diana Spencer; they separated in 1992 and were divorced in 1996; their son, Prince William of Wales, was born in 1982 and their second son, Prince Henry, in 1984. **2 Ray,** real name *Ray Charles Robinson.* born 1930, U.S. singer, pianist, and songwriter, whose work spans jazz, blues, gospel, pop, and country music.

Charles I *n* **1** title as Holy Roman Emperor of **Charlemagne. 2** title as king of France of **Charles II** (Holy Roman Emperor). **3** title as king of Spain of **Charles V** (Holy Roman Emperor). **4** title of **Charles Stuart.** 1600–49, king of England, Scotland, and Ireland (1625–49); son of James I. He ruled for 11 years (1629–40) without parliament, advised by his minister Strafford, until rebellion broke out in Scotland. Conflict with the Long Parliament led to the Civil War and after his defeat at Naseby (1645) he sought refuge with the Scots (1646). He was handed over to the English army under Cromwell (1647) and executed. **5** 1887–1922, emperor of Austria, and, as Charles IV, king of Hungary (1916–18). The last ruler of the Austro-Hungarian monarchy, he was forced to abdicate at the end of World War I.

Charles II *n* **1** known as *Charles the Bald.* 823–877 A.D., Holy Roman Emperor (875–877) and, as Charles I, king of France (843–877). **2** the title as king of France of **Charles III** (Holy Roman Emperor). **3** 1630–85, king of England, Scotland, and Ireland (1660–85) following the Restoration (1660); son of Charles I. He did much to promote commerce, science, and the Navy, but his Roman Catholic sympathies caused widespread distrust. **4** 1661–1700, the last Hapsburg king of Spain: his reign saw the end of Spanish power in Europe.

Charles III *n* **1** known as *Charles the Fat.* 839–888 A.D., Holy Roman Emperor (881–887) and, as Charles II, king of France (884–887). He briefly reunited the empire of Charlemagne. **2** 1716–88, king of Spain (1759–88), who curbed the power of the Church and tried to modernize his country.

Charles IV *n* **1** known as *Charles the Fair.* 1294–1328, king of France (1322–28): brother of Isabella of France, with whom he intrigued against her husband, Edward II of England. **2** 1316–78, king of Bohemia (1346–78) and Holy Roman Emperor (1355–78). **3** 1748–1819, king of Spain (1788–1808), whose reign saw the domination of Spain by Napoleonic France: abdicated. **4** title as king of Hungary of **Charles I** (sense 5).

Charles V *n* **1** known as *Charles the Wise.* 1337–80, king of France (1364–80) during the Hundred Years' War. **2** 1500–58, Holy Roman Emperor (1519–56), king of Burgundy and the Netherlands (1506–55), and, as Charles I, king of Spain (1516–56): his reign saw the empire threatened by Francis I of France, the Turks, and the spread of Protestantism; abdicated.

Charles VI *n* **1** known as *Charles the Mad* or *Charles the Well-Beloved.* 1368–1422, king of France (1380–1422): defeated by Henry V of England at Agincourt (1415), he was forced by the Treaty of Troyes (1420) to recognize Henry as his successor. **2** 1685–1740, Holy Roman Emperor (1711–40). His claim to the Spanish throne (1700) led to the War of the Spanish Succession.

Charles VII *n* **1** 1403–61, king of France (1422–61), son of Charles VI. He was excluded from the French throne by the Treaty of Troyes, but following Joan of Arc's victory over the English at Orléans (1429), was crowned. **2** 1697–1745, Holy Roman Emperor (1742–45) during the War of the Austrian Succession.

Charles IX *n* 1550–74, king of France (1560–74), son of Catherine de' Medici and Henry II: his reign was marked by war between Huguenots and Catholics.

Charles X *n* **1** title of *Charles Gustavus.* 1622–60, king of Sweden, who warred with Poland and Denmark in an attempt to create a unified Baltic state. **2** 1757–1836, king of France (1824–30): his attempt to restore absolutism led to his enforced exile.

Charles XI *n* 1655–97, king of Sweden (1660–97), who established an absolute monarchy and defeated Denmark (1678).

Charles XII *n* 1682–1718, king of Sweden (1697–1718), who inflicted defeats on Denmark, Russia, and Poland during the Great Northern War (1700–21).

Charles XIV *n* the title as king of Sweden and Norway of (Jean Baptiste Jules) **Bernadotte.**

Charles Albert *n* 1798–1849, king of Sardinia-Piedmont (1831–49) during the Risorgimento: abdicated after the failure of his revolt against Austria.

Charles Edward Stuart *n* See (Charles Edward) **Stuart.**

Charles' law *n* the principle that all gases expand equally for the same rise of temperature if they are held at constant pressure: also that the pressures of all gases increase equally for the same rise of temperature if they are held at constant volume. The law is now known to be only approximately true. Also called: **Gay-Lussac's law.** [C18: named after Jacques A. C. *Charles* (1746–1823), French physicist who first formulated it]

Charles Martel (mɑːˈtɛl) *n* grandfather of Charlemagne. ?688–741 A.D., Frankish ruler of Austrasia (715–41), who checked the Muslim invasion of Europe by defeating the Moors at Poitiers (732).

Charles's Wain (weɪn) *n* another name for the **Plough.** [Old English *Carles wægn,* from *Carl* CHARLEMAGNE + *wægn* WAIN]

Charles the Great *n* another name for **Charlemagne.**

charleston (ˈtʃɑːlstən) *n* a fast rhythmic dance of the 1920s, characterized by kicking and by twisting of the legs from the knee down. [C20: named after CHARLESTON, South Carolina]

Charleston (ˈtʃɑːlstən) *n* **1** a city in central West Virginia: the state capital. Pop.: 59 371 (1985 est.). **2** a port in SE South Carolina, on the Atlantic: scene of the first action in the Civil War. Pop.: 76 854 (1994 est.).

Charleville-Mézières (*French* ʃarləvilmezjɛr) *n* twin towns on opposite sides of the River Meuse in NE France. Pop.: 59 440 (1990). See **Mézières.**

charley horse (ˈtʃɑːlɪ) *n U.S. and Canadian informal.* muscle stiffness or cramp following strenuous athletic exercise. [C19: of uncertain origin]

charlie (ˈtʃɑːlɪ) *n Brit. informal.* a silly person; fool. [C20: shortened from *Charlie Hunt,* rhyming slang for CUNT]

Charlie[1] (ˈtʃɑːlɪ) *n Communications.* a code word for the letter *c.*

Charlie[2] *or* **Charley** (ˈtʃɑːlɪ) *n U.S. and Austral. military slang.* a member of the Vietcong or the Vietcong collectively: *Charlie hit us with rockets.* [shortened from *Victor Charlie,* communications code for *VC,* abbreviation of *Vietcong*]

Charlie[3] (ˈtʃɑːlɪ) *n Slang.* cocaine.

charlock (ˈtʃɑːlɒk) *n* **1** Also called: **wild mustard.** a weedy cruciferous Eurasian plant, *Sinapsis arvensis* (or *Brassica kaber*), with hairy stems and foliage and yellow flowers. **2 white charlock.** Also called: **wild radish, runch** (rʌntʃ). a cruciferous plant, *Raphanus raphanistrum,* with yellow, mauve, or white flowers and podlike fruits. [Old English *cerlic,* of obscure origin]

charlotte (ˈʃɑːlət) *n* **1** a baked dessert served hot or cold, commonly made with fruit and layers or a casing of bread or cake crumbs, sponge cake, etc.: *apple charlotte.* **2** short for **charlotte russe.** [C19: from French, from the name *Charlotte*]

Charlotte (ˈʃɑːlət) *n* a city in S North Carolina: the largest city in the state. Pop.: 441 297 (1996 est.).

Charlotte Amalie (ˈʃɑːlət əˈmɑːlɪə) *n* the capital of the Virgin Islands of the United States, a port on St Thomas Island. Pop.: 12 331 (1990). Former name (1921–37): **Saint Thomas.**

Charlottenburg (*German* ʃarˈlɔtənbʊrk) *n* a district of Berlin (of West Berlin until 1990), formerly an independent city. Pop.: 145 564 (1986 est.).

charlotte russe (ruːs) *n* a cold dessert made in a mould with sponge fingers enclosing a mixture of whipped cream, custard, etc. [French: Russian charlotte]

Charlottetown (ˈʃɑːlətˌtaʊn) *n* a port in SE Canada, capital of the province of Prince Edward Island. Pop.: 15 396 (1991).

Charlton (ˈtʃɑːltᵊn) *n* **1 Bobby,** full name *Sir Robert Charlton.* born 1937, English footballer; played for England over 100 times. **2** his brother, **Jack,** full name *John Charlton.* born 1935, English footballer; played for Leeds United (1952–73) and England; manager of the Republic of Ireland soccer team (1986–95).

charm[1] (tʃɑːm) *n* **1** the quality of pleasing, fascinating, or attracting people. **2** a pleasing or attractive feature. **3** a small object worn or kept for supposed magical powers of protection; amulet; talisman. **4** a trinket worn on a bracelet. **5** a magic spell; enchantment. **6** a formula or action used in casting such a spell. **7** *Physics.* a property of certain elementary particles, used to explain some scattering experiments. **8 like a charm.** perfectly; successfully. ◆ *vb* **9** to attract or fascinate; delight greatly. **10** to cast a magic spell on. **11** to protect, influence, or heal, supposedly by magic. **12** (*tr*) to influence or obtain by personal charm: *he charmed them into believing him.* [C13: from Old French *charme,* from Latin *carmen* song, incantation, from *canere* to sing]

charm[2] (tʃɑːm) *n Southwest English dialect.* a loud noise, as of a number of people chattering or of birds singing. [C16: variant of CHIRM]

charmed (tʃɑːmd) *adj* **1** delighted or fascinated: *a charmed audience.* **2** seemingly protected by a magic spell: *he bears a charmed life.* **3** *Physics.* possessing charm: *a charmed quark.*

charmer (ˈtʃɑːmə) *n* **1** an attractive person. **2** a person claiming or seeming to have magical powers.

Charmeuse (ʃɑːˈmuːz; *French* ʃarmøz) *n Trademark.* a lightweight fabric with a satin-like finish.

Charminar (ˌtʃɑːmɪˈnɑː) *n* a 16th-century monument with four minarets at Hyderabad, India.

charming (ˈtʃɑːmɪŋ) *adj* delightful; pleasant; attractive. ▸ **ˈcharmingly** *adv*

charm offensive *n* a concentrated attempt to gain favour or respectability by conspicuously cooperative or obliging behaviour.

charnel (ˈtʃɑːnᵊl) *n* **1** short for **charnel house.** ◆ *adj* **2** ghastly; sepulchral; deathly. [C14: from Old French: burial place, from Latin *carnālis* fleshly, CARNAL]

charnel house *n* (esp. formerly) a building or vault where corpses or bones are deposited.

Charnley (ˈtʃɑːnlɪ) *n* Sir **John.** 1911–82, British surgeon noted for his invention of an artificial hip joint and his development of hip-replacement surgery.

Charollais *or* **Charolais** (ˈʃærəˌleɪ) *n* a breed of large white beef cattle. [C19: from French: named after Monts du *Charollais,* E France]

Charon[1] (ˈkɛərən) *n Greek myth.* the ferryman who brought the dead across the rivers Styx or Acheron to Hades.

Charon[2] (ˈkɛərən) *n* the only known satellite of Pluto, discovered in 1978.

Charpentier (*French* ʃarpɑ̃tje) *n* **1 Gustave** (gystav). 1860–1956, French composer, whose best-known work is the opera *Louise* (1900). **2 Marc-Antoine.** ?1645–1704, French composer, best known for his sacred music, particularly the *Te Deum.*

charpoy (ˈtʃɑːpɔɪ) *or* **charpai** (ˈtʃɑːpaɪ) *n* a bedstead of woven webbing or hemp stretched on a wooden frame on four legs, common in India. [C19: from Urdu *cārpāī*]

charqui (ˈtʃɑːkɪ) *n* meat, esp. beef, cut into strips and dried. [C18: from Spanish, from Quechuan] ▸ **charquid** (ˈtʃɑːkɪd) *adj*

charr (tʃɑː) *n, pl* **charr** *or* **charrs.** a variant spelling of **char** (the fish).

chart (tʃɑːt) *n* **1** a map designed to aid navigation by sea or air. **2** an outline map, esp. one on which weather information is plotted. **3** a sheet giving graphical, tabular, or diagrammatical information. **4** another name for **graph** (sense 1). **5** *Astrology.* another word for **horoscope** (sense 3). **6 the charts.** *Informal.* the lists produced weekly from various sources of the bestselling pop singles and albums or the most popular videos. ◆ *vb* **7** (*tr*) to make a chart of. **8** (*tr*) to make a detailed plan of. **9** (*tr*) to plot or outline the course of. **10** (*intr*) (of a record or video) to appear in the charts (sense 6). [C16: from Latin, from Greek *khartēs* papyrus, literally: something on which to make marks; related to Greek *kharattein* to engrave] ▸ **'chartable** *adj*

charter ('tʃɑːtə) *n* **1** a formal document from the sovereign or state incorporating a city, bank, college, etc., and specifying its purposes and rights. **2** (*sometimes cap.*) a formal document granting or demanding from the sovereign power of a state certain rights or liberties. **3** a document issued by a society or an organization authorizing the establishment of a local branch or chapter. **4** a special privilege or exemption. **5** (*often cap.*) the fundamental principles of an organization; constitution: *the Charter of the United Nations.* **6a** the hire or lease of transportation. **6b** the agreement or contract regulating this. **6c** (*as modifier*): *a charter flight.* **7** *Maritime law.* another word for **charter party.** ◆ *vb* (*tr*) **8** to lease or hire by charter party. **9** to hire (a vehicle, etc.). **10** to grant a charter of incorporation or liberties to (a group or person). [C13: from Old French *chartre,* from Latin *chartula* a little paper, from *charta* leaf of papyrus; see CHART] ▸ **'charterer** *n*

charter colony *n American history.* a colony, such as Virginia or Massachusetts, created by royal charter under the control of an individual, trading company, etc., and exempt from interference by the Crown.

chartered ('tʃɑːtəd) *adj* (of a professional person) having attained certain professional qualifications or standards and acquired membership of a particular professional body.

chartered accountant *n* (in Britain) an accountant who has passed the professional examinations of the Institute of Chartered Accountants in England and Wales, the Institute of Chartered Accountants of Scotland, or the Institute of Chartered Accountants in Ireland. Abbrev.: **CA.**

chartered club *n N.Z.* a private club licensed to serve alcohol to members.

chartered engineer *n* (in Britain) an engineer who is registered with the Engineering Council as having the scientific and technical knowledge and practical experience to satisfy its professional requirements. Abbrev.: **CEng.**

chartered librarian *n* (in Britain) a librarian who has obtained a qualification from the Library Association in addition to a degree or diploma in librarianship.

chartered surveyor *n* (in Britain) a surveyor who is registered with the Royal Institution of Chartered Surveyors as having the qualifications, training, and experience to satisfy their professional requirements.

Charterhouse ('tʃɑːtəˌhaʊs) *n* a Carthusian monastery. [C16: changed by folk etymology from Anglo-French *chartrouse,* after *Chartosse* (now Saint-Pierre-de-Chartreuse), village near Grenoble, France, the original home of the Carthusian order]

Charteris ('tʃɑːtərɪs) *n* **Leslie,** original name *Leslie Charles Bowyer Yin.* 1907–93, British novelist, born in Singapore: created the character Simon Templar, known as The Saint, the central character in many adventure novels.

charter member *n* an original or founder member of a society or organization.

charter party *n* **1** *Maritime law.* an agreement for the hire of all or part of a ship for a specified voyage or period of time. **2** an individual or group that charters a ship, etc.

Chartism ('tʃɑːˌtɪzəm) *n English history.* the principles of the reform movement in England from 1838 to 1848, which included manhood suffrage, payment of Members of Parliament, equal electoral districts, annual parliaments, voting by ballot, and the abolition of property qualifications for MPs. [named after the *People's Charter,* a document which stated their aims] ▸ **'Chartist** *n, adj*

chartist ('tʃɑːtɪst) *n* a stock market specialist who analyses and predicts market trends from graphs of recent price and volume movements of selected securities.

chartless ('tʃɑːtlɪs) *adj* not mapped; uncharted.

chartography (kɑː'tɒgrəfɪ) *n Rare.* a variant spelling of **cartography.** ▸ **char'tographer** *n* ▸ **chartographic** (ˌkɑːtə'græfɪk) *or* **ˌcharto'graphical** *adj* ▸ **ˌcharto'graphically** *adv*

Chartres ('ʃɑːtrə, ʃɑːt; *French* ʃartrə) *n* a city in NW France: Gothic cathedral; market town. Pop.: 41 850 (1990).

chartreuse (ʃɑː'trɜːz; *French* ʃartrøz) *n* **1** either of two liqueurs, green or yellow, made from herbs and flowers. **2a** a colour varying from a clear yellowish-green to a strong greenish-yellow. **2b** (*as adj*): *a chartreuse dress.* [C19: from French, after *La Grande Chartreuse,* monastery near Grenoble, where the liqueur is produced]

chartulary ('tʃɑːtjʊlərɪ) *n, pl* **-laries.** a variant of **cartulary.**

Chartwell ('tʃɑːtˌwel) *n* a house near Westerham in Kent: home for 40 years of Sir Winston Churchill.

charwoman ('tʃɑːˌwʊmən) *n, pl* **-women.** *Brit.* a woman who is hired to clean, tidy, etc., in a house or office.

chary ('tʃeərɪ) *adj* **charier, chariest. 1** wary; careful. **2** choosy; finicky. **3** shy. **4** sparing; mean. [Old English *cearig;* related to *caru* CARE, Old High German *charag* sorrowful]

Charybdis (kə'rɪbdɪs) *n* a ship-devouring monster in classical mythology, identified with a whirlpool off the north coast of Sicily, lying opposite Scylla on the Italian coast. Compare **Scylla.** ▸ **Cha'rybdian** *adj*

chase[1] (tʃeɪs) *vb* **1** to follow or run after (a person, animal, or goal) persistently or quickly. **2** (*tr;* often foll. by *out, away,* or *off*) to force to run (away); drive (out). **3** (*tr*) *Informal.* to court (a member of the opposite sex) in an unsubtle manner. **4** (*tr;* often foll. by *up*) *Informal.* to pursue persistently and energetically in order to obtain results, information, etc.: *chase up the builders and get a delivery date.* **5** (*intr*) *Informal.* to hurry; rush. ◆ *n* **6** the act of chasing; pursuit. **7** any quarry that is pursued. **8** *Brit.* an unenclosed area of land where wild animals are preserved to be hunted. **9** *Brit.* the right to hunt a particular quarry over the land of others. **10 the chase.** the act or sport of hunting. **11** short for **steeplechase. 12** *Real tennis.* a ball that bounces twice, requiring the point to be played again. **13 cut to the chase.** *Informal, chiefly U.S.* to start talking about the important aspects of something. **14 give chase.** to pursue (a person, animal, or thing) actively. [C13: from Old French *chacier,* from Vulgar Latin *captiāre* (unattested), from Latin *captāre* to pursue eagerly, from *capere* to take; see CATCH] ▸ **'chaseable** *adj*

chase[2] (tʃeɪs) *n* **1** *Letterpress printing.* a rectangular steel or cast-iron frame into which metal type and blocks making up pages are locked for printing or platemaking. **2** the part of a gun barrel from the front of the trunnions to the muzzle. **3** a groove or channel, esp. one that is cut in a wall to take a pipe, cable, etc. ◆ *vb* (*tr*) **4** Also: **chamfer.** to cut a groove, furrow, or flute in (a surface, column, etc.). [C17 (in the sense: frame for letterpress matter): probably from French *châsse* frame (in the sense: bore of a cannon, etc.): from Old French *chas* enclosure, from Late Latin *capsus* pen for animals; both from Latin *capsa* CASE[2]]

chase[3] (tʃeɪs) *vb* (*tr*) **1** Also: **enchase.** to ornament (metal) by engraving or embossing. **2** to form or finish (a screw thread) with a chaser. [C14: from Old French *enchasser* ENCHASE]

chaser[1] ('tʃeɪsə) *n* **1** a person or thing that chases. **2** a drink drunk after another of a different kind, as beer after spirits. **3** a cannon on a vessel situated either at the bow (**bow chaser**) or the stern (**stern chaser**) and used during pursuit by or of another vessel.

chaser[2] ('tʃeɪsə) *n* **1** a person who engraves. **2** a lathe cutting tool for accurately finishing a screw thread, having a cutting edge consisting of several repetitions of the thread form.

chasm ('kæzəm) *n* **1** a deep cleft in the ground; abyss. **2** a break in continuity; gap. **3** a wide difference in interests, feelings, etc. [C17: from Latin *chasma,* from Greek *khasma;* related to Greek *khainein* to gape] ▸ **chasmal** ('kæzməl) *or* **'chasmic** *adj*

chasmogamy (kæz'mɒgəmɪ) *adj Botany.* the production of flowers that open, so as to expose the reproductive organs and allow cross-pollination. Compare **cleistogamy.** [C20: from New Latin (*flores*) *chasmogami* from Greek *khasma* CHASM + -GAMY] ▸ **chas'mogamous** *adj*

chassé ('ʃæseɪ) *n* **1** one of a series of gliding steps in ballet in which the same foot always leads. **2** three consecutive dance steps, two fast and one slow, to four beats of music. ◆ *vb* **-sés, -séing, -séd. 3** (*intr*) to perform either of these steps. [C19: from French: a chasing]

chassepot ('ʃæspəʊ; *French* ʃaspo) *n* a breech-loading bolt-action rifle formerly used by the French Army. [C19: named after A. A. *Chassepot* (1833–1905), French gunsmith who invented it]

chasseur (ʃæ'sɜː; *French* ʃasœr) *n* **1** *French Army.* a member of a unit specially trained and equipped for swift deployment. **2** (in some parts of Europe, esp. formerly) a uniformed attendant, esp. one in the livery of a huntsman. ◆ *adj* **3** (*often postpositive*) designating or cooked in a sauce consisting of white wine and mushrooms. [C18: from French: huntsman]

Chassid, Chasid, Hassid, *or* **Hasid** ('hæsɪd; *Hebrew* xə'sid) *n, pl* **Chassidim, Chasidim, Hassidim,** *or* **Hasidim** ('hæsɪˌdiːm, -dɪm; *Hebrew* xasɪ'dim). **1** a sect of Jewish mystics founded in Poland about 1750, characterized by religious zeal and a spirit of prayer, joy, and charity. **2** a Jewish sect of the 2nd century B.C., formed to combat Hellenistic influences. ▸ **Chassidic, Chasidic, Hassidic,** *or* **Hasidic** (hə'sɪdɪk) *adj* ▸ **'Chassidˌism, 'Chasidˌism, 'Hassidˌism,** *or* **'Hasidˌism** *n*

chassis ('ʃæsɪ) *n, pl* **-sis** (-sɪz). **1** the steel frame, wheels, engine, and mechanical parts of a motor vehicle, to which the body is attached. **2** *Electronics.* a mounting for the circuit components of an electrical or electronic device, such as a radio or television. **3** the landing gear of an aircraft. **4** *Obsolete.* a wooden framework for a window, screen, etc. **5** the frame on which a cannon carriage moves backwards and forwards. **6** *Slang.* the body of a person, esp. a woman. [C17 (meaning: window frame): from French *châssis* frame, from Vulgar Latin *capsicum* (unattested), ultimately from Latin *capsa* CASE[2]]

chaste (tʃeɪst) *adj* **1** not having experienced sexual intercourse; virginal. **2** abstaining from unlawful or immoral sexual intercourse. **3** (of conduct, speech, etc.) pure; decent; modest. **4** (of style or taste) free from embellishment; simple; restrained. [C13: from Old French, from Latin *castus* pure; compare CASTE] ▸ **'chastely** *adv* ▸ **'chasteness** *n*

chasten ('tʃeɪsᵊn) *vb* (*tr*) **1** to bring to a state of submission; subdue; tame. **2** to discipline or correct by punishment. **3** to moderate; restrain; temper. [C16: from Old French *chastier,* from Latin *castigāre;* see CASTIGATE] ▸ **'chastener** *n* ▸ **'chasteningly** *adv*

chaste tree *n* a small ornamental verbenaceous tree, *Vitex agnus-castus,* of S Europe and SW Asia, with spikes of pale blue flowers.

chastise (tʃæs'taɪz) *vb* (*tr*) **1** to discipline or punish, esp. by beating. **2** to scold severely. [C14 *chastisen,* irregularly from *chastien* to CHASTEN] ▸ **chas'tisable** *adj* ▸ **chastisement** ('tʃæstɪzmənt, tʃæs'taɪz-) *n* ▸ **chas'tiser** *n*

chastity ('tʃæstɪtɪ) *n* **1** the state of being chaste; purity. **2** abstention from sexual intercourse; virginity or celibacy: *a vow of chastity.* [C13: from Old French *chasteté,* from Latin *castitās,* from *castus* CHASTE]

chastity belt *n* a locking beltlike device with a loop designed to go between a woman's legs in order to prevent her from having sexual intercourse.

chasuble ('tʃæzjʊbᵊl) *n Christianity.* a long sleeveless outer vestment worn by a priest when celebrating Mass. [C13: from French, from Late Latin *casubla* garment with a hood, apparently from *casula* cloak, literally: little house, from Latin *casa* cottage]

chat[1] (tʃæt) *n* **1** informal conversation or talk conducted in an easy familiar manner. **2** any Old World songbird of the subfamily *Turdinae* (thrushes, etc.) having a harsh chattering cry. See also **stonechat, whinchat. 3** any of various North American warblers, such as *Icteria virens* (**yellow-breasted chat**). **4** any of various Australian wrens (family *Muscicapidae*) of the genus *Ephthianura* and other genera. ◆ *vb* **chats, chatting, chatted.** (*intr*) **5** to talk in an easy familiar way. ◆ See also **chat up.** [C16: short for CHATTER]

chat[2] (tʃæt) *n* **1** the catkin of the willow. **2** the flower of the plantain. [C15: from French *chat* cat, referring to the furry appearance]

chateau *or* **château** ('ʃætəʊ; *French* ʃɑto) *n, pl* **-teaux** (-təʊ, -təʊz; *French* -to) *or* **-teaus. 1** a country house, castle, or manor house, esp. in France. **2** (in Quebec) the residence of a seigneur or (formerly) a governor. **3** (in the name of a wine) estate or vineyard. [C18: from French, from Old French *chastel,* from Latin *castellum* fortress, CASTLE]

Chateaubriand (*French* ʃɑtobrijɑ̃) *n* **1 François René** (frɑ̃swa rəne), Vicomte de Chateaubriand. 1768–1848, French writer and statesman: a precursor of the romantic movement in France; his works include *Le Génie du Christianisme* (1802) and *Mémoires d'outre-tombe* (1849–50). **2** a thick steak cut from the fillet of beef.

Châteauroux (*French* ʃɑtoru) *n* a city in central France: tenth-century castle (**Château-Raoul**). Pop.: 52 950 (1990).

Château-Thierry ('ʃætəʊ'tɪərɪ; *French* ʃɑtotjɛri) *n* a town in N central France, on the River Marne: scene of the second battle of the Marne (1918) during World War I. Pop.: 15 830 (1990).

chateau wine *n* a wine produced from any of certain vineyards in the Bordeaux region of France.

chatelain ('ʃætəˌleɪn; *French* ʃɑtlɛ̃) *n* the keeper or governor of a castle. [C16: from French, from Latin *castellānus* occupant of a CASTLE]

chatelaine ('ʃætəˌleɪn; *French* ʃɑtlɛn) *n* **1** (esp. formerly) the mistress of a castle or fashionable household. **2** a chain or clasp worn at the waist by women in the 16th to the 19th centuries, with handkerchief, keys, etc., attached. **3** a decorative pendant worn on the lapel.

Chatham[1] ('tʃætəm) *n* **1** a town in SE England, in N Kent on the River Medway: formerly royal naval dockyard. Pop.: 71 691 (1991). **2** a city in SE Canada, in SE Ontario on the Thames River. Pop.: 43 557 (1991).

Chatham[2] ('tʃætəm) *n* **1st Earl of.** title of the elder (William) **Pitt.**

Chatham Island *n* another name for **San Cristóbal** (sense 1).

Chatham Islands *pl n* a group of islands in the S Pacific Ocean, forming a county of South Island, New Zealand: consists of the main islands of Chatham, Pitt, and several rocky islets. Chief settlement: Waitangi. Pop.: 769 (1991). Area: 963 sq. km (372 sq. miles).

chatline ('tʃætˌlaɪn) *n* a telephone service enabling callers to join in general conversation with each other.

chatoyant (ʃə'tɔɪənt) *adj* **1** having changeable lustre; twinkling. **2** (of a gem, esp. a cabochon) displaying a band of light reflected off inclusions of other minerals. ◆ *n* **3** a gemstone with a changeable lustre, such as a **cat's eye.** [C18: from French, from *chatoyer* to gleam like a cat's eyes, from *chat* CAT[1]] ▸ **cha'toyancy** *n*

chat show *n Brit.* a television or radio show in which guests are interviewed informally. Also called: **talk show.**

Chatsworth House ('tʃætswɜːθ) *n* a mansion near Bakewell in Derbyshire: seat of the Dukes of Devonshire; built (1687–1707) in the classical style.

Chattanooga (ˌtʃætəˈnuːgə) *n* a city in SE Tennessee, on the Tennessee River: scene of two battles during the Civil War, in which the North defeated the Confederates, cleared Tennessee, and opened the way to Georgia (1863). Pop.: 150 425 (1996 est.).

chattel ('tʃætəl) *n* **1** (*often pl*) *Property law.* **1a chattel personal.** an item of movable personal property, such as furniture, domestic animals, etc. **1b chattel real.** an interest in land less than a freehold, such as a lease. **2 goods and chattels.** personal property. [C13: from Old French *chatel* personal property, from Medieval Latin *capitāle* wealth; see CAPITAL[1]]

chattel house *n* (esp. in Barbados) a movable wooden dwelling, usually set on a foundation of loose stones on rented land.

chattel mortgage *n U.S. and Canadian.* a mortgage on movable personal property.

chatter ('tʃætə) *vb* **1** to speak (about unimportant matters) rapidly and incessantly; prattle. **2** (*intr*) (of birds, monkeys, etc.) to make rapid repetitive high-pitched noises resembling human speech. **3** (*intr*) (of the teeth) to click together rapidly through cold or fear. **4** (*intr*) to make rapid intermittent contact with a component, as in machining, causing irregular cutting. ◆ *n* **5** idle or foolish talk; gossip. **6** the high-pitched repetitive noise made by a bird, monkey, etc. **7** the rattling of objects, such as parts of a machine. **8** the undulating pattern of marks in a machined surface from the vibration of the tool or workpiece. [C13: of imitative origin] ▸ **'chattery** *adj*

chatterbox ('tʃætəˌbɒks) *n Informal.* a person who talks constantly, esp. about trivial matters.

chatterer ('tʃætərə) *n* **1** someone or something that chatters. **2** another name for **cotinga.**

chattering classes *n Journalese, often derogatory.* (usually preceded by *the*) the educated sections of society, considered as enjoying discussion of political, social, and cultural issues.

chatter mark *n* **1** any of a series of grooves, pits, and scratches on the surface of a rock, usually made by the movement of a glacier. **2** a mark or series of marks on a workpiece.

Chatterton ('tʃætətən) *n* **Thomas.** 1752–70, British poet; author of spurious medieval verse and prose: he committed suicide at the age of 17.

chatty ('tʃætɪ) *adj* **-tier, -tiest. 1** full of trivial conversation; talkative. **2** informal and friendly; gossipy: *a chatty letter.* ▸ **'chattily** *adv* ▸ **'chattiness** *n*

chat up *vb* (*tr, adv*) *Brit. informal.* **1** to talk flirtatiously to (a person), esp. with the intention of seducing him or her. **2** to talk persuasively to (a person), esp. with an ulterior motive.

Chaucer ('tʃɔːsə) *n* **Geoffrey.** ?1340–1400, English poet, noted for his narrative skill, humour, and insight, particularly in his most famous work, *The Canterbury Tales.* He was influenced by the continental tradition of rhyming verse. His other works include *Troilus and Criseyde, The Legende of Good Women,* and *The Parlement of Foules.*

Chaucerian (tʃɔː'sɪərɪən) *adj* **1** of, relating to, or characteristic of the writings of Chaucer. ◆ *n* **2** an imitator of Chaucer, esp. one of a group of 15th-century Scottish writers who took him as a model. **3a** an admirer of Chaucer's works. **3b** a specialist in the study or teaching of Chaucer.

chaudfroid *French.* (ʃofrwa) *n* a sweet or savoury jellied sauce used to coat cold meat, chicken, etc. [literally: hot-cold (because prepared as hot dish, but served cold)]

chauffer *or* **chaufer** ('tʃɔːfə) *n* a small portable heater or stove. [C19: from French *chauffoir,* from *chauffer* to heat]

chauffeur ('ʃəʊfə, ʃəʊ'fɜː) *n* **1** a person employed to drive a car. ◆ *vb* **2** to act as driver for (a person): *he chauffeured me to the stadium; he chauffeurs for the Duke.* [C20: from French, literally: stoker, from *chauffer* to heat] ▸ **chauffeuse** (ʃəʊ'fɜːz) *fem n*

chaulmoogra (tʃɔːl'muːgrə) *n* **1** a tropical Asian tree, *Taraktogenos* (or *Hydnocarpus*) *kurzii:* family *Flacourtiaceae.* **2** oil from the seed of this tree, used in treating leprosy. **3** any of several similar or related trees. [from Bengali *cāulmugrā,* from *cāul* rice + *mugrā* hemp]

chaunt (tʃɔːnt) *n, vb* a less common variant of **chant.** ▸ **'chaunter** *n*

chausses (ʃəʊs) *n* (*functioning as sing*) a tight-fitting medieval garment covering the feet and legs, usually made of chain mail. [C15: from Old French *chauces,* plural of *chauce* leg-covering, from Medieval Latin *calcea,* from Latin *calceus* shoe, from *calx* heel]

chautauqua (ʃə'tɔːkwə) *n* (in the U.S., formerly) a summer school or educational meeting held in the summer. [C19: named after *Chautauqua,* a lake in New York near which such a school was first held]

chauvinism ('ʃəʊvɪˌnɪzəm) *n* **1** aggressive or fanatical patriotism; jingoism. **2** enthusiastic devotion to a cause. **3** smug irrational belief in the superiority of one's own race, party, sex, etc.: *male chauvinism.* [C19: from French *chauvinisme,* after Nicolas *Chauvin,* legendary French soldier under Napoleon, noted for his vociferous and unthinking patriotism] ▸ **'chauvinist** *n* ▸ **ˌchauvin'istic** *adj* ▸ **ˌchauvin'istically** *adv*

Chavannes (*French* ʃavan) *n* **Puvis de.** See (Pierre Cécile) **Puvis de Chavannes.**

chaw (tʃɔː) *Dialect.* ◆ *vb* **1** to chew (tobacco), esp. without swallowing it. ◆ *n* **2** something chewed, esp. a plug of tobacco. ▸ **'chawer** *n*

chayote (tʃɑː'jəʊteɪ, tʃaɪ'əʊtɪ) *n* **1** a tropical American cucurbitaceous climbing plant, *Sechium edule,* that has edible pear-shaped fruit enclosing a single enormous seed. **2** the fruit of this plant, which is cooked and eaten as a vegetable. [from Spanish, from Nahuatl *chayotli*]

chazan, hazan, *or* ***hazzan*** *Hebrew.* (xa'zan; *English* 'hɑːzən) *n, pl* ***chazanim*** (xaza'nim; *English* hɑː'zɔːniːm) *or English* ***chazans.*** a person who leads synagogue services, esp. as a profession; cantor.

ChB *abbrev. for* Bachelor of Surgery. [Latin: *Chirurgiae Baccalaureus*]

ChE *abbrev. for* Chemical Engineer.

CHE (tʃiː) *n* (in New Zealand) *acronym for* Crown Health Enterprise: an agency supervising health expenditure in a district.

cheap (tʃiːp) *adj* **1** costing relatively little; inexpensive; good value. **2** charging low prices: *a cheap hairdresser.* **3** of poor quality; shoddy: *cheap furniture; cheap and nasty.* **4** worth relatively little: *promises are cheap.* **5** not worthy of respect; vulgar. **6** ashamed; embarrassed: *to feel cheap.* **7** stingy; miserly. **8** *Informal.* mean; despicable: *a cheap liar.* **9 dirt cheap.** *Informal.* extremely inexpensive. ◆ *n* **10 on the cheap.** *Brit. informal.* at a low cost. ◆ *adv* **11** at very little cost. [Old English *ceap* barter, bargain, price, property; related to Old Norse *kaup* bargain, Old High German *kouf* trade, Latin *caupō* innkeeper] ▸ **'cheapish** *adj* ▸ **'cheaply** *adv* ▸ **'cheapness** *n*

cheapen ('tʃiːpən) *vb* **1** to make or become lower in reputation, quality, etc.; degrade or be degraded. **2** to make or become cheap or cheaper. ▸ **'cheapener** *n*

cheap-jack *Informal.* ◆ *n* **1** a person who sells cheap and shoddy goods. ◆ *adj* **2** shoddy or inferior. [C19: from CHEAP + *Jack* (name used to typify a person)]

cheapo ('tʃiːpəʊ) *adj, n Informal.* very cheap and possibly shoddy.

cheapskate ('tʃiːpˌskeɪt) *n Informal.* a miserly person.

cheat (tʃiːt) *vb* **1** to deceive or practise deceit, esp. for one's own gain; trick or swindle (someone). **2** (*intr*) to obtain unfair advantage by trickery, as in a game of cards. **3** (*tr*) to escape or avoid (something unpleasant) by luck or cunning: *to cheat death.* **4** (when *intr,* usually foll. by *on*) *Informal.* to be sexually unfaithful to (one's wife, husband, or lover). ◆ *n* **5** a person who cheats. **6** a deliberately dishonest transaction, esp. for gain; fraud. **7** *Informal.* sham. **8** *Law.* the obtaining of another's property by fraudulent means. **9** the usual U.S. name for **rye-brome.** [C14: short for ESCHEAT] ▸ **'cheatable** *adj* ▸ **'cheater** *n* ▸ **'cheatingly** *adv*

Cheb (*Czech* xɛp) *n* a town in the W Czech Republic, in W Bohemia on the Ohře River: 12th-century castle where Wallenstein was murdered (1634); a centre of the Sudeten-German movement after World War I. Pop.: 31 847 (1991). German name: **Eger.**

Cheboksary (*Russian* tʃɪbak'sari) *n* a port in W central Russia on the River Volga: capital of the Chuvash Republic. Pop.: 450 000 (1995 est.).

Chebyshev's inequality ('tʃɛbɪˌʃɒfs) *n Statistics.* the fundamental theorem that the probability that a random variable differs from its mean by more than k standard deviations is less than or equal to $1/k^2$. [named after P. L. *Chebyshev* (1821–94), Russian mathematician]

Chechen (tʃɪ'tʃɛn) *n, pl* **-chens** *or* **-chen.** a member of a people of Russia, speaking a Circassian language and chiefly inhabiting the Chechen Republic.

Chechen Republic *n* a constituent republic of S Russia, on the N slopes of the Caucasus Mountains: major oil and natural gas resources; formed an Autonomous Republic with Ingushetia from 1936 until 1944 and from 1957 until

1991; separated from Ingushetia in 1992; fighting between Chechen separatists and Russian forces (1994–96). Capital: Grozny. Pop. (including Ingushetia): 1 234 000 (1995 est.). Area (including Ingushetia): 19 300 sq. km (7450 sq. miles). Also called: **Chechenia** (tʃɪˈtʃɛnɪə), **Chechnya** (tʃɪˈtʃnɪə).

check (tʃɛk) *vb* **1** to pause or cause to pause, esp. abruptly. **2** (*tr*) to restrain or control: *to check one's tears.* **3** (*tr*) to slow the growth or progress of; retard. **4** (*tr*) to rebuke or rebuff. **5** (when *intr,* often foll. by *on* or *up on*) to examine, investigate, or make an inquiry into (facts, a product, etc.) for accuracy, quality, or progress, esp. rapidly or informally. **6** (*tr*) *Chiefly U.S. and Canadian.* to mark off so as to indicate approval, correctness, or preference. Usual Brit. word: **tick. 7** (*intr;* often foll. by *with*) *Chiefly U.S. and Canadian.* to correspond or agree: *this report checks with the other.* **8** (*tr*) *Chiefly U.S., Canadian, and N.Z.* to leave in or accept (clothing or property) for temporary custody. **9** *Chess.* to place (an opponent's king) in check. **10** (*tr*) to mark with a pattern of squares or crossed lines. **11** to crack or cause to crack. **12** *Agriculture.* short for **checkrow. 13** (*tr*) *Ice hockey.* to impede (an opponent). **14** (*intr*) *Hunting.* (of hounds) to pause in the pursuit of quarry while relocating a lost scent. **15** (*intr;* foll. by *at*) *Falconry.* to change from one quarry to another while in flight. **16** (*intr*) to decline the option of opening the betting in a round of poker. **17** **check the helm.** *Nautical.* to swing back the helm of a vessel to prevent it from turning too quickly or too far. ◆ *n* **18** a break in progress; stoppage. **19** a restraint or rebuff. **20a** a person or thing that restrains, halts, etc. **20b** (*as modifier*): *a check line.* **21a** a control, esp. a rapid or informal one, designed to ensure accuracy, progress, etc. **21b** (*as modifier*): *a check list.* **22** a means or standard to ensure against fraud or error. **23** the U.S. word for **tick**[1]. **24** the U.S. spelling of **cheque. 25** *Chiefly U.S.* the bill in a restaurant. **26** *Chiefly U.S. and Canadian.* a ticket or tag used to identify clothing or property deposited for custody. **27** a pattern of squares or crossed lines. **28** a single square in such a pattern. **29a** fabric with a pattern of squares or crossed lines. **29b** (*as modifier*): *a check suit.* **30** *Chess.* the state or position of a king under direct attack, from which it must be moved or protected by another piece. **31** a small crack, as one in veneer or one that occurs in timber during seasoning. **32** part of the action of a piano that arrests the backward motion of a hammer after it has struck a string and holds it until the key is released. **33** a chip or counter used in some card and gambling games. **34** *Hunting.* a pause by the hounds in the pursuit of their quarry owing to loss of its scent. **35** *Angling.* a ratchet fitted to a fishing reel to check the free running of the line. **36** *Ice hockey.* the act of impeding an opponent with one's body or stick. **37** **in check.** under control or restraint. ◆ *interj* **38** *Chess.* a call made to an opponent indicating that his king is in check. **39** *Chiefly U.S. and Canadian.* an expression of agreement. ◆ See also **check in, check off, check out, checkup.** [C14: from Old French *eschec* a check at chess, hence, a pause (to verify something), via Arabic from Persian *shāh* the king! (in chess)] ▸ **ˈcheckable** *adj*

check digit *n Computing.* a digit derived from and appended to a string of data digits, used to detect corruption of the data string during transmission or transcription.

checked (tʃɛkt) *adj* **1** having a pattern of small squares. **2** *Phonetics.* (of a syllable) ending in a consonant.

checker[1] (ˈtʃɛkə) *n, vb* **1** the usual U.S. spelling of **chequer.** ◆ *n* **2** *Textiles.* a variant spelling of **chequer** (sense 2). **3** the U.S. and Canadian name for **draughtsman** (sense 3). ◆ See also **checkers.**

checker[2] (ˈtʃɛkə) *n Chiefly U.S. and Canadian.* **1** a cashier, esp. in a supermarket. **2** an attendant in a cloakroom, left-luggage office, etc.

checkerberry (ˈtʃɛkəbərɪ, -brɪ) *n, pl* **-ries. 1** the fruit of any of various plants, esp. the wintergreen (*Gaultheria procumbens*). **2** any plant bearing this fruit.

checkerbloom (ˈtʃɛkəˌbluːm) *n* a Californian malvaceous plant, *Sidalcea malvaeflora,* with pink or purple flowers.

checkerboard (ˈtʃɛkəˌbɔːd) *n* the U.S. and Canadian name for a **draughtboard.**

checkers (ˈtʃɛkəz) *n* (*functioning as sing*) the U.S. and Canadian name for **draughts.**

check in *vb* (*adv*) **1** (*intr*) to record one's arrival, as at a hotel or for work; sign in or report. **2** (*tr*) to register the arrival of (passengers, etc.). ◆ *n* **check-in. 3a** the formal registration of arrival, as at an airport or a hotel. **3b** (*as modifier*): *check-in time.* **4** the place where one registers arrival at an airport, etc.

checking account *n* the U.S. name for **current account.**

check list *n* a list of items, facts, names, etc., to be checked or referred to for comparison, identification, or verification.

checkmate (ˈtʃɛkˌmeɪt) *n* **1** *Chess.* **1a** the winning position in which an opponent's king is under attack and unable to escape. **1b** the move by which this position is achieved. **2** utter defeat. ◆ *vb* (*tr*) **3** *Chess.* to place (an opponent's king) in checkmate. **4** to thwart or render powerless. ◆ *interj* **5** *Chess.* a call made when placing an opponent's king in checkmate. [C14: from Old French *eschec mat,* from Arabic *shāh māt,* the king is dead; see CHECK]

check off *vb* (*tr, adv*) **1** to mark with a tick. **2** to deduct (union contributions) directly from an employee's pay. ◆ *n* **check-off. 3** a procedure whereby an employer deducts union contributions directly from an employee's pay and pays the money to the union.

check out *vb* (*adv*) **1** (*intr*) to pay the bill and depart, esp. from a hotel. **2** (*intr*) to depart from a place; record one's departure from work. **3** to investigate or prove to be in order after investigation: *the police checked out all the statements; their credentials checked out.* **4** (*tr*) *Informal.* to have a look at; inspect: *check out the wally in the pink shirt.* ◆ *n* **checkout. 5a** the latest time for vacating a room in a hotel, etc. **5b** (*as modifier*): *checkout time.* **6** a counter, esp. in a supermarket, where customers pay.

checkpoint (ˈtʃɛkˌpɔɪnt) *n* a place, as at a frontier or in a motor rally, where vehicles or travellers are stopped for official identification, inspection, etc.

checkrail (ˈtʃɛkˌreɪl) *n Brit.* another word for **guardrail** (sense 2).

checkrein (ˈtʃɛkˌreɪn) *n* the usual U.S. word for **bearing rein.**

checkroom (ˈtʃɛkˌruːm, -ˌrʊm) *n* the U.S. and Canadian name for **left-luggage office.**

checkrow (ˈtʃɛkˌrəʊ) *U.S. agriculture.* ◆ *n* **1** a row of plants, esp. corn, in which the spaces between adjacent plants are equal to those between adjacent rows to facilitate cultivation. ◆ *vb* **2** (*tr*) to plant in checkrows.

checks and balances *pl n Government, chiefly U.S.* competition and mutual restraint among the various branches of government.

checkup (ˈtʃɛkˌʌp) *n* **1** an examination to see if something is in order. **2** *Med.* a medical examination, esp. one taken at regular intervals to verify a normal state of health or discover a disease in its early stages. ◆ *vb* **check up. 3** (*intr, adv* sometimes foll. by *on*) to investigate or make an inquiry into (a person's character, evidence, etc.), esp. when suspicions have been aroused.

check valve *n* a valve that closes by fluid pressure to prevent return flow. Also called: **nonreturn valve.**

checky (ˈtʃɛkɪ) *adj* (*usually postpositive*) *Heraldry.* having squares of alternating tinctures or furs; checked.

Cheddar (ˈtʃɛdə) *n* **1** (*sometimes not cap.*) any of several types of smooth hard yellow or whitish cheese. **2** a village in SW England, in N Somerset: situated near **Cheddar Gorge,** a pass through the Mendip Hills renowned for its stalactitic caverns and rare limestone flora. Pop.: 4484 (1991).

cheddite (ˈtʃɛdaɪt, ˈʃɛd-) *n* an explosive made by mixing a powdered chlorate or perchlorate with a fatty substance, such as castor oil. [C20: from *Chedde* town in Savoy, France, where it was first made]

cheder *or* ***heder*** *Hebrew.* (ˈxɛdɛr; *English* ˈheɪdə) *n, pl* ***chadarim*** (xadaˈriːm) *or English* **cheders.** *Judaism.* **1** (in Western countries) elementary religious education classes, usually outside normal school hours. **2** more traditionally, a full-time elementary religious school. **3** *Informal.* a place of corrective instruction; prison. [literally: room]

chee-chee (ˈtʃiːˌtʃiː) *n* a less common spelling of **chichi**[2].

cheek (tʃiːk) *n* **1a** either side of the face, esp. that part below the eye. **1b** either side of the oral cavity; side of the mouth. Related adjs.: **buccal, genal, malar. 2** *Informal.* impudence; effrontery. **3** (*often pl*) *Informal.* either side of the buttocks. **4** (*often pl*) a side of a door jamb. **5** *Nautical.* one of the two fore-and-aft supports for the trestletrees on a mast of a sailing vessel, forming part of the hounds. **6** one of the jaws of a vice. **7** **cheek by jowl.** close together; intimately linked. **8** **turn the other cheek.** to be submissive and refuse to retaliate even when provoked or treated badly. **9** **with (one's) tongue in (one's) cheek.** See **tongue** (sense 19). ◆ *vb* **10** (*tr*) *Informal.* to speak or behave disrespectfully to; act impudently towards. [Old English *ceace;* related to Middle Low German *kāke,* Dutch *kaak*] ▸ **ˈcheekless** *adj*

cheekbone (ˈtʃiːkˌbəʊn) *n* the nontechnical name for **zygomatic bone.** Related adj: **malar.**

cheekpiece (ˈtʃiːkˌpiːs) *n* either of the two straps of a bridle that join the bit to the crownpiece.

cheek pouch *n* a membranous pouch inside the mouth of many rodents and some other mammals: used for holding food.

cheeky (ˈtʃiːkɪ) *adj* **cheekier, cheekiest.** disrespectful in speech or behaviour; impudent: *a cheeky child.* ▸ **ˈcheekily** *adv* ▸ **ˈcheekiness** *n*

cheep (tʃiːp) *n* **1** the short weak high-pitched cry of a young bird; chirp. ◆ *vb* **2** (*intr*) (of young birds) to utter characteristic shrill sounds. ▸ **ˈcheeper** *n*

cheer (tʃɪə) *vb* **1** (usually foll. by *up*) to make or become happy or hopeful; comfort or be comforted. **2** to applaud with shouts. **3** (when *tr,* sometimes foll. by *on*) to encourage (a team, person, etc.) with shouts, esp. in contests. ◆ *n* **4** a shout or cry of approval, encouragement, etc., often using such words as **hurrah!** or **rah! rah! rah! 5** **three cheers.** three shouts of hurrah given in unison by a group to honour someone or celebrate something. **6** happiness; good spirits. **7** state of mind; spirits (archaic, except in the phrases **be of good cheer, with good cheer**). **8** *Archaic.* provisions for a feast; fare. ◆ See also **cheers.** [C13 (in the sense: face, welcoming aspect): from Old French *chere,* from Late Latin *cara* face, from Greek *kara* head] ▸ **ˈcheerer** *n* ▸ **ˈcheeringly** *adv*

cheerful (ˈtʃɪəfʊl) *adj* **1** having a happy disposition; in good spirits. **2** pleasantly bright; gladdening: *a cheerful room.* **3** hearty; ungrudging; enthusiastic: *cheerful help.* ▸ **ˈcheerfully** *adv* ▸ **ˈcheerfulness** *n*

cheerio (ˌtʃɪərɪˈəʊ) *sentence substitute. Informal, chiefly Brit.* **1** a farewell greeting. **2** a drinking toast. ◆ *n* **3** *N.Z.* a type of small sausage.

cheerleader (ˈtʃɪəˌliːdə) *n* a person who leads a crowd in formal cheers, esp. at sports events.

cheerless (ˈtʃɪəlɪs) *adj* dreary, gloomy, or pessimistic. ▸ **ˈcheerlessly** *adv* ▸ **ˈcheerlessness** *n*

cheerly (ˈtʃɪəlɪ) *adj, adv Archaic or nautical.* cheerful or cheerfully.

cheers (tʃɪəz) *sentence substitute. Informal, chiefly Brit.* **1** a drinking toast. **2** goodbye! cheerio! **3** thanks!

cheery (ˈtʃɪərɪ) *adj* **cheerier, cheeriest.** showing or inspiring cheerfulness. ▸ **ˈcheerily** *adv* ▸ **ˈcheeriness** *n*

cheese[1] (tʃiːz) *n* **1** the curd of milk separated from the whey and variously prepared as a food. **2** a mass or complete cake of this substance. **3** any of various substances of similar consistency, etc.: *lemon cheese.* **4** **big cheese.** *Slang.* an important person. **5** **as alike** (*or* **different**) **as chalk and cheese.** See **chalk** (sense 6). [Old English *cēse,* from Latin *cāseus* cheese; related to Old Saxon *kāsi*]

cheese[2] (tʃiːz) *vb Slang.* **1** (*tr*) to stop; desist. **2** (*intr*) *Prison slang.* to act in a grovelling manner. [C19: of unknown origin]

cheeseboard (ˈtʃiːzˌbɔːd) *n* a board from which cheese is served at a meal.

cheeseburger (ˈtʃiːzˌbɜːɡə) *n* a hamburger cooked with a slice of cheese on top of it.

cheesecake (ˈtʃiːzˌkeɪk) *n* **1** a rich tart with a biscuit base, filled with a mixture of cream cheese, cream, sugar, and often sultanas, sometimes having a fruit topping. 2 *Slang.* women displayed for their sex appeal, as in photographs in magazines, newspapers, or films. Compare **beefcake.**

cheesecloth ('tʃi:z,klɒθ) *n* a loosely woven cotton cloth formerly used only for wrapping cheese.

cheese cutter *n* 1 a board with a wire attached for cutting cheese. 2 *Nautical.* a keel that may be drawn up into the boat when not in use. 3 a nautical peaked cap worn without a badge.

cheesed off *adj* (*usually postpositive*) *Brit. slang.* bored, disgusted, or angry. [C20: from CHEESE[2]]

cheese-head *adj* denoting or relating to a screw or bolt with a cylindrical slotted head.

cheese mite *n* a white soft-bodied free-living mite, *Tyrophagus* (or *Tyroglyphus*) *longior,* sometimes found in decaying cheese.

cheesemonger ('tʃi:z,mʌŋgə) *n* a person dealing in cheese, butter, etc.

cheeseparing ('tʃi:z,peərɪŋ) *adj* 1 penny-pinching; stingy. ◆ *n* **2a** a paring of cheese rind. **2b** anything similarly worthless. 3 stinginess.

cheese skipper *n* a dipterous fly, *Piophila casei,* whose larvae feed on cheese and move by jumping: family *Piophilidae.*

cheese straw *n* a long thin cheese-flavoured strip of pastry.

cheesewood ('tʃi:z,wʊd) *n Austral. Rare.* the tough yellowish wood of Australian trees of the genus *Pittosporum:* family *Pittosporaceae.*

cheesy ('tʃi:zɪ) *adj* **cheesier, cheesiest.** 1 like cheese in flavour, smell, or consistency. 2 *Informal.* (of a smile) broad but possibly insincere: *a big cheesy grin.* 3 *Informal.* banal or trite; in poor taste. ▸ **'cheesiness** *n*

cheetah *or* **chetah** ('tʃi:tə) *n* a large feline mammal, *Acinonyx jubatus,* of Africa and SW Asia: the swiftest mammal, having very long legs, nonretractile claws, and a black-spotted light-brown coat. [C18: from Hindi *cītā,* from Sanskrit *citrakāya* tiger, from *citra* bright, speckled + *kāya* body]

Cheever ('tʃi:və) *n* **John.** 1912–82, U.S. novelist and short-story writer. His novels include *The Wapshot Chronicle* (1957) and *Bullet Park* (1969).

chef (ʃɛf) *n* a cook, esp. the principal cook in a restaurant. [C19: from French, from Old French *chief* head, CHIEF]

chef-d'oeuvre *French.* (ʃɛdœvrə) *n, pl* ***chefs-d'oeuvre*** (ʃɛdœvrə). a masterpiece.

Chefoo ('tʃi:'fu:) *n* another name for **Yantai.**

Che Guevara (tʃeɪ gə'vɑ:rə; *Spanish* tʃe ge'βara) *n* See **Guevara.**

cheiro- *combining form.* a variant spelling of **chiro-.**

Cheiron ('kaɪrɒn, -rən) *n* a variant spelling of **Chiron.**

Cheju ('tʃe'dʒu:) *n* a volcanic island in the N East China Sea, southwest of Korea: constitutes a province (Cheju-do) of South Korea. Capital: Cheju. Pop.: 258 509 (1995). Area: 1792 sq. km (692 sq. miles). Also called: **Quelpart.**

Cheka *Russian.* ('tʃɛka) *n Russian history.* the secret police set up in 1917 by the Bolshevik government: reorganized in the Soviet Union in Dec. 1922 as the GPU. [C20: from Russian, acronym of *Chrezvychainaya Komissiya* Extraordinary Commission (to combat Counter-Revolution)]

Chekhov *or* **Chekov** ('tʃɛkɒf; *Russian* 'tʃɛxəf) *n* **Anton Pavlovich** (an'tɔn 'pavləvitʃ). 1860–1904, Russian dramatist and short-story writer. His plays include *The Seagull* (1896), *Uncle Vanya* (1900), *The Three Sisters* (1901), and *The Cherry Orchard* (1904). ▸ **Chekhovian** *or* **Chekovian** (tʃɛ'kəʊvɪən) *adj*

Chekiang ('tʃɛ'kjæŋ, -kaɪ'æŋ) *n* a variant transliteration of the Chinese name for **Zhejiang.**

chela[1] ('ki:lə) *n, pl* **lae** (-li:). a large pincer-like claw of such arthropods as the crab and scorpion. [C17: New Latin, from Greek *khēlē* claw] ▸ **cheliferous** (kɪ'lɪfərəs) *adj*

chela[2] ('tʃeɪlə) *n Hinduism.* a disciple of a religious teacher. [C19: from Hindi *celā,* from Sanskrit *ceta* servant, slave] ▸ **'chela,ship** *n*

chelate ('ki:leɪt) *n* 1 *Chem.* a chemical compound whose molecules contain a closed ring of atoms of which one is a metal atom. ◆ *adj* 2 *Zoology.* of or possessing chelae. 3 *Chem.* of or denoting a chelate. ◆ *vb* 4 (*intr*) *Chem.* to form a chelate. [C20: from CHELA[1]] ▸ **che'lation** *n*

chelating agent *n* a chemical compound that coordinates with a metal to form a chelate, often used to trap or remove heavy metal ions.

chelicera (kɪ'lɪsərə) *n, pl* **-erae** (-ə,ri:). one of a pair of appendages on the head of spiders and other arachnids: often modified as food-catching claws. [C19: from New Latin, from French *chélicère,* from *chél-* (see CHELA[1]) + *-cère* from Greek *keras* horn] ▸ **che'liceral** *adj*

chelicerate (kɪ'lɪsə,reɪt) *adj* 1 of, relating to, or belonging to the *Chelicerata,* a subphylum of arthropods, including arachnids and the horseshoe crab, in which the first pair of limbs are modified as chelicerae. ◆ *n* 2 any arthropod belonging to the *Chelicerata.*

cheliform ('ki:lɪ,fɔ:m) *adj* shaped like a chela; pincer-like.

Chellean ('ʃɛlɪən) *n, adj Archaeol.* (*no longer in technical usage*) another word for **Abbevillian.** [C19: from French *chelléen,* from *Chelles,* France, where various items were found]

Chelmsford ('tʃɛlmzfəd) *n* a town in SE England, administrative centre of Essex: market town. Pop.: 197 451 (1991).

cheloid ('ki:lɔɪd) *n Pathol.* a variant spelling of **keloid.** ▸ **che'loidal** *adj*

chelone (kə'ləʊnɪ) *n* any plant of the hardy N American genus *Chelone,* grown for its white, rose, or purple flower spikes: family *Scrophulariaceae.* [New Latin, from Greek *chelōnē* a tortoise, from a fancied resemblance between a tortoise's head and the shape of the flower]

chelonian (kɪ'ləʊnɪən) *n* 1 any reptile of the order *Chelonia,* including the tortoises and turtles, in which most of the body is enclosed in a protective bony capsule. ◆ *adj* 2 of, relating to, or belonging to the *Chelonia.* [C19: from New Latin *Chelōnia,* from Greek *khelōnē* tortoise]

chelp (tʃɛlp) *vb* (*intr*) *Northern and Midland English dialect.* 1 (esp. of women or children) to chatter or speak out of turn: *she's always chelping at the teacher.* 2 (of birds) to squeak or chirp. [C19: perhaps from *ch(irp)* + *(y)elp*]

Chelsea ('tʃɛlsɪ) *n* a residential district of SW London, in the Royal Borough of Kensington and Chelsea: site of the Chelsea Royal Hospital for old and invalid soldiers (**Chelsea Pensioners**).

Chelsea bun *n* a rolled yeast currant bun decorated with sugar.

Cheltenham ('tʃɛltᵊnəm) *n* 1 a town in W England, in central Gloucestershire: famous for its schools, racecourse, and saline springs (discovered in 1716). Pop.: 91 301 (1991). 2 a style of type.

Chelyabinsk (*Russian* tʃɪ'ljabinsk) *n* an industrial city in SW Russia. Pop.: 1 086 000 (1995 est.).

Chelyuskin (*Russian* tʃɪ'ljuskin) *n* **Cape.** a cape in N central Russia, in N Siberia at the end of the Taimyr Peninsula: the northernmost point of Asia.

chem. *abbrev. for:* 1 chemical. 2 chemist. 3 chemistry.

chem- *combining form.* variant of **chemo-** before a vowel.

chemautotroph (,ki:məʊ'ɔ:tətrəʊf, ,kɛm-) *n Biology.* an organism, such as a bacterium, that obtains its energy from inorganic reactions using simple compounds, such as ammonia or carbon dioxide. ▸ **chemautotrophic** (,ki:məʊ,ɔ:tə'trɒfɪk, ,kɛm-) *adj*

chemical ('kɛmɪkᵊl) *n* 1 any substance used in or resulting from a reaction involving changes to atoms or molecules. ◆ *adj* 2 of or used in chemistry: *chemical balance.* 3 of, made from, or using chemicals: *chemical fertilizer.* ▸ **'chemically** *adv*

chemical bond *n* a mutual attraction between two atoms resulting from a redistribution of their outer electrons. See also **covalent bond, electrovalent bond, coordinate bond.**

chemical engineering *n* the branch of engineering concerned with the design, operation, maintenance, and manufacture of the plant and machinery used in industrial chemical processes. ▸ **chemical engineer** *n*

chemical equation *n* a representation of a chemical reaction using symbols of the elements to indicate the amount of substance, usually in moles, of each reactant and product.

chemical machining *n* the shaping of a metal part by controlled removal of unwanted metal by a flow of chemical solutions.

chemical potential *n* a thermodynamic function of a substance in a system that is the partial differential of the Gibbs function of the system with respect to the number of moles of the substance. Symbol: μ

chemical reaction *n* a process that involves changes in the structure and energy content of atoms, molecules, or ions but not their nuclei. Compare **nuclear reaction.**

chemical warfare *n* warfare in which chemicals other than explosives are used as weapons, esp. warfare using asphyxiating or nerve gases, poisons, defoliants, etc.

chemico- *combining form.* chemical: *chemicophysical.*

chemiluminescence (,kɛmɪ,lu:mɪ'nɛsəns) *n* the phenomenon in which a chemical reaction leads to the emission of light without incandescence. ▸ **,chemi,lumi'nescent** *adj*

chemin de fer (ʃə'mæn də 'fɛə; *French* ʃəmɛ̃dfɛr) *n* a gambling game, a variation of baccarat. [French: railway, referring to the fast tempo of the game]

chemiosmosis (,kɛmɪɒz'məʊsɪs) *n Biochem.* the mechanism by which the synthesis and utilization of the biochemical energy source ATP is regulated: the energy generated by oxidative phosphorylation generates a proton gradient across the membrane of the mitochondrion that drives the enzymic resynthesis of ATP.

chemise (ʃə'mi:z) *n* 1 an unwaisted loose-fitting dress hanging straight from the shoulders. 2 a loose shirtlike undergarment. ◆ Also called: **shift.** [C14: from Old French: shirt, from Late Latin *camisa,* perhaps of Celtic origin]

chemisette (,ʃɛmɪ'zɛt) *n* an underbodice of lawn, lace, etc., worn to fill in a low-cut dress. [C19: from French, diminutive of CHEMISE]

chemism ('kɛmɪzəm) *n Obsolete.* chemical action.

chemisorb (,kɛmɪ'sɔ:b) *or* **chemosorb** *vb* (*tr*) to take up (a substance) by chemisorption.

chemisorption (,kɛmɪ'sɔ:pʃən) *n* an adsorption process in which an adsorbate is held on the surface of an adsorbent by chemical bonds.

chemist ('kɛmɪst) *n* 1 *Brit.* a shop selling medicines, cosmetics, etc. 2 *Brit.* a qualified dispenser of prescribed medicines. 3 a person studying, trained in, or engaged in chemistry. 4 an obsolete word for **alchemist.** [C16: from earlier *chimist,* from New Latin *chimista,* shortened from Medieval Latin *alchimista* ALCHEMIST]

chemistry ('kɛmɪstrɪ) *n, pl* **-tries.** 1 the branch of physical science concerned with the composition, properties, and reactions of substances. See also **inorganic chemistry, organic chemistry, physical chemistry.** 2 the composition, properties, and reactions of a particular substance. 3 the nature and effects of any complex phenomenon: *the chemistry of humour.* 4 *Informal.* a reaction, taken to be instinctual, between two persons. [C17: from earlier *chimistrie,* from *chimist* CHEMIST]

chemmy ('ʃɛmɪ) *n Cards.* short for **chemin de fer.**

Chemnitz (*German* 'kɛmnɪts) *n* a city in E Germany, in Saxony, at the foot of the Erzgebirge: textiles, engineering. Pop.: 266 737 (1996 est.). Also called (1953–90): **Karl-Marx-Stadt.**

chemo-, chemi-, *or before a vowel* **chem-** *combining form.* indicating that chemicals or chemical reactions are involved: *chemotherapy.* [New Latin, from Late Greek *khēmeia;* see ALCHEMY]

chemoattractant (,kɛməʊə'træktənt) *n* a chemical substance that provokes chemotaxis, esp. one that causes a bacterium to move in the direction in which its concentration is increasing.

chemoheterotroph (,ki:məʊ'hɛtərəʊtrəʊf, ,kɛm-) *n Biology.* an organism that obtains its energy from the oxidation of organic compounds. ▸ **chemoheterotrophic** (,ki:məʊ,hɛtərəʊ'trɒfɪk ,kɛm-) *adj*

chemokinesis (,kɛməʊkaɪ'ni:sɪs) *n Immunol.* the random movement of cells, such as leucocytes, stimulated by substances in their environment.

chemonasty ('kɛməʊˌnæstɪ) *n Botany.* the nastic movement of a plant in response to a chemical stimulus.
chemoprophylaxis (ˌkɛməʊˌprəʊfə'læksɪs, -ˌprɒfə-) *n* the prevention of disease using chemical drugs. ► **ˌchemoˌprophy'lactic** *adj*
chemoreceptor (ˌkɛməʊrɪ'sɛptə) *or* **chemoceptor** *n* a sensory receptor in a biological cell membrane to which an external molecule binds to generate a smell or taste sensation.
chemosmosis (ˌkɛmɒz'məʊsɪs) *n* a chemical reaction between two compounds after osmosis through an intervening semipermeable membrane. ► **chemosmotic** (ˌkɛmɒz'mɒtɪk) *adj*
chemosphere ('kɛməˌsfɪə) *n Meteorol.* another name for **thermosphere.** ► **chemospheric** (ˌkɛmə'sfɛrɪk) *adj*
chemostat ('kiːməʊˌstæt, 'kɛm-) *n* an apparatus for growing bacterial cultures at a constant rate by controlling the supply of nutrient medium.
chemosynthesis (ˌkɛməʊ'sɪnθɪsɪs) *n* the formation of organic material by certain bacteria using energy derived from simple chemical reactions. ► **chemosynthetic** (ˌkɛməʊsɪn'θɛtɪk) *adj* ► **ˌchemosyn'thetically** *adv*
chemotaxis (ˌkɛməʊ'tæksɪs) *n* the movement of a microorganism or cell in response to a chemical stimulus. ► **ˌchemo'tactic** *adj* ► **ˌchemo'tactically** *adv*
chemotherapy (ˌkiːməʊ'θɛrəpɪ, kiːmə-) *n* treatment of disease, esp. cancer, by means of chemical agents. Compare **radiotherapy.** ► **ˌchemo'therapist** *n*
chemotropism (ˌkɛməʊ'trəʊˌpɪzəm) *n* the growth response of an organism, esp. a plant, to a chemical stimulus. ► **chemotropic** (ˌkɛməʊ'trɒpɪk) *adj* ► **ˌchemo'tropically** *adv*
chempaduk ('tʃɛmpəˌdʌk) *n* **1** an evergreen moraceous tree, *Artocarpus champeden* (or *A. integer*), of Malaysia, similar to the jackfruit. **2** the fruit of this tree, edible when cooked, having yellow starchy flesh and a leathery rind. [from Malay]
Chemulpo (ˌtʃɛmul'pəʊ) *n* a former name of **Inchon.**
chemurgy ('kɛmɜːdʒɪ) *n* the branch of chemistry concerned with the industrial use of organic raw materials, esp. materials of agricultural origin. ► **chem'urgic** *or* **chem'urgical** *adj*
Chenab (tʃɪ'næb) *n* a river rising in the Himalayas and flowing southwest to the Sutlej River in Pakistan. Length: 1087 km (675 miles).
Cheng-chiang ('tʃɛŋ'tʃæŋ) *n* a variant transliteration of the Chinese name for **Jinjiang.**
Chengchow *or* **Cheng-chou** ('tʃɛŋ'tʃaʊ) *n* a variant transliteration of the Chinese name for **Zhengzhou.**
Chengde, Chengteh, *or* **Ch'eng-te** ('tʃɛŋ'teɪ) *n* a city in NE China, in Hebei on the Luan River: summer residence of the Manchu emperors. Pop.: 246 799 (1990 est.).
Chengdu, Chengtu, *or* **Ch'eng-tu** ('tʃɛŋ'tuː) *n* a city in S central China, capital of Sichuan province. Pop.: 2 810 000 (1991 est.).
Chénier (*French* ʃenje) *n* **1 André** (**Marie de**) (ɑ̃dre). 1762–94, French poet; his work was influenced by the ancient Greek elegiac poets. He was guillotined during the French Revolution. **2** his brother, **Marie-Joseph** (**Blaise de**). 1764–1811, French dramatist and politician. He wrote patriotic songs and historical plays, such as *Charles IX* (1789).
chenille (ʃə'niːl) *n* **1** a thick soft tufty silk or worsted velvet cord or yarn used in embroidery and for trimmings, etc. **2** a fabric of such yarn. **3** a rich and hard-wearing carpet of such fabric. [C18: from French, literally: hairy caterpillar, from Latin *canicula,* diminutive of *canis* dog]
Chennai (tʃɪ'naɪ) *n* the official name for **Madras.**
chenopod ('kiːnəˌpɒd, 'kɛn-) *n* any flowering plant of the family *Chenopodiaceae,* which includes the beet, mangel-wurzel, spinach, and goosefoot. [C16: from Greek *khēn* goose + *pous* foot] ► **chenopodiaceous** (ˌkiːnəˌpəʊdɪ'eɪʃəs,ˌkɛn-) *adj*
cheongsam ('tʃɒŋ'sæm) *n* a straight dress, usually of silk or cotton, with a stand-up collar and a slit in one side of the skirt, worn by Chinese women. [from Chinese (Cantonese), variant of Mandarin *ch'ang shan* long jacket]
Cheops ('kiːɒps) *n* original name *Khufu.* Egyptian king of the fourth dynasty (?2613–?2494 B.C.), who built the largest pyramid at El Gîza.
Chephren ('kɛfrən) *n* See **Khafre.**
Chepstow ('tʃɛpstəʊ) *n* a town in S Wales, in Monmouthshire on the River Wye: tourism, light industry. Pop.: 9461 (1991).
cheque *or U.S.* **check** (tʃɛk) *n* **1** a bill of exchange drawn on a bank by the holder of a current account; into a bank account, if crossed, or payable on demand, if uncrossed. **2** *Austral. and N.Z.* the total sum of money received for contract work or a crop. **3** *Austral. and N.Z.* wages. [C18: from CHECK, in the sense: a means of verification]
cheque account *n* an account at a bank or a building society upon which cheques can be drawn.
chequebook *or U.S.* **checkbook** ('tʃɛkˌbʊk) *n* a book containing detachable blank cheques and issued by a bank or building society to holders of cheque accounts.
chequebook journalism *n* the practice of securing exclusive rights to material for newspaper stories by paying a high price for it, regardless of any moral implications such as paying people to boast of criminal or morally reprehensible activities.
cheque card *n* a card issued by a bank or building society, guaranteeing payment of a customer's cheques up to a stated value.
chequer *or U.S.* **checker** ('tʃɛkə) *n* **1** any of the marbles, pegs, or other pieces used in the game of Chinese chequers. **2a** a pattern consisting of squares of different colours, textures, or materials. **2b** one of the squares in such a pattern. ♦ *vb (tr)* **3** to make irregular in colour or character; variegate. **4** to mark off with alternating squares of colour. ♦ See also **chequers.** [C13: chessboard, from Anglo-French *escheker,* from *eschec* CHECK]
chequerboard ('tʃɛkəˌbɔːd) *n* another name for a **draughtboard.**
chequered *or esp. U.S.* **checkered** ('tʃɛkəd) *adj* marked by fluctuations of fortune (esp. in the phrase **a chequered career**).
chequered flag *n* the black-and-white checked flag traditionally shown to the winner and all finishers at the end of a motor race by a senior race official.
chequers ('tʃɛkəz) *n (functioning as sing)* another name for **draughts.**
Chequers ('tʃɛkəz) *n* an estate and country house in S England, in central Buckinghamshire: the official country residence of the British prime minister.
chequing account ('tʃɛkɪŋ) *n* the Canadian name for **current account.**
Cher (*French* ʃɛr) *n* **1** a department of central France, in E Centre region. Capital: Bourges. Pop.: 321 100 (1995). Area: 7304 sq. km (2849 sq. miles). **2** a river in central France, rising in the Massif Central and flowing northwest to the Loire. Length: 354 km (220 miles).
Cherbourg ('ʃɛəbʊəg; *French* ʃɛrbur) *n* a port in NW France, on the English Channel. Pop.: 28 773 (1990).
Cheremiss *or* **Cheremis** (ˌtʃɛərə'mɪs, -'miːs; 'tʃɛərəˌmɪs, -ˌmiːs) *n* **1** (*pl* **-miss** *or* **-mis**) a member of an Ugrian people of the Volga region, esp. of the Mari El Republic. **2** Also called: **Mari.** the language of this people, belonging to the Finno-Ugric family.
Cherenkov *or* **Cerenkov** (tʃɪ'rɛŋkɒf; *Russian* tʃɪ'rjenkəf) *n* **Pavel Alekseyevich** ('pavɪl alɪk'sjejɪvɪtʃ). 1904–90, Soviet physicist: noted for work on the effects produced by high-energy particles: shared Nobel prize for physics 1958.
Cherenkov radiation *n* the electromagnetic radiation produced when a charged particle moves through a medium at a greater velocity than the velocity of light in that medium. [C20: named after P. A. CHERENKOV]
Cheribon ('tʃɪərəˌbɒn) *n* a variant spelling of **Tjirebon.**
cherish ('tʃɛrɪʃ) *vb (tr)* **1** to show great tenderness for; treasure. **2** to cling fondly to (a hope, idea, etc.); nurse: *to cherish ambitions.* [C14: from Old French *cherir,* from *cher* dear, from Latin *cārus*] ► **'cherishable** *adj* ► **'cherisher** *n* ► **'cherishingly** *adv*
Chernenko (tʃɜː'ɲɛŋkəʊ) *n* **Konstantin** (**Ustinovich**) (kənstan'tin). 1911–85, Soviet statesman; general secretary of the Soviet Communist Party (1984–85).
Chernigov ('tʃɜːnɪgɒf) *n* a city in the N central Ukraine, on the River Desna: tyres, pianos, consumer goods. Pop.: 312 000 (1996 est.).
Chernobyl (tʃɜː'nəʊbᵊl, -nɒbᵊl) *n* a town in the N Ukraine; site of a nuclear power station accident in 1986.
Chernovtsy (*Russian* tʃɪrnaf'tsi) *n* a city in the Ukraine on the Prut River: formerly under Polish, Austro-Hungarian, and Romanian rule; part of the Soviet Union (1947–91). Pop.: 261 000 (1996 est.). German name: **Czernowitz.** Romanian name: **Cernăuţi.**
chernozem *or* **tschernosem** ('tʃɜːnəʊˌzɛm) *n* a black soil, rich in humus and carbonates, in cool or temperate semiarid regions, as the grasslands of Russia. [from Russian, contraction of *chernaya zemlya* black earth]
Cherokee ('tʃɛrəˌkiː, ˌtʃɛrə'kiː) *n* **1** (*pl* **-kees** *or* **-kee**) a member of a North American Indian people formerly living in and around the Appalachian Mountains, now chiefly in Oklahoma; one of the Iroquois peoples. **2** the language of this people, belonging to the Iroquoian family.
Cherokee rose *n* an evergreen climbing Chinese rose, *Rosa laevigata,* that now grows wild in the southern U.S., having large white fragrant flowers.
cheroot (ʃə'ruːt) *n* a cigar with both ends cut off squarely. [C17: from Tamil *curuttu* curl, roll]
cherry ('tʃɛrɪ) *n, pl* **-ries. 1** any of several trees of the rosaceous genus *Prunus,* such as *P. avium* (**sweet cherry**), having a small fleshy rounded fruit containing a hard stone. See also **bird cherry. 2** the fruit or wood of any of these trees. **3** any of various unrelated plants, such as the ground cherry and Jerusalem cherry. **4a** a bright red colour; cerise. **4b** (*as adj*)*: a cherry coat.* **5** *Taboo slang.* virginity or the hymen as its symbol. **6** (*modifier*) of or relating to the cherry fruit or wood: *cherry tart.* [C14: back formation from Old English *ciris* (mistakenly thought to be plural), ultimately from Late Latin *ceresia,* perhaps from Latin *cerasus* cherry tree, from Greek *kerasios*] ► **'cherry-ˌlike** *adj*
cherry brandy *n* a red liqueur made of brandy flavoured with cherries.
cherry laurel *n* a Eurasian rosaceous evergreen shrub, *Prunus laurocerasus,* having glossy aromatic leaves, white flowers, and purplish-black fruits.
cherry-pick *vb (tr)* to choose or take the best or most profitable of (a number of things), esp. for one's own benefit or gain: *to cherry-pick the best routes.*
cherry picker *n* a hydraulic crane, esp. one mounted on a lorry, that has an elbow joint or telescopic arm supporting a basket-like platform enabling a person to service high power lines or to carry out similar operations above the ground.
cherry-pie *n* a widely planted garden heliotrope, *Heliotropium peruvianum.*
cherry plum *n* a small widely planted Asian rosaceous tree, *Prunus cerasifera,* with white flowers and red or yellow cherry-like fruit. Also called: **myrobalan.**
cherry tomato *n* a miniature tomato not much bigger than a cherry.
chersonese ('kɜːsəˌniːs) *n* **a** a poetic or rhetorical word for **peninsula. b** (*cap. when part of a name*)*: Thracian Chersonese.* [C17: from Latin, from Greek *khersonēsos,* from *khersos* dry (land) + *nēsos* island]
chert (tʃɜːt) *n* a microcrystalline form of silica usually occurring as bands or layers of pebbles in sedimentary rock. Formula: SiO_2. Varieties include flint, lyddite (Lydian stone). Also called: **hornstone.** [C17: of obscure origin] ► **'cherty** *adj*
Chertsey ('tʃɜːtsɪ) *n* a town in S England, in N Surrey on the River Thames. Pop.: 11 786 (1991).
cherub ('tʃɛrəb) *n, pl* **cherubs** *or* **cherubim** ('tʃɛrəbɪm, -ubɪm). **1** *Theol.* a member of the second order of angels, whose distinctive gift is knowledge, often represented as a winged child or winged head of a child. **2** an innocent or sweet child. [Old English, from Hebrew *kĕrūbh*] ► **cherubic** (tʃə'ruːbɪk) *or* **che'rubical** *adj* ► **che'rubically** *adv*
Cherubini (ˌkɛrʊ'biːnɪ) *n* (**Maria**) **Luigi** (**Carlo Zenobio Salvatore**) (lu'iːdʒi).

1760–1842, Italian composer, noted particularly for his church music and his operas.

chervil ('tʃɜ:vɪl) *n* **1** an aromatic umbelliferous Eurasian plant, *Anthriscus cerefolium,* with small white flowers and aniseed-flavoured leaves used as herbs in soups and salads. **2 bur chervil.** a similar and related plant, *Anthriscus caucalis.* **3** a related plant, *Chaerophyllum temulentum,* having a hairy purple-spotted stem. [Old English *cerfelle,* from Latin *caerephylla,* plural of *caerephyllum* chervil, from Greek *khairephullon,* from *khairein* to enjoy + *phullon* leaf]

chervonets (tʃə'vɔ:nɛts) *n* (formerly) a Soviet monetary unit and gold coin worth ten roubles. [from Old Russian *červonyi,* from Old Polish *czerwony* golden, purple]

Cherwell ('tʃɑ:wəl) *n* **1st Viscount**, title of *Frederick Alexander Lindemann* ('lɪndəmən). 1886–1957, British physicist, born in Germany, noted for his research on heat capacity, aeronautics, and atomic physics. He was scientific adviser to Winston Churchill during World War II.

Ches. *abbrev. for* Cheshire.

Chesapeake Bay ('tʃɛsə,pi:k) *n* the largest inlet of the Atlantic in the coast of the U.S.: bordered by Maryland and Virginia.

Cheshire[1] ('tʃɛʃə, 'tʃɛʃɪə) *n* a county of NW England: low-lying and undulating, bordering on the Pennines in the east; mainly agricultural. Administrative centre: Chester. Pop.: 975 600 (1994 est.). Area: 2328 sq. km (899 sq. miles). Abbrev.: **Ches.**

Cheshire[2] ('tʃɛʃə) *n* Group Captain (**Geoffrey**) **Leonard.** 1917–92, British philanthropist: awarded the Victoria Cross in World War II; founded the Leonard Cheshire Foundation Homes for the Disabled: married Susan Ryder.

Cheshire cheese *n* a mild-flavoured cheese with a crumbly texture, originally made in Cheshire.

Cheshunt ('tʃɛʃənt) *n* a town in SE England, in SE Hertfordshire: a dormitory town of London. Pop.: 51 998 (1991).

Cheshvan *or* **Heshvan** (xeʃ'van) *n* (in the Jewish calendar) the eighth month of the year according to biblical reckoning and the second month of the civil year, usually falling within October and November. Also called: **Marcheshvan.** [from Hebrew]

chess[1] (tʃɛs) *n* a game of skill for two players using a chessboard on which chessmen are moved. Initially each player has one king, one queen, two rooks, two bishops, two knights, and eight pawns, which have different types of moves according to kind. The object is to checkmate the opponent's king. [C13: from Old French *esches,* plural of *eschec* check (at chess); see CHECK]

chess[2] (tʃɛs) *n U.S.* a less common name for **rye-brome.** [C18: of unknown origin]

chess[3] (tʃɛs) *n, pl* **chess** *or* **chesses.** a floorboard of the deck of a pontoon bridge. [C15 (in the sense: layer, tier): from Old French *chasse* frame, from Latin *capsa* box]

chessboard ('tʃɛs,bɔ:d) *n* a square board divided into 64 squares of two alternating colours, used for playing chess or draughts.

chessel ('tʃɛsᵊl) *n* a mould used in cheese-making. [C18: probably from CHEESE[1] + WELL[2]]

chessman ('tʃɛs,mæn, -mən) *n, pl* **-men.** any of the eight pieces and eight pawns used by each player in a game of chess. [C17: back formation from *chessmen,* from Middle English *chessemeyne* chess company, from *meynie, menye* company, body of men, from Old French *meyné*]

chesspiece ('tʃɛs,pi:s) *n* any of the eight pieces (excluding the pawns) used by each player in a game of chess.

chest (tʃɛst) *n* **1a** the front part of the trunk from the neck to the belly. Related adj: **pectoral. 1b** (*as modifier*): *a chest cold.* **2 get (something) off one's chest.** *Informal.* to unburden oneself of troubles, worries, etc., by talking about them. **3** a box, usually large and sturdy, used for storage or shipping: *a tea chest.* **4** Also: **'chestful.** the quantity a chest holds. **5** *Rare.* **5a** the place in which a public or charitable institution deposits its funds. **5b** the funds so deposited. **6** a sealed container or reservoir for a gas: *a wind chest; a steam chest.* [Old English *cest,* from Latin *cista* wooden box, basket, from Greek *kistē* box] ► **'chested** *adj*

Chester ('tʃɛstə) *n* a city in NW England, administrative centre of Cheshire, on the River Dee: intact surrounding walls; 16th- and 17th-century double-tier shops. Pop.: 80 110 (1991). Latin name: **Deva.**

chesterfield ('tʃɛstə,fi:ld) *n* **1** a man's knee-length overcoat, usually with a fly front to conceal the buttons and having a velvet collar. **2** a large tightly stuffed sofa, often upholstered in leather, with straight upholstered arms of the same height as the back. [C19: named after a 19th-century Earl of *Chesterfield*]

Chesterfield[1] ('tʃɛstə,fi:ld) *n* an industrial town in N central England, in Derbyshire: famous 14th-century church with twisted spire. Pop.: 71 945 (1991).

Chesterfield[2] ('tʃɛstə,fi:ld) *n* **Philip Dormer Stanhope,** 4th Earl of Chesterfield. 1694–1773, English statesman and writer, noted for his elegance, suavity, and wit; author of *Letters to His Son* (1774).

Chesterfieldian (,tʃɛstə'fi:ldɪən) *adj* of or like Lord Chesterfield; suave; elegant; polished.

Chesterton ('tʃɛstətᵊn) *n* **G**(**ilbert**) **K**(**eith**). 1874–1936, English essayist, novelist, poet, and critic.

chestnut ('tʃɛs,nʌt) *n* **1** any N temperate fagaceous tree of the genus *Castanea,* such as *C. sativa* (**sweet** or **Spanish chestnut**), which produce flowers in long catkins and nuts in a prickly bur. Compare **horse chestnut, water chestnut, dwarf chestnut. 2** the edible nut of any of these trees. **3** the hard wood of any of these trees, used in making furniture, etc. **4a** a reddish-brown to brown colour. **4b** (*as adj*): *chestnut hair.* **5** a horse of a yellow-brown or golden-brown colour. **6** a small horny callus on the inner surface of a horse's leg. **7** *Informal.* an old or stale joke. [C16: from earlier *chesten nut: chesten,* from Old French *chastaigne,* from Latin *castanea,* from Greek *kastanea*]

chest of drawers *n* a piece of furniture consisting of a frame, often on short legs, containing a set of drawers.

chest of viols *n* a set of viols of different sizes, usually six in number, used in consorts.

chest-on-chest *n* another term for **tallboy.**

chest voice *or* **register** *n* a voice of the lowest speaking or singing register. Compare **head voice.**

chesty ('tʃɛstɪ) *adj* **chestier, chestiest.** *Informal.* **1** *Brit.* suffering from or symptomatic of chest disease: *a chesty cough.* **2** having a large well-developed chest or bosom. ► **'chestiness** *n*

chetah ('tʃi:tə) *n* a variant spelling of **cheetah.**

Chetnik ('tʃɛtnɪk, tʃɛt'ni:k) *n* **1** a Serbian nationalist belonging to a group that fought against the Turks before World War I and engaged in guerrilla warfare during both World Wars. **2** a member of a Serbian nationalist paramilitary group fighting to retain Serbian influence in the countries which formerly constituted Yugoslavia. [from Serbian *četnik,* from *četa* troop]

cheval-de-frise (ʃə,vældə'fri:z) *n, pl* **chevaux-de-frise** (ʃə,vəʊdə'fri:z). **1** a portable barrier of spikes, etc., used to obstruct the passage of cavalry. **2** a row of spikes or broken glass set as an obstacle on top of a wall. [C17: from French, literally: horse from Friesland (where it was first used)]

cheval glass (ʃə'væl) *n* a full-length mirror mounted so as to swivel within a frame. [C19: from French *cheval* support (literally: horse)]

chevalier (,ʃɛ'vælɪə) *n* **1** a member of certain orders of merit, such as the French Legion of Honour. **2** *French history.* **2a** a mounted soldier or knight, esp. a military cadet. **2b** the lowest title of rank in the old French nobility. **3** an archaic word for **knight. 4** a chivalrous man; gallant. [C14: from Old French, from Medieval Latin *caballārius* horseman, CAVALIER]

Chevalier *n* **1** (,ʃɛvə'lɪə). **Albert.** 1861–1923, British music hall entertainer, remembered for his cockney songs. **2** (,ʃɛ'vælɪə; *French* ʃəvalje). **Maurice** (mɔris). 1888–1972, French singer and film actor.

chevet (ʃə'veɪ) *n* a semicircular or polygonal east end of a church, esp. a French Gothic church, often with a number of attached apses. [C19: from French: pillow, from Latin *capitium,* from *caput* head]

Cheviot ('tʃi:vɪət, 'tʃɛv-) *n* **1** a large British breed of sheep reared for its wool. **2** (*often not cap.*) a rough twill-weave woollen suiting fabric.

Cheviot Hills *pl n* a range of hills on the border between England and Scotland, mainly in Northumberland.

Chevra Kadisha *Hebrew.* (*Hebrew* xɛv'rɑ kadɪ'ʃɑ; *Yiddish* 'xɛvrə ka'dɪʃə) *n* a Jewish burial society, usually composed of unpaid volunteers who provide funerals for members of their congregation. [literally: Holy Company]

chèvre ('ʃɛvrə) *n* any cheese made from goats' milk. [C20: from French, literally: goat]

chevrette (ʃə'vrɛt) *n* **1** the skin of a young goat. **2** the leather made from this skin. [C18: from French: kid, from *chèvre* goat, from Latin *capra*]

chevron ('ʃɛvrən) *n* **1** *Military.* a badge or insignia consisting of one or more V-shaped stripes to indicate a noncommissioned rank or length of service. **2** *Heraldry.* an inverted V-shaped charge on a shield, one of the earliest ordinaries found in English arms. **3** (*usually pl*) a pattern of horizontal black and white V-shapes on a road sign indicating a sharp bend. **4** any V-shaped pattern or device. **5** Also called: **dancette.** an ornamental moulding having a zigzag pattern. [C14: from Old French, ultimately from Latin *caper* goat; compare Latin *capreoli* two pieces of wood forming rafters (literally: little goats)]

chevrotain ('ʃɛvrə,teɪn, -tɪn) *n* any small timid ruminant artiodactyl mammal of the genera *Tragulus* and *Hyemoschus,* of S and SE Asia: family *Tragulidae.* They resemble rodents, and the males have long tusklike upper canines. Also called: **mouse deer.** [C18: from French, from Old French *chevrot* kid, from *chèvre* goat, from Latin *capra,* feminine of *caper* goat]

chevy ('tʃɛvɪ) *n, vb* a variant of **chivy.**

chew (tʃu:) *vb* **1** to work the jaws and teeth in order to grind (food); masticate. **2** to bite repeatedly: *she chewed her nails anxiously.* **3** (*intr*) to use chewing tobacco. **4 chew the fat** *or* **rag.** *Slang.* **4a** to argue over a point. **4b** to talk idly; gossip. ◆ *n* **5** the act of chewing. **6** something that is chewed: *a chew of tobacco.* ◆ See also **chew out, chew over, chew up.** [Old English *ceowan;* related to Old High German *kiuwan,* Dutch *kauwen,* Latin *gingīva* a gum] ► **'chewable** *adj* ► **'chewer** *n*

Chewa ('tʃeɪwə) *n* **1** (*pl* **-was** *or* **-wa**) a member of a Negroid people of Malawi, E Zambia, and N Zimbabwe, related to the Bemba. **2** the language of this people. See **Chichewa.**

chewie ('tʃu:ɪ) *n Austral. informal.* chewing gum.

chewing gum *n* a preparation for chewing, usually made of flavoured and sweetened chicle or such substitutes as polyvinyl acetate.

chew out *vb* (*tr, adv*) *Informal, chiefly U.S. and Canadian.* to reprimand.

chew over *vb* (*tr, adv*) to consider carefully; ruminate on.

chew up *vb* (*tr, adv*) **1** to damage or destroy (something) by or as by chewing or grinding. **2** (*usually passive*) *Slang.* to cause (a person) to be nervous or worried: *he was all chewed up about the interview.*

chewy ('tʃu:ɪ) *adj* **chewier, chewiest.** of a consistency requiring chewing; somewhat firm and sticky.

Cheyenne[1] (ʃaɪ'æn) *n* **1** (*pl* **-enne** *or* **-ennes**) a member of a North American Indian people of the western Plains, now living chiefly in Montana and Oklahoma. **2** the language of this people, belonging to the Algonquian family. [via Canadian French from Dakota *Shaiyena,* from *shaia* to speak incoherently, from *sha* red + *ya* to speak]

Cheyenne[2] (ʃaɪ'æn, -'ɛn) *n* a city in SE Wyoming, capital of the state. Pop.: 50 008 (1990).

Cheyne-Stokes breathing ('tʃeɪn'stəʊks) *n Pathol.* alternating shallow and deep breathing, as in comatose patients. [C19: named after John *Cheyne*

(1777–1836), Scottish physician, and William *Stokes* (1804–78), Irish physician]

chez *French.* (ʃe) *prep* **1** at the home of. **2** with, among, or in the manner of.

chg. *Commerce, finance, etc. abbrev. for* charge.

chi[1] (kaɪ) *n* the 22nd letter of the Greek alphabet (Χ, χ), a consonant, transliterated as *ch* or rarely *kh.*

chi[2] *or* **ch'i** (tʃiː) *or* **qi** *n* (*sometimes cap.*) (in Oriental medicine, martial arts, etc.) vital energy believed to circulate round the body in currents. [Chinese, literally: energy]

chiack *or* **chyack** ('tʃaɪæk) *Austral. informal.* ◆ *vb* (*tr.*) **1** to tease or banter. ◆ *n* **2** good-humoured banter. [C19: from *chi-hike,* a shout or greeting]

Chian ('kaɪən) *adj* **1** of or relating to Chios. ◆ *n* **2** a native or inhabitant of Chios.

Chiang Ch'ing ('tʃæŋ 'tʃɪŋ) *n* a variant transliteration of the Chinese name for **Jiang Qing.**

Chiang Ching-kuo ('tʃæŋ tʃɪŋ'kwəʊ) *or* **Jiang Jing Guo** *n* 1910–88, Chinese statesman; the son of Chiang Kai-shek. He was prime minister of Taiwan (1971–78); president (1978–88).

Chiang Kai-shek ('tʃæŋ kaɪ'ʃek) *or* **Jiang Jie Shi** *n* original name *Chiang Chung-cheng,* 1887–1975, Chinese general: president of China (1928–31; 1943–49) and of the Republic of China (Taiwan) (1950–75). As chairman of the Kuomintang, he allied with the Communists against the Japanese (1937–45), but in the Civil War that followed was forced to withdraw to Taiwan after his defeat by the Communists (1949).

chianti (kɪ'æntɪ) *n* (*sometimes cap.*) a dry red wine produced in the Chianti region of Italy.

Chianti (*Italian* 'kjanti) *pl n* a mountain range in central Italy, in Tuscany, rising over 870 m (2900 ft.): part of the Apennines.

Chiapas (*Spanish* 'tʃjapas) *n* a state of S Mexico: mountainous and forested; Maya ruins in the northeast; rich mineral resources. Capital: Tuxtla Gutiérrez. Pop.: 3 606 828 (1995 est.). Area: 73 887 sq. km (28 816 sq. miles).

chiaroscuro (kɪˌɑːrə'skʊərəʊ) *n, pl* **-ros. 1** the artistic distribution of light and dark masses in a picture. **2** monochrome painting using light and dark only, as in grisaille. [C17: from Italian, from *chiaro* CLEAR + *oscuro* OBSCURE] ▸ **chiˌaro'scurist** *n* ▸ **chiˌaro'scurism** *n*

chiasma (kaɪ'æzmə) *or* **chiasm** ('kaɪæzəm) *n, pl* **-mas, -mata** (-mətə), *or* **-asms. 1** *Cytology.* the cross-shaped connection produced by the crossing over of pairing chromosomes during meiosis. **2** *Anatomy.* the crossing over of two parts or structures, such as the fibres of the optic nerves in the brain. [C19: from Greek *khiasma* wooden crosspiece, from *khiazein* to mark with an X, from *khi* CHI[1]] ▸ **chi'asmal** *or* **chi'asmic** *adj*

chiasmus (kaɪ'æzməs) *n, pl* **-mi** (-maɪ). *Rhetoric.* reversal of the order of words in the second of two parallel phrases: *he came in triumph and in defeat departs.* [C19: from New Latin, from Greek *khiasmos* crisscross arrangement; see CHIASMA] ▸ **chiastic** (kaɪ'æstɪk) *adj*

chiastolite (kaɪ'æstəˌlaɪt) *n* a variety of andalusite containing carbon impurities. Also called: **macle.** [C19: from German *Chiastolith,* from Greek *khiastos* crossed, marked with a chi + *lithos* stone]

Chiba ('tʃiːba) *n* an industrial city in central Japan, in SE Honshu on Tokyo Bay. Pop.: 856 882 (1995).

Chibchan ('tʃɪbtʃən) *n* **1** a family of Indian languages found in Colombia and elsewhere in South America. ◆ *adj* **2** belonging or relating to this family of languages.

chibouk *or* **chibouque** (tʃɪ'buːk) *n* a Turkish tobacco pipe with an extremely long stem. [C19: from French *chibouque,* from Turkish *çubuk* pipe]

chic (ʃiːk, ʃɪk) *adj* **1** (esp. of fashionable clothes, women, etc.) stylish or elegant. ◆ *n* **2** stylishness, esp. in dress; modishness; fashionable good taste. [C19: from French, of uncertain origin] ▸ **'chicly** *adv*

Chicago (ʃɪ'kɑːgəʊ) *n* a port in NE Illinois, on Lake Michigan: the third largest city in the U.S.; it is a major railway and air traffic centre. Pop.: 2 721 547 (1996 est.).

chicalote (ˌtʃiːkɑː'ləʊteɪ) *n* a poppy, *Argemone platyceras,* of the southwestern U.S. and Mexico with prickly leaves and white or yellow flowers. [from Spanish, from Nahuatl *chicalotl*]

chicane (ʃɪ'keɪn) *n* **1** a bridge or whist hand without trumps. **2** *Motor racing.* a short section of sharp narrow bends formed by barriers placed on a motor-racing circuit to provide an additional test of driving skill. **3** a less common word for **chicanery.** ◆ *vb* **4** (*tr*) to deceive or trick by chicanery. **5** (*tr*) to quibble about; cavil over. **6** (*intr*) to use tricks or chicanery. [C17: from French *chicaner* to quibble, of obscure origin] ▸ **chi'caner** *n*

chicanery (ʃɪ'keɪnərɪ) *n, pl* **-eries. 1** verbal deception or trickery, esp. in legal quibbling; dishonest or sharp practice. **2** a trick, deception, or quibble.

chicano (tʃɪ'kɑːnəʊ) *n, pl* **-nos.** *U.S.* an American citizen of Mexican origin. [C20: from Spanish *mejicano* Mexican]

chiccory ('tʃɪkərɪ) *n, pl* **-ries.** a variant spelling of **chicory.**

Chichagof Island ('tʃɪtʃəˌgɔːf) *n* an island of Alaska, in the Alexander Archipelago. Area: 5439 sq. km (2100 sq. miles).

Chichen Itzá (*Spanish* tʃi'tʃen it'sa) *n* a village in Yucatán state in Mexico: site of important Mayan ruins.

Chichester[1] ('tʃɪtʃɪstə) *n* a city in S England, administrative centre of West Sussex: Roman ruins; 11th-century cathedral; Festival Theatre. Pop.: 26 572 (1991).

Chichester[2] ('tʃɪtʃɪstə) *n* Sir **Francis.** 1901–72, British yachtsman, who sailed alone round the world in *Gipsy Moth IV* (1966–67).

Chichewa (tʃɪ'tʃeɪwə) *n* the language of the Chewa people of central Africa, widely used as a lingua franca in Malawi. It belongs to the Bantu group of the Niger-Congo family.

chichi[1] ('ʃiːˌʃiː) *adj* **1** affectedly pretty or stylish. ◆ *n* **2** the quality of being affectedly pretty or stylish. [C20: from French]

chichi[2] ('tʃiːˌtʃiː) *n, pl* **chichis.** (in India, formerly) **a** a person of mixed British and Indian descent; Anglo-Indian. **b** (*as modifier*): *a chichi accent.* ◆ Also (less common): **chee-chee.** [C18: perhaps from Hindi *chhī-chhī,* literally: dirt, or perhaps imitative of their supposed singsong speech]

Chichihaerh *or* **Ch'i-ch'i-haerh** ('tʃiːˌtʃiː'hɑː) *n* a variant transliteration of the Chinese name for **Qiqihar.**

chick (tʃɪk) *n* **1** the young of a bird, esp. of a domestic fowl. **2** *Slang.* a girl or young woman, esp. an attractive one. **3** a young child: used as a term of endearment. [C14: short for CHICKEN]

chickabiddy ('tʃɪkəˌbɪdɪ) *n, pl* **-dies.** a term of endearment, esp. for a child. [C18: from CHICK + BIDDY[1]]

chickadee ('tʃɪkəˌdiː) *n* any of various small North American songbirds of the genus *Parus,* such as *P. atricapillus* (**black-capped chickadee**), typically having grey-and-black plumage: family *Paridae* (titmice). [C19: imitative of its note]

chickaree ('tʃɪkəˌriː) *n* another name for **American red squirrel** (see **squirrel** (sense 1)).

Chickasaw ('tʃɪkəˌsɔː) *n* **1** (*pl* **-saws** *or* **-saw**) a member of a North American Indian people of N Mississippi. **2** the language of this people, belonging to the Muskogean family and closely related to Choctaw.

chicken ('tʃɪkɪn) *n* **1** a domestic fowl bred for its flesh or eggs, esp. a young one. **2** the flesh of such a bird used for food. **3** any of various similar birds, such as a prairie chicken. **4** *Slang.* a cowardly person. **5** *Slang.* a young inexperienced person. **6** *Informal.* any of various, often dangerous, games or challenges in which the object is to make one's opponent lose his nerve. **7 count one's chickens before they are hatched.** to be overoptimistic in acting on expectations which are not yet fulfilled. **8 like a headless chicken.** *Brit. informal.* disorganized and uncontrolled. **9 no (spring) chicken.** *Slang.* no longer young: *she's no chicken.* ◆ *adj* **10** *Slang.* easily scared; cowardly; timid. [Old English *ciecen;* related to Old Norse *kjūklingr* gosling, Middle Low German *küken* chicken]

chicken breast *n Pathol.* another name for **pigeon breast.** ▸ **ˌchicken-'breasted** *adj*

chicken feed *n Slang.* a trifling amount of money.

chicken-hearted *or* **chicken-livered** *adj* easily frightened; cowardly. ▸ **ˌchicken-'heartedly** *adv* ▸ **ˌchicken-'heartedness** *n*

chicken louse *n* a louse, *Menopon pallidum* (or *gallinae*); a parasite of poultry: order *Mallophaga* (bird lice).

chicken out *vb* (*intr, adv*) *Informal.* to fail to do something through fear or lack of conviction.

chickenpox ('tʃɪkɪnˌpɒks) *n* a highly communicable viral disease most commonly affecting children, characterized by slight fever and the eruption of a rash.

chicken wire *n* wire netting with a hexagonal mesh.

chickpea ('tʃɪkˌpiː) *n* **1** a bushy leguminous plant, *Cicer arietinum,* cultivated for its edible pealike seeds in the Mediterranean region, central Asia, and Africa. **2** the seed of this plant. ◆ Also called: **garbanzo.** [C16 *ciche peasen,* from *ciche* (from French *chiche,* from Latin *cicer* chickpea) + *peasen;* see PEA]

chickweed ('tʃɪkˌwiːd) *n* **1** any of various caryophyllaceous plants of the genus *Stellaria,* esp. *S. media,* a common garden weed with small white flowers. **2 mouse-ear chickweed.** any of various similar and related plants of the genus *Cerastium.*

Chiclayo (*Spanish* tʃi'klajo) *n* a city in NW Peru. Pop.: 668 066 (1995).

chicle ('tʃɪkᵊl) *n* a gumlike substance obtained from the sapodilla; the main ingredient of chewing gum. Also called: **chicle gum.** [from Spanish, from Nahuatl *chictli*]

chico ('tʃiːkəʊ) *n, pl* **-cos.** another name for **greasewood** (sense 1).

chicory ('tʃɪkərɪ) *n, pl* **-ries. 1** Also called: **succory.** a blue-flowered plant, *Cichorium intybus,* cultivated for its leaves, which are used in salads, and for its roots: family *Compositae* (composites). **2** the root of this plant, roasted, dried, and used as a coffee substitute. ◆ Compare **endive.** [C15: from Old French *chicorée,* from Latin *cichorium,* from Greek *kikhōrion*]

chide (tʃaɪd) *vb* **chides, chiding, chided** *or* **chid; chided, chid** *or* **chidden. 1** to rebuke or scold. **2** (*tr*) to goad into action. [Old English *cīdan*] ▸ **'chider** *n* ▸ **'chidingly** *adv*

chief (tʃiːf) *n* **1** the head, leader, or most important individual in a group or body of people. **2** another word for **chieftain** (sense 1). **3** *Heraldry.* the upper third of a shield. **4 in chief.** primarily; especially. ◆ *adj* **5** (*prenominal*) **5a** most important; principal. **5b** highest in rank or authority. ◆ *adv* **6** *Archaic.* principally. [C13: from Old French, from Latin *caput* head]

Chief Education Officer *n Brit.* an official who is the chief administrative officer of a Local Education Authority. Also called: **Director of Education.**

chief executive *n* the person with overall responsibility for the efficient running of a company, organization, etc.

chief justice *n* **1** (in any of several Commonwealth countries) the judge presiding over a supreme court. **2** (in the U.S.) the presiding judge of a court composed of a number of members. ◆ See also **Lord Chief Justice.** ▸ **chief justiceship** *n*

chiefly ('tʃiːflɪ) *adv* **1** especially or essentially; above all. **2** in general; mainly; mostly. ◆ *adj* **3** of or relating to a chief or chieftain.

Chief of Staff *n* **1** the senior staff officer under the commander of a major military formation or organization. **2** the senior officer of each service of the armed forces. Abbrevs.: **C of S, COS.**

chief petty officer *n* the senior naval rank for personnel without commissioned or warrant rank. Abbrev.: **CPO.**

Chief Rabbi *n* the chief religious minister of a national Jewish community.

chieftain ('tʃiːftən, -tɪn) *n* **1** the head or leader of a tribe or clan. **2** the chief of a group of people. [C14: from Old French *chevetaine,* from Late Latin *capitāneus* commander; see CAPTAIN] ▸ **'chieftaincy** *or* **'chieftain,ship** *n*

chief technician *n* a noncommissioned officer in the Royal Air Force junior to a flight sergeant.

chiel (tʃiːl) *n Scot.* a young man; lad. [C14: a Scot. variant of CHILD]

Chiengmai ('tʃɪɛŋ'maɪ) *or* **Chiang Mai** *n* a town in NW Thailand: teak, silver, silk industries: university (1964). Pop.: 170 397 (1993 est.).

Ch'ien-lung (tʃɪ'æn'lʊŋ) *n* a variant transliteration of the Chinese name for **Qian Long.**

chiffchaff ('tʃɪf,tʃæf) *n* a common European warbler, *Phylloscopus collybita,* with a yellowish-brown plumage. [C18: imitative of its call]

chiffon (ʃɪ'fɒn, 'ʃɪfɒn) *n* **1** a fine transparent or almost transparent plain-weave fabric of silk, nylon, etc. **2** (*often pl*) *Now rare.* feminine finery. ◆ *adj* **3** made of chiffon. **4** (of soufflés, pies, cakes, etc.) having a very light fluffy texture. [C18: from French, from *chiffe* rag; probably related to CHIP] ▸ **'chiffony** *adj*

chiffonier *or* **chiffonnier** (,ʃɪfə'nɪə) *n* **1** a tall, elegant chest of drawers, originally intended for holding needlework. **2** a wide low open-fronted cabinet, sometimes fitted with two grille doors and shelves. [C19: from French, from *chiffon* rag; see CHIFFON]

Chifley ('tʃɪflɪ) *n* **Joseph Benedict.** 1885–1951, Australian statesman; prime minister of Australia (1945–49).

chigetai (,tʃɪgɪ'taɪ) *n* a variety of the Asiatic wild ass, *Equus hemionus,* of Mongolia. Also spelled: **dziggetai.** [from Mongolian *tchikhitei* long-eared, from *tchikhi* ear]

chigger ('tʃɪgə) *n* **1** Also called: **chigoe, redbug.** *U.S. and Canadian.* the parasitic larva of any of various free-living mites of the family *Trombidiidae,* which causes intense itching of human skin. **2** another name for the **chigoe** (sense 1).

chignon ('ʃiːnjɒn; *French* ʃiɲɔ̃) *n* an arrangement of long hair in a roll or knot at the back of the head. [C18: from French, from Old French *chaignon* link, from *chaine* CHAIN; influenced also by Old French *tignon* coil of hair, from *tigne,* moth, from Latin *tinea* moth] ▸ **'chignoned** *adj*

chigoe ('tʃɪgəʊ) *n* **1** Also called: **chigger, jigger, sand flea.** a tropical flea, *Tunga penetrans,* the female of which lives on or burrows into the skin of its host, which includes man. **2** another name for **chigger** (sense 1). [C17: from Carib *chigo*]

Chigwell ('tʃɪgwəl) *n* a town in S England, in W Essex. Pop.: 10 332 (1991).

Chihli ('tʃiːliː) *n* **Gulf of.** another name for the **Bohai.**

Chihuahua (tʃɪ'waːwaː, -wə) *n* **1** a state of N Mexico: mostly high plateau; important mineral resources, with many silver mines. Capital: Chihuahua. Pop.: 2 792 989 (1995 est.). Area: 247 087 sq. km (153 194 sq. miles). **2** a city in N Mexico, capital of Chihuahua state. Pop.: 516 153 (1990). **3** a breed of tiny dog originally from Mexico, having short smooth hair, large erect ears, and protruding eyes.

chilblain ('tʃɪl,bleɪn) *n Pathol.* (*usually pl*) an inflammation of the fingers, toes, or ears, caused by prolonged exposure to moisture and cold. Technical name: **pernio.** [C16: from CHILL (n) + BLAIN] ▸ **'chil,blained** *adj*

child (tʃaɪld) *n, pl* **children. 1a** a boy or girl between birth and puberty. **1b** (*as modifier*): *child labour.* **2** a baby or infant. **3** an unborn baby. Related prefix: **paedo-. 4 with child.** another term for **pregnant. 5** a human offspring; a son or daughter. Related adj: **filial. 6** a childish or immature person. **7** a member of a family or tribe; descendant: *a child of Israel.* **8** a person or thing regarded as the product of an influence or environment: *a child of nature.* **9** *Midland and western English dialect.* a female infant. [Old English *cild;* related to Gothic *kilthei* womb, Sanskrit *jathara* belly, *jartu* womb] ▸ **'childless** *adj* ▸ **'childlessness** *n* ▸ **'childly** *adj*

child abuse *n* physical, sexual, or emotional ill-treatment or neglect of a child, esp. by those responsible for its welfare. See also **nonaccidental injury.**

child-abuse register *n Social welfare.* (in Britain) a list of children deemed to be at risk of abuse or injury from their parents or guardians, compiled and held by a local authority, area health authority, or NSPCC Special Unit. Also called: **NAI register.**

child-bearing *n* **a** the act or process of carrying and giving birth to a child. **b** (*as modifier*): *of child-bearing age.*

childbed ('tʃaɪld,bɛd) *n* **a** (often preceded by *in*) the condition of giving birth to a child. **b** (*as modifier*): *childbed fever.*

child benefit *n* (in Britain and New Zealand) a regular government payment to the parents of children up to a certain age.

childbirth ('tʃaɪld,bɜːθ) *n* the act of giving birth to a child. Related adj: **obstetric.**

childcare ('tʃaɪld,kɛə) *n Brit.* **1** care provided for children without homes (or with a seriously disturbed home life) by a local authority. **2** care and supervision of children whose parents are working, provided by a childminder or local authority.

childe (tʃaɪld) *n Archaic.* a young man of noble birth. [C13: variant of CHILD]

childermas ('tʃɪldə,mæs) *n Archaic.* Holy Innocents Day, Dec. 28. [Old English *cylda-mæsse,* from *cildra,* genitive plural of CHILD, + *mæsse* MASS]

Childers ('tʃɪldəz) *n* (**Robert**) **Erskine.** 1870–1922, Irish politician, executed by the Irish Free State for his IRA activities: author of the spy story *The Riddle of the Sands* (1903).

child guidance *n* the counselling of emotionally disturbed children.

childhood ('tʃaɪldhʊd) *n* the condition of being a child; the period of life before puberty.

childish ('tʃaɪldɪʃ) *adj* **1** in the manner of, belonging to, or suitable to a child. **2** foolish or petty; puerile: *childish fears.* ▸ **'childishly** *adv* ▸ **'childishness** *n*

child labour *n* the full-time employment of children below a minimum age laid down by statute.

childlike ('tʃaɪld,laɪk) *adj* like or befitting a child, as in being innocent, trustful, etc. Compare **childish** (sense 2).

child minder *n* a person who looks after children, esp. those whose parents are working.

children ('tʃɪldrən) *n* the plural of **child.**

Children's Panel *n* (in Scotland) a group of representatives of relevant agencies, with the power to deal with a child under sixteen who is in criminal or family trouble. Its hearings are private and replace most of the functions of juvenile courts.

child's play *n Informal.* something that is easy to do.

chile ('tʃɪlɪ) *n* a variant spelling of **chilli.**

Chile ('tʃɪlɪ) *n* a republic in South America, on the Pacific, with a total length of about 4090 km (2650 miles) and an average width of only 177 km (110 miles): gained independence from Spain in 1818; the government of President Allende (elected 1970) attempted the implementation of Marxist policies within a democratic system until overthrown by a military coup (1973); democracy restored 1988. Chile consists chiefly of the Andes in the east, the Atacama Desert in the north, a central fertile region, and a huge S region of almost uninhabitable mountains, glaciers, fjords, and islands; an important producer of copper, iron ore, nitrates, etc. Language: Spanish. Religion: Roman Catholic majority. Currency: peso. Capital: Santiago. Pop.: 14 822 000 (1998 est.). Area: 756 945 sq. km (292 256 sq. miles). ▸ **'Chilean** *adj, n*

Chile pine *n* another name for the **monkey puzzle.**

Chile saltpetre *or* **nitre** *n* a naturally occurring form of sodium nitrate: a soluble white or colourless mineral occurring in arid regions, esp. in Chile and Peru. Also called: **soda nitre.**

chiliad ('kɪlɪ,æd) *n* **1** a group of one thousand. **2** one thousand years. [C16: from Greek *khilias,* from *khilioi* a thousand] ▸ **,chili'adal** *or* **,chili'adic** *adj*

chiliasm ('kɪlɪ,æzəm) *n Christian theol.* another term for **millenarianism** or the **millennium.** [C17: from Greek *khiliasmos,* from *khilioi* a thousand] ▸ **'chili,ast** *n* ▸ **,chili'astic** *adj*

Chilkoot Pass ('tʃɪlkuːt) *n* a mountain pass in North America between SE Alaska and NW British Columbia, over the Coast Range.

chill (tʃɪl) *n* **1** a moderate coldness. **2** a sensation of coldness resulting from a cold or damp environment, or from a sudden emotional reaction. **3** a feverish cold. **4** a check on enthusiasm or joy. **5** a metal plate placed in a sand mould to accelerate cooling and control local grain growth. **6** another name for **bloom**[1] (sense 9). ◆ *adj* **7** another word for **chilly.** ◆ *vb* **8** to make or become cold. **9** (*tr*) to cool or freeze (food, drinks, etc.). **10** (*tr*) **10a** to depress (enthusiasm, etc.). **10b** to discourage. **11** (*tr*) to cool (a casting or metal object) rapidly in order to prevent the formation of large grains in the metal. **12** (*intr*) *Slang, chiefly U.S.* to relax; calm oneself. ◆ See also **chill out.** [Old English *ciele;* related to *calan* to COOL, Latin *gelidus* icy] ▸ **'chillingly** *adv* ▸ **'chillness** *n*

Chillán (*Spanish* tʃi'ʎan) *n* a city in central Chile. Pop.: 157 083 (1995 est.).

chiller ('tʃɪlə) *n* **1** *Informal.* short for **spine-chiller. 2** *N.Z.* a refrigerated storage area for meat.

chilli *or* **chili** ('tʃɪlɪ) *n, pl* **chillies** *or* **chilies.** the small red hot-tasting pod of a type of capsicum used for flavouring sauces, pickles, etc. [C17: from Spanish *chile,* from Nahuatl *chilli*]

chilli con carne (kɒn 'kaːnɪ) *n* a highly seasoned Mexican dish of meat, onions, beans, and chilli powder. [from Spanish *chile con carne* chilli with meat]

chilli powder *n* ground chilli blended with other spices.

chilli sauce *n* a highly seasoned sauce made of tomatoes cooked with chilli and other spices and seasonings.

Chillon (ʃɪ'lɒn; *French* ʃijɔ̃) *n* a castle in W Switzerland, in Vaud at the E end of Lake Geneva.

chill out *Informal.* ◆ *vb* **1** (*intr, adv*) to relax, esp. after energetic dancing at a rave. ◆ *adj* **chill-out. 2** suitable for relaxation after energetic dancing: *a chill-out area; chill-out music.*

chillum ('tʃɪləm) *n* a short pipe, usually of clay, used esp. for smoking cannabis. [C18: from Hindi *cilam,* from Persian *chilam*]

chilly ('tʃɪlɪ) *adj* **-lier, -liest. 1** causing or feeling cool or moderately cold. **2** without warmth; unfriendly. **3** (of people) sensitive to cold. ▸ **'chilliness** *n*

chilly bin *n N.Z. informal.* a portable insulated container with provision for packing food and drink in ice.

Chiloé Island (,tʃɪləʊ'eɪ) *n* an island administered by Chile, off the W coast of South America in the Pacific Ocean: timber. Pop.: 116 000 (1984 est.). Area: 8394 sq. km (3240 sq. miles).

chilopod ('kaɪlə,pɒd) *n* any arthropod of the class *Chilopoda,* which includes the centipedes. See also **myriapod.** [C19: from New Latin *Chilopoda,* from Greek *kheilos* lip + *pous* foot; referring to the modification of the first pair of legs into jawlike claws] ▸ **chilopodan** (kaɪ'lɒpədᵊn) *n, adj* ▸ **chi'lopodous** *adj*

Chilpancingo (*Spanish* tʃilpan'θiŋgo) *n* a town in S Mexico, capital of Guerrero state, in the Sierra Madre del Sur. Pop.: 136 243 (1990).

Chiltern Hills ('tʃɪltən) *pl n* a range of low chalk hills in SE England extending northwards from the Thames valley. Highest point: 260 m (852 ft.).

Chiltern Hundreds *pl n* (in Britain) short for **Stewardship of the Chiltern Hundreds;** a nominal office that an MP applies for in order to resign his seat.

Chilung *or* **Chi-lung** ('tʃiː'lʊŋ) *n* a port in N Taiwan: fishing and industrial centre. Pop.: 374 874 (1997 est.). Also called: **Keelung, Kilung.**

chimaera (kaɪ'mɪərə, kɪ-) *n* **1** any tapering smooth-skinned cartilaginous deep-sea fish of the subclass *Holocephali* (or *Bradyodonti*), esp. any of the genus *Chimaera.* They have a skull in which the upper jaw is fused to the cranium. See also **rabbitfish** (sense 1). **2** *Greek myth.* a variant spelling of **chimera** (sense 1).

chimb (tʃaɪm) *n* a variant spelling of **chime**[2].

Chimborazo (ˌtʃɪmbəˈrɑːzəʊ, -ˈreɪ-; *Spanish* tʃimboˈraθo) *n* an extinct volcano in central Ecuador, in the Andes: the highest peak in Ecuador. Height: 6267 m (20 561 ft.).

Chimbote (*Spanish* tʃimˈbote) *n* a port in N central Peru: contains Peru's first steelworks (1958), using hydroelectric power from the Santa River. Pop.: 268 979 (1993).

chime[1] (tʃaɪm) *n* **1** an individual bell or the sound it makes when struck. **2** (*often pl*) the machinery employed to sound a bell in this way. **3** Also called: **bell.** a percussion instrument consisting of a set of vertical metal tubes of graduated length, suspended in a frame and struck with a hammer. **4** a harmonious or ringing sound: *the chimes of children's laughter.* **5** agreement; concord. ◆ *vb* **6a** to sound (a bell) or (of a bell) to be sounded by a clapper or hammer. **6b** to produce (music or sounds) by chiming. **7** (*tr*) to indicate or show (time or the hours) by chiming. **8** (*tr*) to summon, announce, or welcome by ringing bells. **9** (*intr; foll. by with*) to agree or harmonize. **10** to speak or recite in a musical or rhythmic manner. [C13: probably shortened from earlier *chymbe bell,* ultimately from Latin *cymbalum* CYMBAL] ▸ **ˈchimer** *n*

chime[2], **chimb** (tʃaɪm), *or* **chine** *n* the projecting edge or rim of a cask or barrel. [Old English *cimb-;* related to Middle Low German *kimme* outer edge, Swedish *kimb*]

chime in *vb* (*intr, adv*) *Informal.* **1** to join in or interrupt (a conversation), esp. repeatedly and unwelcomely. **2** to voice agreement.

chimera *or* **chimaera** (kaɪˈmɪərə, kɪ-) *n* **1** (*often cap.*) *Greek myth.* a fire-breathing monster with the head of a lion, body of a goat, and tail of a serpent. **2** a fabulous beast made up of parts taken from various animals. **3** a wild and unrealistic dream or notion. **4** *Biology.* an organism, esp. a cultivated plant, consisting of at least two genetically different kinds of tissue as a result of mutation, grafting, etc. [C16: from Latin *chimaera,* from Greek *khimaira* she-goat, from *khimaros* he-goat]

chimere (tʃɪˈmɪə, ʃɪ-), **chimer,** *or* **chimar** (ˈtʃɪmə, ˈʃɪm-) *n Anglican Church.* a sleeveless red or black gown, part of a bishop's formal dress though not a vestment. [C14: perhaps from Medieval Latin *chimēra* (see CHIMERA) and related to Spanish *zamarra* sheepskin coat]

chimerical (kaɪˈmɛrɪkəl, kɪ-) *or* **chimeric** *adj* **1** wildly fanciful; imaginary. **2** given to or indulging in fantasies. ▸ **chiˈmerically** *adv* ▸ **chiˈmericalness** *n*

Chimkent (tʃɪmˈkɛnt) *n* a city in S Kazakhstan; a major railway junction. Pop.: 397 600 (1995 est.).

chimney (ˈtʃɪmnɪ) *n* **1** a vertical structure of brick, masonry, or steel that carries smoke or steam away from a fire, engine, etc. **2** another name for **flue**[1] (sense 1). **3** short for **chimney stack. 4** an open-ended glass tube fitting around the flame of an oil or gas lamp in order to exclude draughts. **5** *Brit.* a fireplace, esp. an old and large one. **6** *Geology.* **6a** the part of a mineral deposit that consists of the most valuable ore. **6b** the vent of a volcano. **7** *Mountaineering.* a vertical fissure large enough for a person's body to enter. **8** anything resembling a chimney in shape or function. [C14: from Old French *cheminée,* from Late Latin *camīnāta,* from Latin *camīnus* furnace, from Greek *kaminos* fireplace, oven]

chimney breast *n* the wall or walls that surround the base of a chimney or fireplace.

chimney corner *n* a recess that contains a seat in a large open fireplace; inglenook.

chimneypiece (ˈtʃɪmnɪˌpiːs) *n* another name (esp. Brit.) for **mantelpiece** (sense 1).

chimneypot (ˈtʃɪmnɪˌpɒt) *n* a short pipe on the top of a chimney, which increases the draught and directs the smoke upwards.

chimney stack *n* the part of a chimney that rises above the roof of a building.

chimney swallow *n* **1** another name for **common swallow** (see **swallow**[2]). **2** a less common name for **chimney swift.**

chimney sweep *or* **sweeper** *n* a person whose job is the cleaning out of soot from chimneys.

chimney swift *n* a North American swift, *Chaetura pelagica,* that nests in chimneys and similar hollows.

chimp (tʃɪmp) *n Informal.* short for **chimpanzee.**

chimpanzee (ˌtʃɪmpænˈziː) *n* a gregarious and intelligent anthropoid ape, *Pan troglodytes,* inhabiting forests in central W Africa. [C18: from Kongo dialect]

chin (tʃɪn) *n* **1** the protruding part of the lower jaw. **2** the front part of the face below the lips. Related adjs.: **genial, menal. 3 keep one's chin up.** to keep cheerful under difficult circumstances. Sometimes shortened to **chin up! 4 take it on the chin.** *Informal.* to face squarely up to a defeat, adversity, etc. ◆ *vb* **chins, chinning, chinned. 5** *Gymnastics.* to raise one's chin to (a horizontal bar, etc.) when hanging by the arms. [Old English *cinn;* related to Old Norse *kinn,* Old High German *kinni,* Latin *gena* cheek, Old Irish *gin* mouth, Sanskrit *hanu*]

Chin. *abbrev. for:* **1** China. **2** Chinese.

china[1] (ˈtʃaɪnə) *n* **1** ceramic ware of a type originally from China. **2** any porcelain or similar ware. **3** cups, saucers, etc., collectively. **4** (*modifier*) made of china. [C16 *chiny,* from Persian *chīnī*]

china[2] (ˈtʃaɪnə) *n Brit. and S. African informal.* a friend or companion. [C19: originally Cockney rhyming slang: *china plate, mate*]

China (ˈtʃaɪnə) *n* **1 People's Republic of.** Also called: **Communist China, Red China.** a republic in E Asia: the third largest and the most populous country in the world; the oldest continuing civilization (beginning over 2000 years B.C.); republic established in 1911 after the overthrow of the Manchu dynasty by Sun Yat-sen; People's Republic formed in 1949; pro-democracy demonstrations violently suppressed in 1989; contains vast deserts, steppes, great mountain ranges (Himalayas, Kunlun, Tian Shan, and Nan Shan), a central rugged plateau, and intensively cultivated E plains. Language: Chinese in various dialects, the chief of which is Mandarin. Religion: nonreligious majority; Buddhist and Taoist minorities. Currency: yuan. Capital: Beijing. Pop.: 1 242 980 000 (1998 est.). Area: 9 560 990 sq. km (3 691 502 sq. miles). **2 Republic of.** Also called: **Nationalist China, Taiwan.** a republic (recognized as independent by 28 other nations) in E Asia occupying the island of Taiwan, 13 nearby islands, and 64 islands of the Penghu (Pescadores) group: established in 1949 by the Nationalist government of China under Chiang Kai-shek after its expulsion by the Communists from the mainland; under U.S. protection 1954–79; lost its seat at the U.N. to the People's Republic of China in 1971; state of war with the People's Republic of China formally ended in 1991. Language: Mandarin Chinese. Religion: nonreligious majority, Buddhist and Taoist minorities. Currency: New Taiwan dollar. Capital: Taipei. Pop.: 21 463 000 (1996). Area: 35 981 sq. km (13 892 sq. miles). Former name: **Formosa.** Related adj: **Sinitic.**

China aster *n* a Chinese plant, *Callistephus chinensis,* widely cultivated for its aster-like flowers: family *Compositae* (composites).

china bark *n* another name for **cinchona** (sense 2).

chinaberry (ˈtʃaɪnəbərɪ) *n, pl* **-ries. 1** Also called: **China tree, azedarach.** a spreading Asian meliaceous tree, *Melia azedarach,* widely grown in the U.S. for its ornamental white or purple flowers and beadlike yellow fruits. **2** another name for **soapberry. 3** the fruit of any of these trees.

china clay *or* **stone** *n* another name for **kaolin.**

Chinagraph (ˈtʃaɪnəˌgrɑːf, -ˌgræf) *n Trademark.* **a** a coloured pencil used for writing on china, glass, etc. **b** (*as modifier*): *a Chinagraph pencil.*

China ink *n* another name for **Indian ink.**

Chinaman (ˈtʃaɪnəmən) *n, pl* **-men. 1** *Archaic or derogatory.* a native or inhabitant of China. **2** (*often not cap.*) *Cricket.* a ball bowled by a left-handed bowler to a right-handed batsman that spins from off to leg.

Chinan *or* **Chi-nan** (ˈtʃiːˈnæn) *n* a variant transliteration of the Chinese name for **Jinan.**

China rose *n* **1** a rosaceous shrub, *Rosa chinensis* (or *R. indica*), with red, pink, or white fragrant flowers: the ancestor of many cultivated roses. **2** a related dwarf plant, *Rosa semperflorens,* having crimson flowers. **3** another name for **hibiscus.**

China Sea *n* part of the Pacific Ocean off the coast of China: divided by Taiwan into the East China Sea in the north and the South China Sea in the south.

china stone *n* **1** a type of kaolinized granitic rock containing unaltered plagioclase. **2** any of certain limestones having a very fine grain and smooth texture.

Chinatown (ˈtʃaɪnəˌtaʊn) *n* a quarter of any city or town outside China with a predominantly Chinese population.

China tree *n* another name for **chinaberry** (sense 1).

chinaware (ˈtʃaɪnəˌwɛə) *n* **1** articles made of china, esp. those made for domestic use. **2** (*modifier*) made of china.

chin ball *n N.Z.* a device fastened under the chin of a bull to mark cows he has mounted.

chincapin (ˈtʃɪŋkəpɪn) *n* a variant spelling of **chinquapin.**

chinch (tʃɪntʃ) *n Southern U.S.* another name for a **bedbug.** [C17: from Spanish *chinche,* from Latin *cīmex* bug]

chinch bug *n* **1** a black-and-white tropical American heteropterous insect, *Blissus leucopterus,* that is very destructive to grasses and cereals in the U.S.: family *Lygaeidae.* **2** a related and similar European insect, *Ischnodemus sabuleti.*

chincherinchee (ˌtʃɪntʃərɪnˈtʃiː, -ˈrɪntʃɪ) *n* a bulbous South African liliaceous plant, *Ornithogalum thyrsoides,* having long spikes of white or yellow long-lasting flowers. [of unknown origin]

chinchilla (tʃɪnˈtʃɪlə) *n* **1** a small gregarious hystricomorph rodent, *Chinchilla laniger,* inhabiting mountainous regions of South America: family *Chinchillidae.* It has a stocky body and is bred in captivity for its soft silvery grey fur. **2** the highly valued fur of this animal. **3 mountain chinchilla.** Also called: **mountain viscacha.** any of several long-tailed rodents of the genus *Lagidium,* having coarse poor quality fur. **4** a thick napped woollen cloth used for coats. [C17: from Spanish, perhaps from Aymara]

chin-chin *sentence substitute. Informal.* a greeting, farewell, or toast. [C18: from Chinese (Peking) *ch'ing-ch'ing* please-please]

Chin-Chou *or* **Chin-chow** (ˈtʃɪnˈtʃaʊ) *n* a variant transliteration of the Chinese name for **Jinzhou.**

chin cough *n* another name for **whooping cough.** [C16: changed (through influence from CHINE[1] and CHIN) from earlier *chink-cough,*from CHINK[2] + COUGH]

Chindit (ˈtʃɪndɪt) *n* a member of the Allied forces commanded by Orde Wingate fighting behind the Japanese lines in Burma (1943–45). [C20: from Burmese *chinthé* a fabulous lion a symbol of which was their badge; adoption of title perhaps influenced by CHINDWIN]

Chindwin (ˈtʃɪnˈdwɪn) *n* a river in N Myanmar, rising in the Kumôn Range and flowing northwest then south to the Irrawaddy, of which it is the main tributary. Length: about 966 km (600 miles).

chine[1] (tʃaɪn) *n* **1** the backbone. **2** the backbone of an animal with adjoining meat, cut for cooking. **3** a ridge or crest of land. **4** (in some boats) a corner-like intersection where the bottom meets the side. ◆ *vb* **5** (*tr*) to cut (meat) along or across the backbone. [C14: from Old French *eschine,* of Germanic origin; compare Old High German *scina* needle, shinbone; see SHIN[1]]

chine[2] (tʃaɪn) *n* another word for **chime**[2].

chine[3] (tʃaɪn) *n Southern English dialect.* a deep fissure in the wall of a cliff. [Old English *cīnan* to crack]

chiné (ˈʃiːneɪ) *adj Textiles.* having a mottled pattern. [C19: from French *chiner* to make in the Chinese fashion, from *Chine* China]

Chinee (tʃaɪˈniː) *n Informal.* a Chinaman.

Chinese (tʃaɪˈniːz) *adj* **1** of, relating to, or characteristic of China, its people, or their languages. ◆ *n* **2** (*pl* **-nese**) a native or inhabitant of China or a descendant of one. **3** any of the languages of China belonging to the Sino-Tibetan family, sometimes regarded as dialects of one language. They share a single writing system that is not phonetic but ideographic. A phonetic system using the Roman alphabet was officially adopted by the Chinese government in 1966. See also **Mandarin Chinese, Pekingese, Cantonese**. Related prefix: **Sino-**.

Chinese block *n* a percussion instrument consisting of a hollow wooden block played with a drumstick.

Chinese cabbage *n* **1** Also called: **pe-tsai cabbage.** a Chinese plant, *Brassica pekinensis,* that is related to the cabbage and has crisp edible leaves growing in a loose cylindrical head. **2** Also called: **pak-choi cabbage.** a similar and related plant, *Brassica chinensis.*

Chinese chequers *n* (*functioning as sing*) a board game played with marbles or pegs.

Chinese Chippendale *n* **a** a branch of Chippendale style in which Chinese styles and motifs are used. **b** (*as modifier*): *a Chinese Chippendale cabinet.*

Chinese copy *n* an exact copy of an original.

Chinese eddo *n* another name for **taro.**

Chinese Empire *n* China as ruled by the emperors until the establishment of the republic in 1911–12.

Chinese gooseberry *n* another name for **kiwi fruit.**

Chinese ink *n* another name for **Indian ink.**

Chinese lantern *n* **1** a collapsible lantern made of thin coloured paper. **2** an Asian solanaceous plant, *Physalis franchetii,* cultivated for its attractive orange-red inflated calyx. See also **winter cherry.**

Chinese leaves *pl n* the edible leaves of a Chinese cabbage.

Chinese puzzle *n* **1** an intricate puzzle, esp. one consisting of boxes within boxes. **2** a complicated problem.

Chinese red *n* **a** a bright red colour. **b** (*as adj*): *a Chinese-red bag.*

Chinese restaurant syndrome *n* a group of symptoms such as dizziness, headache, and flushing thought to be caused in some people by consuming large amounts of monosodium glutamate, esp. as used in Chinese food.

Chinese Revolution *n* **1** the overthrow of the last Manchu emperor and the establishment of a republic in China (1911–12). **2** the transformation of China (esp. in the 1940s and 1950s) under the Chinese Communist Party.

Chinese sacred lily *n* a Chinese amaryllidaceous plant, *Narcissus tazetta orientalis,* widely grown as a house plant for its fragrant yellow and white flowers. See also **polyanthus** (sense 2).

Chinese Turkestan *n* the E part of the central Asian region of Turkestan: corresponds generally to the present-day Xinjiang Uygur Autonomous Region of China.

Chinese wall *n* **1** a notional barrier between the parts of a business, esp. between the market makers and brokers of a stock-exchange business, across which no information should pass to the detriment of clients. **2** an insurmountable obstacle.

Chinese water deer *n* a small Chinese or Korean deer, *Hydropotes inermis,* having tusks and no antlers: introduced into England and France.

Chinese water torture *n* a form of torture in which water is made to drip onto a victim's forehead to drive him insane.

Chinese wax *or* **treewax** ('triː,wæks) *n* a yellowish wax secreted by an oriental scale insect, *Ceroplastes ceriferus,* and used commercially.

Chinese whispers *n* (*functioning as sing*) **1** a game in which a message is passed on, in a whisper, by each of a number of people, so that the final version of the message is often radically changed from the original. **2** any situation where information is passed on in turn by a number of people, often becoming distorted in the process.

Chinese white *n* white zinc oxide, formerly used in paints. Also called: **zinc white.**

Chinese windlass *n* another name for **differential windlass.**

Chinese wood oil *n* another name for **tung oil.**

Ching *or* **Ch'ing** (tʃɪŋ) *adj* of, relating to, or designating the Manchu dynasty (1644–1912) of China.

Chinghai *or* **Ch'ing-hai** ('tʃɪŋ'haɪ) *n* a variant transliteration of the Chinese name for **Qinghai.**

Chingtao *or* **Ch'ing-tao** ('tʃɪŋ'taʊ) *n* a variant transliteration of the Chinese name for **Qingdao.**

Ch'ing-yüan ('tʃɪŋ'juːɑːn) *n* a former name of **Baoding.**

Chin Hills (tʃɪn) *pl n* a mountainous region of W Myanmar; part of the Arakan Yoma system. Highest peak: Mount Victoria, 3053 m (10 075 ft.).

Chin-Hsien ('tʃɪn'ʃjen) *n* the former name (1913–47) of **Jinzhou.**

chink[1] (tʃɪŋk) *n* **1** a small narrow opening, such as a fissure or crack. **2 chink in one's armour.** a small but fatal weakness. ♦ *vb* **3** (*tr*) *Chiefly U.S. and Canadian.* to fill up or make cracks in. [C16: perhaps variant of earlier *chine,* from Old English *cine* crack; related to Middle Dutch *kene,* Danish *kin*] ▸ **'chinky** *adj*

chink[2] (tʃɪŋk) *vb* **1** to make or cause to make a light ringing sound, as by the striking of glasses or coins. ♦ *n* **2** such a sound. [C16: of imitative origin]

Chink (tʃɪŋk) *or* **Chinky** ('tʃɪŋkɪ) *n, pl* **Chinks** *or* **Chinkies,** *adj* a derogatory term for **Chinese.** [C20: probably from *Chinese,* influenced by CHINK[1] (referring to the characteristic shape of the Chinese eye)]

chinkapin ('tʃɪŋkəpɪn) *n* a variant spelling of **chinquapin.**

Chinkiang ('tʃɪn'kjæŋ, -kaɪ'æŋ) *n* a variant transliteration of the Chinese name for **Jinjiang.**

chinless ('tʃɪnlɪs) *adj* **1** having a receding chin. **2** weak or ineffectual.

chinless wonder *n Brit. informal.* a person, esp. an upper-class one, lacking strength of character.

chino ('tʃiːnəʊ) *n, pl* **-nos.** *U.S.* a durable cotton twill cloth. [C20: from American Spanish, of obscure origin]

Chino- *combining form.* of or relating to China. See also **Sino-.**

chinoiserie (ʃiːn,wɑːzə'riː, -'wɑːzərɪ) *n* **1** a style of decorative or fine art based on imitations of Chinese motifs. **2** an object or objects in this style. [French, from *chinois* CHINESE; see -ERY]

chinook (tʃɪ'nuːk, -'nʊk) *n* **1** Also called: **snow eater.** a warm dry southwesterly wind blowing down the eastern slopes of the Rocky Mountains. **2** Also called: **wet chinook.** a warm moist wind blowing onto the Washington and Oregon coasts from the sea. [C19: from Salish *c'inuk*]

Chinook (tʃɪ'nuːk, -'nʊk) *n* **1** (*pl* **-nook** *or* **-nooks**) a North American Indian people of the Pacific coast near the Columbia River. **2** the language of this people, probably forming a separate branch of the Penutian phylum.

Chinook Jargon *n* a pidgin language containing elements of North American Indian languages, English, and French: formerly used among fur traders and Indians on the NW coast of North America.

Chinook salmon *n* a Pacific salmon, *Oncorhynchus tschawytscha,* valued as a food fish. Also called: **quinnat salmon, king salmon.**

chinos ('tʃiːnəʊz) *pl n* trousers made of chino.

chinquapin, chincapin, *or* **chinkapin** ('tʃɪŋkəpɪn) *n* **1** a dwarf chestnut tree, *Castanea pumila,* of the eastern U.S., yielding edible nuts. **2** Also called: **giant chinquapin.** a large evergreen fagaceous tree, *Castanopsis chrysophylla,* of W North America. **3** the nut of either of these trees. ♦ Compare **water chinquapin.** [C17: of Algonquian origin; compare Algonquian *chechinkamin* chestnut]

chintz (tʃɪnts) *n* **1** a printed, patterned cotton fabric, with glazed finish. **2** a painted or stained Indian calico. [C17: from Hindi *chīnt,* from Sanskrit *citra* gaily-coloured]

chintzy ('tʃɪntsɪ) *adj* **chintzier, chintziest. 1** of, resembling, or covered with chintz. **2** *Brit. informal.* typical of the decor associated with the use of chintz soft furnishings, as in a country cottage.

chinwag ('tʃɪn,wæg) *n Brit. informal.* a chat or gossipy conversation.

chionodoxa (kaɪ,ɒnə'dɒksə) *n* any plant of the liliaceous genus *Chionodoxa,* of S Europe and W Asia. See **glory-of-the-snow.** [C19: New Latin, from Greek *khiōn* snow + *doxa* glory]

Chios ('kaɪɒs, -əʊs, 'kiː-) *n* **1** an island in the Aegean Sea, off the coast of Turkey: belongs to Greece. Capital: Chios. Pop.: 52 184 (1991). Area: 904 sq. km (353 sq. miles). **2** a port on the island of Chios: in ancient times, one of the 12 Ionian city-states. Pop.: 54 000 (1995 est.). Modern Greek name: **Khíos.**

chip (tʃɪp) *n* **1** a small piece removed by chopping, cutting, or breaking. **2** a mark left after a small piece has been chopped, cut, or broken off something. **3** (in some games) a counter used to represent money. **4** a thin strip of potato fried in deep fat. **5** the U.S., Canadian, and Australian name for **crisp** (sense 10). **6** a small piece or thin slice of food. **7** *Sport.* a shot, kick, etc., lofted into the air, esp. over an obstacle or an opposing player's head, and travelling only a short distance. **8** *Electronics.* a tiny wafer of semiconductor material, such as silicon, processed to form a type of integrated circuit or component such as a transistor. **9** a thin strip of wood or straw used for making woven hats, baskets, etc. **10** *N.Z.* a container for soft fruit, made of thin sheets of wood; punnet. **11 chip off the old block.** *Informal.* a person who resembles one of his or her parents in behaviour. **12 have a chip on one's shoulder.** *Informal.* to be aggressively sensitive about a particular thing or bear a grudge. **13 have had one's chips.** *Brit. informal.* to be defeated, condemned to die, killed, etc. **14 when the chips are down.** *Informal.* at a time of crisis or testing. ♦ *vb* **chips, chipping, chipped. 15** to break small pieces from or become broken off in small pieces: *will the paint chip?* **16** (*tr*) to break or cut into small pieces: *to chip ice.* **17** (*tr*) to shape by chipping. **18** *Sport.* to strike or kick (a ball) in a high arc. [Old English *cipp* (n), *cippian* (vb), of obscure origin] ▸ **'chipper** *n*

chip-based ('tʃɪp,beɪst) *adj* (of electronic equipment or components) using or incorporating microchips.

chip basket *n* **1** a wire basket for holding potato chips, etc., while frying in deep fat. **2** a basket made of thin strips of wood, used esp. for packing fruit.

chipboard ('tʃɪp,bɔːd) *n* a thin rigid sheet made of compressed wood chips bound with a synthetic resin.

chip in *vb* (*adv*) *Informal.* **1** to contribute (money, time, etc.) to a cause or fund. **2** (*intr*) to interpose a remark or interrupt with a remark.

chip log *n Nautical.* a log for determining a vessel's speed, consisting of a wooden chip tossed overboard at the end of a line that is marked off in lengths of 47 feet 3 inches; the speed is calculated by counting the number of such intervals that pass overboard in a 28-second interval.

chipmunk ('tʃɪp,mʌŋk) *n* any burrowing sciurine rodent of the genera *Tamias* of E North America and *Eutamias* of W North America and Asia, typically having black-striped yellowish fur and cheek pouches for storing food. [C19: of Algonquian origin; compare Ojibwa *atchitamon* squirrel, literally: headfirst, referring to its method of descent from trees]

chipolata (,tʃɪpə'lɑːtə) *n Chiefly Brit.* a small sausage in a narrow casing. [via French from Italian *cipollata* an onion-flavoured dish, from *cipolla* onion]

chip pan *n* a deep pan for frying potato chips, etc.

Chippendale ('tʃɪpᵊn,deɪl) *n* **1 Thomas.** ?1718–79, English cabinet-maker and furniture designer. ♦ *adj* **2** (of furniture) designed by, made by, or in the style of Thomas Chippendale, characterized by the use of Chinese and Gothic motifs, cabriole legs, and massive carving.

chipper[1] ('tʃɪpə) *adj Informal.* **1** cheerful; lively. **2** smartly dressed.

chipper[2] ('tʃɪpər) *n Irish and Scot. informal.* a fish-and-chip shop.

Chippewa ('tʃɪpɪ,wɑː) *or* **Chippeway** ('tʃɪpɪ,weɪ) *n, pl* **-was, -wa** *or* **-ways, -way.** another name for **Ojibwa.**

chipping ('tʃɪpɪŋ) *n* another name for **chip** (sense 1).

chipping sparrow *n* a common North American sparrow, *Spizella passerina,* having brown-and-grey plumage and a white eye stripe.

chippy[1] ('tʃɪpɪ) *n, pl* **-pies. 1** *Brit. informal.* a fish-and-chip shop. **2** *Brit. and N.Z.* a slang word for **carpenter. 3** *N.Z.* a potato crisp. [C19: from CHIP (n)]

chippy[2] ('tʃɪpɪ) *adj* **-pier, -piest.** *Informal.* resentful or oversensitive about being perceived as inferior: *a chippy miner's son.* [C20: from CHIP (sense 12)] ▸ **'chippiness** *n*

chippy[3] *or* **chippie** ('tʃɪpɪ) *n, pl* **-pies.** an informal name for **chipmunk** or **chipping sparrow.**

chippy[4] *or* **chippie** ('tʃɪpɪ) *n, pl* **-pies.** *Informal, chiefly U.S. and Canadian.* a promiscuous woman. [C19: perhaps from CHIP (n)]

chippy[5] ('tʃɪpɪ) *adj* **-pier, -piest.** belligerent or touchy. [C19: from CHIP (n), sense probably developing from: as dry as a chip of wood, hence irritable, touchy]

chip shot *n Golf.* a short approach shot to the green, esp. one that is lofted.

Chirac (*French* ʃirak) *n* **Jacques (René)** (ʒɑk). born 1932, French Gaullist politician: president of France from 1995; prime minister (1974–76 and 1986–88); mayor of Paris (1977–95).

chirality (kaɪ'rælɪtɪ) *n* the configuration or handedness (left or right) of an asymmetric, optically active chemical compound. Also called: **dissymmetry.** [C19: from Greek *kheir* hand + -AL[1] + -ITY] ▸ **'chiral** *adj*

Chirico (*Italian* 'kiːriko) *n* **Giorgio de** ('dʒordʒo de). 1888–1978, Italian artist born in Greece: profoundly influenced the surrealist movement.

chirm (tʃɜːm) *n* **1** the chirping of birds. ◆ *vb* **2** (*intr*) (esp. of a bird) to chirp. [Old English *cierm* noise; related to Old Saxon *karm*]

chiro- *or* **cheiro-** *combining form.* indicating the hand; of or by means of the hand: *chiromancy; chiropractic.* [via Latin from Greek *kheir* hand]

chirography (kaɪ'rɒɡrəfɪ) *n* another name for **calligraphy.** ▸ **chi'rographer** *n* ▸ **chirographic** (ˌkaɪrə'ɡræfɪk) *or* **ˌchiro'graphical** *adj*

chiromancy ('kaɪrəˌmænsɪ) *n* another word for **palmistry.** ▸ **'chiroˌmancer** *n*

Chiron *or* **Cheiron** ('kaɪrɒn, -rən) *n* **1** *Greek myth.* a wise and kind centaur who taught many great heroes in their youth, including Achilles, Actaeon, and Jason. **2** a minor planet, discovered by Charles Kowal in 1977, revolving round the sun between the orbits of Saturn and Uranus.

chironomid (kaɪ'rɒnəmɪd) *n* **1** a member of the *Chironomidae,* a family of nonbiting midges. ◆ *adj* **2** of or relating to this family. [C19: from New Latin *chironomus,* from Greek *kheironomos* a gesturer, from *kheir* hand + *nomos* manager + -ID[2]]

chiropody (kɪ'rɒpədɪ) *n* the treatment of the feet, esp. the treatment of corns, verrucas, etc. ▸ **chi'ropodist** *n* ▸ **chiropodial** (ˌkaɪrəʊ'pəʊdɪəl) *adj*

chiropractic (ˌkaɪrə'præktɪk) *n* a system of treating bodily disorders by manipulation of the spine and other parts, based on the belief that the cause is the abnormal functioning of a nerve. [C20: from CHIRO- + *-practic,* from Greek *praktikos* effective, PRACTICAL] ▸ **'chiroˌpractor** *n*

chiropteran (kaɪ'rɒptərən) *adj* **1** of, relating to, or belonging to the *Chiroptera,* an order of placental mammals comprising the bats. ◆ *n* **2** Also called: **chiropter** (kaɪ'rɒptə) a bat.

chirp (tʃɜːp) *vb* (*intr*) **1** (esp. of some birds and insects) to make a short high-pitched sound. **2** to speak in a lively fashion. ◆ *n* **3** a chirping sound, esp. that made by a bird. [C15 (as *chirpinge,* gerund): of imitative origin] ▸ **'chirper** *n*

CHIRP (tʃɜːp) *n acronym for* Confidential Human Incidents Reporting Programme: a system, run by the RAF Institute of Medicine, by which commercial pilots can comment on safety trends without the knowledge of their employers.

chirpy ('tʃɜːpɪ) *adj* **chirpier, chirpiest.** *Informal* cheerful; lively. ▸ **'chirpily** *adv* ▸ **'chirpiness** *n*

chirr, chirre, *or* **churr** (tʃɜː) *vb* **1** (*intr*) (esp. of certain insects, such as crickets) to make a shrill trilled sound. ◆ *n* **2** the sound of chirring. [C17: of imitative origin]

chirrup ('tʃɪrəp) *vb* (*intr*) **1** (esp. of some birds) to chirp repeatedly. **2** to make clucking sounds with the lips. ◆ *n* **3** such a sound. [C16: variant of CHIRP] ▸ **'chirruper** *n* ▸ **'chirrupy** *adj*

chirurgeon (kaɪ'rɜːdʒən) *n* an archaic word for **surgeon.** [C13: from Old French *cirurgeon*] ▸ **chi'rurgery** *n*

chisel ('tʃɪzᵊl) *n* **1a** a hand tool for working wood, consisting of a flat steel blade with a cutting edge attached to a handle of wood, plastic, etc. It is either struck with a mallet or used by hand. **1b** a similar tool without a handle for working stone or metal. ◆ *vb* **-els, -elling, -elled** *or U.S.* **-els, -eling, -eled. 2** to carve (wood, stone, metal, etc.) or form (an engraving, statue, etc.) with or as with a chisel. **3** *Slang.* to cheat or obtain by cheating. [C14: via Old French, from Vulgar Latin *cīsellus* (unattested), from Latin *caesus* cut, from *caedere* to cut]

chiselled *or U.S.* **chiseled** ('tʃɪzəld) *adj* **1** carved or formed with or as if with a chisel. **2** clear-cut: *finely chiselled features.*

chiseller ('tʃɪzᵊlə) *n* **1** a person who uses a chisel. **2** *Informal.* a cheat. **3** *Dublin slang.* a child.

Chishima (ˌtʃiːʃiː'ma) *n* the Japanese name for the **Kuril Islands.**

Chisimaio (ˌkiːzɪ'mɑːjəʊ) *n* a port in S Somalia, on the Indian Ocean. Pop.: 200 000 (1987 est.). Also called: **Kismayu.**

Chişinău (kiʃi'nəu) *n* the Romanian name for **Kishinev.**

chi-square distribution ('kaɪˌskwɛə) *n Statistics.* a continuous single-parameter distribution derived as a special case of the gamma distribution and used esp. to measure goodness of fit and to test hypotheses and obtain confidence intervals for the variance of a normally distributed variable.

chi-square test *n Statistics.* a test derived from the chi-square distribution to compare the goodness of fit of theoretical and observed frequency distributions or to compare nominal data derived from unmatched groups of subjects.

chit[1] (tʃɪt) *n* **1** a voucher for a sum of money owed, esp. for food or drink. **2** Also called: **chitty** ('tʃɪtɪ) *Chiefly Brit.* **2a** a note or memorandum. **2b** a requisition or receipt. [C18: from earlier *chitty,* from Hindi *cittha* note, from Sanskrit *citra* brightly-coloured]

chit[2] (tʃɪt) *n Facetious or derogatory.* a pert, impudent, or self-confident girl or child. [C14 (in the sense: young of an animal, kitten): of obscure origin]

Chita (*Russian* tʃi'ta) *n* an industrial city in SE Russia, on the Trans-Siberian railway. Pop.: 322 000 (1995 est.).

chital ('tʃiːtᵊl) *n* another name for **axis**[2] (the deer). [from Hindi]

chitarrone (ˌkɪtɑː'rəʊnɪ, ˌtʃɪt-) *n, pl* **-ni** (-nɪ). a large lute with a double neck in common use during the baroque period, esp. in Italy. [Italian, from *chitarra,* from Greek *kithara* lyre]

chitchat ('tʃɪtˌtʃæt) *n* **1** talk of a gossipy nature. ◆ *vb* **-chats, -chatting, -chatted. 2** (*intr*) to gossip.

chitin ('kaɪtɪn) *n* a polysaccharide that is the principal component of the exoskeletons of arthropods and of the bodies of fungi. [C19: from French *chitine,* from Greek *khitōn* CHITON + -IN] ▸ **'chitinous** *adj* ▸ **'chitinˌoid** *adj*

chiton ('kaɪtᵊn, -tɒn) *n* **1** (in ancient Greece and Rome) a loose woollen tunic worn knee length by men and full length by women. **2** Also called: **coat-of-mail shell.** any small primitive marine mollusc of the genus *Chiton* and related genera, having an elongated body covered with eight overlapping shell plates: class *Amphineura.* [C19: from Greek *khitōn* coat of mail, of Semitic origin; related to Hebrew *kethōnet*]

Chittagong ('tʃɪtəˌɡɒŋ) *n* a port in E Bangladesh, on the Bay of Bengal: industrial centre. Pop.: 1 599 000 (1991).

chitter ('tʃɪtə) *vb* (*intr*) **1** *Chiefly U.S.* to twitter or chirp. **2** a dialect word for **shiver**[1] or (of the teeth) **chatter.** [C14: of imitative origin]

chitterlings ('tʃɪtəlɪŋz), **chitlins** ('tʃɪtlɪnz), *or* **chitlings** ('tʃɪtlɪŋz) *pl n* (*sometimes sing*) the intestines of a pig or other animal prepared as a dish. [C13: of uncertain origin; perhaps related to Middle High German *kutel*]

chiv (tʃɪv, ʃɪv) *or* **shiv** (ʃɪv) *Slang.* ◆ *n* **1** a knife. ◆ *vb* **chivs, chivving, chivved** *or* **shivs, shivving, shivved. 2** to stab (someone). [C17: perhaps from Romany *chiv* blade]

chivalrous ('ʃɪvəlrəs) *adj* **1** gallant; courteous. **2** involving chivalry. [C14: from Old French *chevalerous,* from CHEVALIER] ▸ **'chivalrously** *adv* ▸ **'chivalrousness** *n*

chivalry ('ʃɪvəlrɪ) *n, pl* **-ries. 1** the combination of qualities expected of an ideal knight, esp. courage, honour, justice, and a readiness to help the weak. **2** courteous behaviour, esp. towards women. **3** the medieval system and principles of knighthood. **4** knights, noblemen, etc., collectively. [C13: from Old French *chevalerie,* from CHEVALIER] ▸ **'chivalric** *adj*

chivaree (ˌʃɪvə'riː, 'ʃɪvəˌriː) *n* a U.S. spelling of **charivari.**

chive (tʃaɪv) *n* a small Eurasian purple-flowered alliaceous plant, *Allium schoenoprasum,* whose long slender hollow leaves are used in cooking to flavour soups, stews, etc. Also called: **chives.** [C14: from Old French *cive,* ultimately from Latin *caepa* onion]

chivy, chivvy ('tʃɪvɪ), *or* **chevy** *Brit.* ◆ *vb* **chivies, chivying, chivied, chivvies, chivvying, chivvied,** *or* **chevies, chevying, chevied. 1** (*tr*) to harass or nag. **2** (*tr*) to hunt. **3** (*intr*) to run about. ◆ *n, pl* **chivies, chivvies,** *or* **chevies. 4** a hunt. **5** *Obsolete.* a hunting cry. [C19: variant of *chevy,* probably from *Chevy Chase,* title of a Scottish border ballad]

Chkalov (*Russian* 'tʃkaləf) *n* the former name (1938–57) of **Orenburg.**

Chladni figure ('klɑːdnɪ) *n Physics.* a pattern formed by fine powder placed on a vibrating surface, used to display the positions of nodes and antinodes. [C19: named after Ernst *Chladni* (1756–1827), German physicist]

chlamydate ('klæmɪˌdeɪt) *adj* (of some molluscs) possessing a mantle. [C19: from Latin *chlamydātus* wearing a mantle, from Greek *khlamus* mantle]

chlamydeous (klə'mɪdɪəs) *adj* (of plants) relating to or possessing sepals and petals.

chlamydia (klə'mɪdɪə) *n* any virus-like bacterium of the genus *Chlamydia,* responsible for such diseases as trachoma, psittacosis, and some sexually transmitted diseases. [C20: New Latin, from Greek *khlamus* mantle + -IA]

chlamydospore (klæ'mɪdəˌspɔː) *n* a thick-walled asexual spore of many fungi: capable of surviving adverse conditions.

chloanthite (kləʊ'ænθaɪt) *n* a form of nickel arsenide having commercial importance as a nickel ore. [C19: from Greek *khloanthēs* budding, sprouting + -ITE[1]]

chloasma (kləʊ'æzmə) *n, pl* **chloasmata** (kləʊ'æzmətə) *Med.* the appearance on a person's skin, esp. of the face, of patches of darker colour: associated with hormonal changes caused by liver disease or the use of oral contraceptives. [C19: from New Latin, from Greek *khloasma* greenness]

Chlodwig ('kloːtvɪç) *n* the German name for **Clovis I.**

Chloe ('kləʊɪ) *n* See **Daphnis and Chloe.**

chlor- *combining form.* a variant of **chloro-** before a vowel.

chloracne (klɔː'ræknɪ) *n* a disfiguring skin disease that results from contact with or ingestion or inhalation of certain chlorinated aromatic hydrocarbons. [C20: from CHLORO- + ACNE]

chloral ('klɔːrəl) *n* **1** a colourless oily liquid with a pungent odour, made from chlorine and acetaldehyde and used in preparing chloral hydrate and DDT; trichloroacetaldehyde. **2** short for **chloral hydrate.**

chloral hydrate *n* a colourless crystalline soluble solid produced by the reaction of chloral with water and used as a sedative and hypnotic; 2,2,2-trichloro-1,1-ethanediol. Formula: $CCl_3CH(OH)_2$.

chlorambucil (klɔː'ræmbjʊsɪl) *n* a drug derived from nitrogen mustard, administered orally in the treatment of leukaemia and other malignant diseases. Formula: $C_{14}H_{19}Cl_2NO_2$.

chloramine ('klɔːrəˌmiːn) *n* **1** an unstable colourless liquid with a pungent odour, made by the reaction of sodium hypochlorite and ammonia. Formula: NH_2Cl. **2** any compound produced by replacing hydrogen atoms in an azo or amine group with chlorine atoms.

chloramphenicol (ˌklɔːræm'fenɪˌkɒl) *n* a broad-spectrum antibiotic used esp. in treating typhoid fever and rickettsial infections: obtained from the bacterium *Streptomyces venezuelae* or synthesized. Formula: $C_{11}H_{12}N_2O_5Cl_2$. [C20: from CHLORO- + AM(IDO)- + PHE(NO)- + NI(TRO)- + (GLY)COL]

chlorate ('klɔːˌreɪt, -rɪt) *n* any salt of chloric acid, containing the monovalent ion ClO_3^-.

chlordane ('klɔːdeɪn) *or* **chlordan** ('klɔːdæn) *n* a white insoluble toxic solid existing in several isomeric forms and usually used, as an insecticide, in the form of a brown impure liquid. Formula: $C_{10}H_6Cl_8$. [C20: from CHLORO- + (IN)D(ENE) + -ANE]

chlordiazepoxide (ˌklɔːdaɪˌeɪzɪ'pɒksaɪd) *n* a chemical compound used as a tranquillizer and muscle relaxant and in the treatment of alcoholism. Formula: $C_{16}H_{14}ClN_3O$.

chlorella (klɔː'rɛlə, klə-) *n* any microscopic unicellular green alga of the genus *Chlorella:* some species are used in the preparation of human food. [C19: from New Latin, from CHLORO- + Latin *-ella,* diminutive suffix]

chlorenchyma (klə'rɛŋkɪmə) *n* plant tissue consisting of parenchyma cells that contain chlorophyll. [C19: from CHLOR(OPHYLL) + -ENCHYMA]

chlorhexidine (klɔː'hɛksɪdiːn) *n* an antiseptic compound used in skin cleansers, mouthwashes, etc. [C20: from CHLOR(O)- + HEX(ANE) + -I(DE) + (AM)INE]

chloric ('klɔːrɪk) *adj* of or containing chlorine in the pentavalent state.

chloric acid *n* a strong acid with a pungent smell, known only in solution and in the form of chlorate salts. Formula: $HClO_3$.

chloride ('klɔːraɪd) *n* **1** any salt of hydrochloric acid, containing the chloride ion Cl^-. **2** any compound containing a chlorine atom, such as methyl chloride (chloromethane), CH_3Cl. ▸ **chloridic** (klə'rɪdɪk) *adj*

chloride of lime *or* **chlorinated lime** *n* another name for **bleaching powder.**

chlorinate ('klɔːrɪˌneɪt) *vb* (*tr*) **1** to combine or treat (a substance) with chlorine. **2** to disinfect (water) with chlorine. ▸ **ˌchlorin'ation** *n* ▸ **'chlorinˌator** *n*

chlorine ('klɔːriːn) *or* **chlorin** ('klɔːrɪn) *n* a toxic pungent greenish-yellow gas of the halogen group; the 15th most abundant element in the earth's crust, occurring only in the combined state, mainly in common salt: used in the manufacture of many organic chemicals, in water purification, and as a disinfectant and bleaching agent. Symbol: Cl; atomic no.: 17; atomic wt.: 35.4527; valency: 1, 3, 5, or 7; density: 3.214 kg/m^3; relative density: 1.56; melting pt.: −101.03°C; boiling pt.: −33.9°C. [C19 (coined by Sir Humphrey Davy): from CHLORO- + -INE², referring to its colour]

chlorite¹ ('klɔːraɪt) *n* any of a group of green soft secondary minerals consisting of the hydrated silicates of aluminium, iron, and magnesium in monoclinic crystalline form: common in metamorphic rocks. [C18: from Latin *chlōrītis* precious stone of a green colour, from Greek *khlōritis,* from *khlōros* greenish yellow] ▸ **chloritic** (klɔː'rɪtɪk) *adj*

chlorite² ('klɔːraɪt) *n* any salt of chlorous acid, containing the monovalent ion ClO_2^-.

chloro- *or before a vowel* **chlor-** *combining form.* **1** indicating the colour green: *chlorophyll.* **2** chlorine: *chloroform.*

chloroacetic acid (ˌklɔːrəʊə'siːtɪk) *or* **chloracetic acid** (ˌklɔːrə'siːtɪk) *n* **1** a colourless crystalline soluble strong acid prepared by chlorinating acetic acid and used as an intermediate in the manufacture of many chemicals; monochloracetic acid. Formula: $CH_2ClCOOH$. **2** either of two related compounds: **dichloracetic acid,** $CHCl_2COOH$, or **trichloracetic acid,** CCl_3COOH.

chlorobenzene (ˌklɔːrəʊ'bɛnziːn) *n* a colourless volatile flammable insoluble liquid with an almond-like odour, made from chlorine and benzene and used as a solvent and in the preparation of many organic compounds, esp. phenol and DDT. Formula: C_6H_5Cl.

chlorofluorocarbon (ˌklɔːrəˌflʊərəʊ'kɑːbᵊn) *n Chemistry.* any of various gaseous compounds of carbon, hydrogen, chlorine, and fluorine, used as refrigerants, aerosol propellants, solvents, and in foam: some cause a breakdown of ozone in the earth's atmosphere. Abbrev.: **CFC.**

chloroform ('klɔːrəˌfɔːm) *n* a heavy volatile liquid with a sweet taste and odour, used as a solvent and cleansing agent and in refrigerants: formerly used as an inhalation anaesthetic. Systematic name: **trichloromethane.** Formula: $CHCl_3$. [C19: from CHLORO- + FORM(YL) (in an obsolete sense that applied to a CH radical)]

chlorohydrin (ˌklɔːrəʊ'haɪdrɪn) *n* **1** any of a class of organic compounds containing a hydroxyl group and a chlorine atom. **2** a colourless unstable hygroscopic liquid that is used mainly as a solvent; 3-chloropropane-1,2-diol. Formula: $CH_2OHCHOHCH_2Cl$. [C20: from CHLORO- + HYDRO- + -IN]

Chloromycetin (ˌklɔːrəʊmaɪ'siːtɪn) *n Trademark.* a brand of **chloramphenicol.**

chlorophyll *or U.S.* **chlorophyl** ('klɔːrəfɪl) *n* the green pigment of plants, occurring in chloroplasts, that traps the energy of sunlight for photosynthesis and exists in several forms, the most abundant being **chlorophyll a** ($C_{55}H_{72}O_5N_4Mg$): used as a colouring agent in medicines or food (**E140**). ▸ **'chloroˌphylloid** *adj* ▸ **ˌchloro'phyllous** *adj*

chlorophytum (ˌklɔːrə'faɪtəm) *n* any plant of the genus *Chlorophytum,* esp. *C. elatum variegatum,* grown as a pot plant for its long narrow leaves with a light central stripe, and characterized by the production of offsets at the end of long scapes: family *Liliaceae.* Also called: **spider plant.** [New Latin, from Greek *chlōros* green + *phyton* plant]

chloropicrin (ˌklɔːrəʊ'pɪkrɪn) *or* **chlorpicrin** (klɔː'pɪkrɪn) *n* a colourless insoluble toxic lachrymatory liquid used as a pesticide and a tear gas; nitrotrichloromethane. Formula: CCl_3NO_2. [C20: from CHLORO- + PICRO- + -IN]

chloroplast ('klɔːrəʊˌplæst) *n* a plastid containing chlorophyll and other pigments, occurring in plants that carry out photosynthesis. ▸ **ˌchloro'plastic** *adj*

chloroprene ('klɔːrəʊˌpriːn) *n* a colourless liquid derivative of butadiene that is used in making neoprene rubbers; 2-chloro-1,2-butadiene. Formula: $CH_2{:}CHCCl{:}CH_2$. [C20: from CHLORO- + (ISO)PRENE]

chloroquine ('klɔːrəʊˌkwiːn) *n* a synthetic drug administered orally to treat malaria. Formula: $C_{18}H_{26}ClN_3$. [C20: from CHLORO- + QUIN(OLINE)]

chlorosis (klɔː'rəʊsɪs) *n* **1** Also called: **greensickness.** *Pathol.* a disorder, formerly common in adolescent girls, characterized by pale greenish-yellow skin, weakness, and palpitation and caused by insufficient iron in the body. **2** *Botany.* a deficiency of chlorophyll in green plants caused by mineral deficiency, lack of light, disease, etc., the leaves appearing uncharacteristically pale. [C17: from CHLORO- + -OSIS] ▸ **chlorotic** (klɔː'rɒtɪk) *adj*

chlorothiazide (ˌklɔːrə'θaɪəˌzaɪd) *n* a diuretic drug administered orally in the treatment of chronic heart and kidney disease and hypertension. Formula: $C_7H_6ClN_3O_4S_2$. [C20: from CHLORO- + THI(O)- + (DI)AZ(INE + DIOX)IDE]

chlorous ('klɔːrəs) *adj* **1** of or containing chlorine in the trivalent state. **2** of or containing chlorous acid.

chlorous acid *n* an unstable acid that is a strong oxidizing agent. Formula: $HClO_2$.

chlorpromazine (klɔː'prɒməˌziːn) *n* a drug derived from phenothiazine, used as a sedative and tranquillizer, esp. in psychotic disorders. Formula: $C_{17}H_{19}ClN_2S$. [C20: from CHLORO- + PRO(PYL + A)M(INE) + AZINE]

chlorpropamide (klɔː'prəʊpəˌmaɪd) *n* a drug that reduces blood glucose and is administered orally in the treatment of diabetes. Formula: $C_{10}H_{13}ClN_2O_3S$.

chlortetracycline (klɔːˌtɛtrə'saɪkliːn) *n* an antibiotic used in treating many bacterial and rickettsial infections and some viral infections: obtained from the bacterium *Streptomyces aureofaciens.* Formula: $C_{22}H_{23}ClN_2O_8$.

chlorthalidone (klɔː'θælɪdəʊn) *n* a diuretic used in the treatment of oedema, hypertension, and diabetes insipidus. [C20: from CHLOR(O)- + TH(IAZINE) + -AL³ + -ID(E) + -ONE]

ChM *abbrev. for* Master of Surgery. [Latin *Chirurgiae Magister*]

chm. *abbrev. for:* **1** Also: **chmn.** chairman. **2** checkmate.

choanocyte ('kəʊənəˌsaɪt) *n* any of the flagellated cells in sponges that maintain a flow of water through the body. A collar of protoplasm surrounds the base of the flagellum. Also called: **collar cell.** [C19: from Greek *khoanē* funnel (from *khein* to pour) + -CYTE]

choc-ice ('tʃɒkˌaɪs) *n* an ice cream covered with a thin layer of chocolate.

chock (tʃɒk) *n* **1** a block or wedge of wood used to prevent the sliding or rolling of a heavy object. **2** *Nautical.* **2a** a fairlead consisting of a ringlike device with an opening at the top through which a rope is placed. **2b** a cradle-like support for a boat, barrel, etc. **3** *Mountaineering.* See **nut** (sense 10). ♦ *vb* (*tr*) **4** (usually foll. by *up*) *Brit.* to cram full: *chocked up with newspapers.* **5** to fit with or secure by a chock. **6** to support (a boat, barrel, etc.) on chocks. ♦ *adv* **7** as closely or tightly as possible: *chock against the wall.* [C17: of uncertain origin; perhaps related to Old French *çoche* log; compare Provençal *soca* tree stump]

chock-a-block *adj, adv* **1** filled to capacity; in a crammed state. **2** *Nautical.* with the blocks brought close together, as when a tackle is pulled as tight as possible.

chocker ('tʃɒkə) *adj* **1** *Informal.* full up; packed. **2** *Brit. slang.* irritated; fed up. [C20: from CHOCK-A-BLOCK]

chock-full, choke-full, *or* **chuck-full** *adj* (*postpositive*) completely full. [C17 *choke-full;* see CHOKE, FULL]

chockstone ('tʃɒkˌstəʊn) *n Mountaineering.* **1** a stone securely jammed in a crack. It may vary in size from a pebble to a large boulder. **2** another name for **chock** (sense 3).

choco *or* **chocko** ('tʃɒkəʊ) *n, pl* **-os.** *Austral. slang.* (in World War II) **a** a member of the citizen army; militiaman. **b** a conscript. [C20: shortened from *chocolate soldier*]

chocoholic *or* **chocaholic** (ˌtʃɒkə'hɒlɪk) *n Informal.* **a** someone who is very fond of eating chocolate. **b** (*as modifier*): *the chocoholic British.* [C20: from CHOCO(LATE) + -HOLIC]

chocolate ('tʃɒkəlɪt, 'tʃɒklɪt, -lət) *n* **1** a food preparation made from roasted ground cacao seeds, usually sweetened and flavoured. **2** a drink or sweetmeat made from this. **3a** a moderate to deep brown colour. **3b** (*as adj*): *a chocolate carpet.* [C17: from Spanish, from Aztec *xocolatl,* from *xococ* sour, bitter + *atl* water] ▸ **'chocolaty** *adj*

chocolate-box *n* (*modifier*) *Informal.* sentimentally pretty or appealing.

choctaw ('tʃɒktɔː) *n Ice skating.* a turn from the inside edge of one skate to the outside edge of the other or vice versa. [C19: after CHOCTAW]

Choctaw ('tʃɒktɔː) *n* **1** (*pl* **-taws** *or* **-taw**) a member of a North American Indian people of Alabama. **2** the language of this people, belonging to the Muskogean family. [C18: from Choctaw *Chahta*]

Chogyal ('tʃɒgjɑːl) *n* the title of the ruler of Sikkim.

choice (tʃɔɪs) *n* **1** the act or an instance of choosing or selecting. **2** the opportunity or power of choosing. **3** a person or thing chosen or that may be chosen: *he was a possible choice.* **4** an alternative action or possibility: *what choice did I have?* **5** a supply from which to select: *a poor choice of shoes.* ♦ *adj* **6** of superior quality; excellent: *choice wine.* **7** carefully chosen, appropriate: *a few choice words will do the trick.* **8** vulgar or rude: *choice language.* [C13: from Old French *chois,* from *choisir* to CHOOSE] ▸ **'choicely** *adv* ▸ **'choiceness** *n*

choir (kwaɪə) *n* **1** an organized group of singers, esp. for singing in church services. **2a** the part of a cathedral, abbey, or church in front of the altar, lined on both sides with benches, and used by the choir and clergy. Compare **chancel.** **2b** (*as modifier*): *choir stalls.* **3** a number of instruments of the same family playing together: *a brass choir.* **4** Also called: **choir organ.** one of the manuals on an organ controlling a set of soft sweet-toned pipes. Compare **great** (sense 21), **swell** (sense 16). **5** any of the nine orders of angels in medieval angelology. Archaic spelling: **quire.** [C13 *quer,* from Old French *cuer,* from Latin CHORUS] ▸ **'choirˌlike** *adj*

choirboy ('kwaɪəˌbɔɪ) *n* one of a number of young boys who sing the treble part in a church choir.

choir loft *n* a gallery in a cathedral, abbey, or church used by the choir.

choirmaster ('kwaɪəˌmɑːstə) *n* a person who trains, leads, or conducts a choir.

choir school *n* (in Britain) a school, esp. a preparatory school attached to a cathedral, college, etc., offering general education to boys whose singing ability is good.

Choiseul[1] (*French* ʃwazœl) *n* an island in the SW Pacific Ocean, in the Solomon Islands: hilly and densely forested. Area: 3885 sq. km (1500 sq. miles).

Choiseul[2] (*French* ʃwazœl) *n* **Étienne François** (etjɛn frɑ̃swa), Duc de. 1719–85, French statesman; foreign minister (1758–70).

choke (tʃəʊk) *vb* **1** (*tr*) to hinder or stop the breathing of (a person or animal), esp. by constricting the windpipe or by asphyxiation. **2** (*intr*) to have trouble or fail in breathing, swallowing, or speaking. **3** (*tr*) to block or clog up (a passage, pipe, street, etc.). **4** (*tr*) to retard the growth or action of: *the weeds are choking my plants.* **5** (*tr*) to suppress (emotion): *she choked her anger.* **6** (*intr*) *Slang.* to die. **7** (*tr*) to enrich the petrol-air mixture by reducing the air supply to (a carburettor, petrol engine, etc.). **8** (*intr*) (esp. in sport) to be seized with tension and fail to perform well. ◆ *n* **9** the act or sound of choking. **10** a device in the carburettor of a petrol engine that enriches the petrol-air mixture by reducing the air supply. **11** any constriction or mechanism for reducing the flow of a fluid in a pipe, tube, etc. **12** Also called: **choke coil.** *Electronics.* an inductor having a relatively high impedance, used to prevent the passage of high frequencies or to smooth the output of a rectifier. **13** the inedible centre of the head of an artichoke. ◆ See also **choke back, choke up.** [Old English *ācēocian,* of Germanic origin; related to CHEEK] ▸ **'chokeable** *adj* ▸ **'choky** *or* **'chokey** *adj*

choke back *or* **down** *vb* (*tr, adv*) to suppress (anger, tears, etc.).

chokeberry ('tʃəʊkbərɪ, -brɪ) *n, pl* **-ries. 1** any of various North American rosaceous shrubs of the genus *Aronia.* **2** the red or purple bitter fruit of any of these shrubs.

chokebore ('tʃəʊkˌbɔː) *n* **1** a shotgun bore that becomes narrower towards the muzzle so that the shot is not scattered. **2** a shotgun having such a bore.

choke chain *n* a collar and lead for a dog so designed that if the dog drags on the lead the collar tightens round its neck.

chokecherry ('tʃəʊkˌtʃɛrɪ) *n, pl* **-ries. 1** any of several North American species of cherry, esp. *Prunus virginiana,* having very astringent dark red or black fruit. **2** the fruit of any of these trees.

choke coil *n* another name for **choke** (sense 12).

choked (tʃəʊkt) *adj Brit. informal.* annoyed or disappointed.

chokedamp ('tʃəʊkˌdæmp) *n* another word for **blackdamp.**

choke-full *adj* a less common spelling of **chock-full.**

choker ('tʃəʊkə) *n* **1** a woman's high collar, popular esp. in the late 19th century. **2** any neckband or necklace worn tightly around the throat. **3** a high clerical collar; stock. **4** a person who chokes. **5** something that causes a person to choke.

choke up *vb* (*tr, adv*) **1** to block (a drain, pipe, etc.) completely. **2** *Informal.* (*usually passive*) to overcome (a person) with emotion, esp. without due cause.

chokey *or* **choky** ('tʃəʊkɪ) *n Brit.* a slang word for **prison.** [C17: from Anglo-Indian, from Hindi *caukī* a shed or lockup]

choko ('tʃəʊkəʊ) *n, pl* **-kos.** the cucumber-like fruit of a tropical American cucurbitaceous vine, *Sechium edule:* eaten as a vegetable in the Caribbean, Australia, and New Zealand. [C18: from a Brazilian Indian name]

cholagogue ('kɒləgɒg) *n* a drug or other substance that promotes the flow of bile from the gall bladder into the duodenum. ▸ **ˌchola'gogic** *adj*

cholangiography (kəˌlændʒɪ'ɒgrəfɪ) *n* radiographic examination of the bile ducts after the introduction into them of a contrast medium.

chole- *or before a vowel* **chol-** *combining form.* indicating bile or gall: *cholesterol.* [from Greek *kholē*]

cholecalciferol (ˌkəʊlɪkæl'sɪfəˌrɒl) *n* a compound occurring naturally in fish-liver oils, used to treat rickets. Formula: $C_{27}H_{44}O$. Also called: **vitamin D_3.** See also **calciferol.**

cholecyst ('kɒlɪsɪst) *n Rare.* another name for **gall bladder.**

cholecystectomy (ˌkɒlɪsɪ'stɛktəmɪ) *n, pl* **-mies.** surgical removal of the gall bladder.

cholecystitis (ˌkɒlɪsɪs'taɪtɪs) *n* inflammation of the gall bladder, due to bacterial infection or the presence of gallstones.

cholecystography (ˌkɒlɪsɪs'tɒgrəfɪ) *n Med.* radiography of the gall bladder after administration of a contrast medium.

cholecystokinin (ˌkɒlɪˌsɪstə'kaɪnɪn) *n* a hormone secreted by duodenal cells that stimulates the contraction of the gall bladder and secretion of pancreatic enzymes. Also called: **pancreozymin.**

cholent ('tʃɒlənt) *n Judaism.* a meal usually consisting of a stew of meat, potatoes, and pulses prepared before the Sabbath on Friday and left to cook until eaten for Sabbath lunch.

choler ('kɒlə) *n* **1** anger or ill humour. **2** *Archaic.* one of the four bodily humours; yellow bile. See **humour** (sense 8). **3** *Obsolete.* biliousness. [C14: from Old French *colère,* from Medieval Latin *cholera,* from Latin: jaundice, CHOLERA]

cholera ('kɒlərə) *n* an acute intestinal infection characterized by severe diarrhoea, cramp, etc.: caused by ingestion of water or food contaminated with the bacterium *Vibrio comma.* Also called: **Asiatic cholera, epidemic cholera, Indian cholera.** [C14: from Latin, from Greek *kholera* jaundice, from *kholē* bile] ▸ **'choleˌroid** *adj*

choleric ('kɒlərɪk) *adj* **1** bad-tempered. **2** bilious or causing biliousness. ▸ **'cholerically** *or* **'cholericly** *adv*

cholesterol (kə'lɛstəˌrɒl) *n* a sterol found in all animal tissues, blood, bile, and animal fats: a precursor of other body steroids. A high level of cholesterol in the blood is implicated in some cases of atherosclerosis, leading to heart disease. Former name: **cholesterin** (kə'lɛstərɪn). Formula: $C_{27}H_{45}OH$. [C19: from CHOLE- + Greek *stereos* hard, solid, so called because first observed in gallstones]

cholesterolaemia *or U.S.* **cholesterolemia** (kəˌlɛstərə'liːmɪə) *n* the presence of abnormally high levels of cholesterol in the blood.

Chol Hamoed *Hebrew.* (*Hebrew* xol hɑ'moed; *Yiddish* xaʊl hə'maʊəd) *n Judaism.* the middle days of the festivals of Passover and Sukkoth, on which necessary work is permitted. [literally: the weekdays of the festival]

choli ('kəʊlɪ) *n, pl* **-lis.** a short-sleeved bodice, as worn by Indian women. [from Hindi]

cholic acid ('kəʊlɪk) *n* a crystalline insoluble acid present in bile: used as an emulsifying agent and an intermediate in the synthesis of organic compounds. Formula: $C_{24}H_{40}O_5$. [C19: from Greek *kholikos;* see CHOLE-]

choline ('kəʊliːn, -ɪn, 'kɒl-) *n* a colourless viscous soluble alkaline substance present in animal tissues, esp. as a constituent of lecithin: used as a supplement to the diet of poultry and in medicine for preventing the accumulation of fat in the liver. Formula: $[(CH_3)_3NCH_2CH_2OH]^+OH^-$. [C19: from CHOLE- + -INE[2], so called because of its action in the liver]

cholinergic (ˌkəʊlɪ'nɜːdʒɪk) *adj* **1** denoting nerve fibres that release acetylcholine when stimulated. **2** of or relating to the type of chemical activity associated with acetylcholine and similar substances. [C20: from (ACETYL)CHOLIN(E) + Greek *ergon* work]

cholinesterase (ˌkəʊlɪ'nɛstəˌreɪs, ˌkɒl-) *n* an enzyme that hydrolyses acetylcholine to choline and acetic acid.

cholla ('tʃəʊljɑː; *Spanish* 'tʃoʎa) *n* any of several spiny cacti of the genus *Opuntia* that grow in the southwestern U.S. and Mexico and have cylindrical stem segments. See also **prickly pear.** [Mexican Spanish, from Spanish: head, perhaps from Old French (dialect) *cholle* ball, of Germanic origin]

chollers ('tʃɒləz) *pl n Northeast English dialect.* the jowls or cheeks. [C18: perhaps from Old English *ceolur* throat. See JOWL[2]]

Cholon (tʃə'lʌn; *French* ʃɔlɔ̃) *n* a city in S Vietnam: a suburb of Ho Chi Minh City.

Cholula (*Spanish* tʃo'lula) *n* a town in S Mexico, in Puebla state: ancient ruins, notably a pyramid, 53 m (177 ft.) high. Pop.: 37 791 (1990).

chometz *Hebrew.* (*Hebrew* xa'mɛtʒ; *Yiddish* 'xomətʒ) *n* a variant spelling of **chametz.**

chomophyte ('kɒməʊˌfaɪt) *n* any plant that grows on rocky ledges or in fissures and crevices.

chomp (tʃɒmp) *or* **chump** *vb* **1** to chew (food) noisily; champ. ◆ *n* **2** the act or sound of chewing in this manner. [variant of CHAMP[1]]

Chomsky ('tʃɒmskɪ) *n* (**Avram**) **Noam** ('nəʊəm). born 1928, U.S. linguist and political critic. His theory of language structure, transformational generative grammar, superseded the behaviourist view of Bloomfield. ▸ **'Chomskyan** *or* **'ChomskyˌIte** *n, adj*

chon (tʃɒn) *n, pl* **chon.** a North and South Korean monetary unit worth one hundredth of a won.

chondral ('kɒndrəl) *adj* of or relating to cartilage.

chondrichthyan (kɒn'drɪkθɪən) *n Zoology.* a technical name for a **cartilaginous fish.** [New Latin, from Greek *khondros* grain, cartilage + *ikhthus* fish]

chondrify ('kɒndrɪˌfaɪ) *vb* **-fies, -fying, -fied.** to become or convert into cartilage. ▸ **ˌchondrifi'cation** *n*

chondrin ('kɒndrɪn) *n* a resilient translucent bluish-white substance that forms the matrix of cartilage.

chondriosome ('kɒndrɪəˌsəʊm) *n* another name for **mitochondrion.** ▸ **ˌchondrio'somal** *adj*

chondrite ('kɒndraɪt) *n* a stony meteorite consisting mainly of silicate minerals in the form of chondrules. Compare **achondrite.** ▸ **chondritic** (kɒn'drɪtɪk) *adj*

chondro-, chondri-, *or before a vowel* **chondr-** *combining form.* **1** indicating cartilage: *chondroma.* **2** grain or granular: *chondrule.* [from Greek *khondros* grain, cartilage]

chondroma (kɒn'drəʊmə) *n, pl* **-mas** *or* **-mata** (-mətə). *Pathol.* a benign cartilaginous growth or neoplasm. ▸ **chon'dromatous** *adj*

chondroskeleton ('kɒndrəʊˌskɛlɪtən) *n* the cartilaginous part of the skeleton of vertebrates.

chondrule ('kɒndruːl) *n* one of the small spherical masses of mainly silicate minerals present in chondrites.

Chŏngjin *or* **Chungjin** ('tʃʌŋ'dʒɪn) *n* a port in E North Korea, on the Sea of Japan. Pop.: 520 000 (1987 est.).

Chongqing ('tʃʊŋ'tʃɪŋ), **Chungking,** *or* **Ch'ung-ch'ing** *n* a port in SW China, in Sichuan province at the confluence of the Yangtze and Jialing rivers: site of a city since the 3rd millennium B.C.; wartime capital of China (1938–45); major trade centre for W China. Pop.: 2 980 000 (1991 est.). Also called: **Pahsien.**

Chŏnju ('tʃʌn'dʒuː) *n* a city in SW South Korea: centre of large rice-growing region. Pop.: 563 406 (1995).

choo-choo ('tʃuːˌtʃuː) *n Brit.* a child's name for a railway train. [C20: of imitative origin]

choof off (tʃʊf) *vb* (*intr, adv*) *Austral. slang.* to go away; make off.

chook (tʃʊk) *vb* **1** See **jook.** ◆ *n* **2** Also called: **'chookie.** *Informal, chiefly Austral. and N.Z.* a hen or chicken.

choom (tʃʊm) *n* (*often cap.*) *Old-fashioned Austral. slang.* an Englishman.

choose (tʃuːz) *vb* **chooses, choosing, chose, chosen. 1** to select (a person, thing, course of action, etc.) from a number of alternatives. **2** (*tr; takes a clause as object or an infinitive*) to consider it desirable or proper: *I don't choose to read that book.* **3** (*intr*) to like; please: *you may stand if you choose.* **4 cannot choose but.** to be obliged to: *we cannot choose but vote for him.* **5 nothing** *or* **little to choose between.** (of two people or objects) almost equal. [Old English *ceosan;* related to Old Norse *kjōsa,* Old High German *kiosan*] ▸ **'chooser** *n*

choosy ('tʃu:zɪ) *adj* **choosier, choosiest.** *Informal.* particular in making a choice; difficult to please.

chop[1] (tʃɒp) *vb* **chops, chopping, chopped. 1** (often foll. by *down* or *off*) to cut (something) with a blow from an axe or other sharp tool. **2** (*tr*) to produce or make in this manner: *to chop firewood.* **3** (*tr;* often foll. by *up*) to cut into pieces. **4** (*tr*) *Brit. informal.* to dispense with or reduce. **5** (*intr*) to move quickly or violently. **6** *Tennis, cricket, etc.* to hit (a ball) sharply downwards. **7** *Boxing, karate, etc.* to punch or strike (an opponent) with a short sharp blow. **8** *West African.* an informal word for **eat.** ◆ *n* **9** a cutting blow. **10** the act or an instance of chopping. **11** a piece chopped off. **12** a slice of mutton, lamb, or pork, generally including a rib. **13** *Austral. and N.Z. slang.* a share (esp. in the phrase **get** *or* **hop in for one's chop**). **14** *West African.* an informal word for **food. 15** *Austral. and N.Z.* a competition of skill and speed in chopping logs. **16** *Sport.* a sharp downward blow or stroke. **17 not much chop.** *Austral. and N.Z. informal.* not much good; poor. **18 the chop.** *Slang.* dismissal from employment. [C16: variant of CHAP[1]]

chop[2] (tʃɒp) *vb* **chops, chopping, chopped. 1** (*intr*) to change direction suddenly; vacillate (esp. in the phrase **chop and change**). **2** *Obsolete.* to barter. **3 chop logic.** to use excessively subtle or involved logic or argument. [Old English *ceapian* to barter; see CHEAP, CHAPMAN]

chop[3] (tʃɒp) *n* a design stamped on goods as a trademark, esp. in the Far East. [C17: from Hindi *chhāp*]

chop chop *adv* pidgin English for **quickly.** [C19: from Chinese dialect; related to Cantonese *kap kap*]

chopfallen ('tʃɒpˌfɔ:lən) *adj* a variant of **chapfallen.**

chophouse[1] ('tʃɒpˌhaʊs) *n* a restaurant specializing in steaks, grills, chops, etc.

chophouse[2] ('tʃɒpˌhaʊs) *n* (formerly) a customs house in China.

Chopin ('ʃɒpæn; *French* ʃɔpɛ̃) *n* **Frédéric** (**François**) (frederik). 1810–49, Polish composer and pianist active in France, who wrote chiefly for the piano: noted for his harmonic imagination and his lyrical and melancholy qualities.

chopine (tʃɒ'pi:n) *or* **chopin** ('tʃɒpɪn) *n* a sandal-like shoe on tall wooden or cork bases popular in the 18th century. [C16: from Old Spanish *chapín,* probably imitative of the sound made by the shoe when walking]

chopper ('tʃɒpə) *n* **1** *Chiefly Brit.* a small hand axe. **2** a butcher's cleaver. **3** a person or thing that cuts or chops. **4** an informal name for a **helicopter. 5** *Chiefly Brit.* a slang name for **penis. 6** a device for periodically interrupting an electric current or beam of radiation to produce a pulsed current or beam. See also **vibrator** (sense 2). **7** a type of bicycle or motorcycle with very high handlebars and an elongated saddle. **8** *Slang, chiefly U.S.* a sub-machine-gun.

chopper tool *n* a core tool of flint or stone, with a transverse cutting edge, characteristic of cultures in Asia and parts of the Middle East and Europe.

choppy ('tʃɒpɪ) *adj* **-pier, -piest.** (of the sea, weather, etc.) fairly rough. ▸ **'choppily** *adv* ▸ **'choppiness** *n*

chops (tʃɒps) *pl n* **1** the jaws or cheeks; jowls. **2** the mouth. **3** *Music slang.* **3a** embouchure. **3b** *Jazz.* skill. **4 lick one's chops.** *Informal.* to anticipate with pleasure. [C16: of uncertain origin]

chopsticks ('tʃɒpstɪks) *pl n* a pair of thin sticks, of ivory, wood, etc., used as eating utensils by the Chinese, Japanese, etc. [C17: from pidgin English, from *chop* quick, of Chinese dialect origin + STICK[1]]

chop suey ('su:ɪ) *n* a Chinese-style dish originating in the U.S., consisting of meat or chicken, bean sprouts, etc., stewed and served with rice. [C19: from Chinese (Cantonese) *tsap sui* odds and ends]

choragus (kɔ:'reɪgəs) *n, pl* **-gi** (-dʒaɪ) *or* **-guses. 1** (in ancient Greek drama) **1a** the leader of a chorus. **1b** a sponsor of a chorus. **2** a conductor of a festival. [C17: from Latin, from Greek *khoragos,* from *khoros* CHORUS + *agein* to lead] ▸ **choragic** (kɔ:'rædʒɪk, -'reɪ-) *adj*

choral *adj* ('kɔ:rəl). **1** relating to, sung by, or designed for a chorus or choir. ◆ *n* (kɒ'rɑ:l). **2** a variant spelling of **chorale.** ▸ **'chorally** *adv*

chorale *or* **choral** (kɒ'rɑ:l) *n* **1** a slow stately hymn tune, esp. of the Lutheran Church. **2** *Chiefly U.S.* a choir or chorus. [C19: from German *Choralgesang,* translation of Latin *cantus chorālis* choral song]

chorale prelude *n* a composition for organ using a chorale as a cantus firmus or as the basis for variations.

chord[1] (kɔ:d) *n* **1** *Maths.* **1a** a straight line connecting two points on a curve or curved surface. **1b** the line segment lying between two points of intersection of a straight line and a curve or curved surface. **2** *Engineering.* one of the principal members of a truss, esp. one that lies along the top or the bottom. **3** *Anatomy.* a variant spelling of **cord. 4** an emotional response, esp. one of sympathy: *the story struck the right chord.* **5** an imaginary straight line joining the leading edge and the trailing edge of an aerofoil. **6** *Archaic.* the string of a musical instrument. [C16: from Latin *chorda,* from Greek *khordē* gut, string; see CORD] ▸ **'chorded** *adj*

chord[2] (kɔ:d) *n* **1** the simultaneous sounding of a group of musical notes, usually three or more in number. See **concord** (sense 4), **discord** (sense 3). ◆ *vb* **2** (*tr*) to provide (a melodic line) with chords. [C15: short for ACCORD; spelling influenced by CHORD[1]] ▸ **'chordal** *adj*

chordate ('kɔ:ˌdeɪt) *n* **1** any animal of the phylum *Chordata,* including the vertebrates and protochordates, characterized by a notochord, dorsal tubular nerve cord, and pharyngeal gill slits. ◆ *adj* **2** of, relating to, or belonging to the *Chordata.* [C19: from Medieval Latin *chordata;* see CHORD[1] + -ATE[1]]

chording ('kɔ:dɪŋ) *n Music.* **1** the distribution of chords throughout a piece of harmony. **2** the intonation of a group of instruments or voices.

chordophone ('kɔ:dəˌfəʊn) *n* any musical instrument producing sounds through the vibration of strings, such as the piano, harp, violin, or guitar.

chord symbol *n Music.* any of a series of letters and numerals, used as a shorthand indication of chords, esp. in jazz, folk, or pop music: *B7 indicates the dominant seventh chord in the key of E.*

chordwise ('kɔ:dˌwaɪz) *adv* **1** in the direction of an aerofoil chord. ◆ *adj* **2** moving in this direction: *chordwise force.*

chore (tʃɔ:) *n* **1** a small routine task, esp. a domestic one. **2** an unpleasant task. [C19: variant of Middle English *chare;* related to CHAR[3]]

-chore *n combining form.* (in botany) indicating a plant distributed by a certain means: *anemochore.* [from Greek *khōrein* to move] ▸ **-chorous** *or* **-choric** *adj combining form.*

chorea (kɒ'rɪə) *n* a disorder of the central nervous system characterized by uncontrollable irregular brief jerky movements. See **Huntington's disease, Sydenham's chorea.** [C19: from New Latin, from Latin: dance, from Greek *khoreia,* from *khoros* dance; see CHORUS] ▸ **cho'real** *or* **cho'reic** *adj*

choreo- *combining form.* indicating the art of dancing or ballet: *choreodrama; choreography.* [from Greek *khoreios,* from *khoros* dance]

choreodrama (ˌkɔ:rɪəʊ'drɑ:mə) *n Dancing.* dance drama performed by a group.

choreograph ('kɒrɪəˌgræf) *vb* (*tr*) to compose the steps and dances for (a piece of music or ballet).

choreography (ˌkɒrɪ'ɒgrəfɪ) *or* **choregraphy** (kɒ'rɛgrəfɪ) *n* **1** the composition of dance steps and sequences for ballet and stage dancing. **2** the steps and sequences of a ballet or dance. **3** the notation representing such steps. **4** the art of dancing. [C18: from Greek *khoreia* dance + -GRAPHY] ▸ ˌ**chore'ographer** *or* **cho'regrapher** *n* ▸ **choreographic** (ˌkɒrɪə'græfɪk) *or* **choregraphic** (ˌkɒrə'græfɪk) *adj* ▸ ˌ**choreo'graphically** *or* ˌ**chore'graphically** *adv*

choriamb ('kɒrɪˌæmb) *or* **choriambus** (ˌkɒrɪ'æmbəs) *n, pl* **-ambs** *or* **-ambi** (-'æmbaɪ). *Prosody.* a metrical foot used in classical verse consisting of four syllables, two short ones between two long ones (-⌣⌣-). [C19: from Late Latin *choriambus,* from Greek *khoriambos,* from *khoreios* trochee, of a chorus, from *khoros* CHORUS] ▸ ˌ**chori'ambic** *adj*

choric ('kɒrɪk) *adj* of, like, for, or in the manner of a chorus, esp. of singing, dancing, or the speaking of verse.

chorion ('kɔ:rɪən) *n* the outer of two membranes (see also **amnion**) that form a sac around the embryonic reptile, bird, or mammal: contributes to the placenta in mammals. [C16: from Greek *khorion* afterbirth] ▸ ˌ**chori'onic** *or* '**chorial** *adj*

chorionic gonadotrophin *n* a hormone secreted by the chorionic villi of the placenta in mammals, esp. **human chorionic gonadotrophin.** It promotes the secretion of progesterone by the corpus luteum and its presence in the urine is an indication of pregnancy.

chorionic villus sampling *n* a method of diagnosing genetic disorders early in pregnancy by the removal by catheter through the cervix or abdomen of a tiny sample of tissue from the chorionic villi. Abbrev.: **CVS.**

chorister ('kɒrɪstə) *n* a singer in a choir, esp. a choirboy. [C14: from Medieval Latin *chorista*]

chorizo (tʃɔ:'ri:zəʊ) *n, pl* **-zos.** a kind of highly seasoned pork sausage of Spain or Mexico. [C19: Spanish]

C horizon *n* the layer of a soil profile immediately below the B horizon and above the bedrock, composed of weathered rock little affected by soil-forming processes.

Chorley ('tʃɔ:lɪ) *n* a town in NW England, in S Lancashire: cotton textiles. Pop.: 33 536 (1991).

chorography (kɒ'rɒgrəfɪ) *n Geography.* **1** the technique of mapping regions. **2** a description or map of a region, as opposed to a small area. [C16: via Latin from Greek *khōrographia,* from *khōros* place, country + -GRAPHY] ▸ **cho'rographer** *n* ▸ **chorographic** (ˌkɒrə'græfɪk) *or* ˌ**choro'graphical** *adj* ▸ ˌ**choro'graphically** *adv*

choroid ('kɔ:rɔɪd) *or* **chorioid** ('kɔ:rɪˌɔɪd) *adj* **1** resembling the chorion, esp. in being vascular. ◆ *n* **2** the brownish vascular membrane of the eyeball between the sclera and the retina. [C18: from Greek *khoroeidēs,* erroneously for *khorioeidēs,* from CHORION]

choroid plexus *n* a multilobed vascular membrane, projecting into the cerebral ventricles, that secretes cerebrospinal fluid.

chorology (kə'rɒlədʒɪ) *n* **1** the study of the causal relations between geographical phenomena occurring within a particular region. **2** the study of the spatial distribution of organisms. [C20: from German *Chorologie,* from Greek *khōros* place + -LOGY] ▸ **cho'rologist** *n*

choropleth ('kɔ:rəˌplɛθ) *n* **a** a symbol or marked area on a map denoting the distribution of some property. **b** (*as modifier*) *a choropleth map.* [C20: from Gk *khōra* place + *plēthos* multitude]

chortle ('tʃɔ:tᵊl) *vb* **1** (*intr*) to chuckle gleefully. ◆ *n* **2** a gleeful chuckle. [C19: coined (1871) by Lewis Carroll in *Through the Looking-glass;* probably a blend of CHUCKLE + SNORT] ▸ **'chortler** *n*

chorus ('kɔ:rəs) *n, pl* **-ruses. 1** a large choir of singers or a piece of music composed for such a choir. **2** a body of singers or dancers who perform together, in contrast to principals or soloists. **3** a section of a song in which a soloist is joined by a group of singers, esp. in a recurring refrain. **4** an intermediate section of a pop song, blues, etc., as distinct from the verse. **5** *Jazz.* any of a series of variations on a theme. **6** (in ancient Greece) **6a** a lyric poem sung by a group of dancers, originally as a religious rite. **6b** an ode or series of odes sung by a group of actors. **7a** (in classical Greek drama) the actors who sang the chorus and commented on the action of the play. **7b** actors playing a similar role in any drama. **8a** (esp. in Elizabethan drama) the actor who spoke the prologue, etc. **8b** the part of the play spoken by this actor. **9** a group of people or animals producing words or sounds simultaneously. **10** any speech, song, or other utterance produced by a group of people or animals simultaneously: *a chorus of sighs; the dawn chorus.* **11 in chorus.** in unison. ◆ *vb* **12** to speak, sing, or utter (words, etc.) in unison. [C16: from Latin, from Greek *khoros*]

chorus girl *n* a girl who dances or sings in the chorus of a musical comedy, revue, etc.

chorusmaster ('kɔːrəsˌmɑːstə) *n* the conductor of a choir.

chorus pedal *n Music.* an electronic device that creates the effect of more than one sound from a single source by combining a short delay with slight deviations in pitch.

Chorzów (*Polish* 'xɔʒuf) *n* an industrial city in SW Poland: under German administration from 1794 to 1921. Pop.: 125 800 (1996 est.). German name: **Königshütte.**

chose[1] (tʃəʊz) *vb* the past tense of **choose.**

chose[2] (ʃəʊz) *n Law.* an article of personal property. [C17: from French: thing, from Latin *causa* cause, case, reason]

chosen ('tʃəʊzᵊn) *vb* **1** the past participle of **choose.** ◆ *adj* **2** selected or picked out, esp. for some special quality.

Chosen ('tʃəʊ'sɛn) *n* the official name for **Korea** as a Japanese province (1910–45).

chosen people *pl n* any of various peoples believing themselves to be chosen by God, esp. the Jews.

Chosŏn ('tʃəʊ'sɒn) *n* the Korean name for **North Korea.**

Chota Nagpur ('tʃəʊtə 'nɑːgpʊə) *n* a plateau in E India, in Bihar state: forested, with rich mineral resources and much heavy industry; produces chiefly lac (world's leading supplier), coal (half India's total output), and mica.

chott (ʃɒt) *n* a variant spelling of **shott.**

chou (ʃuː) *n, pl* **choux** (ʃuː). **1** a type of cabbage. **2** a rosette. **3** a round cream bun. [C18 (a bun): from French, from Latin *caulis* cabbage]

Chou (tʃəʊ) *or* **Zhou** *n* the imperial dynasty of China from about 1126 to 255 B.C.

Chou En-lai (ɛn'laɪ) *or* **Zhou En Lai** *n* 1898–1976, Chinese Communist statesman; foreign minister of the People's Republic of China (1949–58) and premier (1949–76).

chough (tʃʌf) *n* **1** a large black passerine bird, *Pyrrhocorax pyrrhocorax,* of parts of Europe, Asia, and Africa, with a long downward-curving red bill: family *Corvidae* (crows). **2 alpine chough.** a smaller related bird, *Pyrrhocorax graculus,* with a shorter yellow bill. [C14: of uncertain origin; probably related to Old French *cauwe,* Old English *cēo*]

choux pastry (ʃuː) *n* a very light pastry made with eggs, used for eclairs, etc. [partial translation of French *pâte choux* cabbage dough (from its round shape)]

chow (tʃaʊ) *n* **1** *Informal.* food. **2** short for **chow-chow** (sense 1).

chow-chow *n* **1** a thick-coated breed of the spitz type of dog with a curled tail, originally from China. Often shortened to **chow. 2** a Chinese preserve of ginger, orange peel, etc. in syrup. **3** a mixed vegetable pickle. [C19: from pidgin English, probably based on Mandarin Chinese *cha* miscellaneous]

chowder ('tʃaʊdə) *n* a thick soup or stew containing clams or fish. [C18: from French *chaudière* kettle, from Late Latin *caldāria;* see CAULDRON]

chow mein (meɪn) *n* a Chinese-American dish, consisting of mushrooms, meat, shrimps, etc., served with fried noodles. [from Chinese (Cantonese), variant of Mandarin *ch'ao mien* fried noodles]

Chr. *abbrev. for:* **1** Christ. **2** Christian.

chrematistic (ˌkriːmə'tɪstɪk) *adj* of, denoting, or relating to money-making. [C18: from Greek, from *khrēmatizein* to make money, from *khrēma* money] ▸ **ˌchrema'tistics** *n*

chresard ('krɛsəd) *n* the amount of water present in the soil that is available to plants. [C20: from Greek *khrēsis* use (from *khrēsthai* to use) + *ardein* to water]

chrestomathy (krɛs'tɒməθɪ) *n, pl* **-thies.** *Rare.* a collection of literary passages, used in the study of language. [C19: from Greek *khrēstomatheia,* from *khrēstos* useful + *mathein* to learn] ▸ **chrestomathic** (ˌkrɛstəʊ'mæθɪk) *adj*

Chrétien (*French* kretjɛ̃) *n* **(Joseph Jacques) Jean.** born 1934, Canadian Liberal politician; prime minister of Canada from 1993.

Chrétien de Troyes (*French* kretjɛ̃ də trwa) *n* 12th century, French poet, who wrote the five Arthurian romances *Erec; Cligès; Lancelot, le chevalier de la charette; Yvain, le chevalier au lion;* and *Perceval, le conte del Graal* (?1155–?1190), the first courtly romances.

chrism *or* **chrisom** ('krɪzəm) *n* a mixture of olive oil and balsam used for sacramental anointing in the Greek Orthodox and Roman Catholic Churches. [Old English *crisma,* from Medieval Latin, from Greek *khrisma* unction, from *khriein* to anoint] ▸ **chrismal** ('krɪzməl) *adj*

chrismation (ˌkrɪz'meɪʃən) *n Greek Orthodox Church.* a rite of initiation involving anointing with chrism and taking place at the same time as baptism.

chrismatory ('krɪzmətərɪ, -trɪ) *n, pl* **-ries.** *R.C. Church.* a small receptacle containing the three kinds of consecrated oil used in the sacraments.

chrisom ('krɪzəm) *n* **1** *Christianity.* a white robe put on an infant at baptism and formerly used as a burial shroud if the infant died soon afterwards. **2** *Archaic.* an infant wearing such a robe. **3** a variant spelling of **chrism.**

Chrissie ('krɪsɪ) *n Chiefly Austral.* a slang name for **Christmas.**

Christ (kraɪst) *n* **1** Jesus of Nazareth (Jesus Christ), regarded by Christians as fulfilling Old Testament prophecies of the Messiah. **2** the Messiah or anointed one of God as the subject of Old Testament prophecies. **3** an image or picture of Christ. ◆ *interj* **4** *Taboo slang.* an oath expressing annoyance, surprise, etc. ◆ See also **Jesus.** [Old English *Crīst,* from Latin *Chrīstus,* from Greek *khristos* anointed one (from *khriein* to anoint), translating Hebrew *māshīah* MESSIAH] ▸ **'Christly** *adj*

Christadelphian (ˌkrɪstə'dɛlfɪən) *n* **1** a member of a Christian millenarian sect founded in the U.S. about 1848, holding that only the just will enter eternal life, that the wicked will be annihilated, and that the ignorant, the unconverted, and infants will not be raised from the dead. ◆ *adj* **2** of or relating to this body or its beliefs and practices. [C19: from Late Greek *khristadelphos,* from *khristos* CHRIST + *adelphos* brother]

Christchurch ('kraɪstˌtʃɜːtʃ) *n* **1** a city in New Zealand, on E South Island: manufacturing centre of a rich agricultural region. Pop. (urban area): 313 969 (1996). **2** a town and resort in S England, in SE Dorset. Pop.: 36 379 (1991).

christcross ('krɪsˌkrɒs) *n Archaic.* **1a** the mark of a cross formerly placed in front of the alphabet in hornbooks. **1b** the alphabet itself. **2** a cross used in place of a signature by someone unable to sign his name.

christen ('krɪsᵊn) *vb (tr)* **1** to give a Christian name to in baptism as a sign of incorporation into a Christian Church. **2** another word for **baptize. 3** to give a name to (anything), esp. with some ceremony. **4** *Informal.* to use for the first time. [Old English *cristnian,* from *Crīst* CHRIST] ▸ **'christener** *n*

Christendom ('krɪsᵊndəm) *n* **1** the collective body of Christians throughout the world or throughout history. **2** an obsolete word for **Christianity.**

christening ('krɪsᵊnɪŋ) *n* the Christian sacrament of baptism or the ceremony in which this is conferred.

Christhood ('kraɪsthʊd) *n* the state of being the Christ, the anointed one of God.

Christian[1] ('krɪstʃən) *n* **1a** a person who believes in and follows Jesus Christ. **1b** a member of a Christian Church or denomination. **2** *Informal.* a person who possesses Christian virtues, esp. practical ones. ◆ *adj* **3** of, relating to, or derived from Jesus Christ, his teachings, example, or his followers. **4** (*sometimes not cap.*) exhibiting kindness or goodness. ▸ **'christianly** *adj, adv*

Christian[2] ('krɪstʃən) *n* **Charlie.** 1919–42, U.S. jazz guitarist.

Christian IV ('krɪstʃən; *Danish* 'kresdjan) *n* 1577–1648, king of Denmark and Norway (1588–1648): defeated in the Thirty Years' War (1629) and by Sweden (1645).

Christian X *n* 1890–1947, king of Denmark (1912–47) and Iceland (1918–44).

Christian Action *n* an inter-Church movement formed in 1946 to promote Christian ideals in society at large.

Christian Brothers *pl n R.C. Church.* a religious congregation of laymen founded in France in 1684 for the education of the poor. Also called: **Brothers of the Christian Schools.**

Christian Democracy *n* the beliefs, principles, practices, or programme of a Christian Democratic party. ▸ **Christian Democratic** *adj*

Christian Democrat *n* **1** a member or supporter of a Christian Democratic party. ◆ *adj* **2** of or relating to a Christian Democratic party.

Christian Democratic Party *n* any of various political parties in Europe and Latin America which combine moderate conservatism with historical links to the Christian Church.

Christian Era *n* the period beginning with the year of Christ's birth. Dates in this era are labelled A.D., those previous to it B.C. Also called: **Common Era.**

Christiania (ˌkrɪstɪ'ɑːnɪə) *n* a former name (1624–1877) of **Oslo.**

Christianity (ˌkrɪstɪ'ænɪtɪ) *n* **1** the Christian religion. **2** Christian beliefs, practices or attitudes. **3** a less common word for **Christendom** (sense 1).

Christianize *or* **Christianise** ('krɪstʃəˌnaɪz) *vb* **1** *(tr)* to make Christian or convert to Christianity. **2** *(tr)* to imbue with Christian principles, spirit, or outlook. ▸ **ˌChristiani'zation** *or* **ˌChristiani'sation** *n* ▸ **'Christianˌizer** *or* **'Christianˌiser** *n*

Christian name *n* a personal name formally given to Christians at christening. The term is loosely used to mean any person's first name as distinct from his or her surname. Also called: **first name, forename, given name.**

Christiansand ('krɪstʃənˌsænd; *Norwegian* kristian'san) *n* a variant spelling of **Kristiansand.**

Christian Science *n* the religious system and teaching of the Church of Christ, Scientist. It was founded by Mary Baker Eddy (1866) and emphasizes spiritual healing and the unreality of matter. ▸ **Christian Scientist** *n*

Christie ('krɪstɪ) *n* **1** Dame **Agatha (Mary Clarissa).** 1890–1976, British author of detective stories, many featuring Hercule Poirot, and several plays, including *The Mousetrap* (1952). **2 John (Reginald Halliday).** 1898–1953, British murderer. His trial influenced legislation regarding the death penalty after he was found guilty of a murder for which Timothy Evans had been hanged. **3 Linford** ('lɪnfəd). born 1960, British athlete: Commonwealth (1990), Olympic (1992), World (1993), and European (1994) 100 metres gold medallist.

Christina (krɪ'stiːnə) *n* 1626–89, queen of Sweden (1632–54), daughter of Gustavus Adolphus, noted particularly for her patronage of literature.

Christine de Pisan (*French* krɪstin də pizɑ̃) *n* ?1364–?1430, French poet and prose writer, born in Venice. Her works include ballads, rondeaux, lays, and a biography of Charles V of France.

Christlike ('kraɪstˌlaɪk) *adj* resembling or showing the spirit of Jesus Christ. ▸ **'Christˌlikeness** *n*

Christmas ('krɪsməs) *n* **1a** the annual commemoration by Christians of the birth of Jesus Christ on Dec. 25. **1b** Also called: **Christmas Day.** Dec. 25, observed as a day of secular celebrations when gifts and greetings are exchanged. **1c** (*as modifier*): *Christmas celebrations.* **2** Also called: **Christmas Day.** (in England, Wales and Ireland) Dec. 25, one of the four quarter days. Compare **Lady Day, Midsummer's Day, Michaelmas. 3** Also called: **Christmastide.** the season of Christmas extending from Dec. 24 (Christmas Eve) to Jan. 6 (the festival of the Epiphany or Twelfth Night). [Old English *Crīstes mæsse* MASS of CHRIST]

Christmas beetle *n* any of various greenish-gold Australian scarab beetles of the genus *Anoplognathus,* which are common in summer.

Christmas box *n* a tip or present given at Christmas, esp. to postmen, tradesmen, etc.

Christmas cactus *n* a Brazilian cactus, *Schlumbergera* (formerly *Zygocactus*) *truncatus,* widely cultivated as an ornamental for its showy red flowers.

Christmas card *n* a greeting card sent at Christmas.

Christmas disease *n* a relatively mild type of haemophilia, caused by lack of a protein (**Christmas factor**) implicated in the process of blood clotting. [C20: named after S. *Christmas,* the first patient suffering from the disease who was examined in detail]

Christmas Eve *n* the evening or the whole day before Christmas Day.

Christmas Island *n* **1** the former name (until 1981) of **Kiritimati. 2** an island in the Indian Ocean, south of Java: administered by Singapore (1900–58), now by Australia; phosphate mining. Pop.: 2500 (1994 est.). Area: 135 sq. km (52 sq. miles).

Christmas pudding *n Brit.* a rich steamed pudding containing suet, dried fruit, spices, brandy, etc., served at Christmas. Also called: **plum pudding.**

Christmas rose *n* an evergreen ranunculaceous plant, *Helleborus niger,* of S Europe and W Asia, with white or pinkish winter-blooming flowers. Also called: **hellebore, winter rose.**

Christmas stocking *n* a stocking hung up by children on Christmas Eve for Santa Claus to fill with presents.

Christmassy ('krɪsməsɪ) *adj* of, relating to, or suitable for Christmas.

Christmastide ('krɪsməs,taɪd) *n* another name for **Christmas** (sense 3).

Christmas tree *n* **1** an evergreen tree or an imitation of one, decorated as part of Christmas celebrations. **2** Also called: **Christmas bush.** *Austral.* any of various trees or shrubs flowering at Christmas and used for decoration.

Christo- *combining form.* indicating or relating to Christ: *Christology.*

Christoff ('krɪstɒf) *n* **Boris.** 1919–93, Bulgarian bass-baritone, noted esp. for his performance in the title role of Mussorgsky's *Boris Godunov.*

Christology (krɪ'stɒlədʒɪ, kraɪ-) *n* the branch of theology concerned with the person, attributes, and deeds of Christ. ▸ **Christological** (,krɪstə'lɒdʒɪk°l) *adj* ▸ **Chris'tologist** *n*

Christophe (*French* kristɔf) *n* **Henri** (ɑ̃ri). 1767–1820, Haitian revolutionary leader; king of Haiti (1811–20).

Christopher ('krɪstəfə) *n* **Saint.** 3rd century A.D., Christian martyr; patron saint of travellers.

Christ's-thorn *n* any of several plants of SW Asia, such as *Paliurus spina-christi* and the jujube, that have thorny stems and are popularly believed to have been used for Christ's Crown of Thorns.

Christy *or* **Christie** ('krɪstɪ) *n, pl* **-ties.** *Skiing.* a turn in which the body is swung sharply round with the skis parallel, originating in Norway and used for stopping, slowing down, or changing direction quickly. **[C20:** shortened from CHRISTIANIA**]**

chroma ('krəʊmə) *n* **1** the attribute of a colour that enables an observer to judge how much chromatic colour it contains irrespective of achromatic colour present. See also **saturation** (sense 4). **2** (in colour television) the colour component in a composite coded signal. **[C19:** from Greek *khrōma* colour**]**

chromakey ('krəʊmə,ki:) *n* (in colour television) a special effect in which a coloured background can be eliminated and a different background substituted. Also called: **colour separation overlay.**

chromate ('krəʊ,meɪt) *n* any salt or ester of chromic acid. Simple chromate salts contain the divalent ion, CrO_4^{2-}, and are orange.

chromatic (krə'mætɪk) *adj* **1** of, relating to, or characterized by a colour or colours. **2** *Music.* **2a** involving the sharpening or flattening of notes or the use of such notes in chords and harmonic progressions. **2b** of or relating to the chromatic scale or an instrument capable of producing it: *a chromatic harmonica.* **2c** of or relating to chromaticism. Compare **diatonic. [C17:** from Greek *khrōmatikos,* from *khrōma* colour**]** ▸ **chro'matically** *adv* ▸ **chro'maticism** *n*

chromatic aberration *n* a defect in a lens system in which different wavelengths of light are focused at different distances because they are refracted through different angles. It produces a blurred image with coloured fringes.

chromatic adaptation *n Botany.* the alteration by photosynthesizing organisms of the proportions of their photosynthetic pigments in response to the intensity and colour of the available light, as shown by algae in the littoral zone, which change from green to red as the zone is descended.

chromatic colour *n Physics.* a formal term for **colour** (sense 2).

chromaticity (,krəʊmə'tɪsɪtɪ) *n* the quality of a colour or light with reference to its purity and its dominant wavelength.

chromaticity coordinates *pl n Physics.* three numbers used to specify a colour, each of which is equal to one of the three tristimulus values divided by their sum. Symbols: *x, y, z.*

chromaticity diagram *n Physics.* a diagram in which values of two chromaticity coordinates are marked on a pair of rectangular axes, a point in the plane of these axes representing the chromaticity of any colour.

chromaticness (krəʊ'mætɪknɪs) *n Physics.* the attribute of colour that involves both hue and saturation.

chromatics (krəʊ'mætɪks) *or* **chromatology** (,krəʊmə'tɒlədʒɪ) *n* (*functioning as sing*) the science of colour. ▸ **chromatist** ('krəʊmətɪst) *or* **,chroma'tologist** *n*

chromatic scale *n* a twelve-note scale including all the semitones of the octave.

chromatid ('krəʊmətɪd) *n* either of the two strands into which a chromosome divides during mitosis. They separate to form daughter chromosomes at anaphase.

chromatin ('krəʊmətɪn) *n Cytology.* the part of the nucleus that consists of DNA, RNA, and proteins, forms the chromosomes, and stains with basic dyes. See also **euchromatin, heterochromatin.** ▸ **,chroma'tinic** *adj* ▸ **'chroma,toid** *adj*

chromato- *or before a vowel* **chromat-** *combining form.* **1** indicating colour or coloured: *chromatophore.* **2** indicating chromatin: *chromatolysis.* **[**from Greek *khrōma, khrōmat-* colour**]**

chromatogram ('krəʊmətə,græm, krəʊ'mæt-) *n* **1** a column or strip of material containing constituents of a mixture separated by chromatography. **2** a graph showing the quantity of a substance leaving a chromatography column as a function of time.

chromatography (,krəʊmə'tɒgrəfɪ) *n* the technique of separating and analysing the components of a mixture of liquids or gases by selective adsorption in, for example, a column of powder (**column chromatography**) or on a strip of paper (**paper chromatography**). See also **gas chromatography.** ▸ **,chroma'tographer** *n* ▸ **chromatographic** (,krəʊmətə'græfɪk) *adj* ▸ **,chromato'graphically** *adv*

chromatology (,krəʊmə'tɒlədʒɪ) *n* another name for **chromatics.**

chromatolysis (,krəʊmə'tɒlɪsɪs) *n Cytology.* the dissolution of chromatin in injured cells.

chromatophore ('krəʊmətə,fɔ:) *n* **1** a cell in the skin of frogs, chameleons, etc., in which pigment is concentrated or dispersed, causing the animal to change colour. **2** another name for **chromoplast.** ▸ **,chromato'phoric** *or* **chromatophorous** (,krəʊmə'tɒfərəs) *adj*

chrome (krəʊm) *n* **1a** another word for **chromium,** esp. when present in a pigment or dye. **1b** (*as modifier*): *a chrome dye.* **2** anything plated with chromium, such as fittings on a car body. **3** a pigment or dye that contains chromium. ◆ *vb* **4** to plate or be plated with chromium, usually by electroplating. **5** to treat or be treated with a chromium compound, as in dyeing or tanning. **[C19:** via French from Greek *khrōma* colour**]**

-chrome *n and adj combining form.* colour, coloured, or pigment: *monochrome.* **[**from Greek *khrōma* colour**]**

chrome alum *n* a violet-red crystalline substance, used as a mordant in dyeing. Formula: $KCr(SO_4)_2.12H_2O$.

chrome dioxide *n* another name for **chromium dioxide.**

chrome green *n* **1** any green pigment made by mixing lead chromate with Prussian blue. **2** any green pigment containing chromic oxide.

chromel ('krəʊmel) *n* a nickel-based alloy containing about 10 per cent chromium, used in heating elements. **[C20:** from CHRO(MIUM) + ME(TA)L**]**

chrome red *n* any red pigment used in paints, consisting of a mixture of lead chromate and lead oxide; basic lead chromate.

chrome steel *n* any of various hard rust-resistant steels containing chromium. Also called: **chromium steel.**

chrome tape *n* magnetic recording tape coated with chrome dioxide.

chrome yellow *n* any yellow pigment consisting of lead chromate mixed with lead sulphate.

chromic ('krəʊmɪk) *adj* **1** of or containing chromium in the trivalent state. **2** of or derived from chromic acid.

chromic acid *n* an unstable dibasic oxidizing acid known only in solution and in the form of chromate salts. Formula: H_2CrO_4.

chrominance ('krəʊmɪnəns) *n* **1** the quality of light that causes the sensation of colour. It is determined by comparison with a reference source of the same brightness and of known chromaticity. **2** the information that defines the colour (hue and saturation) of a television image, but not the brightness. **[C20:** from CHROMO- + LUMINANCE**]**

chromite ('krəʊmaɪt) *n* **1** a brownish-black mineral consisting of a ferrous chromic oxide in cubic crystalline form, occurring principally in basic igneous rocks: the only commercial source of chromium and its compounds. Formula: $FeCr_2O_4$. **2** a salt of chromous acid.

chromium ('krəʊmɪəm) *n* a hard grey metallic element that takes a high polish, occurring principally in chromite: used in steel alloys and electroplating to increase hardness and corrosion-resistance. Symbol: Cr; atomic no.: 24; atomic wt.: 51.9961; valency: 2, 3, or 6; relative density: 7.18–7.20; melting pt.: 1863±20°C; boiling pt.: 2672°C. **[C19:** from New Latin, from French: CHROME**]**

chromium dioxide *n* a chemical compound used as a magnetic coating on cassette tapes; chromium(IV) oxide. Formula: CrO_2. Also called (*not in technical usage*) **chrome dioxide.**

chromium steel *n* another name for **chrome steel.**

chromo ('krəʊməʊ) *n, pl* **-mos.** short for **chromolithograph.**

chromo- *or before a vowel* **chrom-** *combining form.* **1** indicating colour, coloured, or pigment: *chromogen.* **2** indicating chromium: *chromyl.* **[**from Greek *khrōma* colour**]**

chromogen ('krəʊmədʒən) *n* **1** a compound that forms coloured compounds on oxidation. **2** a substance that can be converted to a dye. **3** a bacterium that produces a pigment.

chromogenic (,krəʊmə'dʒenɪk) *adj* **1** producing colour. **2** of or relating to a chromogen. **3** *Photog.* involving the use of chromogens rather than silver halide during processing to produce the image: *chromogenic film.*

chromolithograph (,krəʊməʊ'lɪθə,grɑ:f, -,græf) *n* a picture produced by chromolithography.

chromolithography (,krəʊməʊlɪ'θɒgrəfɪ) *n* the process of making coloured prints by lithography. ▸ **,chromoli'thographer** *n* ▸ **chromolithographic** (,krəʊməʊlɪθə'græfɪk) *adj*

chromomere ('krəʊmə,mɪə) *n Cytology.* any of the dense areas of chromatin along the length of a chromosome during the early stages of cell division.

chromonema (,krəʊmə'ni:mə) *n, pl* **-mata** (-mətə). *Cytology.* **1** the coiled mass of threads within a nucleus at cell division. **2** a coiled chromatin thread within a single chromosome. **[C20:** from CHROMO- + Greek *nēma* thread, yarn**]** ▸ **,chromo'nemal, chromonematic** (,krəʊməʊnɪ'mætɪk), *or* **,chromo'nemic** *adj*

chromophore ('krəʊmə,fɔ:) *n* a group of atoms in a chemical compound that are responsible for the colour of the compound. ▸ **,chromo'phoric** *or* **,chromo'phorous** *adj*

chromoplast ('krəʊmə,plæst) *n* a coloured plastid in a plant cell, esp. one containing carotenoids.

chromoprotein (,krəʊməʊ'prəʊti:n) *n* any of a group of conjugated proteins, such as haemoglobin, in which the protein is joined to a coloured group, usually a metallic porphyrin.

chromosome ('krəʊmə,səʊm) *n* any of the microscopic rod-shaped structures that appear in a cell nucleus during cell division, consisting of nucleoprotein arranged into units (genes) that are responsible for the transmission of hereditary characteristics. See also **homologous chromosomes.** ▸ **ˌchromoˈsomal** *adj* ▸ **ˌchromoˈsomally** *adv*

chromosome band *n* any of the transverse bands that appear on a chromosome after staining. The banding pattern is unique to each type of chromosome, allowing characterization.

chromosome map *n* a graphic representation of the positions of genes on chromosomes, obtained by observation of chromosome bands or by determining the degree of linkage between genes. See also **genetic map.** ▸ **chromosome mapping** *n*

chromosome number *n* the number of chromosomes present in each somatic cell, which is constant for any one species of plant or animal. In the reproductive cells this number is halved. See also **diploid** (sense 1), **haploid.**

chromosphere (ˈkrəʊməˌsfɪə) *n* a gaseous layer of the sun's atmosphere extending from the photosphere to the corona and visible during a total eclipse of the sun. ▸ **chromospheric** (ˌkrəʊməˈsfɛrɪk) *adj*

chromous (ˈkrəʊməs) *adj* of or containing chromium in the divalent state.

chromyl (ˈkrəʊməl) *n* (*modifier*) of, consisting of, or containing the divalent radical CrO_2.

chron. *or* **chronol.** *abbrev. for:* **1** chronological. **2** chronology.

Chron. *Bible. abbrev. for* Chronicles.

chronaxie *or* **chronaxy** (ˈkrəʊnæksɪ) *n Physiol.* the minimum time required for excitation of a nerve or muscle when the stimulus is double the minimum (threshold) necessary to elicit a basic response. Compare **rheobase.** [C20: from French, from CHRONO- + Greek *axia* worth, from *axios* worthy, of equal weight]

chronic (ˈkrɒnɪk) *adj* **1** continuing for a long time; constantly recurring. **2** (of a disease) developing slowly, or of long duration. Compare **acute** (sense 7). **3** inveterate; habitual: *a chronic smoker.* **4** *Informal.* **4a** very bad: *the play was chronic.* **4b** very serious: *he left her in a chronic condition.* [C15: from Latin *chronicus* relating to time, from Greek *khronikos,* from *khronos* time] ▸ **ˈchronically** *adv* ▸ **chronicity** (krɒˈnɪsɪtɪ) *n*

chronic fatigue syndrome *n* a condition characterized by painful muscles and general weakness, sometimes persisting long after a viral illness. Also called: **myalgic encephalomyelitis, postviral syndrome.** Abbrev.: **CFS.**

chronicle (ˈkrɒnɪkᵊl) *n* **1** a record or register of events in chronological order. ◆ *vb* **2** (*tr*) to record in or as if in a chronicle. [C14: from Anglo-French *cronicle,* via Latin *chronica* (pl), from Greek *khronika* annals, from *khronikos* relating to time; see CHRONIC] ▸ **ˈchronicler** *n*

chronicle play *n* a drama based on a historical subject.

Chronicles (ˈkrɒnɪkᵊlz) *n* (*functioning as sing*) either of two historical books (**I** and **II Chronicles**) of the Old Testament.

chrono- *or before a vowel* **chron-** *combining form.* indicating time: *chronology; chronometer.* [from Greek *khronos* time]

chronobiology (ˌkrɒnəbaɪˈɒlədʒɪ, ˌkrəʊnə-) *n* the branch of biology concerned with the periodicity occurring in living organisms. See also **biological clock, circadian.** ▸ **ˌchronobiˈologist** *n*

chronogram (ˈkrɒnəˌgræm, ˈkrəʊnə-) *n* **1** a phrase or inscription in which letters such as M, C, X, L and V can be read as Roman numerals giving a date. **2** a record kept by a chronograph. ▸ **chronogrammatic** (ˌkrɒnəʊgrəˈmætɪk) *or* **ˌchronogramˈmatical** *adj* ▸ **ˌchronogramˈmatically** *adv*

chronograph (ˈkrɒnəˌgrɑːf, -ˌgræf, ˈkrəʊnə-) *n* **1** an accurate instrument for recording small intervals of time. **2** any timepiece, esp. a wristwatch designed for maximum accuracy. ▸ **chronographer** (krəˈnɒgrəfə) *n* ▸ **chronographic** (ˌkrɒnəˈgræfɪk) *adj* ▸ **ˌchronoˈgraphically** *adv*

chronological (ˌkrɒnəˈlɒdʒɪkᵊl, ˌkrəʊ-) *or* **chronologic** *adj* **1** (esp. of a sequence of events) arranged in order of occurrence. **2** relating to or in accordance with chronology. ▸ **ˌchronoˈlogically** *adv*

chronology (krəˈnɒlədʒɪ) *n, pl* **-gies. 1** the determination of the proper sequence of past events. **2** the arrangement of dates, events, etc., in order of occurrence. **3** a table or list of events arranged in order of occurrence. ▸ **chroˈnologist** *n*

chronometer (krəˈnɒmɪtə) *n* a timepiece designed to be accurate in all conditions of temperature, pressure, etc., used esp. at sea. ▸ **chronometric** (ˌkrɒnəˈmɛtrɪk) *or* **ˌchronoˈmetrical** *adj* ▸ **ˌchronoˈmetrically** *adv*

chronometry (krəˈnɒmɪtrɪ) *n* the science or technique of measuring time with extreme accuracy.

chronon (ˈkrəʊnɒn) *n* a unit of time equal to the time that a photon would take to traverse the diameter of an electron: about 10^{-24} seconds.

chronoscope (ˈkrɒnəˌskəʊp, ˈkrəʊnə-) *n* an instrument that registers small intervals of time on a dial, cathode-ray tube, etc. ▸ **chronoscopic** (ˌkrɒnəˈskɒpɪk, ˌkrəʊnə-) *adj* ▸ **ˌchronoˈscopically** *adv*

-chroous *or* **-chroic** *adj combining form.* coloured in a specified way: *isochroous.* [from Greek *khrōs* skin, complexion, colour]

chrysalid (ˈkrɪsəlɪd) *n* **1** another name for **chrysalis.** ◆ *adj also* **chrysalidal** (krɪˈsælɪdᵊl). **2** of or relating to a chrysalis.

chrysalis (ˈkrɪsəlɪs) *n, pl* **chrysalises** *or* **chrysalides** (krɪˈsælɪˌdiːz). **1** the obtect pupa of a moth or butterfly. **2** anything in the process of developing. [C17: from Latin *chrȳsallis,* from Greek *khrusallis,* from *khrusos* gold, of Semitic origin; compare Hebrew *harūz* gold]

chrysanthemum (krɪˈsænθəməm) *n* **1** any widely cultivated plant of the genus *Chrysanthemum,* esp. *C. morifolium* of China, having brightly coloured showy flower heads: family *Compositae* (composites). **2** any other plant of the genus *Chrysanthemum,* such as oxeye daisy. [C16: from Latin: marigold, from Greek *khrusanthemon,* from *khrusos* gold + *anthemon* flower]

chrysarobin (ˌkrɪsəˈrəʊbɪn) *n* a tasteless odourless powder containing anthraquinone derivatives of araroba, formerly used medicinally to treat chronic skin conditions. [C20: from CHRYSO- (referring to its golden colour) + ARAROBA + -IN]

chryselephantine (ˌkrɪselɪˈfæntɪn) *adj* (of ancient Greek statues) made of or overlaid with gold and ivory. [C19: from Greek *khruselephantinos,* from *khrusos* gold + *elephas* ivory; see ELEPHANT]

chryso- *or before a vowel* **chrys-** *combining form.* indicating gold or the colour of gold: *chryselephantine; chrysolite.* [from Greek *khrusos* gold]

chrysoberyl (ˈkrɪsəˌbɛrɪl) *n* a rare very hard greenish-yellow mineral consisting of beryllium aluminate in orthorhombic crystalline form and occurring in coarse granite: used as a gemstone in the form of cat's eye and alexandrite. Formula: $BeAl_2O_4$.

chrysolite (ˈkrɪsəˌlaɪt) *n* a brown or yellowish-green olivine consisting of magnesium iron silicate: used as a gemstone (see **peridot**). Formula: $(Mg,Fe)_2SiO_4$. ▸ **chrysolitic** (ˌkrɪsəˈlɪtɪk) *adj*

chrysoprase (ˈkrɪsəˌpreɪz) *n* an apple-green variety of chalcedony: a gemstone. [C13 *crisopace,* from Old French, from Latin *chrȳsoprasus,* from Greek *khrusoprasos,* from CHRYSO- + *prason* leek]

Chrysostom (ˈkrɪsəstəm) *n* Saint **John.** ?345–407 A.D., Greek patriarch; archbishop of Constantinople (398–404). Feast day: Sept. 13 or Nov. 13.

chrysotile (ˈkrɪsətɪl) *n* a green, grey, or white fibrous mineral, a variety of serpentine, that is an important source of commercial asbestos. Formula: $Mg_3Si_2O_5(OH)_4$. [C20: from CHRYSO- + Greek *tilos* something plucked, shred, thread, from *tillein* to pluck]

chs. *abbrev. for* chapters.

chthonian (ˈθəʊnɪən) *or* **chthonic** (ˈθɒnɪk) *adj* of or relating to the underworld. [C19: from Greek *khthonios* in or under the earth, from *khthōn* earth]

Chuang-tzu (ˈtʃwæŋ ˈtsuː) *n* a variant transliteration of the Chinese name for **Zhuangzi.**

chub (tʃʌb) *n, pl* **chub** *or* **chubs. 1** a common European freshwater cyprinid game fish, *Leuciscus* (or *Squalius*) *cephalus,* having a cylindrical dark greenish body. **2** any of various North American fishes, esp. certain whitefishes and minnows. [C15: of unknown origin]

Chubb (tʃʌb) *n Trademark.* a type of patent lock containing a device that sets the bolt immovably if the lock is picked.

chubby (ˈtʃʌbɪ) *adj* **-bier, -biest.** (esp. of the human form) plump and round. [C17: perhaps from CHUB, with reference to the plump shape of the fish] ▸ **ˈchubbiness** *n*

Chu Chiang (ˈtʃuː ˈkjæŋ, kaɪˈæŋ) *n* a variant transliteration of the Chinese name for the **Zhu Jiang.**

Ch'ü Ch'iu-pai (ˈtʃuː ˈtʃjuːˈbeɪ) *n* a variant transliteration of the Chinese name for **Qu Qiu Bai.**

chuck[1] (tʃʌk) *vb* (*mainly tr*) **1** *Informal.* to throw. **2** to pat affectionately, esp. under the chin. **3** (sometimes foll. by *in* or *up*) *Informal.* to give up; reject: *he chucked up his job; she chucked her boyfriend.* **4** (*intr*) (usually foll. by *up*) *Slang. chiefly U.S.* to vomit. **5 chuck off at.** *Austral. and N.Z. informal.* to abuse or make fun of. ◆ *n* **6** a throw or toss. **7** a playful pat under the chin. **8 the chuck.** *Informal.* dismissal. ◆ See also **chuck in, chuck out.** [C16: of unknown origin]

chuck[2] (tʃʌk) *n* **1** Also called: **chuck steak.** a cut of beef extending from the neck to the shoulder blade. **2a** Also called: **three jaw chuck.** a device that holds a workpiece in a lathe or tool in a drill, having a number of adjustable jaws geared to move in unison to centralize the workpiece or tool. **2b** Also called: **four jaw chuck, independent jaw chuck.** a similar device having independently adjustable jaws for holding an unsymmetrical workpiece. [C17: variant of CHOCK]

chuck[3] (tʃʌk) *vb* **1** (*intr*) a less common word for **cluck** (sense 2). ◆ *n* **2** a clucking sound. **3** a term of endearment. [C14 *chukken* to cluck, of imitative origin]

chuck[4] (tʃʌk) *n Canadian W coast.* **1** a large body of water. **2** short for **saltchuck** (the sea). [C19: from Chinook Jargon, from Nootka *chauk*]

chuck-full *adj* a less common spelling of **chock-full.**

chuckie (ˈtʃʌkɪ) *n Scot. and N.Z.* a small stone. [probably from CHUCK[1]]

chuck in *vb* (*adv*) *Informal.* **1** (*tr*) *Brit.* to abandon or give up: *chuck in a hopeless attempt.* **2** (*intr*) *Austral.* to contribute to the cost of something.

chuckle (ˈtʃʌkᵊl) *vb* (*intr*) **1** to laugh softly or to oneself. **2** (of animals, esp. hens) to make a clucking sound. ◆ *n* **3** a partly suppressed laugh. [C16: probably from CHUCK[3]] ▸ **ˈchuckler** *n* ▸ **ˈchucklingly** *adv*

chucklehead (ˈtʃʌkᵊlˌhɛd) *n Informal.* a stupid person; blockhead; dolt. ▸ **ˈchuckleˌheaded** *adj* ▸ **ˈchuckleˌheadedness** *n*

chuck out *vb* (*tr, adv;* often foll. by *of*) *Informal.* to eject forcibly (from); throw out (of): *he was chucked out of the lobby.*

chuck wagon *n* a wagon carrying provisions and cooking utensils for men, such as cowboys, who work in the open. [C19: perhaps from CHUCK[2] (beef, food)]

chuckwalla (ˈtʃʌkˌwɒlə) *n* a lizard, *Sauromalus obesus,* that has an inflatable body and inhabits desert regions of the southwestern U.S.: family *Iguanidae* (iguanas). [from Mexican Spanish *chacahuala,* from Shoshonean *tcaxxwal*]

chuck-will's-widow *n* a large North American nightjar, *Caprimulgus carolinensis,* similar to the whippoorwill.

chuddar, chudder, chuddah, *or* **chador** (ˈtʃʌdə) *n* a large shawl or veil worn by Muslim or Hindu women that covers them from head to foot. [from Hindi *caddar,* from Persian *chaddar*]

Chudskoye Ozero (*Russian* ˈtʃutskəjɪ ˈɔzɪrə) *n* the Russian name for Lake **Peipus.**

chufa (ˈtʃuːfə) *n* a sedge, *Cyperus esculentus,* of warm regions of the Old World, with nutlike edible tubers. [C19: from Old Spanish: a morsel, joke, from *chufar* to joke, from *chuflar* to deride, ultimately from Latin *sībilāre* to whistle]

chuff[1] (tʃʌf) *n* **1** a puffing sound of or as if of a steam engine. ◆ *vb* **2** (*intr*) to move while emitting such sounds: *the train chuffed on its way.* [C20: of imitative origin]

chuff[2] (tʃʌf) *n Dialect.* a boor; churl; sullen fellow. [C17: from obsolete *chuff* (n) fat cheek, of obscure origin]

chuff[3] (tʃʌf) *vb (tr; usually passive) Brit. slang.* to please or delight: *he was chuffed by his pay rise.* [probably from *chuff* (adj) pleased, happy (earlier: chubby), from C16 *chuff* (obsolete n) a fat cheek, of unknown origin] ► **'chuffed** *adj*

chug (tʃʌg) *n* **1** a short dull sound, esp. one that is rapidly repeated, such as that made by an engine. ◆ *vb* **chugs, chugging, chugged. 2** (*intr*) (of an engine, etc.) to operate while making such sounds. [C19: of imitative origin]

chukar (tʃʌ'kɑː) *n* a common Indian partridge, *Alectoris chukar* (or *graeca*), having red legs and bill and a black-barred sandy plumage. [from Hindi *cakor,* from Sanskrit *cakora,* probably of imitative origin]

Chukchi *or* **Chukchee** ('tʃuktʃɪ) *n* **1** (*pl* **-chi, -chis** *or* **-chee, -chees**) a member of a people of the Chukchi Peninsula. **2** the language of this people, related only to some of the smaller aboriginal languages of Siberia.

Chukchi Peninsula ('tʃuktʃɪ) *n* a peninsula in the extreme NE of Russia, in NE Siberia: mainly tundra. Also called: **Chukots Peninsula** ('tʃukɒts).

Chukchi Sea *n* part of the Arctic Ocean, north of the Bering Strait between Asia and North America. Russian name: **Chukotskoye More** (tʃu'kɔtskəji 'mɔrji). Also called: **Chukots Sea** ('tʃukɒts).

Chu Kiang ('tʃuː 'kjæŋ, kaɪ'æŋ) *n* a variant transliteration of the Chinese name for the **Zhu Jiang.**

chukka *or U.S.* **chukker** ('tʃʌkə) *n Polo.* a period of continuous play, generally lasting 7½ minutes. [C20: from Hindi *cakkar,* from Sanskrit *cakra* wheel, circle]

chukka boot *or* **chukka** ('tʃʌkə) *n* an ankle-high boot made of suede or rubber and worn for playing polo.

chum[1] (tʃʌm) *n* **1** *Informal.* a close friend. ◆ *vb* **chums, chumming, chummed. 2** (*intr;* usually foll. by *up with*) to be or become an intimate friend (of). **3** (*tr*) *Scot.* to accompany: *I'll chum you home.* [C17 (meaning: a person sharing rooms with another): probably shortened from *chamber fellow,* originally student slang (Oxford); compare CRONY]

chum[2] (tʃʌm) *n Angling, chiefly U.S. and Canadian.* chopped fish, meal, etc., used as groundbait. [C19: origin uncertain]

chum[3] (tʃum) *n* a Pacific salmon, *Oncorhynchus keta.* [from Chinook Jargon *tsum* spots, marks, from Chinook]

chumash *Hebrew.* (*Hebrew* xu'maʃ; *Yiddish* 'xuməʃ) *n Judaism.* a printed book containing one of the Five Books of Moses. [literally: a fifth (part of the Torah)]

chummy ('tʃʌmɪ) *adj* **-mier, -miest.** *Informal.* friendly. ► **'chummily** *adv* ► **'chumminess** *n*

chump[1] (tʃʌmp) *n* **1** *Informal.* a stupid person. **2** a thick heavy block of wood. **3a** the thick blunt end of anything, esp. of a piece of meat. **3b** (*as modifier*): *a chump chop.* **4** *Brit. slang.* the head (esp. in the phrase **off one's chump**). [C18: perhaps a blend of CHUNK and LUMP[1]]

chump[2] (tʃʌmp) *vb* a less common word for **chomp.**

chumping ('tʃʌmpɪŋ) *n Yorkshire dialect.* collecting wood for bonfires on Guy Fawkes Day. [from CHUMP[1] (sense 2)]

chunder ('tʃʌndə) *Slang, chiefly Austral.* ◆ *vb* (*intr*) **1** to vomit. ◆ *n* **2** vomit. [C20: of uncertain origin]

chunderous ('tʃʌndərəs) *adj Austral. slang.* nauseating.

Chungjin ('tʃʌŋ'dʒɪn) *n* a variant spelling of **Chŏngjin.**

Chungking ('tʃuŋ'kɪŋ, 'tʃʌŋ-) *or* **Ch'ung-ch'ing** ('tʃuŋ'tʃɪŋ, 'tʃʌŋ-) *n* a variant transliteration of the Chinese name for **Chongqing.**

chunk (tʃʌŋk) *n* **1** a thick solid piece, as of meat, wood, etc. **2** a considerable amount. [C17: variant of CHUCK[2]]

chunking ('tʃʌŋkɪŋ) *n Psychol.* the grouping together of a number of items by the mind, after which they can be remembered as a single item, such as a word or a musical phrase.

chunky ('tʃʌŋkɪ) *adj* **chunkier, chunkiest. 1** thick and short. **2** consisting of or containing thick pieces: *chunky dog food.* **3** *Chiefly Brit.* (of clothes, esp. knitwear) made of thick bulky material. ► **'chunkily** *adv* ► **'chunkiness** *n*

Chunnel ('tʃʌnᵊl) *n Informal.* a rail tunnel beneath the English Channel, linking England and France, opened in 1994. [C20: from CH(ANNEL) + (T)UNNEL]

chunter ('tʃʌntə) *vb* (*intr* often foll. by *on*) *Brit. informal.* to mutter or grumble incessantly in a meaningless fashion. [C16: probably of imitative origin]

chupatti *or* **chupatty** (tʃə'pætɪ, -'pʌtɪ, -'pɑːtɪ) *n, pl* **-patti, -pattis, -patties.** variant spellings of **chapati.**

chuppah *or* **huppah** ('hupə) *n Judaism.* **1** the canopy under which a marriage is performed. **2** the wedding ceremony as distinct from the celebration. [from Hebrew]

Chuquisaca (*Spanish* tʃuki'saka) *n* the former name (until 1839) of **Sucre**[1].

Chur (*German* kuːr) *n* a city in E Switzerland, capital of Grisons canton. Pop.: 30 236 (1990). Ancient name: **Curia Rhaetorum** ('kuːrɪə riː'təurəm, 'kjuː-). French name: **Coire.**

Churban *or* **Hurban** *Hebrew.* (*Hebrew* xuːr'bɑn; *Yiddish* 'xuːrbᵊn) *n Judaism.* **1** the destruction of the Temple in Jerusalem, first by the Babylonians in 587 B.C. and again by the Romans in 70 A.D. **2** another name for **holocaust** (sense 2). [literally: destruction]

church (tʃɜːtʃ) *n* **1** a building designed for public forms of worship, esp. Christian worship. **2** an occasion of public worship. **3** the clergy as distinguished from the laity. **4** (*usually cap.*) institutionalized forms of religion as a political or social force: *conflict between Church and State.* **5** (*usually cap.*) the collective body of all Christians. **6** (*often cap.*) a particular Christian denomination or group of Christian believers. **7** (*often cap.*) the Christian religion. **8** (in Britain) the practices or doctrines of the Church of England and similar denominations. Compare **chapel** (sense 4b). Related adj: **ecclesiastical.** ◆ *vb* (*tr*) **9** *Church of England.* to bring (someone, esp. a woman after childbirth) to church for special ceremonies. **10** *U.S.* to impose church discipline upon. [Old English *cirice,* from Late Greek *kurikon,* from Greek *kuriakon* (*dōma*) the Lord's (house), from *kuriakos* of the master, from *kurios* master, from *kuros* power]

Church Army *n* a voluntary Anglican organization founded in 1882 to assist the parish clergy.

Church Commissioners *pl n Brit.* a group of representatives of Church and State that administers the endowments and property of the Church of England.

churchgoer ('tʃɜːtʃˌgəuə) *n* **1** a person who attends church regularly. **2** an adherent of an established Church in contrast to a Nonconformist. ► **'church-ˌgoing** *n, adj*

Churchill[1] ('tʃɜːtʃɪl) *n* **1** a river in E Canada, rising in SE Labrador and flowing north and southeast over Churchill Falls, then east to the Atlantic. Length: about 1000 km (600 miles). Former name: **Hamilton River. 2** a river in central Canada, rising in NW Saskatchewan and flowing east through several lakes to Hudson Bay. Length: about 1600 km (1000 miles).

Churchill[2] ('tʃɜːtʃɪl) *n* **1 Charles.** 1731–64, British poet, noted for his polemical satires. His works include *The Rosciad* (1761) and *The Prophecy of Famine* (1763). **2 John.** See (1st Duke of) **Marlborough. 3** Lord **Randolph.** 1849–95, British Conservative politician: secretary of state for India (1885–86) and chancellor of the Exchequer and leader of the House of Commons (1886). **4** his son, Sir **Winston** (**Leonard Spencer**). 1874–1965, British Conservative statesman, orator, and writer, noted for his leadership during World War II. He held various posts under both Conservative and Liberal governments, including 1st Lord of the Admiralty (1911–15), before becoming prime minister (1940–45; 1951–55). His writings include *The World Crisis* (1923–29), *Marlborough* (1933–38), *The Second World War* (1948–54), and *History of the English-Speaking Peoples* (1956–58): Nobel prize for literature 1953.

Churchill Falls *pl n* a waterfall in E Canada, in SW Labrador on the Churchill River: site of one of the largest hydroelectric power projects in the world. Height: 75 m (245 ft.). Former name: **Grand Falls.**

church key *n U.S.* a device with a triangular point at one end for making holes in the tops of cans.

churchly ('tʃɜːtʃlɪ) *adj* appropriate to, associated with, or suggestive of church life and customs. ► **'churchliness** *n*

churchman ('tʃɜːtʃmən) *n, pl* **-men. 1** a clergyman. **2** a male practising member of a church. ► **'churchmanly** *adj* ► **'churchmanˌship** *n*

church mode *n Music.* a less common name for **mode** (sense 3a).

Church of Christ, Scientist *n* the official name for the **Christian Scientists.**

Church of England *n* the reformed established state Church in England, Catholic in order and basic doctrine, with the Sovereign as its temporal head.

Church of Jesus Christ of Latter-Day Saints *n* the official name for the Mormon Church.

Church of Rome *n* another name for the **Roman Catholic Church.**

Church of Scotland *n* the established church in Scotland, Calvinist in doctrine and Presbyterian in constitution.

church parade *n* a parade by servicemen or members of a uniformed organization for the purposes of attending religious services.

Church Slavonic *or* **Slavic** *n* Old Church Slavonic, esp. as preserved in the liturgical use of the Orthodox church.

church text *n* a heavy typeface in Gothic style.

churchwarden (ˌtʃɜːtʃ'wɔːdᵊn) *n* **1** *Church of England, Episcopal Church.* one of two assistants of a parish priest who administer the secular affairs of the church. **2** a long-stemmed tobacco pipe made of clay.

churchwoman ('tʃɜːtʃˌwumən) *n, pl* **-women.** a female practising member of a church.

churchy ('tʃɜːtʃɪ) *adj* **churchier, churchiest. 1** like a church, church service, etc. **2** excessively religious.

churchyard ('tʃɜːtʃˌjɑːd) *n* the grounds surrounding a church, usually used as a graveyard.

churchyard beetle *n* a blackish nocturnal ground beetle, *Blaps mucronata,* found in cellars and similar places.

churidars ('tʃuːrɪˌdɑːz) *pl n* long tight-fitting trousers, worn by Indian men and women. Also called: **churidar pyjamas.** [from Hindi]

churinga (tʃə'rɪŋgə) *n, pl* **-ga** *or* **-gas.** a sacred amulet of the native Australians. [from a native Australian language]

churl (tʃɜːl) *n* **1** a surly ill-bred person. **2** *Archaic.* a farm labourer. **3** a variant spelling of **ceorl.** [Old English *ceorl;* related to Old Norse *karl,* Middle Low German *kerle,* Greek *gerōn* old man]

churlish ('tʃɜːlɪʃ) *adj* **1** rude or surly. **2** of or relating to peasants. **3** miserly. ► **'churlishly** *adv* ► **'churlishness** *n*

churn (tʃɜːn) *n* **1** *Brit.* a large container for milk. **2** a vessel or machine in which cream or whole milk is vigorously agitated to produce butter. **3** any similar device. ◆ *vb* **4a** to stir or agitate (milk or cream) in order to make butter. **4b** to make (butter) by this process. **5** (sometimes foll. by *up*) to move or cause to move with agitation: *ideas churned in his head.* **6** (of a bank, broker, etc.) to encourage an investor or policyholder to change investments, endowment policies, etc., to increase commissions at the client's expense. **7** (of a government) to pay benefits to a wide category of people and claw it back by taxation from the well off. **8** to promote the turnover of existing subscribers leasing, and new subscribers joining, a cable television system. [Old English *ciern;* related to Old Norse *kjarni,* Middle Low German *kerne* churn, German dialect *Kern* cream] ► **'churner** *n*

churning ('tʃɜːnɪŋ) *n* **1** the quantity of butter churned at any one time. **2** the act, process, or effect of someone or something that churns.

churn out *vb (tr, adv) Informal.* **1** to produce (something) at a rapid rate: *to churn out ideas.* **2** to perform (something) mechanically: *to churn out a song.*

churr (tʃɜː) *vb, n* a variant spelling of **chirr.**

churrigueresque (ˌtʃʊərɪgəˈrɛsk) *or* **churrigueresco** *adj* of or relating to a style of baroque architecture of Spain in the late 17th and early 18th centuries. [C19: from Spanish *churrigueresco* in the style of José *Churriguera* (1650–1725), Spanish architect and sculptor]

chute[1] (ʃuːt) *n* **1** an inclined channel or vertical passage down which water, parcels, coal, etc., may be dropped. **2** a steep slope, used as a slide as for toboggans. **3** a slide into a swimming pool. **4** a narrow passageway through which animals file for branding, spraying, etc. **5** a rapid or waterfall. [C19: from Old French *cheoite,* feminine past participle of *cheoir* to fall, from Latin *cadere;* in some senses, a variant spelling of SHOOT]

chute[2] (ʃuːt) *n, vb Informal.* short for **parachute.** ▸ **ˈchutist** *n*

Chu Teh (ˈtʃuː ˈteɪ) *or* **Zhu De** *n* 1886–1976, Chinese military leader and politician; he became commander in chief of the Red Army (1931) and was chairman of the Standing Committee of the National People's Congress of the People's Republic of China (1959–76).

chutney (ˈtʃʌtnɪ) *n* a pickle of Indian origin, made from fruit, vinegar, spices, sugar, etc.: *mango chutney.* [C19: from Hindi *catnī,* of uncertain origin]

chutzpah *or* **hutzpah** (ˈxʊtspə) *n Informal.* shameless audacity; impudence. [C20: from Yiddish]

Chuvash (tʃʊˈvɑːʃ) *n* **1** (*pl* **-vash** *or* **-vashes**) a member of a Mongoloid people of Russia, living chiefly in the middle Volga region. **2** the language of this people, generally classed within the Turkic branch of the Altaic family.

Chuvash Republic *n* a constituent republic of W central Russia, in the middle Volga valley: generally low-lying with undulating plains and large areas of forest. Capital: Cheboksary. Pop.: 1 361 000 (1995 est.). Area: 18 300 sq. km (7064 sq. miles). Also called: **Chuvashia** (tʃuːˈvɑːʃɪə).

Chu Xi *or* **Chu Hsi** (ˈtʃuː ˈsiː) *n* 1130–1200, Chinese philosopher, known for his neo-Confucian commentaries the *Ssu shu* or *Four Books.*

chyack (ˈtʃaɪæk) *vb* a variant spelling of **chiack.**

chyle (kaɪl) *n* a milky fluid composed of lymph and emulsified fat globules, formed in the small intestine during digestion. [C17: from Late Latin *chȳlus,* from Greek *khulos* juice pressed from a plant; related to Greek *khein* to pour] ▸ **chylaceous** (kaɪˈleɪʃəs) *or* **ˈchylous** *adj*

chylomicron (ˌkaɪləʊˈmaɪkrɒn) *n Biochem.* a minute droplet of fat, found in blood and chyle, that is the form in which dietary fat is carried in these fluids.

chyme (kaɪm) *n* the thick fluid mass of partially digested food that leaves the stomach. [C17: from Late Latin *chȳmus,* from Greek *khumos* juice; compare CHYLE] ▸ **ˈchymous** *adj*

chymosin (ˈkaɪməsɪn) *n* another name for **rennin.** [C20: from CHYME + -OSE[2] + -IN]

chymotrypsin (ˌkaɪməʊˈtrɪpsɪn) *n* a powerful proteolytic enzyme secreted from the pancreas in the form of chymotrypsinogen, being converted to the active form by trypsin. [C20: from CHYME + TRYPSIN]

chymotrypsinogen (ˌkaɪməʊtrɪpˈsɪnədʒɪn) *n* the inactive precursor of chymotrypsin. [C20: from CHYMOTRYPSIN + -GEN]

chypre *French.* (ʃiprə) *n* a perfume made from sandalwood. [literally: Cyprus, where it perhaps originated]

Ci *symbol for* curie.

CI 1 *abbrev. for* Channel Islands. **2** *international car registration for* Côte d'Ivoire.

CIA *abbrev. for* Central Intelligence Agency; a federal U.S. bureau created in 1947 to coordinate and conduct espionage and intelligence activities.

ciabatta (tʃəˈbætə) *n* a type of open-textured bread made with olive oil. [C20: from Italian, literally: slipper]

Ciano (ˈtʃɑːnəʊ) *n* **Galeazzo,** full name *Conte Galeazzo Ciano di Cortellazzo.* 1903–44, Italian fascist politician; minister of foreign affairs (1936–43) and son-in-law of Mussolini, whose supporters shot him.

ciao *Italian.* (tʃau) *sentence substitute.* an informal word for **hello** or **goodbye.**

CIB (in New Zealand) *abbrev. for* Criminal Investigation Branch (of New Zealand police).

Cibber (ˈsɪbə) *n* **Colley** (ˈkɒlɪ). 1671–1757, English actor and dramatist; poet laureate (1730–57).

ciborium (sɪˈbɔːrɪəm) *n, pl* **-ria** (-rɪə). *Christianity.* **1** a goblet-shaped lidded vessel used to hold consecrated wafers in Holy Communion. **2** a freestanding canopy fixed over an altar and supported by four pillars. [C17: from Medieval Latin, from Latin: drinking cup, from Greek *kibōrion* cup-shaped seed vessel of the Egyptian lotus, hence, a cup]

cicada (sɪˈkɑːdə) *or* **cicala** *n, pl* **-das, -dae** (-diː) *or* **-las, -le** (-leɪ). any large broad insect of the homopterous family *Cicadidae,* most common in warm regions. Cicadas have membranous wings and the males produce a high-pitched drone by vibration of a pair of drumlike abdominal organs. [C19: from Latin]

cicala (sɪˈkɑːlə; *Italian* tʃiˈkala) *n, pl* **-las** *or* **-le** (-leɪ; *Italian* -le). another name for **cicada.** [C19: from Italian, from Latin: CICADA]

cicatricle (ˈsɪkəˌtrɪkᵊl) *n* **1** *Zoology.* the blastoderm in the egg of a bird. **2** *Biology.* any small scar or mark. [C17: from Latin *cicātrīcula* a little scar, from CICATRIX]

cicatrix (ˈsɪkətrɪks) *n, pl* **cicatrices** (ˌsɪkəˈtraɪsiːz). **1** the tissue that forms in a wound during healing; scar. **2** a scar on a plant indicating the former point of attachment of a part, esp. a leaf. [C17: from Latin: scar, of obscure origin] ▸ **cicatricial** (ˌsɪkəˈtrɪʃəl) *adj* ▸ **cicatricose** (sɪˈkætrɪˌkəʊs, ˈsɪkə-) *adj*

cicatrize *or* **cicatrise** (ˈsɪkəˌtraɪz) *vb* (of a wound or defect in tissue) to close or be closed by scar formation; heal. ▸ **ˌcicaˈtrizant** *or* **ˌcicaˈtrisant** *adj* ▸ **ˌcicatriˈzation** *or* **ˌcicatriˈsation** *n* ▸ **ˈcicaˌtrizer** *or* **ˈcicaˌtriser** *n*

cicely (ˈsɪsəlɪ) *n, pl* **-lies.** short for **sweet cicely.** [C16: from Latin *seselis,* from Greek, of obscure origin; influenced in spelling by the English proper name *Cicely*]

cicero (ˈsɪsəˌrəʊ) *n, pl* **-ros.** a measure for type that is somewhat larger than the pica. [C19: from its first being used in a 15th-century edition of CICERO]

Cicero (ˈsɪsəˌrəʊ) *n* **Marcus Tullius** (ˈmɑːkəs ˈtʌlɪəs). 106–43 B.C., Roman consul, orator, and writer. He foiled Catiline's conspiracy (63) and was killed by Mark Antony's agents after he denounced Antony in the *Philippics.* His writings are regarded as a model of Latin prose. Formerly known in English as **Tully.**

cicerone (ˌsɪsəˈrəʊnɪ, ˌtʃɪtʃ-) *n, pl* **-nes** *or* **-ni** (-nɪ). a person who conducts and informs sightseers. [C18: from Italian: antiquarian scholar, guide, after CICERO, alluding to the eloquence and erudition of these men]

Ciceronian (ˌsɪsəˈrəʊnɪən) *adj* **1** of or resembling Cicero or his rhetorical style; eloquent. **2** (of literary style) characterized by the use of antithesis and long periods.

cichlid (ˈsɪklɪd) *n* **1** any tropical freshwater percoid fish of the family *Cichlidae,* which includes the mouthbrooders. Cichlids are popular aquarium fishes. ◆ *adj* **2** of, relating to, or belonging to the *Cichlidae.* [C19: from New Latin *Cichlidae,* ultimately from Greek *kikhlē* a sea fish] ▸ **ˈcichloid** *adj*

cicisbeo *Italian.* (tʃitʃizˈbeːo) *n, pl* **-bei** (-ˈbeːi). the escort or lover of a married woman, esp. in 18th-century Italy. [C18: Italian, of uncertain origin]

Cid (sɪd; *Spanish* θið) *n* **El** *or* **the.** original name *Rodrigo Díaz de Vivar.* ?1043–99, Spanish soldier and hero of the wars against the Moors.

CID (in Britain) *abbrev. for* Criminal Investigation Department; the detective division of a police force.

-cide *n combining form.* **1** indicating a person or thing that kills: *insecticide.* **2** indicating a killing; murder: *homicide.* [from Latin *-cīda* (agent), *-cīdium* (act), from *caedere* to kill] ▸ **-cidal** *adj combining form.*

cider *or* **cyder** (ˈsaɪdə) *n* **1** Also called (U.S.): **hard cider.** an alcoholic drink made from the fermented juice of apples. **2** Also called: **sweet cider.** *U.S. and Canadian.* an unfermented drink made from apple juice. [C14: from Old French *cisdre,* via Medieval Latin, from Late Greek *sikera* strong drink, from Hebrew *shēkhār*]

ci-devant *French.* (sidəvɑ̃) *adj* (esp. of an office-holder) former; recent. [literally: heretofore]

Cie *abbrev. for* compagnie. [French: company]

CIE *abbrev. for:* **1** Commission Internationale de l'Éclairage. [French: International Lighting Commission] **2** Companion of the Indian Empire. **3** (in the Irish Republic) Coras Iompair Eireann. [Irish Gaelic: Transport Organization of Ireland]

Cienfuegos (*Spanish* θienˈfueɣos) *n* a port in S Cuba, on **Cienfuegos Bay.** Pop.: 132 038 (1994 est.).

c.i.f. *or* **CIF** *abbrev. for* cost, insurance, and freight (included in the price quoted).

c.i.f.c.i. *abbrev. for* cost, insurance, freight, commission, and interest (included in the price quoted).

CIFE (in Britain) *abbrev. for* Colleges and Institutes for Further Education.

cig (sɪg) *or* **ciggy** (ˈsɪgɪ) *n, pl* **cigs** *or* **ciggies.** *Informal.* a cigarette.

cigar (sɪˈgɑː) *n* a cylindrical roll of cured tobacco leaves, for smoking. [C18: from Spanish *cigarro,* perhaps from Mayan *sicar* to smoke]

cigarette *or U.S. (sometimes)* **cigaret** (ˌsɪgəˈrɛt) *n* a short tightly rolled cylinder of tobacco, wrapped in thin paper and often having a filter tip, for smoking. Shortened forms: **cig, ciggy.** [C19: from French, literally: a little CIGAR]

cigarette card *n* a small picture card, formerly given away with cigarettes, now collected as a hobby.

cigarette end *n* the part of a cigarette that is held in the mouth and that remains unsmoked after it is finished.

cigarette holder *n* a mouthpiece of wood, ivory, etc., used for holding a cigarette while it is smoked.

cigarette lighter *n* See **lighter**[1].

cigarette paper *n* a piece of thin paper rolled around tobacco to form a cigarette.

cigarillo (ˌsɪgəˈrɪləʊ) *n, pl* **-los.** a small cigar, often only slightly larger than a cigarette.

CIGS (in Britain, formerly) *abbrev. for* Chief of the Imperial General Staff.

cilia (ˈsɪlɪə) *n* the plural of **cilium.**

ciliary (ˈsɪlɪərɪ) *adj* **1** of or relating to cilia. **2** of or relating to the ciliary body.

ciliary body *n* the part of the vascular tunic of the eye that connects the choroid with the iris.

ciliate (ˈsɪlɪɪt, -eɪt) *adj* **1** Also: **ˈciliˌated.** possessing or relating to cilia: *a ciliate epithelium.* **2** of or relating to protozoans of the phylum *Ciliophora,* which have an outer layer of cilia. ◆ *n* **3** a protozoan of the phylum *Ciliophora.* ▸ **ˌciliˈation** *n*

cilice (ˈsɪlɪs) *n* a haircloth fabric or garment. [Old English *cilic,* from Latin *cilicium* shirt made of Cilician goats' hair, from Greek *kilikion,* from *Kilikia* CILICIA]

Cilicia (sɪˈlɪʃɪə) *n* an ancient region and former kingdom of SE Asia Minor, between the Taurus Mountains and the Mediterranean: corresponds to the region around present-day Adana. ▸ **Ciˈlician** *adj, n*

Cilician Gates *pl n* a pass in S Turkey, over the Taurus Mountains. Turkish name: **Gülek Bogaz.**

ciliolate (ˈsɪlɪəlɪt, -ˌleɪt) *adj* covered with minute hairs, as some plants. [C19: from New Latin *ciliolum,* diminutive of CILIUM]

cilium (ˈsɪlɪəm) *n, pl* **cilia** (ˈsɪlɪə). **1** any of the short threads projecting from the surface of a cell, organism, etc., whose rhythmic beating causes movement of the organism or of the surrounding fluid. **2** the technical name for **eyelash.** [C18: New Latin, from Latin: (lower) eyelid, eyelash]

cill (sɪl) *n Brit.* a variant spelling (used in the building industry) for **sill** (senses 1–4).

Çiller ('ʃɪlə) *n* **Tansu** ('tænzuː). born 1945, Turkish politician; prime minister (1993–96).

CIM *abbrev. for:* **1** computer input on microfilm. **2** computer integrated manufacture.

Cimabue (*Italian* tʃimaˈbuːe) *n* **Giovanni** (dʒoˈvanni). ?1240–?1302, Italian painter of the Florentine school, who anticipated the movement, led by Giotto, away from the Byzantine tradition in art towards a greater naturalism.

Cimarosa (ˌtʃiːməˈrəʊzə) *n* **Domenico.** 1749–1801, Italian composer, chiefly remembered for his opera buffa *The Secret Marriage* (1792).

cimbalom *or* **cymbalom** ('tsɪmbələm) *n* a type of dulcimer, esp. of Hungary. See **dulcimer** (sense 1). [C19: Hungarian, from Italian *cembalo;* see CEMBALO]

Cimbri ('sɪmbriː, 'kɪm-) *pl n* a Germanic people from N Jutland who migrated southwards in the 2nd century B.C.: annihilated by Marius in the Po valley (101 B.C.). ► **Cimbrian** ('sɪmbrɪən) *n, adj* ► **'Cimbric** *adj*

Ciment Fondu ('siːmɒŋ fɒnˈduː; *French* simɑ̃ fɔ̃dy) *n Trademark.* a type of quick-hardening refractory cement having a high alumina content. Also called: **aluminous cement.**

cimetidine (saɪˈmetɪdiːn) *n* a drug used to suppress the formation of acid by the stomach and so to encourage the healing of gastric and duodenal ulcers. Formula: $C_{10}H_{16}$-N_6S.

cimex ('saɪmɛks) *n, pl* **cimices** ('sɪmɪˌsiːz). any of the heteropterous insects of the genus *Cimex,* esp. the bedbug. [C16: from Latin: bug]

Cimmerian (sɪˈmɪərɪən) *adj* **1** (*sometimes not cap.*) very dark; gloomy. ♦ *n* **2** *Greek myth.* one of a people who lived in a land of darkness at the edge of the world.

Cimon ('saɪmən) *n* died 449 B.C., Athenian military and naval commander: defeated the Persians at Eurymedon (?466).

C in C *or* **C.-in-C.** *Military. abbrev. for* Commander in Chief.

cinch[1] (sɪntʃ) *n* **1** *Slang.* an easy task. **2** *Slang.* a certainty. **3** a U.S. and Canadian name for **girth** (sense 3). **4** *Informal.* a firm grip. ♦ *vb* **5** (often foll. by *up*) *U.S. and Canadian.* to fasten a girth around (a horse). **6** (*tr*) *Informal.* to make sure of. **7** (*tr*) *Informal.* to get a firm grip on. [C19: from Spanish *cincha* saddle girth, from Latin *cingula* girdle, from *cingere* to encircle]

cinch[2] (sɪntʃ) *n* a card game in which the five of trumps ranks highest. [C19: probably from CINCH[1]]

cinchona (sɪŋˈkəʊnə) *n* **1** any tree or shrub of the South American rubiaceous genus *Cinchona,* esp. *C. calisaya,* having medicinal bark. **2** Also called: **cinchona bark, Peruvian bark, calisaya, china bark.** the dried bark of any of these trees, which yields quinine and other medicinal alkaloids. **3** any of the drugs derived from cinchona bark. [C18: New Latin, named after the Countess of *Chinchón* (1576–1639), vicereine of Peru] ► **cinchonic** (sɪŋˈkɒnɪk) *adj*

cinchonidine (sɪŋˈkɒnɪˌdiːn) *n* an alkaloid that is a stereoisomer of cinchonine, with similar properties and uses.

cinchonine ('sɪŋkəˌniːn) *n* an insoluble crystalline alkaloid isolated from cinchona bark and used as a substitute for quinine. Formula: $C_{19}H_{22}N_2O$.

cinchonism ('sɪŋkəˌnɪzəm) *n* a condition resulting from an excessive dose of cinchona bark or its alkaloids, characterized chiefly by headache, ringing in the ears, and vomiting.

cinchonize *or* **cinchonise** ('sɪŋkəˌnaɪz) *vb* (*tr*) to treat (a patient) with cinchona or one of its alkaloids, esp. quinine. ► **ˌcinchoniˈzation** *or* **ˌcinchoniˈsation** *n*

Cincinnati (ˌsɪnsɪˈnætɪ) *n* a city in SW Ohio, on the Ohio River. Pop.: 345 818 (1996 est.).

Cincinnatus (ˌsɪnsɪˈnɑːtəs) *n* **Lucius Quinctius** ('luːsɪəs 'kwɪŋktɪəs). ?519–438 B.C., Roman general and statesman, regarded as a model of simple virtue; dictator of Rome during two crises (458; 439), retiring to his farm after each one.

cincture ('sɪŋktʃə) *n* something that encircles or surrounds, esp. a belt, girdle, or border. [C16: from Latin *cinctūra,* from *cingere* to gird]

cinder ('sɪndə) *n* **1** a piece of incombustible material left after the combustion of coal, coke, etc.; clinker. **2** a piece of charred material that burns without flames; ember. **3** Also called: **sinter.** any solid waste from smelting or refining. **4** (*pl*) fragments of volcanic lava; scoriae. ♦ *vb* **5** (*tr*) *Rare.* to burn to cinders. [Old English *sinder;* related to Old Norse *sindr,* Old High German *sintar,* Old Slavonic *sedra* stalactite] ► **'cindery** *adj*

cinder block *n* the usual U.S. name for **breeze block.**

Cinderella (ˌsɪndəˈrɛlə) *n* **1** a girl who achieves fame after being obscure. **2a** a poor, neglected, or unsuccessful person or thing. **2b** (*as modifier*): *a Cinderella service within the NHS.* **3** (*modifier*) relating to dramatic success: *a Cinderella story.* [C19: after *Cinderella,* the heroine of a fairy tale who is aided by a fairy godmother]

cinder track *n* a racetrack covered with fine cinders.

cine- *combining form.* indicating motion picture or cinema: *cine camera; cinephotography.*

cineaste ('sɪnɪˌæst) *n* an enthusiast for films. [C20: French, from CINEMA + *-aste,* as *-ast* in *enthusiast*]

cine camera ('sɪnɪ) *n Brit.* a camera in which a strip of film moves past the lens, usually to give 16 or 24 exposures per second, thus enabling moving pictures to be taken. U.S. and Canadian term: **movie camera.**

cine film *n Brit.* photographic film, wound on a spool, usually 8, 16, or 35 millimetres wide, up to several hundred metres long, and having one or two lines of sprocket holes along its length enabling it to be used in a cine camera. U.S. and Canadian term: **movie film.**

cinema ('sɪnɪmə) *n* **1** *Chiefly Brit.* **1a** a place designed for the exhibition of films. **1b** (*as modifier*): *a cinema seat.* **2 the cinema. 2a** the art or business of making films. **2b** films collectively. [C19 (earlier spelling: *kinema*): shortened from CINEMATOGRAPH] ► **cinematic** (ˌsɪnɪˈmætɪk) *adj* ► **ˌcineˈmatically** *adv*

CinemaScope ('sɪnɪməˌskəʊp) *n Trademark.* an anamorphic process of wide-screen film projection in which an image of approximately twice the usual width is squeezed into a 35mm frame and then screened by a projector having complementary lenses.

cinematheque (ˌsɪnɪməˈtɛk) *n* a small intimate cinema. [C20: from French *cinémathèque* film library, from CINEMA + (*biblio*)*thèque* library]

cinematograph (ˌsɪnɪˈmætəˌgrɑːf, -ˌgræf) *Chiefly Brit.* ♦ *n* **1** a combined camera, printer, and projector. ♦ *vb* **2** to take pictures (of) with a film camera. [C19 (earlier spelling: *kinematograph*): from Greek *kinēmat-, kinēma* motion + -GRAPH] ► **cinematographer** (ˌsɪnɪməˈtɒgrəfə) *n* ► **cinematographic** (ˌsɪnɪˌmætəˈgræfɪk) *adj* ► **ˌcineˌmatoˈgraphically** *adv* ► **ˌcinemaˈtography** *n*

cinéma vérité (*French* sinema verite) *n* films characterized by subjects, actions, etc., that have the appearance of real life. [French, literally: cinema truth]

cineol ('sɪnɪˌɒl) *or* **cineole** ('sɪnɪˌəʊl) *n* another name for **eucalyptol.** [C19: changed from New Latin *oleum cinae,* literally: oil of wormseed]

Cinerama (ˌsɪnəˈrɑːmə) *n Trademark.* wide-screen presentation of films using either three separate 35mm projectors or one 70mm projector to produce an image on a large deeply curved screen.

cineraria (ˌsɪnəˈrɛərɪə) *n* a plant, *Senecio cruentus,* of the Canary Islands, widely cultivated for its blue, purple, red, or variegated daisy-like flowers: family *Compositae* (composites). [C16: from New Latin, from Latin *cinerārius* of ashes, from *cinis* ashes; from its downy leaves]

cinerarium (ˌsɪnəˈrɛərɪəm) *n, pl* **-raria** (-ˈrɛərɪə). a place for keeping the ashes of the dead after cremation. [C19: from Latin, from *cinerārius* relating to ashes; see CINERARIA] ► **cinerary** ('sɪnərərɪ) *adj*

cinerator ('sɪnəˌreɪtə) *n* another name (esp. U.S.) for **cremator** (sense 1). ► **ˌcineˈration** *n*

cinereous (sɪˈnɪərɪəs) *or* **cineritious** (ˌsɪnəˈrɪʃəs) *adj* **1** of a greyish colour. **2** resembling or consisting of ashes. [C17: from Latin *cinereus,* from *cinis* ashes]

cinerin ('sɪnərɪn) *n* either of two similar organic compounds found in pyrethrum and used as insecticides. Formulas: $C_{20}H_{28}O_3$ (**cinerin I**), $C_{21}H_{28}O_5$ (**cinerin II**). [C20: from Latin *ciner-, cinis* ashes + -IN]

cingulum ('sɪŋgjʊləm) *n, pl* **-la** (-lə). *Anatomy.* a girdle-like part, such as the ridge round the base of a tooth or the band of fibres connecting parts of the cerebrum. [C19: from Latin: belt, from *cingere* to gird] ► **cingulate** ('sɪŋgjʊlɪt, -ˌleɪt) *or* **'cinguˌlated** *adj*

Cinna ('sɪnə) *n* **Lucius Cornelius** ('luːsɪəs kɔːˈniːlɪəs). died 84 B.C., Roman patrician; an opponent of Sulla.

cinnabar ('sɪnəˌbɑː) *n* **1** a bright red or brownish-red mineral form of mercuric sulphide (mercury(II) sulphide), found close to areas of volcanic activity and hot springs. It is the main commercial source of mercury. Formula: HgS. Crystal structure: hexagonal. **2** the red form of mercuric sulphide (mercury(II) sulphide), esp. when used as a pigment. **3** a bright red to reddish-orange; vermilion. **4** a large red-and-black European moth, *Callimorpha jacobaeae:* family *Arctiidae* (tiger moths, etc.). [C15: from Old French *cenobre,* from Latin *cinnābaris,* from Greek *kinnabari,* of Oriental origin]

cinnamic acid (sɪˈnæmɪk) *n* a white crystalline water-insoluble weak organic acid existing in two isomeric forms; 3-phenylpropenoic acid. The *trans-* form occurs naturally and its esters are used in perfumery. Formula: $C_6H_5CH{:}CHCOOH$. [C19: from CINNAM(ON) + -IC; from its being found in cinnamon oil]

cinnamon ('sɪnəmən) *n* **1** a tropical Asian lauraceous tree, *Cinnamomum zeylanicum,* having aromatic yellowish-brown bark. **2** the spice obtained from the bark of this tree, used for flavouring food and drink. **3 Saigon cinnamon.** an E Asian lauraceous tree, *Cinnamomum loureirii,* the bark of which is used as a cordial and to relieve flatulence. **4** any of several similar or related trees or their bark. See **cassia** (sense 2). **5** a light yellowish brown. [C15: from Old French *cinnamome,* via Latin and Greek, from Hebrew *qinnamown*] ► **cinˈnamic** *or* **cinnamonic** (ˌsɪnəˈmɒnɪk) *adj*

cinnamon bear *n* a reddish-brown variety of the American black bear. See **black bear** (sense 1).

cinnamon sedge *n* an angler's name for a small caddis fly, *Limnephilus lunatus,* having pale hind wings, that frequents sluggish water.

cinnamon stone *n* another name for **hessonite.**

cinquain (sɪŋˈkeɪn, 'sɪŋkeɪn) *n* a stanza of five lines. [C18 (in the sense: a military company of five): from French *cinq* five, from Latin *quinque;* compare QUATRAIN]

cinque (sɪŋk) *n* the number five in cards, dice, etc. [C14: from Old French *cinq* five]

cinquecento (ˌtʃɪŋkwɪˈtʃɛntəʊ) *n* the 16th century, esp. in reference to Italian art, architecture, or literature. [C18: Italian, shortened from *milcinquecento* 1500] ► **ˌcinqueˈcentist** *n*

cinquefoil ('sɪŋkˌfɔɪl) *n* **1** any plant of the N temperate rosaceous genus *Potentilla,* typically having five-lobed compound leaves. **2** an ornamental carving in the form of five arcs arranged in a circle and separated by cusps. **3** *Heraldry.* a charge representing a five-petalled flower. [C13 *sink foil,* from Old French *cincfoille,* from Latin *quinquefolium* plant with five leaves, translating Greek *pentaphullon* from *pente* five + *phullon* leaf]

Cinque Ports (sɪŋk) *pl n* an association of ports on the SE coast of England, originally consisting of Hastings, Romney, Hythe, Dover, and Sandwich, which from late Anglo-Saxon times provided ships for the king's service in return for the profits of justice in their courts. The Cinque Ports declined with the growth of other ports and surrendered their charters in 1685.

Cintra ('sɪntrə) *n* the former name for **Sintra.**

Cinzano (tʃɪnˈzɑːnəʊ) *n Trademark.* an Italian vermouth.

CIO *U.S. abbrev. for* Congress of Industrial Organizations. See also **AFL-CIO.**

Cipango (sɪˈpæŋɡəʊ) *n* (in medieval legend) an island E of Asia: called Zipangu by Marco Polo and sought by Columbus; identified with Japan.

cipher *or* **cypher** (ˈsaɪfə) *n* **1** a method of secret writing using substitution or transposition of letters according to a key. **2** a secret message. **3** the key to a secret message. **4** an obsolete name for **zero** (sense 1). **5** any of the Arabic numerals (0, 1, 2, 3, etc., to 9) or the Arabic system of numbering as a whole. **6** a person or thing of no importance; nonentity. **7** a design consisting of interwoven letters; monogram. **8** *Music.* a defect in an organ resulting in the continuous sounding of a pipe, the key of which has not been depressed. ◆ *vb* **9** to put (a message) into secret writing. **10** (*intr*) (of an organ pipe) to sound without having the appropriate key depressed. **11** *Rare.* to perform (a calculation) arithmetically. [C14: from Old French *cifre* zero, from Medieval Latin *cifra,* from Arabic *sifr* zero, empty]

cipolin (ˈsɪpəlɪn) *n* an Italian marble with alternating white and green streaks. [C18: from French, from Italian *cipollino* a little onion, from *cipolla* onion, from Late Latin *cēpulla,* diminutive of Latin *cēpa* onion; from its likeness to the layers of an onion]

cir. *or* **circ.** *abbrev. for:* **1** (preceding a date) circa. **2** circular. **3** circulation. **4** circumference.

circa (ˈsɜːkə) *prep* (used with a date) at the approximate time of: *circa 1182* B.C. Abbrevs.: **c, ca.** [Latin: about; related to Latin *circus* circle, CIRCUS]

circadian (sɜːˈkeɪdɪən) *adj* of or relating to biological processes that occur regularly at about 24-hour intervals, even in the absence of periodicity in the environment. See also **biological clock.** [C20: from Latin *circa* about + *diēs* day]

Circassia (sɜːˈkæsɪə) *n* a region of S Russia, on the Black Sea north of the Caucasus Mountains.

Circassian (sɜːˈkæsɪən) *n* **1** a native of Circassia. **2** a language or languages spoken in Circassia, belonging to the North-West Caucasian family. See also **Adygei, Kabardian.** ◆ *adj also* **Circassic. 3** relating to Circassia, its people, or language.

Circe (ˈsɜːsɪ) *n Greek myth.* an enchantress who detained Odysseus on her island and turned his men into swine. ▸ **Circean** (sɜːˈsɪən) *adj*

circinate (ˈsɜːsɪˌneɪt) *adj* **1** *Botany.* (of part of a plant, such as a young fern) coiled so that the tip is at the centre. **2** *Anatomy.* resembling a ring or a circle. [C19: from Latin *circināre* to make round, from *circinus* pair of compasses, from *circus,* see CIRCUS] ▸ **ˈcirciˌnately** *adv*

Circinus (ˈsɜːsɪnəs) *n, Latin genitive* **Circini** (ˈsɜːsɪˌnaɪ). a small faint constellation in the S hemisphere close to Centaurus and the Southern Cross. [C19: from Latin, a pair of compasses]

circle (ˈsɜːkᵊl) *n* **1** a closed plane curve every point of which is equidistant from a given fixed point, the centre. Equation: $(x-h)^2 + (y-k)^2 = r^2$ where r is the radius and (h, k) are the coordinates of the centre; area: πr^2; circumference: $2\pi r$. **2** the figure enclosed by such a curve. **3** *Theatre.* the section of seats above the main level of the auditorium, usually comprising the dress circle and the upper circle. **4** something formed or arranged in the shape of a circle. **5** a group of people sharing an interest, activity, upbringing, etc.; set: *golf circles; a family circle.* **6** a domain or area of activity, interest, or influence. **7** a circuit. **8** a process or chain of events or parts that forms a connected whole; cycle. **9** a parallel of latitude. See also **great circle, small circle. 10** the ring of a circus. **11** one of a number of Neolithic or Bronze Age rings of standing stones, such as Stonehenge, found in Europe and thought to be associated with some form of ritual or astronomical measurement. **12** *Hockey.* See **striking circle. 13** a circular argument. See **vicious circle** (sense 2). **14 come full circle.** to arrive back at one's starting point. See also **vicious circle. 15 go** *or* **run round in circles.** to engage in energetic but fruitless activity. ◆ *vb* **16** to move in a circle (around): *we circled the city by car.* **17** (*tr*) to enclose in a circle; encircle. [C14: from Latin *circulus* a circular figure, from *circus* ring, circle] ▸ **ˈcircler** *n*

circlet (ˈsɜːklɪt) *n* a small circle or ring, esp. a circular ornament worn on the head. [C15: from Old French *cerclet* a little CIRCLE]

circlip (ˈsɜːˌklɪp) *n Engineering.* a flat spring ring split at one point so that it can be sprung open, passed over a shaft or spindle, and allowed to close into a closely fitting annular recess to form a collar on the shaft. A similar design can be closed to pass into a bore and allowed to spring out into an annular recess to form a shoulder in the bore. Also called: **retaining ring.**

Circlorama (ˌsɜːkləˈrɑːmə) *n Trademark.* a system of film projection in which a number of projectors and screens are employed to produce a picture that surrounds the viewer.

circs (sɜːks) *n Brit. informal.* short for **circumstances** (see **circumstance** (sense 1)).

circuit (ˈsɜːkɪt) *n* **1a** a complete route or course, esp. one that is curved or circular or that lies around an object. **1b** the area enclosed within such a route. **2** the act of following such a route: *we made three circuits of the course.* **3a** a complete path through which an electric current can flow. **3b** (*as modifier*): *a circuit diagram.* **4a** a periodical journey around an area, as made by judges, salesmen, etc. **4b** the route traversed or places visited on such a journey. **4c** the persons making such a journey. **5** an administrative division of the Methodist Church comprising a number of neighbouring churches. **6** *English law.* one of six areas into which England is divided for the administration of justice. **7** a number of theatres, cinemas, etc., under one management or in which the same film is shown or in which a company of performers plays in turn. **8** *Sport.* **8a** a series of tournaments in which the same players regularly take part: *the international tennis circuit.* **8b** (usually preceded by *the*) the contestants who take part in such a series. **9** *Chiefly Brit.* a motor racing track, usually of irregular shape. ◆ *vb* **10** to make or travel in a circuit around (something). [C14: from Latin *circuitus* a going around, from *circumīre,* from *circum* around + *īre* to go] ▸ **ˈcircuital** *adj*

circuit binding *n* a style of limp-leather binding, used esp. for Bibles and prayer books, in which the edges of the cover bend over to protect the edges of the pages.

circuit board *n* short for **printed circuit board.** See **printed circuit.**

circuit breaker *n* a device that under abnormal conditions, such as a short circuit, stops the flow of current in an electrical circuit. Sometimes shortened to **breaker.** Compare **fuse**² (sense 6).

circuit judge *n Brit.* a judge presiding over a county court or crown court.

circuitous (səˈkjuːɪtəs) *adj* indirect and lengthy; roundabout: *a circuitous route.* ▸ **cirˈcuitously** *adv* ▸ **cirˈcuitousness** *n*

circuit rider *n U.S. and Canadian.* (formerly) a minister of religion who preached from place to place along an established circuit.

circuitry (ˈsɜːkɪtrɪ) *n* **1** the design of an electrical circuit. **2** the system of circuits used in an electronic device.

circuit training *n* a form of athletic training in which a number of exercises are performed in turn.

circuity (səˈkjuːɪtɪ) *n, pl* **-ties.** (of speech, reasoning, etc.) a roundabout or devious quality.

circular (ˈsɜːkjʊlə) *adj* **1** of, involving, resembling, or shaped like a circle. **2** circuitous. **3** (of arguments) futile because the truth of the premises cannot be established independently of the conclusion. **4** travelling or occurring in a cycle. **5** (of letters, announcements, etc.) intended for general distribution. ◆ *n* **6** a printed or duplicated advertisement or notice for mass distribution. ▸ **circularity** (ˌsɜːkjʊˈlærɪtɪ) *or* **ˈcircularness** *n* ▸ **ˈcircularly** *adv*

circular breathing *n* a technique for sustaining a phrase on a wind instrument, using the cheeks to force air out of the mouth while breathing in through the nose.

circular function *n* another name for **trigonometric function** (sense 1).

circularize *or* **circularise** (ˈsɜːkjʊləˌraɪz) *vb* (*tr*) **1** to distribute circulars to. **2** to canvass or petition (people), as for support, votes, etc., by distributing letters, etc. **3** to make circular. ▸ **ˌcirculariˈzation** *or* **ˌcirculariˈsation** *n* ▸ **ˈcircularˌizer** *or* **ˈcircularˌiser** *n*

circular measure *n* the measurement of an angle in radians.

circular mil *n* a unit of area of cross section of wire, equal to the area of a circle whose diameter is one thousandth of an inch. 1 circular mil is equal to 0.785×10^{-6} square inch or 0.2×10^{-9} square metre.

circular polarization *n* a transformation of electromagnetic radiation (esp. light) to a form in which the vector representing the instantaneous intensity of the electric field describes a circle about the direction of propagation at any point in the path of the radiation.

circular saw *n* a power-driven saw in which a circular disc with a toothed edge is rotated at high speed.

circular triangle *n* a triangle in which each side is the arc of a circle.

circulate (ˈsɜːkjʊˌleɪt) *vb* **1** to send, go, or pass from place to place or person to person: *don't circulate the news.* **2** to distribute or be distributed over a wide area. **3** to move or cause to move through a circuit, system, etc., returning to the starting point: *blood circulates through the body.* **4** to move in a circle: *the earth circulates around the sun.* [C15: from Latin *circulārī* to assemble in a circle, from *circulus* CIRCLE] ▸ **ˈcircuˌlative** *adj* ▸ **ˈcircuˌlator** *n* ▸ **ˈcirculatory** *adj*

circulating decimal *n* another name for **recurring decimal.**

circulating library *n* **1** another name (esp. U.S.) for **lending library. 2** a small library circulated in turn to a group of schools or other institutions. **3** a rare name for **subscription library.**

circulating medium *n Finance.* currency serving as a medium of exchange.

circulation (ˌsɜːkjʊˈleɪʃən) *n* **1** the transport of oxygenated blood through the arteries to the capillaries, where it nourishes the tissues, and the return of oxygen-depleted blood through the veins to the heart, where the cycle is renewed. **2** the flow of sap through a plant. **3** any movement through a closed circuit. **4** the spreading or transmission of something to a wider group of people or area. **5** (of air and water) free movement within an area or volume. **6a** the distribution of newspapers, magazines, etc. **6b** the number of copies of an issue of such a publication that are distributed. **7** *Library science.* **7a** a book loan, as from a library lending department. **7b** each loan transaction of a particular book. **7c** the total issue of library books over a specified period. **8** a rare term for **circulating medium. 9 in circulation. 9a** (of currency) serving as a medium of exchange. **9b** (of people) active in a social or business context.

circulatory system *n Anatomy, zoology.* the system concerned with the transport of blood and lymph, consisting of the heart, blood vessels, lymph vessels, etc.

circum- *prefix* around; surrounding; on all sides: *circumlocution; circumrotate.* [from Latin *circum* around, from *circus* circle]

circumambient (ˌsɜːkəmˈæmbɪənt) *adj* surrounding. [C17: from Late Latin *circumambīre,* from CIRCUM- + *ambīre* to go round] ▸ **ˌcircumˈambience** *or* **ˌcircumˈambiency** *n*

circumambulate (ˌsɜːkəmˈæmbjʊˌleɪt) *vb* **1** to walk around (something). **2** (*intr*) to avoid the point. [C17: from Late Latin CIRCUM- + *ambulāre* to walk] ▸ **ˌcircumˌambuˈlation** *n* ▸ **ˌcircumˈambuˌlator** *n* ▸ **ˌcircumˈambulatory** *adj*

circumbendibus (ˌsɜːkəmˈbɛndɪbəs) *n Humorous.* a circumlocution. [C17: coined from CIRCUM- + BEND¹, with a pseudo-Latin ending]

circumcise (ˈsɜːkəmˌsaɪz) *vb* (*tr*) **1** to remove the foreskin of (a male). **2** to incise surgically the skin over the clitoris of (a female). **3** to remove the clitoris of (a female). **4** to perform the religious rite of circumcision on (someone). [C13: from Latin *circumcīdere,* from CIRCUM- + *caedere* to cut] ▸ **ˈcircumˌciser** *n*

circumcision (ˌsɜːkəmˈsɪʒən) *n* **1a** surgical removal of the foreskin of males. **1b** surgical incision into the skin covering the clitoris in females. **1c** removal of the clitoris. **2** the act of circumcision, performed as a religious rite by Jews and Muslims. 3 *R.C. Church.* the festival celebrated on Jan. 1 in commemoration of the circumcision of Jesus.

circumference (səˈkʌmfərəns) *n* 1 the boundary of a specific area or geometric figure, esp. of a circle. 2 the length of a closed geometric curve, esp. of a circle. The circumference of a circle is equal to the diameter multiplied by π. [C14: from Old French *circonference,* from Latin *circumferre* to carry around, from CIRCUM- + *ferre* to bear] ► **circumferential** (səˌkʌmfəˈrɛnʃəl) *adj* ► **cirˌcumferˈentially** *adv*

circumflex (ˈsɜːkəmˌflɛks) *n* 1 a mark (^) placed over a vowel to show that it is pronounced with rising and falling pitch, as in ancient Greek, as a long vowel rather than a short one, as in French, or with some other different quality. ◆ *adj* 2 (of certain nerves, arteries, or veins) bending or curving around. [C16: from Latin *circumflexus,* from *circumflectere* to bend around, from CIRCUM- + *flectere* to bend] ► **ˌcircumˈflexion** *n*

circumfluous (səˈkʌmfluəs) *adj* 1 Also: **cirˈcumfluent.** flowing all around. 2 surrounded by or as if by water. [C17: from Latin *circumfluere* to flow around, from CIRCUM- + *fluere* to flow] ► **cirˈcumfluence** *n*

circumfuse (ˌsɜːkəmˈfjuːz) *vb* (*tr*) 1 to pour or spread (a liquid, powder, etc.) around. 2 to surround with a substance, such as a liquid. [C16: from Latin *circumfūsus,* from *circumfundere* to pour around, from CIRCUM- + *fundere* to pour] ► **circumfusion** (ˌsɜːkəmˈfjuːʒən) *n*

circumlocution (ˌsɜːkəmləˈkjuːʃən) *n* 1 an indirect way of expressing something. 2 an indirect expression. ► **circumlocutory** (ˌsɜːkəmˈlɒkjutərɪ, -trɪ) *adj*

circumlunar (ˌsɜːkəmˈluːnə) *adj* around or revolving around the moon: *a circumlunar orbit.*

circumnavigate (ˌsɜːkəmˈnævɪˌgeɪt) *vb* (*tr*) to sail or fly completely around. ► **ˌcircumˈnavigable** *adj* ► **ˌcircumˌnaviˈgation** *n* ► **ˌcircumˈnaviˌgator** *n*

circumnutate (ˌsɜːkəmˈnjuːteɪt) *vb* (*intr*) (of the tip of a plant stem) to grow in an irregular curve, ellipse, or spiral. [C19: from CIRCUM- + *-nutate,* from Latin *nūtāre* to nod repeatedly, sway] ► **ˌcircumnuˈtation** *n*

circumpolar (ˌsɜːkəmˈpəulə) *adj* 1 (of a star or constellation) visible above the horizon at all times at a specified locality on the earth's surface. 2 surrounding or located at or near either of the earth's poles.

circumscissile (ˌsɜːkəmˈsɪsaɪl) *adj* (of the dry dehiscent fruits of certain plants) opening completely by a transverse split. [C19: from CIRCUM- + Latin *scissilis* capable of splitting, from *scindere* to split]

circumscribe (ˌsɜːkəmˈskraɪb, ˈsɜːkəmˌskraɪb) *vb* (*tr*) 1 to restrict within limits. 2 to mark or set the bounds of. 3 to draw a geometric construction around (another construction) so that the two are in contact but do not intersect. Compare **inscribe** (sense 4). 4 to draw a line round. [C15: from Latin *circumscrībere,* from CIRCUM- + *scrībere* to write] ► **ˌcircumˈscribable** *adj* ► **ˌcircumˈscriber** *n*

circumscription (ˌsɜːkəmˈskrɪpʃən) *n* 1 the act of circumscribing or the state of being circumscribed. 2 something that limits or encloses. 3 a circumscribed space. 4 an inscription around a coin or medal. ► **ˌcircumˈscriptive** *adj* ► **ˌcircumˈscriptively** *adv*

circumsolar (ˌsɜːkəmˈsəulə) *adj* surrounding or rotating around the sun.

circumspect (ˈsɜːkəmˌspɛkt) *adj* cautious, prudent, or discreet. [C15: from Latin *circumspectus,* from CIRCUM- + *specere* to look] ► **ˌcircumˈspection** *n* ► **ˌcircumˈspective** *adj* ► **ˈcircumˌspectly** *adv*

circumstance (ˈsɜːkəmstəns) *n* 1 (*usually pl*) a condition of time, place, etc., that accompanies or influences an event or condition. 2 an incident or occurrence, esp. a chance one. 3 accessory information or detail. 4 formal display or ceremony (archaic except in the phrase **pomp and circumstance**). 5 **under** *or* **in no circumstances.** in no case; never. 6 **under the circumstances.** because of conditions; this being the case. 7 **in good** (*or* **bad**) **circumstances.** (of a person) in a good (or bad) financial situation. ◆ *vb* (*tr*) 8 to place in a particular condition or situation. 9 *Obsolete.* to give in detail. [C13: from Old French *circonstance,* from Latin *circumstantia,* from *circumstāre* to stand around, from CIRCUM- + *stāre* to stand]

circumstantial (ˌsɜːkəmˈstænʃəl) *adj* 1 of or dependent on circumstances. 2 fully detailed. 3 incidental. ► **ˌcircumˌstantiˈality** *n* ► **ˌcircumˈstantially** *adv*

circumstantial evidence *n* indirect evidence that tends to establish a conclusion by inference. Compare **direct evidence.**

circumstantiate (ˌsɜːkəmˈstænʃɪˌeɪt) *vb* (*tr*) to support by giving particulars. ► **ˌcircumˌstantiˈation** *n*

circumvallate (ˌsɜːkəmˈvæleɪt) *vb* (*tr*) to surround with a defensive fortification. [C19: from Latin *circumvallāre,* from CIRCUM- + *vallum* rampart] ► **ˌcircumvalˈlation** *n*

circumvent (ˌsɜːkəmˈvɛnt) *vb* (*tr*) 1 to evade or go around. 2 to outwit. 3 to encircle (an enemy) so as to intercept or capture. [C15: from Latin *circumvenīre,* from CIRCUM- + *venīre* to come] ► **ˌcircumˈventer** *or* **ˌcircumˈventor** *n* ► **ˌcircumˈvention** *n* ► **ˌcircumˈventive** *adj*

circumvolution (ˌsɜːkəmvəˈluːʃən) *n* 1 the act of turning, winding, or folding around a central axis. 2 a single complete turn, cycle, or fold. 3 anything winding or sinuous. 4 a roundabout course or procedure. [C15: from Medieval Latin *circumvolūtiō,* from Latin *circumvolvere,* from CIRCUM- + *volvere* to roll] ► **ˌcircumvoˈlutory** *adj*

circus (ˈsɜːkəs) *n, pl* **-cuses.** 1 a travelling company of entertainers such as acrobats, clowns, trapeze artistes, and trained animals. 2 a public performance given by such a company. 3 an oval or circular arena, usually tented and surrounded by tiers of seats, in which such a performance is held. 4 a travelling group of professional sportsmen: *a cricket circus.* 5 (in ancient Rome) **5a** an open-air stadium, usually oval or oblong, for chariot races or public games. **5b** the games themselves. 6 *Brit.* **6a** an open place, usually circular, in a town, where several streets converge. **6b** (*cap. when part of a name*): *Piccadilly Circus.* 7 *Informal.* noisy or rowdy behaviour. 8 *Informal.* a person or group of people whose behaviour is wild, disorganized, or (esp. unintentionally) comic. [C16: from Latin, from Greek *kirkos* ring]

Circus Maximus (ˈmæksɪməs) *n* an amphitheatre in Rome, used in ancient times for chariot races, public games, etc.

ciré (ˈsɪəreɪ) *adj* 1 (of fabric) treated with a heat or wax process to make it smooth. ◆ *n* 2 such a surface on a fabric. 3 a fabric having such a surface. [C20: French, from *cirer* to wax, from *cire,* from Latin *cēra* wax]

Cirenaica (ˌsaɪrəˈneɪɪkə, ˌsɪrə-) *n* a variant spelling of **Cyrenaica.**

Cirencester (ˈsaɪrənˌsɛstə) *n* a market town in S England, in Gloucestershire: Roman amphitheatre. Pop.: 15 221 (1991). Latin name: **Corinium.**

cire perdue *French.* (sir pɛrdy) *n* a method of casting bronze, in which a mould is formed around a wax pattern, which is subsequently melted and drained away. [literally: lost wax]

cirque (sɜːk) *n* 1 Also called: **corrie, cwm.** a semicircular or crescent-shaped basin with steep sides and a gently sloping floor formed in mountainous regions by the erosive action of ice. 2 *Archaeol.* an obsolete term for **circle** (sense 11). 3 *Poetic.* a circle, circlet, or ring. [C17: from French, from Latin *circus* ring, circle, CIRCUS]

cirrate (ˈsɪreɪt), **cirrose,** *or* **cirrous** *adj Biology.* bearing or resembling cirri. [C19: from Latin *cirrātus* curled, from CIRRUS]

cirrhosis (sɪˈrəusɪs) *n* any of various progressive diseases of the liver, characterized by death of liver cells, irreversible fibrosis, etc.: caused by inadequate diet, excessive alcohol, chronic infection, etc. Also called: **cirrhosis of the liver.** [C19: New Latin, from Greek *kirrhos* orange-coloured + -OSIS; referring to the appearance of the diseased liver] ► **cirˈrhosed** *adj* ► **cirrhotic** (sɪˈrɒtɪk) *adj*

cirri (ˈsɪraɪ) *n* the plural of **cirrus.**

cirripede (ˈsɪrɪˌpiːd) *or* **cirriped** (ˈsɪrɪˌpɛd) *n* 1 any marine crustacean of the subclass *Cirripedia,* including the barnacles, the adults of which are sessile or parasitic. ◆ *adj* 2 of, relating to, or belonging to the *Cirripedia.*

cirro- *or* **cirri-** *combining form.* indicating cirrus or cirri: *cirrocumulus; cirriped.*

cirrocumulus (ˌsɪrəuˈkjuːmjuləs) *n, pl* **-li** (-ˌlaɪ). *Meteorol.* a high cloud of ice crystals grouped into small separate globular masses, usually occurring above 6000 metres (20 000 feet). See also **mackerel sky.**

cirrose (ˈsɪrəus, sɪˈrəus) *or* **cirrous** (ˈsɪrəs) *adj* 1 *Biology.* another word for **cirrate.** 2 characteristic of cirrus clouds.

cirrostratus (ˌsɪrəuˈstrɑːtəs) *n, pl* **-ti** (-taɪ). a uniform layer of cloud above about 6000 metres (20 000 feet). ► **ˌcirroˈstrative** *adj*

cirrus (ˈsɪrəs) *n, pl* **-ri** (-raɪ). 1 *Meteorol.* a thin wispy fibrous cloud at high altitudes, composed of ice particles. 2 a plant tendril or similar part. 3 *Zoology.* **3a** a slender tentacle or filament in barnacles and other marine invertebrates. **3b** a hairlike structure in other animals, such as a filament on the appendage of an insect or a barbel of a fish. [C18: from Latin: curl, tuft, fringe]

cirsoid (ˈsɜːsɔɪd) *adj Pathol.* resembling a varix. Also: **varicoid.** [C19: from Greek *kirsoeidēs,* from *kirsos* swollen vein + -OID]

cis- *prefix* 1 on this or the near side of: *cisalpine.* 2 (often in italics) indicating that two groups of atoms in an unsaturated compound lie on the same side of a double bond: *cis*-butadiene. Compare **trans-** (sense 5). [from Latin]

CIS *abbrev. for* Commonwealth of Independent States.

cisalpine (sɪsˈælpaɪn) *adj* 1 on this (the southern) side of the Alps, as viewed from Rome. 2 relating to a movement in the Roman Catholic Church to minimize the authority of the pope and to emphasize the independence of branches of the Church. Compare **ultramontane** (sense 2).

Cisalpine Gaul *n* (in the ancient world) that part of Gaul between the Alps and the Apennines.

Ciscaucasia (ˌsɪskɔːˈkeɪzɪə, -ʒə) *n* the part of Caucasia north of the Caucasus Mountains.

cisco (ˈsɪskəu) *n, pl* **-coes** *or* **-cos.** any of various whitefish, esp. *Coregonus artedi* (also called **lake herring**), of cold deep lakes of North America. [C19: short for Canadian French *ciscoette,* from Ojibwa *pemitewiskawet* fish with oily flesh]

Ciskei (ˈsɪskaɪ) *n* (formerly) a Bantustan in SE South Africa; granted independence in 1981 but this was not recognized outside South Africa; abolished in 1993. Capital: Bisho.

cislunar (sɪsˈluːnə) *adj* of or relating to the space between the earth and the moon. Compare **translunar.**

cismontane (sɪsˈmɒnteɪn) *adj* on this (the writer's or speaker's) side of the mountains, esp. the Alps. Compare **ultramontane** (sense 1). [C18: from Latin CIS- + *montānus* of the mountains, from *mōns* mountain]

cispadane (ˈsɪspəˌdeɪn, sɪsˈpeɪdeɪn) *adj* on this (the southern) side of the River Po, as viewed from Rome. Compare **transpadane.** [from Latin CIS- + *Padānus* of the Po]

cisplatin (sɪsˈplætɪn) *n* a cytotoxic drug that acts by preventing DNA replication and hence cell divisions, used in the treatment of tumours of the ovary and testis. [C20: from CIS- + PLATIN(UM)]

cissing (ˈsɪsɪŋ) *n Building trades.* the appearance of pinholes, craters, etc., in paintwork due to poor adhesion of the paint to the surface.

cissoid (ˈsɪsɔɪd) *n* 1 a geometric curve whose two branches meet in a cusp at the origin and are asymptotic to a line parallel to the *y*-axis. Its equation is $y^2(2a - x)=x^3$ where 2a is the distance between the *y*-axis and this line. ◆ *adj* 2 contained between the concave sides of two intersecting curves. Compare **sistroid.** [C17: from Greek *kissoeidēs,* literally: ivy-shaped, from *kissos* ivy]

cissus (ˈsɪsəs) *n* any plant of the climbing genus *Cissus,* some species of which, esp. the kangaroo vine (*C. antarctica*) from Australia, are grown as greenhouse or house plants for their shiny green or mottled leaves: family *Vitaceae.* [New Latin, from Greek *kissos* ivy]

cissy (ˈsɪsɪ) *n* a variant spelling of **sissy.**

cist[1] (sɪst) *n* a wooden box for holding ritual objects used in ancient Rome and Greece. [C19: from Latin *cista* box, chest, basket, from Greek *kistē*]

cist[2] (sɪst) *or* **kist** *n Archaeol.* a box-shaped burial chamber made from stone slabs or a hollowed tree trunk. [C19: from Welsh: chest, from Latin *cista* box; see CIST[1]]

cistaceous (sɪ'steɪʃəs) *adj* of, relating to, or belonging to the *Cistaceae,* a family of shrubby or herbaceous plants that includes the rockroses. [C19: from New Latin *Cistaceae,* from Greek *kistos* rockrose]

Cistercian (sɪ'stɜːʃən) *n* **a** a member of a Christian order of monks and nuns founded in 1098, which follows an especially strict form of the Benedictine rule. Also called: **White Monk. b** (*as modifier*): *a Cistercian monk.* [C17: from French *Cistercien,* from Medieval Latin *Cisterciānus,* from *Cistercium* (modern *Cîteaux*), original home of the order]

cistern ('sɪstən) *n* **1** a tank for the storage of water, esp. on or within the roof of a house or connected to a WC. **2** an underground reservoir for the storage of a liquid, esp. rainwater. **3** *Anatomy.* another name for **cisterna.** [C13: from Old French *cisterne,* from Latin *cisterna* underground tank, from *cista* box] ▸ **cisternal** (sɪ'stɜːnᵊl) *adj*

cisterna (sɪ'stɜːnə) *n, pl* **-nae** (-niː). a sac or partially closed space containing body fluid, esp. lymph or cerebrospinal fluid. [New Latin, from Latin; see CISTERN]

cis-trans test ('sɪs'trɑːnz) *n Genetics.* a test to define the unit of genetic function, based on whether two mutations of the same character occur in a single chromosome (the cis position) or in different cistrons in each chromosome of a homologous pair (the trans position). [C20: see CIS-, TRANS-]

cistron ('sɪstrən) *n Genetics.* the section of a chromosome that controls a single function; a functional gene. [C20: from *cis-trans;* see CIS-TRANS TEST]

cistus ('sɪstəs) *n* any plant of the genus *Cistus.* See **rockrose.** [C16: New Latin, from Greek *kistos*]

CIT (in New Zealand) *abbrev. for* Central Institute of Technology.

cit. *abbrev. for:* **1** citation. **2** cited. **3** citizen.

citadel ('sɪtədᵊl, -ˌdɛl) *n* **1** a stronghold within or close to a city. **2** any strongly fortified building or place of safety; refuge. **3** a specially strengthened part of the hull of a warship. **4** (*often cap.*) the headquarters of the Salvation Army. [C16: from Old French *citadelle,* from Old Italian *cittadella* a little city, from *cittade* city, from Latin *cīvitās*]

citation (saɪ'teɪʃən) *n* **1** the quoting of a book or author in support of a fact. **2** a passage or source cited for this purpose. **3** a listing or recounting, as of facts. **4** an official commendation or award, esp. for bravery or outstanding service, work, etc., usually in the form of a formal statement made in public. **5** *Law.* **5a** an official summons to appear in court. **5b** the document containing such a summons. **6** *Law.* the quoting of decided cases to serve as guidance to a court. ▸ **citatory** ('saɪtətərɪ, -trɪ) *adj*

cite (saɪt) *vb* (*tr*) **1** to quote or refer to (a passage, book, or author) in substantiation as an authority, proof, or example. **2** to mention or commend (a soldier, etc.) for outstanding bravery or meritorious action. **3** to summon to appear before a court of law. **4** to enumerate: *he cited the king's virtues.* [C15: from Old French *citer* to summon, from Latin *citāre* to rouse, from *citus* quick, from *ciēre* to excite] ▸ **'citable** *or* **'citeable** *adj* ▸ **'citer** *n*

CITES *abbrev. for* Convention on International Trade in Endangered Species.

cithara ('sɪθərə) *or* **kithara** *n* a stringed musical instrument of ancient Greece and elsewhere, similar to the lyre and played with a plectrum. [C18: from Greek *kithara*]

cither ('sɪθə) *or* **cithern** ('sɪθən) *n* variants of **cittern.** [C17: from Latin *cithara,* from Greek *kithara* lyre]

citified *or* **cityfied** ('sɪtɪˌfaɪd) *adj Often derogatory.* having the customs, manners, or dress of city people.

citify *or* **cityfy** ('sɪtɪˌfaɪ) *vb* **-fies, -fying, -fied.** (*tr*) **1** to cause to conform to or adopt the customs, habits, or dress of city people. **2** to make urban. ▸ **ˌcitifi'cation** *or* **ˌcityfi'cation** *n*

citizen ('sɪtɪzᵊn) *n* **1** a native registered or naturalized member of a state, nation, or other political community. Compare **alien. 2** an inhabitant of a city or town. **3** a native or inhabitant of any place. **4** a civilian, as opposed to a soldier, public official, etc. Related adj: **civil.** [C14: from Anglo-French *citesein,* from Old French *citeien,* from *cité* CITY] ▸ **citizeness** ('sɪtɪzənɪs, -ˌnɛs) *fem n* ▸ **'citizenly** *adj*

citizenry ('sɪtɪzənrɪ) *n, pl* **-ries.** citizens collectively.

Citizens' Band *n* a range of radio frequencies assigned officially for use by the public for private communication. Abbrev.: **CB.**

Citizen's Charter *n* (in Britain) a government document setting out standards of service for public and private sector bodies, such as schools, hospitals, railway companies, water and energy suppliers, etc.

citizenship ('sɪtɪzənˌʃɪp) *n* **1** the condition or status of a citizen, with its rights and duties. **2** a person's conduct as a citizen: *an award for good citizenship.*

Citlaltépetl (ˌsiːtlɑːl'teɪpetᵊl) *n* a volcano in SE Mexico, in central Veracruz state: the highest peak in the country. Height: 5699 m (18 698 ft.). Spanish name: **Pico de Orizaba** (piko de ori'saba).

citole ('sɪtəʊl, sɪ'təʊl) *n* a rare word for **cittern.** [C14: from Old French, probably from Latin *cithara* CITHER]

citral ('sɪtrəl) *n* a yellow volatile liquid with a lemon-like odour, found in oils of lemon grass, orange, and lemon and used in perfumery: a terpene aldehyde consisting of the *cis-* isomer (**citral-a** or **geranial**) and the *trans-* isomer (**citral-b** or **neral**). Formula: $(CH_3)_2C{:}CH(CH_2)_2C(CH_3){:}CHCHO$. [C19: from CITR(US) + -AL[3]]

citrate ('sɪtreɪt, -rɪt; 'saɪtreɪt) *n* any salt or ester of citric acid. Salts of citric acid are used in beverages and pharmaceuticals. [C18: from CITR(US) + -ATE[1]]

citreous ('sɪtrɪəs) *adj* of a greenish-yellow colour; citron.

citric ('sɪtrɪk) *adj* of or derived from citrus fruits or citric acid.

citric acid *n* a water-soluble weak tribasic acid found in many fruits, esp. citrus fruits, and used in pharmaceuticals and as a flavouring (**E330**). It is extracted from citrus fruits or made by fermenting molasses and is an intermediate in carbohydrate metabolism. Formula: $CH_2(COOH)C(OH)(COOH)CH_2COOH$.

citric acid cycle *n* another name for **Krebs cycle.**

citriculture ('sɪtrɪˌkʌltʃə) *n* the cultivation of citrus fruits. ▸ **ˌcitri'culturist** *n*

citrin ('sɪtrɪn) *n* another name for **vitamin P.**

citrine ('sɪtrɪn) *n* **1** a brownish-yellow variety of quartz: a gemstone; false topaz. **2** the yellow colour of a lemon.

citron ('sɪtrən) *n* **1** a small Asian rutaceous tree, *Citrus medica,* having lemon-like fruit with a thick aromatic rind. See also **citron wood. 2** the fruit of this tree. **3** Also called: **citron melon.** a variety of watermelon, *Citrullus vulgaris citroides,* that has an inedible fruit with a hard rind. **4** the rind of either of these fruits, candied and used for decoration and flavouring of foods. **5** a greenish-yellow colour. [C16: from Old French, from Old Provençal, from Latin *citrus* citrus tree]

citronella (ˌsɪtrə'nɛlə) *n* **1** Also called: **citronella grass.** a tropical Asian grass, *Cymbopogon* (or *Andropogon*) *nardus,* with bluish-green lemon-scented leaves. **2** Also called: **citronella oil.** the yellow aromatic oil obtained from this grass, used in insect repellents, soaps, perfumes, etc. [C19: New Latin, from French *citronnelle* lemon balm, from *citron* lemon]

citronellal (ˌsɪtrə'nɛlæl) *n* a colourless slightly water-soluble liquid with a lemon-like odour, a terpene aldehyde found esp. in citronella and certain eucalyptus oils: used as a flavouring and in soaps and perfumes. Formula: $(CH_3)_2C{:}CH(CH_2)_2CH(CH_3)CH_2CHO$. Also called: **rhodinal.**

citron wood *n* **1** the wood of the citron tree. **2** the wood of the sandarac.

citrulline ('sɪtrəˌliːn) *n* an amino acid that occurs in watermelons and is an intermediate in the formation of urea. Formula: $NH_2CONH(CH_2)_3CHNH_2COOH$. [C20: from Medieval Latin *citrullus* a kind of watermelon, from Latin *citron,* referring to its colour]

citrus ('sɪtrəs) *n, pl* **-ruses. 1** any tree or shrub of the tropical and subtropical rutaceous genus *Citrus,* which includes the orange, lemon, lime, grapefruit, citron, and calamondin. ♦ *adj also* **citrous. 2** of, relating to, or belonging to the genus *Citrus* or to the fruits of plants of this genus. [C19: from Latin: citrus tree, sandarac tree; related to Greek *kedros* cedar]

Città del Vaticano (tʃit'ta del vati'kaːno) *n* the Italian name for **Vatican City.**

cittern ('sɪtɜːn), **cither,** *or* **cithern** *n* a medieval stringed instrument resembling a lute but having wire strings and a flat back. Compare **gittern.** [C16: perhaps a blend of CITHER + GITTERN]

city ('sɪtɪ) *n, pl* **cities. 1** any large town or populous place. **2** (in Britain) a large town that has received this title from the Crown: usually the seat of a bishop. **3** (in the U.S.) an incorporated urban centre with its own government and administration established by state charter. **4** (in Canada) a similar urban municipality incorporated by the provincial government. **5** an ancient Greek city-state; polis. **6** the people of a city collectively. **7** (*modifier*) in or characteristic of a city: *a city girl; city habits.* ♦ Related adjs.: **civic, urban, municipal.** [C13: from Old French *cité,* from Latin *cīvitās* citizenship, state, from *cīvis* citizen]

City ('sɪtɪ) *n* **the. 1** short for **City of London:** the original settlement of London on the N bank of the Thames; a municipality governed by the Lord Mayor and Corporation. Resident pop.: 5893 (1981). **2** the area in central London in which the United Kingdom's major financial business is transacted. **3** the various financial institutions located in this area.

City and Guilds of London Institute *n* (in Britain) an examining body for technical and craft skills, many of the examinations being at a lower standard than for a degree. Often shortened to **City and Guilds.**

city blues *n* (*functioning as sing*) *Jazz.* another name for **urban blues.**

City Code *n* (in Britain) short for **City Code on Takeovers and Mergers:** a code laid down in 1968 (later modified) to control takeover bids and mergers.

City Company *n* (in Britain) a corporation that represents one of the historic trade guilds of London.

city desk *n* **1** *Brit.* the department of a newspaper office dealing with financial and commercial news. **2** *U.S. and Canadian.* the department of a newspaper office dealing with local news.

city editor *n* (on a newspaper) **1** *Brit.* the editor in charge of financial and commercial news. **2** *U.S. and Canadian.* the editor in charge of local news.

city father *n* a person who is active or prominent in the public affairs of a city, such as an alderman.

city hall *n* **1** the building housing the administrative offices of a city or municipal government. **2** *Chiefly U.S. and Canadian.* **2a** municipal government. **2b** the officials of a municipality collectively. **3** *U.S. informal.* bureaucracy.

city manager *n* (in the U.S.) an administrator hired by a municipal council to manage its affairs. See also **council-manager plan.**

City of God *n* **1** *Christianity.* heaven conceived of as the New Jerusalem. **2** the Church in contrast to the world, as described by St Augustine.

city planning *n* the U.S. term for **town planning.** ▸ **city planner** *n*

cityscape ('sɪtɪskeɪp) *n* an urban landscape; view of a city.

city slicker *n Informal.* **1** a person with the sophistication often attributed to city people. **2** a smooth tricky untrustworthy person.

city-state *n* a state consisting of a sovereign city and its dependencies. Among the most famous are the great independent cities of the ancient world, such as Athens, Sparta, Carthage, and Rome.

city technology college *n* (in Britain) a type of senior secondary school specializing in technological subjects, set up in inner-city areas with funding from industry as well as the government. Abbrev.: **CTC.**

Ciudad Bolívar (*Spanish* θiu'ðað bo'liβar) *n* a port in E Venezuela, on the Orinoco River: accessible to ocean-going vessels. Pop.: 225 340 (1990). Former name (1764–1846): **Angostura.**

Ciudad Guayana (*Spanish* θiu'ðað gwa'jana) *n* an industrial conurbation in E Venezuela, on the River Orinoco: iron and steel processing, gold mining. Pop.: 453 047 (1990). Former name: **Santo Tomé de Guayana.**

Ciudad Juárez (*Spanish* θiu'ðað 'xwareθ) *n* a city in N Mexico, in Chihuahua state on the Río Grande, opposite El Paso, Texas. Pop.: 789 522 (1990). Former name (until 1888): **El Paso del Norte** (ɛl 'paso del 'nɔrte).

Ciudad Real (*Spanish* θiu'ðað re'al) *n* a market town in S central Spain. Pop.: 59 400 (1991).

Ciudad Trujillo (*Spanish* θiu'ðað tru'xiʎo) *n* the former name (1936–61) of **Santo Domingo.**

Ciudad Victoria (*Spanish* θiu'ðað bik'torja) *n* a city in E central Mexico, capital of Tamaulipas state. Pop.: 194 996 (1990).

civ. *abbrev. for:* **1** civil. **2** civilian.

civet ('sɪvɪt) *n* **1** any catlike viverrine mammal of the genus *Viverra* and related genera, of Africa and S Asia, typically having blotched or spotted fur and secreting a powerfully smelling fluid from anal glands. **2** the yellowish fatty secretion of such an animal, used as a fixative in the manufacture of perfumes. **3** the fur of such an animal. **4** short for **palm civet.** [C16: from Old French *civette,* from Italian *zibetto,* from Arabic *zabād* civet perfume]

civic ('sɪvɪk) *adj* of or relating to a city, citizens, or citizenship: *civic duties.* [C16: from Latin *cīvicus,* from *cīvis* citizen] ► **'civically** *adv*

civic centre *n Brit.* the public buildings of a town, including recreational facilities and offices of local administration.

civics ('sɪvɪks) *n* (*functioning as sing*) **1** the study of the rights and responsibilities of citizenship. **2** *U.S. and Canadian.* the study of government and its workings.

civic university *n* (in Britain) a university originally instituted as a higher education college serving a particular city.

civies ('sɪvɪz) *pl n Informal.* a variant spelling of **civvies.**

civil ('sɪvᵊl) *adj* **1** of the ordinary life of citizens as distinguished from military, legal, or ecclesiastical affairs. **2** of or relating to the citizen as an individual: *civil rights.* **3** of or occurring within the state or between citizens: *civil strife.* **4** polite or courteous: *a civil manner.* **5** a less common word for **civic.** **6** of or in accordance with Roman law. **7** relating to the private rights of citizens. [C14: from Old French, from Latin *cīvīlis,* from *cīvis* citizen] ► **'civilly** *adv* ► **'civilness** *n*

civil day *n* another name for **calendar day.** See **day** (sense 1).

civil death *n Law.* (formerly) the loss of all civil rights because of a serious conviction. See also **attainder.**

civil defence *n* the organizing of civilians to deal with enemy attacks.

civil disobedience *n* a refusal to obey laws, pay taxes, etc.: a nonviolent means of protesting or of attempting to achieve political goals.

civil engineer *n* a person qualified to design, construct, and maintain public works, such as roads, bridges, harbours, etc. ► **civil engineering** *n*

civilian (sɪ'vɪljən) *n* **a** a person whose primary occupation is civil or nonmilitary. **b** (*as modifier*): *civilian life.* [C14 (originally: a practitioner of civil law): from *civile* (from the Latin phrase *jūs cīvīle* civil law) + -IAN]

civilianize *or* **civilianise** (sɪ'vɪljə,naɪz) *vb* (*tr*) to change the status of (an armed force, a base, etc.) from military to nonmilitary.

civility (sɪ'vɪlɪtɪ) *n, pl* **-ties. 1** politeness or courtesy, esp. when formal. **2** (*often pl*) an act of politeness.

civilization *or* **civilisation** (,sɪvɪlaɪ'zeɪʃən) *n* **1** a human society that has highly developed material and spiritual resources and a complex cultural, political, and legal organization; an advanced state in social development. **2** the peoples or nations collectively who have achieved such a state. **3** the total culture and way of life of a particular people, nation, region, or period: *classical civilization.* **4** the process of bringing or achieving civilization. **5** intellectual, cultural, and moral refinement. **6** cities or populated areas, as contrasted with sparsely inhabited areas, deserts, etc.

civilize *or* **civilise** ('sɪvɪ,laɪz) *vb* (*tr*) **1** to bring out of savagery or barbarism into a state characteristic of civilization. **2** to refine, educate, or enlighten. ► **'civi,lizable** *or* **'civi,lisable** *adj* ► **'civi,lizer** *or* **'civi,liser** *n*

civilized *or* **civilised** ('sɪvɪ,laɪzd) *adj* **1** having a high state of culture and social development. **2** cultured; polite.

civil law *n* **1** the law of a state relating to private and civilian affairs. **2** the body of law in force in ancient Rome, esp. the law applicable to private citizens. **3** any system of law based on the Roman system as distinguished from the common law and canon law. **4** the law of a state as distinguished from international law.

civil liberty *n* the right of an individual to certain freedoms of speech and action.

civil list *n* (in Britain) the annuities voted by Parliament for the support of the royal household and the royal family.

civil marriage *n Law.* a marriage performed by some official other than a clergyman.

civil rights *pl n* **1** the personal rights of the individual citizen, in most countries upheld by law, as in the U.S. **2** (*modifier*) of, relating to, or promoting equality in social, economic, and political rights.

civil servant *n* a member of the civil service.

civil service *n* **1** the service responsible for the public administration of the government of a country. It excludes the legislative, judicial, and military branches. Members of the civil service have no official political allegiance and are not generally affected by changes of governments. **2** the members of the civil service collectively.

civil war *n* war between parties, factions, or inhabitants of different regions within the same nation.

Civil War *n* **1** *English history.* the conflict between Charles I and the Parliamentarians resulting from disputes over their respective prerogatives. Parliament gained decisive victories at Marston Moor in 1644 and Naseby in 1645, and Charles was executed in 1649. **2** *U.S. history.* the war fought from 1861 to 1865 between the North and the South, sparked off by Lincoln's election as president but with deep-rooted political and economic causes, exacerbated by the slavery issue. The advantages of the North in terms of population, finance, and communications brought about the South's eventual surrender at Appomattox.

civil year *n* another name for **calendar year.** See **year** (sense 1).

civism ('sɪvɪzəm) *n Rare.* good citizenship. [C18: from French *civisme,* from Latin *cīvis* citizen]

civvy ('sɪvɪ) *n, pl* **civvies** *or* **civies.** *Slang.* **1** a civilian. **2** (*pl*) civilian dress as opposed to uniform. **3 civvy street.** civilian life.

CJ *abbrev. for* Chief Justice.

CJA (in Britain) *abbrev. for* Criminal Justice Act.

CJD *abbrev. for* Creutzfeldt-Jakob disease.

CKD (in New Zealand) *abbrev. for* Completely Knocked Down: used of a car imported in parts, for local assembly.

cl *symbol for* centilitre.

Cl *the chemical symbol for* chlorine.

CL *international car registration for* Sri Lanka (formerly Ceylon).

cl. *abbrev. for:* **1** class. **2** classification. **3** clerk. **4** cloth. **5** clergyman.

clabby-doo (,klæbɪ'du:) *n Scot.* a variant of **clappy-doo.**

clachan (*Gaelic* 'klaxən; *English* 'klæ-) *n Scot. and Irish dialect.* a small village; hamlet. [C15: from Scottish Gaelic: probably from *clach* stone]

clack (klæk) *vb* **1** to make or cause to make a sound like that of two pieces of wood hitting each other. **2** (*intr*) to jabber. **3** a less common word for **cluck.** ◆ *n* **4** a short sharp sound. **5** a person or thing that produces this sound. **6** chatter. **7** Also called: **clack valve.** a simple nonreturn valve using either a hinged flap or a ball. [C13: probably from Old Norse *klaka* to twitter, of imitative origin] ► **'clacker** *n*

Clackmannan (klæk'mænən) *n* a town in E central Scotland, in Clackmannanshire. Pop.: 3420 (1991).

Clackmannanshire (klæk'mænən,ʃɪə, -ʃə) *n* a council area and historical county of central Scotland; became part of the Central region in 1975 but reinstated as an independent unitary authority in 1996; mainly agricultural. Administrative centre: Alloa. Pop.: 47 900 (1996 est.). Area: 142 sq. km (55 sq. miles).

Clacton *or* **Clacton-on-Sea** ('klæktən) *n* a town and resort in SE England, in E Essex. Pop.: 45 065 (1991).

Clactonian (klæk'təunɪən) *n* **1** one of the Lower Palaeolithic cultures found in England, characterized by the use of chopper tools. ◆ *adj* **2** of, designating, or relating to this culture. [after CLACTON, Essex, where the tools of this culture were first found]

clad[1] (klæd) *vb* a past participle of **clothe.** [Old English *clāthode* clothed, from *clāthian* to CLOTHE]

clad[2] (klæd) *vb* **clads, cladding, clad.** (*tr*) to bond a metal to (another metal), esp. to form a protective coating. [C14 (in the obsolete sense: to clothe): special use of CLAD[1]]

Claddagh ring ('klædə) *n Irish.* any of various elaborately designed rings, esp. one in the shape of two hands embracing a heart, given as a token of lasting affection. [from *Claddagh,* a small fishing village on the edge of Galway city]

cladding ('klædɪŋ) *n* **1** the process of protecting one metal by bonding a second metal to its surface. **2** the protective coating so bonded to metal. **3** the material used for the outside facing of a building, etc.

clade (kleɪd) *n Biology.* a group of organisms considered as having evolved from a common ancestor. [C20: from Greek *klados* branch, shoot]

cladistics (klə'dɪstɪks) *n* (*functioning as sing*) *Biology.* a method of grouping animals by measurable likenesses or homologues. [C20: New Latin, from Greek *klādos* branch, shoot] ► **cladism** ('klædɪzəm) *n* ► **cladist** ('klædɪst) *n*

cladoceran (klə'dɒsərən) *n* **1** any minute freshwater crustacean of the order *Cladocera,* which includes the water fleas. ◆ *adj* **2** of, relating to, or belonging to the *Cladocera.* [C19: from New Latin *Cladocera,* from Greek *klados* shoot + *keras* horn]

cladode ('klædəud) *n Botany.* a flattened stem resembling and functioning as a leaf, as in butcher's-broom. Also called: **cladophyll, phylloclade.** [C19: from New Latin *cladōdium,* from Late Greek *kladōdēs* having many shoots]

cladogram ('kleɪdəu,græm) *n Biology.* a diagram illustrating the development of a clade by homologues. [C20: from CLADE + -O- + -GRAM]

cladophyll ('klædəfɪl) *n* another name for **cladode.** [C19: from Greek *klados* branch + *phullon* leaf]

claes (klez) *pl n* a Scot. word for **clothes.**

claggy ('klægɪ) *adj* **-gier, -giest.** *Chiefly dialect.* stickily clinging, as mud. [C16: from dialect *clag* to daub, clot, of unknown origin]

claim (kleɪm) *vb* (*mainly tr*) **1** to demand as being due or as one's property; assert one's title or right to: *he claimed the record.* **2** (*takes a clause as object or an infinitive*) to assert as a fact; maintain against denial: *he claimed to be telling the truth.* **3** to call for or need; deserve: *this problem claims our attention.* **4** to take: *the accident claimed four lives.* ◆ *n* **5** an assertion of a right; a demand for something as due. **6** an assertion of something as true, real, or factual: *he made claims for his innocence.* **7** a right or just title to something; basis for demand: *a claim to fame.* **8 lay claim to** *or* **stake a claim to.** to assert one's possession of or right to. **9** anything that is claimed, esp. in a formal or legal manner, such as a piece of land staked out by a miner. **10a** a demand for payment in connection with an insurance policy, etc. **10b** the sum of money demanded. [C13: from Old French *claimer* to call, appeal, from Latin *clāmāre* to shout] ► **'claimable** *adj* ► **'claimant** *or* **'claimer** *n*

claiming race *n U.S. and Canadian horse racing.* a race in which each owner declares beforehand the price at which his horse will be offered for sale after the race.

Clair (*French* klɛr) *n* **René** (rəne), real name *René Chomette.* 1898–1981, French film director; noted for his comedies including *An Italian Straw Hat* (1928) and pioneering sound films such as *Sous les toits de Paris* (1930); later films include *Les Belles de nuit* (1952).

clairaudience (ˌklɛərˈɔːdɪəns) *n Psychol.* the postulated ability to hear sounds beyond the range of normal hearing. Compare **clairvoyance.** [C19: from French *clair* clear + AUDIENCE, after CLAIRVOYANCE]

clair-obscure (ˌklɛərəbˈskjʊə) *n* another word for **chiaroscuro.** [C18: from French, literally: clear-obscure]

clairvoyance (klɛəˈvɔɪəns) *n* **1** the alleged power of perceiving things beyond the natural range of the senses. See also **extrasensory perception. 2** keen intuitive understanding. [C19: from French: clear-seeing, from *clair* clear, from Latin *clārus* + *voyance,* from *voir* to see, from Latin *vidēre*]

clairvoyant (klɛəˈvɔɪənt) *adj* **1** of, possessing, or relating to clairvoyance. **2** having great insight or second sight. ◆ *n* **3** a person claiming to have the power to foretell future events. ▸ **clairˈvoyantly** *adv*

clam[1] (klæm) *n* **1** any of various burrowing bivalve molluscs of the genera *Mya, Venus,* etc. Many species, such as the quahog and soft-shell clam, are edible and *Tridacna gigas* is the largest known bivalve, nearly 1.5 metres long. **2** the edible flesh of such a mollusc. **3** *Informal.* a reticent person. ◆ *vb* **clams, clamming, clammed. 4** (*intr*) *Chiefly U.S.* to gather clams. ◆ See also **clam up.** [C16: from earlier *clamshell,* that is, shell that clamps; related to Old English *clamm* fetter, Old High German *klamma* constriction; see CLAMP[1]]

clam[2] (klæm) *vb* **clams, clamming, clammed.** a variant of **clem.**

clamant (ˈkleɪmənt) *adj* **1** noisy. **2** calling urgently. [C17: from Latin *clāmāns,* from *clāmāre* to shout]

clamatorial (ˌklæməˈtɔːrɪəl) *adj* of or relating to the American flycatchers (family *Tyrannidae*). See **flycatcher** (sense 2). [C19: from New Latin *clāmātōres,* plural of Latin *clāmātor* one who shouts; see CLAMANT]

clambake (ˈklæmˌbeɪk) *n U.S. and Canadian.* **1** a picnic, often by the sea, at which clams, etc., are baked. **2** an informal party.

clamber (ˈklæmbə) *vb* **1** (usually foll. by *up, over,* etc.) to climb (something) awkwardly, esp. by using both hands and feet. ◆ *n* **2** a climb performed in this manner. [C15: probably a variant of CLIMB] ▸ **ˈclamberer** *n*

clammy (ˈklæmɪ) *adj* **-mier, -miest. 1** unpleasantly sticky; moist: *clammy hands.* **2** (of the weather, atmosphere, etc.) close; humid. [C14: from Old English *clǣman* to smear; related to Old Norse *kleima,* Old High German *kleimen*] ▸ **ˈclammily** *adv* ▸ **ˈclamminess** *n*

clamour *or U.S.* **clamor** (ˈklæmə) *n* **1** a loud persistent outcry, as from a large number of people. **2** a vehement expression of collective feeling or outrage: *a clamour against higher prices.* **3** a loud and persistent noise: *the clamour of traffic.* ◆ *vb* **4** (*intr;* often foll. by *for* or *against*) to make a loud noise or outcry; make a public demand. **5** (*tr*) to move, influence, or force by outcry: *the people clamoured him out of office.* [C14: from Old French *clamour,* from Latin *clāmor,* from *clāmāre* to cry out] ▸ **ˈclamourer** *or U.S.* **ˈclamorer** *n* ▸ **ˈclamorous** *adj* ▸ **ˈclamorously** *adv* ▸ **ˈclamorousness** *n*

clamp[1] (klæmp) *n* **1** a mechanical device with movable jaws with which an object can be secured to a bench or with which two objects may be secured together. **2** a means by which a fixed joint may be strengthened. **3** *Nautical.* a horizontal beam fastened to the ribs for supporting the deck beams in a wooden vessel. ◆ *vb* (*tr*) **4** to fix or fasten with or as if with a clamp. **5** to immobilize (a car) by means of a wheel clamp. **6** to inflict or impose forcefully: *they clamped a curfew on the town.* [C14: from Dutch or Low German *klamp;* related to Old English *clamm* bond, fetter, Old Norse *kleppr* lump]

clamp[2] (klæmp) *Brit. agriculture. n* **1** a mound formed out of a harvested root crop, covered with straw and earth to protect it from winter weather. **2** a pile of bricks ready for processing in a furnace. ◆ *vb* **3** (*tr*) to enclose (a harvested root crop) in a mound. [C16: from Middle Dutch *klamp* heap; related to CLUMP]

clamp down *vb* (*intr, adv;* often foll. by *on*) **1** to behave repressively; attempt to suppress something regarded as undesirable. ◆ *n* **clampdown. 2** a sudden restrictive measure.

clamper (ˈklæmpə) *n* a spiked metal frame fastened to the sole of a shoe to prevent slipping on ice.

clamshell (ˈklæmˌʃɛl) *n* **1** *Chiefly U.S.* a dredging bucket that is hinged like the shell of a clam. **2** *Aeronautics.* **2a** an aircraft cockpit canopy hinged at the front and rear. **2b** the hinged door of a cargo aircraft. **2c** another name for **eyelid** (sense 2). **3** any of a variety of objects hinged like the shell of a clam, such as a container for takeaway food, a portable computer, etc.

clam up *vb* (*intr, adv*) *Informal.* to keep or become silent or withhold information.

clamworm (ˈklæmˌwɜːm) *n* the U.S. name for the **ragworm.**

clan (klæn) *n* **1** a group of people interrelated by ancestry or marriage. **2** a group of families with a common surname and a common ancestor, acknowledging the same leader, esp. among the Scots and the Irish. **3** a group of people united by common characteristics, aims, or interests. [C14: from Scottish Gaelic *clann* family, descendants, from Latin *planta* sprout, PLANT[1]]

clandestine (klænˈdɛstɪn) *adj* secret and concealed, often for illicit reasons; furtive. [C16: from Latin *clandestīnus,* from *clam* secretly; related to Latin *celāre* to hide] ▸ **clanˈdestinely** *adv* ▸ **clanˈdestineness** *n*

clang (klæŋ) *vb* **1** to make or cause to make a loud resounding noise, as metal when struck. **2** (*intr*) to move or operate making such a sound. ◆ *n* **3** a resounding metallic noise. **4** the harsh cry of certain birds. [C16: from Latin *clangere*]

clang association *n Psychol.* the association made between two words because they sound similar; for example *cling* and *ring.*

clanger (ˈklæŋə) *n* **1** *Informal.* a conspicuous mistake (esp. in the phrase **drop a clanger**). **2** something that clangs or causes a clang. [C20: from CLANG, referring to a mistake whose effects seem to clang]

clangour *or U.S.* **clangor** (ˈklæŋgə, ˈklæŋə) *n* **1** a loud resonant often-repeated noise. **2** an uproar. ◆ *vb* **3** (*intr*) to make or produce a loud resonant noise. [C16: from Latin *clangor* a noise, from *clangere* to CLANG] ▸ **ˈclangorous** *adj* ▸ **ˈclangorously** *adv*

clank (klæŋk) *n* **1** an abrupt harsh metallic sound. ◆ *vb* **2** to make or cause to make such a sound. **3** (*intr*) to move or operate making such a sound. [C17: of imitative origin] ▸ **ˈclankingly** *adv*

clannish (ˈklænɪʃ) *adj* **1** of or characteristic of a clan. **2** tending to associate closely within a limited group to the exclusion of outsiders; cliquish. ▸ **ˈclannishly** *adv* ▸ **ˈclannishness** *n*

clansman (ˈklænzmən) *or* (*fem*) **clanswoman** *n, pl* **-men** *or* **-women.** a person belonging to a clan.

clap[1] (klæp) *vb* **claps, clapping, clapped. 1** to make or cause to make a sharp abrupt sound, as of two nonmetallic objects struck together. **2** to applaud (someone or something) by striking the palms of the hands together sharply. **3** (*tr*) to strike (a person) lightly with an open hand, in greeting, encouragement, etc. **4** (*tr*) to place or put quickly or forcibly: *they clapped him into jail.* **5** (of certain birds) to flap (the wings) noisily. **6** (*tr;* foll. by *up* or *together*) to contrive or put together hastily: *they soon clapped up a shed.* **7 clap eyes on.** *Informal.* to catch sight of. **8 clap hold of.** *Informal.* to grasp suddenly or forcibly. ◆ *n* **9** the sharp abrupt sound produced by striking the hands together. **10** the act of clapping, esp. in applause: *he deserves a good clap.* **11** a sudden sharp sound, esp. of thunder. **12** a light blow. **13** *Archaic.* a sudden action or mishap. [Old English *clæppan;* related to Old High German *klepfen,* Middle Dutch *klape* rattle, Dutch *klepel* clapper; all of imitative origin]

clap[2] (klæp) *n* (usually preceded by *the*) a slang word for **gonorrhoea.** [C16: from Old French *clapoir* venereal sore, from *clapier* brothel, from Old Provençal, from *clap* heap of stones, of obscure origin]

clapboard (ˈklæpˌbɔːd, ˈklæbəd) *n* **1a** a long thin timber board with one edge thicker than the other, used esp. in the U.S. and Canada in wood-frame construction by lapping each board over the one below. **1b** (*as modifier*): *a clapboard house.* ◆ *vb* **2** (*tr*) to cover with such boards. [C16: partial translation of Low German *klappholt,* from *klappen* to crack + *holt* wood; related to Dutch *claphout;* see BOARD]

Clapham Sect (ˈklæpəm) *n* a group of early 19th-century Church of England evangelicals advocating personal piety, the abolition of slavery, etc. [C19: named after *Clapham,* a district of London]

clap-net *n* a net, used esp. by entomologists, that can be closed instantly by pulling a string.

clap on *vb* (*tr*) to don hastily: *they clapped on their armour.*

clapped out *adj* (**clapped-out** *when prenominal*) *Brit., Austral., and N.Z. informal.* (esp. of machinery) worn out; dilapidated.

clapper (ˈklæpə) *n* **1** a person or thing that claps. **2** a contrivance for producing a sound of clapping, as for scaring birds. **3** Also called: **tongue.** a small piece of metal suspended within a bell that causes it to sound when made to strike against its side. **4** a slang word for **tongue** (sense 1). **5 go** (**run, move**) **like the clappers.** *Brit. informal.* to move extremely fast.

clapperboard (ˈklæpəˌbɔːd) *n* a pair of boards clapped together during film shooting in order to aid sound synchronization.

clapper bridge *n* a primitive type of bridge in which planks or slabs of stone rest on piles of stones.

clapperclaw (ˈklæpəˌklɔː) *vb* (*tr*) *Archaic.* **1** to claw or scratch with the hands and nails. **2** to revile; abuse. [C16: perhaps from CLAPPER + CLAW] ▸ **ˈclapperˌclawer** *n*

clappy-doo (ˌklæpɪˈduː) *or* **clabby-doo** *n Scot.* a large black mussel. [C19: probably from Scottish Gaelic *clab* enormous mouth + *dubh* black]

Clapton (ˈklæptən) *n* **Eric.** born 1945, British rock guitarist, noted for his virtuoso style, his work with the Yardbirds (1963–65), Cream (1966–68), and, with Derek and the Dominos, the album *Layla* (1970).

claptrap (ˈklæpˌtræp) *n Informal.* **1** contrived but foolish talk. **2** insincere and pretentious talk: *politicians' claptrap.* [C18 (in the sense: something contrived to elicit applause): from CLAP[1] + TRAP[1]]

claque (klæk) *n* **1** a group of people hired to applaud. **2** a group of fawning admirers. [C19: from French, from *claquer* to clap, of imitative origin]

clarabella *or* **claribella** (ˌklærəˈbɛlə) *n* an eight-foot flute stop on an organ. [C19: from Latin *clāra,* feminine of *clārus* clear + *bella,* feminine of *bellus* beautiful]

Clare[1] (klɛə) *n* a county of W Republic of Ireland, in Munster between Galway Bay and the Shannon estuary. County town: Ennis. Pop.: 94 000 (1996). Area: 3188 sq. km (1231 sq. miles).

Clare[2] (klɛə) *n* **John.** 1793–1864, English poet, noted for his descriptions of country life, particularly in *The Shepherd's Calendar* (1827) and *The Rural Muse* (1835). He was confined in a lunatic asylum from 1837.

clarence (ˈklærəns) *n* a closed four-wheeled horse-drawn carriage, having a glass front. [C19: named after the Duke of *Clarence* (1765–1837)]

Clarenceux (ˈklærənsuː) *n Heraldry.* the second King-of-Arms in England.

clarendon (ˈklærəndən) *n Printing.* a style of boldface roman type. [C20: named after the Clarendon Press at Oxford University]

Clarendon[1] (ˈklærəndən) *n* a village near Salisbury in S England: site of a council held by Henry II in 1164 that produced a code of laws (the **Constitutions of Clarendon**) defining relations between church and state.

Clarendon[2] (ˈklærəndən) *n* **1st Earl of,** title of *Edward Hyde.* 1609–74, English statesman and historian; chief adviser to Charles II (1660–67); author of *History of the Rebellion and Civil Wars in England* (1704–07).

Clarendon Code *n English history.* four acts passed by the Cavalier Parliament between 1661 and 1665 to deal with the religious problems of the Restoration. [C17: named after Edward Hyde, first Earl of CLARENDON, who was not, however, a supporter of the code]

Clare of Assisi *n* **Saint.** 1194–1253, Italian nun; founder of the Franciscan Order of Poor Clares. Feast day: Aug. 11.

claret ('klærət) *n* **1** *Chiefly Brit.* a red wine, esp. one from the Bordeaux district of France. **2a** a purplish-red colour. **2b** (*as adj*): *a claret carpet.* [C14: from Old French (*vin*) *claret* clear (wine), from Medieval Latin *clārātum,* from *clārāre* to make clear, from Latin *clārus* CLEAR]

claret cup *n* an iced drink made of claret, brandy, lemon, sugar, and sometimes sherry, Curaçao, etc.

clarify ('klærɪˌfaɪ) *vb* **-fies, -fying, -fied. 1** to make or become clear or easy to understand. **2** to make or become free of impurities. **3** to make (fat, butter, etc.) clear by heating, etc., or (of fat, etc.) to become clear as a result of such a process. [C14: from Old French *clarifier,* from Late Latin *clārificāre,* from Latin *clārus* clear + *facere* to make] ▸ **ˌclarifiˈcation** *n* ▸ **ˈclariˌfier** *n*

clarinet (ˌklærɪˈnɛt) *n Music.* **1** a keyed woodwind instrument with a cylindrical bore and a single reed. It is a transposing instrument, most commonly pitched in A or B flat. Obsolete name: **clarionet** (ˌklærɪəˈnɛt). **2** an orchestral musician who plays the clarinet. [C18: from French *clarinette,* probably from Italian *clarinetto,* from *clarino* trumpet] ▸ **ˌclariˈnettist** *or* **ˌclariˈnetist** *n*

clarino (klæˈriːnəʊ) *Music. adj* **1** of or relating to a high passage for the trumpet in 18th-century music. ◆ *n, pl* **-nos** *or* **-ni** (-nɪ). **2** the high register of the trumpet. **3** an organ stop similar to the high register of the trumpet. **4** a trumpet or clarion.

clarion ('klærɪən) *n* **1** a four-foot reed stop of trumpet quality on an organ. **2** an obsolete, high-pitched, small-bore trumpet. **3** the sound of such an instrument or any similar sound. ◆ *adj* **4** (*prenominal*) clear and ringing; inspiring: *a clarion call to action.* ◆ *vb* **5** to proclaim loudly. [C14: from Medieval Latin *clāriō* trumpet, from Latin *clārus* clear]

clarity ('klærɪtɪ) *n* **1** clearness, as of expression. **2** clearness, as of water. [C16: from Latin *clāritās,* from *clārus* CLEAR]

Clark (klɑːk) *n* **1 James,** known as *Jim.* 1936–68, Scottish racing driver; World Champion (1963, 1965). **2 Kenneth,** Baron Clark of Saltwood. 1903–83, English art historian: his books include *Civilization* (1969), which he first presented as a television series. **3 William.** 1770–1838, U.S. explorer and frontiersman: best known for his expedition to the Pacific Northwest (1804–06) with Meriwether Lewis.

Clark cell *n Physics.* a cell having a mercury anode surrounded by a paste of mercuric sulphate and a zinc cathode in a saturated solution of zinc sulphate. Formerly used as a standard, its emf is 1.4345 volts. [C19: named after Hosiah Clark (died 1898), English scientist]

Clarke (klɑːk) *n* **1** Sir **Arthur C(harles).** born 1917, British science-fiction writer, who helped to develop the first communications satellites. He scripted the film *2001, A Space Odyssey* (1968). **2 Austin.** 1896–1974, Irish poet and verse dramatist. His work includes the poem *The Vengeance of Fionn* (1917) and the play *The Son of Learning* (1927). **3 Jeremiah.** ?1673–1707, English composer and organist, best known for his *Trumpet Voluntary,* formerly attributed to Purcell. **4 Kenneth Harry.** born 1940, British Conservative politician: secretary of state for health (1988–90); secretary of state for education (1990–92); home secretary (1992–93); chancellor of the exchequer (1993–97). **5 Marcus (Andrew Hislop).** 1846–81, Australian novelist born in England, noted for his novel *For the Term of His Natural Life,* published in serial form (1870–72); other works include *Twixt Shadow and Shine* (1875).

clarkia ('klɑːkɪə) *n* any North American onagraceous plant of the genus *Clarkia:* cultivated for their red, purple, or pink flowers. [C19: New Latin, named after William CLARK, who discovered it]

Clarkson ('klɑːksən) *n* **Thomas.** 1760–1846, British campaigner for the abolition of slavery.

claro ('klɑːrəʊ) *n, pl* **-ros** *or* **-roes.** a mild light-coloured cigar. [from Spanish: CLEAR]

clarsach ('klɑrsəx, 'klɑːsək) *n* the Celtic harp of Scotland and Ireland. [C15: *clareschaw,* from Scottish Gaelic *clarsach,* Irish Gaelic *cláirsach* harp]

clarts (klɑːts; *Scot.* klærts) *pl n Scot. and northern English dialect.* lumps of mud, esp. on shoes. [of unknown origin] ▸ **ˈclarty** *adj*

clary ('klɛərɪ) *n, pl* **claries.** any of several European plants of the genus *Salvia,* having aromatic leaves and blue flowers: family *Labiatae* (labiates). [C14: from earlier *sclarreye,* from Medieval Latin *sclareia,* of obscure origin]

-clase *n combining form.* (in mineralogy) indicating a particular type of cleavage: *plagioclase.* [via French from Greek *klasis* a breaking, from *klan* to break]

clash (klæʃ) *vb* **1** to make or cause to make a loud harsh sound, esp. by striking together. **2** (*intr*) to be incompatible; conflict. **3** (*intr*) to engage together in conflict or contest. **4** (*intr*) (of dates or events) to coincide. **5** (*intr*) (of colours) to look ugly or inharmonious together. ◆ *n* **6** a loud harsh noise. **7** a collision or conflict. **8** *Scot.* gossip; tattle. [C16: of imitative origin] ▸ **ˈclasher** *n* ▸ **ˈclashingly** *adv*

clasp (klɑːsp) *n* **1** a fastening, such as a catch or hook, used for holding things together. **2** a firm grasp, hold, or embrace. **3** *Military.* a bar or insignia on a medal ribbon, to indicate either a second award or the battle, campaign, or reason for its award. ◆ *vb* (*tr*) **4** to hold in a firm grasp. **5** to grasp firmly with the hand. **6** to fasten together with or as if with a clasp. [C14: of uncertain origin; compare Old English *clyppan* to embrace] ▸ **ˈclasper** *n*

claspers ('klɑːspəz) *pl n Zoology.* **1** a paired organ of male insects, used to clasp the female during copulation. **2** a paired organ of male sharks and related fish, used to assist the transfer of spermatozoa into the body of the female during copulation.

clasp knife *n* a large knife with one or more blades or other devices folding into the handle.

class (klɑːs) *n* **1** a collection or division of people or things sharing a common characteristic, attribute, quality, or property. **2** a group of persons sharing a similar social position and certain economic, political, and cultural characteristics. **3** (in Marxist theory) a group of persons sharing the same relationship to the means of production. **4a** the pattern of divisions that exist within a society on the basis of rank, economic status, etc. **4b** (*as modifier*): *the class struggle; class distinctions.* **5a** a group of pupils or students who are taught and study together. **5b** a meeting of a group of students for tuition. **6** *Chiefly U.S.* a group of students who graduated in a specified year: *the class of '53.* **7** (*in combination and as modifier*) *Brit.* a grade of attainment in a university honours degree: *second-class honours.* **8** one of several standards of accommodation in public transport. See also **first class, second class, third class. 9a** *Informal.* excellence or elegance, esp. in dress, design, or behaviour: *that girl's got class.* **9b** (*as modifier*): *a class act.* **10a** outstanding speed and stamina in a racehorse. **10b** (*as modifier*): *the class horse in the race.* **11** *Biology.* any of the taxonomic groups into which a phylum is divided and which contains one or more orders. *Amphibia, Reptilia,* and *Mammalia* are three classes of phylum *Chordata.* **12** *Maths, logic.* **12a** another name for **set**[2] (sense 3). **12b proper class.** a class which cannot itself be a member of other classes. **13 in a class of its own** *or* **in a class by oneself.** unequalled; unparalleled. ◆ *vb* **14** to have or assign a place within a group, grade, or class. [C17: from Latin *classis* class, rank, fleet; related to Latin *calāre* to summon] ▸ **ˈclassable** *adj* ▸ **ˈclasser** *n*

class. *abbrev. for:* **1** classic(al). **2** classification. **3** classified.

class-A amplifier *n* an electronic amplifier in which the output current flows for the whole of the input signal cycle.

class action *n U.S. law* a legal action undertaken by one or more people representing the interests of a large group of people with the same grievance.

class-B amplifier *n* an electronic amplifier in which the output flows for half of the input signal cycle.

class-C amplifier *n* an electronic amplifier in which the output current flows for less than half of the input cycle.

class-conscious *adj* aware of belonging to a particular social rank or grade, esp. in being hostile or proud because of class distinctions. ▸ **ˌclass-ˈconsciousness** *n*

classic ('klæsɪk) *adj* **1** of the highest class, esp. in art or literature. **2** serving as a standard or model of its kind; definitive. **3** adhering to an established set of rules or principles in the arts or sciences: *a classic proof.* **4** characterized by simplicity, balance, regularity, and purity of form; classical. **5** of lasting interest or significance. **6** continuously in fashion because of its simple and basic style: *a classic day dress.* ◆ *n* **7** an author, artist, or work of art of the highest excellence. **8** a creation or work considered as definitive. **9** *Horse racing.* **9a** any of the five principal races for three-year-old horses in Britain, namely the One Thousand Guineas, Two Thousand Guineas, Derby, Oaks, and Saint Leger. **9b** a race equivalent to any of these in other countries. ◆ See also **classics.** [C17: from Latin *classicus* of the first rank, from *classis* division, rank, CLASS]

classical ('klæsɪkᵊl) *adj* **1** of, relating to, or characteristic of the ancient Greeks and Romans or their civilization, esp. in the period of their ascendancy. **2** designating, following, or influenced by the art or culture of ancient Greece or Rome: *classical architecture.* **3** *Music.* **3a** of, relating to, or denoting any music or its period of composition marked by stability of form, intellectualism, and restraint. Compare **romantic** (sense 5). **3b** accepted as a standard: *the classical suite.* **3c** denoting serious art music in general. Compare **pop**[2]. **4** *Music.* of or relating to a style of music composed, esp. at Vienna, during the late 18th and early 19th centuries. This period is marked by the establishment, esp. by Haydn and Mozart, of sonata form. **5** denoting or relating to a style in any of the arts characterized by emotional restraint and conservatism: *a classical style of painting.* See **classicism** (sense 1). **6** well versed in the art and literature of ancient Greece and Rome. **7** (of an education) based on the humanities and the study of Latin and Greek. **8** *Physics.* **8a** not involving the quantum theory or the theory of relativity: *classical mechanics.* **8b** obeying the laws of Newtonian mechanics or 19th-century physics: *a classical gas.* **9** another word for **classic** (senses 2, 4). **10** (of a logical or mathematical system) according with the law of excluded middle, so that every statement is known to be either true or false even if it is not known which. ▸ **ˌclassiˈcality** *or* **ˈclassicalness** *n* ▸ **ˈclassically** *adv*

classical college *n* (in Quebec) a college offering a programme that emphasizes the classics and leads to university entrance.

classical conditioning *n Psychol.* the alteration in responding that occurs when two stimuli are regularly paired in close succession: the response originally given to the second stimulus comes to be given to the first. See also **conditioned response.**

classical probability *n* another name for **mathematical probability.**

Classical school *n* economic theory based on the works of Adam Smith and David Ricardo, which explains the creation of wealth and advocates free trade.

classic blues *n* (*functioning as sing or pl*) *Jazz.* a type of city blues performed by a female singer accompanied by a small group.

classicism ('klæsɪˌsɪzəm) *or* **classicalism** ('klæsɪkəˌlɪzəm) *n* **1** a style based on the study of Greek and Roman models, characterized by emotional restraint and regularity of form, associated esp. with the 18th century in Europe; the antithesis of romanticism. Compare **neoclassicism. 2** knowledge or study of the culture of ancient Greece and Rome. **3a** a Greek or Latin form or expression. **3b** an expression in a modern language, such as English, that is modelled on a Greek or Latin form.

classicist ('klæsɪsɪst) *or* **classicalist** ('klæsɪkəlɪst) *n* **1a** a student of ancient Latin and Greek. **1b** a person who advocates the study of ancient Latin and Greek. **2** an adherent of classicism in literature or art. ▸ **ˌclassiˈcistic** *adj*

classicize *or* **classicise** ('klæsɪˌsaɪz) *vb* **1** (*tr*) to make classic. **2** (*intr*) to imitate classical style.

classics ('klæsɪks) *pl n* **1 the.** a body of literature regarded as great or lasting, esp. that of ancient Greece or Rome. **2 the.** the ancient Greek and Latin languages. **3** (*functioning as sing*) ancient Greek and Roman culture considered as a subject for academic study.

classification (ˌklæsɪfɪ'keɪʃən) *n* **1** systematic placement in categories. **2** one of the divisions in a system of classifying. **3** *Biology.* **3a** the placing of animals and plants in a series of increasingly specialized groups because of similarities in structure, origin, etc., that indicate a common relationship. The major groups are kingdom, phylum (in animals) or division (in plants), class, order, family, genus, and species. **3b** the study of the principles and practice of this process; taxonomy. **4** *Government.* the designation of an item of information as being secret and not available to people outside a restricted group. [C18: from French; see CLASS, -IFY, -ATION] ► ˌ**classifi'cational** *adj* ► ˌ**classifi'catory** *adj*

classification schedule *n Library science.* the printed scheme of a system of classification.

classified ('klæsɪˌfaɪd) *adj* **1** arranged according to some system of classification. **2** *Government.* (of information) not available to people outside a restricted group, esp. for reasons of national security. **3** (of information) closely concealed or secret. **4** (of advertisements in newspapers, etc.) arranged according to type. **5** *Brit.* (of newspapers) containing sports results, esp. football results. **6** (of British roads) having a number in the national road system. If the number is preceded by an M the road is a motorway, if by an A it is a first-class road, and if by a B it is a secondary road.

classify ('klæsɪˌfaɪ) *vb* **-fies, -fying, -fied.** (*tr*) **1** to arrange or order by classes; categorize. **2** *Government.* to declare (information, documents, etc.) of possible aid to an enemy and therefore not available to people outside a restricted group. [C18: back formation from CLASSIFICATION] ► '**classiˌfiable** *adj* ► '**classiˌfier** *n*

class interval *n Statistics.* one of the intervals into which the range of a variable of a distribution is divided, esp. one of the divisions of the base line of a bar chart or histogram.

classis ('klæsɪs) *n, pl* **classes** ('klæsiːz). (in some Reformed Churches) **1** a governing body of elders or pastors. **2** the district or group of local churches directed by such a body. [C16: from Latin; see CLASS]

classless ('klɑːslɪs) *adj* **1** not belonging to or forming a class. **2** characterized by the absence of economic and social distinctions. ► '**classlessness** *n*

class list *n* (in Britain) a list categorizing students according to the class of honours they have obtained in their degree examination.

class mark *n* **1** *Statistics.* a value within a class interval, esp. its midpoint or the nearest integral value, used to represent the interval for computational convenience. **2** Also called: **class number.** *Library science.* a symbol on a book or other publication indicating its subject field, shelf position, etc.

classmate ('klɑːsˌmeɪt) *n* a friend or contemporary of the same class in a school, college, etc.

classroom ('klɑːsˌruːm, -ˌrʊm) *n* a room in which classes are conducted, esp. in a school or college.

class struggle *n* **the.** *Marxism.* the continual conflict between the capitalist and working classes for economic and political power. Also called: **class war.**

classy ('klɑːsɪ) *adj* **classier, classiest.** *Slang.* elegant; stylish. ► '**classily** *adv* ► '**classiness** *n*

clastic ('klæstɪk) *adj* **1** (of sedimentary rock, etc.) composed of fragments of pre-existing rock that have been transported some distance from their points of origin. **2** *Biology.* dividing into parts: *a clastic cell.* **3** able to be dismantled for study or observation: *a clastic model of the brain.* [C19: from Greek *klastos* shattered, from *klan* to break]

clathrate ('klæθreɪt) *adj* **1** *Botany.* resembling a net or lattice. ◆ *n* **2** *Chem.* a solid compound in which molecules of one substance are physically trapped in the crystal lattice of another. [C17: from Latin *clāthrāre* to provide with a lattice, from Greek *klēthra,* from *klaithron* a bar]

clatter ('klætə) *vb* **1** to make or cause to make a rattling noise, esp. as a result of movement. **2** (*intr*) to chatter. ◆ *n* **3** a rattling sound or noise. **4** a noisy commotion, such as one caused by loud chatter. [Old English *clatrung* clattering (gerund); related to Dutch *klateren* to rattle, German *klatschen* to smack, Norwegian *klattra* to knock] ► '**clatterer** *n* ► '**clatteringly** *adv* ► '**clattery** *adj*

Claude (klɔːd; *French* klod) *n* **Albert.** 1898–1983, U.S. cell biologist, born in Belgium: shared the Nobel prize for physiology or medicine (1974) for work on microsomes and mitochondria.

Claudel (*French* klodɛl) *n* **Paul** (**Louis Charles Marie**) (pɔl). 1868–1955, French dramatist, poet, and diplomat, whose works testify to his commitment to the Roman Catholic faith. His plays include *L'Annonce faite à Marie* (1912) and *Le Soulier de satin* (1919–24).

Claude Lorrain (*French* klod lɔrɛ̃) *n* real name *Claude Gelée.* 1600–82, French painter, esp. of idealized landscapes, noted for his subtle depiction of light.

claudication (ˌklɔːdɪ'keɪʃən) *n* **1** limping; lameness. **2** *Pathol.* short for **intermittent claudication.** [C18: from Latin *claudicātiō,* from *claudicāre,* from *claudus* lame]

Claudius ('klɔːdɪəs) *n* full name *Tiberius Claudius Drusus Nero Germanicus.* 10 B.C.–54 A.D., Roman emperor (41–54); invaded Britain (43); poisoned by his fourth wife, Agrippina.

Claudius II *n* full name *Marcus Aurelius Claudius,* called *Gothicus.* 214–270 A.D., Roman emperor (268–270).

clause (klɔːz) *n* **1** *Grammar.* a group of words, consisting of a subject and a predicate including a finite verb, that does not necessarily constitute a sentence. See also **main clause, subordinate clause, coordinate clause. 2** a section of a legal document such as a contract, will, or draft statute. [C13: from Old French, from Medieval Latin *clausa* a closing (of a rhetorical period), back formation from Latin *clausula,* from *claudere* to close] ► '**clausal** *adj*

Clausewitz (*German* 'klauzəvɪts) *n* **Karl von** (karl fɔn). 1780–1831, Prussian general, noted for his works on military strategy, esp. *Vom Kriege* (1833).

Clausius (*German* 'klauziʊs) *n* **Rudolf Julius** ('ruːdɔlf 'juːliʊs). 1822–88, German physicist and mathematician. He enunciated the second law of thermodynamics (1850) and developed the kinetic theory of gases.

claustral ('klɔːstrəl) *adj* a less common variant of **cloistral.**

claustrophobia (ˌklɔːstrə'fəʊbɪə, ˌklɒs-) *n* an abnormal fear of being closed in or of being in a confined space. [C19: from *claustro-,* from Latin *claustrum* CLOISTER + -PHOBIA] ► '**claustroˌphobe** *n* ► ˌ**claustro'phobic** *adj* ► ˌ**claustro'phobically** *adv*

clavate ('kleɪveɪt, -vɪt) *or* **claviform** *adj* shaped like a club with the thicker end uppermost. [C19: from Latin *clāva* club] ► '**clavately** *adv*

clave[1] (kleɪv, klɑːv) *n Music.* one of a pair of hardwood sticks struck together to make a hollow sound, esp. to mark the beat of Latin-American dance music. [C20: from American Spanish, from Latin *clavis* key]

clave[2] (kleɪv) *vb Archaic.* a past tense of **cleave.**

clave[3] (kleɪv) *n Zoology.* a clublike thickening at the upper end of an organ, esp. of the antenna of an insect. [C19: from Latin *clāva* club]

claver ('kleɪvə) *Scot. vb* (*intr*) **1** to talk idly; gossip. ◆ *n* **2** (*often pl*) idle talk; gossip. [C13: of uncertain origin]

clavicembalo (ˌklævɪ'tʃɛmbələʊ) *n, pl* **-los.** another name for **harpsichord.** [C18: from Italian, from Medieval Latin *clāvis* key + *cymbalum* CYMBAL]

clavichord ('klævɪˌkɔːd) *n* a keyboard instrument consisting of a number of thin wire strings struck from below by brass tangents. The instrument is noted for its delicate tones, since the tangents do not rebound from the string until the key is released. [C15: from Medieval Latin *clāvichordium,* from Latin *clāvis* key + *chorda* string, CHORD[1]] ► '**claviˌchordist** *n*

clavicle ('klævɪkᵊl) *n* **1** either of the two bones connecting the shoulder blades with the upper part of the breastbone. Nontechnical name: **collarbone. 2** the corresponding structure in other vertebrates. [C17: from Medieval Latin *clāvicula,* from Latin *clāvis* key] ► **clavicular** (klə'vɪkjʊlə) *adj* ► **claviculate** (klə'vɪkjʊˌleɪt) *adj*

clavicorn ('klævɪˌkɔːn) *n* **1** any beetle of the group *Clavicornia,* including the ladybirds, characterized by club-shaped antennae. ◆ *adj* **2** of, relating to, or belonging to the *Clavicornia.* [C19: from New Latin *Clavicornia,* from Latin *clāva* club + *cornū* horn]

clavier (klə'vɪə, 'klævɪə) *n* **a** any keyboard instrument. **b** the keyboard itself. [C18: from French: keyboard, from Old French (in the sense: key bearer), from Latin *clāvis* key]

claviform ('klævɪˌfɔːm) *adj* another word for **clavate.** [C19: from Latin *clāva* club]

Clavius ('kleɪvɪəs) *n* one of the largest of the craters on the moon, about 230 kilometres (145 miles) in diameter, whose walls have peaks up to 5700 metres (19 000 feet) above the floor. It lies in the SE quadrant.

claw (klɔː) *n* **1** a curved pointed horny process on the end of each digit in birds, some reptiles, and certain mammals. **2** a corresponding structure in some invertebrates, such as the pincer of a crab. **3** a part or member like a claw in function or appearance. **4** *Botany.* the narrow basal part of certain petals and sepals. ◆ *vb* **5** to scrape, tear, or dig (something or someone) with claws, etc. **6** (*tr*) to create by scratching as with claws: *to claw an opening.* [Old English *clawu;* related to Old High German *kluwi,* Sanskrit *glau-* ball, sphere] ► '**clawer** *n* ► '**clawless** *adj*

claw back *vb* (*tr, adv*) **1** to get back (something) with difficulty. **2** to recover (a sum of money), esp. by taxation or a penalty. ◆ *n* **clawback. 3** the recovery of a sum of money, esp. by taxation or a penalty. **4** the sum so recovered.

claw hammer *n* a hammer with a cleft at one end of the head for extracting nails. Also called: **carpenter's hammer.**

claw hatchet *n* a hatchet with a claw at one end of its head for extracting nails.

claw off *vb* (*adv, usually tr*) *Nautical.* to avoid the dangers of (a lee shore or other hazard) by beating.

claw setting *n Brit.* a jewellery setting with clawlike prongs. U.S. equivalent: **Tiffany setting.**

clay (kleɪ) *n* **1** a very fine-grained material that consists of hydrated aluminium silicate, quartz, and organic fragments and occurs as sedimentary rocks, soils, and other deposits. It becomes plastic when moist but hardens on heating and is used in the manufacture of bricks, cement, ceramics, etc. Related adj: **figuline. 2** earth or mud in general. **3** *Poetic.* the material of the human body. ◆ *vb* **4** (*tr*) to cover or mix with clay. [Old English *clǣg;* related to Old High German *klīa,* Norwegian *kli,* Latin *glūs* glue, Greek *gloios* sticky oil] ► '**clayey,** '**clayish,** *or* '**clayˌlike** *adj*

Clay (kleɪ) *n* **1 Cassius.** See **Muhammad Ali. 2 Henry.** 1777–1852, U.S. statesman and orator; secretary of state (1825–29).

claybank ('kleɪˌbæŋk) *n U.S.* **a** a dull brownish-orange colour. **b** (*as adj*): *a claybank horse.*

clay court *n* a tennis court with a playing surface topped by a layer of crushed shale, brick, or stone.

clay mineral *n* any of a group of minerals consisting of hydrated aluminium silicates: the major constituents of clays.

claymore ('kleɪˌmɔː; *Scot.* ˌkle'mor) *n* a large two-edged broadsword used formerly by Scottish Highlanders. [C18: from Gaelic *claidheamh mōr* great sword]

claypan ('kleɪˌpæn) *n* a layer of stiff impervious clay situated just below the surface of the ground, which holds water after heavy rain.

clay pigeon *n* **1** a disc of baked clay hurled into the air from a machine as a target to be shot at. **2** *U.S. slang.* a person in a defenceless position; sitting duck.

clay road *n N.Z.* an unsealed and unmetalled road in a rural area.

claystone ('kleɪˌstəʊn) *n* a compact very fine-grained rock consisting of consolidated clay particles.

claytonia (kleɪˈtəʊnɪə) *n* any low-growing North American succulent portulaceous plant of the genus *Claytonia*. [C18: named after John *Clayton* (1693–1773), American botanist]

-cle *suffix forming nouns*. indicating smallness: *cubicle; particle*. [via Old French from Latin *-culus*. See -CULE]

clean (kliːn) *adj* **1** without dirt or other impurities; unsoiled. **2** without anything in it or on it: *a clean page*. **3** without extraneous or foreign materials. **4** without defect, difficulties, or problems: *a clean test flight*. **5a** (of a nuclear weapon) producing little or no radioactive fallout or contamination. **5b** uncontaminated. Compare **dirty** (sense 11). **6** (of a wound, etc.) having no pus or other sign of infection. **7** pure; morally sound. **8** without objectionable language or obscenity: *a clean joke*. **9** (of printer's proofs, etc.) relatively free from errors; easily readable: *clean copy*. **10** thorough or complete: *a clean break*. **11** dexterous or adroit: *a clean throw*. **12** *Sport*. played fairly and without fouls. **13** simple in design: *a ship's clean lines*. **14** *Aeronautics*. causing little turbulence; streamlined. **15** (of an aircraft) having no projections, such as rockets, flaps, etc., into the airstream. **16** honourable or respectable. **17** habitually neat. **18** (esp. of a driving licence) showing or having no record of offences. **19** *Slang*. **19a** innocent; not guilty. **19b** not carrying illegal drugs, weapons, etc. **20** *Nautical*. (of a vessel) **20a** having its bottom clean. **20b** having a satisfactory bill of health. **21** *Old Testament*. **21a** (of persons) free from ceremonial defilement. **21b** (of animals, birds, and fish) lawful to eat. **22** *New Testament*. morally and spiritually pure. ♦ *vb* **23** to make or become free of dirt, filth, etc.: *the stove cleans easily*. **24** (*tr*) to remove in making clean: *to clean marks off the wall*. **25** (*tr*) to prepare (fish, poultry, etc.) for cooking: *to clean a chicken*. ♦ *adv* **26** in a clean way; cleanly. **27** *Not standard*. (intensifier): *clean forgotten; clean dead*. **28 clean bowled**. *Cricket*. bowled by a ball that breaks the wicket without hitting the batsman or his bat. **29 come clean**. *Informal*. to make a revelation or confession. ♦ *n* **30** the act or an instance of cleaning: *he gave his shoes a clean*. **31 clean sweep**. See **sweep** (sense 33). ♦ See also **clean out, clean up**. [Old English *clǣne*; related to Old Frisian *klēne* small, neat, Old High German *kleini*] ► ˈ**cleanable** *adj* ► ˈ**cleanness** *n*

clean-cut *adj* **1** clearly outlined; neat: *clean-cut lines of a ship*. **2** definite: *a clean-cut decision in boxing*.

cleaner (ˈkliːnə) *n* **1** a person, device, chemical agent, etc., that removes dirt, as from clothes or carpets. **2** (*usually pl*) a shop, etc. that provides a dry-cleaning service. **3 take (a person) to the cleaners**. *Informal*. to rob or defraud (a person) of all of his money.

clean-limbed *adj* having well-proportioned limbs.

cleanly *adv* (ˈkliːnlɪ). **1** in a fair manner. **2** easily or smoothly: *the screw went into the wood cleanly*. ♦ *adj* (ˈklɛnlɪ), **-lier, -liest**. **3** habitually clean or neat. ► **cleanlily** (ˈklɛnlɪlɪ) *adv* ► **cleanliness** (ˈklɛnlɪnɪs) *n*

clean out *vb* (*tr, adv*) **1** (foll. by *of* or *from*) to remove (something) (from or away from). **2** *Slang*. to leave (someone) with no money: *gambling had cleaned him out*. **3** *Informal*. to exhaust (stocks, goods, etc.) completely.

cleanse (klɛnz) *vb* (*tr*) **1** to remove dirt, filth, etc., from. **2** to remove guilt from. [Old English *clǣnsian*; related to Middle Low German *klēnsen*; see CLEAN] ► ˈ**cleansable** *adj*

cleanser (ˈklɛnzə) *n* a cleansing agent, such as a detergent.

clean-shaven *adj* (of men) having the facial hair shaved off.

clean sheet *n Sport*. an instance of conceding no goals or points in a match or competition (esp. in the phrase **keep a clean sheet**).

cleanskin (ˈkliːnˌskɪn) *n Austral*. **1** an unbranded animal. **2** *Slang*. a person without a criminal record.

Cleanthes (klɪˈænθiːz) *n* ?300–?232 B.C., Greek philosopher: succeeded Zeno as head of the Stoic school.

clean up *vb* (*adv*) **1** to rid (something) of dirt, filth, or other impurities. **2** to make (someone or something) orderly or presentable. **3** (*tr*) to rid (a place) of undesirable people or conditions: *the campaign against vice had cleaned up the city*. **4** (*intr*) *Informal*. to make a great profit. ♦ *n* **cleanup**. **5a** the process of cleaning up or eliminating something. **5b** (*as modifier*): *a cleanup campaign*. **6** *Informal, chiefly U.S*. a great profit.

clean wool *n* wool that has been scoured to remove wax.

clear (klɪə) *adj* **1** free from darkness or obscurity; bright. **2** (of weather) free from dullness or clouds. **3** transparent: *clear water*. **4** even and pure in tone or colour: *clear blue*. **5** without discoloration, blemish, or defect: *a clear skin*. **6** easy to see or hear; distinct. **7** free from doubt or confusion: *his instructions are not clear*. **8** (*postpositive*) certain in the mind; sure: *are you clear?* **9** evident or obvious: *it is clear that he won't come now*. **10** (of sounds or the voice) not harsh or hoarse. **11** serene; calm. **12** without qualification or limitation; complete: *a clear victory*. **13** free of suspicion, guilt, or blame: *a clear conscience*. **14** free of obstruction; open: *a clear passage*. **15** free from debt or obligation. **16** (of money, profits, etc.) without deduction; net. **17** emptied of freight or cargo. **18** (of timber) having a smooth, unblemished surface. **19** Also: **in clear**. (of a message, etc.) not in code. **20** Also: **light**. *Phonetics*. denoting an (l) in whose articulation the main part of the tongue is brought forward giving the sound of a front-vowel timbre. **21** *Showjumping*. (of a round) ridden without any fences being knocked down or any points being lost. ♦ *adv* **22** in a clear or distinct manner. **23** completely or utterly. **24** (*postpositive*; often foll. by *of*) not in contact (with); free: *stand clear of the gates*. ♦ *n* **25** a clear space. **26** another word for **clearance**. **27 in the clear**. **27a** free of suspicion, guilt, or blame. **27b** *Sport*. able to receive a pass without being tackled. ♦ *vb* **28** to make or become free from darkness, obscurity, etc. **29** (*intr*) **29a** (of the weather) to become free from dullness, fog, rain, etc. **29b** (of mist, fog, etc.) to disappear. **30** (*tr*) to free from impurity or blemish. **31** (*tr*) to free from doubt or confusion: *to clear one's mind*. **32** (*tr*) to rid of objects, obstructions, etc. **33** (*tr*) to make or form (a path, way, etc.) by removing obstructions. **34** (*tr*) to free or remove (a person or thing) from something, such as suspicion, blame, or guilt. **35** (*tr*) to move or pass by or over without contact or involvement: *he cleared the wall easily*. **36** (*tr*) to rid (the throat) of phlegm or obstruction. **37** (*tr*) to make or gain (money) as profit. **38** (*tr*; often foll. by *off*) to discharge or settle (a debt). **39** (*tr*) to free (a debtor) from obligation. **40** (*intr*) (of a cheque) to pass through one's bank and be charged against one's account. **41** *Banking*. to settle accounts by exchanging (commercial documents) in a clearing house. **42** to permit (ships, aircraft, cargo, passengers, etc.) to unload, disembark, depart, etc., after fulfilling the customs and other requirements, or (of ships, etc.) to be permitted to unload, etc. **43** to obtain or give (clearance). **44** (*tr*) to obtain clearance from. **45** (*tr*) to make microscope specimens transparent by immersion in a fluid such as xylene. **46** (*tr*) to permit (a person, company, etc.) to see or handle classified information. **47** (*tr*) *Military, etc*. **47a** to achieve transmission of (a signalled message) and acknowledgment of its receipt at its destination. **47b** to decode (a message, etc.). **48** (*tr*) *Sport*. to hit, kick, carry, or throw (the ball) out of the defence area. **49** (*tr*) *Computing*. to remove data from a storage device and replace it with particular characters that usually indicate zero. **50** (*tr*) *N.Z*. to remove (trees, scrub, etc.) from land. **51 clear the air**. See **air** (sense 10). **52 clear the decks**. to prepare for action, as by removing obstacles from a field of activity or combat. ♦ See also **clear away, clear off, clear out, clear up**. [C13 *clere*, from Old French *cler*, from Latin *clārus* clear, bright, brilliant, illustrious] ► ˈ**clearable** *adj* ► ˈ**clearer** *n* ► ˈ**clearly** *adv* ► ˈ**clearness** *n*

clearance (ˈklɪərəns) *n* **1a** the process or an instance of clearing: *slum clearance*. **1b** (*as modifier*): *a clearance order*. **2** space between two parts in motion or in relative motion. **3** permission for an aircraft, ship, passengers, etc., to proceed. **4** *Banking*. the exchange of commercial documents drawn on the members of a clearing house. **5a** the disposal of merchandise at reduced prices. **5b** (*as modifier*): *a clearance sale*. **6** *Sport*. **6a** the act of hitting or kicking a ball out of the defensive area, as in football. **6b** an instance of this. **7** the act of clearing an area of land of its inhabitants by mass eviction. See **Highland Clearances**. **8** *Dentistry*. the extraction of all of a person's teeth. **9** a less common word for **clearing**.

clear away *vb* (*adv*) to remove (objects) from (the table) after a meal.

clearcole (ˈklɪəkəʊl) *n* **1** a type of size containing whiting. ♦ *vb* **2** (*tr*) to paint (a wall) with this size. [C19: from French *claire colle* clear size]

clear-cut *adj* (**clear cut** *when postpositive*). **1** definite; not vague: *a clear-cut proposal*. **2** clearly outlined. ♦ *vb* **3** (*tr*) another term for **clear-fell**.

clear-eyed *adj* **1** discerning; perceptive. **2** having clear eyes or sharp vision.

clear-fell *vb* (*tr*) to cut down all of the trees in (a wood, part of a wood, or throughout an area of land).

clear-headed *adj* mentally alert; sensible; judicious. ► ˌ**clear-ˈheadedly** *adv* ► ˌ**clear-ˈheadedness** *n*

clearing (ˈklɪərɪŋ) *n* an area with few or no trees or shrubs in wooded or overgrown land.

clearing bank *n* (in Britain) any bank that makes use of the central clearing house in London for the transfer of credits and cheques between banks.

clearing house *n* **1** *Banking*. an institution where cheques and other commercial papers drawn on member banks are cancelled against each other so that only net balances are payable. **2** a central agency for the collection and distribution of information or materials.

clearing sale *n Austral*. the auction of plant, stock, and effects of a country property, esp. after the property has changed hands.

clear off *vb* (*intr, adv*) *Informal*. to go away: often used imperatively.

clear out *vb* (*adv*) **1** (*intr*) *Informal*. to go away: often used imperatively. **2** (*tr*) to remove and sort the contents of (a room, container, etc.). **3** (*tr*) *Slang*. to leave (someone) with no money. **4** (*tr*) *Slang*. to exhaust (stocks, goods, etc.) completely.

clear-sighted *adj* **1** involving accurate perception or judgment: *a clear-sighted compromise*. **2** having clear vision. ► ˌ**clear-ˈsightedly** *adv* ► ˌ**clear-ˈsightedness** *n*

clearstory (ˈklɪəˌstɔːrɪ) *n* a variant spelling of **clerestory**. ► ˈ**clearˌstoried** *adj*

clear up *vb* (*adv*) **1** (*tr*) to explain or solve (a mystery, misunderstanding, etc.). **2** to put (a place or thing that is disordered) in order. **3** (*intr*) (of the weather) to become brighter. ♦ *n* **clear-up** (ˈklɪərˌʌp). **4** the act or an instance of clearing up.

clearway (ˈklɪəˌweɪ) *n* **1** *Brit*. a stretch of road on which motorists may stop only in an emergency. **2** an area at the end of a runway over which an aircraft taking off makes its initial climb: it is under the control of the airport.

clearwing *or* **clearwing moth** (ˈklɪəˌwɪŋ) *n* any moth of the family *Sesiidae* (or *Aegeriidae*), characterized by the absence of scales from the greater part of the wings. They are day-flying and some, such as the **hornet clearwing** (*Sesia apiformis*), resemble wasps and other hymenopterans.

cleat (kliːt) *n* **1** a wedge-shaped block, usually of wood, attached to a structure to act as a support. **2** a device consisting of two hornlike prongs projecting horizontally in opposite directions from a central base, used for securing lines on vessels, wharves, etc. **3** a short length of angle iron used as a bracket. **4** a piece of metal, leather, etc., attached to the sole of a shoe to prevent wear or slipping. **5** a small triangular-shaped nail used in glazing. **6** any of the main cleavage planes in a coal seam. ♦ *vb* (*tr*) **7** to supply or support with a cleat or cleats. **8** to secure (a line) on a cleat. [C14: of Germanic origin, compare Old High German *chlōz* clod, lump, Dutch *kloot* ball]

cleavage (ˈkliːvɪdʒ) *n* **1** *Informal*. the separation between a woman's breasts, esp. as revealed by a low-cut dress. **2** a division or split. **3** (of crystals) the act of splitting or the tendency to split along definite planes so as to yield smooth surfaces. **4** Also called: **segmentation**. *Embryol*. (in animals) the repeated division of a fertilized ovum into a solid ball of cells (a morula), which later becomes hollow (a blastula). **5** the breaking of a chemical bond in a molecule to give smaller molecules or radicals. **6** *Geology.* the natural splitting of certain rocks, such as slates, into thin plates.

cleave[1] (kliːv) *vb* **cleaves, cleaving; cleft, cleaved,** *or* **clove; cleft, cleaved,** *or* **cloven. 1** to split or cause to split, esp. along a natural weakness. **2** (*tr*) to make by or as if by cutting: *to cleave a path.* **3** (when *intr,* foll. by *through*) to penetrate or traverse. [Old English *clēofan;* related to Old Norse *kljūfa,* Old High German *klioban,* Latin *glūbere* to peel] ▸ **'cleavable** *adj* ▸ **,cleava'bility** *n*

cleave[2] (kliːv) *vb* (*intr;* foll. by *to*) to cling or adhere. [Old English *cleofian;* related to Old High German *klebēn* to stick]

cleaver ('kliːvə) *n* a heavy knife or long-bladed hatchet, esp. one used by butchers.

cleavers ('kliːvəz) *n* (*functioning as sing*) a Eurasian rubiaceous plant, *Galium aparine,* having small white flowers and prickly stems and fruits. Also called: **goosegrass, hairif, sticky willie.** [Old English *clīfe;* related to *clīfan* to CLEAVE[2]]

cleck[1] (klɛk) *vb* (*tr*) *Scot.* **1** (of birds) to hatch. **2** to lay or hatch (a plot or scheme). [C15: from Old Norse *klekja*]

cleck[2] (klɛk) *South Wales dialect. vb* **1** (*intr;* often foll. by *on*) to gossip (about); tell (on). ◆ *n* **2** (*often pl*) a piece of gossip. [from Welsh, from *clecan* to gossip, and *clec* gossip] ▸ **'clecky** *adj*

cleek *or* **cleik** (kliːk) *n* **1** *Chiefly Scot.* a large hook, such as one used to land fish. **2** *Golf.* a former name for a club, corresponding to the modern No. 1 or No. 2 iron, used for long low shots. [C15: of uncertain origin]

Cleese (kliːz) *n* **John (Marwood).** born 1939, British comedy writer and actor, noted for the TV series *Monty Python's Flying Circus* (1969–74) and *Fawlty Towers* (1975, 1978). His films include *A Fish Called Wanda* (1988) and *Fierce Creatures* (1997).

Cleethorpes ('kliːθɔːps) *n* a resort in E England, in North East Lincolnshire unitary authority, Lincolnshire. Pop.: 32 719 (1991).

clef (klɛf) *n* one of several symbols placed on the left-hand side beginning of each stave indicating the pitch of the music written after it. See also **alto clef, bass clef, C clef, soprano clef, tenor clef, treble clef.** [C16: from French: key, clef, from Latin *clāvis;* related to Latin *claudere* to close]

cleft (klɛft) *vb* **1** the past tense and a past participle of **cleave**[1]. ◆ *n* **2** a fissure or crevice. **3** an indentation or split in something, such as the chin, palate, etc. ◆ *adj* **4** split; divided. **5** (of leaves) having one or more incisions reaching nearly to the midrib. [Old English *geclyft* (n); related to Old High German *kluft* tongs, German *Kluft* gap, fissure; see CLEAVE[1]]

cleft palate *n* a congenital crack or fissure in the midline of the hard palate, often associated with a harelip.

cleg (klɛg) *n* another name for a **horsefly,** esp. one of the genus *Haematopota.* [C15: from Old Norse *kleggi*]

cleidoic egg (klaɪ'dəʊɪk) *n* the egg of birds and insects, which is enclosed in a protective shell limiting the exchange of water, gases, etc. [C20: from Greek *kleidoun* to lock up, from *kleid-, kleis* key]

Cleisthenes ('klaɪsθə,niːz) *n* 6th century B.C., Athenian statesman: democratized the political structure of Athens.

cleistogamy (klaɪ'stɒgəmɪ) *n* self-pollination and fertilization of an unopened flower, as in the violet. Compare **chasmogamy.** ▸ **cleis'togamous** *or* **cleistogamic** (,klaɪstə'gæmɪk) *adj*

Cleland ('klɛlənd) *n* **John.** 1709–89, British writer, best known for his bawdy novel *Fanny Hill* (1748–49).

clem (klɛm) *or* **clam** *vb* **clems, clemming, clemmed** *or* **clams, clamming, clammed.** (when *tr, usually passive*) *English dialect.* to be hungry or cause to be hungry. [C16: of Germanic origin; related to Dutch, German *klemmen* to pinch, cramp; compare Old English *beclemman* to shut in]

clematis ('klɛmətɪs, klə'meɪtɪs) *n* any N temperate ranunculaceous climbing plant or erect shrub of the genus *Clematis,* having plumelike fruits. Many species are cultivated for their large colourful flowers. See also **traveller's joy.** [C16: from Latin, from Greek *klēmatis* climbing plant, brushwood, from *klēma* twig]

Clemenceau (*French* klemɑ̃so) *n* **Georges Eugène Benjamin** (ʒɔrʒ œʒɛn bɛ̃ʒamɛ̃). 1841–1929, French statesman; prime minister of France (1906–09; 1917–20); negotiated the Treaty of Versailles (1919).

clemency ('klɛmənsɪ) *n, pl* **-cies. 1** mercy or leniency. **2** mildness, esp. of the weather. [C15: from Latin *clēmentia,* from *clēmēns* gentle]

Clemens ('klɛmənz) *n* **Samuel Langhorne** ('læŋ,hɔːn). See (Mark) **Twain.**

clement ('klɛmənt) *adj* **1** merciful. **2** (of the weather) mild. [C15: from Latin *clēmēns* mild; probably related to Greek *klinein* to lean] ▸ **'clemently** *adv*

Clement I ('klɛmənt) *n* **Saint,** called *Clement of Rome.* pope (?88–?97 A.D.). Feast day: Nov. 23.

Clement V *n* original name *Bertrand de Got.* ?1264–1314, pope (1305–14): removed the papal seat from Rome to Avignon in France (1309).

Clement VII *n* original name *Giulio de' Medici.* 1478–1534, pope (1523–34): refused to authorize the annulment of the marriage of Henry VIII of England to Catherine of Aragon (1533).

clementine ('klɛmən,tiːn, -,taɪn) *n* a citrus fruit thought to be either a variety of tangerine or a hybrid between a tangerine and sweet orange. [C20: from French *clémentine,* perhaps from the female Christian name]

Clementines ('klɛmən,tiːnz, -,taɪnz) *pl n R.C. Church.* an official compilation of decretals named after Clement V and issued in 1317 which forms part of the Corpus Juris Canonici.

Clement of Alexandria *n* **Saint.** original name *Titus Flavius Clemens.* ?150–?215 A.D., Greek Christian theologian: head of the catechetical school at Alexandria; teacher of Origen. Feast day: Dec. 5.

clench (klɛntʃ) *vb* (*tr*) **1** to close or squeeze together (the teeth, a fist, etc.) tightly. **2** to grasp or grip firmly. ◆ *n* **3** a firm grasp or grip. **4** a device that grasps or grips, such as a clamp. ◆ *n, vb* **5** another word for **clinch.** [Old English *beclencan,* related to Old High German *klenken* to tie, Middle High German *klank* noose, Dutch *klinken* rivet]

cleome (klɪ'əʊmɪ) *n* any herbaceous or shrubby plant of the mostly tropical capparidaceous genus *Cleome,* esp. *C. spinosa,* cultivated for their clusters of white or purplish flowers with long stamens. [C19: New Latin, of obscure origin]

Cleon ('kliːɒn) *n* died 422 B.C., Athenian demagogue and military leader.

cleopatra (,kliːə'pætrə, -'pɑː-) *n* a yellow butterfly, *Gonepteryx cleopatra,* the male of which has its wings flushed with orange.

Cleopatra (,kliːə'pætrə, -'pɑː-) *n* ?69–30 B.C., queen of Egypt (51–30), renowned for her beauty: the mistress of Julius Caesar and later of Mark Antony. She killed herself with an asp to avoid capture by Octavian (Augustus).

Cleopatra's Needle *n* either of two Egyptian obelisks, originally set up at Heliopolis about 1500 B.C.: one was moved to the Thames Embankment, London, in 1878, the other to Central Park, New York, in 1880.

clepe (kliːp) *vb* **clepes, cleping; cleped** (kliːpt, klɛpt), **clept, ycleped,** *or* **yclept.** (*tr*) *Archaic.* to call by the name of. [Old English *cleopian;* related to Middle Low German *kleperen* to rattle]

clepsydra ('klɛpsɪdrə) *n, pl* **-dras** *or* **-drae** (-,driː). an ancient device for measuring time by the flow of water or mercury through a small aperture. Also called: **water clock.** [C17: from Latin, from Greek *klepsudra,* from *kleptein* to steal + *hudōr* water]

cleptomania (,klɛptəʊ'meɪnɪə, -'meɪnjə) *n* a variant spelling of **kleptomania.** ▸ **,clepto'mani,ac** *n*

clerestory *or* **clearstory** ('klɪə,stɔːrɪ) *n, pl* **-ries. 1** a row of windows in the upper part of the wall of a church that divides the nave from the aisle, set above the aisle roof. **2** the part of the wall in which these windows are set. Compare **blindstorey.** [C15: from CLEAR + STOREY] ▸ **'clere,storied** *or* **'clear,storied** *adj*

clergy ('klɜːdʒɪ) *n, pl* **-gies.** the collective body of men and women ordained as religious ministers, esp. of the Christian Church. Related adjs.: **clerical, pastoral.** [C13: from Old French *clergie,* from *clerc* ecclesiastic, CLERK]

clergyman ('klɜːdʒɪmən) *n, pl* **-men.** a member of the clergy.

cleric ('klɛrɪk) *n* a member of the clergy. [C17: from Church Latin *clēricus* priest, CLERK]

clerical ('klɛrɪkᵊl) *adj* **1** relating to or associated with the clergy: *clerical dress.* **2** of or relating to office clerks or their work: *a clerical error.* **3** supporting or advocating clericalism. ▸ **'clerically** *adv*

clerical collar *n* a stiff white collar with no opening at the front that buttons at the back of the neck; the distinctive mark of the clergy in certain Churches. Informal name: **dog collar.**

clericalism ('klɛrɪkᵊ,lɪzəm) *n* **1** a policy of upholding the power of the clergy. **2** the power of the clergy esp. when excessively strong. ▸ **'clericalist** *n*

clericals ('klɛrɪkᵊlz) *pl n* the distinctive dress of a clergyman.

clerihew ('klɛrɪ,hjuː) *n* a form of comic or satiric verse, consisting of two couplets of metrically irregular lines, containing the name of a well-known person. [C20: named after Edmund *Clerihew* Bentley (1875–1956), English writer who invented it]

clerk (klɑːk; *U.S. and Canadian* klɜːrk) *n* **1** a worker, esp. in an office, who keeps records, files, etc. **2 clerk to the justices.** (in England) a legally qualified person who sits in court with lay justices to advise them on points of law. **3** an employee of a court, legislature, board, corporation, etc., who keeps records and accounts, etc.: *a town clerk.* **4** Also called: **clerk of the House.** *Brit.* a senior official of the House of Commons. **5** Also called: **clerk in holy orders.** a cleric. **6** *U.S. and Canadian.* short for **salesclerk. 7** Also called: **desk clerk.** *U.S. and Canadian.* a hotel receptionist. **8** *Archaic.* a scholar. ◆ *vb* **9** (*intr*) to serve as a clerk. [Old English *clerc,* from Church Latin *clēricus,* from Greek *klērikos* cleric, relating to the heritage (alluding to the Biblical Levites, whose inheritance was the Lord), from *klēros* heritage] ▸ **'clerkdom** *n* ▸ **'clerkish** *adj* ▸ **'clerkship** *n*

clerkess (klɑː'kɛs) *n* a female office clerk.

clerkly ('klɑːklɪ) *adj* **-lier, -liest. 1** of or like a clerk. **2** *Obsolete.* learned. ◆ *adv* **3** *Obsolete.* in the manner of a clerk. ▸ **'clerkliness** *n*

clerk of works *n* an employee who supervises building work in progress or the upkeep of existing buildings.

Clermont-Ferrand (*French* klɛrmɔ̃ferɑ̃) *n* a city in S central France: capital of Puy-de-Dôme department; industrial centre. Pop.: 140 167 (1990).

cleruchy ('klɛə,ruːkɪ) *n, pl* **-chies.** (in the ancient world) a special type of Athenian colony, in which settlers (**cleruchs**) retained their Athenian citizenship and the community remained a political dependency of Athens. ▸ **cleruchial** (klɪ'ruːkɪəl) *adj*

cleveite ('kliːvaɪt) *n* a crystalline variety of the mineral uraninite. [C19: named after P. T. *Cleve* (1840–1905), Swedish chemist; see -ITE[1]]

Cleveland[1] ('kliːvlənd) *n* **1** a former county of NE England formed in 1974 from parts of E Durham and N Yorkshire; replaced in 1996 by the unitary authorities of Hartlepool (Durham), Stockton-on-Tees (Durham), Middlesbrough (North Yorkshire) and Redcar and Cleveland (North Yorkshire). **2** a port in NE Ohio, on Lake Erie: major heavy industries. Pop.: 498 246 (1996 est.). **3** a hilly region of NE England, extending from the **Cleveland Hills** to the River Tees.

Cleveland[2] ('kliːvlənd) *n* **Stephen Grover.** 1837–1908, U.S. Democratic politician; the 22nd and 24th president of the U.S. (1885–89; 1893–97).

clever ('klɛvə) *adj* **1** displaying sharp intelligence or mental alertness. **2** adroit or dexterous, esp. with the hands. **3** smart in a superficial way. **4** *Brit. informal.* sly; cunning. **5** (*predicative; used with a negative*) *Dialect.* healthy; fit. [C13 *cliver* (in the sense: quick to seize, adroit), of uncertain origin] ▸ **'cleverish** *adj* ▸ **'cleverly** *adv* ▸ **'cleverness** *n*

clever-clever *adj Informal.* clever in a showy manner; artful; overclever.

clever Dick *or* **cleverdick** ('klɛvə,dɪk) *n Informal.* a person considered to have an unwarrantably high opinion of his own ability or knowledge.

clevis ('klɛvɪs) *n* the U-shaped component of a shackle for attaching a drawbar to a plough or similar implement. [C16: related to CLEAVE[1]]

clew (klu:) *n* **1** a ball of thread, yarn, or twine. **2** *Nautical.* either of the lower corners of a square sail or the after lower corner of a fore-and-aft sail. **3** (*usually pl*) the rigging of a hammock. **4** a rare variant of **clue.** ◆ *vb* **5** (*tr*) to coil or roll into a ball. [Old English *cliewen* (vb); related to Old High German *kliu* ball]

clew line *n Nautical.* any of several lines fastened to the clews of a square sail and used for furling it.

clew up *vb* (*adv*) *Nautical.* to furl (a square sail) by gathering its clews up to the yard by means of clew lines.

clianthus (klɪ'ænθəs) *n* any Australian or New Zealand plant of the leguminous genus *Clianthus,* with ornamental clusters of slender scarlet flowers. [C19: New Latin, probably from Greek *klei-, kleos* glory + *anthos* flower]

cliché ('kli:ʃeɪ) *n* **1** a word or expression that has lost much of its force through overexposure, as for example the phrase: *it's got to get worse before it gets better.* **2** an idea, action, or habit that has become trite from overuse. **3** *Printing, chiefly Brit.* a stereotype or electrotype plate. [C19: from French, from *clicher* to stereotype; imitative of the sound made by the matrix when it is dropped into molten metal] ▸ **'clichéd** *or* **'cliché'd** *adj*

Clichy (kli:'ʃi:) *n* an industrial suburb of NW Paris: residence of the Merovingian kings (7th century). Pop.: 48 204 (1990). Official name: **Clichy-la-Garenne** (*French* kliʃilagarɛn).

click (klɪk) *n* **1** a short light often metallic sound. **2a** the locking member of a ratchet mechanism, such as a pawl or detent. **2b** the movement of such a mechanism between successive locking positions. **3** *Phonetics.* any of various stop consonants, found in Khoisan and as borrowings in southern Bantu languages, that are produced by the suction of air into the mouth. **4** *U.S. and Canadian slang.* a kilometre. ◆ *vb* **5** to make or cause to make a clicking sound: *to click one's heels.* **6** (usually foll. by *on*) *Computing.* to press and release (a button on a mouse) or to select (a particular function) by pressing and releasing a button on a mouse. **7** (*intr*) *Slang.* to be a great success: *that idea really clicked.* **8** (*intr*) *Informal.* to become suddenly clear: *it finally clicked when her name was mentioned.* **9** (*intr*) *Slang.* to go or fit together with ease: *they clicked from their first meeting.* [C17: of imitative origin] ▸ **'clicker** *n*

click beetle *n* any beetle of the family *Elateridae,* which have the ability to right themselves with a snapping movement when placed on their backs. Also called: **snapping beetle, skipjack.** See also **wireworm.**

clicker ('klɪkə) *n* **1** a person or thing that clicks. **2** *Informal.* a foreman in a shoe factory or printing works.

client ('klaɪənt) *n* **1** a person, company, etc., that seeks the advice of a professional man or woman. **2** a customer. **3** a person who is registered with or receiving services or financial aid from a welfare agency. **4** *Computing.* a program or work station that requests data or information from a server. **5** a person depending on another's patronage. [C14: from Latin *cliēns* retainer, dependant; related to Latin *clīnāre* to lean] ▸ **cliental** (klaɪ'ɛntᵊl) *adj*

client-centred therapy *n Psychol.* a form of psychotherapy in which the therapist makes no attempt to interpret what the patient says but encourages him to develop his own attitudes and insights, often by questioning him.

clientele (,kli:ɒn'tɛl) *or* **clientage** ('klaɪəntɪdʒ) *n* customers or clients collectively. [C16: from Latin *clientēla,* from *cliēns* CLIENT]

Clifden nonpareil ('klɪftᵊn) *n* a handsome nocturnal moth, *Catocala fraxini,* that is brown with bluish patches on the hindwings: related to the red underwing.

cliff (klɪf) *n* a steep high rock face, esp. one that runs along the seashore and has the strata exposed. [Old English *clif;* related to Old Norse *kleif,* Middle Low German *klēf,* Dutch *klif;* see CLEAVE[2]] ▸ **'cliffy** *adj*

cliffhanger ('klɪf,hæŋə) *n* **1a** a situation of imminent disaster usually occurring at the end of each episode of a serialized film. **1b** the serialized film itself. **2** a situation that is dramatic or uncertain. ▸ **'cliff,hanging** *adj*

cliff swallow *n* an American swallow, *Petrochelidon pyrrhonota,* that has a square-tipped tail and builds nests of mud on cliffs, walls, etc.

climacteric (klaɪ'mæktərɪk, ,klaɪmæk'tɛrɪk) *n* **1** a critical event or period. **2** another name for **menopause. 3** the period in the life of a man corresponding to the menopause, chiefly characterized by diminished sexual activity. **4** *Botany.* the period during which certain fruits, such as apples, ripen, marked by a rise in the rate of respiration. ◆ *adj also* **climacterical** (,klaɪmæk'tɛrɪkᵊl). **5** involving a crucial event or period. [C16: from Latin *clīmactēricus,* from Greek *klimaktērikos,* from *klimakter* rung of a ladder, from *klimax* ladder; see CLIMAX] ▸ **,climac'terically** *adv*

climactic (klaɪ'mæktɪk) *or* **climactical** *adj* consisting of, involving, or causing a climax. ▸ **cli'mactically** *adv*

USAGE See at **climate.**

climate ('klaɪmɪt) *n* **1** the long-term prevalent weather conditions of an area, determined by latitude, position relative to oceans or continents, altitude, etc. **2** an area having a particular kind of climate. **3** a prevailing trend or current of feeling: *the political climate.* [C14: from Late Latin *clima,* from Greek *klima* inclination, region; related to Greek *klinein* to lean] ▸ **climatic** (klaɪ'mætɪk), **cli'matical,** *or* **'climatal** *adj* ▸ **cli'matically** *adv*

USAGE *Climatic* is sometimes wrongly used where *climactic* is meant. *Climatic* is properly used to talk about things relating to climate; *climactic* is used to describe something which forms a climax.

climatic zone *n* any of the eight principal zones, roughly demarcated by lines of latitude, into which the earth can be divided on the basis of climate.

climatology (,klaɪmə'tɒlədʒɪ) *n* the study of climates. ▸ **climatologic** (,klaɪmətə'lɒdʒɪk) *or* **,climato'logical** *adj* ▸ **,climato'logically** *adv* ▸ **,clima'tologist** *n*

climax ('klaɪmæks) *n* **1** the most intense or highest point of an experience or of a series of events: *the party was the climax of the week.* **2** a decisive moment in a dramatic or other work. **3** a rhetorical device by which a series of sentences, clauses, or phrases are arranged in order of increasing intensity. **4** *Ecology.* the stage in the development of a community during which it remains stable under the prevailing environmental conditions. **5** Also called: **sexual climax.** (esp. in referring to women) another word for **orgasm.** ◆ *vb* **6** to reach or bring to a climax. [C16: from Late Latin, from Greek *klimax* ladder]

climb (klaɪm) *vb* (*mainly intr*) **1** (*also tr;* often foll. by *up*) to go up or ascend (stairs, a mountain, etc.). **2** (often foll. by *along*) to progress with difficulty: *to climb along a ledge.* **3** to rise to a higher point or intensity: *the temperature climbed.* **4** to incline or slope upwards: *the road began to climb.* **5** to ascend in social position. **6** (of plants) to grow upwards by twining, using tendrils or suckers, etc. **7** *Informal.* (foll. by *into*) to put (on) or get (into). **8** to be a climber or mountaineer. ◆ *n* **9** the act or an instance of climbing. **10** a place or thing to be climbed, esp. a route in mountaineering. ◆ Related adj: **scansorial.** [Old English *climban;* related to Old Norse *klembra* to squeeze, Old High German *climban* to clamber] ▸ **'climbable** *adj*

climb down *vb* (*intr, adv*) **1** to descend. **2** (often foll. by *from*) to retreat (from an opinion, position, etc.). ◆ *n* **climb-down. 3** a retreat from an opinion, etc.

climber ('klaɪmə) *n* **1** a person or thing that climbs. **2** a plant that lacks rigidity and grows upwards by twining, scrambling, or clinging with tendrils and suckers. **3** *Chiefly Brit.* short for **social climber.**

climbing fish *or* **perch** *n* an Asian labyrinth fish, *Anabas testudineus,* that resembles a perch and can travel over land on its spiny gill covers and pectoral fins.

climbing frame *n* a structure of wood or metal tubing used by children for climbing.

climbing irons *pl n* spiked steel frames worn on the feet to assist in climbing trees, ice slopes, etc.

climbing wall *n Mountaineering.* a specially constructed wall with recessed and projecting holds to give practice in rock climbing; a feature of many sports centres.

clime (klaɪm) *n Poetic.* a region or its climate. [C16: from Late Latin *clima;* see CLIMATE]

clinandrium (klɪ'nændrɪəm) *n, pl* **-dria** (-drɪə). *Botany.* a cavity in the upper part of the column of an orchid flower that contains the anthers. Also called: **androclinium.** [C19: from New Latin, literally: bed for stamen, from Greek *klinē* couch + *anēr* man + -IUM]

clinch (klɪntʃ) *vb* **1** (*tr*) to secure (a driven nail) by bending the protruding point over. **2** (*tr*) to hold together in such a manner: *to clinch the corners of the frame.* **3** (*tr*) to settle (something, such as an argument, bargain, etc.) in a definite way. **4** (*tr*) *Nautical.* to fasten by means of a clinch. **5** (*intr*) to engage in a clinch, as in boxing or wrestling. ◆ *n* **6** the act of clinching. **7a** a nail with its point bent over. **7b** the part of such a nail, etc., that has been bent over. **8** *Boxing, wrestling, etc.* an act or an instance in which one or both competitors hold on to the other to avoid punches, regain wind, etc. **9** *Slang.* a lovers' embrace. **10** *Nautical.* a loop or eye formed in a line by seizing the end to the standing part. ◆ Also (for senses 1, 2, 4, 7, 8, 10): **clench.** [C16: variant of CLENCH]

clincher ('klɪntʃə) *n* **1** *Informal.* something decisive, such as a fact, score, etc. **2** a person or thing that clinches.

cline (klaɪn) *n* a continuous variation in form between members of a species having a wide variable geographical or ecological range. [C20: from Greek *klinein* to lean] ▸ **'clinal** *adj* ▸ **'clinally** *adv*

-cline *n combining form.* indicating a slope: *anticline.* [back formation from INCLINE] ▸ **-clinal** *adj combining form.*

cling (klɪŋ) *vb* **clings, clinging, clung.** (*intr*) **1** (often foll. by *to*) to hold fast or adhere closely (to something), as by gripping or sticking. **2** (foll. by *together*) to remain in contact (with each other). **3** to be or remain physically or emotionally close: *to cling to outmoded beliefs.* ◆ *n* **4** *Agriculture, chiefly U.S.* the tendency of cotton fibres in a sample to stick to each other. **5** *Agriculture.* diarrhoea or scouring in animals. **6** short for **clingstone.** [Old English *clingan;* related to CLENCH] ▸ **'clinger** *n* ▸ **'clingingly** *adv* ▸ **'clingy** *adj* ▸ **'clinginess** *or* **'clingingness** *n*

clingfilm ('klɪŋ,fɪlm) *n* a thin polythene material that clings closely to any surface around which it is placed: used for wrapping food.

clingfish ('klɪŋ,fɪʃ) *n, pl* **-fish** *or* **-fishes.** any small marine teleost fish of the family *Gobiesocidae,* having a flattened elongated body with a sucking disc beneath the head for clinging to rocks, etc.

clinging vine *n U.S. and Canadian informal.* a woman who displays excessive emotional dependence on a man.

clingstone ('klɪŋ,stəʊn) *n* **a** a fruit, such as certain peaches, in which the flesh tends to adhere to the stone. **b** (*as modifier*): *a clingstone peach.* ◆ Compare **freestone** (sense 2).

clinic ('klɪnɪk) *n* **1** a place in which outpatients are given medical treatment or advice, often connected to a hospital. **2** a similar place staffed by physicians or surgeons specializing in one or more specific areas: *eye clinic.* **3** *Brit.* a private hospital or nursing home. **4** the teaching of medicine to students at the bedside. **5** *U.S.* a place where medical lectures are given. **6** *U.S.* a clinical lecture. **7** *Chiefly U.S. and Canadian.* a group or centre that offers advice or instruction: *a vocational clinic.* [C17: from Latin *clīnicus* one on a sickbed, from Greek, from *klinē* bed]

clinical ('klɪnɪkᵊl) *adj* **1** of or relating to a clinic. **2** of or relating to the bedside of a patient, the course of his disease, or the observation and treatment of patients directly: *a clinical lecture; clinical medicine.* **3** scientifically detached; strictly objective: *a clinical attitude to life.* **4** plain, simple, and usually unattractive: *clinical furniture.* ▸ **'clinically** *adv* ▸ **'clinicalness** *n*

clinical psychology *n* the branch of psychology that studies and treats mental illness and mental retardation.

clinical thermometer *n* a finely calibrated thermometer for determining the temperature of the body, usually placed under the tongue or in the rectum.

clinician (klɪˈnɪʃən) *n* a physician, psychiatrist, etc., who specializes in clinical work as opposed to one engaged in laboratory or experimental studies.

clink[1] (klɪŋk) *vb* **1** to make or cause to make a light and sharply ringing sound. ◆ *n* **2** a light and sharply ringing sound. **3** *Brit.* a pointed steel tool used for breaking up the surface of a road before it is repaired. **[C14:** perhaps from Middle Dutch *klinken;* related to Old Low German *chlanch,* German *Klang* sound**]**

clink[2] (klɪŋk) *n* a slang word for **prison**. **[C16:** after *Clink,* name of a prison in Southwark, London**]**

clinker (ˈklɪŋkə) *n* **1** the ash and partially fused residues from a coal-fired furnace or fire. **2** Also called: **clinker brick.** a hard brick used as a paving stone. **3** a partially vitrified brick or mass of brick. **4** *Slang, chiefly U.S.* something of poor quality, such as a film. **5** *U.S. and Canadian slang.* a mistake or fault, esp. a wrong note in music. ◆ *vb* **6** *(intr)* to form clinker during burning. **[C17:** from Dutch *klinker* a type of brick, from obsolete *klinckaerd,* literally: something that clinks (referring to the sound produced when one was struck), from *klinken* to CLINK[1]**]**

clinker-built *or* **clincher-built** *adj* (of a boat or ship) having a hull constructed with each plank overlapping that below. Also called: **lapstrake.** Compare **carvel-built. [C18** *clinker* a nailing together, probably from CLINCH**]**

clinkstone (ˈklɪŋkˌstəʊn) *n* a variety of phonolite that makes a metallic sound when struck.

clino- *or before a vowel* **clin-** *combining form.* indicating a slope or inclination: *clinometer.* **[**from New Latin, from Greek *klinein* to slant, lean**]**

clinometer (klaɪˈnɒmɪtə) *n* an instrument used in surveying for measuring an angle of inclination. ▸ **clinometric** (ˌklaɪnəˈmɛtrɪk) *or* ˌ**clinoˈmetrical** *adj* ▸ **cliˈnometry** *n*

clinopyroxene (ˌklaɪnəʊpaɪˈrɒksiːn) *n* a member of the pyroxene group of minerals having a monoclinic crystal structure, such as augite, diopside, or jadeite.

clinostat (ˈklaɪnəʊˌstæt) *n* an apparatus for studying tropisms in plants, usually a rotating disc to which the plant is attached so that it receives an equal stimulus on all sides.

clinquant (ˈklɪŋkənt) *adj* **1** glittering, esp. with tinsel. ◆ *n* **2** tinsel or imitation gold leaf. **[C16:** from French, from *clinquer* to clink, from Dutch *klinken,* of imitative origin**]**

clint (klɪnt) *n Physical geography.* **1** a section of a limestone pavement separated from adjacent sections by solution fissures. See **grike. 2** any small surface exposure of hard or flinty rock, as on a hillside or in a stream bed. **[C12:** from Danish and Swedish *klint,* from Old Swedish *klinter,* related to Icelandic *klettr* rock**]**

Clinton (ˈklɪntən) *n* **Bill,** full name *William Jefferson.* born 1946, U.S. Democrat politician; 42nd president of the U.S. from 1993; re-elected in 1996.

clintonia (klɪnˈtəʊnɪə) *n* any temperate liliaceous plant of the genus *Clintonia,* having white, greenish-yellow, or purplish flowers, broad ribbed leaves, and blue berries. **[C19:** named after De Witt *Clinton* (1769–1828), U.S. politician and naturalist**]**

Clio (ˈklaɪəʊ) *n Greek myth.* the Muse of history. **[C19:** from Latin, from Greek *Kleiō,* from *kleein* to celebrate**]**

cliometrics (ˌklaɪəʊˈmɛtrɪks) *n (functioning as sing)* the study of economic history using statistics and computer analysis. **[C20:** CLIO + (ECONO)METRICS**]** ▸ ˌ**clioˈmetric** *or* ˌ**clioˈmetrical** *adj* ▸ **cliometrician** (ˌklaɪəʊməˈtrɪʃən) *n*

clip[1] (klɪp) *vb* **clips, clipping, clipped.** *(mainly tr)* **1** *(also intr)* to cut, snip, or trim with or as if with scissors or shears, esp. in order to shorten or remove a part. **2** *Brit.* to punch (a hole) in something, esp. a ticket. **3** to curtail or cut short. **4** to move a short section from (a film, etc.). **5** to shorten (a word). **6** *(intr)* to trot or move rapidly, esp. over a long distance: *a horse clipping along the road.* **7** *Informal.* to strike with a sharp, often slanting, blow. **8** *Slang.* to obtain (money) by deception or cheating. **9 clip (someone's) wings. 9a** to restrict (someone's) freedom. **9b** to thwart (someone's) ambition. ◆ *n* **10** the act or process of clipping. **11** something clipped off. **12** an extract from a film, newspaper, etc. **13** *Informal.* a sharp, often slanting, blow. **14** *Informal.* speed: *a rapid clip.* **15** *Austral. and N.Z.* the total quantity of wool shorn, as in one place, season, etc. **16** another word for **clipped form. [C12:** from Old Norse *klippa* to cut; related to Low German *klippen***]** ▸ **ˈclippable** *adj*

clip[2] (klɪp) *n* **1** any of various small implements used to hold loose articles together or to attach one article to another. **2** an article of jewellery that can be clipped onto a dress, hat, etc. **3** short for **paperclip** or **cartridge clip. 4** the pointed flange on a horseshoe that secures it to the front part of the hoof. ◆ *vb* **clips, clipping, clipped.** *(tr)* **5** to hold together tightly, as with a clip. **6** *Archaic or dialect.* to embrace. **[**Old English *clyppan* to embrace; related to Old Frisian *kleppa,* Lithuanian *glebiu***]**

clip art *n* a large collection of simple drawings stored in a computer from which items can be selected for incorporation into documents.

clipboard (ˈklɪpˌbɔːd) *n* **1** a portable writing board with a spring clip at the top for holding paper. **2** a temporary storage area in desktop publishing where text or graphics are held after the cut command or the copy command.

clip-clop *n* the sound made by a horse's hooves.

clip-fed *adj* (of an automatic firearm) loaded from a cartridge clip.

clip joint *n Slang.* a place, such as a nightclub or restaurant, in which customers are overcharged.

clip on *vb* **1** *(tr)* to attach by means of a clip. **2** *(intr)* to be attached by means of a clip: *this clips on here.* ◆ *adj* **clip-on. 3** designed to be attached by means of a clip: *a clip-on bow tie.* ◆ *pl n* **clip-ons. 4** sunglasses designed to be clipped on to a person's spectacles.

clipped (klɪpt) *adj* (of speech or voice) abrupt and distinct.

clipped form *n* a shortened form of a word, as for example *doc* for *doctor.*

clipper (ˈklɪpə) *n* **1** any fast sailing ship. **2** a person or thing that cuts or clips. **3** something, such as a horse or sled, that moves quickly. **4** *Electronics.* another word for **limiter.**

clippers (ˈklɪpəz) *or* **clips** *pl n* **1** a hand tool with two cutting blades for clipping fingernails, hedges, etc. **2** a hairdresser's tool, operated either by hand or electrically, with one fixed and one reciprocating set of teeth for cutting short hair.

clippie (ˈklɪpɪ) *n Brit. informal.* a bus conductress.

clipping (ˈklɪpɪŋ) *n* **1** something cut out or trimmed off, esp. an article from a newspaper; cutting. **2** the distortion of an audio or visual signal in which the tops of peaks with a high amplitude are cut off, caused by, for example, overloading of amplifier circuits. ◆ *adj* **3** *(prenominal) Informal.* fast: *a clipping pace.*

clipshears (ˈklɪpˌʃiːrz) *or* **clipshear** (ˈklɪpˌʃiːr) *n* a Scot. dialect name for an **earwig. [**from the resemblance of the forceps at the tip of its abdomen to shears**]**

clique (kliːk, klɪk) *n* a small, exclusive group of friends or associates. **[C18:** from French, perhaps from Old French: latch, from *cliquer* to click; suggestive of the necessity to exclude nonmembers**]** ▸ **ˈcliquey** *or* **ˈcliquy** *adj* ▸ **ˈcliquish** *adj* ▸ **ˈcliquishly** *adv* ▸ **ˈcliquishness** *n*

clishmaclaver (ˌklɪʃməˈkleɪvə) *n Scot.* idle talk; gossip. **[C16:** from *clish-clash,* reduplication of CLASH + CLAVER**]**

Clisthenes (ˈklaɪsθəˌniːz) *n* a variant spelling of **Cleisthenes.**

clitellum (klɪˈtɛləm) *n, pl* **-la** (-lə). a thickened saddle-like region of epidermis in earthworms and leeches whose secretions bind copulating worms together and later form a cocoon around the eggs. **[C19:** from New Latin, from Latin *clītellae* (plural) packsaddle**]**

clitic (ˈklɪtɪk) *adj* **1** (of a word) incapable of being stressed, usually pronounced as if part of the word that follows or precedes it: for example, in French, *me, te,* and *le* are clitic pronouns. See also **proclitic, enclitic.** ◆ *n* **2** a clitic word. **[C20:** back formation from ENCLITIC and PROCLITIC**]**

clitoridectomy (ˌklɪtərɪˈdɛktəmɪ) *n* surgical removal of the clitoris: a form of female circumcision, esp. practised as a religious or ethnic rite.

clitoris (ˈklɪtərɪs, ˈklaɪ-) *n* a part of the female genitalia consisting of a small elongated highly sensitive erectile organ at the front of the vulva: homologous with the penis. **[C17:** from New Latin, from Greek *kleitoris;* related to Greek *kleiein* to close**]** ▸ **ˈclitoral** *adj*

Clive (klaɪv) *n* **Robert,** Baron Clive of Plassey. 1725–74, British general and statesman, whose victory at Plassey (1757) strengthened British control in India.

Cliveden (ˈklɪvdən) *n* a mansion in Buckinghamshire, on the N bank of the Thames near Maidenhead: formerly the home of Nancy Astor and the scene of gatherings of politicians and others (known as the **Cliveden Set**); now a hotel.

Cllr *abbrev. for* Councillor.

cloaca (kləʊˈeɪkə) *n, pl* **-cae** (-kiː). **1** a cavity in the pelvic region of most vertebrates, except higher mammals, and certain invertebrates, into which the alimentary canal and the genital and urinary ducts open. **2** a sewer. **[C18:** from Latin: sewer; related to Greek *kluzein* to wash out**]** ▸ **cloˈacal** *adj*

cloacitis (ˌkləʊəˈsaɪtɪs) *n Vet. science.* inflammation of the cloaca in domestic fowl.

cloak (kləʊk) *n* **1** a wraplike outer garment fastened at the throat and falling straight from the shoulders. **2** something that covers or conceals. ◆ *vb (tr)* **3** to cover with or as if with a cloak. **4** to hide or disguise. **[C13:** from Old French *cloque,* from Medieval Latin *clocca* cloak, bell; referring to the bell-like shape**]**

cloak-and-dagger *n (modifier)* characteristic of or concerned with intrigue and espionage.

cloakroom (ˈkləʊkˌruːm, -ˌrʊm) *n* **1** a room in which hats, coats, luggage, etc., may be temporarily deposited. **2** *Brit.* a euphemistic word for **lavatory.**

clobber[1] (ˈklɒbə) *vb (tr) Slang.* **1** to beat or batter. **2** to defeat utterly. **3** to criticize severely. **[C20:** of unknown origin**]**

clobber[2] (ˈklɒbə) *n Brit. slang.* personal belongings, such as clothes and accessories. **[C19:** of unknown origin**]**

clobber[3] (ˈklɒbə) *vb (tr)* to paint over existing decoration on (pottery). **[C19** (originally in the sense: to patch up): of uncertain origin; perhaps related to CLOBBER[2]**]**

clobbering machine *n N.Z. informal.* pressure to conform with accepted standards.

cloche (klɒʃ) *n* **1** a bell-shaped cover used to protect young plants. **2** a woman's almost brimless close-fitting hat, typical of the 1920s and 1930s. **[C19:** from French: bell, from Medieval Latin *clocca***]**

clock[1] (klɒk) *n* **1** a timepiece, usually free-standing, hanging, or built into a tower, having mechanically or electrically driven pointers that move constantly over a dial showing the numbers of the hours. Compare **digital clock, watch** (sense 7). **2** any clocklike device for recording or measuring, such as a taximeter or pressure gauge. **3** the downy head of a dandelion that has gone to seed. **4** an electrical circuit which generates pulses at a predetermined rate and interval. **5** *Computing.* an electronic pulse generator that transmits streams of regular pulses to which various parts of the computer and its operations are synchronized. **6** short for **time clock. 7 around** *or* **round the clock.** all day and all night. **8** (usually preceded by *the*) an informal word for **speedometer** or **mileometer. 9** *Brit.* a slang word for **face. 10 against the clock. 10a** under pressure, as to meet a deadline. **10b** (in certain sports, such as show jumping) timed by a stop clock: *the last round will be against the clock.* **11 put the clock back.** to regress. ◆ *vb* **12** *(tr) Brit., Austral. and N.Z. slang.* to strike, esp. on the face or head. **13** *(tr) Brit. slang.* to see or notice. **14** *(tr)* to record time as with a stopwatch, esp. in the calculation of speed. **15** *Electronics.* to feed a clock pulse to (a digital device) in order to cause it to switch to a new state.

◆ See also **atomic clock, biological clock, clock off, clock on, clock up.** [C14: from Middle Dutch *clocke* clock, from Medieval Latin *clocca* bell, ultimately of Celtic origin] ▸ **'clocker** *n* ▸ **'clock,like** *adj*

clock[2] (klɒk) *n* an ornamental design either woven in or embroidered on the side of a stocking. [C16: from Middle Dutch *clocke*, from Medieval Latin *clocca* bell]

clock golf *n* a putting game played on a circular area on a lawn.

clockmaker ('klɒk,meɪkə) *n* a person who makes or mends clocks, watches, etc.

clock off *or* **out** *vb* (*intr, adv*) to depart from work, esp. when it involves registering the time of departure on a card.

clock on *or* **in** *vb* (*intr, adv*) to arrive at work, esp. when it involves registering the time of arrival on a card.

clock up *vb* (*tr, adv*) to record or register: *this car has clocked up 80 000 miles.*

clock-watcher *n* an employee who checks the time in anticipation of a break or of the end of the working day.

clockwise ('klɒk,waɪz) *adv, adj* in the direction that the hands of a clock rotate; from top to bottom towards the right when seen from the front.

clockwork ('klɒk,wɜːk) *n* **1** the mechanism of a clock. **2** any similar mechanism, as in a wind-up toy. **3 like clockwork.** with complete regularity and precision.

clod (klɒd) *n* **1** a lump of earth or clay. **2** earth, esp. when heavy or in hard lumps. **3** Also called: **clodpole, clod poll, clodpate.** a dull or stupid person. **4** a cut of beef taken from the shoulder. [Old English *clod-* (occurring in compound words) lump; related to CLOUD] ▸ **'cloddy** *adj* ▸ **'cloddish** *adj* ▸ **'cloddishly** *adv* ▸ **'cloddishness** *n*

clodhopper ('klɒd,hɒpə) *n Informal.* **1** a clumsy person; lout. **2** (*usually pl*) a large heavy shoe or boot. ▸ **'clod,hopping** *adj*

clog (klɒg) *vb* **clogs, clogging, clogged. 1** to obstruct or become obstructed with thick or sticky matter. **2** (*tr*) to encumber; hinder; impede. **3** (*tr*) to fasten a clog or impediment to (an animal, such as a horse). **4** (*intr*) to adhere or stick in a mass. **5** *Slang.* (in soccer) to foul (an opponent). ◆ *n* **6a** any of various wooden or wooden-soled shoes. **6b** (*as modifier*): *clog dance.* **7** a heavy block, esp. of wood, fastened to the leg of a person or animal to impede motion. **8** something that impedes motion or action; hindrance. **9 pop one's clogs.** *Slang.* to die. [C14 (in the sense: block of wood): of unknown origin] ▸ **'cloggy** *adj* ▸ **'clogginess** *n*

cloisonné (klwɑː'zɒneɪ; *French* klwazɔne) *n* **1a** a design made by filling in with coloured enamel an outline of flattened wire put on edge. **1b** the method of doing this. ◆ *adj* **2** of, relating to, or made by cloisonné. [C19: from French, from *cloisonner* to divide into compartments, from *cloison* partition, ultimately from Latin *claudere* to CLOSE[2]]

cloister ('klɔɪstə) *n* **1** a covered walk, usually around a quadrangle in a religious institution, having an open arcade or colonnade on the inside and a wall on the outside. **2** (*sometimes pl*) a place of religious seclusion, such as a monastery. **3** life in a monastery or convent. ◆ *vb* **4** (*tr*) to confine or seclude in or as if in a monastery. [C13: from Old French *cloistre*, from Medieval Latin *claustrum* monastic cell, from Latin: bolt, barrier, from *claudere* to close; influenced in form by Old French *cloison* partition] ▸ **'cloister-,like** *adj*

cloistered ('klɔɪstəd) *adj* **1** secluded or shut up from the world. **2** living in a monastery or nunnery. **3** (of a building, courtyard, etc.) having or provided with a cloister.

cloistral ('klɔɪstrəl) *or* **claustral** *adj* of, like, or characteristic of a cloister.

clomb (kləʊm) *vb Archaic.* a past tense and past participle of **climb.**

clomiphene ('kləʊmɪ,fiːn) *n* a drug that stimulates the production of egg cells in the ovary: used to treat infertility in women.

clomp (klɒmp) *n, vb* a less common word for **clump** (senses 2, 7).

clone (kləʊn) *n* **1** a group of organisms or cells of the same genetic constitution that are descended from a common ancestor by asexual reproduction, as by cuttings, grafting, etc., in plants. **2** Also called: **gene clone.** a segment of DNA that has been isolated and replicated by laboratory manipulation: used to analyse genes and manufacture their products (proteins). **3** *Informal.* a person or thing bearing a very close resemblance to another person or thing. **4** *Slang.* **4a** a mobile phone that has been given the electronic identity of an existing mobile phone, so that calls made on it are charged to the owner of that phone. **4b** any similar object or device, such as a credit card, that has been given the electronic identity of another device, usu. in order to commit theft. ◆ *vb* **5** to produce or cause to produce a clone. **6** *Informal.* to produce near copies (of a person or thing). **7** (*tr*) *Slang.* to give (a mobile phone, etc.) the electronic identity of an existing mobile phone (or other device), so that calls, purchases, etc. made with it are charged to the original owner. [C20: from Greek *klōn* twig, shoot; related to *klan* to break] ▸ **'clonal** *adj* ▸ **'clonally** *adv*

clonk (klɒŋk) *vb* **1** (*intr*) to make a loud dull thud. **2** (*tr*) *Informal.* to hit. ◆ *n* **3** a loud thudding sound. [C20: of imitative origin]

Clonmel (klɒn'mɛl) *n* the county town of Co. Tipperary, Republic of Ireland; birthplace of Laurence Sterne; meat processing and enamelware. Pop.: 14 500 (1991).

Clontarf (klɒn'tɑːf) *n* **Battle of.** a battle fought in 1014, near Dublin, in the Republic of Ireland, in which the Danes were defeated by the Irish but the Irish king, Brian Boru, was killed.

clonus ('kləʊnəs) *n* a type of convulsion characterized by rapid contraction and relaxation of a muscle. [C19: from New Latin, from Greek *klonos* turmoil] ▸ **clonic** ('klɒnɪk) *adj* ▸ **clonicity** (klɒ'nɪsɪtɪ) *n*

clop (klɒp) *vb* **clops, clopping, clopped. 1** (*intr*) to make or move along with a sound as of a horse's hooves striking the ground. ◆ *n* **2** a sound of this nature. [C20: of imitative origin]

cloqué ('klɒkeɪ) *n* **a** a fabric with an embossed surface. **b** (*as modifier*): *a cloqué dress.* [from French, literally: blistered]

close[1] (kləʊs) *adj* **1** near in space or time; in proximity. **2** having the parts near together; dense: *a close formation.* **3** down or near to the surface; short: *a close haircut.* **4** near in relationship: *a close relative.* **5** intimate or confidential: *a close friend.* **6** almost equal or even: *a close contest.* **7** not deviating or varying greatly from a model or standard: *a close resemblance; a close translation.* **8** careful, strict, or searching: *a close study.* **9** (of a style of play in football, hockey, etc.) characterized by short passes. **10** confined or enclosed. **11** shut or shut tight. **12** oppressive, heavy, or airless: *a close atmosphere.* **13** strictly guarded: *a close prisoner.* **14** neat or tight in fit: *a close cap.* **15** secretive or reticent. **16** miserly; not generous, esp. with money. **17** (of money or credit) hard to obtain; scarce. **18** restricted as to public admission or membership. **19** hidden or secluded. **20** Also: **closed.** restricted or prohibited as to the type of game or fish able to be taken. **21** Also: **closed, narrow.** *Phonetics.* denoting a vowel pronounced with the lips relatively close together. ◆ *adv* **22** closely; tightly. **23** near or in proximity. **24 close to the wind.** *Nautical.* sailing as nearly as possible towards the direction from which the wind is blowing. See also **wind**[1] (sense 26). [C13: from Old French *clos* close, enclosed, from Latin *clausus* shut up, from *claudere* to close] ▸ **'closely** *adv* ▸ **'closeness** *n*

close[2] (kləʊz) *vb* **1** to put or be put in such a position as to cover an opening; shut: *the door closed behind him.* **2** (*tr*) to bar, obstruct, or fill up (an entrance, a hole, etc.): *to close a road.* **3** to bring the parts or edges of (a wound, etc.) together or (of a wound, etc.) to be brought together. **4** (*intr*; foll. by *on, over,* etc.) to take hold: *his hand closed over the money.* **5** to bring or be brought to an end; terminate. **6** to complete (an agreement, a deal, etc.) successfully or (of an agreement, deal, etc.) to be completed successfully. **7** to cease or cause to cease to render service: *the shop closed at six.* **8** (*intr*) *Stock Exchange.* to have a value at the end of a day's trading, as specified: *steels closed two points down.* **9** to complete an electrical circuit. **10** (*tr*) *Nautical.* to pass near. **11** (*tr*) *Archaic.* to enclose or shut in. **12 close one's eyes. 12a** *Euphemistic.* to die. **12b** (often foll. by *to*) to ignore. ◆ *n* **13** the act of closing. **14** the end or conclusion: *the close of the day.* **15** a place of joining or meeting. **16** (kləʊs). *Law.* private property, usually enclosed by a fence, hedge, or wall. **17** (kləʊs). *Brit.* a courtyard or quadrangle enclosed by buildings or an entry leading to such a courtyard. **18** (kləʊs). *Brit.* (*cap. when part of a street name*) a small quiet residential road: *Hillside Close.* **19** *Brit.* a field. **20** (kləʊs). the precincts of a cathedral or similar building. **21** (kləʊs) *Scot.* the entry from the street to a tenement building. **22** *Music.* another word for **cadence.** A perfect cadence is called a **full close,** an imperfect one a **half close. 23** *Archaic or rare.* an encounter in battle; grapple. ◆ See also **close down, close in, close out, close-up, close with.** ▸ **closer** ('kləʊzə) *n*

close call (kləʊs) *n* another expression for **close shave.**

close company (kləʊs) *n Brit.* a company under the control of its directors or fewer than five independent participants. Also called: **closed company.**

closed (kləʊzd) *adj* **1** blocked against entry; shut. **2** restricted; exclusive. **3** not open to question or debate. **4** (of a hunting season, etc.) close. **5** *Maths.* **5a** (of a curve or surface) completely enclosing an area or volume. **5b** (of a set) having members that can be produced by a specific operation on other members of the same set: *the integers are a closed set under multiplication.* **6** Also: **checked.** *Phonetics.* **6a** denoting a syllable that ends in a consonant. **6b** another word for **close**[1] (sense 21). **7** not open to public entry or membership: *a closed society.*

closed book *n* **1** something deemed unknown or incapable of being understood. **2** a matter that has been finally concluded and admits of no further consideration.

closed-captioned *adj* (of a video recording) having subtitles which appear on screen only if the cassette is played through a special decoder.

closed chain *n Chem.* another name for **ring**[1] (sense 18).

closed circuit *n* a complete electrical circuit through which current can flow when a voltage is applied. Compare **open circuit.**

closed-circuit television *n* a television system in which signals are transmitted from the television camera to the receivers by cables or telephone links forming a closed circuit, as used in shops, hospitals, etc.

closed community *n Ecology.* a plant community that does not allow for further colonization, all the available niches being occupied.

closed corporation *n U.S.* a corporation the stock of which is owned by a small number of persons and is rarely traded on the open market. Also: **close corporation.**

closed cycle *n Engineering.* a heat engine in which the working substance is continuously circulated and does not need replenishment.

closed-door *adj* private; barred to members of the public: *a closed-door meeting.*

closed game *n Chess.* a relatively complex game involving closed ranks and files and permitting only nontactical positional manoeuvring. Compare **open game.**

close down (kləʊz) *vb* (*adv*) **1** to cease or cause to cease operations: *the shop closed down.* **2** (*tr*) *Sport.* to mark or move towards (an opposing player) in order to prevent him or her running with the ball or making or receiving a pass. ◆ *n* **close-down** ('kləʊz,daʊn). **3** a closure or stoppage of operations, esp. in a factory. **4** *Brit. radio, television.* the end of a period of broadcasting, esp. late at night.

closed primary *n U.S. government.* a primary in which only members of a particular party may vote. Compare **open primary.**

closed scholarship *n* a scholarship for which only certain people, such as those from a particular school or with a particular surname, are eligible.

closed sentence *n Logic.* a formula that contains no free occurrence of any variable. Compare **open sentence.**

closed set *n Maths.* **1** a set that includes all the values obtained by application of a given operation to its members. **2** a topological set containing all its own limit points. **3** an interval on the real line including its end points, as [0, 1], the set of reals between and including 0 and 1.

closed shop *n* (formerly) an industrial establishment in which there exists a contract between a trade union and the employer permitting the employment of the union's members only. Compare **open shop, union shop.**

close-fisted (ˌkləʊsˈfɪstɪd) *adj* very careful with money; mean. ▸ ˌ**close-ˈfistedness** *n*

close-grained (ˌkləʊsˈgreɪnd) *adj* (of wood) dense or compact in texture.

close harmony (kləʊs) *n* a type of singing in which all the parts except the bass lie close together and are confined to the compass of a tenth.

close-hauled (ˌkləʊsˈhɔːld) *adj Nautical.* with the sails flat, so as to sail as close to the wind as possible.

close in (kləʊz) *vb* (*intr, adv*) **1** (of days) to become shorter with the approach of winter. **2** (foll. by *on* or *upon*) to advance (on) so as to encircle or surround.

close-knit (ˌkləʊsˈnɪt) *adj* closely united, esp. by social ties.

close-lipped (ˌkləʊsˈlɪpt) *or* **close-mouthed** (ˌkləʊsˈmaʊðd, -ˈmaʊθt) *adj* not talking or revealing much.

close out (kləʊz) *vb* (*adv*) to terminate (a client's or other account) on which the margin is inadequate or exhausted, usually by sale of securities to realize cash.

close punctuation (kləʊs) *n* punctuation in which many commas, full stops, etc., are used. Compare **open punctuation.**

close quarters (kləʊs) *pl n* **1** a narrow cramped space or position. **2 at close quarters. 2a** engaged in hand-to-hand combat. **2b** in close proximity; very near together.

close season (kləʊs) *or* **closed season** *n* **1** the period of the year when it is prohibited to kill certain game or fish. **2** *Sport.* the period of the year when there is no domestic competition.

close shave (kləʊs) *n Informal.* a narrow escape.

close-stool (ˈkləʊsˌstuːl) *n* a wooden stool containing a covered chamber pot.

closet (ˈklɒzɪt) *n* **1** a small cupboard or recess. **2** a small private room. **3** short for **water closet. 4** (*modifier*) private or secret. **5** (*modifier*) suited or appropriate for use in private: *closet meditations.* **6** (*modifier*) *U.S. and Canadian.* based on or devoted to theory; speculative: *a closet strategist.* ◆ *vb* **-sets, -seting, -seted. 7** (*tr*) to shut up or confine in a small private room, esp. for conference or meditation. [C14: from Old French, from *clos* enclosure; see CLOSE[1]]

closet drama *n Chiefly U.S.* **a** drama suitable for reading rather than performing. **b** a play of this kind.

closet queen *n Informal.* a man who is homosexual but does not admit the fact.

close-up (ˈkləʊsˌʌp) *n* **1** a photograph or film or television shot taken at close range. **2** a detailed or intimate view or examination: *a close-up of modern society.* ◆ *vb* **close up** (kləʊz) (*adv*). **3** to shut entirely. **4** (*intr*) to draw together: *the ranks closed up.* **5** (*intr*) (of wounds) to heal completely.

close with (kləʊz) *vb* (*intr, prep*) to engage in battle with (an enemy).

closing time (ˈkləʊzɪŋ) *n* the time at which pubs must legally stop selling alcoholic drinks.

clostridium (klɒˈstrɪdɪəm) *n, pl* **-iums** *or* **-ia** (-ɪə). any anaerobic typically rod-shaped bacterium of the genus *Clostridium,* occurring in soil and the intestines of man and animals: family *Bacillaceae.* The genus includes the species causing botulism and tetanus. [C20: from New Latin, literally: small spindle, from Greek *klōstēr* spindle, from *klōthein* to spin; see -IUM] ▸ **closˈtridial** *or* **closˈtridian** *adj*

closure (ˈkləʊʒə) *n* **1** the act of closing or the state of being closed. **2** an end or conclusion. **3** something that closes or shuts, such as a cap or seal for a container. **4** (in a deliberative body) a procedure by which debate may be halted and an immediate vote taken. See also **cloture, guillotine, gag rule. 5** *Geology.* the vertical distance between the crest of an anticline and the lowest contour that surrounds it. **6** *Phonetics.* the obstruction of the breath stream at some point along the vocal tract, such as the complete occlusion preliminary to the articulation of a stop. **7** *Logic.* **7a** the closed sentence formed from a given open sentence by prefixing universal or existential quantifiers to bind all its free variables. **7b** the process of forming such a closed sentence. **8** *Maths.* **8a** the smallest closed set containing a given set. **8b** the operation of forming such a set. **9** *Psychol.* the tendency, first noted by Gestalt psychologists, to see an incomplete figure like a circle with a gap in it as more complete than it is. ◆ *vb* **10** (*tr*) (in a deliberative body) to end (debate) by closure. [C14: from Old French, from Late Latin *clausūra* bar, from Latin *claudere* to close]

clot (klɒt) *n* **1** a soft thick lump or mass: *a clot of blood.* **2** *Brit. informal.* a stupid person; fool. ◆ *vb* **clots, clotting, clotted. 3** to form or cause to form into a soft thick lump or lumps. [Old English *clott,* of Germanic origin; compare Middle Dutch *klotte* block, lump] ▸ **ˈclottish** *adj*

cloth (klɒθ) *n, pl* **cloths** (klɒθs, klɒðz). **1a** a fabric formed by weaving, felting or knitting wool, cotton, etc. **1b** (*as modifier*): *a cloth bag.* **2** a piece of such fabric used for a particular purpose, as for a dishcloth. **3** (usually preceded by *the*) **3a** the clothes worn by a clergyman. **3b** the clergy. **4** *Obsolete.* clothing. **5** *Nautical.* any of the panels of a sail. **6** *Chiefly Brit.* a piece of coloured fabric, used on the stage as scenery. **7** *West African.* a garment in a traditional non-European style. [Old English *clāth;* related to Old Frisian *klēth,* Middle High German *kleit* cloth, clothing]

clothbound (ˈklɒθˌbaʊnd) *adj* (of a book) bound in stiff boards covered in cloth.

cloth cap *n Brit.* **1** Also called: **flat cap.** a flat woollen cap with a stiff peak. **2** *Informal.* **2a** a symbol of working-class ethos or origin. **2b** (*as modifier*): *cloth-cap attitudes.*

clothe (kləʊð) *vb* **clothes, clothing, clothed** *or* **clad.** (*tr*) **1** to dress or attire (a person). **2** to provide with clothing or covering. **3** to conceal or disguise. **4** to endow or invest. [Old English *clāthian,* from *clāth* CLOTH; related to Old Norse *klætha*]

cloth-eared *adj Informal.* **1** deaf. **2** insensitive.

clothes (kləʊðz) *pl n* **1a** articles of dress. **1b** (*as modifier*): *clothes brush.* Related adj: **vestiary. 2** *Chiefly Brit.* short for **bedclothes.** [Old English *clāthas,* plural of *clāth* CLOTH]

clotheshorse (ˈkləʊðzˌhɔːs) *n* **1** a frame on which to hang laundry for drying or airing. **2** *Informal.* a dandy.

clothesline (ˈkləʊðzˌlaɪn) *n* a piece of rope, cord, or wire on which clean washing is hung to dry or air.

clothes moth *n* any of various tineid moths, esp. *Tineola bisselliella,* the larvae of which feed on wool or fur.

clothes peg *n* a small wooden or plastic clip for attaching washing to a clothesline.

clothes pole *n* **1** a post to which a clothesline is attached. Also called: **clothes post. 2** *Scot., U.S.* another term for **clothes prop.**

clothes-press *n* a piece of furniture for storing clothes, usually containing wide drawers and a cabinet.

clothes prop *n* a long wooden pole with a forked end, used to raise a line of washing to enable it to catch the breeze.

clothier (ˈkləʊðɪə) *n* a person who makes, sells, or deals in clothes or cloth.

clothing (ˈkləʊðɪŋ) *n* **1** garments collectively. **2** something that covers or clothes.

Clotho (ˈkləʊθəʊ) *n Greek myth.* one of the three Fates, spinner of the thread of life. [Latin, from Greek *Klōtho,* one who spins, from *klōthein* to spin]

cloth of gold *n* cloth woven from silk threads interspersed with gold.

Clotilda (kləˈtɪldə) *n* ?475–?545 A.D., wife of Clovis I of the Franks, whom she converted (496) to Christianity.

clotted cream *n Brit.* a thick cream made from scalded milk, esp. in SW England. Also called: **Devonshire cream.**

clotting factor *n* any one of a group of substances, including factor VIII, the presence of which in the blood is essential for blood clotting to occur. Also called: **coagulation factor.**

cloture (ˈkləʊtʃə) *n* **1** closure in the U.S. Senate. ◆ *vb* **2** (*tr*) to end (debate) in the U.S. Senate by cloture. [C19: from French *clôture,* from Old French CLOSURE]

cloud (klaʊd) *n* **1** a mass of water or ice particles visible in the sky, usually white or grey, from which rain or snow falls when the particles coagulate. See also **cirrus, cumulonimbus, cumulus, stratus. 2** any collection of particles visible in the air, esp. of smoke or dust. **3** a large number of insects or other small animals in flight. **4** something that darkens, threatens, or carries gloom. **5** *Jewellery.* a cloudlike blemish in a transparent stone. **6 in the clouds.** not in contact with reality. **7 under a cloud. 7a** under reproach or suspicion. **7b** in a state of gloom or bad temper. **8 on cloud nine.** *Informal.* elated; very happy. ◆ *vb* **9** (when *intr,* often foll. by *over* or *up*) to make or become cloudy, overcast, or indistinct. **10** (*tr*) to make obscure; darken. **11** (*tr*) to confuse or impair: *emotion clouded his judgment.* **12** to make or become gloomy or depressed. **13** (*tr*) to place under or render liable to suspicion or disgrace. **14** to render (liquids) milky or dull or (of liquids) to become milky or dull. **15** to become or render mottled or variegated. [C13 (in the sense: a mass of vapour): from Old English *clūd* rock, hill; probably related to CLOD] ▸ **ˈcloudless** *adj* ▸ **ˈcloudlessly** *adv* ▸ **ˈcloudlessness** *n* ▸ **ˈcloudˌlike** *adj*

cloudberry (ˈklaʊdbərɪ, -brɪ) *n, pl* **-ries.** a creeping Eurasian herbaceous rosaceous plant, *Rubus chamaemorus,* with white flowers and orange berry-like fruits (drupelets).

cloudburst (ˈklaʊdˌbɜːst) *n* a heavy downpour.

cloud chamber *n Physics.* an apparatus for detecting high-energy particles by observing their tracks through a chamber containing a supersaturated vapour. Each particle ionizes molecules along its path and small droplets condense on them to produce a visible track. Also called: **Wilson cloud chamber.**

cloud-cuckoo-land *or* **cloudland** (ˈklaʊdˌlænd) *n* a realm of fantasy, dreams, or impractical notions.

clouded yellow *n* See **yellow** (sense 6).

cloudlet (ˈklaʊdlɪt) *n* a small cloud.

cloud rack *n* a group of moving clouds.

cloudscape (ˈklaʊdskeɪp) *n* **1** a picturesque formation of clouds. **2** a picture or photograph of such a formation.

cloudy (ˈklaʊdɪ) *adj* **cloudier, cloudiest. 1** covered with cloud or clouds. **2** of or like a cloud or clouds. **3** streaked or mottled like a cloud. **4** opaque or muddy. **5** obscure or unclear. **6** troubled by gloom or depression: *his face had a cloudy expression.* ▸ **ˈcloudily** *adv* ▸ **ˈcloudiness** *n*

Clouet (*French* kluɛ) *n* **François** (frɑ̃swa), ?1515–72, and his father, **Jean** (ʒɑ̃), ?1485–?1540, French portrait painters.

clough (klʌf) *n Dialect.* a gorge or narrow ravine. [Old English *clōh*]

Clough (klʌf) *n* **1 Arthur Hugh.** 1819–61, British poet, author of *Amours de Voyage* (1858) and *Dipsychus* (1865). **2 Brian.** born 1935, English footballer and manager.

clout (klaʊt) *n* **1** *Informal.* a blow with the hand or a hard object. **2** power or influence, esp. in politics. **3** *Archery.* **3a** the target used in long-distance shooting. **3b** the centre of this target. **3c** a shot that hits the centre. **4** Also called: **clout nail.** a short, flat-headed nail used esp. for attaching sheet metal to wood. **5** *Brit. dialect.* **5a** a piece of cloth: *a dish clout.* **5b** a garment. **5c** a patch. ◆ *vb* (*tr*) **6** *Informal.* to give a hard blow to, esp. with the hand. **7** to patch with a piece of cloth or leather. [Old English *clūt* piece of metal or cloth, *clūtian* to patch (C14: to strike with the hand); related to Dutch *kluit* a lump, and to CLOD] ▸ **ˈclouter** *n*

clove[1] (kləʊv) *n* **1** a tropical evergreen myrtaceous tree, *Eugenia aromatica,* native to the East Indies but cultivated elsewhere, esp. Zanzibar. **2** the dried unopened flower buds of this tree, used as a pungent fragrant spice. [C14: from

Old French *clou de girofle,* literally: nail of clove, *clou* from Latin *clāvus* nail + *girofle* clove tree]

clove[2] (kləʊv) *n* any of the segments of a compound bulb that arise from the axils of the scales of a large bulb. [Old English *clufu* bulb; related to Old High German *klovolouh* garlic; see CLEAVE[1]]

clove[3] (kləʊv) *vb* a past tense of **cleave**[1].

clove hitch *n* a knot or hitch used for securing a rope to a spar, post, or larger rope.

Clovelly (klə'vɛlɪ) *n* a village in SW England, in Devon on the Bristol Channel: famous for its steep cobbled streets: tourism, fishing. Pop.: 500 (1989).

cloven ('kləʊvᵊn) *vb* **1** a past participle of **cleave**[1]. ◆ *adj* **2** split; cleft; divided.

cloven hoof *or* **foot** *n* **1** the divided hoof of a pig, goat, cow, deer, or related animal, which consists of the two middle digits of the foot. **2** the mark or symbol of Satan. ▸ ˌ**cloven-'hoofed** *or* ˌ**cloven-'footed** *adj*

clove oil *n* a volatile pale-yellow aromatic oil obtained from clove flowers, formerly much used in confectionery, dentistry, and microscopy. Also called: **oil of cloves.**

clove pink *n* another name for **carnation** (sense 1).

clover ('kləʊvə) *n* **1** any plant of the papilionaceous genus *Trifolium,* having trifoliate leaves and dense flower heads. Many species, such as red clover, white clover, and alsike, are grown as forage plants. **2** any of various similar or related plants. **3 sweet clover.** another name for **melilot. 4 pin clover.** another name for **alfilaria. 5 in clover.** *Informal.* in a state of ease or luxury. [Old English *clāfre;* related to Old High German *klēo,* Middle Low German *klēver,* Dutch *klāver*]

cloverleaf ('kləʊvəˌliːf) *n, pl* **-leaves. 1** an arrangement of connecting roads, resembling a four-leaf clover in form, that joins two intersecting main roads. **2** (*modifier*) in the shape or pattern of a leaf of clover.

cloverleaf aerial *n* a type of aerial, having three or four similar coplanar loops arranged symmetrically around an axis, to which in-phase signals are fed.

Clovis I ('kləʊvɪs) *n* German name *Chlodwig.* ?466–511 A.D., king of the Franks (481–511), who extended the Merovingian kingdom to include most of Gaul and SW Germany.

clovis point ('kləʊvɪs) *n* a concave-based flint projectile dating from the 10th millennium B.C., found throughout most of Central and North America.

clown (klaʊn) *n* **1** a comic entertainer, usually grotesquely costumed and made up, appearing in the circus. **2** any performer who elicits an amused response. **3** someone who plays jokes or tricks. **4** a person who acts in a comic or buffoonlike manner. **5** a coarse clumsy rude person; boor. **6** *Archaic.* a countryman or rustic. ◆ *vb* (*intr*) **7** to perform as a clown. **8** to play jokes or tricks. **9** to act foolishly. [C16: perhaps of Low German origin; compare Frisian *klönne,* Icelandic *klunni* clumsy fellow] ▸ '**clownery** *n* ▸ '**clownish** *adj* ▸ '**clownishly** *adv* ▸ '**clownishness** *n*

cloxacillin (ˌklɒksə'sɪlɪn) *n* a semisynthetic penicillin used to treat staphylococcal infections due to penicillin-resistant organisms.

cloy (klɔɪ) *vb* to make weary or cause weariness through an excess of something initially pleasurable or sweet. [C14 (originally: to nail, hence, to obstruct): from earlier *acloyen,* from Old French *encloer,* from Medieval Latin *inclavāre,* from Latin *clāvāre* to nail, from *clāvus* a nail] ▸ '**cloying** *adj* ▸ '**cloyingly** *adv*

cloze test (kləʊz) *n* a test of the ability to comprehend text in which the reader has to supply the missing words that have been removed from the text at regular intervals. [altered from *close* to complete a pattern (in Gestalt theory)]

club (klʌb) *n* **1** a stout stick, usually with one end thicker than the other, esp. one used as a weapon. **2** a stick or bat used to strike the ball in various sports, esp. golf. See **golf club** (sense 1). **3** short for **Indian club. 4** a group or association of people with common aims or interests: *a wine club.* **5a** the room, building, or facilities used by such a group. **5b** (*in combination*): *clubhouse.* **6** a building in which elected, fee-paying members go to meet, dine, read, etc. **7** a commercial establishment in which people can drink and dance; disco. See also **nightclub. 8** *Chiefly Brit.* an organization, esp. in a shop, set up as a means of saving. **9** *Brit.* an informal word for **friendly society. 10a** the black trefoil symbol on a playing card. **10b** a card with one or more of these symbols or (*when pl*) the suit of cards so marked. **11** *Nautical.* **11a** a spar used for extending the clew of a gaff topsail beyond the peak of the gaff. **11b** short for **club foot** (sense 3). **12 in the club.** *Brit. slang.* pregnant. **13 on the club.** *Brit. slang.* away from work due to sickness, esp. when receiving sickness benefit. ◆ *vb* **clubs, clubbing, clubbed. 14** (*tr*) to beat with or as if with a club. **15** (often foll. by *together*) to gather or become gathered into a group. **16** (often foll. by *together*) to unite or combine (resources, efforts, etc.) for a common purpose. **17** (*tr*) to use (a rifle or similar firearm) as a weapon by holding the barrel and hitting with the butt. **18** (*intr*) *Nautical.* to drift in a current, reducing speed by dragging anchor. [C13: from Old Norse *klubba,* related to Middle High German *klumpe* group of trees, CLUMP, Old English *clympre* lump of metal] ▸ '**clubbing** *n*

clubbable *or* **clubable** ('klʌbəbᵊl) *adj* suitable to be a member of a club; sociable. ▸ ˌ**clubba'bility** *or* ˌ**cluba'bility** *n*

clubbed (klʌbd) *adj* having a thickened end, like a club.

clubber ('klʌbə) *n* a person who regularly frequents nightclubs and similar establishments.

clubby ('klʌbɪ) *adj* **-bier, -biest. 1** sociable, esp. effusively so. **2** exclusive or cliquish. ▸ '**clubbily** *adv*

club class *n* **1** a class of air travel which is less luxurious than first class but more luxurious than economy class. ◆ *adj* **2 club-class.** of or relating to this class of travel.

club foot *n* **1** a congenital deformity of the foot, esp. one in which the foot is twisted so that most of the weight rests on the heel. Technical name: **talipes. 2** a foot so deformed. **3** *Nautical.* a boom attached to the foot of a jib. ▸ ˌ**club-'footed** *adj*

club hand *n* **1** a deformity of the hand, analogous to club foot. **2** a hand so deformed. ▸ ˌ**club-'handed** *adj*

clubhaul ('klʌbˌhɔːl) *vb Nautical.* to force (a sailing vessel) onto a new tack, esp. in an emergency, by fastening a lee anchor to the lee quarter, dropping the anchor as the vessel comes about, and hauling in the anchor cable to swing the stern to windward.

clubhouse ('klʌbˌhaʊs) *n* the premises of a sports or other club, esp. a golf club.

clubland ('klʌblənd) *n* (in Britain) the area of London around St. James's, which contains most of the famous London clubs.

club line *n Printing.* See **orphan** (sense 3).

clubman ('klʌbmən) *or* (*fem*) **clubwoman** *n, pl* **-men** *or* **-women.** a person who is an enthusiastic member of a club or clubs.

club moss *n* any mosslike tracheophyte plant of the phylum *Lycopodophyta,* having erect or creeping stems covered with tiny overlapping leaves.

club root *n* a disease of cabbages and related plants, caused by the fungus *Plasmodiophora brassicae,* in which the roots become thickened and distorted.

club sandwich *n* a sandwich consisting of three or more slices of toast or bread with a filling.

cluck (klʌk) *n* **1** the low clicking sound made by a hen or any similar sound. ◆ *vb* **2** (*intr*) (of a hen) to make a clicking sound. **3** (*tr*) to call or express (a feeling) by making a similar sound. [C17: of imitative origin]

clucky ('klʌkɪ) *adj Austral. informal.* (of a woman) **1** wishing to have a baby. **2** excessively protective towards her children.

clue (kluː) *n* **1** something that helps to solve a problem or unravel a mystery. **2 not to have a clue. 2a** to be completely baffled. **2b** to be completely ignorant or incompetent. ◆ *vb* **clues, cluing, clued. 3** (*tr;* usually foll. by *in* or *up*) to provide with helpful information. ◆ *n, vb* **4** a variant spelling of **clew.** [C15: variant of CLEW]

clued-up *adj Informal.* shrewd; well-informed.

clueless ('kluːlɪs) *adj Slang.* helpless; stupid.

Cluj (kluʃ, kluːʒ) *n* an industrial city in NW Romania, on the Someşul-Mic River: former capital of Transylvania. Pop.: 326 017 (1994 est.). German name: **Klausenburg.** Hungarian name: **Kolozsvár.**

clumber spaniel ('klʌmbə) *n* a type of thickset spaniel having a broad heavy head. Often shortened to **clumber.** [C19: named after *Clumber,* stately home of the Dukes of Newcastle where the breed was developed]

clump (klʌmp) *n* **1** a cluster, as of trees or plants. **2** a dull heavy tread or any similar sound. **3** an irregular mass: *a clump of hair or earth.* **4** an inactive mass of microorganisms, esp. a mass of bacteria produced as a result of agglutination. **5** an extra sole on a shoe. **6** *Slang.* a blow. ◆ *vb* **7** (*intr*) to walk or tread heavily. **8** to gather or be gathered into clumps, clusters, clots, etc. **9** to cause (bacteria, blood cells, etc.) to collect together or (of bacteria, etc.) to collect together. **10** (*tr*) *Slang.* to punch (someone). [Old English *clympe;* related to Middle Dutch *klampe* heap of hay, Middle Low German *klampe* CLAMP[2], Swedish *klimp* small lump] ▸ '**clumpy** *adj* ▸ '**clumpiness** *n*

clumsy ('klʌmzɪ) *adj* **-sier, -siest. 1** lacking in skill or physical coordination. **2** awkwardly constructed or contrived. [C16 (in obsolete sense: benumbed with cold; hence, awkward): perhaps from C13 dialect *clumse* to benumb, probably from Scandinavian; compare Swedish dialect *klumsig* numb] ▸ '**clumsily** *adv* ▸ '**clumsiness** *n*

clung (klʌŋ) *vb* the past tense and past participle of **cling.**

clunk (klʌŋk) *n* **1** a blow or the sound of a blow. **2** a dull metallic sound. **3** a dull or stupid person. **4** *Chiefly Scot.* **4a** the gurgling sound of a liquid. **4b** the sound of a cork being removed from a bottle. ◆ *vb* **5** to make or cause to make such a sound. [C19: of imitative origin]

clunky ('klʌŋkɪ) *adj* **clunkier, clunkiest. 1** making a clunking noise. **2** *Informal.* ponderously ungraceful or unsophisticated: *clunky boots.* **3** awkward or unsophisticated: *then you guffaw at clunky dialogue.*

Cluny ('kluːnɪ; *French* klyni) *n* a town in E central France: reformed Benedictine order founded here in 910; important religious and cultural centre in the Middle Ages. Pop.: 4724 (1990). ▸ '**Cluniac** *adj*

Cluny lace *n* a strong heavy silk and cotton bobbin lace made at Cluny or elsewhere.

clupeid ('kluːpɪɪd) *n* **1** any widely distributed soft-finned teleost fish of the family *Clupeidae,* typically having oily flesh, and including the herrings, sardines, shad, etc. ◆ *adj* **2** of, relating to, or belonging to the family *Clupeidae.* [C19: from New Latin *Clupeidae,* from Latin *clupea* small river fish]

clupeoid ('kluːpɪˌɔɪd) *adj* **1** of, relating to, or belonging to the *Isospondyli* (or *Clupeiformes*), a large order of soft-finned fishes, including the herrings, salmon, and tarpon. ◆ *n* **2** any fish belonging to the order *Isospondyli.* [C19: from Latin *clupea* small fish + -OID]

cluster ('klʌstə) *n* **1** a number of things growing, fastened, or occurring close together. **2** a number of persons or things grouped together. **3** *U.S. Military.* a metal insignia worn on a medal ribbon to indicate a second award or a higher class of a decoration or order. **4** *Military.* **4a** a group of bombs dropped in one stick, esp. fragmentation and incendiary bombs. **4b** the basic unit of mines used in laying a minefield. **5** *Astronomy.* an aggregation of stars or galaxies moving together through space. **6** a group of two or more consecutive vowels or consonants. **7** *Statistics.* a naturally occurring subgroup of a population used in stratified sampling. **8** *Chem.* **8a** a chemical compound or molecule containing groups of metal atoms joined by metal-to-metal bonds. **8b** the group of linked metal atoms present. ◆ *vb* **9** to gather or be gathered in clusters. [Old English *clyster;* related to Low German *Kluster;* see CLOD, CLOT] ▸ '**clustered** *adj* ▸ '**clusteringly** *adv* ▸ '**clustery** *adj*

cluster bomb *n* a bomb that throws out a number of smaller bombs or antipersonnel projectiles when it explodes.

cluster fly *n* a dipterous fly, *Pollenia rudis,* that tends to gather in large numbers in attics in the autumn: family *Calliphoridae.* The larvae are parasitic in earthworms.

clutch[1] (klʌtʃ) *vb* **1** (*tr*) to seize with or as if with hands or claws. **2** (*tr*) to grasp or hold firmly. **3** (*intr;* usually foll. by *at*) to attempt to get hold or possession (of). ◆ *n* **4** a device that enables two revolving shafts to be joined or disconnected as required, esp. one that transmits the drive from the engine to the gearbox in a vehicle. **5** a device for holding fast. **6** a firm grasp. **7** a hand, claw, or talon in the act of clutching: *in the clutches of a bear.* **8** (*often pl*) power or control: *in the clutches of the Mafia.* **9** Also called: **clutch bag.** a handbag without handles. [Old English *clyccan;* related to Old Frisian *kletsie* spear, Swedish *klyka* clasp, fork]

clutch[2] (klʌtʃ) *n* **1** a hatch of eggs laid by a particular bird or laid in a single nest. **2** a brood of chickens. **3** *Informal.* a group, bunch, or cluster. ◆ *vb* **4** (*tr*) to hatch (chickens). [C17 (Northern English dialect) *cletch,* from Old Norse *klekja* to hatch]

Clutha ('klu:θə) *n* a river in New Zealand, the longest river in South Island; rising in the Southern Alps it flows southeast to the Pacific. Length: 338 km (210 miles).

clutter ('klʌtə) *vb* **1** (*usually tr;* often foll. by *up*) to strew or amass (objects) in a disorderly manner. **2** (*intr*) to move about in a bustling manner. **3** (*intr*) to chatter or babble. ◆ *n* **4** a disordered heap or mass of objects. **5** a state of disorder. **6** unwanted echoes that confuse the observation of signals on a radar screen. [C15 *clotter,* from *clotteren* to CLOT]

Clwyd ('klu:ɪd) *n* a former county in NE Wales, formed in 1974 from Flintshire, most of Denbighshire, and part of Merionethshire; replaced in 1996 by Flintshire, Denbighshire, Wrexham county borough, and part of Conwy county borough.

Clyde (klaɪd) *n* **1 Firth of.** an inlet of the Atlantic in SW Scotland. Length: 103 km (64 miles). **2** a river in S Scotland, rising in South Lanarkshire and flowing northwest to the Firth of Clyde: formerly extensive shipyards. Length: 170 km (106 miles).

Clydebank (ˌklaɪd'bæŋk, 'klaɪdˌbæŋk) *n* a town in W Scotland, in West Dunbartonshire on the north bank of the River Clyde. Pop.: 29 171 (1991).

Clydesdale ('klaɪdzˌdeɪl) *n* a heavy powerful breed of carthorse, originally from Scotland.

clype (kləɪp) *Scot. vb* (*intr*) **1** to tell tales; be an informer. ◆ *n* **2** a person who tells tales. [C15: from Old English *clipian, cleopian;* see CLEPE]

clypeus ('klɪpɪəs) *n, pl* **clypei** ('klɪpɪˌaɪ). a cuticular plate on the head of some insects between the labrum and the frons. [C19: from New Latin, from Latin *clipeus* round shield] ▸ **'clypeal** *adj* ▸ **clypeate** ('klɪpɪˌeɪt) *adj*

clyster ('klɪstə) *n Med.* a former name for **enema.** [C14: from Greek *klustēr,* from *kluzein* to rinse]

Clytemnestra *or* **Clytaemnestra** (ˌklaɪtɪm'nɛstrə) *n Greek myth.* the wife of Agamemnon, whom she killed on his return from the Trojan War.

cm *symbol for* centimetre.

Cm *the chemical symbol for* curium.

Cmdr *Military. abbrev. for* Commander.

CMEA *abbrev. for* Council for Mutual Economic Assistance. See **Comecon.**

CMG *abbrev. for* Companion of St. Michael and St. George (a Brit. title).

cml *abbrev. for* commercial.

CMOS ('si:mɒs) *adj Computing. acronym for* complementary metal oxide silicon: *CMOS memory.*

CMV *abbrev. for* cytomegalovirus.

C/N, c/n, *or* **cn** *Commerce. abbrev. for* credit note.

CNAA (in Britain) *abbrev. for* the Council for National Academic Awards: a degree-awarding body separate from the universities.

CNAR *abbrev. for* compound net annual rate.

CND (in Britain) *abbrev. for* Campaign for Nuclear Disarmament.

cnemis ('ni:mɪs) *n Anatomy, zoology.* the shin or tibia. [from Greek *knēmē* leg] ▸ **'cnemial** *adj*

cnidarian (naɪ'dɛərɪən, knaɪ-) *n* **1** any invertebrate of the phylum *Cnidaria,* which comprises the coelenterates. ◆ *adj* **2** of, relating to, or belonging to the *Cnidaria.* [C20: from New Latin *Cnidaria,* from Greek *knidē* nettle]

cnidoblast ('naɪdəʊˌblɑ:st, 'knaɪ-) *n Zoology.* any of the cells of a coelenterate that contain nematocysts. [C19: from New Latin *cnida,* from Greek *knidē* nettle + -BLAST]

Cnidus ('naɪdəs, 'knaɪ-) *n* an ancient Greek city in SW Asia Minor: famous for its school of medicine.

Cnossus ('nɒsəs, 'knɒs-) *n* a variant spelling of **Knossos.**

CNS *abbrev. for* central nervous system.

Cnut (kə'nju:t) *n* a variant spelling of **Canute.**

Co *the chemical symbol for* cobalt.

CO *abbrev. for:* **1** Commanding Officer. **2** Commonwealth Office. **3** conscientious objector. **4** *U.S. zip code for* Colorado. **5** *international car registration number for* Colombia.

Co. *or* **co.** *abbrev. for:* **1** (*esp. in names of business organizations*) Company. **2 and co.** (kəʊ) *Informal.* and the rest of them: *Harold and co.*

Co. *abbrev. for* County.

co- *prefix* **1** together; joint or jointly; mutual or mutually: *coproduction.* **2** indicating partnership or equality: *cofounder; copilot.* **3** to the same or a similar degree: *coextend.* **4** (in mathematics and astronomy) of the complement of an angle: *cosecant; codeclination.* [from Latin, reduced form of COM-]

c/o *abbrev. for:* **1** care of. **2** *Book-keeping.* carried over.

CoA *abbrev. for* coenzyme A.

coacervate (kəʊ'æsəvɪt, -ˌveɪt) *n* either of two liquid phases that may separate from a hydrophilic sol, each containing a different concentration of a dispersed solid. [C17: from Latin *coacervāre* to heap up, from *acervus* a heap] ▸ **coˌacer'vation** *n*

coach (kəʊtʃ) *n* **1** a vehicle for several passengers, used for transport over long distances, sightseeing, etc. **2** a large four-wheeled enclosed carriage, usually horse-drawn. **3** a railway carriage carrying passengers. **4** a trainer or instructor: *a drama coach.* **5** a tutor who prepares students for examinations. ◆ *vb* **6** to give tuition or instruction to (a pupil). **7** (*tr*) to transport in a bus or coach. [C16: from French *coche,* from Hungarian *kocsi szekér* wagon of Kocs, village in Hungary where coaches were first made; in the sense: to teach, probably from the idea that the instructor carried his pupils] ▸ **'coacher** *n*

coach bolt *n* a large round-headed bolt used esp. to secure wood to masonry. Also called (chiefly U.S. and Canadian): **carriage bolt.**

coach box *n* the seat of a coachman on a horse-drawn carriage or coach.

coach-built *adj* (of a vehicle) having specially built bodywork. ▸ **'coach-ˌbuilder** *n*

coach dog *n* a former name for **Dalmatian.**

coach house *n* **1** a building in which a coach is kept. **2** Also called: **coaching house, coaching inn.** *History.* an inn along a coaching route at which horses were changed.

coach line *n* a decorative line on the bodywork of a motor vehicle. Also called: **carriage line.**

coachman ('kəʊtʃmən) *n, pl* **-men. 1** the driver of a coach or carriage. **2** a fishing fly with white wings and a brown hackle.

coach screw *n* a large screw with a square head used in timber work in buildings, etc.

coachwood ('kəʊtʃˌwʊd) *n* an Australian tree, *Ceratopetalum apetalum,* yielding light aromatic wood used for furniture, turnery, etc.

coachwork ('kəʊtʃˌwɜ:k) *n* **1** the design and manufacture of car bodies. **2** the body of a car.

coaction[1] (kəʊ'ækʃən) *n* **1** any relationship between organisms within a community. **2** joint action. [C17: CO- + ACTION] ▸ **co'active** *adj* ▸ **co'actively** *adv* ▸ **ˌcoac'tivity** *n*

coaction[2] (kəʊ'ækʃən) *n Obsolete.* a force or compulsion, either to compel or restrain. [C14: from Late Latin *coāctiō,* from Latin *cōgere* to constrain, compel]

coadjutant (kəʊ'ædʒətənt) *adj* **1** cooperating. ◆ *n* **2** a helper.

coadjutor (kəʊ'ædʒʊtə) *n* **1** a bishop appointed as assistant to a diocesan bishop. **2** *Rare.* an assistant. [C15: via Old French from Latin *co-* together + *adjūtor* helper, from *adjūtāre* to assist, from *juvāre* to help] ▸ **co'adjutress** *or* **co'adjutrix** *fem n*

coadunate (kəʊ'ædjʊnɪt, -ˌneɪt) *adj Biology.* another word for **connate** (sense 3). [C19: from Late Latin *coadūnāre* to join together, from Latin *adūnāre* to join to, from *ūnus* one] ▸ **coˌadu'nation** *n* ▸ **co'aduˌnative** *adj*

coagulant (kəʊ'ægjʊlənt) *or* **coagulator** (kəʊ'ægjʊˌleɪtə) *n* a substance that aids or produces coagulation.

coagulase (kəʊ'ægjʊˌleɪz) *n* any enzyme that causes coagulation of blood.

coagulate *vb* (kəʊ'ægjʊˌleɪt). **1** to cause (a fluid, such as blood) to change into a soft semisolid mass or (of such a fluid) to change into such a mass; clot; curdle. **2** *Chem.* to separate or cause to separate into distinct constituent phases. ◆ *n* (kəʊ'ægjʊlɪt, -ˌleɪt). **3** the solid or semisolid substance produced by coagulation. [C16: from Latin *coāgulāre* to make (a liquid) curdle, from *coāgulum* rennet, from *cōgere* to drive together] ▸ **co'agulable** *adj* ▸ **coˌagula'bility** *n* ▸ **coˌagu'lation** *n* ▸ **coagulative** (kəʊ'ægjʊlətɪv) *adj*

coagulation factor *n Med.* another name for **clotting factor.**

coagulum (kəʊ'ægjʊləm) *n, pl* **-la** (-lə). any coagulated mass; clot; curd. [C17: from Latin: curdling agent; see COAGULATE]

Coahuila (*Spanish* koa'wila) *n* a state of N Mexico: mainly plateau, crossed by several mountain ranges that contain rich mineral resources. Capital: Saltillo. Pop.: 2 172 136 (1995 est.). Area: 151 571 sq. km (59 112 sq. miles).

coal (kəʊl) *n* **1a** a compact black or dark-brown carbonaceous rock consisting of layers of partially decomposed vegetation deposited in the Carboniferous period: a fuel and a source of coke, coal gas, and coal tar. See also **anthracite, bituminous coal, lignite, peat**[1]. **1b** (*as modifier*): *coal cellar; coal merchant; coal mine; coal dust.* **2** one or more lumps of coal. **3** short for **charcoal. 4 coals to Newcastle.** something supplied where it is already plentiful. **5 haul (someone) over the coals.** to reprimand (someone). ◆ *vb* **6** to take in, provide with, or turn into coal. [Old English *col;* related to Old Norse *kol,* Old High German *kolo,* Old Irish *gūal*] ▸ **'coaly** *adj*

coaler ('kəʊlə) *n* **1** a ship, train, etc., used to carry or supply coal. **2** a person who sells or supplies coal.

coalesce (ˌkəʊə'lɛs) *vb* (*intr*) to unite or come together in one body or mass; merge; fuse; blend. [C16: from Latin *coalēscere* from CO- + *alēscere* to increase, from *alere* to nourish] ▸ **ˌcoa'lescence** *n* ▸ **ˌcoa'lescent** *adj*

coalface ('kəʊlˌfeɪs) *n* the exposed seam of coal in a mine.

coalfield ('kəʊlˌfi:ld) *n* an area rich in deposits of coal.

coalfish ('kəʊlˌfɪʃ) *n, pl* **-fish** *or* **-fishes.** a dark-coloured gadoid food fish, *Pollachius virens,* occurring in northern seas. Also called (Brit.): **saithe, coley.**

coal gas *n* a mixture of gases produced by the distillation of bituminous coal and used for heating and lighting: consists mainly of hydrogen, methane, and carbon monoxide.

coal heaver *n* a workman who moves coal.

coal hole *n Brit. informal.* a small coal cellar.

coalition (ˌkəʊə'lɪʃən) *n* **1a** an alliance or union between groups, factions, or parties, esp. for some temporary and specific reason. **1b** (*as modifier*): *a coalition government.* **2** a fusion or merging into one body or mass. [C17: from Medieval Latin *coalitiō,* from Latin *coalēscere* to COALESCE] ▸ **ˌcoa'litional** *adj* ▸ **ˌcoa'litionist** *or* **ˌcoa'litioner** *n*

Coal Measures *pl n* **the.** a series of coal-bearing rocks formed in the upper Carboniferous period; the uppermost series of the Carboniferous system.

coal miner's lung *n* an informal name for **anthracosis.**

coal oil *n* **1** *U.S. and Canadian.* petroleum or a refined product from petroleum, esp. kerosene. **2** a crude oil produced, together with coal gas, during the distillation of bituminous coal.

Coalport ('kəʊl,pɔːt) *n Antiques.* a white translucent bone china having richly coloured moulded patterns, made in the 19th century at Coalport near Shrewsbury.

coal pot *n* a cooking device using charcoal, consisting of a raised iron bowl and a central grid.

Coal Sack *n* a dark nebula in the Milky Way close to the Southern Cross.

coal scuttle *n* a domestic metal container for coal.

coal tar *n* a black tar, produced by the distillation of bituminous coal, that can be further distilled to yield benzene, toluene, xylene, anthracene, phenol, etc.

coal-tar pitch *n* a residue left by the distillation of coal tar: a mixture of hydrocarbons and finely divided carbon used as a binder for fuel briquettes, road surfaces, and carbon electrodes.

coal tit *n* a small European songbird, *Parus ater,* having a black head with a white patch on the nape: family *Paridae* (tits).

coaming ('kəʊmɪŋ) *n* a raised frame around the cockpit or hatchway of a vessel for keeping out water. [C17: of unknown origin]

coaptation (,kəʊæp'teɪʃən) *n* the joining or reuniting of two surfaces, esp. the ends of a broken bone or the edges of a wound. [C16: from Late Latin *coaptātiō* a meticulous joining together, from Latin *co-* together + *aptāre* to fit]

coarctate (kəʊ'ɑːkteɪt) *adj* **1** (of a pupa) enclosed in a hard barrel-shaped case (puparium), as in the housefly. **2** crowded or pressed together; constricted. ◆ *vb* (*intr*) **3** *Pathol.* (esp. of the aorta) to become narrower; become constricted. [C15: from Latin *coarctāre,* to press together, from *artus* tight] ▸ **,coarc'tation** *n*

coarse (kɔːs) *adj* **1** rough in texture, structure, etc.; not fine: *coarse sand.* **2** lacking refinement or taste; indelicate; vulgar: *coarse jokes.* **3** of inferior quality; not pure or choice. **4** (of a metal) not refined. **5** (of a screw) having widely spaced threads. [C14: of unknown origin] ▸ **'coarsely** *adv* ▸ **'coarseness** *n*

coarse fish *n* a freshwater fish that is not a member of the salmon family. Compare **game fish.** ▸ coarse fishing *n*

coarse-grained *adj* **1** having a large or coarse grain. **2** (of a person) having a coarse nature; gross.

coarsen ('kɔːsᵊn) *vb* to make or become coarse.

coast (kəʊst) *n* **1a** the line or zone where the land meets the sea or some other large expanse of water. **1b** (*in combination*): *coastland.* Related adj: **littoral. 2** *Brit.* the seaside. **3** *U.S.* **3a** a slope down which a sledge may slide. **3b** the act or an instance of sliding down a slope. **4** *Obsolete.* borderland or frontier. **5 the coast is clear.** *Informal.* the obstacles or dangers are gone. ◆ *vb* **6** to move or cause to move by momentum or force of gravity. **7** (*intr*) to proceed without great effort: *to coast to victory.* **8** to sail along (a coast). [C13: from Old French *coste* coast, slope, from Latin *costa* side, rib] ▸ **'coastal** *adj* ▸ **'coastally** *adv*

coaster ('kəʊstə) *n* **1** *Brit.* a vessel or trader engaged in coastal commerce. **2** a small tray, sometimes on wheels, for holding a decanter, wine bottle, etc. **3** a person or thing that coasts. **4** a protective disc or mat for glasses or bottles. **5** *U.S.* short for **roller coaster. 6** *West African.* a European resident on the coast.

Coaster ('kəʊstə) *n N.Z.* a person from the West Coast of the South Island, New Zealand.

coastguard ('kəʊst,gɑːd) *n* **1** a maritime force which aids shipping, saves lives at sea, prevents smuggling, etc. **2** Also called: **coastguardsman.** a member of such a force.

coastline ('kəʊst,laɪn) *n* the outline of a coast, esp. when seen from the sea, or the land adjacent to it.

Coast Mountains *pl n* a mountain range in Canada, on the Pacific coast of British Columbia. Highest peak: Mount Waddington, 4043 m (13 266 ft.).

coat (kəʊt) *n* **1** an outdoor garment with sleeves, covering the body from the shoulder to waist, knee, or foot. **2** any similar garment, esp. one forming the top to a suit. **3** a layer that covers or conceals a surface: *a coat of dust.* **4** the hair, wool, or fur of an animal. **5** short for **coat of arms. 6 on the coat.** *Austral.* in disfavour. ◆ *vb* **7** (*tr;* often foll. by *with*) to cover (with) a layer or covering. **8** (*tr*) to provide with a coat. [C16: from Old French *cote* of Germanic origin; compare Old Saxon *kotta,* Old High German *kozzo*]

coat armour *n Heraldry.* **1** coat of arms. **2** an emblazoned surcoat.

Coatbridge ('kəʊt,brɪdʒ; *Scot.* ,kəʊt'brɪdʒ) *n* an industrial town in central Scotland, in North Lanarkshire. Pop.: 43 617 (1991).

coat dress *n* **1** a lightweight button-through garment that can be worn either as a dress or as a coat. **2** formerly, a dress tailored and styled like a coat.

coated ('kəʊtɪd) *adj* **1** covered with an outer layer, film, etc. **2** (of paper) having a coating of a mineral, esp. china clay, to provide a very smooth surface. **3** (of textiles) having been given a plastic or other surface. **4** *Photog., optics.* another word for **bloomed.**

coatee (kəʊ'tiː, 'kəʊtiː) *n Chiefly Brit.* a short coat, esp. for a baby.

Coates (kəʊts) *n* **Joseph Gordon.** 1878–1943, New Zealand statesman; prime minister of New Zealand (1925–28).

coat hanger *n* a curved piece of wood, wire, plastic, etc., fitted with a hook and used to hang up clothes.

coati (kəʊ'ɑːtɪ), **coati-mondi,** *or* **coati-mundi** (kəʊ,ɑːtɪ'mʌndɪ) *n, pl* **-tis** *or* **-dis.** any omnivorous mammal of the genera *Nasua* and *Nasuella,* of Central and South America: family *Procyonidae,* order *Carnivora* (carnivores). They are related to but larger than the raccoons, having a long flexible snout and a brindled coat. [C17: from Portuguese *coatí,* from Tupi, literally: belt-nosed, from *cua* belt + *tim* nose]

coating ('kəʊtɪŋ) *n* **1** a layer or film spread over a surface for protection or decoration. **2** a heavy fabric suitable for coats. **3** *Midland English dialect.* a severe rebuke; ticking-off.

coat of arms *n* **1** the heraldic bearings of a person, family, or corporation. **2** a surcoat decorated with family or personal bearings.

coat of mail *n* a protective garment made of linked metal rings (mail) or of overlapping metal plates; hauberk.

coat-of-mail shell *n* another name for **chiton** (sense 2).

coat-tail *n* **1** the long tapering tails at the back of a man's tailed coat. **2 on someone's coat-tails.** thanks to the popularity or success of someone else.

coauthor (kəʊ'ɔːθə) *n* **1** a person who shares the writing of a book, article, etc., with another. ◆ *vb* **2** (*tr*) to be the joint author of (a book, article, etc.).

coax[1] (kəʊks) *vb* **1** to seek to manipulate or persuade (someone) by tenderness, flattery, pleading, etc. **2** (*tr*) to obtain by persistent coaxing. **3** (*tr*) to work on or tend (something) carefully and patiently so as to make it function as one desires: *he coaxed the engine into starting.* **4** (*tr*) *Obsolete.* to caress. **5** (*tr*) *Obsolete.* to deceive. [C16: verb formed from obsolete noun *cokes* fool, of unknown origin] ▸ **'coaxer** *n* ▸ **'coaxingly** *adv*

coax[2] ('kəʊæks) *n* short for **coaxial cable.**

coaxial (kəʊ'æksɪəl) *or* **coaxal** (kəʊ'æksᵊl) *adj* **1** having or mounted on a common axis. **2** *Geometry.* (of a set of circles) having the same radical axis. **3** *Electronics.* formed from, using, or connected to a coaxial cable.

coaxial cable *n* a cable consisting of an inner insulated core of stranded or solid wire surrounded by an outer insulated flexible wire braid, used esp. as a transmission line for radio-frequency signals. Often shortened to **coax.**

cob[1] (kɒb) *n* **1** a male swan. **2** a thickset type of riding and draught horse. **3** short for **corncob, corncob pipe,** or **cobnut. 4** *Brit.* another name for **hazel** (sense 1). **5** a small rounded lump or heap of coal, ore, etc. **6** *Brit. and N.Z.* a building material consisting of a mixture of clay and chopped straw. **7** Also called: **cob loaf.** *Brit.* a round loaf of bread. ◆ *vb* **cobs, cobbing, cobbed. 8** (*tr*) *Brit. informal.* to beat, esp. on the buttocks. [C15: of uncertain origin; probably related to Icelandic *kobbi* seal; see CUB]

cob[2] *or* **cobb** (kɒb) *n* an archaic or dialect name for a **gull,** esp. the greater black-backed gull (*Larus marinus*). [C16: of Germanic origin; related to Dutch *kob, kobbe*]

cobaea (kəʊ'biːə) *n* any climbing shrub of the tropical American genus *Cobaea,* esp. *C. scandens,* grown for its large trumpet-shaped purple or white flowers: family *Polemoniaceae.* [named after Bernabé *Cobo* (1572–1659), Jesuit missionary and naturalist]

cobalt ('kəʊbɔːlt) *n* a brittle hard silvery-white element that is a ferromagnetic metal: occurs principally in cobaltite and smaltite and is widely used in alloys. The radioisotope **cobalt-60,** with a half-life of 5.3 years, is used in radiotherapy and as a tracer. Symbol: Co; atomic no.: 27; atomic wt.: 58.93320; valency: 2 or 3; relative density: 8.9; melting pt.: 1495°C; boiling pt.: 2928°C. [C17: German *Kobalt,* from Middle High German *kobolt* goblin; from the miners' belief that malicious goblins placed it in the silver ore]

cobalt bloom *n* another name for **erythrite** (sense 1).

cobalt blue *n* **1** Also called: **Thénard's blue.** any greenish-blue pigment containing cobalt aluminate, usually made by heating cobaltous sulphate, aluminium oxide, and phosphoric acid together. **2a** a deep blue to greenish-blue colour. **2b** (*as adj*): *a cobalt-blue car.*

cobalt bomb *n* **1** a cobalt-60 device used in radiotherapy. **2** a nuclear weapon consisting of a hydrogen bomb encased in cobalt, which releases large quantities of radioactive cobalt-60 into the atmosphere.

cobaltic (kəʊ'bɔːltɪk) *adj* of or containing cobalt, esp. in the trivalent state.

cobaltite (kəʊ'bɔːltaɪt, 'kəʊbɔːl,taɪt) *or* **cobaltine** ('kəʊbɔːl,tiːn, -tɪn) *n* a rare silvery-white mineral consisting of cobalt arsenic sulphide in cubic crystalline form: a major ore of cobalt, used in ceramics. Formula: CoAsS.

cobaltous (kəʊ'bɔːltəs) *adj* of or containing cobalt in the divalent state.

cobber ('kɒbə) *n Austral., archaic, and N.Z.* a friend; mate: used as a term of address to males. [C19: from dialect *cob* to take a liking to someone]

Cobbett ('kɒbɪt) *n* **William.** 1763–1835, English journalist and social reformer; founded *The Political Register* (1802); author of *Rural Rides* (1830).

cobble[1] ('kɒbᵊl) *n* **1** short for **cobblestone. 2** *Geology.* a rock fragment, often rounded, with a diameter of 64–256 mm and thus smaller than a boulder but larger than a pebble. ◆ *vb* **3** (*tr*) to pave (a road) with cobblestones. ◆ See also **cobbles.** [C15 (in *cobblestone*): from COB[1]] ▸ **'cobbled** *adj*

cobble[2] ('kɒbᵊl) *vb* (*tr*) **1** to make or mend (shoes). **2** to put together clumsily. [C15: back formation from COBBLER[1]]

cobbler[1] ('kɒblə) *n* a person who makes or mends shoes. [C13 (as surname): of unknown origin]

cobbler[2] ('kɒblə) *n* **1** a sweetened iced drink, usually made from fruit and wine or liqueur. **2** *Chiefly U.S.* a hot dessert made of fruit covered with a rich cake-like crust. [C19: (for sense 1) perhaps shortened from *cobbler's punch;* (for both senses) compare *cobble* (vb)]

cobblers ('kɒbləz) *Brit. taboo slang. pl n* **1** rubbish; nonsense: *a load of old cobblers.* **2** another word for **testicles.** ◆ *interj* **3** an exclamation of strong disagreement. [C20: from rhyming slang *cobblers' awls* balls]

cobbler's pegs (pegz) *pl n* a common Australian weed, *Bidens pilosa,* with spiky peglike awns.

cobbler's wax *n* a resin used for waxing thread.

cobbles ('kɒbᵊlz) *pl n* **1** coal in small rounded lumps. **2** cobblestones.

cobblestone ('kɒbᵊl,stəʊn) *n* a rounded stone used for paving. Sometimes shortened to **cobble.** Compare **sett.**

Cobden ('kɒbdən) *n* **Richard.** 1804–65, British economist and statesman: with John Bright a leader of the successful campaign to abolish the Corn Laws (1846).

cobelligerent (,kəʊbɪ'lɪdʒərənt) *n* a country fighting in a war on the side of another country.

Cóbh (kəuv) *n* a port in S Republic of Ireland, in SE Co. Cork: port of call for Atlantic liners. Pop.: 6200 (1991). Former name (1849–1922): **Queenstown.**

Cobham ('kɒbəm) *n* **Lord,** title of (Sir John) **Oldcastle.**

cobia ('kəubɪə) *n* a large dark-striped percoid game fish, *Rachycentron canadum,* of tropical and subtropical seas: family *Rachycentridae.* [of unknown origin]

coble ('kəub(ə)l, 'kɒb(ə)l) *n Scot. and northern English* a small single-masted flat-bottomed fishing boat. [C13: probably of Celtic origin; compare Welsh *ceubal* skiff]

Coblenz (*German* 'ko:blɛnts) *n* a variant spelling of **Koblenz.**

cob money *n* crude silver coins issued in the Spanish colonies of the New World from about 1600 until 1820.

cobnut ('kɒb,nʌt) *or* **cob** *n* other names for a **hazelnut.** [C16: from earlier *cobylle nut;* see COBBLE[1], NUT]

COBOL *or* **Cobol** ('kəu,bɒl) *n* a high-level computer programming language designed for general commercial use. [C20: *co(mmon) b(usiness) o(riented) l(anguage)*]

cobra ('kəubrə) *n* **1** any highly venomous elapid snake of the genus *Naja,* such as *N. naja* (**Indian cobra**), of tropical Africa and Asia. When alarmed they spread the skin of the neck region into a hood. **2** any related snake, such as the king cobra. [C19: from Portuguese *cobra (de capello)* snake (with a hood), from Latin *colubra* snake]

cobra de capello (di: kə'pɛləu) *n, pl* **cobras de capello.** a cobra, *Naja tripudians,* that has ringlike markings on the body and exists in many varieties in S and SE Asia.

coburg ('kəu,bɜ:g) *n* (*sometimes cap.*) a rounded loaf with a cross cut on the top. Also called: **coburg loaf.** [C19: apparently named in honour of Prince Albert (of SAXE-COBURG-GOTHA)]

Coburg ('kəubɜ:g; *German* 'ko:bʊrk) *n* a city in E Germany, in N Bavaria. Pop.: 44 690 (1991).

cobweb ('kɒb,wɛb) *n* **1** a web spun by certain spiders, esp. those of the family *Theridiidae,* often found in the corners of disused rooms. **2** a single thread of such a web. **3** something like a cobweb, as in its flimsiness or ability to trap. [C14: *cob,* from *coppe,* from Old English *(ātor)coppe* spider; related to Middle Dutch *koppe* spider, Swedish (dialect) *etterkoppa*] ▸ **'cob,webbed** *adj* ▸ **'cob,webby** *adj*

cobwebs ('kɒb,wɛbz) *pl n* **1** mustiness, confusion, or obscurity. **2** *Informal.* stickiness of the eyelids experienced upon first awakening.

coca ('kəukə) *n* **1** either of two shrubs, *Erythroxylon coca* or *E. truxiuense,* native to the Andes: family *Erythroxylaceae.* **2** the dried leaves of these shrubs and related plants, which contain cocaine and are chewed by the peoples of the Andes for their stimulating effects. [C17: from Spanish, from Quechuan *kúka*]

Coca-Cola (,kəukə'kəulə) *n* **1** *Trademark.* a carbonated soft drink flavoured with coca leaves, cola nuts, caramel, etc. **2** (*modifier*) denoting the spread of American culture and values to other parts of the world: *Coca-Cola generation.*

cocaine *or* **cocain** (kə'keɪn) *n* an addictive narcotic drug derived from coca leaves or synthesized, used medicinally as a topical anaesthetic. Formula: $C_{17}H_{21}NO_4$. [C19: from COCA + -INE[1]]

cocainize *or* **cocainise** (kəu'keɪ,naɪz, 'kəukə,naɪz) *vb* (*tr*) to anaesthetize with cocaine. ▸ **,cocaini'zation** *or* **co,caini'sation** *n*

cocci ('kɒksaɪ) *n* the plural of **coccus.**

coccid ('kɒksɪd) *n* any homopterous insect of the superfamily *Coccoidea,* esp. any of the family *Coccidae,* which includes the scale insects. [C19: from New Latin *Coccidae;* see COCCUS]

coccidioidomycosis (kɒk,sɪdɪ,ɔɪdəumaɪ'kəusɪs) *n* a disease of the skin or viscera, esp. the lungs, caused by infection with the fungus *Coccidioides immitis.* [C20: from New Latin *Coccidioides* + -O- + MYCOSIS]

coccidiosis (kɒk,sɪdɪ'əusɪs) *n* any disease of domestic and other animals caused by parasitic protozoa of the order *Coccidia.* One species, *Isospora hominis,* occasionally infects humans. [C19: from New Latin; see COCCUS, -OSIS]

cocciferous (kɒk'sɪfərəs) *adj* (of plants) **1** supporting the cochineal insect. **2** *Obsolete.* bearing berries.

coccolith ('kɒkəlɪθ) *n* any of the round calcareous plates in chalk formations: formed the outer layer of extinct unicellular plankton. [C19: New Latin, from Greek *kokkos* berry + *lithos* stone]

coccus ('kɒkəs) *n, pl* **-ci** (-saɪ). **1** any spherical or nearly spherical bacterium, such as a staphylococcus. Compare **bacillus** (sense 1), **spirillum** (sense 1). **2** the part of a fruit that contains one seed and separates from the whole fruit at maturity. **3** any of the scale insects of the genus *Coccus.* [C18: from New Latin, from Greek *kokkos* berry, grain] ▸ **'coccoid, 'coccal,** *or* **coccic** ('kɒksɪk) *adj* ▸ **'coccous** *adj*

coccyx ('kɒksɪks) *n, pl* **coccyges** (kɒk'saɪdʒi:z). a small triangular bone at the end of the spinal column in man and some apes, representing a vestigial tail. [C17: from New Latin, from Greek *kokkux* cuckoo, of imitative origin; from the likeness of the bone to a cuckoo's beak] ▸ **coccygeal** (kɒk'sɪdʒɪəl) *adj*

Cochabamba (*Spanish* kotʃa'βamba) *n* a city in central Bolivia. Pop.: 448 756 (1993 est.).

co-channel ('kəu,tʃæn(ə)l) *adj* denoting or relating to a radio transmission that is on the same frequency channel as another: *co-channel interference.*

Cochin ('kəutʃɪn, 'kɒtʃ-) *n* **1** a region and former state of SW India: part of Kerala state since 1956. **2** a port in SW India, on the Malabar Coast: the first European settlement in India, founded by Vasco da Gama in 1502: shipbuilding, engineering. Pop.: 564 589 (1991). **3** a large breed of domestic fowl with dense plumage and feathered legs.

Cochin China *n* a former French colony of Indochina (1862–1948): now the part of Vietnam that lies south of Phan Thiet.

cochineal (,kɒtʃɪ'ni:l, 'kɒtʃɪ,ni:l) *n* **1** Also called: **cochineal insect.** a Mexican homopterous insect, *Dactylopius coccus,* that feeds on cacti. **2** a crimson substance obtained from the crushed bodies of these insects, used for colouring food and for dyeing. **3a** the colour of this dye. **3b** (*as adj*): *cochineal shoes.* [C16: from Old Spanish *cochinilla,* from Latin *coccineus* scarlet-coloured, from *coccum* cochineal kermes, from Greek *kokkos* kermes berry]

Cochise (kəu'tʃi:s, -'tʃi:z) *n* died 1874, Apache Indian chief.

cochlea ('kɒklɪə) *n, pl* **-leae** (-lɪ,i:). the spiral tube, shaped like a snail's shell, that forms part of the internal ear, converting sound vibrations into nerve impulses. [C16: from Latin: snail, spiral, from Greek *kokhlias;* probably related to Greek *konkhē* CONCH] ▸ **'cochlear** *adj*

cochlear implant ('kɒklɪə) *n* a device that stimulates the acoustic nerve in the inner ear in order to produce some form of hearing in people who are deaf from inner ear disease.

cochleate ('kɒklɪ,eɪt, -lɪɪt) *or* **cochleated** *adj Biology.* shaped like a snail's shell; spirally twisted.

cock[1] (kɒk) *n* **1** the male of the domestic fowl. **2a** any other male bird. **2b** the male of certain other animals, such as the lobster. **2c** (*as modifier*): *a cock sparrow.* **3** short for **stopcock** or **weathercock. 4** a taboo slang word for **penis. 5a** the hammer of a firearm. **5b** its position when the firearm is ready to be discharged. **6** *Brit. informal.* a friend, mate, or fellow. **7** a jaunty or significant tilting or turning upwards: *a cock of the head.* **8** *Brit. informal.* nonsense. ◆ *vb* **9** (*tr*) to set the firing pin, hammer, or breech block of (a firearm) so that a pull on the trigger will release it and thus fire the weapon. **10** (*tr*) to set the shutter mechanism of (a camera) so that the shutter can be tripped by pressing the shutter-release button. **11** (*tr; sometimes foll. by up*) to raise in an alert or jaunty manner. **12** (*intr*) to stick or stand up conspicuously. ◆ See also **cockup.** [Old English *cocc* (referring to the male fowl; the development of C15 sense spout, tap, and other transferred senses is not clear), ultimately of imitative origin; related to Old Norse *kokkr,* French *coq,* Late Latin *coccus*]

cock[2] (kɒk) *n* **1** a small, cone-shaped heap of hay, straw, etc. ◆ *vb* **2** (*tr*) to stack (hay, straw, etc.) in such heaps. [C14 (in Old English, *cocc* is attested in place names): perhaps of Scandinavian origin; compare Norwegian *kok,* Danish dialect *kok*]

cockabully (kɒkə'bʊlɪ) *n* any of several small freshwater fish of New Zealand. [from Maori *kokopu*]

cockade (kɒ'keɪd) *n* a feather or ribbon worn on military headwear. [C18: changed from earlier *cockard,* from French *cocarde,* feminine of *cocard* arrogant, strutting, from *coq* COCK[1]] ▸ **cock'aded** *adj*

cock-a-doodle-doo (,kɒkə,du:d(ə)l'du:) *interj* an imitation or representation of a cock crowing.

cock-a-hoop *adj* (*usually postpositive*) **1** in very high spirits. **2** boastful. **3** askew; confused. [C16: perhaps from the phrase *to set the cock a hoop* to live prodigally, literally: to put a cock on a *hoop,* a full measure of grain]

Cockaigne *or* **Cockayne** (kɒ'keɪn) *n Medieval legend.* an imaginary land of luxury and idleness. [C14: from Old French *cocaigne,* from Middle Low German *kōkenje* small CAKE (of which the houses in the imaginary land are built); related to Spanish *cucaña,* Italian *cuccagna*]

cock-a-leekie (,kɒkə'li:kɪ) *n* a variant of **cockieleekie.**

cockalorum (,kɒkə'lɔ:rəm) *n* **1** a self-important little man. **2** bragging talk; crowing. [C18: from COCK[1] + *-alorum,* a variant of Latin genitive plural ending *-orum;* perhaps intended to suggest: the cock of all cocks]

cockamamie (,kɒkə'meɪmɪ) *adj Slang, chiefly U.S.* ridiculous or nonsensical: *a cockamamie story.* [C20: in an earlier sense: a paper transfer, prob. a variant of DECALCOMANIA]

cock-and-bull story *n Informal.* an obviously improbable story, esp. a boastful one or one used as an excuse.

cockatiel *or* **cockateel** (,kɒkə'ti:l) *n* a crested Australian parrot, *Leptolophus hollandicus,* having a greyish-brown and yellow plumage. [C19: from Dutch *kaketielje,* from Portuguese *cacatilha* a little cockatoo, from *cacatua* COCKATOO]

cockatoo (,kɒkə'tu:, 'kɒkə,tu:) *n, pl* **-toos. 1** any of various parrots of the genus *Kakatoe* and related genera, such as *K. galerita* (**sulphur-crested cockatoo**), of Australia and New Guinea. They have an erectile crest and most of them are light-coloured. **2** *Austral. and N.Z.* a small farmer or settler. **3** *Austral. informal.* a lookout during some illegal activity. [C17: from Dutch *kaketoe,* from Malay *kakatua*]

cockatrice ('kɒkətrɪs, -,traɪs) *n* **1** a legendary monster, part snake and part cock, that could kill with a glance. **2** another name for **basilisk** (sense 1). [C14: from Old French *cocatris,* from Medieval Latin *cocatrix,* from Late Latin *calcātrix* trampler, tracker (translating Greek *ikhneumon* ICHNEUMON), from Latin *calcāre* to tread, from *calx* heel]

Cockayne (kɒ'keɪn) *n* a variant spelling of **Cockaigne.**

cockboat ('kɒk,bəut) *or* **cockleboat** *n* any small boat. [C15 *cokbote,* perhaps ultimately from Late Latin *caudica* dug-out canoe, from Latin *caudex* tree trunk]

cockchafer ('kɒk,tʃeɪfə) *n* any of various Old World scarabaeid beetles, esp. *Melolontha melolontha* of Europe, whose larvae feed on crops and grasses. Also called: **May beetle, May bug.** [C18: from COCK[1] + CHAFER]

Cockcroft ('kɒk,krɒft) *n* Sir **John Douglas.** 1897–1967, English nuclear physicist. With E. T. S. Walton, he produced the first artificial transmutation of an atomic nucleus (1932) and shared the Nobel prize for physics 1951.

cockcrow ('kɒk,krəu) *or* **cockcrowing** *n* daybreak.

cocked hat *n* **1** a hat with opposing brims turned up and caught together in order to give two points (bicorn) or three points (tricorn). **2 knock into a cocked hat.** *Slang.* to outdo or defeat.

cocker[1] ('kɒkə) *n* **1** a devotee of cockfighting. **2** short for **cocker spaniel.**

cocker[2] ('kɒkə) *vb* **1** (*tr*) *Rare.* to pamper or spoil by indulgence. ◆ *n* **2** *Brit. informal.* a mate (esp. in the phrase **old cocker**). [C15: perhaps from COCK[1] with the sense: to make a cock (i.e. pet) of]

Cocker ('kɒkə) *n* **1 Edward.** 1631–75, English arithmetician. **2 according to Cocker.** reliable or reliably; correct or correctly.
cockerel ('kɒkərəl, 'kɒkrəl) *n* a young domestic cock, usually less than a year old. [C15: diminutive of COCK[1]]
Cockerell ('kɒkərəl) *n* Sir **Christopher Sydney.** 1910–99, British engineer, who invented the hovercraft.
cocker spaniel *n* a small compact breed of spaniel having sleek silky fur, a domed head, and long fringed ears. [C19 *cocker*, from *cocking* hunting woodcocks]
cockeye ('kɒk,aɪ) *n Informal.* an eye affected with strabismus or one that squints.
cockeye bob *or* **cockeyed bob** *n Austral. slang.* a sudden storm or cyclone.
cockeyed ('kɒk,aɪd) *adj Informal.* **1** afflicted with cross-eye, squint, or any other visible abnormality of the eyes. **2** appearing to be physically or logically abnormal, absurd, etc.; crooked; askew: *cockeyed ideas.* **3** drunk.
cock feather *n Archery.* the odd-coloured feather set on the shaft of an arrow at right angles to the nock. Compare **shaft feather.**
cockfight ('kɒk,faɪt) *n* a fight between two gamecocks fitted with sharp metal spurs. ► **'cock,fighting** *n*
cockhorse (,kɒk'hɔːs) *n* another name for **rocking horse** or **hobbyhorse.**
cockieleekie, cockyleeky, *or* **cock-a-leekie** ('kɒkə'liːkɪ) *n Scot.* a soup made from a fowl boiled with leeks.
cockiness ('kɒkɪnɪs) *n* conceited self-assurance.
cockle[1] ('kɒkᵊl) *n* **1** any sand-burrowing bivalve mollusc of the family *Cardiidae*, esp. *Cardium edule* (**edible cockle**) of Europe, typically having a rounded shell with radiating ribs. **2** any of certain similar or related molluscs. **3** short for **cockleshell** (sense 1). **4** a wrinkle or puckering, as in cloth or paper. **5** a small furnace or stove. **6 cockles of one's heart.** one's deepest feelings (esp. in the phrase **warm the cockles of one's heart**). ♦ *vb* **7** to contract or cause to contract into wrinkles. [C14: from Old French *coquille* shell, from Latin *conchӯlium* shellfish, from Greek *konkhulion*, diminutive of *konkhule* mussel; see CONCH]
cockle[2] ('kɒkᵊl) *n* any of several plants, esp. the corn cockle, that grow as weeds in cornfields.
cockleboat ('kɒkᵊl,bəʊt) *n* another word for **cockboat.**
cocklebur ('kɒkᵊl,bɜː) *n* **1** any coarse weed of the genus *Xanthium*, having spiny burs: family *Compositae* (composites). **2** the bur of any of these plants.
cockleshell ('kɒkᵊl,ʃɛl) *n* **1** the shell of the cockle. **2** any of the valves of the shells of certain other bivalve molluscs, such as the scallop. **3** any small light boat. **4** a badge worn by pilgrims.
cockloft ('kɒk,lɒft) *n* a small loft, garret, or attic.
cockney ('kɒknɪ) *n* **1** (*often cap.*) a native of London, esp. of the working class born in the East End, speaking a characteristic dialect of English. Traditionally defined as someone born within the sound of the bells of St. Mary-le-Bow church. **2** the urban dialect of London or its East End. **3** *Austral.* a young snapper fish. ♦ *adj* **4** characteristic of cockneys or their dialect of English. [C14: from *cokeney*, literally: cock's egg, later applied contemptuously to townsmen, from *cokene*, genitive plural of *cok* COCK[1] + *ey* EGG[1]] ► **'cockneyish** *adj*
cockneyfy *or* **cocknify** ('kɒknɪ,faɪ) *vb* **-fies, -fying, -fied.** (*tr*) to cause (one's speech, manners, etc.) to fit the stereotyped idea of a cockney. ► **,cockneyfi'cation** *or* **,cocknifi'cation** *n*
cockneyism ('kɒknɪ,ɪzəm) *n* a characteristic of speech or custom peculiar to cockneys.
cock-of-the-rock *n* either of two tropical South American birds, *Rupicola rupicola* or *R. peruviana*, having an erectile crest and (in the male) a brilliant red or orange plumage: family *Cotingidae* (cotingas).
cock of the walk *n Informal.* a person who asserts himself in a strutting pompous way.
cockpit ('kɒk,pɪt) *n* **1** the compartment in a small aircraft in which the pilot, crew, and sometimes the passengers sit. Compare **flight deck** (sense 1). **2** the driver's compartment in a racing car. **3** *Nautical.* **3a** an enclosed or recessed area towards the stern of a small vessel from which it is steered. **3b** (formerly) an apartment in a warship used as quarters for junior officers and as a first-aid station during combat. **4** the site of numerous battles or campaigns. **5** an enclosure used for cockfights.
cockroach ('kɒk,rəʊtʃ) *n* any insect of the suborder *Blattodea* (or *Blattaria*), such as *Blatta orientalis* (**oriental cockroach** or **black beetle**): order *Dictyoptera*. They have an oval flattened body with long antennae and biting mouthparts and are common household pests. See also **German cockroach, mantis.** [C17: from Spanish *cucaracha*, of obscure origin]
cockscomb *or* **coxcomb** ('kɒks,kəʊm) *n* **1** the comb of a domestic cock. **2** an amaranthaceous garden or pot plant, *Celosia cristata*, with yellow, crimson, or purple feathery plumelike flowers in a broad spike resembling the comb of a cock. **3** any similar species of *Celosia*. **4** *Informal.* a conceited dandy.
cocksfoot ('kɒks,fʊt) *n, pl* **-foots.** a perennial Eurasian grass, *Dactylis glomerata*, cultivated as a pasture grass in North America and South Africa.
cockshot ('kɒk,ʃɒt) *n* another name for **cockshy.**
cockshy ('kɒk,ʃaɪ) *n, pl* **-shies.** *Brit.* **1** a target aimed at in throwing games. **2** the throw itself. ♦ Often shortened to **shy.** [C18: from shying (throwing objects at) a cock, which was given as a prize to the person who hit it]
cockspur ('kɒk,spɜː) *n* **1** a spur on the leg of a cock. **2** an annual grass, *Echinochloa crus-galli*, widely distributed in tropical and warm temperate regions. **3** a small thorny North American hawthorn tree, *Crataegus crus-galli.*
cocksure (,kɒk'ʃʊə, -'ʃɔː) *adj* overconfident; arrogant. [C16: of uncertain origin] ► **,cock'surely** *adv* ► **,cock'sureness** *n*
cockswain ('kɒksən, -,sweɪn) *n* a variant spelling of **coxswain.**
cocktail[1] ('kɒk,teɪl) *n* **1a** any mixed drink with a spirit base, usually drunk before meals. **1b** (*as modifier*): *the cocktail hour.* **2** an appetizer of seafood, mixed fruits, etc. **3** any combination of diverse elements, esp. one considered potent. **4** (*modifier*) appropriate for formal occasions: *a cocktail dress.* [C19: of unknown origin]
cocktail[2] ('kɒk,teɪl) *n* **1** a horse with a docked tail. **2** an animal of unknown or mixed breeding. **3** *Archaic.* a person of little breeding pretending to be a gentleman. [C19: originally *cocktailed* (adj) having a tail like a cock's]
cocktail lounge *n* a room in a hotel, restaurant, etc., where cocktails or other alcoholic drinks are served.
cocktail stick *n* a small pointed stick used for holding cherries, olives, etc., in cocktails, and for serving snacks, such as small sausages.
cockup ('kɒk,ʌp) *n* **1** *Brit. slang.* something done badly. ♦ *vb* **cock up.** (*tr, adv*) **2** (of an animal) to raise (its ears), esp. in an alert manner. **3** *Brit. slang.* to botch.
cocky[1] ('kɒkɪ) *adj* **cockier, cockiest.** excessively proud of oneself. ► **'cockily** *adv*
cocky[2] ('kɒkɪ) *n, pl* **cockies.** *Austral. informal.* **1** short for **cockatoo** (sense 2). **2** a farmer whose farm is regarded as small or of little account.
cockyleeky ('kɒkə'liːkɪ) *n* a variant spelling of **cockieleekie.**
cocky's joy *n Austral. slang.* golden syrup.
coco ('kəʊkəʊ) *n, pl* **-cos.** short for **coconut** or **coconut palm.** [C16: from Portuguese *coco* grimace; from the likeness of the three holes of the nut to a face]
cocoa ('kəʊkəʊ) *or* **cacao** *n* **1** a powder made from cocoa beans after they have been roasted, ground, and freed from most of their fatty oil. **2** a hot or cold drink made from cocoa and milk or water. **3a** a light to moderate brown colour. **3b** (*as adj*): *cocoa paint.* [C18: altered from CACAO]
cocoa bean *n* the seed of the cacao.
cocoa butter *n* a yellowish-white waxy solid that is obtained from cocoa beans and used for confectionery, soap, etc.
coco de mer (də 'mɛə) *n* **1** a palm tree, *Lodoicea maldivica*, of the Seychelles, producing a large fruit containing a two-lobed edible nut. **2** the nut of this palm. ♦ Also called: **double coconut.** [French: coconut of the sea]
coconut *or* **cocoanut** ('kəʊkə,nʌt) *n* **1** the fruit of the coconut palm, consisting of a thick fibrous oval husk inside which is a thin hard shell enclosing edible white meat. The hollow centre is filled with a milky fluid (**coconut milk**). **2a** the meat of the coconut, often shredded and used in cakes, curries, etc. **2b** (*as modifier*): *coconut cake.* [C18: see COCO]
coconut butter *n* a solid form of coconut oil.
coconut ice *n* a sweetmeat made from desiccated coconut and sugar.
coconut matting *n* a form of coarse matting made from the fibrous husk of the coconut.
coconut oil *n* the fatty oil obtained from the meat of the coconut and used for making soap, cosmetics, etc.
coconut palm *n* a tall palm tree, *Cocos nucifera*, widely planted throughout the tropics, having coconuts as fruits. Also called: **coco palm, coconut tree.**
coconut shy *n* a fairground stall in which balls are thrown to knock coconuts off stands.
cocoon (kə'kuːn) *n* **1a** a silky protective envelope secreted by silkworms and certain other insect larvae, in which the pupae develop. **1b** a similar covering for the eggs of the spider, earthworm, etc. **2** a protective spray covering used as a seal on machinery. **3** a cosy warm covering. ♦ *vb* **4** (*tr*) to wrap in a cocoon. [C17: from French *cocon*, from Provençal *coucoun* eggshell, from *coco* shell, from Latin *coccum* kermes berry, from Greek *kokkos* grain, seed, berry; compare COCCUS]
cocopan ('kəʊkəʊ,pæn) *n* (in South Africa) a small wagon running on narrow-gauge railway lines used in mines. Also called: **hopper.** [C20: from Zulu *'ngkumbana* short truck]
Cocos Islands ('kəʊkɒs, 'kəʊkəs) *pl n* a group of 27 coral islands in the Indian Ocean, southwest of Java: a Territory of Australia since 1955. Pop.: 593 (1993). Area: 13 sq. km (5 sq. miles). Also called: **Keeling Islands.**
cocotte (kəʊ'kɒt, kə-; *French* kɔkɔt) *n* **1** a small fireproof dish in which individual portions of food are cooked and served. **2** a prostitute or promiscuous woman. [C19: from French, from nursery word for a hen, feminine of *coq* COCK[1]]
cocoyam ('kəʊkəʊ,jæm) *n* **1** either of two food plants of West Africa, the taro or the yantia, both of which have edible underground stems. **2** the underground stem of either of these plants. [C20: from COCOA + YAM]
Cocteau (*French* kɔkto) *n* **Jean** (ʒɑ̃). 1889–1963, French dramatist, novelist, poet, critic, designer, and film director. His works include the novel *Les Enfants terribles* (1929) and the play *La Machine infernale* (1934).
cocuswood ('kəʊkəs,wʊd) *n* **1** wood from the tropical American leguminous tree *Brya ebenus*, used for inlaying, turnery, musical instruments, etc. **2** the source of this wood, an important timber tree in parts of the Caribbean. ♦ Also called: **Jamaican ebony, West Indian ebony.**
cod[1] (kɒd) *n, pl* **cod** *or* **cods. 1** any of the gadoid food fishes of the genus *Gadus*, esp. *G. morhua* (or *G. callarias*), which occurs in the North Atlantic and has a long body with three rounded dorsal fins: family *Gadidae*. They are also a source of cod-liver oil. **2** any other fish of the family *Gadidae* (see **gadid**). [C13: probably of Germanic origin; compare Old High German *cutte*]
cod[2] (kɒd) *n* **1** *Brit. and U.S. dialect.* a pod or husk. **2** *Taboo.* an obsolete word for **scrotum. 3** *Obsolete.* a bag or envelope. [Old English *codd* husk, bag; related to Old Norse *koddi*, Danish *kodde*]
cod[3] (kɒd) *vb* **cods, codding, codded.** (*tr*) **1** *Brit. and Irish slang.* to make fun of; tease. **2** *Brit. and Irish slang.* to play a trick on; fool. ♦ *n* **3** *Brit. and Irish slang.* a hoax or trick. **4** *Irish slang.* a fraud; hoaxer: *he's an old cod.* ♦ *adj* (*prenominal*) **5** *Brit. slang.* mock; sham: *cod Latin.* [C19: perhaps from earlier *cod* a fool, perhaps shortened from CODGER]

cod[4] (kɒd) *n Northern English dialect.* a fellow; chap: *he's a nice old cod.* [of unknown origin]
Cod *n* **Cape.** See **Cape Cod.**
COD *abbrev. for:* **1** cash on delivery. **2** (in the U.S.) collect on delivery.
Cod. *or* **cod.** *abbrev. for* codex.
coda (ˈkəʊdə) *n* **1** *Music.* the final, sometimes inessential, part of a musical structure. **2** a concluding part of a literary work, esp. a summary at the end of a novel of further developments in the lives of the characters. [C18: from Italian: tail, from Latin *cauda*]
cod-act *vb (intr) Irish informal.* to play tricks; fool. [from COD[3] + ACT]
codder[1] (ˈkɒdə) *n* a cod fisherman or his boat.
codder[2] (ˈkɒdə) *n Yorkshire dialect.* the leader of a team of workers on a press at a steelworks. [perhaps from COD[4]]
coddle (ˈkɒdᵊl) *vb (tr)* **1** to treat with indulgence. **2** to cook (something, esp. eggs) in water just below the boiling point. ◆ *n* **3** *Irish dialect.* stew made from ham and bacon scraps. [C16: of obscure origin; perhaps related to CAUDLE] ▸ **ˈcoddler** *n*
code (kəʊd) *n* **1** a system of letters or symbols, and rules for their association by means of which information can be represented or communicated for reasons of secrecy, brevity, etc.: *binary code; Morse code.* See also **genetic code. 2** a message in code. **3** a symbol used in a code. **4** a conventionalized set of principles, rules, or expectations: *a code of behaviour.* **5** a system of letters or digits used for identification or selection purposes. ◆ *vb (tr)* **6** to translate, transmit, or arrange into a code. [C14: from French, from Latin *cōdex* book, CODEX]
codec (ˈkəʊˌdɛk) *n Electronics.* a set of equipment that encodes an analogue speech or video signal in digital form for transmission purposes and at the receiving end converts such a digital signal into a form close to its original. [C20: from CO(DE) + DEC(ODE)]
codeclination (ˌkəʊdɛklɪˈneɪʃən) *n* another name for **polar distance.**
codeine (ˈkəʊdiːn) *n* a white crystalline alkaloid prepared mainly from morphine and having a similar but milder action. It is used as an analgesic, a sedative, and to relieve coughing. Formula: $C_{18}H_{21}NO_3$. [C19: from Greek *kōdeia* head of a poppy, from *kōos* hollow place + -INE[2]]
Code Napoléon *French.* (kɔd napɔleɔ̃) *n* the civil code of France, promulgated between 1804 and 1810, comprising the main body of French civil law. English name: **Napoleonic Code.**
cod end *n Sea fishing.* the narrow end of a tapered trawl net. [from COD[2]]
coder (ˈkəʊdə) *n* **1** a person or thing that codes. **2** *Electronics.* a device for transforming normal signals into a special coded form.
Co. Derry *abbrev. for* County Londonderry.
codetermination (ˌkəʊdɪtɜːmɪˈneɪʃən) *n* joint participation of management and employees or employees' trade union representatives in some decisions.
codeword (ˈkəʊdˌwɜːd) *n* (esp. in military use) a word used to identify a classified plan, operation, etc. Also: **codename.**
codex (ˈkəʊdɛks) *n, pl* **codices** (ˈkəʊdɪˌsiːz, ˈkɒdɪ-). **1** a volume, in book form, of manuscripts of an ancient text. **2** *Obsolete.* a legal code. [C16: from Latin: tree trunk, wooden block, book]
Codex Juris Canonici (ˈkəʊdɛks ˈdʒʊərɪs kəˈnɒnɪˌsaɪ) *n* the official code of canon law in force in the Roman Catholic Church; introduced in 1918 and revised in 1983. See also **Corpus Juris Canonici.** [Latin: book of canon law]
codfish (ˈkɒdˌfɪʃ) *n, pl* **-fish** *or* **-fishes.** a cod, esp. *Gadus morhua.*
codger (ˈkɒdʒə) *n Informal.* a man, esp. an old or eccentric one: a term of affection or mild derision (often in the phrase **old codger**). [C18: probably variant of CADGER]
codices (ˈkəʊdɪˌsiːz, ˈkɒdɪ-) *n* the plural of **codex.**
codicil (ˈkɒdɪsɪl) *n* **1** *Law.* a supplement modifying a will or revoking some provision of it. **2** an additional provision; appendix. [C15: from Late Latin *cōdicillus,* literally: a little book, diminutive of CODEX] ▸ **codicillary** (ˌkɒdɪˈsɪlərɪ) *adj*
codicology (ˌkəʊdɪˈkɒlədʒɪ) *n* the study of manuscripts. [C20: via French from Latin *codic-,* CODEX + -LOGY] ▸ **codicological** (ˌkəʊdɪkəˈlɒdʒɪkᵊl) *adj*
codification (ˌkəʊdɪfɪˈkeɪʃən, ˌkɒ-) *n* **1** systematic organization of methods, rules, etc. **2** *Law.* the collection into one body of the principles of a system of law.
codify (ˈkəʊdɪˌfaɪ, ˈkɒ-) *vb* **-fies, -fying, -fied.** *(tr)* to organize or collect together (laws, rules, procedures, etc.) into a system or code. ▸ **ˈcodiˌfier** *n*
codling[1] (ˈkɒdlɪŋ) *or* **codlin** (ˈkɒdlɪn) *n* **1** any of several varieties of long tapering apples used for cooking. **2** any unripe apple. [C15 *querdlyng,* of uncertain origin]
codling[2] (ˈkɒdlɪŋ) *n* a codfish, esp. a young one.
codling moth *or* **codlin moth** *n* a tortricid moth, *Carpocapsa pomonella,* the larvae of which are a pest of apples.
codlins-and-cream *n* an onagraceous plant, *Epilobium hirsutum,* native to Europe and Asia and introduced into North America, having purplish-red flowers and hairy stems and leaves. Also called: **hairy willowherb.**
cod-liver oil *n* an oil extracted from the livers of cod and related fish, rich in vitamins A and D and used to treat deficiency of these vitamins.
codology (kɒdˈɒlədʒɪ) *n Irish informal.* the art or practice of bluffing or deception.
codomain (ˌkəʊdəʊˈmeɪn) *n Maths.* another name for **range** (sense 8).
codominant (kəʊˈdɒmɪnənt) *adj Genetics.* (of genes) having both alleles expressed equally in the phenotype of the organism. ▸ **coˈdominance** *n*
codon (ˈkəʊdɒn) *n Genetics, biochem.* a unit that consists of three adjacent bases on a DNA molecule and that determines the position of a specific amino acid in a protein molecule during protein synthesis. [C20: from CODE + -ON]
codpiece (ˈkɒdˌpiːs) *n* a bag covering the male genitals, attached to hose or breeches by laces, etc., worn in the 15th and 16th centuries. [C15: from COD[2] + PIECE]
co-driver *n* one of two drivers who take turns to drive a car, esp. in a rally.
codswallop (ˈkɒdzˌwɒləp) *n Brit. slang.* nonsense. [C20: of unknown origin]
Co. Durham *abbrev. for* County Durham.
cod war *n* any of three disputes that occurred in 1958, 1972–73, and 1975–76 between Britain and Iceland, concerning Iceland's unilateral extension of her fishing limits.
Cody (ˈkəʊdɪ) *n* **William Frederick.** the real name of **Buffalo Bill.**
Coe (kəʊ) *n* **Sebastian.** born 1956, English middle-distance runner and Conservative politician: winner of the 1500 metres in the 1980 and 1984 Olympic Games; holds 1000 m record; held records at 800 m, 1500 m, and a mile: member of parliament (1992–97).
co-ed (ˌkəʊˈɛd) *adj* **1** coeducational. ◆ *n* **2** *U.S.* a female student in a coeducational college or university. **3** *Brit.* a school or college providing coeducation.
coedit (kəʊˈɛdɪt) *vb (tr)* to edit (a book, newspaper, etc.) jointly. ▸ **coˈeditor** *n*
coeducation (ˌkəʊɛdjʊˈkeɪʃən) *n* instruction in schools, colleges, etc., attended by both sexes. ▸ **ˌcoeduˈcational** *adj* ▸ **ˌcoeduˈcationally** *adv*
coefficient (ˌkəʊɪˈfɪʃənt) *n* **1** *Maths.* **1a** a numerical or constant factor in an algebraic term: *the coefficient of the term 3xyz is 3.* **1b** the product of all the factors of a term excluding one or more specified variables: *the coefficient of x in 3axyz is 3ayz.* **2** *Physics.* a number that is the value of a given substance under specified conditions. [C17: from New Latin *coefficiēns,* from Latin *co-* together + *efficere* to EFFECT]
coefficient of expansion *n* the amount of expansion (or contraction) per unit length of a material resulting from one degree change in temperature. Also called: **expansivity.**
coefficient of friction *n Mechanical engineering.* the force required to move two sliding surfaces over each other, divided by the force holding them together. It is reduced once the motion has started.
coefficient of variation *n Statistics.* a measure of the relative variation of distribution independent of the units of measurement; the standard deviation divided by the mean, sometimes expressed as a percentage.
coel- *prefix* indicating a cavity within a body or a hollow organ or part: *coelacanth; coelenterate; coelenteron.* [New Latin, from Greek *koilos* hollow]
coelacanth (ˈsiːləˌkænθ) *n* a primitive marine bony fish of the genus *Latimeria* (subclass *Crossopterygii*), having fleshy limblike pectoral fins and occurring off the coast of E Africa: thought to be extinct until a living specimen was discovered in 1938. [C19: from New Latin *coelacanthus,* literally: hollow spine, from COEL- + Greek *akanthos* spine]
coelenterate (sɪˈlɛntəˌreɪt, -rɪt) *n* **1** any invertebrate of the phylum *Cnidaria* (formerly *Coelenterata*), having a saclike body with a single opening (mouth), which occurs in polyp and medusa forms. Coelenterates include the hydra, jellyfishes, sea anemones, and corals. ◆ *adj* **2** (loosely) any invertebrate of the phyla *Cnidaria* or *Ctenophora.* **3** of or relating to coelenterates. [C19: from New Latin *Coelenterata,* hollow-intestined (creatures); see COEL-, ENTERON] ▸ **coelenteric** (ˌsiːlɛnˈtɛrɪk) *adj*
coelenteron (sɪˈlɛntəˌrɒn) *n, pl* **-tera** (-tərə). the simple saclike body cavity of a coelenterate.
coeliac *or U.S.* **celiac** (ˈsiːlɪˌæk) *adj* of or relating to the abdomen. [C17: from Latin *coeliacus,* from Greek *koiliakos,* from *koilia* belly]
coeliac disease *n* a chronic intestinal disorder of young children caused by sensitivity to the protein gliadin contained in the gluten of cereals, characterized by distention of the abdomen and frothy and pale foul-smelling stools.
coelom *or esp. U.S.* **celom** (ˈsiːləʊm, -ləm) *n* the body cavity of many multicellular animals, situated in the mesoderm and containing the digestive tract and other visceral organs. [C19: from Greek *koilōma* cavity, from *koilos* hollow; see COEL-] ▸ **coelomic** *or esp. U.S.* **celomic** (sɪˈlɒmɪk) *adj*
coelostat (ˈsiːləˌstæt) *n* an astronomical instrument consisting of a plane mirror mounted parallel to the earth's axis and rotated about this axis once every two days so that light from a celestial body, esp. the sun, is reflected onto a second mirror, which reflects the beam into a telescope. Compare **siderostat.** [C19: *coelo-,* from Latin *caelum* heaven, sky + -STAT]
coemption (kəʊˈɛmpʃən) *n* the buying up of the complete supply of a commodity. [C14: from Latin *coemptiōnem* a buying together]
Coen (kuːn) *n* **Jan Pieterszoon.** 1587–1629, Dutch colonial administrator; governor general of the Dutch East Indies (1618–23, 1627–29).
coenacle (ˈsɛnəkᵊl) *n* a variant spelling of **cenacle.**
coenesthesia, cenesthesia (ˌsiːnɪsˈθiːzɪə) *or* **coenesthesis, cenesthesis** (ˌsiːnɪsˈθiːsɪs) *n Psychol.* general awareness of one's own body. ▸ **coenesthetic** *or* **cenesthetic** (ˌsiːnɪsˈθɛtɪk) *adj*
coeno- *or (before a vowel)* **coen-** *combining form.* common: *coenocyte.* [New Latin, from Greek *koinos* common]
coenobite *or* **cenobite** (ˈsiːnəʊˌbaɪt) *n* a member of a religious order following a communal rule of life. Compare **eremite.** [C17: from Old French or Ecclesiastical Latin, from Greek *koinobion* convent, from *koinos* common + *bios* life] ▸ **coenobitic** (ˌsiːnəʊˈbɪtɪk), **ˌcoenoˈbitical** *or* **ˌcenoˈbitic, ˌcenoˈbitical** *adj*
coenocyte (ˈsiːnəʊˌsaɪt) *n Botany.* a mass of protoplasm containing many nuclei and enclosed by a cell wall: occurs in many fungi and some algae. ▸ **coenocytic** (ˌsiːnəˈsɪtɪk) *adj*
coenosarc (ˈsiːnəʊˌsɑːk) *n* a system of protoplasmic branches connecting the polyps of colonial organisms such as corals. [C19: from COENO- + Greek *sarx* flesh]
coenosteum (sɪˈnɒstɪəm) *n Zoology.* the calcareous skeleton of a hydrocoral or a coral colony.
coenurus (siːˈnjʊərəs) *n, pl* **-ri** (-raɪ). an encysted larval form of the tapeworm *Multiceps,* containing many encapsulated heads. In sheep it can cause the gid, and when eaten by dogs it develops into several adult forms. [C19: from New

Latin, from COENO- + Greek *oura* tail, literally: common tail, referring to the single body with its many heads]

coenzyme (kəʊ'enzaɪm) *n Biochem.* a nonprotein organic molecule that forms a complex with certain enzymes and is essential for their activity. See also **apoenzyme.**

coenzyme A *n* a constituent of biological cells that functions as the agent of acylation in metabolic reactions. Abbrev.: **CoA.**

coenzyme Q *n* a quinone derivative, present in biological cells, that functions as an electron carrier in the electron transport chain. Also called: **ubiquinone.**

coequal (kəʊ'i:kwəl) *adj* **1** of the same size, rank, etc. ◆ *n* **2** a person or thing equal with another. ▸ **coequality** (ˌkəʊɪ'kwɒlɪtɪ) *or* **co'equalness** *n* ▸ **co'equally** *adv*

coerce (kəʊ'ɜ:s) *vb (tr)* to compel or restrain by force or authority without regard to individual wishes or desires. [C17: from Latin *coercēre* to confine, restrain, from *co-* together + *arcēre* to enclose] ▸ **co'ercer** *n* ▸ **co'ercible** *adj*

coercimeter (ˌkəʊɜ:'sɪmɪtə) *n* an instrument used for measurement of coercive force.

coercion (kəʊ'ɜ:ʃən) *n* **1** the act or power of coercing. **2** government by force. ▸ **co'ercionist** *n* ▸ **coercive** (kəʊ'ɜ:sɪv) *adj* ▸ **co'ercively** *adv* ▸ **co'erciveness** *n*

coercive force *n* a measure of the magnetization of a ferromagnetic material as expressed by the external magnetic field strength necessary to demagnetize it. Measured in amperes per metre. Compare **coercivity.**

coercivity (ˌkəʊɜ:'sɪvɪtɪ) *n* the magnetic-field strength necessary to demagnetize a ferromagnetic material that is magnetized to saturation. It is measured in amperes per metre. Compare **coercive force.**

coessential (ˌkəʊɪ'senʃəl) *adj Christianity.* being one in essence or nature: a term applied to the three persons of the Trinity. ▸ **coessentiality** (ˌkəʊɪˌsenʃɪ'ælɪtɪ) *or* **ˌcoes'sentialness** *n* ▸ **ˌcoes'sentially** *adv*

coetaneous (ˌkəʊɪ'teɪnɪəs) *adj Rare.* of the same age or period. [C17: from Latin *coaetāneus*, from *co-* same + *aetās* age] ▸ **ˌcoe'taneously** *adv* ▸ **ˌcoe'taneousness** *n*

coeternal (ˌkəʊɪ'tɜ:nᵊl) *adj* existing together eternally. ▸ **ˌcoe'ternally** *adv*

coeternity (ˌkəʊɪ'tɜ:nɪtɪ) *n* existence for, from, or in eternity with another being.

Coetzee ('kɜ:tzɪ) *n* **J(ohn) M(ichael).** born 1940, South African novelist: his works include *Life and Times of Michael K* (1983), *Age of Iron* (1990), and *The Master of Petersburg* (1994).

Coeur (kɜ:; *French* kœr) *n* **Jacques.** ?1395–1456, French merchant; councillor and court banker to Charles VII of France.

Coeur de Lion ('kɜ: də 'li:ən; *French* kœr dəljɔ̃) *n* Lion Heart: an epithet applied to **Richard I** (of England).

coeval (kəʊ'i:vᵊl) *adj* **1** of or belonging to the same age or generation. ◆ *n* **2** a contemporary. [C17: from Late Latin *coaevus* from Latin *co-* + *aevum* age] ▸ **coevality** (ˌkəʊɪ'vælɪtɪ) *n* ▸ **co'evally** *adv*

coexecutor (ˌkəʊɪg'zekjʊtə) *n Law.* a person acting jointly with another or others as executor. ▸ **ˌcoex'ecutrix** *fem n*

coexist (ˌkəʊɪg'zɪst) *vb (intr)* **1** to exist together at the same time or in the same place. **2** to exist together in peace. ▸ **ˌcoex'istence** *n* ▸ **ˌcoex'istent** *adj*

coextend (ˌkəʊɪk'stend) *vb* to extend or cause to extend equally in space or time. ▸ **ˌcoex'tension** *n*

coextensive (ˌkəʊɪk'stensɪv) *adj* of the same limits or extent. ▸ **ˌcoex'tensively** *adv*

cofactor ('kəʊˌfæktə) *n* **1** *Maths.* a number associated with an element in a determinant, equal to the determinant formed by removing the row and column in which the element appears from the given determinant. Also called: **signed minor.** See **minor. 2** *Biochem.* a nonprotein substance that forms a complex with certain enzymes and is essential for their activity. It may be a metal ion or a coenzyme.

C of C *abbrev. for* Chamber of Commerce.

C of E *abbrev. for* Church of England.

coff (kɒf) *vb* **coffs, coffing, coffed** *or* **coft.** *Scot.* to buy; purchase. [C15: from the past participle of obsolete *copen* to buy, of Low German origin; compare German *kaufen* to buy]

coffee ('kɒfɪ) *n* **1a** a drink consisting of an infusion of the roasted and ground or crushed seeds of the coffee tree. **1b** *(as modifier): coffee grounds.* **2** Also called: **coffee beans.** the beanlike seeds of the coffee tree, used to make this beverage. **3** short for **coffee tree. 4a** a medium to dark brown colour. **4b** *(as adj): a coffee carpet.* [C16: from Italian *caffè*, from Turkish *kahve*, from Arabic *qahwah* coffee, wine]

coffee bag *n* a small bag containing ground coffee beans, infused to make coffee.

coffee bar *n* a café; snack bar.

coffee cup *n* a cup from which coffee may be drunk, usually smaller than a teacup.

coffee house *n* a place where coffee is served, esp. one that was a fashionable meeting place in 18th-century London.

coffee mill *n* a machine for grinding roasted coffee beans.

coffee morning *n* a social event (often held in order to raise money) at which coffee is served.

coffee nut *n* **1** the fruit of the Kentucky coffee tree. **2** another name for **Kentucky coffee tree.**

coffeepot ('kɒfɪˌpɒt) *n* a pot in which coffee is brewed or served.

coffee shop *n* a shop where coffee is sold or drunk.

coffee table *n* a low table, on which newspapers, etc., may be placed and coffee served.

coffee-table book *n* a book designed to be looked at rather than read.

coffee tree *n* **1** any of several rubiaceous trees of the genus *Coffea*, esp. *C. arabica*, the seeds of which are used in the preparation of the beverage coffee. **2** short for **Kentucky coffee tree.**

coffer ('kɒfə) *n* **1** a chest, esp. for storing valuables. **2** *(usually pl)* a store of money. **3** Also called: **caisson, lacuna.** an ornamental sunken panel in a ceiling, dome, etc. **4** a watertight box or chamber. **5** short for **cofferdam.** ◆ *vb (tr)* **6** to store, as in a coffer. **7** to decorate (a ceiling, dome, etc.) with coffers. [C13: from Old French *coffre*, from Latin *cophinus* basket, from Greek *kophinos*]

cofferdam ('kɒfəˌdæm) *n* **1** a watertight structure that encloses an area under water, pumped dry to enable construction work to be carried out. **2** (on a ship) a compartment separating two bulkheads or floors, as for insulation or to serve as a barrier against the escape of gas or oil. ◆ Often shortened to **coffer.**

coffin ('kɒfɪn) *n* **1** a box in which a corpse is buried or cremated. **2** the part of a horse's foot that contains the coffin bone. ◆ *vb* **3** *(tr)* to place in or as in a coffin. **4** *Engineering.* another name for **flask** (sense 6). [C14: from Old French *cofin*, from Latin *cophinus* basket; see COFFER]

coffin bone *n* the terminal phalangeal bone inside the hoof of the horse and similar animals.

coffin nail *n* a slang term for **cigarette.**

coffle ('kɒfᵊl) *n* (esp. formerly) a line of slaves, beasts, etc., fastened together. [C18: from Arabic *qāfilah* caravan]

C of I *abbrev. for* Church of Ireland.

C of S *abbrev. for:* **1** Chief of Staff. **2** Church of Scotland.

cog[1] (kɒg) *n* **1** any of the teeth or projections on the rim of a gearwheel. **2** a gearwheel, esp. a small one. **3** a person or thing playing a small part in a large organization or process. ◆ *vb* **cogs, cogging, cogged. 4** *(tr) Metallurgy.* to roll (cast-steel ingots) to convert them into blooms. [C13: of Scandinavian origin; compare Danish *kogge*, Swedish *kugge*, Norwegian *kug*]

cog[2] (kɒg) *vb* **cogs, cogging, cogged.** *Slang.* to cheat (in a game, esp. dice), as by loading a dice. [C16: originally a dice-playing term, of unknown origin]

cog[3] (kɒg) *n* **1** a tenon that projects from the end of a timber beam for fitting into a mortise. ◆ *vb* **cogs, cogging, cogged. 2** *(tr)* to join (pieces of wood) with cogs. [C19: of uncertain origin]

cog. *abbrev. for* cognate.

cogent ('kəʊdʒənt) *adj* compelling belief or assent; forcefully convincing. [C17: from Latin *cōgent-*, *cōgēns*, driving together, from *cōgere*, from *co-* together + *agere* to drive] ▸ **'cogency** *n* ▸ **'cogently** *adv*

coggle ('kɒgᵊl) *vb (intr) Scot.* to wobble or rock; be unsteady. [of uncertain origin] ▸ **'coggly** *adj*

cogitable ('kɒdʒɪtəbᵊl) *adj Rare.* conceivable.

cogitate ('kɒdʒɪˌteɪt) *vb* to think deeply about (a problem, possibility, etc.); ponder. [C16: from Latin *cōgitāre*, from *co-* (intensive) + *agitāre* to turn over, AGITATE] ▸ **'cogiˌtatingly** *adv* ▸ **ˌcogi'tation** *n* ▸ **'cogiˌtator** *n*

cogitative ('kɒdʒɪtətɪv) *adj* **1** capable of thinking. **2** thoughtful. ▸ **'cogitatively** *adv* ▸ **'cogitativeness** *n*

cogito, ergo sum *Latin.* ('kɒgɪˌtəʊ 'ɜ:gəʊ 'sʊm) I think, therefore I am; the basis of Descartes' philosophy.

Cognac ('kɒnjæk; *French* kɔɲak) *n* **1** a town in SW France: centre of the district famed for its brandy. Pop.: 21 000 (latest est.). **2** *(sometimes not cap.)* a high-quality grape brandy.

cognate ('kɒgneɪt) *adj* **1** akin; related: *cognate languages.* **2** related by blood or descended from a common maternal ancestor. Compare **agnate. 3 cognate object.** *Grammar.* a noun functioning as the object of a verb to which it is etymologically related, as in *think a thought* or *sing a song.* ◆ *n* **4** something that is cognate with something else. [C17: from Latin *cognātus*, from *co-* same + *gnātus* born, variant of *nātus*, past participle of *nāscī* to be born] ▸ **'cognately** *adv* ▸ **'cognateness** *n* ▸ **cog'nation** *n*

cognition (kɒg'nɪʃən) *n* **1** the mental act or process by which knowledge is acquired, including perception, intuition, and reasoning. **2** the knowledge that results from such an act or process. [C15: from Latin *cognitiō*, from *cognōscere* from *co-* (intensive) + *nōscere* to learn; see KNOW] ▸ **cog'nitional** *adj* ▸ **cognitive** ('kɒgnɪtɪv) *adj*

cognitive dissonance *n Psychol.* an uncomfortable mental state resulting from conflicting cognitions; usually resolved by changing some of the cognitions.

cognitive ethology *n* a branch of ethology concerned with the influence of conscious awareness and intention on the behaviour of an animal.

cognitive map *n Psychol.* a mental map of one's environment.

cognitive psychology *n* the psychological study of higher mental processes, including thinking and perception.

cognitive science *n* the scientific study of cognition, including elements of the traditional disciplines of philosophy, psychology, semantics, and linguistics, together with artificial intelligence and computer science.

cognitive therapy *n Psychol.* a form of psychotherapy in which the patient is encouraged to change the way he sees the world and himself: used particularly to treat depression.

cognitivism ('kɒgnɪtɪˌvɪzəm) *n Philosophy.* the meta-ethical thesis that moral judgments state facts and so are either true or false. Compare **emotivism, prescriptivism.** See also **naturalism** (sense 4), **non-naturalism.**

cognizable *or* **cognisable** ('kɒgnɪzəbᵊl, 'kɒnɪ-) *adj* **1** perceptible. **2** *Law.* susceptible to the jurisdiction of a court. ▸ **'cognizably** *or* **'cognisably** *adv*

cognizance *or* **cognisance** ('kɒgnɪzəns, 'kɒnɪ-) *n* **1** knowledge; acknowledgment. **2 take cognizance of.** to take notice of; to acknowledge, esp. officially. **3** the range or scope of knowledge or perception. **4** *Law.* **4a** the right of a court to hear and determine a cause or matter. **4b** knowledge of certain facts upon which the court must act without requiring proof. **4c** *Chiefly U.S.* confession. **5** *Heraldry.* a distinguishing badge or bearing. [C14: from Old French *conoissance*, from *conoistre* to know, from Latin *cognōscere* to learn; see COGNITION]

cognizant *or* **cognisant** ('kɒgnɪzənt, 'kɒnɪ-) *adj* (usually foll. by *of*) aware; having knowledge.
cognize *or* **cognise** ('kɒgnaɪz, kɒg'naɪz) *vb* (*tr*) to perceive, become aware of, or know.
cognomen (kɒg'nəumɛn) *n, pl* **-nomens** *or* **-nomina** (-'nɒmɪnə, -'nəu-). (originally) an ancient Roman's third name or nickname, which later became his family name. See also **agnomen, nomen, praenomen.** [C19: from Latin: additional name, from *co-* together + *nōmen* name; influenced in form by *cognōscere* to learn] ▸ **cognominal** (kɒg'nɒmɪnᵊl, -'nəu-) *adj* ▸ **cog'nominally** *adv*
cognoscenti (ˌkɒnjəu'ʃɛntɪ, ˌkɒgnəu-) *or* **conoscenti** *pl n, sing* **-te** (-ti:). (*sometimes sing*) people with informed appreciation of a particular field, esp. in the fine arts; connoisseurs. [C18: from obsolete Italian (modern *conoscente*), from Latin *cognōscere* to know, learn about]
cogon ('kəugəun) *n* any of the coarse tropical grasses of the genus *Imperata,* esp. *I. cylindrica* and *I. exaltata* of the Philippines, which are used for thatching. [from Spanish *cogón,* from Tagalog *kugon*]
cog railway *or* **cogway** ('kɒgˌweɪ) *n Chiefly U.S.* other terms for **rack railway.**
cogwheel ('kɒgˌwi:l) *n* another name for **gearwheel.**
cohabit (kəu'hæbɪt) *vb* (*intr*) to live together as husband and wife, esp. without being married. [C16: via Late Latin, from Latin *co-* together + *habitāre* to live] ▸ **ˌcohabi'tee, co'habitant,** *or* **co'habiter** *n*
cohabitation (kəuˌhæbɪ'teɪʃən) *n* **1** the state or condition of living together as husband and wife without being married. **2** (of political parties) the state or condition of cooperating for specific purposes without forming a coalition.
coheir (kəu'ɛə) *n* a person who inherits jointly with others. ▸ **co'heiress** *fem n*
Cohen[1] ('kəuən) *n* **Stanley.** born 1922, U.S. biochemist: shared the Nobel prize for physiology or medicine 1986.
Cohen[2] (kɒ'hɛn, kəɪn) *n* a variant spelling of **Kohen.**
cohere (kəu'hɪə) *vb* (*intr*) **1** to hold or stick firmly together. **2** to be connected logically; be consistent. **3** *Physics.* to be held together by the action of molecular forces. [C16: from Latin *cohaerēre* from *co-* together + *haerēre* to cling, adhere]
coherence (kəu'hɪərəns) *or* **coherency** *n* **1** logical or natural connection or consistency. **2** another word for **cohesion** (sense 1).
coherent (kəu'hɪərənt) *adj* **1** capable of logical and consistent speech, thought, etc. **2** logical; consistent and orderly. **3** cohering or sticking together. **4** *Physics.* (of two or more waves) having the same phase or a fixed phase difference: *coherent light.* **5** (of a system of units) consisting only of units the quotient or product of any two of which yield the unit of the resultant quantity. ▸ **co'herently** *adv*
coherer (kəu'hɪərə) *n Physics.* an electrical component formerly used to detect radio waves, consisting of a tube containing loosely packed metal particles. The waves caused the particles to cohere, thereby changing the current through the circuit.
cohesion (kəu'hi:ʒən) *n* **1** the act or state of cohering; tendency to unite. **2** *Physics.* the force that holds together the atoms or molecules in a solid or liquid, as distinguished from adhesion. **3** *Botany.* the fusion in some plants of flower parts, such as petals, that are usually separate. [C17: from Latin *cohaesus* stuck together, past participle of *cohaerēre* to COHERE]
cohesionless soil *n* any free-running type of soil, such as sand or gravel, whose strength depends on friction between particles. Also called: **frictional soil.** Compare **cohesive soil.**
cohesive (kəu'hi:sɪv) *adj* **1** characterized by or causing cohesion. **2** tending to cohere or stick together. ▸ **co'hesively** *adv* ▸ **co'hesiveness** *n*
cohesive soil *n* sticky soil such as clay or clayey silt whose strength depends on the surface tension of capillary water. Compare **cohesionless soil.**
coho ('kəuhəu) *n, pl* **-ho** *or* **-hos.** a Pacific salmon, *Oncorhynchus kisutch.* Also called: **silver salmon.** [origin unknown; probably from an American Indian language]
cohobate ('kəuhəuˌbeɪt) *vb* (*tr*) *Pharmacol.* to redistil (a distillate), esp. by allowing it to mingle with the remaining matter. [C17: from New Latin *cohobāre,* perhaps from Arabic *ka'aba* to repeat an action]
cohort ('kəuhɔ:t) *n* **1** one of the ten units of between 300 and 600 men in an ancient Roman Legion. **2** any band of warriors or associates: *the cohorts of Satan.* **3** *Chiefly U.S.* an associate or follower. **4** *Biology.* a taxonomic group that is a subdivision of a subclass (usually of mammals) or subfamily (of plants). **5** *Statistics.* a group of people with a statistic in common, esp. having been born in the same year. [C15: from Latin *cohors* yard, company of soldiers; related to *hortus* garden]
cohosh ('kəuhɒʃ, kəu'hɒʃ) *n* any of several North American plants, such as the **blue cohosh** (*Caulophyllum thalictroides:* family *Leonticaceae*) and **black cohosh** (*Cimicifuga racemosa:* family *Ranunculaceae*). [C18: probably of Algonquian origin]
COHSE ('kəuzɪ) *n* (formerly, in Britain) *acronym for* Confederation of Health Service Employees.
cohune (kəu'hu:n) *n* a tropical American feather palm, *Attalea* (or *Orbignya*) *cohune,* whose large oily nuts yield an oil similar to coconut oil. Also called: **cohune palm.** See also **coquilla nut.** [C19: from American Spanish, from South American Indian *ókhún*]
COI (in Britain) *abbrev. for* Central Office of Information.
coif (kɔɪf) *n* **1** a close-fitting cap worn under a veil, worn in the Middle Ages by many women but now only by nuns. **2** any similar cap, such as a leather cap worn under a chain-mail hood. **3** (formerly in England) the white cap worn by a serjeant at law. **4** a base for the elaborate women's headdresses of the 16th century. **5** (kwɑ:f) a less common word for **coiffure** (sense 1). ◆ *vb* **coifs, coiffing, coiffed.** (*tr*) **6** to cover with or as if with a coif. **7** (kwɑ:f). to arrange (the hair). [C14: from Old French *coiffe,* from Late Latin *cofea* helmet, cap, of obscure origin]
coiffeur (kwɑ:'fɜ:; *French* kwafœr) *n* a hairdresser. ▸ **coiffeuse** (kwɑ:'fɜ:z; *French* kwaføz) *fem n*
coiffure (kwɑ:'fjuə; *French* kwafyr) *n* **1** a hairstyle. **2** an obsolete word for **headdress.** ◆ *vb* **3** (*tr*) to dress or arrange (the hair).
coign *or* **coigne** (kɔɪn) *n* variant spellings of **quoin.**
coign of vantage *n* an advantageous position or stance for observation or action.
coil[1] (kɔɪl) *vb* **1** to wind or gather (ropes, hair, etc.) into loops or (of rope, hair, etc.) to be formed in such loops. **2** (*intr*) to move in a winding course. ◆ *n* **3** something wound in a connected series of loops. **4** a single loop of such a series. **5** an arrangement of pipes in a spiral or loop, as in a condenser. **6** an electrical conductor wound into the form of a spiral, sometimes with a soft iron core, to provide inductance or a magnetic field. See also **induction coil.** **7** an intrauterine contraceptive device in the shape of a coil. **8** the transformer in a petrol engine that supplies the high voltage to the sparking plugs. [C16: from Old French *coillir* to collect together; see CULL] ▸ **'coiler** *n*
coil[2] (kɔɪl) *n* the troubles and activities of the world (in the Shakespearean phrase **this mortal coil**). [C16: of unknown origin]
coil spring *n* a helical spring formed from wire.
Coimbatore (ˌkɔ:ɪmbə'tɔ:) *n* an industrial city in SW India, in W Tamil Nadu. Pop.: 816 321 (1991).
Coimbra (*Portuguese* 'kuimbrə) *n* a city in central Portugal: capital of Portugal from 1190 to 1260; seat of the country's oldest university. Pop.: 96 140 (1991).
coin (kɔɪn) *n* **1** a metal disc or piece used as money. **2** metal currency, as opposed to securities, paper currency, etc. Related adj: **nummary.** **3** *Architect.* a variant spelling of **quoin.** **4** **pay (a person) back in (his) own coin.** to treat (a person) in the way that he has treated others. ◆ *vb* **5** (*tr*) to make or stamp (coins). **6** (*tr*) to make into a coin. **7** (*tr*) to fabricate or invent (words, etc.). **8** (*tr*) *Informal.* to make (money) rapidly (esp. in the phrase **coin it in**). **9** **to coin a phrase.** said ironically after one uses a cliché. **10** **the other side of the coin.** the opposite view of a matter. [C14: from Old French: stamping die, from Latin *cuneus* wedge] ▸ **'coinable** *adj* ▸ **'coiner** *n*
coinage ('kɔɪnɪdʒ) *n* **1** coins collectively. **2** the act of striking coins. **3** the currency of a country. **4** the act of inventing something, esp. a word or phrase. **5** a newly invented word, phrase, usage, etc.
coin box *n* the part of a coin-operated machine into which coins are placed.
coincide (ˌkəuɪn'saɪd) *vb* (*intr*) **1** to occur or exist simultaneously. **2** to be identical in nature, character, etc. **3** to agree. [C18: from Medieval Latin *coincidere,* from Latin *co-* together + *incidere* to occur, befall, from *cadere* to fall]
coincidence (kəu'ɪnsɪdəns) *n* **1** a chance occurrence of events remarkable either for being simultaneous or for apparently being connected. **2** the fact, condition, or state of coinciding. **3** (*modifier*) *Electronics.* of or relating to a circuit that produces an output pulse only when both its input terminals receive pulses within a specified interval: *coincidence gate.* Compare **anticoincidence.**
coincident (kəu'ɪnsɪdənt) *adj* **1** having the same position in space or time. **2** (usually *postpositive* and foll. by *with*) in exact agreement; consonant.
coincidental (kəuˌɪnsɪ'dɛntᵊl) *adj* of or happening by a coincidence; fortuitous. ▸ **coˌinci'dentally** *adv*
coin-op ('kɔɪnˌɒp) *n* a launderette or other service installation in which the machines are operated by the insertion of coins.
coinsurance (ˌkəuɪn'ʃuərəns, -'ʃɔ:-) *n* **1** a method of insurance by which property is insured for a certain percentage of its value by a commercial insurance policy while the owner assumes liability for the remainder. **2** joint insurance held by two or more persons.
coinsure (ˌkəuɪn'ʃuə, -'ʃɔ:) *vb* **1** (*intr*) to take out coinsurance. **2** to insure (property) jointly with another. ▸ **ˌcoin'surer** *n*
Cointreau ('kwɑ:ntrəu) *n Trademark.* a colourless liqueur with orange flavouring.
coir (kɔɪə) *n* the fibre prepared from the husk of the coconut, used in making rope and matting. [C16: from Malayalam *kāyar* rope, from *kāyaru* to be twisted]
Coire (kwar) *n* the French name for **Chur.**
coit (kɔɪt) *n Austral. slang.* buttocks; backside. Also: **quoit.** [C20: perhaps a variant and special use of QUOIT, referring to roundness]
coitus ('kəuɪtəs) *or* **coition** (kəu'ɪʃən) *n* technical terms for **sexual intercourse.** [C18 *coitus:* from Latin: a uniting, from *coīre* to meet, from *īre* to go] ▸ **'coital** *adj*
coitus interruptus (ˌɪntə'rʌptəs) *n* the deliberate withdrawal of the penis from the vagina before ejaculation.
coitus reservatus (ˌrɛzə'vɑ:təs) *n* the deliberate delaying or avoidance of orgasm during intercourse.
cojones *Spanish.* (ko'xones) *pl n* **1** testicles. **2** manly courage.
coke[1] (kəuk) *n* **1** a solid-fuel product containing about 80 per cent of carbon produced by distillation of coal to drive off its volatile constituents: used as a fuel and in metallurgy as a reducing agent for converting metal oxides into metals. **2** any similar material, such as the layer formed in the cylinders of a car engine by incomplete combustion of the fuel. ◆ *vb* **3** to become or convert into coke. [C17: probably a variant of C14 northern English dialect *colk* core, of obscure origin]
coke[2] (kəuk) *n Slang.* short for **cocaine.**
Coke[1] (kəuk) *n Trademark.* short for **Coca-Cola.**
Coke[2] (kuk, kəuk) *n* **1** Sir **Edward.** 1552–1634, English jurist, noted for his defence of the common law against encroachment from the Crown: the Petition of Right (1628) was largely his work. **2** (kuk) **Thomas William,** 1st Earl of Leicester, known as *Coke of Holkham.* 1752–1842, English agriculturist: pio-

neered agricultural improvement and considerably improved productivity at his Holkham estate in Norfolk.

cokuloris (ˌkɒkəˈlɔːrɪs) *n Films.* a palette with irregular holes, placed between lighting and camera to prevent glare. **[C20:** of unknown origin**]**

col (kɒl; *French* kɔl) *n* **1** the lowest point of a ridge connecting two mountain peaks, often constituting a pass. **2** *Meteorol.* a pressure region between two anticyclones and two depressions, associated with variable weather. **[C19:** from French: neck, col, from Latin *collum* neck**]**

col. *abbrev. for:* **1** colour(ed). **2** column.

Col. *abbrev. for:* **1** Colombia(n). **2** Colonel. **3** *Bible.* Colossians.

col-[1] *prefix* a variant of **com-** before *l: collateral.*

col-[2] *prefix* a variant of **colo-** before a vowel: *colectomy.*

cola[1] *or* **kola** (ˈkəʊlə) *n* **1** either of two tropical sterculiaceous trees, *Cola nitida* or *C. acuminata,* widely cultivated in tropical regions for their seeds (see **cola nut**). **2** a sweet carbonated drink flavoured with cola nuts. **[C18:** from *kola,* probably variant of Mandingo *kolo* nut**]**

cola[2] (ˈkəʊlə) *n* a plural of **colon**[1] (sense 3) or **colon**[2].

colander (ˈkɒləndə, ˈkʌl-) *or* **cullender** *n* a pan with a perforated bottom for straining or rinsing foods. **[C14** *colyndore,* probably from Old Provençal *colador,* via Medieval Latin, from Late Latin *cōlāre* to filter, from Latin *cōlum* sieve**]**

cola nut *n* any of the seeds of the cola tree, which contain caffeine and theobromine and are used medicinally and in the manufacture of soft drinks.

colatitude (kəʊˈlætɪˌtjuːd) *n Astronomy, navigation.* the complement of the celestial latitude.

Colbert (*French* kɔlbɛr) *n* **1 Claudette** (klɔːˈdet). real name *Lily Claudette Chauchoin.* 1903–96, U.S. film actress, born in France. Her Hollywood comedies include *Three-Cornered Moon* (1933) and *It Happened One Night* (1934). **2 Jean Baptiste** (ʒɑ̃ batist). 1619–83, French statesman; chief minister to Louis XIV: reformed the taille and pursued a mercantilist policy, creating a powerful navy and merchant fleet and building roads and canals.

colcannon (kəlˈkænən, ˈkɒlˌkænən) *n* a dish, originating in Ireland, of potatoes and cabbage or other greens boiled and mashed together. **[C18:** from Irish Gaelic *cál ceannann,* literally: white-headed cabbage**]**

Colchester (ˈkəʊltʃɪstə) *n* a town in E England, in NE Essex. Pop.: 96 063 (1991). Latin name: **Camulodunum** (ˌkæmjʊləʊˈdjuːnəm, ˌkæmʊləʊˈduːnəm).

colchicine (ˈkɒltʃɪˌsiːn, -sɪn, ˈkɒlkɪ-) *n* a pale-yellow crystalline alkaloid extracted from seeds or corms of the autumn crocus. It is used in the treatment of gout and to create polyploid plants by inhibiting chromosome separation during meiosis. Formula: $C_{22}H_{25}NO_6$. **[C19:** from COLCHICUM + -INE[2]**]**

colchicum (ˈkɒltʃɪkəm, ˈkɒlkɪ-) *n* **1** any Eurasian liliaceous plant of the genus *Colchicum,* such as the autumn crocus. **2** the dried seeds or corms of the autumn crocus: a source of colchicine. **[C16:** from Latin, from Greek *kolkhikon,* from *kolkhikos* of COLCHIS**]**

Colchis (ˈkɒlkɪs) *n* an ancient country on the Black Sea south of the Caucasus; the land of Medea and the Golden Fleece in Greek mythology.

colcothar (ˈkɒlkəˌθɑː) *n* a finely powdered form of ferric oxide produced by heating ferric sulphate and used as a pigment and as jewellers' rouge. Also called: **crocus. [C17:** from French *colcotar,* from Spanish *colcótar,* from Arabic dialect *qulqutār***]**

cold (kəʊld) *adj* **1** having relatively little warmth; of a rather low temperature: *cold weather; cold hands.* **2** without sufficient or proper warmth: *this meal is cold.* **3** lacking in affection, enthusiasm, or warmth of feeling: *a cold manner.* **4** not affected by emotion; objective: *cold logic.* **5** dead. **6** sexually unresponsive or frigid. **7** lacking in freshness: *a cold scent; cold news.* **8** chilling to the spirit; depressing. **9** (of a colour) having violet, blue, or green predominating; giving no sensation of warmth. **10** *Metallurgy.* denoting or relating to a process in which work-hardening occurs as a result of the plastic deformation of a metal at too low a temperature for annealing to take place. **11** (of a process) not involving heat, in contrast with traditional methods: *cold typesetting; cold technology.* **12** *Informal.* (of a seeker) far from the object of a search. **13** denoting the contacting of potential customers, voters, etc., without previously approaching them in order to establish their interest: *cold mailing.* **14 cold comfort.** little or no comfort. **15 cold steel.** the use of bayonets, knives, etc., in combat. **16 from cold.** without advance notice; without giving preparatory information. **17 in cold blood.** showing no passion; deliberately; ruthlessly. **18 leave (someone) cold.** *Informal.* to fail to excite (someone): *the performance left me cold.* **19 throw** (*or* **pour**) **cold water on.** *Informal.* to be unenthusiastic about or discourage. ◆ *n* **20** the absence of heat regarded as a positive force: *the cold took away our breath.* **21** the sensation caused by loss or lack of heat. **22 (out) in the cold.** *Informal.* neglected; ignored. **23** an acute viral infection of the upper respiratory passages characterized by discharge of watery mucus from the nose, sneezing, etc. **24 catch a cold.** *Slang.* to make a loss; lose one's investment. ◆ *adv* **25** *Informal.* without preparation: *he played his part cold.* **26** *Informal, chiefly U.S. and Canadian.* thoroughly; absolutely: *she turned him down cold.* **[**Old English *ceald;* related to Old Norse *kaldr,* Gothic *kalds,* Old High German *kalt;* see COOL**]** ► **ˈcoldish** *adj* ► **ˈcoldly** *adv* ► **ˈcoldness** *n*

cold-blooded *adj* **1** having or showing a lack of feeling or pity: *a cold-blooded killing.* **2** *Informal.* particularly sensitive to cold. **3** (of all animals except birds and mammals) having a body temperature that varies with that of the surroundings. Technical term: **poikilothermic.** ► **ˌcold-ˈbloodedly** *adv* ► **ˌcold-ˈbloodedness** *n*

cold call *n* a call made by a salesman on a potential customer without making an appointment. ► **cold calling** *n*

cold cathode *n Electronics.* a cathode from which electrons are emitted at an ambient temperature, due to a high potential gradient at the surface.

cold chisel *n* a toughened steel chisel.

cold cream *n* an emulsion of water and fat used cosmetically for softening and cleansing the skin.

cold cuts *pl n* cooked meats sliced and served cold.

cold-drawn *adj* (of metal wire, bars, etc.) having been drawn unheated through a die to reduce dimensions, toughen, and improve surface finish.

cold duck *n* an alcoholic beverage made from equal parts of burgundy and champagne.

cold feet *pl n Informal.* loss or lack of courage or confidence.

cold fish *n* an unemotional and unfriendly person.

cold frame *n* an unheated wooden frame with a glass top, used to protect young plants from the cold.

cold front *n Meteorol.* **1** the boundary line between a warm air mass and the cold air pushing it from beneath and behind as it moves. **2** the line on the earth's surface where the cold front meets it. ◆ Compare **warm front.**

cold-hearted *adj* lacking in feeling or warmth; unkind. ► **ˌcold-ˈheartedly** *adv* ► **ˌcold-ˈheartedness** *n*

coldie (ˈkəʊldɪ) *n Austral. slang.* a cold can or bottle of beer.

Colditz (ˈkəʊldɪts) *n* a town in E Germany, on the River Mulde: during World War II its castle was used as a top-security camp for Allied prisoners of war; many daring escape attempts, some successful, were made.

cold light *n* light emitted at low temperatures from a source that is not incandescent, such as fluorescence, phosphorescence, bioluminescence, or triboluminescence.

cold moulding *n* the production of moulded articles from resins that polymerize chemically.

cold pack *n* **1a** a method of lowering the body temperature by wrapping a person in a sheet soaked in cold water. **1b** the sheet so used. **2** a tinning process in which raw food is packed in cans or jars and then heated.

cold-pressed *adj* (of an unrefined oil such as olive oil) produced by pressing the parent seed, nut, or grain at the lowest possible temperature without any further pressing.

cold-rolled *adj* (of metal sheets, etc.) having been rolled without heating, producing a smooth surface finish.

cold rubber *n* synthetic rubber made at low temperatures (about 5°C). It is stronger than that made at higher temperatures and is used for car tyres.

cold shoulder *Informal.* ◆ *n* **1** (often preceded by *the*) a show of indifference; a slight. ◆ *vb* **cold-shoulder.** (*tr*) **2** to treat with indifference.

cold snap *n* a sudden short spell of cold weather.

cold sore *n* a cluster of blisters at the margin of the lips that sometimes accompanies the common cold, caused by a viral infection. Technical name: **herpes labialis.**

cold start *n Computing.* the reloading of a program or operating system.

cold storage *n* **1** the storage of things in an artificially cooled place for preservation. **2** *Informal.* a state of temporary suspension: *to put an idea into cold storage.*

Coldstream (ˈkəʊldˌstriːm) *n* a town in SE Scotland, in Scottish Borders on the English border: the Coldstream Guards were formed here (1660). Pop.: 1746 (1991).

cold sweat *n Informal.* a bodily reaction to fear or nervousness, characterized by chill and moist skin.

cold turkey *n* **1** *Slang.* a method of curing drug addiction by abrupt withdrawal of all doses. **2** the withdrawal symptoms, esp. nausea and shivering, brought on by this method.

cold war *n* a state of political hostility and military tension between two countries or power blocs, involving propaganda, subversion, threats, economic sanctions, and other measures short of open warfare, esp. that between the American and Soviet blocs after World War II (the **Cold War**).

cold warrior *n* a person who engages in or promotes a cold war.

cold wave *n* **1** *Meteorol.* a sudden spell of low temperatures over a wide area, often following the passage of a cold front. **2** *Hairdressing.* a permanent wave made by chemical agents applied at normal temperatures.

cold-weld *vb* (*tr*) to join (two metal surfaces) without heat by forcing them together so that the oxide films are broken and adhesion occurs. ► **cold welding** *n*

cold work *n* **1** the craft of shaping metal without heat. ◆ *vb* **cold-work.** (*tr*) **2** to shape (metal) in this way.

cole (kəʊl) *n* any of various plants of the genus *Brassica,* such as the cabbage and rape. Also called: **colewort. [**Old English *cāl,* from Latin *caulis* plant stalk, cabbage**]**

Cole (kəʊl) *n* **Nat 'King'**, real name *Nathaniel Adams Cole.* 1917–65, U.S. popular singer and jazz pianist.

colectomy (kəˈlɛktəmɪ) *n, pl* **-mies.** surgical removal of part or all of the colon.

Coleman (ˈkəʊlmən) *n* **Ornette** (ɔːˈnɛt). born 1930, U.S. avant-garde jazz alto saxophonist and multi-instrumentalist.

colemanite (ˈkəʊlməˌnaɪt) *n* a colourless or white glassy mineral consisting of hydrated calcium borate in monoclinic crystalline form. It occurs with and is a source of borax. Formula: $Ca_2B_6O_{11}.5H_2O$. **[C19:** named after William T. *Coleman* (1824–93), American pioneer, owner of the mine in which it was discovered**]**

Colenso (kəˈlɛnzəʊ) *n* **John William.** 1814–83, British churchman; Anglican bishop of Natal from 1853: charged with heresy for questioning the accuracy of the Pentateuch.

coleopter (ˌkɒlɪˈɒptə) *n Aeronautics.* an aircraft that has an annular wing with the fuselage and engine on the centre line.

coleopteran (ˌkɒlɪˈɒptərən) *n also* **coleopteron. 1** any of the insects of the cosmopolitan order *Coleoptera,* in which the forewings are modified to form shell-like protective elytra. The order includes the beetles and weevils. ◆ *adj also* **coleopterous. 2** of, relating to, or belonging to the order *Coleoptera.* **[C18:** from New Latin *Coleoptera,* from Greek *koleoptera,* from *koleopteros* sheath-winged, from *koleon* sheath + *pteron* wing**]**

coleoptile (ˌkɒlɪˈɒptaɪl) *n* a protective sheath around the plumule in grasses. [C19: from New Latin *coleoptilum,* from Greek *koleon* sheath + *ptilon* down, soft plumage]

coleorhiza (ˌkɒlɪəˈraɪzə) *n, pl* **-zae** (-ziː). a protective sheath around the radicle in grasses. [C19: from New Latin, from Greek *koleon* sheath + *rhiza* root]

Coleraine (ˈkəʊlˈreɪn) *n* a district in N Northern Ireland, in Co. Londonderry. Pop.: 50 438 (1991). Area: 485 sq. km (187 sq. miles).

Coleridge (ˈkəʊlərɪdʒ) *n* **Samuel Taylor.** 1772–1834, English Romantic poet and critic, noted for poems such as *The Rime of the Ancient Mariner* (1798), *Kubla Khan* (1816), and *Christabel* (1816), and for his critical work *Biographia Literaria* (1817).

Coleridge-Taylor (ˌkəʊlərɪdʒˈteɪlə) *n* **Samuel.** 1875–1912, British composer, best known for his trilogy of oratorios *Song of Hiawatha* (1898–1900).

coleslaw (ˈkəʊlˌslɔː) *n* a salad of shredded cabbage, mayonnaise, carrots, onions, etc. [C19: from Dutch *koolsla,* from *koolsalade,* literally: cabbage salad]

colestipol (kəˈlɛstɪˌpɒl) *n* a drug that reduces the level of cholesterol in the blood: used, together with dietary restriction of cholesterol, to treat selected patients with hypercholesterolaemia and so prevent atherosclerosis.

Colet (ˈkɒlɪt) *n* **John.** ?1467–1519, English humanist and theologian; founder of St. Paul's School, London (1509).

coletit (ˈkəʊlˌtɪt) *n* another name for **coal tit.**

Colette (kɒˈlɛt) *n* full name *Sidonie Gabrielle Claudine Colette.* 1873–1954, French novelist; her works include *Chéri* (1920), *Gigi* (1944), and the series of *Claudine* books.

coleus (ˈkəʊlɪəs) *n, pl* **-uses.** any plant of the Old World genus *Coleus:* cultivated for their variegated leaves, typically marked with red, yellow, or white: family *Labiatae* (labiates). [C19: from New Latin, from Greek *koleos,* variant of *koleon* sheath; from the way in which the stamens are joined]

colewort (ˈkəʊlˌwɜːt) *n* another name for **cole.**

coley (ˈkəʊlɪ, ˈkɒlɪ) *n Brit.* any of various edible fishes, esp. the coalfish.

colic (ˈkɒlɪk) *n* a condition characterized by acute spasmodic abdominal pain, esp. that caused by inflammation, distention, etc., of the gastrointestinal tract. [C15: from Old French *colique,* from Late Latin *cōlicus* ill with colic, from Greek *kōlon,* variant of *kolon* COLON[2]] ▸ **ˈcolicky** *adj*

colicroot (ˈkɒlɪkˌruːt) *n* **1** either of two North American liliaceous plants, *Aletris farinosa* or *A. aurea,* having tubular white or yellow flowers and a bitter root formerly used to relieve colic. **2** any of various other plants formerly used to relieve colic.

colicweed (ˈkɒlɪkˌwiːd) *n* any of several plants of the genera *Dicentra* or *Corydalis,* such as the squirrel corn and Dutchman's-breeches: family *Fumariaceae.*

coliform bacteria (ˈkɒlɪfɔːm) *pl n* a large group of bacteria that inhabit the intestinal tract of man and animals and may cause disease.

Coligny *or* **Coligni** (*French* kɔliɲi) *n* **Gaspard de** (gaspar də), Seigneur de Châtillon. 1519–72, French Huguenot leader.

Colima (*Spanish* koˈlima) *n* **1** a state of SW Mexico, on the Pacific coast: mainly a coastal plain, rising to the foothills of the Sierra Madre, with important mineral resources. Capital: Colima. Pop.: 487 324 (1995 est.). Area: 5455 sq. km (2106 sq. miles). **2** a city in SW Mexico, capital of Colima state, on the Colima River. Pop.: 106 967 (1990). **3 Nevado de.** a volcano in SW Mexico, in Jalisco state. Height: 4339 m (14 235 ft.).

coliseum (ˌkɒlɪˈsɪəm) *or* **colosseum** *n* a large building, such as a stadium or theatre, used for entertainments, sports, etc. [C18: from Medieval Latin *Colisseum,* variant of COLOSSEUM]

colitis (kɒˈlaɪtɪs, kə-) *or* **colonitis** (ˌkɒləˈnaɪtɪs) *n* inflammation of the colon. ▸ **colitic** (kɒˈlɪtɪk) *adj*

coll. *abbrev. for:* **1** colleague. **2** collection. **3** collector. **4** college. **5** collegiate. **6** colloquial.

collaborate (kəˈlæbəˌreɪt) *vb (intr)* **1** (often foll. by *on, with,* etc.) to work with another or others on a joint project. **2** to cooperate as a traitor, esp. with an enemy occupying one's own country. [C19: from Late Latin *collabōrāre,* from Latin *com-* together + *labōrāre* to work] ▸ **colˌlaboˈration** *n* ▸ **colˈlaborative** *adj* ▸ **colˈlaboˌrator** *or* **colˌlaboˈrationist** *n*

collage (kəˈlɑːʒ, kɒ-; *French* kɔlaʒ) *n* **1** an art form in which compositions are made out of pieces of paper, cloth, photographs, and other miscellaneous objects, juxtaposed and pasted on a dry ground. **2** a composition made in this way. **3** any work, such as a piece of music, created by combining unrelated styles. [C20: French, from *coller* to stick, from *colle* glue, from Greek *kolla*] ▸ **colˈlagist** *n*

collagen (ˈkɒlədʒən) *n* a fibrous scleroprotein of connective tissue and bones that is rich in glycine and proline and yields gelatine on boiling. [C19: from Greek *kolla* glue + -GEN] ▸ **collagenic** (ˌkɒləˈdʒɛnɪk) *or* **collagenous** (kəˈlædʒənəs) *adj*

collapsar (kɒˈlæpsɑː) *n Astronomy.* another name for **black hole.**

collapse (kəˈlæps) *vb* **1** *(intr)* to fall down or cave in suddenly: *the whole building collapsed.* **2** *(intr)* to fail completely: *his story collapsed on investigation.* **3** *(intr)* to break down or fall down from lack of strength. **4** to fold (furniture, etc.) compactly or (of furniture, etc.) to be designed to fold compactly. ◆ *n* **5** the act or instance of suddenly falling down, caving in, or crumbling. **6** a sudden failure or breakdown. [C18: from Latin *collāpsus,* from *collābī* to fall in ruins, from *lābī* to fall] ▸ **colˈlapsible** *or* **colˈlapsable** *adj* ▸ **colˌlapsiˈbility** *n*

collar (ˈkɒlə) *n* **1** the part of a garment around the neck and shoulders, often detachable or folded over. **2** any band, necklace, garland, etc., encircling the neck: *a collar of flowers.* **3** a band or chain of leather, rope, or metal placed around an animal's neck to restrain, harness, or identify it. **4** *Biology.* a marking or structure resembling a collar, such as that found around the necks of some birds or at the junction of a stem and a root. **5** a section of a shaft or rod having a locally increased diameter to provide a bearing seat or a locating ring. **6** a cut of meat, esp. bacon, taken from around the neck of an animal. **7 hot under the collar.** *Informal.* aroused with anger, annoyance, etc. ◆ *vb (tr)* **8** to put a collar on; furnish with a collar. **9** to seize by the collar. **10** *Informal.* to seize; arrest; detain. [C13: from Latin *collāre* neckband, neck chain, collar, from *collum* neck]

collarbone (ˈkɒləˌbəʊn) *n* the nontechnical name for **clavicle.**

collar cell *n* another name for **choanocyte.**

collard (ˈkɒləd) *n* **1** a variety of the cabbage, *Brassica oleracea acephala,* having a crown of edible leaves. See also **kale. 2** the leaves of this plant, eaten as a vegetable. [C18: variant of COLEWORT]

collared dove *n* a European dove, *Streptopelia decaocto,* having a brownish-grey plumage with a black band on the back of the neck.

collarette (ˌkɒləˈrɛt) *n* a woman's fur or lace collar.

collat. *abbrev. for* collateral.

collate (kɒˈleɪt, kə-) *vb (tr)* **1** to examine and compare (texts, statements, etc.) in order to note points of agreement and disagreement. **2** (in library work) to check the number and order of (the pages of a book). **3** *Bookbinding.* **3a** to check the sequence of (the sections of a book) after gathering. **3b** a nontechnical word for **gather** (sense 9). **4** (often foll. by *to*) *Christianity.* to appoint (an incumbent) to a benefice. [C16: from Latin *collātus* brought together (past participle of *conferre* to gather), from *com-* together + *lātus,* past participle of *ferre* to bring]

collateral (kɒˈlætərəl, kə-) *n* **1a** security pledged for the repayment of a loan. **1b** *(as modifier): a collateral loan.* **2** a person, animal, or plant descended from the same ancestor as another but through a different line. ◆ *adj* **3** situated or running side by side. **4** descended from a common ancestor but through different lines. **5** serving to support or corroborate. **6** aside from the main issue. **7** uniting in tendency. [C14: from Medieval Latin *collaterālis,* from Latin *com-* together + *laterālis* of the side, from *latus* side] ▸ **colˈlaterally** *adv*

collateral damage *n Military.* unintentional damage to civil property and civilian casualties, caused by military operations.

collation (kɒˈleɪʃən, kə-) *n* **1** the act or process of collating. **2** a description of the technical features of a book. **3** *R.C. Church.* a light meal permitted on fast days. **4** any light informal meal. **5** the appointment of a clergyman to a benefice.

collative (kɒˈleɪtɪv, ˈkɒlə-) *adj* **1** involving collation. **2** (of benefices) presented or held by collation.

collator (kɒˈleɪtə, kəʊ-; ˈkɒleɪtə, ˈkəʊ-) *n* **1** a person or machine that collates texts or manuscripts. **2** *Computing.* a device for matching or checking punched cards in separate files and for merging two or more files sorted into the same ordered sequence.

colleague (ˈkɒliːg) *n* a fellow worker or member of a staff, department, profession, etc. [C16: from French *collègue,* from Latin *collēga* one selected at the same time as another, from *com-* together + *lēgāre* to choose]

collect[1] (kəˈlɛkt) *vb* **1** to gather together or be gathered together. **2** to accumulate (stamps, books, etc.) as a hobby or for study. **3** *(tr)* to call for or receive payment of (taxes, dues, etc.). **4** *(tr)* to regain control of (oneself, one's emotions, etc.) as after a shock or surprise: *he collected his wits.* **5** *(tr)* to fetch: *collect your own post.* **6** *(intr;* sometimes foll. by *on) Slang.* to receive large sums of money, as from an investment: *he really collected when the will was read.* **7** *(tr) Austral. and N.Z. informal.* to collide with; be hit by. **8 collect on delivery.** the U.S. term for **cash on delivery.** ◆ *adv, adj* **9** *U.S.* (of telephone calls) on a reverse-charge basis. ◆ *n* **10** *Austral. informal.* a winning bet. [C16: from Latin *collēctus* collected, from *colligere* to gather together, from *com-* together + *legere* to gather]

collect[2] (ˈkɒlɛkt) *n Christianity.* a short Church prayer generally preceding the lesson or epistle in Communion and other services. [C13: from Medieval Latin *collecta* (from the phrase *ōrātiō ad collēctam* prayer at the (people's) assembly), from Latin *colligere* to COLLECT[1]]

collectable *or* **collectible** (kəˈlɛktəbᵊl) *adj* **1** (of antiques, objets d'art, etc.) of interest to a collector. ◆ *n* **2** any object regarded as being of interest to a collector.

collectanea (ˌkɒlɛkˈteɪnɪə) *pl n* a collection of excerpts from one or more authors; miscellany; anthology. [C18: from Latin, from *collectāneus* assembled, from *colligere* to COLLECT[1]]

collected (kəˈlɛktɪd) *adj* **1** in full control of one's faculties; composed. **2** assembled in totality or brought together into one volume or a set of volumes: *the collected works of Dickens.* **3** (of a horse or a horse's pace) controlled so that movement is in short restricted steps: *a collected canter.* ▸ **colˈlectedly** *adv* ▸ **colˈlectedness** *n*

collection (kəˈlɛkʃən) *n* **1** the act or process of collecting. **2** a number of things collected or assembled together. **3** a selection of clothes, esp. as presented by a particular designer for a specified season. **4** something gathered into a mass or pile; accumulation: *a collection of rubbish.* **5** a sum of money collected or solicited, as in church. **6** removal, esp. regular removal of letters from a postbox. **7** *(often pl)* (at Oxford University) a college examination or an oral report by a tutor.

collective (kəˈlɛktɪv) *adj* **1** formed or assembled by collection. **2** forming a whole or aggregate. **3** of, done by, or characteristic of individuals acting in co-operation. ◆ *n* **4a** a cooperative enterprise or unit, such as a collective farm. **4b** the members of such a cooperative. **5** short for **collective noun.** ▸ **colˈlectively** *adv* ▸ **colˈlectiveness** *n*

collective agreement *n* a negotiated agreement, which is not enforceable at law, between an employer and employees' representatives, covering rates of pay or terms and conditions of employment, or both.

collective bargaining *n* negotiation between one or more trade unions and one or more employers or an employers' organization on the incomes and working conditions of the employees.

collective farm *n* (chiefly in Communist countries) a farm or group of farms managed and owned, through the state, by the community. Russian name: **kolkhoz.**

collective fruit *n* another name for **multiple fruit.**

collective memory *n* the shared memories of a group, family, race, etc.

collective noun *n* a noun that is singular in form but that refers to a group of people or things.

USAGE Collective nouns are usually used with singular verbs: *the family is on holiday; General Motors is mounting a big sales campaign.* In British usage, however, plural verbs are sometimes employed in this context, esp. where reference is being made to a collection of individual objects or persons rather than to the group as a unit: *the family are all on holiday.* Care should be taken that the same collective noun is not treated as both singular and plural in the same sentence: *the family is well and sends its best wishes* or *the family are all well and send their best wishes,* but not *the family is well and send their best wishes.*

collective ownership *n* ownership by a group for the benefit of members of that group.

collective pitch lever *n* a lever in a helicopter to change the angle of attack of all the rotor blades simultaneously, causing it to rise or descend. Compare **cyclic pitch lever.**

collective security *n* a system of maintaining world peace and security by concerted action on the part of the nations of the world.

collective unconscious *n Psychol.* (in Jungian psychological theory) a part of the unconscious mind incorporating patterns of memories, instincts, and experiences common to all mankind. These patterns are inherited, may be arranged into archetypes, and are observable through their effects on dreams, behaviour, etc.

collectivism (kəˈlɛktɪˌvɪzəm) *n* **1** the principle of ownership of the means of production, by the state or the people. **2** a social system based on this principle. ▸ **colˈlectivist** *n* ▸ **colˌlectivˈistic** *adj*

collectivity (ˌkɒlɛkˈtɪvɪtɪ) *n, pl* **-ties. 1** the quality or state of being collective. **2** a collective whole or aggregate. **3** people regarded as a whole.

collectivize *or* **collectivise** (kəˈlɛktɪˌvaɪz) *vb (tr)* to organize according to the principles of collectivism. ▸ **colˌlectiviˈzation** *or* **colˌlectiviˈsation** *n*

collector (kəˈlɛktə) *n* **1** a person or thing that collects. **2** a person employed to collect debts, rents, etc. **3** the head of a district administration in India. **4** a person who collects or amasses objects as a hobby. **5** *Electronics.* the region in a transistor into which charge carriers flow from the base. ▸ **colˈlectorˌship** *n*

collectorate (kəˈlɛktərɪt) *n* the office of a collector in India.

collector's item *or* **piece** *n* a thing regarded as being exquisite or rare and thus worthy of the interest of one who collects such things.

colleen (ˈkɒliːn, kɒˈliːn) *n* **1** an Irish word for **girl. 2** an Irish girl. [C19: from Irish Gaelic *cailín* a girl, a young unmarried woman]

college (ˈkɒlɪdʒ) *n* **1** an institution of higher education; part of a university. **2** a school or an institution providing specialized courses or teaching: *a college of music.* **3** the building or buildings in which a college is housed. **4** the staff and students of a college. **5** an organized body of persons with specific rights and duties: *an electoral college.* See also **Sacred College. 6** a body of clerics living in community and supported by endowment. **7** *Chiefly Brit.* an obsolete slang word for **prison.** [C14: from Latin *collēgium* company, society, band of associates, from *collēga;* see COLLEAGUE]

college of advanced technology *n Brit.* (formerly) a college offering degree or equivalent courses in technology, with research facilities. In the mid-1960s these were granted university status. Abbrev.: **CAT.**

college of arms *n* any of several institutions in the United Kingdom having a royal charter to deal with matters of heraldry, grant armorial bearings, record and trace genealogies, etc. Also called: **herald's college.**

College of Cardinals *n R.C. Church.* the collective body of cardinals having the function of electing and advising the pope.

college of education *n Brit.* a professional training college for teachers.

College of Justice *n* the official name for the Scottish Court of Session; the supreme court of Scotland.

college pudding *n Brit.* a baked or steamed suet pudding containing dried fruit and spice.

collegial (kəˈliːdʒɪəl) *adj* **1** of or relating to a college. **2** having authority or power shared among a number of people associated as colleagues. ▸ **colˈlegially** *adv*

collegian (kəˈliːdʒɪən) *n* a current member of a college; student.

collegiate (kəˈliːdʒɪɪt) *adj* **1** Also: **collegial.** of or relating to a college or college students. **2** (of a university) composed of various colleges of equal standing. ◆ *n* **3** *Canadian.* short for **collegiate institute.**

collegiate church *n* **1** *R.C. Church, Church of England.* a church that has an endowed chapter of canons and prebendaries attached to it but that is not a cathedral. **2** *U.S. Protestantism.* one of a group of churches presided over by a body of pastors. **3** *Scot. Protestantism.* a church served by two or more ministers. **4** a large church endowed in the Middle Ages to become a school. **5** a chapel either endowed by or connected with a college.

collegiate institute *n Canadian.* (in certain provinces) a large secondary school meeting set requirements in terms of courses, facilities, and specialist staff.

collegium (kəˈliːdʒɪəm) *n, pl* **-giums** *or* **-gia** (-dʒɪə). **1** (in the former Soviet Union) a board in charge of a department. **2** another term for **College of Cardinals** or **Sacred College.** [Latin: COLLEGE]

col legno (ˈkɒl ˈlegnəʊ, ˈleɪnjəʊ) *adv Music.* to be played (on a stringed instrument) by striking the strings with the back of the bow. [Italian: with the wood]

collembolan (kəˈlɛmbələn) *n* **1** any small primitive wingless insect of the order *Collembola,* which comprises the springtails. ◆ *adj* **2** of, relating to, or belonging to the *Collembola.* [C19: from New Latin *Collembola,* from Greek *kolla* glue + *embolon* peg, wedge]

collenchyma (kəˈlɛŋkɪmə) *n* a strengthening and supporting tissue in plants, consisting of elongated living cells whose walls are thickened with cellulose and pectins. [C19: New Latin, from Greek *kolla* glue + *enkhuma* infusion] ▸ **collenchymatous** (ˌkɒlənˈkɪmətəs) *adj*

Colles' fracture (ˈkɒlɪs) *n* a fracture of the radius just above the wrist, with backward and outward displacement of the hand. [C19: named after Abraham *Colles* (died 1843), Irish surgeon]

collet (ˈkɒlɪt) *n* **1** (in a jewellery setting) a band or coronet-shaped claw that holds an individual stone. **2** *Mechanical engineering.* an externally tapered sleeve made in two or more segments and used to grip a shaft passed through its centre when the sleeve is compressed by being inserted in a tapered hole. **3** *Horology.* a small collar that supports the inner end of the hairspring. ◆ *vb* **4** *(tr) Jewellery.* to mount in a collet. [C16: from Old French: a little collar, from *col* neckband, neck, from Latin *collum* neck]

colleterial gland (ˌkɒlɪˈtɪərɪəl) *n Zoology.* a paired accessory reproductive gland, present in most female insects, secreting a sticky substance that forms either the egg cases or the cement that binds the eggs to a surface. [C19: from New Latin *colleterium* glue-secreting organ, from Greek *kolla* glue + -AL[1]]

colliculus (kɒˈlɪkjʊləs) *n, pl* **-li.** *Anatomy.* a small elevation, as on the surface of the optic lobe of the brain. [C19: New Latin]

collide (kəˈlaɪd) *vb (intr)* **1** to crash together with a violent impact. **2** to conflict in attitude, opinion, or desire; clash; disagree. [C17: from Latin *collīdere* to clash together, from *com-* together + *laedere* to strike, wound]

collider (kəˈlaɪdə) *n Physics.* a particle accelerator in which beams of particles are made to collide.

collie (ˈkɒlɪ) *n* any of several silky-coated breeds of dog developed for herding sheep and cattle. See **Border collie, rough collie, bearded collie.** [C17: Scottish, probably from earlier *colie* black with coal dust, from *cole* COAL]

collier (ˈkɒlɪə) *n Chiefly Brit.* **1** a coal miner. **2a** a ship designed to transport coal. **2b** a member of its crew. [C14: from COAL + -IER]

colliery (ˈkɒljərɪ) *n, pl* **-lieries.** *Chiefly Brit.* a coal mine.

colligate (ˈkɒlɪˌgeɪt) *vb (tr)* **1** to connect or link together; tie; join. **2** to relate (isolated facts, observations, etc.) by a general hypothesis. [C16: from Latin *colligāre* to fasten together, from *com-* together + *ligāre* to bind] ▸ **ˌcolliˈgation** *n*

colligative (kəˈlɪgətɪv) *adj* (of a physical property of a substance) depending on the concentrations of atoms, ions, and molecules that are present rather than on their nature.

collimate (ˈkɒlɪˌmeɪt) *vb (tr)* **1** to adjust the line of sight of (an optical instrument). **2** to use a collimator on (a beam of radiation or particles). **3** to make parallel or bring into line. [C17: from New Latin *collimāre,* erroneously for Latin *collīneāre* to aim, from *com-* (intensive) + *līneāre,* from *līnea* line] ▸ **ˌcolliˈmation** *n*

collimator (ˈkɒlɪˌmeɪtə) *n* **1** a small telescope attached to a larger optical instrument as an aid in fixing its line of sight. **2** an optical system of lenses and slits producing a nondivergent beam of light, usually for use in spectroscopes. **3** any device for limiting the size and angle of spread of a beam of radiation or particles.

collinear (kɒˈlɪnɪə) *adj* **1** lying on the same straight line. **2** having a common line. ▸ **collinearity** (ˌkɒlɪnɪˈærɪtɪ) *n* ▸ **colˈlinearly** *adv*

collins (ˈkɒlɪnz) *n* a tall fizzy iced drink made with gin, vodka, rum, etc., mixed with fruit juice, soda water, and sugar. [C20: probably after the proper name *Collins*]

Collins (ˈkɒlɪnz) *n* **1 Michael.** 1890–1922, Irish republican revolutionary: a leader of Sinn Féin; member of the Irish delegation that negotiated the treaty with Great Britain (1921) that established the Irish Free State. **2 (William) Wilkie.** 1824–89, British author, noted particularly for his suspense novel *The Moonstone* (1868). **3 William.** 1721–59, British poet, noted for his odes; regarded as a precursor of romanticism.

collinsia (kəˈlɪnsɪə, -zɪə) *n* a North American plant of the scrophulariaceous genus *Collinsia,* having blue, white, or purple flowers. [C19: New Latin, named after Zaccheus *Collins* (1764–1831), American botanist]

Collins Street Farmer *n Austral. slang.* a businessman who invests in farms, land, etc. Also called: **Pitt Street Farmer.** [C20: after a principal business street in Melbourne]

collision (kəˈlɪʒən) *n* **1** a violent impact of moving objects; crash. **2** the conflict of opposed ideas, wishes, attitudes, etc.: *a collision of interests.* **3** *Physics.* an event in which two or more bodies or particles come together with a resulting exchange of energy and change of direction. [C15: from Late Latin *collīsiō* from Latin *collīdere* to COLLIDE]

collocate (ˈkɒləˌkeɪt) *vb (tr)* to group or place together in some system or order. [C16: from Latin *collocāre,* from *com-* together + *locāre* to place, from *locus* place]

collocation (ˌkɒləˈkeɪʃən) *n* a grouping together of things in a certain order, as of the words in a sentence.

collocutor (ˈkɒləˌkjuːtə) *n* a person who talks or engages in conversation with another.

collodion (kəˈləʊdɪən) *or* **collodium** (kəˈləʊdɪəm) *n* a colourless or yellow syrupy liquid that consists of a solution of pyroxylin in ether and alcohol: used in medicine and in the manufacture of photographic plates, lacquers, etc. [C19: from New Latin *collōdium,* from Greek *kollōdēs* glutinous, from *kolla* glue]

collogue (kɒˈləʊg) *vb* **collogues, colloguing, collogued.** *(intr;* usually foll. by *with)* to confer confidentially; intrigue or conspire. [C16: perhaps from obsolete *colleague* (vb) to be or act as a colleague, conspire, influenced by Latin *colloquī* to talk with; see COLLEAGUE]

colloid ('kɒlɔɪd) *n* **1** Also called: **colloidal solution** *or* **suspension.** a mixture having particles of one component, with diameters between 10^{-7} and 10^{-9} metre, suspended in a continuous phase of another component. The mixture has properties between those of a solution and a fine suspension. **2** the solid suspended phase in such a mixture. **3** *Obsolete.* a substance that in solution does not penetrate a semipermeable membrane. Compare **crystalloid** (sense 2). **4** *Physiol.* a gelatinous substance of the thyroid follicles that holds the hormonal secretions of the thyroid gland. ♦ *adj* **5** *Pathol.* of or relating to the gluelike translucent material found in certain degenerating tissues. **6** of, denoting, or having the character of a colloid. [C19: from Greek *kolla* glue + -OID] ▸ **col'loidal** *adj* ▸ **colloidality** (ˌkɒlɔɪ'dælɪtɪ) *n*

collop ('kɒləp) *n Dialect.* **1** a slice of meat. **2** a small piece of anything. [C14: of Scandinavian origin; compare Swedish *kalops* meat stew]

colloq. *abbrev. for* colloquial(ly).

colloquial (kə'ləʊkwɪəl) *adj* **1** of or relating to conversation. **2** denoting or characterized by informal or conversational idiom or vocabulary. Compare **informal.** ▸ **col'loquially** *adv* ▸ **col'loquialness** *n*

colloquialism (kə'ləʊkwɪəˌlɪzəm) *n* **1** a word or phrase appropriate to conversation and other informal situations. **2** the use of colloquial words and phrases.

colloquium (kə'ləʊkwɪəm) *n, pl* **-quiums** *or* **-quia** (-kwɪə). **1** an informal gathering for discussion. **2** an academic seminar. [C17: from Latin: conversation, conference, COLLOQUY]

colloquy ('kɒləkwɪ) *n, pl* **-quies.** **1** a formal conversation or conference. **2** a literary work in dialogue form. **3** an informal conference on religious or theological matters. [C16: from Latin *colloquium* from *colloquī* to talk with, from *com-* together + *loquī* to speak] ▸ **'colloquist** *n*

collotype ('kɒləʊˌtaɪp) *n* **1** Also called: **photogelatine process.** a method of lithographic printing from a flat surface of hardened gelatine: used mainly for fine-detail reproduction in monochrome or colour. **2** a print made using this process. [C19: from Greek *kolla* glue + TYPE] ▸ **collotypic** (ˌkɒlə'tɪpɪk) *adj*

collude (kə'luːd) *vb* (*intr*) to conspire together, esp. in planning a fraud; connive. [C16: from Latin *collūdere,* literally: to play together, hence, conspire together, from *com-* together + *lūdere* to play] ▸ **col'luder** *n*

collusion (kə'luːʒən) *n* **1** secret agreement for a fraudulent purpose; connivance; conspiracy. **2** a secret agreement between opponents at law in order to obtain a judicial decision for some wrongful or improper purpose. [C14: from Latin *collūsiō,* from *collūdere* to COLLUDE] ▸ **col'lusive** *adj*

colluvium (kə'luːvɪəm) *n, pl* **-via** (-vɪə) *or* **-viums.** a mixture of rock fragments from the bases of cliffs. [Latin: collection of filth, from *colluere* to wash thoroughly, from *com-* (intensive) + *luere* to wash] ▸ **col'luvial** *adj*

colly ('kɒlɪ) *Archaic or dialect.* ♦ *n, pl* **-lies.** **1** soot or grime, such as coal dust. ♦ *vb* **collies, collying, collied.** **2** (*tr*) to begrime; besmirch. [C16: ultimately from Old English *col* COAL]

collyrium (kɒ'lɪrɪəm) *n, pl* **-lyria** (-'lɪrɪə) *or* **-lyriums.** a technical name for **eyewash** (sense 1). [C16: from Latin, from Greek *kollurion* poultice, eye salve]

collywobbles ('kɒlɪˌwɒbᵊlz) *pl n* (usually preceded by *the*) *Slang.* **1** an upset stomach. **2** acute diarrhoea. **3** an intense feeling of nervousness. [C19: probably from New Latin *cholera morbus* the disease cholera, influenced through folk etymology by COLIC and WOBBLE]

Colmar (*French* kɔlmar) *n* a city in NE France: annexed to Germany 1871–1919 and 1940–45; textile industry. Pop.: 63 498 (1990). German name: **Kolmar.**

Colo. *abbrev. for* Colorado.

colo- *or before a vowel* **col-** *combining form.* indicating the colon: *colostomy; colotomy.*

coloboma (ˌkɒlə'bəʊmə) *n* a structural defect of the eye, esp. in the choroid, retina, or iris. [C19: New Latin, from Greek *kolobōma* a part taken away in mutilation, from *kolobos* cut short]

colobus ('kɒləbəs) *n* any leaf-eating arboreal Old World monkey of the genus *Colobus,* of W and central Africa, having a slender body, long silky fur, long tail, and reduced or absent thumbs. [C19: New Latin, from Greek *kolobos* cut short; referring to its thumb]

colocynth ('kɒləsɪnθ) *n* **1** a cucurbitaceous climbing plant, *Citrullus colocynthis,* of the Mediterranean region and Asia, having bitter-tasting fruit. **2** the dried fruit pulp of this plant, used as a strong purgative. ♦ Also called: **bitter apple.** [C17: from Latin *colocynthis,* from Greek *kolokunthis,* from *kolokunthē* gourd, of obscure origin]

cologarithm (kəʊ'lɒgəˌrɪðəm) *n* the logarithm of the reciprocal of a number; the negative value of the logarithm: *the cologarithm of 4 is log ¼.* Abbrev.: **colog.**

cologne (kə'ləʊn) *n* a perfumed liquid or solid made of fragrant essential oils and alcohol. Also called: **Cologne water, eau de Cologne.** [C18: *Cologne water,* from COLOGNE, where it was first manufactured (1709)]

Cologne (kə'ləʊn) *n* an industrial city and river port in W Germany, in North Rhine-Westphalia on the Rhine: important commercially since ancient times; university (1388). Pop.: 965 697 (1996 est.). German name: **Köln.**

Colomb-Béchar (*French* kɔlɔ̃beʃar) *n* the former name of **Béchar.**

Colombes (*French* kɔlɔ̃b) *n* an industrial and residential suburb of NW Paris. Pop.: 79 060 (1990).

Colombia (kə'lɒmbɪə) *n* a republic in NW South America: inhabited by Chibchas and other Indians before Spanish colonization in the 16th century; independence won by Bolívar in 1819; became the Republic of Colombia in 1886. It consists chiefly of a hot swampy coastal plain, separated by ranges of the Andes from the pampas and the equatorial forests of the Amazon basin in the east. Language: Spanish. Religion: Roman Catholic majority. Currency: peso. Capital: Bogotá. Pop.: 35 652 000 (1996). Area: 1 138 908 sq. km (439 735 sq. miles). ▸ **Co'lombian** *adj, n*

Colombo (kə'lʌmbəʊ) *n* the capital and chief port of Sri Lanka, on the W coast, with one of the largest artificial harbours in the world. Pop.: 615 000 (1990 est.).

colon[1] ('kəʊlən) *n* **1** (*pl* **-lons**) the punctuation mark : , usually preceding an explanation or an example of what has gone before, a list, or an extended quotation. **2** (*pl* **-lons**) this mark used for certain other purposes, such as expressions of time, as in *2:45 p.m.,* or when a ratio is given in figures, as in *5:3.* **3** (*pl* **-la** (-lə)) (in classical prosody) a part of a rhythmic period with two to six feet and one principal accent or ictus. [C16: from Latin, from Greek *kōlon* limb, hence part of a strophe, clause of a sentence]

colon[2] ('kəʊlən) *n, pl* **-lons** *or* **-la** (-lə). the part of the large intestine between the caecum and the rectum. [C16: from Latin: large intestine, from Greek *kolon*]

colon[3] (kə'lɒn; *French* kɔlɔ̃) *n* a colonial farmer or plantation owner, esp. in a French colony. [French: colonist, from Latin *colōnus,* from *colere* to till, inhabit]

colón (kəʊ'ləʊn; *Spanish* ko'lon) *n, pl* **-lons** *or* **-lones** (*Spanish* -'lones). **1** the standard monetary unit of Costa Rica, divided into 100 céntimos. **2** the standard monetary unit of El Salvador, divided into 100 centavos. [C19: American Spanish, from Spanish, after Cristóbal *Colón* Christopher Columbus]

Colón (kɒ'lɒn; *Spanish* ko'lən) *n* **1** a port in Panama, at the Caribbean entrance to the Panama Canal. Chief Caribbean port. Pop.: 137 825 (1992 est.). Former name: **Aspinwall.** **2 Archipiélago de** (ˌartʃi'pjelaɣo ðe). the official name of the **Galápagos Islands.**

colonel ('kɜːnᵊl) *n* an officer of land or air forces junior to a brigadier but senior to a lieutenant colonel. [C16: via Old French, from Old Italian *colonnello* column of soldiers, from *colonna* COLUMN] ▸ **'colonelcy** *or* **'colonelˌship** *n*

Colonel Blimp *n* See **blimp**[2].

colonial (kə'ləʊnɪəl) *adj* **1** of, characteristic of, relating to, possessing, or inhabiting a colony or colonies. **2** (*often cap.*) characteristic of or relating to the 13 British colonies that became the United States of America (1776). **3** (*often cap.*) of or relating to the colonies of the British Empire. **4** denoting, relating to, or having the style of Neoclassical architecture used in the British colonies in America in the 17th and 18th centuries. **5** of or relating to the period of Australian history before Federation (1901). **6** (of organisms such as corals and bryozoans) existing as a colony of polyps. **7** (of animals and plants) having become established in a community in a new environment. ♦ *n* **8** a native of a colony. ▸ **co'lonially** *adv*

colonial experience *n Austral. history.* experience of farming, etc., gained by a young Englishman in colonial Australia. ▸ **colonial experiencer** *n*

colonial goose *n N.Z.* an old-fashioned name for stuffed roast mutton.

colonialism (kə'ləʊnɪəˌlɪzəm) *n* the policy and practice of a power in extending control over weaker peoples or areas. Also called: **imperialism.** ▸ **co'lonialist** *n, adj*

colonic (kə'lɒnɪk) *adj* **1a** *Anatomy.* of or relating to the colon. **1b** *Med.* relating to irrigation of the colon for cleansing purposes. ♦ *n* **2** *Med.* irrigation of the colon by injecting large amounts of fluid high into the colon: *a high colonic.*

Colonies ('kɒlənɪz) *pl n* **the.** **1** *Brit.* the subject territories formerly in the British Empire. **2** *U.S. history.* the 13 states forming the original United States of America when they declared their independence (1776). These were Connecticut, North and South Carolina, Delaware, Georgia, New Hampshire, New York, Maryland, Massachusetts, Pennsylvania, Rhode Island, Virginia, and New Jersey.

colonist ('kɒlənɪst) *n* **1** a person who settles or colonizes an area. **2** an inhabitant or member of a colony.

colonitis (ˌkɒlə'naɪtɪs) *n Pathol.* another word for **colitis.**

colonize *or* **colonise** ('kɒləˌnaɪz) *vb* **1** to send colonists to or establish a colony in (an area). **2** to settle in (an area) as colonists. **3** (*tr*) to transform (a community) into a colony. **4** (of plants and animals) to become established in (a new environment). ▸ **'coloˌnizable** *or* **'coloˌnisable** *adj* ▸ **ˌcoloni'zation** *or* **ˌcoloni'sation** *n* ▸ **'coloˌnizer** *or* **'coloˌniser** *n*

colonnade (ˌkɒlə'neɪd) *n* **1** a set of evenly-spaced columns. **2** a row of regularly spaced trees. [C18: from French, from *colonne* COLUMN; on the model of Italian *colonnato,* from *colonna* column] ▸ **ˌcolon'naded** *adj*

colonoscope (kə'lɒnəˌskəʊp) *n* an instrument for examining the colon, consisting of a flexible lighted tube that is inserted in the colon to look for abnormalities and to remove them or take tissue samples. [C20: from COLON[2] + -O- + -SCOPE] ▸ **colonoscopy** (ˌkɒlən'ɒskəpɪ) *n*

Colonsay ('kɒlənseɪ, -zeɪ) *n* an island in W Scotland, in the Inner Hebrides. Area: about 41 sq. km (16 sq. miles).

colony ('kɒlənɪ) *n, pl* **-nies.** **1** a body of people who settle in a country distant from their homeland but maintain ties with it. **2** the community formed by such settlers. **3** a subject territory occupied by a settlement from the ruling state. **4a** a community of people who form a national, racial, or cultural minority: *an artists' colony; the American colony in London.* **4b** the area itself. **5** *Zoology.* **5a** a group of the same type of animal or plant living or growing together. **5b** an interconnected group of polyps of a colonial organism. **6** *Bacteriol.* a group of bacteria, fungi, etc., derived from one or a few spores, esp. when grown on a culture medium. [C16: from Latin *colōnia,* from *colere* to cultivate, inhabit]

colony-stimulating factor *n Immunol.* any of a number of substances, secreted by the bone marrow, that cause stem cells to proliferate and differentiate, forming colonies of specific blood cells. Synthetic forms are being tested for their ability to reduce the toxic effects of chemotherapy. Abbrev.: **CSF.**

colophon ('kɒləˌfɒn, -fən) *n* **1** a publisher's emblem on a book. **2** (formerly) an inscription at the end of a book showing the title, printer, date, etc. [C17: via Late Latin, from Greek *kolophōn* a finishing stroke]

colophony (kɒ'lɒfənɪ) *n* another name for **rosin** (sense 1). [C14: from Latin *Colophōnia rēsina* resin from Colophon]

coloquintida (ˌkɒləˈkwɪntɪdə) *n* another name for **colocynth.** [C14: from Medieval Latin, from *colocynthid-* COLOCYNTH]

color (ˈkʌlə) *n, vb* the U.S. spelling of **colour.** ▸ **ˈcolorable** *adj* ▸ **ˈcolorer** *n* ▸ **ˈcolorful** *adj* ▸ **ˈcoloring** *n* ▸ **ˈcolorist** *n* ▸ **ˈcolorless** *adj*

Colorado (ˌkɒləˈrɑːdəʊ) *n* **1** a state of the central U.S.: consists of the Great Plains in the east and the Rockies in the west; drained chiefly by the Colorado, Arkansas, South Platte, and Rio Grande Rivers. Capital: Denver. Pop.: 3 892 644 (1997 est.). Area: 269 998 sq. km (104 247 sq. miles). Abbrevs.: **Colo.** or (with zip code) **CO** **2** a river in SW North America, rising in the Rocky Mountains and flowing southwest to the Gulf of California: famous for the 1600 km (1000 miles) of canyons along its course. Length: about 2320 km (1440 miles). **3** a river in central Texas, flowing southeast to the Gulf of Mexico. Length: about 1450 km (900 miles). **4** a river in central Argentina, flowing southeast to the Atlantic. Length: about 850 km (530 miles). [Spanish, literally: red, from Latin *colōrātus* coloured, tinted red; see COLOUR]

Colorado beetle *n* a black-and-yellow beetle, *Leptinotarsa decemlineata,* that is a serious pest of potatoes, feeding on the leaves: family *Chrysomelidae.* Also called: **potato beetle.**

Colorado Desert *n* an arid region of SE California and NW Mexico, West of the Colorado River. Area: over 5000 sq. km (2000 sq. miles).

Colorado ruby *n* a fire-red form of garnet found in Colorado and other parts of North America.

Colorado Springs *n* a city and resort in central Colorado. Pop.: 345 127 (1996 est.).

Colorado topaz *n* **1** a tawny-coloured form of topaz found in Colorado. **2** quartz of a similar colour.

colorant (ˈkʌlərənt) *n* any substance that imparts colour, such as a pigment, dye, or ink; colouring matter.

coloration *or* **colouration** (ˌkʌləˈreɪʃən) *n* **1** arrangement of colour and tones; colouring. **2** the colouring or markings of insects, birds, etc. See also **apatetic, aposematic, cryptic. 3** unwanted extraneous variations in the frequency response of a loudspeaker or listening environment.

coloratura (ˌkɒlərəˈtʊərə) *or* **colorature** (ˈkɒlərəˌtjʊə) *n Music.* **1a** (in 18th- and 19th-century arias) a florid virtuoso passage. **1b** (*as modifier*): *a coloratura aria.* **2** Also called: **coloratura soprano.** a lyric soprano who specializes in such music. [C19: from obsolete Italian, literally: colouring, from Latin *colōrāre* to COLOUR]

colorectal (ˌkəʊləʊˈrɛktᵊl) *adj* of or relating to the colon and rectum.

colorific (ˌkʌləˈrɪfɪk) *adj* producing, imparting, or relating to colour.

colorimeter (ˌkʌləˈrɪmɪtə) *n* **1** Also called: **tintometer.** an apparatus for determining the concentration of a solution of a coloured substance by comparing the intensity of its colour with that of a standard solution or with standard colour slides. **2** any apparatus for measuring the quality of a colour by comparison with standard colours or combinations of colours. ▸ **colorimetric** (ˌkʌlərɪˈmɛtrɪk) *or* **ˌcoloriˈmetrical** *adj* ▸ **ˌcoloriˈmetrically** *adv* ▸ **ˌcolorˈimetry** *n*

Colossae (kəˈlɒsiː) *n* an ancient city in SW Phrygia in Asia Minor: seat of an early Christian Church.

colossal (kəˈlɒsᵊl) *adj* **1** of immense size; huge; gigantic. **2** (in figure sculpture) approximately twice life-size. Compare **heroic** (sense 7). **3** Also: **giant.** *Architect.* of or relating to the order of columns and pilasters that extend more than one storey in a façade. ▸ **coˈlossally** *adv*

colosseum (ˌkɒləˈsɪəm) *n* a variant spelling of **coliseum.**

Colosseum (ˌkɒləˈsɪəm) *n* an amphitheatre in Rome built about 75–80 A.D.

Colossian (kəˈlɒʃən) *n* **1** a native or inhabitant of Colossae. **2** *New Testament.* any of the Christians of Colossae to whom St. Paul's Epistle was addressed.

Colossians (kəˈlɒʃənz) *n* (*functioning as sing*) a book of the New Testament (in full **The Epistle of Paul the Apostle to the Colossians**).

colossus (kəˈlɒsəs) *n, pl* **-si** (-saɪ) *or* **-suses.** something very large, esp. a statue. [C14: from Latin, from Greek *kolossos*]

Colossus of Rhodes *n* a giant bronze statue of Apollo built on Rhodes in about 292–280 B.C.; destroyed by an earthquake in 225 B.C.; one of the Seven Wonders of the World.

colostomy (kəˈlɒstəmɪ) *n, pl* **-mies.** the surgical formation of an opening from the colon onto the surface of the body, which functions as an anus.

colostrum (kəˈlɒstrəm) *n* the thin milky secretion from the nipples that precedes and follows true lactation. It consists largely of serum and white blood cells. [C16: from Latin, of obscure origin] ▸ **coˈlostral** *adj*

colotomy (kəˈlɒtəmɪ) *n, pl* **-mies.** a colonic incision.

colour *or U.S.* **color** (ˈkʌlə) *n* **1a** an attribute of things that results from the light they reflect, transmit, or emit in so far as this light causes a visual sensation that depends on its wavelengths. **1b** the aspect of visual perception by which an observer recognizes this attribute. **1c** the quality of the light producing this aspect of visual perception. **1d** (*as modifier*): *colour vision.* **2** Also called: **chromatic colour. 2a** a colour, such as red or green, that possesses hue, as opposed to achromatic colours such as white or black. **2b** (*as modifier*): *a colour television; a colour film.* Compare **black-and-white** (sense 2). **3** a substance, such as a dye, pigment, or paint, that imparts colour to something. **4a** the skin complexion of a person, esp. as determined by his race. **4b** (*as modifier*): *colour prejudice; colour problem.* **5** the use of all the hues in painting as distinct from composition, form, and light and shade. **6** the quantity and quality of ink used in a printing process. **7** the distinctive tone of a musical sound; timbre. **8** vividness, authenticity, or individuality: *period colour.* **9** semblance or pretext (esp. in the phrases **take on a different colour, under colour of**). **10** *U.S.* a precious mineral particle, esp. gold, found in auriferous gravel. **11** *Physics.* one of three characteristics of quarks, designated red, blue, or green, but having only a remote formal relationship with the physical sensation. ◆ *vb* **12** to give or apply colour to (something). **13** (*tr*) to give a convincing or plausible appearance to (something, esp. to that which is spoken or recounted): *to colour an alibi.* **14** (*tr*) to influence or distort (something, esp. a report or opinion): *anger coloured her judgment.* **15** (*intr;* often foll. by *up*) to become red in the face, esp. when embarrassed or annoyed. **16** (*intr*) (esp. of ripening fruit) to change hue. ◆ See also **colours.** [C13: from Old French *colour* from Latin *color* tint, hue]

colourable (ˈkʌlərəbᵊl) *adj* **1** capable of being coloured. **2** appearing to be true; plausible: *a colourable excuse.* **3** pretended; feigned: *colourable affection.* ▸ **ˌcolouraˈbility** *or* **ˈcolourableness** *n* ▸ **ˈcolourably** *adv*

colour bar *n* discrimination against people of a different race, esp. as practised by Whites against Blacks.

colour-blind *adj* **1** of or relating to any defect in the normal ability to distinguish certain colours. See **deuteranopia, protanopia, tritanopia. 2** not discriminating on grounds of skin colour or ethnic origin. ▸ **colour blindness** *n*

colour code *n* a system of easily distinguishable colours, as for the identification of electrical wires or resistors.

colour contrast *n Psychol.* the change in the appearance of a colour surrounded by another colour; for example, grey looks bluish if surrounded by yellow.

coloured (ˈkʌləd) *adj* **1** possessing colour. **2** having a strong element of fiction or fantasy; distorted (esp. in the phrase **highly coloured**).

Coloured (ˈkʌləd) *n, pl* **Coloureds** *or* **Coloured. 1** an individual who is not a White person, esp. a Black person. **2** Also called: **Cape Coloured.** (in South Africa) a person of racially mixed parentage or descent. ◆ *adj* **3** designating or relating to a Coloured person or Coloured people: *a Coloured gentleman.*

USAGE The use of *Coloured* to refer to a person who is not White can be offensive and should be avoided.

colourfast (ˈkʌləˌfɑːst) *adj* (of a fabric) having a colour that does not run or change when washed or worn. ▸ **ˈcolourˌfastness** *n*

colour filter *n Photog.* a thin layer of coloured gelatine, glass, etc., that transmits light of certain colours or wavelengths but considerably reduces the transmission of others.

colourful (ˈkʌləfʊl) *adj* **1** having intense colour or richly varied colours. **2** vivid, rich, or distinctive in character. ▸ **ˈcolourfully** *adv* ▸ **ˈcolourfulness** *n*

colour guard *n* a military guard in a parade, ceremony, etc., that carries and escorts the flag or regimental colours.

colour index *n* **1** *Astronomy.* the difference between the photographic magnitude and the visual magnitude of a star, indicating its colour and temperature. **2** *Geology.* the sum of the dark or coloured minerals of a rock, expressed as a percentage of the total minerals. **3** *Chem., physics.* a systematic arrangement of colours according to their hue, saturation, and brightness.

colouring (ˈkʌlərɪŋ) *n* **1** the process or art of applying colour. **2** anything used to give colour, such as dye, paint, etc. **3** appearance with regard to shade and colour. **4** arrangements of colours and tones, as in the markings of birds and animals. **5** the colour of a person's features or complexion. **6** a false or misleading appearance.

colourist (ˈkʌlərɪst) *n* **1** a person who uses colour, esp. an artist. **2** a person who colours photographs, esp. black-and-white ones. ▸ **ˌcolourˈistic** *adj*

colourize, colourise, *or U.S.* **colorize** (ˈkʌləˌraɪz) *vb* (*tr*) to add colour electronically to (an old black-and-white film). ▸ **ˌcolouriˈzation, -iˈsation** *or U.S.* **ˌcoloriˈzation** *n*

colourless (ˈkʌləlɪs) *adj* **1** without colour. **2** lacking in interest: *a colourless individual.* **3** grey or pallid in tone or hue. **4** without prejudice; neutral. ▸ **ˈcolourlessly** *adv* ▸ **ˈcolourlessness** *n*

colour line *n* the social separation of racial groups within a community (esp. in the phrase **to cross the colour line**).

colourman (ˈkʌləmən) *n, pl* **-men.** a person who deals in paints.

colour phase *n* **1** a seasonal change in the coloration of some animals. **2** an abnormal variation in the coloration shown by a group of animals within a species.

colourpoint cat (ˈkʌləˌpɔɪnt) *n* a Persian cat with the colouring of a Siamese. U.S. name: **Himalayan cat.**

colour-reversal *n* (*modifier*) *Photog.* (of film or photographic paper) designed to produce a positive image directly from a positive subject.

colours (ˈkʌləz) *pl n* **1a** the flag that indicates nationality. **1b** *Military.* the ceremony of hoisting or lowering the colours. **2** a pair of silk flags borne by a military unit, esp. British, comprising the **Queen's Colour** showing the unit's crest, and the **Regimental Colour** showing the crest and battle honours. **3** true nature or character (esp. in the phrase **show one's colours**). **4** a distinguishing badge or flag, as of an academic institution. **5** *Sport, Brit.* a badge or other symbol denoting membership of a team, esp. at a school or college. **6** *Informal.* a distinguishing embroidered patch denoting membership of a motorcycle gang. **7 nail one's colours to the mast. 7a** to refuse to admit defeat. **7b** to declare openly one's opinions or allegiances.

colour scheme *n* a planned combination or juxtaposition of colours, as in interior decorating.

colour separation *n Printing.* the division of a coloured original into cyan, magenta, yellow, and black so that plates may be made for print reproduction. Separation may be achieved by electronic scanning or by photographic techniques using filters to isolate each colour.

colour separation overlay *n* another term for **chromakey.**

colour sergeant *n* a sergeant who carries the regimental, battalion, or national colours, as in a colour guard.

colour subcarrier (ˈsʌbˌkærɪə) *n* a component of a colour television signal on which is modulated the colour or chrominance information.

colour supplement *n Brit.* an illustrated magazine accompanying a newspaper, esp. a Sunday newspaper.

colour temperature *n Physics.* the temperature of a black-body radiator at which it would emit radiation of the same chromaticity as the light under consideration.

colourwash ('kʌlə,wɒʃ) *n* **1** a coloured distemper. ◆ *vb* (*tr*) **2** to paint with colourwash.

colourway ('kʌlə,weɪ) *n* one of several different combinations of colours in which a given pattern is printed on fabrics, wallpapers, etc.

coloury *or* **colory** ('kʌlərɪ) *adj* possessing colour.

-colous *adj combining form.* inhabiting or living on: *arenicolous.* [from Latin *-cola* inhabitant + -OUS; related to *colere* to inhabit]

colpitis (kɒl'paɪtɪs) *n Pathol.* another name for **vaginitis.** [C19: from Greek *kolpos* bosom, womb, vagina + -ITIS]

colpo- *or before a vowel* **colp-** *combining form.* indicating the vagina: *colpitis; colpotomy.* [from Greek *kolpos* womb]

colporteur ('kɒl,pɔːtə; *French* kɔlpɔrtœr) *n* a hawker of books, esp. bibles. [C18: from French, from *colporter,* probably from Old French *comporter* to carry (see COMPORT); influenced through folk etymology by *porter à col* to carry on one's neck] ▸ **'col,portage** *n*

colposcope ('kɒlpə,skəup) *n* an instrument for examining the cervix, esp. for early signs of cancer. [C20: from COLPO- + -SCOPE]

colpotomy (kəl'pɒtəmɪ) *n* a surgical incision into the wall of the vagina. [C20: from COLPO- + -TOMY]

colt (kəult) *n* **1** a male horse or pony under the age of four. **2** an awkward or inexperienced young person. **3** *Sport.* **3a** a young and inexperienced player. **3b** a member of a junior team. [Old English *colt* young ass, of obscure origin; compare Swedish dialect *kult* young animal, boy]

Colt (kəult) *n Trademark.* a type of revolver, pistol, etc. [C19: named after Samuel *Colt* (1814–62), American inventor]

colter ('kəultə) *n* a variant spelling (esp. U.S.) of **coulter.**

coltish ('kəultɪʃ) *adj* **1** inexperienced; unruly. **2** playful and lively. ▸ **'coltishly** *adv* ▸ **'coltishness** *n*

Coltrane (kɒl'treɪn) *n* **John** (**William**). 1926–67, U.S. jazz tenor and soprano saxophonist and composer.

coltsfoot ('kəults,fut) *n, pl* **-foots.** a European plant, *Tussilago farfara,* with yellow daisy-like flowers and heart-shaped leaves: a common weed: family *Compositae* (composites).

colubrid ('kɒljubrɪd) *n* **1** any snake of the family *Colubridae,* including many harmless snakes, such as the grass snake and whip snakes, and some venomous types. ◆ *adj* **2** of, relating to, or belonging to the *Colubridae.* [C19: from New Latin *Colubridae,* from Latin *coluber* snake]

colubrine ('kɒlju,braɪn, -brɪn) *adj* **1** of or resembling a snake. **2** of, relating to, or belonging to the *Colubrinae,* a subfamily of harmless colubrid snakes. [C16: from Latin *colubrīnus,* from *coluber* snake]

colugo (kə'luːgəu) *n, pl* **-gos.** another name for **flying lemur.** [from a native word in Malaya]

Colum ('kɒləm) *n* **Padraic** ('pɑːdrɪk). 1881–1972, Irish lyric poet, resident in the U.S. (1914–72).

Columba[1] (kə'lʌmbə) *n, Latin genitive* **Columbae** (kə'lʌmbiː), as in *Alpha Columbae.* a small constellation in the S hemisphere south of Orion. [Latin, literally: dove]

Columba[2] (kə'lʌmbə) *n* **Saint.** ?521–597 A.D., Irish missionary: founded the monastery at Iona (563) from which the Picts were converted to Christianity. Feast day: June 9.

columbarium (,kɒləm'bɛərɪəm) *n, pl* **-ia** (-ɪə). **1** another name for a **dovecote.** **2** a vault having niches for funeral urns. **3** a hole in a wall into which a beam is inserted. [C18: from Latin, from *columba* dove]

Columbia[1] (kə'lʌmbɪə) *n* **1** a river in NW North America, rising in the Rocky Mountains and flowing through British Columbia, then west to the Pacific. Length: about 1930 km (1200 miles). **2** a city in central South Carolina, on the Congaree River: the state capital. Pop.: 112 773 (1996 est.).

Columbia[2] (kə'lʌmbɪə) *n* the first test vehicle of the NASA space shuttle fleet to prove the possibility of routine access to space for scientific and commercial ventures.

Columbian (kə'lʌmbɪən) *adj* **1** of or relating to the United States. **2** relating to Christopher Columbus. ◆ *n* **3** a size of printer's type, approximately equal to 16 point; two-line Brevier.

columbic (kə'lʌmbɪk) *adj* another word for **niobic.**

columbine[1] ('kɒləm,baɪn) *n* any plant of the ranunculaceous genus *Aquilegia,* having purple, blue, yellow, or red flowers with five spurred petals. Also called: **aquilegia.** [C13: from Medieval Latin *columbīna herba* dovelike plant, from Latin *columbīnus* dovelike, from the resemblance of the flower to a group of doves]

columbine[2] ('kɒləm,baɪn) *adj* of, relating to, or resembling a dove. [C14: from Old French *colombin,* from Latin *columbīnus* dovelike, from *columba* dove]

Columbine ('kɒləm,baɪn) *n* **1** (originally) the character of a servant girl in commedia dell'arte. **2** (later) the sweetheart of Harlequin in English pantomime.

columbite (kə'lʌmbaɪt) *n* a black mineral consisting of a mixed niobium and tantalum oxide of iron and manganese in orthorhombic crystalline form: occurs in coarse granite, often with tantalite, and is an ore of niobium and tantalum. Formula: $(Fe, Mn)(Nb,Ta)_2O_6$. Also called: **niobite.** [C19: from COLUMBIUM + -ITE[1]]

columbium (kə'lʌmbɪəm) *n* the former name of **niobium.** [C19: from New Latin, from *Columbia,* the United States of America]

columbous (kə'lʌmbəs) *adj* another word for **niobous.**

Columbus[1] (kə'lʌmbəs) *n* **1** a city in central Ohio: the state capital. Pop.: 657 053 (1996 est.). **2** a city in W Georgia, on the Chattahoochee River. Pop.: 182 828 (1996 est.).

Columbus[2] (kə'lʌmbəs) *n* **Christopher.** Spanish name *Cristóbal Colón,* Italian name *Cristoforo Colombo.* 1451–1506, Italian navigator and explorer in the service of Spain, who discovered the New World (1492).

Columbus Day *n* Oct. 12, a legal holiday in most states of the U.S.: the date of Columbus' landing in the West Indies (Caribbean) in 1492.

columella (,kɒlju'mɛlə) *n, pl* **-lae** (-liː). **1** *Biology.* **1a** the central part of the spore-producing body of some fungi and mosses. **1b** any similar columnar structure. **2** Also called: **columella auris** ('ɔːrɪs). a small rodlike bone in the middle ear of frogs, reptiles, and birds that transmits sound to the inner ear: homologous to the mammalian stapes. [C16: from Latin: diminutive of *columna* COLUMN] ▸ **,colu'mellar** *adj*

column ('kɒləm) *n* **1** an upright post or pillar usually having a cylindrical shaft, a base, and a capital. **2a** a form or structure in the shape of a column: *a column of air.* **2b** a monument. **3** a row, line, or file, as of people in a queue. **4** *Military.* a narrow formation in which individuals or units follow one behind the other. **5** *Journalism.* **5a** any of two or more vertical sections of type on a printed page, esp. on a newspaper page. **5b** a regular article or feature in a paper: *the fashion column.* **6** a vertical array of numbers or mathematical terms. **7** *Botany.* a long structure in the flower of an orchid, consisting of the united stamens and style. **8** *Anatomy, zoology.* any elongated structure, such as a tract of grey matter in the spinal cord or the stalk of a crinoid. [C15: from Latin *columna,* from *columen* top, peak; related to Latin *collis* hill] ▸ **columnar** (kə'lʌmnə) *adj* ▸ **'columned** *or* **columnated** ('kɒləm,neɪtɪd) *adj*

columniation (kə,lʌmnɪ'eɪʃən) *n* the arrangement of architectural columns.

column inch *n* a unit of measurement for advertising space, one inch deep and one column wide.

columnist ('kɒləmɪst, -əmnɪst) *n* a journalist who writes a regular feature in a newspaper: *a gossip columnist.*

colure (kə'luə, 'kəuluə) *n* either of two great circles on the celestial sphere, one of which passes through the celestial poles and the equinoxes and the other through the poles and the solstices. [C16: from Late Latin *colūrī* (plural), from Greek *kolourai* cut short, dock-tailed, from *kolos* docked + *oura* tail; so called because the view of the lower part is curtailed]

Colwyn Bay ('kɒlwɪn) *n* a town and resort in N Wales, in Conwy county borough. Pop.: 29 883 (1991).

coly ('kəulɪ) *n, pl* **-lies.** any of the arboreal birds of the genus *Colius,* family *Coliidae,* and order *Coliiformes,* of southern Africa. They have a soft hairlike plumage, crested head, and very long tail. Also called: **mousebird.** [C19: from New Latin *colius,* probably from Greek *kolios* woodpecker]

colza ('kɒlzə) *n* another name for **rape**[2]. [C18: via French (Walloon) *kolzat* from Dutch *koolzaad,* from *kool* cabbage, COLE + *zaad* SEED]

colza oil *n* the oil obtained from the seeds of the rape plant and used in making lubricants and synthetic rubber.

COM (kɒm) *n* **a** a process in which a computer output is converted direct to microfiche or film, esp. 35 or 16 millimetre film. **b** (*as modifier*): *a COM machine.* [(*C*)*omputer* (*O*)*utput on* (*M*)*icrofilm*]

com. *abbrev. for:* **1** comedy. **2** comic. **3** commerce. **4** commercial. **5** committee.

Com. *abbrev. for:* **1** Commander. **2** committee. **3** Commodore. **4** Communist.

com- *or* **con-** *prefix* together; with; jointly: *commingle.* [from Latin *com-;* related to *cum* with. In compound words of Latin origin, *com-* becomes *col-* and *cor-* before *l* and *r, co-* before *gn, h,* and most vowels, and *con-* before consonants other than *b, p,* and *m.* Although its sense in compounds of Latin derivation is often obscured, it means: together, with, etc. (*combine, compile*); similar (*conform*); extremely, completely (*consecrate*)]

coma[1] ('kəumə) *n, pl* **-mas.** a state of unconsciousness from which a person cannot be aroused, caused by injury to the head, rupture of cerebral blood vessels, narcotics, poisons, etc. [C17: from medical Latin, from Greek *kōma* heavy sleep; related to Greek *koitē* bed, perhaps to Middle Irish *cuma* grief]

coma[2] ('kəumə) *n, pl* **-mae** (-miː). **1** *Astronomy.* the luminous cloud surrounding the frozen solid nucleus in the head of a comet, formed by vaporization of part of the nucleus when the comet is close to the sun. **2** *Botany.* **2a** a tuft of hairs attached to the seed coat of some seeds. **2b** the terminal crown of leaves of palms and moss stems. **3** *Optics.* a type of lens defect characterized by the formation of a diffuse pear-shaped image from a point object. [C17: from Latin: hair of the head, from Greek *komē*] ▸ **'comal** *adj*

Coma Berenices ('kəumə ,bɛrɪ'naɪsiːz) *n, Latin genitive* **Comae Berenices** ('kəumiː). a faint constellation in the N hemisphere between Ursa Major and Boötes containing the **Coma Cluster,** a cluster of approximately 10 000 galaxies, at a mean distance of 220 million light years. [from Latin, literally: Berenice's hair, named after *Berenice* (died 221 B.C.), consort of Ptolemy III]

Comanche (kə'mæntʃɪ) *n* **1** (*pl* **-ches** *or* **-che**) a member of a North American Indian people, formerly ranging from the River Platte to the Mexican border, now living in Oklahoma. **2** the language of this people, belonging to the Shoshonean subfamily of the Uto-Aztecan family.

Comanchean (kə'mæntʃɪən) (in North America) ◆ *adj* **1** of or relating to the early part of the Cretaceous system and period. ◆ *n* **2** the strata and time corresponding to the early Cretaceous.

Comaneci (,kɒmə'nɛtʃɪ) *n* **Nadia.** born 1961, Romanian gymnast; gold medal winner in the 1976 Olympic Games: defected to the U.S. in 1989.

comate ('kəumeɪt) *adj Botany.* **1** having tufts of hair; hairy. **2** having or relating to a coma. [C17: from Latin *comātus,* from *coma* hair]

comatose ('kəumə,təus, -,təuz) *adj* **1** in a state of coma. **2** torpid; lethargic. ▸ **'coma,tosely** *adv*

comatulid (kə'mætjulɪd) *or* **comatula** *n, pl* **-lids** *or* **-lae** (-liː). any of a group of crinoid echinoderms, including the feather stars, in which the adults are free-swimming. [C19: from New Latin *Comatulidae,* from *Comatula* type genus, from Latin *comātus* hairy]

comb (kəum) *n* **1** a toothed device of metal, plastic, wood, etc., used for disentangling or arranging hair. **2** a tool or machine that separates, cleans, and straightens wool, cotton, etc. **3** *Austral. and N.Z.* the fixed cutter on a sheep-shearing machine. **4** anything resembling a toothed comb in form or function. **5** the fleshy deeply serrated outgrowth on the top of the heads of certain birds, esp. the domestic fowl. **6** anything resembling the comb of a bird. **7** a curry-comb. **8** a honeycomb. **9** the row of fused cilia in a ctenophore. **10 go over** (*or* **through**) **with a fine-tooth(ed) comb.** to examine very thoroughly. ◆ *vb* **11** (*tr*) to use a comb on. **12** (when *tr*, often foll. by *through*) to search or inspect with great care: *the police combed the woods.* ◆ See also **comb out.** [Old English *camb;* related to Old Norse *kambr,* Old High German *camb*]

comb. *abbrev. for* combining.

combat *n* ('kɒmbæt, -bət, 'kʌm-). **1** a fight, conflict, or struggle. **2a** an action fought between two military forces. **2b** (*as modifier*): *a combat jacket.* **3 single combat.** a fight between two individuals; duel. **4 close** *or* **hand-to-hand combat.** fighting at close quarters. ◆ *vb* (kəm'bæt; 'kɒmbæt, 'kʌm-). **-bats, -bating, -bated. 5** (*tr*) to fight or defy. **6** (*intr;* often foll. by *with* or *against*) to struggle or strive (against); be in conflict (with): *to combat against disease.* [C16: from French, from Old French *combattre,* from Vulgar Latin *combattere* (unattested), from Latin *com-* with + *battuere* to beat, hit] ▸ **com'batable** *adj* ▸ **com'bater** *n*

combatant ('kɒmbətᵊnt, 'kʌm-) *n* **1** a person or group engaged in or prepared for a fight, struggle, or dispute. ◆ *adj* **2** engaged in or ready for combat.

combat fatigue *n* another term for **battle fatigue.**

combative ('kɒmbətɪv, 'kʌm-) *adj* eager or ready to fight, argue, etc.; aggressive. ▸ **'combatively** *adv* ▸ **'combativeness** *n*

combe *or* **comb** (ku:m) *n* variant spellings of **coomb.**

comber ('kəʊmə) *n* **1** a person, tool, or machine that combs wool, flax, etc. **2** a long curling wave; roller.

combination (ˌkɒmbɪ'neɪʃən) *n* **1** the act of combining or state of being combined. **2** a union of separate parts, qualities, etc. **3** an alliance of people or parties; group having a common purpose. **4a** the set of numbers that opens a combination lock. **4b** the mechanism of this type of lock. **5** *Brit.* a motorcycle with a sidecar attached. **6** *Maths.* **6a** an arrangement of the numbers, terms, etc., of a set into specified groups without regard to order in the group: *the combinations of a, b, and c, taken two at a time, are ab, bc, ac.* **6b** a group formed in this way. The number of combinations of *n* objects taken *r* at a time is $n!/[(n-r)!r!]$. Symbol: $_nC_r$. Compare **permutation** (sense 1). **7** the chemical reaction of two or more compounds, usually to form one other compound. **8** *Chess.* a tactical manoeuvre involving a sequence of moves and more than one piece. ◆ See also **combinations.** ▸ **ˌcombi'national** *adj*

combination lock *n* a type of lock that can only be opened when a set of dials releasing the tumblers of the lock are turned to show a specific sequence of numbers.

combination room *n Brit.* (at Cambridge University) a common room.

combinations (ˌkɒmbɪ'neɪʃənz) *pl n Brit.* a one-piece woollen undergarment with long sleeves and legs. Often shortened to **combs** *or* **coms.** U.S. and Canadian term: **union suit.**

combination tone *n* another term for **resultant tone.**

combinative ('kɒmbɪˌneɪtɪv, -nətɪv), **combinatorial** (ˌkɒmbɪnə'tɔ:rɪəl), *or* **combinatory** ('kɒmbɪnətərɪ, -trɪ) *adj* **1** resulting from being, tending to be, or able to be joined or mixed together. **2** *Linguistics.* (of a sound change) occurring only in specific contexts or as a result of some other factor, such as change of stress within a word. Compare **isolative** (sense 1).

combinatorial analysis *n* the branch of mathematics concerned with the theory of enumeration, or combinations and permutations, in order to solve problems about the possibility of constructing arrangements of objects which satisfy specified conditions. Also called: **combinatorics** (ˌkɒmbɪnə'tɔ:rɪks).

combine *vb* (kəm'baɪn). **1** to integrate or cause to be integrated; join together. **2** to unite or cause to unite to form a chemical compound. **3** *Agriculture.* to harvest (crops) with a combine harvester. ◆ *n* ('kɒmbaɪn). **4** *Agriculture.* short for **combine harvester. 5** an association of enterprises, esp. in order to gain a monopoly of a market. **6** an association of business corporations, political parties, sporting clubs, etc., for a common purpose. [C15: from Late Latin *combīnāre,* from Latin *com-* together + *bīnī* two by two] ▸ **com'binable** *adj* ▸ **comˌbina'bility** *n* ▸ **com'biner** *n*

combine harvester ('kɒmbaɪn) *n* a machine that simultaneously cuts, threshes, and cleans a standing crop of grain.

combings ('kəʊmɪŋz) *pl n* **1** the loose hair, wool, etc., removed by combing, esp. that of animals. **2** the unwanted loose short fibres removed in combing cotton, etc.

combining form *n* a linguistic element that occurs only as part of a compound word, such as *anthropo-* in *anthropology.*

comb jelly *n* another name for a **ctenophore.**

combo ('kɒmbəʊ) *n, pl* **-bos. 1** a small group of musicians, esp. of jazz musicians. **2** *Informal.* any combination.

comb out *vb* (*tr, adv*) **1** to remove (tangles or knots) from (the hair) with a comb. **2** to isolate and remove for a purpose. **3** to survey carefully; examine systematically. ◆ *n* **comb-out. 4** an act of combing out.

combust (kəm'bʌst) *adj* **1** *Astrology.* (of a star or planet) invisible for a period between 24 and 30 days each year due to its proximity to the sun. ◆ *vb* **2** *Chem.* to burn.

combustible (kəm'bʌstəbᵊl) *adj* **1** capable of igniting and burning. **2** easily annoyed; excitable. ◆ *n* **3** a combustible substance. ▸ **comˌbusti'bility** *or* **com'bustibleness** *n* ▸ **com'bustibly** *adv*

combustion (kəm'bʌstʃən) *n* **1** the process of burning. **2** any process in which a substance reacts with oxygen to produce a significant rise in temperature and the emission of light. **3** a chemical process in which two compounds, such as sodium and chlorine, react together to produce heat and light. **4** a process in which a compound reacts slowly with oxygen to produce little heat and no light. [C15: from Old French, from Latin *combūrere* to burn up, from *com-* (intensive) + *ūrere* to burn] ▸ **com'bustive** *n, adj*

combustion chamber *n* an enclosed space in which combustion takes place, such as the space above the piston in the cylinder head of an internal-combustion engine or the chambers in a gas turbine or rocket engine in which fuel and oxidant burn.

combustor (kəm'bʌstə) *n* the combustion system of a jet engine or ramjet, comprising the combustion chamber, the fuel injection apparatus, and the igniter.

comdg *Military. abbrev. for* commanding.

Comdr *Military. abbrev. for* Commander.

Comdt *Military. abbrev. for* Commandant.

come (kʌm) *vb* **comes, coming, came, come.** (*mainly intr*) **1** to move towards a specified person or place: *come to my desk.* **2** to arrive by movement or by making progress. **3** to become perceptible: *light came into the sky.* **4** to occur in the course of time: *Christmas comes but once a year.* **5** to exist or occur at a specific point in a series: *your turn comes next.* **6** to happen as a result: *no good will come of this.* **7** to originate or be derived: *good may come of evil.* **8** to occur to the mind: *the truth suddenly came to me.* **9** to extend or reach: *she comes up to my shoulder.* **10** to be produced or offered: *that dress comes in red only.* **11** to arrive at or be brought into a particular state or condition: *you will soon come to grief; the new timetable comes into effect on Monday.* **12** (foll. by *from*) to be or have been a resident or native (of): *I come from London.* **13** to become: *your wishes will come true.* **14** (*tr; takes an infinitive*) to be given awareness: *I came to realize its enormous value.* **15** (of grain) to germinate. **16** *Taboo slang.* to have an orgasm. **17** (*tr*) *Brit. informal.* to play the part of: *don't come the fine gentleman with me.* **18** (*tr*) *Brit. informal.* to cause or produce: *don't come that nonsense again.* **19** (*subjunctive use*) when (a specified time or event has arrived or begun): *she'll be sixteen come Sunday; come the revolution, you'll be the first to go.* **20 as...as they come.** the most characteristic example of a class or type. **21 come again?** *Informal.* what did you say? **22 come and.** (*imperative or dependent imperative*) to move towards a particular person or thing or accompany a person with some specified purpose: *come and see what I've found.* **23 come clean.** *Informal.* to make a revelation or confession. **24 come good.** *Informal.* to recover and perform well after a bad start or setback. **25 come it.** *Slang.* **25a** to pretend; act a part. **25b** to exaggerate. **25c** (often foll. by *over*) to try to impose (upon). **25d** to divulge a secret; inform the police. **26 come to light.** to be revealed. **27 come to light with.** *Austral. and N.Z. informal.* to find or produce. **28 come to pass.** *Archaic.* to take place. **29 how come?** *Informal.* what is the reason that? ◆ *interj* **30** an exclamation expressing annoyance, irritation, etc.: *come now! come come!* ◆ *n* **31** *Taboo slang.* semen. ◆ See also **come about, come across, come along, come at, come away, comeback, come between, come by, comedown, come forward, come in, come into, come of, come off, come on, come out, come over, come round, come through, come to, come up, come upon.** [Old English *cuman;* related to Old Norse *koma,* Gothic *qiman,* Old High German *queman* to come, Sanskrit *gámati* he goes]

come about *vb* (*intr, adv*) **1** to take place; happen. **2** *Nautical.* to change tacks.

come across *vb* (*intr*) **1** (*prep*) to meet or find by accident. **2** (*adv*) (of a person or his words) to communicate the intended meaning or impression. **3** (often foll. by *with*) to provide what is expected.

come-all-ye (kə'mɔ:ljə, -ji:) *n* a street ballad or folk song. [C19: from the common opening words *come all ye* (*young maidens, loyal heroes, etc.*) ...]

come along *vb* **1** (*intr, adv*) to progress: *how's your French coming along?* **2 come along! 2a** hurry up! **2b** make an effort! ◆ *n* **come-along. 3** *U.S. and Canadian informal.* a hand tool consisting of a ratchet lever, cable, and pulleys, used for moving heavy loads by hand or for tightening wire.

come at *vb* (*intr, prep*) **1** to discover or reach (facts, the truth, etc.). **2** to attack (a person): *he came at me with an axe.* **3** *Austral. slang.* to agree to do (something). **4** (*usually used with a negative*) *Austral. slang.* to stomach, tolerate: *I couldn't come at it.* **5** *Austral. slang.* to presume; impose: *what are you coming at?*

come-at-able *adj* an informal expression for **accessible.**

come away *vb* (*intr, adv*) **1** to become detached. **2** (foll. by *with*) to leave (with).

comeback ('kʌmˌbæk) *n Informal.* **1** a return to a former position, status, etc. **2** a return or response, esp. recriminatory. **3** a quick reply; retort. ◆ *vb* **come back.** (*intr, adv*) **4** to return. **5** to become fashionable again. **6** to reply after a period of consideration: *I'll come back to you on that next week.* **7** *U.S. and Canadian.* to argue back; retort. **8 come back to** (**someone**). (of something forgotten) to return to (someone's) memory.

come between *vb* (*intr, prep*) to cause the estrangement or separation of (two people): *nothing could come between the two lovers.*

come by *vb* (*intr, prep*) to find or obtain (a thing), esp. accidentally: *do you ever come by any old books?*

Comecon ('kɒmɪˌkɒn) *n* (formerly) an association of Soviet-oriented Communist nations, founded in 1949 to coordinate economic development, etc.; it was disbanded in 1991 when free-market policies were adopted by its members. Also: **CMEA.** [C20: *Co(uncil for) M(utual) Econ(omic Assistance)*]

comedian (kə'mi:dɪən) *n* **1** an entertainer who specializes in jokes, comic skits, etc. **2** an actor in comedy. **3** an amusing or entertaining person: sometimes used ironically.

comedic (kə'mi:dɪk) *adj* of or relating to comedy.

Comédie Française *French.* (kɔmedi frɑ̃sɛz) *n* the French national theatre, founded in Paris in 1680.

comedienne (kəˌmi:dɪ'ɛn) *n* a female comedian.

comedo ('kɒmɪˌdəʊ) *n, pl* **comedos** *or* **comedones** (ˌkɒmɪ'dəʊni:z). *Pathol.*

the technical name for **blackhead.** [C19: from New Latin, from Latin: glutton, from *comedere* to eat up, from *com-* (intensive) + *edere* to eat]

comedown ('kʌm,daʊn) *n* **1** a decline in position, status, or prosperity. **2** *Informal.* a disappointment. **3** *Slang.* a depressed or unexcited state. ◆ *vb* **come down.** (*intr, adv*) **4** to come to a place regarded as lower. **5** to lose status, wealth, etc. (esp. in the phrase **to come down in the world**). **6** to reach a decision: *the report came down in favour of a pay increase.* **7** (often foll. by *to*) to be handed down or acquired by tradition or inheritance. **8** *Brit.* to leave college or university. **9** (foll. by *with*) to succumb (to illness or disease). **10** (foll. by *on*) to rebuke or criticize harshly. **11** (foll. by *to*) to amount in essence (to): *it comes down to two choices.* **12** *Slang.* to lose the effects of a drug and return to a normal or more normal state. **13** *Austral. informal.* (of a river) to flow in flood.

comedy ('kɒmɪdɪ) *n, pl* **-dies. 1** a dramatic or other work of light and amusing character. **2** the genre of drama represented by works of this type. **3** (in classical literature) a play in which the main characters and motive triumph over adversity. **4** the humorous aspect of life or of events. **5** an amusing event or sequence of events. **6** humour or comic style: *the comedy of Chaplin.* [C14: from Old French *comédie,* from Latin *cōmoedia,* from Greek *kōmōidia,* from *kōmos* village festival + *aeidein* to sing]

comedy of manners *n* **1** a comedy dealing with the way of life and foibles of a social group. **2** the genre represented by works of this type.

come forward *vb* (*intr, adv*) **1** to offer one's services; volunteer. **2** to present oneself.

come-hither *adj* (*usually prenominal*) *Informal.* alluring; seductive: *a come-hither look.*

come in *vb* (*intr, mainly adv*) **1** to enter, used in the imperative when admitting a person. **2** to prove to be: *it came in useful.* **3** to become fashionable or seasonable. **4** *Cricket.* to begin an innings. **5** *Athletics, horse racing, etc.* to finish a race (in a certain position). **6** (of a politician or political party) to win an election. **7** *Radio, television.* to be received: *news is coming in of a big fire in Glasgow.* **8** (of money) to be received as income. **9** to play a role; advance one's interests: *where do I come in?* **10** (foll. by *for*) to be the object of: *the Chancellor came in for a lot of criticism in the Commons.*

come into *vb* (*intr, prep*) **1** to enter. **2** to inherit. **3 come into one's own.** to become fulfilled: *she really came into her own when she got divorced.*

comely ('kʌmlɪ) *adj* **-lier, -liest.** good-looking; attractive. [Old English *cȳmlīc* beautiful; related to Old High German *cūmi* frail, Middle High German *komlīche* suitably] ▸ **'comeliness** *n*

Comenius (kə'meɪnɪəs) *n* **John Amos,** Czech name *Jan Amos Komensky.* 1592–1670, Czech educational reformer.

come of *vb* (*intr, prep*) **1** to be descended from. **2** to result from: *nothing came of his experiments.*

come off *vb* (*intr, mainly adv*) **1** (*also prep*) to fall (from), losing one's balance. **2** to become detached or be capable of being detached. **3** (*prep*) to be removed from (a price, tax, etc.): *will anything come off income tax in the budget?* **4** (*copula*) to emerge from or as if from a trial or contest: *he came off the winner.* **5** *Informal.* to take place or happen. **6** *Informal.* to have the intended effect; succeed: *his jokes did not come off.* **7** *Taboo slang.* to have an orgasm. **8 come off it!** *Informal.* stop trying to fool me!

come on *vb* (*intr, mainly adv*) **1** (of power, a water supply, etc.) to become available; start running or functioning. **2** to make or show progress; develop: *my plants are coming on nicely.* **3** to advance, esp. in battle. **4** to begin: *she felt a cold coming on; a new bowler has come on.* **5** *Theatre.* to make an entrance on stage. **6** to be considered, esp. in a court of law. **7** (*prep*) See **come upon. 8 come on! 8a** hurry up! **8b** cheer up! pull yourself together! **8c** make an effort! **8d** don't exaggerate! stick to the facts! **9** to attempt to give a specified impression: *he came on like a hard man.* **10 come on strong.** to make a forceful or exaggerated impression. **11 come on to.** *Informal.* to make sexual advances to. ◆ *n* **come-on. 12** *Informal.* anything that serves as a lure or enticement.

come out *vb* (*intr, adv*) **1** to be made public or revealed: *the news of her death came out last week.* **2** to make a debut in society or on stage. **3a** Also: **come out of the closet.** to declare openly that one is a homosexual. **3b** to reveal or declare any habit or practice formerly concealed. **4** *Chiefly Brit.* to go on strike. **5** to declare oneself: *the government came out in favour of scrapping the project.* **6** to be shown visibly or clearly: *you came out very well in the photos.* **7** to yield a satisfactory solution: *these sums just won't come out.* **8** to be published: *the paper comes out on Fridays.* **9** (foll. by *in*) to become covered with: *you're coming out in spots.* **10** (foll. by *with*) to speak or declare openly: *you can rely on him to come out with the facts.*

come over *vb* (*intr*) **1** (*adv*) (of a person or his words) to communicate the intended meaning or impression: *he came over very well.* **2** (*adv*) to change allegiances: *some people came over to our side in the war.* **3** *Informal.* to undergo or feel a particular sensation: *I came over funny.* ◆ *n* **comeover. 4** (in the Isle of Man) a person who has come over from the mainland of Britain to settle.

comer ('kʌmə) *n* **1** (*in combination*) a person who comes: *all-comers; newcomers.* **2** *Informal.* a potential success.

come round *or* **around** *vb* (*intr, adv*) **1** to be restored to life or consciousness. **2** to change or modify one's mind or opinion.

comestible (kə'mɛstɪbᵊl) *n* **1** (*usually pl*) food. ◆ *adj* **2** a rare word for **edible.** [C15: from Late Latin *comestibilis,* from *comedere* to eat up; see COMEDO]

comet ('kɒmɪt) *n* a celestial body that travels around the sun, usually in a highly elliptical orbit: thought to consist of a solid frozen nucleus part of which vaporizes on approaching the sun to form a gaseous luminous coma and a long luminous tail. [C13: from Old French *comète,* from Latin *comēta,* from Greek *komētēs* long-haired, from *komē* hair] ▸ **'cometary** *or* **cometic** (kɒ'mɛtɪk) *adj*

come through *vb* (*intr*) **1** (*adv*) to emerge successfully. **2** (*prep*) to survive (an illness, setback, etc.).

come to *vb* (*intr*) **1** (*adv* or *prep and reflexive*) to regain consciousness or return to one's normal state. **2** (*adv*) *Nautical.* to slow a vessel or bring her to a stop. **3** (*prep*) to amount to (a sum of money): *your bill comes to four pounds.* **4** (*prep*) to arrive at (a certain state): *what is the world coming to?*

come up *vb* (*intr, adv*) **1** to come to a place regarded as higher. **2** (of the sun) to rise. **3** to begin: *a wind came up.* **4** to be regurgitated or vomited. **5** to present itself or be discussed: *that question will come up again.* **6** *Brit.* to begin a term, esp. one's first term, at a college or university. **7** to appear from out of the ground: *my beans have come up early this year.* **8** *Informal.* to win: *have your premium bonds ever come up?* **9 come up against.** to be faced with; come into conflict or competition with. **10 come up to.** to equal or meet a standard: *that just doesn't come up to scratch.* **11 come up with.** to produce or find: *she always comes up with the right answer.*

come upon *vb* (*intr, prep*) to meet or encounter unexpectedly: *I came upon an old friend in the street today.*

comeuppance (,kʌm'ʌpəns) *n Informal.* just retribution. [C19: from *come up* (in the sense: to appear before a judge or court for judgment)]

comfit ('kʌmfɪt, 'kɒm-) *n* a sugar-coated sweet containing a nut or seed. [C15: from Old French, from Latin *confectum* something prepared, from *conficere* to produce; see CONFECT]

comfort ('kʌmfət) *n* **1** a state of ease or well-being. **2** relief from affliction, grief, etc. **3** a person, thing, or event that brings solace or ease. **4** *Obsolete.* support. **5** (*usually pl*) something that affords physical ease and relaxation. ◆ *vb* (*tr*) **6** to ease the pain of; soothe; cheer. **7** to bring physical ease to. [C13: from Old French *confort,* from Late Latin *confortāre* to strengthen very much, from Latin *con-* (intensive) + *fortis* strong] ▸ **'comforting** *adj* ▸ **'comfortingly** *adv* ▸ **'comfortless** *adj* ▸ **'comfortlessly** *adv* ▸ **'comfortlessness** *n*

comfortable ('kʌmftəbᵊl, 'kʌmfətəbᵊl) *adj* **1** giving comfort or physical relief. **2** at ease. **3** free from affliction or pain. **4** (of a person or situation) relaxing. **5** *Informal.* having adequate income. **6** *Informal.* (of income) adequate to provide comfort. ▸ **'comfortableness** *n* ▸ **'comfortably** *adv*

comforter ('kʌmfətə) *n* **1** a person or thing that comforts. **2** *Chiefly Brit.* a woollen scarf. **3** a baby's dummy. **4** *U.S.* a quilted bed covering.

Comforter ('kʌmfətə) *n Christianity.* an epithet of the Holy Spirit. [C14: translation of Latin *consolātor,* representing Greek *paraklētos;* see PARACLETE]

comfort station *n U.S.* a public lavatory and rest room.

comfort zone *n* a situation or position in which a person feels secure, comfortable, or in control: *women are forcing men out of the comfort zone.*

comfrey ('kʌmfrɪ) *n* any hairy Eurasian boraginaceous plant of the genus *Symphytum,* having blue, purplish-pink, or white flowers. [C15: from Old French *cunfirie,* from Latin *conferva* water plant; see CONFERVA]

comfy ('kʌmfɪ) *adj* **-fier, -fiest.** *Informal.* short for **comfortable.**

comic ('kɒmɪk) *adj* **1** of, relating to, characterized by, or characteristic of comedy. **2** (*prenominal*) acting in, writing, or composing comedy: *a comic writer.* **3** humorous; funny. ◆ *n* **4** a person who is comic, esp. a comic actor; comedian. **5** a book or magazine containing comic strips. **6** (*usually pl*) *Chiefly U.S. and Canadian.* comic strips in newspapers, etc. [C16: from Latin *cōmicus,* from Greek *kōmikos* relating to COMEDY]

comical ('kɒmɪkᵊl) *adj* **1** causing laughter. **2** ludicrous; laughable. ▸ **'comically** *adv* ▸ **'comicalness** *n*

comic opera *n* a play largely set to music, employing comic effects or situations. See also **opéra bouffe, opera buffa.**

comic strip *n* a sequence of drawings in a newspaper, magazine, etc., relating a humorous story or an adventure. Also called: **strip cartoon.**

Comines *or* **Commines** (*French* kɔmin) *n* **Philippe de** (filip də). ?1447–?1511, French diplomat and historian, noted for his *Mémoires* (1489–98).

Cominform ('kɒmɪn,fɔːm) *n* short for **Communist Information Bureau:** established 1947 to exchange information among nine European Communist parties and coordinate their activities; dissolved in 1956.

coming ('kʌmɪŋ) *adj* **1** (*prenominal*) (of time, events, etc.) approaching or next: *this coming Thursday.* **2** promising (esp. in the phrase **up and coming**). **3** of future importance: *this is the coming thing.* **4 coming up!** *Informal.* an expression used to announce that a meal is about to be served. **5 have it coming to one.** *Informal.* to deserve what one is about to suffer. **6 not know whether one is coming or going.** to be totally confused. ◆ *n* **7** arrival or approach. **8** (*often cap.*) the return of Christ in glory. See also **Second Coming.**

Comintern *or* **Komintern** ('kɒmɪn,tɜːn) *n* short for **Communist International;** an international Communist organization founded by Lenin in Moscow in 1919 and dissolved in 1943; it degenerated under Stalin into an instrument of Soviet politics. Also called: **Third International.**

comitia (kə'mɪʃɪə) *n* an ancient Roman assembly that elected officials and exercised judicial and legislative authority. [C17: from Latin *comitium* assembly, from *com-* together + *īre* to go] ▸ **comitial** (kə'mɪʃəl) *adj*

comity ('kɒmɪtɪ) *n, pl* **-ties. 1** mutual civility; courtesy. **2** short for **comity of nations. 3** the policy whereby one religious denomination refrains from proselytizing the members of another. [C16: from Latin *cōmitās,* from *cōmis* affable, obliging, of uncertain origin]

comity of nations *n* the friendly recognition accorded by one nation to the laws and usages of another.

comm. *abbrev. for:* **1** commerce. **2** commercial. **3** committee. **4** commonwealth.

comma ('kɒmə) *n* **1** the punctuation mark , indicating a slight pause in the spoken sentence and used where there is a listing of items or to separate a nonrestrictive clause or phrase from a main clause. **2** *Music.* a minute interval. **3** short for **comma butterfly.** [C16: from Latin, from Greek *komma* clause, from *koptein* to cut]

comma bacillus *n* a comma-shaped bacterium, *Vibrio comma,* that causes cholera in man: family *Spirillaceae.*

comma butterfly *n* an orange-brown European vanessid butterfly, *Polygonia c-album,* with a white comma-shaped mark on the underside of each hind wing.

command (kəˈmɑːnd) *vb* **1** (when *tr, may take a clause as object or an infinitive*) to order, require, or compel. **2** to have or be in control or authority over (a person, situation, etc.). **3** (*tr*) to have knowledge or use of: *he commands the language.* **4** (*tr*) to receive as due or because of merit: *his nature commands respect.* **5** to dominate (a view, etc.) as from a height. ◆ *n* **6** an order; mandate. **7** the act of commanding. **8** the power or right to command. **9** the exercise of the power to command. **10** ability or knowledge; control: *a command of French.* **11** *Chiefly military.* the jurisdiction of a commander. **12** a military unit or units commanding a specific area or function, as in the RAF. **13** *Brit.* **13a** an invitation from the monarch. **13b** (*as modifier*): *a command performance.* **14** *Computing.* a word or phrase that can be selected from a menu or typed after a prompt in order to carry out an action. [C13: from Old French *commander,* from Latin *com-* (intensive) + *mandāre* to entrust, enjoin, command]

commandant (ˈkɒmənˌdænt, -ˌdɑːnt) *n* an officer commanding a place, group, or establishment.

command economy *n* an economy in which business activities and the allocation of resources are determined by government order rather than market forces. Also called: **planned economy.**

commandeer (ˌkɒmənˈdɪə) *vb* (*tr*) **1** to seize for public or military use. **2** to seize arbitrarily. [C19: from Afrikaans *kommandeer,* from French *commander* to COMMAND]

commander (kəˈmɑːndə) *n* **1** an officer in command of a military formation or operation. **2** a naval commissioned rank junior to captain but senior to lieutenant commander. **3** the second in command of larger British warships. **4** someone who holds authority. **5** a high-ranking member of some knightly or fraternal orders. **6** an officer responsible for a district of the Metropolitan Police in London. **7** *History.* the administrator of a house, priory, or landed estate of a medieval religious order. ▸ **comˈmanderˌship** *n*

commander in chief *n, pl* **commanders in chief. 1** the officer holding supreme command of the forces in an area or operation. **2** the officer holding command of a major subdivision of one military service.

command guidance *n* a method of controlling a missile during flight by transmitting information to it.

commanding (kəˈmɑːndɪŋ) *adj* (*usually prenominal*) **1** being in command. **2** having the air of authority: *a commanding voice.* **3** (of a position, situation, etc.) exerting control. **4** (of a height, viewpoint, etc.) overlooking; advantageous. ▸ **comˈmandingly** *adv*

commanding officer *n* an officer in command of a military unit.

command language *n Computing.* the language used to access a computer system.

commandment (kəˈmɑːndmənt) *n* **1** a divine command, esp. one of the Ten Commandments of the Old Testament. **2** *Literary.* any command.

command module *n* the cone-shaped module used as the living quarters in an Apollo spacecraft and functioning as the splashdown vehicle.

commando (kəˈmɑːndəʊ) *n, pl* **-dos** *or* **-does. 1a** an amphibious military unit trained for raiding. **1b** a member of such a unit. **2** the basic unit of the Royal Marine Corps. **3** (originally) an armed force raised by Boers during the Boer War. **4** (*modifier*) denoting or relating to a commando or force of commandos: *a commando raid; a commando unit.* [C19: from Afrikaans *kommando,* from Dutch *commando* command, from French *commander* to COMMAND]

commando operation *n Surgery.* a major operation for treatment of cancer of the head and neck, involving removal of many facial structures and subsequent surgical reconstruction.

command paper *n* (in Britain) a government document that is presented to Parliament, in theory by royal command. See also **green paper, white paper.**

command performance *n* a performance of a play, opera, etc., at the request of a ruler or of royalty.

command post *n Military.* the position from which a unit commander and his staff exercise command.

commeasure (kəˈmɛʒə) *vb* (*tr*) to coincide with in degree, extent, quality, etc. ▸ **comˈmeasurable** *adj*

commedia dell'arte (*Italian* kɔmˈmeːdia delˈlarte) *n* a form of popular comedy developed in Italy during the 16th to 18th centuries, with stock characters such as Punchinello, Harlequin, and Columbine, in situations improvised from a plot outline. [Italian, literally: comedy of art]

comme il faut *French.* (kɔm il fo) correct or correctly.

commemorate (kəˈmɛməˌreɪt) *vb* (*tr*) to honour or keep alive the memory of. [C16: from Latin *commemorāre* be mindful of, from *com-* (intensive) + *memorāre* to remind, from *memor* mindful] ▸ **comˈmemorative** *or* **comˈmemoratory** *adj* ▸ **comˈmemoratively** *adv* ▸ **comˈmemoˌrator** *n*

commemoration (kəˌmɛməˈreɪʃən) *n* **1** the act or an instance of commemorating. **2** a ceremony or service in memory of a person or event. ▸ **comˌmemoˈrational** *adj*

commence (kəˈmɛns) *vb* to start or begin; come or cause to come into being, operation, etc. [C14: from Old French *comencer,* from Vulgar Latin *cominitiāre* (unattested), from Latin *com-* (intensive) + *initiāre* to begin, from *initium* a beginning] ▸ **comˈmencer** *n*

commencement (kəˈmɛnsmənt) *n* **1** the beginning; start. **2a** *U.S. and Canadian.* a ceremony for the presentation of awards at secondary schools. **2b** *U.S.* a ceremony for the conferment of academic degrees.

commend (kəˈmɛnd) *vb* (*tr*) **1** to present or represent as being worthy of regard, confidence, kindness, etc.; recommend. **2** to give in charge; entrust. **3** to express a good opinion of; praise. **4** to give the regards of: *commend me to your aunt.* [C14: from Latin *commendāre* to commit to someone's care, from *com-* (intensive) + *mandāre* to entrust] ▸ **comˈmendable** *adj* ▸ **comˈmendableness** *n* ▸ **comˈmendably** *adv* ▸ **comˈmendatory** *adj*

commendam (kəˈmɛndæm) *n* **1** the temporary holding of an ecclesiastical benefice. **2** a benefice so held. [C16: from Medieval Latin phrase *dare in commendam* to give in trust, from *commenda* trust, back formation from Latin *commendāre* to entrust, COMMEND]

commendation (ˌkɒmɛnˈdeɪʃən) *n* **1** the act or an instance of commending; praise. **2** an award.

commensal (kəˈmɛnsəl) *adj* **1** (of two different species of plant or animal) living in close association without being interdependent. **2** *Rare.* of or relating to eating together, esp. at the same table: *commensal pleasures.* ◆ *n* **3** a commensal plant or animal. **4** *Rare.* a companion at table. [C14: from Medieval Latin *commensālis,* from Latin *com-* together + *mensa* table] ▸ **comˈmensalism** *n* ▸ **commensality** (ˌkɒmɛnˈsælɪtɪ) *n* ▸ **comˈmensally** *adv*

commensurable (kəˈmɛnsərəbəl, -ʃə-) *adj* **1** *Maths.* **1a** having a common factor. **1b** having units of the same dimensions and being related by whole numbers: *hours and minutes are commensurable.* **2** well-proportioned; proportionate. ▸ **comˌmensuraˈbility** *n* ▸ **comˈmensurably** *adv*

commensurate (kəˈmɛnsərɪt, -ʃə-) *adj* **1** having the same extent or duration. **2** corresponding in degree, amount, or size; proportionate. **3** able to be measured by a common standard; commensurable. [C17: from Late Latin *commēnsūrātus,* from Latin *com-* same + *mēnsurāre* to MEASURE] ▸ **comˈmensurately** *adv* ▸ **comˈmensurateness** *n* ▸ **commensuration** (kəˌmɛnsəˈreɪʃən, -ʃə-) *n*

comment (ˈkɒmɛnt) *n* **1** a remark, criticism, or observation. **2** talk or gossip. **3** a note explaining or criticizing a passage in a text. **4** explanatory or critical matter added to a text. ◆ *vb* **5** (when *intr,* often foll. by *on;* when *tr,* takes a clause as object) to remark or express an opinion. **6** (*intr*) to write notes explaining or criticizing a text. [C15: from Latin *commentum* invention, from *comminiscī* to contrive, related to *mens* mind] ▸ **ˈcommenter** *n*

commentary (ˈkɒməntərɪ, -trɪ) *n, pl* **-taries. 1** an explanatory series of notes or comments. **2** a spoken accompaniment to a broadcast, film, etc., esp. of a sporting event. **3** an explanatory essay or treatise on a text. **4** (*usually pl*) a personal record of events or facts: *the commentaries of Caesar.* ▸ **commentarial** (ˌkɒmənˈtɛərɪəl) *adj*

commentate (ˈkɒmənˌteɪt) *vb* **1** (*intr*) to serve as a commentator. **2** (*tr*) *U.S.* to make a commentary on (a text, event, etc.).

USAGE The verb *commentate,* derived from *commentator,* is sometimes used as a synonym for *comment on* or *provide a commentary for.* It is not yet fully accepted as standard, though widespread in sports reporting and journalism.

commentator (ˈkɒmənˌteɪtə) *n* **1** a person who provides a spoken commentary for a broadcast, film, etc., esp. of a sporting event. **2** a person who writes notes on a text, event, etc.

commerce (ˈkɒmɜːs) *n* **1** the activity embracing all forms of the purchase and sale of goods and services. **2** social relations and exchange, esp. of opinions, attitudes, etc. [C16: from Latin *commercium* trade, from *commercārī,* from *mercārī* to trade, from *merx* merchandise]

commercial (kəˈmɜːʃəl) *adj* **1** of, connected with, or engaged in commerce; mercantile. **2** sponsored or paid for by an advertiser: *commercial television.* **3** having profit as the main aim: *commercial music.* **4** (of goods, chemicals, etc.) of unrefined quality or presentation and produced in bulk for use in industry. ◆ *n* **5** a commercially sponsored advertisement on radio or television. ▸ **commerciality** (kəˌmɜːʃɪˈælɪtɪ) *n* ▸ **comˈmercially** *adv*

commercial art *n* graphic art for commercial uses such as advertising, packaging, etc. ▸ **commercial artist** *n*

commercial bank *n* a bank primarily engaged in making short-term loans from funds deposited in current accounts.

commercial break *n* an interruption in a radio or television programme for the broadcasting of advertisements.

commercial college *n* a college providing tuition in commercial skills, such as shorthand and book-keeping.

commercialism (kəˈmɜːʃəˌlɪzəm) *n* **1** the spirit, principles, or procedure of commerce. **2** exclusive or inappropriate emphasis on profit. ▸ **comˈmercialist** *n* ▸ **comˌmercialˈistic** *adj*

commercialize *or* **commercialise** (kəˈmɜːʃəˌlaɪz) *vb* (*tr*) **1** to make commercial in aim, methods, or character. **2** to exploit for profit, esp. at the expense of quality. ▸ **comˌmercialiˈzation** *or* **comˌmercialiˈsation** *n*

commercial paper *n* a short-term negotiable document, such as a bill of exchange, promissory note, etc., calling for the transference of a specified sum of money at a designated date.

commercial traveller *n* another name for a **travelling salesman.**

commercial vehicle *n* a vehicle for carrying goods or (less commonly) passengers.

commère (ˈkɒmɛə; *French* kɔmɛr) *n* a female compere. [French, literally: godmother, from COM- + *mère* mother; see COMPERE]

commie *or* **commy** (ˈkɒmɪ) *n, pl* **-mies,** *adj Informal and derogatory.* short for **communist.**

commination (ˌkɒmɪˈneɪʃən) *n* **1** the act or an instance of threatening punishment or vengeance. **2** *Church of England.* a recital of prayers, including a list of God's judgments against sinners, in the office for Ash Wednesday. [C15: from Latin *comminātiō,* from *comminārī* to menace, from *com-* (intensive) + *minārī* to threaten] ▸ **comminatory** (ˈkɒmɪnətərɪ, -trɪ) *adj*

Commines (*French* kɔmin) *n* a variant spelling of (Philippe de) **Comines.**

commingle (kɒˈmɪŋgəl) *vb* to mix or be mixed; blend.

comminute (ˈkɒmɪˌnjuːt) *vb* **1** to break (a bone) into several small fragments. **2** to divide (property) into small lots. **3** (*tr*) to pulverize. [C17: from Latin *com-*

minuere, from *com-* (intensive) + *minuere* to reduce; related to MINOR] ▸ ˌcommiˈnution *n*

comminuted fracture *n* a fracture in which the bone is splintered or fragmented.

commis (ˈkɒmɪs, ˈkɒmɪ) *n, pl* **-mis.** **1** an agent or deputy. ◆ *adj* **2** (of a waiter or chef) apprentice. [C16 (meaning: deputy): from French, from *commettre* to employ, COMMIT]

commiserate (kəˈmɪzəˌreɪt) *vb* (when *intr,* usually foll. by *with*) to feel or express sympathy or compassion (for). [C17: from Latin *commiserārī,* from *com-* together + *miserārī* to bewail, pity, from *miser* wretched] ▸ **comˈmiserable** *adj* ▸ **comˌmiserˈation** *n* ▸ **comˈmiserative** *adj* ▸ **comˈmiseratively** *adv* ▸ **comˈmiserˌator** *n*

commissaire (ˌkɒmɪˈsɛə) *n* (in professional cycle racing) a referee who travels in an open-topped car with the riders to witness any infringement of the rules. [from French: see COMMISSARY]

commissar (ˈkɒmɪˌsɑː, ˌkɒmɪˈsɑː) *n* (in the former Soviet Union) **1** Also called: **political commissar.** an official of the Communist Party responsible for political education, esp. in a military unit. **2** Also called: **People's Commissar.** (before 1946) the head of a government department. Now called: **minister.** [C20: from Russian *kommissar,* from German, from Medieval Latin *commissārius* COMMISSARY]

commissariat (ˌkɒmɪˈsɛərɪət) *n* **1** (in the former Soviet Union) a government department before 1946. Now called: **ministry. 2a** a military department in charge of food supplies, equipment, etc. **2b** the offices of such a department. **3** food supplies. [C17: from New Latin *commissāriātus,* from Medieval Latin *commissārius* COMMISSARY]

commissary (ˈkɒmɪsərɪ) *n, pl* **-saries. 1** *U.S.* a shop supplying food or equipment, as in a military camp. **2** *U.S. army.* an officer responsible for supplies and food. **3** *U.S.* a snack bar or restaurant in a film studio. **4** a representative or deputy, esp. an official representative of a bishop. [C14: from Medieval Latin *commissārius* official in charge, from Latin *committere* to entrust, COMMIT] ▸ **commissarial** (ˌkɒmɪˈsɛərɪəl) *adj* ▸ **ˈcommissaryˌship** *n*

commission (kəˈmɪʃən) *n* **1** a duty or task committed to a person or group to perform. **2** authority to undertake or perform certain duties or functions. **3** a document granting such authority. **4** *Military.* **4a** a document conferring a rank on an officer. **4b** the rank or authority thereby granted. **5** a group of people charged with certain duties: *a commission of inquiry.* **6** a government agency or board empowered to exercise administrative, judicial, or legislative authority. See also **Royal Commission. 7a** the authority given to a person or organization to act as an agent to a principal in commercial transactions. **7b** the fee allotted to an agent for services rendered. **8** the state of being charged with specific duties or responsibilities. **9** the act of committing a sin, crime, etc. **10** something, esp. a sin, crime, etc., that is committed. **11** good working condition or (esp. of a ship) active service (esp. in the phrases **in** *or* **into commission, out of commission**). **12** *U.S.* the head of a department of municipal government. ◆ *vb* **13** (*tr*) to grant authority to; charge with a duty or task. **14** (*tr*) *Military.* to confer a rank on or authorize an action by. **15** (*tr*) to equip and test (a ship) for active service. **16** to make or become operative or operable: *the plant is due to commission next year.* **17** (*tr*) to place an order for (something): *to commission a portrait.* [C14: from Old French, from Latin *commissiō* a bringing together, from *committere* to COMMIT] ▸ **comˈmissional** *or* **comˈmissionary** *adj*

commissionaire (kəˌmɪʃəˈnɛə) *n Chiefly Brit.* a uniformed doorman at a hotel, theatre, etc. [C18: from French, from COMMISSION]

commissioned officer *n* a military officer holding a commission, such as Second Lieutenant in the British Army, Acting Sub-Lieutenant in the Royal Navy, Pilot Officer in the Royal Air Force, and officers of all ranks senior to these.

commissioner (kəˈmɪʃənə) *n* **1** a person authorized to perform certain tasks or endowed with certain powers. **2** *Government.* **2a** any of several types of civil servant. **2b** an ombudsman. ◆ See also **Health Service Commissioner, Parliamentary Commissioner. 3** a member of a commission. ▸ **comˈmissionerˌship** *n*

Commissioner for Local Administration *n* (in Britain) the official name for a local ombudsman who investigates personal complaints of maladministration by police, water, or local authorities, referred through a local-government councillor, and who can require the offending authority to state its intention to make redress.

commissioner for oaths *n* a solicitor authorized to authenticate oaths on sworn statements.

Commission for Racial Equality *n* (in Britain) a body of fourteen members appointed by the Home Secretary under the Race Relations Act 1976 to enforce the provisions of that Act. Abbrev.: **CRE.**

commission plan *n* (in the U.S.) a system of municipal government that combines legislative and executive authority in a commission of five or six elected members.

commissure (ˈkɒmɪˌsjʊə) *n* **1** a band of tissue linking two parts or organs, such as the nervous tissue connecting the right and left sides of the brain in vertebrates. **2** any of various joints between parts, as between the carpels, leaf lobes, etc., of a plant. [C15: from Latin *commissūra* a joining together, from *committere* COMMIT] ▸ **commissural** (kəˈmɪsjʊrəl, ˌkɒmɪˈsjʊərəl) *adj*

commit (kəˈmɪt) *vb* **-mits, -mitting, -mitted.** (*tr*) **1** to hand over, as for safekeeping; charge; entrust: *to commit a child to the care of its aunt.* **2 commit to memory.** to learn by heart; memorize. **3** to confine officially or take into custody: *to commit someone to prison.* **4** (*usually passive*) to pledge or align (oneself), as to a particular cause, action, or attitude: *a committed radical.* **5** to order (forces) into action. **6** to perform (a crime, error, etc.); do; perpetrate. **7** to surrender, esp. for destruction: *she committed the letter to the fire.* **8** to refer (a bill, etc.) to a committee of a legislature. [C14: from Latin *committere* to join, from *com-* together + *mittere* to put, send] ▸ **comˈmittable** *adj* ▸ **comˈmitter** *n*

commitment (kəˈmɪtmənt) *n* **1** the act of committing or pledging. **2** the state of being committed or pledged. **3** an obligation, promise, etc. that restricts one's freedom of action. **4** the referral of a bill to a committee or legislature. **5** Also called (esp. formerly): **mittimus.** *Law.* a written order of a court directing that a person be imprisoned. **6** the official consignment of a person to a mental hospital or prison. **7** commission or perpetration, esp. of a crime. **8** a future financial obligation or contingent liability. ◆ Also called (esp. for senses 5 and 6): **committal** (kəˈmɪtᵊl).

commitment fee *n* a charge made by a bank, in addition to interest, to make a loan available to a potential borrower.

committed facility *n* an agreement by a bank to provide a customer with funds up to a specified limit at a specified rate of interest.

committee *n* **1** (kəˈmɪtɪ). a group of people chosen or appointed to perform a specified service or function. **2** (ˌkɒmɪˈtiː). (formerly) a person to whom the care of a mentally incompetent person or his property was entrusted by a court. See also **receiver** (sense 2). [C15: from *committen* to entrust + -EE]

committeeman (kəˈmɪtɪmən, -ˌmæn) *n, pl* **-men.** *Chiefly U.S.* a member of one or more committees. ▸ **comˈmitteeˌwoman** *fem n*

Committee of the Whole House *n* (in Britain) an informal sitting of the House of Commons to discuss and amend a bill.

commix (kɒˈmɪks) *vb* a rare word for **mix.** [C15: back formation from *commixt* mixed together; see MIX] ▸ **comˈmixture** *n*

commo (ˈkɒməʊ) *n, pl* **-mos,** *adj Austral. slang.* short for **communist.**

commode (kəˈməʊd) *n* **1** a piece of furniture, usually highly ornamented, containing drawers or shelves. **2** a bedside table with a cabinet below for a chamber pot or washbasin. **3** a movable piece of furniture, sometimes in the form of a chair, with a hinged flap concealing a chamber pot. **4** a woman's high-tiered headdress of lace, worn in the late 17th century. [C17: from French, from Latin *commodus* COMMODIOUS]

commodious (kəˈməʊdɪəs) *adj* **1** (of buildings, rooms, etc.) large and roomy; spacious. **2** *Archaic.* suitable; convenient. [C15: from Medieval Latin *commodiōsus,* from Latin *commodus* convenient, from *com-* with + *modus* measure] ▸ **comˈmodiously** *adv* ▸ **comˈmodiousness** *n*

commodity (kəˈmɒdɪtɪ) *n, pl* **-ties. 1** an article of commerce. **2** something of use, advantage, or profit. **3** *Economics.* an exchangeable unit of economic wealth, esp. a primary product or raw material. **4** *Obsolete.* **4a** a quantity of goods. **4b** convenience or expediency. [C14: from Old French *commodité,* from Latin *commoditās* suitability, benefit; see COMMODIOUS]

commodore (ˈkɒməˌdɔː) *n* **1** *Brit.* a naval rank junior to rear admiral and senior to captain. **2** the senior captain of a shipping line. **3** the officer in command of a convoy of merchant ships. **4** the titular head of a yacht or boat club. [C17: probably from Dutch *commandeur,* from French, from Old French *commander* to COMMAND]

Commodus (kəˈməʊdəs, ˈkɒmədəs) *n* **Lucius Aelius Aurelius** (ˈluːsɪəs ˈiːlɪəs ɔːˈriːlɪəs), son of Marcus Aurelius. 161–192 A.D., Roman emperor (180–192), noted for his tyrannical reign.

common (ˈkɒmən) *adj* **1** belonging to or shared by two or more people: *common property.* **2** belonging to or shared by members of one or more nations or communities; public: *a common culture.* **3** of ordinary standard; average: *common decency.* **4** prevailing; widespread: *common opinion.* **5** widely known or frequently encountered; ordinary: *a common brand of soap.* **6** widely known and notorious: *a common nuisance.* **7** *Derogatory.* considered by the speaker to be low-class, vulgar, or coarse: *a common accent.* **8** (*prenominal*) having no special distinction, rank, or status: *the common man.* **9** *Maths.* **9a** having a specified relationship with a group of numbers or quantities: *common denominator.* **9b** (of a tangent) tangential to two or more circles. **10** *Prosody.* (of a syllable) able to be long or short, or (in nonquantitative verse) stressed or unstressed. **11** *Grammar.* (in certain languages) denoting or belonging to a gender of nouns, esp. one that includes both masculine and feminine referents: *Latin* sacerdos *is common.* **12** *Anatomy.* **12a** having branches: *the common carotid artery.* **12b** serving more than one function: *the common bile duct.* **13** *Christianity.* of or relating to the common of the Mass or divine office. **14 common or garden.** *Informal.* ordinary; unexceptional. ◆ *n* **15** (*sometimes pl*) a tract of open public land, esp. one now used as a recreation area. **16** *Law.* the right to go onto someone else's property and remove natural products, as by pasturing cattle or fishing (esp. in the phrase **right of common**). **17** *Christianity.* **17a** a form of the proper of the Mass used on festivals that have no special proper of their own. **17b** the ordinary of the Mass. **18** *Archaic.* the ordinary people; the public, esp. those undistinguished by rank or title. **19 in common.** mutually held or used with another or others. ◆ See also **commons.** [C13: from Old French *commun,* from Latin *commūnis* general, universal] ▸ **ˈcommonness** *n*

commonable (ˈkɒmənəbᵊl) *adj* **1** (of land) held in common. **2** *English history.* (esp. of sheep and cattle) entitled to be pastured on common land.

commonage (ˈkɒmənɪdʒ) *n* **1** *Chiefly law.* **1a** the use of something, esp. a pasture, in common with others. **1b** the right to such use. **2** the state of being held in common. **3** something held in common, such as land. **4** another word for **commonalty** (sense 1).

commonality (ˌkɒməˈnælɪtɪ) *n, pl* **-ties. 1** the fact of being common to more than one individual; commonness. **2** another word for **commonalty** (sense 1).

commonalty (ˈkɒmənəltɪ) *n, pl* **-ties. 1** the ordinary people as distinct from those with authority, rank, or title, esp. when considered as a political and social unit or estate of the realm. Compare **third estate. 2** the members of an incorporated society. [C13: from Old French *comunalte,* from *comunal* communal]

common carrier *n* a person or firm engaged in the business of transporting goods or passengers.
common chord *n Music.* a chord consisting of the keynote, a major or minor third, and a perfect fifth: *the notes G, B, and D form the common chord of G major.*
common cold *n* a mild viral infection of the upper respiratory tract, characterized by sneezing, coughing, watery eyes, nasal congestion, etc.
common denominator *n* **1** an integer exactly divisible by each denominator of a group of fractions: 1/3, 1/4, and 1/6 have a common denominator of 12. **2** a belief, attribute, etc., held in common by members of a class or group.
common divisor *n* another name for **common factor.**
Common Entrance *n* (in Britain) an entrance examination for a public school, usually taken at the age of 13.
commoner ('kɒmənə) *n* **1** a person who does not belong to the nobility. **2** a person who has a right in or over common land jointly with another or others. **3** *Brit.* a student at a university or other institution who is not on a scholarship.
Common Era *n* another name for **Christian Era.**
common factor *n* a number or quantity that is a factor of each member of a group of numbers or quantities: *5 is a common factor of 15 and 20.* Also called: **common divisor.**
common fee *n* (in Australia) the agreed usual charge for any medical service, which determines the amount of reimbursement under the federal health scheme.
common fraction *n* another name for **simple fraction.**
common good *n* the part of the property of a Scottish burgh, in the form of land or funds, that is at the disposal of the community.
common ground *n* an agreed basis, accepted by both or all parties, for identifying issues in an argument.
common knowledge *n* something widely or generally known.
common law *n* **1** the body of law based on judicial decisions and custom, as distinct from statute law. **2** the law of a state that is of general application, as distinct from regional customs. **3 common-law.** (*modifier*) denoting a marriage deemed to exist after a couple have cohabited for several years: *common-law marriage; common-law wife.*
common logarithm *n* a logarithm to the base ten. Usually written log or $\log_{10}$. Compare **natural logarithm.**
commonly ('kɒmənlɪ) *adv* **1** usually; ordinarily: *he was commonly known as Joe.* **2** *Derogatory.* in a coarse or vulgar way: *she dresses commonly.*
Common Market *n* **the.** a former Western European economic association, originally composed by the Treaty of Rome (1958) of Belgium, France, West Germany, Italy, Luxembourg, and the Netherlands, joined in 1973 by the United Kingdom, the Irish Republic, and Denmark, in 1981 by Greece, in 1986 by Spain and Portugal, and in 1990 by the former East Germany; replaced in 1993 by the European Union. Official name: **European Community.**
common measure *n* **1** another term for **common time. 2** the usual stanza form of a ballad, consisting of four iambic lines rhyming a b c b or a b a b.
common metre *n* a stanza form, used esp. for hymns, consisting of four lines, two of eight syllables alternating with two of six.
common multiple *n* an integer or polynomial that is a multiple of each integer or polynomial in a group: *20 is a common multiple of 2, 4, 5, 10.*
common noun *n Grammar.* a noun that refers to each member of a whole class sharing the features connoted by the noun, as for example *planet, orange,* and *drum.* Compare **proper noun.**
commonplace ('kɒmən,pleɪs) *adj* **1** ordinary; everyday: *commonplace duties.* **2** dull and obvious; trite: *commonplace prose.* ◆ *n* **3** something dull and trite, esp. a remark; platitude; truism. **4** a passage in a book marked for inclusion in a commonplace book, etc. **5** an ordinary or common thing. **[C16:** translation of Latin *locus commūnis* argument of wide application, translation of Greek *koinos topos*] ▸ **'common,placeness** *n*
commonplace book *n* a notebook in which quotations, poems, remarks, etc., that catch the owner's attention are entered.
common pleas *n* short for **Court of Common Pleas.**
common prayer *n* the liturgy of public services of the Church of England, esp. Morning and Evening Prayer.
common room *n Chiefly Brit.* a sitting room in schools, colleges, etc., for the relaxation of students or staff.
commons ('kɒmənz) *n* **1** (*functioning as pl*) people not of noble birth viewed as forming a political order. **2** (*functioning as pl*) the lower classes as contrasted to the ruling classes of society; the commonalty. **3** (*functioning as sing*) *Brit.* a building or hall for dining, recreation, etc., usually attached to a college. **4** (*usually functioning as pl*) *Brit.* food or rations (esp. in the phrase **short commons**).
Commons ('kɒmənz) *n* **the.** See **House of Commons.**
common seal *n* the official seal of a corporate body.
common sense *n* **1** plain ordinary good judgment; sound practical sense. ◆ *adj* **common-sense;** *also* **common-sensical. 2** inspired by or displaying sound practical sense.
common stock *n* the U.S. name for **ordinary shares.**
common time *n Music.* a time signature indicating four crotchet beats to the bar; four-four time. Symbol: C
commonweal ('kɒmən,wiːl) *n Archaic.* **1** the good of the community. **2** another name for **commonwealth.**
commonwealth ('kɒmən,welθ) *n* **1** the people of a state or nation viewed politically; body politic. **2** a state or nation in which the people possess sovereignty; republic. **3** the body politic organized for the general good. **4** a group of persons united by some common interest. **5** *Obsolete.* the general good; public welfare.
Commonwealth ('kɒmən,welθ) *n* **the. 1** Official name: **the Commonwealth of Nations.** an association of sovereign states, most of which are or at some time were ruled by Britain. All member states recognize the reigning British sovereign as **Head of the Commonwealth. 2a** the republic that existed in Britain from 1649 to 1660. **2b** the part of this period up to 1653, when Cromwell became Protector. **3** the official designation of Australia, four states of the U.S. (Kentucky, Massachusetts, Pennsylvania, and Virginia), and Puerto Rico.
Commonwealth Day *n* the anniversary of Queen Victoria's birth, May 24, celebrated (now on the second Monday in March) as a holiday in many parts of the Commonwealth. Former name: **Empire Day.**
Commonwealth of Independent States *n* a loose organization of former Soviet republics, excluding the Baltic States, formed in 1991. Abbrev.: **CIS.**
commotion (kə'məʊʃən) *n* **1** violent disturbance; upheaval. **2** political insurrection; disorder. **3** a confused noise; din. **[C15:** from Latin *commōtiō,* from *commovēre* to throw into disorder, from *com-* (intensive) + *movēre* to MOVE] ▸ **com'motional** *adj*
commove (kə'muːv) *vb* (*tr*) *Rare.* **1** to disturb; stir up. **2** to agitate or excite emotionally.
comms (kɒmz) *pl n Informal.* communications.
communal ('kɒmjʊnᵊl) *adj* **1** belonging or relating to a community as a whole. **2** relating to different groups within a society: *communal strife.* **3** of or relating to a commune or a religious community. ▸ **communality** (,kɒmjʊ'nælɪtɪ) *n* ▸ **'communally** *adv*
communal aerial *or* **antenna** *n* a television or radio receiving aerial from which received signals are distributed by cable to several outlets.
communalism ('kɒmjʊnə,lɪzəm) *n* **1** a system or theory of government in which the state is seen as a loose federation of self-governing communities. **2** an electoral system in which ethnic groups vote separately for their own representatives. **3** loyalty to the interests of one's own ethnic group rather than to society as a whole. **4** the practice or advocacy of communal living or ownership. ▸ **'communalist** *n* ▸ **,communal'istic** *adj*
communalize *or* **communalise** ('kɒmjʊnə,laɪz) *vb* (*tr*) to render (something) the property of a commune or community. ▸ **,communali'zation** *or* **,communali'sation** *n* ▸ **'communal,izer** *or* **'communal,iser** *n*
communard ('kɒmjʊ,nɑːd) *n* a member of a commune.
Communard ('kɒmjʊ,nɑːd) *n* any person who participated in or supported the Paris Commune formed after the Franco-Prussian War in 1871. **[C19:** from French]
communautaire (*French* kɔmynotɛr) *adj* supporting the principles of the European Community (now the European Union). **[**lit.: community (as modifier)**]**
commune[1] *vb* (kə'mjuːn). (*intr;* usually foll. by *with*) **1** to talk or converse intimately. **2** to experience strong emotion or spiritual feelings (for): *to commune with nature.* ◆ *n* ('kɒmjuːn). **3** intimate conversation; exchange of thoughts; communion. **[C13:** from Old French *comuner* to hold in common, from *comun* COMMON**]**
commune[2] (kə'mjuːn) *vb* (*intr*) *Christianity, chiefly U.S.* to partake of Communion. **[C16:** back formation from COMMUNION**]**
commune[3] ('kɒmjuːn) *n* **1** a group of families or individuals living together and sharing possessions and responsibilities. **2** any small group of people having common interests or responsibilities. **3** the smallest administrative unit in Belgium, France, Italy, and Switzerland, governed by a mayor and council. **4** the government or inhabitants of a commune. **5** a medieval town enjoying a large degree of autonomy. **[C18:** from French, from Medieval Latin *commūnia,* from Latin: things held in common, from *commūnis* COMMON**]**
Commune ('kɒmjuːn) *n French history.* **1** See **Paris Commune. 2** a committee that governed Paris during the French Revolution and played a leading role in the Reign of Terror: suppressed 1794.
communicable (kə'mjuːnɪkəbᵊl) *adj* **1** capable of being communicated. **2** (of a disease or its causative agent) capable of being passed on readily. ▸ **com,municа'bility** *or* **com'municableness** *n* ▸ **com'municably** *adv*
communicant (kə'mjuːnɪkənt) *n* **1** *Christianity.* a person who receives Communion. **2** a person who communicates or informs. ◆ *adj* **3** communicating.
communicate (kə'mjuːnɪ,keɪt) *vb* **1** to impart (knowledge) or exchange (thoughts, feelings, or ideas) by speech, writing, gestures, etc. **2** (*tr;* usually foll. by *to*) to allow (a feeling, emotion, etc.) to be sensed (by), willingly or unwillingly; transmit (to): *the dog communicated his fear to the other animals.* **3** (*intr*) to have a sympathetic mutual understanding. **4** (*intr;* usually foll. by *with*) to make or have a connecting passage or route; connect. **5** (*tr*) to transmit (a disease); infect. **6** (*intr*) *Christianity.* to receive or administer Communion. **[C16:** from Latin *commūnicāre* to share, from *commūnis* COMMON**]** ▸ **com'muni,cator** *n* ▸ **com'municatory** *adj*
communicating (kə'mjuːnɪ,keɪtɪŋ) *adj* making or having a direct connection from one room to another: *the suite is made up of three communicating rooms.*
communication (kə,mjuːnɪ'keɪʃən) *n* **1** the act or an instance of communicating; the imparting or exchange of information, ideas, or feelings. **2** something communicated, such as a message, letter, or telephone call. **3a** (*usually pl; sometimes functioning as sing*) the study of ways in which human beings communicate, including speech, gesture, telecommunication systems, publishing and broadcasting media, etc. **3b** (*as modifier*): *communication theory.* **4** a connecting route, passage, or link. **5** (*pl*) *Military.* the system of routes and facilities by which forces, supplies, etc., are moved up to or within an area of operations.
communication cord *n Brit.* a cord or chain in a train which may be pulled by a passenger to stop the train in an emergency.
communication interface *n* an electronic circuit, usually designed to a

specific standard, that enables one machine to telecommunicate with another machine.

communications satellite *n* an artificial satellite used to relay radio, television, and telephone signals around the earth, usually in geostationary orbit.

communicative (kəˈmjuːnɪkətɪv) *adj* **1** inclined or able to communicate readily; talkative. **2** of or relating to communication. ► **comˈmunicatively** *adv* ► **comˈmunicativeness** *n*

communion (kəˈmjuːnjən) *n* **1** an exchange of thoughts, emotions, etc. **2** possession or sharing in common; participation. **3** (foll. by *with*) strong emotional or spiritual feelings (for): *communion with nature.* **4** a religious group or denomination having a common body of beliefs, doctrines, and practices. **5** the spiritual union held by Christians to exist between individual Christians and Christ, their Church, or their fellow Christians. **[C14:** from Latin *commūniō* general participation, from *commūnis* COMMON**]** ► **comˈmunional** *adj* ► **comˈmunionally** *adv*

Communion (kəˈmjuːnjən) *n Christianity.* **1** the act of participating in the Eucharist. **2** the celebration of the Eucharist, esp. the part of the service during which the consecrated elements are received. **3a** the consecrated elements of the Eucharist. **3b** (*as modifier*): *Communion cup.* ◆ Also called: **Holy Communion.**

communion of saints *n Christianity.* the spiritual fellowship of all true Christians, living and dead.

communiqué (kəˈmjuːnɪˌkeɪ) *n* an official communication or announcement, esp. to the press or public. **[C19:** from French, from *communiquer* to COMMUNICATE**]**

communism (ˈkɒmjʊˌnɪzəm) *n* **1** advocacy of a classless society in which private ownership has been abolished and the means of production and subsistence belong to the community. **2** any social, economic, or political movement or doctrine aimed at achieving such a society. **3** (*usually cap.*) a political movement based upon the writings of Marx that considers history in terms of class conflict and revolutionary struggle, resulting eventually in the victory of the proletariat and the establishment of a socialist order based on public ownership of the means of production. See also **Marxism, Marxism-Leninism, socialism. 4** (*usually cap.*) a social order or system of government established by a ruling Communist Party, esp. in the former Soviet Union. **5** (*often cap.*) *Chiefly U.S.* any leftist political activity or thought, esp. when considered to be subversive. **6** communal living; communalism. **[C19:** from French *communisme,* from *commun* COMMON**]**

communist (ˈkɒmjʊnɪst) *n* **1** a supporter of any form of communism. **2** (*often cap.*) a supporter of Communism or a Communist movement or state. **3** (*often cap.*) a member of a Communist party. **4** a person who practises communal living; communalist. **5** another name for **Communard.** ◆ *adj* **6** of, characterized by, favouring, or relating to communism; communistic.

Communist China *n* another name for (the People's Republic of) **China.**

communistic (ˌkɒmjʊˈnɪstɪk) *adj* of, characteristic of, or relating to communism. ► **ˌcommuˈnistically** *adv*

Communist Manifesto *n* a political pamphlet written by Marx and Engels in 1848: a fundamental statement of Marxist principles.

Communist Party *n* **1** (in non-Communist countries) a political party advocating Communism. **2** (in Communist countries) the single official party of the state, composed of those who officially espouse Communism.

communitarian (kəˌmjuːnɪˈtɛərɪən) *n* **1** a member of a communist community. **2** an advocate of communalism.

community (kəˈmjuːnɪtɪ) *n, pl* **-ties. 1a** the people living in one locality. **1b** the locality in which they live. **1c** (*as modifier*): *community spirit.* **2** a group of people having cultural, religious, ethnic, or other characteristics in common: *the Protestant community.* **3** a group of nations having certain interests in common. **4** the public in general; society. **5** common ownership or participation. **6** similarity or agreement: *community of interests.* **7** (in Wales since 1974 and Scotland since 1975) the smallest unit of local government; a subdivision of a district. **8** *Ecology.* a group of interdependent plants and animals inhabiting the same region and interacting with each other through food and other relationships. **[C14:** from Latin *commūnitās,* from *commūnis* COMMON**]**

community association *n* (in Britain) an organization of people and groups working for the common good of a neighbourhood, usually operating under a written constitution registered with the Charity Commissioners.

community care *n Social welfare.* **1** help available to persons living in their own homes, rather than services provided in residential institutions. **2** the policy of transferring responsibility for people in need from large, often isolated, state institutions to their relatives and local welfare agencies.

community centre *n* a building used by members of a community for social gatherings, educational activities, etc.

community charge *n* (formerly in Britain) a flat-rate charge paid by each adult in a community to their local authority in place of rates. Also called: **poll tax.**

community chest *n U.S.* a fund raised by voluntary contribution for local welfare activities.

community college *n* **1** *Brit.* another term for **village college. 2** *Chiefly U.S. and Canadian.* a nonresidential college offering two-year courses of study. **3** *N.Z.* an adult education college with trade classes.

community council *n* (in Scotland and Wales) an independent voluntary local body set up to attend to local interests and organize community activities.

community education *n* the provision of a wide range of educational and special interest courses and activities by a local authority.

community home *n* (in Britain) **1** a home provided by a local authority for children who cannot remain with parents or relatives, or be placed with foster parents. **2** a boarding school for young offenders. Former name: **approved school.** Formal name: **community home with education on the premises.** Abbrev.: **CHE.**

Community of Sovereign Republics *n* a political and economic union formed in 1996 by Russia and Belarus.

community policing *n* the assigning of the same one or two policemen to a particular area so that they become familiar with the residents and the residents with them, as a way of reducing crime.

Community Programme *n* a government scheme to provide temporary work for people unemployed for over a year. Abbrev.: **CP.** See also **STEP, TOPS, YOP, YTS.**

community relations *pl n* **1** the particular state of affairs in an area where potentially conflicting ethnic, religious, cultural, political, or linguistic groups live together: *community relations in this neighbourhood were strained before the riots.* **2a** social engineering or mediating work with conflicting groups: *he spent ten years in community relations.* **2b** (*as modifier*): *a community-relations officer.*

community school *n Brit.* a school offering some nonacademic activities related to life in a particular community and often serving as a community centre.

community service *n* **1** voluntary work, intended to be for the common good, usually done as part of an organized scheme. **2** See **community-service order.**

community-service order *n* (in Britain) a court order requiring an offender over seventeen years old to do unpaid socially beneficial work under supervision instead of going to prison.

community singing *n* singing, esp. of hymns, by a large gathering of people.

communize *or* **communise** (ˈkɒmjʊˌnaɪz) *vb* (*tr*) (*sometimes cap.*) **1** to make (property) public; nationalize. **2** to make (a person or country) communist. ► **ˌcommuniˈzation** *or* **ˌcommuniˈsation** *n*

commutable (kəˈmjuːtəbᵊl) *adj* **1** *Law.* (of a punishment) capable of being reduced in severity. **2** able to be exchanged. ► **comˌmutaˈbility** *or* **comˈmutableness** *n*

commutate (ˈkɒmjʊˌteɪt) *vb* (*tr*) **1** to reverse the direction of (an electric current). **2** to convert (an alternating current) into a direct current.

commutation (ˌkɒmjʊˈteɪʃən) *n* **1** a substitution or exchange. **2a** the replacement of one method of payment by another. **2b** the payment substituted. **3** the reduction in severity of a penalty imposed by law. **4** the process of commutating an electric current. **5** *U.S.* the travelling done by a commuter.

commutation ticket *n* a U.S. name for **season ticket.**

commutative (kəˈmjuːtətɪv, ˈkɒmjʊˌteɪtɪv) *adj* **1** relating to or involving substitution. **2** *Maths, logic.* **2a** (of an operator) giving the same result irrespective of the order of the arguments; thus disjunction and addition are commutative but implication and subtraction are not. **2b** relating to this property: *the commutative law of addition.* ► **comˈmutatively** *adv*

commutator (ˈkɒmjʊˌteɪtə) *n* **1** a device used to reverse the direction of flow of an electric current. **2** the segmented metal cylinder or disc mounted on the armature shaft of an electric motor, generator, etc., used to make electrical contact with the rotating coils and ensure unidirectional current flow.

commute (kəˈmjuːt) *vb* **1** (*intr*) to travel some distance regularly between one's home and one's place of work. **2** (*tr*) to substitute; exchange. **3** (*tr*) *Law.* to reduce (a sentence) to one less severe. **4** to pay (an annuity) at one time, esp. with a discount, instead of in instalments. **5** (*tr*) to transform; change: *to commute base metal into gold.* **6** (*intr*) to act as or be a substitute. **7** (*intr*) to make a substitution; change. ◆ *n* **8** *U.S.* a journey made by commuting. **[C17:** from Latin *commūtāre* to replace, from *com-* mutually + *mūtāre* to change**]** ► **comˈmutable** *adj* ► **comˈmutableness** *or* **comˌmutaˈbility** *n*

commuter (kəˈmjuːtə) *n* **a** a person who travels to work over an appreciable distance, usually from the suburbs to the centre of a city. **b** (*as modifier*): *the commuter belt.*

Comnenus (kɒmˈniːnəs) *n* an important Byzantine family from which the imperial dynasties of Constantinople (1057–59; 1081–1185) and Trebizond (1204–1461) derived.

Como (ˈkəʊməʊ; *Italian* ˈkɔːmo) *n* a city in N Italy, in Lombardy at the SW end of **Lake Como**: tourist centre. Pop.: 96 900 (1995 est.). Latin name: **Comum** (ˈkəʊmʊm).

comodo *or* **commodo** (kəˈməʊdəʊ) *adj, adv Music.* (to be performed) at a convenient relaxed speed. **[**Italian: comfortable, from Latin *commodus,* convenient; see COMMODIOUS**]**

Comorin (ˈkɒmərɪn) *n* **Cape.** a headland at the southernmost point of India, in Tamil Nadu state.

Comoros (ˈkɒməˌrəʊz, kəˈmɔːrəʊz) *pl n* a republic consisting of three volcanic islands in the Indian Ocean, off the NW coast of Madagascar; a French territory from 1947; became independent in 1976 except for Mayotte, the fourth island in the group, which chose to remain French. Official languages: Comorian, French, and Arabic; Swahili is used commercially. Religion: Muslim. Currency: franc. Capital: Moroni. Pop.: 546 000 (1998 est.). Area: 1862 sq. km (719 sq. miles). Official name: **Federal Islamic Republic of the Comoros.**

comose (ˈkəʊməʊs, kəʊˈməʊs) *adj Botany.* another word for **comate. [C18:** from Latin *comōsus* hairy, from *coma* long hair; see COMA[2]**]**

comp (kɒmp) *Informal.* ◆ *n* **1** a compositor. **2** an accompanist. **3** an accompaniment. **4** a competition. ◆ *vb* **5** (*intr*) to work as a compositor in the printing industry. **6** to play an accompaniment (to).

comp. *abbrev. for:* **1** companion. **2** comparative. **3** compare. **4** compiled. **5** compiler. **6** complete. **7** composer. **8** composition. **9** compositor. **10** compound. **11** comprehensive. **12** comprising.

compact[1] *adj* (kəmˈpækt). **1** closely packed together; dense. **2** neatly fitted into a restricted space. **3** concise; brief. **4** well constructed; solid; firm. **5** (foll. by *of*) composed or made up (of). **6** *Maths, logic.* (of a relation) having the property that for any pair of elements such that *a* is related to *b*, there is some element *c* such that *a* is related to *c* and *c* to *b*, as *less than* on the rational numbers. **7** *U.S. and Canadian.* (of a car) small and economical. ◆ *vb* (kəm'pækt). (*tr*) **8** to pack or join closely together; compress; condense. **9** (foll. by *of*) to create or form by pressing together: *sediment compacted of three types of clay.* **10** *Metallurgy.* to compress (a metal powder) to form a stable product suitable for sintering. ◆ *n* ('kɒmpækt). **11** a small flat case containing a mirror, face powder, etc., designed to be carried in a woman's handbag. **12** *U.S. and Canadian.* a comparatively small and economical car. **13** *Metallurgy.* a mass of metal prepared for sintering by cold-pressing a metal powder. **[C16:** from Latin *compactus,* from *compingere* to put together, from *com-* together + *pangere* to fasten**]** ▸ **com'pacter** *n* ▸ **com'paction** *n* ▸ **com'pactly** *adv* ▸ **com'pactness** *n*

compact[2] ('kɒmpækt) *n* an official contract or agreement. **[C16:** from Latin *compactum,* from *compacīscī* to agree, from *com-* together + *pacīscī* to contract; see PACT**]**

compact camera ('kɒmpækt) *n* a simple 35 mm snapshot camera not having interchangeable lenses or through-the-lens focusing but sometimes having automatic focusing, exposure, and winding. Sometimes shortened to **compact.**

compact disc ('kɒmpækt) *n* a small digital audio disc on which sound is recorded as a series of metallic pits enclosed in PVC; the disc is spun by the compact disc player and read by an optical laser system. Also called: **compact audio disc.** Abbrevs.: **CD, CAD.**

compact disc player *n* a machine with a laser beam for playing compact discs.

compactify (kəm'pæktɪˌfaɪ) *vb* **-fies, -fying, -fied.** to make or become compact; esp. of higher dimensions in space-time, to become tightly curved so as to be unobservable under normal circumstances. ▸ **com'pactifiˌcation** *n*

compact video disc *n* a compact laser disc that plays both pictures and sound. Abbrev.: **CDV.**

compadre (kɒm'pɑːdreɪ, kəm-) *n Southwestern U.S.* a masculine friend. **[**from Spanish: godfather, from Medieval Latin *compater,* from Latin *com-* with + *pater* father**]**

compages (kəm'peɪdʒiːz) *n* (*functioning as sing*) a structure or framework. **[C17:** from Latin, from *com-* together + *pag-,* from *pangĕre* to fasten**]**

compander (kəm'pændə) *n* a system for improving the signal-to-noise ratio of a signal at a transmitter or recorder by first compressing the volume range of the signal and then restoring it to its original amplitude level at the receiving or reproducing apparatus. **[C20:** from COM(PRESSOR) + (EX)PANDER**]**

companion[1] (kəm'pænjən) *n* **1** a person who is an associate of another or others; comrade. **2** (esp. formerly) an employee, usually a woman, who provides company for an employer, esp. an elderly woman. **3a** one of a pair; match. **3b** (*as modifier*): *a companion volume.* **4** a guidebook or handbook. **5** a member of the lowest rank of any of certain orders of knighthood. **6** *Astronomy.* the fainter of the two components of a double star. ◆ *vb* **7** (*tr*) to accompany or be a companion to. **[C13:** from Late Latin *compāniō,* literally: one who eats bread with another, from Latin *com-* with + *pānis* bread**]** ▸ **com'panionless** *adj*

companion[2] (kəm'pænjən) *n Nautical.* **a** a raised frame on an upper deck with windows to give light to the deck below. **b** (*as modifier*): *a companion ladder.* **[C18:** from Dutch *kompanje* quarterdeck, from Old French *compagne,* from Old Italian *compagna* pantry, perhaps ultimately from Latin *pānis* bread**]**

companionable (kəm'pænjənəbᵊl) *adj* suited to be a companion; sociable. ▸ **com'panionableness** *or* **comˌpaniona'bility** *n* ▸ **com'panionably** *adv*

companionate (kəm'pænjənɪt) *adj* **1** resembling, appropriate to, or acting as a companion. **2** harmoniously suited.

companion set *n* a set of fire irons on a stand.

companionship (kəm'pænjənˌʃɪp) *n* the relationship of friends or companions; fellowship.

companionway (kəm'pænjənˌweɪ) *n* a stairway or ladder leading from one deck to another in a boat or ship.

company ('kʌmpənɪ) *n, pl* **-nies. 1** a number of people gathered together; assembly. **2** the fact of being with someone; companionship: *I enjoy her company.* **3** a social visitor or visitors; guest or guests. **4** a business enterprise. **5** the members of an enterprise not specifically mentioned in the enterprise's title. Abbrevs.: **Co., co. 6** a group of actors, usually including business and technical personnel. **7** a small unit of troops, usually comprising two or more platoons. **8** the officers and crew of a ship. **9** a unit of Girl Guides. **10** *English history.* a medieval guild. **11 keep** *or* **bear company. 11a** to accompany (someone). **11b** (esp. of lovers) to associate with each other; spend time together. **12 part company. 12a** to end a friendship or association, esp. as a result of a quarrel; separate. **12b** (foll. by *with*) to leave; go away (from); be separated (from). ◆ *vb* **-nies, -nying, -nied. 13** *Archaic.* to keep company or associate (with someone). **[C13:** from Old French *compaignie,* from *compain* companion, fellow, from Late Latin *compāniō;* see COMPANION[1]**]**

company doctor *n* **1** a businessman or accountant who specializes in turning ailing companies into profitable enterprises. **2** a physician employed by a company to look after its staff and to advise on health matters.

company man *n* an employee who puts allegiance to the company for which he works above personal opinion or friendship.

company secretary *n Brit.* an officer of an incorporated company who has certain legal obligations.

company sergeant major *n Military.* the senior Warrant Officer II in a British or Commonwealth regiment or battalion, responsible under the company second in command for all aspects of duty and discipline of the NCOs and men in that subunit. Abbrev.: **CSM.** Compare **regimental sergeant major.** See also **warrant officer.**

company town *n U.S. and Canadian.* a town built by a company for its employees.

company union *n Chiefly U.S. and Canadian.* an unaffiliated union of workers usually restricted to a single business enterprise.

compar. *abbrev. for* comparative.

comparable ('kɒmpərəbᵊl) *adj* **1** worthy of comparison. **2** able to be compared (with). ▸ **ˌcompara'bility** *or* **'comparableness** *n* ▸ **'comparably** *adv*

comparative (kəm'pærətɪv) *adj* **1** denoting or involving comparison: *comparative literature.* **2** judged by comparison; relative: *a comparative loss of prestige.* **3** *Grammar.* denoting the form of an adjective that indicates that the quality denoted is possessed to a greater extent. In English the comparative form of an adjective is usually marked by the suffix *-er* or the word *more.* Compare **positive** (sense 10), **superlative** (sense 2). ◆ *n* **4** the comparative form of an adjective. ▸ **com'paratively** *adv* ▸ **com'parativeness** *n*

comparative judgment *n Psychol.* any judgment about whether there is a difference between two or more stimuli. Compare **absolute judgment.**

comparative psychology *n* the study of the similarities and differences in the behaviour of different species.

comparator (kəm'pærətə) *n* **1** any instrument used to measure a property of a system by comparing it with a standard system. **2** an electric circuit that compares two signals and gives an indication of the extent of their dissimilarity.

compare (kəm'pɛə) *vb* **1** (*tr;* usually foll. by *to*) to regard or represent as analogous or similar; liken: *the general has been compared to Napoleon.* **2** (*tr;* usually foll. by *with*) to examine in order to observe resemblances or differences: *to compare rum with gin.* **3** (*intr;* usually foll. by *with*) to be of the same or similar quality or value: *gin compares with rum in alcoholic content.* **4** (*intr*) to bear a specified relation of quality or value when examined: *this car compares badly with the other.* **5** (*intr;* usually foll. by *with*) to correspond to: *profits were £3.2 million. This compares with £2.6 million last year.* **6** (*tr*) *Grammar.* to give the positive, comparative, and superlative forms of (an adjective). **7** (*intr*) *Archaic.* to compete or vie. **8 compare notes.** to exchange opinions. ◆ *n* **9** comparison or analogy (esp. in the phrase **beyond compare**). **[C15:** from Old French *comparer,* from Latin *comparāre* to couple together, match, from *compar* equal to one another, from *com-* together + *par* equal; see PAR**]** ▸ **com'parer** *n*

comparison (kəm'pærɪsᵊn) *n* **1** the act or process of comparing. **2** the state of being compared. **3** comparable quality or qualities; likeness: *there was no comparison between them.* **4** a rhetorical device involving comparison, such as a simile. **5** Also called: **degrees of comparison.** *Grammar.* the listing of the positive, comparative, and superlative forms of an adjective or adverb. **6 bear** *or* **stand comparison (with).** to be sufficiently similar in class or range to be compared with (something else), esp. favourably.

compartment (kəm'pɑːtmənt) *n* **1** one of the sections into which an area, esp. an enclosed space, is divided or partitioned. **2** any separate part or section: *a compartment of the mind.* **3** a small storage space; locker. **[C16:** from French *compartiment,* ultimately from Late Latin *compartīrī* to share, from Latin *com-* with + *partīrī* to apportion, from *pars* PART**]** ▸ **compartmental** (ˌkɒmpɑːt'mɛntᵊl) *adj* ▸ **ˌcompart'mentally** *adv*

compartmentalize *or* **compartmentalise** (ˌkɒmpɑːt'mɛntᵊˌlaɪz) *vb* (*usually tr*) to put or divide into (compartments, categories, etc.), esp. to an excessive degree. ▸ **ˌcompartˌmentali'zation** *or* **ˌcompartˌmentali'sation** *n*

compass ('kʌmpəs) *n* **1** an instrument for finding direction, usually having a magnetized needle which points to magnetic north swinging freely on a pivot. **2** (*often pl*) Also called: **pair of compasses.** an instrument used for drawing circles, measuring distances, etc., that consists of two arms, joined at one end, one arm of which serves as a pivot or stationary reference point, while the other is extended or describes a circle. **3** limits or range: *within the compass of education.* **4** *Music.* the interval between the lowest and highest note attainable by a voice or musical instrument. **5** *Archaic.* a circular course. ◆ *vb* (*tr*) **6** to encircle or surround; hem in. **7** to comprehend or grasp mentally. **8** to achieve; attain; accomplish. **9** *Obsolete.* to plot. **[C13:** from Old French *compas,* from *compasser* to measure, from Vulgar Latin *compassāre* (unattested) to pace out, ultimately from Latin *passus* step**]** ▸ **'compassable** *adj*

compass card *n* a compass in the form of a card that rotates so that "0°" or "North" points to magnetic north.

compassion (kəm'pæʃən) *n* a feeling of distress and pity for the suffering or misfortune of another, often including the desire to alleviate it. **[C14:** from Old French, from Late Latin *compassiō* fellow feeling, from *compatī* to suffer with, from Latin *com-* with + *patī* to bear, suffer**]**

compassionate (kəm'pæʃənət) *adj* **1** showing or having compassion. **2 compassionate leave.** leave granted, esp. to a serviceman, on the grounds of bereavement, family illness, etc. ▸ **com'passionately** *adv* ▸ **com'passionateness** *n*

compassion fatigue *n* the inability to react sympathetically to a crisis, disaster, etc., because of overexposure to previous crises, disasters, etc.

compass plant *n* **1** Also called: **rosinweed.** a tall plant, *Silphium laciniatum,* of central North America, that has yellow flowers and lower leaves that tend to align themselves at right angles to the strongest light, esp. in a north-south plane: family *Compositae* (composites). **2** any of several similar plants.

compass rose *n* a circle or decorative device printed on a map or chart showing the points of the compass measured from true north and usually magnetic north.

compass saw *n* a hand saw with a narrow tapered blade for making a curved cut.

compass window *n Architect.* a bay window having a semicircular shape.

compatible (kəm'pætəbᵊl) *adj* **1** (usually foll. by *with*) able to exist together harmoniously. **2** (usually foll. by *with*) consistent or congruous: *her deeds were not compatible with her ideology.* **3** (of plants) **3a** capable of forming successful grafts. **3b** capable of self-fertilization. **4** (of pieces of machinery, computer equipment, etc.) capable of being used together without special modification or adaptation: *a PC-compatible disc.* [C15: from Medieval Latin *compatibilis,* from Late Latin *compatī* to be in sympathy with; see COMPASSION] ▸ **com,pati'bility** *or* **com'patibleness** *n* ▸ **com'patibly** *adv*

compatriot (kəm'pætrɪət) *n* a fellow countryman. [C17: from French *compatriote,* from Late Latin *compatriōta;* see PATRIOT] ▸ **com,patri'otic** *adj* ▸ **com'patriotism** *n*

compeer ('kɒmpɪə) *n* **1** a person of equal rank, status, or ability; peer. **2** a companion or comrade. [C13: from Old French *comper,* from Medieval Latin *compater* godfather; see COMPADRE]

compel (kəm'pɛl) *vb* **-pels, -pelling, -pelled.** (*tr*) **1** to cause (someone) by force (to be or do something). **2** to obtain by force; exact: *to compel obedience.* **3** to overpower or subdue. **4** *Archaic.* to herd or drive together. [C14: from Latin *compellere* to drive together, from *com-* together + *pellere* to drive] ▸ **com'pellable** *adj* ▸ **com'pellably** *adv* ▸ **com'peller** *n*

compellation (,kɒmpɛ'leɪʃən) *n* a rare word for **appellation.** [C17: from Latin *compellātiō,* from *compellāre* to accost, from *appellāre* to call]

compelling (kəm'pɛlɪŋ) *adj* **1** arousing or denoting strong interest, esp. admiring interest. **2** (of an argument, evidence, etc.) convincing.

compendious (kəm'pɛndɪəs) *adj* containing or stating the essentials of a subject in a concise form; succinct. ▸ **com'pendiously** *adv* ▸ **com'pendiousness** *n*

compendium (kəm'pɛndɪəm) *n, pl* **-diums** *or* **-dia** (-dɪə). **1** *Brit.* a book containing a collection of useful hints. **2** *Brit.* a selection, esp. of different games or other objects in one container. **3** a concise but comprehensive summary of a larger work. [C16: from Latin: a saving, literally: something weighed, from *pendere* to weigh]

compensable (kəm'pɛnsəbᵊl) *adj Chiefly U.S.* entitled to compensation or capable of being compensated.

compensate ('kɒmpɛn,seɪt) *vb* **1** to make amends to (someone), esp. for loss or injury. **2** (*tr*) to serve as compensation or damages for (injury, loss, etc.). **3** to offset or counterbalance the effects of (a force, weight, movement, etc.) so as to nullify the effects of an undesirable influence and produce equilibrium. **4** (*intr*) to attempt to conceal or offset one's shortcomings by the exaggerated exhibition of qualities regarded as desirable. [C17: from Latin *compēnsāre,* from *pensāre,* from *pendere* to weigh] ▸ **compensatory** ('kɒmpɛn,seɪtərɪ, kəm'pɛnsətərɪ, -trɪ) *or* **compensative** ('kɒmpɛn,seɪtɪv, kəm'pɛnsə-) *adj* ▸ **'compen,sator** *n*

compensated semiconductor *n Physics.* a semiconductor in which donors and acceptors are related in such a way that their opposing electrical effects are partially cancelled.

compensation (,kɒmpɛn'seɪʃən) *n* **1** the act or process of making amends for something. **2** something given as reparation for loss, injury, etc.; indemnity. **3** the automatic movements made by the body to maintain balance. **4** the attempt to conceal or offset one's shortcomings by the exaggerated exhibition of qualities regarded as desirable. **5** *Biology.* abnormal growth and increase in size in one organ in response to the removal or inactivation of another. ▸ **,compen'sational** *adj*

compensation order *n* (in Britain) the requirement of a court that an offender pay compensation for injury, loss, or damage resulting from an offence, either in preference to or as well as a fine.

compensation point *n Botany.* the concentration of atmospheric carbon dioxide at which the rate of carbon dioxide uptake by a photosynthesizing plant is exactly balanced by its rate of carbon dioxide release in respiration.

compensatory finance *n* another name for **deficit financing.**

comper ('kɒmpə) *n Informal.* a person who regularly enters competitions in newspapers, magazines, etc., esp. competitions offering consumer goods as prizes. [C20: COMP(ETITION) + -ER[1]] ▸ **'comping** *n*

compere ('kɒmpɛə) *Brit.* ◆ *n* **1** a master of ceremonies who introduces cabaret, television acts, etc. ◆ *vb* **2** to act as a compere (for). [C20: from French, literally: godfather; see COMPEER, COMPADRE]

compete (kəm'piːt) *vb* (*intr;* often foll. by *with*) to contend (against) for profit, an award, athletic supremacy, etc.; engage in a contest (with). [C17: from Late Latin *competere* to strive together, from Latin: to meet, come together, agree, from *com-* together + *petere* to seek]

competence ('kɒmpɪtəns) *n* **1** the condition of being capable; ability. **2** a sufficient income to live on. **3** the state of being legally competent or qualified. **4** *Embryol.* the ability of embryonic tissues to react to external conditions in a way that influences subsequent development. **5** *Linguistics.* (in transformational grammar) the form of the human language faculty, independent of its psychological embodiment in actual human beings. Compare **performance** (sense 7), **langue, parole** (sense 5).

competency ('kɒmpɪtənsɪ) *n, pl* **-cies. 1** *Law.* capacity to testify in a court of law; eligibility to be sworn. **2** a less common word for **competence** (senses 1, 2).

competent ('kɒmpɪtənt) *adj* **1** having sufficient skill, knowledge, etc.; capable. **2** suitable or sufficient for the purpose: *a competent answer.* **3** *Law.* (of a witness) having legal capacity; qualified to testify, etc. **4** (*postpositive;* foll. by *to*) belonging as a right; appropriate. [C14: from Latin *competēns,* from *competere* to be competent; see COMPETE] ▸ **'competently** *adv* ▸ **'competentness** *n*

competition (,kɒmpɪ'tɪʃən) *n* **1** the act of competing; rivalry. **2** a contest in which a winner is selected from among two or more entrants. **3** a series of games, sports events, etc. **4** the opposition offered by a competitor or competitors. **5** a competitor or competitors offering opposition. **6** *Ecology.* the struggle between individuals of the same or different species for food, space, light, etc., when these are inadequate to supply the needs of all.

competitive (kəm'pɛtɪtɪv) *adj* **1** involving or determined by rivalry: *competitive sports.* **2** sufficiently low in price or high in quality to be successful against commercial rivals. **3** relating to or characterized by an urge to compete: *a competitive personality.* ▸ **com'petitively** *adv* ▸ **com'petitiveness** *n*

competitive exclusion *n Ecology.* the dominance of one species over another when both are competing for the same resources, etc.

competitor (kəm'pɛtɪtə) *n* a person, group, team, firm, etc., that vies or competes; rival.

Compiègne (*French* kɔ̃pjɛɲ) *n* a city in N France, on the Oise River: scene of the armistice at the end of World War I (1918) and of the Franco-German armistice of 1940. Pop.: 44 703 (1990).

compilation (,kɒmpɪ'leɪʃən) *n* **1** something collected or compiled, such as a list, report, etc. **2** the act or process of collecting or compiling.

compilation film *n* film from an archive used in a film or documentary to give a feeling of the relevant period.

compile (kəm'paɪl) *vb* (*tr*) **1** to make or compose from other materials or sources: *to compile a list of names.* **2** to collect or gather for a book, hobby, etc. **3** *Computing.* to create (a set of machine instructions) from a high-level programming language, using a compiler. [C14: from Latin *compīlāre* to pile together, plunder, from *com-* together + *pīlāre* to thrust down, pack]

compiler (kəm'paɪlə) *n* **1** a person who collects or compiles something. **2** a computer program by which a high-level programming language, such as COBOL or FORTRAN, is converted into machine language that can be acted upon by a computer. Compare **assembler.**

complacency (kəm'pleɪsənsɪ) *or* **complacence** *n, pl* **-cencies** *or* **-cences. 1** a feeling of satisfaction, esp. extreme self-satisfaction; smugness. **2** an obsolete word for **complaisance.**

complacent (kəm'pleɪsᵊnt) *adj* **1** pleased or satisfied, esp. extremely self-satisfied. **2** an obsolete word for **complaisant.** [C17: from Latin *complacēns* very pleasing, from *complacēre* to be most agreeable to, from *com-* (intensive) + *placēre* to please] ▸ **com'placently** *adv*

complain (kəm'pleɪn) *vb* (*intr*) **1** to express resentment, displeasure, etc., esp. habitually; grumble. **2** (foll. by *of*) to state the presence of pain, illness, etc., esp. in the hope of sympathy: *she complained of a headache.* [C14: from Old French *complaindre,* from Vulgar Latin *complangere* (unattested), from Latin *com-* (intensive) + *plangere* to bewail] ▸ **com'plainer** *n* ▸ **com'plainingly** *adv*

complainant (kəm'pleɪnənt) *n Law.* a person who makes a complaint, usually before justices; plaintiff.

complaint (kəm'pleɪnt) *n* **1** the act of complaining; an expression of grievance. **2** a cause for complaining; grievance. **3** a mild ailment. **4** *English law.* a statement by which a civil proceeding in a magistrates' court is commenced.

complaisance (kəm'pleɪzəns) *n* **1** deference to the wishes of others; willing compliance. **2** an act of willing compliance.

complaisant (kəm'pleɪzᵊnt) *adj* showing a desire to comply or oblige; polite. [C17: from French *complaire,* from Latin *complacēre* to please greatly; compare COMPLACENT] ▸ **com'plaisantly** *adv*

complanate (kəm'pleɪneɪt) *adj Botany.* having a flattened or compressed aspect.

compleat (kəm'pliːt) *adj* an archaic spelling of **complete,** used in the titles of handbooks, in imitation of *The Compleat Angler* by Izaak Walton.

complect (kəm'plɛkt) *vb* (*tr*) *Archaic.* to interweave or entwine. [C16: from Latin *complectī;* see COMPLEX]

complected (kəm'plɛktɪd) *adj* (*in combination*) a U.S. dialect word for **complexioned.**

complement *n* ('kɒmplɪmənt). **1** a person or thing that completes something. **2** one of two parts that make up a whole or complete each other. **3** a complete amount, number, etc. (often in the phrase **full complement**). **4** the officers and crew needed to man a ship. **5** *Grammar.* **5a** a noun phrase that follows a copula or similar verb, as for example *an idiot* in the sentence *He is an idiot.* **5b** a clause that serves as the subject or direct object of a verb or the direct object of a preposition, as for example *that he would be early* in the sentence *I hoped that he would be early.* **6** *Maths.* the angle that when added to a specified angle produces a right angle. **7** *Logic, maths.* the class of all things, or of all members of a given universe of discourse, that are not members of a given set. **8** *Music.* the inverted form of an interval that, when added to the interval, completes the octave: *the sixth is the complement of the third.* **9** *Immunol.* a group of proteins in the blood serum that, when activated by antibodies, causes destruction of alien cells, such as bacteria. ◆ *vb* ('kɒmplɪ,mɛnt). **10** (*tr*) to add to, make complete, or form a complement to. [C14: from Latin *complēmentum,* from *complēre* to fill up, from *com-* (intensive) + *plēre* to fill]

USAGE Avoid confusion with **compliment.**

complementarity (,kɒmplɪmən'tærɪtɪ) *n, pl* **-ties. 1** a state or system that involves complementary components. **2** *Physics.* the principle that the complete description of a phenomenon in microphysics requires the use of two distinct theories that are complementary to each other. See also **duality** (sense 2).

complementary (,kɒmplɪ'mɛntərɪ, -trɪ) *or* **complemental** *adj* **1** acting as or forming a complement; completing. **2** forming a satisfactory or balanced whole. **3** forming a mathematical complement: *sine and cosine are complementary functions.* **4** *Maths, logic.* (of a pair of sets, functions, etc.) mutually exclusive and exhaustive, each being the complement of the other. **5** (of genes) producing an effect in association with other genes. **6** involving or using the treatments and techniques of complementary medicine. ▸ **,comple'mentarily** *or* **,comple'mentally** *adv* ▸ **,comple'mentariness** *n*

complementary angle *n* either of two angles whose sum is 90°. Compare **supplementary angle.**

complementary colour *n* one of any pair of colours, such as yellow and blue, that give white or grey when mixed in the correct proportions.

complementary DNA *n* a form of DNA artificially synthesized from a messenger RNA template and used in genetic engineering to produce gene clones. Abbrev.: **cDNA.**

complementary gene *n* one of a pair of genes, each from different loci, that together are required for the expression of a certain characteristic.

complementary medicine *n* another name for **alternative medicine.**

complementary wavelength *n Physics.* the wavelength of monochromatic light that could be mixed in suitable proportions with a given coloured light so as to produce some specified achromatic light.

complementation (ˌkɒmplɪmenˈteɪʃən) *n* **1** the act or process of forming a complement. **2** *Genetics.* the combination of two homologous chromosomes, each with a different recessive mutant gene, in a single cell to produce a normal phenotype. The deficiency of one homologue is supplied by the normal allele of the other.

complement fixation test *n Med.* a serological test for detecting the presence of a specific antibody or antigen, used in the diagnosis of syphilis, etc.

complementizer (ˈkɒmplɪmənˌtaɪzə) *n Generative grammar.* a word or morpheme that serves to introduce a complement clause or a reduced form of such a clause, as *that* in *I wish that he would leave.*

complete (kəmˈpliːt) *adj* **1** having every necessary part or element; entire. **2** ended; finished. **3** (*prenominal*) thorough; absolute: *he is a complete rogue.* **4** perfect in quality or kind: *he is a complete scholar.* **5** (of a logical system) constituted such that a contradiction arises on the addition of any proposition that cannot be deduced from the axioms of the system. Compare **consistent** (sense 5). **6** (of flowers) having sepals, petals, stamens, and carpels. **7** *Archaic.* expert or skilled; accomplished. ◆ *vb* (*tr*) **8** to make whole or perfect. **9** to end; finish. **10** (in land law) to pay any outstanding balance on a contract for the conveyance of land in exchange for the title deeds, so that the ownership of the land changes hands. **11** *American football.* (of a quarterback) to make a forward pass successfully. [C14: from Latin *complētus,* past participle of *complēre* to fill up; see COMPLEMENT] ▸ **comˈpletely** *adv* ▸ **comˈpleteness** *n* ▸ **comˈpleter** *n* ▸ **comˈpletion** *n* ▸ **comˈpletive** *adj*

completist (kəmˈpliːtɪst) *n* a person who collects objects or memorabilia obsessively: *ardent John Wayne completists.*

complex (ˈkɒmplɛks) *adj* **1** made up of various interconnected parts; composite. **2** (of thoughts, writing, etc.) intricate or involved. **3** *Grammar.* **3a** (of a word) containing at least one bound form. **3b** (of a noun phrase) containing both a lexical noun and an embedded clause, as for example the italicized parts of the following sentence: I didn't know *the man who served me.* **3c** (of a sentence) formed by subordination of one clause to another. **4** *Maths.* **4a** of or involving one or more complex numbers. **4b** consisting of a real and an imaginary part, either of which can be zero. ◆ *n* **5** a whole made up of interconnected or related parts: *a building complex.* **6** *Psychoanal.* a group of emotional ideas or impulses that have been banished from the conscious mind but that continue to influence a person's behaviour. **7** *Informal.* an obsession or excessive fear: *he's got a complex about cats.* **8** Also called: **coordination compound.** a chemical compound in which molecules, groups, or ions are attached to a central metal atom, esp. a transition metal atom, by coordinate bonds. **9** any chemical compound in which one molecule is linked to another by a coordinate bond. [C17: from Latin *complexus,* from *complectī* to entwine, from *com-* together + *plectere* to braid] ▸ **ˈcomplexly** *adv* ▸ **ˈcomplexness** *n*

USAGE *Complex* is sometimes wrongly used where *complicated* is meant. *Complex* is properly used to say only that something consists of several parts. It should not be used to say that, because something consists of many parts, it is difficult to understand or analyse.

complex conjugate *n Maths.* the complex number whose imaginary part is the negation of that of a given complex number, the real parts of both numbers being equal: *a* – *ib is the complex conjugate of a* + *ib.*

complex fraction *n Maths.* a fraction in which the numerator or denominator or both contain fractions. Also called: **compound fraction.**

complexion (kəmˈplɛkʃən) *n* **1** the colour and general appearance of a person's skin, esp. of the face. **2** aspect, character, or nature: *the general complexion of a nation's finances.* **3** *Obsolete.* **3a** the temperament of a person. **3b** the temperature and general appearance of the body. [C14: from medical Latin *complexiō* one's bodily characteristics, from Latin: a combination, from *complectī* to embrace; see COMPLEX] ▸ **comˈplexional** *adj*

complexioned (kəmˈplɛkʃənd) *adj* (*in combination*) of a specified complexion: *light-complexioned.*

complexity (kəmˈplɛksɪtɪ) *n, pl* **-ties. 1** the state or quality of being intricate or complex. **2** something intricate or complex; complication.

complex number *n* any number of the form $a + bi$, where a and b are real numbers and $i = \sqrt{-1}$. See **number** (sense 1).

complexometric titration (kəmˌplɛksəʊˈmetrɪk) *n Chem.* a titration in which a complex is formed, usually by the use of a chelating agent, such as EDTA, the end point being marked by a sharp decrease in the concentration of metal ions.

complexone (kəmˈplɛksəʊn) *n Chem.* any chelating agent, such as EDTA, used for the analytical determination of metals.

complex salt *n* a salt that contains one or more complex ions. Compare **double salt.**

complex sentence *n Grammar.* a sentence containing at least one main clause and one subordinate clause.

complex wave *n Physics.* a waveform consisting of a fundamental frequency with superimposed harmonics.

compliance (kəmˈplaɪəns) *or* **compliancy** *n* **1** the act of complying; acquiescence. **2** a disposition to yield to or comply with others. **3** a measure of the ability of a mechanical system to respond to an applied vibrating force, expressed as the reciprocal of the system's stiffness. Symbol: *C*

compliance officer *n* a specialist, usually a lawyer, employed by a financial group operating in a variety of fields and for multiple clients to ensure that no conflict of interest arises and that all obligations and regulations are complied with.

compliant (kəmˈplaɪənt) *or* **compliable** *adj* complying, obliging, or yielding. ▸ **comˈpliantly** *or* **comˈpliably** *adv* ▸ **comˈpliantness** *or* **comˈpliableness** *n*

complicacy (ˈkɒmplɪkəsɪ) *n, pl* **-cies.** a less common word for **complexity.**

complicate *vb* (ˈkɒmplɪˌkeɪt). **1** to make or become complex. ◆ *adj* (ˈkɒmplɪkɪt). **2** *Biology.* folded on itself: *a complicate leaf.* **3** a less common word for **complicated.** [C17: from Latin *complicāre* to fold together, from *plicāre* to fold]

complicated (ˈkɒmplɪˌkeɪtɪd) *adj* made up of intricate parts or aspects that are difficult to understand or analyse. ▸ **ˈcompliˌcatedly** *adv* ▸ **ˈcompliˌcatedness** *n*

complication (ˌkɒmplɪˈkeɪʃən) *n* **1** a condition, event, etc., that is complex or confused. **2** the act or process of complicating. **3** a situation, event, or condition that complicates or frustrates: *her coming was a serious complication.* **4** a disease or disorder arising as a consequence of another disease.

complice (ˈkɒmplɪs, ˈkʌm-) *n Obsolete.* an associate or accomplice. [C15: from Old French, from Late Latin *complex* partner, associate, from Latin *complicāre* to fold together; see COMPLICATE]

complicity (kəmˈplɪsɪtɪ) *n, pl* **-ties. 1** the fact or condition of being an accomplice, esp. in a criminal act. **2** a less common word for **complexity.**

compliment *n* (ˈkɒmplɪmənt). **1** a remark or act expressing respect, admiration, etc. **2** (*usually pl*) a greeting of respect or regard. ◆ *vb* (ˈkɒmplɪˌmɛnt). (*tr*) **3** to express admiration of; congratulate or commend. **4** to express or show respect or regard for, esp. by a gift. [C17: from French, from Italian *complimento,* from Spanish *cumplimiento,* from *cumplir* to complete, do what is fitting, be polite]

USAGE Avoid confusion with **complement.**

complimentary (ˌkɒmplɪˈmɛntərɪ, -trɪ) *adj* **1** conveying, containing, or resembling a compliment. **2** expressing praise; flattering. **3** given free, esp. as a courtesy or for publicity purposes. ▸ **ˌcompliˈmentarily** *adv*

compline (ˈkɒmplɪn, -plaɪn) *or* **complin** (ˈkɒmplɪn) *n R.C. Church.* the last of the seven canonical hours of the divine office. [C13: from Old French *complie,* from Medieval Latin *hōra complēta,* literally: the completed hour, from Latin *complēre* to fill up, COMPLETE]

complot *Archaic.* ◆ *n* (ˈkɒmplɒt). **1** a plot or conspiracy. ◆ *vb* (kəmˈplɒt), **-plots, -plotting, -plotted. 2** to plot together; conspire. [C16: from Old French, of unknown origin] ▸ **comˈplotter** *n*

comply (kəmˈplaɪ) *vb* **-plies, -plying, -plied.** (*intr*) **1** (usually foll. by *with*) to act in accordance with rules, wishes, etc.; be obedient (to). **2** *Obsolete.* to be obedient or complaisant. [C17: from Italian *complire,* from Spanish *cumplir* to complete; see COMPLIMENT] ▸ **comˈplier** *n*

compo (ˈkɒmpəʊ) *n, pl* **-pos. 1** a mixture of materials, such as mortar, plaster, etc. **2** *Austral. and N.Z. informal.* compensation, esp. for injury or loss of work. ◆ *adj* **3** *Military.* intended to last for several days: *compo rations; a compo pack.* [short for *composition, compensation, composite*]

component (kəmˈpəʊnənt) *n* **1** a constituent part or aspect of something more complex: *a component of a car.* **2** Also called: **element.** any electrical device, such as a resistor, that has distinct electrical characteristics and that may be connected to other electrical devices to form a circuit. **3** *Maths.* **3a** one of a set of two or more vectors whose resultant is a given vector. **3b** the projection of this given vector onto a specified line. **4** one of the minimum number of chemically distinct constituents necessary to describe fully the composition of each phase in a system. See **phase rule.** ◆ *adj* **5** forming or functioning as a part or aspect; constituent. [C17: from Latin *compōnere* to put together, from *pōnere* to place, put] ▸ **componential** (ˌkɒmpəˈnɛnʃəl) *adj*

compony (kəmˈpəʊnɪ) *or* **componé** (kəmˈpəʊneɪ) *adj* (*usually postpositive*) *Heraldry.* made up of alternating metal and colour, colour and fur, or fur and metal. [C16: from Old French *componé,* from *copon* piece, COUPON]

comport (kəmˈpɔːt) *vb* **1** (*tr*) to conduct or bear (oneself) in a specified way. **2** (*intr;* foll. by *with*) to agree (with); correspond (to). [C16: from Latin *comportāre* to bear, collect, from *com-* together + *portāre* to carry]

comportment (kəmˈpɔːtmənt) *n* conduct; bearing.

compose (kəmˈpəʊz) *vb* (*mainly tr*) **1** to put together or make up by combining; put in proper order. **2** to be the component elements of. **3** to produce or create (a musical or literary work). **4** (*intr*) to write music. **5** to calm (someone, esp. oneself); make quiet. **6** to adjust or settle (a quarrel, etc.). **7** to order the elements of (a painting, sculpture, etc.); design. **8** *Printing.* to set up (type). [C15: from Old French *composer,* from Latin *compōnere* to put in place; see COMPONENT]

composed (kəmˈpəʊzd) *adj* (of people) calm; tranquil; serene. ▸ **composedly** (kəmˈpəʊzɪdlɪ) *adv* ▸ **comˈposedness** *n*

composer (kəmˈpəʊzə) *n* **1** a person who composes music. **2** a person or machine that composes anything, esp. type for printing.

composing room *n* the room in a printing establishment in which type is set.

composing stick *n Printing.* a metal holder of adjustable width in which a compositor sets a line of type at a time by hand; now rarely used.

composite (ˈkɒmpəzɪt) *adj* **1** composed of separate parts; compound. **2** of, relating to, or belonging to the plant family *Compositae.* **3** *Maths.* capable of being factorized: *a composite function.* **4** (*sometimes cap.*) denoting or relating to one of the five classical orders of architecture: characterized by a combination of the Ionic and Corinthian styles. See also **Doric, Tuscan.** ◆ *n* **5** something composed of separate parts; compound. **6** any plant of the family *Compositae,* typically having flower heads composed of ray flowers (e.g. dandelion), disc flowers (e.g. thistle), or both (e.g. daisy). **7** a material, such as reinforced concrete, made of two or more distinct materials. **8** a proposal that has been composited. ◆ *vb* ('kɒmpəˌzaɪt) **9** (*tr*) to merge related motions from local branches of (a political party, trade union, etc.) so as to produce a manageable number of proposals for discussion at national level. **[C16:** from Latin *compositus* well arranged, from *compōnere* to collect, arrange; see COMPONENT**]** ▸ **'compositely** *adv* ▸ **'compositeness** *n*

composite colour signal *n* a colour television signal in which luminance and two chrominance components are encoded into a single signal.

composite number *n* an integer that can be factorized into two or more other integers. Compare **prime number.**

composite photograph *n* a photograph formed by superimposing two or more separate photographs.

composite school *n Eastern Canadian.* a secondary school offering both academic and nonacademic courses.

composition (ˌkɒmpə'zɪʃən) *n* **1** the act of putting together or making up by combining parts or ingredients. **2** something formed in this manner or the resulting state or quality; a mixture. **3** the parts of which something is composed or made up; constitution. **4** a work of music, art, or literature. **5** the harmonious arrangement of the parts of a work of art in relation to each other and to the whole. **6** a piece of writing undertaken as an academic exercise in grammatically acceptable writing; an essay. **7** *Printing.* the act or technique of setting up type. **8** *Linguistics.* the formation of compound words. **9** *Logic.* the fallacy of inferring that the properties of the part are also true of the whole, as *every member of the team has won a prize, so the team will win a prize.* **10a** a settlement by mutual consent, esp. a legal agreement whereby the creditors agree to accept partial payment of a debt in full settlement. **10b** the sum so agreed. **11** *Chem.* the nature and proportions of the elements comprising a chemical compound. **[C14:** from Old French, from Latin *compositus;* see COMPOSITE, -ION**]** ▸ **ˌcompo'sitional** *adj*

composition of forces *n* the combination of two or more forces into a single equivalent force (the resultant).

compositor (kəm'pɒzɪtə) *n Printing.* a person who sets and corrects type and generally assembles text and illustrations for printing. Sometimes shortened to **comp.** ▸ **compositorial** (kəmˌpɒzɪ'tɔːrɪəl) *adj*

compos mentis *Latin.* ('kɒmpəs 'mɛntɪs) *adj* (*postpositive*) of sound mind; sane.

compossible (kɒm'pɒsɪbᵊl) *adj Rare.* possible in coexistence with something else.

compost ('kɒmpɒst) *n* **1** a mixture of organic residues such as decomposed vegetation, manure, etc., used as a fertilizer. **2** a mixture, as of sand, peat, and charcoal, in which plants are grown, esp. in pots. **3** *Rare.* a compound or mixture. ◆ *vb* (*tr*) **4** to make (vegetable matter) into compost. **5** to fertilize with compost. **[C14:** from Old French *compost,* from Latin *compositus* put together; see COMPOSITE**]**

Compostela (*Spanish* kɔmpɔs'tela) *n* See **Santiago de Compostela.**

composure (kəm'pəʊʒə) *n* calmness, esp. of the mind; tranquillity; serenity.

compotation (ˌkɒmpə'teɪʃən) *n Rare.* the act of drinking together in a company. **[C16:** from Latin *compōtātiō,* translation of Greek SYMPOSIUM**]** ▸ **'compoˌtator** *n*

compote ('kɒmpəʊt; *French* kɔ̃pɔt) *n* a dish of fruit stewed with sugar or in a syrup and served hot or cold. **[C17:** from French *composte,* from Latin *composita,* feminine of *compositus* put in place; see COMPOSITE**]**

compound[1] *n* ('kɒmpaʊnd). **1** a substance that contains atoms of two or more chemical elements held together by chemical bonds. **2** any combination of two or more parts, aspects, etc. **3** a word formed from two existing words or combining forms. ◆ *vb* (kəm'paʊnd). (*mainly tr*) **4** to mix or combine so as to create a compound or other product. **5** to make by combining parts, elements, aspects, etc.: *to compound a new plastic.* **6** to intensify by an added element: *his anxiety was compounded by her crying.* **7** *Finance.* to calculate or pay (interest) on both the principal and its accrued interest. **8** (*also intr*) to come to an agreement in (a quarrel, dispute, etc.). **9** (*also intr*) to settle (a debt, promise, etc.) for less than what is owed; compromise. **10** *Law.* to agree not to prosecute in return for a consideration: *to compound a crime.* **11** *Electrical engineering.* to place duplex windings on the field coil of (a motor or generator), one acting as a shunt, the other being in series with the main circuit, thus making the machine self-regulating. ◆ *adj* ('kɒmpaʊnd). **12** composed of or created by the combination of two or more parts, elements, etc. **13** (of a word) consisting of elements that are also words or productive combining forms. **14** (of a sentence) formed by coordination of two or more sentences. **15** (of a verb or the tense, mood, etc., of a verb) formed by using an auxiliary verb in addition to the main verb: *the future in English is a compound tense involving the use of such auxiliary verbs as "shall" and "will".* **16** *Music.* **16a** denoting a time in which the number of beats per bar is a multiple of three: *six-four is an example of compound time.* **16b** (of an interval) greater than an octave. **17** *Zoology.* another word for **colonial** (sense 6). **18** (of a steam engine, turbine, etc.) having multiple stages in which the steam or working fluid from one stage is used in a subsequent stage. **19** (of a piston engine) having a supercharger powered by a turbine in the exhaust stream. **[C14:** from earlier *compounen,* from Old French *compondre* to collect, set in order, from Latin *compōnere***]** ▸ **com'poundable** *adj* ▸ **com'pounder** *n*

compound[2] ('kɒmpaʊnd) *n* **1** (esp. formerly in South Africa) an enclosure, esp. on the mines, containing the living quarters for Black workers. **2** any similar enclosure, such as a camp for prisoners of war. **3** (formerly in India, China, etc.) the enclosure in which a European's house or factory stood. **[C17:** by folk etymology (influenced by COMPOUND[1]) from Malay *kampong* village**]**

compound annual return *n* the total return available from an investment, deposit, etc., when the interest earned is used to augment the capital. Abbrev.: **CAR.**

compound engine *n* **1** a steam engine in which the steam is expanded in more than one stage, first in a high-pressure cylinder and then in one or more low-pressure cylinders. **2** a reciprocating engine in which the exhaust gases are expanded in a turbine to drive a supercharger.

compound eye *n* the convex eye of insects and some crustaceans, consisting of numerous separate light-sensitive units (ommatidia). See also **ocellus.**

compound fault *n Geology.* a series of closely spaced faults.

compound flower *n* a flower head made up of many small flowers appearing as a single bloom, as in the daisy.

compound fraction *n* another name for **complex fraction.**

compound fracture *n* a fracture in which the broken bone either pierces the skin or communicates with an open wound.

compound interest *n* interest calculated on both the principal and its accrued interest. Compare **simple interest.**

compound leaf *n* a leaf consisting of two or more leaflets borne on the same leafstalk.

compound lens *n* another term for **lens** (sense 2).

compound microscope *n* an instrument for magnifying small objects, consisting of a lens of short focal length for forming an image that is further magnified by a second lens of longer focal length. Compare **simple microscope.**

compound number *n* a quantity expressed in two or more different but related units: *3 hours 10 seconds is a compound number.*

compound sentence *n* a sentence containing at least two coordinate clauses.

compound time *n* See **compound** (sense 16).

comprador *or* **compradore** (ˌkɒmprə'dɔː) *n* (formerly in China and some other Asian countries) a native agent of a foreign enterprise. **[C17:** from Portuguese: buyer, from Late Latin *comparātor,* from Latin *comparāre* to purchase, from *parāre* to prepare**]**

comprehend (ˌkɒmprɪ'hɛnd) *vb* **1** to perceive or understand. **2** (*tr*) to comprise or embrace; include. **[C14:** from Latin *comprehendere,* from *prehendere* to seize**]**

comprehensible (ˌkɒmprɪ'hɛnsəbᵊl) *adj* capable of being comprehended. ▸ **ˌcompreˌhensi'bility** *or* **ˌcompre'hensibleness** *n* ▸ **ˌcompre'hensibly** *adv*

comprehension (ˌkɒmprɪ'hɛnʃən) *n* **1** the act or capacity of understanding. **2** the state of including or comprising something; comprehensiveness. **3** *Education.* an exercise consisting of a previously unseen passage of text with related questions, designed to test a student's understanding esp. of a foreign language. **4** *Logic, obsolete.* the attributes implied by a given concept or term; connotation.

comprehensive (ˌkɒmprɪ'hɛnsɪv) *adj* **1** of broad scope or content; including all or much. **2** (of a car insurance policy) providing protection against most risks, including third-party liability, fire, theft, and damage. **3** having the ability to understand. **4** of, relating to, or being a comprehensive school. ◆ *n* **5** short for **comprehensive school.** ▸ **ˌcompre'hensively** *adv* ▸ **ˌcompre'hensiveness** *n*

comprehensive school *n* **1** *Chiefly Brit.* a secondary school for children of all abilities from the same district. **2** *Eastern Canadian.* another name for **composite school.**

compress *vb* (kəm'prɛs). **1** (*tr*) to squeeze together or compact into less space; condense. ◆ *n* ('kɒmprɛs). **2** a wet or dry cloth or gauze pad with or without medication, applied firmly to some part of the body to relieve discomfort, reduce fever, drain a wound, etc. **3** a machine for packing material, esp. cotton, under pressure. **[C14:** from Late Latin *compressāre,* from Latin *comprimere,* from *premere* to press**]** ▸ **com'pressible** *adj* ▸ **com'pressibleness** *n* ▸ **com'pressibly** *adv*

compressed (kəm'prɛst) *adj* **1** squeezed together or condensed. **2** (of the form of flatfishes, certain plant parts, etc.) flattened laterally along the whole length.

compressed air *n* air at a higher pressure than atmospheric pressure: used esp. as a source of power for machines.

compressibility (kəmˌprɛsɪ'bɪlɪtɪ) *n* **1** the ability to be compressed. **2** *Physics.* the reciprocal of the bulk modulus; the ratio of volume strain to stress at constant temperature. Symbol: *k*

compression (kəm'prɛʃən) *n* **1** Also called: **compressure** (kəm'prɛʃə). the act of compressing or the condition of being compressed. **2** an increase in pressure of the charge in an engine or compressor obtained by reducing its volume.

compression-ignition engine *n* a type of internal-combustion engine, such as a diesel, in which ignition occurs as a result of the rise in temperature caused by compression of the mixture in the cylinder.

compression ratio *n* the ratio of the volume enclosed by the cylinder of an internal-combustion engine at the beginning of the compression stroke to the volume enclosed at the end of it.

compressive (kəm'prɛsɪv) *adj* compressing or having the power or capacity to compress. ▸ **com'pressively** *adv*

compressor (kəm'prɛsə) *n* **1** any reciprocating or rotating device that compresses a gas. **2** the part of a gas turbine that compresses the air before it enters the combustion chambers. **3** any muscle that causes compression of any part or structure. **4** a medical instrument for holding down a part of the body. **5** an electronic device for reducing the variation in signal amplitude in a transmission system. Compare **expander, compander.**

comprise (kəm'praɪz) *vb* (*tr*) **1** to include; contain. **2** to constitute the whole of; consist of: *her singing comprised the entertainment.* **[C15:** from French *compris* included, understood, from *comprendre* to COMPREHEND**]** ▸ **com'prisable** *adj* ▸ **com'prisal** *n*

USAGE The use of *of* after *comprise* should be avoided: *the library comprises* (not *comprises of*) *500,000 books and manuscripts.*

compromise ('kɒmprəˌmaɪz) *n* **1** settlement of a dispute by concessions on both or all sides. **2** the terms of such a settlement. **3** something midway between two or more different things. **4** an exposure of one's good name, reputation, etc., to injury. ◆ *vb* **5** to settle (a dispute) by making concessions. **6** (*tr*) to expose (a person or persons) to disrepute. **7** (*tr*) to prejudice unfavourably; weaken: *his behaviour compromised his chances.* **8** (*tr*) *Obsolete.* to pledge mutually. [C15: from Old French *compromis,* from Latin *comprōmissum* mutual agreement to accept the decision of an arbiter, from *comprōmittere,* from *prōmittere* to promise] ▸ **'compro,miser** *n* ▸ **'compro,misingly** *adv*

compte rendu *French.* (kɔ̃t rɑ̃dy) *n, pl* ***comptes rendus*** (kɔ̃t rɑ̃dy). **1** a short review or notice, esp. of a book. **2** a statement of account. [literally: account rendered]

Comptometer (kɒmp'tɒmɪtə) *n Trademark.* a high-speed calculating machine: superseded by electronic calculators.

Compton *n* **1** ('kɒmptən). **Arthur Holly.** 1892–1962, U.S. physicist, noted for his research on X-rays, gamma rays, and nuclear energy: Nobel prize for physics 1927. **2** ('kʌmptən). **Denis.** 1918–97, English cricketer, who played for Middlesex and England (1937–57); broke two records in 1947 scoring 3816 runs and 18 centuries in one season.

Compton-Burnett ('kɒmptənbɜː'nɛt, -'bɜːnɪt) *n* Dame **Ivy.** 1884–1969, English novelist. Her novels include *Men and Wives* (1931) and *Mother and Son* (1955).

Compton effect *n* a phenomenon in which a collision between a photon and a particle results in an increase in the kinetic energy of the particle and a corresponding increase in the wavelength of the photon. [C20: named after A. H. COMPTON]

comptroller (kən'trəʊlə) *n* a variant spelling of **controller** (sense 2), esp. as a title of any of various financial executives. ▸ **comp'troller,ship** *n*

compulsion (kəm'pʌlʃən) *n* **1** the act of compelling or the state of being compelled. **2** something that compels. **3** *Psychiatry.* an inner drive that causes a person to perform actions, often of a trivial and repetitive nature, against his will. See also **obsession.** [C15: from Old French, from Latin *compellere* to COMPEL]

compulsive (kəm'pʌlsɪv) *adj* **1** relating to or involving compulsion. ◆ *n* **2** *Psychiatry.* an individual who is subject to a psychological compulsion. ▸ **com'pulsively** *adv* ▸ **com'pulsiveness** *n*

compulsory (kəm'pʌlsərɪ) *adj* **1** required by regulations or laws; obligatory: *compulsory education.* **2** involving or employing compulsion; compelling; necessary; essential. ▸ **com'pulsorily** *adv* ▸ **com'pulsoriness** *n*

compulsory purchase *n* purchase of a house or other property by a local authority or government department for public use or to make way for development, regardless of whether or not the owner wishes to sell.

compunction (kəm'pʌŋkʃən) *n* a feeling of remorse, guilt, or regret. [C14: from Church Latin *compunctiō,* from Latin *compungere* to sting, from *com-* (intensive) + *pungere* to puncture; see POINT] ▸ **com'punctious** *adj* ▸ **com'punctiously** *adv*

compurgation (,kɒmpɜː'geɪʃən) *n Law.* (formerly) a method of trial whereby a defendant might be acquitted if a sufficient number of persons swore to his innocence. [C17: from Medieval Latin *compurgātiō,* from Latin *compurgāre* to purify entirely, from *com-* (intensive) + *purgāre* to PURGE] ▸ **'compur,gator** *n* ▸ **com'purgatory** *or* **com,purga'torial** *adj*

computation (,kɒmpjʊ'teɪʃən) *n* a calculation involving numbers or quantities. ▸ **,compu'tational** *adj*

computational fluid dynamics *n* (*functioning as sing*) the prediction of the effects of fluid motion past objects by numerical methods rather than model experiments.

compute (kəm'pjuːt) *vb* **1** to calculate (an answer, result, etc.), often with the aid of a computer. ◆ *n* **2** calculation; computation (esp. in the phrase **beyond compute**). [C17: from Latin *computāre,* from *putāre* to think] ▸ **com'putable** *adj* ▸ **com,puta'bility** *n*

computed tomography *n Med.* another name (esp. U.S.) for **computerized tomography.**

computer (kəm'pjuːtə) *n* **1a** a device, usually electronic, that processes data according to a set of instructions. The **digital computer** stores data in discrete units and performs arithmetical and logical operations at very high speed. The **analog computer** has no memory and is slower than the digital computer but has a continuous rather than a discrete input. The **hybrid computer** combines some of the advantages of digital and analog computers. **1b** (*as modifier*): *computer technology.* Related prefix: **cyber-**. **2** a person who computes or calculates.

computer-aided design *n* the use of computer techniques in designing products, esp. involving the use of computer graphics. Abbrev.: **CAD.**

computer-aided engineering *n* the use of computers to automate manufacturing processes. Abbrev.: **CAE.**

computer architecture *n* the structure, behaviour, and design of computers.

computerate (kəm'pjuːtərɪt) *adj* able to use computers. [C20: COMPUTER + -ATE[1], by analogy with *literate*]

computer conferencing *n* the conduct of meetings by the use of computer-based telecommunications.

computer dating *n* the use of computers by dating agencies to match their clients.

computer game *n* any of various games, recorded on cassette or disc for use in a home computer, that are played by manipulating a mouse, joystick, or the keys on the keyboard of a computer in response to the graphics on the screen.

computer graphics *n* (*functioning as sing*) the use of a computer to produce and manipulate pictorial images on a video screen, as in animation techniques or the production of audiovisual aids.

computerize *or* **computerise** (kəm'pjuːtə,raɪz) *vb* **1** (*tr*) to cause (certain operations) to be performed by a computer, esp. as a replacement for human labour. **2** (*intr*) to install a computer. **3** (*tr*) to control or perform (operations within a system) by means of a computer. **4** (*tr*) to process or store (information) by means of or in a computer. ▸ **com,puteri'zation** *or* **com,puteri'sation** *n*

computerized tomography *n Med.* a radiological technique that produces images of cross sections through a patient's body. Also called (esp. U.S.): **computed tomography.** Abbrev.: **CT.** See also **CT scanner.**

computer language *n* another term for **programming language.**

computer literate *adj* able to use computers. ▸ **computer literacy** *n*

computer science *n* the study of computers and their application.

computer typesetting *n* a system for the high-speed composition of type by a device driven by punched paper tape or magnetic tape that has been processed by a computer.

computing (kəm'pjuːtɪŋ) *n* **1** the activity of using computers and writing programs for them. **2** the study of computers and their implications. ◆ *adj* of or relating to computers: *computing skills.*

Comr *abbrev. for* Commissioner.

comrade ('kɒmreɪd, -rɪd) *n* **1** an associate or companion. **2** a fellow member of a political party, esp. a fellow Communist or socialist. [C16: from French *camarade,* from Spanish *camarada* group of soldiers sharing a billet, from *cámara* room, from Latin; see CAMERA, CHAMBER] ▸ **'comradely** *adj* ▸ **'comrade,ship** *n*

Comrades Marathon *n* **the.** *S. African.* an annual long-distance race run each June from Durban to Pietermaritzburg, a distance of approximately 90 kilometres (56 miles). Often shortened to **the Comrades.**

Comsat ('kɒmsæt) *n Trademark.* short for **communications satellite.**

comstockery ('kʌm,stɒkərɪ, 'kɒm-) *n U.S.* immoderate censorship on grounds of immorality. [C20: coined by G. B. Shaw (1905) after Anthony *Comstock* (1844–1915), U.S. moral crusader, who founded the Society for the Suppression of Vice]

Comstock Lode ('kʌm,stɒk, 'kɒm-) *n* an extensive gold and silver vein in W Nevada, near Virginia City. [C19: named after T. P. *Comstock* (1820–70), American prospector]

Comte (*French* kɔ̃t) *n* (**Isidore**) **Auguste** (**Marie François**) (ogyst). 1798–1857, French mathematician and philosopher; the founder of positivism. ▸ **Comtism** ('kɔːn,tɪzəm) *n* ▸ **'Comtist** *or* **'Comtian** *adj, n*

Comus ('kəʊməs) *n* (in late Roman mythology) a god of revelry. [C17: from Latin, from Greek *kōmos* a revel]

Com. Ver. *abbrev. for* Common Version (of the Bible).

con[1] (kɒn) *Informal.* ◆ *n* **1a** short for **confidence trick.** **1b** (*as modifier*): *con man.* ◆ *vb* **cons, conning, conned.** **2** (*tr*) to swindle or defraud. [C19: from CONFIDENCE]

con[2] (kɒn) *n* (*usually pl*) **1** an argument or vote against a proposal, motion, etc. **2** a person who argues or votes against a proposal, motion, etc. ◆ Compare **pro[1]**. See also **pros and cons.** [from Latin *contrā* against, opposed to]

con[3] (kɒn) *n Slang.* short for **convict.**

con[4] *or* (*esp. U.S.*) **conn** (kɒn) *Nautical.* ◆ *vb* **cons** *or* **conns, conning, conned.** **1** (*tr*) to direct the steering of (a vessel). ◆ *n* **2** the place where a person who cons a vessel is stationed. [C17 *cun,* from earlier *condien* to guide, from Old French *conduire,* from Latin *condūcere;* see CONDUCT]

con[5] (kɒn) *vb* **cons, conning, conned.** (*tr*) *Archaic.* to study attentively or learn (esp. in the phrase **con by rote**). [C15: variant of CAN[1] in the sense: to come to know]

con[6] (kɒn) *prep Music.* with. [Italian]

con. *abbrev. for:* **1** concerto. **2** conclusion. **3** connection. **4** consolidated. **5** continued. **6** contra. [Latin: against]

Con. *abbrev. for:* **1** Conformist. **2** Conservative. **3** Consul.

con- *prefix* a variant of **com-**.

conacre (kʌ'neːkər) *n Irish.* farming land let for a season or for eleven months. [C19: from CORN[1] + ACRE]

Conakry *or* **Konakri** (*French* kɔnakri) *n* the capital of Guinea, a port on the island of Tombo. Pop.: 1 508 000 (1995 est.).

con amore (kɒn æ'mɔːrɪ) *adj, adv Music.* (to be performed) lovingly. [C19: from Italian: with love]

Conan Doyle ('kəʊnən 'dɔɪl, 'kɒnən) *n* Sir **Arthur.** 1859–1930, British author of detective stories and historical romances and the creator of *Sherlock Holmes.*

conation (kəʊ'neɪʃən) *n* the element in psychological processes that tends towards activity or change and appears as desire, volition, and striving. [C19: from Latin *cōnātiō* an attempting, from *cōnārī* to try] ▸ **co'national** *adj*

conative ('kɒnətɪv, 'kəʊ-) *adj* **1** *Grammar.* denoting an aspect of verbs in some languages used to indicate the effort of the agent in performing the activity described by the verb. **2** of or relating to conation.

conatus (kəʊ'neɪtəs) *n, pl* **-tus.** **1** an effort or striving of natural impulse. **2** (esp. in the philosophy of Spinoza) the tendency of all things to persist in their own being. [C17: from Latin: effort, from *cōnārī* to try]

con brio (kɒn 'briːəʊ) *adj, adv Music.* (to be performed) with liveliness or spirit, as in the phrase **allegro con brio.** [Italian: with energy]

conc. *abbrev. for:* **1** concentrate. **2** concentrated. **3** concentration. **4** concerning. **5** concerto.

concatenate (kɒn'kætɪ,neɪt) *vb* **1** (*tr*) to link or join together, esp. in a chain or series. ◆ *adj* **2** linked or joined together. [C16: from Late Latin *concatēnāre* from Latin *com-* together + *catēna* CHAIN]

concatenation (kɒn,kætɪ'neɪʃən) *n* **1** a series of interconnected events, concepts, etc. **2** the act of linking together or the state of being joined. **3** *Logic.* a function that forms a single string of symbols from two given strings by placing the second after the first.

concave ('kɒnkeɪv, kɒn'keɪv) *adj* **1** curving inwards. **2** *Physics.* having one or two surfaces curved or ground in the shape of a section of the interior of a sphere, paraboloid, etc.: *a concave lens.* **3** *Maths.* (of a polygon) containing an interior angle greater than 180°. **4** an obsolete word for **hollow.** ◆ *vb* **5** (*tr*) to make concave. ◆ Compare **convex.** [C15: from Latin *concavus* arched, from *cavus* hollow] ▸ **'concavely** *adv* ▸ **'concaveness** *n*

concavity (kɒn'kævɪtɪ) *n, pl* **-ties. 1** the state or quality of being concave. **2** a concave surface or thing; cavity.

concavo-concave (kɒn,keɪvəʊkɒn'keɪv) *adj* (esp. of a lens) having both sides concave; biconcave.

concavo-convex *adj* **1** having one side concave and the other side convex. **2** (of a lens) having a concave face with greater curvature than the convex face. Compare **convexo-concave** (sense 2).

conceal (kən'siːl) *vb* (*tr*) **1** to keep from discovery; hide. **2** to keep secret. [C14: from Old French *conceler,* from Latin *concēlāre,* from *com-* (intensive) + *cēlāre* to hide] ▸ **con'cealable** *adj* ▸ **con'cealer** *n* ▸ **con'cealment** *n*

concede (kən'siːd) *vb* **1** (when *tr, may take a clause as object*) to admit or acknowledge (something) as true or correct. **2** to yield or allow (something, such as a right). **3** (*tr*) to admit as certain in outcome: *to concede an election.* [C17: from Latin *concēdere,* from *cēdere* to give way, CEDE] ▸ **con'cededly** *adv* ▸ **con'ceder** *n*

conceit (kən'siːt) *n* **1** a high, often exaggerated, opinion of oneself or one's accomplishments; vanity. **2** *Literary.* an elaborate image or far-fetched comparison, esp. as used by the English Metaphysical poets. **3** *Archaic.* **3a** a witty expression. **3b** fancy; imagination. **3c** an idea. **4** *Obsolete.* a small ornament. ◆ *vb* (*tr*) **5** *Northern English dialect.* to like or be able to bear (something, such as food or drink). **6** *Obsolete.* to think or imagine. [C14: from CONCEIVE]

conceited (kən'siːtɪd) *adj* **1** having a high or exaggerated opinion of oneself or one's accomplishments. **2** *Archaic.* fanciful. **3** *Obsolete.* witty or intelligent. ▸ **con'ceitedly** *adv* ▸ **con'ceitedness** *n*

conceivable (kən'siːvəbᵊl) *adj* capable of being understood, believed, or imagined; possible. ▸ **con,ceiva'bility** *or* **con'ceivableness** *n* ▸ **con'ceivably** *adv*

conceive (kən'siːv) *vb* **1** (when *intr,* foll. by *of;* when *tr, often takes a clause as object*) to have an idea (of); imagine; think. **2** (*tr; takes a clause as object or an infinitive*) to hold as an opinion; believe. **3** (*tr*) to develop or form, esp. in the mind: *she conceived a passion for music.* **4** to become pregnant with (young). **5** (*tr*) *Rare.* to express in words. [C13: from Old French *conceivre,* from Latin *concipere* to take in, from *capere* to take] ▸ **con'ceiver** *n*

concelebrate (kən'sɛlɪ,breɪt) *vb Christianity.* to celebrate (the Eucharist or Mass) jointly with one or more other priests. [C16: from Latin *concelebrāre*] ▸ **con,cele'bration** *n*

concent (kən'sɛnt) *n Archaic.* a concord, as of sounds, voices, etc. [C16: from Latin *concentus* harmonious sounds, from *concinere* to sing together, from *canere* to sing]

concentrate ('kɒnsən,treɪt) *vb* **1** to come or cause to come to a single purpose or aim: *to concentrate one's hopes on winning.* **2** to make or become denser or purer by the removal of certain elements, esp. the solvent of a solution. **3** (*tr*) to remove rock or sand from (an ore) to make it purer. **4** (*intr;* often foll. by *on*) to bring one's faculties to bear (on); think intensely (about). ◆ *n* **5** a concentrated material or solution: *tomato concentrate.* [C17: back formation from CONCENTRATION, ultimately from Latin *com-* same + *centrum* CENTRE] ▸ **'concen,trator** *n*

concentration (,kɒnsən'treɪʃən) *n* **1** intense mental application; complete attention. **2** the act or process of concentrating. **3** something that is concentrated. **4** the strength of a solution, esp. the amount of dissolved substance in a given volume of solvent, usually expressed in moles per cubic metre or cubic decimetre (litre). Symbol: *c* **5** the process of increasing the concentration of a solution. **6** *Military.* **6a** the act of bringing together military forces. **6b** the application of fire from a number of weapons against a target. **7** *Economics.* the degree to which the output or employment in an industry is accounted for by only a few firms. **8** another name (esp. U.S.) for **Pelmanism.**

concentration camp *n* a guarded prison camp in which nonmilitary prisoners are held, esp. one of those in Nazi Germany in which millions were exterminated.

concentrative ('kɒnsən,treɪtɪv) *adj* tending to concentrate; characterized by concentration. ▸ **'concen,tratively** *adv* ▸ **'concen,trativeness** *n*

concentre (kɒn'sɛntə) *vb* to converge or cause to converge on a common centre; concentrate. [C16: from French *concentrer;* see CONCENTRATE]

concentric (kən'sɛntrɪk) *adj* having a common centre: *concentric circles.* Compare **eccentric** (sense 3). [C14: from Medieval Latin *concentricus,* from Latin *com-* same + *centrum* CENTRE] ▸ **con'centrically** *adv* ▸ **concentricity** (,kɒnsən'trɪsɪtɪ) *n*

Concepción (*Spanish* konθep'θjon) *n* an industrial city in S central Chile. Pop.: 350 268 (1995 est.).

concept ('kɒnsɛpt) *n* **1** an idea, esp. an abstract idea: *the concepts of biology.* **2** *Philosophy.* a general idea or notion that corresponds to some class of entities and that consists of the characteristic or essential features of the class. **3** *Philosophy.* **3a** the conjunction of all the characteristic features of something. **3b** a theoretical construct within some theory. **3c** a directly intuited object of thought. **3d** the meaning of a predicate. **4** (*modifier*) (of a product, esp. a car) created as an exercise to demonstrate the technical skills and imagination of the designers, and not intended for mass production or sale. [C16: from Latin *conceptum* something received or conceived, from *concipere* to take in, CONCEIVE]

conceptacle (kən'sɛptəkᵊl) *n* a flask-shaped cavity containing the reproductive organs in some algae and fungi. [C17: from Latin *conceptāculum* receptacle, from *concipere* to receive, CONCEIVE]

conception (kən'sɛpʃən) *n* **1** something conceived; notion, idea, design, or plan. **2** the description under which someone considers something: *her conception of freedom is wrong.* **3** the fertilization of an ovum by a sperm in the Fallopian tube followed by implantation in the womb. **4** origin or beginning: *from its conception the plan was a failure.* **5** the act or power of forming notions; invention. [C13: from Latin *conceptiō,* from *concipere* to CONCEIVE] ▸ **con'ceptional** *or* **con'ceptive** *adj*

conceptual (kən'sɛptjʊəl) *adj* **1** relating to or concerned with concepts; abstract. **2** concerned with the definitions or relations of the concepts of some field of enquiry rather than with the facts. ▸ **con'ceptually** *adv*

conceptual art *n* art in which the idea behind a particular work, and the means of producing it, are more important than the finished work.

conceptualism (kən'sɛptjʊə,lɪzəm) *n* **1** the philosophical theory that the application of general words to a variety of objects reflects the existence of some mental entity through which the application is mediated and which constitutes the meaning of the term. Compare **nominalism, realism, Platonism. 2** the philosophical view that there is no reality independent of our conception of it, or (as in Kant) that the intellect is not a merely passive recipient of experience but rather imposes a structure on it. ▸ **con'ceptualist** *n* ▸ **con,ceptual'istic** *adj*

conceptualize *or* **conceptualise** (kən'sɛptjʊə,laɪz) *vb* to form (a concept or concepts) out of observations, experience, data, etc. ▸ **con,ceptuali'zation** *or* **con,ceptuali'sation** *n*

concern (kən'sɜːn) *vb* (*tr*) **1** to relate to; be of importance or interest to; affect. **2** (usually foll. by *with* or *in*) to involve or interest (oneself): *he concerns himself with other people's affairs.* ◆ *n* **3** something that affects or is of importance to a person; affair; business. **4** regard for or interest in a person or a thing: *he felt a strong concern for her.* **5** anxiety, worry, or solicitude. **6** important bearing or relation: *his news has great concern for us.* **7** a commercial company or enterprise. **8** *Informal.* a material thing, esp. one of which one has a low opinion. [C15: from Late Latin *concernere* to mingle together, from Latin *com-* together + *cernere* to sift, distinguish]

concerned (kən'sɜːnd) *adj* **1** (*postpositive*) interested, guilty, involved, or appropriate: *I shall find the boy concerned and punish him.* **2** worried, troubled, or solicitous. ▸ **concernedly** (kən'sɜːnɪdlɪ) *adv* ▸ **con'cernedness** *n*

concerning (kən'sɜːnɪŋ) *prep* **1** about; regarding; on the subject of. ◆ *adj* **2** worrying or troublesome.

concernment (kən'sɜːnmənt) *n* **1** *Rare.* affair or business; concern. **2** *Archaic.* a matter of importance.

concert *n* ('kɒnsɜːt, -sət). **1a** a performance of music by players or singers that does not involve theatrical staging. Compare **recital** (sense 1). **1b** (*as modifier*): *a concert version of an opera.* **2** agreement in design, plan, or action. **3 in concert. 3a** acting in a co-ordinated fashion with a common purpose. **3b** (of musicians, esp. rock musicians) performing live. ◆ *vb* (kən'sɜːt). **4** to arrange or contrive (a plan) by mutual agreement. [C16: from French *concerter* to bring into agreement, from Italian *concertare,* from Late Latin *concertāre* to work together, from Latin: to dispute, debate, from *certāre* to contend]

concertante (,kɒntʃə'tæntɪ) *Music.* ◆ *adj* **1** characterized by contrasting alternating tutti and solo passages. ◆ *n, pl* **-ti** (-tɪ). **2** a composition characterized by such contrasts. [C18: from Italian, from *concertare* to perform a concert, from *concerto* CONCERT]

concerted (kən'sɜːtɪd) *adj* **1** mutually contrived, planned, or arranged; combined (esp. in the phrases **concerted action, concerted effort**). **2** *Music.* arranged in parts for a group of singers or players. ▸ **con'certedly** *adv*

Concertgebouw (*Dutch* kɔn'sɛrtxəbɔu) *n* a concert hall in Amsterdam, inaugurated in 1888: the **Concertgebouw Orchestra,** established in 1888, has been independent of the hall since World War II.

concertgoer ('kɒnsɜːt,gəʊə) *n* a person who attends concerts of music.

concert grand *n* a full-size grand piano, usually around 7 feet in length. Compare **baby grand, boudoir grand.**

concertina (,kɒnsə'tiːnə) *n* **1** a small hexagonal musical instrument of the reed organ family in which metallic reeds are vibrated by air from a set of bellows operated by the player's hands. Notes are produced by pressing buttons. ◆ *vb* **-nas, -naing, -naed. 2** (*intr*) to collapse or fold up like a concertina. [C19: CONCERT + *-ina*] ▸ **,concer'tinist** *n*

concertino (,kɒntʃə'tiːnəʊ) *n, pl* **-ni** (-nɪ). **1** the small group of soloists in a concerto grosso. Compare **ripieno. 2** a short concerto. [C19: from Italian: a little CONCERTO]

concertize *or* **concertise** ('kɒnsə,taɪz) *vb* (*intr*) (esp. of a soloist or conductor) to give concerts.

concertmaster ('kɒnsət,mɑːstə) *n* a U.S. and Canadian word for **leader** (of an orchestra).

concerto (kən'tʃɛətəʊ) *n, pl* **-tos** *or* **-ti** (-tɪ). **1** a composition for an orchestra and one or more soloists. The classical concerto usually consisted of several movements, and often a candenza. See also **sonata** (sense 1), **symphony** (sense 1). **2** another word for **ripieno.** [C18: from Italian: CONCERT]

concerto grosso ('grɒsəʊ) *n, pl* **concerti grossi** ('grɒsɪ) *or* **concerto grossos.** a composition for an orchestra and a group of soloists, chiefly of the baroque period. [Italian, literally: big concerto]

concert overture *n* See **overture** (sense 1c).

concert party *n* **1** a musical entertainment popular in the early 20th century, esp. one at a British seaside resort. **2** *Stock Exchange, informal.* a group of individuals or companies who secretly agree to purchase shares separately in a particular company, which they plan to amalgamate later into a single holding: a malpractice that is illegal in some countries.

concert pitch *n* **1** the frequency of 440 hertz assigned to the A above middle C. See **pitch**[1] (sense 28b), **international pitch. 2** *Informal.* a state of extreme readiness.

concertstück (kən'sɜːt,ʃtuːk) *n Music.* **1** a composition in concerto style but shorter than a full concerto. 2 (loosely) a piece suitable for concert performance. [from German *Konzertstück* a concertino]

concert tuning *n Music.* the standard tuning for a guitar: E A D G B E.

concession (kən'sɛʃən) *n* **1** the act of yielding or conceding, as to a demand or argument. **2** something conceded. **3** *Brit.* a reduction in the usual price of a ticket granted to a special group of customers: *a student concession.* **4** any grant of rights, land, or property by a government, local authority, corporation, or individual. **5** the right, esp. an exclusive right, to market a particular product in a given area. **6** *U.S. and Canadian.* **6a** the right to maintain a subsidiary business on a lessor's premises. **6b** the premises so granted or the business so maintained. **6c** a free rental period for such premises. **7** *Canadian.* (chiefly in Ontario and Quebec) **7a** a land subdivision in a township survey. **7b** another name for a **concession road.** [C16: from Latin *concessiō* an allowing, from *concēdere* to CONCEDE] ▸ **con'cessible** *adj*

concessionaire (kən,sɛʃə'nɛə), **concessioner** (kən'sɛʃənə), or **concessionary** *n* someone who holds or operates a concession.

concessionary (kən'sɛʃənərɪ) *adj* **1** of, granted, or obtained by a concession. ◆ *n, pl* **-aries. 2** another word for **concessionaire.**

concession road *n Canadian.* (esp. in Ontario) one of a series of roads separating concessions in a township.

concessive (kən'sɛsɪv) *adj* **1** implying or involving concession; tending to concede. **2** *Grammar.* a conjunction, preposition, phrase, or clause describing a state of affairs that might have been expected to rule out what is described in the main clause but in fact does not: *"Although" in the sentence "Although they had been warned, they refused to take care" is a concessive conjunction.* [C18: from Late Latin *concēssīvus,* from Latin *concēdere* to CONCEDE]

conch (kɒŋk, kɒntʃ) *n, pl* **conchs** (kɒŋks) *or* **conches** ('kɒntʃɪz). **1** any of various tropical marine gastropod molluscs of the genus *Strombus* and related genera, esp. *S. gigas* (giant conch), characterized by a large brightly coloured spiral shell. **2** the shell of such a mollusc, used as a trumpet. **3** *Architect.* another name for **concha** (sense 2). [C16: from Latin *concha,* from Greek *konkhē* shellfish]

concha ('kɒŋkə) *n, pl* **-chae** (-kiː). **1** any bodily organ or part resembling a shell in shape, such as the external ear. **2** Also called: **conch.** *Architect.* the half dome of an apse. ▸ **'conchal** *adj*

conchie *or* **conchy** ('kɒntʃɪ) *n, pl* **-chies.** *Informal.* short for **conscientious objector.**

conchiferous (kɒŋ'kɪfərəs) *adj* **1** (esp. of molluscs) having or producing a shell. **2** (of rocks) containing shells.

conchiolin (kɒŋ'kaɪəlɪn) *n* a fibrous insoluble protein that forms the basic structure of the shells of molluscs. Formula: $C_{30}H_{48}O_{11}N_9$. [C19: from CONCH; see -IN]

Conchobar ('kɒŋkəuwə, 'kɒnuə) *n* (in Irish legend) a king of Ulster at about the beginning of the Christian era. See also **Deirdre.**

conchoid ('kɒŋkɔɪd) *n Geometry.* a plane curve consisting of two branches situated about a line to which they are asymptotic, so that a line from a fixed point (the pole) intersecting both branches is of constant length between asymptote and either branch. Equation: $(x - a)^2(x^2 + y^2) = b^2x^2$ where a is the distance between the pole and a vertical asymptote and b is the length of the constant segment.

conchoidal (kɒŋ'kɔɪdᵊl) *adj* **1** (of the fracture of minerals and rocks) having smooth shell-shaped convex and concave surfaces. **2** (of minerals and rocks, such as flint) having such a fracture. ▸ **con'choidally** *adv*

conchology (kɒŋ'kɒlədʒɪ) *n* the study and collection of mollusc shells. ▸ **conchological** (,kɒŋkə'lɒdʒɪkᵊl) *adj* ▸ **con'chologist** *n*

concierge (,kɒnsɪ'ɛəʒ; *French* kɔ̃sjɛrʒ) *n* (esp. in France) a caretaker of a block of flats, hotel, etc., esp. one who lives on the premises. [C17: from French, ultimately from Latin *conservus,* from *servus* slave]

conciliar (kən'sɪlɪə) *adj* of, from, or by means of a council, esp. an ecclesiastical one. ▸ **con'ciliarly** *adv*

conciliate (kən'sɪlɪ,eɪt) *vb (tr)* **1** to overcome the hostility of; placate; win over. **2** to win or gain (favour, regard, etc.), esp. by making friendly overtures. **3** *Archaic.* to make compatible; reconcile. [C16: from Latin *conciliāre* to bring together, from *concilium* COUNCIL] ▸ **con'ciliable** *adj* ▸ **con'cili,ator** *n*

conciliation (kən,sɪlɪ'eɪʃən) *n* **1** the act or process of conciliating. **2** a method of helping the parties in a dispute to reach agreement, esp. divorcing or separating couples to part amicably.

conciliatory (kən'sɪljətərɪ, -trɪ) *or* **conciliative** (kən'sɪljətɪv) *adj* intended to placate or reconcile. ▸ **con'ciliatorily** *adv* ▸ **con'ciliatoriness** *n*

concinnity (kən'sɪnɪtɪ) *n, pl* **-ties.** a harmonious arrangement of parts, esp. in literary works, speeches, etc. [C16: from Latin *concinnitās* a skilful combining of various things, from *concinnāre* to adjust, of obscure origin] ▸ **con'cinnous** *adj*

concise (kən'saɪs) *adj* expressing much in few words; brief and to the point. [C16: from Latin *concīsus* cut up, cut short, from *concīdere* to cut to pieces, from *caedere* to cut, strike down] ▸ **con'cisely** *adv* ▸ **con'ciseness** *n*

concision (kən'sɪʒən) *n* the quality of being concise; brevity; terseness.

conclave ('kɒnkleɪv, 'kɒŋ-) *n* **1** a confidential or secret meeting. **2** *R.C. Church.* **2a** the closed apartments where the college of cardinals elects a new pope. **2b** a meeting of the college of cardinals for this purpose. [C14: from Medieval Latin *conclāve,* from Latin: cage, place that may be locked, from *clāvis* key] ▸ **'conclavist** *n*

conclude (kən'kluːd) *vb (mainly tr)* **1** *(also intr)* to come or cause to come to an end or conclusion. **2** *(takes a clause as object)* to decide by reasoning; deduce: *the judge concluded that the witness had told the truth.* **3** to arrange finally; settle: *to conclude a treaty; it was concluded that he should go.* **4** *Obsolete.* to confine. [C14: from Latin *conclūdere* to enclose, end, from *claudere* to close] ▸ **con'cluder** *n*

conclusion (kən'kluːʒən) *n* **1** end or termination. **2** the last main division of a speech, lecture, essay, etc. **3** the outcome or result of an act, process, event, etc. (esp. in the phrase **a foregone conclusion**). **4** a final decision or judgment; resolution (esp. in the phrase **come to a conclusion**). **5** *Logic.* **5a** a statement that purports to follow from another or others (the **premises**) by means of an argument. **5b** a statement that does validly follow from given premises. **6** *Law.* **6a** an admission or statement binding on the party making it; estoppel. **6b** the close of a pleading or of a conveyance. **7 in conclusion.** lastly; to sum up. **8 jump to conclusions.** to come to a conclusion prematurely, without sufficient thought or on incomplete evidence. [C14: via Old French from Latin; see CONCLUDE, -ION]

conclusive (kən'kluːsɪv) *adj* **1** putting an end to doubt; decisive; final. **2** approaching or involving an end or conclusion. ▸ **con'clusively** *adv* ▸ **con'clusiveness** *n*

concoct (kən'kɒkt) *vb (tr)* **1** to make by combining different ingredients. **2** to invent; make up; contrive. [C16: from Latin *concoctus* cooked together, from *concoquere,* from *coquere* to cook] ▸ **con'cocter** *or* **con'coctor** *n* ▸ **con'coctive** *adj*

concoction (kən'kɒkʃən) *n* **1** the act or process of concocting. **2** something concocted. **3** an untruth; lie.

concomitance (kən'kɒmɪtəns) *n* **1** existence or occurrence together or in connection with another. **2** a thing that exists in connection with another. **3** *Christian theol.* the doctrine that the body and blood of Christ are present in the Eucharist.

concomitant (kən'kɒmɪtənt) *adj* **1** existing or occurring together; associative. ◆ *n* **2** a concomitant act, person, etc. [C17: from Late Latin *concomitārī* to accompany, from *com-* with + *comes* companion, fellow] ▸ **con'comitantly** *adv*

concord ('kɒnkɔːd, 'kɒŋ-) *n* **1** agreement or harmony between people or nations; amity. **2** a treaty establishing peaceful relations between nations. **3** agreement or harmony between things, ideas, etc. **4** *Music.* a combination of musical notes, esp. one containing a series of consonant intervals. Compare **discord** (sense 3). **5** *Grammar.* another word for **agreement** (sense 6). [C13: from Old French *concorde,* from Latin *concordia,* from *concors* of the same mind, harmonious, from *com-* same + *cor* heart]

Concord ('kɒŋkəd) *n* **1** a town in NE Massachusetts: scene of one of the opening military actions (1775) of the War of American Independence. Pop.: 17 080 (1990). **2** a city in New Hampshire, the state capital: printing, publishing. Pop.: 36 364 (1992).

concordance (kən'kɔːdᵊns) *n* **1** a state or condition of agreement or harmony. **2** a book that indexes the principal words in a literary work, often with the immediate context and an account of the meaning. **3** an index produced by computer or machine, alphabetically listing every word in a text. **4** an alphabetical list of subjects or topics.

concordant (kən'kɔːdᵊnt) *adj* being in agreement: harmonious. ▸ **con'cordantly** *adv*

concordat (kɒn'kɔːdæt) *n* a pact or treaty, esp. one between the Vatican and another state concerning the interests of religion in that state. [C17: via French, from Medieval Latin *concordātum,* from Latin: something agreed, from *concordāre* to be of one mind; see CONCORD]

Concorde ('kɒnkɔːd, 'kɒŋ-) *n* the first commercial supersonic airliner. Of Anglo-French construction, it is capable of cruising at over 2160 km per hr (1200 mph).

Concord grape ('kɒŋkəd, 'kɒnkɔːd) *n* a variety of grape with purple-black fruit covered with a bluish bloom. [C19: discovered at CONCORD, Mass.]

concours d'élégance *French.* (kɔ̃kur delegɑ̃s) *n* a parade of cars or other vehicles, prizes being awarded to the most elegant, best designed, or best turned-out.

concourse ('kɒnkɔːs, 'kɒŋ-) *n* **1** a crowd; throng. **2** a coming together; confluence: *a concourse of events.* **3** a large open space for the gathering of people in a public place. **4** *Chiefly U.S.* a ground for sports, racing, athletics, etc. [C14: from Old French *concours,* ultimately from Latin *concurrere* to run together, from *currere* to run]

concrescence (kən'krɛsəns) *n Biology.* a growing together of initially separate parts or organs. [C17: from Latin *concrēscentia,* from *concrēscere* to grow together, from *crēscere* to grow; see CRESCENT] ▸ **con'crescent** *adj*

concrete ('kɒnkriːt) *n* **1a** a construction material made of a mixture of cement, sand, stone, and water that hardens to a stonelike mass. **1b** *(as modifier): a concrete slab.* **2** *Physics.* a mass formed by the coalescence of separate particles. ◆ *adj* **3** relating to a particular instance or object; specific as opposed to general: *a concrete example.* **4a** relating to or characteristic of things capable of being perceived by the senses, as opposed to abstractions. **4b** *(as n): the concrete.* **5** formed by the coalescence of particles; condensed; solid. ◆ *vb* **6** *(tr)* to construct in or cover with concrete. **7** (kən'kriːt). to become or cause to become solid; coalesce. [C14: from Latin *concrētus* grown together, hardened, from *concrēscere;* see CONCRESCENCE] ▸ **'concretely** *adv* ▸ **'concreteness** *n* ▸ **con'cretive** *adj* ▸ **con'cretively** *adv*

concrete music *n* music consisting of an electronically modified montage of tape-recorded sounds.

concrete noun *n* a noun that refers to a material object, as for example *horse.* Compare **abstract noun.**

concrete number *n* a number referring to a particular object or objects, as in *three dogs, ten men.*

concrete poetry *n* poetry in which the visual form of the poem is used to convey meaning.

concretion (kən'kriːʃən) *n* **1** the act or process of coming or growing together; coalescence. **2** a solid or solidified mass. **3** something made real, tangible, or specific. **4** any of various rounded or irregular mineral masses that are different in composition from the sedimentary rock that surrounds them. **5** *Pathol.* another word for **calculus.** ▸ **con'cretionary** *adj*

concretize *or* **concretise** ('kɒnkrɪˌtaɪz, 'kɒŋ-) *vb* (*tr*) to render concrete; make real or specific; give tangible form to. ▸ **ˌconcreti'zation** *or* **ˌconcreti'sation** *n*

concubinage (kɒn'kjuːbɪnɪdʒ) *n* **1** cohabitation without legal marriage. **2** the state of living as a concubine.

concubine ('kɒŋkjʊˌbaɪn, 'kɒn-) *n* **1** (in polygamous societies) a secondary wife, usually of lower social rank. **2** a woman who cohabits with a man. [C13: from Old French, from Latin *concubīna,* from *concumbere* to lie together, from *cubare* to lie] ▸ **concubinary** (kɒŋ'kjubɪnərɪ) *n, adj*

concupiscence (kən'kjuːpɪsəns) *n* strong desire, esp. sexual desire. [C14: from Church Latin *concupiscentia,* from Latin *concupiscere* to covet ardently, from *cupere* to wish, desire] ▸ **con'cupiscent** *adj*

concur (kən'kɜː) *vb* **-curs, -curring, -curred.** (*intr*) **1** to agree; be of the same mind; be in accord. **2** to combine, act together, or cooperate. **3** to occur simultaneously; coincide. **4** *Rare.* to converge. [C15: from Latin *concurrere* to run together, from *currere* to run] ▸ **con'curringly** *adv*

concurrence (kən'kʌrəns) *n* **1** the act of concurring. **2** agreement in opinion; accord; assent. **3** cooperation or combination. **4** simultaneous occurrence; coincidence. **5** *Geometry.* a point at which three or more lines intersect. ◆ Also (for senses 1–4): **concurrency.**

concurrent (kən'kʌrənt) *adj* **1** taking place at the same time or in the same location. **2** cooperating. **3** meeting at, approaching, or having a common point: *concurrent lines.* **4** having equal authority or jurisdiction. **5** in accordance or agreement; harmonious. ◆ *n* **6** something joint or contributory; a concurrent circumstance or cause. ▸ **con'currently** *adv*

concurrent engineering *n* a method of designing and marketing new products in which development stages are run in parallel rather than in series, to reduce lead times and costs. Also called: **interactive engineering.**

concurrent processing *n* the ability of a computer to process two or more programs in parallel.

concuss (kən'kʌs) *vb* (*tr*) **1** to injure (the brain) by a violent blow, fall, etc. **2** to shake violently; agitate; disturb. [C16: from Latin *concussus* violently shaken, from *concutere* to disturb greatly, from *quatere* to shake]

concussion (kən'kʌʃən) *n* **1** a jarring of the brain, caused by a blow or a fall, usually resulting in loss of consciousness. **2** any violent shaking; jarring. ▸ **con'cussive** *adj*

Condé (*French* kɔ̃de) *n* **Prince de** (prɛ̃ də), title of *Louis II de Bourbon, Duc d'Enghien,* called *the Great Condé.* 1621–86, French general, who led Louis XIV's armies against the Fronde (1649) but joined the Fronde in a new revolt (1650–52). He later fought for both France and Spain.

condemn (kən'dɛm) *vb* (*tr*) **1** to express strong disapproval of; censure. **2** to pronounce judicial sentence on. **3** to demonstrate the guilt of: *his secretive behaviour condemned him.* **4** to judge or pronounce unfit for use: *that food has been condemned.* **5** to compel or force into a particular state or activity: *his disposition condemned him to boredom.* [C13: from Old French *condempner,* from Latin *condemnāre,* from *damnāre* to condemn; see DAMN] ▸ **condemnable** (kən'dɛməbᵊl) *adj* ▸ **con'demnably** *adv* ▸ **ˌcondem'nation** *n* ▸ **condemnatory** (ˌkɒndɛm'neɪtərɪ, kən'dɛmnətərɪ, -trɪ) *adj* ▸ **con'demner** *n* ▸ **con'demningly** *adv*

condemned cell *n* a prison cell in which a person condemned to death awaits execution.

condensate (kən'dɛnseɪt) *n* a substance formed by condensation, such as a liquid from a vapour.

condensation (ˌkɒndɛn'seɪʃən) *n* **1** the act or process of condensing, or the state of being condensed. **2** anything that has condensed from a vapour, esp. on a window. **3** *Chem.* a type of reaction in which two organic molecules combine to form a larger molecule as well as a simple molecule such as water, methanol, etc. **4** anything that has been shortened, esp. an abridged version of a book. **5** *Psychoanal.* **5a** the fusion of two or more ideas, etc., into one symbol, occurring esp. in dreams. **5b** the reduction of many experiences into one word or action, as in a phobia. ▸ **ˌconden'sational** *adj*

condensation trail *n* another name for **vapour trail.**

condense (kən'dɛns) *vb* **1** (*tr*) to increase the density of; compress. **2** to reduce or be reduced in volume or size; make or become more compact. **3** to change or cause to change from a gaseous to a liquid or solid state. **4** *Chem.* to undergo or cause to undergo condensation. [C15: from Latin *condēnsāre,* from *dēnsāre* to make thick, from *dēnsus* DENSE] ▸ **con'densable** *or* **con'densible** *adj* ▸ **conˌdensa'bility** *or* **conˌdensi'bility** *n*

condensed (kən'dɛnst) *adj* **1** (of printers' type) narrower than usual for a particular height. Compare **expanded** (sense 1). **2** *Botany.* designating an inflorescence in which the flowers are crowded together and are almost or completely sessile. **3** *Chem.* designating a polycyclic ring system in a molecule in which two rings share two or more common atoms, as in naphthalene. Also: **fused.**

condensed matter *n Physics.* **a** crystalline and amorphous solids and liquids, including liquid crystals, glasses, polymers, and gels. **b** (*as modifier*): *condensed-matter physics.*

condensed milk *n* milk reduced by evaporation to a thick concentration, with sugar added. Compare **evaporated milk.**

condenser (kən'dɛnsə) *n* **1a** an apparatus for reducing gases to their liquid or solid form by the abstraction of heat. **1b** a device for abstracting heat, as in a refrigeration unit. **2** a lens that concentrates light into a small area. **3** another name for **capacitor.** **4** a person or device that condenses.

condescend (ˌkɒndɪ'sɛnd) *vb* (*intr*) **1** to act graciously towards another or others regarded as being on a lower level; behave patronizingly. **2** to do something that one regards as below one's dignity. [C14: from Church Latin *condēscendere* to stoop, condescend, from Latin *dēscendere* to DESCEND]

condescendence (ˌkɒndɪ'sɛndəns) *n* **1** *Scots Law.* a statement of facts presented by the plaintiff in a cause. **2** a less common word for **condescension.**

condescending (ˌkɒndɪ'sɛndɪŋ) *adj* showing or implying condescension by stooping to the level of one's inferiors, esp. in a patronizing way. ▸ **ˌconde'scendingly** *adv*

condescension (ˌkɒndɪ'sɛnʃən) *n* the act or an instance of behaving in a patronizing way.

condign (kən'daɪn) *adj* (esp. of a punishment) fitting; deserved. [C15: from Old French *condigne,* from Latin *condignus,* from *dignus* worthy] ▸ **con'dignly** *adv*

Condillac (*French* kɔ̃dijak) *n* **Étienne Bonnot de** (etjɛn bɔno də). 1715–80, French philosopher. He developed Locke's view that all knowledge derives from the senses in his *Traité des sensations* (1754).

condiment ('kɒndɪmənt) *n* any spice or sauce such as salt, pepper, mustard, etc. [C15: from Latin *condīmentum* seasoning, from *condīre* to pickle]

condition (kən'dɪʃən) *n* **1** a particular state of being or existence; situation with respect to circumstances: *the human condition.* **2** something that limits or restricts something else; a qualification: *you may enter only under certain conditions.* **3** (*pl*) external or existing circumstances: *conditions were right for a takeover.* **4** state of health or physical fitness, esp. good health (esp. in the phrases **in condition, out of condition**). **5** an ailment or physical disability: *a heart condition.* **6** something indispensable to the existence of something else: *your happiness is a condition of mine.* **7** something required as part of an agreement or pact; terms: *the conditions of the lease are set out.* **8** *Law.* **8a** a declaration or provision in a will, contract, etc., that makes some right or liability contingent upon the happening of some event. **8b** the event itself. **9** *Logic.* a statement whose truth is either required for the truth of a given statement (a **necessary condition**) or sufficient to guarantee the truth of the given statement (a **sufficient condition**). See **sufficient** (sense 2), **necessary** (sense 3e). **10** *Maths, logic.* a presupposition, esp. a restriction on the domain of quantification, indispensable to the proof of a theorem and stated as part of it. **11** *Statistics.* short for **experimental condition.** **12** rank, status, or position in life. **13 on** (*or* **upon**) **condition that.** (*conj*) provided that. ◆ *vb* (*mainly tr*) **14** *Psychol.* **14a** to alter the response of (a person or animal) to a particular stimulus or situation. **14b** to establish a conditioned response in (a person or animal). **15** to put into a fit condition or state. **16** to improve the condition of (one's hair) by use of special cosmetics. **17** to accustom or inure. **18** to subject to a condition. **19** (*intr*) *Archaic.* to make conditions. [C14: from Latin *conditiō,* from *condīcere* to discuss, agree together, from *con-* together + *dīcere* to say]

conditional (kən'dɪʃənᵊl) *adj* **1** depending on other factors; not certain. **2** *Grammar.* (of a clause, conjunction, form of a verb, or whole sentence) expressing a condition on which something else is contingent: *"If he comes" is a conditional clause in the sentence "If he comes I shall go".* **3a** (of an equation or inequality) true for only certain values of the variable: $x^2 - 1 = x + 1$ is a conditional equation, only true for $x = 2$ or -1. **3b** (of an infinite series) convergent, but becoming divergent when the absolute values of the terms are considered. **4** Also: **hypothetical.** *Logic.* (of a proposition) consisting of two component propositions associated by the words *if…then* so that the proposition is false only when the antecedent is true and the consequent false. Usually written: $p \rightarrow q$ or $p \supset q$, where p is the antecedent, q the consequent, and $\rightarrow$ or $\supset$ symbolizes *implies.* ◆ *n* **5** *Grammar.* **5a** a conditional form of a verb. **5b** a conditional clause or sentence. **6** *Logic.* a conditional proposition. ▸ **conˌdition'ality** *n* ▸ **con'ditionally** *adv*

conditional access *n* the encryption of television programme transmissions so that only authorized subscribers with suitable decoding apparatus may have access to them.

conditionalization *or* **conditionalisation** (kənˌdɪʃənᵊlaɪ'zeɪʃən) *n Logic.* the derivation from an argument of a conditional statement with the conjunction of the premises as antecedent and the conclusion as consequent. If the argument is valid conditionalization yields a truth.

conditional probability *n Statistics.* the probability of one event, *A,* occurring given that another, *B,* is already known to have occurred: written *P(A/B)* and equal to *P(A and B)/P(B).*

condition code register *n Computing.* a hardware register used for storing the current values of the condition codes.

condition codes *pl n* a set of single bits that indicate specific conditions within a computer. The values of the condition codes are often determined by the outcome of a prior software operation and their principal use is to govern choices between alternative instruction sequences.

conditioned (kən'dɪʃənd) *adj* **1** *Psychol.* of or denoting a response that has been learned. Compare **unconditioned.** **2** (foll. by *to*) accustomed; inured; prepared by training.

conditioned response *n Psychol.* a response that is transferred from the second to the first of a pair of stimuli. See **classical conditioning.** A well-known Pavlovian example is salivation by a dog when it hears a bell ring, because food has always been presented when the bell has been rung previously. Also called (esp. formerly): **conditioned reflex.** See also **unconditioned response.**

conditioned stimulus *n Psychol.* a stimulus to which an organism has learned to make a response by classical conditioning. Compare **unconditioned stimulus.**

conditioned suppression *n Psychol.* the reduction in the frequency of a learned response, e.g. pressing a bar for water, that occurs when a stimulus previously associated with pain is present.

conditioner (kən'dɪʃənə) *n* **1** a person or thing that conditions. **2** a substance, esp. a cosmetic, applied to something to improve its condition: *hair conditioner.*

conditioning (kən'dɪʃənɪŋ) *n* **1** *Psychol.* the learning process by which the behaviour of an organism becomes dependent on an event occurring in its environment. See also **classical conditioning, instrumental learning.** ♦ *adj* **2** (of a shampoo, cosmetic, etc.) intended to improve the condition of something: *a conditioning rinse.*

condo ('kɒndəʊ) *n, pl* **-dos.** *U.S. and Canadian informal.* a condominium building or apartment.

condole (kən'dəʊl) *vb* (*intr;* foll. by *with*) to express sympathy with someone in grief, pain, etc. **[C16:** from Church Latin *condolēre* to suffer pain (with another), from Latin *com-* together + *dolēre* to grieve, feel pain**]** ► **con'dolatory** *adj* ► **con'doler** *n* ► **con'dolingly** *adv*

condolence (kən'dəʊləns) *or* **condolement** *n* (*often pl*) an expression of sympathy with someone in grief, etc.

con dolore (kɒn dɒ'lɔːrɪ) *adj, adv Music.* (to be performed) in a sad manner. **[**Italian: with sorrow**]**

condom ('kɒndəm) *n* a sheathlike covering of thin rubber worn on the penis or in the vagina during sexual intercourse to prevent conception or infection. **[C18:** of unknown origin**]**

condominium (ˌkɒndə'mɪnɪəm) *n, pl* **-ums. 1** joint rule or sovereignty. **2** a country ruled by two or more foreign powers. **3** *U.S. and Canadian.* **3a** an apartment building in which each apartment is individually wholly owned and the common areas are jointly owned. **3b** the title under which an apartment in such a building is owned. Sometimes shortened to **condo.** Compare **cooperative** (sense 5). **[C18:** from New Latin, from Latin *com-* together + *dominium* ownership; see DOMINION**]**

condone (kən'dəʊn) *vb* (*tr*) **1** to overlook or forgive (an offence). **2** *Law.* (esp. of a spouse) to pardon or overlook (an offence, usually adultery). **[C19:** from Latin *condōnāre* to remit a debt, from *com-* (intensive) + *dōnāre* to DONATE**]** ► **con'donable** *adj* ► **condonation** (ˌkɒndəʊ'neɪʃən) *n* ► **con'doner** *n*

condor ('kɒndɔː) *n* either of two very large rare New World vultures, *Vultur gryphus* (**Andean condor**), which has black plumage with white around the neck, and *Gymnogyps californianus* (**California condor**), which is similar but nearly extinct. **[C17:** from Spanish *cóndor,* from Quechuan *kuntur***]**

Condorcet (*French* kɔ̃dɔrsɛ) *n* **Marie Jean Antoine Nicolas de Caritat,** Marquis de. 1743–94, French philosopher and politician. His works include *Sketch for a Historical Picture of the Progress of the Human Mind* (1795).

condottiere (ˌkɒndɒ'tjɛərɪ) *n, pl* **-ri** (-riː). a commander or soldier in a professional mercenary company in Europe from the 13th to the 16th centuries. **[C18:** from Italian, from *condotto* leadership, from *condurre* to lead, from Latin *condūcere;* see CONDUCT**]**

conduce (kən'djuːs) *vb* (*intr;* foll. by *to*) to lead or contribute (to a result). **[C15:** from Latin *condūcere* to lead together, from *com-* together + *dūcere* to lead**]** ► **con'ducer** *n* ► **con'ducible** *adj* ► **con'ducingly** *adv*

conducive (kən'djuːsɪv) *adj* (when *postpositive,* foll. by *to*) contributing, leading, or tending. ► **con'duciveness** *n*

conduct *n* ('kɒndʌkt). **1** the manner in which a person behaves; behaviour. **2** the way of managing a business, affair, etc.; handling. **3** *Rare.* the act of guiding or leading. **4** *Rare.* a guide or leader. ♦ *vb* (kən'dʌkt). **5** (*tr*) to accompany and guide (people, a party, etc.) (esp. in the phrase **conducted tour**). **6** (*tr*) to lead or direct (affairs, business, etc.); control. **7** (*tr*) to do or carry out: *conduct a survey.* **8** (*tr*) to behave or manage (oneself): *the child conducted himself well.* **9** Also (esp. U.S.): **direct.** to control or guide (an orchestra, choir, etc.) by the movements of the hands or a baton. **10** to transmit (heat, electricity, etc.): *metals conduct heat.* **[C15:** from Medieval Latin *conductus* escorted, from Latin: drawn together, from *condūcere* to CONDUCE**]** ► **con'ductible** *adj* ► **conˌducti'bility** *n*

conductance (kən'dʌktəns) *n* the ability of a system to conduct electricity, measured by the ratio of the current flowing through the system to the potential difference across it; the reciprocal of resistance. It is measured in reciprocal ohms, mhos, or siemens. Symbol: G

conducting tissue *n Botany.* another name for **vascular tissue.**

conductiometric titration (kənˌdʌktɪəʊ'mɛtrɪk) *n Chem.* a titration technique in which the end-point is determined by measuring the conductance of the solution.

conduction (kən'dʌkʃən) *n* **1** the transfer of energy by a medium without bulk movement of the medium itself: *heat conduction, electrical conduction, sound conduction.* Compare **convection** (sense 1). **2** the transmission of an electrical or chemical impulse along a nerve fibre. **3** the act of conveying or conducting, as through a pipe. **4** *Physics.* another name for **conductivity** (sense 1). ► **con'ductional** *adj*

conduction band *n* See **energy band.**

conductive (kən'dʌktɪv) *adj* of, denoting, or having the property of conduction. ► **con'ductively** *adv*

conductive education *n* an educational system, developed in Hungary by András Petö, in which teachers (**conductors**) teach children and adults with motor disorders to function independently, by guiding them to attain their own goals in their own way.

conductivity (ˌkɒndʌk'tɪvɪtɪ) *n, pl* **-ties. 1** Also called: **conduction.** the property of transmitting heat, electricity, or sound. **2** a measure of the ability of a substance to conduct electricity; the reciprocal of resistivity. Symbol: κ Formerly called: **specific conductance. 3** See **thermal conductivity.**

conductivity water *n* water that has a conductivity of less than 0.043×10^{-6} $S\ cm^{-1}$.

conductor (kən'dʌktə) *n* **1** an official on a bus who collects fares, checks tickets, etc. **2** Also called: (esp. U.S.): **director.** a person who conducts an orchestra, choir, etc. **3** a person who leads or guides. **4** *U.S. and Canadian.* a railway official in charge of a train. **5** a substance, body, or system that conducts electricity, heat, etc. **6** See **lightning conductor.** ► **con'ductorˌship** *n* ► **conductress** (kən'dʌktrɪs) *fem n*

conduit ('kɒndɪt, -djuɪt) *n* **1** a pipe or channel for carrying a fluid. **2** a rigid tube or duct for carrying and protecting electrical wires or cables. **3** an agency or means of access, communication, etc. **4** *Botany.* a water-transporting element in a plant; a xylem vessel or a tracheid. **5** a rare word for **fountain. [C14:** from Old French, from Medieval Latin *conductus* channel, aqueduct, from Latin *condūcere* to lead, CONDUCE**]**

conduplicate (kɒn'djuːplɪkɪt) *adj Botany.* folded lengthways on itself: *conduplicate leaves in the bud.* **[C18:** from Latin *conduplicāre* to double; see DUPLICATE**]** ► **conˌdupli'cation** *n*

condyle ('kɒndɪl) *n* the rounded projection on the articulating end of a bone, such as the ball portion of a ball-and-socket joint. **[C17:** from Latin *condylus* knuckle, joint, from Greek *kondulos***]** ► **'condylar** *adj*

condyloid ('kɒndɪˌlɔɪd) *adj* of or resembling a condyle.

condyloma (ˌkɒndɪ'ləʊmə) *n, pl* **-mas** *or* **-mata** (-mətə). a skin tumour near the anus or genital organs, esp. as a result of syphilis. **[C17:** from New Latin, from Greek *kondulōma,* from *kondulos* CONDYLE + -OMA**]** ► **condylomatous** (ˌkɒndɪ'lɒmətəs, -'ləʊ-) *adj*

cone (kəʊn) *n* **1a** a geometric solid consisting of a plane base bounded by a closed curve, usually a circle or an ellipse, every point of which is joined to a fixed point, the vertex, lying outside the plane of the base. A **right circular cone** has a vertex perpendicularly above or below the centre of a circular base. Volume of a cone: $\frac{1}{3}\pi r^2 h$, where *r* is the radius of the base and *h* is the height of the cone. **1b** a geometric surface formed by a line rotating about the vertex and connecting the peripheries of two closed plane bases, usually circular or elliptical, above and below the vertex. See also **conic section. 2** anything that tapers from a circular section to a point, such as a wafer shell used to contain ice cream. **3a** the reproductive body of conifers and related plants, made up of overlapping scales, esp. the mature **female cone,** whose scales each bear a seed. **3b** a similar structure in horsetails, club mosses, etc. Technical name: **strobilus. 4** a small cone-shaped bollard used as a temporary traffic marker on roads. **5** Also called: **retinal cone.** any one of the cone-shaped cells in the retina of the eye, sensitive to colour and bright light. ♦ *vb* **6** (*tr*) to shape like a cone or part of a cone. **[C16:** from Latin *cōnus,* from Greek *kōnus* pine cone, geometrical cone**]**

coneflower ('kəʊnˌflaʊə) *n* any North American plant of the genera *Rudbeckia, Ratibida,* and *Echinacea,* which have rayed flowers with a conelike centre: family *Compositae* (composites). See also **black-eyed Susan.**

cone off *vb* (*tr, adv*) *Brit.* to close (one carriageway of a motorway) by placing warning cones across it.

cone shell *n* any of various tropical marine gastropod molluscs of the genus *Conus* and related genera, having a smooth conical shell. Sometimes shortened to **cone.**

con espressione (*Italian* kɔn ˌespres'sjone) *adj, adv Music.* (to be performed) with feeling; expressively. **[**Italian, literally: with expression**]**

Conestoga wagon (ˌkɒnɪ'stəʊgə) *n U.S. and Canadian.* a large heavy horse-drawn covered wagon used in the 19th century. **[C19:** after *Conestoga,* Pennsylvania, where it was first made**]**

coney ('kəʊnɪ) *n* a variant spelling of **cony.**

Coney Island ('kəʊnɪ) *n* an island off the S shore of Long Island, New York: site of a large amusement park.

conf. *abbrev. for:* **1** confer. **[**Latin: compare**] 2** conference. **3** confessor.

confab ('kɒnfæb) *Informal.* ♦ *n* **1** a conversation or chat. ♦ *vb* **-fabs, -fabbing, -fabbed. 2** (*intr*) to converse.

confabulate (kən'fæbjʊˌleɪt) *vb* (*intr*) **1** to talk together; converse; chat. **2** *Psychiatry.* to replace the gaps left by a disorder of the memory with imaginary remembered experiences consistently believed to be true. See also **paramnesia. [C17:** from Latin *confābulārī,* from *fābulārī* to talk, from *fābula* a story; see FABLE**]** ► **conˌfabu'lation** *n* ► **con'fabuˌlator** *n* ► **con'fabulatory** *adj*

confect (kən'fɛkt) *vb* (*tr*) **1** to prepare by combining ingredients. **2** to make; construct. **[C16:** from Latin *confectus* prepared, from *conficere* to accomplish, from *com-* (intensive) + *facere* to make**]**

confection (kən'fɛkʃən) *n* **1** the act or process of compounding or mixing. **2** any sweet preparation of fruit, nuts, etc., such as a preserve or a sweet. **3** *Old-fashioned.* an elaborate article of clothing, esp. for women. **4** *Informal.* anything regarded as overelaborate or frivolous: *the play was merely an ingenious confection.* **5** a medicinal drug sweetened with sugar, honey, etc. **[C14:** from Old French, from Latin *confectiō* a preparing, from *conficere* to produce; see CONFECT**]**

confectionary (kən'fɛkʃənərɪ) *n, pl* **-aries. 1** a place where confections are kept or made. **2** a rare word for **confection.** ♦ *adj* **3** of or characteristic of confections.

confectioner (kən'fɛkʃənə) *n* a person who makes or sells sweets or confections.

confectioners' sugar *n* the U.S. term for **icing sugar.**

confectionery (kən'fɛkʃənərɪ) *n, pl* **-eries. 1** sweets and other confections collectively. **2** the art or business of a confectioner.

Confed. *abbrev. for:* **1** Confederate. **2** Confederation.

confederacy (kən'fɛdərəsɪ, -'fɛdrəsɪ) *n, pl* **-cies. 1** a union or combination of peoples, states, etc.; alliance; league. **2** a combination of groups or individuals for unlawful purposes. **[C14:** from Anglo-French *confederacie,* from Late Latin *confoederātiō* agreement, CONFEDERATION**]** ► **con'federal** *adj*

Confederacy (kən'fɛdərəsɪ, -'fɛdrəsɪ) *n* **the.** another name for the **Confederate States of America.**

confederate *n* (kən'fɛdərɪt, -'fɛdrɪt). **1** a nation, state, or individual that is part of a confederacy. **2** someone who is part of a conspiracy; accomplice. ♦ *adj* (kən'fɛdərɪt, -'fɛdrɪt). **3** united in a confederacy; allied. ◆ *vb* (kən'fɛdə,reɪt). **4** to form into or become part of a confederacy. [C14: from Late Latin *confoederātus,* from *confoederāre* to unite by a league, from Latin *com-* together + *foedus* treaty]

Confederate (kən'fɛdərɪt, -'fɛdrɪt) *adj* **1** of, supporting, or relating to the Confederate States of America. ◆ *n* **2** a supporter of the Confederate States of America.

Confederate States of America *pl n U.S. history.* the 11 Southern states (Alabama, Arkansas, Florida, Georgia, North Carolina, South Carolina, Texas, Virginia, Tennessee, Louisiana, and Mississippi) that seceded from the Union in 1861, precipitating a civil war with the North. The Confederacy was defeated in 1865 and the South reincorporated into the U.S.

confederation (kən,fɛdə'reɪʃən) *n* **1** the act or process of confederating or the state of being confederated. **2** a loose alliance of political units. The union of the Swiss cantons is the oldest surviving confederation. Compare **federation. 3** (esp. in Canada) another name for a **federation.** ▸ **con,feder'ation,ism** *n* ▸ **con,feder'ationist** *n* ▸ **con'federative** *adj*

Confederation (kən,fɛdə'reɪʃən) *n* **1 the.** *U.S. history.* the original 13 states of the United States of America constituted under the Articles of Confederation and superseded by the more formal union established in 1789. **2** the federation of Canada, formed with four original provinces in 1867 and since joined by eight more.

confer (kən'fɜː) *vb* **-fers, -ferring, -ferred. 1** (*tr;* foll. by *on* or *upon*) to grant or bestow (an honour, gift, etc.). **2** (*intr*) to hold or take part in a conference or consult together. **3** (*tr*) an obsolete word for **compare.** [C16: from Latin *conferre* to gather together, compare, from *com-* together + *ferre* to bring] ▸ **con'ferment** *or* **con'ferral** *n* ▸ **con'ferrable** *adj* ▸ **con'ferrer** *n*

conferee *or* **conferree** (,kɒnfɜː'riː) *n* **1** a person who takes part in a conference. **2** a person on whom an honour or gift is conferred.

conference ('kɒnfərəns, -frəns) *n* **1** a meeting for consultation, exchange of information, or discussion, esp. one with a formal agenda. **2** a formal meeting of two or more states, political groups, etc., esp. to discuss differences or formulate common policy. **3** an assembly of the clergy or of clergy and laity of any of certain Protestant Christian Churches acting as representatives of their denomination: *the Methodist conference.* **4** *Sport, U.S. and Canadian.* a league or division of clubs or teams. **5** *Rare.* an act of bestowal. [C16: from Medieval Latin *conferentia,* from Latin *conferre* to bring together; see CONFER] ▸ **conferential** (,kɒnfə'rɛnʃəl) *adj*

conference call *n* a special telephone facility by which three or more people using conventional or cellular phones can be linked up to speak to one another.

Conference pear ('kɒnfərəns, -frəns) *n* a variety of pear that has sweet and juicy fruit.

conferva (kɒn'fɜːvə) *n, pl* **-vae** (-viː) *or* **-vas.** any of various threadlike green algae, esp. any of the genus *Tribonema,* typically occurring in fresh water. [C18: from Latin: a water plant, from *confervēre* to grow together, heal, literally: to seethe, from *fervēre* to boil; named with reference to its reputed healing properties] ▸ **con'ferval** *adj* ▸ **con'fervoid** *n, adj*

confess (kən'fɛs) *vb* (when *tr, may take a clause as object*) **1** (when *intr,* often foll. by *to*) to make an acknowledgment or admission (of faults, misdeeds, crimes, etc.). **2** (*tr*) to admit or grant to be true; concede. **3** *Christianity, chiefly R.C. Church.* to declare (one's sins) to God or to a priest as his representative, so as to obtain pardon and absolution. [C14: from Old French *confesser,* from Late Latin *confessāre,* from Latin *confessus* confessed, from *confitērī* to admit, from *fatērī* to acknowledge; related to Latin *fārī* to speak] ▸ **con'fessable** *adj*

confessant (kən'fɛsᵊnt) *n Christianity, chiefly R.C. Church.* a person who makes a confession.

confessedly (kən'fɛsɪdlɪ) *adv* (*sentence modifier*) by admission or confession; avowedly.

confession (kən'fɛʃən) *n* **1** the act of confessing. **2** something confessed. **3** an acknowledgment or declaration, esp. of one's faults, misdeeds, or crimes. **4** *Christianity, chiefly R.C. Church.* the act of a penitent accusing himself of his sins. **5 confession of faith.** a formal public avowal of religious beliefs. **6** a religious denomination or sect united by a common system of beliefs. ▸ **con'fessionary** *adj*

confessional (kən'fɛʃənᵊl) *adj* **1** of, like, or suited to a confession. ◆ *n* **2** *Christianity, chiefly R.C. Church.* a small stall, usually enclosed and divided by a screen or curtain, where a priest hears confessions. **3** a book of penitential prayers.

confessor (kən'fɛsə) *n* **1** *Christianity, chiefly R.C. Church.* a priest who hears confessions and sometimes acts as a spiritual counsellor. **2** *History.* a person who bears witness to his Christian religious faith by the holiness of his life, esp. in resisting threats or danger, but does not suffer martyrdom. **3** a person who makes a confession.

confetti (kən'fɛtɪ) *n* small pieces of coloured paper thrown on festive occasions, esp. at the bride and groom at weddings. [C19: from Italian, plural of *confetto,* originally, a bonbon; see COMFIT]

confidant *or* (*fem*) **confidante** (,kɒnfɪ'dænt, 'kɒnfɪ,dænt) *n* a person to whom private matters are confided. [C17: from French *confident,* from Italian *confidente,* n use of adj: trustworthy, from Latin *confīdens* CONFIDENT]

confide (kən'faɪd) *vb* **1** (usually foll. by *in;* when *tr, may take a clause as object*) to disclose (secret or personal matters) in confidence (to); reveal in private (to). **2** (*intr;* foll. by *in*) to have complete trust. **3** (*tr*) to entrust into another's keeping. [C15: from Latin *confīdere,* from *fīdere* to trust; related to Latin *foedus* treaty] ▸ **con'fider** *n*

confidence ('kɒnfɪdəns) *n* **1** a feeling of trust in a person or thing: *I have confidence in his abilities.* **2** belief in one's own abilities; self-assurance. **3** trust or a trustful relationship: *take me into your confidence.* **4** something confided or entrusted; secret. **5 in confidence.** as a secret.

confidence interval *n Statistics.* an interval of values bounded by **confidence limits** within which the true value of a population parameter is stated to lie with a specified probability.

confidence level *n Statistics.* a measure of the reliability of a result. A confidence level of 95 per cent or 0.95 means that there is a probability of at least 95 per cent that the result is reliable. Compare **significance** (sense 4).

confidence man *or* **trickster** *n* another name for **con man.**

confidence trick *or U.S. and Canadian* **confidence game** *n* a swindle involving money, goods, etc., in which the victim's trust is won by the swindler. Informal shortened forms: **con trick,** *U.S. and Canadian* **con game.**

confident ('kɒnfɪdənt) *adj* **1** (*postpositive;* foll. by *of*) having or showing confidence or certainty; sure: *confident of success.* **2** sure of oneself; bold. **3** presumptuous; excessively bold. [C16: from Latin *confīdens* trusting, having self-confidence, from *confīdere* to have complete trust in; see CONFIDE] ▸ **'confidently** *adv*

confidential (,kɒnfɪ'dɛnʃəl) *adj* **1** spoken, written, or given in confidence; secret; private. **2** entrusted with another's confidence or secret affairs: *a confidential secretary.* **3** suggestive of or denoting intimacy: *a confidential approach.* ▸ **,confi,denti'ality** *or* **,confi'dentialness** *n* ▸ **,confi'dentially** *adv*

confiding (kən'faɪdɪŋ) *adj* unsuspicious; trustful. ▸ **con'fidingly** *adv* ▸ **con'fidingness** *n*

configuration (kən,fɪgjʊ'reɪʃən) *n* **1** the arrangement of the parts of something. **2** the external form or outline achieved by such an arrangement. **3** *Physics, chem.* **3a** Also called: **conformation.** the shape of a molecule as determined by the arrangement of its atoms. **3b** the structure of an atom or molecule as determined by the arrangement of its electrons and nucleons. **4** *Psychol.* the unit or pattern in perception studied by Gestalt psychologists. **5** *Computing.* the particular choice of hardware items and their interconnection that make up a particular computer system. [C16: from Late Latin *configūrātiō* a similar formation, from *configūrāre* to model on something, from *figūrāre* to shape, fashion] ▸ **con,figu'rational** *or* **con'figurative** *adj* ▸ **con,figu'rationally** *adv*

confine *vb* (kən'faɪn). (*tr*) **1** to keep or close within bounds; limit; restrict. **2** to keep shut in; restrict the free movement of: *arthritis confined him to bed.* ◆ *n* ('kɒnfaɪn). **3** (*often pl*) a limit; boundary. [C16: from Medieval Latin *confīnāre* from Latin *confīnis* adjacent, from *fīnis* end, boundary] ▸ **con'finable** *or* **con'fineable** *adj* ▸ **'confineless** *adj* ▸ **con'finer** *n*

confined (kən'faɪnd) *adj* **1** enclosed or restricted; limited. **2** in childbed; undergoing childbirth. ▸ **confinedly** (kən'faɪnɪdlɪ) *adv* ▸ **con'finedness** *n*

confinement (kən'faɪnmənt) *n* **1** the act of confining or the state of being confined. **2** the period from the onset of labour to the birth of a child. **3** *Physics.* another name for **containment** (sense 3).

confirm (kən'fɜːm) *vb* (*tr*) **1** (*may take a clause as object*) to prove to be true or valid; corroborate; verify. **2** (*may take a clause as object*) to assert for a second or further time, so as to make more definite: *he confirmed that he would appear in court.* **3** to strengthen or make more firm: *his story confirmed my doubts.* **4** to make valid by a formal act or agreement; ratify. **5** to administer the rite of confirmation to. [C13: from Old French *confermer,* from Latin *confirmāre,* from *firmus* FIRM[1]] ▸ **con'firmable** *adj* ▸ **con'firmatory** *or* **con'firmative** *adj* ▸ **con'firmer** *n*

confirmand ('kɒnfə,mænd) *n* a candidate for confirmation.

confirmation (,kɒnfə'meɪʃən) *n* **1** the act of confirming. **2** something that confirms; verification. **3** a rite in several Christian churches that confirms a baptized person in his faith and admits him to full participation in the church. **4** (in the philosophy of science) the relationship between an observation and the theory which it supposedly renders more probable. Compare **hypothetico-deductive.**

confirmed (kən'fɜːmd) *adj* **1** (*prenominal*) long-established in a habit, way of life, etc.: *a confirmed bachelor.* **2** having received the rite of confirmation. **3** (of a disease) another word for **chronic.** ▸ **confirmedly** (kən'fɜːmɪdlɪ) *adv* ▸ **confirmedness** (kən'fɜːmɪdnɪs, -'fɜːmd-) *n*

confiscable (kən'fɪskəbᵊl) *adj* subject or liable to confiscation or seizure.

confiscate ('kɒnfɪ,skeɪt) *vb* (*tr*) **1** to seize (property), esp. for public use and esp. by way of a penalty. ◆ *adj* **2** seized or confiscated; forfeit. **3** having lost or been deprived of property through confiscation. [C16: from Latin *confiscāre* to seize for the public treasury, from *fiscus* basket, treasury] ▸ **,confis'cation** *n* ▸ **'confis,cator** *n* ▸ **confiscatory** (kən'fɪskətərɪ, -trɪ) *adj*

confit *French.* (kɔ̃fi) *n Cookery.* a preserve: *a confit of duck.* [literally: preserve]

Confiteor (kən'fɪtɪ,ɔː) *n R.C. Church.* a prayer consisting of a general confession of sinfulness and an entreaty for forgiveness. [C13: from Latin: I confess; from the beginning of the Latin prayer of confession]

confiture ('kɒnfɪ,tjʊə) *n* a confection, preserve of fruit, etc. [C19: from French, from Old French *confire* to prepare, from Latin *conficere* to produce; see CONFECT]

conflagrant (kən'fleɪgrənt) *adj Rare.* burning fiercely.

conflagration (,kɒnflə'greɪʃən) *n* a large destructive fire. [C16: from Latin *conflagrātiō,* from *conflagrāre* to be burnt up, from *com-* (intensive) + *flagrāre* to burn; related to Latin *fulgur* lightning] ▸ **'confla,grative** *adj*

conflate (kən'fleɪt) *vb* (*tr*) to combine or blend (two things, esp. two versions of a text) so as to form a whole. [C16: from Latin *conflāre* to blow together, from *flāre* to blow] ▸ **con'flation** *n*

conflict *n* ('kɒnflɪkt). **1** a struggle or clash between opposing forces; battle. **2** a state of opposition between ideas, interests, etc.; disagreement or controversy. **3** a clash, as between two appointments made for the same time. **4** *Psychol.* opposition between two simultaneous but incompatible wishes or drives, sometimes leading to a state of emotional tension and thought to be responsible for neuroses. ◆ *vb* (kən'flɪkt). (*intr*) **5** to come into opposition; clash. **6** to fight. [C15: from Latin *conflictus,* from *confligere* to combat, from *fligere* to strike] ▸ **con'fliction** *n* ▸ **con'flictive** *or* **con'flictory** *adj*

conflicting (kən'flɪktɪŋ) *adj* clashing; contradictory: *conflicting rumours.* ▸ **con'flictingly** *adv*

confluence ('kɒnfluəns) *or* **conflux** ('kɒnflʌks) *n* **1** a merging or flowing together, esp. of rivers. **2** a gathering together, esp. of people.

confluent ('kɒnfluənt) *adj* **1** flowing together or merging. ◆ *n* **2** a stream that flows into another, usually of approximately equal size. [C17: from Latin *confluēns,* from *confluere* to flow together, from *fluere* to flow]

confocal (kɒn'fəʊkᵊl) *adj* having a common focus or common foci: *confocal ellipses.*

confocal microscope *n* a light microscope with an optical system designed to reject background from matter outside the focal plane and therefore allowing images of different sections of a specimen to be obtained.

conform (kən'fɔːm) *vb* **1** (*intr;* usually foll. by *to*) to comply in actions, behaviour, etc., with accepted standards or norms. **2** (*intr;* usually foll. by *with*) to be in accordance; fit in: *he conforms with my idea of a teacher.* **3** to make or become similar in character or form. **4** (*intr*) to comply with the practices of an established church, esp. the Church of England. **5** (*tr*) to bring (oneself, ideas, etc.) into harmony or agreement. [C14: from Old French *conformer,* from Latin *confirmāre* to establish, strengthen, from *firmāre* to make firm, from *firmus* FIRM[1]] ▸ **con'former** *n* ▸ **con'formingly** *adv*

conformable (kən'fɔːməbᵊl) *adj* **1** corresponding in character; similar. **2** obedient; submissive. **3** (foll. by *to*) in agreement or harmony (with); consistent (with). **4** (of rock strata) lying in a parallel arrangement so that their original relative positions have remained undisturbed. **5** *Maths.* (of two matrices) related so that the number of columns in one is equal to the number of rows in the other. ▸ **con,forma'bility** *or* **con'formableness** *n* ▸ **con'formably** *adv*

conformal (kən'fɔːməl) *adj* **1** *Maths.* **1a** (of a transformation) preserving the angles of the depicted surface. **1b** (of a parameter) relating to such a transformation. **2** Also called: **orthomorphic.** (of a map projection) maintaining true shape over a small area and scale in every direction. [C17: from Late Latin *conformālis* having the same shape, from Latin *com-* same + *forma* shape]

conformation (,kɒnfɔː'meɪʃən) *n* **1** the general shape or outline of an object; configuration. **2** the arrangement of the parts of an object. **3** the act or state of conforming. **4** *Chem.* **4a** another name for **configuration** (sense 3a). **4b** one of the configurations of a molecule that can easily change its shape and can consequently exist in equilibrium with molecules of different configuration. ▸ **,confor'mational** *adj*

conformational analysis *n Chem.* the study of the spatial arrangement of atoms or groups of atoms in a molecule and the way in which this influences chemical behaviour.

conformist (kən'fɔːmɪst) *n* **1** a person who adopts the attitudes, behaviour, dress, etc. of the group to which he belongs. **2** a person who complies with the practices of an established church, esp. the Church of England. ◆ *adj* **3** of a conforming nature or character.

conformity (kən'fɔːmɪtɪ) *or* **conformance** *n, pl* **-ities** *or* **-ances. 1** compliance in actions, behaviour, etc., with certain accepted standards or norms. **2** correspondence or likeness in form or appearance; congruity; agreement. **3** compliance with the practices of an established church.

confound (kən'faʊnd) *vb* (*tr*) **1** to astound or perplex; bewilder. **2** to mix up; confuse. **3** to treat mistakenly as similar to or identical with (one or more other things). **4** (kɒn'faʊnd) to curse or damn (usually as an expletive in the phrase **confound it!**). **5** to contradict or refute (an argument, etc.). **6** to rout or defeat (an enemy). **7** *Obsolete.* to waste. [C13: from Old French *confondre,* from Latin *confundere* to mingle, pour together, from *fundere* to pour] ▸ **con'foundable** *adj* ▸ **con'founder** *n*

confounded (kən'faʊndɪd) *adj* **1** bewildered; confused. **2** (*prenominal*) *Informal.* execrable; damned. ▸ **con'foundedly** *adv* ▸ **con'foundedness** *n*

confraternity (,kɒnfrə'tɜːnɪtɪ) *n, pl* **-ties.** a group of men united for some particular purpose, esp. Christian laymen organized for religious or charitable service; brotherhood. [C15: from Medieval Latin *confrāternitās;* see CONFRÈRE, FRATERNITY] ▸ **,confra'ternal** *adj*

confrère ('kɒnfreə) *n* a fellow member of a profession, fraternity, etc. [C15: from Old French, from Medieval Latin *confrāter* fellow member, from Latin *frāter* brother]

confront (kən'frʌnt) *vb* (*tr*) **1** (usually foll. by *with*) to present or face (with something), esp. in order to accuse or criticize. **2** to face boldly; oppose in hostility. **3** to be face to face with; be in front of. **4** to bring together for comparison. [C16: from Medieval Latin *confrontārī* to stand face to face with, from *frons* forehead] ▸ **con'fronter** *n*

confrontation (,kɒnfrʌn'teɪʃən) *or Archaic* **confrontment** (kɒn'frʌntmənt) *n* **1** the act or an instance of confronting. **2** a situation of mutual hostility between two powers or nations without open warfare. **3** a state of conflict between two antagonistic forces, creeds, or ideas etc. ▸ **,confron'tational** *adj*

Confucian (kən'fjuːʃən) *adj* **1** of or relating to the doctrines of Confucius. ◆ *n* **2** a follower of Confucius.

Confucianism (kən'fjuːʃə,nɪzəm) *n* the ethical system of Confucius, emphasizing moral order, the humanity and virtue of China's ancient rulers, and gentlemanly education. ▸ **Con'fucianist** *n*

Confucius (kən'fjuːʃəs) *n* Chinese name *Kong Zi* or *K'ung Fu-tse.* 551–479 B.C., Chinese philosopher and teacher of ethics (see **Confucianism**). His doctrines were compiled after his death under the title *The Analects of Confucius.*

con fuoco (kɒn fuː'əʊkəʊ) *adj, adv Music.* (to be performed) in a fiery manner. [Italian: with fire]

confuse (kən'fjuːz) *vb* (*tr*) **1** to bewilder; perplex. **2** to mix up (things, ideas, etc.); jumble. **3** to make unclear: *he confused his talk with irrelevant details.* **4** to fail to recognize the difference between; mistake (one thing) for another. **5** to disconcert; embarrass. **6** to cause to become disordered: *the enemy ranks were confused by gas.* [C18: back formation from *confused,* from Latin *confūsus* mingled together, from *confundere* to pour together; see CONFOUND] ▸ **con'fusable** *adj* ▸ **con,fusa'bility** *n* ▸ **con'fused** *adj* ▸ **confusedly** (kən'fjuːzɪdlɪ, -'fjuːzd-) *adv* ▸ **con'fusedness** *n* ▸ **con'fusing** *adj* ▸ **con'fusingly** *adv*

confused elderly *adj Social welfare.* **a** old and no longer having mental abilities sufficient for independent living. **b** (*as collective n;* preceded by *the*): *the confused elderly.*

confusion (kən'fjuːʒən) *n* **1** the act of confusing or the state of being confused. **2** disorder; jumble. **3** bewilderment; perplexity. **4** lack of clarity; indistinctness. **5** embarrassment; abashment. ▸ **con'fusional** *adj*

confute (kən'fjuːt) *vb* (*tr*) **1** to prove (a person or thing) wrong, invalid, or mistaken; disprove. **2** *Obsolete.* to put an end to. [C16: from Latin *confūtāre* to check, silence] ▸ **con'futable** *adj* ▸ **confutation** (,kɒnfjʊ'teɪʃən) *n* ▸ **con'futative** *adj* ▸ **con'futer** *n*

cong. *abbrev. for:* **1** *Pharmacol.* congius. [Latin: gallon] **2** congregation.

Cong. *abbrev. for:* **1** Congregational. **2** Congress. **3** Congressional.

conga ('kɒŋgə) *n* **1** a Latin American dance of three steps and a kick to each bar, usually performed by a number of people in single file. **2** Also called: **conga drum.** a large tubular bass drum, used chiefly in Latin American and funk music and played with the hands. ◆ *vb* **-gas, -gaing, -gaed. 3** (*intr*) to perform this dance. [C20: from American Spanish, feminine of *congo* belonging to the CONGO]

congé ('kɒnʒeɪ) *n* **1** permission to depart or dismissal, esp. when formal. **2** a farewell. **3** *Architect.* a concave moulding. See also **cavetto.** [C16: from Old French *congié,* from Latin *commeātus* leave of absence, from *meātus* movement, from *meāre* to go, pass]

congeal (kən'dʒiːl) *vb* **1** to change or cause to change from a soft or fluid state to a firm or solid state. **2** to form or cause to form into a coagulated mass; curdle; jell. **3** (*intr*) (of ideas) to take shape or become fixed in form. [C14: from Old French *congeler,* from Latin *congelāre,* from *com-* together + *gelāre* to freeze] ▸ **con'gealable** *adj* ▸ **con'gealer** *n* ▸ **con'gealment** *n*

congelation (,kɒndʒɪ'leɪʃən) *n* **1** the process of congealing. **2** something formed by this process.

congener (kən'dʒiːnə, 'kɒndʒɪnə) *n* **1** a member of a class, group, or other category, esp. any animal of a specified genus. **2** a by-product formed in alcoholic drinks during the fermentation process, which largely determines the flavour and colour of the drink. [C18: from Latin, from *com-* same + *genus* kind]

congeneric (,kɒndʒɪ'nɛrɪk) *or* **congenerous** (kɒn'dʒɛnərəs) *adj* belonging to the same group, esp. (of animals or plants) belonging to the same genus.

congenial (kən'dʒiːnjəl, -nɪəl) *adj* **1** friendly, pleasant, or agreeable: *a congenial atmosphere to work in.* **2** having a similar disposition, tastes, etc.; compatible; sympathetic. [C17: from CON- (same) + GENIAL[1]] ▸ **congeniality** (kən,dʒiːnɪ'ælɪtɪ) *or* **con'genialness** *n* ▸ **con'genially** *adv*

congenic (kən'dʒɛnɪk) *adj Genetics.* (of inbred animal cells) genetically identical except for a single gene locus.

congenital (kən'dʒɛnɪtᵊl) *adj* **1** denoting or relating to any nonhereditary condition, esp. an abnormal condition, existing at birth: *congenital blindness.* **2** *Informal.* complete, as if from birth: *a congenital idiot.* [C18: from Latin *congenitus* born together with, from *genitus* born, from *gignere* to bear, beget] ▸ **con'genitally** *adv* ▸ **con'genitalness** *n*

conger ('kɒŋgə) *n* any large marine eel of the family *Congridae,* esp. *Conger conger,* occurring in temperate and tropical coastal waters. [C14: from Old French *congre,* from Latin *conger,* from Greek *gongros* sea eel]

congeries (kɒn'dʒɪəriːz) *n* (*functioning as sing or pl*) a collection of objects or ideas; mass; heap. [C17: from Latin, from *congerere* to pile up, from *gerere* to carry]

congest (kən'dʒɛst) *vb* **1** to crowd or become crowded to excess; overfill. **2** to overload or clog (an organ or part) with blood or (of an organ or part) to become overloaded or clogged with blood. **3** (*tr; usually passive*) to block (the nose) with mucus. [C16: from Latin *congestus* pressed together, from *congerere* to assemble; see CONGERIES] ▸ **con'gested** *adj* ▸ **con'gestible** *adj* ▸ **con'gestion** *n* ▸ **con'gestive** *adj*

congius ('kɒndʒɪəs) *n, pl* **-gii** (-dʒɪ,aɪ). **1** *Pharmacol.* a unit of liquid measure equal to 1 Imperial gallon. **2** an ancient Roman unit of liquid measure equal to about 0.7 Imperial gallon or 0.84 U.S. gallon. [C14: from Latin, probably from Greek *konkhos* liquid measure, CONCH]

conglobate ('kɒŋgləʊ,beɪt) *vb* **1** to form into a globe or ball. ◆ *adj* **2** a rare word for **globular.** [C17: from Latin *conglobāre* to gather into a ball, from *globāre* to make round, from *globus* a sphere] ▸ **,conglo'bation** *n*

conglomerate *n* (kən'glɒmərɪt). **1** a thing composed of heterogeneous elements; mass. **2** any coarse-grained sedimentary rock consisting of rounded fragments of rock embedded in a finer matrix. Compare **agglomerate** (sense 3). **3** a large corporation consisting of a group of companies dealing in widely diversified goods, services, etc. ◆ *vb* (kən'glɒmə,reɪt). **4** to form into a cluster or mass. ◆ *adj* (kən'glɒmərɪt). **5** made up of heterogeneous elements; massed. **6** (of sedimentary rocks) consisting of rounded fragments within a finer matrix. [C16: from Latin *conglomerāre* to roll up, from *glomerāre* to wind into a ball, from *glomus* ball of thread]

conglomeration (kən,glɒmə'reɪʃən) *n* **1** a conglomerate mass. **2** a mass of miscellaneous things. **3** the act of conglomerating or the state of being conglomerated.

conglutinant (kən'gluːtɪnənt) *adj* (of the edges of a wound or fracture) promoting union; adhesive.

conglutinate (kən'gluːtɪ,neɪt) *vb* **1** to cause (the edges of a wound or fracture) to join during the process of healing or (of the edges of a wound or fracture) to join during this process. **2** to stick or become stuck together. [C16: from Latin *conglūtināre* to glue together, from *glūtināre* to glue, from *glūten* GLUE] ▸ **con,gluti'nation** *n* ▸ **con'glutinative** *adj*

Congo ('kɒŋgəʊ) *n* **1 People's Republic of the.** a republic in W Central Africa: formerly the French colony of Middle Congo, part of French Equatorial Africa, it became independent in 1960; consists mostly of equatorial forest, with savanna and extensive swamps; drained chiefly by the Rivers Congo and Ubangi. Official language: French. Religion: Christian majority. Currency: franc. Capital: Brazzaville. Pop.: 2 658 000 (1998 est.). Area: 342 000 sq. km (132 018 sq. miles). Former names: **Middle Congo** (until 1958), **Congo-Brazzaville. 2 Democratic Republic of the.** a republic in S central Africa, with a narrow strip of land along the Congo estuary leading to the Atlantic in the west: Congo Free State established in 1885, with Leopold II of Belgium as absolute monarch; became the Belgian Congo colony in 1908; gained independence in 1960, followed by civil war and the secession of Katanga (until 1963); President Mobutu Sese Seko seized power in 1965; declared a one-party state in 1978; Sese Seko, accused of corruption on a massive scale, was overthrown by rebels in 1997. The country consists chiefly of the Congo basin, with large areas of dense tropical forest and marshes, and the Mitumba highlands reaching over 5000 m (16 000 ft.) in the east. Official language: French. Religion: Christian majority, animist minority. Currency: Congolese franc. Capital: Kinshasa. Pop.: 49 001 000 (1998 est.). Area: 2 344 116 sq. km (905 063 sq. miles). Former names: **Congo Free State** (1885–1908), **Belgian Congo** (1908–60), **Congo-Kinshasa** (1960–71), **Zaïre** (1971–97). **3** the second longest river in Africa, rising as the Lualaba on the Katanga plateau in the Democratic Republic of the Congo and flowing in a wide northerly curve to the Atlantic: forms the border between the People's Republic of the Congo and the Democratic Republic of the Congo. Length: about 4800 km (3000 miles). Area of basin: about 3 000 000 sq. km (1 425 000 sq. miles). Former (Zaïrese) name (1971–97): **Zaïre. 4** a variant spelling of **Kongo** (the people and language). ▸ **Congolese** (,kɒŋgə'li:z) *adj, n*

congo eel *or* **snake** *n* an aquatic salamander, *Amphiuma means,* having an eel-like body with gill slits and rudimentary limbs and inhabiting still muddy waters in the southern U.S.: family *Amphiumidae.*

Congo Free State *n* a former name (1885–1908) of (**Democratic Republic of the**) **Congo** (sense 2).

Congo red *n* a brownish-red soluble powder, used as a dye, a diagnostic indicator, a biological stain, and a chemical indicator. Formula: $C_{32}H_{22}N_6O_6S_2Na_2$.

congou ('kɒŋgu:) *or* **congo** ('kɒŋgəʊ) *n* a kind of black tea from China. [C18: from Chinese (Amoy) *kong hu tē* tea prepared with care]

congrats (kən'græts) *or* (*Chiefly Brit.*) **congratters** (kən'grætəz) *pl n, sentence substitute.* informal shortened forms of **congratulations.**

congratulate (kən'grætjʊ,leɪt) *vb* (*tr*) **1** (usually foll. by *on*) to communicate pleasure, approval, or praise to (a person or persons); compliment. **2** (often foll. by *on*) to consider (oneself) clever or fortunate (as a result of): *she congratulated herself on her tact.* **3** *Obsolete.* to greet; salute. [C16: from Latin *congrātulārī,* from *grātulārī* to rejoice, from *grātus* pleasing] ▸ **con,gratu'lation** *n* ▸ **con'gratu,lator** *n* ▸ **con'gratulatory** *or* **con'gratulative** *adj*

congratulations (kən,grætjʊ'leɪʃənz) *pl n, sentence substitute.* expressions of pleasure or joy; felicitations.

congregant ('kɒŋgrɪgənt) *n* a member of a congregation, esp. a Jewish congregation.

congregate *vb* ('kɒŋgrɪ,geɪt). **1** to collect together in a body or crowd; assemble. ♦ *adj* ('kɒŋgrɪgɪt, -,geɪt). **2** collected together; assembled. **3** relating to collecting; collective. [C15: from Latin *congregāre* to collect into a flock, from *grex* flock] ▸ **'congre,gative** *adj* ▸ **'congre,gativeness** *n* ▸ **'congre,gator** *n*

congregation (,kɒŋgrɪ'geɪʃən) *n* **1** a group of persons gathered for worship, prayer, etc., esp. in a church or chapel. **2** the act of congregating or collecting together. **3** a group of people, objects, etc., collected together; assemblage. **4** the group of persons habitually attending a given church, chapel, etc. **5** *R.C. Church.* **5a** a society of persons who follow a common rule of life but who are bound only by simple vows. **5b** an administrative subdivision of the papal curia. **5c** an administrative committee of bishops for arranging the business of a general council. **6** *Chiefly Brit.* an assembly of senior members of a university.

congregational (,kɒŋgrɪ'geɪʃən^əl) *adj* **1** of or relating to a congregation. **2** (*usually cap.*) of, relating to, or denoting the Congregational Church, its members, or its beliefs. ▸ **,congre'gationally** *adv*

Congregational Church *n* any evangelical Protestant Christian Church that is governed according to the principles of Congregationalism. In 1972 the majority of churches in the Congregational Church in England and Wales voted to become part of the United Reformed Church.

Congregationalism (,kɒŋgrɪ'geɪʃənə,lɪzəm) *n* a system of Christian doctrines and ecclesiastical government in which each congregation is self-governing and maintains bonds of faith with other similar local congregations. ▸ **,Congre'gationalist** *adj, n*

congress ('kɒŋgres) *n* **1** a meeting or conference, esp. of representatives of a number of sovereign states. **2** a national legislative assembly. **3** a society or association. **4** sexual intercourse. [C16: from Latin *congressus* from *congredī* to meet with, from *com-* together + *gradī* to walk, step]

Congress ('kɒŋgres) *n* **1** the bicameral federal legislature of the U.S., consisting of the House of Representatives and the Senate. **2** this body during any two-year term. **3** Also called: **Congress Party.** (in India) a major political party, which controlled the Union government from 1947 to 1977. Official name: **Indian National Congress.** ▸ **Con'gressional** *adj*

congressional (kən'greʃən^əl) *adj* of or relating to a congress. ▸ **con'gressionalist** *n* ▸ **con'gressionally** *adv*

Congressional district *n* (in the U.S.) an electoral division of a state, entitled to send one member to the U.S. House of Representatives.

Congressional Medal of Honor *n* See **Medal of Honor.**

Congressional Record *n* (in the U.S.) the government journal that publishes all proceedings of Congress.

Congressman ('kɒŋgresmən) *or* (*fem*) **Congresswoman** *n, pl* **-men** *or* **-women.** (in the U.S.) a member of Congress, esp. of the House of Representatives.

Congress of Industrial Organizations *n* (in the U.S.) a federation of industrial unions formed in 1935. It united with the AFL in 1955 to form the AFL-CIO. Abbrev.: **CIO.**

Congress of Vienna *n* the European conference held at Vienna from 1814–15 to settle the territorial problems left by the Napoleonic Wars.

Congreve ('kɒŋgri:v) *n* **William.** 1670–1729, English dramatist, a major exponent of Restoration comedy; author of *Love for Love* (1695) and *The Way of the World* (1700).

congruence ('kɒŋgrʊəns) *or* **congruency** *n* **1** the quality or state of corresponding, agreeing, or being congruent. **2** *Maths.* the relationship between two integers, *x* and *y,* such that their difference, with respect to another integer called the modulus, *n,* is a multiple of the modulus. Usually written $x \equiv y$ (mod *n*), as in $25 \equiv 11$ (*mod 7*).

congruent ('kɒŋgrʊənt) *adj* **1** agreeing; corresponding; congruous. **2** having identical shapes so that all parts correspond: *congruent triangles.* Compare **similar** (sense 2). **3** of or concerning two integers related by a congruence. [C15: from Latin *congruere* to meet together, agree] ▸ **'congruently** *adv*

congruous ('kɒŋgrʊəs) *adj* **1** corresponding or agreeing. **2** suitable; appropriate. [C16: from Latin *congruus* suitable, harmonious; see CONGRUENT] ▸ **congruity** (kən'gru:ɪtɪ) *or* **'congruousness** *n* ▸ **'congruously** *adv*

conic ('kɒnɪk) *adj also* **conical. 1a** having the shape of a cone. **1b** of or relating to a cone. ♦ *n* **2** another name for **conic section.** ♦ See also **conics.** [C16: from New Latin, from Greek *kōnikos,* from *kōnos* CONE] ▸ **'conically** *adv*

conic projection *or* **conical projection** *n* a map projection on which the earth is shown as projected onto a cone with its apex over one of the poles and with parallels of latitude radiating from this apex.

conics ('kɒnɪks) *n* (*functioning as sing*) the branch of geometry concerned with the parabola, ellipse, and hyperbola.

conic section *n* one of a group of curves formed by the intersection of a plane and a right circular cone. It is either a circle, ellipse, parabola, or hyperbola, depending on the eccentricity, *e,* which is constant for a particular curve: $e = 0$ for a circle; $e<1$ for an ellipse; $e = 1$ for a parabola; $e>1$ for a hyperbola. Often shortened to **conic.**

conidiophore (kəʊ'nɪdɪə,fɔ:) *n* a simple or branched hypha that bears spores (conidia) in such fungi as *Penicillium.* [C19: from CONIDIUM + -PHORE] ▸ **conidiophorous** (kəʊ,nɪdɪ'ɒfərəs, kə-) *adj*

conidium (kəʊ'nɪdɪəm) *n, pl* **-nidia** (-'nɪdɪə). an asexual spore formed at the tip of a specialized hypha (conidiophore) in fungi such as *Penicillium.* [C19: from New Latin, from Greek *konis* dust + -IUM] ▸ **co'nidial** *or* **co'nidian** *adj*

conifer ('kəʊnɪfə, 'kɒn-) *n* any gymnosperm tree or shrub of the phylum *Coniferophyta,* typically bearing cones and evergreen leaves. The group includes the pines, spruces, firs, larches, yews, junipers, cedars, cypresses, and sequoias. [C19: from Latin, from *cōnus* CONE + *ferre* to bear]

coniferous (kə'nɪfərəs, kɒ-) *adj* of, relating to, or belonging to the plant phylum *Coniferophyta.* See **conifer.**

coniine ('kəʊnɪ,i:n, -nɪɪn, -ni:n), **conin** ('kəʊnɪn), *or* **conine** ('kəʊni:n, -nɪn) *n* a colourless poisonous soluble liquid alkaloid found in hemlock; 2-propylpiperidine. Formula: $C_5H_{10}NC_3H_7$. Also called: **cicutine** ('sɪkjʊti:n), **conicine** ('kəʊnɪsi:n). [C19: from CONIUM + -INE[2]]

coniology (,kəʊnɪ'ɒlədʒɪ) *n* a variant spelling of **koniology.**

Coniston Water ('kɒnɪstən) *n* a lake in NW England, in Cumbria: scene of the establishment of world water speed records by Sir Malcolm Campbell (1939) and his son Donald Campbell (1959). Length: 8 km (5 miles).

conium ('kəʊnɪəm) *n* **1** either of the two N temperate plants of the umbelliferous genus *Conium,* esp. hemlock. **2** an extract of either of these plants, used to treat spasmodic disorders. [C19: from Late Latin: hemlock, from Greek *kōneion;* perhaps related to Greek *kōnos* CONE]

conj. *abbrev. for:* **1** *Grammar.* conjugation, conjunction, *or* conjunctive. **2** *Astronomy.* conjunction.

conjectural (kən'dʒektʃərəl) *adj* involving or inclined to conjecture. ▸ **con'jecturally** *adv*

conjecture (kən'dʒektʃə) *n* **1** the formation of conclusions from incomplete evidence; guess. **2** the inference or conclusion so formed. **3** *Obsolete.* interpretation of occult signs. ♦ *vb* **4** to infer or arrive at (an opinion, conclusion, etc.) from incomplete evidence. [C14: from Latin *conjectūra* an assembling of facts, from *conjicere* to throw together, from *jacere* to throw] ▸ **con'jecturable** *adj* ▸ **con'jecturably** *adv* ▸ **con'jecturer** *n*

conjoin (kən'dʒɔɪn) *vb* to join or become joined. [C14: from Old French *conjoindre,* from Latin *conjungere,* from *jungere* to JOIN] ▸ **con'joiner** *n*

conjoined twins *pl n* the technical name for **Siamese twins.**

conjoint (kən'dʒɔɪnt) *adj* united, joint, or associated. ▸ **con'jointly** *adv*

conjugal ('kɒndʒʊg^əl) *adj* of or relating to marriage or the relationship between husband and wife: *conjugal rights.* [C16: from Latin *conjugālis,* from *conjunx* wife or husband, from *conjungere* to unite; see CONJOIN] ▸ **conjugality** (,kɒndʒʊ'gælɪtɪ) *n* ▸ **'conjugally** *adv*

conjugant ('kɒndʒʊgənt) *n* either of a pair of organisms or gametes undergoing conjugation.

conjugate *vb* ('kɒndʒʊ,geɪt). **1** (*tr*) *Grammar.* to inflect (a verb) systematically; state or set out the conjugation of (a verb). **2** (*intr*) (of a verb) to undergo inflection according to a specific set of rules. **3** (*tr*) to join (two or more substances) together, esp. in such a way that the resulting substance may easily be turned back into its original components. **4** (*intr*) *Biology.* to undergo conjugation. **5** (*tr*) *Obsolete.* to join together, esp. in marriage. ◆ *adj* ('kɒndʒʊgɪt, -ˌgeɪt). **6** joined together in pairs; coupled. **7** *Maths.* **7a** (of two angles) having a sum of 360°. **7b** (of two complex numbers) differing only in the sign of the imaginary part as 4 + 3i and 4 − 3i. **7c** (of two algebraic numbers) being roots of the same irreducible algebraic equation with rational coefficients: *$3 \pm 2\sqrt{2}$ are conjugate algebraic numbers, being roots of $x^2 - 6x + 1$.* **7d** (of two elements of a determinant) interchanged when the rows and columns are interchanged. **7e** (of two arcs) forming a complete circle or other closed curved figure. **8** *Chem.* of, denoting, or concerning the state of equilibrium in which two liquids can exist as two separate phases that are both solutions. The liquid that is the solute in one phase is the solvent in the other. **9** another word for **conjugated. 10** *Chem.* (of acids and bases) related by loss or gain of a proton: *Cl^- is the conjugate base of HCl; HCl is the conjugate acid of Cl^-.* **11** *Physics.* (of points connected with a lens) having the property that an object placed at one point will produce an image at the other point. **12** (of a compound leaf) having one pair of leaflets. **13** (of words) cognate; related in origin. ◆ *n* ('kɒndʒʊgɪt). **14** one of a pair or set of conjugate substances, values, quantities, words, etc. [C15: from Latin *conjugāre* to join together, from *com-* together + *jugāre* to marry, connect, from *jugum* a yoke] ▸ **'conjugable** *adj* ▸ **'conjugately** *adv* ▸ **'conjugateness** *n* ▸ **'conjuˌgative** *adj* ▸ **'conjuˌgator** *n*

conjugated ('kɒndʒʊˌgeɪtɪd) *adj* **1** *Chem.* **1a** (of a molecule, compound, or substance) containing two or more double bonds alternating with single bonds. **1b** (of a double bond) separated from another double bond by one single bond. **2** *Chem.* formed by the union of two compounds: *a conjugated protein.* ◆ Also: **conjugate.**

conjugated protein *n* a biochemical compound consisting of a sequence of amino acids making up a simple protein to which another nonprotein group (a prosthetic group), such as a carbohydrate or lipid group, is attached.

conjugation (ˌkɒndʒʊ'geɪʃən) *n* **1** *Grammar.* **1a** inflection of a verb for person, number, tense, voice, mood, etc. **1b** the complete set of the inflections of a given verb. **2** a joining, union, or conjunction. **3** a type of sexual reproduction in ciliate protozoans involving the temporary union of two individuals and the subsequent migration and fusion of the gametic nuclei. **4** the union of gametes, esp. isogametes, as in some algae and fungi. **5** the pairing of chromosomes in the early phase of a meiotic division. **6** *Chem.* the existence of alternating double or triple bonds in a chemical compound, with consequent electron delocalization over part of the molecule. ▸ **ˌconju'gational** *adj* ▸ **ˌconju'gationally** *adv*

conjunct *adj* (kən'dʒʌŋkt, 'kɒndʒʌŋkt). **1** joined; united. **2** *Music.* relating to or denoting two adjacent degrees of a scale. ◆ *n* **3** *Logic.* one of the propositions or formulas in a conjunction. [C15: from Latin *conjunctus*, from *conjugere* to unite; see CONJOIN] ▸ **con'junctly** *adv*

conjunction (kən'dʒʌŋkʃən) *n* **1** the act of joining together; combination; union. **2** simultaneous occurrence of events; coincidence. **3** any word or group of words, other than a relative pronoun, that connects words, phrases, or clauses; for example *and* and *while*. Abbrev.: **conj.** See also **coordinating conjunction, subordinating conjunction. 4** *Astronomy.* **4a** the position of a planet or the moon when it is in line with the sun as seen from the earth. The inner planets are in **inferior conjunction** when the planet is between the earth and the sun and in **superior conjunction** when the sun lies between the earth and the planet. Compare **opposition** (sense 8a). **4b** the apparent proximity or coincidence of two celestial bodies on the celestial sphere. **5** *Astrology.* an exact aspect of 0° between two planets, etc., an orb of 8° being allowed. Compare **opposition** (sense 9) and **square** (sense 10). **6** *Logic.* **6a** the operator that forms a compound sentence from two given sentences, and corresponds to the English *and.* **6b** a sentence so formed. Usually written *p&q*, *p∧q*, or *p.q.*, where *p,q* are the component sentences, it is true only when both these are true. **6c** the relation between such sentences. ▸ **con'junctional** *adj* ▸ **con'junctionally** *adv*

conjunction-reduction *n Transformational grammar.* a rule that reduces coordinate sentences, applied, for example, to convert *John lives in Ireland and Brian lives in Ireland* into *John and Brian live in Ireland.*

conjunctiva (ˌkɒndʒʌŋk'taɪvə) *n, pl* **-vas** *or* **-vae** (-viː). the delicate mucous membrane that covers the eyeball and the under surface of the eyelid. [C16: from New Latin *membrāna conjunctīva* the conjunctive membrane, from Late Latin *conjunctīvus* CONJUNCTIVE] ▸ **ˌconjunc'tival** *adj*

conjunctive (kən'dʒʌŋktɪv) *adj* **1** joining; connective. **2** joined. **3** of or relating to conjunctions or their use. **4** *Logic.* relating to, characterized by, or containing a conjunction. ◆ *n* **5** a less common word for **conjunction** (sense 3). [C15: from Late Latin *conjunctīvus*, from Latin *conjungere* to CONJOIN] ▸ **con'junctively** *adv*

conjunctive eye movement *n* any movement of both eyes in the same direction.

conjunctivitis (kənˌdʒʌŋktɪ'vaɪtɪs) *n* inflammation of the conjunctiva.

conjuncture (kən'dʒʌŋktʃə) *n* **1** a combination of events, esp. a critical one. **2** *Rare.* a union; conjunction. ▸ **con'junctural** *adj*

conjuration (ˌkɒndʒʊ'reɪʃən) *n* **1** a magic spell; incantation. **2** a less common word for **conjuring. 3** *Archaic.* supplication; entreaty.

conjure ('kʌndʒə) *vb* **1** (*intr*) to practise conjuring or be a conjuror. **2** (*intr*) to call upon supposed supernatural forces by spells and incantations. **3** (kən'dʒʊə). (*tr*) to appeal earnestly or strongly to: *I conjure you to help me.* **4 a name to conjure with. 4a** a person thought to have great power or influence. **4b** any name that excites the imagination. [C13: from Old French *conjurer* to plot, from Latin *conjūrāre* to swear together, form a conspiracy, from *jūrāre* to swear]

conjure up *vb* (*tr, adv*) **1** to present to the mind; evoke or imagine: *he conjured up a picture of his childhood.* **2** to call up or command (a spirit or devil) by an incantation.

conjuring ('kʌndʒərɪŋ) *n* **1** the performance of tricks that appear to defy natural laws. ◆ *adj* **2** denoting or relating to such tricks or entertainment.

conjuror *or* **conjurer** ('kʌndʒərə) *n* **1** a person who practises conjuring, esp. for people's entertainment. **2** a person who practises magic; sorcerer.

conk (kɒŋk) *Slang.* ◆ *vb* **1** to strike (someone) a blow, esp. on the head or nose. ◆ *n* **2** a punch or blow, esp. on the head or nose. **3** the head or (esp. Brit. and N.Z.) the nose. [C19: probably changed from CONCH]

conker ('kɒŋkə) *n* an informal name for **horse chestnut** (sense 2).

conkers ('kɒŋkəz) *n* (*functioning as sing*) *Brit.* a game in which a player swings a horse chestnut (conker), threaded onto a string, against that of another player to try to break it. [C19: from dialect *conker* snail shell, originally used in the game]

conk out *vb* (*intr, adv*) *Informal.* **1** (of machines, cars, etc.) to fail suddenly. **2** to tire suddenly or collapse, as from exhaustion. [C20: of uncertain origin]

con man *n Informal.* **1** a person who swindles another by means of a confidence trick. **2** a plausible character. ◆ More formal term: **confidence man.**

con moto (kɒn 'məʊtəʊ) *adj, adv Music.* (to be performed) in a brisk or lively manner. [Italian, literally: with movement]

conn (kɒn) *vb, n* a variant spelling (esp. U.S.) of **con**[4].

Conn (kɒn) *n* 2nd century A.D., king of Leinster and high king of Ireland.

Conn. *abbrev. for* Connecticut.

Connacht ('kɒnət) *n* a province and ancient kingdom of NW Republic of Ireland: consists of the counties of Galway, Leitrim, Mayo, Roscommon, and Sligo. Pop.: 433 000 (1996). Area: 17 122 sq. km (6611 sq. miles). Former name: **Connaught.**

connate ('kɒneɪt) *adj* **1** existing in a person or thing from birth; congenital or innate. **2** allied or associated in nature or origin; cognate: *connate qualities.* **3** Also called: **coadunate.** *Biology.* (of similar parts or organs) closely joined or united together by growth. **4** *Geology.* (of fluids) produced or originating at the same time as the rocks surrounding them: *connate water.* [C17: from Late Latin *connātus* born at the same time, from Latin *nātus*, from *nāscī* to be born] ▸ **'connately** *adv* ▸ **'connateness** *n*

connatural (kə'nætʃərəl) *adj* **1** having a similar nature or origin. **2** congenital or innate; connate. ▸ **con'naturally** *adv*

Connaught ('kɒnɔːt) *n* the former name of **Connacht.**

connect (kə'nɛkt) *vb* **1** to link or be linked together; join; fasten. **2** (*tr*) to relate or associate: *I connect him with my childhood.* **3** (*tr*) to establish telephone communications with or between. **4** (*intr*) to be meaningful or meaningfully related. **5** (*intr*) (of two public vehicles, such as trains or buses) to have the arrival of one timed to occur just before the departure of the other, for the convenient transfer of passengers. **6** (*intr*) *Informal.* to hit, punch, kick, etc., solidly. **7** (*intr*) *U.S. and Canadian informal.* to be successful. **8** (*intr*) *Slang.* to find a source of drugs, esp. illegal drugs. [C17: from Latin *connectere* to bind together, from *nectere* to bind, tie] ▸ **con'nectible** *or* **con'nectable** *adj* ▸ **con'nector** *or* **con'necter** *n*

connected (kə'nɛktɪd) *adj* **1** joined or linked together. **2** (of speech) coherent and intelligible. **3** *Logic, maths.* (of a relation) such that either it or its converse holds between any two members of its domain. ▸ **con'nectedly** *adv*

Connecticut (kə'nɛtɪkət) *n* **1** a state of the northeastern U.S., in New England. Capital: Hartford. Pop.: 3 269 858 (1997 est.). Area: 12 973 sq. km (5009 sq. miles). Abbrevs.: **Conn.** or (with zip code) **CT** **2** a river in the northeastern U.S., rising in N New Hampshire and flowing south to Long Island Sound. Length: 651 km (407 miles).

connecting rod *n* **1** a rod or bar for transmitting motion, esp. one that connects a rotating part to a reciprocating part. **2** such a rod that connects the piston to the crankshaft in an internal-combustion engine or reciprocating pump. See also **big end, little end. 3** a similar rod that connects the crosshead of a steam engine to the crank. ◆ Often shortened to **con rod.**

connection *or* **connexion** (kə'nɛkʃən) *n* **1** the act or state of connecting; union. **2** something that connects, joins, or relates; link or bond. **3** a relationship or association. **4** logical sequence in thought or expression; coherence. **5** the relation of a word or phrase to its context: *in this connection the word has no political significance.* **6** (*often pl*) an acquaintance, esp. one who is influential or has prestige. **7** a relative, esp. if distant and related by marriage. **8a** an opportunity to transfer from one train, bus, aircraft, ship, etc., to another. **8b** the vehicle, aircraft, etc., scheduled to provide such an opportunity. **9** (*pl*) *N.Z.* the persons owning or controlling a racehorse. **10** a link, usually a wire or metallic strip, between two components in an electric circuit. **11** a communications link between two points, esp. by telephone. **12** *Slang.* a supplier of illegal drugs, such as heroin. **13** *Rare.* sexual intercourse. **14** *Rare.* a small sect or religious group united by a body of distinct beliefs or practices. ▸ **con'nectional** *or* **con'nexional** *adj*

connectionism (kə'nɛkʃənɪzəm) *n Psychol.* the theory that the connections between brain cells mediate thought and govern behaviour.

connective (kə'nɛktɪv) *adj* **1** serving to connect or capable of connecting. ◆ *n* **2** a thing that connects. **3** *Grammar, logic.* **3a** a less common word for **conjunction** (sense 3). **3b** any word that connects phrases, clauses, or individual words. **3c** a symbol used in a formal language in the construction of compound sentences from simpler sentences, corresponding to terms such as *or, and, not,* etc., in ordinary speech. **4** *Botany.* the tissue of a stamen that connects the two lobes of the anther. **5** *Anatomy.* a nerve-fibre bundle connecting two nerve centres. ▸ **con'nectively** *adv* ▸ **connectivity** (ˌkɒnɛk'tɪvɪtɪ) *n*

connective tissue *n* an animal tissue developed from the embryonic mesoderm that consists of collagen or elastic fibres, fibroblasts, fatty cells, etc., within a jelly-like matrix. It supports organs, fills the spaces between them, and forms tendons and ligaments.

Connemara (ˌkɒnɪˈmɑːrə) *n* a barren coastal region of W Republic of Ireland, in Co. Galway: consists of quartzite mountains, peat bogs, and many lakes.

Connery (ˈkɒnərɪ) *n* **Sean**, real name *Thomas Connery*. born 1929, Scottish film actor, who played James Bond in such films as *Goldfinger* (1964). His later films include *The Name of the Rose* (1986), *Indiana Jones and the Last Crusade* (1989), and *Playing by Heart* (1999).

conning tower (ˈkɒnɪŋ) *n* **1** Also called: **sail**. a superstructure of a submarine, used as the bridge when the vessel is on the surface. **2** the armoured pilot house of a warship. [C19: see CON[4]]

conniption (kəˈnɪpʃən) *n* (*often pl*) *U.S. and Canadian slang*. a fit of rage or tantrums. [C19: arbitrary pseudo-Latin coinage]

connivance (kəˈnaɪvəns) *n* **1** the act or fact of conniving. **2** *Law*. the tacit encouragement of or assent to another's wrongdoing, esp. (formerly) of the petitioner in a divorce suit to the respondent's adultery.

connive (kəˈnaɪv) *vb* (*intr*) **1** to plot together, esp. secretly; conspire. **2** (foll. by *at*) *Law*. to give assent or encouragement (to the commission of a wrong). [C17: from French *conniver*, from Latin *connīvēre* to blink, hence, leave uncensured; *-nīvēre* related to *nictāre* to wink] ▸ **conˈniver** *n* ▸ **conˈnivingly** *adv*

connivent (kəˈnaɪvənt) *adj* (of parts of plants and animals) touching without being fused, as some petals, insect wings, etc. [C17: from Latin *connīvēns*, from *connīvēre* to shut the eyes, CONNIVE] ▸ **conˈniventty** *adv*

connoisseur (ˌkɒnɪˈsɜː) *n* a person with special knowledge or appreciation of a field, esp. in the arts. [C18: from French, from Old French *conoiseor*, from *connoistre* to know, from Latin *cognōscere*] ▸ **ˌconnoisˈseurship** *n*

Connolly (ˈkɒnəlɪ) *n* **1 Billy**. born 1942, Scottish comedian. **2 Cyril (Vernon)**. 1903–74, British critic and writer, founder and editor of *Horizon* (1939–50): his books include *Enemies of Promise* (1938). **3 James**. 1868–1916, Irish labour leader: executed by the British for his part in the Easter Rising (1916).

Connors (ˈkɒnəz) *n* **Jimmy**. born 1952, U.S. tennis player: Wimbledon champion 1974 and 1982; U.S. champion 1974, 1976, 1978, 1982, and 1983.

connotation (ˌkɒnəˈteɪʃən) *n* **1** an association or idea suggested by a word or phrase; implication. **2** the act or fact of connoting. **3** *Logic*. another name for **intension** (sense 1). ▸ **connotative** (ˈkɒnəˌteɪtɪv, kəˈnəʊtə-) *or* **conˈnotive** *adj* ▸ **ˈconnoˌtatively** *or* **conˈnotively** *adv*

connote (kɒˈnəʊt) *vb* (*tr; often takes a clause as object*) **1** (of a word, phrase, etc.) to imply or suggest (associations or ideas) other than the literal meaning: *the word "maiden" connotes modesty*. **2** to involve as a consequence or condition. [C17: from Medieval Latin *connotāre*, from *notāre* to mark, make a note, from *nota* mark, sign, note]

connubial (kəˈnjuːbɪəl) *adj* of or relating to marriage; conjugal: *connubial bliss*. [C17: from Latin *cōnūbiālis* from *cōnūbium* marriage, from *com-* together + *nūbere* to marry] ▸ **conˌnubiˈality** *n* ▸ **conˈnubially** *adv*

conodont (ˈkəʊnədɒnt, ˈkɒn-) *n* any of various small Palaeozoic toothlike fossils derived from an extinct unknown animal. [C19: from Greek *kōnos* CONE + -ODONT]

conoid (ˈkəʊnɔɪd) *n* **1** a geometric surface formed by rotating a parabola, ellipse, or hyperbola about one axis. ◆ *adj also* **conoidal** (kəʊˈnɔɪdᵊl). **2** conical, cone-shaped. [C17: from Greek *kōnoeidēs*, from *kōnos* CONE] ▸ **coˈnoidally** *adv*

conoscenti (ˌkɒnəʊˈʃɛntɪ) *pl n, sing* **-te** (-tiː). a variant spelling of **cognoscenti**.

conquer (ˈkɒŋkə) *vb* **1** to overcome (an enemy, army, etc.); defeat. **2** to overcome (an obstacle, feeling, desire, etc.); surmount. **3** (*tr*) to gain possession or control of by or as if by force or war; win. **4** (*tr*) to gain the love, sympathy, etc., of (someone) by seduction or force of personality. [C13: from Old French *conquerre*, from Vulgar Latin *conquērere* (unattested) to obtain, from Latin *conquīrere* to search for, collect, from *quaerere* to seek] ▸ **ˈconquerable** *adj* ▸ **ˈconquerableness** *n* ▸ **ˈconquering** *adj* ▸ **ˈconqueror** *n*

Conqueror (ˈkɒŋkərə) *n* **William the**. See **William I**.

conquest (ˈkɒnkwest, ˈkɒŋ-) *n* **1** the act or an instance of conquering or the state of having been conquered; victory. **2** a person, thing, etc., that has been conquered or won. **3** the act or art of gaining a person's compliance, love, etc., by seduction or force of personality. **4** a person, whose compliance, love, etc., has been won over by seduction or force of personality. [C13: from Old French *conqueste*, from Vulgar Latin *conquēsta* (unattested), from Latin *conquīsīta*, feminine past participle of *conquīrere* to seek out, procure; see CONQUER]

Conquest (ˈkɒnkwest, ˈkɒŋ-) *n* **the**. See **Norman Conquest**.

conquian (ˈkɒŋkɪən) *n* another word for **cooncan**.

conquistador (kɒnˈkwɪstəˌdɔː; *Spanish* konkistaˈðor) *n, pl* **-dors** *or* **-dores** (*Spanish* -ˈðores). an adventurer or conqueror, esp. one of the Spanish conquerors of the New World in the 16th century. [C19: from Spanish, from *conquistar* to conquer; see CONQUEST]

Conrad (ˈkɒnræd) *n* **Joseph**. real name *Teodor Josef Konrad Korzeniowski*. 1857–1924, British novelist born in Poland, noted for sea stories such as *The Nigger of the Narcissus* (1897) and *Lord Jim* (1900) and novels of politics and revolution such as *Nostromo* (1904) and *Under Western Eyes* (1911).

con rod *n* short for **connecting rod**.

cons. *abbrev. for:* **1** consecrated. **2** consigned. **3** consignment. **4** consolidated. **5** consonant. **6** constitutional. **7** construction. **8** consulting.

Cons. *or* **cons.** *abbrev. for:* **1** Conservative. **2** Constitution. **3** Consul.

consanguinity (ˌkɒnsæŋˈgwɪnɪtɪ) *n* **1** relationship by blood; kinship. **2** close affinity or connection. **3** *Geology*. (of rocks) similarity of origin, as shown by common mineral and chemical compositions and often texture. [C14: see CON-, SANGUINE] ▸ **ˌconsanˈguineous** *or* **conˈsanguine** *adj* ▸ **ˌconsanˈguineously** *adv*

conscience (ˈkɒnʃəns) *n* **1a** the sense of right and wrong that governs a person's thoughts and actions. **1b** regulation of one's actions in conformity to this sense. **1c** a supposed universal faculty of moral insight. **2** conscientiousness; diligence. **3** a feeling of guilt or anxiety: *he has a conscience about his unkind action*. **4** *Obsolete*. consciousness. **5 in (all) conscience**. **5a** with regard to truth and justice. **5b** certainly. **6 on one's conscience**. causing feelings of guilt or remorse. [C13: from Old French, from Latin *conscientia* knowledge, consciousness, from *conscīre* to know; see CONSCIOUS] ▸ **ˈconscienceless** *adj*

conscience clause *n* a clause in a law or contract exempting persons with moral scruples.

conscience money *n* money paid voluntarily to compensate for dishonesty, esp. money paid voluntarily for taxes formerly evaded.

conscience-stricken *adj* feeling anxious or guilty. Also: **conscience-smitten**.

conscientious (ˌkɒnʃɪˈɛnʃəs) *adj* **1** involving or taking great care; painstaking; diligent. **2** governed by or done according to conscience. ▸ **ˌconsciˈentiously** *adv* ▸ **ˌconsciˈentiousness** *n*

conscientious objector *n* a person who refuses to serve in the armed forces on the grounds of conscience.

conscionable (ˈkɒnʃənəbᵊl) *adj Obsolete*. acceptable to one's conscience. [C16: from *conscions*, obsolete form of CONSCIENCE] ▸ **ˈconscionableness** *n* ▸ **ˈconscionably** *adv*

conscious (ˈkɒnʃəs) *adj* **1a** alert and awake; not sleeping or comatose. **1b** aware of one's surroundings, one's own thoughts and motivations, etc. **2a** aware of and giving value or emphasis to a particular fact or phenomenon: *I am conscious of your great kindness to me*. **2b** (*in combination*): *clothes-conscious*. **3** done with full awareness; deliberate: *a conscious effort; conscious rudeness*. **4a** denoting or relating to a part of the human mind that is aware of a person's self, environment, and mental activity and that to a certain extent determines his choices of action. **4b** (*as n*): *the conscious is only a small part of the mind*. ◆ Compare **unconscious**. [C17: from Latin *conscius* sharing knowledge, from *com-* with + *scīre* to know] ▸ **ˈconsciously** *adv* ▸ **ˈconsciousness** *n*

consciousness raising *n* **a** the process of developing awareness in a person or group of a situation regarded as wrong or unjust, with the aim of producing active participation in changing it. **b** (*as modifier*): *a consciousness-raising group*.

conscript *n* (ˈkɒnskrɪpt). **1a** a person who is enrolled for compulsory military service. **1b** (*as modifier*): *a conscript army*. ◆ *vb* (kənˈskrɪpt). **2** (*tr*) to enrol (youths, civilians, etc.) for compulsory military service. [C15: from Latin *conscrīptus*, past participle of *conscrībere* to write together in a list, enrol, from *scrībere* to write]

conscript fathers *pl n Literary*. august legislators, esp. Roman senators.

conscription (kənˈskrɪpʃən) *n* compulsory military service.

consecrate (ˈkɒnsɪˌkreɪt) *vb* (*tr*) **1** to make or declare sacred or holy; sanctify. **2** to dedicate (one's life, time, etc.) to a specific purpose. **3** to ordain (a bishop). **4** *Christianity*. to sanctify (bread and wine) for the Eucharist to be received as the body and blood of Christ. **5** to cause to be respected or revered; venerate: *time has consecrated this custom*. ◆ *adj* **6** *Archaic*. consecrated. [C15: from Latin *consecrāre*, from *com-* (intensive) + *sacrāre* to devote, from *sacer* sacred] ▸ **ˌconseˈcration** *n* ▸ **ˈconseˌcrator** *n* ▸ **consecratory** (ˌkɒnsɪˈkreɪtərɪ) *or* **ˈconseˌcrative** *adj*

Consecration (ˌkɒnsɪˈkreɪʃən) *n R.C. Church*. the part of the Mass after the sermon during which the bread and wine are believed to change into the Body and Blood of Christ.

consecution (ˌkɒnsɪˈkjuːʃən) *n* **1** a sequence or succession of events or things. **2** a logical sequence of deductions; inference. [C16: from Latin *consecūtiō*, from *consequī* to follow up, pursue]

consecutive (kənˈsɛkjʊtɪv) *adj* **1** (of a narrative, account, etc.) following chronological sequence. **2** following one another without interruption; successive. **3** characterized by logical sequence. **4** *Music*. another word for **parallel** (sense 3). **5** *Grammar*. expressing consequence or result: *consecutive clauses*. [C17: from French *consécutif*, from Latin *consecūtus* having followed, from *consequī* to pursue] ▸ **conˈsecutively** *adv* ▸ **conˈsecutiveness** *n*

consensual (kənˈsɛnsjʊəl) *adj* **1** *Law*. (of a contract, agreement, etc.) existing by consent. **2** *Law*. (of a sexual activity) performed with the consent of all parties involved. **3** (of certain reflex actions of a part of the body) responding to stimulation of another part. ▸ **conˈsensually** *adv* [from CONSENSUS + -AL[1]]

consensus (kənˈsɛnsəs) *n* general or widespread agreement (esp. in the phrase **consensus of opinion**). [C19: from Latin, from *consentīre* to feel together, agree; see CONSENT]

USAGE Since *consensus* refers to a collective opinion, the words *of opinion* in the phrase *consensus of opinion* are redundant and should therefore be avoided.

consensus sequence *n Biochem*. a DNA sequence common to different organisms and having a similar function in each.

consent (kənˈsɛnt) *vb* **1** to give assent or permission (to do something); agree; accede. **2** (*intr*) *Obsolete*. to be in accord; agree in opinion, feelings, etc. ◆ *n* **3** acquiescence to or acceptance of something done or planned by another; permission. **4** accordance or harmony in opinion; agreement (esp. in the phrase **with one consent**). **5 age of consent**. the lowest age at which the law recognizes the right of a person, esp. a girl, to consent to sexual intercourse. [C13: from Old French *consentir*, from Latin *consentīre* to feel together, agree, from *sentīre* to feel] ▸ **conˈsenter** *n* ▸ **conˈsenting** *adj*

consentaneous (ˌkɒnsɛnˈteɪnɪəs) *adj Rare*. **1** (foll. by *to*) accordant or consistent (with). **2** done by general consent. [C17: from Latin *consentāneus*, from *consentīre* to CONSENT] ▸ **ˌconsenˈtaneously** *adv* ▸ **consentaneity** (kənˌsɛntəˈniːɪtɪ) *or* **ˌconsenˈtaneousness** *n*

consentient (kənˈsɛnʃənt) *adj* being in agreement; united in opinion. ▸ **conˈsentience** *n*

consenting adult *n Brit.* a male person over the age of eighteen, who may legally engage in homosexual behaviour in private.

consequence ('kɒnsɪkwəns) *n* **1** a result or effect of some previous occurrence. **2** an unpleasant result (esp. in the phrase **take the consequences**). **3** significance or importance: *it's of no consequence; a man of consequence.* **4** *Logic.* **4a** a conclusion reached by reasoning. **4b** the conclusion of an argument. **4c** the relations between the conclusion and the premises of a valid argument. **5** the relation between an effect and its cause. **6 in consequence.** as a result.

consequences ('kɒnsɪkwənsɪz) *pl n* (*functioning as sing*) *Brit.* a game in which each player writes down a part of a story, folds over the paper, and passes it on to another player who continues the story. After several stages, the resulting (nonsensical) stories are read out.

consequent ('kɒnsɪkwənt) *adj* **1** following as an effect or result. **2** following as a logical conclusion or by rational argument. **3** (of a river) flowing in the direction of the original slope of the land or dip of the strata. ◆ *n* **4** something that follows something else, esp. as a result. **5** *Logic.* the resultant clause in a conditional sentence. **6 affirming the consequent.** *Logic.* the fallacy of inferring the antecedent of a conditional sentence, given the truth of the conditional and its consequent, as *if John is six feet tall, he's more than five feet: he's more than five feet so he's six feet.* **7** an obsolete term for **denominator** (sense 1). **[**C15: from Latin *consequēns* following closely, from *consequī* to pursue**]**

USAGE See at **consequential.**

consequential (ˌkɒnsɪ'kwɛnʃəl) *adj* **1** important or significant. **2** self-important; conceited. **3** following as a consequence; resultant, esp. indirectly: *consequential loss.* ▸ **ˌconseˌquenti'ality** *or* **ˌconse'quentialness** *n* ▸ **ˌconse'quentially** *adv*

USAGE Although both *consequential* and *consequent* can refer to something which happens as the result of something else, *consequent* is more common in this sense in modern English: *the new measures were put into effect, and the consequent protest led to the dismissal of those responsible.*

consequentialism (ˌkɒnsɪ'kwɛnʃəˌlɪzəm) *n Ethics.* the doctrine that an action is right or wrong according as its consequences are good or bad.

consequently ('kɒnsɪkwəntlɪ) *adv, sentence connector.* as a result or effect; therefore; hence.

conservancy (kən'sɜːvənsɪ) *n, pl* **-cies. 1** (in Britain) a court or commission with jurisdiction over a river, port, area of countryside, etc. **2** another word for **conservation** (sense 2).

conservation (ˌkɒnsə'veɪʃən) *n* **1** the act or an instance of conserving or keeping from change, loss, injury, etc. **2a** protection, preservation, and careful management of natural resources and of the environment. **2b** (*as modifier*): *a conservation area.* ▸ **ˌconser'vational** *adj*

conservationist (ˌkɒnsə'veɪʃənɪst) *n* a person who advocates or strongly promotes preservation and careful management of natural resources and of the environment.

conservation of charge *n* the principle that the total charge of any isolated system is constant and independent of changes that take place within the system.

conservation of energy *n* the principle that the total energy of any isolated system is constant and independent of any changes occurring within the system.

conservation of mass *n* the principle that the total mass of any isolated system is constant and is independent of any chemical and physical changes taking place within the system.

conservation of momentum *n* the principle that the total linear or angular momentum in any isolated system is constant, provided that no external force is applied.

conservation of parity *n* the principle that the parity of the total wave function describing a system of elementary particles is conserved. In fact it is not conserved in weak interactions.

conservatism (kən'sɜːvəˌtɪzəm) *n* **1** opposition to change and innovation. **2** a political philosophy advocating the preservation of the best of the established order in society and opposing radical change.

Conservatism (kən'sɜːvəˌtɪzəm) *n* (in Britain, Canada, etc.) **1** the form of conservatism advocated by the Conservative Party. **2** the policies, doctrines, or practices of the Conservative Party.

conservative (kən'sɜːvətɪv) *adj* **1** favouring the preservation of established customs, values, etc., and opposing innovation. **2** of, characteristic of, or relating to conservatism. **3** tending to be moderate or cautious: *a conservative estimate.* **4** conventional in style or type: *a conservative suit.* **5** *Med.* (of treatment) designed to alleviate symptoms. Compare **radical** (sense 4). **6** *Physics.* (of a field of force, system, etc.) doing work by moving an object or particle but being independent of the path along which the object or particle is displaced: *electrostatic fields of force are conservative.* ◆ *n* **7** a person who is reluctant to change or consider new ideas; conformist. **8** a supporter or advocate of conservatism. ◆ *adj, n* **9** a less common word for **preservative.** ▸ **con'servatively** *adv* ▸ **con'servativeness** *n*

Conservative (kən'sɜːvətɪv) (in Britain, Canada, and elsewhere) ◆ *adj* **1** of, supporting, or relating to a Conservative Party. **2** of, relating to, or characterizing Conservative Judaism. ◆ *n* **3** a supporter or member of a Conservative Party.

Conservative Judaism *n* a movement reacting against the radicalism of Reform Judaism, rejecting extreme change and advocating moderate relaxations of traditional Jewish law, by an extension of the process by which its adherents claim traditional orthodox Judaism evolved. Compare **Orthodox Judaism, Reform Judaism.**

Conservative Party *n* **1** (in Britain) the major right-wing party, which developed from the Tories in the 1830s. It advocates a mixed economy, and encourages property owning and free enterprise. In full: **Conservative and Unionist Party. 2** (in Canada) short for **Progressive Conservative Party. 3** (in other countries) any of various political parties generally opposing change.

conservatoire (kən'sɜːvəˌtwɑː) *n* an institution or school for instruction in music. Also called: **conservatory. [**C18: from French: CONSERVATORY**]**

conservator ('kɒnsəˌveɪtə, kən'sɜːvə-) *n* a person who conserves or keeps safe; custodian, guardian, or protector.

conservatorium (kənˌsɜːvə'tɔːrɪəm) *n Austral.* the usual term for **conservatoire.**

conservatory (kən'sɜːvətrɪ) *n, pl* **-tories. 1** a greenhouse, esp. one attached to a house. **2** another word for **conservatoire.** ◆ *adj* **3** preservative.

conserve *vb* (kən'sɜːv). (*tr*) **1** to keep or protect from harm, decay, loss, etc. **2** to preserve (a foodstuff, esp. fruit) with sugar. ◆ *n* ('kɒnsɜːv, kən'sɜːv). **3** a preparation of fruit in sugar, similar to jam but usually containing whole pieces of fruit. **[**(vb) C14: from Latin *conservāre* to keep safe, from *servāre* to save, protect; (n) C14: from Medieval Latin *conserva,* from Latin *conservāre***]** ▸ **con'servable** *adj* ▸ **con'server** *n*

Consett ('kɒnsɪt) *n* a town in N England, in N Durham. Pop.: 21 153 (1991).

consider (kən'sɪdə) *vb* (*mainly tr*) **1** (*also intr*) to think carefully about or ponder on (a problem, decision, etc.); contemplate. **2** (*may take a clause as object*) to judge, deem, or have as an opinion: *I consider him a fool.* **3** to have regard for; respect: *consider your mother's feelings.* **4** to look at; regard: *he considered her face.* **5** (*may take a clause as object*) to bear in mind as possible or acceptable: *when buying a car consider this make.* **6** to describe or discuss: *in this programme we consider the traffic problem.* **7** (*may take a clause as object*) to keep in mind and make allowances (for): *consider his childhood.* **[**C14: from Latin *consīderāre* to inspect closely, literally: to observe the stars, from *sīdus* star**]** ▸ **con'siderer** *n*

considerable (kən'sɪdərəb^{ə}l) *adj* **1** large enough to reckon with: *a considerable quantity.* **2** a lot of; much: *he had considerable courage.* **3** worthy of respect: *a considerable man in the scientific world.* ▸ **con'siderably** *adv*

considerate (kən'sɪdərɪt) *adj* **1** thoughtful towards other people; kind. **2** *Rare.* carefully thought out; considered. ▸ **con'siderately** *adv* ▸ **con'siderateness** *n*

consideration (kənˌsɪdə'reɪʃən) *n* **1** the act or an instance of considering; deliberation; contemplation. **2 take into consideration.** to bear in mind; consider. **3 under consideration.** being currently discussed or deliberated. **4** a fact or circumstance to be taken into account when making a judgment or decision. **5 on no consideration.** for no reason whatsoever; never. **6** thoughtfulness for other people; kindness. **7** payment for a service; recompense; fee. **8** thought resulting from deliberation; opinion. **9** *Law.* the promise, object, etc., given by one party to persuade another to enter into a contract. **10** estimation; esteem. **11 in consideration of. 11a** because of. **11b** in return for.

considered (kən'sɪdəd) *adj* **1** presented or thought out with care: *a considered opinion.* **2** (*qualified by a preceding adverb*) esteemed: *highly considered.*

considering (kən'sɪdərɪŋ) *prep* **1** in view of. ◆ *adv* **2** *Informal.* all in all; taking into account the circumstances: *it's not bad considering.* ◆ *conj* **3** (*subordinating*) in view of the fact that.

consign (kən'saɪn) *vb* (*mainly tr*) **1** to hand over or give into the care or charge of another; entrust. **2** to commit irrevocably: *he consigned the papers to the flames.* **3** to commit for admittance: *to consign someone to jail.* **4** to address or deliver (goods) for sale, disposal, etc.: *it was consigned to his London address.* **5** (*intr*) *Obsolete.* to assent; agree. **[**C15: from Old French *consigner,* from Latin *consignāre* to put one's seal to, sign, from *signum* mark, SIGN**]** ▸ **con'signable** *adj* ▸ **ˌconsign'ation** *n*

consignee (ˌkɒnsaɪ'niː) *n* a person, agent, organization, etc., to which merchandise is consigned.

consignment (kən'saɪnmənt) *n* **1** the act of consigning; commitment. **2** a shipment of goods consigned. **3 on consignment.** for payment by the consignee after sale: *he made the last shipment on consignment.*

consignor (kən'saɪnə, ˌkɒnsaɪ'nɔː) *or* **consigner** (kən'saɪnə) *n* a person, enterprise, etc., that consigns goods.

consist (kən'sɪst) *vb* (*intr*) **1** (foll. by *of*) to be composed (of); be formed (of): *syrup consists of sugar and water.* **2** (foll. by *in* or *of*) to have its existence (in); lie (in); be expressed (by): *his religion consists only in going to church.* **3** to be compatible or consistent; accord. **[**C16: from Latin *consistere* to halt, stand firm, from *sistere* to stand, cause to stand; related to *stāre* to STAND**]**

consistency (kən'sɪstənsɪ) *or* **consistence** *n, pl* **-encies** *or* **-ences. 1** agreement or accordance with facts, form, or characteristics previously shown or stated. **2** agreement or harmony between parts of something complex; compatibility. **3** degree of viscosity or firmness. **4** the state or quality of holding or sticking together and retaining shape. **5** conformity with previous attitudes, behaviour, practice, etc.

consistent (kən'sɪstənt) *adj* **1** showing consistency; not self-contradictory. **2** (*postpositive;* foll. by *with*) in agreement or harmony; accordant. **3** steady; even: *consistent growth.* **4** *Maths.* (of two or more equations) satisfied by at least one common set of values of the variables: $x + y = 4$ *and* $x - y = 2$ *are consistent.* **5** *Logic.* **5a** (of a set of statements) capable of all being true at the same time or under the same interpretation. **5b** (of a formal system) not permitting the deduction of a contradiction from the axioms. Compare **complete** (sense 5). **6** *Obsolete.* stuck together; cohering. ▸ **con'sistently** *adv*

consistory (kən'sɪstərɪ) *n, pl* **-ries. 1** *Church of England.* **1a** the court of a diocese (other than Canterbury) administering ecclesiastical law. **1b** the area in a church where the consistory meets. **2** *R.C. Church.* an assembly of the cardinals and the pope. **3** (in certain Reformed Churches) the governing body of a local congregation or church. **4** *Archaic.* a council or assembly. **[**C14: from Old French *consistorie,* from Medieval Latin *consistōrium* ecclesiastical tribunal, ultimately from Latin *consistere* to stand still] ▸ **consistorial** (ˌkɒnsɪˈstɔːrɪəl) *or* ˌ**consisˈtorian** *adj*

consociate *vb* (kənˈsəʊʃɪˌeɪt). **1** to enter into or bring into friendly association. ◆ *adj* (kənˈsəʊʃɪɪt, -ˌeɪt). **2** associated or united. ◆ *n* (kənˈsəʊʃɪɪt, -ˌeɪt). **3** an associate or partner. [C16: from Latin *consociāre,* from *socius* partner] ▸ **conˌsociˈation** *n*

consocies (kənˈsəʊʃiːz) *n, pl* **-cies.** *Ecology.* a natural community with a single dominant species. [C20: from CONSOCIATE + SPECIES]

consolation (ˌkɒnsəˈleɪʃən) *n* **1** the act of consoling or state of being consoled; solace. **2** a person or thing that is a source of comfort in a time of suffering, grief, disappointment, etc. ▸ **consolatory** (kənˈsɒlətərɪ, -trɪ) *adj*

consolation prize *n* a prize given to console a loser of a game.

console[1] (kənˈsəʊl) *vb* to serve as a source of comfort to (someone) in disappointment, loss, sadness, etc. [C17: from Latin *consōlārī,* from *sōlārī* to comfort; see SOLACE] ▸ **conˈsolable** *adj* ▸ **conˈsoler** *n* ▸ **conˈsolingly** *adv*

console[2] (ˈkɒnsəʊl) *n* **1** an ornamental bracket, esp. one used to support a wall fixture, bust, etc. **2** the part of an organ comprising the manuals, pedals, stops, etc. **3** a unit on which the controls of an electronic system are mounted. **4** a cabinet for a television, gramophone, etc., designed to stand on the floor. **5** See **console table.** [C18: from French, shortened from Old French *consolateur* one that provides support, hence, supporting bracket, from Latin *consōlātor* a comforter; see CONSOLE[1]]

console table (ˈkɒnsəʊl) *n* a table with one or more curved legs of bracket-like construction, designed to stand against a wall.

consolidate (kənˈsɒlɪˌdeɪt) *vb* **1** to form or cause to form into a solid mass or whole; unite or be united. **2** to make or become stronger or more stable. **3** *Military.* to strengthen or improve one's control over (a situation, force, newly captured area, etc.). [C16: from Latin *consolidāre* to make firm, from *solidus* strong, SOLID] ▸ **conˈsoliˌdator** *n*

Consolidated Fund *n Brit.* a fund into which tax revenue is paid in order to meet standing charges, esp. interest payments on the national debt.

consolidation (kənˌsɒlɪˈdeɪʃən) *n* **1** the act of consolidating or state of being consolidated. **2** something that is consolidated or integrated. **3** *Law.* **3a** the combining of two or more actions at law. **3b** the combination of a number of Acts of Parliament into one codifying statute. **4** *Geology.* the process, including compression and cementation, by which a loose deposit is transformed into a hard rock. **5** *Psychol.* the process in the brain that makes the memory for an event enduring; the process is thought to continue for some time after the event. ▸ **conˈsoliˌdative** *adj*

consolidation loan *n* a single loan which is taken out to pay off several separate existing loans.

consols (ˈkɒnsɒlz, kənˈsɒlz) *pl n* irredeemable British government securities carrying annual interest rates of two and a half or four per cent. Also called: **bank annuities.** [short for *consolidated stock*]

consolute (ˈkɒnsəˌluːt) *adj* **1** (of two or more liquids) mutually soluble in all proportions. **2** (of a substance) soluble in each of two conjugate liquids. **3** of or concerned with the particular state in which two partially miscible liquids become totally miscible. [C20: from Late Latin *consolūtus,* from Latin *con-* together + *solvere* to dissolve]

consommé (kənˈsɒmeɪ, ˈkɒnsɒˌmeɪ; *French* kɔ̃sɔme) *n* a clear soup made from meat or chicken stock. [C19: from French, from *consommer* to finish, use up, from Latin *consummāre;* so called because all the goodness of the meat goes into the liquid]

consonance (ˈkɒnsənəns) *or* **consonancy** *n, pl* **-nances** *or* **-nancies. 1** agreement, harmony, or accord. **2** *Prosody.* similarity between consonants, but not between vowels, as between the *s* and *t* sounds in *sweet silent thought.* Compare **assonance** (sense 1). **3** *Music.* **3a** an aesthetically pleasing sensation or perception associated with the interval of the octave, the perfect fourth and fifth, the major and minor third and sixth, and chords based on these intervals. Compare **dissonance** (sense 3). **3b** an interval or chord producing this sensation.

consonant (ˈkɒnsənənt) *n* **1** a speech sound or letter of the alphabet other than a vowel; a stop, fricative, or continuant. ◆ *adj* **2** (*postpositive;* foll. by *with* or *to*) consistent; in agreement. **3** harmonious in tone or sound. **4** *Music.* characterized by the presence of a consonance. **5** being or relating to a consonant. [C14: from Latin *consonāns,* from *consonāre* to sound at the same time, be in harmony, from *sonāre* to sound] ▸ **ˈconsonantly** *adv*

consonantal (ˌkɒnsəˈnæntᵊl) *adj* **1** relating to, functioning as, or constituting a consonant, such as the semivowel *w* in English *work.* **2** consisting of or characterized by consonants: *a consonantal cluster.* ▸ ˌ**consoˈnantally** *adv*

con sordino *adv Music.* See **sordino** (sense 3).

consort *vb* (kənˈsɔːt). **1** (*intr;* usually foll. by *with*) to keep company (with undesirable people); associate. **2** (*intr*) to agree or harmonize. **3** (*tr*) *Rare.* to combine or unite. ◆ *n* (ˈkɒnsɔːt). **4** (esp. formerly) **4a** a small group of instruments, either of the same type, such as viols, (a **whole consort**) or of different types (a **broken consort**). **4b** (*as modifier*): *consort music.* **5** the husband or wife of a reigning monarch. **6** a partner or companion, esp. a husband or wife. **7** a ship that escorts another. **8** *Obsolete.* **8a** companionship or association. **8b** agreement or accord. [C15: from Old French, from Latin *consors* sharer, partner, from *sors* lot, fate, portion] ▸ **conˈsortable** *adj* ▸ **conˈsorter** *n*

consortium (kənˈsɔːtɪəm) *n, pl* **-tia** (-tɪə). **1** an association of financiers, companies, etc., esp. one formed for a particular purpose. **2** *Law.* the right of husband or wife to the company, assistance, and affection of the other. [C19: from Latin: community of goods, partnership; see CONSORT] ▸ **conˈsortial** *adj*

conspecific (ˌkɒnspɪˈsɪfɪk) *adj* (of animals or plants) belonging to the same species.

conspectus (kənˈspɛktəs) *n* **1** an overall view; survey. **2** a summary; résumé. [C19: from Latin: a viewing, from *conspicere* to observe, from *specere* to look]

conspicuous (kənˈspɪkjʊəs) *adj* **1** clearly visible; obvious or showy. **2** attracting attention because of a striking quality or feature: *conspicuous stupidity.* [C16: from Latin *conspicuus,* from *conspicere* to perceive; see CONSPECTUS] ▸ **conˈspicuously** *adv* ▸ **conˈspicuousness** *n*

conspicuous consumption *n* spending in a lavish or ostentatious way, esp. to impress others with one's wealth.

conspiracy (kənˈspɪrəsɪ) *n, pl* **-cies. 1** a secret plan or agreement to carry out an illegal or harmful act, esp. with political motivation; plot. **2** the act of making such plans in secret. ▸ **conˈspirator** *n* ▸ **conspiratorial** (kənˌspɪrəˈtɔːrɪəl) *or* **conˈspiratory** *adj* ▸ **conˌspiraˈtorially** *adv*

conspiracy theory *n* the belief that the government or a covert organization is responsible for an event that is unusual or unexplained, esp. when any such involvement is denied.

conspire (kənˈspaɪə) *vb* (when *intr,* sometimes foll. by *against*) **1** to plan or agree on (a crime or harmful act) together in secret. **2** (*intr*) to act together towards some end as if by design: *the elements conspired to spoil our picnic.* [C14: from Old French *conspirer,* from Latin *conspīrāre* to plot together, literally: to breathe together, from *spīrāre* to breathe] ▸ **conˈspirer** *n* ▸ **conˈspiringly** *adv*

con spirito (kɒn ˈspɪrɪtəʊ) *adj, adv Music.* (to be performed) in a spirited or lively manner (also in the phrases **allegro con spirito, presto con spirito**). [Italian: with spirit]

const. *abbrev. for:* **1** constant. **2** constitution.

constable (ˈkʌnstəbᵊl, ˈkɒn-) *n* **1** (in Britain, Australia, Canada, New Zealand, etc.) a police officer of the lowest rank. **2** any of various officers of the peace, esp. one who arrests offenders, serves writs, etc. **3** the keeper or governor of a royal castle or fortress. **4** (in medieval Europe) the chief military officer and functionary of a royal household, esp. in France and England. **5** an officer of a hundred in medieval England, originally responsible for raising the military levy but later assigned other administrative duties. [C13: from Old French, from Late Latin *comes stabulī* officer in charge of the stable, from Latin *comes* comrade + *stabulum* dwelling, stable; see also COUNT[2]] ▸ **ˈconstableˌship** *n*

Constable (ˈkʌnstəbᵊl) *n* **John.** 1776–1837, English landscape painter, noted particularly for his skill in rendering atmospheric effects of changing light.

constabulary (kənˈstæbjʊlərɪ) *Chiefly Brit.* ◆ *n, pl* **-laries. 1** the police force of a town or district. ◆ *adj* **2** of or relating to constables, constabularies, or their duties.

Constance (ˈkɒnstəns) *n* **1** a city in S Germany, in Baden-Württemberg on Lake Constance: tourist centre. Pop.: 72 860 (1989 est.). German name: **Konstanz. 2 Lake.** a lake in W Europe, bounded by S Germany, W Austria, and N Switzerland, through which the Rhine flows. Area: 536 sq. km. (207 sq. miles). German name: **Bodensee.**

constancy (ˈkɒnstənsɪ) *n* **1** the quality of having a resolute mind, purpose, or affection; steadfastness. **2** freedom from change or variation; stability. **3** *Psychol.* the perceptual phenomenon in which attributes of an object appear to remain the same in a variety of different presentations, e.g., a given object looks roughly the same size regardless of its distance from the observer. **4** *Ecology.* the frequency of occurrence of a particular species in sample plots from a plant community.

constant (ˈkɒnstənt) *adj* **1** fixed and invariable; unchanging. **2** continual or continuous; incessant: *constant interruptions.* **3** resolute in mind, purpose, or affection; loyal. ◆ *n* **4** something that is permanent or unchanging. **5** a specific quantity that is always invariable: *the velocity of light is a constant.* **6a** *Maths.* a symbol representing an unspecified number that remains invariable throughout a particular series of operations. **6b** *Physics.* a theoretical or experimental quantity or property that is considered invariable throughout a particular series of calculations or experiments. **7** See **logical constant.** [C14: from Old French, from Latin *constāns* standing firm, from *constāre* to be steadfast, from *stāre* to stand] ▸ **ˈconstantly** *adv*

Constant (*French* kɔ̃stɑ̃) *n* **Benjamin** (bɛ̃ʒamɛ̃). real name *Henri Benjamin Constant de Rebecque.* 1767–1830, French writer and politician: author of the psychological novel *Adolphe* (1816).

Constanţa (*Romanian* konˈstantsa) *n* a port and resort in SE Romania, on the Black Sea: founded by the Greeks in the 6th century B.C. and rebuilt by Constantine the Great (4th century); exports petroleum. Pop.: 348 575 (1994 est.).

constantan (ˈkɒnstənˌtæn) *n* an alloy of copper (60 per cent) and nickel (40 per cent). It has a high resistivity that does not vary significantly with temperature and is used in resistors and, with copper, in thermocouples. [C20: formed from CONSTANT]

Constantia (kɒnˈstænʃə) *n S. African.* **1** a region of the Cape Peninsula. **2** any of several red or white wines produced around Constantia.

Constantine (ˈkɒnstənˌtaɪn; *French* kɔ̃stɑ̃tin) *n* a walled city in NE Algeria: built on an isolated rock; military and trading centre. Pop.: 440 842 (1987).

Constantine I (ˈkɒnstənˌtaɪn, -ˌtiːn) *n* **1** known as *Constantine the Great.* Latin name *Flavius Valerius Aurelius Constantinus.* ?280–337 A.D., first Christian Roman emperor (306–337): moved his capital to Byzantium, which he renamed Constantinople (330). **2** 1868–1923, king of Greece (1913–17; 1920–22): deposed (1917), recalled by a plebiscite (1920), but forced to abdicate again (1922) after defeat by the Turks.

Constantine II *n* official title *Constantine XIII.* born 1940, king of Greece (1964–73): went into exile when the army seized power in 1967. He was officially deposed in 1973 and Greece became a republic.

Constantine VII *n* known as *Porphyrogenitus.* 905–59 A.D., Byzantine emperor (913–59) and scholar: his writings are an important source for Byzantine history.

Constantine XI *n* 1404–53, last Byzantine emperor (1448–53): killed when Constantinople was captured by the Turks.

Constantinople (ˌkɒnstæntɪˈnəʊpᵊl) *n* the former name (330–1926) of **Istanbul.**

constatation (ˌkɒnstəˈteɪʃən) *n* **1** the process of verification. **2** a statement or assertion. [C20: from French, from *constater* to verify, from Latin *constat* it is certain; see CONSTANT]

constellate (ˈkɒnstɪˌleɪt) *vb* to form into clusters in or as if in constellations.

constellation (ˌkɒnstɪˈleɪʃən) *n* **1a** any of the 88 groups of stars as seen from the earth and the solar system, many of which were named by the ancient Greeks after animals, objects, or mythological persons. **1b** an area on the celestial sphere containing such a group. **2** a gathering of brilliant or famous people or things. **3** *Psychoanal.* a group of ideas felt to be related. [C14: from Late Latin *constellātiō*, from Latin *com-* together + *stella* star] ▸ **ˌconstelˈlational** *adj* ▸ **constellatory** (kənˈstelətərɪ, -trɪ) *adj*

consternate (ˈkɒnstəˌneɪt) *vb* (*tr; usually passive*) to fill with anxiety, dismay, dread, or confusion. [C17: from Latin *consternāre*, from *sternere* to lay low, spread out]

consternation (ˌkɒnstəˈneɪʃən) *n* a feeling of anxiety, dismay, dread, or confusion.

constipate (ˈkɒnstɪˌpeɪt) *vb* (*tr*) to cause constipation in. [C16: from Latin *constīpāre* to press closely together, from *stīpāre* to crowd together] ▸ **ˈconstiˌpated** *adj*

constipation (ˌkɒnstɪˈpeɪʃən) *n* infrequent or difficult evacuation of the bowels, with hard faeces, caused by functional or organic disorders or improper diet.

constituency (kənˈstɪtjʊənsɪ) *n, pl* **-cies. 1** the whole body of voters who elect one representative to a legislature or all the residents represented by one deputy. **2a** a district that sends one representative to a legislature. **2b** (*as modifier*): *constituency organization.*

constituent (kənˈstɪtjʊənt) *adj* (*prenominal*) **1** forming part of a whole; component. **2** having the power to frame a constitution or to constitute a government (esp. in the phrases **constituent assembly, constituent power**). **3** *Becoming rare.* electing or having the power to elect. ◆ *n* **4** a component part; ingredient. **5** a resident of a constituency, esp. one entitled to vote. **6** *Chiefly law.* a person who appoints another to act for him, as by power of attorney. **7** *Linguistics.* a word, phrase, or clause forming a part of a larger construction. Compare **immediate constituent, ultimate constituent.** [C17: from Latin *constituēns* setting up, from *constituere* to establish, CONSTITUTE] ▸ **conˈstituently** *adv*

constitute (ˈkɒnstɪˌtjuːt) *vb* (*tr*) **1** to make up; form; compose: *the people who constitute a jury.* **2** to appoint to an office or function: *a legally constituted officer.* **3** to set up (a school or other institution) formally; found. **4** *Law.* to give legal form to (a court, assembly, etc.). **5** *Law, obsolete.* to set up or enact (a law). [C15: from Latin *constituere*, from *com-* (intensive) + *statuere* to place] ▸ **ˈconstiˌtuter** *or* **ˈconstiˌtutor** *n*

constitution (ˌkɒnstɪˈtjuːʃən) *n* **1** the act of constituting or state of being constituted. **2** the way in which a thing is composed; physical make-up; structure. **3** the fundamental political principles on which a state is governed, esp. when considered as embodying the rights of the subjects of that state. **4** (*often cap.*) (in certain countries, esp. Australia and the U.S.) a statute embodying such principles. **5** a person's state of health. **6** a person's disposition of mind; temperament.

constitutional (ˌkɒnstɪˈtjuːʃənᵊl) *adj* **1** denoting, characteristic of, or relating to a constitution. **2** authorized by or subject to a constitution. **3** of or inherent in the physical make-up or basic nature of a person or thing: *a constitutional weakness.* **4** beneficial to one's general physical wellbeing. ◆ *n* **5** a regular walk taken for the benefit of one's health. ▸ **ˌconstiˈtutionally** *adv*

constitutionalism (ˌkɒnstɪˈtjuːʃənəˌlɪzəm) *n* **1** the principles, spirit, or system of government in accord with a constitution, esp. a written constitution. **2** adherence to or advocacy of such a system or such principles. ▸ **ˌconstiˈtutionalist** *n*

constitutionality (ˌkɒnstɪˌtjuːʃəˈnælɪtɪ) *n* the quality or state of being in accord with a constitution.

constitutional monarchy *n* a monarchy governed according to a constitution that limits and defines the powers of the sovereign. Also called: **limited monarchy.**

constitutional psychology *n* a school of thought postulating that the personality of an individual is dependent on the type of his physique (somatotype).

constitutional strike *n* a stoppage of work by the workforce of an organization, with the approval of the trade union concerned, in accordance with the dispute procedure laid down in a collective agreement between the parties.

constitutive (ˈkɒnstɪˌtjuːtɪv) *adj* **1** having power to enact, appoint, or establish. **2** *Chem.* (of a physical property) determined by the arrangement of atoms in a molecule rather than by their nature. **3** *Biochem.* (of an enzyme) formed continuously, irrespective of the cell's needs. **4** another word for **constituent** (sense 1). ▸ **ˈconstiˌtutively** *adv*

constr. *abbrev. for* construction.

constrain (kənˈstreɪn) *vb* (*tr*) **1** to compel or force, esp. by persuasion, circumstances, etc.; oblige. **2** to restrain by or as if by force; confine. [C14: from Old French *constreindre*, from Latin *constringere* to bind together, from *stringere* to bind] ▸ **conˈstrainer** *n*

constrained (kənˈstreɪnd) *adj* embarrassed, unnatural, or forced: *a constrained smile.* ▸ **constrainedly** (kənˈstreɪnɪdlɪ) *adv*

constraint (kənˈstreɪnt) *n* **1** compulsion, force, or restraint. **2** repression or control of natural feelings or impulses. **3** a forced unnatural manner; inhibition. **4** something that serves to constrain; restrictive condition: *social constraints kept him silent.* **5** *Linguistics.* any very general restriction on a sentence formation rule.

constrict (kənˈstrɪkt) *vb* (*tr*) **1** to make smaller or narrower, esp. by contracting at one place. **2** to hold in or inhibit; limit. [C18: from Latin *constrictus* compressed, from *constringere* to tie up together; see CONSTRAIN]

constriction (kənˈstrɪkʃən) *n* **1** a feeling of tightness in some part of the body, such as the chest. **2** the act of constricting or condition of being constricted. **3** something that is constricted. **4** *Genetics.* a localized narrow region of a chromosome, esp. at the centromere. ▸ **conˈstrictive** *adj* ▸ **conˈstrictively** *adv* ▸ **conˈstrictiveness** *n*

constrictor (kənˈstrɪktə) *n* **1** any of various nonvenomous snakes, such as the pythons, boas, and anaconda, that coil around and squeeze their prey to kill it. **2** any muscle that constricts or narrows a canal or passage; sphincter. **3** a person or thing that constricts.

constringe (kənˈstrɪndʒ) *vb* (*tr*) *Rare.* to shrink or contract. [C17: from Latin *constringere* to bind together; see CONSTRAIN] ▸ **conˈstringency** *n* ▸ **conˈstringent** *adj*

constringence (kənˈstrɪndʒəns) *n Physics.* inverse of the dispersive power of a medium.

construct *vb* (kənˈstrʌkt). (*tr*) **1** to put together substances or parts, esp. systematically, in order to make or build (a building, bridge, etc.); assemble. **2** to compose or frame mentally (an argument, sentence, etc.). **3** *Geometry.* to draw (a line, angle, or figure) so that certain requirements are satisfied. ◆ *n* (ˈkɒnstrʌkt). **4** something formulated or built systematically. **5** a complex idea resulting from a synthesis of simpler ideas. **6** *Psychol.* a model devised on the basis of observation, designed to relate what is observed to some theoretical framework. [C17: from Latin *constructus* piled up, from *construere* to heap together, build, from *struere* to arrange, erect] ▸ **conˈstructible** *adj* ▸ **conˈstructor** *or* **conˈstructer** *n*

construction (kənˈstrʌkʃən) *n* **1** the process or act of constructing or manner in which a thing is constructed. **2** the thing constructed; a structure. **3a** the business or work of building dwellings, offices, etc. **3b** (*as modifier*): *a construction site.* **4** an interpretation or explanation of a law, text, action, etc.: *they put a sympathetic construction on her behaviour.* **5** *Grammar.* a group of words that together make up one of the constituents into which a sentence may be analysed; a phrase or clause. **6** *Geometry.* a drawing of a line, angle, or figure satisfying certain conditions, used in solving a problem or proving a theorem. **7** an abstract work of art in three dimensions or relief. See also **constructivism** (sense 1). ▸ **conˈstructional** *adj* ▸ **conˈstructionally** *adv*

constructionist (kənˈstrʌkʃənɪst) *n U.S.* a person who interprets constitutional law in a certain way, esp. strictly.

constructive (kənˈstrʌktɪv) *adj* **1** serving to build or improve; positive: *constructive criticism.* **2** *Law.* deduced by inference or construction; not expressed but inferred. **3** *Law.* having an implied legal effect: *constructive notice.* **4** another word for **structural.** ▸ **conˈstructively** *adv* ▸ **conˈstructiveness** *n*

constructive dismissal *n* a course of action taken by an employer that is detrimental to an employee and designed to leave the employee with no option but to resign.

constructivism (kənˈstrʌktɪˌvɪzəm) *n* **1** a movement in abstract art evolved in Russia after World War I, primarily by Naum Gabo, which explored the use of movement and machine-age materials in sculpture and had considerable influence on modern art and architecture. **2** *Philosophy.* the theory that mathematical entities do not exist independently of our construction of them. Compare **intuitionism** (sense 4), **finitism.** ▸ **conˈstructivist** *adj, n*

construe (kənˈstruː) *vb* **-strues, -struing, -strued.** (*mainly tr*) **1** to interpret the meaning of (something): *you can construe that in different ways.* **2** (*may take a clause as object*) to discover by inference; deduce. **3** to analyse the grammatical structure of; parse (esp. a Latin or Greek text as a preliminary to translation). **4** to combine (words) syntactically. **5** (*also intr*) *Old-fashioned.* to translate literally, esp. aloud as an academic exercise. ◆ *n* **6** *Old-fashioned.* something that is construed, such as a piece of translation. [C14: from Latin *construere* to pile up; see CONSTRUCT] ▸ **conˈstruable** *adj* ▸ **conˌstruaˈbility** *n* ▸ **conˈstruer** *n*

consubstantial (ˌkɒnsəbˈstænʃəl) *adj Christian theol.* (esp. of the three persons of the Trinity) regarded as identical in substance or essence though different in aspect. [C15: from Church Latin *consubstantiālis*, from Latin COM- + *substantia* SUBSTANCE] ▸ **ˌconsubˌstantiˈality** *n* ▸ **ˌconsubˈstantially** *adv*

consubstantiate (ˌkɒnsəbˈstænʃɪˌeɪt) *vb* (*intr*) *Christian theol.* (of the Eucharistic bread and wine and Christ's body and blood) to undergo consubstantiation.

consubstantiation (ˌkɒnsəbˌstænʃɪˈeɪʃən) *n Christian theol.* (in the belief of High-Church Anglicans) **1** the doctrine that after the consecration of the Eucharist the substance of the body and blood of Christ coexists within the substance of the consecrated bread and wine. **2** the mystical process by which this is believed to take place during consecration. ◆ Compare **transubstantiation.**

consuetude (ˈkɒnswɪˌtjuːd) *n* an established custom or usage, esp. one having legal force. [C14: from Latin *consuētūdō*, from *consuēscere* to accustom, from CON- + *suēscere* to be wont] ▸ **ˌconsueˈtudinary** *adj*

consul (ˈkɒnsᵊl) *n* **1** an official appointed by a sovereign state to protect its commercial interests and aid its citizens in a foreign city. **2** (in ancient Rome) either of two annually elected magistrates who jointly exercised the highest authority in the republic. **3** (in France from 1799 to 1804) any of the three chief magistrates of the First Republic. [C14: from Latin, from *consulere* to CONSULT] ▸ **consular** (ˈkɒnsjʊlə) *adj* ▸ **ˈconsulˌship** *n*

consular agent *n* a consul of one of the lower grades.

consulate (ˈkɒnsjʊlɪt) *n* **1** the business premises or residence of a consul. **2** government by consuls. **3** the office or period of office of a consul or consuls. **4** (*often cap.*) **4a** the government of France by the three consuls from 1799 to 1804. **4b** this period of French history. **5** (*often cap.*) **5a** the consular government of the Roman republic. **5b** the office or rank of a Roman consul.

consul general *n, pl* **consuls general.** a consul of the highest grade, usually stationed in a city of considerable commercial importance.

consult (kən'sʌlt) *vb* **1** (when *intr,* often foll. by *with*) to ask advice from (someone); confer with (someone). **2** (*tr*) to refer to for information: *to consult a map.* **3** (*tr*) to have regard for (a person's feelings, interests, etc.) in making decisions or plans; consider. **4** (*intr*) to make oneself available to give professional advice, esp. at scheduled times and for a fee. **[C17:** from French *consulter,* from Latin *consultāre* to reflect, take counsel, from *consulere* to consult**]** ▸ **con'sultable** *adj* ▸ **con'sulter** *or* **con'sultor** *n*

consultant (kən'sʌltᵊnt) *n* **1a** a physician, esp. a specialist, who is asked to confirm a diagnosis. **1b** a physician or surgeon holding the highest appointment in a particular branch of medicine or surgery in a hospital. **2** a specialist who gives expert advice or information. **3** a person who asks advice in a consultation. ▸ **con'sultancy** *n*

consultation (ˌkɒnsᵊl'teɪʃən) *n* **1** the act or procedure of consulting. **2** a conference for discussion or the seeking of advice, esp. from doctors or lawyers.

consultative (kən'sʌltətɪv), **consultatory** (kən'sʌltətərɪ, -trɪ), *or* **consultive** *adj* available for, relating to, or involving consultation; advisory. ▸ **con'sultatively** *adv*

consulting (kən'sʌltɪŋ) *adj* (*prenominal*) acting in an advisory capacity on professional matters: *a consulting engineer.*

consulting room *n* a room in which a doctor, esp. a general practitioner, sees his patients.

consumable (kən'sjuːməbᵊl) *adj* **1** capable of being consumed. ◆ *n* **2** (*usually pl*) goods intended to be bought and used; consumer goods.

consume (kən'sjuːm) *vb* **1** (*tr*) to eat or drink. **2** (*tr; often passive*) to engross or obsess. **3** (*tr*) to use up; expend: *my car consumes little oil.* **4** to destroy or be destroyed by burning, decomposition, etc.: *fire consumed the forest.* **5** (*tr*) to waste or squander: *the time consumed on that project was excessive.* **6** (*passive*) to waste away. **[C14:** from Latin *consūmere* to devour, from *com-* (intensive) + *sūmere* to take up, from *emere* to take, purchase**]** ▸ **con'suming** *adj* ▸ **con'sumingly** *adv*

consumedly (kən'sjuːmɪdlɪ) *adv Old-fashioned.* (intensifier): *a consumedly fascinating performance.*

consumer (kən'sjuːmə) *n* **1** a person who acquires goods and services for his or her own personal needs. Compare **producer** (sense 6). **2** a person or thing that consumes. **3** (*usually pl*) *Ecology.* an organism, esp. an animal, within a community that feeds upon plants or other animals. See also **decomposer, producer** (sense 8).

consumer durable *n* a manufactured product that has a relatively long useful life, such as a car or a television.

consumer goods *pl n* goods that satisfy personal needs rather than those required for the production of other goods or services. Compare **capital goods.**

consumerism (kən'sjuːməˌrɪzəm) *n* **1** protection of the interests of consumers. **2** advocacy of a high rate of consumption and spending as a basis for a sound economy. ▸ **con'sumerist** *n, adj*

consummate *vb* ('kɒnsəˌmeɪt). **1** (*tr*) to bring to completion or perfection; fulfil. **2** (*tr*) to complete (a marriage) legally by sexual intercourse. ◆ *adj* (kən'sʌmɪt, 'kɒnsəmɪt). **3** accomplished or supremely skilled: *a consummate artist.* **4** (*prenominal*) (intensifier): *a consummate fool.* **[C15:** from Latin *consummāre* to complete, from *summus* highest, utmost**]** ▸ **con'summately** *adv* ▸ **ˌconsum'mation** *n* ▸ **'consumˌmative** *or* **con'summatory** *adj* ▸ **'consumˌmator** *n*

consummatory behaviour (kən'sʌmətərɪ) *n Psychol.* any behaviour that leads directly to the satisfaction of an innate drive, e.g. eating or drinking.

consumption (kən'sʌmpʃən) *n* **1** the act of consuming or the state of being consumed, esp. by eating, burning, etc. **2** *Economics.* expenditure on goods and services for final personal use. **3** the quantity consumed. **4** *Pathol.* a condition characterized by a wasting away of the tissues of the body, esp. as seen in tuberculosis of the lungs. **[C14:** from Latin *consumptiō* a wasting, from *consūmere* to CONSUME**]**

consumptive (kən'sʌmptɪv) *adj* **1** causing consumption; wasteful; destructive. **2** *Pathol.* relating to or affected with consumption, esp. tuberculosis of the lungs. ◆ *n* **3** *Pathol.* a person who suffers from consumption. ▸ **con'sumptively** *adv* ▸ **con'sumptiveness** *n*

cont. *abbrev. for:* **1** containing. **2** contents. **3** continent(al). **4** continued.

contact *n* ('kɒntækt). **1** the act or state of touching physically. **2** the state or fact of close association or communication (esp. in the phrases **in contact, make contact**). **3a** a junction of two or more electrical conductors. **3b** the part of the conductors that makes the junction. **3c** the part of an electrical device to which such connections are made. **4** an acquaintance, esp. one who might be useful in business, as a means of introduction, etc. **5** any person who has been exposed to a contagious disease. **6** *Photog.* See **contact print.** **7** (*usually pl*) an informal name for **contact lens.** **8** (*modifier*) of or relating to irritation or inflammation of the skin caused by touching the causative agent: *contact dermatitis.* **9** (*modifier*) denoting an insecticide or herbicide that kills on contact, rather than after ingestion or absorption. **10** (*modifier*) of or maintaining contact. **11** (*modifier*) requiring or involving (physical) contact: *the contact sport of boxing.* ◆ *vb* ('kɒntækt, kən'tækt). **12** (when *intr,* often foll. by *with*) to put, come, or be in association, touch, or communication. ◆ *interj* **13** *Aeronautics.* (formerly) a call made by the pilot to indicate that an aircraft's ignition is switched on and that the engine is ready for starting by swinging the propeller. **[C17:** from Latin *contactus,* from *contingere* to touch on all sides, pollute, from *tangere* to touch**]** ▸ **contactual** (kɒn'tæktjʊəl) *adj* ▸ **con'tactually** *adv*

contactable (kɒn'tæktəbᵊl) *adj* able to be communicated with: *the manager is not contactable at the moment.*

contact flight *n* **1** a flight in which the pilot remains in sight of land or water. **2** air navigation by observation of prominent landmarks, beacons, etc.

contact lens *n* a thin convex lens, usually of plastic, which floats on the layer of tears in front of the cornea to correct defects of vision.

contact man *n* an intermediary or go-between.

contactor (kɒn'tæktə) *n* a type of switch for repeatedly opening and closing an electric circuit. Its operation can be mechanical, electromagnetic, or pneumatic.

contact print *n* a photographic print made by exposing the printing paper through a negative placed directly onto it.

contagion (kən'teɪdʒən) *n* **1** the transmission of disease from one person to another by direct or indirect contact. **2** a contagious disease. **3** another name for **contagium.** **4** a corrupting or harmful influence that tends to spread; pollutant. **5** the spreading of an emotional or mental state among a number of people: *the contagion of mirth.* **[C14:** from Latin *contāgiō* a touching, infection, from *contingere;* see CONTACT**]**

contagious (kən'teɪdʒəs) *adj* **1** (of a disease) capable of being passed on by direct contact with a diseased individual or by handling clothing, etc., contaminated with the causative agent. Compare **infectious.** **2** (of an organism) harbouring or spreading the causative agent of a transmissible disease. **3** causing or likely to cause the same reaction or emotion in several people; catching; infectious: *her laughter was contagious.* ▸ **con'tagiously** *adv* ▸ **con'tagiousness** *n*

contagious abortion *n* another name for **brucellosis.**

contagium (kən'teɪdʒɪəm) *n, pl* **-gia** (-dʒɪə). *Pathol.* the specific virus or other direct cause of any infectious disease. **[C17:** from Latin, variant of *contāgiō* CONTAGION**]**

contain (kən'teɪn) *vb* (*tr*) **1** to hold or be capable of holding or including within a fixed limit or area: *this contains five pints.* **2** to keep (one's feelings, behaviour, etc.) within bounds; restrain. **3** to consist of; comprise: *the book contains three different sections.* **4** *Military.* to prevent (enemy forces) from operating beyond a certain level or area. **5** to be a multiple of, leaving no remainder: *6 contains 2 and 3.* **[C13:** from Old French *contenir,* from Latin *continēre,* from *com-* together + *tenēre* to hold**]** ▸ **con'tainable** *adj*

container (kən'teɪnə) *n* **1** an object used for or capable of holding, esp. for transport or storage, such as a carton, box, etc. **2a** a large cargo-carrying standard-sized container that can be loaded from one mode of transport to another. **2b** (*as modifier*): *a container port; a container ship.*

containerize *or* **containerise** (kən'teɪnəˌraɪz) *vb* (*tr*) **1** to convey (cargo) in standard-sized containers. **2** to adapt (a port or transportation system) to the use of standard-sized containers. ▸ **conˌtaineri'zation** *or* **conˌtaineri'sation** *n*

containment (kən'teɪnmənt) *n* **1** the act or condition of containing, esp. of restraining the ideological or political power of a hostile country or the operations of a hostile military force. **2** (from 1947 to the mid-1970s) a principle of U.S. foreign policy that sought to prevent the expansion of Communist power. **3** Also called: **confinement.** *Physics.* the process of preventing the plasma in a controlled thermonuclear reaction from reaching the walls of the reaction vessel, usually by confining it within a configuration of magnetic fields. See **magnetic bottle.**

contaminate *vb* (kən'tæmɪˌneɪt). (*tr*) **1** to make impure, esp. by touching or mixing; pollute. **2** to make radioactive by the addition of radioactive material. ◆ *adj* (kən'tæmɪnɪt, -ˌneɪt). **3** *Archaic.* contaminated. **[C15:** from Latin *contamināre* to defile; related to Latin *contingere* to touch**]** ▸ **con'taminable** *adj* ▸ **con'taminant** *n* ▸ **con'taminative** *adj* ▸ **con'tamiˌnator** *n*

contamination (kənˌtæmɪ'neɪʃən) *n* **1** the act or process of contaminating or the state of being contaminated. **2** something that contaminates. **3** *Linguistics.* the process by which one word or phrase is altered because of mistaken associations with another word or phrase; for example, the substitution of *irregardless* for *regardless* by association with such words as *irrespective.*

contango (kən'tæŋgəʊ) *n, pl* **-gos.** **1** (formerly, on the London Stock Exchange) postponement of payment for and delivery of stock from one account day to the next. **2** the fee paid for such a postponement. ◆ Also called: **carry-over, continuation.** Compare **backwardation.** ◆ *vb* **-goes, -going, -goed.** **3** (*tr*) to arrange such a postponement of payment (for): *my brokers will contango these shares.* **[C19:** apparently an arbitrary coinage based on CONTINUE**]**

contd *abbrev. for* continued.

conte *French.* (kɔ̃t) *n* a tale or short story, esp. of adventure.

Conté ('kɒnteɪ; *French* kɔ̃te) *n Trademark.* a hard crayon used by artists, etc., made of clay and graphite and often coloured a reddish-brown. Also called: **conté-crayon.** **[C19:** named after N.J. *Conté,* 18th-century French chemist**]**

contemn (kən'tɛm) *vb* (*tr*) *Formal.* to treat or regard with contempt; scorn. **[C15:** from Latin *contemnere,* from *temnere* to slight**]** ▸ **contemner** (kən'tɛmnə, -'tɛmə) *n* ▸ **contemnible** (kən'tɛmnɪbᵊl) *adj* ▸ **con'temnibly** *adv*

contemp. *abbrev. for* contemporary.

contemplate ('kɒntɛmˌpleɪt, -təm-) *vb* (*mainly tr*) **1** to think about intently and at length; consider calmly. **2** (*intr*) to think intently and at length, esp. for spiritual reasons; meditate. **3** to look at thoughtfully; observe pensively. **4** to have in mind as a possibility: *to contemplate changing jobs.* **[C16:** from Latin *contemplāre,* from *templum* TEMPLE[1]**]** ▸ **'contemˌplator** *n*

contemplation (ˌkɒntɛm'pleɪʃən, -təm-) *n* **1** thoughtful or long consideration or observation. **2** spiritual meditation esp. (in Christian religious practice) concentration of the mind and soul upon God. Compare **meditation.** **3** purpose or intention.

contemplative ('kɒntɛmˌpleɪtɪv, -təm-; kən'tɛmplə-) *adj* **1** denoting, concerned with, or inclined to contemplation; meditative. ◆ *n* **2** a person dedicated to religious contemplation or to a way of life conducive to this. ▸ **'contemˌplatively** *adv* ▸ **'contemˌplativeness** *n*

contemporaneous (kənˌtɛmpə'reɪnɪəs) *adj* existing, beginning, or occurring in the same period of time. ► **contemporaneity** (kən,tempərə'niːɪtɪ) *or* **con,tempo'raneousness** *n* ► **con,tempo'raneously** *adv*

contemporary (kən'tɛmprərɪ) *adj* **1** belonging to the same age; living or occurring in the same period of time. **2** existing or occurring at the present time. **3** conforming to modern or current ideas in style, fashion, design, etc. **4** having approximately the same age as one another. ♦ *n, pl* **-raries. 5** a person living at the same time or of approximately the same age as another. **6** something that is contemporary. **7** *Journalism.* a rival newspaper. [C17: from Medieval Latin *contemporārius,* from Latin *com-* together + *temporārius* relating to time, from *tempus* time] ► **con'temporarily** *adv* ► **con'temporariness** *n*

USAGE Since *contemporary* can mean either of the same period or of the present period, it is best to avoid this word where ambiguity might arise, as in *a production of* Othello *in contemporary dress. Modern dress* or *Elizabethan dress* should be used in this example to avoid ambiguity.

contemporize *or* **contemporise** (kən'tɛmpə,raɪz) *vb* to be or make contemporary; synchronize.

contempt (kən'tɛmpt) *n* **1** the attitude or feeling of a person towards a person or thing that he considers worthless or despicable; scorn. **2** the state of being scorned; disgrace (esp. in the phrase **hold in contempt**). **3** wilful disregard of or disrespect for the authority of a court of law or legislative body: *contempt of court.* [C14: from Latin *contemptus* a despising, from *contemnere* to CONTEMN]

contemptible (kən'tɛmptəbᵊl) *adj* deserving or worthy of contempt; despicable. ► **con,tempti'bility** *or* **con'temptibleness** *n* ► **con'temptibly** *adv*

contemptuous (kən'tɛmptjʊəs) *adj* (when *predicative,* often foll. by *of*) showing or feeling contempt; disdainful. ► **con'temptuously** *adv* ► **con'temptuousness** *n*

contend (kən'tɛnd) *vb* **1** (*intr;* often foll. by *with*) to struggle in rivalry, battle, etc.; vie. **2** to argue earnestly; debate. **3** (*tr; may take a clause as object*) to assert or maintain. [C15: from Latin *contendere* to strive, from *com-* with + *tendere* to stretch, aim] ► **con'tender** *n* ► **con'tendingly** *adv*

content[1] ('kɒntɛnt) *n* **1** (*often pl*) everything that is inside a container: *the contents of a box.* **2** (*usually pl*) **2a** the chapters or divisions of a book. **2b** a list, printed at the front of a book, of chapters or divisions together with the number of the first page of each. **3** the meaning or significance of a poem, painting, or other work of art, as distinguished from its style or form. **4** all that is contained or dealt with in a discussion, piece of writing, etc.; substance. **5** the capacity or size of a thing. **6** the proportion of a substance contained in an alloy, mixture, etc.: *the lead content of petrol.* [C15: from Latin *contentus* contained, from *continēre* to CONTAIN]

content[2] (kən'tɛnt) *adj* (*postpositive*) **1** mentally or emotionally satisfied with things as they are. **2** assenting to or willing to accept circumstances, a proposed course of action, etc. ♦ *vb* **3** (*tr*) to make (oneself or another person) content or satisfied: *to content oneself with property.* ♦ *n* **4** peace of mind; mental or emotional satisfaction. ♦ *interj* **5** *Brit.* (in the House of Lords) a formal expression of assent, as opposed to the expression **not content.** [C14: from Old French, from Latin *contentus* contented, that is, having restrained desires, from *continēre* to restrain] ► **con'tently** *adv* ► **con'tentment** *n*

content-addressable storage *n Computing.* another name for **associative storage.**

contented (kən'tɛntɪd) *adj* accepting one's situation or life with equanimity and satisfaction. ► **con'tentedly** *adv* ► **con'tentedness** *n*

contention (kən'tɛnʃən) *n* **1** a struggling between opponents; competition. **2** dispute in an argument (esp. in the phrase **bone of contention**). **3** a point asserted in argument. [C14: from Latin *contentiō* exertion, from *contendere* to CONTEND]

contentious (kən'tɛnʃəs) *adj* **1** tending to argue or quarrel. **2** causing or characterized by dispute; controversial. **3** *Law.* relating to a cause or legal business that is contested, esp. a probate matter. ► **con'tentiously** *adv* ► **con'tentiousness** *n*

content word ('kɒntɛnt) *n* a word to which an independent meaning can be given by reference to a world outside any sentence in which the word may occur. Compare **function word, lexical meaning.**

conterminous (kən'tɜːmɪnəs), **conterminal,** *or* **coterminous** (kəʊ'tɜːmɪnəs) *adj* **1** enclosed within a common boundary. **2** meeting at the ends; without a break or interruption. [C17: from Latin *conterminus,* from CON- + *terminus* end, boundary] ► **con'terminously, con'terminally,** *or* **co'terminously** *adv*

contest *n* ('kɒntɛst). **1** a formal game or match in which two or more people, teams, etc., compete and attempt to win. **2** a struggle for victory between opposing forces or interests. ♦ *vb* (kən'tɛst). **3** (*tr*) to try to disprove; call in question. **4** (when *intr,* foll. by *with* or *against*) to fight, dispute, or contend (with): *contest an election.* [C16: from Latin *contestārī* to introduce a lawsuit, from *testis* witness] ► **con'testable** *adj* ► **con'testableness** *or* **con,testa'bility** *n* ► **con'testably** *adv* ► **,contes'tation** *n* ► **con'tester** *n* ► **con'testingly** *adv*

contestant (kən'tɛstənt) *n* a person who takes part in a contest; competitor.

context ('kɒntɛkst) *n* **1** the parts of a piece of writing, speech, etc., that precede and follow a word or passage and contribute to its full meaning: *it is unfair to quote out of context.* **2** the conditions and circumstances that are relevant to an event, fact, etc. [C15: from Latin *contextus* a putting together, from *contexere* to interweave, from *com-* together + *texere* to weave, braid]

contextual (kən'tɛkstjʊəl) *adj* relating to, dependent on, or using context: *contextual criticism of a book.* ► **con'textually** *adv*

contextualize *or* **contextualise** (kən'tɛkstjʊə,laɪz) *vb* (*tr*) to state the social, grammatical, or other context of; put into context.

contexture (kən'tɛkstʃə) *n* **1** the fact, process, or manner of weaving or of being woven together. **2** the arrangement of assembled parts; structure. **3** an interwoven structure; fabric. ► **con'textural** *adj*

contiguous (kən'tɪgjʊəs) *adj* **1** touching along the side or boundary; in contact. **2** physically adjacent; neighbouring. **3** preceding or following in time. [C17: from Latin *contiguus,* from *contingere* to touch; see CONTACT] ► **contiguity** (,kɒntɪ'gjuːɪtɪ) *or* **con'tiguousness** *n* ► **con'tiguously** *adv*

continent[1] ('kɒntɪnənt) *n* **1** one of the earth's large land masses (Asia, Australia, Africa, Europe, North and South America, and Antarctica). **2** that part of the earth's crust that rises above the oceans and is composed of sialic rocks. Including the continental shelves, the continents occupy 30 per cent of the earth's surface. **3** *Obsolete.* **3a** mainland as opposed to islands. **3b** a continuous extent of land. [C16: from the Latin phrase *terra continens* continuous land, from *continēre;* see CONTAIN] ► **continental** (,kɒntɪ'nɛntᵊl) *adj* ► **,conti'nentally** *adv*

continent[2] ('kɒntɪnənt) *adj* **1** able to control urination and defecation. **2** exercising self-restraint, esp. from sexual activity; chaste. [C14: from Latin *continent-,* present participle of *continēre;* see CONTAIN] ► **'continence** *or* **'continency** *n* ► **'continently** *adv*

Continent ('kɒntɪnənt) *n* **the.** the mainland of Europe as distinguished from the British Isles.

Continental (,kɒntɪ'nɛntᵊl) *adj* **1** of or characteristic of Europe, excluding the British Isles. **2** of or relating to the 13 original British North American colonies during and immediately after the War of American Independence. ♦ *n* **3** (*sometimes not cap.*) an inhabitant of Europe, excluding the British Isles. **4** a regular soldier of the rebel army during the War of American Independence. **5** *U.S. History.* a currency note issued by the Continental Congress. ► **,Conti'nental,ism** *n* ► **,Conti'nentalist** *n*

continental breakfast *n* a light breakfast of coffee and rolls.

continental climate *n* a climate characterized by hot summers, cold winters, and little rainfall, typical of the interior of a continent.

Continental Congress *n* the assembly of delegates from the North American rebel colonies held during and after the War of American Independence. It issued the Declaration of Independence (1776) and framed the Articles of Confederation (1777).

continental crust *n Geology.* that part of the earth's crust that underlies the continents and continental shelves.

continental divide *n* the watershed of a continent, esp. (*often caps.*) the principal watershed of North America, formed by the Rocky Mountains.

continental drift *n Geology.* the theory that the earth's continents move gradually over the surface of the planet on a substratum of magma. The present-day configuration of the continents is thought to be the result of the fragmentation of a single landmass, Pangaea, that existed 200 million years ago. See also **plate tectonics.**

continental quilt *n Brit.* a quilt, stuffed with down or a synthetic material and containing pockets of air, used as a bed cover in place of the top sheet and blankets. Also called: **duvet,** (Austral.) **doona.**

continental shelf *n* the sea bed surrounding a continent at depths of up to about 200 metres (100 fathoms), at the edge of which the **continental slope** drops steeply to the ocean floor.

Continental System *n* **the.** Napoleon's plan in 1806 to blockade Britain by excluding her ships from ports on the mainland of Europe.

contingence (kən'tɪndʒəns) *n* **1** the state of touching or being in contact. **2** another word for **contingency.**

contingency (kən'tɪndʒənsɪ) *n, pl* **-cies. 1a** a possible but not very likely future event or condition; eventuality. **1b** (*as modifier*): *a contingency plan.* **2** something dependent on a possible future event. **3** a fact, event, etc., incidental to or dependent on something else. **4** (in systemic grammar) **4a** modification of the meaning of a main clause by use of a bound clause introduced by a binder such as *if, when, though,* or *since.* Compare **adding** (sense 3). **4b** (*as modifier*): *a contingency clause.* **5** *Logic.* **5a** the state of being contingent. **5b** a contingent statement. **6** dependence on chance; uncertainty. **7** *Statistics.* **7a** the degree of association between theoretical and observed common frequencies of two graded or classified variables. It is measured by the chi-square test. **7b** (*as modifier*): *a contingency table; the contingency coefficient.*

contingency table *n Statistics.* an array having the frequency of occurrence of certain events in each of a number of samples.

contingent (kən'tɪndʒənt) *adj* **1** (when *postpositive,* often foll. by *on* or *upon*) dependent on events, conditions, etc., not yet known; conditional. **2** *Logic.* (of a proposition) true under certain conditions, false under others; not necessary. **3** (in systemic grammar) denoting contingency (sense 4). **4** *Metaphysics.* (of some being) existing only as a matter of fact; not necessarily existing. **5** happening by chance or without known cause; accidental. **6** that may or may not happen; uncertain. ♦ *n* **7** a part of a military force, parade, etc. **8** a representative group distinguished by common origin, interests, etc., that is part of a larger group or gathering. **9** a possible or chance occurrence. [C14: from Latin *contingere* to touch, fall to one's lot, befall; see also CONTACT] ► **con'tingently** *adv*

continual (kən'tɪnjʊəl) *adj* **1** recurring frequently, esp. at regular intervals. **2** occurring without interruption; continuous in time. [C14: from Old French *continuel,* from Latin *continuus* uninterrupted, from *continēre* to hold together, CONTAIN] ► **con,tinu'ality** *or* **con'tinualness** *n* ► **con'tinually** *adv*

USAGE See at **continuous.**

continuance (kən'tɪnjʊəns) *n* **1** the act or state of continuing. **2** the duration of an action, condition, etc. **3** *U.S.* the postponement or adjournment of a legal proceeding.

continuant (kən'tɪnjʊənt) *Phonetics.* ♦ *n* **1** a speech sound, such as (l), (r), (f), or (s), in which the closure of the vocal tract is incomplete, allowing the continuous passage of the breath. ♦ *adj* **2** relating to or denoting a continuant.

continuation (kənˌtɪnju'eɪʃən) *n* **1** a part or thing added, esp. to a book or play, that serves to continue or extend; sequel. **2** a renewal of an interrupted action, process, etc.; resumption. **3** the act or fact of continuing without interruption; prolongation. **4** another word for **contango** (senses 1, 2).

continuative (kən'tɪnjuətɪv) *adj* **1** serving or tending to continue. **2** *Grammar.* **2a** (of any word, phrase, or clause) expressing continuation. **2b** (of verbs) another word for **progressive** (sense 8). ◆ *n* **3** a continuative word, phrase, or clause. ▸ **con'tinuatively** *adv*

continuator (kən'tɪnjuˌeɪtə) *n* a person who continues something, esp. the work of someone else.

continue (kən'tɪnjuː) *vb* **-ues, -uing, -ued. 1** (when *tr, may take an infinitive*) to remain or cause to remain in a particular condition, capacity, or place. **2** (when *tr, may take an infinitive*) to carry on uninterruptedly (a course of action); persist in (something): *he continued running.* **3** (when *tr, may take an infinitive*) to resume after an interruption: *we'll continue after lunch.* **4** to draw out or be drawn out; prolong or be prolonged: *continue the chord until it meets the tangent.* **5** (*tr*) *Law, chiefly Scots.* to postpone or adjourn (legal proceedings). **[C14:** from Old French *continuer,* from Latin *continuāre* to join together, from *continuus* CONTINUOUS**]** ▸ **con'tinuable** *adj* ▸ **con'tinuer** *n* ▸ **con'tinuingly** *adv*

continued fraction *n* a number plus a fraction whose denominator contains a number and a fraction whose denominator contains a number and a fraction, and so on.

continuity (ˌkɒntɪ'njuːɪtɪ) *n, pl* **-ties. 1** logical sequence, cohesion, or connection. **2** a continuous or connected whole. **3** the comprehensive script or scenario of detail and movement in a film or broadcast. **4** the continuous projection of a film, using automatic rewind.

continuity announcer *n* a person who makes linking announcements betweeen programmes to give continuity to a television or radio broadcast channel.

continuity girl *or* **man** *n* a girl or man whose job is to ensure continuity and consistency, esp. in matters of dress, make-up, etc., in successive shots of a film, esp. when these shots are filmed on different days.

continuo (kən'tɪnjuˌəʊ) *n, pl* **-os. 1** *Music.* **1a** a shortened form of **basso continuo** (see **thorough bass**). **1b** (*as modifier*): *a continuo accompaniment.* **2** the thorough-bass part as played on a keyboard instrument, often supported by a cello, bassoon, etc. **[**Italian, literally: continuous**]**

continuous (kən'tɪnjuəs) *adj* **1** prolonged without interruption; unceasing: *a continuous noise.* **2** in an unbroken series or pattern. **3** *Maths.* (of a function or curve) changing gradually in value as the variable changes in value. At any value $x = a$ of the continuous function $f(x)$, $\lim_{x \to a} f(x) = f(a)$. At every value a of the independent variable, the difference between $f(x)$ and $f(a)$ approaches zero as x approaches a when f is a continuous function. Compare **discontinuous** (sense 2). See also **limit** (sense 5). **4** *Statistics.* (of a variable) having a continuum of possible values so that its distribution requires integration rather than summation to determine its cumulative probability. Compare **discrete** (sense 3). **5** *Grammar.* another word for **progressive** (sense 8). **[C17:** from Latin *continuus,* from *continēre* to hold together, CONTAIN**]** ▸ **con'tinuously** *adv* ▸ **con'tinuousness** *n*

USAGE Both *continual* and *continuous* can be used to say that something continues without interruption, but only *continual* can correctly be used to say that something keeps happening repeatedly.

continuous assessment *n* the assessment of a pupil's progress throughout a course of study rather than exclusively by examination at the end of it.

continuous creation *n* **1** the theory that matter is being created continuously in the universe. See **steady-state theory. 2** the theory that animate matter is being continuously created from inanimate matter.

continuous processing *n* the systems in a plant or factory for the manufacturing of products, treating of materials, etc., that have been designed to run continuously and are often computer-controlled. Compare **batch processing.**

continuous spectrum *n* a spectrum that contains or appears to contain all wavelengths over a wide portion of its range. The emission spectrum of incandescent solids is continuous; spectra consisting of a large number of lines may appear continuous.

continuous stationery *n Computing.* paper that is perforated between pages and folded concertina fashion, used in dot-matrix, line, and daisywheel printers.

continuous waves *pl n* radio waves generated as a continuous train of oscillations having a constant frequency and amplitude. Abbrev: **CW.**

continuum (kən'tɪnjuəm) *n, pl* **-tinua** (-'tɪnjuə) *or* **-tinuums. 1** a continuous series or whole, no part of which is perceptibly different from the adjacent parts. **2** *Maths.* a set of elements between any two of which a third element can always be inserted: *a continuum of real numbers.* **[C17:** from Latin, neuter of *continuus* CONTINUOUS**]**

conto ('kɒntəʊ; *Portuguese* 'kõːtu) *n, pl* **-tos** (-təʊz; *Portuguese* -tuʃ). **1** a Portuguese monetary unit worth 1000 escudos. **2** an unofficial Brazilian monetary unit worth 1000 cruzeiros (now replaced by the real). **[C17:** from Portuguese, from Late Latin *computus* calculation, from *computāre* to reckon, COMPUTE; see COUNT[1]**]**

contort (kən'tɔːt) *vb* to twist or bend severely out of place or shape, esp. in a strained manner. **[C15:** from Latin *contortus* intricate, obscure, from *contorquēre* to whirl around, from *torquēre* to twist, wrench**]** ▸ **con'tortive** *adj*

contorted (kən'tɔːtɪd) *adj* **1** twisted out of shape. **2** (esp. of petals and sepals in a bud) twisted so that they overlap on one side. ▸ **con'tortedly** *adv* ▸ **con'tortedness** *n*

contortion (kən'tɔːʃən) *n* **1** the act or process of contorting or the state of being contorted. **2** a twisted shape or position. **3** something twisted or out of the ordinary in character, meaning, etc: *mental contortions.* ▸ **con'tortional** *adj* ▸ **con'tortioned** *adj*

contortionist (kən'tɔːʃənɪst) *n* **1** a performer who contorts his body for the entertainment of others. **2** a person who twists or warps meaning or thoughts: *a verbal contortionist.* ▸ **conˌtortion'istic** *adj*

contour ('kɒntʊə) *n* **1** the outline of a mass of land, figure, or body; a defining line. **2a** See **contour line. 2b** (*as modifier*): *a contour map.* **3** (*often pl*) the shape or surface, esp. of a curving form: *the contours of her body were full and round.* **4** (*modifier*) shaped to fit the form of something: *a contour chair.* ◆ *vb* (*tr*) **5** to shape so as to form the contour of something. **6** to mark contour lines on. **7** to construct (a road, railway, etc.) to follow the outline of the land. **[C17:** from French, from Italian *contorno,* from *contornare* to sketch, from *tornare* to TURN**]**

contour feather *n* any of the feathers that cover the body of an adult bird, apart from the wings and tail, and determine its shape.

contour interval *n* the difference in altitude represented by the space between two contour lines on a map.

contour line *n* a line on a map or chart joining points of equal height or depth. Often shortened to **contour.**

contour ploughing *n* ploughing following the contours of the land, to minimize the effects of erosion.

contr. *abbrev. for:* **1** contraction. **2** contralto.

contra- *prefix* **1** against; contrary; opposing; contrasting: *contraceptive; contradistinction.* **2** (in music) pitched below: *contrabass.* **[**from Latin, from *contrā* against**]**

contraband ('kɒntrəˌbænd) *n* **1a** goods that are prohibited by law from being exported or imported. **1b** illegally imported or exported goods. **2** illegal traffic in such goods; smuggling. **3** Also called: **contraband of war.** *International law.* goods that a neutral country may not supply to a belligerent. **4** (during the American Civil War) a Black slave captured by the Union forces or one who escaped to the Union lines. ◆ *adj* **5** (of goods) **5a** forbidden by law from being imported or exported. **5b** illegally imported or exported. **[C16:** from Spanish *contrabanda,* from Italian *contrabando* (modern *contrabbando*), from Medieval Latin *contrabannum,* from CONTRA- + *bannum* ban, of Germanic origin**]** ▸ **'contraˌbandist** *n*

contrabass (ˌkɒntrə'beɪs) *n* **1** a member of any of various families of musical instruments that is lower in pitch than the bass. **2** another name for **double bass.** ◆ *adj* **3** of or denoting the instrument of a family that is lower than the bass. ▸ **contrabassist** (ˌkɒntrə'beɪsɪst, -'bæs-) *n*

contrabassoon (ˌkɒntrəbə'suːn) *n* the largest instrument in the oboe family, pitched an octave below the bassoon; double bassoon. ▸ **ˌcontrabas'soonist** *n*

contraception (ˌkɒntrə'sɛpʃən) *n* the intentional prevention of conception by artificial or natural means. Artificial methods in common use include preventing the sperm from reaching the ovum (using condoms, diaphragms, etc.), inhibiting ovulation (using oral contraceptive pills), preventing implantation (using intrauterine devices), killing the sperm (using spermicides), and preventing the sperm from entering the seminal fluid (by vasectomy). Natural methods include the rhythm method and coitus interruptus. Compare **birth control, family planning. [C19:** from CONTRA- + CONCEPTION**]**

contraceptive (ˌkɒntrə'sɛptɪv) *adj* **1** relating to or used for contraception; able or tending to prevent impregnation. ◆ *n* **2** any device that prevents or tends to prevent conception.

contract *vb* (kən'trækt). **1** to make or become smaller, narrower, shorter, etc.: *metals contract as the temperature is reduced.* **2** ('kɒntrækt). (when *intr,* sometimes foll. by *for;* when *tr, may take an infinitive*) to enter into an agreement with (a person, company, etc.) to deliver (goods or services) or to do (something) on mutually agreed and binding terms, often in writing. **3** to draw or be drawn together; coalesce or cause to coalesce. **4** (*tr*) to acquire, incur, or become affected by (a disease, liability, debt, etc.). **5** (*tr*) to shorten (a word or phrase) by the omission of letters or syllables, usually indicated in writing by an apostrophe. **6** *Phonetics.* to unite (two vowels) or (of two vowels) to be united within a word or at a word boundary so that a new long vowel or diphthong is formed. **7** (*tr*) to wrinkle or draw together (the brow or a muscle). **8** (*tr*) to arrange (a marriage) for; betroth. ◆ *n* ('kɒntrækt). **9** a formal agreement between two or more parties. **10** a document that states the terms of such an agreement. **11** the branch of law treating of contracts. **12** marriage considered as a formal agreement. **13** See **contract bridge. 14** *Bridge.* **14a** (in the bidding sequence before play) the highest bid, which determines trumps and the number of tricks one side must try to make. **14b** the number and suit of these tricks. **15** *Slang.* **15a** a criminal agreement to kill a particular person in return for an agreed sum of money. **15b** (*as modifier*): *a contract killing.* **[C16:** from Latin contractus agreement, something drawn up, from *contrahere* to draw together, from *trahere* to draw**]** ▸ **con'tractible** *adj* ▸ **con'tractibly** *adv*

contract bridge ('kɒntrækt) *n* the most common variety of bridge, in which the declarer receives points counting towards game and rubber only for tricks he bids as well as makes, any overtricks receiving bonus points. Compare **auction bridge.**

contractile (kən'træktaɪl) *adj* having the power to contract or to cause contraction. ▸ **contractility** (ˌkɒntræk'tɪlɪtɪ) *n*

contraction (kən'trækʃən) *n* **1** an instance of contracting or the state of being contracted. **2** *Physiol.* any normal shortening or tensing of an organ or part, esp. of a muscle, e.g. during childbirth. **3** *Pathol.* any abnormal tightening or shrinking of an organ or part. **4** a shortening of a word or group of words, often marked in written English by an apostrophe: *I've come* for *I have come.* ▸ **con'tractive** *adj* ▸ **con'tractively** *adv* ▸ **con'tractiveness** *n*

contract of employment *n* a written agreement between an employer and an employee, that, taken together with the rights of each under statute and common law, determines the employment relations between them.

contractor ('kɒntræktə, kən'træk-) *n* **1** a person or firm that contracts to supply materials or labour, esp. for building. **2** something that contracts, esp. a muscle. **3** *Law.* a person who is a party to a contract. **4** the declarer in bridge.

contract out *vb* (*intr, adv*) *Brit.* to agree not to participate in something, esp. the state pension scheme.

contractual (kən'træktjuəl) *adj* of the nature of or assured by a contract. ► **con'tractually** *adv*

contracture (kən'træktʃə) *n* a disorder in which a skeletal muscle is permanently tightened (contracted), most often caused by spasm or paralysis of the antagonist muscle that maintains normal muscle tension.

contradance ('kɒntrəˌdɑːns) *n* a variant spelling of **contredanse.**

contradict (ˌkɒntrə'dɪkt) *vb* **1** (*tr*) to affirm the opposite of (a proposition, statement, etc.). **2** (*tr*) to declare (a proposition, statement, etc.) to be false or incorrect; deny. **3** (*intr*) to be argumentative or contrary. **4** (*tr*) to be inconsistent with (a proposition, theory, etc.): *the facts contradicted his theory.* **5** (*intr*) (of two or more facts, principles, etc.) to be at variance; be in contradiction. **[C16:** from Latin *contrādīcere,* from CONTRA- + *dīcere* to speak, say**]** ► **ˌcontra'dictable** *adj* ► **ˌcontra'dicter** *or* **ˌcontra'dictor** *n* ► **ˌcontra'dictive** *or* **ˌcontra'dictious** *adj* ► **ˌcontra'dictively** *or* **ˌcontra'dictiously** *adv* ► **ˌcontra'dictiveness** *or* **ˌcontra'dictiousness** *n*

contradiction (ˌkɒntrə'dɪkʃən) *n* **1** the act of going against; opposition; denial. **2** a declaration of the opposite or contrary. **3** a statement that is at variance with itself (often in the phrase **a contradiction in terms**). **4** conflict or inconsistency, as between events, qualities, etc. **5** a person or thing containing conflicting qualities. **6** *Logic.* a statement that is false under all circumstances; necessary falsehood.

contradictory (ˌkɒntrə'dɪktərɪ) *adj* **1** inconsistent; incompatible. **2** given to argument and contention: *a contradictory person.* **3** *Logic.* (of a pair of statements) unable both to be true or both to be false under the same circumstances. Compare **contrary** (sense 5), **subcontrary** (sense 1). ♦ *n, pl* **-ries. 4** *Logic.* a statement that cannot be true when a given statement is true or false when it is false. ► **ˌcontra'dictorily** *adv* ► **ˌcontra'dictoriness** *n*

contradistinction (ˌkɒntrədɪ'stɪŋkʃən) *n* a distinction made by contrasting different qualities. ► **ˌcontradis'tinctive** *adj* ► **ˌcontradis'tinctively** *adv*

contradistinguish (ˌkɒntrədɪ'stɪŋgwɪʃ) *vb* (*tr*) to differentiate by means of contrasting or opposing qualities.

contraflow ('kɒntrəˌfləʊ) *n Brit.* two-way traffic on one carriageway of a motorway, esp. to allow maintenance work to be carried out or an accident to be cleared.

contrail ('kɒntreɪl) *n* another name for **vapour trail. [C20:** from CON(DENSATION) + TRAIL**]**

contraindicate (ˌkɒntrə'ɪndɪˌkeɪt) *vb* (*tr; usually passive*) *Med.* to advise against or indicate the possible danger of (a drug, treatment, etc.). ► **ˌcontra'indicant** *n* ► **ˌcontraˌindi'cation** *n*

contralateral (ˌkɒntrə'lætərəl) *adj Anatomy, zoology.* relating to or denoting the opposite side of a body, structure, etc.

contralto (kən'træltəʊ, -'trɑːl-) *n, pl* **-tos** *or* **-ti** (-tɪ). **1** the lowest female voice, usually having a range of approximately from F a fifth below middle C to D a ninth above it. In the context of a choir often shortened to **alto. 2** a singer with such a voice. ♦ *adj* **3** of or denoting a contralto: *the contralto part.* **[C18:** from Italian; see CONTRA-, ALTO**]**

contraposition (ˌkɒntrəpə'zɪʃən) *n* **1** the act of placing opposite or against, esp. in contrast or antithesis. **2** *Logic.* the derivation of the contrapositive of a given categorial proposition.

contrapositive (ˌkɒntrə'pɒzɪtɪv) *adj* **1** placed opposite or against. ♦ *n* **2** *Logic.* **2a** a conditional statement derived from another by negating and interchanging antecedent and consequent. **2b** a categorial proposition obtained from another, esp. validly, by any of a number of operations including negation, transferring the terms, changing their quality, and also possibly weakening from universal to particular.

contrapposto (ˌkɒntrə'pɒstəʊ) *n, pl* **-tos.** (in the visual arts) a curving or asymmetrical arrangement of the human figure with the shoulders, hips, and legs in different planes. **[C20:** from Italian, from the past participle of *contrapporre,* from Latin *contra* CONTRA- + *pōnere* to place**]**

contraption (kən'træpʃən) *n Informal, often facetious or derogatory.* a device or contrivance, esp. one considered strange, unnecessarily intricate, or improvised. **[C19:** perhaps from CON(TRIVANCE) + TRAP[1] + (INVEN)TION**]**

contrapuntal (ˌkɒntrə'pʌnt^{ə}l) *adj Music.* characterized by counterpoint. **[C19:** from Italian *contrappunto* COUNTERPOINT + -AL[1]**]** ► **ˌcontra'puntally** *adv*

contrapuntist (ˌkɒntrə'pʌntɪst) *or* **contrapuntalist** *n Music.* a composer skilled in counterpoint.

contrariety (ˌkɒntrə'raɪətɪ) *n, pl* **-ties. 1** opposition between one thing and another; disagreement. **2** an instance of such opposition; inconsistency; discrepancy. **3** *Logic.* the relationship between two contraries.

contrarily *adv* **1** (kən'trɛərɪlɪ). in a perverse or obstinate manner. **2** ('kɒntrərɪlɪ). on the other hand; from the opposite point of view. **3** ('kɒntrərɪlɪ). in an opposite, adverse, or unexpected way.

contrarious (kən'trɛərɪəs) *adj Rare.* **1** (of people or animals) perverse or obstinate. **2** (of conditions) unfavourable. ► **con'trariously** *adv* ► **con'trariousness** *n*

contrariwise ('kɒntrərɪˌwaɪz) *adv* **1** from a contrasting point of view; on the other hand. **2** in the reverse way or direction. **3** (kən'trɛərɪˌwaɪz). in a contrary manner.

contrary ('kɒntrərɪ) *adj* **1** opposed in nature, position, etc.: *contrary ideas.* **2** (kən'trɛərɪ). perverse; obstinate. **3** (esp. of wind) adverse; unfavourable. **4** (of plant parts) situated at right angles to each other. **5** *Logic.* (of a pair of propositions) related so that they cannot both be true at once, although they may both be false together. Compare **subcontrary** (sense 1), **contradictory** (sense 3). ♦ *n, pl* **-ries. 6** the exact opposite (esp. in the phrase **to the contrary**). **7 on the contrary.** quite the reverse; not at all. **8** either of two exactly opposite objects, facts, or qualities. **9** *Logic.* a statement that cannot be true when a given statement is true. ♦ *adv* (usually foll. by *to*) **10** in an opposite or unexpected way: *contrary to usual belief.* **11** in conflict (with) or contravention (of): *contrary to nature.* **[C14:** from Latin *contrārius* opposite, from *contrā* against**]** ► **con'trariness** *n*

contrast *vb* (kən'trɑːst). **1** (often foll. by *with*) to distinguish or be distinguished by comparison of unlike or opposite qualities. ♦ *n* ('kɒntrɑːst). **2** distinction or emphasis of difference by comparison of opposite or dissimilar things, qualities, etc. (esp. in the phrases **by contrast, in contrast to** *or* **with**). **3** a person or thing showing notable differences when compared with another. **4** (in painting) the effect of the juxtaposition of different colours, tones, etc. **5a** (of a photographic emulsion) the degree of density measured against exposure used. **5b** the extent to which adjacent areas of an optical image, esp. on a television screen or in a photographic negative or print, differ in brightness. **6** *Psychol.* the phenomenon that when two different but related stimuli are presented close together in space and/or time they are perceived as being more different than they really are. **[C16:** (n): via French from Italian, from *contrastare* (vb), from Latin *contra-* against + *stare* to stand**]** ► **con'trastable** *adj* ► **con'trastably** *adv* ► **con'trasting** *adj* ► **con'trastive** *adj* ► **con'trastively** *adv*

contrast medium *n Med.* a radiopaque substance, such as barium sulphate, used to increase the contrast of an image in radiography.

contrasty (kən'trɑːstɪ) *adj* (of a photograph or subject) having sharp gradations in tone, esp. between light and dark areas.

contrasuggestible (ˌkɒntrəsə'dʒɛstɪb^{ə}l) *adj Psychol.* responding or tending to respond to a suggestion by doing or believing the opposite. ► **ˌcontrasugˌgesti'bility** *n* ► **ˌcontrasug'gestion** *n*

contravallation (ˌkɒntrəvə'leɪʃən) *n* fortifications built by besiegers around the place besieged. **[C17:** from CONTRA- + Latin *vallātiō* entrenchment; compare French *contrevallation***]**

contravene (ˌkɒntrə'viːn) *vb* (*tr*) **1** to come into conflict with or infringe (rules, laws, etc.). **2** to dispute or contradict (a statement, proposition, etc.). **[C16:** from Late Latin *contrāvenīre,* from Latin CONTRA- + *venīre* to come**]** ► **ˌcontra'vener** *n* ► **contravention** (ˌkɒntrə'vɛnʃən) *n*

contrayerva (ˌkɒntrə'jɜːvə) *n* the root of any of several tropical American moraceous plants of the genus *Dorstenia,* esp. *D. contrayerva,* used as a stimulant and tonic. **[C17:** from Spanish *contrayerba,* from CONTRA- + *yerba* grass, (poisonous) plant, from Latin *herba;* referring to the belief that it was an antidote to poisons**]**

contredanse *or* **contradance** ('kɒntrəˌdɑːns) *n* **1** a courtly Continental version of the English country dance, similar to the quadrille. **2** music written for or in the rhythm of this dance. **[C19:** from French, changed from English *country dance; country* altered to French *contre* (opposite) by folk etymology (because the dancers face each other)**]**

contre-jour ('kɒntrəˌʒʊə) *n Photog.* **a** the technique of taking photographs into the light, with the light source behind the subject. **b** (*as modifier*): *a contre-jour shot.* **[C20:** from French, literally: against day(light)**]**

contretemps ('kɒntrəˌtɑːn; *French* kɔ̃trətɑ̃) *n, pl* **-temps. 1** an awkward or difficult situation or mishap. **2** *Fencing.* a feint made with the purpose of producing a counterthrust from one's opponent. **3** a small disagreement that is rather embarrassing. **[C17:** from French, from *contre* against + *temps* time, from Latin *tempus***]**

contrib. *abbrev. for:* **1** contribution. **2** contributor.

contribute (kən'trɪbjuːt) *vb* (often foll. by *to*) **1** to give (support, money, etc.) for a common purpose or fund. **2** to supply (ideas, opinions, etc.) as part of a debate or discussion. **3** (*intr*) to be partly instrumental (in) or responsible (for): *drink contributed to the accident.* **4** to write (articles) for a publication. **[C16:** from Latin *contribuere* to collect, from *tribuere* to grant, bestow**]** ► **con'tributable** *adj* ► **con'tributive** *adj* ► **con'tributively** *adv* ► **con'tributiveness** *n*

contribution (ˌkɒntrɪ'bjuːʃən) *n* **1** the act of contributing. **2** something contributed, such as money or ideas. **3** an article, story, etc., contributed to a newspaper or other publication. **4** *Insurance.* a portion of the total liability incumbent on each of two or more companies for a risk with respect to which all of them have issued policies. **5** *Archaic.* a levy, esp. towards the cost of a war.

contributor (kən'trɪbjʊtə) *n* **1** a person who contributes, esp. one who writes for a newspaper or one who makes a donation to a cause, etc. **2** something that is a factor in or is partly responsible for something: *alcohol was a contributor to his death.*

contributory (kən'trɪbjʊtərɪ, -trɪ) *adj* **1** (often foll. by *to*) sharing in or being partly responsible (for the cause of something): *a contributory factor.* **2** giving or donating to a common purpose or fund. **3** of, relating to, or designating an insurance or pension scheme in which the premiums are paid partly by the employer and partly by the employees who benefit from it. **4** liable or subject to a tax or levy. ♦ *n, pl* **-ries. 5** a person or thing that contributes. **6** *Company law.* a member or former member of a company liable to contribute to the assets on the winding-up of the company.

contributory negligence *n Law.* failure by an injured person to have taken proper precautions to prevent an accident.

con trick *n Informal.* a shortened form of **confidence trick.**

contrite (kən'traɪt, 'kɒntraɪt) *adj* **1** full of guilt or regret; remorseful. **2** arising from a sense of shame or guilt: *contrite promises.* **3** *Theol.* remorseful for past sin and resolved to avoid future sin. **[C14:** from Latin *contrītus* worn out, from *conterere* to bruise, from *terere* to grind] ► **con'tritely** *adv* ► **con'triteness** *n*

contrition (kən'trɪʃən) *n* **1** deeply felt remorse; penitence. **2** *Christianity.* detestation of past sins and a resolve to make amends, either from love of God (**perfect contrition**) or from hope of heaven (**imperfect contrition**).

contrivance (kən'traɪvəns) *n* **1** something contrived, esp. an ingenious device; contraption. **2** the act or faculty of devising or adapting; inventive skill or ability. **3** an artificial rather than natural selection or arrangement of details, parts, etc. **4** an elaborate or deceitful plan or expedient; stratagem.

contrive (kən'traɪv) *vb* **1** (*tr*) to manage (something or to do something), esp. by means of a trick; engineer: *he contrived to make them meet.* **2** (*tr*) to think up or adapt ingeniously or elaborately: *he contrived a new mast for the boat.* **3** to plot or scheme (treachery, evil, etc.). [C14: from Old French *controver,* from Late Latin *contropāre* to represent by figures of speech, compare, from Latin *com-* together + *tropus* figure of speech, TROPE] ► **con'trivable** *adj* ► **con'triver** *n*

contrived (kən'traɪvd) *adj* obviously planned, artificial, or lacking in spontaneity; forced; unnatural.

control (kən'trəʊl) *vb* **-trols, -trolling, -trolled.** (*tr*) **1** to command, direct, or rule: *to control a country.* **2** to check, limit, curb, or regulate; restrain: *to control one's emotions; to control a fire.* **3** to regulate or operate (a machine). **4** to verify (a scientific experiment) by conducting a parallel experiment in which the variable being investigated is held constant or is compared with a standard. **5a** to regulate (financial affairs). **5b** to examine and verify (financial accounts). **6** to restrict or regulate the authorized supply of (certain substances, such as drugs). ◆ *n* **7** power to direct or determine: *under control; out of control.* **8** a means of regulation or restraint; curb; check: *a frontier control.* **9** (*often pl*) a device or mechanism for operating a car, aircraft, etc. **10** a standard of comparison used in a statistical analysis or scientific experiment. **11a** a device that regulates the operation of a machine. A **dynamic control** is one that incorporates a governor so that it responds to the output of the machine it regulates. **11b** (*as modifier*): *control panel; control room.* **12** *Spiritualism.* an agency believed to assist the medium in a séance. **13** Also called: **control mark.** a letter, or letter and number, printed on a sheet of postage stamps, indicating authenticity, date, and series of issue. **14** one of a number of checkpoints on a car rally, orienteering course, etc., where competitors check in and their time, performance, etc., is recorded. [C15: from Old French *conteroller* to regulate, from *contrerolle* duplicate register, system of checking, from *contre-* COUNTER- + *rolle* ROLL] ► **con'trollable** *adj* ► **con,trolla'bility** *or* **con'trollableness** *n* ► **con'trollably** *adv*

control account *n Accounting.* an account to which are posted the debit and credit totals of other accounts, usually in preparation of financial statements.

control chart *n Statistics.* a chart on which observed values of a variable are plotted, usually against the expected value of the variable and its allowable deviation, so that excessive variations in the quality, quantity, etc., of the variable can be detected.

control column *n* a lever or pillar, usually fitted with a handwheel, used to control the movements of an aircraft. Also called: **control stick, joy stick.**

control commands *pl n* keyed instructions conveyed to a computer by using the control key in conjunction with the standard keys.

control experiment *n* an experiment designed to check or correct the results of another experiment by removing the variable or variables operating in that other experiment. The comparison obtained is an indication or measurement of the effect of the variables concerned.

control grid *n Electronics.* another name for **grid** (sense 6), esp. in a tetrode or pentode.

control group *n* any group used as a control in a statistical experiment, esp. a group of patients who receive either a placebo or a standard drug during an investigation of the effects of another drug on other patients.

control key *n* a key on the keyboard of a computer that is used in conjunction with the standard keys in order to initiate a specific function, such as editing.

controller (kən'trəʊlə) *n* **1** a person who directs, regulates, or restrains. **2** Also called: **comptroller.** a business executive or government officer who is responsible for financial planning, control, etc. **3** the equipment concerned with controlling the operation of an electrical device. ► **con'troller,ship** *n*

controlling interest *n* a quantity of shares in a business that is sufficient to ensure control over its direction.

control rod *n* one of a number of rods or tubes containing a neutron absorber, such as boron, that can be inserted into or retracted from the core of a nuclear reactor in order to control its rate of reaction.

control stick *n* the lever by which a pilot controls the lateral and longitudinal movements of an aircraft. Also called: **control column, joy stick.**

control surface *n* a movable surface, such as a rudder, elevator, aileron, etc., that controls an aircraft or rocket.

control tower *n* a tower at an airport from which air traffic is controlled.

controversy ('kɒntrə,vɜːsɪ, kən'trɒvəsɪ) *n, pl* **-sies.** dispute, argument, or debate, esp. one concerning a matter about which there is strong disagreement and esp. one carried on in public or in the press. [C14: from Latin *contrōversia,* from *contrōversus* turned in an opposite direction, from CONTRA- + *vertere* to turn] ► **controversial** (,kɒntrə'vɜːʃəl) *adj* ► **,contro'versial,ism** *n* ► **,contro'versialist** *n* ► **,contro'versially** *adv*

controvert ('kɒntrə,vɜːt, ,kɒntrə'vɜːt) *vb* (*tr*) **1** to deny, refute, or oppose (some argument or opinion). **2** to argue or wrangle about. [C17: from Latin *contrōversus;* see CONTROVERSY] ► **'contro,verter** *n* ► **,contro'vertible** *adj* ► **,contro'vertibly** *adv*

contumacious (,kɒntjʊ'meɪʃəs) *adj* stubbornly resistant to authority; wilfully obstinate. ► **,contu'maciously** *adv* ► **,contu'maciousness** *n*

contumacy ('kɒntjʊməsɪ) *n, pl* **-cies.** **1** obstinate and wilful rebelliousness or resistance to authority; insubordination; disobedience. **2** the wilful refusal of a person to appear before a court or to comply with a court order. [C14: from Latin *contumācia,* from *contumāx* obstinate; related to *tumēre* to swell, be proud]

contumely ('kɒntjʊmɪlɪ) *n, pl* **-lies.** **1** scornful or insulting language or behaviour. **2** a humiliating or scornful insult. [C14: from Latin *contumēlia* invective, from *tumēre* to swell, as with wrath] ► **contumelious** (,kɒntjʊ'miːlɪəs) *adj* ► **,contu'meliously** *adv* ► **,contu'meliousness** *n*

contuse (kən'tjuːz) *vb* (*tr*) to injure (the body) without breaking the skin; bruise. [C15: from Latin *contūsus* bruised, from *contundere* to grind, from *tundere* to beat, batter] ► **con'tusive** *adj*

contusion (kən'tjuːʒən) *n* an injury in which the skin is not broken; bruise. ► **con'tusioned** *adj*

conundrum (kə'nʌndrəm) *n* **1** a riddle, esp. one whose answer makes a play on words. **2** a puzzling question or problem. [C16: of unknown origin]

conurbation (,kɒnɜː'beɪʃən) *n* a large densely populated urban sprawl formed by the growth and coalescence of individual towns or cities. [C20: from CON- + *-urbation,* from Latin *urbs* city; see URBAN]

conure ('kɒnjʊə) *n* any of various small American parrots of the genus *Aratinga* and related genera. [C19: from New Latin *conurus,* from Greek *kōnos* CONE + *oura* tail]

conus ('kəʊnəs) *n, pl* **-ni.** *Anatomy, zoology.* any of several cone-shaped structures, such as the conus medullaris, the lower end of the spinal cord.

convalesce (,kɒnvə'lɛs) *vb* (*intr*) to recover from illness, injury, or the aftereffects of a surgical operation, esp. by resting. [C15: from Latin *convalēscere,* from *com-* (intensive) + *valēscere* to grow strong, from *valēre* to be strong]

convalescence (,kɒnvə'lɛsəns) *n* **1** gradual return to health after illness, injury, or an operation, esp. through rest. **2** the period during which such recovery occurs. ► **,conva'lescent** *n, adj* ► **,conva'lescently** *adv*

convection (kən'vɛkʃən) *n* **1** a process of heat transfer through a gas or liquid by bulk motion of hotter material into a cooler region. Compare **conduction** (sense 1). **2** *Meteorol.* the process by which masses of relatively warm air are raised into the atmosphere, often cooling and forming clouds, with compensatory downward movements of cooler air. **3** *Geology.* the slow circulation of subcrustal material, thought to be the mechanism by which tectonic plates are moved. [C19: from Late Latin *convectiō* a bringing together, from Latin *convehere* to bring together, gather, from *vehere* to bear, carry] ► **con'vectional** *adj* ► **con'vective** *adj*

convector (kən'vɛktə) *n* a space-heating device from which heat is transferred to the surrounding air by convection.

convenance *French.* (kõvnɑ̃s) *n* suitable behaviour; propriety. [from *convenir* to be suitable, from Latin *convenīre;* see CONVENIENT]

convene (kən'viːn) *vb* **1** to gather, call together, or summon, esp. for a formal meeting. **2** (*tr*) to order to appear before a court of law, judge, tribunal, etc. [C15: from Latin *convenīre* to assemble, from *venīre* to come]

convener *or* **convenor** (kən'viːnə) *n* **1** a person who convenes or chairs a meeting, committee, etc., esp. one who is specifically elected to do so: *a convener of shop stewards.* **2** the chairman and civic head of certain Scottish councils. Compare **provost** (sense 3). ► **con'venership** *or* **con'venorship** *n*

convenience (kən'viːnɪəns) *n* **1** the state or quality of being suitable or opportune: *the convenience of the hour.* **2** a convenient time or situation. **3 at your convenience.** at a time suitable to you. **4 at your earliest convenience.** *Formal.* as soon as possible. **5** usefulness, comfort, or facility. **6** an object that is particularly useful, esp. a labour-saving device. **7** *Euphemistic, chiefly Brit.* a lavatory, esp. a public one. **8 make a convenience of.** to take advantage of; impose upon.

convenience food *n* food that needs little preparation, especially food that has been pre-prepared and preserved for long-term storage.

convenience store *n* a shop that has long opening hours, caters to local tastes, and is conveniently situated.

convenient (kən'viːnɪənt) *adj* **1** suitable for one's purpose or needs; opportune. **2** easy to use. **3** close by or easily accessible; handy. [C14: from Latin *conveniēns* appropriate, fitting, from *convenīre* to come together, be in accord with, from *venīre* to come] ► **con'veniently** *adv*

convent ('kɒnvənt) *n* **1** a building inhabited by a religious community, usually of nuns. **2** the religious community inhabiting such a building. **3** Also called: **convent school.** a school in which the teachers are nuns. [C13: from Old French *covent,* from Latin *conventus* meeting, from *convenīre* to come together; see CONVENE]

conventicle (kən'ventɪk^əl) *n* **1** a secret or unauthorized assembly for worship. **2** a small meeting house or chapel for a religious assembly, esp. of Nonconformists or Dissenters. [C14: from Latin *conventiculum* a meeting, from *conventus;* see CONVENT] ► **con'venticler** *n*

convention (kən'venʃən) *n* **1a** a large formal assembly of a group with common interests, such as a political party or trade union. **1b** the persons attending such an assembly. **2** *U.S. politics.* an assembly of delegates of one party to select candidates for office. **3** *Diplomacy.* an international agreement second only to a treaty in formality: *a telecommunications convention.* **4** any agreement, compact, or contract. **5** the most widely accepted or established view of what is thought to be proper behaviour, good taste, etc. **6** an accepted rule, usage, etc.: *a convention used by printers.* **7** *Bridge.* Also called: **conventional.** a bid or play not to be taken at its face value, which one's partner can interpret according to a prearranged bidding system. [C15: from Latin *conventiō* an assembling, agreeing]

conventional (kən'venʃən^əl) *adj* **1** following the accepted customs and proprieties, esp. in a way that lacks originality: *conventional habits.* **2** established by accepted usage or general agreement. **3** of or relating to a convention or assembly. 4 *Law.* based upon the agreement or consent of parties. 5 *Arts.* represented in a simplified or generalized way; conventionalized. 6 (of weapons, warfare, etc.) not nuclear. ◆ *n* 7 *Bridge.* another word for **convention** (sense 7). ► **con'ventionally** *adv*

conventionalism (kən'vɛnʃənə,lɪzəm) *n* 1 advocacy of or conformity to that which is established. 2 something conventional. 3 *Philosophy.* a theory that moral principles are not enshrined in the nature of things but merely reflect customary practice. 4 *Philosophy.* the theory that meaning is a matter of convention and thus that scientific laws merely reflect such general linguistic agreement. ► **con'ventionalist** *n*

conventionality (kən,vɛnʃə'nælɪtɪ) *n, pl* **-ties.** 1 the quality or characteristic of being conventional, esp. in behaviour, thinking, etc. 2 (*often pl*) something conventional, esp. a normal or accepted rule of behaviour; propriety.

conventionalize *or* **conventionalise** (kən'vɛnʃənə,laɪz) *vb* (*tr*) 1 to make conventional. 2 to simplify or stylize (a design, decorative device, etc.). ► **con,ventionali'zation** *or* **con,ventionali'sation** *n*

conventual (kən'vɛntjʊəl) *adj* 1 of, belonging to, or characteristic of a convent. ◆ *n* 2 a member of a convent. ► **con'ventually** *adv*

converge (kən'vɜːdʒ) *vb* 1 to move or cause to move towards the same point. 2 to meet or cause to meet; join. 3 (*intr*) (of opinions, effects, etc.) to tend towards a common conclusion or result. 4 (*intr*) *Maths.* (of an infinite series) to approach a finite limit as the number of terms increases. 5 (*intr*) (of animals and plants during evolutionary development) to undergo convergence. [C17: from Late Latin *convergere,* from Latin *com-* together + *vergere* to incline]

convergence (kən'vɜːdʒəns) *n* 1 Also called: **con'vergency.** the act, degree, or a point of converging. 2 concurrence of opinions, results, etc. 3 *Maths.* the property or manner of approaching a finite limit, esp. of an infinite series: *conditional convergence.* 4 the combining of different forms of electronic technology, such as data processing and word processing converging into information processing. 5 Also called: **convergent evolution.** the evolutionary development of a superficial resemblance between unrelated animals that occupy a similar environment, as in the evolution of wings in birds and bats. 6 *Meteorol.* an accumulation of air in a region that has a greater inflow than outflow of air, often giving rise to vertical air currents. See also **Intertropical Convergence Zone.** 7 the turning of the eyes inwards in order to fixate an object nearer than that previously being fixated. Compare **divergence** (sense 6).

convergence zone *n Geology.* a zone where tectonic plates collide, typified by earthquakes, mountain formation, and volcanic activity.

convergent (kən'vɜːdʒənt) *adj* 1 (of two or more lines, paths, etc.) moving towards or meeting at some common point. 2 (of forces, ideas, etc.) tending towards the same result; merging. 3 *Maths.* (of an infinite series) having a finite limit.

convergent thinking *n Psychol.* analytical, usually deductive, thinking in which ideas are examined for their logical validity or in which a set of rules is followed, e.g. in arithmetic.

conversable (kən'vɜːsəbᵊl) *adj* 1 easy or pleasant to talk to. 2 able or inclined to talk. ► **con'versableness** *n* ► **con'versably** *adv*

conversant (kən'vɜːsᵊnt) *adj* (*usually postpositive* and foll. by *with*) experienced (in), familiar (with), or acquainted (with). ► **con'versance** *or* **con'versancy** *n* ► **con'versantly** *adv*

conversation (,kɒnvə'seɪʃən) *n* 1 the interchange through speech of information, ideas, etc.; spoken communication. 2 **make conversation.** to talk in an artificial way. Related adj: **colloquial.**

conversational (,kɒnvə'seɪʃənᵊl) *adj* 1 of, using, or in the manner of conversation. 2 inclined to or skilled in conversation; conversable. ► **,conver'sationally** *adv*

conversational implicature *n Logic, philosophy.* another term for **implicature.**

conversationalist (,kɒnvə'seɪʃənəlɪst) *or* **conversationist** *n* a person who enjoys or excels in conversation.

conversation piece *n* 1 something, esp. an unusual object, that provokes conversation. 2 (esp. in 18th-century Britain) a group portrait in a landscape or domestic setting. 3 a play emphasizing dialogue.

conversazione *Italian.* (konversat'tsjone; *English* ,kɒnvə,sætsɪ'əʊnɪ) *n, pl* ***-zioni*** (*Italian* -'tsjoni) *or* ***-ziones*** (*English* -tsɪ'əʊniːz). a social gathering for discussion of the arts, literature, etc. [C18: literally: conversation]

converse[1] *vb* (kən'vɜːs). (*intr;* often foll. by *with*) 1 to engage in conversation (with). 2 to commune spiritually (with). 3 *Obsolete.* 3a to associate; consort. 3b to have sexual intercourse. ◆ *n* ('kɒnvɜːs). 4 conversation (often in the phrase **hold converse with**). 5 *Obsolete.* 4a fellowship or acquaintance. 4b sexual intercourse. [C16: from Old French *converser,* from Latin *conversārī* to keep company with, from *conversāre* to turn constantly, from *vertere* to turn] ► **con'verser** *n*

converse[2] ('kɒnvɜːs) *adj* 1 (*prenominal*) reversed; opposite; contrary. ◆ *n* 2 something that is opposite or contrary. 3 *Logic.* 3a a categorical proposition obtained from another by the transposition of subject and predicate, as *no bad man is bald* from *no bald man is bad.* 3b a proposition so derived, possibly by weakening a universal proposition to the corresponding particular, as *some socialists are rich* from *all rich men are socialists.* 4 *Logic, maths.* a relation that holds between two relata only when a given relation holds between them in reverse order: thus *father of* is the converse of *son of.* [C16: from Latin *conversus* turned around; see CONVERSE[1]] ► **con'versely** *adv*

conversion (kən'vɜːʃən) *n* 1a a change or adaptation in form, character, or function. 1b something changed in one of these respects. 2 a change to another attitude or belief, as in a change of religion. 3 *Maths.* a change in the units or form of a number or expression: *the conversion of miles to kilometres involves multiplying by 1.61.* 4 *Logic.* a form of inference by which one proposition is obtained as the converse of another proposition. 5 *Law.* 5a unauthorized dealing with or the assumption of rights of ownership to another's personal property. 5b the changing of real property into personalty or personalty into realty. 6 *Rugby.* a score made after a try by kicking the ball over the crossbar from a place kick. 7 *Physics.* a change of fertile material to fissile material in a reactor. 8a an alteration to a car engine to improve its performance. 8b (*as modifier*): *a conversion kit.* 9 material alteration to the structure or fittings of a building undergoing a change in function or legal status. 10 *N.Z.* the unauthorized appropriation of a motor vehicle. [C14: from Latin *conversiō* a turning around; see CONVERT] ► **con'versional** *or* **con'versionary** *adj*

conversion disorder *n* a psychological disorder in which severe physical symptoms like blindness or paralysis appear with no apparent physical cause.

convert *vb* (kən'vɜːt). (*mainly tr*) 1 to change or adapt the form, character, or function of; transform. 2 to cause (someone) to change in opinion, belief, etc. 3 to change (a person or his way of life, etc.) for the better. 4 (*intr*) to admit of being changed (into): *the table converts into a tray.* 5 (*also intr*) to change or be changed into another chemical compound or physical state: *to convert water into ice.* 6 *Law.* 6a to assume unlawful proprietary rights over (personal property). 6b to change (property) from realty into personalty or vice versa. 7 (*also intr*) *Rugby.* to make a conversion after (a try). 8 *Logic.* to transpose the subject and predicate of (a proposition) by conversion. 9 to change (a value or measurement) from one system of units to another. 10 to exchange (a security or bond) for something of equivalent value. ◆ *n* ('kɒnvɜːt). 11 a person who has been converted to another belief, religion, etc. [C13: from Old French *convertir,* from Latin *convertere* to turn around, alter, transform, from *vertere* to turn] ► **con'vertive** *adj*

converter *or* **convertor** (kən'vɜːtə) *n* 1 a person or thing that converts. 2 *Physics.* 2a a device for converting alternating current to direct current or vice versa. 2b a device for converting a signal from one frequency to another. 3 a vessel in which molten metal is refined, using a blast of air or oxygen. See also **Bessemer converter, L-D converter.** 4 short for **converter reactor.** 5 *Computing.* a device for converting one form of coded information to another, such as an analogue-to-digital converter.

converter reactor *n* a nuclear reactor for converting one fuel into another, esp. one that transforms fertile material into fissionable material. Compare **breeder reactor.**

convertible (kən'vɜːtəbᵊl) *adj* 1 capable of being converted. 2 (of a car) having a folding or removable roof. 3 *Finance.* 3a a bond or debenture that can be converted to ordinary or preference shares on a fixed date at a fixed price. 3b (of a paper currency) exchangeable on demand for precious metal to an equivalent value. ◆ *n* 4 a car with a folding or removable roof. ► **con,verti'bility** *or* **con'vertibleness** *n* ► **con'vertibly** *adv*

convertiplane, convertaplane, *or* **convertoplane** (kən'vɜːtə,pleɪn) *n* an aircraft that can land and take off vertically by temporarily directing its propulsive thrust downwards.

convertite ('kɒnvə,taɪt) *n Archaic.* a convert, esp. a reformed prostitute.

convex ('kɒnvɛks, kɒn'vɛks) *adj* 1 curving or bulging outwards. 2 *Physics.* having one or two surfaces curved or ground in the shape of a section of the exterior of a sphere, paraboloid, ellipsoid, etc.: *a convex lens.* 3 *Maths.* (of a polygon) containing no interior angle greater than 180°. ◆ *vb* 4 (*tr*) to make convex. ◆ Compare **concave.** [C16: from Latin *convexus* vaulted, rounded] ► **'convexly** *adv*

convexity (kən'vɛksɪtɪ) *n, pl* **-ties.** 1 the state or quality of being convex. 2 a convex surface, object, etc.; bulge.

convexo-concave (kən,vɛksəʊkɒn'keɪv) *adj* 1 having one side convex and the other side concave. 2 (of a lens) having a convex face with greater curvature than the concave face. Compare **concavo-convex** (sense 2).

convexo-convex *adj* (esp. of a lens) having both sides convex; biconvex.

convey (kən'veɪ) *vb* (*tr*) 1 to take, carry, or transport from one place to another. 2 to communicate (a message, information, etc.). 3 (of a channel, path, etc.) to conduct, transmit, or transfer. 4 *Law.* to transmit or transfer (the title to property). 5 *Archaic.* to steal. [C13: from Old French *conveier,* from Medieval Latin *conviāre* to escort, from Latin *com-* with + *via* way] ► **con'veyable** *adj*

conveyance (kən'veɪəns) *n* 1 the act of conveying. 2 a means of transport. 3 *Law.* 3a a transfer of the legal title to property. 3b the document effecting such a transfer. ► **con'veyancer** *n*

conveyancing (kən'veɪənsɪŋ) *n* the branch of law dealing with the transfer of ownership of property.

conveyor *or* **conveyer** (kən'veɪə) *n* 1 a person or thing that conveys. 2 short for **conveyor belt.**

conveyor belt *n* a flexible endless strip of fabric or linked plates driven by rollers and used to transport objects, esp. in a factory.

convict *vb* (kən'vɪkt). (*tr*) 1 to pronounce (someone) guilty of an offence. ◆ *n* ('kɒnvɪkt). 2 a person found guilty of an offence against the law, esp. one who is sentenced to imprisonment. 3 a person serving a prison sentence. ◆ *adj* (kən'vɪkt). 4 *Obsolete.* convicted. [C14: from Latin *convictus* convicted of crime, from *convincere* to prove guilty, CONVINCE] ► **con'victable** *or* **con'victible** *adj*

conviction (kən'vɪkʃən) *n* 1 the state or appearance of being convinced. 2 a fixed or firmly held belief, opinion, etc. 3 the act of convincing. 4 the act or an instance of convicting or the state of being convicted. 5 **carry conviction.** to be convincing. ► **con'victional** *adj*

convictive (kən'vɪktɪv) *adj* able or serving to convince or convict. ► **con'victively** *adv*

convince (kən'vɪns) *vb* (*tr*) 1 (*may take a clause as object*) to make (someone) agree, understand, or realize the truth or validity of something; persuade. 2 *Chiefly U.S.* to persuade (someone) to do something. 3 *Obsolete.* 3a to overcome. 3b to prove guilty. [C16: from Latin *convincere* to demonstrate incontrovertibly, from *com-* (intensive) + *vincere* to overcome, conquer] ▸ **con'vincement** *n* ▸ **con'vincer** *n* ▸ **con'vincible** *adj*

USAGE The use of *convince* to talk about persuading someone to do something is considered by many British speakers to be wrong or unacceptable.

convincing (kən'vɪnsɪŋ) *adj* **1** credible or plausible. **2** *Chiefly law.* persuading by evidence or argument. ▸ **con'vincingly** *adv* ▸ **con'vincingness** *n*

convivial (kən'vɪvɪəl) *adj* sociable; jovial or festive: *a convivial atmosphere.* [C17: from Late Latin *convīviālis* pertaining to a feast, from Latin *convīvium,* a living together, banquet, from *vīvere* to live] ▸ **con'vivialist** *n* ▸ **con,vivi'ality** *n* ▸ **con'vivially** *adv*

convocation (,kɒnvə'keɪʃən) *n* **1** a large formal assembly, esp. one specifically convened. **2** the act of convoking or state of being convoked. **3** *Church of England.* either of the synods of the provinces of Canterbury or York. **4** *Episcopal Church.* **4a** an assembly of the clergy and part of the laity of a diocese. **4b** a district represented at such an assembly. **5** (*sometimes cap.*) (in some British universities) a legislative assembly composed mainly of graduates. **6** (in India) a degree-awarding ceremony. **7** (in Australia and New Zealand) the graduate membership of a university. ▸ **,convo'cational** *adj* ▸ **'convo,cator** *n*

convoke (kən'vəʊk) *vb* (*tr*) to call (a meeting, assembly, etc.) together; summon. [C16: from Latin *convocāre,* from *vocāre* to call] ▸ **convocative** (kən'vɒkətɪv) *adj* ▸ **con'voker** *n*

convolute ('kɒnvə,luːt) *vb* (*tr*) **1** to form into a twisted, coiled, or rolled shape. ◆ *adj* **2** *Botany.* rolled longitudinally upon itself: *a convolute petal.* **3** another word for **convoluted** (sense 2). [C18: from Latin *convolūtus* rolled up, from *convolvere* to roll together, from *volvere* to turn] ▸ **'convo,lutely** *adv*

convoluted ('kɒnvə,luːtɪd) *adj* **1** (esp. of meaning, style, etc.) difficult to comprehend; involved. **2** wound together; coiled. ▸ **'convo,lutedly** *adv* ▸ **'convo,lutedness** *n*

convolution (,kɒnvə'luːʃən) *n* **1** a twisting together; a turn, twist, or coil. **2** an intricate, involved, or confused matter or condition. **3** Also called: **gyrus.** any of the numerous convex folds or ridges of the surface of the brain. ▸ **,convo'lutional** *or* **,convo'lutionary** *adj*

convolve (kən'vɒlv) *vb* to wind or roll together; coil; twist. [C16: from Latin *convolvere;* see CONVOLUTE]

convolvulaceous (kən,vɒlvjʊ'leɪʃəs) *adj* of, relating to, or belonging to the *Convolvulaceae,* a family of plants having trumpet-shaped flowers and typically a climbing, twining, or prostrate habit: includes bindweed, morning-glory, and sweet potato.

convolvulus (kən'vɒlvjʊləs) *n, pl* **-luses** *or* **-li** (-,laɪ). any typically twining herbaceous convolvulaceous plant of the genus *Convolvulus,* having funnel-shaped flowers and triangular leaves. See also **bindweed.** [C16: from Latin: bindweed; see CONVOLUTE]

convoy ('kɒnvɔɪ) *n* **1** a group of merchant ships with an escort of warships. **2** a group of land vehicles assembled to travel together. **3** the act of travelling or escorting by convoy (esp. in the phrase **in convoy**). ◆ *vb* **4** (*tr*) to escort while in transit. [C14: from Old French *convoier* to CONVEY]

convulsant (kən'vʌlsənt) *adj* **1** producing convulsions. ◆ *n* **2** a drug that produces convulsions. [C19: from French, from *convulser* to CONVULSE]

convulse (kən'vʌls) *vb* **1** (*tr*) to shake or agitate violently. **2** (*tr*) to cause (muscles) to undergo violent spasms or contractions. **3** (*intr; often foll. by with*) *Informal.* to shake or be overcome (with violent emotion, esp. laughter). **4** (*tr*) to disrupt the normal running of (a country, etc.): *student riots have convulsed India.* [C17: from Latin *convulsus,* from *convellere* to tear up, from *vellere* to pluck, pull] ▸ **con'vulsive** *adj* ▸ **con'vulsively** *adv* ▸ **con'vulsiveness** *n*

convulsion (kən'vʌlʃən) *n* **1** a violent involuntary contraction of a muscle or muscles. **2** a violent upheaval, disturbance, or agitation, esp. a social one. **3** (*usually pl*) *Informal.* uncontrollable laughter: *I was in convulsions.* ▸ **con'vulsionary** *adj*

Conwy ('kɒnwɪ) *n* **1** a market town and resort in N Wales, in Conwy county borough on the estuary of the River Conwy: medieval town walls, 13th-century castle. Pop.: 13 627 (1991). Former name: **Conway. 2** a county borough in N Wales, created in 1996 from parts of Gwynedd and Clwyd. Pop.: 70 200 (1996 est.). Area: 1130 sq. km (436 sq. miles).

cony *or* **coney** ('kəʊnɪ) *n, pl* **-nies** *or* **-neys. 1** a rabbit or fur made from the skin of a rabbit. **2** (in the Bible) another name for the **hyrax,** esp. the Syrian rock hyrax. **3** another name for the **pika. 4** *Archaic.* a fool or dupe. [C13: back formation from *conies,* from Old French *conis,* plural of *conil,* from Latin *cunīculus* rabbit]

Conybeare ('kɒnɪ,bɪə, 'kʌn-) *n* **William Daniel.** 1787–1857, British geologist. He summarized all that was known about rocks at the time in *Outlines of the Geology of England and Wales* (1822).

coo (kuː) *vb* **coos, cooing, cooed. 1** (*intr*) (of doves, pigeons, etc.) to make a characteristic soft throaty call. **2** (*tr*) to speak in a soft murmur. **3** (*intr*) to murmur lovingly (esp. in the phrase **bill and coo**). ◆ *n* **4** the sound of cooing. ◆ *interj* **5** *Brit. slang.* an exclamation of surprise, awe, etc. ▸ **'cooer** *n* ▸ **'cooingly** *adv*

Cooch Behar *or* **Kuch Bihar** (kuːtʃ bɪ'hɑː) *n* **1** a former state of NE India: part of West Bengal since 1950. **2** a city in India, in NE West Bengal: capital of the former state of Cooch Behar. Pop.: 62 500 (latest est.).

cooee *or* **cooey** ('kuːiː) *interj* **1** a call used to attract attention, esp. (originally) a long loud high-pitched call on two notes used in the Australian bush. ◆ *vb* **cooees, cooeeing, cooeed** *or* **cooeys, cooeying, cooeyed. 2** (*intr*) to utter this call. ◆ *n* **3** *Austral. and N.Z. informal.* calling distance (esp. in the phrase **within (a) cooee (of)**). [C19: from a native Australian language]

cook (kʊk) *vb* **1** to prepare (food) by the action of heat, as by boiling, baking, etc., or (of food) to become ready for eating through such a process. Related adj: **culinary. 2** to subject or be subjected to the action of intense heat: *the town cooked in the sun.* **3** (*tr*) *Slang.* to alter or falsify (something, esp. figures, accounts, etc.): *to cook the books.* **4** (*tr*) *Slang.* to spoil or ruin (something). **5** (*intr*) *Slang.* to happen (esp. in the phrase **what's cooking?**). **6** (*tr*) *Slang.* to prepare (any of several drugs) by heating. **7** (*intr*) *Music slang.* to play vigorously: *the band was cooking.* **8 cook someone's goose.** *Informal.* **8a** to spoil a person's plans. **8b** to bring about someone's ruin, downfall, etc. ◆ *n* **9** a person who prepares food for eating, esp. as an occupation. ◆ See also **cook up.** [Old English *cōc* (n), from Latin *coquus* a cook, from *coquere* to cook] ▸ **'cookable** *adj*

Cook[1] (kʊk) *n* **Mount. 1** Official name: **Aorangi-Mount Cook.** a mountain in New Zealand, in the South Island, in the Southern Alps: the highest peak in New Zealand. Height: 3764 m (12 349 ft.). **2** a mountain in SE Alaska, in the St. Elias Mountains. Height: 4194 m (13 760 ft.).

Cook[2] (kʊk) *n* **1** Captain **James.** 1728–79, British navigator and explorer: claimed the E coast of Australia for Britain, circumnavigated New Zealand, and discovered several Pacific and Atlantic islands (1768–79). **2** Sir **Joseph.** 1860–1947, Australian statesman, born in England: prime minister of Australia (1913–14). **3 Peter (Edward).** 1937–95, British comedy actor and writer, noted esp. for his partnership (1960–73) with Dudley Moore. **4 Robin,** full name *Robert Finlayson Cook.* born 1946, British Labour politician; foreign secretary from 1997. **5 Thomas.** 1808–92, British travel agent; innovator of conducted excursions and founder of the travel agents Thomas Cook and Son.

cook-chill *n* a method of food preparation used by caterers, in which cooked dishes are chilled rapidly and reheated as required.

cooker ('kʊkə) *n* **1** an apparatus, usually of metal and heated by gas, electricity, oil, or solid fuel, for cooking food; stove. **2** *Brit.* any large sour apple used in cooking.

cookery ('kʊkərɪ) *n* **1** the art, study, or practice of cooking. **2** *U.S.* a place for cooking. **3** *Canadian.* a cookhouse at a mining or lumber camp.

cookery book *or* **cookbook** ('kʊk,bʊk) *n* a book containing recipes and instructions for cooking.

cook-general *n, pl* **cooks-general.** *Brit.* (formerly, esp. in the 1920s and '30s) a domestic servant who did cooking and housework.

cookhouse ('kʊk,haʊs) *n* a place for cooking, esp. a camp kitchen.

cookie *or* **cooky** ('kʊkɪ) *n, pl* **-ies. 1** the U.S. and Canadian word for **biscuit. 2** a Scot. word for **bun. 3** *Informal.* a person: *smart cookie.* **4 that's the way the cookie crumbles.** *Informal.* matters are inevitably or unalterably so. [C18: from Dutch *koekje,* diminutive of *koek* cake]

Cook Inlet *n* an inlet of the Pacific on the coast of S Alaska: part of the Gulf of Alaska.

Cook Island Maori *n N.Z.* a dialect of Maori spoken in the Cook Islands.

Cook Islands *pl n* a group of islands in the SW Pacific, an overseas territory of New Zealand: consists of the **Lower Cooks** and the **Northern Cooks.** Capital: Avarua, on Rarotonga. Pop.: 18 500 (1994). Area: 234 sq. km (90 sq. miles).

cookout ('kʊk,aʊt) *n U.S. and Canadian.* a party where a meal is cooked and eaten out of doors.

cook shop *n* **1** *Brit.* a shop that sells cookery equipment. **2** *U.S.* a restaurant.

Cookson ('kʊksən) *n* Dame **Catherine.** 1906–98, British novelist, known for her popular novels set in northeast England.

Cook's tour *n Informal.* a rapid but extensive tour or survey of anything. [C19: after Thomas COOK[2]]

Cookstown ('kʊkstaʊn) *n* a district of central Northern Ireland, in Co. Tyrone. Pop.: 31 082 (1991). Area: 622 sq. km (240 sq. miles).

Cook Strait *n* the strait between North and South Islands, New Zealand. Width: 26 km (16 miles).

cook up *vb* (*tr, adv*) **1** *Informal.* to concoct or invent (a story, alibi, etc.). **2** to prepare (a meal), esp. quickly. **3** *Slang.* to prepare (a drug) for use by heating, as by dissolving heroin in a spoon. ◆ *n* **cook-up. 4** (in the Caribbean) a dish consisting of mixed meats, rice, shrimps, and sometimes vegetables.

cool (kuːl) *adj* **1** moderately cold: *a cool day.* **2** comfortably free of heat: *a cool room.* **3** producing a pleasant feeling of coldness: *a cool shirt.* **4** able to conceal emotion; calm: *a cool head.* **5** lacking in enthusiasm, affection, cordiality, etc.: *a cool welcome.* **6** calmly audacious or impudent. **7** *Informal.* (esp. of numbers, sums of money, etc.) without exaggeration; actual: *a cool ten thousand.* **8** (of a colour) having violet, blue, or green predominating; cold. **9** (of jazz) characteristic of the late 1940s and early 1950s, economical and rhythmically relaxed. **10** *Informal.* sophisticated or elegant, esp. in an unruffled way. **11** *Informal.* excellent; marvellous. ◆ *adv* **12** *Not standard.* in a cool manner; coolly. ◆ *n* **13** coolness: *the cool of the evening.* **14** *Slang.* calmness; composure (esp. in the phrases **keep** *or* **lose one's cool**). **15** *Slang.* unruffled elegance or sophistication. ◆ *vb* **16** (usually foll. by *down* or *off*) to make or become cooler. **17** (usually foll. by *down* or *off*) to lessen the intensity of (anger or excitement) or (of anger or excitement) to become less intense; calm down. **18 cool it.** (*usually imperative*) *Slang.* to calm down; take it easy. **19 cool one's heels.** to wait or be kept waiting. ◆ See also **cool out.** [Old English *cōl;* related to Old Norse *kōlna,* Old High German *kuoli;* see COLD, CHILL] ▸ **'coolingly** *adv* ▸ **'coolingness** *n* ▸ **'coolish** *adj* ▸ **'coolly** *adv* ▸ **'coolness** *n*

coolabah *or* **coolibah** ('kuːlə,bɑː) *n* an Australian myrtaceous tree, *Eucalyptus microtheca,* that grows along rivers and has smooth bark and long narrow leaves. [from a native Australian language]

coolamon ('kuːləmɒn) *n Austral.* a shallow dish of wood or bark, used for carrying water. [C19: from a native Australian language]

coolant ('kuːlənt) *n* **1** a fluid used to cool a system or to transfer heat from one part of it to another. **2** a liquid, such as an emulsion of oil, water, and soft soap, used to lubricate and cool the workpiece and cutting tool during machining.

cool bag *or* **box** *n* an insulated container used to keep food cool on picnics, to carry frozen food, etc.

cool drink *n S. African.* any soft drink.

cooler ('kuːlə) *n* **1** a container, vessel, or apparatus for cooling, such as a heat exchanger. **2** a slang word for **prison. 3** a drink consisting of wine, fruit juice, and carbonated water.

Cooley's anaemia ('ku:lɪz) *n* another name for **thalassaemia.** [named after Thomas B. *Cooley* (1871–1945), U.S. paediatrician who reported on it in children in the Mediterranean area]

Coolgardie safe (ku:l'gɑ:dɪ) *n* a cupboard with wetted hessian walls for keeping food cool: used esp. in Australia. Sometimes shortened to **Coolgardie.** [named after *Coolgardie,* Western Australia, perhaps because of resemblance to COOL and GUARD]

Coolidge ('ku:lɪdʒ) *n* **(John) Calvin.** 1872–1933, 30th president of the U.S. (1923–29).

coolie *or* **cooly** ('ku:lɪ) *n, pl* **-ies. 1** a cheaply hired unskilled Oriental labourer. **2** *Derogatory.* an Indian living in South Africa. [C17: from Hindi *kulī,* probably of Dravidian origin; related to Tamil *kūli* hire, hireling]

cooling-off period *n* **1** a period during which the contending sides to a dispute reconsider their options before taking further action. **2** a period, often 14 days, that begins when a sale contract or life-assurance policy is received by a member of the public, during which the contract or policy can be cancelled without loss.

cooling tower *n* a tall hollow structure in which steam is condensed or water that is used as a coolant in some industrial process is allowed to cool for reuse by trickling down a surface.

cool out *vb (intr, adv) Caribbean.* to relax and cool down.

coolth (ku:lθ) *n* coolness. [C16: originally dialect, from COOL + -TH[1]]

coom *or* **coomb** (ku:m) *n Dialect, chiefly Scot. and northern English.* waste material, such as dust from coal, grease from axles, etc. [C16 (meaning: soot): probably a variant of CULM[1]]

Coomaraswamy (ku:ˌmɑ:rə'swɑ:mɪ) *n* **Ananda (Kentish).** 1877–1947, Ceylonese art historian and interpreter of Indian culture to the West.

coomb, combe, coombe, *or* **comb** (ku:m) *n* **1** *Chiefly southern English* a short valley or deep hollow, esp. in chalk areas. **2** *Chiefly northern English* another name for a **cirque.** [Old English *cumb* (in place names), perhaps of Celtic origin; compare Old French *combe* small valley, also probably of Celtic origin]

coon (ku:n) *n* **1** *Informal.* short for **raccoon. 2** *Offensive slang.* a Black or a native Australian. **3** *S. African. offensive* a person of mixed race.

cooncan ('ku:nˌkæn) *or* **conquian** *n* a card game for two players, similar to rummy. [C19: from (Mexican) Spanish *con quién* with whom?, apparently with reference to the forming and declaring of sequences and sets of cards]

coonhound ('ku:nˌhaʊnd) *n* another name for **raccoon dog** (sense 2).

coon's age *n U.S. slang.* a long time.

coonskin ('ku:nˌskɪn) *n* **1** the pelt of a raccoon. **2** a raccoon cap with the tail hanging at the back. **3** *U.S.* an overcoat made of raccoon.

coontie ('ku:ntɪ) *n* **1** an evergreen plant, *Zamia floridana* of S Florida, related to the cycads and having large dark green leathery leaves: family *Zamiaceae.* **2** a starch derived from the underground stems of this plant. [C19: from Seminole *kunti* flour from this plant]

coop[1] (ku:p) *n* **1** a cage or small enclosure for poultry or small animals. **2** a small narrow place of confinement, esp. a prison cell. **3** a wicker basket for catching fish. ◆ *vb* **4** *(tr; often foll. by up or in)* to confine in a restricted area. [C15: probably from Middle Low German *kūpe* basket, tub; related to Latin *cūpa* cask, vat]

coop[2] *or* **co-op** ('kəʊˌɒp) *n* a cooperative, cooperative society, or shop run by a cooperative society.

coop. *or* **co-op.** *abbrev. for* cooperative.

cooper ('ku:pə) *n* **1** Also called: **hooper.** a person skilled in making and repairing barrels, casks, etc. ◆ *vb* **2** *(tr)* to make or mend (barrels, casks, etc.). **3** *(intr)* to work as a cooper. [C13: from Middle Dutch *cūper* or Middle Low German *kūper;* see COOP[1]]

Cooper ('ku:pə) *n* **1 Anthony Ashley.** See (Earl of) **Shaftesbury. 2 Gary,** real name *Frank James Cooper.* 1901–61, U.S. film actor; his many films include *Sergeant York* (1941) and *High Noon* (1952), for both of which he won Oscars. **3 Henry.** born 1934, British boxer; European heavyweight champion (1964; 1968–71). **4 James Fenimore.** 1789–1851, U.S. novelist, noted for his stories of American Indians, esp. *The Last of the Mohicans* (1826). **5 Leon Neil.** born 1930, U.S. physicist, noted for his work on the theory of superconductivity. He shared the Nobel prize for physics 1972. **6 Samuel.** 1609–72, English miniaturist.

cooperage ('ku:pərɪdʒ) *n* **1** Also called: **coopery.** the craft, place of work, or products of a cooper. **2** the labour fee charged by a cooper.

cooperate *or* **co-operate** (kəʊ'ɒpəˌreɪt) *vb (intr)* **1** to work or act together. **2** to be of assistance or be willing to assist. **3** *Economics.* (of firms, workers, consumers, etc.) to engage in economic cooperation. [C17: from Late Latin *cooperārī* to work with, combine, from Latin *operārī* to work] ▸ **co'operˌator** *or* **co-'operˌator** *n*

cooperation *or* **co-operation** (kəʊˌɒpə'reɪʃən) *n* **1** joint operation or action. **2** assistance or willingness to assist. **3** *Economics.* the combination of consumers, workers, farmers, etc., in activities usually embracing production, distribution, or trade. **4** *Ecology.* beneficial but inessential interaction between two species in a community. ▸ **coˌoper'ationist** *or* **co-ˌoper'ationist** *n*

cooperative *or* **co-operative** (kəʊ'ɒpərətɪv, -'ɒprə-) *adj* **1** willing to cooperate; helpful. **2** acting in conjunction with others; cooperating. **3a** (of an enterprise, farm, etc.) owned collectively and managed for joint economic benefit. **3b** (of an economy or economic activity) based on collective ownership and cooperative use of the means of production and distribution. ◆ *n* **4** a cooperative organization. **5** Also called: **cooperative apartment.** *U.S.* a block of flats belonging to a corporation in which shares are owned in proportion to the relative value of the flat occupied. Sometimes shortened to **coop.** Compare **condominium** (sense 3). ▸ **co'operatively** *or* **co-'operatively** *adv* ▸ **co'operativeness** *or* **co-'operativeness** *n*

cooperative bank *n* a U.S. name for **building society.**

cooperative farm *n* **1** a farm that is run in cooperation with others in the purchasing and using of machinery, stock, etc., and in the marketing of produce through its own institutions (**farmers' cooperatives**). **2** a farm that is owned by a cooperative society. **3** a farm run on a communal basis, such as a kibbutz. **4** another name for **collective farm.**

Cooperative Party *n* (in Great Britain) a political party supporting the cooperative movement and linked with the Labour Party: founded in 1917.

cooperative society *n* a commercial enterprise owned and managed by and for the benefit of customers or workers. Often shortened to **coop, co-op.**

cooperativity (kəʊˌɒpərə'tɪvɪtɪ) *n Biochem., chem.* an interaction between structural units within a molecule or between molecules in an assemblage that enables the system to respond more sharply to an external change than would isolated units.

Cooper Creek *n* an intermittent river in E central Australia, in the Channel Country: rises in central Queensland and flows generally southwest, reaching Lake Eyre only during wet-year floods; scene of the death of the explorers Burke and Wills in 1861; the surrounding basin provides cattle pastures after the floods subside. Total length: 1420 km (880 miles).

Cooper pair *n Physics.* a pair of weakly bound electrons responsible for the transfer of charge in a superconducting material. [C20: named after Leon Neil COOPER]

Cooper's hawk *n* a small North American hawk, *Accipiter cooperii,* having a bluish-grey back and wings and a reddish-brown breast. [C19: named after William *Cooper* (died 1864), American naturalist]

coopery ('ku:pərɪ) *n, pl* **-eries.** another word for **cooperage** (sense 1).

coopt *or* **co-opt** (kəʊ'ɒpt) *vb (tr)* **1** to add (someone) to a committee, board, etc., by the agreement of the existing members. **2** to appoint summarily; commandeer. [C17: from Latin *cooptāre* to elect, from *optāre* to choose] ▸ **co'option, co-'option** *or* **ˌcoop'tation, ˌco-op'tation** *n* ▸ **co'optative** *or* **co-'optative** *adj*

Coopworth ('ku:pˌwɜ:θ) *n* a New Zealand breed of sheep derived from the Romney Marsh.

coordinal *or* **co-ordinal** (kəʊ'ɔ:dɪnᵊl) *adj* (of animals or plants) belonging to the same order.

coordinate *or* **co-ordinate** *vb* (kəʊ'ɔ:dɪˌneɪt). **1** *(tr)* to organize or integrate (diverse elements) in a harmonious operation. **2** to place (things) in the same class or order, or (of things) to be placed in the same class or order. **3** *(intr)* to work together, esp. harmoniously. **4** *(intr)* to take or be in the form of a harmonious order. **5** *Chem.* to form or cause to form a coordinate bond. ◆ *n* (kəʊ'ɔ:dɪnɪt, -ˌneɪt) **6** *Maths.* any of a set of numbers that defines the location of a point in space with reference to a system of axes. See **Cartesian coordinates, polar coordinates. 7** a person or thing equal in rank, type, etc. ◆ *adj* (kəʊ'ɔ:dɪnɪt, -ˌneɪt). **8** of, concerned with, or involving coordination. **9** of the same rank, type, etc. **10** of or involving the use of coordinates: *coordinate geometry.* ◆ See also **coordinates.** ▸ **co'ordinately** *or* **co-'ordinately** *adv* ▸ **co'ordinateness** *or* **co-'ordinateness** *n* ▸ **co'ordinative** *or* **co-'ordinative** *adj* ▸ **co'ordiˌnator** *or* **co-'ordiˌnator** *n*

coordinate bond *n* a type of covalent chemical bond in which both the shared electrons are provided by one of the atoms. Also called: **dative bond, semipolar bond.**

coordinate clause *n* one of two or more clauses in a sentence having the same status and introduced by coordinating conjunctions. Compare **subordinate clause.**

coordinate geometry *n* another term for **analytical geometry.**

coordinates (kəʊ'ɔ:dɪnɪts, -ˌneɪts) *pl n* clothes of matching or harmonious colours and design, suitable for wearing together. Compare **separates.**

coordinating conjunction *n* a conjunction that introduces coordinate clauses, such as *and, but,* and *or.* Compare **subordinating conjunction.**

coordination *or* **co-ordination** (kəʊˌɔ:dɪ'neɪʃən) *n* balanced and effective interaction of movement, actions, etc. [C17: from Late Latin *coordinātiō,* from Latin *ordinātiō* an arranging; see ORDINATE]

coordination compound *n* another name for **complex** (sense 8).

coordination number *n Chem.* the number of coordinated species surrounding the central atom in a complex or crystal.

Coorg (kʊəg) *n* a former province of SW India: since 1956 part of Karnataka state.

coorie ('ku:rɪ) *vb (intr) Scot.* a variant spelling of **courie.**

coot (ku:t) *n* **1** any aquatic bird of the genus *Fulica,* esp. *F. atra* of Europe and Asia, having lobed toes, dark plumage, and a white bill with a frontal shield: family *Rallidae* (rails, crakes, etc.). **2** a foolish person, esp. an old man (often in the phrase **old coot**). [C14: probably from Low German; compare Dutch *koet*]

cootch *or* **cwtch** (kʊtʃ) *South Wales dialect.* ◆ *n* **1** a hiding place. **2** a room, shed, etc., used for storage: *a coal cootch.* ◆ *vb* **3** *(tr)* to hide. **4** (often foll. by *up*) to cuddle or be cuddled. **5** *(tr)* to clasp (someone or something) to oneself. [from French *couche* COUCH, probably influenced by Welsh *cwt* hut]

cootie ('ku:tɪ) *n U.S. and N.Z.* a slang name for the **body louse.** See **louse** (sense 1). Also called (N.Z.) **kutu.** [C20: perhaps from Malay or Maori *kutu* louse]

cop[1] (kɒp) *Slang.* ◆ *n* **1** another name for **policeman. 2** *Brit.* an arrest (esp. in the phrase **a fair cop**). **3** an instance of plagiarism. ◆ *vb* **cops, copping, copped.** *(tr)* **4** to seize or catch. **5** to steal. **6** to buy, steal, or otherwise obtain (illegal drugs). Compare **score** (sense 26). **7** to suffer (a punishment): *you'll cop a clout if you do that!* Also in the phrase **cop it. 8 cop it sweet.** *Austral. slang.* **8a** to accept a penalty without complaint. **8b** to have good fortune. ◆ See also

cop out. [C18: (vb) perhaps from obsolete *cap* to arrest, from Old French *caper* to seize; sense 1, back formation from COPPER[2]]

cop[2] (kɒp) *n* **1** a conical roll of thread wound on a spindle. **2** *Now chiefly dialect.* the top or crest, as of a hill. [Old English *cop, copp* top, summit, of uncertain origin; perhaps related to Old English *copp* CUP]

cop[3] (kɒp) *n Brit. slang.* (*usually used with a negative*) worth or value: *that work is not much cop.* [C19: n use of COP[1] (in the sense: to catch, hence something caught, something of value)]

COP (in New Zealand) *abbrev. for* Certificate of Proficiency: a pass in a university subject.

copacetic, copasetic *or* **copesetic, copesettic** (ˌkəʊpəˈsɛtɪk) *adj U.S. and Canadian slang.* very good; excellent; completely satisfactory. [C20: of unknown origin]

copaiba (kəʊˈpaɪbə) *or* **copaiva** (kəʊˈpaɪvə) *n* a transparent yellowish viscous oleoresin obtained from certain tropical South American trees of the caesalpiniaceous genus *Copaifera:* used in varnishes and ointments. Also called: **copaiba balsam, copaiba resin.** [C18: via Spanish via Portuguese from Tupi]

copal (ˈkəʊpᵊl, -pæl) *n* a hard aromatic resin, yellow, orange, or red in colour, obtained from various tropical trees and used in making varnishes and lacquers. [C16: from Spanish, from Nahuatl *copalli* resin]

copalm (ˈkəʊˌpɑːm) *n* **1** the aromatic brown resin obtained from the sweet gum tree. **2** another name for the **sweet gum.** [C19: from Louisiana French, from Mexican Spanish *copalme;* see COPAL, PALMATE]

Copán (*Spanish* koˈpan) *n* a town in W Honduras: site of a ruined Mayan city. Pop.: 21 200 (1991).

coparcenary (kəʊˈpɑːsənərɪ) *or* **coparceny** (kəʊˈpɑːsɪnɪ) *n Law.* a form of joint ownership of property, esp. joint heirship. Also called: **parcenary.**

coparcener (kəʊˈpɑːsɪnə) *n Law.* a person who inherits an estate as coheir with others. Also called: **parcener.**

copartner (kəʊˈpɑːtnə) *n* a partner or associate, esp. an equal partner in business.

copartnership (kəʊˈpɑːtnəʃɪp) *n* **1** a partnership or association between two equals, esp. in a business enterprise. **2** a form of industrial democracy in which the employees of an organization are partners in the company and share in part of its profits.

cope[1] (kəʊp) *vb* **1** (*intr;* foll. by *with*) to contend (against). **2** (*intr*) to deal successfully with or handle a situation; manage: *she coped well with the problem.* **3** (*tr*) *Archaic.* **3a** to deal with. **3b** to meet in battle. [C14: from Old French *coper* to strike, cut, from *coup* blow; see COUP[1]]

cope[2] (kəʊp) *n* **1** a large ceremonial cloak worn at solemn liturgical functions by priests of certain Christian sects. **2** any covering shaped like a cope. ◆ *vb* **3** (*tr*) to dress (someone) in a cope. [Old English *cāp,* from Medieval Latin *cāpa,* from Late Latin *cappa* hooded cloak; see CAP]

cope[3] (kəʊp) *vb* (*tr*) **1** to provide (a wall) with a coping. **2** to join (two moulded timber members). ◆ *n* **3** another name for **coping.** [C17: probably from French *couper* to cut; see COPE[1]]

copeck (ˈkəʊpɛk) *n* a variant spelling of **kopeck.**

Copenhagen (ˌkəʊpənˈheɪgən, -ˈhɑː-; ˈkəʊpənˌheɪ-, -ˌhɑː-) *n* the capital of Denmark, a port on Zealand and Amager Islands on a site inhabited for some 6000 years: exports chiefly agricultural products; iron and steel works; university (1479). Pop. (urban area): 1 362 264 (1996 est.). Danish name: **København.**

Copenhagen blue *n* **a** a greyish-blue colour. **b** (*as adj*): *Copenhagen-blue markings.*

Copenhagen interpretation *n* an interpretation of quantum mechanics developed by Niels Bohr and his colleagues at the University of Copenhagen, based on the concept of wave–particle duality and the idea that the observation influences the result of an experiment.

copepod (ˈkəʊpɪˌpɒd) *n* **1** any minute free-living or parasitic crustacean of the subclass *Copepoda* of marine and fresh waters: an important constituent of plankton. ◆ *adj* **2** of, relating to, or belonging to the *Copepoda.* [C19: from New Latin *Copepoda,* from Greek *kōpē* oar + *pous* foot]

coper (ˈkəʊpə) *n* a horse-dealer. [C17 (a dealer, chapman): from dialect *cope* to buy, barter, from Low German; related to Dutch *koopen* to buy]

Copernican system *n* the theory published in 1543 by Copernicus which stated that the earth and the planets rotated around the sun and which opposed the Ptolemaic system.

Copernicus[1] (kəˈpɜːnɪkəs) *n* **Nicolaus** (ˌnɪkəˈleɪəs). Polish name *Mikolaj Kopernik.* 1473–1543, Polish astronomer, whose theory of the solar system (the **Copernican system**) was published in 1543. ▸ **Coˈpernican** *adj*

Copernicus[2] (kəˈpɜːnɪkəs) *n* a conspicuous crater on the moon, over 4000 metres deep and 90 kilometres in diameter, from which a system of rays emanates.

copestone (ˈkəʊpˌstəʊn) *n* **1** Also called: **coping stone.** a stone used to form a coping. **2** Also called: **capstone.** the stone at the top of a building, wall, etc.

copier (ˈkɒpɪə) *n* **1** a person or device that copies. **2** another word for **copyist.**

copilot (ˈkəʊˌpaɪlət) *n* a second or relief pilot of an aircraft.

coping (ˈkəʊpɪŋ) *n* the sloping top course of a wall, usually made of masonry or brick. Also called: **cope.**

coping saw *n* a handsaw with a U-shaped frame used for cutting curves in a material too thick for a fret saw.

coping stone *n* another word for **copestone** (sense 1).

copious (ˈkəʊpɪəs) *adj* **1** abundant; extensive in quantity. **2** having or providing an abundant supply. **3** full of words, ideas, etc.; profuse. [C14: from Latin *cōpiōsus* well supplied, from *cōpia* abundance, from *ops* wealth] ▸ **ˈcopiously** *adv* ▸ **ˈcopiousness** *n*

copita (*Spanish* koˈpita; *English* kəˈpiːtə) *n* **1** a tulip-shaped sherry glass. **2** a glass of sherry. [diminutive of *copa* cup]

coplanar (kəʊˈpleɪnə) *adj* lying in the same plane: *coplanar lines.* ▸ **ˌcoplaˈnarity** *n*

Copland (ˈkəʊplənd) *n* **Aaron.** 1900–90, U.S. composer of orchestral and chamber music, ballets, and film music.

Copley (ˈkɒplɪ) *n* **John Singleton.** 1738–1815, U.S. painter.

copolymer (kəʊˈpɒlɪmə) *n* a chemical compound of high molecular weight formed by uniting the molecules of two or more different compounds (monomers). Compare **polymer, oligomer.**

copolymerize *or* **copolymerise** (kəʊˈpɒlɪməˌraɪz) *vb* to react (two compounds) together to produce a copolymer. ▸ **coˌpolymeriˈzation** *or* **coˌpolymeriˈsation** *n*

cop out *Slang.* ◆ *vb* **1** (*intr, adv*) to fail to assume responsibility or to commit oneself. ◆ *n* **cop-out. 2** an instance of avoiding responsibility or commitment. **3** a person who acts in this way. [C20: probably from COP[1]]

copper[1] (ˈkɒpə) *n* **1a** a malleable ductile reddish metallic element occurring as the free metal, copper glance, and copper pyrites: used as an electrical and thermal conductor and in such alloys as brass and bronze. Symbol: Cu; atomic no.: 29; atomic wt.: 63.546; valency: 1 or 2; relative density: 8.96; melting pt.: 1084.87±0.2°C; boiling pt.: 2563°C. Related adjs.: **cupric, cuprous.** Related prefix: **cupro-. 1b** (*as modifier*): *a copper coin.* **2a** the reddish-brown colour of copper. **2b** (*as adj*): *copper hair.* **3** *Informal.* any copper or bronze coin. **4** *Chiefly Brit.* a large vessel, formerly of copper, used for boiling or washing. **5** any of various small widely distributed butterflies of the genera *Lycaena, Heodes,* etc., typically having reddish-brown wings: family *Lycaenidae.* ◆ *vb* **6** (*tr*) to coat or cover with copper. [Old English *coper,* from Latin *Cyprium aes* Cyprian metal, from Greek *Kupris* Cyprus] ▸ **ˈcoppery** *adj*

copper[2] (ˈkɒpə) *n* a slang word for **policeman.** Often shortened to **cop.** [C19: from COP[1] (vb) + -ER[1]]

copperas (ˈkɒpərəs) *n* a less common name for **ferrous sulphate.** [C14: *coperose,* via Old French from Medieval Latin *cuperosa,* perhaps originally in the phrase *aqua cuprosa* copper water]

copper beech *n* a cultivated variety of European beech that has reddish leaves.

Copper Belt *n* a region of Central Africa, along the border between Zambia and the Democratic Republic of the Congo: rich deposits of copper.

copper-bottomed *adj* reliable, esp. financially reliable. [from the former practice of coating the bottoms of ships with copper to prevent the timbers rotting]

copper-fasten *vb* (*tr*) *Irish.* to make (a bargain or agreement) binding.

copperhead (ˈkɒpəˌhɛd) *n* **1** a venomous reddish-brown snake, *Agkistrodon contortrix,* of the eastern U.S.: family *Crotalidae* (pit vipers). **2** a venomous reddish-brown Australian elapid snake, *Denisonia superba.* **3** *U.S. informal.* a Yankee supporter of the South during the Civil War.

copperplate (ˈkɒpəˌpleɪt) *n* **1** a polished copper plate on which a design has been etched or engraved. **2** a print taken from such a plate. **3** a fine handwriting based upon that used on copperplate engravings.

copper pyrites (ˈpaɪraɪts) *n* (*functioning as sing*) another name for **chalcopyrite.**

coppersmith (ˈkɒpəˌsmɪθ) *n* **1** a person who works copper or copper alloys. **2** an Asian barbet (a bird), *Megalaima haemacephala,* the call of which has a ringing metallic note.

copper sulphate *n* a copper salt found naturally as chalcanthite and made by the action of sulphuric acid on copper oxide. It usually exists as blue crystals of the pentahydrate that form a white anhydrous powder when heated: used as a mordant, in electroplating, and in plant sprays. Formula: $CuSO_4$.

coppice (ˈkɒpɪs) *n* **1** a thicket or dense growth of small trees or bushes, esp. one regularly trimmed back to stumps so that a continual supply of small poles and firewood is obtained. ◆ *vb* **2** (*tr*) to trim back (trees or bushes) to form a coppice. **3** (*intr*) to form a coppice. [C14: from Old French *copeiz,* from *couper* to cut] ▸ **ˈcoppiced** *adj* ▸ **ˈcoppicing** *n*

Coppola (ˈkɒpələ) *n* **Francis Ford.** born 1939, U.S. film director. His films include *The Godfather* (1972), *Apocalypse Now* (1979), and *Tucker* (1988).

copra (ˈkɒprə) *n* the dried, oil-yielding kernel of the coconut. [C16: from Portuguese, from Malayalam *koppara,* probably from Hindi *khoprā* coconut]

copro- *or before a vowel* **copr-** *combining form.* indicating dung or obscenity: *coprology.* [from Greek *kopros* dung]

coprocessor (ˌkəʊˈprəʊsɛsə) *n Computing.* a microprocessor circuit that operates alongside and supplements the capabilities of the main processor, providing, for example, high-speed arithmetic.

coprolalia (ˌkɒprəˈleɪlɪə) *n* obsessive use of obscene or foul language.

coprolite (ˈkɒprəˌlaɪt) *n* any of various rounded stony nodules thought to be the fossilized faeces of Mesozoic reptiles. ▸ **coprolitic** (ˌkɒprəˈlɪtɪk) *adj*

coprology (kɒpˈrɒlədʒɪ) *n* preoccupation with excrement. Also called: **scatology.**

coprophagous (kɒˈprɒfəgəs) *adj* (esp. of certain beetles) feeding on dung. ▸ **copˈrophagy** *n*

coprophilia (ˌkɒprəʊˈfɪlɪə) *n* an abnormal interest in faeces and their evacuation.

coprophilous (kəˈprɒfɪləs) *or* **coprophilic** (ˌkɒprəʊˈfɪlɪk) *adj* growing in or on dung.

coprosma (kəˈprɒzmə) *n* any shrub of the Australasian rubiaceous genus *Coprosma:* sometimes planted for ornament. [C19: New Latin, from Greek *kopros* excrement + *osmē* smell]

coprozoic (ˌkɒprəʊˈzəʊɪk) *adj* (of animals) living in dung.

copse (kɒps) *n* another word for **coppice** (sense 1). [C16: by shortening from COPPICE]

Copt (kɒpt) *n* **1** a member of the Coptic Church. **2** an Egyptian descended from the ancient Egyptians. [C17: from Arabic *qubt* Copts, from Coptic *kyptios* Egyptian, from Greek *Aiguptios,* from *Aiguptos* Egypt]

copter *or* **'copter** ('kɒptə) *n Informal.* short for **helicopter.**

Coptic ('kɒptɪk) *n* **1** an Afro-Asiatic language, written in the Greek alphabet but descended from ancient Egyptian. It was extinct as a spoken language by about 1600 A.D. but survives in the Coptic Church. ◆ *adj* **2** of or relating to this language. **3** of or relating to the Copts.

Coptic Church *n* the ancient Christian Church of Egypt.

copula ('kɒpjʊlə) *n, pl* **-las** *or* **-lae** (-ˌliː). **1** a verb, such as *be, seem,* or *taste,* that is used merely to identify or link the subject with the complement of a sentence. Copulas may serve to link nouns (or pronouns), as in *he became king,* nouns (or pronouns) and adjectival complements, as in *sugar tastes sweet,* or nouns (or pronouns) and adverbial complements, as in *John is in jail.* **2** anything that serves as a link. **3** *Logic.* the often unexpressed link between the subject and predicate terms of a categorial proposition, as *are* in *all men are mortal.* [C17: from Latin: bond, connection, from *co-* together + *apere* to fasten] ▸ **'copular** *adj*

copulate ('kɒpjʊˌleɪt) *vb* (*intr*) to perform sexual intercourse. [C17: from Latin *copulāre* to join together; see COPULA] ▸ **ˌcopu'lation** *n* ▸ **'copulatory** *adj*

copulative ('kɒpjʊlətɪv) *adj* **1** serving to join or unite. **2** of or characteristic of copulation. **3** *Grammar.* (of a verb) having the nature of a copula. ▸ **'copulatively** *adv*

copy ('kɒpɪ) *n, pl* **copies. 1** an imitation or reproduction of an original. **2** a single specimen of something that occurs in a multiple edition, such as a book, article, etc. **3a** matter to be reproduced in print. **3b** written matter or text as distinct from graphic material in books, newspapers, etc. **4** the words used to present a promotional message in an advertisement. **5** *Journalism, informal.* suitable material for an article or story: *disasters are always good copy.* **6** *Archaic.* a model to be copied, esp. an example of penmanship. ◆ *vb* **copies, copying, copied. 7** (when *tr,* often foll. by *out*) to make a copy or reproduction of (an original). **8** (*tr*) to imitate as a model. **9** (*intr*) to imitate unfairly. [C14: from Medieval Latin *cōpia* an imitation, something copied, from Latin: abundance, riches; see COPIOUS]

copybook ('kɒpɪˌbʊk) *n* **1** a book of specimens, esp. of penmanship, for imitation. **2** *Chiefly U.S.* a book for or containing documents. **3 blot one's copybook.** *Informal.* to spoil one's reputation by making a mistake, offending against social customs, etc. **4** (*modifier*) trite or unoriginal: *copybook sentiments.*

copycat ('kɒpɪˌkæt) *n Informal.* **a** a person, esp. a child, who imitates or copies another. **b** (*as modifier*): *copycat murders.*

copy desk *n Journalism.* a desk where copy is edited.

copy-edit *vb Journalism, etc.* to prepare (copy) for printing by styling, correcting, etc. ▸ **copy editor** *n*

copygraph ('kɒpɪˌgrɑːf, -ˌgræf) *n* another name for **hectograph.**

copyhold ('kɒpɪˌhəʊld) *n Law.* (formerly) **a** a tenure less than freehold of land in England evidenced by a copy of the Court roll. **b** land held in this way.

copyholder ('kɒpɪˌhəʊldə) *n* **1** *Printing.* one who reads aloud from the copy as the proof corrector follows the reading in the proof. **2** *Printing.* a device that holds copy in place for the compositor. **3** *Law.* (formerly) a person who held land by copyhold tenure.

copyist ('kɒpɪɪst) *n* **1** a person who makes written copies; transcriber. **2** a person who imitates or copies.

copyread ('kɒpɪˌriːd) *vb* **-reads, -reading, -read.** *U.S.* to subedit.

copyreader ('kɒpɪˌriːdə) *n U.S.* a person who edits and prepares newspaper copy for publication; subeditor.

copyright ('kɒpɪˌraɪt) *n* **1** the exclusive right to produce copies and to control an original literary, musical, or artistic work, granted by law for a specified number of years (in Britain, usually 70 years from the death of the author, composer, etc., or from the date of publication if later). Symbol: © ◆ *adj* **2** (of a work, etc.) subject to or controlled by copyright. ◆ *vb* **3** (*tr*) to take out a copyright on. ▸ **'copyˌrightable** *adj* ▸ **'copyˌrighter** *n*

copyright deposit library *n* one of six libraries legally entitled to receive a gratis copy of every book published in the United Kingdom: the British Library, Bodleian, Cambridge University, Trinity College in Dublin, Scottish National Library, and National Library of Wales.

copytaker ('kɒpɪˌteɪkə) *n* (esp. in a newspaper office) a person employed to type reports as journalists dictate them over the telephone.

copy taster *n* a person who selects or approves text for publication, esp. in a periodical.

copy typist *n* a typist whose job is to type from written or typed drafts rather than dictation.

copywriter ('kɒpɪˌraɪtə) *n* a person employed to write advertising copy. ▸ **'copyˌwriting** *n*

coq au vin *French.* (kɔk o vɛ̃) *n* chicken stewed with red wine, onions, etc. [literally: cock with wine]

coquelicot ('kəʊklɪˌkəʊ) *n* another name for **corn poppy.** [C18: from French: crow of a cock, from its resemblance to a cock's comb]

coquet (kəʊ'kɛt, kɒ-) *vb* **-quets, -quetting, -quetted.** (*intr*) **1** to behave flirtatiously. **2** to dally or trifle. [C17: from French: a gallant, literally: a little cock, from *coq* cock]

coquetry ('kəʊkɪtrɪ, 'kɒk-) *n, pl* **-ries.** flirtation.

coquette (kəʊ'kɛt, kɒ'kɛt) *n* **1** a woman who flirts. **2** any hummingbird of the genus *Lophornis,* esp. the crested Brazilian species *L. magnifica.* [C17: from French, feminine of COQUET] ▸ **co'quettish** *adj* ▸ **co'quettishly** *adv* ▸ **co'quettishness** *n*

coquilla nut (kɒ'kiːljə) *n* the nut of a South American palm tree, *Attalea funifera,* having a hard brown shell used for carving. See also **cohune.** [C19: from Portuguese *coquilho,* diminutive of *côco* coconut; see COCO]

coquille (*French* kɔkij) *n* **1** any dish, esp. seafood, served in a scallop shell: *Coquilles St. Jacques.* **2** a scallop shell, or dish resembling a shell. **3** *Fencing.* a bell-shaped hand guard on a foil. [French, literally: shell, from Latin *conchȳlium* mussel; see COCKLE[1]]

coquimbite (kɒ'kɪmbaɪt) *n Mineralogy.* hydrated ferric sulphate found in certain rocks and in volcanic fumaroles. [C19: from *Coquimbo,* Chilean province where it was originally found, + -ITE[1]]

coquina (kɒ'kiːnə) *n* a soft limestone containing shells, corals, etc., that occurs in parts of the U.S. [C19: from Spanish: shellfish, probably from *concha* shell, CONCH]

coquito (kɒ'kiːtəʊ) *n, pl* **-tos.** a Chilean palm tree, *Jubaea spectabilis,* yielding edible nuts and a syrup. [C19: from Spanish: a little coco palm, from *coco* coco palm]

cor (kɔː) *interj Brit. slang.* an exclamation of surprise, amazement, or admiration. [C20: corruption of *God*]

cor. *abbrev. for:* **1** corner. **2** cornet. **3** coroner.

Cor. *Bible. abbrev. for* Corinthians.

coraciiform (ˌkɒrə'saɪɪˌfɔːm) *adj* of, relating to, or belonging to the *Coraciiformes,* an order of birds including the kingfishers, bee-eaters, hoopoes, and hornbills. [C20: from New Latin *Coracias* name of genus, from Greek *korakias* a chough + -I- + -FORM; related to Greek *korax* raven]

coracle ('kɒrək°l) *n* a small roundish boat made of waterproofed hides stretched over a wicker frame. [C16: from Welsh *corwgl;* related to Irish *curach* boat]

coracoid ('kɒrəˌkɔɪd) *n* a paired ventral bone of the pectoral girdle in vertebrates. In mammals it is reduced to a peg (the **coracoid process**) on the scapula. [C18: from New Latin *coracoīdēs,* from Greek *korakoeidēs* like a raven, curved like a raven's beak, from *korax* raven]

coral ('kɒrəl) *n* **1** any marine mostly colonial coelenterate of the class *Anthozoa* having a calcareous, horny, or soft skeleton. See also **stony coral, sea fan. 2a** the calcareous or horny material forming the skeleton of certain of these animals. **2b** (*as modifier*): *a coral reef.* See also **red coral. 3a** a rocklike aggregation of certain of these animals or their skeletons, forming an island or reef. **3b** (*as modifier*): *a coral island.* **4a** an object made of coral, esp. a piece of jewellery. **4b** (*as modifier*): *a coral necklace.* **5a** a deep-pink to yellowish-pink colour. **5b** (*as adj*): *coral lipstick.* **6** the roe of a lobster or crab, which becomes pink when cooked. [C14: from Old French, from Latin *corāllium,* from Greek *korallion,* probably of Semitic origin]

coral fern *n Austral.* a scrambling fern of the genus *Gleichenia,* having repeatedly forked fronds.

coralline ('kɒrəˌlaɪn) *adj* **1** Also: **coralloid.** of, relating to, or resembling coral. **2** of the colour of coral. ◆ *n* **3** any of various red algae impregnated with calcium carbonate, esp. any of the genus *Corallina.* **4** any of various animals that resemble coral, such as certain sponges. [C16: from Late Latin *corallīnus* coral red, from Latin *corāllium* CORAL]

corallite ('kɒrəlaɪt) *n* the skeleton of a coral polyp.

coralloid ('kɒrəlɔɪd) *adj* of or resembling coral.

coral reef *n* a marine ridge or reef consisting of coral and other organic material consolidated into limestone.

coralroot ('kɒrəlˌruːt) *n* any N temperate leafless orchid of the genus *Corallorhiza,* with small yellow-green or purple flowers and branched roots resembling coral.

Coral Sea *n* the SW arm of the Pacific, between Australia, New Guinea, and Vanuatu.

coral snake *n* **1** any venomous elapid snake of the genus *Micrurus* and related genera, of tropical and subtropical America, marked with red, black, yellow, and white transverse bands. **2** any of various other brightly coloured elapid snakes of Africa and SE Asia.

coral tree *n Austral.* any of various thorny trees of the papilionaceous genus *Erythrina,* having bright red flowers and reddish shiny seeds.

coram populo Latin. ('kɔːræm 'pɒpʊˌləʊ) *adv* in the presence of the people; publicly.

cor anglais ('kɔːr 'ɑːŋgleɪ) *n, pl* **cors anglais** ('kɔːz 'ɑːŋgleɪ). *Music.* a woodwind instrument, the alto of the oboe family. It is a transposing instrument in F. Range: two and a half octaves upwards from E on the third space of the bass staff. Also called: **English horn.** [C19: from French: English horn]

Corantijn ('kɒranˌtejn) *n* the Dutch name of **Courantyne.**

coranto (kɒ'ræntəʊ) *n, pl* **-tos.** a variant of **courante.**

corban ('kɔːbᵊn; *Hebrew* kɔr'ban) *n* **1** *Old Testament.* a gift to God. **2** *New Testament, Judaism.* the Temple treasury or a consecration or gift to it (Matthew 27:6; Mark 7:11). [C14: from Late Latin, from Greek *korban,* from Hebrew *qorbān* offering, literally: a drawing near]

corbeil *or* **corbeille** ('kɔːbᵊl; *French* kɔrbɛj) *n Architect.* a carved ornament in the form of a basket of fruit, flowers, etc. [C18: from French *corbeille* basket, from Late Latin *corbicula* a little basket, from Latin *corbis* basket]

corbel ('kɔːbᵊl) *Architect.* ◆ *n* **1** Also called: **truss.** a bracket, usually of stone or brick. ◆ *vb* **-bels, -belling, -belled** *or U.S.* **-bels, -beling, -beled. 2** (*tr*) to lay (a stone or brick) so that it forms a corbel. [C15: from Old French, literally: a little raven, from Medieval Latin *corvellus,* from Latin *corvus* raven]

corbelling *or U.S.* **corbeling** ('kɔːbəlɪŋ) *n* a set of corbels stepped outwards, one above another.

corbel out *or* **off** *vb* (*tr, adv*) to support on corbels.

Corbett ('kɔːbət) *n Mountaineering.* any separate mountain peak between 2500 feet and 3000 feet high: originally used of Scotland only, but now sometimes extended to other parts of the British Isles.

corbicula (kɔː'bɪkjʊlə) *n, pl* **-lae** (-ˌliː). the technical name for **pollen basket.** [C19: from Late Latin, diminutive of Latin *corbis* basket]

corbie ('kɔːbɪ; *Scot.* 'kɔːrbɪ) *n* a Scot. name for **raven**[1] or **crow**[1]. [C15: from Old French *corbin,* from Latin *corvīnus* CORVINE]

corbie gable *n Architect.* a gable having corbie-steps.

corbie-step *or* **corbel step** *n Architect.* any of a set of steps on the top of a gable. Also called: **crow step.**

cor blimey ('kɔː 'blaɪmɪ) *or* **gorblimey** *interj Brit. slang.* an exclamation of surprise or annoyance. [C20: corruption of *God blind me*]

Corbusier (*French* kɔrbyzje) *n* **Le.** See **Le Corbusier.**

Corby ('kɔːbɪ) *n* a town in central England, in N Northamptonshire: designated a new town in 1950. Pop.: 49 053 (1991).

Corcovado *n* **1** (*Spanish* korko'βaðo). a volcano in S Chile, in the Andes. Height: 2300 m (7546 ft.). **2** (*Portuguese* korku'vaːdu). a mountain in SE Brazil, in SW Rio de Janeiro city. Height: 704 m (2310 ft.).

Corcyra (kɔː'saɪərə) *n* the ancient name for **Corfu.**

cord (kɔːd) *n* **1** string or thin rope made of several twisted strands. **2** a length of woven or twisted strands of silk, etc., sewn on clothing or used as a belt. **3** a ribbed fabric, esp. corduroy. **4** any influence that binds or restrains. **5** the U.S. and Canadian name for **flex** (sense 1). **6** *Anatomy.* any part resembling a string or rope: *the spinal cord.* **7** a unit of volume for measuring cut wood, equal to 128 cubic feet. ◆ *vb* (*tr*) **8** to bind or furnish with a cord or cords. **9** to stack (wood) in cords. [C13: from Old French *corde,* from Latin *chorda* cord, from Greek *khordē;* see CHORD[1]] ▸ **'corder** *n* ▸ **'cord,like** *adj*

cordage ('kɔːdɪdʒ) *n* **1** *Nautical.* the lines and rigging of a vessel. **2** an amount of wood measured in cords.

cordate ('kɔːdeɪt) *adj* heart-shaped: *a cordate leaf; cordate shells.* ▸ **'cordately** *adv*

Corday (*French* kɔrdɛ) *n* **Charlotte** (ʃarlɔt), full name *Marie Anne Charlotte Corday d'Armont.* 1768–93, French Girondist revolutionary, who assassinated Marat.

corded ('kɔːdɪd) *adj* **1** bound or fastened with cord. **2** (of a fabric) ribbed. **3** (of muscles) standing out like cords.

Cordelier (,kɔːdɪ'lɪə) *n R.C. Church.* a Franciscan friar of the order of the Friars Minor. [C19: from Old French *cordelle,* literally: a little cord, from the knotted cord girdles that they wear]

Cordeliers (,kɔːdɪ'lɪəz) *n* **the.** a political club founded in 1790 and meeting at an old Cordelier convent in Paris.

cord grass *n* a coarse perennial grass of the genus *Spartina,* characteristically growing in mud or marsh. Also called: **rice grass.**

cordial ('kɔːdɪəl) *adj* **1** warm and friendly: *a cordial greeting.* **2** giving heart; stimulating. ◆ *n* **3** a drink with a fruit base, usually sold in concentrated form and diluted with water before being drunk: *lime cordial.* **4** another word for **liqueur.** [C14: from Medieval Latin *cordiālis,* from Latin *cor* heart] ▸ **'cordially** *adv* ▸ **'cordialness** *n*

cordiality (,kɔːdɪ'ælɪtɪ) *n, pl* **-ties.** warmth of feeling.

cordierite ('kɔːdɪə,raɪt) *n* a grey or violet-blue dichroic mineral that consists of magnesium aluminium iron silicate in orthorhombic crystalline form and is found in metamorphic rocks. Formula: $(MgFe_2)Al_4Si_5O_{18}$. Also called: **dichroite, iolite.** [C19: named after Pierre L. A. *Cordier* (1777–1861), French geologist who described it]

cordiform ('kɔːdɪ,fɔːm) *adj* heart-shaped. [C19: from Latin *cor* heart]

cordillera (,kɔːdɪl'jɛərə) *n* a series of parallel ranges of mountains, esp. in the northwestern U.S. [C18: from Spanish, from *cordilla,* literally: a little cord, from *cuerda* mountain range, CORD] ▸ **,cordil'leran** *adj*

Cordilleras (,kɔːdɪl'jɛərəz; *Spanish* korði'ʎeras) *pl n* **the.** the complex of mountain ranges on the W side of the Americas, extending from Alaska to Cape Horn and including the Andes and the Rocky Mountains.

cordite ('kɔːdaɪt) *n* any of various explosive materials used for propelling bullets, shells, etc., containing cellulose nitrate, sometimes mixed with nitroglycerine, plasticizers, and stabilizers. [C19: from CORD + -ITE[1], referring to its stringy appearance]

cordless ('kɔːdlɪs) *adj* (of an electrical device) operated by an internal battery so that no connection to mains supply or other apparatus is needed.

cordless telephone *n* a portable battery-powered telephone with a short-range radio link to a fixed base unit.

cordoba ('kɔːdəbə) *n* the standard monetary unit of Nicaragua, divided into 100 centavos. [Spanish *córdoba,* named in honour of Francisco Fernández de CÓRDOBA]

Córdoba[1] (*Spanish* 'korðoβa) *n* **1** a city in central Argentina: university (1613). Pop.: 1 208 713 (1991). **2** a city in S Spain, on the Guadalquivir River: centre of Moorish Spain (711–1236). Pop.: 323 138 (1995 est.). English name: **Cordova.**

Córdoba[2] *or* **Córdova** (*Spanish* 'korðoβa) *n* **Francisco Fernández de** (fran'θisko fɛr'nandeθ de). died 1518, Spanish soldier and explorer, who discovered Yucatán.

cordon ('kɔːdᵊn) *n* **1** a chain of police, soldiers, ships, etc., stationed around an area. **2** a ribbon worn as insignia of honour or rank. **3** a cord or ribbon worn as an ornament or fastening. **4** Also called: **string course, belt course, table.** *Architect.* an ornamental projecting band or continuous moulding along a wall. **5** *Horticulture.* a form of fruit tree consisting of a single stem bearing fruiting spurs, produced by cutting back all lateral branches. ◆ *vb* **6** (*tr;* often foll. by *off*) to put or form a cordon (around); close (off). [C16: from Old French, literally: a little cord, from *corde* string, CORD]

cordon bleu (*French* kɔrdɔ̃ blø) *n* **1** *French history.* **1a** the sky-blue ribbon worn by members of the highest order of knighthood under the Bourbon monarchy. **1b** a knight entitled to wear the cordon bleu. **2** any very high distinction. ◆ *adj* **3** of or denoting food prepared to a very high standard. [French, literally: blue ribbon]

cordon sanitaire *French.* (kɔrdɔ̃ saniter) *n* **1** a guarded line serving to cut off an infected area. **2** a line of buffer states, esp. when protecting a nation from infiltration or attack. [C19: literally: sanitary line]

Cordova ('kɔːdəvə) *n* the English name for **Córdoba**[1] (sense 2).

cordovan ('kɔːdəvᵊn) *n* a fine leather now made principally from horsehide, isolated from the skin layers above and below it and tanned. [C16: from Spanish *cordobán* (n), from *cordobán* (adj) of CÓRDOBA]

Cordovan ('kɔːdəvᵊn) *n* **1** a native or inhabitant of Córdoba, Spain. ◆ *adj* **2** of or relating to Córdoba, Spain.

cords (kɔːdz) *pl n* trousers, esp. jeans, made of corduroy.

corduroy ('kɔːdə,rɔɪ, ,kɔːdə'rɔɪ) *n* **a** a heavy cotton pile fabric with lengthways ribs. **b** (*as modifier*): *a corduroy coat.* ◆ See also **corduroys.** [C18: perhaps from the proper name *Corderoy*]

corduroy road *n* a road across swampy ground, made of logs laid transversely.

corduroys (,kɔːdə'rɔɪz, 'kɔːdə,rɔɪz) *pl n* trousers or breeches of corduroy.

cordwain ('kɔːd,weɪn) *n* an archaic name for **cordovan.** [C12 *cordewan,* from Old French *cordoan,* from Old Spanish *cordovan* CORDOVAN]

cordwainer ('kɔːd,weɪnə) *n Archaic.* a shoemaker or worker in cordovan leather. ▸ **'cord,wainery** *n*

cordwood ('kɔːd,wʊd) *n* wood that has been cut into lengths of four feet so that it can be stacked in cords.

core (kɔː) *n* **1** the central part of certain fleshy fruits, such as the apple or pear, consisting of the seeds and supporting parts. **2a** the central, innermost, or most essential part of something: *the core of the argument.* **2b** (*as modifier*): *the core meaning.* **3** a piece of magnetic material, such as soft iron, placed inside the windings of an electromagnet or transformer to intensify and direct the magnetic field. **4** *Geology.* the central part of the earth, beneath the mantle, consisting mainly of iron and nickel. **5** a cylindrical sample of rock, soil, etc., obtained by the use of a hollow drill. **6** shaped body of material (in metal casting usually of sand) supported inside a mould to form a cavity of predetermined shape in the finished casting. **7** *Physics.* the region of a nuclear reactor in which the reaction takes place. **8** a layer of wood serving as a backing for a veneer. **9** *Computing.* **9a** a ferrite ring formerly used in a computer memory to store one bit of information. **9b** short for **core store. 9c** (*as modifier*): *core memory.* **10** *Archaeol.* a lump of stone or flint from which flakes or blades have been removed. **11** *Physics.* the nucleus together with all complete electron shells of an atom. ◆ *vb* **12** (*tr*) to remove the core from (fruit). [C14: of uncertain origin] ▸ **'coreless** *adj*

CORE (kɔː) *n* (in the U.S.) *acronym for* Congress of Racial Equality.

coreferential (,kəʊrɛfə'rɛnʃəl) *adj Philosophy.* (of more than one linguistic expression) designating the same individual or class.

coreligionist (,kəʊrɪ'lɪdʒənɪst) *n* an adherent of the same religion as another.

corella (kə'rɛlə) *n* any of certain white Australian cockatoos of the genus *Kakatoe.* [C19: probably from native Australian *carall*]

Corelli (kɒ'rɛlɪ) *n* **1** (*Italian* ko'rɛlli) *n* **Arcangelo** (ar'kandʒelo). 1653–1713, Italian violinist and composer of sonatas and concerti grossi. **2 Marie,** real name *Mary Mackay.* 1854–1924, British novelist. Her melodramatic works include *The Sorrows of Satan* (1895) and *The Murder of Delicia* (1896).

coreopsis (,kɒrɪ'ɒpsɪs) *n* any plant of the genus *Coreopsis,* of America and tropical Africa, cultivated for their yellow, brown, or yellow-and-red daisy-like flowers: family *Compositae* (composites). Also called: **calliopsis.** Compare **caryopsis.** [C18: from New Latin, from Greek *koris* bedbug + -OPSIS; so called from the appearance of the seed]

co-respondent (,kəʊrɪ'spɒndənt) *n Law.* a person cited in divorce proceedings, who is alleged to have committed adultery with the respondent. ▸ **,co-re'spondency** *n*

co-respondent shoes *pl n* men's two-coloured shoes, usually black and white or brown and white. Also called: **co-respondents.**

core store *n* an obsolete type of computer memory made up of a matrix of cores.

core subjects *pl n Brit. education.* three foundation subjects (English, mathematics, and science) that are compulsory throughout each key stage in the National Curriculum.

core time *n* See **flexitime.**

corf (kɔːf) *n, pl* **corves.** *Brit.* a wagon or basket used formerly in mines. [C14: from Middle Dutch *corf* or Middle Low German *korf,* probably from Latin *corbis* basket]

Corfam ('kɔːfæm) *n Trademark.* a synthetic water-repellent material used as a substitute for shoe leather.

Corfu (kɔː'fuː) *n* **1** an island in the Ionian Sea, in the Ionian Islands: forms, with neighbouring islands, a department of Greece. Pop.: 107 592 (1991). Area: 641 sq. km (247 sq. miles). **2** a port on E Corfu island. Pop.: 105 000 (1995 est.). Modern Greek name: **Kérkyra.** Ancient name: **Corcyra.**

corgi ('kɔːgɪ) *n* either of two long-bodied short-legged sturdy breeds of dog, the Cardigan and the Pembroke. Also called: **Welsh corgi.** [C20: from Welsh, from *cor* dwarf + *ci* dog]

Cori ('kɔːrɪ) *n* **Carl Ferdinand.** 1896–1984, U.S. biochemist, born in Bohemia; shared a Nobel prize for physiology or medicine (1947) with his wife **Gerty Theresa Radnitz Cori** (1896–1957) and Bernardo Houssay, for elucidating the stages of glycolysis.

coriaceous (,kɒrɪ'eɪʃəs) *or* **corious** *adj* of or resembling leather. [C17: from Late Latin *coriāceus* from *corium* leather]

coriander (,kɒrɪ'ændə) *n* a European umbelliferous plant, *Coriandrum sativum,* widely cultivated for its aromatic seeds and leaves, used in flavouring food, etc. [C14: from Old French *coriandre,* from Latin *coriandrum,* from Greek *koriannon,* of uncertain origin]

Corinth ('kɒrɪnθ) *n* **1** a port in S Greece, in the NE Peloponnese: the modern town is near the site of the ancient city, the largest and richest of the city-states after Athens. Pop.: 29 600 (1995 est.). Modern Greek name: **Kórinthos. 2** a region of ancient Greece, occupying most of the Isthmus of Corinth and part of the NE Peloponnese. **3 Gulf of.** Also called: Gulf of **Lepanto.** an inlet of the Ionian Sea between the Peloponnese and central Greece. **4 Isthmus of.** a narrow strip of land between the Gulf of Corinth and the Saronic Gulf: crossed by the **Corinth Canal,** making navigation possible between the gulfs.

Corinthian (kəˈrɪnθɪən) *adj* **1** of, characteristic of, or relating to Corinth. **2** of, denoting, or relating to one of the five classical orders of architecture: characterized by a bell-shaped capital having carved ornaments based on acanthus leaves. See also **Ionic, Doric, Composite, Tuscan. 3** given to luxury; dissolute. **4** ornate and elaborate. ♦ *n* **5** a native or inhabitant of Corinth. **6** an amateur sportsman. **7** *Rare.* a man about town, esp. one who is dissolute.

Corinthians (kəˈrɪnθɪənz) *n* (*functioning as sing*) either of two books of the New Testament (in full **The First and Second Epistles of Paul the Apostle to the Corinthians**).

Coriolanus (ˌkɒrɪəˈleɪnəs) *n* **Gaius Marcius** (ˈgaɪəs ˈmɑːsɪəs). 5th century B.C., a legendary Roman general, who allegedly led an army against Rome but was dissuaded from conquering it by his mother and wife.

Coriolis force (ˌkɒrɪˈəʊlɪs) *n* a hypothetical force postulated to explain a deflection in the path of a body moving relative to the earth when observed from the earth. The deflection (**Coriolis effect**) is due to the earth's rotation and is to the left in the S hemisphere and to the right in the N hemisphere. [C19: named after Gaspard G. *Coriolis* (1792–1843), French civil engineer]

corious (ˈkɒrɪəs) *adj* a variant of **coriaceous.**

corium (ˈkɔːrɪəm) *n, pl* **-ria** (-rɪə). **1** Also called: **derma, dermis.** the deep inner layer of the skin, beneath the epidermis, containing connective tissue, blood vessels, and fat. **2** *Entomol.* the leathery basal part of the forewing of hemipterous insects. [C19: from Latin: rind, skin, leather]

corixid (kəˈrɪksɪd) *n* **1** any heteropterous water bug of the vegetarian family *Corixidae,* typified by *Corixa punctata,* common in sluggish waters. The forelegs have become modified and are used in stridulation, as by the **water singer** (*Micronecta poweri*). See also **water boatman.** ♦ *adj* **2** of or relating to the Corixidae. [from New Latin *corixa,* from Greek *koris* bedbug]

cork (kɔːk) *n* **1** the thick light porous outer bark of the cork oak, used widely as an insulator and for stoppers for bottles, casks, etc. **2** a piece of cork or other material used as a stopper. **3** an angling float. **4** Also called: **phellem.** *Botany.* a protective layer of dead impermeable cells on the outside of the stems and roots of woody plants, produced by the outer layer of the cork cambium. ♦ *adj* **5** made of cork. Related adj: **suberose.** ♦ *vb* (*tr*) **6** to stop up (a bottle, cask, etc.) with or as if with a cork; fit with a cork. **7** (often foll. by *up*) to restrain: *to cork up the emotions.* **8** to black (the face, hands, etc.) with burnt cork. [C14: probably from Arabic *qurq,* from Latin *cortex* bark, especially of the cork oak] ▸ **ˈcorkˌlike** *adj*

Cork (kɔːk) *n* **1** a county of SW Republic of Ireland, in Munster province: crossed by ridges of low mountains; scenic coastline. County town: Cork. Pop.: 420 000 (1996). Area: 7459 sq. km (2880 sq. miles). **2** a port in S Republic of Ireland, county town of Co. Cork, at the mouth of the River Lee: seat of the University College of Cork (1849). Pop.: 127 253 (1991). Gaelic name: **Corcaigh.**

corkage (ˈkɔːkɪdʒ) *n* a charge made at a restaurant for serving wine, etc., bought off the premises.

corkboard (ˈkɔːkˌbɔːd) *n* a thin slab made of granules of cork, used as a floor or wall finish and as an insulator.

cork cambium *n* a layer of meristematic cells in the cortex of the stems and roots of woody plants, the outside of which gives rise to cork cells and the inside to secondary cortical cells (phelloderm). Also called: **phellogen.**

corked (kɔːkt) *adj* **1** Also: **ˈcorky.** (of a wine) tainted through having a cork containing excess tannin. **2** (*postpositive*) *Brit.* a slang word for **drunk.**

corker (ˈkɔːkə) *n* **1** *Slang.* **1a** something or somebody striking or outstanding: *that was a corker of a joke.* **1b** an irrefutable remark that puts an end to discussion. **2** a person or machine that inserts corks.

corking (ˈkɔːkɪŋ) *adj* (*prenominal*) *Brit. slang.* excellent.

cork oak *n* an evergreen Mediterranean oak tree, *Quercus suber,* with a porous outer bark from which cork is obtained. Also called: **cork tree.**

Corkonian (kɔːˈkəʊnɪən, kərˈkɔːnɪən) *n* a native or inhabitant of the city of Cork.

corkscrew (ˈkɔːkˌskruː) *n* **1** a device for drawing corks from bottles, typically consisting of a pointed metal spiral attached to a handle or screw mechanism. **2** *Boxing slang.* a blow that ends with a twist of the fist, esp. one intended to cut the opponent. **3** (*modifier*) resembling a corkscrew in shape. ♦ *vb* **4** to move or cause to move in a spiral or zigzag course.

cork-tipped (ˈkɔːkˌtɪpt) *adj* (of a cigarette) having a filter of cork or some material resembling cork.

corkwing (ˈkɔːkˌwɪŋ) *n* a greenish or bluish European fish of the wrasse family, *Ctenolabrus melops.* [of uncertain origin]

corkwood (ˈkɔːkˌwʊd) *n* **1** a small tree, *Leitneria floridana,* of the southeastern U.S., having very lightweight porous wood: family *Leitneriaceae.* **2** any other tree with light porous wood. **3** the wood of any of these trees.

corm (kɔːm) *n* an organ of vegetative reproduction in plants such as the crocus, consisting of a globular stem base swollen with food and surrounded by papery scale leaves. Compare **bulb** (sense 1). [C19: from New Latin *cormus,* from Greek *kormos* tree trunk from which the branches have been lopped] ▸ **ˈcormous** *adj*

cormel (ˈkɔːməl) *n* a new small corm arising from the base of a fully developed one.

cormophyte (ˈkɔːməˌfaɪt) *n* any of the *Cormophyta,* a major division (now obsolete) of plants having a stem, root, and leaves: includes the mosses, ferns, and seed plants. [C19: from Greek *kormos* tree trunk + -PHYTE] ▸ **cormophytic** (ˌkɔːməˈfɪtɪk) *adj*

cormorant (ˈkɔːmərənt) *n* any aquatic bird of the family *Phalacrocoracidae,* of coastal and inland waters, having a dark plumage, a long neck and body, and a slender hooked beak: order *Pelecaniformes* (pelicans, etc.). [C13: from Old French *cormareng,* from *corp* raven, from Latin *corvus* + *-mareng* of the sea, from Latin *mare* sea]

corn[1] (kɔːn) *n* **1** *Brit.* **1a** any of various cereal plants, esp. the predominant crop of a region, such as wheat in England and oats in Scotland and Ireland. **1b** the seeds of such plants, esp. after harvesting. **1c** a single seed of such plants; a grain. **2** the usual U.S., Canadian, Austral., and N.Z. name for **maize.** See also **sweet corn** (sense 1), **popcorn** (sense 1). **3a** the plants producing these kinds of grain considered as a growing crop: *spring corn.* **3b** (*in combination*): *a cornfield.* **4** short for **corn whisky. 5** *Slang.* an idea, song, etc., regarded as banal or sentimental. **6** *Archaic or dialect.* any hard particle or grain. ♦ *vb* (*tr*) **7** to feed (animals) with corn, esp. oats. **8a** to preserve in brine. **8b** to salt. **9** to plant corn on. [Old English *corn;* related to Old Norse, Old High German *corn,* Gothic *kaúrn,* Latin *grānum,* Sanskrit *jīrṇá* fragile]

corn[2] (kɔːn) *n* **1** a hardening or thickening of the skin around a central point in the foot, caused by pressure or friction. **2 tread on (someone's) corns.** *Brit. informal.* to offend or hurt (someone) by touching on a sensitive subject or encroaching on his privileges. [C15: from Old French *corne* horn, from Latin *cornū*]

cornaceous (kɔːˈneɪʃəs) *adj* of, relating to, or belonging to the *Cornaceae,* a family of temperate plants, mostly trees and shrubs, including dogwood, cornel, and spotted laurel (see **laurel** (sense 5)). [C19: from New Latin *Cornaceae,* from *Cornus* genus name, from Latin: CORNEL]

cornball (ˈkɔːnˌbɔːl) *Chiefly U.S.* ♦ *n* **1** a person given to mawkish or unsophisticated behaviour. ♦ *adj* **2** another word for **corny.** [C20: from *corn ball* a sweet consisting of a ball of popcorn and molasses]

corn borer *n* the larva of the pyralid moth *Pyrausta nubilalis,* native to S and Central Europe: in E North America a serious pest of maize.

corn bread *n* a kind of bread made from maize meal. Also called: **Indian bread.**

corn bunting *n* a heavily built European songbird, *Emberiza calandra,* with a streaked brown plumage: family *Emberizidae* (buntings).

corn circle *n* another name for **crop circle.**

corncob (ˈkɔːnˌkɒb) *n* **1** the core of an ear of maize, to which kernels are attached. **2** short for **corncob pipe.**

corncob pipe *n* a pipe made from a dried corncob.

corncockle (ˈkɔːnˌkɒkᵊl) *n* a European caryophyllaceous plant, *Agrostemma githago,* that has reddish-purple flowers and grows in cornfields and by roadsides.

corncrake (ˈkɔːnˌkreɪk) *n* a common Eurasian rail, *Crex crex,* of fields and meadows, with a buff speckled plumage and reddish wings.

corncrib (ˈkɔːnˌkrɪb) *n Chiefly U.S. and Canadian.* a ventilated building for the storage of unhusked maize.

corn dolly *n* a decorative figure made by plaiting straw.

cornea (ˈkɔːnɪə) *n, pl* **-neas** (-nɪəz) *or* **-neae** (-nɪˌiː). the convex transparent membrane that forms the anterior covering of the eyeball and is continuous with the sclera. [C14: from Medieval Latin *cornea tēla* horny web, from Latin *cornū* HORN] ▸ **ˈcorneal** *adj*

corn earworm *n U.S.* the larva of the noctuid moth *Heliothis armigera,* which feeds on maize and many other crop plants. See also **bollworm.**

corned (kɔːnd) *adj* (esp. of beef) cooked and then preserved or pickled in salt or brine, now often canned.

Corneille (*French* kɔrnɛj) *n* **Pierre** (pjɛr). 1606–84, French tragic dramatist often regarded as the founder of French classical drama. His plays include *Médée* (1635), *Le Cid* (1636), *Horace* (1640), and *Polyeucte* (1642).

cornel (ˈkɔːnᵊl) *n* any cornaceous plant of the genus *Cornus,* such as the dogwood and dwarf cornel. [C16: probably from Middle Low German *kornelle,* from Old French *cornelle,* from Vulgar Latin *cornicula* (unattested), from Latin *cornum* cornel cherry, from *cornus* cornel tree]

cornelian (kɔːˈniːlɪən) *n* a variant spelling of **carnelian.**

corneous (ˈkɔːnɪəs) *adj* horny; hornlike. [C17: from Latin *corneus* horny, from *cornū* HORN]

corner (ˈkɔːnə) *n* **1** the place, position, or angle formed by the meeting of two converging lines or surfaces. **2** a projecting angle of a solid object or figure. **3** the place where two streets meet. **4** any small, secluded, secret, or private place. **5** a dangerous or awkward position, esp. from which escape is difficult: *a tight corner.* **6** any part, region or place, esp. a remote place. **7** something used to protect or mark a corner, as of the hard cover of a book. **8** *Commerce.* a monopoly over the supply of a commodity so that its market price can be controlled. **9** *Soccer, hockey, etc.* a free kick or shot from the corner of the field, taken against a defending team when the ball goes out of play over their goal line after last touching one of their players. **10** either of two opposite angles of a boxing ring in which the opponents take their rests. **11** *Mountaineering.* a junction between two rock faces forming an angle of between 60° and 120°. U.S. name: **dihedral. 12 cut corners.** to do something in the easiest and shortest way, esp. at the expense of high standards. **13 (just) round the corner.** close at hand. **14 turn the corner.** to pass the critical point (in an illness, etc.). **15** (*modifier*) located on a corner: *a corner shop.* **16** (*modifier*) suitable or designed for a corner: *a corner table.* **17** *Logic.* either of a pair of symbols used in the same way as ordinary quotation marks to indicate quasi quotation. See **quasi-quotation.** ♦ *vb* **18** (*tr*) to manoeuvre (a person or animal) into a position from which escape is difficult or impossible: *finally they cornered the fox.* **19** (*tr*) to furnish or provide with corners. **20** (*tr*) to place in or move into a corner. **21** (*tr*) **21a** to acquire enough of (a commodity) to attain control of the market. **21b** Also: **engross.** to attain control of (a market) in such a manner. Compare **forestall** (sense 3). **22** (*intr*) (of vehicles, etc.) to turn a corner. **23** (*intr*) *U.S.* to be situated on a corner. **24** (*intr*) (in soccer, etc.) to take a corner. [C13: from Old French *corniere,* from Latin *cornū* point, extremity, HORN]

Corner *n* **the.** *Informal.* an area in central Australia, at the junction of the borders of Queensland and South Australia.
cornerback ('kɔːnəˌbæk) *n American football.* a defensive back.
cornerstone ('kɔːnəˌstəʊn) *n* **1** a stone at the corner of a wall, uniting two intersecting walls; quoin. **2** a stone placed at the corner of a building during a ceremony to mark the start of construction. **3** a person or thing of prime importance; basis: *the cornerstone of the whole argument.*
cornerwise ('kɔːnəˌwaɪz) *or* **cornerways** ('kɔːnəˌweɪz) *adv, adj* with a corner in front; diagonally.
cornet ('kɔːnɪt) *n* **1** Also called: **cornet à pistons** ('kɔːnɪt ə 'pɪstənz; *French* kɔrnɛ a pistɔ̃). a three-valved brass instrument of the trumpet family. Written range: about two and a half octaves upwards from E below middle C. It is a transposing instrument in B flat or A. **2** a person who plays the cornet. **3** a variant spelling of **cornett. 4** a cone-shaped paper container for sweets, etc. **5** *Brit.* a cone-shaped wafer container for ice cream. **6** (formerly) the lowest rank of commissioned cavalry officer in the British army. **7** *S. African.* short for **field cornet. 8** a starched and wired muslin or lace cap worn by women from the 12th to the 15th centuries. **9** the large white headdress of some nuns. [C14: from Old French, from *corn,* from Latin *cornū* HORN]
cornetcy ('kɔːnɪtsɪ) *n, pl* **-cies.** *Obsolete.* the commission or rank of a cornet.
cornetist *or* **cornettist** (kɔː'nɛtɪst) *n* a person who plays the cornet.
cornett (kɔː'nɛt) *or* **cornet** *n* a musical instrument consisting of a straight or curved tube of wood or ivory having finger holes like a recorder and a cup-shaped mouthpiece like a trumpet. [from Old French *cornet* a little horn, from *corn* horn, from Latin *cornū*]
corn exchange *n* a building where corn is bought and sold.
corn factor *n* a person who deals in corn.
cornfield ('kɔːnˌfiːld) *n* a field planted with cereal crops.
cornflakes ('kɔːnˌfleɪks) *pl n* a breakfast cereal made from toasted maize, eaten with milk, sugar, etc.
cornflour ('kɔːnˌflaʊə) *n* a fine starchy maize flour, used esp. for thickening sauces. U.S. and Canadian name: **cornstarch.**
cornflower ('kɔːnˌflaʊə) *n* a Eurasian herbaceous plant, *Centaurea cyanus,* with blue, purple, pink, or white flowers, formerly a common weed in cornfields: family *Compositae* (composites). Also called: **bluebottle.** See also **bachelor's-buttons.**
Cornforth ('kɔːnˌfɔːθ) *n* Sir **John Warcup.** born 1917, Australian chemist, who shared the 1975 Nobel prize for chemistry with Vladimir Prelog for their work on stereochemistry.
cornhusk ('kɔːnˌhʌsk) *n U.S. and Canadian.* the outer protective covering of an ear of maize; the chaff.
cornice ('kɔːnɪs) *n* **1** *Architect.* **1a** the top projecting mouldings of an entablature. **1b** a continuous horizontal projecting course or moulding at the top of a wall, building, etc. **2** an overhanging ledge of snow formed by the wind on the edge of a mountain ridge, cliff, or corrie. ◆ *vb* **3** *(tr) Architect.* to furnish or decorate with or as if with a cornice. [C16: from Old French, from Italian, perhaps from Latin *cornix* crow, but influenced also by Latin *corōnis* decorative flourish used by scribes, from Greek *korōnis,* from *korōnē* curved object, CROWN]
corniche ('kɔːnɪʃ) *n* a coastal road, esp. one built into the face of a cliff. [C19: from *corniche road,* originally the coastal road between Nice and Monte Carlo; see CORNICE]
corniculate (kɔː'nɪkjʊˌleɪt, -lɪt) *adj* **1** having horns or hornlike projections. **2** relating to or resembling a horn. [C17: from Latin *corniculātus* horned, from *corniculum* a little horn, from *cornū* HORN]
Cornish ('kɔːnɪʃ) *adj* **1** of, relating to, or characteristic of Cornwall, its inhabitants, their former language, or their present-day dialect of English. ◆ *n* **2** a former language of Cornwall, belonging to the S Celtic branch of the Indo-European family and closely related to Breton: extinct by 1800. **3 the.** *(functioning as pl)* the natives or inhabitants of Cornwall. ▸ **'Cornishman** *n*
Cornish pasty ('pæstɪ) *n Cookery.* a pastry case with a filling of meat and vegetables.
Cornish split *n* another term for **Devonshire split.**
Corn Laws *pl n* the laws introduced in Britain in 1804 to protect domestic farmers against foreign competition by the imposition of a heavy duty on foreign corn: repealed in 1846. See also **Anti-Corn Law League.**
corn lily *n* any of several South African iridaceous plants of the genus *Ixia,* which have coloured lily-like flowers.
corn marigold *n* an annual plant, *Chrysanthemum segetum,* with yellow daisy-like flower heads: a common weed of cultivated land: family *Compositae* (composites).
corn meal *n* meal made from maize. Also called: **Indian meal.**
Corno (*Italian* 'kɔrno) *n* **Monte** ('monte). a mountain in central Italy: the highest peak in the Apennines. Height: 2912 m (9554 ft.).
corn oil *n* an oil prepared from maize, used in cooking and in making soaps, lubricants, etc.
corn on the cob *n* a cob of maize, boiled and eaten as a vegetable.
corn-picker *n Chiefly U.S. and Canadian.* a machine for removing ears of maize from the standing stalks, often also equipped to separate the corn from the husk and shell.
corn pone *n Southern U.S.* corn bread, esp. a plain type made with water. Sometimes shortened to **pone.**
corn poppy *n* a poppy, *Papaver rhoeas,* that has bright red flowers and grows in cornfields. Since World War I it has been the symbol of fallen soldiers. Also called: **coquelicot, Flanders poppy, field poppy.**
corn rose *n Brit., archaic.* any of several red-flowered weeds of cornfields, such as the corn poppy.
corn row (rəʊ) *n* a Black, originally African, hair-style in which the hair is plaited in close parallel rows, resembling furrows in a ploughed field.
corn salad *n* any valerianaceous plant of the genus *Valerianella,* esp. the European species *V. locusta,* which often grows in cornfields and whose leaves are sometimes used in salads. Also called: **lamb's lettuce.**
corn shock *n* a stack or bundle of bound or unbound corn piled upright for curing or drying.
corn shuck *n U.S. and Canadian.* the husk of an ear of maize.
corn silk *n U.S. and Canadian.* the silky tuft of styles and stigmas at the tip of an ear of maize, formerly used as a diuretic.
corn smut *n* **1** an ascomycetous parasitic fungus, *Ustilago zeae,* that causes gall-like deformations on maize grain. **2** the condition produced by this fungus.
corn snow *n Skiing, U.S. and Canadian.* granular snow formed by alternate freezing and thawing.
cornstalk ('kɔːnˌstɔːk) *n* **1** a stalk or stem of corn. **2** *Austral. slang.* a tall thin man.
cornstarch ('kɔːnˌstɑːtʃ) *n* the U.S. and Canadian name for **cornflour.**
cornstone ('kɔːnˌstəʊn) *n* a mottled green and red limestone.
corn syrup *n* syrup prepared from maize.
cornu ('kɔːnjuː) *n, pl* **-nua** (-njʊə). *Anatomy.* a part or structure resembling a horn or having a hornlike pattern, such as a cross section of the grey matter of the spinal cord. [C17: from Latin: a horn] ▸ **'cornual** *adj*
cornucopia (ˌkɔːnjʊ'kəʊpɪə) *n* **1** *Greek myth.* the horn of Amalthea, the goat that suckled Zeus. **2** a representation of such a horn in painting, sculpture, etc., overflowing with fruit, vegetables, etc.; horn of plenty. **3** a great abundance; overflowing supply. **4** a horn-shaped container. [C16: from Late Latin, from Latin *cornū cōpiae* horn of plenty] ▸ **ˌcornu'copian** *adj*
cornute (kɔː'njuːt) *or* **cornuted** *adj Biology.* having or resembling cornua; hornlike: *the cornute process of a bone.* [C17: from Latin *cornūtus* horned, from *cornū* HORN]
Cornwall ('kɔːnˌwɔːl, -wəl) *n* a county of SW England: hilly, with a deeply indented coastline. Administrative centre: Truro. Pop.: 479 600 (1994 est.). Area: 3564 sq. km (1376 sq. miles).
Cornwallis (kɔːn'wɒlɪs) *n* **Charles,** 1st Marquis Cornwallis. 1738–1805, British general in the War of American Independence: commanded forces defeated at Yorktown (1781): defeated Tipu Sahib (1791): governor general of Bengal (1786–93, 1805): negotiated the Treaty of Amiens (1801).
corn whisky *n* whisky made from maize.
corny ('kɔːnɪ) *adj* **cornier, corniest.** *Slang.* **1** trite or banal. **2** sentimental or mawkish. **3** abounding in corn. [C16 (C20 in the sense rustic, banal): from CORN[1] + -Y[1]]
corody *or* **corrody** ('kɒrədɪ) *n, pl* **-dies.** *History.* **1** (originally) the right of a lord to receive free quarters from his vassal. **2** an allowance for maintenance. [C15: from Medieval Latin *corrōdium* something provided, from Old French *corroyer* to provide, of Germanic origin]
corol. *or* **coroll.** *abbrev. for* corollary.
corolla (kə'rɒlə) *n* the petals of a flower collectively, forming an inner floral envelope. Compare **calyx.**
corollaceous (ˌkɒrə'leɪʃəs) *adj* of, relating to, resembling, or having a corolla.
corollary (kə'rɒlərɪ) *n, pl* **-laries. 1** a proposition that follows directly from the proof of another proposition. **2** an obvious deduction. **3** a natural consequence or result. ◆ *adj* **4** consequent or resultant. [C14: from Latin *corollārium* money paid for a garland, from Latin *corolla* garland, from *corōna* CROWN]
Coromandel Coast (ˌkɒrə'mænd[ə]l) *n* the SE coast of India, along the Bay of Bengal, extending from Point Calimere to the mouth of the Krishna River.
corona (kə'rəʊnə) *n, pl* **-nas** *or* **-nae** (-niː). **1** a circle of light around a luminous body, usually the moon. **2** Also called: **aureole.** the outermost region of the sun's atmosphere, visible as a faint halo during a solar eclipse. **3** *Architect.* the flat vertical face of a cornice just above the soffit. **4** something resembling a corona or halo. **5** a circular chandelier suspended from the roof of a church. **6** *Botany.* **6a** the trumpet-shaped part of the corolla of daffodils and similar plants; the crown. **6b** a crown of leafy outgrowths from inside the petals of some flowers. **7** *Anatomy.* a crownlike structure, such as the top of the head. **8** *Zoology.* the head or upper surface of an animal, such as the body of an echinoid or the disc and arms of a crinoid. **9** a long cigar with blunt ends. **10** *Physics.* short for **corona discharge.** [C16: from Latin: crown, from Greek *korōnē* anything curved; related to Greek *korōnis* wreath, *korax* crow, Latin *curvus* curved]
Corona Australis (ɒ'streɪlɪs) *n, Latin genitive* **Coronae Australis** (kə'rəʊniː). a small faint constellation in the S hemisphere between Ara and Pavo. [literally: Southern crown]
Corona Borealis (ˌbɔːrɪ'eɪlɪs) *n, Latin genitive* **Coronae Borealis** (kə'rəʊniː). a small compact constellation in the N hemisphere lying between Boötes and Hercules. [literally: Northern crown]
coronach ('kɒrənəx, -nək) *n Scot. or Irish.* a dirge or lamentation for the dead. [C16: from Scottish Gaelic *corranach;* related to Irish *rānadh* a crying]
corona discharge *n* an electrical discharge appearing on and around the surface of a charged conductor, caused by ionization of the surrounding gas. Also called: **corona.** See also **Saint Elmo's fire.**
coronagraph *or* **coronograph** (kə'rəʊnəˌgrɑːf, -ˌgræf) *n* an optical instrument used to simulate an eclipse of the sun so that the faint solar corona can be studied.
coronal *n* ('kɒrən[ə]l). **1** *Poetic.* a circlet for the head; crown. **2** a wreath or garland. **3** *Anatomy.* short for **coronal suture.** ◆ *adj* (kə'rəʊn[ə]l). **4** of or relating to a corona or coronal. **5** *Phonetics.* a less common word for **retroflex.** [C16: from Late Latin *corōnālis* belonging to a CROWN]
coronal suture *n* the serrated line across the skull between the frontal bone and the parietal bones.

coronary ('kɒrənərɪ) *adj* **1** *Anatomy.* designating blood vessels, nerves, ligaments, etc., that encircle a part or structure. ♦ *n, pl* **-naries. 2** short for **coronary thrombosis.** [C17: from Latin *corōnārius* belonging to a wreath or crown; see CORONA]

coronary artery *n* either of two arteries branching from the aorta and supplying blood to the heart.

coronary bypass *n* the surgical bypass of a narrowed or blocked coronary artery by grafting a section of a healthy blood vessel taken from another part of the patient's body.

coronary heart disease *n* any heart disorder caused by disease of the coronary arteries.

coronary insufficiency *n* inadequate circulation of blood through the coronary arteries, characterized by attacks of angina pectoris.

coronary thrombosis *n* a condition of interrupted blood flow to the heart due to a blood clot in a coronary artery, usually as a consequence of atherosclerosis: characterized by intense pain. Sometimes shortened to: **coronary.** Compare **myocardial infarction.**

coronation (ˌkɒrəˈneɪʃən) *n* the act or ceremony of crowning a monarch. [C14: from Old French, from *coroner* to crown, from Latin *corōnāre*]

coroner ('kɒrənə) *n* a public official responsible for the investigation of violent, sudden, or suspicious deaths. The investigation (**coroner's inquest**) is held in the presence of a jury (**coroner's jury**). See also **procurator fiscal.** Compare **medical examiner.** [C14: from Anglo-French *corouner* officer in charge of the pleas of the Crown, from Old French *corone* CROWN] ▸ **'coronerˌship** *n*

coronet ('kɒrənɪt) *n* **1** any small crown, esp. one worn by princes or peers as a mark of rank. **2** a woman's jewelled circlet for the head. **3** the margin between the skin of a horse's pastern and the horn of the hoof. **4** the knob at the base of a deer's antler. **5** *Heraldry.* a support for a crest shaped like a crown. [C15: from Old French *coronete* a little crown, from *corone* CROWN]

coroneted (ˌkɒrəˈnɛtɪd) *adj* **1** wearing a coronet. **2** belonging to the peerage.

Corot (*French* kɔro) *n* **Jean Baptiste Camille** (ʒɑ̃ batist kamij). 1796–1875, French landscape and portrait painter.

co-routine ('kəuruːˌtiːn) *n Computing.* a section of a computer program similar to but differing from a subroutine in that it can be left and re-entered at any point.

corozo (kəˈrəuzəu) *n, pl* **-zos.** a tropical American palm, *Corozo oleifera,* whose seeds yield a useful oil. [C18: via Spanish from an Indian name]

corp. *abbrev. for:* **1** corporation. **2** corporal.

corpora ('kɔːpərə) *n* the plural of **corpus.**

corporal[1] ('kɔːpərəl, -prəl) *adj* **1** of or relating to the body; bodily. **2** an obsolete word for **corporeal.** [C14: from Latin *corporālis* of the body, from *corpus* body] ▸ ˌ**corpoˈrality** *n* ▸ **'corporally** *adv*

corporal[2] ('kɔːpərəl, -prəl) *n* **1** a noncommissioned officer junior to a sergeant in the army, air force, or marines. **2** (in the Royal Navy) a petty officer who assists the master-at-arms. [C16: from Old French, via Italian, from Latin *caput* head; perhaps also influenced in Old French by *corps* body (of men)] ▸ **'corporalˌship** *n*

corporal[3] ('kɔːpərəl, -prəl) *or* **corporale** (ˌkɔːpəˈreɪlɪ) *n* a white linen cloth on which the bread and wine are placed during the Eucharist. [C14: from Medieval Latin *corporāle pallium* eucharistic altar cloth, from Latin *corporālis* belonging to the body, from *corpus* body (of Christ)]

Corporal of Horse *n* a noncommissioned rank in the British Household Cavalry above that of sergeant and below that of staff sergeant.

corporal punishment *n* punishment of a physical nature, such as caning, flogging, or beating.

corporate ('kɔːpərɪt, -prɪt) *adj* **1** forming a corporation; incorporated. **2** of or belonging to a corporation or corporations: *corporate finance.* **3** of or belonging to a united group; joint. [C15: from Latin *corporātus* made into a body, from *corporāre,* from *corpus* body] ▸ **'corporately** *adv*

corporate anorexia *n* a malaise of a business organization resulting from making too many creative people redundant in a cost-cutting exercise.

corporate culture *n* the distinctive ethos of an organization that influences the level of formality, loyalty, and general behaviour of its employees.

corporate identity *or* **image** *n* the way an organization is presented to or perceived by its members and the public.

corporate raider *n Finance.* a person or organization that acquires a substantial holding of the shares of a company in order to take it over or to force its management to act in a desired way.

corporate restructuring *n* a change in the business strategy of an organization resulting in diversification, closing parts of the business, etc., to increase its long-term profitability.

corporate venturing *n Finance.* the provision of venture capital by one company for another in order to obtain information about the company requiring capital or as a step towards acquiring it.

corporation (ˌkɔːpəˈreɪʃən) *n* **1** a group of people authorized by law to act as an individual and having its own powers, duties, and liabilities. **2** Also called: **municipal corporation.** the municipal authorities of a city or town. **3** a group of people acting as one body. **4** See **public corporation. 5** *Informal.* a large paunch or belly.

corporation tax *n* a British tax on the profits of a company or other incorporated body.

corporatism ('kɔːpərɪtɪzəm, -prɪtɪzəm) *n* the organization of a state on a corporative basis. ▸ **'corporatist** *n, adj*

corporative ('kɔːpərətɪv, -prətɪv) *adj* **1** of or characteristic of a corporation. **2** (of a state) organized into and governed by corporations of individuals involved in any given profession, industry, etc.

corporator ('kɔːpəˌreɪtə) *n* a member of a corporation.

corporeal (kɔːˈpɔːrɪəl) *adj* **1** of the nature of the physical body; not spiritual. **2** of a material nature; physical. [C17: from Latin *corporeus,* from *corpus* body] ▸ **corˌporeˈality** *or* **corˈporealness** *n* ▸ **corˈporeally** *adv*

corporeity (ˌkɔːpəˈriːɪtɪ) *n* bodily or material nature or substance; physical existence; corporeality.

corposant ('kɔːpəˌzænt) *n* another name for **Saint Elmo's fire.** [C17: from Portuguese *corpo-santo,* literally: holy body, from Latin *corpus sanctum*]

corps (kɔː) *n, pl* **corps** (kɔːz). **1** a military formation that comprises two or more divisions and additional support arms. **2** a military body with a specific function: *intelligence corps; medical corps.* **3** a body of people associated together: *the diplomatic corps.* [C18: from French, from Latin *corpus* body]

corps de ballet ('kɔː də 'bæleɪ; *French* kɔr də balɛ) *n* the members of a ballet company who dance together in a group.

corps diplomatique (ˌdɪpləumæˈtiːk) *n* another name for **diplomatic corps.** Abbrev.: **CD.**

corpse (kɔːps) *n* **1** a dead body, esp. of a human being; cadaver. ♦ *vb* **2** *Theatre slang.* to laugh or cause to laugh involuntarily or inopportunely while on stage. [C14: from Old French *corps* body, from Latin *corpus* body]

corpsman ('kɔːmən) *n, pl* **-men.** *U.S. military.* a medical orderly or stretcher-bearer.

corpulent ('kɔːpjulənt) *adj* physically bulky; fat. [C14: from Latin *corpulentus* fleshy] ▸ **'corpulence** *or* **'corpulency** *n* ▸ **'corpulently** *adv*

cor pulmonale (kɔː pʌlməˈnɑːlɪ) *n* pulmonary heart disease: a serious heart condition in which there is enlargement and failure of the right ventricle resulting from lung disease. [New Latin]

corpus ('kɔːpəs) *n, pl* **-pora** (-pərə). **1** a collection or body of writings, esp. by a single author or on a specific topic: *the corpus of Dickens' works.* **2** the main body, section, or substance of something. **3** *Anatomy.* **3a** any distinct mass or body. **3b** the main part of an organ or structure. **4** *Linguistics.* a body of data, esp. the finite collection of grammatical sentences of a language that a linguistic theory seeks to describe by means of an algorithm. **5** a capital or principal sum, as contrasted with a derived income. **6** *Obsolete.* a human or animal body, esp. a dead one. [C14: from Latin: body]

corpus callosum (kəˈləusəm) *n, pl* **corpora callosa** (kəˈləusə). the band of white fibres that connects the cerebral hemispheres in mammals. [New Latin, literally: callous body]

corpus cavernosum (ˌkævəˈnəusəm) *n, pl* **corpora cavernosa.** either of two masses of erectile tissue in the penis of mammals. [New Latin, literally: cavernous body]

Corpus Christi[1] ('krɪstɪ) *n Chiefly R.C. Church.* a festival in honour of the Eucharist, observed on the Thursday after Trinity Sunday. [C14: from Latin: body of Christ]

Corpus Christi[2] ('krɪstɪ) *n* a port in S Texas, on **Corpus Christi Bay,** an inlet of the Gulf of Mexico. Pop.: 280 260 (1996 est.).

corpuscle ('kɔːpʌsᵊl) *n* **1** any cell or similar minute body that is suspended in a fluid, esp. any of the **red blood corpuscles** (see **erythrocyte**) or **white blood corpuscles** (see **leucocyte**). **2** *Anatomy.* the encapsulated ending of a sensory nerve. **3** *Physics.* a discrete particle such as an electron, photon, ion, or atom. **4** Also called: **corpuscule** (kɔːˈpʌskjuːl). any minute particle. [C17: from Latin *corpusculum* a little body, from *corpus* body] ▸ **corpuscular** (kɔːˈpʌskjulə) *adj*

corpuscular theory *n* the theory, originally proposed by Newton, and revived with the development of the quantum theory, that light consists of a stream of particles. See **photon.** Compare **wave theory.**

corpus delicti (dɪˈlɪktaɪ) *n Law.* the body of facts that constitute an offence. [New Latin, literally: the body of the crime]

corpus juris ('dʒuərɪs) *n* a body of law, esp. the laws of a nation or state. [from Late Latin, literally: a body of law]

Corpus Juris Canonici (kəˈnɒnɪˌsaɪ) *n R.C. Church.* the official compilation of canon law published by authority of Gregory XIII in 1582, superseded by the Codex Juris Canonici in 1918. See also **Clementines, Decretals, Decretum, Extravagantes, Sext.** [Medieval Latin, literally: body of canon law]

Corpus Juris Civilis (sɪˈvaɪlɪs) *n Law.* the body of Roman or civil law consolidated by Justinian in the 6th century A.D. It consists of four parts, the Institutes, Digest, Code, and Novels. [New Latin, literally: body of civil law]

corpus luteum ('luːtɪəm) *n, pl* **corpora lutea** ('luːtɪə). a yellow glandular mass of tissue that forms in a Graafian follicle following release of an ovum. It secretes progesterone, a hormone necessary to maintain pregnancy. [New Latin, literally: yellow body]

corpus luteum hormone *n* another name for **progesterone.**

corpus spongiosum (ˌspʌndʒɪˈəusəm) *n* a mass of tissue that, with the corpora cavernosa, forms the erectile tissue of the penis of mammals. [New Latin, literally: spongy body]

corpus striatum (straɪˈeɪtəm) *n, pl* **corpora striata** (straɪˈeɪtə). a striped mass of white and grey matter situated in front of the thalamus in each cerebral hemisphere. [New Latin, literally: striated body]

corpus vile ('kɔːpəs 'vaɪlɪ) *n, pl* **corpora vilia** ('kɔːpərə 'vɪlɪə) *Latin.* a person or thing fit only to be the object of an experiment. [literally: worthless body]

corr. *abbrev. for:* **1** correct. **2** corrected. **3** correction. **4** correspondence. **5** correspondent. **6** corresponding.

corrade (kɒˈreɪd) *vb* (of rivers, streams, etc.) to erode (land) by the abrasive action of rock particles. [C17: from Latin *corrādere* to scrape together, from *rādere* to scrape]

corral (kɒˈrɑːl) *n* **1** *Chiefly U.S. and Canadian.* an enclosure for confining cattle or horses. **2** *Chiefly U.S.* (formerly) a defensive enclosure formed by a ring of covered wagons. ♦ *vb* **-rals, -ralling, -ralled.** (*tr*) *U.S. and Canadian.* **3** to drive into and confine in or as in a corral. **4** *Informal.* to capture. [C16: from Spanish, from Vulgar Latin *currāle* (unattested) area for vehicles, from Latin *currus* wagon, from *currere* to run]

corrasion (kəˈreɪʒən) *n* erosion of a rock surface by rock fragments transported over it by water, wind, or ice. Compare **abrasion** (sense 3), **attrition** (sense 4). ► **corrasive** (kəˈreɪsɪv) *adj*

correa (ˈkɒrɪə, kəˈriːə) *n* an Australian evergreen shrub of the genus *Correa*, with large showy tubular flowers. [C19: after Jose Francesco *Correa* da Serra (1750–1823), Portuguese botanist]

correct (kəˈrɛkt) *vb* (*tr*) **1** to make free from errors. **2** to indicate the errors in. **3** to rebuke or punish in order to set right or improve: *to correct a child; to stand corrected.* **4** to counteract or rectify (a malfunction, ailment, etc.): *these glasses will correct your sight.* **5** to adjust or make conform, esp. to a standard. ◆ *adj* **6** free from error; true; accurate: *the correct version.* **7** in conformity with accepted standards: *correct behaviour.* [C14: from Latin *corrigere* to make straight, put in order, from *com-* (intensive) + *regere* to rule] ► **corˈrectable** *or* **corˈrectible** *adj* ► **corˈrectly** *adv* ► **corˈrectness** *n* ► **corˈrector** *n*

correction (kəˈrɛkʃən) *n* **1** the act or process of correcting. **2** something offered or substituted for an error; an improvement. **3** the act or process of punishing; reproof. **4** a number or quantity added to or subtracted from a scientific or mathematical calculation or observation to increase its accuracy.

correctional (kəˈrɛkʃənəl) *adj Chiefly U.S.* of or relating to the punishment and rehabilitation of criminals: *a correctional facility.*

correctitude (kəˈrɛktɪˌtjuːd) *n* the quality of correctness, esp. conscious correctness in behaviour.

corrective (kəˈrɛktɪv) *adj* **1** tending or intended to correct. ◆ *n* **2** something that tends or is intended to correct. ► **corˈrectively** *adv*

Correggio (*Italian* korˈreddʒo) *n* **Antonio Allegri da** (anˈtɔːnjo alˈleːgri da). 1494–1534, Italian painter, noted for his striking use of perspective and foreshortening.

Corregidor (kəˈrɛgɪˌdɔː) *n* an island at the entrance to Manila Bay, in the Philippines: site of the defeat of American forces by the Japanese (1942) in World War II.

correl. *abbrev. for* correlative.

correlate (ˈkɒrɪˌleɪt) *vb* **1** to place or be placed in a mutual, complementary, or reciprocal relationship. **2** (*tr*) to establish or show a correlation. ◆ *adj* **3** having a mutual, complementary, or reciprocal relationship. ◆ *n* **4** either of two things mutually or reciprocally related. ► **ˈcorreˌlatable** *adj*

correlation (ˌkɒrɪˈleɪʃən) *n* **1** a mutual or reciprocal relationship between two or more things. **2** the act or process of correlating or the state of being correlated. **3** *Statistics.* the extent of correspondence between the ordering of two variables. Correlation is positive or direct when two variables move in the same direction and negative or inverse when they move in opposite directions. [C16: from Medieval Latin *correlātiō,* from *com-* together + *relātiō,* RELATION] ► **ˌcorreˈlational** *adj*

correlation coefficient *n Statistics.* a statistic measuring the degree of correlation between two variables as by dividing their covariance by the square root of the product of their variances. The closer the correlation coefficient is to 1 or −1 the greater the correlation; if it is random, the coefficient is zero. See also **Pearson's correlation coefficient, Spearman's rank-order coefficient.**

correlative (kɒˈrɛlətɪv) *adj* **1** in mutual, complementary, or reciprocal relationship; corresponding. **2** denoting words, usually conjunctions, occurring together though not adjacently in certain grammatical constructions, as for example *neither* and *nor* in such sentences as *he neither ate nor drank.* ◆ *n* **3** either of two things that are correlative. **4** a correlative word. ► **corˈrelatively** *adv* ► **corˈrelativeness** *or* **corˌrelaˈtivity** *n*

correspond (ˌkɒrɪˈspɒnd) *vb* (*intr*) **1** (usually foll. by *with* or *to*) to conform, be in agreement, or be consistent or compatible (with); tally (with). **2** (usually foll. by *to*) to be similar or analogous in character or function. **3** (usually foll. by *with*) to communicate by letter. [C16: from Medieval Latin *corrēspondēre,* from Latin *respondēre* to RESPOND] ► **ˌcorreˈspondingly** *adv*

USAGE See at **similar.**

correspondence (ˌkɒrɪˈspɒndəns) *n* **1** the act or condition of agreeing or corresponding. **2** similarity or analogy. **3** agreement or conformity. **4a** communication by the exchange of letters. **4b** the letters so exchanged.

correspondence column *n* a section of a newspaper or magazine in which are printed readers' letters to the editor.

correspondence school *n* an educational institution that offers tuition (**correspondence courses**) by post.

correspondent (ˌkɒrɪˈspɒndənt) *n* **1** a person who communicates by letter or by letters. **2** a person employed by a newspaper, etc., to report on a special subject or to send reports from a foreign country. **3** a person or firm that has regular business relations with another, esp. one in a different part of the country or abroad. **4** something that corresponds to another. ◆ *adj* **5** similar or analogous.

Corrèze (*French* kɔrɛz) *n* a department of central France, in Limousin region. Capital: Tulle. Pop.: 236 300 (1995). Area: 5888 sq. km (2296 sq. miles).

corrida (koˈrriða) *n* the Spanish word for **bullfight.** [Spanish, from the phrase *corrida de toros,* literally: a running of bulls, from *correr* to run, from Latin *currere*]

corridor (ˈkɒrɪˌdɔː) *n* **1** a hallway or passage connecting parts of a building. **2** a strip of land or airspace that affords access, either from a landlocked country to the sea (such as the **Polish corridor,** 1919-39, which divided Germany) or from a state to an exclave (such as the **Berlin corridor,** 1945–90, which passed through the former East Germany). **3** a passageway connecting the compartments of a railway coach. **4** **corridors of power.** the higher echelons of government, the Civil Service, etc., considered as the location of power and influence. **5** a flight path that affords safe access for intruding aircraft. **6** the path that a spacecraft must follow when re-entering the atmosphere, above which lift is insufficient and below which heating effects are excessive. [C16: from Old French, from Old Italian *corridore,* literally: place for running, from *correre* to run, from Latin *currere*]

corrie (ˈkɒrɪ) *n* **1** (in Scotland) a circular hollow on a hillside. **2** *Geology.* another name for **cirque** (sense 1). [C18: from Gaelic *coire* cauldron, kettle]

Corriedale (ˈkɒrɪˌdeɪl) *n* a breed of sheep reared for both wool and meat, originally developed in New Zealand.

corrie-fisted (ˌkɒrɪˈfɪstɪd) *adj Scot. dialect.* left-handed. [C20: from earlier *car, ker* left hand or side, from Gaelic *cearr* left or wrong hand]

Corrientes (*Spanish* koˈrrjentes) *n* a port in NE Argentina, on the Paraná River. Pop.: 258 103 (1991).

corrigendum (ˌkɒrɪˈdʒɛndəm) *n, pl* **-da** (-də). **1** an error to be corrected. **2** (*sometimes pl*) Also called: **erratum.** a slip of paper inserted into a book after printing, listing errors and corrections. [C19: from Latin: that which is to be corrected, from *corrigere* to CORRECT]

corrigible (ˈkɒrɪdʒɪbᵊl) *adj* **1** capable of being corrected. **2** submissive or submitting to correction. [C15: from Old French, from Medieval Latin *corrigibilis,* from Latin *corrigere* to set right, CORRECT] ► **ˌcorrigiˈbility** *n* ► **ˈcorrigibly** *adv*

corrival (kəˈraɪvᵊl) *n, vb* a rare word for **rival.** [C16: from Old French, from Late Latin *corrīvālis,* from Latin *com-* together, mutually + *rīvālis* RIVAL] ► **corˈrivalry** *n*

corroborant (kəˈrɒbərənt) *adj Archaic.* **1** serving to corroborate. **2** strengthening.

corroborate *vb* (kəˈrɒbəˌreɪt). **1** (*tr*) to confirm or support (facts, opinions, etc.), esp. by providing fresh evidence: *the witness corroborated the accused's statement.* ◆ *adj* (kəˈrɒbərɪt). *Archaic.* **2** serving to corroborate a fact, an opinion, etc. **3** (of a fact) corroborated. [C16: from Latin *corrōborāre* to invigorate, from *rōborāre* to make strong, from *rōbur* strength, literally: oak] ► **corˌroboˈration** *n* ► **corroborative** (kəˈrɒbərətɪv) *or* **corˌroboˈratory** *adj* ► **corˈroboratively** *adv* ► **corˈroboˌrator** *n*

corroboree (kəˈrɒbərɪ) *n Austral.* **1** a native assembly of sacred, festive, or warlike character. **2** *Informal.* any noisy gathering. [C19: from a native Australian language]

corrode (kəˈrəʊd) *vb* **1** to eat away or be eaten away, esp. by chemical action as in the oxidation or rusting of a metal. **2** (*tr*) to destroy gradually; consume: *his jealousy corroded his happiness.* [C14: from Latin *corrōdere* to gnaw to pieces, from *rōdere* to gnaw; see RODENT, RAT] ► **corˈrodant** *or* **corˈrodent** *n* ► **corˈroder** *n* ► **corˈrodible** *adj* ► **corˌrodiˈbility** *n*

corrody (ˈkɒrədɪ) *n, pl* **-dies.** a variant spelling of **corody.**

corrosion (kəˈrəʊʒən) *n* **1** a process in which a solid, esp. a metal, is eaten away and changed by a chemical action, as in the oxidation of iron in the presence of water by an electrolytic process. **2** slow deterioration by being eaten or worn away. **3** the condition produced by or the product of corrosion.

corrosive (kəˈrəʊsɪv) *adj* **1** (esp. of acids or alkalis) capable of destroying solid materials. **2** tending to eat away or consume. **3** cutting; sarcastic: *a corrosive remark.* ◆ *n* **4** a corrosive substance, such as a strong acid or alkali. ► **corˈrosively** *adv* ► **corˈrosiveness** *n*

corrosive sublimate *n* another name for **mercuric chloride.**

corrugate *vb* (ˈkɒrʊˌgeɪt). **1** (*usually tr*) to fold or be folded into alternate furrows and ridges. ◆ *adj* (ˈkɒrʊgɪt, -ˌgeɪt). **2** folded into furrows and ridges; wrinkled. [C18: from Latin *corrūgāre,* from *rūga* a wrinkle] ► **ˌcorruˈgation** *n*

corrugated iron *n* a thin structural sheet made of iron or steel, formed with alternating ridges and troughs.

corrugated paper *n* a packaging material made from layers of heavy paper, the top layer of which is grooved and ridged.

corrugator (ˈkɒrʊˌgeɪtə) *n* a muscle whose contraction causes wrinkling of the brow.

corrupt (kəˈrʌpt) *adj* **1** lacking in integrity; open to or involving bribery or other dishonest practices: *a corrupt official; corrupt practices in an election.* **2** morally depraved. **3** putrid or rotten. **4** contaminated; unclean. **5** (of a text or manuscript) made meaningless or different in meaning from the original by scribal errors or alterations. **6** (of computer programs or data) containing errors. ◆ *vb* **7** to become or cause to become dishonest or disloyal. **8** to debase or become debased morally; deprave. **9** (*tr*) to infect or contaminate; taint. **10** (*tr*) to cause to become rotten. **11** (*tr*) to alter (a text, manuscript, etc.) from the original. **12** (*tr*) *Computing.* to introduce errors into (data or a program). [C14: from Latin *corruptus* spoiled, from *corrumpere* to ruin, literally: break to pieces, from *rumpere* to break] ► **corˈrupter** *or* **corˈruptor** *n* ► **corˈruptive** *adj* ► **corˈruptively** *adv* ► **corˈruptly** *adv* ► **corˈruptness** *n*

corruptible (kəˈrʌptəbᵊl) *adj* susceptible to corruption; capable of being corrupted. ► **corˌruptiˈbility** *or* **corˈruptibleness** *n* ► **corˈruptibly** *adv*

corruption (kəˈrʌpʃən) *n* **1** the act of corrupting or state of being corrupt. **2** moral perversion; depravity. **3** dishonesty, esp. bribery. **4** putrefaction or decay. **5** alteration, as of a manuscript. **6** an altered form of a word. ► **corˈruptionist** *n*

corsac (ˈkɔːsæk) *n* a fox, *Vulpes corsac,* of central Asia. [C19: from a Turkic language]

corsage (kɔːˈsɑːʒ) *n* **1** a flower or small bunch of flowers worn pinned to the lapel, bosom, etc., or sometimes carried by women. **2** the bodice of a dress. [C15: from Old French, from *cors* body, from Latin *corpus*]

corsair (ˈkɔːsɛə) *n* **1** a pirate. **2** a privateer, esp. of the Barbary Coast. [C15: from Old French *corsaire* pirate, from Medieval Latin *cursārius,* from Latin *cursus* a running, COURSE]

corse (kɔːs) *n* an archaic word for **corpse.**

Corse (kɔrs) *n* the French name for **Corsica.**

corselet (ˈkɔːslɪt) *n* **1** Also spelt: **corslet.** a piece of armour for the top part of the body. **2** a one-piece foundation garment, usually combining a brassiere and a corset. [C15: from Old French, from *cors* bodice of a garment, from Latin *corpus* body]

corset (ˈkɔːsɪt) *n* **1a** a stiffened, elasticated, or laced foundation garment, worn esp. by women, that usually extends from below the chest to the hips, providing support for the spine and stomach and shaping the figure. **1b** a similar garment worn because of injury, weakness, etc., by either sex. **2** *Informal.* a restriction or limitation, esp. government control of bank lending. **3** a stiffened outer bodice worn by either sex, esp. in the 16th century. ◆ *vb* **4** (*tr*) to dress or enclose in, or as in, a corset. [C14: from Old French, literally: a little bodice; see CORSELET]

corsetière (ˌkɔːsɛtɪ'ɛə, kɔːˌsɛt-) *or* (*masc*) **corsetier** (ˌkɔːsɪ'tɪə) *n* a person who makes and fits corsets.

corsetry ('kɔːsɪtrɪ) *n* **1** the making of or dealing in corsets. **2** corsets considered collectively.

Corsica ('kɔːsɪkə) *n* an island in the Mediterranean, west of N Italy: forms, with 43 islets, a region of France; mountainous; settled by Greeks in about 560 B.C.; sold by Genoa to France in 1768. Capital: Ajaccio. Pop.: 259 700 (1995). Area: 8682 sq. km (3367 sq. miles). French name: **Corse.** ▸ **'Corsican** *adj, n*

CORSO ('kɔːsəʊ) *n* (in New Zealand) *acronym for* Council of Organizations for Relief Services Overseas.

cortege *or* **cortège** (kɔː'teɪʒ) *n* **1** a formal procession, esp. a funeral procession. **2** a train of attendants; retinue. [C17: from French, from Italian *corteggio,* from *corteggiare* to attend, from *corte* COURT]

Cortes ('kɔːtɛz; *Spanish* 'kortes) *n* the national assembly of Spain and (until 1910) Portugal. [C17: from Spanish, literally: courts, plural of *corte* court, from Latin *cohors* COHORT]

Cortés ('kɔːtɛz; *Spanish* kor'tes) *or* **Cortez** (kɔː'tɛz) *n* **Hernando** (ɛr'nando) *or* **Hernán** (ɛr'nan). 1485–1547, Spanish conquistador: defeated the Aztecs and conquered Mexico (1523).

cortex ('kɔːtɛks) *n, pl* **-tices** (-tɪˌsiːz). **1** *Anatomy.* the outer layer of any organ or part, such as the grey matter in the brain that covers the cerebrum (**cerebral cortex**) or the outer part of the kidney (**renal cortex**). **2** *Botany.* **2a** the unspecialized tissue in plant stems and roots between the vascular bundles and the epidermis. **2b** the outer layer of a part such as the bark of a stem. [C17: from Latin: bark, outer layer] ▸ **cortical** ('kɔːtɪkᵊl) *adj* ▸ **'cortically** *adv*

corticate ('kɔːtɪkɪt, -ˌkeɪt) *or* **corticated** *adj* (of plants, seeds, etc.) having a bark, husk, or rind. [C19: from Latin *corticātus* covered with bark] ▸ **ˌcorti'cation** *n*

cortico- *or before a vowel* **cortic-** *combining form.* indicating the cortex: *corticotrophin.*

corticolous ((kɔː'tɪkələs) *adj Biology.* living or growing on the surface of bark.

corticosteroid (ˌkɔːtɪkəʊ'stɪərɔɪd) *or* **corticoid** *n* **1** any steroid hormone produced by the adrenal cortex that affects carbohydrate, protein, and electrolyte metabolism, gonad function, and immune response. **2** any similar synthetic substance, used in treating inflammatory and allergic diseases. ◆ See **glucocorticoid, mineralocorticoid.**

corticosterone (ˌkɔːtɪ'kɒstəˌrəʊn) *n* a glucocorticoid hormone secreted by the adrenal cortex. Formula: $C_{21}H_{30}O_4$. See also **corticosteroid.** [C20: from CORTICO- + STER(OL) + -ONE]

corticotrophic (ˌkɔːtɪkəʊ'trəʊfɪk) *or* **corticotropic** (ˌkɔːtɪkəʊ'trɒpɪk) *adj* stimulating the adrenal cortex; adrenocorticotrophic.

corticotrophin (ˌkɔːtɪkəʊ'trəʊfɪn) *n* another name for **adrenocorticotrophic hormone.** See **ACTH.**

cortisol ('kɔːtɪˌsɒl) *n* another name for **hydrocortisone.** [C20: from CORTIS(ONE) + -OL[2]]

cortisone ('kɔːtɪˌsəʊn, -ˌzəʊn) *n* a glucocorticoid hormone, the synthetic form of which has been used in treating rheumatoid arthritis, allergic and skin diseases, leukaemia, etc.; 17-hydroxy-11-dehydrocorticosterone. Formula: $C_{21}H_{28}O_5$. [C20: shortened from CORTICOSTERONE]

Cortona (kɔː'təʊnə; *Italian* kor'tona) *n* a town in Italy, in Tuscany: Roman and Etruscan remains, 15th-century cathedral. Pop.: 22 700 (1987 est.).

Cortot (*French* korto) *n* **Alfred** (alfrɛd). 1877–1962, French pianist, born in Switzerland.

corundum (kə'rʌndəm) *n* a white, grey, blue, green, red, yellow, or brown mineral, found in metamorphosed shales and limestones, in veins, and in some igneous rocks. It is used as an abrasive and as gemstone; the red variety is ruby, the blue is sapphire. Composition: aluminium oxide. Formula: Al_2O_3. Crystal structure: hexagonal (rhombohedral). [C18: from Tamil *kuruntam;* related to Sanskrit *kuruvinda* ruby]

Corunna (kə'rʌnə) *n* the English name for **La Coruña.**

coruscate ('kɒrəˌskeɪt) *vb* (*intr*) to emit flashes of light; sparkle. [C18: from Latin *coruscāre* to flash, vibrate]

coruscation (ˌkɒrə'skeɪʃən) *n* **1** a gleam or flash of light. **2** a sudden or striking display of brilliance, wit, etc.

corvée ('kɔːveɪ) *n* **1** *European history.* a day's unpaid labour owed by a feudal vassal to his lord. **2** the practice or an instance of forced labour. [C14: from Old French, from Late Latin *corrogāta* contribution, from Latin *corrogāre* to collect, from *rogāre* to ask]

corves (kɔːvz) *n* the plural of **corf.**

corvette (kɔː'vɛt) *n* a lightly armed escort warship. [C17: from Old French, perhaps from Middle Dutch *corf* basket, small ship, from Latin *corbis* basket]

corvine ('kɔːvaɪn) *adj* **1** of, relating to, or resembling a crow. **2** of, relating to, or belonging to the passerine bird family *Corvidae,* which includes the crows, raven, rook, jackdaw, magpies, and jays. [C17: from Latin *corvīnus* ravenlike, from *corvus* a raven]

Corvo ('kɔːvəʊ) *n* **Baron.** See (Frederick William) **Rolfe.**

Corvus ('kɔːvəs) *n, Latin genitive* **Corvi** ('kɔːvaɪ). a small quadrilateral-shaped constellation in the S hemisphere, lying between Virgo and Hydra. [Latin: raven]

Corybant ('kɒrɪˌbænt) *n, pl* **Corybants** *or* **Corybantes** (ˌkɒrɪ'bæntiːz). *Classical myth.* a wild attendant of the goddess Cybele. [C14: from Latin *Corybās,* from Greek *Korubas,* probably of Phrygian origin] ▸ **ˌCory'bantian, ˌCory'bantic** *or* **ˌCory'bantine** *adj*

corydalis (kə'rɪdəlɪs) *n* any erect or climbing plant of the N temperate genus *Corydalis,* having finely-lobed leaves and spurred yellow or pinkish flowers: family *Fumariaceae.* Also called: **fumitory.** [C19: from New Latin, from Greek *korudallis* variant of *korudos* crested lark, from *korus* helmet, crest; alluding to the appearance of the flowers]

Corydon ('kɒrɪdᵊn, -ˌdɒn) *n* (in pastoral literature) a shepherd or rustic: used as a proper name.

corymb ('kɒrɪmb, -rɪm) *n* an inflorescence in the form of a flat-topped flower cluster with the oldest flowers at the periphery. This type of raceme occurs in the candytuft. [C18: from Latin *corymbus,* from Greek *korumbos* cluster] ▸ **'corymbed** *adj* ▸ **co'rymbose** *or* **co'rymbous** *adj* ▸ **co'rymbosely** *adv*

coryphaeus (ˌkɒrɪ'fiːəs) *n, pl* **-phaei** (-'fiːaɪ). **1** (in ancient Greek drama) the leader of the chorus. **2** *Archaic or literary.* a leader of a group. [C17: from Latin, from Greek *koruphaios* leader, from *koruphē* summit]

coryphée (ˌkɒrɪ'feɪ) *n* a leading dancer of a corps de ballet. [C19: from French, from Latin *coryphaeus* CORYPHAEUS]

coryza (kə'raɪzə) *n* acute inflammation of the mucous membrane of the nose, with discharge of mucus; a head cold. [C17: from Late Latin: catarrh, from Greek *koruza*]

cos[1] *or* **cos lettuce** (kɒs) *n* a variety of lettuce with a long slender head and crisp leaves. Compare **cabbage lettuce.** Usual U.S. and Canadian name: **romaine.** [C17: named after *Kos,* the Aegean island of its origin]

cos[2] (kɒz) *abbrev. for* cosine.

Cos (kɒs) *n* a variant spelling of **Kos.**

COS *abbrev. for* Chief of Staff.

Cos. *or* **cos.** *abbrev. for:* **1** Companies. **2** Counties.

c.o.s. *or* **COS** *abbrev. for* cash on shipment.

Cosa Nostra ('kəʊsə 'nɒstrə) *n* the branch of the Mafia that operates in the U.S. [Italian, literally: our thing]

cosec ('kəʊsɛk) *abbrev. for* cosecant.

cosecant (kəʊ'siːkənt) *n* (of an angle) a trigonometric function that in a right-angled triangle is the ratio of the length of the hypotenuse to that of the opposite side; the reciprocal of sine. Abbrev.: **cosec.**

cosech ('kəʊsetʃ, -sɛk) *n* hyperbolic cosecant; a hyperbolic function that is the reciprocal of sinh.

coseismal (kəʊ'saɪzməl) *or* **coseismic** *adj* **1** of or designating points at which earthquake waves are felt at the same time. **2** (of a line on a map) connecting such points. ◆ *n* **3** such a line on a map.

Cosenza (*Italian* ko'zɛntsa) *n* a city in S Italy, in Calabria. Pop.: 104 480 (1990).

coset ('kəʊˌsɛt) *n Maths.* a set that when added to another set produces a specified larger set.

Cosgrave ('kɒzgreɪv) *n* **1 Liam** ('liːəm). born 1920, Irish statesman; prime minister of the Republic of Ireland (1973–77). **2** his father, **W(illiam) T(homas).** 1880–1965, Irish statesman; first president of the Irish Free State (1922–32).

cosh[1] (kɒʃ) *Brit.* ◆ *n* **1** a blunt weapon, often made of hard rubber; bludgeon. **2** an attack with such a weapon. ◆ *vb* (*tr*) **3** to hit with such a weapon, esp. on the head. [C19: from Romany *kosh,* from *koshter* skewer, stick]

cosh[2] (kɒʃ, 'kɒs'eɪtʃ) *n* hyperbolic cosine; a hyperbolic function, $\cosh z = ½(e^z + e^{-z})$, related to cosine by the expression $\cosh iz = \cos z$, where $i = \sqrt{-1}$. [C19: from COS(INE) + H(YPERBOLIC)]

cosher ('kɒʃə) *vb Irish.* **1** (*tr*) to pamper or coddle. **2** (*intr*) to live or be entertained at the expense of another.

cosignatory (kəʊ'sɪgnətərɪ, -trɪ) *n, pl* **-ries. 1** a person, country, etc., that signs a document jointly with others. ◆ *adj* **2** signing jointly with another or others.

Cosimo I (*Italian* 'kɔːzimo) *n* See (Cosimo I) **Medici.**

cosine ('kəʊˌsaɪn) *n* (of an angle) **1** a trigonometric function that in a right-angled triangle is the ratio of the length of the adjacent side to that of the hypotenuse; the sine of the complement. **2** a function that in a circle centred at the origin of a Cartesian coordinate system is the ratio of the abscissa of a point on the circumference to the radius of the circle. ◆ Abbrev.: **cos.** [C17: from New Latin *cosinus;* see CO-, SINE[1]]

COSLA ('kɒzlə) *n acronym for* Convention of Scottish Local Authorities.

cosmetic (kɒz'mɛtɪk) *n* **1** any preparation applied to the body, esp. the face, with the intention of beautifying it. ◆ *adj* **2** serving or designed to beautify the body, esp. the face. **3** having no other function than to beautify: *cosmetic illustrations in a book.* **4** *Slightly derogatory.* designed to cover up a greater flaw or deficiency; superficial: *their resignation is a cosmetic exercise.* [C17: from Greek *kosmētikos,* from *kosmein* to arrange, from *kosmos* order] ▸ **cos'metically** *adv* ▸ **cosˌmeti'cology** *n*

cosmetician (ˌkɒzmɪ'tɪʃən) *n* a person who makes, sells, or applies cosmetics.

cosmetic surgery *n* surgery performed to improve the appearance, rather than for medical reasons.

cosmic ('kɒzmɪk) *adj* **1** of or relating to the whole universe: *cosmic laws.* **2** occurring or originating in outer space, esp. as opposed to the vicinity of the earth, the solar system, or the local galaxy: *cosmic rays.* **3** immeasurably extended in space or time; vast. **4** *Rare.* harmonious. ▸ **'cosmically** *adv*

cosmic dust *n* fine particles of solid matter occurring throughout interstellar space and often collecting into clouds of extremely low density. See also **nebula** (sense 1).

cosmic rays *pl n* radiation consisting of atomic nuclei, esp. protons, of very high energy that reach the earth from outer space. Also called: **cosmic radiation.**

cosmic string *n* any of a number of linear defects in space–time postulated in certain theories of cosmology to exist in the universe as a consequence of the big bang.

cosmine ('kɒzmiːn) *or* **cosmin** *n Zoology.* a substance resembling dentine,

forming the outer layer of cosmoid scales. [C20: from Greek *kosmos* arrangement + -INE[1]]
cosmo- *or before a vowel* **cosm-** *combining form.* indicating the world or universe: *cosmology; cosmonaut; cosmography.* [from Greek: COSMOS]
cosmodrome ('kɒzmə,drəʊm) *n* a site, esp. one in the former Soviet Union, from which spacecraft are launched.
cosmogony (kɒz'mɒgənɪ) *n, pl* **-nies. 1** the study of the origin and development of the universe or of a particular system in the universe, such as the solar system. **2** a theory of such an origin or evolution. [C17: from Greek *kosmogonia,* from COSMO- + *gonos* creation] ► **cos'mogonal** *adj* ► **cosmogonic** (,kɒzmə'gɒnɪk) *or* **,cosmo'gonical** *adj* ► **cos'mogonist** *n*
cosmography (kɒz'mɒgrəfɪ) *n* **1** a representation of the world or the universe. **2** the science dealing with the whole order of nature. ► **cos'mographer** *or* **cos'mographist** *n* ► **cosmographic** (,kɒzmə'græfɪk) *or* **,cosmo'graphical** *adj* ► **,cosmo'graphically** *adv*
cosmoid ('kɒzmɔɪd) *adj* (of the scales of coelacanths and lungfish) consisting of two inner bony layers and an outer layer of cosmine. [C20: from COSM(INE) + -OID]
cosmological argument *n Philosophy.* one of the arguments that purport to prove the existence of God from empirical facts about the universe, esp. the argument to the existence of a first cause. Compare **ontological argument** (sense 1), **teleological argument.**
cosmological principle *n Astronomy.* the theory that the universe is uniform, homogenous, and isotropic, and therefore appears the same from any position.
cosmology (kɒz'mɒlədʒɪ) *n* **1** the philosophical study of the origin and nature of the universe. **2** the branch of astronomy concerned with the evolution and structure of the universe. **3** a particular account of the origin or structure of the universe: *Ptolemaic cosmology.* ► **cosmological** (,kɒzmə'lɒdʒɪkᵊl) *or* **,cosmo'logic** *adj* ► **,cosmo'logically** *adv* ► **cos'mologist** *n*
cosmonaut ('kɒzmə,nɔːt) *n* an astronaut, esp. in the former Soviet Union. [C20: from Russian *kosmonavt,* from COSMO- + Greek *nautēs* sailor; compare ARGONAUT]
cosmopolis (kɒz'mɒpəlɪs) *n* an international city. [C19: see COSMO-, POLIS[1]]
cosmopolitan (,kɒzmə'pɒlɪtᵊn) *n* **1** a person who has lived and travelled in many countries, esp. one who is free of national prejudices. ◆ *adj* **2** having interest in or familiar with many parts of the world. **3** sophisticated or urbane. **4** composed of people or elements from all parts of the world or from many different spheres. **5** (of plants or animals) widely distributed. [C17: from French, ultimately from Greek *kosmopolitēs,* from *kosmo-* COSMO- + *politēs* citizen] ► **,cosmo'politanism** *n*
cosmopolite (kɒz'mɒpə,laɪt) *n* **1** a less common word for **cosmopolitan** (sense 1). **2** an animal or plant that occurs in most parts of the world. ► **cos'mopolit,ism** *n*
cosmos ('kɒzmɒs) *n* **1** the world or universe considered as an ordered system. **2** any ordered system. **3** harmony; order. **4** (*pl* **-mos** *or* **-moses**) any tropical American plant of the genus *Cosmos,* cultivated as garden plants for their brightly coloured flowers: family *Compositae* (composites). [C17: from Greek *kosmos* order, world, universe]
Cosmos ('kɒzmɒs) *n Astronautics.* any of various types of Soviet satellite, including Cosmos 1 (launched 1962) and nearly 2000 subsequent satellites.
Cosmotron ('kɒzmə,trɒn) *n* a large synchrotron for accelerating protons to high energies (of the order of 1 GeV). [C20: from COSM(IC RAY) + -TRON]
coss (kɒs) *n* another name for **kos.**
Cossack ('kɒsæk) *n* **1** (formerly) any of the free warrior-peasants of chiefly East Slavonic descent who lived in communes, esp. in the Ukraine, and served as cavalry under the tsars. ◆ *adj* **2** of, relating to, or characteristic of the Cossacks: *a Cossack dance.* [C16: from Russian *kazak* vagabond, of Turkic origin]
cossack hat *n* a warm brimless hat of fur or sheepskin.
cosset ('kɒsɪt) *vb* (*tr*) **-sets, -seting, -seted. 1** to pamper; coddle; pet. ◆ *n* **2** any pet animal, esp. a lamb. [C16: of unknown origin]
cossie ('kɒzɪ) *n* an informal name for a swimming costume.
cost (kɒst) *n* **1** the price paid or required for acquiring, producing, or maintaining something, usually measured in money, time, or energy; expense or expenditure; outlay. **2** suffering or sacrifice; loss; penalty: *count the cost to your health; I know to my cost.* **3a** the amount paid for a commodity by its seller: *to sell at cost.* **3b** (*as modifier*): *the cost price.* **4** (*pl*) *Law.* the expenses of judicial proceedings. **5 at any cost** *or* **at all costs.** regardless of cost or sacrifice involved. **6 at the cost of.** at the expense of losing. ◆ *vb* **costs, costing, cost. 7** (*tr*) to be obtained or obtainable in exchange for (money or something equivalent); be priced at: *the ride cost one pound.* **8** to cause or require the expenditure, loss, or sacrifice (of): *the accident cost him dearly.* **9** to estimate the cost of (a product, process, etc.) for the purposes of pricing, budgeting, control, etc. [C13: from Old French (n), from *coster* to cost, from Latin *constāre* to stand at, cost, from *stāre* to stand] ► **'costless** *adj*
costa ('kɒstə) *n, pl* **-tae** (-tiː). **1** the technical name for **rib**[1] (sense 1). **2** a riblike part, such as the midrib of a plant leaf. [C19: from Latin: rib, side, wall] ► **'costal** *adj*
Costa Brava ('kɒstə 'brɑːvə) *n* a coastal region of NE Spain along the Mediterranean, extending from Barcelona to the French border: many resorts.
cost accounting *n* the recording and controlling of all the expenditures of an enterprise in order to facilitate control of separate activities. Also called: **management accounting.** ► **cost accountant** *n*
co-star *n* **1** an actor who shares star billing with another. ◆ *vb* **-stars, -starring, -starred. 2** (*intr;* often foll. by *with*) to share star billing (with another actor). **3** (*tr*) to present as sharing top billing: *the film co-starred Mae West and W. C. Fields.*
costard ('kʌstəd) *n* **1** an English variety of apple tree. **2** the large ribbed apple of this tree. **3** *Archaic, humorous.* a slang word for **head.** [C14: from Anglo-Norman, from Old French *coste* rib]
Costa Rica ('kɒstə 'riːkə) *n* a republic in Central America: gained independence from Spain in 1821; mostly mountainous and volcanic, with extensive forests. Official language: Spanish. Official religion: Roman Catholic. Currency: colón. Capital: San José. Pop.: 3 533 000 (1998 est.). Area: 50 900 sq. km (19 652 sq. miles). ► **Costa Rican** *adj, n*
costate ('kɒsteɪt) *adj* **1** *Anatomy.* having ribs. **2** (of leaves) having veins or ridges, esp. parallel ones. [C19: from Late Latin *costātus,* from Latin *costa* rib]
cost-benefit *adj* denoting or relating to a method of assessing a project that takes into account its costs and its benefits to society as well as the revenue it generates: *a cost-benefit analysis; the project was assessed on a cost-benefit basis.*
cost centre *n* a unit, such as a department of a company, to which costs may be allocated for cost accounting purposes.
cost-effective *adj* providing adequate financial return in relation to outlay. ► **cost-effectiveness** *n*
Costello (kɒ'stɛləʊ) *n* **Elvis,** real name *Declan McManus.* born 1954, British rock singer and songwriter. His recordings include *This Year's Model* (1978), "Oliver's Army" (1979), and *Spike* (1989).
Costermansville ('kɒstəmənz,vɪl) *n* the former name (until 1966) of **Bukavu.**
costermonger ('kɒstə,mʌŋgə) *or* **coster** *n Brit., rare.* a person who sells fruit, vegetables, etc., from a barrow. [C16: *coster-,* from COSTARD + MONGER]
costive ('kɒstɪv) *adj* **1** having constipation; constipated. **2** sluggish. **3** niggardly. [C14: from Old French *costivé,* from Latin *constipātus;* see CONSTIPATE] ► **'costively** *adv* ► **'costiveness** *n*
costly ('kɒstlɪ) *adj* **-lier, -liest. 1** of great price or value; expensive. **2** entailing great loss or sacrifice: *a costly victory.* **3** splendid; lavish. ► **'costliness** *n*
costmary ('kɒst,mɛərɪ) *n, pl* **-maries.** a herbaceous plant, *Chrysanthemum balsamita,* native to Asia. Its fragrant leaves were used as a seasoning and to flavour ale: family *Compositae* (composites). Also called: **alecost.** [C15 *costmarie,* from Latin *costum* aromatic plant + *Marie* (the Virgin) Mary]
Costner ('kɒstnə) *n* **Kevin.** born 1955, U.S. film actor: his films include *Robin Hood: Prince of Thieves* (1990), *Dances with Wolves* (1990; also directed), *JFK* (1991), *Waterworld* (1995), and *Message in a Bottle* (1999).
cost of living *n* **1a** the basic cost of the food, clothing, shelter, and fuel necessary to maintain life, esp. at a standard regarded as basic or minimal. **1b** (*as modifier*): *the cost-of-living index.* **2** the average expenditure of a person or family in a given period.
costotomy (kɒ'stɒtəmɪ) *n, pl* **-mies.** surgical incision into a rib.
cost-plus *n* **a** a method of establishing a selling price in which an agreed percentage is added to the cost price to cover profit. **b** (*as modifier*): *cost-plus pricing.*
cost-push inflation *n* See **inflation.**
costrel ('kɒstrəl) *n Obsolete.* a flask, usually of earthenware or leather. [C14: from Old French *costerel,* from *coste* side, rib, from Latin *costa*]
cost rent *n* (in Britain) the rent of a dwelling calculated on the cost of providing and maintaining the property without allowing for a profit.
costume ('kɒstjuːm) *n* **1** a complete style of dressing, including all the clothes, accessories, etc., worn at one time, as in a particular country or period; dress: *national costume.* **2** *Old-fashioned.* a woman's suit. **3** a set of clothes, esp. unusual or period clothes, worn in a play by an actor or at a fancy dress ball: *a jester's costume.* **4** short for **swimming costume.** ◆ *vb* (*tr*) **5** to furnish the costumes for (a show, film, etc.). **6** to dress (someone) in a costume. [C18: from French, from Italian: dress, habit, CUSTOM]
costume jewellery *n* jewellery that is decorative but has little intrinsic value.
costume piece *n* any theatrical production, film, television presentation, etc., in which the performers wear the costumes of a former age. Also called: **costume drama.**
costumier (kɒ'stjuːmɪə) *or* **costumer** (kɒ'stjuːmə) *n* a person or firm that makes or supplies theatrical or fancy costumes.
cosy *or U.S.* **cozy** ('kəʊzɪ) *adj* **-sier, -siest** *or U.S.* **-zier, -ziest. 1** warm and snug. **2** intimate; friendly. **3** convenient, esp. for devious purposes: *a cosy deal.* ◆ *n, pl* **-sies** *or U.S.* **-zies. 4** a cover for keeping things warm: *egg cosy.* [C18: from Scots, of unknown origin] ► **'cosily** *or U.S.* **'cozily** *adv* ► **'cosiness** *or U.S.* **'coziness** *n*
cosy along *vb* **-sies, -sying, -sied.** (*tr, adv*) to reassure (someone), esp. with false assurances.
cosy up *or U.S.* **cozy up** *vb* (*intr,* often foll. by *to*) *Chiefly U.S. and Canadian.* **1** to seek to become intimate or to ingratiate oneself (with someone). **2** to draw close to (somebody or something) for warmth or for affection; snuggle up.
cot[1] (kɒt) *n* **1** a child's boxlike bed, usually incorporating vertical bars. **2** a collapsible or portable bed. **3** a light bedstead. **4** *Nautical.* a hammock-like bed with a stiff frame. [C17: from Hindi *khāt* bedstead, from Sanskrit *khátvā,* of Dravidian origin; related to Tamil *kattil* bedstead]
cot[2] (kɒt) *n* **1** *Literary or archaic.* a small cottage. **2** Also called: **cote. 2a** a small shelter, esp. one for pigeons, sheep, etc. **2b** (*in combination*): *dovecot.* **3** another name for **fingerstall.** [Old English *cot;* related to Old Norse *kot* little hut, Middle Low German *cot*]
cot[3] (kɒt) *abbrev. for* cotangent.
cotan ('kəʊ,tæn) *abbrev. for* cotangent.
cotangent (kəʊ'tændʒənt) *n* (of an angle) a trigonometric function that in a right-angled triangle is the ratio of the length of the adjacent side to that of the opposite side; the reciprocal of tangent. Abbrevs.: **cot, cotan, ctn.** ► **cotangential** (,kəʊtæn'dʒɛnʃəl) *adj*
cot case *n Austral.* & *N.Z.* **1** a person confined to bed through illness. **2** *Humorous.* a person who is incapacitated by drink.
cot death *n* the unexplained sudden death of an infant during sleep. Technical

name: **sudden infant death syndrome.** Also called (U.S. and Canadian): **crib death.**

cote[1] (kəʊt) *or* **cot** *n* **1a** a small shelter for pigeons, sheep, etc. **1b** (*in combination*): *dovecote.* **2** *Dialect, chiefly Brit.* a small cottage. [Old English *cote;* related to Low German *Kote;* see COT[2]]

cote[2] (kəʊt) *vb* (*tr*) *Archaic.* to pass by, outstrip, or surpass. [C16: perhaps from Old French *costoier* to run alongside, from *coste* side; see COAST]

Côte d'Azur (*French* kot dazyr) *n* the Mediterranean coast of France, including the French Riviera: forms an administrative region with Provence.

Côte d'Ivoire (*French* kot divwar) *n* a republic in West Africa, on the Gulf of Guinea: Portuguese trading for ivory and slaves began in the 16th century; made a French protectorate in 1842 and became independent in 1960; major producer of coffee and cocoa. Official language: French. Religion: Muslim majority, with animist, atheist, and Roman Catholic minorities. Currency: franc. Capital: Yamoussoukro (administrative); Abidjan (legislative). Pop.: 15 446 000 (1998 est.). Area: 319 820 sq. km (123 483 sq. miles). Former name (until 1986): **the Ivory Coast.**

Côte-d'Or (*French* kotdɔr) *n* a department of E central France, in NE Burgundy. Capital: Dijon. Pop.: 507 300 (1995). Area: 8787 sq. km (3427 sq. miles).

cotemporary (kəʊ'tempərərɪ) *adj* a variant of **contemporary.**

cotenant (kəʊ'tenənt) *n* a person who holds property jointly or in common with others. ▸ **co'tenancy** *n*

coterie ('kəʊtərɪ) *n* a small exclusive group of friends or people with common interests; clique. [C18: from French, from Old French: association of tenants, from *cotier* (unattested) cottager, from Medieval Latin *cotārius* COTTER[2]; see COT[2]]

coterminous (kəʊ'tɜːmɪnəs) *or* **conterminous** *adj* **1** having a common boundary; bordering; contiguous. **2** coextensive or coincident in range, time, scope, etc.

Côtes-d'Armor (*French* kotdarmɔr) *n* a department of W France, on the N coast of Brittany. Capital: St Brieuc. Pop.: 536 600 (1995). Area: 6878 sq. km (2656 sq. miles). Former name: **Côtes-du-Nord.**

Côtes-du-Nord (*French* kotdynɔr) *n* the former name of **Côtes-d'Armor.**

coth (kɒθ) *n* hyperbolic cotangent; a hyperbolic function that is the ratio of cosh to sinh, being the reciprocal of tanh. [C20: from COT(ANGENT) + H(YPERBOLIC)]

cothurnus (kəʊ'θɜːnəs) *or* **cothurn** ('kəʊθɜːn, kəʊ'θɜːn) *n, pl* **-thurni** (-'θɜːnaɪ) *or* **-thurns.** the buskin worn in ancient Greek tragedy. [C18: from Latin, from Greek *kothornos*]

cotidal (kəʊ'taɪdᵊl) *adj* (of a line on a tidal chart) joining points at which high tide occurs simultaneously.

cotillion *or* **cotillon** (kə'tɪljən, kəʊ-) *n* **1** a French formation dance of the 18th century. **2** *U.S.* a quadrille. **3** *U.S.* a complicated dance with frequent changes of partners. **4** *U.S. and Canadian.* a formal ball, esp. one at which debutantes are presented. [C18: from French *cotillon* dance, from Old French: petticoat, from *cote* COAT]

cotinga (kə'tɪŋgə) *n* any tropical American passerine bird of the family *Cotingidae,* such as the umbrella bird and the cock-of-the-rock, having a broad slightly hooked bill. Also called: **chatterer.**

Cotman ('kɒtmən) *n* **John Sell.** 1782–1842, English landscape watercolourist and etcher.

cotoneaster (kəˌtəʊnɪ'æstə) *n* any Old World shrub of the rosaceous genus *Cotoneaster:* cultivated for their small ornamental white or pinkish flowers and red or black berries. [C18: from New Latin, from Latin *cotōneum* QUINCE]

Cotonou (ˌkəʊtə'nuː) *n* the chief port and official capital of Benin, on the Bight of Benin. Pop.: 750 000 (1994 est.).

Cotopaxi (*Spanish* koto'paksi) *n* a volcano in central Ecuador, in the Andes: the world's highest active volcano. Height: 5896 m (19 344 ft.).

cotquean ('kɒtˌkwiːn) *n Archaic.* **1** a coarse woman. **2** a man who does housework. [C16: see COT[2], QUEAN]

cotransport (kəʊ'trænsˌpɔːt) *n Biochem.* the transport of one solute across a membrane from a region of low concentration of another solute to a region of high concentration of that solute. See **active transport.**

co-trimoxazole (ˌkəʊtrɪ'mɒksəzəʊl) *n* an antibiotic consisting of a mixture of trimethoprim (an antiseptic) and sulphamethoxazole (a sulpha drug): used esp. to treat infections of the urinary tract.

Cotswold ('kɒtsˌwəʊld, -wəld) *n* a breed of sheep with long wool that originated in the Cotswolds.

Cotswolds ('kɒtsˌwəʊldz, -wəldz) *pl n* a range of low hills in SW England, mainly in Gloucestershire: formerly a centre of the wool industry.

cotta ('kɒtə) *n R.C. Church.* a short form of surplice. [C19: from Italian: tunic, from Medieval Latin; see COAT]

cottage ('kɒtɪdʒ) *n* **1** a small simple house, esp. in a rural area. **2** *U.S. and Canadian.* a small house in the country or at a resort, used for holiday purposes. **3** *U.S.* one of several housing units, as at a hospital, for accommodating people in groups. **4** *Slang.* a public lavatory. [C14: from COT[2]]

cottage cheese *n* a mild loose soft white cheese made from skimmed milk curds.

cottage flat *n Brit.* any of the flats in a two-storey house that is divided into four flats, two on each floor.

cottage hospital *n Brit.* a small rural hospital.

cottage industry *n* an industry in which employees work in their own homes, often using their own equipment.

cottage loaf *n Brit.* a loaf consisting of two round pieces, the smaller of which sits on top of the larger.

cottage piano *n* a small upright piano.

cottage pie *n Brit.* another term for **shepherd's pie.**

cottager ('kɒtɪdʒə) *n* **1** a person who lives in a cottage. **2** a rural labourer. **3** *Chiefly Canadian.* a person holidaying in a cottage, esp. an owner and seasonal resident of a cottage in a resort area. **4** *History.* another name for **cotter**[2].

cottaging ('kɒtɪdʒɪŋ) *n Brit.* homosexual activity between men in a public lavatory. [C20: from COTTAGE (sense 4)]

Cottbus (*German* 'kɔtbʊs) *n* an industrial city in E Germany, in Brandenburg on the Spree River. Pop.: 123 214 (1996 est.).

cotter[1] ('kɒtə) *Machinery.* ◆ *n* **1** any part, such as a pin, wedge, key, etc., that is used to secure two other parts so that relative motion between them is prevented. **2** short for **cotter pin.** ◆ *vb* **3** (*tr*) to secure (two parts) with a cotter. [C14: shortened from *cotterel,* of unknown origin]

cotter[2] ('kɒtə) *n* **1** Also called: **cottier.** *English history.* a villein in late Anglo-Saxon and early Norman times occupying a cottage and land in return for labour. **2** Also called: **cottar.** a peasant occupying a cottage and land in the Scottish Highlands under the same tenure as an Irish cottier. ◆ See also **cottier** (sense 2), **cottager** (sense 1). [C14: from Medieval Latin *cotārius,* from Middle English *cote* COT[2]]

cotter pin *n Machinery.* **1** a split pin secured, after passing through holes in the parts to be attached, by spreading the ends. **2** a tapered pin threaded at the smaller end and secured by a nut after insertion.

Cottian Alps ('kɒtɪən) *pl n* a mountain range in SW Europe, between NW Italy and SE France: part of the Alps. Highest peak: Monte Viso, 3841 m (12 600 ft.).

cottid ('kɒtɪd) *n* any fish of the scorpaenoid family *Cottidae,* typically possessing a large head, tapering body, and spiny fins, including the pogge, sea scorpion, bullhead, father lasher, and cottus. [from New Latin *Cottidae,* from *cottus,* from Greek *kottos,* the name of an unidentified river fish]

cottier ('kɒtɪə) *n* **1** another name for **cotter**[2] (sense 1). **2** (in Ireland) a peasant farming a smallholding under **cottier tenure** (the holding of not more than half an acre at a rent of not more than five pounds a year). **3** another name for **cottager** (sense 1). [C14: from Old French *cotier;* see COTE[1], COTERIE]

cotton ('kɒtᵊn) *n* **1** any of various herbaceous plants and shrubs of the malvaceous genus *Gossypium,* such as **sea-island cotton,** cultivated in warm climates for the fibre surrounding the seeds and the oil within the seeds. **2** the soft white downy fibre of these plants: used to manufacture textiles. **3** cotton plants collectively, as a cultivated crop. **4a** a cloth or thread made from cotton fibres. **4b** (*as modifier*): *a cotton dress.* **5** any substance, such as kapok (**silk cotton**), resembling cotton but obtained from other plants. ◆ See also **cotton on, cotton to.** [C14: from Old French *coton,* from Arabic dialect *qutun,* from Arabic *qutn*] ▸ **'cottony** *adj*

Cotton ('kɒtᵊn) *n* **Henry.** 1907–87, British golfer: three times winner of the British Open.

cottonade (ˌkɒtᵊ'neɪd) *n* a coarse fabric of cotton or mixed fibres, used for work clothes, etc. [C19: from French *cotonnade,* from *coton* COTTON + -ADE]

cotton belt *n* a belt of land in the southeastern U.S. that specializes in the production of cotton.

cotton bush *n Austral.* any of various downy chenopodiaceous shrubs, esp. *Kochia aphylla,* which is used to feed livestock.

cotton cake *n* cottonseed meal compressed into nuts or cubes of various sizes for feeding to animals.

cotton candy *n* the U.S. and Canadian name for **candyfloss.**

cotton flannel *n* a plain-weave or twill-weave fabric with nap on one side only. Also called: **Canton flannel.**

cotton grass *n* any of various N temperate and arctic grasslike bog plants of the cyperaceous genus *Eriophorum,* whose clusters of long silky hairs resemble cotton tufts. Also called: **bog cotton.**

cottonmouth ('kɒtᵊnˌmaʊθ) *n* another name for the **water moccasin.**

cotton on *vb* (*intr, adv;* often foll. by *to*) *Informal.* **1** to perceive the meaning (of). **2** to make use (of).

cotton picker *n* **1** a machine for harvesting cotton fibre. **2** a person who picks ripe cotton fibre from the plants.

cotton-picking *adj U.S. and Canadian slang.* (intensifier qualifying something undesirable): *you cotton-picking layabout!*

cotton sedge *n Canadian.* another name for **cotton grass.**

cottonseed ('kɒtᵊnˌsiːd) *n, pl* **-seeds** *or* **-seed.** the seed of the cotton plant: a source of oil and fodder.

cottonseed meal *n* the residue of cottonseed kernels from which oil has been extracted, used as fodder or fertilizer.

cottonseed oil *n* a yellowish or dark red oil with a nutlike smell, extracted or expelled from cottonseed, used in cooking and in the manufacture of paints, soaps, etc.

cotton stainer *n* any of various heteropterous insects of the genus *Dysdercus:* serious pests of cotton, piercing and staining the cotton bolls: family *Pyrrhocoridae.*

cottontail ('kɒtᵊnˌteɪl) *n* any of several common rabbits of the genus *Sylvilagus,* such as *S. floridanus* (**eastern cottontail**), of American woodlands.

cotton to *vb* (*intr, prep*) *U.S. and Canadian informal.* **1** to become friendly with. **2** to approve of.

cotton waste *n* refuse cotton yarn, esp. when used as a cleaning material.

cottonweed ('kɒtᵊnˌwiːd) *n* **1** a downy perennial plant, *Otanthus maritimus,* of European coastal regions, having small yellow flowers surrounded by large hairy bracts: family *Compositae* (composites). **2** any of various similar plants.

cottonwood ('kɒtᵊnˌwʊd) *n* any of several North American poplars, esp. *Populus deltoides,* whose seeds are covered with cottony hairs.

cotton wool *n* **1** Also called: **purified cotton.** *Chiefly Brit.* bleached and sterilized cotton from which the gross impurities, such as the seeds and waxy matter, have been removed: used for surgical dressings, tampons, etc. Usual U.S. term: **absorbent cotton. 2** cotton in the natural state. **3** *Brit. informal.* **3a** a state of pampered comfort and protection. **3b** (*as modifier*): *a cotton-wool existence.*

cottony-cushion scale *n* a small scale insect, *Icerya purchasi,* that is a pest of citrus trees in California: it is controlled by introducing an Australian ladybird, *Rodolia cardinalis,* into affected areas.

cottus ('kɒtəs) *n* a scorpaenoid fish of the family *Cottidae;* the type genus, having four yellowish knobs on its head. See also **cottid.**

cotyledon (ˌkɒtɪ'liːdᵊn) *n* **1** a simple embryonic leaf in seed-bearing plants, which, in some species, forms the first green leaf after germination. **2** a tuft of villi on the mammalian placenta. [C16: from Latin: a plant, navelwort, from Greek *kotulēdōn,* from *kotulē* cup, hollow] ▸ ˌ**coty'ledonous** *or* ˌ**coty'ledoˌnoid** *adj* ▸ ˌ**coty'ledonal** *adj* ▸ ˌ**coty'ledonary** *adj*

cotyloid ('kɒtɪˌlɔɪd) *or* **cotyloidal** *Anatomy.* ◆ *adj* **1a** shaped like a cup. **1b** of or relating to the acetabulum. ◆ *n* **2** a small bone forming part of the acetabular cavity in some mammals. [C18: from Greek *kotuloeidēs* cup-shaped, from *kotulē* a cup]

cotype ('kəʊˌtaɪp) *n Biology.* an additional type specimen from the same brood as the original type specimen.

coucal ('kuːkæl, -kᵊl) *n* any ground-living bird of the genus *Centropus,* of Africa, S Asia, and Australia, having long strong legs: family *Cuculidae* (cuckoos). [C19: from French, perhaps from *couc(ou)* cuckoo + *al(ouette)* lark]

couch (kaʊtʃ) *n* **1** a piece of upholstered furniture, usually having a back and armrests, for seating more than one person. **2** a bed, esp. one used in the daytime by the patients of a doctor or a psychoanalyst. **3** a frame upon which barley is malted. **4** a priming layer of paint or varnish, esp. in a painting. **5** *Papermaking.* **5a** a board on which sheets of handmade paper are dried by pressing. **5b** a felt blanket onto which sheets of partly dried paper are transferred for further drying. **5c** a roll on a papermaking machine from which the wet web of paper on the wire is transferred to the next section. **6** *Archaic.* the lair of a wild animal. ◆ *vb* **7** *(tr)* to express in a particular style of language: *couched in an archaic style.* **8** (when *tr, usually reflexive or passive*) to lie down or cause to lie down for or as for sleep. **9** *(intr) Archaic.* to lie in ambush; lurk. **10** *(tr)* to spread (barley) on a frame for malting. **11** *(intr)* (of decomposing leaves) to lie in a heap or bed. **12** *(tr)* to embroider or depict by couching. **13** *(tr)* to lift (sheets of handmade paper) onto the board on which they will be dried. **14** *(tr) Surgery.* to remove (a cataract) by downward displacement of the lens of the eye. **15** *(tr) Archaic.* to lower (a lance) into a horizontal position. [C14: from Old French *couche* a bed, lair, from *coucher* to lay down, from Latin *collocāre* to arrange, from *locāre* to place; see LOCATE] ▸ **'coucher** *n*

couchant ('kaʊtʃənt) *adj (usually postpositive) Heraldry.* in a lying position: *a lion couchant.* [C15: from French: lying, from Old French *coucher* to lay down; see COUCH]

couchette (kuː'ʃɛt) *n* a bed in a railway carriage, esp. one converted from seats. [C20: from French, diminutive of *couche* bed]

couch grass (kaʊtʃ, kuːtʃ) *n* a grass, *Agropyron repens,* with a yellowish-white creeping underground stem by which it spreads quickly: a troublesome weed. Sometimes shortened to **couch.** Also called: **scutch grass, twitch grass, quitch grass.**

couching ('kaʊtʃɪŋ) *n* **a** a method of embroidery in which the thread is caught down at intervals by another thread passed through the material from beneath. **b** a pattern or work done by this method.

couch potato *n Slang.* a lazy person whose recreation consists chiefly of watching television and videos.

cou-cou ('kuːkuː, 'kʊkuː) *n* a preparation of boiled corn meal and okras stirred to a stiff consistency with a **cou-cou stick:** eaten in the Caribbean. [of uncertain origin]

coudé (kuː'deɪ) *adj* (of a reflecting telescope) having plane mirrors positioned to reflect light from the primary mirror along the axis onto a photographic plate or spectroscope. [French, literally: bent in the shape of an elbow, from *coude* an elbow]

Coué (*French* kue) *n* **Émile** (emil). 1857–1926, French psychologist and pharmacist: advocated psychotherapy by autosuggestion. ▸ **Couéism** ('kuːeɪˌɪzəm) *n*

cougar ('kuːgə) *n* another name for **puma.** [C18: from French *couguar,* from Portuguese *cuguardo,* from Tupi *suasuarana,* literally: deerlike, from *suasú* deer + *rana* similar to]

cough (kɒf) *vb* **1** *(intr)* to expel air abruptly and explosively through the partially closed vocal chords. **2** *(intr)* to make a sound similar to this. **3** *(tr)* to utter or express with a cough or coughs. **4** *(intr) Slang.* to confess to a crime. ◆ *n* **5** an act, instance, or sound of coughing. **6** a condition of the lungs or throat that causes frequent coughing. [Old English *cohhetten;* related to Middle Dutch *kochen,* Middle High German *kūchen* to wheeze; probably of imitative origin] ▸ **'cougher** *n*

cough drop *n* a lozenge to relieve a cough.

cough mixture *n* any medicine that relieves coughing.

cough up *vb (adv)* **1** *Informal.* to surrender (money, information, etc.), esp. reluctantly. **2** *(tr)* to bring into the mouth or eject (phlegm, food, etc.) by coughing.

could (kʊd) *vb* (takes an infinitive without *to* or an implied infinitive) used as an auxiliary: **1** to make the past tense of **can**[1]. **2** to make the subjunctive mood of **can**[1], esp. used in polite requests or in conditional sentences: *could I see you tonight? she'd telephone if she could.* **3** to indicate suggestion of a course of action: *you could take the car tomorrow if it's raining.* **4** (often foll. by *well*) to indicate a possibility: *he could well be a spy.* [Old English *cūthe;* influenced by WOULD, SHOULD; see CAN[1]]

couldn't ('kʊdᵊnt) *contraction of* could not.

couldst (kʊdst) *vb Archaic.* the form of **could** used with the pronoun *thou* or its relative form.

coulee ('kuːleɪ, -lɪ) *n* **1a** a flow of molten lava. **1b** such lava when solidified. **2** *Western U.S. and Canadian.* a steep-sided ravine formed by heavy rain or melting snow. **3** a small intermittent stream in such a ravine. [C19: from Canadian French *coulée* a flow, from French, from *couler* to flow, from Latin *cōlāre* to sift, purify; see COLANDER]

coulibiaca (ˌkuːlɪ'bjɑːkə) *n* a variant spelling of **koulibiaca.**

coulis ('kuːliː) *n* a thin purée of vegetables, fruit, etc., usually served as a sauce surrounding a dish. [C20: French, literally: purée]

coulisse (kuː'liːs) *n* **1** Also called: **cullis.** a timber member grooved to take a sliding panel, such as a sluicegate, portcullis, or stage flat. **2a** a flat piece of scenery situated in the wings of a theatre; wing flat. **2b** a space between wing flats. **3** part of the Paris Bourse where unofficial securities are traded. Compare **parquet** (sense 4). [C19: from French: groove, from Old French *couleïce* PORTCULLIS]

couloir ('kuːlwɑː; *French* kulwar) *n* a deep gully on a mountain side, esp. in the French Alps. [C19: from French: corridor, from *couler* to pour; see COULEE]

coulomb ('kuːlɒm) *n* the derived SI unit of electric charge; the quantity of electricity transported in one second by a current of 1 ampere. Symbol: C [C19: named after C.A. de COULOMB]

Coulomb ('kuːlɒm; *French* kulɔ̃) *n* **Charles Augustin de** (ʃarl ogystɛ̃ də). 1736–1806, French physicist: made many discoveries in the field of electricity and magnetism.

Coulomb field *n* the electrostatic field around an electrically charged body or particle. The interaction between two such fields produces **Coulomb force.**

Coulomb's law *n* the principle that the force of attraction or repulsion between two point electric charges is directly proportional to the product of the charges and inversely proportional to the square of the distance between them. The law also holds for magnetic poles.

coulometer (kuː'lɒmɪtə) *or* **coulombmeter** ('kuːlɒmˌmiːtə) *n* an electrolytic cell for measuring the magnitude of an electric charge by determining the total amount of decomposition resulting from the passage of the charge through the cell. Also called: **voltameter.** [C19: from COULOMB + METER[3]] ▸ **coulometric** (ˌkuːlə'mɛtrɪk) *adj* ▸ **cou'lometry** *n*

coulter ('kəʊltə) *n* a blade or sharp-edged disc attached to a plough so that it cuts through the soil vertically in advance of the ploughshare. Also (esp. U.S.): **colter.** [Old English *culter,* from Latin: ploughshare, knife]

coumarin *or* **cumarin** ('kuːmərɪn) *n* a white vanilla-scented crystalline ester, used in perfumes and flavourings and as an anticoagulant. Formula: $C_9H_6O_2$. [C19: from French *coumarine,* from *coumarou* tonka-bean tree, from Spanish *cumarú,* from Tupi] ▸ **'coumaric** *or* **'cumaric** *adj*

coumarone ('kuːməˌrəʊn) *n* another name for **benzofuran.** [C19: from COUMAR(IN) + -ONE]

council ('kaʊnsəl) *n* **1** an assembly of people meeting for discussion, consultation, etc.: *an emergency council.* **2** a body of people elected or appointed to serve in an administrative, legislative, or advisory capacity: *a student council.* **3** *Brit.* (*sometimes cap.;* often preceded by *the*) the local governing authority of a town, county, etc. **4** a meeting or the deliberation of a council. **5** *(modifier)* of, relating to, provided for, or used by a local council: *a council chamber; council offices.* **6** *(modifier) Brit.* provided by a local council, esp. (of housing) at a subsidized rent: *a council house; a council estate.* **7** *Austral.* an administrative or legislative assembly, esp. the upper house of a state parliament in Australia. **8** *Christianity.* an assembly of bishops, theologians, and other representatives of several churches or dioceses, convened for regulating matters of doctrine or discipline. [C12: from Old French *concile,* from Latin *concilium* assembly, from *com-* together + *calāre* to call; influenced also by Latin *consilium* advice, COUNSEL]

USAGE Avoid confusion with **counsel.**

council area *n* any of the 32 unitary authorities into which Scotland has been divided for administrative purposes since April 1996.

councillor *or U.S.* **councilor** ('kaʊnsələ) *n* a member of a council. ▸ **'councillorˌship** *or U.S.* **'councilorˌship** *n*

USAGE Avoid confusion with **counsellor.**

councilman ('kaʊnsəlmən) *n, pl* **-men.** *Chiefly U.S.* a member of a council, esp. of a town or city; councillor.

council-manager plan *n* (in the U.S.) a system of local government with an elected legislative council and an appointed administrative manager. See also **city manager.**

Council of Europe *n* an association of European states, established in 1949 to promote unity between its members, defend human rights, and increase social and economic progress.

Council of States *n* another name for **Rajya Sabha.**

Council of Trent *n* the council of the Roman Catholic Church that met between 1545 and 1563 at Trent in S Tyrol. Reacting against the Protestants, it reaffirmed traditional Catholic beliefs and formulated the ideals of the Counter-Reformation.

council of war *n* **1** an assembly of military leaders in wartime. **2** an emergency meeting to formulate a plan.

councilor ('kaʊnsələ) *n* **1** a variant U.S. spelling of **councillor.** **2** an archaic spelling of **counsellor.** ▸ **'councilorˌship** *n*

council school *n Brit.* (esp. formerly) any school maintained by the state.

council tax *n* (in Britain) a tax, based on the relative value of property, levied to fund local council services.

counsel ('kaʊnsəl) *n* **1** advice or guidance on conduct, behaviour, etc. **2** discussion, esp. on future procedure; consultation: *to take counsel with a friend.* **3** a person whose advice or guidance is or has been sought. **4** a barrister or group of barristers engaged in conducting cases in court and advising on legal matters: *counsel for the prosecution.* **5** a policy or plan. **6** *Christianity.* any of the **counsels of perfection** or **evangelical counsels,** namely poverty, chastity, and obedience. **7 counsel of perfection.** excellent but unrealizable advice. **8** private opinions or plans (esp. in the phrase **keep one's own counsel**). **9** *Ar-*

chaic. wisdom; prudence. ◆ *vb* **-sels, -selling, -selled** *or U.S.* **-sels, -seling, -seled. 10** (*tr*) to give advice or guidance to. **11** (*tr; often takes a clause as object*) to recommend the acceptance of (a plan, idea, etc.); urge. **12** (*intr*) *Archaic.* to take counsel; consult. [C13: from Old French *counseil,* from Latin *consilium* deliberating body; related to CONSUL, CONSULT] ► **'counsellable** *or U.S.* **'counselable** *adj*

USAGE Avoid confusion with **council.**

counselling *or U.S.* **counseling** ('kaunsəlɪŋ) *n* guidance offered by social workers, doctors, etc., to help a person resolve social or personal problems.

counsellor *or U.S.* **counselor** ('kaunsələ) *n* **1** a person who gives counsel; adviser. **2** a person, such as a social worker, who is involved in counselling. **3** Also called: **counselor-at-law.** *U.S.* a lawyer, esp. one who conducts cases in court; attorney. **4** a senior British diplomatic officer. **5** a U.S. diplomatic officer ranking just below an ambassador or minister. **6** a person who advises students or others on personal problems or academic and occupational choice. ► **'counsellor,ship** *or U.S.* **'counselor,ship** *n*

USAGE Avoid confusion with **councillor.**

count[1] (kaunt) *vb* **1** to add up or check (each unit in a collection) in order to ascertain the sum; enumerate: *count your change.* **2** (*tr*) to recite numbers in ascending order up to and including. **3** (*tr;* often foll. by *in*) to take into account or include: *we must count him in.* **4 not counting.** excluding. **5** (*tr*) to believe to be; consider; think; deem: *count yourself lucky.* **6** (*intr*) to recite or list numbers in ascending order either in units or groups: *to count in tens.* **7** (*intr*) to have value, importance, or influence: *this picture counts as a rarity.* **8** (*intr;* often foll. by *for*) to have a certain specified value or importance: *the job counts for a lot.* **9** (*intr*) *Music.* to keep time by counting beats. ◆ *n* **10** the act of counting or reckoning. **11** the number reached by counting; sum. **12** *Law.* a paragraph in an indictment containing a distinct and separate charge. **13** *Physics.* the total number of photons or ionized particles detected by a counter. **14 keep count.** to keep a record of items, events, etc. **15 lose count.** to fail to keep an accurate record of items, events, etc. **16** *Boxing, wrestling.* the act of telling off a number of seconds by the referee, as when a boxer has been knocked down or a wrestler pinned by his opponent. **17 out for the count.** *Boxing.* knocked out and unable to continue after a count of ten by the referee. **18 take the count.** *Boxing.* to be unable to continue after a count of ten. **19** *Archaic.* notice; regard; account. ◆ See also **count against, countdown, count on, count out.** [C14: from Anglo-French *counter,* from Old French *conter,* from Latin *computāre* to calculate, COMPUTE]

count[2] (kaunt) *n* **1** a nobleman in any of various European countries having a rank corresponding to that of a British earl. **2** any of various officials in the late Roman Empire and under various Germanic kings in the early Middle Ages. **3** a man who has received an honour (**papal knighthood**) from the Pope in recognition of good deeds, achievements, etc. [C16: from Old French *conte,* from Late Latin *comes* occupant of a state office, from Latin: overseer, associate, literally: one who goes with, from COM- with + *īre* to go] ► **'count,ship** *n*

countable ('kauntəbəl) *adj* **1** capable of being counted. **2** *Maths., logic.* able to be counted using the natural numbers; finite or denumerable. **3** *Linguistics.* denoting a count noun.

count against *vb* (*intr, prep*) to have influence to the disadvantage of: *your bad timekeeping will count against you.*

countdown ('kaunt,daun) *n* **1** the act of counting backwards to time a critical operation exactly, such as the launching of a rocket or the detonation of explosives. ◆ *vb* **count down.** (*intr, adv*) **2** to count numbers backwards towards zero, esp. in timing such a critical operation.

countenance ('kauntɪnəns) *n* **1** the face, esp. when considered as expressing a person's character or mood: *a pleasant countenance.* **2** support or encouragement; sanction. **3** composure; self-control (esp. in the phrases **keep** *or* **lose one's countenance; out of countenance**). ◆ *vb* (*tr*) **4** to support or encourage; sanction. **5** to tolerate; endure. [C13: from Old French *contenance* mien, behaviour, from Latin *continentia* restraint, control; see CONTAIN] ► **'countenancer** *n*

counter[1] ('kauntə) *n* **1** a horizontal surface, as in a shop or bank, over which business is transacted. **2** (in some cafeterias) a long table on which food is served to customers. **3a** a small flat disc of wood, metal, or plastic, used in various board games. **3b** a similar disc or token used as an imitation coin. **4** a person or thing that may be used or manipulated. **5** a skating figure consisting of three circles. **6 under the counter.** (**under-the-counter** when prenominal) (of the sale of goods, esp. goods in short supply) clandestine, surreptitious, or illegal; not in an open manner. **7 over the counter.** (**over-the-counter** when prenominal) (of security transactions) through a broker rather than on a stock exchange. [C14: from Old French *comptouer,* ultimately from Latin *computāre* to COMPUTE]

counter[2] ('kauntə) *n* **1** a person who counts. **2** an apparatus that records the number of occurrences of events. **3** any instrument for detecting or counting ionizing particles or photons. See **Geiger counter, scintillation counter, crystal counter. 4** *Electronics.* another name for **scaler** (sense 2). [C14: from Old French *conteor,* from Latin *computātor;* see COUNT[1]]

counter[3] ('kauntə) *adv* **1** in a contrary direction or manner. **2** in a wrong or reverse direction. **3 run counter to.** to have a contrary effect or action to. ◆ *adj* **4** opposing; opposite; contrary. ◆ *n* **5** something that is contrary or opposite to some other thing. **6** an act, effect, or force that opposes another. **7** a return attack, such as a blow in boxing. **8** *Fencing.* a parry in which the foils move in a circular fashion. **9** the portion of the stern of a boat or ship that overhangs the water aft of the rudder. **10** Also called: **void.** *Printing.* the inside area of a typeface that is not type high, such as the centre of an "o", and therefore does not print. **11** the part of a horse's breast under the neck and between the shoulders. **12** a piece of leather forming the back of a shoe. ◆ *vb* **13** to say or do (something) in retaliation or response. **14** (*tr*) to move, act, or perform in a manner or direction opposite to (a person or thing). **15** to return the attack of (an opponent). [C15: from Old French *contre,* from Latin *contrā* against]

counter- *prefix* **1** against; opposite; contrary: *counterattack.* **2** complementary; corresponding: *counterfoil.* **3** duplicate or substitute: *counterfeit.* [via Norman French from Latin *contrā* against, opposite; see CONTRA-]

counteract (,kauntər'ækt) *vb* (*tr*) to oppose, neutralize, or mitigate the effects of by contrary action; check. ► **,counter'action** *n* ► **,counter'active** *adj* ► **,counter'actively** *adv*

counterattack ('kauntərə,tæk) *n* **1** an attack in response to an attack. ◆ *vb* **2** to make a counterattack (against).

counterattraction ('kauntərə,trækʃən) *n* a rival attraction.

counterbalance *n* ('kauntə,bæləns). **1** a weight or force that balances or offsets another. ◆ *vb* (,kauntə'bæləns). (*tr*) **2** to act as a counterbalance. ◆ Also: **counterpoise.**

counterblast ('kauntə,blɑːst) *n* **1** an aggressive response to a verbal attack. **2** a blast that counteracts another.

counterchange (,kauntə'tʃeɪndʒ) *vb* (*tr*) **1** to change parts, qualities, etc. **2** *Poetic.* to chequer, as with contrasting colours.

countercharge ('kauntə,tʃɑːdʒ) *n* **1** a charge brought by an accused person against the accuser. **2** *Military.* a retaliatory charge. ◆ *vb* **3** (*tr*) to make a countercharge against.

countercheck *n* ('kauntə,tʃɛk). **1** a check or restraint, esp. one that acts in opposition to another. **2** a restraint that reinforces another restraint. **3** a double check, as for accuracy. ◆ *vb* (,kauntə'tʃɛk). (*tr*) **4** to oppose by counteraction. **5** to control or restrain by a second check. **6** to double-check.

counterclaim ('kauntə,kleɪm) *Chiefly law.* ◆ *n* **1** a claim set up in opposition to another, esp. by the defendant in a civil action against the plaintiff. ◆ *vb* **2** to set up (a claim) in opposition to another claim. ► **,counter'claimant** *n*

counterclockwise (,kauntə'klɒk,waɪz) *or* **contraclockwise** *adv, adj* the U.S. and Canadian equivalent of **anticlockwise.**

counterconditioning (,kauntərkən'dɪʃənɪŋ) *n Psychol.* the conditioning of a response that is incompatible with some previously learned response; for example, in psychotherapy an anxious person might be taught relaxation, which is incompatible with anxiety.

counterculture ('kauntə,kʌltʃə) *n* an alternative culture, deliberately at variance with the social norm.

counterespionage (,kauntər'ɛspɪə,nɑːʒ) *n* activities designed to detect and counteract enemy espionage.

counterexample ('kauntərɪg,zɑːmpəl) *n* an example or fact that is inconsistent with a hypothesis and may be used in argument against it.

counterfactual (,kauntə'fæktʃuəl) *Logic.* ◆ *adj* **1** expressing what has not happened but could, would, or might under differing conditions. ◆ *n* **2** a conditional statement in which the first clause is a past tense subjunctive statement expressing something contrary to fact, as in: *if she had hurried she would have caught the bus.*

counterfeit ('kauntəfɪt) *adj* **1** made in imitation of something genuine with the intent to deceive or defraud; forged. **2** simulated; sham: *counterfeit affection.* ◆ *n* **3** an imitation designed to deceive or defraud. **4** *Archaic.* an impostor; cheat. ◆ *vb* **5** (*tr*) to make a fraudulent imitation of. **6** (*intr*) to make counterfeits. **7** to feign; simulate. **8** (*tr*) to imitate; copy. [C13: from Old French *contrefait,* from *contrefaire* to copy, from *contre-* COUNTER- + *faire* to make, from Latin *facere*] ► **'counterfeiter** *n*

counterfoil ('kauntə,fɔɪl) *n Brit.* the part of a cheque, postal order, receipt, etc., detached and retained as a record of the transaction. Also called (esp. U.S. and Canadian): **stub.**

counterfort ('kauntə,fɔːt) *n Civil engineering.* a strengthening buttress at right angles to a retaining wall, bonded to it to provide stability. [from a partial translation of French *contrefort,* from *contre* counter + *fort* strength; see FORT]

counterglow ('kauntə,gləu) *n* another name for **gegenschein.**

counterinsurgency (,kauntərɪn'sɜːdʒənsɪ) *n* action taken by a government to counter the activities of rebels, guerrillas, etc.

counterintelligence (,kauntərɪn'tɛlɪdʒəns) *n* **1** activities designed to frustrate enemy espionage. **2** intelligence collected about enemy espionage.

counterirritant (,kauntər'ɪrɪtənt) *n* **1** an agent that causes a superficial irritation of the skin and thereby relieves inflammation of deep structures. ◆ *adj* **2** producing a counterirritation. ► **,counter,irri'tation** *n*

counter jumper *n Old-fashioned derogatory.* a sales assistant in a shop.

countermand *vb* (,kauntə'mɑːnd). (*tr*) **1** to revoke or cancel (a command, order, etc.). **2** to order (forces, etc.) to return or retreat; recall. ◆ *n* ('kauntə,mɑːnd). **3** a command revoking another. [C15: from Old French *contremander,* from *contre-* COUNTER- + *mander* to command, from Latin *mandāre;* see MANDATE]

countermarch ('kauntə,mɑːtʃ) *vb* **1** *Chiefly military.* **1a** to march or cause to march back along the same route. **1b** to change the order of soldiers during a march. ◆ *n* **2** the act or instance of countermarching. **3** a reversal of method, conduct, etc.

countermeasure ('kauntə,mɛʒə) *n* action taken to oppose, neutralize, or retaliate against some other action.

countermine *n* ('kauntə,maɪn). **1** *Military.* a tunnel dug to defeat similar activities by an enemy. **2** a plot to frustrate another plot. ◆ *vb* (,kauntə'maɪn). **3** to frustrate by countermeasures. **4** *Military.* to take measures to defeat the underground operations of (an enemy). **5** *Military.* to destroy enemy mines in (an area) with mines of one's own.

countermove ('kauntə,muːv) *n* **1** an opposing move. ◆ *vb* **2** to make or do (something) as an opposing move. ► **'counter,movement** *n*

counteroffensive ('kauntərə,fɛnsɪv) *n* a series of attacks by a defending force against an attacking enemy.

counteroffer ('kaʊntər,ɒfə) *n* a response to a bid in which a seller amends his original offer, making it more favourable to the buyer.
counterpane ('kaʊntə,peɪn) *n* another word for **bedspread.** [C17: from obsolete *counterpoint* (influenced by *pane* coverlet), changed from Old French *coutepointe* quilt, from Medieval Latin *culcita puncta* quilted mattress]
counterpart ('kaʊntə,pɑːt) *n* **1** a person or thing identical to or closely resembling another. **2** one of two parts that complement or correspond to each other. **3** a person acting opposite another in a play. **4** a duplicate, esp. of a legal document; copy.
counterparty ('kaʊntə,pɑːtɪ) *n* a person who is a party to a contract.
counterparty risk *n* the risk that a person who is a party to a contract will default on their obligations under that contract.
counterplot ('kaʊntə,plɒt) *n* **1** a plot designed to frustrate another plot. ◆ *vb* **-plots, -plotting, -plotted. 2** (*tr*) to oppose with a counterplot. **3** (*intr*) to devise or carry out a counterplot.
counterpoint ('kaʊntə,pɔɪnt) *n* **1** the technique involving the simultaneous sounding of two or more parts or melodies. **2** a melody or part combined with another melody or part. See also **descant** (sense 1). **3** the musical texture resulting from the simultaneous sounding of two or more melodies or parts. **4 strict counterpoint.** the application of the rules of counterpoint as an academic exercise. **5** a contrasting or interacting element, theme, or item; foil. **6** *Prosody.* the use of a stress or stresses at variance with the regular metrical stress. ◆ *vb* **7** (*tr*) to set in contrast. ◆ Related adj: **contrapuntal.** [C15: from Old French *contrepoint,* from *contre-* COUNTER- + *point* dot, note in musical notation, that is, an accompaniment set against the notes of a melody]
counterpoise ('kaʊntə,pɔɪz) *n* **1** a force, influence, etc., that counterbalances another. **2** a state of balance; equilibrium. **3** a weight that balances another. **4** a radial array of metallic wires, rods, or tubes arranged horizontally around the base of a vertical aerial to increase its transmitting efficiency. ◆ *vb* (*tr*) **5** to oppose with something of equal effect, weight, or force; offset. **6** to bring into equilibrium. **7** *Archaic.* to consider (one thing) carefully in relation to another.
counterpoise bridge *n* another name for **bascule bridge** (see **bascule** (sense 1)).
counterproductive (,kaʊntəprə'dʌktɪv) *adj* tending to hinder or act against the achievement of an aim.
counterproof ('kaʊntə,pruːf) *n Printing.* a reverse impression of a newly printed proof of an engraving made by laying it while wet upon plain paper and passing it through the press.
counterproposal ('kaʊntəprə,pəʊzᵊl) *n* a proposal offered as an alternative to a previous proposal.
counterpunch ('kaʊntə,pʌntʃ) *Boxing.* ◆ *vb* (*intr*) **1** to punch an attacking opponent; return an attack. ◆ *n* **2** a return punch.
Counter-Reformation (,kaʊntə,rɛfə'meɪʃən) *n* the reform movement of the Roman Catholic Church in the 16th and early 17th centuries considered as a reaction to the Protestant Reformation.
counter-revolution (,kaʊntə,rɛvə'luːʃən) *n* a revolution opposed to a previous revolution and aimed at reversing its effects. ► **,counter-,revo'lutionist** *n*
counter-revolutionary (,kaʊntə,rɛvə'luːʃənərɪ, -nrɪ) *n, pl* **-aries. 1** a person opposed to revolution. **2** a person who opposes a specific revolution or revolutionary government. ◆ *adj* **3** characterized by opposition to a revolution or revolutions in general.
counterscarp ('kaʊntə,skɑːp) *n Fortifications.* the outer side of the ditch of a fort. Compare **escarp** (sense 1).
countershading (,kaʊntə'ʃeɪdɪŋ) *n* (in the coloration of certain animals) a pattern, serving as camouflage, in which dark colours occur on parts of the body exposed to the light and pale colours on parts in the shade.
countershaft ('kaʊntə,ʃɑːft) *n* an intermediate shaft that is driven by, but rotates in the opposite direction to, a main shaft, esp. in a gear train.
countersign *vb* ('kaʊntə,saɪn, ,kaʊntə'saɪn). **1** (*tr*) to sign (a document already signed by another). ◆ *n* ('kaʊntə,saɪn). **2** Also called: **countersignature.** the signature so written. **3** a secret sign given in response to another sign. **4** *Chiefly military.* a password.
countersink ('kaʊntə,sɪŋk) *vb* **-sinks, -sinking, -sank, -sunk.** (*tr*) **1** to enlarge the upper part of (a hole) in timber, metal, etc., so that the head of a bolt or screw can be sunk below the surface. **2** to drive (a screw) or sink (a bolt) into such an enlarged hole. ◆ *n* **3** Also called: **countersink bit.** a tool for countersinking. **4** a countersunk depression or hole.
counterspy ('kaʊntə,spaɪ) *n, pl* **-spies.** a spy working against or investigating enemy espionage.
counterstain ('kaʊntə,steɪn) *vb Microscopy.* **1** to apply two or more stains in sequence to (a specimen to be examined), each of which colours a different tissue. **2** (*tr; usually passive*) to apply (one of a series of stains) to a specimen to be examined: *haematoxylin is counterstained with eosin.*
countersubject ('kaʊntə,sʌbdʒɪkt) *n Music.* (in a fugue) the theme in one voice that accompanies the statement of the subject in another.
countertenor (,kaʊntə'tɛnə) *n* **1** an adult male voice with an alto range. **2** a singer with such a voice.
counterterrorism (,kaʊntə'tɛrə,rɪzəm) *n* an act or acts of terrorism committed in revenge or retaliation for a previous terrorist act. ► **,counter'terrorist** *adj*
countertrade ('kaʊntə,treɪd) *n* **1** international trade in which payment is made in goods rather than currency. ◆ *vb* (*tr*) **2** to buy or sell goods by countertrade: *countertrading weapons for coffee beans.*
countertype ('kaʊntə,taɪp) *n* **1** an opposite type. **2** a corresponding type.
countervail (,kaʊntə'veɪl, 'kaʊntə,veɪl) *vb* **1** (when *intr,* usually foll. by *against*) to act or act against with equal power or force. **2** (*tr*) to make up for; compensate; offset. [C14: from Old French *contrevaloir,* from Latin *contrā valēre,* from *contrā* against + *valēre* to be strong]
countervailing duty *n* an extra import duty imposed by a country on certain imports, esp. to prevent dumping or to counteract subsidies in the exporting country.
counterweigh (,kaʊntə'weɪ) *vb* another word for **counterbalance.**
counterweight ('kaʊntə,weɪt) *n* a counterbalancing weight, influence, or force. ► **'counter,weighted** *adj*
counterword ('kaʊntə,wɜːd) *n* a word widely used in a sense much looser than its original meaning, such as *tremendous* or *awful.*
counterwork ('kaʊntə,wɜːk) *n* **1** work done in opposition to other work. **2** defensive fortifications put up against attack. ► **'counter,worker** *n*
countess ('kaʊntɪs) *n* **1** the wife or widow of a count or earl. **2** a woman of the rank of count or earl.
counting house *n Rare, chiefly Brit.* a room or building used by the accountants of a business.
countless ('kaʊntlɪs) *adj* innumerable; myriad.
count noun *n Linguistics, logic.* a noun that can be qualified by the indefinite article, and may be used in the plural, as *telephone* and *thing* but not *airs and graces* or *bravery.* Compare **mass noun, sortal.**
count on *vb* (*intr, prep*) to rely or depend on.
count out *vb* (*tr, adv*) **1** *Informal.* to leave out; exclude: *count me out!* **2** (of a boxing referee) to judge (a floored boxer) to have failed to recover within the specified time. See **count**[1] (sense 16). **3** to count (something) aloud.
count palatine *n, pl* **counts palatine.** *History.* **1** (in the Holy Roman Empire) **1a** originally an official who administered the king's domains or his justice. **1b** later, a count who exercised royal authority in his own domains. **2** (in England and Ireland) an earl or other lord of a county palatine. **3** (in the late Roman Empire) a palace official who exercised judicial authority.
countrified *or* **countryfied** ('kʌntrɪ,faɪd) *adj* in the style, manners, etc., of the country; rural.
country ('kʌntrɪ) *n, pl* **-tries. 1** a territory distinguished by its people, culture, language, geography, etc. **2** an area of land distinguished by its political autonomy; state. **3** the people of a territory or state: *the whole country rebelled.* **4** an area associated with a particular person: *Burns country.* **5a** the part of the land that is away from cities or industrial areas; rural districts. **5b** (*as modifier*): *country cottage.* **5c** (*in combination*): *a countryman.* Related adj: **pastoral, rural. 6** short for **country music. 7** *Archaic.* a particular locality or district. **8 up country.** away from the coast or the capital. **9** one's native land or nation of citizenship. **10** (usually preceded by *the*) *Brit. informal.* the outlying area or area furthest from the finish of a sports ground or racecourse. **11** (*modifier*) rough; uncouth; rustic: *country manners.* **12 across country.** not keeping to roads, etc. **13 go** *or* **appeal to the country.** *Chiefly Brit.* to dissolve Parliament and hold an election. **14 unknown country.** an unfamiliar topic, place, matter, etc. [C13: from Old French *contrée,* from Medieval Latin *contrāta,* literally: that which lies opposite, from Latin *contrā* opposite]
country and western *n* **1** another name for **country music. 2** a fusion of cowboy songs and Appalachian music. **3** (*as modifier*): *country-and-western music.* Abbrev.: **C & W.**
country blues *n* (*sometimes functioning as sing*) acoustic folk blues with a guitar accompaniment. Compare **urban blues.**
country club *n* a club in the country, having sporting and social facilities.
country code *n* a code of good practice recommended to those who use the countryside for recreational purposes.
country cousin *n* an unsophisticated person from the country, esp. one regarded as an object of amusement.
country dance *n* a type of folk dance in which couples are arranged in sets and perform a series of movements, esp. facing one another in a line. ► **country dancing** *n*
country gentleman *n* a rich man with an estate in the country.
country house *n* a large house in the country, esp. a mansion belonging to a wealthy family.
countryman ('kʌntrɪmən) *n, pl* **-men. 1** a person who lives in the country. **2** a person from a particular country or from one's own country (esp. in the phrase **fellow countryman**). ► **'country,woman** *fem n*
country music *n* a type of 20th-century popular music based on White folk music of the southeastern U.S. Sometimes shortened to **country.**
country park *n Brit.* an area of countryside, usually not less than 10 hectares, set aside for public recreation: often funded by a Countryside Commission grant.
country rock[1] *n* the rock surrounding a mineral vein or igneous intrusion.
country rock[2] *n* a style of rock music influenced by country and western.
country seat *n* a large estate or property in the country.
countryside ('kʌntrɪ,saɪd) *n* a rural area or its population.
Countryside Commission *n* **1** (in England and Wales) an organization concerned with conservation of the natural beauty of the landscape and the provision of recreational facilities in the countryside. **2 Countryside Commission for Scotland.** an organization performing a similar function in Scotland.
county ('kaʊntɪ) *n, pl* **-ties. 1a** any of the administrative or geographic subdivisions of certain states, esp. any of the major units into which England and Wales are or have been divided for purposes of local government. **1b** (*as modifier*): *county cricket.* **2** *N.Z.* an electoral division in a rural area. **3** *Obsolete.* the lands under the jurisdiction of a count or earl. ◆ *adj* **4** *Brit. informal.* having the characteristics and habits of the inhabitants of country houses and estates, esp. an upper-class accent and an interest in horses, dogs, etc. [C14: from Old French *conté* land belonging to a count, from Late Latin *comitātus* office of a count, from *comes* COUNT[2]]
county borough *n* **1** (in England and Wales from 1888 to 1974 and in Wales

from 1996) a borough administered independently of any higher tier of local government. **2** (in the Republic of Ireland) any of the four largest boroughs, governed independently of the administrative county around it by an elected council that constitutes an all-purpose authority.

county court *n* (in England) a local court exercising limited jurisdiction in civil matters.

county palatine *n, pl* **counties palatine.** **1** the lands of a count palatine. **2** (in England and Ireland) a county in which the earl or other lord exercised many royal powers, esp. judicial authority.

county seat *n Chiefly U.S.* another term for **county town.**

county town *n* the town in which a county's affairs are or were administered.

coup[1] (ku:) *n* **1** a brilliant and successful stroke or action. **2** short for **coup d'état.** [C18: from French: blow, from Latin *colaphus* blow with the fist, from Greek *kolaphos*]

coup[2] *or* **cowp** (kaʊp) *Scot.* ◆ *vb* **1** to turn or fall over. ◆ *n* **2** a rubbish tip. [C15: perhaps identical with obsolete *cope* to strike; see COPE[1]]

coup[3] (kaʊp) *vb Scot.* to barter; traffic; deal. [C14: from Old Norse *kaupa* to buy]

coup de foudre *French.* (ku də fudrə) *n, pl* ***coups de foudre*** (ku də fudrə). a sudden and amazing action or event. [literally: lightning flash]

coup de grâce *French.* (ku də grɑs) *n, pl* ***coups de grâce*** (ku də grɑs). **1** a mortal or finishing blow, esp. one delivered as an act of mercy to a sufferer. **2** a final or decisive stroke. [literally: blow of mercy]

coup de main *French.* (ku də mɛ̃) *n, pl* ***coups de main*** (ku də mɛ̃). *Chiefly military.* an attack that achieves complete surprise. [literally: blow with the hand]

coup d'état (ˈku: deɪˈtɑ:; *French* ku deta) *n, pl* **coups d'état** (ˈku:z deɪˈtɑ:; *French* ku deta). a sudden violent or illegal seizure of government. [French, literally: stroke of state]

coup de théâtre *French.* (ku də teɑtrə) *n, pl* ***coups de théâtre*** (ku də teɑtrə). **1** a dramatic turn of events, esp. in a play. **2** a sensational device of stagecraft. **3** a stage success. [literally: stroke of the theatre]

coup d'oeil *French.* (ku dœj) *n, pl* ***coups d'oeil*** (ku dœj). a quick glance. [literally: stroke of the eye]

coupe (ku:p) *n* **1** a dessert of fruit and ice cream, usually served in a glass goblet. **2** a dish or stemmed glass bowl designed for this dessert. [C19: from French: goblet, CUP]

coupé (ˈku:peɪ) *n* **1** Also called: **fixed-head coupé.** a four-seater car with a fixed roof, a sloping back, and usually two doors. Compare **drophead coupé.** **2** a four-wheeled horse-drawn carriage with two seats inside and one outside for the driver. **3** an end compartment in a European railway carriage with seats on one side only. [C19: from French, short for *carosse coupé,* literally: cut-off carriage, from *couper* to cut, from *coup* blow, stroke]

Couperin (*French* kuprɛ̃) *n* **François** (frɑ̃swa). 1668–1733, French composer, noted for his harpsichord suites and organ music.

couple (ˈkʌpᵊl) *n* **1** two people who regularly associate with each other or live together: *an engaged couple.* **2** (*functioning as sing or pl*) two people considered as a pair, for or as if for dancing, games, etc. **3** *Chiefly hunting or coursing.* **3a** a pair of collars joined by a leash, used to attach hounds to one another. **3b** two hounds joined in this way. **3c** the unit of reckoning for hounds in a pack: *twenty and a half couple.* **4** a pair of equal and opposite parallel forces that have a tendency to produce rotation with a turning moment equal to the product of either force and the perpendicular distance between them. **5** *Physics.* **5a** two dissimilar metals, alloys, or semiconductors in electrical contact, across which a voltage develops. See **thermocouple.** **5b** Also called: **galvanic couple.** two dissimilar metals or alloys in electrical contact that when immersed in an electrolyte act as the electrodes of an electrolytic cell. **6** a connector or link between two members, such as a tie connecting a pair of rafters in a roof. **7 a couple of.** (*functioning as sing or pl*) **7a** a combination of two; a pair of: *a couple of men.* **7b** *Informal.* a small number of; a few: *a couple of days.* ◆ *pron* **8** (usually preceded by *a; functioning as sing or pl*) two; a pair: *give him a couple.* ◆ *vb* **9** (*tr*) to connect (two things) together or to connect (one thing) to (another): *to couple railway carriages.* **10** (*tr*) to do (two things) simultaneously or alternately: *he couples studying with teaching.* **11** to form or be formed into a pair or pairs. **12** to associate, put, or connect together: *history is coupled with sociology.* **13** to link (two circuits) by electromagnetic induction. **14** (*intr*) to have sexual intercourse. **15** to join or be joined in marriage; marry. **16** (*tr*) to attach (two hounds to each other). [C13: from Old French: a pair, from Latin *cōpula* a bond; see COPULA]

coupledom (ˈkʌpᵊldəm) *n* the state of living as a couple, esp. when regarded as being interested in each other to the exclusion of the outside world.

coupler (ˈkʌplə) *n* **1** a link or rod transmitting power between two rotating mechanisms or a rotating part and a reciprocating part. **2** *Music.* a device on an organ or harpsichord connecting two keys, two manuals, etc., so that both may be played at once. **3** *Electronics.* a device, such as a transformer, used to couple two or more electrical circuits. **4** a U.S. and Canadian word for **coupling** (sense 2).

couplet (ˈkʌplɪt) *n* two successive lines of verse, usually rhymed and of the same metre. [C16: from French, literally: a little pair; see COUPLE]

coupling (ˈkʌplɪŋ) *n* **1** a mechanical device that connects two things. **2** a device for connecting railway cars or trucks together. **3** the part of the body of a horse, dog, or other quadruped that lies between the forequarters and the hindquarters. **4** *Electronics.* the act or process of linking two or more circuits so that power can be transferred between them usually by mutual induction, as in a transformer, or by means of a capacitor or inductor common to both circuits. See also **direct coupling.** **5** *Physics.* an interaction between different properties of a system, such as a group of atoms or nuclei, or between two or more systems. **6** *Genetics.* the occurrence of two specified nonallelic genes from the same parent on the same chromosome.

coupon (ˈku:pɒn) *n* **1a** a detachable part of a ticket or advertisement entitling the holder to a discount, free gift, etc. **1b** a detachable slip usable as a commercial order form. **1c** a voucher given away with certain goods, a certain number of which are exchangeable for goods offered by the manufacturers. **2** one of a number of detachable certificates attached to a bond, esp. a bearer bond, the surrender of which entitles the bearer to receive interest payments. **3** one of several detachable cards used for making hire-purchase payments. **4** a ticket issued to facilitate rationing. **5** *Brit.* a detachable entry form for any of certain competitions, esp. football pools. [C19: from French, from Old French *colpon* piece cut off, from *colper* to cut, variant of *couper;* see COPE[1]]

courage (ˈkʌrɪdʒ) *n* **1** the power or quality of dealing with or facing danger, fear, pain, etc. **2 the courage of one's convictions.** the confidence to act in accordance with one's beliefs. **3 take one's courage in both hands.** to nerve oneself to perform an action. **4** *Obsolete.* mind; disposition; spirit. [C13: from Old French *corage,* from *cuer* heart, from Latin *cor*]

courageous (kəˈreɪdʒəs) *adj* possessing or expressing courage. ▸ **couˈrageously** *adv* ▸ **couˈrageousness** *n*

courante (kuˈrɑ:nt) *n Music.* **1** an old dance in quick triple time **2** a movement of a (mostly) 16th- to 18th-century suite based on this. ◆ Also called (esp. for the dance): **coranto.** [C16: from French, literally: running, feminine of *courant,* present participle of *courir* to run, from Latin *currere*]

Courantyne (ˈkɔ:rən,taɪn) *n* a river in N South America, rising in S Guyana and flowing north to the Atlantic, forming the boundary between Guyana and Surinam. Length: 765 km (475 miles). Dutch name: **Corantijn.**

courbaril (ˈkʊəbərɪl) *n* a tropical American leguminous tree, *Hymenaea courbaril.* Its wood is a useful timber and its gum is a source of copal. Also called: **West Indian locust.** [C18: from a native American name]

Courbet (*French* kurbɛ) *n* **Gustave** (gystav). 1819–77, French painter, a leader of the realist movement; noted for his depiction of contemporary life.

Courbevoie (*French* kurbəvwa) *n* an industrial suburb of Paris, on the Seine. Pop.: 54 500 (latest est.).

coureur de bois (*French* kurœr də bwa) *n, pl* **coureurs de bois** (kurœr də bwa). *Canadian history.* a French Canadian woodsman or Métis who traded with Indians for furs. [Canadian French: trapper (literally: wood-runner)]

courgette (kʊəˈʒɛt) *n* a small variety of vegetable marrow, cooked and eaten as a vegetable. U.S., Canadian, and Austral. name: **zucchini.** [from French, diminutive of *courge* marrow, gourd]

courie *or* **coorie** (ˈku:rɪ) *vb* (*intr*) *Scot.* (often foll. by *doun*) to nestle or snuggle. [C19: from *coor* a Scot. word for COWER]

courier (ˈkʊərɪə) *n* **1** a special messenger, esp. one carrying diplomatic correspondence. **2** a person who makes arrangements for or accompanies a group of travellers on a journey or tour. ◆ *vb* **3** (*tr*) to send (a parcel, letter, etc.) by courier. [C16: from Old French *courrier,* from Old Latin *corriere,* from *correre* to run, from Latin *currere*]

courlan (ˈkʊələn) *n* another name for **limpkin.** [C19: from French, variant of *courliri,* from Galibi *kurliri*]

Courland *or* **Kurland** (ˈkʊələnd) *n* a region of Latvia, between the Gulf of Riga and the Lithuanian border. Latvian name: **Kurzeme.**

Cournand (ˈkʊənənd, -nænd; *French* kurnɑ̃) *n* **André** (**Frederic**). 1895–1988, U.S. physician, born in France: shared the 1956 Nobel prize for physiology or medicine for his work on heart catheterization.

Courrèges (*French* kurɛʒ) *n* **André** (ɑ̃dre). born 1923, French couturier: helped to launch unisex fashion in the mid-1960s.

course (kɔ:s) *n* **1** a continuous progression from one point to the next in time or space; onward movement: *the course of his life.* **2** a route or direction followed: *they kept on a southerly course.* **3a** the path or channel along which something moves: *the course of a river.* **3b** (*in combination*)*: a watercourse.* **4** an area or stretch of land or water on which a sport is played or a race is run: *a golf course.* **5** a period of time; duration: *in the course of the next hour.* **6** the usual order of and time required for a sequence of events; regular procedure: *the illness ran its course.* **7** a mode of conduct or action: *if you follow that course, you will fail.* **8** a connected series of events, actions, etc. **9a** a prescribed number of lessons, lectures, etc., in an educational curriculum. **9b** the material covered in such a curriculum. **10** a prescribed regimen to be followed for a specific period of time: *a course of treatment.* **11** a part of a meal served at one time: *the fish course.* **12** a continuous, usually horizontal, layer of building material, such as a row of bricks, tiles, etc. **13** *Nautical.* any of the sails on the lowest yards of a square-rigged ship. **14** *Knitting.* the horizontal rows of stitches. Compare **wale**[1] (sense 2b.). **15** (in medieval Europe) a charge by knights in a tournament. **16a** a hunt by hounds relying on sight rather than scent. **16b** a match in which two greyhounds compete in chasing a hare. **17** the part or function assigned to an individual bell in a set of changes. **18** *Archaic.* a running race. **19 as a matter of course.** as a natural or normal consequence, mode of action, or event. **20 the course of nature.** the ordinary course of events. **21 in course of.** in the process of: *the ship was in course of construction.* **22 in due course.** at some future time, esp. the natural or appropriate time. **23 of course.** **23a** (*adv*) as expected; naturally. **23b** (*sentence substitute*) certainly; definitely. **24 run** (*or* **take**) **its course.** (of something) to complete its development or action. ◆ *vb* **25** (*intr*) to run, race, or flow, esp. swiftly and without interruption. **26** to cause (hounds) to hunt by sight rather than scent or (of hounds) to hunt (a quarry) thus. **27** (*tr*) to run through or over; traverse. **28** (*intr*) to take a direction; proceed on a course. ◆ See also **courses.** [C13: from Old French *cours,* from Latin *cursus* a running, from *currere* to run]

courser[1] (ˈkɔ:sə) *n* **1** a person who courses hounds or dogs, esp. greyhounds. **2** a hound or dog trained for coursing.

courser[2] (ˈkɔ:sə) *n Literary.* a swift horse; steed. [C13: from Old French *coursier,* from *cours* COURSE]

courser[3] (ˈkɔ:sə) *n* a terrestrial plover-like shore bird, such as *Cursorius cursor* (cream-coloured courser), of the subfamily *Cursoriinae* of desert and semidesert regions of the Old World: family *Glareolidae*, order *Charadriiformes*. [C18: from Latin *cursōrius* suited for running, from *cursus* COURSE]

courses ('kɔːsɪz) *pl n* (*sometimes sing*) *Physiol.* another word for **menses.**

coursework ('kɔːsˌwɜːk) *n* written or oral work completed by a student within a given period, which is assessed as an integral part of an educational course.

coursing ('kɔːsɪŋ) *n* **1** hunting with hounds or dogs that follow their quarry by sight. **2** a sport in which hounds are matched against one another in pairs for the hunting of hares by sight.

court (kɔːt) *n* **1** an area of ground wholly or partly surrounded by walls or buildings. **2** *Brit.* (*cap. when part of a name*) **2a** a block of flats: *Selwyn Court.* **2b** a mansion or country house. **2c** a short street, sometimes closed at one end. **3** a space inside a building, sometimes surrounded with galleries. **4a** the residence, retinues, or household of a sovereign or nobleman. **4b** (*as modifier*): *a court ball.* **5** a sovereign or prince and his retinue, advisers, etc. **6** any formal assembly, reception, etc., held by a sovereign or nobleman with his courtiers. **7** homage, flattering attention, or amorous approaches (esp. in the phrase **pay court to someone**). **8** *Law.* **8a** a tribunal having power to adjudicate in civil, criminal, military, or ecclesiastical matters. **8b** the regular sitting of such a judicial tribunal. **8c** the room or building in which such a tribunal sits. **9a** a marked outdoor or enclosed area used for any of various ball games, such as tennis, squash, etc. **9b** a marked section of such an area: *the service court.* **10a** the board of directors or council of a corporation, company, etc. **10b** *Chiefly Brit.* the supreme council of some universities. **11** a branch of any of several friendly societies. **12 go to court.** to take legal action. **13 hold court.** to preside over admirers, attendants, etc. **14 out of court. 14a** without a trial or legal case: *the case was settled out of court.* **14b** too unimportant for consideration. **14c** *Brit.* so as to ridicule completely (in the phrase **laugh out of court**). **15 the ball is in your court.** you are obliged to make the next move. ◆ *vb* **16** to attempt to gain the love of (someone); woo. **17** (*tr*) to pay attention to (someone) in order to gain favour. **18** (*tr*) to try to obtain (fame, honour, etc.). **19** (*tr*) to invite, usually foolishly, as by taking risks: *to court disaster.* **20** *Old-fashioned.* to be conducting a serious emotional relationship usually leading to marriage. [C12: from Old French, from Latin *cohors* COHORT]

Court (kɔːt) *n* **Margaret** (née *Smith*). born 1942, Australian tennis player: Australian champion 1960–66, 1969–71, and 1973; U.S. champion 1962, 1965, 1969–70, and 1973; Wimbledon champion 1963, 1965, and 1970.

court-bouillon ('kʊət'buːjɒn; *French* kurbujɔ̃) *n* a stock made from root vegetables, water, and wine or vinegar, used primarily for poaching fish. [from French, from *court* short, from Latin *curtus* + *bouillon* broth, from *bouillir* to BOIL[1]]

court card *n* (in a pack of playing cards) a king, queen, or jack of any suit. U.S. equivalent: **face card.** [C17: altered from earlier *coat-card,* from the decorative coats worn by the figures depicted]

court circular *n* (in countries having a monarchy) a daily report of the activities, engagements, etc., of the sovereign, published in a national newspaper.

court cupboard *n* a wooden stand with two or three tiers, used in the 16th and 17th centuries to display pewter, silver, etc.

court dress *n* the formal clothing worn at court.

Courtelle (kɔː'tɛl) *n Trademark.* a synthetic acrylic fibre resembling wool.

courteous ('kɜːtɪəs) *adj* polite and considerate in manner. [C13 *corteis,* literally: with courtly manners, from Old French; see COURT] ▸ **'courteously** *adv* ▸ **'courteousness** *n*

courtesan *or* **courtezan** (ˌkɔːtɪ'zæn) *n* (esp. formerly) a prostitute, or the mistress of a man of rank. [C16: from Old French *courtisane,* from Italian *cortigiana* female courtier, from *cortigiano* courtier, from *corte* COURT]

courtesy ('kɜːtɪsɪ) *n, pl* **-sies. 1** politeness; good manners. **2** a courteous gesture or remark. **3** favour or consent (esp. in the phrase **by courtesy of**). **4** common consent as opposed to right (esp. in the phrase **by courtesy**). See also **courtesy title. 5** ('kɜːtsɪ). an archaic spelling of **curtsy.** [C13 *curteisie,* from Old French, from *corteis* COURTEOUS]

courtesy light *n* the interior light in a motor vehicle.

courtesy title *n* any of several titles having no legal significance, such as those borne by the children of peers.

court hand *n* a style of handwriting formerly used in English law courts.

courthouse ('kɔːtˌhaʊs) *n* a public building in which courts of law are held.

courtier ('kɔːtɪə) *n* **1** an attendant at a court. **2** a person who seeks favour in an ingratiating manner. [C13: from Anglo-French *courteour* (unattested), from Old French *corteier* to attend at court]

court-leet *n* the full name for **leet**[1] (sense 1).

courtly ('kɔːtlɪ) *adj* **-lier, -liest. 1** of or suitable for a royal court. **2** refined in manner. **3** ingratiating. ▸ **'courtliness** *n*

courtly love *n* a tradition represented in Western European literature between the 12th and the 14th centuries, idealizing love between a knight and a revered (usually married) lady.

court martial *n, pl* **court martials** *or* **courts martial. 1** a military court that tries persons subject to military law. ◆ *vb* **court-martial, -tials, -tialling, -tialled** *or U.S.* **-tials, -tialing, -tialed. 2** (*tr*) to try by court martial.

Court of Appeal *n* a branch of the Supreme Court of Judicature that hears appeals from the High Court in both criminal and civil matters and from the county and crown courts.

Court of Common Pleas *n* **1** *English law.* (formerly) a superior court exercising jurisdiction in civil actions between private citizens. **2** *U.S. law.* (in some states) a court exercising original and general jurisdiction.

Court of Exchequer *n* (formerly) an English civil court where Crown revenue cases were tried. Also called: **Exchequer.**

court of first instance *n* a court in which legal proceedings are begun or first heard.

court of honour *n* a military court that is instituted to investigate matters involving personal honour.

court of inquiry *n* **1** *Brit.* a group of people appointed to investigate the causes of a disaster, accident, etc. **2** a military court set up to inquire into a military matter.

Court of Justiciary *n* short for **High Court of Justiciary.**

Court of Session *n* the supreme civil court in Scotland.

Court of St James's *n* the official name of the royal court of Britain.

court plaster *n* a plaster, composed of isinglass on silk, formerly used to cover superficial wounds. [C18: so called because formerly used by court ladies for beauty spots]

Courtrai (*French* kurtrɛ) *n* a town in W Belgium, in West Flanders on the Lys River: the largest producer of linen in W Europe. Pop.: 76 040 (1995 est.). Flemish name: **Kortrijk.**

court roll *n History.* the register of land holdings, etc., of a manorial court.

courtroom ('kɔːtˌruːm, -ˌrʊm) *n* a room in which the sittings of a law court are held.

courtship ('kɔːtʃɪp) *n* **1** the act, period, or art of seeking the love of someone with intent to marry. **2** the seeking or soliciting of favours. **3** *Obsolete.* courtly behaviour.

court shoe *n* a low-cut shoe for women, having no laces or straps.

court tennis *n* the U.S. term for **real tennis.**

courtyard ('kɔːtˌjɑːd) *n* an open area of ground surrounded by walls or buildings; court.

couscous ('kuːskuːs) *n* a spicy dish, originating from North Africa, consisting of steamed semolina served with a meat stew. [C17: via French from Arabic *kouskous,* from *kaskasa* to pound until fine]

cousin ('kʌzᵊn) *n* **1** Also called: **first cousin, cousin-german, full cousin.** the child of one's aunt or uncle. **2** a relative who has descended from one of one's common ancestors. A person's **second cousin** is the child of one of his parents' first cousins. A person's **third cousin** is the child of one of his parents' second cousins. A **first cousin once removed** (or loosely **second cousin**) is the child of one's first cousin. **3** a member of a group related by race, ancestry, interests, etc.: *our Australian cousins.* **4** a title used by a sovereign when addressing another sovereign or a nobleman. [C13: from Old French *cosin,* from Latin *consōbrīnus* cousin, from *sōbrīnus* cousin on the mother's side; related to *soror* sister] ▸ **'cousinˌhood** *or* **'cousinˌship** *n* ▸ **'cousinly** *adj, adv*

Cousin (*French* kuzɛ̃) *n* **Victor** (viktɔr). 1792–1867, French philosopher and educational reformer.

Cousteau (*French* kusto) *n* **Jacques Yves** (ʒɑk iv). 1910–97, French underwater explorer.

couteau (kuː'təʊ) *n, pl* **-teaux** (-'təʊz). a large two-edged knife used formerly as a weapon. [C17: from Old French *coutel,* from Latin *cultellus* a little knife, from *culter* knife, ploughshare]

couth (kuːθ) *adj* **1** *Facetious.* refined. **2** *Archaic.* familiar; known. [Old English *cūth* known, past participle of *cunnan* to know; sense 1, back formation from UNCOUTH]

couthie *or* **couthy** ('kuːθɪ) *adj Scot.* **1** sociable; friendly; congenial. **2** comfortable; snug. **3** plain; homely; unsophisticated: *a couthie saying.* [C13: see COUTH, UNCOUTH]

couture (kuː'tʊə; *French* kutyr) *n* **a** high-fashion designing and dressmaking. **b** (*as modifier*): *couture clothes.* [from French: sewing, dressmaking, from Old French *cousture* seam, from Latin *consuere* to stitch together, from *suere* to sew]

couturier (kuː'tʊərɪˌeɪ; *French* kutyrje) *n* a person who designs, makes, and sells fashion clothes for women. [from French: dressmaker; see COUTURE] ▸ **couturière** (kuːˌtʊːrɪ'ɛə; *French* kutyrjɛr) *fem n*

couvade (kuː'vɑːd; *French* kuvad) *n Anthropol.* a custom in certain cultures of treating the husband of a woman giving birth as if he were bearing the child. [C19: from French, from *couver* to hatch, from Latin *cubāre* to lie down]

couvert (kuˈvɛə) *n* another word for **cover** (sense 32). [C18: from French]

COV *abbrev. for:* **1** *Statistics.* covariance. **2** *Genetics.* crossover value.

covalency (kəʊ'veɪlənsɪ) *or U.S.* **covalence** *n* **1** the formation and nature of covalent bonds. **2** the number of covalent bonds that a particular atom can make with other atoms in forming a molecule. ▸ **co'valent** *adj* ▸ **co'valently** *adv*

covalent bond *n* a type of chemical bond involving the sharing of electrons between atoms in a molecule, esp. the sharing of a pair of electrons by two adjacent atoms.

covariance (kəʊ'vɛərɪəns) *n Statistics.* a measure of the association between two random variables, equal to the expected value of the product of the deviations from the mean of the two variables, and estimated by the sum of products of deviations from the sample mean for associated values of the two variables, divided by the number of sample points. Written as: *Cov (X, Y).*

cove[1] (kəʊv) *n* **1** a small bay or inlet, usually between rocky headlands. **2** a narrow cavern formed in the sides of cliffs, mountains, etc., usually by erosion. **3** a sheltered place. **4** Also called: **coving.** *Architect.* a concave curved surface between the wall and ceiling of a room. ◆ *vb* **5** (*tr*) to form an architectural cove in. [Old English *cofa;* related to Old Norse *kofi,* Old High German *kubisi* tent]

cove[2] (kəʊv) *n* **1** *Old-fashioned slang, Brit. and Austral.* a fellow; chap. **2** *Austral. history.* an overseer of convict labourers. [C16: probably from Romany *kova* thing, person]

coven ('kʌvᵊn) *n* **1** a meeting of witches. **2** a company of 13 witches. [C16: probably from Old French *covin* group, ultimately from Latin *convenīre* to come together; compare CONVENT]

covenant ('kʌvənənt) *n* **1** a binding agreement; contract. **2** *Law.* **2a** an agreement in writing under seal, as to pay a stated annual sum to a charity. **2b** a particular clause in such an agreement, esp. in a lease. **3** (in early English law) an action in which damages were sought for breach of a sealed agreement. **4** *Bible.* God's promise to the Israelites and their commitment to worship him alone. ◆ *vb* **5** to agree to a covenant (concerning). [C13: from Old French, from *covenir* to agree, from Latin *convenīre* to come together, make an agreement; see CONVENE] ▸ **covenantal** (ˌkʌvəˈnæntᵊl) *adj* ▸ **ˌcoveˈnantally** *adv*

Covenant (ˈkʌvənənt) *n Scottish history.* any of the bonds entered into by Scottish Presbyterians to defend their religion, esp. one in 1638 (**National Covenant**) and one of 1643 (**Solemn League and Covenant**).

covenantee (ˌkʌvənənˈtiː) *n* the person to whom the promise in a covenant is made.

Covenanter (ˈkʌvənəntə, ˌkʌvəˈnæntə) *n* a person upholding the National Covenant of 1638 or the Solemn League and Covenant of 1643 between Scotland and England to establish and defend Presbyterianism.

covenantor *or* **covenanter** (ˈkʌvənəntə) *n* a party who makes a promise and who is to perform the obligation expressed in a covenant.

Covent Garden (ˈkʌvənt, ˈkɒv-) *n* **1** a district of central London: famous for its former fruit, vegetable, and flower market, now a shopping precinct. **2** the Royal Opera House (built 1858) in Covent Garden.

Coventry (ˈkɒvəntrɪ) *n* **1** a city in central England, in Coventry unitary authority, West Midlands: devastated in World War II; modern cathedral (1954–62); industrial centre, esp. for motor vehicles. Pop.: 299 316 (1991). **2** a unitary authority in central England, in West Midlands. Pop.: 303 600 (1995 est.). Area: 97 sq. km (37 sq. miles). **3 send to Coventry.** to ostracize or ignore.

cover (ˈkʌvə) *vb* (*mainly tr*) **1** to place or spread something over so as to protect or conceal. **2** to provide with a covering; clothe. **3** to put a garment, esp. a hat, on (the body or head). **4** to extend over or lie thickly on the surface of; spread: *snow covered the fields.* **5** to bring upon (oneself); invest (oneself) as if with a covering: *covered with shame.* **6** (sometimes foll. by *up*) to act as a screen or concealment for; hide from view. **7** *Military.* to protect (an individual, formation, or place) by taking up a position from which fire may be returned if those being protected are fired upon. **8** (*also intr*, often foll. by *for*) to assume responsibility for (a person or thing): *to cover for a colleague in his absence.* **9** (*intr;* foll. by *for* or *up for*) to provide an alibi (for). **10** to have as one's territory: *this salesman covers your area.* **11** to travel over: *to cover three miles a day.* **12** (*tr*) to have or place in the aim and within the range of (a firearm). **13** to include or deal with: *his talk covered all aspects of the subject.* **14** (of an asset or income) to be sufficient to meet (a liability or expense). **15a** to insure against loss, risk, etc. **15b** to provide for (loss, risk, etc.) by insurance. **16** (*also intr*) *Finance.* to purchase (securities, etc.) in order to meet contracts, esp. short sales. **17** to deposit (an equivalent stake) in a bet or wager. **18** (*also intr*) to play a card higher in rank than (one played beforehand by another player). **19** to act as reporter or photographer on (a news event, etc.) for a newspaper or magazine: *to cover sports events.* **20** *Sport.* to guard or protect (an opponent, team-mate, or area). **21** *Music.* to record a cover version of. **22** (of a male animal, esp. a horse) to copulate with (a female animal). **23** (of a bird) to brood (eggs). ◆ *n* **24** anything that covers, spreads over, protects, or conceals. **25** woods or bushes providing shelter or a habitat for wild creatures. **26a** a blanket used on a bed for warmth. **26b** another word for **bedspread. 27** *Finance.* liquid assets, reserves, or guaranteed income sufficient to discharge a liability, meet an expenditure, etc. **28** a pretext, disguise, or false identity: *the thief sold brushes as a cover.* **29** *Insurance.* another word for **coverage** (sense 3). **30** an envelope or package for sending through the post: *under plain cover.* **31** *Philately.* **31a** an entire envelope that has been postmarked. **31b on cover.** (of a postage stamp) kept in this form by collectors. **32** an individual table setting, esp. in a restaurant. **33** *Sport.* the guarding or protection of an opponent, team-mate, or area. **34** Also called: **cover version.** a version by a different artist of a previously recorded musical item. **35** *Cricket.* **35a** (*often pl*) the area more or less at right angles to the pitch on the off side and usually about halfway to the boundary: *to field in the covers.* **35b** (*as modifier*): *a cover drive by a batsman.* **35c** Also called: **cover point.** a fielder in such a position. **36** *Ecology.* the percentage of the ground surface covered by a given species of plant. **37 break cover.** (esp. of game animals) to come out from a shelter or hiding place. **38 take cover.** to make for a place of safety or shelter. **39 under cover.** protected, concealed, or in secret: *under cover of night.* ◆ See also **cover-up.** [C13: from Old French *covrir,* from Latin *cooperīre* to cover completely, from *operīre* to cover over] ▸ **ˈcoverable** *adj* ▸ **ˈcoverer** *n* ▸ **ˈcoverless** *adj*

coverage (ˈkʌvərɪdʒ) *n* **1** the amount or extent to which something is covered. **2** *Journalism.* the amount and quality of reporting or analysis given to a particular subject or event. **3** the extent of the protection provided by insurance. **4** *Finance.* **4a** the value of liquid assets reserved to meet liabilities. **4b** the ratio of liquid assets to specific liabilities. **4c** the ratio of total net profit to distributed profit in a company. **5** the section of the public reached by a medium of communication.

coverall (ˈkʌvərˌɔːl) *n* **1** a thing that covers something entirely. **2** (*usually pl*) protective outer garments for the body.

cover charge *n* a sum of money charged in a restaurant for each individual customer in addition to the cost of food and drink.

cover crop *n* a crop planted between main crops to prevent leaching or soil erosion or to provide green manure.

Coverdale (ˈkʌvəˌdeɪl) *n* **Miles.** 1488–1568, the first translator of the complete Bible into English (1535).

covered wagon *n U.S. and Canadian.* a large wagon with an arched canvas top, used formerly for prairie travel.

cover girl *n* a girl, esp. a glamorous one, whose picture appears on the cover of a newspaper or magazine.

cover glass *n* a thin square of mounted glass used to protect a photographic slide.

covering (ˈkʌvərɪŋ) *n* another word for **cover** (sense 24).

covering letter *n* an accompanying letter sent as an explanation, introduction, or record.

coverlet (ˈkʌvəlɪt) *n* another word for **bedspread.**

Coverley (ˈkʌvəlɪ) *n* See **Sir Roger de Coverley.**

covermount (ˈkʌvəˌmaʊnt) *Marketing.* ◆ *n* **1** an item attached to the front of a magazine as a gift. ◆ *vb* **2** (*tr*) to attach (an item) to the front of a magazine as a gift.

cover note *n Brit.* a certificate issued by an insurance company stating that a policy is operative: used as a temporary measure between the commencement of cover and the issue of the policy.

cover point *n Cricket.* **a** a fielding position in the covers. **b** a fielder in this position.

covers (ˈkəʊvɜːs) *abbrev. for* coversed sine.

coversed sine (ˈkəʊvɜːst) *n* a trigonometric function equal to one minus the sine of the specified angle. Abbrev.: **covers.**

cover-shoulder *n* a type of blouse worn in Ghana.

cover slip *n* a very thin piece of glass placed over a specimen on a glass slide that is to be examined under a microscope.

covert (ˈkʌvət) *adj* **1** concealed or secret: *covert jealousy.* **2** *Law.* See **feme covert.** Compare **discovert.** ◆ *n* **3** a shelter or disguise. **4** a thicket or woodland providing shelter for game. **5** short for **covert cloth. 6** *Ornithol.* any of the small feathers on the wings and tail of a bird that surround the bases of the larger feathers. **7** a flock of coots. [C14: from Old French: covered, from *covrir* to COVER] ▸ **ˈcovertly** *adv* ▸ **ˈcovertness** *n*

covert cloth *n* a twill-weave cotton or worsted suiting fabric. Sometimes shortened to **covert.**

covert coat *n Brit.* a short topcoat worn for hunting.

coverture (ˈkʌvətʃə) *n* **1** *Law.* the condition or status of a married woman considered as being under the protection and influence of her husband. **2** *Rare.* shelter, concealment, or disguise. [C13: from Old French, from *covert* covered; see COVERT]

cover-up *n* **1** concealment or attempted concealment of a mistake, crime, etc. ◆ *vb* **cover up.** (*adv*) **2** (*tr*) to cover completely. **3** (when *intr,* often foll. by *for*) to attempt to conceal (a mistake or crime): *she tried to cover up for her friend.* **4** (*intr*) *Boxing.* to defend the body and head with the arms.

cover version *n* another name for **cover** (sense 34).

cove stripe *n Nautical.* a decorative stripe painted along the sheer strake of a vessel, esp. of a sailing boat.

covet (ˈkʌvɪt) *vb* (*tr*) **-vets, -veting, -veted.** to wish, long, or crave for (something, esp. the property of another person). [C13: from Old French *coveitier,* from *coveitié* eager desire, ultimately from Latin *cupiditās* CUPIDITY] ▸ **ˈcovetable** *adj* ▸ **ˈcoveter** *n*

covetous (ˈkʌvɪtəs) *adj* (*usually postpositive* and foll. by *of*) jealously eager for the possession of something (esp. the property of another person). ▸ **ˈcovetously** *adv* ▸ **ˈcovetousness** *n*

covey (ˈkʌvɪ) *n* **1** a small flock of grouse or partridge. **2** a small group, as of people. [C14: from Old French *covee,* from *cover* to sit on, hatch; see COUVADE]

Covilhã (*Portuguese* kuviˈʎɑ̃) *n* **Pero da** (ˈpeːrʊ da). ?1460–?1526, Portuguese explorer, who established relations between Portugal and Ethiopia.

covin (ˈkʌvɪn) *n Law.* a conspiracy between two or more persons to act to the detriment or injury of another. [C14: from Old French; see COVEN, CONVENE]

cow[1] (kaʊ) *n* **1** the mature female of any species of cattle, esp. domesticated cattle. **2** the mature female of various other mammals, such as the elephant, whale, and seal. **3** (*not in technical use*) any domestic species of cattle. **4** *Informal.* a disagreeable woman. **5** *Austral. and N.Z. slang.* something objectionable (esp. in the phrase **a fair cow**). **6 till the cows come home.** *Informal.* for a very long time; effectively for ever. [Old English *cū;* related to Old Norse *kȳr,* Old High German *kuo,* Latin *bōs,* Greek *bous,* Sanskrit *gāūs*]

cow[2] (kaʊ) *vb* (*tr*) to frighten or overawe, as with threats. [C17: from Old Norse *kūga* to oppress, related to Norwegian *kue,* Swedish *kuva*]

cowage *or* **cowhage** (ˈkaʊɪdʒ) *n* **1** a tropical climbing leguminous plant, *Stizolobium* (or *Mucuna*) *pruriens,* whose bristly pods cause severe itching and stinging. **2** the pods of this plant or the stinging hairs covering them. [C17: from Hindi *kavāch,* of obscure origin]

cowal (ˈkaʊəl) *n Austral.* a shallow lake or swampy depression supporting vegetation. [from a native Australian language]

coward (ˈkaʊəd) *n* a person who shrinks from or avoids danger, pain, or difficulty. [C13: from Old French *cuard,* from *coue* tail, from Latin *cauda;* perhaps suggestive of a frightened animal with its tail between its legs]

Coward (ˈkaʊəd) *n* Sir **Noël (Pierce).** 1899–1973, English dramatist, actor, and composer, noted for his sophisticated comedies, which include *Private Lives* (1930) and *Blithe Spirit* (1941).

cowardice (ˈkaʊədɪs) *n* lack of courage in facing danger, pain, or difficulty.

cowardly (ˈkaʊədlɪ) *adj* of or characteristic of a coward; lacking courage. ▸ **ˈcowardliness** *n*

cow bail *n* See **bail**[3] (sense 3).

cowbane (ˈkaʊˌbeɪn) *n* **1** Also called: **water hemlock.** any of several N temperate poisonous umbelliferous marsh plants of the genus *Cicuta,* esp. *C. virosa,* having clusters of small white flowers. **2** a similar and related plant, *Oxypolis rigidior* of the southeastern and central U.S. **3** any umbelliferous plant reputed to be poisonous to cattle.

cowbell (ˈkaʊˌbɛl) *n* **1** a bell hung around a cow's neck so that the cow can be easily located. **2** a metal percussion instrument usually mounted on the bass drum or hand-held and struck with a drumstick. **3** *U.S.* another name for **bladder campion.**

cowberry (ˈkaʊbərɪ, -brɪ) *n, pl* **-ries. 1** a creeping ericaceous evergreen shrub, *Vaccinium vitis-idaea,* of N temperate and arctic regions, with pink or red flowers and edible slightly acid berries. **2** the berry of this plant. ◆ Also called: **red whortleberry.**

cowbind ('kaʊ,baɪnd) *n* any of various bryony plants, esp. the white bryony.

cowbird ('kaʊ,bɜːd) *n* any of various American orioles of the genera *Molothrus, Tangavius,* etc., esp. *M. ater* (common or brown-headed cowbird). They have a dark plumage and short bill.

cowboy ('kaʊ,bɔɪ) *n* **1** Also called: **'cow,hand.** a hired man who herds and tends cattle, usually on horseback, esp. in the western U.S. **2** a conventional character of Wild West folklore, films, etc., esp. one involved in fighting Indians. **3** *Informal.* **3a** a person who is an irresponsible or unscrupulous operator in business. **3b** (*as modifier*): *cowboy contractors; cowboy shop steward.* **4** *Austral.* a man or boy who tends cattle. ▸ **'cow,girl** *fem n*

cowcatcher ('kaʊ,kætʃə) *n U.S. and Canadian.* a metal frame on the front of a locomotive to clear the track of animals or other obstructions.

cow cocky *n, pl* **cow cockies.** *Austral. and N.Z.* a one-man dairy farmer.

Cowdrey ('kaʊdrɪ) *n* **(Michael) Colin,** Baron. born 1932, English cricketer. He played for Kent and in 114 Test matches (captaining England 27 times).

cower ('kaʊə) *vb (intr)* to crouch or cringe, as in fear. [C13: from Middle Low German *kūren* to lie in wait; related to Swedish *kura* to lie in wait, Danish *kure* to squat]

Cowes (kaʊz) *n* a town in S England, on the Isle of Wight: famous for its annual regatta. Pop.: 16 335 (1991).

cowfeteria (,kaʊfɪ'tɪərɪə) *n N.Z. informal.* a calf feeder with multiple teats. [from a blend of *cow* and *cafeteria*]

cowfish ('kaʊ,fɪʃ) *n, pl* **-fish** *or* **-fishes. 1** any trunkfish, such as *Lactophrys quadricornis,* having hornlike spines over the eyes. **2** (loosely) any of various large aquatic animals, such as a sea cow.

Cow Gum *n Trademark.* a colourless adhesive based on a natural rubber solution.

cowherb ('kaʊ,hɜːb) *n* a European caryophyllaceous plant, *Saponaria vaccaria,* having clusters of pink flowers: a weed in the U.S. See also **soapwort.**

cowherd ('kaʊ,hɜːd) *n* a person employed to tend cattle.

cowhide ('kaʊ,haɪd) *n* **1** the hide of a cow. **2** the leather made from such a hide. ◆ Also called: **cowskin.**

Cowichan sweater ('kaʊɪtʃən) *n Canadian.* a heavy sweater of grey, unbleached wool with distinctive designs that were originally black-and-white but are now sometimes coloured: knitted originally by Cowichan Indians in British Columbia. Also called: **Cowichan Indian sweater, siwash, siwash sweater.**

cowitch ('kaʊ,ɪtʃ) *n* another name for **cowage.** [C17: alteration of COWAGE by folk etymology]

cowk (kaʊk) *vb (intr) Northeast Scot. dialect.* to retch or feel nauseated. [of obscure origin]

cowl (kaʊl) *n* **1** a hood, esp. a loose one. **2** the hooded habit of a monk. **3** a cover fitted to a chimney to increase ventilation and prevent draughts. **4** the part of a car body that supports the windscreen and the bonnet. **5** *Aeronautics.* another word for **cowling.** ◆ *vb (tr)* **6** to cover or provide with a cowl. **7** to make a monk of. [Old English *cugele,* from Late Latin *cuculla* cowl, from Latin *cucullus* covering, cap, hood]

Cowley ('kaʊlɪ) *n* **Abraham.** 1618–67, English poet and essayist, who introduced the Pindaric ode to English literature.

cowlick ('kaʊ,lɪk) *n* a tuft of hair over the forehead.

cowling ('kaʊlɪŋ) *n* a streamlined metal covering, esp. one fitted around an aircraft engine. Also called: **cowl.** Compare **fairing**[1].

cowl neckline *n* a neckline of women's clothes loosely folded over and sometimes resembling a folded hood.

cowman ('kaʊmən) *n, pl* **-men. 1** *Brit.* another name for **cowherd. 2** *U.S. and Canadian.* a man who owns cattle; rancher.

co-worker *n* a fellow worker; associate.

cow parsley *n* a common Eurasian umbelliferous hedgerow plant, *Anthriscus sylvestris,* having umbrella-shaped clusters of white flowers. Also called: **keck.**

cow parsnip *n* any tall coarse umbelliferous plant of the genus *Heracleum,* such as *H. sphondylium* of Europe and Asia, having thick stems and flattened clusters of white or purple flowers. Also called: **hogweed, keck.**

cowpat ('kaʊ,pæt) *n* a single dropping of cow dung.

cowpea ('kaʊ,piː) *n* **1** a leguminous tropical climbing plant, *Vigna sinensis,* producing long pods containing edible pealike seeds: grown for animal fodder and sometimes as human food. **2** Also called: **black-eyed pea.** the seed of this plant.

Cowper ('kuːpə, 'kaʊ-) *n* **William.** 1731–1800, English poet, noted for his nature poetry, such as in *The Task* (1785), and his hymns.

Cowper's glands *pl n* two small yellowish glands near the prostate that secrete a mucous substance into the urethra during sexual stimulation in males. Compare **Bartholin's glands.** [C18: named after William *Cowper* (1666–1709), English anatomist who discovered them]

cow pillow *n* (in India) a large cylindrical pillow stuffed with cotton and used for reclining rather than sleeping.

cow pony *n* a horse used by cowboys when herding.

cowpox ('kaʊ,pɒks) *n* a contagious viral disease of cows characterized by vesicles on the skin, esp. on the teats and udder. Inoculation of humans with this virus provides temporary immunity to smallpox.

cowpuncher ('kaʊ,pʌntʃə) *or* **cowpoke** ('kaʊ,pəʊk) *n U.S. and Canadian.* informal words for **cowboy.**

cowrie *or* **cowry** ('kaʊrɪ) *n, pl* **-ries. 1** any marine gastropod mollusc of the mostly tropical family *Cypraeidae,* having a glossy brightly marked shell with an elongated opening. **2** the shell of any of these molluscs, esp. the shell of *Cypraea moneta* **(money cowry),** used as money in parts of Africa and S Asia. [C17: from Hindi *kaurī,* from Sanskrit *kaparda,* of Dravidian origin; related to Tamil *kōtu* shell]

cow shark *n* any large primitive shark, esp. *Hexanchus griseum,* of the family *Hexanchidae* of warm and temperate waters. Also called: **six-gilled shark.**

cowskin ('kaʊ,skɪn) *n* another word for **cowhide.**

cowslip ('kaʊ,slɪp) *n* **1** Also called: **paigle.** a primrose, *Primula veris,* native to temperate regions of the Old World, having fragrant yellow flowers. **2** *U.S. and Canadian.* another name for **marsh marigold.** [Old English *cūslyppe;* see COW[1], SLIP[3]]

cow tree *n* a South American moraceous tree, *Brosimum galactodendron,* producing latex used as a substitute for milk.

cox (kɒks) *n* **1** a coxswain, esp. of a racing eight or four. ◆ *vb* **2** to act as coxswain of (a boat). ▸ **'coxless** *adj*

Cox (kɒks) *n* **David.** 1783–1859, English landscape painter.

coxa ('kɒksə) *n, pl* **coxae** ('kɒksiː). **1** a technical name for the hipbone or hip joint. **2** the basal segment of the leg of an insect. [C18: from Latin: hip] ▸ **'coxal** *adj*

coxalgia (kɒk'sældʒɪə) *n* **1** pain in the hip joint. **2** disease of the hip joint causing pain. [C19: from COXA + -ALGIA] ▸ **cox'algic** *adj*

coxcomb ('kɒks,kəʊm) *n* **1** a variant spelling of **cockscomb. 2** *Archaic.* a foppish man. **3** *Obsolete.* the cap, resembling a cock's comb, worn by a jester.

coxcombry ('kɒks,kəʊmrɪ) *n, pl* **-ries.** conceited arrogance or foppishness.

Coxsackie virus (kʊk'sɑːkɪ) *n* any of various viruses that occur in the intestinal tract of man and cause diseases, some of which resemble poliomyelitis. [C20: after *Coxsackie,* a town in New York state, where the virus was first found]

Cox's Orange Pippin ('pɪpɪn) *n* a variety of eating apple with sweet flesh and a red-tinged green skin. Often shortened to **Cox.** [C19: named after R. *Cox,* its English propagator]

coxswain ('kɒksən, -,sweɪn) *n* the helmsman of a lifeboat, racing shell, etc. Also called: **cockswain.** [C15: from *cock* a ship's boat + SWAIN]

coy (kɔɪ) *adj* **1** (usually of a woman) affectedly demure, esp. in a playful or provocative manner. **2** shy; modest. **3** evasive, esp. in an annoying way. [C14: from Old French *coi* reserved, from Latin *quiētus* QUIET] ▸ **'coyish** *adj* ▸ **'coyly** *adv* ▸ **'coyness** *n*

Coy. *Military. abbrev. for* company.

coyote ('kɔɪəʊt, kɔɪ'əʊt, kɔɪ'əʊtɪ) *n, pl* **-otes** *or* **-ote. 1** Also called: **prairie wolf.** a predatory canine mammal, *Canis latrans,* related to but smaller than the wolf, roaming the deserts and prairies of North America. **2** (in American Indian legends of the West) a trickster and culture hero represented as a man or as an animal. [C19: from Mexican Spanish, from Nahuatl *coyotl*]

coyotillo (,kəʊjəʊ'tiːljəʊ) *n, pl* **-los.** a thorny poisonous rhamnaceous shrub, *Karwinskia humboldtiana* of Mexico and the southwestern U.S., the berries of which cause paralysis. [Mexican Spanish, literally: a little COYOTE]

Coypel (*French* kwapɛl) *n* **Antoine.** 1661–1722, French baroque painter, noted esp. for his large biblical compositions.

coypu ('kɔɪpuː) *n, pl* **-pus** *or* **-pu. 1** an aquatic South American hystricomorph rodent, *Myocastor coypus,* introduced into Europe: family *Capromyidae.* It resembles a small beaver with a ratlike tail and is bred in captivity for its soft grey underfur. **2** the fur of this animal. ◆ Also called: **nutria.** [C18: from American Spanish *coipú,* from Araucanian *kóypu*]

coz (kʌz) *n* an archaic word for **cousin:** used chiefly as a term of address.

cozen ('kʌzᵊn) *vb* to cheat or trick (someone). [C16: cant term perhaps related to COUSIN] ▸ **'cozenage** *n* ▸ **'cozener** *n*

cozy ('kəʊzɪ) *adj* **-zier, -ziest.** *n* the usual U.S. spelling of **cosy.** ▸ **'cozily** *adv* ▸ **'coziness** *n*

cp *abbrev. for:* **1** candlepower. **2** chemically pure.

CP *abbrev. for:* **1** Canadian Press. **2** *Military.* Command Post. **3** Common Prayer. **4** Communist Party. **5** (in Britain) Community Programme. **6** Court of Probate.

cp. *abbrev. for* compare.

CPA (in the U.S.) *abbrev. for* certified public accountant.

CPAG (in Britain) *abbrev. for* Child Poverty Action Group.

cpd *Zoology, botany, chem. abbrev. for* compound.

cpi *abbrev. for* characters per inch.

CPI *abbrev. for* consumer price index.

Cpl *abbrev. for* Corporal.

CP/M *n* an operating system widely used on microcomputers to enable a wide range of software from many suppliers to be run on them.

CPO *abbrev. for* Chief Petty Officer.

CPR *abbrev. for* cardiopulmonary resuscitation.

CPRE *abbrev. for* Council for the Protection of Rural England.

cps *abbrev. for:* **1** *Physics.* cycles per second. **2** *Computing.* characters per second.

CPS (in England and Wales) *abbrev for.* Crown Prosecution Service.

CPSA (in Britain) *abbrev. for* Civil and Public Services Association.

CPSU *abbrev. for* (formerly) Communist Party of the Soviet Union.

CPU *Computing. abbrev. for* central processing unit.

CPVE (in Britain) *abbrev. for* Certificate of Pre-vocational Education: a certificate awarded for completion of a broad-based course of study offered as a less advanced alternative to traditional school-leaving qualifications.

CQ 1 *Telegraphy, telephony.* a symbol transmitted by an amateur radio operator requesting two-way communication with any other amateur radio operator listening. **2** *Military. abbrev. for* charge of quarters.

CQSW (in Britain) *abbrev. for* Certificate of Qualification in Social Work.

Cr 1 *abbrev. for* Councillor. **2** *the chemical symbol for* chromium.

CR *abbrev. for:* **1** Community of the Resurrection. **2** Costa Rica. ◆ **3** *international car registration for* Costa Rica.

cr. *abbrev. for:* **1** credit. **2** creditor.

crab[1] (kræb) *n* **1** any chiefly marine decapod crustacean of the genus *Cancer* and related genera (section *Brachyura*), having a broad flattened carapace covering the cephalothorax, beneath which is folded the abdomen. The first pair of limbs are modified as pincers. See also **fiddler crab, soft-shell crab, pea crab, oyster crab.** Related adj: **cancroid. 2** any of various similar or related arthropods, such as the hermit crab and horseshoe crab. **3** short for **crab louse. 4** a manoeuvre in which an aircraft flies slightly into the crosswind to compensate for drift. **5** a mechanical lifting device, esp. the travelling hoist of a gantry crane. **6** *Wrestling.* See **Boston crab. 7 catch a crab.** *Rowing.* to make a stroke in which the oar either misses the water or digs too deeply, causing the rower to fall backwards. ◆ *vb* **crabs, crabbing, crabbed. 8** (*intr*) to hunt or catch crabs. **9** (*tr*) to fly (an aircraft) slightly into a crosswind to compensate for drift. **10** (*intr*) *Nautical.* to move forwards with a slight sideways motion, as to overcome an offsetting current. **11** (*intr*) to move sideways. ◆ See also **crabs.** [Old English *crabba;* related to Old Norse *krabbi,* Old High German *krebiz* crab, Dutch *krabben* to scratch]

crab[2] (kræb) *Informal.* ◆ *vb* **crabs, crabbing, crabbed. 1** (*intr*) to find fault; grumble. **2** (*tr*) *Chiefly U.S.* to spoil (esp. in the phrase **crab someone's act**). ◆ *n* **3** an irritable person. **4 draw the crabs.** *Austral.* to attract unwelcome attention. [C16: probably back formation from CRABBED]

crab[3] (kræb) *n* short for **crab apple.** [C15: perhaps of Scandinavian origin; compare Swedish *skrabbe* crab apple]

Crab (kræb) *n* **the.** the constellation Cancer, the fourth sign of the zodiac.

crab apple *n* **1** any of several rosaceous trees of the genus *Malus* that have white, pink, or red flowers and small sour apple-like fruits. **2** the fruit of any of these trees, used to make jam.

Crabbe (kræb) *n* **George.** 1754–1832, English narrative poet, noted for his depiction of impoverished rural life in *The Village* (1783) and *The Borough* (1810).

crabbed (ˈkræbɪd) *adj* **1** surly; irritable; perverse. **2** (esp. of handwriting) cramped and hard to decipher. [C13: probably from CRAB[1] (from its wayward gait), influenced by CRAB (APPLE) (from its tartness)] ▸ **ˈcrabbedly** *adv* ▸ **ˈcrabbedness** *n*

crabber (ˈkræbə) *n* **1** a crab fisherman. **2** a boat used for crab-fishing.

crabby (ˈkræbɪ) *adj* **-bier, -biest.** bad-tempered.

crab canon *n Music.* a canon in which the imitating voice repeats the notes of the theme in reverse order. Also called **retrograde canon, canon cancrizans.** [from the mistaken medieval notion that crabs move backwards]

crab grass *n* any of several coarse weedy grasses of the genus *Digitaria,* which grow in warm regions and tend to displace other grasses in lawns.

crab louse *n* a parasitic louse, *Pthirus* (or *Phthirus*) *pubis,* that infests the pubic region in man.

Crab Nebula *n* the expanding remnant of the supernova observed in 1054 A.D., lying in the constellation Taurus at an approximate distance of 5000 light years.

crabs (kræbz) *n* (*sometimes functioning as sing*) the lowest throw in a game of chance, esp. two aces in dice. [plural of CRAB[1]]

crabstick (ˈkræbˌstɪk) *n* **1** a stick, cane, or cudgel made of crab-apple wood. **2** *Informal.* a bad-tempered person.

crabwise (ˈkræbˌwaɪz) *adj, adv* (of motion) sideways; like a crab.

crabwood (ˈkræbˌwʊd) *n* **1** a tropical American meliaceous tree, *Carapa guianensis.* **2** the wood of this tree, used for construction.

CRAC *abbrev. for* Careers Research and Advisory Centre.

crack (kræk) *vb* **1** to break or cause to break without complete separation of the parts: *the vase was cracked but unbroken.* **2** to break or cause to break with a sudden sharp sound; snap: *to crack a nut.* **3** to make or cause to make a sudden sharp sound: *to crack a whip.* **4** to cause (the voice) to change tone or become harsh or (of the voice) to change tone, esp. to a higher register; break. **5** *Informal.* to fail or cause to fail. **6** to yield or cause to yield: *to crack under torture.* **7** (*tr*) to hit with a forceful or resounding blow. **8** (*tr*) to break into or force open: *to crack a safe.* **9** (*tr*) to solve or decipher (a code, problem, etc.). **10** (*tr*) *Informal.* to tell (a joke, etc.). **11** to break (a molecule) into smaller molecules or radicals by the action of heat, as in the distillation of petroleum. **12** (*tr*) to open (esp. a bottle) for drinking: *let's crack another bottle.* **13** (*intr*) *Scot., northern English dialect.* to chat; gossip. **14** (*tr*) *Informal.* to achieve (esp. in the phrase **crack it**). **15** (*tr*) *Austral. informal.* to find or catch: *to crack a wave in surfing.* **16 crack a smile.** *Informal.* to break into a smile. **17 crack hardy** *or* **hearty.** *Austral. and N.Z. informal.* to disguise one's discomfort, etc.; put on a bold front. ◆ *n* **18** a sudden sharp noise. **19** a break or fracture without complete separation of the two parts: *a crack in the window.* **20** a narrow opening or fissure. **21** *Informal.* a resounding blow. **22** a physical or mental defect; flaw. **23** a moment or specific instant: *the crack of day.* **24** a broken or cracked tone of voice, as a boy's during puberty. **25** (often foll. by *at*) *Informal.* an attempt; opportunity to try: *he had a crack at the problem.* **26** *Slang.* a gibe; wisecrack; joke. **27** *Slang.* a person that excels. **28** *Scot., northern English dialect.* a talk; chat. **29** *Slang.* a processed form of cocaine hydrochloride used as a stimulant. It is highly addictive. **30** *Informal, chiefly Irish.* fun; informal entertainment; *the crack was great in here last night.* **31** *Obsolete slang.* a burglar or burglary. **32 crack of dawn. 32a** the very instant that the sun rises. **32b** very early in the morning. **33 a fair crack of the whip.** *Informal.* a fair chance or opportunity. **34 crack of doom.** doomsday; the end of the world; the Day of Judgment. ◆ *adj* **35** (*prenominal*) *Slang.* first-class; excellent: *a crack shot.* ◆ See also **crack down, crack up.** [Old English *cracian;* related to Old High German *krahhōn,* Dutch *kraken,* Sanskrit *gárjati* he roars]

crackbrain (ˈkrækˌbreɪn) *n* a person who is insane.

crackbrained (ˈkrækˌbreɪnd) *adj* insane, idiotic, or crazy.

crack down *vb* (*intr, adv;* often foll. by *on*) **1** to take severe measures (against); become stricter (with). ◆ *n* **crackdown. 2** severe or repressive measures.

cracked (krækt) *adj* **1** damaged by cracking. **2** *Informal.* crazy.

cracked wheat *n* whole wheat cracked between rollers so that it will cook more quickly.

cracker (ˈkrækə) *n* **1** a decorated cardboard tube that emits a bang when pulled apart, releasing a toy, a joke, or a paper hat. **2** short for **firecracker. 3** a thin crisp biscuit, usually unsweetened. **4** a person or thing that cracks. **5** *U.S.* another word for **poor White. 6** *Brit. slang.* a thing or person of notable qualities or abilities. **7 not worth a cracker.** *Austral. and N.Z. informal.* worthless; useless.

cracker-barrel *adj U.S.* rural; rustic; homespun: *a cracker-barrel philosopher.*

crackerjack (ˈkrækəˌdʒæk) *Informal.* ◆ *adj* **1** excellent. ◆ *n* **2** a person or thing of exceptional quality or ability. [C20: changed from CRACK (first-class) + JACK[1] (man)]

crackers (ˈkrækəz) *adj* (*postpositive*) *Brit.* a slang word for **insane.**

cracket (ˈkrækɪt) *n Dialect.* **1** a low stool, often one with three legs. **2** a box for a miner to kneel on when working a low seam. [variant of CRICKET[3]]

crackhead (ˈkrækˌhed) *n Slang.* a person addicted to the drug crack.

cracking (ˈkrækɪŋ) *adj* **1** (*prenominal*) *Informal.* fast; vigorous (esp. in the phrase **a cracking pace**). **2 get cracking.** *Informal.* to start doing something quickly or do something with increased speed. ◆ *adv, adj* **3** *Brit. informal.* first-class; excellent: *a cracking good match.* ◆ *n* **4** the process in which molecules are cracked, esp. the oil-refining process in which heavy oils are broken down into hydrocarbons of lower molecular weight by heat or catalysis. See also **catalytic cracker.**

crackjaw (ˈkrækˌdʒɔː) *Informal.* ◆ *adj* **1** difficult to pronounce. ◆ *n* **2** a word or phrase that is difficult to pronounce.

crackle (ˈkrækəl) *vb* **1** to make or cause to make a series of slight sharp noises, as of paper being crushed or of a wood fire burning. **2** (*tr*) to decorate (porcelain or pottery) by causing a fine network of cracks to appear in the glaze. **3** (*intr*) to abound in vivacity or energy. ◆ *n* **4** the act or sound of crackling. **5** intentional crazing in the glaze of a piece of porcelain or pottery. **6** Also called: **ˈcrackleˌware.** porcelain or pottery so decorated.

crackling (ˈkræklɪŋ) *n* the crisp browned skin of roast pork.

cracknel (ˈkræknəl) *n* **1** a type of hard plain biscuit. **2** (*often pl*) *U.S. and Canadian.* crisply fried bits of fat pork. [C15: perhaps from Old French *craquelin,* from Middle Dutch *krākelinc,* from *krāken* to CRACK]

crackpot (ˈkrækˌpɒt) *Informal.* ◆ *n* **1** an eccentric person; crank. ◆ *adj* **2** (*usually prenominal*) eccentric; crazy.

cracksman (ˈkræksmən) *n, pl* **-men.** *Slang.* a burglar, esp. a safe-breaker.

crack up *vb* (*adv*) **1** (*intr*) to break into pieces. **2** (*intr*) *Informal.* to undergo a physical or mental breakdown. **3** (*tr*) *Informal.* to present or report, esp. in glowing terms: *it's not all it's cracked up to be.* **4** *Informal, chiefly U.S. and Canadian.* to laugh or cause to laugh uproariously or uncontrollably. ◆ *n* **crackup. 5** *Informal.* a physical or mental breakdown.

crack willow *n* **1** a species of commonly grown willow, *Salix fragilis,* with branches that snap easily. **2** any of various related willows.

Cracow (ˈkrækaʊ, -əʊ, -ɒf) *n* an industrial city in S Poland, on the River Vistula: former capital of the country (1320–1609); university (1364). Pop.: 746 000 (1995 est.). Polish name: **Kraków.** German name: **Krakau.**

-cracy *n combining form.* indicating a type of government or rule: *plutocracy; mobocracy.* See also **-crat.** [from Greek *-kratia,* from *kratos* power]

cradle (ˈkreɪdəl) *n* **1** a baby's bed with enclosed sides, often with a hood and rockers. **2** a place where something originates or is nurtured during its early life: *the cradle of civilization.* **3** the earliest period of life: *they knew each other from the cradle.* **4** a frame, rest, or trolley made to support or transport a piece of equipment, aircraft, ship, etc. **5** a platform, cage, or trolley, in which workmen are suspended on the side of a building or ship. **6** the part of a telephone on which the handset rests when not in use. **7** another name for **creeper** (sense 5). **8** *Agriculture.* **8a** a framework of several wooden fingers attached to a scythe to gather the grain into bunches as it is cut. **8b** a scythe equipped with such a cradle; cradle scythe. **8c** a collar of wooden fingers that prevents a horse or cow from turning its head and biting itself. **9** Also called: **rocker.** a boxlike apparatus for washing rocks, sand, etc., containing gold or gem stones. **10** *Engraving.* a tool that produces the pitted surface of a copper mezzotint plate before the design is engraved upon it. **11** a framework used to prevent the bedclothes from touching a sensitive part of an injured person. **12 from the cradle to the grave.** throughout life. ◆ *vb* **13** (*tr*) to rock or place in or as if in a cradle; hold tenderly. **14** (*tr*) to nurture in or bring up from infancy. **15** (*tr*) to replace (the handset of a telephone) on the cradle. **16** to reap (grain) with a cradle scythe. **17** (*tr*) to wash (soil bearing gold, etc.) in a cradle. **18** *Lacrosse.* to keep (the ball) in the net of the stick, esp. while running with it. [Old English *cradol;* related to Old High German *kratto* basket] ▸ **ˈcradler** *n*

cradle cap *n* a form of seborrhoea of the scalp common in young babies. Technical name: **crusta lactea.**

cradle snatcher *n Informal.* someone who marries or has an affair with a much younger person.

cradlesong (ˈkreɪdəlˌsɒŋ) *n* another word for **lullaby.**

cradling (ˈkreɪdlɪŋ) *n Architect.* a framework of iron or wood, esp. as used in the construction of a ceiling.

craft (krɑːft) *n* **1** skill or ability, esp. in handiwork. **2** skill in deception and trickery; guile; cunning. **3** an occupation or trade requiring special skill, esp. manual dexterity. **4a** the members of such a trade, regarded collectively. **4b** (*as modifier*): *a craft guild.* **5** a single vessel, aircraft, or spacecraft. **6** (*functioning as pl*) ships, boats, aircraft, or spacecraft collectively. ◆ *vb* **7** (*tr*) to make or fashion with skill, esp. by hand. [Old English *cræft* skill, strength; related to Old Norse *kraptr* power, skill, Old High German *kraft*]

craft apprenticeship *n* a period of training for a skilled trade in industry, such as for a plumber or electrician.

craftsman (ˈkrɑːftsmən) *n, pl* **-men. 1** a member of a skilled trade; someone who practises a craft; artisan. **2** Also called: (*fem*) **craftswoman.** an artist

skilled in the techniques of an art or craft. ▸ **'craftsmanly** *adj* ▸ **'craftsman,ship** *n*
craft union *n* a labour organization membership of which is restricted to workers in a specified trade or craft. Compare **industrial union.**
crafty ('krɑːftɪ) *adj* **craftier, craftiest. 1** skilled in deception; shrewd; cunning. **2** *Archaic.* skilful. ▸ **'craftily** *adv* ▸ **'craftiness** *n*
crag (kræg) *n* a steep rugged rock or peak. [C13: of Celtic origin; related to Old Welsh *creik* rock]
Crag (kræg) *n* a formation of shelly sandstone in E England, deposited during the Pliocene and Pleistocene epochs.
craggy ('krægɪ) *or U.S.* **cragged** ('krægɪd) *adj* **-gier, -giest. 1** having many crags. **2** (of the face) rugged; rocklike. ▸ **'craggily** *adv* ▸ **'cragginess** *n*
cragsman ('krægzmən) *n, pl* **-men.** a rock climber.
craig (kreg, kreɪg) *n* a Scot. word for **crag.**
Craig (kreɪg) *n* **Edward Gordon.** 1872–1966, English theatrical designer, actor, and director. His nonrealistic scenic design greatly influenced theatre in Europe and the U.S.
Craigavon (ˌkreɪg'ævᵊn) *n* a district in central Northern Ireland, in Co. Armagh. Pop.: 78 100 (1995 est.). Area: 279 sq. km (108 sq. miles).
Craigie ('kreɪgɪ) *n* Sir **William A(lexander).** 1867–1957, Scottish lexicographer; joint editor of the *Oxford English Dictionary* (1901–33), and of *A Dictionary of American English on Historical Principles* (1938–44).
Craiova (*Romanian* kra'jova) *n* a city in SW Romania, on the Jiul River. Pop.: 306 825 (1994 est.).
crake (kreɪk) *n Zoology.* any of several rails that occur in the Old World, such as the corncrake and the spotted crake. [C14: from Old Norse *krāka* crow or *krākr* raven, of imitative origin]
cram (kræm) *vb* **crams, cramming, crammed. 1** (*tr*) to force (people, material, etc.) into (a room, container, etc.) with more than it can hold; stuff. **2** to eat or cause to eat more than necessary. **3** *Informal.* to study or cause to study (facts, etc.), esp. for an examination, by hastily memorizing. ◆ *n* **4** the act or condition of cramming. **5** a crush. [Old English *crammian;* related to Old Norse *kremja* to press]
Cram (kræm) *n* **Steve.** born 1960, English middle-distance runner: European 1500 m champion (1981, 1986); world 1500 m champion (1983).
crambo ('kræmbəʊ) *n* a word game in which one team says a rhyme or rhyming line for a word or line given by the other team. [C17: from earlier *crambe,* probably from Latin *crambē repetīta* cabbage repeated, hence an old story, a rhyming game, from Greek *krambē*]
cram-full *adj* stuffed full.
crammer ('kræmə) *n* a person or school that prepares pupils for an examination, esp. pupils who have already failed that examination.
cramoisy *or* **cramoisie** ('kræmɔɪzɪ, -əzɪ) *Archaic.* ◆ *adj* **1** of a crimson colour. ◆ *n* **2** crimson cloth. [C15: from Old French *cramoisi,* from Arabic *qirmizī* red obtained from kermes; see CRIMSON, KERMES]
cramp[1] (kræmp) *n* **1** a painful involuntary contraction of a muscle, typically caused by overexertion, heat, or chill. **2** temporary partial paralysis of a muscle group: *writer's cramp.* **3** (*usually pl in the U.S. and Canada*) severe abdominal pain. ◆ *vb* **4** (*tr*) to affect with or as if with a cramp. [C14: from Old French *crampe,* of Germanic origin; compare Old High German *krampho*]
cramp[2] (kræmp) *n* **1** Also called: **cramp iron.** a strip of metal with its ends bent at right angles, used to bind masonry. **2** a device for holding pieces of wood while they are glued; clamp. **3** something that confines or restricts. **4** a confined state or position. ◆ *vb* (*tr*) **5** to secure or hold with a cramp. **6** to confine, hamper, or restrict. **7 cramp (someone's) style.** *Informal.* to prevent (a person) from using his abilities or acting freely and confidently. [C15: from Middle Dutch *crampe* cramp, hook, of Germanic origin; compare Old High German *khramph* bent; see CRAMP[1]]
cramp ball *n* a hard round blackish ascomycetous fungus, *Daldinia concentrica,* characteristically found on the bark of ash trees and formerly carried to ward off cramp. The specific name refers to the concentric rings revealed if the fungus is sliced.
cramped (kræmpt) *adj* **1** closed in; restricted. **2** (esp. of handwriting) small and irregular; difficult to read.
cramper ('kræmpə) *n Curling.* a spiked metal plate used as a brace for the feet in throwing the stone.
crampon ('kræmpən) *n* **1** one of a pair of pivoted steel levers used to lift heavy objects; grappling iron. **2** (*often pl*) one of a pair of frames each with 10 or 12 metal spikes, strapped to boots for climbing or walking on ice or snow. ◆ *vb* **3** to climb using crampons. [C15: from French, from Middle Dutch *crampe* hook; see CRAMP[2]]
cran (kræn) *n* a unit of capacity used for measuring fresh herring, equal to 37.5 gallons. [C18: of uncertain origin]
Cranach (*German* 'kraːnax) *n* **Lucas** ('luːkas), known as *the Elder,* real name *Lucas Müller.* 1472–1553, German painter, etcher, and designer of woodcuts.
cranage ('kreɪnɪdʒ) *n* **1** the use of a crane. **2** a fee charged for such use.
cranberry ('krænbərɪ, -brɪ) *n, pl* **-ries. 1** any of several trailing ericaceous shrubs of the genus *Vaccinium,* such as the European *V. oxycoccus,* that bear sour edible red berries. **2** the berry of this plant, used to make sauce or jelly. [C17: from Low German *kraanbere,* from *kraan* CRANE + *bere* BERRY]
cranberry bush *or* **tree** *n* a North American caprifoliaceous shrub or small tree, *Viburnum trilobum,* producing acid red fruit.
crane (kreɪn) *n* **1** any large long-necked long-legged wading bird of the family *Gruidae,* inhabiting marshes and plains in most parts of the world except South America, New Zealand, and Indonesia: order *Gruiformes.* See also **demoiselle** (sense 1), **whooping crane. 2** (*not in ornithological use*) any similar bird, such as a heron. **3** a device for lifting and moving heavy objects, typically consisting of a pivoted boom rotating about a vertical axis with lifting gear suspended from the end of the boom. See also **gantry. 4** *Films.* a large trolley carrying a boom, on the end of which is mounted a camera. ◆ *vb* **5** (*tr*) to lift or move (an object) by or as if by a crane. **6** to stretch out (esp. the neck), as to see over other people's heads. **7** (*intr*) (of a horse) to pull up short before a jump. [Old English *cran;* related to Middle High German *krane,* Latin *grūs,* Greek *géranos*]
Crane (kreɪn) *n* **1** (**Harold**) **Hart.** 1899–1932, U.S. poet; author of *The Bridge* (1930). **2 Stephen.** 1871–1900, U.S. novelist and short-story writer, noted particularly for his novel *The Red Badge of Courage* (1895). **3 Walter.** 1845–1915, British painter, illustrator of children's books, and designer of textiles and wallpaper.
crane fly *n* any dipterous fly of the family *Tipulidae,* having long legs, slender wings, and a narrow body. Also called (Brit.): **daddy-longlegs.**
cranesbill ('kreɪnz,bɪl) *n* any of various plants of the genus *Geranium,* having pink or purple flowers and long slender beaked fruits: family *Geraniaceae.* See also **herb Robert, storksbill.**
cranial ('kreɪnɪəl) *adj* of or relating to the skull. ▸ **'cranially** *adv*
cranial index *n* the ratio of the greatest length to the greatest width of the cranium, multiplied by 100: used in comparative anthropology. Compare **cephalic index.**
cranial nerve *n* any of the 12 paired nerves that have their origin in the brain and reach the periphery through natural openings in the skull.
craniate ('kreɪnɪɪt, -ˌeɪt) *adj* **1** having a skull or cranium. ◆ *adj, n* **2** another word for **vertebrate.**
cranio- *or before a vowel* **crani-** *combining form.* indicating the cranium or cranial: *craniotomy.*
craniology (ˌkreɪnɪ'ɒlədʒɪ) *n* the branch of science concerned with the shape and size of the human skull, esp. with reference to variations between different races. ▸ **craniological** (ˌkreɪnɪə'lɒdʒɪkᵊl) *adj* ▸ **ˌcranio'logically** *adv* ▸ **ˌcrani'ologist** *n*
craniometer (ˌkreɪnɪ'ɒmɪtə) *n* an instrument for measuring the cranium or skull.
craniometry (ˌkreɪnɪ'ɒmɪtrɪ) *n* the study and measurement of skulls. ▸ **craniometric** (ˌkreɪnɪə'mɛtrɪk) *or* **ˌcranio'metrical** *adj* ▸ **ˌcranio'metrically** *adv* ▸ **ˌcrani'ometrist** *n*
craniotomy (ˌkreɪnɪ'ɒtəmɪ) *n, pl* **-mies. 1** surgical incision into the skull, esp. to expose the brain for neurosurgery. **2** surgical crushing of a fetal skull to extract a dead fetus.
cranium ('kreɪnɪəm) *n, pl* **-niums** *or* **-nia** (-nɪə). **1** the skull of a vertebrate. **2** the part of the skull that encloses the brain. Nontechnical name: **brainpan.** [C16: from Medieval Latin *crānium* skull, from Greek *kranion*]
crank[1] (kræŋk) *n* **1** a device for communicating motion or for converting reciprocating motion into rotary motion or vice versa. It consists of an arm projecting from a shaft, often with a second member attached to it parallel to the shaft. **2** Also called: **crank handle, starting handle.** a handle incorporating a crank, used to start an engine or motor. **3** *Informal.* **3a** an eccentric or odd person, esp. someone who stubbornly maintains unusual views. **3b** *U.S. and Canadian.* a bad-tempered person. ◆ *vb* **4** (*tr*) to rotate (a shaft) by means of a crank. **5** (*tr*) to start (an engine, motor, etc.) by means of a crank handle. **6** (*tr*) to bend, twist, or make into the shape of a crank. **7** (*intr*) *Obsolete.* to twist or wind. ◆ See also **crank up.** [Old English *cranc;* related to Middle Low German *krunke* wrinkle, Dutch *krinkel* CRINKLE]
crank[2] (kræŋk) *or* **cranky** *adj* (of a sailing vessel) easily keeled over by the wind; tender. [C17: of uncertain origin; perhaps related to CRANK[1]]
crankcase ('kræŋk,keɪs) *n* the metal housing that encloses the crankshaft, connecting rods, etc., in an internal-combustion engine, reciprocating pump, etc.
Cranko ('kræŋkəʊ) *n* **John.** 1927–73, British choreographer, born in South Africa: director of the Stuttgart Ballet (1961–73).
crankpin ('kræŋk,pɪn) *n* a short cylindrical bearing surface fitted between two arms of a crank and set parallel to the main shaft of the crankshaft.
crankshaft ('kræŋk,ʃɑːft) *n* a shaft having one or more cranks, esp. the main shaft of an internal-combustion engine to which the connecting rods are attached.
crank up *vb* (*tr*) *Slang.* **1** to increase (loudness, output, etc.): *he cranked up his pace.* **2** to set in motion or invigorate: *news editors have to crank up tired reporters.* **3** (*intr, adv*) to inject a narcotic drug.
cranky[1] ('kræŋkɪ) *adj* **crankier, crankiest. 1** *Informal.* eccentric. **2** *Chiefly U.S., Canadian, and Irish informal.* fussy and bad-tempered. **3** shaky; out of order. **4** full of bends and turns. **5** *Dialect.* unwell. ▸ **'crankily** *adv* ▸ **'crankiness** *n*
cranky[2] ('kræŋkɪ) *adj* **crankier, crankiest.** *Nautical.* another word for **crank**[2].
Cranmer ('krænmə) *n* **Thomas.** 1489–1556, the first Protestant archbishop of Canterbury (1533–56) and principal author of the Book of Common Prayer. He was burnt as a heretic by Mary I.
crannog ('krænəg) *or* **crannoge** ('krænədʒ) *n* an ancient Celtic lake or bog dwelling dating from the late Bronze Age to the 16th century A.D., often fortified and used as a refuge. [C19: from Irish Gaelic *crannóg,* from Old Irish *crann* tree]
cranny ('krænɪ) *n, pl* **-nies.** a narrow opening, as in a wall or rock face; chink; crevice (esp. in the phrase **every nook and cranny**). [C15: from Old French *cran* notch, fissure; compare CRENEL] ▸ **'crannied** *adj*
Cranwell ('krænwəl) *n* a village in E England, in Lincolnshire: Royal Air Force College (1920).
crap[1] (kræp) *n* **1** a losing throw in the game of craps. **2** another name for **craps.** [C20: back formation from CRAPS]
crap[2] (kræp) *Slang* ◆ *n* **1** nonsense. **2** rubbish. **3** a taboo word for **faeces.** ◆ *vb* **craps, crapping, crapped. 4** (*intr*) to defecate. [C15 *crappe* chaff, from Middle Dutch, probably from *crappen* to break off]
crapaud ('kræpəʊ, 'krɑː-) *n Caribbean.* a frog or toad. [from French: toad]

crape (kreɪp) *n* **1** a variant spelling of **crepe**. **2** crepe, esp. when used for mourning clothes. **3** a band of black crepe worn in mourning. ▸ **'crapy** *adj*

crape myrtle *or* **crepe myrtle** *n* an oriental lythraceous shrub, *Lagerstroemia indica,* cultivated in warm climates for its pink, red, or white flowers.

crap out *vb* (*intr, adv*) **1** *U.S. slang.* to make a losing throw in craps. **2** *U.S. slang.* to fail; withdraw. **3** *U.S. slang.* to rest. **4** *Slang.* to fail to do or attempt something through fear.

crappie ('kræpɪ) *n, pl* **-pies.** either of two North American freshwater percoid food and game fishes, *Pomoxis nigromaculatus* (**black crappie**) or *P. annularis* (**white crappie**): family *Centrarchidae* (sunfishes, etc.). [C19: from Canadian French *crapet*]

craps (kræps) *n* (*usually functioning as sing*) **1** a gambling game using two dice, in which a player wins the bet if 7 or 11 is thrown first, and loses if 2, 3, or 12 is thrown. **2 shoot craps.** to play this game. [C19: probably from *crabs* lowest throw at dice, plural of CRAB[1]]

crapshooter ('kræp,ʃuːtə) *n U.S.* a person who plays the game of craps.

crapulent ('kræpjʊlənt) *or* **crapulous** ('kræpjʊləs) *adj* **1** given to or resulting from intemperance. **2** suffering from intemperance; drunken. [C18: from Late Latin *crāpulentus* drunk, from Latin *crāpula,* from Greek *kraipalē* drunkenness, headache resulting therefrom] ▸ **'crapulence** *n* ▸ **'crapulently** *or* **'crapulously** *adv* ▸ **'crapulousness** *n*

craquelure ('krækəluə) *n* a network of fine cracks on old paintings caused by the deterioration of pigment or varnish. [C20: from French, from *craqueler* to crackle, from *craquer* to crack, of imitative origin]

crash[1] (kræʃ) *vb* **1** to make or cause to make a loud noise as of solid objects smashing or clattering. **2** to fall or cause to fall with force, breaking in pieces with a loud noise as of solid objects smashing. **3** (*intr*) to break or smash in pieces with a loud noise. **4** (*intr*) to collapse or fail suddenly: *this business is sure to crash.* **5** to cause (an aircraft) to hit land or water violently resulting in severe damage or (of an aircraft) to hit land or water in this way. **6** to cause (a car, etc.) to collide with another car or other object or (of two or more cars) to be involved in a collision. **7** to move or cause to move violently or noisily: *to crash through a barrier.* **8** *Brit. informal.* short for **gate-crash. 9** (*intr*) (of a computer system or program) to fail suddenly and completely because of a malfunction. **10** (*intr*) *Slang.* another term for **crash out.** ♦ *n* **11** an act or instance of breaking and falling to pieces. **12** a sudden loud noise: *the crash of thunder.* **13** a collision, as between vehicles. **14** a sudden descent of an aircraft as a result of which it hits land or water. **15** the sudden collapse of a business, stock exchange, etc., esp. one causing further financial failure. **16** (*modifier*) **16a** requiring or using intensive effort and all possible resources in order to accomplish something quickly: *a crash programme.* **16b** sudden or vigorous: *a crash halt; a crash tackle.* ♦ See also **crash out.** [C14: probably from *crasen* to smash, shatter + *dasshen* to strike violently, DASH[1]; see CRAZE] ▸ **'crasher** *n*

crash[2] (kræʃ) *n* a coarse cotton or linen cloth used for towelling, curtains, etc. [C19: from Russian *krashenina* coloured linen]

Crashaw ('kræʃɔː) *n* **Richard.** 1613–49, English religious poet, noted esp. for the *Steps to the Temple* (1646).

crash barrier *n* a barrier erected along the centre of a motorway, around a racetrack, etc., for safety purposes.

crash dive *n* **1** a sudden steep dive from the surface by a submarine. ♦ *vb* **crash-dive. 2** (usually of an aircraft) to descend steeply and rapidly, before hitting the ground. **3** to perform or cause to perform a crash dive.

crash helmet *n* a padded helmet worn for motorcycling, flying, bobsleighing, etc., to protect the head in a crash.

crashing ('kræʃɪŋ) *adj* (*prenominal*) *Informal.* (intensifier) (esp. in the phrase **a crashing bore**).

crash-land *vb* to land (an aircraft) in an emergency causing damage or (of an aircraft) to land in this way. ▸ **'crash-,landing** *n*

crash out *vb* (*intr, adv*) *Slang.* **1a** to go to sleep. **1b** to spend the night (in a place): *we crashed out at John's place.* **2** to pass out.

crash pad *n Slang.* a place to sleep or live temporarily.

crash team *n* a medical team with special equipment able to be mobilized quickly to treat cardiac arrest.

crash-test *vb* (*tr*) to test (a new product) for safety and reliability by finding out its breaking point under pressure, heat, etc.

crashworthiness ('kræʃ,wɜːðɪnɪs) *n* the ability of a vehicle structure to withstand a crash. ▸ **'crash,worthy** *adj*

crasis ('kreɪsɪs) *n, pl* **-ses** (-siːz). the fusion or contraction of two adjacent vowels into one. Also called: **syneresis.** [C17: from Greek *krasis* a mingling, from *kerannunai* to mix]

crass (kræs) *adj* stupid; gross. [C16: from Latin *crassus* thick, dense, gross] ▸ **'crassly** *adv* ▸ **'crassness** *or* **'crassi,tude** *n*

crassulacean acid metabolism (,kræsjʊ'leɪʃən) *n* the full name for **CAM** (sense 2).

crassulaceous (,kræsjʊ'leɪʃəs) *adj* of, relating to, or belonging to the *Crassulaceae,* a family of herbaceous or shrubby flowering plants with fleshy succulent leaves, including the houseleeks and stonecrops. [C19: from New Latin *Crassula* name of genus, from Medieval Latin: stonecrop, from Latin *crassus* thick]

Crassus ('kræsəs) *n* **Marcus Licinius** ('mɑːkəs lɪ'sɪnɪəs). ?115–53 B.C., Roman general; member of the first triumvirate with Caesar and Pompey.

-crat *n combining form.* indicating a person who takes part in or is a member of a form of government or class: *democrat; technocrat.* See also **-cracy.** [from Greek *-kratēs,* from *-kratia* -CRACY] ▸ **-cratic** *or* **-critical** *adj combining form.*

cratch (krætʃ) *n* a rack for holding fodder for cattle, etc. [C14: from Old French: CRÈCHE]

crate (kreɪt) *n* **1** a fairly large container, usually made of wooden slats or wickerwork, used for packing, storing, or transporting goods. **2** *Slang.* an old car, aeroplane, etc. ♦ *vb* **3** (*tr*) to pack or place in a crate. [C16: from Latin *crātis* wickerwork, hurdle] ▸ **'crater** *n* ▸ **'crateful** *n*

crater ('kreɪtə) *n* **1** the bowl-shaped opening at the top or side of a volcano or top of a geyser through which lava and gases are emitted. **2** a similarly shaped depression formed by the impact of a meteorite or exploding bomb. **3** any of the circular or polygonal walled formations covering the surface of the moon and some other planets, formed probably either by volcanic action or by the impact of meteorites. They can have a diameter of up to 240 kilometres (150 miles) and a depth of 8900 metres (29 000 feet). **4** a pit in an otherwise smooth surface. **5** a large open bowl with two handles, used for mixing wines, esp. in ancient Greece. ♦ *vb* **6** to make or form craters in (a surface, such as the ground). [C17: from Latin: mixing bowl, crater, from Greek *kratēr,* from *kerannunai* to mix] ▸ **'cratered** *adj* ▸ **'craterless** *adj* ▸ **'crater-,like** *adj*

Crater ('kreɪtə) *n, Latin genitive* **Crateris** ('kreɪtərɪs). a small faint constellation in the S hemisphere lying between Virgo and Hydra.

craton ('kreɪtᵊn) *n Geology.* a stable part of the earth's crust or lithosphere that has not been deformed significantly for many millions, even hundreds of millions, of years. See **shield** (sense 7). [C20: from Greek *kratos* strength] ▸ **cratonic** (krə'tɒnɪk) *adj*

cratur ('kretər) *n Irish and Scot.* **1 the.** whisky or whiskey: *a drop of the cratur.* **2** a person. [from CREATURE]

craunch (krɔːntʃ) *vb* a dialect word for **crunch.** ▸ **'craunchable** *adj* ▸ **'craunchy** *adj* ▸ **'craunchiness** *n*

cravat (krə'væt) *n* a scarf of silk or fine wool, worn round the neck, esp. by men. [C17: from French *cravate,* from Serbo-Croat *Hrvat* Croat; so called because worn by Croats in the French army during the Thirty Years' War]

crave (kreɪv) *vb* **1** (when *intr,* foll. by *for* or *after*) to desire intensely; long (for). **2** (*tr*) to need greatly or urgently. **3** (*tr*) to beg or plead for. [Old English *crafian;* related to Old Norse *krefja* to demand, *kræfr* strong; see CRAFT] ▸ **'craver** *n*

craven ('kreɪvᵊn) *adj* **1** cowardly; mean-spirited. ♦ *n* **2** a coward. [C13 *cravant,* probably from Old French *crevant* bursting, from *crever* to burst, die, from Latin *crepāre* to burst, crack] ▸ **'cravenly** *adv* ▸ **'cravenness** *n*

craving ('kreɪvɪŋ) *n* an intense desire or longing.

craw (krɔː) *n* **1** a less common word for **crop** (sense 6). **2** the stomach of an animal. **3 stick in one's craw** *or* **throat.** *Informal.* to be difficult, or against one's conscience, for one to accept, utter, or believe. [C14: related to Middle High German *krage,* Middle Dutch *crāghe* neck, Icelandic *kragi* collar]

crawfish ('krɔː,fɪʃ) *n, pl* **-fish** *or* **-fishes.** a variant (esp. U.S.) of **crayfish** (esp. sense 2).

Crawford ('krɔːfəd) *n* **1 Joan,** real name *Lucille le Sueur.* 1908–77, U.S. film actress, who portrayed ambitious women in such films as *Mildred Pierce* (1945). **2 Michael,** real name *Michael Dumbell Smith.* born 1942, British actor.

crawl[1] (krɔːl) *vb* (*intr*) **1** to move slowly, either by dragging the body along the ground or on the hands and knees. **2** to proceed or move along very slowly or laboriously: *the traffic crawled along the road.* **3** to act or behave in a servile manner; fawn; cringe. **4** to be or feel as if overrun by something unpleasant, esp. crawling creatures: *the pile of refuse crawled with insects.* **5** (of insects, worms, snakes, etc.) to move with the body close to the ground. **6** to swim the crawl. ♦ *n* **7** a slow creeping pace or motion. **8** Also called: **Australian crawl, front crawl.** *Swimming.* a stroke in which the feet are kicked like paddles while the arms reach forward and pull back through the water. [C14: probably from Old Norse *krafla* to creep; compare Swedish *kravla,* Middle Low German *krabbelen* to crawl, Old Norse *krabbi* CRAB[1]] ▸ **'crawlingly** *adv*

crawl[2] (krɔːl) *n* an enclosure in shallow, coastal water for fish, lobsters, etc. [C17: from Dutch *kraal* KRAAL]

crawler ('krɔːlə) *n* **1** *Slang.* a servile flatterer. **2** a person or animal that crawls. **3** *U.S.* an informal name for an **earthworm. 4** (*pl*) a baby's overalls; rompers.

crawler lane *n* a lane on an uphill section of a motorway reserved for slow vehicles.

Crawley ('krɔːlɪ) *n* a town in S England, in NE West Sussex: designated a new town in 1956. Pop.: 88 203 (1991).

crawling ('krɔːlɪŋ) *n* a defect in freshly applied paint or varnish characterized by bare patches and ridging.

crawling peg *n* a method of stabilizing exchange rates, prices, etc., by maintaining a fixed level for a specified period or until the level has persisted at an upper or lower limit for a specified period and then permitting a predetermined incremental rise or fall.

crawly ('krɔːlɪ) *adj* **crawlier, crawliest.** *Informal.* feeling or causing a sensation like creatures crawling on one's skin.

craw-thumper *n Irish informal.* an ostentatiously pious person. [C18: in the sense: breast-beater, from CRAW]

Craxi ('kræksɪ) *n* **Bettino** (be'tiːno). born 1934, Italian socialist statesman; prime minister (1983–87).

cray (kreɪ) *n Austral. and N.Z. informal.* a crayfish.

crayfish ('kreɪ,fɪʃ) *or esp. U.S.* **crawfish** *n, pl* **-fish** *or* **-fishes. 1** any freshwater decapod crustacean of the genera *Astacus* and *Cambarus,* resembling a small lobster. **2** any of various similar crustaceans, esp. the spiny lobster. [C14: *cray,* by folk etymology, from Old French *crevice* crab, from Old High German *krebiz* + FISH]

crayon ('kreɪən, -ɒn) *n* **1** a small stick or pencil of charcoal, wax, clay, or chalk mixed with coloured pigment. **2** a drawing made with crayons. ♦ *vb* **3** to draw or colour with crayons. [C17: from French, from *craie,* from Latin *crēta* chalk] ▸ **'crayonist** *n*

craythur *n Irish.* **1** ('kreːθər) **the.** a variant of **cratur** (sense 1). **2** ('kreːtʃər) a variant of **cratur** (sense 2). [from Irish Gaelic *Créatur* creature]

craze (kreɪz) *n* **1** a short-lived current fashion. **2** a wild or exaggerated enthusiasm: *a craze for chestnuts.* **3** mental disturbance; insanity. ◆ *vb* **4** to make or become mad. **5** *Ceramics, metallurgy.* to develop or cause to develop a fine network of cracks. **6** (*tr*) *Brit. dialect or obsolete.* to break. **7** (*tr*) *Archaic.* to weaken. [C14 (in the sense: to break, shatter): probably of Scandinavian origin; compare Swedish *krasa* to shatter, ultimately of imitative origin]

crazed (kreɪzd) *adj* **1** driven insane. **2** (of porcelain or pottery) having a fine network of cracks in the glaze.

crazy ('kreɪzɪ) *adj* **-zier, -ziest. 1** *Informal.* insane. **2** fantastic; strange; ridiculous: *a crazy dream.* **3** (*postpositive;* foll. by *about* or *over*) *Informal.* extremely fond (of). **4** *Slang.* very good or excellent. ▸ **'crazily** *adv* ▸ **'craziness** *n*

crazy bone *n* a U.S. name for **funny bone.**

crazy golf *n* a putting game in which the ball has to be played via various obstacles.

Crazy Horse *n* Indian name *Ta-Sunko-Witko.* ?1849–77, Sioux Indian chief, remembered for his attempts to resist White settlement in Sioux territory.

crazy paving *n Brit.* a form of paving, as for a path, made of slabs of stone of irregular shape fitted together.

crazy quilt *n* a patchwork quilt made from assorted pieces of material of irregular shape, size, and colour.

CRE (in Britain) *abbrev. for* Commission for Racial Equality.

creak (kri:k) *vb* **1** to make or cause to make a harsh squeaking sound. **2** (*intr*) to make such sounds while moving: *the old car creaked along.* ◆ *n* **3** a harsh squeaking sound. [C14: variant of CROAK, of imitative origin] ▸ **'creaky** *adj* ▸ **'creakily** *adv* ▸ **'creakiness** *n* ▸ **'creakingly** *adv*

cream (kri:m) *n* **1a** the fatty part of milk, which rises to the top if the milk is allowed to stand. **1b** (*as modifier*): *cream buns.* **2** anything resembling cream in consistency: *shoe cream; beauty cream.* **3** the best one or most essential part of something; pick: *the cream of the bunch; the cream of the joke.* **4** a soup containing cream or milk: *cream of chicken soup.* **5** any of various dishes, cakes, biscuits, etc., resembling or containing cream. **6** a confection made of fondant or soft fudge, often covered in chocolate. **7 cream sherry.** a full-bodied sweet sherry. **8a** a yellowish-white colour. **8b** (*as adj*): *cream wallpaper.* ◆ *vb* **9** (*tr*) to skim or otherwise separate the cream from (milk). **10** (*tr*) to beat (foodstuffs, esp. butter and sugar) to a light creamy consistency. **11** (*intr*) to form cream. **12** (*tr*) to add or apply cream or any creamlike substance to: *to cream one's face; to cream coffee.* **13** (*tr;* sometimes foll. by *off*) to take away the best part of. **14** (*tr*) to prepare or cook (vegetables, chicken, etc.) with cream or milk. **15** to allow (milk) to form a layer of cream on its surface or (of milk) to form such a layer. **16** (*tr*) *Slang, chiefly U.S., Canadian, & Austral.* to beat thoroughly. **17** (*intr*) *Taboo slang.* (of men) to ejaculate, as during orgasm. [C14: from Old French *cresme,* from Late Latin *crāmum* cream, of Celtic origin; influenced by Church Latin *chrisma* unction, CHRISM] ▸ **'cream,like** *adj*

cream cheese *n* a smooth soft white cheese made from soured cream or milk.

cream cracker *n Brit.* a crisp unsweetened biscuit, often eaten with cheese.

creamcups ('kri:m,kʌps) *n* (*functioning as sing or pl*) a Californian papaveraceous plant, *Platystemon californicus,* with small cream-coloured or yellow flowers on long flower stalks.

creamer ('kri:mə) *n* **1** a vessel or device for separating cream from milk. **2** a powdered substitute for cream, used in coffee. **3** *Chiefly U.S. and Canadian.* a small jug or pitcher for serving cream.

creamery ('kri:mərɪ) *n, pl* **-eries. 1** an establishment where milk and cream are made into butter and cheese. **2** a place where dairy products are sold. **3** a place where milk is left to stand until the cream rises to the top.

creamlaid ('kri:m,leɪd) *adj* (of laid paper) cream-coloured and of a ribbed appearance.

cream of tartar *n* another name for **potassium hydrogen tartrate,** esp. when used in baking powders.

cream puff *n* **1** a shell of light pastry with a custard or cream filling. **2** *Informal.* an effeminate man.

cream sauce *n* a white sauce made from cream, butter, etc.

cream soda *n* a carbonated soft drink flavoured with vanilla.

cream tea *n* afternoon tea including bread or scones served with clotted cream and jam.

creamware ('kri:m,wɛə) *n* a type of earthenware with a deep cream body developed about 1720 and widely produced. See also **Queensware.**

creamwove ('kri:m,wəʊv) *adj* (of wove paper) cream-coloured and even-surfaced.

creamy ('kri:mɪ) *adj* **creamier, creamiest. 1** resembling cream in colour, taste, or consistency. **2** containing cream. ▸ **'creamily** *adv* ▸ **'creaminess** *n*

crease[1] (kri:s) *n* **1** a line or mark produced by folding, pressing, or wrinkling. **2** a wrinkle or furrow, esp. on the face. **3** *Cricket.* any three lines near each wicket marking positions for the bowler or batsman. See also **bowling crease, popping crease, return crease. 4** *Ice hockey.* the small rectangular area in front of each goal cage. **5** Also called: **goal crease.** *Lacrosse.* the circular area surrounding the goal. ◆ *vb* **6** to make or become wrinkled or furrowed. **7** (*tr*) to graze with a bullet, causing superficial injury. **8** (often foll. by *up*) *Slang.* to be or cause to be greatly amused. [C15: from earlier *crēst;* probably related to Old French *cresté* wrinkled] ▸ **'creaseless** *adj* ▸ **'creaser** *n* ▸ **'creasy** *adj*

crease[2] (kri:s) *n* a rare spelling of **kris.**

crease-resistant *adj* (of a fabric, garment, etc.) designed to remain uncreased when subjected to wear or use.

create (kri:'eɪt) *vb* **1** (*tr*) to cause to come into existence. **2** (*tr*) to invest with a new honour, office, or title; appoint. **3** (*tr*) to be the cause of: *these circumstances created the revolution.* **4** (*tr*) to act (a role) in the first production of a play. **5** (*intr*) to be engaged in creative work. **6** (*intr*) *Brit. slang.* to make a fuss or uproar. [C14 *creat* created, from Latin *creātus,* from *creāre* to produce, make] ▸ **cre'atable** *adj*

creatine ('kri:ə,ti:n, -tɪn) *or* **creatin** ('kri:ətɪn) *n* an important metabolite involved in many biochemical reactions and present in many types of living cells. [C19: *creat-* from Greek *kreas* flesh + -INE[2]]

creatinine (kri:'ætə,ni:n) *n* an anhydride of creatine that is abundant in muscle and excreted in the urine. [C19: from German *Kreatinin,* from *Kreatin* CREATINE + *-in* -INE[2]]

creation (kri:'eɪʃən) *n* **1** the act or process of creating. **2** the fact of being created or produced. **3** something that has been brought into existence or created, esp. a product of human intelligence or imagination. **4** the whole universe, including the world and all the things in it. **5** an unusual or striking garment or hat. ▸ **cre'ational** *adj*

Creation (kri:'eɪʃən) *n Theol.* **1** (often preceded by *the*) God's act of bringing the universe into being. **2** the universe as thus brought into being by God.

creationism (kri:'eɪʃə,nɪzəm) *n* **1** the belief that God brings individual human souls into existence at conception or birth. Compare **traducianism. 2** the doctrine that ascribes the origins of all things to God's acts of creation rather than to evolution. ▸ **cre'ationist** *n* ▸ **cre,ation'istic** *adj*

creative (kri:'eɪtɪv) *adj* **1** having the ability or power to create. **2** characterized by originality of thought or inventiveness; having or showing imagination: *a creative mind.* **3** designed to or tending to stimulate the imagination or invention: *creative toys.* ▸ **cre'atively** *adv* ▸ **cre'ativeness** *n* ▸ **,crea'tivity** *n*

creator (kri:'eɪtə) *n* a person or thing that creates; originator. ▸ **cre'ator,ship** *n* ▸ **cre'atress** *or* **cre'atrix** *fem n*

Creator (kri:'eɪtə) *n* (usually preceded by *the*) an epithet of God.

creature ('kri:tʃə) *n* **1** a living being, esp. an animal. **2** something that has been created, whether animate or inanimate: *a creature of the imagination.* **3** a human being; person: used as a term of scorn, pity, or endearment. **4** a person who is dependent upon another; tool or puppet. [C13: from Church Latin *creātūra,* from Latin *creāre* to create] ▸ **'creatural** *or* **'creaturely** *adj* ▸ **'creatureliness** *n*

creature comforts *pl n* material things or luxuries that help to provide for one's bodily comfort.

crèche (krɛʃ, kreɪʃ; *French* krɛʃ) *n* **1** *Chiefly Brit.* **1a** a day nursery for very young children. **1b** a supervised play area provided for young children for short periods. **2** a tableau of Christ's Nativity. **3** a foundling home or hospital. [C19: from Old French: manger, crib, ultimately of Germanic origin; compare Old High German *kripja* crib]

Crécy ('krɛsɪ; *French* kresi) *n* a village in N France: scene of the first decisive battle of the Hundred Years' War when the English defeated the French (1346). Official name: **Crécy-en-Ponthieu** (-ɑ̃pɔ̃tjø). English name: **Cressy.**

cred (krɛd) *n Slang.* short for **credibility** (esp. in the phrase **street cred**).

credence ('kri:dᵊns) *n* **1** acceptance or belief, esp. with regard to the truth of the evidence of others: *I cannot give credence to his account.* **2** something supporting a claim to belief; recommendation; credential (esp. in the phrase **letters of credence**). **3** short for **credence table.** [C14: from Medieval Latin *crēdentia* trust, credit, from Latin *crēdere* to believe]

credence table *n* **1** a small sideboard, originally one at which food was tasted for poison before serving. **2** *Christianity.* a small table or ledge on which the bread, wine, etc., are placed before being consecrated in the Eucharist.

credendum (krɪ'dɛndəm) *n, pl* **-da** (-də). (*often pl*) *Christianity.* an article of faith. [Latin: a thing to be believed, from *crēdere* to believe]

credent ('kri:dᵊnt) *adj Obsolete.* believing or believable. [C17: from Latin *crēdēns* believing]

credential (krɪ'dɛnʃəl) *n* **1** something that entitles a person to confidence, authority, etc. **2** (*pl*) a letter or certificate giving evidence of the bearer's identity or competence. ◆ *adj* **3** entitling one to confidence, authority, etc. [C16: from Medieval Latin *crēdentia* credit, trust; see CREDENCE] ▸ **cre'dentialed** *adj*

credenza (krɪ'dɛnzə) *n* another name for **credence table.** [Italian: see CREDENCE]

credibility gap *n* a disparity between claims or statements made and the evident facts of the situation or circumstances to which they relate.

credible ('krɛdɪbᵊl) *adj* **1** capable of being believed. **2** trustworthy or reliable: *the latest claim is the only one to involve a credible witness.* [C14: from Latin *crēdibilis,* from Latin *crēdere* to believe] ▸ **'credibleness** *or* **,credi'bility** *n* ▸ **'credibly** *adv*

credit ('krɛdɪt) *n* **1** commendation or approval, as for an act or quality: *she was given credit for her work.* **2** a person or thing serving as a source of good influence, repute, ability, etc.: *a credit to the team.* **3** the quality of being believable or trustworthy: *that statement had credit.* **4** influence or reputation coming from the approval or good opinion of others: *he acquired credit within the community.* **5** belief in the truth, reliability, quality, etc., of someone or something: *I would give credit to that philosophy.* **6** a sum of money or equivalent purchasing power, as at a shop, available for a person's use. **7a** the positive balance in a person's bank account. **7b** the sum of money that a bank makes available to a client in excess of any deposit. **8a** the practice of permitting a buyer to receive goods or services before payment. **8b** the time permitted for paying for such goods or services. **9** reputation for solvency and commercial or financial probity, inducing confidence among creditors. **10** *Accounting.* **10a** acknowledgment of an income, liability, or capital item by entry on the right-hand side of an account. **10b** the right-hand side of an account. **10c** an entry on this side. **10d** the total of such entries. **10e** (*as modifier*): *credit entries.* Compare **debit** (sense 1). **11** *Education.* **11a** a distinction awarded to an examination candidate obtaining good marks. **11b** a section of an examination syllabus satisfactorily completed, as in higher and professional education. **12 letter of credit.** an order authorizing a named person to draw money from correspondents of the issuer. **13 on credit.** with payment to be made at a future date. ◆ *vb* (*tr*) **-dits, -diting, -dited. 14** (foll. by *with*) to ascribe (to); give credit (for): *they credited him with the discovery.* **15** to accept as true; believe. **16** to do credit to. **17** *Accounting.* **17a** to enter (an item) as a credit in an account. **17b** to acknowledge (a payer) by making such an entry. Compare **debit** (sense 2). **18** to award a credit to (a student). ◆ See also **credits.** [C16: from Old French *crédit,* from Italian *credito,* from Latin *crēditum* loan, from *crēdere* to believe] ▸ **'creditless** *adj*

creditable ('krɛdɪtəbᵊl) *adj* **1** deserving credit, honour, etc.; praiseworthy. **2** *Obsolete.* credible. ▸ **'creditableness** *or* **,credita'bility** *n* ▸ **'creditably** *adv*

credit account *n Brit.* a credit system by means of which customers may obtain goods and services before payment. Also called: **charge account.**

credit card *n* a card issued by banks, businesses, etc., enabling the holder to obtain goods and services on credit.

credit line *n* **1** an acknowledgment of origin or authorship, as in a newspaper or film. **2** Also called: **line of credit.** *U.S. and Canadian.* the maximum credit that a customer is allowed.

creditor ('krɛdɪtə) *n* a person or commercial enterprise to whom money is owed. Compare **debtor.**

credit rating *n* an evaluation of the creditworthiness of an individual or business enterprise.

credit-reference agency *n* an agency, other than a bank, that specializes in providing credit ratings of people or organizations.

credits ('krɛdɪts) *pl n* a list of those responsible for the production of a film or television programme.

credit squeeze *n* the control of credit facilities as an instrument of economic policy, associated with restrictions on bank loans and overdrafts, raised interest rates, etc.

credit standing *n* reputation for discharging financial obligations.

credit transfer *n* a method of settling a debt by transferring money through a bank or post office, esp. for those who do not have cheque accounts.

credit union *n* a cooperative association whose members can obtain low-interest loans out of their combined savings.

creditworthy ('krɛdɪt,wɜːðɪ) *adj* (of an individual or business enterprise) adjudged as meriting credit on the basis of such factors as earning power, previous record of debt repayment, etc. ▸ **'credit,worthiness** *n*

credo ('kriːdəʊ, 'kreɪ-) *n, pl* **-dos.** any formal or authorized statement of beliefs, principles, or opinions.

Credo ('kriːdəʊ, 'kreɪ-) *n, pl* **-dos. 1** the Apostles' Creed or the Nicene Creed. **2** a musical setting of the Creed. [C12: from Latin, literally: I believe; first word of the Apostles' and Nicene Creeds]

credulity (krɪ'djuːlɪtɪ) *n* disposition to believe something on little evidence; gullibility.

credulous ('krɛdjʊləs) *adj* **1** tending to believe something on little evidence. **2** arising from or characterized by credulity: *credulous beliefs.* [C16: from Latin *crēdulus,* from *crēdere* to believe] ▸ **'credulously** *adv* ▸ **'credulousness** *n*

cree (kriː) *n South Wales and southwest English dialect.* temporary immunity from the rules of a game: said by children. [of unknown origin]

Cree (kriː) *n* **1** (*pl* **Cree** *or* **Crees**) a member of a North American Indian people living in Ontario, Saskatchewan, and Manitoba. **2** the language of this people, belonging to the Algonquian family. **3** a syllabic writing system of this and certain other languages. [from first syllable of Canadian French *Christianaux,* probably based on Ojibwa *Kenistenoag* (tribal name)]

creed (kriːd) *n* **1** a concise, formal statement of the essential articles of Christian belief, such as the Apostles' Creed or the Nicene Creed. **2** any statement or system of beliefs or principles. [Old English *crēda,* from Latin *crēdo* I believe] ▸ **'creedal** *or* **'credal** *adj*

Creed (kriːd) *n* **Frederick.** 1871–1957, Canadian inventor, resident in Scotland from 1897, noted for his invention of the teleprinter, first used in 1912.

creek (kriːk) *n* **1** *Chiefly Brit.* a narrow inlet or bay, esp. of the sea. **2** *U.S., Canadian, Austral., and N.Z.* a small stream or tributary. **3 up the creek.** *Slang.* in trouble; in a difficult position. [C13: from Old Norse *kriki* nook; related to Middle Dutch *krēke* creek, inlet]

Creek (kriːk) *n* **1** (*pl* **Creek** *or* **Creeks**) a member of a confederacy of North American Indian peoples formerly living in Georgia and Alabama, now chiefly in Oklahoma. **2** any of the languages of these peoples, belonging to the Muskhogean family.

creel (kriːl) *n* **1** a wickerwork basket, esp. one used to hold fish. **2** a wickerwork trap for catching lobsters, etc. **3** the framework on a spinning machine that holds the bobbins. **4** *West Yorkshire dialect.* a wooden frame suspended from a ceiling, used for drying clothes. [C15: from Scottish, of obscure origin]

creep (kriːp) *vb* **creeps, creeping, crept.** (*intr*) **1** to crawl with the body near to or touching the ground. **2** to move slowly, quietly, or cautiously. **3** to act in a servile way; fawn; cringe. **4** to move or slip out of place, as from pressure or wear. **5** (of plants) to grow along the ground or over rocks, producing roots, suckers, or tendrils at intervals. **6** (of a body or substance) to become permanently deformed as a result of an applied stress, often when combined with heating. **7** to develop gradually: *creeping unrest.* **8** to have the sensation of something crawling over the skin. **9** (of metals) to undergo slow plastic deformation. ◆ *n* **10** the act of creeping or a creeping movement. **11** *Slang.* a person considered to be obnoxious or servile. **12** the continuous permanent deformation of a body or substance as a result of stress or heat. **13** *Geology.* the gradual downwards movement of loose rock material, soil, etc., on a slope. **14** a slow relative movement of two adjacent parts, structural components, etc. **15** slow plastic deformation of metals. ◆ See also **creeps.** [Old English *crēopan;* related to Old Frisian *kriāpa,* Old Norse *krjūpa,* Middle Low German *krūpen*]

creeper ('kriːpə) *n* **1** a person or animal that creeps. **2** a plant, such as the ivy or periwinkle, that grows by creeping. **3** the U.S. and Canadian name for the **tree creeper. 4** a hooked instrument for dragging deep water. **5** Also called: **cradle.** a flat board or framework mounted on casters, used to lie on when working under cars. **6** Also called: **daisycutter.** *Cricket.* a bowled ball that keeps low or travels along the ground. **7** either of a pair of low iron supports for logs in a hearth. **8** *Informal.* a shoe with a soft sole.

creepie ('kriːpɪ, 'krɪp-) *n Chiefly Scot.* a low stool.

creeping bent grass *n* a grass, *Agrostris palustris,* grown as a pasture grass in Europe and North America: roots readily from the stem.

creeping Jennie ('dʒɛnɪ) *or U.S. and Canadian* **creeping Charlie** *n* other names for **moneywort.**

creeping Jesus *n Derogatory slang.* **1** an obsequious or servile person. **2** a hypocritically religious person.

creeping thistle *n* a weedy Eurasian thistle, *Cirsium arvense,* common as a fast-spreading weed in the U.S. U.S. and Canadian name: **Canada thistle.**

creeps (kriːps) *pl n* (preceded by *the*) *Informal.* a feeling of fear, repulsion, disgust, etc.

creepy ('kriːpɪ) *adj* **creepier, creepiest. 1** *Informal.* having or causing a sensation of repulsion, horror, or fear, as of creatures crawling on the skin. **2** creeping; slow-moving. ▸ **'creepily** *adv* ▸ **'creepiness** *n*

creepy-crawly *Brit. informal.* ◆ *n, pl* **-crawlies. 1** a small crawling creature. ◆ *adj* **2** feeling or causing a sensation as of creatures crawling on one's skin.

creese (kriːs) *n* a rare spelling of **kris.**

cremate (krɪ'meɪt) *vb* (*tr*) to burn up (something, esp. a corpse) and reduce to ash. [C19: from Latin *cremāre*] ▸ **cre'mation** *n* ▸ **cre'mationism** *n* ▸ **cre'mationist** *n*

cremator (krɪ'meɪtə) *n* **1** Also called (esp. U.S.): **cinerator.** *Brit.* a furnace for cremating corpses. **2** a person who operates such a furnace.

crematorium (,krɛmə'tɔːrɪəm) *n, pl* **-riums** *or* **-ria** (-rɪə). *Brit.* a building in which corpses are cremated.

crematory ('krɛmətərɪ, -trɪ) *adj* **1** of or relating to cremation or crematoriums. ◆ *n, pl* **-ries. 2** another word (esp. U.S.) for **crematorium.**

crème (krɛm, kriːm, kreɪm) *n* **1** cream. **2** any of various sweet liqueurs: *crème de moka.* ◆ *adj* **3** (of a liqueur) rich and sweet.

crème brûlée *French.* (krɛm bryle) *n* a cream or custard dessert covered with caramelized sugar. [literally, burnt cream]

crème caramel *n* a dessert made of eggs, sugar, milk, etc., topped with caramel. Also called: **caramel cream.**

crème de cacao ('krɛm də kɑː'kɑːəʊ, 'kəʊkəʊ;'kriːm, 'kreɪm) *n* a sweet liqueur with a chocolate flavour. [French, literally: cream of cacao]

crème de la crème *French.* (krɛm də la krɛm) *n* the very best. [literally: cream of the cream]

crème de menthe ('krɛm də 'mɛnθ, 'mɪnt; 'kriːm,'kreɪm) *n* a liqueur flavoured with peppermint, usually bright green in colour. [French, literally: cream of mint]

crème fraîche ('krɛm 'frɛʃ) *n* thickened and slightly fermented cream. [French, literally: fresh cream]

Cremona (*Italian* kre'moːna) *n* a city in N Italy, in Lombardy on the River Po: noted for the manufacture of fine violins in the 16th–18th centuries. Pop.: 75 160 (1990).

crenate ('kriːneɪt) *or* **crenated** *adj* having a scalloped margin, as certain leaves. [C18: from New Latin *crēnātus,* from Medieval Latin, probably from Late Latin *crēna* a notch] ▸ **'crenately** *adv*

crenation (krɪ'neɪʃən) *or* **crenature** ('krɛnə,tjʊə,'kriː-) *n* **1** any of the rounded teeth or the notches between them on a crenate structure. **2** a crenate formation or condition.

crenel ('krɛnᵊl) *or* **crenelle** (krɪ'nɛl) *n* **1** any of a set of openings formed in the top of a wall or parapet and having slanting sides, as in a battlement. **2** another name for **crenation.** [C15: from Old French, literally: a little notch, from *cren* notch, from Late Latin *crēna*]

crenellate *or U.S.* **crenelate** ('krɛnɪ,leɪt) *vb* (*tr*) **1** to supply with battlements. **2** to form square indentations in (a moulding, etc.). [C19: from Old French *creneler,* from CRENEL] ▸ **'crenel,lated** *or U.S.* **'crenel,ated** *adj* ▸ **,crenel'lation** *or U.S.* **,crenel'ation** *n*

crenulate ('krɛnjʊ,leɪt, -lɪt) *or* **crenulated** *adj* having a margin very finely notched with rounded projections, as certain leaves. [C18: from New Latin *crēnulātus,* from *crēnula,* literally: a little notch; see CRENEL]

crenulation (,krɛnjʊ'leɪʃən) *n* **1** any of the teeth or notches of a crenulate structure. **2** a crenulate formation.

creodont ('kriːə,dɒnt) *n* any of a group of extinct Tertiary mammals some of which are thought to have been the ancestors of modern carnivores: order *Carnivora.* [C19: from New Latin *Creodonta,* from Greek *kreas* flesh + *odōn* tooth]

creole ('kriːəʊl) *n* **1** a language that has its origin in extended contact between two language communities, one of which is generally European. It incorporates features from each and constitutes the mother tongue of a community. Compare **pidgin.** ◆ *adj* **2** denoting, relating to, or characteristic of creole. **3** (of a sauce or dish) containing or cooked with tomatoes, green peppers, onions, etc. [C17: via French and Spanish probably from Portuguese *crioulo* slave born in one's household, person of European ancestry born in the colonies, probably from *criar* to bring up, from Latin *creāre* to CREATE]

Creole ('kriːəʊl) *n* **1** (*sometimes not cap.*) (in the Caribbean and Latin America) **1a** a native-born person of European, esp. Spanish, ancestry. **1b** a native-born person of mixed European and African ancestry who speaks a French or Spanish creole. **1c** a native-born Black person as distinguished from one brought from Africa. **2** (in Louisiana and other Gulf States of the U.S.) a native-born person of French ancestry. **3** the creolized French spoken in Louisiana, esp. in New Orleans. ◆ *adj* **4** of, relating to, or characteristic of any of these peoples.

creolized *or* **creolised** ('kriːə,laɪzd) *adj* (of a language) incorporating a considerable range of features from one or more unrelated languages, as the result of contact between language communities.

Creon ('kriːɒn) *n Greek myth.* the successor to Oedipus as king of Thebes; the brother of Jocasta. See also **Antigone.**

creophagous (krɪ'ɒfəgəs) *adj* flesh-eating or carnivorous. [C19: from Greek *kreophagos,* from *kreas* flesh + *-phagein* to consume] ▶ **creophagy** (krɪ'ɒfədʒɪ) *n*

creosol ('kriːəˌsɒl) *n* a colourless or pale yellow insoluble oily liquid with a smoky odour and a burning taste; 2-methoxy-4-methylphenol: an active principle of creosote. Formula: $CH_3O(CH_3)C_6H_3OH$. [C19: from CREOS(OTE) + -OL[1]]

creosote ('krɪəˌsəʊt) *n* **1** a colourless or pale yellow liquid mixture with a burning taste and penetrating odour distilled from wood tar, esp. from beechwood, contains creosol and other phenols, and is used as an antiseptic. **2** Also called: **coal-tar creosote.** a thick dark liquid mixture prepared from coal tar, containing phenols: used as a preservative for wood. ◆ *vb* **3** to treat (wood) with creosote. [C19: from Greek *kreas* flesh + *sōtēr* preserver, from *sōzein* to keep safe] ▶ **creosotic** (ˌkrɪə'sɒtɪk) *adj*

creosote bush *n* a shrub, *Larrea* (or *Covillea*) *tridentata* of the western U.S. and Mexico, that has resinous leaves with an odour resembling creosote: family *Zygophyllaceae.* Also called: **greasewood.**

crepe *or* **crape** (kreɪp) *n* **1a** a light cotton, silk, or other fabric with a fine ridged or crinkled surface. **1b** (*as modifier*): *a crepe dress.* **2** a black armband originally made of this, worn as a sign of mourning. **3** a very thin pancake, often rolled or folded around a filling. **4** short for **crepe paper** or **crepe rubber.** ◆ *vb* **5** (*tr*) to cover or drape with crepe. [C19: from French *crêpe,* from Latin *crispus* curled, uneven, wrinkled]

crepe de Chine (kreɪp də ʃiːn) *n* **a** a very thin crepe of silk or a similar light fabric. **b** (*as modifier*): *a crepe-de-Chine blouse.* [C19: from French: Chinese crepe]

crepe hair *n* artificial hair, usually plaited and made of wool or vegetable fibre, used in theatrical make-up.

crepe paper *n* thin crinkled coloured paper, resembling crepe and used for decorations.

creperie ('krepərɪ, 'kreɪp-) *n* an eating establishment that specializes in pancakes; pancake house.

crepe rubber *n* **1** a type of crude natural rubber in the form of colourless or pale yellow crinkled sheets, prepared by pressing bleached coagulated latex through corrugated rollers: used for the soles of shoes and in making certain surgical and medical goods. Sometimes shortened to **crepe.** Compare **smoked rubber. 2** a similar synthetic rubber.

crêpe suzette (kreɪp suː'zet) *n, pl* **crêpes suzettes.** (*sometimes pl*) an orange-flavoured pancake flambéed in a liqueur or brandy.

crepitate ('krepɪˌteɪt) *vb* (*intr*) to make a rattling or crackling sound; rattle or crackle. [C17: from Latin *crepitāre*] ▶ **'crepitant** *adj*

crepitation (ˌkrepɪ'teɪʃən) *n* **1** the act of crepitating. **2** *Zoology.* the sudden expulsion of an acrid fluid by some beetles as a means of self-defence. **3** another name for **crepitus.**

crepitus ('krepɪtəs) *n* **1** a crackling chest sound heard in pneumonia and other lung diseases. **2** the grating sound of two ends of a broken bone rubbing together. ◆ Also called: **crepitation.** [C19: from Latin, from *crepāre* to crack, creak]

crept (krept) *vb* the past tense and past participle of **creep.**

crepuscular (krɪ'pʌskjʊlə) *adj* **1** of or like twilight; dim. **2** (of certain insects, birds, and other animals) active at twilight or just before dawn. [C17: from Latin *crepusculum* dusk, from *creper* dark]

crepy *or* **crepey** ('kreɪpɪ) *adj* (esp. of the skin) having a dry wrinkled appearance like crepe.

Cres. *abbrev. for* Crescent.

crescendo (krɪ'ʃendəʊ) *n, pl* **-dos** *or* **-di** (-dɪ). **1** *Music.* **1a** a gradual increase in loudness or the musical direction or symbol indicating this. Abbrev.: **cresc.** Symbol: < (written over the music affected). **1b** (*as modifier*): *a crescendo passage.* **2** a gradual increase in loudness or intensity: *the rising crescendo of a song.* **3** a peak of noise or intensity: *the cheers reached a crescendo.* ◆ *vb* **-does, -doing, -doed. 4** (*intr*) to increase in loudness or force. ◆ *adv* **5** with a crescendo. [C18: from Italian, literally: increasing, from *crescere* to grow, from Latin]

crescent ('kresᵊnt, -zᵊnt) *n* **1** the biconcave shape of the moon in its first or last quarters. **2** any shape or object resembling this. **3** *Chiefly Brit.* **3a** a crescent-shaped street, often lined with houses of the same style. **3b** (*cap. when part of a name*): *Pelham Crescent.* **4** *Heraldry.* a crescent moon, used as the cadency mark of a second son. **5** (*often cap.* and preceded by *the*) **5a** the emblem of Islam or Turkey. **5b** Islamic or Turkish power. ◆ *adj* **6** *Archaic or poetic.* increasing or growing. [C14: from Latin *crescēns* increasing, from *crescere* to grow] ▶ **crescentic** (krə'sentɪk) *adj*

cresol ('kriːsɒl) *n* an aromatic compound derived from phenol, existing in three isomeric forms: found in coal tar and creosote and used in making synthetic resins and as an antiseptic and disinfectant; hydroxytoluene. Formula: $C_6H_4(CH_3)OH$. Also called: **cresylic acid.** Systematic name: **methylphenol.**

cress (kres) *n* any of various cruciferous plants of the genera *Lepidium, Cardamine, Arabis,* etc., having pungent-tasting leaves often used in salads and as a garnish. See also **watercress, garden cress.** [Old English *cressa;* related to Old High German *cresso* cress, *kresan* to crawl]

Cressent (*French* kresɑ̃) *n* **Charles.** 1685–1768, French cabinetmaker, noted esp. for his marquetry using coloured woods.

cresset ('kresɪt) *n History.* a metal basket mounted on a pole in which oil or pitch was burned for illumination. [C14: from Old French *craisset,* from *craisse* GREASE]

Cressida ('kresɪdə), **Criseyde,** *or* **Cressid** *n* (in medieval adaptations of the story of Troy) a lady who deserts her Trojan lover Troilus for the Greek Diomedes.

Cressy ('kresɪ) *n Rare.* the English name for **Crécy.**

crest (krest) *n* **1** a tuft or growth of feathers, fur, or skin along the top of the heads of some birds, reptiles, and other animals. **2** something resembling or suggesting this. **3** the top, highest point, or highest stage of something. **4** a ridge on the neck of a horse, dog, lion, etc. **5** the mane or hair growing from this ridge. **6** an ornamental piece, such as a plume, on top of a helmet. **7** *Heraldry.* a symbol of a family or office, usually representing a beast or bird, borne in addition to a coat of arms and used in medieval times to decorate the helmet. **8** a ridge along the top of a roof, wall, etc. **9** a ridge along the surface of a bone. **10** Also called: **cresting.** *Archery.* identifying rings painted around an arrow shaft. ◆ *vb* **11** (*intr*) to come or rise to a high point. **12** (*tr*) to lie at the top of; cap. **13** (*tr*) to go to or reach the top of (a hill, wave, etc.). [C14: from Old French *creste,* from Latin *crista*] ▶ **'crested** *adj* ▶ **'crestless** *adj*

CREST (krest) *n* an electronic share-settlement system, created by the Bank of England and owned by 69 firms, that began operations in 1996. [C20: from *CrestCo,* the name of the operating company]

cresta run ('krestə) *n* **a** an activity involving travelling at high speed in a toboggan down a steep narrow passage of compacted snow and ice. **b** the passage itself.

crested dog's-tail *n* a common wiry perennial grass, *Cynosurus cristatus,* of meadows and pasture. [C19: named from the fancied resemblance between its one-sided flower spike and a dog's feathery tail]

crested tit *n* a small European songbird, *Parus cristatus,* that has a greyish-brown plumage with a prominent speckled black-and-white crest: family *Paridae* (tits).

crestfallen ('krestˌfɔːlən) *adj* dejected, depressed, or disheartened. ▶ **'crestˌfallenly** *adv*

cresting ('krestɪŋ) *n* **1** an ornamental ridge along the top of a roof, wall, etc. **2** *Furniture.* a shaped decorative toprail or horizontal carved ornament surmounting a chair, mirror, etc.

cresylic (krɪ'sɪlɪk) *adj* of, concerned with, or containing creosote or cresol. [C19: from CRE(O)S(OTE) + -YL + -IC]

cretaceous (krɪ'teɪʃəs) *adj* consisting of or resembling chalk. [C17: from Latin *crētāceus,* from *crēta,* literally: Cretan earth, that is, chalk] ▶ **cre'taceously** *adv*

Cretaceous (krɪ'teɪʃəs) *adj* **1** of, denoting, or formed in the last period of the Mesozoic era, between the Jurassic and Tertiary periods, lasting 65 million years during which chalk deposits were formed and flowering plants first appeared. ◆ *n* **2 the.** the Cretaceous period or rock system.

Crete (kriːt) *n* a mountainous island in the E Mediterranean, the largest island of Greece: of archaeological importance for the ruins of Minoan civilization. Capital: Canea (Khaniá). Pop.: 540 054 (1991). Area: 8331 sq. km (3216 sq. miles). Modern Greek name: **Kríti.** ▶ **'Cretan** *adj, n*

cretic ('kriːtɪk) *n Prosody.* a metrical foot consisting of three syllables, the first long, the second short, and the third long (-⏑-). Also called: **amphimacer.** Compare **amphibrach.** [C16: from Latin *crēticus* consisting of the amphimacer, literally: Cretan, from Greek *krētikos,* from *Krētē* CRETE]

cretin ('kretɪn) *n* **1** a person afflicted with cretinism: a mentally retarded dwarf with wide-set eyes, a broad flat nose, and protruding tongue. **2** a person considered to be extremely stupid. [C18: from French *crétin,* from Swiss French *crestin,* from Latin *Chrīstiānus* CHRISTIAN[1], alluding to the humanity of such people, despite their handicaps] ▶ **'cretinˌoid** *adj* ▶ **'cretinous** *adj*

cretinism ('kretɪˌnɪzəm) *n* a condition arising from a deficiency of thyroid hormone, present from birth, characterized by dwarfism and mental retardation. See also **myxoedema.**

cretonne (kre'tɒn, 'kretɒn) *n* **a** a heavy cotton or linen fabric with a printed design, used for furnishing. **b** (*as modifier*): *cretonne chair covers.* [C19: from French, from *Creton* Norman village where it originated]

Creuse (*French* krøz) *n* a department of central France, in Limousin region. Capital: Guéret. Pop.: 127 100 (1995). Area: 5606 sq. km (2186 sq. miles).

Creutzfeldt-Jakob disease ('krɔɪtsfelt 'jɑːkɒp) *n Pathol.* a fatal slow-developing disease that affects the central nervous system, characterized by mental deterioration and loss of coordination of the limbs. It is thought to be caused by an abnormal prion protein in the brain. [C20: named after Hans G. *Creutzfeldt* (1885–1964) and Alfons *Jakob* (1884–1931), German physicians]

crevasse (krɪ'væs) *n* **1** a deep crack or fissure, esp. in the ice of a glacier. **2** *U.S.* a break in a river embankment. ◆ *vb* **3** (*tr*) *U.S.* to make a break or fissure in (a dyke, wall, etc.). [C19: from French: CREVICE]

crevice ('krevɪs) *n* a narrow fissure or crack; split; cleft. [C14: from Old French *crevace,* from *crever* to burst, from Latin *crepāre* to crack]

crew[1] (kruː) *n* (*sometimes functioning as pl*) **1** the men who man a ship, boat, aircraft, etc. **2** *Nautical.* a group of people assigned to a particular job or type of work. **3** *Informal.* a gang, company, or crowd. ◆ *vb* **4** to serve on (a ship) as a member of the crew. [C15 *crue* (military) reinforcement, from Old French *creue* augmentation, from Old French *creistre* to increase, from Latin *crescere*]

crew[2] (kruː) *vb* a past tense of **crow**[2].

crew cut *n* a closely cropped haircut for men, originating in the U.S. [C20: from the style of haircut worn by the boat crews at Harvard and Yale Universities]

Crewe (kruː) *n* a town in NW England, in Cheshire: major railway junction. Pop.: 63 351 (1991).

crewel ('kruːɪl) *n* a loosely twisted worsted yarn, used in fancy work and embroidery. [C15: of unknown origin] ▶ **'crewelist** *n* ▶ **'crewelˌwork** *n*

crew neck *n* a plain round neckline in sweaters. ▶ **'crew-ˌneck** *or* **'crew-ˌnecked** *adj*

crib (krɪb) *n* **1** a child's bed with slatted wooden sides; cot. **2** a cattle stall or pen. **3** a fodder rack or manger. **4** a bin or granary for storing grain, etc. **5** a small crude cottage or room. **6** *N.Z.* a weekend cottage: term is South Island usage only. **7** any small confined space. **8** *Informal.* a brothel. **9** a wicker basket. **10** a representation of the manger in which the infant Jesus was laid at birth. **11** *Informal.* a theft, esp. of another's writing or thoughts. **12** Also called (esp. U.S.): **pony.** *Informal, chiefly Brit.* a translation of a foreign text or a list of answers used by students, often illicitly, as an aid in lessons, examinations, etc. **13** short for **cribbage. 14** *Cribbage.* the discard pile. **15** Also called: **cribwork.** a framework of heavy timbers laid in layers at right angles to one another, used in the construction of foundations, mines, etc. **16** a storage area for floating logs contained by booms. **17** *Austral. and N.Z.* a packed lunch taken to work. ◆ *vb* **cribs, cribbing, cribbed. 18** (*tr*) to put or enclose in or as if in a crib; furnish with a crib. **19** (*tr*) *Informal.* to steal (another's writings or thoughts). **20** (*intr*) *Informal.* to copy either from a crib or from someone else during a lesson or examination. **21** (*tr*) to line (a construction hole) with timber beams, logs, or planks. **22** (*intr*) *Informal.* to grumble. [Old English *cribb;* related to Old Saxon *kribbia,* Old High German *krippa;* compare Middle High German *krēbe* basket] ▸ **'cribber** *n*

cribbage ('krɪbɪdʒ) *n* a game of cards for two to four, in which players try to win a set number of points before their opponents. Often shortened to **crib.** [C17: of uncertain origin]

cribbage board *n* a board, with pegs and holes, used for scoring at cribbage.

crib-biting *n* a harmful habit of horses in which the animal leans on the manger or seizes it with the teeth and swallows a gulp of air. ▸ **'crib-,biter** *n*

crib death *n* the U.S. and Canadian term for **cot death.**

cribellum (krɪ'bɛləm) *n, pl* **-la** (-lə). a sievelike spinning organ in certain spiders that occurs between the spinnerets. [C19: New Latin, from Late Latin *cribellum,* diminutive of Latin *cribrum* a sieve]

cribriform ('krɪbrɪ,fɔːm) *or* **cribrous** ('krɪbrəs) *or* **cribrose** ('kraɪ,brəʊs) *adj Anatomy, botany.* pierced with holes; sievelike. [C18: from New Latin *crībriformis,* from Latin *crībrum* a sieve + -FORM]

crib-wall *n N.Z.* a supporting wall constructed by laying cribs at right angles to each other, as in cribwork.

cribwork ('krɪb,wɜːk) *n* another name for **crib** (sense 15).

Crichton ('kraɪtᵊn) *n* **James.** 1560–82, Scottish scholar and writer, called *the Admirable Crichton* because of his talents.

crick[1] (krɪk) *Informal.* ◆ *n* **1** a painful muscle spasm or cramp, esp. in the neck or back. ◆ *vb* **2** (*tr*) to cause a crick in (the neck, back, etc.). [C15: of uncertain origin]

crick[2] (krɪk) *n U.S. and Canadian.* a dialect word for **creek** (sense 2).

Crick (krɪk) *n* **Francis Harry Compton.** born 1916, English molecular biologist: helped to discover the helical structure of DNA; Nobel prize for physiology or medicine shared with James Watson and Maurice Wilkins 1962.

cricket[1] ('krɪkɪt) *n* **1** any insect of the orthopterous family *Gryllidae,* having long antennae and, in the males, the ability to produce a chirping sound (stridulation) by rubbing together the leathery forewings. **2** any of various related insects, such as the mole cricket. [C14: from Old French *criquet,* from *criquer* to creak, of imitative origin]

cricket[2] ('krɪkɪt) *n* **1a** a game played by two teams of eleven players on a field with a wicket at either end of a 22-yard pitch, the object being for one side to score runs by hitting a hard leather-covered ball with a bat while the other side tries to dismiss them by bowling, catching, running them out, etc. **1b** (*as modifier*): *a cricket bat.* **2 not cricket.** *Informal.* not fair play. ◆ *vb* (*intr*) **3** to play cricket. [C16: from Old French *criquet* goalpost, wicket, of uncertain origin] ▸ **'cricketer** *n*

cricket[3] ('krɪkɪt) *n* a small low stool. [C17: of unknown origin]

cricoid ('kraɪkɔɪd) *adj* **1** of or relating to the ring-shaped lowermost cartilage of the larynx. ◆ *n* **2** this cartilage. [C18: from New Latin *cricoīdes,* from Greek *krikoeidēs* ring-shaped, from *krikos* ring]

cri de coeur (kriː də kɜː) *n, pl* **cris de coeur.** a cry from the heart; heartfelt or sincere appeal. [C20: altered from French *cri du coeur*]

crier ('kraɪə) *n* **1** a person or animal that cries. **2** (formerly) an official who made public announcements, esp. in a town or court. **3** a person who shouts advertisements about the goods he is selling.

crikey ('kraɪkɪ) *interj Slang.* an expression of surprise. [C19: euphemistic for *Christ!*]

crim (krɪm) *n, adj Austral. and N.Z. slang.* short for **criminal.**

crim. *abbrev. for* criminal.

crim. con. *Law. abbrev. for* criminal conversation.

crime (kraɪm) *n* **1** an act or omission prohibited and punished by law. **2a** unlawful acts in general: *a wave of crime.* **2b** (*as modifier*): *crime wave.* **3** an evil act. **4** *Informal.* something to be regretted: *it is a crime that he died young.* [C14: from Old French, from Latin *crīmen* verdict, accusation, crime]

Crimea (kraɪ'mɪə) *n* a peninsula and autonomous region in the Ukraine between the Black Sea and the Sea of Azov: a former autonomous republic of the Soviet Union (1921–45), part of the Ukrainian SSR from 1945 until 1991. Russian name: **Krym.** ▸ **Cri'mean** *adj, n*

Crimean War *n* the war fought mainly in the Crimea between Russia on one side and Turkey, France, Sardinia, and Britain on the other (1853-56).

crime passionnel (*French* krim pasjɔnɛl) *n, pl* **crimes passionnels.** a crime committed from passion, esp. sexual passion. Also called: **crime of passion.** [from French]

crime sheet *n Mil.* a record of an individual's offences against regulations.

criminal ('krɪmɪnᵊl) *n* **1** a person charged with and convicted of crime. **2** a person who commits crimes for a living. ◆ *adj* **3** of, involving, or guilty of crime. **4** (*prenominal*) of or relating to crime or its punishment: *criminal court; criminal lawyer.* **5** *Informal.* senseless or deplorable: *a criminal waste of money.* [C15: from Late Latin *crīminālis;* see CRIME, -AL[1]] ▸ **'criminally** *adv*

criminal conversation *n* **1** (formerly) a common law action brought by a husband by which he claimed damages against an adulterer. **2** another term for **adultery.**

criminality (,krɪmɪ'nælɪtɪ) *n, pl* **-ties. 1** the state or quality of being criminal. **2** (*often pl*) *Now rare.* a criminal act or practice.

criminalize *or* **criminalise** ('krɪmɪnə,laɪz) *vb* (*tr*) to declare (an action or activity) criminal. ▸ **,criminali'zation** *or* **,criminali'sation** *n*

criminal law *n* the body of law dealing with the constitution of offences and the punishment of offenders.

criminate ('krɪmɪ,neɪt) *vb* (*tr*) *Rare.* **1** to charge with a crime; accuse. **2** to condemn or censure (an action, event, etc.). **3** short for **incriminate.** [C17: from Latin *crīminārī* to accuse] ▸ **,crimi'nation** *n* ▸ **'criminative** *or* **criminatory** ('krɪmɪnətərɪ, -trɪ) *adj* ▸ **'crimi,nator** *n*

criminology (,krɪmɪ'nɒlədʒɪ) *n* the scientific study of crime, criminal behaviour, law enforcement, etc. See also **penology.** [C19: from Latin *crimin-* CRIME, -LOGY] ▸ **criminological** (,krɪmɪnə'lɒdʒɪkᵊl) *or* **,crimino'logic** *adj* ▸ **,crimino'logically** *adv* ▸ **,crimi'nologist** *n*

crimmer ('krɪmə) *n* a variant spelling of **krimmer.**

crimp[1] (krɪmp) *vb* (*tr*) **1** to fold or press into ridges. **2** to fold and pinch together (something, such as the edges of two pieces of metal). **3** to curl or wave (the hair) tightly, esp. with curling tongs. **4** to decorate (the edge of pastry) by pinching with the fingers to give a fluted effect. **5** to gash (fish or meat) with a knife to make the flesh firmer and crisper when cooked. **6** to bend or mould (leather) into shape, as for shoes. **7** *Metallurgy.* to bend the edges of (a metal plate) before forming into a cylinder. **8** *Informal, chiefly U.S.* to hinder. ◆ *n* **9** the act or result of folding or pressing together or into ridges. **10** a tight wave or curl in the hair. **11** a crease or fold in a metal sheet. **12** the natural wave of wool fibres. [Old English *crympan;* related to *crump* bent, Old Norse *kreppa* to contract, Old High German *crumpf,* Old Swedish *crumb* crooked; see CRAMP[1]] ▸ **'crimper** *n* ▸ **'crimpy** *adj*

crimp[2] (krɪmp) *n* **1** (formerly) a person who swindled or pressganged men into naval or military service. ◆ *vb* **2** to recruit by coercion or under false pretences. [C17: of unknown origin]

crimple ('krɪmpᵊl) *vb* to crumple, wrinkle, or curl.

Crimplene ('krɪmpliːn) *n Trademark.* a synthetic material similar to Terylene, characterized by its crease-resistance.

crimson ('krɪmzən) *n* **1a** a deep or vivid red colour. **1b** (*as adj*): *a crimson rose.* ◆ *vb* **2** to make or become crimson. **3** (*intr*) to blush. [C14: from Old Spanish *cremesin,* from Arabic *qirmizi* red of the kermes, from *qirmiz* KERMES] ▸ **'crimsonness** *n*

cringe (krɪndʒ) *vb* (*intr*) **1** to shrink or flinch, esp. in fear or servility. **2** to behave in a servile or timid way. **3** *Informal.* **3a** to wince in embarrassment or distaste. **3b** to experience a sudden feeling of embarrassment or distaste. ◆ *n* **4** the act of cringing. **5 the cultural cringe.** *Austral.* subservience to overseas cultural standards. [Old English *cringan* to yield in battle; related to Old Norse *krangr* weak, Middle High German *krenken* to weaken] ▸ **'cringer** *n* ▸ **'cringingly** *adv*

cringe-making *or* **cringeworthy** ('krɪndʒ,wɜːðɪ) *adj Brit. informal.* causing feelings of acute embarrassment or distaste.

cringle ('krɪŋgᵊl) *n* an eye at the edge of a sail, usually formed from a thimble or grommet. [C17: from Low German *Kringel* small RING[1]; see CRANK[1], CRINKLE]

crinite[1] ('kraɪnaɪt) *adj Biology.* covered with soft hairs or tufts. [C16: from Latin *crīnītus* hairy, from *crīnis* hair]

crinite[2] ('kraɪnaɪt, 'krɪn-) *n* short for **encrinite.** [C19: from Greek *krinon* lily + -ITE[1]]

crinkle ('krɪŋkᵊl) *vb* **1** to form or cause to form wrinkles, twists, or folds. **2** to make or cause to make a rustling noise. ◆ *n* **3** a wrinkle, twist, or fold. **4** a rustling noise. [Old English *crincan* to bend, give way; related to Middle Dutch *krinkelen* to crinkle, Middle High German *krank* weak, ill, *krenken* to weaken]

crinkleroot ('krɪŋkᵊl,ruːt) *n* any of several species of the toothwort *Dentaria,* esp. *D. diphylla* of E North America, which has a fleshy pungent rhizome and clusters of white or pinkish flowers: family *Cruciferae* (crucifers).

crinkly ('krɪŋklɪ) *adj* **1** wrinkled; crinkled. ◆ *n, pl* **-lies. 2** *Slang.* an old person.

crinkum-crankum ('krɪŋkəm'kræŋkəm) *n* a fanciful name for any object that is full of twists and turns. [C18: coinage based on CRANK[1]]

crinoid ('kraɪnɔɪd, 'krɪn-) *n* **1** any primitive echinoderm of the class *Crinoidea,* having delicate feathery arms radiating from a central disc. The group includes the free-swimming feather stars, the sessile sea lilies, and many stemmed fossil forms. ◆ *adj* **2** of, relating to, or belonging to the *Crinoidea.* **3** shaped like a lily. [C19: from Greek *krinoeidēs* lily-like] ▸ **cri'noidal** *adj*

crinoline ('krɪnᵊlɪn) *n* **1** a stiff fabric, originally of horsehair and linen used in lining garments. **2** a petticoat stiffened with this, worn to distend skirts, esp. in the mid-19th century. **3** a framework of steel hoops worn for the same purpose. [C19: from French, from Italian *crinolino,* from *crino* horsehair, from Latin *crīnis* hair + *lino* flax, from Latin *līnum*]

crinum ('kraɪnəm) *n* any plant of the mostly tropical amaryllidaceous genus *Crinum,* having straplike leaves and clusters of lily-like flowers. Also called: **crinum lily.** [Latin: lily, from Greek *krinon*]

criollo (kriː'əʊləʊ; *Spanish* 'krjoʎo) *n, pl* **-los** (-ləʊz; *Spanish* -ʎos). **1** a native or inhabitant of Latin America of European descent, esp. of Spanish descent. **2a** any of various South American breeds of domestic animal. **2b** (*as modifier*): *a criollo pony.* **3** a high-quality variety of cocoa. ◆ *adj* **4** of, relating to, or characteristic of a criollo or criollos. [Spanish: native; see CREOLE]

crios (krɪs) *n Irish.* a multicoloured woven woollen belt traditionally worn by men in the Aran Islands. [Irish Gaelic]

cripes (kraɪps) *interj Old-fashioned slang.* an expression of surprise. [C20: euphemistic for *Christ!*]

Crippen ('krɪpᵊn) *n* **Hawley Harvey,** known as *Doctor Crippen.* 1862–1910,

U.S. doctor living in England: executed for poisoning his wife; the first criminal to be apprehended by the use of radiotelegraphy.

cripple ('krɪp^əl) *n* **1** *Offensive.* a person who is lame. **2** *Offensive.* a person who is or seems disabled or deficient in some way: *a mental cripple.* **3** *U.S. dialect.* a dense thicket, usually in marshy land. ◆ *vb* **4** (*tr*) to make a cripple of; disable. [Old English *crypel;* related to *crēopan* to CREEP, Old Frisian *kreppel* a cripple, Middle Low German *kröpel*] ▸ **'crippler** *n*

Cripple Creek *n* a village in central Colorado: gold-mining centre since 1891, once the richest in the world.

crippling ('krɪplɪŋ) *adj* damaging or injurious. ▸ **'cripplingly** *adv*

Cripps (krɪps) *n* Sir (**Richard**) **Stafford.** 1889–1952, British Labour statesman; Chancellor of the Exchequer (1947–50).

Criseyde (krɪ'seɪdə) *n* a variant of **Cressida.**

crisis ('kraɪsɪs) *n, pl* **-ses** (-si:z). **1** a crucial stage or turning point in the course of something, esp. in a sequence of events or a disease. **2** an unstable period, esp. one of extreme trouble or danger in politics, economics, etc. **3** *Pathol.* a sudden change, for better or worse, in the course of a disease. [C15: from Latin: decision, from Greek *krisis,* from *krinein* to decide]

crisp (krɪsp) *adj* **1** dry and brittle. **2** fresh and firm: *crisp lettuce.* **3** invigorating or bracing: *a crisp breeze.* **4** clear; sharp: *crisp reasoning.* **5** lively or stimulating: *crisp conversation.* **6** clean and orderly; neat: *a crisp appearance.* **7** concise and pithy; terse: *a crisp reply.* **8** wrinkled or curly: *crisp hair.* ◆ *vb* **9** to make or become crisp. ◆ *n* **10** *Brit.* a very thin slice of potato fried and eaten cold as a snack. **11** something that is crisp. [Old English, from Latin *crispus* curled, uneven, wrinkled] ▸ **'crisply** *adv* ▸ **'crispness** *n*

crispate ('krɪspeɪt, -pɪt), **crispated,** *or* **crisped** *adj* having a curled or waved appearance. [C19: from Latin *crispāre* to curl]

crispation (krɪ'speɪʃən) *n* **1** the act of curling or state of being curled. **2** any slight muscular spasm or contraction that gives a creeping sensation. **3** a slight undulation, such as a ripple on the surface of water.

crispbread ('krɪsp,brɛd) *n* a thin dry biscuit made of wheat or rye.

crisper ('krɪspə) *n* a compartment in a refrigerator for storing salads, vegetables, etc., in order to keep them fresh.

Crispi (*Italian* 'krispi) *n* **Francesco** (fran'tʃesko). 1819–1901, Italian statesman; premier (1887–91; 1893–96).

Crispin ('krɪspɪn) *n* **Saint,** 3rd century A.D., legendary Roman Christian martyr, with his brother **Crispinian** (krɪ'spɪnɪən): they are the patron saints of shoemakers. Feast day: Oct. 25.

crispy ('krɪspɪ) *adj* **crispier, crispiest. 1** crisp. **2** having waves or curls. ▸ **'crispily** *adv* ▸ **'crispiness** *n*

crisscross ('krɪs,krɒs) *vb* **1** to move or cause to move in a crosswise pattern. **2** to mark with or consist of a pattern of crossing lines. ◆ *adj* **3** (esp. of a number of lines) crossing one another in different directions. ◆ *n* **4** a pattern made of crossing lines. **5** a U.S. term for **noughts and crosses.** ◆ *adv* **6** in a crosswise manner or pattern.

crissum ('krɪsəm) *n, pl* **-sa** (-sə). the area or feathers surrounding the cloaca of a bird. [C19: from New Latin, from Latin *crissāre* to move the haunches] ▸ **'crissal** *adj*

crista ('krɪstə) *n, pl* **-tae** (-ti:). *Biology.* a structure resembling a ridge or crest, as on the inner membrane of a mitochondrion. [C20: from Latin: CREST]

cristate ('krɪsteɪt) *or* **cristated** *adj* **1** having a crest. **2** forming a crest. [C17: from Latin *cristātus,* from *crista* CREST]

cristobalite (krɪs'təubə,laɪt) *n* a white microcrystalline mineral consisting of silica and occurring in volcanic rocks. Formula: SiO_2. [C19: from German, named after Cerro San *Cristóbal,* Mexico, where it was discovered]

crit. *abbrev. for:* **1** *Med.* critical. **2** criticism.

criterion (kraɪ'tɪərɪən) *n, pl* **-ria** (-rɪə) *or* **-rions. 1** a standard by which something can be judged or decided. **2** *Philosophy.* a defining characteristic of something. [C17: from Greek *kritērion* from *kritēs* judge, from *krinein* to decide]

USAGE *Criteria,* the plural of *criterion,* is not acceptable as a singular noun: *this criterion is not valid; these criteria are not valid.*

critic ('krɪtɪk) *n* **1** a person who judges something. **2** a professional judge of art, music, literature, etc. **3** a person who often finds fault and criticizes. [C16: from Latin *criticus,* from Greek *kritikos* capable of judging, from *kritēs* judge; see CRITERION]

critical ('krɪtɪk^əl) *adj* **1** containing or making severe or negative judgments. **2** containing careful or analytical evaluations: *a critical dissertation.* **3** of or involving a critic or criticism. **4** of or forming a crisis; crucial; decisive: *a critical operation.* **5** urgently needed: *critical medical supplies.* **6** *Informal.* so seriously injured or ill as to be in danger of dying. **7** *Physics.* of, denoting, or concerned with a state in which the properties of a system undergo an abrupt change: *a critical temperature.* **8 go critical.** (of a nuclear power station or reactor) to reach a state in which a nuclear-fission chain reaction becomes self-sustaining. ▸ **'critically** *adv* ▸ **'criticalness** *n*

critical angle *n* **1** the smallest possible angle of incidence for which light rays are totally reflected at an interface between substances of different refractive index. **2** another name for **stalling angle.**

critical apparatus *n* the variant readings, footnotes, etc. found in a scholarly work or a critical edition of a text. Also called: **apparatus criticus.**

critical constants *pl n* the physical constants that express the properties of a substance in its critical state. See **critical pressure, critical temperature.**

critical damping *n Physics.* the minimum amount of viscous damping that results in a displaced system returning to its original position without oscillation. Symbol: C_c

criticality (,krɪtɪ'kælɪtɪ) *n* **1** the state of being critical. **2** *Physics.* the condition in a nuclear reactor when the fissionable material can sustain a chain reaction by itself.

critical mass *n* the minimum mass of fissionable material that can sustain a nuclear chain reaction.

critical path analysis *n* a technique for planning complex projects by analysing alternative systems with reference to the critical path, which is the sequence of stages requiring the longest time. Compare **programme evaluation and review technique.**

critical period *n Psychol.* a period in a lifetime during which a specific stage of development usually occurs. If it fails to do so, it cannot readily occur afterwards.

critical point *n* **1** *Physics.* **1a** the point on a phase diagram that represents the critical state of a substance. **1b** another name for **critical state. 2** *Maths.* the U.S. name for **stationary point.**

critical pressure *n* the pressure of a gas or the saturated vapour pressure of a substance in its critical state.

critical region *n* that part of a statistical distribution in which the probability of a given hypothesis is less than the chosen significance level, so that the hypothesis would be rejected.

critical state *n* the state of a substance in which two of its phases have the same temperature, pressure, and volume. Also called: **critical point.**

critical temperature *n* the temperature of a substance in its critical state. A gas can only be liquefied by pressure alone at temperatures below its critical temperature.

critical volume *n* the volume occupied by one mole or unit mass of a substance in its critical state.

criticism ('krɪtɪ,sɪzəm) *n* **1** the act or an instance of making an unfavourable or severe judgment, comment, etc. **2** the analysis or evaluation of a work of art, literature, etc. **3** the occupation of a critic. **4** a work that sets out to evaluate or analyse. **5** Also called: **textual criticism.** the investigation of a particular text, with related material, in order to establish an authentic text.

criticize *or* **criticise** ('krɪtɪ,saɪz) *vb* **1** to judge (something) with disapproval; censure. **2** to evaluate or analyse (something). ▸ **'criti,cizable** *or* **'criti,cisable** *adj* ▸ **'criti,cizer** *or* **'criti,ciser** *n* ▸ **'criti,cizingly** *or* **'criti,cisingly** *adv*

critique (krɪ'ti:k) *n* **1** a critical essay or commentary, esp. on artistic work. **2** the act or art of criticizing. [C17: from French, from Greek *kritikē,* from *kritikos* able to discern]

critter ('krɪtə) *n U.S. and Canadian.* a dialect word for **creature.**

CRO *abbrev. for:* **1** cathode-ray oscilloscope. **2** (in Britain) Community Relations Officer. **3** Criminal Records Office.

Croagh Patrick (kro:x) *n* a mountain in NW Republic of Ireland, in Mayo: a place of pilgrimage as Saint Patrick is said to have prayed and fasted there. Height: 765 m (2510 ft.).

croak (krəuk) *vb* **1** (*intr*) (of frogs, crows, etc.) to make a low, hoarse cry. **2** to utter (something) in this manner: *he croaked out the news.* **3** (*intr*) to grumble or be pessimistic. **4** *Slang.* **4a** (*intr*) to die. **4b** (*tr*) to kill. ◆ *n* **5** a low hoarse utterance or sound. [Old English *crācettan;* related to Old Norse *krāka* a crow; see CREAK] ▸ **'croaky** *adj* ▸ **'croakily** *adv* ▸ **'croakiness** *n*

croaker ('krəukə) *n* **1** an animal, bird, etc., that croaks. **2** any of various mainly tropical marine sciaenid fishes, such as *Umbrina roncador* (**yellowfin croaker**), that utter croaking noises. **3** a grumbling person.

Croat ('krəuæt) *n* **1a** a native or inhabitant of Croatia. **1b** a speaker of Croatian. ◆ *n, adj* **2** another word for **Croatian.**

Croatia (krəu'eɪʃə) *n* a republic in SE Europe: settled by Croats in the 7th century; belonged successively to Hungary, Turkey, and Austria; formed part of Yugoslavia (1918–91); became independent in 1991 but was invaded by Serbia and fighting continued until 1995; involved in the civil war in Bosnia-Herzegovina (1991–95). Language: Croatian. Religion: Roman Catholic majority. Currency: kuna. Capital: Zagreb. Pop.: 4 672 000 (1998 est.). Area: 55 322 sq. km (21 359 sq. miles). Croatian name: **Hrvatska.**

Croatian (krəu'eɪʃən) *adj* **1** of, relating to, or characteristic of Croatia, its people, or their language. ◆ *n* **2** the language that is spoken in Croatia, a dialect of Serbo-Croat (Croato-Serb). **3a** a native or inhabitant of Croatia. **3b** a speaker of Croatian.

Croato-Serb (krəu'eɪtəu-sɜ:b) another name for **Serbo-Croat.**

croc *abbrev. for* **crocodile** (senses 1–3).

Croce (*Italian* 'kro:tʃe) *n* **Benedetto** (bene'detto). 1866–1952, Italian philosopher, critic, and statesman: an opponent of Fascism, he helped re-establish liberalism in postwar Italy.

crocein ('krəusɪɪn) *n* any one of a group of red or orange acid azo dyes. [C20: from Latin *croceus* yellow + -IN]

crochet ('krəuʃeɪ, -ʃɪ) *vb* **-chets** (-ʃeɪz, -ʃɪz), **-cheting** (-ʃeɪɪŋ, -ʃɪɪŋ), **-cheted** (-ʃeɪd, -ʃɪd). **1** to make (a piece of needlework, a garment, etc.) by looping and intertwining thread with a hooked needle (**crochet hook**). ◆ *n* **2** work made by crocheting. **3** *Architect.* another name for **crocket. 4** *Zoology.* a hooklike structure of insect larvae that aids locomotion. [C19: from French *crochet,* diminutive of *croc* hook, probably of Scandinavian origin] ▸ **'crocheter** *n*

crocidolite (krəu'sɪdə,laɪt) *n* a blue fibrous amphibole mineral consisting of sodium iron silicate: a variety of asbestos used in cement products and pressure piping. [C19: from Greek *krokis* nap on woollen cloth + -LITE]

crock[1] (krɒk) *n* **1** an earthen pot, jar, etc. **2** a piece of broken earthenware. [Old English *crocc* pot; related to Old Norse *krukka* jug, Middle Low German *krūke* pot]

crock[2] (krɒk) *n* **1** *Slang, chiefly Brit.* a person or thing, such as a car, that is old or decrepit (esp. in the phrase **old crock**). **2** an old broken-down horse or ewe. ◆ *vb* **3** *Slang, chiefly Brit.* to become or cause to become weak or disabled. [C15: originally Scottish; related to Norwegian *krake* unhealthy animal, Dutch *kraak* decrepit person or animal]

crock[3] (krɒk) *n* **1** *Dialect, chiefly Brit.* soot or smut. **2** colour that rubs off fabric. ◆ *vb* **3** (*tr*) *Dialect, chiefly Brit.* to soil with or as if with soot. **4** (*intr*) (of a dyed fabric) to release colour when rubbed, as a result of imperfect dyeing. [C17: probably from CROCK[1]]

crocked (krɒkt) *adj Slang.* **1** *Brit.* injured. **2** *U.S. and Canadian.* drunk.

crockery ('krɒkərɪ) *n* china dishes, earthen vessels, etc., collectively.

crocket ('krɒkɪt) *n* a carved ornament in the form of a curled leaf or cusp, used in Gothic architecture. Also called: **crochet.** [C17: from Anglo-French *croket* a little hook, from *croc* hook, of Scandinavian origin]

Crockett ('krɒkɪt) *n* **David,** known as *Davy Crockett.* 1786–1836, U.S. frontiersman, politician, and soldier.

Crockford ('krɒkfəd) *n* short for *Crockford's Clerical Directory,* the standard directory of living Anglican clergy. [C19: named after John *Crockford* (1823–65), clerk to Edward William Cox (1809–79), a lawyer who devised the directory]

crocodile ('krɒkə,daɪl) *n* **1** any large tropical reptile, such as *C. niloticus* (**African crocodile**), of the family *Crocodylidae:* order *Crocodilia* (crocodilians). They have a broad head, tapering snout, massive jaws, and a thick outer covering of bony plates. **2** any other reptile of the order *Crocodilia;* a crocodilian. **3a** leather made from the skin of any of these animals. **3b** (*as modifier*): *crocodile shoes.* **4** *Brit. informal.* a line of schoolchildren walking two by two. [C13: via Old French, from Latin *crocodīlus,* from Greek *krokodeilos* lizard, ultimately from *krokē* pebble + *drilos* worm; referring to its fondness for basking on shingle]

crocodile bird *n* an African courser, *Pluvianus aegyptius,* that lives close to rivers and is thought to feed on insects parasitic on crocodiles.

crocodile clip *n* a clasp with serrated interlocking edges used for making electrical connections.

Crocodile River *n* **1** a river in N South Africa, rising north of Johannesburg and flowing north-westerly into the Marico River on the Botswanan border; a tributary of the Limpopo. **2** a river that rises in NE South Africa, in the Kruger National Park and flows south-easterly into Mozambique.

crocodile tears *pl n* an insincere show of grief; false tears. [from the belief that crocodiles wept over their prey to allure further victims]

crocodilian (,krɒkə'dɪlɪən) *n* **1** any large predatory reptile of the order *Crocodilia,* which includes the crocodiles, alligators, and caymans. They live in or near water and have a long broad snout, powerful jaws, a four-chambered heart, and socketed teeth. ◆ *adj* **2** of, relating to, or belonging to the *Crocodilia.* **3** of, relating to, or resembling a crocodile.

crocoite ('krəʊkəʊ,aɪt) *or* **crocoisite** (krəʊ'kəʊɪ,saɪt, 'krəʊkwə,saɪt) *n* a rare orange secondary mineral consisting of lead chromate in monoclinic crystalline form. Formula: $PbCrO_4$. Also called: **red-lead ore.** [C19: from Greek *krokoeis* saffron-coloured, golden + -ITE[1]]

crocosmia (krə'kɒzmɪə) *n* any plant of the cormous S. African genus *Crocosmia,* including the plant known to gardeners as montbretia, a cross between *C. anrea* and *C. pottsii,* with graceful orange or yellow flowers: family *Iridaceae.* [New Latin, from Greek *krokos* saffron + *osmē* smell, from the odour of the dried flowers when wetted]

crocus ('krəʊkəs) *n, pl* **-cuses. 1** any plant of the iridaceous genus *Crocus,* widely cultivated in gardens, having white, yellow, or purple flowers. See also **autumn crocus. 2** another name for **jeweller's rouge.** ◆ *adj* **3** of a saffron yellow colour. [C17: from New Latin, from Latin *crocus,* from Greek *krokos* saffron, of Semitic origin]

Croesus ('kri:səs) *n* **1** died ?546 B.C., the last king of Lydia (560–546), noted for his great wealth. **2** any very rich man.

croft (krɒft) *n Brit.* **1** a small enclosed plot of land, adjoining a house, worked by the occupier and his family, esp. in Scotland. **2** *Lancashire dialect.* a patch of wasteland, formerly one used for bleaching fabric in the sun. [Old English *croft;* related to Middle Dutch *krocht* hill, field, Old English *creopan* to CREEP]

crofter ('krɒftə) *n Brit.* an owner or tenant of a small farm, esp. in Scotland or northern England.

crofting ('krɒftɪŋ) *n Brit.* the system or occupation of working land in crofts.

Crohn's disease (krəʊnz) *n* inflammation, thickening, and ulceration of any of various parts of the intestine, esp. the ileum. Also called: **regional enteritis.** See also **Johne's disease.** [C20: named after B. B. *Crohn* (1884–1983), U.S. physician]

croissant ('krwʌsɒŋ; *French* krwasɑ̃) *n* a flaky crescent-shaped bread roll made of a yeast dough similar to puff pastry. [French, literally: crescent]

Croix de Guerre *French.* (krwa də gɛr) *n* a French military decoration awarded for gallantry in battle: established 1915. [literally: cross of war]

Cro-Magnon man ('krəʊ'mænjɒn, -'mægnɒn) *n* an early type of modern man, *Homo sapiens,* who lived in Europe during late Palaeolithic times, having tall stature, long head, and a relatively large cranial capacity. [C19: named after the cave (Cro-Magnon), Dordogne, France, where the remains were first found]

crombec ('krɒmbɛk) *n* any African Old World warbler of the genus *Sylvietta,* having colourful plumage. [C19: via French from Dutch *krom* crooked + *bek* BEAK[1]]

Crome (krəʊm) *n* **John,** known as *Old Crome.* 1768–1821, English landscape painter and etcher.

Cromer[1] ('krəʊmə) *n* a resort in E England, on the Norfolk coast: fishing. Pop.: 7267 (1991).

Cromer[2] ('krəʊmə) *n* **1st Earl of,** title of (Evelyn) **Baring.**

cromlech ('krɒmlɛk) *n* **1** a circle of prehistoric standing stones. **2** (no longer in technical usage) a megalithic chamber tomb or dolmen. [C17: from Welsh, from *crom,* feminine of *crwm* bent, arched + *llech* flat stone]

Crompton ('krɒmptən) *n* **1 Richmal,** full name *Richmal Crompton Lamburn.* 1890–1969, British children's author, best known for her *Just William* stories. **2 Samuel.** 1753–1827, British inventor of the spinning mule (1779).

Cromwell ('krɒmwəl, -wɛl) *n* **1 Oliver.** 1599–1658, English general and statesman. A convinced Puritan, he was an effective leader of the parliamentary army in the Civil War. After the execution of Charles I he quelled the Royalists in Scotland and Ireland, and became Lord Protector of the Commonwealth (1653–58). **2** his son, **Richard.** 1626–1712, Lord Protector of the Commonwealth (1658–59). **3 Thomas,** Earl of Essex. ?1485–1540, English statesman. He was secretary to Cardinal Wolsey (1514), after whose fall he became chief adviser to Henry VIII. He drafted most of the Reformation legislation, securing its passage through parliament, the power of which he thereby greatly enhanced. He was executed after losing Henry's favour. ► **Cromwellian** (krɒm'wɛlɪən) *adj, n*

Cromwell Current ('krɒmwɛl, -wəl) *n* an equatorial Pacific current, flowing eastward from the Hawaiian Islands to the Galápagos Islands. [C20: named after T. *Cromwell* (1922–58), U.S. oceanographer]

crone (krəʊn) *n* a witchlike old woman. [C14: from Old Northern French *carogne* carrion, ultimately from Latin *caro* flesh]

Cronin ('krəʊnɪn) *n* **1 A(rchibald) J(oseph).** 1896–1981, British novelist and physician. His works include *Hatter's Castle* (1931), *The Judas Tree* (1961), and *Dr Finlay's Casebook,* a TV series based on his medical experiences. **2 James Watson.** born 1931, U.S. physicist; shared the Nobel prize for physics (1980) for his work on parity conservation in weak interactions.

cronk (krɒŋk) *adj Austral.* unfit; unsound. [C19: compare CRANK[2]]

Cronus ('krəʊnəs), **Cronos,** *or* **Kronos** ('krəʊnɒs) *n Greek myth.* a Titan, son of Uranus (sky) and Gaea (earth), who ruled the world until his son Zeus dethroned him. Roman counterpart: **Saturn.**

crony ('krəʊnɪ) *n, pl* **-nies.** a friend or companion. [C17: student slang (Cambridge), from Greek *khronios* of long duration, from *khronos* time]

cronyism ('krəʊnɪ,ɪzəm) *n* the practice of appointing friends to high-level, esp. political, posts regardless of their suitability.

crook (krʊk) *n* **1** a curved or hooked thing. **2** a staff with a hooked end, such as a bishop's crosier or shepherd's staff. **3** a turn or curve; bend. **4** *Informal.* a dishonest person, esp. a swindler or thief. **5** the act or an instance of crooking or bending. **6** Also called: **shank.** a piece of tubing added to a brass instrument in order to obtain a lower harmonic series. ◆ *vb* **7** to bend or curve or cause to bend or curve. ◆ *adj* **8** *Austral. and N.Z. informal.* **8a** ill. **8b** of poor quality. **8c** unpleasant; bad. **9 go (off) crook.** *Austral. and N.Z. informal.* to lose one's temper. **10 go crook at** *or* **on.** *Austral. and N.Z. informal.* to rebuke or upbraid. [C12: from Old Norse *krokr* hook; related to Swedish *krok,* Danish *krog* hook, Old High German *krācho* hooked tool]

crookback ('krʊk,bæk) *n* a rare word for **hunchback.** ► **'crook,backed** *adj*

crooked ('krʊkɪd) *adj* **1** bent, angled or winding. **2** set at an angle; not straight. **3** deformed or contorted. **4** *Informal.* dishonest or illegal. **5 crooked on.** (*also* krʊkt) *Austral. informal.* hostile or averse to. ► **'crookedly** *adv* ► **'crookedness** *n*

Crookes (krʊks) *n* Sir **William.** 1832–1919, English chemist and physicist: he investigated the properties of cathode rays and invented a type of radiometer and the lens named after him.

Crookes lens *n* a type of lens, used in sunglasses, that is made from glass containing cerium. It reduces the transmission of ultraviolet radiation.

Crookes radiometer *n Physics.* a type of radiometer consisting of an evacuated glass bulb containing a set of lightweight vanes, each blackened on one side. The vanes are mounted on a vertical axis and revolve when light, or other radiant energy, falls on them.

Crookes space *n* a dark region near the cathode in some low-pressure gas-discharge tubes. Also called: **Crookes dark space.**

Crookes tube *n* a type of cathode-ray tube in which the electrons are produced by a glow discharge in a low-pressure gas.

croon (kru:n) *vb* **1** to sing or speak in a soft low tone. ◆ *n* **2** a soft low singing or humming. [C14: via Middle Dutch *crōnen* to groan; compare Old High German *chrōnan* to chatter, Latin *gingrīre* to cackle (of geese)] ► **'crooner** *n*

crop (krɒp) *n* **1** the produce of cultivated plants, esp. cereals, vegetables, and fruit. **2a** the amount of such produce in any particular season. **2b** the yield of some other farm produce: *the lamb crop.* **3** a group of products, thoughts, people, etc., appearing at one time or in one season: *a crop of new publications.* **4** the stock of a thonged whip. **5** short for **riding crop. 6a** a pouchlike expanded part of the oesophagus of birds, in which food is stored or partially digested before passing on to the gizzard. **6b** a similar structure in insects, earthworms, and other invertebrates. **7** the entire tanned hide of an animal. **8** a short cropped hairstyle. See also **Eton crop. 9** a notch in or a piece cut out of the ear of an animal. **10** the act of cropping. ◆ *vb* **crops, cropping, cropped.** (*mainly tr*) **11** to cut (hair, grass, etc.) very short. **12** to cut and collect (mature produce) from the land or plant on which it has been grown. **13** to clip part of (the ear or ears) of (an animal), esp. as a means of identification. **14** (*also intr*) to cause (land) to bear or (of land) to bear or yield a crop: *the land cropped well.* **15** (of herbivorous animals) to graze on (grass or similar vegetation). **16** *Photog.* to cut off or mask unwanted edges or areas of (a negative or print). ◆ See also **crop out, crop up.** [Old English *cropp;* related to Old Norse *kroppr* rump, body, Old High German *kropf* goitre, Norwegian *kröypa* to bend]

crop circle *n* any of various patterns, usually wholly or partly consisting of ring shapes, formed by the unexplained flattening of cereals growing in a field.

crop-dusting *n* the spreading of fungicide, etc. on crops in the form of dust, often from an aircraft.

crop-eared *adj* having the ears or hair cut short.

crop out *vb* (*intr, adv*) (of a formation of rock strata) to appear or be exposed at the surface of the ground; outcrop.

cropper ('krɒpə) *n* **1** a person who cultivates or harvests a crop. **2a** a cutting machine for removing the heads from castings and ingots. **2b** a guillotine for cutting lengths of bar or strip. **3** a machine for shearing the nap from cloth. **4** a plant or breed of plant that will produce a certain kind of crop under specified conditions: *a poor cropper on light land.* **5** (*often cap.*) a variety of domestic pigeon with a puffed-out crop. **6 come a cropper.** *Informal.* **6a** to fall heavily. **6b** to fail completely.

crop rotation *n* the system of growing a sequence of different crops on the same ground so as to maintain or increase its fertility.

crop up *vb* (*intr, adv*) *Informal.* to occur or appear, esp. unexpectedly.

croquet ('krəʊkeɪ, -kɪ) *n* **1** a game for two to four players who hit a wooden ball through iron hoops with mallets in order to hit a peg. **2** the act of croqueting. ◆ *vb* **-quets** (-keɪz, -kɪz), **-queting** (-keɪɪŋ, -kɪɪŋ), **-queted** (-keɪd, -kɪd). **3** to drive away (another player's ball) by hitting one's own ball when the two are in contact. [C19: perhaps from French dialect, variant of CROCHET (little hook)]

croquette (krəʊ'kɛt, krɒ-) *n* a savoury cake of minced meat, fish, etc., fried in breadcrumbs. [C18: from French, from *croquer* to crunch, of imitative origin]

crore (krɔː) *n* (in Indian English) ten million. [C17: from Hindi *karōr,* from Prakrit *krodi*]

Crosby[1] ('krɒzbɪ) *n* a town in NW England, in Sefton unitary authority, Merseyside. Pop.: 52 869 (1991).

Crosby[2] ('krɒzbɪ) *n* **Bing,** real name *Harry Lillis Crosby.* 1904–77, U.S. singer and film actor; famous for his style of crooning: best known for the song "White Christmas" from the film *Holiday Inn* (1942).

crosier *or* **crozier** ('krəʊʒə) *n* **1** a staff surmounted by a crook or cross, carried by bishops as a symbol of pastoral office. **2** the tip of a young plant, esp. a fern frond, that is coiled into a hook. [C14: from Old French *crossier* staff bearer, from *crosse* pastoral staff, literally: hooked stick, of Germanic origin]

Crosland ('krɒslənd) *n* **Anthony.** 1918–77, British Labour politician and socialist theorist, author of *The Future of Socialism* (1957).

cross (krɒs) *n* **1** a structure or symbol consisting essentially of two intersecting lines or pieces at right angles to one another. **2** a wooden structure used as a means of execution, consisting of an upright post with a transverse piece to which people were nailed or tied. **3** a representation of the Cross used as an emblem of Christianity or as a reminder of Christ's death. **4** any mark or shape consisting of two intersecting lines, esp. such a symbol (×) used as a signature, point of intersection, error mark, etc. **5** a sign representing the Cross made either by tracing a figure in the air or by touching the forehead, breast, and either shoulder in turn. **6** any conventional variation of the Christian symbol, used emblematically, decoratively, or heraldically, such as a Maltese, tau, or Greek cross. **7** *Heraldry.* any of several charges in which one line crosses or joins another at right angles. **8** a cruciform emblem awarded to indicate membership of an order or as a decoration for distinguished service. **9** (*sometimes cap.*) Christianity or Christendom, esp. as contrasted with non-Christian religions: *Cross and Crescent.* **10** the place in a town or village where a cross has been set up. **11** a pipe fitting, in the form of a cross, for connecting four pipes. **12** *Biology.* **12a** the process of crossing; hybridization. **12b** an individual produced as a result of this process. **13** a mixture of two qualities or types: *he's a cross between a dictator and a saint.* **14** an opposition, hindrance, or misfortune; affliction (esp. in the phrase **bear one's cross**). **15** *Slang.* a match or game in which the outcome has been rigged. **16** *Slang.* a fraud or swindle. **17** *Boxing.* a straight punch delivered from the side, esp. with the right hand. **18** *Football.* the act or an instance of kicking or passing the ball from a wing to the middle of the field. **19 on the cross.** **19a** diagonally. **19b** *Slang.* dishonestly. ◆ *vb* **20** (sometimes foll. by *over*) to move or go across (something); traverse or intersect: *we crossed the road.* **21a** to meet and pass: *the two trains crossed.* **21b** (of each of two letters in the post) to be dispatched before receipt of the other. **22** (*tr;* usually foll. by *out, off,* or *through*) to cancel with a cross or with lines; delete. **23** (*tr*) to place or put in a form resembling a cross: *to cross one's legs.* **24** (*tr*) to mark with a cross or crosses. **25** (*tr*) *Brit.* to draw two parallel lines across the face of (a cheque) and so make it payable only into a bank account. **26** (*tr*) **26a** to trace the form of the Cross, usually with the thumb or index finger upon (someone or something) in token of blessing. **26b** to make the sign of the Cross upon (oneself). **27** (*intr*) (of telephone lines) to interfere with each other so that three or perhaps four callers are connected together at one time. **28** to cause fertilization between (plants or animals of different breeds, races, varieties, etc.). **29** (*tr*) to oppose the wishes or plans of; thwart: *his opponent crosses him at every turn.* **30** *Football.* to kick or pass (the ball) from a wing to the middle of the field. **31** (*tr*) *Nautical.* to set (the yard of a square sail) athwartships. **32 cross a bridge when one comes to it.** to deal with matters, problems, etc., as they arise; not to anticipate difficulties. **33 cross one's fingers.** to fold one finger across another in the hope of bringing good luck: *keep your fingers crossed.* **34 cross one's heart.** to promise or pledge, esp. by making the sign of a cross over one's heart. **35 cross one's mind.** to occur to one briefly or suddenly. **36 cross someone's palm.** to give someone money. **37 cross the path** (**of**). to meet or thwart (someone). **38 cross swords.** to argue or fight. ◆ *adj* **39** angry; ill-humoured; vexed. **40** lying or placed across; transverse: *a cross timber.* **41** involving interchange; reciprocal. **42** contrary or unfavourable. **43** another word for **crossbred** (sense 1). **44** a Brit. slang word for **dishonest.** [Old English *cros,* from Old Irish *cross* (unattested), from Latin *crux;* see CRUX] ▶ **'crosser** *n* ▶ **'crossly** *adv* ▶ **'crossness** *n*

Cross[1] (krɒs) *n* **the. 1** the cross on which Jesus Christ was crucified. **2** the Crucifixion of Jesus.

Cross[2] (krɒs) *n* **Richard Assheton,** 1st Viscount. 1823–1914, British Conservative statesman, home secretary (1874–80); noted for reforms affecting housing, public health, and the employment of women and children in factories.

cross- *combining form.* **1** indicating action from one individual, group, etc., to another: *cross-cultural; cross-fertilize; cross-refer.* **2** indicating movement, position, etc., across something (sometimes implying interference, opposition, or contrary action): *crosscurrent; crosstalk.* **3** indicating a crosslike figure or intersection: *crossbones.* [from CROSS (in various senses)]

crossandra (krɒ'sɑːndrə) *n* any shrub of the free-flowering mostly African genus *Crossandra,* grown in greenhouses for their large yellow, lilac, or orange flowers: family *Acanthaceae.* [New Latin, from Greek *krossos* fringed + *andros,* genitive of *anēr* man, male (from the fringed anthers)]

cross assembler *n* an assembler that runs on a computer other than the one for which it assembles programs.

crossbar ('krɒs,bɑː) *n* **1** a horizontal bar, line, stripe, etc. **2** a horizontal beam across a pair of goalposts. **3** a horizontal bar mounted on vertical posts used in athletics or show-jumping. **4** the horizontal bar on a man's bicycle that joins the handlebar and saddle supports.

crossbeam ('krɒs,biːm) *n* a beam that spans from one support to another.

cross bedding *n Geology.* layering within one or more beds in a series of rock strata that does not run parallel to the plane of stratification. Also called: **false bedding.**

cross-bench *n* (*usually pl*) *Brit.* a seat in Parliament occupied by a neutral or independent member. ▶ **'cross-,bencher** *n*

crossbill ('krɒs,bɪl) *n* any of various widely distributed finches of the genus *Loxia,* such as *L. curvirostra,* that occur in coniferous woods and have a bill with crossed mandible tips for feeding on conifer seeds.

crossbones ('krɒs,bəʊnz) *pl n* See **skull and crossbones.**

crossbow ('krɒs,bəʊ) *n* a type of medieval bow fixed transversely on a wooden stock grooved to direct a square-headed arrow (quarrel). ▶ **'cross,bowman** *n*

crossbred ('krɒs,brɛd) *adj* **1** (of plants or animals) produced as a result of cross-breeding. ◆ *n* **2** a crossbred plant or animal, esp. an animal resulting from a cross between two pure breeds. Compare **grade** (sense 9), **purebred** (sense 2).

crossbreed ('krɒs,briːd) *vb* **-breeds, -breeding, -bred. 1** Also: **interbreed.** to breed (animals or plants) using parents of different races, varieties, breeds, etc. ◆ *n* **2** the offspring produced by such a breeding.

cross-buttock *n* a wrestling throw in which the hips are used as a fulcrum to throw an opponent.

crosscheck (,krɒs'tʃɛk) *vb* **1** to verify (a fact, report, etc.) by considering conflicting opinions or consulting other sources. **2** (in ice hockey) to check illegally, as by chopping at an opponent's arms or stick. ◆ *n* **3** the act or an instance of crosschecking.

cross colour *n* distortion in a colour television receiver in which high-frequency luminance detail is interpreted as colour information and reproduced as flashes of spurious colour.

cross-correlation *n Statistics.* the correlation between two sequences of random variables in a time series.

cross-country *adj, adv* **1** by way of fields, woods, etc., as opposed to roads: *cross-country running.* **2** across a country: *a cross-country railway.* ◆ *n* **3** a long race held over open ground.

cross-cultural *adj* involving or bridging the differences between cultures.

crosscurrent ('krɒs,kʌrənt) *n* **1** a current in a river or sea flowing across another current. **2** a conflicting tendency moving counter to the usual trend.

cross-curricular *adj Brit. education.* denoting or relating to an approach to a topic that includes contributions from several different disciplines and viewpoints.

crosscut ('krɒs,kʌt) *adj* **1** cut at right angles or obliquely to the major axis. ◆ *n* **2** a transverse cut or course. **3** a less common word for **short cut. 4** *Mining.* a tunnel through a vein of ore or from the shaft to a vein. ◆ *vb* **-cuts, -cutting, -cut. 5** to cut across. **6** Also: **intercut.** *Films.* to link (two sequences or two shots) so that they appear to be taking place at the same time.

crosscut file *n* a file having two intersecting rows of teeth.

crosscut saw *n* a saw for cutting timber across the grain.

cross-dating *n Archaeol.* a method of dating objects, remains, etc., by comparison and correlation with other sites and levels.

cross-dressing *n* **1** transvestism. See **transvestite. 2** the wearing of clothes normally associated with the opposite sex. ▶ **,cross-'dresser** *n*

crosse (krɒs) *n* a light staff with a triangular frame to which a network is attached, used in playing lacrosse. [French, from Old French *croce* CROSIER]

cross-examine *vb* (*tr*) **1** *Law.* to examine (a witness for the opposing side), as in attempting to discredit his testimony. Compare **examine-in-chief. 2** to examine closely or relentlessly. ▶ **'cross-ex,ami'nation** *n* ▶ **'cross-ex'aminer** *n*

cross-eye *n* a turning inwards towards the nose of one or both eyes, caused by abnormal alignment. See also **strabismus.** ▶ **'cross-,eyed** *adj*

cross-fade *vb Radio, television.* to fade in (one sound or picture source) as another is being faded out.

cross-fertilization *n* **1** fertilization by the fusion of male and female gametes from different individuals of the same species. Compare **self-fertilization. 2** (*not in technical use*) cross-pollination. ▶ **'cross-'fertile** *adj*

cross-fertilize *vb* to subject or be subjected to cross-fertilization.

crossfire ('krɒs,faɪə) *n* **1** *Military, etc.* converging fire from one or more positions. **2** a lively exchange of ideas, opinions, etc.

cross-garnet *n* a hinge with a long horizontal strap fixed to the face of a door and a short vertical leaf fixed to the door frame.

cross-grained *adj* **1** (of timber) having the fibres arranged irregularly or in a direction that deviates from the axis of the piece. **2** perverse, cantankerous, or stubborn.

cross hairs *pl n* two fine mutually perpendicular lines or wires that cross in the focal plane of a theodolite, gunsight, or other optical instrument and are used to define the line of sight. Also called: **cross wires.**

crosshatch ('krɒs,hætʃ) *vb Drawing.* to shade or hatch (forms, figures, etc.) with two or more sets of parallel lines that cross one another. ▶ **'cross,hatching** *n*

crosshead ('krɒs,hɛd) *n* **1** *Printing.* a subsection or paragraph heading printed within the body of the text. **2** a block or beam, usually restrained by sliding bearings in a reciprocating mechanism, esp. the junction piece between the piston rod and connecting rod of an engine. **3** *Nautical.* a bar fixed across the top of the rudder post to which the tiller is attached. **4** a block, rod, or beam fixed at the head of any part of a mechanism.

cross-index *n* **1** a note or notes referring the reader to other material. ◆ *vb* **2** (*intr*) (of a note in a book) to refer to related material. **3** to provide or be provided with cross-indexes.

crossing ('krɒsɪŋ) *n* **1** the place where one thing crosses another. **2** a place, often shown by markings, lights, or poles, where a street, railway, etc., may be crossed. **3** the intersection of the nave and transept in a church. **4** the act or instance of travelling across something, esp. the sea. **5** the act or process of cross-breeding.

crossing over *n Biology.* the interchange of sections between pairing homologous chromosomes during the diplotene stage of meiosis. It results in the rearrangement of genes and produces variation in the inherited characteristics of the offspring. See also **linkage** (sense 4).

crossjack ('krɒs,dʒæk; *Nautical* 'krɔ:dʒɪk, 'krɒdʒ-) *n Nautical.* a square sail on a ship's mizzenmast.

cross-legged ('krɒs'lɛgɪd, -'lɛgd) *adj* **1** sitting with the legs bent and the knees pointing outwards. **2** standing or sitting with one leg crossed over the other.

crosslet *or* **cross crosslet** ('krɒslɪt) *n Heraldry.* a cross having a smaller cross near the end of each arm. [C16 *croslet* a little CROSS]

cross-link *or* **cross-linkage** *n* a chemical bond, atom, or group of atoms that connects two adjacent chains of atoms in a large molecule such as a polymer or protein.

Crossman ('krɒsmən) *n* **Richard** (**Howard Stafford**). 1907–74, British Labour politician. His diaries, published posthumously as the *Crossman Papers* (1975), revealed details of cabinet discussions.

cross-match *n Immunology.* to test the compatibility of (a donor's and recipient's blood) by checking that the red cells of each do not agglutinate in the other's serum.

cross-nodal *adj* having to do with interaction between the senses.

cross of Lorraine *n* a cross with two horizontal bars above and below the midpoint of the vertical bar, the lower longer than the upper.

Cross of Valour *n* the highest Canadian award for bravery. Abbrev.: **CV**.

crossopterygian (krɒ,sɒptə'rɪdʒɪən) *n* **1** any bony fish of the subclass *Crossopterygii,* having fleshy limblike pectoral fins. The group, now mostly extinct, contains the ancestors of the amphibians. See also **coelacanth.** ◆ *adj* **2** of, relating to, or belonging to the *Crossopterygii.* [C19: from New Latin *Crossopterygii,* from Greek *krossoi* fringe, tassels + *pterugion* a little wing, from *pterux* wing]

crossover ('krɒs,əʊvə) *n* **1** a place at which a crossing is made. **2** *Genetics.* **2a** another term for **crossing over. 2b** a chromosomal structure or character resulting from crossing over. **3** *Railways.* a point of transfer between two main lines. **4** short for **crossover network. 5** a recording, book, or other product that becomes popular in a genre other than its own. ◆ *adj* **6** (of music, fashion, art, etc.) combining two distinct styles. **7** (of a performer, writer, recording, book, etc.) having become popular in more than one genre.

crossover network *n* an electronic network in a loudspeaker system that separates the signal into two or more frequency bands, the lower frequencies being fed to a woofer, the higher frequencies to a tweeter.

crossover value *n Genetics.* the percentage of offspring showing recombination among the total offspring of a given cross. It indicates the amount of crossing over that has occurred and therefore the relative positions of the genes on the chromosomes. Abbrev.: **COV**.

crosspatch ('krɒs,pætʃ) *n Informal.* a peevish bad-tempered person. [C18: from CROSS + obsolete *patch* fool]

crosspiece ('krɒs,pi:s) *n* a transverse beam, joist, etc.

cross-ply *adj* (of a motor tyre) having the fabric cords in the outer casing running diagonally to stiffen the sidewalls. Compare **radial-ply.**

cross-pollinate *vb* to subject or be subjected to cross-pollination.

cross-pollination *n* the transfer of pollen from the anthers of one flower to the stigma of another flower by the action of wind, insects, etc. Compare **self-pollination.**

cross press *n* a fall in wrestling using the weight of the body to pin an opponent's shoulders to the floor.

cross product *n Maths.* **1** another name for **vector product. 2** another name for **Cartesian product.**

cross protection *n Botany.* the protection against a viral infection given to a plant by its prior inoculation with a related but milder virus.

cross-purpose *n* **1** a contrary aim or purpose. **2 at cross-purposes.** conflicting; opposed; disagreeing.

cross-question *vb* (*tr*) **1** to cross-examine. ◆ *n* **2** a question asked in cross-examination. ▸ **'cross-'questioning** *n*

cross-refer *vb* to refer from one part of something, esp. a book, to another.

cross-reference *n* **1** a reference within a text to another part of the text. ◆ *vb* **2** to cross-refer.

cross relation *n* another term (esp. U.S.) for **false relation.**

Cross River *n* a state of SE Nigeria, on the Gulf of Guinea. Capital: Calabar. Pop.: 2 085 926 (1995 est.). Area: 20 156 sq. km (7782 sq. miles). Former name (until 1976): **South-Eastern State.**

crossroad ('krɒs,rəʊd) *n U.S. and Canadian.* **1** a road that crosses another road. **2** Also called: **'cross,way.** a road that crosses from one main road to another.

crossroads ('krɒs,rəʊdz) *n* (*functioning as sing*) **1** an area or the point at which two or more roads cross each other. **2** the point at which an important choice has to be made (esp. in the phrase **at the crossroads**).

Crossroads care attendant scheme *n Social welfare.* (in Britain) a service providing paid attendants for disabled people who need continuous supervision. [so named because the idea arose out of criticism of the plight of a disabled character in the TV serial *Crossroads*]

crossruff ('krɒs,rʌf) *Bridge, whist.* ◆ *n* **1** the alternate trumping of each other's leads by two partners, or by declarer and dummy. ◆ *vb* **2** (*intr*) to trump alternately in two hands of a partnership.

cross section *n* **1** *Maths.* a plane surface formed by cutting across a solid, esp. perpendicular to its longest axis. **2** a section cut off in this way. **3** the act of cutting anything in this way. **4** a random selection or sample, esp. one regarded as representative: *a cross section of the public.* **5** *Surveying.* a vertical section of a line of ground at right angles to a survey line. **6** *Physics.* a measure of the probability that a collision process will result in a particular reaction. It is expressed by the effective area that one participant presents as a target for the other. ▸ **'cross-'sectional** *adj*

cross-slide *n* the part of a lathe or planing machine on which the tool post is mounted and across which it slides at right angles to the bed of the lathe.

cross-stitch *n* **1** an embroidery stitch made by two stitches forming a cross. **2** embroidery worked with this stitch. ◆ *vb* **3** to embroider (a piece of needlework) with cross-stitch.

crosstalk ('krɒs,tɔ:k) *n* **1** unwanted signals in one channel of a communications system as a result of a transfer of energy from one or more other channels. **2** *Brit.* rapid or witty talk or conversation.

cross-town *adj U.S. and Canadian.* going across or following a route across a town: *a cross-town bus.*

cross training *n* training in two or more sports to improve performance, esp. on one's main sport.

crosstree ('krɒs,tri:) *n Nautical.* either of a pair of wooden or metal braces on the head of a mast to support the topmast, etc.

cross vine *n* a woody bignoniaceous vine, *Bignonia capreolata,* of the south-eastern U.S., having large trumpet-shaped reddish flowers.

crosswalk ('krɒs,wɔ:k) *n* the U.S. and Canadian name for **pedestrian crossing.**

crosswind ('krɒs,wɪnd) *n* a wind that blows at right angles to the direction of travel.

cross wires *pl n* another name for **cross hairs.**

crosswise ('krɒs,waɪz) *or* **crossways** ('krɒs,weɪz) *adj, adv* **1** across; transversely. **2** in the shape of a cross.

crossword puzzle ('krɒs,wɜ:d) *n* a puzzle in which the solver deduces words suggested by numbered clues and writes them into corresponding boxes in a grid to form a vertical and horizontal pattern. Sometimes shortened to **crossword.**

crosswort ('krɒs,wɜ:t) *n* a herbaceous perennial Eurasian rubiaceous plant, *Galium cruciata,* with pale yellow flowers and whorls of hairy leaves. Also called: **mugwort.**

crostini (krɒ'sti:ni:) *pl n* pieces of toasted bread served with a savoury topping. [Italian: literally, little crusts]

crotal *or* **crottle** ('krɒtᵊl) *n Scot.* any of various lichens used in dyeing wool, esp. for the manufacture of tweeds. [Gaelic *crotal*]

crotch (krɒtʃ) *n* **1** Also called (Brit.): **crutch. 1a** the angle formed by the inner sides of the legs where they join the human trunk. **1b** the human external genitals or the genital area. **1c** the corresponding part of a pair of trousers, pants, etc. **2** a forked region formed by the junction of two members. **3** a forked pole or stick. [C16: probably variant of CRUTCH] ▸ **crotched** (krɒtʃt) *adj*

crotchet ('krɒtʃɪt) *n* **1** *Music.* a note having the time value of a quarter of a semibreve. Usual U.S. and Canadian name: **quarter note. 2** a small hook or hooklike device. **3** a perverse notion. **4** *Zoology.* a small notched or hooked process, as in an insect. [C14: from Old French *crochet,* literally: little hook, from *croche* hook; see CROCKET]

crotchety ('krɒtʃɪtɪ) *adj* **1** *Informal.* cross; irritable; contrary. **2** full of crotchets. ▸ **'crotchetiness** *n*

croton ('krəʊtᵊn) *n* **1** any shrub or tree of the chiefly tropical euphorbiaceous genus *Croton,* esp. *C. tiglium,* the seeds of which yield croton oil. **2** any of various tropical plants of the related genus *Codiaeum,* esp. *C. variegatum pictum,* a house plant with variegated foliage. [C18: from New Latin, from Greek *krotōn* tick, castor-oil plant (whose berries resemble ticks)]

Croton bug *n U.S.* another name for the **German cockroach.** [C19: named after the *Croton* river, whose water was piped to New York City in 1842]

Crotone (*Italian* kro'to:ne) *n* a town in S Italy, on the coast of Calabria: founded in about 700 B.C. by the Achaeans; chemical works and zinc-smelting. Pop.: 61 326 (1988 est.).

crotonic acid (krəʊ'tɒnɪk) *n* a colourless crystalline insoluble unsaturated carboxylic acid produced by oxidation of crotonaldehyde and used in organic synthesis; *trans*-2-butenoic acid. Formula: $CH_3CH{:}CHCOOH$.

croton oil *n* a yellowish-brown oil obtained from the plant *Croton tiglium,* formerly used as a drastic purgative. See also **croton** (sense 1).

crottle ('krɒtᵊl) *n* a variant spelling of **crotal.**

crouch (kraʊtʃ) *vb* **1** (*intr*) to bend low with the limbs pulled up close together, esp. (of an animal) in readiness to pounce. **2** (*intr*) to cringe, as in humility or fear. **3** (*tr*) to bend (parts of the body), as in humility or fear. ◆ *n* **4** the act of stooping or bending. [C14: perhaps from Old French *crochir* to become bent like a hook, from *croche* hook]

croup[1] (kru:p) *n* a throat condition, occurring usually in children, characterized by a hoarse cough and laboured breathing, resulting from inflammation and partial obstruction of the larynx. [C16 *croup* to cry hoarsely, probably of imitative origin] ▸ **'croupous** *or* **'croupy** *adj*

croup[2] *or* **croupe** (kru:p) *n* the hindquarters of a quadruped, esp. a horse. [C13: from Old French *croupe;* related to German *Kruppe*]

croupier ('kru:pɪə; *French* krupje) *n* a person who deals cards, collects bets, etc., at a gaming table. [C18: literally: one who rides behind another, from French *croupe* CROUP[2]]

crouse (kru:s) *adj Scot. and northern English dialect.* lively, confident, or saucy. [C14 (Scottish and Northern) English: from Middle Low German *krūs* twisted, curled, confused]

croute (kru:t) *n* a small round of toasted bread on which a savoury mixture is served. [from French *croûte* CRUST]

crouton ('kru:tɒn) *n* a small piece of fried or toasted bread, usually served in soup. [French: diminutive of *croûte* CRUST]

crow[1] (krəʊ) *n* **1** any large gregarious songbird of the genus *Corvus,* esp. *C. corone* (**carrion crow**) of Europe and Asia: family *Corvidae.* Other species are the raven, rook, and jackdaw and all have a heavy bill, glossy black plumage, and rounded wings. Related adj: **corvine. 2** any of various other corvine birds, such as the jay, magpie, and nutcracker. **3** any of various similar birds of other families. **4** short for **crowbar. 5 as the crow flies.** as directly as possible. **6 eat crow.** *U.S. and Canadian informal.* to be forced to do something humiliating. **7 stone the crows.** *(interj) Brit. and Austral. slang.* an expression of surprise, dismay, etc. [Old English *crāwa;* related to Old Norse *krāka,* Old High German *krāia,* Dutch *kraai*]

crow[2] (krəʊ) *vb (intr)* **1** (past tense **crowed** *or* **crew**) to utter a shrill squawking sound, as a cock. **2** (often foll. by *over*) to boast one's superiority. **3** (esp. of babies) to utter cries of pleasure. ◆ *n* **4** the act or an instance of crowing. [Old English *crāwan;* related to Old High German *krāen,* Dutch *kraaien*] ▸ **'crower** *n* ▸ **'crowingly** *adv*

Crow (krəʊ) *n* **1** (*pl* **Crows** *or* **Crow**) a member of a North American Indian people living in E Montana. **2** the language of this people, belonging to the Siouan family.

crowbar ('krəʊˌbɑ:) *n* a heavy iron lever with one pointed end, and one forged into a wedge shape.

crowberry ('krəʊbərɪ, -brɪ) *n, pl* **-ries. 1** a low-growing N temperate evergreen shrub, *Empetrum nigrum,* with small purplish flowers and black berry-like fruit: family *Empetraceae.* **2** any of several similar or related plants. **3** the fruit of any of these plants.

crow-bill *n* a type of forceps used to extract bullets, etc., from wounds.

crow blackbird *n* another name for **grackle.**

crowboot ('krəʊˌbu:t) *n* a type of Eskimo boot made of fur and leather.

crowd[1] (kraʊd) *n* **1** a large number of things or people gathered or considered together. **2** a particular group of people, esp. considered as a social or business set: *the crowd from the office.* **3a** (preceded by *the*) the common people; the masses. **3b** *(as modifier): crowd ideas.* ◆ *vb* **4** *(intr)* to gather together in large numbers; throng. **5** *(tr)* to press together into a confined space. **6** *(tr)* to fill to excess; fill by pushing into. **7** *(tr) Informal.* to urge or harass by urging. **8 crowd on sail.** *Nautical.* to hoist as much sail as possible. **9 follow the crowd.** to conform with the majority. [Old English *crūdan;* related to Middle Low German *krūden* to molest, Middle Dutch *crūden* to push, Norwegian *kryda* to swarm] ▸ **'crowded** *adj* ▸ **'crowdedly** *adv* ▸ **'crowdedness** *n* ▸ **'crowder** *n*

crowd[2] (kraʊd) *n Music.* an ancient bowed stringed instrument; crwth. [C13: from Welsh *crwth*]

crowdie ('kraʊdɪ) *n Scot.* **1** a porridge of meal and water; brose. **2** a cheese-like dish made by straining the whey from soured milk and beating up the remaining curd with salt. [C17: of unknown origin]

crowd puller *n Informal.* a person, object, event, etc., that attracts a large audience.

crowfoot ('krəʊˌfʊt) *n, pl* **-foots. 1** any of several plants of the genus *Ranunculus,* such as *R. sceleratus* and *R. aquatilis* (**water crowfoot**) that have yellow or white flowers and divided leaves resembling the foot of a crow. See also **buttercup. 2** any of various other plants that have leaves or other parts resembling a bird's foot. **3** *pl* **-feet.** *Nautical.* a bridle-like arrangement of lines rove through a wooden block or attached to a ring for supporting an awning from above. **4** *pl* **-feet.** *Military.* another name for **caltrop.**

crown (kraʊn) *n* **1** an ornamental headdress denoting sovereignty, usually made of gold embedded with precious stones. **2** a wreath or garland for the head, awarded as a sign of victory, success, honour, etc. **3** (*sometimes cap.*) monarchy or kingship. **4** an award, distinction, or title, given as an honour to reward merit, victory, etc. **5** anything resembling or symbolizing a crown, such as a sergeant major's badge or a heraldic bearing. **6a** *History.* a coin worth 25 pence (five shillings). **6b** any of several continental coins, such as the krona or krone, with a name meaning *crown.* **7** the top or summit of something, esp. of a rounded object: *crown of a hill; crown of the head.* **8** the centre part of a road, esp. when it is cambered. **9** *Botany.* **9a** the leaves and upper branches of a tree. **9b** the junction of root and stem, usually at the level of the ground. **9c** another name for **corona** (sense 6). **10** *Zoology.* **10a** the cup and arms of a crinoid, as distinct from the stem. **10b** the crest of a bird. **11** the outstanding quality, achievement, state, etc.: *the crown of his achievements.* **12a** the enamel-covered part of a tooth above the gum. **12b artificial crown.** a substitute crown, usually of gold, porcelain, or acrylic resin, fitted over a decayed or broken tooth. **13** the part of a cut gem above the girdle. **14** *Horology.* a knurled knob for winding a watch. **15** the part of an anchor where the arms are joined to the shank. **16** the highest part of an arch or vault. **17** a standard size of printing paper, 15 by 20 inches. ◆ *vb (tr)* **18** to put a crown on the head of, symbolically vesting with royal title, powers, etc. **19** to place a crown, wreath, garland, etc., on the head of. **20** to place something on or over the head or top of: *he crowned the pie with cream.* **21** to confer a title, dignity, or reward upon: *he crowned her best cook.* **22** to form the summit or topmost part of: *the steeple crowned the tower.* **23** to cap or put the finishing touch to a series of events: *to crown it all it rained, too.* **24** *Draughts.* to promote (a draught) to a king by placing another draught on top of it, as after reaching the end of the board. **25** to attach a crown to (a tooth). **26** *Slang.* to hit over the head. [C12: from Old French *corone,* from Latin *corōna* wreath, crown, from Greek *korōnē* crown, something curved] ▸ **'crownless** *adj*

Crown (kraʊn) *n* (*sometimes not cap.;* usually preceded by *the*) **1** the sovereignty or realm of a monarch. **2a** the government of a constitutional monarchy. **2b** *(as modifier): Crown property.*

Crown Agent *n* **1** a member of a board appointed by the Minister for Overseas Development to provide financial, commercial, and professional services for a number of overseas governments and international bodies. **2** *Scot.* (*not caps.*) a solicitor dealing with criminal prosecutions.

crown and anchor *n* a game played with dice marked with crowns and anchors.

Crown attorney *n Canadian.* a lawyer who acts for the Crown, esp. as prosecutor in a criminal court.

crown cap *n Brit.* an airtight metal seal crimped on the top of most bottled beers, ciders, mineral waters, etc.

crown colony *n* a British colony whose administration and legislature is controlled by the Crown.

crown court *n English law.* a court of criminal jurisdiction holding sessions in towns throughout England and Wales at which circuit judges hear and determine cases.

Crown Derby *n* **1** a type of porcelain manufactured at Derby from 1784–1848. **2** *Trademark.* shortened form of Royal Crown Derby.

crowned head *n* a monarch: *the crowned heads of Europe.*

crowner ('kraʊnə) *n* a promotional label consisting of a shaped printed piece of card or paper attached to a product on display.

crown ether *n Chem.* a type of cyclic ether consisting of a ring of carbon and oxygen atoms, with two carbon atoms between each oxygen atom.

crown glass *n* **1** another name for **optical crown. 2** an old form of window glass made by blowing a globe and spinning it until it formed a flat disc.

crown graft *n Horticulture.* a type of graft in which the scion is inserted at the crown of the stock.

crown green *n* a type of bowling green in which the sides are lower than the middle.

crown imperial *n* a liliaceous garden plant, *Fritillaria imperialis,* with a cluster of leaves and orange bell-shaped flowers at the top of the stem.

crowning ('kraʊnɪŋ) *n Obstetrics.* the stage of labour when the infant's head is passing through the vaginal opening.

crown-jewel option *n Informal.* an option given by a company subjected to an unwelcome takeover bid to a friendly firm, allowing this firm to buy one or more of its best businesses if the bid succeeds.

crown jewels *pl n* the jewellery, including the regalia, used by a sovereign on a state occasion.

crownland ('kraʊnˌlænd) *n* a large administrative division of the former empire of Austria-Hungary.

crown land *n* **1** (in the United Kingdom) land belonging to the Crown. **2** public land in some dominions of the Commonwealth.

crown lens *n* a lens made of optical crown, esp. the optical-crown part of a compound achromatic lens.

Crown Office *n* (in England) an office of the Queen's Bench Division of the High Court that is responsible for administration and where actions are entered for trial.

crown-of-thorns *n* **1** a starfish, *Acanthaster planci,* that has a spiny test and feeds on living coral in coral reefs. **2** Also called: **Christ's thorn.** a thorny euphorbiaceous Madagascan shrub, *Euphorbia splendens,* cultivated as a hedging shrub or pot plant, having flowers with scarlet bracts.

crownpiece ('kraʊnˌpi:s) *n* **1** the piece forming or fitting the top of something. **2** the strap of a bridle that goes over a horse's head behind the ears.

crown prince *n* the male heir to a sovereign throne.

crown princess *n* **1** the wife of a crown prince. **2** the female heir to a sovereign throne.

Crown Prosecution Service *n* (in England and Wales) an independent prosecuting body, established in 1986, that decides whether cases brought by the police should go to the courts: headed by the Director of Public Prosecutions. Compare **procurator fiscal.** Abbrev.: **CPS.**

Crown prosecutor *n Canadian.* another name for **Crown attorney.**

crown roast *n* a roast consisting of ribs of lamb or pork arranged in a crown shape.

crown saw *n* a hollow cylinder with cutting teeth forming a rotary saw for trepanning.

crown vetch *n* a trailing papilionaceous European plant, *Coronilla varia,* with clusters of white or pink flowers: cultivated in North America as a border plant. Also called (U.S.): **axseed** ('æksi:d).

crown wheel *n* **1** *Horology.* the wheel next to the winding knob that has one set of teeth at right angles to the other. **2** the larger of the two gears in a bevel gear.

crownwork ('kraʊnˌwɜ:k) *n* **1a** the manufacture of artificial crowns for teeth. **1b** such an artificial crown or crowns. **2** *Fortifications.* a covering or protective outwork.

crow's-foot *n, pl* **-feet. 1** (*often pl*) a wrinkle at the outer corner of the eye. **2** an embroidery stitch with three points, used esp. as a finishing at the end of a seam. **3** a system of diverging short ropes to distribute the pull of a single rope, used esp. in balloon and airship riggings.

crow's-nest *n* a lookout platform high up on a ship's mast.

crow step *n* another term for **corbie-step.**

Croydon ('krɔɪdᵊn) *n* a borough in S Greater London (since 1965): formerly important for its airport (1915–59). Pop.: 326 800 (1994 est.). Area: 87 sq. km (33 sq. miles).

croze (krəuz) *n* **1** the recess cut at the end of a barrel or cask to receive the head. **2** a tool for cutting this recess. [C17: probably from Old French *crues* a hollow]

crozier ('krəuʒə) *n* a variant spelling of **crosier**.

CRP (in India) *abbrev. for* Central Reserve Police.

CRT *abbrev. for:* **1** cathode-ray tube. **2** (in Britain) composite rate tax: a system of paying interest to savers by which a rate of tax for a period, such as one financial year, is determined in advance, and interest is paid net of tax which is deducted at source.

cru (kru:; *French* kry) *n Winemaking.* (in France) a vineyard, group of vineyards, or wine-producing region. [from French: production, from *crû*, past participle of *croître* to grow]

cruces ('kru:si:z) *n* a plural of **crux**.

crucial ('kru:ʃəl) *adj* **1** involving a final or supremely important decision or event; decisive; critical. **2** *Informal.* very important. **3** *Slang.* very good. [C18: from French, from Latin *crux* CROSS] ▸ **'crucially** *adv*

crucian ('kru:ʃən) *n* a European cyprinid fish, *Carassius carassius,* with a dark-green back, a golden-yellow undersurface, and reddish dorsal and tail fins: an aquarium fish. [C18: from Low German *Karusse*]

cruciate ('kru:ʃɪɪt, -ˌeɪt) *adj* shaped or arranged like a cross: *cruciate petals.* [C17: from New Latin *cruciātus,* from Latin *crux* cross] ▸ **'cruciately** *adv*

crucible ('kru:sɪbᵊl) *n* **1** a vessel in which substances are heated to high temperatures. **2** the hearth at the bottom of a metallurgical furnace in which the metal collects. **3** a severe trial or test. [C15 *corusible,* from Medieval Latin *crūcibulum* night lamp, crucible, of uncertain origin]

Crucible ('kru:sɪbᵊl) *n* **the.** a Sheffield theatre, venue of the annual world professional snooker championship.

crucible steel *n* a high-quality steel made by melting wrought iron, charcoal, and other additives in a crucible.

crucifer ('kru:sɪfə) *n* **1** any plant of the family *Cruciferae,* having a corolla of four petals arranged like a cross and a fruit called a siliqua. The family includes the brassicas, mustard, cress, and wallflower. **2** a person who carries a cross. [C16: from Late Latin, from Latin *crux* cross + *ferre* to carry]

cruciferous (kru:'sɪfərəs) *adj* of, relating to, or belonging to the plant family *Cruciferae.* See **crucifer** (sense 1).

crucifix ('kru:sɪfɪks) *n* a cross or image of a cross with a figure of Christ upon it. [C13: from Church Latin *crucifixus* the crucified Christ, from *crucifīgere* to CRUCIFY]

crucifixion (ˌkru:sɪ'fɪkʃən) *n* a method of putting to death by nailing or binding to a cross, normally by the hands and feet, which was widespread in the ancient world.

Crucifixion (ˌkru:sɪ'fɪkʃən) *n* **1** (usually preceded by *the*) the crucifying of Christ at Calvary, regarded by Christians as the culminating redemptive act of his ministry. **2** a picture or representation of this.

cruciform ('kru:sɪˌfɔ:m) *adj* **1** shaped like a cross. ◆ *n* **2** a geometric curve, shaped like a cross, that has four similar branches asymptotic to two mutually perpendicular pairs of lines. Equation: $x^2y^2 - a^2x^2 - a^2y^2 = 0$, where $x = y = \pm a$ are the four lines. [C17: from Latin *crux* cross + -FORM] ▸ **'cruciˌformly** *adv*

crucify ('kru:sɪˌfaɪ) *vb* **-fies, -fying, -fied.** (*tr*) **1** to put to death by crucifixion. **2** *Slang.* to defeat, ridicule, etc., totally: *the critics crucified his performance.* **3** to treat very cruelly; torment. **4** to subdue (passion, lust, etc.); mortify. [C13: from Old French *crucifier,* from Late Latin *crucifīgere* to crucify, to fasten to a cross, from Latin *crux* cross + *fīgere* to fasten] ▸ **'cruciˌfier** *n*

cruck (krʌk) *n* one of a pair of curved wooden timbers supporting the end of the roof in certain types of building. [C19: variant of CROOK (n)]

crud (krʌd) *Slang.* ◆ *n* **1** a sticky substance, esp. when dirty and encrusted. **2** an undesirable residue from a process, esp. one inside a nuclear reactor. **3** something or someone that is worthless, disgusting, or contemptible. **4** (sometimes preceded by *the*) a disease; rot. ◆ *interj* **5** an expression of disgust, disappointment, etc. [C14: earlier form of CURD] ▸ **'cruddy** *adj*

crude (kru:d) *adj* **1** lacking taste, tact, or refinement; vulgar: *a crude joke.* **2** in a natural or unrefined state. **3** lacking care, knowledge, or skill: *a crude sketch.* **4** (*prenominal*) stark; blunt: *the crude facts.* **5** (of statistical data) unclassified or unanalysed. **6** *Archaic.* unripe. ◆ *n* **7** short for **crude oil.** [C14: from Latin *crūdus* bloody, raw; related to Latin *cruor* blood] ▸ **'crudely** *adv* ▸ **'crudity** *or* **'crudeness** *n*

Cruden ('kru:dᵊn) *n* **Alexander.** 1701–70, Scottish bookseller and compiler of a well-known biblical concordance (1737).

crude oil *n* petroleum before it has been refined.

crudités (ˌkru:dɪ'teɪ) *pl n* a selection of raw vegetables, usually cut into strips or small chunks and served, with a dip, as an hors d'oeuvre. [C20: from French, plural of *crudité,* literally: rawness]

cruel ('kru:əl) *adj* **1** causing or inflicting pain without pity: *a cruel teacher.* **2** causing pain or suffering: *a cruel accident.* [C13: from Old French, from Latin *crūdēlis,* from *crūdus* raw, bloody] ▸ **'cruelly** *adv* ▸ **'cruelness** *n*

cruelty ('kru:əltɪ) *n, pl* **-ties. 1** deliberate infliction of pain or suffering. **2** the quality or characteristic of being cruel. **3** a cruel action. **4** *Law.* conduct that causes danger to life or limb or a threat to bodily or mental health, on proof of which a decree of divorce may be granted.

cruelty-free *adj* (of a cosmetic or other product) developed without being tested on animals.

cruet ('kru:ɪt) *n* **1** a small container for holding pepper, salt, vinegar, oil, etc., at table. **2** a set of such containers, esp. on a stand. **3** *Christianity.* either of a pair of small containers for the wine and water used in the Eucharist. [C13: from Anglo-French, diminutive of Old French *crue* flask, of Germanic origin; compare Old Saxon *krūka,* Old English *crūce* pot]

Cruft (krʌft) *n* **Charles.** 1852–1938, British dog breeder, who organized the first (1886) of the annual dog shows known as Cruft's.

Cruikshank ('krʊkˌʃæŋk) *n* **George.** 1792–1878, English illustrator and caricaturist.

cruise (kru:z) *vb* **1** (*intr*) to make a trip by sea in a liner for pleasure, usually calling at a number of ports. **2** to sail or travel over (a body of water) for pleasure in a yacht, cruiser, etc. **3** (*intr*) to search for enemy vessels in a warship. **4** (*intr*) (of a vehicle, aircraft, or vessel) to travel at a moderate and efficient speed. **5** (*intr*) *Informal.* to search the streets or other public places for a sexual partner. ◆ *n* **6** an act or instance of cruising, esp. a trip by sea. [C17: from Dutch *kruisen* to cross, from *cruis* CROSS; related to French *croiser* to cross, cruise, Spanish *cruzar,* German *kreuzen*]

cruise control *n* a system in a road vehicle that automatically maintains a selected speed until cancelled.

cruise missile *n* an air-breathing low-flying subsonic missile that is continuously powered and guided throughout its flight and carries a warhead.

cruiser ('kru:zə) *n* **1** a high-speed, long-range warship of medium displacement, armed with medium calibre weapons or missiles. **2** Also called: **cabin cruiser.** a pleasure boat, esp. one that is power-driven and has a cabin. **3** any person or thing that cruises. **4** *Boxing.* short for **cruiserweight** (see **light heavyweight**).

cruiserweight ('kru:zəˌweɪt) *n Boxing.* another term (esp. Brit.) for **light heavyweight.**

cruiseway ('kru:zˌweɪ) *n* a canal used for recreational purposes.

cruizie, cruzie, *or* **crusie** ('kru:zɪ) *n Scot.* an oil lamp. [C18: perhaps from *cruset* crucible, from French *creuset*]

cruller *or* **kruller** ('krʌlə) *n U.S. and Canadian.* a light sweet ring-shaped cake, fried in deep fat. [C19: from Dutch *krulle,* from *krullen* to CURL]

crumb (krʌm) *n* **1** a small fragment of bread, cake, or other baked foods. **2** a small piece or bit: *crumbs of information.* **3** the soft inner part of bread. **4** *Slang.* a contemptible person. ◆ *vb* **5** (*tr*) to prepare or cover (food) with breadcrumbs. **6** to break into small fragments. ◆ *adj* **7** (esp. of pie crusts) made with a mixture of biscuit crumbs, sugar, etc. [Old English *cruma;* related to Middle Dutch *krome,* Middle High German *krūme,* Latin *grūmus* heap of earth] ▸ **'crumber** *n*

crumble ('krʌmbᵊl) *vb* **1** to break or be broken into crumbs or fragments. **2** (*intr*) to fall apart or away: *his resolution crumbled.* ◆ *n* **3** *Brit.* a baked pudding consisting of a crumbly mixture of flour, fat, and sugar over stewed fruit: *apple crumble.* [C16: variant of *crimble,* of Germanic origin; compare Low German *krömeln,* Dutch *kruimelen*]

crumbly ('krʌmblɪ) *adj* **-blier, -bliest.** easily crumbled or crumbling. ▸ **'crumbliness** *n*

crumbs (krʌmz) *interj Slang.* an expression of dismay or surprise. [C20: euphemistic for *Christ!*]

crumby ('krʌmɪ) *adj* **crumbier, crumbiest. 1** full of or littered with crumbs. **2** soft, like the inside of bread. **3** a variant spelling of **crummy**[1].

crumhorn *or* **krummhorn** ('krʌmˌhɔ:n) *n* a medieval woodwind instrument of bass pitch, consisting of an almost cylindrical tube curving upwards and blown through a double reed covered by a pierced cap. [C17 *cromorne, krumhorn,* from German *Krummhorn:* curved horn]

Crummock Water ('krʌmək) *n* a lake in NW England, in Cumbria in the Lake District. Length: 4 km (2.5 miles).

crummy[1] ('krʌmɪ) *adj* **-mier, -miest.** *Slang.* **1** of little value; inferior; contemptible. **2** unwell or depressed: *to feel crummy.* [C19: variant spelling of CRUMBY]

crummy[2] ('krʌmɪ) *n, pl* **-mies.** *Canadian.* a lorry that carries loggers to work from their camp. [probably originally meaning: makeshift camp, from CRUMMY[1]]

crump (krʌmp) *vb* **1** (*intr*) to thud or explode with a loud dull sound. **2** (*tr*) to bombard with heavy shells. ◆ *n* **3** a crunching, thudding, or exploding noise. [C17: of imitative origin]

crumpet ('krʌmpɪt) *n Chiefly Brit.* **1** a light soft yeast cake full of small holes on the top side, eaten toasted and buttered. **2** (in Scotland) a large flat sweetened cake made of batter. **3** *Slang.* women collectively. **4 a piece of crumpet.** *Slang.* a sexually desirable woman. **5 not worth a crumpet.** *Austral. slang.* utterly worthless. [C17: of uncertain origin]

crumple ('krʌmpᵊl) *vb* **1** (when *intr,* often foll. by *up*) to collapse or cause to collapse: *his courage crumpled.* **2** (when *tr,* often foll. by *up*) to crush or cause to be crushed so as to form wrinkles or creases. **3** (*intr*) to shrink; shrivel. ◆ *n* **4** a loose crease or wrinkle. [C16: from obsolete *crump* to bend; related to Old High German *krimpfan* to wrinkle, Old Norse *kreppa* to contract] ▸ **'crumply** *adj*

crumple zones *pl n* parts of a motor vehicle, at the front and the rear, that are designed to crumple in a collision, thereby absorbing the impact.

crunch (krʌntʃ) *vb* **1** to bite or chew (crisp foods) with a crushing or crackling sound. **2** to make or cause to make a crisp or brittle sound: *the snow crunched beneath his feet.* ◆ *n* **3** the sound or act of crunching. **4 the crunch.** *Informal.* the critical moment or situation. ◆ *adj* **5** *Informal.* critical; decisive: *crunch time.* ◆ Also: **craunch.** [C19: changed (through influence of MUNCH) from earlier *craunch,* of imitative origin] ▸ **'crunchable** *adj* ▸ **'crunchy** *adj* ▸ **'crunchily** *adv* ▸ **'crunchiness** *n*

crunchie ('krʌntʃɪ) *n S. African derogatory slang.* another name for an **Afrikaner.**

crunode ('kru:nəud) *n* a point at which two branches of a curve intersect, each branch having a distinct tangent; node. [C19: *cru-* from Latin *crux* cross + NODE]

cruor (kruɔ:) *n, pl* **cruores** ('kruɔ:ri:z). *Med.* a blood clot.

crupper ('krʌpə) *n* **1** a strap from the back of a saddle that passes under the horse's tail to prevent the saddle from slipping forwards. **2** the part of the horse's rump behind the saddle. [C13: from Old French *crupiere,* from *crupe* CROUP[2]]

crura ('krʊərə) *n* the plural of **crus.**

crural ('krʊərəl) *adj* of or relating to the leg or thigh. [C16: from Latin *crūrālis,* from *crūs* leg, shin]

crus (krʌs) *n, pl* **crura** ('krʊərə). **1** *Anatomy.* the leg, esp. from the knee to the foot. **2** (*usually pl*) leglike parts or structures. [C17: from Latin: leg]

crusade (kruː'seɪd) *n* **1** (*often cap.*) any of the military expeditions undertaken in the 11th, 12th, and 13th centuries by the Christian powers of Europe to recapture the Holy Land from the Muslims. **2** (formerly) any holy war undertaken on behalf of a religious cause. **3** a vigorous and dedicated action or movement in favour of a cause. ◆ *vb* (*intr*) **4** to campaign vigorously for something. **5** to go on a crusade. [C16: from earlier *croisade,* from Old French *crois* cross, from Latin *crux;* influenced also by Spanish *cruzada,* from *cruzar* to take up the cross] ▸ **cru'sader** *n*

crusado (kruː'seɪdəʊ) *or* **cruzado** (kruː'zeɪdəʊ; *Portuguese* kru'zaːdu) *n, pl* **-does** *or* **-dos** (-dəʊz; *Portuguese* -duʃ). a former gold or silver coin of Portugal bearing on its reverse the figure of a cross. [C16: literally, marked with a cross, from *cruzar* to bear a cross; see CRUSADE]

cruse (kruːz) *n* a small earthenware container used, esp. formerly, for liquids. [Old English *crūse;* related to Middle High German *krūse,* Dutch *kroes* jug]

crush (krʌʃ) *vb* (*mainly tr*) **1** to press, mash, or squeeze so as to injure, break, crease, etc. **2** to break or grind (rock, ore, etc.) into small particles. **3** to put down or subdue, esp. by force: *to crush a rebellion.* **4** to extract (juice, water, etc.) by pressing: *to crush the juice from a lemon.* **5** to oppress harshly. **6** to hug or clasp tightly: *he crushed her to him.* **7** to defeat or humiliate utterly, as in argument or by a cruel remark. **8** (*intr*) to crowd; throng. **9** (*intr*) to become injured, broken, or distorted by pressure. ◆ *n* **10** a dense crowd, esp. at a social occasion. **11** the act of crushing; pressure. **12** a drink or pulp prepared by or as if by crushing fruit: *orange crush.* **13** *Informal.* **13a** an infatuation: *she had a crush on him.* **13b** the person with whom one is infatuated. [C14: from Old French *croissir,* of Germanic origin; compare Gothic *kriustan* to gnash; see CRUNCH] ▸ **'crushable** *adj* ▸ **,crusha'bility** *n* ▸ **'crusher** *n*

crush bar *n* a bar at a theatre for serving drinks during the intervals of a play.

crush barrier *n* a barrier erected to separate sections of large crowds in order to prevent crushing.

crusie ('kruːzɪ) *n* a variant spelling of **cruizie.**

Crusoe ('kruːsəʊ, -zəʊ) *n* **Robinson.** See **Robinson Crusoe.**

crust (krʌst) *n* **1a** the hard outer part of bread. **1b** a piece of bread consisting mainly of this. **2** the baked shell of a pie, tart, etc. **3** any hard or stiff outer covering or surface: *a crust of ice.* **4** the solid outer shell of the earth, with an average thickness of 30–35 km in continental regions and 5 km beneath the oceans, forming the upper part of the lithosphere and lying immediately above the mantle, from which it is separated by the Mohorovičić discontinuity. See also **sial, sima. 5** the dry covering of a skin sore or lesion; scab. **6** a layer of acid potassium tartrate deposited by some wine, esp. port, on the inside of the bottle. **7** the hard outer layer of such organisms as lichens and crustaceans. **8** *Slang.* impertinence. **9** *Brit., Austral., and N.Z. slang.* a living (esp. in the phrase **earn a crust**). ◆ *vb* **10** to cover with or acquire a crust. **11** to form or be formed into a crust. [C14: from Latin *crūsta* hard surface, rind, shell]

crustacean (krʌ'steɪʃən) *n* **1** any arthropod of the mainly aquatic class *Crustacea,* typically having a carapace hardened with lime and including the lobsters, crabs, shrimps, woodlice, barnacles, copepods, and water fleas. ◆ *adj also* **crustaceous. 2** of, relating to, or belonging to the *Crustacea.* [C19: from New Latin *crūstāceus* hard-shelled, from Latin *crūsta* shell, CRUST]

crustaceous (krʌ'steɪʃəs) *adj* **1** forming, resembling, or possessing a surrounding crust or shell. **2** *Zoology.* another word for **crustacean** (sense 2).

crustal ('krʌstᵊl) *adj* of or relating to the earth's crust.

crustose ('krʌstəʊs) *adj Biology.* having a crustlike appearance: *crustose lichens.*

crusty ('krʌstɪ) *adj* **crustier, crustiest. 1** having or characterized by a crust, esp. having a thick crust. **2** having a rude or harsh character or exterior; surly; curt: *a crusty remark.* ◆ *n, pl* **crusties. 3** *Slang.* a dirty type of punk or hippy whose lifestyle involves travelling and squatting. ▸ **'crustily** *adv* ▸ **'crustiness** *n*

crutch (krʌtʃ) *n* **1** a long staff of wood or metal having a rest for the armpit, for supporting the weight of the body. **2** something that supports or sustains: *a crutch to the economy.* **3** *Brit.* another word for **crotch** (sense 1). **4** *Nautical.* **4a** a forked support for a boom or oar, etc. **4b** a brace for reinforcing the frames at the stern of a wooden vessel. ◆ *vb* **5** (*tr*) to support or sustain (a person or thing) as with a crutch. **6** *Austral. and N.Z. slang.* to clip (wool) from the hindquarters of a sheep. [Old English *crycc;* related to Old High German *krucka,* Old Norse *krykkja;* see CROSIER, CROOK]

Crutched Friar (krʌtʃt, 'krʌtʃɪd) *n* a member of a mendicant order, suppressed in 1656. [C16: *crutched,* variant of *crouched,* literally: crossed, referring to the cross worn on their habits]

crutchings ('krʌtʃɪŋz) *pl n Austral. and N.Z.* the wool clipped from a sheep's hindquarters.

crux (krʌks) *n, pl* **cruxes** *or* **cruces** ('kruːsiːz). **1** a vital or decisive stage, point, etc. (often in the phrase **the crux of the matter**). **2** a baffling problem or difficulty. **3** *Mountaineering.* the most difficult and often decisive part of a climb or pitch. **4** a rare word for **cross.** [C18: from Latin: cross]

Crux (krʌks) *n, Latin genitive* **Crucis** ('kruːsɪs). the more formal name for the **Southern Cross.**

crux ansata (æn'seɪtə) *n, pl* **cruces ansatae** (æn'seɪtiː). another term for **ankh.** [New Latin, literally: cross with a handle]

Cruyff (krɔɪf; *Dutch* krœjf) *n* **Johan** (joː'hɑn). born 1947, Dutch footballer: one of the world's leading strikers; played for Ajax of Amsterdam (1965–73) and Barcelona (1973–78); captained the Dutch team in the 1974 World Cup.

cruzado (kruː'zeɪdəʊ; *Portuguese* kru'zaːdu) *n, pl* **-does** *or* **-dos** (-dəʊz; *Portuguese* -duʃ). **1** a former standard monetary unit of Brazil, replaced by the cruzeiro. **2** another name for **crusado.** [C16: literally marked with a cross, from *cruzar* to bear a cross; see CRUSADE]

cruzeiro (kruː'zɛərəʊ; *Portuguese* kru'zeiru) *n, pl* **-ros** (-rəʊz; *Portuguese* -ruʃ). a former monetary unit of Brazil, replaced by the cruzeiro real. [Portuguese: from *cruz* CROSS]

cruzeiro real *n* a former monetary unit of Brazil, replaced by the **real**[3] (sense 1).

cruzie ('kruːzɪ) *n* a variant spelling of **cruizie.**

crwth (kruːθ) *n* an ancient stringed instrument of Celtic origin similar to the cithara but bowed in later types. [Welsh; compare Middle Irish *crott* harp]

cry (kraɪ) *vb* **cries, crying, cried. 1** (*intr*) to utter inarticulate sounds, esp. when weeping; sob. **2** (*intr*) to shed tears; weep. **3** (*intr;* usually foll. by *out*) to scream or shout in pain, terror, etc. **4** (*tr;* often foll. by *out*) to utter or shout (words of appeal, exclamation, fear, etc.). **5** (*intr;* often foll. by *out*) (of animals, birds, etc.) to utter loud characteristic sounds. **6** (*tr*) to hawk or sell by public announcement: *to cry newspapers.* **7** to announce (something) publicly or in the streets. **8** (*intr;* foll. by *for*) to clamour or beg. **9** *Scot.* to call. **10 cry for the moon.** to desire the unattainable. **11 cry one's eyes** *or* **heart out.** to weep bitterly. **12 cry quits** (*or* **mercy**). to give up a task, fight, etc. ◆ *n, pl* **cries. 13** the act or sound of crying; a shout, exclamation, scream, or wail. **14** the characteristic utterance of an animal or bird: *the cry of gulls.* **15** *Scot.* a call. **16** *Archaic.* an oral announcement, esp. one made by town criers. **17** a fit of weeping. **18** *Hunting.* the baying of a pack of hounds hunting their quarry by scent. **19** a pack of hounds. **20 a far cry. 20a** a long way. **20b** something very different. **21 in full cry.** (esp. of a pack of hounds) in hot pursuit of a quarry. ◆ See also **cry down, cry off, cry out, cry up.** [C13: from Old French *crier,* from Latin *quirītāre* to call for help]

crybaby ('kraɪ,beɪbɪ) *n, pl* **-bies.** a person, esp. a child, given to frequent crying or complaint.

cry down *vb* (*tr, adv*) **1** to belittle; disparage. **2** to silence by making a greater noise: *to cry down opposition.*

crying ('kraɪɪŋ) *adj* (*prenominal*) notorious; lamentable (esp. in the phrase **crying shame**).

cryo- *combining form.* indicating low temperature; frost, cold, or freezing: *cryogenics; cryosurgery.* [from Greek *kruos* icy cold, frost]

cryobiology (,kraɪəʊbaɪ'ɒlədʒɪ) *n* the branch of biology concerned with the study of the effects of very low temperatures on organisms. ▸ **,cryobi'ologist** *n*

cryocable (,kraɪəʊ'keɪbᵊl) *n* a highly conducting electrical cable cooled with a refrigerant such as liquid nitrogen.

cry off *vb* (*intr*) *Informal.* to withdraw from or cancel (an agreement or arrangement).

cryogen ('kraɪədʒən) *n* a substance used to produce low temperatures; a freezing mixture.

cryogenics (,kraɪə'dʒɛnɪks) *n* (*functioning as sing*) the branch of physics concerned with the production of very low temperatures and the phenomena occurring at these temperatures. ▸ **,cryo'genic** *adj*

cryoglobulin (,kraɪəʊ'glɒbjʊlɪn) *n Med.* an abnormal immunoglobulin, present in the blood in certain diseases, that precipitates below about 10°C, obstructing small blood vessels in the fingers and toes.

cryohydrate (,kraɪəʊ'haɪdreɪt) *n* a crystalline substance containing water and a salt in definite proportions: a eutectic crystallizing below the freezing point of water.

cryolite ('kraɪə,laɪt) *n* a white or colourless mineral consisting of a fluoride of sodium and aluminium in monoclinic crystalline form: used in the production of aluminium, glass, and enamel. Formula: Na_3AlF_6.

cryometer (kraɪ'ɒmɪtə) *n* a thermometer for measuring low temperatures. ▸ **cry'ometry** *n*

cryonics (kraɪ'ɒnɪks) *n* (*functioning as sing*) the practice of freezing a human corpse in the hope of restoring it to life in the future.

cryophilic (,kraɪə'fɪlɪk) *adj Biology.* able to thrive at low temperatures.

cryophyte ('kraɪə,faɪt) *n* an organism, esp. an alga or moss, that grows on snow or ice.

cryoplankton (,kraɪəʊ'plæŋktən) *n* minute organisms, esp. algae, living in ice, snow, or icy water.

cryoprecipitate (,kraɪəʊprɪ'sɪpɪteɪt) *n* a precipitate obtained by controlled thawing of a previously frozen substance. Factor VIII, for treating haemophilia, is often obtained as a cryoprecipitate from frozen blood.

cryoscope ('kraɪə,skəʊp) *n* any instrument used to determine the freezing point of a substance.

cryoscopy (kraɪ'ɒskəpɪ) *n, pl* **-pies.** the determination of freezing points, esp. for the determination of molecular weights by measuring the lowering of the freezing point of a solvent when a known quantity of solute is added. ▸ **cryoscopic** (,kraɪə'skɒpɪk) *adj*

cryostat ('kraɪə,stæt) *n* an apparatus for maintaining a constant low temperature or a vessel in which a substance is stored at a low temperature.

cryosurgery (,kraɪəʊ'sɜːdʒərɪ) *n* surgery involving the local destruction of tissues by quick freezing for therapeutic benefit.

cryotherapy (,kraɪəʊ'θɛrəpɪ) *or* **crymotherapy** (,kraɪməʊ'θɛrəpɪ) *n* medical treatment in which all or part of the body is subjected to cold temperatures, as by means of ice packs.

cryotron ('kraɪə,trɒn) *n* a miniature switch working at the temperature of liquid helium and depending for its action on the production and destruction of superconducting properties in the conductor.

cry out *vb* (*intr, adv*) **1** to scream or shout aloud, esp. in pain, terror, etc. **2** (*often foll. by for*) *Informal.* to demand in an obvious manner: *our inner cities* *are crying out for redevelopment.* **3 for crying out loud.** *Informal.* an exclamation of anger or dismay.

crypt (krɪpt) *n* **1** a cellar, vault, or underground chamber, esp. beneath a church, where it is often used as a chapel, burial place, etc. **2** *Anatomy.* any pitlike recess or depression. **[C18:** from Latin *crypta,* from Greek *kruptē* vault, secret place, from *kruptos* hidden, from *kruptein* to hide**]** ► **'cryptal** *adj*

cryptaesthesia *or U.S.* **cryptesthesia** (ˌkrɪptəsˈθiːzɪə) *n Psychol.* another term for **extrasensory perception.**

cryptanalysis (ˌkrɪptəˈnælɪsɪs) *n* the study of codes and ciphers; cryptography. **[**C20: from CRYPTOGRAPH + ANALYSIS**]** ► **cryptanalytic** (ˌkrɪptænəˈlɪtɪk) *adj* ► **crypt'analyst** *n*

cryptic (ˈkrɪptɪk) *or* **cryptical** *adj* **1** hidden; secret; occult. **2** (esp. of comments, sayings, etc.) obscure in meaning. **3** (of the coloration of animals) tending to conceal by disguising or camouflaging the shape. **[C17:** from Late Latin *crypticus,* from Greek *kruptikos,* from *kruptos* concealed; see CRYPT**]** ► **'cryptically** *adv*

crypto- *or before a vowel* **crypt-** *combining form.* secret, hidden, or concealed: *cryptography; crypto-fascist.* **[**New Latin, from Greek *kruptos* hidden, from *kruptein* to hide**]**

cryptobiont (ˌkrɪptəʊˈbaɪɒnt) *n* any organism that exhibits cryptobiosis.

cryptobiosis (ˌkrɪptəʊbaɪˈəʊsɪs) *n Zoology.* a temporary state in an organism in which metabolic activity is absent or undetectable.

cryptoclastic (ˌkrɪptəʊˈklæstɪk) *adj* (of minerals and rocks) composed of microscopic fragments.

cryptocrystalline (ˌkrɪptəʊˈkrɪstəlaɪn) *adj* (of rocks) composed of crystals that can be distinguished individually only by the use of a polarizing microscope.

cryptogam (ˈkrɪptəʊˌgæm) *n* (in former plant classification schemes) any organism that does not produce seeds, including algae, fungi, mosses, and ferns. Compare **phanerogam. [C19:** from New Latin *Cryptogamia,* from CRYPTO- + Greek *gamos* marriage**]** ► **ˌcrypto'gamic** *or* **cryptogamous** (krɪpˈtɒgəməs) *adj*

cryptogenic (ˌkrɪptəʊˈdʒɛnɪk) *adj* (esp. of diseases) of unknown or obscure origin.

cryptograph (ˈkrɪptəʊˌgræf, -ˌgrɑːf) *n* **1** something written in code or cipher. **2** a code using secret symbols (**cryptograms**). **3** a device for translating text into cipher, or vice versa.

cryptography (krɪpˈtɒgrəfɪ) *or* **cryptology** (krɪpˈtɒlədʒɪ) *n* the science or study of analysing and deciphering codes, ciphers, etc.; cryptanalysis. ► **cryp'tographer, cryp'tographist,** *or* **cryp'tologist** *n* ► **cryptographic** (ˌkrɪptəˈgræfɪk) *or* **ˌcrypto'graphical** *adj* ► **ˌcrypto'graphically** *adv*

cryptomeria (ˌkrɪptəʊˈmɪərɪə) *n* a coniferous tree, *Cryptomeria japonica,* of China and Japan, with curved needle-like leaves and small round cones: family *Taxodiaceae.* **[C19:** from New Latin, from CRYPTO- + Greek *meros* part; so called because the seeds are hidden by scales**]**

cryptometer (krɪpˈtɒmɪtə) *n* an instrument used to determine the opacity of pigments and paints.

cryptophyte (ˈkrɪptəˌfaɪt) *n* any perennial plant that bears its buds below the soil or water surface. ► **cryptophytic** (ˌkrɪptəˈfɪtɪk) *adj*

cryptorchid (krɪpˈtɔːkɪd) *n* **1** an animal or human in which the testes fail to descend into the scrotum. ◆ *adj* **2** denoting or relating to such an individual. **[**from CRYPTO- + *orchid,* from Greek *orkhis* testicle**]** ► **cryp'torchidˌism** *n*

cryptosporidium (ˌkrɪptəʊspɒˈrɪdɪəm) *n* any parasitic sporozoan protozoan of the genus *Cryptosporidium,* species of which are parasites of animals and can be transmitted to humans, causing severe abdominal pain and diarrhoea.

cryptozoic (ˌkrɪptəʊˈzəʊɪk) *adj* (of animals) living in dark places, such as holes, caves, and beneath stones.

Cryptozoic (ˌkrɪptəʊˈzəʊɪk) *adj* **1** of or relating to that part of geological time represented by rocks in which the evidence of life is slight and the life forms are primitive; pre-Phanerozoic. ◆ *n* **2 the.** the Cryptozoic era. ◆ See also **Precambrian.** Compare **Phanerozoic.**

cryptozoite (ˌkrɪptəʊˈzəʊaɪt) *n* a malarial parasite at the stage of development in its host before it enters the red blood cells.

cryptozoology (ˌkrɪptəʊzəʊˈɒlədʒɪ, -zuː-) *n* the study of creatures, such as the Loch Ness monster, whose existence has not been scientifically proved.

cryst. *abbrev. for:* **1** crystalline. **2** Also: **crystall.** crystallography.

crystal (ˈkrɪstᵊl) *n* **1** a piece of solid substance, such as quartz, with a regular shape in which plane faces intersect at definite angles, due to the regular internal structure of its atoms, ions, or molecules. **2** a single grain of a crystalline substance. **3** anything resembling a crystal, such as a piece of cut glass. **4a** a highly transparent and brilliant type of glass, often used in cut-glass tableware, ornaments, etc. **4b** (*as modifier*)*: a crystal chandelier.* **5** something made of or resembling crystal. **6** crystal glass articles collectively. **7** *Electronics.* **7a** a crystalline element used in certain electronic devices as a detector, oscillator, transducer, etc. **7b** (*as modifier*)*: crystal pick-up; crystal detector.* **8** a transparent cover for the face of a watch, usually of glass or plastic. **9** (*modifier*) of or relating to a crystal or the regular atomic arrangement of crystals: *crystal structure; crystal lattice.* ◆ *adj* **10** resembling crystal; transparent: *crystal water.* **[**Old English *cristalla,* from Latin *crystallum,* from Greek *krustallos* ice, crystal, from *krustainein* to freeze**]**

crystal ball *n* the glass globe used in crystal gazing.

crystal class *n Crystallog.* any of 32 possible types of crystals, classified according to their rotational symmetry about axes through a point. Also called: **point group.**

crystal counter *n* an instrument for detecting and measuring the intensity of high-energy radiation, in which particles collide with a crystal and momentarily increase its conductivity.

crystal detector *n Electronics.* a demodulator, used esp. in early radio receivers, consisting of a thin metal wire in point contact with a semiconductor crystal.

crystal form *n Crystallog.* a symmetrical set of planes in space, associated with a crystal, having the same symmetry as the crystal class. Compare **crystal habit.**

crystal gazing *n* **1** the act of staring into a crystal globe (**crystal ball**) supposedly in order to arouse visual perceptions of the future, etc. **2** the act of trying to predict something. ► **crystal gazer** *n*

crystal habit *n Crystallog.* the external shape of a crystal. Compare **crystal form.**

crystal healing *n* (in alternative therapy) the use of the supposed power of crystals to affect the human energy field.

crystal lattice *n* the regular array of points about which the atoms, ions, or molecules composing a crystal are centred.

crystalline (ˈkrɪstəˌlaɪn) *adj* **1** having the characteristics or structure of crystals. **2** consisting of or containing crystals. **3** made of or like crystal; transparent; clear. ► **crystallinity** (ˌkrɪstəˈlɪnɪtɪ) *n*

crystalline lens *n* a biconvex transparent elastic structure in the eye situated behind the iris, serving to focus images on the retina.

crystallite (ˈkrɪstəˌlaɪt) *n* any of the minute rudimentary or imperfect crystals occurring in many glassy rocks. ► **crystallitic** (ˌkrɪstəˈlɪtɪk) *adj*

crystallize, crystalize *or* **crystallise, crystalise** (ˈkrɪstəˌlaɪz) *vb* **1** to form or cause to form crystals; assume or cause to assume a crystalline form or structure. **2** to coat or become coated with sugar: *crystallized fruit.* **3** to give a definite form or expression to (an idea, argument, etc.) or (of an idea, argument, etc.) to assume a recognizable or definite form. ► **'crystalˌlizable, 'crystalˌizable** *or* **'crystalˌlisable, 'crystalˌisable** *adj* ► **ˌcrystalˌliza'bility, ˌcrystalˌiza'bility** *or* **ˌcrystalˌlisa'bility, ˌcrystalˌisa'bility** *n* ► **ˌcrystalli'zation, ˌcrystali'zation** *or* **ˌcrystalli'sation, ˌcrystali'sation** *n* ► **'crystalˌlizer, 'crystalˌizer** *or* **'crystalˌliser, 'crystalˌiser** *n*

crystallo- *or before a vowel* **crystall-** *combining form.* crystal: *crystallography.*

crystallography (ˌkrɪstəˈlɒgrəfɪ) *n* the science concerned with the formation, properties, and structure of crystals. ► **ˌcrystal'lographer** *n* ► **crystallographic** (ˌkrɪstələʊˈgræfɪk) *adj* ► **ˌcrystallo'graphically** *adv*

crystalloid (ˈkrɪstəˌlɔɪd) *adj* **1** resembling or having the appearance or properties of a crystal or crystalloid. ◆ *n* **2** a substance that in solution can pass through a semipermeable membrane. Compare **colloid** (sense 3). **3** *Botany.* any of numerous crystals of protein occurring in certain seeds and other storage organs. ► **ˌcrystal'loidal** *adj*

crystal microphone *n* a microphone that uses a piezoelectric crystal to convert sound energy into electrical energy.

crystal nucleus *n Chem.* the tiny crystal that forms at the onset of crystallization.

Crystal Palace *n* a building of glass and iron designed by Joseph Paxton to house the Great Exhibition of 1851. Erected in Hyde Park, London, it was moved to Sydenham (1852–53): destroyed by fire in 1936.

crystal pick-up *n* a record-player pick-up in which the current is generated by the deformation of a piezoelectric crystal caused by the movements of the stylus.

crystal set *n* an early form of radio receiver having a crystal detector to demodulate the radio signals but no amplifier, therefore requiring earphones.

crystal system *n Crystallog.* any of six, or sometimes seven, classifications of crystals depending on their symmetry. The classes are cubic, tetragonal, hexagonal, orthorhombic, monoclinic, and triclinic. Sometimes an additional system, trigonal, is distinguished, although this is usually included in the hexagonal system. See also **crystal class.**

crystal violet *n* another name for **gentian violet.**

cry up *vb* (*tr, adv*) to praise highly; extol.

Cs *the chemical symbol for* caesium.

CS *abbrev. for:* **1** Also: **cs.** capital stock. **2** chartered surveyor. **3** Christian Science. **4** Christian Scientist. **5** Civil Service. **6** Also: **cs.** Court of Session. **7** (formerly) *international car registration for* Czechoslovakia.

cs. *abbrev. for* case.

CSA (in Britain) *abbrev. for* Child Support Agency.

CSB *abbrev. for* chemical stimulation of the brain.

csc *abbrev. for* cosecant.

CSC *abbrev. for* Civil Service Commission.

CSCE *abbrev. for* (formerly) Conference for Security and Cooperation in Europe.

csch *n* a U.S. form of **cosech.**

CSE (in Britain) *abbrev. for* Certificate of Secondary Education; a series of examinations the first grade of pass of which is an equivalent to a GCE O level.

CSEU *abbrev. for* Confederation of Shipbuilding and Engineering Unions.

CSF *abbrev. for:* **1** *Physiol.* cerebrospinal fluid. **2** *Immunol.* colony-stimulating factor.

CS gas *n* a gas causing tears, salivation, and painful breathing, used in civil disturbances; *ortho*-chlorobenzal malononitrile. Formula: $C_6H_4ClCH{:}C(CN)_2$. **[C20:** from the surname initials of its U.S. inventors, Ben Carson and Roger Staughton**]**

CSIRO (in Australia) *abbrev. for* Commonwealth Scientific and Industrial Research Organization.

CSM (in Britain) *abbrev. for* Company Sergeant-Major.

C-spanner *n* a sickle-shaped spanner having a projection at the end of the curve, used for turning large narrow nuts that have an indentation into which the projection on the spanner fits.

CSR (in Australia) *abbrev. for* Colonial Sugar Refining Company.

CSS (in Britain) *abbrev. for* Certificate in Social Service.

CST *abbrev. for* Central Standard Time.

CSU (in Britain) *abbrev. for* Civil Service Union.
CSV *abbrev. for* Community Service Volunteer.
CSYS (in Scotland) *abbrev. for* Certificate of Sixth Year Studies.
ct *abbrev. for:* **1** cent. **2** court.
CT *abbrev. for:* **1** central time. **2** Connecticut. **3** computerized tomography (see also **CT scanner**).
ct. *abbrev. for* certificate.
CTC (in Britain) *abbrev. for* city technology college.
ctenidium (tɪ'nɪdɪəm) *n, pl* **-ia** (-ɪə). one of the comblike respiratory gills of molluscs. [C19: New Latin, from Greek *ktenidion,* diminutive of *kteis* comb]
ctenoid ('ti:nɔɪd, 'ten-) *adj Biology.* toothed like a comb, as the scales of perches. [C19: from Greek *ktenoeidēs,* from *kteis* comb + *-oeidēs* -OID]
ctenophore ('tɛnəˌfɔ:, 'ti:nə-) *n* any marine invertebrate of the phylum *Ctenophora,* including the sea gooseberry and Venus's-girdle, whose body bears eight rows of fused cilia, for locomotion. Also called: **comb jelly.** [C19: from New Latin *ctenophorus,* from Greek *kteno-, kteis* comb + -PHORE] ▸ **ctenophoran** (tɪ'nɒfərən) *adj, n*
Ctesiphon ('tɛsɪˌfɒn) *n* an ancient city on the River Tigris about 100 km (60 miles) above Babylon. First mentioned in 221 B.C., it was destroyed in the 7th and 8th centuries A.D.
ctn *abbrev. for* cotangent.
CTO *Philately. abbrev. for* cancelled to order (of postage stamps); postmarked in sheets for private sale.
CTR *abbrev. for* Control Traffic Zone: an area established about an aerodrome or airport to afford protection to aircraft entering or leaving the terminal area.
ctr. *abbrev. for* centre.
cts *abbrev. for* cents.
cts. *abbrev. for* certificates.
CT scanner *n* computerized tomography scanner: an X-ray machine that can produce stereographic images. Former name: **CAT scanner.**
CTV *abbrev. for* Canadian Television Network Limited.
Cu *the chemical symbol for* copper. [from Late Latin *cuprum*]
cu. *abbrev. for* cubic.
cub (kʌb) *n* **1** the young of certain animals, such as the lion, bear, etc. **2** a young or inexperienced person. ◆ *vb* **cubs, cubbing, cubbed. 3** to give birth to (cubs). [C16: perhaps from Old Norse *kubbi* young seal; see COB[1]] ▸ **'cubbish** *adj* ▸ **'cubbishly** *adv*
Cub (kʌb) *n* short for **Cub Scout.**
Cuba ('kju:bə) *n* a republic and the largest island in the Caribbean, at the entrance to the Gulf of Mexico: became a Spanish colony after its discovery by Columbus in 1492; gained independence after the Spanish-American War of 1898 but remained subject to U.S. influence until declared a people's republic under Castro in 1960; subject of an international crisis in 1962, when the U.S. blockaded the island in order to compel the Soviet Union to dismantle its nuclear missile base. Sugar comprises about 80 per cent of total exports but the economy has been devastated by loss of trade following the collapse of the Soviet Union and by a U.S. trade embargo. Language: Spanish. Religion: nonreligious majority. Currency: peso. Capital: Havana. Pop.: 11 116 000 (1998 est.). Area: 110 922 sq. km (42 827 sq. miles). ▸ **'Cuban** *adj, n*
cubage ('kju:bɪdʒ) *n* another word for **cubature** (sense 2).
Cuba libre ('kju:bə 'li:brə) *n Chiefly U.S.* a drink of rum, cola, lime juice, and ice. [Spanish, literally: free Cuba, a toast during the Cuban War of Independence]
cubane ('kju:beɪn) *n* **a** a rare octahedral hydrocarbon formed by eight CH groups, each of which is situated at the corner of a cube. Formula: C_8H_8. **b** (*as modifier*): *cubane chemistry.* [C20: from CUBE[1] + -ANE]
Cuban heel *n* a moderately high heel for a shoe or boot.
cubature ('kju:bətʃə) *n* **1** the determination of the cubic contents of something. **2** Also called: **cubage.** cubic contents. [C17: from CUBE[1] + *-ature,* on the model of *quadrature*]
cubbyhole ('kʌbɪˌhəʊl) *n* **1** a small enclosed space or room. **2** any small compartment, such as a pigeonhole. ◆ Often shortened to **cubby** ('kʌbɪ). [C19: from dialect *cub* cattle pen; see COVE[1]]
cube[1] (kju:b) *n* **1** a solid having six plane square faces in which the angle between two adjacent sides is a right angle. **2** the product of three equal factors: the cube of 2 is $2 \times 2 \times 2$ (usually written 2^3). **3** something in the form of a cube: *a bath cube.* ◆ *vb* **4** to raise (a number or quantity) to the third power. **5** (*tr*) to measure the cubic contents of. **6** (*tr*) to make, shape, or cut (something, esp. food) into cubes. **7** (*tr*) *U.S. and Canadian.* to tenderize (meat) by scoring into squares or by pounding with a device which has a surface of metal cubes. [C16: from Latin *cubus* die, cube, from Greek *kubos*] ▸ **'cuber** *n*
cube[2] ('kju:beɪ) *n* **1** any of various tropical American plants, esp. any of the leguminous genus *Lonchocarpus,* the roots of which yield rotenone. **2** an extract from the roots of these plants: a fish poison and insecticide. [American Spanish *cubé,* of unknown origin]
cubeb ('kju:bɛb) *n* **1** a SE Asian treelike piperaceous woody climbing plant, *Piper cubeba,* with brownish berries. **2** the unripe spicy fruit of this plant, dried and used as a stimulant and diuretic and sometimes smoked in cigarettes. [C14: from Old French *cubebe,* from Medieval Latin *cubēba,* from Arabic *kubābah*]
cube root *n* the number or quantity whose cube is a given number or quantity: 2 is the cube root of 8 (usually written $\sqrt[3]{8}$ or $8^{1/3}$).
cubic ('kju:bɪk) *adj* **1** having the shape of a cube. **2a** having three dimensions. **2b** denoting or relating to a linear measure that is raised to the third power: *a cubic metre.* Abbrevs.: **cu., c. 3** *Maths.* of, relating to, or containing a variable to the third power or a term in which the sum of the exponents of the variables is three. **4** Also: **isometric, regular.** *Crystallog.* relating to or belonging to the crystal system characterized by three equal perpendicular axes. The unit cell of cubic crystals is a cube with a lattice point at each corner (**simple cubic**) and one in the cube's centre (**body-centred cubic**), or a lattice point at each corner and one at the centre of each face (**face-centred cubic**). ◆ *n* **5** *Maths.* **5a** a cubic equation, such as $x^3 + x + 2 = 0$. **5b** a cubic term or expression.
cubical ('kju:bɪk^əl) *adj* **1** of or related to volume: *cubical expansion.* **2** shaped like a cube. **3** of or involving the third power. ▸ **'cubically** *adv* ▸ **'cubicalness** *n*
cubicle ('kju:bɪk^əl) *n* a partially or totally enclosed section of a room, as in a dormitory. [C15: from Latin *cubiculum,* from *cubāre* to lie down, lie asleep]
cubic measure *n* a system of units for the measurement of volumes, based on the cubic inch, the cubic centimetre, etc.
cubiculum (kju:'bɪkjʊləm) *n, pl* **-la** (-lə). an underground burial chamber in Imperial Rome, such as those found in the catacombs. [C19: from Latin: CUBICLE]
cubiform ('kju:bɪˌfɔ:m) *adj* having the shape of a cube.
cubism ('kju:bɪzəm) *n* (*often cap.*) a French school of painting, collage, relief, and sculpture initiated in 1907 by Picasso and Braque, which amalgamated viewpoints of natural forms into a multifaceted surface of geometrical planes. ▸ **'cubist** *adj, n* ▸ **cu'bistic** *adj* ▸ **cu'bistically** *adv*
cubit ('kju:bɪt) *n* an ancient measure of length based on the length of the forearm. [C14: from Latin *cubitum* elbow, cubit]
cubital ('kju:bɪt^əl) *adj* of or relating to the forearm.
cuboid ('kju:bɔɪd) *adj also* **cuboidal** (kju:'bɔɪd^əl). **1** shaped like a cube; cubic. **2** of or denoting the cuboid bone. ◆ *n* **3** the cubelike bone of the foot; the outer distal bone of the tarsus. **4** *Maths.* a geometric solid whose six faces are rectangles; rectangular parallelepiped.
Cu-bop ('kju:ˌbɒp) *n Jazz.* music of the 1940s in which Cuban rhythms are combined with bop. Compare **Afro-Cuban.**
cub reporter *n* a trainee reporter on a newspaper.
Cub Scout *or* **Cub** *n* a member of a junior branch (for those aged 8–11 years) of the Scout Association.
Cuchulain, Cuchulainn, *or* **Cuchullain** (ku:'kʌlɪn, kʊ'xʊlɪn) *n Celtic myth.* a legendary hero of Ulster.
cucking stool ('kʌkɪŋ) *n History.* a stool to which suspected witches, scolds, etc., were tied and pelted or ducked into water as a punishment. Compare **ducking stool.** [C13 *cucking stol,* literally: defecating chair, from *cukken* to defecate; compare Old Norse *kúkr* excrement]
cuckold ('kʌkəld) *n* **1** a man whose wife has committed adultery, often regarded as an object of scorn. ◆ *vb* **2** (*tr*) to make a cuckold of. [C13 *cukeweld,* from Old French *cucuault,* from *cucu* CUCKOO; perhaps an allusion to the parasitic cuckoos that lay their eggs in the nests of other birds] ▸ **'cuckoldry** *n*
cuckoo ('kʊku:) *n, pl* **-oos. 1** any bird of the family *Cuculidae,* having pointed wings, a long tail, and zygodactyl feet: order *Cuculiformes.* Many species, including the **European cuckoo** (*Cuculus canorus*), lay their eggs in the nests of other birds and have a two-note call. **2** *Informal.* an insane or foolish person. ◆ *adj* **3** *Informal.* insane or foolish. ◆ *interj* **4** an imitation or representation of the call of a cuckoo. ◆ *vb* **-oos, -ooing, -ooed. 5** (*tr*) to repeat over and over. **6** (*intr*) to make the sound imitated by the word *cuckoo.* [C13: from Old French *cucu,* of imitative origin; related to German *kuckuck,* Latin *cucūlus,* Greek *kokkux*]
cuckoo bee *n* any of several species of parasitic or inquiline bee the queen of which lays her eggs in the nest of the bumblebee or other species, sometimes killing the host queen, leaving her eggs to be raised by the workers of the nest.
cuckoo clock *n* a clock in which a mechanical cuckoo pops out with a sound like a cuckoo's call when the clock strikes.
cuckooflower ('kʊku:ˌflaʊə) *n* another name for **lady's-smock** and **ragged robin.**
cuckoopint ('kʊku:ˌpaɪnt) *n* a European aroid plant, *Arum maculatum,* with arrow-shaped leaves, a spathe marked with purple, a pale purple spadix, and scarlet berries. Also called: **lords-and-ladies,** (chiefly U.S.) **wake-robin.**
cuckoo shrike *n* any Old World tropical songbird of the family *Campephagidae,* typically having a strong notched bill, long rounded tail, and pointed wings. See also **minivet.**
cuckoo spit *n* a white frothy mass on the stems and leaves of many plants, produced by froghopper larvae (**cuckoo spit insects**) which feed on the plant juices. Also called: **frog spit.**
cuculiform (kjʊ'kju:lɪˌfɔ:m) *adj* of, relating to, or belonging to the order *Cuculiformes,* which includes the cuckoos. [from Latin *cucūlus* cuckoo + -FORM]
cucullate ('kju:kəˌleɪt, -lɪt) *adj* shaped like a hood or having a hoodlike part: *cucullate sepals.* [C18: from Late Latin *cucullātus,* from Latin *cucullus* hood, cap] ▸ **'cuculˌlately** *adv*
cucumber ('kju:ˌkʌmbə) *n* **1** a creeping cucurbitaceous plant, *Cucumis sativus,* cultivated in many forms for its edible fruit. Compare **squirting cucumber. 2** the cylindrical fruit of this plant, which has hard thin green rind and white crisp flesh. **3** any of various similar or related plants or their fruits. **4 cool as a cucumber.** very calm; self-possessed. [C14: from Latin *cucumis,* of unknown origin]
cucumber tree *n* **1** any of several American trees or shrubs of the genus *Magnolia,* esp. *M. acuminata,* of E and central North America, having cup-shaped greenish flowers and cucumber-shaped fruits. **2** an E Asian tree, *Averrhoa bilimbi,* with edible fruits resembling small cucumbers: family *Averrhoaceae.* See also **carambola.**
cucurbit (kju:'kɜ:bɪt) *n* any creeping flowering plant of the mainly tropical and subtropical family *Cucurbitaceae,* which includes the pumpkin, cucumber, squashes, and gourds. [C14: from Old French, from Latin *cucurbita* gourd, cup] ▸ **cuˌcurbi'taceous** *adj*
Cúcuta (*Spanish* 'kukuta) *n* a city in E Colombia: commercial centre of a coffee-producing region. Pop.: 589 196 (1997 est.). Official name: **San José de Cúcuta** (san xo'se ðe).
cud (kʌd) *n* **1** partially digested food regurgitated from the first stomach of cattle

and other ruminants to the mouth for a second chewing. **2 chew the cud.** to reflect or think over something. [Old English *cudu,* from *cwidu* what has been chewed; related to Old Norse *kvātha* resin (for chewing), Old High German *quiti* glue, Sanskrit *jatu* rubber]

cudbear ('kʌd,bɛə) *n* another name for **orchil.** [C18: whimsical alteration of *Cuthbert,* the Christian name of Dr Gordon, 18th-century Scot who patented the dye. See CUDDY[2]]

cuddle ('kʌdᵊl) *vb* **1** to hold (another person or thing) close or (of two people, etc.) to hold each other close, as for affection, comfort, or warmth; embrace; hug. **2** (*intr;* foll. by *up*) to curl or snuggle up into a comfortable or warm position. ♦ *n* **3** a close embrace, esp. when prolonged. [C18: of uncertain origin] ▸ **'cuddlesome** *adj* ▸ **'cuddly** *adj*

cuddy[1] ('kʌdɪ) *n, pl* **-dies. 1** a small cabin in a boat. **2** a small room, cupboard, etc. [C17: perhaps from Dutch *kajute;* compare Old French *cahute*]

cuddy[2] *or* **cuddie** ('kʌdɪ) *n, pl* **-dies.** *Dialect, chiefly Scot.* a donkey or horse. [C18: probably from *Cuddy,* nickname for *Cuthbert*]

cuddy[3] ('kʌdɪ) *n* a young coalfish. [C18: of unknown origin]

cudgel ('kʌdʒəl) *n* **1** a short stout stick used as a weapon. **2 take up the cudgels.** (often foll. by *for* or *on behalf of*) to join in a dispute, esp. to defend oneself or another. ♦ *vb* **-els, -elling, -elled** *or U.S.* **-els, -eling, -eled. 3** (*tr*) to strike with a cudgel or similar weapon. **4 cudgel one's brains.** to think hard about a problem. [Old English *cycgel;* related to Middle Dutch *koghele* stick with knob] ▸ **'cudgeller** *n*

cudgerie ('kʌdʒərɪ) *n Austral.* **1** a large tropical rutaceous tree, *Flindersia schottina,* having light-coloured wood. **2** Also called: **pink poplar.** an anacardiaceous rainforest tree, *Euroschinus falcatus.*

Cudlipp ('kʌdlɪp) *n* **Hugh,** Baron. 1913–98, British newspaper editor, a pioneer of tabloid journalism: editorial director of the *Daily Mirror* (1952–63).

cudweed ('kʌd,wiːd) *n* **1** any of various temperate woolly plants of the genus *Gnaphalium,* having clusters of whitish or yellow button-like flowers: family *Compositae* (composites). **2** any of several similar and related plants of the genus *Filago,* esp. *F. germanica.*

Cudworth ('kʌdwəθ) *n* **Ralph.** 1617–88, English philosopher and theologian. His works include *True Intellectual System of the Universe* (1678) and *A Treatise concerning Eternal and Immutable Morality* (1731).

cue[1] (kjuː) *n* **1a** (in the theatre, films, music, etc.) anything spoken or done that serves as a signal to an actor, musician, etc., to follow with specific lines or action. **1b on cue.** at the right moment. **2** a signal or reminder to do something. **3** *Psychol.* the part of any sensory pattern that is identified as the signal for a response. **4** the part, function, or action assigned to or expected of a person. ♦ *vb* **cues, cueing, cued. 5** (*tr*) to give a cue or cues to (an actor). **6** (usually foll. by *in* or *into*) to signal (to something or somebody) at a specific moment in a musical or dramatic performance: *to cue in a flourish of trumpets.* **7** (*tr*) to give information or a reminder to (someone). **8** (*intr*) to signal the commencement of filming, as with the word "Action!" [C16: probably from name of the letter *q,* used in an actor's script to represent Latin *quando* when]

cue[2] (kjuː) *n* **1** *Billiards, etc.* a long tapered shaft with a leather tip, used to drive the balls. **2** hair caught at the back forming a tail or braid. **3** *U.S.* a variant spelling of **queue.** ♦ *vb* **cues, cueing, cued. 4** to drive (a ball) with a cue. **5** (*tr*) to twist or tie (the hair) into a cue. [C18: variant of QUEUE]

cue ball *n Billiards, etc.* the ball struck by the cue, as distinguished from the object balls.

cue bid *n Contract bridge.* a bid in a suit made to show an ace or a void in that suit.

cueing ('kjuːɪŋ) *n* another name for **foldback.**

Cuenca (*Spanish* 'kweŋka) *n* **1** a city in SW Ecuador: university (1868). Pop.: 255 028 (1997 est.). **2** a town in central Spain: prosperous in the Middle Ages for its silver and textile industries. Pop.: 45 800 (1991).

Cuernavaca (*Spanish* kwerna'βaka) *n* a city in S central Mexico, capital of Morelos state: resort with nearby Cacahuamilpa Caverns. Pop.: 279 187 (1990).

cuesta ('kwɛstə) *n* a long low ridge with a steep scarp slope and a gentle back slope, formed by the differential erosion of strata of differing hardness. [Spanish: shoulder, from Latin *costa* side, rib]

cuff[1] (kʌf) *n* **1** the part of a sleeve nearest the hand, sometimes turned back and decorative. **2** the part of a gauntlet or glove that extends past the wrist. **3** the U.S., Canadian, and Australian name for **turn-up** (sense 5). **4 off the cuff.** *Informal.* improvised; extemporary. ♦ See also **cuffs.** [C14 *cuffe* glove, of obscure origin]

cuff[2] (kʌf) *vb* **1** (*tr*) to strike with an open hand. ♦ *n* **2** a blow of this kind. [C16: of obscure origin]

cuff link *n* one of a pair of linked buttons, used to join the buttonholes on the cuffs of a shirt.

cuffs (kʌfs) *pl n Informal.* short for **handcuffs.**

Cufic ('kuːfɪk, 'kjuː-) *n, adj* a variant spelling of **Kufic.**

Cuiabá *or* **Cuyabá** (*Portuguese* kuia'ba) *n* **1** a port in W Brazil, capital of Mato Grosso state, on the Cuibá River. Pop.: 252 784 (1991). **2** a river in SW Brazil, rising on the Mato Grosso plateau and flowing southwest into the São Lourenço River. Length: 483 km (300 miles).

cui bono *Latin.* (kwiː 'bəʊnəʊ) for whose benefit? for what purpose?

cuirass (kwɪ'ræs) *n* **1** a piece of armour, of leather or metal covering the chest and back. **2** a hard outer protective covering of some animals, consisting of shell, plate, or scales. **3** any similar protective covering, as on a ship. ♦ *vb* **4** (*tr*) to equip with a cuirass. [C15: from French *cuirasse,* from Late Latin *coriacea,* from *coriaceus* made of leather, from Latin *corium* leather]

cuirassier (,kwɪrə'sɪə) *n* a mounted soldier, esp. of the 16th century, who wore a cuirass.

cuir-bouilli (,kwɪəbuː'jiː) *n* a type of leather hardened by soaking in wax, used for armour before the 14th century. [French, literally: boiled leather]

Cuisenaire rod (,kwɪzə'nɛə) *n Trademark.* one of a set of rods of various colours and lengths representing different numbers, used to teach arithmetic to young children. [C20: named after Emil-Georges *Cuisenaire* (?1891–1976), Belgian educationalist]

cuisine (kwɪ'ziːn) *n* **1** a style or manner of cooking: *French cuisine.* **2** the food prepared by a restaurant, household, etc. [C18: from French, literally: kitchen, from Late Latin *coquīna,* from Latin *coquere* to cook]

cuisine minceur *French* (kɥizin mɛ̃sœr) *n* a style of cooking, originating in France, that limits the use of starch, sugar, butter, and cream traditionally used in French cookery. [literally: slimness cooking]

cuisse (kwɪs) *or* **cuish** (kwɪʃ) *n* a piece of armour for the thigh. [C15: back formation from *cuisses* (plural), from Old French *cuisseaux* thigh guards, from *cuisse* thigh, from Latin *coxa* hipbone]

Culbertson ('kʌlbətsᵊn) *n* **Ely** ('iːlaɪ). 1891–1955, U.S. authority on contract bridge.

culch *or* **cultch** (kʌltʃ) *n* **1** a mass of broken stones, shells, and gravel that forms the basis of an oyster bed. **2** the oyster spawn attached to such a structure. **3** *Dialect.* refuse; rubbish. [C17: perhaps ultimately from Old French *culche* bed, COUCH]

culchie ('kʌltʃɪ) *n Irish informal.* a rough labouring countryman. [of unknown origin]

cul-de-sac ('kʌldə,sæk, 'kʊl-) *n, pl* **culs-de-sac** *or* **cul-de-sacs. 1** a road with one end blocked off; dead end. **2** an inescapable position. **3** any tube-shaped bodily cavity or pouch closed at one end, such as the caecum. [C18: from French, literally: bottom of the bag]

-cule *suffix forming nouns.* indicating smallness: *animalcule.* [from Latin *-culus,* diminutive suffix; compare -CLE]

Culebra Cut (kuː'lebrə) *n* the former name of the **Gaillard Cut.**

culet ('kjuːlɪt) *n* **1** *Jewellery.* the flat face at the bottom of a gem. **2** either of the plates of armour worn at the small of the back. [C17: from obsolete French, diminutive of *cul,* from Latin *cūlus* bottom]

culex ('kjuːlɛks) *n, pl* **-lices** (-lɪ,siːz). any mosquito of the genus *Culex,* such as *C. pipiens,* the common mosquito. [C15: from Latin: midge, gnat; related to Old Irish *cuil* gnat]

Culham ('kʌləm) *n* a village in S central England, in Oxfordshire: site of the UK centre for thermonuclear reactor research and of the Joint European Torus (JET) programme.

Culiacán (*Spanish* kulja'kan) *n* a city in NW Mexico, capital of Sinaloa state. Pop.: 415 046 (1990).

culicid (kjuː'lɪsɪd) *n* **1** any dipterous insect of the family *Culicidae,* which comprises the mosquitos. ♦ *adj* **2** of, relating to, or belonging to the *Culicidae.* [C19: from New Latin *Culicidae,* from Latin *culex* gnat, CULEX]

culinary ('kʌlɪnərɪ) *adj* of, relating to, or used in the kitchen or in cookery. [C17: from Latin *culīnārius,* from *culīna* kitchen] ▸ **'culinarily** *adv*

cull (kʌl) *vb* (*tr*) **1** to choose or gather the best or required examples. **2** to take out (an animal, esp. an inferior one) from a herd. **3** to reduce the size of (a herd or flock) by killing a proportion of its members. **4** to gather (flowers, fruit, etc.). ♦ *n* **5** the act or product of culling. **6** an inferior animal taken from a herd or group. [C15: from Old French *coillir* to pick, from Latin *colligere;* see COLLECT[1]]

cullender ('kʌlɪndə) *n* a variant of **colander.**

culler (kʌlə) *n* **1** a person employed to cull animals. **2** *Austral. and N.Z.* an animal, esp. a sheep, designated for culling.

cullet ('kʌlɪt) *n* waste glass for melting down to be reused. [C17: perhaps variant of COLLET (literally: little neck, referring to the glass neck of newly blown bottles, etc.)]

cullis ('kʌlɪs) *n* **1** a gutter in or at the eaves of a roof. **2** another word for **coulisse** (sense 1). [C19: from French *coulisse* channel, groove; see COULISSE]

Culloden (kə'lɒdᵊn) *n* a moor near Inverness in N Scotland: site of a battle in 1746 in which government troops under the Duke of Cumberland defeated the Jacobites under Prince Charles Edward Stuart.

cully ('kʌlɪ) *n, pl* **-lies.** *Slang.* pal; mate. [C17: of unknown origin]

culm[1] (kʌlm) *n Mining.* **1** coal-mine waste. **2** inferior anthracite. [C14: probably related to COAL]

culm[2] (kʌlm) *n* the hollow jointed stem of a grass or sedge. [C17: from Latin *culmus* stalk; see HAULM]

Culm *or* **Culm Measures** *n* a formation consisting mainly of shales and sandstone deposited during the Carboniferous period in parts of Europe. [C19: from CULM[1]]

culmiferous (kʌl'mɪfərəs) *adj* (of grasses) having a hollow jointed stem.

culminant ('kʌlmɪnənt) *adj* highest or culminating.

culminate ('kʌlmɪ,neɪt) *vb* **1** (when *intr,* usually foll. by *in*) to end or cause to end, esp. to reach or bring to a final or climactic stage. **2** (*intr*) (of a celestial body) to cross the meridian of the observer. [C17: from Late Latin *culmināre* to reach the highest point, from Latin *culmen* top]

culmination (,kʌlmɪ'neɪʃən) *n* **1** the final, highest, or decisive point. **2** the act of culminating. **3** *Astronomy.* the highest or lowest altitude attained by a heavenly body as it crosses the meridian.

culottes (kjuː'lɒts) *pl n* women's flared trousers cut to look like a skirt. [C20: from French, literally: breeches, from *cul* bottom; see CULET]

culpa ('kʊlpɑː) *n, pl* **-pae** (-piː). **1** *Civil law.* an act of neglect. **2** a fault; sin; guilt. [Latin: fault]

culpable ('kʌlpəbᵊl) *adj* deserving censure; blameworthy. [C14: from Old French *coupable,* from Latin *culpābilis,* from *culpāre* to blame, from *culpa* fault] ▸ **,culpa'bility** *or* **'culpableness** *n* ▸ **'culpably** *adv*

culpable homicide *n Scots Law.* manslaughter.

Culpeper ('kʌlpɛpə) *n* **Nicholas.** 1616–54, English herbalist and astrologer;

his unauthorized translation (1649) of the College of Physicians' *Pharmacopoeia* and his *Herbal* (1653) popularized herbalism.

culprit ('kʌlprɪt) *n* **1** *Law.* a person awaiting trial, esp. one who has pleaded not guilty. **2** the person responsible for a particular offence, misdeed, etc. [C17: from Anglo-French *cul-,* short for *culpable* guilty + *prit* ready, indicating that the prosecution was ready to prove the guilt of the one charged]

cult (kʌlt) *n* **1** a specific system of religious worship, esp. with reference to its rites and deity. **2** a sect devoted to such a system. **3** a quasi-religious organization using devious psychological techniques to gain and control adherents. **4** *Sociol.* a group having an exclusive ideology and ritual practices centred on sacred symbols, esp. one characterized by lack of organizational structure. **5** intense interest in and devotion to a person, idea, or activity: *the cult of yoga.* **6** the person, idea, etc., arousing such devotion. **7a** something regarded as fashionable or significant by a particular group. **7b** (*as modifier*): *a cult show.* **8** (*modifier*) of, relating to, or characteristic of a cult or cults: *a cult figure.* [C17: from Latin *cultus* cultivation, refinement, from *colere* to till] ► **'cultism** *n* ► **'cultist** *n*

cultch (kʌltʃ) *n* a variant spelling of **culch.**

cultic ('kʌltɪk) *adj* of or relating to a religious cult.

cultigen ('kʌltɪdʒən) *n* a species of plant that is known only as a cultivated form and did not originate from a wild type. [C20: from CULTI(VATED) + -GEN]

cultish ('kʌltɪʃ) *or* **culty** ('kʌltɪ) *adj* intended to appeal to a small group of fashionable people.

cultivable ('kʌltɪvəbᵊl) *or* **cultivatable** ('kʌltɪˌveɪtəbᵊl) *adj* (of land) capable of being cultivated. [C17: from French, from Old French *cultiver* to CULTIVATE] ► **ˌcultiva'bility** *n*

cultivar ('kʌltɪˌvɑː) *n* a variety of a plant that was produced from a natural species and is maintained by cultivation. [C20: from CULTI(VATED) + VAR(IETY)]

cultivate ('kʌltɪˌveɪt) *vb* (*tr*) **1** to till and prepare (land or soil) for the growth of crops. **2** to plant, tend, harvest, or improve (plants) by labour and skill. **3** to break up (land or soil) with a cultivator or hoe. **4** to improve or foster (the mind, body, etc.) as by study, education, or labour. **5** to give special attention to: *to cultivate a friendship; to cultivate a hobby.* **6** to give or bring culture to (a person, society, etc.); civilize. [C17: from Medieval Latin *cultivāre* to till, from Old French *cultiver,* from Medieval Latin *cultīvus* cultivable, from Latin *cultus* cultivated, from *colere* to till, toil over]

cultivated ('kʌltɪˌveɪtɪd) *adj* **1** cultured, refined, or educated. **2** (of land or soil) **2a** subjected to tillage or cultivation. **2b** tilled and broken up. **3** (of plants) specially bred or improved by cultivation.

cultivation (ˌkʌltɪ'veɪʃən) *n* **1** *Agriculture.* **1a** the planting, tending, improving, or harvesting of crops or plants. **1b** the preparation of ground to promote their growth. **2** development, esp. through education, training, etc. **3** culture or sophistication, esp. social refinement.

cultivator ('kʌltɪˌveɪtə) *n* **1** a farm implement equipped with shovels, blades, etc., used to break up soil and remove weeds. **2** a person or thing that cultivates. **3** a person who grows, tends, or improves plants or crops.

cultrate ('kʌltreɪt) *or* **cultrated** *adj* shaped like a knife blade: *cultrate leaves.* [C19: from Latin *cultrātus,* from *culter* knife]

cultural ('kʌltʃərəl) *adj* **1** of or relating to artistic or social pursuits or events considered to be valuable or enlightened. **2** of or relating to a culture or civilization. **3** (of certain varieties of plant) obtained by specialized breeding. ► **'culturally** *adv*

cultural anthropology *n* the branch of anthropology dealing with cultural as opposed to biological and racial features. ► **cultural anthropologist** *n*

cultural lag *or* **culture lag** *n* the difference in the rate of change between two parts of a culture.

Cultural Revolution *n* (in China) a mass movement (1965–68), in which the youthful Red Guard played a prominent part. It was initiated by Mao Tse-tung to destroy the power of the bureaucrats and to revolutionize the attitudes and behaviour of the people. Also called: **Great Proletarian Cultural Revolution.**

culture ('kʌltʃə) *n* **1** the total of the inherited ideas, beliefs, values, and knowledge, which constitute the shared bases of social action. **2** the total range of activities and ideas of a group of people with shared traditions, which are transmitted and reinforced by members of the group: *the Mayan culture.* **3** a particular civilization at a particular period. **4** the artistic and social pursuits, expression, and tastes valued by a society or class, as in the arts, manners, dress, etc. **5** the enlightenment or refinement resulting from these pursuits. **6** the cultivation of plants, esp. by scientific methods designed to improve stock or to produce new ones. **7** *Stockbreeding.* the rearing and breeding of animals, esp. with a view to improving the strain. **8** the act or practice of tilling or cultivating the soil. **9** *Biology.* **9a** the experimental growth of microorganisms, such as bacteria and fungi, in a nutrient substance (see **culture medium**), usually under controlled conditions. **9b** a group of microorganisms grown in this way. ◆ *vb* (*tr*) **10** to cultivate (plants or animals). **11** to grow (microorganisms) in a culture medium. [C15: from Old French, from Latin *cultūra* a cultivating, from *colere* to till; see CULT] ► **'culturist** *n* ► **'cultureless** *adj*

cultured ('kʌltʃəd) *adj* **1** showing or having good taste, manners, upbringing, and education. **2** artificially grown or synthesized: *cultured pearls.*

cultured pearl *n* a pearl induced to grow in the shell of an oyster or clam, by the insertion of a small object around which layers of nacre are deposited.

culture-free test *n* a test (usually for intelligence) that does not put anyone taking it at a disadvantage, for instance, as regards material or cultural background.

culture medium *n* a nutritive substance, such as an agar gel, in which cultures of bacteria and fungi are grown.

culture shock *n Sociol.* the feelings of isolation, rejection, etc., experienced when one culture is brought into sudden contact with another, as when a primitive tribe is confronted by modern civilization.

culture vulture *n Informal.* a person considered to be excessively, and often pretentiously, interested in the arts.

cultus ('kʌltəs) *n, pl* **-tuses** *or* **-ti** (-taɪ). *Chiefly R.C. Church.* another word for **cult** (sense 1). [C17: from Latin: a toiling over something, refinement, CULT]

culver ('kʌlvə) *n* an archaic or poetic name for **pigeon**[1] or **dove**[1]. [Old English *culfre,* from Latin *columbula* a little dove, from *columba* dove]

culverin ('kʌlvərɪn) *n* **1** a long-range medium to heavy cannon used during the 15th, 16th, and 17th centuries. **2** a medieval musket. [C15: from Old French *coulevrine,* from *couleuvre,* from Latin *coluber* serpent]

Culver's root *or* **physic** ('kʌlvəz) *n* **1** a tall North American scrophulariaceous plant, *Veronicastrum virginicum,* having spikes of small white or purple flowers. **2** the dried roots of this plant, formerly used as a cathartic and emetic. [C19: named after a Dr *Culver,* 18th-century American physician]

culvert ('kʌlvət) *n* **1** a drain or covered channel that crosses under a road, railway, etc. **2** a channel for an electric cable. [C18: of unknown origin]

Culzean Castle (kə'leɪn) *n* a Gothic Revival castle near Ayr in South Ayrshire, in SW Scotland: designed by Robert Adam (1772–92); includes a room dedicated to General Eisenhower.

cum (kʌm) *prep* used between two nouns to designate an object of a combined nature: *a kitchen-cum-dining room.* [Latin: with, together with, along with]

cumacean (kjʊ'meɪʃᵊn) *n* **1** any small malacostracan marine crustacean of the *Cumacea* family, mostly dwelling on the sea bed but sometimes found among the plankton. ◆ *adj* **2** of, relating to, or belonging to the *Cumacea.* [C19: from New Latin *cuma,* from Greek *kuma* (see CYMA) + -EAN]

Cumae ('kjuːmiː) *n* the oldest Greek colony in Italy, founded about 750 B.C. near Naples. ► **Cu'maean** *adj*

Cumaná (*Spanish* kuma'na) *n* a city in NE Venezuela: founded in 1523; the oldest European settlement in South America. Pop.: 212 432 (1990).

cumber ('kʌmbə) *vb* (*tr*) **1** to obstruct or hinder. **2** *Obsolete.* to inconvenience. ◆ *n* **3** a hindrance or burden. [C13: probably from Old French *combrer* to impede, prevent, from *combre* barrier; see ENCUMBER] ► **'cumberer** *n*

Cumberland[1] ('kʌmbələnd) *n* (until 1974) a county of NW England, now part of Cumbria.

Cumberland[2] ('kʌmbələnd) *n* **1 Richard.** 1631–1718, English theologian and moral philosopher; bishop of Peterborough (1691–1718). **2 William Augustus,** Duke of Cumberland, known as *Butcher Cumberland.* 1721–65, English soldier, younger son of George II, noted for his defeat of Charles Edward Stuart at Culloden (1746) and his subsequent ruthless destruction of Jacobite rebels.

Cumbernauld (ˌkʌmbə'nɔːld) *n* a town in central Scotland, in E central Strathclyde region, northeast of Glasgow: developed as a new town since 1956. Pop.: 50 700 (latest est.).

cumbersome ('kʌmbəsəm) *or* **cumbrous** ('kʌmbrəs) *adj* **1** awkward because of size, weight, or shape: *cumbersome baggage.* **2** difficult because of extent or complexity: *cumbersome accounts.* [C14: *cumber,* short for ENCUMBER + -SOME[1]] ► **'cumbersomely** *or* **'cumbrously** *adv* ► **'cumbersomeness** *or* **'cumbrousness** *n*

cumbrance ('kʌmbrəns) *n* **1** a burden, obstacle, or hindrance. **2** trouble or bother.

Cumbria ('kʌmbrɪə) *n* (since 1974) a county of NW England comprising the former counties of Westmorland and Cumberland together with N Lancashire: includes the Lake District mountain area and surrounding coastal lowlands with the Pennine uplands in the extreme east. Administrative centre: Carlisle. Pop.: 490 200 (1994 est.). Area: 6810 sq. km (2629 sq. miles). ► **'Cumbrian** *adj, n*

Cumbrian Mountains ('kʌmbrɪən) *pl n* a mountain range in NW England, in Cumbria. Highest peak: Scafell Pike, 978 m (3210 ft.).

cum dividend *adv* (of shares, etc.) with the right to current dividend. Compare **ex dividend.** [*cum,* from Latin: with]

cum grano salis *Latin.* (kʊm 'grɑːnəʊ 'sɑːlɪs) *adv* with a grain of salt; not too literally.

cumin *or* **cummin** ('kʌmɪn) *n* **1** an umbelliferous Mediterranean plant, *Cuminum cyminum,* with finely divided leaves and small white or pink flowers. **2** the aromatic seeds (collectively) of this plant, used as a condiment and a flavouring. [C12: from Old French, from Latin *cumīnum,* from Greek *kuminon,* of Semitic origin; compare Hebrew *kammōn*]

cum laude (kʌm 'lɔːdɪ, kʊm 'laʊdeɪ) *adv Chiefly U.S.* with praise: the lowest of three designations for above-average achievement in examinations. Compare **magna cum laude, summa cum laude.** [Latin]

cummerbund *or* **kummerbund** ('kʌməˌbʌnd) *n* a wide sash, worn with a dinner jacket. [C17: from Hindi *kamarband,* from Persian, from *kamar* loins, waist + *band* band]

Cummings ('kʌmɪŋz) *n* **Edward Estlin** ('estlɪn), (preferred typographical representation of name **e e cummings**). 1894–1962, U.S. poet.

cum new *adv, adj* (of shares, etc.) with the right to take up any scrip issue or rights issue. Compare **ex new.**

cumquat ('kʌmkwɒt) *n* a variant spelling of **kumquat.**

cumshaw ('kʌmʃɔː) *n* (used, esp. formerly, by beggars in Chinese ports) a present or tip. [C19: from pidgin English, from Chinese (Amoy) *kam siā,* from Mandarin *kan hsieh* grateful thanks]

cumulate *vb* ('kjuːmjʊˌleɪt). **1** to accumulate. **2** (*tr*) to combine (two or more sequences) into one. ◆ *adj* ('kjuːmjʊlɪt, -ˌleɪt). **3** heaped up. [C16: from Latin *cumulāre* from *cumulus* heap] ► **'cumulately** *adv* ► **ˌcumu'lation** *n*

cumulative ('kjuːmjʊlətɪv) *adj* **1** growing in quantity, strength, or effect by successive additions or gradual steps: *cumulative pollution.* **2** gained by or resulting from a gradual building up: *cumulative benefits.* **3** *Finance.* **3a** (of preference shares) entitling the holder to receive any arrears of dividend before any dividend is distributed to ordinary shareholders. **3b** (of dividends or interest) intended to be accumulated if not paid when due. **4** *Statistics.* **4a** (of a frequency) including all values of a variable either below or above a specified value. **4b** (of error) tending to increase as the sample size is increased. ► **'cumulatively** *adv* ► **'cumulativeness** *n*

cumulative distribution function *n Statistics.* a function defined on the sample space of a distribution and taking as its value at each point the probability that the random variable has that value or less. The function $F(x) = P(X \leq x)$ where X is the random variable, which is the sum or integral of the probability density function of the distribution. Sometimes shortened to **distribution function.**

cumulative evidence *n Law.* additional evidence reinforcing testimony previously given.

cumulative voting *n* a system of voting in which each elector has as many votes as there are candidates in his constituency. Votes may all be cast for one candidate or distributed among several.

cumulet ('kju:mjulɪt) *n* (*sometimes cap.*) a variety of domestic fancy pigeon, pure white or white with light red markings. [C19: from CUMULUS]

cumuliform ('kju:mjulɪˌfɔ:m) *adj* resembling a cumulus cloud.

cumulonimbus (ˌkju:mjuləʊ'nɪmbəs) *n, pl* **-bi** (-baɪ) *or* **-buses.** *Meteorol.* a cumulus cloud of great vertical extent, the top often forming an anvil shape and the bottom being dark coloured, indicating rain or hail: associated with thunderstorms.

cumulostratus (ˌkju:mjuləʊ'streɪtəs) *n, pl* **-ti** (-taɪ). *Meteorol.* another name for **stratocumulus.**

cumulous ('kju:mjuləs) *adj* resembling or consisting of cumulus clouds.

cumulus ('kju:mjuləs) *n, pl* **-li** (-ˌlaɪ). **1** a bulbous or billowing white or dark grey cloud associated with rising air currents. Compare **cirrus** (sense 1), **stratus. 2** *Histology.* the mass of cells surrounding a recently ovulated egg cell in a Graafian follicle. [C17: from Latin: mass]

Cunaxa (kju:'næksə) *n* the site near the lower Euphrates where Artaxerxes II defeated Cyrus the Younger in 401 B.C.

cunctation (kʌŋk'teɪʃən) *n Rare.* delay. [C16: from Latin *cunctātiō* a hesitation, from *cunctārī* to delay] ► **cunctative** ('kʌŋktətɪv) *adj* ► **cunc'tator** *n*

cuneal ('kju:nɪəl) *adj* wedge-shaped; cuneiform. [C16: from New Latin *cuneālis,* from *cuneus* wedge]

cuneate ('kju:nɪɪt, -ˌeɪt) *adj* wedge-shaped: cuneate leaves are attached at the narrow end. [C19: from Latin *cuneāre* to make wedge-shaped, from *cuneus* a wedge] ► **'cuneately** *adv*

cuneiform ('kju:nɪˌfɔ:m) *adj* **1** Also: **cuneal.** wedge-shaped. **2** of, relating to, or denoting the wedge-shaped characters employed in the writing of several ancient languages of Mesopotamia and Persia, esp. Sumerian, Babylonian, etc. **3** of or relating to a tablet in which this script is employed. **4** of or relating to any of the three tarsal bones. ♦ *n* **5** cuneiform characters or writing. **6** any one of the three tarsal bones. [C17: probably from Old French *cunéiforme,* from Latin *cuneus* wedge]

Cuneo (*Italian* 'ku:neo) *n* a city in NW Italy, in Piedmont. Pop.: 55 840 (1990).

cunjevoi ('kʌndʒɪˌvɔɪ) *n Austral.* **1** an aroid plant, *Alocasia macrorrhiza,* of tropical Asia and Australia, cultivated for its edible rhizome. **2** a sea squirt. [C19: from a native Australian language]

cunnilingus (ˌkʌnɪ'lɪŋgəs) *or* **cunnilinctus** (ˌkʌnɪ'lɪŋktəs) *n* a sexual activity in which the female genitalia are stimulated by the partner's lips and tongue. Compare **fellatio.** [C19: from New Latin, from Latin *cunnus* vulva + *lingere* to lick]

cunning ('kʌnɪŋ) *adj* **1** crafty and shrewd, esp. in deception; sly: *cunning as a fox.* **2** made with or showing skill or cleverness; ingenious. ♦ *n* **3** craftiness, esp. in deceiving; slyness. **4** cleverness, skill, or ingenuity. [Old English *cunnende;* related to *cunnan* to know (see CAN[1]), *cunnian* to test, experience, Old Norse *kunna* to know] ► **'cunningly** *adv* ► **'cunningness** *n*

Cunningham ('kʌnɪŋəm) *n* **Merce** (mɜ:s). born 1919, U.S. dancer and choreographer. His experimental ballets include *Suit for Five* (1956) and *Travelogue* (1977).

Cunninghame Graham ('kʌnɪŋəm 'greɪəm) *n* **R**(**obert**) **B**(**ontine**). 1852–1936, Scottish traveller, writer, and politician, noted for his essays and short stories: first president (1928) of the Scottish Nationalist Party.

Cunobelinus (kju:ˌnɒbə'laɪnəs) *n* also called *Cymbeline.* died ?42 A.D., British ruler of the Catuvellauni tribe (?10–?42); founder of Colchester (?10).

cunt (kʌnt) *n Taboo.* **1** the female genitals. **2** *Offensive slang.* a woman considered sexually. **3** *Offensive slang.* a mean or obnoxious person. [C13: of Germanic origin; related to Old Norse *kunta,* Middle Low German *kunte*]

cup (kʌp) *n* **1** a small open container, usually having one handle, used for drinking from. **2** the contents of such a container: *that cup was too sweet.* **3** Also called: **teacup, cupful.** a unit of capacity used in cooking equal to approximately half a pint, 8 fluid ounces, or about one quarter of a litre. **4** something resembling a cup in shape or function, such as the flower base of some plants of the rose family or a cuplike bodily organ. **5** either of two cup-shaped parts of a brassiere, designed to support the breasts. **6** a cup-shaped trophy awarded as a prize. **7** *Brit.* **7a** a sporting contest in which a cup is awarded to the winner. **7b** (*as modifier*): *a cup competition.* **8** a mixed drink with one ingredient as a base, usually served from a bowl: *claret cup.* **9** *Golf.* the hole or metal container in the hole on a green. **10** the chalice or the consecrated wine used in the Eucharist. **11** one's lot in life. **12 in one's cups.** drunk. **13 one's cup of tea.** *Informal.* one's chosen or preferred thing, task, company, etc.: *she's not my cup of tea.* ♦ *vb* **cups, cupping, cupped.** (*tr*) **14** to form (something, such as the hands) into the shape of a cup. **15** to put into or as if into a cup. **16** to draw blood to the surface of the body of (a person) by using a cupping glass. [Old English *cuppe,* from Late Latin *cuppa* cup, alteration of Latin *cūpa* cask] ► **'cupˌlike** *adj*

cupbearer ('kʌpˌbɛərə) *n* an attendant who fills and serves wine cups, as in a royal household.

cupboard ('kʌbəd) *n* a piece of furniture or a recessed area of a room, with a door concealing storage space.

cupboard love *n* a show of love inspired only by some selfish or greedy motive.

cupcake ('kʌpˌkeɪk) *n* a small cake baked in a cup-shaped foil or paper case.

cupel ('kju:pᵊl, kju'pɛl) *n* **1** a refractory pot in which gold or silver is refined. **2** a small porous bowl made of bone ash in which gold and silver are recovered from a lead button during assaying. ♦ *vb* **-pels, -pelling, -pelled** *or U.S.* **-pels, -peling, -peled. 3** (*tr*) to refine (gold or silver) by means of cupellation. [C17: from French *coupelle,* diminutive of *coupe* CUP] ► **'cupeller** *n*

cupellation (ˌkju:pɪ'leɪʃən) *n* **1** the process of recovering precious metals from lead by melting the alloy in a cupel and oxidizing the lead by means of an air blast. **2** the manufacture of lead oxide by melting and oxidizing lead.

Cup Final *n* **1** (often preceded by *the*) the annual final of the FA Cup soccer competition, played at Wembley, or the Scottish Cup, played at Hampden Park. **2** (*often not cap.*) the final of any cup competition.

Cupid ('kju:pɪd) *n* **1** the Roman god of love, represented as a winged boy with a bow and arrow. Greek counterpart: **Eros. 2** (*not cap.*) any similar figure, esp. as represented in Baroque art. [C14: from Latin *Cupīdō,* from *cupīdō* desire, from *cupidus* desirous; see CUPIDITY]

cupidity (kju:'pɪdɪtɪ) *n* strong desire, esp. for possessions or money; greed. [C15: from Latin *cupiditās,* from *cupidus* eagerly desiring, from *cupere* to long for]

Cupid's bow *n* a shape of the upper lip considered to resemble Cupid's double-curved bow.

cupid's dart *n* another name for **catananche.**

cupola ('kju:pələ) *n* **1** a roof or ceiling in the form of a dome. **2** a small structure, usually domed, on the top of a roof or dome. **3** a protective dome for a gun on a warship. **4** a vertical air-blown coke-fired cylindrical furnace in which iron is remelted for casting. [C16: from Italian, from Late Latin *cūpula* a small cask, from Latin *cūpa* tub] ► **cupolated** ('kju:pəˌleɪtɪd) *adj*

cuppa *or* **cupper** ('kʌpə) *n Brit. informal.* a cup of tea.

cupped (kʌpt) *adj* hollowed like a cup; concave.

cupping ('kʌpɪŋ) *n Med.* the process of applying a cupping glass to the skin.

cupping glass *n Med.* a glass vessel from which air can be removed by suction or heat to create a partial vacuum: formerly used in drawing blood to the surface of the skin for slow bloodletting. Also called: **artificial leech.**

cupreous ('kju:prɪəs) *adj* **1** of, consisting of, containing, or resembling copper; coppery. **2** of the reddish-brown colour of copper. [C17: from Late Latin *cupreus,* from *cuprum* COPPER[1]]

cupressus (kju'prɛsəs) *n* any tree of the genus *Cupressus.* See **cypress**[1].

cupric ('kju:prɪk) *adj* of or containing copper in the divalent state. [C18: from Late Latin *cuprum* copper]

cupriferous (kju:'prɪfərəs) *adj* (of a substance such as an ore) containing or yielding copper.

cuprite ('kju:praɪt) *n* a red secondary mineral consisting of cuprous oxide in cubic crystalline form: a source of copper. Formula: Cu_2O.

cupro-, cupri-, *or before a vowel* **cupr-** *combining form.* indicating copper: *cupronickel; cuprite.* [from Latin *cuprum*]

cupronickel (ˌkju:prəʊ'nɪkᵊl) *n* any ductile corrosion-resistant copper alloy containing up to 40 per cent nickel: used in coins, condenser tubes, turbine blades, etc.

cuprous ('kju:prəs) *adj* of or containing copper in the monovalent state.

cuprum ('kju:prəm) *n* an obsolete name for **copper.** [Latin: COPPER[1]]

cup tie *n Sport.* an eliminating match or round between two teams in a cup competition.

cup-tied *adj Sport.* **1** (of a team) unable to play another fixture because of involvement in a cup tie. **2** (of a player) unable to play in a cup tie because of some disallowance.

cupula ('kʌpjulə) *n, pl* **-lae** (-li:). *Anatomy, zoology.* a dome-shaped structure, esp. the sensory structure within the semicircular canals of the ear.

cupulate ('kju:pjuˌleɪt) *or* **cupular** ('kju:pjulə) *adj* **1** shaped like a small cup. **2** (of plants or animals) having cupules.

cupule ('kju:pju:l) *n Biology.* a cup-shaped part or structure, such as the cup around the base of an acorn. [C19: from Late Latin *cūpula;* see CUPOLA]

cur (kɜ:) *n* **1** any vicious dog, esp. a mongrel. **2** a despicable or cowardly person. [C13: shortened from *kurdogge;* probably related to Old Norse *kurra* to growl]

cur. *abbrev. for* currency.

curable ('kjuərəbᵊl) *adj* capable of being cured. ► ˌ**cura'bility** *or* **'curableness** *n* ► **'curably** *adv*

Curaçao (ˌkjuərə'səʊ) *n* **1** an island in the Caribbean, the largest in the Netherlands Antilles. Capital: Willemstad. Pop.: 149 376 (1994 est.). Area: 444 sq. km (171 sq. miles). **2** an orange-flavoured liqueur originally made there.

curacy ('kjuərəsɪ) *n, pl* **-cies.** the office or position of curate.

Cur. adv vult *abbrev.* See **CAV.**

curagh *Gaelic.* ('kʌrəx; 'kʌrə) *n* a variant spelling of **currach.**

curare *or* **curari** (kju'rɑ:rɪ) *n* **1** black resin obtained from certain tropical South American trees, acting on the motor nerves to cause muscular paralysis: used medicinally as a muscle relaxant and by South American Indians as an arrow poison. **2** any of various trees of the genera *Chondrodendron* and *Strychnos* from which this resin is obtained. [C18: from Portuguese and Spanish, from Carib *kurari*]

curarine ('kjuərəˌri:n) *n* an alkaloid extracted from curare, used as a muscle relaxant in surgery. Formula: $C_{19}H_{26}ON_2$.

curarize *or* **curarise** ('kjuərəˌraɪz) *vb* (*tr*) to paralyse or treat with curare. ► ˌ**curari'zation** *or* ˌ**curari'sation** *n*

curassow ('kjuərəˌsəʊ) *n* any gallinaceous ground-nesting bird of the family *Cracidae,* of S North, Central, and South America. Curassows have long legs and tails and, typically, a distinctive crest of curled feathers. See also **guan.** [C17: anglicized variant of CURAÇAO (island)]

curate[1] ('kjʊərɪt) *n* **1** a clergyman appointed to assist a parish priest. **2** a clergyman who has the charge of a parish (**curate-in-charge**). **3** *Irish.* an assistant barman. [C14: from Medieval Latin *cūrātus,* from *cūra* spiritual oversight, CURE]

curate[2] (kjʊə'reɪt) *vb (tr)* to be in charge of (an art exhibition or museum). [C20: back formation from CURATOR]

curate's egg *n* something that has both good and bad parts. [C20: derived from a cartoon in *Punch* (November, 1895) in which a timid curate, who has been served a bad egg while breakfasting with his bishop, says that parts of the egg are excellent]

curative ('kjʊərətɪv) *adj* **1** able or tending to cure. ◆ *n* **2** anything able to heal or cure. ▸ **'curatively** *adv* ▸ **'curativeness** *n*

curator (kjʊə'reɪtə) *n* **1** the administrative head of a museum, art gallery, or similar institution. **2** *Law, chiefly Scot.* a guardian of a minor, mentally ill person, etc. [C14: from Latin: one who cares, from *cūrāre* to care for, from *cūra* care] ▸ **curatorial** (,kjʊərə'tɔːrɪəl) *adj* ▸ **cu'rator,ship** *n*

curb (kɜːb) *n* **1** something that restrains or holds back. **2** any enclosing framework, such as a wall of stones around the top of a well. **3a** Also called: **curb bit.** a horse's bit with an attached chain or strap, which checks the horse. **3b** Also called: **curb chain.** the chain or strap itself. **4** a hard swelling on the hock of a horse. ◆ *vb (tr)* **5** to control with or as if with a curb; restrain. ◆ See also **kerb.** [C15: from Old French *courbe* curved piece of wood or metal, from Latin *curvus* curved]

curbing ('kɜːbɪŋ) *n* the U.S. spelling of **kerbing.**

curb roof *n* a roof having two or more slopes on each side of the ridge. See also **mansard** (sense 1), **gambrel roof** (sense 2).

curbstone ('kɜːb,stəʊn) *n* the U.S. spelling of **kerbstone.**

curch (kɜːtʃ) *n* a woman's plain cap or kerchief. Also called: **curchef.** [C15: probably back formation from *courcheis* (plural), from Old French *couvrechies,* plural of *couvrechef* KERCHIEF]

curculio (kɜː'kjuːlɪ,əʊ) *n, pl* **-lios.** any of various American weevils, esp. *Conotrachelus nenuphar* (**plum curculio**), a pest of fruit trees. [C18: from Latin: grain weevil]

curcuma ('kɜːkjʊmə) *n* any tropical Asian tuberous plant of the genus *Curcuma,* such as *C. longa,* which is the source of turmeric, and *C. zedoaria,* which is the source of zedoary: family *Zingiberaceae.* [C17: from New Latin, from Arabic *kurkum* turmeric]

curd (kɜːd) *n* **1** *(often pl)* a substance formed from the coagulation of milk by acid or rennet, used in making cheese or eaten as a food. **2** something similar in consistency. ◆ *vb* **3** to turn into or become curd. [C15: from earlier *crud,* of unknown origin] ▸ **'curdy** *adj* ▸ **'curdiness** *n*

curd cheese *n* a mild white cheese made from skimmed milk curds, smoother and fattier than cottage cheese.

curdle ('kɜːdᵊl) *vb* **1** to turn or cause to turn into curd. **2 curdle someone's blood.** to fill someone with fear. [C16 *(crudled,* past participle): from CURD] ▸ **'curdler** *n*

cure (kjʊə) *vb* **1** *(tr)* to get rid of (an ailment, fault, or problem); heal. **2** *(tr)* to restore to health or good condition. **3** *(intr)* to bring about a cure. **4** *(tr)* to preserve (meat, fish, etc.) by salting, smoking, etc. **5** *(tr)* **5a** to treat or finish (a substance) by chemical or physical means. **5b** to vulcanize (rubber). **6** *(tr)* to assist the hardening of (concrete, mortar, etc.) by keeping it moist. ◆ *n* **7** a return to health, esp. after specific treatment. **8** any course of medical therapy, esp. one proved effective in combating a disease. **9** a means of restoring health or improving a condition, situation, etc. **10** the spiritual and pastoral charge of a parish: *the cure of souls.* **11** a process or method of preserving meat, fish, etc., by salting, pickling, or smoking. [(n) C13: from Old French, from Latin *cūra* care; in ecclesiastical sense, from Medieval Latin *cūra* spiritual charge; (vb) C14: from Old French *curer,* from Latin *cūrāre* to attend to, heal, from *cūra* care] ▸ **'cureless** *adj* ▸ **'curer** *n*

curé ('kjʊəreɪ) *n* a parish priest in France. [French, from Medieval Latin *cūrātus;* see CURATE[1]]

cure-all *n* something reputed to cure all ailments.

curettage ('kjʊərɪ'tɑːʒ, kjʊə'retɪdʒ) *or* **curettement** (kjʊə'retmənt) *n* the process of [illegible]ng a curette. See also **D and C.**

curette *or* **curet** (kjʊə'ret) *n* **1** a surgical instrument for removing dead tissue, growths, etc., from the walls of certain body cavities. ◆ *vb* **-rettes** *or* **-rets, -retting, -retted. 2** *(tr)* to scrape or clean with such an instrument. [C18: from French, from *curer* to heal, make clean; see CURE]

curfew ('kɜːfjuː) *n* **1** an official regulation setting restrictions on movement, esp. after a specific time at night. **2** the time set as a deadline by such a regulation. **3** (in medieval Europe) **3a** the ringing of a bell to prompt people to extinguish fires and lights. **3b** the time at which the curfew bell was rung. **3c** the bell itself. [C13: from Old French *cuevrefeu,* literally: cover the fire]

curia ('kjʊərɪə) *n, pl* **-riae** (-rɪ,iː). **1** *(sometimes cap.)* the papal court and government of the Roman Catholic Church. **2** (in ancient Rome) **2a** any of the ten subdivisions of the Latin, Sabine, or Etruscan tribes. **2b** a meeting place of such a subdivision. **2c** the senate house of Rome. **2d** the senate of an Italian town under Roman administration. **3** (in the Middle Ages) a court held in the king's name. See also **Curia Regis.** [C16: from Latin, from Old Latin *coviria* (unattested), from CO- + *vir* man] ▸ **'curial** *adj*

Curia Regis ('riːdʒɪs) *n, pl* **Curiae Regis.** (in Norman England) the king's court, which performed all functions of government. [Latin, literally: council of the king]

curie ('kjʊərɪ, -riː) *n* a unit of radioactivity equal to 3.7×10^{10} disintegrations per second. Symbol: Ci [C20: named after Pierre CURIE]

Curie ('kjʊərɪ, -riː; *French* kyri) *n* **1 Marie** (mari). 1867–1934, French physicist and chemist, born in Poland: discovered with her husband Pierre the radioactivity of thorium, and discovered and isolated radium and polonium. She shared a Nobel prize for physics (1903) with her husband and Henri Becquerel, and was awarded a Nobel prize for chemistry (1911). **2** her husband, **Pierre** (pjɛr). 1859–1906, French physicist and chemist.

Curie point *or* **temperature** *n* the temperature above which a ferromagnetic substance loses its ferromagnetism and becomes paramagnetic. [C20: named after Pierre CURIE]

Curie's law *n* the principle that the magnetic susceptibility of a paramagnetic substance is inversely proportional to its thermodynamic temperature. See also **Curie-Weiss law.**

Curie-Weiss law *n* the principle that the magnetic susceptibility of a paramagnetic substance is inversely proportional to the difference between its temperature and its Curie point. [C20: named after Pierre CURIE and Pierre-Ernest *Weiss* (died 1940), French physicist]

curio ('kjʊərɪ,əʊ) *n, pl* **-rios.** a small article valued as a collector's item, esp. something fascinating or unusual. [C19: shortened from CURIOSITY]

curiosa (,kjʊərɪ'əʊsə) *n (functioning as pl)* **1** curiosities. **2** books on strange subjects, esp. erotica. [New Latin: from Latin *cūriōsus* CURIOUS]

curiosity (,kjʊərɪ'ɒsɪtɪ) *n, pl* **-ties. 1** an eager desire to know; inquisitiveness. **2a** the quality of being curious; strangeness. **2b** *(as modifier): the ring had curiosity value only.* **3** something strange or fascinating. **4** a rare or strange object; curio. **5** *Obsolete.* fastidiousness.

curious ('kjʊərɪəs) *adj* **1** eager to learn; inquisitive. **2** over inquisitive; prying. **3** interesting because of oddness or novelty; strange; unexpected. **4** *Rare.* (of workmanship, etc.) highly detailed, intricate, or subtle. **5** *Obsolete.* fastidious or hard to please. [C14: from Latin *cūriōsus* taking pains over something, from *cūra* care] ▸ **'curiously** *adv* ▸ **'curiousness** *n*

Curitiba (,kʊərɪ'tiːbə) *n* a city in SE Brazil, capital of Paraná state: seat of the University of Paraná (1946). Pop.: 841 882 (1991).

curium ('kjʊərɪəm) *n* a silvery-white metallic transuranic element artificially produced from plutonium. Symbol: Cm; atomic no.: 96; half-life of most stable isotope, ^{247}Cm: 1.6×10^7 years; valency: 3 and 4; relative density: 13.51 (calculated); melting pt.: 1345±400°C. [C20: New Latin, named after Pierre and Marie CURIE]

curl (kɜːl) *vb* **1** *(intr)* (esp. of hair) to grow into curves or ringlets. **2** *(tr; sometimes foll. by up)* to twist or roll (something, esp. hair) into coils or ringlets. **3** (often foll. by *up*) to become or cause to become spiral-shaped or curved; coil: *the heat made the leaves curl up.* **4** *(intr)* to move in a curving or twisting manner. **5** *(intr)* to play the game of curling. **6 curl one's lip.** to show contempt, as by raising a corner of the lip. ◆ *n* **7** a curve or coil of hair. **8** a curved or spiral shape or mark, as in wood. **9** the act of curling or state of being curled. **10** any of various plant diseases characterized by curling of the leaves. **11** Also called: **rot, rotation.** *Maths.* a vector quantity associated with a vector field that is the vector product of the operator ∇ and a vector function ***A***, where $\nabla = \mathbf{i}\partial/\partial x + \mathbf{j}\partial/\partial y + \mathbf{k}\partial/\partial z$, ***i, j,*** and ***k*** being unit vectors. Usually written curl ***A***, rot ***A***. Compare **divergence** (sense 4), **gradient** (sense 4). ◆ See also **curl up.** [C14: probably from Middle Dutch *crullen* to curl; related to Middle High German *krol* curly, Middle Low German *krūs* curly]

curled paperwork *n* another name for **rolled paperwork.**

curler ('kɜːlə) *n* **1** any of various pins, clasps, or rollers used to curl or wave hair. **2** a person or thing that curls. **3** a person who plays curling.

curlew ('kɜːljuː) *n* any large shore bird of the genus *Numenius,* such as *N. arquata* of Europe and Asia: family *Scolopacidae* (sandpipers, etc.), order *Charadriiformes.* They have a long downward-curving bill and occur in northern and arctic regions. Compare **stone curlew.** [C14: from Old French *corlieu,* perhaps of imitative origin]

curlew sandpiper *n* a common Eurasian sandpiper, *Calidris ferruginea,* having a brick-red breeding plumage and a greyish winter plumage.

curli ('kɜːlɪ) *pl n Bacteriol.* curled hairlike processes on the surface of the bacterium *Escherichia coli* by means of which the bacterium adheres to and infects wounds. [C20: from *curl(ed)* (PIL)I]

curlicue ('kɜːlɪ,kjuː) *n* an intricate ornamental curl or twist. [C19: from CURLY + CUE[2]]

curling ('kɜːlɪŋ) *n* a game played on ice, esp. in Scotland, in which heavy stones with handles (**curling stones**) are slid towards a target (**tee**).

curling tongs *pl n* a metal scissor-like device that is heated, so that strands of hair may be twined around it in order to form curls. Also called: **curling iron, curling irons, curling pins.**

curlpaper ('kɜːl,peɪpə) *n* a strip of paper used to roll up and set a section of hair, usually wetted, into a curl.

curl up *vb (adv)* **1** *(intr)* to adopt a reclining position with the legs close to the body and the back rounded. **2** to become or cause to become spiral-shaped or curved. **3** *(intr)* to retire to a quiet cosy setting: *to curl up with a good novel.* **4** *Brit. informal.* to be or cause to be embarrassed or disgusted (esp. in the phrase **curl up and die**).

curly ('kɜːlɪ) *adj* **curlier, curliest. 1** tending to curl; curling. **2** having curls. **3** (of timber) having irregular curves or waves in the grain. **4** *Austral. and N.Z.* difficult to counter or answer: *a curly question.* ▸ **'curliness** *n*

curmudgeon (kɜː'mʌdʒən) *n* a surly or miserly person. [C16: of unknown origin] ▸ **cur'mudgeonly** *adj*

Curnow (kɜːnaʊ) *n* (**Thomas**) **Allen** (**Monro**) born 1911, New Zealand poet and anthologist.

currach, curagh, *or* ***curragh*** *Gaelic.* ('kʌrəx, 'kʌrə) *n* a Scot. or Irish name for **coracle.** [C15: from Irish Gaelic *currach;* compare CORACLE]

currajong ('kʌrə,dʒɒŋ) *n* a variant spelling of **kurrajong.**

currant ('kʌrənt) *n* **1** a small dried seedless grape of the Mediterranean region, used in cooking. **2** any of several mainly N temperate shrubs of the genus *Ribes,* esp. *R. rubrum* (redcurrant) and *R. nigrum* (blackcurrant): family *Grossulariaceae.* See also **gooseberry** (sense 1). **3** the small acid fruit of any of these plants. [C16: shortened from *rayson of Corannte* raisin of Corinth]

currant bun *n* **1** *Brit.* a sweet bun containing currants. **2** *Scot.* another name for **black bun.**

currawong ('kʌrə,wɒŋ) *n* any Australian crowlike songbird of the genus *Strepera,* having black, grey, and white plumage: family *Cracticidae.* Also called: **bell magpie.** [from a native Australian name]

currency ('kʌrənsɪ) *n, pl* **-cies. 1** a metal or paper medium of exchange that is in current use in a particular country. **2** general acceptance or circulation; prevalence: *the currency of ideas.* **3** the period of time during which something is valid, accepted, or in force. **4** the act of being passed from person to person. **5** *Austral.* (formerly) the local medium of exchange, esp. in the colonies, as distinct from sterling. **6** *Austral. slang.* (formerly) the native-born Australians, as distinct from the British immigrants. [C17: from Medieval Latin *currentia,* literally: a flowing, from Latin *currere* to run, flow]

currency note *n* another name for **treasury note** (sense b).

current ('kʌrənt) *adj* **1** of the immediate present; in progress: *current events.* **2** most recent; up-to-date: *the current issue of a magazine.* **3** commonly known, practised, or accepted; widespread: *a current rumour.* **4** circulating and valid at present: *current coins.* ◆ *n* **5** (esp. of water or air) a steady usually natural flow. **6** a mass of air, body of water, etc., that has a steady flow in a particular direction. **7** the rate of flow of such a mass. **8** Also called: **electric current.** *Physics.* **8a** a flow of electric charge through a conductor. **8b** the rate of flow of this charge. It is usually measured in amperes. Symbol: I **9** a general trend or drift: *currents of opinion.* [C13: from Old French *corant,* literally: running, from *corre* to run, from Latin *currere*] ▸ **'currently** *adv* ▸ **'currentness** *n*

current account *n* **1** an account at a bank or building society against which cheques may be drawn at any time. U.S. name: **checking account.** Canadian name: **chequing account. 2** *Economics.* that part of the balance of payments composed of the balance of trade and the invisible balance. Compare **capital account** (sense 1).

current assets *pl n* cash and operating assets that are convertible into cash within a year. Also called: **floating assets.** Compare **fixed assets.**

current-cost accounting *n* a method of accounting that values assets at their current replacement cost rather than their original cost. It is often used in times of high inflation. Compare **historical-cost accounting.**

current density *n* the ratio of the electric current flowing at a particular point in a conductor to the cross-sectional area of the conductor taken perpendicular to the current flow at that point. It is measured in amperes per square metre. Symbol: J

current efficiency *n Physics.* the ratio of the actual mass of a substance liberated from an electrolyte by the passage of current to the theoretical mass liberated according to Faraday's law.

current expenses *pl n* noncapital and usually recurrent expenditures necessary for the operation of a business.

current liabilities *pl n* business liabilities maturing within a year.

curricle ('kʌrɪkᵊl) *n* a two-wheeled open carriage drawn by two horses side by side. [C18: from Latin *curriculum* from *currus* chariot, from *currere* to run]

curriculum (kə'rɪkjʊləm) *n, pl* **-la** (-lə) *or* **-lums. 1** a course of study in one subject at a school or college. **2** a list of all the courses of study offered by a school or college. **3** any programme or plan of activities. [C19: from Latin: course, from *currere* to run] ▸ **cur'ricular** *adj*

curriculum vitae ('vi:taɪ, 'vaɪti:) *n, pl* **curricula vitae.** an outline of a person's educational and professional history, usually prepared for job applications. Abbrev.: **CV.** [Latin, literally: the course of one's life]

currier ('kʌrɪə) *n* a person who curries leather. [C14: from Old French *corier,* from Latin *coriārius* a tanner, from *corium* leather]

curriery ('kʌrɪərɪ) *n, pl* **-eries.** the trade, work, or place of occupation of a currier.

currish ('kɜ:rɪʃ) *adj* of or like a cur; rude or bad-tempered. ▸ **'currishly** *adv* ▸ **'currishness** *n*

curry[1] ('kʌrɪ) *n, pl* **-ries. 1** a spicy dish of oriental, esp. Indian, origin that is made in many ways but usually consists of meat or fish prepared in a hot piquant sauce. **2** curry seasoning or sauce. **3 give someone curry.** *Austral. slang.* to assault (a person) verbally or physically. ◆ *vb* **-ries, -rying, -ried. 4** (*tr*) to prepare (food) with curry powder or sauce. [C16: from Tamil *kari* sauce, relish]

curry[2] ('kʌrɪ) *vb* **-ries, -rying, -ried.** (*tr*) **1** to beat vigorously, as in order to clean. **2** to dress and finish (leather) after it has been tanned to make it strong, flexible, and waterproof. **3** to groom (a horse). **4 curry favour.** to ingratiate oneself, esp. with superiors. [C13: from Old French *correer* to make ready, from Vulgar Latin *conrēdāre* (unattested), from *rēdāre* (unattested) to provide, of Germanic origin]

Curry ('kʌrɪ) *n* **John (Anthony).** 1949–94, British ice skater: won the figure-skating gold medal in the 1976 Olympic Games.

currycomb ('kʌrɪ,kəʊm) *n* a square comb consisting of rows of small teeth, used for grooming horses.

curry powder *n* a mixture of finely ground pungent spices, such as turmeric, cumin, coriander, ginger, etc., used in making curries.

curry puff *n* (in eastern cookery) a type of pie or pasty consisting of a pastry case containing curried meat and vegetables.

curse (kɜ:s) *n* **1** a profane or obscene expression of anger, disgust, surprise, etc.; oath. **2** an appeal to a supernatural power for harm to come to a specific person, group, etc. **3** harm resulting from an appeal to a supernatural power: *to be under a curse.* **4** something that brings or causes great trouble or harm. **5** a saying, charm, effigy, etc., used to invoke a curse. **6** an ecclesiastical censure of excommunication. **7** (preceded by *the*) *Informal.* menstruation or a menstrual period. ◆ *vb* **curses, cursing, cursed** *or* (*Archaic*) **curst. 8** (*intr*) to utter obscenities or oaths. **9** (*tr*) to abuse (someone) with obscenities or oaths. **10** (*tr*) to invoke supernatural powers to bring harm to (someone or something). **11** (*tr*) to bring harm upon. **12** (*tr*) another word for **excommunicate.** [Old English *cursian* to curse, from *curs* a curse] ▸ **'curser** *n*

cursed ('kɜ:sɪd, kɜ:st) *or* **curst** *adj* **1** under a curse. **2** deserving to be cursed; detestable; hateful. ▸ **'cursedly** *adv* ▸ **'cursedness** *n*

curses ('kɜ:sɪz) *interj Often facetious.* an expression of disappointment or dismay.

cursive ('kɜ:sɪv) *adj* **1** of or relating to handwriting in which letters are formed and joined in a rapid flowing style. **2** *Printing.* of or relating to typefaces that resemble handwriting. ◆ *n* **3** a cursive letter or printing type. **4** a manuscript written in cursive letters. [C18: from Medieval Latin *cursīvus* running, ultimately from Latin *currere* to run] ▸ **'cursively** *adv*

cursor ('kɜ:sə) *n* **1** the sliding part of a measuring instrument, esp. a transparent sliding square on a slide rule. **2** any of various means, typically a flashing bar or underline, of identifying a particular position on a computer screen, such as the insertion point for text.

cursorial (kɜ:'sɔ:rɪəl) *adj Zoology.* adapted for running: *a cursorial skeleton; cursorial birds.*

cursory ('kɜ:sərɪ) *adj* hasty and usually superficial; quick: *a cursory check.* [C17: from Late Latin *cursōrius* of running, from Latin *cursus* a course, from *currere* to run] ▸ **'cursorily** *adv* ▸ **'cursoriness** *n*

curst (kɜ:st) *vb* **1** *Archaic.* a past tense and past participle of **curse.** ◆ *adj* **2** a variant of **cursed.**

curt (kɜ:t) *adj* **1** rudely blunt and brief; abrupt: *a curt reply.* **2** short or concise. [C17: from Latin *curtus* cut short, mutilated] ▸ **'curtly** *adv* ▸ **'curtness** *n*

curtail (kɜ:'teɪl) *vb* (*tr*) to cut short; abridge. [C16: changed (through influence of TAIL[1]) from obsolete *curtal* to dock; see CURTAL] ▸ **cur'tailer** *n* ▸ **cur'tailment** *n*

curtail step ('kɜ:teɪl) *n* the step or steps at the foot of a flight of stairs, widened at one or both ends and terminated with a scroll.

curtain ('kɜ:tᵊn) *n* **1** a piece of material that can be drawn across an opening or window, to shut out light or to provide privacy. **2** a barrier to vision, access, or communication: *a curtain of secrecy.* **3** a hanging cloth or similar barrier for concealing all or part of a theatre stage from the audience. **4** (often preceded by *the*) the end of a scene of a play, opera, etc., marked by the fall or closing of the curtain. **5** the rise or opening of the curtain at the start of a performance. ◆ *vb* **6** (*tr; sometimes foll. by off*) to shut off or conceal with or as if with a curtain. **7** (*tr*) to provide (a window, etc.) with curtains. ◆ See also **curtains.** [C13: from Old French *courtine,* from Late Latin *cortīna* enclosed place, curtain, probably from Latin *cohors* courtyard]

curtain call *n* the appearance of performers at the end of a theatrical performance to acknowledge applause.

curtain lecture *n* a scolding or rebuke given in private, esp. by a wife to her husband. [alluding to the curtained beds where such rebukes were once given]

curtain-raiser *n* **1** *Theatre.* a short dramatic piece presented before the main play. **2** any preliminary event: *the debate was a curtain-raiser to the election.*

curtains ('kɜ:tᵊnz) *pl n Informal.* death or ruin; the end: *if the enemy see us it will be curtains for us.*

curtain speech *n* **1** a talk given in front of the curtain after a stage performance, often by the author or an actor. **2** the final speech of an act or a play.

curtain wall *n* **1** a non-load-bearing external wall attached to a framed structure, often one that is prefabricated. **2** a low wall outside the outer wall of a castle, serving as a first line of defence.

curtal ('kɜ:tᵊl) *Obsolete.* ◆ *adj* **1** cut short. **2** (of friars) wearing a short frock. ◆ *n* **3** an animal whose tail has been docked. **4** something that is cut short. [C16: from Old French *courtault* animal whose tail has been docked, from *court* short, from Latin *curtus;* see CURT]

curtal axe *n* an obsolete term for **cutlass.** [C16: alteration by folk etymology of Old French *coutelas* CUTLASS; see CURTAL]

curtana (kɜ:'tɑ:nə) *n* the unpointed sword carried before an English sovereign at a coronation as an emblem of mercy. [C15: from Anglo-Latin, from Old French *cortain,* the name of Roland's sword, which was broken at the point, ultimately from Latin *curtus* short]

curtate ('kɜ:teɪt) *adj* shortened. [C17: from Late Latin *curtāre* to shorten, from Latin *curtus* cut short; see CURT]

curtilage ('kɜ:tɪlɪdʒ) *n* the enclosed area of land adjacent to a dwelling house. [C14: from Old French *cortillage,* from *cortil* a little yard, from *cort* COURT]

Curtin ('kɜ:tɪn) *n* **John Joseph.** 1885–1945, Australian statesman; prime minister of Australia (1941–45).

curtsy *or* **curtsey** ('kɜ:tsɪ) *n, pl* **-sies** *or* **-seys. 1** a formal gesture of greeting and respect made by women in which the knees are bent, the head slightly bowed, and the skirt held outwards. ◆ *vb* **-sies, -sying, -sied** *or* **-seys, -seying, -seyed. 2** (*intr*) to make a curtsy. [C16: variant of COURTESY]

curule ('kjʊəru:l) *adj* (in ancient Rome) of the highest rank, esp. one entitled to use a curule chair. [C16: from Latin *curūlis* of a chariot, from *currus* chariot, from *currere* to run]

curule chair *n* an upholstered folding seat with curved legs used by the highest civil officials of ancient Rome.

curvaceous (kɜ:'veɪʃəs) *adj Informal.* (esp. of a woman) having shapely curves or a well-rounded body. ▸ **cur'vaceously** *adv*

curvature ('kɜ:vətʃə) *n* **1** something curved or a curved part of a thing. **2** any normal or abnormal curving of a bodily part: *curvature of the spine.* **3** *Geometry.* the change in inclination of a tangent to a curve over unit length of arc. For a circle or sphere it is the reciprocal of the radius. See also **radius of curva-**

ture, centre of curvature. **4** the act of curving or the state or degree of being curved or bent.

curve (kɜːv) *n* **1** a continuously bending line that has no straight parts. **2** something that curves or is curved, such as a bend in a road or the contour of a woman's body. **3** the act or extent of curving; curvature. **4** *Maths.* **4a** a system of points whose coordinates satisfy a given equation; a locus of points. **4b** the graph of a function with one independent variable. **5** a line representing data, esp. statistical data, on a graph: *an unemployment curve.* **6** short for **French curve.** ◆ *vb* **7** to take or cause to take the shape or path of a curve; bend. ◆ Related adj: **sinuous.** [C15: from Latin *curvāre* to bend, from *curvus* crooked] ▸ **curvedly** ('kɜːvɪdlɪ) *adv* ▸ **'curvedness** *n* ▸ **'curvy** *adj*

curve ball *n* **1** *Baseball.* a ball pitched in a curving path so as to make it more difficult to hit. **2** *Informal.* something deceptive: *his wholesome image was a curve ball thrown to deceive the public.*

curvet (kɜː'vɛt) *n* **1** *Dressage.* a low leap with all four feet off the ground. ◆ *vb* **-vets, -vetting, -vetted** *or* **-vets, -veting, -veted.** **2** *Dressage.* to make or cause to make such a leap. **3** (*intr*) to prance or frisk about. [C16: from Old Italian *corvetta,* from Old French *courbette,* from *courber* to bend, from Latin *curvāre*]

curvilinear (ˌkɜːvɪ'lɪnɪə) *or* **curvilineal** *adj* **1** consisting of, bounded by, or characterized by a curved line. **2** along a curved line: *curvilinear motion.* **3** *Maths.* (of a set of coordinates) determined by or determining a system of three orthogonal surfaces. ▸ **ˌcurviˌline'arity** *n* ▸ **ˌcurvi'linearly** *adv*

Curzon ('kɜːzᵊn) *n* **1** Sir **Clifford.** 1907–82, English pianist. **2 George Nathaniel,** 1st Marquis Curzon of Kedleston. 1859–1925, British Conservative statesman; viceroy of India (1898–1905).

Cusack ('kjuːsæk) *n* **Cyril (James).** 1910–93, Irish actor.

Cusanus (kjuː'seɪnəs) *n* **Nicholas.** See **Nicholas of Cusa.**

Cusco (*Spanish* 'kusko) *n* a variant of **Cuzco.**

cuscus ('kʌskʌs) *n, pl* **-cuses.** any of several large nocturnal phalangers of the genus *Phalanger,* of N Australia, New Guinea, and adjacent islands, having dense fur, prehensile tails, large eyes, and a yellow nose. [C17: New Latin, probably from a native name in New Guinea]

cusec ('kjuːsɛk) *n* a unit of flow equal to 1 cubic foot per second. 1 cusec is equivalent to 0.028 317 cubic metre per second. [C20: from *cu(bic foot per) sec(ond)*]

Cush *or* **Kush** (kʌʃ, kʊʃ) *n Old Testament.* **1** the son of Ham and brother of Canaan (Genesis 10:6). **2** the country of the supposed descendants of Cush (ancient Ethiopia), comprising approximately Nubia and the modern Sudan, and the territory of southern (or Upper) Egypt.

cushat ('kʌʃət) *n* another name for **wood pigeon.** [Old English *cūscote;* perhaps related to *sceōtan* to shoot]

cushie-doo (ˌkʊʃɪ'duː) *n* a Scot. name for a **wood pigeon.** Often shortened to **cushie.** [from CUSHAT + DOO]

Cushing ('kʊʃɪŋ) *n* **Harvey Williams.** 1869–1939, U.S. neurosurgeon: identified a pituitary tumour as a cause of the disease named after him.

Cushing's disease *or* **syndrome** *n* a rare condition caused by excess corticosteroid hormones in the body, characterized chiefly by obesity of the trunk and face, high blood pressure, fatigue, and loss of calcium from the bones. [C20: named after H. W. CUSHING]

cushion ('kʊʃən) *n* **1** a bag made of cloth, leather, plastic, etc., filled with feathers, air, or other yielding substance, used for sitting on, leaning against, etc. **2** something resembling a cushion in function or appearance, esp. one to support or pad or to absorb shock. **3** the resilient felt-covered rim of a billiard table. **4** another name for **pillow** (sense 2). **5** short for **air cushion.** **6** a capital, used in Byzantine, Romanesque, and Norman architecture, in the form of a bowl with a square top. ◆ *vb* (*tr*) **7** to place on or as on a cushion. **8** to provide with cushions. **9** to protect, esp. against hardship or change. **10a** to check the motion of (a mechanism) gently, esp. by the compression of trapped fluid in a cylinder. **10b** to provide with a means of absorbing shock. [from Latin *culcita* mattress] ▸ **'cushiony** *adj*

cushion plant *n* a type of low-growing plant having many closely spaced short upright shoots, typical of alpine and arctic habitats.

Cushitic (kʊ'ʃɪtɪk) *n* **1** a group of languages of Somalia, Ethiopia, NE Kenya, and adjacent regions: a subfamily within the Afro-Asiatic family of languages. ◆ *adj* **2** denoting, relating to, or belonging to this group of languages.

cushy ('kʊʃɪ) *adj* **cushier, cushiest.** *Informal.* easy; comfortable: *a cushy job.* [C20: from Hindi *khush* pleasant, from Persian *khōsh*]

cusk (kʌsk) *n, pl* **cusks** *or* **cusk.** the usual Eastern U.S. and Canadian name for the **torsk.** [C17: probably alteration of *tusk* of Scandinavian origin; compare Old Norse *thorskr* codfish]

CUSO ('kjuːsəʊ) *n acronym for* Canadian University Services Overseas; an organization that sends students to work as volunteers in developing countries.

cusp (kʌsp) *n* **1** any of the small elevations on the grinding or chewing surface of a tooth. **2** any of the triangular flaps of a heart valve. **3** a point or pointed end. **4** Also called: **spinode.** *Geom.* a point at which two arcs of a curve intersect and at which the two tangents are coincident. **5** *Architect.* a carving at the meeting place of two arcs. **6** *Astronomy.* either of the points of a crescent moon or of a satellite or inferior planet in a similar phase. **7** *Astrology.* any division between houses or signs of the zodiac. [C16: from Latin *cuspis* point, pointed end]

cuspate ('kʌspɪt, -peɪt), **cuspated,** *or* **cusped** (kʌspt) *adj* **1** having a cusp or cusps. **2** shaped like a cusp; cusplike.

cuspid ('kʌspɪd) *n* a tooth having one point; canine tooth.

cuspidate ('kʌspɪˌdeɪt), **cuspidated,** *or* **cuspidal** ('kʌspɪdᵊl) *adj* **1** having a cusp or cusps. **2** (esp. of leaves) narrowing to a point. [C17: from Latin *cuspidāre* to make pointed, from *cuspis* a point]

cuspidation (ˌkʌspɪ'deɪʃən) *n Architect.* decoration using cusps.

cuspidor ('kʌspɪˌdɔː) *n* another word (esp. U.S.) for **spittoon.** [C18: from Portuguese, from *cuspir* to spit, from Latin *conspuere,* from *spuere* to spit]

cuss (kʌs) *Informal.* ◆ *n* **1** a curse; oath. **2** a person or animal, esp. an annoying one. ◆ *vb* **3** another word for **curse** (senses 8, 9).

cussed ('kʌsɪd) *adj Informal.* **1** another word for **cursed.** **2** obstinate. **3** annoying: *a cussed nuisance.* ▸ **'cussedly** *adv* ▸ **'cussedness** *n*

custard ('kʌstəd) *n* **1** a baked sweetened mixture of eggs and milk. **2** a sauce made of milk and sugar and thickened with cornflour. [C15: alteration of Middle English *crustade* kind of pie, probably from Old Provençal *croustado,* from *crosta* CRUST]

custard apple *n* **1** a West Indian tree, *Annona reticulata:* family *Annonaceae.* **2** the large heart-shaped fruit of this tree, which has a fleshy edible pulp. **3** any of several related trees or fruits, esp. the papaw and sweetsop. ◆ Also called (for senses 1, 2): **bullock's heart.**

custard pie *n* **a** a flat, open pie filled with real or artificial custard, as thrown in slapstick comedy. **b** (*as modifier*): *custard-pie humour.*

custard powder *n* a powder containing cornflour, sugar, etc., for thickening milk to make a yellow sauce. See **custard** (sense 2).

Custer ('kʌstə) *n* **George Armstrong.** 1839–76, U.S. cavalry general: Civil War hero, killed fighting the Sioux Indians at Little Bighorn, Montana.

custodian (kʌ'stəʊdɪən) *n* **1** a person who has custody, as of a prisoner, ward, etc. **2** a guardian or keeper, as of an art collection, etc.

custodianship (kʌ'stəʊdɪənʃɪp) *n* **1** the condition of being a custodian. **2** (in Britain) a legal basis for the care of children under the Children's Act 1975, midway between fostering and adoption, devised for children settled in long-term foster care or living permanently with relatives or a step-parent.

custody ('kʌstədɪ) *n, pl* **-dies. 1** the act of keeping safe or guarding, esp. the right of guardianship of a minor. **2** the state of being held by the police; arrest (esp. in the phrases **in custody, take into custody**). [C15: from Latin *custōdia,* from *custōs* guard, defender] ▸ **custodial** (kʌ'stəʊdɪəl) *adj*

custom ('kʌstəm) *n* **1** a usual or habitual practice; typical mode of behaviour. **2** the long-established habits or traditions of a society collectively; convention: *custom dictates good manners.* **3a** a practice which by long-established usage has come to have the force of law. **3b** such practices collectively (esp. in the phrase **custom and practice**). **4** habitual patronage, esp. of a shop or business. **5** the customers of a shop or business collectively. **6** (in feudal Europe) a tribute paid by a vassal to his lord. ◆ *adj* **7** made to the specifications of an individual customer (often in the combinations **custom-built, custom-made**). **8** specializing in goods so made. ◆ See also **customs.** [C12: from Old French *costume,* from Latin *consuētūdō,* from *consuēscere* to grow accustomed to, from *suēscere* to be used to]

customable ('kʌstəməbᵊl) *adj* subject to customs.

customary ('kʌstəmərɪ, -təmrɪ) *adj* **1** in accordance with custom or habitual practice; usual; habitual. **2** *Law.* **2a** founded upon long continued practices and usage rather than law. **2b** (of land, esp. a feudal estate) held by custom. ◆ *n, pl* **-aries. 3a** a statement in writing of customary laws and practices. **3b** a body of such laws and customs. ▸ **'customarily** *adv* ▸ **'customariness** *n*

custom-built *adj* (of cars, houses, etc.) made according to the specifications of an individual buyer.

customer ('kʌstəmə) *n* **1** a person who buys. **2** *Informal.* a person with whom one has dealings: *a cool customer.*

custom house *or* **customs house** *n* a government office, esp. at a port, where customs are collected and ships cleared for entry.

customize *or* **customise** ('kʌstəˌmaɪz) *vb* (*tr*) to make (something) according to a customer's individual requirements.

custom-made *adj* (of suits, dresses, etc.) made according to the specifications of an individual buyer.

customs ('kʌstəmz) *n* (*functioning as sing or pl*) **1** duty on imports or exports. **2** the government department responsible for the collection of these duties. **3** the part of a port, airport, frontier station, etc., where baggage and freight are examined for dutiable goods and contraband. **4** the procedure for examining baggage and freight, paying duty, etc. **5** (*as modifier*): *customs officer.*

customs union *n* an association of nations which promotes free trade within the union and establishes common tariffs on trade with nonmember nations.

custos ('kʌstɒs) *n, pl* **custodes** (kʌ'stəʊdiːz). a superior in the Franciscan religious order. Also called (in England): **guardian.** [C15: from Latin: keeper, guard]

custumal ('kʌstjʊməl) *n, adj* another word for **customary** (senses 2, 3). [C16: from Medieval Latin *custumālis* relating to CUSTOM]

cut (kʌt) *vb* **cuts, cutting, cut. 1** to open up or incise (a person or thing) with a sharp edge or instrument; gash. **2** (of a sharp instrument) to penetrate or incise (a person or thing). **3** to divide or be divided with or as if with a sharp instrument: *cut a slice of bread.* **4** (*intr*) to use a sharp-edged instrument or an instrument that cuts. **5** (*tr*) to trim or prune by or as if by clipping: *to cut hair.* **6** (*tr*) to reap or mow (a crop, grass, etc.). **7** (*tr*) to geld or castrate. **8** (*tr;* sometimes foll. by *out*) to make, form, or shape by cutting: *to cut a suit.* **9** (*tr*) to hollow or dig out; excavate: *to cut a tunnel through the mountain.* **10** to strike (an object) sharply. **11** (*tr*) *Sport.* to hit (a ball) with a downward slicing stroke so as to impart spin or cause it to fall short. **12** *Cricket.* to hit (the ball) to the off side, usually between cover and third man, with a roughly horizontal bat. **13** to hurt or wound the feelings of (a person), esp. by malicious speech or action. **14** (*tr*) *Informal.* to refuse to recognize; snub. **15** (*tr*) *Informal.* to absent oneself from (an activity, location, etc.), esp. without permission or in haste: *to cut class.* **16** (*tr*) to abridge, shorten, or edit by excising a part or parts. **17** (*tr;* often foll. by *down*) to lower, reduce, or curtail: *to cut losses.* **18** (*tr*) to dilute or weaken: *heroin that was cut with nontoxic elements.* **19** (*tr*) to dissolve or break up: *to cut fat.* **20** (when *intr,* foll. by *across* or *through*) to cross or traverse: *the footpath cuts through the field.* **21** (*intr*) to make a sharp or sudden change in direction; veer. **22** to grow (teeth) through the gums or (of teeth) to appear through the gums. **23** (*intr*) *Films.* **23a** to call a halt to a shooting sequence. **23b** (foll. by *to*) to move quickly to another scene. **24** *Films.* to edit (film). **25** (*tr*) to switch off (a light, car engine, etc.). **26** (*tr*) (of a performer, recording company, etc.) to make (a record or tape of a song, concert, performance, etc.). **27** *Cards.* **27a** to divide (the pack) at random into two parts after shuffling. **27b** (*intr*) to pick cards from a spread pack to decide dealer, partners, etc. **28** (*tr*) to remove (material) from an object by means of a chisel, lathe, etc. **29** (*tr*) (of a tool) to bite into (an object). **30** (*intr*) (of a horse) to injure the leg just above the hoof by a blow from the opposite foot. **31 cut a caper** *or* **capers. 31a** to skip or jump playfully. **31b** to act or behave playfully; frolic. **32 cut both ways. 32a** to have both good and bad effects. **32b** to affect both sides of something, as two parties in an argument, etc. **33 cut a dash.** to behave or dress showily or strikingly; make a stylish impression. **34 cut (a person) dead.** *Informal.* to ignore (a person) completely. **35 cut a (good, poor, etc.) figure.** to appear or behave in a specified manner. **36 cut and run.** *Informal.* to make a rapid escape. **37 cut it fine.** *Informal.* to allow little margin of time, space, etc. **38 cut corners.** to do something in the easiest or shortest way, esp. at the expense of high standards: *we could finish this project early only if we cut corners.* **39 cut loose.** to free or become freed from restraint, custody, anchorage, etc. **40 cut no ice.** *Informal.* to fail to make an impression. **41 cut one's losses.** to give up spending time, money, or energy on an unprofitable or unsuccessful activity. **42 cut one's teeth on.** *Informal.* **42a** to use at an early age or stage. **42b** to practise on. ◆ *adj* **43** detached, divided, or separated by cutting. **44** *Botany.* incised or divided: *cut leaves.* **45** made, shaped, or fashioned by cutting. **46** reduced or diminished by or as if by cutting: *cut prices.* **47** gelded or castrated. **48** weakened or diluted. **49** *Brit.* a slang word for **drunk. 50** hurt; resentful. **51 cut and dried.** *Informal.* settled or arranged in advance. **52 cut lunch.** *Austral. and N.Z.* a sandwich lunch carried from home to work, school, etc. ◆ *n* **53** the act of cutting. **54** a stroke or incision made by cutting; gash. **55** a piece or part cut off, esp. a section of food cut from the whole: *a cut of meat.* **56** the edge of anything cut or sliced. **57** a passage, channel, path, etc., cut or hollowed out. **58** an omission or deletion, esp. in a text, film, or play. **59** a reduction in price, salary, etc. **60** a decrease in government finance in a particular department or area, usually leading to a reduction of services, staff numbers, etc. **61** short for **power cut. 62** *Chiefly U.S. and Canadian.* a quantity of timber cut during a specific time or operation. **63** *Informal.* a portion or share. **64** *Informal.* a straw, slip of paper, etc., used in drawing lots. **65** the manner or style in which a thing, esp. a garment, is cut; fashion. **66a** *Irish informal.* a person's general appearance: *I didn't like the cut of him.* **66b** *Irish derogatory.* a dirty or untidy condition: *look at the cut of your shoes.* **67** a direct route; short cut. **68** the U.S. name for **block** (sense 15). **69** *Sport.* the spin of a cut ball. **70** *Cricket.* a stroke made with the bat in a roughly horizontal position. **71** *Films.* an immediate transition from one shot to the next, brought about by splicing the two shots together. **72** *Informal.* an individual piece of music on a record; track. **73** words or an action that hurt another person's feelings. **74** a refusal to recognize an acquaintance; snub. **75** *Informal, chiefly U.S.* an unauthorized absence, esp. from a school class. **76** *Chem.* a fraction obtained in distillation, as in oil refining. **77** the metal removed in a single pass of a machine tool. **78a** the shape of the teeth of a file. **78b** their coarseness or fineness. **79** *Brit.* a stretch of water, esp. a canal. **80 a cut above.** *Informal.* superior (to); better (than). ◆ See also **cut across, cut along, cutback, cut down, cut in, cut off, cut out, cut up.** [C13: probably of Scandinavian origin; compare Norwegian *kutte* to cut, Icelandic *kuti* small knife]

cut across *vb* (*prep*) **1** (*intr*) to be contrary to ordinary procedure or limitations: *opinion on European integration still cuts clean across party lines.* **2** to cross or traverse, making a shorter route: *she cut across the field quickly.*

cut along *vb* (*intr, adv*) *Brit. informal.* to hurry off.

cut-and-cover *adj* designating a method of constructing a tunnel by excavating a cutting to the required depth and then backfilling the excavation over the tunnel roof.

cut and paste *n* a technique used in word processing by which a section of text can be moved within a document.

cut and thrust *n* **1** *Fencing.* using both the blade and the point of a sword. **2** (in argument, debate, etc.) a lively and spirited exchange of ideas or opinions.

cutaneous (kju:'teɪnɪəs) *adj* of, relating to, or affecting the skin. [C16: from New Latin *cutāneus,* from Latin *cutis* skin; see HIDE[2]] ► **cu'taneously** *adv*

cutaway ('kʌtəˌweɪ) *n* **1** a man's coat cut diagonally from the front waist to the back of the knees. **2a** a drawing or model of a machine, engine, etc., in which part of the casing is omitted to reveal the workings. **2b** (*as modifier*): *a cutaway model.* **3** *Films, television.* a shot separate from the main action of a scene, to emphasize something or to show simultaneous events.

cutback ('kʌtˌbæk) *n* **1** a decrease or reduction. **2** another word (esp. U.S.) for **flashback.** ◆ *vb* **cut back** (*adv*) **3** (*tr*) to shorten by cutting off the end; prune. **4** (when *intr,* foll. by *on*) to reduce or make a reduction (in). **5** (*intr*) *Chiefly U.S.* (in films) to show an event that took place earlier in the narrative; flash back.

cutch (kʌtʃ) *n* another name for **catechu.**

Cutch (kʌtʃ) *n* a variant spelling of **Kutch.**

cutcherry *or* **cutchery** ('kʌtʃərɪ) *n, pl* **-cherries** *or* **-cheries.** (formerly in India) government offices and law courts collectively. [C17: from Hindi *Kachachrī*]

cut down *vb* (*adv*) **1** (*tr*) to fell. **2** (when *intr,* often foll. by *on*) to reduce or make a reduction (in): *to cut down on drink.* **3** (*tr*) to remake (an old garment) in order to make a smaller one. **4** (*tr*) to kill: *he was cut down in battle.* **5 cut (a person) down to size.** to reduce in importance or decrease the conceit of.

cute (kju:t) *adj* **1** appealing or attractive, esp. in a pretty way. **2** *Informal.* affecting cleverness or prettiness. **3** clever; shrewd. [C18 (in the sense: clever): shortened from ACUTE] ► **'cutely** *adv* ► **'cuteness** *n*

cutesy ('kju:tsɪ) *adj* **cutesier, cutesiest.** *Informal, chiefly U.S.* affectedly cute or coy.

cut glass *n* **1a** glass, esp. bowls, vases, etc., decorated by facet-cutting or grinding. **1b** (*as modifier*): *a cut-glass vase.* **2** (*modifier*) (of an accent) upper-class; refined.

Cuthbert ('kʌθbət) *n* **Saint.** ?635–87A.D., English monk; bishop of Lindisfarne. Feast day: March 20.

cuticle ('kju:tɪk[ə]l) *n* **1** dead skin, esp. that round the base of a fingernail or toenail. **2** another name for **epidermis. 3** any covering layer or membrane. **4** the protective layer, containing cutin, that covers the epidermis of higher plants. **5** the hard protective layer covering the epidermis of many invertebrates. [C17: from Latin *cutīcula* diminutive of *cutis* skin] ► **cuticular** (kju:'tɪkjʊlə) *adj*

cuticula (kju:'tɪkjʊlə) *n, pl* **-lae** (-li:). *Anatomy.* cuticle. [C18: from Latin; see CUTICLE]

cutie *or* **cutey** ('kju:tɪ) *n Slang.* a person regarded as appealing or attractive, esp. a girl or woman.

cut in *vb* (*adv*) **1** (*intr;* often foll. by *on*) Also: **cut into.** to break in or interrupt. **2** (*intr*) to interrupt a dancing couple to dance with one of them. **3** (*intr*) (of a driver, motor vehicle, etc.) to draw in front of another vehicle leaving too little space. **4** (*tr*) *Informal.* to allow to have a share. **5** (*intr*) to take the place of a person in a card game. ◆ *n* **cut-in. 6** *Films.* a separate shot or scene inserted at a relevant point.

cutin ('kju:tɪn) *n* a waxy waterproof substance, consisting of derivatives of fatty acids, that is the main constituent of the plant cuticle. [C19: from Latin *cutis* skin + -IN]

cutinize *or* **cutinise** ('kju:tɪˌnaɪz) *vb* to become or cause to become covered or impregnated with cutin. ► **ˌcutini'zation** *or* **ˌcutini'sation** *n*

cutis ('kju:tɪs) *n, pl* **-tes** (-ti:z) *or* **-tises.** *Anatomy.* a technical name for the **skin.** [C17: from Latin: skin]

cutlass ('kʌtləs) *n* a curved, one-edged sword formerly used by sailors. [C16: from French *coutelas,* from *coutel* knife, from Latin *cultellus* a small knife, from *culter* knife; see COULTER]

cutlass fish *n U.S.* another name for the **hairtail** (the fish).

cutler ('kʌtlə) *n* a person who makes or sells cutlery. [C14: from French *coutelier,* ultimately from Latin *culter* knife; see CUTLASS]

cutlery ('kʌtlərɪ) *n* **1** implements used for eating, such as knives, forks, and spoons. **2** instruments used for cutting. **3** the art or business of a cutler.

cutlet ('kʌtlɪt) *n* **1** a piece of meat taken esp. from the best end of neck of lamb, pork, etc. **2** a flat croquette of minced chicken, lobster, etc. [C18: from Old French *costelette,* literally: a little rib, from *coste* rib, from Latin *costa*]

cut off *vb* (*tr, adv*) **1** to remove by cutting. **2** to intercept or interrupt something, esp. a telephone conversation. **3** to discontinue the supply of: *to cut off the water.* **4** to bring to an end. **5** to deprive of rights; disinherit: *she was cut off without a penny.* **6** to sever or separate: *she was cut off from her family.* **7** to occupy a position so as to prevent or obstruct (a retreat or escape). ◆ *n* **cutoff. 8a** the act of cutting off; limit or termination. **8b** (*as modifier*): *the cutoff point.* **9** *Chiefly U.S.* a route or way that is shorter than the usual one; short cut. **10** a device to terminate the flow of a fluid in a pipe or duct. **11** the remnant of metal, plastic, etc., left after parts have been machined or trimmed. **12** *Electronics.* **12a** the value of voltage, frequency, etc., below or above which an electronic device cannot function efficiently. **12b** (*as modifier*): *cutoff voltage.* **13** a channel cutting across the neck of a meander, which leaves an oxbow lake. **14** another name for **oxbow** (the lake).

cut out *vb* (*adv*) **1** (*tr*) to delete or remove. **2** (*tr*) to shape or form by cutting: *to cut out a dress.* **3** (*tr; usually passive*) to suit or equip for: *you're not cut out for this job.* **4** (*intr*) (of an engine, etc.) to cease to operate suddenly. **5** (*tr*) *Printing.* to remove the background from a photograph or drawing to make the outline of the subject stand out. **6** (*intr*) (of an electrical device) to switch off, usually automatically. **7** (*tr*) *Informal.* to oust and supplant (a rival). **8** (*intr*) (of a person) to be excluded from a card game. **9** (*tr*) *Informal.* to cease doing something, esp. something undesirable (esp. in the phrase **cut it out**). **10** (*tr*) *Soccer.* to intercept (a pass). **11** (*tr*) to separate (cattle) from a herd. **12** (*intr*) *Austral. and N.Z.* to end or finish: *the road cuts out at the creek.* **13 have one's work cut out.** to have as much work as one can manage. ◆ *n* **cutout. 14** something that has been or is intended to be cut out from something else. **15** a photograph or drawing from which the background has been cut away. **16** a device that switches off or interrupts an electric circuit, esp. a switch acting as a safety device. **17** an impressed stamp cut out from an envelope for collecting purposes. **18** *Austral. slang.* the end of shearing.

cut-price *or esp. U.S.* **cut-rate** *adj* **1** available at prices or rates below the standard price or rate. **2** (*prenominal*) offering goods or services at prices below the standard price: *a cut-price shop.*

cutpurse ('kʌtˌpɜ:s) *n* an archaic word for **pickpocket.**

CUTS (kʌts) *n acronym for* Computer Users' Tape System.

cut sheet feed *n Computing.* the automatic movement of single sheets of paper through the platen of the printer.

cut string *n* another name for **bridgeboard.**

Cuttack (kʌ'tæk) *n* a city in NE India, in E Orissa near the mouth of the Mahanadi River: former state capital until 1948. Pop.: 403 418 (1991).

cutter ('kʌtə) *n* **1** a person or thing that cuts, esp. a person who cuts cloth for clothing. **2** a sailing boat with its mast stepped further aft so as to have a larger foretriangle than that of a sloop. **3** a ship's boat, powered by oars or sail, for carrying passengers or light cargo. **4** a small lightly armed boat, as used in the enforcement of customs regulations. **5** a pig weighing between 68 and 82 kg, from which fillets and larger joints are cut.

cut-throat *n* **1** a person who cuts throats; murderer. **2** Also called: **cut-throat razor.** *Brit.* a razor with a long blade that usually folds into the handle. U.S. name: **straight razor.** ◆ *adj* **3** bloodthirsty or murderous; cruel. **4** fierce or relentless in competition: *cut-throat prices.* **5** (of some games) played by three people: *cut-throat poker.*

cutting ('kʌtɪŋ) *n* **1** a piece cut off from the main part of something. **2** *Horticulture.* **2a** a method of vegetative propagation in which a part of a plant, such as a stem or leaf, is induced to form its own roots. **2b** a part separated for this purpose. **3** Also called (esp. U.S. and Canadian): **clipping.** an article, photograph, etc., cut from a newspaper or other publication. **4** the editing process by which a film is cut and made. **5** an excavation in a piece of high land for a road, railway, etc., enabling it to remain at approximately the same level. **6** *Irish informal.* sharp-wittedness: *there is no cutting in him.* **7** (*modifier*) designed for or adapted to cutting; edged; sharp: *a cutting tool.* ◆ *adj* **8** keen; piercing: *a cutting wind.* **9** tending to hurt the feelings: *a cutting remark.* ► **'cuttingly** *adv*

cutting compound *n Engineering.* a mixture, such as oil, water, and soap, used for cooling drills and other cutting tools.

cutting edge *n* the leading position in any field; forefront: *on the cutting edge of space technology.*

cutting grass *n* a W African name for **cane rat** (sense 1).

cutting horse *n U.S. and Canadian.* a saddle horse trained for use in separating an individual animal, such as a cow, from a herd.

cuttle ('kʌtᵊl) *n* **1** short for **cuttlefish** or **cuttlebone. 2 little cuttle.** a small cuttlefish, *Sepiola atlantica,* often found on beaches. [Old English *cudele;* related to Old High German *kiot* bag, Norwegian dialect *kaule* cuttle, Old English *codd* bag]

cuttlebone ('kʌtᵊl,bəʊn) *n* the internal calcareous shell of the cuttlefish, used as a mineral supplement to the diet of cage-birds and as a polishing agent.

cuttlefish ('kʌtᵊl,fɪʃ) *n, pl* **-fish** *or* **-fishes.** any cephalopod mollusc of the genus *Sepia* and related genera, which occur near the bottom of inshore waters and have a broad flattened body: order *Decapoda* (decapods). Sometimes shortened to **cuttle.** See also **squid.**

cutty ('kʌtɪ) *Scot. and northern English dialect.* ◆ *adj* **1** short or cut short. ◆ *n, pl* **-ties. 2** something cut short, such as a spoon or short-stemmed tobacco pipe. **3** an immoral girl or woman (in Scotland used as a general term of abuse for a woman). **4** a short thickset girl. [C18 (Scottish and northern English): from CUT (vb)]

cutty grass *n* a species of sedge, *Cyperus ustulatus,* of New Zealand with sharp leaves.

Cutty Sark *n* a three-masted merchant clipper built in 1869: now kept at Greenwich, London. [named after the witch in Robert Burns' poem *Tam O'Shanter,* who wore only a *cutty sark* (short shirt)]

cutty stool *n* (formerly in Scotland) the church seat on which an unchaste person sat while being harangued by the minister.

cut up *vb* (*tr, adv*) **1** to cut into pieces. **2** to inflict injuries on. **3** (*usually passive*) *Informal.* to affect the feelings of deeply. **4** *Informal.* to subject to severe criticism. **5 cut up rough.** *Brit. informal.* to become angry or bad-tempered. ◆ *n* **cut-up 6** *Informal, chiefly U.S.* a joker or prankster.

cut-up technique *n* a technique of writing involving cutting up lines or pages of prose and rearranging these fragments, popularized by the novelist William Burroughs.

cutwater ('kʌt,wɔːtə) *n* the forward part of the stem of a vessel, which cuts through the water.

cutwork ('kʌt,wɜːk) *n* openwork embroidery in which the pattern is cut away from the background.

cutworm ('kʌt,wɜːm) *n* the caterpillar of various noctuid moths, esp. those of the genus *Argrotis,* which is a pest of young crop plants in North America.

cuvée (kuː'veɪ) *n* an individual batch or blend of wine. [C19: from French, literally: put in a cask, from *cuve* cask]

cuvette (kjuː'vɛt) *n* a shallow dish or vessel for holding liquid. [C17: from French, diminutive of *cuve* cask, from Latin *cupa*]

Cuvier ('kjuːvɪeɪ; *French* kyvje) *n* **Georges** (**Jean-Leopold-Nicolas-Frédéric**) (ʒɔrʒ), Baron. 1769–1832, French zoologist and statesman; founder of the sciences of comparative anatomy and palaeontology.

Cuxhaven ('kʊks,hɑːvᵊn; *German* kʊks'haːfən) *n* a port in NW Germany, at the mouth of the River Elbe. Pop.: 55 250 (1989 est.).

Cuyabá (*Portuguese* kuja'ba) *n* a variant spelling of **Cuiabá.**

Cuyp *or* **Kuyp** (kaɪp; *Dutch* kœip) *n* **Aelbert** ('aːlbert). 1620–91, Dutch painter of landscapes and animals.

Cuzco (*Spanish* 'kuθko) *or* **Cusco** *n* a city in S central Peru: former capital of the Inca Empire, with extensive Inca remains; university (1692). Pop.: 255 568 (1993).

CV *abbrev. for:* **1** curriculum vitae. **2** (in Canada) Cross of Valour.

CVA *abbrev. for* cerebrovascular accident.

CVO *abbrev. for* Commander of the Royal Victorian Order.

CVS *abbrev. for:* **1** (in Britain) Council of Voluntary Service. **2** chorionic villus sampling.

CW 1 *Radio. abbrev. for* continuous waves. ◆ *n* **2a** an informal term for **Morse code. 2b** (*as modifier*): *his CW speed is 30 words per minute.* **3** *abbrev. for* chemical weapons and chemical warfare.

CWA (in Australia) *abbrev. for* Country Women's Association.

Cwlth *abbrev. for* Commonwealth.

cwm (kuːm) *n* **1** (in Wales) a valley. **2** *Geology.* another name for **cirque** (sense 1).

Cwmbran (,kuːm'brɑːn) *n* a new town in SE Wales, in Torfaen county borough, developed in the 1950s. Pop.: 46 021 (1991).

c.w.o. *or* **CWO** *abbrev. for* cash with order.

CWS *abbrev. for* Cooperative Wholesale Society.

cwt *abbrev. for* hundredweight. [*c,* from the Latin numeral *C* one hundred (*centum*)]

CY *international car registration for* Cyprus.

-cy *suffix.* **1** (*forming nouns from adjectives ending in -t, -tic, -te, and -nt*) indicating state, quality, or condition: *plutocracy; lunacy; intimacy; infancy.* **2** (*forming abstract nouns from other nouns*) rank or office: *captaincy.* [via Old French from Latin *-cia, -tia,* Greek *-kia, -tia,* abstract noun suffixes]

cyan ('saɪæn, 'saɪən) *n* **1** a highly saturated green-blue that is the complementary colour of red and forms, with magenta and yellow, a set of primary colours. ◆ *adj* **2** of this colour: *a cyan filter.* [C19: from Greek *kuanos* dark blue]

cyan- *combining form.* a variant of **cyano-** before a vowel: *cyanamide; cyanide.*

cyanamide (saɪ'ænə,maɪd, -mɪd) *or* **cyanamid** (saɪ'ænəmɪd) *n* **1** Also called: **cyanogenamide** (,saɪənəʊ'dʒɛnə,maɪd, -mɪd). a white or colourless crystalline soluble weak dibasic acid, which can be hydrolysed to urea. Formula: H_2NCN. **2** a salt or ester of cyanamide. **3** short for **calcium cyanamide.**

cyanate ('saɪə,neɪt) *n* any salt or ester of cyanic acid, containing the ion ^{-}OCN or the group –OCN.

cyanic acid (saɪ'ænɪk) *n* a colourless poisonous volatile liquid acid that hydrolyses readily to ammonia and carbon dioxide. Formula: HOCN. Compare **isocyanic acid, fulminic acid.**

cyanide ('saɪə,naɪd) *or* **cyanid** ('saɪənɪd) *n* **1** any salt of hydrocyanic acid. Cyanides contain the ion CN^- and are extremely poisonous. **2** another name (not in technical usage) for **nitrile.** ► **,cyani'dation** *n*

cyanide process *n* a process for recovering gold and silver from ores by treatment with a weak solution of sodium cyanide. Also called: **cyaniding.**

cyanine ('saɪə,niːn) *or* **cyanin** ('saɪənɪn) *n* **1** a blue dye used to extend the sensitivity of photographic emulsions to colours other than blue and ultraviolet. **2** any of a class of chemically related dyes, used for the same purpose.

cyanite ('saɪə,naɪt) *n* a grey, green, or blue mineral consisting of aluminium silicate in triclinic crystalline form. It occurs in metamorphic rocks and is used as a refractory. Formula: Al_2SiO_5. ► **cyanitic** (,saɪə'nɪtɪk) *adj*

cyano- *or before a vowel* **cyan-** *combining form.* **1** blue or dark blue: *cyanotype.* **2** indicating cyanogen: *cyanohydrin.* **3** indicating cyanide. [from Greek *kuanos* (adj) dark blue, (n) dark blue enamel, lapis lazuli]

cyanobacteria (,saɪənəʊbæk'tɪərɪə) *pl n, sing* **-rium** (-rɪəm). a group of bacteria (phylum *Cyanobacteria*) containing a blue photosynthetic pigment and formerly regarded as algae. Former name: **blue-green algae.**

cyanocobalamin (,saɪənəʊkəʊ'bæləmɪn) *n* a complex red crystalline compound, containing cyanide and cobalt and occurring in liver: lack of it in the tissues leads to pernicious anaemia. Formula: $C_{63}H_{88}O_{14}N_{14}PCo$. Also called: **vitamin B_{12}.** [C20: from CYANO- + COBAL(T) + (VIT)AMIN]

cyanogen (saɪ'ænədʒɪn) *n* an extremely poisonous colourless flammable gas with an almond-like odour: has been used in chemical warfare. Formula: $(CN)_2$. [C19: from French *cyanogène;* see CYANO-, -GEN; so named because it is one of the constituents of Prussian blue]

cyanogenesis (,saɪənəʊ'dʒɛnɪsɪs) *n Botany.* the release by certain plants, such as cherry laurel, of hydrogen cyanide, esp. after wounding or invasion by pathogens.

cyanohydrin (,saɪənəʊ'haɪdrɪn) *n* any of a class of organic compounds containing a cyanide group and a hydroxyl group bound to the same carbon atom.

cyanophyte (saɪ'ænəfaɪt) *n* a former name for a cyanobacterium. See **cyanobacteria.**

cyanosis (,saɪə'nəʊsɪs) *n Pathol.* a bluish-purple discoloration of skin and mucous membranes usually resulting from a deficiency of oxygen in the blood. ► **cyanotic** (,saɪə'nɒtɪk) *adj*

cyanotype (saɪ'ænə,taɪp) *n* another name for **blueprint** (sense 1).

Cybele ('sɪbɪlɪ) *n Classical myth.* the Phrygian goddess of nature, mother of all living things and consort of Attis; identified with the Greek Rhea or Demeter.

cyber- *combining form.* indicating computers: *cyberphobia.* [C20: back formation from CYBERNETICS]

cybercafé ('saɪbə,kæfeɪ, -,kæfɪ) *n* a café with computer equipment that gives public access to the Internet.

cybernate ('saɪbə,neɪt) *vb* to control (a manufacturing process) with a servomechanism or (of a process) to be controlled by a servomechanism. [C20: from CYBER(NETICS) + -ATE[1]] ► **,cyber'nation** *n*

cybernetics (,saɪbə'nɛtɪks) *n* (*functioning as sing*) the branch of science concerned with control systems in electronic and mechanical devices and the extent to which useful comparisons can be made between man-made and biological systems. See also **feedback** (sense 1). [C20: from Greek *kubernētēs* steersman, from *kubernan* to steer, control] ► **,cyber'netic** *adj* ► **,cyber'neticist** *n*

cyberpet (,saɪbə'pɛt) *n* an electronic toy that simulates the activities of a pet, requiring the owner to feed, discipline, and entertain it.

cyberphobia (,saɪbə'fəʊbɪə) *n* an irrational fear of computers. ► **,cyber'phobic** *adj*

cyberpunk ('saɪbə,pʌŋk) *n* **1** a genre of science fiction that features rebellious computer hackers and is set in a dystopian society integrated by computer networks. **2** a writer of cyberpunk.

cyberspace ('saɪbə,speɪs) *n* all of the data stored in a large computer or network represented as a three-dimensional model through which a virtual-reality user can move.

cyborg ('saɪ,bɔːg) *n* (in science fiction) a living being whose powers are enhanced by computer implants. [C20: from *cyb(ernetic) org(anism)*]

cycad ('saɪkæd) *n* any tropical or subtropical gymnosperm plant of the phylum *Cycadophyta,* having an unbranched stem with fernlike leaves crowded at the top. See also **sago palm** (sense 2). [C19: from New Latin *Cycas* name of genus, from Greek *kukas,* scribe's error for *koïkas,* from *koïx* a kind of palm, probably of Egyptian origin] ► **,cyca'daceous** *adj*

Cyclades ('sɪklə,diːz) *pl n* a group of over 200 islands in the S Aegean Sea, forming a department of Greece. Capital: Hermoupolis (Siros). Pop.: 94 005 (1991).

Area: 2572 sq. km (993 sq. miles). Modern Greek name: **Kikládhes.** ► **Cycladic** (sɪ'klædɪk) *adj*

cyclamate ('saɪklə,meɪt, 'sɪklə,meɪt) *n* a salt or ester of cyclamic acid. Certain of the salts have a very sweet taste and were formerly used as food additives and sugar substitutes. [C20: *cycl(ohexyl-sulph)amate*]

cyclamen ('sɪkləmən, -,mɛn) *n* **1** any Old World plant of the primulaceous genus *Cyclamen,* having nodding white, pink, or red flowers, with reflexed petals. See also **sowbread.** ◆ *adj* **2** of a dark reddish-purple colour. [C16: from Medieval Latin, from Latin *cyclamīnos,* from Greek *kuklaminos,* probably from *kuklos* circle, referring to the bulb-like roots]

cycle ('saɪkᵊl) *n* **1** a recurring period of time in which certain events or phenomena occur and reach completion or repeat themselves in a regular sequence. **2** a completed series of events that follows or is followed by another series of similar events occurring in the same sequence. **3** the time taken or needed for one such series. **4** a vast period of time; age; aeon. **5** a group of poems or prose narratives forming a continuous story about a central figure or event: *the Arthurian cycle.* **6** a series of miracle plays: *the Chester cycle.* **7** a group or sequence of songs (see **song cycle**). **8** short for **bicycle, tricycle, motorcycle,** etc. **9** *Astronomy.* the orbit of a celestial body. **10** a recurrent series of events or processes in plants and animals: *a life cycle; a growth cycle.* **11** *Physics.* a continuous change or a sequence of changes in the state of a system that leads to the restoration of the system to its original state after a finite period of time. **12** one of a series of repeated changes in the magnitude of a periodically varying quantity, such as current or voltage. **13** *Computing.* **13a** a set of operations that can be both treated and repeated as a unit. **13b** the time required to complete a set of operations. **13c** one oscillation of the regular voltage waveform used to synchronize processes in a digital computer. **14** (in generative grammar) the set of cyclic rules. ◆ *vb* **15** (*tr*) to process through a cycle or system. **16** (*intr*) to move in or pass through cycles. **17** to travel by or ride a bicycle or tricycle. [C14: from Late Latin *cyclus,* from Greek *kuklos* cycle, circle, ring, wheel; see WHEEL] ► **'cycling** *n, adj*

cycle of erosion *n* the hypothetical sequence of modifications to the earth's surface by erosion, from the original uplift of the land to the ultimate low plain, usually divided into the youthful, mature, and old stages.

cyclic ('saɪklɪk, 'sɪklɪk) *or* **cyclical** ('saɪklɪkᵊl, 'sɪklɪkᵊl) *adj* **1** recurring or revolving in cycles. **2** (of an organic compound) containing a closed saturated or unsaturated ring of atoms. See also **heterocyclic** and **homocyclic. 3** *Botany.* **3a** arranged in whorls: *cyclic petals.* **3b** having parts arranged in this way: *cyclic flowers.* **4** *Music.* of or relating to a musical form consisting of several movements sharing thematic material. **5** *Geometry.* (of a polygon) having vertices that lie on a circle. **6** (in generative grammar) denoting one of a set of transformational rules all of which must apply to a clause before any one of them applies to any clause in which the first clause is embedded. ► **'cyclically** *adv*

cyclical unemployment *n* unemployment caused by fluctuations in the level of economic activity inherent in trade cycles.

cyclic AMP *n* cyclic adenosine monophosphate: a constituent of biological cells, responsible for triggering processes that are dependent on hormones.

cyclic pitch lever *n* a lever in a helicopter to change the angle of attack of individual rotor blades, causing the helicopter to move forwards, backwards, or sideways. Compare **collective pitch lever.**

cycling shorts *pl n* tight-fitting shorts reaching partway to the knee for cycling, sport, etc.

cyclist ('saɪklɪst) *or U.S.* **cycler** *n* a person who rides or travels by bicycle, motorcycle, etc.

cyclo- *or before a vowel* **cycl-** *combining form.* **1** indicating a circle or ring: *cyclotron.* **2** denoting a cyclic compound: *cyclohexane.* [from Greek *kuklos* CYCLE]

cycloalkane (,saɪkləʊ'ælkeɪn) *n* any saturated hydrocarbon similar to an alkane but having a cyclic molecular structure and the general formula C_nH_{2n}. Also called: **cycloparaffin.**

cyclo-cross *n* **a** a form of cycle race held over rough ground. **b** this sport.

cyclogiro ('saɪkləʊ,dʒaɪrəʊ) *n Aeronautics.* an aircraft lifted and propelled by pivoted blades rotating parallel to roughly horizontal transverse axes.

cyclograph ('saɪkləʊ,grɑːf, -,græf) *n* another name for **arcograph.**

cyclohexane (,saɪkləʊ'hɛkseɪn, ,sɪk-) *n* a colourless insoluble flammable liquid cycloalkane with a pungent odour, made by hydrogenation of benzene and used as a paint remover and solvent. Formula: C_6H_{12}.

cyclohexanone (,saɪkləʊ'hɛksə,nəʊn) *n* a colourless liquid used as a solvent for cellulose lacquers. Formula: $C_6H_{10}O$.

cycloid ('saɪklɔɪd) *adj* **1** resembling a circle. **2** (of fish scales) rounded, thin, and smooth-edged, as those of the salmon. **3** *Psychiatry.* (of a type of personality) characterized by exaggerated swings of mood between elation and depression. See also **cyclothymia.** ◆ *n* **4** *Geometry.* the curve described by a point on the circumference of a circle as the circle rolls along a straight line. Compare **trochoid** (sense 1). **5** a fish that has cycloid scales. ► **cy'cloidal** *adj* ► **cy'cloidally** *adv*

cyclometer (saɪ'klɒmɪtə) *n* a device that records the number of revolutions made by a wheel and hence the distance travelled. ► **cy'clometry** *n*

cyclone ('saɪkləʊn) *n* **1** another name for **depression** (sense 6). **2** a violent tropical storm; hurricane. ◆ *adj* **3** *Austral. and N.Z. Trademark.* (of fencing) made of interlaced wire and metal. [C19: from Greek *kuklōn* a turning around, from *kukloein* to revolve, from *kuklos* wheel] ► **cyclonic** (saɪ'klɒnɪk), **cy'clonical,** *or* **'cyclonal** *adj* ► **cy'clonically** *adv*

cyclonite ('saɪklə,naɪt) *n* a white crystalline insoluble explosive prepared by the action of nitric acid on hexamethylenetetramine; cyclotrimethylenetrinitramine: used in bombs and shells. Formula: $C_3H_6N_6O_6$. [C20: from CYCLO- + *(trimethylene-tri)nit(ramin)e*]

cycloparaffin (,saɪkləʊ'pærəfɪn, ,sɪk-) *n* another name for **cycloalkane.**

Cyclopean (,saɪkləʊ'piːən, saɪ'kləʊpɪən) *adj* **1** of, relating to, or resembling the Cyclops. **2** denoting, relating to, or having the kind of masonry used in preclassical Greek architecture, characterized by large dry undressed blocks of stone.

cyclopedia *or* **cyclopaedia** (,saɪkləʊ'piːdɪə) *n* a less common word for **encyclopedia.** ► **,cyclo'pedic** *or* **,cyclo'paedic** *adj* ► **,cyclo'pedist** *or* **,cyclo'paedist** *n*

cyclopentadiene (,saɪkləʊ,pentə'daɪiːn) *n* a colourless liquid unsaturated cyclic hydrocarbon obtained in the cracking of petroleum hydrocarbons and the distillation of coal tar: used in the manufacture of plastics and insecticides. Formula: C_5H_6.

cyclopentane (,saɪkləʊ'penteɪn, ,sɪk-) *n* a colourless insoluble cycloalkane found in petroleum and used mainly as a solvent. Formula: C_5H_{10}.

cyclophosphamide (,saɪkləʊ'fɒsfə,maɪd) *n* an alkylating agent used in the treatment of leukaemia and lymphoma. [C20: from CYCLO- + PHOSPH(ORUS) + AMIDE]

cycloplegia (,saɪkləʊ'pliːdʒɪə, ,sɪk-) *n* paralysis of the muscles that adjust the shape of the lens of the eye, resulting in loss of ability to focus. ► **,cyclo'plegic** *adj*

cyclopropane (,saɪkləʊ'prəʊpeɪn, ,sɪk-) *n* a colourless flammable gaseous hydrocarbon, used in medicine as an anaesthetic; trimethylene. It is a cycloalkane with molecules containing rings of three carbon atoms. Formula: C_3H_6; boiling pt.: −34°C.

cyclops ('saɪklɒps) *n, pl* **cyclops** *or* **cyclopes** (saɪ'kləʊpiːz). any copepod of the genus *Cyclops,* characterized by having one eye.

Cyclops ('saɪklɒps) *n, pl* **Cyclopes** (saɪ'kləʊpiːz) *or* **Cyclopses.** *Classical myth.* one of a race of giants having a single eye in the middle of the forehead, encountered by Odysseus in the *Odyssey.* See also **Polyphemus.** [C15: from Latin *Cyclōps,* from Greek *Kuklōps,* literally: round eye, from *kuklos* circle + *ōps* eye]

cyclorama (,saɪkləʊ'rɑːmə) *n* **1** Also called: **panorama.** a large picture, such as a battle scene, on the interior wall of a cylindrical room, designed to appear in natural perspective to a spectator in the centre. **2** *Theatre.* **2a** a curtain or wall curving along the back of a stage, usually painted to represent the sky and serving to enhance certain lighting effects. **2b** any set of curtains that enclose the back and sides of a stage setting. [C19: CYCLO- + Greek *horama* view, sight, on the model of *panorama*] ► **cycloramic** (,saɪkləʊ'ræmɪk) *adj*

cyclosis (saɪ'kləʊsɪs) *n, pl* **-ses** (-siːz). *Biology.* the circulation of cytoplasm or cell organelles, such as food vacuoles in some protozoans. [C19: from Greek *kuklōsis* an encircling, from *kukloun* to surround, from *kuklos* circle]

cyclosporin-A (,saɪkləʊ'spɔːrɪn) *n* a drug extracted from a fungus and used in transplant surgery to suppress the body's immune mechanisms, and so prevent rejection of an organ.

cyclostome ('saɪklə,stəʊm, 'sɪk-) *n* **1** any primitive aquatic jawless vertebrate of the class *Cyclostomata,* such as the lamprey and hagfish, having a round sucking mouth and pouchlike gills. ◆ *adj* **2** of, relating to, or belonging to the class *Cyclostomata.* ◆ Also: **marsipobranch.** ► **cyclostomate** (saɪ'klɒstəmɪt, -,meɪt) *or* **cyclostomatous** (,saɪkləʊ'stɒmətəs, -'stəʊmə-, ,sɪk-) *adj*

cyclostyle ('saɪklə,staɪl) *n* **1** a kind of pen with a small toothed wheel, used for cutting minute holes in a specially prepared stencil. Copies of the design so formed can be printed on a duplicator by forcing ink through the holes. **2** an office duplicator using a stencil prepared in this way. ◆ *vb* **3** (*tr*) to print on a duplicator using such a stencil. ► **'cyclo,styled** *adj*

cyclothymia (,saɪkləʊ'θaɪmɪə, ,sɪk-) *n Psychiatry.* a condition characterized by periodical swings of mood between excitement and depression, activity and inactivity. See also **manic-depressive.** ► **,cyclo'thymic** *or* **,cyclo'thymi,ac** *adj, n*

cyclotron ('saɪklə,trɒn) *n* a type of particle accelerator in which the particles spiral inside two D-shaped hollow metal electrodes under the effect of a strong vertical magnetic field, gaining energy by a high-frequency voltage applied between these electrodes.

cyder ('saɪdə) *n* a variant spelling (esp. Brit.) of **cider.**

Cydnus ('sɪdnəs) *n* the ancient name for the (River) **Tarsus.**

cyesis (saɪ'iːsɪs) *n, pl* **-ses** (-siːz). *Med.* the technical name for **pregnancy.** [from Greek *kuēsis*]

cygnet ('sɪgnɪt) *n* a young swan. [C15 *sygnett,* from Old French *cygne* swan, from Latin *cygnus,* from Greek *kuknos*]

Cygnus ('sɪgnəs) *n, Latin genitive* **Cygni** ('sɪgnaɪ). a constellation in the N hemisphere lying between Pegasus and Draco in the Milky Way. The constellation contains the expanding supernova remnant, the **Cygnus Loop.** It may also contain a black hole. [Latin: swan; see CYGNET]

cyl. *abbrev. for:* **1** cylinder. **2** cylindrical.

cylinder ('sɪlɪndə) *n* **1** a solid consisting of two parallel planes bounded by identical closed curves, usually circles, that are interconnected at every point by a set of parallel lines, usually perpendicular to the planes. Volume: *base area* × *length.* **2** a surface formed by a line moving round a closed plane curve at a fixed angle to it. **3** any object shaped like a cylinder. **4** the chamber in a reciprocating internal-combustion engine, pump, or compressor within which the piston moves. See also **cylinder block. 5** the rotating mechanism of a revolver, situated behind the barrel and containing cartridge chambers. **6** *Printing.* any of the rotating drums on a printing press. **7** Also called: **cylinder seal.** a cylindrical seal of stone, clay, or precious stone decorated with linear designs, found in the Middle East and Balkans: dating from about 6000 B.C. **8** Also called: **hot-water cylinder.** *Brit.* a vertical cylindrical tank for storing hot water, esp. an insulated one made of copper used in a domestic hot-water system. **9 firing on all cylinders.** working or performing at full capability. ◆ *vb* **10** (*tr*) to provide (a system) with cylinders. [C16: from Latin *cylindrus,* from Greek *kulindros* a roller, from *kulindein* to roll] ► **'cylinder-,like** *adj*

cylinder barrel *n Engineering.* the metal casting containing a cylinder of a reciprocating internal-combustion engine.
cylinder block *n* the metal casting containing the cylinders and cooling channels or fins of a reciprocating internal-combustion engine. Sometimes shortened to **block.**
cylinder head *n* the detachable metal casting that fits onto the top of a cylinder block. In an engine it contains part of the combustion chamber and in an overhead-valve four-stroke engine it houses the valves and their operating mechanisms. Sometimes shortened to **head.**
cylinder press *n Printing.* another name for **flat-bed press.**
cylindrical (sɪ'lɪndrɪkᵊl) *or* **cylindric** *adj* of, shaped like, or characteristic of a cylinder. ▸ **cy,lindri'cality** *or* **cy'lindricalness** *n* ▸ **cy'lindrically** *adv*
cylindrical coordinates *pl n* three coordinates defining the location of a point in three-dimensional space in terms of its polar coordinates (r, θ) in one plane, usually the (x, y) plane, and its perpendicular distance, z, measured from this plane.
cylindroid ('sɪlɪn,drɔɪd) *n* **1** a cylinder with an elliptical cross section. ♦ *adj* **2** resembling a cylinder.
cylix ('saɪlɪks, 'sɪl-) *n, pl* **-lices** (-lɪ,siːz). a variant of **kylix.**
cyma ('saɪmə) *n, pl* **-mae** (-miː) *or* **-mas. 1** either of two mouldings having a double curve, part concave and part convex. **Cyma recta** has the convex part nearer the wall and **cyma reversa** has the concave part nearer the wall. **2** *Botany.* a variant of **cyme.** [C16: from New Latin, from Greek *kuma* something swollen, from *kuein* to be pregnant]
cymar (sɪ'mɑː) *n* a woman's short fur-trimmed jacket, popular in the 17th and 18th centuries. [C17: variant of *simar,* from French *simarre,* perhaps ultimately from Basque *zamar* sheepskin]
cymatium (sɪ'meɪtɪəm, -ʃɪəm) *n, pl* **-tia** (-tɪə, -ʃɪə). *Architect.* the top moulding of a classical cornice or entablature. [C16: see CYMA]
cymbal ('sɪmbᵊl) *n* a percussion instrument of indefinite pitch consisting of a thin circular piece of brass, which vibrates when clashed together with another cymbal or struck with a stick. [Old English *cymbala,* from Medieval Latin, from Latin *cymbalum,* from Greek *kumbalon,* from *kumbē* something hollow] ▸ **'cymbaler, ,cymbal'eer,** *or* **'cymbalist** *n* ▸ **'cymbal-,like** *adj*
cymbalo ('sɪmbə,ləʊ) *n, pl* **-los.** another name for **dulcimer.** [from Italian; see CYMBAL]
Cymbeline ('sɪmbəliːn) *n* See **Cunobelinus.**
cyme (saɪm) *n* an inflorescence in which the first flower is the terminal bud of the main stem and subsequent flowers develop as terminal buds of lateral stems. [C18: from Latin *cȳma* cabbage sprout, from Greek *kuma* anything swollen; see CYMA] ▸ **cymiferous** (saɪ'mɪfərəs) *adj*
cymene ('saɪmiːn) *n* a colourless insoluble liquid with an aromatic odour that exists in three isomeric forms; methylpropylbenzene: used as solvents and for making synthetic resins. The *para-* isomer is present in several essential oils. Formula: $CH_3C_6H_4CH(CH_3)_2$. [C19: *cym-* from Greek *kuminon* CUMIN + -ENE]
cymogene ('saɪmə,dʒiːn) *n U.S.* a mixture of volatile flammable hydrocarbons, mainly butane, obtained in the distillation of petroleum. [C19: from CYMENE + -GENE]
cymograph ('saɪmə,grɑːf, -,græf) *n* **1** a variant of **kymograph. 2** an instrument for tracing the outline of an architectural moulding. ▸ **cymographic** (,saɪmə'græfɪk) *adj*
cymoid ('saɪmɔɪd) *adj Architect., botany.* resembling a cyme or cyma.
cymophane ('saɪmə,feɪn) *n* a yellow or green opalescent variety of chrysoberyl. [C19: from Greek *kuma* wave, undulation + -PHANE]
cymose ('saɪməʊs, -məʊz, saɪ'məʊs) *adj* having the characteristics of a cyme. ▸ **'cymosely** *adv*
Cymric *or* **Kymric** ('kɪmrɪk) *n* **1** the Welsh language. **2** the Brythonic group of Celtic languages. ♦ *adj* **3** of or relating to the Cymry, any of their languages, Wales, or the Welsh.
Cymru (*Welsh* kum'ri) *n* the Welsh name for **Wales.**
Cymry *or* **Kymry** ('kɪmrɪ) *n* **the.** (*functioning as pl*) **1** the Brythonic branch of the Celtic people, comprising the present-day Welsh, Cornish, and Bretons. See **Brythonic. 2** the Welsh people. [Welsh: the Welsh]
Cynewulf, Kynewulf ('kɪnɪ,wʊlf), *or* **Cynwulf** ('kɪn,wʊlf) *n* ?8th century A.D., Anglo-Saxon poet; author of *Juliana, The Ascension, Elene,* and *The Fates of the Apostles.*
cynghanedd (kʌŋ'hanɛð) *n* a complex system of rhyme and alliteration used in Welsh verse. [from Welsh]
cynic ('sɪnɪk) *n* **1** a person who believes the worst about people or the outcome of events. ♦ *adj* **2** a less common word for **cynical. 3** *Astronomy.* of or relating to Sirius, the Dog Star. [C16: via Latin from Greek *Kunikos,* from *kuōn* dog]
Cynic ('sɪnɪk) *n* a member of a sect founded by Antisthenes that scorned worldly things and held that self-control was the key to the only good.
cynical ('sɪnɪkᵊl) *adj* **1** distrustful or contemptuous of virtue, esp. selflessness in others; believing the worst of others, esp. that all acts are selfish. **2** sarcastic; mocking. **3** showing contempt for accepted standards of behaviour, esp. of honesty or morality: *the politician betrayed his promises in a cynical way.* ▸ **'cynically** *adv* ▸ **'cynicalness** *n*
cynicism ('sɪnɪ,sɪzəm) *n* **1** the attitude or beliefs of a cynic. **2** a cynical action, remark, idea, etc.
Cynicism ('sɪnɪ,sɪzəm) *n* the doctrines of the Cynics.
cynopodous (saɪ'nɒpədəs) *adj* (of some mammals, such as dogs) having claws that do not retract. [from New Latin, from Greek *kuōn* dog + -PODOUS]
cynosure ('sɪnə,zjʊə, -ʃʊə) *n* **1** a person or thing that attracts notice, esp. because of its brilliance or beauty. **2** something that serves as a guide. [C16: from Latin *Cynosūra* the constellation of Ursa Minor, from Greek *Kunosoura,* from *kuōn* dog + *oura* tail] ▸ **,cyno'sural** *adj*
Cynthia ('sɪnθɪə) *n* another name for **Artemis** (Diana).
cyperaceous (,saɪpə'reɪʃəs) *adj* of, relating to, or belonging to the *Cyperaceae,* a family of grasslike flowering plants with solid triangular stems, including the sedges, bulrush, cotton grass, and certain rushes. Some are grown as water plants or as ornamental grasses; and *Cyperus papyrus* is the papyrus plant. Compare **juncaceous.** [C19: from New Latin *Cypērus* type genus, from Latin *cypēros* a kind of rush, from Greek *kupeiros* marsh plant, probably of Semitic origin]
cypher ('saɪfə) *n, vb* a variant spelling of **cipher.**
cy pres (siː preɪ) *n Law.* the doctrine that the intention of a donor or testator should be carried out as closely as practicable when literal compliance is impossible. [C15: from Anglo-French, literally: as near (as possible, etc.)]
cypress[1] ('saɪprəs) *n* **1** any coniferous tree of the N temperate genus *Cupressus,* having dark green scalelike leaves and rounded cones: family *Cupressaceae.* **2** any of several similar and related trees, such as the widely cultivated *Chamaecyparis lawsoniana* (**Lawson's cypress**), of the western U.S. **3** any of various other coniferous trees, esp. the swamp cypress. **4** the wood of any of these trees. [Old English *cypresse,* from Latin *cyparissus,* from Greek *kuparissos;* related to Latin *cupressus*]
cypress[2] *or* **cyprus** ('saɪprəs) *n* a fabric, esp. a fine silk, lawn, or crepelike material, often black and worn as mourning. [C14 *cyprus* from the island of CYPRUS]
cypress pine *n* any coniferous tree of the Australian genus *Callitrus,* having leaves in whorls and yielding valuable timber: family *Cupressaceae.*
cypress vine *n* a tropical American convolvulaceous climbing plant, *Quamoclit pennata,* having finely divided compound leaves and scarlet or white tubular flowers.
Cyprian[1] ('sɪprɪən) *adj* **1** of or relating to Cyprus. **2** of or resembling the ancient orgiastic worship of Aphrodite on Cyprus. ♦ *n* **3** (*often not cap.*) *Obsolete.* a licentious person, esp. a prostitute or dancer. ♦ *n, adj* **4** another word for **Cypriot.**
Cyprian[2] ('sɪprɪən) *n* **Saint.** ?200–258 A.D., bishop of Carthage and martyr. Feast day: Sept. 26 or 16.
cyprinid (sɪ'praɪnɪd, 'sɪprɪnɪd) *n* **1** any teleost fish of the mainly freshwater family *Cyprinidae,* typically having toothless jaws and cycloid scales and including such food and game fishes as the carp, tench, roach, rudd, and dace. ♦ *adj* **2** of, relating to, or belonging to the *Cyprinidae.* **3** resembling a carp; cyprinoid. [C19: from New Latin *Cyprīnidae,* from Latin *cyprīnus* carp, from Greek *kuprinos*]
cyprinodont (sɪ'prɪnə,dɒnt, sɪ'praɪ-) *n* **1** any small tropical or subtropical soft-finned fish of the mostly marine family *Cyprinodontidae,* resembling carp but having toothed jaws. The group includes the guppy, killifish, swordtail, and topminnow. ♦ *adj* **2** of, relating to, or belonging to the *Cyprinodontidae.* [C19: from Latin *cyprīnus* carp (see CYPRINID) + -ODONT]
cyprinoid ('sɪprɪ,nɔɪd, sɪ'praɪnɔɪd) *adj* **1** of, relating to, or belonging to the *Cyprinoidea,* a large suborder of teleost fishes including the cyprinids, characins, electric eels, and loaches. **2** of, relating to, or resembling the carp. ♦ *n* **3** any fish belonging to the *Cyprinoidea.* [C19: from Latin *cyprīnus* carp]
Cypriot ('sɪprɪət) *or* **Cypriote** ('sɪprɪ,əʊt) *n* **1** a native, citizen, or inhabitant of Cyprus. **2** the dialect of Ancient or Modern Greek spoken in Cyprus. ♦ *adj* **3** denoting or relating to Cyprus, its inhabitants, or dialects.
cypripedium (,sɪprɪ'piːdɪəm) *n* **1** any orchid of the genus *Cypripedium,* having large flowers with an inflated pouchlike lip. See also **lady's-slipper. 2** any cultivated tropical orchid of the genus *Paphiopedilum,* having yellow, green, or brownish-purple waxy flowers. [C18: from New Latin, from Latin *Cypria* the Cyprian, that is, Venus + *pēs* foot (that is, Venus' slipper)]
Cyprus ('saɪprəs) *n* an island in the E Mediterranean: ceded to Britain by Turkey in 1878 and made a colony in 1925; became an independent republic in 1960 as a member of the Commonwealth; invaded by Turkey in 1974 following a Greek-supported military coup, leading to the virtual partition of the island. In 1983 the Turkish-controlled northern sector declared itself to be an independent state as the Turkish Republic of Northern Cyprus but failed to receive international recognition. Attempts by the U.N. to broker a reunification agreement have failed. Languages: Greek and Turkish. Religions: Greek Orthodox and Muslim. Currency: pound and Turkish lira. Capital: Nicosia. Pop. (Greek): 657 000 (1996); (Turkish): 110 000 (1996). Area: 9251 sq. km (3571 sq. miles).
cypsela ('sɪpsɪlə) *n, pl* **-lae** (-,liː). the dry one-seeded fruit of the daisy and related plants, which resembles an achene but is surrounded by a calyx sheath. [C19: from New Latin, from Greek *kupselē* chest, hollow vessel]
Cyrano de Bergerac (*French* sirano də bɛrʒərak) *n* **Savinien** (savinjɛ̃). 1619–55, French writer and soldier, famous as a duellist and for his large nose. He became widely known through the verse drama *Cyrano de Bergerac* (1897) by Edmond Rostand.
Cyrenaic (,saɪrə'neɪɪk, ,sɪrə-) *adj* **1** (in the ancient world) of or relating to the city of Cyrene or the territory of Cyrenaica. **2** of or relating to the philosophical school founded by Aristippus in Cyrene that held pleasure to be the highest good. ♦ *n* **3** an inhabitant of Cyrene or Cyrenaica. **4** a follower of the Cyrenaic school of philosophy.
Cyrenaica *or* **Cirenaica** (,saɪrə'neɪɪkə,,sɪrə-) *n* a region and former province (1951–63) of E Libya: largely desert; settled by the Greeks in about 630 B.C.; ruled successively by the Egyptians, Romans, Arabs, Turks, and Italians. Area: 855 370 sq. km (330 258 sq. miles).
Cyrene (saɪ'riːnɪ) *n* an ancient Greek city of N Africa, near the coast of Cyrenaica: famous for its medical school.
Cyril ('sɪrəl) *n* **Saint.** ?827–869 A.D., Greek Christian theologian, missionary to the Moravians and inventor of the Cyrillic alphabet; he and his brother Saint Methodius were called *the Apostles of the Slavs.* Feast day: Feb 14 or May 11.
Cyrillic (sɪ'rɪlɪk) *adj* **1** denoting or relating to the alphabet derived from that of the Greeks, supposedly by Saint Cyril, for the writing of Slavonic languages:

now used primarily for Russian, Bulgarian, and the Serbian dialect of Serbo-Croat. ◆ *n* **2** this alphabet.

Cyril of Alexandria *n* **Saint.** ?375–444 A.D., Christian theologian and patriarch of Alexandria. Feast day: June 27 or June 9.

Cyrus ('saɪrəs) *n* **1** known as *Cyrus the Great* or *Cyrus the Elder.* died ?529 B.C., king of Persia and founder of the Persian empire. **2** called *the Younger.* died 401 B.C., Persian satrap of Lydia: revolted against his brother Artaxerxes II, but was killed at the battle of Cunaxa. See also **anabasis, katabasis.**

cyst (sɪst) *n* **1** *Pathol.* any abnormal membranous sac or blisterlike pouch containing fluid or semisolid material. **2** *Anat.* any normal sac or vesicle in the body. **3** a thick-walled protective membrane enclosing a cell, larva, or organism. **[**C18: from New Latin *cystis,* from Greek *kustis* pouch, bag, bladder**]**

-cyst *n combining form.* indicating a bladder or sac: *otocyst.* **[**from Greek *kustis* bladder**]**

cystectomy (sɪ'stɛktəmɪ) *n, pl* **-mies. 1** surgical removal of the gall bladder or of part of the urinary bladder. **2** surgical removal of any abnormal cyst.

cysteine ('sɪstɪˌiːn, -ɪn) *n* a sulphur-containing amino acid, present in proteins, that oxidizes on exposure to air to form cystine. Formula: $HSCH_2CH(NH_2)COOH$. **[**C19: variant of CYSTINE**]** ▸ **ˌcyste'inic** *adj*

cystic ('sɪstɪk) *adj* **1** of, relating to, or resembling a cyst. **2** having or enclosed within a cyst; encysted. **3** relating to the gall bladder or urinary bladder.

cysticercoid (ˌsɪstɪ'sɜːkɔɪd) *n* the larva of any of certain tapeworms, which resembles a cysticercus but has a smaller bladder.

cysticercus (ˌsɪstɪ'sɜːkəs) *n, pl* **-ci** (-saɪ). an encysted larval form of many tapeworms, consisting of a head (scolex) inverted in a fluid-filled bladder. See also **hydatid** (sense 1), **coenurus. [**C19: from New Latin, from Greek *kustis* pouch, bladder + *kerkos* tail**]**

cystic fibrosis *n* an inheritable disease of the exocrine glands, controlled by a recessive gene: affected children inherit defective alleles from both parents. It is characterized by chronic infection of the respiratory tract and by pancreatic insufficiency.

cystine ('sɪstiːn, -tɪn) *n* a sulphur-containing amino acid present in proteins: yields two molecules of cysteine on reduction. Formula: $HOOCCH(NH_2)CH_2SSCH_2CH(NH_2)COOH$. **[**C19: see CYSTO- (bladder), -INE[2]; named from its being discovered in a type of urinary calculus**]**

cystitis (sɪ'staɪtɪs) *n* inflammation of the urinary bladder.

cysto- *or before a vowel* **cyst-** *combining form.* indicating a cyst or bladder: *cystocarp; cystoscope.*

cystocarp ('sɪstəˌkɑːp) *n* a reproductive body in red algae, developed after fertilization and consisting of filaments bearing carpospores. ▸ **ˌcysto'carpic** *adj*

cystocele ('sɪstəˌsiːl) *n Pathol.* a hernia of the urinary bladder, esp. one protruding into the vagina.

cystogenous (sɪs'tɒdʒɪnəs) *adj Biology.* forming or secreting cysts.

cystography (sɪs'tɒgrəfɪ) *n* radiography of the urinary bladder using a contrast medium.

cystoid ('sɪstɔɪd) *adj* **1** resembling a cyst or bladder. ◆ *n* **2** a tissue mass, such as a tumour, that resembles a cyst but lacks an outer membrane.

cystolith ('sɪstəlɪθ) *n* **1** a knoblike deposit of calcium carbonate in the epidermal cells of such plants as the stinging nettle. **2** *Pathol.* a urinary calculus.

cystoscope ('sɪstəˌskəʊp) *n* a slender tubular medical instrument for examining the interior of the urethra and urinary bladder. ▸ **cystoscopic** (ˌsɪstə'skɒpɪk) *adj* ▸ **cystoscopy** (sɪs'tɒskəpɪ) *n*

cystotomy (sɪ'stɒtəmɪ) *n, pl* **-mies. 1** surgical incision into the gall bladder or urinary bladder. **2** surgical incision into the capsule of the lens of the eye.

cytaster (saɪ'tæstə, 'saɪtæs-) *n Cytology.* another word for **aster** (sense 3). **[**C19: from CYTO- + ASTER**]**

-cyte *n combining form.* indicating a cell: *spermatocyte.* **[**from New Latin *-cyta,* from Greek *kutos* container, body, hollow vessel**]**

Cythera (sɪ'θɪərə) *n* **1** a Greek island off the SE coast of the Peloponnese: in ancient times a centre of the worship of Aphrodite. Pop.: 3500 (latest est.). Area: about 285 sq. km (110 sq. miles). **2** the chief town of this island, on the S coast. Pop.: 300 (latest est.). ◆ Modern Greek name: **Kíthira.**

Cytherea (ˌsɪθə'riːə) *n* another name for **Aphrodite** (Venus). ▸ **ˌCyther'ean** *adj*

cytidine ('sɪtɪˌdaɪn) *n Biochem.* a nucleoside formed by the condensation of cytosine and ribose. **[**C20: from CYTO- + -IDE + -INE[2]**]**

cytidylic acid (ˌsɪtɪ'dɪlɪk) *n* a nucleotide consisting of cytosine, ribose or deoxyribose, and a phosphate group. It is a constituent of DNA or RNA. Also called: **cytidine monophosphate.**

cyto- *combining form.* indicating a cell: *cytolysis; cytoplasm.* **[**from Greek *kutos* vessel, container; related to *kuein* to contain**]**

cytochemistry (ˌsaɪtəʊ'kɛmɪstrɪ) *n* the chemistry of living cells. ▸ **ˌcyto'chemical** *adj*

cytochrome ('saɪtəʊˌkrəʊm) *n* any of a group of naturally occurring compounds, consisting of iron, a protein, and a porphyrin, that are important in cell oxidation-reduction reactions.

cytochrome reductase *n* another name for **flavoprotein.**

cytogenesis (ˌsaɪtəʊ'dʒɛnɪsɪs) *or* **cytogeny** (saɪ'tɒdʒənɪ) *n* the origin and development of plant and animal cells.

cytogenetics (ˌsaɪtəʊdʒɪ'nɛtɪks) *n (functioning as sing)* the branch of genetics that correlates the structure of chromosomes with heredity and variation. ▸ **ˌcytoge'netic** *adj* ▸ **ˌcytoge'netically** *adv* ▸ **ˌcytoge'neticist** *n*

cytokine ('saɪtəʊˌkaɪn) *n* any of various proteins, secreted by cells, that carry signals to neighbouring cells. Cytokines include interferon.

cytokinesis (ˌsaɪtəʊkɪ'niːsɪs, -kaɪ-) *n* division of the cytoplasm of a cell, occurring at the end of mitosis or meiosis.

cytokinin (ˌsaɪtəʊ'kaɪnɪn) *n* any of a group of plant hormones that promote cell division and retard ageing in plants. Also called: **kinin.**

cytology (saɪ'tɒlədʒɪ) *n* **1** the study of plant and animal cells, including their structure, function, and formation. **2** the detailed structure of a tissue, as revealed by microscopic examination. ▸ **cytological** (ˌsaɪtə'lɒdʒɪk[ə]l) *adj* ▸ **ˌcyto'logically** *adv* ▸ **cy'tologist** *n*

cytolysin (saɪ'tɒlɪsɪn) *n* a substance that can partially or completely destroy animal cells.

cytolysis (saɪ'tɒlɪsɪs) *n Cytology.* the dissolution of cells, esp. by the destruction of their membranes. ▸ **cytolytic** (ˌsaɪtə'lɪtɪk) *adj*

cytomegalovirus (ˌsaɪtəʊ'mɛgələʊˌvaɪrəs) *n* a virus, related to the herpes viruses, that may cause serious disease in patients whose immune systems are compromised and the birth of handicapped children to pregnant women infected with it. Abbrev.: **CMV.**

cytoplasm ('saɪtəʊˌplæzəm) *n* the protoplasm of a cell contained within the cell membrane but excluding the nucleus: contains organelles, vesicles, and other inclusions. ▸ **ˌcyto'plasmic** *adj*

cytoplast ('saɪtəʊˌplɑːst, -ˌplæst) *n* the intact cytoplasm of a single cell. ▸ **cytoplastic** (ˌsaɪtəʊ'plæstɪk) *adj*

cytosine ('saɪtəsɪn) *n* a white crystalline pyrimidine occurring in nucleic acids; 6-amino-2-hydroxy pyrimidine. Formula: $C_4H_5N_3O$. See also **DNA, RNA. [**C19: from CYTO- + -OSE[2] + -INE[2]**]**

cytoskeleton (ˌsaɪtəʊ'skɛlɪtən) *n* a network of fibrous proteins that governs the shape and movement of a biological cell.

cytosol ('saɪtəʊˌsɒl) *n* the solution of proteins and metabolites inside a biological cell, in which the organelles are suspended.

cytotaxis (ˌsaɪtəʊ'tæksɪs) *n Biology.* movement of cells due to external stimulation.

cytotaxonomy (ˌsaɪtəʊtæk'sɒnəmɪ) *n* classification of organisms based on cell structure, esp. the number, shape, etc., of the chromosomes. ▸ **ˌcytoˌtaxo'nomic** *adj* ▸ **ˌcytotax'onomist** *n*

cytotoxic (ˌsaɪtəʊ'tɒksɪk) *adj* poisonous to living cells: denoting certain drugs used in the treatment of leukaemia and other cancers. ▸ **cytotoxicity** (ˌsaɪtəʊ'tɒksɪsɪtɪ) *n*

cytotoxin (ˌsaɪtəʊ'tɒksɪn) *n* any substance that is poisonous to living cells.

Cyzicus ('sɪzɪkəs) *n* an ancient Greek colony in NW Asia Minor on the S shore of the Sea of Marmara: site of Alcibiades' naval victory over the Peloponnesians (410 B.C.).

CZ *international car registration for* the Czech Republic.

czar (zɑː) *n* a variant spelling (esp. U.S.) of **tsar.** ▸ **'czardom** *n*

czardas ('tʃɑːdæʃ) *n* **1** a Hungarian national dance of alternating slow and fast sections. **2** a piece of music composed for or in the rhythm of this dance. **[**from Hungarian *csárdás***]**

czarevitch ('zɑːrɪvɪtʃ) *n* a variant spelling (esp. U.S.) of **tsarevitch.**

czarevna (zɑː'rɛvnə) *n* a variant spelling (esp. U.S.) of **tsarevna.**

czarina (zɑː'riːnə) *or* **czaritza** (zɑː'rɪtsə) *n* variant spellings (esp. U.S.) of **tsarina** or **tsaritsa.**

czarism ('zɑːrɪzəm) *n* a variant spelling (esp. U.S.) of **tsarism.**

czarist ('zɑːrɪst) *adj, n* a variant spelling (esp. U.S.) of **tsarist.**

Czech (tʃɛk) *adj* **1a** of, relating to, or characteristic of the Czech Republic, its people, or its language. **1b** of, relating to, or characteristic of Bohemia and Moravia, their people, or their language. **1c** (loosely) of, relating to, or characteristic of the former Czechoslovakia or its people. ◆ *n* **2** the official language of the Czech Republic, belonging to the West Slavonic branch of the Indo-European family; also spoken in Slovakia. Czech and Slovak are closely related and mutually intelligible. **3a** a native or inhabitant of the Czech Republic. **3b** a native or inhabitant of Bohemia or Moravia. **3c** (loosely) a native, inhabitant, or citizen of the former Czechoslovakia. **[**C19: from Polish, from Czech *Čech***]**

Czech. *abbrev. for:* **1** Czechoslovak. **2** Czechoslovakian. **3** Czechoslovakia.

Czechoslovak (ˌtʃɛkəʊ'sləʊvæk) *adj* **1** of, relating to, or characteristic of the former Czechoslovakia, its peoples, or their languages. ◆ *n* **2** (loosely) either of the two mutually intelligible languages of the former Czechoslovakia; Czech or Slovak.

Czechoslovakia (ˌtʃɛkəʊsləʊ'vækɪə) *n* a former republic in central Europe: formed after the defeat of Austria-Hungary (1918) as a nation of Czechs in Bohemia and Moravia and Slovaks in Slovakia; occupied by Germany from 1939 until its liberation by the Soviet Union in 1945; became a people's republic under the Communists in 1948; invaded by Warsaw Pact troops in 1968, ending Dubček's attempt to liberalize communism; in 1989 popular unrest led to the resignation of the politburo and the formation of a non-Communist government. It consisted of two federal republics, the **Czech Republic** and the **Slovak Republic**, which became independent in 1993. Czech name: **Československo.** ▸ **ˌCzechoslo'vakian** *adj, n*

Czech Republic *n* a country in central Europe; formed part of Czechoslovakia until 1993; mostly wooded, with lowlands surrounding the River Morava, rising to the Bohemian plateau in the W and to highlands in the N. Language: Czech. Religion: Christian majority. Currency: koruna. Capital: Prague. Pop.: 10 302 000 (1998 est.). Area: 78 864 sq. km (30 450 sq. miles).

Czernowitz ('tʃɛrnovɪts) *n* the German name for **Chernovtsy.**

Czerny (*German* 'tʃɛrni) *n* **Karl** (karl). 1791–1857, Austrian pianist, composer, and teacher, noted for his studies.

Częstochowa (*Polish* tʃɛ̃stɔ'xɔva) *n* an industrial city in S Poland, on the River Warta: pilgrimage centre. Pop.: 259 500 (1996 est.).

Dd

d *or* **D** (diː) *n, pl* **d's, D's,** *or* **Ds. 1** the fourth letter and third consonant of the modern English alphabet. **2** a speech sound represented by this letter, usually a voiced alveolar stop, as in *dagger.* **3** the semicircle on a billiards table having a radius of 11½ inches and its straight edge in the middle of the baulk line.

d *symbol for:* **1** *Physics.* density or relative density. **2** *Maths.* a small increment in a given variable or function: used to indicate a derivative of one variable with respect to another, as in d*y*/d*x*. **3** *Chess.* See **algebraic notation.**

D *symbol for:* **1** *Music.* **1a** a note having a frequency of 293.66 hertz (**D above middle C**) or this value multiplied or divided by any power of 2; the second note of the scale of C major. **1b** a key, string, or pipe producing this note. **1c** the major or minor key having this note as its tonic. **2** *Chem.* deuterium. **3** *Maths.* the first derivative of a function, as in $D(x^3 + x^2) = 3x^2 + 2x$. **4** *Physics.* dispersion. **5** *Aeronautics.* drag. **6a** a semiskilled or unskilled manual worker, or a trainee or apprentice to a skilled worker. **6b** (as modifier): *D worker.* ◆ See also **occupation groupings.** ◆ **7** *the Roman numeral for* 500. See **Roman numerals.** ◆ **8** *international car registration for* Germany. [from German *Deutschland*]

D *or* **D.** *abbrev. for* Deutsch: indicating the serial number in the catalogue (1951) of the musical compositions of Schubert made by Otto Deutsch (1883–1967).

2,4-D *n* a synthetic auxin widely used as a weedkiller; 2,4-dichlorophenoxyacetic acid.

d. *abbrev. for:* **1** date. **2** (in animal pedigrees) dam. **3** daughter. **4** day. **5** degree. **6** delete. **7** *Brit. currency before decimalization.* penny *or* pennies. [Latin *denarius*] **8** depart(s). **9** diameter. **10** died. **11** dinar(s). **12** dollar(s). **13** dose. **14** drachma(s).

D. *abbrev. for:* **1** *U.S. politics.* Democrat(ic). **2** *Government.* Department. **3** Deus. [Latin: God] **4** dinar(s). **5** *Optics.* diopter. **6** Director. **7** Dominus. [Latin: Lord] **8** Don (a Spanish title). **9** Duchess. **10** Duke. **11** Dutch.

'd *contraction of* would *or* had: *I'd; you'd.*

DA *abbrev. for:* **1** (in the U.S.) District Attorney. **2** Diploma of Art. **3** duck's arse (hairstyle).

D/A *or* **d.a.** *abbrev. for:* **1** deposit account. **2** *Commerce.* documents against acceptance.

dab[1] (dæb) *vb* **dabs, dabbing, dabbed. 1** to touch lightly and quickly. **2** (*tr*) to daub with short tapping strokes: *to dab the wall with paint.* **3** (*tr*) to apply (paint, cream, etc.) with short tapping strokes. ◆ *n* **4** a small amount, esp. of something soft or moist: *a dab of ink.* **5** a small light stroke or tap, as with the hand. **6** (*often pl*) *Chiefly Brit.* a slang word for **fingerprint.** [C14: of imitative origin]

dab[2] (dæb) *n* **1** a small common European brown flatfish, *Limanda limanda,* covered with rough toothed scales: family *Pleuronectidae:* a food fish. **2** (*often pl*) any of various other small flatfish, esp. flounders. ◆ Compare **sand dab.** [C15: from Anglo-French *dabbe,* of uncertain origin]

dab[3] (dæb) *n Brit. informal.* See **dab hand.** [C17: perhaps from DAB[1] (vb)]

dabber ('dæbə) *n* a pad used by printers for applying ink by hand.

dabble ('dæbᵊl) *vb* **1** to dip, move, or splash (the fingers, feet, etc.) in a liquid. **2** (*intr; usually foll. by in, with,* or *at*) to deal (with) or work (at) frivolously or superficially; play (at). **3** (*tr*) to daub, mottle, splash, or smear: *his face was dabbled with paint.* [C16: probably from Dutch *dabbelen;* see DAB[1]] ▸ **'dabbler** *n*

dabchick ('dæbˌtʃɪk) *n* any of several small grebes of the genera *Podiceps* and *Podilymbus,* such as *Podiceps ruficollis* of the Old World. [C16: probably from Old English *dop* to dive + CHICK; see DEEP, DIP]

dab hand *n Brit. informal.* a person who is particularly skilled at something; expert: *a dab hand at chess.*

dabster ('dæbstə) *n* **1** *Brit.* a dialect word for **dab hand. 2** *U.S. informal.* an incompetent or amateurish worker; bungler. [C18: from DAB[1] + -STER]

da capo (dɑː 'kɑːpəʊ) *adj, adv Music.* to be repeated (in whole or part) from the beginning. Abbrev.: **DC.** See also **fine**[3]. [C18: from Italian, literally: from the head]

Dacca ('dækə) *n* the former name (until 1982) of **Dhaka.**

dace (deɪs) *n, pl* **dace** *or* **daces. 1** a European freshwater cyprinid fish, *Leuciscus leuciscus,* with a slender bluish-green body. **2** any of various similar fishes. [C15: from Old French *dars* DART, probably referring to its swiftness]

dacha *or* **datcha** ('dætʃə) *n* a country house or cottage in Russia. [from Russian: a giving, gift]

Dachau (*German* 'daxau) *n* a town in S Germany, in Bavaria: site of a Nazi concentration camp. Pop.: 33 200 (latest est.).

dachshund ('dæksˌhʊnd; *German* 'dakshʊnt) *n* a long-bodied short-legged breed of dog. [C19: from German, from *Dachs* badger + *Hund* dog, HOUND[1]]

Dacia ('deɪsɪə) *n* an ancient region bounded by the Carpathians, the Tisza, and the Danube, roughly corresponding to modern Romania. United under kings from about 60 B.C., it later contained the Roman province of the same name (about 105 to 270 A.D.). ▸ **'Dacian** *adj, n*

dacoit (də'kɔɪt) *n* (in India and Myanmar) a member of a gang of armed robbers. [C19: from Hindi *dakait,* from *dākā* robbery]

dacoity (də'kɔɪtɪ) *n, pl* **-coities.** (in India and Myanmar) robbery by an armed gang.

Dacron ('deɪkrɒn, 'dæk-) *n* the U.S. name (trademark) for **Terylene.**

dactyl ('dæktɪl) *n* **1** Also called: **dactylic.** *Prosody.* a metrical foot of three syllables, one long followed by two short (–⏑⏑). Compare **bacchius. 2** *Zoology.* any digit of a vertebrate. [C14: via Latin from Greek *daktulos* finger, dactyl, comparing the finger's three joints to the three syllables]

dactylic (dæk'tɪlɪk) *adj* **1** of, relating to, or having a dactyl: *dactylic verse.* ◆ *n* **2** a variant of **dactyl** (sense 1). ▸ **dac'tylically** *adv*

dactylo- *or before a vowel* **dactyl-** *combining form.* finger or toe: *dactylogram.* [from Greek *daktulos* finger]

dactylogram (dæk'tɪləˌɡræm) *n Chiefly U.S.* a technical term for **fingerprint.**

dactylography (ˌdæktɪ'lɒɡrəfɪ) *n Chiefly U.S.* the scientific study of fingerprints for purposes of identification. ▸ **ˌdacty'lographer** *n* ▸ **dactylographic** (dækˌtɪlə'ɡræfɪk) *adj*

dactylology (ˌdæktɪ'lɒlədʒɪ) *n, pl* **-gies.** the method of using manual sign language, as in communicating with the deaf.

dad (dæd) *n* an informal word for **father.** [C16: childish word; compare Greek *tata,* Sanskrit *tatas*]

Dada ('dɑːdɑː) *or* **Dadaism** ('dɑːdɑːˌɪzəm) *n* a nihilistic artistic movement of the early 20th century in W Europe and the U.S., founded on principles of irrationality, incongruity, and irreverence towards accepted aesthetic criteria. [C20: from French, from a children's word for hobbyhorse, the name being arbitrarily chosen] ▸ **'Dadaist** *n, adj* ▸ **ˌDada'istic** *adj* ▸ **ˌDada'istically** *adv*

Dad and Dave (dæd ən deɪv) *n Austral.* stereotypes of the unsophisticated rural dweller before World War II. [from characters in the stories of STEELE RUDD]

Dadd (dæd) *n* **Richard.** 1817–86, British painter of mythological and fairy scenes. He was committed to an asylum for patricide.

daddy ('dædɪ) *n, pl* **-dies. 1** an informal word for **father. 2 the daddy.** *Slang, chiefly U.S., Canadian, and Austral.* the supreme or finest example: *the daddy of them all.*

daddy-longlegs *n* **1** *Brit.* an informal name for a **crane fly. 2** *U.S. and Canadian.* an informal name for **harvestman** (sense 2).

dado ('deɪdəʊ) *n, pl* **-does** *or* **-dos. 1** the lower part of an interior wall that is decorated differently from the upper part. **2** *Architect.* the part of a pedestal between the base and the cornice. ◆ *vb* **3** (*tr*) to provide with a dado. [C17: from Italian: die, die-shaped pedestal, perhaps from Arabic *dad* game]

Dadra and Nagar Haveli (də'drɑː; 'nʌɡə ə'velɪ) *n* a union territory of W India, on the Gulf of Cambay: until 1961 administratively part of Portuguese Damão. Capital: Silvassa. Pop.: 153 000 (1994 est.). Area: 489 sq. km (191 sq. miles).

dae (de) *vb* a Scot. word for **do**[1].

daedal *or* **dedal** ('diːdᵊl) *adj Literary.* skilful or intricate. [C16: via Latin from Greek *daidalos;* see DAEDALUS]

Daedalus ('diːdələs) *n Greek myth.* an Athenian architect and inventor who built the labyrinth for Minos on Crete and fashioned wings for himself and his son Icarus to flee the island. ▸ **Daedalian, Daedalean** (dɪ'deɪlɪən) *or* **Daedalic** (dɪ'dælɪk) *adj*

daemon ('diːmən) *or* **daimon** *n* **1** a demigod. **2** the guardian spirit of a place or person. **3** a variant spelling of **demon** (sense 3). ▸ **daemonic** (diː'mɒnɪk) *adj*

daff[1] (dæf) *n Informal.* short for **daffodil.**

daff[2] (dɑːf) *vb* (*intr*) *Chiefly Scot.* to frolic; play the fool. [C16: from obsolete *daff* fool, of uncertain origin]

daffodil ('dæfədɪl) *n* **1** Also called: **Lent lily.** a widely cultivated Eurasian amaryllidaceous plant, *Narcissus pseudonarcissus,* having spring-blooming yellow flowers. **2** any other plant of the genus *Narcissus.* **3a** a brilliant yellow colour. **3b** (*as adj*)*: daffodil paint.* **4** a daffodil, or a representation of one, as a national emblem of Wales. [C14: from Dutch *de affodil* the asphodel, from Medieval Latin *affodillus,* variant of Latin *asphodelus* ASPHODEL]

daffy ('dæfɪ) *adj* **daffier, daffiest.** *Informal.* another word for **daft** (senses 1, 2). [C19: from obsolete *daff* fool; see DAFT]

daft (dɑːft) *adj Chiefly Brit.* **1** *Informal.* foolish, simple, or stupid. **2** a slang word for **insane. 3** *Informal.* (*postpositive;* foll. by *about*) extremely fond (of). **4** *Slang.* frivolous; giddy. [Old English *gedæfte* gentle, foolish; related to Middle Low German *ondaft* incapable] ▸ **'daftly** *adv* ▸ **'daftness** *n*

Dafydd ap Gruffudd (*Welsh* 'dævɪθ æp 'ɡrɪfɪθ) *n.* died 1283, Welsh leader. Claiming the title Prince of Wales (1282), he led an unsuccessful revolt against Edward I: executed.

Dafydd ap Gwilym (*Welsh* 'dævɪθ æp 'ɡwɪlɪm) *n* ?1320–?1380, Welsh poet.

dag[1] (dæɡ) *n* **1** short for **daglock.** ◆ *vb* **dags, dagging, dagged. 2** to cut the daglock away from (a sheep). [C18: of obscure origin] ▸ **'dagger** *n*

dag[2] (dæɡ) *n Austral. and N.Z. informal.* **1** a character; eccentric. **2** a person who is untidily dressed. **3** a person with a good sense of humour. [back formation from DAGGY]

Da Gama (də 'ɡɑːmə) *n* See (Vasco da) **Gama.**

Dagan ('dɑːɡən) *n* an earth god of the Babylonians and Assyrians.

Dagenham ('dægənəm) *n* part of the Greater London borough of Barking and Dagenham: motor-vehicle manufacturing.

Dagestan Republic (ˌdɑːgɪ'stɑːn) *n* a constituent republic of S Russia, on the Caspian Sea: annexed from Persia in 1813; rich mineral resources. Capital: Makhachkala. Pop.: 2 009 000 (1995 est.). Area: 50 278 sq. km (19 416 sq. miles). Also called: **Dagestan** or **Daghestan.**

dagga ('daxə, 'dɑːgə) *n S. African informal.* a local name for marijuana. **[C19:** from Afrikaans, from Khoikhoi *dagab*]

dagger ('dægə) *n* **1** a short stabbing weapon with a pointed blade. **2** Also called: **obelisk.** a character (†) used in printing to indicate a cross reference, esp. to a footnote. **3 at daggers drawn.** in a state of open hostility. **4 look daggers.** to glare with hostility; scowl. ◆ *vb* (*tr*) **5** to mark with a dagger. **6** *Archaic.* to stab with a dagger. **[C14:** of uncertain origin]

daggerboard ('dægəˌbɔːd) *n* a light bladelike board inserted into the water through a slot in the keel of a boat to reduce keeling and leeway. Compare **centreboard.**

daggy ('dægɪ) *adj Austral. and N.Z. informal.* untidy; dishevelled. [from DAG[1]]

daglock ('dægˌlɒk) *n* a dung-caked lock of wool around the hindquarters of a sheep. **[C17:** see DAG[1], LOCK[2]]

dago ('deɪgəʊ) *n, pl* **-gos** *or* **-goes.** *Derogatory.* a member of a Latin race, esp. a Spaniard or Portuguese. **[C19:** alteration of *Diego,* a common Spanish name]

dagoba ('dɑːgəbə) *n* a dome-shaped shrine containing relics of the Buddha or a Buddhist saint. **[C19:** from Sinhalese *dāgoba,* from Sanskrit *dhātugarbha* containing relics]

Dagon ('deɪgɒn) *n Bible.* a god worshipped by the Philistines, represented as half man and half fish. **[C14:** via Latin and Greek from Hebrew *Dāgōn,* literally: little fish]

Daguerre (*French* dagɛr) *n* **Louis Jacques Mandé** (lwi ʒak mɑ̃de). 1789–1851, French inventor, who devised one of the first practical photographic processes (1838).

daguerreotype (də'gɛrəʊˌtaɪp) *n* **1** one of the earliest photographic processes, in which the image was produced on iodine-sensitized silver and developed in mercury vapour. **2** a photograph formed by this process. ▸ **da'guerreoˌtyper** *or* **da'guerreoˌtypist** *n* ▸ **da'guerreoˌtypy** *n*

dah (dɑː) *n* the long sound used in combination with the short sound *dit,* in the spoken representation of Morse and other telegraphic codes. Compare **dash**[1] (sense 14).

dahabeah, dahabeeyah, *or* **dahabiah** (ˌdɑːhə'biːə) *n* a houseboat used on the Nile. [from Arabic *dhahabīyah,* literally: the golden one (that is, gilded barge)]

Dahl (dɑːl) *n* **Roald** ('rəʊəld). 1916–90, British writer with Norwegian parents, noted for his short stories and such children's books as *Charlie and the Chocolate Factory* (1964).

dahlia ('deɪljə) *n* **1** any herbaceous perennial plant of the Mexican genus *Dahlia,* having showy flowers and tuberous roots, esp. any horticultural variety derived from *D. pinnata:* family *Compositae* (composites). **2** the flower or root of any of these plants. **[C19:** named after Anders *Dahl,* 18th-century Swedish botanist; see -IA]

Dahna ('dɑːxnɑː) *n* another name for **Rub' al Khali.**

Dahomey (də'həʊmɪ) *n* the former name (until 1975) of **Benin.**

Dáil Éireann ('dɑːl 'eːrɪn) *or* **Dáil** *n* (in the Republic of Ireland) the lower chamber of parliament. See also **Oireachtas.** [from Irish *dáil* assembly (from Old Irish *dāl*) + *Éireann* of Eire]

dailies ('deɪlɪz) *pl n Films.* another word for **rushes.**

daily ('deɪlɪ) *adj* **1** of or occurring every day or every weekday: *a daily paper.* **2 earn one's daily bread.** to earn one's living. **3 the daily round.** the usual activities of one's day. ◆ *n, pl* **-lies. 4** a daily publication, esp. a newspaper. **5** Also called: **daily help.** *Brit.* another name for a **charwoman.** ◆ *adv* **6** every day. **7** constantly; often. [Old English *dæglīc;* see DAY, -LY[1]]

daily double *n Horse racing.* a single bet on the winners of two named races in any one day's racing.

Daimler ('deɪmlə) *n* **Gottlieb (Wilhelm)** (*German* 'gɔtliːp 'vɪlhɛlm). 1834–1900, German engineer and car manufacturer, who collaborated with Nikolaus Otto in inventing the first internal-combustion engine (1876).

daimon ('daɪmɒn) *n* a variant of **daemon** or **demon** (sense 3). ▸ **dai'monic** *adj*

daimyo *or* **daimio** ('daɪmjəʊ) *n, pl* **-myo, -myos** *or* **-mio, -mios.** (in Japan) one of the territorial magnates who dominated much of the country from about the 11th to the 19th century. [from Japanese, from Ancient Chinese *d'âi miäng* great name]

daimyo bond *n* a bearer bond issued in Japan and the eurobond market by the World Bank.

dainty ('deɪntɪ) *adj* **-tier, -tiest. 1** delicate or elegant: *a dainty teacup.* **2** pleasing to the taste; choice; delicious: *a dainty morsel.* **3** refined, esp. excessively genteel; fastidious. ◆ *n, pl* **-ties. 4** a choice piece of food, esp. a small cake or sweet; delicacy. **[C13:** from Old French *deintié,* from Latin *dignitās* DIGNITY] ▸ **'daintily** *adv* ▸ **'daintiness** *n*

daiquiri ('daɪkɪrɪ, 'dæk-) *n, pl* **-ris.** *Chiefly U.S. and Canadian.* an iced drink containing rum, lime juice, and syrup or sugar. **[C20:** named after *Daiquiri,* rum-producing town in Cuba]

Dairen (daɪ'rɛn) *n* a former name of **Dalian.**

dairy ('dɛərɪ) *n, pl* **dairies. 1** a company that supplies milk and milk products. **2a** a shop that sells provisions, esp. milk and milk products. **2b** *N.Z.* a shop that remains open outside normal trading hours. **3** a room or building where milk and cream are stored or made into butter and cheese. **4a** (*modifier*) of or relating to the production of milk and milk products: *dairy cattle.* **4b** (*in combination*): *a dairymaid; a dairyman.* **5** (*modifier*) containing milk or milk products: *dairy produce.* **[C13** *daierie,* from Old English *dǣge* servant girl, one who kneads bread; see DOUGH, LADY]

dairy factory *n N.Z.* a factory making butter, cheese, lactose, etc. from milk collected from surrounding farming areas.

dairying ('dɛərɪɪŋ) *n* the business of producing, processing, and selling dairy products.

dairymaid ('dɛərɪˌmeɪd) *n* (esp. formerly) a girl or woman who works in a dairy, esp. one who milks cows and makes butter and cheese on a farm.

dairyman ('dɛərɪmən) *n, pl* **-men.** a man who works in a dairy or deals in dairy products.

dais ('deɪɪs, deɪs) *n* a raised platform, usually at one end of a hall, used by speakers, etc. **[C13:** from Old French *deis,* from Latin *discus* DISCUS]

daisy ('deɪzɪ) *n, pl* **-sies. 1** a small low-growing European plant, *Bellis perennis,* having a rosette of leaves and flower heads of yellow central disc flowers and pinkish-white outer ray flowers: family *Compositae* (composites). **2** Also called: **oxeye daisy, marguerite, moon daisy.** a Eurasian composite plant, *Chrysanthemum leucanthemum,* having flower heads with a yellow centre and white outer rays. **3** any of various other composite plants having conspicuous ray flowers, such as the Michaelmas daisy and Shasta daisy. **4** *Slang.* an excellent person or thing. **5 pushing up the daisies.** dead and buried. [Old English *dægesēge* day's eye] ▸ **'daisied** *adj*

daisy bush *n* any of various shrubs of the genus *Olearia,* of Australia and New Zealand, with daisy-like flowers: family *Compositae* (composites).

daisy chain *n* a garland made, esp. by children, by threading daisies together.

daisycutter ('deɪzɪˌkʌtə) *n Cricket.* a ball bowled so that it rolls along the ground towards the batsman.

daisywheel ('deɪzɪˌwiːl) *n Computing.* a component of a computer printer in the shape of a wheel with many spokes that prints characters using a disk with characters around the circumference as the print element. Also called: **printwheel.**

dak (dɑːk) *or* **dawk** (dɔːk) *n* (in India, formerly) **a** a system of mail delivery or passenger transport by relays of bearers or horses stationed at intervals along a route. **b** (*as modifier*): *dak bearers.* **[C18:** from Hindi *dāk,* from Sanskrit *drāk* quickly]

Dak. *abbrev. for* Dakota.

Dakar ('dækə) *n* the capital and chief port of Senegal, on the SE side of Cape Verde peninsula. Pop.: 1 500 000 (1995 est.).

dak bungalow *n* (in India, formerly) a house where travellers on a dak route could be accommodated.

Dakin's solution ('deɪkɪnz) *n* a dilute solution containing sodium hypochlorite and boric acid, used as an antiseptic in the treatment of wounds. **[C20:** named after Henry D. *Dakin* (1880–1952), English chemist]

Dakota (də'kəʊtə) *n* a former territory of the U.S.: divided into the states of North Dakota and South Dakota in 1889. ▸ **Da'kotan** *adj, n*

dal[1] (dɑːl) *n* **1** split grain, a common foodstuff in India; pulse. **2** a variant spelling of **dhal.**

dal[2] *symbol for* decalitre(s).

Daladier (*French* daladje) *n* **Édouard** (edwar). 1884–1970, French radical socialist statesman; premier of France (1933; 1934; 1938–40) and signatory of the Munich Pact (1938).

Dalai Lama ('dælaɪ 'lɑːmə) *n* **1** (until 1959) the chief lama and ruler of Tibet. **2** born 1935, the 14th holder of this office (1940), who fled to India (1959): Nobel peace prize 1989. [from Mongolian *dalai* ocean; see LAMA]

dalasi (də'lɑːsɪ) *n* the standard monetary unit of The Gambia, divided into 100 bututs. [from a Gambian native name]

dale (deɪl) *n* an open valley, usually in an area of low hills. [Old English *dæl;* related to Old Frisian *del,* Old Norse *dalr,* Old High German *tal* valley]

Dale (deɪl) *n* Sir **Henry Hallet.** 1875–1968, English physiologist: shared a Nobel prize for physiology or medicine in 1936 with Otto Loewi for their work on the chemical transmission of nerve impulses.

Dalek ('dɑːlɛk) *n* any of a set of fictional robot-like creations that are aggressive, mobile, and produce rasping staccato speech. **[C20:** from a children's television series, *Dr Who*]

d'Alembert (*French* dalɑ̃bɛr) *n* See (Jean le Rond d') **Alembert.**

d'Alembert's principle *n Physics.* the principle that for a moving body the external forces are in equilibrium with the inertial forces; a generalization of Newton's third law of motion. **[C18:** named after Jean Le Rond d'ALEMBERT]

Dalén (da'leːn) *n* **Nils Gustaf.** 1869–1937, Swedish engineer, inventor of an automatic light-controlled valve known as 'Solventil'. Nobel prize for physics 1912.

Dales (deɪlz) *pl n* (*sometimes not cap.*) **the.** short for the **Yorkshire Dales.**

dalesman ('deɪlzmən) *n, pl* **-men.** a person living in a dale, esp. in the dales of N England.

daleth *or* **daled** ('dɑːlɪd; *Hebrew* 'dalɛt) *n* the fourth letter of the Hebrew alphabet (ד), transliterated as *d* or, when final, *dh.* [Hebrew]

Dalglish (dæl'gliːʃ, dəl-) *n* **Kenny,** born 1951, Scottish footballer: a striker, he played for Celtic (1968–77) and for Liverpool (1977–89): manager of Liverpool (1985–91), of Blackburn Rovers (1991–95), and of Newcastle United (1997–98): Scotland's most-capped footballer.

dalgyte ('dælgaɪt) *n Austral.* another name for **bilby.**

Dalhousie (dæl'haʊzɪ) *n* **1 9th Earl of,** title of *George Ramsay.* 1770–1838, British general; governor of the British colonies in Canada (1819–28). **2** his son, **1st Marquis and 10th Earl of,** title of *James Andrew Broun Ramsay.* 1812–60, British statesman: governor general of India (1848–56).

Dali ('dɑːlɪ; *Spanish* da'li:) *n* **Salvador** ('sælvədɔː). 1904–89, Spanish surrealist painter.

Dalian (dɑːl'jɛn) *or* **Talien** (tɑːl'jɛn) *n* a city in NE China, at the end of the Liaodong Peninsula: with the adjoining city of Lü-shun comprises the port complex of Lüda. Pop.: 2 330 000 (1993). Former name: **Dairen.**

Dallapiccola (*Italian* dalla'pikkola) *n* **Luigi** (lu'i:dʒi). 1904–75, Italian composer of twelve-tone music. His works include the opera *Il Prigioniero* (1944–48) and the ballet *Marsia* (1948).

Dallas ('dæləs) *n* a city in NE Texas, on the Trinity River: scene of the assassination of President John F. Kennedy (1963). Pop.: 1 053 292 (1996 est.).

dalles ('dæləs, dælz) *pl n Canadian.* a stretch of a river between high rock walls, with rapids and dangerous currents. **[**from Canadian French, from French (Normandy dialect): sink; compare DALE**]**

dalliance ('dælıəns) *n* **1** waste of time in frivolous action or in dawdling. **2** an archaic word for **flirtation.**

dally ('dælı) *vb* **-lies, -lying, -lied.** (*intr*) **1** to waste time idly; dawdle. **2** (usually foll. by *with*) to deal frivolously or lightly with; trifle; toy: *to dally with someone's affections.* **[C14:** from Anglo-French *dalier* to gossip, of uncertain origin**]** ▸ **'dallier** *n*

Dalmatia (dæl'meıʃə) *n* a region of W Croatia along the Adriatic: mountainous, with many offshore islands.

Dalmatian (dæl'meıʃən) *n* **1** Also called (esp. formerly): **carriage dog, coach dog.** a large breed of dog having a short smooth white coat with black or (in liver-spotted dalmatians) brown spots. **2** a native or inhabitant of Dalmatia. ◆ *adj* **3** of or relating to Dalmatia or its inhabitants.

dalmatic (dæl'mætık) *n* **1** a wide-sleeved tunic-like vestment open at the sides, worn by deacons and bishops. **2** a similar robe worn by a king at his coronation. **[C15:** from Late Latin *dalmatica* (*vestis*) Dalmatian (robe) (originally made of Dalmatian wool)**]**

Dalriada (dæl'rıədə) *n* a former Gaelic kingdom (5th century A.D.–9th century A.D.) comprising Argyll, parts of the Inner Hebrides, and parts of modern Antrim. **[**named after the *Dalriada* family, its founders**]**

dal segno ('dæl 'sɛnjəʊ) *adj, adv Music.* (of a piece of music) to be repeated from the point marked with a sign to the word *fine.* Abbrev.: **DS.** See also **fine**[3]. **[**Italian, literally: from the sign**]**

dalton ('dɔ:ltən) *n* another name for **atomic mass unit. [C20:** named after J. DALTON**]**

Dalton ('dɔ:ltən) *n* **John.** 1766–1844, English chemist and physicist, who formulated the modern form of the atomic theory and the law of partial pressures for gases. He also gave the first accurate description of colour blindness, from which he suffered.

daltonism ('dɔ:ltə,nızəm) *n* colour blindness, esp. the confusion of red and green. **[C19:** from French *daltonisme,* after J. DALTON**]** ▸ **daltonic** (dɔ:l'tɒnık) *adj*

Dalton plan *or* **system** *n* a system devised to encourage pupils to learn and develop at their own speed, using libraries and other sources to complete long assignments. **[C20:** named after *Dalton,* Massachusetts, where the plan was used in schools**]**

Dalton's atomic theory *n Chem.* the theory that matter consists of indivisible particles called atoms and that atoms of a given element are all identical and can neither be created nor destroyed. Compounds are formed by combination of atoms in simple ratios to give compound atoms (molecules). The theory was the basis of modern chemistry. **[C19:** named after J. DALTON**]**

Dalton's law *n* the principle that the pressure exerted by a mixture of gases in a fixed volume is equal to the sum of the pressures that each gas would exert if it occupied the whole volume. Also called: **Dalton's law of partial pressures. [C19:** named after J. DALTON**]**

dam[1] (dæm) *n* **1** a barrier of concrete, earth, etc., built across a river to create a body of water, as for a domestic water supply. **2** a reservoir of water created by such a barrier. **3** something that resembles or functions as a dam. ◆ *vb* **dams, damming, dammed. 4** (*tr;* often foll. by *up*) to obstruct or restrict by or as if by a dam. **[C12:** probably from Middle Low German; compare Old Icelandic *damma* to block up**]**

dam[2] (dæm) *n* the female parent of an animal, esp. of domestic livestock. **[C13:** variant of DAME**]**

dam[3] (dæm) *interj, adv, adj* a variant spelling of **damn** (senses 1–4); often used in combination, as in **damfool, damme, dammit.**

dam[4] *symbol for* decametre(s).

Dam (*Danish* dam) *n* (**Carl Peter**) **Henrik** ('hɛnrəg). 1895–1976, Danish biochemist who discovered vitamin K (1934): Nobel prize for physiology or medicine 1943.

damage ('dæmıdʒ) *n* **1** injury or harm impairing the function or condition of a person or thing. **2** loss of something desirable. **3** *Informal.* cost; expense (esp. in the phrase **what's the damage?**). ◆ *vb* **4** (*tr*) to cause damage to. **5** (*intr*) to suffer damage. **[C14:** from Old French, from Latin *damnum* injury, loss, fine**]** ▸ **'damageable** *adj* ▸ **,damagea'bility** *n* ▸ **'damager** *n* ▸ **'damaging** *adj* ▸ **'damagingly** *adv*

damages ('dæmıdʒız) *pl n Law.* money to be paid as compensation to a person for injury, loss, etc.

daman ('dæmən) *n* a rare name for the **hyrax,** esp. the Syrian rock hyrax. See also **cony** (sense 2). **[**from Arabic *damān Isrā'īl* sheep of Israel**]**

Daman (dɑ:'mɑ:n) *n* a coastal town in W India, the chief town of Daman and Diu. Pop.: 26 895 (1991 est.). Portuguese name: **Damão.**

Daman and Diu (dɑ:'mɑ:n; 'di:u:) *n* a union territory in W India: formerly a district of Portuguese India (1559–1961) then part of the union territory of Goa, Daman, and Diu (1961–87). Area: 112 sq. km (43 sq. miles). Pop.: 111 000 (1994 est.).

Damanhûr (,dɑ:mən'hʊə) *n* a city in NE Egypt, in the Nile delta. Pop.: 222 000 (1992 est.).

Damão (də'mɐ̃u) *n* the Portuguese name for **Daman,** a former Portuguese settlement now in **Daman and Diu.**

damar ('dæmə) *n* a variant spelling of **dammar.**

Damara (də'mɑ:rə) *n* **1** (*pl* **-ras** *or* **-ra**) Also called: **Bergdama.** a member of a Negroid people of South West Africa. **2** the language of this people, a dialect of Nama.

Damaraland (də'mɑ:rə,lænd) *n* a plateau region of central Namibia, the traditional homeland of the Damara people.

damascene ('dæmə,si:n, ,dæmə'si:n) *vb* **1** (*tr*) to ornament (metal, esp. steel) by etching or by inlaying, usually with gold or silver. ◆ *n* **2** a design or article produced by this process. ◆ *adj* **3** of or relating to this process. **[C14:** from Latin *damascēnus* of Damascus**]**

Damascene ('dæmə,si:n, ,dæmə'si:n) *adj* **1** of or relating to Damascus. ◆ *n* **2** a native or inhabitant of Damascus. **3** a variety of domestic fancy pigeon with silvery plumage.

Damascus (də'mɑ:skəs, -'mæs-) *n* the capital of Syria, in the southwest: reputedly the oldest city in the world, having been inhabited continuously since before 2000 B.C. Pop.: 1 549 932 (1994 est.). Arabic names: **Dimashq, Esh Sham** (ɛʃ ʃæm).

Damascus steel *or* **damask steel** *n History.* a hard flexible steel with wavy markings caused by forging the metal in strips: used for sword blades.

damask ('dæməsk) *n* **1a** a reversible fabric, usually silk or linen, with a pattern woven into it. It is used for table linen, curtains, etc. **1b** table linen made from this. **1c** (*as modifier*): *a damask tablecloth.* **2** short for **Damascus steel. 3** the wavy markings on such steel. **4a** the greyish-pink colour of the damask rose. **4b** (*as adj*): *damask wallpaper.* ◆ *vb* **5** (*tr*) another word for **damascene** (sense 1). **[C14:** from Medieval Latin *damascus,* from Damascus, where this fabric was originally made**]**

damask rose *n* a rose, *Rosa damascena,* native to Asia and cultivated for its pink or red fragrant flowers, which are used to make the perfume attar. **[C16:** from Medieval Latin *rosa damascēna* rose of Damascus**]**

Dam Busters *pl n* **the.** the members of the special squadron of the RAF who carried out a bombing raid in May 1943 to destroy the Sorpe, Ede, and Moehne dams thereby flooding the Ruhr valley and disrupting German industry. See also **Wallis**[2].

dame (deım) *n* **1** (formerly) a woman of rank or dignity; lady. **2** a nun who has taken the vows of her order, esp. a Benedictine. **3** *Archaic, chiefly Brit.* a matronly or elderly woman. **4** *Slang, chiefly U.S. and Canadian.* a woman. **5** Also called: **pantomime dame.** *Brit.* the role of a comic old woman in a pantomime, usually played by a man. **[C13:** from Old French, from Latin *domina* lady, mistress of a household**]**

Dame (deım) *n* (in Britain) **1** the title of a woman who has been awarded the Order of the British Empire or any of certain other orders of chivalry. **2** the legal title of the wife or widow of a knight or baronet, placed before her name: *Dame Judith.* Compare **Lady.**

dame school *n* (formerly) a small school, often in a village, usually run by an elderly woman in her own home to teach young children to read and write.

dame's violet, dame's rocket, *or* **damewort** ('deım,wɜ:t) *n* a Eurasian cruciferous hairy perennial plant, *Hesperis matronalis,* cultivated in gardens for its mauve or white fragrant flowers.

Damien (*French* damjɛ̃) *n* **Joseph** (ʒozɛf), known as *Father Damien.* 1840–89, Belgian Roman Catholic missionary to the leper colony at Molokai, Hawaii.

Damietta (,dæmı'ɛtə) *n* a town in NE Egypt, in the Nile delta: important medieval commercial centre. Pop.: 113 000 (1991). Arabic name: **Dumyat.**

dammar, damar, *or* **dammer** ('dæmə) *n* any of various resins obtained from SE Asian trees, esp. of the genera *Agathis* (conifers) and *Shorea* (family *Dipterocarpaceae*): used for varnishes, lacquers, bases for oil paints, etc. **[C17:** from Malay *damar* resin**]**

dammit ('dæmıt) *interj* a contracted form of *damn it.*

damn (dæm) *interj* **1** *Slang.* an exclamation of annoyance (often in exclamatory phrases such as **damn it! damn you!** etc.). **2** *Informal.* an exclamation of surprise or pleasure (esp. in the exclamatory phrase **damn me!**). ◆ *adj* **3** (*prenominal*) *Slang.* deserving damnation; detestable. ◆ *adv, adj* (*prenominal*) **4** *Slang.* (intensifier): *damn fool; a damn good pianist.* ◆ *adv* **5 damn all.** *Slang.* absolutely nothing. ◆ *vb* (*mainly tr*) **6** to condemn as bad, worthless, etc. **7** to curse. **8** to condemn to eternal damnation. **9** (*often passive*) to doom to ruin; cause to fail: *the venture was damned from the start.* **10** (*also intr*) to prove (someone) guilty: *damning evidence.* **11** to swear (at) using the word *damn.* **12 as near as damn it.** *Brit. informal.* as near as possible; very near. **13 damn with faint praise.** to praise so unenthusiastically that the effect is condemnation. ◆ *n* **14** *Slang.* something of negligible value; jot (esp. in the phrase **not worth a damn**). **15 not give a damn.** *Informal.* to be unconcerned; not care. **[C13:** from Old French *dampner,* from Latin *damnāre* to injure, condemn, from *damnum* loss, injury, penalty**]**

damnable ('dæmnəbᵊl) *adj* **1** execrable; detestable. **2** liable to or deserving damnation. ▸ **'damnableness** *or* **,damna'bility** *n*

damnably ('dæmnəblı) *adv* **1** in a detestable manner. **2** (intensifier): *it was damnably unfair.*

damnation (dæm'neıʃən) *n* **1** the act of damning or state of being damned. **2** a cause or instance of being damned. ◆ *interj* **3** an exclamation of anger, disappointment, etc.

damnatory ('dæmnətərı, -trı) *adj* threatening or occasioning condemnation.

damned (dæmd) *adj* **1a** condemned to hell. **1b** (*as n*): *the damned.* ◆ *adv, adj Slang.* **2** (intensifier): *a damned good try; a damned liar; I should damned well think so!* **3** used to indicate amazement, disavowal, or refusal (in such phrases as **I'll be damned** and **damned if I care**).

damnedest ('dæmdıst) *n Informal.* utmost; best (esp. in the phrases **do** or **try one's damnedest**).

damnify ('dæmnı,faı) *vb* **-fies, -fying, -fied.** (*tr*) *Law.* to cause loss or damage to (a person); injure. [C16: from Old French *damnifier,* ultimately from Latin *damnum* harm, + *facere* to make] ▸ ˌ**damnifiˈcation** *n*

Damocles (ˈdæməˌkliːz) *n Classical legend.* a sycophant forced by Dionysius, tyrant of Syracuse, to sit under a sword suspended by a hair to demonstrate that being a king was not the happy state Damocles had said it was. See also **Sword of Damocles.** ▸ ˌ**Damoˈclean** *adj*

Damodar (ˈdæməˌdɑː) *n* a river in NE India, rising in Bihar and flowing east through West Bengal to the Hooghly River: the **Damodar Valley** is an important centre of heavy industry.

damoiselle, damosel, *or* **damozel** (ˌdæməˈzɛl) *n* archaic variants of **damsel.**

Damon and Pythias (ˈdeɪmən) *n Classical legend.* two friends noted for their mutual loyalty. Damon offered himself as a hostage for Pythias, who was to be executed for treason by Dionysius of Syracuse. When Pythias returned to save his friend's life, he was pardoned.

damp (dæmp) *adj* **1** slightly wet, as from dew, steam, etc. **2** *Archaic.* dejected. ◆ *n* **3** slight wetness; moisture; humidity. **4** rank air or poisonous gas, esp. in a mine. See also **firedamp. 5** a discouragement; damper. **6** *Archaic.* dejection. ◆ *vb (tr)* **7** to make slightly wet. **8** (often foll. by *down*) to stifle or deaden: *to damp one's ardour.* **9** (often foll. by *down*) to reduce the flow of air to (a fire) to make it burn more slowly or to extinguish it. **10** *Physics.* to reduce the amplitude of (an oscillation or wave). **11** *Music.* to muffle (the sound of an instrument). ◆ See also **damp off.** [C14: from Middle Low German *damp* steam; related to Old High German *demphen* to cause to steam] ▸ ˈ**dampish** *adj* ▸ ˈ**damply** *adv* ▸ ˈ**dampness** *n*

dampcourse (ˈdæmpˌkɔːs) *n* a horizontal layer of impervious material in a brick wall, fairly close to the ground, to stop moisture rising. Also called: **damp-proof course.**

dampen (ˈdæmpən) *vb* **1** to make or become damp. **2** *(tr)* to stifle; deaden. ▸ ˈ**dampener** *n*

damper (ˈdæmpə) *n* **1** a person, event, or circumstance that depresses or discourages. **2 put a damper on.** to produce a depressing or inhibiting effect on. **3** a movable plate to regulate the draught in a stove or furnace flue. **4** a device to reduce electronic, mechanical, acoustic, or aerodynamic oscillations in a system. **5** *Music.* the pad in a piano or harpsichord that deadens the vibration of each string as its key is released. **6** *Chiefly Austral. and N.Z.* any of various unleavened loaves and scones, typically cooked on an open fire.

Dampier (ˈdæmpɪə) *n* **William.** 1652–1715, English navigator, pirate, and writer: sailed around the world twice.

damping (ˈdæmpɪŋ) *n* **1** moistening or wetting. **2** stifling, as of spirits. **3** *Electronics.* the introduction of resistance into a resonant circuit with the result that the sharpness of response at the peak of a frequency is reduced. **4** *Engineering.* any method of dispersing energy in a vibrating system.

damping off *n* any of various diseases of plants, esp. the collapse and death of seedlings caused by the parasitic fungus *Pythium debaryanum* and related fungi in conditions of excessive moisture.

damp off *vb (intr, adv)* (of plants, seedlings, shoots, etc.) to be affected by damping off.

damp-proof *vb Building trades.* **1** to protect against the incursion of damp by adding a dampcourse or by coating with a moisture-resistant preparation. ◆ *adj* **2** protected against damp or causing protection against damp: *a damp-proof course.*

damsel (ˈdæmzᵊl) *n Archaic or poetic.* a young unmarried woman; maiden. [C13: from Old French *damoisele,* from Vulgar Latin *domnicella* (unattested) young lady, from Latin *domina* mistress; see DAME]

damsel bug *n* any of various bugs of the carnivorous family *Nabiidae,* related to the bedbugs but feeding on other insects. The larvae of some species mimic and associate with ants.

damselfish (ˈdæmzᵊlˌfɪʃ) *n, pl* **-fish** *or* **-fishes.** any small tropical percoid fish of the family *Pomacentridae,* having a brightly coloured deep compressed body. See also **anemone fish.**

damselfly (ˈdæmzᵊlˌflaɪ) *n, pl* **-flies.** any insect of the suborder *Zygoptera,* similar to but smaller than dragonflies and usually resting with the wings closed over the back: order *Odonata.*

damson (ˈdæmzən) *n* **1** a small rosaceous tree, *Prunus domestica instititia* (or *P. instititia*), cultivated for its blue-black edible plumlike fruit and probably derived from the bullace. See also **plum**[1] (sense 1). **2** the fruit of this tree. [C14: from Latin *prūnum Damascēnum* Damascus plum]

damson cheese *n* thick damson jam.

dan[1] (dæn) *n* a small buoy used as a marker at sea. Also called: **dan buoy.** [C17: of unknown origin]

dan[2] (dæn) *n Judo, karate, etc.* **1** any one of the 10 black-belt grades of proficiency. **2** a competitor entitled to dan grading. ◆ Compare **kyu.** [Japanese]

Dan[1] (dæn) *n* an archaic title of honour, equivalent to *Master* or *Sir: Dan Chaucer.*

Dan[2] (dæn) *n Old Testament.* **1a** the fourth son of Jacob (Genesis 30:1–6). **1b** the tribe descended from him. **2** a city in the northern territory of Canaan.

Dan. *abbrev. for:* **1** *Bible.* Daniel. **2** Danish.

Dana (ˈdeɪnə) *n* **James Dwight** (dwaɪt). 1813–95, American geologist; noted for his work *The System of Mineralogy* (1837).

Danaë (ˈdæneɪˌiː) *n Greek myth.* the mother of Perseus by Zeus, who came to her in prison as a shower of gold.

Danaides (dəˈneɪɪˌdiːz) *pl n, sing* **Danaid.** *Greek myth.* the fifty daughters of Danaüs. All but Hypermnestra murdered their bridegrooms and were punished in Hades by having to pour water perpetually into a jar with a hole in the bottom. ▸ **Danaidean** (ˌdænɪˈɪdɪən, ˌdænɪəˈdiːən) *adj*

Da Nang (dɑː næŋ) *n* a port in central Vietnam, on the South China Sea. Pop.: 382 674 (1992 est.). Former name: **Tourane.**

Danaüs (ˈdænɪəs) *n Greek myth.* a king of Argos who told his fifty daughters, the Danaides, to kill their bridegrooms on their wedding night.

Danby (ˈdænbɪ) *n* **1 1st Earl of,** title of *Thomas Osborne.* 1631–1712, English politician; Lord Treasurer (1673–78): regarded as the founder of the Tory party. Also called (from 1694): **1st Duke of Leeds. 2 Francis.** 1793–1861, Irish painter of romantic landscapes and historical subjects.

dance (dɑːns) *vb* **1** *(intr)* to move the feet and body rhythmically, esp. in time to music. **2** *(tr)* to perform (a particular dance). **3** *(intr)* to skip or leap, as in joy, etc. **4** to move or cause to move in a light rhythmic way. **5 dance attendance on (someone).** to attend (someone) solicitously or obsequiously. ◆ *n* **6** a series of rhythmic steps and movements, usually in time to music. Related adj: **Terpsichorean. 7** an act of dancing. **8a** a social meeting arranged for dancing; ball. **8b** *(as modifier): a dance hall.* **9** a piece of music in the rhythm of a particular dance form, such as a waltz. **10** dancelike movements made by some insects and birds, esp. as part of a behaviour pattern. **11 lead (someone) a dance.** *Brit. informal.* to cause (someone) continued worry and exasperation; play up. [C13: from Old French *dancier*] ▸ ˈ**danceable** *adj* ▸ ˈ**dancer** *n* ▸ ˈ**dancing** *n, adj*

dancehall (ˈdɑːnsˌhɔːl) *n* a style of dance-oriented reggae, originating in the late 1980s.

dance of death *n* a pictorial, literary, or musical representation, current esp. in the Middle Ages, of a dance in which living people, in order of social precedence, are led off to their graves, by a personification of death. Also called (French): **danse macabre.**

dancette (dɑːnˈsɛt) *n* another name for **chevron** (sense 5).

dancing girl *n* a professional female dancer who dances to entertain customers at a club, theatre, etc.

D and C *n Med.* dilation and curettage; a therapeutic or diagnostic procedure in obstetrics and gynaecology involving dilation of the cervix and curettage of the cavity of the uterus, as for abortion.

dandelion (ˈdændɪˌlaɪən) *n* **1** a plant, *Taraxacum officinale,* native to Europe and Asia and naturalized as a weed in North America, having yellow rayed flowers and deeply notched basal leaves, which are used for salad or wine: family *Compositae* (composites). **2** any of several similar related plants. [C15: from Old French *dent de lion,* literally: tooth of a lion, referring to its leaves]

dander[1] (ˈdændə) *n* **1** small particles or scales of hair or feathers. **2 get one's** (*or* **someone's**) **dander up.** *Informal.* to become or cause to become annoyed or angry. [C19: changed from DANDRUFF]

dander[2] (ˈdændə; *Scot.* ˈdændər) *Scot. and northern English dialect.* ◆ *n* **1** a stroll. ◆ *vb* **2** *(intr)* to stroll. [C19: of unknown origin]

Dandie Dinmont (ˈdændɪ ˈdɪnmɒnt) *n* a breed of small terrier with a long coat and drooping ears. Also called: **Dandie Dinmont terrier.** [C19: named after a character who owned two terriers in *Guy Mannering* (1815), a novel by Sir Walter Scott]

dandify (ˈdændɪˌfaɪ) *vb* **-fies, -fying, -fied.** *(tr)* to dress like or cause to resemble a dandy. ▸ ˌ**dandifiˈcation** *n*

dandiprat (ˈdændɪˌpræt) *n* **1** a small English coin minted in the 16th century. **2** *Archaic.* **2a** a small boy. **2b** an insignificant person. [C16: of unknown origin]

dandle (ˈdændᵊl) *vb (tr)* **1** to move (a young child, etc.) up and down (on the knee or in the arms). **2** to pet; fondle. [C16: of uncertain origin] ▸ ˈ**dandler** *n*

Dandolo (*Italian* ˈdandolo) *n* **Enrico.** *c.* 1108–1205, Venetian statesman; doge (1192–1205). During the fourth Crusade he won Greek colonies for Venice.

dandruff (ˈdændrəf) *n* loose scales of dry dead skin shed from the scalp. Also called (now rarely): **dandriff.** [C16: *dand-,* of unknown origin + *-ruff,* probably from Middle English *roufe* scab, from Old Norse *hrūfa*] ▸ ˈ**dandruffy** *adj*

dandy[1] (ˈdændɪ) *n, pl* **-dies. 1** a man greatly concerned with smartness of dress; beau. **2** a yawl or ketch. ◆ *adj* **-dier, -diest. 3** *Informal.* very good or fine. [C18: perhaps short for *jack-a-dandy*] ▸ ˈ**dandily** *adv* ▸ ˈ**dandyish** *adj* ▸ ˈ**dandyism** *n*

dandy[2] (ˈdændɪ) *n* another name for **dengue.**

dandy-brush *n* a stiff brush used for grooming a horse.

dandy roll *or* **roller** *n* a light roller used in the manufacture of certain papers to produce watermarks.

Dane (deɪn) *n* **1** a native, citizen, or inhabitant of Denmark. **2** any of the Vikings who invaded England from the late 8th to the 11th century A.D.

Danegeld (ˈdeɪnˌgɛld) *or* **Danegelt** (ˈdeɪnˌgɛlt) *n* the tax first levied in the late 9th century in Anglo-Saxon England to provide protection money for or to finance forces to oppose Viking invaders. [C11: from *Dan* Dane + *geld* tribute; see YIELD]

Danelaw *or* **Danelagh** (ˈdeɪnˌlɔː) *n* the northern, central and eastern parts of Anglo-Saxon England in which Danish law and custom were observed. [Old English *Dena lagu* Danes' law; term revived in the 19th century]

danewort (ˈdeɪnˌwɜːt) *n* a caprifoliaceous shrub, *Sambucus ebulus,* native to Europe and Asia and having serrated leaves and white flowers. See also **elder**[2].

dang (dæŋ) *interj, adv, adj* a euphemistic word for **damn** (senses 1–4).

danger (ˈdeɪndʒə) *n* **1** the state of being vulnerable to injury, loss, or evil; risk. **2** a person or thing that may cause injury, pain, etc. **3** *Obsolete.* power. **4 in danger of.** liable to. **5 on the danger list.** critically ill in hospital. [C13: *daunger* power, hence power to inflict injury, from Old French *dongier* (from Latin *dominium* ownership) blended with Old French *dam* injury, from Latin *damnum*] ▸ ˈ**dangerless** *adj*

danger money *n* extra money paid to compensate for the risks involved in certain dangerous jobs.

dangerous ('deɪndʒərəs) *adj* causing danger; perilous. ▸ **'dangerously** *adv* ▸ **'dangerousness** *n*

dangle ('dæŋgᵊl) *vb* **1** to hang or cause to hang freely: *his legs dangled over the wall.* **2** (*tr*) to display as an enticement: *the hope of a legacy was dangled before her.* ◆ *n* **3** the act of dangling or something that dangles. **[C16:** perhaps from Danish *dangle,* probably of imitative origin**]** ▸ **'dangler** *n* ▸ **'danglingly** *adv*

dangling participle *n Grammar.* another name (esp. U.S. and Canadian) for **misplaced modifier.**

Dani ('dɑːnɪ) *n* **1** (*pl* **Dani** ('dɑːnɪ)). a member of a New Guinea people living in the central highlands of West Irian. **2** the language of this people, probably related to other languages of New Guinea.

Daniel[1] ('dænjəl) *n* **1** *Old Testament.* **1a** a youth who was taken into the household of Nebuchadnezzar, received guidance and apocalyptic visions from God, and was given divine protection when thrown into the lions' den. **1b** the book that recounts these experiences and visions (in full **The Book of the Prophet Daniel**). **2** (often preceded by *a*) a wise upright person. **[**sense 2: referring to Daniel in the Apocryphal *Book of Susanna***]**

Daniel[2] ('dænjəl) *n* **Samuel.** ?1562–1619, English poet and writer: author of the sonnet sequence *Delia* (1592).

Daniell cell ('dænjəl) *n Physics.* a type of cell having a zinc anode in dilute sulphuric acid separated by a porous barrier from a copper cathode in copper sulphate solution. It has an emf of 1.1 volts. **[C19:** named after John *Daniell* (1790–1845), English scientist**]**

danio ('deɪnɪˌəʊ) *n, pl* **-os.** any brightly coloured tropical freshwater cyprinid fish of the genus *Danio* and related genera: popular aquarium fishes. **[C19:** from New Latin, of obscure origin**]**

Danish ('deɪnɪʃ) *adj* **1** of, relating to, or characteristic of Denmark, its people, or their language. ◆ *n* **2** the official language of Denmark, belonging to the North Germanic branch of the Indo-European family.

Danish blue *n* a strong-tasting white cheese with blue veins.

Danish loaf *n Brit.* a large white loaf with a centre split having the top crust dusted with flour, esp. one baked on the sole of the oven.

Danish pastry *n* a rich puff pastry filled with apple, almond paste, icing, etc.

Danish West Indies *pl n* the former possession of Denmark in the W Lesser Antilles, sold to the U.S. in 1917 and since then named the **Virgin Islands of the United States.**

dank (dæŋk) *adj* (esp. of cellars, caves, etc.) unpleasantly damp and chilly. **[C14:** probably of Scandinavian origin; compare Swedish *dank* marshy spot**]** ▸ **'dankly** *adv* ▸ **'dankness** *n*

Dankworth ('dæŋkwɜːθ) *n* **John** (**Philip William**). born 1927, British jazz composer, bandleader, and saxophonist: married to Cleo Laine.

Danmark ('danmarg) *n* the Danish name for **Denmark.**

D'Annunzio (*Italian* dan'nuntsjo) *n* **Gabriele** (ga'brjɛːle). 1863–1938, Italian poet, dramatist, novelist, national hero, and Fascist. His works include the poems in *Alcione* (1904) and the drama *La Figlia di Iorio* (1904).

danny ('dænɪ) *or* **donny** *n, pl* **-nies.** *Dialect.* the hand (used esp. when addressing children). **[**probably from *dandy,* childish pronunciation of HAND**]**

Dano-Norwegian (ˌdeɪnəʊnɔː'wiːdʒən) *n* another name for **Bokmål.**

danse macabre *French.* (dɑ̃s makɑbrə) *n* another name for **dance of death.**

danseur *French.* (dɑ̃sœr) *or* (*fem*) ***danseuse*** (dɑ̃søz) *n* a ballet dancer.

Dante ('dæntɪ, 'dɑːnteɪ; *Italian* 'dante) *n* full name **Dante Alighieri** (*Italian* ali'gjɛːri). 1265–1321, Italian poet famous for *La Divina Commedia* (?1309–?1320), an allegorical account of his journey through Hell, Purgatory, and Paradise, guided by Virgil and his idealized love Beatrice. His other works include *La Vita Nuova* (?1292), in which he celebrates his love for Beatrice. ▸ **Dantean** ('dæntɪən, dæn'tiːən) *or* **Dantesque** (dæn'tɛsk) *adj*

danthonia (dæn'θəʊnɪə) *n* any of various grasses of Australia and New Zealand having narrow leaves and small terminal panicles of densely crowded florets. **[**named after E. *Danthoine,* French botanist**]**

Danton ('dæntən; *French* dɑ̃tɔ̃) *n* **Georges Jacques** (ʒɔrʒ ʒɑk). 1759–94, French revolutionary leader: a founder member of the Committee of Public Safety (1793) and minister of justice (1792–94). He was overthrown by Robespierre and guillotined.

Danube ('dænjuːb) *n* a river in central and SE Europe, rising in the Black Forest in Germany and flowing to the Black Sea. Length: 2859 km (1776 miles). German name: **Donau.** Czech name: **Dunaj.** Hungarian name: **Duna.** Serbo-Croat name: **Dunav** ('dunaf). Romanian name: **Dunărea.** ▸ **Danubian** (dæn'juːbɪən) *adj*

Danzig ('dænsɪg; *German* 'dantsɪç) *n* **1** the German name for **Gdańsk. 2** a rare variety of domestic fancy pigeon originating in this area.

dap[1] (dæp) *vb* **daps, dapping, dapped. 1** *Angling.* to fish with a natural or artificial fly on a floss silk line so that the wind makes the fly bob on and off the surface of the water. **2** (*intr*) (as of a bird) to dip lightly into water. **3** to bounce or cause to bounce. **[C17:** of imitative origin**]**

dap[2] (dæp) *n Southwest Brit. dialect.* another word for **plimsoll. [C20:** probably special use of DAP[1] (in the sense: to bounce, skip)**]**

DAP *Computing. abbrev. for* distributed array processor.

daphne ('dæfnɪ) *n* any shrub of the Eurasian thymelaeaceous genus *Daphne,* such as the mezereon and spurge laurel: ornamentals with shiny evergreen leaves and clusters of small bell-shaped flowers. See also **laurel** (sense 4). **[**via Latin from Greek: laurel**]**

Daphne ('dæfnɪ) *n Greek myth.* a nymph who was saved from the amorous attentions of Apollo by being changed into a laurel tree.

daphnia ('dæfnɪə) *n* any water flea of the genus *Daphnia,* having a rounded body enclosed in a transparent shell and bearing branched swimming antennae. **[C19:** from New Latin, probably from DAPHNE**]**

Daphnis ('dæfnɪs) *n Greek myth.* a Sicilian shepherd, the son of Hermes and a nymph, who was regarded as the inventor of pastoral poetry.

Daphnis and Chloe *n* two lovers in pastoral literature, esp. in a prose idyll attributed to the Greek writer Longus.

Da Ponte (*Italian* dɑ 'pɔnte) *n* **Lorenzo** (lo'rɛntso), real name *Emmanuele Conegliano.* 1749–1838, Italian writer; Mozart's librettist for *The Marriage of Figaro* (1786), *Don Giovanni* (1787), and *Cosi fan tutte* (1790).

dapper ('dæpə) *adj* **1** neat and spruce in dress and bearing; trim. **2** small and nimble. **[C15:** from Middle Dutch: active, nimble**]** ▸ **'dapperly** *adv* ▸ **'dapperness** *n*

dapple ('dæpᵊl) *vb* **1** to mark or become marked with spots or patches of a different colour; mottle. ◆ *n* **2** mottled or spotted markings. **3** a dappled horse, etc. ◆ *adj* **4** marked with dapples or spots. **[C14:** of unknown origin**]**

dapple-grey *n* a horse with a grey coat having spots of darker colour.

Dapsang (dʌp'sʌŋ) *n* another name for **K2.**

dapsone ('dæpˌsəʊn) *n* an antibiotic drug used to treat leprosy and certain types of dermatitis. Formula: $C_{12}H_{12}N_2O_2S$. **[C20:** from *d(i)a(minodi)p(henyl) s(ulph)one***]**

DAR *abbrev. for* Daughters of the American Revolution.

daraf ('dæræf) *n Physics.* a unit of elastance equal to a reciprocal farad. **[C20:** reverse spelling of FARAD**]**

darbies ('dɑːbɪz) *pl n Brit.* a slang term for **handcuffs. [C16:** perhaps from the phrase *Father Derby's* or *Father Darby's bonds,* a rigid agreement between a usurer and his client**]**

d'Arblay ('dɑːbleɪ) *n* **Madame.** married name of (Fanny) **Burney.**

Darby ('dɑːbɪ) *n* **Abraham.** 1677–1717, British iron manufacturer: built the first coke-fired blast furnace (1709).

Darby and Joan ('dɑːbɪ) *n* **1** an ideal elderly married couple living in domestic harmony. **2 Darby and Joan Club.** a club for elderly people. **[C18:** a couple in an 18th-century English ballad**]**

darcy ('dɑːsɪ) *n Geology.* a unit expressing the permeability coefficient of rock. Symbol: D **[**named after Henri-Philibert-Gaspard *Darcy* (1803–58), French hydraulic engineer**]**

Darcy ('dɑːsɪ) *n* (**James**) **Les**(**lie**). 1895–1917, Australian boxer and folk hero, who lost only five professional fights and was never knocked out, considered a martyr after his death from septicaemia during a tour of the United States.

Dard (dɑːd) *n* a member of any of the Indo-European peoples speaking a Dardic language.

Dardan ('dɑːdᵊn) *or* **Dardanian** (dɑː'deɪnɪən) *n* another name for a **Trojan.**

Dardanelles (ˌdɑːdə'nɛlz) *n* the strait between the Aegean and the Sea of Marmara, separating European from Asian Turkey. Ancient name: **Hellespont.**

Dardanus ('dɑːdənəs) *n Classical myth.* the son of Zeus and Electra who founded the royal house of Troy.

Dardic ('dɑːdɪk) *adj* **1** belonging or relating to a group of languages spoken in Kashmir, N Pakistan, and E Afghanistan, regarded as a subbranch of the Indic branch of the Indo-European family but showing certain Iranian characteristics. ◆ *n* **2** this group of languages.

dare (dɛə) *vb* **1** (*tr*) to challenge (a person to do something) as proof of courage. **2** (can take an infinitive with or without *to*) to be courageous enough to try (to do something): *she dares to dress differently from the others; you wouldn't dare!* **3** (*tr*) *Rare.* to oppose without fear; defy. **4 I dare say.** Also: **I daresay. 4a** (it is) quite possible (that). **4b** probably: used as sentence substitute. ◆ *n* **5** a challenge to do something as proof of courage. **6** something done in response to such a challenge. **[**Old English *durran;* related to Old High German *turran* to venture**]** ▸ **'darer** *n*

USAGE When used negatively or interrogatively, *dare* does not usually add *-s: he dare not come; dare she come?* When used negatively in the past tense, however, *dare* usually adds *-d: he dared not come.*

daredevil ('dɛəˌdɛvᵊl) *n* **1** a recklessly bold person. ◆ *adj* **2** reckless; daring; bold. ▸ **'dareˌdevilry** *or* **'dareˌdeviltry** *n*

Dar es Salaam ('dɑːr ɛs sə'lɑːm) *n* the chief port of Tanzania, on the Indian Ocean: capital of German East Africa (1891–1916); capital of Tanzania until 1983 when it was replaced by Dodoma; university (1963). Pop.: 1 360 850 (1988).

Darfur (dɑː'fʊə) *n* a region of the W Sudan; an independent kingdom until conquered by Egypt in 1874.

darg (dɑːg) *n Scot. and northern English dialect.* a day's work. **[C15:** formed by syncope from *day-work***]**

dargah *or* **durgah** ('dɜːgɑː) *n* the tomb of a Muslim saint; a Muslim shrine. **[**Persian**]**

daric ('dærɪk) *n* a gold coin of ancient Persia. Compare **siglos. [C16:** from Greek *Dareikos,* probably after Darius I of Persia**]**

Darien ('dɛərɪən, 'dæ-) *n* **1** the E part of the Isthmus of Panama, between the **Gulf of Darien** on the Caribbean coast and the Gulf of San Miguel on the Pacific coast; chiefly within the republic of Panama but extending also into Colombia: site of a disastrous attempt to establish a Scottish colony in 1698. **2 Isthmus of.** the former name of the Isthmus of **Panama.** ◆ Spanish name: **Darién** (da'rjen).

daring ('dɛərɪŋ) *adj* **1** bold or adventurous; reckless. ◆ *n* **2** courage in taking risks; boldness. ▸ **'daringly** *adv*

Dario (*Spanish* da'rio) *n* **Rubén** (ru'βen), real name *Félix Rubén Garcia Sarmiento.* 1867–1916, Nicaraguan poet whose poetry includes *Prosas Profanas* (1896).

dariole ('dærɪˌəʊl) *n* **1** Also called: **dariole mould.** a small cup-shaped mould used for making individual sweet or savoury dishes. **2** a dish prepared in such a mould. **[C14:** from Old French**]**

Darius I (də'raɪəs) *n* known as *Darius the Great,* surname *Hystaspis.* ?550–486 B.C., king of Persia (521–486), who extended the Persian empire and crushed the revolt of the Ionian city states (500). He led two expeditions against Greece but was defeated at Marathon (490).

Darius III *n* died 330 B.C., last Achaemenid king of Persia (336–330), who was defeated by Alexander the Great.

Darjeeling (dɑːˈdʒiːlɪŋ) *n* **1** a town in NE India, in West Bengal in the Himalayas, at an altitude of about 2250 m (7500 ft.). Pop.: 73 090 (1991). **2** a high-quality black tea grown in the mountains around Darjeeling.

dark (dɑːk) *adj* **1** having little or no light: *a dark street.* **2** (of a colour) reflecting or transmitting little light: *dark brown.* Compare **light**[1] (sense 29), **medium** (sense 2). **3a** (of complexion, hair colour, etc.) not fair or blond; swarthy; brunette. **3b** (*in combination*): *dark-eyed.* **4** gloomy or dismal. **5** sinister; evil: *a dark purpose.* **6** sullen or angry: *a dark scowl.* **7** ignorant or unenlightened: *a dark period in our history.* **8** secret or mysterious: *keep it dark.* **9** *Phonetics.* denoting an (l) pronounced with a velar articulation giving back vowel resonance. In English, *l* is usually dark when final or preconsonantal. Compare **light**[1] (sense 30). ◆ *n* **10** absence of light; darkness. **11** night or nightfall. **12** a dark place, patch, or shadow. **13** a state of ignorance (esp. in the phrase **in the dark**). ◆ *vb* **14** an archaic word for **darken**. [Old English *deorc;* related to Old High German *terchennen* to hide] ► **ˈdarkish** *adj* ► **ˈdarkly** *adv* ► **ˈdarkness** *n*

Dark Ages *pl n* **the.** *European history.* **1** the period from about the late 5th century A.D. to about 1000 A.D., once considered an unenlightened period. **2** (occasionally) the whole medieval period.

Dark Continent *n* **the.** a term for Africa when it was relatively unexplored.

dark current *n* the residual current produced by a photoelectric device when not illuminated.

darken (ˈdɑːkən) *vb* **1** to make or become dark or darker. **2** to make or become gloomy, angry, or sad: *his mood darkened.* **3 darken (someone's) door.** (*usually used with a negative*) to visit someone: *never darken my door again!* ► **ˈdarkener** *n*

dark-field illumination *n* illumination of the field of a microscope from the side so that the specimen is viewed against a dark background.

dark-field microscope *n* another name for an **ultramicroscope.**

dark glasses *pl n* spectacles with lenses tinted to reduce transmitted light.

dark horse *n* **1** a competitor in a race or contest about whom little is known; an unknown. **2** a person who reveals little about himself or his activities, esp. one who has unexpected talents or abilities. **3** *U.S. politics.* a candidate who is unexpectedly nominated or elected.

dark lantern *n* a lantern having a sliding shutter or panel to dim or hide the light.

darkle (ˈdɑːkᵊl) *vb Archaic or literary.* **1** to grow dark; darken. **2** (*intr*) to appear dark or indistinct. [C19: back formation from DARKLING]

darkling (ˈdɑːklɪŋ) *Poetic.* ◆ *adv, adj* **1** in the dark or night. ◆ *adj* **2** darkening or almost dark; obscure. [C15: from DARK + -LING[2]]

dark matter *n Astronomy.* matter known to make up a substantial part of the mass of the universe, but not detectable by its absorption or emission of electromagnetic radiation.

dark nebula *n* a type of nebula that is observed by its blocking of radiation from other sources. See **nebula.**

dark reaction *n Botany.* the stage of photosynthesis involving the reduction of carbon dioxide and the dissociation of water, using chemical energy stored in ATP: does not require the presence of light. Compare **light reaction.**

darkroom (ˈdɑːkˌruːm, -ˌrʊm) *n* a room in which photographs are processed in darkness or safe light.

darksome (ˈdɑːksəm) *adj Literary.* dark or darkish.

dark star *n* an invisible star known to exist only from observation of its radio, infrared, or other spectrum or of its gravitational effect, such as an invisible component of a binary or multiple star.

darky, darkie, *or* **darkey** (ˈdɑːkɪ) *n, pl* **darkies** *or* **darkeys.** *Informal.* **1** an offensive word for a Black. **2** *Austral.* an offensive word for a native Australian.

Darlan (*French* darlɑ̃) *n* **Jean Louis Xavier François** (ʒɑ̃ lwi gzavje frɑ̃swa). 1881–1942, French admiral and member of the Vichy government. He co-operated with the Allies after their invasion of North Africa; assassinated.

darling (ˈdɑːlɪŋ) *n* **1** a person very much loved: often used as a term of address. **2** a favourite: *the teacher's darling.* ◆ *adj* (*prenominal*) **3** beloved. **4** much admired; pleasing: *a darling hat.* [Old English *dēorling;* see DEAR, -LING[1]]

Darling (ˈdɑːlɪŋ) *n* **Grace.** 1815–42, English national heroine, famous for her rescue (1838) of some shipwrecked sailors with her father, a lighthouse keeper.

Darling Downs *pl n* a plateau in NE Australia, in SE Queensland: a vast agricultural and stock-raising area.

Darling Range *n* a ridge in SW Western Australia, parallel to the coast. Highest point: about 582 m (1669 ft.).

Darling River *n* a river in SE Australia, rising in the Eastern Highlands and flowing southwest to the Murray River. Length: 2740 km (1702 miles).

Darlington (ˈdɑːlɪŋtən) *n* **1** an industrial town in NE England in Darlington unitary authority, S Durham: developed mainly with the opening of the Stockton-Darlington railway (1825). Pop.: 86 767 (1991). **2** a unitary authority in NE England, in Durham. Pop.: 101 106 (1997 est.). Area: 198 sq. km (77 sq. miles).

Darmstadt (ˈdɑːmstæt; *German* ˈdarmʃtat) *n* an industrial city in central Germany, in Hesse: former capital of the grand duchy of Hesse-Darmstadt (1567–1945). Pop.: 138 980 (1996 est.).

darn[1] (dɑːn) *vb* **1** to mend (a hole or a garment) with a series of crossing or interwoven stitches. ◆ *n* **2** a patch of darned work on a garment. **3** the process or act of darning. [C16: probably from French (Channel Islands dialect) *darner;* compare Welsh, Breton *darn* piece] ► **ˈdarner** *n* ► **ˈdarning** *n*

darn[2] (dɑːn) *interj, adj, adv, n* a euphemistic word for **damn** (senses 1–4, 15).

darned (dɑːnd) *adv, adj Slang.* **1** (intensifier): *this darned car won't start; a darned good shot.* ◆ *adj* **2** another word for **damned** (senses 2, 3).

darnel (ˈdɑːnᵊl) *n* any of several grasses of the genus *Lolium,* esp. *L. temulentum,* that grow as weeds in grain fields in Europe and Asia. [C14: probably related to French (Walloon dialect) *darnelle,* of obscure origin]

darning egg *or* **mushroom** *n* a rounded piece of wood or plastic used in darning to support the fabric around the hole.

darning needle *n* **1** a long needle with a large eye used for darning. **2** *U.S. and Canadian.* a dialect name for a **dragonfly.**

Darnley (ˈdɑːnlɪ) *n* **Lord.** title of *Henry Stuart* (or *Stewart*). 1545–67, Scottish nobleman; second husband of Mary, Queen of Scots and father of James I of England. After murdering his wife's secretary, Rizzio (1566), he was himself assassinated (1567).

darogha (dɑːˈrəʊgɑː) *n* (in India and Pakistan) **1** a manager. **2** an inspector. [Urdu]

dart (dɑːt) *n* **1** a small narrow pointed missile that is thrown or shot, as in the game of darts. **2** a sudden quick movement. **3** *Zoology.* a slender pointed structure, as in snails for aiding copulation or in nematodes for penetrating the host's tissues. **4** a tapered tuck made in dressmaking. ◆ *vb* **5** to move or throw swiftly and suddenly; shoot: *she darted across the room.* ◆ See also **darts.** [C14: from Old French, of Germanic origin; related to Old English *daroth* spear, Old High German *tart* dart] ► **ˈdarting** *adj* ► **ˈdartingly** *adv*

dartboard (ˈdɑːtˌbɔːd) *n* a circular piece of wood, cork, etc., used as the target in the game of darts. It is divided into numbered sectors with central inner and outer bull's-eyes.

darter (ˈdɑːtə) *n* **1** Also called: **anhinga, snakebird.** any aquatic bird of the genus *Anhinga* and family *Anhingidae,* of tropical and subtropical inland waters, having a long slender neck and bill: order *Pelecaniformes* (pelicans, cormorants, etc.). **2** any small brightly coloured North American freshwater fish of the genus *Etheostoma* and related genera: family *Percidae* (perches).

Dartford (ˈdɑːtfəd) *n* a town in SE England, in NW Kent. Pop.: 59 411 (1991).

Dartmoor (ˈdɑːtˌmʊə) *n* **1** a moorland plateau in SW England, in SW Devon: a national park since 1951. Area: 945 sq. km (365 sq. miles). **2** a prison in SW England, on Dartmoor: England's main prison for long-term convicts. **3** a small strong breed of pony, originally from Dartmoor. **4** a hardy coarse-woolled breed of sheep originally from Dartmoor.

Dartmouth (ˈdɑːtməθ) *n* **1** a port in SW England, in S Devon: Royal Naval College (1905). Pop.: 5676 (1991). **2** a city in SE Canada, in S Nova Scotia, on Halifax Harbour: oil refineries and shipyards. Pop.: 67 798 (1991).

darts (dɑːts) *n* (*functioning as sing*) any of various competitive games in which darts are thrown at a dartboard.

Darwin[1] (ˈdɑːwɪn) *n* a port in N Australia, capital of the Northern Territory: destroyed by a cyclone in 1974 but rebuilt on the same site. Pop.: 78 100 (1994). Former name (1869–1911): **Palmerston.**

Darwin[2] (ˈdɑːwɪn) *n* **1 Charles** (**Robert**). 1809–82, English naturalist who formulated the theory of evolution by natural selection, expounded in *On the Origin of Species* (1859) and applied to man in *The Descent of Man* (1871). **2** his grandfather, **Erasmus.** 1731–1802, English physician and poet; author of *Zoonomia, or the Laws of Organic Life* (1794–96), anticipating Lamarck's views on evolution. **3** Sir **George Howard,** son of Charles Darwin. 1845–1912, English astronomer and mathematician noted for his work on tidal friction.

Darwinian (dɑːˈwɪnɪən) *adj* **1** of or relating to Charles Darwin or his theory of evolution. ◆ *n* **2** a person who accepts, supports, or uses this theory.

Darwinism (ˈdɑːwɪˌnɪzəm) *or* **Darwinian theory** *n* the theory of the origin of animal and plant species by evolution through a process of natural selection. Compare **Lamarckism.** See also **Neo-Darwinism.** ► **ˈDarwinist** *or* **ˈDarwinite** *n, adj* ► **ˌDarwinˈistic** *adj*

Darwin's finches *pl n* the finches of the subfamily *Geospizinae* of the Galapagos Islands, showing great variation in bill structure and feeding habits: provided Darwin with evidence to support his theory of evolution.

dash[1] (dæʃ) *vb* (*mainly tr*) **1** to hurl; crash: *he dashed the cup to the floor; the waves dashed against the rocks.* **2** to mix: *white paint dashed with blue.* **3** (*intr*) to move hastily or recklessly; rush: *he dashed to her rescue.* **4** (usually foll. by *off* or *down*) to write (down) or finish (off) hastily. **5** to destroy; frustrate: *his hopes were dashed.* **6** to daunt (someone); cast down; discourage: *he was dashed by her refusal.* ◆ *n* **7** a sudden quick movement; dart. **8** a small admixture: *coffee with a dash of cream.* **9** a violent stroke or blow. **10** the sound of splashing or smashing: *the dash of the waves.* **11** panache; style: *he rides with dash.* **12 cut a dash.** See **cut** (sense 33). **13** the punctuation mark ►, used singly in place of a colon, esp. to indicate a sudden change of subject or grammatical anacoluthon, or in pairs to enclose a parenthetical remark. **14** the symbol (—) used, in combination with the symbol *dot* (·), in the written representation of Morse and other telegraphic codes. Compare **dah. 15** *Athletics.* another word (esp. U.S. and Canadian) for **sprint. 16** *Informal.* short for **dashboard.** [Middle English *dasche, dasse*]

dash[2] (dæʃ) *interj Informal.* a euphemistic word for **damn** (senses 1, 2).

dash[3] (dæʃ) *W. African.* ◆ *n* **1** a gift, commission, tip, or bribe. ◆ *vb* **2** to give (a dash) to someone. [C16: perhaps from Fanti]

dashboard (ˈdæʃˌbɔːd) *n* **1** Also called (Brit.): **fascia.** the instrument panel in a car, boat, or aircraft. Sometimes shortened to **dash. 2** *Obsolete.* a board at the side of a carriage or boat to protect against splashing.

dasheen (dæˈʃiːn) *n* another name for **taro.** [C19: perhaps changed from French (*chou*) *de Chine* (cabbage) of China]

dasher (ˈdæʃə) *n* the plunger in a churn, often with paddles attached.

dashiki (dɑːˈʃiːkɪ) *n* a large loose-fitting buttonless upper garment worn esp. by Blacks in the U.S., Africa, and the Caribbean. [C20: of W African origin]

dashing ('dæʃɪŋ) *adj* **1** spirited; lively: *a dashing young man.* **2** stylish; showy: *a dashing hat.* ► **'dashingly** *adv*

Dashing White Sergeant *n* a lively Scottish dance for sets of six people.

dashpot ('dæʃ,pɒt) *n* a device for damping vibrations; the vibrating part is attached to a piston moving in a liquid-filled cylinder. [C20: from DASH[1] + POT[1]]

Dasht-i-Kavir *or* **Dasht-e-Kavir** (,dæʃtiːkæ'vɪə) *n* a salt waste on the central plateau of Iran: a treacherous marsh beneath a salt crust. Also called: **Kavir Desert.**

Dasht-i-Lut *or* **Dasht-e-Lut** (,dæʃtiː'luːt) *n* a desert plateau in central and E central Iran.

Dassehra ('dæsəræ) *n* an annual Hindu festival celebrated on the 10th lunar day of Navaratri; images of the goddess Durga are immersed in water.

dassie ('dæsɪ) *n* another name for a **hyrax,** esp. the rock hyrax. [C19: from Afrikaans]

dastard ('dæstəd) *n Archaic.* a contemptible sneaking coward. [C15 (in the sense: dullard): probably from Old Norse *dæstr* exhausted, out of breath]

dastardly ('dæstədlɪ) *adj* mean and cowardly. ► **'dastardliness** *n*

dasypaedal (,dæsɪ'piːdᵊl) *adj* (of the young of some species of birds after hatching) having a covering of down. [from Greek *dasus* shaggy + *pais, paid-* child]

dasyure ('dæsɪ,jʊə) *n* any small carnivorous marsupial, such as *Dasyurus quoll* (**eastern dasyure**), of the subfamily *Dasyurinae,* of Australia, New Guinea, and adjacent islands. See also **Tasmanian devil.** [C19: from New Latin *Dasyūrus,* from Greek *dasus* shaggy + *oura* tail; see DENSE]

DAT *abbrev. for* digital audio tape.

dat. *abbrev. for* dative.

data ('deɪtə, 'dɑːtə) *pl n* **1** a series of observations, measurements, or facts; information. **2** Also called: **information.** *Computing.* the information operated on by a computer program. [C17: from Latin, literally: (things) given, from *dare* to give]

USAGE Although now often used as a singular noun, *data* is properly a plural.

data bank *n* a store of a large amount of information, esp. in a form that can be handled by a computer.

database ('deɪtə,beɪs) *n* **1** a systematized collection of data that can be accessed immediately and manipulated by a data-processing system for a specific purpose. **2** *Informal.* any large store of information: *a database of knowledge.*

database management *n* the maintenance of information stored in a computer system.

data capture *n* any process for converting information into a form that can be handled by a computer.

data dictionary *n Computing.* an index of data held in a database and used to assist in the access to data. Also called: **data directory.**

dataflow architecture ('deɪtə,fləʊ, 'dɑːtə-) *n* a means of arranging computer data processing in which operations are governed by the data present and the processing it requires rather than by a prewritten program that awaits data to be processed.

data pen *n* a device for reading or scanning magnetically coded data on labels, packets, etc.

data processing *n* **a** a sequence of operations performed on data, esp. by a computer, in order to extract information, reorder files, etc. **b** (*as modifier*): *a data-processing centre.* See also **automatic data processing.**

data protection *n* (in Britain) safeguards for individuals relating to personal data stored on a computer.

datary ('deɪtərɪ) *n, pl* **-ries.** *R.C. Church.* the head of the **dataria** (deɪ'tɛərɪə), the papal office that assesses candidates for benefices reserved to the Holy See. [C16: from Medieval Latin *datārius* official who dated papal letters, from Late Latin *data* DATE[1]]

data set *n Computing.* another name for **file**[1] (sense 7).

data structure *n* an organized form, such as an array list or string, in which connected data items are held in a computer.

datcha ('dætʃə) *n* a variant spelling of **dacha.**

date[1] (deɪt) *n* **1** a specified day of the month: *today's date is October 27.* **2** the particular day or year of an event: *the date of the Norman Conquest was 1066.* **3** (*pl*) the years of a person's birth and death or of the beginning and end of an event or period. **4** an inscription on a coin, letter, etc., stating when it was made or written. **5a** an appointment for a particular time, esp. with a person of the opposite sex: *she has a dinner date.* **5b** the person with whom the appointment is made. **6** the present moment; now (esp. in the phrases **to date, up to date**). ♦ *vb* **7** (*tr*) to mark (a letter, coin, etc.) with the day, month, or year. **8** (*tr*) to assign a date of occurrence or creation to. **9** (*intr;* foll. by *from* or *back to*) to have originated (at a specified time): *his decline dates from last summer.* **10** (*tr*) to reveal the age of: *that dress dates her.* **11** to make or become old-fashioned: *some good films hardly date at all.* **12** *Informal, chiefly U.S. and Canadian.* **12a** to be a boyfriend or girlfriend of (someone of the opposite sex). **12b** to accompany (a member of the opposite sex) on a date. [C14: from Old French, from Latin *dare* to give, as in the phrase *epistula data Romae* letter handed over at Rome] ► **'datable** *or* **'dateable** *adj* ► **'dateless** *adj*

USAGE See at **year.**

date[2] (deɪt) *n* **1** the fruit of the date palm, having sweet edible flesh and a single large woody seed. **2** short for **date palm.** [C13: from Old French, from Latin, from Greek *daktulos* finger]

dated ('deɪtɪd) *adj* **1** unfashionable; outmoded. **2** (of a security) having a fixed date for redemption.

Datel ('deɪ,tɛl) *n Trademark.* a British Telecom service providing for the direct transmission of data from one computer to another. [C20: from DA(TA) + TEL(EX)]

dateless ('deɪtlɪs) *adj* **1** likely to remain fashionable, relevant, or interesting regardless of age; timeless. **2** having no date or limit.

dateline ('deɪt,laɪn) *n Journalism.* the date and location of a story, placed at the top of an article.

date line *n* (*often caps.*) short for **International Date Line.**

date palm *n* a feather palm, *Phoenix dactylifera,* native to Syria but grown in other tropical regions for its edible fruit (dates).

date rape *n* **1** the act or an instance of a man raping a woman while they are on a date together. **2** an act of sexual intercourse regarded as tantamount to rape, esp. if the woman was encouraged to drink excessively or was subjected to undue pressure.

date stamp *n* **1** an adjustable rubber stamp for recording the date. **2** an inked impression made by this.

dating ('deɪtɪŋ) *n* any of several techniques, such as radioactive dating, dendrochronology, or varve dating, for establishing the age of rocks, palaeontological or archaeological specimens, etc.

dating agency *n* an agency that provides introductions to people seeking a companion with similar interests.

dative ('deɪtɪv) *Grammar.* ♦ *adj* **1** denoting a case of nouns, pronouns, and adjectives used to express the indirect object, to identify the recipients, and for other purposes. ♦ *n* **2a** the dative case. **2b** a word or speech element in this case. [C15: from Latin *datīvus,* from *dare* to give; translation of Greek *dotikos*] ► **datival** (deɪ'taɪvᵊl) *adj* ► **'datively** *adv*

dative bond *n Chem.* another name for **coordinate bond.**

dato ('dɑːtəʊ) *n, pl* **-tos.** the chief of any of certain Muslim tribes in the Philippine Islands. [C19: from Spanish, ultimately from Malay *dato'* grandfather]

datolite ('dætə,laɪt) *n* a colourless mineral consisting of a hydrated silicate of calcium and boron in monoclinic crystalline form, occurring in cavities in igneous rocks. Formula: $CaBSiO_4(OH)$. [C19: *dato-* from Greek *dateisthai* to divide + -LITE]

Datuk (dæ'tʊk) *n* (in Malaysia) a title denoting membership of a high order of chivalry. [from Malay *datu* chief] ► **Datin** (dæ'tiːn) *fem n*

datum ('deɪtəm, 'dɑːtəm) *n, pl* **-ta** (-tə). **1** a single piece of information; fact. **2** a proposition taken for granted, often in order to construct some theoretical framework upon it; a given. See also **sense datum.** [C17: from Latin: something given; see DATA]

datum plane, level, *or* **line** *n Surveying.* the horizontal plane from which heights and depths are calculated.

datura (də'tjʊərə) *n* any of various chiefly Indian solanaceous plants of the genus *Datura,* such as the moonflower and thorn apple, having large trumpet-shaped flowers, prickly pods, and narcotic properties. [C16: from New Latin, from Hindi *dhatūra* jimson weed, from Sanskrit *dhattūra*]

DATV *abbrev. for* digitally assisted television: a technique in which special digital signals are transmitted with an analogue picture signal to assist the receiver to display the picture to the best advantage.

daub (dɔːb) *vb* **1** (*tr*) to smear or spread (paint, mud, etc.), esp. carelessly. **2** (*tr*) to cover or coat (with paint, plaster, etc.) carelessly. **3** to paint (a picture) clumsily or badly. ♦ *n* **4** an unskilful or crude painting. **5** something daubed on, esp. as a wall covering. See also **wattle and daub. 6** a smear (of paint, mud, etc.). **7** the act of daubing. [C14: from Old French *dauber* to paint, whitewash, from Latin *dealbāre,* from *albāre* to whiten, from *albus* white] ► **'dauber** *n* ► **'dauby** *adj*

daube (dəʊb) *n* a braised meat stew. [from French]

daubery ('dɔːbərɪ) *n* **1** the act or an instance of daubing. **2** an unskilful painting.

Daubigny (*French* dobiɲi) *n* **Charles François** (ʃarl frɑ̃swa). 1817–78, French landscape painter associated with the Barbizon School.

daud (dɔːd, dɒd) *n Scot.* a lump or chunk of something. [C18: from earlier *dad* to strike, of unknown origin]

Daudet (*French* dodɛ) *n* **Alphonse** (alfɔ̃s). 1840–97, French novelist, short-story writer, and dramatist: noted particularly for his humorous sketches of Provençal life, as in *Lettres de mon moulin* (1866).

Daugava ('dauga,va) *n* the Latvian name for the Western **Dvina.**

Daugavpils (*Latvian* 'daugaf,pils) *n* a city in SE Latvia on the Western Dvina River: founded in 1274 by Teutonic Knights; ruled by Poland (1559–1772) and Russia (1772–1915); retaken by the Russians in 1940. Pop.: 118 500 (1996 est.). German name (until 1893): **Dünaburg.** Former Russian name (1893–1920): **Dvinsk.**

daughter ('dɔːtə) *n* **1** a female offspring; a girl or woman in relation to her parents. **2** a female descendant. **3** a female from a certain country, etc., or one closely connected with a certain environment, etc.: *a daughter of the church.* ♦ Related adj: **filial. 4** (*often cap.*) *Archaic.* a form of address for a girl or woman. ♦ (*modifier*) **5** *Biology.* denoting a cell or unicellular organism produced by the division of one of its own kind. **6** *Physics.* (of a nuclide) formed from another nuclide by radioactive decay. [Old English *dohtor;* related to Old High German *tohter* daughter, Greek *thugatēr,* Sanskrit *duhitá*] ► **'daughterhood** *n* ► **'daughterless** *adj* ► **'daughter-,like** *adj* ► **'daughterliness** *n* ► **'daughterly** *adj*

daughter-in-law *n, pl* **daughters-in-law.** the wife of one's son.

Daughters of the American Revolution *n* **the.** an organization of women descended from patriots of the period of the War of Independence. Abbrev.: **DAR.**

Daumier (*French* domje) *n* **Honoré** (ɔnɔre). 1808–79, French painter and lithographer, noted particularly for his political and social caricatures.

daunt (dɔːnt) *vb* (*tr; often passive*) **1** to intimidate. **2** to dishearten. [C13: from Old French *danter,* changed from *donter* to conquer, from Latin *domitāre* to tame] ► **'daunter** *n* ► **'daunting** *adj* ► **'dauntingly** *adv*

dauntless ('dɔːntlɪs) *adj* bold; fearless; intrepid. ► **'dauntlessly** *adv* ► **'dauntlessness** *n*

dauphin ('dɔːfɪn; *French* dofɛ̃) *n* (1349–1830) the title of the direct heir to the

French throne; the eldest son of the king of France. [C15: from Old French: originally a family name; adopted as a title by the Counts of Vienne and later by the French crown princes]

dauphine ('dɔːfiːn; *French* dofin) *or* **dauphiness** ('dɔːfɪnɪs) *n French history.* the wife of a dauphin.

Dauphiné (*French* dofine) *n* a former province of SE France: its rulers, the Counts of Vienne, assumed the title of *dauphin;* annexed to France in 1457.

daur (dɔːr) *vb* a Scot. word for **dare.**

Davao (da'vaːo) *n* a port in the S Philippines, in SE Mindanao. Pop.: 960 910 (1994 est.).

daven ('dɑvən) *vb (intr) Judaism.* **1** to pray. **2** to lead prayers. [from Yiddish]

Davenant ('dævənənt) *n* Sir **William.** 1606–68, English dramatist and poet: poet laureate (1638–68). His plays include *Love and Honour* (1634).

davenport ('dævən,pɔːt) *n* **1** *Chiefly Brit.* a tall narrow desk with a slanted writing surface and drawers at the side. **2** *U.S. and Canadian.* a large sofa, esp. one convertible into a bed. [C19: sense 1 said to be named after Captain *Davenport* who commissioned the first ones]

Daventry ('dævəntrɪ) *n* a town in central England, in Northamptonshire: light industries, site of an important international radio transmitter. Pop.: 18 099 (1991).

David ('deɪvɪd) *n* **1** the second king of the Hebrews (about 1000–962 B.C.), who united Israel as a kingdom with Jerusalem as its capital. **2 Elizabeth.** 1914–92, British cookery writer. Her books include *Mediterranean Food* (1950) and *An Omelette and a Glass of Wine* (1984). **3** (*French* david). **Jacques Louis** (ʒɑk lwi). 1748–1825, French neoclassical painter of such works as the *Oath of the Horatii* (1784), *Death of Socrates* (1787), and *The Intervention of the Sabine Women* (1799). He actively supported the French Revolution and became court painter to Napoleon Bonaparte in 1804; banished at the Bourbon restoration. **4 Saint.** 6th century A.D., Welsh bishop; patron saint of Wales. Feast day: March 1.

David I *n* 1084–1153, king of Scotland (1124–53) who supported his niece Matilda's claim to the English throne and unsuccessfully invaded England on her behalf.

David II *n* 1324–71, king of Scotland (1329–71): he was forced into exile in France (1334–41) by Edward de Baliol; captured following the battle of Neville's Cross (1346), and imprisoned by the English (1346–57).

Davies ('deɪvɪs) *n* **1** Sir **John.** 1569–1626, English poet, author of *Orchestra or a Poem of Dancing* (1596) and the philosophical poem *Nosce Teipsum* (1599). **2** Sir **Peter Maxwell.** born 1934, English composer whose operas include *Taverner* (1967) and *The Martyrdom of St Magnus* (1977). He has written four symphonies (1976, 1980, 1983, and 1989), a violin concerto (1985), and much orchestral music. **3** (**William**) **Robertson.** 1913–95, Canadian novelist and dramatist. His novels include *Leaven of Malice* (1954), *The Rebel Angels* (1981), *What's Bred in the Bone* (1985), and *Murther and Walking Spirits* (1991). **4 W(illiam) H(enry).** 1871–1940, Welsh poet, noted also for his *Autobiography of a Super-tramp* (1908).

da Vinci (də 'vɪntʃɪ) *n* See **Leonardo da Vinci.**

Davis ('deɪvɪs) *n* **1 Bette** ('bɛtɪ), real name *Ruth Elizabeth Davis.* 1908–89, U.S. film actress, whose films include *Of Human Bondage* (1934), *Jezebel* (1938) for which she won an Oscar, *Now Voyager* (1942), *Whatever Happened to Baby Jane?* (1962), *The Nanny* (1965), and *Death on the Nile* (1978). **2** Sir **Colin (Rex).** born 1927, English conductor, noted for his interpretation of the music of Berlioz. **3 Jefferson.** 1808–89, president of the Confederate States of America during the Civil War (1861–65). **4 Joe.** 1901–78, English billiards and snooker player: world champion from 1927 to 1946. **5 John.** Also called: **John Davys.** ?1550–1605, English navigator: discovered the Falkland Islands (1592); searched for a Northwest Passage. **6 Miles (Dewey).** 1926–91, U.S. jazz trumpeter and composer. **7 Steve.** born 1957, English snooker player: world champion 1981, 1983–84, 1987–89.

Davis Cup *n* **1** an annual international lawn tennis championship for men's teams. **2** the trophy awarded for this. [C20: after Dwight F. *Davis* (1879–1945), American civic leader who donated the cup]

Davisson ('deɪvɪsən) *n* **Clinton Joseph.** 1881–1958, U.S. physicist, noted for his discovery of electron diffraction; shared the Nobel prize for physics in 1937.

Davis Strait *n* a strait between Baffin Island, in Canada, and Greenland. [named after John DAVIS]

davit ('dævɪt, 'deɪ-) *n* a cranelike device, usually one of a pair, fitted with a tackle for suspending or lowering equipment, esp. a lifeboat. [C14: from Anglo-French *daviot,* diminutive of *Davi* David]

Davos ('dævɒs) *n* a mountain resort in Switzerland: winter sports, site of the Parsenn ski run. Pop.: 10 500 (1990). Height: about 1560 m (5118 ft.). Romansh name: **Tarau.**

Davy ('deɪvɪ) *n* Sir **Humphry.** 1778–1829, English chemist who isolated sodium, magnesium, chlorine, and other elements and suggested the electrical nature of chemical combination. He invented the **Davy lamp.**

Davy Jones *n* **1** Also called: **Davy Jones's locker.** the ocean's bottom, esp. when regarded as the grave of those lost or buried at sea. **2** the spirit or devil of the sea. [C18: of unknown origin]

Davy lamp *n* See **safety lamp.** [C19: named after Sir H. DAVY, who invented it]

daw (dɔː) *n* an archaic, dialect, or poetic name for a **jackdaw.** [C15: related to Old High German *taha*]

dawdle ('dɔːdᵊl) *vb* **1** (*intr*) to be slow or lag behind. **2** (when *tr,* often foll. by *away*) to waste (time); trifle. [C17: of uncertain origin] ▸ **'dawdler** *n* ▸ **'dawdlingly** *adv*

Dawes (dɔːz) *n* **Charles Gates.** 1865–1951, U.S. financier, diplomat, and statesman, who devised the Dawes Plan for German reparations payments after World War I; vice president of the U.S. (1925–29); Nobel peace prize 1925.

dawk (dɔːk) *n* a variant spelling of **dak.**

Dawkins ('dɔːkɪnz) *n* **Richard.** born 1941, British zoologist, noted for such works as *The Selfish Gene* (1976), *The Blind Watchmaker* (1986), and *River Out of Eden* (1995).

dawn (dɔːn) *n* **1** daybreak; sunrise. Related adj: **auroral. 2** the sky when light first appears in the morning. **3** the beginning of something. ◆ *vb* (*intr*) **4** to begin to grow light after the night. **5** to begin to develop, appear, or expand. **6** (usually foll. by *on* or *upon*) to begin to become apparent (to). [Old English *dagian* to dawn; see DAY] ▸ **'dawn,like** *adj*

dawn chorus *n* the singing of large numbers of birds at dawn.

dawney ('dɑːniː) *adj Irish.* (of a person) dull or slow; listless. [of unknown origin]

dawn raid *n Stock Exchange.* an unexpected attempt to acquire a substantial proportion of a company's shares at the start of a day's trading as a preliminary to a takeover bid.

dawn redwood *n* a deciduous conifer, *Metasequoia glyptostroboides,* native to China but planted in other regions as an ornamental tree: family *Taxodiaceae.* Until recently it was thought to be extinct.

Dawson ('dɔːsᵊn) *n* a town in NW Canada, in the Yukon on the Yukon River: a boom town during the Klondike gold rush (at its height in 1899). Pop.: 1988 (1995 est.).

Dawson Creek *n* a town in W Canada, in NE British Columbia: SE terminus of the Alaska Highway. Pop.: 10 981 (1991).

day (deɪ) *n* **1** Also called: **civil day.** the period of time, the **calendar day,** of 24 hours' duration reckoned from one midnight to the next. **2** the period of light between sunrise and sunset, as distinguished from the night. **3** the part of a day occupied with regular activity, esp. work: *he took a day off.* **4** (*sometimes pl*) a period or point in time: *he was a good singer in his day; in days gone by; any day now.* **5** the period of time, the **sidereal day,** during which the earth makes one complete revolution on its axis relative to a particular star. The **mean sidereal day** lasts 23 hours 56 minutes 4.1 seconds of the mean solar day. **6** the period of time, the **solar day,** during which the earth makes one complete revolution on its axis relative to the sun. The **mean solar day** is the average length of the apparent solar day and is some four minutes (3 minutes 56.5 seconds of sidereal time) longer than the sidereal day. **7** the period of time taken by a specified planet to make one complete rotation on its axis: *the Martian day.* **8** (*often cap.*) a day designated for a special observance, esp. a holiday: *Christmas Day.* **9 all in a day's work.** part of one's normal activity; no trouble. **10 at the end of the day.** in the final reckoning. **11 day of rest.** the Sabbath; Sunday. **12 end one's days.** to pass the end of one's life. **13 every dog has his day.** one's luck will come. **14 in this day and age.** nowadays. **15 it's early days.** it's too early to tell how things will turn out. **16 late in the day. 16a** very late (in a particular situation). **16b** too late. **17 that will be the day. 17a** I look forward to that. **17b** that is most unlikely to happen. **18** a time of success, recognition, power, etc.: *his day will soon come.* **19** a struggle or issue at hand: *the day is lost.* **20a** the ground surface over a mine. **20b** (*as modifier*): *the day level.* **21 from day to day.** without thinking of the future. **22 call it a day.** to stop work or other activity. **23 day after day.** without respite; relentlessly. **24 day by day.** gradually or progressively; daily: *he weakened day by day.* **25 day in, day out.** every day and all day long. **26 from Day 1** *or* **Day One.** from the very beginning. **27 one of these days.** at some future time. **28** (*modifier*) of, relating to, or occurring in the day: *the day shift.* ◆ Related adj: **diurnal.** See also **days.** [Old English *dæg;* related to Old High German *tag,* Old Norse *dagr*]

Day (deɪ) *n* Sir **Robin.** born 1923, British radio and television journalist, noted esp. for his political interviews.

Dayak ('daɪæk) *n, pl* **-aks** *or* **-ak.** a variant spelling of **Dyak.**

dayan (dɑ'jɑn, 'dɑjən) *n Judaism.* a senior rabbi, esp. one who sits in a religious court. [from Hebrew, literally: judge]

Dayan (daɪ'jɑːn) *n* **Moshe** ('mɒʃe). 1915–81, Israeli soldier and statesman; minister of defence (1967; 1969–74) and foreign minister (1977–79).

day bed *n* a narrow bed, with a head piece and sometimes a foot piece and back, on which to recline during the day.

day blindness *n* a nontechnical name for **hemeralopia.**

daybook ('deɪ,bʊk) *n Book-keeping.* a book in which the transactions of each day are recorded as they occur.

dayboy ('deɪ,bɔɪ) *n Brit.* a boy who attends a boarding school daily, but returns home each evening.

daybreak ('deɪ,breɪk) *n* the time in the morning when light first appears; dawn; sunrise.

daycare ('deɪ,kɛə) *n Social welfare.* **1** *Brit.* occupation, treatment, or supervision during the working day for people who might be at risk if left on their own, or whose usual carers need daytime relief. **2** *Brit.* welfare services provided by a local authority, health service, or voluntary body during the day. Compare **residential care. 3** *N.Z.* short for **daycare centre.**

daycare centre *n* another name (esp. U.S. and N.Z.) for **day nursery.**

daycentre ('deɪ,sɛntə) *or* **day centre** *n Social welfare.* (in Britain) **1** a building used for daycare or other welfare services. See also **drop-in centre. 2** the enterprise itself, including staff, users, and organization.

day-clean *n Caribbean and West African informal.* the time after first dawn when the sun begins to shine; clear daybreak.

daydream ('deɪ,driːm) *n* **1** a pleasant dreamlike fantasy indulged in while awake; idle reverie. **2** a pleasant scheme or wish that is unlikely to be fulfilled; pipe dream. ◆ *vb* **3** (*intr*) to have daydreams; indulge in idle fantasy. ▸ **'day,dreamer** *n* ▸ **'day,dreamy** *adj*

dayflower ('deɪ,flaʊə) *n* any of various tropical and subtropical plants of the genus *Commelina,* having jointed creeping stems, narrow pointed leaves, and blue or purplish flowers which wilt quickly: family *Commelinaceae.*

dayfly ('deɪˌflaɪ) *n, pl* **-flies.** another name for a **mayfly.**
Day-Glo *n Trademark.* **a** a brand of fluorescent colouring materials, as of paint. **b** (*as modifier*): *Day-Glo colours.*
day hospital *n Brit.* part of a hospital that offers therapeutic services, where patients usually attend all day but go home or to a hospital ward at night.
day labourer *n* an unskilled worker hired and paid by the day.
Day-Lewis ('deɪ'luːɪs) *or* **Day Lewis** *n* **C(ecil).** 1904–72, British poet, critic, and (under the pen name *Nicholas Blake*) author of detective stories; poet laureate (1968–72).
daylight ('deɪˌlaɪt) *n* **1a** light from the sun. **1b** (*as modifier*): *daylight film.* **2** the period when it is light; daytime. **3** daybreak. **4 see daylight. 4a** to understand something previously obscure. **4b** to realize that the end of a difficult task is approaching. ◆ See also **daylights.**
daylight lamp *n Physics.* a lamp whose light has a range of wavelengths similar to that of natural sunlight.
daylight robbery *n Informal.* blatant overcharging.
daylights ('deɪˌlaɪts) *pl n* consciousness or wits (esp. in the phrases **scare, knock,** or **beat the (living) daylights out of someone**).
daylight-saving time *n* time set usually one hour ahead of the local standard time, widely adopted in the summer to provide extra daylight in the evening. Also called (in the U.S.): **daylight time.** ◆ See also **British Summer Time.**
day lily *n* **1** any widely cultivated Eurasian liliaceous plant of the genus *Hemerocallis,* having large yellow, orange, or red lily-like flowers, which typically last for only one day and are immediately succeeded by others. **2** the flower of any of these plants.
daylong ('deɪˌlɒŋ) *adj, adv* lasting the entire day; all day.
day name *n W African.* a name indicating a person's day of birth.
day-neutral *adj* (of plants) having an ability to mature and bloom that is not affected by day length.
day nursery *n Social welfare, Brit. and N.Z.* an establishment offering daycare to preschool children, enabling their parents to work full time or have extended relief if child care is a problem. Also called (N.Z.): **daycare centre.**
Day of Atonement *n* another name for **Yom Kippur.**
Day of Judgment *n* another name for **Judgment Day.**
day of reckoning *n* a time when the effects of one's past mistakes or misdeeds catch up with one.
day release *n Brit.* a system whereby workers are released for part-time education without loss of pay.
day return *n* a reduced fare for a journey (by train, etc.) travelling both ways in one day.
day room *n* a communal living room in a residential institution such as a hospital.
days (deɪz) *adv Informal.* during the day, esp. regularly: *he works days.*
day school *n* **1** a private school taking day students only. Compare **boarding school. 2** a school giving instruction during the daytime. Compare **night school.**
day shift *n* **1** a group of workers who work a shift during the daytime in an industry or occupation where a night shift or a back shift is also worked. **2** the period worked. ◆ See also **back shift.**
Days of Awe *pl n Judaism.* another name for **High Holidays.** [a literal translation of YAMIM NORA'IM]
days of grace *pl n* days permitted by custom for payment of a promissory note, bill of exchange, etc., after it falls due.
dayspring ('deɪˌsprɪŋ) *n* a poetic word for **dawn.**
daystar ('deɪˌstɑː) *n* **1** a poetic word for the **sun. 2** another word for the **morning star.**
daytime ('deɪˌtaɪm) *n* the time between dawn and dusk; the day as distinct from evening or night.
day-to-day *adj* routine; everyday: *day-to-day chores.*
Dayton ('deɪtᵊn) *n* an industrial city in SW Ohio: aviation research centre. Pop.: 172 947 (1996 est.).
Daytona Beach (deɪ'təʊnə) *n* a city in NE Florida, on the Atlantic: a resort with a beach of hard white sand, used since 1903 for motor speed trials. Pop.: 61 921 (1990).
day trip *n* a journey made to and from a place within one day. ▸ **'day-ˌtripper** *n*
Da Yunhe ('dæ 'juːnhə) *n* Pinyin transliteration of the Chinese name for the **Grand Canal** (sense 1).
daze (deɪz) *vb (tr)* **1** to stun or stupefy, esp. by a blow or shock. **2** to bewilder, amaze, or dazzle. ◆ *n* **3** a state of stunned confusion or shock (esp. in the phrase **in a daze**). [C14: from Old Norse *dasa-,* as in *dasast* to grow weary] ▸ **dazedly** ('deɪzɪdlɪ) *adv*
dazzle ('dæzᵊl) *vb* **1** (*usually tr*) to blind or be blinded partially and temporarily by sudden excessive light. **2** to amaze, as with brilliance: *she was dazzled by his wit; she dazzles in this film.* ◆ *n* **3** bright light that dazzles. **4** bewilderment caused by glamour, brilliance, etc.: *the dazzle of fame.* [C15: from DAZE] ▸ **'dazzling** *adj* ▸ **'dazzlingly** *adv*
dB *or* **db** *symbol for* decibel *or* decibels.
DBE *abbrev. for* Dame (Commander of the Order) of the British Empire (a Brit. title).
Dbh *or* **DBH** *Forestry. abbrev. for* diameter at breast height.
DBib *abbrev. for* Douay Bible.
DBMS *abbrev. for* database management system.
DBS *abbrev. for:* **1** direct broadcasting by satellite. **2** direct broadcasting satellite.
dbx *or* **DBX** *n Trademark. Electronics.* a noise-reduction system that works as a compander across the full frequency spectrum.
DC *abbrev. for:* **1** *Music.* da capo. **2** Detective Constable. **3** direct current. Compare **AC. 4** district commissioner. **5** Also: **D.C.** District of Columbia.
DCB *abbrev. for* Dame Commander of the Order of the Bath (a Brit. title).
DCC *abbrev. for* digital compact cassette.
DCF *Account. abbrev. for* discounted cash flow.
DCL *abbrev. for* Doctor of Civil Law.
DCM *Brit. military. abbrev. for* Distinguished Conduct Medal.
DCMG *abbrev. for* Dame Commander of the Order of St Michael and St George (a Brit. title).
DCVO *abbrev. for* Dame Commander of the Royal Victorian Order (a Brit. title).
DD *abbrev. for:* **1** Also: **dd.** direct debit. **2** Doctor of Divinity.
D-day *n* **1** the day, June 6, 1944, on which the Allied invasion of Europe began. **2** the day on which any large-scale operation is planned to start. [C20: from *D(ay)-day;* compare H-HOUR]
DDR *abbrev. for* Deutsche Demokratische Republik (the former East Germany; GDR).
DDS *abbrev. for:* **1** Dewey Decimal System. **2** Doctor of Dental Surgery.
DDSc *abbrev. for* Doctor of Dental Science.
DDT *n* dichlorodiphenyltrichloroethane; a colourless odourless substance used as an insecticide. It is toxic to animals and is known to accumulate in the tissues. It is now banned in the UK.
de, De *or before a vowel* **d', D'** (də) of; from: occurring as part of some personal names and originally indicating place of origin: *Simon de Montfort; D'Arcy; de la Mare.* [from Latin *dē;* see DE-]
DE *abbrev. for:* **1** (in Britain) Department of Employment. **2** Delaware.
de- *prefix forming verbs and verbal derivatives.* **1** removal of or from something specified: *deforest; dethrone.* **2** reversal of something: *decode; decompose; desegregate.* **3** departure from: *decamp.* [from Latin, from *dē* (prep) from, away from, out of, etc. In compound words of Latin origin, *de-* also means away, away from (*decease*); down (*degrade*); reversal (*detect*); removal (*defoliate*); and is used intensively (*devote*) and pejoratively (*detest*)]
deacon ('diːkən) *n Christianity.* **1** (in the Roman Catholic and other episcopal churches) an ordained minister ranking immediately below a priest. **2** (in Protestant churches) a lay official appointed or elected to assist the minister, esp. in secular affairs. **3** *Scot.* the president of an incorporated trade or body of craftsmen in a burgh. ◆ Related adj: **diaconal.** [Old English, ultimately from Greek *diakonos* servant] ▸ **'deaconˌship** *n*
deaconess ('diːkənɪs) *n Christianity.* (in the early church and in some modern Churches) a female member of the laity with duties similar to those of a deacon.
deaconry ('diːkənrɪ) *n, pl* **-ries. 1** the office or status of a deacon. **2** deacons collectively.
deactivate (diː'æktɪˌveɪt) *vb* **1** (*tr*) to make (a bomb, etc.) harmless or inoperative. **2** (*intr*) to become less radioactive. **3** (*tr*) *U.S.* to end the active status of (a military unit). **4** *Chem.* to return or cause to return from an activated state to a normal or ground state. ▸ **deˌacti'vation** *n* ▸ **de'actiˌvator** *n*
dead (dɛd) *adj* **1a** no longer alive. **1b** (*as n*): *the dead.* **2** not endowed with life; inanimate. **3** no longer in use, valid, effective, or relevant: *a dead issue; a dead language.* **4** unresponsive or unaware; insensible: *he is dead to my strongest pleas.* **5** lacking in freshness, interest, or vitality: *a dead handshake.* **6** devoid of physical sensation; numb: *his gums were dead from the anaesthetic.* **7** resembling death; deathlike: *a dead sleep.* **8** no longer burning or hot: *dead coals.* **9** (of flowers or foliage) withered; faded. **10** (*prenominal*) (intensifier): *a dead stop; a dead loss.* **11** *Informal.* very tired. **12** *Electronics.* **12a** drained of electric charge; discharged: *the battery was dead.* **12b** not connected to a source of potential difference or electric charge. **13** lacking acoustic reverberation: *a dead sound; a dead surface.* **14** *Sport.* (of a ball, etc.) out of play. **15** unerring; accurate; precise (esp. in the phrase **a dead shot**). **16** lacking resilience or bounce: *a dead ball.* **17** *Printing.* **17a** (of type) set but no longer needed for use. Compare **standing** (sense 7). **17b** (of copy) already composed. **18** not yielding a return; idle: *dead capital.* **19** *Informal.* certain to suffer a terrible fate; doomed: *you're dead if your mother catches you at that.* **20** (of colours) not glossy or bright; lacklustre. **21** stagnant: *dead air.* **22** *Military.* shielded from view, as by a geographic feature or environmental condition: *a dead zone; dead space.* **23 dead as a doornail.** *Informal.* completely dead. **24 dead from the neck up.** *Informal.* stupid or unintelligent. **25 dead in the water.** *Informal.* unsuccessful, and with little hope of future success: *the talks are now dead in the water.* **26 dead to the world.** *Informal.* unaware of one's surroundings, esp. fast asleep or very drunk. **27 leave for dead. 27a** to abandon. **27b** *Informal.* to surpass or outdistance by far. **28 wouldn't be seen dead (in, at, etc.).** *Informal.* to refuse to wear, to go (to), etc. ◆ *n* **29** a period during which coldness, darkness, or some other quality associated with death is at its most intense: *the dead of winter.* ◆ *adv* **30** (intensifier): *dead easy; stop dead; dead level.* **31 dead on.** exactly right. [Old English *dēad;* related to Old High German *tōt,* Old Norse *dauthr;* see DIE[1]] ▸ **'deadness** *n*
dead-and-alive *adj Brit.* (of a place, activity, or person) dull; uninteresting.
dead-ball line *n Rugby.* a line not more than 22 metres behind the goal line at each end of the field beyond which the ball is out of play.
deadbeat ('dɛdˌbiːt) *n* **1** *Informal.* a lazy or socially undesirable person. **2** a high grade escapement used in pendulum clocks. **3** (*modifier*) (of a clock escapement) having a beat without any recoil. **4** (*modifier*) *Physics.* **4a** (of a system) returning to an equilibrium position with little or no oscillation. **4b** (of an instrument or indicator) indicating a true reading without oscillation.
dead beat *adj Informal.* tired out; exhausted.
deadboy ('dɛdˌbɔɪ) *n* See **deadman** (sense 2).
dead-cat bounce *n Stock Exchange informal.* a temporary recovery in prices following a substantial fall as a result of speculators buying stocks they have already sold rather than as a result of a genuine reversal of the downward trend.
dead centre *n* **1** the exact top (**top dead centre**) or bottom (**bottom dead centre**) of the piston stroke in a reciprocating engine or pump. **2** a pointed rod

mounted in the tailstock of a lathe to support a workpiece. ◆ Also called: **dead point.**

dead duck *n Slang.* a person or thing doomed to death, failure, etc., esp. because of a mistake or misjudgment.

deaden ('dɛdᵊn) *vb* **1** to make or become less sensitive, intense, lively, etc; damp or be damped down; dull. **2** (*tr*) to make acoustically less resonant: *he deadened the room with heavy curtains.* ► **'deadener** *n* ► **'deadening** *adj*

dead end *n* **1** another name for **cul-de-sac. 2** a situation in which further progress is impossible. **3** (*as modifier*): *a dead-end street; a dead-end job.*

deadeye ('dɛd,aɪ) *n* **1** *Nautical.* either of a pair of disclike wooden blocks, supported by straps in grooves around them, between which a line is rove so as to draw them together to tighten a shroud. Compare **bull's-eye** (sense 9). **2** *Informal, chiefly U.S.* an expert marksman.

deadfall ('dɛd,fɔːl) *n* a type of trap, used esp. for catching large animals, in which a heavy weight falls to crush the prey. Also called: **downfall.**

dead fingers *n* (*functioning as sing.*) *Med.* a disease of users of pneumatic drills, characterized by anaesthesia of the fingertips and cyanosis.

dead hand *n* **1** an oppressive or discouraging influence or factor: *the dead hand of centralized control.* **2** *Law.* a less common word for **mortmain.**

deadhead ('dɛd,hɛd) *n* **1** a dull unenterprising person. **2** a person who uses a free ticket, as for a train, the theatre, etc. **3** *U.S. and Canadian.* a train, etc., travelling empty. **4** *U.S. and Canadian.* a totally or partially submerged log floating in a lake, etc. ◆ *vb* **5** (*tr*) to cut off withered flowers from (a plant). **6** (*intr*) *U.S. and Canadian.* to drive an empty bus, train, etc.

Dead Heart *n* (usually preceded by *the*) *Austral.* the remote interior of Australia. [C20: from the title *The Dead Heart of Australia* (1906) by J. W. Gregory (1864–1932), British geologist]

dead heat *n* **a** a race or contest in which two or more participants tie for first place. **b** a tie between two or more contestants in any position.

dead key *n* a key on the keyboard of a typewriter which does not automatically advance the carriage when depressed.

dead leg *n Informal.* temporary loss of sensation in the leg, caused by a blow to a muscle.

dead letter *n* **1** a letter that cannot be delivered or returned because it lacks adequate directions. **2** a law or ordinance that is no longer enforced but has not been formally repealed. **3** *Informal.* anything considered no longer worthy of consideration.

dead letter box *or* **drop** *n* a place where messages and other material can be left and collected secretly without the sender and the recipient meeting.

deadlight ('dɛd,laɪt) *n* **1** *Nautical.* **1a** a bull's-eye let into the deck or hull of a vessel to admit light to a cabin. **1b** a shutter of wood or metal for sealing off a porthole or cabin window. **2** a skylight designed not to be opened.

deadline ('dɛd,laɪn) *n* a time limit for any activity.

dead load *n* the intrinsic invariable weight of a structure, such as a bridge. Also called: **dead weight.** Compare **live load.**

deadlock ('dɛd,lɒk) *n* **1** a state of affairs in which further action between two opposing forces is impossible; stalemate. **2** a tie between opposite sides in a contest. **3** a lock having a bolt that can be opened only with a key. ◆ *vb* **4** to bring or come to a deadlock.

dead loss *n* **1** *Informal.* a person, thing, or situation that is completely useless or unprofitable. **2** a complete loss for which no compensation is received.

deadly ('dɛdlɪ) *adj* **-lier, -liest. 1** likely to cause death: *deadly poison; deadly combat.* **2** *Informal.* extremely boring. ◆ *adv, adj* **3** like death in appearance or certainty: *deadly pale; a deadly sleep.* ► **'deadliness** *n*

deadly nightshade *n* a poisonous Eurasian solanaceous plant, *Atropa belladonna,* having dull purple bell-shaped flowers and small very poisonous black berries. Also called: **belladonna, dwale.**

deadly sins *pl n Theol.* the sins of pride, covetousness, lust, envy, gluttony, anger, and sloth.

deadman ('dɛd,mæn) *n, pl* **-men. 1** *Civil engineering.* a heavy plate, wall, or block buried in the ground that acts as an anchor for a retaining wall, sheet pile, etc., by a tie connecting the two. **2** *Mountaineering.* a metal plate with a wire loop attached for thrusting into firm snow to serve as a belay point, a smaller version being known as a **deadboy.**

dead man's fingers *n* (*functioning as sing*) a soft coral, *Alcyonium digitatum,* with long finger-like polyps.

dead man's handle *or* **pedal** *n* a safety switch on a piece of machinery, such as a train, that allows operation only while depressed by the operator.

dead march *n* a piece of solemn funeral music played to accompany a procession, esp. at military funerals.

dead-nettle *n* any Eurasian plant of the genus *Lamium,* such as *L. alba* (white dead-nettle), having leaves resembling nettles but lacking stinging hairs: family *Labiatae* (labiates).

deadpan ('dɛd,pæn) *adj, adv* with a deliberately emotionless face or manner: *deadpan humour.*

dead point *n* another name for **dead centre.**

dead reckoning *n* a method of establishing one's position using the distance and direction travelled rather than astronomical observations.

Dead Sea *n* a lake between Israel and Jordan, 397 m (1302 ft.) below sea level: the lowest lake in the world, with no outlet and very high salinity. Area: 1020 sq. km (394 sq. miles).

Dead Sea Scrolls *pl n* a collection of manuscripts in Hebrew and Aramaic discovered in caves near the Dead Sea between 1947 and 1956. They are widely held to have been written between about 100 B.C. and 68 A.D. and provide important biblical evidence.

dead set *adv* **1** absolutely: *he is dead set against going to Spain.* ◆ *n* **2** the motionless position of a dog when pointing with its muzzle towards game. ◆ *adj* **3** (of a hunting dog) in this position. ◆ *interj* **4** *Austral. slang.* an expression of affirmation: *dead set, I worked from dawn to dusk.*

dead-smooth file *n Engineering.* the smoothest grade of file commonly used.

dead soldier *or* **marine** *n Informal.* an empty beer or spirit bottle.

dead stock *n* farm equipment. Compare **livestock.**

dead time *n Electronics.* the interval of time immediately following a stimulus, during which an electrical device, component, etc., is insensitive to a further stimulus.

dead weight *n* **1** a heavy weight or load. **2** an oppressive burden; encumbrance. **3** the difference between the loaded and the unloaded weights of a ship. **4** another name for **dead load. 5** (in shipping) freight chargeable by weight rather than by bulk.

Dead White European Male *or* **Dead White Male** *n* a man whose importance and talents may have been exaggerated because he belonged to a historically dominant gender and ethnic group.

deadwood ('dɛd,wʊd) *n* **1** dead trees or branches. **2** *Informal.* a useless person; encumbrance. **3** *Nautical.* a filler piece between the keel and the stern of a wooden vessel.

deaf (dɛf) *adj* **1a** partially or totally unable to hear. **1b** (*as collective n;* preceded by *the*): *the deaf.* ◆ See also **tone-deaf. 2** refusing to heed: *deaf to the cries of the hungry.* [Old English *dēaf;* related to Old Norse *daufr*] ► **'deafly** *adv* ► **'deafness** *n*

USAGE See at **disabled.**

deaf aid *n* another name for **hearing aid.**

deaf-and-dumb *Offensive.* ◆ *adj* **1** unable to hear or speak. ◆ *n* **2** a deaf-mute person.

deafblind ('dɛf'blaɪnd) *adj* **a** unable to hear or see. **b** (*as collective n;* preceded by *the*): *the deafblind.*

deafen ('dɛfᵊn) *vb* (*tr*) to make deaf, esp. momentarily, as by a loud noise. ► **'deafeningly** *adv*

deaf-mute *n* **1** a person who is unable to hear or speak. See also **mute**[1] (sense 7), **mutism** (sense 2b). ◆ *adj* **2** unable to hear or speak. [C19: translation of French *sourd-muet*] ► **'deaf-,muteness** *or* **'deaf-,mutism** *n*

deaf without speech *adj* **a** (usually of a prelingually deaf person) able to utter sounds but not speak. **b** (*as collective n;* preceded by *the*): *the deaf without speech.*

Deak ('dɛɑːk) *n* **Ferenc** ('fɛrɛnts). 1803–76, Hungarian statesman: minister of justice following the 1848 Hungarian uprising. The Austro-Hungarian dual monarchy was largely his creation.

Deakin ('diːkɪn) *n* **Alfred.** 1856–1919, Australian statesman. He was a leader of the movement for Australian federation; prime minister of Australia (1903–04; 1905–08; 1909–10).

deal[1] (diːl) *vb* **deals, dealing, dealt** (dɛlt). **1** (*intr*) (foll. by *in*) to engage (in) commercially: *to deal in upholstery.* **2** (often foll. by *out*) to apportion (something, such as cards) to a number of people; distribute. **3** (*tr*) to give (a blow) to (someone); inflict. **4** (*intr*) *Slang.* to sell any illegal drug. ◆ *n* **5** *Informal.* a bargain, transaction, or agreement. **6** a particular type of treatment received, esp. as the result of an agreement: *a fair deal.* **7** an indefinite amount, extent, or degree (esp. in the phrases **good** *or* **great deal**). **8** *Cards.* **8a** the process of distributing the cards. **8b** a player's turn to do this. **8c** a single round in a card game. **9** See **big deal.** ◆ See also **deal with.** [Old English *dǣlan,* from *dǣl* a part; compare Old High German *teil* a part, Old Norse *deild* a share]

deal[2] (diːl) *n* **1** a plank of softwood timber, such as fir or pine, or such planks collectively. **2** the sawn wood of various coniferous trees, such as that from the Scots pine (**red deal**) or from the Norway Spruce (**white deal**). ◆ *adj* **3** of fir or pine. [C14: from Middle Low German *dele* plank; see THILL]

Deal (diːl) *n* a town in SE England, in Kent, on the English Channel: two 16th-century castles: tourism, light industries. Pop.: 28 504 (1991).

dealate ('diːeɪ,leɪt, -lɪt) *or* **dealated** ('diːeɪ,leɪtɪd) *adj* (of ants and other insects) having lost their wings, esp. by biting or rubbing them off after mating. [from DE- + ALATE] ► **,dea'lation** *n*

dealer ('diːlə) *n* **1** a person or firm engaged in commercial purchase and sale; trader: *a car dealer.* **2** *Cards.* the person who distributes the cards. **3** *Slang.* a person who sells illegal drugs. ► **'dealer,ship** *n*

dealfish ('diːl,fɪʃ) *n, pl* **-fish** *or* **-fishes.** any deep-sea teleost fish of the genus *Trachipterus,* esp. *T. arcticus,* related to the ribbonfishes and having a very long tapelike body and a fan-shaped tail fin.

dealings ('diːlɪŋz) *pl n* (*sometimes sing*) transactions or business relations.

dealt (dɛlt) *vb* the past tense and past participle of **deal**[1].

deal with *vb* (*tr, adv*) **1** to take action on: *to deal with each problem in turn.* **2** to punish: *the headmaster will deal with the culprit.* **3** to be concerned with: *the book deals with Dutch art.* **4** to conduct oneself (towards others), esp. with regard to fairness: *he can be relied on to deal fairly with everyone.* **5** to do business with: *the firm deals with many overseas suppliers.*

deaminate (diː'æmɪ,neɪt) *or* **deaminize, deaminise** *vb* (*tr*) to remove one or more amino groups from (a molecule). ► **de,ami'nation, de,amini'zation** *or* **de,amini'sation** *n*

dean (diːn) *n* **1** the chief administrative official of a college or university faculty. **2** (at Oxford and Cambridge universities) a college fellow with responsibility for undergraduate discipline. **3** *Chiefly Church of England.* the head of a chapter of canons and administrator of a cathedral or collegiate church. **4** *R.C. Church.* the cardinal bishop senior by consecration and head of the college of cardinals. ◆ Related adj: **decanal.** See also **rural dean.** [C14: from Old French *deien,* from Late Latin *decānus* one set over ten persons, from Latin *decem* ten] ► **'dean,ship** *n*

Dean[1] (diːn) *n* **Forest of.** a forest in W England, in Gloucestershire, between the Rivers Severn and Wye: formerly a royal hunting ground.

Dean[2] (diːn) *n* **1 Christopher.** See **Torvill and Dean. 2 James** (**Byron**).

1931–55, U.S. film actor, who became a cult figure; his films include *East of Eden* and *Rebel Without a Cause* (both 1955). He died in a car crash.

deanery ('di:nərɪ) *n, pl* **-eries.** **1** the office or residence of dean. **2** the group of parishes presided over by a rural dean.

de-anglicization *or* **de-anglicisation** *n* (in Ireland) the elimination of English influence, language, customs, etc.

Dean of Faculty *n* the president of the Faculty of Advocates in Scotland.

dean of guild *n* the titular head of the guild or merchant company in a Scots burgh, who formerly exercised jurisdiction over all building in the burgh in the **Dean of Guild Court.**

dear (dɪə) *adj* **1** beloved; precious. **2** used in conventional forms of address preceding a title or name, as in *Dear Sir* or *my dear Mr Smith.* **3** (*postpositive;* foll. by *to*) important; close: *a wish dear to her heart.* **4a** highly priced. **4b** charging high prices. **5** appealing or pretty: *what a dear little ring!* **6 for dear life.** urgently or with extreme vigour or desperation. ◆ *interj* **7** used in exclamations of surprise or dismay, such as *Oh dear!* and *dear me!* ◆ *n* **8** (*often used in direct address*) someone regarded with affection and tenderness; darling. ◆ *adv* **9** dearly: *his errors have cost him dear.* [Old English *dēore;* related to Old Norse *dȳrr*] ▸ **'dearness** *n*

Dearborn ('dɪəbən, -ˌbɔ:n) *n* a city in SE Michigan, near Detroit: automobile industry. Pop.: 91 418 (1996 est.).

Dear John letter *n Informal.* a letter from a girl breaking off a love affair.

dearly ('dɪəlɪ) *adv* **1** very much: *I would dearly like you to go.* **2** affectionately. **3** at a great cost.

dearth (dɜ:θ) *n* an inadequate amount, esp. of food; scarcity. [C13: *derthe,* from *dēr* DEAR]

deary *or* **dearie** ('dɪərɪ) *n* **1** (*pl* **dearies**) *Informal.* a term of affection: now often sarcastic or facetious. **2 deary** *or* **dearie me!** an exclamation of surprise or dismay.

deasil ('di:zᵊl, 'di:ʃᵊl) *Scot.* ◆ *adv* **1** in the direction of the apparent course of the sun; clockwise. ◆ *n* **2** motion in this direction. ◆ Compare **withershins.** [C18: Scot. Gaelic *deiseil*]

death (dɛθ) *n* **1** the permanent end of all functions of life in an organism or some of its cellular components. **2** an instance of this: *his death ended an era.* **3** a murder or killing: *he had five deaths on his conscience.* **4** termination or destruction: *the death of colonialism.* **5** a state of affairs or an experience considered as terrible as death: *your constant nagging will be the death of me.* **6** a cause or source of death. **7** (*usually cap.*) a personification of death, usually a skeleton or an old man holding a scythe. **8a to death** *or* **to the death.** until dead: *bleed to death; a fight to the death.* **8b to death.** excessively: *bored to death.* **9 at death's door.** likely to die soon. **10 catch one's death** (**of cold**). *Informal.* to contract a severe cold. **11 do to death. 11a** to kill. **11b** to overuse (a joke, etc.) so that it no longer has any effect. **12 in at the death. 12a** present when an animal that is being hunted is caught and killed. **12b** present at the finish or climax. **13 like death warmed up.** *Informal.* very ill. **14 like grim death.** as if afraid of one's life. **15 put to death.** to kill deliberately or execute. ◆ Related adjs.: **fatal, lethal, mortal.** ◆ Related prefixes: **necro-, thanato-.** [Old English *dēath;* related to Old High German *tōd* death, Gothic *dauthus*]

death adder *n* a venomous Australian elapid snake, *Acanthophis antarcticus,* resembling an adder.

deathbed ('dɛθˌbɛd) *n* **1a** the bed in which a person is about to die. **1b** (*as modifier*): *a deathbed conversion.* **2 on one's deathbed.** about to die.

deathblow ('dɛθˌbləʊ) *n* a thing or event that destroys life or hope, esp. suddenly.

death camp *n* a concentration camp in which the conditions are so brutal that few prisoners survive, or one to which prisoners are sent for execution.

death cap *or* **angel** *n* a poisonous woodland saprotrophic basidiomycetous fungus, *Amanita phalloides,* differing from the edible mushroom (*Agaricus*) only in its white gills (pinkish-brown in *Agaricus*) and the presence of a volva. See also **amanita.**

death cell *n* a prison cell for criminals sentenced to death.

death certificate *n* a legal document issued by a qualified medical practitioner certifying the death of a person and stating the cause if known.

death-dealing *adj* fatal; lethal.

death duty *n* a tax on property inheritances: in Britain, replaced in 1975 by capital transfer tax and since 1986 by inheritance tax. Also called: **estate duty.**

death futures *pl n* life insurance policies of terminally ill people that are bought speculatively for a lump sum by a company, enabling it to collect the proceeds of the policies when the sufferers die.

death grant *n* (in the British National Insurance scheme) a grant payable to a relative, executor, etc., after the death of a person.

death knell *or* **bell** *n* **1** something that heralds death or destruction. **2** a bell rung to announce a death.

deathless ('dɛθlɪs) *adj* immortal, esp. because of greatness; everlasting. ▸ **'deathlessly** *adv* ▸ **'deathlessness** *n*

deathly ('dɛθlɪ) *adj* **1** deadly. **2** resembling death: *a deathly quiet.* ▸ **'deathliness** *n*

death mask *n* a cast of a person's face taken shortly after death. Compare **life mask.**

death penalty *n* (often preceded by *the*) capital punishment.

death rate *n* the ratio of deaths in a specified area, group, etc., to the population of that area, group, etc. Also called (esp. U.S.): **mortality rate.**

death rattle *n* a low-pitched gurgling sound sometimes made by a dying person, caused by air passing through an accumulation of mucus in the trachea.

death ray *n* an imaginary ray capable of killing.

death row *or* **house** *n U.S.* the part of a prison where those sentenced to death are confined.

death seat *n U.S. and Austral. slang.* the seat beside the driver of a vehicle.

death's-head *n* a human skull or a representation of one.

death's-head moth *n* a European hawk moth, *Acherontia atropos,* having markings resembling a human skull on its upper thorax.

deathtrap ('dɛθˌtræp) *n* a building, vehicle, etc., that is considered very unsafe.

Death Valley *n* a desert valley in E California and W Nevada: the lowest, hottest, and driest area of the U.S. Lowest point: 86 m (282 ft.) below sea level. Area: about 3885 sq. km (1500 sq. miles).

death-valley curve *n* a curve on a graph showing how the capital of a new company plotted against time declines sharply as the venture capital is used up before income reaches predicted levels.

death warrant *n* **1** the official authorization for carrying out a sentence of death. **2 sign one's** (**own**) **death warrant.** to cause one's own destruction.

deathwatch ('dɛθˌwɒtʃ) *n* **1** a vigil held beside a dying or dead person. **2 deathwatch beetle.** a beetle, *Xestobium rufovillosum,* whose woodboring larvae are a serious pest. The adult produces a rapid tapping sound with its head that was once popularly supposed to presage death. See also **anobiid.**

death wish *n* (in Freudian psychology) the desire for self-annihilation. See also **Thanatos.**

Deauville ('dəʊvi:l; *French* dovil) *n* a town and resort in NW France: casino. Pop.: 4770 (latest est.).

deave (di:v) *vb* (*tr*) *Scot.* **1** to deafen. **2** to bewilder or weary (a person) with noise. [Old English *dēafian*]

deb (dɛb) *n Informal.* short for **debutante.**

deb. *abbrev. for* debenture.

debacle (deɪ'bɑ:kᵊl, dɪ-) *n* **1** a sudden disastrous collapse or defeat, esp. one involving a disorderly retreat; rout. **2** the breaking up of ice in a river during spring or summer, often causing flooding. **3** a violent rush of water carrying along debris. [C19: from French *débâcle,* from Old French *desbacler* to unbolt, ultimately from Latin *baculum* rod, staff]

debag (di:'bæg) *vb* **-bags, -bagging, -bagged.** (*tr*) *Brit. slang.* to remove the trousers from (someone) by force.

debar (dɪ'bɑ:) *vb* **-bars, -barring, -barred.** (*tr;* usually foll. by *from*) to exclude from a place, a right, etc.; bar. ▸ **de'barment** *n*

USAGE See at **disbar.**

debark[1] (dɪ'bɑ:k) *vb* a less common word for **disembark.** [C17: from French *débarquer,* from *dé-* DIS-[1] + *barque* BARQUE] ▸ **debarkation** (ˌdi:bɑ:'keɪʃən) *n*

debark[2] (di:'bɑ:k) *vb* (*tr*) to remove the bark from (a tree).

debase (dɪ'beɪs) *vb* (*tr*) to lower in quality, character, or value, as by adding cheaper metal to coins; adulterate. [C16: see DE-, BASE[2]] ▸ **debasedness** (dɪ'beɪsɪdnɪs) *n* ▸ **de'basement** *n* ▸ **de'baser** *n* ▸ **de'basingly** *adv*

debatable *or* **debateable** (dɪ'beɪtəbᵊl) *adj* **1** open to question; disputable. **2** *Law.* in dispute, as land or territory to which two parties lay claim.

debate (dɪ'beɪt) *n* **1** a formal discussion, as in a legislative body, in which opposing arguments are put forward. **2** discussion or dispute. **3** the formal presentation and opposition of a specific motion, followed by a vote. ◆ *vb* **4** to discuss (a motion), esp. in a formal assembly. **5** to deliberate upon (something): *he debated with himself whether to go.* [C13: from Old French *debatre* to discuss, argue, from Latin *battuere*] ▸ **de'bater** *n*

debauch (dɪ'bɔ:tʃ) *vb* **1** (when *tr, usually passive*) to lead into a life of depraved self-indulgence. **2** (*tr*) to seduce (a woman). ◆ *n* **3** an instance or period of extreme dissipation. [C16: from Old French *desbaucher* to corrupt, literally: to shape (timber) roughly, from *bauch* beam, of Germanic origin] ▸ **debauchedly** (dɪ'bɔ:tʃɪdlɪ) *adv* ▸ **de'bauchedness** *n* ▸ **de'baucher** *n* ▸ **de'bauchery** *or* **de'bauchment** *n*

debauchee (ˌdɛbɔ:'tʃi:, -ɔ:'ʃi:) *n* a man who leads a life of reckless drinking, promiscuity, and self-indulgence.

debe ('dɛbɛ) *n E African.* a tin. [C20: from Swahili]

de Beauvoir (*French* də bovwar) *n* See (Simone de) **Beauvoir.**

debenture (dɪ'bɛntʃə) *n* **1** Also called: **debenture bond.** a long-term bond, bearing fixed interest and usually unsecured, issued by a company or governmental agency. **2** a certificate acknowledging the debt of a stated sum of money to a specified person. **3** a customs certificate providing for a refund of excise or import duty. [C15: from Latin phrase *dēbentur mihi* there are owed to me, from *dēbēre* to owe] ▸ **de'bentured** *adj*

debilitate (dɪ'bɪlɪˌteɪt) *vb* (*tr*) to make feeble; weaken. [C16: from Latin *dēbilitāre,* from *dēbilis* weak] ▸ **de'bilitating** *adj* ▸ **deˌbili'tation** *n*

debility (dɪ'bɪlɪtɪ) *n, pl* **-ties.** weakness or infirmity.

debit ('dɛbɪt) *Accounting.* ◆ *n* **1a** acknowledgment of a sum owing by entry on the left side of an account. **1b** the left side of an account. **1c** an entry on this side. **1d** the total of such entries. **1e** (*as modifier*): *a debit balance.* Compare **credit** (sense 10). ◆ *vb* **-its, -iting, -ited. 2** (*tr*) **2a** to record (an item) as a debit in an account. **2b** to charge (a person or his account) with a debt. Compare **credit** (sense 17). [C15: from Latin *dēbitum* DEBT]

debit card *n* an embossed plastic card issued by a bank or building society to enable its customers to pay for goods or services by inserting it into a computer-controlled device at the place of sale, which is connected through the telephone network to the bank or building society. It may also function as a credit card or cash card.

debonair *or* **debonnaire** (ˌdɛbə'nɛə) *adj* (esp. of a man or his manner) **1** suave and refined. **2** carefree; light-hearted. **3** courteous and cheerful; affable. [C13: from Old French *debonaire,* from *de bon aire* having a good disposition] ▸ **ˌdebo'nairly** *adv* ▸ **ˌdebo'nairness** *n*

Deborah ('dɛbərə, -brə) *n Old Testament.* **1** a prophetess and judge of Israel who fought the Canaanites (Judges 4, 5). **2** Rebecca's nurse (Genesis 35:8).

debouch (dɪ'baʊtʃ) *vb* **1** (*intr*) (esp. of troops) to move into a more open space, as from a narrow or concealed place. **2** (*intr*) (of a river, glacier, etc.) to flow from a valley into a larger area or body. ◆ *n* **3** Also called: **débouché** (*French* debuʃe). *Fortifications.* an outlet or passage, as for the exit of troops. [C18: from French *déboucher,* from *dé-* DIS-[1] + *bouche* mouth, from Latin *bucca* cheek]

debouchment (dɪˈbaʊtʃmənt) *n* **1** the act or an instance of debouching. **2** Also called: **debouchure** (ˌdeɪbuːˈʃʊə). an outlet, mouth, or opening.

Debrecen (ˈdɛbrɛtsɛn) *n* a city in E Hungary: seat of the revolutionary government of 1849. Pop.: 210 000 (1997 est.).

Debrett (dəˈbrɛt) *n* a list of the British aristocracy. In full: **Debrett's Peerage.** [C19: after J. *Debrett* (c. 1750–1822), London publisher who first issued it]

débridement (dɪˈbriːdmənt, deɪ-) *n* the surgical removal of dead tissue or cellular debris from the surface of a wound. [C19: from French, from Old French *desbrider* to unbridle, from *des-* DE- + *bride* BRIDLE]

debrief (diːˈbriːf) *vb* (of a soldier, astronaut, diplomat, etc.) to make or (of his superiors) to elicit a report after a mission or event. Compare **brief** (sense 13).

debris *or* **débris** (ˈdeɪbrɪ, ˈdɛbrɪ) *n* **1** fragments or remnants of something destroyed or broken; rubble. **2** a collection of loose material derived from rocks, or an accumulation of animal or vegetable matter. [C18: from French, from obsolete *debrisier* to break into pieces, from *bruisier* to shatter, of Celtic origin]

debris bug *n* a bug of the family *Cimicidae* found where vegetable debris accumulates and feeding on small arthropods like springtails: related to the bedbugs.

de Broglie (*French* də brɔj) *n* See (Louis Victor de) **Broglie.**

de Broglie waves (də ˈbrəʊglɪ) *pl n Physics.* the set of waves that represent the behaviour of an elementary particle, or some atoms and molecules, under certain conditions. The **de Broglie wavelength,** λ, is given by λ = *h*/*mv,* where *h* is the Planck constant, *m* the mass, and *v* the velocity of the particle. Also called: **matter waves.** [C20: named after Louis Victor DE BROGLIE]

Debs (dɛbz) *n* **Eugene Victor.** 1855–1926, U.S. labour leader; five times Socialist presidential candidate (1900–20).

debt (dɛt) *n* **1** something that is owed, such as money, goods, or services. **2 bad debt.** a debt that has little or no prospect of being paid. **3** an obligation to pay or perform something; liability. **4** the state of owing something, esp. money, or of being under an obligation (esp. in the phrases **in debt, in (someone's) debt**). [C13: from Old French *dette,* from Latin *dēbitum,* from *dēbēre* to owe, from DE- + *habēre* to have; English spelling influenced by the Latin etymon] ▸ **ˈdebtless** *adj*

debt of honour *n* a debt that is morally but not legally binding, such as one contracted in gambling.

debtor (ˈdɛtə) *n* a person or commercial enterprise that owes a financial obligation. Compare **creditor.**

debt swap *n* See **swap** (sense 4).

debud (diːˈbʌd) *vb* **-buds, -budding, -budded.** another word for **disbud.**

debug (diːˈbʌg) *Informal.* ◆ *vb* **-bugs, -bugging, -bugged.** (*tr*) **1** to locate and remove concealed microphones from (a room, etc.). **2** to locate and remove defects in (a device, system, plan, etc.). **3** to remove insects from. ◆ *n* **4a** something, esp. a computer program, that locates and removes defects in (a device, system, etc.) **4b** (*as modifier*): *a debug program.* [C20: from DE- + BUG[1]]

debunk (diːˈbʌŋk) *vb* (*tr*) *Informal.* to expose the pretensions or falseness of, esp. by ridicule. [C20: from DE- + BUNK[2]] ▸ **deˈbunker** *n*

deburr (diːˈbɜː) *vb* (*tr*) **1** to remove burrs from (a workpiece). **2** *Textiles.* to remove dirt and debris from (raw wool).

debus (diːˈbʌs) *vb* **debuses, debusing, debused** *or* **debusses, debussing, debussed.** to unload (goods) or (esp. of troops) to alight from a bus.

Debussy (dəˈbjuːsɪ, ˈdeɪbjuːsɪ; *French* dəbysi) *n* (**Achille**) **Claude** (klod). 1862–1918, French composer and critic, the creator of impressionism in music and a profound influence on contemporary composition. His works include *Prélude à l'après-midi d'un faune* (1894) and *La Mer* (1905) for orchestra, the opera *Pelléas et Mélisande* (1902), and many piano pieces and song settings.

debut (ˈdeɪbjuː, ˈdɛbjuː) *n* **1a** the first public appearance of an actor, musician, etc., or the first public presentation of a show. **1b** (*as modifier*): *debut album.* **2** the presentation of a debutante. ◆ *vb* (*intr*) **3** to make a debut. [C18: from French *début,* from Old French *desbuter* to play first (hence: make one's first appearance), from *des-* DE- + *but* goal, target; see BUTT[2]]

debutante (ˈdɛbjʊˌtɑːnt, -ˌtænt) *n* **1** a young woman of upper-class background who is presented to society, usually at a formal ball. **2** a girl or young woman regarded as being upper-class, wealthy, and of a frivolous or snobbish social set. [C19: from French, from *débuter* to lead off in a game, make one's first appearance; see DEBUT]

Debye (*Dutch* dəˈbɛiə) *n* **Peter Joseph Wilhelm.** 1884–1966, Dutch chemist and physicist, working in the U.S.: Nobel prize for chemistry (1936) for his work on dipole moments.

dec. *abbrev. for:* **1** deceased. **2** declaration. **3** declension. **4** declination. **5** decrease. **6** *Music.* decrescendo.

Dec. *abbrev. for* December.

deca-, deka- *or before a vowel* **dec-, dek-** *prefix* denoting ten: *decagon.* In conjunction with scientific units the symbol **da** is used. [from Greek *deka*]

decade (ˈdɛkeɪd, dɪˈkeɪd) *n* **1** a period of ten consecutive years. **2** a group or series of ten. [C15: from Old French, from Late Latin *decad-, decas,* from Greek *dekas,* from *deka* ten] ▸ **deˈcadal** *adj*

decadence (ˈdɛkədəns) *or* **decadency** *n* **1** deterioration, esp. of morality or culture; decay; degeneration. **2** the state reached through such a process. [C16: from French, from Medieval Latin *dēcadentia,* literally: a falling away; see DECAY]

decadent (ˈdɛkədənt) *adj* **1** characterized by decay or decline, as in being self-indulgent or morally corrupt. **2** belonging to a period of decline in artistic standards. ◆ *n* **3** a decadent person. **4** (*often cap.*) one of a group of French and English writers of the late 19th century whose works were characterized by refinement of style and a tendency toward the artificial and abnormal. ▸ **ˈdecadently** *adv*

decaf (ˈdiːkæf) *Informal.* ◆ *n* **1** decaffeinated coffee. ◆ *adj* **2** decaffeinated.

decaffeinate (dɪˈkæfɪˌneɪt) *vb* (*tr*) to remove all or part of the caffeine from (coffee, tea, etc.).

decagon (ˈdɛkəˌgɒn) *n* a polygon having ten sides. ▸ **decagonal** (dɪˈkægənᵊl) *adj* ▸ **deˈcagonally** *adv*

decahedron (ˌdɛkəˈhiːdrən) *n* a solid figure having ten plane faces. See also **polyhedron.** ▸ ˌ**decaˈhedral** *adj*

decal (dɪˈkæl, ˈdiːkæl) *n* **1** short for **decalcomania.** ◆ *vb* **2** to transfer (a design) by decalcomania.

decalcify (diːˈkælsɪˌfaɪ) *vb* **-fies, -fying, -fied.** (*tr*) to remove calcium or lime from (bones, teeth, etc.). ▸ **decalcification** (diːˌkælsɪfɪˈkeɪʃən) *n* ▸ **deˈcalciˌfier** *n*

decalcomania (dɪˌkælkəˈmeɪnɪə) *n* **1** the art or process of transferring a design from prepared paper onto another surface, such as china, glass or paper. **2** a design so transferred. [C19: from French *décalcomanie,* from *décalquer* to transfer by tracing, from *dé-* DE- + *calquer* to trace + *-manie* -MANIA]

decalescence (ˌdiːkəˈlɛsᵊns) *n* the absorption of heat when a metal is heated through a particular temperature range, caused by a change in internal crystal structure. [C19: from Late Latin *dēcalēscere* to become warm, from Latin DE- + *calescere,* from *calēre* to be warm] ▸ ˌ**decaˈlescent** *adj*

decalitre *or U.S.* **decaliter** (ˈdɛkəˌliːtə) *n* ten litres. One decalitre is equal to about 2.2 imperial gallons. Symbol: **dal**

Decalogue (ˈdɛkəˌlɒg) *n* another name for the **Ten Commandments.** [C14: from Church Latin *decalogus,* from Greek, from *deka* ten + *logos* word]

decametre *or U.S.* **decameter** (ˈdɛkəˌmiːtə) *n* ten metres. Symbol: **dam**

decamp (dɪˈkæmp) *vb* (*intr*) **1** to leave a camp; break camp. **2** to depart secretly or suddenly; abscond. ▸ **deˈcampment** *n*

decanal (dɪˈkeɪnᵊl) *adj* **1** of or relating to a dean or deanery. **2** (of part of a choir) on the same side of a cathedral, etc., as the dean; on the S side of the choir. ◆ Compare **cantorial.** [C18: from Medieval Latin *decānālis, decānus* DEAN] ▸ **deˈcanally** *or* **decanically** (dɪˈkænɪkəlɪ) *adv*

decane (ˈdɛkeɪn) *n* a liquid alkane hydrocarbon existing in several isomeric forms. Formula: $C_{10}H_{22}$. [C19: from DECA- + -ANE]

decanedioic acid (ˌdɛkeɪndaɪˈəʊɪk) *n* a white crystalline carboxylic acid obtained by heating castor oil with sodium hydroxide, used in the manufacture of polyester resins and rubbers and plasticizers. Formula: $HOOC(CH_2)_8COOH$. Also called: **sebacic acid.**

decani (dɪˈkeɪnaɪ) *adj, adv Music.* to be sung by the decanal side of a choir. Compare **cantoris.** [Latin: genitive of *decānus*]

decanoic acid (ˌdɛkəˈnəʊɪk) *n* a white crystalline insoluble carboxylic acid with an unpleasant odour, used in perfumes and for making fruit flavours. Formula: $C_9H_{19}COOH$. Also called: **capric acid.**

decant (dɪˈkænt) *vb* **1** to pour (a liquid, such as wine) from one container to another, esp. without disturbing any sediment. **2** (*tr*) to rehouse (people) while their homes are being rebuilt or refurbished. [C17: from Medieval Latin *dēcanthāre,* from *canthus* spout, rim; see CANTHUS]

decanter (dɪˈkæntə) *n* a stoppered bottle, usually of glass, into which a drink, such as wine, is poured for serving.

decapitate (dɪˈkæpɪˌteɪt) *vb* (*tr*) to behead. [C17: from Late Latin *dēcapitāre,* from Latin DE- + *caput* head] ▸ **deˌcapiˈtation** *n* ▸ **deˈcapiˌtator** *n*

decapod (ˈdɛkəˌpɒd) *n* **1** any crustacean of the mostly marine order *Decapoda,* having five pairs of walking limbs: includes the crabs, lobsters, shrimps, prawns, and crayfish. **2** any cephalopod mollusc of the order *Decapoda,* having a ring of eight short tentacles and two longer ones: includes the squids and cuttlefish. ◆ *adj* **3** of, relating to, or belonging to either of these orders. **4** (of any other animal) having ten limbs. ▸ **decapodal** (dɪˈkæpədᵊl), **deˈcapodan,** *or* **deˈcapodous** *adj*

Decapolis (dɪˈkæpəlɪs) *n* a league of ten cities, including Damascus, in the northeast of ancient Palestine: established in 63 B.C. by Pompey and governed by Rome.

decapsulate (diːˈkæpsjʊˌleɪt) *vb* (*tr*) *Med.* to remove a capsule from (a part or organ, esp. the kidney). ▸ **deˌcapsuˈlation** *n*

decarbonate (diːˈkɑːbəˌneɪt) *vb* (*tr*) to remove carbon dioxide from (a solution, substance, etc.). ▸ **deˌcarbonˈation** *n* ▸ **deˈcarbonˌator** *n*

decarbonize *or* **decarbonise** (diːˈkɑːbəˌnaɪz) *vb* (*tr*) to remove carbon from (the walls of the combustion chamber of an internal-combustion engine). Also: **decoke, decarburize.** ▸ **deˌcarboniˈzation** *or* **deˌcarboniˈsation** *n* ▸ **deˈcarbonˌizer** *or* **deˈcarbonˌiser** *n*

decarboxylase (ˌdiːkɑːˈbɒksɪˌleɪs) *n* an enzyme that catalyses the removal of carbon dioxide from a compound.

decarboxylation (ˌdiːkɑːˌbɒksəˈleɪʃən) *n* the removal or loss of a carboxyl group from an organic compound.

decarburize *or* **decarburise** (diːˈkɑːbjʊˌraɪz) *vb* another word for **decarbonize.** ▸ **deˌcarburiˈzation, deˌcarburiˈsation,** *or* **deˌcarbuˈration** *n*

decare (ˈdɛkɛə, dɛˈkɛə) *n* ten ares or 1000 square metres. [C19: from French *décare;* see DECA-, ARE[2]]

decastyle (ˈdɛkəˌstaɪl) *n Architect.* a portico consisting of ten columns.

decasyllable (ˈdɛkəˌsɪləbᵊl) *n* a word or line of verse consisting of ten syllables. ▸ **decasyllabic** (ˌdɛkəsɪˈlæbɪk) *adj*

decathlon (dɪˈkæθlɒn) *n* an athletic contest for men in which each athlete competes in ten different events. Compare **pentathlon.** [C20: from DECA- + Greek *athlon* contest, prize; see ATHLETE] ▸ **deˈcathlete** *n*

Decatur (dəˈkeɪtə) *n* **Stephen.** 1779–1820, U.S. naval officer, noted for his raid on Tripoli harbour (1804) and his role in the War of 1812.

decay (dɪˈkeɪ) *vb* **1** to decline or cause to decline gradually in health, prosperity, excellence, etc.; deteriorate; waste away. **2** to rot or cause to rot as a result of bacterial, fungal, or chemical action; decompose. **3** (*intr*) Also: **disintegrate.** *Physics.* **3a** (of an atomic nucleus) to undergo radioactive disintegration. **3b** (of an elementary particle) to transform into two or more different elementary particles. **4** (*intr*) *Physics.* (of a stored charge, magnetic flux, etc.) to decrease gradually when the source of energy has been removed. ♦ *n* **5** the process of decline, as in health, mentality, beauty, etc. **6** the state brought about by this process. **7** decomposition, as of vegetable matter. **8** rotten or decayed matter: *the dentist drilled out the decay.* **9** *Physics.* **9a** See **radioactive decay. 9b** a spontaneous transformation of an elementary particle into two or more different particles. **10** *Physics.* a gradual decrease of a stored charge, magnetic flux, current, etc., when the source of energy has been removed. See also **time constant. 11** *Music.* the fading away of a note. [C15: from Old Northern French *decaïr,* from Late Latin *dēcadere,* literally: to fall away, from Latin *cadere* to fall] ► **de'cayable** *adj*

Deccan ('dɛkən) *n* **the. 1** a plateau in S India, between the Eastern Ghats, the Western Ghats, and the Narmada River. **2** the whole Indian peninsula south of the Narmada River.

decd *abbrev. for* deceased.

decease (dɪ'si:s) *n* **1** a more formal word for **death.** ♦ *vb* **2** (*intr*) a more formal word for **die**[1]. [C14 (n): from Old French *deces,* from Latin *dēcēdere* to depart]

deceased (dɪ'si:st) *adj* **a** a more formal word for **dead** (sense 1). **b** (*as n*): *the deceased.*

decedent (dɪ'si:dᵊnt) *n Law, chiefly U.S.* a deceased person. [C16: from Latin *dēcēdēns* departing; see DECEASE]

deceit (dɪ'si:t) *n* **1** the act or practice of deceiving. **2** a statement, act, or device intended to mislead; fraud; trick. **3** a tendency to deceive. [C13: from Old French *deceite,* from *deceivre* to DECEIVE]

deceitful (dɪ'si:tful) *adj* full of deceit. ► **de'ceitfully** *adv* ► **de'ceitfulness** *n*

deceive (dɪ'si:v) *vb* (*tr*) **1** to mislead by deliberate misrepresentation or lies. **2** to delude (oneself). **3** to be unfaithful to (one's sexual partner). **4** *Archaic.* to disappoint: *his hopes were deceived.* [C13: from Old French *deceivre,* from Latin *dēcipere* to ensnare, cheat, from *capere* to take] ► **de'ceivable** *adj* ► **de'ceivably** *adv* ► **de'ceivableness** *or* **de,ceiva'bility** *n* ► **de'ceiver** *n* ► **de'ceiving** *n, adj* ► **de'ceivingly** *adv*

decelerate (di:'sɛlə,reɪt) *vb* to slow down or cause to slow down. [C19: from DE- + ACCELERATE] ► **de,celer'ation** *n* ► **de'celer,ator** *n*

decelerometer (dɪ,sɛlə'rɒmɪtə) *n* an instrument for measuring deceleration.

December (dɪ'sɛmbə) *n* the twelfth and last month of the year, consisting of 31 days. [C13: from Old French *decembre,* from Latin *december* the tenth month (the Roman year originally began with March), from *decem* ten]

Decembrist (dɪ'sɛmbrɪst) *n Russian history.* a participant in the unsuccessful revolt against Tsar Nicolas I in Dec. 1825. [C19: translation of Russian *dekabrist*]

decemvir (dɪ'sɛmvə) *n, pl* **-virs** *or* **-viri** (-vɪ,ri:). **1** (in ancient Rome) a member of a board of ten magistrates, esp. either of the two commissions established in 451 and 450 B.C. to revise the laws. **2** a member of any governing body composed of ten men. [C17: from Latin, from *decem* ten + *virī* men] ► **de'cemviral** *adj*

decemvirate (dɪ'sɛmvɪrɪt, -,reɪt) *n* **1** a board of decemvirs. **2** the rule or rank of decemvirs.

decenary *or* **decennary** (dɪ'sɛnərɪ) *adj History.* of or relating to a tithing. [C13: from Medieval Latin *decēna* a tithing, from *decem* ten]

decencies ('di:sᵊnsɪz) *pl n* **1 the.** those things that are considered necessary for a decent life. **2** another word for **proprieties.**

decency ('di:sᵊnsɪ) *n, pl* **-cies. 1** conformity to the prevailing standards of propriety, morality, modesty, etc. **2** the quality of being decent.

decennial (dɪ'sɛnɪəl) *adj* **1** lasting for ten years. **2** occurring every ten years. ♦ *n* **3** a tenth anniversary or its celebration. ► **de'cennially** *adv*

decennium (dɪ'sɛnɪəm) *or* **decennary** (dɪ'sɛnərɪ) *n, pl* **-niums, -nia** (-nɪə), *or* **-naries.** a less common word for **decade** (sense 1). [C17: from Latin, from *decem* ten + *annus* year]

decent ('di:sᵊnt) *adj* **1** polite or respectable: *a decent family.* **2** proper and suitable; fitting: *a decent burial.* **3** conforming to conventions of sexual behaviour; not indecent. **4** free of oaths, blasphemy, etc.: *decent language.* **5** good or adequate: *a decent wage.* **6** *Informal.* kind; generous: *he was pretty decent to me.* **7** *Informal.* sufficiently clothed to be seen by other people: *are you decent?* [C16: from Latin *decēns* suitable, from *decēre* to be fitting] ► **'decently** *adv* ► **'decentness** *n*

decentralize *or* **decentralise** (di:'sɛntrə,laɪz) *vb* **1** to reorganize (a government, industry, etc.) into smaller more autonomous units. **2** to disperse (a concentration, as of industry or population). ► **de'centralist** *n, adj* ► **de,centrali'zation** *or* **de,centrali'sation** *n*

decentralized processing *n Computing.* the use of word processing or data processing units in stand-alone or localized situations.

deception (dɪ'sɛpʃən) *n* **1** the act of deceiving or the state of being deceived. **2** something that deceives; trick.

deceptive (dɪ'sɛptɪv) *adj* **1** likely or designed to deceive; misleading: *appearances can be deceptive.* **2** *Music.* (of a cadence) another word for **interrupted** (sense 3). ► **de'ceptively** *adv* ► **de'ceptiveness** *n*

decerebrate *vb* (di:'sɛrɪ,breɪt). **1** (*tr*) to remove the brain or a large section of the brain or to cut the spinal cord at the level of the brain stem of (a person or animal). ♦ *n* (di:'sɛrɪbrɪt). **2** a decerebrated individual. [C19: from DE- + CEREBRO- + -ATE[1]] ► **de,cere'bration** *n*

decern (dɪ'sɜ:n) *vb* (*tr*) **1** *Scots Law.* to decree or adjudge. **2** an archaic spelling of **discern.** [C15: from Old French *decerner,* from Latin *dēcernere* to judge, from *cernere* to discern]

deci- *prefix* denoting one tenth; 10^{-1}: *decimetre.* Symbol: d [from French *déci-,* from Latin *decimus* tenth]

deciare ('dɛsɪ,ɛə) *n* one tenth of an are or 10 square metres. [C19: from French *déciare;* see DECI-, ARE[2]]

decibel ('dɛsɪ,bɛl) *n* **1** a unit for comparing two currents, voltages, or power levels, equal to one tenth of a bel. **2** a similar unit for measuring the intensity of a sound. It is equal to ten times the logarithm to the base ten of the ratio of the intensity of the sound to be measured to the intensity of some reference sound, usually the lowest audible note of the same frequency. Abbrev.: **dB.** See also **perceived noise decibel.**

decidable (dɪ'saɪdəbᵊl) *adj* **1** able to be decided. **2** *Logic.* (of a formal theory) having the property that it is possible by a mechanistic procedure to determine whether or not any well-formed formula is a theorem.

decide (dɪ'saɪd) *vb* **1** (*may take a clause or an infinitive as object;* when *intr,* sometimes foll. by *on* or *about*) to reach a decision: *decide what you want; he decided to go.* **2** (*tr*) to cause (a person) to reach a decision: *the weather decided me against going.* **3** (*tr*) to determine or settle (a contest or question): *he decided his future plans.* **4** (*tr*) to influence decisively the outcome of (a contest or question): *Borg's stamina decided the match.* **5** (*intr;* foll. by *for* or *against*) to pronounce a formal verdict. [C14: from Old French *decider,* from Latin *dēcīdere,* literally: to cut off, from *caedere* to cut]

decided (dɪ'saɪdɪd) *adj* (*prenominal*) **1** unmistakable: *a decided improvement.* **2** determined; resolute: *a girl of decided character.* ► **de'cidedly** *adv* ► **de'cidedness** *n*

decider (dɪ'saɪdə) *n* the point, goal, game, etc., that determines who wins a match or championship.

decidua (dɪ'sɪdjuə) *n, pl* **-ciduas** *or* **-ciduae** (-'sɪdju,i:). the specialized mucous membrane that lines the uterus of some mammals during pregnancy: is shed, with the placenta, at parturition. [C18: from New Latin, from Latin *dēciduus* falling down; see DECIDUOUS] ► **de'cidual** *or* **de'ciduate** *adj*

deciduous (dɪ'sɪdjuəs) *adj* **1** (of trees and shrubs) shedding all leaves annually at the end of the growing season. Compare **evergreen** (sense 1). **2** (of antlers, wings, teeth, etc.) being shed at the end of a period of growth. **3** *Rare.* impermanent; transitory. Compare **evergreen** (sense 2). [C17: from Latin *dēciduus* falling off, from *dēcidere* to fall down, from *cadere* to fall] ► **de'ciduously** *adv* ► **de'ciduousness** *n*

decile ('dɛsɪl, -aɪl) *n Statistics.* **a** one of nine actual or notional values of a variable dividing its distribution into ten groups with equal frequencies: the ninth decile is the value below which 90% of the population lie. See also **percentile. b** a tenth part of a distribution. [C17: from DECA- + -ILE]

decilitre *or U.S.* **deciliter** ('dɛsɪ,li:tə) *n* one tenth of a litre. Symbol: **dl**

decillion (dɪ'sɪljən) *n* **1** (in Britain, France, and Germany) the number represented as one followed by 60 zeros (10^{60}). **2** (in the U.S. and Canada) the number represented as one followed by 33 zeros (10^{33}). [C19: from Latin *decem* ten + *-illion* as in *million*] ► **de'cillionth** *adj*

decimal ('dɛsɪməl) *n* **1** Also called: **decimal fraction.** a fraction that has a denominator of a power of ten, the power depending on or deciding the decimal place. It is indicated by a decimal point to the left of the numerator, the denominator being omitted. Zeros are inserted between the point and the numerator, if necessary, to obtain the correct decimal place. **2** any number used in the decimal system. ♦ *adj* **3a** relating to or using powers of ten. **3b** of the base ten. **4** (*prenominal*) expressed as a decimal. [C17: from Medieval Latin *decimālis* of tithes, from Latin *decima* a tenth, from *decem* ten] ► **'decimally** *adv*

decimal classification *n* another term for **Dewey Decimal System.**

decimal currency *n* a system of currency in which the monetary units are parts or powers of ten.

decimal fraction *n* another name for **decimal** (sense 1).

decimalize *or* **decimalise** ('dɛsɪmə,laɪz) *vb* to change (a system, number, etc.) to the decimal system: *Britain has decimalized her currency.* ► **,decimali'zation** *or* **,decimali'sation** *n*

decimal place *n* **1** the position of a digit after the decimal point, each successive position to the right having a denominator of an increased power of ten: *in 0.025, 5 is in the third decimal place.* **2** the number of digits to the right of the decimal point: *3.142 is a number given to three decimal places.* Compare **significant figures** (sense 2).

decimal point *n* a full stop or a raised full stop placed between the integral and fractional parts of a number in the decimal system.

USAGE Conventions relating to the use of the decimal point are confused. The IX General Conference on Weights and Measures resolved in 1948 that the decimal point should be a point on the line or a comma, but not a centre dot. It also resolved that figures could be grouped in threes about the decimal point, but that no point or comma should be used for this purpose. These conventions are adopted in this dictionary. However, the Decimal Currency Board recommended that for sums of money the centre dot should be used as the decimal point and that the comma should be used as the thousand marker. Moreover, in some countries the position is reversed, the comma being used as the decimal point and the dot as the thousand marker.

decimal system *n* **1** the number system in general use, having a base of ten, in which numbers are expressed by combinations of the ten digits 0 to 9. **2** a system of measurement, such as the metric system, in which the multiple and submultiple units are related to a basic unit by powers of ten.

decimate ('dɛsɪ,meɪt) *vb* (*tr*) **1** to destroy or kill a large proportion of: *a plague decimated the population.* **2** (esp. in the ancient Roman army) to kill every tenth man of (a mutinous section). [C17: from Latin *decimāre,* from *decimus* tenth, from *decem* ten] ► **,deci'mation** *n* ► **'deci,mator** *n*

USAGE One talks about the whole of something being *decimated,* not a part: *disease decimated the population,* not *disease decimated most of the population.*

decimetre *or U.S.* **decimeter** (ˈdɛsɪˌmiːtə) *n* one tenth of a metre. Symbol: **dm** ▸ **decimetric** (ˌdɛsɪˈmɛtrɪk) *adj*

decipher (dɪˈsaɪfə) *vb (tr)* **1** to determine the meaning of (something obscure or illegible). **2** to convert from code into plain text; decode. ▸ **deˈcipherable** *adj* ▸ **deˌcipheraˈbility** *n* ▸ **deˈcipherer** *n* ▸ **deˈcipherment** *n*

decision (dɪˈsɪʒən) *n* **1** a judgment, conclusion, or resolution reached or given; verdict. **2** the act of making up one's mind. **3** firmness of purpose or character; determination. [C15: from Old French, from Latin *dēcīsiō,* literally: a cutting off; see DECIDE] ▸ **deˈcisional** *adj*

decision support system *n* a system in which one or more computers and computer programs assist in decision-making by providing information.

decision table *n* a table within a computer program that specifies the actions to be taken when certain conditions arise.

decision theory *n Statistics.* the study of strategies for decision making under conditions of uncertainty in such a way as to maximize the expected utility. See also **game theory.**

decision tree *n* a treelike diagram illustrating the choices available to a decision maker, each possible decision and its estimated outcome being shown as a separate branch of the tree.

decisive (dɪˈsaɪsɪv) *adj* **1** influential; conclusive: *a decisive argument.* **2** characterized by the ability to make decisions, esp. quickly; resolute. ▸ **deˈcisively** *adv* ▸ **deˈcisiveness** *n*

deck (dɛk) *n* **1** *Nautical.* any of various platforms built into a vessel: *a promenade deck; the poop deck.* **2** a similar floor or platform, as in a bus. **3a** the horizontal platform that supports the turntable and pick-up of a record player. **3b** See **tape deck.** **4** *Chiefly U.S.* a pack of playing cards. **5** Also called: **pack.** *Computing.* a collection of punched cards relevant to a particular program. **6** **clear the decks.** *Informal.* to prepare for action, as by removing obstacles from a field of activity or combat. **7** **hit the deck.** *Informal.* **7a** to fall to the floor or ground, esp. in order to avoid injury. **7b** to prepare for action. **7c** to get out of bed. ◆ *vb (tr)* **8** (often foll. by *out*) to dress or decorate. **9** to build a deck on (a vessel). **10** *Slang.* to knock (a person) to the floor or ground. ◆ See also **deck over.** [C15: from Middle Dutch *dec* a covering; related to THATCH] ▸ **ˈdecker** *n*

deck-access *adj* (of a block of flats) having a continuous inset balcony at each level onto which the front door of each flat on that level opens.

deck beam *n Nautical.* a stiffening deck member supported at its extremities by knee connections to frames or bulkheads.

deck bridge *n Civil engineering.* a bridge with an upper horizontal beam that carries the roadway.

deck chair *n* a folding chair for use out of doors, consisting of a wooden frame suspending a length of canvas.

deck crane *n Nautical.* a deck-mounted crane used for loading and unloading cargo.

deck department *n* the part of a ship's crew, from the captain down, concerned with running the ship but not with heavy machinery or catering.

Decker (ˈdɛkə) *n* a variant spelling of (Thomas) **Dekker.**

-decker *adj (in combination):* having a certain specified number of levels or layers: *a double-decker bus.*

deck hand *n* **1** a seaman assigned various duties, such as mooring and cargo handling, on the deck of a ship. **2** (in Britain) a seaman over 17 years of age who has seen sea duty for at least one year. **3** a helper aboard a yacht.

deckhouse (ˈdɛkˌhaʊs) *n* a houselike cabin on the deck of a ship.

deckle *or* **deckel** (ˈdɛkᵊl) *n* **1** a frame used to contain pulp on the mould in the making of handmade paper. **2** Also called: **deckle strap.** a strap on each edge of the moving web of paper on a paper-making machine that fixes the width of the paper. **3** See **deckle edge.** [C19: from German *Deckel* lid, from *decken* to cover]

deckle edge *n* **1** the rough edge of handmade paper, caused by pulp seeping between the mould and the deckle: often left as ornamentation in fine books and writing papers. **2** a trimmed edge imitating this. ▸ **ˈdeckle-ˈedged** *adj*

deck officer *n* a ship's officer who is part of the deck crew.

deck over *vb (tr)* to complete the construction of the upper deck between the bulwarks of (a vessel).

deck shoe *n* **1** a rubber-soled leather shoe worn when boating. **2** a casual cloth or soft leather shoe resembling this.

deck tennis *n* a game played on board ship in which a quoit is tossed to and fro across a high net on a small court resembling a tennis court.

decl. *Grammar. abbrev. for* declension.

declaim (dɪˈkleɪm) *vb* **1** to make (a speech, statement, etc.) loudly and in a rhetorical manner. **2** to speak lines from (a play, poem, etc.) with studied eloquence; recite. **3** *(intr;* foll. by *against)* to protest (against) loudly and publicly. [C14: from Latin *dēclāmāre,* from *clāmāre* to call out] ▸ **deˈclaimer** *n*

declamation (ˌdɛkləˈmeɪʃən) *n* **1** a rhetorical or emotional speech, made esp. in order to protest or condemn; tirade. **2** a speech, verse, etc., that is or can be spoken. **3** the act or art of declaiming. **4** *Music.* the artistry or technique involved in singing recitative passages.

declamatory (dɪˈklæmətərɪ, -trɪ) *adj* **1** relating to or having the characteristics of a declamation. **2** merely rhetorical; empty and bombastic. ▸ **deˈclamatorily** *adv*

declarant (dɪˈklɛərənt) *n Chiefly law.* a person who makes a declaration.

declaration (ˌdɛkləˈreɪʃən) *n* **1** an explicit or emphatic statement. **2** a formal statement or announcement; proclamation. **3** the act of declaring. **4** the ruling of a judge or court on a question of law, esp. in the chancery division of the High Court. **5** *Law.* an unsworn statement of a witness admissible in evidence under certain conditions. See also **statutory declaration.** **6** *Cricket.* the voluntary closure of an innings before all ten wickets have fallen. **7** *Contract bridge.* the final contract. **8** a statement or inventory of goods, etc., submitted for tax assessment: *a customs declaration.* **9** *Cards.* an announcement of points made after taking a trick, as in bezique.

Declaration of Independence *n* **1** the proclamation made by the second American Continental Congress on July 4, 1776, which asserted the freedom and independence of the 13 Colonies from Great Britain. **2** the document formally recording this proclamation.

declarative (dɪˈklærətɪv) *adj* making or having the nature of a declaration. ▸ **deˈclaratively** *adv*

declarator (dɪˈklærətə) *n Scots Law.* an action seeking to have some right, status, etc., judicially ascertained.

declaratory (dɪˈklærətərɪ, -trɪ) *adj* **1** another word for **declarative.** **2** *Law.* **2a** (of a statute) stating the existing law on a particular subject; explanatory. **2b** (of a decree or judgment) stating the rights of the parties without specifying the action to be taken. ▸ **deˈclaratorily** *adv*

declare (dɪˈklɛə) *vb (mainly tr)* **1** *(may take a clause as object)* to make clearly known or announce officially: *to declare one's interests; war was declared.* **2** to state officially that (a person, fact, etc.) is as specified: *he declared him fit.* **3** *(may take a clause as object)* to state emphatically; assert. **4** to show, reveal, or manifest: *the heavens declare the glory of God.* **5** *(intr;* often foll. by *for* or *against)* to make known one's choice or opinion. **6** to make a complete statement of (dutiable goods, etc.). **7** *(also intr) Cards.* **7a** to display (a card or series of cards) on the table so as to add to one's score. **7b** to decide (the trump suit) by making the final bid. **8** *(intr) Cricket.* to close an innings voluntarily before all ten wickets have fallen. **9** to authorize the payment of (a dividend) from corporate net profit. [C14: from Latin *dēclārāre* to make clear, from *clārus* bright, clear] ▸ **deˈclarable** *adj*

declarer (dɪˈklɛərə) *n* **1** a person who declares. **2** *Bridge.* the player who, as first bidder of the suit of the final contract, plays both hands of the partnership.

declass (diːˈklɑːs) *vb (tr)* to lower in social status or position; degrade.

déclassé (*French* deklɑse) *adj* having lost social standing or status. [C19: from French *déclasser* to DECLASS] ▸ **déclassée** *fem adj*

declassify (diːˈklæsɪˌfaɪ) *vb* **-fies, -fying, -fied.** *(tr)* to release (a document or information) from the security list. ▸ **deˈclassiˌfiable** *adj* ▸ **deˌclassifiˈcation** *n*

declension (dɪˈklɛnʃən) *n* **1** *Grammar.* **1a** inflection of nouns, pronouns, or adjectives for case, number, and gender. **1b** the complete set of the inflections of such a word: *"puella" is a first-declension noun in Latin.* **2** a decline or deviation from a standard, belief, etc. **3** a downward slope or bend. [C15: from Latin *dēclīnātiō,* literally: a bending aside, hence variation, inflection; see DECLINE] ▸ **deˈclensional** *adj* ▸ **deˈclensionally** *adv*

declinate (ˈdɛklɪˌneɪt, -nɪt) *adj* (esp. of plant parts) descending from the horizontal in a curve; drooping.

declination (ˌdɛklɪˈneɪʃən) *n* **1** *Astronomy.* the angular distance in degrees of a star, planet, etc., from the celestial equator measured north (positive) or south (negative) along the great circle passing through the celestial poles and the body. Symbol: δ Compare **right ascension.** **2** See **magnetic declination.** **3** a refusal, esp. a courteous or formal one. ▸ ˌ**decliˈnational** *adj*

decline (dɪˈklaɪn) *vb* **1** to refuse to do or accept (something), esp. politely. **2** *(intr)* to grow smaller; diminish: *demand has declined over the years.* **3** to slope or cause to slope downwards. **4** *(intr)* to deteriorate gradually, as in quality, health, or character. **5** *Grammar.* to state or list the inflections of (a noun, adjective, or pronoun), or (of a noun, adjective, or pronoun) to be inflected for number, case, or gender. Compare **conjugate** (sense 1). ◆ *n* **6** gradual deterioration or loss. **7** a movement downward or towards something smaller; diminution. **8** a downward slope; declivity. **9** *Archaic.* any slowly progressive disease, such as tuberculosis. [C14: from Old French *decliner* to inflect, turn away, sink, from Latin *dēclīnāre* to bend away, inflect grammatically] ▸ **deˈclinable** *adj* ▸ **deˈcliner** *n*

declinometer (ˌdɛklɪˈnɒmɪtə) *n* an instrument for measuring magnetic declination.

declivity (dɪˈklɪvɪtɪ) *n, pl* **-ties.** a downward slope, esp. of the ground. Compare **acclivity.** [C17: from Latin *dēclīvitās,* from DE- + *clīvus* a slope, hill] ▸ **deˈclivitous** *adj*

declutch (dɪˈklʌtʃ) *vb (intr)* to disengage the clutch of a motor vehicle.

decoct (dɪˈkɒkt) *vb* to extract (the essence or active principle) from (a medicinal or similar substance) by boiling. [C15: see DECOCTION]

decoction (dɪˈkɒkʃən) *n* **1** *Pharmacol.* the extraction of the water-soluble substances of a drug or medicinal plants by boiling. **2** the essence or liquor resulting from this. [C14: from Old French, from Late Latin *dēcoctiō,* from *dēcoquere* to boil down, from *coquere* to COOK]

decode (diːˈkəʊd) *vb* **1** to convert (a message, text, etc.) from code into ordinary language. **2** *Computing.* to convert (coded characters) from one form to another, as from binary-coded decimals to decimal numbers. Compare **encode** (sense 2). **3** *Electronics.* to convert (a coded electrical signal) into normal analogue components. **4** to analyse and understand the construction of words and phrases, esp. in a foreign language. ▸ **deˈcoder** *n*

decoke (diːˈkəʊk) *vb (tr)* another word for **decarbonize.**

decollate (dɪˈkɒleɪt, ˈdɛkəˌleɪt, ˌdiːkəˈleɪt) *vb* **1** to separate (continuous stationery, etc.) into individual forms. **2** an archaic word for **decapitate.** [C16: from Latin *dēcollāre* to behead, from DE- + *collum* neck] ▸ ˌ**decolˈlation** *n* ▸ **ˈdecolˌlator** *n*

décolletage (ˌdeɪkɒlˈtɑːʒ; *French* dekɔltaʒ) *n* a low-cut neckline or a woman's garment with a low neck. [C19: from French; see DÉCOLLETÉ]

décolleté (deɪˈkɒlteɪ; *French* dekɔlte) *adj* **1** (of a woman's garment) low-cut. **2**

wearing a low-cut garment. ◆ *n* **3** a low-cut neckline. [C19: from French *décolleter* to cut out the neck (of a dress), from *collet* collar]

decolonize *or* **decolonise** (diːˈkɒləˌnaɪz) *vb* (*tr*) to grant independence to (a colony). ▸ **deˌcoloniˈzation** *or* **deˌcoloniˈsation** *n*

decolorant (diːˈkʌlərənt) *adj* **1** able to decolour or bleach. ◆ *n* **2** a substance that decolours.

decolour (diːˈkʌlə), **decolorize,** *or* **decolorise** *vb* (*tr*) to deprive of colour, as by bleaching. ▸ **deˌcolorˈation** *n* ▸ **deˌcoloriˈzation** *or* **deˌcoloriˈsation** *n*

decommission (ˌdiːkəˈmɪʃən) *vb* (*tr*) to dismantle or remove from service (a nuclear reactor, weapon, ship, etc. which is no longer required).

decompensation (diːˌkɒmpɛnˈseɪʃən) *n Pathol.* inability of an organ, esp. the heart, to maintain its function due to overload caused by a disease.

decompose (ˌdiːkəmˈpəʊz) *vb* **1** to break down (organic matter) or (of organic matter) to be broken down into constituent elements by bacterial or fungal action; rot. **2** *Chem.* to break down or cause to break down into simpler chemical compounds. **3** to break up or separate into constituent parts. **4** (*tr*) *Maths.* to express in terms of a number of independent simpler components, as a set as a canonical union of disjoint subsets, or a vector into orthogonal components. ▸ **ˌdecomˈposable** *adj* ▸ **ˌdecomˌposaˈbility** *n* ▸ **decomposition** (ˌdiːkɒmpəˈzɪʃən) *n*

decomposer (ˌdiːkəmˈpəʊzə) *n Ecology.* any organism in a community, such as a bacterium or fungus, that breaks down dead tissue into its constituent parts. See also **consumer** (sense 3), **producer** (sense 8).

decompound (ˌdiːkəmˈpaʊnd) *adj* **1** (of a compound leaf) having leaflets consisting of several distinct parts. **2** made up of one or more compounds. ◆ *vb* **3** a less common word for **decompose. 4** *Obsolete.* to mix with or form from one or more compounds.

decompress (ˌdiːkəmˈprɛs) *vb* **1** to relieve (a substance) of pressure or (of a substance) to be relieved of pressure. **2** to return (a diver, caisson worker, etc.) to a condition of normal atmospheric pressure from a condition of increased pressure or (of a diver, etc.) to be returned to such a condition. ▸ **ˌdecomˈpression** *n* ▸ **ˌdecomˈpressive** *adj*

decompression chamber *n* a chamber in which the pressure of air can be varied slowly for returning people from abnormal pressures to atmospheric pressure without inducing decompression sickness.

decompression sickness *or* **illness** *n* a disorder characterized by severe pain in muscles and joints, cramp, and difficulty in breathing, caused by a sudden and sustained decrease in air pressure. Also called: **caisson disease, aeroembolism.** Nontechnical name: **the bends.**

decongestant (ˌdiːkənˈdʒɛstənt) *adj* **1** relieving congestion, esp. nasal congestion. ◆ *n* **2** a decongestant drug.

deconsecrate (diːˈkɒnsɪˌkreɪt) *vb* (*tr*) to transfer (a church) to secular use. ▸ **deˌconseˈcration** *n*

deconstruct (ˌdiːkənˈstrʌkt) *vb* (*tr*) **1** to apply the theories of deconstruction to (a text, film, etc.). **2** to expose or dismantle the existing structure in (a system, organization, etc.).

deconstruction (ˌdiːkənˈstrʌkʃən) *n* a technique of literary analysis that regards meaning as resulting from the differences between words rather than their reference to the things they stand for. Different meanings are discovered by taking apart the structure of the language used and exposing the assumption that words have a fixed reference point beyond themselves.

decontaminate (ˌdiːkənˈtæmɪˌneɪt) *vb* (*tr*) to render (an area, building, object, etc.) harmless by the removal, distribution, or neutralization of poisons, radioactivity, etc. ▸ **ˌdeconˈtaminant** *n* ▸ **ˌdeconˌtamiˈnation** *n* ▸ **ˌdeconˈtaminative** *adj* ▸ **ˌdeconˈtamiˌnator** *n*

decontrol (ˌdiːkənˈtrəʊl) *vb* **-trols, -trolling, -trolled.** (*tr*) to free of restraints or controls, esp. government controls: *to decontrol prices.*

décor *or* **decor** (ˈdeɪkɔː) *n* **1** a style or scheme of interior decoration, furnishings, etc., as in a room or house. **2** stage decoration; scenery. [C19: from French, from *décorer* to DECORATE]

decorate (ˈdɛkəˌreɪt) *vb* **1** (*tr*) to make more attractive by adding ornament, colour, etc. **2** to paint or wallpaper (a room, house, etc.). **3** (*tr*) to confer a mark of distinction, esp. a military medal, upon. **4** (*tr*) to evaporate a metal film onto (a crystal) in order to display dislocations in structure. [C16: from Latin *decorāre,* from *decus* adornment; see DECENT]

Decorated style *or* **architecture** *n* a 14th-century style of English architecture characterized by the ogee arch, geometrical tracery, and floral decoration.

decoration (ˌdɛkəˈreɪʃən) *n* **1** an addition that renders something more attractive or ornate; adornment. **2** the act, process, or art of decorating. **3** a medal, badge, etc., conferred as a mark of honour.

decorative (ˈdɛkərətɪv, ˈdɛkrətɪv) *adj* serving to decorate or adorn; ornamental. ▸ **ˈdecoratively** *adv* ▸ **ˈdecorativeness** *n*

decorator (ˈdɛkəˌreɪtə) *n* **1** *Brit.* a person whose profession is the painting and wallpapering of buildings. **2** a person who decorates. **3** See **interior decorator** (sense 1).

decorous (ˈdɛkərəs) *adj* characterized by propriety in manners, conduct, etc. [C17: from Latin *decōrus,* from *decor* elegance] ▸ **ˈdecorously** *adv* ▸ **ˈdecorousness** *n*

decorticate (diːˈkɔːtɪˌkeɪt) *vb* **1** (*tr*) to remove the bark or some other outer layer from. **2** *Surgery.* to remove the cortex of (an organ or part). [C17: from Latin *dēcorticāre,* from DE- + *-corticāre,* from *cortex* bark] ▸ **deˌcortiˈcation** *n* ▸ **deˈcortiˌcator** *n*

decorum (dɪˈkɔːrəm) *n* **1** propriety, esp. in behaviour or conduct. **2** a requirement of correct behaviour in polite society. [C16: from Latin: propriety]

decoupage (ˌdeɪkuːˈpɑːʒ) *n* **1** the art or process of decorating a surface with shapes or illustrations cut from paper, card, etc. **2** anything produced by this technique. [C20: from French, from *découper* to cut out, from DE- + *couper* to cut]

decouple (ˌdiːˈkʌpᵊl) *vb* (*tr*) to separate (joined or coupled subsystems) thereby enabling them to exist and operate separately.

decoupling (diːˈkʌplɪŋ) *n* **1** the separation of previously linked systems so that they may operate independently. **2** *Electronics.* the reduction or avoidance of undesired distortion or oscillations in a circuit, caused by unwanted common coupling between two or more circuits.

decoy *n* (ˈdiːkɔɪ, dɪˈkɔɪ). **1** a person or thing used to beguile or lead someone into danger; lure. **2** *Military.* something designed to deceive an enemy or divert his attention. **3** a bird or animal, or an image of one, used to lure game into a trap or within shooting range. **4** an enclosed space or large trap, often with a wide funnelled entrance, into which game can be lured for capture. ◆ *vb* (dɪˈkɔɪ). **5** to lure or be lured by or as if by means of a decoy. [C17: probably from Dutch *de kooi,* literally: the cage, from Latin *cavea* CAGE] ▸ **deˈcoyer** *n*

decrease *vb* (dɪˈkriːs). **1** to diminish or cause to diminish in size, number, strength, etc. ◆ *n* (ˈdiːkriːs, dɪˈkriːs). **2** the act or process of diminishing; reduction. **3** the amount by which something has been diminished. [C14: from Old French *descreistre,* from Latin *dēcrescere* to grow less, from DE- + *crescere* to grow] ▸ **deˈcreasingly** *adv*

decree (dɪˈkriː) *n* **1** an edict, law, etc., made by someone in authority. **2** an order or judgment of a court made after hearing a suit, esp. in matrimonial proceedings. See **decree nisi, decree absolute.** ◆ *vb* **decrees, decreeing, decreed. 3** to order, adjudge, or ordain by decree. [C14: from Old French *decre,* from Latin *dēcrētum* ordinance, from *dēcrētus* decided, past participle of *dēcernere* to determine; see DECERN] ▸ **deˈcreeable** *adj* ▸ **deˈcreer** *n*

decree absolute *n* the final decree in divorce proceedings, which leaves the parties free to remarry. Compare **decree nisi.**

decree nisi (ˈnaɪsaɪ) *n* a provisional decree, esp. in divorce proceedings, which will later be made absolute unless cause is shown why it should not. Compare **decree absolute.**

decreet (dɪˈkriːt) *n Scots Law.* the final judgment or sentence of a court. [C14: *decret:* from Old French, from Latin *dēcrētum* DECREE]

decrement (ˈdɛkrɪmənt) *n* **1** the act of decreasing; diminution. **2** *Maths.* a negative increment. **3** *Physics.* a measure of the damping of an oscillator, expressed by the ratio of the amplitude of a cycle to its amplitude after one period. [C17: from Latin *dēcrēmentum,* from *dēcrescere* to DECREASE]

decrepit (dɪˈkrɛpɪt) *adj* **1** enfeebled by old age; infirm. **2** broken down or worn out by hard or long use; dilapidated. [C15: from Latin *dēcrepitus,* from *crepāre* to creak] ▸ **deˈcrepitly** *adv* ▸ **deˈcrepiˌtude** *n*

decrepitate (dɪˈkrɛpɪˌteɪt) *vb* **1** (*tr*) to heat (a substance, such as a salt) until it emits a crackling sound or until this sound stops. **2** (*intr*) (esp. of a salt) to crackle, as while being heated. [C17: from New Latin *dēcrepitāre,* from Latin *crepitāre* to crackle, from *crepāre* to creak] ▸ **deˌcrepiˈtation** *n*

decresc. *Music. abbrev. for* decrescendo.

decrescendo (ˌdiːkrɪˈʃɛndəʊ) *n, adj* another word for **diminuendo.** [Italian, from *decrescere* to DECREASE]

decrescent (dɪˈkrɛsənt) *adj* (esp. of the moon) decreasing; waning. [C17: from Latin *dēcrescēns* growing less; see DECREASE] ▸ **deˈcrescence** *n*

decretal (dɪˈkriːtᵊl) *n* **1** *R.C. Church.* a papal edict on doctrine or church law. ◆ *adj* **2** of or relating to a decretal or a decree. [C15: from Old French, from Late Latin *dēcrētālis;* see DECREE] ▸ **deˈcretalist** *n*

Decretals (dɪˈkriːtᵊlz) *pl n R.C. Church.* a compilation of decretals, esp. the authoritative compilation (**Liber Extra**) of Gregory IX (1234) which forms part of the Corpus Juris Canonici.

Decretum (dɪˈkriːtəm) *n R.C. Church.* the name given to various collections of canon law, esp. that made by the monk Gratian in the 12th century, which forms the first part of the Corpus Juris Canonici.

decriminalize *or* **decriminalise** (diːˈkrɪmənᵊˌlaɪz) *vb* (*tr*) to remove (an action) from the legal category of criminal offence: *to decriminalize the possession of marijuana.* ▸ **ˌdecriminaliˈzation** *or* **ˌdecriminaliˈsation** *n*

decry (dɪˈkraɪ) *vb* **-cries, -crying, -cried.** (*tr*) **1** to express open disapproval of; disparage. **2** to depreciate by proclamation: *to decry obsolete coinage.* [C17: from Old French *descrier,* from *des-* DIS-[1] + *crier* to CRY] ▸ **deˈcrial** *n* ▸ **deˈcrier** *n*

decrypt (diːˈkrɪpt) *vb* (*tr*) **1** to decode (a message) with or without previous knowledge of its key. **2** to make intelligible (a television or other signal) that has been deliberately distorted for transmission. [C20: from DE- + *crypt,* as in CRYPTIC] ▸ **deˈcrypted** *adj* ▸ **deˈcryption** *n*

decubitus (dɪˈkjuːbɪtəs) *n Med.* the posture adopted when lying down. [C19: Latin, past participle of *decumbere* to lie down] ▸ **deˈcubital** *adj*

decubitus ulcer *n* a chronic ulcer of the skin and underlying tissues caused by prolonged pressure on the body surface of bedridden patients. Nontechnical names: **bedsore, pressure sore.**

decumbent (dɪˈkʌmbənt) *adj* **1** lying down or lying flat. **2** *Botany.* (of certain stems) lying flat with the tip growing upwards. [C17: from Latin *dēcumbēns,* present participle of *dēcumbere* to lie down] ▸ **deˈcumbence** *or* **deˈcumbency** *n* ▸ **deˈcumbently** *adv*

decuple (ˈdɛkjʊpᵊl) *vb* **1** (*tr*) to increase by ten times. ◆ *n* **2** an amount ten times as large as a given reference. ◆ *adj* **3** increasing tenfold. [C15: from Old French, from Late Latin *decuplus* tenfold, from Latin *decem* ten]

decurion (dɪˈkjʊərɪən) *n* (in the Roman Empire) **1** a local councillor. **2** the commander of a troop of ten cavalrymen. [C14: from Latin *decuriō,* from *decuria* company of ten, from *decem* ten]

decurrent (dɪˈkʌrənt) *adj Botany.* extending down the stem, esp. (of a leaf) having the base of the blade extending down the stem as two wings. [C15: from Latin *dēcurrere* to run down, from *currere* to run] ▸ **deˈcurrently** *adv*

decurved (diːˈkɜːvd) *adj* bent or curved downwards: *a decurved bill; decurved petals.*

decury (ˈdɛkjʊərɪ) *n, pl* **-ries.** (in ancient Rome) a body of ten men. [C16: from Latin *decuria;* see DECURION]

decussate *vb* (dɪˈkʌseɪt). **1** to cross or cause to cross in the form of the letter X; intersect. ◆ *adj* (dɪˈkʌseɪt, dɪˈkʌsɪt). **2** in the form of the letter X; crossed; intersected. **3** *Botany.* (esp. of leaves) arranged in opposite pairs, with each pair at right angles to the one above and below it. [C17: from Latin *decussāre,* from *decussis* the number ten, from *decem* ten] ▸ **deˈcussately** *adv* ▸ **ˌdecusˈsation** *n*

dedal (ˈdiːdᵊl) *adj* a variant spelling (esp. U.S.) of **daedal.**

dedans *French.* (dədɑ̃) *n Real Tennis.* the open gallery at the server's end of the court. [literally: interior]

Dedéagach, Dedeagatch, *or* **Dedeağaç** (ˈdɛdeɪɑːˈgɑːtʃ) *n* a former name (until the end of World War I) of **Alexandroúpolis.**

Dedekind (*German* ˈdedəˌkɪnt) *n* (**Julius Wilhelm**) **Richard** (ˈjuːlɪʊs ˈvɪlhelm ˈrɪxɑːt). 1831–1916, German mathematician, who devised a way (the **Dedekind cut**) of according irrational and rational numbers the same status.

dedicate (ˈdɛdɪˌkeɪt) *vb* (*tr*) **1** (often foll. by *to*) to devote (oneself, one's time, etc.) wholly to a special purpose or cause; commit wholeheartedly or unreservedly. **2** (foll. by *to*) to address or inscribe (a book, artistic performance, etc.) to a person, cause, etc. as a token of affection or respect. **3** (foll. by *to*) to request or play (a record) on radio for another person as a greeting. **4** to assign or allocate to a particular project, function, etc. **5** to set apart for a deity or for sacred uses; consecrate. ◆ *adj* **6** an archaic word for **dedicated.** [C15: from Latin *dēdicāre* to announce, from *dicāre* to make known, variant of *dīcere* to say] ▸ **ˌdedicaˈtee** *n* ▸ **ˈdediˌcator** *n* ▸ **dedicatory** (ˈdɛdɪˌkeɪtərɪ, ˈdɛdɪkətərɪ, -trɪ) *or* **ˈdediˌcative** *adj*

dedicated (ˈdɛdɪˌkeɪtɪd) *adj* **1** devoted to a particular purpose or cause: *a dedicated man.* **2** assigned or allocated to a particular project, function, etc.: *a dedicated transmission line; dedicated parking space.* **3** *Computing.* designed to fulfil one function: *a dedicated microprocessor.*

dedication (ˌdɛdɪˈkeɪʃən) *n* **1** the act of dedicating or the state of being dedicated. **2** an inscription or announcement prefixed to a book, piece of music, etc., dedicating it to a person or thing. **3** complete and wholehearted devotion, esp. to a career, ideal, etc. **4** a ceremony in which something, such as a church, is dedicated. ▸ **ˌdediˈcational** *adj*

de dicto *Latin.* (ˈdeɪˈdɪktəʊ) *adj Logic, philosophy.* relating to the expression of a belief, possibility, etc., rather than to the individuals mentioned, as in *the number of the planets is the number of satellites of the sun,* the truth of which is independent of what number that is. Compare **de re.** See also **Electra paradox.** [literally: about the saying]

dedifferentiation (diːˌdɪfəˌrɛnʃɪˈeɪʃən) *n* the reversion of the cells of differentiated tissue to a less specialized form.

deduce (dɪˈdjuːs) *vb* (*tr*) **1** (*may take a clause as object*) to reach (a conclusion about something) by reasoning; conclude (that); infer. **2** *Archaic.* to trace the origin, course, or derivation of. [C15: from Latin *dēdūcere* to lead away, derive, from DE- + *dūcere* to lead] ▸ **deˈducible** *adj* ▸ **deˌduciˈbility** *or* **deˈducibleness** *n*

deduct (dɪˈdʌkt) *vb* (*tr*) to take away or subtract (a number, quantity, part, etc.): *income tax is deducted from one's wages.* [C15: from Latin *dēductus,* past participle of *dēdūcere* to DEDUCE]

deductible (dɪˈdʌktɪbᵊl) *adj* **1** capable of being deducted. **2** *U.S. and Canadian.* short for **tax-deductible.** ◆ *n* **3** *Insurance.* the U.S. and Canadian name for **excess** (sense 6). ▸ **deˌductiˈbility** *n*

deduction (dɪˈdʌkʃən) *n* **1** the act or process of deducting or subtracting. **2** something, esp. a sum of money, that is or may be deducted. **3a** the process of reasoning typical of mathematics and logic, whose conclusions follow necessarily from their premises. **3b** an argument of this type. **3c** the conclusion of such an argument. **4** *Logic.* **4a** a systematic method of deriving conclusions that cannot be false when the premises are true, esp. one amenable to formalization and study by the science of logic. **4b** an argument of this type. Compare **induction** (sense 4).

deduction theorem *n Logic.* the property of many formal systems that the conditional derived from a valid argument by taking the conjunction of the premises as antecedent and the conclusion as consequent is true.

deductive (dɪˈdʌktɪv) *adj* of or relating to deduction: *deductive reasoning.* ▸ **deˈductively** *adv*

de Duve (də dyːv) *n* **Christian.** born 1917, Belgian biochemist, who discovered lysosomes: shared the Nobel prize (1974) for his work in cell biology.

dee (diː) *vb* a Scot. word for **die**[1].

Dee[1] (diː) *n* **1** a river in N Wales and NW England, rising in S Gwynedd and flowing east and north to the Irish Sea. Length: about 112 km (70 miles). **2** a river in NE Scotland, rising in the Cairngorms and flowing east to the North Sea. Length: about 140 km (87 miles). **3** a river in S Scotland, flowing south to the Solway Firth. Length: about 80 km (50 miles).

Dee[2] (diː) *n* **John.** 1527–1608, English mathematician, astrologer, and magician: best known for his preface (1570) to the first edition of Euclid in English.

deed (diːd) *n* **1** something that is done or performed; act. **2** a notable achievement; feat; exploit. **3** action or performance, as opposed to words. **4** *Law.* a formal legal document signed, witnessed, and delivered to effect a conveyance or transfer of property or to create a legal obligation or contract. ◆ *vb* **5** (*tr*) *U.S. and Canadian.* to convey or transfer (property) by deed. [Old English *dēd;* related to Old High German *tāt,* Gothic *gadeths;* see DO[1]]

deed box *n* a lockable metal box for storing documents.

deed poll *n Law.* a deed made by one party only, esp. one by which a person changes his name.

deejay (ˈdiːˌdʒeɪ) *n* an informal name for **disc jockey.** [C20: from the initials DJ]

deek (diːk) *vb* (*tr; imperative*) *Edinburgh and Northumbrian dialect.* to look at: *deek that!* [perhaps of Romany origin]

deem (diːm) *vb* (*tr*) to judge or consider: *I do not deem him worthy of this honour.* [Old English *dēman;* related to Old High German *tuomen* to judge, Gothic *domjan;* see DOOM]

de-emphasize *or* **de-emphasise** (diːˈɛmfəˌsaɪz) *vb* (*tr*) to remove emphasis from.

deemster (ˈdiːmstə) *n* the title of one of the two justices in the Isle of Man. Also called: **dempster.** ▸ **ˈdeemsterˌship** *n*

de-energize *or* **de-energise** (diːˈɛnəˌdʒaɪz) *vb* (*tr*) *Electrical engineering.* to disconnect (an electrical circuit) from its source. ▸ **de-ˌenergiˈzation** *or* **de-ˌenergiˈsation** *n*

deep (diːp) *adj* **1** extending or situated relatively far down from a surface: *a deep pool.* **2** extending or situated relatively far inwards, backwards, or sideways: *a deep border of trees.* **3** *Cricket.* relatively far from the pitch: *the deep field; deep third man.* **4a** (*postpositive*) of a specified dimension downwards, inwards, or backwards: *six feet deep.* **4b** (*in combination*): *a six-foot-deep trench.* **5** coming from or penetrating to a great depth: *a deep breath.* **6** difficult to understand or penetrate; abstruse. **7** learned or intellectually demanding: *a deep discussion.* **8** of great intensity; extreme: *deep happiness; deep trouble.* **9** (*postpositive;* foll. by *in*) absorbed or enveloped (by); engrossed or immersed (in): *deep in study; deep in debt.* **10** very cunning or crafty; devious: *a deep plot.* **11** mysterious or obscure: *a deep secret.* **12** (of a colour) having an intense or dark hue. **13** low in pitch or tone: *a deep voice.* **14 go off the deep end.** *Informal.* **14a** to lose one's temper; react angrily. **14b** *Chiefly U.S.* to act rashly. **15 in deep water.** in a tricky position or in trouble. **16 throw** (**someone**) **in at the deep end.** See **end** (sense 28). ◆ *n* **17** any deep place on land or under water, esp. below 6000 metres (3000 fathoms). **18 the deep. 18a** a poetic term for the **ocean. 18b** *Cricket.* the area of the field relatively far from the pitch. **19** the most profound, intense, or central part: *the deep of winter.* **20** a vast extent, as of space or time. **21** *Nautical.* one of the intervals on a sounding lead, one fathom apart. ◆ *adv* **22** far on in time; late: *they worked deep into the night.* **23** profoundly or intensely. **24 deep down.** *Informal.* in reality, esp. as opposed to appearance: *she is a very kind person deep down.* **25 deep in the past.** long ago. [Old English *dēop;* related to Old High German *tiof* deep, Old Norse *djupr*] ▸ **ˈdeeply** *adv* ▸ **ˈdeepness** *n*

deep-discount bond *n* a fixed-interest security that pays little or no interest but is issued at a substantial discount to its redemption value, thus largely substituting capital gain for income.

deep-dish pie *n Chiefly U.S. and Canadian.* a pie baked in a deep dish and having only a top crust.

deep-dyed *adj Usually derogatory.* thoroughgoing; absolute; complete.

deepen (ˈdiːpᵊn) *vb* to make or become deep, deeper, or more intense. ▸ **ˈdeepener** *n*

deepfreeze (ˌdiːpˈfriːz) *n* **1** a type of refrigerator in which food, etc., is stored for long periods at temperatures below freezing. **2** storage in or as if in a deepfreeze. **3** *Informal.* a state of suspended activity. ◆ *vb* **deep-freeze, -freezes, -freezing, -froze, -frozen. 4** (*tr*) to freeze or keep in or as if in a deepfreeze.

deep-fry *vb* **-fries, -frying, -fried.** to cook (fish, potatoes, etc.) in sufficient hot fat to cover the food entirely.

deep kiss *n* another name for **French kiss.**

deep-laid *adj* (of a plot or plan) carefully worked out and kept secret.

deep-litter *n* (*modifier*) *Poultry farming.* **1** denoting a system in which a number of hens are housed in one covered enclosure, within which they can move about freely, on a layer of straw or wood shavings several centimetres deep: *deep-litter system.* **2** kept in or produced by the deep-litter method: *deep-litter eggs.*

deep-rooted *or* **deep-seated** *adj* (of ideas, beliefs, prejudices, etc.) firmly fixed, implanted, or held; ingrained.

deep-sea *n* (*modifier*) of, found in, or characteristic of the deep parts of the sea: *deep-sea fishing.*

deep-set *adj* (of the eyes) deeply set into the face.

deep-six *vb* (*tr*) *U.S. slang.* to dispose of (something, such as documents) completely; destroy. [C20: from *six feet deep,* the traditional depth for a grave]

Deep South *n* the SE part of the U.S., esp. South Carolina, Georgia, Alabama, Mississippi, and Louisiana.

deep space *n* any region of outer space beyond the system of the earth and moon.

deep structure *n Generative grammar.* a representation of a sentence at a level where logical or grammatical relations are made explicit, before transformational rules have been applied. Compare **surface structure.**

deep therapy *n* radiotherapy with very penetrating short-wave radiation.

deep throat *n* an anonymous source of secret information. [C20: from the code name of such a source in the Watergate scandal; a reference to the title of a pornographic film]

deer (dɪə) *n, pl* **deer** *or* **deers. 1** any ruminant artiodactyl mammal of the family *Cervidae,* including reindeer, elk, muntjacs, and roe deer, typically having antlers in the male. Related adj: **cervine. 2** (in N Canada) another name for **caribou.** [Old English *dēor* beast; related to Old High German *tior* wild beast, Old Norse *dȳr*]

deergrass (ˈdɪəˌgrɑːs) *n* a perennial cyperaceous plant, *Trichophorum caespitosum,* that grows in dense tufts in peat bogs of temperate regions.

deerhound (ˈdɪəˌhaʊnd) *n* a very large rough-coated breed of dog of the greyhound type.

deer lick *n* a naturally or artificially salty area of ground where deer come to lick the salt.

deer mouse *n* any of various mice of the genus *Peromyscus,* esp. *P. maniculatus,* of North and Central America, having brownish fur with white underparts: family *Cricetidae.* See also **white-footed mouse.** [so named because of its agility]

deerskin ('dɪə,skɪn) *n* **a** the hide of a deer. **b** (*as modifier*): *a deerskin jacket.*

deerstalker ('dɪə,stɔːkə) *n* **1** Also called: **stalker.** a person who stalks deer, esp. in order to shoot them. **2** a hat, peaked in front and behind, with earflaps usually turned up and tied together on the top. ▸ **'deer,stalking** *adj, n*

de-escalate (diː'ɛskə,leɪt) *vb* to reduce the level or intensity of (a crisis, etc.). ▸ **de-,esca'lation** *n*

def (dɛf) *adj Slang.* very good, esp. of hip-hop. [C20: perhaps from *definitive*]

def. *abbrev. for:* **1** defective. **2** defence. **3** defendant. **4** deferred. **5** definite. **6** definition.

deface (dɪ'feɪs) *vb* (*tr*) to spoil or mar the surface, legibility, or appearance of; disfigure. ▸ **de'faceable** *adj* ▸ **de'facement** *n* ▸ **de'facer** *n*

de facto (deɪ 'fæktəʊ) *adv* **1** in fact. ◆ *adj* **2** existing in fact, whether legally recognized or not: *a de facto regime.* Compare **de jure.** ◆ *n, pl* **-tos. 3** *Austral. and N.Z.* a de facto husband or wife. [C17: Latin]

defaecate ('dɛfɪ,keɪt) *vb* a variant spelling of **defecate.**

defalcate ('diːfæl,keɪt) *vb* (*intr*) *Law.* to misuse or misappropriate property or funds entrusted to one. [C15: from Medieval Latin *dēfalcāre* to cut off, from Latin DE- + *falx* sickle] ▸ **,defal'cation** *n* ▸ **'defal,cator** *n*

defamation (,dɛfə'meɪʃən) *n* **1** *Law.* the injuring of a person's good name or reputation. Compare **libel, slander. 2** the act of defaming or state of being defamed.

defamatory (dɪ'fæmətərɪ, -trɪ) *adj* injurious to someone's name or reputation. ▸ **de'famatorily** *adv*

defame (dɪ'feɪm) *vb* (*tr*) **1** to attack the good name or reputation of; slander; libel. **2** *Archaic.* to indict or accuse. [C14: from Old French *defamer,* from Latin *dēfāmāre,* from *diffāmāre* to spread by unfavourable report, from *fāma* FAME] ▸ **de'famer** *n*

default (dɪ'fɔːlt) *n* **1** a failure to act, esp. a failure to meet a financial obligation or to appear in a court of law at a time specified. **2** absence: *he lost the chess game by default.* **3 in default of.** through or in the lack or absence of. **4 judgment by default.** *Law.* a judgment in the plaintiff's favour when the defendant fails to plead or to appear. **5** lack, want, or need. **6** (*also* 'diːfɔːlt). *Computing.* **6a** the preset selection of an option offered by a system, which will always be followed except when explicitly altered. **6b** (*as modifier*): *default setting.* ◆ *vb* **7** (*intr;* often foll. by *on* or *in*) to fail to make payment when due. **8** (*intr*) to fail to fulfil or perform an obligation, engagement, etc: *to default in a sporting contest.* **9** *Law.* to lose (a case) by failure to appear in court. [C13: from Old French *defaute,* from *defaillir* to fail, from Vulgar Latin *dēfallīre* (unattested) to be lacking]

defaulter (dɪ'fɔːltə) *n* **1** a person who defaults. **2** *Chiefly Brit.* a person, esp. a soldier, who has broken the disciplinary code of his service.

defeasance (dɪ'fiːzᵊns) *n Chiefly law.* **1** the act or process of rendering null and void; annulment. **2a** a condition, the fulfilment of which renders a deed void. **2b** the document containing such a condition. [C14: from Old French, from *desfaire* to DEFEAT]

defeasible (dɪ'fiːzəbᵊl) *adj* **1** *Law.* (of an estate or interest in land) capable of being defeated or rendered void. **2** *Philosophy.* (of a judgment, opinion, etc.) having a presupposition in its favour but open to revision if countervailing evidence becomes known. Compare **incorrigible** (sense 3). ▸ **de'feasibleness** *or* **de,feasi'bility** *n*

defeat (dɪ'fiːt) *vb* (*tr*) **1** to overcome in a contest or competition; win a victory over. **2** to thwart or frustrate: *this accident has defeated all his hopes of winning.* **3** *Law.* to render null and void; annul. ◆ *n* **4** the act of defeating or state of being defeated. **5** an instance of defeat. **6** overthrow or destruction. **7** *Law.* an annulment. [C14: from Old French *desfait,* from *desfaire* to undo, ruin, from *des-* DIS-[1] + *faire* to do, from Latin *facere*] ▸ **de'feater** *n*

defeatism (dɪ'fiːtɪzəm) *n* a ready acceptance or expectation of defeat. ▸ **de'featist** *n, adj*

defecate *or* **defaecate** ('dɛfɪ,keɪt) *vb* **1** (*intr*) to discharge waste from the body through the anus. **2** (*tr*) to clarify or remove impurities from (a solution, esp. of sugar). [C16: from Latin *dēfaecāre* to cleanse from dregs, from DE- + *faex* sediment, dregs] ▸ **,defe'cation** *or* **,defae'cation** *n* ▸ **'defe,cator** *or* **'defae,cator** *n*

defect *n* (dɪ'fɛkt, 'diːfɛkt). **1** a lack of something necessary for completeness or perfection; shortcoming; deficiency. **2** an imperfection, failing, or blemish. **3** *Crystallog.* a local deviation from regularity in the crystal lattice of a solid. See also **point defect, dislocation** (sense 3). ◆ *vb* (dɪ'fɛkt). **4** (*intr*) to desert one's country, cause, allegiance, etc., esp. in order to join the opposing forces. [C15: from Latin *dēfectus,* from *dēficere* to forsake, fail; see DEFICIENT] ▸ **de'fector** *n*

defection (dɪ'fɛkʃən) *n* **1** the act or an instance of defecting. **2** abandonment of duty, allegiance, principles, etc.; backsliding. **3** another word for **defect** (senses 1, 2).

defective (dɪ'fɛktɪv) *adj* **1** having a defect or flaw; imperfect; faulty. **2** (of a person) below the usual standard or level, esp. in intelligence. **3** *Grammar.* (of a word) lacking the full range of inflections characteristic of its form class, as for example *must,* which has no past tense. ▸ **de'fectively** *adv* ▸ **de'fectiveness** *n*

defence *or U.S.* **defense** (dɪ'fɛns) *n* **1** resistance against danger, attack, or harm; protection. **2** a person or thing that provides such resistance. **3** a plea, essay, speech, etc., in support of something; vindication; justification. **4a** a country's military measures or resources. **4b** (*as modifier*): *defence spending.* **5** *Law.* a defendant's denial of the truth of the allegations or charge against him. **6** *Law.* the defendant and his legal advisers collectively. Compare **prosecution. 7** *Sport.* **7a** the action of protecting oneself, one's goal, or one's allotted part of the playing area against an opponent's attacks. **7b** the method of doing this. **7c** (usually preceded by *the*) the players in a team whose function is to do this. **8** *American football.* (usually preceded by *the*) **8a** the team that does not have possession of the ball. **8b** the members of a team that play in such circumstances. **9** *Psychoanal.* See **defence mechanism. 10** (*pl*) fortifications. [C13: from Old French, from Late Latin *dēfensum,* past participle of *dēfendere* to DEFEND] ▸ **de'fenceless** *or U.S.* **de'fenseless** *adj* ▸ **de'fencelessly** *or U.S.* **de'fenselessly** *adv* ▸ **de'fencelessness** *or U.S.* **de'fenselessness** *n*

defence in depth *n Military.* the act or practice of positioning successive mutually supporting lines of defence in a given area.

defence mechanism *n* **1** *Psychoanal.* a usually unconscious mental process designed to reduce the anxiety, shame, etc., associated with instinctive desires. **2** *Physiol.* the protective response of the body against disease organisms.

defend (dɪ'fɛnd) *vb* **1** to protect (a person, place, etc.) from harm or danger; ward off an attack on. **2** (*tr*) to support in the face of criticism, esp. by argument or evidence. **3** to represent (a defendant) in court in a civil or criminal action. **4** *Sport.* to guard or protect (oneself, one's goal, etc.) against attack. **5** (*tr*) to protect (a championship or title) against a challenge. [C13: from Old French *defendre,* from Latin *dēfendere* to ward off, from DE- + *-fendere* to strike] ▸ **de'fendable** *adj* ▸ **de'fender** *n*

defendant (dɪ'fɛndənt) *n* **1** a person against whom an action or claim is brought in a court of law. Compare **plaintiff.** ◆ *adj* **2** making a defence; defending.

Defender of the Faith *n* the title conferred upon Henry VIII by Pope Leo X in 1521 in recognition of the King's pamphlet attacking Luther's doctrines and retained by subsequent monarchs of England. Latin: ***Fidei Defensor.***

defenestration (diː,fɛnɪ'streɪʃən) *n* the act of throwing someone out of a window. [C17: from New Latin *dēfenestrātiō,* from Latin DE- + *fenestra* window]

defensible (dɪ'fɛnsɪbᵊl) *adj* capable of being defended, as in war, an argument, etc. ▸ **de,fensi'bility** *or* **de'fensibleness** *n* ▸ **de'fensibly** *adv*

defensive (dɪ'fɛnsɪv) *adj* **1** intended, suitable, or done for defence, as opposed to offence. **2** rejecting criticisms of oneself or covering up one's failings. ◆ *n* **3** a position of defence. **4 on the defensive.** in an attitude or position of defence, as in being ready to reject criticism. ▸ **de'fensively** *adv* ▸ **de'fensiveness** *n*

defensive medicine *n* the practice by a doctor of ordering extensive tests in order to minimize liability if accused of negligence.

defer[1] (dɪ'fɜː) *vb* **-fers, -ferring, -ferred.** (*tr*) to delay or cause to be delayed until a future time; postpone. [C14: from Old French *differer* to be different, postpone; see DIFFER] ▸ **de'ferrable** *or* **de'ferable** *adj* ▸ **de'ferrer** *n*

defer[2] (dɪ'fɜː) *vb* **-fers, -ferring, -ferred.** (*intr;* foll. by *to*) to yield (to) or comply (with) the wishes or judgments of another. [C15: from Latin *dēferre,* literally: to bear down, from DE- + *ferre* to bear]

deference ('dɛfərəns) *n* **1** submission to or compliance with the will, wishes, etc., of another. **2** courteous regard; respect. [C17: from French *déférence;* see DEFER[2]]

deferent[1] ('dɛfərənt) *adj* another word for **deferential.**

deferent[2] ('dɛfərənt) *adj* **1** (esp. of a bodily nerve, vessel, or duct) conveying an impulse, fluid, etc., outwards, down, or away; efferent. ◆ *n* **2** *Astronomy.* (in the Ptolemaic system) a circle centred on the earth around which the centre of the epicycle was thought to move. [C17: from Latin *dēferre; see* DEFER[2]]

deferential (,dɛfə'rɛnʃəl) *adj* marked by or showing deference or respect; respectful. ▸ **,defer'entially** *adv*

deferment (dɪ'fɜːmənt) *or* **deferral** (dɪ'fɜːrəl) *n* the act of deferring or putting off until another time; postponement.

deferred (dɪ'fɜːd) *adj* **1** withheld over a certain period; postponed: *a deferred payment.* **2** (of shares) ranking behind other types of shares for dividend.

deferred annuity *n* an annuity that commences not less than one year after the final purchase premium. Compare **immediate annuity.**

deferred sentence *n Law.* a sentence that is postponed for a specific period to allow a court to examine the conduct of the offender during the deferment. Compare **suspended sentence.**

defervescence (,dɛfə'vɛsəns) *n Med.* **1** the abatement of a fever. **2** the period during which this occurs.

defiance (dɪ'faɪəns) *n* **1** open or bold resistance to or disregard for authority, opposition, or power. **2** a challenging attitude or behaviour; challenge.

defiant (dɪ'faɪənt) *adj* marked by resistance or bold opposition, as to authority; challenging. ▸ **de'fiantly** *adv*

defibrillation (dɪ,faɪbrɪ'leɪʃən, -fɪb-) *n Med.* the application of an electric current to the heart to restore normal rhythmic contractions after a heart attack caused by fibrillation.

defibrillator (dɪ'faɪbrɪ,leɪtə, -'fɪb-) *n Med.* an apparatus for stopping fibrillation of the heart by application of an electric current to the chest wall or directly to the heart.

deficiency (dɪ'fɪʃənsɪ) *n, pl* **-cies. 1** the state or quality of being deficient. **2** a lack or insufficiency; shortage. **3** another word for **deficit. 4** *Biology.* the absence of a gene or a region of a chromosome normally present.

deficiency disease *n* **1** *Med.* any condition, such as pellagra, beriberi, or scurvy, produced by a lack of vitamins or other essential substances. Compare **avitaminosis. 2** *Botany.* any disease caused by lack of essential minerals.

deficient (dɪ'fɪʃənt) *adj* **1** lacking some essential; incomplete; defective. **2** inadequate in quantity or supply; insufficient. [C16: from Latin *dēficiēns* lacking, from *dēficere* to fall short; see DEFECT] ▸ **de'ficiently** *adv*

deficit ('dɛfɪsɪt, dɪ'fɪsɪt) *n* **1** the amount by which an actual sum is lower than that expected or required. **2a** an excess of liabilities over assets. **2b** an excess of expenditures over revenues during a certain period. **2c** an excess of payments over receipts on the balance of payments. [C18: from Latin, literally: there is lacking, from *dēficere* to be lacking]

deficit financing *n* government spending in excess of revenues so that a budget deficit is incurred, which is financed by borrowing: recommended by Keynesian economists in order to increase economic activity and reduce unemployment. Also called: **compensatory finance, pump priming.**

de fide *Latin.* (diː ˈfaɪdɪ) *adj R.C. Church.* (of a doctrine) belonging to the essentials of the faith, esp. by virtue of a papal ruling. [literally: from faith]

defilade (ˌdɛfɪˈleɪd) *Military fortifications.* ◆ *n* **1** protection provided by obstacles against enemy crossfire from the rear, or observation. **2** the disposition of defensive fortifications to produce this protection. ◆ *vb (tr)* **3** to provide protection for by defilade. [C19: see DE-, ENFILADE]

defile[1] (dɪˈfaɪl) *vb (tr)* **1** to make foul or dirty; pollute. **2** to tarnish or sully the brightness of; taint; corrupt. **3** to damage or sully (someone's good name, reputation, etc.). **4** to make unfit for ceremonial use; desecrate. **5** to violate the chastity of. [C14: from earlier *defoilen* (influenced by *filen* to FILE[3]), from Old French *defouler* to trample underfoot, abuse, from DE- + *fouler* to tread upon; see FULL[2]] ▸ **deˈfilement** *n* ▸ **deˈfiler** *n*

defile[2] (ˈdiːfaɪl, dɪˈfaɪl) *n* **1** a narrow pass or gorge, esp. one between two mountains. **2** a single file of soldiers, etc. ◆ *vb* **3** *Chiefly military.* to march or cause to march in single file. [C17: from French *défilé*, from *défiler* to file off, from *filer* to march in a column, from Old French: to spin, from *fil* thread, from Latin *fīlum*]

define (dɪˈfaɪn) *vb (tr)* **1** to state precisely the meaning of (words, terms, etc.). **2** to describe the nature, properties, or essential qualities of. **3** to determine the boundary or extent of. **4** (*often passive*) to delineate the form or outline of: *the shape of the tree was clearly defined by the light behind it.* **5** to fix with precision; specify. [C14: from Old French *definer* to determine, from Latin *dēfīnīre* to set bounds to, from *fīnīre* to FINISH] ▸ **deˈfinable** *adj* ▸ **deˌfinaˈbility** *n* ▸ **deˈfinably** *adv* ▸ **deˈfiner** *n*

definiendum (dɪˌfɪnɪˈɛndəm) *n, pl* **-da** (-də). something to be defined, esp. the term or phrase to be accounted for in a dictionary entry. Compare **definiens.** [Latin]

definiens (dɪˈfɪnɪənz) *n, pl* **definientia** (dɪˌfɪnɪˈɛnʃə). the word or words used to define or give an account of the meaning of another word, as in a dictionary entry. Compare **definiendum.** [Latin: defining]

definite (ˈdɛfɪnɪt) *adj* **1** clearly defined; exact; explicit. **2** having precise limits or boundaries. **3** known for certain; sure: *it is definite that they have won.* **4** *Botany.* **4a** denoting a type of growth in which the main stem ends in a flower, as in a cymose inflorescence; determinate. **4b** (esp. of flower parts) limited or fixed in number in a given species. [C15: from Latin *dēfīnītus* limited, distinct; see DEFINE] ▸ **ˈdefiniteness** *n* ▸ **definitude** (dɪˈfɪnɪˌtjuːd) *n*

definite article *n Grammar.* a determiner that expresses specificity of reference, such as *the* in English. Compare **indefinite article.**

definite description *n* **1** a description that is modified by the definite article or a possessive, such as *the woman in white* or *Rosemary's baby.* **2** a similar plural expression, such as *the kings of Scotland.*

definite integral *n Maths.* **a** the evaluation of the indefinite integral between two limits, representing the area between the given function and the *x*-axis between these two values of *x*. **b** the expression for that function, $\int_a^b f(x)dx$, where $f(x)$ is the given function and $x = a$ and $x = b$ are the limits of integration. Where $F(x) = \int f(x)dx$, the indefinite integral, $\int_a^b f(x)dx = F(b)-F(a)$.

definitely (ˈdɛfɪnɪtlɪ) *adv* **1** in a definite manner. **2** (*sentence modifier*) certainly: *he said he was coming, definitely.* ◆ *sentence substitute.* **3** unquestionably: used to confirm an assumption by a questioner.

definition (ˌdɛfɪˈnɪʃən) *n* **1** a formal and concise statement of the meaning of a word, phrase, etc. **2** the act of defining a word, phrase, etc. **3** specification of the essential properties of something, or of the criteria which uniquely identify it. **4** the act of making clear or definite. **5** the state or condition of being clearly defined or definite. **6** a measure of the clarity of an optical, photographic, or television image as characterized by its sharpness and contrast. ▸ **ˌdefiˈnitional** *adj*

definitive (dɪˈfɪnɪtɪv) *adj* **1** serving to decide or settle finally; conclusive. **2** most reliable, complete, or authoritative: *the definitive reading of a text.* **3** serving to define or outline. **4** *Zoology.* fully developed; complete: *the definitive form of a parasite.* **5a** (of postage stamps) permanently on sale. **5b** (*as n*) a definitive postage stamp. ◆ *n* **6** *Grammar.* a word indicating specificity of reference, such as the definite article or a demonstrative adjective or pronoun. ▸ **deˈfinitively** *adv* ▸ **deˈfinitiveness** *n*

deflagrate (ˈdɛfləˌgreɪt, ˈdiː-) *vb* to burn or cause to burn with great heat and light. [C18: from Latin *dēflagrāre*, from DE- + *flagrāre* to burn] ▸ **ˌdeflaˈgration** *n*

deflate (dɪˈfleɪt) *vb* **1** to collapse or cause to collapse through the release of gas. **2** (*tr*) to take away the self-esteem or conceit from. **3** *Economics.* to cause deflation of (an economy, the money supply, etc.). [C19: from DE- + (IN)FLATE] ▸ **deˈflator** *n*

deflation (dɪˈfleɪʃən) *n* **1** the act of deflating or state of being deflated. **2** *Economics.* a reduction in the level of total spending and economic activity resulting in lower levels of output, employment, investment, trade, profits, and prices. Compare **disinflation. 3** *Geology.* the removal of loose rock material, sand, and dust by the wind. ▸ **deˈflationary** *adj* ▸ **deˈflationist** *n, adj*

deflationary gap *n Economics.* a situation in which total spending in an economy is insufficient to buy all the output that can be produced with full employment.

deflect (dɪˈflɛkt) *vb* to turn or cause to turn aside from a course; swerve. [C17: from Latin *dēflectere*, from *flectere* to bend] ▸ **deˈflector** *n*

deflection *or* **deflexion** (dɪˈflɛkʃən) *n* **1** the act of deflecting or the state of being deflected. **2** the amount of deviation. **3** the change in direction of a light beam as it crosses a boundary between two media with different refractive indexes. **4** a deviation of the indicator of a measuring instrument from its zero position. **5** the movement of a structure or structural member when subjected to a load. ▸ **deˈflective** *adj*

deflexed (dɪˈflɛkst, ˈdiːflɛkst) *adj* (of leaves, petals, etc.) bent sharply outwards and downwards.

deflocculate (dɪˈflɒkjʊˌleɪt) *vb (tr)* **1** to disperse, forming a colloid or suspension. **2** to prevent flocculation of (a colloid or suspension). ▸ **deˌflocculation** *n* ▸ **deˈflocculant** *n*

defloration (ˌdiːflɔːˈreɪʃən) *n* the act of deflowering. [C15: from Late Latin *dēflōrātiō*; see DE-, FLOWER]

deflower (diːˈflaʊə) *vb (tr)* **1** to deprive of virginity, esp. by rupturing the hymen through sexual intercourse. **2** to despoil of beauty, innocence, etc.; mar; violate. **3** to rob or despoil of flowers. ▸ **deˈflowerer** *n*

Defoe (dɪˈfəʊ) *n* **Daniel.** ?1660–1731, English novelist, journalist, spymaster, and pamphleteer, noted particularly for his novel *Robinson Crusoe* (1719). His other novels include *Moll Flanders* (1722) and *A Journal of the Plague Year* (1722).

defoliant (diːˈfəʊlɪənt) *n* a chemical sprayed or dusted onto trees to cause their leaves to fall, esp. to remove cover from an enemy in warfare.

defoliate *vb* (diːˈfəʊlɪˌeɪt). **1** to deprive (a plant) of its leaves, as by the use of a herbicide, or (of a plant) to shed its leaves. ◆ *adj* (diːˈfəʊlɪɪt). **2** (of a plant) having shed its leaves. [C18: from Medieval Latin *dēfoliāre*, from Latin DE- + *folium* leaf] ▸ **deˌfoliˈation** *n* ▸ **deˈfoliˌator** *n*

deforce (dɪˈfɔːs) *vb (tr) Property law.* **1** to withhold (property, esp. land) wrongfully or by force from the rightful owner. **2** to eject or keep forcibly from possession of property. [C13: from Anglo-French, from *deforcer*] ▸ **deˈforcement** *n*

deforest (diːˈfɒrɪst) *vb (tr)* to clear of trees. Also: **disforest.** ▸ **deˌforesˈtation** *n* ▸ **deˈforester** *n*

De Forest (də ˈfɒrɪst) *n* **Lee.** 1873–1961, U.S. inventor of telegraphic, telephonic, and radio equipment: patented the first triode valve (1907).

deform (dɪˈfɔːm) *vb* **1** to make or become misshapen or distorted. **2** (*tr*) to mar the beauty of; disfigure. **3** (*tr*) to subject or be subjected to a stress that causes a change of dimensions. [C15: from Latin *dēfōrmāre*, from DE- + *forma* shape, beauty] ▸ **deˈformable** *adj* ▸ **deˌformaˈbility** *n* ▸ **deˈformer** *n*

deformation (ˌdiːfɔːˈmeɪʃən) *n* **1** the act of deforming; distortion. **2** the result of deforming; a change in form, esp. for the worse. **3** a change in the dimensions of an object resulting from a stress.

deformed (dɪˈfɔːmd) *adj* **1** disfigured or misshapen. **2** morally perverted; warped. ▸ **deformedly** (dɪˈfɔːmɪdlɪ) *adv* ▸ **deˈformedness** *n*

deformity (dɪˈfɔːmɪtɪ) *n, pl* **-ties. 1** a deformed condition; disfigurement. **2** *Pathol.* an acquired or congenital distortion of an organ or part. **3** a deformed person or thing. **4** a defect, esp. of the mind or morals; depravity.

defraud (dɪˈfrɔːd) *vb (tr)* to take away or withhold money, rights, property, etc., from (a person) by fraud; cheat; swindle. ▸ **defraudation** (ˌdiːfrɔːˈdeɪʃən) *or* **deˈfraudment** *n* ▸ **deˈfrauder** *n*

defray (dɪˈfreɪ) *vb (tr)* to furnish or provide money for (costs, expenses, etc.); pay. [C16: from Old French *deffroier* to pay expenses, from *de-* DIS-[1] + *frai* expenditure, originally: cost incurred through breaking something, from Latin *frangere* to break] ▸ **deˈfrayable** *adj* ▸ **deˈfrayal** *or* **deˈfrayment** *n* ▸ **deˈfrayer** *n*

defrock (diːˈfrɒk) *vb (tr)* to deprive (a person in holy orders) of ecclesiastical status; unfrock.

defrost (diːˈfrɒst) *vb* **1** to make or become free of frost or ice. **2** to thaw, esp. through removal from a refrigerator.

defroster (diːˈfrɒstə) *n* a device by which the de-icing process of a refrigerator is accelerated, usually by circulating the refrigerant without the expansion process.

deft (dɛft) *adj* quick and neat in movement; nimble; dexterous. [C13 (in the sense: gentle): see DAFT] ▸ **ˈdeftly** *adv* ▸ **ˈdeftness** *n*

defunct (dɪˈfʌŋkt) *adj* **1** no longer living; dead or extinct. **2** no longer operative or valid. [C16: from Latin *dēfungī* to discharge (one's obligations), die; see DE-, FUNCTION] ▸ **deˈfunctive** *adj* ▸ **deˈfunctness** *n*

defuse *or U.S. (sometimes)* **defuze** (diːˈfjuːz) *vb (tr)* **1** to remove the triggering device of (a bomb, etc.). **2** to remove the cause of tension from (a crisis, etc.).

USAGE Avoid confusion with **diffuse.**

defy (dɪˈfaɪ) *vb* **-fies, -fying, -fied.** (*tr*) **1** to resist (a powerful person, authority, etc.) openly and boldly. **2** to elude, esp. in a baffling way: *his actions defy explanation.* **3** *Formal.* to challenge or provoke (someone to do something judged to be impossible); dare: *I defy you to climb that cliff.* **4** *Archaic.* to invite to do battle or combat. [C14: from Old French *desfier*, from *des-* DE- + *fier* to trust, from Latin *fīdere*] ▸ **deˈfier** *n*

deg. *abbrev. for* degree.

dégagé *French.* (degaʒe) *adj* **1** unconstrained in manner; casual; relaxed. **2** uninvolved; detached.

degas (diːˈgæs) *vb* **-gases** *or* **-gasses, -gassing, -gassed. 1** (*tr*) to remove gas from (a container, vacuum tube, liquid, adsorbent, etc.). **2** (*intr*) to lose adsorbed or absorbed gas by desorption. ▸ **deˈgasser** *n*

Degas (ˈdeɪgɑː; *French* dəgɑ) *n* **Hilaire Germain Edgar** (ilɛr ʒɛrmɛ̃ ɛdgar). 1834–1917, French impressionist painter and sculptor, noted for his brilliant draughtsmanship and ability to convey movement, esp. in his studies of horse racing and ballet dancers.

De Gasperi (*Italian* de ˈgasperi) *n* **Alcide** (alˈtʃiːde). 1881–1954, Italian statesman; prime minister (1945–53). An antifascist, he led the Christian Democratic party during World War II from the Vatican City.

de Gaulle (*French* də gol) *n* **Charles** (**André Joseph Marie**) (ʃarl). 1890–1970,

French general and statesman. During World War II, he refused to accept Pétain's armistice with Germany and founded the Free French movement in England (1940). He was head of the provisional governments (1944–46) and, as first president of the Fifth Republic (1959–69), he restored political and economic stability to France.

degauss (diː'gaʊs, -'gɔːs) *vb (tr)* **1** to neutralize the magnetic field of a ship's hull (as a protection against magnetic mines) using equipment producing an opposing magnetic field. **2** another word for **demagnetize.**

degearing (diː'gɪərɪŋ) *n Finance.* the process in which a company replaces some or all of its fixed-interest loan stock with ordinary shares.

degeneracy (dɪ'dʒɛnərəsɪ) *n, pl* **-cies. 1** the act or state of being degenerate. **2** the process of becoming degenerate. **3** *Physics.* the number of degenerate quantum states of a particular orbital, degree of freedom, etc.

degenerate *vb* (dɪ'dʒɛnəˌreɪt). *(intr)* **1** to become degenerate. **2** *Biology.* (of organisms or their parts) to become less specialized or functionally useless. ◆ *adj* (dɪ'dʒɛnərɪt). **3** having declined or deteriorated to a lower mental, moral, or physical level; debased; degraded; corrupt. **4** *Physics.* **4a** (of the constituents of a system) having the same energy but different wave functions. **4b** (of a semiconductor) containing a similar number of electrons in the conduction band to the number of electrons in the conduction band of metals. **4c** (of a resonant device) having two or more modes of equal frequency. **5** (of a code) containing symbols that represent more than one letter, figure, etc. **6** (of a plant or animal) having undergone degeneration. ◆ *n* (dɪ'dʒɛnərɪt). **7** a degenerate person. **[C15:** from Latin *dēgenerāre,* from *dēgener* departing from its kind, ignoble, from DE- + *genus* origin, race] ▸ **de'generately** *adv* ▸ **de'generateness** *n*

degenerate matter *n Astrophysics.* the highly compressed state of a star's matter when its atoms virtually touch in the final stage of its evolution into a white dwarf.

degeneration (dɪˌdʒɛnə'reɪʃən) *n* **1** the process of degenerating. **2** the state of being degenerate. **3** *Biology.* the loss of specialization, function, or structure by organisms and their parts, as in the development of vestigial organs. **4a** impairment or loss of the function and structure of cells or tissues, as by disease or injury, often leading to death (necrosis) of the involved part. **4b** the resulting condition. **5** *Electronics.* negative feedback of a signal.

degenerative (dɪ'dʒɛnəˌreɪtɪv) *adj* (of a disease or condition) getting steadily worse.

degenerative joint disease *n* another name for **osteoarthritis.**

deglutinate (diː'gluːtɪˌneɪt) *vb (tr)* to extract the gluten from (a cereal, esp. wheat). **[C17:** from Latin *dēglūtināre* to unglue, from DE- + *glūtināre,* from *glūten* GLUE] ▸ **deˌgluti'nation** *n*

deglutition (ˌdiːgluː'tɪʃən) *n* the act of swallowing. **[C17:** from French *déglutition,* from Late Latin *dēglūtīre* to swallow down, from DE- + *glutīre* to swallow]

degradable (dɪ'greɪdəbᵊl) *adj* **1** (of waste products, packaging materials, etc.) capable of being decomposed chemically or biologically. See also **biodegradable. 2** capable of being degraded. ▸ **deˌgrada'bility** *n*

degradation (ˌdɛgrə'deɪʃən) *n* **1** the act of degrading or the state of being degraded. **2** a state of degeneration, squalor, or poverty. **3** some act, constraint, etc., that is degrading. **4** the wearing down of the surface of rocks, cliffs, etc., by erosion, weathering, or some other process. **5** *Chem.* a breakdown of a molecule into atoms or smaller molecules. **6** *Physics.* an irreversible process in which the energy available to do work is decreased. **7** *R.C. Church.* the permanent unfrocking of a priest.

degrade (dɪ'greɪd) *vb* **1** *(tr)* to reduce in worth, character, etc.; disgrace; dishonour. **2** (diː'greɪd). *(tr)* to reduce in rank, status, or degree; remove from office; demote. **3** *(tr)* to reduce in strength, quality, intensity, etc. **4** to reduce or be reduced by erosion or down-cutting, as a land surface or bed of a river. Compare **aggrade. 5** *Chem.* to decompose or be decomposed into atoms or smaller molecules. **[C14:** from Late Latin *dēgradāre,* from Latin DE- + *gradus* rank, degree] ▸ **de'grader** *n*

degrading (dɪ'greɪdɪŋ) *adj* causing humiliation; debasing. ▸ **de'gradingly** *adv* ▸ **de'gradingness** *n*

degrease (diː'griːs) *vb (tr)* to remove grease from.

degree (dɪ'griː) *n* **1** a stage in a scale of relative amount or intensity: *a high degree of competence.* **2** an academic award conferred by a university or college on successful completion of a course or as an honorary distinction (**honorary degree**). **3** any of three categories of seriousness of a burn. See **burn**[1] (sense 22). **4** (in the U.S.) any of the categories into which a crime is divided according to its seriousness: *first-degree murder.* **5** *Genealogy.* a step in a line of descent, used as a measure of the closeness of a blood relationship. **6** *Grammar.* any of the forms of an adjective used to indicate relative amount or intensity: in English they are *positive, comparative,* and *superlative.* **7** *Music.* any note of a diatonic scale relative to the other notes in that scale: *D is the second degree of the scale of C major.* **8** a unit of temperature on a specified scale: *the normal body temperature of man is 36.8 degrees Celsius.* Symbol: ° See also **Celsius scale, Fahrenheit scale. 9** a measure of angle equal to one three-hundred-and-sixtieth of the angle traced by one complete revolution of a line about one of its ends. Symbol: ° See also **minute**[1] (sense 2), **second**[2] (sense 2). Compare **radian. 10a** a unit of latitude or longitude, divided into 60 minutes, used to define points on the earth's surface or on the celestial sphere. **10b** a point or line defined by units of latitude and/or longitude. Symbol: ° **11** a unit on any of several scales of measurement, as for alcohol content or specific gravity. Symbol: ° **12** *Maths.* **12a** the highest power or the sum of the powers of any term in a polynomial or by itself: $x^4 + x + 3$ *and* xyz^2 *are of the fourth degree.* **12b** the greatest power of the highest order derivative in a differential equation. **13** *Obsolete.* a step; rung. **14** *Archaic.* a stage in social status or rank. **15 by degrees.** little by little; gradually. **16 to a degree.** somewhat; rather. **17 degrees of frost.** See **frost** (sense 3). **[C13:** from Old French *degre,* from Latin DE- + *gradus* step, GRADE] ▸ **de'greeless** *adj*

degree day *n* a day on which university degrees are conferred.

degree-day *n* a unit used in estimating fuel requirements in heating buildings. It is equal to a fall of temperature of 1 degree below the mean outside temperature (usually taken as 18°C) for one day.

degree of freedom *n* **1** *Physics.* one of the minimum number of parameters necessary to describe a state or property of a system. **2** one of the independent components of motion (translation, vibration, and rotation) of an atom or molecule. **3** *Chem.* one of a number of intensive properties that can be independently varied without changing the number of phases in a system. See also **phase rule. 4** *Statistics.* one of the independent unrestricted random variables constituting a statistic.

degression (dɪ'grɛʃən) *n* **1** a decrease by stages. **2** a gradual decrease in the tax rate on amounts below a specified sum. **[C15:** from Medieval Latin *dēgressiō* descent, from Latin *dēgredī* to go down, from DE- + *gradī* to take steps, go]

degust (dɪ'gʌst) *or* **degustate** (dɪ'gʌsteɪt) *vb (tr) Rare.* to taste, esp. with care or relish; savour. **[C17:** from Latin *dēgustāre,* from *gustāre,* from *gustus* a tasting, taste] ▸ **degustation** (ˌdiːgʌ'steɪʃən) *n*

de Havilland (də 'hævɪlənd) *n* Sir **Geoffrey.** 1882–1965, British aircraft designer. He produced many military aircraft and the first jet airliners.

dehisce (dɪ'hɪs) *vb (intr)* (of fruits, anthers, etc.) to burst open spontaneously, releasing seeds, pollen, etc. **[C17:** from Latin *dēhiscere* to split open, from DE- + *hiscere* to yawn, gape]

dehiscent (dɪ'hɪsənt) *adj* (of fruits, anthers, etc.) opening spontaneously to release seeds or pollen. ▸ **de'hiscence** *n*

dehorn (diː'hɔːn) *vb (tr)* **1** to remove or prevent the growth of the horns of (cattle, sheep, or goats). **2** to cut back (the larger limbs of a tree) drastically. ▸ **de'horner** *n*

Dehra Dun ('dɛərə 'duːn) *n* a city in N India, in NW Uttar Pradesh: Indian military academy (1932). Pop.: 270 159 (1991).

dehumanize *or* **dehumanise** (diː'hjuːməˌnaɪz) *vb (tr)* **1** to deprive of human qualities. **2** to render mechanical, artificial, or routine. ▸ **deˌhumani'zation** *or* **deˌhumani'sation** *n*

dehumidifier (ˌdiːhjuː'mɪdɪˌfaɪə) *n* a device for reducing the moisture content of the atmosphere.

dehumidify (ˌdiːhjuː'mɪdɪˌfaɪ) *vb* **-fies, -fying, -fied.** *(tr)* to remove water from (something, esp. the air). ▸ **ˌdehuˌmidifi'cation** *n*

dehydrate (diː'haɪdreɪt, ˌdiːhaɪ'dreɪt) *vb* **1** to lose or cause to lose water; make or become anhydrous. **2** to lose or cause to lose hydrogen atoms and oxygen atoms in the proportions in which they occur in water, as in a chemical reaction. **3** to lose or deprive of water, as the body or tissues. ▸ **ˌdehy'dration** *n* ▸ **de'hydrator** *n*

dehydrogenase (diː'haɪdrədʒəˌneɪz) *n* an enzyme, such as any of the respiratory enzymes, that activates oxidation-reduction reactions by transferring hydrogen from substrate to acceptor.

dehydrogenate (diː'haɪdrədʒəˌneɪt), **dehydrogenize,** *or* **dehydrogenise** (diː'haɪdrədʒəˌnaɪz) *vb (tr)* to remove hydrogen from. ▸ **deˌhydroge'nation, deˌhydrogeni'zation,** *or* **deˌhydrogeni'sation** *n*

dehydroretinol (diːˌhaɪdrəʊ'rɛtɪnɒl) *n* another name for **vitamin** $\mathbf{A_2}$.

dehypnotize *or* **dehypnotise** (diː'hɪpnəˌtaɪz) *vb (tr)* to bring out of the hypnotic state. ▸ **deˌhypnoti'zation** *or* **deˌhypnoti'sation** *n*

Deianira (ˌdiːə'naɪərə, ˌdeɪə-) *n Greek myth.* a sister of Meleager and wife of Hercules. She unintentionally killed Hercules by dipping his tunic in the poisonous blood of the Centaur Nessus, thinking it to be a love charm.

de-ice (diː'aɪs) *vb* to free or be freed of ice.

de-icer (diː'aɪsə) *n* **1** a mechanical or thermal device designed to melt or stop the formation of ice on an aircraft, usually fitted to the aerofoil surfaces. Compare **anti-icer. 2** a chemical or other substance used for this purpose, esp. an aerosol that can be sprayed on car windscreens to remove ice or frost.

deicide ('diːɪˌsaɪd) *n* **1** the act of killing a god. **2** a person who kills a god. **[C17:** from ecclesiastical Latin *deicida,* from Latin *deus* god; see -CIDE] ▸ **ˌdei'cidal** *adj*

deictic ('daɪktɪk) *adj* **1** *Logic.* proving by direct argument. Compare **elenctic.** ◆ *n* **2** another word for **indexical** (sense 2). **[C17:** from Greek *deiktikos* concerning proof, from *deiknunai* to show] ▸ **'deictically** *adv*

deid (diːd) *adj* a Scot. word for **dead.**

deif (diːf) *adj* a Scot. word for **deaf.**

deific (diː'ɪfɪk, deɪ-) *adj* **1** making divine or exalting to the position of a god. **2** divine or godlike.

deification (ˌdiːɪfɪ'keɪʃən, ˌdeɪ-) *n* **1** the act or process of exalting to the position of a god. **2** the state or condition of being deified.

deiform ('diːɪˌfɔːm) *adj* having the form or appearance of a god; sacred or divine.

deify ('diːɪˌfaɪ, 'deɪɪ-) *vb* **-fies, -fying, -fied.** *(tr)* **1** to exalt to the position of a god or personify as a god. **2** to accord divine honour or worship to. **3** to exalt in an extreme way; idealize. **[C14:** from Old French *deifier,* from Late Latin *deificāre,* from Latin *deus* god + *facere* to make] ▸ **'deiˌfier** *n*

Deighton ('deɪtᵊn) *n* **Len.** born 1929, British thriller writer. His books include *The Ipcress File* (1962), *Bomber* (1970), and the trilogy *Berlin Game, Mexico Set,* and *London Match* (1983–85).

deign (deɪn) *vb* **1** *(intr)* to think it fit or worthy of oneself (to do something); condescend: *he will not deign to speak to us.* **2** *(tr) Archaic.* to vouchsafe: *he deigned no reply.* **[C13:** from Old French *deignier,* from Latin *dignārī* to consider worthy, from *dignus* worthy]

Dei gratia *Latin.* ('diːɪ 'greɪʃɪə, 'deɪɪ 'grɑːtɪə) *adv* by the grace of God.

deil (diːl) *n* a Scot. word for **devil.**

Deimos ('deɪmɒs) *n* the smaller of the two satellites of Mars and the more distant from the planet. Approximate diameter: 13 km. Compare **Phobos.**

deindex (diː'ɪndɛks) *vb (tr)* to cause to become no longer index-linked.

deindividuation (diːˌɪndɪvɪdjuˈeɪʃən) *n Psychol.* the loss of a person's sense of individuality and personal responsibility.

deindustrialization *or* **deindustrialisation** (ˌdiːɪnˌdʌstrɪəlaɪˈzeɪʃən) *n* the decline in importance of manufacturing industry in the economy of a nation or area. ▸ **ˌdeinˈdustrialˌize** *or* **ˌdeinˈdustrialˌise** *vb*

de-ionize *or* **de-ionise** (diːˈaɪəˌnaɪz) *vb (tr)* to remove ions from (water, etc.), esp. by ion exchange. ▸ **deˌioniˈzation** *or* **deˌioniˈsation** *n*

deipnosophist (daɪpˈnɒsəfɪst) *n Rare.* a person who is a master of dinner-table conversation. [C17: from Greek *deipnosophistai,* title of a Greek work by Athenaeus (3rd century), describing learned discussions at a banquet, from *deipnon* meal + *sophistai* wise men; see SOPHIST]

Deirdre (ˈdɪədrɪ) *n Irish myth.* a beautiful girl who was raised by Conchobar to be his wife but eloped with Naoise. When Conchobar treacherously killed Naoise she took her own life: often used to symbolize Ireland. See also **Naoise.**

deism (ˈdiːɪzəm, ˈdeɪ-) *n* belief in the existence of God based solely on natural reason, without reference to revelation. Compare **theism.** [C17: from French *déisme,* from Latin *deus* god] ▸ **ˈdeist** *n, adj* ▸ **deˈistic** *or* **deˈistical** *adj* ▸ **deˈistically** *adv*

deity (ˈdiːɪtɪ, ˈdeɪ-) *n, pl* **-ties. 1** a god or goddess. **2** the state of being divine; godhead. **3** the rank, status, or position of a god. **4** the nature or character of God. [C14: from Old French, from Late Latin *deitās,* from Latin *deus* god]

Deity (ˈdiːɪtɪ, ˈdeɪ-) *n* **the.** the Supreme Being; God.

deixis (ˈdaɪksɪs) *n Grammar.* the use or reference of a deictic word. [C20: from Greek, from *deiknunai* to show]

déjà vu (ˈdeɪʒæ ˈvuː; *French* deʒa vy) *n* the experience of perceiving a new situation as if it had occurred before. It is sometimes associated with exhaustion or certain types of mental disorder. [literally: already seen]

deject (dɪˈdʒɛkt) *vb* **1** *(tr)* to have a depressing effect on; dispirit; dishearten. ◆ *adj* **2** *Archaic.* downcast; dejected. [C15: from Latin *dēicere* to cast down, from DE- + *iacere* to throw]

dejecta (dɪˈdʒɛktə) *pl n* waste products excreted through the anus; faeces. [C19: New Latin: things cast down; see DEJECT]

dejected (dɪˈdʒɛktɪd) *adj* miserable; despondent; downhearted. ▸ **deˈjectedly** *adv* ▸ **deˈjectedness** *n*

dejection (dɪˈdʒɛkʃən) *n* **1** lowness of spirits; depression; melancholy. **2a** faecal matter evacuated from the bowels; excrement. **2b** the act of defecating; defecation.

de jure (deɪ ˈdʒʊəreɪ) *adv* according to law; by right; legally. Compare **de facto.** [Latin]

deka- *or* **dek-** *combining form.* variants of **deca-.**

Dekker *or* **Decker** (ˈdɛkə) *n* **Thomas.** ?1572–?1632, English dramatist and pamphleteer, noted particularly for his comedy *The Shoemaker's Holiday* (1600) and his satirical pamphlet *The Gull's Hornbook* (1609).

dekko (ˈdɛkəʊ) *n, pl* **-kos.** *Brit. slang.* a look; glance; view (esp. in the phrase **take a dekko (at)**). [C19: from Hindi *dekho!* look! from *dekhnā* to see]

de Klerk (də ˈklɜːk) *n* **F(rederik) W(illem).** born 1936, South African statesman; president (1989–94), second executive deputy president (1994–97). In 1990 he legalized the ANC and released Nelson Mandela from prison, and initiated the abolition of apartheid: Nobel peace prize 1993 jointly with Mandela.

de Kooning (də ˈkuːnɪŋ) *n* **Willem.** See (Willem de) **Kooning.**

del (dɛl) *n Maths.* the differential operator $\boldsymbol{i}(\partial/\partial x) + \boldsymbol{j}(\partial/\partial y) + \boldsymbol{k}(\partial/\partial z)$, where ***i, j,*** and ***k*** are unit vectors in the *x, y,* and *z* directions. Symbol: ∇ Also called: **nabla.**

del. *abbrev. for* delegate.

Del. *abbrev. for* Delaware.

de la Beche (də læ biːtʃ) *n* **Henry.** 1796–1855, English geologist. His work led to the founding of the Geological Survey (1835).

Delacroix (*French* dəlakrwa) *n* **(Ferdinand Victor) Eugène** (øʒɛn). 1798–1863, French romantic painter whose use of colour and free composition influenced impressionism. His paintings of historical and contemporary scenes include *The Massacre at Chios* (1824).

Delagoa Bay (ˌdɛləˈgəʊə) *n* an inlet of the Indian Ocean, in S Mozambique. Official name: **Baía de Lourenço Marques.**

delaine (dəˈleɪn) *n* a sheer wool or wool and cotton fabric. [C19: from French *mousseline de laine* muslin of wool]

de la Mare (də lɑː mɛə) *n* **Walter (John).** 1873–1956, English poet and novelist, noted esp. for his evocative verse for children. His works include the volumes of poetry *The Listeners and Other Poems* (1912) and *Peacock Pie* (1913) and the novel *Memoirs of a Midget* (1921).

delaminate (diːˈlæmɪˌneɪt) *vb* to divide or cause to divide into thin layers. ▸ **deˌlamiˈnation** *n*

Delaroche (*French* dəlarɔʃ) *n* **(Hippolyte) Paul.** 1797–1859, French painter of portraits and sentimental historical scenes, such as *The Children of Edward IV in the Tower* (1830).

delate (dɪˈleɪt) *vb (tr)* **1** (formerly) to bring a charge against; denounce; impeach. **2** *Rare.* to report (an offence, etc.). **3** *Obsolete.* to make known or public. [C16: from Latin *dēlātus,* from *dēferre* to bring down, report, indict, from DE- + *ferre* to bear] ▸ **deˈlation** *n* ▸ **deˈlator** *n*

Delaunay (*French* dəlonɛ) *n* **Robert** (rɔbɛr). 1885–1941, French painter, whose abstract use of colour characterized Orphism, an attempt to introduce more colour into austere forms of Cubism.

Delaware[1] (ˈdɛləˌwɛə) *n* **1** *(pl* **-wares** *or* **-ware)** a member of a North American Indian people formerly living near the Delaware River. **2** the language of this people, belonging to the Algonquian family.

Delaware[2] (ˈdɛləˌwɛə) *n* **1** a state of the northeastern U.S., on the Delmarva Peninsula: mostly flat and low-lying, with hills in the extreme north and cypress swamps in the extreme south. Capital: Dover. Pop.: 731 581 (1997 est.). Area: 5004 sq. km (1932 sq. miles). Abbrevs.: **Del.** or (with zip code) **DE 2** a river in the northeastern U.S., rising in the Catskill Mountains and flowing south into **Delaware Bay,** an inlet of the Atlantic. Length 660 km (410 miles). ▸ **ˌDelaˈwarean** *adj*

Delaware[3] (ˈdɛləˌwɛə) *n* an American variety of grape that has sweet light red fruit.

De La Warr (ˈdɛləˌwɛə) *n* **Baron,** title of *Thomas West,* known as *Lord Delaware.* 1577–1618, English administrator in America; first governor of Virginia (1610).

delay (dɪˈleɪ) *vb* **1** *(tr)* to put off to a later time; defer. **2** *(tr)* to slow up, hinder, or cause to be late; detain. **3** *(intr)* to be irresolute or put off doing something; procrastinate. **4** *(intr)* to linger; dawdle. ◆ *n* **5** the act or an instance of delaying or being delayed. **6** the interval between one event and another; lull; interlude. [C13: from Old French *delaier,* from *des-* off + *laier,* variant of *laissier* to leave, from Latin *laxāre* to loosen, from *laxus* slack, LAX] ▸ **deˈlayer** *n*

delayed action *or* **delay action** *n* **a** a device for operating a mechanism, such as a camera shutter, a short time after setting. **b** *(as modifier): a delayed-action fuse.*

delayed drop *n Aeronautics.* a parachute descent with the opening of the parachute delayed, usually for a predetermined period.

delayed neutron *n* a neutron produced in a nuclear reactor by the breakdown of a fission product and released a short time after neutrons produced in the primary process.

delayed opening *n Aeronautics.* the automatic opening of a parachute after a predetermined delay to allow the parachutist to reach a particular height.

delayering (diːˈleɪərɪŋ) *n* the process of pruning the administrative structure of a large organization by reducing the number of tiers in its hierarchy.

delaying action *n* a measure or measures taken to gain time, as when weaker military forces harass the advance of a superior enemy without coming to a pitched battle.

delay line *n* a device in which a known delay time is introduced in the transmission of a signal. An **acoustic delay line** delays a sound wave by circulating it through a liquid or solid medium.

Delbrück (delˈbryk) *n* **Max.** 1906–81, U.S. molecular biologist, born in Germany. Noted for his work on bacteriophages, he shared the Nobel prize for physiology or medicine in 1969.

dele (ˈdiːlɪ) *n, pl* **deles. 1** a sign (δ) indicating that typeset matter is to be deleted. Compare **stet.** ◆ *vb* **deles, deleing, deled. 2** *(tr)* to mark (matter to be deleted) with a dele. [C18: from Latin: delete (imperative), from *dēlēre* to destroy, obliterate; see DELETE]

delectable (dɪˈlɛktəbᵊl) *adj* highly enjoyable, esp. pleasing to the taste; delightful. [C14: from Latin *dēlectābilis,* from *dēlectāre* to DELIGHT] ▸ **deˈlectableness** *or* **deˌlectaˈbility** *n* ▸ **deˈlectably** *adv*

delectation (ˌdiːlɛkˈteɪʃən) *n* pleasure; enjoyment.

Deledda (*Italian* deˈlɛdda) *n* **Grazia** (ˈgrattsja). 1875–1936, Italian novelist, noted for works, such as *La Madre* (1920), on peasant life in Sardinia: Nobel prize for literature 1926.

delegacy (ˈdɛlɪgəsɪ) *n, pl* **-cies. 1** a less common word for **delegation** (senses 1, 2). **2a** an elected standing committee at some British universities. **2b** a department or institute of a university: *a delegacy of Education.*

delegate *n* (ˈdɛlɪˌgeɪt, -gɪt). **1** a person chosen or elected to act for or represent another or others, esp. at a conference or meeting. **2** *U.S. government.* a representative of a territory in the U.S. House of Representatives. ◆ *vb* (ˈdɛlɪˌgeɪt). **3** to give or commit (duties, powers, etc.) to another as agent or representative; depute. **4** *(tr)* to send, authorize, or elect (a person) as agent or representative. **5** *(tr) Chiefly U.S.* to assign (a person owing a debt to oneself) to one's creditor in substitution for oneself. [C14: from Latin *dēlēgāre* to send on a mission, from *lēgāre* to send, depute; see LEGATE] ▸ **delegable** (ˈdɛlɪgəbᵊl) *adj*

delegation (ˌdɛlɪˈgeɪʃən) *n* **1** a person or group chosen to represent another or others. **2** the act of delegating or state of being delegated. **3** *U.S. politics.* all the members of Congress from one state.

de Lesseps (*French* də lɛsɛps) *n* **Vicomte.** title of (Ferdinand Marie) **Lesseps.**

delete (dɪˈliːt) *vb (tr)* to remove (something printed or written); erase; cancel; strike out. [C17: from Latin *dēlēre* to destroy, obliterate]

deleterious (ˌdɛlɪˈtɪərɪəs) *adj* harmful; injurious; hurtful. [C17: from New Latin *dēlētērius,* from Greek *dēlētērios* injurious, destructive, from *dēleisthai* to hurt] ▸ **ˌdeleˈteriously** *adv* ▸ **ˌdeleˈteriousness** *n*

deletion (dɪˈliːʃən) *n* **1** the act of deleting or fact of being deleted. **2** a deleted passage, word, etc., in a piece of text. **3** the loss or absence of a section of a chromosome.

Delft (dɛlft) *n* **1** a town in the SW Netherlands, in South Holland province. Pop.: 91 941 (1994). **2** Also called: **ˈdelftware.** tin-glazed earthenware made in Delft since the 17th century, typically having blue decoration on a white ground. **3** a similar earthenware made in England.

Delgado (dɛlˈgɑːdəʊ) *n* **Cape.** a headland on the extreme NE coast of Mozambique.

Delhi (ˈdɛlɪ) *n* **1** the capital of India, in the N central part, on the Jumna river: consists of **Old Delhi** (a walled city reconstructed in 1639 on the site of former cities of Delhi, which date from the 15th century B.C.) and **New Delhi** to the south, chosen as the capital in 1912, replacing Calcutta; university (1922). Pop.: (total) 9 882 000 (1995). **2** an administrative division (National Capital Territory) of N India, formerly a Union Territory. Capital: Delhi. Area: 1483 sq. km (572 sq. miles). Pop.: 10 865 000 (1994 est.).

deli (ˈdɛlɪ) *n, pl* **delis.** an informal word for **delicatessen.**

Delian (ˈdiːlɪən) *n* **1** a native or inhabitant of Delos. ◆ *adj* **2** of or relating to Delos. **3** of or relating to Delius.

Delian League *or* **Confederacy** *n* an alliance of ancient Greek states formed in 478–77 B.C. to fight Persia.

deliberate *adj* (dɪˈlɪbərɪt). **1** carefully thought out in advance; planned; studied; intentional: *a deliberate insult.* **2** careful or unhurried in speech or action: *a deliberate pace.* ◆ *vb* (dɪˈlɪbəˌreɪt). **3** to consider (something) deeply; ponder; think over. [C15: from Latin *dēlīberāre* to consider well, from *lībrāre* to weigh, from *lībra* scales] ▸ **deˈliberately** *adv* ▸ **deˈliberateness** *n* ▸ **deˈliberˌator** *n*

deliberation (dɪˌlɪbəˈreɪʃən) *n* **1** thoughtful, careful, or lengthy consideration. **2** (*often pl*) formal discussion and debate, as of a committee, jury, etc. **3** care, thoughtfulness, or absence of hurry, esp. in movement or speech.

deliberative (dɪˈlɪbərətɪv) *adj* **1** involved in, organized for, or having the function of deliberating: *a deliberative assembly.* **2** characterized by or resulting from deliberation: *a deliberative conclusion.* ▸ **deˈliberatively** *adv* ▸ **deˈliberativeness** *n*

Delibes (*French* dəlib) *n* (**Clément Philibert**) **Léo** (leo). 1836–91, French composer, noted particularly for his ballets *Coppélia* (1870) and *Sylvia* (1876), and the opera *Lakmé* (1883).

delicacy (ˈdɛlɪkəsɪ) *n, pl* **-cies. 1** fine or subtle quality, character, construction, etc.: *delicacy of craftsmanship.* **2** fragile, soft, or graceful beauty. **3** something that is considered choice to eat, such as caviar. **4** fragile construction or constitution; frailty. **5** refinement of feeling, manner, or appreciation: *the delicacy of the orchestra's playing.* **6** fussy or squeamish refinement, esp. in matters of taste, propriety, etc. **7** need for tactful or sensitive handling. **8** accuracy or sensitivity of response or operation, as of an instrument. **9** (in systemic grammar) the level of detail at which a linguistic description is made; the degree of fine distinction in a linguistic description. **10** *Obsolete.* gratification, luxury, or voluptuousness.

delicate (ˈdɛlɪkɪt) *adj* **1** exquisite, fine, or subtle in quality, character, construction, etc. **2** having a soft or fragile beauty. **3** (of colour, tone, taste, etc.) pleasantly subtle, soft, or faint. **4** easily damaged or injured; lacking robustness, esp. in health; fragile. **5** precise, skilled, or sensitive in action or operation: *a delicate mechanism.* **6** requiring tact and diplomacy. **7** sensitive in feeling or manner; showing regard for the feelings of others. **8** excessively refined; squeamish. ◆ *n* **9** *Archaic.* a delicacy; dainty. [C14: from Latin *dēlicātus* affording pleasure, from *dēliciae* (pl) delight, pleasure; see DELICIOUS] ▸ **ˈdelicately** *adv* ▸ **ˈdelicateness** *n*

delicatessen (ˌdɛlɪkəˈtɛsᵊn) *n* **1** a shop selling various foods, esp. unusual or imported foods, already cooked or prepared. **2** such foods. [C19: from German *Delikatessen,* literally: delicacies, pl of *Delikatesse* a delicacy, from French *délicatesse*]

delicious (dɪˈlɪʃəs) *adj* **1** very appealing to the senses, esp. to the taste or smell. **2** extremely enjoyable or entertaining: *a delicious joke.* [C13: from Old French, from Late Latin *dēliciōsus,* from Latin *dēliciae* delights, charms, from *dēlicere* to entice; see DELIGHT] ▸ **deˈliciously** *adv* ▸ **deˈliciousness** *n*

delict (dɪˈlɪkt, ˈdiːlɪkt) *n* **1** *Law, chiefly Scots.* a wrongful act for which the person injured has the right to a civil remedy. See also **tort. 2** *Roman law.* a civil wrong redressable by compensation or punitive damages. [C16: from Latin *dēlictum* a fault, crime, from *dēlinquere* to fail, do wrong; see DELINQUENCY]

delight (dɪˈlaɪt) *vb* **1** (*tr*) to please greatly. **2** (*intr;* foll. by *in*) to take great pleasure (in). ◆ *n* **3** extreme pleasure or satisfaction; joy. **4** something that causes this: *music was always his delight.* [C13: from Old French *delit,* from *deleitier* to please, from Latin *dēlectāre,* from *dēlicere* to allure, from DE- + *lacere* to entice; see DELICIOUS; English spelling influenced by *light*] ▸ **deˈlighter** *n*

delighted (dɪˈlaɪtɪd) *adj* **1** (often foll. by an infinitive) extremely pleased (to do something): *I'm delighted to hear it!* ◆ *sentence substitute.* **2** I should be delighted to! ▸ **deˈlightedly** *adv* ▸ **deˈlightedness** *n*

delightful (dɪˈlaɪtfʊl) *adj* giving great delight; very pleasing, beautiful, charming, etc. ▸ **deˈlightfully** *adv* ▸ **deˈlightfulness** *n*

Delilah (dɪˈlaɪlə) *n* **1** Samson's Philistine mistress, who deprived him of his strength by cutting off his hair (Judges 16:4–22). **2** a voluptuous and treacherous woman; temptress.

delimit (diːˈlɪmɪt) *or* **delimitate** *vb* (*tr*) to mark or prescribe the limits or boundaries of; demarcate. ▸ **deˌlimiˈtation** *n* ▸ **deˈlimitative** *adj*

delineate (dɪˈlɪnɪˌeɪt) *vb* (*tr*) **1** to trace the shape or outline of; sketch. **2** to represent pictorially, as by making a chart or diagram; depict. **3** to portray in words, esp. with detail and precision; describe. [C16: from Latin *dēlīneāre* to sketch out, from *līnea* LINE[1]] ▸ **deˈlineable** *adj* ▸ **deˌlineˈation** *n* ▸ **deˈlineative** *adj*

delineator (dɪˈlɪnɪˌeɪtə) *n* a tailor's pattern, adjustable for different sizes.

delinquency (dɪˈlɪŋkwənsɪ) *n, pl* **-cies. 1** an offence or misdeed, usually of a minor nature, esp. one committed by a young person. See **juvenile delinquency. 2** failure or negligence in duty or obligation; dereliction. **3** a delinquent nature or delinquent behaviour. [C17: from Late Latin *dēlinquentia* a fault, offence, from Latin *dēlinquere* to transgress, from DE- + *linquere* to forsake]

delinquent (dɪˈlɪŋkwənt) *n* **1** someone, esp. a young person, guilty of delinquency. See **juvenile delinquent. 2** *Archaic.* a person who fails in an obligation or duty. ◆ *adj* **3** guilty of an offence or misdeed, esp. one of a minor nature. **4** failing in or neglectful of duty or obligation. [C17: from Latin *dēlinquēns* offending; see DELINQUENCY] ▸ **deˈlinquently** *adv*

deliquesce (ˌdɛlɪˈkwɛs) *vb* (*intr*) **1** (esp. of certain salts) to dissolve gradually in water absorbed from the air. **2** (of a plant stem) to form many branches. [C18: from Latin *dēliquēscere* to melt away, become liquid, from DE- + *liquēscere* to melt, from *liquēre* to be liquid]

deliquescence (ˌdɛlɪˈkwɛsᵊns) *n* **1** the process of deliquescing. **2** a solution formed when a solid or liquid deliquesces. ▸ ˌ**deliˈquescent** *adj*

delirious (dɪˈlɪrɪəs) *adj* **1** affected with delirium. **2** wildly excited, esp. with joy or enthusiasm. ▸ **deˈliriously** *adv* ▸ **deˈliriousness** *n*

delirium (dɪˈlɪrɪəm) *n, pl* **-liriums, -liria** (-ˈlɪrɪə). **1** a state of excitement and mental confusion, often accompanied by hallucinations, caused by high fever, poisoning, brain injury, etc. **2** violent excitement or emotion; frenzy. [C16: from Latin: madness, from *dēlīrāre,* literally: to swerve from a furrow, hence be crazy, from DE- + *līra* ridge, furrow] ▸ **deˈliriant** *adj*

delirium tremens (ˈtrɛmɛnz, ˈtriː-) *n* a severe psychotic condition occurring in some persons with chronic alcoholism, characterized by delirium, tremor, anxiety, and vivid hallucinations. Abbrevs.: **DT's** (informal), **dt.** [C19: New Latin, literally: trembling delirium]

delitescence (ˌdɛlɪˈtɛsᵊns) *n* the sudden disappearance of a lesion or of the signs and symptoms of a disease. [C18: from Latin *dēlitēscens,* present participle of *dēlitēscere* to lurk, from *latēscere* to become hidden, from *latēre* to be hidden; see LATENT] ▸ ˌ**deliˈtescent** *adj*

Delius (ˈdiːlɪəs) *n* **Frederick.** 1862–1934, English composer, who drew inspiration from folk tunes and the sounds of nature. His works include the opera *A Village Romeo and Juliet* (1901), *A Mass of Life* (1905), and the orchestral variations *Brigg Fair* (1907).

deliver (dɪˈlɪvə) *vb* (*mainly tr*) **1** to carry (goods, etc.) to a destination, esp. to carry and distribute (goods, mail, etc.) to several places: *to deliver letters; our local butcher delivers.* **2** (often foll. by *over* or *up*) to hand over, transfer, or surrender. **3** (often foll. by *from*) to release or rescue (from captivity, harm, corruption, etc.). **4** (*also intr*) **4a** to aid in the birth of (offspring). **4b** to give birth to (offspring). **4c** (usually foll. by *of*) to aid or assist (a female) in the birth (of offspring). **4d** (*passive;* foll. by *of*) to give birth (to offspring). **5** to utter or present (a speech, oration, idea, etc.). **6** short for **deliver the goods:** see sense 11, below. **7** to utter (an exclamation, noise, etc.): *to deliver a cry of exultation.* **8** to discharge or release (something, such as a blow or shot) suddenly. **9** *Chiefly U.S.* to cause (voters, constituencies, etc.) to support a given candidate, cause, etc.: *can you deliver the Bronx?* **10 deliver oneself of.** to speak with deliberation or at length: *to deliver oneself of a speech.* **11 deliver the goods.** *Informal.* to produce or perform something promised or expected. [C13: from Old French *delivrer,* from Late Latin *dēlīberāre* to set free, from Latin DE- + *līberāre* to free] ▸ **deˈliverable** *adj* ▸ **deˌliveraˈbility** *n* ▸ **deˈliverer** *n*

deliverance (dɪˈlɪvərəns) *n* **1** a formal pronouncement or expression of opinion. **2** rescue from moral corruption or evil; salvation. **3** another word for **delivery** (senses 3–5).

delivery (dɪˈlɪvərɪ) *n, pl* **-eries. 1a** the act of delivering or distributing goods, mail, etc. **1b** something that is delivered. **1c** (*as modifier*): *a delivery service.* **2** the act of giving birth to a child: *she had an easy delivery.* **3** manner or style of utterance, esp. in public speaking or recitation: *the chairman had a clear delivery.* **4** the act of giving or transferring or the state of being given or transferred. **5** the act of rescuing or state of being rescued; liberation. **6** *Sport.* **6a** the act or manner of bowling or throwing a ball. **6b** the ball so delivered: *a fast delivery.* **7** an actual or symbolic handing over of property, a deed, etc. **8** the discharge rate of a compressor or pump.

delivery van *n* a small van used esp. for delivery rounds. U.S. and Canadian name: **panel truck.**

dell (dɛl) *n* a small, esp. wooded hollow. [Old English; related to Middle Low German *delle* valley; compare DALE]

della Robbia (*Italian* ˈdɛlla ˈrobbja) *n* See (Luca della) **Robbia.**

Deller (ˈdɛlə) *n* **Alfred** (**George**). 1912–79, British countertenor.

Del Mar (dɛl ˈmɑː) *n* **Norman.** 1919–94, British conductor, associated esp. with 20th-century British music.

Delmarva Peninsula (dɛlˈmɑːvə) *n* a peninsula of the northeast U.S., between Chesapeake Bay and the Atlantic.

delocalize *or* **delocalise** (diːˈləukᵊˌlaɪz) *vb* (*tr*) **1** to remove from the usual locality. **2** to free from local influences. ▸ **deˌlocaliˈzation** *or* **deˌlocaliˈsation** *n*

Delorme (*French* dəlɔrm) *or* **de l'Orme** *n* **Philibert** (filibɛr). ?1510–70, French Renaissance architect of the Tuileries, Paris.

Delors (dəlɔː) *n* **Jacques** (**Lucien Jean**). born 1925, French politician and economist, President of the European Commission (1985–94): originator of the **Delors plan** for closer European union.

Delos (ˈdiːlɒs) *n* a Greek island in the SW Aegean Sea, in the Cyclades: a commercial centre in ancient times; the legendary birthplace of Apollo and Artemis. Area: about 5 sq. km (2 sq. miles). Modern Greek name: **Dhílos.**

de los Angeles (*Spanish* de los ˈaŋxeles) *n* **Victoria** (bikˈtorja). born 1923, Spanish soprano.

delouse (diːˈlaus, -ˈlauz) *vb* (*tr*) to rid (a person or animal) of lice as a sanitary measure.

Delphi (ˈdɛlfɪ) *n* an ancient Greek city on the S slopes of Mount Parnassus: site of the most famous oracle of Apollo.

Delphic (ˈdɛlfɪk) *or* **Delphian** *adj* **1** of or relating to Delphi or its oracle or temple. **2** obscure or ambiguous.

Delphic oracle *n* the oracle of Apollo at Delphi that gave answers held by the ancient Greeks to be of great authority but also noted for their ambiguity. Related word: **Pythian.**

delphinium (dɛlˈfɪnɪəm) *n, pl* **-iums** *or* **-ia** (-ɪə). any ranunculaceous plant of the genus *Delphinium:* many varieties are cultivated as garden plants for their spikes of blue, pink, or white spurred flowers. See also **larkspur.** [C17: New Latin, from Greek *delphinion* larkspur, from *delphis* DOLPHIN, referring to the shape of the nectary]

Delphinus (dɛlˈfaɪnəs) *n, Latin genitive* **Delphini** (dɛlˈfaɪnaɪ). a small constellation in the N hemisphere, between Pegasus and Sagitta. [C17: from Latin: DOLPHIN]

Delphi technique *n* a forecasting or decision-making technique that makes use of written questionnaires to eliminate the influence of personal relationships and the domination of committees by strong personalities.

Delsarte system (ˈdɛlsɑːt) *n* a method of teaching drama and dancing based on the exercises of Alexandre Delsarte (1811–71), famous teacher at the Paris Conservatoire.

del Sarto (*Italian* dɛl 'sarto) *n* See (Andrea del) **Sarto.**

delta ('dɛltə) *n* **1** the fourth letter in the Greek alphabet (Δ or δ), a consonant transliterated as *d*. **2** an object resembling a capital delta in shape. **3** (*cap. when part of name*) the flat alluvial area at the mouth of some rivers where the mainstream splits up into several distributaries: *the Mississippi Delta.* **4** *Maths.* a finite increment in a variable. [C16: via Latin from Greek, of Semitic origin; compare Hebrew *dāleth*] ▸ **deltaic** (dɛl'teɪɪk) *or* **'deltic** *adj*

Delta ('dɛltə) *n* **1** (*foll. by the genitive case of a specified constellation*) usually the fourth brightest star in a constellation. **2** any of a group of U.S. launch vehicles used to put unmanned satellites into orbit. **3** *Communications.* a code word for the letter *d*.

delta connection *n* a connection used in a three-phase electrical system in which three elements in series form a triangle, the supply being input and output at the three junctions. Compare **star connection.**

delta iron *n* an allotrope of iron that exists between 1400°C and the melting point of iron and has the same structure as alpha iron.

delta particle *n Physics.* a very short-lived hyperon.

delta ray *n* a particle, esp. an electron, ejected from matter by ionizing radiation.

delta rhythm *or* **wave** *n Physiol.* the normal electrical activity of the cerebral cortex during deep sleep, occurring at a frequency of 1 to 4 hertz and detectable with an electroencephalograph. See also **brain wave.**

delta stock *n* any of the fourth rank of active securities on the Stock Exchange. Market makers need not display prices of these securities continuously and any prices displayed are taken only as an indication rather than an offer to buy or sell.

delta wing *n* a triangular sweptback aircraft wing.

deltiology (ˌdɛltɪ'ɒlədʒɪ) *n* the collection and study of picture postcards. [C20: from Greek *deltion*, diminutive of *deltos* a writing tablet + -LOGY] ▸ **ˌdelti'ologist** *n*

deltoid ('dɛltɔɪd) *n* **1** the thick muscle forming the rounded contour of the outer edge of the shoulder and acting to raise the arm. ◆ *adj* **2** shaped like a Greek capital delta, Δ; triangular. [C18: from Greek *deltoeidēs* triangular, from DELTA]

delude (dɪ'lu:d) *vb* (*tr*) **1** to deceive the mind or judgment of; mislead; beguile. **2** *Rare.* to frustrate (hopes, expectations, etc.). [C15: from Latin *dēlūdere* to mock, play false, from DE- + *lūdere* to play] ▸ **de'ludable** *adj* ▸ **de'luder** *n* ▸ **de'ludingly** *adv*

deluge ('dɛlju:dʒ) *n* **1** a great flood of water. **2** torrential rain; downpour. **3** an overwhelming rush or number: *a deluge of requests.* ◆ *vb* (*tr*) **4** to flood, as with water; soak, swamp, or drown. **5** to overwhelm or overrun; inundate. [C14: from Old French, from Latin *dīluvium* a washing away, flood, from *dīluere* to wash away, drench, from *di-* DIS-[1] + *-luere*, from *lavere* to wash]

Deluge ('dɛlju:dʒ) *n* **the.** another name for the **Flood.**

delusion (dɪ'lu:ʒən) *n* **1** a mistaken or misleading opinion, idea, belief, etc.: *he has delusions of grandeur.* **2** *Psychiatry.* a belief held in the face of evidence to the contrary, that is resistant to all reason. See also **illusion, hallucination. 3** the act of deluding or state of being deluded. ▸ **de'lusional** *adj* ▸ **de'lusive** *adj* ▸ **de'lusively** *adv* ▸ **de'lusiveness** *n* ▸ **delusory** (dɪ'lu:sərɪ) *adj*

de luxe (də 'lʌks, 'lʊks) *adj* **1** (esp. of products, articles for sale, etc.) rich, elegant, or sumptuous; superior in quality, number of accessories, etc.: *the de luxe model of a car.* ◆ *adv* **2** *Chiefly U.S.* in a luxurious manner. [C19: from French, literally: of luxury]

Delvaux (dɛlvə) *n* **Paul.** 1897–1994, Belgian surrealist painter: his works portray dreamlike figures in mysterious settings.

delve (dɛlv) *vb* (*mainly intr; often foll. by in or into*) **1** to inquire or research deeply or intensively (for information, etc.): *he delved in the Bible for quotations.* **2** to search or rummage (in a drawer, the pockets, etc.). **3** (esp. of an animal) to dig or burrow deeply (into the ground, etc.). **4** (*also tr*) *Archaic or dialect.* to dig or turn up (earth, a garden, etc.), as with a spade. [Old English *delfan*; related to Old High German *telban* to dig, Russian *dolbit* to hollow out with a chisel] ▸ **'delver** *n*

Dem. *U.S. abbrev. for* Democrat(ic).

demagnetize *or* **demagnetise** (di:'mægnəˌtaɪz) *vb* to lose magnetic properties or remove magnetic properties from. Also: **degauss.** ▸ **deˌmagneti'zation** *or* **deˌmagneti'sation** *n* ▸ **de'magnetˌizer** *or* **de'magnetˌiser** *n*

demagogic (ˌdɛmə'gɒgɪk) *or* **demagogical** *adj* of, characteristic of, relating to, or resembling a demagogue. ▸ **ˌdema'gogically** *adv*

demagogue *or U.S.* (*sometimes*) **demagog** ('dɛməˌgɒg) *n* **1** a political agitator who appeals with crude oratory to the prejudice and passions of the mob. **2** (esp. in the ancient world) any popular political leader or orator. [C17: from Greek *dēmagōgos* people's leader, from *dēmos* people + *agein* to lead]

demagoguery (ˌdɛmə'gɒgərɪ) *or* **demagoguism** ('dɛməˌgɒgɪzəm) *n* the methods, practices, or rhetoric of a demagogue.

demagogy ('dɛməˌgɒgɪ) *n, pl* **-gogies. 1** demagoguery. **2** rule by a demagogue or by demagogues. **3** a group of demagogues.

de-man *vb* (*tr*) **-mans, -manning, -manned.** *Brit.* to reduce the workforce of (a plant, industry, etc.).

demand (dɪ'mɑ:nd) *vb* (*tr; may take a clause as object or an infinitive*) **1** to request peremptorily or urgently. **2** to require or need as just, urgent, etc.: *the situation demands attention.* **3** to claim as a right; exact: *his parents demanded obedience of him.* **4** *Law.* to make a formal legal claim to (property, esp. realty). ◆ *n* **5** an urgent or peremptory requirement or request. **6** something that requires special effort or sacrifice: *a demand on one's time.* **7** the act of demanding something or the thing demanded: *the kidnappers' demand was a million pounds.* **8** an insistent question or query. **9** *Economics.* **9a** willingness and ability to purchase goods and services. **9b** the amount of a commodity that consumers are willing and able to purchase at a specified price. Compare **supply**[1] (sense 9). **10** *Law.* a formal legal claim, esp. to real property. **11 in demand.** sought after; popular. **12 on demand.** as soon as requested: *a draft payable on demand.* [C13: from Anglo-French *demaunder*, from Medieval Latin *dēmandāre*, from Latin: to commit to, from DE- + *mandāre* to command, entrust; see MANDATE] ▸ **de'mandable** *adj* ▸ **de'mander** *n*

demandant (dɪ'mɑ:ndənt) *n Law.* (formerly) the plaintiff in an action relating to real property. [C14: from Old French, from *demander* to DEMAND]

demand bill *or* **draft** *n* a bill of exchange that is payable on demand. Also called: **sight bill.**

demand deposit *n* a bank deposit from which withdrawals may be made without notice. Compare **time deposit.**

demand feeding *n* the practice of feeding a baby whenever it seems to be hungry, rather than at set intervals.

demanding (dɪ'mɑ:ndɪŋ) *adj* requiring great patience, skill, etc.: *a demanding job.* ▸ **de'mandingly** *adv*

demand loan *n* another name for **call loan.**

demand management *n Economics.* the regulation of total spending in an economy to required levels, attempted by a government esp. in order to avoid unemployment or inflation: a measure advocated by Keynesian economists.

demand note *n* a promissory note payable on demand.

demand-pull inflation *n* See **inflation** (sense 2).

demantoid (dɪ'mæntɔɪd) *n* a bright green variety of andradite garnet. [C19: from German, from obsolete *Demant* diamond, from Old French *diamant* + -OID]

demarcate ('di:mɑ:ˌkeɪt) *vb* (*tr*) **1** to mark, fix, or draw the boundaries, limits, etc., of. **2** to separate or distinguish between (areas with unclear boundaries). ▸ **'demarˌcator** *n*

demarcation *or* **demarkation** (ˌdi:mɑ:'keɪʃən) *n* **1** the act of establishing limits or boundaries. **2** a limit or boundary. **3a** a strict separation of the kinds of work performed by members of different trade unions. **3b** (*as modifier*): *demarcation dispute.* **4** separation or distinction (often in the phrase **line of demarcation**). [C18: Latinized version of Spanish *demarcación*, from *demarcar* to appoint the boundaries of, from *marcar* to mark, from Italian *marcare*, of Germanic origin; see MARK[1]]

démarche *French.* (demarʃ) *n* **1** a move, step, or manoeuvre, esp. in diplomatic affairs. **2** a representation or statement of views, complaints, etc., to a public authority. [C17: literally: walk, gait, from Old French *demarcher* to tread, trample; see DE-, MARCH[1]]

demarket (di:'mɑ:kɪt) *vb* to discourage consumers from buying (a particular product), either because it is faulty or because it could jeopardize the seller's reputation.

dematerialize *or* **dematerialise** (di:mə'tɪərɪəˌlaɪz) *vb* (*intr*) **1** to cease to have material existence, as in science fiction or spiritualism. **2** to disappear without trace; vanish. ▸ **demaˌteriali'zation** *or* **demaˌteriali'sation** *n*

Demavend ('dɛməvɛnd) *n* **Mount.** a volcanic peak in N Iran, in the Elburz Mountains. Height: 5601 m (18 376 ft.).

deme (di:m) *n* **1a** (in preclassical Greece) the territory inhabited by a tribe. **1b** (in ancient Attica) a geographical unit of local government. **2** *Biology.* a group of individuals within a species that possess particular characteristics of cytology, genetics, etc. [C19: from Greek *dēmos* district in local government, the populace]

demean[1] (dɪ'mi:n) *vb* (*tr*) to lower (oneself) in dignity, status, or character; humble; debase. [C17: see DE-, MEAN[2]; on the model of *debase*]

demean[2] (dɪ'mi:n) *vb* (*tr*) *Rare.* to behave or conduct (oneself) in a specified way. [C13: from Old French *demener*, from DE- + *mener* to lead, drive, from Latin *mināre* to drive (animals), from *minārī* to use threats]

demeanour *or U.S.* **demeanor** (dɪ'mi:nə) *n* **1** the way a person behaves towards others; conduct. **2** bearing, appearance, or mien. [C15: see DEMEAN[2]]

dement (dɪ'mɛnt) *vb* **1** (*intr*) to deteriorate mentally, esp. because of old age. **2** (*tr*) *Rare.* to drive mad; make insane. [C16: from Late Latin *dēmentāre* to drive mad, from Latin DE- + *mēns* mind]

demented (dɪ'mɛntɪd) *adj* mad; insane. ▸ **de'mentedly** *adv* ▸ **de'mentedness** *n*

dementia (dɪ'mɛnʃə, -ʃɪə) *n* a state of serious emotional and mental deterioration, of organic or functional origin. [C19: from Latin: madness; see DEMENT]

dementia praecox ('pri:kɒks) *n* a former name for **schizophrenia.** [C19: New Latin, literally: premature dementia]

demerara (ˌdɛmə'rɛərə, -'rɑ:rə) *n* **1** brown crystallized cane sugar from the Caribbean and nearby countries. **2** a highly flavoured rum used mainly for blending purposes. [C19: named after *Demerara*, a region of Guyana]

Demerara (ˌdɛmə'rɛərə, -'rɑ:rə) *n* **the.** a river in Guyana, rising in the central forest area and flowing north to the Atlantic at Georgetown. Length: 346 km (215 miles).

demerger (di:'mɜ:dʒə) *n* the separation of two or more companies which have previously been merged. ▸ **de'merge** *vb*

demerit (di:'mɛrɪt, 'di:ˌmɛrɪt) *n* **1** something, esp. conduct, that deserves censure. **2** *U.S. and Canadian.* a mark given against a person for failure or misconduct, esp. in schools or the armed forces. **3** a fault or disadvantage. [C14 (originally: worth, later specialized to mean: something worthy of blame): from Latin *dēmerērī* to deserve] ▸ **deˌmeri'torious** *adj* ▸ **deˌmeri'toriously** *adv*

demersal (dɪ'mɜ:s°l) *adj* living or occurring on the bottom of a sea or a lake: *demersal fish.* [C19: from Latin *dēmersus* submerged (from *dēmergere* to plunge into, from *mergere* to dip) + -AL[1]]

demesne (dɪ'meɪn, -'mi:n) *n* **1** land, esp. surrounding a house or manor, retained by the owner for his own use. **2** *Property law.* the possession and use of one's own property or land. **3** the territory ruled by a state or a sovereign;

realm; domain. **4** a region or district; domain. [C14: from Old French *demeine;* see DOMAIN]

Demeter (dɪ'miːtə) *n Greek myth.* the goddess of agricultural fertility and protector of marriage and women. Roman counterpart: **Ceres.**

demi- *prefix* **1** half: *demirelief.* Compare **hemi-, semi-** (sense 1). **2** of less than full size, status, or rank: *demigod.* [via French from Medieval Latin *dīmedius,* from Latin *dīmīdius* half, from *dis-* apart + *medius* middle]

demibastion (ˌdɛmɪ'bæstɪən) *n Fortifications.* half a bastion, having only one flank, at right angles to the wall.

demicanton (ˌdɛmɪ'kæntɒn, -kæn'tɒn) *n* either of the two parts of certain Swiss cantons.

demigod ('dɛmɪˌgɒd) *n* **1a** a mythological being who is part mortal, part god. **1b** a lesser deity. **2** a person with outstanding or godlike attributes. [C16: translation of Latin *sēmideus*] ▸ **'demiˌgoddess** *fem n*

demijohn ('dɛmɪˌdʒɒn) *n* a large bottle with a short narrow neck, often with small handles at the neck and encased in wickerwork. [C18: probably by folk etymology from French *dame-jeanne,* from *dame* lady + *Jeanne* Jane]

demilitarize *or* **demilitarise** (diː'mɪlɪtəˌraɪz) *vb (tr)* **1** to remove any military presence or function in (an area): *demilitarized zone.* **2** to free of military character, purpose, etc.: *11 regiments were demilitarized.* ▸ **deˌmilitari'zation** *or* **deˌmilitari'sation** *n*

De Mille (də 'mɪl) *n* **Cecil B(lount).** 1881–1959, U.S. film producer and director.

demilune ('dɛmɪˌluːn, -ˌljuːn) *n* **1** *Fortifications.* an outwork in front of a fort, shaped like a crescent moon. **2** a crescent-shaped object or formation; half-moon. [C18: from French, literally: half-moon]

demimondaine (ˌdɛmɪ'mɒndeɪn; *French* dəmimɔ̃dɛn) *n* a woman of the demimonde. [C19: from French]

demimonde (ˌdɛmɪ'mɒnd; *French* dəmimɔ̃d) *n* **1** (esp. in the 19th century) those women considered to be outside respectable society, esp. on account of sexual promiscuity. **2** any social group considered to be not wholly respectable. [C19: from French, literally: half-world]

demineralize *or* **demineralise** (diː'mɪnərəˌlaɪz) *vb (tr)* to remove dissolved salts from (a liquid, esp. water). ▸ **deˌminerali'zation** *or* **deˌminerali'sation** *n*

demi-pension *French.* (dəmipɑ̃sjɔ̃) *n* another name for **half board.**

Demirel (*Turkish* dɛmɪ'rɛl) *n* **Süleyman** (sylei'mɑn). born 1924, Turkish statesman; president from 1993 and prime minister of Turkey (1965–71; 1975–77; 1977–78; 1979–80; 1991–93).

demirelief (ˌdɛmɪrɪ'liːf) *n* a less common term for **mezzo-relievo.**

demirep ('dɛmɪˌrɛp) *n Rare.* a woman of bad repute, esp. a prostitute. [C18: from DEMI- + REP(UTATION)]

demise (dɪ'maɪz) *n* **1** failure or termination: *the demise of one's hopes.* **2** a euphemistic or formal word for **death. 3** *Property law.* **3a** a transfer of an estate by lease. **3b** the passing or transfer of an estate on the death of the owner. **4** the immediate transfer of sovereignty to a successor upon the death, abdication, etc., of a ruler (esp. in the phrase **demise of the crown**). ◆ *vb* **5** to transfer or be transferred by inheritance, will, or succession. **6** *(tr) Property law.* to transfer (an estate, etc.) for a limited period; lease. **7** *(tr)* to transfer (sovereignty, a title, etc.) by or as if by the death, deposition, etc., of a ruler. [C16: from Old French, feminine of *demis* dismissed, from *demettre* to send away, from Latin *dīmittere;* see DISMISS] ▸ **de'misable** *adj*

demi-sec (ˌdɛmɪ'sɛk) *adj* (of wine, esp. champagne) medium-sweet. [C20: from French, from *demi* half + *sec* dry]

demisemiquaver ('dɛmɪˌsɛmɪˌkweɪvə) *n Music.* a note having the time value of one thirty-second of a semibreve. Usual U.S. and Canadian name: **thirty-second note.**

demission (dɪ'mɪʃən) *n Rare.* relinquishment of or abdication from an office, responsibility, etc. [C16: from Anglo-French *dimissioun,* from Latin *dīmissiō* a dismissing; see DISMISS]

demist (diː'mɪst) *vb* to free or become free of condensation through evaporation produced by a heater and/or blower. ▸ **de'mister** *n*

demit (dɪ'mɪt) *vb* **-mits, -mitting, -mitted.** *Archaic and Scot.* **1** to resign (an office, position, etc.). **2** *(tr)* to dismiss. [C16: from Latin *dīmittere* to send forth, discharge, renounce, from DI-[2] + *mittere* to send]

demitasse ('dɛmɪˌtæs; *French* dəmitɑs) *n* a small cup used to serve coffee, esp. after a meal. [C19: French, literally: half-cup]

demiurge ('dɛmɪˌɜːdʒ, 'diː-) *n* **1a** (in the philosophy of Plato) the creator of the universe. **1b** (in Gnostic and some other philosophies) the creator of the universe, supernatural but subordinate to the Supreme Being. **2** (in ancient Greece) a magistrate with varying powers found in any of several states. [C17: from Church Latin *dēmiūrgus,* from Greek *dēmiourgos* skilled workman, literally: one who works for the people, from *dēmos* people + *ergon* work] ▸ **ˌdemi'urgeous, ˌdemi'urgic,** *or* **ˌdemi'urgical** *adj* ▸ **ˌdemi'urgically** *adv*

demiveg ('dɛmɪˌvɛdʒ) Informal. ◆ *n* **1** a person who eats poultry and fish, but no red meat. ◆ *adj* **2** denoting a person who eats poultry and fish, but no red meat. [C20: from DEMI- + VEG(ETARIAN)]

demivierge ('dɛmɪˌvjɛəʒ) *n* a woman who engages in promiscuous sexual activity but retains her virginity. [C20: French, literally: half-virgin]

demivolt *or* **demivolte** ('dɛmɪˌvɒlt) *n Dressage.* a half turn on the hind legs.

demo ('dɛməʊ) *n, pl* **-os.** *Informal.* **1** short for **demonstration** (sense 4). **2** a demonstration record or tape, used for audition purposes. **3** *U.S.* short for **demonstrator** (sense 3).

demo- *or before a vowel* **dem-** *combining form.* indicating people or population: *demography.* [from Greek *dēmos*]

demob (diː'mɒb) *Brit. informal.* ◆ *vb* **-mobs, -mobbing, -mobbed. 1** short for **demobilize.** ◆ *n* **2a** short for **demobilization. 2b** *(as modifier): a demob suit.* **3** a soldier who has been demobilized.

demobilize *or* **demobilise** (diː'məʊbɪˌlaɪz) *vb* to disband, as troops, etc. ▸ **deˌmobili'zation** *or* **deˌmobili'sation** *n*

democracy (dɪ'mɒkrəsɪ) *n, pl* **-cies. 1** government by the people or their elected representatives. **2** a political or social unit governed ultimately by all its members. **3** the practice or spirit of social equality. **4** a social condition of classlessness and equality. **5** the common people, esp. as a political force. [C16: from French *démocratie,* from Late Latin *dēmocratia,* from Greek *dēmokratia* government by the people; see DEMO-, -CRACY]

democrat ('dɛməˌkræt) *n* **1** an advocate of democracy; adherent of democratic principles. **2** a member or supporter of a democratic party or movement.

Democrat ('dɛməˌkræt) *n* (in the U.S.) a member or supporter of the Democratic Party. ▸ **ˌDemo'cratic** *adj*

democratic (ˌdɛmə'krætɪk) *adj* **1** of, characterized by, derived from, or relating to the principles of democracy. **2** upholding or favouring democracy or the interests of the common people. **3** popular with or for the benefit of all: *democratic sports.* ▸ **ˌdemo'cratically** *adv*

democratic centralism *n* the Leninist principle that policy should be decided centrally by officials, who are nominally democratically elected.

democratic deficit *n* any situation in which there is believed to be a lack of democratic accountability and control over the decision-making process.

Democratic Party *n U.S. politics.* the older and more liberal of the two major political parties, so named since 1840. Compare **Republican Party.**

Democratic-Republican Party *n U.S. history.* the antifederalist party originally led by Thomas Jefferson, which developed into the modern Democratic Party.

Democratic Republic of the Congo *n* **the.** See **Congo** (sense 2).

democratize *or* **democratise** (dɪ'mɒkrəˌtaɪz) *vb (tr)* to make democratic. ▸ **deˌmocrati'zation** *or* **deˌmocrati'sation** *n*

Democritus (dɪ'mɒkrɪtəs) *n* ?460–?370 B.C., Greek philosopher who developed the atomist theory of matter of his teacher, Leucippus. See also **atomism.**

démodé *French.* (demɔde) *adj* out of fashion; outmoded. [French, from *dé-* out of + *mode* style, fashion]

demodulate (diː'mɒdjʊˌleɪt) *vb* to carry out demodulation on (a wave or signal). ▸ **de'moduˌlator** *n*

demodulation (ˌdiːmɒdjʊ'leɪʃən) *n Electronics.* the act or process by which an output wave or signal is obtained having the characteristics of the original modulating wave or signal; the reverse of modulation.

Demogorgon (ˌdiːməʊ'gɔːgən) *n* a mysterious and awesome god in ancient mythology, often represented as ruling in the underworld. [C16: via Late Latin from Greek]

demographics (ˌdɛmə'græfɪks, ˌdiːmə-) *pl n* data resulting from the science of demography; population statistics.

demographic timebomb *n Chiefly Brit.* a predicted shortage of school-leavers and consequently of available workers, caused by an earlier drop in the birth rate, resulting in an older workforce.

demography (dɪ'mɒgrəfɪ) *n* the scientific study of human populations, esp. with reference to their size, structure, and distribution. [C19: from French *démographie,* from Greek *dēmos* the populace; see -GRAPHY] ▸ **de'mographer** *or* **de'mographist** *n* ▸ **demographic** (ˌdɛmə'græfɪk, ˌdiːmə-) *or* **ˌdemo'graphical** *adj* ▸ **ˌdemo'graphically** *adv*

demoiselle (dəmwɑː'zɛl) *n* **1** Also called: **demoiselle crane, Numidian crane.** a small crane, *Anthropoides virgo,* of central Asia, N Africa, and SE Europe, having grey plumage with long black breast feathers and white ear tufts. **2** a less common name for a **damselfly. 3** another name for **damselfish. 4** a literary word for **damsel.** [C16: from French: young woman; see DAMSEL]

de Molina (*Spanish* ðe mo'lina) *n* See **Tirso de Molina.**

demolish (dɪ'mɒlɪʃ) *vb (tr)* **1** to tear down or break up (buildings, etc.). **2** to destroy; put an end to (an argument, etc.). **3** *Facetious.* to eat up: *she demolished the whole cake!* [C16: from French *démolir,* from Latin *dēmōlīrī* to throw down, destroy, from DE- + *mōlīrī* to strive, toil, construct, from *mōles* mass, bulk] ▸ **de'molisher** *n* ▸ **de'molishment** *n*

demolition (ˌdɛmə'lɪʃən, ˌdiː-) *n* **1** the act of demolishing or state of being demolished. **2** *Chiefly military.* **2a** destruction by explosives. **2b** *(as modifier): a demolition charge.* ▸ **ˌdemo'litionist** *n, adj*

demolitions (ˌdɛmə'lɪʃənz, ˌdiː-) *pl n Chiefly military.* **a** explosives, as when used to blow up bridges, etc. **b** *(as modifier): a demolitions expert.*

demon ('diːmən) *n* **1** an evil spirit or devil. **2** a person, habit, obsession, etc., thought of as evil, cruel, or persistently tormenting. **3** Also called: **daemon, daimon.** an attendant or ministering spirit; genius: *the demon of inspiration.* **4a** a person who is extremely skilful in, energetic at, or devoted to a given activity, esp. a sport: *a demon at cycling.* **4b** *(as modifier): a demon cyclist.* **5** a variant spelling of **daemon** (sense 1). **6** *Austral. and N.Z. informal, archaic.* a detective or policeman. [C15: from Latin *daemōn* evil spirit, spirit, from Greek *daimōn* spirit, deity, fate; see DAEMON]

demonetarize *or* **demonetarise** (diː'mʌnətəraɪz) *vb (tr)* another word for **demonetize** (sense 1). ▸ **deˌmonetari'zation** *or* **deˌmonetari'sation** *n*

demonetize *or* **demonetise** (diː'mʌnɪˌtaɪz) *vb (tr)* **1** to deprive (a metal) of its capacity as a monetary standard. **2** to withdraw from use as currency. ▸ **deˌmoneti'zation** *or* **deˌmoneti'sation** *n*

demoniac (dɪ'məʊnɪˌæk) *adj also* **demoniacal** (ˌdiːmə'naɪəkᵊl). **1** of, like, or suggestive of a demon; demonic. **2** suggesting inner possession or inspiration: *the demoniac fire of genius.* **3** frantic; frenzied; feverish: *demoniac activity.* ◆ *n* **4** a person possessed by an evil spirit or demon. ▸ **ˌdemo'niacally** *adv*

demonic (dɪ'mɒnɪk) *adj* **1** of, relating to, or characteristic of a demon; fiendish. **2** inspired or possessed by a demon, or seemingly so: *demonic laughter.* ▸ **de'monically** *adv*

demonism ('diːməˌnɪzəm) *n* **1a** belief in the existence and power of demons. **1b** worship of demons. **2** another word for **demonology.** ▸ **'demonist** *n*

demonize *or* **demonise** ('di:mə,naɪz) *vb (tr)* **1** to make into or like a demon. **2** to subject to demonic influence. **3** to mark out or describe as evil or culpable: *the technique of demonizing the enemy in the run-up to war.*

demonolater (,di:mə'nɒlətə) *n* a person who worships demons. [C19: back formation from DEMONOLATRY]

demonolatry (,di:mə'nɒlətrɪ) *n* the worship of demons. [C17: see DEMON, -LATRY]

demonology (,di:mə'nɒlədʒɪ) *n* **1** the study of demons or demonic beliefs. Also called: **demonism. 2** a set of people or things that are disliked or held in low esteem: *the place occupied by Hitler in contemporary demonology.* ▸ **demonological** (,di:mənə'lɒdʒɪkᵊl) *adj* ▸ **,demon'ologist** *n*

demonstrable ('dɛmənstrəbᵊl, dɪ'mɒn-) *adj* able to be demonstrated or proved. ▸ **,demonstra'bility** *or* **'demonstrableness** *n* ▸ **demonstrably** ('dɛmənstrəblɪ, dɪ'mɒn-) *adv*

demonstrate ('dɛmən,streɪt) *vb* **1** *(tr)* to show, manifest, or prove, esp. by reasoning, evidence, etc.: *it is easy to demonstrate the truth of this proposition.* **2** *(tr)* to evince; reveal the existence of: *the scheme later demonstrated a fatal flaw.* **3** *(tr)* to explain or illustrate by experiment, example, etc. **4** *(tr)* to display, operate, and explain the workings of (a machine, product, etc.). **5** *(intr)* to manifest support, protest, etc., by public parades or rallies. **6** *(intr)* to be employed as a demonstrator of machinery, etc. **7** *(intr) Military.* to make a show of force, esp. in order to deceive one's enemy. [C16: from Latin *dēmonstrāre* to point out, from *monstrāre* to show]

demonstration (,dɛmən'streɪʃən) *n* **1** the act of demonstrating. **2** proof or evidence leading to proof. **3** an explanation, display, illustration, or experiment showing how something works. **4** a manifestation of grievances, support, or protest by public rallies, parades, etc. **5** a manifestation of emotion. **6** a show of military force or preparedness. **7** *Maths.* a logical presentation of the assumptions and equations used in solving a problem or proving a theorem. ▸ **,demon'strational** *adj* ▸ **,demon'strationist** *n*

demonstration model *n* a nearly new product, such as a car or washing machine, that has been used only to demonstrate its performance by a dealer and is offered for sale at a discount.

demonstrative (dɪ'mɒnstrətɪv) *adj* **1** tending to manifest or express one's feelings easily or unreservedly. **2** *(postpositive;* foll. by *of)* serving as proof; indicative. **3** involving or characterized by demonstration: *a demonstrative lecture.* **4** conclusive; indubitable: *demonstrative arguments.* **5** *Grammar.* denoting or belonging to a class of determiners used to point out the individual referent or referents intended, such as *this, that, these,* and *those.* Compare **interrogative, relative.** ◆ *n* **6** *Grammar.* a demonstrative word or construction. ▸ **de'monstratively** *adv* ▸ **de'monstrativeness** *n*

demonstrator ('dɛmən,streɪtə) *n* **1** a person who demonstrates equipment, machines, products, etc. **2** a person who takes part in a public demonstration. **3** a piece of merchandise, such as a car that one test-drives, used to display merits or performance to prospective buyers.

demoralize *or* **demoralise** (dɪ'mɒrə,laɪz) *vb (tr)* **1** to undermine the morale of; dishearten: *he was demoralized by his defeat.* **2** to debase morally; corrupt. **3** to throw into confusion. ▸ **de,morali'zation** *or* **de,morali'sation** *n* ▸ **de'moral,izer** *or* **de'moral,iser** *n*

De Morgan's laws *pl n* (in formal logic and set theory) the principles that conjunction and disjunction, or union and intersection, are dual. Thus the negation of *P* & *Q* is equivalent to *not-P* or *not-Q.* [named after Augustus *De Morgan* (1806–71), British mathematician]

demos ('di:mɒs) *n* **1** the people of a nation regarded as a political unit. **2** *Rare.* the common people; masses. [C19: from Greek: the populace; see DEME]

Demosthenes (dɪ'mɒsθə,ni:z) *n* 384–322 B.C., Athenian statesman, orator, and lifelong opponent of the power of Macedonia over Greece.

demote (dɪ'məʊt) *vb (tr)* to lower in rank or position; relegate. [C19: from DE- + (PRO)MOTE] ▸ **de'motion** *n*

demotic (dɪ'mɒtɪk) *adj* **1** of or relating to the common people; popular. **2** of or relating to a simplified form of hieroglyphics used in ancient Egypt by the ordinary literate class outside the priesthood. Compare **hieratic.** ◆ *n* **3** the demotic script of ancient Egypt. [C19: from Greek *dēmotikos* of the people, from *dēmotēs* a man of the people, commoner; see DEMOS] ▸ **de'motist** *n*

Demotic (dɪ'mɒtɪk) *n* **1** the spoken form of Modern Greek, now increasingly used in literature. Compare **Katharevusa.** ◆ *adj* **2** denoting or relating to this.

demount (di:'maʊnt) *vb (tr)* to remove (a motor, gun, etc.) from its mounting or setting. ▸ **de'mountable** *adj*

Dempsey ('dɛmpsɪ) *n* **Jack.** real name *William Harrison Dempsey.* 1895–1983, U.S. boxer; world heavyweight champion (1919–26).

dempster ('dɛmpstə) *n* a variant spelling of **deemster.**

demulcent (dɪ'mʌlsᵊnt) *adj* **1** soothing; mollifying. ◆ *n* **2** a drug or agent that soothes the irritation of inflamed or injured skin surfaces. [C18: from Latin *dēmulcēre* to caress soothingly, from DE- + *mulcēre* to stroke]

demulsify (di:'mʌlsɪ,faɪ) *vb* **-fies, -fying, -fied.** to undergo or cause to undergo a process in which an emulsion is permanently broken down into its constituents. [C20: from DE- + EMULSIFY] ▸ **de,mulsifi'cation** *n* ▸ **de'mulsi,fier** *n*

demur (dɪ'mɜ:) *vb* **-murs, -murring, -murred.** *(intr)* **1** to raise objections or show reluctance; object. **2** *Law.* to raise an objection by entering a demurrer. **3** *Archaic.* to hesitate; delay. ◆ *n also* **demurral** (dɪ'mʌrəl). **4** the act of demurring. **5** an objection raised. **6** *Archaic.* hesitation. [C13: from Old French *demorer,* from Latin *dēmorārī* to loiter, linger, from *morārī* to delay, from *mora* a delay] ▸ **de'murrable** *adj*

demure (dɪ'mjʊə) *adj* **1** sedate; decorous; reserved. **2** affectedly modest or prim; coy. [C14: perhaps from Old French *demorer* to delay, linger; perhaps influenced by *meur* ripe, MATURE] ▸ **de'murely** *adv* ▸ **de'mureness** *n*

demurrage (dɪ'mʌrɪdʒ) *n* **1** the delaying of a ship, railway wagon, etc., caused by the charterer's failure to load, unload, etc., before the time of scheduled departure. **2** the extra charge required as compensation for such delay. **3** a fee charged by the Bank of England for changing bullion into notes. [C17: from Old French *demorage, demourage;* see DEMUR]

demurrer (dɪ'mʌrə) *n* **1** *Law.* a pleading that admits an opponent's point but denies that it is a relevant or valid argument. **2** any objection raised.

demutualize *or* **demutualise** (di:'mju:tʃʊə,laɪz) *vb* to convert (a mutual society, such as a building society) to a public limited company or (of such a society) to be converted. ▸ **,demutuali'zation** *or* **,demutuali'sation** *n*

demy (dɪ'maɪ) *n, pl* **-mies. 1a** a size of printing paper, 17½ by 22½ inches (444.5 × 571.5 mm). **1b** a size of writing paper, 15½ by 20 inches (Brit.) (393.7 × 508 mm) or 16 by 21 inches (U.S.) (406.4 × 533.4 mm). **2** either one of two book sizes, 8½ by 5½ inches (**demy octavo**) or (chiefly Brit.) 11¾ by 8¾ inches (**demy quarto**). [C16: see DEMI-]

demystify (di:'mɪstɪ,faɪ) *vb* **-fies, -fying, -fied.** *(tr)* to remove the mystery from; make clear. ▸ **de,mystifi'cation** *n*

demythologize *or* **demythologise** (,di:mɪ'θɒlə,dʒaɪz) *vb (tr)* **1** to eliminate all mythical elements from (a piece of writing, esp. the Bible) so as to arrive at an essential meaning. **2** to restate (a message, esp. a religious one) in rational terms. ▸ **,demy,thologi'zation** *or* **,demy,thologi'sation** *n*

den (dɛn) *n* **1** the habitat or retreat of a lion or similar wild animal; lair. **2** a small or secluded room in a home, often used for carrying on a hobby. **3** a squalid or wretched room or retreat. **4** a site or haunt: *a den of vice.* **5** *Scot.* a small wooded valley; dingle. **6** *Scot. and northern English dialect.* a place of sanctuary in certain catching games; home or base. ◆ *vb* **dens, denning, denned. 7** *(intr)* to live in or as if in a den. [Old English *denn;* related to Old High German *tenni* threshing floor, early Dutch *denne* low ground, den, cave]

Den. *abbrev. for* Denmark.

denar (dɪ'nɛar) *n* the standard monetary unit of Macedonia, divided into 100 deni.

denarius (dɪ'nɛərɪəs) *n, pl* **-narii** (-'nɛərɪ,aɪ). **1** a silver coin of ancient Rome, often called a penny in translation. **2** a gold coin worth 25 silver denarii. [C16: from Latin: coin originally equal to ten asses, from *dēnārius* (adj) containing ten, from *dēnī* ten each, from *decem* ten]

denary ('di:nərɪ) *adj* **1** calculated by tens; based on ten; decimal. **2** containing ten parts; tenfold. [C16: from Latin *dēnārius* containing ten; see DENARIUS]

denationalize *or* **denationalise** (di:'næʃənᵊ,laɪz) *vb* **1** to return or transfer (an industry, etc.) from public to private ownership. **2** to deprive (an individual, people, institution, etc.) of national character or nationality. ▸ **de,nationali'zation** *or* **de,nationali'sation** *n*

denaturalize *or* **denaturalise** (di:'nætʃrə,laɪz) *vb (tr)* **1** to deprive of nationality. **2** to make unnatural. ▸ **de,naturali'zation** *or* **de,naturali'sation** *n*

denature (di:'neɪtʃə) *or* **denaturize, denaturise** (di:'neɪtʃə,raɪz) *vb (tr)* **1** to change the nature of. **2** to change (a protein) by chemical or physical means, such as the action of acid or heat, to cause loss of solubility, biological activity, etc. **3** to render (something, such as ethanol) unfit for consumption by adding nauseous substances. **4** to render (fissile material) unfit for use in nuclear weapons by addition of an isotope. ▸ **de'naturant** *n* ▸ **de,natur'ation** *n*

denatured alcohol *n Chem.* ethanol rendered unfit for human consumption by the addition of a noxious substance, as in methylated spirits.

denazify (di:'nɑ:tsɪ,faɪ) *vb* **-fies, -fying, -fied.** *(tr)* to free or declare (people, institutions, etc.) freed from Nazi influence or ideology. ▸ **de,nazifi'cation** *n*

Denbighshire ('dɛnbɪ,ʃɪə, -ʃə) *n* a county of N Wales: became part of Clwyd and Gwynedd in 1974; reinstated with different boundaries in 1996: borders the Irish Sea, with the Cambrian Mountains in the south: chiefly agricultural. Administrative centre: Ruthin. Pop.: 91 585 (1996 est.). Area: 844 sq. km (327 sq. miles).

Den Bosch (dən bɒs) *n* another name for **'s Hertogenbosch.**

Dench (dɛntʃ) *n* Dame **Judi (Olivia).** born 1934, British actress and theatre director.

dendriform ('dɛndrɪ,fɔ:m) *adj* branching or treelike in appearance.

dendrite ('dɛndraɪt) *n* **1** Also called: **dendron.** any of the short branched threadlike extensions of a nerve cell, which conduct impulses towards the cell body. **2** a branching mosslike crystalline structure in some rocks and minerals. **3** a crystal that has branched during growth and has a treelike form. [C18: from Greek *dendritēs* relating to a tree] ▸ **dendritic** (dɛn'drɪtɪk) *or* **den'dritical** *adj* ▸ **den'dritically** *adv*

dendro-, dendri-, *or before a vowel* **dendr-** *combining form.* tree: *dendrochronology; dendrite.* [New Latin, from Greek, from *dendron* tree]

dendrochronology (,dɛndrəʊkrə'nɒlədʒɪ) *n* the study of the annual rings of trees, used esp. to date past events. ▸ **dendrochronological** (,dɛndrəʊ,krɒn-ᵊ'lɒdʒɪkᵊl) *adj* ▸ **,dendrochro'nologist** *n*

dendrogram ('dɛndrəʊ,græm) *n* any branching diagram, such as a cladogram, showing the interconnections between things.

dendroid ('dɛndrɔɪd) *or* **dendroidal** (dɛn'drɔɪdᵊl) *adj* **1** freely branching; arborescent; treelike. **2** (esp. of tree ferns) having a tall trunklike stem. [C19: from Greek *dendroeidēs* like a tree]

dendrology (dɛn'drɒlədʒɪ) *n* the branch of botany that is concerned with the natural history of trees and shrubs. ▸ **dendrological** (,dɛndrə'lɒdʒɪkᵊl), **,dendro'logic,** *or* **den'drologous** *adj* ▸ **den'drologist** *n*

dendron ('dɛndrɒn) *n* another name for **dendrite** (sense 1).

dene[1] *or* **dean** (di:n) *n Brit.* a valley, esp. one that is narrow and wooded. [Old English *denu* valley; see DEN]

dene[2] *or* **dean** (di:n) *n Dialect, chiefly southern English.* a sandy stretch of land or dune near the sea. [C13: probably related to Old English *dūn* hill; see DOWN[3]]

Dene ('dɛnɪ, 'dɛneɪ) *pl n* the North American Indian peoples of the Northwest Territories in Canada. The official body representing them is called the Dene Nation. [via French *déné,* from Athapason *dene* people]

Deneb ('dɛnɛb) *n* the brightest star in the constellation Cygnus and one of the brightest but remotest stars in the night sky. Visual magnitude: 1.3; spectral type: A2. [C19: from Arabic *dhanab* a tail]

Denebola (dɪ'nɛbələ) *n* the second brightest star in the constellation Leo. Visual magnitude: 2.2; spectral type: A2. [from Arabic *dhanab al-(asad)* tail of the (lion)]

denegation (ˌdɛnɪ'geɪʃən) *n* a denial, contradiction, or refusal. [C17: from Late Latin *dēnegātiō*, from Latin *dēnegāre* to deny, refuse, from *negāre* to deny]

dene hole *n* a hole or shaft excavated in the chalk of southern England or northern France, of uncertain origin and purpose. [of uncertain origin: perhaps from DENE[1]]

denervate ('dɛnəˌveɪt) *vb* (*tr*) to deprive (a tissue or organ) of its nerve supply. ▸ ˌ**dener'vation** *n*

Deneuve (*French* dənøv) *n* **Catherine**, original name *Catherine Dorléac.* born 1943, French film actress: her films include *Les Parapluies de Cherbourg* (1964), *Belle de Jour* (1967), and *Indochine* (1992).

DEng. *abbrev. for* Doctor of Engineering.

dengue ('dɛŋgɪ) *or* **dandy** ('dændɪ) *n* an acute viral disease transmitted by mosquitoes, characterized by headache, fever, pains in the joints, and skin rash. Also called: **breakbone fever.** [C19: from Spanish, probably of African origin; compare Swahili *kidinga*]

Deng Xiaoping ('dʌŋ 'sjaupɪŋ) *or* **Teng Hsiao-ping** *n* 1904–97, Chinese Communist statesman; deputy prime minister (1973–76; 1977–80) and the dominant figure in the Chinese government from 1977 until his death. He was twice removed from office (1967–73, 1976–77) and rehabilitated. He introduced economic liberalization, but violently suppressed mass demonstrations in favour of political reform, most notably in 1989 when over 2500 demonstrators were killed by the military in Tiananmen Square in Beijing.

Den Haag (dɛn 'haːx) *n* the Dutch name for (The) **Hague.**

Den Helder (*Dutch* dɛn 'hɛldər) *n* a port in the W Netherlands, in North Holland province: fortified by Napoleon in 1811; naval station. Pop.: 61 024 (1994).

deniable (dɪ'naɪəbᵊl) *adj* able to be denied; questionable. ▸ **de'niably** *adv*

denial (dɪ'naɪəl) *n* **1** a refusal to agree or comply with a statement; contradiction. **2** the rejection of the truth of a proposition, doctrine, etc.: *a denial of God's existence.* **3** a negative reply; rejection of a request. **4** a refusal to acknowledge; renunciation; disavowal: *a denial of one's leader.* **5** a psychological process by which painful truths are not admitted into an individual's consciousness. See also **defence mechanism. 6** abstinence; self-denial.

denier[1] *n* **1** ('dɛnɪˌeɪ, 'dɛnjə). a unit of weight used to measure the fineness of silk and man-made fibres, esp. when woven into women's tights, etc. It is equal to 1 gram per 9000 metres. **2** (də'njeɪ, -'nɪə). any of several former European coins of various denominations. [C15: from Old French: coin, from Latin *dēnārius* DENARIUS]

denier[2] (dɪ'naɪə) *n* a person who denies.

denigrate ('dɛnɪˌgreɪt) *vb* **1** (*tr*) to belittle or disparage the character of; defame. **2** a rare word for **blacken.** [C16: from Latin *dēnigrāre* to make very black, defame, from *nigrāre* to blacken, from *niger* black] ▸ ˌ**deni'gration** *n* ▸ '**deniˌgrator** *n*

denim ('dɛnɪm) *n Textiles.* **1a** a hard-wearing twill-weave cotton fabric used for trousers, work clothes, etc. **1b** (*as modifier*): *a denim jacket.* **2a** a similar lighter fabric used in upholstery. **2b** (*as modifier*): *denim cushion covers.* [C17: from French (*serge*) *de Nîmes* (serge) of NÎMES]

denims ('dɛnɪmz) *pl n* jeans or overalls made of denim.

De Niro (də 'nɪərəʊ) *n* **Robert.** born 1943, U.S. film actor. His films include *The Deer Hunter* (1978), *Raging Bull* (1980), *GoodFellas* (1990), *A Bronx Tale* (1993), which he directed, *Ronin* (1998), and *Analyze This* (1999).

Denis ('dɛnɪs; *French* dəni) *n* **1 Maurice** (mɔris). 1870–1943, French painter and writer on art. One of the leading Nabis, he defined a picture as "essentially a flat surface covered with colours assembled in a certain order". **2 Saint.** Also: **Denys.** 3rd century A.D., first bishop of Paris; patron saint of France. Feast day: Oct. 9.

denitrate (diː'naɪtreɪt) *vb* to undergo or cause to undergo a process in which a compound loses a nitro or nitrate group, nitrogen dioxide, or nitric acid. ▸ ˌ**deni'tration** *n*

denitrify (diː'naɪtrɪˌfaɪ) *vb* **-fies, -fying, -fied.** to undergo or cause to undergo loss or removal of nitrogen compounds or nitrogen. ▸ **deˌnitrifi'cation** *n*

denizen ('dɛnɪzən) *n* **1** an inhabitant; occupant; resident. **2** *Brit.* an individual permanently resident in a foreign country where he enjoys certain rights of citizenship. **3** a plant or animal established in a place to which it is not native. **4** a naturalized foreign word. ◆ *vb* **5** (*tr*) to make a denizen. [C15: from Anglo-French *denisein*, from Old French *denzein*, from *denz* within, from Latin *de intus* from within]

Denmark ('dɛnmɑːk) *n* a kingdom in N Europe, between the Baltic and the North Sea: consists of the mainland of Jutland and about 100 inhabited islands (chiefly Zealand, Lolland, Funen, Falster, Langeland, and Bornholm); extended its territory throughout the Middle Ages, ruling Sweden until 1523 and Norway until 1814, and incorporating Greenland as a province from 1953 to 1979; joined the Common Market (now the EU) in 1973; an important exporter of dairy produce. Language: Danish. Religion: Christian, Lutheran majority. Currency: krone. Capital: Copenhagen. Pop.: 5 303 000 (1998 est.). Area: 43 031 sq. km (16 614 sq. miles). Danish name: **Danmark.** Related adj: **Danish.**

Denmark Strait *n* a channel between SE Greenland and Iceland, linking the Arctic Ocean with the Atlantic.

Denning ('dɛnɪŋ) *n* Baron **Alfred Thompson.** 1899–1999, English judge; Master of the Rolls 1962–82.

Dennis ('dɛnɪs) *n* **C(larence) J(ames).** 1876–1938, the poet of the Australian larrikin, esp. in *The Songs of a Sentimental Bloke* (1915) and *The Moods of Ginger Mick* (1916).

denom. *abbrev. for* (religious) denomination.

denominate *vb* (dɪ'nɒmɪˌneɪt). **1** (*tr*) to give a specific name to; designate. ◆ *adj* (dɪ'nɒmɪnɪt, -ˌneɪt). **2** *Maths.* (of a number) representing a multiple of a unit of measurement: *4 is the denominate number in 4 miles.* [C16: from DE- + Latin *nōmināre* to call by name; see NOMINATE] ▸ **de'nominable** *adj*

denomination (dɪˌnɒmɪ'neɪʃən) *n* **1** a group having a distinctive interpretation of a religious faith and usually its own organization. **2** a grade or unit in a series of designations of value, weight, measure, etc.: *coins of this denomination are being withdrawn.* **3** a name given to a class or group; classification. **4** the act of giving a name. **5** a name; designation. [C15: from Latin *dēnōminātiō* a calling by name; see DENOMINATE] ▸ **deˌnomi'national** *adj* ▸ **deˌnomi'nationally** *adv*

denominationalism (dɪˌnɒmɪ'neɪʃənᵊˌlɪzəm) *n* **1** adherence to particular principles, esp. to the tenets of a religious denomination; sectarianism. **2** the tendency to divide or cause to divide into sects or denominations. **3** division into denominations. ▸ **deˌnomi'nationalist** *n, adj*

denominative (dɪ'nɒmɪnətɪv) *adj* **1** giving or constituting a name; naming. **2** *Grammar.* **2a** (of a word other than a noun) formed from or having the same form as a noun. **2b** (*as n*): *the verb "to mushroom" is a denominative.* ▸ **de'nominatively** *adv*

denominator (dɪ'nɒmɪˌneɪtə) *n* **1** the divisor of a fraction, as 8 in ⅞. Compare **numerator** (sense 1). **2** *Archaic.* a person or thing that denominates or designates.

denotation (ˌdiːnəʊ'teɪʃən) *n* **1** the act or process of denoting; indication. **2** a particular meaning, esp. one given explicitly rather than by suggestion. **3a** something designated or referred to. See **referent.** Compare **connotation. 3b** another name for **extension** (sense 11).

denotative (dɪ'nəʊtətɪv) *adj* **1** able to denote; designative. **2** explicit; overt. ▸ **de'notatively** *adv*

denote (dɪ'nəʊt) *vb* (*tr; may take a clause as object*) **1** to be a sign, symbol, or symptom of; indicate or designate. **2** (of words, phrases, expressions, etc.) to have as a literal or obvious meaning. [C16: from Latin *dēnotāre* to mark, from *notāre* to mark, NOTE] ▸ **de'notable** *adj* ▸ **de'notement** *n*

denouement (deɪ'nuːmɒn) *or* **dénouement** (*French* denumɑ̃) *n* **1a** the final clarification or resolution of a plot in a play or other work. **1b** the point at which this occurs. **2** final outcome; solution. [C18: from French, literally: an untying, from *dénouer* to untie, from Old French *desnoer*, from *des-* DE- + *noer* to tie, knot, from Latin *nōdāre*, from *nōdus* a knot; see NODE]

denounce (dɪ'naʊns) *vb* (*tr*) **1** to deplore or condemn openly or vehemently. **2** to give information against; accuse. **3** to announce formally the termination of (a treaty, etc.). **4** *Obsolete.* **4a** to announce (something evil). **4b** to portend. [C13: from Old French *denoncier* to proclaim, from Latin *dēnuntiāre* to make an official proclamation, threaten, from DE- + *nuntiāre* to announce] ▸ **de'nouncement** *n* ▸ **de'nouncer** *n*

de novo *Latin.* (diː 'nəʊvəʊ) *adv* from the beginning; anew.

dense (dɛns) *adj* **1** thickly crowded or closely set: *a dense crowd.* **2** thick; impenetrable: *a dense fog.* **3** *Physics.* having a high density. **4** stupid; dull; obtuse. **5** (of a photographic negative) having many dark or exposed areas. **6** (of an optical glass, colour, etc.) transmitting little or no light. [C15: from Latin *densus* thick; related to Greek *dasus* thickly covered with hair or leaves] ▸ '**densely** *adv* ▸ '**denseness** *n*

densimeter (dɛn'sɪmɪtə) *n Physics.* any instrument for measuring density. ▸ **densimetric** (ˌdɛnsɪ'mɛtrɪk) *adj* ▸ **den'simetry** *n*

densitometer (ˌdɛnsɪ'tɒmɪtə) *n* an instrument for measuring the optical density of a material by directing a beam of light onto the specimen and measuring its transmission or reflection. ▸ **densitometric** (ˌdɛnsɪtə'mɛtrɪk) *adj* ▸ ˌ**densi'tometry** *n*

density ('dɛnsɪtɪ) *n, pl* **-ties. 1** the degree to which something is filled, crowded, or occupied: *high density of building in towns.* **2** obtuseness; stupidity. **3** a measure of the compactness of a substance, expressed as its mass per unit volume. It is measured in kilograms per cubic metre or pounds per cubic foot. Symbol: ρ See also **relative density. 4** a measure of a physical quantity per unit of length, area, or volume. See **charge density, current density. 5** *Physics, photog.* See **transmission density, reflection density.**

density function *n Statistics.* short for **probability density function.**

dent[1] (dɛnt) *n* **1** a hollow or dip in a surface, as one made by pressure or a blow. **2** an appreciable effect, esp. of lessening: *a dent in our resources.* ◆ *vb* **3** to impress or be impressed with a dent or dents. [C13 (in the sense: a stroke, blow): variant of DINT]

dent[2] (dɛnt) *n* **1** a toothlike protuberance, esp. the tooth of a sprocket or gearwheel. **2** *Textiles.* the space between two wires in a loom through which a warp thread is drawn. [C16: from French: tooth]

dent. *abbrev. for:* **1** dental. **2** dentistry.

dental ('dɛntᵊl) *adj* **1** of or relating to the teeth. **2** of or relating to dentistry. **3** *Phonetics.* **3a** pronounced or articulated with the tip of the tongue touching the backs of the upper teeth, as for *t* in French *tout.* **3b** (esp. in the phonology of some languages, such as English) another word for **alveolar.** ◆ *n* **4** *Phonetics.* a dental consonant. [C16: from Medieval Latin *dentālis*, from Latin *dens* tooth]

dental clinic *n N.Z.* a school clinic in which minor dental work is carried out by dental nurses.

dental floss *n* a soft usually flattened often waxed thread for cleaning the teeth and the spaces between them.

dental hygiene *n* the maintenance of the teeth and gums in healthy condition, esp. by proper brushing, the removal of plaque, etc. Also called: **oral hygiene.**

dental hygienist *n* a dentist's assistant skilled in dental hygiene. Also called: **oral hygienist.**

dentalium (dɛnˈteɪlɪəm) *n, pl* **-liums** *or* **-lia** (-lɪə). any scaphopod mollusc of the genus *Dentalium.* See **tusk shell.** [C19: New Latin, from Medieval Latin *dentālis* DENTAL]

dental nurse *n* **1** a dentist's assistant, esp. one who passes instruments, mixes fillings, etc. **2** *N.Z.* a nurse trained to do fillings and carry out other minor dental work on schoolchildren.

dental plaque *n* a filmy deposit on the surface of a tooth consisting of a mixture of mucus, bacteria, food, etc. Also called: **bacterial plaque.**

dental surgeon *n* another name for **dentist.**

dentate (ˈdɛnteɪt) *adj* **1** having teeth or toothlike processes. **2** (of leaves) having a toothed margin. [C19: from Latin *dentātus*] ▸ **ˈdentately** *adv*

dentation (dɛnˈteɪʃən) *n* **1** the state or condition of being dentate. **2** an angular projection or series of projections, as on the margin of a leaf.

dentex (ˈdɛntɛks) *n* a large active predatory sparid fish, *Dentex dentex,* of Mediterranean and E Atlantic waters, having long sharp teeth and powerful jaws. [C19: from Latin *dentix, dentex* from *dens* tooth]

denti- *or before a vowel* **dent-** *combining form.* indicating a tooth: *dentiform; dentine.* [from Latin *dēns, dent-*]

denticle (ˈdɛntɪkᵊl) *n* a small tooth or toothlike part, such as any of the placoid scales of sharks. [C14: from Latin *denticulus*]

denticulate (dɛnˈtɪkjʊlɪt, -ˌleɪt) *adj* **1** *Biology.* very finely toothed: *denticulate leaves.* **2** having denticles. **3** *Architect.* having dentils. [C17: from Latin *denticulātus* having small teeth] ▸ **denˈticulately** *adv*

denticulation (dɛnˌtɪkjʊˈleɪʃən) *n* **1** a denticulate structure. **2** a less common word for **denticle.**

dentiform (ˈdɛntɪˌfɔːm) *adj* shaped like a tooth.

dentifrice (ˈdɛntɪfrɪs) *n* any substance, esp. paste or powder, for use in cleaning the teeth. [C16: from Latin *dentifricium* tooth powder, from *dent-, dens* tooth + *fricāre* to rub]

dentil (ˈdɛntɪl) *n* one of a set of small square or rectangular blocks evenly spaced to form an ornamental row, usually under a classical cornice on a building, piece of furniture, etc. [C17: from French, from obsolete *dentille* a little tooth, from *dent* tooth]

dentilabial (ˌdɛntɪˈleɪbɪəl) *adj* another word for **labiodental.**

dentilingual (ˌdɛntɪˈlɪŋgwəl) *adj* **1** *Phonetics.* pronounced or articulated with the tongue touching the upper teeth. ◆ *n* **2** a consonant so pronounced.

dentine (ˈdɛntiːn) *or* **dentin** (ˈdɛntɪn) *n* the calcified tissue surrounding the pulp cavity of a tooth and comprising the bulk of the tooth. [C19: from DENTI- + -IN] ▸ **ˈdentinal** *adj*

dentist (ˈdɛntɪst) *n* a person qualified to practise dentistry. [C18: from French *dentiste,* from *dent* tooth]

dentistry (ˈdɛntɪstrɪ) *n* the branch of medical science concerned with the diagnosis and treatment of diseases and disorders of the teeth and gums.

dentition (dɛnˈtɪʃən) *n* **1** the arrangement, type, and number of the teeth in a particular species. Man has a **primary dentition** of deciduous teeth and a **secondary dentition** of permanent teeth. **2** teething or the time or process of teething. [C17: from Latin *dentītiō* a teething]

dentoid (ˈdɛntɔɪd) *adj* resembling a tooth.

Denton (ˈdɛntᵊn) *n* a town in NW England, in Tameside unitary authority, Greater Manchester. Pop.: 37 785 (1991).

D'Entrecasteaux Islands (*French* dɑ̃trəkasto) *pl n* a group of volcanic islands in the Pacific, off the SE coast of New Guinea: part of Papua New Guinea. Pop.: 49 167 (1990 est.). Area: 3141 sq. km (1213 sq. miles).

denture (ˈdɛntʃə) *n* (*usually pl*) **1** Also called: **dental plate, false teeth.** a partial or full set of artificial teeth. **2** *Rare.* a set of natural teeth. [C19: from French, from *dent* tooth + -URE]

denuclearize *or* **denuclearise** (dɪˈnjuːklɪəˌraɪz) *vb* (*tr*) to deprive (a country, state, etc.) of nuclear weapons. ▸ **deˌnuclearɪˈzation** *or* **deˌnucleariˈsation** *n*

denudate (ˈdɛnjʊˌdeɪt, dɪˈnjuːdeɪt) *vb* **1** a less common word for **denude.** ◆ *adj* **2** denuded; bare.

denude (dɪˈnjuːd) *vb* (*tr*) **1** to divest of covering; make bare; uncover; strip. **2** to expose (rock) by the erosion of the layers above. [C16: from Latin *dēnūdāre;* see NUDE] ▸ **denudation** (ˌdɛnjʊˈdeɪʃən, ˌdiː-) *n* ▸ **deˈnuder** *n*

denumerable (dɪˈnjuːmərəbᵊl) *adj Maths.* capable of being put into a one-to-one correspondence with the positive integers; countable. ▸ **deˈnumerably** *adv*

denunciate (dɪˈnʌnsɪˌeɪt) *vb* (*tr*) to condemn; denounce. [C16: from Latin *dēnuntiāre;* see DENOUNCE] ▸ **deˈnunciˌator** *n* ▸ **deˈnunciatory** *adj*

denunciation (dɪˌnʌnsɪˈeɪʃən) *n* **1** open condemnation; censure; denouncing. **2** *Law, obsolete.* a charge or accusation of crime made by an individual before a public prosecutor or tribunal. **3** a formal announcement of the termination of a treaty. **4** *Archaic.* an announcement in the form of an impending threat or warning.

Denver (ˈdɛnvə) *n* a city in central Colorado: the state capital. Pop.: 497 840 (1996 est.).

Denver boot *n* a slang name for **wheel clamp.** [C20: from DENVER, Colorado, where the device was first used]

deny (dɪˈnaɪ) *vb* **-nies, -nying, -nied.** (*tr*) **1** to declare (an assertion, statement, etc.) to be untrue: *he denied that he had killed her.* **2** to reject as false; refuse to accept or believe. **3** to withhold; refuse to give. **4** to refuse to fulfil the requests or expectations of: *it is hard to deny a child.* **5** to refuse to acknowledge or recognize; disown; disavow: *the baron denied his wicked son.* **6** to refuse (oneself) things desired. [C13: from Old French *denier,* from Latin *dēnegāre,* from *negāre*]

Denys (ˈdɛnɪs; *French* dəni) *n* **Saint.** a variant spelling of (Saint) **Denis.**

deoch-an-doruis (ˈdjɒxənˈdɒrɪs, dɒx-) *n Scot.* a parting drink or stirrup cup. Also: **doch-an-doris.** [Scottish Gaelic: drink at the door]

deodand (ˈdiːəʊˌdænd) *n English law.* (formerly) a thing that had caused a person's death and was forfeited to the crown for a charitable purpose: abolished 1862. [C16: from Anglo-French *deodande,* from Medieval Latin *deōdandum,* from Latin *Deō dandum* (something) to be given to God, from *deus* god + *dare* to give]

deodar (ˈdiːəʊˌdɑː) *n* **1** a Himalayan cedar, *Cedrus deodara,* with drooping branches. **2** the durable fragrant highly valued wood of this tree. [C19: from Hindi *deodār,* from Sanskrit *devadāru,* literally: wood of the gods, from *deva* god + *dāru* wood]

deodorant (diːˈəʊdərənt) *n* **1a** a substance applied to the body to suppress or mask the odour of perspiration or other body odours. **1b** (*as modifier*): *a deodorant spray.* Compare **antiperspirant. 2** any substance for destroying or masking odours, such as liquid sprayed into the air.

deodorize *or* **deodorise** (diːˈəʊdəˌraɪz) *vb* (*tr*) to remove, disguise, or absorb the odour of, esp. when unpleasant. ▸ **deˌodoriˈzation** *or* **deˌodoriˈsation** *n* ▸ **deˈodorˌizer** *or* **deˈodorˌiser** *n*

Deo gratias *Latin.* (ˈdeɪəʊ ˈgrɑːtɪəs) thanks be to God. Abbrev.: **DG.**

deontic (diːˈɒntɪk) *adj Logic.* **a** of or relating to such ethical concepts as obligation and permissibility. **b** designating the branch of modal logic that deals with the formalization of these concepts. [C19: from Greek *deon* duty, from impersonal *dei* it behoves, it is binding]

deontological (dɪˌɒntəˈlɒdʒɪkᵊl) *adj Philosophy.* (of an ethical theory) regarding obligation as deriving from reason or as residing primarily in certain specific rules of conduct rather than in the maximization of some good.

deontology (ˌdiːɒnˈtɒlədʒɪ) *n* the branch of ethics dealing with duty, moral obligation, and moral commitment. [C19: from Greek *deon* duty (see DEONTIC) + -LOGY] ▸ **ˌdeonˈtologist** *n*

Deo volente *Latin.* (ˈdeɪəʊ vɒˈlɛntɪ) God willing. Abbrev.: **DV.**

deoxidize *or* **deoxidise** (diːˈɒksɪˌdaɪz) *vb* **1** (*tr*) **1a** to remove oxygen atoms from (a compound, molecule, etc.). **1b** another word for **deoxygenate. 2** another word for **reduce** (sense 12). ▸ **deˌoxidiˈzation** *or* **deˌoxidiˈsation** *n* ▸ **deˈoxiˌdizer** *or* **deˈoxiˌdiser** *n*

deoxy- *or* **desoxy-** *combining form.* indicating the presence of less oxygen than in a specified related compound: *deoxyribonucleic acid.*

deoxycorticosterone (diːˌɒksɪˌkɔːtɪkəʊˈstɪərəʊn) *or* **deoxycortone** (diːˌɒksɪˈkɔːtəʊn) *n* a corticosteroid hormone important in maintaining sodium and water balance in the body.

deoxygenate (diːˈɒksɪdʒɪˌneɪt) *or* **deoxygenize, deoxygenise** (diːˈɒksɪdʒɪˌnaɪz) *vb* (*tr*) to remove oxygen from (water, air, etc.). ▸ **deˌoxygenˈation** *n*

deoxyribonuclease (diːˌɒksɪˌraɪbəʊˈnjuːklɪeɪz) *n* the full name for **DNAase.**

deoxyribonucleic acid (diːˌɒksɪˌraɪbəʊnjuːˈkleɪɪk) *or* **desoxyribonucleic acid** *n* the full name for **DNA.**

deoxyribose (diːˌɒksɪˈraɪbəʊs, -bəʊz) *or* **desoxyribose** (dɛsˌɒksɪˈraɪbəʊs, -bəʊz) *n* a pentose sugar obtained by the hydrolysis of DNA. Formula: $C_5H_{10}O_4$.

dep. *abbrev. for:* **1** departs. **2** departure. **3** deponent. **4** deposed. **5** deposit. **6** depot. **7** deputy.

Depardieu (*French* dəpardjø) *n* **Gérard.** born 1948, French film actor. His films include *Jean de Florette* (1986), *Cyrano de Bergerac* (1990), *Green Card* (1991), and *The Man in the Iron Mask* (1997).

depart (dɪˈpɑːt) *vb* (*mainly intr*) **1** to go away; leave. **2** to start out; set forth. **3** (usually foll. by *from*) to deviate; differ; vary: *to depart from normal procedure.* **4** (*tr*) to quit (archaic, except in the phrase **depart this life**). [C13: from Old French *departir,* from DE- + *partir* to go away, divide, from Latin *partīrī* to divide, distribute, from *pars* a part]

departed (dɪˈpɑːtɪd) *adj Euphemistic.* **a** dead; deceased. **b** (*as sing or collective n; preceded by the*): *the departed.*

department (dɪˈpɑːtmənt) *n* **1** a specialized division of a large concern, such as a business, store, or university: *the geography department.* **2** a major subdivision or branch of the administration of a government. **3** a branch or subdivision of learning: *physics is a department of science.* **4** a territorial and administrative division in several countries, such as France. **5** *Informal.* a specialized sphere of knowledge, skill, or activity: *wine-making is my wife's department.* [C18: from French *département,* from *départir* to divide; see DEPART] ▸ **departmental** (ˌdiːpɑːtˈmɛntᵊl) *adj* ▸ **ˌdepartˈmentally** *adv*

departmentalism (ˌdiːpɑːtˈmɛntᵊˌlɪzəm) *n* division into departments, esp. when resulting in impaired efficiency.

departmentalize *or* **departmentalise** (ˌdiːpɑːtˈmɛntᵊˌlaɪz) *vb* (*tr*) to organize into departments, esp. excessively. ▸ **ˌdepartˌmentaliˈzation** *or* **ˌdepartˌmentaliˈsation** *n*

department store *n* a large shop divided into departments selling a great many kinds of goods.

departure (dɪˈpɑːtʃə) *n* **1** the act or an instance of departing. **2** a deviation or variation from previous custom; divergence. **3** a project, course of action, venture, etc.: *selling is a new departure for him.* **4** *Nautical.* **4a** the net distance travelled due east or west by a vessel. **4b** Also called: **point of departure.** the latitude and longitude of the point from which a vessel calculates dead reckoning. **5** a euphemistic word for **death.**

depasture (diːˈpɑːstʃə) *vb* **1** to graze or denude by grazing (a pasture, esp. a meadow specially grown for the purpose). **2** (*tr*) to pasture (cattle or sheep).

depend (dɪˈpɛnd) *vb* (*intr*) **1** (foll. by *on* or *upon*) to put trust (in); rely (on); be sure (of). **2** (usually foll. by *on* or *upon;* often with *it* as subject) to be influenced or determined (by); be resultant (from): *whether you come or not depends on what father says; it all depends on you.* **3** (foll. by *on* or *upon*) to rely (on) for income, support, etc. **4** (foll. by *from*) *Rare.* to hang down; be suspended. **5** to be undecided or pending. [C15: from Old French *dependre,* from Latin *dēpendēre* to hang from, from DE- + *pendēre* to hang]

dependable (dɪˈpɛndəbᵊl) *adj* able to be depended on; reliable; trustworthy. ▸ **de,pendaˈbility** *or* **deˈpendableness** *n* ▸ **deˈpendably** *adv*

dependant (dɪˈpɛndənt) *n* a person who depends on another person, organization, etc., for support, aid, or sustenance, esp. financial support.

USAGE Avoid confusion with **dependent.**

dependence *or U.S. (sometimes)* **dependance** (dɪˈpɛndəns) *n* **1** the state or fact of being dependent, esp. for support or help. **2** reliance; trust; confidence. **3** *Rare.* an object or person relied upon.

dependency *or U.S. (sometimes)* **dependancy** (dɪˈpɛndənsɪ) *n, pl* **-cies. 1** a territory subject to a state on which it does not border. **2** a dependent or subordinate person or thing. **3** *Psychol.* overreliance by a person on another person or on a drug, etc. **4** another word for **dependence.**

dependent *or U.S. (sometimes)* **dependant** (dɪˈpɛndənt) *adj* **1** depending on a person or thing for aid, support, life, etc. **2** *(postpositive;* foll. by *on* or *upon)* influenced or conditioned (by); contingent (on). **3** subordinate; subject: *a dependent prince.* **4** *Obsolete.* hanging down. **5** *Maths.* **5a** (of a variable) having a value depending on that assumed by a related independent variable. **5b** (of a linear equation) having every solution as a solution of one or more given linear equations. ◆ *n* **6** *Grammar.* an element in a phrase or clause that is not the governor. **7** a variant spelling (esp. U.S.) of **dependant.** ▸ **deˈpendently** *adv*

USAGE Avoid confusion with **dependant.**

dependent clause *n Grammar.* another term for **subordinate clause.**

dependent variable *n* **1** a variable in a mathematical equation or statement whose value depends on that taken on by the independent variable: *in "y = f(x)", "y" is the dependent variable.* **2** *Psychol., statistics.* the variable measured by the experimenter. It is controlled by the value of the independent variable, of which it is an index.

depersonalization *or* **depersonalisation** (dɪ,pɜːsnᵊlaɪˈzeɪʃən) *n* **1** the act or an instance of depersonalizing. **2** *Psychiatry.* an abnormal state of consciousness in which the subject feels unreal and detached from himself and the world.

depersonalize *or* **depersonalise** (dɪˈpɜːsnᵊ,laɪz) *vb (tr)* **1** to deprive (a person, organization, system, etc.) of individual or personal qualities; render impersonal. **2** to cause (someone) to lose his sense of personal identity. **[C19:** from DE- + PERSONAL + -IZE**]**

depict (dɪˈpɪkt) *vb (tr)* **1** to represent by or as by drawing, sculpture, painting, etc.; delineate; portray. **2** to represent in words; describe. **[C17:** from Latin *dēpingere,* from *pingere* to paint**]** ▸ **deˈpicter** *or* **deˈpictor** *n* ▸ **deˈpiction** *n* ▸ **deˈpictive** *adj*

depicture (dɪˈpɪktʃə) *vb* a less common word for **depict.**

depilate (ˈdɛpɪ,leɪt) *vb (tr)* to remove the hair from. **[C16:** from Latin *dēpilāre,* from *pilāre* to make bald, from *pilus* hair**]** ▸ **,depiˈlation** *n* ▸ **ˈdepi,lator** *n*

depilatory (dɪˈpɪlətərɪ, -trɪ) *adj* **1** able or serving to remove hair. ◆ *n, pl* **-ries. 2** a chemical that is used to remove hair from the body.

deplane (diːˈpleɪn) *vb (intr) Chiefly U.S. and Canadian.* to disembark from an aeroplane. **[C20:** from DE- + PLANE[1]**]**

deplete (dɪˈpliːt) *vb (tr)* **1** to use up (supplies, money, energy, etc.); reduce or exhaust. **2** to empty entirely or partially. **3** *Med.* to empty or reduce the fluid contents of (an organ or vessel). **[C19:** from Latin *dēplēre* to empty out, from DE- + *plēre* to fill**]** ▸ **deˈpletable** *adj* ▸ **deˈpletion** *n* ▸ **deˈpletive** *or* **deˈpletory** *adj*

depleted uranium *n Chem.* uranium containing a smaller proportion of the isotope uranium–235 than is present in the natural form of uranium.

depletion layer *n Electronics.* a region at the interface between dissimilar zones of conductivity in a semiconductor, in which there are few charge carriers.

deplorable (dɪˈplɔːrəbᵊl) *adj* **1** lamentable: *a deplorable lack of taste.* **2** worthy of censure or reproach; very bad: *deplorable behaviour.* ▸ **deˈplorableness** *or* **de,ploraˈbility** *n* ▸ **deˈplorably** *adv*

deplore (dɪˈplɔː) *vb (tr)* **1** to express or feel sorrow about; lament; regret. **2** to express or feel strong disapproval of; censure. **[C16:** from Old French *deplorer,* from Latin *dēplōrāre* to weep bitterly, from *plōrāre* to weep, lament**]** ▸ **deˈplorer** *n* ▸ **deˈploringly** *adv*

deploy (dɪˈplɔɪ) *vb Chiefly military.* **1** to adopt or cause to adopt a battle formation, esp. from a narrow front formation. **2** *(tr)* to redistribute (forces) to or within a given area. **[C18:** from French *déployer,* from Latin *displicāre* to unfold; see DISPLAY**]** ▸ **deˈployment** *n*

deplume (diːˈpluːm) *vb (tr)* **1** to deprive of feathers; pluck. **2** to deprive of honour, position, wealth, etc. ▸ **,depluˈmation** *n*

depolarize *or* **depolarise** (diːˈpəʊlə,raɪz) *vb* to undergo or cause to undergo a loss of polarity or polarization. ▸ **de,polariˈzation** *or* **de,polariˈsation** *n* ▸ **deˈpolar,izer** *or* **deˈpolar,iser** *n*

depoliticize *or* **depoliticise** (,diːpəˈlɪtɪ,saɪz) *vb (tr)* to deprive of a political nature; render apolitical: *two years on the committee totally depoliticized him.*

depolymerize *or* **depolymerise** (diːˈpɒlɪmə,raɪz) *vb* to break (a polymer) into constituent monomers or (of a polymer) to decompose in this way. ▸ **de,polymeriˈzation** *or* **de,polymeriˈsation** *n*

depone (dɪˈpəʊn) *vb Law, chiefly Scots.* to declare (something) under oath; testify; depose. **[C16:** from Latin *dēpōnere* to put down, from DE- + *pōnere* to put, place**]**

deponent (dɪˈpəʊnənt) *adj* **1** *Grammar.* (of a verb, esp. in Latin) having the inflectional endings of a passive verb but the meaning of an active verb. ◆ *n* **2** *Grammar.* a deponent verb. **3** *Law.* **3a** a person who makes an affidavit. **3b** a person, esp. a witness, who makes a deposition. **[C16:** from Latin *dēpōnēns* putting aside, putting down, from *dēpōnere* to put down, DEPONE**]**

depopulate (dɪˈpɒpjʊ,leɪt) *vb* to be or cause to be reduced in population. ▸ **de,popuˈlation** *n*

deport (dɪˈpɔːt) *vb (tr)* **1** to remove (an alien) forcibly from a country; expel. **2** to carry (an inhabitant) forcibly away from his homeland; transport; exile; banish. **3** to conduct, hold, or behave (oneself) in a specified manner. **[C15:** from French *déporter,* from Latin *dēportāre* to carry away, banish, from DE- + *portāre* to carry**]** ▸ **deˈportable** *adj*

deportation (,diːpɔːˈteɪʃən) *n* **1** the act of expelling an alien from a country; expulsion. **2** the act of transporting someone from his country; banishment.

deportee (,diːpɔːˈtiː) *n* a person deported or awaiting deportation.

deportment (dɪˈpɔːtmənt) *n* the manner in which a person behaves, esp. in physical bearing: *military deportment.* **[C17:** from French *déportement,* from Old French *deporter* to conduct (oneself); see DEPORT**]**

deposal (dɪˈpəʊzᵊl) *n* another word for **deposition** (sense 2).

depose (dɪˈpəʊz) *vb* **1** *(tr)* to remove from an office or position, esp. one of power or rank. **2** *Law.* to testify or give (evidence, etc.) on oath, esp. when taken down in writing; make a deposition. **[C13:** from Old French *deposer* to put away, put down, from Late Latin *dēpōnere* to depose from office, from Latin: to put aside; see DEPONE**]** ▸ **deˈposable** *adj* ▸ **deˈposer** *n*

deposit (dɪˈpɒzɪt) *vb (tr)* **1** to put or set down, esp. carefully or in a proper place; place. **2** to entrust for safekeeping; consign. **3** to place (money) in a bank or similar institution in order to earn interest or for safekeeping. **4** to give (money) in part payment or as security. **5** to lay down naturally; cause to settle: *the river deposits silt.* ◆ *n* **6a** an instance of entrusting money or valuables to a bank or similar institution. **6b** the money or valuables so entrusted. **7** money given in part payment or as security, as when goods are bought on hire-purchase. See also **down payment. 8** a consideration, esp. money, given temporarily as security against loss of or damage to something borrowed or hired. **9** an accumulation of sediments, mineral ores, coal, etc. **10** any deposited material, such as a sediment or a precipitate that has settled out of solution. **11** a coating produced on a surface, esp. a layer of metal formed by electrolysis. **12** a depository or storehouse. **13 on deposit.** payable as the first instalment, as when buying on hire-purchase. **[C17:** from Medieval Latin *dēpositāre,* from Latin *dēpositus* put down**]**

deposit account *n Brit.* a bank account that earns interest and usually requires notice of withdrawal.

depositary (dɪˈpɒzɪtərɪ, -trɪ) *n, pl* **-taries. 1** a person or group to whom something is entrusted for safety or preservation. **2** a variant spelling of **depository** (sense 1).

deposition (,dɛpəˈzɪʃən, ,diːpə-) *n* **1** *Law.* **1a** the giving of testimony on oath. **1b** the testimony so given. **1c** the sworn statement of a witness used in court in his absence. **2** the act or instance of deposing. **3** the act or an instance of depositing. **4** something that is deposited; deposit. **[C14:** from Late Latin *dēpositiō* a laying down, disposal, burying, testimony**]**

Deposition (,dɛpəˈzɪʃən, ,diːpə-) *n* the taking down of Christ's body from the Cross or a representation of this.

depositor (dɪˈpɒzɪtə) *n* a person who places or has money on deposit in a bank or similar organization.

depository (dɪˈpɒzɪtərɪ, -trɪ) *n, pl* **-ries. 1** a store, such as a warehouse, for furniture, valuables, etc.; repository. **2** a variant spelling of **depositary** (sense 1). **[C17** (in the sense: place of a deposit): from Medieval Latin *dēpositōrium;* **C18** (in the sense: depositary): see DEPOSIT, -ORY[1]**]**

depot (ˈdɛpəʊ; *U.S. and Canadian* ˈdiːpəʊ) *n* **1** a storehouse or warehouse. **2** *Military.* **2a** a store for supplies. **2b** a training and holding centre for recruits and replacements. **3** *Chiefly Brit.* a building used for the storage and servicing of buses or railway engines. **4** *U.S. and Canadian.* **4a** a bus or railway station. **4b** *(as modifier): a depot manager.* ◆ *adj* **5** (of a drug or drug dose) designed for gradual release from the site of an injection so as to act over a long period. **[C18:** from French *dépôt,* from Latin *dēpositum* a deposit, trust**]**

deprave (dɪˈpreɪv) *vb (tr)* **1** to make morally bad; corrupt; vitiate. **2** *Obsolete.* to defame; slander. **[C14:** from Latin *dēprāvāre* to distort, corrupt, from DE- + *prāvus* crooked**]** ▸ **depravation** (,dɛprəˈveɪʃən) *n* ▸ **deˈpraver** *n*

depraved (dɪˈpreɪvd) *adj* morally bad or debased; corrupt; perverted. ▸ **depravedness** (dɪˈpreɪvɪdnɪs) *n*

depravity (dɪˈprævɪtɪ) *n, pl* **-ties.** the state or an instance of moral corruption.

deprecate (ˈdɛprɪ,keɪt) *vb (tr)* **1** to express disapproval of; protest against. **2** to depreciate (a person, someone's character, etc.); belittle. **3** *Archaic.* to try to ward off by prayer. **[C17:** from Latin *dēprecārī* to avert, ward off by entreaty, from DE- + *precārī* to PRAY**]** ▸ **ˈdepre,cating** *adj* ▸ **ˈdepre,catingly** *adv* ▸ **,depreˈcation** *n* ▸ **ˈdeprecative** *adj* ▸ **ˈdeprecatively** *adv* ▸ **ˈdepre,cator** *n*

USAGE Avoid confusion with **depreciate.**

deprecatory (ˈdɛprɪkətərɪ) *adj* **1** expressing disapproval; protesting. **2** expressing apology; apologetic. ▸ **ˈdeprecatorily** *adv*

depreciable (dɪˈpriːʃəbᵊl) *adj* **1** *U.S.* able to be depreciated for tax deduction. **2** liable to depreciation.

depreciate (dɪˈpriːʃɪ,eɪt) *vb* **1** to reduce or decline in value or price. **2** *(tr)* to lessen the value of by derision, criticism, etc.; disparage. **[C15:** from Late Latin *dēpretiāre* to lower the price of, from Latin DE- + *pretium* PRICE**]** ▸ **deˈpreci,atingly** *adv* ▸ **deˈpreci,ator** *n* ▸ **depreciatory** (dɪˈpriːʃɪətərɪ, -trɪ) *or* **deˈpreciative** *adj*

USAGE Avoid confusion with **deprecate.**

depreciation (dɪ,priːʃɪˈeɪʃən) *n* **1** *Accounting.* **1a** the reduction in value of a fixed asset due to use, obsolescence, etc. **1b** the amount deducted from gross profit to allow for such reduction in value. **2** *Accounting.* a modified amount permitted for purposes of tax deduction. **3** the act or an instance of depreciating or belittling; disparagement. **4** a decrease in the exchange value of currency against gold or other currencies brought about by excess supply of that currency under conditions of fluctuating exchange rates. Compare **devaluation** (sense 1).

depredate ('dɛprɪˌdeɪt) *vb* (*tr*) *Rare.* to plunder or destroy; pillage. [C17: from Late Latin *dēpraedārī* to ravage, from Latin DE- + *praeda* booty; see PREY] ▸ **'depreˌdator** *n* ▸ **depredatory** ('dɛprɪˌdeɪtərɪ, dɪ'prɛdɪtərɪ, -trɪ) *adj*

depredation (ˌdɛprɪ'deɪʃən) *n* the act or an instance of plundering; robbery; pillage.

depress (dɪ'prɛs) *vb* (*tr*) **1** to lower in spirits; make gloomy; deject. **2** to weaken or lower the force, vigour, or energy of. **3** to lower prices of (securities or a security market). **4** to press or push down. **5** to lower the pitch of (a musical sound). **6** *Obsolete.* to suppress or subjugate. [C14: from Old French *depresser,* from Latin *dēprimere* from DE- + *premere* to PRESS[1]] ▸ **de'pressible** *adj* ▸ **de'pressing** *adj* ▸ **de'pressingly** *adv*

depressant (dɪ'prɛsᵊnt) *adj* **1** *Med.* able to diminish or reduce nervous or functional activity. **2** causing gloom or dejection; depressing. ◆ *n* **3** a depressant drug.

depressed (dɪ'prɛst) *adj* **1** low in spirits; downcast; despondent. **2** lower than the surrounding surface. **3** pressed down or flattened. **4** Also: **distressed.** characterized by relative economic hardship, such as unemployment: *a depressed area.* **5** lowered in force, intensity, or amount. **6** (of plant parts) flattened as though pressed from above. **7** *Zoology.* flattened from top to bottom: *the depressed bill of the spoonbill.*

depression (dɪ'prɛʃən) *n* **1** the act of depressing or state of being depressed. **2** a depressed or sunken place or area. **3** a mental disorder characterized by extreme gloom, feelings of inadequacy, and inability to concentrate. **4** *Pathol.* an abnormal lowering of the rate of any physiological activity or function, such as respiration. **5** an economic condition characterized by substantial and protracted unemployment, low output and investment, etc.; slump. **6** Also called: **cyclone, low.** *Meteorol.* a body of moving air below normal atmospheric pressure, which often brings rain. **7** (esp. in surveying and astronomy) the angular distance of an object, celestial body, etc., below the horizontal plane through the point of observation. Compare **elevation** (sense 11).

Depression (dɪ'prɛʃən) *n* (usually preceded by *the*) the worldwide economic depression of the early 1930s, when there was mass unemployment. Also called: the **Great Depression,** the **Slump.**

depressive (dɪ'prɛsɪv) *adj* **1** tending to depress; causing depression. **2** *Psychol.* tending to be subject to periods of depression. See also **manic-depressive.** ▸ **de'pressively** *adv* ▸ **de'pressiveness** *n*

depressomotor (dɪˌprɛsəʊ'məʊtə) *adj* **1** *Physiol.* retarding motor activity. ◆ *n* **2** a depressomotor drug.

depressor (dɪ'prɛsə) *n* **1** a person or thing that depresses. **2** any muscle that draws down a part. **3** *Med.* an instrument used to press down or aside an organ or part: *a tongue depressor.* **4** Also called: **depressor nerve.** any nerve that when stimulated produces a fall in blood pressure by dilating the arteries or lowering the heartbeat.

depressurize *or* **depressurise** (dɪ'prɛʃəˌraɪz) *vb* (*tr*) to reduce the pressure of a gas inside (a container or enclosed space), as in an aircraft cabin. ▸ **deˌpressuri'zation** *or* **deˌpressuri'sation** *n*

Depretis (*Italian* de'pretis) *n* **Agostino** (ago'sti:no). 1813–87, Italian statesman; prime minister (1876–78; 1878–79; 1881–87). His policy led to the Triple Alliance (1882) between Italy, Austria-Hungary, and Germany.

deprivation (ˌdɛprɪ'veɪʃən) *n* **1** an act or instance of depriving. **2** the state of being deprived: *social deprivation; a cycle of deprivation and violence.*

deprive (dɪ'praɪv) *vb* (*tr*) **1** (foll. by *of*) to prevent from possessing or enjoying; dispossess (of). **2** *Archaic.* to remove from rank or office; depose; demote. [C14: from Old French *depriver,* from Medieval Latin *dēprīvāre,* from Latin DE- + *prīvāre* to deprive of, rob; see PRIVATE] ▸ **de'privable** *adj* ▸ **de'prival** *n* ▸ **de'priver** *n*

deprived (dɪ'praɪvd) *adj* lacking adequate food, shelter, education, etc.: *deprived inner-city areas.*

de profundis *Latin.* (deɪ prɒ'fʊndɪs) *adv* out of the depths of misery or dejection. [from the first words of Psalm 130]

deprogramme *or* **deprogram** (di:'prəʊgræm) *vb* to free (someone) from the effects of indoctrination, esp. by a religious cult or political group.

depside ('dɛpsaɪd, -sɪd) *n* any ester formed by the condensation of the carboxyl group of one phenolic carboxylic acid with the hydroxyl group of another, found in plant cells. [C20: *deps-,* from Greek *depsein* to knead + -IDE]

dept *abbrev. for* department.

Deptford ('dɛtfəd) *n* a district in the Greater London borough of Lewisham, on the S bank of the River Thames: formerly the site of the Royal Naval dockyard.

depth (dɛpθ) *n* **1** the extent, measurement, or distance downwards, backwards, or inwards. **2** the quality of being deep; deepness. **3** intensity or profundity of emotion or feeling. **4** profundity of moral character; penetration; sagacity; integrity. **5** complexity or abstruseness, as of thought or objects of thought. **6** intensity, as of silence, colour, etc. **7** lowness of pitch. **8** *Nautical.* the distance from the top of a ship's keel to the top of a particular deck. **9** (*often pl*) a deep, far, inner, or remote part, such as an inaccessible region of a country. **10** (*often pl*) the deepest, most intense, or most severe part: *the depths of winter.* **11** (*usually pl*) a low moral state; demoralization: *how could you sink to such depths?* **12** (*often pl*) a vast space or abyss. **13** **beyond** *or* **out of one's depth. 13a** in water deeper than one is tall. **13b** beyond the range of one's competence or understanding. **14** **in depth.** thoroughly or comprehensively. See also **in-depth.** [C14: from *dep* DEEP + -TH[1]]

depth charge *or* **bomb** *n* a bomb used to attack submarines that explodes at a pre-set depth of water.

depth gauge *n* a device attached to a drill bit to prevent the hole from exceeding a predetermined depth.

depth of field *n* the range of distance in front of and behind an object focused by an optical instrument, such as a camera or microscope, within which other objects will also appear clear and sharply defined in the resulting image. Compare **depth of focus.**

depth of focus *n* the amount by which the distance between the camera lens and the film can be altered without the resulting image appearing blurred. Compare **depth of field.**

depth psychology *n Psychol.* the study of unconscious motives and attitudes.

depurate ('dɛpjʊˌreɪt) *vb* **1** to cleanse or purify or to be cleansed or purified. **2** to promote the elimination of waste products from (the body). [C17: from Medieval Latin *dēpūrāre,* from Latin DE- + *pūrāre* to purify; see PURE] ▸ **ˌdepu'ration** *n* ▸ **'depuˌrator** *n*

depurative ('dɛpjʊˌreɪtɪv, -rətɪv) *adj* **1** used for or capable of depurating; purifying; purgative. ◆ *n* **2** a depurative substance or agent.

deputation (ˌdɛpjʊ'teɪʃən) *n* **1** the act of appointing a person or body of people to represent or act on behalf of others. **2** a person or, more often, a body of people so appointed; delegation.

depute *vb* (dɪ'pju:t) (*tr*) **1** to appoint as an agent, substitute, or representative. **2** to assign or transfer (authority, duties, etc.) to a deputy; delegate. ◆ *n* ('dɛpju:t). **3** *Scot.* **3a** a deputy. **3b** (*as modifier; usually postpositive*): *sheriff depute.* [C15: from Old French *deputer,* from Late Latin *dēputāre* to assign, allot, from Latin DE- + *putāre* to think, consider]

deputize *or* **deputise** ('dɛpjʊˌtaɪz) *vb* to appoint or act as deputy.

deputy ('dɛpjʊtɪ) *n, pl* **-ties. 1a** a person appointed to act on behalf of or represent another. **1b** (*as modifier*): *the deputy chairman.* **2** a member of the legislative assembly or of the lower chamber of the legislature in various countries, such as France. **3** *Brit. mining.* another word for **fireman** (sense 4). [C16: from Old French *depute,* from *deputer* to appoint; see DEPUTE]

deputy minister *n* (in Canada) the senior civil servant in a government department.

De Quincey (də 'kwɪnsɪ) *n* **Thomas.** 1785–1859, English critic and essayist, noted particularly for his *Confessions of an English Opium Eater* (1821).

der. *abbrev. for:* **1** derivation. **2** derivative.

deracinate (dɪ'ræsɪˌneɪt) *vb* (*tr*) **1** to pull up by or as if by the roots; uproot; extirpate. **2** to remove, as from a natural environment. [C16: from Old French *desraciner,* from *des-* DIS-[1] + *racine* root, from Late Latin *rādīcīna* a little root, from Latin *rādīx* a root] ▸ **deˌraci'nation** *n*

deraign *or* **darraign** (də'reɪn) *vb* (*tr*) *Obsolete.* **1** *Law.* to contest (a claim, suit, etc.). **2** to arrange (soldiers) for battle. [C13: from Old French *deraisnier* to defend, from Vulgar Latin *ratiōnāre* (unattested) to REASON] ▸ **de'raignment** *or* **dar'raignment** *n*

derail (dɪ'reɪl) *vb* **1** to go or cause to go off the rails, as a train, tram, etc. ◆ *n* **2** Also called: **de'railer.** *Chiefly U.S.* a device designed to make rolling stock or locomotives leave the rails to avoid a collision or accident. ▸ **de'railment** *n*

derailleur (də'reɪljə) *n* a mechanism for changing gear on bicycles, consisting of a device that lifts the driving chain from one sprocket wheel to another of different size. [French *dérailleur* derailer]

Derain (*French* dərɛ̃) *n* **André** (ɑ̃dre). 1880–1954, French painter, noted for his Fauvist pictures (1905–08).

derange (dɪ'reɪndʒ) *vb* (*tr*) **1** to disturb the order or arrangement of; throw into disorder; disarrange. **2** to disturb the action or operation of. **3** to make insane; drive mad. [C18: from Old French *desrengier,* from *des-* DIS-[1] + *reng* row, order]

derangement (dɪ'reɪndʒmənt) *n* **1** the act of deranging or state of being deranged. **2** disorder or confusion. **3** *Psychiatry.* a mental disorder or serious mental disturbance.

derate (di:'reɪt) *vb* (*tr*) *Brit.* to assess the value of (some types of property, such as agricultural land) at a lower rate than others for local taxation. ▸ **de'rating** *n*

deration (di:'ræʃən) *vb* (*tr*) to end rationing of (food, petrol, etc.).

Derbent (*Russian* dɪr'bjɛnt) *n* a port in S Russia, in the Dagestan Republic on the Caspian Sea: founded by the Persians in the 6th century. Pop.: 84 000 (1987 est.).

derby ('dɜ:rbɪ) *n, pl* **-bies.** the U.S. and Canadian name for **bowler**[2].

Derby[1] ('dɑ:bɪ; *U.S.* 'dɜ:rbɪ) *n* **1** **the.** an annual horse race run at Epsom Downs, Surrey, since 1780: one of the English flat-racing classics. **2** any of various other horse races. **3** **local Derby.** a football match between two teams from the same area. [C18: named after the twelfth Earl of *Derby* (died 1834), who founded the horse race at Epsom Downs in 1780]

Derby[2] ('dɑ:bɪ) *n* **1** a city in central England, in Derby unitary authority, Derbyshire: engineering industries (esp. aircraft engines and railway rolling stock). Pop.: 223 836 (1991). **2** a unitary authority in central England, in Derbyshire. Pop.: 230 500 (1994 est.). Area: 78 sq. km (30 sq. miles). **3** a firm-textured pale-coloured type of cheese. **4** **sage Derby.** a green-and-white Derby cheese flavoured with sage.

Derby[3] ('dɑ:bɪ) *n* **Earl of.** title of *Edward George Geoffrey Smith Stanley.* 1799–1869, British statesman; Conservative prime minister (1852; 1858–59; 1866–68).

Derbyshire ('dɑ:bɪˌʃɪə, -ʃə) *n* a county of N central England: contains the Peak District and several resorts with mineral springs: the geographical and ceremonial county includes the city of Derby, which became an independent unitary authority in 1997. Administrative centre: Matlock. Pop. (including Derby city): 954 100 (1991). Area (including Derby city): 2631 sq. km (1016 sq. miles).

de re *Latin.* ('deɪ 'reɪ) *adj Logic, philosophy.* (of a belief, possibility, etc.) relating to the individual rather than to an expression, as the necessity of *the number of wonders of the world is prime* since that number, seven, is necessarily prime. Compare **de dicto.** [literally: about the thing]

derecognize *or* **derecognise** (di:'rɛkəgˌnaɪz) *vb* (*tr*) **1** to cease to recognize a trade union as having special negotiating rights within a company or industry. **2** to advise (a trade union) of such action. ▸ **ˌderecogˈnition** *n*

deregister (diːˈredʒɪstə) *vb* to remove (oneself, a car, etc.) from a register. ▸ **ˌderegisˈtration** *n*

deregulate (diːˈrɛgjʊˌleɪt) *vb* (*tr*) to remove regulations or controls from. ▸ **deˌreguˈlation** *n* ▸ **deˈregulator** *n* ▸ **deˈregulatory** *adj*

derelict (ˈdɛrɪlɪkt) *adj* **1** deserted or abandoned, as by an owner, occupant, etc. **2** falling into ruins; neglected; dilapidated. **3** neglectful of duty or obligation; remiss. ◆ *n* **4** a person abandoned or neglected by society; a social outcast or vagrant. **5** property deserted or abandoned by an owner, occupant, etc. **6** a vessel abandoned at sea. **7** a person who is neglectful of duty or obligation. [C17: from Latin *dērelictus* forsaken, from *dērelinquere* to abandon, from DE- + *relinquere* to leave]

dereliction (ˌdɛrɪˈlɪkʃən) *n* **1** deliberate, conscious, or wilful neglect (esp. in the phrase **dereliction of duty**). **2** the act of abandoning or deserting or the state of being abandoned or deserted. **3** *Law.* **3a** accretion of dry land gained by the gradual receding of the sea or by a river changing its course. **3b** the land thus left.

derequisition (diːˌrɛkwɪˈzɪʃən) *vb* (*tr*) to release from military to civilian use.

derestrict (ˌdiːrɪˈstrɪkt) *vb* (*tr*) to render or leave free from restriction, esp. a road from speed limits. ▸ **ˌdereˈstriction** *n*

Dergue (dɜːg) *n* **the.** the socialist ruling body of Ethiopia, established in 1974. [C20: from Amharic, literally, committee]

deride (dɪˈraɪd) *vb* (*tr*) to speak of or treat with contempt, mockery, or ridicule; scoff or jeer at. [C16: from Latin *dērīdēre* to laugh to scorn, from DE- + *rīdēre* to laugh, smile] ▸ **deˈrider** *n* ▸ **deˈridingly** *adv*

de rigueur *French.* (də rigœr; *English* də rɪˈgɜː) *adj* required by etiquette or fashion. [literally: of strictness]

derisible (dɪˈrɪzɪbᵊl) *adj* subject to or deserving of derision; ridiculous.

derision (dɪˈrɪʒən) *n* **1** the act of deriding; mockery; scorn. **2** an object of mockery or scorn. [C15: from Late Latin *dērīsiō,* from Latin *dērīsus;* see DERIDE]

derisive (dɪˈraɪsɪv, -zɪv) *adj* showing or characterized by derision; mocking; scornful. ▸ **deˈrisively** *adv* ▸ **deˈrisiveness** *n*

derisory (dɪˈraɪsərɪ, -zərɪ) *adj* **1** subject to or worthy of derision, esp. because of being ridiculously small or inadequate. **2** another word for **derisive.**

deriv. *abbrev. for:* **1** derivation. **2** derivative. **3** derived.

derivation (ˌdɛrɪˈveɪʃən) *n* **1** the act of deriving or state of being derived. **2** the source, origin, or descent of something, such as a word. **3** something derived; a derivative. **4a** the process of deducing a mathematical theorem, formula, etc., as a necessary consequence of a set of accepted statements. **4b** this sequence of statements. **4c** the operation of finding a derivative. ▸ **ˌderiˈvational** *adj*

derivative (dɪˈrɪvətɪv) *adj* **1** resulting from derivation; derived. **2** based on or making use of other sources; not original or primary. **3** copied from others, esp. slavishly; plagiaristic. ◆ *n* **4** a term, idea, etc., that is based on or derived from another in the same class. **5** a word derived from another word. **6** *Chem.* a compound that is formed from, or can be regarded as formed from, a structurally related compound: *chloroform is a derivative of methane.* **7** *Maths.* **7a** Also called: **differential coefficient, first derivative.** the change of a function, f(*x*), with respect to an infinitesimally small change in the independent variable, *x;* the limit of $[f(a + \Delta x) - f(a)]/\Delta x$, at $x = a$, as the increment, Δx, tends to 0. Symbols: $df(x)/dx$, $f'(x)$, $Df(x)$: *the derivative of* x^n *is* nx^{n-1}. **7b** the rate of change of one quantity with respect to another: *velocity is the derivative of distance with respect to time.* **8** *Finance.* a financial instrument, such as a futures contract or option, the price of which is largely determined by the commodity, currency, share price, interest rate, etc., to which it is linked. **9** *Psychoanal.* an activity that represents the expression of hidden impulses and desires by channelling them into socially acceptable forms. ▸ **deˈrivatively** *adv*

derive (dɪˈraɪv) *vb* **1** (usually foll. by *from*) to draw or be drawn (from) in source or origin; trace or be traced. **2** (*tr*) to obtain by reasoning; deduce; infer. **3** (*tr*) to trace the source or development of. **4** (usually foll. by *from*) to produce or be produced (from) by a chemical reaction. **5** *Maths.* to obtain (a function) by differentiation. [C14: from Old French *deriver* to spring from, from Latin *dērīvāre* draw off, from DE- + *rīvus* a stream] ▸ **deˈrivable** *adj* ▸ **deˈriver** *n*

derived fossil *n* a fossil eroded from a sediment and redeposited in a younger sediment.

derived unit *n* a unit of measurement obtained by multiplication or division of the base units of a system without the introduction of numerical factors.

-derm *n combining form.* indicating skin: *endoderm.* [via French from Greek *derma* skin]

derma[1] (ˈdɜːmə) *n* another name for **corium.** Also: **derm** (dɜːm). [C18: New Latin, from Greek: skin, from *derein* to skin]

derma[2] (ˈdɜːmə) *n* beef or fowl intestine used as a casing for certain dishes, esp. kishke. [from Yiddish *derme,* plural of *darm* intestine, from Old High German *daram;* related to Old English *thearm* gut, Old Norse *tharmr*]

dermal (ˈdɜːməl) *adj* of or relating to the skin.

dermapteran (dɜːˈmæptərən) *n* **1** any insect of the order *Dermaptera,* the earwigs. ◆ *adj* **2** of, relating to, or belonging to this order. [C19: from Greek *derma* (see DERMA[1]) + *pteron* wing]

dermatitis (ˌdɜːməˈtaɪtɪs) *n* inflammation of the skin.

dermato-, derma- *or before a vowel* **dermat-, derm-** *combining form.* indicating skin: *dermatology; dermatome; dermal; dermatitis.* [from Greek *derma* skin]

dermatogen (dəˈmætədʒən, ˈdɜːməˌtəʊdʒən) *n Botany.* a meristem at the apex of stems and roots that gives rise to the epidermis.

dermatoglyphics (ˌdɜːmətəʊˈglɪfɪks) *pl n* **1** the lines forming a skin pattern, esp. on the palms of the hands and soles of the feet. **2** (*functioning as sing*) the study of such skin patterns. [C20: from DERMATO- + Greek *gluphē* a carving; see GLYPH]

dermatoid (ˈdɜːməˌtɔɪd) *adj* resembling skin.

dermatology (ˌdɜːməˈtɒlədʒɪ) *n* the branch of medicine concerned with the skin and its diseases. ▸ **dermatological** (ˌdɜːmətəˈlɒdʒɪkᵊl) *adj* ▸ **ˌdermaˈtologist** *n*

dermatome (ˈdɜːməˌtəʊm) *n* **1** a surgical instrument for cutting thin slices of skin, esp. for grafting. **2** the area of skin supplied by nerve fibres from a single posterior spinal root. **3** *Embryol.* the part of a somite in a vertebrate embryo that gives rise to the dermis. ▸ **dermatomic** (ˌdɜːməˈtɒmɪk) *adj*

dermatophyte (ˈdɜːmətəʊˌfaɪt) *n* any parasitic fungus that affects the skin. ▸ **dermatophytic** (ˌdɜːmətəʊˈfɪtɪk) *adj*

dermatophytosis (ˌdɜːmətəʊfaɪˈtəʊsɪs) *n* a fungal infection of the skin, esp. the feet. See **athlete's foot.**

dermatoplasty (ˈdɜːmətəʊˌplæstɪ) *n* any surgical operation on the skin, esp. skin grafting. ▸ **ˌdermatoˈplastic** *adj*

dermatosis (ˌdɜːməˈtəʊsɪs) *n, pl* **-toses** (-ˈtəʊsiːz). any skin disease.

dermestid (ˌdɜːˈmɛstɪd) *n* any beetle of the family *Dermestidae,* whose members are destructive at both larval and adult stages to a wide range of stored organic materials such as wool, fur, feathers, and meat. They include the bacon (*or* larder), cabinet, carpet, leather, and museum beetles. [C19: from New Latin *dermestida,* from Greek *dermēstēs,* from *derma* skin + *esthiein* to eat]

dermis (ˈdɜːmɪs) *n* another name for **corium.** [C19: New Latin, from EPIDERMIS] ▸ **ˈdermic** *adj*

dermoid (ˈdɜːmɔɪd) *adj* **1** of or resembling skin. ◆ *n* **2** a congenital cystic tumour whose walls are lined with epithelium.

Dermot MacMurrough (ˈdɛːmət məkˈmʌrə) *n* ?1110–71, king of Leinster, who, by enlisting the support of the English to win back his kingdom, was responsible for the English conquest of Ireland.

dernier cri *French.* (dɛrnje kri) *n* **le** (lə). the latest fashion; the last word. [literally: last cry]

dero (ˈdɛrəʊ) *n, pl* **deros.** *Austral. slang.* a tramp or derelict. [C20: shortened from DERELICT]

derogate *vb* (ˈdɛrəˌgeɪt). **1** (*intr;* foll. by *from*) to cause to seem inferior or be in disrepute; detract. **2** (*intr;* foll. by *from*) to deviate in standard or quality; degenerate. **3** (*tr*) to cause to seem inferior, etc.; disparage. **4** (*tr*) to curtail the application of (a law or regulation). ◆ *adj* (ˈdɛrəgɪt, -ˌgeɪt). **5** *Archaic.* debased or degraded. [C15: from Latin *dērogāre* to repeal some part of a law, modify it, from DE- + *rogāre* to ask, propose a law] ▸ **ˈderogately** *adv* ▸ **ˌderoˈgation** *n* ▸ **derogative** (dɪˈrɒgətɪv) *adj* ▸ **deˈrogatively** *adv*

derogatory (dɪˈrɒgətərɪ, -trɪ) *adj* tending or intended to detract, disparage, or belittle; intentionally offensive. ▸ **deˈrogatorily** *adv* ▸ **deˈrogatoriness** *n*

derrick (ˈdɛrɪk) *n* **1** a simple crane having lifting tackle slung from a boom. **2** the framework erected over an oil well to enable drill tubes to be raised and lowered. ◆ *vb* **3** to raise or lower the jib of (a crane). [C17 (in the sense: gallows): from *Derrick,* name of a celebrated hangman at Tyburn]

Derrida (*French* dɛrida) *n* **Jacques.** born 1930, French philosopher and literary critic, regarded as the founder of deconstruction: author of *L'Ecriture et la différence* (1967).

derrière (ˌdɛrɪˈɛə; *French* dɛrjɛr) *n* a euphemistic word for **buttocks.** [C18: literally: behind (prep), from Old French *deriere,* from Latin *dē retrō* from the back]

derring-do (ˈdɛrɪŋˈduː) *n Archaic or literary.* a daring spirit or deed; boldness or bold action. [C16: from Middle English *durring don* daring to do, from *durren* to dare + *don* to do]

derringer *or* **deringer** (ˈdɛrɪndʒə) *n* a short-barrelled pocket pistol of large calibre. [C19: named after Henry *Deringer,* American gunsmith who invented it]

derris (ˈdɛrɪs) *n* any East Indian leguminous woody climbing plant of the genus *Derris,* esp. *D. elliptica,* whose roots yield the compound rotenone. [C19: New Latin, from Greek: covering, leather, from *deros* skin, hide, from *derein* to skin]

derry[1] (ˈdɛrɪ) *n, pl* **-ries.** *Austral. and N.Z.* **have a derry on.** to have a prejudice or grudge against. [C19: probably from *derry down,* a refrain in some folk songs, alluding to the phrase *have a down on;* see DOWN[1]]

derry[2] (ˈdɛrɪ) *n, pl* **-ries.** *Slang.* a derelict house, esp. one used by tramps, drug addicts, etc. [C20: shortened from DERELICT]

Derry (ˈdɛrɪ) *n* **1** a district in NW Northern Ireland, in Co. Londonderry. Pop.: 95 371 (1991). Area: 387 sq. km (149 sq. miles). **2** another name for **Londonderry.**

derv (dɜːv) *n* a Brit. name for **diesel oil** when used for road transport. [C20: from *d(iesel) e(ngine) r(oad) v(ehicle)*]

dervish (ˈdɜːvɪʃ) *n* a member of any of various Muslim orders of ascetics, some of which (**whirling dervishes**) are noted for a frenzied, ecstatic, whirling dance. [C16: from Turkish: beggar, from Persian *darvīsh* mendicant monk] ▸ **ˈdervish-ˌlike** *adj*

Derwent (ˈdɜːwənt) *n* **1** a river in S Australia, in S Tasmania, flowing southeast to the Tasman Sea. Length: 172 km (107 miles). **2** a river in N central England, in N Derbyshire, flowing southeast to the River Trent. Length: 96 km (60 miles). **3** a river in N England, in Yorkshire, rising on the North York Moors and flowing south to the River Ouse. Length: 92 km (57 miles). **4** a river in NW England, in Cumbria, rising on the Borrowdale Fells and flowing north and west to the Irish Sea. Length: 54 km (34 miles).

Derwentwater (ˈdɜːwəntˌwɔːtə) *n* a lake in NW England, in Cumbria in the Lake District. Area: about 8 sq. km (3 sq. miles).

DES (in Britain) *abbrev. for* (former) Department of Education and Science.

Desai (dɛˈsaɪ) *n* **Morarji (Ranchhodji)** (məˈrɑːdʒɪ). 1896–1995, Indian statesman, noted for his asceticism. He founded the Janata party in opposition to Indira Gandhi, whom he defeated in the 1977 election; prime minister of India (1977–79).

desalinate (diːˈsælɪˌneɪt) *or* **desalinize, desalinise** *vb* (*tr*) to remove the salt from (esp. from sea water). Also: **desalt** (diːˈsɔːlt).

desalination (diːˌsælɪˈneɪʃən) *or* **desalinization, desalinisation** *n* the process of removing salt, esp. from sea water so that it can be used for drinking or irrigation.

desaturation (diːˌsætʃəˈreɪʃən) *n Physics.* the addition of white light to a pure colour to produce a paler less saturated colour.

desc. *abbrev. for* descendant.

descant *n* (ˈdɛskænt, ˈdɪs-). **1** Also called: **discant.** a decorative counterpoint added above a basic melody. **2** a comment, criticism, or discourse. ◆ *adj* (ˈdɛskænt,ˈdɪs-) **3** Also: **discant.** of or pertaining to the highest member in common use of a family of musical instruments: *a descant recorder.* ◆ *vb* (dɛsˈkænt, dɪs-). (*intr*) **4** Also: **discant.** (often foll. by *on* or *upon*) to compose or perform a descant (for a piece of music). **5** (often foll. by *on* or *upon*) to discourse at length or make varied comments. **[C14:** from Old Northern French, from Medieval Latin *discanthus,* from Latin DIS-[1] + *cantus* song; see CHANT**]** ▸ **desˈcanter** *n*

Descartes (ˈdeɪˌkɑːt; *French* dekart) *n* **René** (rəne). 1596–1650, French philosopher and mathematician. He provided a mechanistic basis for the philosophical theory of dualism and is regarded as the founder of modern philosophy. He also founded analytical geometry and contributed greatly to the science of optics. His works include *Discours de la méthode* (1637), *Meditationes de Prima Philosophia* (1641), and *Principia Philosophiae* (1644). Related adj: **Cartesian.**

descend (dɪˈsɛnd) *vb* (*mainly intr*) **1** (*also tr*) to move, pass, or go down (a hill, slope, staircase, etc.) **2** (of a hill, slope, or path) to lead or extend down; slope; incline. **3** to move to a lower level, pitch, etc.; fall. **4** (often foll. by *from*) to be connected by a blood relationship (to a dead or extinct individual, race, species, etc.). **5** to be passed on by parents or ancestors; be inherited. **6** to sink or come down in morals or behaviour; lower oneself. **7** (often foll. by *on* or *upon*) to arrive or attack in a sudden or overwhelming way: *their relatives descended upon them last week.* **8** (of the sun, moon, etc.) to move towards the horizon. **[C13:** from Old French *descendre,* from Latin *dēscendere,* from DE- + *scandere* to climb; see SCAN**]** ▸ **desˈcendable** *adj*

descendant (dɪˈsɛndənt) *n* **1** a person, animal, or plant when described as descended from an individual, race, species, etc. **2** something that derives or is descended from an earlier form. ◆ *adj* **3** a variant spelling of **descendent.**

Descendant (dɪˈsɛndənt) *n Astrology.* the point on the ecliptic lying directly opposite the Ascendant.

descendent (dɪˈsɛndənt) *adj* **1** coming or going downwards; descending. **2** deriving by descent, as from an ancestor.

descender (dɪˈsɛndə) *n* **1** a person or thing that descends. **2** *Printing.* the portion of a letter, such as j, p, or y, below the level of the base of an x or n.

descendeur *French.* (desɑ̃dœr) *n Mountaineering.* a shaped metal piece through which the rope can be fed: used to control the rate of descent in abseiling. Also called: **descender. [C20]**

descendible *or* **descendable** (dɪˈsɛndəbᵊl) *adj Law.* capable of being inherited.

descent (dɪˈsɛnt) *n* **1** the act of descending. **2** a downward slope or inclination. **3** a passage, path, or way leading downwards. **4** derivation from an ancestor or ancestral group; lineage. **5** (in genealogy) a generation in a particular lineage. **6** a decline or degeneration. **7** a movement or passage in degree or state from higher to lower. **8** (often foll. by *on*) a sudden and overwhelming arrival or attack. **9** *Property law.* (formerly) the transmission of real property to the heir on an intestacy.

Deschamps (*French* deʃɑ̃) *n* **1 Émile** (*French* emil), full name *Émile Deschamps de Saint-Armand.* 1791–1871, French poet, dramatist, and librettist: a leading figure in the French romantic movement. **2 Eustache** (østaʃ). ?1346–?1406, French poet, noted for his *Miroir de mariage,* a satirical attack on women.

deschool (ˌdiːˈskuːl) *vb* (*tr*) to separate education from the institution of school and operate through the pupil's life experience as opposed to a set curriculum.

descramble (diːˈskræmbᵊl) *vb* to restore (a scrambled signal) to an intelligible form, esp. automatically by the use of electronic devices. ▸ **ˌdeˈscrambler** *n*

describe (dɪˈskraɪb) *vb* (*tr*) **1** to give an account or representation of in words. **2** to pronounce or label: *he has been described as a genius.* **3** to draw a line or figure, such as a circle. **[C15:** from Latin *dēscrībere* to copy off, write out, delineate, from DE- + *scrībere* to write**]** ▸ **deˈscribable** *adj* ▸ **deˈscriber** *n*

description (dɪˈskrɪpʃən) *n* **1** a statement or account that describes; representation in words. **2** the act, process, or technique of describing. **3** sort, kind, or variety: *reptiles of every description.* **4** *Geometry.* the act of drawing a line or figure, such as an arc. **5** *Philosophy.* a noun phrase containing a predicate that may replace a name as the subject of a sentence.

descriptive (dɪˈskrɪptɪv) *adj* **1** characterized by or containing description; serving to describe. **2** *Grammar.* (of an adjective) serving to describe the referent of the noun modified, as for example the adjective *brown* as contrasted with *my* and *former.* **3** relating to or based upon description or classification rather than explanation or prescription: *descriptive linguistics.* ▸ **deˈscriptively** *adv* ▸ **deˈscriptiveness** *n*

descriptive geometry *n* the study of the projection of three-dimensional figures onto a plane surface.

descriptive linguistics *n* (*functioning as sing*) the study of the description of the internal phonological, grammatical, and semantic structures of languages at given points in time without reference to their histories or to one another. Also called: **synchronic linguistics.** Compare **historical linguistics.**

descriptive metaphysics *n* (*functioning as sing*) the philosophical study of the structure of how we think about the world.

descriptive notation *n Chess.* a method of denoting the squares on the chessboard in which each player names the files from the pieces that stand on them at the opening and numbers the ranks away from himself. Compare **algebraic notation.**

descriptive statistics *n* (*functioning as sing*) the use of statistics to describe a set of known data in a clear and concise manner, as in terms of its mean and variance, or diagramatically, as by a histogram. Compare **statistical inference.**

descriptivism (dɪˈskrɪptɪˌvɪzəm) *n Ethics.* the theory that moral utterances have a truth value. Compare **prescriptivism, emotivism.** ▸ **deˈscriptiˌvist** *adj*

descry (dɪˈskraɪ) *vb* **-scries, -scrying, -scried.** (*tr*) **1** to discern or make out; catch sight of. **2** to discover by looking carefully; detect. **[C14:** from Old French *descrier* to proclaim, DECRY**]** ▸ **deˈscrier** *n*

desecrate (ˈdɛsɪˌkreɪt) *vb* (*tr*) **1** to violate or outrage the sacred character of (an object or place) by destructive, blasphemous, or sacrilegious action. **2** to remove the consecration from (a person, object, building, etc.); deconsecrate. **[C17:** from DE- + CONSECRATE**]** ▸ **ˈdeseˌcrator** *or* **ˈdeseˌcrater** *n* ▸ **ˌdeseˈcration** *n*

desegregate (diːˈsɛgrɪˌgeɪt) *vb* to end racial segregation in (a school or other public institution). ▸ **ˌdesegreˈgation** *n* ▸ **ˌdesegreˈgationist** *n, adj*

deselect (ˌdiːsɪˈlɛkt) *vb* (*tr*) **1** *Brit. Politics.* (of a constituency organization) to refuse to select (an existing MP) for re-election. **2** *U.S.* to discharge (a trainee) during the period of training. ▸ **ˌdeseˈlection** *n*

desensitize *or* **desensitise** (diːˈsɛnsɪˌtaɪz) *vb* (*tr*) **1** to render insensitive or less sensitive: *the patient was desensitized to the allergen; to desensitize photographic film.* **2** *Psychol.* to decrease the abnormal fear in (a person) of a situation or object, by exposing him to it either in reality or in his imagination. ▸ **deˌsensitiˈzation** *or* **deˌsensitiˈsation** *n* ▸ **deˈsensiˌtizer** *or* **deˈsensiˌtiser** *n*

desert[1] (ˈdɛzət) *n* **1** a region that is devoid or almost devoid of vegetation, esp. because of low rainfall. **2** an uncultivated uninhabited region. **3** a place which lacks some desirable feature or quality: *a cultural desert.* **4** (*modifier*) of, relating to, or like a desert; infertile or desolate. **[C13:** from Old French, from Church Latin *dēsertum,* from Latin *dēserere* to abandon, literally: to sever one's links with, from DE- + *serere* to bind together**]**

desert[2] (dɪˈzɜːt) *vb* **1** (*tr*) to leave or abandon (a person, place, etc.) without intending to return, esp. in violation of a duty, promise, or obligation. **2** *Military.* to abscond from (a post or duty) with no intention of returning. **3** (*tr*) to fail (someone) in time of need: *his good humour temporarily deserted him.* **4** (*tr*) *Scots Law.* to give up or postpone (a case or charge). **[C15:** from French *déserter,* from Late Latin *dēsertāre,* from Latin *dēserere* to forsake; see DESERT[1]**]** ▸ **deˈserter** *n* ▸ **deˈserted** *adj*

desert[3] (dɪˈzɜːt) *n* **1** (*often pl*) something that is deserved or merited; just reward or punishment. **2** the state of deserving a reward or punishment. **3** virtue or merit. **[C13:** from Old French *deserte,* from *deservir* to DESERVE**]**

desert boots *pl n* ankle-high suede boots with laces and soft soles, worn informally by men and women.

desert cooler *n* (in India) a cooling device in which air is driven by an electric fan through wet grass.

desertification (dɪˌzɜːtɪfɪˈkeɪʃən) *n* a process by which fertile land turns into barren land or desert.

desertion (dɪˈzɜːʃən) *n* **1** the act of deserting or abandoning or the state of being deserted or abandoned. **2** *Law.* wilful abandonment, esp. of one's spouse or children, without consent and in breach of obligations.

desert island *n* a small remote tropical island.

desert lynx *n* another name for **caracal.**

desert oak *n* a tree, *Casuarina decaisneana,* of Central and NW Australia, the timber of which is resistant to termite attack.

desert pea *n* an Australian trailing leguminous plant, *Clianthus formosus,* with scarlet flowers.

desert rat *n* **1** a jerboa, *Jaculus orientalis,* inhabiting the deserts of N Africa. **2** *Brit. informal.* a soldier who served in North Africa with the British 7th Armoured Division in 1941–42.

desert soil *n* a type of soil developed in arid climates, characterized by a lack of leaching and small humus content.

deserve (dɪˈzɜːv) *vb* **1** (*tr*) to be entitled to or worthy of; merit. **2** (*intr;* foll. by *of*) *Obsolete.* to be worthy. **[C13:** from Old French *deservir,* from Latin *dēservīre* to serve devotedly, from DE- + *servīre* to SERVE**]** ▸ **deˈserved** *adj* ▸ **deservedness** (dɪˈzɜːvɪdnɪs) *n* ▸ **deˈserver** *n*

deservedly (dɪˈzɜːvɪdlɪ) *adv* according to merit; justly.

deserving (dɪˈzɜːvɪŋ) *adj* **1** (often *postpositive* and foll. by *of*) worthy, esp. of praise or reward. ◆ *n* **2** *Rare.* a merit or demerit; desert. ▸ **deˈservingly** *adv* ▸ **deˈservingness** *n*

desexualize *or* **desexualise** (diːˈsɛksjʊəˌlaɪz) *vb* (*tr*) to deprive of sexual characteristics by the surgical removal of the testicles or ovaries; castrate or spay. Often shortened to **desex** (diːˈsɛks). ▸ **deˌsexualiˈzation** *or* **deˌsexualiˈsation** *n*

deshabille (ˌdeɪzæˈbiːl) *or* **dishabille** *n* **1** the state of being partly or carelessly dressed. **2** *Archaic.* clothes worn in such a state. **[C17:** from French *déshabillé* undressed, from *dés-* DIS-[1] + *habiller* to dress; see HABILIMENT**]**

de Sica (*Italian* de ˈsiːka) *n* **Vittorio** (vitˈtɔːrjo). 1902–74, Italian film actor and director. His films, in the realist tradition, include *Shoeshine* (1946) and *Bicycle Thieves* (1948).

desiccant (ˈdɛsɪkənt) *adj* **1** desiccating or drying. ◆ *n* **2** a substance, such as calcium oxide, that absorbs water and is used to remove moisture; a drying agent. **[C17:** from Latin *dēsiccāns* drying up; see DESICCATE**]**

desiccate (ˈdɛsɪˌkeɪt) *vb* **1** (*tr*) to remove most of the water from (a substance or material); dehydrate. **2** (*tr*) to preserve (food) by removing moisture; dry. **3**

(*intr*) to become dried up. [C16: from Latin *dēsiccāre* to dry up, from DE- + *siccāre* to dry, from *siccus* dry] ► ˌ**desic'cation** *n* ► '**desiccative** *adj*

desiccated ('dɛsɪˌkeɪtɪd) *adj* **1** dehydrated and powdered: *desiccated coconut.* **2** lacking in spirit or animation.

desiccator ('dɛsɪˌkeɪtə) *n* **1** any apparatus for drying milk, fruit, etc. **2** an airtight box or jar containing a desiccant, used to dry chemicals and protect them from the water vapour in the atmosphere.

desiderata (dɪˌzɪdə'rɑːtə) *n* the plural of **desideratum.**

desiderate (dɪ'zɪdəˌreɪt) *vb* (*tr*) to feel the lack of or need for; long for; miss. [C17: from Latin *dēsīderāre,* from DE- + *sīdus* star; see DESIRE] ► **deˌsider'ation** *n*

desiderative (dɪ'zɪdərətɪv) *adj* **1** feeling or expressing desire. **2** (in certain languages, of a verb) related in form to another verb and expressing the subject's desire or intention to perform the act denoted by the other verb. ◆ *n* **3** a desiderative verb.

desideratum (dɪˌzɪdə'rɑːtəm) *n, pl* **-ta** (-tə). something lacked and wanted. [C17: from Latin; see DESIDERATE]

design (dɪ'zaɪn) *vb* **1** to work out the structure or form of (something), as by making a sketch, outline, pattern, or plans. **2** to plan and make (something) artistically or skilfully. **3** (*tr*) to form or conceive in the mind; invent. **4** (*tr*) to intend, as for a specific purpose; plan. **5** (*tr*) *Obsolete.* to mark out or designate. ◆ *n* **6** a plan, sketch, or preliminary drawing. **7** the arrangement or pattern of elements or features of an artistic or decorative work: *the design of the desk is Chippendale.* **8** a finished artistic or decorative creation. **9** the art of designing. **10** a plan, scheme, or project. **11** an end aimed at or planned for; intention; purpose. **12** (*often pl; often foll. by on or against*) a plot or hostile scheme, often to gain possession of (something) by illegitimate means. **13** a coherent or purposeful pattern, as opposed to chaos: *God's design appears in nature.* **14 argument from design.** *Philosophy.* another name for **teleological argument.** [C16: from Latin *dēsignāre* to mark out, describe, from DE- + *signāre* to mark, from *signum* a mark, SIGN] ► **de'signable** *adj*

designate *vb* ('dɛzɪgˌneɪt). (*tr*) **1** to indicate or specify. **2** to give a name to; style; entitle. **3** to select or name for an office or duty; appoint. ◆ *adj* ('dɛzɪgnɪt, -ˌneɪt). **4** (*immediately postpositive*) appointed, but not yet in office: *a minister designate.* [C15: from Latin *dēsignātus* marked out, defined; see DESIGN] ► '**desigˌnative** *or* **designatory** (ˌdɛzɪg'neɪtərɪ) *adj* ► '**desigˌnator** *n*

designated *adj Logic.* (of a truth value) corresponding to truth in a two-valued logic, or having one of the analogous values in a many-valued logic.

designated driver *n* a person who volunteers not to drink alcohol on a social occasion, so that he or she can safely drive other people who have been drinking.

designated employment *n* (in Britain) any of certain kinds of jobs reserved for handicapped workers under the Disabled Persons (Employment) Act 1944.

designation (ˌdɛzɪg'neɪʃən) *n* **1** something that designates, such as a name or distinctive mark. **2** the act of designating or the fact of being designated.

designedly (dɪ'zaɪnɪdlɪ) *adv* by intention or design; on purpose.

designer (dɪ'zaɪnə) *n* **1** a person who devises and executes designs, as for works of art, clothes, machines, etc. **2** (*modifier*) designed by and bearing the label or signature of a well-known fashion designer: *designer jeans.* **3** (*modifier*) (of things, ideas, etc.) having an appearance of fashionable trendiness: *designer pop songs; designer stubble.* **4** (*modifier*) (of cells, chemicals, etc.) designed (or produced) to perform a specific function or combat a specific problem: *designer insecticide.* **5** a person who devises plots or schemes; intriguer.

designer drug *n* **1** *Med.* a synthetic antibiotic designed to be effective against a particular bacterium. **2** any of various narcotic or hallucinogenic substances manufactured illegally from a range of chemicals.

designing (dɪ'zaɪnɪŋ) *adj* artful and scheming; conniving; crafty. ► **de'signingly** *adv*

desinence ('dɛsɪnəns) *n Grammar.* an ending or termination, esp. an inflectional ending of a word. [C16: from French *désinence,* from Latin *dēsinēns* ending, from *dēsinere* to leave off, from DE- + *sinere* to leave, permit] ► '**desinent** *or* **desinential** (ˌdɛsɪ'nɛnʃəl) *adj*

desirable (dɪ'zaɪərəb^əl) *adj* **1** worthy of desire or recommendation: *a desirable residence.* **2** arousing desire, esp. sexual desire; attractive. ◆ *n* **3** a person or thing that is the object of desire. ► **deˌsira'bility** *or* **de'sirableness** *n* ► **de'sirably** *adv*

desire (dɪ'zaɪə) *vb* (*tr*) **1** to wish or long for; crave; want. **2** to express a wish or make a request for; ask for. ◆ *n* **3** a wish or longing; craving. **4** an expressed wish; request. **5** sexual appetite; lust. **6** a person or thing that is desired. Related adj: **orectic.** [C13: from Old French *desirer,* from Latin *dēsīderāre* to desire earnestly; see DESIDERATE] ► **de'sirer** *n*

desirous (dɪ'zaɪərəs) *adj* (usually *postpositive* and foll. by *of*) having or expressing desire (for); having a wish or longing (for). ► **de'sirously** *adv* ► **de'sirousness** *n*

desist (dɪ'zɪst) *vb* (*intr;* often foll. by *from*) to cease, as from an action; stop or abstain. [C15: from Old French *desister,* from Latin *dēsistere* to leave off, stand apart, from DE- + *sistere* to stand, halt] ► **de'sistance** *or* **de'sistence** *n*

desk (dɛsk) *n* **1** a piece of furniture with a writing surface and usually drawers or other compartments. **2** a service counter or table in a public building, such as a hotel: *information desk.* **3** a support, lectern, or book rest for the book from which services are read in a church. **4** the editorial section of a newspaper, etc., responsible for a particular subject: *the news desk.* **5a** a music stand shared by two orchestral players. **5b** these two players. **6** (*modifier*) **6a** made for use at a desk: *a desk calendar.* **6b** done at a desk: *a desk job.* [C14: from Medieval Latin *desca* table, from Latin *discus* disc, dish]

desk-bound *adj* engaged in or involving sedentary work, as at an office desk.

desk clerk *n U.S. and Canadian.* a hotel receptionist. Also called: **clerk.**

deskill (diː'skɪl) *vb* (*tr*) **1** to mechanize or computerize (a job or process) to such an extent that little human skill is required to do it. **2** to cause (skilled persons or a labour force) to work at a job that does not utilize their skills. ► **de'skilling** *n*

desktop ('dɛskˌtɒp) *n* (*modifier*) denoting a computer system, esp. for word processing, that is small enough to use at a desk.

desktop publishing *n* a means of publishing reports, advertising, etc., to near-typeset quality using a desktop computer and a laser printer. Abbrev.: **DTP.**

desman ('dɛsmən) *n, pl* **-mans.** either of two molelike amphibious mammals, *Desmana moschata* (**Russian desman**) or *Galemys pyrenaicus* (**Pyrenean desman**), having dense fur and webbed feet: family *Talpidae,* order *Insectivora* (insectivores). [C18: from Swedish *desmansråtta,* from *desman* musk (of Germanic origin) + *råtta* rat]

desmid ('dɛsmɪd) *n* any freshwater green alga of the mainly unicellular family *Desmidioideae,* typically constricted into two symmetrical halves. [C19: from New Latin *Desmidium* (genus name), from Greek *desmos* bond, from *dein* to bind] ► **des'midian** *adj*

desmoid ('dɛsmɔɪd) *adj* **1** *Anatomy.* resembling a tendon or ligament. ◆ *n* **2** *Pathol.* a very firm tumour of connective tissue. [C19: from Greek *desmos* band + -OID; see DESMID]

Des Moines (də 'mɔɪn, 'mɔɪnz) *n* **1** a city in S central Iowa: state capital. Pop.: 193 422 (1996 est.). **2** a river in the N central U.S., rising in SW Minnesota and flowing southeast to join the Mississippi. Length: 861 km (535 miles).

Desmond ('dɛzmənd) *n* **15th Earl of,** title of *Gerald Fitzgerald.* died 1583, Anglo-Irish nobleman, who led a Catholic rebellion (1579) against English domination of Ireland.

desmosome ('dɛsməˌsəʊm) *n Cytology.* an attachment between adjacent cells.

Desmoulins (*French* dɛmulɛ̃) *n* (**Lucie Simplice**) **Camille** (**Benoît**) (kamij). 1760–94, French revolutionary leader, pamphleteer, and orator.

desolate *adj* ('dɛsəlɪt). **1** uninhabited; deserted. **2** made uninhabitable; laid waste; devastated. **3** without friends, hope, or encouragement; forlorn, wretched, or abandoned. **4** gloomy or dismal; depressing. ◆ *vb* ('dɛsəˌleɪt). (*tr*) **5** to deprive of inhabitants; depopulate. **6** to make barren or lay waste; devastate. **7** to make wretched or forlorn. **8** to forsake or abandon. [C14: from Latin *dēsōlāre* to leave alone, from DE- + *sōlāre* to make lonely, lay waste, from *sōlus* alone] ► '**desoˌlater** *or* '**desoˌlator** *n* ► '**desolately** *adv* ► '**desolateness** *n*

desolation (ˌdɛsə'leɪʃən) *n* **1** the act of desolating or the state of being desolated; ruin or devastation. **2** solitary misery; wretchedness. **3** a desolate region; barren waste.

desorb (dɪ'sɔːb, -'zɔːb) *vb Chem.* to change from an adsorbed state on a surface to a gaseous or liquid state.

desorption (dɪ'sɔːpʃən, -'zɔːp-) *n* the action or process of desorbing.

De Soto (də 'səʊtəʊ; *Spanish* de 'soto) *n* **Hernando** (ɛr'nando). ?1500–42, Spanish explorer, who discovered the Mississippi River (1541). Also called: **Fernando De Soto** (fɛr'nando).

desoxy- *combining form.* a variant of **deoxy-.**

despair (dɪ'spɛə) *vb* **1** (*intr;* often foll. by *of*) to lose or give up hope: *I despair of his coming.* **2** (*tr*) *Obsolete.* to give up hope of; lose hope in. ◆ *n* **3** total loss of hope. **4** a person or thing that causes hopelessness or for which there is no hope. [C14: from Old French *despoir* hopelessness, from *desperer* to despair, from Latin *dēspērāre,* from DE- + *spērāre* to hope]

despairing (dɪ'spɛərɪŋ) *adj* marked by or resulting from despair; hopeless or desperate. ► **des'pairingly** *adv*

despatch (dɪ'spætʃ) *vb* (*tr*) a less common spelling of **dispatch.** ► **des'patcher** *n*

Despenser (dɪs'pɛnsə) *n* **Hugh le,** Earl of Winchester. 1262–1326, English statesman, a favourite of Edward II. Together with his son **Hugh,** *the Younger* (?1290–1326), he was executed by the king's enemies.

desperado (ˌdɛspə'rɑːdəʊ) *n, pl* **-does** *or* **-dos.** a reckless or desperate person, esp. one ready to commit any violent illegal act. [C17: probably pseudo-Spanish variant of obsolete *desperate* (n) a reckless character]

desperate ('dɛspərɪt, -prɪt) *adj* **1** careless of danger, as from despair; utterly reckless. **2** (of an act) reckless; risky. **3** used or undertaken in desperation or as a last resort: *desperate measures.* **4** critical; very grave: *in desperate need.* **5** (often *postpositive* and foll. by *for*) in distress and having a great need or desire. **6** moved by or showing despair or hopelessness; despairing. [C15: from Latin *dēspērāre* to have no hope; see DESPAIR] ► '**desperately** *adv* ► '**desperateness** *n*

desperation (ˌdɛspə'reɪʃən) *n* **1** desperate recklessness. **2** the act of despairing or the state of being desperate.

despicable ('dɛspɪkəb^əl, dɪ'spɪk-) *adj* worthy of being despised; contemptible; mean. [C16: from Late Latin *dēspicābilis,* from *dēspicārī* to disdain; compare DESPISE] ► ˌ**despica'bility** *or* '**despicableness** *n* ► '**despicably** *adv*

despise (dɪ'spaɪz) *vb* (*tr*) to look down on with contempt; scorn: *he despises flattery.* [C13: from Old French *despire,* from Latin *dēspicere* to look down, from DE- + *specere* to look] ► **de'spiser** *n*

despite (dɪ'spaɪt) *prep* **1** in spite of; undeterred by. ◆ *n* **2** *Archaic.* contempt; insult. **3 in despite of.** (*prep*) *Rare.* in spite of. ◆ *vb* **4** (*tr*) an archaic word for **spite.** [C13: from Old French *despit,* from Latin *dēspectus* contempt; see DESPISE]

despiteful (dɪ'spaɪtfʊl) *or* **despiteous** (dɪ'spɪtɪəs) *adj* an archaic word for **spiteful.** ► **de'spitefully** *adv* ► **de'spitefulness** *n*

despoil (dɪ'spɔɪl) *vb* (*tr*) to strip or deprive by force; plunder; rob; loot. [C13: from Old French *despoillier,* from Latin *dēspoliāre,* from DE- + *spoliāre* to rob (esp. of clothing); see SPOIL] ► **de'spoiler** *n* ► **de'spoilment** *n*

despoliation (dɪˌspəulɪˈeɪʃən) *n* **1** the act of despoiling; plunder or pillage. **2** the state of being despoiled.

despond *vb* **1** (*intr*) (dɪˈspɒnd). to lose heart or hope; become disheartened; despair. ◆ *n* **2** (ˈdɛspɒnd, dɪˈspɒnd). an archaic word for **despondency.** [C17: from Latin *dēspondēre* to promise, make over to, yield, lose heart, from DE- + *spondēre* to promise] ▸ **deˈspondingly** *adv*

despondent (dɪˈspɒndənt) *adj* downcast or disheartened; lacking hope or courage; dejected. ▸ **deˈspondence** *n* ▸ **deˈspondency** *n* ▸ **deˈspondently** *adv*

despot (ˈdɛspɒt) *n* **1** an absolute or tyrannical ruler; autocrat or tyrant. **2** any person in power who acts tyrannically. **3** a title borne by numerous persons of rank in the later Roman, Byzantine, and Ottoman Empires: *the despot of Servia.* [C16: from Medieval Latin *despota,* from Greek *despotēs* lord, master; related to Latin *domus* house] ▸ **despotic** (dɛsˈpɒtɪk) *or* **desˈpotical** *adj* ▸ **desˈpotically** *adv*

despotism (ˈdɛspəˌtɪzəm) *n* **1** the rule of a despot; arbitrary, absolute, or tyrannical government. **2** arbitrary or tyrannical authority or behaviour.

des Prés *or* **Desprez** (*French* de pre) *n* **Josquin** (ʒɔskɛ̃). ?1450–1521, Flemish Renaissance composer of masses, motets, and chansons.

despumate (dɪˈspjuːmeɪt, ˈdɛspjʊˌmeɪt) *vb* **1** (*tr*) to clarify or purify (a liquid) by skimming a scum from its surface. **2** (*intr*) (of a liquid) to form a scum or froth. [C17: from Latin *dēspūmāre* to skim off, from DE- + *spūma* foam, froth] ▸ **ˌdespuˈmation** *n*

desquamate (ˈdɛskwəˌmeɪt) *vb* (*intr*) (esp. of the skin in certain diseases) to peel or come off in scales. [C18: from Latin *dēsquāmāre* to scale off, from DE- + *squāma* a scale] ▸ **ˌdesquaˈmation** *n*

des res (dɛz rɛz) *n* (in estate agents' jargon) a desirable residence.

Dessalines (*French* desalin) *n* **Jean Jacques** (ʒɑ̃ ʒak). ?1758–1806, emperor of Haiti (1804–06) after driving out the French; assassinated.

Dessau (*German* ˈdɛsau) *n* an industrial city in E Germany, in Saxony-Anhalt: capital of Anhalt state from 1340 to 1918. Pop.: 95 100 (1991).

dessert (dɪˈzɜːt) *n* **1** the sweet, usually last course of a meal. **2** *Chiefly Brit.* (esp. formerly) fruit, dates, nuts, etc., served at the end of a meal. [C17: from French, from *desservir* to clear a table, from *des-* DIS-[1] + *servir* to SERVE]

dessertspoon (dɪˈzɜːtˌspuːn) *n* a spoon intermediate in size between a tablespoon and a teaspoon.

dessiatine (ˈdɛsjəˌtiːn) *n* a Russian unit of area equal to approximately 2.7 acres or 10 800 square metres. [C18: from Russian *desyatina,* literally: tithe, from *desyat* ten]

destabilize *or* **destabilise** (diːˈsteɪbɪˌlaɪz) *vb* (*tr*) to undermine or subvert (a government, economy, etc.) so as to cause unrest or collapse. ▸ **ˌdestabiliˈzation** *or* **ˌdestabiliˈsation** *n*

de-Stalinization *or* **de-Stalinisation** (diːˌstɑːlɪnaɪˈzeɪʃən) *n* the elimination of the influence of Stalin.

De Stijl (də staɪl) *n* a group of artists and architects in the Netherlands in the 1920s, including Mondrian and van Doesburg, devoted to neoplasticism and then dada. [Dutch, literally: the style, title of this group's own magazine]

destination (ˌdɛstɪˈneɪʃən) *n* **1** the predetermined end of a journey or voyage. **2** the ultimate end or purpose for which something is created or a person is destined.

destine (ˈdɛstɪn) *vb* (*tr*) to set apart or appoint (for a certain purpose or person, or to do something); intend; design. [C14: from Old French *destiner,* from Latin *dēstināre* to appoint, from DE- + *-stināre,* from *stāre* to stand]

destined (ˈdɛstɪnd) *adj* (*postpositive*) **1** foreordained or certain; meant: *he is destined to be famous.* **2** (usually foll. by *for*) heading (towards a specific destination); directed: *a letter destined for Europe.*

destiny (ˈdɛstɪnɪ) *n, pl* **-nies. 1** the future destined for a person or thing; fate; fortune; lot. **2** the predetermined or inevitable course of events. **3** the ultimate power or agency that predetermines the course of events. [C14: from Old French *destinee,* from *destiner* to DESTINE]

Destiny (ˈdɛstɪnɪ) *n, pl* **-nies.** the power that predetermines events, personified as a goddess.

destitute (ˈdɛstɪˌtjuːt) *adj* **1** lacking the means of subsistence; totally impoverished. **2** (*postpositive;* foll. by *of*) completely lacking; deprived or bereft (of): *destitute of words.* **3** *Obsolete.* abandoned or deserted. [C14: from Latin *dēstitūtus* forsaken, from *dēstituere* to leave alone, from *statuere* to place] ▸ **ˈdestiˌtuteness** *n*

destitution (ˌdɛstɪˈtjuːʃən) *n* **1** the state of being destitute; utter poverty. **2** *Rare.* lack or deficiency.

destrier (ˈdɛstrɪə) *n* an archaic word for **warhorse** (sense 1). [C13: from Old French, from *destre* right hand, from Latin *dextra;* from the fact that a squire led a knight's horse with his right hand]

destroy (dɪˈstrɔɪ) *vb* (*mainly tr*) **1** to ruin; spoil; render useless. **2** to tear down or demolish; break up; raze. **3** to put an end to; do away with; extinguish. **4** to kill or annihilate. **5** to crush, subdue, or defeat. **6** (*intr*) to be destructive or cause destruction. [C13: from Old French *destruire,* from Latin *dēstruere* to pull down, from DE- + *struere* to pile up, build] ▸ **deˈstroyable** *adj*

destroyer (dɪˈstrɔɪə) *n* **1** a small fast lightly armoured but heavily armed warship. **2** a person or thing that destroys.

destroyer escort *n* a lightly armed warship smaller than a destroyer, designed to escort fleets or convoys.

destroying angel *n* a white slender very poisonous basidiomycetous toadstool, *Amanita virosa,* having a pronounced volva, frilled, shaggy stalk, and sickly smell.

destruct (dɪˈstrʌkt) *vb* **1** to destroy (one's own missile or rocket) for safety. **2** (*intr*) (of a missile or rocket) to be destroyed, for safety, by those controlling it; self-destruct. ◆ *n* **3** the act of destructing. ◆ *adj* **4** designed to be capable of destroying itself or the object, system, or installation containing it: *destruct mechanism.*

destructible (dɪˈstrʌktəbᵊl) *adj* capable of being or liable to be destroyed. ▸ **deˌstructiˈbility** *n*

destruction (dɪˈstrʌkʃən) *n* **1** the act of destroying or state of being destroyed; demolition. **2** a cause of ruin or means of destroying. [C14: from Latin *dēstructiō* a pulling down; see DESTROY]

destructionist (dɪˈstrʌkʃənɪst) *n* a person who believes in destruction, esp. of social institutions.

destructive (dɪˈstrʌktɪv) *adj* **1** (often *postpositive* and foll. by *of* or *to*) causing or tending to cause the destruction (of). **2** intended to disprove or discredit, esp. without positive suggestions or help; negative: *destructive criticism.* Compare **constructive** (sense 1). ▸ **deˈstructively** *adv* ▸ **deˈstructiveness** *or* **destructivity** (ˌdiːstrʌkˈtɪvɪtɪ) *n*

destructive distillation *n* the decomposition of a complex substance, such as wood or coal, by heating it in the absence of air and collecting the volatile products.

destructor (dɪˈstrʌktə) *n* **1** a furnace or incinerator for the disposal of refuse, esp. one that uses the resulting heat to generate power. **2** a device used to blow up a dangerously defective missile or rocket after launching.

desuetude (dɪˈsjuːɪˌtjuːd, ˈdɛswɪtjuːd) *n Formal.* the condition of not being in use or practice; disuse: *those ceremonies had fallen into desuetude.* [C15: from Latin *dēsuētūdō,* from *dēsuescere* to lay aside a habit, from DE- + *suescere* to grow accustomed]

desulphurize *or* **desulphurise** (diːˈsʌlfjʊˌraɪz) *vb* to free or become free from sulphur. ▸ **deˌsulphuriˈzation** *or* **deˌsulphuriˈsation** *n* ▸ **deˈsulphurˌizer** *or* **deˈsulphurˌiser** *n*

desultory (ˈdɛsəltərɪ, -trɪ) *adj* **1** passing or jumping from one thing to another, esp. in a fitful way; unmethodical; disconnected. **2** occurring in a random or incidental way; haphazard: *a desultory thought.* [C16: from Latin *dēsultōrius,* relating to one who vaults or jumps, hence superficial, from *dēsilīre* to jump down, from DE- + *salīre* to jump] ▸ **ˈdesultorily** *adv* ▸ **ˈdesultoriness** *n*

DET *abbrev. for* diethyltryptamine, a hallucinogenic drug.

detach (dɪˈtætʃ) *vb* (*tr*) **1** to disengage and separate or remove, as by pulling; unfasten; disconnect. **2** *Military.* to separate (a small unit) from a larger, esp. for a special assignment. [C17: from Old French *destachier,* from *des-* DIS-[1] + *attachier* to ATTACH] ▸ **deˈtachable** *adj* ▸ **deˌtachaˈbility** *n* ▸ **deˈtacher** *n*

detached (dɪˈtætʃt) *adj* **1** disconnected or standing apart; not attached: *a detached house.* **2** having or showing no bias or emotional involvement; disinterested. **3** *Social welfare.* working at the clients' normal location rather than from an office; not dependent on premises for providing a service: *a detached youth worker.* Compare **outreach** (sense 7). **4** *Ophthalmol.* (of the retina) separated from the choroid layer of the eyeball to which it is normally attached, resulting in loss of vision in the affected part.

detachment (dɪˈtætʃmənt) *n* **1** indifference to other people or to one's surroundings; aloofness. **2** freedom from self-interest or bias; disinterest. **3** the act of disengaging or separating something. **4** the condition of being disengaged or separated; disconnection. **5** *Military.* **5a** the separation of a small unit from its main body, esp. of ships or troops. **5b** the unit so detached. **6** *Logic.* the rule whereby the consequent of a true conditional statement, given the truth of its antecedent, may be asserted on its own. See also **modus ponens.**

detail (ˈdiːteɪl) *n* **1** an item or smaller part that is considered separately; particular. **2** an item or circumstance that is insignificant or unimportant: *passengers' comfort was regarded as a detail.* **3** treatment of or attention to items or particulars: *this essay includes too much detail.* **4** items collectively; particulars. **5** a small or accessory section or element in a painting, building, statue, etc., esp. when considered in isolation. **6** *Military.* **6a** the act of assigning personnel for a specific duty, esp. a fatigue. **6b** the personnel selected. **6c** the duty or assignment. **7 go into detail.** to include all or most particulars. **8 in detail.** including all or most particulars or items thoroughly. ◆ *vb* (*tr*) **9** to list or relate fully. **10** *Military.* to select (personnel) for a specific duty. **11** to decorate or elaborate (carving, etc.) with fine delicate drawing or designs. [C17: from French *détail,* from Old French *detailler* to cut in pieces, from *de-* DIS-[1] + *tailler* to cut; see TAILOR]

detail drawing *n* a separate large-scale drawing of a small part or section of a building, machine, etc.

detailed (ˈdiːteɪld) *adj* having many details or giving careful attention to details.

detain (dɪˈteɪn) *vb* (*tr*) **1** to delay; hold back; stop. **2** to confine or hold in custody; restrain. **3** *Archaic.* to retain or withhold. [C15: from Old French *detenir,* from Latin *dētinēre* to hold off, keep back, from DE- + *tenēre* to hold] ▸ **deˈtainable** *adj* ▸ **detainee** (ˌdiːteɪˈniː) *n* ▸ **deˈtainment** *n*

detainer (dɪˈteɪnə) *n Law.* **1** the wrongful withholding of the property of another person. **2a** the detention of a person in custody. **2b** a writ authorizing the further detention of a person already in custody. [C17: from Anglo-French *detener* (n), from *detener* to DETAIN]

detect (dɪˈtɛkt) *vb* (*tr*) **1** to perceive or notice: *to detect a note of sarcasm.* **2** to discover the existence or presence of (esp. something likely to elude observation): *to detect alcohol in the blood.* **3** to extract information from (an electromagnetic wave). **4** *Obsolete.* to reveal or expose (a crime, criminal, etc.). [C15: from Latin *dētectus* uncovered, from *dētegere* to uncover, from DE- + *tegere* to cover] ▸ **deˈtectable** *or* **deˈtectible** *adj* ▸ **deˈtecter** *n*

detection (dɪˈtɛkʃən) *n* **1** the act of discovering or the fact of being discovered: *detection of crime.* **2** the act or process of extracting information, esp. at audio or video frequencies, from an electromagnetic wave. See also **demodulation.**

detective (dɪˈtɛktɪv) *n* **1a** a police officer who investigates crimes. **1b** See private detective. **1c** (*as modifier*): *a detective story*. ◆ *adj* **2** used in or serving for detection. **3** serving to detect.

detector (dɪˈtɛktə) *n* **1** a person or thing that detects. **2** any mechanical sensing device. **3** *Electronics*. a device used in the detection of radio signals.

detent (dɪˈtɛnt) *n* the locking piece of a mechanism, often spring-loaded to check the movement of a wheel in one direction only. See also **pawl**. [C17: from Old French *destente*, a loosening, trigger: see DÉTENTE]

détente (deɪˈtɑːnt; *French* detɑ̃t) *n* the relaxing or easing of tension, esp. between nations. [French, literally: a loosening, from Old French *destendre* to release, from *tendre* to stretch]

detention (dɪˈtɛnʃən) *n* **1** the act of detaining or state of being detained. **2a** custody or confinement, esp. of a suspect awaiting trial. **2b** (*as modifier*): *a detention order*. **3** a form of punishment in which a pupil is detained after school. **4** the withholding of something belonging to or claimed by another. [C16: from Latin *dētentiō* a keeping back; see DETAIN]

detention centre *n* a place where young persons may be detained for short periods by order of a court.

deter (dɪˈtɜː) *vb* **-ters, -terring, -terred**. (*tr*) to discourage (from acting) or prevent (from occurring), usually by instilling fear, doubt, or anxiety. [C16: from Latin *dēterrēre*, from DE- + *terrēre* to frighten] ▸ **deˈterment** *n*

deterge (dɪˈtɜːdʒ) *vb* (*tr*) to wash or wipe away; cleanse: *to deterge a wound*. [C17: from Latin *dētergēre* to wipe away, from DE- + *tergēre* to wipe]

detergency (dɪˈtɜːdʒənsɪ) *or* **detergence** *n* cleansing power.

detergent (dɪˈtɜːdʒənt) *n* **1** a cleansing agent, esp. a surface-active chemical such as an alkyl sulphonate, widely used in industry, laundering, shampoos, etc. ◆ *adj also* **detersive** (dɪˈtɜːsɪv). **2** having cleansing power. [C17: from Latin *dētergēns* wiping off; see DETERGE]

deteriorate (dɪˈtɪərɪəˌreɪt) *vb* **1** to make or become worse or lower in quality, value, character, etc.; depreciate. **2** (*intr*) to wear away or disintegrate. [C16: from Late Latin *dēteriōrāre*, from Latin *dēterior* worse] ▸ **deˌterioˈration** *n* ▸ **deˈteriorative** *adj*

determinable (dɪˈtɜːmɪnəbᵊl) *adj* **1** able to be decided, fixed, or found out. **2** *Law*. liable to termination under certain conditions; terminable. ▸ **deˈterminably** *adv*

determinant (dɪˈtɜːmɪnənt) *adj* **1** serving to determine or affect. ◆ *n* **2** a factor, circumstance, etc., that influences or determines. **3** *Maths*. a square array of elements that represents the sum of certain products of these elements, used to solve simultaneous equations, in vector studies, etc. Compare **matrix** (sense 9).

determinate (dɪˈtɜːmɪnɪt) *adj* **1** definitely limited, defined, or fixed; distinct. **2** a less common word for **determined**. **3a** able to be predicted or deduced. **3b** (of an effect) obeying the law of causality. **4** *Botany*. (of an inflorescence) having the main and branch stems ending in flowers; cymose. **5** (of a structure, stress, etc.) able to be fully analysed or determined. ▸ **deˈterminately** *adv* ▸ **deˈterminateness** *n*

determination (dɪˌtɜːmɪˈneɪʃən) *n* **1** the act or an instance of making a decision. **2** the condition of being determined; resoluteness. **3** the act or an instance of ending an argument by the opinion or decision of an authority. **4** the act or an instance of fixing or settling the quality, limit, position, etc., of something. **5** a decision or opinion reached, rendered, or settled upon. **6** a resolute movement towards some object or end. **7** *Law*. the termination of an estate or interest. **8** *Law*. the decision reached by a court of justice on a disputed matter. **9** *Logic*. **9a** the process of qualifying or limiting a proposition or concept. **9b** the qualifications or limitations used in this process. **10** the condition of embryonic tissues of being able to develop into only one particular tissue or organ in the adult.

determinative (dɪˈtɜːmɪnətɪv) *adj* **1** able to or serving to settle or determine; deciding. ◆ *n* **2** a factor, circumstance, etc., that settles or determines. **3** *Grammar*. a less common word for **determiner**. **4** (in a logographic writing system) a logogram that bears a separate meaning, from which compounds and inflected forms are built up. ▸ **deˈterminatively** *adv* ▸ **deˈterminativeness** *n*

determine (dɪˈtɜːmɪn) *vb* **1** to settle or decide (an argument, question, etc.) conclusively, as by referring to an authority. **2** (*tr*) to ascertain or conclude, esp. after observation or consideration. **3** (*tr*) to shape or influence; give direction to: *experience often determines ability*. **4** (*tr*) to fix in scope, extent, variety, etc.: *the river determined the edge of the property*. **5** to make or cause to make a decision: *he determined never to marry*. **6** (*tr*) *Logic*. to define or limit (a notion) by adding or requiring certain features or characteristics. **7** (*tr*) *Geom*. to fix or specify the position, form, or configuration of: *two points determine a line*. **8** *Chiefly law*. to come or bring to an end, as an estate or interest in land. **9** (*tr*) to decide (a legal action or dispute). [C14: from Old French *determiner*, from Latin *dētermināre* to set boundaries to, from DE- + *termināre* to limit; see TERMINATE]

determined (dɪˈtɜːmɪnd) *adj* of unwavering mind; resolute; firm. ▸ **deˈterminedly** *adv* ▸ **deˈterminedness** *n*

determiner (dɪˈtɜːmɪnə) *n* **1** a word, such as a number, article, personal pronoun, that determines (limits) the meaning of a noun phrase, e.g. *their* in 'their black cat'. **2** a person or thing that determines.

determinism (dɪˈtɜːmɪˌnɪzəm) *n* **1** the philosophical doctrine that all events including human actions and choices are fully determined by preceding events and states of affairs, and so that freedom of choice is illusory. Also called: **necessitarianism**. Compare **free will** (sense 1b). **2** the scientific doctrine that all occurrences in nature take place in accordance with natural laws. **3** the principle in classical mechanics that the values of dynamic variables of a system and of the forces acting on the system at a given time, completely determine the values of the variables at any later time. ▸ **deˈterminist** *n, adj* ▸ **deˌterminˈistic** *adj*

deterrent (dɪˈtɛrənt) *n* **1** something that deters. **2** a weapon or combination of weapons, esp. nuclear, held by one state, etc., to deter attack by another. ◆ *adj* **3** tending or used to deter; restraining. [C19: from Latin *dēterrēns* hindering; see DETER] ▸ **deˈterrence** *n*

detest (dɪˈtɛst) *vb* (*tr*) to dislike intensely; loathe. [C16: from Latin *dētestārī* to curse (while invoking a god as witness), from DE- + *testārī* to bear witness, from *testis* a witness] ▸ **deˈtester** *n*

detestable (dɪˈtɛstəbᵊl) *adj* being or deserving to be abhorred or detested; abominable; odious. ▸ **deˌtestaˈbility** *or* **deˈtestableness** *n* ▸ **deˈtestably** *adv*

detestation (ˌdiːtɛsˈteɪʃən) *n* **1** intense hatred; abhorrence. **2** a person or thing that is detested.

dethrone (dɪˈθrəʊn) *vb* (*tr*) to remove from a throne or deprive of any high position or title; depose: *the champion was dethroned by a young boxer*. ▸ **deˈthronement** *n* ▸ **deˈthroner** *n*

detinue (ˈdɛtɪˌnjuː) *n Law*. an action brought by a plaintiff to recover goods wrongfully detained. [C15: from Old French *detenue*, from *detenir* to DETAIN]

Detmold (ˈdɛtməʊld; *German* ˈdɛtmɔlt) *n* a city in NW Germany, in North Rhine-Westphalia. Pop.: 70 970 (1992 est.).

detonate (ˈdɛtəˌneɪt) *vb* to cause (a bomb, mine, etc.) to explode or (of a bomb, mine, etc.) to explode; set off or be set off. [C18: from Latin *dētonāre* to thunder down, from DE- + *tonāre* to THUNDER]

detonation (ˌdɛtəˈneɪʃən) *n* **1** an explosion or the act of exploding. **2** the spontaneous combustion in an internal-combustion engine of part of the mixture before it has been reached by the flame front, causing the engine to knock. **3** *Physics*. rapid combustion, esp. that occurring within a shock wave. ▸ **ˈdetoˌnative** *adj*

detonator (ˈdɛtəˌneɪtə) *n* **1** a small amount of explosive, as in a percussion cap, used to initiate a larger explosion. **2** a device, such as an electrical generator, used to set off an explosion from a distance. **3** a substance or object that explodes or is capable of exploding.

detour (ˈdiːtʊə) *n* **1** a deviation from a direct, usually shorter route or course of action. ◆ *vb* **2** to deviate or cause to deviate from a direct route or course of action. [C18: from French *détour*, from Old French *destorner* to divert, turn away, from *des-* DE- + *torner* to TURN]

detox (ˈdiːˌtɒks) *Informal*. ◆ *n* **1** treatment designed to rid the body of poisonous substances, esp. alcohol and drugs. ◆ *vb* **2** to undergo treatment to rid the body of poisonous substances, esp. alcohol and drugs. [C20: from (for sense 1) DETOXIFICATION or (for sense 2) DETOXICATE]

detoxicate (diːˈtɒksɪˌkeɪt) *vb* (*tr*) **1** to rid (a patient) of a poison or its effects. **2** to counteract (a poison). [C19: DE- + *-toxicate*, from Latin *toxicum* poison; see TOXIC] ▸ **deˈtoxicant** *adj, n* ▸ **deˌtoxiˈcation** *n*

detoxification centre *n* a place that specializes in the treatment of alcoholism or drug addiction.

detoxify (diːˈtɒksɪˌfaɪ) *vb* **-fies, -fying, -fied**. (*tr*) to remove poison from; detoxicate. ▸ **deˌtoxifiˈcation** *n*

detract (dɪˈtrækt) *vb* **1** (when *intr*, usually foll. by *from*) to take away a part (of); diminish: *her anger detracts from her beauty*. **2** (*tr*) to distract or divert. **3** (*tr*) *Obsolete*. to belittle or disparage. [C15: from Latin *dētractus* drawn away, from *dētrahere* to pull away, disparage, from DE- + *trahere* to drag] ▸ **deˈtractingly** *adv* ▸ **deˈtractive** *or* **deˈtractory** *adj* ▸ **deˈtractively** *adv* ▸ **deˈtractor** *n*

USAGE *Detract* is sometimes wrongly used where *distract* is meant: *a noise distracted* (not *detracted*) *my attention*.

detraction (dɪˈtrækʃən) *n* **1** a person, thing, circumstance, etc., that detracts. **2** the act of discrediting or detracting from another's reputation, esp. by slander; disparagement.

detrain (diːˈtreɪn) *vb* to leave or cause to leave a railway train, as passengers, etc. ▸ **deˈtrainment** *n*

detribalize *or* **detribalise** (diːˈtraɪbəˌlaɪz) *vb* (*tr*) **1** to cause members of a tribe to lose their characteristic customs or social, religious, or other organizational features. **2** to cause tribal people to adopt urban ways of life. ▸ **deˌtribaliˈzation** *or* **deˌtribaliˈsation** *n*

detriment (ˈdɛtrɪmənt) *n* **1** disadvantage or damage; harm; loss. **2** a cause of disadvantage or damage. [C15: from Latin *dētrīmentum*, a rubbing off, hence damage, from *dēterere* to rub away, from DE- + *terere* to rub]

detrimental (ˌdɛtrɪˈmɛntᵊl) *adj* (when *postpositive*, foll. by *to*) harmful; injurious; prejudicial: *smoking can be detrimental to health*. ▸ **ˌdetriˈmentally** *adv*

detrition (dɪˈtrɪʃən) *n* the act of rubbing or wearing away by friction. [C17: from Medieval Latin *dētrītiō*, from Latin *dētrītus* worn away; see DETRIMENT]

detritovore (dɪˈtraɪtəˌvɔː) *n Ecology*. any organism that feeds on detritus.

detritus (dɪˈtraɪtəs) *n* **1** a loose mass of stones, silt, etc., worn away from rocks. **2** an accumulation of disintegrated material or debris. **3** the organic debris formed from the decay of organisms. [C18: from French *détritus*, from Latin *dētrītus* a rubbing away; see DETRIMENT] ▸ **deˈtrital** *adj*

Detroit (dɪˈtrɔɪt) *n* **1** a city in SE Michigan, on the Detroit River: a major Great Lakes port; largest car-manufacturing centre in the world. Pop.: 1 000 272 (1996 est.). **2** a river in central North America, flowing along the U.S.-Canadian border from Lake St Clair to Lake Erie.

de trop *French*. (də tro) *adj* (*postpositive*) not wanted; in the way; superfluous. [literally: of too much]

detrude (dɪˈtruːd) *vb* (*tr*) to force down or thrust away or out. [C16: from Latin *dētrūdere* to push away, from DE- + *trūdere* to thrust] ▸ **detrusion** (dɪˈtruːʒən) *n*

detruncate (diːˈtrʌŋkeɪt) *vb* (*tr*) another word for **truncate**. ▸ **ˌdetrunˈcation** *n*

detumescence (ˌdiːtjuˈmɛsəns) *n* the subsidence of a swelling, esp. the return of a swollen organ, such as the penis, to the flaccid state. [C17: from Latin *dētumescere* to cease swelling, from DE- + *tumescere,* from *tumēre* to swell]

Deucalion (djuːˈkeɪlɪən) *n* the son of Prometheus and, with his wife Pyrrha, the only survivor on earth of a flood sent by Zeus (**Deucalion's flood**). Together, they were allowed to repopulate the world by throwing stones over their shoulders, which became men and women.

deuce[1] (djuːs) *n* **1a** a playing card or dice with two pips or spots; two. **1b** a throw of two in dice. **2** *Tennis, table tennis, etc.* a tied score (in tennis 40-all) that requires one player to gain two successive points to win the game. [C15: from Old French *deus* two, from Latin *duos,* accusative masculine of *duo* two]

deuce[2] (djuːs) *Informal.* ◆ *interj* **1** an expression of annoyance or frustration. ◆ *n* **2 the deuce.** (intensifier): used in such phrases as **what the deuce, where the deuce,** etc. [C17: probably special use of DEUCE[1] (in the sense: lowest throw at dice)]

deuced (ˈdjuːsɪd, djuːst) *Brit. informal.* ◆ *adj* **1** (intensifier, usually qualifying something undesirable) damned; confounded: *he's a deuced idiot.* ◆ *adv* **2** (intensifier): *deuced good luck.* ▸ **ˈdeucedly** *adv*

Deurne (*Flemish* ˈdøːrnə) *n* a town in N Belgium, a suburb of E Antwerp: site of Antwerp airport. Pop.: 80 000 (latest est.).

Deus *Latin.* (ˈdeɪʊs) *n* God. [related to Greek *Zeus*]

deus ex machina *Latin.* (ˈdeɪʊs ɛks ˈmækɪnə) *n* **1** (in ancient Greek and Roman drama) a god introduced into a play to resolve the plot. **2** any unlikely or artificial device serving this purpose. [literally: god out of a machine, translating Greek *theos ek mēkhanēs*]

Deut. *Bible. abbrev. for* Deuteronomy.

deuteragonist (ˌdjuːtəˈrægənɪst) *n* (in ancient Greek drama) the character next in importance to the protagonist, esp. the antagonist. [C19: from Greek *deuteragōnistēs,* from DEUTERO- + *agōnistēs* contestant, actor]

deuteranopia (ˌdjuːtərəˈnəʊpɪə) *n* a form of colour blindness in which there is a tendency to confuse blues and greens, and greens and reds, and in which sensitivity to green is reduced. [C20: New Latin, from DEUTERO- (referring to the theory in which green is the second primary colour) + AN- + Greek *-ops* eye] ▸ **deuteranopic** (ˌdjuːtərəˈnɒpɪk) *adj*

deuterate (ˈdjuːtəˌreɪt) *vb* to treat or combine with deuterium.

deuteride (ˈdjuːtəˌraɪd) *n* a compound of deuterium with some other element. It is analogous to a hydride.

deuterium (djuːˈtɪərɪəm) *n* a stable isotope of hydrogen, occurring in natural hydrogen (156 parts per million) and in heavy water: used as a tracer in chemistry and biology. Symbol: D or ^{2}H; atomic no.: 1; atomic wt.: 2.014; boiling pt.: –249.7°C. [C20: New Latin; see DEUTERO-, -IUM; from the fact that it is the second heaviest hydrogen isotope]

deuterium oxide *n* another name for **heavy water.**

deutero-, deuto- *or before a vowel* **deuter-, deut-** *combining form.* **1** second or secondary: *deuterogamy; deuterium.* **2** (in chemistry) indicating the presence of deuterium. [from Greek *deuteros* second]

deuterogamy (ˌdjuːtəˈrɒgəmɪ) *n* another word for **digamy.** ▸ **ˌdeuterˈogamist** *n*

deuteron (ˈdjuːtəˌrɒn) *n* the nucleus of a deuterium atom, consisting of one proton and one neutron.

Deuteronomist (ˌdjuːtəˈrɒnəmɪst) *n* one of the writers of Deuteronomy.

Deuteronomy (ˌdjuːtəˈrɒnəmɪ) *n* the fifth book of the Old Testament, containing a second statement of the Mosaic Law. [from Late Latin *Deuteronomium,* from Greek *Deuteronomion;* see DEUTERO-, -NOMY] ▸ **Deuteronomic** (ˌdjuːtərəˈnɒmɪk) *adj*

deuterotoky (ˌdjuːtəˈrɒtəkɪ) *n Biology.* parthenogenesis in which both males and females are produced. [from DEUTERO- + *-toky* from Greek *tokos* bringing forth]

deutoplasm (ˈdjuːtəˌplæzəm) *or* **deuteroplasm** (ˈdjuːtərəʊˌplæzəm) *n* nutritive material in a cell, esp. the yolk in a developing ovum. ▸ **ˌdeutoˈplasmic** *or* **ˌdeutoˈplastic** *adj*

Deutsch (dɔɪtʃ; *German* dɔytʃ) *n* **Otto Erich** (ˈɔto ˈeːrɪç). 1883–1967, Austrian music historian and art critic, noted for his catalogue of Schubert's works (1951).

Deutschland (ˈdɔytʃlant) *n* the German name for **Germany.**

Deutschmark (ˈdɔɪtʃˌmɑːk) *or* **Deutsche Mark** (ˈdɔɪtʃə) *n* the standard monetary unit of Germany divided into 100 pfennigs; formerly the standard monetary unit of West Germany. Abbrev.: **DM.**

deutzia (ˈdjuːtsɪə) *n* any saxifragaceous shrub of the genus *Deutzia:* cultivated for their clusters of white or pink spring-blooming flowers. [C19: New Latin, named after Jean *Deutz,* 18th-century Dutch patron of botany]

Deux-Sèvres (*French* døsɛvrə) *n* a department of W France, in Poitou-Charentes region. Capital: Niort. Pop.: 346 800 (1995). Area: 6054 sq. km (2337 sq. miles).

deva (ˈdeɪvə) *n* (in Hinduism and Buddhism) a divine being or god. [C19: from Sanskrit: god]

de Valera (də vəˈlɛərə, -ˈlɪə-) *n* **Eamon** (ˈeɪmən). 1882–1975, Irish statesman; president of Sinn Fein (1917) and of the Dáil (1918–22); formed the Fianna Fáil party (1927); prime minister (1937–48; 1951–54; 1957–59) and president (1959–73) of the Irish Republic.

de Valois (də ˈvælwɑː) *n* See (Ninette de) **Valois**[3].

devaluation (diːˌvæljuːˈeɪʃən) *n* **1** a decrease in the exchange value of a currency against gold or other currencies, brought about by a government. Compare **depreciation** (sense 4). **2** a reduction in value, status, importance, etc.

devalue (diːˈvæljuː) *or* **devaluate** (diːˈvæljuːˌeɪt) *vb* **-values, -valuing, -valued** *or* **-valuates, -valuating, -valuated. 1** to reduce (a currency) or (of a currency) be reduced in exchange value. **2** (*tr*) to reduce the value or worth of (something).

Devanagari (ˌdeɪvəˈnɑːgərɪ) *n* a syllabic script in which Sanskrit, Hindi, and other modern languages of India are written. [C18: from Sanskrit: alphabet of the gods, from *deva* god + *nagari* an Indian alphabet]

devastate (ˈdɛvəˌsteɪt) *vb* (*tr*) **1** to lay waste or make desolate; ravage; destroy. **2** to confound or overwhelm, as with grief or shock. [C17: from Latin *dēvastāre,* from DE- + *vastāre* to ravage; related to *vastus* waste, empty] ▸ **ˌdevasˈtation** *n* ▸ **ˈdevasˌtative** *adj* ▸ **ˈdevasˌtator** *n*

devastating (ˈdɛvəˌsteɪtɪŋ) *adj* extremely effective in a destructive way: *a devastating war; a devastating report on urban deprivation.* ▸ **ˈdevasˌtatingly** *adv*

develop (dɪˈvɛləp) *vb* **1** to come or bring to a later or more advanced or expanded stage; grow or cause to grow gradually. **2** (*tr*) to elaborate or work out in detail. **3** to disclose or unfold (thoughts, a plot, etc.) gradually or (of thoughts, etc.) to be gradually disclosed or unfolded. **4** to come or bring into existence; generate or be generated: *he developed a new faith in God.* **5** (*intr;* often foll. by *from*) to follow as a result (of); ensue (from): *a row developed following the chairman's remarks.* **6** (*tr*) to contract (a disease or illness). **7** (*tr*) to improve the value or change the use of (land), as by building. **8** (*tr*) to exploit or make available the natural resources of (a country or region). **9** (*tr*) *Photog.* **9a** to treat (film, plate, or paper previously exposed to light, or the latent image in such material) with chemical solutions in order to produce a visible image. **9b** to process (photographic material) in order to produce negatives and prints. **10** *Biology.* to progress or cause to progress from simple to complex stages in the growth of an individual or the evolution of a species. **11** (*tr*) to elaborate upon (a musical theme) by varying the melody, key, etc. **12** (*tr*) *Maths.* to expand (a function or expression) in the form of a series. **13** (*tr*) *Geometry.* to project or roll out (a surface) onto a plane without stretching or shrinking any element. **14** *Chess.* to bring (a piece) into play from its initial position on the back rank. **15** (*tr*) *Obsolete.* to disclose or reveal. [C19: from Old French *desveloper* to unwrap, from *des-* DIS-[1] + *veloper* to wrap; see ENVELOP] ▸ **deˈvelopable** *adj*

developer (dɪˈvɛləpə) *n* **1** a person or thing that develops something, esp. a person who develops property. **2** *Photog.* a solution of a chemical reducing agent that converts the latent image recorded in the emulsion of a film or paper into a visible image.

developing agent *n* another name for **developer** (sense 2).

developing country *n* a nonindustrialized poor country that is seeking to develop its resources by industrialization.

developing world *n* another name for **Third World.**

development (dɪˈvɛləpmənt) *n* **1** the act or process of growing, progressing, or developing. **2** the product or result of developing. **3** a fact, event, or happening, esp. one that changes a situation. **4** an area or tract of land that has been developed. **5** Also called: **development section.** the section of a movement, usually in sonata form, in which the basic musical themes are developed. **6** *Chess.* **6a** the process of developing pieces. **6b** the manner in which they are developed. **6c** the position of the pieces in the early part of a game with reference to their attacking potential or defensive efficiency. ▸ **deˌvelopˈmental** *adj* ▸ **deˌvelopˈmentally** *adv*

developmental disorder *n Psychiatry.* any condition, such as autism or dyslexia, that appears in childhood and is characterized by delay in the development of one or more psychological functions, such as language skill.

development area *n* (in Britain) an area suffering from high unemployment and economic depression, because of the decline of its main industries, that is given government help to establish new industries.

development education *n Brit.* an area of study that aims to give pupils an understanding of their involvement in world affairs.

development system *n* a computer system, including hardware and software, that is specifically designed to aid in the development of software and interfaces.

development well *n* (in the oil industry) a well drilled for the production of oil or gas from a field already proven by appraisal drilling to be suitable for exploitation.

Deventer (ˈdeɪvəntə; *Dutch* ˈdeːvəntər) *n* an industrial city in the E Netherlands, in Overijssel province, on the River IJssel: medieval intellectual centre; early centre of Dutch printing. Pop.: 69 079 (1994).

Devereux (ˈdɛvəˌruː) *n* **Robert.** See (2nd Earl of) **Essex.**

devest (dɪˈvɛst) *vb* (*tr*) a rare variant spelling of **divest.**

Devi (ˈdeɪviː) *n* a Hindu goddess and embodiment of the female energy of Siva. [Sanskrit: goddess; see DEVA]

deviance (ˈdiːvɪəns) *n* **1** Also called: **deviancy.** the act or state of being deviant. **2** *Statistics.* a measure of the degree of fit of a statistical model compared to that of a more complete model.

deviant (ˈdiːvɪənt) *adj* **1** deviating, as from what is considered acceptable behaviour. ◆ *n* **2** a person whose behaviour, esp. sexual behaviour, deviates from what is considered to be acceptable.

deviate *vb* (ˈdiːvɪˌeɪt). **1** (*usually intr*) to differ or diverge or cause to differ or diverge, as in belief or thought. **2** (*usually intr*) to turn aside or cause to turn aside; diverge or cause to diverge. **3** (*intr*) *Psychol.* to depart from an accepted standard or convention. ◆ *n, adj* (ˈdiːvɪɪt). **4** another word for **deviant.** [C17: from Late Latin *dēviāre* to turn aside from the direct road, from DE- + *via* road] ▸ **ˈdeviˌator** *n* ▸ **ˈdeviatory** *adj*

deviation (ˌdiːvɪˈeɪʃən) *n* **1** an act or result of deviating. **2** *Statistics.* the difference between an observed value in a series of such values and their arithmetic mean. **3** the error of a compass due to local magnetic disturbances.

deviationism (ˌdiːvɪˈeɪʃəˌnɪzəm) *n* ideological deviation (esp. from orthodox Communism). ▸ **ˌdeviˈationist** *n, adj*

device (dɪˈvaɪs) *n* **1** a machine or tool used for a specific task; contrivance. **2** *Euphemistic.* a bomb. **3** a plan or plot, esp. a clever or evil one; scheme; trick. **4** any ornamental pattern or picture, as in embroidery. **5** computer hardware that is designed for a specific function. **6** a written, printed, or painted design or figure, used as a heraldic sign, emblem, trademark, etc. **7** a particular pattern of words, figures of speech, etc., used in literature to produce an effect on the reader. **8** *Archaic.* the act or process of planning or devising. **9 leave (someone) to his own devices.** to leave (someone) alone to do as he wishes. [C13: from Old French *devis* purpose, contrivance and *devise* difference, intention, from *deviser* to divide, control; see DEVISE]

devil ('dɛvᵊl) *n* **1** *Theol.* (*often cap.*) the chief spirit of evil and enemy of God, often represented as the ruler of hell and often depicted as a human figure with horns, cloven hoofs, and tail. **2** *Theol.* one of the subordinate evil spirits of traditional Jewish and Christian belief. **3** a person or animal regarded as cruel, wicked, or ill-natured. **4** a person or animal regarded as unfortunate or wretched: *that poor devil was ill for months.* **5** a person or animal regarded as clever, daring, mischievous, or energetic. **6** *Informal.* something difficult or annoying. **7** *Christian Science.* the opposite of truth; an error, lie, or false belief in sin, sickness, and death. **8** (in Malaysia) a ghost. **9** a portable furnace or brazier, esp. one used in road-making or one used by plumbers. Compare **salamander** (sense 7). **10** any of various mechanical devices, such as a machine for making wooden screws or a rag-tearing machine. **11** See **printer's devil. 12** *Law.* (in England) a junior barrister who does work for another in order to gain experience, usually for a half fee. **13** *Meteorology.* a small whirlwind in arid areas that raises dust or sand in a column. **14 between the devil and the deep blue sea.** between equally undesirable alternatives. **15 devil of.** *Informal.* (intensifier): *a devil of a fine horse.* **16 give the devil his due.** to acknowledge the talent or the success of an opponent or unpleasant person. **17 go to the devil. 17a** to fail or become dissipated. **17b** (*interj*) used to express annoyance with the person causing it. **18 like the devil.** with great speed, determination, etc. **19 play the devil with.** *Informal.* to make much worse; upset considerably: *the damp plays the devil with my rheumatism.* **20 raise the devil. 20a** to cause a commotion. **20b** to make a great protest. **21 talk** (*or* **speak**) **of the devil!** (*interj*) used when an absent person who has been the subject of conversation appears. **22 the devil!** (intensifier): **22a** used in such phrases as **what the devil, where the devil,** etc. **22b** an exclamation of anger, surprise, disgust, etc. **23 the devil's own.** a very difficult or problematic (thing). **24** (**let**) **the devil take the hindmost.** look after oneself and leave others to their fate. **25 the devil to pay.** problems or trouble to be faced as a consequence of an action. **26 the very devil.** something very difficult or awkward. ◆ *vb* **-ils, -illing, -illed** *or U.S.* **-ils, -iling, -iled. 27** (*tr*) to prepare (esp. meat, poultry, or fish) by coating with a highly flavoured spiced paste or mixture of condiments before cooking. **28** (*tr*) to tear (rags) with a devil. **29** (*intr*) to serve as a printer's devil. **30** (*intr*) *Chiefly Brit.* to do hackwork, esp. for a lawyer or author; perform arduous tasks, often without pay or recognition of one's services. **31** (*tr*) *U.S. informal.* to harass, vex, torment, etc. [Old English *dēofol,* from Latin *diabolus,* from Greek *diabolos* enemy, accuser, slanderer, from *diaballein,* literally: to throw across, hence, to slander]

devilfish ('dɛvᵊl,fɪʃ) *n, pl* **-fish** *or* **-fishes. 1** Also called: **devil ray.** another name for **manta** (the fish). **2** another name for **octopus.**

devilish ('dɛvəlɪʃ, 'dɛvlɪʃ) *adj* **1** of, resembling, or befitting a devil; diabolic; fiendish. ◆ *adv, adj Informal.* **2** (intensifier): *devilish good food; this devilish heat.* ▸ **'devilishly** *adv* ▸ **'devilishness** *n*

devil-may-care *adj* careless or reckless; happy-go-lucky: *a devil-may-care attitude.*

devilment ('dɛvᵊlmənt) *n* devilish or mischievous conduct.

devilry ('dɛvᵊlrɪ) *or* **deviltry** *n, pl* **-ries** *or* **-tries. 1** reckless or malicious fun or mischief. **2** wickedness or cruelty. **3** black magic or other forms of diabolism. [C18: from French *diablerie,* from *diable* DEVIL]

devil's advocate *n* **1** a person who advocates an opposing or unpopular view, often for the sake of argument. **2** *R.C. Church.* the official appointed to put the case against the beatification or canonization of a candidate. Technical name: **promotor fidei** (prəʊ'məʊtɔː fɪ'deɪiː). [translation of New Latin *advocātus diabolī*]

devil's bit *n* short for **devil's bit scabious** (see **scabious**[2] (sense 3)).

devil's coach-horse *n* a large black rove beetle, *Ocypus olens,* with large jaws and ferocious habits.

devil's darning needle *n* a popular name for a **dragonfly.**

devil's food cake *n Chiefly U.S. and Canadian.* a rich chocolate cake.

Devil's Island *n* one of the three Safety Islands, off the coast of French Guiana: formerly a leper colony, then a French penal colony from 1895 until 1938. Area: less than 2 sq. km (1 sq. mile). French name: **Île du Diable.**

devils-on-horseback *n* (*functioning as sing or pl*) a savoury of prunes wrapped in bacon slices and served on toast.

Devine (də'viːn) *n* **George** (**Alexander Cassady**). 1910–65, British stage director and actor: founded (1956) the English Stage Company in London's Royal Court Theatre.

devious ('diːvɪəs) *adj* **1** not sincere or candid; deceitful; underhand. **2** (of a route or course of action) rambling; indirect; roundabout. **3** going astray from a proper or accepted way; erring. [C16: from Latin *dēvius* lying to one side of the road, from DE- + *via* road] ▸ **'deviously** *adv* ▸ **'deviousness** *n*

devisable (dɪ'vaɪzəbᵊl) *adj* **1** *Law.* (of property, esp. realty) capable of being transferred by will. **2** able to be invented, contrived, or devised.

devisal (dɪ'vaɪzᵊl) *n* the act of inventing, contriving, or devising; contrivance.

devise (dɪ'vaɪz) *vb* **1** to work out, contrive, or plan (something) in one's mind. **2** (*tr*) *Law.* to dispose of (property, esp. real property) by will. **3** (*tr*) *Obsolete.* to imagine or guess. ◆ *n Law.* **4a** a disposition of property by will. **4b** the property so transmitted. Compare **bequeath** (sense 1). **5** a will or clause in a will disposing of real property. Compare **bequest** (sense 2). [C15: from Old French *deviser* to divide, apportion, intend, from Latin *dīvidere* to DIVIDE] ▸ **de'viser** *n*

devisee (dɪvaɪ'ziː, ˌdɛvɪ-) *n Property law.* a person to whom property, esp. realty, is devised by will. Compare **legatee.**

devisor (dɪ'vaɪzə) *n Property law.* a person who devises property, esp. realty, by will.

devitalize *or* **devitalise** (diː'vaɪtəˌlaɪz) *vb* (*tr*) to lower or destroy the vitality of; make weak or lifeless: *the war devitalized the economy.* ▸ **deˌvitali'zation** *or* **deˌvitali'sation** *n*

devitrify (diː'vɪtrɪˌfaɪ) *vb* **-fies, -fying, -fied. 1** to change from a vitreous state to a crystalline state. **2** to lose or cause to lose the properties of a glass and become brittle and opaque. ▸ **deˌvitrifi'cation** *n*

Devizes (də'vaɪzəz) *n* a market town in S England, in Wiltshire: agricultural and dairy products. Pop.: 13 205 (1991).

devoice (diː'vɔɪs) *or* **devocalize, devocalise** (diː'vəʊkəˌlaɪz) *vb* (*tr*) *Phonetics.* to make (a voiced speech sound) voiceless.

devoid (dɪ'vɔɪd) *adj* (*postpositive;* foll. by *of*) destitute or void (of); free (from). [C15: originally past participle of *devoid* (*vb*) to remove, from Old French *devoidier,* from *de-* DE- + *voider* to VOID]

devoirs (də'vwɑː; *French* dəvwar) *pl n* (*sometimes sing*) compliments or respects; courteous attentions. [C13: from Old French: duty, from *devoir* to be obliged to, owe, from Latin *dēbēre;* see DEBT]

devolution (ˌdiːvə'luːʃən) *n* **1** the act, fact, or result of devolving. **2** a passing onwards or downwards from one stage to another. **3** another word for **degeneration** (sense 3). **4** a transfer or allocation of authority, esp. from a central government to regional governments or particular interests. [C16: from Medieval Latin *dēvolūtiō* a rolling down, from Latin *dēvolvere* to roll down, sink into; see DEVOLVE] ▸ **ˌdevo'lutionary** *adj* ▸ **ˌdevo'lutionist** *n, adj*

devolve (dɪ'vɒlv) *vb* **1** (foll. by *on, upon, to,* etc.) to pass or cause to pass to a successor or substitute, as duties, power, etc. **2** (*intr;* foll. by *on* or *upon*) *Law.* (of an estate, etc.) to pass to another by operation of law, esp. on intestacy or bankruptcy. **3** (*intr;* foll. by *on* or *upon*) to depend (on): *your argument devolves on how you interpret this clause.* **4** *Archaic.* to roll down or cause to roll down. [C15: from Latin *dēvolvere* to roll down, fall into, from DE- + *volvere* to roll] ▸ **de'volvement** *n*

devon ('dɛvən) *n Austral.* a bland processed meat in sausage form, eaten cold in slices. [named after DEVON]

Devon ('dɛvᵊn) *n* **1** Also called: **Devonshire.** a county of SW England, between the Bristol Channel and the English Channel, including the island of Lundy: hilly, rising to the uplands of Exmoor and Dartmoor, with wooded river valleys and a rugged coastline. Administrative centre: Exeter. Pop.: 1 053 400 (1994 est.). Area: 6712 sq. km (2591 sq. miles). **2** a breed of large red cattle originally from Devon.

Devonian (də'vəʊnɪən) *adj* **1** of, denoting, or formed in the fourth period of the Palaeozoic era, between the Silurian and Carboniferous periods, lasting for 50 million years during which amphibians first appeared. **2** of or relating to Devon. ◆ *n* **3 the.** the Devonian period or rock system.

Devon minnow *n Angling.* a spinning lure intended to imitate the swimming motion of a minnow. Often shortened to **Devon.**

Devonshire ('dɛvᵊnʃɪə, -ʃə) *n* **8th Duke of,** title of *Spencer Compton Cavendish.* 1833–1908, British politician, also known (1858–91) as Lord Hartington. He led the Liberal Party (1874–80) and left it to found the Liberal Unionist Party (1886).

Devonshire cream *n* another name for **clotted cream.**

Devonshire split *n* a kind of yeast bun split open and served with whipped cream or butter and jam. Also called: **Cornish split, split.**

devoré (dəvɒ're) *n* a velvet fabric with a raised pattern created by disintegrating some of the pile with chemicals. [from French, past participle of *dévorer* to devour]

devote (dɪ'vəʊt) *vb* (*tr*) **1** to apply or dedicate (oneself, time, money, etc.) to some pursuit, cause, etc. **2** *Obsolete.* to curse or doom. [C16: from Latin *dēvōtus* devoted, solemnly promised, from *dēvovēre* to vow; see DE-, VOW] ▸ **de'votement** *n*

devoted (dɪ'vəʊtɪd) *adj* **1** feeling or demonstrating loyalty or devotion; ardent; devout. **2** (*postpositive;* foll. by *to*) set apart, dedicated, or consecrated. ▸ **de'votedly** *adv* ▸ **de'votedness** *n*

devotee (ˌdɛvə'tiː) *n* **1** a person ardently enthusiastic about or devoted to something, such as a sport or pastime. **2** a zealous follower of a religion.

devotion (dɪ'vəʊʃən) *n* **1** (often foll. by *to*) strong attachment (to) or affection (for a cause, person, etc.) marked by dedicated loyalty. **2** religious zeal; piety. **3** (*often pl*) religious observance or prayers.

devotional (dɪ'vəʊʃənᵊl) *adj* **1** relating to, characterized by, or conducive to devotion. ◆ *n* **2** (*often pl*) a short religious or prayer service. ▸ **deˌvotion'ality** *or* **de'votionalness** *n* ▸ **de'votionally** *adv*

devour (dɪ'vaʊə) *vb* (*tr*) **1** to swallow or eat up greedily or voraciously. **2** to waste or destroy; consume: *the flames devoured the curtains.* **3** to consume greedily or avidly with the senses or mind: *he devoured the manuscripts.* **4** to engulf or absorb: *the flood devoured the land.* [C14: from Old French *devourer,* from Latin *dēvorāre* to gulp down, from DE- + *vorāre* to consume greedily; see VORACIOUS] ▸ **de'vourer** *n* ▸ **de'vouring** *adj* ▸ **de'vouringly** *adv*

devout (dɪ'vaʊt) *adj* **1** deeply religious; reverent. **2** sincere; earnest; heartfelt: *a devout confession.* [C13: from Old French *devot,* from Late Latin *dēvōtus,* from Latin: faithful; see DEVOTE] ▸ **de'voutly** *adv* ▸ **de'voutness** *n*

De Vries (*Dutch* də 'vriːs) *n* **Hugo** ('hyːxoː). 1848–1935, Dutch botanist, who rediscovered Mendel's laws and developed the mutation theory of evolution.

dew (djuː) *n* **1a** drops of water condensed on a cool surface, esp. at night, from vapour in the air. **1b** (*in combination*): *dewdrop.* **2** something like or suggestive of this, esp. in freshness: *the dew of youth.* **3** small drops of moisture, such as tears. ◆ *vb* **4** (*tr*) *Poetic.* to moisten with or as with dew. [Old English *dēaw;* related to Old High German *tou* dew, Old Norse *dögg*]

dewan *or* **diwan** (dɪ'wɑːn) *n* (formerly in India) the chief minister or finance minister of a state ruled by an Indian prince. [C17: from Hindi *dīwān,* from Persian *dēvan* register, book of accounts; see DIVAN]

Dewar ('djuːə) *n* **1 Donald.** born 1937, Scottish Labour politician; secretary of state for Scotland (1997–99); First Minister of Scotland from 1999. **2** Sir **James.** 1842–1923, Scottish chemist and physicist. He worked on the liquefaction of gases and the properties of matter at low temperature, invented the vacuum flask, and (with Sir Frederick Abel) was the first to prepare cordite.

Dewar flask *n* a type of vacuum flask, esp. one used in scientific experiments to keep liquid air, helium, etc.; Thermos. [C20: named after Sir James DEWAR]

dewberry ('djuːbərɪ, -brɪ) *n, pl* **-ries. 1** any trailing bramble, such as *Rubus hispidus* of North America and *R. caesius* of Europe and NW Asia, having blue-black fruits. **2** the fruit of any such plant.

dewclaw ('djuːˌklɔː) *n* **1** a nonfunctional claw in dogs; the rudimentary first digit. **2** an analogous rudimentary hoof in deer, goats, etc. ▸ **'dewˌclawed** *adj*

dewdrop ('djuːˌdrɒp) *n* **1** a drop of dew. **2** *Brit. euphemistic.* a drop of mucus on the end of one's nose.

de Wet (də 'vɛt) *n* **Christian Rudolf.** 1854–1922, Afrikaner military commander and politician, who led the Orange Free State army in the second Boer War (1899–1902). He was imprisoned for treason (1914) after organizing an Afrikaner nationalist rebellion.

Dewey ('djuːɪ) *n* **John.** 1859–1952, U.S. pragmatist philosopher and educator: an exponent of progressivism in education, he formulated an instrumentalist theory of learning through experience. His works include *The School and Society* (1899), *Democracy and Education* (1916), and *Logic: the Theory of Inquiry* (1938).

Dewey Decimal System *n* a frequently used system of library book classification and arrangement with ten main subject classes. Also called: **decimal classification.** Abbrev.: **DDS.** [C19: named after Melvil *Dewey* (1851–1931), U.S. educator who invented the system]

de Wint (də 'wɪnt) *n* **Peter.** 1784–1849, English landscape painter.

de Witt (də 'wɪt) *n* **Johan.** See (Johan de) **Witt.**

dewlap ('djuːˌlæp) *n* **1** a loose fold of skin hanging from beneath the throat in cattle, dogs, etc. **2** loose skin on an elderly person's throat. [C14 *dewlappe,* from DEW (probably changed by folk etymology from an earlier form of different meaning) + LAP[1] (from Old English *læppa* hanging flap), perhaps of Scandinavian origin; compare Danish *doglæp*] ▸ **'dewˌlapped** *adj*

DEW line (djuː) *n acronym for* distant early warning line, a network of radar stations situated mainly in Arctic regions to give early warning of aircraft or missile attack on North America.

dew point *n* the temperature at which water vapour in the air becomes saturated and dew begins to form.

dew pond *n* a shallow pond, usually man-made, that is kept supplied with water by dew and condensation.

Dewsbury ('djuːzbərɪ, -brɪ) *n* a town in N England, in Kirklees unitary authority, West Yorkshire: woollen industry. Pop.: 50 168 (1991).

dew-worm *n* any large earthworm that is found on the ground at night and is used as fishing bait.

dewy ('djuːɪ) *adj* **dewier, dewiest. 1** moist with or as with dew: *a dewy complexion.* **2** of or resembling dew. **3** *Poetic.* suggesting, falling, or refreshing like dew: *dewy sleep.* ▸ **'dewily** *adv* ▸ **'dewiness** *n*

dewy-eyed *adj* naive, innocent, or trusting, esp. in a romantic or childlike way.

Dexedrine ('dɛksɪˌdriːn) *n* a trademark for **dextroamphetamine.**

dexiotropic (ˌdɛksɪəʊ'trɒpɪk) *adj Embryol.* (of cleavage) spiral; twisting in a spiral fashion from left to right. [C19: from Greek *dexios* right + -TROPIC]

dexter[1] ('dɛkstə) *adj* **1** *Archaic.* of or located on the right side. **2** (*usually postpositive*) *Heraldry.* of, on, or starting from the right side of a shield from the bearer's point of view and therefore on the spectator's left. ◆ Compare **sinister.** [C16: from Latin; compare Greek *dexios* on the right hand]

dexter[2] ('dɛkstə) *n* a small breed of red or black cattle, originally from Ireland. [C19: perhaps from the surname of the original breeder]

Dexter ('dɛkstə) *n* **John.** 1925–90, British actor and theatre director.

dexterity (dɛk'stɛrɪtɪ) *n* **1** physical, esp. manual, skill or nimbleness. **2** mental skill or adroitness: cleverness. **3** *Rare.* the characteristic of being right-handed. [C16: from Latin *dexteritās* aptness, readiness, prosperity; see DEXTER[1]]

dexterous *or* **dextrous** ('dɛkstrəs) *adj* **1** possessing or done with dexterity. **2** a rare word for **right-handed.** ▸ **'dexterously** *or* **'dextrously** *adv* ▸ **'dexterousness** *or* **'dextrousness** *n*

dextral ('dɛkstrəl) *adj* **1** of, relating to, or located on the right side, esp. of the body; right-hand. **2** of or relating to a person who prefers to use his right foot, hand, or eye; right-handed. **3** (of the shells of certain gastropod molluscs) coiling in an anticlockwise direction from the apex; dextrorse. ◆ Compare **sinistral.** ▸ **dextrality** (dɛk'strælɪtɪ) *n* ▸ **'dextrally** *adv*

dextran ('dɛkstrən) *n Biochem.* a polysaccharide produced by the action of bacteria on sucrose: used as a substitute for plasma in blood transfusions. [C19: from DEXTRO- + -AN]

dextrin ('dɛkstrɪn) *or* **dextrine** ('dɛkstrɪn, -triːn) *n* any of a group of sticky substances that are intermediate products in the conversion of starch to maltose: used as thickening agents in foods and as gums. [C19: from French *dextrine;* see DEXTRO-, -IN]

dextro ('dɛkstrəʊ) *adj* short for **dextrorotatory.**

dextro- *or before a vowel* **dextr-** *combining form.* **1** on or towards the right: *dextrorotation.* **2** (in chemistry) indicating a dextrorotatory compound: *dextroglucose.* [from Latin, from *dexter* on the right side]

dextroamphetamine (ˌdɛkstrəʊæm'fɛtəˌmiːn, -mɪn) *n* a dextrorotatory amphetamine, used in medicine.

dextrocardia (ˌdɛkstrəʊ'kɑːdɪə) *n Med.* the abnormal location of the heart in the right side of the chest.

dextroglucose (ˌdɛkstrəʊ'gluːkəʊz, -kəʊs) *n* another name for **dextrose.**

dextrogyrate (ˌdɛkstrəʊ'dʒaɪrɪt, -ˌreɪt) *or* **dextrogyre** ('dɛkstrəʊˌdʒaɪə) *adj* having dextrorotation.

dextrorotation (ˌdɛkstrəʊrəʊ'teɪʃən) *n* a rotation to the right; clockwise rotation, esp. of the plane of polarization of plane-polarized light passing through a crystal, liquid, or solution, as seen by an observer facing the oncoming light. Compare **laevorotation.** ▸ **dextrorotatory** (ˌdɛkstrəʊ'rəʊtətərɪ, -trɪ) *or* **ˌdextro'rotary** *adj*

dextrorse ('dɛkstrɔːs, dɛk'strɔːs) *or* **dextrorsal** (dɛk'strɔːsᵊl) *adj* (of some climbing plants) growing upwards in a spiral from left to right or anticlockwise. Compare **sinistrorse.** [C19: from Latin *dextrorsum* towards the right, from DEXTRO- + *vorsus* turned, variant of *versus,* from *vertere* to turn] ▸ **'dextrorsely** *adv*

dextrose ('dɛkstrəʊz, -trəʊs) *n* a white soluble sweet-tasting crystalline solid that is the dextrorotatory isomer of glucose, occurring widely in fruit, honey, and in the blood and tissue of animals. Formula: $C_6H_{12}O_6$. Also called: **grape sugar, dextroglucose.**

dextrous ('dɛkstrəs) *adj* a variant spelling of **dexterous.** ▸ **'dextrously** *adv* ▸ **'dextrousness** *n*

dey (deɪ) *n* **1** the title given to commanders or (from 1710) governors of the Janissaries of Algiers (1671–1830). **2** a title applied by Western writers to various other Ottoman governors, such as the bey of Tunis. [C17: from French, from Turkish *dayi,* literally: maternal uncle, hence title given to an older person]

Dezhnev (*Russian* dɪʒ'njɔf) *n* **Cape.** a cape in NE Russia at the E end of Chukotski Peninsula: the northeasternmost point of Asia. Former name: **East Cape.**

DF *abbrev. for* Defender of the Faith.

D/F *or* **DF** *Telecomm. abbrev. for:* **1** direction finder. **2** direction finding.

DFC *abbrev. for* Distinguished Flying Cross.

DfEE (in Britain) *abbrev. for* Department for Education and Employment.

DFM *abbrev. for* Distinguished Flying Medal.

dg *or* **dg.** *abbrev. for* decigram.

DG *abbrev. for:* **1** Deo gratias. **2** director-general.

DH (in Britain) *abbrev. for* Department of Health.

DHA (in Britain) *abbrev. for* District Health Authority.

Dhahran (dɑː'rɑːn) *n* a town in E Saudi Arabia: site of the original discovery of oil in the country (1938).

dhak (dɑːk, dɔːk) *n* a tropical Asian leguminous tree, *Butea frondosa,* that has bright red flowers and yields a red resin, used as an astringent. [C19: from Hindi]

Dhaka *or* **Dacca** ('dækə) *n* the capital of Bangladesh, in the E central part: capital of Bengal (1608–39; 1660–1704) and of East Pakistan (1949–71); jute and cotton mills; university (1921). Pop.: 3 839 000 (1991).

dhal, dal, *or* **dholl** (dɑːl) *n* **1** a tropical African and Asian leguminous shrub, *Cajanus cajan,* cultivated in tropical regions for its nutritious pealike seeds. **2** the seed of this shrub. ◆ Also called: **pigeon pea. 3** a curry made from lentils or other pulses. [C17: from Hindi *dāl* split pulse, from Sanskrit *dal* to split]

dhansak ('dænzæk) *n* any of a variety of Indian dishes consisting of meat or vegetables braised with water or stock and lentils. [C20: from Urdu]

dharma ('dɑːmə) *n* **1** *Hinduism.* social custom regarded as a religious and moral duty. **2** *Hinduism.* **2a** the essential principle of the cosmos; natural law. **2b** conduct that conforms with this. **3** *Buddhism.* ideal truth as set forth in the teaching of Buddha. [Sanskrit: habit, usage, law, from *dhārayati* he holds]

dharna *or* **dhurna** ('dʌnə, 'dɑː-) *n* (in India) a method of obtaining justice, as the payment of a debt, by sitting, fasting, at the door of the person from whom reparation is sought. [C18: from Hindi, literally: a placing]

Dhaulagiri (ˌdaʊlə'gɪərɪ) *n* a mountain in W central Nepal, in the Himalayas. Height: 8172 m (26 810 ft.).

Dhílos ('ðilɔs) *n* transliteration of the Modern Greek name for **Delos.**

dhobi ('dəʊbɪ) *n, pl* **-bis.** (in India, Malaya, East Africa, etc., esp. formerly) a washerman. [C19: from Hindi, from *dhōb* washing; related to Sanskrit *dhāvaka* washerman]

dhobi itch *n* a fungal disease of the skin: a type of ringworm chiefly affecting the groin. Also called: **tinea cruris.**

Dhodhekánisos (ðɔðɛ'kanisɔs) *n* a transliteration of the modern Greek name for the **Dodecanese.**

dhole (dəʊl) *n* a fierce canine mammal, *Cuon alpinus,* of the forests of central and SE Asia, having a reddish-brown coat and rounded ears: hunts in packs. [C19: of uncertain origin]

dholl (dɑːl) *n* a variant spelling of **dhal.**

dhoti ('dəʊtɪ), **dhooti, dhootie,** *or* **dhuti** ('duːtɪ) *n, pl* **-tis.** a long loincloth worn by men in India. [C17: from Hindi]

dhow (daʊ) *n* a lateen-rigged coastal Arab sailing vessel with one or two masts. [C19: from Arabic *dāwa*]

DHSS (Britain) *abbrev. for* (former) Department of Health and Social Security.

Di *the chemical symbol for* didymium.

DI *abbrev. for* **1** Defence Intelligence. **2** Detective Inspector. **3** Donor Insemination.

di. *or* **dia.** *abbrev. for* diameter.

di-[1] *prefix* **1** twice; two; double: *dicotyledon.* **2a** containing two specified atoms or groups of atoms: *dimethyl ether; carbon dioxide.* **2b** a nontechnical equivalent of **bi-**[1] (sense 5c). [via Latin from Greek, from *dis* twice, double, related to *duo* two. Compare BI-[1]]

di-[2] *combining form.* variant of **dia-** before a vowel: *diopter.*

dia- *or* **di-** *prefix* **1** through, throughout, or during: *diachronic.* **2** across: *diac-*

tinic. **3** apart: *diacritic.* **4** (in botany) at right angles: *diatropism.* **5** in opposite or different directions: *diamagnetism.* [from Greek *dia* through, between, across, by]

diabase ('daɪəˌbeɪs) *n* **1** *Brit.* an altered dolerite. **2** *U.S.* another name for **dolerite.** [C19: from French, from Greek *diabasis* a crossing over, from *diabainein* to cross over, from DIA- + *bainein* to go] ▸ ˌ**dia'basic** *adj*

diabetes (ˌdaɪə'biːtɪs, -tiːz) *n* any of various disorders, esp. diabetes mellitus, characterized by excretion of an abnormally large amount of urine. [C16: from Latin: siphon, from Greek, literally: a passing through (referring to the excessive urination), from *diabainein* to pass through, cross over; see DIABASE]

diabetes insipidus (ɪn'sɪpɪdəs) *n* a disorder of the pituitary gland causing excessive thirst and excretion of large quantities of dilute urine. [C18: New Latin, literally: insipid diabetes]

diabetes mellitus (mə'laɪtəs) *n* a disorder of carbohydrate metabolism characterized by excessive thirst and excretion of abnormally large quantities of urine containing an excess of sugar, caused by a deficiency of insulin. [C18: New Latin, literally: honey-sweet diabetes]

diabetic (ˌdaɪə'bɛtɪk) *adj* **1** of, relating to, or having diabetes. **2** for the use of diabetics: *diabetic chocolate.* ◆ *n* **3** a person who has diabetes.

diablerie (dɪ'ɑːbləri; *French* djɑbləri) *n* **1** magic or witchcraft connected with devils. **2** demonic lore or esoteric knowledge of devils. **3** the domain of devils. **4** devilry; mischief. [C18: from Old French, from *diable* devil, from Latin *diabolus;* see DEVIL]

diabolic (ˌdaɪə'bɒlɪk) *adj* **1** of, relating to, or proceeding from the devil; satanic. **2** befitting a devil; extremely cruel or wicked; fiendish. **3** very difficult or unpleasant. [C14: from Late Latin *diabolicus,* from Greek *diabolikos,* from *diabolos* DEVIL] ▸ ˌ**dia'bolically** *adv* ▸ ˌ**dia'bolicalness** *n*

diabolical (ˌdaɪə'bɒlɪkᵊl) *adj Informal.* **1** excruciatingly bad; outrageous. **2** (intensifier): *a diabolical liberty.* ▸ ˌ**dia'bolically** *adv* ▸ ˌ**dia'bolicalness** *n*

diabolism (daɪ'æbəˌlɪzəm) *n* **1a** activities designed to enlist the aid of devils, esp. in witchcraft or sorcery. **1b** worship of devils or beliefs and teachings concerning them. **1c** the nature of devils. **2** character or conduct that is devilish or fiendish; devilry. ▸ **di'abolist** *n*

diabolize *or* **diabolise** (daɪ'æbəˌlaɪz) *vb* (*tr*) **1a** to make (someone or something) diabolical. **1b** to subject to the influence of devils. **2** to portray as diabolical.

diabolo (dɪ'æbəˌləʊ) *n, pl* **-los.** **1** a game in which one throws and catches a spinning top on a cord fastened to two sticks held in the hands. **2** the top used in this game.

diacaustic (ˌdaɪə'kɔːstɪk, -'kɒs-) *adj* **1** (of a caustic curve or surface) formed by refracted light rays. ◆ *n* **2** a diacaustic curve or surface. ◆ Compare **catacaustic.**

diacetylmorphine (daɪˌæsətɪl'mɔːfiːn) *n* another name for **heroin.**

diachronic (ˌdaɪə'krɒnɪk) *adj* of, relating to, or studying the development of a phenomenon through time; historical: *diachronic linguistics.* Compare **synchronic.** [C19: from DIA- + Greek *khronos* time]

diachronism (daɪ'ækrəˌnɪzəm) *n Geology.* the passage of a geological formation across time planes, as occurs when a marine sediment laid down by an advancing sea is noticeably younger in the direction of advancement. ▸ **di'achronous** *adj*

diacid (daɪ'æsɪd) *adj* **1** another word for **diacidic.** **2** (of a salt or acid) containing two acidic hydrogen atoms: *NaH_2PO_4 is a diacid salt of phosphoric acid.* ◆ *n* **3** an acid or salt that contains two acidic hydrogen atoms.

diacidic (ˌdaɪə'sɪdɪk) *adj* (of a base, such as calcium hydroxide $Ca(OH)_2$) capable of neutralizing two protons with one of its molecules. Also: **diacid.** Compare **dibasic.**

diaconal (daɪ'ækənᵊl) *adj* of or associated with a deacon or the diaconate. [C17: from Late Latin *diāconālis,* from *diāconus* DEACON]

diaconate (daɪ'ækənɪt, -ˌneɪt) *n* the office, sacramental status, or period of office of a deacon. [C17: from Late Latin *diāconātus;* see DEACON]

diacritic (ˌdaɪə'krɪtɪk) *n* **1** Also called: **diacritical mark.** a sign placed above or below a character or letter to indicate that it has a different phonetic value, is stressed, or for some other reason. ◆ *adj* **2** another word for **diacritical.** [C17: from Greek *diakritikos* serving to distinguish, from *diakrinein,* from DIA- + *krinein* to separate]

diacritical (ˌdaɪə'krɪtɪkᵊl) *adj* **1** of or relating to a diacritic. **2** showing up a distinction. ▸ ˌ**dia'critically** *adv*

diactinic (ˌdaɪæk'tɪnɪk) *adj Physics.* able to transmit photochemically active radiation. ▸ **di'actinism** *n*

diadelphous (ˌdaɪə'dɛlfəs) *adj* **1** (of stamens) having united filaments so that they are arranged in two groups. **2** (of flowers) having diadelphous stamens. [C19: from DI-[1] + Greek *adelphos* brother]

diadem ('daɪəˌdɛm) *n* **1** a royal crown, esp. a light jewelled circlet. **2** royal dignity or power. ◆ *vb* **3** (*tr*) to adorn or crown with or as with a diadem. [C13: from Latin *diadēma,* from Greek: fillet, royal headdress, from *diadein* to bind around, from DIA- + *dein* to bind]

diadem spider *n* a common Eurasian spider, *Araneus diadematus,* that constructs orb webs: family *Argiopidae.*

Diadochi (daɪ'ædəkaɪ) *pl n* the six Macedonian generals who, after the death of Alexander the Great, fought for control of his empire in the **Wars of the Diadochi** (321–281 B.C.). [Greek: successors]

diadochy (daɪ'ædəʊkɪ) *n Geology.* the replacement of one element in a crystal by another. [C20: from Greek *diadochē* succession]

diadromous (daɪ'ædrəməs) *adj* **1** *Botany.* of or possessing a leaf venation in the shape of a fan. **2** (of some fishes) migrating between fresh and salt water. See also **anadromous, catadromous.**

diaeresis *or* **dieresis** (daɪ'ɛrɪsɪs) *n, pl* **-ses** (-ˌsiːz). **1** the mark ¨ , in writing placed over the second of two adjacent vowels to indicate that it is to be pronounced separately rather than forming a diphthong with the first, as in some spellings of *coöperate, naïve,* etc. **2** this mark used for any other purpose, such as to indicate that a special pronunciation is appropriate to a particular vowel. Compare **umlaut.** **3** a pause in a line of verse occurring when the end of a foot coincides with the end of a word. [C17: from Latin *diaeresis,* from Greek *diairesis* a division, from *diairein,* from DIA- + *hairein* to take; compare HERESY] ▸ **diaeretic** *or* **dieretic** (ˌdaɪə'rɛtɪk) *adj*

diag. *abbrev. for* diagram.

diagenesis (ˌdaɪə'dʒɛnɪsɪs) *n* **1** the sum of the physical, chemical, and biological changes that take place in sediments before they become consolidated into rocks, excluding weathering and metamorphic changes. **2** *Chem.* recrystallization of a solid to form large crystal grains from smaller ones. ▸ **diagenetic** (ˌdaɪədʒə'nɛtɪk) *adj*

diageotropism (ˌdaɪədʒɪ'ɒtrəˌpɪzəm) *n* a diatropic response of plant parts, such as rhizomes, to the stimulus of gravity. ▸ **diageotropic** (ˌdaɪəˌdʒiːəʊ'trɒpɪk) *adj*

Diaghilev (*Russian* 'djagɪlif) *n* **Sergei Pavlovich** (sɪr'gjej 'pavləvitʃ). 1872–1929, Russian ballet impresario. He founded (1909) and directed (1909–29) the *Ballet Russe* in Paris, introducing Russian ballet to the West.

diagnose ('daɪəgˌnəʊz) *vb* **1** to determine or distinguish by diagnosis. **2** (*tr*) to examine (a person or thing), as for a disease. ▸ ˌ**diag'nosable** *adj*

diagnosis (ˌdaɪəg'nəʊsɪs) *n, pl* **-ses** (-siːz). **1a** the identification of diseases from the examination of symptoms. **1b** an opinion or conclusion so reached. **2a** thorough analysis of facts or problems in order to gain understanding and aid future planning. **2b** an opinion or conclusion reached through such analysis. **3** a detailed description of an organism, esp. a plant, for the purpose of classification. [C17: New Latin, from Greek: a distinguishing, from *diagignōskein* to distinguish, from *gignōskein* to perceive, KNOW]

diagnostic (ˌdaɪəg'nɒstɪk) *adj* **1** of, relating to, or of value in diagnosis. ◆ *n* **2** *Med.* any symptom that provides evidence for making a specific diagnosis. **3** a diagnosis. ▸ ˌ**diag'nostically** *adv*

diagnostician (ˌdaɪəgnɒs'tɪʃən) *n* a specialist or expert in making diagnoses.

diagnostics (ˌdaɪəg'nɒstɪks) *n* (*functioning as sing*) the art or practice of diagnosis, esp. of diseases.

diagonal (daɪ'ægənᵊl) *adj* **1** *Maths.* connecting any two vertices that in a polygon are not adjacent and in a polyhedron are not in the same face. **2** slanting; oblique. **3** marked with slanting lines or patterns. ◆ *n* **4** *Maths.* a diagonal line or plane. **5** *Chess.* any oblique row of squares of the same colour. **6** cloth marked or woven with slanting lines or patterns. **7** something put, set, or drawn obliquely. **8** another name for **solidus** (sense 1). **9** one front leg and the hind leg on the opposite side of a horse, which are on the ground together when the horse is trotting. [C16: from Latin *diagōnālis,* from Greek *diagōnios,* from DIA- + *gōnia* angle] ▸ **di'agonally** *adv*

diagonal process *n Maths, logic.* a form of argument in which a new member of a set is constructed from a list of its known members by making the *n*th term of the new member differ from the *n*th term of the *n*th member. The new member is thus different from every member of the list.

diagram ('daɪəˌgræm) *n* **1** a sketch, outline, or plan demonstrating the form or workings of something. **2** *Maths.* a pictorial representation of a quantity or of a relationship: *a Venn diagram.* ◆ *vb* **-grams, -gramming, -grammed** *or U.S.* **-grams, -graming, -gramed.** **3** to show in or as if in a diagram. [C17: from Latin *diagramma,* from Greek, from *diagraphein,* from *graphein* to write] ▸ **diagrammatic** (ˌdaɪəgrə'mætɪk) *adj* ▸ ˌ**diagram'matically** *adv*

diagraph ('daɪəˌgrɑːf, -ˌgræf) *n* **1** a device for enlarging or reducing maps, plans, etc. **2** a protractor and scale used in drawing. [C19: from French *diagraphe,* from Greek *diagraphein* to represent with lines; see DIAGRAM]

diakinesis (ˌdaɪəkɪ'niːsɪs, -kaɪ-) *n* the final stage of the prophase of meiosis, during which homologous chromosomes start to separate after crossing over. [C20: from DIA- + Greek *kinēsis* movement]

dial ('daɪəl, daɪl) *n* **1** the face of a watch, clock, chronometer, sundial, etc., marked with divisions representing units of time. **2** the circular graduated disc of various measuring instruments. **3a** the control on a radio or television set used to change the station or channel. **3b** the panel on a radio on which the frequency, wavelength, or station is indicated by means of a pointer. **4** a numbered disc on a telephone that is rotated a set distance for each digit of a number being called. **5** a miner's compass for surveying in a mine. **6** *Brit.* a slang word for **face** (sense 1). ◆ *vb* **dials, dialling, dialled** *or U.S.* **dials, dialing, dialed.** **7** to establish or try to establish a telephone connection with (a subscriber or his number) by operating the dial on a telephone. **8** (*tr*) to indicate, measure, or operate with a dial. [C14: from Medieval Latin *diālis* daily, from Latin *diēs* day] ▸ **'dialler** *n*

dial. *abbrev. for* dialect(al).

dialect ('daɪəˌlɛkt) *n* **a** a form of a language spoken in a particular geographical area or by members of a particular social class or occupational group, distinguished by its vocabulary, grammar, and pronunciation. **b** a form of a language that is considered inferior: *the farmer spoke dialect and was despised by the merchants.* **c** (*as modifier*): *a dialect word.* [C16: from Latin *dialectus,* from Greek *dialektos* speech, dialect, discourse, from *dialegesthai* to converse, from *legein* to talk, speak] ▸ ˌ**dia'lectal** *adj*

dialect atlas *n* another term for **linguistic atlas.**

dialect geography *n* another term for **linguistic geography.** ▸ **dialect geographer** *n*

dialectic (ˌdaɪə'lɛktɪk) *n* **1** disputation or debate, esp. intended to resolve differences between two views rather than to establish one of them as true. **2** *Philosophy.* **2a** the conversational Socratic method of argument. **2b** (in Plato) the highest study, that of the Forms. **3** (in the writings of Kant) the exposure of the contradictions implicit in applying empirical concepts beyond the limits of experience. **4** *Philosophy.* the process of reconciliation of contradiction either of beliefs or in historical processes. See also **Hegelian dialectic, dialectical materialism.** ◆ *adj* **5** of or relating to logical disputation. [C17: from Latin *dialectica,* from Greek *dialektikē (tekhnē)* (the art) of argument; see DIALECT] ▸ ˌ**dialecˈtician** *n*

dialectical (ˌdaɪəˈlɛktɪkᵊl) *adj* of or relating to dialectic or dialectics. ▸ ˌ**diaˈlectically** *adv*

dialectical materialism *n* the economic, political, and philosophical system of Karl Marx and Friedrich Engels that combines traditional materialism and Hegelian dialectic. ▸ **dialectical materialist** *n*

dialectics (ˌdaɪəˈlɛktɪks) *n (functioning as pl or (sometimes) sing)* **1** the study of reasoning or of argumentative methodology. **2** a particular methodology or system; a logic. **3** the application of the Hegelian dialectic or the rationale of dialectical materialism.

dialectology (ˌdaɪəlɛkˈtɒlədʒɪ) *n* the study of dialects and dialectal variations. ▸ **dialectological** (ˌdaɪəˌlɛktəˈlɒdʒɪkᵊl) *adj* ▸ ˌ**diaˌlectoˈlogically** *adv* ▸ ˌ**dialecˈtologist** *n*

dial gauge *n* another name for an **indicator** (sense 6).

diallage (ˈdaɪəlɪdʒ) *n* a green or brownish-black variety of the mineral augite in the form of layers of platelike crystals. [C19: from Greek *diallagē* interchange]

dialling code *n* a sequence of numbers which are dialled for connection with another exchange before an individual subscriber's telephone number is dialled.

dialling tone *or U.S. and Canadian* **dial tone** *n* a continuous sound, either purring or high-pitched, heard over a telephone indicating that a number can be dialled. Compare **ringing tone, engaged tone.**

dialogism (daɪˈæləˌdʒɪzəm) *n* **1** *Logic.* a deduction with one premise and a disjunctive conclusion. **2** *Rhetoric.* a discussion in an imaginary dialogue or discourse.

dialogist (daɪˈælədʒɪst) *n* a person who writes or takes part in a dialogue. ▸ ˌ**dialoˈgistic** *or* ˌ**dialoˈgistical** *adj*

dialogize *or* **dialogise** (daɪˈæləˌdʒaɪz) *vb (intr)* to carry on a dialogue.

dialogue *or U.S. (often)* **dialog** (ˈdaɪəˌlɒg) *n* **1** conversation between two or more people. **2** an exchange of opinions on a particular subject; discussion. **3** the lines spoken by characters in drama or fiction. **4** a particular passage of conversation in a literary or dramatic work. **5** a literary composition in the form of a dialogue. **6** a political discussion between representatives of two nations or groups. ◆ *vb Rare.* **7** *(tr)* to put into the form of a dialogue. **8** *(intr)* to take part in a dialogue; converse. [C13: from Old French *dialoge,* from Latin *dialogus,* from Greek *dialogos,* from *dialegesthai* to converse; see DIALECT] ▸ **dialogic** (ˌdaɪəˈlɒdʒɪk) *adj* ▸ ˈ**diaˌloguer** *n*

dialyse *or U.S.* **dialyze** (ˈdaɪəˌlaɪz) *vb (tr)* to separate by dialysis. ▸ ˈ**diaˌlysable** *or U.S.* ˈ**diaˌlyzable** *adj* ▸ ˌ**diaˌlysaˈbility** *or U.S.* ˌ**diaˌlyzaˈbility** *n* ▸ ˌ**dialyˈsation** *or U.S.* ˌ**dialyˈzation** *n*

dialyser *or U.S.* **dialyzer** (ˈdaɪəˌlaɪzə) *n* a machine that performs dialysis, esp. one that removes impurities from the blood of patients with malfunctioning kidneys; kidney machine.

dialysis (daɪˈælɪsɪs) *n, pl* **-ses** (-ˌsiːz). **1** the separation of small molecules from large molecules and colloids in a solution by the selective diffusion of the small molecules through a semipermeable membrane. **2** *Med.* See **haemodialysis.** [C16: from Late Latin: a separation, from Greek *dialusis* a dissolution, from *dialuein* to tear apart, dissolve, from *luein* to loosen] ▸ **dialytic** (ˌdaɪəˈlɪtɪk) *adj* ▸ ˌ**diaˈlytically** *adv*

diam. *abbrev. for* diameter.

diamagnet (ˈdaɪəˌmægnɪt) *n* a substance exhibiting diamagnetism.

diamagnetic (ˌdaɪəmægˈnɛtɪk) *adj* of, exhibiting, or concerned with diamagnetism. ▸ ˌ**diamagˈnetically** *adv*

diamagnetism (ˌdaɪəˈmægnɪˌtɪzəm) *n* the phenomenon exhibited by substances that have a relative permeability less than unity and a negative susceptibility. It is caused by the orbital motion of electrons in the atoms of the material and is unaffected by temperature. Compare **ferromagnetism, paramagnetism.**

diamanté (ˌdaɪəˈmæntɪ, ˌdɪə-) *adj* **1** decorated with glittering ornaments, such as artificial jewels or sequins. ◆ *n* **2** a fabric so covered. [C20: from French, from *diamanter* to adorn with diamonds, from *diamant* DIAMOND]

diamantine (ˌdaɪəˈmæntaɪn) *adj* of or resembling diamonds. [C17: from French *diamantin,* from *diamant* DIAMOND]

diameter (daɪˈæmɪtə) *n* **1a** a straight line connecting the centre of a geometric figure, esp. a circle or sphere, with two points on the perimeter or surface. **1b** the length of such a line. **2** the thickness of something, esp. with circular cross section. [C14: from Medieval Latin *diametrus,* variant of Latin *diametros,* from Greek: diameter, diagonal, from DIA- + *metron* measure]

diametral (daɪˈæmɪtrəl) *adj* **1** located on or forming a diameter: *diametral plane.* **2** a less common word for **diametric.** ▸ **diˈametrally** *adv*

diametric (ˌdaɪəˈmɛtrɪk) *or* **diametrical** *adj* **1** Also: **diametral.** of, related to, or along a diameter. **2** completely opposed.

diametrically (ˌdaɪəˈmɛtrɪkəlɪ) *adv* completely; utterly (esp. in the phrase **diametrically opposed**).

diamine (ˈdaɪəˌmiːn, -mɪn; ˌdaɪəˈmiːn) *n* any chemical compound containing two amino groups in its molecules.

diamond (ˈdaɪəmənd) *n* **1a** a colourless exceptionally hard mineral (but often tinted yellow, orange, blue, brown, or black by impurities), found in certain igneous rocks (esp. the kimberlites of South Africa). It is used as a gemstone, as an abrasive, and on the working edges of cutting tools. Composition: carbon. Formula: C. Crystal structure: cubic. **1b** *(as modifier): a diamond ring.* Related adj: **diamantine. 2** *Geometry.* **2a** a figure having four sides of equal length forming two acute angles and two obtuse angles; rhombus. **2b** *(modifier)* rhombic. **3a** a red lozenge-shaped symbol on a playing card. **3b** a card with one or more of these symbols or *(when pl)* the suit of cards so marked. **4** *Baseball.* **4a** the whole playing field. **4b** the square formed by the four bases. **5** (formerly) a size of printer's type approximately equal to 4½ point. **6 black diamond.** a figurative name for **coal. 7 rough diamond. 7a** an unpolished diamond. **7b** a person of fine character who lacks refinement and polish. ◆ *vb* **8** *(tr)* to decorate with or as with diamonds. [C13: from Old French *diamant,* from Medieval Latin *diamas,* modification of Latin *adamas* the hardest iron or steel, diamond; see ADAMANT] ▸ ˈ**diamond-ˌlike** *adj*

diamond anniversary *n* a 60th, or occasionally 75th, anniversary.

diamondback (ˈdaɪəmənd,bæk) *n* **1** Also called: **diamondback terrapin** *or* **turtle.** any edible North American terrapin of the genus *Malaclemys,* esp. *M. terrapin,* occurring in brackish and tidal waters and having diamond-shaped markings on the shell: family *Emydidae.* **2** a large North American rattlesnake, *Crotalus adamanteus,* having cream-and-grey diamond-shaped markings.

diamond bird *n* any small insectivorous Australian songbird of the genus *Pardalotus,* having a diamond-patterned plumage. Also called: **pardalote.**

diamond jubilee *n* the celebration of a 60th, or occasionally 75th, anniversary.

diamond point *n* a diamond-tipped engraving tool.

diamond snake *n* a python, *Morelia argus,* of Australia and New Guinea, with yellow diamond-shaped markings.

diamond wedding *n* the 60th, or occasionally the 75th, anniversary of a marriage.

diamond willow *n Canadian.* wood that may come from any species of willow and has a diamond pattern in the grain, used for making walking sticks, table lamps, etc.

diamorphine (ˌdaɪəˈmɔːfiːn) *n* a technical name for **heroin.**

Diana (daɪˈænə) *n* **1** the virginal Roman goddess of the hunt and the moon. Greek counterpart: **Artemis. 2** title *Diana, Princess of Wales,* original name *Lady Diana Frances Spencer.* 1961–97, she married Charles, Prince of Wales, in 1981; they were divorced in 1996.

diandrous (daɪˈændrəs) *adj* (of some flowers or flowering plants) having two stamens.

dianoetic (ˌdaɪənəʊˈɛtɪk) *adj* of or relating to thought, esp. to discursive reasoning rather than intuition. Compare **discursive** (sense 2). [C17: from Greek *dianoētikos,* from *dianoia* the thinking process, an opinion, from DIA- + *noein* to think]

dianoia (ˌdaɪəˈnɔɪə) *n Philosophy.* **1** perception and experience regarded as lower modes of knowledge. Compare **noesis. 2** the faculty of discursive reasoning. [from Greek; see DIANOETIC]

dianthus (daɪˈænθəs) *n, pl* **-thuses.** any Eurasian caryophyllaceous plant of the widely cultivated genus *Dianthus,* such as the carnation, pink, and sweet william. [C19: New Latin, from Greek DI-[1] + *anthos* flower]

diapason (ˌdaɪəˈpeɪzᵊn, -ˈpeɪsᵊn) *n Music.* **1** either of two stops (**open** and **stopped diapason**) usually found throughout the compass of a pipe organ that give it its characteristic tone colour. **2** the compass of an instrument or voice. **3** (chiefly in French usage) **3a** a standard pitch used for tuning, esp. the now largely obsolete one of A above middle C = 435 hertz, known as **diapason normal** (*French* djapazɔ̃ nɔrmal). **3b** a tuning fork or pitch pipe. **4** (in classical Greece) an octave. [C14: from Latin: the whole octave, from Greek: *(hē) dia pasōn (khordōn sumphōnia)* (concord) through all (the notes), from *dia* through + *pas* all] ▸ **diaˈpasonal** *or* **diapasonic** (ˌdaɪəpeɪˈzɒnɪk, -ˈsɒn-) *adj*

diapause (ˈdaɪəˌpɔːz) *n* a period of suspended development and growth accompanied by decreased metabolism in insects and some other animals. It is correlated with seasonal changes. [C19: from Greek *diapausis* pause, from *diapauein* to pause, bring to an end, from DIA- + *pauein* to stop]

diapedesis (ˌdaɪəpəˈdiːsɪs) *n* the passage of blood cells through the unruptured wall of a blood vessel into the surrounding tissues. [C17: New Latin, from Greek: a leaping through, from *diapēdan* to spring through, from DIA- + *pēdan* to leap] ▸ **diapedetic** (ˌdaɪəpəˈdɛtɪk) *adj*

diapente (ˌdaɪəˈpɛntɪ) *n Music.* (in classical Greece) the interval of a perfect fifth. [C14: from Latin, from Greek *dia pente khordōn sumphōnia* concord through five notes, from *dia* through + *pente* five]

diaper (ˈdaɪəpə) *n* **1** the U.S. and Canadian word for **nappy**[1]. **2a** a woven pattern on fabric consisting of a small repeating design, esp. diamonds. **2b** fabric having such a pattern. **2c** such a pattern, used as decoration. ◆ *vb* **3** *(tr)* to decorate with such a pattern. [C14: from Old French *diaspre,* from Medieval Latin *diasprus* made of diaper, from Medieval Greek *diaspros* pure white, from DIA- + *aspros* white, shining]

diaphanous (daɪˈæfənəs) *adj* (usually of fabrics such as silk) fine and translucent. [C17: from Medieval Latin *diaphanus,* from Greek *diaphanēs* transparent, from *diaphainein* to show through, from DIA- + *phainein* to show] ▸ **diˈaphanously** *adv* ▸ **diˈaphanousness** *or* **diaphaneity** (ˌdaɪəfəˈniːɪtɪ) *n*

diaphone (ˈdaɪəˌfəʊn) *n* **1a** the set of all realizations of a given phoneme in a language. **1b** one of any number of corresponding sounds in different dialects of a language. **2** a foghorn that emits a two-toned signal. [C20: from DIA(LECT) + PHONE[2]]

diaphony (daɪˈæfənɪ) *n Music.* **1** a style of two-part polyphonic singing; organum or a freer form resembling it. **2** (in classical Greece) another word for **dissonance** (sense 3). Compare **symphony** (sense 5a). [C17: from Late Latin *diaphōnia,* from Greek, from *diaphōnos* discordant, from DIA- + *phōnē* sound] ▸ **diaphonic** (ˌdaɪəˈfɒnɪk) *adj*

diaphoresis (ˌdaɪəfəˈriːsɪs) *n* **1** a technical name for **perspiration. 2** perceptible and excessive perspiration; sweat. [C17: via Late Latin from Greek, from *diaphorein* to disperse by perspiration, from DIA- + *phorein* to carry, variant of *pherein*]

diaphoretic (ˌdaɪəfəˈrɛtɪk) *adj* **1** relating to or causing perspiration or sweat. ◆ *n* **2** a diaphoretic drug or agent.

diaphototropism (ˌdaɪəfəutəu'trəupɪzəm) *n* growth of a plant or plant part in a direction transverse to that of the light. [C20: from Greek, from DIA- + PHOTOTROPIC] ▸ **diaphototropic** (ˌdaɪəfəutəu'trɒpɪk) *adj*

diaphragm ('daɪəˌfræm) *n* **1** *Anatomy.* any separating membrane, esp. the dome-shaped muscular partition that separates the abdominal and thoracic cavities in mammals. Related adj: **phrenic. 2** a circular rubber or plastic contraceptive membrane placed over the mouth of the uterine cervix before copulation to prevent entrance of sperm. **3** any thin dividing membrane. **4** Also called: **stop.** a disc with a fixed or adjustable aperture to control the amount of light or other radiation entering an optical instrument, such as a camera. **5** a thin disc that vibrates when receiving or producing sound waves, used to convert sound signals to electrical signals or vice versa in telephones, etc. **6** *Chem.* **6a** a porous plate or cylinder dividing an electrolytic cell, used to permit the passage of ions and prevent the mixing of products formed at the electrodes. **6b** a semipermeable membrane used to separate two solutions in osmosis. **7** *Botany.* a transverse plate of cells that occurs in the stems of certain aquatic plants. [C17: from Late Latin *diaphragma,* from Greek, from DIA- + *phragma* fence] ▸ **diaphragmatic** (ˌdaɪəfræg'mætɪk) *adj* ▸ ˌ**diaphrag'matically** *adv*

diaphysis (daɪ'æfɪsɪs) *n, pl* **-ses** (-ˌsiːz). the shaft of a long bone. Compare **epiphysis.** [C19: New Latin, from Greek *diaphusis,* from *diaphuesthai* to grow between, from DIA- + *phuein* to produce] ▸ **diaphysial** (ˌdaɪə'fɪzɪəl) *adj*

diapir ('daɪəˌpɪə) *n Geology.* an anticlinal fold in which the brittle overlying rock has been pierced by material, such as salt, from beneath. [C20: from Greek *diapeirainein* to make holes through, pierce]

diapophysis (ˌdaɪə'pɒfɪsɪs) *n, pl* **-ses** (-ˌsiːz). *Anatomy.* the upper or articular surface of a transverse vertebral process. [C19: New Latin, from DI-[2] + APOPHYSIS] ▸ **diapophysial** (ˌdaɪæpə'fɪzɪəl) *adj*

diapositive (ˌdaɪə'pɒzɪtɪv) *n* a positive transparency; slide.

diarch ('daɪɑːk) *adj Botany.* (of a vascular bundle) having two strands of xylem. [C19: from Greek DI-[1] + *archē* beginning, origin]

diarchy *or* **dyarchy** ('daɪɑːkɪ) *n, pl* **-chies.** government by two states, individuals, etc. ▸ **di'archic, di'archical, di'archal,** *or* **dy'archic, dy'archical, dy'archal** *adj*

diarist ('daɪərɪst) *n* a person who keeps or writes a diary, esp. one that is subsequently published.

diarrhoea *or esp. U.S.* **diarrhea** (ˌdaɪə'rɪə) *n* frequent and copious discharge of abnormally liquid faeces. [C16: from Late Latin, from Greek *diarrhoia,* from *diarrhein* to flow through, from DIA- + *rhein* to flow] ▸ ˌ**diar'rhoeal,** ˌ**diar'rhoeic** *or esp. U.S.* ˌ**diar'rheal,** ˌ**diar'rheic** *adj*

diarthrosis (ˌdaɪɑː'θrəusɪs) *n, pl* **-ses** (-siːz). *Anatomy.* any freely movable joint, such as the shoulder and hip joints. [C16: New Latin, from DI-[2] + Greek *arthrōsis,* from *arthroun* to fasten by a joint, from *arthron* joint] ▸ ˌ**diar'throdial** *adj*

diary ('daɪərɪ) *n, pl* **-ries. 1** a personal record of daily events, appointments, observations, etc. **2** a book for keeping such a record. [C16: from Latin *diārium* daily allocation of food or money, journal, from *diēs* day]

Dias *or* **Diaz** ('diːəs; *Portuguese* 'diəʃ) *n* **Bartholomeu** (ˌbərtulu'meu). ?1450–1500, Portuguese navigator who discovered the sea route from Europe to the East via the Cape of Good Hope (1488).

diascope ('daɪəˌskəup) *n* an optical projector used to display transparencies.

Diaspora (daɪ'æspərə) *n* **1a** the dispersion of the Jews after the Babylonian and Roman conquests of Palestine. **1b** the Jewish communities outside Israel. **1c** the Jews living outside Israel. **1d** the extent of Jewish settlement outside Israel. **2** (in the New Testament) the body of Christians living outside Palestine. **3** (*often not cap.*) a dispersion or spreading, as of people originally belonging to one nation or having a common culture. [C19: from Greek: a scattering, from *diaspeirein* to disperse, from DIA- + *speirein* to scatter, sow; see SPORE]

diaspore ('daɪəˌspɔː) *n* **1** a white, yellowish, or grey mineral consisting of hydrated aluminium oxide in orthorhombic crystalline form, found in bauxite and corundum. Formula: $Al_2O_3.H_2O$. **2** any propagative part of a plant, esp. one that is easily dispersed, such as a spore. [C19: from Greek *diaspora* a scattering, dispersion; see DIASPORA: so named from its dispersion and crackling when highly heated]

diastalsis (ˌdaɪə'stælsɪs) *n, pl* **-ses** (-siːz). *Physiol.* a downward wave of contraction occurring in the intestine during digestion. See also **peristalsis.** [C20: New Latin, from DIA- + (PERI)STALSIS] ▸ ˌ**dia'staltic** *adj*

diastase ('daɪəˌsteɪs, -ˌsteɪz) *n* any of a group of enzymes that hydrolyse starch to maltose. They are present in germinated barley and in the pancreas. See also **amylase.** [C19: from French, from Greek *diastasis* a separation; see DIASTASIS] ▸ ˌ**dia'stasic** *adj*

diastasis (daɪ'æstəsɪs) *n, pl* **-ses** (-ˌsiːz). **1** *Pathol.* **1a** the separation of an epiphysis from the long bone to which it is normally attached without fracture of the bone. **1b** the separation of any two parts normally joined. **2** *Physiol.* the last part of the diastolic phase of the heartbeat. [C18: New Latin, from Greek: a separation, from *diistanai* to separate, from DIA- + *histanai* to place, make stand] ▸ **diastatic** (ˌdaɪə'stætɪk) *adj*

diastema (ˌdaɪə'stiːmə) *n, pl* **-mata** (-mətə). **1** an abnormal space, fissure, or cleft in a bodily organ or part. **2** a gap between the teeth. [C19: New Latin, from Greek: gap, from *diistanai* to separate; see DIASTASIS]

diaster (daɪ'æstə) *n Cytology.* the stage in cell division at which the chromosomes are in two groups at the poles of the spindle before forming daughter nuclei. [C19: from DI-[1] + Greek *astēr* star] ▸ **di'astral** *adj*

diastereoisomer (ˌdaɪəˌsterɪəu'aɪsəmə) *n Chem.* a type of isomer that differs in the spatial arrangement of atoms in the molecule, but is not a mirror image; a stereoisomer that is not an enantiomer.

diastole (daɪ'æstəlɪ) *n* the dilation of the chambers of the heart that follows each contraction, during which they refill with blood. Compare **systole.** [C16: via Late Latin from Greek: an expansion, from *diastellein* to expand, from DIA- + *stellein* to place, bring together, make ready] ▸ **diastolic** (ˌdaɪə'stɒlɪk) *adj*

diastrophism (daɪ'æstrəˌfɪzəm) *n* the process of movement and deformation of the earth's crust that gives rise to large-scale features such as continents, ocean basins, and mountains. See also **orogeny, epeirogeny.** [C19: from Greek *diastrophē* a twisting; see DIA-, STROPHE] ▸ **diastrophic** (ˌdaɪə'strɒfɪk) *adj*

diastyle ('daɪəˌstaɪl) *Architect.* ◆ *adj* **1** having columns about three diameters apart. ◆ *n* **2** a diastyle building. [C16: via Latin from Greek *diastȳlos* having spaced pillars]

diatessaron (ˌdaɪə'tesəˌrɒn) *n* **1** *Music.* (in classical Greece) the interval of a perfect fourth. **2** a conflation of the four Gospels into a single continuous narrative. [C14: from Late Latin, from Greek *dia tessarōn khordōn sumphōnia* concord through four notes, from *dia* through + *tessares* four]

diathermancy (ˌdaɪə'θɜːmənsɪ) *n, pl* **-cies.** the property of transmitting infrared radiation. [C19: from French *diathermansie,* from DIA- + Greek *thermansis* heating, from *thermainein* to heat, from *thermos* hot] ▸ ˌ**dia'thermanous** *adj*

diathermic (ˌdaɪə'θɜːmɪk) *adj* **1** of or relating to diathermy. **2** able to conduct heat; passing heat freely.

diathermy ('daɪəˌθɜːmɪ) *or* **diathermia** (ˌdaɪə'θɜːmɪə) *n* local heating of the body tissues with an electric current for medical or surgical purposes. [C20: from New Latin *diathermia,* from DIA- + Greek *thermē* heat]

diathesis (daɪ'æθɪsɪs) *n, pl* **-ses** (-ˌsiːz). a hereditary or acquired susceptibility of the body to one or more diseases. [C17: New Latin, from Greek: propensity, from *diatithenai* to dispose, from DIA- + *tithenai* to place] ▸ **diathetic** (ˌdaɪə'θetɪk) *adj*

diatom ('daɪətəm, -ˌtɒm) *n* any microscopic unicellular alga of the phylum *Bacillariophyta,* occurring in marine or fresh water singly or in colonies, each cell having a cell wall made of two halves and impregnated with silica. See also **diatomite.** [C19: from New Latin *Diatoma* (genus name), from Greek *diatomos* cut in two, from *diatemnein* to cut through, from DIA- + *temnein* to cut]

diatomaceous (ˌdaɪətə'meɪʃəs) *adj* of, relating to, consisting of, or containing diatoms or their fossil remains.

diatomaceous earth *n* an unconsolidated form of diatomite. Also called: **kieselguhr.**

diatomic (ˌdaɪə'tɒmɪk) *adj* (of a compound or molecule) **a** containing two atoms. **b** containing two characteristic groups or atoms: *ethylene glycol is a diatomic alcohol.* ▸ **diatomicity** (ˌdaɪætə'mɪsɪtɪ) *n*

diatomite (daɪ'ætəˌmaɪt) *n* a soft very fine-grained whitish rock consisting of the siliceous remains of diatoms deposited in small ponds or lakes. It is used as an absorbent, filtering medium, insulator, filler, etc. See also **diatomaceous earth.**

diatonic (ˌdaɪə'tɒnɪk) *adj* **1** of, relating to, or based upon any scale of five tones and two semitones produced by playing the white keys of a keyboard instrument, esp. the natural major or minor scales forming the basis of the key system in Western music. Compare **chromatic** (sense 2). **2** not involving the sharpening or flattening of the notes of the major or minor scale nor the use of such notes as modified by accidentals. [C16: from Late Latin *diatonicus,* from Greek *diatonikos,* from *diatonos* extending, from *diateinein* to stretch out, from DIA- + *teinein* to stretch] ▸ ˌ**dia'tonically** *adv* ▸ **diatonicism** (ˌdaɪə'tɒnɪˌsɪzəm) *n*

diatribe ('daɪəˌtraɪb) *n* a bitter or violent criticism or attack; denunciation. [C16: from Latin *diatriba* learned debate, from Greek *diatribē* discourse, pastime, from *diatribein* to while away, from DIA- + *tribein* to rub]

diatropism (daɪ'ætrəˌpɪzəm) *n* a response of plants or parts of plants to an external stimulus by growing at right angles to the direction of the stimulus. ▸ **diatropic** (ˌdaɪə'trɒpɪk) *adj*

Diaz *n* **1** ('diːəs; *Portuguese* 'diəʃ), **Bartholomeu** (ˌbərtulu'meu). a variant spelling of (Bartholomeu) **Dias. 2** ('diːəs; *Spanish* 'diaθ), **(José de la Cruz) Porfirio** (pər'firjo). 1830–1915, Mexican general and statesman; president of Mexico (1877–80; 1884–1911).

Díaz de Vivar (*Spanish* 'diaθ dɛ bi'βar) *n* **Rodrigo** (rɔ'ðriɣo). the original name of (El) **Cid.**

diazepam (daɪ'æzəˌpæm) *n* a chemical compound used as a tranquillizer and muscle relaxant. Formula: $C_{16}H_{13}ClN_2O$. [C20: from DI-[1] + AZO- + EP(OXIDE) + *-am*]

diazine ('daɪəˌziːn; daɪ'æziːn, -ɪn) *or* **diazin** ('daɪəzɪn, daɪ'æzɪn) *n* any organic compound whose molecules contain a hexagonal ring of four carbon atoms and two nitrogen atoms, esp. any of three isomers with the formula $C_4N_2H_4$. See also **pyrimidine.**

diazo (daɪ'eɪzəu) *adj* **1** of, consisting of, or containing the divalent group, =N:N, or the divalent group, -N:N-: *diazo compound.* See also **azo. 2** Also: **dyeline.** of or relating to the reproduction of documents using the bleaching action of ultraviolet radiation on diazonium salts. ◆ *n, pl* **-os** *or* **-oes. 3** a document produced by this method.

diazole (daɪ'eɪzəul) *n* any organic compound whose molecules contain a pentagonal ring of three carbon atoms and two nitrogen atoms, esp. imidazole (**1,3-diazole**) or pyrazole (**1,1-diazole**).

diazomethane (daɪˌeɪzəu'miːθeɪn) *n* a yellow odourless explosive gas, used as a methylating agent. Formula: CH_2:N:N.

diazonium (ˌdaɪə'zəunɪəm) *n* (*modifier*) of, consisting of, or containing the group, Ar-N:N-, where Ar is an aryl group: *diazonium group or radical; a diazonium compound.* [C19: DIAZO + (AMM)ONIUM]

diazonium salt *n* any of a class of compounds with the general formula $[ArN:N]^-M^+$, where Ar is an aryl group and M is a metal atom; made by the action of nitrous acid on aromatic amines and used in dyeing.

diazotize *or* **diazotise** (daɪ'eɪzəˌtaɪz) *vb* (*tr*) to cause (an aryl amine) to react with nitrous acid to produce a diazonium salt. ▶ **di,azoti'zation** *or* **di,azoti'sation** *n*

dib (dɪb) *vb* **dibs, dibbing, dibbed.** (*intr*) to fish by allowing the bait to bob and dip on the surface. [C17: perhaps alteration of DAB[1]]

dibasic (daɪ'beɪsɪk) *adj* **1** (of an acid, such as sulphuric acid, H_2SO_4) containing two acidic hydrogen atoms. Compare **diacidic. 2** (of a salt) derived by replacing two acidic hydrogen atoms: *dibasic sodium phosphate,* Na_2HPO_4. ▶ **dibasicity** (,daɪbeɪ'sɪsɪtɪ) *n*

dibble[1] ('dɪbᵊl) *n* **1** Also called (esp. Brit.): **dibber** ('dɪbə). a small hand tool used to make holes in the ground for planting or transplanting bulbs, seeds, or roots. ◆ *vb* **2** to make a hole in (the ground) with a dibble. **3** to plant (bulbs, seeds, etc.) with a dibble. [C15: of obscure origin] ▶ **'dibbler** *n*

dibble[2] ('dɪbᵊl) *vb* (*intr*) **1** a variant of **dib. 2** a less common word for **dabble.**

dibbuk ('dɪbək; *Hebrew* di'buk) *n, pl* **-buks** *or* **-bukkim** (*Hebrew* -bu'kim). a variant spelling of **dybbuk.**

dibranchiate (daɪ'bræŋkɪɪt, -,eɪt) *adj* **1** of, relating to, or belonging to the *Dibranchiata,* a group or former order of cephalopod molluscs, including the octopuses, squids, and cuttlefish, having two gills. ◆ *n* **2** any dibranchiate mollusc.

dibromide (daɪ'brəʊmaɪd) *n* a chemical compound that contains two bromine atoms per molecule.

dibs (dɪbz) *pl n* **1** another word for **jacks. 2** a slang word for **money. 3** (foll. by *on*) *Informal.* rights (to) or claims (on): used mainly by children. [C18: shortened from *dibstones* children's game played with knucklebones or pebbles, probably from *dib* to tap, dip, variant of DAB[1]]

dicarboxylic acid (daɪ,kɑːbɒk'sɪlɪk) *n* any carboxylic acid that contains two carboxyl groups per molecule.

dicast ('dɪkæst) *n* (in ancient Athens) a juror in the popular courts chosen by lot from a list of citizens. [C19: from Greek *dikastēs,* from *dikazein* to judge, from *dikē* right, judgment, order] ▶ **di'castic** *adj*

dice (daɪs) *pl n* **1** cubes of wood, plastic, etc., each of whose sides has a different number of spots (1 to 6), used in games of chance and in gambling to give random numbers. **2** (*functioning as sing*) Also called: **die.** one of these cubes. **3** small cubes as of vegetables, chopped meat, etc. **4 no dice.** *Slang, chiefly U.S. and Canadian.* an expression of refusal or rejection. ◆ *vb* **5** to cut (food, etc.) into small cubes. **6** (*intr*) to gamble with or play at a game involving dice. **7** (*intr*) to take a chance or risk (esp. in the phrase **dice with death**). **8** (*tr*) *Austral. informal.* to abandon or reject. **9** (*tr*) to decorate or mark with dicelike shapes. [C14: plural of DIE[2]] ▶ **'dicer** *n*

dicentra (daɪ'sɛntrə) *n* any Asian or North American plant of the genus *Dicentra,* such as bleeding heart and Dutchman's-breeches, having finely divided leaves and ornamental clusters of drooping flowers: family *Fumariaceae.* [C19: New Latin, from Greek *dikentros* having two sharp points, from DI-[1] + *kentron* sharp point, from *kentein* to prick; see CENTRE]

dicephalous (daɪ'sɛfələs) *adj* having two heads. ▶ **di'cephalism** *n*

dicey ('daɪsɪ) *adj* **dicier, diciest.** *Informal, chiefly Brit.* difficult or dangerous; risky; tricky.

dichasium (daɪ'keɪzɪəm) *n, pl* **-sia** (-zɪə). a cymose inflorescence in which each branch bearing a flower gives rise to two other flowering branches, as in the stitchwort. Compare **monochasium.** [C19: New Latin, from Greek *dikhasis* a dividing, from *dikhazein* to divide in two, from *dikha* in two] ▶ **di'chasial** *adj* ▶ **di'chasially** *adv*

dichlamydeous (,daɪklə'mɪdɪəs) *adj* (of a flower) having a corolla and calyx. [C19: from Greek, from DI-[1] + *khlamus* a cloak + -EOUS]

dichloride (daɪ'klɔːraɪd) *n* a compound in which two atoms of chlorine are combined with another atom or group. Also called: **bichloride.**

dichlorodifluoromethane (daɪ,klɔːrəʊdaɪ,flʊərəʊ'miːθeɪn) *n* a colourless nonflammable gas easily liquefied by pressure: used as a propellant in aerosols and fire extinguishers and as a refrigerant. Formula: CCl_2F_2. See also **Freon.**

dichlorodiphenyltrichloroethane (daɪ,klɔːrəʊdaɪ,fiːnaɪltraɪ,klɔːrəʊ'iːθeɪn, -nɪl-; -,fɛn-) *n* the full name for **DDT.**

dichloromethane (daɪ,klɔːrəʊ'miːθeɪn) *n* a noxious colourless liquid widely used as a solvent, e.g. in paint strippers. Formula: CH_2Cl_2. Traditional name: **methylene dichloride.**

dicho- *or before a vowel* **dich-** *combining form.* in two parts; in pairs: *dichotomy.* [from Greek *dikho-,* from *dikha* in two]

dichogamy (daɪ'kɒgəmɪ) *n* the maturation of male and female parts of a flower at different times, preventing self-pollination. Compare **homogamy** (sense 2). ▶ **di'chogamous** *or* **dichogamic** (,daɪkəʊ'gæmɪk) *adj*

dichoptic (daɪ'kɒptɪk) *adj Zoology.* having the eyes distinctly separate.

dichotic (daɪ'kɒtɪk) *adj* relating to or involving the stimulation of each ear simultaneously by different sounds. [DICHO- + -IC]

dichotomize *or* **dichotomise** (daɪ'kɒtə,maɪz) *vb* to divide or become divided into two parts or classifications. ▶ **di'chotomist** *n* ▶ **di,chotomi'zation** *or* **di,chotomi'sation** *n*

dichotomous question *n* a question to which there can only be one of two answers, often "yes" or "no".

dichotomy (daɪ'kɒtəmɪ) *n, pl* **-mies. 1** division into two parts or classifications, esp. when they are sharply distinguished or opposed: *the dichotomy between eastern and western cultures.* **2** *Logic.* the division of a class into two mutually exclusive subclasses: *the dichotomy of married and single people.* **3** *Botany.* a simple method of branching by repeated division into two equal parts. **4** the phase of the moon, Venus, or Mercury when half of the disc is visible. [C17: from Greek *dichotomia;* see DICHO-, -TOMY] ▶ **di'chotomous** *or* **dichotomic** (,daɪkəʊ'tɒmɪk) *adj* ▶ **di'chotomously** *adv*

USAGE *Dichotomy* should always refer to a division of some kind into two groups. It is sometimes used to refer to a puzzling situation which seems to involve a contradiction, but this use is generally thought to be incorrect.

dichroic (daɪ'krəʊɪk) *or* **dichroitic** (,daɪkrəʊ'ɪtɪk) *adj* **1** (of a solution or uniaxial crystal) exhibiting dichroism. **2** another word for **dichromatic.** [C19: from Greek *dikhroos* having two colours, from DI-[1] + *khrōs* colour]

dichroic filter *n* an optical colour filter operating on the principle of wave interference between closely spaced reflecting surfaces, rather than by colour absorption.

dichroism ('daɪkrəʊ,ɪzəm) *n* **1** Also called: **dichromaticism.** a property of a uniaxial crystal, such as tourmaline, of showing a perceptible difference in colour when viewed along two different axes in transmitted white light. See also **pleochroism. 2** a property of certain solutions as a result of which the wavelength (colour) of the light transmitted depends on the concentration of the solution and the length of the path of the light within the solution.

dichroite ('daɪkrəʊ,aɪt) *n* another name for **cordierite.** [C19: from Greek *dikhroos* two-coloured + -ITE[1]]

dichromate (daɪ'krəʊmeɪt) *n* any salt or ester of dichromic acid. Dichromate salts contain the ion $Cr_2O_7^{2-}$ Also called: **bichromate.**

dichromatic (,daɪkrəʊ'mætɪk) *adj* **1** Also: **dichroic.** having or consisting of only two colours. **2** (of animal species) having two different colour varieties that are independent of sex and age. **3** able to perceive only two (instead of three) primary colours and the mixes of these colours. ▶ **dichromatism** (daɪ'krəʊmə,tɪzəm) *n*

dichromaticism (,daɪkrəʊ'mætɪ,sɪzəm) *n* another name for **dichroism** (sense 1).

dichromic (daɪ'krəʊmɪk) *adj* of or involving only two colours; dichromatic.

dichromic acid *n* an unstable dibasic oxidizing acid known only in solution and in the form of dichromate salts. Formula: $H_2Cr_2O_7$.

dichroscope ('daɪkrə,skəʊp) *n* an instrument for investigating the dichroism of solutions or crystals. Also called: **di'chroi,scope, di'chroo,scope.** [C19: from Greek *dikhroos* two-coloured + -SCOPE] ▶ **dichroscopic** (,daɪkrə'skɒpɪk), **,dichroi'scopic,** *or* **,dichroo'scopic** *adj*

dick[1] (dɪk) *n Chiefly U.S.* a slang word for **detective.** [C20: by shortening and alteration from DETECTIVE; probably influenced by proper name *Dick*]

dick[2] (dɪk) *n Slang.* **1** *Brit.* a fellow or person. **2 clever dick.** *Brit.* a person who is obnoxiously opinionated or self-satisfied; know-all. **3** a taboo word for **penis.** [C16 (meaning: fellow): from the name *Dick,* familiar form of *Richard,* applied generally (like *Jack*) to any fellow, lad, etc.; hence, C19: penis]

dickens ('dɪkɪnz) *n Informal.* a euphemistic word for **devil** (used as intensifier in the interrogative phrase **what the dickens**). [C16: from the name *Dickens*]

Dickens ('dɪkɪnz) *n* **Charles (John Huffam),** pen name *Boz.* 1812–70, English novelist, famous for the humour and sympathy of his characterization and his criticism of social injustice. His major works include *The Pickwick Papers* (1837), *Oliver Twist* (1839), *Nicholas Nickleby* (1839), *Old Curiosity Shop* (1840–41), *Martin Chuzzlewit* (1844), *David Copperfield* (1850), *Bleak House* (1853), *Little Dorrit* (1857), and *Great Expectations* (1861).

Dickensian (dɪ'kɛnzɪən) *adj* **1** of Charles Dickens or his works. **2** resembling or suggestive of conditions described in Dickens' novels, esp.: **2a** squalid and poverty-stricken: *working conditions were truly Dickensian.* **2b** characterized by jollity and conviviality: *a Dickensian scene round the Christmas tree.* **3** grotesquely comic, as some of the characters of Dickens.

dicker ('dɪkə) *vb* **1** to trade (goods) by bargaining; barter. **2** (*intr*) to negotiate a political deal. ◆ *n* **3a** a petty bargain or barter. **3b** the item or items bargained or bartered. **4** a political deal or bargain. [C12: ultimately from Latin *decuria* DECURY; related to Middle Low German *dēker* lot of ten hides]

dickhead ('dɪk,hɛd) *n Slang.* a stupid or despicable man or boy. [C20: from DICK[2] (in the sense: penis) + HEAD]

Dickinson ('dɪkɪnsᵊn) *n* **Emily.** 1830–86, U.S. poet, noted for her short mostly unrhymed mystical lyrics.

Dick test (dɪk) *n* a skin test for determining whether a person is immune or susceptible to scarlet fever. [C20: named after George F. *Dick* (1881–1967), U.S. physician who devised it]

dicky[1] *or* **dickey** ('dɪkɪ) *n, pl* **dickies** *or* **dickeys. 1** a woman's false blouse front, worn to fill in the neck of a jacket or low-cut dress. **2** a man's false shirt front, esp. one worn with full evening dress. **3** Also called: **dicky bow.** *Brit.* a bow tie. **4** *Chiefly Brit.* an informal name for **donkey,** esp. a male one. **5** Also called: **'dicky,bird, 'dickey,bird.** a child's word for a **bird,** esp. a small one. **6** a folding outside seat at the rear of some early cars. U.S. and Canadian name: **rumble seat.** [C18 (in the senses: donkey, shirt front): from *Dickey,* diminutive of *Dick* (name); the relationship of the various senses is obscure]

dicky[2] *or* **dickey** ('dɪkɪ) *adj* **dickier, dickiest.** *Brit. informal.* in bad condition; shaky, unsteady, or unreliable: *I feel a bit dicky today.* [C18: perhaps from the name *Dick* in the phrase *as queer as Dick's hatband* feeling ill]

diclinous ('daɪklɪnəs, daɪ'klaɪ-) *adj* (of flowers and flowering plants) unisexual. Compare **monoclinous.** ▶ **'diclinism** *n* ▶ **dicliny** ('daɪklɪnɪ, daɪ'klaɪ-) *n*

Diconal ('daɪkənæl) *n Trademark.* an opiate drug with potent analgesic properties: used to relieve severe pain.

dicotyledon (daɪ,kɒtɪ'liːdᵊn, ,daɪkɒt-) *n* any flowering plant of the class *Dicotyledonae,* having two embryonic seed leaves and leaves with netlike veins. The group includes many herbaceous plants and most families of trees and shrubs. Often shortened to **dicot.** Compare **monocotyledon.** ▶ **,dicoty'ledonous** *adj*

dicrotic (daɪ'krɒtɪk) *or* **dicrotal** ('daɪkrətᵊl) *adj Physiol.* having or relating to a double pulse for each heartbeat. [C19: from Greek *dikrotos* double-beating, from DI-[1] + *krotein* to beat] ▶ **dicrotism** ('daɪkrə,tɪzəm) *n*

dict. *abbrev. for:* **1** dictation. **2** dictator. **3** dictionary.

dicta ('dɪktə) *n* a plural of **dictum.**

Dictaphone ('dɪktə,fəʊn) *n Trademark.* a tape recorder designed for recording dictation and later reproducing it for typing.

dictate *vb* (dɪk'teɪt). **1** to say (messages, letters, speeches, etc.) aloud for mechanical recording or verbatim transcription by another person. **2** (*tr*) to prescribe (commands) authoritatively. **3** (*intr*) to act in a tyrannical manner; seek to impose one's will on others. ◆ *n* ('dɪkteɪt). **4** an authoritative command. **5** a guiding principle or rule: *the dictates of reason.* [C17: from Latin *dictāre* to say repeatedly, order, from *dīcere* to say]

dictation (dɪk'teɪʃən) *n* **1** the act of dictating material to be recorded or taken down in writing. **2** the material dictated. **3** authoritative commands or the act of giving them. ▸ **dic'tational** *adj*

dictator (dɪk'teɪtə) *n* **1a** a ruler who is not effectively restricted by a constitution, laws, recognized opposition, etc. **1b** an absolute, esp. tyrannical, ruler. **2** (in ancient Rome) a person appointed during a crisis to exercise supreme authority. **3** a person who makes pronouncements, as on conduct, fashion, etc., which are regarded as authoritative. **4** a person who behaves in an authoritarian or tyrannical manner. ▸ **dictatress** (dɪk'teɪtrɪs) *or* **dictatrix** ('dɪktətrɪks) *fem n*

dictatorial (ˌdɪktə'tɔːrɪəl) *adj* **1** of or characteristic of a dictator. **2** tending to dictate; tyrannical; overbearing. ▸ **ˌdicta'torially** *adv* ▸ **ˌdicta'torialness** *n*

dictatorship (dɪk'teɪtəˌʃɪp) *n* **1** the rank, office, or period of rule of a dictator. **2** government by a dictator or dictators. **3** a country ruled by a dictator or dictators. **4** absolute or supreme power or authority.

diction ('dɪkʃən) *n* **1** the choice and use of words in writing or speech. **2** the manner of uttering or enunciating words and sounds; elocution. [C15: from Latin *dictiō* a saying, mode of expression, from *dīcere* to speak, say]

dictionary ('dɪkʃənərɪ, -ʃənrɪ) *n, pl* **-aries. 1a** a reference book that consists of an alphabetical list of words with their meanings and parts of speech, and often a guide to accepted pronunciation and syllabification, irregular inflections of words, derived words of different parts of speech, and etymologies. **1b** a similar reference book giving equivalent words in two or more languages. Such dictionaries often consist of two or more parts, in each of which the alphabetical list is given in a different language: *a German-English dictionary.* **1c** (*as modifier*): *a dictionary definition.* See also **glossary, lexicon, thesaurus. 2** a reference book listing words or terms of a particular subject or activity, giving information about their meanings and other attributes: *a dictionary of gardening.* **3** a collection of information or examples with the entries alphabetically arranged: *a dictionary of quotations.* [C16: from Medieval Latin *dictiōnārium* collection of words, from Late Latin *dictiō* word; see DICTION]

dictionary catalogue *n* a catalogue of the authors, titles and subjects of books in one alphabetical sequence.

Dictograph ('dɪktəˌgrɑːf, -ˌgræf) *n Trademark.* a telephonic instrument for secretly monitoring or recording conversations by means of a small, sensitive, and often concealed microphone.

dictum ('dɪktəm) *n, pl* **-tums** *or* **-ta** (-tə). **1** a formal or authoritative statement or assertion; pronouncement. **2** a popular saying or maxim. **3** *Law.* See **obiter dictum.** [C16: from Latin, from *dīcere* to say]

dictyopteran (ˌdɪktɪ'ɒptərən) *n* any insect of the order *Dictyoptera,* which comprises the cockroaches and mantises. [New Latin, from Greek *diktuon* a net, from *dikein* to cast + *pteron* a wing]

dicyclic (daɪ'saɪklɪk) *adj* **1** *Botany.* having the perianth arranged in two whorls; having separate petals and sepals. **2** *Chem.* (of a molecule) containing only two rings of atoms.

dicynodont (daɪ'sɪnəˌdɒnt) *n* any of various extinct Triassic mammal-like reptiles having a single pair of tusklike teeth. [C19: from Greek, from DI-[1] + *kuōn* dog + -ODONT]

did (dɪd) *vb* the past tense of **do**[1].

Didache ('dɪdəˌkiː) *n* a treatise, perhaps of the 1st or early 2nd century A.D., on Christian morality and practices. Also called: the **Teaching of the Twelve Apostles.** [C19: from Greek, literally: a teaching, from *didaskein* to teach]

didactic (dɪ'dæktɪk) *adj* **1** intended to instruct, esp. excessively. **2** morally instructive; improving. **3** (of works of art or literature) containing a political or moral message to which aesthetic considerations are subordinated. [C17: from Greek *didaktikos* skilled in teaching, from *didaskein* to teach] ▸ **di'dactically** *adv* ▸ **di'dacticism** *n*

didactics (dɪ'dæktɪks) *n* (*functioning as sing*) the art or science of teaching.

didactyl (daɪ'dæktɪl) *adj* (esp. of many marsupials) having the hind toes separate. ▸ **di'dactylism** *n*

diddle[1] ('dɪdᵊl) *vb Informal.* **1** (*tr*) to cheat or swindle. **2** (*intr*) an obsolete word for **dawdle.** [C19: back formation from Jeremy *Diddler,* a scrounger in J. Kenney's farce *Raising the Wind* (1803)] ▸ **'diddler** *n*

diddle[2] ('dɪdᵊl) *vb Dialect.* to jerk (an object) up and down or back and forth; shake rapidly. [C17: probably variant of *doderen* to tremble, totter; see DODDER[1]]

diddy ('dɪdɪ) *n, pl* **-dies.** *Dialect.* a female breast or nipple. [C18: from *titty,* diminutive of TIT[2]]

Diderot ('diːdərəʊ; *French* didro) *n* **Denis** (dəni). 1713–84, French philosopher, noted particularly for his direction (1745–72) of the great French *Encyclopédie.*

didgeridoo (ˌdɪdʒərɪ'duː) *n Music.* a deep-toned native Australian wind instrument made from a long hollowed-out piece of wood. [C20: imitative of its sound]

didicoy, diddicoy ('dɪdɪˌkɔɪ), *or* **didakai** ('dɪdəˌkaɪ) *n, pl* **-coys** *or* **-kais.** (in Britain) one of a group of caravan-dwelling roadside people, who live like Gypsies but are not true Romanies. [C19: from Romany]

didn't ('dɪdᵊnt) *contraction of* did not.

dido ('daɪdəʊ) *n, pl* **-dos** *or* **-does.** (*usually pl*) *Informal.* an antic; prank; trick. [C19: originally U.S.: of uncertain origin]

Dido ('daɪdəʊ) *n Classical myth.* a princess of Tyre who founded Carthage and became its queen. Virgil tells of her suicide when abandoned by her lover Aeneas.

didst (dɪdst) *vb Archaic.* (used with the pronoun *thou* or its relative equivalent) a form of the past tense of **do**[1].

didymium (daɪ'dɪmɪəm, dɪ-) *n* **1** a mixture of the metallic rare earths neodymium and praseodymium, once thought to be an element. **2** a mixture of rare earths and their oxides used in colouring glass. [C19: from New Latin, from Greek *didumos* twin + -IUM]

didymous ('dɪdɪməs) *adj Biology.* in pairs or in two parts. [C18: from Greek *didumos* twin, from *duo* two]

didynamous (daɪ'dɪnəməs) *adj* (of plants) having four stamens arranged in two pairs of unequal length, as in the foxglove. [C18: from New Latin *Didynamia* name of former class, from DI-[1] + Greek *dunamis* power, referring to the greater strength of the two long stamens]

die[1] (daɪ) *vb* **dies, dying, died.** (*mainly intr*) **1** (of an organism or its cells, organs, etc.) to cease all biological activity permanently: *she died of pneumonia.* **2** (of something inanimate) to cease to exist; come to an end: *the memory of her will never die.* **3** (often foll. by *away, down,* or *out*) to lose strength, power, or energy, esp. by degrees. **4** (often foll. by *away* or *down*) to become calm or quiet; subside: *the noise slowly died down.* **5** to stop functioning: *the engine died.* **6** to languish or pine, as with love, longing, etc. **7** (usually foll. by *of*) *Informal.* to be nearly overcome (with laughter, boredom, etc.). **8** *Theol.* to lack spiritual life within the soul, thus separating it from God and leading to eternal punishment. **9** (*tr*) to undergo or suffer (a death of a specified kind) (esp. in phrases such as **die a saintly death**). **10** (foll. by *to*) to become indifferent or apathetic (to): *to die to the world.* **11 never say die.** *Informal.* never give up. **12 die hard.** to cease to exist after resistance or a struggle: *old habits die hard.* **13 die in harness.** to die while still working or active, prior to retirement. **14 be dying.** (foll. by *for* or an infinitive) to be eager or desperate (for something or to do something): *I'm dying to see the new house.* **15 to die for.** *Informal.* highly desirable: *a salary to die for.* ◆ See also **dieback, die down, die out.** [Old English *dīegan,* probably of Scandinavian origin; compare Old Norse *deyja,* Old High German *touwen*]

USAGE It was formerly considered incorrect to use the preposition *from* after *die,* but *of* and *from* are now both acceptable: *he died of/from his injuries.*

die[2] (daɪ) *n* **1a** a shaped block of metal or other hard material used to cut or form metal in a drop forge, press, or similar device. **1b** a tool of metal, silicon carbide, or other hard material with a conical hole through which wires, rods, or tubes are drawn to reduce their diameter. **2** an internally-threaded tool for cutting external threads. Compare **tap**[2] (sense 6). **3** a casting mould giving accurate dimensions and a good surface to the object cast. See also **die-cast. 4** *Architect.* the dado of a pedestal, usually cubic. **5** another name for **dice** (sense 2). **6 as straight as a die.** perfectly honest. **7 the die is cast.** the decision that commits a person irrevocably to an action has been taken. [C13 *dee,* from Old French *de,* perhaps from Vulgar Latin *datum* (unattested) a piece in games, n use of past participle of Latin *dare* to play]

dieback ('daɪˌbæk) *n* **1** a disease of trees and shrubs characterized by death of the young shoots, which spreads to the larger branches: caused by injury to the roots or attack by bacteria or fungi. **2** any similar condition of herbaceous plants. ◆ *vb* **die back. 3** (*intr, adv*) (of plants) to suffer from dieback.

die-cast *vb* **-casts, -casting, -cast.** (*tr*) to shape or form (a metal or plastic object) by introducing molten metal or plastic into a reusable mould, esp. under pressure, by gravity, or by centrifugal force. ▸ **'die-ˌcasting** *n*

diecious (daɪ'iːʃəs) *adj* a variant spelling of **dioecious.** ▸ **di'eciously** *adv*

die-cutting *n Printing.* the cutting by machine of paper or card into shapes with sharp steel knives, such as in the manufacture of cardboard boxes.

die down *vb* (*intr, adv*) **1** (of some perennial plants) to wither and die above ground, leaving only the root alive during the winter. **2** to lose strength or power, esp. by degrees. **3** to become calm or quiet.

dièdre *French.* (djedrə) *n Mountaineering.* a large shallow groove or corner in a rock face. [C20: dihedral]

Diefenbaker ('diːfᵊnˌbeɪkə) *n* **John George.** 1895–1979, Canadian Conservative statesman; prime minister of Canada (1957–63).

dieffenbachia (ˌdiːfᵊn'bækɪə) *n* any plant of the tropical American evergreen perennial genus *Dieffenbachia,* some species of which are grown as pot plants for their handsome variegated foliage. The plants are poisonous and the sap is extremely acrid: family *Araceae.* [named after Ernst *Dieffenbach* (died 1855), German horticulturist]

Diégo-Suarez (*French* djegosɥarɛs) *n* the former name of **Antseranana.**

die-hard *n* **1** a person who resists change or who holds onto an untenable position or outdated attitude. **2** (*modifier*) obstinately resistant to change. ▸ **'die-ˌhardism** *n*

dieldrin ('diːldrɪn) *n* a crystalline insoluble substance, consisting of a chlorinated derivative of naphthalene: a contact insecticide the use of which is now restricted as it accumulates in the tissues of animals. Formula: $C_{12}H_8OCl_6$. [C20: from DIEL(S-AL)D(E)R (REACTION) + -IN]

dielectric (ˌdaɪɪ'lɛktrɪk) *n* **1** a substance or medium that can sustain an electric field. **2** a substance or body of very low electrical conductivity; insulator. ◆ *adj* **3** of, concerned with, or having the properties of a dielectric. [from DIA- + ELECTRIC] ▸ **ˌdie'lectrically** *adv*

dielectric constant *n* another name for **relative permittivity.**

dielectric heating *n* a technique in which an insulator is heated by the application of a high-frequency electric field.

dielectric lens *n Physics.* a lens constructed of a material that converges or diverges a beam of electromagnetic radiation of radio frequency.

Diels-Alder reaction ('diːlz'ɔːldə) *n Chem.* a type of chemical reaction in which one organic compound containing conjugated double bonds adds to another containing an ethylenic bond to form a product containing a ring.

[C20: named after Otto *Diels* (1876–1954) and Kurt *Alder* (1902–58), German chemists]

Dien Bien Phu (ˌdjɛn bjɛn 'fuː) *n* a village in NW Vietnam: French military post during the Indochina War; scene of a major defeat of French forces by the Vietminh (1954).

diencephalon (ˌdaɪɛn'sɛfəˌlɒn) *n* the part of the brain that includes the basal ganglia, thalamus, hypothalamus, and associated areas. ▸ **diencephalic** (ˌdaɪɛnsɪ'fælɪk) *adj*

diene ('daɪiːn) *n Chem.* a hydrocarbon that contains two carbon-to-carbon double bonds in its molecules.

-diene *n combining form.* denoting an organic compound containing two double bonds between carbon atoms: *butadiene.* [from DI-[1] + -ENE]

die out *or* **off** *vb* (*intr, adv*) **1** (of a family, race, etc.) to die one after another until few or none are left. **2** to become extinct, esp. after a period of gradual decline.

Dieppe (dɪ'ɛp; *French* djɛp) *n* a port and resort in N France, on the English Channel. Pop.: 36 600 (1990).

dieresis (daɪ'ɛrɪsɪs) *n, pl* **-ses** (-ˌsiːz) a variant spelling of **diaeresis.** ▸ **dieretic** (ˌdaɪə'rɛtɪk) *adj*

diesel ('diːzᵊl) *n* **1** See **diesel engine. 2** a ship, locomotive, lorry, etc., driven by a diesel engine. **3** *Informal.* short for **diesel oil** (*or* **fuel**).

Diesel ('diːzᵊl) *n* **Rudolf** ('ruːdɔlf). 1858–1913, German engineer, who invented the diesel engine (1892).

diesel cycle *n* a four-stroke cycle in which combustion takes place at constant pressure and heat is rejected at constant volume. Compare **Otto cycle.**

diesel-electric *n* **1** a locomotive fitted with a diesel engine driving an electric generator that feeds electric traction motors. ◆ *adj* **2** of or relating to such a locomotive or system.

diesel engine *or* **motor** *n* a type of internal-combustion engine in which atomized fuel oil is sprayed into the cylinder and ignited by compression alone.

diesel-hydraulic *n* **1** a locomotive driven by a diesel engine through hydraulic transmission and torque converters. ◆ *adj* **2** of or relating to such a locomotive or system.

diesel oil *or* **fuel** *n* a fuel obtained from petroleum distillation that is used in diesel engines. It has a relatively low ignition temperature (540°C) and is ignited by the heat of compression. Also called (Brit.): **derv.** See also **cetane number.**

Dies Irae *Latin.* ('diːeɪz 'ɪəraɪ) *n* **1** *Christianity.* a famous Latin hymn of the 13th century, describing the Last Judgment. It is used in the Mass for the dead. **2** a musical setting of this hymn, usually part of a setting of the Requiem. [literally: day of wrath]

diesis ('daɪɪsɪs) *n, pl* **-ses** (-ˌsiːz). **1** *Printing.* another name for **double dagger. 2** *Music.* **2a** (in ancient Greek theory) any interval smaller than a whole tone, esp. a semitone in the Pythagorean scale. **2b** (in modern theory) the discrepancy of pitch in just intonation between an octave and either a succession of four ascending minor thirds (**great diesis**), or a succession of three ascending major thirds (**minor diesis**). [C16: via Latin from Greek: a quarter tone, literally: a sending through, from *diienai;* the double dagger was originally used in musical notation]

dies non ('daɪiːz nɒn) *n Law.* a day on which no legal business may be transacted. Also called: **dies non juridicus** (dʒʊ'rɪdɪkəs). Compare **juridical days.** [C19: shortened from Latin phrase *diēs nōn jūridicus* literally: day which is not juridical, that is, not reserved for legal affairs]

die stamping *n Printing.* the production of words or decoration on a surface by using a steel die so that the printed images stand in relief.

diestock ('daɪˌstɒk) *n* the device holding the dies used to cut an external screw thread.

diestrus (daɪ'iːstrəs) *n* the U.S. spelling of **dioestrus.**

diet[1] ('daɪət) *n* **1a** a specific allowance or selection of food, esp. prescribed to control weight or in disorders in which certain foods are contraindicated: *a salt-free diet; a 900-calorie diet.* **1b** (*as modifier*): *a diet bread.* **2** the food and drink that a person or animal regularly consumes: *a diet of nuts and water.* **3** regular activities or occupations. ◆ *vb* **4** (*usually intr*) to follow or cause to follow a dietary regimen. [C13: from Old French *diete,* from Latin *diaeta,* from Greek *diaita* mode of living, from *diaitan* to direct one's own life] ▸ **'dieter** *n*

diet[2] ('daɪət) *n* **1** (*sometimes cap.*) a legislative assembly in various countries, such as Japan. **2** (*sometimes cap.*) Also called: **Reichstag.** the assembly of the estates of the Holy Roman Empire. **3** *Scots Law.* **3a** the date fixed by a court for hearing a case. **3b** a single session of a court. [C15: from Medieval Latin *diēta* public meeting, probably from Latin *diaeta* DIET[1] but associated with Latin *diēs* day]

dietary ('daɪətərɪ, -trɪ) *adj* **1** of or relating to a diet. ◆ *n, pl* **-taries. 2** a regulated diet. **3** a system of dieting.

dietary fibre *n* fibrous substances in fruits and vegetables, such as the structural polymers of cell walls, consumption of which aids digestion and is believed to help prevent certain diseases. Also called: **roughage.**

dietetic (ˌdaɪɪ'tɛtɪk) *or* **dietetical** *adj* **1** denoting or relating to diet or the regulation of food intake. **2** prepared for special dietary requirements. ▸ **ˌdie'tetically** *adv*

dietetics (ˌdaɪɪ'tɛtɪks) *n* (*functioning as sing*) the scientific study and regulation of food intake and preparation.

diethylene glycol (daɪ'ɛθɪˌliːn 'glaɪkɒl) *n* a colourless soluble liquid used as an antifreeze and solvent. Formula: $(C_2H_4OH)_2O$.

diethyl ether (daɪ'ɛθɪl) *n* a formal name for **ether** (sense 1).

diethylstilboestrol (daɪˌɛθɪlstɪl'bɛstrɒl, -ˌiːθaɪl-) *n* another name for **stilboestrol.**

dietitian *or* **dietician** (ˌdaɪɪ'tɪʃən) *n* a person who specializes in dietetics.

Dietrich (*German* 'diːtrɪç) *n* **Marlene** (mar'leːnə), real name *Maria Magdalene von Losch.* 1901–92, U.S. film actress and cabaret singer, born in Germany.

Dieu et mon droit *French.* (djø e mɔ̃ drwa) God and my right: motto of the Royal Arms of Great Britain.

diff. *abbrev. for:* **1** difference. **2** different.

differ ('dɪfə) *vb* (*intr*) **1** (often foll. by *from*) to be dissimilar in quality, nature, or degree (to); vary (from). **2** (often foll. by *from* or *with*) to be at variance (with); disagree (with). **3** *Dialect.* to quarrel or dispute. **4 agree to differ.** to end an argument amicably while maintaining differences of opinion. [C14: from Latin *differre,* literally: to bear off in different directions, hence scatter, put off, be different, from *dis-* apart + *ferre* to bear]

difference ('dɪfərəns, 'dɪfrəns) *n* **1** the state or quality of being unlike. **2** a specific instance of being unlike. **3** a distinguishing mark or feature. **4** a significant change in a situation: *the difference in her is amazing.* **5** a disagreement or argument: *he had a difference with his wife.* **6** a degree of distinctness, as between two people or things. **7a** the result of the subtraction of one number, quantity, etc., from another. **7b** the single number that when added to the subtrahend gives the minuend; remainder. **8** *Logic.* another name for **differentia. 9** *Maths.* (of two sets) **9a** the set of members of the first that are not members of the second. Symbol: A – B **9b symmetric difference.** the set of members of one but not both of the given sets. Often symbolized: A + B **10** *Heraldry.* an addition to the arms of a family to represent a younger branch. **11 make a difference. 11a** to have an effect. **11b** to treat differently. **12 split the difference. 12a** to settle a dispute by a compromise. **12b** to divide a remainder equally. **13 with a difference.** with some peculiarly distinguishing quality, good or bad. ◆ *vb* (*tr*) **14** *Rare.* to distinguish. **15** *Heraldry.* to add a charge to (arms) to differentiate a branch of a family.

difference threshold *n Psychol.* the minimum difference between two stimuli that is just detectable by a person.

different ('dɪfərənt, 'dɪfrənt) *adj* **1** partly or completely unlike. **2** not identical or the same; other: *he always wears a different tie.* **3** out of the ordinary; unusual. ▸ **'differently** *adv* ▸ **'differentness** *n*

USAGE The constructions *different from, different to,* and *different than* are all found in the works of writers of English during the past. Nowadays, however, the most widely acceptable preposition to use after *different* is *from. Different to* is common in British English, but is considered by some people to be incorrect, or less acceptable. *Different than* is a standard construction in American English, and has the advantage of conciseness when a clause or phrase follows, as in *this result is only slightly different than in the U.S.* As, however, this idiom is not regarded as totally acceptable in British usage, it is preferable either to use *different from: this result is only slightly different from that obtained in the U.S.* or to rephrase the sentence: *this result differs only slightly from that in the U.S.*

differentia (ˌdɪfə'rɛnʃɪə) *n, pl* **-tiae** (-ʃɪˌiː). *Logic.* a feature by which two subclasses of the same class of named objects can be distinguished. Also called: **difference.** [C19: from Latin: diversity, DIFFERENCE]

differentiable (ˌdɪfə'rɛnʃɪəbᵊl) *adj* **1** capable of being differentiated. **2** *Maths.* possessing a derivative. ▸ **ˌdifferˌentia'bility** *n*

differential (ˌdɪfə'rɛnʃəl) *adj* **1** of, relating to, or using a difference. **2** constituting a difference; distinguishing. **3** *Maths.* of, containing, or involving one or more derivatives or differentials. **4** *Physics, engineering.* relating to, operating on, or based on the difference between two opposing effects, motions, forces, etc.: *differential amplifier.* ◆ *n* **5** a factor that differentiates between two comparable things. **6** *Maths.* **6a** an increment in a given function, expressed as the product of the derivative of that function and the corresponding increment in the independent variable. **6b** an increment in a given function of two or more variables, $f(x_1, x_2, \dots x_n)$, expressed as the sum of the products of each partial derivative and the increment in the corresponding variable. **7** an epicyclic gear train that permits two shafts to rotate at different speeds while being driven by a third shaft. See also **differential gear. 8** *Chiefly Brit.* the difference between rates of pay for different types of labour, esp. when forming a pay structure within an industry. **9** (in commerce) a difference in rates, esp. between comparable labour services or transportation routes. ▸ **ˌdiffer'entially** *adv*

differential calculus *n* the branch of calculus concerned with the study, evaluation, and use of derivatives and differentials. Compare **integral calculus.**

differential coefficient *n Maths.* another name for **derivative.**

differential equation *n* an equation containing differentials or derivatives of a function of one independent variable. A **partial differential equation** results from a function of more than one variable.

differential gear *n* the epicyclic gear mounted in the driving axle of a road vehicle that permits one driving wheel to rotate faster than the other, as when cornering.

differential geometry *n* the application of differential calculus to geometrical problems.

differential operator *n* the mathematical operator del ∇, used in vector analysis, where $\nabla = \mathbf{i}\partial/\partial x + \mathbf{j}\partial/\partial y + \mathbf{k}\partial/\partial z$, ***i, j,*** and ***k*** being unit vectors and $\partial/\partial x$, $\partial/\partial y$, and $\partial/\partial z$ the partial derivatives of a function in *x, y,* and *z.*

differential windlass *n* a windlass employing the velocity ratio incurred in unwinding from a small drum while winding onto a larger drum rotating at a common speed. Also called: **Chinese windlass.**

differentiate (ˌdɪfə'rɛnʃɪˌeɪt) *vb* **1** (*tr*) to serve to distinguish between. **2** (when *intr,* often foll. by *between*) to perceive, show, or make a difference (in or between); discriminate. **3** (*intr*) to become dissimilar or distinct. **4** *Maths.* to perform a differentiation on (a quantity, expression, etc.). **5** (*intr*) (of unspecialized cells, etc.) to change during development to more specialized forms. ▸ **ˌdiffer'entiˌator** *n*

differentiation (ˌdɪfəˌrɛnʃɪ'eɪʃən) *n* **1** the act, process, or result of differentiating. **2** *Maths.* an operation used in calculus in which the derivative of a function or variable is determined; the inverse of **integration** (sense 6). **3** any process in which a mixture of materials separates out partially or completely into its constituent parts, as in the cooling and solidification of a magma into two or more different rock types or in the gradual separation of an originally homogeneous earth into crust, mantle, and core.

difficult ('dɪfɪkəlt) *adj* **1** not easy to do; requiring effort: *a difficult job.* **2** not easy to understand or solve; intricate: *a difficult problem.* **3** hard to deal with; troublesome: *a difficult child.* **4** not easily convinced, pleased, or satisfied. **5** full of hardships or trials: *difficult times ahead.* [C14: back formation from DIFFICULTY] ▸ **'difficultly** *adv*

difficulty ('dɪfɪkəltɪ) *n, pl* **-ties. 1** the state or quality of being difficult. **2** a task, problem, etc., that is hard to deal with. **3** (*often pl*) a troublesome or embarrassing situation, esp. a financial one. **4** a dispute or disagreement. **5** (*often pl*) an objection or obstacle: *he always makes difficulties.* **6** a trouble or source of trouble; worry. **7** lack of ease; awkwardness: *he could run only with difficulty.* [C14: from Latin *difficultās,* from *difficilis* difficult, from *dis-* not + *facilis* easy, FACILE]

diffident ('dɪfɪdənt) *adj* lacking self-confidence; timid; shy. [C15: from Latin *diffīdere* to distrust, from *dis-* not + *fīdere* to trust] ▸ **'diffidence** *n* ▸ **'diffidently** *adv*

diffract (dɪ'frækt) *vb* to undergo or cause to undergo diffraction: *to diffract light; the light diffracts at a slit.* ▸ **dif'fractive** *adj* ▸ **dif'fractively** *adv* ▸ **dif'fractiveness** *n*

diffraction (dɪ'frækʃən) *n* **1** *Physics.* a deviation in the direction of a wave at the edge of an obstacle in its path. **2** any phenomenon caused by diffraction and interference of light, such as the formation of light and dark fringes by the passage of light through a small aperture. **3** deflection of sound waves caused by an obstacle or by nonhomogeneity of a medium. [C17: from New Latin *diffractiō* a breaking to pieces, from Latin *diffringere* to shatter, from *dis-* apart + *frangere* to break]

diffraction grating *n* a glass plate or a mirror with a large number of equidistant parallel lines or grooves on its surface. It causes diffraction of transmitted or reflected light, ultraviolet radiation, or X-rays.

diffraction pattern *n Physics.* the distinctive pattern of light and dark fringes, rings, etc., formed by diffraction.

diffractometer (ˌdɪfræk'tɒmɪtə) *n Physics.* an instrument used in studying diffraction, as in the determination of crystal structure by diffraction of X-rays.

diffuse *vb* (dɪ'fjuːz). **1** to spread or cause to spread in all directions. **2** to undergo or cause to undergo diffusion. **3** to scatter or cause to scatter; disseminate; disperse. ◆ *adj* (dɪ'fjuːs). **4** spread out over a wide area. **5** lacking conciseness. **6** (esp. of some creeping stems) spreading loosely over a large area. **7** characterized by or exhibiting diffusion: *diffuse light; diffuse reflection.* **8** *Botany.* (of plant growth) occurring throughout a tissue. [C15: from Latin *diffūsus* spread abroad, from *diffundere* to pour forth, from *dis-* away + *fundere* to pour] ▸ **diffusely** (dɪ'fjuːslɪ) *adv* ▸ **dif'fuseness** *n* ▸ **diffusible** (dɪ'fjuːzəbəl) *adj* ▸ **difˌfusi'bility** *or* **dif'fusibleness** *n*

USAGE Avoid confusion with **defuse.**

diffused junction *n* a semiconductor junction formed by diffusing acceptor or donor impurity atoms into semiconductor material to form regions of p-type or n-type conductivity. See also **photolithography** (sense 2). Compare **alloyed junction.**

diffuser *or* **diffusor** (dɪ'fjuːzə) *n* **1** a person or thing that diffuses. **2** a part of a lighting fixture consisting of a translucent or frosted covering or of a rough reflector: used to scatter the light and prevent glare. **3** a cone, wedge, or baffle placed in front of the diaphragm of a loudspeaker to diffuse the sound waves. **4** a duct, esp. in a wind tunnel or jet engine, that widens gradually in the direction of flow to reduce the speed and increase the pressure of the air or fluid. **5** *Photog.* a light-scattering medium, such as a screen of fine fabric, placed in the path of a source of light to reduce the sharpness of shadows and thus soften the lighting. **6** a perforated plate or similar device for distributing compressed air in the aeration of sewage. **7** a device, attached to a hairdryer, which diffuses the warm air as it comes out.

diffusion (dɪ'fjuːʒən) *n* **1** the act or process of diffusing or being diffused; dispersion. **2** verbosity. **3** *Physics.* **3a** the random thermal motion of atoms, molecules, clusters of atoms, etc., in gases, liquids, and some solids. **3b** the transfer of atoms or molecules by their random motion from one part of a medium to another. **4** *Physics.* the transmission or reflection of electromagnetic radiation, esp. light, in which the radiation is scattered in many directions and not directly reflected or refracted; scattering. **5** Also called: **diffusivity.** *Physics.* the degree to which the directions of propagation of reverberant sound waves differ from point to point in an enclosure. **6** *Anthropol.* the transmission of social institutions, skills, and myths from one culture to another.

diffusion coefficient *or* **constant** *n* the rate at which a diffusing substance is transported between opposite faces of a unit cube of a system when there is unit concentration difference between them. Symbol: *D* Also called: **diffusivity.**

diffusive (dɪ'fjuːsɪv) *adj* characterized by diffusion. ▸ **dif'fusively** *adv* ▸ **dif'fusiveness** *n*

diffusivity (ˌdɪfjuː'sɪvɪtɪ) *n* **1** a measure of the ability of a substance to transmit a difference in temperature; expressed as the thermal conductivity divided by the product of specific heat capacity and density. **2** *Physics.* **2a** the ability of a substance to permit or undergo diffusion. **2b** another name for **diffusion coefficient. 3** another name for **diffusion** (sense 5).

difunctional (daɪ'fʌŋkʃənəl) *Chem.* ◆ *adj* **1** (of a compound) having two sites in the molecule that are highly reactive. ◆ *n* **2** a compound having two sites in the molecule that are highly reactive.

dig (dɪg) *vb* **digs, digging, dug. 1** (when *tr,* often foll. by *up*) to cut into, break up, and turn over or remove (earth, soil, etc.), esp. with a spade. **2** to form or excavate (a hole, tunnel, passage, etc.) by digging, usually with an implement or (of animals) with feet, claws, etc.: *to dig a tunnel.* **3** (often foll. by *through*) to make or force (one's way), esp. by removing obstructions: *he dug his way through the crowd.* **4** (*tr;* often foll. by *out* or *up*) to obtain by digging: *to dig potatoes; to dig up treasure.* **5** (*tr;* often foll. by *out* or *up*) to find or discover by effort or searching: *to dig out unexpected facts.* **6** (*tr;* foll. by *in* or *into*) to thrust or jab (a sharp instrument, weapon, etc.); poke: *he dug his spurs into the horse's side.* **7** (*tr;* foll. by *in* or *into*) to mix (compost, etc.) with soil by digging. **8** (*tr*) *Informal.* to like, understand, or appreciate. **9** (*intr*) *U.S. slang.* to work hard, esp. for an examination. **10** (*intr*) *Brit. informal.* to have lodgings: *I dig in South London.* ◆ *n* **11** the act of digging. **12** a thrust or poke, esp. in the ribs. **13** a cutting or sarcastic remark. **14** *Informal.* an archaeological excavation. ◆ See also **dig in, digs.** [C13 *diggen,* of uncertain origin]

Dig (dɪg) *n N.Z. informal.* short for **Digger** (sense 1).

dig. *abbrev. for* digest (book or summary).

digamma (daɪ'gæmə) *n* a letter of the Greek alphabet (*F*) that became obsolete before the classical period of the language. It represented a semivowel like English *W* and was used as a numeral in later stages of written Greek, and passed into the Roman alphabet as *F.* [C17: via Latin from Greek, from DI-[1] + GAMMA; from its shape, which suggests one gamma upon another]

digamy ('dɪgəmɪ) *n, pl* **-mies.** a second marriage contracted after the termination of the first by death or divorce. Also called: **deuterogamy.** Compare **bigamy.** [C17: from Late Latin *digamia,* from Greek, from DI-[1] + *gamos* marriage] ▸ **'digamist** *n* ▸ **'digamous** *adj*

digastric (daɪ'gæstrɪk) *adj* **1** (of certain muscles) having two fleshy portions joined by a tendon. ◆ *n* **2** a muscle of the mandible that assists in lowering the lower jaw. [C17: from New Latin *digastricus* (with two bellies), from DI-[1] + *gastricus* gastric, from Greek *gastēr* belly]

digenesis (daɪ'dʒɛnɪsɪs) *n Zoology.* another name for **alternation of generations.**

digenetic (ˌdaɪdʒɪ'nɛtɪk) *adj Zoology.* **1** of or relating to digenesis. **2** (of parasites) having two hosts.

digest *vb* (dɪ'dʒɛst, daɪ-). **1** to subject (food) to a process of digestion. **2** (*tr*) to assimilate mentally. **3** *Chem.* to soften or disintegrate or be softened or disintegrated by the action of heat, moisture, or chemicals; decompose. **4** (*tr*) to arrange in a methodical or systematic order; classify. **5** (*tr*) to reduce to a summary. **6** (*tr*) *Archaic.* to tolerate. ◆ *n* ('daɪdʒɛst). **7** a comprehensive and systematic compilation of information or material, often condensed. **8** a magazine, periodical, etc., that summarizes news of current events. **9** a compilation of rules of law based on decided cases. [C14: from Late Latin *dīgesta* writings grouped under various heads, from Latin *dīgerere* to divide, from *di-* apart + *gerere* to bear]

Digest ('daɪdʒɛst) *n Roman law.* an arrangement of excerpts from the writings and opinions of eminent lawyers, contained in 50 books compiled by order of Justinian in the sixth century A.D.

digestant (dɪ'dʒɛstənt, daɪ-) *n* a substance, such as hydrochloric acid or a bile salt, that promotes or aids digestion, esp. one used therapeutically.

digester (dɪ'dʒɛstə, daɪ-) *n* **1** *Chem.* an apparatus or vessel, such as an autoclave, in which digestion is carried out. **2** a less common word for **digestant. 3** a person or thing that digests.

digestible (dɪ'dʒɛstəbəl, daɪ-) *adj* capable of being digested or easy to digest. ▸ **diˌgesti'bility** *or* **di'gestibleness** *n* ▸ **di'gestibly** *adv*

digestif *French.* (diʒɛstif) *n* something, esp. a drink, taken as an aid to digestion, either before or after a meal.

digestion (dɪ'dʒɛstʃən, daɪ-) *n* **1** the act or process in living organisms of breaking down ingested food material into easily absorbed and assimilated substances by the action of enzymes and other agents. Related adj: **peptic. 2** mental assimilation, esp. of ideas. **3** *Bacteriol.* the decomposition of sewage by the action of bacteria. **4** *Chem.* the treatment of material with heat, solvents, chemicals, etc., to cause softening or decomposition. [C14: from Old French, from Latin *digestiō* a dissolving, digestion] ▸ **di'gestional** *adj*

digestive (dɪ'dʒɛstɪv, daɪ-) *or* **digestant** (daɪ'dʒɛstənt) *adj* **1** relating to, aiding, or subjecting to digestion: *a digestive enzyme.* ◆ *n* **2** a less common word for **digestant. 3** short for **digestive biscuit.** ▸ **di'gestively** *adv*

digestive biscuit *n* a round semisweet biscuit made from wholemeal flour.

digged (dɪgd) *vb Archaic.* a past tense of **dig.**

digger ('dɪgə) *n* **1** a person, animal, or machine that digs. **2** a miner, esp. one who digs for gold. **3** a tool or part of a machine used for excavation, esp. a mechanical digger fitted with a head for digging trenches.

Digger ('dɪgə) *n* **1** (*sometimes not cap.*) *Archaic slang.* **1a** an Australian or New Zealander, esp. a soldier: often used as a term of address. **1b** (*as modifier*): *a Digger accent.* **2** one of a number of tribes of America whose diet was largely composed of roots dug out of the ground.

Diggers ('dɪgəz) *pl n* **the.** a radical English Puritan group, led by Gerrard Winstanley, which advocated communal ownership of land (1649–50).

digger wasp *n* any solitary wasp of the families *Sphecidae* and *Pamphilidae* that digs nest holes in the ground, rotten wood, or a hollow stem and stocks them with live insects for the larvae.

diggings ('dɪgɪŋz) *pl n* **1** (*functioning as pl*) material that has been dug out. **2** (*functioning as sing or pl*) a place where mining, esp. gold mining, has taken place. **3** (*functioning as pl*) *Brit. informal.* a less common name for **digs.**

dight (daɪt) *vb* **dights, dighting, dight** *or* **dighted.** (*tr*) *Archaic.* to adorn or equip, as for battle. [Old English *dihtan* to compose, from Latin *dictāre* to DICTATE]

dig in *vb* (*adv*) **1** *Military.* to provide (a defensive position) by digging foxholes, trenches, etc. **2** *Informal.* to entrench (oneself) firmly. **3** (*intr*) *Informal.* to defend or maintain a position firmly, as in an argument. **4** (*intr*) *Informal.* to begin vigorously to eat: *don't wait, just dig in.* **5 dig one's heels in.** *Informal.* to refuse stubbornly to move or be persuaded.

digit ('dɪdʒɪt) *n* **1** a finger or toe. **2** Also called: **figure.** any of the ten Arabic numerals from 0 to 9. **3** another name for **finger** (sense 4). **4** *Astronomy.* one twelfth of the diameter of the sun or moon, used to express the magnitude of an eclipse. [C15: from Latin *digitus* toe, finger]

digital ('dɪdʒɪtᵊl) *adj* **1** of, relating to, resembling, or possessing a digit or digits. **2** performed with the fingers. **3** representing data as a series of numerical values. **4** displaying information as numbers rather than by a pointer moving over a dial: *a digital voltmeter; digital read-out.* **5** *Electronics.* responding to discrete values of input voltage and producing discrete output voltage levels, as in a logic circuit: *digital circuit.* **6** a less common word for **digitate.** ◆ *n* **7** *Music.* one of the keys on the manuals of an organ or on a piano, harpsichord, etc. ▸ **'digitally** *adv*

digital audio tape *n* magnetic tape on which sound is recorded digitally, giving high-fidelity reproduction. Abbrev.: **DAT.**

digital camera *n* a camera that produces digital images that can be stored in a computer, displayed on a screen and printed.

digital clock *or* **watch** *n* a clock or watch in which the hours, minutes, and sometimes seconds are indicated by digits, rather than by hands on a dial. Compare **analogue clock.**

digital compact cassette *n* a magnetic tape cassette on which sound can be recorded in a digital format. Abbrev.: **DCC.**

digital computer *n* an electronic computer in which the input is discrete rather than continuous, consisting of combinations of numbers, letters, and other characters written in an appropriate programming language and represented internally in binary notation. Compare **analog computer.**

digital fount *n* a typeface of which the letter-shapes have been converted into digital form so that they can be used in computer-aided typesetting.

digitalin (ˌdɪdʒɪ'teɪlɪn) *n* a poisonous amorphous white glycoside extracted from digitalis leaves and used in treating heart disease. Formula: $C_{36}H_{56}O_{14}$. [C19: from DIGITAL(IS) + -IN]

digitalis (ˌdɪdʒɪ'teɪlɪs) *n* **1** any Eurasian scrophulariaceous plant of the genus *Digitalis,* such as the foxglove, having bell-shaped flowers and a basal rosette of leaves. **2** a drug prepared from the dried leaves or seeds of the foxglove: a mixture of glycosides used medicinally as a heart stimulant. [C17: from New Latin, from Latin: relating to a finger (referring to the corollas of the flower); based on German *Fingerhut* foxglove, literally: finger-hat]

digitalism ('dɪdʒɪtəˌlɪzəm) *n* a serious condition resulting from digitalis poisoning, characterized by nausea, vomiting, and a disturbance in heart rhythm or rate.

digitalize *or* **digitalise** ('dɪdʒɪtəˌlaɪz) *vb* (*tr*) to administer digitoxin or digoxin to (a patient) for the treatment of certain heart disorders. ▸ **ˌdigitali'zation** *or* **ˌdigitali'sation** *n*

digital mapping *n* a method of preparing maps in which the data is stored in a computer for ease of access and updating. ▸ **digital map** *n*

digital recording *n* a sound recording process that converts audio or analogue signals into a series of pulses that correspond to the voltage level. These can be stored on tape or on any other memory system.

digital television *n* television in which the picture information is transmitted in digital form and decoded at the television receiver.

digital video *n* video output based on digital rather than analogue signals.

digitate ('dɪdʒɪˌteɪt) *or* **digitated** *adj* **1** (of compound leaves) having the leaflets in the form of a spread hand. **2** (of animals) having digits or corresponding parts. ▸ **'digiˌtately** *adv* ▸ **ˌdigi'tation** *n*

digitiform ('dɪdʒɪtɪˌfɔːm) *adj* shaped like a finger.

digitigrade ('dɪdʒɪtɪˌgreɪd) *adj* **1** (of dogs, cats, horses, etc.) walking so that only the toes touch the ground. ◆ *n* **2** a digitigrade animal.

digitize *or* **digitise** ('dɪdʒɪˌtaɪz) *vb* (*tr*) to transcribe (data) into a digital form so that it can be directly processed by a computer. ▸ **ˌdigiti'zation** *or* **ˌdigiti'sation** *n* ▸ **'digiˌtizer** *or* **'digiˌtiser** *n*

digitoxin (ˌdɪdʒɪ'tɒksɪn) *n* a white toxic bitter-tasting glycoside, extracted from digitalis leaves and used in the treatment of heart failure. Formula: $C_{41}H_{64}O_{13}$. [from DIGI(TALIS) + TOXIN]

digitron ('dɪdʒɪˌtrɒn) *n Electronics.* a type of tube, for displaying information, having a common anode and several cathodes shaped in the form of characters, which can be lit by a glow discharge. Also called: **Nixie tube.** [C20: from DIGIT + -TRON]

digitule ('dɪdʒɪtjuːl) *n Zoology.* any small finger-like process.

diglossia (daɪ'glɒsɪə) *n Linguistics.* the existence in a language of a high, or socially prestigious, and a low, or everyday, form, as German and Swiss German in Switzerland. [C20: New Latin, via French, from Greek *diglōssos* speaking two languages: see DIGLOT]

diglot ('daɪglɒt) *adj* **1** a less common word for **bilingual.** ◆ *n* **2** a bilingual book. [C19: from Greek (Attic) *diglōttos,* from DI-[1] + *glōtta* tongue] ▸ **di'glottic** *adj*

dignified ('dɪgnɪˌfaɪd) *adj* characterized by dignity of manner or appearance; stately. ▸ **'digniˌfiedly** *adv* ▸ **'digniˌfiedness** *n*

dignify ('dɪgnɪˌfaɪ) *vb* **-fies, -fying, -fied.** (*tr*) **1** to invest with honour or dignity; ennoble. **2** to add distinction to: *the meeting was dignified by the minister.* **3** to add a semblance of dignity to, esp. by the use of a pretentious name or title: *she dignifies every plant with its Latin name.* [C15: from Old French *dignifier,* from Late Latin *dignificāre,* from Latin *dignus* worthy + *facere* to make]

dignitary ('dɪgnɪtərɪ, -trɪ) *n, pl* **-taries.** a person of high official position or rank, esp. in government or the church.

dignity ('dɪgnɪtɪ) *n, pl* **-ties. 1** a formal, stately, or grave bearing: *he entered with dignity.* **2** the state or quality of being worthy of honour: *the dignity of manual labour.* **3** relative importance; rank: *he is next in dignity to the mayor.* **4** sense of self-importance (often in the phrases **stand** (or **be**) **on one's dignity, beneath one's dignity**). **5** high rank, esp. in government or the church. **6** a person of high rank or such persons collectively. [C13: from Old French *dignite,* from Latin *dignitās* merit, from *dignus* worthy]

digonal (daɪ'gəʊnəl) *adj Maths.* of or relating to a symmetry operation in which the original figure is reconstructed after a 180° turn about an axis.

digoneutic (ˌdaɪgə'njuːtɪk) *adj Zoology.* producing offspring twice yearly. [C19: from DI-[1] + Greek *gonein* to beget] ▸ **ˌdigo'neutism** *n*

digoxin (daɪ'dʒɒksɪn) *n* a glycoside extracted from digitalis leaves and used in the treatment of heart failure.

digraph ('daɪgrɑːf, -græf) *n* a combination of two letters or characters used to represent a single speech sound such as *gh* in English *tough.* Compare **ligature** (sense 5), **diphthong.** ▸ digraphic (daɪ'græfɪk) *adj*

digress (daɪ'gres) *vb* (*intr*) **1** to depart from the main subject in speech or writing. **2** to wander from one's path or main direction. [C16: from Latin *dīgressus* turned aside, from *dīgredī,* from *dis-* apart + *gradī* to go] ▸ **di'gresser** *n*

digression (daɪ'greʃən) *n* an act or instance of digressing from a main subject in speech or writing. ▸ **di'gressional** *adj*

digressive (daɪ'gresɪv) *adj* characterized by digression or tending to digress. ▸ **di'gressively** *adv* ▸ **di'gressiveness** *n*

digs (dɪgz) *pl n Brit. informal.* lodgings. [C19: shortened from DIGGINGS, perhaps referring to where one *digs* or works, but see also DIG IN]

dihedral (daɪ'hiːdrəl) *adj* **1** having or formed by two intersecting planes; two-sided: *a dihedral angle.* ◆ *n* **2** Also called: **dihedron, dihedral angle.** the figure formed by two intersecting planes. **3** the U.S. name for **corner** (sense 11). **4** the upward inclination of an aircraft wing in relation to the lateral axis. Compare **anhedral.**

dihedron (daɪ'hiːdrən) *n* another name for **dihedral** (sense 2).

dihybrid (daɪ'haɪbrɪd) *n Genetics.* the offspring of two individuals that differ with respect to two pairs of genes; an individual heterozygous for two pairs of genes. ▸ **di'hybridism** *n*

dihydric (daɪ'haɪdrɪk) *adj* (of an alcohol) containing two hydroxyl groups per molecule.

Dijon (*French* diʒɔ̃) *n* a city in E France: capital of the former duchy of Burgundy. Pop.: 151 636 (1990).

dik-dik ('dɪkˌdɪk) *n* any small antelope of the genus *Madoqua,* inhabiting semi-arid regions of Africa, having an elongated muzzle and, in the male, small stout horns. [C19: an East African name, probably of imitative origin]

dike (daɪk) *n, vb* a variant spelling of **dyke.**

dikkop ('dɪkəp) *n* a South African name for **stone curlew.** [from Afrikaans, from *dik* thick + *kop* head]

diktat ('dɪktɑːt) *n* **1** decree or settlement imposed, esp. by a ruler or a victorious nation. **2** a dogmatic statement. [German: dictation, from Latin *dictātum,* from *dictāre* to DICTATE]

dilapidate (dɪ'læpɪˌdeɪt) *vb* to fall or cause to fall into ruin or decay. [C16: from Latin *dīlapidāre* to scatter, waste, from *dis-* apart + *lapidāre* to stone, throw stones, from *lapis* stone]

dilapidated (dɪ'læpɪˌdeɪtɪd) *adj* falling to pieces or in a state of disrepair; shabby.

dilapidation (dɪˌlæpɪ'deɪʃən) *n* **1** the state of being or becoming dilapidated. **2** (*often pl*) *Property law.* **2a** the state of disrepair of premises at the end of a tenancy due to neglect. **2b** the extent of repairs necessary to such premises. ▸ **di'lapiˌdator** *n*

dilatancy (daɪ'leɪtənsɪ, dɪ-) *n* a phenomenon caused by the nature of the stacking or fitting together of particles or granules in a heterogeneous system, such as the solidification of certain sols under pressure, and the thixotropy of certain gels.

dilatant (daɪ'leɪtᵊnt, dɪ-) *adj* **1** tending to dilate; dilating. **2** *Physics.* of, concerned with, or exhibiting dilatancy. ◆ *n* **3** something, such as a catheter, that causes dilation.

dilate (daɪ'leɪt, dɪ-) *vb* **1** to expand or cause to expand; make or become wider or larger: *the pupil of the eye dilates in the dark.* **2** (*intr;* often foll. by *on* or *upon*) to speak or write at length; expand or enlarge. [C14: from Latin *dīlātāre* to spread out, amplify, from *dis-* apart + *lātus* wide] ▸ **di'latable** *adj* ▸ **diˌlata'bility** *or* **di'latableness** *n* ▸ **di'lation** *or* **dilatation** (ˌdaɪlə'teɪʃən, ˌdɪ-) *n* ▸ **ˌdila'tational** *adj* ▸ **dilative** (daɪ'leɪtɪv, dɪ-) *adj*

dilatometer (ˌdɪlə'tɒmɪtə) *n* any instrument for measuring changes in dimension: often a glass bulb fitted with a long stopper through which a capillary tube runs, used for measuring volume changes of liquids. ▸ **dilatometric** (ˌdɪlətə'metrɪk) *adj* ▸ **ˌdilato'metrically** *adv* ▸ **ˌdila'tometry** *n*

dilator, dilater (daɪ'leɪtə, dɪ-), *or* **dilatator** (ˌdaɪlə'teɪtə, ˌdɪ-) *n* **1** something that dilates an object, esp. a surgical instrument for dilating a bodily cavity. **2** a muscle that expands an orifice or dilates an organ.

dilatory ('dɪlətərɪ, -trɪ) *adj* **1** tending or inclined to delay or waste time. **2** intended or designed to waste time or defer action. [C15: from Late Latin *dīlātōrius* inclined to delay, from *differre* to postpone; see DIFFER] ▸ **'dilatorily** *adv* ▸ **'dilatoriness** *n*

dildo *or* **dildoe** ('dɪldəʊ) *n, pl* **-dos** *or* **-does.** an object used as a substitute for an erect penis. [C16: of unknown origin]

dilemma (dɪ'lemə, daɪ-) *n* **1** a situation necessitating a choice between two equal, esp. equally undesirable, alternatives. **2** a problem that seems incapable of a solution. **3** *Logic.* a form of argument one of whose premises is the conjunction of two conditional statements and the other of which affirms the disjunction of their antecedents, and whose conclusion is the disjunction of their consequents. Its form is *if p then q and if r then s; either p or r so either q or s.* **4 on the horns of a dilemma. 4a** faced with the choice between two equally unpalatable alternatives. **4b** in an awkward situation. [C16: via Latin from

Greek, from DI-[1] + *lēmma* assumption, proposition, from *lambanein* to take, grasp] ▸ **dilemmatic** (ˌdɪlɪˈmætɪk,ˌdaɪlɪ-) *or* **dil'emmic** *adj*

USAGE The use of *dilemma* to refer to a problem that seems incapable of a solution is considered by some people to be incorrect.

dilettante (ˌdɪlɪˈtɑːntɪ) *n, pl* **-tantes** *or* **-tanti** (-ˈtɑːntɪ). **1** a person whose interest in a subject is superficial rather than professional. **2** a person who loves the arts. ◆ *adj* **3** of or characteristic of a dilettante. **[C18:** from Italian, from *dilettare* to delight, from Latin *dēlectāre*] ▸ **ˌdiletˈtantish** *or* **ˌdiletˈtanteish** *adj* ▸ **ˌdiletˈtantism** *or* **ˌdiletˈtanteism** *n*

Díli *or* **Dilli** (ˈdiːliː) *n* a port in Indonesia, in N Timor: the former capital (until 1976) of Portuguese Timor. Pop.: 60 150 (latest est.).

diligence[1] (ˈdɪlɪdʒəns) *n* **1** steady and careful application. **2** proper attention or care. **3** *Law.* the degree of care required in a given situation. **[C14:** from Latin *dīligentia* care, attentiveness**]**

diligence[2] (ˈdɪlɪʒəns; *French* diliʒɑ̃s) *n History.* a stagecoach. **[C18:** from French, shortened from *carosse de diligence,* literally: coach of speed**]**

diligent (ˈdɪlɪdʒənt) *adj* **1** careful and persevering in carrying out tasks or duties. **2** carried out with care and perseverance: *diligent work.* **[C14:** from Old French, from Latin *dīligere* to value, from *dis-* apart + *legere* to read**]** ▸ **ˈdiligently** *adv*

dill (dɪl) *n* **1** an umbelliferous aromatic Eurasian plant, *Anethum graveolens,* with finely dissected leaves and umbrella-shaped clusters of yellow flowers. **2** the leaves or seedlike fruits of this plant, used for flavouring in pickles, soups, etc., and in medicine. **3** *Informal, chiefly Austral. and N.Z.* a fool; idiot. **[**Old English *dile;* related to Old High German *tilli***]** ▸ **ˈdilly** *adj*

dill pickle *n* a pickled cucumber flavoured with dill.

dilly (ˈdɪlɪ) *n, pl* **-lies.** *Slang, chiefly U.S. and Canadian.* a person or thing that is remarkable. **[C20:** perhaps from girl's proper name *Dilly***]**

dilly bag *n Austral.* a small bag, esp. one made of plaited grass, etc., often used for carrying food. Sometimes shortened to **dilly.** **[**from native Australian *dilly* small bag or basket**]**

dilly-dally (ˌdɪlɪˈdælɪ) *vb* **-lies, -lying, -lied.** (*intr*) *Informal.* to loiter or vacillate. **[C17:** by reduplication from DALLY**]**

diluent (ˈdɪljʊənt) *adj* **1** causing dilution or serving to dilute. ◆ *n* **2** a substance used for or causing dilution. **[C18:** from Latin *dīluēns* dissolving; see DILUTE**]**

dilute (daɪˈluːt) *vb* **1** to make or become less concentrated, esp. by adding water or a thinner. **2** to make or become weaker in force, effect, etc.: *he diluted his story.* ◆ *adj* **3** *Chem.* **3a** (of a solution, suspension, mixture, etc.) having a low concentration or a concentration that has been reduced by admixture. **3b** (of a substance) present in solution, esp. a weak solution in water: *dilute acetic acid.* **[C16:** from Latin *dīluere,* from *dis-* apart + *-luere,* from *lavāre* to wash**]** ▸ **ˌdiluˈtee** *n* ▸ **diˈluter** *n*

dilution (daɪˈluːʃən) *n* **1** the act of diluting or state of being diluted. **2** a diluted solution.

diluvial (daɪˈluːvɪəl, dɪ-) *or* **diluvian** *adj* **1** of or connected with a deluge, esp. with the great Flood described in Genesis. **2** of or relating to diluvium. **[C17:** from Late Latin *dīluviālis;* see DILUVIUM**]**

diluvialism (daɪˈluːvɪəlɪzm) *n* the theory, generally abandoned in the mid-19th century, that the earth's surface was shaped by the biblical flood.

diluvium (daɪˈluːvɪəm, dɪ-) *n, pl* **-via** (-vɪə). *Geology.* a former name for **drift** (sense 12). **[C19:** from Latin: flood, from *dīluere* to wash away; see DILUTE**]**

dim (dɪm) *adj* **dimmer, dimmest. 1** badly illuminated: *a dim room.* **2** not clearly seen; indistinct; faint: *a dim shape.* **3** having weak or indistinct vision: *eyes dim with tears.* **4** lacking in understanding; mentally dull. **5** not clear in the mind; obscure: *a dim memory.* **6** lacking in brilliance, brightness, or lustre: *a dim colour.* **7** tending to be unfavourable; gloomy or disapproving (esp. in the phrase **take a dim view**). ◆ *vb* **dims, dimming, dimmed. 8** to become or cause to become dim. **9** (*tr*) to cause to seem less bright, as by comparison. **10** the U.S. and Canadian word for **dip** (sense 5). **[**Old English *dimm;* related to Old Norse *dimmr* gloomy, dark**]** ▸ **ˈdimly** *adv* ▸ **ˈdimness** *n*

dim. *abbrev. for:* **1** dimension. **2** Also: **dimin.** *Music.* diminuendo. **3** Also: **dimin.** diminutive.

DiMaggio (dɪˈmædʒɪəʊ) *n* **Joe.** 1914–99, U.S. baseball player.

Dimashq (diːˈmæʃk) *n* an Arabic name for **Damascus.**

Dimbleby (ˈdɪmbəlbɪ) *n* **Richard.** 1913–65, British broadcaster.

dime (daɪm) *n* **1** a coin of the U.S. and Canada, worth one tenth of a dollar or ten cents. **2 a dime a dozen.** very cheap or common. **[C14:** from Old French *disme,* from Latin *decimus* tenth, from *decem* ten**]**

dimenhydrinate (ˌdaɪmenˈhaɪdrɪˌneɪt) *n* a white slightly soluble bitter-tasting crystalline substance, used as an antihistamine and for the prevention of nausea, esp. in travel sickness. Formula: $C_{24}H_{28}ClN_5O_3$. **[**from *dime(thyl* + AMI)N(E) + *(diphen)hydr(am)in(e)* + -ATE[1]**]**

dime novel *n U.S.* (formerly) a cheap melodramatic novel, usually in paperback. Also called (esp. Brit.): **penny-dreadful.**

dimension (dɪˈmɛnʃən) *n* **1** (*often pl*) a measurement of the size of something in a particular direction, such as the length, width, height, or diameter. **2** (*often pl*) scope; size; extent: *a problem of enormous dimensions.* **3** aspect: *a new dimension to politics.* **4** *Maths.* the number of coordinates required to locate a point in space. **5** *Physics.* **5a** the product or the quotient of the fundamental physical quantities (such as mass, length, or time) raised to the appropriate power in a derived physical quantity: *the dimensions of velocity are length divided by time.* **5b** the power to which such a fundamental quantity has to be raised in a derived quantity. ◆ *vb* **6** (*tr*) *Chiefly U.S.* **6a** to shape or cut to specified dimensions. **6b** to mark with specified dimensions. **[C14:** from Old French, from Latin *dīmensiō* an extent, from *dīmētīrī* to measure out, from *mētīrī***]** ▸ **diˈmensional** *adj* ▸ **diˌmensionˈality** *n* ▸ **diˈmensionally** *adv* ▸ **diˈmensionless** *adj*

dimer (ˈdaɪmə) *n Chem.* **a** a molecule composed of two identical simpler molecules (monomers). **b** a compound consisting of dimers.

dimercaprol (ˌdaɪməˈkæprɒl) *n* a colourless oily liquid with an offensive smell, used as an antidote to lewisite and similar toxic substances. Formula: $CH_2(SH)CH(SH)CH_2OH$. Also called: **BAL.** **[C20:** by shortening and altering from *dimercaptopropanol***]**

dimerize *or* **-ise** (ˈdaɪməˌraɪz) *vb* to react or cause to react to form a dimer. ▸ **ˌdimeriˈzation** *or* **-iˈsation** *n*

dimerous (ˈdɪmərəs) *adj* **1** consisting of or divided into two segments, as the tarsi of some insects. **2** (of flowers) having their floral parts arranged in whorls of two. **[C19:** from New Latin *dimerus,* from Greek *dimerēs,* from DI-[1] + *meros* part**]** ▸ **ˈdimerism** *n*

dimeter (ˈdɪmɪtə) *n Prosody.* a line of verse consisting of two metrical feet or a verse written in this metre.

dimethylformamide (daɪˌmiːθaɪlˈfɔːməˌmaɪd, -ˌmeθɪ-) *n* a colourless liquid widely used as a solvent and sometimes as a catalyst. Formula: $(CH_3)_2NCHO$. Abbrev.: **DMF.**

dimethylsulphoxide (daɪˌmiːθaɪlsʌlˈfɒksaɪd, -ˌmeθɪl-) *n* a colourless odourless liquid substance used as a solvent and in medicine as an agent to improve the penetration of drugs applied to the skin. Formula: $(CH_3)_2SO$. Abbrev.: **DMSO.**

dimetric (daɪˈmɛtrɪk) *adj Crystallog.* another word for **tetragonal.**

dimidiate *adj* (dɪˈmɪdɪɪt). **1** divided in halves. **2** *Biology.* having one of two sides or parts more developed than the other: *dimidiate antlers.* ◆ *vb* (dɪˈmɪdɪˌeɪt). **3** (*tr*) *Heraldry.* to halve (two bearings) so that they can be represented on the same shield. **[C17:** from Latin *dīmidiāre* to halve, from *dīmidius* half, from *dis-* apart + *medius* middle**]** ▸ **diˌmidiˈation** *n*

diminish (dɪˈmɪnɪʃ) *vb* **1** to make or become smaller, fewer, or less. **2** (*tr*) *Architect.* to cause (a column, etc.) to taper. **3** (*tr*) *Music.* to decrease (a minor or perfect interval) by a semitone. **4** to belittle or be belittled; reduce in authority, status, etc.; depreciate. **[C15:** blend of *diminuen* to lessen (from Latin *dēminuere* to make smaller, from *minuere* to reduce) + archaic *minish* to lessen**]** ▸ **diˈminishable** *adj* ▸ **diˈminishingly** *adv* ▸ **diˈminishment** *n*

diminished (dɪˈmɪnɪʃt) *adj* **1** reduced or lessened; made smaller. **2** *Music.* denoting any minor or perfect interval reduced by a semitone. **3** *Music.* denoting a triad consisting of the root plus a minor third and a diminished fifth. **4** *Music.* (*postpositive*) (esp. in jazz or pop music) denoting a diminished seventh chord having as its root the note specified: *B diminished.*

diminished responsibility *n Law.* a plea under which proof of mental derangement is submitted as demonstrating lack of premeditation and therefore criminal responsibility.

diminished seventh chord *n* a chord often used in an enharmonic modulation and very common in modern music, esp. jazz and pop music, consisting of a diminished triad with an added diminished seventh above the root. Often shortened to **diminished seventh.**

diminishing returns *pl n. Economics.* **1** progressively smaller rises in output resulting from the increased application of a variable input, such as labour, to a fixed quantity, as of capital or land. **2** the increase in the average cost of production that may arise beyond a certain point as a result of increasing the overall scale of production.

diminuendo (dɪˌmɪnjʊˈɛndəʊ) *Music.* ◆ *n, pl* **-dos. 1a** a gradual decrease in loudness or the musical direction indicating this. Abbrev.: **dim.** Symbol: > (written over the music affected). **1b** a musical passage affected by a diminuendo. ◆ *adj* **2** gradually decreasing in loudness. **3** with a diminuendo. ◆ Also: **decrescendo.** **[C18:** from Italian, from *diminuire* to DIMINISH**]**

diminution (ˌdɪmɪˈnjuːʃən) *n* **1** reduction; decrease. **2** *Music.* the presentation of the subject of a fugue, etc., in which the note values are reduced in length. Compare **augmentation** (sense 3). **[C14:** from Latin *dēminūtiō;* see DIMINISH**]**

diminutive (dɪˈmɪnjʊtɪv) *adj* **1** very small; tiny. **2** *Grammar.* **2a** denoting an affix added to a word to convey the meaning *small* or *unimportant* or to express affection, as for example, the suffix *-ette* in French. **2b** denoting a word formed by the addition of a diminutive affix. ◆ *n* **3** *Grammar.* a diminutive word or affix. **4** a tiny person or thing. ◆ Compare (for senses 2, 3) **augmentative.** ▸ **diminutival** (dɪˌmɪnjʊˈtaɪvəl) *adj* ▸ **diˈminutively** *adv* ▸ **diˈminutiveness** *n*

dimissory (dɪˈmɪsərɪ) *adj* **1** granting permission to be ordained: *a bishop's dimissory letter.* **2** granting permission to depart.

Dimitrovo (diˈmitrovo) *n* the former name (1949–62) of **Pernik.**

dimity (ˈdɪmɪtɪ) *n, pl* **-ties. a** a light strong cotton fabric with woven stripes or squares. **b** (*as modifier*): *a dimity bonnet.* **[C15:** from Medieval Latin *dimitum,* from Greek *dimiton,* from DI-[1] + *mitos* thread of the warp**]**

dimmer (ˈdɪmə) *n* **1** a device, such as a rheostat, for varying the current through an electric light and thus changing the illumination. **2** (*often pl*) *U.S.* **2a** a dipped headlight on a road vehicle. **2b** a parking light on a car.

dimorph (ˈdaɪmɔːf) *n* either of two forms of a substance that exhibits dimorphism.

dimorphism (daɪˈmɔːfɪzəm) *n* **1** the occurrence within a plant of two distinct forms of any part, such as the leaves of some aquatic plants. **2** the occurrence in an animal species of two distinct types of individual. **3** a property of certain substances that enables them to exist in two distinct crystalline forms. ▸ **diˈmorphic** *or* **diˈmorphous** *adj*

dimple (ˈdɪmpəl) *n* **1** a small natural dent or crease in the flesh, esp. on the cheeks or chin. **2** any slight depression in a surface. **3** a bubble or dent in glass. ◆ *vb* **4** to make or become dimpled. **5** (*intr*) to produce dimples by smiling. **[C13** *dympull;* compare Old English *dyppan* to dip, German *Tümpel* pool**]** ▸ **ˈdimply** *adj*

dim sum (ˈdɪm ˈsʌm) *n* a Chinese appetizer of steamed dumplings containing various fillings. **[**Cantonese**]**

dimwit ('dɪm,wɪt) *n Informal.* a stupid or silly person. ► ,**dim-'witted** *adj* ► ,**dim-'wittedly** *adv* ► ,**dim-'wittedness** *n*

din[1] (dɪn) *n* **1** a loud discordant confused noise. ◆ *vb* **dins, dinning, dinned. 2** (*tr;* usually foll. by *into*) to instil (into a person) by constant repetition. **3** (*tr*) to subject to a din. **4** (*intr*) to make a din. [Old English *dynn;* compare Old Norse *dynr,* Old High German *tuni*]

din[2] (dɪn) *n Judaism.* **1** a particular religious law; the halacha about something. **2** the ruling of a Beth Din or religious court. [from Hebrew, literally: judgment]

din[3] (diːn) *n Islam.* religion in general, esp. the beliefs and obligations of Islam. [Arabic, related to *dain* debt]

DIN (dɪn) *n* **1** a formerly used logarithmic expression of the speed of a photographic film, plate, etc., given as $-10\log_{10}E$, where *E* is the exposure of a point 0.1 density units above the fog level; high-speed films have high numbers. Compare **ISO rating. 2** a system of standard plugs, sockets, and cables formerly used for interconnecting domestic audio and video equipment. [C20: from German *D(eutsche) I(ndustrie) N(ormen)* German Industry Standard]

Din. *abbrev. for* dinar.

Dinah ('daɪnə) *n* the daughter of Jacob and Leah (Genesis 30:21; 34).

Dinan (*French* dinɑ̃) *n* a town in NW France, in Brittany, on the estuary of the River Rance: medieval buildings, including town walls and castle: tourism, hosiery, cider: Pop.: 14 200 (latest est.).

Dinant (*French* dinɑ̃) *n* a town in S Belgium, on the River Meuse below steep limestone cliffs: 11th-century citadel: famous in the Middle Ages for fine brassware, known as *dinanderie*: tourism, metalwork, biscuits. Pop.: 12 200 (1991).

dinar ('diːnɑː) *n* **1** the standard monetary unit of the following countries. Algeria: divided into 100 centimes. Bahrain: divided into 1000 fils. Bosnia-Herzegovina: divided into 100 paras. Iraq: divided into 1000 fils. Jordan: divided into 1000 fils. Kuwait: divided into 1000 fils. Libya: divided into 1000 dirhams. Sudan. Tunisia: divided into 1000 millimes. Yugoslavia: divided into 100 paras. Abbrev.: **Din., D., d. 2** a coin, esp. one of gold, formerly used in the Middle East. [C17: from Arabic, from Late Greek *dēnarion,* from Latin *dēnārius* DENARIUS]

Dinaric Alps (dɪ'nærɪk, daɪ-) *pl n* a mountain range in W Croatia, Bosnia-Herzegovina, and Serbia: connected with the main Alpine system by the Julian Alps. Highest peak: Troglav, 1913 m (6277 ft.).

d'Indy (*French* dɛ̃di) *n* (**Paul Marie Theodore**) **Vincent.** 1851–1931, French composer. His works include operas, chamber music, and the *Symphony on a French Mountaineer's Song* (1866).

dine (daɪn) *vb* **1** (*intr*) to eat dinner. **2** (*intr;* often foll. by *on, off,* or *upon*) to make one's meal (of): *the guests dined upon roast beef.* **3** (*tr*) *Informal.* to entertain to dinner (esp. in the phrase **to wine and dine someone**). [C13: from Old French *disner,* contracted from Vulgar Latin *disjējūnāre* (unattested) to cease fasting, from *dis-* not + Late Latin *jējūnāre* to fast; see JEJUNE]

dine out *vb* (*intr, adv*) **1** to dine away from home, esp. in a restaurant. **2** (foll. by *on*) to have dinner at the expense of someone else mainly for the sake of one's knowledge or conversation about (a subject or story).

diner ('daɪnə) *n* **1** a person eating a meal, esp. in a restaurant. **2** *Chiefly U.S. and Canadian.* a small restaurant, often at the roadside. **3** a fashionable bar, or a section of one, where food is served.

dineric (dɪ'nɛrɪk) *adj* of or concerned with the interface between immiscible liquids. [C20: from DI-[1] + Late Greek *nēron* water + -IC]

Dinesen ('dɪnɪsᵊn) *n* **Isak** ('aɪzək), pen name of *Baroness Karen Blixen.* 1885–1962, Danish author of short stories in Danish and English, including *Seven Gothic Tales* (1934) and *Winter's Tales* (1942). Her life story was told in the film *Out of Africa* (1986).

dinette (daɪ'nɛt) *n* an alcove or small area for use as a dining room.

ding[1] (dɪŋ) *vb* **1** to ring or cause to ring, esp. with tedious repetition. **2** (*tr*) another word for **din**[1] (sense 2). ◆ *n* **3** an imitation or representation of the sound of a bell. **4** *Austral. informal.* a party or social event. [C13: probably of imitative origin, but influenced by DIN[1] + RING[2]; compare Old Swedish *diunga* to beat]

ding[2] (dɪŋ) *vb Scot.* **1** to strike; dash down. **2** to surpass. [Middle English *dingen*]

Dingaan ('dɪŋgɑːn) *n* died 1840, Zulu chief (1828–40), who fought the Boer colonists in Natal.

Ding an sich (dɪŋ æn sɪk; *German* dɪŋ an zɪç) *n Philosophy.* the thing in itself.

dingbat ('dɪŋ,bæt) *n U.S. slang.* **1** any unnamed object, esp. one used as a missile. **2** a crazy or stupid person. [C19: of unknown origin]

dingbats ('dɪŋ,bæts) *Austral. and N.Z.* ◆ *pl n* **1 the.** *Slang.* delirium tremens. **2 give someone the dingbats.** *Informal.* to make someone nervous. ◆ *adj* **3** *Informal.* crazy or stupid.

ding-dong *n* **1** the sound of a bell or bells, esp. two bells tuned a fourth or fifth apart. **2** an imitation or representation of the sound of a bell. **3a** a violent exchange of blows or words. **3b** (*as modifier*): *a ding-dong battle.* ◆ *adj* **4** sounding or ringing repeatedly. [C16: of imitative origin; see DING[1]]

dinge[1] (dɪndʒ) *n* dinginess. [C19: back formation from DINGY]

dinge[2] (dɪndʒ) *U.S. derogatory slang.* ◆ *n* **1** a Black person. ◆ *adj* **2** of or relating to Black people.

dinge[3] (dɪndʒ) *English dialect and Irish.* ◆ *vb* (*tr*) **1** to make a dent in (something). ◆ *n* **2** a dent. [of unknown origin]

dinges ('dɪŋəs) *n S. African informal.* a jocular word for something whose name is unknown or forgotten; thingumabob. [from Afrikaans, from *ding* thing]

dinghy ('dɪŋɪ) *n, pl* **-ghies.** any small boat, powered by sail, oars, or outboard motor. Also (esp. formerly): **dingy, dingey.** [C19: from Hindi or Bengali *dingi* a little boat, from *dingā* boat]

dingle ('dɪŋgᵊl) *n* a small wooded dell. [C13: of uncertain origin]

dingo ('dɪŋgəʊ) *n, pl* **-goes. 1** a wild dog, *Canis dingo,* of Australia, having a yellowish-brown coat and resembling a wolf. **2** *Austral. slang.* a cheat or coward. ◆ *vb* **-goes, -going, -goed.** (*intr*) *Austral. slang.* **3a** to act in a cowardly manner. **3b** to drop out of something. **4** (foll. by *on*) to let (someone) down. [C18: native Australian name]

dingy ('dɪndʒɪ) *adj* **-gier, -giest. 1** lacking light or brightness; drab. **2** dirty; discoloured. [C18: perhaps from an earlier dialect word related to Old English *dynge* dung] ► **'dingily** *adv* ► **'dinginess** *n*

dining car *n* a railway coach in which meals are served at tables. Also called: **restaurant car.**

dining room *n* a room where meals are eaten.

dinitrobenzene (daɪ,naɪtrəʊ'bɛnziːn, -bɛn'ziːn) *n* a yellow crystalline compound existing in three isomeric forms, obtained by reaction of benzene with nitric and sulphuric acids. The *meta-* form is used in the manufacture of dyes and plastics. Formula: $C_6H_4(NO_2)_2$.

dinitrogen tetroxide (daɪ'naɪtrədʒən) *n* a colourless gaseous substance that exists in equilibrium with nitrogen dioxide. As the temperature is reduced the proportion of the tetroxide increases. Formula: N_2O_4.

dink (dɪŋk) *adj* **1** *Scot. and northern English dialect.* neat or neatly dressed. ◆ *vb* **2** *Austral. and N.Z., chiefly children's slang.* **2a** (*tr*) to carry (a second person) on a horse, bicycle, etc. **2b** (*intr*) (of two people) to travel together on a horse, bicycle, etc. [C16: of unknown origin]

Dinka ('dɪŋkə) *n* **1** (*pl* **-kas** *or* **-ka**) a member of a Nilotic people of the S Sudan, noted for their height, which often reaches seven feet tall: chiefly herdsmen. **2** the language of this people, belonging to the Nilotic group of the Nilo-Saharan family. [from Dinka *jieng* people]

dinkie ('dɪŋkɪ) *n* **1** an affluent married childless person. ◆ *adj* **2** designed for or appealing to dinkies. [C20: from *d(ouble) i(ncome) n(o) k(ids)* + -IE]

dinkum ('dɪŋkəm) *adj Austral. and N.Z. informal.* **1** Also: **dinky-di.** genuine or right (usually preceded by *fair* and used esp. as an interjection): *a fair dinkum offer.* **2 dinkum oil.** *Archaic.* the truth. [C19: from English dialect: work, of unknown origin]

dinky ('dɪŋkɪ) *adj* **dinkier, dinkiest.** *Informal.* **1** *Brit.* small and neat; dainty. **2** *U.S.* inconsequential; insignificant. [C18 (in the sense: dainty): from DINK]

dinna ('dɪnə) *vb Scot.* do not.

dinner ('dɪnə) *n* **1** a meal taken in the evening. **2** a meal taken at midday, esp. when it is the main meal of the day; lunch. **3a** a formal evening meal, as of a club, society, etc. **3b** a public banquet in honour of someone or something. **4** a complete meal at a fixed price in a restaurant; table d'hôte. **5** (*modifier*) of, relating to, or used at dinner: *dinner plate; dinner table; dinner hour.* **6 do like a dinner.** (*usually passive*) *Austral. informal.* to do for, overpower, or outdo. [C13: from Old French *disner;* see DINE]

dinner-dance *n* a formal dinner followed by dancing.

dinner jacket *n* a man's semiformal evening jacket without tails, usually black with a silk facing over the collar and lapels. Abbrevs.: **DJ, dj.** U.S. and Canadian name: **tuxedo.**

dinner lady *n Brit.* a female cook or canteen worker in a school.

dinner service *n* a set of matching plates, dishes, etc., suitable for serving a meal to a certain number of people.

dinoceras (daɪ'nɒsərəs) *n* another name for a **uintathere.** [C19: New Latin, from Greek *deinos* fearful + *keras* horn]

dinoflagellate (,daɪnəʊ'flædʒɪlɪt, -,leɪt) *n* **1** any of a group of unicellular biflagellate aquatic organisms forming a constituent of plankton: now usually classified as a phylum of protoctists (*Dinoflagellata*). ◆ *adj* **2** of or relating to dinoflagellates. [C19: from New Latin *Dinoflagellata,* from Greek *dinos* whirling + FLAGELLUM + -ATE[1]]

dinosaur ('daɪnə,sɔː) *n* **1** any extinct terrestrial reptile of the orders *Saurischia* and *Ornithischia,* many of which were of gigantic size and abundant in the Mesozoic era. See also **saurischian, ornithischian.** Compare **pterosaur, plesiosaur. 2** a person or thing that is considered to be out of date. [C19: from New Latin *dinosaurus,* from Greek *deinos* fearful + *sauros* lizard] ► ,**dino'saurian** *adj*

dinothere ('daɪnə,θɪə) *n* any extinct late Tertiary elephant-like mammal of the genus *Dinotherium* (or *Deinotherium*), having a down-turned jaw with tusks curving downwards and backwards. [C19: from New Latin *dinotherium,* from Greek *deinos* fearful + *thērion,* diminutive of *thēr* beast]

dint (dɪnt) *n* **1 by dint of.** by means or use of: *by dint of hard work.* **2** *Archaic.* a blow or a mark made by a blow. ◆ *vb* **3** (*tr*) to mark with dints. ◆ *n, vb* **4** a variant of **dent**[1]. [Old English *dynt;* related to Old Norse *dyttr* blow] ► **'dintless** *adj*

D'Inzeo (*Italian* din'tsɛːo) *n* **Piero** ('pjɛːro), born 1923, and his brother **Raimondo** (rai'mondo), born 1925, Italian showjumping riders.

dioc. *abbrev. for:* **1** diocesan. **2** diocese.

Dio Cassius ('daɪəʊ 'kæsɪəs) *n* ?155–?230 A.D., Roman historian. His *History of Rome* covers the period of Rome's transition from Republic to Empire.

diocesan (daɪ'ɒsɪsᵊn) *adj* **1** of or relating to a diocese. ◆ *n* **2** the bishop of a diocese.

diocese ('daɪəsɪs) *n* the district under the jurisdiction of a bishop. [C14: from Old French, from Late Latin *diocēsis,* from Greek *dioikēsis* administration, from *dioikein* to manage a household, from *oikos* house]

Dio Chrysostom (*Greek* 'diːo 'krizəstəm) *n* 2nd century A.D., Greek orator and philosopher.

Diocletian (,daɪə'kliːʃən) *n* full name *Gaius Aurelius Valerius Diocletianus.* 245–313 A.D., Roman emperor (284–305), who divided the empire into four administrative units (293) and instigated the last severe persecution of the Christians (303).

diode ('daɪəʊd) *n* **1** a semiconductor device containing one p-n junction, used in circuits for converting alternating current to direct current. More formal name: **semiconductor diode. 2** the earliest and simplest type of electronic valve having two electrodes, an anode and a cathode, between which a current can flow only in one direction. It was formerly widely used as a rectifier and detector but has now been replaced in most electrical circuits by the more efficient and reliable semiconductor diode. [C20: from DI-[1] + -ODE[2]]

Diodorus Siculus (ˌdaɪəˈdɔːrəs ˈsɪkjʊləs) *n* 1st century B.C., Greek historian, noted for his history of the world in 40 books, of which 15 are extant.

dioecious, diecious (daɪˈiːʃəs), *or* **dioicous** (daɪˈɔɪkəs) *adj* (of some plants) having the male and female reproductive organs in separate flowers on separate plants. Compare **monoecious.** [C18: from New Latin *Dioecia* name of class, from DI-[1] + Greek *oikia* house, dwelling] ▸ **diˈoeciously, diˈeciously,** *or* **diˈoicously** *adv* ▸ **diˈoeciousness, diˈeciousness,** *or* **diˈoicousness** *n*

dioestrus *or U.S.* **diestrus** (daɪˈiːstrəs) *n* a period of sexual inactivity between periods of oestrus in animals that have several oestrous cycles in one breeding season.

Diogenes (daɪˈɒdʒɪˌniːz) *n* ?412–?323 B.C., Greek Cynic philosopher, who rejected social conventions and advocated self-sufficiency and simplicity of life.

diol (ˈdaɪɒl) *n Chem.* any of a class of alcohols that have two hydroxyl groups in each molecule. Also called: **glycol, dihydric alcohol.** [from DI-[1] + (ALCOH)OL]

Diomede Islands (ˈdaɪəˌmiːd) *pl n* two small islands in the Bering Strait, separated by the international date line and by the boundary line between the U.S. and Russia.

Diomedes (ˌdaɪəˈmiːdiːz), **Diomede,** *or* **Diomed** (ˈdaɪəˌmɛd) *n Greek myth.* **1** a king of Argos, and suitor of Helen, who fought with the Greeks at Troy. **2** a king of the Bistones in Thrace whose savage horses ate strangers.

Dione[1] (daɪˈəʊnɪ) *n Greek myth.* a Titaness; the earliest consort of Zeus and mother of Aphrodite.

Dione[2] (daɪˈəʊnɪ) *n* one of the larger satellites of the planet Saturn.

Dionysia (ˌdaɪəˈnɪzɪə) *n* (in ancient Greece) festivals of the god Dionysus: a source of Athenian drama.

Dionysiac (ˌdaɪəˈnɪzɪˌæk) *adj* **1** of or relating to Dionysus or his worship. **2** a less common word for **Dionysian.**

Dionysian (ˌdaɪəˈnɪzɪən) *adj* **1** of or relating to Dionysus. **2** (*sometimes not cap.*) (in the philosophy of Nietzsche) of or relating to the set of creative qualities that encompasses spontaneity, irrationality, the rejection of discipline, etc. **3** (*often not cap.*) wild or orgiastic. **4** of or relating to any of the historical characters named Dionysius. ◆ Compare (for senses 2, 3) **Apollonian.**

Dionysius (ˌdaɪəˈnɪsɪəs) *n* called *the Elder.* ?430–367 B.C., tyrant of Syracuse (405–367), noted for his successful campaigns against Carthage and S Italy.

Dionysius Exiguus (ɛgˈzɪgjʊəs) *n* died ?556 A.D., Scythian monk and scholar, who is believed to have introduced the current method of reckoning dates on the basis of the Christian era.

Dionysius of Halicarnassus *n* died ?7 B.C., Greek historian and rhetorician; author of a history of Rome.

Dionysius the Areopagite (ˌærɪˈɒpəˌgaɪt) *n* 1st century A.D., Greek Christian, thought to have been the first Bishop of Athens: long considered the author of influential theological works actually written *c.* 500. See **Pseudo-Dionysius.**

Dionysus *or* **Dionysos** (ˌdaɪəˈnaɪsəs) *n* the Greek god of wine, fruitfulness, and vegetation, worshipped in orgiastic rites. He was also known as the bestower of ecstasy and god of the drama, and identified with Bacchus.

Diophantine equation (ˌdaɪəʊˈfæntaɪn) *n* (in number theory) an equation in more than one variable and with integral coefficients, for which integral solutions are sought.

Diophantus (ˌdaɪəʊˈfæntəs) *n* 3rd century A.D., Greek mathematician, noted for his treatise on the theory of numbers, *Arithmetica.*

diopside (daɪˈɒpsaɪd, -sɪd) *n* a colourless or pale-green pyroxene mineral consisting of calcium magnesium silicate in monoclinic crystalline form: used as a gemstone. Formula: $CaMgSi_2O_6$. [C19: from DI-[2] + Greek *opsis* sight, appearance + -IDE]

dioptase (daɪˈɒpteɪs, -teɪz) *n* a green glassy mineral consisting of hydrated copper silicate in hexagonal crystalline form. Formula: H_2CuSiO_4. [C19: from French, from Greek *dia-* through + *optos* visible]

dioptometer (ˌdaɪɒpˈtɒmɪtə) *n* an instrument for measuring ocular refraction. [from DI-[2] + OPT(IC) + -METER] ▸ **ˌdiopˈtometry** *n*

dioptre *or U.S.* **diopter** (daɪˈɒptə) *n* a unit for measuring the refractive power of a lens: the reciprocal of the focal length of the lens expressed in metres. [C16: from Latin *dioptra* optical instrument, from Greek, from *dia-* through + *opsesthai* to see] ▸ **diˈoptral** *adj*

dioptric (daɪˈɒptrɪk) *or* **dioptrical** *adj* **1** of or concerned with dioptrics. **2** of or denoting refraction or refracted light. ▸ **diˈoptrically** *adv*

dioptrics (daɪˈɒptrɪks) *n* (*functioning as sing*) the branch of geometrical optics concerned with the formation of images by lenses. [C20: from DIOPTRE + -ICS]

Dior (diːˈɔː; *French* djɔr) *n* **Christian** (ˈkrɪstʃən; *French* kristjɑ̃). 1905–57, French couturier, noted for his New Look of narrow waist with a long full skirt (1947); he also created the waistless sack dress.

diorama (ˌdaɪəˈrɑːmə) *n* **1** a miniature three-dimensional scene, in which models of figures are seen against a background. **2** a picture made up of illuminated translucent curtains, viewed through an aperture. **3** a museum display, as of an animal, of a specimen in its natural setting. **4** *Films.* a scene produced by the rearrangement of lighting effects. [C19: from French, from Greek *dia-* through + Greek *horama* view, from *horan* to see] ▸ **dioramic** (ˌdaɪəˈræmɪk) *adj*

diorite (ˈdaɪəˌraɪt) *n* a dark coarse-grained igneous plutonic rock consisting of plagioclase feldspar and ferromagnesian minerals such as hornblende. [C19: from French, from Greek *diorizein* to distinguish (from *dia-* apart + *horizein* to define) + -ITE[1]] ▸ **dioritic** (ˌdaɪəˈrɪtɪk) *adj*

Dioscuri (ˌdaɪɒsˈkjʊərɪ) *pl n* the Greek name for **Castor and Pollux,** when considered together.

dioxan (daɪˈɒksən) *or* **dioxane** (daɪˈɒkseɪn) *n* a colourless insoluble toxic liquid made by heating ethanediol with sulphuric acid; 1,4-diethylene dioxide: used as a solvent, esp. for waxes and cellulose acetate resins. Formula: $(CH_2)_2O(CH_2)_2O$.

dioxide (daɪˈɒksaɪd) *n* **1** any oxide containing two oxygen atoms per molecule, both of which are bonded to an atom of another element. **2** another name for a **peroxide** (sense 4).

dioxin (daɪˈɒksɪn) *n* any of a number of mostly poisonous chemical by-products of the manufacture of certain herbicides and bactericides, esp. the extremely toxic 2,3,7,8 tetrachlorodibenzo-para-dioxin.

dip (dɪp) *vb* **dips, dipping, dipped. 1** to plunge or be plunged quickly or briefly into a liquid, esp. to wet or coat. **2** (*intr*) to undergo a slight decline, esp. temporarily: *sales dipped in November.* **3** (*intr*) to slope downwards: *the land dips towards the river.* **4** (*intr*) to sink or appear to sink quickly: *the sun dipped below the horizon.* **5** (*tr*) to switch (car headlights) from the main to the lower beam. U.S. and Canadian word: **dim. 6** (*tr*) **6a** to immerse (poultry, sheep, etc.) briefly in a liquid chemical to rid them of or prevent infestation by insects, etc. **6b** to immerse (grain, vegetables, or wood) in a preservative liquid. **7** (*tr*) to stain or dye by immersing in a liquid. **8** (*tr*) to baptize (someone) by immersion. **9** (*tr*) to plate or galvanize (a metal, etc.) by immersion in an electrolyte or electrolytic cell. **10** (*tr*) to scoop up a liquid or something from a liquid in the hands or in a container. **11** to lower or be lowered briefly: *she dipped her knee in a curtsy.* **12** (*tr*) to make (a candle) by plunging the wick into melted wax. **13** (*intr*) to plunge a container, the hands, etc., into something, esp. to obtain or retrieve an object: *he dipped in his pocket for money.* **14** (*intr;* foll. by *in* or *into*) to dabble (in); play (at): *he dipped into black magic.* **15** (*intr*) (of an aircraft) to drop suddenly and then regain height. **16** (*intr*) (of a rock stratum or mineral vein) to slope downwards from the horizontal. **17** (*intr; often foll. by for*) (in children's games) to select (a leader, etc.) by reciting any of various rhymes. ◆ *n* **18** the act of dipping or state of being dipped. **19** a brief swim in water. **20a** any liquid chemical preparation in which poultry, sheep, etc. are dipped. **20b** any liquid preservative into which objects, esp. of wood, are dipped. **21** a preparation of dyeing agents into which fabric is immersed. **22** a depression, esp. in a landscape. **23** something taken up by dipping. **24** a container used for dipping; dipper. **25** a momentary sinking down. **26** the angle of slope of rock strata, fault planes, etc., from the horizontal plane. **27** Also called: **angle of dip, magnetic dip, inclination.** the angle between the direction of the earth's magnetic field and the plane of the horizon; the angle that a magnetic needle free to swing in a vertical plane makes with the horizontal. **28** a creamy mixture into which pieces of food are dipped before being eaten. **29** *Surveying.* the angular distance of the horizon below the plane of observation. **30** a candle made by plunging a wick repeatedly into wax. **31** a momentary loss of altitude when flying. **32** (in gymnastics) a chinning exercise on the parallel bars. **33** a slang word for **pickpocket.** ◆ See also **dip into, dip out.** [Old English *dyppan;* related to Old High German *tupfen* to wash, German *taufen* to baptize; see DEEP]

dip. *or* **Dip.** *abbrev. for* diploma.

DipAD (in Britain) *abbrev. for* Diploma in Art and Design.

dip-and-scarp *adj* (of topography) characterized by alternating steeper scarp slopes and gentler dip slopes.

DipChemEng *abbrev. for* Diploma in Chemical Engineering.

dip circle *n* an instrument for measuring dip, consisting of a dip needle with a vertical circular scale of angles. Also called: **inclinometer.**

DipCom *abbrev. for* Diploma of Commerce.

DipEd (in Britain) *abbrev. for* Diploma in Education.

dipeptide (daɪˈpɛptaɪd) *n* a compound consisting of two linked amino acids. See **peptide.**

dipetalous (daɪˈpɛtələs) *adj* another word for **bipetalous.**

dip fault *n Geology.* a fault that runs perpendicular to the strike of the affected rocks (i.e. parallel to the plane of the angle of dip of the rocks).

diphase (ˈdaɪˌfeɪz) *or* **diphasic** *adj Physics.* of, having, or concerned with two phases.

diphasic (daɪˈfeɪzɪk) *adj* **1** *Zoology.* (of parasites) having a free active stage in the life cycle. **2** *Physics.* another word for **diphase.**

diphenyl (daɪˈfiːnaɪl, -nɪl; -ˈfɛnɪl) *n* another name for **biphenyl.**

diphenylamine (daɪˌfiːnaɪləˈmiːn, -ˈæmɪn; -nɪl-; -ˌfɛn-) *n* a colourless insoluble crystalline derivative of benzene, used in the manufacture of dyes, as a stabilizer in plastics, etc. Formula: $(C_6H_5)_2NH$.

diphenylhydantoin sodium (daɪˌfiːnaɪlhaɪˈdæntəʊɪn, -nɪl-, -ˌfɛn-) *n* a white soluble bitter-tasting powder used as an anticonvulsant in the treatment of epilepsy. Formula: $C_{15}H_{11}N_2O_2Na$.

diphosgene (daɪˈfɒzdʒiːn) *n* an oily liquid with an extremely poisonous vapour, made by treating methanol with phosgene and chlorinating the product: has been used in chemical warfare. Formula: $ClCOOCCl_3$.

diphtheria (dɪpˈθɪərɪə, dɪf-) *n* an acute contagious disease caused by the bacillus *Corynebacterium diphtheriae,* producing fever, severe prostration, and difficulty in breathing and swallowing as the result of swelling of the throat and formation of a false membrane. [C19: New Latin, from French *diphthérie,* from Greek *diphthera* leather; from the nature of the membrane] ▸ **diphˈtherial, diphtheritic** (ˌdɪpθəˈrɪtɪk, dɪf-), *or* **diphtheric** (dɪpˈθɛrɪk, dɪf-) *adj* ▸ **ˈdiphtheˌroid** *adj*

diphthong (ˈdɪfθɒŋ, ˈdɪp-) *n* **1** a vowel sound, occupying a single syllable, during the articulation of which the tongue moves from one position to another, causing a continual change in vowel quality, as in the pronunciation of *a* in English *late,* during which the tongue moves from the position of (e) towards (ɪ). **2** a digraph or ligature representing a composite vowel such as this, as *ae* in *Caesar.* [C15: from Late Latin *diphthongus,* from Greek *diphthongos,* from DI-[1] + *phthongos* sound] ▸ **diphˈthongal** *adj*

diphthongize *or* **diphthongise** (ˈdɪfθɒŋˌaɪz, -ˌgaɪz; ˈdɪp-) *vb* (*often passive*) to make (a simple vowel) into a diphthong. ▸ ˌ**diphthongiˈzation** *or* ˌ**diphthongiˈsation** *n*

diphycercal (ˌdɪfɪˈsɜːkᵊl) *adj Ichthyol.* of or possessing a symmetrical or pointed tail with the vertebral column extending to the tip, as in primitive fishes. [C19: from Greek *diphuēs* twofold (from DI-[1] + *phuē* growth) + *kerkos* tail]

diphyletic (ˌdaɪfaɪˈlɛtɪk) *adj* relating to or characterized by descent from two ancestral groups of animals or plants.

diphyllous (daɪˈfɪləs) *adj* (of certain plants) having two leaves.

diphyodont (ˈdɪfɪəʊˌdɒnt) *adj* having two successive sets of teeth, as mammals (including man). Compare **polyphyodont.** [C19: from Greek *diphuēs* double (see DIPHYCERCAL) + -ODONT]

dip into *vb* (*intr, prep*) **1** to draw (upon): *he dipped into his savings.* **2** to read (passages) at random or cursorily in (a book, newspaper, etc.).

dipl. *abbrev. for:* **1** diplomat(ic). **2** Also: **Dip., dip.** diploma.

diplegia (daɪˈpliːdʒə) *n* paralysis of corresponding parts on both sides of the body; bilateral paralysis. ▸ **diˈplegic** *adj*

diplo- *or before a vowel* **dipl-** *combining form.* double: *diplococcus.* [from Greek, from *diploos,* from DI-[1] + *-ploos* -fold]

diplobiont (ˌdɪpləʊˈbaɪɒnt) *n Biology.* an organism that has both haploid and diploid individuals in its life cycle. ▸ ˌ**diplobiˈontic** *adj*

diploblastic (ˌdɪpləʊˈblæstɪk) *adj* (of jellyfish, corals, and other coelenterates) having a body developed from only two germ layers (ectoderm and endoderm). Compare **triploblastic.**

diplocardiac (ˌdɪpləʊˈkɑːdɪˌæk) *adj* (of birds and mammals) having a four-chambered heart, which enables two separate circulations and prevents mixing of the arterial and venous blood.

Diplock court (ˈdɪplɒk) *n* in Northern Ireland, a court of law designed to try cases linked with terrorism. In order to prevent the intimidation of jurors, the court consists of a single judge and no jury. [C20: named after Lord *Diplock,* who introduced the courts in 1972]

diplococcus (ˌdɪpləʊˈkɒkəs) *n, pl* **-cocci** (-ˈkɒksaɪ). any of various spherical Gram-positive bacteria that occur in pairs, esp. any of the genus *Diplococcus,* such as *D. pneumoniae,* which causes pneumonia: family *Lactobacillaceae.* ▸ ˌ**diploˈcoccal** *or* **diplococcic** (ˌdɪpləʊˈkɒksɪk, -ˈkɒkɪk) *adj*

diplodocus (dɪˈplɒdəkəs, ˌdɪpləʊˈdəʊkəs) *n, pl* **-cuses.** any herbivorous quadrupedal late Jurassic dinosaur of the genus *Diplodocus,* characterized by a very long neck and tail and a total body length of 27 metres: suborder *Sauropoda* (sauropods). [C19: from New Latin, from DIPLO- + Greek *dokos* beam]

diploë (ˈdɪpləʊˌiː) *n Anatomy.* the spongy bone separating the two layers of compact bone of the skull. [C17: via New Latin, from Greek: a fold, from *diploos* double]

diploid (ˈdɪplɔɪd) *adj* **1** *Biology.* (of cells or organisms) having paired homologous chromosomes so that twice the haploid number is present. **2** double or twofold. ◆ *n* **3** *Biology.* a diploid cell or organism. ▸ **dipˈloidic** *adj* ▸ ˈ**diploidy** *n*

diploma (dɪˈpləʊmə) *n* **1** a document conferring a qualification, recording success in examinations or successful completion of a course of study. **2** an official document that confers an honour or privilege. [C17: from Latin: official letter or document, literally: letter folded double, from Greek; see DIPLO-]

diplomacy (dɪˈpləʊməsɪ) *n, pl* **-cies. 1** the conduct of the relations of one state with another by peaceful means. **2** skill in the management of international relations. **3** tact, skill, or cunning in dealing with people. [C18: from French *diplomatie,* from *diplomatique* DIPLOMATIC]

diplomat (ˈdɪpləˌmæt) *n* **1** an official, such as an ambassador or first secretary, engaged in diplomacy. **2** a person who deals with people tactfully or skilfully.

diplomate (ˈdɪpləˌmeɪt) *n* any person who has been granted a diploma, esp. a physician certified as a specialist.

diplomatic (ˌdɪpləˈmætɪk) *adj* **1** of or relating to diplomacy or diplomats. **2** skilled in negotiating, esp. between states or people. **3** tactful in dealing with people. **4** of or relating to diplomatics. [C18: from French *diplomatique* concerning the documents of diplomacy, from New Latin *diplōmaticus;* see DIPLOMA] ▸ ˌ**diploˈmatically** *adv*

diplomatic bag *n* a container or bag in which official mail is sent, free from customs inspection, to and from an embassy or consulate.

diplomatic corps *or* **body** *n* the entire body of diplomats accredited to a given state.

diplomatic immunity *n* the immunity from local jurisdiction and exemption from taxation in the country to which they are accredited afforded to diplomats.

diplomatics (ˌdɪpləˈmætɪks) *n* (*functioning as sing*) **1** the critical study of historical documents. **2** a less common word for **diplomacy.**

Diplomatic Service *n* **1** (in Britain) the division of the Civil Service which provides diplomats to represent the U.K. abroad. **2** (*not caps.*) the equivalent institution of any other country.

diplomatist (dɪˈpləʊmətɪst) *n* a less common word for **diplomat.**

diplonema (ˌdɪpləʊˈniːmə) *n Biology.* the stage during meiosis at which the chromosomes are distinctly doubled.

diplont (ˈdɪplɒnt) *n* an animal or plant that has the diploid number of chromosomes in its somatic cells. [C20: DIPLO- + Greek *ōn* being, from *einai* to be] ▸ **dipˈlontic** *adj*

diplopia (dɪˈpləʊpɪə) *n* a visual defect in which a single object is seen in duplicate; double vision. It can be caused by incorrect fixation or by an abnormality in the visual system. [C19: New Latin, from DIPLO- + Greek *ōps* eye] ▸ **diplopic** (dɪˈplɒpɪk) *adj*

diplopod (ˈdɪpləˌpɒd) *n* any arthropod of the class *Diplopoda,* which includes the millipedes.

diplosis (dɪˈpləʊsɪs) *n Biology.* the doubling of the haploid number of chromosomes that occurs during fusion of gametes to form a diploid zygote. [C20: from Greek *diplōsis* doubling, from *diploun* to double, from *diploos* double]

diplostemonous (ˌdɪpləʊˈstiːmənəs, -ˈstem-) *adj* (of plants) having twice as many stamens as petals, esp. with the stamens arranged in two whorls. [C19: from New Latin *diplostemonus* (unattested), from DIPLO- + *-stemonus* relating to a STAMEN]

diplotene (ˈdɪpləʊˌtiːn) *n* the fourth stage of the prophase of meiosis, during which the chromosomes of each bivalent separate, usually with the interchange of genetic material. See also **chiasma** (sense 1), **crossing over.** [C20: from DIPLO- + Greek *tainia* band]

diplozoic (ˌdɪpləˈzəʊɪk) *adj* (of certain animals) bilaterally symmetrical.

DipMet *abbrev. for* Diploma in Metallurgy.

dip needle *n* a magnetized needle pivoted through its centre of gravity able to rotate freely in a vertical plane, used to determine the inclination of the earth's magnetic field. See also **dip circle.**

dipnoan (dɪpˈnəʊən) *adj* **1** of, relating to, or belonging to the *Dipnoi,* a subclass of bony fishes comprising the lungfishes. ◆ *n* **2** any lungfish. [C19: from New Latin *Dipnoi,* from Greek *dipnoos,* double-breathing, from DI-[1] + *pnoē* breathing, air, from *pnein* to breathe]

dipody (ˈdɪpədɪ) *n, pl* **-dies.** *Prosody.* a metrical unit consisting of two feet. [C19: from Late Latin *dipodia,* from Greek DI-[1] + *pous* foot]

dipole (ˈdaɪˌpəʊl) *n* **1** two electric charges or magnetic poles that have equal magnitudes but opposite signs and are separated by a small distance. **2** a molecule in which the centre of positive charge does not coincide with the centre of negative charge. **3** Also called: **dipole aerial.** a directional radio or television aerial consisting of two equal lengths of metal wire or rods, with a connecting wire fixed between them in the form of a T. ▸ **diˈpolar** *adj*

dipole moment *n Chem.* a measure of the polarity in a chemical bond or molecule, equal to the product of one charge and the distance between the charges. Symbol: μ

dip out *vb* (*intr, adv*) *Austral. and N.Z. informal.* (often foll. by *on*) to miss out on or fail to participate in something: *he dipped out in the examination.*

dipper (ˈdɪpə) *n* **1** a ladle used for dipping. **2** Also called: **water ouzel.** any aquatic songbird of the genus *Cinclus* and family *Cinclidae,* esp. *C. cinclus.* They inhabit fast-flowing streams and resemble large wrens. **3** a person or thing that dips, such as the mechanism for directing car headlights downwards. **4** a small metal cup clipped onto a painter's palette for holding diluent or medium. **5** *Archaic.* an Anabaptist. ◆ See also **big dipper.**

dippy (ˈdɪpɪ) *adj* **-pier, -piest.** *Slang.* odd, eccentric, or crazy. [C20: of unknown origin]

dipropellant (ˌdaɪprəˈpɛlənt) *n* another name for **bipropellant.**

diprotodont (daɪˈprəʊtəʊˌdɒnt) *n* any marsupial of the group or suborder *Diprotodontia,* including kangaroos, phalangers, and wombats, having fewer than three upper incisor teeth on each side of the jaw. Compare **polyprotodont.** [C19: from Greek from DI-[1] + PROTO- + -ODONT]

dip-slip fault *n Geology.* a fault on which the movement is along the dip of the fault.

dipsomania (ˌdɪpsəʊˈmeɪnɪə) *n* a compulsive desire to drink alcoholic beverages. [C19: New Latin, from Greek *dipsa* thirst + -MANIA]

dipsomaniac (ˌdɪpsəʊˈmeɪnɪˌæk) *n* **1** any person who has an uncontrollable and recurring urge to drink alcohol. Shortened form: **dipso.** ◆ *adj* **2** relating to or affected with dipsomania. ▸ **dipsomaniacal** (ˌdɪpsəʊməˈnaɪəkᵊl) *adj*

dipstick (ˈdɪpˌstɪk) *n* a graduated rod or strip dipped into a container to indicate the fluid level.

dip switch *n* a device for dipping car headlights.

dipteral (ˈdɪptərəl) *adj Architect.* having a double row of columns.

dipteran (ˈdɪptərən) *or* **dipteron** (ˈdɪptəˌrɒn) *n* **1** any dipterous insect. ◆ *adj* **2** another word for **dipterous** (sense 1).

dipterocarpaceous (ˌdɪptərəʊkɑːˈpeɪʃəs) *adj* of, relating to, or belonging to the *Dipterocarpaceae,* a family of trees chiefly native to Malaysia, having two-winged fruits. Many species yield useful timber and resins. [C19: via New Latin from Greek *dipteros* two-winged + *karpos* fruit]

dipterous (ˈdɪptərəs) *adj* **1** Also: **dipteran.** of, relating to, or belonging to the *Diptera,* a large order of insects having a single pair of wings and sucking or piercing mouthparts. The group includes flies, mosquitoes, craneflies, and midges. **2** *Botany.* having two winglike parts: *a dipterous seed.* [C18: from New Latin, from Greek *dipteros,* from *di-* two + *pteros* wing]

diptych (ˈdɪptɪk) *n* **1** a pair of hinged wooden tablets with waxed surfaces for writing. **2** a painting or carving on two panels, usually hinged like a book. [C17: from Greek *diptukhos* folded together, from DI-[1] + *ptukhos* fold; compare TRIPTYCH]

dir. *abbrev. for* director.

Dirac (dɪˈræk) *n* **Paul Adrien Maurice.** 1902–84, English physicist, noted for his work on the application of relativity to quantum mechanics and his prediction of electron spin and the positron: shared the Nobel prize for physics 1933.

Dirac constant *n* a constant used in quantum mechanics equal to the Planck constant divided by 2π. It has a value of $1.0544 \pm 0.0003 \times 10^{-34}$ joule seconds. Symbol: $\hbar$ or $\underline{h}$ Also called: **crossed-h, h-bar.**

dire (daɪə) *adj* (*usually prenominal*) **1** Also: **direful.** disastrous; fearful. **2** desperate; urgent: *a dire need.* **3** foreboding disaster; ominous: *a dire warning.* [C16: from Latin *dīrus* ominous, fearful; related to Greek *deos* fear] ▸ ˈ**direly** *adv* ▸ ˈ**direness** *n*

direct (dɪˈrɛkt, daɪ-) *vb* (*mainly tr*) **1** to regulate, conduct, or control the affairs of. **2** (*also intr*) to give commands or orders with authority to (a person or group): *he directed them to go away.* **3** to tell or show (someone) the way to a place. **4** to aim, point, or cause to move towards a goal. **5** to address (a letter, parcel, etc.). **6** to address (remarks, words, etc.): *to direct comments at someone.* **7** (*also intr*) to provide guidance to (actors, cameramen, etc.) in the rehearsal of a play or the filming of a motion picture. **8** (*also intr*) **8a** to conduct (a piece of music or musicians), usually while performing oneself. **8b** another word (esp. U.S.) for **conduct** (sense 9). ◆ *adj* **9** without delay or evasion; straightforward: *a direct approach.* **10** without turning aside; uninterrupted; shortest; straight: *a direct route.* **11** without intervening persons or agencies; immediate: *a direct link.* **12** honest; frank; candid: *a direct answer.* **13** (*usually prenominal*) precise; exact: *a direct quotation.* **14** diametrical: *the direct opposite.* **15** in an unbroken line of descent, as from father to son over succeeding generations: *a direct descendant.* **16** (of government, decisions, etc.) by or from the electorate rather than through representatives. **17** *Logic, maths.* (of a proof) progressing from the premises to the conclusion, rather than eliminating the possibility of the falsehood of the conclusion. Compare **indirect proof. 18** *Astronomy.* moving from west to east on the celestial sphere. Compare **retrograde** (sense 4a). **19a** of or relating to direct current. **19b** (of a secondary induced current) having the same direction as the primary current. **20** *Music.* **20a** (of motion) in the same direction. See **motion** (sense 9). **20b** (of an interval or chord) in root position; not inverted. ◆ *adv* **21** directly; straight: *he went direct to the office.* [C14: from Latin *dīrectus;* from *dīrigere* to guide, from *dis-* apart + *regere* to rule] ▸ **diˈrectness** *n*

direct access *n* a method of reading data from a computer file without reading through the file from the beginning as on a disk or drum. Also called: **random access.** Compare **sequential access.**

direct action *n* action such as strikes or civil disobedience, employed by organized labour or other groups to obtain demands from an employer, government, etc.

direct coupling *n Electronics.* conductive coupling between electronic circuits, as opposed to inductive or capacitative coupling. See also **coupling** (sense 4). ▸ **direct coupled** *adj*

direct current *n* a continuous electric current that flows in one direction only, without substantial variation in magnitude. Abbrev.: **DC.** Compare **alternating current.**

direct debit *n* an order given to a bank or building society by a holder of an account, instructing it to pay to a specified person or organization any sum demanded by that person or organization. Compare **standing order.**

direct distance dialing *n* the U.S. and Canadian equivalent of **subscriber trunk dialling.**

direct dye *n* any of a number of dyes that can be applied without the use of a mordant. They are usually azo dyes applied to cotton or rayon from a liquid bath containing an electrolyte such as sodium sulphate.

directed (dɪˈrɛktɪd, daɪ-) *adj Maths.* (of a number, line, or angle) having either a positive or negative sign to distinguish measurement in one direction or orientation from that in the opposite direction or orientation.

direct evidence *n Law.* evidence, usually the testimony of a witness, directly relating to the fact in dispute. Compare **circumstantial evidence.**

direct-grant school *n* (in Britain, formerly) a school financed by endowment, fees, and a state grant conditional upon admittance of a percentage of nonpaying pupils nominated by the local education authority.

direct injection *n* See **solid injection.**

direct input *n* a device, such as a keyboard, used to insert data directly into a computerized system.

direction (dɪˈrɛkʃən, daɪ-) *n* **1** the act of directing or the state of being directed. **2** management, control, or guidance. **3** the work of a stage or film director. **4** the course or line along which a person or thing moves, points, or lies. **5** the course along which a ship, aircraft, etc., is travelling, expressed as the angle between true or magnetic north and an imaginary line through the main fore-and-aft axis of the vessel. **6** the place towards which a person or thing is directed. **7** a line of action; course. **8** the name and address on a letter, parcel, etc. **9** *Music.* the process of conducting an orchestra, choir, etc. **10** *Music.* an instruction in the form of a word or symbol heading or occurring in the body of a passage, movement, or piece to indicate tempo, dynamics, mood, etc. **11** (*modifier*) *Maths.* **11a** (of an angle) being any one of the three angles that a line in space makes with the three positive directions of the coordinate axes. Usually given as α, β, and γ with respect to the *x-, y-,* and *z-* axes. **11b** (of a cosine) being the cosine of any of the direction angles. ◆ See also **directions.**

directional (dɪˈrɛkʃən^{ə}l, daɪ-) *adj* **1** of or relating to a spatial direction. **2** *Electronics.* **2a** having or relating to an increased sensitivity to radio waves, sound waves, nuclear particles, etc., coming from a particular direction. **2b** (of an aerial) transmitting or receiving radio waves more effectively in some directions than in others. **3** *Physics, electronics.* **3a** concentrated in, following, or producing motion in a particular direction. **3b** indicating direction. ▸ **diˌrectionˈality** *n*

directional drilling *n* a method of drilling for oil in which the well is not drilled vertically, as when a number of wells are to be drilled from a single platform to reach different areas of an oil field. Also called: **deviated drilling.**

direction finder *n* a highly directional aerial system that can be used to determine the direction of incoming radio signals, used esp. as a navigation aid. Abbrevs.: **D/F** or **DF** ▸ **direction finding** *n*

directions (dɪˈrɛkʃənz, daɪ-) *pl n* (*sometimes sing*) instructions for doing something or for reaching a place.

directive (dɪˈrɛktɪv, daɪ-) *n* **1** an instruction; order. ◆ *adj* **2** tending to direct; directing. **3** indicating direction.

direct labour *n Commerce.* **1** work that is an essential part of a production process or the provision of a service. Compare **indirect labour. 2** *Brit.* workers who are part of an employer's own labour force rather than hired through a contractor, such as building workers employed by a local authority.

direct lighting *n Electrical engineering.* a lighting system in which a large proportion (at least 90 per cent) of the light is directed downwards.

directly (dɪˈrɛktlɪ, daɪ-) *adv* **1** in a direct manner. **2** at once; without delay. **3** (foll. by *before* or *after*) immediately; just. ◆ *conj* **4** (*subordinating*) as soon as: *we left directly the money arrived.*

direct-mail shot *n Marketing.* the posting of unsolicited sales literature to potential customers' homes or business addresses.

direct marketing *n* selling goods directly to consumers rather than through retailers, usually by mail order, direct-mail shot, newspaper advertising, door-to-door selling, or telephone selling. Also called: **direct selling.**

direct memory access *n* a process in which data may be moved directly to or from the main memory of a computer system by operations not under the control of the central processing unit. Abbrev.: **DMA.**

direct method *n* a method of teaching a foreign language with minimal use of the pupil's native language and of formal grammar.

direct object *n Grammar.* a noun, pronoun, or noun phrase whose referent receives the direct action of a verb. For example, *a book* is the direct object in the sentence *They bought Anne a book.* Compare **indirect object.**

Directoire *French.* (dirɛktwar) *n* **1** *History.* the French Directory. See **Directory.** ◆ *adj* **2** of, in, or relating to a decorative style of the end of the 18th century in France; a form of neoclassicism. **3** characteristic of women's dress during the French Directory, typically an almost transparent dress with the waistline under the bust.

director (dɪˈrɛktə, daɪ-) *n* **1** a person or thing that directs, controls, or regulates. **2** a member of the governing board of a business concern who may or may not have an executive function. **3** a person who directs the affairs of an institution, trust, educational programme, etc. **4** the person responsible for the artistic and technical aspects of making a film or television programme. Compare **producer** (sense 4). **5** *Music.* another word (esp. U.S.) for **conductor** (sense 2). ▸ **ˌdirecˈtorial** *adj* ▸ **ˌdirecˈtorially** *adv* ▸ **diˈrectorˌship** *n* ▸ **diˈrectress** *fem n*

directorate (dɪˈrɛktərɪt, daɪ-) *n* **1** a board of directors. **2** Also: **diˈrectorˌship.** the position of director.

director-general *n, pl* **directors-general.** the head of a large organization such as the CBI or BBC.

Director of Education *n Brit.* another term for **Chief Education Officer.**

Director of Public Prosecutions *n* (in Britain) an official who, as head of the Crown Prosecution Service, is responsible for conducting all criminal prosecutions initiated by the police. Abbrev.: **DPP.**

director's chair *n* a light wooden folding chair with arm rests and a canvas seat and back.

director's cut *n Films.* a version of a film which realizes the artistic aims of the director more fully than the original version.

directory (dɪˈrɛktərɪ, -trɪ; daɪ-) *n, pl* **-ries. 1** a book, arranged alphabetically or classified by trade listing names, addresses, telephone numbers, etc., of individuals or firms. **2** a book or manual giving directions. **3** a book containing the rules to be observed in the forms of worship used in churches. **4** a less common word for **directorate** (sense 2). **5** *Computing.* an area of a disk, Winchester disk, or floppy disk that contains the names and locations of files currently held on that disk. ◆ *adj* **6** directing.

Directory (dɪˈrɛktərɪ, -trɪ; daɪ-) *n* **the.** *History.* the body of five directors in power in France from 1795 until their overthrow by Napoleon in 1799. Also called: **French Directory.**

direct primary *n U.S. government.* a primary in which voters directly select the candidates who will run for office.

direct question *n* a question asked in direct speech, such as *Why did you come?* Compare **indirect question.**

direct-reading *adj* (of an instrument) calibrated so that a given quantity to be measured can be read directly off the scale without the need of a multiplying constant.

directrix (dɪˈrɛktrɪks, daɪ-) *n* **1** *Geometry.* a fixed reference line, situated on the convex side of a conic section, that is used when defining or calculating its eccentricity. **2** a directress. [C17: New Latin, feminine of DIRECTOR]

direct selling *n* another name for **direct marketing.**

direct speech *or esp. U.S.* **direct discourse** *n* the reporting of what someone has said or written by quoting his exact words.

direct tax *n* a tax paid by the person or organization on which it is levied. Compare **indirect tax.** ▸ **direct taxˈation** *n*

dirge (dɜːdʒ) *n* **1** a chant of lamentation for the dead. **2** the funeral service in its solemn or sung forms. **3** any mourning song or melody. [C13: changed from Latin *dīrigē* direct (imperative), opening word of the Latin antiphon used in the office of the dead] ▸ **ˈdirgeful** *adj*

dirham (ˈdɪəræm) *n* **1** the standard monetary unit of Morocco, divided into 100 centimes. **2** the standard monetary unit of the United Arab Emirates, divided into 10 dinars and 100 fils. **3a** a Kuwaiti monetary unit worth one tenth of a dinar and 100 fils. **3b** a Tunisian monetary unit worth one tenth of a dinar and 100 millimes. **3c** a Qatari monetary unit worth one hundredth of a riyal. **3d** a Libyan monetary unit worth one thousandth of a dinar. **4** any of various silver coins minted in North African countries at different periods. [C18: from Arabic, from Latin: DRACHMA]

Dirichlet (*German* diriˈkleː) *n* **Peter Gustav Lejeune** (ˈpeːtər ˈgustaf ləˈʒœn). 1805–59, German mathematician, noted for his work on number theory and calculus.

dirigible (dɪˈrɪdʒɪb^{ə}l) *adj* **1** able to be steered or directed. ◆ *n* **2** another name for **airship.** [C16: from Latin *dīrigere* to DIRECT] ▸ **ˌdirigiˈbility** *n*

dirigisme (diːriːˈʒiːzəm) *n* control by the state of economic and social matters. [C20: from French] ▸ **dirigˈiste** *adj*

diriment (ˈdɪrɪmənt) *adj* **1** (of an impediment to marriage in canon law) totally invalidating. **2** *Rare.* nullifying. [C19: from Latin *dirimēns* separating, from Latin *dirimere* to part, from DIS-[1] + *emere* to obtain]

dirk (dɜːk) *n* **1** a dagger esp. as formerly worn by Scottish Highlanders. ◆ *vb* (*tr*) **2**

to stab with a dirk. [C16: from Scottish *durk*, perhaps from German *dolch* dagger]

dirndl ('dɜːndᵊl) *n* **1** a woman's dress with a full gathered skirt and fitted bodice; originating from Tyrolean peasant wear. **2** a gathered skirt of this kind. [German (Bavarian and Austrian): shortened from *Dirndlkleid*, from *Dirndl* little girl + *Kleid* dress]

dirt (dɜːt) *n* **1** any unclean substance, such as mud, dust, excrement, etc.; filth. **2** loose earth; soil. **3a** packed earth, gravel, cinders, etc., used to make a racetrack. **3b** (*as modifier*): *a dirt track*. **4** *Mining*. the gravel or soil from which minerals are extracted. **5** a person or thing regarded as worthless. **6** obscene or indecent speech or writing. **7** *Slang*. gossip; scandalous information. **8** moral corruption. **9 do (someone) dirt.** *Slang*. to do something vicious to (someone). **10 dish the dirt.** *Informal*. to spread malicious gossip. **11 eat dirt.** *Slang*. to accept insult without complaining. **12 treat someone like dirt.** to have no respect or consideration for someone. [C13: from Old Norse *drit* excrement; related to Middle Dutch *drēte*]

dirt-cheap *adj, adv Informal*. at an extremely low price.

dirt-poor *adj Chiefly U.S.* extremely poor.

dirt road *n* an unsealed country road.

dirty ('dɜːtɪ) *adj* **dirtier, dirtiest. 1** covered or marked with dirt; filthy. **2a** obscene; salacious: *dirty books*. **2b** sexually clandestine: *a dirty weekend*. **3** causing one to become grimy: *a dirty job*. **4** (of a colour) not clear and bright; impure. **5** unfair; dishonest; unscrupulous; unsporting. **6** mean; nasty: *a dirty cheat*. **7** scandalous; unkind: *a dirty rumour*. **8** revealing dislike or anger: *a dirty look*. **9** (of weather) rainy or squally; stormy. **10** (of an aircraft) having projections into the airstream, such as lowered flaps. **11** (of a nuclear weapon) producing a large quantity of radioactive fallout or contamination. Compare **clean** (sense 5). **12 be dirty on.** *Austral. slang*. to be offended by or be hostile towards. **13 dirty dog.** a despicable person. **14 dirty linen.** *Informal*. intimate secrets, esp. those that might give rise to gossip. **15 dirty word. 15a** an obscene word. **15b** something that is regarded with disapproval: *federalism is a dirty word*. **16 dirty work.** unpleasant or illicit activity. **17 do the dirty on.** *Brit. informal*. to behave meanly or unkindly towards. ◆ *vb* **dirties, dirtying, dirtied. 18** to make or become dirty; stain; soil. ► **'dirtily** *adv* ► **'dirtiness** *n*

dirty realism *n* a style of writing, originating in the U.S. in the 1980s, which depicts in great detail the seamier or more mundane aspects of ordinary life. ► **dirty realist** *n*

dirty trick *n* **1** a malicious and contemptible action. **2** (*pl*) **2a** underhand activity and machinations in political or governmental affairs. **2b** (*as modifier*): *dirty-tricks operation*.

dis (dɪs) *vb* a variant spelling of **diss**.

Dis (dɪs) *n* **1** Also called: **Orcus, Pluto.** the Roman god of the underworld. **2** the abode of the dead; underworld. ◆ Greek equivalent: **Hades.**

dis-[1] *prefix* **1** indicating reversal: *disconnect; disembark*. **2** indicating negation, lack, or deprivation: *dissimilar; distrust; disgrace*. **3** indicating removal or release: *disembowel; disburden*. **4** expressing intensive force: *dissever*. [from Latin *dis-* apart; in some cases, via Old French *des-*. In compound words of Latin origin, *dis-* becomes *dif-* before *f* and *di-* before some consonants]

dis-[2] *combining form*. variant of **di-**[1] before *s*: *dissyllable*.

disability (ˌdɪsə'bɪlɪtɪ) *n, pl* **-ties. 1** the condition of being unable to perform a task or function because of a physical or mental impairment. **2** something that disables; handicap. **3** lack of necessary intelligence, strength, etc. **4** an incapacity in the eyes of the law to enter into certain transactions.

disability clause *n* (in life assurance policies) a clause enabling a policyholder to cease payment of premiums without loss of coverage and often to receive a pension or indemnity if he becomes permanently disabled.

disable (dɪs'eɪbᵊl) *vb* (*tr*) **1** to make ineffective, unfit, or incapable, as by crippling. **2** to make or pronounce legally incapable. **3** to switch off (an electronic device). ► **dis'ablement** *n*

disabled (dɪ'seɪbᵊld) *adj* **a** lacking one or more physical powers, such as the ability to walk or to coordinate one's movements, as from the effects of a disease or accident, or through mental impairment. **b** (*as collective n; preceded by the*): *the disabled*. See usage note below.

USAGE The use of *the disabled, the blind*, etc. can be offensive and should be avoided. Instead one should talk about *disabled people, blind people*, etc.

disablement benefit *n* (in the National Insurance scheme) a weekly payment to a person disabled at work.

disabuse (ˌdɪsə'bjuːz) *vb* (*tr; usually foll. by of*) to rid (oneself, another person, etc.) of a mistaken or misguided idea; set right. ► ˌ**disa'busal** *n*

disaccharide (daɪ'sækəˌraɪd, -rɪd) *or* **disaccharid** *n* any of a class of sugars, such as maltose, lactose, and sucrose, having two linked monosaccharide units per molecule.

disaccord (ˌdɪsə'kɔːd) *n* **1** lack of agreement or harmony. ◆ *vb* **2** (*intr*) to be out of agreement; disagree.

disaccredit (ˌdɪsə'kredɪt) *vb* (*tr*) to take away the authorization or credentials of.

disaccustom (ˌdɪsə'kʌstəm) *vb* (*tr; usually foll. by to*) to cause to lose a habit.

disadvantage (ˌdɪsəd'vɑːntɪdʒ) *n* **1** an unfavourable circumstance, state of affairs, thing, person, etc. **2** injury, loss, or detriment. **3** an unfavourable condition or situation (esp. in the phrase **at a disadvantage**). ◆ *vb* **4** (*tr*) to put at a disadvantage; handicap.

disadvantaged (ˌdɪsəd'vɑːntɪdʒd) *adj* socially or economically deprived or discriminated against.

disadvantageous (dɪsˌædvən'teɪdʒəs, ˌdɪsæd-) *adj* unfavourable; detrimental. ► **disˌadvan'tageously** *adv* ► **disˌadvan'tageousness** *n*

disaffect (ˌdɪsə'fekt) *vb* (*tr; often passive*) to cause to lose loyalty or affection; alienate. ► ˌ**disaf'fectedly** *adv* ► ˌ**disaf'fectedness** *n* ► ˌ**disaf'fection** *n*

disaffiliate (ˌdɪsə'fɪlɪˌeɪt) *vb* to sever an affiliation (with); dissociate. ► ˌ**disafˌfili'ation** *n*

disaffirm (ˌdɪsə'fɜːm) *vb* (*tr*) **1** to deny or contradict (a statement). **2** *Law*. **2a** to annul or reverse (a decision). **2b** to repudiate obligations. ► ˌ**disaf'firmance** *or* **disaffirmation** (ˌdɪsæfə'meɪʃən) *n*

disafforest (ˌdɪsə'fɒrɪst) *vb* (*tr*) **1** *English law*. to reduce (land) from the status of a forest to the state of ordinary ground. **2** to remove forests from (land). ► ˌ**disafˌfores'tation** *or* ˌ**disaf'forestment** *n*

disagree (ˌdɪsə'griː) *vb* **-grees, -greeing, -greed.** (*intr*; often foll. by *with*) **1** to dissent in opinion (from another person) or dispute (about an idea, fact, etc.). **2** to fail to correspond; conflict. **3** to be unacceptable (to) or unfavourable (for); be incompatible (with): *curry disagrees with me*. **4** to be opposed (to) in principle.

disagreeable (ˌdɪsə'grɪəbᵊl) *adj* **1** not likable, esp. bad-tempered, offensive, or disobliging: *disagreeable remarks*. **2** not to one's liking; unpleasant: *a disagreeable task*. ► ˌ**disa'greeableness** *or* ˌ**disaˌgreea'bility** *n* ► ˌ**disa'greeably** *adv*

disagreement (ˌdɪsə'griːmənt) *n* **1** refusal or failure to agree. **2** a failure to correspond. **3** an argument or dispute.

disallow (ˌdɪsə'laʊ) *vb* (*tr*) **1** to reject as untrue or invalid. **2** to cancel. ► ˌ**dis-al'lowable** *adj* ► ˌ**disal'lowance** *n*

disambiguate (ˌdɪsæm'bɪgjʊˌeɪt) *vb* (*tr*) to make (an ambiguous expression) unambiguous. ► ˌ**disamˌbigu'ation** *n*

disannul (ˌdɪsə'nʌl) *vb* **-nuls, -nulling, -nulled.** (*tr*) *Chiefly law*. to cancel; make void. ► ˌ**disan'nulment** *n*

disappear (ˌdɪsə'pɪə) *vb* **1** (*intr*) to cease to be visible; vanish. **2** (*intr*) to go away or become lost, esp. secretly or without explanation. **3** (*intr*) to cease to exist, have effect, or be known; become extinct or lost: *the pain has disappeared*. **4** (*tr*) (esp. in South and Central America) to arrest secretly and presumably imprison or kill (a member of an opposing political group). ► ˌ**disap'pearance** *n*

disapplication (ˌdɪsæplɪ'keɪʃən) *n Brit. Education*. a provision for exempting schools or individuals from the requirements of the National Curriculum in special circumstances.

disappoint (ˌdɪsə'pɔɪnt) *vb* (*tr*) **1** to fail to meet the expectations, hopes, desires, or standards of; let down. **2** to prevent the fulfilment of (a plan, intention, etc.); frustrate; thwart. [C15 (originally meaning: to remove from office): from Old French *desapointier*; see DIS-[1], APPOINT] ► ˌ**disap'pointing** *adj* ► ˌ**disap'pointingly** *adv*

disappointed (ˌdɪsə'pɔɪntɪd) *adj* saddened by the failure of an expectation, etc. ► ˌ**disap'pointedly** *adv*

disappointment (ˌdɪsə'pɔɪntmənt) *n* **1** the act of disappointing or the state of being disappointed. **2** a person, thing, or state of affairs that disappoints.

disapprobation (ˌdɪsæprəʊ'beɪʃən) *n* moral or social disapproval.

disapproval (ˌdɪsə'pruːvᵊl) *n* the act or a state or feeling of disapproving; censure; condemnation.

disapprove (ˌdɪsə'pruːv) *vb* **1** (*intr*; often foll. by *of*) to consider wrong, bad, etc. **2** (*tr*) to withhold approval from. ► ˌ**disap'proving** *adj* ► ˌ**disap'provingly** *adv*

disarm (dɪs'ɑːm) *vb* **1** (*tr*) to remove defensive or offensive capability from (a country, army, etc.). **2** (*tr*) to deprive of weapons. **3** (*tr*) to win the confidence or affection of. **4** (*intr*) (of a nation, etc.) to decrease the size and capability of one's armed forces. **5** (*intr*) to lay down weapons. ► **dis'armer** *n*

disarmament (dɪs'ɑːməmənt) *n* **1** the reduction of offensive or defensive fighting capability, as by a nation. **2** the act of disarming or state of being disarmed.

disarming (dɪs'ɑːmɪŋ) *adj* tending to neutralize or counteract hostility, suspicion, etc. ► **dis'armingly** *adv*

disarrange (ˌdɪsə'reɪndʒ) *vb* (*tr*) to throw into disorder. ► ˌ**disar'rangement** *n*

disarray (ˌdɪsə'reɪ) *n* **1** confusion, dismay, and lack of discipline. **2** (esp. of clothing) disorderliness; untidiness. ◆ *vb* (*tr*) **3** to throw into confusion. **4** *Archaic*. to undress.

disarticulate (ˌdɪsɑː'tɪkjʊˌleɪt) *vb* to separate or cause to separate at the joints, esp. those of bones. ► ˌ**disarˌticu'lation** *n* ► ˌ**disar'ticuˌlator** *n*

disassemble (ˌdɪsə'sembᵊl) *vb* (*tr*) to take apart (a piece of machinery, etc.); dismantle. ► ˌ**disas'sembly** *n*

disassembler (ˌdɪsə'semblə) *n Computing*. a computer program that translates machine code into assembly language.

disassociate (ˌdɪsə'səʊʃɪˌeɪt) *vb* a less common word for **dissociate.** ► ˌ**dis-asˌsoci'ation** *n*

disaster (dɪ'zɑːstə) *n* **1** an occurrence that causes great distress or destruction. **2** a thing, project, etc., that fails or has been ruined. [C16 (originally in the sense: malevolent astral influence): from Italian *disastro*, from *dis-* (pejorative) + *astro* star, from Latin *astrum*, from Greek *astron*] ► **dis'astrous** *adj*

disavow (ˌdɪsə'vaʊ) *vb* (*tr*) to deny knowledge of, connection with, or responsibility for. ► ˌ**disa'vowal** *n* ► ˌ**disa'vowedly** *adv* ► ˌ**disa'vower** *n*

disband (dɪs'bænd) *vb* to cease to function or cause to stop functioning, as a unit, group, etc. ► **dis'bandment** *n*

disbar (dɪs'bɑː) *vb* **-bars, -barring, -barred.** (*tr*) *Law*. to deprive of the status of barrister; expel from the Bar. ► **dis'barment** *n*

USAGE *Disbar* is sometimes wrongly used where *debar* is meant: *he was debarred* (not *disbarred*) *from attending meetings*.

disbelief (ˌdɪsbɪ'liːf) *n* refusal or reluctance to believe.

disbelieve (ˌdɪsbɪ'liːv) *vb* **1** (*tr*) to reject as false or lying; refuse to accept as true or truthful. **2** (*intr*; usually foll. by *in*) to have no faith (in): *disbelieve in God*. ► ˌ**disbe'liever** *n* ► ˌ**disbe'lieving** *adj* ► ˌ**disbe'lievingly** *adv*

disbranch (dɪsˈbrɑːntʃ) *vb (tr)* to remove or cut a branch or branches from (a tree).
disbud (dɪsˈbʌd) *or* **debud** (diːˈbʌd) *vb* **-buds, -budding, -budded. 1** to remove superfluous buds, flowers, or shoots from (a plant, esp. a fruit tree). **2** *Vet. science.* to remove the horn buds of (calves, lambs, and kids).
disburden (dɪsˈbɜːdᵊn) *vb* **1** to remove a load from (a person or animal). **2** *(tr)* to relieve (oneself, one's mind, etc.) of a distressing worry or oppressive thought. ▸ **disˈburdenment** *n*
disburse (dɪsˈbɜːs) *vb (tr)* to pay out. [C16: from Old French *desborser,* from *des-* DIS-[1] + *borser* to obtain money, from *borse* bag, from Late Latin *bursa*] ▸ **disˈbursable** *adj* ▸ **disˈbursement** *n* ▸ **disˈburser** *n*
USAGE *Disburse* is sometimes wrongly used where *disperse* is meant: *the police used a water cannon to disperse* (not *disburse*) *the crowd.*
disc *or (now esp. U.S.)* **disk** (dɪsk) *n* **1** a flat circular plate. **2** something resembling or appearing to resemble this: *the sun's disc.* **3** another word for (gramophone) **record. 4** *Anatomy.* any approximately circular flat structure in the body, esp. an intervertebral disc. **5a** the flat receptacle of composite flowers, such as the daisy. **5b** *(as modifier): a disc flower.* **6** the middle part of the lip of an orchid. **7a** Also called: **parking disc.** a marker or device for display in a parked vehicle showing the time of arrival or the latest permitted time of departure or both. **7b** *(as modifier): a disc zone; disc parking.* **8** *Computing.* a variant spelling of **disk** (sense 2). ♦ *vb* **9** to work (land) with a disc harrow. [C18: from Latin *discus,* from Greek *diskos* quoit]
disc. *abbrev. for:* **1** discount. **2** discovered.
discal (ˈdɪskᵊl) *adj Biology, zoology.* relating to or resembling a disc; disclike: *discal cells.*
discalced (dɪsˈkælst) *adj* barefooted: used to denote friars and nuns who wear sandals. [C17: from Latin *discalceātus,* from DIS-[1] + *calceātus* shod, from *calceāre* to provide with shoes, from *calceus* shoe, from *calx* heel]
discant *n* (ˈdɪskænt), *vb* (dɪsˈkænt). a variant of **descant** (senses 1, 3, 4). ▸ **disˈcanter** *n*
discard *vb* (dɪsˈkɑːd). **1** *(tr)* to get rid of as useless or undesirable. **2** *Cards.* to throw out (a card or cards) from one's hand. **3** *Cards.* to play (a card not of the suit led nor a trump) when unable to follow suit. ♦ *n* (ˈdɪskɑːd). **4** a person or thing that has been cast aside. **5** *Cards.* a discarded card. **6** the act of discarding. ▸ **disˈcarder** *n*
disc brake *n* a type of brake in which two calliper-operated pads rub against a flat disc attached to the wheel hub when the brake is applied.
discern (dɪˈsɜːn) *vb* **1** *(tr)* to recognize or perceive clearly. **2** to recognize or perceive (differences). [C14: from Old French *discerner,* from Latin *discernere* to divide, from DIS-[1] (apart) + *cernere* to separate] ▸ **disˈcerner** *n*
discernible *or (rarely)* **discernable** (dɪˈsɜːnəbᵊl) *adj* able to be discerned; perceptible. ▸ **disˈcernibly** *or (rarely)* **disˈcernably** *adv*
discerning (dɪˈsɜːnɪŋ) *adj* having or showing good taste or judgment; discriminating. ▸ **disˈcerningly** *adv*
discernment (dɪˈsɜːnmənt) *n* keen perception or judgment.
disc flower *or* **floret** *n* any of the small tubular flowers at the centre of the flower head of certain composite plants, such as the daisy. Compare **ray flower.**
discharge *vb* (dɪsˈtʃɑːdʒ). **1** *(tr)* to release or allow to go: *the hospital discharged the patient.* **2** *(tr)* to dismiss from or relieve of duty, office, employment, etc. **3** to fire or be fired, as a gun. **4** to pour forth or cause to pour forth: *the boil discharges pus.* **5** *(tr)* to remove (the cargo) from (a boat, etc.); unload. **6** *(tr)* to perform (the duties of) or meet (the demands of an office, obligation, etc.): *he discharged his responsibilities as mayor.* **7** *(tr)* to relieve oneself of (a responsibility, debt, etc.). **8** *(intr) Physics.* **8a** to lose or remove electric charge. **8b** to form an arc, spark, or corona in a gas. **8c** to take or supply electrical current from a cell or battery. **9** *(tr) Law.* to release (a prisoner from custody, etc.). **10** *(tr)* to remove dye from (a fabric), as by bleaching. **11** *(intr)* (of a dye or colour) to blur or run. **12** *(tr) Architect.* **12a** to spread (weight) evenly over a supporting member. **12b** to relieve a member of (excess weight) by distribution of pressure. ♦ *n* (ˈdɪstʃɑːdʒ, dɪsˈtʃɑːdʒ). **13** a person or thing that is discharged. **14a** dismissal or release from an office, job, institution, etc. **14b** the document certifying such release. **15** the fulfilment of an obligation or release from a responsibility or liability. **16** the act of removing a load, as of cargo. **17** a pouring forth of a fluid; emission. **18a** the act of firing a projectile. **18b** the volley, bullet, missile, etc., fired. **19** *Law.* **19a** a release, as of a person held under legal restraint. **19b** an annulment, as of a court order. **20** *Physics.* **20a** the act or process of removing or losing charge or of equalizing a potential difference. **20b** a transient or continuous conduction of electricity through a gas by the formation and movement of electrons and ions in an applied electric field. ▸ **disˈchargeable** *adj* ▸ **disˈcharger** *n*
discharge tube *n Electronics.* an electrical device in which current flow is by electrons and ions in an ionized gas, as in a fluorescent light or neon tube.
disc harrow *n* a harrow with sharp-edged slightly concave discs mounted on horizontal shafts and used to cut clods or debris on the surface of the soil or to cover seed after planting.
disciple (dɪˈsaɪpᵊl) *n* **1** a follower of the doctrines of a teacher or a school of thought. **2** one of the personal followers of Christ (including his 12 apostles) during his earthly life. [Old English *discipul,* from Latin *discipulus* pupil, from *discere* to learn] ▸ **disˈcipleˌship** *n* ▸ **discipular** (dɪˈsɪpjʊlə) *adj*
Disciples of Christ *pl n* a Christian denomination founded in the U.S. in 1809 by Thomas and Alexander Campbell.
disciplinant (ˈdɪsɪˌplɪnənt) *n (often cap.) R.C. Church.* a person belonging to a former order of flagellants in Spain.
disciplinarian (ˌdɪsɪplɪˈnɛərɪən) *n* **1** a person who imposes or advocates discipline. ♦ *adj* **2** a less common word for **disciplinary.**
disciplinary (ˈdɪsɪˌplɪnərɪ) *or* **disciplinarian** *adj* **1** of, promoting, or used for discipline; corrective. **2** relating to a branch of learning: *criticism that crosses disciplinary boundaries.*
discipline (ˈdɪsɪplɪn) *n* **1** training or conditions imposed for the improvement of physical powers, self-control, etc. **2** systematic training in obedience to regulations and authority. **3** the state of improved behaviour, etc., resulting from such training or conditions. **4** punishment or chastisement. **5** a system of rules for behaviour, methods of practice, etc. **6** a branch of learning or instruction. **7** the laws governing members of a Church. **8** a scourge of knotted cords. ♦ *vb (tr)* **9** to improve or attempt to improve the behaviour, orderliness, etc., of by training, conditions, or rules. **10** to punish or correct. [C13: from Latin *disciplīna* teaching, from *discipulus* DISCIPLE] ▸ **ˈdisciˌplinable** *adj* ▸ **disciplinal** (ˌdɪsɪˈplaɪnᵊl, ˈdɪsɪplɪnᵊl) *adj* ▸ **ˈdisciˌpliner** *n*
discission (dɪˈsɪʒən) *n Med.* surgical incision, esp. of a cataract.
disc jockey *n* a person who announces and plays recorded music, esp. pop music, on a radio programme, etc. Abbrevs.: **DJ, dj.**
disclaim (dɪsˈkleɪm) *vb* **1** *(tr)* to deny or renounce (any claim, connection, etc.). **2** *(tr)* to deny the validity or authority of. **3** *Law.* to renounce or repudiate (a legal claim or right). ▸ **disclamation** (ˌdɪskləˈmeɪʃən) *n*
disclaimer (dɪsˈkleɪmə) *n* a repudiation or denial.
disclimax (dɪsˈklaɪmæks) *n Ecology.* a climax community resulting from the activities of man or domestic animals in climatic and other conditions that would otherwise support a different type of community.
disclose (dɪsˈkləʊz) *vb (tr)* **1** to make (information) known. **2** to allow to be seen; lay bare. ▸ **disˈcloser** *n*
disclosing agent *n Dentistry.* a vegetable dye, administered as a liquid or in tablet form (**disclosing tablet**), that stains plaque, making it readily apparent on the teeth.
disclosure (dɪsˈkləʊʒə) *n* **1** something that is disclosed. **2** the act of disclosing; revelation.
disco (ˈdɪskəʊ) *n, pl* **-cos. 1a** an occasion at which typically young people dance to amplified pop records, usually compered by a disc jockey and featuring special lighting effects. **1b** *(as modifier): disco dancing.* **2** a nightclub or other public place where such dances take place. **3** mobile equipment, usually accompanied by a disc jockey who operates it, for providing music for a disco. **4a** a type of dance music designed to be played in discos, with a solid thump on each beat. **4b** *(as modifier): a disco record.* [C20: shortened from DISCOTHEQUE]
discobolus *or* **discobolos** (dɪsˈkɒbələs) *n, pl* **-li** (-ˌlaɪ). **1** (in classical Greece) a discus thrower. **2** a statue of a discus thrower. [C18: from Latin, from Greek *diskobolos,* from *diskos* DISCUS + *-bolos,* from *ballein* to throw]
discography (dɪsˈkɒgrəfɪ) *n* **1** a classified reference list of gramophone records. **2** another word for **discology.** ▸ **disˈcographer** *n*
discoid (ˈdɪskɔɪd) *adj also* **discoidal** (**disɪsˈkɔɪdᵊl**). **1** like a disc. **2** (of a composite flower such as the tansy) consisting of disc flowers only. ♦ *n* **3** a disclike object.
discology (dɪsˈkɒlədʒɪ) *n* the study of gramophone records. ▸ **disˈcologist** *n*
discolour *or U.S.* **discolor** (dɪsˈkʌlə) *vb* to change or cause to change in colour; fade or stain. ▸ **disˌcolorˈation** *or* **disˌcolourˈation** *n* ▸ **disˈcolourment** *or U.S.* **disˈcolorment** *n*
discombobulate (ˌdɪskəmˈbɒbjʊˌleɪt) *vb (tr) Informal, chiefly U.S. and Canadian.* to throw into confusion. [C20: probably a whimsical alteration of DISCOMPOSE or DISCOMFIT]
discomfit (dɪsˈkʌmfɪt) *vb (tr)* **1** to make uneasy, confused, or embarrassed. **2** to frustrate the plans or purpose of. **3** *Archaic.* to defeat in battle. [C14: from Old French *desconfire* to destroy, from *des-* (indicating reversal) + *confire* to make, from Latin *conficere* to produce; see CONFECT] ▸ **disˈcomfiter** *n* ▸ **disˈcomfiture** *n*
discomfort (dɪsˈkʌmfət) *n* **1** an inconvenience, distress, or mild pain. **2** something that disturbs or deprives of ease. ♦ *vb* **3** *(tr)* to make uncomfortable or uneasy.
discomfortable (dɪsˈkʌmfətəbᵊl, -ˈkʌmftə-) *adj Archaic.* tending to deprive of mental or physical ease or comfort.
discommend (ˌdɪskəˈmɛnd) *vb (tr)* **1** *Rare.* to express disapproval of. **2** *Obsolete.* to bring into disfavour. ▸ **ˌdiscomˈmendable** *adj* ▸ **disˌcommenˈdation** *n*
discommode (ˌdɪskəˈməʊd) *vb (tr)* to cause inconvenience or annoyance to; disturb. ▸ **ˌdiscomˈmodious** *adj* ▸ **ˌdiscomˈmodiously** *adv*
discommodity (ˌdɪskəˈmɒdɪtɪ) *n, pl* **-ties. 1** *Economics.* a commodity without utility. **2** *Archaic.* the state or a source of inconvenience.
discommon (dɪsˈkɒmən) *vb (tr) Law.* to deprive (land) of the character and status of common, as by enclosure.
discompose (ˌdɪskəmˈpəʊz) *vb (tr)* **1** to disturb the composure of; disconcert. **2** *Now rare.* to disarrange. ▸ **ˌdiscomˈposedly** *adv* ▸ **ˌdiscomˈposingly** *adv* ▸ **ˌdiscomˈposure** *n*
disconcert (ˌdɪskənˈsɜːt) *vb (tr)* **1** to disturb the composure of. **2** to frustrate or upset. ▸ **ˌdisconˈcerting** *adj* ▸ **ˌdisconˈcertingly** *adv* ▸ **ˌdisconˈcertion** *or* **ˌdisconˈcertment** *n*
disconcerted (ˌdɪskənˈsɜːtɪd) *adj* perturbed, embarrassed, or confused. ▸ **ˌdisconˈcertedly** *adv* ▸ **ˌdisconˈcertedness** *n*
disconfirm (ˌdɪskənˈfɜːm) *vb (tr)* (of a fact or argument) to suggest that a hypothesis is wrong or ill-formulated. ▸ **ˌdisconfirˈmation** *n*
disconformity (ˌdɪskənˈfɔːmɪtɪ) *n, pl* **-ties. 1** lack of conformity; discrepancy. **2** the junction between two parallel series of stratified rocks, representing a considerable period of erosion of the much older underlying rocks before the more recent ones were deposited.
disconnect (ˌdɪskəˈnɛkt) *vb (tr)* to undo or break the connection of or between (something, such as a plug and a socket). ▸ **ˌdisconˈnecter** *n* ▸ **ˌdisconˈnection** *or* **ˌdisconˈnexion** *n* ▸ **ˌdisconˈnective** *adj*
disconnected (ˌdɪskəˈnɛktɪd) *adj* **1** not rationally connected; confused or in-

coherent. **2** not connected or joined. ▸ **ˌdisconˈnectedly** *adv* ▸ **ˌdisconˈnectedness** *n*

disconsolate (dɪsˈkɒnsəlɪt) *adj* **1** sad beyond comfort; inconsolable. **2** disappointed; dejected. [C14: from Medieval Latin *disconsōlātus*, from DIS-[1] + *consōlātus* comforted; see CONSOLE[1]] ▸ **disˈconsolately** *adv* ▸ **disˈconsolateness** *or* **disˌconsoˈlation** *n*

discontent (ˌdɪskənˈtɛnt) *n* **1** Also called: **ˌdisconˈtentment.** lack of contentment, as with one's condition or lot in life. **2** a discontented person. ◆ *adj* **3** dissatisfied. ◆ *vb* **4** (*tr*) to make dissatisfied. ▸ **ˌdisconˈtented** *adj* ▸ **ˌdisconˈtentedly** *adv* ▸ **ˌdisconˈtentedness** *n*

discontinue (ˌdɪskənˈtɪnjuː) *vb* **-ues, -uing, -ued. 1** to come or bring to an end; interrupt or be interrupted; stop. **2** (*tr*) *Law.* to terminate or abandon (an action, suit, etc.). ▸ **ˌdisconˈtinuance** *n* ▸ **ˌdisconˌtinuˈation** *n* ▸ **ˌdisconˈtinuer** *n*

discontinuity (dɪsˌkɒntɪˈnjuːɪtɪ) *n, pl* **-ties. 1** lack of rational connection or cohesion. **2** a break or interruption. **3** *Maths.* **3a** the property of being discontinuous. **3b** the point or the value of the variable at which a curve or function becomes discontinuous. **4** *Geology.* **4a** a zone within the earth where a sudden change in physical properties, such as the velocity of earthquake waves, occurs. Such a zone marks the boundary between the different layers of the earth, as between the core and mantle. See also **Mohorovičić discontinuity. 4b** a surface separating rocks that are not continuous with each other.

discontinuous (ˌdɪskənˈtɪnjʊəs) *adj* **1** characterized by interruptions or breaks; intermittent. **2** *Maths.* (of a function or curve) changing suddenly in value for one or more values of the variable or at one or more points. Compare **continuous** (sense 3). ▸ **ˌdisconˈtinuously** *adv* ▸ **ˌdisconˈtinuousness** *n*

discord *n* (ˈdɪskɔːd). **1** lack of agreement of harmony; strife. **2** harsh confused mingling of sounds. **3** a combination of musical notes containing one or more dissonant intervals. See **dissonance** (sense 3), **concord** (sense 4). ◆ *vb* (dɪsˈkɔːd). **4** (*intr*) to disagree; clash. [C13: from Old French *descort*, from *descorder* to disagree, from Latin *discordāre*, from *discors* at variance, from DIS-[1] + *cor* heart]

discordance (dɪsˈkɔːdᵊns) *or* **discordancy** *n* **1** *Geology.* an arrangement of rock strata in which the older underlying ones dip at a different angle from the younger overlying ones; unconformity. **2** lack of agreement or consonance. **3** variants of **discord.**

discordant (dɪsˈkɔːdᵊnt) *adj* **1** at variance; disagreeing. **2** harsh in sound; inharmonious. ▸ **disˈcordantly** *adv*

discotheque (ˈdɪskəˌtɛk) *n* the full name of **disco.** [C20: from French *discothèque*, from Greek *diskos* disc + -o- + Greek *thēkē* case]

discount *vb* (dɪsˈkaʊnt, ˈdɪskaʊnt). (*mainly tr*) **1** to leave out of account as being unreliable, prejudiced, or irrelevant. **2** to anticipate and make allowance for, often so as to diminish the effect of. **3a** to deduct (a specified amount or percentage) from the usual price, cost, etc. **3b** to reduce (the regular price, cost, etc.) by a stated percentage or amount. **4** to sell or offer for sale at a reduced price. **5** to buy or sell (a bill of exchange, etc.) before maturity, with a deduction for interest determined by the time to maturity and also by risk. **6** (*also intr*) to loan money on (a negotiable instrument that is not immediately payable) with a deduction for interest determined by risk and time to maturity. ◆ *n* (ˈdɪskaʊnt). **7** a deduction from the full amount of a price or debt, as in return for prompt payment or to a special group of customers. See also **cash discount, trade discount. 8** Also called: **discount rate. 8a** the amount of interest deducted in the purchase or sale of or the loan of money on unmatured negotiable instruments. **8b** the rate of interest deducted. **9a** (in the issue of shares) a percentage deducted from the par value to give a reduced amount payable by subscribers. **9b** the amount by which the par value of something, esp. shares, exceeds its market value. Compare **premium** (sense 3). **10** the act or an instance of discounting a negotiable instrument. **11 at a discount. 11a** below the regular price. **11b** (of share values) below par. **11c** held in low regard; not sought after or valued. **12** (*modifier*) offering or selling at reduced prices: *a discount shop.* ▸ **disˈcountable** *adj* ▸ **ˈdiscounter** *n*

discounted cash flow *n Account.* a technique for appraising an investment that takes into account the different values of future returns according to when they will be received. Abbrev.: **DCF.**

discountenance (dɪsˈkaʊntɪnəns) *vb* (*tr*) **1** to make ashamed or confused. **2** to disapprove of. ◆ *n* **3** disapproval.

discount house *n* **1** *Chiefly Brit.* a financial organization engaged in discounting bills of exchange, etc. on a large scale primarily by borrowing call money from commercial banks. **2** *Chiefly U.S.* another name for **discount store.**

discount market *n* the part of the money market consisting of banks, discount houses, and brokers on which bills are discounted.

discount store *n* a shop where goods are sold at a low price.

discourage (dɪsˈkʌrɪdʒ) *vb* (*tr*) **1** to deprive of the will to persist in something. **2** to inhibit; prevent: *this solution discourages rust.* **3** to oppose by expressing disapproval. ▸ **disˈcouragement** *n* ▸ **disˈcourager** *n* ▸ **disˈcouragingly** *adv*

discourse *n* (ˈdɪskɔːs, dɪsˈkɔːs). **1** verbal communication; talk; conversation. **2** a formal treatment of a subject in speech or writing, such as a sermon or dissertation. **3** a unit of text used by linguists for the analysis of linguistic phenomena that range over more than one sentence. **4** *Archaic.* the ability to reason or the reasoning process. ◆ *vb* (dɪsˈkɔːs). **5** (*intr; often foll. by on or upon*) to speak or write (about) formally and extensively. **6** (*intr*) to hold a discussion. **7** (*tr*) *Archaic.* to give forth (music). [C14: from Medieval Latin *discursus* argument, from Latin: a running to and fro, from *discurrere* to run different ways, from DIS-[1] + *currere* to run] ▸ **disˈcourser** *n*

discourteous (dɪsˈkɜːtɪəs) *adj* showing bad manners; impolite; rude. ▸ **disˈcourteously** *adv* ▸ **disˈcourteousness** *n*

discourtesy (dɪsˈkɜːtɪsɪ) *n, pl* **-sies. 1** bad manners; rudeness. **2** a rude remark or act.

discover (dɪˈskʌvə) *vb* (*tr; may take a clause as object*) **1** to be the first to find or find out about: *Fleming discovered penicillin.* **2** to learn about or encounter for the first time; realize: *she discovered the pleasures of wine.* **3** to find after study or search: *I discovered a leak in the tank.* **4** to reveal or make known. ▸ **disˈcoverable** *adj* ▸ **disˈcoverer** *n*

discovered check *n Chess.* check given by moving a man that has been masking a potential check from a bishop, rook, or queen.

discovert (dɪsˈkʌvət) *adj Law.* (of a woman) not under the protection of a husband; being a widow, spinster, or divorcée. [C14: from Old French *descovert*, past participle of *descouvrir* to DISCOVER] ▸ **disˈcoverture** *n*

discovery (dɪˈskʌvərɪ) *n, pl* **-eries. 1** the act, process, or an instance of discovering. **2** a person, place, or thing that has been discovered. **3** *Law.* the compulsory disclosure by a party to an action of relevant documents in his possession.

Discovery Bay *n* an inlet of the Indian Ocean in SE Australia.

disc plough *n* a plough that cuts by means of revolving steel discs.

discredit (dɪsˈkrɛdɪt) *vb* (*tr*) **1** to damage the reputation of. **2** to cause to be disbelieved or distrusted. **3** to reject as untrue or of questionable accuracy. ◆ *n* **4** a person, thing, or state of affairs that causes disgrace. **5** damage to a reputation. **6** lack of belief or confidence.

discreditable (dɪsˈkrɛdɪtəbᵊl) *adj* tending to bring discredit; shameful or unworthy. ▸ **disˈcreditably** *adv*

discreet (dɪˈskriːt) *adj* careful to avoid social embarrassment or distress, esp. by keeping confidences secret; tactful. [C14: from Old French *discret*, from Medieval Latin *discrētus*, from Latin *discernere* to DISCERN] ▸ **disˈcreetly** *adv* ▸ **disˈcreetness** *n*

USAGE Avoid confusion with **discrete.**

discrepancy (dɪˈskrɛpənsɪ) *n, pl* **-cies.** a conflict or variation, as between facts, figures, or claims.

USAGE *Discrepancy* is sometimes wrongly used where *disparity* is meant. A *discrepancy* exists between things which ought to be the same; it can be small but is usually significant. A *disparity* is a large difference between measurable things such as age, rank, or wages.

discrepant (dɪˈskrɛpənt) *adj* inconsistent; conflicting; at variance. [C15: from Latin *discrepāns*, from *discrepāre* to differ in sound, from DIS-[1] + *crepāre* to be noisy] ▸ **disˈcrepantly** *adv*

discrete (dɪsˈkriːt) *adj* **1** separate or distinct in form or concept. **2** consisting of distinct or separate parts. **3** *Statistics.* **3a** (of a variable) having consecutive values that are not infinitesimally close, so that its analysis requires summation rather than integration. **3b** (of a distribution) relating to a discrete variable. Compare **continuous** (sense 4). [C14: from Latin *discrētus* separated, set apart; see DISCREET] ▸ **disˈcretely** *adv* ▸ **disˈcreteness** *n*

USAGE Avoid confusion with **discreet.**

discretion (dɪˈskrɛʃən) *n* **1** the quality of behaving or speaking in such a way as to avoid social embarrassment or distress. **2** freedom or authority to make judgments and to act as one sees fit (esp. in the phrases **at one's own discretion, at the discretion of**). **3 age** *or* **years of discretion.** the age at which a person is considered to be able to manage his own affairs.

discretionary (dɪˈskrɛʃənərɪ, -ənrɪ) *or* **discretional** *adj* having or using the ability to decide at one's own discretion: *discretionary powers.* ▸ **disˈcretionarily** *or* **disˈcretionally** *adv*

discretionary trust *n* a trust in which the beneficiaries' shares are not fixed in the trust deed but are left to the discretion of other persons, often the trustees.

discriminant (dɪˈskrɪmɪnənt) *n* an algebraic expression related to the coefficients of a polynomial equation whose value gives information about the roots of the polynomial: $b^2 - 4ac$ *is the discriminant of* $ax^2 + bx + c = 0$.

discriminate *vb* (dɪˈskrɪmɪˌneɪt). **1** (*intr; usu. foll. by in favour of or against*) to single out a particular person, group, etc., for special favour or, esp., disfavour, often because of a characteristic such as race, colour, sex, intelligence, etc. **2** (when *intr*, foll. by *between* or *among*) to recognize or understand the difference (between); distinguish: *to discriminate right and wrong; to discriminate between right and wrong.* **3** (*intr*) to constitute or mark a difference. **4** (*intr*) to be discerning in matters of taste. ◆ *adj* (dɪˈskrɪmɪnɪt). **5** showing or marked by discrimination. [C17: from Latin *discrīmināre* to divide, from *discrīmen* a separation, from *discernere* to DISCERN] ▸ **disˈcriminately** *adv* ▸ **disˈcrimiˌnator** *n*

discriminating (dɪˈskrɪmɪˌneɪtɪŋ) *adj* **1** able to see fine distinctions and differences. **2** discerning in matters of taste. **3** (of a tariff, import duty, etc.) levied at differential rates in order to favour or discourage imports or exports. ▸ **disˈcrimiˌnatingly** *adv*

discrimination (dɪˌskrɪmɪˈneɪʃən) *n* **1** unfair treatment of a person, racial group, minority, etc.; action based on prejudice. **2** subtle appreciation in matters of taste. **3** the ability to see fine distinctions and differences. **4** *Electronics.* the selection of a signal having a particular frequency, amplitude, phase, etc., effected by the elimination of other signals by means of a discriminator. ▸ **disˌcrimiˈnational** *adj*

discrimination learning *n Psychol.* a learning process in which an organism learns to react differently to different stimuli. Compare **generalization** (sense 3).

discriminator (dɪˈskrɪmɪˌneɪtə) *n* **1** an electronic circuit that converts a frequency or phase modulation into an amplitude modulation for subsequent demodulation. **2** an electronic circuit that has an output voltage only when the amplitude of the input pulses exceeds a predetermined value.

discriminatory (dɪˈskrɪmɪnətərɪ, -trɪ) *or* **discriminative** (dɪˈskrɪmɪnətɪv) *adj* **1** based on or showing prejudice; biased. **2** capable of making fine distinctions. **3** (of a statistical test) unbiased. ▸ **dis'criminatorily** *or* **dis'criminatively** *adv*

discursive (dɪ'skɜːsɪv) *adj* **1** passing from one topic to another, usually in an unmethodical way; digressive. **2** *Philosophy.* of or relating to knowledge obtained by reason and argument rather than intuition. Compare **dianoetic.** [C16: from Medieval Latin *discursīvus,* from Late Latin *discursus* DISCOURSE] ▸ **dis'cursively** *adv* ▸ **dis'cursiveness** *n*

discus ('dɪskəs) *n, pl* **discuses** *or* **disci** ('dɪskaɪ). **1** (originally) a circular stone or plate used in throwing competitions by the ancient Greeks. **2** *Field sports.* **2a** a similar disc-shaped object with a heavy middle thrown by athletes. **2b** (*as modifier*): *a discus thrower.* **3** (preceded by *the*) the event or sport of throwing the discus. **4** a South American cichlid fish, *Symphysodon discus,* that has a compressed coloured body and is a popular aquarium fish. [C17: from Latin, from Greek *diskos* from *dikein* to throw]

discuss (dɪ'skʌs) *vb* (*tr*) **1** to have a conversation about; consider by talking over; debate. **2** to treat (a subject) in speech or writing: *the first three volumes discuss basic principles.* **3** *Facetious, rare.* to eat or drink with enthusiasm. [C14: from Late Latin *discussus* examined, from *discutere* to investigate, from Latin: to dash to pieces, from DIS-[1] + *quatere* to shake, strike] ▸ **dis'cussant** *or* **dis'cusser** *n* ▸ **dis'cussible** *or* **dis'cussable** *adj*

discussion (dɪ'skʌʃən) *n* the examination or consideration of a matter in speech or writing. ▸ **dis'cussional** *adj*

disc wheel *n* a road wheel of a motor vehicle that has a round pressed disc in place of spokes. Compare **wire wheel.**

disdain (dɪs'deɪn) *n* **1** a feeling or show of superiority and dislike; contempt; scorn. ◆ *vb* **2** (*tr; may take an infinitive*) to refuse or reject with disdain. [C13 *dedeyne,* from Old French *desdeign,* from *desdeigner* to reject as unworthy, from Latin *dēdignārī;* see DIS-[1], DEIGN]

disdainful (dɪs'deɪnfʊl) *adj* showing or feeling disdain. ▸ **dis'dainfully** *adv* ▸ **dis'dainfulness** *n*

disease (dɪ'ziːz) *n* **1** any impairment of normal physiological function affecting all or part of an organism, esp. a specific pathological change caused by infection, stress, etc., producing characteristic symptoms; illness or sickness in general. **2** a corresponding condition in plants. **3** any situation or condition likened to this: *the disease of materialism.* Related adj: **pathological.** [C14: from Old French *desaise;* see DIS-[1], EASE]

diseased (dɪ'ziːzd) *adj* having or affected with disease.

diseconomy (ˌdɪsɪ'kɒnəmɪ) *n Economics.* disadvantage, such as lower efficiency or higher average costs, resulting from the scale on which an enterprise produces goods or services.

disembark (ˌdɪsɪm'bɑːk) *vb* to land or cause to land from a ship, aircraft, etc.: *several passengers disembarked; we will disembark the passengers.* ▸ **disembarkation** (dɪsˌɛmbɑː'keɪʃən) *or* ˌ**disem'barkment** *n*

disembarrass (ˌdɪsɪm'bærəs) *vb* (*tr*) **1** to free from embarrassment, entanglement, etc. **2** to relieve or rid of something burdensome. ▸ ˌ**disem'barrassment** *n*

disembodied (ˌdɪsɪm'bɒdɪd) *adj* **1** lacking a body or freed from the body; incorporeal. **2** lacking in substance, solidity, or any firm relation to reality.

disembody (ˌdɪsɪm'bɒdɪ) *vb* **-bodies, -bodying, -bodied.** (*tr*) to free from the body or from physical form. ▸ ˌ**disem'bodiment** *n*

disembogue (ˌdɪsɪm'bəʊg) *vb* **-bogues, -boguing, -bogued. 1** (of a river, stream, etc.) to discharge (water) at the mouth. **2** (*intr*) to flow out. [C16: from Spanish *desembocar,* from *des-* DIS-[1] + *embocar* put into the mouth, from *em-* in + *boca* mouth, from Latin *bucca* cheek] ▸ ˌ**disem'boguement** *n*

disembowel (ˌdɪsɪm'baʊəl) *vb* **-els, -elling, -elled** *or U.S.* **-els, -eling, -eled.** (*tr*) to remove the entrails of. ▸ ˌ**disem'bowelment** *n*

disembroil (ˌdɪsɪm'brɔɪl) *vb* (*tr*) to free from entanglement or a confused situation.

disempower (ˌdɪsɪm'paʊə) *vb* (*tr*) to deprive (a person) of power or authority. ▸ ˌ**disem'powerment** *n*

disenable (ˌdɪsɪ'neɪbᵊl) *vb* (*tr*) to cause to become incapable; prevent. ▸ ˌ**disen'ablement** *n*

disenchant (ˌdɪsɪn'tʃɑːnt) *vb* (*tr;* when passive, foll. by *with* or *by*) to make disappointed or disillusioned: *she is disenchanted with the marriage.* ▸ ˌ**disen'chanted** *adj* ▸ ˌ**disen'chantment** *n*

disencumber (ˌdɪsɪn'kʌmbə) *vb* (*tr*) to free from encumbrances. ▸ ˌ**disen'cumberment** *n*

disendow (ˌdɪsɪn'daʊ) *vb* (*tr*) to take away an endowment from. ▸ ˌ**disen'dower** *n* ▸ ˌ**disen'dowment** *n*

disenfranchise (ˌdɪsɪn'fræntʃaɪz) *or* **disfranchise** *vb* (*tr*) **1** to deprive (a person) of the right to vote or other rights of citizenship. **2** to deprive (a place) of the right to send representatives to an elected body. **3** to deprive (a business concern, etc.) of some privilege or right. **4** to deprive (a person, place, etc.) of any franchise or right. ▸ **disenfranchisement** (ˌdɪsɪn'fræntʃɪzmənt) *or* **dis'franchisement** *n*

disengage (ˌdɪsɪn'geɪdʒ) *vb* **1** to release or become released from a connection, obligation, etc.: *press the clutch to disengage the gears.* **2** *Military.* to withdraw (forces) from close action. **3** *Fencing.* to move (one's blade) from one side of an opponent's blade to another in a circular motion to bring the blade into an open line of attack.

disengagement (ˌdɪsɪn'geɪdʒmənt) *n* **1** the act or process of disengaging or the state of being disengaged. **2** leisure; ease. ▸ ˌ**disen'gaged** *adj*

disentail (ˌdɪsɪn'teɪl) *Property law.* ◆ *vb* **1** to free (an estate) from entail. ◆ *n* **2** the act of disentailing; disentailment. ▸ ˌ**disen'tailment** *n*

disentangle (ˌdɪsɪn'tæŋgᵊl) *vb* **1** to release or become free from entanglement or confusion. **2** (*tr*) to unravel or work out. ▸ ˌ**disen'tanglement** *n*

disenthral *or U.S.* **disenthrall** (ˌdɪsɪn'θrɔːl) *vb* **-thrals, -thralling, -thralled** *or U.S.* **-thralls, -thralling, -thralled.** (*tr*) to set free. ▸ ˌ**disen'thralment** *or U.S.* ˌ**disen'thrallment** *n*

disentitle (ˌdɪsɪn'taɪtᵊl) *vb* (*tr*) to deprive of a title, right, or claim.

disentomb (ˌdɪsɪn'tuːm) *vb* (*tr*) to disinter; unearth.

disentwine (ˌdɪsɪn'twaɪn) *vb* to become or cause to become untwined; unwind.

disepalous (daɪ'sɛpələs) *adj* (of flowers or plants) having two sepals.

disequilibrium (ˌdɪsiːkwɪ'lɪbrɪəm) *n* a loss or absence of equilibrium, esp. in an economy.

disestablish (ˌdɪsɪ'stæblɪʃ) *vb* (*tr*) to deprive (a church, custom, institution, etc.) of established status. ▸ ˌ**dises'tablishment** *n*

disesteem (ˌdɪsɪ'stiːm) *vb* **1** (*tr*) to think little of. ◆ *n* **2** lack of esteem.

diseuse (*French* dizøz) *n* (esp. formerly) an actress who presents dramatic recitals, usually sung accompanied by music. Male counterpart: **diseur** (*French* dizœr). [C19: from French, feminine of *diseur* speaker, from *dire* to speak, from Latin *dīcere*]

disfavour *or U.S.* **disfavor** (dɪs'feɪvə) *n* **1** disapproval or dislike. **2** the state of being disapproved of or disliked. **3** an unkind act. ◆ *vb* **4** (*tr*) to regard or treat with disapproval or dislike.

disfeature (dɪs'fiːtʃə) *vb* (*tr*) to mar the features or appearance of; deface. ▸ **dis'featurement** *n*

disfigure (dɪs'fɪgə) *vb* (*tr*) **1** to spoil the appearance or shape of; deface. **2** to mar the effect or quality of. ▸ **dis'figurer** *n*

disfigurement (dɪs'fɪgəmənt) *or* **disfiguration** *n* **1** something that disfigures. **2** the act of disfiguring or the state of being disfigured.

disforest (dɪs'fɒrɪst) *vb* (*tr*) **1** another word for **deforest. 2** *English law.* a less common word for **disafforest.** ▸ **dis,fores'tation** *n*

disfranchise (dɪs'fræntʃaɪz) *vb* another word for **disenfranchise.**

disfrock (dɪs'frɒk) *vb* another word for **unfrock.**

disgorge (dɪs'gɔːdʒ) *vb* **1** to throw out (swallowed food, etc.) from the throat or stomach; vomit. **2** to discharge or empty of (contents). **3** (*tr*) to yield up unwillingly or under pressure. **4** (*tr*) *Angling.* to remove (a hook) from the mouth or throat of (a fish). ▸ **dis'gorgement** *n*

disgorger (dɪs'gɔːdʒə) *n Angling.* a thin notched metal implement for removing hooks from a fish.

disgrace (dɪs'greɪs) *n* **1** a condition of shame, loss of reputation, or dishonour. **2** a shameful person, thing, or state of affairs. **3** exclusion from confidence or trust: *he is in disgrace with his father.* ◆ *vb* (*tr*) **4** to bring shame upon; be a discredit to. **5** to treat or cause to be treated with disfavour. ▸ **dis'gracer** *n*

disgraceful (dɪs'greɪsfʊl) *adj* shameful; scandalous. ▸ **dis'gracefully** *adv* ▸ **dis'gracefulness** *n*

disgruntle (dɪs'grʌntᵊl) *vb* (*tr; usually passive*) to make sulky or discontented. [C17: DIS-[1] + obsolete *gruntle* to complain; see GRUNT] ▸ **dis'gruntled** *adj* ▸ **dis'gruntlement** *n*

disguise (dɪs'gaɪz) *vb* **1** to modify the appearance or manner in order to conceal the identity of (oneself, someone, or something). **2** (*tr*) to misrepresent in order to obscure the actual nature or meaning: *to disguise the facts.* ◆ *n* **3** a mask, costume, or manner that disguises. **4** the act of disguising or the state of being disguised. [C14: from Old French *desguisier,* from *des-* DIS-[1] + *guise* manner; see GUISE] ▸ **dis'guisable** *adj* ▸ **dis'guised** *adj* ▸ **disguisedly** (dɪs'gaɪzɪdlɪ) *adv* ▸ **dis'guiser** *n*

disgust (dɪs'gʌst) *vb* (*tr*) **1** to sicken or fill with loathing. **2** to offend the moral sense, principles, or taste of. ◆ *n* **3** a great loathing or distaste aroused by someone or something. **4 in disgust.** as a result of disgust. [C16: from Old French *desgouster,* from *des-* DIS-[1] + *gouster* to taste, from *goust* taste, from Latin *gustus*] ▸ **dis'gustedly** *adv* ▸ **dis'gustedness** *n*

disgusting (dɪs'gʌstɪŋ) *adj* loathsome; repugnant. Also (rare): **dis'gustful.** ▸ **dis'gustingly** *adv*

dish (dɪʃ) *n* **1** a container used for holding or serving food, esp. an open shallow container of pottery, glass, etc. **2** the food that is served or contained in a dish. **3** a particular article or preparation of food: *a local fish dish.* **4** Also called: **'dishful.** the amount contained in a dish. **5** something resembling a dish, esp. in shape. **6** a concavity or depression. **7** short for **dish aerial** or **satellite dish aerial. 8** *Informal.* an attractive person. **9** *Informal.* something that one particularly enjoys or excels in. ◆ *vb* (*tr*) **10** to put into a dish. **11** to make hollow or concave. **12** *Brit. informal.* to ruin or spoil: *he dished his chances of getting the job.* ◆ See also **dish out, dish up.** [Old English *disc,* from Latin *discus* quoit, see DISC] ▸ **'dish,like** *adj*

dishabille (ˌdɪsæ'biːl) *n* a variant of **deshabille.**

dish aerial *n* **1** a microwave aerial, used esp. in radar, radio telescopes, and satellite broadcasting, consisting of a parabolic reflector. Formal name: **parabolic aerial.** Often shortened to **dish. 2** short for **satellite dish aerial.** ◆ Also called: **dish antenna.**

disharmony (dɪs'hɑːmənɪ) *n, pl* **-nies. 1** lack of accord or harmony. **2** a situation, circumstance, etc., that is inharmonious. ▸ **disharmonious** (ˌdɪshɑː'məʊnɪəs) *adj* ▸ ˌ**dishar'moniously** *adv*

dishcloth ('dɪʃˌklɒθ) *n* a cloth or rag for washing or drying dishes. Also called (dialect): **dishclout** ('dɪʃˌkluːt).

dishcloth gourd *n* **1** any of several tropical climbing plants of the cucurbitaceous genus *Luffa,* esp. *L. cylindrica,* which is cultivated for ornament and for the fibrous interior of its fruits (see **loofah**). **2** the fruit of any of these plants. ◆ Also called: **vegetable sponge.**

dishearten (dɪs'hɑːtᵊn) *vb* (*tr*) to weaken or destroy the hope, courage, enthusiasm, etc., of. ▸ **dis'hearteningly** *adv* ▸ **dis'heartenment** *n*

dished (dɪʃt) *adj* **1** shaped like a dish; concave. **2** (of a pair of road wheels) arranged so that they are closer to one another at the bottom than at the top. **3** *Informal.* exhausted or defeated.

dishevel (dɪ'ʃɛvᵊl) *vb* **-els, -elling, -elled** *or U.S.* **-els, -eling, -eled.** to disarrange (the hair or clothes) of (someone). [C15: back formation from DISHEVELLED] ▸ **di'shevelment** *n*

dishevelled (dɪ'ʃɛvᵊld) *adj* **1** (esp. of hair) hanging loosely. **2** (of general appearance) unkempt; untidy. [C15 *dischevelee*, from Old French *deschevelé*, from *des-* DIS-[1] + *chevel* hair, from Latin *capillus*]

dishonest (dɪs'ɒnɪst) *adj* not honest or fair; deceiving or fraudulent. ▸ **dis'honestly** *adv*

dishonesty (dɪs'ɒnɪstɪ) *n, pl* **-ties. 1** lack of honesty or fairness; deceit. **2** a deceiving act or statement; fraud.

dishonour *or U.S.* **dishonor** (dɪs'ɒnə) *vb* (*tr*) **1** to treat with disrespect. **2** to fail or refuse to pay (a cheque, bill of exchange, etc.). **3** to cause the disgrace of (a woman) by seduction or rape. ◆ *n* **4** a lack of honour or respect. **5** a state of shame or disgrace. **6** a person or thing that causes a loss of honour: *he was a dishonour to his family*. **7** an insult; affront: *we did him a dishonour by not including him*. **8** refusal or failure to accept or pay a commercial paper. ▸ **dis'honourer** *or U.S.* **dis'honorer** *n*

dishonourable *or U.S.* **dishonorable** (dɪs'ɒnərəbᵊl, -'ɒnrəbᵊl) *adj* **1** characterized by or causing dishonour or discredit. **2** having little or no integrity; unprincipled. ▸ **dis'honourableness** *or U.S.* **dis'honorableness** *n* ▸ **dis'honourably** *or U.S.* **dis'honorably** *adv*

dish out *vb Informal*. **1** (*tr, adv*) to distribute. **2 dish it out.** to inflict punishment: *he can't take it, but he can sure dish it out*.

dishpan ('dɪʃ,pæn) *n Chiefly U.S. and Canadian*. a large pan for washing dishes, pots, etc.

dishtowel ('dɪʃ,taʊəl) *n* another name (esp. U.S. and Canadian) for a **tea towel.**

dish up *vb* (*adv*) **1** to serve (a meal, food, etc.). **2** (*tr*) *Informal*. to prepare or present, esp. in an attractive manner.

dishwasher ('dɪʃ,wɒʃə) *n* **1** an electrically operated machine for washing, rinsing, and drying dishes, cutlery, etc. **2** a person who washes dishes, etc.

dishwater ('dɪʃ,wɔːtə) *n* **1** water in which dishes and kitchen utensils are or have been washed. **2** something resembling this: *that was dishwater, not coffee*.

dishy ('dɪʃɪ) *adj* **dishier, dishiest.** *Informal, chiefly Brit*. good-looking or attractive.

disillusion (,dɪsɪ'luːʒən) *vb* **1** (*tr*) to destroy the ideals, illusions, or false ideas of. ◆ *n also* **disillusionment. 2** the act of disillusioning or the state of being disillusioned. ▸ **,disil'lusioned** *adj*

disincentive (,dɪsɪn'sɛntɪv) *n* **1** something that acts as a deterrent. ◆ *adj* **2** acting as a deterrent: *a disincentive effect on productivity*.

disincline (,dɪsɪn'klaɪn) *vb* to make or be unwilling, reluctant, or averse. ▸ **disinclination** (,dɪsɪnklɪ'neɪʃən) *n*

disinfect (,dɪsɪn'fɛkt) *vb* (*tr*) to rid of microorganisms potentially harmful to man, esp. by chemical means. ▸ **,disin'fection** *n* ▸ **,disin'fector** *n*

disinfectant (,dɪsɪn'fɛktənt) *n* an agent that destroys or inhibits the activity of microorganisms that cause disease.

disinfest (,dɪsɪn'fɛst) *vb* (*tr*) to rid of vermin. ▸ **dis,infes'tation** *n*

disinflation (,dɪsɪn'fleɪʃən) *n Economics*. a reduction or stabilization of the general price level intended to improve the balance of payments without incurring reductions in output, employment, and investment. Compare **deflation** (sense 2).

disinformation (,dɪsɪnfə'meɪʃən) *n* false information intended to deceive or mislead.

disingenuous (,dɪsɪn'dʒɛnjuəs) *adj* not sincere; lacking candour. ▸ **,disin'genuously** *adv* ▸ **,disin'genuousness** *n*

disinherit (,dɪsɪn'hɛrɪt) *vb* (*tr*) **1** *Law*. to deprive (an heir or next of kin) of inheritance or right to inherit. **2** to deprive of a right or heritage. ▸ **,disin'heritance** *n*

disinhibition (,dɪsɪnɪ'bɪʃən, -ɪnhɪ-) *n Psychol*. a temporary loss of inhibition, caused by an outside stimulus such as alcohol or a drug.

disintegrate (dɪs'ɪntɪ,greɪt) *vb* **1** to break or be broken into fragments or constituent parts; shatter. **2** to lose or cause to lose cohesion or unity. **3** (*intr*) to lose judgment or control; deteriorate. **4** *Physics*. **4a** to induce or undergo nuclear fission, as by bombardment with fast particles. **4b** another word for **decay** (sense 3). ▸ **dis'integrable** *adj* ▸ **dis,inte'gration** *n* ▸ **dis'integrative** *adj* ▸ **dis'inte,grator** *n*

disinter (,dɪsɪn'tɜː) *vb* **-ters, -terring, -terred.** (*tr*) **1** to remove or dig up; exhume. **2** to bring (a secret, hidden facts, etc.) to light; expose. ▸ **,disin'terment** *n*

disinterest (dɪs'ɪntrɪst, -tərɪst) *n* **1** freedom from bias or involvement. **2** lack of interest; indifference. ◆ *vb* **3** (*tr*) to free from concern for personal interests.

disinterested (dɪs'ɪntrɪstɪd, -tərɪs-) *adj* **1** free from bias or partiality; objective. **2** not interested. ▸ **dis'interestedly** *adv* ▸ **dis'interestedness** *n*

USAGE Many people consider that the use of *disinterested* to mean not interested is incorrect and that *uninterested* should be used.

disintermediation (dɪs,ɪntə,miːdɪ'eɪʃən) *n Finance*. the elimination of such financial intermediaries as banks and brokers in transactions between principals, often as a result of deregulation and the use of computers.

disinvest (dɪsɪn'vɛst) *vb Economics*. **1** (usually foll. by *in*) to remove investment (from). **2** (*intr*) to reduce the capital stock of an economy or enterprise, as by not replacing obsolete machinery. ▸ **,disin'vestment** *n*

disject (dɪs'dʒɛkt) *vb* (*tr*) to break apart; scatter. [C16: from Latin *disjectus*, from *disjicere* to scatter, from DIS-[1] + *jacere* to throw]

disjecta membra *Latin*. (dɪs'dʒɛktə 'mɛmbrə) *pl n* scattered fragments, esp. parts taken from a writing or writings.

disjoin (dɪs'dʒɔɪn) *vb* to disconnect or become disconnected; separate. ▸ **dis'joinable** *adj*

disjoint (dɪs'dʒɔɪnt) *vb* **1** to take apart or come apart at the joints. **2** (*tr*) to disunite or disjoin. **3** to dislocate or become dislocated. **4** (*tr; usually passive*) to end the unity, sequence, or coherence of. ◆ *adj* **5** *Maths*. (of two sets) having no members in common. **6** *Obsolete*. disjointed.

disjointed (dɪs'dʒɔɪntɪd) *adj* **1** having no coherence; disconnected. **2** separated at the joint. **3** dislocated. ▸ **dis'jointedly** *adv* ▸ **dis'jointedness** *n*

disjunct *adj* (dɪs'dʒʌŋkt). **1** not united or joined. **2** (of certain insects) having deep constrictions between the head, thorax, and abdomen. **3** *Music*. denoting two notes the interval between which is greater than a second. ◆ *n* ('dɪsdʒʌŋkt). **4** *Logic*. one of the propositions or formulas in a disjunction.

disjunction (dɪs'dʒʌŋkʃən) *n* **1** Also called: **dis'juncture.** the act of disconnecting or the state of being disconnected; separation. **2** *Cytology*. the separation of the chromosomes of each homologous pair during the anaphase of meiosis. **3** *Logic*. **3a** the operator that forms a compound sentence from two given sentences and corresponds to the English *or*. **3b** a sentence so formed. Usually written $p \vee q$ where *p*, *q* are the component sentences, it is true (inclusive sense) whenever either or both of the latter are true; the exclusive disjunction, for which there is no symbol, is true when either but not both disjuncts is. **3c** the relation between such sentences.

disjunctive (dɪs'dʒʌŋktɪv) *adj* **1** serving to disconnect or separate. **2** *Grammar*. **2a** denoting a word, esp. a conjunction, that serves to express opposition or contrast: *but* in the sentence *She was poor but she was honest*. **2b** denoting an inflection of pronouns in some languages that is used alone or after a preposition, such as *moi* in French. **3** Also: **alternative.** *Logic*. relating to, characterized by, or containing disjunction. ◆ *n* **4** *Grammar*. **4a** a disjunctive word, esp. a conjunction. **4b** a disjunctive pronoun. **5** *Logic*. a disjunctive proposition; disjunction. ▸ **dis'junctively** *adv*

disk (dɪsk) *n* **1** a variant spelling (esp. U.S. and Canadian) of **disc. 2** Also called: **magnetic disk, hard disk.** *Computing*. a direct-access storage device consisting of a stack of plates coated with a magnetic layer, the whole assembly rotating rapidly as a single unit. Each surface has a read-write head that can move radially to read or write data on concentric tracks. Compare **drum**[1] (sense 9). See also **floppy disk.**

disk crash *n Computing*. the failure of a disk storage system, usually resulting from the read/write head touching the moving disk surface and causing mechanical damage.

disk drive *n Computing*. the controller and mechanism for reading and writing data on computer disks. See also **disk** (sense 2).

diskette (dɪs'kɛt) *n Computing*. another name for **floppy disk.**

Disko ('dɪskəʊ) *n* an island in Davis Strait, off the W coast of Greenland: extensive coal deposits.

disk operating system *n* an operating system used on a computer system with one or more disk drives. Often shortened to: **DOS.**

dislike (dɪs'laɪk) *vb* **1** (*tr*) to consider unpleasant or disagreeable. ◆ *n* **2** a feeling of aversion or antipathy. ▸ **dis'likable** *or* **dis'likeable** *adj*

dislimn (dɪs'lɪm) *vb* (*tr*) *Poetic*. to efface.

dislocate ('dɪslə,keɪt) *vb* (*tr*) **1** to disrupt or shift out of place or position. **2** to displace (an organ or part) from its normal position, esp. a bone from its joint.

dislocation (,dɪslə'keɪʃən) *n* **1** the act of displacing or the state of being displaced; disruption. **2** (esp. of the bones in a joint) the state or condition of being dislocated. **3** a line, plane, or region in which there is a discontinuity in the regularity of a crystal lattice. **4** *Geology*. a less common word for **fault** (sense 6).

dislodge (dɪs'lɒdʒ) *vb* to remove from or leave a lodging place, hiding place, or previously fixed position. ▸ **dis'lodgment** *or* **dis'lodgement** *n*

disloyal (dɪs'lɔɪəl) *adj* not loyal or faithful; deserting one's allegiance or duty. ▸ **dis'loyally** *adv*

disloyalty (dɪs'lɔɪəltɪ) *n, pl* **-ties.** the condition or an instance of being unfaithful or disloyal.

dismal ('dɪzməl) *adj* **1** causing gloom or depression. **2** causing dismay or terror. [C13: from *dismal* (n) list of 24 unlucky days in the year, from Medieval Latin *diēs malī* bad days, from Latin *diēs* day + *malus* bad] ▸ **'dismally** *adv* ▸ **'dismalness** *n*

dismal science *n* **the.** a name for economics coined by Thomas Carlyle.

Dismal Swamp *or* **Great Dismal Swamp** *n* a coastal marshland in SE Virginia and NE North Carolina: partly reclaimed. Area: about 1940 sq. km (750 sq. miles). Area before reclamation: 5200 sq. km (2000 sq. miles).

dismantle (dɪs'mæntᵊl) *vb* (*tr*) **1** to take apart. **2** to demolish or raze. **3** to strip of covering. [C17: from Old French *desmanteler* to remove a cloak from; see MANTLE] ▸ **dis'mantlement** *n* ▸ **dis'mantler** *n*

dismast (dɪs'mɑːst) *vb* (*tr*) to break off the mast or masts of (a sailing vessel). ▸ **dis'mastment** *n*

dismay (dɪs'meɪ) *vb* (*tr*) **1** to fill with apprehension or alarm. **2** to fill with depression or discouragement. ◆ *n* **3** consternation or agitation. [C13: from Old French *desmaiier* (unattested), from *des-* DIS-[1] + *esmayer* to frighten, ultimately of Germanic origin; see MAY[1]] ▸ **dis'maying** *adj*

dismember (dɪs'mɛmbə) *vb* (*tr*) **1** to remove the limbs or members of. **2** to cut to pieces. **3** to divide or partition (something, such as an empire). ▸ **dis'memberer** *n* ▸ **dis'memberment** *n*

dismiss (dɪs'mɪs) *vb* (*tr*) **1** to remove or discharge from employment or service. **2** to send away or allow to go or disperse. **3** to dispel from one's mind; discard; reject. **4** to cease to consider (a subject): *they dismissed the problem*. **5** to decline further hearing to (a claim or action): *the judge dismissed the case*. **6** *Cricket*. to bowl out a side for a particular number of runs. ◆ *sentence substitute*. **7** *Military*. an order to end an activity or give permission to disperse. [C15: from Medieval Latin *dismissus* sent away, variant of Latin *dīmissus*, from *dīmittere*, from *dī-* DIS-[1] + *mittere* to send] ▸ **dis'missible** *adj* ▸ **dis'missive** *adj*

dismissal (dɪsˈmɪsᵊl) *n* **1** an official notice of discharge from employment or service. **2** the act of dismissing or the condition of being dismissed.

dismount (dɪsˈmaʊnt) *vb* **1** to get off a horse, bicycle, etc. **2** (*tr*) to disassemble or remove from a mounting. ◆ *n* **3** the act of dismounting. ▸ **disˈmountable** *adj*

Disney (ˈdɪznɪ) *n* **Walt(er Elias)**. 1901–66, U.S. film producer, who pioneered animated cartoons: noted esp. for his creations *Mickey Mouse* and *Donald Duck* and films such as *Fantasia* (1940). ▸ **ˌDisneyˈesque** *adj*

Disneyland (ˈdɪznɪˌlænd) *n* an amusement park in Anaheim, California, founded by Walt Disney and opened in 1955. **Walt Disney World,** a second amusement park, opened in 1971 near Orlando, Florida.

disobedience (ˌdɪsəˈbiːdɪəns) *n* lack of obedience.

disobedient (ˌdɪsəˈbiːdɪənt) *adj* not obedient; neglecting or refusing to obey. ▸ **ˌdisoˈbediently** *adv*

disobey (ˌdɪsəˈbeɪ) *vb* to neglect or refuse to obey (someone, an order, etc.). ▸ **ˌdisoˈbeyer** *n*

disoblige (ˌdɪsəˈblaɪdʒ) *vb* (*tr*) **1** to disregard the desires of. **2** to slight; insult. **3** *Informal.* to cause trouble or inconvenience to. ▸ **ˌdisoˈbliging** *adj* ▸ **ˌdisoˈbligingly** *adv* ▸ **ˌdisoˈbligingness** *n*

disomic (daɪˈsəʊmɪk) *adj Genetics.* having an extra chromosome in the haploid state that is homologous to an existing chromosome in this set. ▸ **diˈsomy** *n*

disoperation (dɪsˌɒpəˈreɪʃən) *n Ecology.* a relationship between two organisms in a community that is harmful to both.

disorder (dɪsˈɔːdə) *n* **1** a lack of order; disarray; confusion. **2** a disturbance of public order or peace. **3** an upset of health; ailment. **4** a deviation from the normal system or order. ◆ *vb* (*tr*) **5** to upset the order of; disarrange; muddle. **6** to disturb the health or mind of.

disorderly (dɪsˈɔːdəlɪ) *adj* **1** untidy; irregular. **2** uncontrolled; unruly. **3** *Law.* violating public peace or order. ◆ *adv* **4** in an irregular or confused manner. ▸ **disˈorderliness** *n*

disorderly conduct *n Law.* any of various minor offences tending to cause a disturbance of the peace.

disorderly house *n Law.* an establishment in which unruly behaviour habitually occurs, esp. a brothel or a gaming house.

disorganize *or* **disorganise** (dɪsˈɔːgəˌnaɪz) *vb* (*tr*) to disrupt or destroy the arrangement, system, or unity of. ▸ **disˌorganiˈzation** *or* **disˌorganiˈsation** *n* ▸ **disˈorganˌizer** *or* **disˈorganˌiser** *n*

disorientate (dɪsˈɔːrɪenˌteɪt) *or* **disorient** *vb* (*tr*) **1** to cause (someone) to lose his bearings. **2** to perplex; confuse. ▸ **disˌorienˈtation** *n*

disown (dɪsˈəʊn) *vb* (*tr*) to deny any connection with; refuse to acknowledge. ▸ **disˈowner** *n* ▸ **disˈownment** *n*

disparage (dɪˈspærɪdʒ) *vb* (*tr*) **1** to speak contemptuously of; belittle. **2** to damage the reputation of. [C14: from Old French *desparagier,* from *des-* DIS-[1] + *parage* equality, from Latin *par* equal] ▸ **disˈparagement** *n* ▸ **disˈparager** *n* ▸ **disˈparaging** *adj* ▸ **disˈparagingly** *adv*

disparate (ˈdɪspərɪt) *adj* **1** utterly different or distinct in kind. ◆ *n* **2** (*pl*) unlike things or people. [C16: from Latin *disparāre* to divide, from DIS-[1] + *parāre* to prepare; also influenced by Latin *dispar* unequal] ▸ **ˈdisparately** *adv* ▸ **ˈdisparateness** *n*

disparity (dɪˈspærɪtɪ) *n, pl* **-ties. 1** inequality or difference, as in age, rank, wages, etc. **2** dissimilarity.

USAGE See at **discrepancy**.

dispassion (dɪsˈpæʃən) *n* detachment; objectivity.

dispassionate (dɪsˈpæʃənɪt) *adj* devoid of or uninfluenced by emotion or prejudice; objective; impartial. ▸ **disˈpassionately** *adv* ▸ **disˈpassionateness** *n*

dispatch *or* **despatch** (dɪˈspætʃ) *vb* (*tr*) **1** to send off promptly, as to a destination or to perform a task. **2** to discharge or complete (a task, duty, etc.) promptly. **3** *Informal.* to eat up quickly. **4** to murder or execute. ◆ *n* **5** the act of sending off a letter, messenger, etc. **6** prompt action or speed (often in the phrase **with dispatch**). **7** an official communication or report, sent in haste. **8** *Journalism.* a report sent to a newspaper, etc., by a correspondent. **9** murder or execution. [C16: from Italian *dispacciare,* from Provençal *despachar,* from Old French *despeechier* to set free, from *des-* DIS-[1] + *-peechier,* ultimately from Latin *pedica* a fetter] ▸ **disˈpatcher** *n*

dispatch box *n* a case or box used to hold valuables or documents, esp. official state documents.

dispatch case *n* a case used for carrying papers, documents, books, etc., usually flat and stiff.

dispatch rider *n* a horseman or motorcyclist who carries dispatches.

dispel (dɪˈspɛl) *vb* **-pels, -pelling, -pelled.** (*tr*) to disperse or drive away. [C17: from Latin *dispellere,* from DIS-[1] + *pellere* to drive] ▸ **disˈpeller** *n*

dispend (dɪˈspɛnd) *vb* (*tr*) *Obsolete.* to spend. [C14: from Old French *despendre,* from Latin *dispendere* to distribute; see DISPENSE]

dispensable (dɪˈspɛnsəbᵊl) *adj* **1** not essential; expendable. **2** capable of being distributed. **3** (of a law, vow, etc.) able to be relaxed. ▸ **disˌpensaˈbility** *or* **disˈpensableness** *n*

dispensary (dɪˈspɛnsərɪ, -srɪ) *n, pl* **-ries.** a place where medicine and medical supplies are dispensed.

dispensation (ˌdɪspɛnˈseɪʃən) *n* **1** the act of distributing or dispensing. **2** something distributed or dispensed. **3** a system or plan of administering or dispensing. **4** *Chiefly R.C. Church.* **4a** permission to dispense with an obligation of church law. **4b** the document authorizing such permission. **5** any exemption from a rule or obligation. **6** *Christianity.* **6a** the ordering of life and events by God. **6b** a divine decree affecting an individual or group. **6c** a religious system or code of prescriptions for life and conduct regarded as of divine origin. ▸ **ˌdispenˈsational** *adj*

dispensatory (dɪˈspɛnsətərɪ, -trɪ) *n, pl* **-ries. 1** a book listing the composition, preparation, and application of various drugs. ◆ *adj* **2** of or involving dispensation.

dispense (dɪˈspɛns) *vb* **1** (*tr*) to give out or distribute in portions. **2** (*tr*) to prepare and distribute (medicine), esp. on prescription. **3** (*tr*) to administer (the law, etc.). **4** (*intr;* foll. by *with*) to do away (with) or manage (without). **5** to grant a dispensation to (someone) from (some obligation of church law). **6** to exempt or excuse from a rule or obligation. [C14: from Medieval Latin *dispensāre* to pardon, from Latin *dispendere* to weigh out, from DIS-[1] + *pendere* to weigh]

USAGE *Dispense with* is sometimes wrongly used where *dispose of* is meant: *this task can be disposed of* (not *dispensed with*) *quickly and easily.*

dispenser (dɪˈspɛnsə) *n* **1** a device, such as a vending machine, that automatically dispenses a single item or a measured quantity. **2** a person or thing that dispenses.

dispensing optician *n* See **optician.**

dispermous (daɪˈspɜːməs) *adj* (of flowering plants) producing or having two seeds. [C18: from DI-[1] + Greek *sperma* seed]

dispersal (dɪˈspɜːsᵊl) *n* **1** the act of dispersing or the condition of being dispersed. **2** the spread of animals, plants, or seeds to new areas.

dispersal prison *n* a prison organized and equipped to accommodate a proportion of the most dangerous and highest security risk prisoners.

dispersant (dɪsˈpɜːsənt) *n* a liquid or gas used to disperse small particles or droplets, as in an aerosol.

disperse (dɪˈspɜːs) *vb* **1** to scatter; distribute over a wide area. **2** to dissipate or cause to dissipate. **3** to leave or cause to leave a gathering, often in a random manner. **4** to separate or be separated by dispersion. **5** (*tr*) to diffuse or spread (news, information, etc.). **6** to separate (particles) throughout a solid, liquid, or gas, as in the formation of a suspension or colloid. ◆ *adj* **7** of or consisting of the particles in a colloid or suspension: *disperse phase.* [C14: from Latin *dispersus* scattered, from *dispergere* to scatter widely, from DI-[2] + *spargere* to strew] ▸ **dispersedly** (dɪˈspɜːsɪdlɪ) *adv* ▸ **disˈperser** *n*

USAGE See at **disburse.**

dispersion (dɪˈspɜːʃən) *n* **1** another word for **dispersal. 2** *Physics.* **2a** the separation of electromagnetic radiation into constituents of different wavelengths. **2b** a measure of the ability of a substance to separate by refraction, expressed by the first differential of the refractive index with respect to wavelength at a given value of wavelength. Symbol: *D* **3** *Statistics.* the degree to which values of a frequency distribution are scattered around some central point, usually the arithmetic mean or median. **4** *Chem.* a system containing particles dispersed in a solid, liquid, or gas. **5** *Military.* the pattern of fire from a weapon system. **6** the deviation of a rocket from its prescribed path. **7** *Ecology.* the distribution pattern of an animal or a plant population.

Dispersion (dɪˈspɜːʃən) *n* **the.** another name for the **Diaspora.**

dispersion hardening *n* the strengthening of an alloy as a result of the presence of fine particles in the lattice.

dispersive (dɪˈspɜːsɪv) *adj* tending or serving to disperse. ▸ **disˈpersively** *adv* ▸ **disˈpersiveness** *n*

dispersive medium *n Physics.* a substance in which waves of different frequencies travel at different speeds.

dispersoid (dɪˈspɜːsɔɪd) *n Chem.* a system, such as a colloid or suspension, in which one phase is dispersed in another.

dispirit (dɪˈspɪrɪt) *vb* (*tr*) to lower the spirit or enthusiasm of; make downhearted or depressed; discourage. ▸ **disˈpirited** *adj* ▸ **disˈpiritedly** *adv* ▸ **disˈpiritedness** *n* ▸ **disˈpiriting** *adj* ▸ **disˈpiritingly** *adv*

displace (dɪsˈpleɪs) *vb* (*tr*) **1** to move from the usual or correct location. **2** to remove from office or employment. **3** to occupy the place of; replace; supplant. **4** to force (someone) to leave home or country, as during a war. **5** *Chem.* to replace (an atom or group in a chemical compound) by another atom or group. **6** *Physics.* to cause a displacement of (a quantity of liquid, usually water of a specified type and density). ▸ **disˈplaceable** *adj* ▸ **disˈplacer** *n*

displaced person *n* a person forced from his home or country, esp. by war or revolution. Abbrev.: **DP.**

displacement (dɪsˈpleɪsmənt) *n* **1** the act of displacing or the condition of being displaced. **2** the weight or volume displaced by a floating or submerged body in a fluid. **3** *Chem.* another name for **substitution. 4** the volume displaced by the piston of a reciprocating pump or engine. **5** *Psychoanal.* the transferring of emotional feelings from their original object to one that disguises their real nature. **6** *Geology.* the distance any point on one side of a fault plane has moved in relation to a corresponding point on the opposite side. **7** *Astronomy.* an apparent change in position of a body, such as a star. **8** *Maths.* the distance measured in a particular direction from a reference point. Symbol: *s*

displacement activity *n* **1** *Psychol.* behaviour that occurs typically when there is a conflict between motives and that has no relevance to either motive: e.g. head scratching. **2** *Zoology.* the substitution of a pattern of animal behaviour that is different from behaviour relevant to the situation: e.g. preening at an apparently inappropriate time.

displacement ton *n* the full name for **ton**[1] (sense 6).

displant (dɪsˈplɑːnt) *vb* (*tr*) *Obsolete.* **1** to displace. **2** to transplant (a plant).

display (dɪˈspleɪ) *vb* **1** (*tr*) to show or make visible. **2** (*tr*) to disclose or make evident; reveal: *to display anger.* **3** (*tr*) to flaunt in an ostentatious way: *to display military might.* **4** (*tr*) to spread or open out; unfurl or unfold. **5** (*tr*) to give prominence to (headings, captions, etc.) by the use of certain typefaces. **6** (*intr*) *Zoology.* to engage in a display. ◆ *n* **7** the act of exhibiting or displaying; show: *a display of fear.* **8** something exhibited or displayed. **9** an ostentatious or pretentious exhibition: *a display of his accomplishments.* **10a** an arrangement of certain typefaces to give prominence to headings, captions, advertisements, etc. **10b** printed matter that is eye-catching. **11** *Electronics.* **11a** a device capable of representing information visually, as on a cathode-ray tube screen. **11b** the information so presented. **12** *Zoology.* a pattern of behaviour in birds, fishes, etc., by which the animal attracts attention while it is courting the female, defending its territory, etc. **13** (*modifier*) relating to or using typefaces that give prominence to the words they are used to set. [C14: from Anglo-French *despleier* to unfold, from Late Latin *displicāre* to scatter, from DIS-[1] + *plicāre* to fold] ▸ **dis'player** *n*

display advertisement *or* **display ad** *n* an advertisement designed to attract attention by using devices such as conspicuous or elegant typefaces, graphics, etc. See **small advertisement.**

displease (dɪs'pliːz) *vb* to annoy, offend, or cause displeasure to (someone). ▸ **dis'pleasing** *adj* ▸ **dis'pleasingly** *adv*

displeasure (dɪs'plɛʒə) *n* **1** the condition of being displeased. **2** *Archaic.* **2a** pain. **2b** an act or cause of offence. ◆ *vb* **3** an archaic word for **displease.**

displode (dɪs'pləʊd) *vb* an obsolete word for **explode.** [C17: from Latin *displōdere* from DIS-[1] + *plaudere* to clap]

disport (dɪ'spɔːt) *vb* **1** (*tr*) to indulge (oneself) in pleasure. **2** (*intr*) to frolic or gambol. ◆ *n* **3** *Archaic.* amusement. [C14: from Anglo-French *desporter,* from *des-* DIS-[1] + *porter* to carry]

disposable (dɪ'spəʊzəb^{ə}l) *adj* **1** designed for disposal after use: *disposable cups.* **2** available for use if needed: *disposable assets.* ◆ *n* **3** something, such as a baby's nappy, that is designed for disposal. **4** (*pl*) short for **disposable goods.** ▸ **dis,posa'bility** *or* **dis'posableness** *n*

disposable goods *pl n* consumer goods that are used up a short time after purchase, including perishables, newspapers, clothes, etc. Compare **durable goods.** Also called: **disposables.**

disposable income *n* **1** the money a person has available to spend after paying taxes, pension contributions, etc. **2** the total amount of money that the individuals in a community, country, etc., have available to buy consumer goods.

disposal (dɪ'spəʊz^{ə}l) *n* **1** the act or means of getting rid of something. **2** placement or arrangement in a particular order. **3** a specific method of tending to matters, as in business. **4** the act or process of transferring something to or providing something for another. **5** the power or opportunity to make use of someone or something (esp. in the phrase **at one's disposal**). **6** a means of destroying waste products, as by grinding into particles. ◆ Also (for senses 2–5): **disposition.**

dispose (dɪ'spəʊz) *vb* **1** (*intr;* foll. by *of*) **1a** to deal with or settle. **1b** to give, sell, or transfer to another. **1c** to throw out or away. **1d** to consume, esp. hurriedly. **1e** to kill. **2** to arrange or settle (matters) by placing into correct or final condition: *man proposes, God disposes.* **3** (*tr*) to make willing or receptive. **4** (*tr*) to adjust or place in a certain order or position. **5** (*tr;* often foll. by *to*) to accustom or condition. ◆ *n* **6** an obsolete word for **disposal** or **disposition.** [C14: from Old French *disposer,* from Latin *dispōnere* to set in different places, arrange, from DIS-[1] + *pōnere* to place] ▸ **dis'poser** *n*

disposed (dɪ'spəʊzd) *adj* **a** having an inclination as specified (towards something). **b** (*in combination*): *well-disposed.*

disposition (,dɪspə'zɪʃən) *n* **1** a person's usual temperament or frame of mind. **2** a natural or acquired tendency, inclination, or habit in a person or thing. **3** another word for **disposal** (senses 2–5). **4** *Philosophy, logic.* a property that consists not in the present state of an object, but in its propensity to change in a certain way under certain conditions, as brittleness which consists in the propensity to break when struck. Compare **occurrent. 5** *Archaic.* manner of placing or arranging. ▸ **,dispo'sitional** *adj*

dispossess (,dɪspə'zɛs) *vb* (*tr*) to take away possession of something, esp. property; expel. ▸ **,dispos'session** *n* ▸ **,dispos'sessor** *n* ▸ **,dispos'sessory** *adj*

disposure (dɪ'spəʊʒə) *n* a rare word for **disposal** or **disposition.**

dispraise (dɪs'preɪz) *vb* **1** (*tr*) to express disapproval or condemnation of. ◆ *n* **2** the disapproval, etc., expressed. ▸ **dis'praiser** *n* ▸ **dis'praisingly** *adv*

disprize (dɪs'praɪz) *vb* (*tr*) *Archaic.* to scorn; disdain.

disproof (dɪs'pruːf) *n* **1** facts that disprove something. **2** the act of disproving.

disproportion (,dɪsprə'pɔːʃən) *n* **1** lack of proportion or equality. **2** an instance of disparity or inequality. ◆ *vb* **3** (*tr*) to cause to become exaggerated or unequal. ▸ **,dispro'portionable** *adj* ▸ **,dispro'portionableness** *n* ▸ **,dispro'portionably** *adv*

disproportionate *adj* (,dɪsprə'pɔːʃənɪt). **1** out of proportion; unequal. ◆ *vb* (,dɪsprə'pɔːʃə,neɪt). **2** *Chem.* to undergo or cause to undergo disproportionation. ▸ **,dispro'portionately** *adv* ▸ **,dispro'portionateness** *n*

disproportionation (,dɪsprə,pɔːʃə'neɪʃən) *n* a reaction between two identical molecules in which one is reduced and the other oxidized.

disprove (dɪs'pruːv) *vb* (*tr*) to show (an assertion, claim, etc.) to be incorrect. ▸ **dis'provable** *adj* ▸ **dis'proval** *n*

disputable (dɪ'spjuːtəb^{ə}l, 'dɪspjutə-) *adj* capable of being argued; debatable. ▸ **dis,puta'bility** *or* **dis'putableness** *n* ▸ **dis'putably** *adv*

disputant (dɪ'spjuːt^{ə}nt, 'dɪspjutənt) *n* **1** a person who argues; contestant. ◆ *adj* **2** engaged in argument.

disputation (,dɪspju'teɪʃən) *n* **1** the act or an instance of arguing. **2** a formal academic debate on a thesis. **3** an obsolete word for **conversation.**

disputatious (,dɪspju'teɪʃəs) *or* **disputative** (dɪ'spjuːtətɪv) *adj* inclined to argument. ▸ **,dispu'tatiously** *or* **dis'putatively** *adv* ▸ **,dispu'tatiousness** *or* **dis'putativeness** *n*

dispute *vb* (dɪ'spjuːt). **1** to argue, debate, or quarrel about (something). **2** (*tr; may take a clause as object*) to doubt the validity, etc., of. **3** (*tr*) to seek to win; contest for. **4** (*tr*) to struggle against; resist. ◆ *n* (dɪ'spjuːt, 'dɪspjuːt). **5** an argument or quarrel. [C13: from Late Latin *disputāre* to contend verbally, from Latin: to discuss, from DIS-[1] + *putāre* to think] ▸ **dis'puter** *n*

disqualify (dɪs'kwɒlɪ,faɪ) *vb* **-fies, -fying, -fied.** (*tr*) **1** to make unfit or unqualified. **2** to make ineligible, as for entry to an examination. **3** to debar (a player or team) from a sporting contest. **4** to divest or deprive of rights, powers, or privileges: *disqualified from driving.* ▸ **dis'quali,fiable** *adj* ▸ **dis,qualifi'cation** *n* ▸ **dis'quali,fier** *n*

disquiet (dɪs'kwaɪət) *n* **1** a feeling or condition of anxiety or uneasiness. ◆ *vb* **2** (*tr*) to make anxious or upset. ◆ *adj* **3** *Archaic.* uneasy or anxious. ▸ **dis'quietedly** *or* **dis'quietly** *adv* ▸ **dis'quietedness** *or* **dis'quietness** *n* ▸ **dis'quieting** *adj* ▸ **dis'quietingly** *adv*

disquietude (dɪs'kwaɪɪ,tjuːd) *n* a feeling or state of anxiety or uneasiness.

disquisition (,dɪskwɪ'zɪʃən) *n* a formal written or oral examination of a subject. [C17: from Latin *disquīsītiō,* from *disquīrere* to make an investigation, from DIS-[1] + *quaerere* to seek] ▸ **,disqui'sitional** *adj*

Disraeli (dɪz'reɪlɪ) *n* **Benjamin,** 1st Earl of Beaconsfield. 1804–81, British Tory statesman and novelist; prime minister (1868; 1874–80). He gave coherence to the Tory principles of protectionism and imperialism, was responsible for the Reform Bill (1867) and, as prime minister, bought a controlling interest in the Suez Canal. His novels include *Coningsby* (1844) and *Sybil* (1845).

disrate (dɪs'reɪt) *vb* (*tr*) *Naval.* to punish (an officer) by lowering him in rank.

disregard (,dɪsrɪ'gɑːd) *vb* (*tr*) **1** to give little or no attention to; ignore. **2** to treat as unworthy of consideration or respect. ◆ *n* **3** lack of attention or respect. **4** (*often pl*) *Social welfare.* capital or income which is not counted in calculating the amount payable to a claimant for a means-tested benefit. ▸ **,disre'garder** *n* ▸ **,disre'gardful** *adj* ▸ **,disre'gardfully** *adv* ▸ **,disre'gardfulness** *n*

disrelish (dɪs'rɛlɪʃ) *vb* **1** (*tr*) to have a feeling of aversion for; dislike. ◆ *n* **2** such a feeling.

disremember (,dɪsrɪ'mɛmbə) *vb Informal, chiefly U.S.* to fail to recall (someone or something).

disrepair (,dɪsrɪ'pɛə) *n* the condition of being worn out or in poor working order; a condition requiring repairs.

disreputable (dɪs'rɛpjutəb^{ə}l) *adj* **1** having or causing a lack of repute. **2** disordered in appearance. ▸ **dis,reputa'bility** *or* **dis'reputableness** *n* ▸ **dis'reputably** *adv*

disrepute (,dɪsrɪ'pjuːt) *n* a loss or lack of credit or repute.

disrespect (,dɪsrɪ'spɛkt) *n* **1** contempt; rudeness. ◆ *vb* **2** (*tr*) to show lack of respect for. ▸ **,disre'spectful** *adj* ▸ **,disre'spectfully** *adv* ▸ **,disre'spectfulness** *n*

disrespectable (,dɪsrɪ'spɛktəb^{ə}l) *adj* unworthy of respect; not respectable. ▸ **,disre,specta'bility** *n*

disrobe (dɪs'rəʊb) *vb* **1** to remove the clothing of (a person) or (of a person) to undress. **2** (*tr*) to divest of authority, etc. ▸ **dis'robement** *n* ▸ **dis'rober** *n*

disrupt (dɪs'rʌpt) *vb* **1** (*tr*) to throw into turmoil or disorder. **2** (*tr*) to interrupt the progress of (a movement, meeting, etc.). **3** to break or split (something) apart. [C17: from Latin *disruptus* burst asunder, from *dīrumpere* to dash to pieces, from DIS-[1] + *rumpere* to burst] ▸ **dis'rupter** *or* **dis'ruptor** *n* ▸ **dis'ruption** *n*

disruptive (dɪs'rʌptɪv) *adj* involving, causing, or tending to cause disruption. ▸ **dis'ruptively** *adv*

disruptive discharge *n* a sudden large increase in current through an insulating medium resulting from failure of the medium to withstand an applied electric field.

diss *or* **dis** (dɪs) *vb Slang, chiefly U.S.* to treat (someone) with contempt. [C20: originally Black rap slang, short for DISRESPECT]

dissatisfied (dɪs'sætɪs,faɪd) *adj* having or showing dissatisfaction; discontented. ▸ **dis'satis,fiedly** *adv*

dissatisfy (dɪs'sætɪs,faɪ) *vb* **-fies, -fying, -fied.** (*tr*) to fail to satisfy; disappoint. ▸ **,dissatis'faction** *n* ▸ **,dissatis'factory** *adj*

dissect (dɪ'sɛkt, daɪ-) *vb* **1** to cut open and examine the structure of (a dead animal or plant). **2** (*tr*) to examine critically and minutely. [C17: from Latin *dissecāre,* from DIS-[1] + *secāre* to cut] ▸ **dis'sectible** *adj* ▸ **dis'section** *n* ▸ **dis'sector** *n*

dissected (dɪ'sɛktɪd, daɪ-) *adj* **1** *Botany.* in the form of narrow lobes or segments: *dissected leaves.* **2** *Geology.* (of plains) cut by erosion into hills and valleys, esp. following tectonic movements.

disseise *or* **disseize** (dɪs'siːz) *vb* (*tr*) *Property law.* to deprive of seisin; wrongfully dispossess of a freehold interest in land. [C14: from Anglo-Norman *desseisir,* from DIS-[1] + SEIZE] ▸ **dis'seisor** *or* **dis'seizor** *n*

disseisin *or* **disseizin** (dɪs'siːzɪn) *n* the act of disseising or state of being disseised. [C14: from Old French *dessaisine;* see DIS-[1], SEISIN]

disselboom ('dɪsəl,buəm) *n S. African.* the main haulage shaft of a wagon or cart. [from Afrikaans *dissel* shaft + *boom* beam]

dissemble (dɪ'sɛmb^{ə}l) *vb* **1** to conceal (one's real motives, emotions, etc.) by pretence. **2** (*tr*) to pretend; simulate. **3** *Obsolete.* to ignore. [C15: from earlier *dissimulen,* from Latin *dissimulāre;* probably influenced by obsolete *semble* to resemble] ▸ **dis'semblance** *n* ▸ **dis'sembler** *n* ▸ **dis'sembling** *n, adj* ▸ **dis'semblingly** *adv*

disseminate (dɪ'sɛmɪ,neɪt) *vb* (*tr*) to distribute or scatter about; diffuse. [C17: from Latin *dissēmināre,* from DIS-[1] + *sēmināre* to sow, from *sēmen* seed] ▸ **dis,semi'nation** *n* ▸ **dis'seminative** *adj* ▸ **dis'semi,nator** *n*

disseminated sclerosis *n* another name for **multiple sclerosis.**

disseminule (dɪ'sɛmɪ,njuːl) *n* any propagative part of a plant, such as a seed or spore, that helps to spread the species. [C20: from DISSEMINATE + -ULE]

dissension (dɪ'sɛnʃən) *n* disagreement, esp. when leading to a quarrel. [C13: from Latin *dissēnsiō,* from *dissentīre* to dissent]

dissent (dɪ'sɛnt) *vb* (*intr*) **1** to have a disagreement or withhold assent. **2** *Christianity.* to refuse to conform to the doctrines, beliefs, or practices of an established church, and to adhere to a different system of beliefs and practices. ◆ *n* **3** a difference of opinion. **4** *Christianity.* separation from an established church; Nonconformism. **5** the voicing of a minority opinion in announcing the decision on a case at law; dissenting judgment. [C16: from Latin *dissentīre* to disagree, from DIS-[1] + *sentīre* to perceive, feel] ▸ **dis'senter** *n* ▸ **dis'senting** *adj* ▸ **dis'sentingly** *adv*

Dissenter (dɪ'sɛntə) *n Christianity, chiefly Brit.* a Nonconformist or a person who refuses to conform to the established church.

dissentient (dɪ'sɛnʃənt) *adj* **1** dissenting, esp. from the opinion of the majority. ◆ *n* **2** a dissenter. ▸ **dis'sentience** *or* **dis'sentiency** *n* ▸ **dis'sentiently** *adv*

dissentious (dɪ'sɛnʃəs) *adj* argumentative.

dissepiment (dɪ'sɛpɪmənt) *n Biology.* a dividing partition or membrane, such as that between the chambers of a syncarpous ovary. [C18: from Late Latin *dissaepīmentum,* from DIS-[1] + *saepīmentum* hedge, from *saepīre* to enclose] ▸ **dis,sepi'mental** *adj*

dissertate ('dɪsə,teɪt) *vb* (*intr*) *Rare.* to give or make a dissertation. [C18: from Latin *dissertāre* to debate, from *disserere* to examine, from DIS-[1] + *serere* to arrange] ▸ **'disser,tator** *n*

dissertation (,dɪsə'teɪʃən) *n* **1** a written thesis, often based on original research, usually required for a higher degree. **2** a formal discourse. ▸ **,disser'tational** *adj* ▸ **,disser'tationist** *n*

disserve (dɪs'sɜːv) *vb* (*tr*) *Archaic.* to do a disservice to.

disservice (dɪs'sɜːvɪs) *n* an ill turn; wrong; injury, esp. when trying to help. ▸ **dis'serviceable** *adj*

dissever (dɪ'sɛvə) *vb* **1** to break off or become broken off. **2** (*tr*) to divide up into parts. [C13: from Old French *dessevrer,* from Late Latin DIS-[1] + *sēparāre* to SEPARATE] ▸ **dis'severance, dis'severment,** *or* **dis,sever'ation** *n*

dissident ('dɪsɪdənt) *adj* **1** disagreeing; dissenting. ◆ *n* **2** a person who disagrees, esp. one who disagrees with the government. [C16: from Latin *dissidēre* to be remote from, from DIS-[1] + *sedēre* to sit] ▸ **'dissidence** *n* ▸ **'dissidently** *adv*

dissimilar (dɪ'sɪmɪlə) *adj* not alike; not similar; different. ▸ **dis'similarly** *adv*

dissimilarity (,dɪsɪmɪ'lærɪtɪ) *n, pl* **-ties. 1** difference; unlikeness. **2** a point or instance of difference.

dissimilate (dɪ'sɪmɪ,leɪt) *vb* **1** to make or become dissimilar. **2** (usually foll. by *to*) *Phonetics.* to change or displace (a consonant) or (of a consonant) to be changed to or displaced by (another consonant) so that its manner of articulation becomes less similar to a speech sound in the same word. Thus (r) in the final syllable of French *marbre* is dissimilated to (l) in its English form *marble.* [C19: from DIS-[1] + ASSIMILATE] ▸ **dis'similative** *adj* ▸ **dis'similatory** *adj*

dissimilation (,dɪsɪmɪ'leɪʃən) *n* **1** the act or an instance of making dissimilar. **2** *Phonetics.* the alteration or omission of a consonant as a result of being dissimilated. **3** *Biology.* a less common word for **catabolism.**

dissimilitude (,dɪsɪ'mɪlɪ,tjuːd) *n* **1** dissimilarity; difference. **2** a point of difference.

dissimulate (dɪ'sɪmjʊ,leɪt) *vb* to conceal (one's real feelings) by pretence. ▸ **dis,simu'lation** *n* ▸ **dis'simulative** *adj* ▸ **dis'simu,lator** *n*

dissipate ('dɪsɪ,peɪt) *vb* **1** to exhaust or be exhausted by dispersion. **2** (*tr*) to scatter or break up. **3** (*intr*) to indulge in the pursuit of pleasure. [C15: from Latin *dissipāre* to disperse, from DIS-[1] + *supāre* to throw] ▸ **'dissi,pater** *or* **'dissi,pator** *n* ▸ **'dissi,pative** *adj*

dissipated ('dɪsɪ,peɪtɪd) *adj* **1** indulging without restraint in the pursuit of pleasure; debauched. **2** wasted, scattered, or exhausted. ▸ **'dissi,patedly** *adv* ▸ **'dissi,patedness** *n*

dissipation (,dɪsɪ'peɪʃən) *n* **1** the act of dissipating or condition of being dissipated. **2** unrestrained indulgence in physical pleasures, esp. alcohol. **3** excessive expenditure; wastefulness. **4** amusement; diversion.

dissociable (dɪ'səʊʃɪəbᵊl, -ʃə-) *adj* **1** able to be dissociated; distinguishable. **2** incongruous; irreconcilable. **3** (dɪ'səʊʃəbᵊl). Also: **dis'social.** a less common word for **unsociable.** ▸ **dis,socia'bility** *or* **dis'sociableness** *n* ▸ **dis'sociably** *adv*

dissociate (dɪ'səʊʃɪ,eɪt, -sɪ-) *vb* **1** to break or cause to break the association between (people, organizations, etc.). **2** (*tr*) to regard or treat as separate or unconnected. **3** to undergo or subject to dissociation. ▸ **dis'sociative** *adj*

dissociation (dɪ,səʊsɪ'eɪʃən, -ʃɪ-) *n* **1** the act of dissociating or the state of being dissociated. **2** *Chem.* **2a** a reversible chemical change of the molecules of a single compound into two or more other molecules, atoms, ions, or radicals. **2b** any decomposition of the molecules of a single compound into two or more other compounds, atoms, ions, or radicals. **3** separation of molecules or atoms that occurs when a liquid or solid changes to a gas. **4** *Psychiatry.* the separation of a group of mental processes or ideas from the rest of the personality, so that they lead an independent existence, as in cases of multiple personality.

dissociative disorder *n Psychol.* an emotional disorder characterized by fugue states or multiple personality.

dissoluble (dɪ'sɒljʊbᵊl) *adj* a less common word for **soluble.** [C16: from Latin *dissolūbilis,* from *dissolvere* to DISSOLVE] ▸ **dis,solu'bility** *or* **dis'solubleness** *n*

dissolute ('dɪsə,luːt) *adj* given to dissipation; debauched. [C14: from Latin *dissolūtus* loose, from *dissolvere* to DISSOLVE] ▸ **'disso,lutely** *adv* ▸ **'disso,luteness** *n*

dissolution (,dɪsə'luːʃən) *n* **1** the resolution or separation into component parts; disintegration. **2** destruction by breaking up and dispersing. **3** the termination of a meeting or assembly, such as Parliament. **4** the termination of a formal or legal relationship, such as a business enterprise, marriage, etc. **5** the state of being dissolute; dissipation. **6** the act or process of dissolving. ▸ **'disso,lutive** *adj*

dissolve (dɪ'zɒlv) *vb* **1** to go or cause to go into solution: *salt dissolves in water; water dissolves sugar.* **2** to become or cause to become liquid; melt. **3** to disintegrate or disperse. **4** to come or bring to an end. **5** to dismiss (a meeting, parliament, etc.) or (of a meeting, etc.) to be dismissed. **6** to collapse or cause to collapse emotionally: *to dissolve into tears.* **7** to lose or cause to lose distinctness or clarity. **8** (*tr*) to terminate legally, as a marriage, etc. **9** (*intr*) *Films, television.* to fade out one scene and replace with another to make two scenes merge imperceptibly (**fast dissolve**) or slowly overlap (**slow dissolve**) over a period of about three or four seconds. ◆ *n* **10** *Films, television.* a scene filmed or televised by dissolving. [C14: from Latin *dissolvere* to make loose, from DIS-[1] + *solvere* to release] ▸ **dis'solvable** *adj* ▸ **dis,solva'bility** *or* **dis'solvableness** *n* ▸ **dis'solver** *n*

dissolvent (dɪ'zɒlvənt) *n* **1** a rare word for **solvent** (sense 3). ◆ *adj* **2** able to dissolve.

dissonance ('dɪsənəns) *or* **dissonancy** *n* **1** a discordant combination of sounds. **2** lack of agreement or consistency. **3** *Music.* **3a** a sensation commonly associated with all intervals of the second and seventh, all diminished and augmented intervals, and all chords based on these intervals. Compare **consonance** (sense 3). **3b** an interval or chord of this kind.

dissonant ('dɪsənənt) *adj* **1** discordant; cacophonous. **2** incongruous or discrepant. **3** *Music.* characterized by dissonance. [C15: from Latin *dissonāre* to be discordant, from DIS-[1] + *sonāre* to sound] ▸ **'dissonantly** *adv*

dissuade (dɪ'sweɪd) *vb* (*tr*) **1** (often foll. by *from*) to deter (someone) by persuasion from a course of action, policy, etc. **2** to advise against (an action, etc.). [C15: from Latin *dissuādēre,* from DIS-[1] + *suādēre* to persuade] ▸ **dis'suadable** *adj* ▸ **dis'suader** *n* ▸ **dis'suasion** *n* ▸ **dis'suasive** *adj* ▸ **dis'suasively** *adv* ▸ **dis'suasiveness** *n*

dissyllable (dɪ'sɪləbᵊl, 'dɪs,sɪl-, 'daɪsɪl-) *or* **disyllable** ('daɪsɪləbᵊl, dɪ'sɪl-) *n Grammar.* a word of two syllables. ▸ **dissyllabic** (,dɪsɪ'læbɪk,,dɪssɪ-, ,daɪ-) *or* **disyllabic** (,daɪsɪ'læbɪk,,dɪ-) *adj*

dissymmetry (dɪ'sɪmɪtrɪ, dɪs'sɪm-) *n, pl* **-tries. 1** lack of symmetry. **2** the relationship between two objects when one is the mirror image of the other. **3** another name for **chirality.** ▸ **dissymmetric** (,dɪsɪ'mɛtrɪk, ,dɪssɪ-) *or* **,dissym'metrical** *adj* ▸ **,dissym'metrically** *adv*

dist. *abbrev. for:* **1** distant. **2** distinguish(ed). **3** district.

distaff ('dɪstɑːf) *n* **1** the rod on which flax is wound preparatory to spinning. **2** *Figurative.* women's work. [Old English *distæf,* from *dis-* bunch of flax + *stæf* STAFF[1]; see DIZEN]

distaff side *n* the female side or branch of a family. Compare **spear side.**

distal ('dɪstᵊl) *adj Anatomy.* (of a muscle, bone, limb, etc.) situated farthest from the centre, median line, or point of attachment or origin. Compare **proximal.** [C19: from DISTANT + -AL[1]] ▸ **'distally** *adv*

distance ('dɪstəns) *n* **1** the intervening space between two points or things. **2** the length of this gap. **3** the state of being apart in space; remoteness. **4** an interval between two points in time. **5** the extent of progress; advance. **6** a distant place or time: *he lives at a distance from his work.* **7** a separation or remoteness in relationship; disparity. **8 keep one's distance.** to maintain a proper or discreet reserve in respect of another person. **9** *Geom.* **9a** the length of the shortest line segment joining two points. **9b** the length along a straight line or curve. **10** (preceded by *the*) the most distant or a faraway part of the visible scene or landscape. **11** *Horse racing.* **11a** *Brit.* a point on a racecourse 240 yards from the winning post. **11b** *Brit.* any interval of more than 20 lengths between any two finishers in a race. **11c** *U.S.* the part of a racecourse that a horse must reach in any heat before the winner passes the finishing line in order to qualify for later heats. **12 go the distance. 12a** *Boxing.* to complete a bout without being knocked out. **12b** to be able to complete an assigned task or responsibility. **13** the distant parts of a picture, such as a landscape. **14 middle distance. 14a** (in a picture) halfway between the foreground and the horizon. **14b** (in a natural situation) halfway between the observer and the horizon. **15** (*modifier*) *Athletics.* relating to or denoting the longer races, usually those longer than a mile: *a distance runner.* ◆ *vb* (*tr*) **16** to hold or place at a distance. **17** to separate (oneself) mentally or emotionally from something. **18** to outdo; outstrip.

distance learning *n* a teaching system consisting of video, audio, and written material designed for a person to use in studying a subject at home.

distant ('dɪstənt) *adj* **1** far away or apart in space or time. **2** (*postpositive*) separated in space or time by a specified distance. **3** apart in relevance, association, or relationship: *a distant cousin.* **4** coming from or going to a faraway place: *a distant journey.* **5** remote in manner; aloof. **6** abstracted; absent: *a distant look.* [C14: from Latin *distāre* to be distant, from DIS-[1] + *stāre* to stand] ▸ **'distantly** *adv* ▸ **'distantness** *n*

distant early warning *n* a U.S. radar detection system to warn of missile attack. See also **DEW line.**

distaste (dɪs'teɪst) *n* **1** (often foll. by *for*) an absence of pleasure (in); dislike (of); aversion (to): *to look at someone with distaste.* ◆ *vb* **2** (*tr*) an archaic word for **dislike.**

distasteful (dɪs'teɪstfʊl) *adj* unpleasant or offensive. ▸ **dis'tastefully** *adv* ▸ **dis'tastefulness** *n*

distemper[1] (dɪs'tɛmpə) *n* **1** any of various infectious diseases of animals, esp. **canine distemper,** a highly contagious viral disease of dogs, characterized initially by high fever and a discharge from the nose and eyes. See also **hard pad, strangles. 2** *Archaic.* **2a** a disease or disorder. **2b** disturbance. **2c** discontent. ◆ *vb* **3** (*tr*) *Archaic.* to disturb. [C14: from Late Latin *distemperāre* to derange the health of, from Latin DIS-[1] + *temperāre* to mix in correct proportions]

distemper[2] (dɪs'tɛmpə) *n* **1** a technique of painting in which the pigments are mixed with water, glue, size, etc., used for poster, mural, and scene painting. **2** the paint used in this technique or any of various water-based paints, including, in Britain, whitewash. ◆ *vb* **3** (*tr*) to mix (pigments) with water and size. **4** to paint (something) with distemper. [C14: from Medieval Latin *distemperāre* to soak, from Latin DIS-[1] + *temperāre* to mingle]

distend (dɪ'stɛnd) *vb* **1** to expand or be expanded by or as if by pressure from within; swell; inflate. **2** (*tr*) to stretch out or extend. **3** (*tr*) to magnify in importance; exaggerate. [C14: from Latin *distendere,* from DIS-[1] + *tendere* to stretch]

▸ **dis'tender** *n* ▸ **dis'tensible** *adj* ▸ **dis,tensi'bility** *n* ▸ **dis'tension** *or* **dis'tention** *n*

distich ('dıstık) *n Prosody.* a unit of two verse lines, usually a couplet. **[C16:** from Greek *distikhos* having two lines, from DI-[1] + *stikhos* STICH**]** ▸ **'distichal** *adj*

distichous ('dıstıkəs) *adj* (of leaves) arranged in two vertical rows on opposite sides of the stem. ▸ **'distichously** *adv*

distil *or U.S.* **distill** (dıs'tıl) *vb* **-tils** *or* **-tills, -tilling, -tilled. 1** to subject to or undergo distillation. See also **rectify** (sense 2). **2** (sometimes foll. by *out* or *off*) to purify, separate, or concentrate, or be purified, separated, or concentrated by distillation. **3** to obtain or be obtained by distillation: *to distil whisky.* **4** to exude or give off (a substance) in drops or small quantities. **5** (*tr*) to extract the essence of as if by distillation. **[C14:** from Latin *dēstillāre* to distil, from DE- + *stillāre* to drip**]** ▸ **dis'tillable** *adj*

distillate ('dıstılıt, -,leıt) *n* **1** Also called: **distillation.** the product of distillation. **2** a concentrated essence.

distillation (,dıstı'leıʃən) *or* **distillment** *n* **1** the act, process, or product of distilling. **2** the process of evaporating or boiling a liquid and condensing its vapour. **3** purification or separation of mixture by using different evaporation rates or boiling points of their components. See also **fractional distillation. 4** the process of obtaining the essence or an extract of a substance, usually by heating it in a solvent. **5** another name for **distillate** (sense 1). **6** a concentrated essence. ▸ **dis'tillatory** *adj*

distiller (dı'stılə) *n* a person or organization that distils, esp. a company that makes spirits.

distillery (dı'stılərı) *n, pl* **-eries.** a place where alcoholic drinks, etc., are made by distillation.

distinct (dı'stıŋkt) *adj* **1** easily sensed or understood; clear; precise. **2** (when postpositive, foll. by *from*) not the same (as); separate (from); distinguished (from). **3** not alike; different. **4** sharp; clear. **5** recognizable; definite: *a distinct improvement.* **6** explicit; unequivocal. **7** *Maths, logic.* (of a pair of entities) not numerically identical. **8** *Botany.* (of parts of a plant) not joined together; separate. **[C14:** from Latin *distinctus,* from *distinguere* to DISTINGUISH**]** ▸ **dis'tinctly** *adv* ▸ **dis'tinctness** *n*

distinction (dı'stıŋkʃən) *n* **1** the act or an instance of distinguishing or differentiating. **2** a distinguishing feature. **3** the state of being different or distinguishable. **4** special honour, recognition, or fame. **5** excellence of character; distinctive qualities: *a man of distinction.* **6** distinguished appearance. **7** a symbol of honour or rank.

distinctive (dı'stıŋktıv) *adj* **1** serving or tending to distinguish. **2** denoting one of a set of minimal features of a phoneme in a given language that serve to distinguish it from other phonemes. The distinctive features of /p/ in English are that it is voiceless, bilabial, non-nasal, and plosive; /b/ is voiced, bilabial, non-nasal, and plosive: the two differ by the distinctive feature of voice. ▸ **dis'tinctively** *adv* ▸ **dis'tinctiveness** *n*

distinctiveness ratio *n Statistics.* the ratio of the relative frequency of some event in a given sample to that in the general population or another relevant sample.

distingué *French.* (distẽge) *adj* distinguished or noble.

distinguish (dı'stıŋgwıʃ) *vb* (*mainly tr*) **1** (when *intr*, foll. by *between* or *among*) to make, show, or recognize a difference or differences (between or among); differentiate (between). **2** to be a distinctive feature of; characterize. **3** to make out; perceive. **4** to mark for a special honour or title. **5** to make (oneself) noteworthy: *he distinguished himself by his cowardice.* **6** to classify; categorize: *we distinguished three species.* **[C16:** from Latin *distinguere* to separate, discriminate**]** ▸ **dis'tinguishable** *adj* ▸ **dis'tinguishably** *adv* ▸ **dis'tinguisher** *n* ▸ **dis'tinguishing** *adj* ▸ **dis'tinguishingly** *adv*

distinguished (dı'stıŋgwıʃt) *adj* **1** noble or dignified in appearance or behaviour. **2** eminent; famous; celebrated.

distort (dı'stɔːt) *vb* (*tr*) **1** (*often passive*) to twist or pull out of shape; make bent or misshapen; contort; deform. **2** to alter or misrepresent (facts, motives, etc.). **3** *Electronics.* to reproduce or amplify (a signal) inaccurately, changing the shape of the waveform. **[C16:** from Latin *distortus* misshapen, from *distorquēre* to turn different ways, from DIS-[1] + *torquēre* to twist**]** ▸ **dis'torted** *adj* ▸ **dis'tortedly** *adv* ▸ **dis'tortedness** *n* ▸ **dis'torter** *n* ▸ **dis'tortive** *adj*

distortion (dı'stɔːʃən) *n* **1** the act or an instance of distorting or the state of being distorted. **2** something that is distorted. **3** an aberration of a lens or optical system in which the magnification varies with the lateral distance from the axis. **4** *Electronics.* **4a** an undesired change in the shape of an electrical wave or signal. **4b** the result of such a change in waveform, esp. a loss of clarity in radio reception or sound reproduction. **5** *Psychol.* a change in perception so that it does not correspond to reality. **6** *Psychoanal.* the disguising of the meaning of unconscious thoughts so that they may appear in consciousness, e.g. in dreams. ▸ **dis'tortional** *adj*

distr. *abbrev. for:* **1** distribution. **2** distributor.

distract (dı'strækt) *vb* (*tr*) **1** (*often passive*) to draw the attention of (a person) away from something. **2** to divide or confuse the attention of (a person). **3** to amuse or entertain. **4** to trouble greatly. **5** to make mad. **[C14:** from Latin *distractus* perplexed, from *distrahere* to pull in different directions, from DIS-[1] + *trahere* to drag**]** ▸ **dis'tracter** *n* ▸ **dis'tractible** *adj* ▸ **dis,tracti'bility** *n* ▸ **dis'tracting** *adj* ▸ **dis'tractingly** *adv* ▸ **dis'tractive** *adj* ▸ **dis'tractively** *adv*

distracted (dı'stræktıd) *adj* **1** bewildered; confused. **2** mad. ▸ **dis'tractedly** *adv* ▸ **dis'tractedness** *n*

distraction (dı'strækʃən) *n* **1** the act or an instance of distracting or the state of being distracted. **2** something that serves as a diversion or entertainment. **3** an interruption; an obstacle to concentration. **4** mental turmoil or madness.

distrain (dı'streın) *vb Law.* to seize (personal property) by way of distress. **[C13:** from Old French *destreindre,* from Latin *distringere* to impede, from DIS-[1] + *stringere* to draw tight**]** ▸ **dis'trainable** *adj* ▸ **dis'trainment** *n* ▸ **dis'trainor** *or* **dis'trainer** *n*

distrainee (,dıstreı'niː) *n Law.* a person whose property has been seized by way of distraint.

distraint (dı'streınt) *n Law.* the act or process of distraining; distress.

distrait (dı'streı; *French* distrɛ) *adj* absent-minded; abstracted. **[C18:** from French, from *distraire* to DISTRACT**]**

distraught (dı'strɔːt) *adj* **1** distracted or agitated. **2** *Rare.* mad. **[C14:** changed from obsolete *distract* through influence of obsolete *straught,* past participle of STRETCH**]**

distress (dı'strɛs) *vb* (*tr*) **1** to cause mental pain to; upset badly. **2** (*usually passive*) to subject to financial or other trouble. **3** to damage (esp. furniture), as by scratching or denting it, in order to make it appear older than it is. **4** *Law.* a less common word for **distrain. 5** *Archaic.* to compel. ◆ *n* **6** mental pain; anguish. **7** the act of distressing or the state of being distressed. **8** physical or financial trouble. **9 in distress.** (of a ship, aircraft, etc.) in dire need of help. **10** *Law.* **10a** the seizure and holding of property as security for payment of or in satisfaction of a debt, claim, etc.; distraint. **10b** the property thus seized. **10c** *U.S.* (*as modifier*): *distress merchandise.* **[C13:** from Old French *destresse* distress, via Vulgar Latin, from Latin *districtus* divided in mind; see DISTRAIN**]** ▸ **dis'tressful** *adj* ▸ **dis'tressfully** *adv* ▸ **dis'tressfulness** *n* ▸ **dis'tressing** *adj, n* ▸ **dis'tressingly** *adv*

distressed (dı'strɛst) *adj* **1** much troubled; upset; afflicted. **2** in financial straits; poor. **3** (of furniture, fabric, etc.) having signs of ageing artificially applied. **4** *Economics.* another word for **depressed** (sense 4).

distress merchandise *n U.S.* goods sold at reduced prices in order to pay overdue debts, etc.

distress signal *n* a signal by radio, Very light, etc. from a ship or other vessel in need of immediate assistance.

distributary (dı'strıbjutərı, -trı) *n, pl* **-taries.** one of several outlet streams draining a river, esp. on a delta.

distribute (dı'strıbjuːt) *vb* (*tr*) **1** to give out in shares; dispense. **2** to hand out or deliver: *to distribute handbills.* **3** (*often passive*) to spread throughout a space or area: *gulls are distributed along the west coast.* **4** (*often passive*) to divide into classes or categories; classify: *these books are distributed in four main categories.* **5** *Printing.* to return (used type) to the correct positions in the type case. **6** *Logic.* to incorporate in a distributed term of a categorial proposition. **7** *Maths, logic.* to expand an expression containing two operators in such a way that the precedence of the operators is changed; for example, distributing multiplication over addition in $a(b + c)$ yields $ab + ac$. **8** *Obsolete.* to dispense (justice). **[C15:** from Latin *distribuere* from DIS-[1] + *tribuere* to give**]** ▸ **dis'tributable** *adj*

distributed array processor *n* a type of computer system that uses a coordinated array of separate processors applied to a single problem. Abbrev.: **DAP.**

distributed logic *n* a computer system in which remote terminals and electronic devices, distributed throughout the system, supplement the main computer by doing some of the computing or decision making.

distributed practice *n Psychol.* learning with reasonably long intervals between separate occasions of learning. Compare **massed practice.**

distributed systems *pl n* two or more computers linked by telecommunication, each of which can perform independently.

distributed term *n Logic.* a term applying equally to every member of the class it designates, as *doctors* in *no doctors are overworked.*

distributee (dı,strıbjʊ'tiː) *n Law, chiefly U.S.* a person entitled to share in the estate of an intestate.

distribution (,dıstrı'bjuːʃən) *n* **1** the act of distributing or the state or manner of being distributed. **2** a thing or portion distributed. **3** arrangement or location. **4** *Commerce.* the process of physically satisfying the demand for goods and services. **5** *Economics.* the division of the total income of a community among its members, esp. between labour incomes (wages and salaries) and property incomes (rents, interest, and dividends). **6** *Statistics.* the set of possible values of a random variable, or points in a sample space, considered in terms of new theoretical or observed frequency: *a normal distribution.* **7** *Law.* the apportioning of the estate of a deceased intestate among the persons entitled to share in it. **8** *Law.* the lawful division of the assets of a bankrupt among his creditors. **9** *Finance.* **9a** the division of part of a company's profit as a dividend to its shareholders. **9b** the amount paid by dividend in a particular distribution. **10** *Engineering.* the way in which the fuel-air mixture is supplied to each cylinder of a multicylinder internal-combustion engine. ▸ **,distri'butional** *adj*

distribution channel *n Marketing.* the network of organizations, including manufacturers, wholesalers, and retailers, that distributes goods or services to consumers.

distribution function *n* short for **cumulative distribution function.**

distributive (dı'strıbjutıv) *adj* **1** characterized by or relating to distribution. **2** *Grammar.* referring separately to the individual people or items in a group, as the words *each* and *every.* ◆ *n* **3** *Grammar.* a distributive word. ▸ **dis'tributively** *adv* ▸ **dis'tributiveness** *n*

distributive bargaining *n Industrial relations.* a negotiation process aimed at reaching a compromise agreement over how resources may be allocated between the parties.

distributive law *n Maths, logic.* a theorem asserting that one operator can validly be distributed over another. See **distribute** (sense 7).

distributor *or* **distributer** (dı'strıbjutə) *n* **1** a person or thing that distributes. **2** a wholesaler or middleman engaged in the distribution of a category of goods, esp. to retailers in a specific area. **3** the device in a petrol engine that distributes the high-tension voltage to the sparking plugs in the sequence of the firing order.

district ('dɪstrɪkt) *n* **1a** an area of land marked off for administrative or other purposes. **1b** (*as modifier*): *district nurse.* **2** a locality separated by geographical attributes; region. **3** any subdivision of any territory, region, etc. **4** (in England from 1974 and in Wales 1974–96) any of the subdivisions of the nonmetropolitan counties that elects a council responsible for local planning, housing, rates, etc. See also **metropolitan district. 5** (in Scotland until 1975) a landward division of a county. **6** (in Scotland 1975–96) any of the subdivisions of the regions that elected a council responsible for environmental health services, housing, etc. **7** any of the 26 areas into which Northern Ireland has been divided since 1973. Elected district councils are responsible for environmental health services etc. ◆ *vb* **8** (*tr*) to divide into districts. [C17: from Medieval Latin *districtus* area of jurisdiction, from Latin *distringere* to stretch out; see DISTRAIN]

district attorney *n* (in the U.S.) the state prosecuting officer in a specified judicial district.

district court *n* **1** (in Scotland) a court of summary jurisdiction held by a stipendiary magistrate or one or more justices of the peace to deal with minor criminal offences. **2** (in the U.S.) **2a** a federal trial court serving a federal judicial district. **2b** (in some states) a court having general jurisdiction in a state judicial district. **3** (in Australia and New Zealand) a court lower than a high court. Former name: **magistrates' court.**

district court judge *n Austral. and N.Z.* a judge presiding over a lower court. Former name: **magistrate.**

district high school *n N.Z.* a school in a rural area that includes primary and post-primary classes.

district nurse *n* (in Britain) a nurse employed within the National Health Service to attend patients in a particular area, usually by visiting them in their own homes.

District of Columbia *n* a federal district of the eastern U.S., coextensive with the federal capital, Washington. Pop.: 528 964 (1997 est.). Area: 178 sq. km (69 sq. miles). Abbrevs.: **D.C.** or (with zip code) **DC**

distringas (dɪs'trɪŋgæs) *n Law.* (formerly) a writ directing a sheriff to distrain. [from Latin: you shall distrain (the opening word of the writ)]

Distrito Federal (*Portuguese* dis'tritu fede'ral) *n* a district in S central Brazil, containing Brasília: detached from Goiás state in 1960. Pop.: 1 737 800 (1995 est.). Area: 5815 sq. km (2245 sq. miles).

distrix ('dɪstrɪks) *n Med.* the splitting of the ends of hairs. [from Greek DIS-[2] + *thrix* hair]

distrust (dɪs'trʌst) *vb* **1** to regard as untrustworthy or dishonest. ◆ *n* **2** suspicion; doubt. ▸ **dis'truster** *n* ▸ **dis'trustful** *adj* ▸ **dis'trustfully** *adv* ▸ **dis'trustfulness** *n*

disturb (dɪ'stɜːb) *vb* (*tr*) **1** to intrude on; interrupt. **2** to destroy or interrupt the quietness or peace of. **3** to disarrange; muddle. **4** (*often passive*) to upset or agitate; trouble: *I am disturbed at your bad news.* **5** to inconvenience; put out: *don't disturb yourself on my account.* [C13: from Latin *disturbāre*, from DIS-[1] + *turbāre* to confuse] ▸ **dis'turber** *n* ▸ **dis'turbing** *adj* ▸ **dis'turbingly** *adv*

disturbance (dɪ'stɜːbəns) *n* **1** the act of disturbing or the state of being disturbed. **2** an interruption or intrusion. **3** an unruly outburst or tumult. **4** *Law.* an interference with another's rights. **5** *Geology.* a minor movement of the earth causing a small earthquake. **6** *Meteorol.* a small depression. **7** *Psychiatry.* a mental or emotional disorder.

disturbed (dɪ'stɜːbd) *adj Psychiatry.* emotionally upset, troubled, or maladjusted.

disulfiram (ˌdaɪsʌl'fɪərəm) *n* a drug used in the treatment of alcoholism that acts by inducing nausea and vomiting following ingestion of alcohol. [C20: from tetraethylthiu*ram disulf*ide]

disulphate (daɪ'sʌlfeɪt) *n* another name for **pyrosulphate.**

disulphide (daɪ'sʌlfaɪd) *n* any chemical compound containing two sulphur atoms per molecule. Also called (not in technical usage): **bisulphide.**

disulphuric acid (ˌdaɪsʌl'fjʊərɪk) *n* another name for **pyrosulphuric acid.**

disunite (ˌdɪsju'naɪt) *vb* **1** to separate or become separate; disrupt. **2** (*tr*) to set at variance; estrange. ▸ **dis'union** *n* ▸ ˌ**disu'niter** *n*

disunity (dɪs'juːnɪtɪ) *n, pl* **-ties.** dissension or disagreement.

disuse (dɪs'juːs) *n* the condition of being unused; neglect (often in the phrases **in** *or* **into disuse**).

disused (dɪs'juːzd) *adj* no longer used: *a disused mine.*

disutility (ˌdɪsjuː'tɪlɪtɪ) *n, pl* **-ties.** *Economics.* **a** the shortcomings of a commodity or activity in satisfying human wants. **b** the degree to which a commodity or activity fails to satisfy human wants. ◆ Compare **utility** (sense 4).

disyllable ('daɪsɪləb°l, dɪ'sɪl-) *n* a variant of **dissyllable.** ▸ **disyllabic** (ˌdaɪsɪ'læbɪk, ˌdɪ-) *adj*

dit (dɪt) *n* the short sound used, in combination with the long sound *dah*, in the spoken representation of Morse and other telegraphic codes. Compare **dot**[1] (sense 6).

dita ('diːtə) *n* an apocynaceous shrub, *Alstonia scholaris*, of tropical Africa and Asia, having large shiny whorled leaves and medicinal bark. [C19: from Tagalog]

ditch (dɪtʃ) *n* **1** a narrow channel dug in the earth, usually used for drainage, irrigation, or as a boundary marker. **2** any small, natural waterway. **3** *Irish.* a bank made of earth excavated from and placed alongside a drain or stream. **4** *Informal.* either of the gutters at the side of a tenpin bowling lane. **5 last ditch.** a last resort or place of last defence. ◆ *vb* **6** to make a ditch or ditches in (a piece of ground). **7** (*intr*) to edge with a ditch. **8** *Slang.* to crash or be crashed, esp. deliberately, as to avoid more unpleasant circumstances: *he had to ditch the car.* **9** (*tr*) *Slang.* to abandon or discard: *to ditch a girlfriend.* **10** *Slang.* to land (an aircraft) on water in an emergency. **11** (*tr*) *U.S. slang.* to evade: *to ditch the police.* [Old English *dīc*; related to Old Saxon *dīk*, Old Norse *dīki*, Middle High German *tīch* dyke, pond, Latin *fīgere* to stick, see DYKE[1]] ▸ **'ditcher** *n* ▸ **'ditchless** *adj*

ditchwater ('dɪtʃˌwɔːtə) *n* **1** stagnant water. **2** (**as**) **dull as ditchwater.** extremely uninspiring.

ditheism ('daɪθiːˌɪzəm) *n Theol.* **1** the belief in two equal gods. **2** the belief that two equal principles reign over the world, one good and one evil. ▸ **'ditheist** *n* ▸ ˌ**dithe'istic** *adj*

dither ('dɪðə) *vb* (*intr*) **1** *Chiefly Brit.* to be uncertain or indecisive. **2** *Chiefly U.S.* to be in an agitated state. **3** to tremble, as with cold. ◆ *n* **4** *Chiefly Brit.* a state of indecision. **5** a state of agitation. [C17: variant of C14 (northern English dialect) *didder*, of uncertain origin] ▸ **'ditherer** *n* ▸ **'dithery** *adj*

dithionite (daɪ'θaɪəˌnaɪt) *n* any salt of dithionous acid. Also called: **hyposulphite, hydrosulphite.**

dithionous acid (daɪ'θaɪənəs) *n* an unstable dibasic acid known only in solution and in the form of dithionite salts. It is a powerful reducing agent. Formula: $H_2S_2O_4$. Also called: **hyposulphurous acid, hydrosulphurous acid.** [from DI-[1] + *thion-*, from Greek *theion* sulphur + -OUS]

dithyramb ('dɪθɪˌræm, -ˌræmb) *n* **1** (in ancient Greece) a passionate choral hymn in honour of Dionysus; the forerunner of Greek drama. **2** any utterance or a piece of writing that resembles this. [C17: from Latin *dīthyrambus*, from Greek *dithurambos*; related to *iambos* IAMB]

dithyrambic (ˌdɪθɪ'ræmbɪk) *adj* **1** *Prosody.* of or relating to a dithyramb. **2** passionately eloquent. ▸ ˌ**dithy'rambically** *adv*

dittander (dɪ'tændə, 'dɪt°n-) *n* a cruciferous plant, *Lepidium latifolium*, of coastal regions of Europe, N Africa, and SW Asia, with clusters of small white flowers.

dittany ('dɪtənɪ) *n, pl* **-nies. 1** an aromatic Cretan plant, *Origanum dictamnus*, with pink drooping flowers: formerly credited with great medicinal properties: family *Labiatae* (labiates). **2** Also called: **stone mint.** a North American labiate plant, *Cunila origanoides*, with clusters of purplish flowers. **3** another name for **gas plant.** [C14: from Old French *ditan*, from Latin *dictamnus*, from Greek *diktamnon*, perhaps from *Diktē*, mountain in Crete]

ditto ('dɪtəʊ) *n, pl* **-tos. 1** the aforementioned; the above; the same. Used in accounts, lists, etc., to avoid repetition and symbolized by two small marks (,,) known as **ditto marks,** placed under the thing repeated. Abbrev.: **do. 2** *Informal.* **2a** a duplicate. **2b** (*as modifier*): *a ditto copy.* ◆ *adv* **3** in the same way. ◆ **4** *sentence substitute. Informal.* used to avoid repeating or to confirm agreement with an immediately preceding sentence. ◆ *vb* **-tos, -toing, -toed. 5** (*tr*) to copy; repeat. [C17: from Italian (Tuscan dialect), variant of *detto* said, from *dicere* to say, from Latin]

dittography (dɪ'tɒgrəfɪ) *n, pl* **-phies. 1** the unintentional repetition of letters or words. **2** a passage of manuscript demonstrating dittography. ▸ **dittographic** (ˌdɪtə'græfɪk) *adj*

ditty ('dɪtɪ) *n, pl* **-ties.** a short simple song or poem. [C13: from Old French *ditie* poem, from *ditier* to compose, from Latin *dictāre* DICTATE]

ditty bag *n* a sailor's cloth bag for personal belongings or tools. A box used for these purposes is termed a **ditty box.** [C19: perhaps from obsolete *dutty* calico, from Hindi *dhōtī* loincloth, DHOTI]

ditzy *or* **ditsy** ('dɪtzɪ) *adj* **-zier, -ziest** *or* **-sier, -siest.** *Slang.* silly and scatterbrained. [C20: perhaps from DOTTY + DIZZY]

Diu ('diːuː) *n* a small island off the NW coast of India: together with a mainland area, it formed a district of Portuguese India (1535–1961); formerly part of the Indian Union Territory of Goa, Daman, and Diu (1962–87).

diuresis (ˌdaɪju'riːsɪs) *n* excretion of an unusually large quantity of urine. [C17: from New Latin, from Greek *diourein* to urinate]

diuretic (ˌdaɪju'retɪk) *adj* **1** acting to increase the flow of urine. ◆ *n* **2** a drug or agent that increases the flow of urine. ▸ ˌ**diu'retically** *adv* ▸ ˌ**diu'reticalness** *n*

diurnal (daɪ'ɜːn°l) *adj* **1** happening during the day or daily. **2** (of flowers) open during the day and closed at night. **3** (of animals) active during the day. ◆ Compare **nocturnal.** ◆ *n* **4** a service book containing all the canonical hours except matins. [C15: from Late Latin *diurnālis*, from Latin *diurnus*, from *diēs* day] ▸ **di'urnally** *adv*

diurnal parallax *n* See **parallax** (sense 2).

div[1] (dɪv) *n Maths.* short for **divergence** (sense 4).

div[2] (dɪv) *n Prison slang.* a stupid or foolish person. [C20: probably shortened and changed from DEVIANT]

div. *abbrev. for:* **1** divide(d). **2** dividend. **3** division. **4** divorce(d).

diva ('diːvə) *n, pl* **-vas** *or* **-ve** (-vɪ). a highly distinguished female singer; prima donna. [C19: via Italian from Latin: a goddess, from *dīvus* DIVINE]

divagate ('daɪvəˌgeɪt) *vb* (*intr*) *Rare.* to digress or wander. [C16: from Latin DI-[2] + *vagārī* to wander] ▸ ˌ**diva'gation** *n*

divalent (daɪ'veɪlənt, 'daɪˌveɪ-) *adj Chem.* **1** having a valency of two. **2** having two valencies. ◆ Also: **bivalent.** ▸ **di'valency** *n*

divan (dɪ'væn) *n* **1a** a backless sofa or couch, designed to be set against a wall. **1b** a bed resembling such a couch. **2** (esp. formerly) a room for smoking and drinking, as in a coffee shop. **3a** a Muslim law court, council chamber, or counting house. **3b** a Muslim council of state. **4** a collection of poems. **5** (in Muslim law) an account book. ◆ Also called (for senses 2–5): **diwan.** [C16: from Turkish *dīvān*, from Persian *dīwān*]

divaricate *vb* (daɪ'værɪˌkeɪt). **1** (*intr*) (esp. of branches) to diverge at a wide angle. ◆ *adj* (daɪ'værɪkɪt, -ˌkeɪt). **2** branching widely; forked. [C17: from Latin *dīvāricāre* to stretch apart, from DI-[2] + *vāricāre* to stand astride] ▸ **di'varicately** *adv* ▸ **di'varˌcatingly** *adv* ▸ **diˌvari'cation** *n*

divaricator (daɪ'værɪˌkeɪtə) *n Zoology.* a muscle in brachiopods that controls the opening of the shell.

dive (daɪv) *vb* **dives, diving, dived** *or U.S.* **dove, dived.** (*mainly intr*) **1** to plunge headfirst into water. **2** (of a submarine, swimmer, etc.) to submerge under water. **3** (*also tr*) to fly (an aircraft) in a steep nose-down descending path, or (of an aircraft) to fly in such a path. **4** to rush, go, or reach quickly, as in a headlong plunge: *he dived for the ball.* **5** (*also tr; foll. by in or into*) to dip or put (one's hand) quickly or forcefully (into): *to dive into one's pocket.* **6** (usually foll. by *in* or *into*) to involve oneself (in something), as in eating food. ◆ *n* **7** a headlong plunge into water, esp. one of several formalized movements executed as a sport. **8** an act or instance of diving. **9** a steep nose-down descent of an aircraft. **10** *Slang.* a disreputable or seedy bar or club. **11** *Boxing slang.* the act of a boxer pretending to be knocked down or out: *he took a dive in the fourth round.* [Old English *dȳfan;* related to Old Norse *dȳfa* to dip, Frisian *dīvi;* see DEEP, DIP]

dive-bomb *vb* (*tr*) to bomb (a target) using or in the manner of a dive bomber.

dive bomber *n* a military aircraft designed to release its bombs on a target during a steep dive.

dive brake *n* **1** a flap or spoiler extended from the wings of a ground-attack aircraft for controlling a dive. **2** another name for **air brake.**

Divehi ('dɪveɪ) *n* the language of the Maldive Islands, belonging to the Indic branch of the Indo-European family.

diver ('daɪvə) *n* **1** a person or thing that dives. **2** a person who works or explores underwater. **3** any aquatic bird of the genus *Gavia,* family *Gaviidae,* and order *Gaviiformes* of northern oceans, having a straight pointed bill, small wings, and a long body: noted for swiftness and skill in swimming and diving. U.S. and Canadian name: **loon. 4** any of various other diving birds.

diverge (daɪ'vɜːdʒ) *vb* **1** to separate or cause to separate and go in different directions from a point. **2** (*intr*) to be at variance; differ: *our opinions diverge.* **3** (*intr*) to deviate from a prescribed course. **4** (*intr*) *Maths.* (of a series) to have no limit. [C17: from Medieval Latin *dīvergere,* from Latin DI-[2] + *vergere* to turn]

divergence (daɪ'vɜːdʒəns) *n* **1** the act or result of diverging or the amount by which something diverges. **2** the condition of being divergent. **3** *Meteorol.* the outflowing of airstreams from a particular area, caused by expanding air. **4** *Maths.* **4a** the scalar product of the operator, ∇, and a vector function, *A,* where $\nabla = i\partial/\partial x + j\partial/\partial y + k\partial/\partial z$, and *i, j,* and *k* are unit vectors. Usually written: div **A**, ∇*A*, or ∇.**A**. Compare **curl** (sense 11), **gradient** (sense 4). **4b** the property of being divergent. **5** the spreading of a stream of electrons as a result of their mutual electrostatic repulsion. **6** the turning of the eyes outwards in order to fixate an object farther away than that previously being fixated. Compare **convergence** (sense 7). **7** Also called: **divergent evolution.** the evolutionary development of structures or organisms that differ from each other in form and function but have evolved from the same basic structure or organism. Compare **convergence** (sense 5). ◆ Also called (for senses 1, 2): **divergency.**

divergent (daɪ'vɜːdʒənt) *adj* **1** diverging or causing divergence. **2** (of opinions, interests, etc.) different. **3** *Maths.* (of a series) having no limit; not convergent. **4** *Botany.* (of plant organs) farther apart at their tops than at their bases. ▸ **di'vergently** *adv*

USAGE The use of *divergent* to mean different as in *they hold widely divergent views* is considered by some people to be incorrect.

divergent thinking *n Psychol.* thinking in an unusual and unstereotyped way, e.g. to generate several possible solutions to a problem. Compare **convergent thinking.**

divers ('daɪvəz) *determiner Archaic or literary.* **a** various; sundry; some. **b** (*as pronoun; functioning as pl*): *divers of them.* [C13: from Old French, from Latin *dīversus* turned in different directions; see DIVERT]

diverse (daɪ'vɜːs, 'daɪvɜːs) *adj* **1** having variety; assorted. **2** distinct in kind. [C13: from Latin *dīversus;* see DIVERS] ▸ **di'versely** *adv* ▸ **di'verseness** *n*

diversification (daɪˌvɜːsɪfɪ'keɪʃən) *n* **1** *Commerce.* the practice of varying products, operations, etc., in order to spread risk, expand, exploit spare capacity, etc. **2** (in regional planning policies) the attempt to provide regions with an adequate variety of industries. **3** the act of diversifying.

diversiform (daɪ'vɜːsɪˌfɔːm) *adj* having various forms.

diversify (daɪ'vɜːsɪˌfaɪ) *vb* **-fies, -fying, -fied. 1** (*tr*) to create different forms of; variegate; vary. **2** (of an enterprise) to vary (products, operations, etc.) in order to spread risk, expand, etc. **3** to distribute (investments) among several securities in order to spread risk. [C15: from Old French *diversifier,* from Medieval Latin *dīversificāre,* from Latin *dīversus* DIVERSE + *facere* to make] ▸ **di'versiˌfiable** *adj* ▸ **diˌversiˌfia'bility** *n* ▸ **di'versiˌfier** *n*

diversion (daɪ'vɜːʃən) *n* **1** the act of diverting from a specified course. **2** *Chiefly Brit.* an official detour used by traffic when a main route is closed. **3** something that distracts from business, etc.; amusement. **4** *Military.* a feint attack designed to draw an enemy away from the main attack. ▸ **di'versional** *or* **di'versionary** *adj*

diversity (daɪ'vɜːsɪtɪ) *n* **1** the state or quality of being different or varied. **2** a point of difference. **3** *Logic.* the relation that holds between two entities when and only when they are not identical; the property of being numerically distinct.

divert (daɪ'vɜːt) *vb* **1** to turn (a person or thing) aside from a course; deflect. **2** (*tr*) to entertain; amuse. **3** (*tr*) to distract the attention of. [C15: from French *divertir,* from Latin *dīvertere* to turn aside, from DI-[2] + *vertere* to turn] ▸ **di'verter** *n* ▸ **di'vertible** *adj* ▸ **di'verting** *adj* ▸ **di'vertingly** *adv* ▸ **di'vertive** *adj*

diverticulitis (ˌdaɪvəˌtɪkjʊ'laɪtɪs) *n* inflammation of one or more diverticula, esp. of the colon.

diverticulosis (ˌdaɪvəˌtɪkjʊ'ləʊsɪs) *n Pathol.* the presence of several diverticula, esp. in the intestines. [from New Latin, from DIVERTICULUM + -OSIS]

diverticulum (ˌdaɪvə'tɪkjʊləm) *n, pl* **-la** (-lə). any sac or pouch formed by herniation of the wall of a tubular organ or part, esp. the intestines. [C16: from New Latin, from Latin *dēverticulum* by-path, from *dēvertere* to turn aside, from *vertere* to turn] ▸ **ˌdiver'ticular** *adj*

divertimento (dɪˌvɜːtɪ'mɛntəʊ) *n, pl* **-ti** (-tɪ). **1** a piece of entertaining music in several movements, often scored for a mixed ensemble and having no fixed form. **2** an episode in a fugue. ◆ See also **divertissement.** [C18: from Italian]

divertissement (dɪ'vɜːtɪsmənt; *French* divɛrtismɑ̃) *n* **1** a brief entertainment or diversion, usually between the acts of a play. **2** *Music.* **2a** a fantasia on popular melodies; potpourri. **2b** a piece or pieces written to be played during the intervals in a play, opera, etc. **2c** another word for **divertimento.** [C18: from French: entertainment]

Dives ('daɪviːz) *n* **1** a rich man in the parable in Luke 16:19–31. **2** a very rich man.

divest (daɪ'vɛst) *vb* (*tr;* usually foll. by *of*) **1** to strip (of clothes): *to divest oneself of one's coat.* **2** to deprive or dispossess. **3** *Property law.* to take away an estate or interest in property vested (in a person). [C17: changed from earlier DEVEST] ▸ **di'vestible** *adj* ▸ **divestiture** (daɪ'vɛstɪtʃə), **divesture** (daɪ'vɛstʃə), *or* **di'vestment** *n*

divi ('dɪvɪ) *n* an alternative spelling of **divvy**[1].

divide (dɪ'vaɪd) *vb* **1** to separate or be separated into parts or groups; split up; part. **2** to share or be shared out in parts; distribute. **3** to diverge or cause to diverge in opinion or aim: *the issue divided the management.* **4** (*tr*) to keep apart or be a boundary between: *the Rio Grande divides Mexico from the United States.* **5** (*intr*) (in Parliament and similar legislatures) to vote by separating into two groups. **6** to categorize; classify. **7** to calculate the quotient of (one number or quantity) and (another number or quantity) by division: *to divide 50 by 10; to divide 10 into 50; to divide by 10.* **8** (*intr*) to diverge: *the roads divide.* **9** (*tr*) to mark increments of (length, angle, etc.) as by use of an engraving machine. ◆ *n* **10** *Chiefly U.S. and Canadian.* an area of relatively high ground separating drainage basins; watershed. See also **continental divide. 11** a division; split. [C14: from Latin *dīvidere* to force apart, from DI-[2] + *vid-* separate, from the source of *viduus* bereaved, *vidua* WIDOW] ▸ **di'vidable** *adj*

divided (dɪ'vaɪdɪd) *adj* **1** *Botany.* another word for **dissected** (sense 1). **2** split; not united. ▸ **di'videdly** *adv* ▸ **di'videdness** *n*

divided highway *n* the U.S. and Canadian term for **dual carriageway.**

dividend ('dɪvɪˌdɛnd) *n* **1** *Finance.* **1a** a distribution from the net profits of a company to its shareholders. **1b** a pro-rata portion of this distribution received by a shareholder. **2** the share of a cooperative society's surplus allocated at the end of a period to members. **3** *Insurance.* a sum of money distributed from a company's net profits to the holders of certain policies. **4** something extra; bonus. **5** a number or quantity to be divided by another number or quantity. Compare **divisor. 6** *Law.* the proportion of an insolvent estate payable to the creditors. [C15: from Latin *dīvidendum* what is to be divided; see DIVIDE]

dividend cover *n* the number of times that a company's dividends to shareholders could be paid out of its annual profits after tax, used as an indication of the probability that dividends will be maintained in subsequent years.

divider (dɪ'vaɪdə) *n* **1** Also called: **room divider.** a screen or piece of furniture placed so as to divide a room into separate areas. **2** a person or thing that divides. **3** *Electronics.* an electrical circuit with an output that is a well-defined fraction of a given input: *a voltage divider.*

dividers (dɪ'vaɪdəz) *pl n* a type of compass with two pointed arms, used for measuring lines or dividing them.

divi-divi (ˌdɪvɪ'dɪvɪ) *n, pl* **-divis** *or* **-divi. 1** a tropical American caesalpiniaceous tree, *Caesalpinia coriaria.* **2** the pods of this plant, which yield a substance used in tanning leather. [C19: from Spanish, of Cariban origin]

divination (ˌdɪvɪ'neɪʃən) *n* **1** the art, practice, or gift of discerning or discovering future events or unknown things, as though by supernatural powers. **2** a prophecy. **3** a presentiment or guess. ▸ **divinatory** (dɪ'vɪnətərɪ, -trɪ) *adj*

divine (dɪ'vaɪn) *adj* **1** of, relating to, or characterizing God or a deity. **2** godlike. **3** of, relating to, or associated with religion or worship: *the divine liturgy.* **4** of supreme excellence or worth. **5** *Informal.* splendid; perfect. ◆ *n* **6** (*often cap.;* preceded by *the*) another term for **God. 7** a priest, esp. one learned in theology. ◆ *vb* **8** to perceive or understand (something) by intuition or insight. **9** to conjecture (something); guess. **10** to discern (a hidden or future reality) as though by supernatural power. **11** (*tr*) to search for (underground supplies of water, metal, etc.) using a divining rod. [C14: from Latin *dīvīnus,* from *dīvus* a god; related to *deus* a god] ▸ **di'vinable** *adj* ▸ **di'vinely** *adv* ▸ **di'vineness** *n* ▸ **di'viner** *n*

divine office *n* (*sometimes caps.*) the canonical prayers (in the Roman Catholic Church those of the breviary) recited daily by priests, those in religious orders, etc.

divine right of kings *n History.* the concept that the right to rule derives from God and that kings are answerable for their actions to God alone.

divine service *n* a service of the Christian church, esp. one at which no sacrament is given.

diving beetle *n* any of the aquatic predatory beetles of the widely distributed family *Dytiscidae,* characterized by flattened hindlegs adapted for swimming and diving.

diving bell *n* an early diving submersible having an open bottom and being supplied with compressed air.

diving board *n* a platform or springboard from which swimmers may dive.

diving duck *n* any of various ducks, such as the pochard, scaup, redhead, and canvasback, that inhabit bays, estuaries, lakes, etc., and can dive and swim beneath the surface of the water.

diving suit *or* **dress** *n* a waterproof suit used by divers, having a heavy detachable helmet and an air supply.

divining rod *n* a rod, usually a forked hazel twig, said to move or dip when held over ground in which water, metal, etc., is to be found. Also called: **dowsing rod.**

divinity (dɪ'vɪnɪtɪ) *n, pl* **-ties. 1** the nature of a deity or the state of being divine. **2** a god or other divine being. **3** (*often cap.;* preceded by *the*) another term for **God. 4** another word for **theology.**

divinize *or* **divinise** ('dɪvɪ,naɪz) *vb* (*tr*) to make divine; deify. ▸ ,**divini'zation** *or* ,**divini'sation** *n*
divisibility (dɪ,vɪzɪ'bɪlɪtɪ) *n* the capacity of a dividend to be exactly divided by a given number.
divisible (dɪ'vɪzəbᵊl) *adj* capable of being divided, usually with no remainder. ▸ **di'visibleness** *n* ▸ **di'visibly** *adv*
division (dɪ'vɪʒən) *n* **1** the act of dividing or state of being divided. **2** the act of sharing out; distribution. **3** something that divides or keeps apart, such as a boundary. **4** one of the parts, groups, etc., into which something is divided. **5** a part of a government, business, country, etc., that has been made into a unit for administrative, political, or other reasons. **6** a formal vote in Parliament or a similar legislative body. **7** a difference of opinion, esp. one that causes separation. **8** (in sports) a section, category, or class organized according to age, weight, skill, etc. **9** a mathematical operation, the inverse of multiplication, in which the quotient of two numbers or quantities is calculated. Usually written: $a \div b$, $\frac{a}{b}$, a/b. **10a** *Army.* a major formation, larger than a regiment or brigade but smaller than a corps, containing the necessary arms to sustain independent combat. **10b** *Navy.* a group of ships of similar type or a tactical unit of naval aircraft. **10c** *Air Force.* an organization normally comprising two or more wings with required support units. **11** (*pl*) *Navy.* the assembly of all crew members for the captain's inspection. **12** *Biology.* (in traditional classification systems) a major category of the plant kingdom that contains one or more related classes. Compare **phylum** (sense 1). **13** *Horticulture.* any type of propagation in plants in which a new plant grows from a separated part of the original. **14** *Logic.* the fallacy of inferring that the properties of the whole are also true of the parts, as *Britain is in debt, so John Smith is in debt.* **15** (esp. in 17th-century English music) the art of breaking up a melody into quick phrases, esp. over a ground bass. [C14: from Latin *dīvīsiō*, from *dīvidere* to DIVIDE] ▸ **di'visional** *or* **di'visionary** *adj* ▸ **di'visionally** *adv*
divisionism (dɪ'vɪʒə,nɪzəm) *n* the pointillism of Seurat and his followers. ▸ **di'visionist** *n, adj*
division of labour *n* a system of organizing the manufacture of an article in a series of separate specialized operations, each of which is carried out by a different worker or group of workers.
division sign *n* the symbol ÷, placed between the dividend and the divisor to indicate division, as in $12 \div 6 = 2$.
divisive (dɪ'vaɪsɪv) *adj* **1** causing or tending to cause disagreement or dissension. **2** *Archaic.* having the quality of distinguishing. ▸ **di'visively** *adv* ▸ **di'visiveness** *n*
divisor (dɪ'vaɪzə) *n* **1** a number or quantity to be divided into another number or quantity (the dividend). **2** a number that is a factor of another number.
divorce (dɪ'vɔːs) *n* **1** the dissolution of a marriage by judgment of a court or by accepted custom. **2** a judicial decree declaring a marriage to be dissolved. **3** a separation, esp. one that is total or complete. ♦ *vb* **4** to separate or be separated by divorce; give or obtain a divorce (to a couple or from one's spouse). **5** (*tr*) to remove or separate, esp. completely. [C14: from Old French, from Latin *dīvortium* from *dīvertere* to separate; see DIVERT] ▸ **di'vorceable** *adj* ▸ **di'vorcer** *n* ▸ **di'vorcive** *adj*
divorcée (dɪvɔː'siː) *or* (*masc*) **divorcé** (dɪ'vɔːseɪ) *n* a person who has been divorced.
divorcement (dɪ'vɔːsmənt) *n* a less common word for **divorce.**
divot ('dɪvət) *n* a piece of turf dug out of a grass surface, esp. by a golf club or by horses' hooves. [C16: from Scottish, of obscure origin]
divulgate (dɪ'vʌlgeɪt) *vb* (*tr*) *Archaic.* to make publicly known. [C16: from Latin *dīvulgāre;* see DIVULGE] ▸ **di'vulgator** *or* **di'vulgater** *n* ▸ ,**divul'gation** *n*
divulge (daɪ'vʌldʒ) *vb* (*tr; may take a clause as object*) to make known (something private or secret); disclose. [C15: from Latin *dīvulgāre*, from DI-[2] + *vulgāre* to spread among the people, from *vulgus* the common people] ▸ **di'vulgence** *or* **di'vulgement** *n* ▸ **di'vulger** *n*
divulsion (daɪ'vʌlʃən) *n* a tearing or pulling apart. [C17: from Latin *dīvulsiō*, from *dīvulsus* torn apart, from *dīvellere* to rend, from DI-[2] + *vellere* to pull] ▸ **di'vulsive** *adj*
divvy[1] ('dɪvɪ) *Informal.* ♦ *n, pl* **-vies. 1** *Brit.* short for **dividend,** esp. (formerly) one paid by a cooperative society. **2** *U.S. and Canadian.* a share; portion. ♦ *vb* **-vies, -vying, -vied. 3** (*tr;* usually foll. by *up*) to divide and share.
divvy[2] ('dɪvɪ) *n, pl* **-vies.** *Dialect.* a stupid or foolish person.
Diwali (dɪ'wɑːlɪ) *n* a major Hindu religious festival, honouring Lakshmi, the goddess of wealth. Held over the New Year according to the Vikrama calendar, it is marked by feasting, gifts, and the lighting of lamps.
diwan (dɪ'wɑːn) *n* a variant of **dewan** or **divan** (senses 2–5).
dixie ('dɪksɪ) *n* **1** *Chiefly military.* a large metal pot for cooking, brewing tea, etc. **2** a mess tin. [C19: from Hindi *degcī*, diminutive of *degcā* pot]
Dixie ('dɪksɪ) *n* **1** Also called: **Dixieland.** the southern states of the U.S.; the states that joined the Confederacy during the Civil War. **2** a song adopted as a marching tune by the Confederate states during the American Civil War. ♦ *adj* **3** of, relating to, or characteristic of the southern states of the U.S. [C19: perhaps from the nickname of New Orleans, from *dixie* a ten-dollar bill printed there, from French *dix* ten]
Dixieland ('dɪksɪ,lænd) *n* **1** a form of jazz that originated in New Orleans, becoming popular esp. with White musicians in the second decade of the 20th century. **2** a revival of this style in the 1950s. **3** See **Dixie** (sense 1).
DIY *or* **d.i.y.** (in Britain) *abbrev. for* do-it-yourself.
Diyarbakir *or* **Diyarbekir** (diː'jɑːbekɪə) *n* a city in SE Turkey, on the River Tigris: ancient black basalt walls. Pop.: 448 145 (1995 est.). Ancient name: **Amida** (ə'miːdə).
dizen ('daɪzᵊn) *vb* an archaic word for **bedizen.** [C16: from Middle Dutch *dīsen* to dress a distaff with flax; see DISTAFF] ▸ **'dizenment** *n*
dizzy ('dɪzɪ) *adj* **-zier, -ziest. 1** affected with a whirling or reeling sensation; giddy. **2** mentally confused or bewildered. **3** causing or tending to cause vertigo or bewilderment. **4** *Informal.* foolish or flighty. ♦ *vb* **-zies, -zying, -zied. 5** (*tr*) to make dizzy. [Old English *dysig* silly; related to Old High German *tusīg* weak, Old Norse *dos* quiet] ▸ **'dizzily** *adv* ▸ **'dizziness** *n*
DJ *or* **dj** *abbrev. for:* **1** disc jockey. **2** dinner jacket.
Djailolo *or* **Jilolo** (dʒaɪ'ləʊləʊ) *n* the Dutch name for **Halmahera.**
Djaja ('dʒɑːdʒə) *n* a variant spelling of (Mount) **Jaya.**
Djajapura (,dʒɑːdʒɑː'pʊərə) *n* a variant spelling of **Jayapura.**
Djakarta (dʒə'kɑːtə) *n* a variant spelling of **Jakarta.**
Djambi ('dʒæmbɪ) *n* a variant spelling of **Jambi.**
djebel ('dʒɛbᵊl) *n* a variant spelling of **jebel.**
Djerba *or* **Jerba** ('dʒɜːbə) *n* an island off the SE coast of Tunisia, in the Gulf of Gabès: traditionally Homer's land of the lotus-eaters. Pop.: 92 269 (1984). Area: 510 sq. km (197 sq. miles). Ancient name: **Meninx** ('menɪŋks).
Djibouti *or* **Jibouti** (dʒɪ'buːtɪ) *n* **1** a republic in E Africa, on the Gulf of Aden: a French overseas territory (1946–77); became independent in 1977; mainly desert. Official languages: Arabic and French. Religion: Muslim majority. Currency: Djibouti franc. Capital: Djibouti. Pop.: 652 000 (1998 est.). Area: 23 200 sq. km (8950 sq. miles). Former name (until 1977): (Territory of the) **Afars and the Issas. 2** the capital of Djibouti, a port on the Gulf of Aden: an outlet for Ethiopian goods. Pop.: 383 000 (1995).
Djilas ('dʒiːlɑːs) *n* **Milovan.** 1911–95, Yugoslav politician and writer; vice president (1953–54): imprisoned (1956–61, 1962–66) for his criticism of the communist system.
djinni *or* **djinny** (dʒɪ'niː, 'dʒɪnɪ) *n, pl* **djinn** (dʒɪn). variant spellings of **jinni.**
dk *abbrev. for:* **1** dark. **2** deck. **3** dock.
DK *international car registration for* Denmark.
dl *symbol for* decilitre(s).
D/L *abbrev. for* demand loan.
DLitt *or* **DLit** *abbrev. for:* **1** Doctor of Letters. **2** Doctor of Literature. [Latin *Doctor Litterarum*]
DLP (formerly) *abbrev. for* Democratic Labor Party (of Australia).
dlr *abbrev. for* dealer.
dlvy *abbrev. for* delivery.
dm *symbol for* decimetre.
DM *abbrev. for* Deutschmark.
DMA *Computing. abbrev. for* direct memory access.
DMAC *abbrev. for* duobinary multiplexed analogue component: a transmission coding system using duobinary techniques for the digital sound and data components of colour television using satellite broadcasting.
D-mark *or* **D-Mark** *n* short for **Deutschmark.**
DMD *abbrev. for* Duchenne muscular dystrophy.
DMF *abbrev. for* dimethylformamide.
DMK (in India) *abbrev. for* Dravida Munnetra Kazgham: a political party in the state of Tamil Nadu.
DMs *abbrev. for* Doc Martens.
DMS (in Britain) *abbrev. for* Diploma in Management Studies.
DMSO *abbrev. for* dimethylsulphoxide.
DMT *abbrev. for* dimethyltryptamine, a hallucinogenic drug.
DMus *abbrev. for* Doctor of Music.
DMZ *abbrev. for* demilitarized zone.
DNA *n* deoxyribonucleic acid; a nucleic acid that is the main constituent of the chromosomes of all organisms (except some viruses). The DNA molecule consists of two polynucleotide chains in the form of a double helix, containing phosphate and the sugar deoxyribose and linked by hydrogen bonds between the complementary bases adenine and thymine or cytosine and guanine. DNA is self-replicating, plays a central role in protein synthesis, and is responsible for the transmission of hereditary characteristics from parents to offspring. See also **genetic code.**
DNAase (,diːɛn'eɪeɪz) *or* **DNase** (,diːɛn'eɪz) *n* deoxyribonuclease; any of a number of enzymes that hydrolyse DNA. See **endonuclease, exonuclease.**
DNA fingerprinting *or* **profiling** *n* another name for **genetic fingerprinting.**
Dneprodzerzhinsk (*Russian* dnɪprədzɪr'ʒinsk) *n* an industrial city in the E Ukraine on the Dnieper River. Pop.: 281 000 (1996 est.).
Dnepropetrovsk (*Russian* dnɪprəpɪ'trɔfsk) *n* a city in the E central Ukraine on the Dnieper River: a major centre of the metallurgical industry. Pop.: 1 147 000 (1996 est.). Former name (1787–1796, 1802–1926): **Yekaterinoslav.**
Dnieper ('dniːpə) *n* a river in NE Europe, rising in Russia, in the Valdai Hills NE of Smolensk and flowing south to the Black Sea: the third longest river in Europe; a major navigable waterway. Length: 2200 km (1370 miles). Russian name: **Dnepr** ('dnjɛpə).
Dniester ('dniːstə) *n* a river in E Europe, rising in the Ukraine, in the Carpathian Mountains and flowing generally southeast to the Black Sea. Length: 1411 km (877 miles). Russian name: **Dnestr** ('dnjɛstə).
D-notice *n Brit.* an official notice sent to newspapers, prohibiting the publication of certain security information. [C20: from their administrative classification letter]
DNS (in Britain) *abbrev. for* Department for National Savings.
do[1] (duː; *unstressed* dʊ, də) *vb* **does, doing, did, done. 1** to perform or complete (a deed or action): *to do a portrait; the work is done.* **2** (often *intr;* foll. by *for*) to serve the needs of; be suitable for (a person, situation, etc.); suffice: *there isn't much food, but it'll do for the two of us.* **3** (*tr*) to arrange or fix: *you should do the garden now.* **4** (*tr*) to prepare or provide; serve: *this restaurant doesn't do lunch on Sundays.* **5** (*tr*) to make tidy, elegant, ready, etc., as by arranging or adorning: *to do one's hair.* **6** (*tr*) to improve (esp. in the phrase **do something to** *or* **for**). **7** (*tr*) to find an answer to (a problem or puzzle). **8** (*tr*) to translate or

adapt the form or language of: *the book was done into a play.* **9** (*intr*) to conduct oneself: *do as you please.* **10** (*intr*) to fare or manage: *how are you doing these days?* **11** (*tr*) to cause or produce: *complaints do nothing to help.* **12** (*tr*) to give or render: *your portrait doesn't do you justice; do me a favour.* **13** (*tr*) to work at, esp. as a course of study or a profession: *he is doing chemistry; what do you do for a living?* **14** (*tr*) to perform (a play, etc.); act: *they are doing "Hamlet" next week.* **15** (*tr*) to travel at a specified speed, esp. as a maximum: *this car will do 120 mph.* **16** (*tr*) to travel or traverse (a distance): *we did 15 miles on our walk.* **17** (takes an infinitive without *to*) used as an auxiliary before the subject of an interrogative sentence as a way of forming a question: *do you agree? when did John go out?* **18** (takes an infinitive without *to*) used as an auxiliary to intensify positive statements and commands: *I do like your new house; do hurry!* **19** (takes an infinitive without *to*) used as an auxiliary before a negative adverb to form negative statements or commands: *he does not like cheese; do not leave me here alone!* **20** (takes an infinitive without *to*) used as an auxiliary in inverted constructions: *little did he realize that; only rarely does he come in before ten o'clock.* **21** used as an auxiliary to replace an earlier verb or verb phrase to avoid repetition: *he likes you as much as I do.* **22** (*tr*) *Informal.* to visit or explore as a sightseer or tourist: *to do Westminster Abbey.* **23** (*tr*) to wear out; exhaust. **24** (*intr*) to happen (esp. in the phrase **nothing doing**). **25** (*tr*) *Slang.* to serve (a period of time) as a prison sentence: *he's doing three years for burglary; he's doing time.* **26** (*tr*) *Informal.* to cheat or swindle. **27** (*tr*) *Slang.* to rob: *they did three shops last night.* **28** (*tr*) *Slang.* **28a** to arrest. **28b** to convict of a crime. **29** (*tr*) *Austral. informal.* to lose or spend (money) completely. **30** (*tr*) *Slang, chiefly Brit.* to treat violently; assault. **31** (*tr*) *Slang.* to take or use (a drug). **32** (*tr*) *Taboo slang.* (of a male) to have sexual intercourse with. **33 do** (**a**). *Informal.* act like; imitate: *he's a good mimic—he can do all his friends well.* **34 do or die.** to make a final or supreme effort. **35 how do you do?** a conventional formula when being introduced. **36 make do.** to manage with whatever is available. ◆ *n, pl* **dos** *or* **do's. 37** *Slang.* an act or instance of cheating or swindling. **38** *Informal, chiefly Brit. and N.Z.* a formal or festive gathering; party. **39 do's and don'ts.** *Informal.* those things that should or should not be done; rules. ◆ See also **do away with, do by, do down, do for, do in, done, do out, do over, do up, do with, do without.** [Old English *dōn;* related to Old Frisian *duān,* Old High German *tuon,* Latin *abdere* to put away, Greek *tithenai* to place; see DEED, DOOM]

do[2] (dəʊ) *n, pl* **dos.** a variant spelling of **doh.**

DO *abbrev. for:* **1** Doctor of Optometry. **2** Doctor of Osteopathy.

do. *abbrev. for* ditto.

D/O *or* **d.o.** *Commerce. abbrev. for* delivery order.

DOA *abbrev. for* dead on arrival.

doab ('dəʊɑːb) *n* the alluvial land between two converging rivers, esp. the area between the Ganges and Jumna in N India. [C20: from Persian *dōāb,* from *dō* two + *āb* water]

doable ('duːəbᵊl) *adj* capable of being done; practical.

doat (dəʊt) *vb* (*intr*) a variant (now rare) spelling of **dote.**

do away with *vb* (*intr, adv + prep*) **1** to kill or destroy. **2** to discard or abolish.

dobber-in (ˌdɒbər'ɪn) *n Austral. slang.* an informant or traitor. Sometimes shortened to **dobber.**

dobbin ('dɒbɪn) *n* **1** a name for a horse, esp. a workhorse, often used in children's tales, etc. **2** *N.Z.* a trolley for moving loose wool in a woolshed or shearing shed. [C16: from *Robin,* pet form of *Robert*]

dobby ('dɒbɪ) *n, pl* **-bies.** an attachment to a loom, used in weaving small figures. [C17: perhaps from *Dobby,* pet form of *Robert*]

Dobell (dəʊ'bel) *n* Sir **William.** 1899–1970, Australian portrait and landscape painter. Awarded the Archibald prize (1943) for his famous painting of *Joshua Smith* which resulted in a heated clash between the conservatives and the moderns and led to a lawsuit. His other works include *The Cypriot* (1940), *The Billy Boy* (1943), and *Portrait of a strapper* (1941).

Dobell's solution ('dəʊbəlz) *n* a solution of sodium borate, sodium bicarbonate, phenol, and glycerol, used as an astringent or antiseptic wash for the throat and nose. [C19: named after Horace B. *Dobell* (1828–1917), British physician]

Doberman pinscher ('dəʊbəmən 'pɪnʃə) *or* **Doberman** *n* a fairly large slender but muscular breed of dog, originally from Germany, with a glossy black-and-tan coat, a short tail, and erect ears. Also spelt **Dobermann.** [C19: probably named after L. *Dobermann,* 19th-century German dog breeder who bred it + *Pinscher,* a type of terrier, perhaps after *Pinzgau,* district in Austria]

dob in *vb* **dobs, dobbing, dobbed.** (*adv*) *Austral. and N.Z. informal.* **1** (*tr*) to inform against or report, esp. to the police. **2** to contribute to a fund for a specific purpose.

dobla ('dəʊblɑː) *n* a medieval Spanish gold coin, probably worth 20 maravedis. [Spanish, from Latin *dupla,* feminine of *duplus* twofold, DOUBLE]

doblón (də'bləʊn; *Spanish* do'βlon) *n* a variant spelling of **doubloon.** [Spanish; see DOUBLOON]

dobra ('dəʊbrə) *n* the standard monetary unit of São Tomé e Principe.

Dobro ('dəʊbrəʊ) *n, pl* **-bros.** *Trademark.* an acoustic guitar having a metal resonator built into the body.

Dobruja (*Bulgarian* 'dɔbrudʒa) *n* a region of E Europe, between the River Danube and the Black Sea: the north passed to Romania and the south to Bulgaria after the Berlin Congress (1878). Romanian name: **Dobrogea** (do'brodʒea).

dobsonfly ('dɒbsᵊnˌflaɪ) *n, pl* **-flies.** *U.S. and Canadian.* a large North American neuropterous insect, *Corydalis cornutus:* the male has elongated horn-like mouthparts and the larva (a **hellgrammite** or **dobson**) is used as bait by anglers: suborder *Megaloptera.* [C20: origin uncertain, perhaps after the surname *Dobson*]

do by *vb* (*intr, prep*) to treat in the manner specified: *employers do well by hard working employees.*

Dobzhansky (dɒb'ʒænskɪ) *n* **Theodosius.** 1900–75, U.S. biologist, born in Russia, noted for work on evolution and genetic variation.

doc (dɒk) *n Informal.* short for **doctor,** esp. a medical doctor: often used as a term of address.

DOC *abbrev. for* Denominazione di Origine Controllata: used of wines. [Italian, literally: name of origin controlled]

doc. *abbrev. for* document.

docent ('dəʊsᵊnt) *n* **1** a voluntary worker who acts as a guide in a museum, art gallery, etc. **2** (dəʊ'sent; *German* do'tsɛnt) (in the U.S.) a lecturer in some colleges or universities. [C19: from German *Dozent,* from Latin *docēns* from *docēre* to teach] ▶ **'docent,ship** *n*

Docetism ('dəʊsɪˌtɪzəm) *n* (in the early Christian Church) a heresy that the humanity of Christ, his sufferings, and his death were apparent rather than real. [C19: from Medieval Latin *Docētae,* from Greek *Dokētai,* from *dokein* to seem]

DOCG *abbrev. for* Denominazione di Origine Controllata Garantita: used of wines. [Italian, literally: name of origin guaranteed controlled]

doch-an-doris ('dɒxən'dɒrɪs) *n* a variant spelling of **deoch-an-doruis.**

docile ('dəʊsaɪl) *adj* **1** easy to manage, control, or discipline; submissive. **2** *Rare.* ready to learn; easy to teach. [C15: from Latin *docilis* easily taught, from *docēre* to teach] ▶ **'docilely** *adv* ▶ **docility** (dəʊ'sɪlɪtɪ) *n*

dock[1] (dɒk) *n* **1** a wharf or pier. **2** a space between two wharves or piers for the mooring of ships. **3** an area of water that can accommodate a ship and can be closed off to allow regulation of the water level. **4** short for **dry dock. 5** short for **scene dock. 6** *Chiefly U.S. and Canadian.* a platform from which lorries, goods trains, etc., are loaded and unloaded. ◆ *vb* **7** to moor (a vessel) at a dock or (of a vessel) to be moored at a dock. **8** to put (a vessel) into a dry dock for repairs or (of a vessel) to come into a dry dock. **9** (of two spacecraft) to link together in space or link together (two spacecraft) in space. [C14: from Middle Dutch *docke;* perhaps related to Latin *ducere* to lead]

dock[2] (dɒk) *n* **1** the bony part of the tail of an animal, esp. a dog or sheep. **2** the part of an animal's tail left after the major part of it has been cut off. ◆ *vb* (*tr*) **3** to remove (the tail or part of the tail) of (an animal) by cutting through the bone: *to dock a tail; to dock a horse.* **4** to deduct (an amount) from (a person's wages, pension, etc.): *they docked a third of his wages.* [C14: *dok,* of uncertain origin]

dock[3] (dɒk) *n* an enclosed space in a court of law where the accused sits or stands during his trial. [C16: from Flemish *dok* sty]

dock[4] (dɒk) *n* **1** any of various temperate weedy plants of the polygonaceous genus *Rumex,* having greenish or reddish flowers and typically broad leaves. **2** any of several similar or related plants. [Old English *docce;* related to Middle Dutch, Old Danish *docke,* Gaelic *dogha*]

dockage[1] ('dɒkɪdʒ) *n* **1** a charge levied upon a vessel for using a dock. **2** facilities for docking vessels. **3** the practice of docking vessels.

dockage[2] ('dɒkɪdʒ) *n* **1** a deduction, as from a price or wages. **2** *Agriculture.* the seeds of weeds and other waste material in commercial seeds, removable by normal cleaning methods.

docken ('dɒkᵊn) *n Chiefly Scot.* **1** another name for **dock**[4]. **2** something of no value or importance: *not worth a docken.* [C14 *doken,* from Old English *doccan,* pl. of *docce* DOCK[4]]

docker[1] ('dɒkə) *n Brit.* a man employed in the loading or unloading of ships. U.S. and Canadian equivalent: **longshoreman.** See also **stevedore.**

docker[2] ('dɒkə) *n* a person or thing that docks something, such as the tail of a horse.

docket ('dɒkɪt) *n* **1** *Chiefly Brit.* a piece of paper accompanying or referring to a package or other delivery, stating contents, delivery instructions, etc., sometimes serving as a receipt. **2** *Law.* **2a** an official summary of the proceedings in a court of justice. **2b** a register containing such a summary. **3** *Brit.* **3a** a customs certificate declaring that duty has been paid. **3b** a certificate giving particulars of a shipment and allowing its holder to obtain a delivery order. **4** a summary of contents, as in a document. **5** *U.S.* a list of things to be done. **6** *U.S. law.* **6a** a list of cases awaiting trial. **6b** the names of the parties to pending litigation. ◆ *vb* (*tr*) **7** to fix a docket to (a package, etc.). **8** *Law.* **8a** to make a summary of (a document, judgment, etc.). **8b** to abstract and enter in a book or register. **9** to endorse (a document, etc.) with a summary. [C15: of unknown origin]

dockland ('dɒkˌlænd) *n* the area around the docks.

dockyard ('dɒkˌjɑːd) *n* a naval establishment with docks, workshops, etc., for the building, fitting out, and repair of vessels.

Doc Martens (dɒk 'mɑːtənz) *pl n Trademark.* a brand of lace-up boots with thick lightweight resistant soles. In full: **Doctor Martens.** Abbrev.: **DMs.**

doco ('dɒkəʊ) *n, pl* **docos.** *Austral. informal.* short for **documentary.**

doctor ('dɒktə) *n* **1** a person licensed to practise medicine. **2** a person who has been awarded a higher academic degree in any field of knowledge. **3** *Chiefly U.S. and Canadian.* a person licensed to practise dentistry or veterinary medicine. **4** (*often cap.*) Also called: **Doctor of the Church.** a title given to any of several of the leading Fathers or theologians in the history of the Christian Church down to the late Middle Ages whose teachings have greatly influenced orthodox Christian thought. **5** *Angling.* any of various gaudy artificial flies. **6** *Informal.* a person who mends or repairs things. **7** *Slang.* a cook on a ship or at a camp. **8** *Archaic.* a man, esp. a teacher, of learning. **9** a device used for local repair of electroplated surfaces, consisting of an anode of the plating material embedded in an absorbent material containing the solution. **10** (in a paper-making machine) a blade that is set to scrape the roller in order to regulate the thickness of pulp or ink on it. **11 go for the doctor.** *Austral. slang.* to make a great effort or move very fast, esp. in a horse race. **12 what the doctor ordered.** something needed or desired. ◆ *vb* **13** (*tr*) **13a** to give medical treatment to. **13b** to prescribe for (a disease or disorder). **14** (*intr*) *Informal.* to practise medicine: *he doctored in Easter Island for six years.* **15** (*tr*) to repair or mend, esp. in a makeshift manner. **16** (*tr*) to make different in order to deceive, tamper with, falsify, or adulterate. **17** (*tr*) to adapt for a desired end, effect, etc. **18** (*tr*) to castrate (a cat, dog, etc.). **[C14:** from Latin: teacher, from *docēre* to teach**]** ▸ **'doctoral** *or* **doctorial** (dɒk'tɔːrɪəl) *adj*

doctorate ('dɒktərɪt, -trɪt) *n* the highest academic degree in any field of knowledge. Also called: **doctor's degree.**

Doctor of Philosophy *n* a doctorate awarded for original research in any subject except law, medicine, or theology. Abbrevs.: **PhD, DPhil.**

Doctor's Commons *n Informal.* the London building of the College of Advocates and Doctors of Law between 1572 and 1867, in which the ecclesiastical and Admiralty courts were housed.

doctrinaire (ˌdɒktrɪ'nɛə) *adj* **1** stubbornly insistent on the observation of the niceties of a theory, esp. without regard to practicality, suitability, etc. **2** theoretical; impractical. ◆ *n* **3** a person who stubbornly attempts to apply a theory without regard to practical difficulties. ▸ **ˌdoctri'nairism** *or* **ˌdoctri'narism** *n* ▸ **ˌdoctri'narian** *n*

doctrine ('dɒktrɪn) *n* **1** a creed or body of teachings of a religious, political, or philosophical group presented for acceptance or belief; dogma. **2** a principle or body of principles that is taught or advocated. **[C14:** from Old French, from Latin *doctrīna* teaching, from *doctor* see DOCTOR**]** ▸ **doctrinal** (dɒk'traɪnᵊl) *adj* ▸ **doctrinality** (ˌdɒktrɪ'nælɪtɪ) *n* ▸ **doc'trinally** *adv* ▸ **'doctrinism** *n* ▸ **'doctrinist** *n*

doctrine of descent *n* the theory that animals and plants arose by descent from previously existing organisms; theory of evolution.

docudrama ('dɒkjuˌdrɑːmə) *n* a film or television programme based on true events, presented in a dramatized form.

document *n* ('dɒkjumənt). **1** a piece of paper, booklet, etc., providing information, esp. of an official or legal nature. **2** a piece of text, such as a letter or article, stored in a computer as a file for manipulation by document processing software. **3** *Archaic.* evidence; proof. ◆ *vb* ('dɒkjuˌmɛnt). (*tr*) **4** to record or report in detail, as in the press, on television, etc.: *the trial was well documented by the media.* **5** to support (statements in a book) with citations, references, etc. **6** to support (a claim, etc.) with evidence or proof. **7** to furnish (a vessel) with official documents specifying its ownership, registration, weight, dimensions, and function. **[C15:** from Latin *documentum* a lesson, from *docēre* to teach**]**

documentary (ˌdɒkju'mɛntərɪ, -trɪ) *adj* **1** Also: **documental.** consisting of, derived from, or relating to documents. **2** presenting factual material with little or no fictional additions: *the book gives a documentary account of the war.* ◆ *n, pl* **-ries. 3** a factual film or television programme about an event, person, etc., presenting the facts with little or no fiction. ▸ **ˌdocu'mentarily** *adv*

documentation (ˌdɒkjumɛn'teɪʃən) *n* **1** the act of supplying with or using documents or references. **2** the documents or references supplied. **3** the furnishing and use of documentary evidence, as in a court of law. **4** *Computing.* the written comments, graphical illustrations, flowcharts, manuals, etc., supplied with a program or software system.

document reader *n Computing.* a device that reads and inputs into a computer marks and characters on a special form, as by optical or magnetic character recognition.

docu-soap ('dɒkjuˌsəup) *n* a television documentary series in which the lives of the people filmed are presented as entertainment or drama. **[C20:** from DOCU(MENTARY) + SOAP(OPERA)**]**

DOD (in the U.S.) *abbrev. for* Department of Defense.

Dodd (dɒd) *n* **C**(**harles**) **H**(**arold**). 1884–1973, British New Testament scholar. His works include *The Parables of the Kingdom* (1935).

dodder[1] ('dɒdə) *vb* (*intr*) **1** to move unsteadily; totter. **2** to shake or tremble, as from age. **[C17:** variant of earlier *dadder;* related to Norwegian *dudra* to tremble**]** ▸ **'dodderer** *n* ▸ **'doddery** *adj*

dodder[2] ('dɒdə) *n* any rootless parasitic plant of the convolvulaceous genus *Cuscuta,* lacking chlorophyll and having slender twining stems with suckers for drawing nourishment from the host plant, scalelike leaves, and whitish flowers. **[C13:** of Germanic origin; related to Middle Dutch, Middle Low German *dodder,* Middle High German *toter***]**

doddering ('dɒdərɪŋ) *adj* shaky, feeble, or infirm, esp. from old age.

doddle ('dɒdᵊl) *n Brit. informal.* something easily accomplished.

dodeca- *n combining form.* indicating twelve: *dodecagon; dodecahedron; dodecaphonic.* **[**from Greek *dōdeka* twelve**]**

dodecagon (dəu'dɛkəˌgɒn) *n* a polygon having twelve sides. ▸ **dodecagonal** (ˌdəudɛ'kægənᵊl) *adj*

dodecahedron (ˌdəudɛkə'hiːdrən) *n* a solid figure having twelve plane faces. A **regular dodecahedron** has regular pentagons as faces. See also **polyhedron.** ▸ **ˌdodeca'hedral** *adj*

Dodecanese (ˌdəudɪkə'niːz) *pl n* a group of islands in the SE Aegean Sea, forming a department of Greece: part of the Southern Sporades. Capital: Rhodes. Pop.: 162 439 (1991). Area: 2663 sq. km (1028 sq. miles). Modern Greek name: **Dhodhekánisos.**

dodecanoic acid (ˌdəudɛkə'nəuɪk) *n* a crystalline fatty acid found as glycerides in many vegetable oils: used in making soaps, insecticides, and synthetic resins. Formula: $CH_3(CH_2)_{10}COOH$. Also called: **lauric acid. [C20:** from *dodecane* (see DODECA-, -ANE)**]**

dodecaphonic (ˌdəudɛkə'fɒnɪk) *adj* of or relating to the twelve-tone system of serial music. ▸ **ˌdodeca'phonism** *n* ▸ **ˌdodeca'phony** *n*

dodecasyllable (ˌdəudɛkə'sɪləbᵊl) *n Prosody.* a line of twelve syllables.

dodge (dɒdʒ) *vb* **1** to avoid or attempt to avoid (a blow, discovery, etc.), as by moving suddenly. **2** to evade (questions, etc.) by cleverness or trickery. **3** (*intr*) *Change-ringing.* to make a bell change places with its neighbour when sounding in successive changes. **4** (*tr*) *Photog.* to lighten or darken (selected areas on a print) by manipulating the light from an enlarger. ◆ *n* **5** a plan or expedient contrived to deceive. **6** a sudden evasive or hiding movement. **7** a clever contrivance. **8** *Change-ringing.* the act of dodging. **[C16:** of unknown origin**]**

dodge ball *n* a game in which the players form a circle and try to hit opponents in the circle with a large ball.

Dodge City *n* a city in SW Kansas, on the Arkansas River: famous as a frontier town on the Santa Fe Trail. Pop.: 21 130 (1990).

Dodgem ('dɒdʒəm) *n Trademark.* another name for **bumper car.**

dodger ('dɒdʒə) *n* **1** a person who evades or shirks. **2** a shifty dishonest person. **3** a canvas shelter, mounted on a ship's bridge or over the companionway of a sailing yacht to protect the helmsman from bad weather. **4** *Archaic, U.S. and Austral.* a handbill. **5** *Dialect and Austral.* food, esp. bread.

Dodgson ('dɒdʒsən) *n* **Charles Lutwidge** ('lʌtwɪdʒ). the real name of (Lewis) **Carroll.**

dodgy ('dɒdʒɪ) *adj* **dodgier, dodgiest.** *Brit., Austral., and N.Z. informal.* **1** risky, difficult, or dangerous. **2** uncertain or unreliable; tricky.

dodo ('dəudəu) *n, pl* **dodos** *or* **dodoes. 1** any flightless bird, esp. *Raphus cucullatus,* of the recently extinct family *Raphidae* of Mauritius and adjacent islands: order *Columbiformes* (pigeons, etc.). They had a hooked bill, short stout legs, and greyish plumage. See also **ratite. 2** *Informal.* an intensely conservative or reactionary person who is unaware of changing fashions, ideas, etc. **3** (**as**) **dead as a dodo.** (of a person or thing) irretrievably defunct or out of date. **[C17:** from Portuguese *doudo,* from *duodo* stupid**]** ▸ **'dodoism** *n*

Dodoma ('dəudəmə) *n* a city in central Tanzania, the legislative capital of the country. Pop.: 203 833 (1988).

Dodona (dəu'dəunə) *n* an ancient Greek town in Epirus: seat of an ancient sanctuary and oracle of Zeus and later the religious centre of Pyrrhus' kingdom. ▸ **Dodonaean** *or* **Dodonean** (ˌdəudəu'niːən) *adj*

do down *vb* (*tr, adv*) **1** to belittle or humiliate. **2** to deceive or cheat.

doe (dəu) *n, pl* **does** *or* **doe.** the female of the deer, hare, rabbit, and certain other animals. **[**Old English *dā;* related to Old English *dēon* to suck, Sanskrit *dhēnā* cow**]**

Doe (dəu) *n* **1** *Law.* (formerly) the plaintiff in a fictitious action, Doe versus Roe, to test a point of law. See also **Roe. 2 John** *or* **Jane.** *U.S.* an unknown or unidentified male or female person.

DOE (in Britain) *abbrev. for* Department of the Environment.

doek (duk) *n S. African informal.* a square of cloth worn mainly by African women to cover the head, esp. to indicate married status. **[C18:** from Afrikaans: cloth**]**

Doenitz (*German* 'døːnɪts) *n* a variant spelling of (Karl) **Dönitz.**

doer ('duːə) *n* **1** a person or thing that does something or acts in a specified manner: *a doer of good.* **2** an active or energetic person. **3** a thriving animal, esp. a horse.

does (dʌz) *vb* (used with a singular noun or the pronouns *he, she,* or *it*) a form of the present tense (indicative mood) of **do**[1].

doeskin ('dəuˌskɪn) *n* **1** the skin of a deer, lamb, or sheep. **2** a very supple leather made from this skin and used esp. for gloves. **3** a heavy smooth satin-weave or twill-weave cloth. **4** (*modifier*) made of doeskin.

doff (dɒf) *vb* (*tr*) **1** to take off or lift (one's hat) in salutation. **2** to remove (clothing). **[**Old English *dōn of;* see DO[1], OFF; compare DON[1]**]** ▸ **'doffer** *n*

do for *vb* (*prep*) *Informal.* **1** (*tr*) to convict of a crime or offence: *they did him for manslaughter.* **2** (*intr*) to cause the ruin, death, or defeat of: *the last punch did for him.* **3** (*intr*) to do housework for. **4 do well for oneself.** to thrive or succeed.

dog (dɒg) *n* **1a** a domesticated canine mammal, *Canis familiaris,* occurring in many breeds that show a great variety in size and form. **1b** (*as modifier*): *dog biscuit.* **2a** any other carnivore of the family *Canidae,* such as the dingo and coyote. **2b** (*as modifier*): *the dog family.* Related adj: **canine. 3a** the male of animals of the dog family. **3b** (*as modifier*): *a dog fox.* **4** (*modifier*) **4a** spurious, inferior, or useless: *dog Latin.* **4b** (*in combination*): *dogberry.* **5** a mechanical device for gripping or holding, esp. one of the axial slots by which gear wheels or shafts are engaged to transmit torque. **6** *Informal.* a fellow; chap: *you lucky dog.* **7** *Informal.* a man or boy regarded as unpleasant, contemptible, or wretched. **8** *Slang.* an unattractive or boring girl or woman. **9** *U.S. and Canadian informal.* something unsatisfactory or inferior. **10** short for **firedog. 11** any of various atmospheric phenomena. See **fogdog, seadog, sundog. 12 a dog's chance.** no chance at all. **13 a dog's dinner** *or* **breakfast.** *Informal.* something that is messy or bungled. **14 a dog's life.** a wretched existence. **15 dog eat dog.** ruthless competition or self-interest. **16 like a dog's dinner.** *Informal.* dressed smartly or ostentatiously. **17 put on the dog.** *U.S. and Canadian informal.* to behave or dress in an ostentatious or showy manner. ◆ *vb* **dogs, dogging, dogged.** (*tr*) **18** to pursue or follow after like a dog. **19** to trouble; plague: *to be dogged by ill health.* **20** to chase with a dog or dogs. **21** to grip, hold, or secure by a mechanical device. ◆ *adv* **22** (usually in combination) thoroughly; utterly: *dog-tired.* ◆ See also **dogs. [**Old English *docga,* of obscure origin**]** ▸ **'dogˌlike** *adj*

dogbane ('dɒgˌbeɪn) *n* any of several North American apocynaceous plants of the genus *Apocynum,* esp. *A. androsaemifolium,* having bell-shaped white or pink flowers: thought to be poisonous to dogs.

dogberry[1] ('dɒgˌbɛrɪ, -bərɪ, -brɪ) *n, pl* **-ries. 1** any of certain plants that have berry-like fruits, such as the European dogwood or the bearberry. **2** the fruit of any of these plants.

dogberry[2] ('dɒgˌbɛrɪ, -bərɪ, -brɪ) *n, pl* **-ries.** (*sometimes cap.*) a foolish, meddling, and usually old official. **[**after *Dogberry,* character in Shakespeare's *Much Ado about Nothing* (1598)**]** ▸ **'dogberryˌism** *n*

dog biscuit *n* a hard biscuit for dogs.

dog box *n* **1** *Austral. informal.* a compartment in a railway carriage with no corridor. **2** *N.Z. informal.* disgrace; disfavour (in the phrase **in the dog box**).

dogcart ('dɒgˌkɑːt) *n* a light horse-drawn two-wheeled vehicle: originally, one containing a box or section for transporting gun dogs.

dog-catcher *n Now chiefly U.S. and Canadian.* a local official whose job is to catch and impound stray dogs, cats, etc.

dog collar *n* **1** a collar for a dog. **2** an informal name for a **clerical collar. 3** *Informal.* a tight-fitting necklace.

dog days *pl n* **1** the hot period of the summer reckoned in ancient times from the heliacal rising of Sirius (the Dog Star). **2** a period marked by inactivity. [C16: translation of Late Latin *diēs caniculārēs,* translation of Greek *hēmerai kunades*]

doge (dəʊdʒ) *n* (formerly) the chief magistrate in the republics of Venice (until 1797) and Genoa (until 1805). [C16: via French from Italian (Venetian dialect), from Latin *dux* leader] ▸ **'dogeship** *n*

dog-ear *vb* **1** (*tr*) to fold down the corner of (a page). ◆ *n also* **dog's-ear. 2** a folded-down corner of a page.

dog-eared *adj* **1** having dog-ears. **2** shabby or worn.

dog-end *n* an informal name for **cigarette end.**

dog fennel *n* **1** another name for **mayweed. 2** a weedy plant, *Eupatorium capillifolium,* of the southeastern U.S., having divided leaves and greenish rayless flower heads: family *Compositae* (composites).

dogfight ('dɒgˌfaɪt) *n* **1** close quarters combat between fighter aircraft. **2** any rough violent fight.

dogfish ('dɒgˌfɪʃ) *n, pl* **-fish** *or* **-fishes. 1** any of several small spotted European sharks, esp. *Scyliorhinus caniculus* (**lesser spotted dogfish**): family *Scyliorhinidae.* **2** any small shark of the family *Squalidae,* esp. *Squalus acanthias* (**spiny dogfish**), typically having a spine on each dorsal fin. **3** any small smooth-skinned shark of the family *Triakidae,* esp. *Mustelus canis* (**smooth dogfish** or **smooth hound**). **4** a less common name for the **bowfin.**

dogged ('dɒgɪd) *adj* obstinately determined; wilful or tenacious. ▸ **'doggedly** *adv* ▸ **'doggedness** *n*

dogger[1] ('dɒgə) *n* a Dutch fishing vessel with two masts. [C14: probably from Middle Dutch *dogge* trawler]

dogger[2] ('dɒgə) *n* a large concretion of consolidated material occurring in certain sedimentary rocks. [C17: of uncertain origin]

dogger[3] ('dɒgə) *n Austral.* a hunter of dingoes. [C20: from DOG (see sense 2a) + -ER[1]]

Dogger ('dɒgə) *n Geology.* a formation of mid-Jurassic rocks in N England.

Dogger Bank ('dɒgə) *n* an extensive submerged sandbank in the North Sea between N England and Denmark: fishing ground.

doggerel ('dɒgərəl) *or* **dogrel** ('dɒgrəl) *n* **1a** comic verse, usually irregular in measure. **1b** (*as modifier*): *a doggerel rhythm.* **2** nonsense; drivel. [C14 *doggerel* worthless, perhaps from *dogge* DOG]

doggery ('dɒgərɪ) *n, pl* **-geries. 1** surly behaviour. **2** dogs collectively. **3** a mob.

Doggett's Coat and Badge race ('dɒgɪts) *n* an annual rowing race held on the River Thames to commemorate the accession of George I: the winner is presented with a coat bearing an embroidered badge. [C18: after Thomas *Doggett* (1670–1721), British actor who initiated it]

doggish ('dɒgɪʃ) *adj* **1** of or like a dog. **2** surly; snappish. ▸ **'doggishly** *adv* ▸ **'doggishness** *n*

doggo ('dɒgəʊ) *adv Brit. informal.* in hiding and keeping quiet (esp. in the phrase **lie doggo**). [C19: probably from DOG]

doggone ('dɒgɒn) *U.S. and Canadian informal.* ◆ *interj* **1** an exclamation of annoyance, disappointment, etc. ◆ *adj (prenominal), adv* **2** Also: **doggoned.** another word for **damn** (senses 3, 4). [C19: euphemism for *God damn*]

doggy *or* **doggie** ('dɒgɪ) *n, pl* **-gies. 1** a children's word for a dog. ◆ *adj* **2** of, like, or relating to a dog. **3** fond of dogs.

doggy bag *n* a bag into which leftovers from a meal may be put and taken away, supposedly for the diner's dog.

doggy paddle *or* **doggie paddle** *n* **1** a swimming stroke in which the swimmer lies on his front, paddles his hands in imitation of a swimming dog, and beats his legs up and down. ◆ *vb* **doggy-paddle** *or* **doggie-paddle. 2** (*intr*) to swim using the doggy paddle. Also called: **dog paddle.**

dog handler *n* a member of the police force, security organization, etc., who works in collaboration with a specially trained dog.

doghouse ('dɒgˌhaʊs) *n* **1** the U.S. and Canadian name for **kennel**[1]. **2** *Informal.* disfavour (in the phrase **in the doghouse**).

dogie, dogy, *or* **dogey** ('dəʊgɪ) *n, pl* **-gies** *or* **-geys.** *Western U.S. and Canadian.* a motherless calf. [C19: from *dough-guts,* because they were fed on flour and water paste]

dog in the manger *n* **a** a person who prevents others from using something he has no use for. **b** (*as modifier*): *a dog-in-the-manger attitude.*

dog Latin *n* spurious or incorrect Latin.

dogleg ('dɒgˌlɛg) *n* **1a** a sharp bend or angle. **1b** something with a sharp bend. ◆ *vb* **-legs, -legging, -legged. 2** (*intr*) to go off at an angle. ◆ *adj* **3** of or with the shape of a dogleg. ▸ **doglegged** (ˌdɒg'lɛgɪd, 'dɒgˌlɛgd) *adj*

dogleg fence *n Austral.* a fence made of sloping poles supported by forked uprights.

dogma ('dɒgmə) *n, pl* **-mas** *or* **-mata** (-mətə). **1** a religious doctrine or system of doctrines proclaimed by ecclesiastical authority as true. **2** a belief, principle, or doctrine or a code of beliefs, principles, or doctrines: *Marxist dogma.* [C17: via Latin from Greek: opinion, belief, from *dokein* to seem good]

dogman ('dɒgmən) *n, pl* **-men** *Austral.* a person who directs the operation of a crane whilst riding on an object being lifted by it.

dogmatic (dɒg'mætɪk) *or* **dogmatical** *adj* **1a** (of a statement, opinion, etc.) forcibly asserted as if authoritative and unchallengeable. **1b** (of a person) prone to making such statements. **2** of, relating to, or constituting dogma: *dogmatic writings.* **3** based on assumption rather than empirical observation. ▸ **dog'matically** *adv*

dogmatics (dɒg'mætɪks) *n* (*functioning as sing*) the study of religious dogmas and doctrines. Also called: **dogmatic** (*or* **doctrinal**) **theology.**

dogmatist ('dɒgmətɪst) *n* **1** a dogmatic person. **2** a person who formulates dogmas.

dogmatize *or* **dogmatise** ('dɒgməˌtaɪz) *vb* to say or state (something) in a dogmatic manner. ▸ **'dogmatism** *n* ▸ **ˌdogmati'zation** *or* **ˌdogmati'sation** *n* ▸ **'dogmaˌtizer** *or* **'dogmaˌtiser** *n*

do-gooder *n Informal, usually disparaging.* a well-intentioned person, esp. a naive or impractical one. ▸ **ˌdo-'goodery** *n* ▸ **ˌdo-'gooding** *n, adj*

dog paddle *n* another name for **doggy paddle.**

dog rose *n* a prickly wild rose, *Rosa canina,* that is native to Europe and has pink or white delicate scentless flowers. [translation of the Latin name, from Greek; from the belief that its root was effective against the bite of a mad dog]

dogs (dɒgz) *pl n* **1 the.** *Brit. informal.* greyhound racing. **2** *Slang.* the feet. **3** *Marketing informal.* goods with a low market share, which are unlikely to yield substantial profits. **4 go to the dogs.** *Informal.* to go to ruin physically or morally. **5 let sleeping dogs lie.** to leave things undisturbed. **6 throw (someone) to the dogs.** to abandon (someone) to criticism or attack.

Dogs (dɒgz) *n* **Isle of.** a district in the East End of London, bounded on three sides by the River Thames.

dogsbody ('dɒgzˌbɒdɪ) *n, pl* **-bodies. 1** *Informal.* a person who carries out menial tasks for others; drudge. ◆ *vb* **-bodies, -bodying, -bodied. 2** (*intr*) to act as a dogsbody.

dogsled ('dɒgˌslɛd) *n Chiefly U.S. and Canadian.* a sleigh drawn by dogs. Also called: **dog sledge** (Brit.), **dog sleigh.**

dog's mercury *n* a hairy somewhat poisonous euphorbiaceous perennial of the spurge family, *Mercurialis perennis,* having broad lanceolate toothed leaves and small greenish flowers like catkins: often creeping to carpet shady woodlands.

dog's-tail *n* any of several grasses of the genus *Cynosurus,* esp. *C. cristatus* (crested dog's-tail), that are native to Europe and have flowers clustered in a dense narrow spike.

Dog Star *n* **the.** another name for **Sirius.**

dog's-tongue *n* another name for **hound's-tongue.**

dog's-tooth check *or* **dog-tooth check** *n* other names for **hound's-tooth check.**

dog tag *n U.S. slang.* a military personal-identification disc.

dog-tired *adj* (*usually postpositive*) *Informal.* exhausted.

dogtooth ('dɒgˌtu:θ) *n, pl* **-teeth. 1** another name for a **canine** (sense 3). **2** *Architect.* a carved ornament in the form of four leaflike projections radiating from a raised centre, used in England in the 13th century.

dogtooth violet *n* a name for various plants of the liliaceous genus *Erythronium,* esp. the North American *E. americanum,* with yellow nodding flowers, or the European *E. dens-canis,* with purple flowers. Also called: **adders-tongue, fawn lily.**

dog train *n Canadian.* a sleigh drawn by a team of dogs.

dogtrot ('dɒgˌtrɒt) *n* a gently paced trot.

dog tucker *n N.Z.* the meat of a sheep killed on a farm and used as dog food.

dogvane ('dɒgˌveɪn) *n Nautical.* a light windvane consisting of a feather or a piece of cloth or yarn mounted on the side of a vessel. Also called: **telltale.**

dog violet *n* a violet, *Viola canina,* that grows in Europe and N Asia and has blue yellow-spurred flowers.

dogwatch ('dɒgˌwɒtʃ) *n* **1** either of two two-hour watches aboard ship, from four to six p.m. or from six to eight p.m. **2** *N.Z.* a shift from midnight to six a.m. in a mine.

dogwood ('dɒgˌwʊd) *n* any of various cornaceous trees or shrubs of the genus *Cornus,* esp. *C. sanguinea,* a European shrub with clusters of small white flowers and black berries: the shoots are red in winter.

dogy ('dəʊgɪ) *n, pl* **-gies.** a variant spelling of **dogie.**

doh (dəʊ) *n, pl* **dohs. 1** *Music.* (in tonic sol-fa) the first degree of any major scale. **2 up to high doh.** *Informal, chiefly Scot.* extremely excited or keyed up. [C18: from Italian; see GAMUT]

Doha ('dəʊhɑ:, 'dəʊə) *n* the capital and chief port of Qatar, on the E coast of the peninsula. Pop.: 339 471 (1993 est.). Former name: **Bida, El Beda.**

Dohnányi (dɒk'nɑ:njɪ, dɒx-; *Hungarian* 'dohna:nji) *n* **Ernö** ('ɛrnø:) *or* **Ernst von** (ɛrnst fɔn). 1877–1960, Hungarian pianist and composer whose works include *Variations on a Nursery Theme* (1913) for piano and orchestra.

doily, doyley, *or* **doyly** ('dɔɪlɪ) *n, pl* **-lies** *or* **-leys.** a decorative mat of lace or lacelike paper, etc., laid on or under plates. [C18: named after *Doily,* a London draper]

do in *vb (tr, adv) Slang.* **1** to murder or kill. **2** to exhaust.

doing ('du:ɪŋ) *n* **1** an action or the performance of an action: *whose doing is this?* **2** *Informal.* a beating or castigation.

doings ('du:ɪŋz) *pl n* **1** deeds, actions or events. **2** *Brit. and N.Z. informal.* anything of which the name is not known, or euphemistically left unsaid, etc.: *have you got the doings for starting the car?*

Doisy ('dɔɪzɪ) *n* **Edward Adelbert.** 1893–1986, U.S. biochemist. He discovered (1939) the nature of vitamin K and shared a Nobel prize for medicine with Carl Dam (1943).

doit (dɔɪt) *n* **1** a former small copper coin of the Netherlands. **2** a trifle. [C16: from Middle Dutch *duit*]

doited ('dɔɪtɪd) *or* **doitit** ('dɔɪtɪt) *adj Scot.* foolish or childish, as from senility. [C15: probably from *doten* to DOTE]

do-it-yourself *n* **a** the hobby or process of constructing and repairing things oneself. **b** (*as modifier*): *a do-it-yourself kit.*

dojo ('dəʊdʒəʊ) *n, pl* **-jos.** a room or hall for the practice of martial arts. [C20: from Japanese *dōjō* Buddhist seminary, from Sanskrit *bodhi-manda* seat of wisdom]

dol (dɒl) *n* a unit of pain intensity, as measured by dolorimetry. [C20: by shortening, from Latin *dolor* pain]

dol. *abbrev. for:* **1** *Music.* dolce. **2** (*pl* **dols.**) dollar.
dolabriform (dəʊˈlæbrɪˌfɔːm) *or* **dolabrate** (dəʊˈlæbreɪt) *adj Botany.* shaped like a hatchet or axe head. [C18: from Latin *dolābra* pickaxe]
Dolby (ˈdɒlbɪ) *n Trademark.* any of various specialized electronic circuits, esp. those used for noise reduction in tape recorders by functioning as companders on high-frequency signals. [named after R. *Dolby* (born 1933), its U.S. inventor]
dolce (ˈdɒltʃɪ; *Italian* ˈdoltʃe) *adj, adv Music.* (to be performed) gently and sweetly. [Italian: sweet]
dolce far niente *Italian.* (ˈdoltʃe far ˈnjɛnte) *n* pleasant idleness. [literally: sweet doing nothing]
Dolcelatte (ˌdɒltʃiːˈlɑːtɪ) *n* a soft creamy blue-veined cheese made in Italy. [Italian, literally: sweet milk]
dolce vita (ˈdɒltʃɪ ˈviːtə; *Italian* ˈdoltʃeˈvita) *n* a life of luxury. [Italian, literally: sweet life]
doldrums (ˈdɒldrəmz) *n* **the. 1** a depressed or bored state of mind. **2** a state of inactivity or stagnation. **3a** a belt of light winds or calms along the equator. **3b** the weather conditions experienced in this belt, formerly a hazard to sailing vessels. [C19: probably from Old English *dol* DULL, influenced by TANTRUM]
dole[1] (dəʊl) *n* **1** a small portion or share, as of money or food, given to a poor person. **2** the act of giving or distributing such portions. **3** (usually preceded by *the*) *Brit. informal.* money received from the state while out of work. **4 on the dole.** *Brit. informal.* receiving such money. **5** *Archaic.* fate. ◆ *vb* **6** (*tr;* usually foll. by *out*) to distribute, esp. in small portions. [Old English *dāl* share; related to Old Saxon *dēl*, Old Norse *deild*, Gothic *dails*, Old High German *teil;* see DEAL[1]]
dole[2] (dəʊl) *n Archaic.* grief or mourning. [C13: from Old French, from Late Latin *dolus*, from Latin *dolēre* to lament]
dole bludger *n Austral. slang, offensive.* a person who draws unemployment benefit without making any attempt to find work.
doleful (ˈdəʊlfʊl) *adj* dreary; mournful. Archaic word: **dolesome** (ˈdəʊlsəm). ▸ **ˈdolefully** *adv* ▸ **ˈdolefulness** *n*
dolente (dɒˈlɛntɪ) *adj, adv Music.* (to be performed) in a sorrowful manner.
dolerite (ˈdɒləˌraɪt) *n* **1** a dark basic igneous rock consisting of plagioclase feldspar and a pyroxene, such as augite; a coarse-grained basalt. **2** any dark igneous rock whose composition cannot be determined with the naked eye. [C19: from French *dolérite*, from Greek *doleros* deceitful; so called because of the difficulty of determining its composition] ▸ **doleritic** (ˌdɒləˈrɪtɪk) *adj*
Dolgellau (dɒlˈgɛθlaɪ, *Welsh* dɒlˈgɛhlaɪ) *n* a market town and tourist centre in NW Wales, in Gwynedd. Pop.: 2396 (1991).
dolichocephalic (ˌdɒlɪkəʊsɪˈfælɪk) *or* **dolichocephalous** (ˌdɒlɪkəʊˈsɛfələs) *adj* **1** having a head much longer than it is broad, esp. one with a cephalic index under 75. ◆ *n* **2** an individual with such a head. ◆ Compare **brachycephalic, mesocephalic.** ▸ **ˌdolichoˈcephalism** *or* **ˌdolichoˈcephaly** *n*
dolichosaurus (ˌdɒlɪkəʊˈsɔːrəs) *n* any of various extinct Cretaceous aquatic reptiles that had long necks and bodies and well-developed limbs. [C20: from Greek, from *dolikhos* long + -SAUR]
Dolin (ˈdəʊlɪn) *n* Sir **Anton**, real name *Sydney Healey-Kay.* 1904–83, British ballet dancer and choreographer: with Alicia Markova he founded (1949) the London Festival Ballet.
doline *or* **dolina** (dəˈliːnə) *n* a shallow usually funnel-shaped depression of the ground surface formed by solution in limestone regions. [C20: from Russian *dolina*, valley, plain; related to DALE]
D'Oliviera (ˌdɒlɪˈvɪərə) *n* **Basil** (**Lewis**). born 1931, South African cricketer, who played for Worcestershire and England.
doll (dɒl) *n* **1** a small model or dummy of a human being, used as a toy. **2** *Slang.* a pretty girl or woman of little intelligence: sometimes used as a term of address. [C16: probably from *Doll*, pet name for *Dorothy*] ▸ **ˈdollish** *adj* ▸ **ˈdollishly** *adv* ▸ **ˈdollishness** *n*
dollar (ˈdɒlə) *n* **1** the standard monetary unit of the U.S. and its dependencies, divided into 100 cents. **2** the standard monetary unit, comprising 100 cents, of the following countries: Antigua and Barbuda, Australia, the Bahamas, Barbados, Belize, Bermuda, Brunei, Canada, the Cayman Islands, Dominica, Fiji, Grenada, Guyana, Jamaica, Kiribati, Liberia, Malaysia, the Marshall Islands, Micronesia, Namibia, Nauru, New Zealand, Saint Kitts and Nevis, Saint Lucia, Saint Vincent and the Grenadines, Singapore, Solomon Islands, Taiwan, Trinidad and Tobago, Tuvalu, and Zimbabwe. **3** *Brit informal.* (formerly) five shillings or a coin of this value. **4 look** *or* **feel (like) a million dollars.** *Informal.* to look *or* feel extremely well. [C16: from Low German *daler*, from German *Taler, Thaler*, short for *Joachimsthaler* coin made from metal mined in *Joachimsthal* Jachymov, town now in the Czech Republic]
dollarbird (ˈdɒləˌbɜːd) *n* a bird, *Eurystomus orientalis*, of S and SE Asia and Australia, with a round white spot on each wing: family *Coraciidae* (rollers), order *Coraciiformes.*
dollar diplomacy *n Chiefly U.S.* **1** a foreign policy that encourages and protects capital investment and commercial and financial involvement abroad. **2** use of financial power as a diplomatic weapon.
dollarfish (ˈdɒləˌfɪʃ) *n, pl* **-fish** *or* **-fishes.** any of various fishes that have a rounded compressed silvery body, esp. the moonfishes or the American butterfish.
Dollfuss (*German* ˈdɔlfuːs) *n* **Engelbert** (ˈɛŋəlbɛrt). 1892–1934, Austrian statesman, chancellor (1932–34), who was assassinated by Austrian Nazis.
dollop (ˈdɒləp) *Informal.* ◆ *n* **1** a semisolid lump. **2** a large serving, esp. of food. ◆ *vb* **3** (*tr;* foll. by *out*) to serve out (food). [C16: of unknown origin]
doll up *vb* (*tr, adv*) *Slang.* to adorn or dress (oneself or another, esp. a child) in a stylish or showy manner.
dolly (ˈdɒlɪ) *n, pl* **-lies. 1** a child's word for a **doll. 2** *Films, television.* a wheeled support on which a camera may be mounted. **3** a cup-shaped anvil held against the head of a rivet while the other end is being hammered. **4** a shaped block of lead used to hammer dents out of sheet metal. **5** a distance piece placed between the head of a pile and the pile-driver to form an extension to the length of the pile. **6** *Cricket.* a simple catch. **7** Also called: **dolly bird.** *Slang, chiefly Brit.* an attractive and fashionable girl, esp. one who is considered to be unintelligent. ◆ *vb* **-lies, -lying, -lied. 8** *Films, television.* to wheel (a camera) backwards or forwards on a dolly.
Dolly Varden (ˈdɒlɪ ˈvɑːdᵊn) *n* **1** a woman's large-brimmed hat trimmed with flowers. **2** a red-spotted trout, *Salvelinus malma*, occurring in lakes in W North America. [C19: from the name of a character in Dickens' *Barnaby Rudge* (1841)]
dolma (ˈdɒlmə, -mɑː) *n, pl* **dolmas, dolmades** (dɒlˈmɑːdiːz). a vine leaf stuffed with a filling of meat and rice. [C19: Turkish *dolma* literally something filled]
dolman (ˈdɒlmən) *n, pl* **-mans. 1** a long Turkish outer robe. **2** Also called: **dolman jacket.** a hussar's jacket worn slung over the shoulder. **3** a woman's cloak with voluminous capelike sleeves. [C16: via French from German *Dolman*, from Turkish *dolaman* a winding round, from *dolamak* to wind]
dolman sleeve *n* a sleeve that is very wide at the armhole and tapers to a tight wrist.
dolmen (ˈdɒlmɛn) *n* **1** (in British archaeology) a Neolithic stone formation, consisting of a horizontal stone supported by several vertical stones, and thought to be a tomb. **2** (in French archaeology) any megalithic tomb. [C19: from French, probably from Old Breton *tol* table, from Latin *tabula* board + Breton *mēn* stone, of Celtic origin; see TABLE]
Dolmetsch (ˈdɒlmɛtʃ) *n* **Arnold.** 1858–1940, British musician, born in France. He contributed greatly to the revival of interest in early music and instruments.
dolomite (ˈdɒləˌmaɪt) *n* **1** a white mineral often tinted by impurities, found in sedimentary rocks and veins. It is used in the manufacture of cement and as a building stone (marble). Composition: calcium magnesium carbonate. Formula: $CaMg(CO_3)_2$. Crystal structure: hexagonal (rhombohedral). **2** a sedimentary rock resembling limestone but consisting principally of the mineral dolomite. It is an important source of magnesium and its compounds, and is used as a building material and refractory. [C18: named after Déodat de *Dolomieu* (1750–1801), French mineralogist] ▸ **dolomitic** (ˌdɒləˈmɪtɪk) *adj*
Dolomites (ˈdɒləˌmaɪts) *pl n* a mountain range in NE Italy: part of the Alps; formed of dolomitic limestone. Highest peak: Marmolada, 3342 m (10 965 ft.).
dolorimetry (ˌdɒləˈrɪmətrɪ) *n* a technique for measuring the level of pain perception by applying heat to the skin.
doloroso (ˌdɒləˈrəʊsəʊ) *adj, adv Music.* (to be performed) in a sorrowful manner. [Italian: dolorous]
dolorous (ˈdɒlərəs) *adj* causing or involving pain or sorrow. ▸ **ˈdolorously** *adv* ▸ **ˈdolorousness** *n*
dolos (ˈdɒlɒs) *n, pl* **-osse.** *S. African.* a knucklebone of a sheep, buck, etc., used esp. by diviners. [from Afrikaans, possibly from *dollen* play + *os* ox or from *dobbel* dice + *os* ox]
dolostone (ˈdɒləˌstəʊn) *n* rock composed of the mineral dolerite.
dolour *or U.S.* **dolor** (ˈdɒlə) *n Poetic.* grief or sorrow. [C14: from Latin, from *dolēre* to grieve]
dolphin (ˈdɒlfɪn) *n* **1** any of various marine cetacean mammals of the family *Delphinidae*, esp. *Delphinus delphis*, that are typically smaller than whales and larger than porpoises and have a beaklike snout. **2 river dolphin.** any freshwater cetacean of the family *Platanistidae*, inhabiting rivers of North and South America and S Asia. They are smaller than marine dolphins and have a longer narrower snout. **3** Also called: **dorado.** either of two large marine percoid fishes, *Coryphaena hippurus* or *C. equisetis*, that resemble the cetacean dolphins and have an iridescent coloration. **4** *Nautical.* a post or buoy for mooring a vessel. [C13: from Old French *dauphin*, via Latin, from Greek *delphin-*, *delphis*]
dolphinarium (ˌdɒlfɪˈnɛərɪəm) *n* a pool or aquarium for dolphins, esp. one in which they give public displays.
dolphin striker *n Nautical.* a short vertical strut between the bowsprit and a rope or cable (martingale) from the end of the jib boom to the stem or bows, used for maintaining tension and preventing upward movement of the jib boom. Also called: **martingale boom, martingale.**
dolt (dəʊlt) *n* a slow-witted or stupid person. [C16: probably related to Old English *dol* stupid; see DULL] ▸ **ˈdoltish** *adj* ▸ **ˈdoltishly** *adv* ▸ **ˈdoltishness** *n*
dom (dɒm) *n* **1** (*sometimes cap.*) *R.C. Church.* a title given to Benedictine, Carthusian, and Cistercian monks and to certain of the canons regular. **2** (formerly in Portugal and Brazil) a title borne by royalty, princes of the Church, and nobles. [C18 (monastic title): from Latin *dominus* lord]
DOM *abbrev. for:* **1** Deo Optimo Maximo [Latin: to God, the best, the Greatest] **2** Dirty Old Man. ◆ **3** *international car registration for* Dominican Republic.
dom. *abbrev. for:* **1** domain. **2** domestic.
Dom. *R.C. Church. abbrev. for* Dominican.
-dom *suffix forming nouns.* **1** state or condition: *freedom; martyrdom.* **2** rank or office: *earldom.* **3** domain: *kingdom; Christendom.* **4** a collection of persons: *officialdom.* [Old English *-dōm*]
Domagk (*German* ˈdoːmak) *n* **Gerhard** (ˈgeːrhart). 1895–1964, German biochemist: Nobel prize for medicine (1939) for isolating sulphanilamide for treating bacterial infections.
domain (dəˈmeɪn) *n* **1** land governed by a ruler or government. **2** land owned by one person or family. **3** a field or scope of knowledge or activity. **4** a region having specific characteristics or containing certain types of plants or animals. **5** *Austral. and N.Z.* a park or recreation reserve maintained by a public authority, often the government. **6** *Law.* the absolute ownership and right to dispose

of land. See also **demesne, eminent domain.** **7** *Maths.* **7a** the set of values of the independent variable of a function for which the functional value exists: *the domain of sin x is all real numbers.* Compare **range** (sense 8a). **7b** any open set containing at least one point. **8** *Logic.* another term for **universe of discourse** (esp. in the phrase **domain of quantification**). **9** *Philosophy.* range of significance (esp. in the phrase **domain of definition**). **10** Also called: **magnetic domain.** *Physics.* one of the regions in a ferromagnetic solid in which all the atoms have their magnetic moments aligned in the same direction. **11** *Computing.* a group of computers that have the same suffix (**domain name**) in their names on the Internet, specifying the country, type of institution, etc. where they are located. **[C17:** from French *domaine,* from Latin *dominium* property, from *dominus* lord**]**

domatium (dɒ'meɪʃɪəm) *n, pl* **-tia.** *Botany.* a plant cavity inhabited by commensal insects or mites.

dome (dəʊm) *n* **1** a hemispherical roof or vault or a structure of similar form. **2** something shaped like this. **3** *Crystallog.* a crystal form in which two planes intersect along an edge parallel to a lateral axis. **4** a slang word for the **head. 5** *Geology.* another name for **pericline** (sense 2). ◆ *vb (tr)* **6** to cover with or as if with a dome. **7** to shape like a dome. **[C16:** from French, from Italian *duomo* cathedral, from Latin *domus* house**]** ▸ **'dome,like** *adj* ▸ **domical** ('dəʊmɪkᵊl, 'dɒm-) *adj*

dome fastener *n* the usual Canadian name for **press stud.**

Domenichino (*Italian* domeni'ki:no) *n* full name **Domenico Zampieri** (do'me:niko dzam'pjɛ:ri). 1581–1641, Italian Baroque painter, noted for his frescoes and the altarpiece *Last Communion of St Jerome* (1614).

Domenico Veneziano (*Italian* do'me:niko venet'tsja:no) *n* died 1461, Italian painter, noted for the St Lucy Altarpiece.

Dome of the Rock *n* the mosque in Jerusalem, Israel, built in 691 A.D. by caliph 'Abd al-Malik: the third most holy place of Islam; stands on the Temple Mount alongside the **al-Aqsa** mosque. Also called (not in Muslim usage): **Mosque of Omar.**

domesday ('du:mz,deɪ) *n* a variant spelling of **doomsday.**

Domesday Book *or* **Doomsday Book** *n History.* the record of a survey of the land of England carried out by the commissioners of William I in 1086.

domestic (də'mɛstɪk) *adj* **1** of or involving the home or family. **2** enjoying or accustomed to home or family life. **3** (of an animal) bred or kept by man as a pet or for purposes such as the supply of food. **4** of, produced in, or involving one's own country or a specific country: *domestic and foreign affairs.* ◆ *n* **5** a household servant. **6** *Informal.* (esp. in police use) an incident of violence in the home, esp. between a man and a woman. **[C16:** from Old French *domestique,* from Latin *domesticus* belonging to the house, from *domus* house**]** ▸ **do'mestically** *adv*

domesticate (də'mɛstɪ,keɪt) *or U.S.* (*sometimes*) **domesticize** (də'mɛstɪ,saɪz) *vb (tr)* **1** to bring or keep (wild animals or plants) under control or cultivation. **2** to accustom to home life. **3** to adapt to an environment: *to domesticate foreign trees.* ▸ **do'mesticable** *adj* ▸ **do,mesti'cation** *n* ▸ **do'mesticative** *adj* ▸ **do'mesti,cator** *n*

domestic court *n* (in England) a magistrates' court for domestic proceedings, such as matrimonial, guardianship, custodianship, affiliation, or adoption disputes.

domestic fowl *n* a domesticated gallinaceous bird thought to be descended from the red jungle fowl (*Gallus gallus*) and occurring in many varieties. Often shortened to **fowl.**

domesticity (,dəʊmɛ'stɪsɪtɪ) *n, pl* **-ties. 1** home life. **2** devotion to or familiarity with home life. **3** (*usually pl*) a domestic duty, matter, or condition.

domestic science *n* the study of cooking, needlework, and other subjects concerned with household skills.

Domett ('dɒmɪt) *n* **Alfred.** 1811–87, New Zealand poet, colonial administrator, and statesman, born in England: prime minister of New Zealand (1862–63).

domicile ('dɒmɪ,saɪl) *or* **domicil** ('dɒmɪsɪl) *Formal.* ◆ *n* **1** a dwelling place. **2** a permanent legal residence. **3** *Commerce, Brit.* the place where a bill of exchange is to be paid. ◆ *vb also* **domiciliate** (,dɒmɪ'sɪlɪ,eɪt). **4** to establish or be established in a dwelling place. **[C15:** from Latin *domicilium,* from *domus* house**]** ▸ **domiciliary** (,dɒmɪ'sɪlɪərɪ) *adj*

domiciliary care *or* **services** *n Social welfare.* services, such as meals-on-wheels, health visiting, and home help, provided by a welfare agency for people in their own homes.

dominance ('dɒmɪnəns) *n* control; ascendancy.

dominant ('dɒmɪnənt) *adj* **1** having primary control, authority, or influence; governing; ruling. **2** predominant or primary: *the dominant topic of the day.* **3** occupying a commanding position. **4** *Genetics.* **4a** (of a gene) producing the same phenotype in the organism whether its allele is identical or dissimilar. **4b** (of a character) controlled by such a gene. Compare **recessive** (sense 2). **5** *Music.* of or relating to the fifth degree of a scale. **6** *Ecology.* (of a plant or animal species within a community) more prevalent than any other species and determining the appearance and composition of the community. ◆ *n* **7** *Genetics.* **7a** a dominant gene or character. **7b** an organism having such a gene or character. **8** *Music.* **8a** the fifth degree of a scale and the second in importance after the tonic. **8b** a key or chord based on this. **9** *Ecology.* a dominant plant or animal in a community. ▸ **'dominantly** *adv*

dominant hemisphere *n* See **cerebral dominance.**

dominant seventh chord *n* a chord consisting of the dominant and the major third, perfect fifth, and minor seventh above it. Its most natural resolution is to a chord on the tonic.

dominant tenement *n Property law.* the land or tenement with the benefit of an easement over land belonging to another. Compare **servient tenement.**

dominant wavelength *n Physics.* the wavelength of monochromatic light that would give the same visual sensation if combined in a suitable proportion with an achromatic light. See also **complementary wavelength.**

dominate ('dɒmɪ,neɪt) *vb* **1** to control, rule, or govern (someone or something). **2** to tower above (surroundings, etc.); overlook. **3** (*tr; usually passive*) to predominate in (something or someone). **[C17:** from Latin *dominārī* to be lord over, from *dominus* lord**]** ▸ **'domi,nating** *adj* ▸ **'domi,natingly** *adv* ▸ **'dominative** *adj* ▸ **'domi,nator** *n*

domination (,dɒmɪ'neɪʃən) *n* **1** the act of dominating or state of being dominated. **2** authority; rule; control.

dominations (,dɒmɪ'neɪʃənz) *pl n* (*sometimes cap.*) the fourth order of medieval angelology. Also called: **dominions.**

dominatrix (,dɒmɪ'neɪtrɪks) *n, pl* **dominatrices** (,dɒmɪnə'traɪsi:z). **1** a woman who is the dominant sexual partner in a sadomasochistic relationship. **2** a dominant woman. **[C16:** from Latin, fem of *dominātor,* from *dominārī* to be lord over**]**

dominee ('du:mɪnɪ, 'dʊə-) *n* (in South Africa) a minister in any of the Afrikaner Churches. Also called: **predikant. [**from Afrikaans, from Dutch; compare DOMINIE**]**

domineer (,dɒmɪ'nɪə) *vb* (*intr;* often foll. by *over*) to act with arrogance or tyranny; behave imperiously. **[C16:** from Dutch *domineren,* from French *dominer* to DOMINATE**]** ▸ **,domi'neering** *adj* ▸ **,domi'neeringly** *adv* ▸ **,domi'neeringness** *n*

Domingo (*Spanish* do'miŋgo) *n* **Placido** ('plaθiðo). born 1941, Spanish operatic tenor.

Dominic ('dɒmɪnɪk) *n* **Saint.** original name *Domingo de Guzman.* ?1170–1221, Spanish priest; founder of the Dominican order. Feast day: Aug. 7.

Dominica (,dɒmɪ'ni:kə, də'mɪnɪkə) *n* a republic in the E Caribbean, comprising a volcanic island in the Windward Islands group; a former British colony; became independent as a member of the Commonwealth in 1978. Official language: English. Religion: Roman Catholic majority. Currency: East Caribbean dollar. Capital: Roseau. Pop.: 76 400 (1998 est.). Area: 751 sq. km (290 sq. miles). Official name: **Commonwealth of Dominica.**

dominical (də'mɪnɪkᵊl) *adj* **1** of, relating to, or emanating from Jesus Christ as Lord. **2** of or relating to Sunday as the Lord's Day. **[C15:** from Late Latin *dominicālis,* from Latin *dominus* lord**]**

dominical letter *n Christianity.* any one of the letters A to G as used to denote Sundays in a given year in order to determine the church calendar.

Dominican[1] (də'mɪnɪkən) *n* **1a** a member of an order of preaching friars founded by Saint Dominic in 1215; a Blackfriar. **1b** a nun of one of the orders founded under the patronage of Saint Dominic. ◆ *adj* **2** of or relating to Saint Dominic or the Dominican order.

Dominican[2] (də'mɪnɪkən) *adj* **1** of or relating to the Dominican Republic or Dominica. ◆ *n* **2** a native or inhabitant of the Dominican Republic or Dominica.

Dominican Republic *n* a republic in the Caribbean, occupying the eastern half of the island of Hispaniola: colonized by the Spanish after its discovery by Columbus in 1492; gained independence from Spain in 1821. It is generally mountainous, dominated by the Cordillera Central, which rises over 3000 m (10 000 ft.), with fertile lowlands. Language: Spanish. Religion: Roman Catholic majority. Currency: peso. Capital: Santo Domingo. Pop.: 7 883 000 (1998 est.). Area: 48 441 sq. km (18 703 sq. miles). Former name (until 1844): **Santo Domingo.**

dominie ('dɒmɪnɪ) *n* **1** a Scot. word for **schoolmaster. 2** a minister or clergyman: also used as a term of address. **[C17:** from Latin *dominē,* vocative case of *dominus* lord**]**

dominion (də'mɪnjən) *n* **1** rule; authority. **2** the land governed by one ruler or government. **3** sphere of influence; area of control. **4** a name formerly applied to self-governing divisions of the British Empire. **5** (*cap.*) **the.** New Zealand. **6** *Law.* a less common word for **dominium. [C15:** from Old French, from Latin *dominium* ownership, from *dominus* master**]**

Dominion Day *n* the former name for **Canada Day.**

dominions (də'mɪnjənz) *pl n* (*often cap.*) another term for **dominations.**

dominium (də'mɪnɪəm) *or* (*rarely*) **dominion** *n Property law.* the ownership or right to possession of property, esp. realty. **[C19:** from Latin: property, ownership; see DOMINION**]**

domino[1] ('dɒmɪ,nəʊ) *n, pl* **-noes. 1** a small rectangular block used in dominoes, divided on one side into two equal areas, each of which is either blank or marked with from one to six dots. **2** (*modifier*) exhibiting the domino effect: *a domino pattern of takeovers.* ◆ See also **dominoes. [C19:** from French, from Italian, perhaps from *domino!* master, said by the winner**]**

domino[2] ('dɒmɪ,nəʊ) *n, pl* **-noes** *or* **-nos. 1** a large hooded cloak worn with an eye mask at a masquerade. **2** the eye mask worn with such a cloak. **[C18:** from French or Italian, probably from Latin *dominus* lord, master**]**

Domino ('dɒmɪnəʊ) *n* **Fats.** real name *Antoine Domino.* born 1928, U.S. rhythm-and-blues and rock-and-roll pianist, singer, and songwriter. His singles include "Ain't that a Shame" (1955) and "Blueberry Hill" (1956).

domino effect *n* a series of similar or related events occurring as a direct and inevitable result of one initial event. **[C20:** alluding to a row of dominoes, each standing on end, all of which fall when one is pushed: originally used with reference to possible Communist takeovers of countries in SE Asia**]**

dominoes ('dɒmɪ,nəʊz) *n* (*functioning as sing*) any of several games in which matching halves of dominoes are laid together.

Dominus *Latin.* ('dɒmɪnʊs) *n* God or Christ.

Domitian (də'mɪʃən) *n* full name *Titus Flavius Domitianus.* 51–96 A.D., Roman emperor (81–96): instigated a reign of terror (93); assassinated.

Domrémy-la-Pucelle (*French* dɔ̃remilapysɛl) *or* **Domrémy** *n* a village in NE France, in the Vosges: birthplace of Joan of Arc.

don[1] (dɒn) *vb* **dons, donning, donned.** (*tr*) to put on (clothing). [C14: from DO[1] + ON; compare DOFF]

don[2] (dɒn) *n* **1** *Brit.* a member of the teaching staff at a university or college, esp. at Oxford or Cambridge. **2** a Spanish gentleman or nobleman. **3** (in the Mafia) the head of a family. [C17: ultimately from Latin *dominus* lord]

Don[1] (dɒn; *Spanish* don) *n* a Spanish title equivalent to *Mr*: placed before a name to indicate respect. [C16: via Spanish, from Latin *dominus* lord; see DON[2]]

Don[2] (dɒn) *n* **1** a river rising in W Russia, southeast of Tula and flowing generally south, to the Sea of Azov: linked by canal to the River Volga. Length: 1870 km (1162 miles). **2** a river in NE Scotland, rising in the Cairngorm Mountains and flowing east to the North Sea. Length: 100 km (62 miles). **3** a river in N central England, rising in S Yorkshire and flowing northeast to the Humber. Length: about 96 km (60 miles).

Dona (*Portuguese* 'dõːnə) *n* a Portuguese title of address equivalent to *Mrs* or *Madam*: placed before a name to indicate respect. [C19: from Latin *domina* lady, feminine of *dominus* master]

Doña ('dɒnjə; *Spanish* 'doɲa) *n* a Spanish title of address equivalent to *Mrs* or *Madam*: placed before a name to indicate respect. [C17: via Spanish, from Latin *domina;* see DONA]

Donald ('dɒnᵊld) *n* ?1031–1100, king of Scotland (1093–94; 1094–97).

Donar ('dəʊnɑː; *German* 'doːnar) *n* the Germanic god of thunder, corresponding to Thor in Norse mythology.

donate (dəʊ'neɪt) *vb* to give (money, time, etc.), esp. to a charity. ▸ **do'nator** *n*

Donatello (*Italian* dona'tello) *n* real name *Donato di Betto Bardi*. 1386–1466, Florentine sculptor, regarded as the greatest sculptor of the quattrocento, who was greatly influenced by classical sculpture and contemporary humanist theories. His marble relief of *St George Killing the Dragon* (1416–17) shows his innovative use of perspective. Other outstanding works are the classic bronze *David,* and the bronze equestrian monument to Gattamalata, which became the model of subsequent equestrian sculpture.

donation (dəʊ'neɪʃən) *n* **1** the act of giving, esp. to a charity. **2** a contribution. [C15: from Latin *dōnātiō* a presenting, from *dōnāre* to give, from *dōnum* gift]

Donatist ('dəʊnətɪst) *n* a member of a schismatic heretical Christian sect originating in N Africa in 311 A.D., that maintained that it alone constituted the true church. [C15: from Late Latin *Dōnātista* a follower of *Dōnātus,* bishop of Carthage] ▸ **'Dona,tism** *n*

donative ('dəʊnətɪv) *n* **1** a gift or donation. **2** a benefice capable of being conferred as a gift. ◆ *adj* **3** of or like a donation. **4** being or relating to a benefice. [C15: from Latin *dōnātīvum* donation made to soldiers by a Roman emperor, from *dōnāre* to present]

Donatus (dəʊ'nɑːtəs) *n* **1 Aelius** ('iːlɪəs). 4th century A.D., Latin grammarian, who taught Saint Jerome; his textbook *Ars Grammatica* was used throughout the Middle Ages. **2** 4th century A.D., bishop of Carthage; leader of the Donatists, a heretical Christian sect originating in N Africa in 311 A.D.

Donau ('doːnau) *n* the German name for the **Danube.**

Donbass *or* **Donbas** (dɒn'bɑːs) *n* an industrial region in the E Ukraine in the plain of the Rivers Donets and lower Dnieper: the site of a major coalfield. Also called: **Donets Basin.**

Doncaster ('dɒŋkəstə) *n* **1** an industrial town in N England, in Doncaster unitary authority, South Yorkshire, on the River Don. Pop.: 71 595 (1991). **2** a unitary authority in N England, in South Yorkshire. Pop.: 292 500 (1994 est.). Area: 582 sq. km (225 sq. miles).

donder ('dɒndə) *S. African slang.* ◆ *vb* (*tr*) **1** to beat (someone) up. ◆ *n* **2** a wretch; swine. [C19: Afrikaans, from Dutch *donderen* to swear, bully]

done (dʌn) *vb* **1** the past participle of **do**[1]. **2 be** *or* **have done with.** to end relations with. **3 have done.** to be completely finished: *have you done?* **4 that's done it. 4a** an exclamation of frustration when something is ruined. **4b** an exclamation when something is completed. ◆ *interj* **5** an expression of agreement, as on the settlement of a bargain between two parties. ◆ *adj* **6** completed; finished. **7** cooked enough: *done to a turn.* **8** used up: *they had to surrender when the ammunition was done.* **9** socially proper or acceptable: *that isn't done in higher circles.* **10** *Informal.* cheated; tricked. **11 done for.** *Informal.* **11a** dead or almost dead. **11b** in serious difficulty. **12 done in** *or* **up.** *Informal.* physically exhausted.

donee (dəʊ'niː) *n Law.* **1** a person who receives a gift. **2** a person to whom a power of appointment is given. [C16: from DON(OR) + -EE]

Donegal ('dɒnɪ,gɔːl, ,dɒnɪ'gɔːl) *n* a county in NW Republic of Ireland, on the Atlantic: mountainous, with a rugged coastline and many offshore islands. County town: Lifford. Pop.: 129 000 (1996). Area: 4830 sq. km (1865 sq. miles).

doner kebab ('dɒnə) *n* a fast-food dish comprising grilled meat and salad served in pitta bread with chilli sauce. [from Turkish *döner* rotating + KEBAB]

Donets (*Russian* da'njets) *n* a river rising in SW Russia, in the Kursk steppe and flowing southeast, through the Ukraine, to the Don River. Length: about 1078 km (670 miles).

Donets Basin (də'nɛts) *n* another name for the **Donbass.**

Donetsk (*Russian* da'njetsk) *n* a city in the E Ukraine: the chief industrial centre of the Donbass; first ironworks founded by a Welshman, John Hughes (1872), after whom the town was named **Yuzovka** (Hughesovka). Pop.: 1 088 000 (1996 est.). Former names (from 1924 until 1961): **Stalin** or **Stalino.**

dong (dɒŋ) *n* **1** the deep reverberating sound of a large bell. **2** *Austral. and N.Z. informal.* a heavy blow. **3** a slang word for **penis.** ◆ *vb* **4** (*intr*) (of a bell) to make a deep reverberating sound. **5** (*tr*) *Austral. and N.Z. informal.* to strike or punch. [C16: of imitative origin]

dông (dɒŋ) *n* the standard monetary unit of Vietnam. [from Vietnamese]

donga[1] ('dɒŋgə) *n S. African, Austral., and N.Z.* a steep-sided gully created by soil erosion. [C19: Afrikaans, from Nguni *donga* washed out gully]

donga[2] ('dɒŋgə) *n* (in Papua New Guinea) a house or shelter.

dongle ('dɒŋgᵊl) *n Computing.* an electronic device that accompanies a software item to prevent the unauthorized copying of programs.

Dongola ('dɒŋgələ) *n* a small town in the N Sudan, on the Nile: built on the site of Old Dongola, the capital of the Christian Kingdom of Nubia (6th to 14th centuries). Pop.: 5937 (latest est.).

Dongting ('duŋ'tɪŋ), **Tungting,** *or* **Tung-t'ing** *n* a lake in S China, in NE Hunan province: main outlet flows to the Yangtze; rice-growing in winter. Area: (in winter) 3900 sq. km (1500 sq. miles).

Dönitz *or* **Doenitz** (*German* 'døːnɪts) *n* **Karl** (karl). 1891–1980, German admiral; commander in chief of the German navy (1943–45); as head of state after Hitler's death he surrendered to the Allies (May 7, 1945).

Donizetti (,dɒnɪ'zɛtɪ; *Italian* donid'dzetti) *n* **Gaetano** (gae'taːno). 1797–1848, Italian operatic composer: his works include *Lucia di Lammermoor* (1835), *La Fille du régiment* (1840), and *Don Pasquale* (1843).

donjon ('dʌndʒən, 'dɒn-) *n* the heavily fortified central tower or keep of a medieval castle. Also called: **dungeon.** [C14: archaic variant of *dungeon*]

Don Juan ('dɒn 'dʒuːən; *Spanish* don xwan) *n* **1** a legendary Spanish nobleman and philanderer: hero of many poems, plays, and operas, including treatments by de Molina, Molière, Goldoni, Mozart, Byron, and Shaw. **2** a successful seducer of women.

donkey ('dɒŋkɪ) *n* **1** Also called: **ass.** a long-eared domesticated member of the horse family (*Equidae*), descended from the African wild ass (*Equus asinus*). **2** a stupid or stubborn person. **3** *Brit. slang, derogatory.* a footballer known for his or her lack of skill: *the players are a bunch of overpriced and overrated donkeys.* **4 talk the hind leg(s) off a donkey.** to talk endlessly. [C18: perhaps from *dun* dark + *-key,* as in *monkey*]

donkey derby *n* a race in which contestants ride donkeys, esp. at a rural fête.

donkey engine *n* a small auxiliary engine, such as one used for pumping water into the boilers of a steamship.

donkey jacket *n* a hip-length jacket usually made of a thick navy fabric with a waterproof panel across the shoulders.

donkey-lick *vb Austral. slang.* to defeat decisively.

donkey's years *n Informal.* a long time.

donkey vote *n Austral.* a vote on a preferential ballot on which the voter's order of preference follows the order in which the candidates are listed.

donkey-work *n* **1** groundwork. **2** drudgery.

donko ('dɒŋkəʊ) *n, pl* **-kos.** *N.Z. informal.* a tearoom or cafeteria in a factory, wharf area, etc. [origin unknown]

Donleavy (dɒn'liːvɪ) *n* **J(ames) P(atrick).** born 1926, Irish-American novelist. His books include *The Ginger Man* (1956), *The Onion Eaters* (1971), *Are You Listening Rabbi Löw?* (1987), *That Darcy, That Dancer, That Gentleman* (1990), and *The Lady Who Liked Clean Rest Rooms* (1995).

Donna ('dɒnə; *Italian* 'dɔnna) *n* an Italian title of address equivalent to *Madam,* indicating respect. [C17: from Italian, from Latin *domina* lady, feminine of *dominus* lord, master]

Donne (dʌn) *n* **John.** 1573–1631, English metaphysical poet and preacher. He wrote love and religious poems, sermons, epigrams, and elegies.

donnée *or* ***donné*** *French.* (dɔne) *n* **1** a subject or theme. **2** a basic assumption or fact. [literally: (a) given]

donnert ('dɒnərt), **donnard,** *or* **donnered** ('dɒnərd) *adj Scot.* stunned. [C18: from Scottish dialect *donner* to astound, perhaps from Dutch *donderen* to thunder, from Middle Dutch *donder* thunder]

donnish ('dɒnɪʃ) *adj* of or resembling a university don. ▸ **'donnishly** *adv* ▸ **'donnishness** *n*

donny ('dɒnɪ) *n* a variant of **danny.**

donnybrook ('dɒnɪ,brʊk) *n* a rowdy brawl. [C19: after *Donnybrook Fair,* an annual event until 1855 near Dublin]

donor ('dəʊnə) *n* **1** a person who makes a donation. **2** *Med.* any person who voluntarily gives blood, skin, etc., for use in the treatment of another person. **3** *Law.* **3a** a person who makes a gift of property. **3b** a person who bestows upon another a power of appointment over property. **4** the atom supplying both electrons in a coordinate bond. **5** an impurity, such as antimony or arsenic, that is added to a semiconductor material in order to increase its n-type conductivity by contributing free electrons. Compare **acceptor** (sense 2). [C15: from Old French *doneur,* from Latin *dōnātor,* from *dōnāre* to give] ▸ **'donor,ship** *n*

donor card *n* a card carried by a person to show that the bodily organs specified on it may be used for transplants after the person's death.

Don Quixote ('dɒn kiː'həʊtiː, 'kwɪksət; *Spanish* don ki'xote) *n* an impractical idealist. [after the hero of Cervantes' *Don Quixote de la Mancha*]

don't (dəʊnt) *contraction of* do not.

don't know *n* a person who has not reached a definite opinion on a subject, esp. as a response to a questionnaire.

donut ('dəʊnʌt) *n* a variant spelling (esp. U.S.) of **doughnut.**

doo (duː) *n* a Scot. word for **dove**[1] or **pigeon**[1].

doodah ('duːdɑː) *or U.S. and Canadian* **doodad** ('duːdæd) *n Informal.* **1** an unnamed thing, esp. an object the name of which is unknown or forgotten. **2 all of a doodah.** excited; agitated. [C20: of uncertain origin]

doodle ('duːdᵊl) *Informal.* ◆ *vb* **1** to scribble or draw aimlessly. **2** to play or improvise idly. **3** (*intr;* often foll. by *away*) *U.S.* to dawdle or waste time. ◆ *n* **4** a shape, picture, etc., drawn aimlessly. [C20: perhaps from C17 *doodle* a foolish person, but influenced in meaning by DAWDLE; compare Low German *dudeltopf* simpleton] ▸ **'doodler** *n*

doodlebug ('duːdᵊl,bʌg) *n* **1** another name for the **V-1. 2** a diviner's rod. **3** a

U.S. name for an **antlion** (the larva). **4** *U.S.* any of certain insect larvae that resemble the antlion. [C20: probably from DOODLE + BUG[1]]

doo-doo ('du:,du:) *n U.S. and Canadian informal.* a child's word for **excrement.**

doohickey ('du:,hɪkɪ) *n U.S. and Canadian informal.* another name for **doodah** (sense 1).

dook[1] *or* **douk**[1] (dʊk) *n Scot.* a wooden plug driven into a wall to hold a nail, screw, etc. [of unknown origin]

dook[2] *or* **douk**[2] (dʊk) *Scot.* ◆ *vb* **1** to dip or plunge. **2** to bathe. ◆ *n* **3** an instance of dipping, plunging, or bathing. [a Scot. form of DUCK[2]]

dooket ('du:kɪt, 'dʊkɪt) *n Scot.* **1** a dovecote. **2** a small closet or cupboard.

doolally (du:'lælɪ) *adj* in full: **doolally tap.** *Slang.* out of one's mind; crazy. [C19: originally military slang, from *Deolali,* a town near Bombay, the location of a military sanatorium + Hindustani *tap* fever]

doolan ('du:lən) *n N.Z. informal.* a Roman Catholic. [probably from the Irish surname *Doolan*]

Doolittle ('du:lɪtᵊl) *n* **Hilda.** known as *H.D.* 1886–1961, U.S. imagist poet and novelist, living in Europe.

doom (du:m) *n* **1** death or a terrible fate. **2** a judgment or decision. **3** (*sometimes cap.*) another term for the **Last Judgment.** ◆ *vb* **4** (*tr*) to destine or condemn to death or a terrible fate. [Old English *dōm;* related to Old Norse *dōmr* judgment, Gothic *dōms* sentence, Old High German *tuom* condition, Greek *thomos* crowd, Sanskrit *dhāman* custom; see DO[1], DEEM, DEED, -DOM]

doom-laden *adj* conveying a sense of disaster and tragedy.

doom palm *n* a variant spelling of **doum palm.**

doomsday *or* **domesday** ('du:mz,deɪ) *n* **1** (*sometimes cap.*) the day on which the Last Judgment will occur. **2** any day of reckoning. **3** (*modifier*) characterized by predictions of disaster: *doomsday scenario.* [Old English *dōmes dæg* Judgment Day; related to Old Norse *domsdagr*]

Doomsday Book *n* a variant spelling of **Domesday Book.**

doomster ('du:mstə) *n Informal.* **1** a person habitually given to predictions of impending disaster or doom. **2** *Archaic.* a judge.

doomwatch ('du:m,wɒtʃ) *n* **1** surveillance of the environment to warn of and prevent harm to it from human factors such as pollution or overpopulation. **2** a watching for or prediction of impending disaster. ▸ **'doomwatcher** *n*

doomy ('du:mɪ) *adj Informal.* **1** despondent or pessimistic. **2** depressing, frightening, or chilling.

doon *or* **doun** (du:n) *prep, adv, adj* a Scot. word for **down**[1].

doona ('du:nə) *n* the Austral. name for **continental quilt.** [from a trademark]

door (dɔ:) *n* **1a** a hinged or sliding panel for closing the entrance to a room, cupboard, etc. **1b** (*in combination*): *doorbell; doorknob.* **2** a doorway or entrance to a room or building. **3** a means of access or escape: *a door to success.* **4 lay at someone's door.** to lay (the blame or responsibility) on someone. **5 out of doors.** in or into the open air. **6 show someone the door.** to order someone to leave. ◆ See also **next door.** [Old English *duru;* related to Old Frisian *dure,* Old Norse *dyrr,* Old High German *turi,* Latin *forēs,* Greek *thura*]

do-or-die *adj* (*prenominal*) of or involving a determined and sometimes reckless effort to succeed.

doorframe ('dɔ:,freɪm) *n* a frame that supports a door. Also called: **'door,case.**

door furniture *n* locks, handles, etc., designed for use on doors.

doorjamb ('dɔ:,dʒæm) *n* one of the two vertical members forming the sides of a doorframe. Also called: **doorpost.**

doorkeeper ('dɔ:,ki:pə) *n* **1** a person attending or guarding a door or gateway. **2** *R.C. Church.* (formerly) the lowest grade of holy orders.

doorknock ('dɔ:nɒk) *n Austral.* a fund-raising campaign for charity conducted by seeking donations from door to door.

doorman ('dɔ:,mæn, -mən) *n, pl* **-men.** a man employed to attend the doors of certain buildings.

doormat ('dɔ:,mæt) *n* **1** a mat, placed at the entrance to a building, for wiping dirt from shoes. **2** *Informal.* a person who offers little resistance to ill-treatment by others.

Doorn (*Dutch* do:rn) *n* a town in the central Netherlands, in Utrecht province: residence of Kaiser William II of Germany from his abdication (1919) until his death (1941).

doornail ('dɔ:,neɪl) *n* (**as**) **dead as a doornail.** dead beyond any doubt.

Doornik ('do:rnɪk) *n* the Flemish name for **Tournai.**

doorpost ('dɔ:,pəʊst) *n* another name for **doorjamb.**

Doors (dɔ:z) *pl n* **the.** U.S. rock group (1965–73), originally comprising Jim Morrison, Ray Manzarek (born 1935), Robby Krieger (born 1946), and John Densmore (born 1945). See also (Jim) **Morrison.**

doorsill ('dɔ:,sɪl) *n* a horizontal member of wood, stone, etc., forming the bottom of a doorframe.

doorstep ('dɔ:,stɛp) *n* **1** a step in front of a door. **2 on one's doorstep.** very close or accessible. **3** *Informal.* a thick slice of bread. ◆ *vb* **-steps, -stepping, -stepped.** (*tr*) **4** to canvass (a district) or interview (a member of the public) by or in the course of door-to-door visiting.

doorstop ('dɔ:,stɒp) *n* **1** a heavy object, wedge, or other device which prevents an open door from moving. **2** a projecting piece of rubber, etc., fixed to the floor to stop a door from striking a wall.

door to door *adj* (**door-to-door** *when prenominal*), *adv* **1** (of selling, canvassing, etc.) from one house to the next. **2** (of journeys, deliveries, etc.) direct.

doorway ('dɔ:,weɪ) *n* **1** an opening into a building, room, etc., esp. one that has a door. **2** a means of access or escape: *a doorway to freedom.*

dooryard ('dɔ:,jɑ:d) *n U.S. and Canadian.* a yard in front of the front or back door of a house.

do out *vb* (*tr, adv*) *Informal.* **1** to make tidy or clean; redecorate. **2** (foll. by *of*) to deprive (a person) of by swindling or cheating.

do over *vb* (*tr, adv*) **1** *Informal.* to renovate or redecorate. **2** *Brit., Austral., and N.Z. slang.* to beat up; thrash.

doo-wop ('du:,wɒp) *n* rhythm-and-blues harmony vocalizing developed by unaccompanied street-corner groups in the U.S. in the 1950s. [C20: of imitative origin]

dop (dɒp) *n S. African informal.* a tot or small drink, usually alcoholic. [Afrikaans]

dopa ('dəʊpə) *n* See **L-dopa.**

dopamine ('dɒpəmɪn) *n* a chemical found in the brain that acts as a neurotransmitter and is an intermediate compound in the synthesis of noradrenaline. Formula: $(HO)_2C_6(CH_2)_2NH_2$. [from *d(ihydr)o(xy)p(henylethyl)amine*]

dopant ('dəʊpənt) *n* an element or compound used to dope a semiconductor. [C20: see DOPE, -ANT]

dope (dəʊp) *n* **1** any of a number of preparations made by dissolving cellulose derivatives in a volatile solvent, applied to fabric in order to improve strength, tautness, etc. **2** an additive used to improve the properties of something, such as an antiknock compound added to petrol. **3** a thick liquid, such as a lubricant, applied to a surface. **4** a combustible absorbent material, such as sawdust or wood pulp, used to hold the nitroglycerine in dynamite. **5** *Slang.* **5a** any illegal drug, usually cannabis. **5b** (*as modifier*): *a dope fiend.* **6** a drug administered to a racehorse or greyhound to affect its performance. **7** *Informal.* a person considered to be stupid or slow-witted. **8** *Informal.* news or facts, esp. confidential information. **9** *U.S. and Canadian informal.* a photographic developing solution. ◆ *vb* (*tr*) **10** *Electronics.* to add impurities to (a semiconductor) in order to produce or modify its properties. **11** to apply or add dope to. **12** to administer a drug to (oneself or another). **13** (*intr*) to take dope. ◆ *adj* **14** *Slang, chiefly U.S.* excellent. [C19: from Dutch *doop* sauce, from *doopen* to DIP]

dope out *vb* (*tr, adv*) *U.S. slang.* to devise, solve, or contrive: *to dope out a floor plan.*

dope sheet *n Horse racing slang.* a publication giving information on horses running in races.

dopester ('dəʊpstə) *n U.S. and Canadian slang.* a person who makes predictions, esp. in sport or politics.

dopey *or* **dopy** ('dəʊpɪ) *adj* **dopier, dopiest. 1** *Slang.* silly. **2** *Informal.* half-asleep or in a state of semiconsciousness, as when under the influence of a drug. ▸ **'dopily** *adv* ▸ **'dopiness** *n*

doppelgänger ('dɒpᵊl,gɛŋə; *German* 'dɔpəl,gɛŋər) *n Legend.* a ghostly duplicate of a living person. [from German *Doppelgänger,* literally: double-goer]

Dopper ('dɒpə) *n* (in South Africa) a member of the most conservative Afrikaner Church, which practises a strict Calvinism. [C19: from Afrikaans, of unknown origin]

Doppler effect ('dɒplə) *n* a phenomenon, observed for sound waves and electromagnetic radiation, characterized by a change in the apparent frequency of a wave as a result of relative motion between the observer and the source. Also called: **Doppler shift.** [C19: named after C. J. *Doppler* (1803–53), Austrian physicist]

dor (dɔ:) *n* any European dung beetle of the genus *Geotrupes* and related genera, esp. *G. stercorarius,* having a droning flight. [Old English *dora* bumblebee; related to Middle Low German *dorte* DRONE[1]]

dorado (də'rɑ:dəʊ) *n* **1** another name for **dolphin** (sense 3). **2** a S. American river fish of the genus *Salminus* that resembles a salmon.

Dorado (də'rɑ:dəʊ) *n, Latin genitive* **Doradus** (də'rɑ:dəs). a constellation in the S hemisphere lying between Reticulum and Pictor and containing part of the Large Magellanic cloud. [C17: from Spanish, from *dorar* to gild, from Latin DE- + *-aurāre,* from *aurum* gold]

Doráti (də'rɑ:tɪ) *n* **Antal** ('æntæl). 1906–88, U.S. conductor and composer.

Dorcas ('dɔ:kəs) *n* a charitable woman of Joppa (Acts 9:36–42).

Dorcas society *n* a Christian charitable society for women with the aim of providing clothes for the poor.

Dorchester ('dɔ:tʃɪstə) *n* a town in S England, administrative centre of Dorset: associated with Thomas Hardy, esp. as the Casterbridge of his novels. Pop.: 15 037 (1991). Latin name: **Durnovaria** (,djʊrnəʊ'vɛərɪə).

Dordogne (*French* dɔrdɔɲ) *n* **1** a river in SW France, rising in the Auvergne Mountains and flowing southwest and west to join the Garonne river and form the Gironde estuary. Length: 472 km (293 miles). **2** a department of SW France, in Aquitaine region. Capital: Périgueux. Pop.: 388 700 (1995). Area: 9224 sq. km (3597 sq. miles).

Dordrecht (*Dutch* 'dɔrdrɛxt) *n* a port in the SW Netherlands, in South Holland province: chief port of the Netherlands until the 17th century. Pop.: 116 196 (1996 est.). Also called: **Dort.**

Doré (*French* dɔre) *n* (**Paul**) **Gustave** (gystav). 1832–83, French illustrator, whose style tended towards the grotesque. He illustrated the Bible, Dante's *Inferno,* Cervantes' *Don Quixote,* and works by Rabelais.

Dorgon ('dɔ:gɒn) *n* 1612–50, Manchurian prince, who ruled China as regent (1643–50) and helped to establish the Ching dynasty.

Dorian ('dɔ:rɪən) *n* **1** a member of a Hellenic people who invaded Greece around 1100 B.C., overthrew the Mycenaean civilization, and settled chiefly in the Peloponnese. ◆ *adj* **2** of or relating to this people or their dialect of Ancient Greek; Doric. **3** *Music.* of or relating to a mode represented by the ascending natural diatonic scale from D to D. See also **Hypo-.**

Doric ('dɒrɪk) *adj* **1** of or relating to the Dorians, esp. the Spartans, or their dialect of Ancient Greek. **2** of, denoting, or relating to one of the five classical orders of architecture: characterized by a column having no base, a heavy fluted shaft, and a capital consisting of an ovolo moulding beneath a square abacus. See also **Ionic, composite** (sense 4), **Corinthian, Tuscan. 3** (*sometimes not cap.*) rustic. ◆ *n* **4** one of four chief dialects of Ancient Greek, spoken chiefly in the Peloponnese. **5** any rural dialect of English, esp. a Scots one. Compare **Aeolic, Arcadic, Ionic.** See also **Attic** (sense 3).

Doris[1] ('dɒrɪs) *n* (in ancient Greece) **1** a small landlocked area north of the Gulf of Corinth. Traditionally regarded as the home of the Dorians, it was perhaps settled by some of them during their southward migration. **2** the coastal area of Caria in SW Asia Minor, settled by Dorians.

Doris[2] ('dɒrɪs) *n Greek myth.* a sea nymph.

dork (dɔːk) *n Slang.* **1** a stupid or incompetent person. **2** *U.S.* a penis. [C20: of unknown origin] ▸ **'dorky** *adj*

Dorking ('dɔːkɪŋ) *n* a heavy breed of domestic fowl. [C19: after *Dorking,* town in Surrey]

dorm (dɔːm) *n Informal.* short for **dormitory.**

dormant ('dɔːmənt) *adj* **1** quiet and inactive, as during sleep. **2** latent or inoperative. **3** (of a volcano) neither extinct nor erupting. **4** *Biology.* alive but in a resting torpid condition with suspended growth and reduced metabolism. **5** (*usually postpositive*) *Heraldry.* (of a beast) in a sleeping position. ◆ Compare **active, passive.** [C14: from Old French *dormant,* from *dormir* to sleep, from Latin *dormīre*] ▸ **'dormancy** *n*

dormer ('dɔːmə) *n* a construction with a gable roof and a window at its outer end that projects from a sloping roof. Also called: **dormer window.** [C16: from Old French *dormoir,* from Latin *dormītōrium* DORMITORY]

dormie *or* **dormy** ('dɔːmɪ) *adj Golf.* (of a player or side) as many holes ahead of an opponent as there are still to play: *dormie three.* [C19: of unknown origin]

Dormition of the Blessed Virgin *n* another name for **Feast of the Assumption:** see **Assumption.**

dormitory ('dɔːmɪtərɪ, -trɪ) *n, pl* **-ries. 1** a large room, esp. at a school or institution, containing several beds. **2** *U.S.* a building, esp. at a college or camp, providing living and sleeping accommodation. **3** (*modifier*) *Brit.* denoting or relating to an area from which most of the residents commute to work (esp. in the phrase **dormitory suburb**). ◆ Often shortened (for senses 1, 2) to **dorm.** [C15: from Latin *dormītōrium,* from *dormīre* to sleep]

Dormobile ('dɔːməʊˌbiːl) *n Trademark.* a vanlike vehicle specially equipped for living in while travelling.

dormouse ('dɔːˌmaʊs) *n, pl* **-mice.** any small Old World rodent of the family *Gliridae,* esp. the Eurasian *Muscardinus avellanarius,* resembling a mouse with a furry tail. [C15: *dor-,* perhaps from Old French *dormir* to sleep, from Latin *dormīre* + MOUSE]

Dornbirn (*German* 'dɔrnbɪrn) *n* a city in W Austria, in Vorarlberg. Pop.: 40 880 (1991).

dornick[1] ('dɔːnɪk) *or* **dorneck** *n* a heavy damask cloth, formerly used for vestments, curtains, etc. [C15: from *Doornik* Tournai in Belgium where it was first manufactured]

dornick[2] ('dɔːnɪk) *n U.S.* a small stone or pebble. [C15: probably from Irish Gaelic *dornōg,* from *dorn* hand]

doronicum (də'rɒnɪkəm) *n* any plant of the Eurasian and N African genus *Doronicum,* such as leopard's-bane, having yellow daisy-like flower heads: family *Compositae* (composites). [C17: New Latin, from Arabic *dorūnaj*]

Dorothy Dixer (ˌdɒrəθɪ 'dɪksə) *n Austral. informal.* a parliamentary question asked by a member of the government so that the minister may give a prepared answer. [from pen name *Dorothy Dix* of U.S. journalist Elizabeth Meriwether (1870–1951), who wrote a column replying to correspondents' problems]

dorp (dɔːp) *n Archaic except in S. Africa.* a small town or village. [C16: from Dutch: village; related to THORP]

Dorpat ('dɔrpat) *n* the German name for **Tartu.**

dorsad ('dɔːsæd) *adj Anatomy.* towards the back or dorsal aspect. [C19: from Latin *dorsum* back + *ad* to, towards]

dorsal ('dɔːsᵊl) *adj* **1** *Anatomy, zoology.* relating to the back or spinal part of the body. Compare **ventral** (sense 1). **2** *Botany.* of, relating to, or situated on the side of an organ that is directed away from the axis. **3** articulated with the back of the tongue, as the (k) sound in English *coot.* [C15: from Medieval Latin *dorsālis,* from Latin *dorsum* back] ▸ **'dorsally** *adv*

dorsal fin *n* any unpaired median fin on the backs of fishes and some other aquatic vertebrates: maintains balance during locomotion.

Dorset ('dɔːsɪt) *n* a county in SW England, on the English Channel: mainly hilly but low-lying in the east: the geographical and ceremonial county includes Bournemouth and Poole, which became independent unitary authorities in 1997. Administrative centre: Dorchester. Pop. (including unitary authorities): 673 000 (1994 est.). Area (including unitary authorities): 2654 sq. km (1024 sq. miles).

Dorset Down *n* a breed of stocky sheep having a broad head, dark face, and a dense fleece: kept for lamb production.

Dorset Horn *n* a breed of horned sheep with dense fine-textured wool.

dorsiferous (dɔː'sɪfərəs) *adj Botany, zoology, rare.* bearing or carrying (young, spores, etc.) on the back or dorsal surface.

dorsiflexion (ˌdɔːsɪ'flɛkʃən) *n Med.* the bending back of a part, esp. the hand or foot or their digits.

dorsigrade ('dɔːsɪˌgreɪd) *adj* (of animals such as certain armadillos) walking on the backs of the toes. [C19: from Latin, from *dorsum* back + -GRADE]

dorsiventral (ˌdɔːsɪ'vɛntrəl) *adj* **1** (of leaves and similar flat parts) having distinct upper and lower faces. **2** a variant spelling of **dorsoventral.** ▸ dorsiventrality (ˌdɔːsɪvɛn'trælɪtɪ) *n* ▸ ˌ**dorsi'ventrally** *adv*

dorso-, dorsi-, *or before a vowel* **dors-** *combining form.* indicating dorsum or dorsal: *dorsoventral.*

dorsoventral (ˌdɔːsəʊ'vɛntrəl) *adj* **1** relating to both the dorsal and ventral sides; extending from the back to the belly. **2** *Botany.* a variant spelling of **dorsiventral.** ▸ ˌ**dorso'ventrally** *adv*

dorsum ('dɔːsəm) *n, pl* **-sa** (-sə). *Anatomy.* **1** a technical name for the **back. 2** any analogous surface: *the dorsum of the hand.* [C18: from Latin: back]

Dort (*Dutch* dɔrt) *n* another name for **Dordrecht.**

Dortmund ('dɔːtmənd; *German* 'dɔrtmʊnt) *n* an industrial city in W Germany, in North Rhine-Westphalia at the head of the **Dortmund-Ems Canal:** university (1966). Pop.: 598 840 (1998 est.).

dorty ('dɔːtɪ) *adj* **dortier, dortiest.** *Scot.* haughty, or sullen. [C17: from Scottish *dort* peevishness] ▸ **'dortiness** *n*

dory[1] ('dɔːrɪ) *n, pl* **-ries. 1** any spiny-finned marine teleost food fish of the family *Zeidae,* esp. the John Dory, having a deep compressed body. **2** another name for **walleye** (the fish). [C14: from French *dorée* gilded, from *dorer* to gild, from Late Latin *deaurāre,* ultimately from Latin *aurum* gold]

dory[2] ('dɔːrɪ) *n, pl* **-ries.** *U.S. and Canadian.* a flat-bottomed rowing boat with a high bow, stern, and sides. [C18: from Mosquito (an American Indian language of Honduras and Nicaragua) *dóri* dugout]

DOS (dɒs) *n Computing. Trademark. acronym for* disk-operating system, often prefixed, as in MS-DOS and PC-DOS; a computer operating system.

dos-à-dos (ˌdəʊsɪ'dəʊ; *French* dozado) *n* **1** a seat on which the users sit back to back. **2** an alternative spelling of **do-si-do.** [literally: back to back]

dosage ('dəʊsɪdʒ) *n* **1** the administration of a drug or agent in prescribed amounts. **2** the optimum therapeutic dose and optimum interval between doses. **3** another name for **dose** (senses 3, 4).

dose (dəʊs) *n* **1** *Med.* a specific quantity of a therapeutic drug or agent taken at any one time or at specified intervals. **2** *Informal.* something unpleasant to experience: *a dose of influenza.* **3** Also called: **dosage.** the total energy of ionizing radiation absorbed by unit mass of material, esp. of living tissue; usually measured in grays (SI unit) or rads. **4** Also called: **dosage.** a small amount of syrup added to wine, esp. sparkling wine, when the sediment is removed and the bottle is corked. **5** *Slang.* a venereal infection, esp. gonorrhoea. **6 like a dose of salts.** very quickly indeed. ◆ *vb* (*tr*) **7** to administer a dose or doses to (someone). **8** *Med.* to prescribe (a therapeutic drug or agent) in appropriate quantities. **9** (often foll. by *up*) to give (someone, esp. oneself) drugs, medicine, etc., esp. in large quantities. **10** to add syrup to (wine) during bottling. [C15: from French, from Late Latin *dosis,* from Greek: a giving, from *didonai* to give] ▸ **'doser** *n*

dose equivalent *n* a quantity that expresses the probability that exposure to ionizing radiation will cause biological effects. It is usually obtained by multiplying the dose by the quality factor of the radiation, but other factors may be considered. It is measured in sieverts (SI unit) or rems.

dosh (dɒʃ) *n Brit.* a slang word for **money.** [C20: of unknown origin]

do-si-do (ˌdəʊsɪ'dəʊ) *n* **1** a square-dance figure in which dancers pass each other with right shoulders close or touching and circle back to back. ◆ *sentence substitute.* **2** a call instructing dancers to perform such a figure. ◆ Also: **dos-à-dos.** [C20: from DOS-À-DOS]

dosimeter (dəʊ'sɪmiːtə) *or* **dosemeter** ('dəʊsˌmiːtə) *n* an instrument for measuring the dose of X-rays or other radiation absorbed by matter or the intensity of a source of radiation. ▸ **dosimetric** (ˌdəʊsɪ'metrɪk) *adj* ▸ **dosimetrician** (ˌdəʊsɪmə'trɪʃən) *or* **do'simetrist** *n* ▸ **do'simetry** *n*

dosing strip *n* (in New Zealand) an area set aside for treating dogs suspected of having hydatid disease.

Dos Passos ('dɒs 'pæsɒs) *n* **John (Roderigo).** 1896–1970, U.S. novelist of the Lost Generation; author of *Three Soldiers* (1921), *Manhattan Transfer* (1925), and the trilogy *U.S.A.* (1930–36).

doss (dɒs) *Brit. slang.* ◆ *vb* **1** (*intr;* often foll. by *down*) to sleep, esp. in a dosshouse. **2** (*intr;* often foll. by *around*) to pass time aimlessly. ◆ *n* **3** a bed, esp. in a dosshouse. **4** a slang word for **sleep. 5** short for **dosshouse. 6** a task or pastime requiring little effort: *making a film is a bit of a doss.* [C18: of uncertain origin]

dossal *or* **dossel** ('dɒsᵊl) *n* an ornamental hanging, placed at the back of an altar or at the sides of a chancel. [C17: from Medieval Latin *dossāle,* neuter of *dossālis,* variant of *dorsālis* DORSAL]

dosser[1] ('dɒsə) *n Rare.* a bag or basket for carrying objects on the back. [C14: from Old French *dossier,* from Medieval Latin *dorsārium,* from Latin *dorsum* back]

dosser[2] ('dɒsə) *n* **1** *Brit. slang.* a person who sleeps in dosshouses. **2** *Brit. slang.* another word for **dosshouse. 3** *Slang.* a lazy person; idler.

dosshouse ('dɒsˌhaʊs) *n Brit. slang.* a cheap lodging house, esp. one used by tramps. U.S. name: **flophouse.**

dossier ('dɒsɪˌeɪ, -sɪə; *French* dosje) *n* a collection of papers containing information on a particular subject or person. [C19: from French: a file with a label on the back, from *dos* back, from Latin *dorsum*]

dost (dʌst) *vb Archaic or dialect.* (used with the pronoun *thou* or its relative equivalent) a singular form of the present tense (indicative mood) of **do**[1].

Dostoevsky, Dostoyevsky, Dostoevski, *or* **Dostoyevski** (ˌdɒstɔɪ'ɛfskɪ; *Russian* dəstaˈjefskij) *n* **Fyodor Mikhailovich** ('fjɔdər mi'xajləvitʃ). 1821–81, Russian novelist, the psychological perception of whose works has greatly influenced the subsequent development of the novel. His best-known works are *Crime and Punishment* (1866), *The Idiot* (1868), *The Possessed* (1871), and *The Brothers Karamazov* (1879–80).

dot[1] (dɒt) *n* **1** a small round mark made with or as with a pen, etc.; spot; speck; point. **2** anything resembling a dot; a small amount: *a dot of paint.* **3** the mark (·) that appears above the main stem of the letters *i, j.* **4** *Music.* **4a** the symbol (.) placed after a note or rest to increase its time value by half. **4b** this symbol written above or below a note indicating that it must be played or sung staccato. **5** *Maths., logic.* **5a** the symbol (.) indicating multiplication or logical conjunction. **5b** a decimal point. **6** the symbol (·) used, in combination with the symbol for *dash* (—), in the written representation of Morse and other telegraphic codes. Compare **dit. 7 the year dot.** *Informal.* as long ago as can be remembered. **8 on the dot.** at exactly the arranged time. ◆ *vb* **dots, dotting, dotted. 9** (*tr*) to mark or form with a dot: *to dot a letter; a dotted crotchet.* **10** (*tr*) to scatter or intersperse (with dots or something resembling dots): *bushes dotting* *the plain.* **11** (*intr*) to make a dot or dots. **12 dot one's i's and cross one's t's.** to pay meticulous attention to detail. [Old English *dott* head of a boil; related to Old High German *tutta* nipple, Norwegian *dott,* Dutch *dott* lump] ▸ **'dotter** *n*

dot[2] (dɒt) *n Civil law.* a woman's dowry. [C19: from French, from Latin *dōs;* related to *dōtāre* to endow, *dāre* to give] ▸ **dotal** ('dəʊtᵊl) *adj*

dotage ('dəʊtɪdʒ) *n* **1** feebleness of mind, esp. as a result of old age. **2** foolish infatuation. [C14: from DOTE + -AGE]

dotard ('dəʊtəd) *n* a person who is weak-minded, esp. through senility. [C14: from DOTE + -ARD] ▸ **'dotardly** *adj*

dotation (dəʊ'teɪʃən) *n Law.* the act of giving a dowry; endowment. [C14: from Latin *dōtātiō,* from *dōtāre* to endow]

dote *or* (*now rarely*) **doat** (dəʊt) *vb* (*intr*) **1** (foll. by *on* or *upon*) to love to an excessive or foolish degree. **2** to be foolish or weak-minded, esp. as a result of old age. [C13: related to Middle Dutch *doten* to be silly, Norwegian *dudra* to shake] ▸ **'doter** *or* (*now rarely*) **'doater** *n*

doth (dʌθ) *vb Archaic or dialect.* (used with the pronouns *he, she,* or *it* or with a noun) a singular form of the present tense of **do**[1].

dot-matrix printer *n Computing.* a printer in which each character is produced by a subset of an array of needles at the printhead.

dot product *n* another name for **scalar product.**

dotted ('dɒtɪd) *adj* **1** having dots, esp. having a pattern of dots. **2** *Music.* **2a** (of a note) increased to one and a half times its original time value. See **dot**[1] (sense 4). **2b** (of a musical rhythm) characterized by dotted notes. Compare **double-dotted.** See also **notes inégales.**

dotted line *n* **1** a line of dots or dashes on a form or document. **2 sign on the dotted line.** to agree formally, esp. by signing one's name on a document.

dotterel *or* **dottrel** ('dɒtrəl) *n* **1** a rare Eurasian plover, *Eudromias morinellus,* with reddish-brown underparts and white bands around the head and neck. **2** *Austral.* any similar and related bird, esp. of the genus *Charadrius.* **3** *Dialect.* a person who is foolish or easily duped. [C15 *dotrelle;* see DOTE]

dottle *or* **dottel** ('dɒtᵊl) *n* the plug of tobacco left in a pipe after smoking. [C15: diminutive of *dot* lump; see DOT[1]]

dotty ('dɒtɪ) *adj* **-tier, -tiest. 1** *Slang, chiefly Brit.* feeble-minded; slightly crazy. **2** *Brit. slang.* (foll. by *about*) extremely fond (of). **3** marked with dots. [C19: from DOT[1]: sense development of 1 from meaning of "unsteady on one's feet"] ▸ **'dottily** *adv* ▸ **'dottiness** *n*

Dou, Dow, *or* **Douw** (daʊ; *Dutch* dɔu) *n* **Gerard** ('xe:rɑrt). 1613–75, Dutch portrait and genre painter.

Douai ('du:eɪ; *French* dwɛ) *n* an industrial city in N France: the political and religious centre of exiled English Roman Catholics in the 16th and 17th centuries. Pop.: 199 562 (1990).

Douala *or* **Duala** (du'ɑ:lə) *n* the chief port and largest city in W Cameroon, on the Bight of Bonny: capital of the German colony of Kamerun (1901–16). Pop.: 1 200 000 (1992 est.).

Douay Bible *or* **Version** ('du:eɪ) *n* an English translation of the Bible from the Latin Vulgate text completed by Roman Catholic scholars at Douai in 1610.

double ('dʌbᵊl) *adj* (*usually prenominal*) **1** as much again in size, strength, number, etc.: *a double portion.* **2** composed of two equal or similar parts; in a pair; twofold: *a double egg cup.* **3** designed for two users: *a double room.* **4** folded in two; composed of two layers: *double paper.* **5** stooping; bent over. **6** having two aspects or existing in two different ways; ambiguous: *a double meaning.* **7** false, deceitful, or hypocritical: *a double life.* **8** (of flowers) having more than the normal number of petals. **9** *Maths.* **9a** (of a root) being one of two equal roots of a polynomial equation. **9b** (of an integral) having an integrand containing two independent variables requiring two integrations, in each of which one variable is kept constant. **10** *Music.* **10a** (of an instrument) sounding an octave lower than the pitch indicated by the notation: *a double bass.* **10b** (of time) duple, usually accompanied by the direction *alla breve.* ◆ *adv* **11** twice over; twofold. **12** two together; two at a time (esp. in the phrase **see double**). ◆ *n* **13** twice the number, amount, size, etc. **14** a double measure of spirits, such as whisky or brandy. **15** a duplicate or counterpart, esp. a person who closely resembles another; understudy. **16** a wraith or ghostly apparition that is the exact counterpart of a living person; doppelgänger. **17** a sharp turn, esp. a return on one's own tracks. **18** an evasive shift or artifice; trick. **19** an actor who plays two parts in one play. **20** *Bridge.* a call that increases certain scoring points if the last preceding bid becomes the contract. **21** *Billiards, etc.* a strike in which the object ball is struck so as to make it rebound against the cushion to an opposite pocket. **22** a bet on two horses in different races in which any winnings from the horse in the first race are placed on the horse in the later race. **23** (*often cap.*) *Chiefly R.C. Church.* one of the higher-ranking feasts on which the antiphons are recited both before and after the psalms. **24** *Music.* an ornamented variation in 16th and 17th century music. **25** Also called: **double time.** a pace of twice the normal marching speed. **26** *Tennis.* See **double fault. 27a** the narrow outermost ring on a dartboard. **27b** a hit on this ring. **28 at** *or* **on the double. 28a** at twice normal marching speed. **28b** quickly or immediately. ◆ *vb* **29** to make or become twice as much. **30** to bend or fold (material, a bandage, etc.). **31** (*tr;* sometimes foll. by *up*) to clench (a fist). **32** (*tr;* often foll. by *together* or *up*) to join or couple: *he doubled up the team.* **33** (*tr*) to repeat exactly; copy. **34** (*intr*) to play two parts or serve two roles. **35** (*intr*) to turn sharply; follow a winding course. **36** *Nautical.* to sail around (a headland or other point). **37** *Music.* **37a** to duplicate (a voice or instrumental part) either in unison or at the octave above or below it. **37b** (*intr;* usually foll. by *on*) to be capable of performing (upon an instrument additional to one's normal one): *the third trumpeter doubles on cornet.* **38** *Bridge.* to make a call that will double certain scoring points if the preceding bid becomes the contract. **39** *Billiards, etc.* to cause (a ball) to rebound or (of a ball) to rebound from a cushion across or up or down the table. **40** *Chess.* **40a** to cause two pawns of the same colour to be on the same file. **40b** to place both rooks of the same colour on the same rank or the same file. **41** (*intr;* foll. by *for*) to act as substitute (for an actor or actress). **42** (*intr*) to go or march at twice the normal speed. ◆ See also **double back, doubles, double up.** [C13: from Old French, from Latin *duplus* twofold, from *duo* two + *-plus* -FOLD] ▸ **'doubleness** *n* ▸ **'doubler** *n*

double-acting *adj* **1** (of a reciprocating engine or pump) having a piston or pistons that are pressurized alternately on opposite sides. Compare **single-acting. 2** (of a hinge, door, etc.) having complementary actions in opposed directions.

double agent *n* a spy employed by two mutually antagonistic countries, companies, etc.

double-aspect theory *n Philosophy.* a monistic theory that holds that mind and body are not distinct substances but merely different aspects of a single substance.

double back *vb* (*intr, adv*) to go back in the opposite direction (esp. in the phrase **to double back on one's tracks**).

double-bank *vb Austral. and N.Z. informal.* to carry a second person on (a horse, bicycle, etc.). Also: **dub.**

double bar *n Music.* a symbol, consisting of two ordinary bar lines or a single heavy one, that marks the end of a composition or a section within it.

double-barrelled *or U.S.* **double-barreled** *adj* **1** (of a gun) having two barrels. **2** extremely forceful or vehement. **3** *Brit.* (of a surname) having hyphenated parts. **4** serving two purposes; ambiguous: *a double-barrelled remark.*

double bass (beɪs) *n* **1** Also called (U.S.): **bass viol.** a stringed instrument, the largest and lowest member of the violin family. Range: almost three octaves upwards from E in the space between the fourth and fifth leger lines below the bass staff. It is normally bowed in classical music, but it is very common in a jazz or dance band, where it is practically always played pizzicato. Informal name: **bass fiddle.** ◆ *adj* **double-bass. 2** of or relating to an instrument whose pitch lies below that regarded as the bass; contrabass.

double bassoon *n Music.* the lowest and largest instrument in the oboe class; contrabassoon.

double bill *n* a programme or event with two main items.

double bind *n* a situation of conflict from which there is no escape; unresolvable dilemma.

double-blind *adj* of or relating to an experiment to discover reactions to certain commodities, drugs, etc., in which neither the experimenters nor the subjects know the particulars of the test items during the experiments. Compare **single-blind.**

double boiler *n* the U.S. and Canadian name for **double saucepan.**

double bond *n* a type of chemical bond consisting of two covalent bonds linking two atoms in a molecule.

double-breasted *adj* (of a garment) having overlapping fronts such as to give a double thickness of cloth.

double bridle *n* a bridle with four reins coming from a bit with two rings on each side.

double-check *vb* **1** to check twice or again; verify. ◆ *n* **double check. 2** a second examination or verification. **3** *Chess.* a simultaneous check from two pieces brought about by moving one piece to give check and thereby revealing a second check from another piece.

double chin *n* a fold of fat under the chin. ▸ **,double-'chinned** *adj*

double concerto *n* a concerto for two solo instruments.

double cream *n* thick cream with a high fat-content.

double cross *n* a technique for producing hybrid stock, esp. seed for cereal crops, by crossing the hybrids between two different pairs of inbred lines.

double-cross *vb* **1** (*tr*) to cheat or betray. ◆ *n* **2** the act or an instance of double-crossing; betrayal. ▸ **'double-'crosser** *n*

double dagger *n* a character (‡) used in printing to indicate a cross reference, esp. to a footnote. Also called: **diesis, double obelisk.**

double-dealing *n* **a** action characterized by treachery or deceit. **b** (*as modifier*): *double-dealing treachery.* ▸ **'double-'dealer** *n*

double-decker *n* **1** *Chiefly Brit.* a bus with two passenger decks. **2** *Informal.* **2a** a thing or structure having two decks, layers, etc. **2b** (*as modifier*): *a double-decker sandwich.*

double-declutch *vb* (*intr*) *Brit.* to change to a lower gear in a motor vehicle by first placing the gear lever into the neutral position before engaging the desired gear, at the same time releasing the clutch pedal and increasing the engine speed. U.S. term: **double-clutch.**

double decomposition *n* a chemical reaction between two compounds that results in the interchange of one part of each to form two different compounds, as in $AgNO_3 + KI \rightarrow AgI + KNO_3$. Also called: **metathesis.**

double density *Computing.* ◆ *n* **1** a disk with more than the normal capacity for storage. ◆ *adj* **2** (of a floppy disk) having a storage capacity of 360K or 720K, which is double the normal amount.

double digging *n Brit.* a method of digging ground in a series of trenches two spits deep, mixing the soil of the bottom spit with manure, and then transferring the soil from the top spit of one trench to the top spit of the preceding one.

double-dotted *adj Music.* **1** (of a note) increased to one and three quarters of its original time value by the addition of two dots. **2** (of a rhythm) characterized by pairs of notes in which the first one, lengthened by two dots, makes up seven eighths of the time value of the pair.

double drummer *n Austral. informal.* a type of cicada.

double-dumped *adj N.Z.* (of a wool bale) compressed, with two bales occupying the volume-equivalent of one ordinary bale.

double Dutch *n Brit. informal.* incomprehensible talk; gibberish.

double-dyed *adj* **1** confirmed; inveterate: *a double-dyed villain.* **2** dyed twice.

double eagle *n* a former U.S. gold coin, having a nominal value of 20 dollars.

double-edged *adj* **1** acting in two ways; having a dual effect: *a double-edged law.* **2** (of a remark, argument, etc.) having two possible interpretations, esp. applicable both for and against or being really malicious though apparently innocuous. **3** (of a sword, knife, etc.) having a cutting edge on either side of the blade.

double entendre (ˈdʌbᵊl ɑːnˈtɑːndrə, -ˈtɑːnd; *French* dubl ɑ̃tɑ̃drə) *n* **1** a word, phrase, etc., that can be interpreted in two ways, esp. one having one meaning that is indelicate. **2** the type of humour that depends upon such ambiguity. [C17: from obsolete French: double meaning]

double entry *n* **a** a book-keeping system in which any commercial transaction is entered as a debit in one account and as a credit in another. Compare **single entry. b** (*as modifier*): *double-entry book-keeping.*

double exposure *n* **1** the act or process of recording two superimposed images on a photographic medium, usually done intentionally to produce a special effect. **2** the photograph resulting from such an act.

double-faced *adj* **1** (of textiles) having a finished nap on each side; reversible. **2** insincere or deceitful.

double fault *Tennis.* ◆ *n* **1** the serving of two faults in succession, thereby losing a point. ◆ *vb* **double-fault. 2** (*intr*) to serve a double fault.

double feature *n Films.* a programme showing two full-length films. Informal name (U.S.): **twin bill.**

double first *n Brit.* a first-class honours degree in two subjects.

double flat *n* **1** *Music.* **1a** an accidental that lowers the pitch of the following note two semitones. Usual symbol: 𝄫 **1b** a note affected by this accidental. ◆ *adj* **double-flat. 2** (*postpositive*) denoting a note of a given letter name lowered in pitch by two semitones.

double glazing *n* **1** two panes of glass in a window, fitted to reduce the transmission of heat, sound, etc. **2** the fitting of glass in such a manner.

double Gloucester *n* a type of smooth orange-red cheese of mild flavour.

double-header *n* **1** a train drawn by two locomotives coupled together to provide extra power. **2** Also called: **twin bill.** *Sport, U.S. and Canadian.* two games played consecutively by the same teams or by two different teams. **3** *Austral. and N.Z. informal.* a coin with the impression of a head on each side. **4** *Austral. informal.* a double ice-cream cone.

double-helical gear *n* another name for **herringbone gear.**

double helix *n Biochem.* the form of the molecular structure of DNA, consisting of two helical polynucleotide chains linked by hydrogen bonds and coiled around the same axis.

double-hung *adj* (of a window) having two vertical sashes, the upper one sliding in grooves outside those of the lower.

double indemnity *n U.S. and Canadian.* (in life assurance policies) a clause providing for the payment of double the policy's face value in the event of the policyholder's accidental death.

double jeopardy *n Chiefly U.S.* the act of prosecuting a defendant a second time for an offence for which he has already been tried.

double-jointed *adj* having unusually flexible joints permitting an abnormal degree of motion of the parts.

double knit *n* **a** a knitted material made on two sets of needles that produce a double thickness joined with interlocking stitches. **b** (*as modifier*): *a double-knit fabric.*

double knitting *n* **a** a widely used medium thickness of knitting wool. **b** (*as modifier*): *double-knitting wool.*

double-minded *adj Rare.* undecided; vacillating. ▸ **ˌdouble-ˈmindedness** *n*

double negation *n Logic.* the principle that a statement is equivalent to the denial of its negation, as *it is not the case that John is not here* meaning *John is here.*

double negative *n* a syntactic construction, often considered ungrammatical in standard Modern English, in which two negatives are used where one is needed, as in *I wouldn't never have believed it.*

USAGE There are two contexts where double negatives are found. An adjective with negative force is often used with a negative in order to express a nuance of meaning somewhere between the positive and the negative: *he was a not infrequent visitor; it is not an uncommon sight.* Two negatives are also found together where they reinforce each other rather than conflict: *he never went back, not even to collect his belongings.* These two uses of what is technically a double negative are acceptable. A third case, illustrated by *I shouldn't wonder if it didn't rain today,* has the force of a weak positive statement (*I expect it to rain today*) and is common in informal English.

double obelisk *n* another name for **double dagger.**

double or quits *n* a game, throw, toss, etc., to decide whether the stake due is to be doubled or cancelled.

double-park *vb* to park (a car or other vehicle) alongside or directly opposite another already parked by the roadside, thereby causing an obstruction.

double play *n Baseball.* a play in which two runners are put out.

double pneumonia *n* pneumonia affecting both lungs.

double printing *n Photog.* the exposure of the same positive photographic emulsion to two or more negatives, resulting in the superimposition of multiple images after development.

double-quick *adj* **1** very quick; rapid. ◆ *adv* **2** in a very quick or rapid manner.

double-reed *adj* relating to or denoting a wind instrument in which the sounds are produced by air passing over two reeds that vibrate against each other.

double refraction *n* the splitting of a ray of unpolarized light into two unequally refracted rays polarized in mutually perpendicular planes. Also called: **birefringence.**

doubles (ˈdʌbᵊlz) *n* (*functioning as pl*) **a** a game between two pairs of players, as in tennis, badminton, etc. **b** (*as modifier*): *a doubles player.*

double salt *n* a solid solution of two simple salts formed by crystallizing a solution of the two salts. Compare **complex salt.**

double saucepan *n Brit.* a cooking utensil consisting of two saucepans, one fitting inside the other. The bottom saucepan contains water that, while boiling, gently heats food in the upper pan. U.S. and Canadian name: **double boiler.**

double scull *n Rowing.* a racing shell in which two scullers sit one behind the other and pull two oars each. Compare **pair-oar.**

double sharp *n* **1** *Music.* **1a** an accidental that raises the pitch of the following note by two semitones. Usual symbol: 𝄪 **1b** a note affected by this accidental. ◆ *adj* **2** (*immediately postpositive*) denoting a note of a given letter name raised in pitch by two semitones.

double-space *vb* to type (copy) with a full space between lines.

double spread *n Printing.* two facing pages of a publication treated as a single unit.

double standard *n* a set of principles that allows greater freedom to one person or group than to another.

double star *n* two stars, appearing close together when viewed through a telescope; either physically associated (see **binary star**) or not associated (**optical double star**).

double-stop *vb* **-stops, -stopping, -stopped.** to play (two notes or parts) simultaneously on a violin or related instrument by drawing the bow over two strings.

double-system sound recording *n Films.* a system in which picture and sound are taken simultaneously and the sound is recorded separately on magnetic tape.

doublet (ˈdʌblɪt) *n* **1** (formerly) a man's close-fitting jacket, with or without sleeves (esp. in the phrase **doublet and hose.**) **2a** a pair of similar things, esp. two words deriving ultimately from the same source, for example *reason* and *ratio* or *fragile* and *frail.* **2b** one of such a pair. **3** *Jewellery.* a false gem made by welding a thin layer of a gemstone onto a coloured glass base or by fusing two small stones together to make a larger one. **4** *Physics.* **4a** a multiplet that has two members. **4b** a closely spaced pair of related spectral lines. **5** (*pl*) two dice each showing the same number of spots on one throw. **6** *Physics.* two simple lenses designed to be used together, the optical distortion in one being balanced by that in the other. [C14: from Old French, from DOUBLE]

double tackle *n* a lifting or pulling tackle in which a rope is passed around the twin pulleys of a pair of pulley blocks in sequence.

double take *n* (esp. in comedy) a delayed reaction by a person to a remark, situation, etc.

double talk *n* **1** rapid speech with a mixture of nonsense syllables and real words; gibberish. **2** empty, deceptive, or ambiguous talk, esp. by politicians.

doublethink (ˈdʌbᵊlˌθɪŋk) *n* deliberate, perverse, or unconscious acceptance or promulgation of conflicting facts, principles, etc.

double time *n* **1** a doubled wage rate, paid for working on public holidays, etc. **2** *Music.* **2a** a time twice as fast as an earlier section. **2b** two beats per bar. **3** a slow running pace, keeping in step. **4** *U.S. Army.* a fast march of 180 paces to the minute. ◆ *vb* **double-time. 5** to move or cause to move in double time.

doubleton (ˈdʌbᵊltən) *n Bridge, etc.* an original holding of two cards only in a suit.

double-tongue *vb* **-tongues, -tonguing, -tongued.** *Music.* to play (fast staccato passages) on a wind instrument by rapid obstruction and uncovering of the air passage through the lips with the tongue. Compare **single-tongue, triple-tongue.** ▸ double tonguing *n*

double-tongued *adj* deceitful or hypocritical in speech.

double top *n Darts.* a score of double 20.

doubletree (ˈdʌbᵊlˌtriː) *n* a horizontal pivoted bar on a vehicle to the ends of which swingletrees are attached for harnessing two horses side by side.

double up *vb* (*adv*) **1** to bend or cause to bend in two: *he doubled up with the pain.* **2** (*intr*) to share a room or bed designed for one person, family, etc. **3** (*intr*) *Brit.* to use the winnings from one bet as the stake for another. U.S. and Canadian term: **parlay.**

doubloon (dʌˈbluːn) *or* **doblón** *n* **1** a former Spanish gold coin. **2** (*pl*) *Slang.* money. [C17: from Spanish *doblón,* from DOBLA]

doublure (dəˈblʊə; *French* dublyr) *n* a decorative lining of vellum or leather, etc., on the inside of a book cover. [C19: from French: lining, from Old French *doubler* to make double]

doubly (ˈdʌblɪ) *adv* **1** to or in a double degree, quantity, or measure: *doubly careful.* **2** in two ways: *doubly wrong.*

Doubs (*French* du) *n* **1** a department of E France, in Franche-Comté region. Capital: Besançon. Pop.: 493 133 (1994 est.). Area: 5258 sq. km (2030 sq. miles). **2** a river in E France, rising in the Jura Mountains, becoming part of the border between France and Switzerland and flowing generally southwest to the Saône River. Length: 430 km (267 miles).

doubt (daʊt) *n* **1** uncertainty about the truth, fact, or existence of something (esp. in the phrases **in doubt, without doubt, beyond a shadow of doubt,** etc.). **2** (*often pl*) lack of belief in or conviction about something: *all his doubts about the project disappeared.* **3** an unresolved difficulty, point, etc. **4** *Philosophy.* the methodical device, esp. in the philosophy of Descartes, of identifying certain knowledge as the residue after rejecting any proposition which might, however improbably, be false. **5** *Obsolete.* fear. **6 give (someone) the benefit of the doubt.** to presume (someone suspected of guilt) innocent; judge leniently. **7 no doubt.** almost certainly. ◆ *vb* **8** (*tr; may take a clause as object*) to be inclined to disbelieve: *I doubt we are late.* **9** (*tr*) to distrust or be suspicious of: *he doubted their motives.* **10** (*intr*) to feel uncertainty or be undecided. **11** (*tr; may take a clause as object*) *Scot.* to be inclined to believe. **12** (*tr*) *Archaic.* to fear. **13 I wouldn't doubt (someone).** *Irish.* I would expect nothing else from (someone). [C13: from Old French *douter,* from Latin *dubitāre*] ▸ 'doubtable *adj* ▸ 'doubtably *adv* ▸ 'doubter *n* ▸ 'doubtingly *adv*

USAGE Where a clause follows *doubt* in a positive sentence, it was formerly considered correct to use *whether:* (*I doubt whether he will come*), but now *if* and *that* are also acceptable. In negative statements, *doubt* is followed by *that: I do not doubt that he is telling the truth.* In such sentences, *but* (*I do not doubt but that he is telling the truth*) is redundant.

doubtful ('daʊtfʊl) *adj* **1** unlikely; improbable. **2** characterized by or causing doubt; uncertain: *a doubtful answer.* **3** unsettled; unresolved. **4** of questionable reputation or morality. **5** having reservations or misgivings. ▸ **'doubtfully** *adv* ▸ **'doubtfulness** *n*

USAGE It was formerly considered correct to use *whether* after *doubtful (it is doubtful whether he will come),* but now *if* and *that* are also acceptable.

doubting Thomas *n* a person who insists on proof before he will believe anything; sceptic. [after THOMAS (the apostle), who did not believe that Jesus had been resurrected until he had proof]

doubtless ('daʊtlɪs) *adv also* **doubtlessly.** *sentence substitute or sentence modifier.* **1** certainly. **2** probably. ◆ *adj* **3** certain; assured. ▸ **'doubtlessness** *n*

douc (du:k) *n* an Old World monkey, *Pygathrix nemaeus,* of SE Asia, with a bright yellow face surrounded by tufts of reddish-brown fur, a white tail, and white hindquarters: one of the langurs. [C18: from French, from the native name]

douce (du:s) *adj Scot. and northern English dialect.* quiet; sober; sedate. [C14: from Old French, feminine of *dous,* from Latin *dulcis* sweet] ▸ **'doucely** *adv*

douceur (du:'sɜ:; *French* dusœr) *n* **1** a gratuity, tip, or bribe. **2** sweetness. [C17: from French, from Late Latin *dulcor,* from Latin *dulcis* sweet]

douche (du:ʃ) *n* **1** a stream of water or air directed onto the body surface or into a body cavity, for cleansing or medical purposes. **2** the application of such a stream of water or air. **3** an instrument, such as a special syringe, for applying a douche. ◆ *vb* **4** to cleanse or treat or be cleansed or treated by means of a douche. [C18: from French, from Italian *doccia,* pipe; related to Latin *ductus* DUCT]

dough (dəʊ) *n* **1** a thick mixture of flour or meal and water or milk, used for making bread, pastry, etc. **2** any similar pasty mass. **3** a slang word for **money.** [Old English *dāg;* related to Old Norse *deig,* Gothic *daigs,* Old High German *teig* dough, Sanskrit *degdhi* he daubs; see DAIRY, DUFF[1], LADY]

doughboy ('dəʊˌbɔɪ) *n* **1** *U.S. informal.* an infantryman, esp. in World War I. **2** dough that is boiled or steamed as a dumpling.

doughnut *or (esp. U.S.)* **donut** ('dəʊnʌt) *n* **1** a small cake of sweetened dough, often ring-shaped or spherical with a jam or cream filling, cooked in hot fat. **2** anything shaped like a ring, such as the reaction vessel of a thermonuclear reactor. ◆ *vb* **-nuts, -nutting, -nutted. 3** (*tr*) *Informal.* (of Members of Parliament) to surround (a speaker) during the televising of Parliament to give the impression that the chamber is crowded or the speaker is well supported.

doughty ('daʊtɪ) *adj* **-tier, -tiest.** hardy; resolute. [Old English *dohtig;* related to Old High German *toht* worth, Middle Dutch *duchtich* strong, Greek *tukhē* luck] ▸ **'doughtily** *adv* ▸ **'doughtiness** *n*

Doughty ('daʊtɪ) *n* **Charles Montagu.** 1843–1926, English writer and traveller; author of *Travels in Arabia Deserta* (1888).

doughy ('dəʊɪ) *adj* **doughier, doughiest.** resembling dough in consistency, colour, etc.; soft, pallid, or flabby.

Douglas[1] ('dʌgləs) *n* a town and resort on the Isle of Man, capital of the island, on the E coast. Pop.: 22 214 (1991).

Douglas[2] ('dʌgləs) *n* **1 C(lifford) H(ugh).** 1879–1952, British economist, who originated the theory of social credit. **2 Gavin.** ?1474–1522, Scottish poet, the first British translator of the *Aeneid.* **3 Keith (Castellain).** 1920–44, British poet, noted for his poems of World War II: killed in action. **4 (George) Norman.** 1868–1952, British writer, esp. of books on southern Italy such as *South Wind* (1917).

Douglas fir, spruce, *or* **hemlock** *n* a North American pyramidal coniferous tree, *Pseudotsuga menziesii,* widely planted for ornament and for timber, having needle-like leaves and hanging cones: family *Pinaceae.* Also called: **Oregon fir, Oregon pine.** [C19: named after David *Douglas* (1798–1834), Scottish botanist]

Douglas-Home ('dʌgləs'hju:m) *n* Sir **Alexander.** See (Baron Alexander) **Home of the Hirsel.**

Douglas scale *n* an international scale of sea disturbance and swell ranging from 0 to 9 with one figure for disturbance and one for swell. [C20: named after Sir Henry *Douglas* (1876–1939), former director of the British Naval Meteorological Service]

douk (dʊk) *n* a variant spelling of **dook**[1] and **dook**[2].

Doukhobor *or* **Dukhobor** ('du:kəʊˌbɔ:) *n* a member of a Russian sect of Christians that originated in the 18th century. In the late 19th century a large minority emigrated to W Canada, where most Doukhobors now live. [from Russian *dukhoborcy* spirit wrestler, from *dukh* spirit + *borcy* wrestler]

douma *Russian.* ('du:mə) *n* a variant spelling of **duma.**

doum palm *or* **doom palm** (du:m) *n* an Egyptian palm tree, *Hyphaene thebaica,* with a divided trunk and edible apple-sized fruits. [C19 *doum,* via French from Arabic *dawm*]

doun (du:n) *prep, adv, adj* a variant spelling of **doon.**

Dounreay (du:n'reɪ) *n* the site in N Scotland of a nuclear power station, which contained the world's first fast-breeder reactor (1962–77). A prototype fast-breeder operated from 1974 until 1994: a nuclear fuel re-processing plant has also operated at the site.

do up *vb* (*adv; mainly tr*) **1** to wrap and make into a bundle: *to do up a parcel.* **2** to cause the downfall of (a person). **3** to beautify or adorn. **4** (*also intr*) to fasten or be fastened: *this skirt does up at the back.* **5** *Informal.* to renovate or redecorate. **6** *Slang.* to assault.

dour (dʊə, 'daʊə) *adj* **1** sullen. **2** hard or obstinate. [C14: probably from Latin *dūrus* hard] ▸ **'dourly** *adv* ▸ **'dourness** *n*

doura ('dʊərə) *n* a variant of **durra.**

dourine ('dʊəri:n) *n* an infectious disease of horses characterized by swollen glands, inflamed genitals, and paralysis of the hindquarters, caused by the protozoan *Trypanosoma equiperdum* contracted during copulation. [C19: from French, from Arabic *darina* to be dirty, scabby]

Douro ('dʊərəʊ; *Portuguese* 'doru) *n* a river in SW Europe, rising in N central Spain and flowing west to NE Portugal, then south as part of the border between the two countries and finally west to the Atlantic. Length: 895 km (556 miles). Spanish name: **Duero.**

douroucouli (ˌdu:ru:'ku:lɪ) *n* a nocturnal omnivorous New World monkey, *Aotus trivirgatus,* of Central and South America, with large eyes, thick fur, and a round head with pale and dark markings. [from a South American Indian name]

douse[1] *or* **dowse** (daʊs) *vb* **1** to plunge or be plunged into water or some other liquid; duck. **2** (*tr*) to drench with water, esp. in order to wash or clean. **3** (*tr*) to put out (a light, candle, etc.). ◆ *n* **4** an immersion. [C16: perhaps related to obsolete *douse* to strike, of obscure origin] ▸ **'douser** *or* **'dowser** *n*

douse[2] (daʊs) *vb* (*tr*) **1** *Nautical.* to lower (sail) quickly. **2** *Archaic.* to strike or beat. ◆ *n* **3** *Archaic.* a blow. [C16: of uncertain origin; perhaps related to DOUSE[1]]

douzepers ('du:zˌpeəz) *pl n French history.* the 12 great peers of the realm, seen as the symbolic heirs of Charlemagne's 12 chosen peers. [C13: from Old French *douze pers;* see DOZEN, PEER[1]]

DOVAP ('dəʊˌvæp) *n* a tracking system for determining the position and velocity of spacecraft, missiles, etc., based on the Doppler effect. [C20: from *Do(ppler) v(elocity) a(nd) p(osition)*]

dove[1] (dʌv) *n* **1** any of various birds of the family *Columbidae,* having a heavy body, small head, short legs, and long pointed wings: order *Columbiformes.* They are typically smaller than pigeons. Related adj: **columbine. 2** *Politics.* a person opposed to war. Compare **hawk**[1] (sense 3). **3** a gentle or innocent person: used as a term of endearment. **4a** a greyish-brown colour. **4b** (*as adj*): *dove walls.* [Old English *dūfe* (unattested except as a feminine proper name); related to Old Saxon *dūbva,* Old High German *tūba*] ▸ **'doveˌlike** *adj* ▸ **'dovish** *adj*

dove[2] (dəʊv) *vb Chiefly U.S.* a past tense of **dive.**

Dove (dʌv) *n Christianity.* **the.** a manifestation of the Holy Spirit (John 1:32).

dovecote ('dʌvˌkəʊt) *or* **dovecot** ('dʌvˌkɒt) *n* a structure for housing pigeons, often raised on a pole or set on a wall, containing compartments for the birds to roost and lay eggs.

dovekie *or* **dovekey** ('dʌvkɪ) *n* another name for the **little auk** (see **auk**). [C19: Scottish diminutive of DOVE[1]]

dove prion *n* a common petrel, *Pachyptila desolata,* of the southern seas, having a bluish back and white underparts. Also called: **Antarctic prion,** (N.Z. informal) **blue billy.**

Dover ('dəʊvə) *n* **1** a port in SE England, in E Kent on the Strait of Dover: the only one of the Cinque Ports that is still important; a stronghold since ancient times and Caesar's first point of attack in the invasion of Britain (55 B.C.). Pop.: 34 179 (1991). **2 Strait of.** a strait between SE England and N France, linking the English Channel with the North Sea. Width: about 32 km (20 miles). French name: **Pas de Calais. 3** a city in the U.S., the capital of Delaware, founded in 1683: 18th-century buildings. Pop.: 27 630 (1990).

Dover's powder *n* a preparation of opium and ipecacuanha, formerly used to relieve pain, induce sweating, and check spasms. [C19: named after Thomas *Dover* (1660–1742), English physician]

dovetail ('dʌvˌteɪl) *n* **1** a wedge-shaped tenon. **2** Also called: **dovetail joint.** a joint containing such tenons. ◆ *vb* **3** (*tr*) to join by means of dovetails. **4** to fit or cause to fit together closely or neatly: *he dovetailed his arguments to the desired conclusion.*

dovetail saw *n Building trades.* a saw similar to a tenon saw but of smaller size.

Dovzhenko (*Russian* dov'ʒenko) *n* **Aleksandr Petrovitch** (alɪk'sandr pe'trɔvɪtʃ). 1894–1956, Soviet film director. His films include *Zemlya* (1930) and *Ivan* (1932).

Dow (daʊ; *Dutch* dɔu) *n* See (Gerard) **Dou.**

dowable ('daʊəbᵊl) *adj Law.* **1** capable of being endowed. **2** (of a person, esp. a widow) entitled to dower.

dowager ('daʊədʒə) *n* **1a** a widow possessing property or a title obtained from her husband. **1b** (*as modifier*): *the dowager duchess.* **2** a wealthy or dignified elderly woman. [C16: from Old French *douagiere,* from *douage* DOWER]

Dowding ('daʊdɪŋ) *n* Baron **Hugh Caswall Tremenheere,** nicknamed *Stuffy.* 1882–1970, British air chief marshal. As commander in chief of Fighter Command (1936–40), he contributed greatly to the British victory in the Battle of Britain (1940).

dowdy ('daʊdɪ) *adj* **-dier, -diest. 1** (esp. of a woman's dress) drab, unflattering, and old-fashioned. ◆ *n, pl* **-dies. 2** a dowdy woman. [C14: *dowd* slut, of unknown origin] ▸ **'dowdily** *adv* ▸ **'dowdiness** *n* ▸ **'dowdyish** *adj*

dowel ('daʊəl) *n* a wooden or metal peg that fits into two corresponding holes to join two adjacent parts. Also called: **dowel pin.** [C14: from Middle Low German *dövel* plug, from Old High German *tubili;* related to Greek *thuphos* wedge]

doweling *or* **dowelling** ('daʊəlɪŋ, -əlɪŋ) *n Carpentry, cabinetmaking.* **1** the joining of two pieces of wood using dowels. **2** wood or other material in a long thin rod for cutting up into dowels.

Dowell ('daʊəl) *n* **Anthony.** born 1943, British ballet dancer. He became director of the Royal Ballet in 1986.

dower ('daʊə) *n* **1** the life interest in a part of her husband's estate allotted to a widow by law. **2** an archaic word for **dowry** (sense 1). **3** a natural gift or talent. ◆ *vb* **4** (*tr*) to endow. **[C14:** from Old French *douaire,* from Medieval Latin *dōtārium,* from Latin *dōs* gift**]** ► **'dowerless** *adj*

dower house *n* a house set apart for the use of a widow, often on her deceased husband's estate.

dowitcher ('daʊɪtʃə) *n* either of two snipelike shore birds, *Limnodromus griseus* or *L. scolopaceus,* of arctic and subarctic North America: family *Scolopacidae* (sandpipers, etc.), order *Charadriiformes.* **[C19:** of Iroquoian origin**]**

do with *vb* **1 could** *or* **can do with.** to find useful; benefit from: *she could do with a night's sleep.* **2 have to do with.** to be involved in or connected with: *his illness has a lot to do with his failing the exam.* **3 to do with.** concerning; related to. **4 what...do with. 4a** to put or place: *what did you do with my coat?* **4b** to handle or treat: *what are we going to do with these hooligans?* **4c** to fill one's time usefully: *she didn't know what to do with herself when term ended.*

do without *vb* (*intr*) **1** to forgo; manage without: *I can't do without cigarettes.* **2** (*prep*) not to require (uncalled-for comments or advice): *we can do without your criticisms thank you.*

Dow-Jones average ('daʊ'dʒəʊnz) *n U.S.* a daily index of stock-exchange prices based on the average price of a selected number of securities. **[C20:** named after Charles H. *Dow* (died 1902) and Edward D. *Jones* (died 1920), American financial statisticians**]**

Dowland ('daʊlənd) *n* **John.** ?1563–1626, English lutenist and composer of songs and lute music.

down[1] (daʊn) *prep* **1** used to indicate movement from a higher to a lower position: *they went down the mountain.* **2** at a lower or further level or position on, in, or along: *he ran down the street.* ◆ *adv* **3** downwards; at or to a lower level or position: *don't fall down.* **4** (*particle*) used with many verbs when the result of the verb's action is to lower or destroy its object: *pull down; knock down; bring down.* **5** (*particle*) used with several verbs to indicate intensity or completion: *calm down.* **6** immediately: *cash down.* **7** on paper: *write this down.* **8** arranged; scheduled: *the meeting is down for next week.* **9** in a helpless position: *they had him down on the ground.* **10a** away from a more important place: *down from London.* **10b** away from a more northerly place: *down from Scotland.* **10c** (of a member of some British universities) away from the university; on vacation. **10d** in a particular part of a country: *down south.* **11** *Nautical.* (of a helm) having the rudder to windward. **12** reduced to a state of lack or want: *down to the last pound.* **13** lacking a specified amount: *at the end of the day the cashier was ten pounds down.* **14** lower in price: *bacon is down.* **15** including all intermediate terms, grades, people, etc.: *from managing director down to tea-lady.* **16** from an earlier to a later time: *the heirloom was handed down.* **17** to a finer or more concentrated state: *to grind down; boil down.* **18** *Sport.* being a specified number of points, goals, etc. behind another competitor, team, etc.: *six goals down.* **19** (of a person) being inactive, owing to illness: *down with flu.* **20** (*functioning as imperative*) (to dogs): *down Rover!* **21** (*functioning as imperative*) **down with.** wanting the end of somebody or something: *down with the king!* **22 get down on something.** *Austral. and N.Z.* to procure something, esp. in advance of needs or in anticipation of someone else. ◆ *adj* **23** (*postpositive*) depressed or miserable. **24** (*prenominal*) of or relating to a train or trains from a more important place or one regarded as higher: *the down line.* **25** (*postpositive*) (of a device, machine, etc., esp. a computer) temporarily out of action. **26** made in cash: *a down payment.* **27 down to.** the responsibility or fault of: *this defeat was down to me.* ◆ *vb* **28** (*tr*) to knock, push or pull down. **29** (*intr*) to go or come down. **30** (*tr*) *Informal.* to drink, esp. quickly: *he downed three gins.* **31** (*tr*) to bring (someone) down, esp. by tackling. ◆ *n* **32** *American football.* one of a maximum of four consecutive attempts by one team to advance the ball a total of at least ten yards. **33** a descent; downward movement. **34** a lowering or a poor period (esp. in the phrase **ups and downs**). **35 have a down on.** *Informal.* to bear ill will towards (someone or something). **[**Old English *dūne,* short for *adūne,* variant of *of dūne,* literally: from the hill, from *of,* OFF + *dūn* hill; see DOWN[3]**]**

down[2] (daʊn) *n* **1** the soft fine feathers with free barbs that cover the body of a bird and prevent loss of heat. In the adult they lie beneath and between the contour feathers. **2** another name for **eiderdown** (sense 1). **3** *Botany.* a fine coating of soft hairs, as on certain leaves, fruits, and seeds. **4** any growth or coating of soft fine hair, such as that on the human face. **[C14:** of Scandinavian origin; related to Old Norse *dūnn***]**

down[3] (daʊn) *n Archaic.* a hill, esp. a sand dune. ◆ See also **downs** (sense 1), **Downs** (sense 1). **[**Old English *dūn;* related to Old Frisian *dūne,* Old Saxon *dūna* hill, Old Irish *dūn* fortress, Greek *this* sandbank; see DUNE, TOWN**]**

Down[1] (daʊn) *n* **1** a district of SE Northern Ireland, in Co. Down. Pop.: 58 008 (1991). Area: 649 sq. km (250 sq. miles). **2** a historical county of SE Northern Ireland, on the Irish Sea: generally hilly, rising to the Mountains of Mourne: in 1973 it was replaced for administrative purposes by the districts of Ards, Banbridge, Castlereagh, Down, Newry and Mourne, North Down, and part of Lisburn. Area: 2466 sq. km (952 sq. miles).

Down[2] (daʊn) *n* any of various lowland breeds of sheep, typically of stocky build and having dense close wool, originating from various parts of southern England, such as Oxford, Hampshire, etc. See also **Dorset Down.**

down-and-out *adj* **1** without any means of livelihood; impoverished and, often, socially outcast. ◆ *n* **2** a person who is destitute and, often, homeless; a social outcast or derelict.

downbeat ('daʊn,bi:t) *n* **1** *Music.* the first beat of a bar or the downward gesture of a conductor's baton indicating this. Compare **upbeat.** ◆ *adj* **2** *Informal.* depressed; gloomy. **3** *Informal.* relaxed; unemphatic.

down-bow ('daʊn,bəʊ) *n* a downward stroke of the bow from its nut to its tip across a stringed instrument. Compare **up-bow.**

downburst ('daʊn,bɜ:st) *n* a very high-speed downward movement of turbulent air in a limited area for a short time. Near the ground it spreads out from its centre with high horizontal velocities. Also called: **microburst.**

downcast ('daʊn,kɑ:st) *adj* **1** dejected. **2** (esp. of the eyes) directed downwards. ◆ *n* **3** *Mining.* a ventilation shaft. **4** *Geology.* another word for **downthrow.**

downcome ('daʊn,kʌm) *n* **1** *Archaic.* downfall. **2** another name for **downcomer.**

downcomer ('daʊn,kʌmə) *n* a pipe that connects a cistern to a W.C., wash basin, etc. Also called: **downcome.**

downdraught ('daʊn,drɑ:ft) *n* the large-scale downward movement of air in the lee of large objects, mountains, etc.

downer ('daʊnə) *n Slang.* **1** Also called: **down.** a barbiturate, tranquillizer, or narcotic. Compare **upper. 2** a depressing experience. **3** a state of depression: *he's on a downer today.*

downfall ('daʊn,fɔ:l) *n* **1** a sudden loss of position, health, or reputation. **2** a fall of rain, snow, etc., esp. a sudden heavy one. **3** another word for **deadfall.**

downfallen ('daʊn,fɔ:lən) *adj* **1** (of a building, etc.) decrepit. **2** *Chiefly U.S.* (of a person) ruined; fallen.

downgrade ('daʊn,greɪd) *vb* (*tr*) **1** to reduce in importance, esteem, or value, esp. to demote (a person) to a poorer job. **2** to speak of disparagingly. ◆ *n* **3** *Chiefly U.S. and Canadian.* a downward slope, esp. in a road. **4 on the downgrade.** waning in importance, popularity, health, etc.

downhaul ('daʊn,hɔ:l) *n Nautical.* a line for hauling down a sail or for increasing the tension at its luff.

downhearted (,daʊn'hɑ:tɪd) *adj* discouraged; dejected. ► **,down'heartedly** *adv* ► **,down'heartedness** *n*

downhill ('daʊn'hɪl) *adj* **1** going or sloping down. ◆ *adv* **2** towards the bottom of a hill; downwards. **3 go downhill.** *Informal.* to decline; deteriorate. ◆ *n* **4** the downward slope of a hill; descent. **5** a competitive event in which skiers are timed in a downhill run.

downhole ('daʊn,həʊl) *adj* (in the oil industry) denoting any piece of equipment that is used in the well itself.

downhome (,daʊn'həʊm) *adj Slang, chiefly U.S.* of, relating to, or reminiscent of rural life, esp. in the southern U.S.; unsophisticated.

Downing Street ('daʊnɪŋ) *n* **1** a street in W central London, in Westminster: official residences of the British prime minister and the chancellor of the exchequer. **2** *Informal.* the prime minister or the British Government. **[**named after Sir George *Downing* (1623–84), English statesman**]**

download ('daʊn,ləʊd) *vb* (*tr*) **1** to copy or transfer (data or a program) from one computer's memory to that of another, esp. in a network of computers. **2** to broadcast specialist programmes, for such groups as doctors, outside normal broadcasting hours. They are often recorded on video tapes and viewed later.

down-market *adj* relating to commercial products, services, etc., that are cheap, have little prestige, or are poor in quality.

Downpatrick (,daʊn'pætrɪk) *n* a market town in Northern Ireland: reputedly the burial place of Saint Patrick. Pop.: 10 257 (1991).

down payment *n* the deposit paid on an item purchased on hire-purchase, mortgage, etc.

downpipe ('daʊn,paɪp) *n Brit. and N.Z.* a pipe for carrying rainwater from a roof gutter to the ground or to a drain. Also called: **rainwater pipe, drainpipe.** Usual U.S. and Canadian name: **downspout.**

downplay ('daʊn,pleɪ) *vb* (*tr*) to play down; make little of.

downpour ('daʊn,pɔ:) *n* a heavy continuous fall of rain.

downrange ('daʊn'reɪndʒ) *adj, adv* in the direction of the intended flight path of a rocket or missile.

downright ('daʊn,raɪt) *adj* **1** frank or straightforward; blunt: *downright speech.* **2** *Archaic.* directed or pointing straight down. ◆ *adv, adj* (*prenominal*) **3** (intensifier): *a downright certainty; downright rude.* ► **'down,rightly** *adv* ► **'down,rightness** *n*

downs (daʊnz) *pl n* **1** Also called: **downland.** rolling upland, esp. in the chalk areas of S Britain, characterized by lack of trees and used mainly as pasture. **2** *Austral. and N.Z.* a flat grassy area, not necessarily of uplands.

Downs (daʊnz) *n* **the. 1** any of various ranges of low chalk hills in S England, esp. the **South Downs** in Sussex. **2** a roadstead off the SE coast of Kent, protected by the Goodwin Sands.

downshifting ('daʊn,ʃɪftɪŋ) *n* the practice of simplifying one's lifestyle and becoming less materialistic.

downside ('daʊn,saɪd) *n* the disadvantageous aspect of a situation: *the downside of twentieth-century living.*

downsize ('daʊn,saɪz) *vb* **-sizes, -sizing, -sized.** (*tr*) **1** to reduce the operating costs of a company by reducing the number of people it employs. **2** to reduce the size of or produce a smaller version of (something). **3** to upgrade (a computer system) by replacing a mainframe or minicomputer with a network of microcomputers. Compare **rightsize.**

downspout ('daʊn,spaʊt) *n* a U.S. and Canadian name for **downpipe.**

Down's syndrome *n* **a** *Pathol.* a chromosomal abnormality resulting in a flat face and nose, short stubby fingers, a vertical fold of skin at the inner edge of the eye, and mental retardation. Former name: **mongolism. b** (*as modifier*): *a Down's syndrome baby.* **[C19:** after John *Langdon-Down* (1828–96), English physician**]**

downstage ('daʊn'steɪdʒ) *Theatre.* ◆ *adv* **1** at or towards the front of the stage. ◆ *adj* **2** of or relating to the front of the stage. ◆ *n* **3** the front half of the stage.

downstairs ('daʊn'steəz) *adv* **1** down the stairs; to or on a lower floor. ◆ *n* **2a** a lower or ground floor. **2b** (*as modifier*): *a downstairs room.* **3** *Brit. informal, old-fashioned.* the servants of a household collectively. Compare **upstairs** (sense 6).

downstate ('daʊn,steɪt) *U.S.* ◆ *adj* **1** in, or relating to the part of the state away from large cities, esp. the southern part. ◆ *adv* **2** towards the southern part of a state. ◆ *n* **3** the southern part of a state.

downstream ('daʊn'striːm) *adv, adj* **1** in or towards the lower part of a stream; with the current. **2** (in the oil industry) of or for the refining, distribution, or marketing of oil or its derived products. Compare **upstream** (sense 2).

downswing ('daʊn,swɪŋ) *n* **1** a statistical downward trend in business activity, the death rate, etc. **2** *Golf.* the downward movement or line of a club when striking the ball.

downthrow ('daʊn,θrəʊ) *n* **1** the state of throwing down or being thrown down. **2** *Geology.* the sinking of rocks on one side of a fault plane.

downtime ('daʊn,taɪm) *n Commerce.* time during which a machine or plant is not working because it is incapable of production, as when under repair: the term is sometimes used to include all nonproductive time. Compare **idle time.**

down-to-earth *adj* sensible; practical; realistic.

downtown ('daʊn'taʊn) *U.S., Canadian, and N.Z.* ◆ *n* **1** the central or lower part of a city, esp. the main commercial area. ◆ *adv* **2** towards, to, or into this area. ◆ *adj* **3** of, relating to, or situated in the downtown area: *downtown Manhattan.* ▸ **'down'towner** *n*

downtrodden ('daʊn,trɒdᵊn) *or* **downtrod** *adj* **1** subjugated; oppressed. **2** trodden down; trampled.

downturn ('daʊn,tɜːn) *n* a drop or reduction in the success of a business or economy.

down under *Informal.* ◆ *n* **1** Australia or New Zealand. ◆ *adv* **2** in or to Australia or New Zealand.

downward ('daʊnwəd) *adj* **1** descending from a higher to a lower level, condition, position, etc. **2** descending from a beginning. ◆ *adv* **3** a variant of **downwards.** ▸ **'downwardly** *adv* ▸ **'downwardness** *n*

downward mobility *n Sociol.* the movement of an individual, social group, or class to a lower status. Compare **upward mobility.** See also **horizontal mobility, vertical mobility.**

downwards ('daʊnwədz) *or* **downward** *adv* **1** from a higher to a lower place, level, etc. **2** from an earlier time or source to a later: *from the Tudors downwards.*

downwash ('daʊn,wɒʃ) *n* the downward deflection of an airflow, esp. one caused by an aircraft wing.

downwind ('daʊn'wɪnd) *adv, adj* **1** in the same direction towards which the wind is blowing; with the wind from behind. **2** towards or on the side away from the wind; leeward.

downy ('daʊnɪ) *adj* **downier, downiest. 1** covered with soft fine hair or feathers. **2** light, soft, and fluffy. **3** made from or filled with down. **4** resembling downs; undulating. **5** *Brit. slang.* sharp-witted; knowing. ▸ **'downiness** *n*

downy mildew *n* **1** a serious plant disease, characterized by yellowish patches on the undersurface of the leaves, caused by the parasitic fungi of the family *Peronosporaceae,* such as *Peronospora destructor:* affects onions, cauliflower, lettuce, etc. **2** any of the fungi causing this disease. ◆ Compare **powdery mildew.**

dowry ('daʊərɪ) *n, pl* **-ries. 1** the money or property brought by a woman to her husband at marriage. **2** (esp. formerly) a gift made by a man to his bride or her parents. **3** *Christianity.* a sum of money required on entering certain orders of nuns. **4** a natural talent or gift. **5** *Obsolete.* a widow's dower. **[C14:** from Anglo-French *douarie,* from Medieval Latin *dōtārium;* see DOWER**]**

dowsabel ('duːsə,bel, 'daʊs-) *n* an obsolete word for **sweetheart. [C16:** from Latin *Dulcibella* feminine given name, from *dulcis* sweet + *bellus* beautiful**]**

dowse[1] (daʊs) *vb, n* a variant spelling of **douse**[1]. ▸ **'dowser** *n*

dowse[2] (daʊz) *vb* (*intr*) to search for underground water, minerals, etc., using a divining rod; divine. **[C17:** of unknown origin**]** ▸ **'dowser** *n*

dowsing rod ('daʊzɪŋ) *n* another name for **divining rod.**

Dowson ('daʊsᵊn) *n* **Ernest (Christopher).** 1867–1900, English Decadent poet noted for his lyric *Cynara.*

doxastic (dɒks'æstɪk) *adj Logic.* **1** of or relating to belief. **2** denoting the branch of modal logic that studies the concept of belief. **[C18:** from Greek *doxastikos* having an opinion, ultimately from *doxazein* to conjecture**]**

doxographer (,dɒks'ɒgrəfə) *n Rare.* a person who collects the opinions and conjectures of ancient Greek philosophers. **[C19:** from New Latin *doxographus,* from Greek *doxa* opinion, conjecture + *graphos* writer**]** ▸ **,doxo'graphic** *adj* ▸ **,dox'ography** *n*

doxology (dɒk'sɒlədʒɪ) *n, pl* **-gies.** a hymn, verse, or form of words in Christian liturgy glorifying God. **[C17:** from Medieval Latin *doxologia,* from Greek, from *doxologos* uttering praise, from *doxa* praise; see -LOGY**]** ▸ **doxological** (,dɒksə'lɒdʒɪkᵊl) *adj* ▸ **,doxo'logically** *adv*

doxy[1] *or* **doxie** ('dɒksɪ) *n, pl* **doxies.** opinion or doctrine, esp. concerning religious matters. **[C18:** independent use of *-doxy* as in *orthodoxy, heterodoxy***]**

doxy[2] ('dɒksɪ) *n, pl* **doxies.** *Archaic slang.* a prostitute or mistress. **[C16:** probably from Middle Flemish *docke* doll; compare Middle Dutch *docke* doll**]**

doyen ('dɔɪən; *French* dwajɛ̃) *n* the senior member of a group, profession, or society. **[C17:** from French, from Late Latin *decānus* leader of a group of ten; see DEAN**]** ▸ **doyenne** (dɔɪ'en; *French* dwajɛn) *fem n*

Doyle (dɔɪl) *n* See (Sir Arthur) **Conan Doyle.**

doyley ('dɔɪlɪ) *n* a variant spelling of **doily.**

D'Oyly Carte ('dɔɪlɪ kɑːt) *n* **Richard.** 1844–1901, British impresario noted for his productions of the operettas of Gilbert and Sullivan.

doz. *abbrev. for* dozen.

doze (dəʊz) *vb* (*intr*) **1** to sleep lightly or intermittently. **2** (often foll. by *off*) to fall into a light sleep. ◆ *n* **3** a short sleep. **[C17:** probably from Old Norse *dūs* lull; related to Danish *döse* to drowse, Swedish dialect *dusa* slumber**]** ▸ **'dozer** *n*

dozed (dozd, dəʊzd) *adj Chiefly Irish.* (of timber or rubber) rotten or decayed. **[C18:** probably from DOZE**]**

dozen ('dʌzᵊn) *determiner* **1** (preceded by *a* or a numeral) **1a** twelve or a group of twelve: *a dozen eggs; two dozen oranges.* **1b** (*as pronoun; functioning as sing or pl*): *give me a dozen; there are at least a dozen who haven't arrived yet.* ◆ *n, pl* **dozens** *or* **dozen. 2 by the dozen.** in large quantities. **3** See **baker's dozen. 4 talk nineteen to the dozen.** to talk without stopping. ◆ See also **dozens. [C13:** from Old French *douzaine,* from *douze* twelve, from Latin *duodecim,* from *duo* two + *decem* ten**]** ▸ **'dozenth** *adj*

dozens ('dʌzᵊnz) *pl n* (usually foll. by *of*) *Informal.* a lot: *I've got dozens of things to do.*

dozer ('dəʊzə) *n* short for **bulldozer.**

dozy ('dəʊzɪ) *adj* **dozier, doziest. 1** drowsy. **2** *Brit. informal.* stupid. ▸ **'dozily** *adv* ▸ **'doziness** *n*

DP *abbrev. for:* **1** data processing. **2** displaced person.

D/P *Commerce. abbrev. for* documents against presentation.

DPB (in New Zealand) *abbrev. for* domestic purposes benefit: an allowance paid to solo parents.

DPH *abbrev. for* Diploma in Public Health.

DPhil, *or* **DPh** *abbrev. for* Doctor of Philosophy. Also: **PhD.**

dpi *abbrev. for* dots per inch: a measure of the resolution of a typesetting machine, computer screen, etc.

DPM *abbrev. for* Diploma in Psychological Medicine.

DPN *n Biochem.* diphosphopyridine nucleotide; the former name for **NAD.**

DPNH *n Biochem.* the reduced form of DPN; the former name for **NADH.**

DPP (in Britain) *abbrev. for* Director of Public Prosecutions.

dpt *abbrev. for* department.

DPW *abbrev. for* Department of Public Works.

dr *abbrev. for:* **1** debtor. **2** Also: **dr.** dram. **3** drawer.

Dr *abbrev. for:* **1** Doctor. **2** (in street names) Drive.

DR *abbrev. for* **dry riser.**

dr. *abbrev. for:* **1** debit. **2** Also: **dr** dram. **3** drachma.

drab[1] (dræb) *adj* **drabber, drabbest. 1** dull; dingy; shabby. **2** cheerless; dreary: *a drab evening.* **3** of the colour drab. ◆ *n* **4** a light olive-brown colour. **5** a fabric of a dull grey or brown colour. **[C16:** from Old French *drap* cloth, from Late Latin *drappus,* perhaps of Celtic origin**]** ▸ **'drably** *adv* ▸ **'drabness** *n*

drab[2] (dræb) *Archaic.* ◆ *n* **1** a slatternly woman. **2** a whore. ◆ *vb* **drabs, drabbing, drabbed. 3** (*intr*) to consort with prostitutes. **[C16:** of Celtic origin; compare Scottish Gaelic *drabag***]**

drabbet ('dræbɪt) *n Brit.* a yellowish-brown fabric of coarse linen. **[C19:** see DRAB[1]**]**

drabble ('dræbᵊl) *vb* to make or become wet or dirty. **[C14:** from Low German *drabbelen* to paddle in mud; related to DRAB[2]**]**

Drabble ('dræbᵊl) *n* **Margaret.** born 1939, British novelist and editor. Her novels include *The Needle's Eye* (1972), *The Radiant Way* (1987), and *The Gates of Ivory* (1991). She edited the 1985 edition of the *Oxford Companion to Literature.*

dracaena (drə'siːnə) *n* **1** any tropical liliaceous plant of the genus *Dracaena:* some species are cultivated as house plants for their decorative foliage. See also **dragon tree. 2** any of several similar plants of the related genus *Cordyline.* **[C19:** from New Latin, from Latin: she-dragon, from Greek *drakaina,* feminine of *drakōn* DRAGON**]**

drachm (dræm) *n* **1** Also called: **fluid dram.** *Brit.* one eighth of a fluid ounce. **2** *U.S.* another name for **dram** (sense 2). **3** another name for **drachma. [C14:** learned variant of DRAM**]**

drachma ('drækmə) *n, pl* **-mas** *or* **-mae** (-miː). **1** the standard monetary unit of Greece, divided into 100 lepta. **2** *U.S.* another name for **dram** (sense 2). **3** a silver coin of ancient Greece. **4** a unit of weight in ancient Greece. **[C16:** from Latin, from Greek *drakhmē* a handful, from *drassesthai* to seize**]**

drack *or* **drac** (dræk) *adj Austral. slang.* (esp. of a woman) unattractive. **[**perhaps from *Dracula's* Daughter**]**

Draco[1] ('dreɪkəʊ) *n, Latin genitive* **Draconis** (dreɪ'kəʊnɪs). a faint extensive constellation twisting around the N celestial pole and lying between Ursa Major and Cepheus. **[**from Latin, from Greek *drakōn* DRAGON**]**

Draco[2] ('dreɪkəʊ) *n* 7th century B.C., Athenian statesman and lawmaker, whose code of laws (621) prescribed death for almost every offence.

draco lizard ('dreɪkəʊ) *n* another name for **flying lizard.**

dracone ('drækəʊn) *n* a large flexible cylindrical container towed by a ship, used for transporting liquids. **[C20:** from Latin: DRAGON**]**

Draconian (dreɪ'kəʊnɪən) *or* **Draconic** (dreɪ'kɒnɪk) *adj* (*sometimes not cap.*) **1** of or relating to Draco or his code of laws. **2** harsh. ▸ **Dra'conianism** *n* ▸ **Dra'conically** *adv*

draconic (dreɪ'kɒnɪk) *adj* of, like, or relating to a dragon. **[C17:** from Latin *dracō* DRAGON**]** ▸ **dra'conically** *adv*

draff (dræf) *n* the residue of husks after fermentation of the grain used in brewing, used as a food for cattle. **[C13:** from Old Norse *draf;* related to Old High German *trebir,* Russian *drob* fragment; see DRIVEL**]** ▸ **'draffy** *adj*

draft (drɑːft) *n* **1** a plan, sketch, or drawing of something. **2** a preliminary outline of a book, speech, etc. **3** another word for **bill of exchange. 4** a demand or drain on something. **5** the divergent duct leading from a water turbine to its tailrace. **6** *U.S.* selection for compulsory military service. **7** detachment of military personnel from one unit to another. **8** *Commerce.* an allowance on merchandise sold by weight. **9** a line or narrow border that is chiselled on the surface of a stone to serve as a guide for levelling it. **10** *Austral. and N.Z.* a group of livestock separated from the rest of the herd or flock. ◆ *vb* (*tr*) **11** to draw up an outline or sketch for something: *to draft a speech.* **12** to prepare a plan or design of. **13** to detach (military personnel) from one unit to another. **14** *Chiefly U.S.* to select for compulsory military service. **15** to chisel a draft on (stone, etc.). **16** *Austral. and N.Z.* **16a** to select (cattle or sheep) from a herd or flock. **16b** to select (farm stock) for sale. ◆ *n, vb* **17** the usual U.S. spelling of **draught** (senses 1–8, 11). [C16: variant of DRAUGHT] ▸ **'drafter** *n*

draft board *n U.S.* a tribunal responsible for the selection of personnel liable for compulsory military service.

draft dodger *n U.S.* one who evades compulsory military service.

draftee (drɑːf'tiː) *n U.S.* a conscript.

draft-quality printing *n Computing.* low-quality, high-speed output in printed form from a printer linked to a word processor. Compare **letter-quality printing.**

draftsman ('drɑːftsmən) *n, pl* **-men.** the usual U.S. spelling of **draughtsman** (senses 1, 2). ▸ **'draftsmanship** *n*

drafty ('drɑːftɪ) *adj* **draftier, draftiest.** the usual U.S. spelling of **draughty.** ▸ **'draftily** *adv* ▸ **'draftiness** *n*

drag (dræg) *vb* **drags, dragging, dragged. 1** to pull or be pulled with force, esp. along the ground or other surface. **2** (*tr;* often foll. by *away* or *from*) to persuade to come away (from something attractive or interesting): *he couldn't drag himself away from the shop.* **3** to trail or cause to trail on the ground. **4** (*tr*) to move (oneself, one's feet, etc.) with effort or difficulty: *he drags himself out of bed at dawn.* **5** to linger behind. **6** (often foll. by *on* or *out*) to prolong or be prolonged tediously or unnecessarily: *his talk dragged on for hours.* **7** (*tr;* foll. by *out*) to pass (time) in discomfort, poverty, unhappiness, etc.: *he dragged out his few remaining years.* **8** (when *intr,* usually foll. by *for*) to search (the bed of a river, canal, etc.) with a dragnet or hook: *they dragged the river for the body.* **9** (*tr* foll. by *out* or *from*) to crush (clods) or level (a soil surface) by use of a drag. **10** (of hounds) to follow (a fox or its trail) to the place where it has been lying. **11** (*intr*) *Slang.* to draw (on a cigarette, pipe, etc.). **12** *Computing.* to move (a graphics image) from one place to another on the screen by manipulating a mouse with its button held down. **13 drag anchor.** (of a vessel) to move away from its mooring because the anchor has failed to hold. **14 drag one's feet** *or* **heels.** *Informal.* to act with deliberate slowness. **15 drag (someone's) name in the mud.** to disgrace or defame (someone). ◆ *n* **16** the act of dragging or the state of being dragged. **17** an implement, such as a dragnet, dredge, etc., used for dragging. **18** Also called: **drag harrow.** a type of harrow consisting of heavy beams, often with spikes inserted, used to crush clods, level soil, or prepare seedbeds. **19** a sporting coach with seats inside and out, usually drawn by four horses. **20** a braking or retarding device, such as a metal piece fitted to the underside of the wheel of a horse-drawn vehicle. **21** a person or thing that slows up progress. **22** slow progress or movement. **23** *Aeronautics.* the resistance to the motion of a body passing through a fluid, esp. through air: applied to an aircraft in flight, it is the component of the resultant aerodynamic force measured parallel to the direction of air flow. **24** the trail of scent left by a fox or other animal hunted with hounds. **25** an artificial trail of a strong-smelling substance, sometimes including aniseed, drawn over the ground for hounds to follow. **26** See **drag hunt. 27** *Angling.* unnatural movement imparted to a fly, esp. a dry fly, by tension on the angler's line. **28** *Informal.* a person or thing that is very tedious; bore: *exams are a drag.* **29** *Slang.* a car. **30** short for **drag race. 31** *Slang.* **31a** women's clothes worn by a man, usually by a transvestite (esp. in the phrase **in drag**). **31b** (*as modifier*): *a drag club; drag show.* **31c** clothes collectively. **32** *Informal.* a draw on a cigarette, pipe, etc. **33** *U.S. slang.* influence or persuasive power. **34** *Chiefly U.S. slang.* a street or road. ◆ See also **drag down, drag in, drag out of, drag up.** [Old English *dragan* to DRAW; related to Swedish *dragga*]

drag down *vb* (*tr, adv*) to depress or demoralize: *the flu really dragged her down.*

dragée (dræ'ʒeɪ) *n* **1** a sweet made of a nut, fruit, etc., coated with a hard sugar icing. **2** a tiny beadlike sweet used for decorating cakes, etc. **3** a medicinal pill coated with sugar to disguise the taste. [C19: from French; see DREDGE[2]]

draggle ('dræg[ə]l) *vb* **1** to make or become wet or dirty by trailing on the ground; bedraggle. **2** (*intr*) to lag; dawdle. [C16: probably frequentative of DRAG]

draggletailed ('dræg[ə]l,teɪld) *adj Archaic.* (esp. of a woman) bedraggled; besmirched.

draggy ('drægɪ) *adj* **-gier, -giest.** *Slang.* **1** slow or boring: *a draggy party.* **2** dull and listless.

draghound ('dræg,haʊnd) *n* a hound used to follow an artificial trail of scent in a drag hunt.

drag hunt *n* **1** a hunt in which hounds follow an artificial trail of scent. **2** a club that organizes such hunts. ◆ *vb* **drag-hunt. 3** to follow draghounds, esp. on horseback, or cause (draghounds) to follow an artificial trail of scent.

drag in *vb* (*tr, adv*) to introduce or mention (a topic, name, etc.) with slight or no pretext.

dragline ('dræg,laɪn) *n* **1** another word for **dragrope** (sense 2). **2** Also called: **dragline crane, dragline excavator.** a power shovel that operates by being dragged by cables at the end of an arm or jib: used for quarrying, opencast mining, etc.

drag link *n* a link for conveying motion between cranks on parallel shafts that are slightly offset. It is used in cars to connect the steering gear to the steering arm.

dragnet ('dræg,nɛt) *n* **1** a heavy or weighted net used to scour the bottom of a pond, river, etc., as when searching for something. **2** any system of coordinated efforts by police forces to track down wanted persons.

dragoman ('drægəʊmən) *n, pl* **-mans** *or* **-men.** (in some Middle Eastern countries, esp. formerly) a professional interpreter or guide. [C14: from French, from Italian *dragomano,* from Medieval Greek *dragoumanos,* from Arabic *targumān* an interpreter, from Aramaic *tūrgemānā,* of Akkadian origin]

dragon ('drægən) *n* **1** a mythical monster usually represented as breathing fire and having a scaly reptilian body, wings, claws, and a long tail. **2** *Informal.* a fierce or intractable person, esp. a woman. **3** any of various very large lizards, esp. the Komodo dragon. **4** any of various North American aroid plants, esp. the green dragon. **5** *Christianity.* a manifestation of Satan or an attendant devil. **6** a yacht of the International Dragon Class, 8.88m long (29.2 feet), used in racing. **7 chase the dragon.** *Slang.* to smoke opium or heroin. [C13: from Old French, from Latin *dracō,* from Greek *drakōn;* related to *drakos* eye] ▸ **'dragoness** *fem n* ▸ **'dragonish** *adj*

dragonet ('drægənɪt) *n* any small spiny-finned fish of the family *Callionymidae,* having a flat head and a slender tapering brightly coloured body and living at the bottom of shallow seas. [C14 (meaning: small dragon): from French; applied to fish C18]

dragonfly ('drægən,flaɪ) *n, pl* **-flies. 1** any predatory insect of the suborder *Anisoptera,* having a large head and eyes, a long slender body, two pairs of iridescent wings that are outspread at rest, and aquatic larvae: order *Odonata.* See also **damselfly. 2** any other insect of the order *Odonata.*

dragonhead ('drægən,hɛd) *or* **dragon's-head** *n* **1** any plant of the genus *Dracocephalum,* of Europe, Asia, and North America, having dense spikes of white or bluish flowers: family *Labiatae* (labiates). **2** any North American plant of the related genus *Physostegia,* having pink or purplish flowers.

dragon market *n Informal.* any of the emerging markets of the Pacific rim, esp. Indonesia, Malaysia, Thailand, and the Philippines. Compare **tiger market.**

dragonnade (,drægə'neɪd) *n* **1** *History.* the persecution of French Huguenots during the reign of Louis XIV by dragoons quartered in their villages and homes. **2** subjection by military force. ◆ *vb* **3** (*tr*) to subject to persecution by military troops. [C18: from French, from *dragon* DRAGOON]

dragonroot ('drægən,ruːt) *n* **1** a North American aroid plant, *Arisaema dracontium,* having a greenish spathe and a long pointed spadix. **2** the tuberous root of this plant, formerly used in medicine.

dragon's blood *n* **1** a red resinous substance obtained from the fruit of a Malaysian palm, *Daemonorops* (or *Calamus*) *draco:* formerly used medicinally and now used in varnishes and lacquers. **2** any of several similar resins obtained from other trees, esp. from the dragon tree.

dragon's teeth *pl n* **1** *Informal.* concrete antitank obstacles protruding from the ground in rows: used in World War II. **2 sow dragon's teeth.** to take some action that is intended to prevent strife or trouble but that actually brings it about. [sense 2 from the story of CADMUS]

dragon tree *n* a liliaceous tree, *Dracaena draco,* of the Canary Islands, having clusters of sword-shaped leaves at the tips of its branches: a source of dragon's blood.

dragoon (drə'guːn) *n* **1** (originally) a mounted infantryman armed with a carbine. **2** (*sometimes cap.*) a domestic fancy pigeon. **3a** a type of cavalryman. **3b** (*pl; cap. when part of a name*): *the Royal Dragoons.* ◆ *vb* (*tr*) **4** to coerce; force: *he was dragooned into admitting it.* **5** to persecute by military force. [C17: from French *dragon* (special use of DRAGON), soldier armed with a carbine, perhaps suggesting that a carbine, like a dragon, breathed forth fire] ▸ **dra'goonage** *n*

drag out of *vb* (*tr, adv +prep*) to obtain or extract (a confession, statement, etc.), esp. by force: *we dragged the name out of him.* Also: **drag from.**

drag race *n* a type of motor race in which specially built or modified cars or motorcycles are timed over a measured course. ▸ **drag racer** *n* ▸ **drag racing** *n*

dragrope ('dræg,rəʊp) *n* **1** a rope used to drag military equipment, esp. artillery. **2** Also called: **dragline, guide rope.** a rope trailing from a balloon or airship for mooring or braking purposes.

drag sail *n* another term for **sea anchor.**

dragster ('drægstə) *n* a car specially built or modified for drag racing.

drag up *vb* (*tr, adv*) *Informal.* **1** to rear (a child) poorly and in an undisciplined manner. **2** to introduce or revive (an unpleasant fact or story).

drail (dreɪl) *Angling.* ◆ *n* **1** a weighted hook used in trolling. ◆ *vb* **2** (*intr*) to fish with a drail. [C16: apparently from TRAIL, influenced by DRAW]

drain (dreɪn) *n* **1** a pipe or channel that carries off water, sewage, etc. **2** an instance or cause of continuous diminution in resources or energy; depletion. **3** *Surgery.* a device, such as a tube, for insertion into a wound, incision, or bodily cavity to drain off pus, etc. **4** *Electronics.* the electrode region in a field-effect transistor into which majority carriers flow from the interelectrode conductivity channel. **5 down the drain.** wasted. ◆ *vb* **6** (*tr;* often foll. by *off*) to draw off or remove (liquid) from: *to drain water from vegetables; to drain vegetables.* **7** (*intr;* often foll. by *away*) to flow (away) or filter (off). **8** (*intr*) to dry or be emptied as a result of liquid running off or flowing away: *leave the dishes to drain.* **9** (*tr*) to drink the entire contents of (a glass, cup, etc.). **10** (*tr*) to consume or make constant demands on (resources, energy, etc.); exhaust; sap. **11** (*intr*) to disappear or leave, esp. gradually: *the colour drained from his face.* **12** (*tr*) (of a river, etc.) to carry off the surface water from (an area). **13** (*intr*) (of an area) to discharge its surface water into rivers, streams, etc. [Old English *drēahnian;* related to Old Norse *drangr* dry wood; see DRY] ▸ **'drainable** *adj* ▸ **'drainer** *n*

drainage ('dreɪnɪdʒ) *n* **1** the process or a method of draining. **2** a system of watercourses or drains. **3** liquid, sewage, etc., that is drained away.

drainage basin *or* **area** *n* another name for **catchment area.**

draining board *n* a sloping grooved surface at the side of a sink, used for draining washed dishes, etc. Also called: **drainer.**

drainpipe ('dreɪn,paɪp) *n* a pipe for carrying off rainwater, sewage, etc.; downpipe.

drainpipes ('dreɪn,paɪps) *pl n* trousers with very narrow legs.

drain rod *n* one of a series of flexible rods with threaded ends that screw together and can be pushed to and fro in a drain to clear a blockage.

drake[1] (dreɪk) *n* the male of any duck. [C13: perhaps from Low German; compare Middle Dutch *andrake,* Old High German *antrahho*]

drake[2] (dreɪk) *n* **1** *Angling.* an artificial fly resembling a mayfly. **2** *History.* a small cannon. **3** an obsolete word for **dragon.** [Old English *draca,* ultimately from Latin *dracō* DRAGON]

Drake (dreɪk) *n* Sir **Francis.** ?1540–96, English navigator and buccaneer, the first Englishman to sail around the world (1577–80). He commanded a fleet against the Spanish Armada (1588) and contributed greatly to its defeat.

Drakensberg ('drɑːkənzˌbɜːg) *n* a mountain range in southern Africa, extending through Lesotho, E South Africa, and Swaziland. Highest peak: Thabana Ntlenyana, 3482 m (11 425 ft.). Sotho name: **Quathlamba.**

Drake Passage *n* a strait between S South America and the South Shetland Islands, connecting the Atlantic and Pacific Oceans.

Dralon ('dreɪlɒn) *n Trademark.* an acrylic fibre fabric used esp. for upholstery.

dram (dræm) *n* **1** one sixteenth of an ounce (avoirdupois). 1 dram is equivalent to 0.0018 kilogram. **2** Also called: **drachm, drachma.** *U.S.* one eighth of an apothecaries' ounce; 60 grains. 1 dram is equivalent to 0.0039 kilogram. **3** a small amount of an alcoholic drink, esp. a spirit; tot. **4** the standard monetary unit of Armenia, divided into 100 lumas. [C15: from Old French *dragme,* from Late Latin *dragma,* from Greek *drakhmē;* see DRACHMA]

DRAM *or* **D-RAM** ('diːræm) *acronym for* dynamic random access memory: **a** a widely used type of random access memory. See **RAM**[1]. **b** a chip containing such a memory.

drama ('drɑːmə) *n* **1** a work to be performed by actors on stage, radio, or television; play. **2** the genre of literature represented by works intended for the stage. **3** the art of the writing and production of plays. **4** a situation or sequence of events that is highly emotional, tragic, or turbulent. [C17: from Late Latin: a play, from Greek: something performed, from *drān* to do]

Dramamine ('dræməˌmiːn) *n* a trademark for **dimenhydrinate.**

dramatic (drə'mætɪk) *adj* **1** of or relating to drama. **2** like a drama in suddenness, emotional impact, etc. **3** striking; effective. **4** acting or performed in a flamboyant way. **5** *Music.* (of a voice) powerful and marked by histrionic quality. ► **dra'matically** *adv*

dramatic irony *n Theatre.* the irony occurring when the implications of a situation, speech, etc., are understood by the audience but not by the characters in the play.

dramatics (drə'mætɪks) *n* **1** (*functioning as sing or pl*) **1a** the art of acting or producing plays. **1b** dramatic productions. **2** (*usually functioning as pl*) histrionic behaviour.

dramatis personae ('drɑːmətɪs pə'səʊnaɪ) *pl n* (*often functioning as sing*) **1** the characters or a list of characters in a play or story. **2** the main personalities in any situation or event. [C18: from New Latin]

dramatist ('dræmətɪst) *n* a writer of plays; playwright.

dramatization *or* **dramatisation** (ˌdræmətaɪ'zeɪʃən) *n* **1** the reconstruction of an event, novel, story, etc. in a form suitable for dramatic presentation. **2** the art or act of dramatizing.

dramatize *or* **dramatise** ('dræməˌtaɪz) *vb* **1** (*tr*) to put into dramatic form. **2** to express or represent (something) in a dramatic or exaggerated way: *he dramatizes his illness.* ► **'dramaˌtizable** *or* **'dramaˌtisable** *adj* ► **'dramaˌtizer** *or* **'dramaˌtiser** *n*

dramaturge ('dræməˌtɜːdʒ) *n* **1** Also called: **dramaturgist.** a dramatist, esp. one associated with a particular company or theatre. **2** Also called: **dramaturg.** a literary adviser on the staff of a theatre, film corporation, etc., whose responsibilities may include selection and editing of texts, liaison with authors, preparation of printed programmes, and public relations work. [C19: probably from French, from Greek *dramatourgos* playwright, from DRAMA + *ergon* work]

dramaturgy ('dræməˌtɜːdʒɪ) *n* the art and technique of the theatre; dramatics. ► **ˌdrama'turgic** *or* **ˌdrama'turgical** *adj* ► **ˌdrama'turgically** *adv*

Drambuie (dræm'bjuːɪ) *n Trademark.* a liqueur based on Scotch whisky and made exclusively in Scotland from a recipe dating from the 18th century.

Drammen (*Norwegian* 'dramən) *n* a port in S Norway. Pop.: 51 900 (1991).

Drancy (*French* drɑ̃si) *n* a residential suburb of NE Paris. Pop.: 64 363 (1983 est.).

drank (dræŋk) *vb* the past tense of **drink.**

drap (dræp) *n, vb* a Scot. word for **drop.**

drape (dreɪp) *vb* **1** (*tr*) to hang or cover with flexible material or fabric, usually in folds; adorn. **2** to hang or arrange or be hung or arranged, esp. in folds. **3** (*tr*) to place casually and loosely; hang: *she draped her arm over the back of the chair.* ♦ *n* **4** (*often pl*) a cloth or hanging that covers something in folds; drapery. **5** the way in which fabric hangs. ♦ See also **drapes.** [C15: from Old French *draper,* from *drap* piece of cloth; see DRAB[1]] ► **'drapable** *or* **'drapeable** *adj*

draper ('dreɪpə) *n Brit.* a dealer in fabrics and sewing materials.

Draper ('dreɪpə) *n* **1 Henry.** 1837–82, U.S. astronomer, who contributed to stellar classification and spectroscopy. **2** his father, **John William.** 1811–82, U.S. chemist and historian, born in England, made the first photograph of the moon.

drapery ('dreɪpərɪ) *n, pl* **-peries. 1** fabric or clothing arranged and draped. **2** (*often pl*) curtains or hangings that drape. **3** *Brit.* the occupation or shop of a draper. **4** fabrics and cloth collectively. ► **'draperied** *adj*

drapes (dreɪps) *or* **draperies** ('dreɪpərɪz) *pl n Chiefly U.S. and Canadian.* curtains, esp. ones of heavy fabric.

drappie ('dræpɪ) *n Scot.* a little drop, esp. a small amount of spirits.

drastic ('dræstɪk) *adj* extreme or forceful; severe. [C17: from Greek *drastikos,* from *dran* to do, act] ► **'drastically** *adv*

drat (dræt) *interj Slang.* an exclamation of annoyance (also in the phrases **drat it! drat you!** etc.). [C19: probably alteration of *God rot*]

dratted ('drætɪd) *adj* (*prenominal*) *Informal.* wretched; annoying.

draught *or U.S.* **draft** (drɑːft) *n* **1** a current of air, esp. one intruding into an enclosed space. **2a** the act of pulling a load, as by a vehicle or animal. **2b** (*as modifier*): *a draught horse.* **3** the load or quantity drawn. **4** a portion of liquid to be drunk, esp. a dose of medicine. **5** the act or an instance of drinking; a gulp or swallow. **6** the act or process of drawing air, smoke, etc., into the lungs. **7** the amount of air, smoke, etc., inhaled in one breath. **8a** beer, wine, etc., stored in bulk, esp. in a cask, as opposed to being bottled. **8b** (*as modifier*): *draught beer.* **8c on draught.** drawn from a cask or keg. **9** Also called: **draughtsman.** any one of the 12 flat thick discs used by each player in the game of draughts. U.S. and Canadian equivalent: **checker. 10** the depth of a loaded vessel in the water, taken from the level of the waterline to the lowest point of the hull. **11 feel the draught.** to be short of money. ♦ See also **draughts.** [C14: probably from Old Norse *drahtr,* of Germanic origin; related to DRAW] ► **'draughter** *or U.S.* **'drafter** *n*

draughtboard ('drɑːftˌbɔːd) *n* a square board divided into 64 squares of alternating colours, used for playing draughts or chess.

draughts (drɑːfts) *n* (*functioning as sing*) a game for two players using a draughtboard and 12 draughtsmen each. The object is to jump over and capture the opponent's pieces. U.S. and Canadian name: **checkers.** [C14: plural of DRAUGHT (in obsolete sense: a chess move)]

draughtsman *or U.S.* **draftsman** ('drɑːftsmən) *n, pl* **-men. 1** Also called (*fem*): **'draughtsˌwoman.** a person who practises or is qualified in mechanical drawing, employed to prepare detailed scale drawings of machinery, buildings, devices, etc. **2** Also called (*fem*): **'draughtsˌwoman.** a person skilled in drawing. **3** *Brit.* any of the 12 flat thick discs used by each player in the game of draughts. U.S. and Canadian equivalent: **checker.** ► **'draughtsmanˌship** *or U.S.* **'draftsmanˌship** *n*

draughty *or U.S.* **drafty** ('drɑːftɪ) *adj* **draughtier, draughtiest** *or U.S.* **draftier, draftiest.** characterized by or exposed to draughts of air. ► **'draughtily** *or U.S.* **'draftily** *adv* ► **'draughtiness** *or U.S.* **'draftiness** *n*

Drava *or* **Drave** ('drɑːvə) *n* a river in S central Europe, rising in N Italy and flowing east through Austria, then southeast along the southern Hungarian border to join the River Danube. Length: 725 km (450 miles). German name: **Drau** (drau).

Dravidian (drə'vɪdɪən) *n* **1** a family of languages spoken in S and central India and Sri Lanka, including Tamil, Malayalam, Telugu, Kannada, and Gondi. **2** a member of one of the aboriginal races of India, pushed south by the Indo-Europeans and now mixed with them. ♦ *adj* **3** denoting, belonging to, or relating to this family of languages or these peoples.

draw (drɔː) *vb* **draws, drawing, drew, drawn. 1** to cause (a person or thing) to move towards or away by pulling. **2** to bring, take, or pull (something) out, as from a drawer, holster, etc. **3** (*tr*) to extract or pull or take out: *to draw teeth; to draw a card from a pack.* **4** (*tr;* often foll. by *off*) to take (liquid) out of a cask, keg, tank, etc., by means of a tap. **5** (*intr*) to move, go, or proceed, esp. in a specified direction: *to draw alongside.* **6** (*tr*) to attract or elicit: *to draw a crowd; draw attention.* **7** (*tr*) to cause to flow: *to draw blood.* **8** to depict or sketch (a form, figure, picture, etc.) in lines, as with a pencil or pen, esp. without the use of colour; delineate. **9** (*tr*) to make, formulate, or derive: *to draw conclusions, comparisons, parallels.* **10** (*tr*) to write (a legal document) in proper form. **11** (*tr;* sometimes foll. by *in*) to suck or take in (air, liquid, etc.): *to draw a breath.* **12** (*intr*) to induce or allow a draught to carry off air, smoke, etc.: *the flue draws well.* **13** (*tr*) to take or receive from a source: *to draw money from the bank.* **14** (*tr*) to earn: *draw interest.* **15** (*tr*) *Finance.* to write out (a bill of exchange or promissory note): *to draw a cheque.* **16** (*tr*) to choose at random: *to draw lots.* **17** (*tr*) to reduce the diameter of (a wire or metal rod) by pulling it through a die. **18** (*tr*) to shape (a sheet of metal or glass) by rolling, by pulling it through a die or by stretching. **19** *Archery.* to bend (a bow) by pulling the string. **20** to steep (tea) or (of tea) to steep in boiling water. **21** (*tr*) to disembowel: *draw a chicken.* **22** (*tr*) to cause (pus, blood, etc.) to discharge from an abscess or wound. **23** (*intr*) (of two teams, contestants, etc.) to finish a game with an equal number of points, goals, etc.; tie. **24** (*tr*) *Bridge, whist.* to keep leading a suit in order to force out (all outstanding cards). **25 draw trumps.** *Bridge, whist.* to play the trump suit until the opponents have none left. **26** (*tr*) *Billiards.* to cause (the cue ball) to spin back after a direct impact with another ball by applying backspin when making the stroke. **27** (*tr*) to search (a place) in order to find wild animals, game, etc., for hunting. **28** *Golf.* to cause (a golf ball) to move with a controlled right-to-left trajectory or (of a golf ball) to veer gradually from right to left. **29** (*tr*) *Curling.* to deliver (the stone) gently. **30** (*tr*) *Nautical.* (of a vessel) to require (a certain depth) in which to float. **31 draw (a) blank.** to get no results from something. **32 draw and quarter.** to disembowel and dismember (a person) after hanging. **33 draw stumps.** *Cricket.* to close play, as by pulling out the stumps. **34 draw the line (at).** See **line**[1] (sense 51). **35 draw the short straw.** See **short straw. 36 draw the shot.** *Bowls.* to deliver the bowl in such a way that it approaches the jack. ♦ *n* **37** the act of drawing. **38** *U.S.* a sum of money advanced to finance anticipated expenses. **39** an event, occasion, act, etc., that attracts a large audience. **40** a raffle or lottery. **41** something taken or chosen at random, as a ticket in a raffle or lottery. **42** a contest or game ending in a tie. **43** *U.S. and Canadian.* a small natural drainage way or gully. **44** a defect found in metal castings due to the contraction of the metal on solidification. ♦ See also **drawback, draw in, draw off, draw on, draw out, draw up.** [Old English *dragan;* related to Old Norse *draga;* Old Frisian *draga,* Old Saxon *dragan,* Old High German *tragan* to carry] ► **'drawable** *adj*

drawback ('drɔːˌbæk) *n* **1** a disadvantage or hindrance. **2** a refund of customs or excise duty paid on goods that are being exported or used in the production of manufactured exports. ♦ *vb* **draw back.** (*intr, adv;* often foll. by *from*) **3** to retreat; move backwards. **4** to turn aside from an undertaking.

drawbar ('drɔːˌbɑː) *n* a strong metal bar on a tractor, locomotive, etc., bearing a hook or link and pin to attach a trailer, wagon, etc.

drawbridge ('drɔːˌbrɪdʒ) *n* a bridge that may be raised to prevent access or to enable vessels to pass.

drawee (drɔːˈiː) *n* the person or organization on which a cheque or other order for payment is drawn.

drawer (ˈdrɔːə) *n* **1** a person or thing that draws, esp. a draughtsman. **2** a person who draws a cheque. See **draw** (sense 15). **3** a person who draws up a commercial paper. **4** *Archaic.* a person who draws beer, etc., in a bar. **5** (drɔː). a boxlike container in a chest, table, etc., made for sliding in and out.

drawers (drɔːz) *pl n* a legged undergarment for either sex, worn below the waist. Also called: **underdrawers.**

draw-gate *n* the valve that controls a sluice.

draw gear *n Brit.* an apparatus for coupling railway cars.

draw in *vb* (*intr, adv*) **1** (of hours of daylight) to become shorter. **2** (of a train) to arrive at a station.

drawing (ˈdrɔːɪŋ) *n* **1** a picture or plan made by means of lines on a surface, esp. one made with a pencil or pen without the use of colour. **2** a sketch, plan, or outline. **3** the art of making drawings; draughtsmanship.

drawing account *n U.S.* an account out of which an employee, partner, or salesman may make withdrawals to meet expenses or as advances against expected income.

drawing board *n* **1** a smooth flat rectangular board on which paper, canvas, etc., is placed for making drawings. **2 back to the drawing board.** return to an earlier stage in an enterprise because a planned undertaking has failed.

drawing card *n U.S. and Canadian theatre.* a performer, act, etc., certain to attract a large audience.

drawing pin *n Brit.* a short tack with a broad smooth head for fastening papers to a drawing board, etc. U.S. and Canadian name: **thumbtack.**

drawing room *n* **1** a room where visitors are received and entertained; living room; sitting room. **2** *Archaic.* a ceremonial or formal reception, esp. at court.

drawknife (ˈdrɔːˌnaɪf) *or* **drawshave** *n, pl* **-knives** *or* **-shaves.** a woodcutting tool with two handles at right angles to the blade, used to shave wood. U.S. name: **spokeshave.**

drawl (drɔːl) *vb* **1** to speak or utter (words) slowly, esp. prolonging the vowel sounds. ◆ *n* **2** the way of speech of someone who drawls. [C16: probably frequentative of DRAW] ▸ ˈ**drawler** *n* ▸ ˈ**drawling** *adj* ▸ ˈ**drawly** *adj*

drawn (drɔːn) *adj* haggard, tired, or tense in appearance.

drawn butter *n* melted butter often with seasonings.

drawn work *n* ornamental needlework done by drawing threads out of the fabric and using the remaining threads to form lacelike patterns. Also called: **drawn-thread work.**

draw off *vb* (*adv*) **1** (*tr*) to cause (a liquid) to flow from something. **2** to withdraw (troops).

draw on *vb* **1** (*intr, prep*) to use or exploit (a source, fund, etc.): *to draw on one's experience.* **2** (*intr, adv*) to come near: *the time for his interview drew on.* **3** (*tr, prep*) to withdraw (money) from (an account). **4** (*tr, adv*) to put on (clothes). **5** (*tr, adv*) to lead further; entice or encourage: *the prospect of nearing his goal drew him on.*

draw out *vb* (*adv*) **1** to extend or cause to be extended: *he drew out his stay.* **2** (*tr*) to cause (a person) to talk freely: *she's been quiet all evening —see if you can draw her out.* **3** (*tr;* foll. by *of*) Also: **draw from.** to elicit (information) (from): *he managed to draw out of his son where he had been.* **4** (*tr*) to withdraw (money) as from a bank account or a business. **5** (*intr*) (of hours of daylight) to become longer. **6** (*intr*) (of a train) to leave a station. **7** (*tr*) to extend (troops) in line; lead from camp. **8** (*intr*) (of troops) to proceed from camp.

drawplate (ˈdrɔːˌpleɪt) *n* a plate used to reduce the diameter of wire by drawing it through conical holes.

drawstring (ˈdrɔːˌstrɪŋ) *n* **a** a cord, ribbon, etc., run through a hem around an opening, as on the bottom of a sleeve or at the mouth of a bag, so that when it is pulled tighter, the opening closes. **b** (*as modifier*): *a drawstring neckline.*

drawtube (ˈdrɔːˌtjuːb) *n* a tube, such as one of the component tubes of a telescope, fitting coaxially within another tube through which it can slide.

draw up *vb* (*adv*) **1** to come or cause to come to a halt. **2** (*tr*) **2a** to prepare a draft of (a legal document). **2b** to formulate and write out in appropriate form: *to draw up a contract.* **3** (*used reflexively*) to straighten oneself. **4** to form or arrange (a body of soldiers, etc.) in order or formation.

dray[1] (dreɪ) *n* **1a** a low cart without fixed sides, used for carrying heavy loads. **1b** (*in combination*): *a drayman.* **2** any other vehicle or sledge used to carry a heavy load. [Old English *dræge* dragnet; related to Old Norse *draga* load of timber carried on horseback and trailing on the ground; see DRAW]

dray[2] (dreɪ) *n* a variant spelling of **drey.**

drayhorse (ˈdreɪˌhɔːs) *n* a large powerful horse used for drawing a dray.

Drayton (ˈdreɪtᵊn) *n* **Michael.** 1563–1631, English poet. His work includes odes and pastorals, and *Poly-Olbion* (1613–22), on the topography of England.

dread (drɛd) *vb* (*tr*) **1** to anticipate with apprehension or terror. **2** to fear greatly. **3** *Archaic.* to be in awe of. ◆ *n* **4** great fear; horror. **5** an object of terror. **6** *Slang.* a Rastafarian. **7** *Archaic.* deep reverence. ◆ *adj* **8** *Literary.* awesome; awe-inspiring. [Old English *ondrædan;* related to Old Saxon *antdrādan,* Old High German *intrātan*]

dreadful (ˈdrɛdfʊl) *adj* **1** extremely disagreeable, shocking, or bad: *what a dreadful play.* **2** (intensifier): *this is a dreadful waste of time.* **3** causing dread; terrifying. **4** *Archaic.* inspiring awe. ▸ ˈ**dreadfulness** *n*

dreadfully (ˈdrɛdfʊlɪ) *adv* **1** in a shocking, or disagreeable manner. **2** (intensifier): *you're dreadfully kind.*

dreadlocks (ˈdrɛdˌlɒks) *pl n* hair worn in the Rastafarian style of long matted or tightly curled strands.

dreadnought *or* **dreadnaught** (ˈdrɛdˌnɔːt) *n* **1** a battleship armed with heavy guns of uniform calibre. **2** an overcoat made of heavy cloth. **3** *Slang.* a heavyweight boxer. **4** a person who fears nothing.

dream (driːm) *n* **1a** mental activity, usually in the form of an imagined series of events, occurring during certain phases of sleep. **1b** (*as modifier*): *a dream sequence.* **1c** (*in combination*): *dreamland.* Related adj: **oneiric. 2a** a sequence of imaginative thoughts indulged in while awake; daydream; fantasy. **2b** (*as modifier*): *a dream world.* **3** a person or thing seen or occurring in a dream. **4** a cherished hope; ambition; aspiration. **5** a vain hope. **6** a person or thing that is as pleasant, or seemingly unreal as a dream. **7 go like a dream.** to move, develop, or work very well. ◆ *vb* **dreams, dreaming, dreamed** *or* **dreamt** (drɛmt). **8** (*may take a clause as object*) to undergo or experience (a dream or dreams). **9** (*intr*) to indulge in daydreams. **10** (*intr*) to suffer delusions; be unrealistic: *you're dreaming if you think you can win.* **11** (when *intr,* foll. by *of* or *about*) to have an image (of) or fantasy (about) in or as if in a dream. **12** (*intr;* foll. by *of*) to consider the possibility (of): *I wouldn't dream of troubling you.* ◆ See also **dream up.** ◆ *adj* **13** too good to be true; ideal: *dream kitchen.* [Old English *drēam* song; related to Old High German *troum,* Old Norse *draumr,* Greek *thrulos* noise] ▸ ˈ**dreamful** *adj* ▸ ˈ**dreamfully** *adv* ▸ ˈ**dreaming** *n, adj* ▸ ˈ**dreamingly** *adv* ▸ ˈ**dreamless** *adj* ▸ ˈ**dreamlessly** *adv* ▸ ˈ**dreamlessness** *n* ▸ ˈ**dreamˌlike** *adj*

dreamboat (ˈdriːmˌbəʊt) *n Old-fashioned slang.* an exceptionally attractive person or thing, esp. a person of the opposite sex.

dreamer (ˈdriːmə) *n* **1** a person who dreams habitually. **2** a person who lives in or escapes to a world of fantasy or illusion; escapist. **3** *Archaic.* a prophet; visionary.

dreamland (ˈdriːmlænd) *n* an ideal land existing in dreams or in the imagination.

dreamt (drɛmt) *vb* a past tense and past participle of **dream.**

dream ticket *n* a combination of two people, usu. candidates in an election, that is considered to be ideal.

Dreamtime *n* **1** (in the mythology of Australian Aboriginal peoples) a mythical Golden Age of the past. Also called: **alchera** (ˈæltʃərə), **alcheringa. 2** *Austral. informal.* any remote period, out of touch with the actualities of the present.

dream up *vb* (*tr, adv*) to invent by ingenuity and imagination: *to dream up an excuse for leaving.*

dreamy (ˈdriːmɪ) *adj* **dreamier, dreamiest. 1** vague or impractical. **2** resembling a dream in quality. **3** relaxing; gentle: *dreamy music.* **4** *Informal.* wonderful. **5** having dreams, esp. daydreams. ▸ ˈ**dreamily** *adv* ▸ ˈ**dreaminess** *n*

dreary (ˈdrɪərɪ) *adj* **drearier, dreariest. 1** sad or dull; dismal. **2** wearying; boring. **3** *Archaic.* miserable. ◆ Also (literary): **drear.** [Old English *drēorig* gory; related to Old High German *trūreg* sad] ▸ ˈ**drearily** *adv* ▸ ˈ**dreariness** *n*

dreck (drɛk) *n Slang, chiefly U.S.* rubbish; trash. [from Yiddish *drek* filth, dregs] ▸ ˈ**drecky** *adj*

dredge[1] (drɛdʒ) *n* **1** Also called: **dredger.** a machine, in the form of a bucket ladder, grab, or suction device, used to remove material from a riverbed, channel, etc. **2** another name for **dredger**[1] (sense 1). ◆ *vb* **3** to remove (material) from a riverbed, channel, etc., by means of a dredge. **4** (*tr*) to search for (a submerged object) with or as if with a dredge; drag. [C16: perhaps ultimately from Old English *dragan* to DRAW; see DRAG]

dredge[2] (drɛdʒ) *vb* to sprinkle or coat (food) with flour, sugar, etc. [C16: from Old French *dragie,* perhaps from Latin *tragēmata* spices, from Greek]

dredger[1] (ˈdrɛdʒə) *n* **1** Also called: **dredge.** a vessel used for dredging, often bargelike and usually equipped with retractable steel piles that are driven into the bottom for stability. **2** another name for **dredge**[1] (sense 1).

dredger[2] (ˈdrɛdʒə) *n* a container with a perforated top for sprinkling flour, sugar, etc.

dredge up *vb* (*tr, adv*) **1** to bring to notice, esp. with considerable effort and from an obscure, remote, or unlikely source: *to dredge up worthless ideas.* **2** to raise with or as if with a dredge: *they dredged up the corpse from the lake.*

dree (driː) *Scot., literary.* ◆ *vb* **drees, dreeing, dreed. 1** (*tr*) to endure. **2 dree one's weird.** to endure one's fate. ◆ *adj* **3** another word for **dreich.** [Old English *drēogan;* related to Old Norse *drȳgja* to perpetrate]

dreg (drɛg) *n* a small quantity: *not a dreg of pity.* See also **dregs.** [see DREGS]

dreggy (ˈdrɛgɪ) *adj* **-gier, -giest.** like or full of dregs.

D region *or* **layer** *n* the lowest region of the ionosphere, extending from a height of about 60 kilometres to about 90 kilometres: contains a low concentration of free electrons and reflects low-frequency radio waves. See also **ionosphere.**

dregs (drɛgz) *pl n* **1** solid particles that tend to settle at the bottom of some liquids, such as wine or coffee. **2** residue or remains. **3** *Brit. slang.* a despicable person. [C14 *dreg,* from Old Norse *dregg;* compare Icelandic *dreggjar* dregs, Latin *fracēs* oil dregs]

Dreibund *German.* (ˈdraibunt) *n* a triple alliance, esp. that formed between Germany, Austria-Hungary, and Italy (1882–1915). [from *drei* THREE + *Bund* union, alliance]

dreich *or* **dreigh** (driːx) *adj Scot. dialect.* dreary. [Middle English *dreig, drih* enduring, from Old English *drēog* (unattested); see DREE]

dreikanter (ˈdraɪkæntə) *n* a pebble, common in desert areas, typically having three curved faces shaped by wind-blown sand. [C20: from German: three-edged thing]

Dreiser (ˈdraɪsə, -zə) *n* **Theodore** (**Herman Albert**). 1871–1945, U.S. novelist; his works include *Sister Carrie* (1900) and *An American Tragedy* (1925).

drench (drɛntʃ) *vb* (*tr*) **1** to make completely wet; soak. **2** to give liquid medicine to (an animal), esp. by force. ◆ *n* **3** the act or an instance of drenching. **4** a dose of liquid medicine given to an animal. [Old English *drencan* to cause to drink; related to Old High German *trenken*] ▸ ˈ**drencher** *n* ▸ ˈ**drenching** *n, adj*

Drenthe (*Dutch* ˈdrɛntə) *n* a province of the NE Netherlands: a low plateau, with many raised bogs, partially reclaimed; agricultural, with oil deposits. Capital: Assen. Pop.: 457 300 (1996 est.). Area: 2647 sq. km (1032 sq. miles).

drepanid ('drɛpənɪd) *n* any moth of the superfamily *Drepanoidae* (family *Drepanidae*): it comprises the hook-tip moths.

Dresden ('drɛzdᵊn) *n* **1** an industrial city in SE Germany, the capital of Saxony on the River Elbe: it was severely damaged in the Seven Years' War (1760); the baroque city was almost totally destroyed in World War II by Allied bombing (1945). Pop.: 469 110 (1996 est.). ◆ *adj* **2** relating to, designating, or made of Dresden china.

Dresden china *n* porcelain ware, esp. delicate and elegantly decorative objects and figures of high quality, made at Meissen, near Dresden, since 1710.

dress (drɛs) *vb* **1** to put clothes on (oneself or another); attire. **2** (*intr*) **2a** to change one's clothes. **2b** to wear formal or evening clothes. **3** (*tr*) to provide (someone) with clothing; clothe. **4** (*tr*) to arrange merchandise in (a shop window) for effective display. **5** (*tr*) to comb out or arrange (the hair) into position. **6** (*tr*) to apply protective or therapeutic covering to (a wound, sore, etc.). **7** (*tr*) to prepare (food, esp. fowl and fish) for cooking or serving by cleaning, trimming, gutting, etc. **8** (*tr*) to put a finish on (the surface of stone, metal, etc.). **9** (*tr*) to till and cultivate (land), esp. by applying manure, compost, or fertilizer. **10** (*tr*) to prune and trim (trees, bushes, etc.). **11** (*tr*) to groom (an animal, esp. a horse). **12** (*tr*) to convert (tanned hides) into leather. **13** (*tr*) to spay or neuter (an animal). **14** *Angling.* to tie (a fly). **15** *Military.* to bring (troops) into line or (of troops) to come into line (esp. in the phrase **dress ranks**). **16 dress ship.** *Nautical.* to decorate a vessel by displaying all signal flags on lines run from the bow to the stern over the mast trucks. ◆ *n* **17** a one-piece garment for a woman, consisting of a skirt and bodice. **18** complete style of clothing; costume: *formal dress; military dress.* **19** (*modifier*) suitable or required for a formal occasion: *a dress shirt.* **20** the outer covering or appearance, esp. of living things: *trees in their spring dress of leaves.* ◆ See also **dress down, dress up.** [C14: from Old French *drecier,* ultimately from Latin *dīrigere* to DIRECT]

dressage ('drɛsɑːʒ) *n* **1** the method of training a horse to perform manoeuvres in response to the rider's body signals. **2** the manoeuvres performed by a horse trained in this method. [French: preparation, from Old French *dresser* to prepare; see DRESS]

dress circle *n* a tier of seats in a theatre or other auditorium, usually the first gallery above the ground floor.

dress coat *n* a man's formal tailcoat with a cutaway skirt.

dress code *n* a set of rules or guidelines regarding the manner of dress acceptable in an office, restaurant, etc.

dress down *vb* (*tr, adv*) *Informal.* to reprimand severely or scold (a person).

dresser[1] ('drɛsə) *n* **1** a set of shelves, usually also with cupboards or drawers, for storing or displaying dishes, etc. **2** *U.S.* a chest of drawers for storing clothing in a bedroom or dressing room, often having a mirror on the top. [C14 *dressour,* from Old French *dreceore,* from *drecier* to arrange; see DRESS]

dresser[2] ('drɛsə) *n* **1** a person who dresses in a specified way: *a fashionable dresser.* **2** *Theatre.* a person employed to assist actors in putting on and taking off their costumes. **3** a tool used for dressing stone or other materials. **4** *Brit.* a person who assists a surgeon during operations. **5** *Brit.* See **window-dresser.**

dress form *n* an adjustable dummy used in dressmaking that can be made to conform to a person's figure.

dressing ('drɛsɪŋ) *n* **1** a sauce for food, esp. for salad. **2** the U.S. and Canadian name for **stuffing** (sense 2). **3** a covering for a wound, sore, etc. **4** manure or artificial fertilizer spread on land. **5** size used for stiffening textiles. **6** the processes in the conversion of certain rough tanned hides into leather ready for use. ◆ See also **dressings.**

dressing case *n* (esp. formerly) a box or case fitted with all the toilet articles necessary for dressing oneself, arranging one's hair, etc.

dressing-down *n Informal.* a severe scolding or thrashing.

dressing gown *n* a full robe worn before dressing or for lounging.

dressing room *n* **1** *Theatre.* a room backstage for an actor to change clothing and to make up. **2** any room used for changing clothes, such as one at a sports ground or off a bedroom.

dressings ('drɛsɪŋz) *pl n* dressed stonework, mouldings, and carved ornaments used to form quoins, keystones, sills, and similar features.

dressing station *n Military.* a first-aid post close to a combat area.

dressing table *n* a piece of bedroom furniture with a mirror and a set of drawers for clothes, cosmetics, etc.

dressmaker ('drɛsˌmeɪkə) *n* a person whose occupation is making clothes, esp. for women. ▸ **'dressˌmaking** *n*

dress parade *n Military.* a formal parade of sufficient ceremonial importance for the wearing of dress uniform.

dress rehearsal *n* **1** the last complete rehearsal of a play or other work, using costumes, scenery, lighting, etc., as for the first night. **2** any full-scale practice.

dress shield *n* a fabric pad worn under the armpits or attached to the armhole of a garment to prevent sweat from showing on or staining the clothing.

dress shirt *n* a man's shirt, usually white, worn as part of formal evening dress, usually having a stiffened or decorative front.

dress suit *n* a man's evening suit, esp. tails.

dress uniform *n Military.* formal ceremonial uniform.

dress up *vb* (*adv*) **1** to attire (oneself or another) in one's best clothes. **2** to put fancy dress, disguise, etc., on (oneself or another), as in children's games: *let's dress up as ghosts!* **3** (*tr*) to improve the appearance or impression of: *it's no good trying to dress up the facts.*

dressy ('drɛsɪ) *adj* **dressier, dressiest. 1** (of clothes) elegant. **2** (of persons) dressing stylishly. **3** over-elegant. ▸ **'dressily** *adv* ▸ **'dressiness** *n*

drew (druː) *vb* the past tense of **draw.**

drey *or* **dray** (dreɪ) *n* a squirrel's nest. [C17: of unknown origin]

Dreyfus ('dreɪfəs; *French* drɛfys) *n* **Alfred** (alfrɛd). 1859–1935, French army officer, a Jew whose false imprisonment for treason (1894) raised issues of anti-semitism and militarism that dominated French politics until his release (1906).

dribble ('drɪbᵊl) *vb* **1** (*usually intr*) to flow or allow to flow in a thin stream or drops; trickle. **2** (*intr*) to allow saliva to trickle from the mouth. **3** (in soccer, basketball, hockey, etc.) to propel (the ball) by repeatedly tapping it with the hand, foot, or stick. ◆ *n* **4** a small quantity of liquid falling in drops or flowing in a thin stream. **5** a small quantity or supply. **6** an act or instance of dribbling. [C16: frequentative of *drib,* variant of DRIP] ▸ **'dribbler** *n* ▸ **'dribbly** *adj*

driblet *or* **dribblet** ('drɪblɪt) *n* a small quantity or amount, as of liquid. [C17: from obsolete *drib* to fall bit by bit + -LET]

dribs and drabs (drɪbz) *pl n* small sporadic amounts.

dried (draɪd) *vb* the past tense and past participle of **dry.**

drier[1] ('draɪə) *adj* a comparative of **dry.**

drier[2] ('draɪə) *n* a variant spelling of **dryer**[1].

Driesch (*German* driːʃ) *n* **Hans Adolf Eduard** (hans 'aːdɔlf 'ɛduaːd). 1867–1941, German zoologist and embryologist.

driest ('draɪɪst) *adj* a superlative of **dry.**

drift (drɪft) *vb* (*mainly intr*) **1** (*also tr*) to be carried along by or as if by currents of air or water or (of a current) to carry (a vessel, etc.) along. **2** to move aimlessly from place to place or from one activity to another. **3** to wander or move gradually away from a fixed course or point; stray. **4** (*also tr*) (of snow, sand, etc.) to accumulate in heaps or banks or to drive (snow, sand, etc.) into heaps or banks. ◆ *n* **5** something piled up by the wind or current, such as a snowdrift. **6** tendency, trend, meaning, or purport: *the drift of the argument.* **7** a state of indecision or inaction. **8** the extent to which a vessel, aircraft, projectile, etc. is driven off its course by adverse winds, tide, or current. **9** a general tendency of surface ocean water to flow in the direction of the prevailing winds: *North Atlantic Drift.* **10** a driving movement, force, or influence; impulse. **11** a controlled four-wheel skid, used by racing drivers to take bends at high speed. **12** a loose unstratified deposit of sand, gravel, etc., esp. one transported and deposited by a glacier or ice sheet. **13** a horizontal passage in a mine that follows the mineral vein. **14** something, esp. a group of animals, driven along by human or natural agencies: *a drift of cattle.* **15** Also called: **driftpin.** a tapering steel tool driven into holes to enlarge or align them before bolting or riveting. **16** an uncontrolled slow change in some operating characteristic of a piece of equipment, esp. an electronic circuit or component. **17** *Linguistics.* gradual change in a language, esp. in so far as this is influenced by the internal structure of the language rather than by contact with other languages. **18** *S. African.* a ford. **19** *Engineering.* a copper or brass bar used as a punch. [C13: from Old Norse: snowdrift; related to Old High German *trift* pasturage] ▸ **'drifty** *adj*

driftage ('drɪftɪdʒ) *n* **1** the act of drifting. **2** matter carried along or deposited by drifting. **3** the amount by which an aircraft or vessel has drifted from its intended course.

drift anchor *n* another term for **sea anchor.**

drifter ('drɪftə) *n* **1** a person or thing that drifts. **2** a person who moves aimlessly from place to place, usually without a regular job. **3** a boat used for drift-net fishing. **4** *Nautical.* a large jib of thin material used in light breezes.

drift ice *n* masses of ice floating in the open sea.

drift net *n* a large fishing net supported by floats or attached to a drifter that is allowed to drift with the tide or current.

drift transistor *n* a transistor in which the impurity concentration in the base increases from the collector-base junction to the emitter-base junction, producing a resistivity gradient that greatly increases its high-frequency response.

drift tube *n Physics.* a hollow cylindrical electrode to which a radio-frequency voltage is applied in a linear accelerator.

driftwood ('drɪftˌwʊd) *n* wood floating on or washed ashore by the sea or other body of water.

drill[1] (drɪl) *n* **1** a rotating tool that is inserted into a drilling machine or tool for boring cylindrical holes. **2** a hand tool, either manually or electrically operated, for drilling holes. **3** *Military.* **3a** training in procedures or movements, as for ceremonial parades or the use of weapons. **3b** (*as modifier*): *drill hall.* **4** strict and often repetitious training or exercises used as a method of teaching. **5** *Informal.* correct procedure or routine. **6** a marine gastropod mollusc, *Urosalpinx cinera,* closely related to the whelk, that preys on oysters. ◆ *vb* **7** to pierce, bore, or cut (a hole) in (material) with or as if with a drill: *to drill a hole; to drill metal.* **8** to instruct or be instructed in military procedures or movements. **9** (*tr*) to teach by rigorous exercises or training. **10** (*tr*) *Informal.* to hit (a ball) in a straight line at great speed. **11** (*tr*) *Informal.* to riddle with bullets. [C17: from Middle Dutch *drillen;* related to Old High German *drāen* to turn] ▸ **'drillable** *adj* ▸ **'driller** *n*

drill[2] (drɪl) *n* **1** a machine for planting seeds in rows or depositing fertilizer. **2** a small furrow in which seeds are sown. **3** a row of seeds planted using a drill. ◆ *vb* **4** to plant (seeds) by means of a drill. [C18: of uncertain origin; compare German *Rille* furrow] ▸ **'driller** *n*

drill[3] (drɪl) *or* **drilling** *n* a hard-wearing twill-weave cotton cloth, used for uniforms, etc. [C18: variant of German *Drillich,* from Latin *trilīx,* from TRI- + *līcium* thread]

drill[4] (drɪl) *n* an Old World monkey, *Mandrillus leucophaeus,* of W Africa, related to the mandrill but smaller and less brightly coloured. [C17: from a West African word; compare MANDRILL]

drilling mud *n* a mixture of clays, water, and chemicals pumped down the drill string while an oil well is being drilled to lubricate the mechanism, carry away rock cuttings, and maintain pressure so that oil or gas does not escape.

drilling platform *n* a structure, either fixed to the sea bed or mobile, which supports the machinery and equipment (**drilling rig**), together with the stores, required for digging an offshore oil well.

drilling rig *n* **1** the full name for **rig** (sense 6). **2** a mobile drilling platform used for exploratory offshore drilling.

drillmaster ('drɪl,mɑːstə) *n* **1** Also called: **drill sergeant.** a military drill instructor. **2** a person who instructs in a strict manner.

drill press *n* a machine tool for boring holes, having a stand and work table with facilities for lowering the tool to the workpiece.

drillstock ('drɪl,stɒk) *n* the part of a machine tool that holds the shank of a drill or bit; chuck.

drill string *or* **pipe** *n* (in the oil industry) a pipe made of lengths of steel tubing that is attached to the drilling tool and rotates during drilling to form a bore.

drily *or* **dryly** ('draɪlɪ) *adv* in a dry manner.

Drin (drɪn) *n* a river in S Europe, rising in SW Macedonia and flowing north and west, through Albania, into the Adriatic Sea. Length: about 270 km (170 miles).

drink (drɪŋk) *vb* **drinks, drinking, drank** (dræŋk), **drunk** (drʌŋk). **1** to swallow (a liquid); imbibe. **2** (*tr*) to take in or soak up (liquid); absorb: *this plant drinks a lot of water.* **3** (*tr;* usually foll. by *in*) to pay close attention (to); be fascinated (by): *he drank in the speaker's every word.* **4** (*tr*) to bring (oneself into a certain condition) by consuming alcohol. **5** (*tr;* often foll. by *away*) to dispose of or ruin by excessive expenditure on alcohol: *he drank away his fortune.* **6** (*intr*) to consume alcohol, esp. to excess. **7** (when *intr,* foll. by *to*) to drink (a toast) in celebration, honour, or hope (of). **8 drink (someone) under the table.** to be able to drink more intoxicating beverage than (someone). **9 drink the health of.** to salute or celebrate with a toast. **10 drink with the flies.** *Austral. informal.* to drink alone. ◆ *n* **11** liquid suitable for drinking; any beverage. **12** alcohol or its habitual or excessive consumption. **13** a portion of liquid for drinking; draught. **14 the drink.** *Informal.* the sea. [Old English *drincan;* related to Old Frisian *drinka,* Gothic *drigkan,* Old High German *trinkan*] ▸ **'drinkable** *adj*

drink-driving *n* (*modifier*) of or relating to driving a car after drinking alcohol: *drink-driving offences; drink-driving campaign.*

drinker ('drɪŋkə) *n* **1** a person who drinks, esp. a person who drinks alcohol habitually. **2** short for **drinker moth.**

drinker moth *n* a large yellowish-brown bombycid eggar moth, *Philudoria potatoria,* having a stout hairy body, the larvae of which drink dew and feed on grasses. Also called: **drinker.**

drinking fountain *n* a device for providing a flow or jet of drinking water, usually in public places.

drinking-up time *n* (in Britain) a short time allowed for finishing drinks before closing time in a public house.

drinking water *n* water reserved or suitable for drinking.

Drinkwater ('drɪŋk,wɔːtə) *n* **John.** 1882–1937, English dramatist, poet, and critic; author of chronicle plays such as *Abraham Lincoln* (1918) and *Mary Stuart* (1921).

drip (drɪp) *vb* **drips, dripping, dripped. 1** to fall or let fall in drops. ◆ *n* **2** the formation and falling of drops of liquid. **3** the sound made by falling drops. **4** *Architect.* a projection at the front lower edge of a sill or cornice designed to throw water clear of the wall below. **5** *Informal.* an inane, insipid person. **6** *Med.* **6a** the usually intravenous drop-by-drop administration of a therapeutic solution, as of salt or sugar. **6b** the solution administered. [Old English *dryppan,* from *dropa* DROP]

drip-dry *adj* **1** designating clothing or a fabric that will dry relatively free of creases if hung up when wet. ◆ *vb* **-dries, -drying, -dried. 2** to dry or become dry thus.

drip-feed *n* **1** another name for **drip** (sense 6). ◆ *vb* (*tr*) **drip feed. 2** to administer a solution (to someone) by means of a drip-feed. **3** *Informal.* to fund (a new company) in stages rather than by injecting a large sum at its inception.

dripping ('drɪpɪŋ) *n* **1** the fat exuded by roasting meat. **2** (*often pl*) liquid that falls in drops. ◆ *adv* **3** (intensifier): *dripping wet.*

dripping pan *or* **drip pan** *n* a shallow pan placed under roasting meat to catch the dripping.

drippy ('drɪpɪ) *adj* **-pier, -piest. 1** *Informal.* mawkish, insipid, or inane. **2** tending to drip.

dripstone ('drɪp,stəʊn) *n* **1** the form of calcium carbonate existing in stalactites or stalagmites. **2** Also called: **label, hood mould.** *Architect.* a drip made of stone.

drisheen (drɪ'ʃiːn) *n Irish.* a pudding made of sheep's intestines filled with meal and sheep's blood. [C20: from Irish Gaelic *drisín* an animal's intestines]

drive (draɪv) *vb* **drives, driving, drove** (drəʊv), **driven** ('drɪvᵊn). **1** to push, propel, or be pushed or propelled. **2** to control and guide the movement of (a vehicle, draught animal, etc.): *to drive a car.* **3** (*tr*) to compel or urge to work or act, esp. excessively. **4** (*tr*) to goad or force into a specified attitude or state: *work drove him to despair.* **5** (*tr*) to cause (an object) to make or form (a hole, crack, etc.): *his blow drove a hole in the wall.* **6** to move or cause to move rapidly by striking or throwing with force. **7** *Sport.* to hit (a ball) very hard and straight, as (in cricket) with the bat swinging more or less vertically. **8** *Golf.* to strike (the ball) with a driver, as in teeing off. **9** (*tr*) **9a** to chase (game) from cover into more open ground. **9b** to search (an area) for game. **10** to transport or be transported in a driven vehicle. **11** (*intr*) to rush or dash violently, esp. against an obstacle or solid object: *the waves drove against the rock.* **12** (*tr*) to carry through or transact with vigour (esp. in the phrase **drive a hard bargain**). **13** (*tr*) to force (a component) into or out of its location by means of blows or a press. **14** (*tr*) *Mining.* to excavate horizontally. **15** (*tr*) *N.Z.* to fell (a tree or trees) by the impact of another felled tree. **16 drive home. 16a** to cause to penetrate to the fullest extent. **16b** to make clear by special emphasis. ◆ *n* **17** the act of driving. **18** a trip or journey in a driven vehicle. **19a** a road for vehicles, esp. a private road leading to a house. **19b** (*cap. when part of a street name*): *Woodland Drive.* **20** vigorous or urgent pressure, as in business. **21** a united effort, esp. directed towards a common goal: *a charity drive.* **22** *Brit.* a large gathering of persons to play cards, etc. See **beetle drive, whist drive. 23** energy, ambition, or initiative. **24** *Psychol.* a motive or interest, such as sex, hunger, or ambition, that actuates an organism to attain a goal. **25** a sustained and powerful military offensive. **26a** the means by which force, torque, motion, or power is transmitted in a mechanism: *fluid drive.* **26b** (*as modifier*): *a drive shaft.* **27** *Sport.* a hard straight shot or stroke. **28** a search for and chasing of game towards waiting guns. **29** *Electronics.* the signal applied to the input of an amplifier. [Old English *drīfan;* related to Old Frisian *drīva,* Old Norse *drífa,* Gothic *dreiban,* Old High German *trīban*] ▸ **'drivable** *or* **'driveable** *adj* ▸ **,driva'bility** *or* **,drivea'bility** *n*

drive at *vb* (*intr, prep*) *Informal.* to intend or mean: *what are you driving at?*

drive-by shooting *n* an incident in which a person, building, or vehicle is shot at by someone in a moving vehicle. Sometimes shortened to **drive-by.**

drive-in *n Chiefly U.S. and Canadian.* **a** a cinema designed to be used by patrons seated in their cars. **b** (*modifier*) a public facility or service designed for use in such a manner: *a drive-in restaurant; a drive-in bank.*

drivel ('drɪvᵊl) *vb* **-els, -elling, -elled** *or U.S.* **-els, -eling, -eled. 1** to allow (saliva) to flow from the mouth; dribble. **2** (*intr*) to speak foolishly or childishly. ◆ *n* **3** foolish or senseless talk. **4** saliva flowing from the mouth; slaver. [Old English *dreflian* to slaver; see DRAFF] ▸ **'driveller** *n*

driven ('drɪvᵊn) *vb* the past participle of **drive.**

driver ('draɪvə) *n* **1** a person who drives a vehicle. **2 in the driver's seat.** in a position of control. **3** a person who drives animals. **4** a mechanical component that exerts a force on another to produce motion. **5** *Golf.* a club, a No. 1 wood, with a large head and deep face for tee shots. **6** *Electronics.* a circuit whose output provides the input of another circuit. **7** *Computing.* a computer program that controls a device. ▸ **'driverless** *adj*

driver ant *n* any of various tropical African predatory ants of the subfamily *Dorylinae,* which live in temporary nests and travel in vast hordes preying on other animals. See also **army ant.**

drive shaft *n* another name for **propeller shaft.**

drive-thru *n* **a** a takeaway restaurant, bank, etc. designed so that customers can use it without leaving their cars. **b** (*as modifier*): *a drive-thru restaurant.*

drive-time *n* **a** the time of day when many people are driving to or from work, regarded as a broadcasting slot. **b** (*as modifier*): *the daily drive-time show.*

driveway ('draɪv,weɪ) *n* a private road for vehicles, often connecting a house or garage with a public road; drive.

driving ('draɪvɪŋ) *adj* **1** having or moving with force and violence: *driving rain.* **2** forceful or energetic. **3** relating to the controlling of a motor vehicle in motion: *driving test.*

driving chain *n Engineering.* a roller chain that transmits power from one toothed wheel to another. Also called: **drive chain.**

driving licence *n* an official document or certificate authorizing a person to drive a motor vehicle.

driving wheel *n* **1** a wheel, esp. a gear wheel, that causes other wheels to rotate. **2** any wheel of a vehicle that transforms torque into a tractive force.

drizzle ('drɪzᵊl) *n* **1** very light rain, specifically consisting of droplets less than 0.5 mm in diameter. ◆ *vb* **2** (*intr*) to rain lightly. **3** (*tr*) to moisten with tiny droplets. [Old English *drēosan* to fall; related to Old Saxon *driosan,* Gothic *driusan,* Norwegian *drjōsa*] ▸ **'drizzly** *adj*

Drobny ('drɒbnɪ; *Czech* 'drɔbniː) *n* **Jaroslav** ('jærəʊ,slɑːv; *Czech* 'jaroslaf). born 1921, British tennis and ice-hockey player, born in Czechoslovakia: Wimbledon champion 1954: a member of the Czech ice-hockey team in the 1948 Olympic Games.

Drogheda ('drɔɪɪdə) *n* a port in NE Republic of Ireland, in Co. Louth near the mouth of the River Boyne: captured by Cromwell in 1649 and its inhabitants massacred. Pop.: 23 800 (1991).

drogue (drəʊg) *n* **1** any funnel-like device, esp. one of canvas, used as a sea anchor. **2a** a small parachute released behind a jet aircraft to reduce its landing speed. **2b** a small parachute released before a heavier main parachute during the landing of a spacecraft. **3** a device towed behind an aircraft as a target for firing practice. **4** a funnel-shaped device on the end of the refuelling hose of a tanker aircraft, to assist stability and the location of the probe of the receiving aircraft. **5** another name for **windsock.** [C18: probably based ultimately on Old English *dragan* to DRAW]

droit (drɔɪt; *French* drwa) *n, pl* **droits** (drɔɪts; *French* drwa). a legal or moral right or claim; due. [C15: from French: legal right, from Medieval Latin *dīrēctum* law, from Latin: a straight line; see DIRECT]

droit du seigneur (*French* drwa dy sɛɲœr) *n* in feudal times, the right of a lord to have sexual intercourse with a vassal's bride on her wedding night. [from French, literally: the right of the lord]

droll (drəʊl) *adj* amusing in a quaint or odd manner; comical. [C17: from French *drôle* scamp, from Middle Dutch: imp] ▸ **'drollness** *n* ▸ **'drolly** *adv*

drollery ('drəʊlərɪ) *n, pl* **-eries. 1** humour; comedy. **2** *Rare.* a droll act, story, or remark.

Drôme (*French* drom) *n* a department of SE France, in Rhône-Alpes region. Capital: Valence. Pop.: 426 800 (1995). Area: 6561 sq. km (2559 sq. miles).

-drome *n combining form.* **1** a course, racecourse: *hippodrome.* **2** a large place for a special purpose: *aerodrome.* [via Latin from Greek *dromos* race, course]

dromedary ('drʌmədərɪ, -drɪ, 'drɒm-) *n, pl* **-daries. 1** a type of Arabian camel bred for racing and riding, having a single hump and long slender legs. **2** another name for **Arabian camel.** [C14: from Late Latin *dromedārius* (*camēlus*), from Greek *dromas* running]

dromond ('drɒmənd, 'drʌm-) *or* **dromon** ('drɒmən, 'drʌm-) *n* a large swift sailing vessel of the 12th to 15th centuries. [C13: from Anglo-French *dromund,* ultimately from Late Greek *dromōn* light swift ship, from *dromos* a running]

-dromous *adj combining form.* moving or running: *anadromous; catadromous.* [via New Latin from Greek *-dromos,* from *dromos* a running]

drone[1] (drəʊn) *n* **1** a male bee in a colony of social bees, whose sole function is to mate with the queen. **2** *Brit.* a person who lives off the work of others. **3** a pilotless radio-controlled aircraft. [Old English *drān;* related to Old High German *treno* drone, Gothic *drunjus* noise, Greek *tenthrēnē* wasp; see DRONE[2]] ▸ **'dronish** *adj*

drone[2] (drəun) *vb* **1** (*intr*) to make a monotonous low dull sound; buzz or hum. **2** (when *intr,* often foll. by *on*) to utter (words) in a monotonous tone, esp. to talk without stopping. ◆ *n* **3** a monotonous low dull sound. **4** *Music.* **4a** a sustained bass note or chord of unvarying pitch accompanying a melody. **4b** (*as modifier*): *a drone bass.* **5** *Music.* one of the single-reed pipes in a set of bagpipes, used for accompanying the melody played on the chanter. **6** a person who speaks in a low monotonous tone. [C16: related to DRONE[1] and Middle Dutch *drōnen,* German *dröhnen*] ▸ **'droning** *adj* ▸ **'droningly** *adv*

drongo ('drɒŋgəu) *n, pl* **-gos. 1** Also called: **drongo shrike.** any insectivorous songbird of the family *Dicruridae,* of the Old World tropics, having a glossy black plumage, a forked tail, and a stout bill. **2** *Austral. and N.Z. slang.* a slow-witted person. [C19: from Malagasy]

droob (druːb) *n Austral. archaic slang.* a pathetic person. [C20: of unknown origin]

drook (drʊk) *vb* (*tr*) *Scot.* a variant spelling of **drouk.**

drookit ('drʊkɪt) *adj Scot.* a variant spelling of **droukit.**

drool (druːl) *vb* **1** (*intr;* often foll. by *over*) to show excessive enthusiasm (for) or pleasure (in); gloat (over). ◆ *vb, n* **2** another word for **drivel** (senses 1, 2, 4). [C19: probably alteration of DRIVEL]

droop (druːp) *vb* **1** to sag or allow to sag, as from weakness or exhaustion; hang down; sink. **2** (*intr*) to be overcome by weariness; languish; flag. **3** (*intr*) to lose courage; become dejected. ◆ *n* **4** the act or state of drooping. [C13: from Old Norse *drūpa;* see DROP] ▸ **'drooping** *adj* ▸ **'droopingly** *adv*

droopy ('druːpɪ) *adj* hanging or sagging downwards: *a droopy moustache* ▸ **'droopily** *adv* ▸ **'droopiness** *n*

drop (drɒp) *n* **1** a small quantity of liquid that forms or falls in a spherical or pear-shaped mass; globule. **2** a very small quantity of liquid. **3** a very small quantity of anything. **4** something resembling a drop in shape or size, such as a decorative pendant or small sweet. **5** the act or an instance of falling; descent. **6** a decrease in amount or value; slump: *a drop in prices.* **7** the vertical distance that anything may fall. **8** a steep or sheer incline or slope. **9** short for **fruit drop. 10** the act of unloading troops, equipment, or supplies by parachute. **11** (in cable television) a short spur from a trunk cable that feeds signals to an individual house. **12** *Theatre.* See **drop curtain. 13** another word for **trap door** or **gallows. 14** *Chiefly U.S. and Canadian.* a slot or aperture through which an object can be dropped to fall into a receptacle. **15** *Nautical.* the midships height of a sail bent to a fixed yard. Compare **hoist** (sense 6a). **16** *Austral. cricket slang.* a fall of the wicket: *he came in at first drop.* **17** See **drop shot. 18 a drop in the bucket** (*or* **in the ocean**). an amount very small in relation to what is needed or desired. **19 at the drop of a hat.** without hesitation or delay. **20 have had a drop too much.** to be drunk. **21 have the drop on (someone).** *U.S. and N.Z.* to have the advantage over (someone). ◆ *vb* **drops, dropping, dropped. 22** (of liquids) to fall or allow to fall in globules. **23** to fall or allow to fall vertically. **24** (*tr*) to allow to fall by letting go of. **25** to sink or fall or cause to sink or fall to the ground, as from a blow, wound, shot, weariness, etc. **26** (*intr;* foll. by *back, behind,* etc.) to fall, move, or go in a specified manner, direction, etc. **27** (*intr;* foll. by *in, by,* etc.) *Informal.* to pay a casual visit (to). **28** to decrease or cause to decrease in amount or value: *the cost of living never drops.* **29** to sink or cause to sink to a lower position, as on a scale. **30** to make or become less in strength, volume, etc. **31** (*intr*) to sink or decline in health or condition. **32** (*intr;* sometimes foll. by *into*) to pass easily into a state or condition: *to drop into a habit.* **33** (*intr*) to move along gently as with a current of water or air. **34** (*tr*) to allow to pass casually in conversation: *to drop a hint.* **35** (*tr*) to leave out (a word or letter). **36** (*tr*) to set down or unload (passengers or goods). **37** (*tr*) to send or post: *drop me a line.* **38** (*tr*) to discontinue; terminate: *let's drop the matter.* **39** (*tr*) to cease to associate or have to do with. **40** (*tr*) *Slang, chiefly U.S.* to cease to employ: *he was dropped from his job.* **41** (*tr;* sometimes foll. by *in, off,* etc.) *Informal.* to leave or deposit, esp. at a specified place. **42** (of animals) to give birth to (offspring). **43** *Slang, chiefly U.S. and Canadian.* to lose (money), esp. when gambling. **44** (*tr*) to lengthen (a hem, etc.). **45** (*tr*) to unload (troops, equipment, or supplies) by parachute. **46** (*tr*) *Nautical.* to leave behind; sail out of sight of. **47** (*tr*) *Sport.* to omit (a player) from a team. **48** (*tr*) to lose (a score, game, or contest): *the champion dropped his first service game.* **49** (*tr*) *Golf, basketball, etc.* to hit or throw (a ball) into a goal: *he dropped a 30 foot putt.* **50** (*tr*) to hit (a ball) with a drop shot. **51 drop astern.** *Nautical.* to fall back to the stern (of another vessel). **52** (*tr*) *Motor-racing slang.* to spin (the car) and (usually) crash out of the race. **53** (*tr*) *Slang.* to swallow (a drug, esp. a barbiturate or LSD). **54 drop dead!** *Slang.* an exclamation of contempt. ◆ *n, vb* **55** *Rugby.* short for **drop kick** or **drop-kick.** ◆ See also **drop away, drop off, dropout, drops.** [Old English *dropian;* related to Old High German *triofan* to DRIP]

drop away *vb* (*intr, adv*) to fall or go away gradually.

drop cannon *n Billiards.* a shot in which the first object ball joins or gathers with the cue ball and the other object ball, esp. at the top of the table.

drop curtain *n Theatre.* a curtain that is suspended from the flies and can be raised and lowered onto the stage. Also called: **drop cloth, drop.**

drop-dead *adv Informal.* outstandingly or exceptionally: *drop-dead gorgeous.*

drop-dead fee *n* a fee paid to an organization lending money to a company that is hoping to use it to finance a takeover bid. The fee is only paid if the bid fails and interest charges are only incurred if the money is needed.

drop forge *n* **1** Also called: **drop hammer.** a device for forging metal between two dies, one of which is fixed, the other acting by gravity or by steam or hydraulic pressure. ◆ *vb* **drop-forge.** (*tr*) **2** to forge (metal) into (a component) by the use of a drop forge.

drop goal *n Rugby.* a goal scored with a drop kick during the run of play.

drop hammer *n* another name for **drop forge.**

drophead coupé *n Brit.* a two-door four-seater car with a folding roof and a sloping back.

drop-in centre *n Social welfare.* (in Britain) a daycentre run by the social services or a charity that clients may attend on an informal basis.

drop kick *n* **1** a kick in certain sports such as rugby, in which the ball is dropped and kicked as it bounces from the ground. Compare **punt**[2]**, place kick. 2** a wrestling attack, illegal in amateur wrestling, in which a wrestler leaps in the air and kicks his opponent in the face or body with both feet. ◆ *vb* **drop-kick. 3** to kick (a ball, etc.) using a drop kick. **4** to kick (an opponent in wrestling) by the use of a drop kick.

drop leaf *n* **a** a hinged flap on a table that can be raised and supported by a bracket or additional pivoted leg to extend the surface. **b** (*as modifier*): *a drop-leaf table.*

droplet ('drɒplɪt) *n* a tiny drop.

droplight ('drɒpˌlaɪt) *n* an electric light that may be raised or lowered by means of a pulley or other mechanism.

drop lock *n Finance.* a variable-rate bank loan used on international markets that is automatically replaced by a fixed-rate long-term bond if the long-term interest rates fall to a specified level; it thus combines the advantages of a bank loan with those of a bond.

drop off *vb* (*adv*) **1** (*intr*) to grow smaller or less; decline. **2** (*tr*) to allow to alight; set down. **3** (*intr*) *Informal.* to fall asleep. ◆ *n* **drop-off. 4** a steep or vertical descent. **5** a sharp decrease.

dropout ('drɒpˌaʊt) *n* **1** a student who fails to complete a school or college course. **2** a person who rejects conventional society. **3 drop-out.** *Rugby.* a drop kick taken by the defending team to restart play, as after a touchdown. **4 drop-out.** *Electronics.* a momentary loss of signal in a magnetic recording medium as a result of an imperfection in its magnetic coating. ◆ *vb* **drop out.** (*intr, adv;* often foll. by *of*) **5** to abandon or withdraw from (a school, social group, job, etc.).

dropper ('drɒpə) *n* **1** a small tube having a rubber bulb at one end for drawing up and dispensing drops of liquid. **2** a person or thing that drops. **3** *Angling.* a short length of monofilament by which a fly is attached to the main trace or leader above the tail fly. **4** *Austral. and N.Z.* a batten attached to the top wire of a fence to keep the wires apart.

droppings ('drɒpɪŋz) *pl n* the dung of certain animals, such as rabbits, sheep, and birds.

drops (drɒps) *pl n* any liquid medication applied by means of a dropper.

drop scone *n* a flat spongy cake made by dropping a spoonful of batter on a griddle. Also called: **girdlecake, griddlecake, Scotch pancake,** (Scot.) **pancake.**

drop shipment *n* a consignment invoiced to a wholesaler or other middleman but sent directly to the retailer by a manufacturer.

drop shot *n* **1a** *Tennis.* a softly-played return that drops abruptly after clearing the net, intended to give an opponent no chance of reaching the ball and usually achieved by imparting backspin. **1b** *Squash.* a similar shot that stops abruptly after hitting the front wall of the court. **2** a type of shot made by permitting molten metal to percolate through a sieve and then dropping it into a tank of water.

dropsonde ('drɒpsɒnd) *n Meteorol.* a radiosonde dropped by parachute. [C20: DROP + (RADIO)SONDE]

dropsy ('drɒpsɪ) *n* **1** *Pathol.* a condition characterized by an accumulation of watery fluid in the tissues or in a body cavity. **2** *Slang.* a tip or bribe. [C13: shortened from *ydropesie,* from Latin *hydrōpisis,* from Greek *hudrōps,* from *hudōr* water] ▸ **dropsical** ('drɒpsɪkᵊl) *or* **'dropsied** *adj* ▸ **'dropsically** *adv*

drop tank *n* an external aircraft tank, usually containing fuel, that can be detached and dropped in flight.

dropwort ('drɒpˌwɜːt) *n* **1** a Eurasian rosaceous plant, *Filipendula vulgaris,* with finely divided leaves and clusters of white or reddish flowers. See also **meadowsweet** (sense 1). **2 water dropwort.** any of several umbelliferous marsh plants of the genus *Oenanthe,* esp. *O. fistulosa,* with umbrella-shaped clusters of white flowers.

droshky ('drɒʃkɪ) *or* **drosky** ('drɒskɪ) *n, pl* **-kies.** an open four-wheeled horse-drawn passenger carriage, formerly used in Russia. [C19: from Russian *drozhki,* diminutive of *drogi* a wagon, from *droga* shaft]

drosometer (drɒ'sɒmɪtə) *n* an instrument that measures the amount of dew deposited. [C19: from Greek *drosos* dew + -METER]

drosophila (drɒ'sɒfɪlə) *n, pl* **-las** *or* **-lae** (-ˌliː). any small dipterous fly of the genus *Drosophila,* esp. *D. melanogaster,* a species widely used in laboratory genetics studies: family *Drosophilidae.* They feed on plant sap, decaying fruit, etc. Also called: **fruit fly, vinegar fly.** [C19: New Latin, from Greek *drosos* dew, water + *-phila;* see -PHILE]

dross (drɒs) *n* **1** the scum formed, usually by oxidation, on the surfaces of molten metals. **2** worthless matter; waste. [Old English *drōs* dregs; related to Old High German *truosana*] ▸ **'drossy** *adj* ▸ **'drossiness** *n*

drought (draʊt) *n* **1** a prolonged period of scanty rainfall. **2** a prolonged shortage. **3** an archaic or dialect word for **thirst.** Archaic and Scot. form: **drouth** (druːθ). [Old English *drūgoth;* related to Dutch *droogte;* see DRY] ▸ **'droughty** *adj*

drouk *or* **drook** (drʊk) *vb* (*tr*) *Scot.* to drench; soak. [C16: of uncertain origin; compare Old Norse *drukna* to be drowned]

droukit *or* **drookit** ('drʊkɪt) *adj Scot.* drenched; soaked. [from DROUK]

drouthy ('drʊθɪ) *adj Scot.* thirsty or dry.

drove[1] (drəuv) *vb* the past tense of **drive.**

drove[2] (drəuv) *n* **1** a herd of livestock being driven together. **2** (*often pl*) a moving crowd of people. **3** a narrow irrigation channel. **4** Also called: **drove chisel.** a chisel with a broad edge used for dressing stone. ◆ *vb* **5a** (*tr*) to drive (a group of livestock), usually for a considerable distance. **5b** (*intr*) to be employed as a drover. **6** to work (a stone surface) with a drove. **[**Old English *drāf* herd; related to Middle Low German *drēfwech* cattle pasture; see DRIVE, DRIFT**]**

drover ('drəuvə) *n* a person whose occupation is the driving of sheep or cattle, esp. to and from market.

drown (draun) *vb* **1** to die or kill by immersion in liquid. **2** (*tr*) to destroy or get rid of as if by submerging: *he drowned his sorrows in drink.* **3** (*tr*) to drench thoroughly; inundate; flood. **4** (*tr;* sometimes foll. by *out*) to render (a sound) inaudible by making a loud noise. **[C13:** probably from Old English *druncnian;* related to Old Norse *drukna* to be drowned**]** ▸ **'drowner** *n*

drowse (drauz) *vb* **1** to be or cause to be sleepy, dull, or sluggish. ◆ *n* **2** the state of being drowsy. **[C16:** probably from Old English *drūsian* to sink; related to *drēosan* to fall**]**

drowsy ('drauzɪ) *adj* **drowsier, drowsiest. 1** heavy with sleepiness; sleepy. **2** inducing sleep; soporific. **3** sluggish or lethargic; dull. ▸ **'drowsily** *adv* ▸ **'drowsiness** *n*

drub (drʌb) *vb* **drubs, drubbing, drubbed.** (*tr*) **1** to beat as with a stick; cudgel; club. **2** to defeat utterly, as in a contest. **3** to drum or stamp (the feet). **4** to instil with force or repetition: *the master drubbed Latin into the boys.* ◆ *n* **5** a blow, as from a stick. **[C17:** probably from Arabic *dáraba* to beat**]** ▸ **'drubbing** *n*

drudge (drʌdʒ) *n* **1** a person, such as a servant, who works hard at wearisome menial tasks. ◆ *vb* **2** (*intr*) to toil at such tasks. **[C16:** perhaps from *druggen* to toil**]** ▸ **'drudger** *n* ▸ **'drudgingly** *adv*

drudgery ('drʌdʒərɪ) *n, pl* **-eries.** hard, menial, and monotonous work.

drug (drʌg) *n* **1** any synthetic or natural chemical substance used in the treatment, prevention, or diagnosis of disease, or for other medical reasons. Related adj: **pharmaceutical. 2** a chemical substance, esp. a narcotic, taken for the pleasant effects it produces. **3 drug on the market.** a commodity available in excess of the demands of the market. ◆ *vb* **drugs, drugging, drugged.** (*tr*) **4** to mix a drug with (food, drink, etc.). **5** to administer a drug to. **6** to stupefy or poison with or as if with a drug. ◆ Related prefix: **pharmaco-. [C14:** from Old French *drogue,* probably of Germanic origin**]** ▸ **'druggy** *adj*

drug addict *n* any person who is abnormally dependent on narcotic drugs. See **addiction.**

drugget ('drʌgɪt) *n* a coarse fabric used as a protective floor-covering, etc. **[C16:** from French *droguet* useless fabric, from *drogue* trash**]**

druggie ('drʌgɪ) *n Informal.* a drug addict.

druggist ('drʌgɪst) *n* a U.S. and Canadian term for a **pharmacist.**

drugstore ('drʌg,stɔː) *n U.S. and Canadian.* a shop where medical prescriptions are made up and a wide variety of goods and sometimes light meals are sold.

druid ('druːɪd) *n* (*sometimes cap.*) **1** a member of an ancient order of priests in Gaul, Britain, and Ireland in the pre-Christian era. **2** a member of any of several modern movements attempting to revive druidism. **[C16:** from Latin *druides,* of Gaulish origin; compare Old Irish *druid* wizards**]** ▸ **druidess** ('druːɪdɪs) *n fem* ▸ **dru'idic** *or* **dru'idical** *adj* ▸ **'druid,ism** *n*

drum[1] (drʌm) *n* **1** *Music.* a percussion instrument sounded by striking a membrane stretched across the opening of a hollow cylinder or hemisphere. **2 beat the drum for.** *Informal.* to attempt to arouse interest in. **3** the sound produced by a drum or any similar sound. **4** an object that resembles a drum in shape, such as a large spool or a cylindrical container. **5** *Architect.* **5a** one of a number of cylindrical blocks of stone used to construct the shaft of a column. **5b** the wall or structure supporting a dome or cupola. **6** short for **eardrum. 7** Also called: **drumfish.** any of various North American marine and freshwater sciaenid fishes, such as *Equetus pulcher* (**striped drum**), that utter a drumming sound. **8** a type of hollow rotor for steam turbines or axial compressors. **9** *Computing.* a rotating cylindrical device on which data may be stored for later retrieval: now mostly superseded by disks. See **disk** (sense 2). **10** *Archaic.* a drummer. **11 the drum.** *Austral. informal.* the necessary information (esp. in the phrase **give (someone) the drum**). ◆ *vb* **drums, drumming, drummed. 12** to play (music) on or as if on a drum. **13** to beat or tap (the fingers) rhythmically or regularly. **14** (*intr*) (of birds) to produce a rhythmic sound, as by beating the bill against a tree, branch, etc. **15** (*tr;* sometimes foll. by *up*) to summon or call by drumming. **16** (*tr*) to instil by constant repetition: *to drum an idea into someone's head.* ◆ See also **drum out, drum up. [C16:** probably from Middle Dutch *tromme,* of imitative origin**]**

drum[2] (drʌm) *n Scot., Irish.* a narrow ridge or hill. **[C18:** from Scottish Gaelic *druim***]**

drumbeat ('drʌm,biːt) *n* the sound made by beating a drum.

drum brake *n* a type of brake used on the wheels of vehicles, consisting of two pivoted shoes that rub against the inside walls of the brake drum when the brake is applied.

drumfire ('drʌm,faɪə) *n* heavy, rapid, and continuous gunfire, the sound of which resembles rapid drumbeats.

drumfish ('drʌm,fɪʃ) *n, pl* **-fish** *or* **-fishes.** another name for **drum**[1] (sense 7).

drumhead ('drʌm,hɛd) *n* **1** *Music.* the part of a drum that is actually struck with a stick or the hand. **2** the head of a capstan, pierced with holes for the capstan bars. **3** another name for **eardrum.**

drumhead court-martial *n* a military court convened to hear urgent charges of offences committed in action. **[C19:** from the use of a drumhead as a table around which the court-martial was held**]**

drumlin ('drʌmlɪn) *n* a streamlined mound of glacial drift, rounded or elongated in the direction of the original flow of ice. **[C19:** from Irish Gaelic *druim* ridge + *-lin* -LING[1]**]**

drum machine *n* a synthesizer specially programmed to reproduce the sound of drums and other percussion instruments in variable rhythms and combinations selected by the musician; the resulting beat is produced continually until stopped or changed.

drum major *n* the noncommissioned officer, usually of warrant officer's rank, who is appointed to command the corps of drums of a military band and who is in command of both the drums and the band when paraded together.

drum majorette *n* a girl who marches at the head of a procession, twirling a baton.

drummer ('drʌmə) *n* **1** a person who plays a drum or set of drums. **2** *Chiefly U.S.* a salesman, esp. a travelling salesman. **3** *Austral. and N.Z. slang.* the slowest shearer in a team.

Drummond of Hawthornden ('drʌmənd, 'hɔːθɔːndən) *n* **William.** 1585–1649, Scottish poet, historian, and royalist pamphleteer.

drum out *vb* (*tr, adv;* usually foll. by *of*) **a** to expel from a club, association, etc. **b** (formerly) to dismiss from military service to the beat of a drum.

drumstick ('drʌm,stɪk) *n* **1** a stick used for playing a drum. **2** the lower joint of the leg of a cooked fowl.

drum up *vb* (*tr, adv*) to evoke or obtain (support, business, etc.) by solicitation or canvassing.

drunk (drʌŋk) *adj* **1** intoxicated with alcohol to the extent of losing control over normal physical and mental functions. **2** overwhelmed by strong influence or emotion: *drunk with power.* ◆ *n* **3** a person who is drunk or drinks habitually to excess. **4** *Informal.* a drinking bout. **[**Old English *druncen,* past participle of *drincan* to drink; see DRINK**]**

drunkard ('drʌŋkəd) *n* a person who is frequently or habitually drunk.

drunken ('drʌŋkən) *adj* **1** intoxicated with or as if with alcohol. **2** frequently or habitually drunk. **3** (*prenominal*) caused by or relating to alcoholic intoxication: *a drunken brawl.* ▸ **'drunkenly** *adv* ▸ **'drunkenness** *n*

drupe (druːp) *n* an indehiscent fruit consisting of outer epicarp, fleshy or fibrous mesocarp, and stony endocarp enclosing a single seed. It occurs in the peach, plum, and cherry. **[C18:** from Latin *druppa* wrinkled overripe olive, from Greek: olive**]** ▸ **drupaceous** (druː'peɪʃəs) *adj*

drupelet ('druːplɪt) *or* **drupel** ('druːpəl) *n* a small drupe, usually one of a number forming a compound fruit.

Drury Lane ('druərɪ) *n* a street in the West End of London, formerly famous for its theatres.

druse (druːz) *n* **1** an aggregate of small crystals within a cavity, esp. those lining a cavity in a rock or mineral. **2** *Botany.* a globular mass of calcium oxalate crystals formed around an organic core, found in some plant cells. **[C19:** from German, from Old High German *druos* bump**]**

Druse *or* **Druze** (druːz) *n, pl* **Druse** *or* **Druze. a** a member of a religious sect, mainly living in Syria, Lebanon, and Israel, having certain characteristics in common with Muslims. **b** (*as modifier*) *Druse beliefs.* **[C18:** from Arabic *Durūz* the Druses, after *Ismail al-Darazi* Ismail the tailor, 11th-century Muslim leader who founded the sect**]** ▸ **'Drusean, 'Drusian** *or* **'Druzean, 'Druzian** *adj*

dry (draɪ) *adj* **drier, driest** *or* **dryer, dryest. 1** lacking moisture; not damp or wet. **2** having little or no rainfall. **3** not in or under water: *dry land.* **4** having the water drained away or evaporated: *a dry river.* **5** not providing milk: *a dry cow.* **6** (of the eyes) free from tears. **7a** *Informal.* in need of a drink; thirsty. **7b** causing thirst: *dry work.* **8** eaten without butter, jam, etc.: *dry toast.* **9** (of a wine, cider, etc.) not sweet. **10** *Pathol.* not accompanied by or producing a mucous or watery discharge: *a dry cough.* **11** consisting of solid as opposed to liquid substances or commodities. **12** without adornment; plain: *dry facts.* **13** lacking interest or stimulation: *a dry book.* **14** lacking warmth or emotion; cold: *a dry greeting.* **15** (of wit or humour) shrewd and keen in an impersonal, sarcastic, or laconic way. **16** opposed to or prohibiting the sale of alcoholic liquor for human consumption: *a dry area.* **17** *N.Z.* (of a ewe) without a lamb after the mating season. **18** *Electronics.* (of a soldered electrical joint) imperfect because the solder has not adhered to the metal, thus reducing conductance. ◆ *vb* **dries, drying, dried. 19** (when *intr,* often foll. by *off*) to make or become dry or free from moisture. **20** (*tr*) to preserve (meat, vegetables, fruit, etc.) by removing the moisture. ◆ *n, pl* **drys** *or* **dries. 21** *Brit. informal.* a Conservative politician who is considered to be a hard-liner. Compare **wet** (sense 10). **22 the dry.** *Austral. informal.* the dry season. **23** *U.S. and Canadian.* an informal word for **prohibitionist.** ◆ See also **dry out, dry up. [**Old English *drȳge;* related to Old High German *truckan,* Old Norse *draugr* dry wood**]** ▸ **'dryable** *adj* ▸ **'dryness** *n*

dryad ('draɪəd, -æd) *n, pl* **-ads** *or* **-ades** (-ə,diːz). *Greek myth.* a nymph or divinity of the woods. **[C14:** from Latin *Dryas,* from Greek *Druas,* from *drus* tree**]** ▸ **dryadic** (draɪ'ædɪk) *adj*

dry battery *n* an electric battery consisting of two or more dry cells.

dry-bone ore *n* a mining term for **smithsonite.**

dry-bulb thermometer *n* an ordinary thermometer used alongside a wet-bulb thermometer to obtain relative humidity. See also **psychrometer.**

dry cell *n* a primary cell in which the electrolyte is in the form of a paste or is treated in some way to prevent it from spilling. Compare **wet cell.**

dry-clean *vb* (*tr*) to clean (clothing, fabrics, etc.) with a solvent other than water, such as trichloroethylene. ▸ **,dry-'cleaner** *n* ▸ **,dry-'cleaning** *n*

Dryden ('draɪdən) *n* **John.** 1631–1700, English poet, dramatist, and critic of the Augustan period, commonly regarded as the chief exponent of heroic tragedy. His major works include the tragedy *All for Love* (1677), the verse satire *Absalom and Achitophel* (1681), and the *Essay of Dramatick Poesie* (1668).

dry distillation *n* another name for **destructive distillation.**

dry dock *n* **1** a basin-like structure that is large enough to admit a ship and that can be pumped dry for work on the ship's bottom. ◆ *vb* **dry-dock. 2** to put (a ship) into a dry dock, or (of a ship) to go into a dry dock.

dryer[1] ('draɪə) *n* **1** a person or thing that dries. **2** an apparatus for removing moisture by forced draught, heating, or centrifuging. **3** any of certain chemicals added to oils such as linseed oil to accelerate their drying when used as bases in paints, etc.

dryer[2] ('draɪə) *adj* a variant spelling of **drier**[1].

dry farming *n* a system of growing crops in arid or semiarid regions without artificial irrigation, by reducing evaporation and by special methods of tillage. ▸ **dry farmer** *n*

dry fly *n Angling.* **a** an artificial fly designed and prepared to be floated or skimmed on the surface of the water. **b** (*as modifier*): *dry-fly fishing.* ◆ Compare **wet fly.**

dry hole *n* (in the oil industry) a well that is drilled but does not produce oil or gas in commercially worthwhile amounts.

dry ice *n* solid carbon dioxide, which sublimes at −78.5°C: used as a refrigerant, and to create billows of smoke in stage shows. Also called: **carbon dioxide snow.**

drying ('draɪɪŋ) *n* **1** the action or process of making or becoming dry. **2** Also called (not now in technical usage): **seasoning.** the processing of timber until it has a moisture content suitable for the purposes for which it is to be used. ◆ *adj* **3** causing dryness: *a drying wind.*

drying oil *n* one of a number of animal or vegetable oils, such as linseed oil, that harden by oxidation on exposure to air: used as a base for some paints and varnishes.

dry kiln *n* an oven in which cut timber is dried and seasoned.

dry law *n Chiefly U.S.* a law prohibiting the sale of alcoholic beverages.

dryly ('draɪlɪ) *adv* a variant spelling of **drily.**

dry martini *n* a cocktail of between four and ten parts gin to one part dry vermouth.

dry measure *n* a unit or a system of units for measuring dry goods, such as fruit, grains, etc.

dry nurse *n* **1** a nurse who cares for a child without suckling it. Compare **wet nurse.** ◆ *vb* **dry-nurse. 2** to care for (a baby or young child) without suckling.

dryopithecine (ˌdraɪəʊ'pɪθəˌsiːn) *n* any extinct Old World ape of the genus *Dryopithecus,* common in Miocene and Pliocene times: thought to be the ancestors of modern apes. [C20: from New Latin *Dryopithēcus,* from Greek *drus* tree + *pithēkos* ape]

dry out *vb* (*adv*) **1** to make or become dry. **2** to undergo or cause to undergo treatment for alcoholism or drug addiction.

dry point *n* **1** a technique of intaglio engraving with a hard steel needle, without acid, on a copper plate. **2** the sharp steel needle used in this process. **3** an engraving or print produced by this method.

dry riser *n* a vertical pipe, not containing water, having connections on different floors of a building for a fireman's hose to be attached. A fire tender can be connected at the lowest level to make water rise under pressure within the pipe. Abbrev.: **DR.**

dry rot *n* **1** crumbling and drying of timber, bulbs, potatoes, or fruit, caused by saprotrophic basidiomycetous fungi. **2** any fungus causing this decay, esp. of the genus *Merulius.* **3** moral degeneration or corrupt practices, esp. when previously unsuspected.

dry run *n* **1** *Military.* practice in weapon firing without live ammunition. **2** *Informal.* a trial or practice, esp. in simulated conditions; rehearsal.

dry-salt *vb* to preserve (food) by salting and removing moisture.

drysalter ('draɪˌsɔːltə) *n Obsolete.* a dealer in certain chemical products, such as dyestuffs and gums, and in dried, tinned, or salted foods and edible oils.

Drysdale[1] ('draɪzdeɪl) *n* Sir **George Russell.** 1912–81, Australian painter, esp. of landscapes.

Drysdale[2] ('draɪzdeɪl) *n* a New Zealand breed of sheep with hair growing among its wool: bred for its coat which is used in making carpets.

dry steam *n* steam that does not contain droplets of water.

dry-stone *adj* (of a wall) made without mortar.

Dry Tortugas (tɔː'tuːgəz) *n* a group of eight coral islands at the entrance to the Gulf of Mexico: part of Florida.

dry up *vb* (*adv*) **1** (*intr*) to become barren or unproductive; fail: *in middle age his inspiration dried up.* **2** to dry (dishes, cutlery, etc.) with a tea towel after they have been washed. **3** (*intr*) *Informal.* to stop talking or speaking: *when I got on the stage I just dried up; dry up!*

dry valley *n* a valley originally produced by running water but now waterless.

DS *abbrev. for* **1** Also: **ds.** *Music.* dal segno. **2** Detective Sergeant.

DSc *abbrev. for* Doctor of Science.

DSC *Military. abbrev. for* Distinguished Service Cross.

DSIR (in New Zealand) *abbrev. for* Department of Scientific and Industrial Research.

DSM *Military. abbrev. for* Distinguished Service Medal.

DSO *Brit. military. abbrev. for* Distinguished Service Order.

dsp *abbrev. for* decessit sine prole. [Latin: died without issue]

DSS (in Britain) *abbrev. for:* **1** Director of Social Services. **2** Department of Social Security.

DST *abbrev. for* Daylight Saving Time.

DSW (in New Zealand) *abbrev. for* Department of Social Welfare.

DTI (in Britain) *abbrev. for* Department of Trade and Industry.

DTL *Electronics. abbrev. for* diode transistor logic: a stage in the development of electronic logic circuits.

DTP *abbrev. for* desktop publishing.

DT's *Informal. abbrev. for* delirium tremens.

Du. *abbrev. for:* **1** Duke. **2** Dutch.

duad ('djuːæd) *n* a rare word for **pair**[1]. [C17: from Greek *duas* two, a pair]

dual ('djuːəl) *adj* **1** relating to or denoting two. **2** twofold; double. **3** (in the grammar of Old English, Ancient Greek, and certain other languages) denoting a form of a word indicating that exactly two referents are being referred to. **4** *Maths, logic.* (of structures or expressions) having the property that the interchange of certain pairs of terms, and usually the distribution of negation, yields equivalent structures or expressions. ◆ *n* **5** *Grammar.* **5a** the dual number. **5b** a dual form of a word. [C17: from Latin *duālis* concerning two, from *duo* two] ▸ **'dually** *adv*

Duala (du'ɑːlə, -lɑː) *n* **1** (*pl* **-la** *or* **-las**) a member of a Negroid people of W Africa living chiefly in Cameroon. **2** the language of this people, belonging to the Bantu group of the Niger-Congo family.

Dual Alliance *n* **1** the alliance between France and Russia (1893–1917). **2** the secret Austro-German alliance against Russia (1879) later expanded to the Triple Alliance.

dual carriageway *n Brit.* a road on which traffic travelling in opposite directions is separated by a central strip of turf, etc. U.S. and Canadian name: **divided highway.**

dualism ('djuːəˌlɪzəm) *n* **1** the state of being twofold or double. **2** *Philosophy.* the doctrine, as opposed to idealism and materialism, that reality consists of two basic types of substance usually taken to be mind and matter or two basic types of entity, mental and physical. Compare **monism. 3a** the theory that the universe has been ruled from its origins by two conflicting powers, one good and one evil, both existing as equally ultimate first causes. **3b** the theory that there are two personalities, one human and one divine, in Christ. ▸ **'dualist** *n* ▸ **ˌdual'istic** *adj* ▸ **ˌdual'istically** *adv*

duality (djuː'ælɪtɪ) *n, pl* **-ties. 1** the state or quality of being two or in two parts; dichotomy. **2** *Physics.* the principle that in microphysics wave theory and corpuscular theory are complementary. The propagation of electromagnetic radiation is analysed using wave theory but its interaction with matter is described in terms of photons. The condition of particles such as electrons, neutrons, and atoms is described in terms of de Broglie waves. **3** *Geometry.* the interchangeability of the roles of the point and the plane in statements and theorems in projective geometry.

Dual Monarchy *n* the monarchy of Austria-Hungary from 1867 to 1918.

dual-purpose *adj* having or serving two functions.

duathlon (djuː'æθlɒn) *n* an athletic contest in which each athlete competes in running and cycling events. [C20: from DUO- + Greek *athlon* contest]

dub[1] (dʌb) *vb* **dubs, dubbing, dubbed. 1** (*tr*) to invest (a person) with knighthood by the ritual of tapping on the shoulder with a sword. **2** (*tr*) to invest with a title, name, or nickname. **3** (*tr*) to dress (leather) by rubbing. **4** *Angling.* to dress (a fly). ◆ *n* **5** the sound of a drum. [Old English *dubbian;* related to Old Norse *dubba* to dub a knight, Old High German *tubili* plug, peg]

dub[2] (dʌb) *vb* **dubs, dubbing, dubbed.** *Films, television.* **1** to alter the soundtrack of (an old recording, film, etc.). **2** (*tr*) to substitute for the soundtrack of (a film) a new soundtrack, esp. in a different language. **3** (*tr*) to provide (a film or tape) with a soundtrack. **4** (*tr*) to alter (a taped soundtrack) by removing some parts and exaggerating others. ◆ *n* **5** *Films.* the new sounds added. **6a** *Music.* a style of record production associated with reggae, involving the removal or exaggeration of instrumental parts, extensive use of echo, etc. **6b** (*as modifier*): *a dub mix.* [C20: shortened from DOUBLE]

dub[3] (dʌb) *vb* **dubs, dubbing, dubbed.** *Austral. and N.Z. informal.* short for **double-bank.**

dub[4] (dʌb) *U.S. and Canadian informal.* ◆ *n* **1** a clumsy or awkward person or player. ◆ *vb* **dubs, dubbing, dubbed. 2** to bungle (a shot), as in golf. [C19: of uncertain origin]

dub[5] (dʌb) *n Scot. and northern English dialect.* a pool of water; puddle. [C16: Scottish dialect *dubbe;* related to Middle Low German *dobbe*]

dub[6] (dʌb) *vb* **dubs, dubbing, dubbed.** (*intr;* foll. by *in, up,* or *out*) *Slang.* to contribute to the cost of (something); pay. [C19: of obscure origin]

Dubai (duː'baɪ) *n* a sheikhdom in the NE United Arab Emirates, consisting principally of the port of Dubai, on the Persian Gulf: oilfields. Pop.: 548 000 (1993).

du Barry (djuː 'bærɪ; *French* dy bari) *n* **Comtesse** (kɔ̃tɛs), original name *Marie Jeanne Bécu.* ?1743–93, mistress of Louis XV, guillotined in the French Revolution.

dubbin ('dʌbɪn) *or* **dubbing** *n Brit.* a greasy mixture of tallow and oil applied to leather to soften it and make it waterproof. [C18: from *dub* to dress leather; see DUB[1]]

dubbing[1] ('dʌbɪŋ) *n Films.* **1** the replacement of a soundtrack in one language by one in another language. **2** the combination of several soundtracks into a single track. **3** the addition of a soundtrack to a film or broadcast.

dubbing[2] ('dʌbɪŋ) *n* **1** *Angling.* hair or fur spun on waxed silk and added to the body of an artificial fly to give it shape. **2** a variant of **dubbin.**

dubbo ('dʌbəʊ) *Austral. slang.* ◆ *adj* **1** stupid. ◆ *n, pl* **-bos. 2** a stupid person. [of uncertain origin]

Dubček (*Slovak* 'duptʃɛk) *n* **Alexander** ('aleksandᵊr). 1921–92, Czechoslovak statesman. His reforms as first secretary of the Czechoslovak Communist Party (1968–69) prompted the Russian occupation (1968) and his enforced resignation. Following the uprising of 1989 he was elected chairman of the new Czechoslovak Federal Assembly.

du Bellay (*French* dy bɛlɛ) *n* See (Joachim du) **Bellay.**

dubiety (djuː'baɪɪtɪ) *or* **dubiosity** (ˌdjuːbɪ'ɒsɪtɪ) *n, pl* **-ties. 1** the state of being doubtful. **2** a doubtful matter. [C18: from Late Latin *dubietās,* from Latin *dubius* DUBIOUS]

dubious ('djuːbɪəs) *adj* **1** marked by or causing doubt: *a dubious reply.* **2** unsettled in mind; uncertain; doubtful. **3** of doubtful quality; untrustworthy: *a dubious reputation.* **4** not certain in outcome. [C16: from Latin *dubius* wavering] ▸ **'dubiously** *adv* ▸ **'dubiousness** *n*

dubitable ('djuːbɪtəbᵊl) *adj* open to doubt. [C17: from Latin *dubitāre* to DOUBT] ▸ **'dubitably** *adv*

dubitation (ˌdjuːbɪ'teɪʃən) *n* another word for **doubt.**

Dublin ('dʌblɪn) *n* **1** the capital of the Republic of Ireland, on **Dublin Bay:** under English rule from 1171 until 1922; commercial and cultural centre; contains one of the world's largest breweries and exports whiskey, stout, and agricultural produce. Pop.: 478 389 (1991). Gaelic name: **Baile Átha Cliath.** **2** a county in E Republic of Ireland, in Leinster on the Irish Sea: mountainous in the south but low-lying in the north and centre. County seat: Dublin. Pop.: 1 057 000 (1996). Area: 922 sq. km (356 sq. miles). ▸ **'Dubliner** *n*

Dublin Bay prawn *n* a large prawn usually used in a dish of scampi.

Dubna ('dʌbnə) *n* a new town in W Russia, founded in 1956: site of the United Institute of Nuclear Research. Pop.: 66 000 (1990 est.).

dubnium (dʌbnɪəm) *n* a synthetic transactinide element produced in minute quantities by bombarding plutonium with high-energy neon ions. Symbol: Du; atomic no. 105. **[C20:** after DUBNA in Russia, where it was first reported**]**

Dubois (djuː'bwɑː) *n* **W(illiam) E(dward) B(urghardt).** 1868–1963, U.S. Black sociologist, writer, and political activist; a founder of the National Association for the Advancement of Colored People (NAACP).

dubonnet (djuː'bɒneɪ) *n* **a** a dark purplish-red colour. **b** (*as adj*): *a dubonnet coat.* **[**from DUBONNET**]**

Dubonnet (djuː'bɒneɪ) *n Trademark.* a sweet usually red apéritif wine flavoured with quinine and cinchona.

Dubrovnik (dʊ'brɒvnɪk) *n* a port in W Croatia, on the Dalmatian coast: an important commercial centre in the Middle Ages; damaged in 1991 when it was shelled by Serbian artillery. Pop.: 49 730 (1991). Former Italian name (until 1918): **Ragusa.**

Dubuffet (*French* dybyfɛ) *n* **Jean** (ʒɑ̃). 1901–85, French painter, inspired by graffiti and the untrained art of children and psychotics.

ducal ('djuːkᵊl) *adj* of or relating to a duke or duchy. **[C16:** from French, from Late Latin *ducālis* of a leader, from *dux* leader**]** ▸ **'ducally** *adv*

ducat ('dʌkət) *n* **1** any of various former European gold or silver coins, esp. those used in Italy or the Netherlands. **2** (*often pl*) any coin or money. **[C14:** from Old French, from Old Italian *ducato* coin stamped with the doge's image, from *duca* doge, from Latin *dux* leader**]**

Duccio di Buoninsegna (*Italian* 'duttʃo di buonin'seɲɲa) *n* ?1255–?1318, Italian painter; founder of the Sienese school.

duce ('duːtʃɪ; *Italian* 'duːtʃe) *n* leader. **[C20:** from Italian, from Latin *dux***]**

Duce (*Italian* 'duːtʃe) *n* **Il** (il). the title assumed by Benito Mussolini as leader of Fascist Italy (1922–43).

Duchamp (*French* dyʃɑ̃) *n* **Marcel** (marsel). 1887–1968, U.S. painter and sculptor, born in France; noted as a leading exponent of Dada. His best-known work is *Nude Descending a Staircase* (1912).

Duchenne dystrophy (duː'ʃɛn) *or* **Duchenne muscular dystrophy** *n* the most common form of muscular dystrophy, usually affecting only boys. Abbrev.: **DMD.** **[**named after Guillaume *Duchenne* (1806–75), French neurologist**]**

duchess ('dʌtʃɪs) *n* **1** the wife or widow of a duke. **2** a woman who holds the rank of duke in her own right. ◆ *vb* **3** *Austral. informal.* to overwhelm with flattering attention. **[C14:** from Old French *duchesse,* feminine of *duc* DUKE**]**

duchy ('dʌtʃɪ) *n, pl* **duchies.** the territory of a duke or duchess; dukedom. **[C14:** from Old French *duche,* from *duc* DUKE**]**

duck[1] (dʌk) *n, pl* **ducks** *or* **duck. 1** any of various small aquatic birds of the family *Anatidae,* typically having short legs, webbed feet, and a broad blunt bill: order *Anseriformes.* **2** the flesh of this bird, used as food. **3** the female of such a bird, as opposed to the male (drake). **4** any other bird of the family *Anatidae,* including geese, and swans. **5** Also: **ducks.** *Brit. informal.* dear or darling: used as a term of endearment or of general address. See also **ducky. 6** *Informal.* a person, esp. one regarded as odd or endearing. **7** *Cricket.* a score of nothing by a batsman. **8 like water off a duck's back.** *Informal.* without effect. **9 take to something like a duck to water.** *Informal.* to become adept at or attracted to something very quickly. **[**Old English *dūce* duck, diver; related to DUCK[2]**]**

duck[2] (dʌk) *vb* **1** to move (the head or body) quickly downwards or away, esp. so as to escape observation or evade a blow. **2** to submerge or plunge suddenly and often briefly under water. **3** (when *intr,* often foll. by *out*) *Informal.* to dodge or escape (a person, duty, etc.). **4** (*intr*) *Bridge.* to play a low card when possessing a higher one rather than try to win a trick. ◆ *n* **5** the act or an instance of ducking. **[C14:** related to Old High German *tūhhan* to dive, Middle Dutch *dūken***]** ▸ **'ducker** *n*

duck[3] (dʌk) *n* a heavy cotton fabric of plain weave, used for clothing, tents, etc. See also **ducks. [C17:** from Middle Dutch *doek;* related to Old High German *tuoh* cloth**]**

duck[4] (dʌk) *n* an amphibious vehicle used in World War II. **[C20:** from code name DUKW**]**

duck-billed platypus *n* an amphibious egg-laying mammal, *Ornithorhynchus anatinus,* of E Australia, having dense fur, a broad bill and tail, and webbed feet: family *Ornithorhynchidae.* Sometimes shortened to **duckbill, platypus.** See also **monotreme.**

duckboard ('dʌk,bɔːd) *n* a board or boards laid so as to form a floor or path over wet or muddy ground.

duck-egg blue *n* **a** a pale greenish-blue colour. **b** (*as adj*): *duck-egg blue walls.*

duckfoot quote ('dʌkfʊt) *n Printing.* a chevron-shaped quotation mark (≪ or ≫) used in Europe. Also called: **guillemet.**

duck hawk *n* a variety of peregrine falcon, *Falco peregrinus anatum,* occurring in North America.

ducking stool *n History.* a chair or stool used for the punishment of offenders by plunging them into water.

duckling ('dʌklɪŋ) *n* a young duck.

ducks (dʌks) *pl n* clothing made of duck, esp. white trousers for sports.

ducks and drakes *n* (*functioning as sing*) **1** a game in which a flat stone is bounced across the surface of water. **2 make ducks and drakes of** *or* **play (at) ducks and drakes with.** to use recklessly; squander or waste.

duck's arse *n* a hairstyle in which the hair is swept back to a point at the nape of the neck, resembling a duck's tail. Also called: **DA.**

duck shove *vb Austral. and N.Z. informal.* to evade responsibility. ▸ **duck shover** *n* ▸ **duck shoving** *n*

duck soup *n U.S. slang.* something that is easy to do.

duckweed ('dʌk,wiːd) *n* any of various small stemless aquatic plants of the family *Lemnaceae,* esp. any of the genus *Lemna,* that have rounded leaves and occur floating on still water in temperate regions.

ducky *or* **duckie** ('dʌkɪ) *Informal.* ◆ *n, pl* **duckies. 1** *Brit.* darling or dear: used as a term of endearment among women, but now often used in imitation of the supposed usage of homosexual men. ◆ *adj* **2** delightful; fine.

duct (dʌkt) *n* **1** a tube, pipe, or canal by means of which a substance, esp. a fluid or gas, is conveyed. **2** any bodily passage, esp. one conveying secretions or excretions. **3** a narrow tubular cavity in plants, often containing resin or some other substance. **4** Also called: **conduit.** a channel or pipe carrying electric cable or wires. **5** a passage through which air can flow, as in air conditioning. **6** the ink reservoir in a printing press. **[C17:** from Latin *ductus* a leading (in Medieval Latin: aqueduct), from *dūcere* to lead**]** ▸ **'ductless** *adj*

ductile ('dʌktaɪl) *adj* **1** (of a metal, such as gold or copper) able to sustain large deformations without fracture and able to be hammered into sheets or drawn out into wires. **2** able to be moulded; pliant; plastic. **3** easily led or influenced; tractable. **[C14:** from Old French, from Latin *ductilis,* from *dūcere* to lead**]** ▸ **'ductilely** *adv* ▸ **ductility** (dʌk'tɪlɪtɪ) *or* **'ductileness** *n*

ductless gland *n Anatomy.* See **endocrine gland.**

ductule ('dʌktjuːl) *n Anatomy, zoology.* a small duct.

dud (dʌd) *Informal.* ◆ *n* **1** a person or thing that proves ineffectual or a failure. **2** a shell, etc., that fails to explode. **3** (*pl*) *Old-fashioned.* clothes or other personal belongings. ◆ *adj* **4** failing in its purpose or function: *a dud cheque.* **[C15** (in the sense: an article of clothing, a thing, used disparagingly): of unknown origin**]**

dude (duːd, djuːd) *n Informal.* **1** *Western U.S. and Canadian.* a city dweller, esp. one holidaying on a ranch. **2** *Chiefly U.S. and Canadian.* a dandy. **3** *U.S. and Canadian.* a person: often used to any male in direct address. **[C19:** of unknown origin**]** ▸ **'dudish** *adj* ▸ **'dudishly** *adv*

dudeen (duː'diːn) *n* a clay pipe with a short stem. **[C19:** from Irish *dúidín* a little pipe, from *dúd* pipe**]**

dude ranch *n U.S. and Canadian.* a ranch used as a holiday resort offering activities such as riding and camping.

dudgeon[1] ('dʌdʒən) *n* anger or resentment (archaic, except in the phrase **in high dudgeon**). **[C16:** of unknown origin**]**

dudgeon[2] ('dʌdʒən) *n* **1** *Obsolete.* a wood used in making the handles of knives, daggers, etc. **2** *Archaic.* a dagger, knife, etc., with a dudgeon hilt. **[C15:** from Anglo-Norman *digeon,* of obscure origin**]**

Dudley[1] ('dʌdlɪ) *n* **1** a town in W central England, in Dudley unitary authority, West Midlands: wrought-iron industry. Pop.: 192 171 (1991). **2** a unitary authority in W central England, in West Midlands. Pop.: 312 200 (1994 est.). Area: 98 sq. km (38 sq. miles).

Dudley[2] ('dʌdlɪ) *n* **Robert.** See (Earl of) **Leicester.**

due (djuː) *adj* **1** (*postpositive*) immediately payable. **2** (*postpositive*) owed as a debt, irrespective of any date for payment. **3** requisite; fitting; proper. **4** (*prenominal*) adequate or sufficient; enough. **5** (*postpositive*) expected or appointed to be present or arrive: *the train is now due.* **6 due to.** attributable to or caused by. ◆ *n* **7** something that is owed, required, or due. **8 give (a person) his due.** to give or allow what is deserved or right. ◆ *adv* **9** directly or exactly; straight: *a course due west.* ◆ See also **dues. [C13:** from Old French *deu,* from *devoir* to owe, from Latin *debēre;* see DEBT, DEBIT**]**

USAGE The use of *due to* as a compound preposition *(the performance has been cancelled due to bad weather)* was formerly considered incorrect, but is now acceptable.

due bill *n Chiefly U.S.* a document acknowledging indebtedness, exchangeable for goods or services.

duel ('djuːəl) *n* **1** a prearranged combat with deadly weapons between two people following a formal procedure in the presence of seconds and traditionally fought until one party was wounded or killed, usually to settle a quarrel involving a point of honour. **2** a contest or conflict between two persons or parties. ◆ *vb* **duels, duelling, duelled** *or U.S.* **duels, dueling, dueled.** (*intr*) **3** to fight in a duel. **4** to contest closely. **[C15:** from Medieval Latin *duellum,* from Latin, poetical variant of *bellum* war; associated by folk etymology with Latin *duo* two**]** ▸ **'dueller** *or* **'duellist** *n*

duello (djuː'ɛləʊ) *n, pl* **-los. 1** the art of duelling. **2** the code of rules for duelling. **[C16:** from Italian; see DUEL**]**

duenna (djuː'ɛnə) *n* (in Spain and Portugal, etc.) an elderly woman retained by a family to act as governess and chaperon to young girls. **[C17:** from Spanish *dueña,* from Latin *domina* lady, feminine of *dominus* master**]**

due process of law *n* the administration of justice in accordance with established rules and principles.

Duero ('duero) *n* the Spanish name for the **Douro.**

dues (djuːz) *pl n* (*sometimes sing*) charges, as for membership of a club or organization; fees: *trade-union dues.*

duet (djuː'ɛt) *n* **1** Also called (esp. for instrumental compositions): **duo.** a musical composition for two performers or voices. **2** an action or activity performed by a pair of closely connected individuals. **[C18:** from Italian *duetto* a little duet, from *duo* duet, from Latin: two**]** ▸ **du'ettist** *n*

duff[1] (dʌf) *n* **1** a thick flour pudding, often flavoured with currants, citron, etc., and boiled in a cloth bag: *plum duff.* **2 up the duff.** *Slang.* pregnant. **[C19:** Northern English variant of DOUGH**]**

duff[2] (dʌf) *vb* (*tr*) **1** *Slang.* to change the appearance of or give a false appearance to (old or stolen goods); fake. **2** *Austral. slang.* to steal (cattle), altering the brand. **3** Also: **sclaff.** *Golf, informal.* to bungle (a shot) by hitting the ground behind the ball. ◆ *adj* **4** *Brit. informal.* bad or useless, as by not working out or operating correctly; dud: *a duff idea; a duff engine.* ◆ See also **duff up.** [C19: probably back formation from DUFFER]

duff[3] (dʌf) *n Slang.* the rump or buttocks. [C20: special use of DUFF[1]]

duffel *or* **duffle** (ˈdʌfᵊl) *n* **1** a heavy woollen cloth with a thick nap. **2** *Chiefly U.S. and Canadian.* equipment or supplies, esp. those of a camper. [C17: after *Duffel,* Belgian town]

duffel bag *n* a cylindrical drawstring canvas bag, originally used esp. by sailors for carrying personal articles.

duffel coat *n* a knee-length or short wool coat, usually with a hood and fastened with toggles.

duffer (ˈdʌfə) *n* **1** *Informal.* a dull or incompetent person. **2** *Slang.* something worthless. **3** *Dialect.* a peddler or hawker. **4** *Austral. slang.* **4a** a mine that proves unproductive. **4b** a person who steals cattle. [C19: of uncertain origin]

duff up *vb (tr, adv) Brit. slang.* to beat or thrash (a person) severely.

Du Fu (ˈduː ˈfuː) *or* **Tu Fu** *n* 712–770 A.D., Chinese poet of the Tang dynasty.

Dufy (*French* dyfi) *n* **Raoul** (raul). 1877–1953, French painter and designer whose style is characterized by swift calligraphic draughtsmanship and bright colouring.

dug[1] (dʌg) *vb* the past tense and past participle of **dig.**

dug[2] (dʌg) *n* **1** the nipple, teat, udder, or breast of a female mammal. **2** a human breast, esp. when old and withered. [C16: of Scandinavian origin; compare Danish *dægge* to coddle, Gothic *daddjan* to give suck]

dug[3] (dʌg) *n* a Scot. word for **dog.**

du Gard (*French* dy gar) *n* See (Roger) **Martin du Gard.**

dugite (ˈduːgaɪt) *n* a medium-sized venomous snake, *Pseudonaja affinis,* of Central and W Australia, having a small head and slender olive-coloured body with black specks.

dugong (ˈduːgɒŋ) *n* a whalelike sirenian mammal, *Dugong dugon,* occurring in shallow tropical waters from E Africa to Australia: family *Dugongidae.* [C19: from Malay *duyong*]

dugout (ˈdʌgˌaʊt) *n* **1** a canoe made by hollowing out a log. **2** *Military.* a covered excavation dug to provide shelter. **3** *Slang.* a retired officer, former civil servant, etc., recalled to employment. **4** (at a sports ground) the covered bench where managers, trainers, etc. sit and players wait when not on the field.

Du Guesclin (*French* dy geklɛ̃) *n* **Bertrand** (bɛrtrɑ̃). ?1320–80, French military leader; as constable of France (1370–80), he helped to drive the English from France.

Duhamel (*French* dyamɛl) *n* **Georges** (ʒɔrʒ). 1884–1966, French novelist, poet, and dramatist; author of *La Chronique des Pasquier* (1933–45).

duiker *or* **duyker** (ˈdaɪkə) *n, pl* **-kers** *or* **-ker. 1** Also called: **duikerbok** (ˈdaɪkəbɒk). any small antelope of the genera *Cephalophus* and *Sylvicapra,* occurring throughout Africa south of the Sahara, having short straight backward-pointing horns, pointed hooves, and an arched back. **2** *S. African.* any of several cormorants, esp. the long-tailed shag (*Phalacrocorax africanus*). [C18: via Afrikaans from Dutch *duiker* diver, from *duiken* to dive; see DUCK[2]]

Duisburg (*German* ˈdyːsbʊrk) *n* an industrial city in NW Germany, in North Rhine-Westphalia at the confluence of the Rivers Rhine and Ruhr: one of the world's largest and busiest inland ports; university (1972). Pop.: 535 250 (1996 est.).

duka (ˈduːka) *n E African.* a shop; store. [C20: from Swahili]

Dukas (*French* dykɑ) *n* **Paul** (pɔl). 1865–1935, French composer best known for the orchestral scherzo *The Sorcerer's Apprentice* (1897).

duke (djuːk) *n* **1** a nobleman of high rank: in the British Isles standing above the other grades of the nobility. **2** the prince or ruler of a small principality or duchy. Related adj: **ducal.** [C12: from Old French *duc,* from Latin *dux* leader]

dukedom (ˈdjuːkdəm) *n* **1** another name for a **duchy. 2** the title, rank, or position of a duke.

dukes (djuːks) *pl n Slang.* the fists. [C19: from *Duke of Yorks* rhyming slang for *forks* (fingers)]

Dukhobor (ˈduːkəʊˌbɔː) *pl n* a variant spelling of **Doukhobor.**

dukkha (ˈdukə) *n* (in Theravada Buddhism) the belief that all things are suffering, due to the desire to seek permanence or recognise the self when neither exist: one of the three basic characteristics of existence. Sanskrit word: **duhkha.** Compare **anatta, anicca.** [Pali, literally: suffering, illness]

Dulbecco (dʌlˈbɛkəʊ; *Italian* dʌlˈbekko) *n* **Renato.** born 1914, U.S. physician and molecular biologist, born in Italy: shared the Nobel prize for physiology or medicine (1975) for cancer research.

dulcet (ˈdʌlsɪt) *adj* (of a sound) soothing or pleasant; sweet. [C14: from Latin *dulcis* sweet] ▸ **ˈdulcetly** *adv* ▸ **ˈdulcetness** *n*

dulciana (ˌdʌlsɪˈɑːnə) *n* a sweet-toned organ stop, controlling metal pipes of narrow scale. [C18: from Latin *dulcis* sweet]

dulcify (ˈdʌlsɪˌfaɪ) *vb* **-fies, -fying, -fied.** (*tr*) **1** *Rare.* to make pleasant or agreeable. **2** a rare word for **sweeten.** [C16: from Late Latin *dulcificāre,* from Latin *dulcis* sweet + *facere* to make] ▸ **ˌdulcifiˈcation** *n*

dulcimer (ˈdʌlsɪmə) *n Music.* **1** a tuned percussion instrument consisting of a set of strings of graduated length stretched over a sounding board and struck with a pair of hammers. **2** an instrument used in U.S. folk music, consisting of an elliptical body, a fretted fingerboard, and usually three strings plucked with a goose quill. [C15: from Old French *doulcemer,* from Old Italian *dolcimelo,* from *dolce* sweet, from Latin *dulcis* + *-melo,* perhaps from Greek *melos* song]

dulcinea (ˌdʌlsɪˈnɪə) *n* a man's sweetheart. [C18: from the name of Don Quixote's mistress Dulcinea del Toboso in Cervantes' novel; from Spanish *dulce* sweet]

dulia (ˈdjuːlɪə) *n* the veneration accorded to saints in the Roman Catholic and Eastern Churches, as contrasted with hyperdulia and latria. [C17: from Medieval Latin: service, from Greek *douleia* slavery, from *doulos* slave]

dull (dʌl) *adj* **1** slow to think or understand; stupid. **2** lacking in interest. **3** lacking in perception or the ability to respond; insensitive. **4** lacking sharpness; blunt. **5** not acute, intense, or piercing. **6** (of weather) not bright or clear; cloudy. **7** not active, busy, or brisk. **8** lacking in spirit or animation; listless. **9** (of colour) lacking brilliance or brightness; sombre. **10** not loud or clear; muffled. **11** *Med.* (of sound elicited by percussion, esp. of the chest) not resonant. ◆ *vb* **12** to make or become dull. [Old English *dol;* related to Old Norse *dul* conceit, Old High German *tol* foolish, Greek *tholeros* confused] ▸ **ˈdullish** *adj* ▸ **ˈdullness** *or* **ˈdulness** *n* ▸ **ˈdully** *adv*

dullard (ˈdʌləd) *n* a dull or stupid person.

Dulles (ˈdʌlɪs) *n* **John Foster.** 1888–1959, U.S. statesman and lawyer; secretary of state (1953–59).

dullsville (ˈdʌlzvɪl) *n Slang.* **1** a thing, place, or activity that is boring or dull. **2** the state of being bored.

dulosis (djuːˈləʊsɪs) *n* a practice of some ants, in which one species forces members of a different species to do the work of the colony. Also called: **helotism.** [C20: from Greek: enslavement, from *doulos* slave] ▸ **dulotic** (djuːˈlɒtɪk) *adj*

dulse (dʌls) *n* any of several seaweeds, esp. *Rhodymenia palmata,* that occur on rocks and have large red edible fronds. [C17: from Old Irish *duilesc* seaweed]

Duluth (dəˈluːθ) *n* a port in E Minnesota, at the W end of Lake Superior. Pop.: 83 699 (1996 est.).

Dulwich (ˈdʌlɪtʃ) *n* a residential district in the Greater London borough of Southwark: site of an art gallery and the public school, Dulwich College.

duly (ˈdjuːlɪ) *adv* **1** in a proper or fitting manner. **2** at the proper time; punctually. [C14: see DUE, -LY[2]]

duma *or* ***douma*** *Russian.* (ˈduːmə) *n Russian history.* **1** (*usually cap.*) the elective legislative assembly established by Tsar Nicholas II in 1905: overthrown by the Bolsheviks in 1917. **2** (before 1917) any official assembly or council. **3** short for **State Duma,** the lower chamber of the Russian parliament. [C20: from *duma* thought, of Germanic origin; related to Gothic *dōms* judgment]

Dumas (*French* dymɑ) *n* **1 Alexandre** (alɛksɑ̃drə), known as *Dumas père.* 1802–70, French novelist and dramatist, noted for his historical romances *The Count of Monte Cristo* (1844) and *The Three Musketeers* (1844). **2** his son, **Alexandre,** known as *Dumas fils.* 1824–95, French novelist and dramatist, noted esp. for the play he adapted from an earlier novel, *La Dame aux camélias* (1852). **3 Jean-Baptiste André** (ʒɑ̃batistɑ̃dre). 1800–84, French chemist, noted for his research on vapour density and atomic weight.

Du Maurier (djuː ˈmɒrɪˌeɪ) *n* **1** Dame **Daphne.** 1907–89, English novelist; author of *Rebecca* (1938) and *My Cousin Rachel* (1951). **2** her grandfather, **George Louis Palmella Busson** (ˈpælmɛlə ˈbjuːsᵊn). 1834–96, English novelist, caricaturist, and illustrator; author of *Peter Ibbetson* (1891) and *Trilby* (1894). **3** his son, Sir **Gerald** (**Hubert Edward**). 1873–1934, British actor-manager: father of Daphne Du Maurier.

dumb (dʌm) *adj* **1** lacking the power to speak, either because of defects in the vocal organs or because of hereditary deafness; mute. **2** lacking the power of human speech: *dumb animals.* **3** temporarily lacking or bereft of the power to speak: *struck dumb.* **4** refraining from speech; uncommunicative. **5** producing no sound; silent: *a dumb piano.* **6** made, done, or performed without speech. **7** *Informal.* **7a** slow to understand; dim-witted. **7b** foolish; stupid. See also **dumb down.** [Old English; related to Old Norse *dumbr,* Gothic *dumbs,* Old High German *tump*] ▸ **ˈdumbly** *adv* ▸ **ˈdumbness** *n*

dumb ague *n* an irregular form of malarial fever (ague) lacking the typically symptomatic chill.

Dumbarton (dʌmˈbɑːtᵊn) *n* a town in W Scotland, in West Dunbartonshire near the confluence of the Rivers Leven and Clyde: centred around the **Rock of Dumbarton,** an important stronghold since ancient times; engineering and distilling. Pop.: 21 962 (1991).

Dumbarton Oaks (ˈdʌmˌbɑːtᵊn) *n* an estate in the District of Columbia in the U.S.: scene of conferences in 1944 concerned with creating the United Nations.

dumbbell (ˈdʌmˌbɛl) *n* **1** *Gymnastics, etc.* an exercising weight consisting of a single bar with a heavy ball or disc at either end. **2** *Dog training.* a small wooden object shaped like this used for the dog to retrieve. **3** *Slang, chiefly U.S. and Canadian.* a fool.

dumb-cane *n* a West Indian aroid plant, *Dieffenbachia seguine,* chewing the stem of which induces speechlessness by paralysing the throat muscles.

dumb down *vb* (*tr*) to make less intellectually demanding or sophisticated: *the alleged dumbing down of BBC radio.*

dumbfound *or* **dumfound** (dʌmˈfaʊnd) *vb* (*tr*) to strike dumb with astonishment; amaze. [C17: from DUMB + (CON)FOUND]

dumb show *n* **1** a part of a play acted in pantomime, popular in early English drama. **2** meaningful gestures; mime.

dumbstruck (ˈdʌmˌstrʌk) *or* **dumbstricken** (ˈdʌmˌstrɪkᵊn) *adj* temporarily deprived of speech through shock or surprise.

dumbwaiter (ˈdʌmˌweɪtə) *n* **1** *Brit.* **1a** a stand placed near a dining table to hold food. **1b** a revolving circular tray placed on a table to hold food. U.S. and Canadian name: **lazy Susan. 2** a lift for carrying food, rubbish, etc., between floors.

dumdum (ˈdʌmˌdʌm) *n* a soft-nosed or hollow-nosed small-arms bullet that expands on impact and inflicts extensive laceration. Also called: **dumdum bullet.** [C19: named after *Dum-Dum,* town near Calcutta where these bullets were made]

dumela (dumɛla) *sentence substitute. S. African.* hello; good morning. [Sotho]

Dumfries (dʌmˈfriːs) *n* a town in S Scotland on the River Nith, administrative centre of Dumfries and Galloway. Pop.: 32 136 (1991).

Dumfries and Galloway *n* a council area in SW Scotland: created in 1975 from the counties of Dumfries, Kirkcudbright, and Wigtown; became a unitary authority in 1996; chiefly agricultural. Administrative centre: Dumfries. Pop.: 147 900 (1993 est.). Area: 6439 sq. km (2486 sq. miles).

Dumfriesshire (dʌm'fri:s,ʃɪə, -ʃə) *n* (until 1975) a county in S Scotland, on the Solway Firth, now part of Dumfries and Galloway.

dummy ('dʌmɪ) *n, pl* **-mies. 1** a figure representing the human form, used for displaying clothes, in a ventriloquist's act, as a target, etc. **2a** a copy or imitation of an object, often lacking some essential feature of the original. **2b** (*as modifier*): *a dummy drawer.* **3** *Slang.* a stupid person; fool. **4** *Derogatory, slang.* a person without the power of speech; mute. **5** *Informal.* a person who says or does nothing. **6a** a person who appears to act for himself while acting on behalf of another. **6b** (*as modifier*): *a dummy buyer.* **7** *Military.* a weighted round without explosives, used in drill and training. **8** *Bridge.* **8a** the hand exposed on the table by the declarer's partner and played by the declarer. **8b** the declarer's partner. **9a** a prototype of a proposed book, indicating the general appearance and dimensions of the finished product. **9b** a designer's layout of a page indicating the positions for illustrations, etc. **10** a feigned pass or move in a sport such as football or rugby. **11** *Brit.* a rubber teat for babies to suck or bite on. U.S. and Canadian equivalent: **pacifier. 12** (*modifier*) counterfeit; sham. **13** (*modifier*) (of a card game) played with one hand exposed or unplayed. ◆ *vb* **-mies, -mying, -mied. 14** to prepare a dummy of (a proposed book, page, etc.). **15** Also: **sell (someone) a dummy.** *Sport.* to use a dummy pass in order to trick (an opponent). **[C16:** see DUMB, -Y[3]**]**

dummy head *n* a model of the human head with a microphone in each ear intended to receive sound in binaural and surround sound reproduction and transmission.

dummy load *n* a resistive component that absorbs all the output power of an electrical generator or radio transmitter in order to simulate working conditions for test purposes.

dummy run *n* a practice or rehearsal; trial run.

dummy variable *n* a variable or constant appearing in a mathematical expression that can be replaced by any arbitrary variable or constant, not occurring in the expression, without affecting the value of the whole.

Du Mont ('dju:,mɒnt) *n* **Allen Balcom.** 1901–65, U.S. inventor and electronics manufacturer. He developed the cathode-ray tube used in television sets and oscilloscopes.

dumortierite (dju:'mɔ:tɪə,raɪt) *n* a hard fibrous blue or green mineral consisting of hydrated aluminium borosilicate. Formula: $Al_8BSi_3O_{19}(OH)$. **[C19:** named after Eugène *Dumortier,* 19th-century French palaeontologist who discovered it**]**

dump[1] (dʌmp) *vb* **1** to drop, fall, or let fall heavily or in a mass. **2** (*tr*) to empty (objects or material) out of a container. **3** to unload, empty, or make empty (a container), as by tilting or overturning. **4** (*tr*) *Informal.* to dispose of. **5** (*tr*) to dispose of (waste, esp. radioactive nuclear waste) in the sea or on land. **6** *Commerce.* **6a** to market (goods) in bulk and at low prices. **6b** to offer for sale large quantities of (goods) on foreign markets at low prices in order to maintain a high price in the home market and obtain a share of the foreign markets. **7** (*tr*) to store (supplies, arms, etc.) temporarily. **8** (*intr*) *Slang, chiefly U.S.* to defecate. **9** (*tr*) *Surfing.* (of a wave) to hurl a swimmer or surfer down. **10** (*tr*) *Austral. and N.Z.* to compact (bales of wool) by hydraulic pressure. **11** (*tr*) *Computing.* to record (the contents of part or all of the memory) on a storage device, such as magnetic tape, at a series of points during a computer run. ◆ *n* **12a** a place or area where waste materials are dumped. **12b** (*in combination*): *rubbish dump.* **13** a pile or accumulation of rubbish. **14** the act of dumping. **15** *Informal.* a dirty or unkempt place. **16** *Military.* a place where weapons, supplies, etc., are stored. **17** *Slang, chiefly U.S.* an act of defecation. ◆ See also **dump on. [C14:** probably of Scandinavian origin; compare Norwegian *dumpa* to fall suddenly, Middle Low German *dumpeln* to duck**]** ► **'dumper** *n*

dump[2] (dʌmp) *n Obsolete.* a mournful song; lament. **[C16:** see DAMP**]**

dump bin *n* **1** a free-standing unit in a bookshop in which the books of a particular publisher are displayed. **2** a container in a shop in which goods are heaped, often in a disorderly fashion.

dumpling ('dʌmplɪŋ) *n* **1** a small ball of dough cooked and served with stew. **2** a pudding consisting of a round pastry case filled with fruit: *apple dumpling.* **3** *Informal.* a short plump person. **[C16:** *dump-,* perhaps variant of LUMP[1] + -LING[1]**]**

dump on *vb* (*intr, prep*) *Informal, chiefly U.S.* to abuse or criticize.

dump orbit *n* an earth orbit into which communications satellites may be moved at the end of their operational lives, where there is no risk of their interference or collision with working satellites in the normal orbits. Also called: **graveyard orbit.**

dumps (dʌmps) *pl n Informal.* a state of melancholy or depression (esp. in the phrase **down in the dumps**). **[C16:** probably from Middle Dutch *domp* haze, mist; see DAMP**]**

dump truck *or* **dumper-truck** *n* a small truck used on building sites, having a load-bearing container at the front that can be tipped up to unload the contents.

dumpy[1] ('dʌmpɪ) *adj* **dumpier, dumpiest.** short and plump; squat. **[C18:** perhaps related to DUMPLING**]** ► **'dumpily** *adv* ► **'dumpiness** *n*

dumpy[2] ('dʌmpɪ) *or* **dumpish** ('dʌmpɪʃ) *adj Rare.* in low spirits; depressed; morose. **[C17:** from C16 *dump;* see DUMPS**]**

dumpy level *n Surveying.* a levelling instrument consisting of a horizontal telescope with various rotational arrangements and a spirit level.

Dumyat (dum'jæt) *n* the Arabic name for **Damietta.**

dun[1] (dʌn) *vb* **duns, dunning, dunned. 1** (*tr*) to press or importune (a debtor) for the payment of a debt. ◆ *n* **2** a person, esp. a hired agent, who importunes another for the payment of a debt. **3** a demand for payment, esp. one in writing. **[C17:** of unknown origin**]**

dun[2] (dʌn) *n* **1** a brownish-grey colour. **2** a horse of this colour. **3** *Angling.* **3a** an immature adult mayfly (the subimago), esp. one of the genus *Ephemera.* **3b** an artificial fly imitating this or a similar fly. ◆ *adj* **dunner, dunnest. 4** of a dun colour. **5** dark and gloomy. **[**Old English *dunn;* related to Old Norse *dunna* wild duck, Middle Irish *doun* dark; see DUSK**]**

Duna ('dunɔ) *n* the Hungarian name for the **Danube.**

Dünaburg ('dy:naburk) *n* the German name (until 1893) for **Daugavpils.**

Dunaj ('dunaj) *n* the Czech name for the **Danube.**

Dunant (*French* dynɑ̃) *n* **Jean Henri** (ʒɑ̃ ɑ̃ri). 1828–1910, Swiss humanitarian, founder of the International Red Cross (1864): shared the Nobel peace prize 1901.

Dunărea ('dunərja) *n* the Romanian name for the **Danube.**

Dunbar[1] (dʌn'bɑ:) *n* a port and resort in SE Scotland, in East Lothian: scene of Cromwell's defeat of the Scots (1650). Pop.: 6518 (1991).

Dunbar[2] (dʌn'bɑ:) *n* **William.** ?1460–?1520, Scottish poet, noted for his satirical, allegorical, and elegiac works.

Dunbartonshire (dʌn'bɑ:tᵊnʃɪə, -ʃə) *n* a historical county of W Scotland: became part of Strathclyde region in 1975; administered since 1996 by the council areas of East Dunbartonshire and West Dunbartonshire.

Duncan ('dʌŋkən) *n* **Isadora** (,ɪzə'dɔ:rə). 1878–1927, U.S. dancer and choreographer, who influenced modern ballet by introducing greater freedom of movement.

Duncan I ('dʌŋkən) *n* died 1040, king of Scotland (1034–40); killed by Macbeth.

Duncan Phyfe *or* **Fife** (faɪf) *n* (*modifier*) *U.S. furniture.* of or in the manner of Duncan Phyfe, esp. in that which followed the Sheraton and Directoire styles.

dunce (dʌns) *n* a person who is stupid or slow to learn. **[C16:** from *Dunses* or *Dunsmen,* term of ridicule applied to the followers of John DUNS SCOTUS especially by 16th-century humanists**]** ► **'dunce,like** *adj*

dunce cap *or* **dunce's cap** *n* a conical paper hat, formerly placed on the head of a dull child at school.

Dundalk (dʌn'dɔ:k) *n* a town in NE Republic of Ireland, on **Dundalk Bay:** county town of Co. Louth. Pop.: 25 800 (1991).

Dundee[1] (dʌn'di:) *n* **1** a port in E Scotland, in City of Dundee council area, on the Firth of Tay: centre of the former British jute industry. Pop.: 158 981 (1991). **2 City of.** a council area in E Scotland. Pop.: 167 600 (1996 est.). Area: 65 sq. km (25 sq. miles). ► **Dundonian** (dʌn'dəunɪən) *n, adj*

Dundee[2] (dʌn'di:) *n* **1st Viscount,** title of *John Graham of Claverhouse.* ?1649–89, Scottish Jacobite leader, who died from his wounds after winning the battle of Killiecrankie.

Dundee cake *n Chiefly Brit.* a fairly rich fruit cake decorated with almonds.

dunderhead ('dʌndə,hɛd) *n* a stupid or slow-witted person; dunce. Also called: **dunderpate. [C17:** probably from Dutch *donder* thunder + HEAD; compare BLOCKHEAD**]** ► **'dunder,headed** *adj* ► **'dunder,headedness** *n*

dune (dju:n) *n* a mound or ridge of drifted sand, occurring on the sea coast and in deserts. **[C18:** via Old French from Middle Dutch *dūne;* see DOWN[3]**]**

Dunedin (dʌn'i:dɪn) *n* a port in New Zealand, on SE South Island: founded (1848) by Scottish settlers. Pop. (urban area): 113 500 (1995 est.).

Dunfermline (dʌn'fɜ:mlɪn) *n* a city in E Scotland, in SW Fife: ruined palace, a former residence of Scottish kings. Pop.: 55 083 (1991).

dung (dʌŋ) *n* **1a** excrement, esp. of animals; manure. **1b** (*as modifier*): *dung cart.* **2** something filthy. ◆ *vb* **3** (*tr*) to cover (ground) with manure. **[**Old English: prison; related to Old High German *tunc* cellar roofed with dung, Old Norse *dyngja* manure heap**]** ► **'dungy** *adj*

Dungannon (dʌn'gænən) *n* a district of S Northern Ireland, in Co. Tyrone. Pop.: 45 428 (1991). Area: 783 sq. km (302 sq. miles).

dungaree (,dʌŋgə'ri:) *n* **1** a coarse cotton fabric used chiefly for work clothes, etc. **2** (*pl*) **2a** a suit of workman's overalls made of this material consisting of trousers with a bib attached. **2b** a casual garment resembling this, usually worn by women or children. **3** *U.S.* trousers. **[C17:** from Hindi *dungrī,* after *Dungrī,* district of Bombay, where this fabric originated**]**

dung beetle *or* **chafer** *n* any of the various beetles of the family *Scarabaeidae* and related families that feed on or breed in dung.

Dungeness (,dʌndʒə'nɛs) *n* a low shingle headland on the S coast of England, in Kent: two nuclear power stations: automatic lighthouse.

dungeon ('dʌndʒən) *n* **1** a close prison cell, often underground. **2** a variant of **donjon. [C14:** from Old French *donjon;* related to Latin *dominus* master**]**

dung fly *n* any of various muscid flies of the subfamily *Cordilurinae,* such as the predatory **yellow dung fly** (*Scatophaga stercoraria*), that frequents cowpats to feed and lay its eggs.

dunghill ('dʌŋ,hɪl) *n* **1** a heap of dung. **2** a foul place, condition, or person.

dunite ('dʌnaɪt) *n* an ultrabasic igneous rock consisting mainly of olivine. **[C19:** named after Dun Mountain, a mountain in New Zealand where it is abundant**]**

duniwassal ('du:nɪ,wɑ:sᵊl) *n* (in Scotland) a minor nobleman. **[C16:** from Gaelic *duine* man +*uasal* noble**]**

dunk (dʌŋk) *vb* **1** to dip (bread, etc.) in tea, soup, etc., before eating. **2** to submerge or be submerged in liquid. **[C20:** from Pennsylvania Dutch, from Middle High German *dunken,* from Old High German *dunkōn;* see DUCK[2], TINGE**]** ► **'dunker** *n*

Dunker ('dʌŋkə) *or* **Dunkard** ('dʌŋkəd) *n* a member of the German Baptist Brethren. **[C18:** from German *Tunker* ducker**]**

Dunkerque (*French* dœ̃kɛrk) *n* a port in N France, on the Strait of Dover: scene of the evacuation of British and other Allied troops after the fall of France in 1940; industrial centre with an oil refinery and naval shipbuilding yards. Pop.: 190 879 (1990). English name: **Dunkirk** (dʌn'kɜ:k).

Dún Laoghaire (du:n 'lɪərɪ) *n* a port in E Republic of Ireland, on Dublin Bay. Pop.: 185 400 (1991). Former names: **Dunleary** (until 1821), **Kingstown** (1821–1921).

dunlin ('dʌnlɪn) *n* a small sandpiper, *Calidris* (or *Erolia*) *alpina,* of northern and arctic regions, having a brown back and black breast in summer. Also called: **red-backed sandpiper.** [C16: DUN[2] + -LING[1]]

Dunlop ('dʌnlɒp) *n* **John Boyd.** 1840–1921, Scottish veterinary surgeon, who devised the first successful pneumatic tyre, which was manufactured by the company named after him.

dunnage ('dʌnɪdʒ) *n* loose material used for packing cargo. [C14: of uncertain origin]

dunnakin ('dʌnəkɪn) *n Dialect.* a lavatory. Also called: **dunny.** [of obscure origin; but perhaps related to DUNG]

dunnite ('dʌnaɪt) *n* an explosive containing ammonium picrate. [C20: named after Colonel B. W. *Dunn* (1860–1936), American army officer who invented it]

dunno (dʌ'nəʊ, dʊ-, də-) *Slang. contraction of* (I) do not know.

dunnock ('dʌnək) *n* another name for **hedge sparrow.** [C15: from DUN[2] + -OCK]

dunny ('dʌnɪ) *n, pl* **-nies. 1** *Scot. dialect.* a cellar or basement. **2** *Dialect.* another word for **dunnakin. 3** *Austral. and N.Z. informal.* **3a** an outside lavatory. **3b** (*as modifier*): *a dunny roll; a dunny seat.* [C20: of obscure origin; but see DUNNAKIN]

Dunois (*French* dynwa) *n* **Jean** (ʒɑ̃), Comte de Dunois, known as *the Bastard of Orléans.* ?1403–68, French military commander, who defended Orléans against the English until the siege was raised by Joan of Arc (1429).

Dunoon (də'nu:n) *n* a town and resort in W Scotland, in Argyll and Bute, on the Firth of Clyde. Pop.: 9038 (1991).

Dunsany (dʌn'seɪnɪ) *n* **18th Baron,** title of *Edward John Moreton Drax Plunkett.* 1878–1957, Irish dramatist and short-story writer.

Dunsinane (dʌn'sɪnən) *n* a hill in central Scotland, in the Sidlaw Hills: the ruined fort at its summit is regarded as Macbeth's castle. Height: 308 m (1012 ft.).

USAGE The pronunciation ('dʌnsɪˌneɪn) is used in Shakespeare's *Macbeth* for the purposes of rhyme.

Duns Scotus ('dʌnz 'skɒtəs) *n* **John.** ?1265–1308, Scottish scholastic theologian and Franciscan priest: opposed the theology of St. Thomas Aquinas. See also **Scotism.**

Dunstable[1] ('dʌnstəbᵊl) *n* an industrial town in SE central England, in Bedfordshire. Pop.: 49 666 (1991).

Dunstable[2] ('dʌnstəbᵊl) *n* **John.** died 1453, English composer, esp. of motets and mass settings, noted for his innovations in harmony and rhythm.

Dunstan ('dʌnstən) *n* **Saint.** ?909–988 A.D., English prelate and statesman; archbishop of Canterbury (959–988). He revived monasticism in England on Benedictine lines and promoted education. Feast day: May 19.

dunt (dʌnt, dʊnt) *Scot. and northern English dialect.* ◆ *n* **1** a blow; thump. **2** the injury caused by such a blow. ◆ *vb* **3** to strike or hit. [C15: perhaps variant of DINT]

Duntroon (dʌn'tru:n) *n* a suburb of Canberra: seat of the Royal Military College of Australia.

duo ('dju:əʊ) *n, pl* **duos** *or* **dui** ('dju:i:). **1** *Music.* **1a** a pair of performers. **1b** another word for **duet. 2** a pair of actors, entertainers, etc. **3** *Informal.* a pair of closely connected individuals. [C16: via Italian from Latin: two]

duo- *combining form.* indicating two: *duotone.* [from Latin]

duobinary (ˌdju:əʊ'baɪnərɪ) *adj* denoting a communications system for coding digital data in which three data bands are used, 0, +1, −1. Compare **binary notation.**

duodecimal (ˌdju:əʊ'desɪməl) *adj* **1** relating to twelve or twelfths. ◆ *n* **2** a twelfth. **3** one of the numbers used in a duodecimal number system. ▸ ˌ**duo'decimally** *adv*

duodecimo (ˌdju:əʊ'desɪˌməʊ) *n, pl* **-mos. 1** a book size resulting from folding a sheet of paper into twelve leaves. Also called: **twelvemo.** Often written: **12mo, 12°. 2** a book of this size. [C17: from Latin phrase *in duodecimō* in twelfth, from *duodecim* twelve]

duodenary (ˌdju:ə'di:nərɪ) *adj* of or relating to the number 12; duodecimal. [C17: from Latin *duodēnārius* containing twelve]

duodenitis (ˌdju:əʊdɪ'naɪtɪs) *n* inflammation of the duodenum.

duodenum (ˌdju:əʊ'di:nəm) *n, pl* **-na** (-nə) *or* **-nums.** the first part of the small intestine, between the stomach and the jejunum. [C14: from Medieval Latin, shortened from *intestinum duodenum digitorum* intestine of twelve fingers' length, from Latin *duodēnī* twelve each] ▸ ˌ**duo'denal** *adj*

duologue *or U.S.* (*sometimes*) **duolog** ('dju:əˌlɒg) *n* **1** a part or all of a play in which the speaking roles are limited to two actors. **2** a less common word for **dialogue.**

duopoly (dju'ɒpəlɪ) *n* a situation in which control of a commodity or service in a particular market is vested in just two producers or suppliers. ▸ **duopolistic** (djuˌɒpə'lɪstɪk) *adj*

duotone ('dju:əˌtəʊn) *n Printing.* **1** a process for producing halftone illustrations using two shades of a single colour or black and a colour. **2** a picture produced by this process.

dup (dʌp) *vb* **dups, dupping, dupped.** (*tr*) *Archaic or dialect.* to open. [C16: contraction of DO[1] + UP]

dup. *abbrev. for* duplicate.

Duparc (*French* dypark) *n* **Henri** (ɑ̃ri), full name *Marie Eugène Henri Fouques Duparc.* 1848–1933, French composer of songs noted for their sad brooding quality.

dupatta (dʊ'pʌtə) *n* a scarf worn in India.

dupe (dju:p) *n* **1** a person who is easily deceived. **2** a person who unwittingly serves as the tool of another person or power. ◆ *vb* **3** (*tr*) to deceive, esp. by trickery; make a dupe or tool of; cheat; fool. [C17: from French, from Old French *duppe,* contraction of *de huppe* of (a) hoopoe (from Latin *upupa*); from the bird's reputation for extreme stupidity] ▸ **'dupable** *adj* ▸ ˌ**dupa'bility** *n* ▸ **'duper** *n* ▸ **'dupery** *n*

dupion ('dju:pɪən, -'pi:ɒn) *n* a silk fabric made from the threads of double cocoons. [C19: from French *doupion,* from Italian *doppione* double]

duple ('dju:pᵊl) *adj* **1** a less common word for **double. 2** *Music.* (of time or music) having two beats in a bar. [C16: from Latin *duplus* twofold, double]

Dupleix (*French* dyplɛks) *n* Marquis **Joseph François** (ʒozɛf frɑ̃swa). 1697–1763, French governor general in India (1742–54). His plan to establish a French empire in India was frustrated by Clive.

Duplessis-Mornay (*French* dyplɛsimɔrnɛ) *n* a variant of (Philippe de) **Mornay.**

duplet ('dju:plɪt) *n* **1** a pair of electrons shared between two atoms in a covalent bond. **2** *Music.* a group of two notes played in the time of three.

duple time *n* musical time with two beats in each bar.

duplex ('dju:plɛks) *n* **1** *U.S. and Canadian.* a duplex apartment or house. **2** a double-stranded region in a nucleic acid molecule. ◆ *adj* **3** having two parts. **4** *Machinery.* having pairs of components of independent but identical function. **5** permitting the transmission of simultaneous signals in both directions in a radio, telecommunications, or computer channel. [C19: from Latin: twofold, from *duo* two + *-plex* -FOLD] ▸ **du'plexity** *n*

duplex apartment *n U.S. and Canadian.* an apartment on two floors.

duplex chain *n Engineering.* a roller chain having two sets of rollers linked together, used for heavy-duty applications.

duplex house *n U.S. and Canadian.* a house divided into two separate dwellings. Also called (U.S.): **semidetached.**

duplicate *adj* ('dju:plɪkɪt). **1** copied exactly from an original. **2** identical. **3** existing as a pair or in pairs; twofold. ◆ *n* ('dju:plɪkɪt). **4** an exact copy; double. **5** something additional or supplementary of the same kind. **6** two exact copies (esp. in the phrase **in duplicate**). ◆ *vb* ('dju:plɪˌkeɪt). **7** (*tr*) to make a replica of. **8** (*tr*) to do or make again. **9** (*tr*) to make in a pair; make double. **10** (*intr*) *Biology.* to reproduce by dividing into two identical parts: *the chromosomes duplicated in mitosis.* [C15: from Latin *duplicāre* to double, from *duo* two + *plicāre* to fold] ▸ **duplicable** ('dju:plɪkəbᵊl) *adj* ▸ ˌ**duplica'bility** *n* ▸ **'duplicately** *adv* ▸ **'duplicative** *adj*

duplicate bridge *n* a form of contract bridge, esp. at clubs and in competitions, in which the hands are kept as dealt and played by different players. The partners with the highest average score are the winners. Also called: **board bridge.** Compare **rubber bridge.**

duplication (ˌdju:plɪ'keɪʃən) *n* **1** the act of duplicating or the state of being duplicated. **2** a copy; duplicate. **3** *Genetics.* a mutation in which there are two or more copies of a gene or of a segment of a chromosome.

duplicator ('dju:plɪˌkeɪtə) *n* an apparatus for making replicas of an original, such as a machine using a stencil wrapped on an ink-loaded drum.

duplicident (dju:'plɪsɪdənt) *adj* (of certain animals, such as rabbits) having two pairs of incisors in the upper jaw.

duplicity (dju:'plɪsɪtɪ) *n, pl* **-ties.** deception; double-dealing. [C15: from Old French *duplicite,* from Late Latin *duplicitās* a being double, from Latin DUPLEX] ▸ **du'plicitous** *adj*

dupondius (dju:'pɒndɪəs) *n, pl* **-dii** (-dɪˌaɪ). a brass coin of ancient Rome worth half a sesterce. [from Latin, from *duo* two + *pondus* weight]

duppy ('dʌpɪ) *n, pl* **-pies.** *Caribbean.* a spirit or ghost. [C18: probably of African origin]

du Pré (du: preɪ) *n* **Jacqueline.** 1945–87, English cellist. Multiple sclerosis ended her performing career (1973) after which she became a cello teacher.

Dupré (*French* dypre) *n* **Marcel** (marsɛl). 1886–1971, French organist and composer, noted as an improviser.

Duque de Caxias (*Portuguese* 'du:ke 'də: kə'ʃiəʃ) *n* a city in SE Brazil, near Rio de Janeiro. Pop.: 325 903 (1991).

Dur. *abbrev. for* Durham.

durable ('djʊərəbᵊl) *adj* long-lasting; enduring: *a durable fabric.* [C14: from Old French, from Latin *dūrābilis,* from *dūrāre* to last; see ENDURE] ▸ ˌ**dura'bility** *or* **'durableness** *n* ▸ **'durably** *adv*

durable goods *pl n* goods, such as most producer goods and some consumer goods, that require infrequent replacement. Compare **disposable goods, perishables.** Also called: **durables.**

durable press *n* **a** another term for **permanent press. b** (*as modifier*): *durable-press skirts.*

dural ('djʊərəl) *adj* relating to or affecting the dura mater.

Duralumin (djʊ'ræljʊmɪn) *n Trademark.* a light strong aluminium alloy containing 3.5–4.5 per cent of copper with small quantities of silicon, magnesium, and manganese; used in aircraft manufacture.

dura mater ('djʊərə 'meɪtə) *n* the outermost and toughest of the three membranes (see **meninges**) covering the brain and spinal cord. Often shortened to **dura.** [C15: from Medieval Latin, hard mother]

duramen (djʊ'reɪmɛn) *n* another name for **heartwood.** [C19: from Latin: hardness, from *dūrāre* to harden]

Durán (dju'ræn) *n* **Roberto.** born 1951, Panamanian boxer.

durance ('djʊərəns) *n Archaic or literary.* **1** imprisonment. **2** duration. [C15: from Old French, from *durer* to last, from Latin *dūrāre*]

Durance (*French* dyrɑ̃s) *n* a river in S France, rising in the Alps and flowing generally southwest into the Rhône. Length: 304 km (189 miles).

Durango (djʊ'ræŋgəʊ; *Spanish* du'raŋgo) *n* **1** a state in N central Mexico: high plateau, with the Sierra Madre Occidental in the west; irrigated agriculture (esp. cotton) and rich mineral resources. Capital: Durango. Pop.: 1 430 964 (1995 est.). Area: 119 648 sq. km (46 662 sq. miles). **2** a city in NW central Mexico, capital of Durango state: mining centre. Pop.: 348 036 (1990). Official name: **Victoria de Durango.**

Durante (də'ræntɪ) *n* **Jimmy,** known as *Schnozzle.* 1893–1980, U.S. comedian.

Duras (*French* dyra) *n* **Marguerite**, real name *Marguerite Donnadieu*. 1914–96, French novelist born in Giadinh, Indochina (now in Vietnam). Her works include *The Sea Wall* (1950), *Practicalities* (1990), *Écrire* (1993), and the script for the film *Hiroshima mon amour* (1960).

duration (dju'reɪʃən) *n* the length of time that something lasts or continues. [C14: from Medieval Latin *dūrātiō*, from Latin *dūrāre* to last] ▸ **du'rational** *adj*

durative ('djʊərətɪv) *Grammar*. ◆ *adj* **1** denoting an aspect of verbs that includes the imperfective and the progressive. ◆ *n* **2a** the durative aspect of a verb. **2b** a verb in this aspect.

Durazzo (du'rattso) *n* the Italian name for **Durrës**.

Durban ('dɜːbᵊn) *n* a port in E South Africa, in E KwaZulu/Natal province on the Indian Ocean: University of Natal (1909); resort and industrial centre, with oil refineries, shipbuilding yards, etc. Pop.: 715 669 (1991).

durbar ('dɜːbɑː, ˌdɜː'bɑː) *n* **a** (formerly) the court of a native ruler or a governor in India and British Colonial West Africa. **b** a levee at such a court. [C17: from Hindi *darbār* court, from Persian, from *dar* door + *bār* entry, audience]

Düren (*German* 'dyːrən) *n* a city in W Germany, in North Rhine-Westphalia. Pop.: 83 150 (1989 est.).

Dürer (*German* 'dyːrər) *n* **Albrecht** ('albrɛçt). 1471–1528, German painter and engraver, regarded as the greatest artist of the German Renaissance and noted particularly as a draughtsman and for his copper engravings and woodcuts.

duress (djʊ'rɛs, djʊə-) *n* **1** compulsion by use of force or threat; constraint; coercion (often in the phrase **under duress**). **2** *Law*. the illegal exercise of coercion. **3** confinement; imprisonment. [C14: from Old French *duresse*, from Latin *dūritia* hardness, from *dūrus* hard]

Durex ('djʊərɛks) *n, pl* **-rex**. *Trademark*. **1** a brand of condom. **2** *Austral*. a brand of adhesive tape.

Durga ('dʊəgæ) *n Hinduism*. the goddess Parvati portrayed as a warrior: renowned for slaying the buffalo demon, Mahisha. [from Sanskrit: the inaccessible one]

durgah ('dɜːgɑː) *n* a variant spelling of **dargah**.

Durga Puja (ˌdʊəgæ 'puːdʒə) *n* another name for **Navaratri**. [from Sanskrit DURGA + *puja* worship]

Durgapur ('dɜːgəˌpʊə) *n* a city in NE India, in West Bengal: heavy industry, including steelworks. Pop.: 425 836 (1991).

Durham ('dʌrəm) *n* **1** a county of NE England, on the North Sea: rises to the N Pennines in the west: the geographical and ceremonial county includes the unitary authorities of Hartlepool and Stockton-on-Tees (both part of Cleveland until 1996) and Darlington (created in 1997). Administrative centre: Durham. Pop. (including unitary authorities): 874 809 (1994 est.). Area (including unitary authorities): 2722 sq. km (1051 sq. miles). Abbrev.: **Dur. 2** a city in NE England, administrative centre of Co. Durham, on the River Wear: Norman cathedral; 11th-century castle (founded by William the Conqueror), now occupied by the University of Durham (1832). Pop.: 36 937 (1991). **3** a variety of shorthorn cattle. See **shorthorn**.

durian *or* **durion** ('djʊərɪən) *n* **1** a SE Asian bombacaceous tree, *Durio zibethinus*, having edible oval fruits with a hard spiny rind. **2** the fruit of this tree, which has an offensive smell but a pleasant taste: supposedly an aphrodisiac. [C16: from Malay, from *duri* thorn]

duricrust ('djʊərɪˌkrʌst) *n* a hard crust formed by the precipitation of minerals from water on or in soil from semiarid regions.

during ('djʊərɪŋ) *prep* **1** concurrently with (some other activity): *kindly don't sleep during my lectures!* **2** within the limit of (a period of time): *during the day*. [C14: from *duren* to last, ultimately from Latin *dūrāre* to last]

Durkheim ('dɜːkhaɪm; *French* dyrkɛm) *n* **Émile** (emil). 1858–1917, French sociologist, whose pioneering works include *De la Division du travail social* (1893).

durmast *or* **durmast oak** ('dɜːˌmɑːst) *n* **1** Also called: **sessile oak**. a large Eurasian oak tree, *Quercus petraea*, with lobed leaves and sessile acorns. Compare **pedunculate oak. 2** the heavy elastic wood of this tree, used in building and cabinetwork. [C18: probably alteration of *dun mast*; see DUN², MAST²]

durn (dɜːn) *interj, adj, adv, n* a U.S. variant of **darn²**.

duro ('dʊərəʊ) *n, pl* **-ros**. the silver peso of Spain or Spanish America. [from Spanish, shortened from *peso duro* hard peso, ultimately from Latin *dūrus* hard]

Duroc ('djʊərɒk) *n* an American breed of red lard pig. [C19: from *Duroc*, name of a stallion owned by the man who developed this breed]

durra ('dʌrə), **doura**, *or* **dourah** ('dʊərə) *n* an Old World variety of sorghum, *Sorghum vulgare durra*, with erect hairy flower spikes and round seeds: cultivated for grain and fodder. Also called: **Guinea corn, Indian millet**. [C18: from Arabic *dhurah* grain]

Durrell ('dʌrəl) *n* **1 Gerald (Malcolm)**. 1925–95, British zoologist and writer: his books include *The Bafut Beagles* (1954), *My Family and Other Animals* (1956), and *The Aye-aye and I* (1992). **2** his brother, **Lawrence (George)**. 1912–90, British poet and novelist; author of *The Alexandria Quartet* of novels, consisting of *Justine* (1957), *Balthazar* (1958), *Mountolive* (1958), and *Clea* (1960). Later works include *The Avignon Quintet* of novels (1974–85).

Dürrenmatt ('dyrənmat) *n* **Friedrich** ('friːdrɪç). 1921–90, Swiss dramatist and writer of detective stories, noted for his grotesque and paradoxical treatment of the modern world: author of *The Visit* (1956) and *The Physicists* (1962).

Durrës ('durrəs) *n* a port in W Albania, on the Adriatic. Pop.: 86 900 (1991 est.). Ancient names: **Epidamnus** (ɛpɪ'dæmnəs), **Dyrrachium** (də'reɪkɪəm). Italian name: **Durazzo**.

durrie ('dʌrɪ) *n* a cotton carpet made in India, often in rectangular pieces fringed at the ends: sometimes used as a sofa cover, wall hanging, etc. [from Hindi *darī*]

durry ('dʌrɪ) *n, pl* **-ries**. *Austral. slang*. a cigarette. [from DURRIE]

durst (dɜːst) *vb* a past tense of **dare**.

Duruflé (*French* dyrufle) *n* **Maurice** (mɔris). 1902–86, French composer and organist, best known for his *Requiem* (1947).

durum *or* **durum wheat** ('djʊərəm) *n* a variety of wheat, *Triticum durum*, with a high gluten content, cultivated mainly in the Mediterranean region, and used chiefly to make pastas. [C20: short for New Latin *trīticum dūrum*, literally: hard wheat]

durzi ('dɜːzɪ) *n* an Indian tailor. [C19: from Hindi, from Persian *darzi* from *darz* sewing]

Duse (*Italian* 'duːze) *n* **Eleonora** (ˌɛlɪə'nɔːrə). 1858–1924, Italian actress, noted as a tragedienne.

Dushanbe (duː'ʃɑːnbɪ) *n* the capital of Tajikistan; a cultural centre. Pop.: 524 000 (1994 est.). Former name (1929–61): **Stalinabad**.

dusk (dʌsk) *n* **1** twilight or the darker part of twilight. **2** *Poetic*. gloom; shade. ◆ *adj* **3** *Poetic*. shady; gloomy. ◆ *vb* **4** *Poetic*. to make or become dark. [Old English *dox*; related to Old Saxon *dosan* brown, Old High German *tusin* yellow, Norwegian *dusmen* misty, Latin *fuscus* dark brown]

dusky ('dʌskɪ) *adj* **duskier, duskiest**. **1** dark in colour; swarthy or dark-skinned. **2** dim. ▸ **'duskily** *adv* ▸ **'duskiness** *n*

Düsseldorf ('dʊsəlˌdɔːf; *German* 'dysəldɔrf) *n* an industrial city in W Germany, capital of North Rhine-Westphalia, on the Rhine: commercial centre of the Rhine-Ruhr industrial area. Pop.: 571 030 (1996 est.).

dust (dʌst) *n* **1** dry fine powdery material, such as particles of dirt, earth or pollen. **2** a cloud of such fine particles. **3** the powdery particles to which something is thought to be reduced by death, decay, or disintegration. **4a** the mortal body of man. **4b** the corpse of a dead person. **5** the earth; ground. **6** *Informal*. a disturbance; fuss (esp. in the phrases **kick up a dust, raise a dust**). **7** something of little or no worth. **8** *Informal*. (in mining parlance) silicosis or any similar respiratory disease. **9** short for **gold dust**. **10** ashes or household refuse. **11 bite the dust. 11a** to fail completely or cease to exist. **11b** to fall down dead. **12 dust and ashes**. something that is very disappointing. **13 shake the dust off one's feet**. to depart angrily or contemptuously. **14 throw dust in the eyes of**. to confuse or mislead. ◆ *vb* **15** (*tr*) to sprinkle or cover (something) with (dust or some other powdery substance): *to dust a cake with sugar; to dust sugar onto a cake*. **16** to remove dust by wiping, sweeping, or brushing. **17** *Archaic*. to make or become dirty with dust. ◆ See also **dust down, dust-up**. [Old English *dūst*; related to Danish *dyst* flour dust, Middle Dutch *dūst* dust, meal dust, Old High German *tunst* storm] ▸ **'dustless** *adj*

dust-bath *n* the action of a bird of driving dust into its feathers, which may dislodge parasites.

dustbin ('dʌstˌbɪn) *n* a large, usually cylindrical container for rubbish, esp. one used by a household. U.S. and Canadian names: **garbage can, trash can**.

dust bowl *n* a semiarid area in which the surface soil is exposed to wind erosion and dust storms occur.

Dust Bowl *n* **the**. the area of the south central U.S. that became denuded of topsoil by wind erosion during the droughts of the mid-1930s.

dustcart ('dʌstˌkɑːt) *n* a road vehicle for collecting domestic refuse. U.S. and Canadian name: **garbage truck**.

dust coat *n Brit*. a loose lightweight coat worn for early open motor-car riding. U.S. name: **duster**.

dust cover *n* **1** another name for **dustsheet**. **2** another name for **dust jacket**. **3** a perspex cover for the turntable of a record player.

dust devil *n* a strong miniature whirlwind that whips up dust, litter, leaves, etc., into the air.

dust down *vb* (*tr, adv*). **1** to remove dust from by brushing or wiping. **2** to reprimand severely. ▸ **dusting down** *n*

duster ('dʌstə) *n* **1** a cloth used for dusting furniture, etc. U.S. name: **dust cloth**. **2** a machine for blowing out dust over trees or crops. **3** a person or thing that dusts.

duster coat *n* a woman's loose summer coat with wide sleeves and no buttons, popular in the mid-20th century.

dust explosion *n* an explosion caused by the ignition of an inflammable dust, such as flour or sawdust, in the air.

dusting-powder *n* fine powder (such as talcum powder) used to absorb moisture, etc.

dust jacket *or* **cover** *n* a removable paper cover used to protect a bound book. Also called: **book jacket, jacket**.

dustman ('dʌstmən) *n, pl* **-men**. *Brit*. a man whose job is to collect domestic refuse.

dustpan ('dʌstˌpæn) *n* a short-handled hooded shovel into which dust is swept from floors, etc.

dustsheet ('dʌstˌʃiːt) *n Brit*. a large cloth or sheet used for covering furniture to protect it from dust. Also called: **dust cover**.

dust shot *n* the smallest size of shot for a shotgun.

dust storm *n* a windstorm that whips up clouds of dust.

dust-up *Informal*. ◆ *n* **1** a quarrel, fight, or argument. ◆ *vb* **dust up**. **2** (*tr, adv*) to attack or assault (someone).

dusty ('dʌstɪ) *adj* **dustier, dustiest**. **1** covered with or involving dust. **2** like dust in appearance or colour. **3** (of a colour) tinged with grey; pale: *dusty pink*. **4 a dusty answer**. an unhelpful or bad-tempered reply. **5 not so dusty**. *Informal*. not too bad; fairly well: often in response to the greeting *how are you?* ▸ **'dustily** *adv* ▸ **'dustiness** *n*

dusty miller *n* **1** Also called: **snow-in-summer**. a caryophyllaceous plant, *Cerastium tomentosum*, of SE Europe and Asia, having white flowers and downy stems and leaves: cultivated as a rock plant. **2** a plant, *Artemisia stelleriana*, of NE Asia and E North America, having small yellow flower heads and downy stems and leaves: family *Compositae* (composites). **3** any of various other downy plants, such as the rose campion.

dutch (dʌtʃ) *n Cockney slang.* wife. [C19: short for *duchess*]

Dutch (dʌtʃ) *n* **1** the language of the Netherlands, belonging to the West Germanic branch of the Indo-European family and quite closely related to German and English. See also **Flemish, Afrikaans. 2 the Dutch.** (*functioning as pl*) the natives, citizens, or inhabitants of the Netherlands. **3** See **Pennsylvania Dutch. 4** See **double Dutch. 5 in Dutch.** *Slang.* in trouble. ◆ *adj* **6** of, relating to, or characteristic of the Netherlands, its inhabitants, or their language. ◆ *adv* **7 go Dutch.** *Informal.* to share expenses equally.

Dutch auction *n* an auction in which the price is lowered by stages until a buyer is found.

Dutch barn *n Brit.* a farm building consisting of a steel frame and a curved roof.

Dutch cap *n* **1** a woman's lace cap with triangular flaps, characteristic of Dutch national dress. **2** a contraceptive device for women. See **diaphragm** (sense 2).

Dutch courage *n* **1** false courage gained from drinking alcohol. **2** alcoholic drink.

Dutch disease *n* the deindustrialization of an economy as a result of the discovery of a natural resource, as that which occurred in Holland with the exploitation of North Sea Oil, which raised the value of the Dutch currency, making its exports uncompetitive and causing its industry to decline.

Dutch doll *n* a jointed wooden doll.

Dutch door *n* the U.S. and Canadian name for **stable door.**

Dutch East Indies *n* **the.** a former name (1798–1945) of **Indonesia.** Also called: **Netherlands East Indies.**

Dutch elm *n* a widely planted hybrid elm tree, *Ulmus hollandica,* with spreading branches and a short trunk.

Dutch elm disease *n* a disease of elm trees caused by the fungus *Ceratocystis ulmi* and characterized by withering of the foliage and stems and eventual death of the tree.

Dutch gold *n* another name for **Dutch metal.**

Dutch Guiana *or* **Netherlands Guiana** *n* the former name of **Surinam.**

Dutch hoe *n* a type of hoe in which the head consists of a two-edged crossblade attached to two prongs or of a single pressing of this shape.

Dutchman ('dʌtʃmən) *n, pl* **-men. 1** a native, citizen, or inhabitant of the Netherlands. **2** a piece of wood, metal, etc., used to repair or patch faulty workmanship. **3** *S. African, often derogatory.* an Afrikaaner.

Dutchman's-breeches *n* (*functioning as sing*) a North American plant, *Dicentra cucullaria,* with finely divided basal leaves and pink flowers: family *Fumariaceae.* Also called: **colicweed.**

Dutchman's-pipe *n* a woody climbing plant, *Aristolochia sipho,* of the eastern U.S., cultivated for its greenish-brown mottled flowers, which are shaped like a curved pipe: family *Aristolochiaceae.*

Dutch mattress *n* another name for **mattress** (sense 2).

Dutch medicine *n S. African.* patent medicine, esp. made of herbs.

Dutch metal *or* **gold** *n* a substitute for gold leaf, consisting of thin sheets of copper that have been turned yellow by exposure to the fumes of molten zinc.

Dutch New Guinea *n* a former name (until 1963) of **Irian Jaya.**

Dutch oven *n* **1** an iron or earthenware container with a cover used for stews, etc. **2** a metal box, open in front, for cooking in front of an open fire.

Dutch Reformed Church *n* any of the three Calvinist Churches to which most Afrikaans-speaking South Africans belong.

Dutch rise *n N.Z.* an increase in wages that is of no benefit to the recipient.

Dutch rush *n* (*sometimes not cap.*) a horsetail, *Equisetum hyemale,* whose siliceous stems have been used for polishing and scouring pots and pans. Also called: **scouring rush.**

Dutch treat *n Informal.* an entertainment, meal, etc., where each person pays for himself.

Dutch uncle *n Informal.* a person who criticizes or reproves frankly and severely.

Dutch West Indies *pl n* **the.** a former name of the **Netherlands Antilles.**

Dutch wife *n* a long hard bolster used, esp. in the tropics, to support one's uppermost knee when sleeping on one's side.

duteous ('dju:tɪəs) *adj Formal or archaic.* dutiful; obedient. ▸ **'duteously** *adv* ▸ **'duteousness** *n*

dutiable ('dju:tɪəbᵊl) *adj* (of goods) liable to duty. ▸ **ˌdutia'bility** *n*

dutiful ('dju:tɪfʊl) *adj* **1** exhibiting or having a sense of duty. **2** characterized by or resulting from a sense of duty: *a dutiful answer.* ▸ **'dutifully** *adv* ▸ **'dutifulness** *n*

Dutton ('dʌtᵊn) *n* **Clarence Edward.** 1841–1912, American geologist who first developed the theory of isostasy.

duty ('dju:tɪ) *n, pl* **-ties. 1** a task or action that a person is bound to perform for moral or legal reasons. **2** respect or obedience due to a superior, older persons, etc.: *filial duty.* **3** the force that binds one morally or legally to one's obligations. **4** a government tax, esp. on imports. **5** *Brit.* **5a** the quantity of work for which a machine is designed. **5b** a measure of the efficiency of a machine. **6** the quantity of water necessary to irrigate an area of land to grow a particular crop. **7a** a job or service allocated. **7b** (*as modifier*): *duty rota.* **8 do duty for.** to act as a substitute for. **9 on** (*or* **off**) **duty.** at (*or* not at) work. [C13: from Anglo-French *dueté,* from Old French *deu* DUE]

duty-bound *adj* morally obliged as a matter of duty.

duty-free *adj, adv* **1** with exemption from customs or excise duties. ◆ *n* **2** goods sold in a duty-free shop.

duty-free shop *n* a shop, esp. one at an airport or on board a ship, that sells perfume, tobacco, etc., at duty-free prices.

duty officer *n* an officer (in the armed forces, police, etc.) on duty at a particular time.

duumvir (dju:'ʌmvə) *n, pl* **-virs** *or* **-viri** (-vɪˌri:). **1** *Roman history.* one of two coequal magistrates or officers. **2** either of two men who exercise a joint authority. [C16: from Latin, from *duo* two + *vir* man]

duumvirate (dju:'ʌmvɪrɪt) *n* the office of or government by duumvirs.

Duvalier (*French* dyvalje) *n* **1 François** (frɑ̃swa), known as *Papa Doc.* 1907–71, president of Haiti (1957–71). **2** his son, **Jean-Claude** (ʒɑ̃klod), known as *Baby Doc.* born 1951, Haitian statesman; president of Haiti 1971–86; deposed and exiled.

duvet ('du:veɪ) *n* **1** another name for **continental quilt. 2** Also called: **duvet jacket.** a down-filled jacket used esp. by mountaineers. [C18: from French, from earlier *dumet,* from Old French *dum* DOWN[2]]

duvetyn, duvetine, *or* **duvetyne** ('dju:vəˌti:n) *n* a soft napped velvety fabric of cotton, silk, wool, or rayon. [C20: from French *duvetine,* from *duvet* down + -INE[1]]

Du Vigneaud (du: 'vi:njəʊ) *n* **Vincent.** 1901–78, U.S. biochemist: Nobel prize for chemistry (1955) for his synthesis of the hormones oxytocin and vasopressin.

dux (dʌks) *n* (in Scottish and certain other schools) the top pupil in a class or school. [Latin: leader]

duyker ('daɪkə) *n* a variant spelling of **duiker.**

DV *abbrev. for:* **1** Deo volente. [Latin: God willing] **2** Douay Version (of the Bible).

dvandva ('dvɑ:ndvɑ:) *n* **1** a class of compound words consisting of two elements having a coordinate relationship as if connected by *and.* **2** a compound word of this type, such as *Austro-Hungarian, tragicomic.* [from Sanskrit *dvamdva* a pair, from the reduplication of *dva* TWO]

Dvina (*Russian* dvi'na) *n* **1 Northern.** a river in NW Russia, formed by the confluence of the Sukhona and Yug Rivers and flowing northwest to *Dvina Bay* in the White Sea. Length: 750 km (466 miles). Russian name: **Severnaya Dvina. 2 Western.** a river rising in W Russia, in the Valdai Hills and flowing south and southwest then northwest to the Gulf of Riga. Length: 1021 km (634 miles). Russian name: **Zapadnaya Dvina** ('zapədnəjə). Latvian name: **Daugava.**

Dvina Bay *or* **Dvina Gulf** *n* an inlet of the White Sea, off the coast of NW Russia.

Dvinsk (dvinsk) *n* transliteration of the former Russian name for **Daugavpils.**

DVLA (in Britain) *abbrev. for* Driver and Vehicle Licensing Agency.

DVM *abbrev. for* Doctor of Veterinary Medicine.

Dvořák ('dvɔ:ʒæk; *Czech* 'dvɔrʒa:k) *n* **Antonín** ('antɔnji:n), known as *Anton Dvořák.* 1841–1904, Czech composer, much of whose work reflects the influence of folk music. His best-known work is the *Symphony No. 9 From the New World* (1893).

D/W *abbrev. for* dock warrant.

dwaal (dwɑ:l) *n S. African.* a state of befuddlement. [Afrikaans]

dwale (dweɪl) *n* another name for **deadly nightshade.** [C14: perhaps of Scandinavian origin]

dwam (dwɑ:m) *or* **dwaum** (dwɔ:m) *Scot.* ◆ *n* **1** a stupor or daydream (esp. in the phrase **in a dwam**). ◆ *vb* **2** (*intr*) to faint or fall ill. [Old English *dwolma* confusion]

dwang (dwæŋ) *n Scot. and N.Z.* another name for **nogging** (sense 1). [C19: Scot.; compare Dutch *dwang* force, Middle Low German *dwanc*]

dwarf (dwɔ:f) *n, pl* **dwarfs** *or* **dwarves** (dwɔ:vz). **1** an abnormally undersized person, esp. one with a large head and short arms and legs. Compare **midget. 2a** an animal or plant much below the average height for the species. **2b** (*as modifier*): *a dwarf tree.* **3** (in folklore) a small ugly manlike creature, often possessing magical powers. **4** *Astronomy.* short for **dwarf star.** ◆ *vb* **5** to become or cause to become comparatively small in size, importance, etc. **6** (*tr*) to stunt the growth of. [Old English *dweorg;* related to Old Norse *dvergr,* Old High German *twerc*] ▸ **'dwarfish** *adj* ▸ **'dwarfishly** *adv* ▸ **'dwarfishness** *n*

dwarf bean *n* another name for **French bean.**

dwarf chestnut *n* **1** the edible nut of the chinquapin tree. **2** another name for **chinquapin** (sense 1).

dwarf cornel *n* an arctic and subarctic cornaceous plant, *Chamaepericlymenum suecicum* (or *Cornus suecica*), having small purple flowers surrounded by petal-like bracts.

dwarfism ('dwɔ:fɪzəm) *n* the condition of being a dwarf.

dwarf male *n* a male animal that is much smaller, and often internally simpler, than its female counterpart. Dwarf males are commonly carried by the female, as in species of angler fish.

dwarf mallow *n* a European malvaceous plant, *Malva neglecta* (or *M. rotundifolia*), having rounded leaves and small pinkish-white flowers.

dwarf star *n* any unevolved star, such as the sun, lying in the main sequence of the Hertzsprung-Russell diagram. Also called **main-sequence star.** See also **red dwarf, white dwarf.**

dweeb (dwi:b) *n Slang, chiefly U.S.* a stupid or uninteresting person. [C20: of unknown origin]

dwell (dwel) *vb* **dwells, dwelling, dwelt** (dwɛlt) *or* **dwelled.** (*intr*) **1** *Formal, literary.* to live as a permanent resident. **2** to live (in a specified state): *to dwell in poverty.* ◆ *n* **3** a regular pause in the operation of a machine. **4** a flat or constant-radius portion on a linear or rotary cam. [Old English *dwellan* to seduce, get lost; related to Old Saxon *bidwellian* to prevent, Old Norse *dvelja,* Old High German *twellen* to prevent] ▸ **'dweller** *n*

dwelling ('dwelɪŋ) *n Formal, literary.* a place of residence.

dwell on *or* **upon** *vb* (*intr, prep*) to think, speak, or write at length: *he dwells on his misfortunes.*

dwelt (dwɛlt) *vb* a past tense of **dwell.**

Dwem (dwem) *n acronym for* **Dead White European Male.**

dwindle ('dwɪndᵊl) *vb* to grow or cause to grow less in size, intensity, or number; diminish or shrink gradually. [C16: from Old English *dwīnan* to waste away; related to Old Norse *dvīna* to pine away]

dwt *abbrev. for:* **1** deadweight tonnage. **2** Also **dwt.** *Obsolete.* pennyweight. [*d*, from Latin *denarius* penny]

DX *Telegraphy, telephony.* **1** *symbol for* long distance. **2** (of a radio station) indicating that it is far away.

DX code *n Photog.* a code on a film cassette that automatically adjusts the film-speed setting on a suitably equipped camera to the correct ISO rating. [C20: from *d(aylight) (e)x(posure)*]

Dy *the chemical symbol for* dysprosium.

DY *international car registration for* Benin.

dyad ('daɪæd) *n* **1** *Maths.* an operator that is the unspecified product of two vectors. It can operate on a vector to produce either a scalar or vector product. **2** an atom or group that has a valency of two. **3** a group of two; couple. [C17: from Late Latin *dyas*, from Greek *duas* two, a pair]

dyadic (daɪ'ædɪk) *adj* **1** of or relating to a dyad. **2** relating to or based on two; twofold. **3** *Logic, maths.* (of a relation, predicate, etc.) relating two terms; binary. Compare **monadic, polyadic.** ◆ *n* **4** *Maths.* the sum of two or more dyads.

Dyak *or* **Dayak** ('daɪæk) *n, pl* **-aks** *or* **-ak.** a member of a Malaysian people of the interior of Borneo: noted for their long houses. [from Malay *Dayak* upcountry, from *darat* land]

dyarchy ('daɪɑːkɪ) *n, pl* **-chies.** a variant spelling of **diarchy.** ► **dy'archic, dy'archical,** *or* **dy'archal** *adj*

dybbuk ('dɪbək; *Hebrew* di'buk) *n, pl* **-buks** *or* **-bukkim** (*Hebrew* -bu'kim). *Judaism.* (in the folklore of the cabala) the soul of a dead sinner that has transmigrated into the body of a living person. [from Yiddish *dibbūk* devil, from Hebrew *dibbūq*; related to *dābhaq* to hang on, cling]

dye (daɪ) *n* **1** a staining or colouring substance, such as a natural or synthetic pigment. **2** a liquid that contains a colouring material and can be used to stain fabrics, skins, etc. **3** the colour or shade produced by dyeing. ◆ *vb* **dyes, dyeing, dyed. 4** (*tr*) to impart a colour or stain to (something, such as fabric or hair) by or as if by the application of a dye. [Old English *dēagian*, from *dēag* a dye; related to Old High German *tugōn* to change, Lettish *dūkans* dark] ► **'dyable** *or* **'dyeable** *adj* ► **'dyer** *n*

dyed-in-the-wool *adj* **1** extreme or unchanging in attitude, opinion, etc. **2** (of a fabric) made of dyed yarn.

dyeing ('daɪɪŋ) *n* the process or industry of colouring yarns, fabric, etc.

dyeline ('daɪˌlaɪn) *adj* another word for **diazo** (sense 2).

dyer's-greenweed *or esp. U.S.* **dyer's-broom** *n* a small Eurasian papilionaceous shrub, *Genista tinctoria*, whose yellow flowers yield a yellow dye, formerly mixed with woad to produce the colour Kendal green. Also called: **woadwaxen, woodwaxen.**

dyer's rocket *n* a Eurasian resedaceous plant, *Reseda luteola*, with a spike of yellowish-green flowers and long narrow leaves: formerly cultivated as the source of a yellow dye, used with woad to make Lincoln green. Also called: **weld.**

dyer's-weed *n* any of several plants that yield a dye, such as woad, dyer's rocket, and dyer's-greenweed.

dyestuff ('daɪˌstʌf) *n* a substance that can be used as a dye or from which a dye can be obtained.

dyewood ('daɪˌwʊd) *n* any wood, such as brazil, from which dyes and pigments can be obtained.

Dyfed ('dʌvɛd) *n* a former county in SW Wales: created in 1974 from Cardiganshire, Pembrokeshire, and Carmarthenshire; in 1996 it was replaced by Pembrokeshire, Carmarthenshire, and Ceredigion.

dying ('daɪɪŋ) *vb* **1** the present participle of **die**[1]. ◆ *adj* **2** relating to or occurring at the moment of death: *a dying wish.*

dyke[1] *or* **dike** (daɪk) *n* **1** an embankment constructed to prevent flooding, keep out the sea, etc. **2** a ditch or watercourse. **3** a bank made of earth excavated for and placed alongside a ditch. **4** *Scot.* a wall, esp. a dry-stone wall. **5** a barrier or obstruction. **6** a vertical or near-vertical wall-like body of igneous rock intruded into cracks in older rock. **7** *Austral. and N.Z. informal.* **7a** a lavatory. **7b** (*as modifier*): *a dyke roll.* ◆ *vb* **8** *Civil engineering.* an embankment or wall built to confine a river to a particular course. **9** (*tr*) to protect, enclose, or drain (land) with a dyke. [C13: modification of Old English *dīc* ditch; compare Old Norse *dīki* ditch]

dyke[2] *or* **dike** (daɪk) *n Slang.* a lesbian. [C20: of unknown origin]

Dylan ('dɪlən) *n* **Bob.** real name *Robert Allen Zimmerman.* born 1941, U.S. rock singer and songwriter, also noted for his acoustic protest songs in the early 1960s. His albums include *The Freewheelin' Bob Dylan* (1963), *Highway 61 Revisited* (1965), *Blonde on Blonde* (1966), *John Wesley Harding* (1968), *Blood on the Tracks* (1974), *Oh Mercy* (1989), and *Time Out of Mind* (1997).

dynameter (daɪ'næmɪtə) *n* an instrument for determining the magnifying power of telescopes.

dynamic (daɪ'næmɪk) *adj* **1** of or concerned with energy or forces that produce motion, as opposed to *static.* **2** of or concerned with dynamics. **3** Also: **dynamical.** characterized by force of personality, ambition, energy, new ideas, etc. **4** *Music.* of, relating to, or indicating dynamics: *dynamic marks.* **5** *Computing.* (of a memory) needing its contents refreshed periodically. Compare **static** (sense 8). [C19: from French *dynamique*, from Greek *dunamikos* powerful, from *dunamis* power, from *dunasthai* to be able] ► **dy'namically** *adv*

dynamic psychology *n Psychol.* any system of psychology that emphasizes the interaction between different motives, emotions, and drives.

dynamic range *n* the range of signal amplitudes over which an electronic communications channel can operate within acceptable limits of distortion. The range is determined by system noise at the lower end and by the onset of overload at the upper end.

dynamics (daɪ'næmɪks) *n* **1** (*functioning as sing*) the branch of mechanics concerned with the forces that change or produce the motions of bodies. Compare **statics, kinematics. 2** (*functioning as sing*) the branch of mechanics that includes statics and kinetics. See **statics, kinetics. 3** (*functioning as sing*) the branch of any science concerned with forces. **4** those forces that produce change in any field or system. **5** *Music.* **5a** the various degrees of loudness called for in performance. **5b** Also called: **dynamic marks, dynamic markings.** directions and symbols used to indicate degrees of loudness.

dynamism ('daɪnəˌmɪzəm) *n* **1** *Philosophy.* any of several theories that attempt to explain phenomena in terms of an immanent force or energy. Compare **mechanism** (sense 5), **vitalism. 2** the forcefulness of an energetic personality. ► **'dynamist** *n* ► **ˌdyna'mistic** *adj*

dynamite ('daɪnəˌmaɪt) *n* **1** an explosive consisting of nitroglycerine or ammonium nitrate mixed with kieselguhr, sawdust, or wood pulp. **2** *Informal.* a spectacular or potentially dangerous person or thing. ◆ *vb* **3** (*tr*) to mine or blow up with dynamite. [C19 (coined by Alfred Nobel): from DYNAMO- + -ITE[1]] ► **'dynaˌmiter** *n*

dynamo ('daɪnəˌməʊ) *n, pl* **-mos. 1** a device for converting mechanical energy into electrical energy, esp. one that produces direct current. Compare **generator** (sense 1). **2** *Informal.* an energetic hard-working person. [C19: short for *dynamoelectric machine*]

dynamo- *or sometimes before a vowel* **dynam-** *combining form.* indicating power: *dynamoelectric; dynamite.* [from Greek, from *dunamis* power]

dynamoelectric (ˌdaɪnəməʊɪ'lɛktrɪk) *or* **dynamoelectrical** *adj* of or concerned with the interconversion of mechanical and electrical energy.

dynamometer (ˌdaɪnə'mɒmɪtə) *n* any of a number of instruments for measuring power or force.

dynamometry (ˌdaɪnə'mɒmɪtrɪ) *n* **1** the science of power measurement. **2** the manufacture and use of dynamometers. ► **dynamometric** (ˌdaɪnəməʊ'mɛtrɪk) *or* **ˌdynamo'metrical** *adj*

dynamotor ('daɪnəˌməʊtə) *n* an electrical machine having a single magnetic field and two independent armature windings of which one acts as a motor and the other a generator: used to convert direct current from an accumulator into alternating current.

dynast ('dɪnəst, -æst) *n* a ruler, esp. a hereditary one. [C17: from Latin *dynastēs*, from Greek *dunastēs*, from *dunasthai* to be powerful]

dynasty ('dɪnəstɪ) *n, pl* **-ties. 1** a sequence of hereditary rulers: *an Egyptian dynasty.* **2** any sequence of powerful leaders of the same family: *the Kennedy dynasty.* [C15: via Late Latin from Greek *dunasteia*, from *dunastēs* DYNAST] ► **dynastic** (dɪ'næstɪk) *or* **dy'nastical** *adj* ► **dy'nastically** *adv*

dynatron oscillator ('daɪnəˌtrɒn) *n Electronics.* an oscillator containing a tetrode in which the screen grid is more positive than the anode, causing the anode current to decrease as its voltage increases. [C20: from DYNA(MO)- + -TRON]

dyne (daɪn) *n* the cgs unit of force; the force that imparts an acceleration of 1 centimetre per second per second to a mass of 1 gram. 1 dyne is equivalent to 10^{-5} newton or 7.233×10^{-5} poundal. [C19: from French, from Greek *dunamis* power, force]

dynode ('daɪnəʊd) *n* an electrode onto which a beam of electrons can fall, causing the emission of a greater number of electrons by secondary emission. They are used in photomultipliers to amplify the signal.

dys- *prefix* **1** diseased, abnormal, or faulty: *dysentery; dyslexia.* **2** difficult or painful: *dysuria.* **3** unfavourable or bad: *dyslogistic.* [via Latin from Greek *dus-*]

dysarthria (dɪs'ɑːθrɪə) *n* imperfect articulation of speech caused by damage to the nervous system. [from DYS- + *arthria* from Greek *arthron* articulation]

dyscalculia (ˌdɪskæl'kjuːlɪə) *n* severe difficulty in making simple mathematical calculations, due to cerebral disease or injury. [C20: from DYS- + Latin *calculare* to calculate]

dyscrasia (dɪs'kreɪzɪə) *n Obsolete.* any abnormal physiological condition, esp. of the blood. [C19: New Latin, from Medieval Latin: an imbalance of humours, from Greek, from DYS- + *-krasia*, from *krasis* a mixing]

dysentery ('dɪsᵊntrɪ) *n* infection of the intestine with bacteria or amoebae, marked chiefly by severe diarrhoea with the passage of mucus and blood. [C14: via Latin from Greek *dusenteria*, from *dusentera*, literally: bad bowels, from DYS- + *enteron* intestine] ► **dysenteric** (ˌdɪsᵊn'tɛrɪk) *adj*

dysfunction (dɪs'fʌŋkʃən) *n* **1** *Med.* any disturbance or abnormality in the function of an organ or part. **2** (esp. of a family) failure to show the characteristics or fulfil the purposes accepted as normal or beneficial.

dysfunctional (dɪs'fʌŋkʃənᵊl) *adj* **1** *Med.* (of an organ or part) not functioning normally. **2** (esp. of a family) characterized by a breakdown of normal or beneficial relationships between members of the group.

dysgenic (dɪs'dʒɛnɪk) *adj* **1** of, relating to, or contributing to a degeneration or deterioration in the fitness and quality of a race or strain. **2** of or relating to dysgenics.

dysgenics (dɪs'dʒɛnɪks) *n* (*functioning as sing*) the study of factors capable of reducing the quality of a race or strain, esp. the human race. Also called: **cacogenics.**

dysgraphia (dɪs'græfɪə) *n* inability to write correctly, caused by disease of part of the brain.

dyskinesia (dɪskɪ'niːzɪə) *n* involuntary repetitive movements, such as those occurring in chorea. [DYS- + *-kinesia* from Greek *kinesis* movement]

dyslalia (dɪs'leɪlɪə) *n* defective speech characteristic of those affected by aphasia.

dyslexia (dɪs'lɛksɪə) *n* a developmental disorder which can cause learning difficulty in one or more of the areas of reading, writing, and numeracy. Nontechnical name: **word blindness.** [from DYS- + *-lexia* from Greek *lexis* word] ► **dyslectic** (dɪs'lɛktɪk) *adj, n* ► **dys'lexic** *adj*

dyslogistic (ˌdɪslə'dʒɪstɪk) *adj Rare.* disapproving. [C19: from DYS- + *-logistic,* as in *eulogistic*] ▸ ˌ**dyslo'gistically** *adv*

dysmenorrhoea *or esp. U.S.* **dysmenorrhea** (ˌdɪsmɛnə'rɪə, dɪsˌmɛn-) *n* abnormally difficult or painful menstruation. ▸ ˌ**dysmenor'rhoeal** *or esp. U.S.* ˌ**dysmenor'rheal** *adj*

dysmorphophobia (dɪsˌmɔːfəʊ'fəʊbɪə) *n* an obsessive fear that one's body, or any part of it, is repulsive or may become so.

dyspepsia (dɪs'pɛpsɪə) *or* **dyspepsy** (dɪs'pɛpsɪ) *n* indigestion or upset stomach. [C18: from Latin, from Greek *duspepsia,* from DYS- + *pepsis* digestion]

dyspeptic (dɪs'pɛptɪk) *adj also* **dyspeptical. 1** relating to or suffering from dyspepsia. **2** irritable. ◆ *n* **3** a person suffering from dyspepsia. ▸ **dys'peptically** *adv*

dysphagia (dɪs'feɪdʒɪə) *n* difficulty in swallowing, caused by obstruction or spasm of the oesophagus. [C18: New Latin, from DYS- + Greek *-phagos;* see PHAGO-] ▸ **dysphagic** (dɪs'fædʒɪk) *adj*

dysphasia (dɪs'feɪzɪə) *n* a disorder of language caused by a brain lesion. [see DYS- + -PHASIA] ▸ **dys'phasic** *adj, n*

dysphemism ('dɪsfɪˌmɪzəm) *n* **1** substitution of a derogatory or offensive word or phrase for an innocuous one. **2** the word or phrase so substituted. [C19: DYS- + EUPHEMISM] ▸ ˌ**dysphe'mistic** *adj*

dysphonia (dɪs'fəʊnɪə) *n* any impairment in the ability to speak normally, as from spasm or strain of the vocal cords. [C18: New Latin, from Greek: harshness of sound, from DYS- + *-phōnia* -PHONY] ▸ **dysphonic** (dɪs'fɒnɪk) *adj*

dysphoria (dɪs'fɔːrɪə) *n* a feeling of being ill at ease. [C20: New Latin, from Greek DYS- + *-phoria,* from *pherein* to bear] ▸ **dysphoric** (dɪs'fɒrɪk) *adj*

dysplasia (dɪs'pleɪzɪə) *n* abnormal development of an organ or part of the body, including congenital absence. [C20: New Latin, from DYS- + *-plasia,* from Greek *plasis* a moulding] ▸ **dysplastic** (dɪs'plæstɪk) *adj*

dyspnoea *or U.S.* **dyspnea** (dɪsp'niːə) *n* difficulty in breathing or in catching the breath. Compare **eupnoea.** [C17: via Latin from Greek *duspnoia,* from DYS- + *pnoē* breath, from *pnein* to breathe] ▸ **dysp'noeal, dysp'noeic** *or U.S.* **dysp'neal, dysp'neic** *adj*

dyspraxia (dɪs'præksɪə) *n Pathol.* an impairment in the control of the motor system. [DYS- + PRAX(IS) + -IA]

dysprosium (dɪs'prəʊsɪəm) *n* a soft silvery-white metallic element of the lanthanide series: used in laser materials and as a neutron absorber in nuclear control rods. Symbol: Dy; atomic no.: 66; atomic wt.: 162.50; valency: 3; relative density: 8.551; melting pt.: 1412°C; boiling pt.: 2567°C. [C20: New Latin, from Greek *dusprositos* difficult to get near + -IUM]

dyssynergia (dɪsɪ'nɜːdʒɪə) *n* muscular incoordination caused by a brain disorder. [from DYS- + Greek *synergia* cooperation]

dystaxia (dɪs'tæksɪə) *n Pathol.* lack of muscular coordination resulting in shaky limb movements and unsteady gait. [from DYS- + Greek *-taxia,* from *tassein* to put in order]

dysteleology (ˌdɪstelɪ'ɒlədʒɪ, -tiːlɪ-) *n Philosophy.* the denial of purpose in life. Compare **teleology.** ▸ **dysˌteleo'logical** *adj* ▸ ˌ**dystele'ologist** *n*

dysthymia (dɪs'θaɪmɪə) *n Psychiatry.* **1** the characteristics of the neurotic and introverted, including anxiety, depression, and compulsive behaviour. **2** *Obsolete.* a relatively mild depression. [C19: New Latin, from Greek *dusthumia,* from DYS- + *thumos* mind] ▸ **dys'thymic** *adj*

dysthymic disorder *n* a psychiatric disorder characterized by generalized depression that lasts for at least a year.

dystocia (dɪs'təʊʃə) *n Med.* abnormal, slow, or difficult childbirth, usually because of disordered or ineffective contractions of the uterus. [New Latin, from Greek, from *dus-* (see DYS-) + *tokos* childbirth + -IA] ▸ **dys'tocial** *adj*

dystonia (dɪs'təʊnɪə) *n* a neurological disorder, caused by disease of the basal ganglia, in which the muscles of the trunk, shoulders, and neck go into spasm, so that the head and limbs are held in unnatural positions. [from DYS- + *-tonia* from Greek *tonos* tension, from *teinen* to stretch]

dystopia (dɪs'təʊpɪə) *n* an imaginary place where everything is as bad as it can be. [C19 (coined by J. S. Mill): from DYS- + UTOPIA] ▸ **dys'topian** *adj, n*

dystrophin ('dɪstrəfɪn) *n* a protein, the absence of which is believed to cause muscular dystrophy.

dystrophy ('dɪstrəfɪ) *or* **dystrophia** (dɪ'strəʊfɪə) *n* **1** any of various bodily disorders, characterized by wasting of tissues. See also **muscular dystrophy. 2** *Ecology.* a condition of lake water when it is too acidic and poor in oxygen to support life, resulting from excessive humus content. [C19: New Latin *dystrophia,* from DYS- + Greek *trophē* food] ▸ **dystrophic** (dɪs'trɒfɪk) *adj*

dysuria (dɪs'jʊərɪə) *n* difficult or painful urination. [C14: via Latin from Greek *dusouria,* from DYS- + -URIA] ▸ **dys'uric** *adj*

dytiscid (dɪ'tɪsɪd, daɪ-) *n* **1** any carnivorous aquatic beetle of the family *Dytiscidae,* having large flattened back legs used for swimming. ◆ *adj* **2** of, relating to, or belonging to the *Dytiscidae.* [C19: from New Latin *Dytiscus* genus name, changed from Greek *dutikos* able to dive, from *duein* to dive]

Dyula (diː'uːlə, 'djuːlə) *n* **1** (*pl* **-la** *or* **-las**) a member of a negroid people of W Africa, living chiefly in the rain forests of the Ivory Coast, where they farm rice, etc. **2** the language of this people, belonging to the Mande branch of the Niger-Congo family.

DZ *international car registration for* Algeria. [from Arabic *Djazïr*]

dz. *abbrev. for* dozen.

Dzaudzhikau (dzəudʒi'kau) *n* the former name (1944–54) of **Ordzhonikidze.**

Dzerzhinsk (*Russian* dzɪr'ʒinsk) *n* an industrial city and port in central Russia. Pop.: 285 000 (1995 est.).

Dzhambul (*Russian* dʒam'bul) *n* the former name (1938–91) of **Auliye-Ata.**

dziggetai ('dʒɪgɪˌtaɪ) *n* a variant of **chigetai.**

dzo (zəʊ) *n, pl* **dzos** *or* **dzo.** a variant spelling of **zo.**

Dzongka *or* **Dzongkha** ('zɒŋkə) *n* the official language of Bhutan: a dialect of Tibetan.

Dzungaria (dzʊŋ'gɛərɪə, zʊŋ-) *n* a variant transliteration of the Chinese name for **Junggar Pendi.**

Ee

e *or* **E** (iː) *n, pl* **e's, E's,** *or* **Es. 1** the fifth letter and second vowel of the modern English alphabet. **2** any of several speech sounds represented by this letter, in English as in *he, bet,* or *below.*

e *symbol for:* **1** *Maths.* a transcendental number, fundamental to mathematics, that is the limit of $(1 + 1/n)^n$ as *n* increases to infinity: used as the base of natural logarithms. Approximate value: 2.718 282...; relation to π: $e^{\pi i} = -1$, where i = $\sqrt{-1}$. **2** electron. **3** *Chess.* See **algebraic notation.**

E *symbol for:* **1** earth. **2** East. **3** English. **4** Egypt(ian). **5** exa-. **6** *Music.* **6a** a note having a frequency of 329.63 hertz (**E above middle C**) or this value multiplied or divided by any power of 2; the third note of the scale of C major. **6b** a key, string, or pipe producing this note. **6c** the major or minor key having this note as its tonic. **7** *Physics.* **7a** energy. **7b** electric field strength. **7c** electromotive force. **7d** Young's modulus (of elasticity). **8** *Logic.* a universal negative categorical proposition, such as *no pigs can fly:* often symbolized as **SeP.** Compare **A, I**[2], **O**[1]. [from Latin *(n)e(go)* I deny] **9a** a person without a regular income, or who is dependent on the state on a long-term basis because of unemployment, sickness, old age, etc. **9b** (*as modifier*): *E worker.* ◆ See also **occupation groupings.** ◆ **10** *international car registration for* Spain. [from Spanish *España*]

e. *abbrev. for:* **1** engineer(ing). **2** *Telephony.* Erlang.

E. *abbrev. for* Earl.

e-[1] *prefix forming verbs and verbal derivatives.* **1** out: *eviscerate; egest.* **2** away: *elapse; elongate.* **3** outside: *evaginate.* **4** completely: *evaporate.* **5** without: *ebracteate.* [from Latin ē- away; related to EX-[1]]

e-[2] *prefix* electronic: *e-mail; e-money.*

E- *prefix* used with numbers indicating a standardized system within the European Union, as of recognized food additives or standard pack sizes. See also **E number.**

ea. *abbrev. for* each.

each (iːtʃ) *determiner* **1a** every (one) of two or more considered individually: *each day; each person.* **1b** (*as pronoun*): *each gave according to his ability.* ◆ *adv* **2** for, to, or from each one; apiece: *four apples each.* [Old English *ǣlc;* related to Old High German *ēogilīh,* Old Frisian *ellik,* Dutch *elk*]

USAGE *Each* is a singular pronoun and should be used with a singular form of a verb: *each of the candidates was* (not *were*) *interviewed separately.* See also at **either.**

each other *pron* used when the action, attribution, etc., is reciprocal: *furious with each other.*

USAGE *Each other* and *one another* are interchangeable in modern British usage.

each way *adj, adv Horse racing etc., chiefly Brit.* (of a bet) made on the same runner or contestant to win or come second or third in a race. Also: **both ways.** U.S. term: **across-the-board.**

EACSO (iːˈɑːksəʊ) *n acronym for* East African Common Services Organization.

Eadred (ˈɛdrɪd) *n* died 955 A.D., king of England (946–55): regained Northumbria (954) from the Norwegian king Eric Bloodaxe.

Eadwig (ˈɛdwɪg) *or* **Edwy** (ˈɛdwɪ) *n* died 959 A.D., king of England (955–57).

eager[1] (ˈiːgə) *adj* **1** (*postpositive;* often foll. by *to* or *for*) impatiently desirous (of); anxious or avid (for): *he was eager to see her departure.* **2** characterized by or feeling expectancy or great desire: *an eager look.* **3** *Archaic.* tart or biting; sharp. [C13: from Old French *egre,* from Latin *acer* sharp, keen] ▸ **ˈeagerly** *adv* ▸ **ˈeagerness** *n*

eager[2] (ˈeɪgə) *n* a variant spelling of **eagre.**

eager beaver *n Informal.* a person who displays conspicuous diligence, esp. one who volunteers for extra work.

eagle (ˈiːgᵊl) *n* **1** any of various birds of prey of the genera *Aquila, Harpia,* etc. (see **golden eagle, harpy eagle**), having large broad wings and strong soaring flight: family *Accipitridae* (hawks, etc.). See also **sea eagle.** Related adj: **aquiline. 2** a representation of an eagle used as an emblem, etc., esp. representing power: *the Roman eagle.* **3** a standard, seal, etc., bearing the figure of an eagle. **4** *Golf.* a score of two strokes under par for a hole. **5** a former U.S. gold coin worth ten dollars: withdrawn from circulation in 1934. **6** the shoulder insignia worn by a U.S. full colonel or equivalent rank. ◆ *vb* **7** *Golf.* to score two strokes under par for a hole. [C14: from Old French *aigle,* from Old Provençal *aigla,* from Latin *aquila,* perhaps from *aquilus* dark]

eagle-eyed *adj* having keen or piercing eyesight.

eagle-hawk *n* a large aggressive Australian eagle, *Aquila audax.* Also called: **wedge-tailed eagle.**

eagle owl *n* a large owl, *Bubo bubo,* of Europe and Asia. It has brownish speckled plumage and large ear tufts.

eagle ray *n* any of various rays of the family *Myliobatidae,* related to the stingrays but having narrower pectoral fins and a projecting snout with heavily browed eyes.

eaglestone (ˈiːgᵊlˌstəʊn) *n* a hollow oval nodule of clay ironstone, formerly thought to have magical properties.

eaglet (ˈiːglɪt) *n* a young eagle.

eaglewood (ˈiːgᵊlˌwʊd) *n* **1** an Asian thymelaeaceous tree, *Aquilaria agallocha,* having fragrant wood that yields a resin used as a perfume. **2** the wood of this tree. ◆ Also called: **aloes, aloes wood, agalloch, lignaloes.**

eagre *or* **eager** (ˈeɪgə) *n* a tidal bore, esp. of the Humber or Severn estuaries. [C17: perhaps from Old English *ēagor* flood; compare Old English *ēa* river, water]

EAK *international car registration for* (East Africa) Kenya.

Eakins (ˈiːkɪnz) *n* **Thomas.** 1844–1916, U.S. painter of portraits and sporting life: a noted realist.

ealdorman (ˈɔːldəmən) *n, pl* **-men.** an official of Anglo-Saxon England, appointed by the king, who was responsible for law, order, and justice in his shire and for leading his local fyrd in battle. [Old English *ealdor* lord + MAN]

Ealing (ˈiːlɪŋ) *n* a borough of W Greater London, formed in 1965 from Acton, Ealing, and Southall. Pop.: 289 800 (1994 est.). Area: 55 sq. km (21 sq. miles).

EAM *n* (in World War II) the leftist resistance in German-occupied Greece. [C20: from Modern Greek *Ethniko Apeleutherotiko Metopo* National Liberation Front]

-ean *suffix forming adjectives.* a variant of **-an:** *Caesarean.*

E & OE *abbrev. for* errors and omissions excepted.

ear[1] (ɪə) *n* **1** the organ of hearing and balance in higher vertebrates and of balance only in fishes. In man and other mammals it consists of three parts (see **external ear, middle ear, internal ear**). Related adjs.: **aural, otic. 2** the outermost cartilaginous part of the ear (pinna) in mammals, esp. man. **3** the sense of hearing. **4** sensitivity to musical sounds, poetic diction, etc.: *he has an ear for music.* **5** attention, esp. favourable attention; consideration; heed (esp. in the phrases **give ear to, lend an ear**). **6** an object resembling the external ear in shape or position, such as a handle on a jug. **7** Also called (esp. Brit.): **earpiece.** a display box at the head of a newspaper page, esp. the front page, for advertisements, etc. **8 all ears.** very attentive; listening carefully. **9 by ear.** without reading from written music. **10 fall on deaf ears.** to be ignored or pass unnoticed. **11 have hard ears.** *Caribbean.* to be stubbornly disobedient. **12 a flea in one's ear.** *Informal.* a sharp rebuke. **13 have the ear of.** to be in a position to influence: *he has the ear of the president.* **14 in one ear and out the other.** heard but unheeded. **15 keep** (*or* **have**) **one's ear to the ground.** to be or try to be well informed about current trends and opinions. **16 make a pig's ear of.** *Informal.* to ruin disastrously. **17 one's ears are burning.** one is aware of being the topic of another's conversation. **18 out on one's ear.** *Informal.* dismissed unceremoniously. **19 play by ear. 19a** to act according to the demands of a situation rather than to a plan; improvise. **19b** to perform a musical piece on an instrument without written music. **20 prick up one's ears.** to start to listen attentively; become interested. **21 set by the ears.** to cause disagreement or commotion. **22 a thick ear.** *Informal.* a blow on the ear delivered as punishment, in anger, etc. **23 turn a deaf ear.** to be deliberately unresponsive. **24 up to one's ears.** *Informal.* deeply involved, as in work or debt. **25 wet behind the ears.** *Informal.* inexperienced; naive; immature. [Old English *ēare;* related to Old Norse *eyra,* Old High German *ōra,* Gothic *ausō,* Greek *ous,* Latin *auris*] ▸ **ˈearless** *adj* ▸ **ˈearˌlike** *adj*

ear[2] (ɪə) *n* **1** the part of a cereal plant, such as wheat or barley, that contains the seeds, grains, or kernels. ◆ *vb* **2** (*intr*) (of cereal plants) to develop such parts. [Old English *ēar;* related to Old High German *ahar,* Old Norse *ax,* Gothic *ahs* ear, Latin *acus* chaff, Greek *akros* pointed]

earache (ˈɪərˌeɪk) *n* pain in the middle or inner ear. Technical name: **otalgia.** Compare **otitis.**

earbash (ˈɪəˌbæʃ) *vb* (*intr*) *Austral. and N.Z. slang.* to talk incessantly. ▸ **ˈearˌbasher** *n* ▸ **ˈearˌbashing** *n*

eardrop (ˈɪəˌdrɒp) *n* a pendant earring.

eardrops (ˈɪəˌdrɒps) *pl n* liquid medication for inserting into the external ear.

eardrum (ˈɪəˌdrʌm) *n* the nontechnical name for **tympanic membrane.**

eared (ɪəd) *adj* **a** having an ear or ears. **b** (*in combination*): *long-eared; two-eared.*

eared seal *n* any seal of the pinniped family *Otariidae,* typically having visible earflaps and conspicuous hind limbs that can be used for locomotion on land. Compare **earless seal.**

earflap (ˈɪəˌflæp) *n* **1** Also called: **earlap.** either of two pieces of fabric or fur attached to a cap, which can be let down to keep the ears warm. **2** *Zoology.* a small flap of skin forming the pinna of such animals as seals.

earful (ˈɪəfʊl) *n Informal.* **1** something heard or overheard. **2** a rebuke or scolding, esp. a lengthy or severe one.

Earhart (ˈɛəˌhɑːt) *n* **Amelia.** 1898–1937, U.S. aviator: the first woman to fly the Atlantic (1928). She disappeared on a Pacific flight (1937).

earing (ˈɪərɪŋ) *n Nautical.* a line fastened to a corner of a sail for reefing. [C17: from EAR[1] + -ING[1] or perhaps RING[1]]

earl (ɜːl) *n* **1** (in the British Isles) a nobleman ranking below a marquess and above a viscount. Female equivalent: **countess. 2** (in Anglo-Saxon England) a royal governor of any of the large divisions of the kingdom, such as Wessex. [Old English *eorl;* related to Old Norse *jarl* chieftain, Old Saxon *erl* man]

earlap (ˈɪəˌlæp) *n* **1** another word for **earflap** (sense 1). **2** *Rare.* **2a** the external ear. **2b** the ear lobe. [C16: from EAR[1] + LAP[1]]

earldom ('ɜːldəm) *n* **1** the rank, title, or dignity of an earl or countess. **2** the lands of an earl or countess.

earless seal *n* any seal of the pinniped family *Phocidae,* typically having rudimentary hind limbs, no external earflaps, and a body covering of hair with no underfur. Also called: **hair seal.** Compare **eared seal.**

Earl Grey *n* a variety of China tea flavoured with oil of bergamot.

Earl Marshal *n* an officer of the English peerage who presides over the College of Heralds and organizes royal processions and other important ceremonies.

ear lobe *n* the fleshy lower part of the external ear.

early ('ɜːlɪ) *adj* **-lier, -liest,** *adv* **1** before the expected or usual time. **2** occurring in or characteristic of the first part of a period or sequence. **3** occurring in or characteristic of a period far back in time. **4** occurring in the near future. **5 at the earliest.** not before the time or date mentioned. **6 early days.** too soon to tell how things will turn out. [Old English *ǣrlīce,* from *ǣr* ERE + *-līce* -LY[2]; related to Old Norse *arliga*] ▸ **'earliness** *n*

early bird *n Informal.* a person who rises early or arrives in good time.

Early Bird *n* one of a number of communications satellites, the first of which was launched in 1965 into a stationary orbit and provided telephone channels between Europe and the U.S. See also **Intelsat.**

Early Christian *adj* denoting or relating to the style of architecture that started in Italy in the 3rd century A.D. and spread through the Roman empire until the 5th century.

early closing *n Brit.* **1a** the shutting of most of the shops in a town one afternoon each week. **1b** (*as adj*): *early-closing day.* **2** the day on which this happens: *Thursday is early closing in Aylesbury.*

Early English *n* a style of architecture used in England in the 12th and 13th centuries, characterized by lancet arches, narrow openings, and plate tracery.

early music *n* **1** music of the Middle Ages and Renaissance, sometimes also including music of the baroque and early classical periods. ◆ (*modifier*) **early-music 2** of or denoting an approach to musical performance emphasizing the use of period instruments and historically researched scores and playing techniques: *the early-music movement.*

early purple orchid *n* a Eurasian orchid, *Orchis mascula,* with purplish-crimson flowers and stems marked with blackish-purple spots.

Early Renaissance *n* **the.** the period from about 1400 to 1500 in European, esp. Italian, painting, sculpture, and architecture, when naturalistic styles and humanist theories were evolved from the study of classical sources, notably by Donatello, Masaccio, and Alberti.

early warning *n* advance notice of some impending event or development.

early warning system *n* a network of radar and communications units intended to detect at the earliest possible moment an attack by enemy aircraft or missiles.

earmark ('ɪəˌmɑːk) *vb* (*tr*) **1** to set aside or mark out for a specific purpose. **2** to make an identification mark on the ear of (a domestic animal). ◆ *n* **3** a mark of identification on the ear of a domestic animal. **4** any distinguishing mark or characteristic.

earmuff ('ɪəˌmʌf) *n* one of a pair of pads of fur or cloth, joined by a headband, for keeping the ears warm.

earn (ɜːn) *vb* **1** to gain or be paid (money or other payment) in return for work or service. **2** (*tr*) to acquire, merit, or deserve through behaviour or action: *he has earned a name for duplicity.* **3** (*tr*) (of securities, investments, etc.) to gain (interest, return, profit, etc.). [Old English *earnian;* related to Old High German *arnēn* to reap, Old Saxon *asna* salary, tithe] ▸ **'earner** *n*

earned income *n* income derived from paid employment and comprising mainly wages and salaries.

earnest[1] ('ɜːnɪst) *adj* **1** serious in mind or intention: *an earnest student.* **2** showing or characterized by sincerity of intention: *an earnest promise.* **3** demanding or receiving serious attention. ◆ *n* **4 in earnest.** with serious or sincere intentions. [Old English *eornost;* related to Old High German *ernust* seriousness, Old Norse *ern* energetic, efficient, Gothic *arniba* secure] ▸ **'earnestly** *adv* ▸ **'earnestness** *n*

earnest[2] ('ɜːnɪst) *n* **1** a part or portion of something given in advance as a guarantee of the remainder. **2** Also called: **earnest money.** *Contract law.* something given, usually a nominal sum of money, to confirm a contract. **3** any token of something to follow; pledge; assurance. [C13: from Old French *erres* pledges, plural of *erre* earnest money, from Latin *arrha,* shortened from *arrabō* pledge, from Greek *arrabon,* from Hebrew *'ērābhōn* pledge, from *'ārabh* he pledged]

earnings ('ɜːnɪŋz) *pl n* **1** money or other payment earned. **2** the profits of an enterprise.

Earnings Related Supplement *or* **Benefit** *n* (formerly, in the British National Insurance scheme) a payment based on earnings in the previous tax year, payable (in addition to unemployment or sickness benefit) for about six months to a sick or unemployed person. Abbrev.: **ERS.**

EAROM ('ɪərɒm) *n Computing. acronym for* electrically alterable read only memory.

earphone ('ɪəˌfəʊn) *n* a device for converting electric currents into sound waves, held close to or inserted into the ear.

earpiece ('ɪəˌpiːs) *n* the earphone in a telephone receiver.

ear piercing *n* **1** the making of a hole in the lobe of an ear, using a sterilized needle, so that an earring may be worn fastened in the hole. ◆ *adj* **ear-piercing. 2** so loud or shrill as to hurt the ears.

earplug ('ɪəˌplʌg) *n* a small piece of soft material, such as wax, placed in the ear to keep out noise or water.

earring ('ɪəˌrɪŋ) *n* an ornament for the ear, usually clipped onto the lobe or fastened through a hole pierced in the lobe.

ear shell *n* another name for the **abalone.**

earshot ('ɪəˌʃɒt) *n* the range or distance within which sound may be heard (esp. in the phrases **within earshot, out of earshot**).

ear-splitting *adj* so loud or shrill as to hurt the ears.

earth (ɜːθ) *n* **1** (*sometimes cap.*) the third planet from the sun, the only planet on which life is known to exist. It is not quite spherical, being flattened at the poles, and consists of three geological zones, the core, mantle, and thin outer crust. The surface, covered with large areas of water, is enveloped by an atmosphere principally of nitrogen (78 per cent), oxygen (21 per cent), and some water vapour. The age is estimated at over four thousand million years. Distance from sun: 149.6 million kilometres; equatorial diameter: 12 756 km; mass: 5.976×10^{24} kg; sidereal period of axial rotation: 23 hours 56 minutes 4 seconds; sidereal period of revolution: 365.256 days. Related adjs: **terrestrial, tellurian, telluric, terrene. 2** the inhabitants of this planet: *the whole earth rejoiced.* **3** the dry surface of this planet as distinguished from sea or sky; land; ground. **4** the loose soft material that makes up a large part of the surface of the ground and consists of disintegrated rock particles, mould, clay, etc.; soil. **5** worldly or temporal matters as opposed to the concerns of the spirit. **6** the hole in which a burrowing animal, esp. a fox, lives. **7** *Chem.* See **rare earth, alkaline earth. 8a** a connection between an electrical circuit or device and the earth, which is at zero potential. **8b** a terminal to which this connection is made. U.S. and Canadian equivalent: **ground. 9** Also called: **earth colour.** any of various brown pigments composed chiefly of iron oxides. **10** (*modifier*) *Astrology.* of or relating to a group of three signs of the zodiac, Taurus, Virgo, and Capricorn. Compare **air** (sense 19), **fire** (sense 24), **water** (sense 12). **11 cost the earth.** *Informal.* to be very expensive. **12 come back** *or* **down to earth.** to return to reality from a fantasy or daydream. **13 on earth.** used as an intensifier in such phrases as **what on earth, who on earth,** etc. **14 run to earth. 14a** to hunt (an animal, esp. a fox) to its earth and trap it there. **14b** to find (someone) after searching. ◆ *vb* **15** (*intr*) (of a hunted fox) to go to ground. **16** (*tr*) to connect (a circuit, device, etc.) to earth. ◆ See also **earth up.** [Old English *eorthe;* related to Old Norse *jorth,* Old High German *ertha,* Gothic *airtha,* Greek *erā*]

earthborn ('ɜːθˌbɔːn) *adj Chiefly poetic.* **1** of earthly origin. **2** human; mortal.

earthbound ('ɜːθˌbaʊnd) *adj* **1** confined to the earth. **2** lacking in imagination; pedestrian or dull. **3** moving or heading towards the earth.

earth closet *n* a type of lavatory in which earth is used to cover excreta.

earthen ('ɜːθən) *adj* (*prenominal*) **1** made of baked clay: *an earthen pot.* **2** made of earth.

earthenware ('ɜːθənˌwɛə) *n* **a** vessels, etc., made of baked clay. **b** (*as adj*): *an earthenware pot.*

earth-grazer *n* an asteroid in an orbit that takes it close to the earth. Also called: **near-earth asteroid.**

earth inductor compass *n* a compass that depends on the current induced in a coil revolving in the earth's magnetic field. Also called: **inductor compass.**

earthlight ('ɜːθˌlaɪt) *n* another name for **earthshine.**

earthling ('ɜːθlɪŋ) *n* (esp. in poetry or science fiction) an inhabitant of the earth; human being. [C16: from EARTH + LING[1]]

earthly ('ɜːθlɪ) *adj* **-lier, -liest. 1** of or characteristic of the earth as opposed to heaven; material or materialistic; worldly. **2** (*usually used with a negative*) *Informal.* conceivable or possible; feasible (in such phrases as **not an earthly** (**chance**), etc.). ▸ **'earthliness** *n*

earthman ('ɜːθˌmæn) *n, pl* **-men.** (esp. in science fiction) an inhabitant or native of the earth.

earth mother *n* **1** (in various mythologies) **1a** a female goddess considered as the source of fertility and life. **1b** the earth personified. **2** *Informal.* a sensual or fecund woman.

earthnut ('ɜːθˌnʌt) *n* **1** Also called: **pignut.** a perennial umbelliferous plant, *Conopodium majus,* of Europe and Asia, having edible dark brown tubers. **2** any of various plants having an edible root, tuber, underground pod, or similar part, such as the peanut or truffle.

earth pillar *n* a landform consisting of a column of clay or earth capped and protected from erosion by a boulder.

earthquake ('ɜːθˌkweɪk) *n* a sudden release of energy in the earth's crust or upper mantle, usually caused by movement along a fault plane or by volcanic activity and resulting in the generation of seismic waves which can be destructive. Related adj: **seismic.**

earth return *n* the return path for an electrical circuit made by connections to earth at each end.

earthrise ('ɜːθˌraɪz) *n* the rising of the earth above the lunar horizon, as seen from the moon or a spacecraft.

earth science *n* any of various sciences, such as geology, geography, and geomorphology, that are concerned with the structure, age, and other aspects of the earth.

Earthshaker ('ɜːθˌʃeɪkə) *n* **the.** *Classical myth.* Poseidon (or Neptune) in his capacity as the bringer of earthquakes.

earthshaking ('ɜːθˌʃeɪkɪŋ) *adj Informal.* of enormous importance or consequence; momentous.

earthshine ('ɜːθˌʃaɪn) *or* **earthlight** *n* the ashen light reflected from the earth, which illuminates the new moon when it is not receiving light directly from the sun.

earthstar ('ɜːθˌstɑː) *n* any of various basidiomycetous saprotrophic woodland fungi of the genus *Geastrum,* whose brown onion-shaped reproductive body splits into a star shape to release the spores.

earth up *vb* (*tr, adv*) to cover (part of a plant, esp. the stem) with soil in order to protect from frost, light, etc.

earthward ('ɜːθwəd) *adj* **1** directed towards the earth. ◆ *adv* **2** a variant of **earthwards.**

earthwards ('ɜːθwədz) *or* **earthward** *adv* towards the earth.
earth wax *n* another name for **ozocerite.**
earthwork ('ɜːθˌwɜːk) *n* **1** excavation of earth, as in engineering construction. **2** a fortification made of earth.
earthworm ('ɜːθˌwɜːm) *n* any of numerous oligochaete worms of the genera *Lumbricus, Allolobophora, Eisenia,* etc., which burrow in the soil and help aerate and break up the ground. Related adj: **lumbricoid.**
earthy ('ɜːθɪ) *adj* **earthier, earthiest. 1** of, composed of, or characteristic of earth. **2** robust, lusty, or uninhibited. **3** unrefined, coarse, or crude. **4** an archaic word for **worldly** (sense 1). **5** *Electrical engineering.* on the earthed side of an electrical circuit, but not necessarily with a direct current connection to earth. ► **'earthily** *adv* ► **'earthiness** *n*
ear trumpet *n* a trumpet-shaped instrument that amplifies sounds and is held to the ear: an old form of hearing aid.
earwax ('ɪəˌwæks) *n* the nontechnical name for **cerumen.**
earwig ('ɪəˌwɪg) *n* **1** any of various insects of the order *Dermaptera,* esp. *Forficula auricularia* (**common European earwig**), which typically have an elongated body with small leathery forewings, semicircular membranous hindwings, and curved forceps at the tip of the abdomen. ♦ *vb* **-wigs, -wigging, -wigged. 2** *Informal.* to eavesdrop. **3** (*tr*) *Archaic.* to attempt to influence (a person) by private insinuation. **[**Old English *ēarwicga,* from *ēare* EAR[1] + *wicga* beetle, insect; probably from a superstition that the insect crept into human ears**]**
earwigging ('ɪəˌwɪgɪŋ) *n Informal.* a scolding or harangue: *I'll give him an earwigging about that.*
EAS *Aeronautics. abbrev. for* equivalent air speed.
ease (iːz) *n* **1** freedom from discomfort, worry, or anxiety. **2** lack of difficulty, labour, or awkwardness; facility. **3** rest, leisure, or relaxation. **4** freedom from poverty or financial embarrassment; affluence: *a life of ease.* **5** lack of restraint, embarrassment, or stiffness: *his ease of manner disarmed us.* **6 at ease. 6a** *Military.* (of a standing soldier, etc.) in a relaxed position with the feet apart rather than at attention. **6b** a command to adopt such a position. **6c** in a relaxed attitude or frame of mind. ♦ *vb* **7** to make or become less burdensome. **8** (*tr*) to relieve (a person) of worry or care; comfort. **9** (*tr*) to make comfortable or give rest to. **10** (*tr*) to make less difficult; facilitate. **11** to move or cause to move into, out of, etc., with careful manipulation: *to ease a car into a narrow space.* **12** (when *intr,* often foll. by *off* or *up*) to lessen or cause to lessen in severity, pressure, tension, or strain; slacken, loosen, or abate. **13 ease oneself** *or* **ease nature.** *Archaic, euphemistic.* to urinate or defecate. **14 ease the helm.** *Nautical.* to relieve the pressure on the rudder of a vessel, esp. by bringing the bow into the wind. **[**C13: from Old French *aise* ease, opportunity, from Latin *adjacēns* neighbouring (area); see ADJACENT**]** ► **'easer** *n*
easeful ('iːzfʊl) *adj* characterized by or bringing ease; peaceful; tranquil. ► **'easefully** *adv* ► **'easefulness** *n*
easel ('iːzᵊl) *n* a frame, usually in the form of an upright tripod, used for supporting or displaying an artist's canvas, blackboard, etc. **[**C17: from Dutch *ezel* ASS[1]; related to Gothic *asilus,* German *Esel,* Latin *asinus* ass**]**
easement ('iːzmənt) *n* **1** *Property law.* the right enjoyed by a landowner of making limited use of his neighbour's land, as by crossing it to reach his own property. **2** the act of easing or something that brings ease.
easily ('iːzɪlɪ) *adv* **1** with ease; without difficulty or exertion. **2** by far; beyond question; undoubtedly: *he is easily the best in the contest.* **3** probably; almost certainly: *he may easily come first.*
USAGE See at **easy.**
easiness ('iːzɪnɪs) *n* **1** the quality or condition of being easy to accomplish, do, obtain, etc. **2** ease or relaxation of manner; nonchalance.
east (iːst) *n* **1** one of the four cardinal points of the compass, 90° clockwise from north and 180° from west. **2** the direction along a parallel towards the sunrise, at 90° to north; the direction of the earth's rotation. **3 the east.** (*often cap.*) any area lying in or towards the east. Related adj: **oriental. 4** *Cards.* (*usually cap.*) the player or position at the table corresponding to east on the compass. ♦ *adj* **5** situated in, moving towards, or facing the east. **6** (esp. of the wind) from the east. ♦ *adv* **7** in, to, or towards the east. **8** *Archaic.* (of the wind) from the east. ♦ Symbol: E **[**Old English *ēast;* related to Old High German *ōstar* to the east, Old Norse *austr,* Latin *aurora* dawn, Greek *eōs,* Sanskrit *usās* dawn, morning**]**
East (iːst) *n* **the. 1** the continent of Asia regarded as culturally distinct from Europe and the West; the Orient. **2** the countries under Communist rule and formerly under Communist rule, lying mainly in the E hemisphere. Compare **West**[1] (sense 2). **3** (in the U.S.) **3a** the area north of the Ohio and east of the Mississippi. **3b** the area north of Maryland and east of the Alleghenies. ♦ *adj* **4a** of or denoting the eastern part of a specified country, area, etc. **4b** (*as part of a name*): *East Sussex.* ► **'Eastern** *adj*
East Africa *n* a region of Africa comprising Kenya, Uganda, and Tanzania. ► **East African** *adj, n*
East African Community *n* an association established in 1967 by Kenya, Uganda, and Tanzania to promote closer economic and social ties between member states: dissolved in 1977.
East Anglia *n* **1** a region of E England south of the Wash: consists of Norfolk and Suffolk, and parts of Essex and Cambridgeshire. **2** an Anglo-Saxon kingdom that consisted of Norfolk and Suffolk in the 6th century A.D.; became a dependency of Mercia in the 8th century. ► **East Anglian** *adj, n*
East Ayrshire *n* a council area of SW Scotland, comprising the E part of the historical county of Ayrshire: part of Strathclyde region from 1975 to 1996: chiefly agricultural. Administrative centre: Kilmarnock. Pop.: 123 820 (1996 est.). Area: 1252 sq. km (483 sq. miles).
East Bengal *n* the part of the former Indian province of Bengal assigned to Pakistan in 1947 (now Bangladesh). ► **East Bengali** *adj, n*
East Berlin *n* (formerly) the part of Berlin under East German control. ► **East Berliner** *n*
eastbound ('iːstˌbaʊnd) *adj* going or leading towards the east.
Eastbourne ('iːstˌbɔːn) *n* a resort in SE England, in East Sussex on the English Channel. Pop.: 83 200 (1991 est.).
east by north *n* **1** one point on the compass north of east, 78° 45′ clockwise from north. ♦ *adj, adv* **2** in, from, or towards this direction.
east by south *n* **1** one point on the compass south of east, 101° 15′ clockwise from north. ♦ *adj, adv* **2** in, from, or towards this direction.
East Cape *n* **1** the easternmost point of New Guinea, on Milne Bay. **2** the easternmost point of New Zealand, on North Island. **3** the former name for Cape **Dezhnev.**
East China Sea *n* part of the N Pacific, between the E coast of China and the Ryukyu Islands.
east coast fever *n* a disease of cattle, endemic in east and central Africa, caused by a parasite, *Theileria parva,* that is carried by ticks.
East Dunbartonshire *n* a council area of central Scotland to the N of Glasgow: part of Strathclyde region from 1975 until 1996: mainly agricultural and residential. Administrative centre: Kirkintilloch. Pop.: 110 220 (1996 est.). Area: 172 sq. km (66 sq. miles).
East End *n* **the.** a densely populated part of E London containing former industrial and dock areas. ► **East Ender** *n*
Easter ('iːstə) *n* **1** the most important festival of the Christian Church, commemorating the Resurrection of Christ: falls on the Sunday following the first full moon after the vernal equinox. **2** Also called: **Easter Sunday, Easter Day.** the day on which this festival is celebrated. **3** the period between Good Friday and Easter Monday. Related adj: **Paschal. [**Old English *ēastre,* after a Germanic goddess *Eostre;* related to Old High German *ōstarūn* Easter, Old Norse *austr* to the EAST, Old Slavonic *ustru* like summer**]**
Easter cactus *n* a Brazilian cactus, *Rhipsalidopsis gaertneri,* widely cultivated as an ornamental for its showy red flowers.
Easter egg *n* an egg given to children at Easter, usually a chocolate egg or a hen's egg with its shell painted.
Easter Island *n* an isolated volcanic island in the Pacific, 3700 km (2300 miles) west of Chile, of which it is a dependency: discovered on Easter Sunday, 1722; annexed by Chile in 1888; noted for the remains of an aboriginal culture, which includes gigantic stone figures. Pop.: 2000 (1988 est.). Area: 166 sq. km (64 sq. miles). Also called: **Rapa Nui.** ► **Easter Islander** *n*
Easter-ledges *n* **1** (*functioning as sing*) another name for **bistort** (sense 1). **2 Easter-ledge pudding.** *Northern English dialect.* a pudding made from the young leaves of the bistort.
Easter lily *n* any of various lilies, esp. *Lilium longiflorum,* that have large showy white flowers.
easterly ('iːstəlɪ) *adj* **1** of, relating to, or situated in the east. ♦ *adv, adj* **2** towards or in the direction of the east. **3** from the east: *an easterly wind.* ♦ *n, pl* **-lies. 4** a wind from the east.
eastern ('iːstən) *adj* **1** situated in or towards the east. **2** facing or moving towards the east.
Eastern Cape *n* a province of S South Africa; formed in 1994 from part of the former Cape Province: service industries, agriculture, and mining. Capital: Bisho. Pop.: 6 481 300 (1995 est.). Area: 169 600 sq. km (65 483 sq. miles).
Eastern Church *n* **1** any of the Christian Churches of the former Byzantine Empire. **2** any Church owing allegiance to the Orthodox Church and in communion with the Greek patriarchal see of Constantinople. **3** any Church, including Uniat Churches, having Eastern forms of liturgy and institutions.
Easterner ('iːstənə) *n* (*sometimes not cap.*) a native or inhabitant of the east of any specified region, esp. of the Orient or of the eastern states of the U.S.
Eastern Ghats *pl n* a mountain range in S India, parallel to the Bay of Bengal: united with the Western Ghats by the Nilgiri Hills; forms the E margin of the Deccan plateau.
eastern hemisphere *n* (*often caps.*) **1** that half of the globe containing Europe, Asia, Africa, and Australia, lying east of the Greenwich meridian. **2** the lands in this, esp. Asia.
easternmost ('iːstənˌməʊst) *adj* situated or occurring farthest east.
Eastern Orthodox Church *n* another name for the **Orthodox Church.**
Eastern rite *n* the rite and liturgy of an Eastern Church or of a Uniat Church.
Eastern Roman Empire *n* the eastern of the two empires created by the division of the Roman Empire in 395 A.D. See also **Byzantine Empire.**
Eastern Standard Time *n* one of the standard times used in North America, five hours behind Greenwich Mean Time. Abbrev.: **EST.**
Eastern Townships *n* an area of central Canada, in S Quebec: consists of 11 townships south of the St Lawrence.
Easter Rising *n* an armed insurrection in Dublin in 1916 against British rule in Ireland: the insurgents proclaimed the establishment of an independent Irish republic before surrendering, sixteen of the leaders later being executed.
Easter term *n* the term at the Inns of Court following the Hilary term.
Eastertide ('iːstəˌtaɪd) *n* the Easter season.
East Flanders *n* a province of W Belgium: low-lying, with reclaimed land in the northeast: textile industries. Capital: Ghent. Pop.: 1 351 777 (1996 est.). Area: 2979 sq. km (1150 sq. miles).
East Germanic *n* a subbranch of the Germanic languages: now extinct. The only member of which records survive is Gothic.
East Germany *n* a former republic in N central Europe: established in 1949 and declared a sovereign state by the Soviet Union in 1954; Communist regime replaced by a multiparty democracy in 1989; reunited with West Germany in 1990. Official name: **German Democratic Republic.** Abbrevs.: **DDR, GDR.** See also **Germany.** ► **East German** *adj, n*
East India Company *n* **1** the company chartered in 1600 by the British gov-

ernment to trade in the East Indies: after being driven out by the Dutch it developed trade with India until the Indian Mutiny (1857), when the Crown took over the administration: the company was dissolved in 1874. **2** any similar trading company, such as any of those founded by the Dutch, French, and Danes in the 17th and 18th centuries.

East Indian *n* **1** *Caribbean.* an immigrant to the countries of the Caribbean (West Indies) who is of Indian origin; an Asian West Indian. ◆ *adj* **2** *U.S. and Canadian.* of, relating to, or originating in the East Indies.

East Indies *pl n* **the. 1** the Malay Archipelago, including or excluding the Philippines. **2** SE Asia in general.

easting ('iːstɪŋ) *n* **1** *Nautical.* the net distance eastwards made by a vessel moving towards the east. **2** *Cartography.* **2a** the distance eastwards of a point from a given meridian indicated by the first half of a map grid reference. **2b** a longitudinal grid line. Compare **northing** (sense 3).

East Kilbride (kɪl'braɪd) *n* a town in W Scotland, in South Lanarkshire near Glasgow: designated a new town in 1947. Pop.: 70 422 (1991).

Eastleigh ('iːst,liː) *n* a town in S England, in S Hampshire: railway engineering industry. Pop.: 49 934 (1991).

East London *n* a port in S South Africa, in S Eastern Cape province. Pop.: 102 325 (1991).

East Lothian *n* a council area and historical county of E central Scotland, on the Firth of Forth and the North Sea: part of Lothian region from 1975 to 1996: chiefly agricultural. Administrative centre: Haddington. Pop.: 85 640 (1996 est.). Area: 678 sq. km (262 sq. miles).

Eastman ('iːstmən) *n* **George.** 1854–1932, U.S. manufacturer of photographic equipment: noted for the introduction of roll film and developments in colour photography.

east-northeast *n* **1** the point on the compass or the direction midway between northeast and east, 67° 30′ clockwise from north. ◆ *adj, adv* **2** in, from, or towards this direction. ◆ Symbol: ENE

East Pakistan *n* the former name (until 1971) of **Bangladesh.** ▸ **East Pakistani** *adj, n*

East Prussia *n* a former province of NE Germany on the Baltic Sea: separated in 1919 from the rest of Germany by the Polish Corridor and Danzig: in 1945 Poland received the south part, the Soviet Union the north. German name: **Ostpreussen** (ɔst'prɔysən). ▸ **East Prussian** *adj, n*

East Renfrewshire *n* a council area of W central Scotland, comprising part of the historical county of Renfrewshire; part of Strathclyde region from 1975 to 1996: chiefly agricultural and residential. Administrative centre: Giffnock. Pop.: 86 780 (1996 est.). Area: 173 sq. km (67 sq. miles).

East Riding of Yorkshire *n* a county of NE England, a historical division of Yorkshire on the North Sea and the Humber estuary: became part of Humberside in 1974; reinstated as an independent unitary authority in 1996, with a separate authority for Kingston upon Hull: chiefly agricultural and low-lying, with various industries in Hull. Administrative centre: Beverley. Pop. (including Hull): 595 440 (1996 est.). Area (including Hull): 1819 sq. km (704 sq. miles).

east-southeast *n* **1** the point on the compass or the direction midway between east and southeast, 112° 30′ clockwise from north. ◆ *adj, adv* **2** in, from, or towards this direction. ◆ Symbol: ESE

East Sussex *n* a county of SE England comprising part of the former county of Sussex: mainly undulating agricultural land, with the South Downs and seaside resorts in the south: Brighton and Hove became an independent unitary authority in 1997 but is part of the geographical and ceremonial county. Administrative centre: Lewes. Pop. (including Brighton and Hove): 726 500 (1994 est.). Area (including Brighton and Hove): 1795 sq. km (693 sq. miles).

East Timor *n* See **Portuguese Timor.**

eastward ('iːstwəd) *adj* **1** situated or directed towards the east. ◆ *adv* **2** a variant of **eastwards.** ◆ *n* **3** the eastward part, direction, etc. ▸ **'eastwardly** *adv, adj*

eastwards ('iːstwədz) *or* **eastward** *adv* towards the east.

Eastwood ('iːstwʊd) *n* **Clint.** born 1930, U.S. film actor and director. His films as an actor include *The Good The Bad and The Ugly* (1966), *Dirty Harry* (1971), and as actor and director *Play Misty for Me* (1971), *Unforgiven* (1993), and *True Crime* (1999). He was mayor of Carmel, California (1985–88).

easy ('iːzɪ) *adj* **easier, easiest. 1** not requiring much labour or effort; not difficult; simple: *an easy job.* **2** free from pain, care, or anxiety: *easy in one's mind.* **3** not harsh or restricting; lenient: *easy laws.* **4** tolerant and undemanding; easy-going: *an easy disposition.* **5** readily influenced or persuaded; pliant: *she was an easy victim of his wiles.* **6** not tight or constricting; loose: *an easy fit.* **7** not strained or extreme; moderate; gentle: *an easy pace; an easy ascent.* **8** *Economics.* **8a** readily obtainable. **8b** (of a market) characterized by low demand or excess supply with prices tending to fall. Compare **tight** (sense 10). **9** *Informal.* ready to fall in with any suggestion made; not predisposed: *he is easy about what to do.* **10** *Slang.* sexually available. **11 easy on the eye.** *Informal.* pleasant to look at; attractive, esp. sexually. **12 woman of easy virtue.** a sexually available woman, esp. a prostitute. ◆ *adv* **13** *Informal.* in an easy or relaxed manner. **14 easy does it.** *Informal.* go slowly and carefully; be careful. **15 go easy on. 15a** to use in moderation. **15b** to treat leniently. **16 stand easy.** *Military.* a command to soldiers standing at ease that they may relax further. **17 take it easy. 17a** to avoid stress or undue hurry. **17b** to remain calm; not become agitated or angry. ◆ *vb* **easies, easying, easied. 18** (*usually imperative*) Also: **easy-oar.** to stop rowing. [C12: from Old French *aisié*, past participle of *aisier* to relieve, EASE]

USAGE *Easy* is not used as an adverb by careful speakers and writers except in certain set phrases: *to take it easy; easy does it.* Where a fixed expression is not involved, the usual adverbial form of *easy* is preferred: *this polish goes on more easily* (not *easier*) *than the other.*

easy-care *adj* (esp. of a fabric or garment) hardwearing, practical, and requiring no special treatment during washing, cleaning, etc.

easy chair *n* a comfortable upholstered armchair.

easy game *or* **easy mark** *n Informal.* a person who is easily deceived or taken advantage of.

easy-going ('iːzɪ'gəʊɪŋ) *adj* **1** relaxed in manner or attitude; inclined to be excessively tolerant. **2** moving at a comfortable pace: *an easy-going horse.*

easy meat *n Informal.* **1** someone easily seduced or deceived. **2** something easy to get or do.

easy money *n* **1** money made with little effort, sometimes dishonestly. **2** *Commerce.* money that can be borrowed at a low interest rate.

Easy Street *n* (*sometimes not caps.*) *Informal.* a state of financial security.

eat (iːt) *vb* **eats, eating, ate, eaten. 1** to take into the mouth and swallow (food, etc.), esp. after biting and chewing. **2** (*tr;* often foll. by *away* or *up*) to destroy as if by eating: *the damp had eaten away the woodwork.* **3** (often foll. by *into*) to use up or waste: *taxes ate into his inheritance.* **4** (often foll. by *into* or *through*) to make (a hole, passage, etc.) by eating or gnawing: *rats ate through the floor.* **5** to take or have (a meal or meals): *we always eat at six.* **6** (*tr*) to include as part of one's diet: *he doesn't eat fish.* **7** (*tr*) *Informal.* to cause to worry; make anxious: *what's eating you?* **8** (*tr*) *Taboo slang.* to perform cunnilingus or fellatio upon. **9 I'll eat my hat if.** *Informal.* to be greatly surprised if (something happens that proves one wrong). **10 eat one's heart out.** to brood or pine with grief or longing. **11 eat one's words.** to take back something said; recant; retract. **12 eat out of (someone's) hand.** to be entirely obedient to (someone). **13 eat (someone) out of house and home.** to ruin (someone, esp. one's parent or one's host) by consuming all his food. ◆ See also **eat out, eats, eat up.** [Old English *etan;* related to Gothic *itan,* Old High German *ezzan,* Latin *edere,* Greek *edein,* Sanskrit *admi*] ▸ **'eater** *n*

EAT *international car registration for* (East Africa) Tanzania.

eatable ('iːtəbᵊl) *adj* fit or suitable for eating; edible.

eatables ('iːtəbᵊlz) *pl n* (*sometimes sing*) food.

eatage ('iːtɪdʒ) *n Northern English dialect.* grazing rights.

eaten ('iːtᵊn) *vb* the past participle of **eat.**

eatery ('iːtərɪ) *n, pl* **-eries** (-ərɪz) *Informal.* a restaurant or eating house.

eating ('iːtɪŋ) *n* **1** food, esp. in relation to its quality or taste: *this fruit makes excellent eating.* ◆ *adj* **2** relating to or suitable for eating, esp. uncooked: *eating pears.* **3** relating to or for eating: *an eating house.*

eat out *vb* (*intr, adv*) to eat away from home, esp. in a restaurant.

eats (iːts) *pl n Informal.* articles of food; provisions.

eat up *vb* (*adv, mainly tr*) **1** (*also intr*) to eat or consume entirely: often used as an exhortation to children. **2** *Informal.* to listen to with enthusiasm or appreciation: *the audience ate up the speaker's every word.* **3** (*often passive*) *Informal.* to affect grossly: *she was eaten up by jealousy.* **4** *Informal.* to travel (a distance) quickly: *we just ate up the miles.*

EAU *international car registration for* (East Africa) Uganda.

eau de Cologne (əʊ də kə'ləʊn) *n* See **cologne.** [French, literally: water of Cologne]

eau de Javelle (əʊ də ʒæ'vɛl, ʒə-; *French* od ʒavɛl) *n* another name for **Javel water.**

eau de nil (əʊ də niːl) *n, adj* **a** a pale yellowish-green colour. **b** (*as adj*): *eau-de-nil walls.* [French, literally: water of (the) Nile]

eau de vie (əʊ də viː; *French* od vi) *n* brandy or other spirits. [French, literally: water of life]

eaves (iːvz) *pl n* the edge of a roof that projects beyond the wall. [Old English *efes;* related to Gothic *ubizwa* porch, Greek *hupsos* height]

eavesdrop ('iːvz,drɒp) *vb* **-drops, -dropping, -dropped.** (*intr*) to listen secretly to the private conversation of others. [C17: back formation from earlier *evesdropper,* from Old English *yfesdrype* water dripping from the eaves; see EAVES, DROP; compare Old Norse *upsardropi*] ▸ **'eaves,dropper** *n*

ebb (ɛb) *vb* (*intr*) **1** (of tide water) to flow back or recede. Compare **flow** (sense 9). **2** to fall away or decline. ◆ *n* **3a** the flowing back of the tide from high to low water or the period in which this takes place. **3b** (*as modifier*): *the ebb tide.* Compare **flood** (sense 3). **4 at a low ebb.** in a state or period of weakness, lack of vigour, or decline. [Old English *ebba;* related to Old Norse *efja* river bend, Gothic *ibuks* moving backwards, Old High German *ippihōn* to roll backwards, Middle Dutch *ebbe* ebb]

Ebbinghaus ('ɛbɪŋhaʊs) *n* **Hermann** ('hɛrman). 1850–1909, German experimental psychologist who undertook the first systematic and large-scale studies of memory and devised tests using nonsense syllables.

Ebbw Vale ('ɛbuː veɪl) *n* a town in S Wales, in Blaenau Gwent county borough: a former coal mining centre. Pop.: 19 484 (1991).

EBCDIC ('ɛpsɪ,dɪk) *n acronym for* extended binary-coded decimal-interchange code: a computer code for representing alphanumeric characters.

Eberhard (*German* 'eːbər,hart) *n* **Johann August** (jo'han'augʊst). 1739–1809, German philosopher and lexicographer, best known for his German dictionary (1795–1802).

Ebert (*German* 'eːbərt) *n* **Friedrich** ('friːdrɪç). 1871–1925, German Social Democratic statesman; first president of the German Republic (1919–25).

Eblis ('ɛblɪs) *n* the chief evil jinni in Islamic mythology. [Arabic *Iblīs,* from Greek *diabolos* slanderer, DEVIL]

E-boat *n* (in World War II) a fast German boat carrying guns and torpedoes. [from *enemy* boat]

Ebola virus disease (iː'bəʊlə) *n* a severe infectious disease characterized by fever, vomiting, and internal bleeding. Compare **Marburg disease.** [C20: named after the *Ebola* river, N Democratic Republic of the Congo (formerly Zaïre), where an outbreak occurred in 1976]

ebon ('ɛbᵊn) *n, adj* a poetic word for **ebony.** [C14: from Latin *hebenus;* see EBONY]

ebonite ('ɛbəˌnaɪt) *n* another name for **vulcanite.**
ebonize *or* **ebonise** ('ɛbəˌnaɪz) *vb* (*tr*) to stain or otherwise finish in imitation of ebony.
ebony ('ɛbənɪ) *n, pl* **-onies. 1** any of various tropical and subtropical trees of the genus *Diospyros,* esp. *D. ebenum* of S India, that have hard dark wood: family *Ebenaceae.* See also **persimmon. 2** the wood of such a tree, much used for cabinetwork. **3a** a black colour, sometimes with a dark olive tinge. **3b** (*as adj*): *an ebony skin.* [C16: *hebeny,* from Late Latin *ebeninus* from Greek *ebeninos,* from *ebenos* ebony, of Egyptian origin]
Ebor. ('iːbɔː) *abbrev. for* Eboracensis. [Latin: (Archbishop) of York]
Eboracum (iː'bɒrəkəm, ˌiːbɔː'rɑːkəm) *n* the Roman name for **York**[1] (sense 1).
ebracteate (ɪ'bræktɪˌeɪt, -tɪt) *adj* (of plants) having no bracts. [C19: from New Latin *ebracteātus;* see E-[1], BRACTEATE]
EBRD *abbrev. for* European Bank for Reconstruction and Development.
Ebro ('iːbrəʊ; *Spanish* 'eβro) *n* the second largest river in Spain, rising in the Cantabrian Mountains and flowing southeast to the Mediterranean. Length: 910 km (565 miles).
EBU *abbrev. for* European Broadcasting Union.
ebullient (ɪ'bʌljənt, ɪ'bʊl-) *adj* **1** overflowing with enthusiasm or excitement; exuberant. **2** boiling. [C16: from Latin *ēbullīre* to bubble forth, be boisterous, from *bullīre* to BOIL[1]] ▸ **e'bullience** *or* **e'bulliency** *n* ▸ **e'bulliently** *adv*
ebulliometer (ɪˌbʌlɪ'ɒmɪtə) *n Physics.* a device used to determine the boiling point of a solution. ▸ **eˌbulli'ometry** *n*
ebullioscopy (ɪˌbʌlɪ'ɒskəpɪ, ɪˌbʊl-) *n Chem.* a technique for finding molecular weights of substances by measuring the extent to which they change the boiling point of a solvent. [C19: from *ebullioscope,* from Latin *ebullire* to boil over + -SCOPE] ▸ **ebullioscopic** (ɪˌbʌlɪə'skɒpɪk, ɪˌbʊl-) *adj* ▸ **eˌbullio'scopically** *adv*
ebullition (ˌɛbə'lɪʃən) *n* **1** the process of boiling. **2** a sudden outburst, as of intense emotion. [C16: from Late Latin *ēbullītiō;* see EBULLIENT]
eburnation (ˌiːbə'neɪʃən, ˌɛb-) *n* a degenerative condition of bone or cartilage characterized by unusual hardness. [C19: from Latin *eburnus* of ivory, from *ebur* ivory]
EBV *abbrev. for* Epstein-Barr virus.
EC *abbrev. for:* **1** European Community (now called European Union). **2** (in London postal code) East Central. ◆ **3** *international car registration for* Ecuador.
ec- *combining form.* out from; away from: *ecbolic; eccentric; ecdysis.* [from Greek *ek* (before a vowel *ex*) out of, away from; see EX-[1]]
ecad ('iːkæd) *n* an organism whose form has been affected by its environment. [C20: from EC(OLOGY) + -AD[1]]
ecarinate (iː'kærɪnɪt) *adj Biology.* having no carina or keel. [E-[1] + CARINATE]
écarté (eɪ'kɑːteɪ; *French* ekarte) *n* **1** a card game for two, played with 32 cards and king high. **2** *Ballet.* **2a** a body position in which one arm and the same leg are extended at the side of the body. **2b** (*as adj*): *the écarté position.* [C19: from French, from *écarter* to discard, from *carte* CARD[1]]
ECB *abbrev. for* European Central Bank.
Ecbatana (ɛk'bætənə) *n* an ancient city in Iran, on the site of modern Hamadān; capital of Media and royal residence of the Persians and Parthians.
ecbolic (ɛk'bɒlɪk) *adj* **1** hastening labour or abortion. ◆ *n* **2** a drug or agent that hastens labour or abortion. [C18: from Greek *ekbolē* a throwing out, from *ekballein* to throw out, from *ballein* to throw]
Ecce Homo ('ɛkeɪ 'haʊməʊ, 'ɛksɪ) *n* a picture or sculpture of Christ crowned with thorns. [Latin: behold the man, the words of Pontius Pilate to his accusers (John 19:5)]
eccentric (ɪk'sɛntrɪk) *adj* **1** deviating or departing from convention, esp. in a bizarre manner; irregular or odd. **2** situated away from the centre or the axis. **3** not having a common centre: *eccentric circles.* Compare **concentric. 4** not precisely circular. ◆ *n* **5** a person who deviates from normal forms of behaviour esp. in a bizarre manner. **6** a device for converting rotary motion to reciprocating motion. [C16: from Medieval Latin *eccentricus,* from Greek *ekkentros* out of centre, from *ek-* EX-[1] + *kentron* centre] ▸ **ec'centrically** *adv*
eccentricity (ˌɛksɛn'trɪsɪtɪ) *n, pl* **-ties. 1** unconventional or irregular behaviour. **2** deviation from a circular path or orbit. **3** a measure of the elongation of an elliptical orbit, esp. of a planet or satellite: the distance between the foci divided by the length of the major axis. **4** *Geometry.* a number that expresses the shape of a conic section: the ratio of the distance of a point on the curve from a fixed point (the focus) to the distance of the point from a fixed line (the directrix). **5** the degree of displacement of the geometric centre of a part from the true centre, esp. of the axis of rotation of a wheel.
ecchymosis (ˌɛkɪ'məʊsɪs) *n, pl* **-ses** (-siːz). discoloration of the skin through bruising. [C16: from New Latin, from Greek *ekkhumōsis,* from *ekkhumousthai* to pour out, from *khumos* juice] ▸ **ecchymosed** ('ɛkɪˌməʊzd, -ˌməʊst) *or* **ecchymotic** (ˌɛkɪ'mɒtɪk) *adj*
eccl. *or* **eccles.** *abbrev. for* ecclesiastic(al).
Eccles[1] ('ɛkəlz) *n* a town in NW England, in Salford unitary authority, Greater Manchester. Pop.: 36 000 (1991).
Eccles[2] ('ɛkəlz) *n* Sir **John Carew.** 1903–97, Australian physiologist: shared the Nobel prize for physiology (1963) with A. L. Hodgkin and A. F. Huxley for their work on conduction of nervous impulses.
Eccles. *or* **Eccl.** *Bible. abbrev. for* Ecclesiastes.
Eccles cake *n Brit.* a pastry with a filling of dried fruit.
ecclesia (ɪ'kliːzɪə) *n, pl* **-siae** (-zɪˌiː). **1** (in formal Church usage) a congregation. **2** the assembly of citizens of an ancient Greek state. [C16: from Medieval Latin, from Late Greek *ekklēsia* assembly, from *ekklētos* called, from *ekkalein* to call out, from *kalein* to call]
ecclesiast. *abbrev. for* ecclesiastical.
Ecclesiastes (ɪˌkliːzɪ'æstiːz) *n* (*functioning as sing*) a book of the Old Testament, probably written about 250 B.C. [via Late Latin, from Greek *ekklēsiastēs* member of the assembly; see ECCLESIA]
ecclesiastic (ɪˌkliːzɪ'æstɪk) *n* **1** a clergyman or other person in holy orders. ◆ *adj* **2** of or associated with the Christian Church or clergy.
ecclesiastical (ɪˌkliːzɪ'æstɪkəl) *adj* of or relating to the Christian Church. ▸ **ecˌclesi'astically** *adv*
Ecclesiastical Commissioners *pl n* the administrators of the properties of the Church of England from 1836 to 1948, when they were combined with Queen Anne's Bounty to form the Church Commissioners.
ecclesiasticism (ɪˌkliːzɪ'æstɪˌsɪzəm) *n* exaggerated attachment to the practices or principles of the Christian Church.
Ecclesiasticus (ɪˌkliːzɪ'æstɪkəs) *n* one of the books of the Apocrypha, written around 180 B.C. and also called **the Wisdom of Jesus, the son of Sirach.**
ecclesiolatry (ɪˌkliːzɪ'ɒlətrɪ) *n* obsessional devotion to ecclesiastical traditions. ▸ **ecˌclesi'olater** *n*
ecclesiology (ɪˌkliːzɪ'ɒlədʒɪ) *n* **1** the study of the Christian Church. **2** the study of Church architecture and decoration. ▸ **ecclesiological** (ɪˌkliːzɪə'lɒdʒɪkəl) *adj* ▸ **ecˌclesio'logically** *adv* ▸ **ecˌclesi'ologist** *n*
Ecclus. *Bible. abbrev. for* Ecclesiasticus.
eccremocarpus (ˌɛkrəmə'kɑːpəs) *n* any plant of the evergreen climbing genus *Eccremocarpus,* esp. *E. scaber,* grown for its decorative pinnate foliage and bright orange-red bell flowers: family *Bignoniaceae.* [New Latin, from Greek *ekkremēs* suspended + *karpos* fruit]
eccrine ('ɛkrɪn) *adj* of or denoting glands that secrete externally, esp. the numerous sweat glands on the human body. Compare **apocrine.** [from Greek *ekkrinein* to secrete, from *ek-* EC- + *krinein* to separate]
eccrinology (ˌɛkrɪ'nɒlədʒɪ) *n* the branch of medical science concerned with secretions of the eccrine glands.
ecdemic (ɛk'dɛmɪk) *adj* not indigenous or endemic; foreign: *an ecdemic disease.*
ecdysiast (ɛk'dɪzɪˌæst) *n* a facetious word for **stripper** (sense 1). [C20: (coined by H. L. Mencken) from ECDYSIS + *-ast,* variant of -IST]
ecdysis ('ɛkdɪsɪs) *n, pl* **-ses** (-ˌsiːz). the periodic shedding of the cuticle in insects and other arthropods or the outer epidermal layer in reptiles. See also **ecdysone.** [C19: New Latin, from Greek *ekdusis,* from *ekduein* to strip, from *ek-* EX-[1] + *duein* to put on] ▸ **ec'dysial** *adj*
ecdysone (ɛk'daɪˌsəʊn) *n* a hormone secreted by the prothoracic gland of insects that controls ecdysis and stimulates metamorphosis. [C20: from German *ecdyson,* from Greek *ekdusis;* see ECDYSIS]
ecesis (ɪ'siːsɪs) *n* the establishment of a plant in a new environment. [C20: from Greek *oikēsis* a dwelling in, from *oikein* to inhabit; related to *oikos* a house]
ECG *abbrev. for:* **1** electrocardiogram. **2** electrocardiograph.
echard ('ɛkɑːd) *n* water that is present in the soil but cannot be absorbed or otherwise utilized by plants. [C20: from Greek *ekhein* to hold back + *ardein* to water]
Echegaray y Eizaguirre (*Spanish* etʃeɣa'rai i eiθa'ɣirre) *n* **José** (xo'se). 1832–1916, Spanish dramatist, statesman, and mathematician. His plays include *Madman or Saint* (1877); Nobel prize for literature 1904.
echelon ('ɛʃəˌlɒn) *n* **1** a level of command, responsibility, etc. (esp. in the phrase **the upper echelons**). **2** *Military.* **2a** a formation in which units follow one another but are offset sufficiently to allow each unit a line of fire ahead. **2b** a group formed in this way. **3** *Physics.* a type of diffraction grating consisting of a series of plates of equal thickness arranged stepwise with a constant offset. ◆ *vb* **4** to assemble in echelon. [C18: from French *échelon,* literally: rung of a ladder, from Old French *eschiele* ladder, from Latin *scāla;* see SCALE[3]]
echeveria (ˌɛtʃɪ'vɪərɪə) *n* any of various tropical American crassulaceous plants of the genus *Echeveria,* cultivated for their colourful foliage. [named after M. *Echeveri,* 19th-century Mexican botanical artist]
echidna (ɪ'kɪdnə) *n, pl* **-nas** *or* **-nae** (-niː). any of the spine-covered monotreme mammals of the genera *Tachyglossus* of Australia and *Zaglossus* of New Guinea: family *Tachyglossidae.* They have a long snout and claws for hunting ants and termites. Also called: **spiny anteater.** [C19: from New Latin, from Latin: viper, from Greek *ekhidna*]
echinate ('ɛkɪˌneɪt) *or* **echinated** *adj Biology.* covered with spines, bristles, or bristle-like outgrowths.
echino- *or before a vowel* **echin-** *combining form* indicating spiny or prickly: *echinoderm.* [from New Latin, via Latin from Greek *ekhinos* sea urchin, hedgehog]
echinococcus (ɪˌkaɪnə'kɒkəs) *n* any of the tapeworms constituting the genus *Echinococcus,* the larvae of which are parasitic in man and domestic animals.
echinoderm (ɪ'kaɪnəʊˌdɜːm) *n* any of the marine invertebrate animals constituting the phylum *Echinodermata,* characterized by tube feet, a calcite body-covering (test), and a five-part symmetrical body. The group includes the starfish, sea urchins, and sea cucumbers. ▸ **eˌchino'dermal** *or* **eˌchino'dermatous** *adj*
echinoid (ɪ'kaɪnɔɪd, 'ɛkə-) *n* **1** any of the echinoderms constituting the class *Echinoidea,* typically having a rigid ovoid body. The class includes the sea urchins and sand dollars. ◆ *adj* **2** of or belonging to this class.
echinus (ɪ'kaɪnəs) *n, pl* **-ni** (-naɪ). **1** *Architect.* an ovolo moulding between the shaft and the abacus of a Doric column. **2** any of the sea urchins of the genus *Echinus,* such as *E. esculentus* (**edible sea urchin**) of the Mediterranean. [C14: from Latin, from Greek *ekhinos*]
echium ('ɛkɪəm) *n* any plant of the Mediterranean genus *Echium* whose bell-shaped flowers are borne on single-sided spikes in a wide variety of colours; *E. vulgare* is viper's bugloss: family *Boraginaceae.* [New Latin, from Greek *echion,* from *echis* viper, from its use as an antidote to a viper bite]
echo ('ɛkəʊ) *n, pl* **-oes. 1a** the reflection of sound or other radiation by a reflect-

ing medium, esp. a solid object. **1b** the sound so reflected. **2** a repetition or imitation, esp. an unoriginal reproduction of another's opinions. **3** something that evokes memories, esp. of a particular style or era. **4** (*sometimes pl*) an effect that continues after the original cause has disappeared; repercussion: *the echoes of the French Revolution.* **5** a person who copies another, esp. one who obsequiously agrees with another's opinions. **6a** the signal reflected by a radar target. **6b** the trace produced by such a signal on a radar screen. **7** the repetition of certain sounds or syllables in a verse line. **8** the quiet repetition of a musical phrase. **9** Also called: **echo organ** *or* **echo stop.** a manual or stop on an organ that controls a set of quiet pipes that give the illusion of sounding at a distance. **10** an electronic effect in recorded music that adds vibration or resonance. ◆ *vb* **-oes, -oing, -oed. 11** to resound or cause to resound with an echo: *the cave echoed their shouts.* **12** (*intr*) (of sounds) to repeat or resound by echoes; reverberate. **13** (*tr*) (of persons) to repeat (words, opinions, etc.), in imitation, agreement, or flattery. **14** (*tr*) (of things) to resemble or imitate (another style, earlier model, etc.). **15** (*tr*) (of a computer) to display (a character) on the screen of a visual display unit as a response to receiving that character from a keyboard entry. [C14: via Latin from Greek *ēkhō;* related to Greek *ēkhē* sound] ▸ **'echoing** *adj* ▸ **'echoless** *adj* ▸ **'echo-ˌlike** *adj*

Echo[1] ('ɛkəʊ) *n* either of two U.S. passive communications satellites, the first of which was launched in 1960.

Echo[2] ('ɛkəʊ) *n Greek myth.* a nymph who, spurned by Narcissus, pined away until only her voice remained.

Echo[3] ('ɛkəʊ) *n Communications.* code word for the letter *e.*

echocardiography (ˌɛkəʊkɑːdɪ'ɒgrəfɪ) *n* examination of the heart using ultrasound techniques.

echo chamber *n* a room with walls that reflect sound. It is used to make acoustic measurements and as a source of reverberant sound to be mixed with direct sound for recording or broadcasting. Also called: **reverberation chamber.**

echography (ɛ'kɒgrəfɪ) *n* medical examination of the internal structures of the body by means of ultrasound.

echoic (ɛ'kəʊɪk) *adj* **1** characteristic of or resembling an echo. **2** onomatopoeic; imitative.

echoic memory *n Psychol.* the ability to recapture the exact impression of a sound shortly after the sound has finished. Compare **iconic memory.**

echoism ('ɛkəʊˌɪzəm) *n* **1** onomatopoeia as a source of word formation. **2** phonetic assimilation of one vowel to the vowel in the preceding syllable.

echolalia (ˌɛkəʊ'leɪlɪə) *n Psychiatry.* the tendency to repeat mechanically words just spoken by another person: can occur in cases of brain damage, mental retardation, and schizophrenia. [C19: from New Latin, from ECHO + Greek *lalia* talk, chatter, from *lalein* to chatter] ▸ **echolalic** (ˌɛkəʊ'lælɪk) *adj*

echolocation (ˌɛkəʊləʊ'keɪʃən) *n* determination of the position of an object by measuring the time taken for an echo to return from it and its direction.

echo plate *n* (in sound recording or broadcasting) an electromechanical device for producing echo and reverbation effects.

echopraxia (ˌɛkəʊ'præksɪə) *or* **echopraxis** *n* the involuntary imitation of the actions of others.

echo sounder *n* a navigation and position-finding device that determines depth by measuring the time taken for a pulse of high-frequency sound to reach the sea bed or a submerged object and for the echo to return. ▸ **echo sounding** *n*

echovirus ('ɛkəʊˌvaɪrəs) *or* **ECHO virus** *n* any of a group of viruses that can cause symptoms of mild meningitis, the common cold, or infections of the intestinal and respiratory tracts. [C20: from the initials of *Enteric Cytopathic Human Orphan* ("orphan" because originally believed to be unrelated to any disease) + VIRUS]

echt *German.* (ɛçt; *English* ɛkt) *adj* real; genuine; authentic.

Eck (ɛk) *n* **Johann** (jo'han), original name *Johann Mayer.* 1486–1543, German Roman Catholic theologian; opponent of Luther and the Reformation.

Eckert ('ɛkət) *n* **John Presper.** 1919–95, U.S. electronics engineer: built the first electronic computer with John W. Mauchly in 1946.

Eckhart (*German* 'ɛkhart) *n* **Johannes** (jo'hanəs), called *Meister Eckhart.* ?1260–?1327, German Dominican theologian, mystic, and preacher.

éclair (eɪ'klɛə, ɪ'klɛə) *n* a finger-shaped cake of choux pastry, usually filled with cream and covered with chocolate. [C19: from French, literally: lightning (probably so called because it does not last long), from *éclairer,* from Latin *clārāre*to make bright, from *clārus* bright]

eclampsia (ɪ'klæmpsɪə) *n Pathol.* a toxic condition of unknown cause that sometimes develops in the last three months of pregnancy, characterized by high blood pressure, abnormal weight gain and convulsions. Compare **pre-eclampsia.** [C19: from New Latin, from Greek *eklampsis* a shining forth, from *eklampein,* from *lampein* to shine] ▸ **ec'lamptic** *adj*

éclat (eɪ'klɑː; *French* ekla) *n* **1** brilliant or conspicuous success, effect, etc. **2** showy display; ostentation. **3** social distinction. **4** approval; acclaim; applause. [C17: from French, from *éclater* to burst; related to Old French *esclater* to splinter, perhaps of Germanic origin; compare SLIT]

eclectic (ɪ'klɛktɪk, ɛ'klɛk-) *adj* **1** (in art, philosophy, etc.) selecting what seems best from various styles, doctrines, ideas, methods, etc. **2** composed of elements drawn from a variety of sources, styles, etc. ◆ *n* **3** a person who favours an eclectic approach, esp. in art or philosophy. [C17: from Greek *eklektikos,* from *eklegein* to select, from *legein* to gather] ▸ **ec'lectically** *adv*

eclecticism (ɪ'klɛktɪˌsɪzəm, ɛ'klɛk-) *n* **1** an eclectic system or method. **2** the use or advocacy of such a system.

eclipse (ɪ'klɪps) *n* **1** the total or partial obscuring of one celestial body by another. A **solar eclipse** occurs when the moon passes between the sun and the earth; a **lunar eclipse** when the earth passes between the sun and the moon. See also **total eclipse, partial eclipse, annular eclipse.** Compare **occultation. 2** the period of time during which such a phenomenon occurs. **3** any dimming or obstruction of light. **4** a loss of importance, power, fame, etc., esp. through overshadowing by another. ◆ *vb* (*tr*) **5** to cause an eclipse of. **6** to cast a shadow upon; darken; obscure. **7** to overshadow or surpass in importance, power, etc. [C13: back formation from Old English *eclypsis,* from Latin *eclīpsis,* from Greek *ekleipsis* a forsaking, from *ekleipein* to abandon, from *leipein* to leave] ▸ **e'clipser** *n*

eclipse plumage *n* seasonal plumage that occurs in certain birds after the breeding plumage and before the winter plumage: is characterized by dull coloration.

eclipsing binary *or* **variable** *n* a binary star whose orbital plane lies in or near the line of sight so that one component is regularly eclipsed by its companion. See also **variable star.**

eclipsis (ɪ'klɪpsɪs) *n Linguistics.* **1** a rare word for **ellipsis** (sense 1). **2** (in Gaelic) phonetic change of an initial consonant under the influence of a preceding word. Unvoiced plosives become voiced, while voiced plosives are changed to nasals.

ecliptic (ɪ'klɪptɪk) *n* **1** *Astronomy.* **1a** the great circle on the celestial sphere representing the apparent annual path of the sun relative to the stars. It is inclined at 23.45° to the celestial equator. The **poles of the ecliptic** lie on the celestial sphere due north and south of the plane of the ecliptic. **1b** (*as modifier*): *the ecliptic plane.* **2** an equivalent great circle, opposite points of which pass through the Tropics of Cancer and Capricorn, on the terrestrial globe. ◆ *adj* **3** of or relating to an eclipse. ▸ **e'cliptically** *adv*

eclogite ('ɛkləˌdʒaɪt) *n* a rare coarse-grained basic rock consisting of large bright red garnets in a greenish mixture of pyroxene, quartz, feldspar, etc. Its origin is thought to be intermediate between igneous and metamorphic. [C19: from Greek *eklogē* a selection]

eclogue ('ɛklɒg) *n* a pastoral or idyllic poem, usually in the form of a conversation or soliloquy. [C15: from Latin *ecloga* short poem, collection of extracts, from Greek *eklogē* selection, from *eklegein* to select; see ECLECTIC]

eclosion (ɪ'kləʊʒən) *n* the emergence of an insect larva from the egg or an adult from the pupal case. [C19: from French *éclosion,* from *éclore* to hatch, ultimately from Latin *exclūdere* to shut out, EXCLUDE]

eco ('iːkəʊ) *n* **a** short for **ecology. b** (*as modifier*): *an eco group.*

Eco ('ɛkəʊ) *n* **Umberto.** born 1932, Italian semiologist and writer. His novels include *The Name of the Rose* (1981) and *Foucault's Pendulum* (1988).

eco- *combining form.* denoting ecology or ecological: *ecocide; ecosphere.*

ecocentric (ˌiːkəʊ'sentrɪk) *adj* having a serious concern for environmental issues: *ecocentric management.*

ecocide ('iːkəˌsaɪd, 'ɛkə-) *n* total destruction of an area of the natural environment, esp. by human agency.

ecofriendly ('iːkəʊˌfrɛndlɪ) *adj* having a beneficial effect on the environment or at least not causing environmental damage.

ecol. *abbrev. for:* **1** ecological. **2** ecology.

E.coli (iː'kəʊlaɪ) *n* short for *Escherichia coli,* see ***Escherichia.***

ecological (ˌiːkə'lɒdʒɪkᵊl) *adj* **1** of or relating to ecology. **2** (of a practice, policy, product, etc.) tending to benefit or cause minimal damage to the environment. ▸ **ˌeco'logically** *adv*

ecology (ɪ'kɒlədʒɪ) *n* **1** the study of the relationships between living organisms and their environment. **2** the set of relationships of a particular organism with its environment. **3 human ecology.** the study of the relationships between human groups and their physical environment. ◆ Also called (for senses 1, 2): **bionomics.** [C19: from German *Ökologie,* from Greek *oikos* house (hence, environment)] ▸ **e'cologist** *n*

e-commerce *or* **ecommerce** ('iːˌkɒmɜːs) *n* business transactions conducted on the Internet. [C20: from E-[2] + COMMERCE]

econ. *abbrev. for:* **1** economical. **2** economics. **3** economy.

econometrics (ɪˌkɒnə'mɛtrɪks) *n* (*functioning as sing*) the application of mathematical and statistical techniques to economic problems and theories. ▸ **eˌcono'metric** *or* **eˌcono'metrical** *adj* ▸ **econometrician** (ɪˌkɒnəmə'trɪʃən) *or* **eˌcono'metrist** *n*

economic (ˌiːkə'nɒmɪk, ˌɛkə-) *adj* **1** of or relating to an economy, economics, or finance: *economic development; economic theories.* **2** *Brit.* capable of being produced, operated, etc., for profit; profitable: *the firm is barely economic.* **3** concerning or affecting material resources or welfare: *economic pests.* **4** concerned with or relating to the necessities of life; utilitarian. **5** a variant of **economical. 6** *Informal.* inexpensive; cheap.

economical (ˌiːkə'nɒmɪkᵊl, ˌɛkə-) *adj* **1** using the minimum required; not wasteful of time, effort, resources, etc.: *an economical car; an economical style.* **2** frugal; thrifty: *she was economical by nature.* **3** a variant of **economic** (senses 1–4). **4** *Euphemistic.* deliberately withholding information (esp. in the phrase **economical with the truth**).

economically (ˌiːkə'nɒmɪkəlɪ, ˌɛkə-) *adv* **1** with economy or thrift; without waste. **2** with regard to the economy of a person, country, etc.

economic determinism *n* a doctrine that states that all cultural, social, political, and intellectual activities are a product of the economic organization of society.

economic geography *n* the study of the geographical distribution of economic resources and their use.

economic geology *n* the study of how geological deposits can be used as economic resources.

economic indicator *n* a statistical measure representing an economic variable: *the retail price index is an economic indicator of the actual level of prices.*

economic rent *n* **1** *Economics.* a payment to a factor of production (land, labour, or capital) in excess of that needed to keep it in its present use. **2** (in Britain) the rent of a dwelling based on recouping the costs of providing it plus a profit sufficient to motivate the landlord to let it.

economics (ˌiːkəˈnɒmɪks, ˌɛkə-) *n* **1** (*functioning as sing*) the social science concerned with the production and consumption of goods and services and the analysis of the commercial activities of a society. See also **macroeconomics, microeconomics. 2** (*pl*) financial aspects: *the economics of the project are very doubtful.*

economic sanctions *pl n* any actions taken by one nation or group of nations to harm the economy of another nation or group, often to force a political change.

economic zone *n* another term for **exclusive economic zone.**

economism (ɪˈkɒnəˌmɪzəm) *n* **1a** a political theory that regards economics as the main factor in society, ignoring or reducing to simplistic economic terms other factors such as culture, nationality, etc. **1b** the belief that the main aim of a political group, trade union, etc., is to improve the material living standards of its members. **2** (*often cap.*) (in Tsarist Russia) a political belief that the sole concern of the working classes should be with improving their living conditions and not with political reforms.

economist (ɪˈkɒnəmɪst) *n* **1** a specialist in economics. **2** *Archaic.* a person who advocates or practises frugality.

economize *or* **economise** (ɪˈkɒnəˌmaɪz) *vb* (often foll. by *on*) to limit or reduce (expense, waste, etc.). ▶ **eˌconomiˈzation** *or* **eˌconomiˈsation** *n*

economizer *or* **economiser** (ɪˈkɒnəˌmaɪzə) *n* **1** a device that uses the waste heat from a boiler flue to preheat the feed water. **2** a person or thing that economizes.

Economo's disease (ɪˈkɒnəməʊz) *n Pathol.* another name for **sleeping sickness** (sense 2). [C20: named after K. von *Economo* (1876–1931), Austrian neurologist]

economy (ɪˈkɒnəmɪ) *n, pl* **-mies. 1** careful management of resources to avoid unnecessary expenditure or waste; thrift. **2** a means or instance of this; saving. **3** sparing, restrained, or efficient use, esp. to achieve the maximum effect for the minimum effort: *economy of language.* **4a** the complex of human activities concerned with the production, distribution, and consumption of goods and services. **4b** a particular type or branch of such production, distribution, and consumption: *a socialist economy; an agricultural economy.* **5** the management of the resources, finances, income, and expenditure of a community, business enterprise, etc. **6a** a class of travel in aircraft, providing less luxurious accommodation than first class at a lower fare. **6b** (*as modifier*): *economy class.* **7** (*modifier*) offering or purporting to offer a larger quantity for a lower price: *economy pack.* **8** the orderly interplay between the parts of a system or structure: *the economy of nature.* **9** *Philosophy.* the principle that, of two competing theories, the one with less ontological presupposition is to be preferred. **10** *Archaic.* the management of household affairs; domestic economy. [C16: via Latin from Greek *oikonomia* domestic management, from *oikos* house + *-nomia,* from *nemein* to manage]

economy of scale *n Economics.* a fall in average costs resulting from an increase in the scale of production.

ecophysiology (ˌiːkəʊˌfɪzɪˈɒlədʒɪ) *n* the study of the ways in which organisms are adapted to their environment.

écorché (ˌeɪkɔːˈʃeɪ) *n* an anatomical figure without the skin, so that the muscular structure is visible. [C19: French, literally: skinned]

ecospecies (ˈiːkəʊˌspiːʃiːz, -ˌspiːsiːz; ˈɛkəʊ-) *n Ecology.* a species of plant or animal that can be divided into several ecotypes. [C20: from ECO(LOGY) + SPECIES] ▶ **ecospecific** (ˌiːkəʊspɪˈsɪfɪk, ˌɛkəʊ-) *adj*

ecosphere (ˈiːkəʊˌsfɪə, ˈɛkəʊ-) *n* the parts of the universe, esp. on the earth, in which life can exist.

écossaise (ˌeɪkɒˈseɪz; *French* ekɔsɛz) *n* **1** a lively dance in two-four time. **2** the tune for such a dance. [C19: French, literally: Scottish (dance)]

ecosystem (ˈiːkəʊˌsɪstəm, ˈɛkəʊ-) *n Ecology.* a system involving the interactions between a community and its non-living environment. [C20: from ECO(LOGY) + SYSTEM]

ecoterrorist (ˈiːkəʊˌtɛrərɪst) *n* a person who uses violence in order to achieve environmentalist aims. [C20: from ECO- + TERRORIST]

ecotone (ˈiːkəˌtəʊn, ˈɛkə-) *n* the zone between two major ecological communities. [C20: from ECO(LOGY) + *-tone,* from Greek *tonos* tension, TONE] ▶ **ˈecoˌtonal** *adj*

ecotourism (ˈiːkəʊˌtʊərɪzəm) *n* tourism which is designed to contribute to the protection of the environment or at least minimize damage to it, often involving travel to areas of natural interest in developing countries or participation in environmental projects. ▶ **ˈecoˌtourist** *n*

ecotype (ˈiːkəˌtaɪp, ˈɛkə-) *n Ecology.* a group of organisms within a species that are adapted to different environmental conditions and therefore differ from one another in structure and physiology. ▶ **ecotypic** (ˌiːkəˈtɪpɪk, ˌɛkə-) *adj* ▶ **ˌecoˈtypically** *adv*

ECOWAS (ɛˈkəʊəs) *n acronym for* Economic Community of West African States; an economic association established in 1975 among Benin, Burkina-Faso (then called Upper Volta), The Gambia, Ghana, Guinea, Guinea-Bissau, Ivory Coast, Liberia, Mali, Mauritania, Niger, Nigeria, Senegal, Sierra Leone, and Togo.

ECR *abbrev. for* efficient consumer response: the use of point-of-sale data to initiate the reordering of stock from a supplier.

écraseur (ˌeɪkrɑːˈzɜː) *n* a surgical device consisting of a heavy wire loop placed around a part to be removed and tightened until it cuts through. [C19: from French, from *écraser* to crush]

ecru (ˈɛkruː, ˈeɪkruː) *n* **1** a greyish-yellow to a light greyish colour; the colour of unbleached linen. ◆ *adj* **2** of the colour ecru. [C19: from French, from *é-* (intensive) + *cru* raw, from Latin *crūdus;* see CRUDE]

ECS *abbrev. for* European Communications Satellite.

ECSC *abbrev. for* European Coal and Steel Community.

ecstasy (ˈɛkstəsɪ) *n, pl* **-sies. 1** (*often pl*) a state of exalted delight, joy, etc.; rapture. **2** intense emotion of any kind: *an ecstasy of rage.* **3** *Psychol.* overpowering emotion characterized by loss of self-control and sometimes a temporary loss of consciousness: often associated with orgasm, religious mysticism, and the use of certain drugs. **4** *Archaic.* a state of prophetic inspiration, esp. of poetic rapture. **5** *Slang.* 3,4-methylenedioxymethamphetamine: a powerful drug that acts as a stimulant and can produce hallucinations. [C14: from Old French *extasie,* via Medieval Latin from Greek *ekstasis* displacement, trance, from *existanai* to displace, from *ex-* out + *histanai* to cause to stand]

ecstatic (ɛkˈstætɪk) *adj* **1** in a trancelike state of great rapture or delight. **2** showing or feeling great enthusiasm: *ecstatic applause.* ◆ *n* **3** a person who has periods of intense trancelike joy. ▶ **ecˈstatically** *adv*

ecstatics (ɛkˈstætɪks) *pl n* fits of delight or rapture.

ECT *abbrev. for* electroconvulsive therapy.

ectasia (ɛkˈteɪzɪə) *or* **ectasis** (ˈɛktəsɪs) *n Pathol.* the distension or dilation of any part of the body. ▶ **ecˈtatic** *adj*

ecthyma (ˈɛkθɪmə) *n Pathol.* a local inflammation of the skin characterized by flat ulcerating pustules. [C19: from New Latin, from Greek *ekthuma* pustule, from *ekthuein* to break out, from *ek-* out + *thuein* to seethe]

ecto- *combining form.* indicating outer, outside, external: *ectoplasm.* [from Greek *ektos* outside, from *ek, ex* out]

ectoblast (ˈɛktəʊˌblæst) *n* another name for **ectoderm** or **epiblast.** ▶ **ˌectoˈblastic** *adj*

ectocrine (ˈɛktəʊˌkriːn, -krɪn) *n* a substance that is released by an organism into the external environment and influences the development, behaviour, etc., of members of the same or different species. [C20: from ECTO- + *-crine,* as in *endocrine*]

ectoderm (ˈɛktəʊˌdɜːm) *or* **exoderm** *n* the outer germ layer of an animal embryo, which gives rise to epidermis and nervous tissue. See also **mesoderm** and **endoderm.** ▶ **ˌectoˈdermal** *or* **ˌectoˈdermic** *adj*

ectoenzyme (ˌɛktəʊˈɛnzaɪm) *n* any of a group of enzymes secreted from the cells in which they are produced into the surrounding medium; extracellular enzyme. Also called: **exoenzyme.**

ectogenesis (ˌɛktəʊˈdʒɛnəsɪs) *n* the growth of an organism outside the body in which it would normally be found, such as the growth of an embryo outside the mother's body or the growth of bacteria outside the body of a host. ▶ **ˌectogeˈnetic, ˌectoˈgenic,** *or* **ectogenous** (ɛkˈtɒdʒɪnəs) *adj* ▶ **ˌectoˈgenically** *adv*

ectomere (ˈɛktəʊˌmɪə) *n Embryol.* any of the blastomeres that later develop into ectoderm. ▶ **ectomeric** (ˌɛktəʊˈmɛrɪk) *adj*

ectomorph (ˈɛktəʊˌmɔːf) *n* a person with a thin body build: said to be correlated with cerebrotonia. Compare **endomorph, mesomorph.** ▶ **ˌectoˈmorphic** *adj* ▶ **ˈectoˌmorphy** *n*

-ectomy *n combining form.* indicating surgical excision of a part: *appendectomy.* [from New Latin *-ectomia,* from Greek *ek-* out + -TOMY]

ectoparasite (ˌɛktəʊˈpærəˌsaɪt) *n* a parasite, such as the flea, that lives on the outer surface of its host. Also called: **exoparasite.** ▶ **ectoparasitic** (ˌɛktəʊˌpærəˈsɪtɪk) *adj*

ectophyte (ˈɛktəʊˌfaɪt) *n* a parasitic plant that lives on the surface of its host. ▶ **ectophytic** (ˌɛktəʊˈfɪtɪk) *adj*

ectopia (ɛkˈtəʊpɪə) *n Med.* congenital displacement or abnormal positioning of an organ or part. [C19: from New Latin, from Greek *ektopos* out of position, from *ek-* out of + *topos* place] ▶ **ectopic** (ɛkˈtɒpɪk) *adj*

ectopic pregnancy *n Pathol.* the abnormal development of a fertilized egg outside the cavity of the uterus, usually within a Fallopian tube.

ectoplasm (ˈɛktəʊˌplæzəm) *n* **1** *Cytology.* the outer layer of cytoplasm that differs in many cells from the inner cytoplasm (see **endoplasm**) in being a clear gel. **2** *Spiritualism.* the substance supposedly emanating from the body of a medium during trances. ▶ **ˌectoˈplasmic** *adj*

ectoproct (ˈɛktəʊˌprɒkt) *n, adj* another word for **bryozoan.** [from ECTO- + *-proct,* from Greek *prōktos* rectum]

ectosarc (ˈɛktəʊˌsɑːk) *n Zoology.* the ectoplasm of an amoeba or any other protozoan. [C19: ECTO- + *-sarc,* from Greek *sarx* flesh] ▶ **ˌectoˈsarcous** *adj*

ectotrophic (ˌɛktəʊˈtrɒfɪk) *adj Botany.* denoting a type of mycorrhiza in which the fungus forms a layer on the outside of the roots of the plant. Compare **endotrophic.**

ectype (ˈɛkˌtaɪp) *n* **1** a copy as distinguished from a prototype. **2** *Architect.* a cast embossed or in relief. [C17: from Greek *ektupos* worked in relief, from *ek-* out of + *tupos* mould; see TYPE] ▶ **ectypal** (ˈɛktɪpᵊl) *adj*

écu (eɪˈkjuː; *French* eky) *n* **1** any of various former French gold or silver coins. **2** a small shield. [C18: from Old French *escu,* from Latin *scūtum* shield]

ECU (ˈeɪkjuː; *or sometimes* ˈiːˈsiːˈjuː) *n acronym for* European Currency Unit: a unit of currency based on the composite value of several different currencies in the European Union and functioning both as the reserve asset and accounting unit of the European Monetary System.

Ecua. *abbrev. for* Ecuador.

Ecuador (ˈɛkwəˌdɔː) *n* a republic in South America, on the Pacific: under the Incas when Spanish colonization began in 1532; gained independence in 1822; declared a republic in 1830. It consists chiefly of a coastal plain in the west, separated from the densely forested upper Amazon basin (Oriente) by ranges and plateaus of the Andes. Official language: Spanish; Quechua is also widely spoken. Religion: Roman Catholic majority. Currency: sucre. Capital: Quito. Pop.: 12 175 000 (1998 est.). Area: 283 560 sq. km (109 483 sq. miles). ▶ **ˌEcuaˈdorean** *adj, n*

ecumenical, oecumenical (ˌiːkjʊˈmɛnɪkᵊl, ˌɛk-) *or* **ecumenic, oecumenic** *adj* **1** of or relating to the Christian Church throughout the world, esp. with regard to its unity. **2a** tending to promote unity among Churches. **2b** of or relating to the international movement initiated among non-Catholic Churches in 1910 aimed at Christian unity: embodied, since 1937, in the World Council of Churches. 3 *Rare.* universal; general; worldwide. [C16: via Late Latin from Greek *oikoumenikos,* from *oikein* to inhabit, from *oikos* house] ▸ ˌecu'menically *or* ˌoecu'menically *adv*

ecumenical council *n* an assembly of bishops and other ecclesiastics representative of the Christian Church throughout the world. Roman Catholic canon law states that an ecumenical council must be convened by the pope.

ecumenism (ɪ'kju:məˌnɪzəm, 'ɛkjum-), **ecumenicism** (ˌi:kju'mɛnˌsɪkɪzəm, ˌɛk-) *or* **ecumenicalism** *n* the aim of unity among all Christian churches throughout the world.

écurie (*French* ekyri) *n* a team of motor-racing cars. [C20: French, literally: a stable]

eczema ('ɛksɪmə) *n Pathol.* a skin inflammation with lesions that scale, crust, or ooze a serous fluid, often accompanied by intense itching or burning. [C18: from New Latin, from Greek *ekzema,* from *ek-* out + *zein* to boil; see YEAST] ▸ **eczematous** (ɛk'sɛmətəs) *adj*

ed. *abbrev. for:* **1** edited. **2** (*pl* **eds.**) edition. **3** (*pl* **eds.**) editor. **4** education.

-ed[1] *suffix.* forming the past tense of most English verbs. [Old English *-de, -ede, -ode, -ade*]

-ed[2] *suffix.* forming the past participle of most English verbs. [Old English *-ed, -od, -ad*]

-ed[3] *suffix forming adjectives from nouns.* possessing or having the characteristics of: *salaried; red-blooded.* [Old English *-ede*]

edacious (ɪ'deɪʃəs) *adj Chiefly humorous.* devoted to eating; voracious; greedy. [C19: from Latin *edāx* voracious, from *edere* to eat] ▸ **e'daciously** *adv* ▸ **edacity** (ɪ'dæsɪtɪ) *or* **e'daciousness** *n*

Edam ('i:dæm) *n* **1** a town in the NW Netherlands, in North Holland province, on the IJsselmeer: cheese, light manufacturing. Pop.: 24 572 (1989). **2** a hard round mild-tasting Dutch cheese, yellow in colour with a red outside covering.

edaphic (ɪ'dæfɪk) *adj* of or relating to the physical and chemical conditions of the soil, esp. in relation to the plant and animal life it supports. Compare **biotic** (sense 2). [C20: from Greek *edaphos* bottom, soil] ▸ **e'daphically** *adv*

Edberg ('ɛdbɜ:g) *n* **Stefan.** born 1966, Swedish tennis player: Wimbledon champion 1988, 1990.

EDC *abbrev. for* European Defence Community.

Edda ('ɛdə) *n* **1** Also called: **Elder Edda, Poetic Edda.** a collection of mythological Old Norse poems made in the 12th century. **2** Also called: **Younger Edda, Prose Edda.** a treatise on versification together with a collection of Scandinavian myths, legends, and poems compiled by Snorri Sturluson. [C18: Old Norse] ▸ **Eddaic** (ɛ'deɪɪk) *adj*

Eddery ('ɛdərɪ) *n* **Patrick,** known as *Pat.* born 1952, Irish jockey.

Eddington ('ɛdɪŋtən) *n* Sir **Arthur Stanley.** 1882–1944, English astronomer and physicist, noted for his research on the motion, internal constitution, and luminosity of stars and for his elucidation of the theory of relativity.

eddo *or* **Chinese eddo** ('ɛdəʊ) *n, pl* **eddoes.** other names for **taro.**

eddy ('ɛdɪ) *n, pl* **-dies. 1** a movement in a stream of air, water, or other fluid in which the current doubles back on itself causing a miniature whirlwind or whirlpool. **2** a deviation from or disturbance in the main trend of thought, life, etc., esp. one that is relatively unimportant. ◆ *vb* **-dies, -dying, -died. 3** to move or cause to move against the main current. [C15: probably of Scandinavian origin; compare Old Norse *itha;* related to Old English *ed-* again, back, Old High German *it-*]

Eddy ('ɛdɪ) *n* **Mary Baker.** 1821–1910, U.S. religious leader; founder of the Christian Science movement (1866).

eddy current *n* an electric current induced in a massive conductor, such as the core of an electromagnet, transformer, etc., by an alternating magnetic field. Also called: **Foucault current.**

Eddystone Rocks ('ɛdɪstən) *n* a dangerous group of rocks at the W end of the English Channel, southwest of Plymouth: lighthouse.

Ede ('eɪdə) *n* a city in the central Netherlands, in Gelderland province. Pop.: 98 220 (1994).

Edelman ('ɛd°lmən) *n* **Gerald Maurice.** born 1929, U.S. biochemist: he shared the Nobel prize for physiology or medicine (1972) with Rodney Porter for determining the structure of antibodies.

edelweiss ('eɪd°lˌvaɪs) *n* a small alpine flowering plant, *Leontopodium alpinum,* having white woolly oblong leaves and a tuft of attractive floral leaves surrounding the flowers: family *Compositae* (composites). [C19: German, literally: noble white]

edema (ɪ'di:mə) *n, pl* **-mata** (-mətə). the usual U.S. spelling of **oedema.** ▸ **edematous** (ɪ'dɛmətəs) *or* **e'demaˌtose** *adj*

Eden[1] ('i:d°n) *n* **1** Also called: **Garden of Eden.** *Old Testament.* the garden in which Adam and Eve were placed at the Creation. **2** a delightful place, region, dwelling, etc.; paradise. **3** a state of great delight, happiness, or contentment; bliss. [C14: from Late Latin, from Hebrew *'ēdhen* place of pleasure] ▸ **Edenic** (i:'dɛnɪk) *adj*

Eden[2] ('i:d°n) *n* Sir (**Robert**) **Anthony,** Earl of Avon. 1897–1977, British Conservative statesman; foreign secretary (1935–38; 1940–45; 1951–55) and prime minister (1955–57). He resigned after the controversy caused by the occupation of the Suez Canal zone by British and French forces (1956).

edentate (i:'dɛnteɪt) *n* **1** any of the placental mammals that constitute the order *Edentata,* which inhabit tropical regions of Central and South America. The order includes anteaters, sloths, and armadillos. ◆ *adj* **2** of, relating to, or belonging to the order *Edentata.* [C19: from Latin *ēdentātus* lacking teeth, from *ēdentāre* to render toothless, from *e-* out + *dēns* tooth]

edentulous (i:'dɛntʃuləs) *or* **edentulate** (i:'dɛntʃulɪt) *adj* having no teeth.

Edessa (ɪ'dɛsə) *n* **1** an ancient city on the N edge of the Syrian plateau, founded as a Macedonian colony by Seleucus I: a centre of early Christianity. Modern name: **Urfa. 2** a market town in Greece: ancient capital of Macedonia. Pop.: 15 980 (1981). Ancient name: **Aegae** ('i:gi:). Modern Greek name: **Édhessa.**

Edgar ('ɛdgə) *n* **1** 944–975 A.D., king of Mercia and Northumbria (957–975) and of England (959–975). **2** ?1074–1107, king of Scotland (1097–1107), fourth son of Malcolm III. He overthrew his uncle Donald to gain the throne. **3 David.** born 1948, British dramatist, noted for political plays such as *Destiny* (1976) and *Maydays* (1983): he adapted (1980) *Nicholas Nickleby* and (1991) *Dr Jekyll and Mr Hyde* for the RSC.

Edgar Atheling ('æθɪlɪŋ) *n* ?1050–?1125, grandson of Edmund II; Anglo-Saxon pretender to the English throne in 1066.

edge (ɛdʒ) *n* **1** the border, brim, or margin of a surface, object, etc. **2** a brink or verge: *the edge of a cliff; the edge of a breakthrough.* **3** a line along which two faces or surfaces of a solid meet. **4** the sharp cutting side of a blade. **5** keenness, sharpness, or urgency: *the walk gave an edge to his appetite.* **6** force, effectiveness, or incisiveness: *the performance lacked edge.* **7** *Dialect.* **7a** a cliff, ridge, or hillside. **7b** (*cap.*) (in place names): *Hade Edge.* **8 have the edge on** *or* **over.** to have a slight advantage or superiority (over). **9 on edge. 9a** nervously irritable; tense. **9b** nervously excited or eager. **10 set (someone's) teeth on edge.** to make (someone) acutely irritated or uncomfortable. ◆ *vb* **11** (*tr*) to provide an edge or border for. **12** (*tr*) to shape or trim (the edge or border of something), as with a knife or scissors: *to edge a pie.* **13** to push (one's way, someone, something, etc.) gradually, esp. edgeways. **14** (*tr*) *Cricket.* to hit (a bowled ball) with the edge of the bat. **15** (*tr*) to tilt (a ski) sideways so that one edge digs into the snow. **16** (*tr*) to sharpen (a knife, etc.). [Old English *ecg;* related to Old Norse *egg,* Old High German *ecka* edge, Latin *aciēs* sharpness, Greek *akis* point] ▸ **'edgeless** *adj* ▸ **'edger** *n*

Edgehill (ˌɛdʒ'hɪl) *n* a ridge in S Warwickshire: site of the indecisive first battle between Charles I and the Parliamentarians (1642) in the Civil War.

edge tool *n* a tool with one or more cutting edges.

edgeways ('ɛdʒˌweɪz) *or esp. U.S. and Canadian.* **edgewise** ('ɛdʒˌwaɪz) *adv* **1** with the edge forwards or uppermost: *they carried the piano in edgeways.* **2** on, by, with, or towards the edge: *he held it edgeways.* **3 get a word in edgeways.** (*usually used with a negative*) to succeed in interrupting a conversation in which someone else is talking incessantly.

Edgeworth ('ɛdʒwɜ:θ) *n* **Maria.** 1767–1849, Anglo-Irish novelist: her works include *Castle Rackrent* (1800) and *The Absentee* (1812).

edging ('ɛdʒɪŋ) *n* **1** anything placed along an edge to finish it, esp. as an ornament, fringe, or border on clothing or along a path in a garden. **2** the act of making an edge. ◆ *adj* **3** relating to or used for making an edge: *edging shears.*

edgy ('ɛdʒɪ) *adj* **-ier, -iest. 1** (*usually postpositive*) nervous, irritable, tense, or anxious. **2** (of paintings, drawings, etc.) excessively defined. ▸ **'edgily** *adv* ▸ **'edginess** *n*

edh (ɛð) *or* **eth** *n* a character of the runic alphabet (ð) used to represent the voiced dental fricative as in *then, mother, bathe.* It is used in modern phonetic transcription for the same purpose. Compare **theta** (sense 2), **thorn** (sense 5).

Édhessa (*Greek* 'ɛðɛsa) *n* transliteration of the Modern Greek name for **Edessa.**

EDI *abbrev. for* electronic data interchange: an interactive electronic system that enables a supplier and a customer to communicate efficiently.

edible ('ɛdɪb°l) *adj* fit to be eaten; eatable. [C17: from Late Latin *edibilis,* from Latin *edere* to eat] ▸ ˌ**edi'bility** *or* **'edibleness** *n*

edibles ('ɛdɪb°lz) *pl n* articles fit to eat; food.

edict ('i:dɪkt) *n* **1** a decree, order, or ordinance issued by a sovereign, state, or any other holder of authority. **2** any formal or authoritative command, proclamation, etc. [C15: from Latin *ēdictum,* from *ēdīcere* to declare] ▸ **e'dictal** *adj* ▸ **e'dictally** *adv*

Edict of Nantes *n* the law granting religious and civil liberties to the French Protestants, promulgated by Henry IV in 1598 and revoked by Louis XIV in 1685.

edification (ˌɛdɪfɪ'keɪʃən) *n* **1** improvement, instruction, or enlightenment, esp. when morally or spiritually uplifting. **2** the act of edifying or state of being edified. ▸ ˌ**edifi'catory** *adj*

edifice ('ɛdɪfɪs) *n* **1** a building, esp. a large or imposing one. **2** a complex or elaborate institution or organization. [C14: from Old French, from Latin *aedificium,* from *aedificāre* to build; see EDIFY] ▸ **edificial** (ˌɛdɪ'fɪʃəl) *adj*

edify ('ɛdɪˌfaɪ) *vb* **-fies, -fying, -fied.** (*tr*) to improve the morality, intellect, etc., of, esp. by instruction. [C14: from Old French *edifier,* from Latin *aedificāre* to construct, from *aedēs* a dwelling, temple + *facere* to make] ▸ **'ediˌfier** *n* ▸ **'ediˌfying** *adj* ▸ **'ediˌfyingly** *adv*

edile ('i:daɪl) *n* a variant spelling of **aedile.**

Edinburgh[1] ('ɛdɪnbərə, -brə) *n* **1** the capital of Scotland and seat of the Scottish Parliament, in City of Edinburgh council area on the S side of the Firth of Forth: became the capital in the 15th century; castle; universities (1583, 1966); commercial and cultural centre, noted for its annual festival. Pop.: 401 910 (1991). **2 City of.** a council area in central Scotland, created from part of Lothian region in 1996. Pop.: 447 550 (1996 est.). Area: 262 sq. km (101 sq. miles).

Edinburgh[2] ('ɛdɪnbərə, -brə) *n* **Duke of,** title of Prince *Philip Mountbatten.* born 1921, husband of Elizabeth II of Great Britain and Northern Ireland.

Edirne (ɛ'dirnɛ) *n* a city in NW Turkey: a Thracian town, rebuilt and renamed by the Roman emperor Hadrian. Pop.: 117 331 (1995 est.). Former name: **Adrianople.**

Edison ('ɛdɪs°n) *n* **Thomas Alva.** 1847–1931, U.S. inventor. He patented more than a thousand inventions, including the phonograph, the incandescent electric lamp, the microphone, and the kinetoscope.

edit ('ɛdɪt) *vb* (*tr*) **1** to prepare (text) for publication by checking and improving its accuracy, clarity, etc. **2** to be in charge of (a publication, esp. a periodical): *he edits the local newspaper.* **3** to prepare (a film, tape, etc.) by rearrangement, selection, or rejection of previously filmed or taped material. **4** (*tr*) to modify (a computer file) by, for example, deleting, inserting, moving, or copying text. **5** (often foll. by *out*) to remove (incorrect or unwanted matter), as from a manuscript or film. ◆ *n* 6 *Informal.* an act of editing: *give the book a final edit.* [C18: back formation from EDITOR]

edit. *abbrev. for:* 1 edited. 2 edition. 3 editor.

edition (ɪ'dɪʃən) *n* 1 *Printing.* 1a the entire number of copies of a book, newspaper, or other publication printed at one time from a single setting of type. 1b a single copy from this number: *a first edition; the evening edition.* 2 one of a number of printings of a book or other publication, issued at separate times with alterations, amendments, etc. Compare **impression** (sense 6). 3a an issue of a work identified by its format: *a leather-bound edition of Shakespeare.* 3b an issue of a work identified by its editor or publisher: *the Oxford edition of Shakespeare.* ◆ *vb* 4 (*tr*) to produce multiple copies of (an original work of art). [C16: from Latin *ēditiō* a bringing forth, publishing, from *ēdere* to give out; see EDITOR]

editio princeps (ɪ'dɪʃɪəʊ 'prɪnsɛps) *n, pl* **editiones principes** (ɪˌdɪʃɪ'əʊniːz 'prɪnsɪˌpiːz). *Latin.* the first printed edition of a work.

editor ('ɛdɪtə) *n* 1 a person who edits written material for publication. 2 a person in overall charge of the editing and often the policy of a newspaper or periodical. 3 a person in charge of one section of a newspaper or periodical: *the sports editor.* 4 *Films.* 4a a person who makes a selection and arrangement of individual shots in order to construct the flowing sequence of images for a film. 4b a device for editing film, including a viewer and a splicer. 5 *Television, radio.* a person in overall control of a programme that consists of various items, such as a news or magazine style programme. 6 a computer program that facilitates the deletion or insertion of data to information already stored in a computer. [C17: from Late Latin: producer, exhibitor, from *ēdere* to give out, publish, from *ē-* out + *dāre* to give] ▸ **'editorˌship** *n*

editorial (ˌɛdɪ'tɔːrɪəl) *adj* 1 of or relating to editing or editors. 2 of, relating to, or expressed in an editorial. 3 of or relating to the content of a publication rather than its commercial aspects. ◆ *n* 4 an article in a newspaper, etc., expressing the opinion of the editor or the publishers. ▸ **ˌedi'torialist** *n* ▸ **ˌedi'torially** *adv*

editorialize *or* **editorialise** (ˌɛdɪ'tɔːrɪəˌlaɪz) *vb* (*intr*) 1 to express an opinion in or as in an editorial. 2 to insert one's personal opinions into an otherwise objective account. ▸ **ˌediˌtoriali'zation** *or* **ˌediˌtoriali'sation** *n* ▸ **ˌedi'toriˌalˌizer** *or* **ˌedi'torialˌiser** *n*

editor in chief *n* the controlling editor of a publication.

EDM *Surveying. abbrev. for* electronic distance measurement.

Edmonton ('ɛdməntən) *n* a city in W Canada, capital of Alberta: oil industry. Pop.: 616 741 (1991).

Edmund ('ɛdmənd) *n* **Saint**, also called *Saint Edmund Rich.* 1175–1240, English churchman: archbishop of Canterbury (1234–40). Feast day: Nov. 16.

Edmund I *n* ?922–946 A.D., king of England (940–946).

Edmund II *n* called *Edmund Ironside.* ?980–1016, king of England in 1016. His succession was contested by Canute and they divided the kingdom between them.

Edo ('ɛdəʊ) *n* 1 (*pl* **Edo** *or* **Edos**) a member of a Negroid people of SW Nigeria around Benin, noted for their 16th-century bronze sculptures. 2 Also called: **Bini.** the language of this people, belonging to the Kwa branch of the Niger-Congo family.

Edom ('iːdəm) *n* 1 a nomadic people descended from Esau. 2 the son of Esau who was the supposed ancestor of this nation. 3 the ancient kingdom of this people, situated between the Dead Sea and the Gulf of Aqaba.

Edomite ('iːdəˌmaɪt) *n* 1 an inhabitant of the ancient kingdom of Edom, whose people were hostile to the Israelites in Old Testament times. 2 the ancient Semitic language of this people, closely related to Hebrew. ▸ **'Edomˌitish** *or* **Edomitic** (ˌiːdə'mɪtɪk) *adj*

EDT (in the U.S. and Canada) *abbrev. for* Eastern Daylight Time.

EDTA *n* ethylenediaminetetra-acetic acid; a colourless crystalline slightly soluble organic compound used in inorganic chemistry and biochemistry. It is a powerful chelating agent used to stabilize bleach in detergents. Formula: $[(HOOCCH_2)_2NCH_2]_2$.

educ. *abbrev. for:* 1 educated. 2 education(al).

educable ('ɛdjʊkəbᵊl) *or* **educatable** ('ɛdjʊˌkeɪtəbᵊl) *adj* capable of being trained or educated; able to learn. ▸ **ˌeduca'bility** *or* **ˌeduˌcata'bility** *n*

educate ('ɛdjʊˌkeɪt) *vb* (*mainly tr*) 1 (*also intr*) to impart knowledge by formal instruction to (a pupil); teach. 2 to provide schooling for (children): *I have educated my children at the best schools.* 3 to improve or develop (a person, judgment, taste, skills, etc.). 4 to train for some particular purpose or occupation. [C15: from Latin *ēducāre* to rear, educate, from *dūcere* to lead]

educated ('ɛdjʊˌkeɪtɪd) *adj* 1 having an education, esp. a good one. 2 displaying culture, taste, and knowledge; cultivated. 3 (*prenominal*) based on experience or information (esp. in the phrase **an educated guess**).

education (ˌɛdjʊ'keɪʃən) *n* 1 the act or process of acquiring knowledge, esp. systematically during childhood and adolescence. 2 the knowledge or training acquired by this process: *his education has been invaluable to him.* 3 the act or process of imparting knowledge, esp. at a school, college, or university: *education is my profession.* 4 the theory of teaching and learning: *a course in education.* 5 a particular kind of instruction or training: *a university education; consumer education.*

educational (ˌɛdjʊ'keɪʃənᵊl) *adj* 1 providing knowledge; instructive or informative: *an educational toy.* 2 of or relating to education. ▸ **ˌedu'cationally** *adv*

educationalist (ˌɛdjʊ'keɪʃənəlɪst) *or* **educationist** *n* a specialist in educational theory or administration.

educational psychology *n* the study of methods of training and teaching and their effectiveness, and of the problems experienced in learning formal material; in particular, the study of how to help people, esp. school children, with learning problems to overcome their difficulties.

Educational Welfare Officer *n* (in Britain) a local education authority worker whose job it is to find out whether difficulties outside school are contributing to a child's classroom problems or irregular attendance and who may intervene to help the child to benefit more from schooling. Former names: **school attendance officer, truancy officer.**

educative ('ɛdjʊkətɪv) *adj* producing or resulting in education: *an educative experience.*

educator ('ɛdjʊˌkeɪtə) *n* 1 a person who educates; teacher. 2 a specialist in education; educationalist.

educatory ('ɛdjʊkətərɪ, -trɪ; ˌɛdjʊ'keɪtərɪ, -trɪ) *adj* educative or educational: *an educatory procedure.*

educe (ɪ'djuːs) *vb* (*tr*) *Rare.* 1 to evolve or develop, esp. from a latent or potential state. 2 to draw out or elicit (information, solutions, etc.). [C15: from Latin *ēdūcere* to draw out, from *ē-* out + *dūcere* to lead] ▸ **e'ducible** *adj* ▸ **eductive** (ɪ'dʌktɪv) *adj*

educt ('iːdʌkt) *n* a substance separated from another substance without chemical change. Compare **product** (sense 4). [C18: from Latin *ēductus;* see EDUCE]

eduction (ɪ'dʌkʃən) *n* 1 something educed. 2 the act or process of educing. 3 the exhaust stroke of a steam or internal-combustion engine. Compare **induction.** [C17: from Latin *ēductiō*, from *ēdūcere* to EDUCE]

edulcorate (ɪ'dʌlkəˌreɪt) *vb* (*tr*) to free from soluble impurities by washing. [C17: from Medieval Latin *ēdulcorāre,* from Late Latin *dulcor* sweetness] ▸ **eˌdulco'ration** *n*

edutainment (ˌɛdjʊ'teɪnmənt) *n* the presentation of informative or educational material in an entertaining style. [C20: from EDU(CATION) + (ENTER)TAINMENT]

Edward[1] ('ɛdwəd) *n* **Lake.** a lake in central Africa, between Uganda and the Democratic Republic of the Congo (formerly Zaïre) in the Great Rift Valley: empties through the Semliki River into Lake Albert. Area: about 2150 sq. km (830 sq. miles). Former official name: **Lake Amin.**

Edward[2] ('ɛdwəd) *n* 1 known as *the Black Prince.* 1330–76, Prince of Wales, the son of Edward III of England. He won victories over the French at Crécy (1346) and Poitiers (1356) in the Hundred Years' War. 2 **Prince.** born 1964, Earl of Wessex, third son of Elizabeth II of Great Britain and Northern Ireland. In 1999 he married Sophie Rhys-Jones (born 1965).

Edward I *n* 1239–1307, king of England (1272–1307); son of Henry III. He conquered Wales (1284) but failed to subdue Scotland.

Edward II *n* 1284–1327, king of England (1307–27); son of Edward I. He invaded Scotland but was defeated by Robert Bruce at Bannockburn (1314). He was deposed by his wife Isabella and Roger Mortimer; died in prison.

Edward III *n* 1312–77, king of England (1327–77); son of Edward II. His claim to the French throne in right of his mother Isabella provoked the Hundred Years' War (1337).

Edward IV *n* 1442–83, king of England (1461–70; 1471–83); son of Richard, duke of York. He defeated Henry VI in the Wars of the Roses and became king (1461). In 1470 Henry was restored to the throne, but Edward recovered the crown by his victory at Tewkesbury.

Edward V *n* 1470–?83, king of England in 1483; son of Edward IV. He was deposed by his uncle, Richard, Duke of Gloucester (Richard III), and is thought to have been murdered with his brother in the Tower of London.

Edward VI *n* 1537–53, king of England (1547–53), son of Henry VIII and Jane Seymour. His uncle the Duke of Somerset was regent until 1552, when he was executed. Edward then came under the control of Dudley, Duke of Northumberland.

Edward VII *n* 1841–1910, king of Great Britain and Ireland (1901–10); son of Queen Victoria.

Edward VIII *n* 1894–1972, king of Great Britain and Ireland in 1936; son of George V and brother of George VI. He abdicated in order to marry an American divorcée, Mrs Wallis Simpson (1896–1986); created Duke of Windsor (1937).

Edwardian (ɛd'wɔːdɪən) *adj* denoting, relating to, or having the style of life, architecture, dress, etc., current in Britain during the reign of Edward VII. ▸ **Ed'wardianism** *n*

Edwards ('ɛdwədz) *n* 1 **Gareth (Owen).** born 1947, Welsh Rugby Union footballer: halfback for Wales (1967–78) and the British Lions (1968–74). 2 **Jonathan.** 1703–58, American Calvinist theologian and metaphysician; author of *The Freedom of the Will* (1754).

Edward the Confessor *n* **Saint.** ?1002–66, king of England (1042–66); son of Ethelred II; founder of Westminster Abbey. Feast day: Oct. 13.

Edward the Elder *n* died 924 A.D., king of England (899–924), son of Alfred the Great.

Edward the Martyr *n* **Saint.** ?963–978 A.D., king of England (975–78), son of Edgar: murdered. Feast day: March 18.

Edwin ('ɛdwɪn) *n* ?585–633 A.D., king of Northumbria (617–633) and overlord of all England except Kent.

ee (iː) *n, pl* **een** (iːn) a Scot. word for **eye**[1].

EE *abbrev. for:* 1 Early English. 2 electrical engineer(ing). 3 (in New Zealand) ewe equivalent.

e.e. *abbrev. for* errors excepted.

-ee *suffix forming nouns.* 1 indicating a person who is the recipient of an action (as opposed, esp. in legal terminology, to the agent, indicated by *-or* or *-er*): *assignee; grantee; lessee.* 2 indicating a person in a specified state or condition: *absentee; employee.* 3 indicating a diminutive form of something: *bootee.* [via Old French *-e, -ee,* past participial endings, from Latin *-ātus, -āta* -ATE[1]]

EE & MP *abbrev. for* Envoy Extraordinary and Minister Plenipotentiary.

EEC *abbrev. for* European Economic Community (now called European Union).

EEG *abbrev. for:* 1 electroencephalogram. 2 electroencephalograph.

eejit ('iːdʒɪt) *n* a Scot. and Irish word for **idiot** (sense 2).

eel (iːl) *n* 1 any teleost fish of the order *Apodes* (or *Anguilliformes*), such as the

European freshwater species *Anguilla anguilla,* having a long snakelike body, a smooth slimy skin, and reduced fins. **2** any of various other animals with a long body and smooth skin, such as the mud eel and the electric eel. **3** an evasive or untrustworthy person. [Old English *ǣl;* related to Old Frisian *ēl,* Old Norse *āll,* Old High German *āl*] ▸ **'eel-,like** *adj* ▸ **'eely** *adj*

eelgrass ('iːl,grɑːs) *n* **1** any of several perennial submerged marine plants of the genus *Zostera,* esp. *Z. marina,* having grasslike leaves: family *Zosteraceae.* **2** another name for **tape grass.**

eelpout ('iːl,paʊt) *n* **1** any marine eel-like blennioid fish of the family *Zoarcidae,* such as *Zoarces viviparus* (**viviparous eelpout** or blenny). **2** another name for **burbot.** [Old English *ǣlepūte;* related to Middle Dutch *aalpuit*]

eelworm ('iːl,wɜːm) *n* any of various nematode worms, esp. the wheatworm and the vinegar eel.

e'en (iːn) *adv, n Poetic or archaic.* a contraction of **even**[2] or **evening.**

e'er (ɛə) *adv Poetic or archaic.* a contraction of **ever.**

-eer *or* **-ier** *suffix.* **1** (*forming nouns*) indicating a person who is concerned with or who does something specified: *auctioneer; engineer; profiteer; mutineer.* **2** (*forming verbs*) to be concerned with something specified: *electioneer.* [from Old French *-ier,* from Latin *-arius* -ARY]

eerie ('ɪərɪ) *adj* **eerier, eeriest.** (esp. of places, an atmosphere, etc.) mysteriously or uncannily frightening or disturbing; weird; ghostly. [C13: originally Scottish and Northern English, probably from Old English *earg* cowardly, miserable] ▸ **'eerily** *adv* ▸ **'eeriness** *n*

EETPU (in Britain) *abbrev. for* Electrical, Electronic, Telecommunications, and Plumbing Union.

eff (ɛf) *vb* **1** euphemism for **fuck** (esp. in the phrase **eff off**). **2 eff and blind.** *Slang.* to use obscene language. ▸ **'effing** *n, adj*

effable ('ɛfəbᵊl) *adj Archaic.* capable of being expressed in words. [C17: from Old French, from Late Latin *effābilis,* from Latin *effārī,* from *ex-* out + *fārī* to speak]

efface (ɪ'feɪs) *vb* (*tr*) **1** to obliterate or make dim: *to efface a memory.* **2** to make (oneself) inconspicuous or humble through modesty, cowardice, or obsequiousness. **3** to rub out (a line, drawing, etc.); erase. [C15: from French *effacer,* literally: to obliterate the face; see FACE] ▸ **ef'faceable** *adj* ▸ **ef'facement** *n* ▸ **ef'facer** *n*

effect (ɪ'fɛkt) *n* **1** something that is produced by a cause or agent; result. **2** power or ability to influence or produce a result; efficacy: *with no effect.* **3** the condition of being operative (esp. in the phrases **in** or **into effect**): *the law comes into effect at midnight.* **4 take effect.** to become operative or begin to produce results. **5** basic meaning or purpose (esp. in the phrase **to that effect**). **6** an impression, usually one that is artificial or contrived (esp. in the phrase **for effect**). **7** a scientific phenomenon: *the Doppler effect.* **8 in effect. 8a** in fact; actually. **8b** for all practical purposes. **9** the overall impression or result: *the effect of a painting.* ◆ *vb* **10** (*tr*) to cause to occur; bring about; accomplish. ◆ See also **effects.** [C14: from Latin *effectus* a performing, tendency, from *efficere* to accomplish, from *facere* to do] ▸ **ef'fecter** *n* ▸ **ef'fectible** *adj*

effective (ɪ'fɛktɪv) *adj* **1** productive of or capable of producing a result. **2** in effect; operative: *effective from midnight.* **3** producing a striking impression; impressive: *an effective entrance.* **4** (*prenominal*) actual rather than theoretical; real: *the effective income after deductions.* **5** (of a military force, etc.) equipped and prepared for action. **6** *Physics.* (of an alternating quantity) having a value that is the square root of the mean of the squares of the magnitude measured at each instant over a defined period of time, usually one cycle. ◆ *n* **7** a serviceman who is equipped and prepared for action. ▸ **ef'fectively** *adv* ▸ **ef'fectiveness** *n*

effector *or* **effecter** (ɪ'fɛktə) *n Physiol.* a nerve ending that terminates in a muscle or gland and provides neural stimulation causing contraction or secretion.

effects (ɪ'fɛkts) *pl n* **1** Also called: **personal effects.** personal property or belongings. **2** lighting, sounds, etc., to accompany and enhance a stage, film, or broadcast production.

effectual (ɪ'fɛktjʊəl) *adj* **1** capable of or successful in producing an intended result; effective. **2** (of documents, agreements, etc.) having legal force. ▸ **ef,fectu'ality** *or* **ef'fectualness** *n*

effectually (ɪ'fɛktjʊəlɪ) *adv* **1** with the intended effect; thoroughly. **2** to all practical purposes; in effect.

effectuate (ɪ'fɛktjʊ,eɪt) *vb* (*tr*) to cause to happen; effect; accomplish. ▸ **ef,fectu'ation** *n*

effeminate (ɪ'fɛmɪnɪt) *adj* **1** (of a man or boy) displaying characteristics regarded as typical of a woman; not manly. **2** lacking firmness or vigour: *an effeminate piece of writing.* [C14: from Latin *effēmināre* to make into a woman, from *fēmina* woman] ▸ **ef'feminacy** *or* **ef'feminateness** *n* ▸ **ef'feminately** *adv*

effendi (ɛ'fɛndɪ) *n, pl* **-dis. 1** (in the Ottoman Empire) a title of respect used to address men of learning or social standing. **2** (in Turkey since 1934) the oral title of address equivalent to *Mr.* [C17: from Turkish *efendi* master, from Modern Greek *aphentēs,* from Greek *authentēs* lord, doer; see AUTHENTIC]

efferent ('ɛfərənt) *adj* carrying or conducting outwards from a part or an organ of the body, esp. from the brain or spinal cord. Compare **afferent.** [C19: from Latin *efferre* to bear off, from *ferre* to bear] ▸ **'efference** *n* ▸ **'efferently** *adv*

effervesce (,ɛfə'vɛs) *vb* (*intr*) **1** (of a liquid) to give off bubbles of gas. **2** (of a gas) to issue in bubbles from a liquid. **3** to exhibit great excitement, vivacity, etc. [C18: from Latin *effervescere* to foam up, from *fervescere* to begin to boil, from *fervēre* to boil, ferment] ▸ **,effer'vescible** *adj* ▸ **,effer'vescingly** *adv*

effervescent (,ɛfə'vɛsᵊnt) *adj* **1** (of a liquid) giving off bubbles of gas; bubbling. **2** high-spirited; vivacious. ▸ **,effer'vescence** *n* ▸ **,effer'vescently** *adv*

effete (ɪ'fiːt) *adj* **1** weak, ineffectual, or decadent as a result of overrefinement: *an effete academic.* **2** exhausted of vitality or strength; worn out; spent. **3** (of animals or plants) no longer capable of reproduction. [C17: from Latin *effētus* having produced young, hence, exhausted by bearing, from *fētus* having brought forth; see FETUS] ▸ **ef'fetely** *adv* ▸ **ef'feteness** *n*

efficacious (,ɛfɪ'keɪʃəs) *adj* capable of or successful in producing an intended result; effective as a means, remedy, etc. [C16: from Latin *efficāx* powerful, efficient, from *efficere* to achieve; see EFFECT] ▸ **,effi'caciously** *adv* ▸ **efficacy** ('ɛfɪkəsɪ) *or* **,effi'caciousness** *n*

efficiency (ɪ'fɪʃənsɪ) *n, pl* **-cies. 1** the quality or state of being efficient; competence; effectiveness. **2** the ratio of the useful work done by a machine, engine, device, etc., to the energy supplied to it, often expressed as a percentage. See also **thermal efficiency.**

efficiency apartment *n U.S.* a small flat or bedsit.

efficient (ɪ'fɪʃənt) *adj* **1** functioning or producing effectively and with the least waste of effort; competent. **2** *Philosophy.* producing a direct effect; causative. [C14: from Latin *efficiēns* effecting] ▸ **ef'ficiently** *adv*

efficient cause *n Philosophy.* that which produces an effect by a causal process. Compare **final cause.** See also **cause** (sense 7).

effigy ('ɛfɪdʒɪ) *n, pl* **-gies. 1** a portrait of a person, esp. as a monument or architectural decoration. **2** a crude representation of someone, used as a focus for contempt or ridicule and often hung up or burnt in public (often in the phrases **burn** or **hang in effigy**). [C18: from Latin *effigiēs,* from *effingere* to form, portray, from *fingere* to shape] ▸ **effigial** (ɪ'fɪdʒɪəl) *adj*

effleurage (,ɛflɜː'rɑːʒ) *n* **1** a light stroking technique used in massage. ◆ *vb* **2** (*intr*) to massage using this movement. [C19: from French *effleurer* to stroke lightly]

effloresce (,ɛflɔː'rɛs) *vb* (*intr*) **1** to burst forth into or as if into flower; bloom. **2** to become powdery by loss of water or crystallization. **3** to become encrusted with powder or crystals as a result of chemical change or the evaporation of a solution. [C18: from Latin *efflōrēscere* to blossom, from *flōrēscere,* from *flōs* flower]

efflorescence (,ɛflɔː'rɛsᵊns) *n* **1** a bursting forth or flowering. **2** *Chem., geology.* **2a** the process of efflorescing. **2b** the powdery substance formed as a result of this process, esp. on the surface of rocks. **3** any skin rash or eruption. ▸ **,efflo'rescent** *adj*

effluence ('ɛflʊəns) *or* **efflux** ('ɛflʌks) *n* **1** the act or process of flowing out. **2** something that flows out.

effluent ('ɛflʊənt) *n* **1** liquid discharged as waste, as from an industrial plant or sewage works. **2** radioactive waste released from a nuclear power station. **3** a stream that flows out of another body of water. **4** something that flows out or forth. ◆ *adj* **5** flowing out or forth. [C18: from Latin *effluere* to run forth, from *fluere* to flow]

effluvium (ɛ'fluːvɪəm) *n, pl* **-via** (-vɪə) *or* **-viums.** an unpleasant smell or exhalation, as of gaseous waste or decaying matter. [C17: from Latin: a flowing out; see EFFLUENT] ▸ **ef'fluvial** *adj*

effort ('ɛfət) *n* **1** physical or mental exertion, usually considerable when unqualified: *the rock was moved with effort.* **2** a determined attempt: *our effort to save him failed.* **3** achievement; creation: *a great literary effort.* **4** *Physics.* an applied force acting against inertia. [C15: from Old French *esfort,* from *esforcier* to force, ultimately from Latin *fortis* strong; see FORCE[1]] ▸ **'effortful** *adj*

effort bargain *n* a bargain in which the reward to an employee is based on the effort that the employee puts in.

effortless ('ɛfətlɪs) *adj* **1** requiring or involving little effort; easy. **2** *Archaic.* making little effort; passive. ▸ **'effortlessly** *adv* ▸ **'effortlessness** *n*

effrontery (ɪ'frʌntərɪ) *n, pl* **-ies.** shameless or insolent boldness; impudent presumption; audacity; temerity. [C18: from French *effronterie,* from Old French *esfront* barefaced, shameless, from Late Latin *effrons,* literally: putting forth one's forehead; see FRONT]

effulgent (ɪ'fʌldʒənt) *adj* radiant; brilliant. [C18: from Latin *effulgēre* to shine forth, from *fulgēre* to shine] ▸ **ef'fulgence** *n* ▸ **ef'fulgently** *adv*

effuse *vb* (ɪ'fjuːz). **1** to pour or flow out. **2** to spread out; diffuse. **3** (*intr*) to talk profusely, esp. in an excited manner. **4** to cause (a gas) to flow or (of a gas) to flow under pressure. ◆ *adj* (ɪ'fjuːs). **5** *Botany.* (esp. of an inflorescence) spreading out loosely. [C16: from Latin *effūsus* poured out, from *effundere* to shed, from *fundere* to pour]

effusiometer (ɪ,fjuːzɪ'ɒmɪtə) *n Physics.* an apparatus for determining rates of effusion of gases, usually used for measuring molecular weights.

effusion (ɪ'fjuːʒən) *n* **1** an unrestrained outpouring in speech or words. **2** the act or process of being poured out. **3** something that is poured out. **4** the flow of a gas through a small aperture under pressure, esp. when the density is such that the mean distance between molecules is large compared to the diameter of the aperture. **5** *Med.* **5a** the escape of blood or other fluid into a body cavity or tissue. **5b** the fluid that has escaped.

effusive (ɪ'fjuːsɪv) *adj* **1** extravagantly demonstrative of emotion; gushing. **2** (of rock) formed by the solidification of magma. ▸ **ef'fusively** *adv* ▸ **ef'fusiveness** *n*

Efik ('ɛfɪk) *n* **1** (*pl* **Efiks** *or* **Efik**) a member of a subgroup of the Ibibio people of SE Nigeria. **2** the language spoken by this people, variously classified as belonging to the Benue-Congo or Kwa divisions of the Niger-Congo family.

EFIS *Aeronautics. abbrev. for* electronic flight information systems.

EFL *abbrev. for* English as a Foreign Language.

eft[1] (ɛft) *n* **1** a dialect or archaic name for a **newt. 2** any of certain terrestrial newts, such as *Diemictylus viridescens* (**red eft**) of eastern North America. [Old English *efeta*]

eft[2] (ɛft) *adv Archaic.* **a** again. **b** afterwards. [Old English; see AFT, AFTER]

EFTA ('ɛftə) *n acronym for* European Free Trade Association; established in 1960 to eliminate trade tariffs on industrial products; now comprises Norway, Switzerland, Iceland, and Liechtenstein. Free trade was established between EFTA and the EC (now EU) in 1984. In 1994 EFTA (excluding Switzerland) and the EU together created the European Economic Area (EEA).

EFTPOS ('ɛftpɒs) *acronym for* electronic funds transfer at point of sale.

EFTS *Computing. abbrev. for* electronic funds transfer system.

eftsoons (ɛft'su:nz) *adv Archaic.* **1** soon afterwards. **2** repeatedly. [Old English *eft sōna,* literally: afterwards soon]

Eg. *abbrev. for:* **1** Egypt(ian). **2** Egyptology.

e.g., eg, *or* **eg.** *abbrevs. for* exempli gratia. [Latin: for example]

egad (ɪ'gæd, i:'gæd) *interj Archaic.* a mild oath or expression of surprise. [C17: probably variant of *Ah God!*]

egalitarian (ɪˌgælɪ'tɛərɪən) *adj* **1** of, relating to, or upholding the doctrine of the equality of mankind and the desirability of political, social, and economic equality. ♦ *n* **2** an adherent of egalitarian principles. [C19: alteration of *equalitarian,* through influence of French *égal* EQUAL] ▸ **eˌgali'tarianˌism** *n*

Egas Moniz (*Portuguese* 'egas 'monɪz) *n* **Antonio Caetanio de Abreu Freire.** 1874–1955, Portuguese neurologist: shared the Nobel prize for physiology or medicine (1949) with Walter Hess for their development of prefrontal leucotomy.

Egbert ('ɛgbɜ:t) *n* ?775–839 A.D., king of Wessex (802–839); first overlord of all England (829–830).

Eger *n* **1** (*Hungarian* 'ɛgɛr). a city in N central Hungary. Pop.: 60 000 (1995 est.). **2** ('e:gər). the German name for **Cheb.**

Egeria (ɪ'dʒɪərɪə) *n* a female adviser. [C17: name of the mythical adviser of Numa Pompilius, king of Rome]

egest (i:'dʒɛst) *vb* (*tr*) to excrete (waste material). [C17: from Latin *ēgerere* to carry out, from *gerere* to carry] ▸ **e'gestion** *n* ▸ **e'gestive** *adj*

egesta (i:'dʒɛstə) *pl n* anything egested, as waste material from the body; excrement. [C18: from Latin, literally: (things) carried out; see EGEST]

egg[1] (ɛg) *n* **1** the oval or round reproductive body laid by the females of birds, reptiles, fishes, insects, and some other animals, consisting of a developing embryo, its food store, and sometimes jelly or albumen, all surrounded by an outer shell or membrane. **2** Also called: **egg cell.** any female gamete; ovum. **3** the egg of the domestic hen used as food. **4** something resembling an egg, esp. in shape or in being in an early stage of development. **5 good** (*or* **bad**) **egg.** *Old-fashioned informal.* **5a** a good (or bad) person. **5b** an exclamation of delight (or dismay). **6 lay an egg.** *Slang, chiefly U.S. and Canadian.* **6a** to make a joke or give a performance, etc., that fails completely. **6b** (of a joke, performance, etc.) to fail completely; flop. **7 put** *or* **have all one's eggs in one basket.** to stake everything on a single venture. **8 teach one's grandmother to suck eggs.** to presume to teach someone something that he knows already. **9 with egg on one's face.** *Informal.* made to look ridiculous. ♦ *vb* (*tr*) **10** to dip (food) in beaten egg before cooking. **11** *U.S. informal.* to throw eggs at. [C14: from Old Norse *egg;* related to Old English *ǣg,* Old High German *ei*]

egg[2] (ɛg) *vb* (*tr;* usually foll. by *on*) to urge or incite, esp. to daring or foolish acts. [Old English *eggian,* from Old Norse *eggja* to urge; related to Old English *ecg* EDGE, Middle Low German *eggen* to harrow]

egg and dart, egg and tongue, *or* **egg and anchor** *n* (in architecture and cabinetwork) **a** an ornamental moulding in which a half egg shape alternates with a dart, tongue, or anchor shape. **b** (*as modifier*): *egg-and-dart moulding.*

egg-and-spoon race *n* a race in which runners carry an egg balanced in a spoon.

eggbeater ('ɛgˌbi:tə) *n* **1** Also called: **'eggˌwhisk.** a kitchen utensil for beating eggs, whipping cream, etc.; whisk. **2** *Chiefly U.S. and Canadian.* an informal name for **helicopter.**

egg cup *n* a small cuplike container, used for holding a boiled egg while it is being eaten.

egger *or* **eggar** ('ɛgə) *n* any of various widely distributed moths of the family *Lasiocampidae,* such as *Lasiocampa quercus* (**oak egger**) of Europe, having brown bodies and wings. [C18: from EGG[1], from the egg-shaped cocoon]

egghead ('ɛgˌhɛd) *n Informal.* an intellectual; highbrow.

eggler ('ɛglə) *n Archaic or dialect.* an egg dealer: sometimes itinerant.

eggnog (ˌɛg'nɒg) *n* a drink that can be served hot or cold, made of eggs, milk, sugar, spice, and brandy, rum, or other spirit. Also called: **egg flip.** [C19: from EGG[1] + NOG[1]]

eggplant ('ɛgˌplɑ:nt) *n* another name (esp. U.S., Canadian, and Austral.) for **aubergine** (sense 1).

egg roll *n* a Chinese-American dish consisting of egg dough filled with a minced mixture of pork, bamboo shoots, onions, etc., and browned in deep fat.

eggs Benedict *n* a dish consisting of toast, covered with a slice of ham, poached egg, and hollandaise sauce.

eggshell ('ɛgˌʃɛl) *n* **1** the hard porous protective outer layer of a bird's egg, consisting of calcite and protein. **2** a yellowish-white colour. **3** a type of paper with a slightly rough finish. **4** (*modifier*) (of paint) having a very slight sheen. **5 walk on eggshells.** to be very cautious or diplomatic for fear of upsetting someone. ♦ *adj* **6** of a yellowish-white colour.

eggshell porcelain *or* **china** *n* a type of very thin translucent porcelain originally made in China.

egg slice *n* a spatula for removing omelettes, fried eggs, etc., from a pan.

egg spoon *n* a small spoon for eating a boiled egg.

egg timer *n* a device, typically a miniature hourglass, for timing the boiling of an egg.

egg tooth *n* (in embryo birds and reptiles) a temporary tooth or (in birds) projection of the beak used for piercing the eggshell.

egg white *n* the white of an egg; albumen.

Egham ('ɛgəm) *n* a town in S England, in N Surrey on the River Thames. Pop.: 23 816 (1991).

egis ('i:dʒɪs) *n* a rare spelling of **aegis.**

eglandular (i:'glændjʊlə) *adj* having no glands. [E-[1] + GLANDULAR]

eglantine ('ɛglənˌtaɪn) *n* another name for **sweetbrier.** [C14: from Old French *aiglent,* ultimately from Latin *acus* needle, from *acer* sharp, keen]

EGM *abbrev. for* extraordinary general meeting.

Egmont[1] ('ɛgmɒnt) *n* an extinct volcano in New Zealand, in W central North Island in the **Egmont National Park:** an almost perfect cone. Height: 2518 m (8261 ft.).

Egmont[2] ('ɛgmɒnt) *n* **Lamoral** (lamo'ral), Count of Egmont, Prince of Gavre. 1522–68, Flemish statesman and soldier. He attempted to secure limited reforms and religious tolerance in the Spanish government of the Netherlands, refused to join William the Silent's rebellion, but was nevertheless executed for treason by the Duke of Alva.

ego ('i:gəʊ, 'ɛgəʊ) *n, pl* **egos. 1** the self of an individual person; the conscious subject. **2** *Psychoanal.* the conscious mind, based on perception of the environment from birth onwards: responsible for modifying the antisocial instincts of the id and itself modified by the conscience (superego). **3** one's image of oneself; morale: *to boost one's ego.* **4** egotism; conceit. [C19: from Latin: I]

egocentric (ˌi:gəʊ'sɛntrɪk, ˌɛg-) *adj* **1** regarding everything only in relation to oneself; self-centred; selfish. **2** *Philosophy.* pertaining to a theory in which everything is considered in relation to the self: *an egocentric universe.* ♦ *n* **3** a self-centred person; egotist. ▸ **ˌegocen'tricity** *n*

egocentrism (ˌi:gəʊ'sɛntrɪzəm, ˌɛgəʊ-) *n* **1** the condition or fact of being egocentric. **2** *Psychol.* a stage in a child's development characterized by lack of awareness that other people's points of view differ from his own.

ego ideal *n Psychoanal.* an internal ideal of personal perfection that represents what one wants to be rather than what one ought to be and is derived from one's early relationship with one's parents. See also **superego.**

egoism ('i:gəʊˌɪzəm, 'ɛg-) *n* **1** concern for one's own interests and welfare. **2** *Ethics.* the theory that the pursuit of one's own welfare is the highest good. Compare **altruism. 3** self-centredness; egotism.

egoist ('i:gəʊɪst, 'ɛg-) *n* **1** a person who is preoccupied with his own interests; a selfish person. **2** a conceited person; egotist. **3** *Ethics.* a person who lives by the values of egoism. ▸ **ˌego'istic** *or* **ˌego'istical** *adj* ▸ **ˌego'istically** *adv*

Egoli (ɛ'gəʊlɪ) *S. African.* an informal name for **Johannesburg.** [from Zulu *eGoli* place of gold]

egomania (ˌi:gəʊ'meɪnɪə, ˌɛg-) *n Psychiatry.* **1** obsessive love for oneself and regard for one's own needs. **2** any action dictated by this point of view. ▸ **ˌego'maniˌac** *n* ▸ **egomaniacal** (ˌi:gəʊmə'naɪk°l, ˌɛg-) *adj*

egotism ('i:gəˌtɪzəm, 'ɛgə-) *n* **1** an inflated sense of self-importance or superiority; self-centredness. **2** excessive reference to oneself. [C18: from Latin *ego* I + -ISM]

egotist ('i:gətɪst, 'ɛg-) *n* **1** a conceited boastful person. **2** a self-interested person; egoist. ▸ **ˌego'tistic** *or* **ˌego'tistical** *adj* ▸ **ˌego'tistically** *adv*

ego trip *Informal.* ♦ *n* **1** something undertaken to boost or draw attention to a person's own image or appraisal of himself. ♦ *vb* **ego-trip, -trips, -tripping, -tripped.** (*intr*) **2** to act in this way.

egregious (ɪ'gri:dʒəs, -dʒɪəs) *adj* **1** outstandingly bad; flagrant: *an egregious lie.* **2** *Archaic.* distinguished; eminent. [C16: from Latin *ēgregius* outstanding (literally: standing out from the herd), from *ē-* out + *grex* flock, herd] ▸ **e'gregiously** *adv* ▸ **e'gregiousness** *n*

egress *n* ('i:grɛs). **1** Also called: **egression.** the act of going or coming out; emergence. **2** a way out, such as a path; exit. **3** the right or permission to go out or depart. **4** *Astronomy.* another name for **emersion** (sense 2). ♦ *vb* (ɪ'grɛs). (*intr*) **5** to go forth; issue. [C16: from Latin *ēgredī* to come forth, depart, from *gradī* to move, step]

egret ('i:grɪt) *n* any of various wading birds of the genera *Egretta, Hydranassa,* etc., that are similar to herons but usually have a white plumage and, in the breeding season, long feathery plumes (see **aigrette**): family *Ardeidae,* order *Ciconiiformes.* [C15: from Old French *aigrette,* from Old Provençal *aigreta,* from *aigron* heron, of Germanic origin; compare Old High German *heigaro* HERON]

Egypt ('i:dʒɪpt) *n* a republic in NE Africa, on the Mediterranean and Red Sea: its history dates back about 5000 years. Occupied by the British from 1882, it became an independent kingdom in 1922 and a republic in 1953. Over 96 per cent of the total area is desert, with the chief areas of habitation and cultivation in the Nile delta and valley. Cotton is the main export. Official language: Arabic. Official religion: Muslim; Sunni majority. Currency: pound. Capital: Cairo. Pop.: 63 261 000 (1998 est.). Area: 997 739 sq. km (385 229 sq. miles). Official name: **Arab Republic of Egypt.** Former official name (1958–71): **United Arab Republic.**

Egypt. *abbrev. for* Egyptian.

Egyptian (ɪ'dʒɪpʃən) *adj* **1** of, relating to, or characteristic of Egypt, its inhabitants, or their dialect of Arabic. **2** of, relating to, or characteristic of the ancient Egyptians, their language, or culture. **3** (of type) having square slab serifs. **4** *Archaic.* of or relating to the Gypsies. ♦ *n* **5** a native or inhabitant of Egypt. **6** a member of an indigenous non-Semitic people who established an advanced civilization in Egypt that flourished from the late fourth millennium B.C. **7** the extinct language of the ancient Egyptians, belonging to the Afro-Asiatic family of languages. It is recorded in hieroglyphic inscriptions, the earliest of which date from before 3000 B.C. It was extinct by the fourth century A.D. See also **Coptic. 8** a large size of drawing paper. **9** an archaic name for a **Gypsy.**

Egyptian jasper *n* a type of jasper, generally with zones of colour, found in desert regions of Egypt.

Egyptology (ˌi:dʒɪp'tɒlədʒɪ) *n* the study of the archaeology and language of ancient Egypt. ▸ **Egyptological** (ɪˌdʒɪptə'lɒdʒɪk°l) *adj* ▸ **ˌEgyp'tologist** *n*

eh (eɪ) *interj* an exclamation used to express questioning surprise or to seek the repetition or confirmation of a statement or question: *Eh? What did you say?*

EHF *abbrev. for* extremely high frequency.

EHO (in Britain) *abbrev. for* Environmental Health Officer.

Ehrenburg *or* **Erenburg** ('ɛərən,bɜːg; *Russian* ɪrɪn'burk) *n* **Ilya Grigorievich** (ilj'ja gri'gɔrjɪvitʃ). 1891–1967, Soviet novelist and journalist. His novel *The Thaw* (1954) was the first published in the Soviet Union to deal with repression under Stalin.

Ehrlich (*German* 'eːrlɪç) *n* **Paul** (paul). 1854–1915, German bacteriologist, noted for his pioneering work in immunology and chemotherapy and for his discovery of a remedy for syphilis: Nobel prize for physiology or medicine 1908.

EI *abbrev. for:* **1** East Indian. **2** East Indies.

Eichendorff (*German* 'aiçəndɔrf) *n* **Joseph** ('joːzɛf), Freiherr von. 1788–1857, German poet and novelist, regarded as one of the greatest German romantic lyricists.

Eichler (*German* 'aiçlər) *n* **August Wilhelm** ('ɑʊgʊst 'vilhɛlm). 1839–87, German botanist: devised the system on which modern plant classification is based.

Eichmann (*German* 'aiçman) *n* **(Karl) Adolf** ('aːdɔlf). 1902–62, Austrian Nazi official, who took a leading role in organizing the extermination of the European Jews. He escaped to Argentina after World War II, but was captured and executed in Israel as a war criminal.

eider *or* **eider duck** ('aɪdə) *n* any of several sea ducks of the genus *Somateria*, esp. *S. mollissima*, and related genera, which occur in the N hemisphere. The male has black and white plumage, and the female is the source of eiderdown. [C18: from Old Norse *æthr;* related to Swedish *ejder*, Dutch, German *Eider*]

eiderdown ('aɪdə,daʊn) *n* **1** the breast down of the female eider duck, with which it lines the nest, used for stuffing pillows, quilts, etc. **2** a thick warm cover for a bed, made of two layers of material enclosing a soft filling. **3** *U.S.* a warm cotton fabric having a woollen nap.

eidetic (aɪ'dɛtɪk) *adj Psychol.* **1** (of visual, or sometimes auditory, images) exceptionally vivid and allowing detailed recall of something previously perceived: thought to be common in children. **2** relating to or subject to such imagery. [C20: from Greek *eidētikos*, from *eidos* shape, form] ▸ **ei'detically** *adv*

eidolon (aɪ'dəʊlɒn) *n, pl* **-la** (-lə) *or* **-lons. 1** an unsubstantial image; apparition; phantom. **2** an ideal or idealized figure. [C19: from Greek: phantom, IDOL]

Eifel ('aɪfəl; *German* 'aifəl) *n* a plateau region in W Germany, between the River Moselle and the Belgian frontier: quarrying.

Eiffel ('aɪfᵊl; *French* ɛfɛl) *n* **Alexandre Gustave** (alɛksɑ̃drə gystav). 1832–1923, French engineer.

Eiffel Tower ('aɪfᵊl) *n* a tower in Paris: designed by A. G. Eiffel; erected for the 1889 Paris Exposition. Height: 300 m (984 ft.), raised in 1959 to 321 m (1052 ft.).

Eigen (*German* 'aigən) *n* **Manfred.** born 1927, German physical chemist: shared the Nobel prize for chemistry (1967) for developing his relaxation technique for studying fast reactions.

eigen- *n combining form.* characteristic; proper: *eigenvalue.* [from German, literally: own]

eigenfrequency ('aɪgən,friːkwənsɪ) *n, pl* **-cies.** *Physics.* a resonance frequency of a system.

eigenfunction ('aɪgən,fʌŋkʃən) *n Maths, physics.* a function satisfying a differential equation, esp. an allowed function for a system in wave mechanics.

eigentone ('aɪgən,təʊn) *n* a characteristic acoustic resonance frequency of a system.

eigenvalue ('aɪgən,væljuː) *n Maths, physics.* one of the particular values of a certain parameter for which a differential equation has an eigenfunction. In wave mechanics an eigenvalue is equivalent to the energy of a quantum state of a system.

Eiger (*German* 'aigər) *n* a mountain in central Switzerland, in the Bernese Alps. Height: 3970 m (13 025 ft.).

eight (eɪt) *n* **1** the cardinal number that is the sum of one and seven and the product of two and four. See also **number** (sense 1). **2** a numeral, 8, VIII, etc., representing this number. **3** *Music.* the numeral 8 used as the lower figure in a time signature to indicate that the beat is measured in quavers. **4** the amount or quantity that is one greater than seven. **5** something representing, represented by, or consisting of eight units, such as a playing card with eight symbols on it. **6** *Rowing.* **6a** a racing shell propelled by eight oarsmen. **6b** the crew of such a shell. **7** Also called: **eight o'clock.** eight hours after noon or midnight. **8 have one over the eight.** *Slang.* to be drunk. **9** See **figure of eight.** ◆ *determiner* **10a** amounting to eight. **10b** (*as pronoun*): *I could only find eight.* ◆ Related prefixes: **octa-, octo-.** [Old English *eahta;* related to Old High German *ahto*, Old Norse *ātta*, Old Irish *ocht*, Latin *octō*, Greek *okto*, Sanskrit *astau*]

eight ball *n U.S. and Canadian.* **1** (in pool) the black ball, marked with the number eight. **2 behind the eight ball.** in a difficult situation; snookered.

eighteen ('eɪ'tiːn) *n* **1** the cardinal number that is the sum of ten and eight and the product of two and nine. See also **number** (sense 1). **2** a numeral, 18, XVIII, etc., representing this number. **3** the amount or quantity that is eight more than ten. **4** something represented by, representing, or consisting of 18 units. **5** (*functioning as sing or pl*) a team of 18 players in Australian Rules football. ◆ *determiner* **6a** amounting to eighteen: *eighteen weeks.* **6b** (*as pronoun*): *eighteen of them knew.* [Old English *eahtatēne;* related to Old Norse *attjan*, Old High German *ahtozehan*]

eighteenmo ('eɪ'tiːnməʊ) *n, pl* **-mos. 1** Also called: **octodecimo.** a book size resulting from folding a sheet of paper into 18 leaves or 36 pages. Often written: **18mo, 18°. 2** a book of this size.

eighteenth ('eɪ'tiːnθ) *adj* **1** (*usually prenominal*) **1a** coming after the seventeenth in numbering or counting order, position, time, etc.; being the ordinal number of *eighteen:* often written 18th. **1b** (*as n*): *come on the eighteenth.* ◆ *n* **2a** one of 18 approximately equal parts of something. **2b** (*as modifier*): *an eighteenth part.* **3** the fraction that is equal to one divided by 18 (1/18).

eightfold ('eɪt,fəʊld) *adj* **1** equal to or having eight times as many or as much. **2** composed of eight parts. ◆ *adv* **3** by or up to eight times as much.

eighth (eɪtθ) *adj* **1** (*usually prenominal*) **1a** coming after the seventh and before the ninth in numbering or counting order, position, time, etc.; being the ordinal number of *eight:* often written 8th. **1b** (*as n*): *the eighth in line.* ◆ *n* **2a** one of eight equal or nearly equal parts of an object, quantity, measurement, etc. **2b** (*as modifier*): *an eighth part.* **3** the fraction equal to one divided by eight (1/8). **4** another word for **octave.** ◆ *adv* **5** Also: **'eighthly.** after the seventh person, position, event, etc.

eighth note *n* the usual U.S. and Canadian name for **quaver** (sense 4).

eightieth ('eɪtɪɪθ) *adj* **1** (*usually prenominal*) **1a** being the ordinal number of *eighty* in numbering or counting order, position, time, etc.: often written 80th. **1b** (*as n*): *the eightieth in succession.* ◆ *n* **2a** one of 80 approximately equal parts of something. **2b** (*as modifier*): *an eightieth part.* **3** the fraction equal to one divided by 80 (1/80).

eightsome reel ('eɪtsəm) *n* a Scottish dance for eight people.

eightvo ('eɪtvəʊ) *n, pl* **-vos.** *Bookbinding.* another word for **octavo.**

eighty ('eɪtɪ) *n, pl* **-ies. 1** the cardinal number that is the product of ten and eight. See also **number** (sense 1). **2** a numeral, 80, LXXX, etc., representing this number. **3** (*pl*) the numbers 80-89, esp. the 80th to the 89th year of a person's life or of a particular century. **4** the amount or quantity that is eight times as big as ten. **5** something represented by, representing, or consisting of 80 units. ◆ *determiner* **6a** amounting to eighty: *eighty pages of nonsense.* **6b** (*as pronoun*): *eighty are expected.* [Old English *eahtatig;* related to Old Frisian *achtig*, Old High German *ahtozug*]

Eijkman (*Dutch* 'ɛikmɑn) *n* **Christiaan** ('kriːstiː,aːn). 1858–1930, Dutch physician, who discovered that beriberi is caused by nutritional deficiency: Nobel prize for physiology or medicine 1929.

eikon ('aɪkɒn) *n* a variant spelling of **icon.**

Eilat, Elat, *or* **Elath** (eɪ'lɑːt) *n* a port in S Israel, on the Gulf of Aqaba: Israel's only outlet to the Red Sea. Pop.: 26 010 (1989 est.).

Eileen Donan Castle ('eɪliːn 'dɒnən) *n* a castle near the Kyle of Lochalsh in Highland, Scotland: built in the 13th century; famous for its picturesque setting.

eina ('eɪ,nɑː) *interj S. African.* an exclamation of sudden pain. [C19: Afrikaans, from Khoi]

Eindhoven ('aɪnt,həʊvᵊn, *Dutch* 'ɛinthoːvə) *n* a city in the SE Netherlands, in North Brabant province: radio and electrical industry. Pop.: 197 055 (1995 est.).

einkorn ('aɪn,kɔːn) *n* a variety of wheat, *Triticum monococcum*, of Greece and SW Asia, having pale red kernels, and cultivated in hilly regions as grain for horses. [C20: from German, literally: one kernel]

Einstein ('aɪnstaɪn) *n* **Albert.** 1879–1955, U.S. physicist and mathematician, born in Germany. He formulated the special theory of relativity (1905) and the general theory of relativity (1916), and made major contributions to the quantum theory, for which he was awarded the Nobel prize for physics in 1921. He was noted also for his work for world peace. ▸ **Ein'steinian** *adj*

einsteinium (aɪn'staɪnɪəm) *n* a metallic transuranic element artificially produced from plutonium. Symbol: Es; atomic no.: 99; half-life of most stable isotope, ^{252}Es: 276 days. [C20: New Latin, named after Albert EINSTEIN]

Einstein shift *n Astronomy.* a small displacement towards the red in the spectra, caused by the interaction between the radiation and the gravitational field of a massive body, such as the sun.

Einstein's law *n* **1** the principle that mass (m) and energy (E) are equivalent according to the equation $E = mc^2$, where c is the velocity of light. **2** the principle that the maximum energy of a photoelectron is $h\nu - \Phi$, where ν is the frequency of the incident radiation, h is the Planck constant, and Φ is the work function.

Einthoven (*Dutch* 'ɛɪnthoːvə) *n* **Willem.** 1860–1927, Dutch physiologist. A pioneer of electrocardiography, he was awarded the Nobel prize for physiology or medicine in 1924.

Eire ('ɛərə) *n* **1** the Irish Gaelic name for **Ireland**[1]: often used to mean the **Republic of Ireland. 2** a former name for the **Republic of Ireland** (1937–49).

eirenic (aɪ'riːnɪk) *adj* a variant spelling of **irenic.**

eirenicon *or* **irenicon** (aɪ'riːnɪ,kɒn) *n* a proposition that attempts to harmonize conflicting viewpoints. [C19: from Greek, from *eirēnikos* of or concerning peace, from *eirēnē* peace]

EIS *abbrev. for* Educational Institute of Scotland.

eisegesis (,aɪsə'dʒiːsɪs) *n, pl* **-ses** (-siːz). the interpretation of a text, esp. a biblical text, using one's own ideas. Compare **exegesis.** [C19: from Greek *eis* into, in + *-egesis*, as in EXEGESIS]

Eisenach (*German* 'aizənax) *n* a city in central Germany, in Thuringia: birthplace of Johann Sebastian Bach. Pop.: 48 361 (1989 est.).

Eisenhower ('aɪzən,haʊə) *n* **Dwight David,** known as *Ike.* 1890–1969, U.S. general and Republican statesman; Supreme Commander of the Allied Expeditionary Force (1943–45) and 34th president of the U.S. (1953–61). He commanded Allied forces in Europe and North Africa (1942), directed the invasion of Italy (1943), and was Supreme Commander of the combined land forces of NATO (1950–52).

Eisenstadt (*German* 'aizənʃtat) *n* a town in E Austria, capital of Burgenland province: Hungarian until 1921. Pop.: 10 506 (1991).

Eisenstaedt ('aɪzᵊn,stæt) *n* **Alfred.** 1898–1995, U.S. photographer, born in Germany.

Eisenstein ('aɪzᵊn,staɪn; *Russian* ejzɪn'ʃtjejn) *n* **Sergei Mikhailovich** (sɪr'gjej mi'xajləvitʃ). 1898–1948, Soviet film director. His films include *Battleship Potemkin* (1925), *Alexander Nevsky* (1938), and *Ivan the Terrible* (1944).

Eisk *or* **Eysk** (*Russian* jejsk) *n* variant transliterations of the Russian name for **Yeisk.**

eisteddfod (aɪˈstɛdfəd; *Welsh* aɪˈstɛðvɒd) *n, pl* **-fods** *or* **-fodau** (*Welsh* aɪˌstɛðˈvɒdaɪ). any of a number of annual festivals in Wales, esp. the **Royal National Eisteddfod,** in which competitions are held in music, poetry, drama, and the fine arts. [C19: from Welsh, literally: session, from *eistedd* to sit (from *sedd* seat) + *-fod,* from *bod* to be] ▸ **ˌeisteddˈfodic** *adj*

either (ˈaɪðə, ˈiːðə) *determiner* **1a** one or the other (of two): *either coat will do.* **1b** (*as pronoun*): *either is acceptable.* **2** both one and the other: *there were ladies at either end of the table.* ◆ *conj* **3** (*coordinating*) used preceding two or more possibilities joined by *"or"*: *you may have either cheese or a sweet.* ◆ *adv* (*sentence modifier*) **4** (*used with a negative*) used to indicate that the clause immediately preceding is a partial reiteration of a previous clause: *John isn't a liar, but he isn't exactly honest either.* [Old English *ǣgther,* short for *ǣghwæther* each of two; related to Old Frisian *ēider,* Old High German *ēogihweder;* see EACH, WHETHER]

USAGE *Either* is followed by a singular verb in good usage: *either is good; either of these books is useful.* Care should be taken to avoid ambiguity when using *either* to mean *both* or *each,* as in the following sentence: *a ship could be moored on either side of the channel.* Agreement between the verb and its subject in *either...or...* constructions follows the pattern given for *neither...nor...* See at **neither.**

either-or *adj* presenting an unavoidable need to choose between two alternatives: *an either-or situation.*

ejaculate *vb* (ɪˈdʒækjʊˌleɪt). **1** to eject or discharge (semen) in orgasm. **2** (*tr*) to utter abruptly; blurt out. ◆ *n* (ɪˈdʒækjʊlɪt). **3** another word for **semen.** [C16: from Latin *ējaculārī* to hurl out, from *jaculum* javelin, from *jacere* to throw] ▸ **eˈjacuˌlator** *n*

ejaculation (ɪˌdʒækjʊˈleɪʃən) *n* **1** an abrupt emphatic utterance or exclamation. **2** a discharge of semen. ▸ **eˈjaculatory** *or* **eˈjaculative** *adj*

ejaculatio praecox (ɪˌdʒækjʊˈleɪʃɪəʊ ˈpriːkɒks) *n* premature ejaculation during sexual intercourse. [Latin]

eject (ɪˈdʒɛkt) *vb* **1** (*tr*) to drive or force out; expel or emit. **2** (*tr*) to compel (a person) to leave; evict; dispossess. **3** (*tr*) to dismiss, as from office. **4** (*intr*) to leave an aircraft rapidly, using an ejection seat or capsule. **5** (*tr*) *Psychiatry.* to attribute (one's own motivations and characteristics) to others. [C15: from Latin *ejicere,* from *jacere* to throw] ▸ **eˈjection** *n*

ejecta (ɪˈdʒɛktə) *pl n* matter thrown out by an erupting volcano. [C19: Latin, literally: (things) ejected; see EJECT]

ejection seat *or* **ejector seat** *n* a seat, esp. as fitted to military aircraft, that is fired by a cartridge or rocket to eject the occupant from the aircraft in an emergency.

ejective (ɪˈdʒɛktɪv) *adj* **1** relating to or causing ejection. **2** *Phonetics.* (of a plosive or fricative consonant, as in some African languages) pronounced with a glottal stop. ◆ *n* **3** *Phonetics.* an ejective consonant. ▸ **eˈjectively** *adv*

ejectment (ɪˈdʒɛktmənt) *n* **1** *Property law.* (formerly) an action brought by a wrongfully dispossessed owner seeking to recover possession of his land. **2** the act of ejecting or state of being ejected; dispossession.

ejector (ɪˈdʒɛktə) *n* **1** a person or thing that ejects. **2** the mechanism in a firearm that ejects the empty cartridge or shell after firing.

Ekaterinburg (*Russian* jɪkətɪrimˈburk) *n* a variant transliteration of the Russian name for **Yekaterinburg.**

Ekaterinodar (*Russian* jɪkətɪrinaˈdar) *n* the former name (until 1920) of **Krasnodar.**

Ekaterinoslav (*Russian* jɪkətɪrinaˈslaf) *n* the former name (1787–96, 1802–1926) of **Dnepropetrovsk.**

eke[1] (iːk) *vb* (*tr*) *Archaic.* to increase, enlarge, or lengthen. [Old English *eacan;* related to Old Norse *auka* to increase, Latin *augēre* to increase]

eke[2] (iːk) *sentence connector. Archaic.* also; moreover. [Old English *eac;* related to Old Norse, Gothic *auk* also, Old High German *ouh,* Latin *autem* but, *aut* or]

eke out *vb* (*tr, adv*) **1** to make (a supply) last, esp. by frugal use: *they eked out what little food was left.* **2** to support (existence) with difficulty and effort. **3** to add to (something insufficient), esp. with effort: *to eke out an income with evening work.*

ekistics (ɪˈkɪstɪks) *n* (*functioning as sing*) the science or study of human settlements. [C20: from Greek *oikistikos* of or concerning settlements, from *oikizein* to settle (a colony), from *oikos* a house] ▸ **eˈkistic** *or* **eˈkistical** *adj* ▸ **ˌekisˈtician** *n*

Ekman (*Swedish* ˈɛkman) *n* **Vagn Walfrid** (vayᵊn wɑːlfriːd). 1874–1954, Swedish oceanographer: discoverer of the **Ekman Spiral** (a complex interaction on the surface of the sea between wind, rotation of the earth, and friction forces) and the **Ekman layer** (the thin top layer of the sea that flows at 90° to the wind direction).

ekpwele (ɛkˈpweleɪ) *or* **ekuele** (eɪˈkweɪleɪ) *n, pl* **-le** (-leɪ). a former monetary unit of Equatorial Guinea. [from the native name in Equatorial Guinea]

el (ɛl) *n U.S. informal.* a shortened form of **elevated railway** *or* **railroad.**

El Aaiún (ɛl aɪˈjuːn) *n* a city in Morocco, in Western Sahara: the capital of the former Spanish Sahara; port facilities begun in 1967 at **Playa de El Aaiún,** 20 km (12 miles) away, following the discovery of rich phosphate deposits. Pop.: 136 950 (1994).

elaborate *adj* (ɪˈlæbərɪt). **1** planned or executed with care and exactness; detailed. **2** marked by complexity, ornateness, or detail. ◆ *vb* (ɪˈlæbəˌreɪt). **3** (*intr;* usually foll. by *on* or *upon*) to add information or detail (to an account); expand (upon). **4** (*tr*) to work out in detail; develop. **5** (*tr*) to make more complicated or ornate. **6** (*tr*) to produce by careful labour; create. **7** (*tr*) *Physiol.* to change (food or simple substances) into more complex substances for use in the body. [C16: from Latin *ēlabōrāre* to take pains, from *labōrāre* to toil] ▸ **eˈlaborately** *adv* ▸ **eˈlaborateness** *n* ▸ **eˌlaboˈration** *n* ▸ **elaborative** (ɪˈlæbərətɪv) *adj* ▸ **eˈlaboˌrator** *n*

elaeoptene (ˌɛlɪˈɒptiːn) *n* a variant spelling of **eleoptene.**

Elagabalus (ˌɛləˈgæbələs, ˌiːlə-) *n* a variant of **Heliogabalus.**

El Alamein *or* **Alamein** (ɛl ˈæləˌmeɪn) *n* a village on the N coast of Egypt, about 112 km (70 miles) west of Alexandria: scene of a decisive Allied victory over the Axis forces (1942).

Elam (ˈiːləm) *n* an ancient kingdom east of the River Tigris: established before 4000 B.C.; probably inhabited by a non-Semitic people.

Elamite (ˈiːləˌmaɪt) *n* **1** an inhabitant of the ancient kingdom of Elam. **2** Also called: **Elamitic, Susian.** the extinct language of this people, of no known relationship, recorded in cuneiform inscriptions dating from the 25th to the 4th centuries B.C. ◆ *adj* **3** of or relating to Elam, its people, or their language.

élan (eɪˈlɑːn, eɪˈlæn; *French* elɑ̃) *n* a combination of style and vigour: *he performed the concerto with élan.* [C19: from French, from *élancer* to throw forth, ultimately from Latin *lancea* LANCE]

eland (ˈiːlənd) *n* **1** a large spiral-horned antelope, *Taurotragus oryx,* inhabiting bushland in eastern and southern Africa. It has a dewlap and a hump on the shoulders and is light brown with vertical white stripes. **2 giant eland.** a similar but larger animal, *T. derbianus,* living in wooded areas of central and W Africa. [C18: via Afrikaans from Dutch *eland* elk; related to Old Slavonic *jeleni* stag, Greek *ellos* fawn]

élan vital *French.* (elɑ̃ vital) *n* a creative principle held by Henri Bergson to be present in all organisms and responsible for evolution. Compare **Bergsonism.** [literally: vital impetus]

elapid (ˈɛləpɪd) *n* **1** any venomous snake of the mostly tropical family *Elapidae,* having fixed poison fangs at the front of the upper jaw and including the cobras, coral snakes, and mambas. ◆ *adj* **2** of, relating to, or belonging to the *Elapidae.* [C19: from New Latin *Elapidae,* from Medieval Greek *elaps, elops* a fish, sea serpent; perhaps related to Greek *lepis* scale]

elapse (ɪˈlæps) *vb* (*intr*) (of time) to pass by. [C17: from Latin *ēlābī* to slip away, from *lābī* to slip, glide]

Elara (ɛˈlærə) *n Astronomy.* a small satellite of Jupiter in an intermediate orbit.

elasmobranch (ɪˈlæsməˌbræŋk, ɪˈlæz-) *n* **1** any cartilaginous fish of the subclass *Elasmobranchii* (or *Selachii*), which includes the sharks, rays, dogfish, and skates. ◆ *adj* **2** of, relating to, or belonging to the *Elasmobranchii.* ◆ Also called: **selachian.** [C19: from New Latin *elasmobranchii,* from Greek *elasmos* metal plate + *brankhia* gills]

elasmosaur (ɪˈlæzməˌsɔː) *n* a very long-necked extinct marine reptile: a type of plesiosaur. [C19: from Greek *elasmos* metal plate + *sauros* lizard]

elastance (ɪˈlæstəns) *n Physics.* the reciprocal of capacitance. It is measured in reciprocal farads (darafs). [C19: from ELASTIC + -ANCE]

elastane (ɪˈlæsteɪn) *n* a synthetic fibre characterized by its ability to revert to its original shape after being stretched.

elastase (ɪˈlæsteɪs) *n* an enzyme that digests elastin.

elastic (ɪˈlæstɪk) *adj* **1** (of a body or material) capable of returning to its original shape after compression, expansion, stretching, or other deformation. **2** capable of adapting to change: *an elastic schedule.* **3** quick to recover from fatigue, dejection, etc.; buoyant. **4** springy or resilient: *an elastic walk.* **5** (of gases) capable of expanding spontaneously. **6** *Physics.* (of collisions) involving no overall change in translational kinetic energy. **7** made of elastic. ◆ *n* **8** tape, cord, or fabric containing interwoven strands of flexible rubber or similar substance allowing it to stretch and return to its original shape. **9** *Chiefly U.S. and Canadian.* something made of elastic, such as a rubber band or a garter. [C17: from New Latin *elasticus* impulsive, from Greek *elastikos,* from *elaunein* to beat, drive] ▸ **eˈlastically** *adv*

elasticate (ɪˈlæstɪˌkeɪt) *vb* (*tr*) to insert elastic sections or thread into (a fabric or garment): *an elasticated waistband.* ▸ **eˌlastiˈcation** *n*

elastic band *n* another name for **rubber band.**

elasticity (ɪlæˈstɪsɪtɪ, ˌiːlæ-) *n* **1** the property of a body or substance that enables it to resume its original shape or size when a distorting force is removed. See also **elastic limit. 2** the state or quality of being elastic; flexibility or buoyancy. **3** a measure of the sensitivity of demand for goods or services to changes in price or other marketing variables, such as advertising.

elasticize *or* **elasticise** (ɪˈlæstɪˌsaɪz) *vb* (*tr*) **1** to make elastic. **2** another word for **elasticate.**

elastic limit *n* the greatest stress that can be applied to a material without causing permanent deformation.

elastic modulus *n* another name for **modulus of elasticity.**

elastic rebound *n Geology.* a theory of earthquakes that envisages gradual deformation of the fault zone without fault slippage until friction is overcome, when the fault suddenly slips to produce the earthquake.

elastin (ɪˈlæstɪn) *n Biochem.* a fibrous scleroprotein constituting the major part of elastic tissue, such as the walls of arteries. [C19: from ELASTIC + -IN]

elastivity (ɪlæˈstɪvɪtɪ) *n Physics.* a measure of the resistance of a substance to an electric field; the reciprocal of the permittivity of a dielectric.

elastomer (ɪˈlæstəmə) *n* any material, such as natural or synthetic rubber, that is able to resume its original shape when a deforming force is removed. [C20: from ELASTIC + -MER] ▸ **elastomeric** (ɪˌlæstəˈmɛrɪk) *adj*

Elastoplast (ɪˈlæstəˌplɑːst) *n Trademark.* a gauze surgical dressing backed by adhesive tape.

Elat *or* **Elath** (eɪˈlɑːt) *n* variant spellings of **Eilat.**

elate (ɪˈleɪt) *vb* (*tr*) to fill with high spirits, exhilaration, pride or optimism. [C16: from Latin *ēlāt-* stem of past participle of *efferre* to bear away, from *ferre* to carry] ▸ **eˈlated** *adj* ▸ **eˈlatedly** *adv* ▸ **eˈlatedness** *n*

elater (ˈɛlətə) *n* **1** an elaterid beetle. **2** *Botany.* a spirally thickened filament, occurring in liverwort capsules and horsetails, thought to aid dispersal of spores.

[C17: via New Latin from Greek: driver, from *elaunein* to beat, drive; compare ELASTIC]

elaterid (ɪ'lætərɪd) *n* **1** any of the beetles constituting the widely distributed family *Elateridae* (click beetles). The group includes the wireworms and certain fireflies. ♦ *adj* **2** of, relating to, or belonging to the family *Elateridae*. [C19: from New Latin *Elateridae*, from ELATER]

elaterin (ɪ'lætərɪn) *n* a white crystalline substance found in elaterium, used as a purgative. [C19: from ELATERIUM + -IN]

elaterite (ɪ'lætəˌraɪt) *n* a dark brown naturally occurring bitumen resembling rubber. [C19: from ELATER + -ITE[1]]

elaterium (ˌɛlə'tɪərɪəm) *n* a greenish sediment prepared from the juice of the squirting cucumber, used as a purgative. [C16: from Latin, from Greek *elatērion* squirting cucumber, from *elatērios* purgative, from *elaunein* to drive]

elation (ɪ'leɪʃən) *n* joyfulness or exaltation of spirit, as from success, pleasure, or relief; high spirits.

elative ('iːlətɪv) *adj* **1** (in the grammar of Finnish and other languages) denoting a case of nouns expressing a relation of motion or direction, usually translated by the English prepositions *out of* or *away from*. Compare **illative** (sense 3). ♦ *n* **2a** the elative case. **2b** an elative word or speech element. [C19: from Latin *ēlātus*, past participle of *efferre* to carry out; see ELATE]

E layer *n* another name for **E region**.

Elba ('ɛlbə) *n* a mountainous island off the W coast of Italy, in the Mediterranean: Napoleon Bonaparte's first place of exile (1814–15). Pop.: 27 722 (1991 est.). Area: 223 sq. km (86 sq. miles).

Elbe (ɛlb; *German* 'ɛlbə) *n* a river in central Europe, rising in the N Czech Republic and flowing generally northwest through Germany to the North Sea at Hamburg. Length: 1165 km (724 miles). Czech name: **Labe**.

Elbert ('ɛlbət) *n* **Mount.** a mountain in central Colorado, in the Sawatch range. Height: 4399 m (14 431 ft.).

Elbląg (*Polish* 'ɛlblɔŋk) *n* a port in N Poland: metallurgical industries. Pop.: 128 700 (1996 est.). German name: **Elbing** ('ɛlbɪŋ).

elbow ('ɛlbəʊ) *n* **1** the joint between the upper arm and the forearm, formed by the junction of the radius and ulna with the humerus. **2** the corresponding joint or bone of birds or mammals. **3** the part of a garment that covers the elbow. **4** something resembling an elbow, such as a sharp bend in a road or river. **5 at one's elbow.** within easy reach. **6 out at elbow(s).** ragged or impoverished. **7 up to the elbows with** *or* **in.** busily occupied with; deeply immersed in. ♦ *vb* **8** to make (one's way) by shoving, jostling, etc. **9** (*tr*) to knock or shove with or as if with the elbow. **10** (*tr*) to reject; dismiss (esp. in the phrases **give** *or* **get the elbow**). [Old English *elnboga;* see ELL[2], BOW[2]; related to Old Norse *olbogi*, Old High German *elinbogo*]

elbow grease *n Facetious.* vigorous physical labour, esp. hard rubbing.

elbowroom ('ɛlbəʊˌruːm, -ˌrʊm) *n* sufficient scope to move or function.

Elbrus (ɪl'bruːs) *n* a mountain in SW Russia, on the border with Georgia, in the Caucasus Mountains, with two extinct volcanic peaks: the highest mountain in Europe. Height: 5642 m (18 510 ft.).

Elburz Mountains (ɛl'bʊəz) *pl n* a mountain range in N Iran, parallel to the SW and S shores of the Caspian Sea. Highest peak: Mount Demavend, 5601 m (18 376 ft.).

El Capitan (ɛl ˌkæpɪ'tæn) *n* a mountain in E central California, in the Sierra Nevada: a monolith with a precipice rising over 1100 m (3600 ft.) above the floor of the Yosemite Valley. Height: 2306 m (7564 ft.).

Elche (*Spanish* 'ɛltʃe) *n* a town in S Spain, in Valencia: noted for Iberian and Roman archaeological finds and the medieval religious drama performed there annually: fruit growing, esp. dates, pomegranates, figs. Pop.: 192 424 (1995 est.).

El Cid Campeador (*Spanish* ɛl θið kampea'ðɔr) *n* See (El) **Cid**.

eld (ɛld) *n Archaic.* **1** old age. **2** olden days; antiquity. [Old English *eldu;* related to Old Norse *elli;* see OLD]

elder[1] ('ɛldə) *adj* **1** born earlier; senior. Compare **older**. **2** (in piquet and similar card games) denoting or relating to the nondealer (the **elder hand**), who has certain advantages in the play. **3** *Archaic.* **3a** prior in rank, position, or office. **3b** of a previous time; former. ♦ *n* **4** an older person; one's senior. **5** *Anthropol.* a senior member of a tribe who has influence or authority. **6** (in certain Protestant Churches) a lay office having teaching, pastoral, or administrative functions. **7** another word for **presbyter**. [Old English *eldra*, comparative of *eald* OLD; related to Old Norse *ellri*, Old High German *altiro*, Gothic *althiza*] ▸ **'elderˌship** *n*

elder[2] ('ɛldə) *n* **1** Also called: **elderberry**. any of various caprifoliaceous shrubs or small trees of the genus *Sambucus*, having clusters of small white flowers and red, purple, or black berry-like fruits. **2** any of various unrelated plants, such as box elder and marsh elder. ♦ Compare **alder**. [Old English *ellern;* related to Old Norse *elrir*, Old High German *erlīn*, Old Slavonic *jelĭcha*, Latin *alnus*]

elderberry ('ɛldəˌbɛrɪ) *n, pl* **-ries. 1** the berry-like fruit of the elder, used for making wines, jellies, etc. **2** another name for **elder**[2] (sense 1).

Elder Brethren *pl n* the senior members of the governing body of Trinity House.

elderly ('ɛldəlɪ) *adj* (of people) **a** quite old; past middle age. **b** (*as collective n* preceded by *the*): *the elderly*. Related adj: **geriatric**. ▸ **'elderliness** *n*

elder statesman *n* an old, experienced, and eminent person, esp. a politician, whose advice is often sought.

eldest ('ɛldɪst) *adj* being the oldest, esp. the oldest surviving child of the same parents. [Old English *eldesta*, superlative of *eald* OLD]

ELDO ('ɛldəʊ) *n acronym for* European Launcher Development Organization.

Eldon ('ɛldən) *n* **1st Earl of**, title of *John Scott*. 1751–1838, British statesman and jurist; Lord Chancellor (1801–06, 1807–27): an inflexible opponent of parliamentary reform, Catholic emancipation, and the abolition of slavery.

El Dorado (ɛl dɒ'rɑːdəʊ; *Spanish* ɛl do'raðo) *n* **1** a fabled city in South America, rich in treasure and sought by Spanish explorers in the 16th century. **2** Also: **ˌeldo'rado.** any place of great riches or fabulous opportunity. [C16: from Spanish, literally: the gilded (place)]

eldritch *or* **eldrich** ('ɛldrɪtʃ) *adj Poetic, Scot.* unearthly; weird. [C16: perhaps from Old English *ælf* ELF + *rīce* realm; see RICH]

Elea ('iːlɪə) *n* (in ancient Italy) a Greek colony on the Tyrrhenian coast of Lucana.

Eleanor of Aquitaine ('ɛlɪnə, -ˌnɔː) *n* ?1122–1204, queen of France (1137–52) by her marriage to Louis VII and queen of England (1154–89) by her marriage to Henry II; mother of the English kings Richard I and John.

Eleanor of Castile ('ɛlɪnə, -ˌnɔː) *n* 1246–90, Spanish wife of Edward I of England. **Eleanor Crosses** were erected at each place at which her body rested between Nottingham, where she died, and London, where she is buried.

Eleatic (ˌɛlɪ'ætɪk) *adj* **1** denoting or relating to a school of philosophy founded in Elea in Greece in the 6th century B.C. by Xenophanes, Parmenides, and Zeno. It held that one pure immutable Being is the only object of knowledge and that information obtained by the senses is illusory. ♦ *n* **2** a follower of this school. ▸ **Eleaticism** (ˌɛlɪ'ætɪˌsɪzəm) *n*

elecampane (ˌɛlɪkæm'peɪn) *n* a perennial flowering plant, *Inula helenium*, of Europe, Asia, and North America having large hairy leaves and narrow yellow petals: family *Compositae* (composites). [C16: from Medieval Latin *enula campāna*, from *enula* (from Greek *helenion*) + *campānus* of the field]

elect (ɪ'lɛkt) *vb* **1** (*tr*) to choose (someone) to be (a representative or a public official) by voting: *they elected him Mayor.* **2** to select; choose: *to elect to die rather than surrender.* **3** (*tr*) (of God) to select or predestine for the grace of salvation. ♦ *adj* **4** (*immediately postpositive*) voted into office but not yet installed: *the president elect.* **5a** chosen or choice; selected or elite. **5b** (*as collective n* preceded by *the*): *the elect.* **6** *Christianity.* **6a** selected or predestined by God to receive salvation; chosen. **6b** (*as collective n* preceded by *the*): *the elect.* [C15: from Latin *ēligere* to select, from *legere* to choose] ▸ **e'lectable** *adj*

elect. *or* **elec.** *abbrev. for:* **1** electric(al). **2** electricity.

election (ɪ'lɛkʃən) *n* **1** the selection by vote of a person or persons from among candidates for a position, esp. a political office. **2** a public vote on an official proposition. **3** the act or an instance of choosing. **4** *Christianity.* **4a** the doctrine of Calvin that God chooses certain individuals for salvation without reference to their faith or works. **4b** the doctrine of Arminius and others that God chooses for salvation those who, by grace, persevere in faith and works.

electioneer (ɪˌlɛkʃə'nɪə) *vb* (*intr*) **1** to be active in a political election or campaign. ♦ *n* **2** a person who engages in this activity. ▸ **eˌlection'eering** *n, adj*

elective (ɪ'lɛktɪv) *adj* **1** of or based on selection by vote: *elective procedure.* **2** selected by vote: *an elective official.* **3** having the power to elect. **4** open to choice; optional: *an elective course of study.* ♦ *n* **5** an optional course or hospital placement undertaken by a medical student. ▸ **e'lectively** *adv* ▸ **electivity** (ˌiːlɛk'tɪvɪtɪ) *or* **e'lectiveness** *n*

elector (ɪ'lɛktə) *n* **1** someone who is eligible to vote in the election of a government. **2** (*often cap.*) a member of the U.S. electoral college. **3** (*often cap.*) (in the Holy Roman Empire) any of the German princes entitled to take part in the election of a new emperor. ▸ **e'lectorˌship** *n*

electoral (ɪ'lɛktərəl) *adj* relating to or consisting of electors. ▸ **e'lectorally** *adv*

electoral college *n* **1** (*often caps.*) *U.S.* a body of electors chosen by the voters who formally elect the president and vice president. **2** any body of electors with similar functions.

electorate (ɪ'lɛktərɪt) *n* **1** the body of all qualified voters. **2** the rank, position, or territory of an elector of the Holy Roman Empire. **3** *Austral. and N.Z.* the area represented by a Member of Parliament. **4** *Austral. and N.Z.* the voters in a constituency.

Electra (ɪ'lɛktrə) *n Greek myth.* the daughter of Agamemnon and Clytemnestra. She persuaded her brother Orestes to avenge their father by killing his murderess Clytemnestra and her lover Aegisthus.

Electra complex *n Psychoanal.* the sexual attachment of a female child to her father. See also **penis envy**.

Electra paradox *n Logic.* the supposed paradox that one may know something to be true of an object under one description but not another, as when Electra knew that Orestes was her brother but not that the man before her was her brother although he was Orestes. This shows the predicate "knows" to be intensional, that Electra's knowledge here is de dicto, and that the statement of it yields an opaque context. See also **de dicto**.

electret (ɪ'lɛktrət) *n* a permanently polarized dielectric material; its electric field is similar to the magnetic field of a permanent magnet. [C20: from *electr(icity* + *magn)et*]

electric (ɪ'lɛktrɪk) *adj* **1** of, derived from, produced by, producing, transmitting, or powered by electricity: *electric current; an electric cord; an electric blanket; an electric fence; an electric fire.* **2** (of a musical instrument) amplified electronically: *an electric guitar; an electric mandolin.* **3** very tense or exciting; emotionally charged: *an electric atmosphere.* ♦ *n* **4** *Informal.* an electric train, car, etc. **5** *Brit. informal.* electricity or electrical power. **6** (*pl*) an electric circuit or electric appliances. [C17: from New Latin *electricus* amber-like (because friction causes amber to become charged), from Latin *ēlectrum* amber, from Greek *ēlektron*, of obscure origin]

USAGE See at **electronic**.

electrical (ɪ'lɛktrɪk[ə]l) *adj* of, relating to, or concerned with electricity. ▸ **e'lectrically** *adv*

USAGE See at **electronic**.

electrical engineering *n* the branch of engineering concerned with the practical applications of electricity. ▸ **electrical engineer** *n*

electric-arc furnace *n* another name for **arc furnace.**
electric-arc welding *n* another name for **arc welding.**
electric blanket *n* a blanket that contains an electric heating element, used to warm a bed.
electric blue *n, adj* **a** a strong metallic blue colour. **b** (*as adj*): *an electric-blue evening dress.*
electric chair *n* (in the U.S.) **a** an electrified chair for executing criminals. **b** (usually preceded by *the*) execution by this method.
electric charge *n* another name for **charge** (sense 25).
electric circuit *n Physics.* another name for **circuit** (sense 3a).
electric constant *n* the permittivity of free space, which has the value 8.854 185 × 10^{-12} farad per metre. Symbol: ε_0 Also called: **absolute permittivity.**
electric current *n* another name for **current** (sense 8).
electric discharge *n Physics.* another name for **discharge** (sense 20b).
electric-discharge lamp *n* another name for **fluorescent lamp.**
electric displacement *n Physics.* the charge per unit area displaced across a layer of conductor in an electric field. Symbol: *D* Also called: **electric flux density.**
electric eel *n* an eel-like freshwater cyprinoid fish, *Electrophorus electricus,* of N South America, having electric organs in the body: family *Electrophoridae.*
electric eye *n* another name for **photocell.**
electric field *n* a field of force surrounding a charged particle within which another charged particle experiences a force. Compare **magnetic field.**
electric field strength *n* the strength or intensity of an electric field at any point, usually measured in volts per metre. Symbol: *E*
electric fire *n* a device that provides heat for a room from an incandescent electric element.
electric flux *n* the amount of electricity displaced across a given area in a dielectric. Symbol: Ψ
electric flux density *n* another name for **electric displacement.**
electric furnace *n* any furnace in which the heat is provided by an electric current.
electric guitar *n* an electrically amplified guitar, used mainly in pop music. Compare **acoustic guitar.**
electric hare *n* (in greyhound racing) a model of a hare, mounted on an electrified rail, which the dogs chase.
electrician (ɪlɛk'trɪʃən, ˌiːlɛk-) *n* a person whose occupation is the installation, maintenance, and repair of electrical devices.
electricity (ɪlɛk'trɪsɪtɪ, ˌiːlɛk-) *n* **1** any phenomenon associated with stationary or moving electrons, ions, or other charged particles. **2** the science concerned with electricity. **3** an electric current or charge: *a motor powered by electricity.* **4** emotional tension or excitement, esp. between or among people.
electric motor *n* a device that converts electrical energy to mechanical torque.
electric needle *n* a surgical instrument for cutting tissue by the application of a high-frequency current.
electric organ *n* **1** *Music.* **1a** a pipe organ operated by electrical means. **1b** another name for **electronic organ. 2** *Zoology.* a small group of modified muscle cells on the body of certain fishes, such as the electric eel, that gives an electric shock to any animal touching them.
electric potential *n* **a** the work required to transfer a unit positive electric charge from an infinite distance to a given point. **b** the potential difference between the point and some other reference point. Symbol: *V* or ϕ Sometimes shortened to **potential.**
electric ray *n* any ray of the order *Torpediniformes,* of tropical and temperate seas, having a flat rounded body with an electric organ in each of the fins, close to the head.
electric shock *n* the physiological reaction, characterized by pain and muscular spasm, to the passage of an electric current through the body. It can affect the respiratory system and heart rhythm. Sometimes shortened to **shock.**
electric storm *n* a violent atmospheric disturbance in which the air is highly charged with static electricity, causing a storm. Compare **thunderstorm.**
electric strength *n* the maximum voltage sustainable by an insulating material, after which it loses its insulating properties.
electric susceptibility *n* another name for **susceptibility** (sense 4a).
electrify (ɪ'lɛktrɪˌfaɪ) *vb* **-fies, -fying, -fied.** (*tr*) **1** to adapt or equip (a system, device, etc.) for operation by electrical power. **2** to charge with or subject to electricity. **3** to startle or excite intensely; shock or thrill. ► **e'lectriˌfiable** *adj* ► **eˌlectrifi'cation** *n* ► **e'lectriˌfier** *n*
electro (ɪ'lɛktrəʊ) *n, pl* **-tros.** short for **electroplate** or **electrotype.**
electro- *or sometimes before a vowel* **electr-** *combining form.* **1** electric or electrically: *electrocardiograph; electrocute.* **2** electrolytic: *electroanalysis.* [from New Latin, from Latin *ēlectrum* amber, from Greek *ēlektron*]
electroacoustic (ɪˌlɛktrəʊə'kuːstɪk) *adj* another word for **acoustoelectronic.**
electroanalysis (ɪˌlɛktrəʊə'nælɪsɪs) *n* chemical analysis by electrolysis or electrodeposition. ► **electroanalytic** (ɪˌlɛktrəʊˌænə'lɪtɪk) *or* **eˌlectroˌana'lytical** *adj*
electrocardiogram (ɪˌlɛktrəʊ'kɑːdɪəʊˌgræm) *n* a tracing of the electric currents that initiate the heartbeat, used to diagnose possible heart disorders. Abbrev.: **ECG.**
electrocardiograph (ɪˌlɛktrəʊ'kɑːdɪəʊˌgrɑːf, -ˌgræf) *n* an instrument for recording the electrical activity of the heart. Abbrev.: **ECG.** ► **eˌlectroˌcardio'graphic** *adj* ► **eˌlectroˌcardio'graphically** *adv* ► **electrocardiography** (ɪˌlɛktrəʊˌkɑːdɪ'ɒgrəfɪ) *n*
electrochemical equivalent *n* the mass of an element liberated from its ions or converted into them by one coulomb of electric charge.
electrochemical series *n* another name for **electromotive series.**
electrochemistry (ɪˌlɛktrəʊ'kɛmɪstrɪ) *n* the branch of chemistry concerned with the study of electric cells and electrolysis. ► **electrochemical** (ɪˌlɛktrəʊ'kɛmɪkᵊl) *adj* ► **eˌlectro'chemically** *adv* ► **eˌlectro'chemist** *n*
electrochromatography (ɪˌlɛktrəʊkrəʊmə'tɒgrəfɪ) *n* chromatography effected by the influence of an applied electric field. ► **eˌlectrochro'matic** *adj*
electroconvulsive therapy (ɪˌlɛktrəʊkən'vʌlsɪv) *n Med.* the treatment of certain psychotic conditions by passing an electric current through the brain to induce coma or convulsions. Abbrev.: **ECT.** Also called: **electroshock therapy.** See also **shock therapy.**
electrocorticogram (ɪˌlɛktrəʊ'kɔːtɪkəʊˌgræm) *n* a record of brain waves obtained by placing electrodes directly on the surface of the exposed cerebral cortex. Compare **electroencephalogram, electroencephalograph.**
electrocute (ɪ'lɛktrəˌkjuːt) *vb* (*tr*) **1** to kill as a result of an electric shock. **2** *U.S.* to execute in the electric chair. [C19: from ELECTRO- + (exe)cute] ► **eˌlectro'cution** *n*
electrocyte (ɪ'lɛktrəʊˌsaɪt) *n Zoology.* a specialized muscle or nerve cell that generates electricity, as found in an electric organ.
electrode (ɪ'lɛktrəʊd) *n* **1** a conductor through which an electric current enters or leaves an electrolyte, an electric arc, or an electronic valve or tube. **2** an element in a semiconducting device that emits, collects, or controls the movement of electrons or holes.
electrode efficiency *n Chem.* the ratio of the amount of metal deposited in an electrolytic cell to that theoretically deposited according to Faraday's laws.
electrodeposit (ɪˌlɛktrəʊdɪ'pɒzɪt) *vb* **1** (*tr*) to deposit (a metal) by electrolysis. ◆ *n* **2** the deposit so formed. ► **electrodeposition** (ɪˌlɛktrəʊˌdɛpə'zɪʃən) *n*
electrode potential *n Chem.* the potential difference developed when an electrode of an element is placed in a solution containing ions of that element.
electrodialysis (ɪˌlɛktrəʊdaɪ'ælɪsɪs) *n* dialysis in which electrolytes are removed from a colloidal solution by a potential difference between two electrodes separated by one or more membranes.
electrodynamic (ɪˌlɛktrəʊdaɪ'næmɪk) *adj* **1** operated by an electromotive force between current-carrying coils: *an electrodynamic wattmeter.* **2** of or relating to electrodynamics.
electrodynamics (ɪˌlɛktrəʊdaɪ'næmɪks) *n* (*functioning as sing*) the branch of physics concerned with the interactions between electrical and mechanical forces.
electrodynamometer (ɪˌlɛktrəʊˌdaɪnə'mɒmɪtə) *n* an instrument that uses the interaction of the magnetic fields of two coils to measure electric current, voltage, or power.
electroencephalogram (ɪˌlɛktrəʊɛn'sɛfələˌgræm) *n Med.* the tracing obtained from an electroencephalograph. Abbrev.: **EEG.**
electroencephalograph (ɪˌlɛktrəʊɛn'sɛfələˌgrɑːf, -ˌgræf) *n* an instrument for recording the electrical activity of the brain, usually by means of electrodes placed on the scalp: used to diagnose tumours of the brain, to study brain waves, etc. Abbrev.: **EEG.** See also **brain wave.** ► **eˌlectroenˌcephalo'graphic** *adj* ► **eˌlectroenˌcephalo'graphically** *adv* ► **electroencephalography** (ɪˌlɛktrəʊɛnˌsɛfə'lɒgrəfɪ) *n*
electroendosmosis (ɪˌlɛktrəʊˌɛndɒz'məʊsɪs, -dɒs-) *n* another name for **electro-osmosis.**
electrofluor (ɪ'lɛktrəʊˌfluːɔː) *n Physics.* a transparent material that stores electrical energy and subsequently releases it as light. [C20: from ELECTRO- + FLUOR(ESCENCE)]
electroform (ɪ'lɛktrəˌfɔːm) *vb* to form (a metallic object) by electrolytic deposition on a mould or matrix.
electrogen (ɪ'lɛktrəʊˌdʒɛn) *n* a molecule that emits electrons when it is illuminated. ► **eˌlectro'genic** *adj*
electrograph (ɪ'lɛktrəʊˌgrɑːf, -ˌgræf) *n* **1** an apparatus for engraving metal printing cylinders, esp. in gravure printing. **2** the equipment used for the electrical transmission of pictures. **3a** a recording electrometer. **3b** a graph produced by this instrument. **4** a visual record of the surface composition of a metal, obtained by placing an electrolyte-soaked paper over the metal and passing a current through the paper to an electrode on the other side. ► **electrographic** (ɪˌlɛktrəʊ'græfɪk) *adj* ► **eˌlectro'graphically** *adv* ► **electrography** (ɪlɛk'trɒgrəfɪ, ˌiːlɛk-) *n*
electrojet (ɪ'lɛktrəʊˌdʒɛt) *n* a narrow belt of fast-moving ions in the ionosphere, under the influence of the earth's magnetic field, causing auroral displays.
electrokinetic (ɪˌlɛktrəʊkɪ'nɛtɪk, -kaɪ-) *adj* of or relating to the motion of charged particles and its effects.
electrokinetics (ɪˌlɛktrəʊkɪ'nɛtɪks, -kaɪ-) *n* (*functioning as sing*) the branch of physics concerned with the motion of charged particles.
electroluminescence (ɪˌlɛktrəʊˌluːmɪ'nɛsᵊns) *n Physics.* **a** the emission of light by a phosphor when activated by an alternating field or by a gas when activated by an electric discharge. **b** the light emitted by this process. ► **eˌlectroˌlumi'nescent** *adj*
electrolyse *or U.S.* **electrolyze** (ɪ'lɛktrəʊˌlaɪz) *vb* (*tr*) **1** to decompose (a chemical compound) by electrolysis. **2** to destroy (living tissue, such as hair roots) by electrolysis. [C19: back formation from ELECTROLYSIS on pattern of *analyse*] ► **eˌlectroly'sation** *or U.S.* **eˌlectroly'zation** *n* ► **e'lectroˌlyser** *or U.S.* **e'lectroˌlyzer** *n*
electrolysis (ɪlɛk'trɒlɪsɪs) *n* **1** the conduction of electricity by a solution or melt, esp. the use of this process to induce chemical changes. **2** the destruction of living tissue, such as hair roots, by an electric current, usually for cosmetic reasons. [C19: from ELECTRO- + -LYSIS]
electrolyte (ɪ'lɛktrəʊˌlaɪt) *n* **1** a solution or molten substance that conducts electricity. **2a** a chemical compound that dissociates in solution into ions. **2b** any of the ions themselves.
electrolytic (ɪˌlɛktrəʊ'lɪtɪk) *adj* **1** *Physics.* **1a** of, concerned with, or produced

by electrolysis or electrodeposition. **1b** of, relating to, or containing an electrolyte. ◆ *n* 2 *Electronics.* Also called: **electrolytic capacitor.** a small capacitor consisting of two electrodes separated by an electrolyte. ▶ **e,lectro'lytically** *adv*

electrolytic cell *n* any device in which electrolysis occurs. Sometimes shortened to **cell.**

electrolytic gas *n* a mixture of two parts of hydrogen and one part of oxygen by volume, formed by the electrolysis of water.

electromagnet (ɪˌlɛktrəʊ'mægnɪt) *n* a magnet consisting of an iron or steel core wound with a coil of wire, through which a current is passed.

electromagnetic (ɪˌlɛktrəʊmæg'nɛtɪk) *adj* **1** of, containing, or operated by an electromagnet: *an electromagnetic pump.* **2** of, relating to, or consisting of electromagnetism: *electromagnetic moment.* **3** of or relating to electromagnetic radiation: *the electromagnetic spectrum.* ▶ **e,lectromag'netically** *adv*

electromagnetic field *n* a field of force equivalent to an electric field and a magnetic field at right angles to each other and to the direction of propagation.

electromagnetic interaction *or* **force** *n Physics.* an interaction between charged particles arising from their electric and magnetic fields; its strength is about 100 times weaker than the strong interaction. See **interaction** (sense 2), **electroweak interaction.**

electromagnetic moment *n* a measure of the magnetic strength of a magnet or current-carrying coil, expressed as the torque produced when the magnet or coil is set with its axis perpendicular to unit magnetic flux density. It is measured in ampere metres squared. Symbol: m Also called: **magnetic moment.** Compare **magnetic dipole moment.**

electromagnetic pump *n* a device for pumping liquid metals by placing a pipe between the poles of an electromagnet and passing a current through the liquid metal.

electromagnetic radiation *n* radiation consisting of an electric and magnetic field at right angles to each other and to the direction of propagation. It does not require a supporting medium and travels through empty space at 2.9979×10^8 metres per second. See also **photon.**

electromagnetics (ɪˌlɛktrəʊmæg'nɛtɪks) *n* (*functioning as sing*) *Physics.* another name for **electromagnetism** (sense 2).

electromagnetic spectrum *n* the complete range of electromagnetic radiation from the longest radio waves (wavelength 10^5 metres) to the shortest gamma radiation (wavelength 10^{-13} metre).

electromagnetic unit *n* any unit that belongs to a system of electrical cgs units in which the magnetic constant is given the value of unity and is taken as a pure number. Abbrevs.: **EMU, e.m.u.** Compare **electrostatic unit.**

electromagnetic wave *n* a wave of energy propagated in an electromagnetic field. See also **electromagnetic radiation.**

electromagnetism (ɪˌlɛktrəʊ'mægnɪˌtɪzəm) *n* **1** magnetism produced by an electric current. **2** Also called: **electromagnetics.** the branch of physics concerned with magnetism produced by electric currents and with the interaction of electric and magnetic fields.

electromechanical (ɪˌlɛktrəʊmɪ'kænɪkᵊl) *adj* of, relating to, or concerning an electrically operated mechanical device. ▶ **e,lectrome'chanically** *adv*

electromerism (ɪˌlɛktrəʊ'mɛrɪzəm) *n Chem.* a type of tautomerism in which the isomers (**electromers**) differ in the distribution of charge in their molecules. [C20: from ELECTRO- + (iso)merism]

electrometallurgy (ɪˌlɛktrəʊmɪ'tælədʒɪ, -'mɛtəˌlɜːdʒɪ) *n* metallurgy involving the use of electric-arc furnaces, electrolysis, and other electrical operations. ▶ **e,lectro,metal'lurgical** *adj* ▶ **e,lectromet'allurgist** *n*

electrometer (ɪlɛk'trɒmɪtə, ˌiːlɛk-) *n* an instrument for detecting or determining the magnitude of a potential difference or charge by the electrostatic forces between charged bodies. ▶ **electrometric** (ɪˌlɛktrəʊ'mɛtrɪk) *or* **e,lectro'metrical** *adj* ▶ **e,lectro'metrically** *adv* ▶ **elec'trometry** *n*

electromotive (ɪˌlɛktrəʊ'məʊtɪv) *adj* of, concerned with, producing, or tending to produce an electric current.

electromotive force *n Physics.* **a** a source of energy that can cause a current to flow in an electrical circuit or device. **b** the rate at which energy is drawn from this source when unit current flows through the circuit or device, measured in volts. Abbrevs.: **emf, EMF.** Symbol: *E* Compare **potential difference.**

electromotive series *n Chem.* a series of the metals, together with hydrogen, ranged in the order of their electrode potentials.

electromyography (ɪˌlɛktrəʊmaɪ'ɒgrəfɪ) *n Med.* a technique for recording the electrical activity of muscles: used in the diagnosis of nerve and muscle disorders.

electron (ɪ'lɛktrɒn) *n* a stable elementary particle present in all atoms, orbiting the nucleus in numbers equal to the atomic number of the element; a lepton with a negative charge of 1.6022×10^{-19} coulomb, a rest mass of 9.1096×10^{-31} kilogram, a radius of 2.818×10^{-15} metre, and a spin of ½. [C19: from ELECTRO- + -ON]

electron affinity *n* a measure of the ability of an atom or molecule to form a negative ion, expressed as the energy released when an electron is attached. Symbol: *A*

electron capture *n Physics.* the transformation of an atomic nucleus in which an electron from the atom is spontaneously absorbed into the nucleus. A proton is changed into a neutron, thereby reducing the atomic number by one. A neutrino is emitted. The process may be detected by the consequent emission of the characteristic X-rays of the resultant element. Former name: **K-capture.**

electronegative (ɪˌlɛktrəʊ'nɛgətɪv) *adj* **1** having a negative electric charge. **2** (of an atom, group, molecule, etc.) tending to gain or attract electrons and form negative ions or polarized bonds. Compare **electropositive.**

electronegativity (ɪˌlɛktrəʊˌnɛgə'tɪvɪtɪ) *n* **1** the state of being electronegative. **2** a measure of the ability of a specified atom to attract electrons in a molecule.

electron gun *n* a heated cathode with an associated system of electrodes and coils for producing and focusing a beam of electrons, used esp. in cathode-ray tubes.

electronic (ɪlɛk'trɒnɪk, ˌiːlɛk-) *adj* **1** of, concerned with, using, or operated by devices, such as transistors or valves, in which electrons are conducted through a semiconductor, free space, or gas. **2** of or concerned with electronics. **3** of or concerned with electrons or an electron: *an electronic energy level in a molecule.* **4** involving or concerned with the representation, storage, or transmission of information by electronic systems: *electronic mail; electronic shopping.* ▶ **elec'tronically** *adv*

USAGE *Electronic* is used to refer to equipment, such as television sets, computers, etc., in which the current is controlled by transistors, valves, and similar components and also to the components themselves. *Electrical* is used in a more general sense, often to refer to the use of electricity as a whole as opposed to other forms of energy: *electrical engineering; an electrical appliance. Electric,* in many cases used interchangeably with *electrical,* is often restricted to the description of particular devices or to concepts relating to the flow of current: *electric fire; electric charge.*

electronic configuration *n Chem.* the arrangement of electrons in the orbitals of an atom or molecule.

electronic countermeasures *n Military.* (in electronic warfare) actions intended to interfere with an enemy's use of electromagnetic radiation equipment.

electronic editing *n Radio, television.* editing of a sound or vision tape recording by electronic rerecording rather than by physical cutting.

electronic file cabinet *n Computing.* a device, controlled by software, for the storage and retrieval of information.

electronic flash *n Photog.* an electronic device for producing a very bright flash of light by means of an electric discharge in a gas-filled tube.

electronic flight information systems *pl n* (in an aircraft) the computer-operated visual displays on the flight deck, showing information about the aircraft's state and performance in flight.

electronic funds transfer at point of sale *n* a system for debiting a retail sale direct to the customer's bank, building-society, or credit-card account by means of a computer link using the telephone network. Acronym: **EFTPOS.**

electronic game *n* any of various small hand-held computerized games, usually battery operated, having a small screen on which graphics are displayed and buttons to operate the game.

electronic graphics *pl n* (on television) the production of graphic designs and text by electronic means.

electronic ignition *n* any system that uses an electronic circuit to supply the voltage to the sparking plugs of an internal-combustion engine.

electronic keyboard *n* a typewriter keyboard used to operate an electronic device such as a computer, word processor, etc.

electronic mail *n* the transmission and distribution of messages, information, facsimiles of documents, etc., from one computer terminal to another. Abbrevs.: **E-mail, e-mail, email.**

electronic mailbox *n* a device used to store electronic mail.

electronic music *n* a form of music consisting of sounds produced by oscillating electric currents either controlled from an instrument panel or keyboard or prerecorded on magnetic tape.

electronic office *n* integrated computer systems designed to handle office work.

electronic organ *n Music.* an electrophonic instrument played by means of a keyboard, in which sounds are produced and amplified by any of various electronic or electrical means. See also **synthesizer.**

electronic organizer *n* See **personal organizer** (sense 2).

electronic point of sale *n* a computerized system for recording sales in retail shops, using a laser scanner at the cash till to read bar codes on the packages of the items sold. Acronym: **EPOS.**

electronic publishing *n* the publication of information on magnetic tape, disks, etc., so that it can be accessed by a computer.

electronics (ɪlɛk'trɒnɪks, ˌiːlɛk-) *n* **1** (*functioning as sing*) the science and technology concerned with the development, behaviour, and applications of electronic devices and circuits. **2** (*functioning as pl*) the circuits and devices of a piece of electronic equipment: *the electronics of a television set.*

electronic surveillance *n* **1** the use of such electronic devices as television monitors, video cameras, etc., to prevent burglary, shop lifting, break-ins, etc. **2** monitoring events, conversations, etc., at a distance by electronic means, esp. by such covert means as wire tapping or bugging.

electronic tag *n* another name for **tag**[1] (sense 2).

electronic transfer of funds *n* the transfer of money from one bank or building-society account to another by means of a computer link using the telephone network. Abbrev.: **ETF.**

electronic warfare *n* the military use of electronics to prevent or reduce an enemy's effective use and to protect friendly use of electromagnetic radiation equipment.

electron lens *n* a system, such as an arrangement of electrodes or magnets, that produces a field for focusing a beam of electrons.

electron micrograph *n* a photograph of a specimen taken through an electron microscope.

electron microscope *n* a powerful type of microscope that uses electrons, rather than light, and electron lenses to produce a magnified image.

electron multiplier *n Physics.* a device for amplifying and measuring a flux of electrons. Each electron hits an anode surface and releases secondary electrons that are accelerated to a second surface; after several such stages a measurable pulse of current is obtained.

electron optics *n* (*functioning as sing*) the study and use of beams of electrons and of their deflection and focusing by electric and magnetic fields.

electron paramagnetic resonance *n Physics.* another name for **electron spin resonance.** Abbrev.: **EPR.**

electron probe microanalysis *n* a technique for the analysis of a very small amount of material by bombarding it with a narrow beam of electrons and examining the resulting X-ray emission spectrum.

electron spin resonance *n* a technique for investigating paramagnetic substances by subjecting them to high-frequency radiation in a strong magnetic field. Changes in the spin of unpaired electrons cause radiation to be absorbed at certain frequencies. Abbrev.: **ESR.** See also **nuclear magnetic resonance.**

electron telescope *n* an astronomical telescope with an attachment for converting the infrared radiation emitted from the surface of planets into a visible image.

electron transport *n Biochem.* the metabolic process in mitochondria or chloroplasts, in which electrons are transferred in stages from energy-rich compounds to molecular oxygen with liberation of energy.

electron tube *n* an electrical device, such as a valve, in which a flow of electrons between electrodes takes place. Sometimes shortened to **tube.**

electronvolt (ɪˌlɛktrɒnˈvəʊlt) *n* a unit of energy equal to the work done on an electron accelerated through a potential difference of 1 volt. 1 electronvolt is equivalent to 1.602×10^{-19} joule. Symbol: eV

electro-osmosis *n* movement of liquid through a capillary tube or membrane under the influence of an electric field: used in controlling rising damp. Also called: **electroendosmosis.**

electropalatography (ɪˌlɛktrəʊˌpæləˈtɒgrəfɪ) *n* the study of the movements of the tongue during speech using touch-sensitive electrodes in the mouth linked to a computer.

electrophilic (ɪˌlɛktrəʊˈfɪlɪk) *adj Chem.* having or involving an affinity for negative charge. Electrophilic reagents (**electrophiles**) are atoms, molecules, and ions that behave as electron acceptors. Compare **nucleophilic.** ▸ **electrophile** (ɪˈlɛktrəʊˌfaɪl) *n*

electrophone (ɪˈlɛktrəˌfəʊn) *n Music.* any instrument whose sound is produced by the oscillation of an electric current, such as an electronic organ, synthesizer, etc. ▸ **electrophonic** (ɪˌlɛktrəˈfɒnɪk) *adj*

electrophoresis (ɪˌlɛktrəʊfəˈriːsɪs) *n* the motion of charged particles in a colloid under the influence of an applied electric field. Also called: **cataphoresis.** ▸ **electrophoretic** (ɪˌlɛktrəʊfəˈrɛtɪk) *adj*

electrophorus (ɪlɛkˈtrɒfərəs, ˌiːlɛk-) *n* an apparatus for generating static electricity. It consists of an insulating plate charged by friction and used to charge a metal plate by induction. **[C18:** from ELECTRO- + *-phorus,* from Greek *-phoros* bearing, from *pherein* to bear**]**

electrophotography (ɪˌlɛktrəʊˌfəˈtɒgrəfɪ) *n* photography in which an image is transferred onto paper by means of electrical rather than chemical processes. ▸ **eˌlectroˌphotoˈgraphic** *adj*

electrophysiology (ɪˌlɛktrəʊˌfɪzɪˈɒlədʒɪ) *n* the branch of medical science concerned with the electrical activity associated with bodily processes. ▸ **eˌlectroˌphysioˈlogical** *adj* ▸ **eˌlectroˌphysiˈologist** *n*

electroplate (ɪˈlɛktrəʊˌpleɪt) *vb* **1** (*tr*) to plate (an object) by electrolysis. ◆ *n* **2** electroplated articles collectively, esp. when plated with silver. ◆ *adj* **3** coated with metal by electrolysis; electroplated. ▸ **eˈlectroˌplater** *n*

electropositive (ɪˌlɛktrəʊˈpɒzɪtɪv) *adj* **1** having a positive electric charge. **2** (of an atom, group, molecule, etc.) tending to release electrons and form positive ions or polarized bonds. Compare **electronegative.**

electroreceptor (ɪˈlɛktrəʊrɪˌsɛptə) *n Zoology.* an organ, present in some fishes, that detects electrical discharges.

electrorheology (ɪˌlɛktrəʊrɪˈɒlədʒɪ) *n* **1** the study of the flow of fluids under the influence of electric fields. **2** the way in which fluid flow is influenced by an electric field. ▸ **eˌlectrorheoˈlogical** *adj*

electroscope (ɪˈlɛktrəʊˌskəʊp) *n* an apparatus for detecting an electric charge, typically consisting of a rod holding two gold foils that separate when a charge is applied. ▸ **electroscopic** (ɪˌlɛktrəʊˈskɒpɪk) *adj*

electroshock therapy (ɪˈlɛktrəʊˌʃɒk) *n* another name for **electroconvulsive therapy.**

electrostatic (ɪˌlɛktrəʊˈstætɪk) *adj* **1** of, concerned with, producing, or caused by static electricity. **2** concerned with electrostatics. ▸ **eˌlectroˈstatically** *adv*

electrostatic field *n* an electric field associated with a static electric field.

electrostatic generator *n* any device for producing a high voltage by building up a charge of static electricity.

electrostatic lens *n* an electron lens consisting of a system of metal electrodes, the electrostatic field of which focuses the charged particles.

electrostatic precipitation *n Chem.* the removal of suspended solid particles from a gas by giving them an electric charge and attracting them to charged plates.

electrostatics (ɪˌlɛktrəʊˈstætɪks) *n* (*functioning as sing*) the branch of physics concerned with static electricity.

electrostatic unit *n* any unit that belongs to a system of electrical cgs units in which the electric constant is given the value of unity and is taken as a pure number. Abbrevs.: **ESU, e.s.u.** Compare **electromagnetic unit.**

electrostriction (ɪˌlɛktrəʊˈstrɪkʃən) *n* the change in dimensions of a dielectric occurring as an elastic strain when an electric field is applied.

electrosurgery (ɪˌlɛktrəʊˈsɜːdʒərɪ) *n* the surgical use of electricity, as in cauterization. ▸ **eˌlectroˈsurgical** *adj*

electrotechnics (ɪˌlɛktrəʊˈtɛknɪks) *n* (*functioning as sing*) another name for **electrotechnology.** ▸ **eˌlectroˈtechnical** *adj* ▸ **eˌlectrotechˈnician** *n*

electrotechnology (ɪˌlɛktrəʊtɛkˈnɒlədʒɪ) *n* the technological use of electric power.

electrotherapeutics (ɪˌlɛktrəʊˌθɛrəˈpjuːtɪks) *n* (*functioning as sing*) the branch of medical science concerned with the use of electrotherapy. ▸ **eˌlectroˌtheraˈpeutic** *or* **eˌlectroˌtheraˈpeutical** *adj*

electrotherapy (ɪˌlɛktrəʊˈθɛrəpɪ) *n* treatment in which electric currents are passed through the tissues to stimulate muscle function in paralysed patients. ▸ **eˌlectroˈtherapist** *n*

electrothermal (ɪˌlɛktrəʊˈθɜːməl) *or* **electrothermic** (ɪˌlɛktrəʊˈθɜːmɪk) *adj* concerned with both electricity and heat, esp. the production of electricity by heat.

electrothermal printer (ɪˌlɛktrəʊˈθɜːməl) *n Computing.* a printer that produces characters by burning the image on specially coated paper. Also called: **thermal printer.**

electrotint (ɪˈlɛktrəʊˌtɪnt) *n* a printing block made by drawing on a metal plate with varnish and electrolytically depositing a layer of metal on the nonvarnished areas of the plate.

electrotonus (ɪlɛkˈtrɒtənəs, ˌiːlɛk-) *n Physiol.* the change in the state of irritability and conductivity of a nerve or muscle caused by the passage of an electric current. **[C19:** from New Latin, from ELECTRO- + Latin *tonus* TONE**]** ▸ **electrotonic** (ɪˌlɛktrəʊˈtɒnɪk) *adj*

electrotype (ɪˈlɛktrəʊˌtaɪp) *n* **1** a duplicate printing plate made by electrolytically depositing a layer of copper or nickel onto a mould of the original. Sometimes shortened to **electro.** ◆ *vb* **2** (*tr*) to make an electrotype of (printed matter, illustrations, etc.). ▸ **eˈlectroˌtyper** *n*

electrovalency (ɪˌlɛktrəʊˈveɪlənsɪ) *or* **electrovalence** *n Chem.* the valency of a substance in forming ions, equal to the number of electrons gained or lost. ▸ **eˌlectroˈvalent** *adj* ▸ **eˌlectroˈvalently** *adv*

electrovalent bond *n* a type of chemical bond in which one atom loses an electron to form a positive ion and the other atom gains the electron to form a negative ion. The resulting ions are held together by electrostatic attraction. Also called: **ionic bond.** Compare **covalent bond.**

electroweak interaction (ɪˌlɛktrəʊˈwiːk) *n Physics.* a type of fundamental interaction combining both the electromagnetic interaction and the weak interaction. See also **electromagnetic interaction, weak interaction.**

electrum (ɪˈlɛktrəm) *n* an alloy of gold (55–88 per cent) and silver used for jewellery and ornaments. **[C14:** from Latin, from Greek *ēlektron* amber**]**

electuary (ɪˈlɛktjʊərɪ) *n, pl* **-aries.** *Med.* a paste taken orally, containing a drug mixed with syrup or honey. **[C14:** from Late Latin *ēlectuārium,* probably from Greek *ekleikton* electuary, from *ekleikhein* to lick out, from *leikhein* to lick**]**

eleemosynary (ˌɛlɪiːˈmɒsɪnərɪ) *adj* **1** of, concerned with, or dependent on charity. **2** given as an act of charity. **[C17:** from Church Latin *eleēmosyna* ALMS**]**

elegance (ˈɛlɪgəns) *or* **elegancy** *n, pl* **-gances** *or* **-gancies. 1** dignified grace in appearance, movement, or behaviour. **2** good taste in design, style, arrangement, etc. **3** something elegant; a refinement.

elegant (ˈɛlɪgənt) *adj* **1** tasteful in dress, style, or design. **2** dignified and graceful in appearance, behaviour, etc. **3** cleverly simple; ingenious: *an elegant solution to a problem.* **[C16:** from Latin *ēlegāns* tasteful, related to *ēligere* to select; see ELECT**]** ▸ **ˈelegantly** *adv*

elegiac (ˌɛlɪˈdʒaɪək) *adj* **1** resembling, characteristic of, relating to, or appropriate to an elegy. **2** lamenting; mournful; plaintive. **3** denoting or written in elegiac couplets or elegiac stanzas. ◆ *n* **4** (*often pl*) an elegiac couplet or stanza. ▸ **ˌeleˈgiacally** *adv*

elegiac couplet *n Classical prosody.* a couplet composed of a dactylic hexameter followed by a dactylic pentameter.

elegiac stanza *n Prosody.* a quatrain in iambic pentameters with alternate lines rhyming.

elegize *or* **elegise** (ˈɛlɪˌdʒaɪz) *vb* **1** to compose an elegy or elegies (in memory of). **2** (*intr*) to write elegiacally. ▸ **ˈelegist** *n*

elegy (ˈɛlɪdʒɪ) *n, pl* **-gies. 1** a mournful or plaintive poem or song, esp. a lament for the dead. **2** poetry or a poem written in elegiac couplets or stanzas. **[C16:** via French and Latin from Greek *elegeia,* from *elegos* lament sung to flute accompaniment**]**

USAGE Avoid confusion with **eulogy.**

Eleia (ˈiːlɪə) *n* a variant spelling of **Elia**[1].

elem. *abbrev. for:* **1** element(s). **2** elementary.

element (ˈɛlɪmənt) *n* **1** any of the 118 known substances (of which 93 occur naturally) that consist of atoms with the same number of protons in their nuclei. Compare **compound**[1] (sense 1). **2** one of the fundamental or irreducible components making up a whole. **3** a cause that contributes to a result; factor. **4** any group that is part of a larger unit, such as a military formation. **5** a small amount; hint: *an element of sarcasm in her voice.* **6** a distinguishable section of a social group: *he belonged to the stable element in the expedition.* **7** the most favourable environment for an animal or plant. **8** the situation in which a person is happiest or most effective (esp. in the phrases **in** or **out of one's element**). **9** the resistance wire and its former that constitute the electrical heater in a cooker, heater, etc. **10** *Electronics.* another name for **component** (sense 2). **11** one of the four substances thought in ancient and medieval cosmology to constitute the universe (earth, air, water, or fire). **12** (*pl*) atmospheric conditions or forces, esp. wind, rain, and cold: *exposed to the elements.* **13** (*pl*) the first principles of a subject. **14** *Geometry.* a point, line, plane, or part of a geometric figure. **15** *Maths.* **15a** any of the terms in the array of a determinant or matrix. **15b** one of the infinitesimally small quantities summed by an integral, often represented by the expression following the integral sign: *in* $\int_a^b f(x)dx$, $f(x)dx$ *is an element of area.* **16** *Maths, logic.* one of the objects or numbers that together constitute a set. **17** *Christianity.* the bread or wine consecrated in the Eucharist. **18** *Astronomy.* any of the numerical quantities, such as the major axis or eccentricity, used in describing the orbit of a planet, satellite, etc. **19** one of the vertical or horizontal rods forming a television or VHF radio receiving aerial. 20 *Physics.* a component of a compound lens. [C13: from Latin *elementum* a first principle, alphabet, element, of uncertain origin]

elemental (ˌɛlɪˈmɛntᵊl) *adj* **1** fundamental; basic; primal: *the elemental needs of man.* **2** motivated by or symbolic of primitive and powerful natural forces or passions: *elemental rites of worship.* **3** of or relating to earth, air, water, and fire considered as elements. **4** of or relating to atmospheric forces, esp. wind, rain, and cold. **5** of, relating to, or denoting a chemical element. ♦ *n* **6** *Rare.* a spirit or force that is said to appear in physical form. ▸ **ˌeleˈmentally** *adv* ▸ **ˌeleˈmentalˌism** *n*

elementary (ˌɛlɪˈmɛntərɪ, -trɪ) *adj* **1** not difficult; simple; rudimentary. **2** of or concerned with the first principles of a subject; introductory or fundamental. **3** *Maths.* (of a function) having the form of an algebraic, exponential, trigonometric, or a logarithmic function, or any combination of these. **4** *Chem.* another word for **elemental** (sense 5). ▸ **ˌeleˈmentarily** *adv* ▸ **ˌeleˈmentariness** *n*

elementary particle *n* any of several entities, such as electrons, neutrons, or protons, that are less complex than atoms and are regarded as the constituents of all matter. Also called: **fundamental particle.**

elementary school *n* **1** *Brit.* a former name for **primary school. 2** Also called (in the U.S.): **grade school, grammar school.** *U.S. and Canadian.* a state school in which instruction is given for the first six to eight years of a child's education.

elemi (ˈɛlɪmɪ) *n, pl* **-mis.** any of various fragrant resins obtained from tropical trees, esp. trees of the family *Burseraceae:* used in making varnishes, ointments, inks, etc. [C16: via Spanish from Arabic *al-lāmi* the elemi]

elenchus (ɪˈlɛŋkəs) *n, pl* **-chi** (-kaɪ). *Logic.* **1** refutation of an argument by proving the contrary of its conclusion, esp. syllogistically. **2 Socratic elenchus.** the drawing out of the consequences of a position in order to show them to be contrary to some accepted position. [C17: from Latin, from Greek *elenkhos* refutation, from *elenkhein* to put to shame, refute]

elenctic (ɪˈlɛŋktɪk) *adj Logic.* refuting an argument by proving the falsehood of its conclusion. Compare **deictic** (sense 1).

eleoptene *or* **elaeoptene** (ˌɛlɪˈɒptiːn) *n* the liquid part of a volatile oil. [C20: from Greek *elaion* oil + *ptēnos* having wings, volatile; related to Greek *petesthai* to fly]

elephant (ˈɛlɪfənt) *n, pl* **-phants** *or* **-phant. 1** either of the two proboscidean mammals of the family *Elephantidae.* The **African elephant** (*Loxodonta africana*) is the larger species, with large flapping ears and a less humped back than the **Indian elephant** (*Elephas maximus*), of S and SE Asia. **2** *Chiefly Brit.* a size of writing paper, 23 by 28 inches. [C13: from Latin *elephantus,* from Greek *elephas* elephant, ivory, of uncertain origin] ▸ **ˈelephanˌtoid** *adj*

elephant bird *n* another name for **aepyornis.**

elephant grass *n* any of various stout tropical grasses or grasslike plants, esp. *Pennisetum purpureum,* and *Typha elephantina,* a type of reed mace.

elephantiasis (ˌɛlɪfənˈtaɪəsɪs) *n Pathol.* a complication of chronic filariasis, in which nematode worms block the lymphatic vessels, usually in the legs or scrotum, causing extreme enlargement of the affected area. See also **filariasis.** [C16: via Latin from Greek, from *elephas* ELEPHANT + -IASIS] ▸ **elephantiasic** (ˌɛlɪˌfæntɪˈæsɪk, -fənˈtaɪəsɪk) *adj*

elephantine (ˌɛlɪˈfæntaɪn) *adj* **1** denoting, relating to, or characteristic of an elephant or elephants. **2** huge, clumsy, or ponderous.

elephant seal *n* either of two large earless seals, *Mirounga leonina* of southern oceans or *M. angustirostris* of the N Atlantic, the males of which have a long trunklike snout.

elephant's-ear *n* **1** any aroid plant of the genus *Colocasia,* of tropical Asia and Polynesia, having very large heart-shaped leaves: grown for ornament and for their edible tubers. See also **taro. 2** any of various cultivated begonias with large showy leaves.

elephant's-foot *or* **elephant foot** *n* a monocotyledonous plant, *Testudinaria elephantipes,* of southern Africa, with a very large starchy tuberous stem, covered in corky scales: family *Dioscoreaceae.*

elephant shrew *n* any small active African mammal of the family *Macroscelididae* and order *Macroscelidea,* having an elongated nose, large ears, and long hind legs.

Eleusinian mysteries *pl n* a mystical religious festival, held in September at Eleusis in classical times, in which initiates celebrated Persephone, Demeter, and Dionysus.

Eleusis (ɪˈluːsɪs) *n* a town in Greece, in Attica about 23 km (14 miles) west of Athens, of which it is now an industrial suburb. Modern Greek name: **Elevsís.** ▸ **Eleusinian** (ˌɛljuˈsɪnɪən) *n, adj*

elev. *or* **el.** *abbrev. for* elevation.

elevate (ˈɛlɪˌveɪt) *vb* (*tr*) **1** to move to a higher place. **2** to raise in rank or status; promote. **3** to put in a cheerful mood; elate. **4** to put on a higher cultural plane; uplift: *to elevate the tone of a conversation.* **5** to raise the axis of a gun. **6** to raise the intensity or pitch of (the voice). **7** *R.C. Church.* to lift up (the Host) at Mass for adoration. [C15: from Latin *ēlevāre* from *levāre* to raise, from *levis* (adj) light] ▸ **ˌeleˈvatory** *adj*

elevated (ˈɛlɪˌveɪtɪd) *adj* **1** raised to or being at a higher level. **2** inflated or lofty; exalted: *an elevated opinion of oneself.* **3** in a cheerful mood; elated. **4** *Informal.* slightly drunk. ♦ *n* **5** *U.S.* short for **elevated railway** *or* **railroad.**

elevated railway *or* **railroad** *n U.S.* an urban railway track built on supports above a road.

elevation (ˌɛlɪˈveɪʃən) *n* **1** the act of elevating or the state of being elevated. **2** the height of something above a given or implied place, esp. above sea level. **3** a raised area; height. **4** nobleness or grandeur; loftiness: *elevation of thought.* **5** a drawing to scale of the external face of a building or structure. Compare **plan** (sense 3), **ground plan** (sense 1). **6** the external face of a building or structure. **7** a ballet dancer's ability to leap high. **8** *R.C. Church.* the lifting up of the Host at Mass for adoration. **9** *Astronomy.* another name for **altitude** (sense 3). **10** the angle formed between the muzzle of a gun and the horizontal. **11** *Surveying.* the angular distance between the plane through a point of observation and an object above it. Compare **depression** (sense 7). **12** *Linguistics.* another term for **amelioration.** ▸ **ˌeleˈvational** *adj*

elevator (ˈɛlɪˌveɪtə) *n* **1** a person or thing that elevates. **2** a mechanical hoist for raising something, esp. grain or coal, often consisting of a chain of scoops linked together on a conveyor belt. **3** the U.S. and Canadian name for **lift**[1] (sense 17a). **4** *Chiefly U.S. and Canadian.* a large granary equipped with an elevator and, usually, facilities for cleaning and grading the grain. **5** any muscle that raises a part of the body. **6** a surgical instrument for lifting a part of the body. **7** a control surface on the tailplane of an aircraft, for making it climb or descend.

eleven (ɪˈlɛvᵊn) *n* **1** the cardinal number that is the sum of ten and one. **2** a numeral 11, XI, etc., representing this number. **3** something representing, represented by, or consisting of 11 units. **4** (*functioning as sing or pl*) a team of 11 players in football, cricket, hockey, etc. **5** Also called: **eleven o'clock.** eleven hours after noon or midnight. ♦ *determiner* **6a** amounting to eleven: *eleven chances.* **6b** (*as pronoun*): *have another eleven today.* [Old English *endleofan;* related to Old Norse *ellefo,* Gothic *ainlif,* Old Frisian *andlova,* Old High German *einlif*]

eleven-plus *n* (esp. formerly) an examination, taken by children aged 11 or 12, that determines the type of secondary education a child will be given.

elevenses (ɪˈlɛvᵊnzɪz) *pl n* (*sometimes functioning as sing*) *Brit. informal.* a light snack, usually with tea or coffee, taken in mid-morning.

eleventh (ɪˈlɛvᵊnθ) *adj* **1** (*usually prenominal*) **1a** coming after the tenth in numbering or counting order, position, time, etc.; being the ordinal number of *eleven:* often written 11th. **1b** (*as pronoun*): *the eleventh in succession.* ♦ *n* **2a** one of 11 equal or nearly equal parts of an object, quantity, measurement, etc. **2b** (*as modifier*): *an eleventh part.* **3** the fraction equal to one divided by 11 (1/11). **4** *Music.* **4a** an interval of one octave plus one fourth. **4b** See **eleventh chord.**

eleventh chord *n* a chord much used in jazz, consisting of a major or minor triad upon which are superimposed the seventh, ninth, and eleventh above the root.

eleventh hour *n* **a** the latest possible time; last minute. **b** (*as modifier*): *an eleventh-hour decision.*

elevon (ˈɛlɪˌvɒn) *n* an aircraft control surface that combines the functions of an elevator and aileron, usually fitted to tailless or delta-wing aircraft. [C20: from ELEV(ATOR + AILER)ON]

Elevsís (ˌɛlɛfˈsis) *n* transliteration of the Modern Greek name for **Eleusis.**

elf (ɛlf) *n, pl* **elves** (ɛlvz). **1** (in folklore) one of a kind of legendary beings, usually characterized as small, manlike, and mischievous. **2** a mischievous or whimsical child. [Old English *ælf;* related to Old Norse *elfr* elf, Middle Low German *alf* incubus, Latin *albus* white] ▸ **ˈelfˌlike** *adj*

ELF *abbrev. for* extremely low frequency.

El Faiyûm (ɛl faɪˈjuːm) *or* **Al Faiyûm** (æl faɪˈjuːm) *n* a city in N Egypt: a site of towns going back at least to the 12th dynasty. Pop.: 250 000 (1992 est.).

elf-cup *n* any of various cup-shaped ascomycetous fungi of the order *Pezizales,* often strikingly coloured, such as the **orange-peel elf-cup** (*Aleuria aurantia*), that is bright orange inside and dirty white outside, and the **scarlet elf-cup** (*Sarcoscypha coccinea*).

El Ferrol (*Spanish* ɛl feˈrrɔl) *n* a port in NW Spain, on the Atlantic: fortified naval base, with a deep natural harbour. Pop.: 82 371 (1991). Official name (since 1939): **El Ferrol del Caudillo** (dɛl kauˈðiʎo).

elfin (ˈɛlfɪn) *adj* **1** of, relating to, or like an elf or elves. **2** small, delicate, and charming.

elfish (ˈɛlfɪʃ) *or* **elvish** *adj* **1** of, relating to, or like an elf or elves; charmingly mischievous or sprightly; impish. ♦ *n* **2** the supposed language of elves. ▸ **ˈelfishly** *or* **ˈelvishly** *adv* ▸ **ˈelfishness** *or* **ˈelvishness** *n*

elfland (ˈɛlfˌlænd) *n* another name for **fairyland.**

elflock (ˈɛlfˌlɒk) *n* a lock of hair, fancifully regarded as having been tangled by the elves.

Elgar (ˈɛlgɑː) *n* Sir **Edward (William).** 1857–1934, English composer, whose works include the *Enigma Variations* (1899), the oratorio *The Dream of Gerontius* (1900), two symphonies, a cello concerto, and a violin concerto.

Elgin (ˈɛlgɪn) *n* a market town in NE Scotland, the administrative centre of Moray, on the River Lossie: ruined 13th-century cathedral: distilling, engineering. Pop.: 19 027 (1991).

Elgin marbles *pl n* a group of 5th-century B.C. Greek sculptures originally decorating the Parthenon in Athens, brought to England by Thomas Bruce, seventh Earl of Elgin (1766–1841), and now at the British Museum.

El Gîza (ɛl ˈgiːzə) *n* a city in NE Egypt, on the W bank of the Nile opposite Cairo: nearby are the Great Pyramid of Cheops (Khufu) and the Sphinx. Pop.: 2 144 000 (1992 est.).

Elgon (ˈɛlgɒn) *n* **Mount.** an extinct volcano in E Africa, on the Kenya-Uganda border. Height: 4321 m (14 178 ft.).

El Greco (ɛl ˈgrɛkəʊ) *n* real name *Domenikos Theotocopoulos.* 1541–1614, Spanish painter, born in Crete; noted for his elongated human forms and dramatic use of colour.

Eli (ˈiːlaɪ) *n Old Testament.* the highest priest at Shiloh and teacher of Samuel (I Samuel 1–3).

Elia[1] *or* **Eleia** (ˈiːlɪə) *n* a department of SW Greece, in the W Peloponnese: in ancient times most of the region formed the state of Elis. Pop.: 179 429 (1991). Area: 2681 sq. km (1035 sq. miles). Modern Greek name: **Ilía.**

Elia[2] (ˈiːlɪə) *n* the pen name of (Charles) **Lamb.**

Eliade (*Romanian* eˈljaːde) *n* **Mircea.** 1907–86, Romanian scholar and writer, noted for his study of religious symbolism. His works include *Patterns of Comparative Religion* (1949).

Elias (ɪ'laɪəs) *n Bible.* the Douay spelling of **Elijah.**

elicit (ɪ'lɪsɪt) *vb (tr)* **1** to give rise to; evoke: *to elicit a sharp retort.* **2** to bring to light: *to elicit the truth.* [C17: from Latin *ēlicere* to lure forth, from *licere* to entice] ▸ **e'licitable** *adj* ▸ **e,lici'tation** *n* ▸ **e'licitor** *n*

elide (ɪ'laɪd) *vb Phonetics.* to undergo or cause to undergo elision. [C16: from Latin *ēlīdere* to knock, from *laedere* to hit, wound] ▸ **e'lidible** *adj*

eligible ('ɛlɪdʒəbᵊl) *adj* **1** fit, worthy, or qualified, as for an office or function. **2** desirable and worthy of being chosen, esp. as a spouse: *an eligible young man.* [C15: from Late Latin *ēligibilis* able to be chosen, from *ēligere* to ELECT] ▸ **,eligi'bility** *n* ▸ **'eligibly** *adv*

Elijah (ɪ'laɪdʒə) *n Old Testament.* a Hebrew prophet of the 9th century B.C., who was persecuted for denouncing Ahab and Jezebel. (I Kings 17–21: 21; II Kings 1–2:18).

Elikón (ɛli'kɔn) *n* transliteration of the Modern Greek name for **Helicon.**

eliminate (ɪ'lɪmɪ,neɪt) *vb (tr)* **1** to remove or take out; get rid of. **2** to reject as trivial or irrelevant; omit from consideration. **3** to remove (a competitor, team, etc.) from a contest, usually by defeat. **4** *Slang.* to murder in a cold-blooded manner. **5** *Physiol.* to expel (waste matter) from the body. **6** *Maths.* to remove (an unknown variable) from two or more simultaneous equations. [C16: from Latin *ēlīmināre* to turn out of the house, from *e-* out + *līmen* threshold] ▸ **e'liminable** *adj* ▸ **e,limina'bility** *n* ▸ **e'liminant** *n* ▸ **e'liminative** *or* **e'liminatory** *adj* ▸ **e'limi,nator** *n*

USAGE *Eliminate* is sometimes wrongly used to talk about avoiding the repetition of something undesirable: *we must prevent* (not *eliminate*) *further mistakes of this kind.*

elimination (ɪ,lɪmɪ'neɪʃən) *n* **1** the act of eliminating or the state of being eliminated. **2** *Logic.* (qualified by the name of an operation) a syntactic rule specifying the conditions under which a formula or statement containing the specified operation may permit the derivation of others that do not contain it: *conjunction-elimination; universal elimination.* **3** *Chem.* a type of chemical reaction involving the loss of a simple molecule, such as water or carbon dioxide.

Eliot ('ɛlɪət) *n* **1 George,** real name *Mary Ann Evans.* 1819–80, English novelist, noted for her analysis of provincial Victorian society. Her best-known novels include *Adam Bede* (1859), *The Mill on the Floss* (1860), *Silas Marner* (1861), and *Middlemarch* (1872). **2** Sir **John.** 1592–1632, English statesman, a leader of parliamentary opposition to Charles I. **3 T(homas) S(tearns).** 1888–1965, British poet, dramatist, and critic, born in the U.S. His poetry includes *Prufrock and Other Observations* (1917), *The Waste Land* (1922), *Ash Wednesday* (1930), and *Four Quartets* (1943). Among his verse plays are *Murder in the Cathedral* (1935), *The Family Reunion* (1939), *The Cocktail Party* (1950), and *The Confidential Clerk* (1954): Nobel prize for literature 1948.

Elis ('iːlɪs) *n* an ancient city-state of SW Greece, in the NW Peloponnese: site of the ancient Olympic games.

ELISA (ɪ'laɪzə) *n acronym for* enzyme-linked immunosorbent assay: an immunological technique for accurately measuring the amount of a substance, for example in a blood sample.

Elisabeth (ɪ'lɪzəbəθ) *n* a variant spelling of **Elizabeth**[2] (sense 1).

Élisabethville (ɪ'lɪzəbəθ,vɪl) *n* the former name (until 1966) of **Lubumbashi.**

Elisavetgrad (*Russian* jɪliza'vjetgrət) *n* a former name (until 1924) of **Kirovograd.**

Elisavetpol (*Russian* jɪliza'vjetpəlj) *n* a former name (until 1920) of **Kirovabad.**

Elisha (ɪ'laɪʃə) *n Old Testament.* a Hebrew prophet of the 9th century B.C.: successor of Elijah (II Kings 3–9).

elision (ɪ'lɪʒən) *n* **1** the omission of a syllable or vowel at the beginning or end of a word, esp. when a word ending with a vowel is next to one beginning with a vowel. **2** any omission of a part or parts. [C16: from Latin *ēlīsiō,* from *ēlīdere* to ELIDE]

elite *or* **élite** (ɪ'liːt, eɪ-) *n* **1** (*sometimes functioning as pl*) the most powerful, rich, gifted, or educated members of a group, community, etc. **2** Also called: **twelve pitch.** a typewriter typesize having 12 characters to the inch. ◆ *adj* **3** of, relating to, or suitable for an elite; exclusive. [C18: from French, from Old French *eslit* chosen, from *eslire* to choose, from Latin *ēligere* to ELECT]

elitism (ɪ'liːtɪzəm, eɪ-) *n* **1a** the belief that society should be governed by a select group of gifted and highly educated individuals. **1b** such government. **2** pride in or awareness of being one of an elite group. ▸ **e'litist** *adj, n*

elixir (ɪ'lɪksə) *n* **1** an alchemical preparation supposed to be capable of prolonging life indefinitely (**elixir of life**) or of transmuting base metals into gold. **2** anything that purports to be a sovereign remedy; panacea. **3** an underlying principle; quintessence. **4** a liquid containing a medicinal drug with syrup, glycerine, or alcohol added to mask its unpleasant taste. [C14: from Medieval Latin, from Arabic *al iksīr* the elixir, probably from Greek *xērion* powder used for drying wounds, from *xēros* dry]

Eliz. *abbrev. for* Elizabethan.

Elizabeth[1] (ɪ'lɪzəbəθ) *n* **1** a city in NE New Jersey, on Newark Bay. Pop.: 110 149 (1996 est.). **2** a town in SE South Australia, near Adelaide. Pop.: 34 000 (latest est.).

Elizabeth[2] (ɪ'lɪzəbəθ) *n* **1 Saint.** Also: **Elisabeth.** *New Testament.* the wife of Zacharias, mother of John the Baptist, and kinswoman of the Virgin Mary. Feast day: Nov. 5 or 8. **2** pen name *Carmen Sylva.* 1843–1916, queen of Romania (1881–1914) and author. **3** Russian name *Yelizaveta Petrovna.* 1709–62, empress of Russia (1741–62); daughter of Peter the Great. **4** title *the Queen Mother;* original name Lady *Elizabeth Bowes-Lyon.* born 1900, queen of Great Britain and Northern Ireland (1936–52) as the wife of George VI; mother of Elizabeth II.

Elizabeth I *n* 1533–1603, queen of England (1558–1603); daughter of Henry VIII and Anne Boleyn. She established the Church of England (1559) and put an end to Catholic plots, notably by executing Mary Queen of Scots (1587) and defeating the Spanish Armada (1588). Her reign was notable for commercial growth, maritime expansion, and the flourishing of literature, music, and architecture.

Elizabeth II *n* born 1926, queen of Great Britain and Northern Ireland from 1952; daughter of George VI.

Elizabethan (ɪ,lɪzə'biːθən) *adj* **1** of, characteristic of, or relating to England or its culture in the age of Elizabeth I or to the United Kingdom or its culture in the age of Elizabeth II. **2** of, relating to, or designating a style of architecture used in England during the reign of Elizabeth I, characterized by moulded and sculptured ornament based on German and Flemish models. ◆ *n* **3** a person who lived in England during the reign of Elizabeth I.

Elizabethan sonnet *n* another term for **Shakespearean sonnet.**

Elizabeth of Hungary *n* **Saint.** 1207–31, Hungarian princess who devoted herself to charity and asceticism. Feast day: Nov. 17 and 19.

elk (ɛlk) *n, pl* **elks** *or* **elk. 1** a large deer, *Alces alces,* of N Europe and Asia, having large flattened palmate antlers: also occurs in North America, where it is called a moose. **2 American elk.** another name for **wapiti. 3** a stout pliable waterproof leather made from calfskin or horsehide. [Old English *eolh;* related to Old Norse *elgr,* Old High German *elaho,* Latin *alcēs,* Greek *alkē, elaphos* deer]

El Khalil (æl xɒ'liːl) *n* transliteration of the Arabic name for **Hebron.**

elkhound ('ɛlk,haʊnd) *n* a powerful breed of dog of the spitz type with a thick grey coat and tightly curled tail. Also called: **Norwegian elkhound.**

ell[1] (ɛl) *n* an obsolete unit of length equal to approximately 45 inches. [Old English *eln* the forearm (the measure originally being from the elbow to the fingertips); related to Old High German*elina,* Latin *ulna,* Greek *ōlenē*]

ell[2] (ɛl) *n* **1** an extension to a building, usually at right angles and located at one end. **2** a pipe fitting, pipe, or tube with a sharp right-angle bend. [C20: a spelling of *L,* indicating a right angle]

Ellás (ɛ'las) *n* transliteration of the Modern Greek name for **Greece.**

Ellenborough ('ɛlənbrə) *n* **Earl of,** title of *Edward Law.* 1780–1871, British colonial administrator: governor general of India (1742–44).

Ellesmere Island ('ɛlzmɪə) *n* a Canadian island in the Arctic Ocean: part of the Northwest Territories; mountainous, with many glaciers. Area: 212 688 sq. km (82 119 sq. miles).

Ellesmere Port *n* a port in NW England, in NW Cheshire on the Mersey estuary and Manchester Ship Canal. Pop.: 64 504 (1991).

Ellice Islands ('ɛlɪs) *pl n* the former name (until 1975) of **Tuvalu.**

Ellington ('ɛlɪŋtən) *n* **Duke,** nickname of *Edward Kennedy Ellington.* 1899–1974, U.S. jazz composer, pianist, and conductor, famous for such works as "Mood Indigo" and "Creole Love Call".

ellipse (ɪ'lɪps) *n* a closed conic section shaped like a flattened circle and formed by an inclined plane that does not cut the base of the cone. Standard equation: $x^2/a^2 + y^2/b^2 = 1$, where $2a$ and $2b$ are the lengths of the major and minor axes. Area: πab. [C18: back formation from ELLIPSIS]

ellipsis (ɪ'lɪpsɪs) *n, pl* **-ses** (-siːz). **1** Also called: **eclipsis.** omission of parts of a word or sentence. **2** *Printing.* a sequence of three dots (...) indicating an omission in text. [C16: from Latin, from Greek *elleipsis* omission, from *elleipein* to leave out, from *leipein* to leave]

ellipsoid (ɪ'lɪpsɔɪd) *n* **a** a geometric surface, symmetrical about the three coordinate axes, whose plane sections are ellipses or circles. Standard equation: $x^2/a^2 + y^2/b^2 + z^2/c^2 = 1$, where $\pm a$, $\pm b$, $\pm c$ are the intercepts on the *x*-, *y*-, and *z*-axes. **b** a solid having this shape: *the earth is an ellipsoid.* ▸ **ellipsoidal** (ɪlɪp'sɔɪdᵊl, ,ɛl-) *adj*

ellipsoid of revolution *n* a geometric surface produced by rotating an ellipse about one of its two axes and having circular plane surfaces perpendicular to the axis of revolution. Also called: **spheroid.**

elliptical (ɪ'lɪptɪkᵊl) *adj* **1** relating to or having the shape of an ellipse. **2** relating to or resulting from ellipsis. **3** (of speech, literary style, etc.) **3a** very condensed or concise, often so as to be obscure or ambiguous. **3b** circumlocutory or long-winded. ◆ Also (for senses 1 and 2): **elliptic.** ▸ **el'liptically** *adv* ▸ **el'lipticalness** *n*

USAGE The use of *elliptical* to mean *circumlocutory* should be avoided as it may be interpreted wrongly as meaning *condensed* or *concise.*

elliptic geometry *n* another name for **Riemannian geometry.**

ellipticity (ɪlɪp'tɪsɪtɪ, ,ɛl-) *n* the degree of deviation from a circle or sphere of an elliptical or ellipsoidal shape or path, measured as the ratio of the major to the minor axes.

Ellis ('ɛlɪs) *n* **1 Alexander John.** 1814–90, English philologist: made the first systematic survey of the phonology of British dialects. **2 (Henry) Havelock** ('hævlɒk). 1859–1939, English essayist: author of works on the psychology of sex.

elm (ɛlm) *n* **1** any ulmaceous tree of the genus *Ulmus,* occurring in the N hemisphere, having serrated leaves and winged fruits (samaras): cultivated for shade, ornament, and timber. **2** the hard heavy wood of this tree. ◆ See also **slippery elm, wahoo**[1]**, wych-elm.** [Old English *elm;* related to Old Norse *almr,* Old High German *elm,* Latin *ulmus*]

El Mansûra (ɛl mæn'sʊərə) *or* **Al Mansûrah** *n* a city in NE Egypt: scene of a battle (1250) in which the Crusaders were defeated by the Mamelukes and Louis IX of France was captured; cotton-manufacturing centre. Pop.: 371 000 (1992 est.).

El Minya (ɛl 'mɪnjə) *n* a river port in central Egypt on the Nile. Pop.: 208 000 (1992 est.).

El Misti (ɛl 'miːstiː) *n* a volcano in S Peru, in the Andes. Height: 5852 m (19 199 ft.).

El Niño (ɛl 'niːnjəʊ) *n Meteorol.* a warming of the eastern tropical Pacific occurring every few years, which disrupts the weather pattern of the region. [from Spanish: The Child, i.e. Christ, referring to its original occurrence at Christmas time]

El Obeid (el əʊ'beɪd) *n* a city in the central Sudan, in Kordofan province: scene of the defeat of a British and Egyptian army by the Mahdi (1883). Pop.: 228 096 (1993).

elocute ('ɛlə,kju:t) *vb* (*intr*) *Facetious.* to speak as if practising elocution; declaim. [C19: back formation from ELOCUTION]

elocution (,ɛlə'kju:ʃən) *n* the art of public speaking, esp. of voice production, delivery, and gesture. [C15: from Latin *ēlocūtiō* a speaking out, from *ēloquī*, from *loquī* to speak] ▸ **,elo'cutionary** *adj* ▸ **,elo'cutionist** *n*

Elohim (ɛ'ləʊhɪm, ,ɛləʊ'hi:m) *n* *Old Testament.* a Hebrew word for God or gods. [C17: from Hebrew *'Elōhīm*, plural (used to indicate uniqueness) of *'Elōah* God; probably related to *'El* God]

Elohist (ɛ'ləʊhɪst) *n* *Old Testament.* the supposed author or authors of one of the four main strands of text of the Pentateuch, identified chiefly by the use of the word *Elohim* for God instead of *YHVH* (Jehovah).

eloign *or* **eloin** (ɪ'lɔɪn) *vb* (*tr*) *Archaic.* to remove (oneself, one's property, etc.) to a distant place. [C16: from Anglo-French *esloigner* to go far away; related to Latin *longē* (adv) far; compare ELONGATE] ▸ **e'loigner** *or* **e'loiner** *n* ▸ **e'loignment** *or* **e'loinment** *n*

elongate ('i:lɒŋgeɪt) *vb* **1** to make or become longer; stretch. ◆ *adj* **2** long and narrow; slender: *elongate leaves.* **3** lengthened or tapered. [C16: from Late Latin *ēlongāre* to keep at a distance, from *ē-* away + Latin *longē* (adv) far, but also later: to lengthen, as if from *ē-* + Latin *longus* (adj) long]

elongation (,i:lɒŋ'geɪʃən) *n* **1** the act of elongating or state of being elongated; lengthening. **2** something that is elongated. **3** *Astronomy.* the difference between the celestial longitude of the sun and that of a planet or the moon.

elope (ɪ'ləʊp) *vb* (*intr*) to run away secretly with a lover, esp. in order to marry. [C16: from Anglo-French *aloper*, perhaps from Middle Dutch *lōpen* to run; see LOPE] ▸ **e'lopement** *n* ▸ **e'loper** *n*

eloquence ('ɛləkwəns) *n* **1** ease in using language to best effect. **2** powerful and effective language. **3** the quality of being persuasive or moving.

eloquent ('ɛləkwənt) *adj* **1** (of speech, writing, etc.) characterized by fluency and persuasiveness. **2** visibly or vividly expressive, as of an emotion: *an eloquent yawn.* [C14: from Latin *ēloquēns*, from *ēloquī* to speak out, from *loquī* to speak] ▸ **'eloquently** *adv*

El Paso (ɛl 'pæsəʊ) *n* a city in W Texas, on the Rio Grande opposite Ciudad Juárez, Mexico. Pop.: 599 865 (1996 est.).

El Salvador (ɛl 'sælvə,dɔ:) *n* a republic in Central America, on the Pacific: colonized by the Spanish from 1524; declared independence in 1841, becoming a republic in 1856. It consists of coastal lowlands rising to a central plateau. Coffee constitutes about half of the total exports. Official language: Spanish. Religion: Roman Catholic majority. Currency: colón. Capital: San Salvador. Pop.: 5 752 000 (1998 est.). Area: 21 393 sq. km (8236 sq. miles). ▸ **,Salva'doran, ,Salva'dorean,** *or* **,Salva'dorian** *adj, n*

Elsan ('ɛlsæn) *n* *Trademark.* a type of portable lavatory in which chemicals are used to kill bacteria and deodorize the sludge. [C20: from the initials of *E. L. Jackson*, the manufacturer + SAN(ITATION)]

Elsass ('ɛlzas) *n* the German name for **Alsace.**

Elsass-Lothringen ('ɛlzas'lo:trɪŋən) *n* the German name for **Alsace-Lorraine.**

else (ɛls) *determiner* (*postpositive; used after an indefinite pronoun or an interrogative*) **1** in addition; more: *there is nobody else here.* **2** other; different: *where else could he be?* ◆ *adv* **3 or else. 3a** if not, then: *go away or else I won't finish my work today.* **3b** or something terrible will result: used as a threat: *sit down, or else!* [Old English *elles*, genitive of *el-* strange, foreign; related to Old High German *eli-* other, Gothic *alja*, Latin *alius*, Greek *allos*]

elsewhere (,ɛls'wɛə) *adv* in or to another place; somewhere else. [Old English *elles hwǣr*; see ELSE, WHERE]

Elsinore ('ɛlsɪ,nɔ:, ,ɛlsɪ'nɔ:) *n* the English name for **Helsingør.**

ELT *abbrev. for* English Language Teaching: the teaching of English specifically to students whose native language is not English.

Elton ('ɛltᵊn) *n* **Charles Sutherland.** 1900–91, British zoologist: initiated the study of animal ecology.

Éluard (*French* elɥar) *n* **Paul** (pɔl), real name *Eugène-Émile-Paul Grindel.* 1895–1952, French surrealist poet, noted for his political and love poems.

eluate ('ɛlju:,eɪt) *n* a solution of adsorbed material in the eluent obtained during the process of elution.

elucidate (ɪ'lu:sɪ,deɪt) *vb* to make clear (something obscure or difficult); clarify. [C16: from Late Latin *ēlūcidāre* to enlighten; see LUCID] ▸ **e,luci'dation** *n* ▸ **e'luci,dative** *or* **e'luci,datory** *adj* ▸ **e'luci,dator** *n*

elude (ɪ'lu:d) *vb* (*tr*) **1** to escape or avoid (capture, one's pursuers, etc.), esp. by cunning. **2** to avoid fulfilment of (a responsibility, obligation, etc.); evade. **3** to escape discovery, or understanding by; baffle: *the solution eluded her.* [C16: from Latin *ēlūdere* to deceive, from *lūdere* to play] ▸ **e'luder** *n* ▸ **elusion** (ɪ'lu:ʒən) *n*

USAGE *Elude* is sometimes wrongly used where *allude* is meant: *he was alluding* (not *eluding*) *to his previous visit to the city.*

eluent *or* **eluant** ('ɛlju:ənt) *n* a solvent used for eluting.

Elul (ɛ'lu:l) *n* (in the Jewish calendar) the sixth month of the year according to biblical reckoning and the twelfth month of the civil year, usually falling within August and September. [from Hebrew]

elusive (ɪ'lu:sɪv) *adj* **1** difficult to catch: *an elusive thief.* **2** preferring or living in solitude and anonymity. **3** difficult to remember: *an elusive thought.* ▸ **e'lusively** *adv* ▸ **e'lusiveness** *n*

USAGE See at **illusory.**

elusory (ɪ'lu:sərɪ) *adj* **1** avoiding the issue; evasive: *elusory arguments.* **2** difficult to grasp mentally; elusive: *elusory ideas.*

elute (i:'lu:t, ɪ'lu:t) *vb* (*tr*) to wash out (a substance) by the action of a solvent, as in chromatography. [C18: from Latin *ēlūtus* rinsed out, from *ēluere* to wash clean, from *luere* to wash, LAVE] ▸ **e'lution** *n*

elutriate (ɪ'lu:trɪ,eɪt) *vb* (*tr*) to purify or separate (a substance or mixture) by washing and straining or decanting. [C18: from Latin *ēlūtriāre* to wash out, from *ēluere*, from *ē-* out + *lavere* to wash] ▸ **e,lutri'ation** *n* ▸ **e'lutri,ator** *n*

eluviation (ɪ,lu:vɪ'eɪʃən) *n* the process by which material suspended in water is removed from one layer of soil to another by the action of rainfall or chemical decomposition. [C20: from ELUVIUM]

eluvium (ɪ'lu:vɪəm) *n, pl* **-via** (-vɪə). a mass of sand, silt, etc.: a product of the erosion of rocks that has remained in its place of origin. [C19: New Latin, from Latin *ēluere* to wash out] ▸ **e'luvial** *adj*

elver ('ɛlvə) *n* a young eel, esp. one migrating up a river from the sea. See also **leptocephalus.** [C17: variant of *eelfare* migration of young eels, literally: eel-journey; see EEL, FARE]

elves (ɛlvz) *n* the plural of **elf.**

elvish ('ɛlvɪʃ) *adj* a variant of **elfish.**

Ely ('i:lɪ) *n* **1** a cathedral city in E England, in E Cambridgeshire on the River Ouse. Pop.: 10 329 (1991). **2 Isle of.** a former county of E England, part of Cambridgeshire since 1965.

Elyot ('ɛlɪət) *n* Sir **Thomas.** ?1490–1546, English scholar and diplomat; author of *The Boke named the Governour* (1531), a treatise in English on education.

Elysée (eɪ'li:zeɪ) *n* a palace in Paris, in the Champs Elysées: official residence of the president of France.

Elysian (ɪ'lɪzɪən) *adj* **1** of or relating to Elysium. **2** *Literary.* delightful; glorious; blissful.

Elysium (ɪ'lɪzɪəm) *n* **1** Also called: **Elysian fields.** *Greek myth.* the dwelling place of the blessed after death. See also **Islands of the Blessed. 2** a state or place of perfect bliss. [C16: from Latin, from Greek *Ēlusion pedion* Elysian (that is, blessed) fields]

elytron ('ɛlɪ,trɒn) *or* **elytrum** ('ɛlɪtrəm) *n, pl* **-tra** (-trə). either of the horny front wings of beetles and some other insects, which cover and protect the hind wings. [C18: from Greek *elutron* sheath, covering] ▸ **'ely,troid** *or* **'elytrous** *adj*

em (ɛm) *n* *Printing.* **1** Also called: **mutton, mut.** the square of a body of any size of type, used as a unit of measurement. **2** Also called: **pica em, pica.** a unit of measurement used in printing, equal to one sixth of an inch. [C19: from the name of the letter *M*]

em- *prefix* a variant of **en-**[1] and **en-**[2] before *b, m,* and *p.*

'em (əm) *pron* an informal variant of **them.**

emaciate (ɪ'meɪsɪ,eɪt) *vb* (*usually tr*) to become or cause to become abnormally thin. [C17: from Latin *ēmaciāre* to make lean, from *macer* thin] ▸ **e'maci,ated** *adj* ▸ **e,maci'ation** *n*

E-mail, e-mail, *or* **email** ('i:meɪl) *n* **1** short for **electronic mail.** ◆ *vb* (*tr*) **2** to contact (a person) by electronic mail. **3** to send (a message, document, etc.) by electronic mail.

emanate ('ɛmə,neɪt) *vb* **1** (*intr;* often foll. by *from*) to issue or proceed from or as from a source. **2** (*tr*) to send forth; emit. [C18: from Latin *ēmānāre* to flow out, from *mānāre* to flow] ▸ **emanative** ('ɛmənətɪv) *adj* ▸ **'ema,nator** *n* ▸ **emanatory** ('ɛmə,neɪtərɪ, -trɪ) *adj*

emanation (,ɛmə'neɪʃən) *n* **1** an act or instance of emanating. **2** something that emanates or is produced; effusion. **3** a gaseous product of radioactive decay, such as radon. ▸ **,ema'national** *adj*

emancipate (ɪ'mænsɪ,peɪt) *vb* (*tr*) **1** to free from restriction or restraint, esp. social or legal restraint. **2** (*often passive*) to free from the inhibitions imposed by conventional morality. **3** to liberate (a slave) from bondage. [C17: from Latin *ēmancipāre* to give independence (to a son), from *mancipāre* to transfer property, from *manceps* a purchaser; see MANCIPLE] ▸ **e'manci,pated** *adj* ▸ **e'manci,pative** *adj* ▸ **e'mancipist** *or* **e'manci,pator** *n* ▸ **emancipatory** (ɪ'mænsɪpətərɪ, -trɪ) *adj*

emancipation (ɪ,mænsɪ'peɪʃən) *n* **1** the act of freeing or state of being freed; liberation. **2** *Informal.* freedom from inhibition and convention. ▸ **e,manci'pationist** *n*

emarginate (ɪ'mɑ:dʒɪ,neɪt) *or* **emarginated** *adj* having a notched tip or edge: *emarginate leaves.* [C17: from Latin *ēmargināre* to deprive of its edge, from *margō* MARGIN] ▸ **e'margi,nately** *adv* ▸ **e,margi'nation** *n*

emasculate *vb* (ɪ'mæskju,leɪt). (*tr*) **1** to remove the testicles of; castrate; geld. **2** to deprive of vigour, effectiveness, etc. **3** *Botany.* to remove the stamens from (a flower) to prevent self-pollination for the purposes of plant breeding. ◆ *adj* (ɪ'mæskjʊlɪt, -,leɪt). **4** castrated; gelded. **5** deprived of strength, effectiveness, etc. [C17: from Latin *ēmasculāre*, from *masculus* male; see MASCULINE] ▸ **e,mascu'lation** *n* ▸ **e'masculative** *or* **e'masculatory** *adj* ▸ **e'mascu,lator** *n*

embalm (ɪm'bɑ:m) *vb* (*tr*) **1** to treat (a dead body) with preservatives, as by injecting formaldehyde into the blood vessels, to retard putrefaction. **2** to preserve or cherish the memory of. **3** *Poetic.* to give a sweet fragrance to. [C13: from Old French *embaumer;* see BALM] ▸ **em'balmer** *n* ▸ **em'balmment** *n*

embank (ɪm'bæŋk) *vb* (*tr*) to protect, enclose, or confine (a waterway, road, etc.) with an embankment.

embankment (ɪm'bæŋkmənt) *n* a man-made ridge of earth or stone that carries a road or railway or confines a waterway. See also **levee**[1].

embargo (ɛm'bɑ:gəʊ) *n, pl* **-goes. 1** a government order prohibiting the departure or arrival of merchant ships in its ports. **2** any legal stoppage of commerce: *an embargo on arms shipments.* **3** a restraint, hindrance, or prohibition. ◆ *vb* **-goes, -going, -goed.** (*tr*) **4** to lay an embargo upon. **5** to seize for use by the state. [C16: from Spanish, from *embargar*, from Latin IM- + *barra* BAR[1]]

embark (ɛm'bɑ:k) *vb* **1** to board (a ship or aircraft). **2** (*intr;* usually foll. by *on* or *upon*) to commence or engage (in) a new project, venture, etc. [C16: via

French from Old Provençal *embarcar,* from EM- + *barca* boat, BARQUE] ▸ ˌem**bar'kation** *n* ▸ **em'barkment** *n*

embarras de richesses *French.* (ɑ̃bara də riʃɛs) *n* a superfluous abundance of options, from which one finds it difficult to select. Also called: ***embarras de choix*** (də ʃwa). [C18: literally: embarrassment of riches]

embarrass (ɪm'bærəs) *vb* (*mainly tr*) **1** (*also intr*) to feel or cause to feel confusion or self-consciousness; disconcert; fluster. **2** (*usually passive*) to involve in financial difficulties. **3** *Archaic.* to make difficult; complicate. **4** *Archaic.* to impede; obstruct; hamper. [C17 (in the sense: to impede): via French and Spanish from Italian *imbarrazzare,* from *imbarrare* to confine within bars; see EN-[1], BAR[1]] ▸ **em'barrassed** *adj* ▸ **em'barrassedly** *adv* ▸ **em'barrassing** *adj* ▸ **em'barrassingly** *adv*

embarrassment (ɪm'bærəsmənt) *n* **1** the state of being embarrassed. **2** something that embarrasses. **3** a financial predicament. **4** an excessive amount; superfluity.

embassy ('ɛmbəsɪ) *n, pl* **-sies. 1** the residence or place of official business of an ambassador. **2** an ambassador and his entourage collectively. **3** the position, business, or mission of an ambassador. **4** any important or official mission, duty, etc., esp. one undertaken by an agent. [C16: from Old French *ambassee,* from Old Italian *ambasciata,* from Old Provençal *ambaisada,* ultimately of Germanic origin; see AMBASSADOR]

embattle (ɪm'bætᵊl) *vb* (*tr*) **1** to deploy (troops) for battle. **2** to strengthen or fortify (a position, town, etc.). **3** to provide (a building) with battlements. [C14: from Old French *embataillier;* see EN-[1], BATTLE]

embattled (ɪm'bætᵊld) *adj* **1** prepared for or engaged in conflict, controversy, or battle. **2** *Heraldry.* having an indented edge resembling battlements.

embay (ɪm'beɪ) *vb* (*tr*) (*usually passive*) **1** to form into a bay. **2** to enclose in or as if in a bay. **3** (esp. of the wind) to force (a ship, esp. a sailing ship) into a bay.

embayment (ɪm'beɪmənt) *n* a shape resembling a bay.

Embden-Meyerhof pathway *n* the metabolic reaction sequence in glycolysis by which glucose is converted to pyruvic acid with production of ATP. [C20: named after Gustav *Embden* (1874–1933) and Otto *Meyerhof* (1884–1951), German biochemists]

embed (ɪm'bɛd) *vb* **-beds, -bedding, -bedded. 1** (usually foll. by *in*) to fix or become fixed firmly and deeply in a surrounding solid mass: *to embed a nail in wood.* **2** (*tr*) to surround closely: *hard rock embeds the roots.* **3** (*tr*) to fix or retain (a thought, idea, etc.) in the mind. **4** (*tr*) *Grammar.* to insert (a subordinate clause) into a sentence. ◆ Also: **imbed.** ▸ **em'bedment** *n*

embellish (ɪm'bɛlɪʃ) *vb* (*tr*) **1** to improve or beautify by adding detail or ornament; adorn. **2** to make (a story) more interesting by adding detail. **3** to provide (a melody, part, etc.) with ornaments. See **ornament** (sense 5). [C14: from Old French *embelir,* from *bel* beautiful, from Latin *bellus*] ▸ **em'bellisher** *n* ▸ **em'bellishment** *n*

ember ('ɛmbə) *n* **1** a glowing or smouldering piece of coal or wood, as in a dying fire. **2** the fading remains of a past emotion: *the embers of his love.* [Old English *ǣmyrge;* related to Old Norse *eimyrja* ember, *eimr* smoke, Old High German *eimuria* ember]

Ember days *pl n R.C. and Anglican Church.* any of four groups of three days (always Wednesday, Friday, and Saturday) of prayer and fasting, the groups occurring after Pentecost, after the first Sunday of Lent, after the feast of St Lucy (Dec. 13), and after the feast of the Holy Cross (Sept. 14). [Old English *ymbrendǣg,* from *ymbren,* perhaps from *ymbryne* a (recurring) period, from *ymb* around + *ryne* a course + *dǣg* day]

ember goose *n* (*not in ornithological use*) another name for the **great northern diver.** [C18: from Norwegian *emmer-gaas*]

Ember week *n* a week in which Ember days fall.

embezzle (ɪm'bɛzᵊl) *vb* to convert (money or property entrusted to one) fraudulently to one's own use. [C15: from Anglo-French *embeseiller* to destroy, from Old French *beseiller* to make away with, of uncertain origin] ▸ **em'bezzlement** *n* ▸ **em'bezzler** *n*

embitter (ɪm'bɪtə) *vb* (*tr*) **1** to make (a person) resentful or bitter. **2** to aggravate (an already hostile feeling, difficult situation, etc.). ▸ **em'bittered** *adj* ▸ **em'bitterer** *n* ▸ **em'bitterment** *n*

emblaze (ɪm'bleɪz) *vb* (*tr*) *Archaic.* **1** to cause to light up; illuminate. **2** to set fire to.

emblazon (ɪm'bleɪzᵊn) *vb* (*tr*) **1** to describe, portray, or colour (arms) according to the conventions of heraldry. **2** to portray heraldic arms on (a shield, one's notepaper, etc.). **3** to make bright or splendid, as with colours, flowers, etc. **4** to glorify, praise, or extol, often so as to attract great publicity: *his feat was emblazoned on the front page.* ▸ **em'blazonment** *n*

emblazonry (ɪm'bleɪzᵊnrɪ) *n* another name for **blazonry.**

emblem ('ɛmbləm) *n* **1** a visible object or representation that symbolizes a quality, type, group, etc., esp. the concrete symbol of an abstract idea: *the dove is an emblem of peace.* **2** an allegorical picture containing a moral lesson, often with an explanatory motto or verses, esp. one printed in an **emblem book.** [C15: from Latin *emblēma* raised decoration, mosaic, from Greek, literally: something inserted, from *emballein* to insert, from *ballein* to throw] ▸ ˌem**blem'atic** *or* ˌ**emblem'atical** *adj* ▸ ˌ**emblem'atically** *adv*

emblematize (ɛm'blɛməˌtaɪz), **emblemize** ('ɛmbləˌmaɪz), *or* **emblematise, emblemise** *vb* (*tr*) **1** to function as an emblem of; symbolize. **2** to represent by or as by an emblem.

emblements ('ɛmbləmənts) *pl n Law.* **1** annual crops and vegetable products cultivated by man's labour. **2** the profits from such crops. [C15: from Old French *emblaement,* from *emblaer* to sow with grain, from Medieval Latin *imblādāre,* from *blāda* grain, of Germanic origin; compare Old English *blǣd* grain]

embody (ɪm'bɒdɪ) *vb* **-bodies, -bodying, -bodied.** (*tr*) **1** to give a tangible, bodily, or concrete form to (an abstract concept). **2** to be an example of or express (an idea, principle, etc.), esp. in action: *his gentleness embodies a Christian ideal.* **3** (often foll. by *in*) to collect or unite in a comprehensive whole, system, etc.; comprise; include: *all the different essays were embodied in one long article.* **4** to invest (a spiritual entity) with a body or with bodily form; render incarnate. ▸ **em'bodiment** *n*

embolden (ɪm'bəʊldᵊn) *vb* (*tr*) to encourage; make bold.

embolectomy (ˌɛmbə'lɛktəmɪ) *n, pl* **-mies.** the surgical removal of an embolus that is blocking a blood vessel.

embolic (ɛm'bɒlɪk) *adj* **1** of or relating to an embolus or embolism. **2** *Embryol.* of, relating to, or resulting from invagination.

embolism ('ɛmbəˌlɪzəm) *n* **1** the occlusion of a blood vessel by an embolus. **2** *Botany.* the blocking of a xylem vessel by an air bubble. **3** the insertion of one or more days into a calendar, esp. the Jewish calendar; intercalation. **4** *R.C. Church.* a prayer inserted in the canon of the Mass between the Lord's Prayer and the breaking of the bread. **5** another name (not in technical use) for **embolus.** [C14: from Medieval Latin *embolismus,* from Late Greek *embolismos* intercalary; see EMBOLUS] ▸ ˌ**embo'lismic** *adj*

embolize *or* **embolise** ('ɛmbəˌlaɪz) *vb* (*tr*) to cause embolism in (a blood vessel). ▸ ˌ**emboli'zation** *or* ˌ**emboli'sation** *n*

embolus ('ɛmbələs) *n, pl* **-li** (-ˌlaɪ). material, such as part of a blood clot or an air bubble, that is transported by the blood stream until it becomes lodged within a small vessel and impedes the circulation. Compare **thrombus.** [C17: via Latin from Greek *embolos* stopper, from *emballein* to insert, from *ballein* to throw; see EMBLEM]

emboly ('ɛmbəlɪ) *n, pl* **-lies.** another name for **invagination** (sense 3). [C19: from Greek *embolē* an insertion, from *emballein* to throw in; see EMBLEM]

embonpoint *French.* (ɑ̃bɔ̃pwɛ̃) *n* **1** plumpness or stoutness. ◆ *adj* **2** plump; stout. [C18: from phrase *en bon point* in good condition]

embosom (ɪm'bʊzəm) *vb* (*tr*) *Archaic.* **1** to enclose or envelop, esp. protectively. **2** to clasp to the bosom; hug. **3** to cherish.

emboss (ɪm'bɒs) *vb* **1** to mould or carve (a decoration or design) on (a surface) so that it is raised above the surface in low relief. **2** to cause to bulge; make protrude. [C14: from Old French *embocer,* from EM- + *boce* BOSS[2]] ▸ **em'bossed** *adj* ▸ **em'bosser** *n* ▸ **em'bossment** *n*

embothrium (ɪm'bɒθrɪəm) *n* any evergreen shrub of the genus *Embothrium,* esp. *E. coccineum,* native to South America but widely cultivated as an ornamental for its scarlet flowers: family *Proteaceae.* [C19: from EM- + Greek *bothrion* small pit (referring to its anthers)]

embouchure (ˌɒmbʊ'ʃʊə) *n* **1** the mouth of a river or valley. **2** *Music.* **2a** the correct application of the lips and tongue in playing a wind instrument. **2b** the mouthpiece of a wind instrument. [C18: from French, from Old French *emboucher* to put to one's mouth, from *bouche* mouth, from Latin *bucca* cheek]

embourgeoisement (*French* ɑ̃burʒwaz'mɑ̃) *n* the process of becoming middle class; the assimilation into the middle class of traditionally working-class people. [from French, from EN-[1] + BOURGEOIS[1]]

embow (ɪm'bəʊ) *vb* (*tr*) to design or create (a structure) in the form of an arch or vault. ▸ **em'bowed** *adj* ▸ **em'bowment** *n*

embowel (ɪm'baʊəl) *vb Obsolete.* **1** to bury or embed deeply. **2** another word for **disembowel.**

embower (ɪm'baʊə) *vb* (*tr*) *Archaic.* to enclose in or as in a bower.

embrace[1] (ɪm'breɪs) *vb* (*mainly tr*) **1** (*also intr*) (of a person) to take or clasp (another person) in the arms, or (of two people) to clasp each other, as in affection, greeting, etc.; hug. **2** to accept (an opportunity, challenge, etc.) willingly or eagerly. **3** to take up (a new idea, faith, etc.); adopt: *to embrace Judaism.* **4** to comprise or include as an integral part: *geology embraces the science of mineralogy.* **5** to encircle or enclose: *an island embraced by the ocean.* ◆ *n* **6** the act of embracing. **7** (*often pl*) *Euphemistic.* sexual intercourse. [C14: from Old French *embracier,* from EM- + *brace* a pair of arms, from Latin *bracchia* arms] ▸ **em'braceable** *adj* ▸ **em'bracement** *n* ▸ **em'bracer** *n*

embrace[2] (ɪm'breɪs) *vb* (*tr*) *Criminal law.* to commit or attempt to commit embracery against (a jury, etc.). [C15: back formation from EMBRACEOR]

embraceor *or* **embracer** (ɪm'breɪsə) *n Criminal law.* a person guilty of embracery. [C15: from Old French *embraseor,* from *embraser* to instigate, literally: to set on fire, from *braser* to burn, from *brese* live coals]

embracery (ɪm'breɪsərɪ) *n Criminal law.* the offence of attempting by corrupt means to influence a jury or juror, as by bribery or threats.

embranchment (ɪm'brɑːntʃmənt) *n* **1** the process of branching out, esp. by a river. **2** a branching out or ramification, as of a river or mountain range.

embrangle (ɪm'bræŋgᵊl) *vb* (*tr*) *Rare.* to confuse or entangle. [C17: from EM- + obsolete *brangle* to wrangle, perhaps a blend of BRAWL[1] + WRANGLE] ▸ **em'branglement** *n*

embrasure (ɪm'breɪʒə) *n* **1** *Fortifications.* an opening or indentation, as in a battlement, for shooting through. **2** an opening forming a door or window, having splayed sides that increase the width of the opening in the interior. [C18: from French, from obsolete *embraser* to widen, of uncertain origin] ▸ **em'brasured** *adj*

embrocate ('ɛmbrəʊˌkeɪt) *vb* (*tr*) to apply a liniment or lotion to (a part of the body). [C17: from Medieval Latin *embrocāre,* from *embrocha* poultice, from Greek *embrokhē* lotion, infusion, from *brokhē* a moistening]

embrocation (ˌɛmbrəʊ'keɪʃən) *n* a drug or agent for rubbing into the skin; liniment.

embroider (ɪm'brɔɪdə) *vb* **1** to do decorative needlework (upon). **2** to add fictitious or fanciful detail to (a story). **3** to add exaggerated or improbable details to (an account of an event, etc.). [C15: from Old French *embroder;* see *em-* EN-[1], BROIDER] ▸ **em'broiderer** *n*

embroidery (ɪm'brɔɪdərɪ) *n, pl* **-deries. 1** decorative needlework done usually on loosely woven cloth or canvas, often being a picture or pattern. **2** elaboration or exaggeration, esp. in writing or reporting; embellishment.

embroil (ɪm'brɔɪl) *vb* (*tr*) **1** to involve (a person, oneself, etc.) in trouble, conflict, or argument. **2** to throw (affairs) into a state of confusion or disorder; complicate; entangle. [C17: from French *embrouiller,* from *brouiller* to mingle, confuse] ▸ **em'broiler** *n* ▸ **em'broilment** *n*

embrue (ɪm'bru:) *vb* **-brues, -bruing, -brued.** a variant spelling of **imbrue.** ▸ **em'bruement** *n*

embryectomy (ˌɛmbrɪ'ɛktəmɪ) *n, pl* **-mies.** the surgical removal of an embryo.

embryo ('ɛmbrɪˌəʊ) *n, pl* **-bryos. 1** an animal in the early stages of development following cleavage of the zygote and ending at birth or hatching. **2** the human product of conception up to approximately the end of the second month of pregnancy. Compare **fetus. 3** a plant in the early stages of development: in higher plants, the plumule, cotyledons, and radicle within the seed. **4** an undeveloped or rudimentary state (esp. in the phrase **in embryo**). **5** something in an early stage of development: *an embryo of an idea.* [C16: from Late Latin, from Greek *embruon,* from *bruein* to swell] ▸ **'embryˌoid** *adj*

embryogeny (ˌɛmbrɪ'ɒdʒɪnɪ) *n* **1** Also called: **embryogenesis** (ˌɛmbrɪəʊ'dʒɛnəsɪs). the formation and development of an embryo. **2** the study of these processes. ▸ **embryogenic** (ˌɛmbrɪəʊ'dʒɛnɪk) *adj*

embryol. *abbrev. for* embryology.

embryology (ˌɛmbrɪ'ɒlədʒɪ) *n* **1** the branch of science concerned with the study of embryos. **2** the structure and development of the embryo of a particular organism. ▸ **embryological** (ˌɛmbrɪə'lɒdʒɪkᵊl) *or* **ˌembryo'logic** *adj* ▸ **ˌembryo'logically** *adv* ▸ **ˌembry'ologist** *n*

embryonic (ˌɛmbrɪ'ɒnɪk) *or* **embryonal** ('ɛmbrɪənᵊl) *adj* **1** of or relating to an embryo. **2** in an early stage; rudimentary; undeveloped. ▸ **ˌembry'onically** *adv*

embryo sac *n* the structure within a plant ovule that contains the egg cell; the megaspore of seed plants: contains the embryo plant and endosperm after fertilization.

embus (ɪm'bʌs) *vb* **-buses, -busing, -bused** *or* **-busses, -bussing, -bussed.** *Military.* to cause (troops) to board or (of troops) to board a transport vehicle.

embusqué *French.* (ɑ̃byske) *n, pl* ***-qués*** (-ke). a man who avoids military conscription by obtaining a government job. [C20: from *embusquer* to lie in ambush, shirk]

emcee (ˌɛm'si:) *Informal.* ◆ *n* **1** a master of ceremonies. ◆ *vb* **-cees, -ceeing, -ceed. 2** to act as master of ceremonies (for or at). [C20: from the abbreviation MC]

em dash *or* **rule** *n Printing.* a dash (—) one em long.

Emden (*German* 'ɛmdən) *n* a port in NW Germany, in Lower Saxony at the mouth of the River Ems. Pop.: 51 100 (1991).

-eme *suffix forming nouns. Linguistics.* indicating a minimal distinctive unit of a specified type in a language: *morpheme; phoneme.* [C20: via French, abstracted from PHONEME]

emend (ɪ'mɛnd) *vb* (*tr*) to make corrections or improvements in (a text) by critical editing. [C15: from Latin *ēmendāre* to correct, from *ē-* out + *mendum* a mistake] ▸ **e'mendable** *adj*

emendation (ˌi:mɛn'deɪʃən) *n* **1** a correction or improvement in a text. **2** the act or process of emending. ▸ **'emenˌdator** *n* ▸ **emendatory** (ɪ'mɛndətərɪ, -trɪ) *adj*

emerald ('ɛmərəld, 'ɛmrəld) *n* **1** a green transparent variety of beryl: highly valued as a gem. **2a** the clear green colour of an emerald. **2b** (*as adj*): *an emerald carpet.* **3** (formerly) a size of printer's type approximately equal to 6½ point. **4** short for **emerald moth.** [C13: from Old French *esmeraude,* from Latin *smaragdus,* from Greek *smaragdos;* related to Sanskrit *marakata* emerald]

Emerald Isle *n* a poetic name for **Ireland**[1].

emerald moth *n* any of various green geometrid moths, esp. the **large emerald** (*Geometra papilionaria*) a handsome pale green moth with white wavy markings.

emerge (ɪ'mɜ:dʒ) *vb* (*intr;* often foll. by *from*) **1** to come up to the surface of or rise from water or other liquid. **2** to come into view, as from concealment or obscurity: *he emerged from the cave.* **3** (foll. by *from*) to come out (of) or live (through a difficult experience): *he emerged from his ordeal with dignity.* **4** to become apparent: *several interesting things emerged from the report.* [C17: from Latin *ēmergere* to rise up from, from *mergere* to dip] ▸ **e'merging** *adj*

emergence (ɪ'mɜ:dʒəns) *n* **1** the act or process of emerging. **2** an outgrowth, such as a prickle, that contains no vascular tissue and does not develop into stem, leaf, etc.

emergency (ɪ'mɜ:dʒənsɪ) *n, pl* **-cies. 1a** an unforeseen or sudden occurrence, esp. of a danger demanding immediate remedy or action. **1b** (*as modifier*): *an emergency exit.* **2a** a patient requiring urgent treatment. **2b** (*as modifier*): *an emergency ward.* **3 state of emergency.** a condition, declared by a government, in which martial law applies, usually because of civil unrest or natural disaster. **4** *N.Z.* a player selected to stand by to replace an injured member of a team; reserve.

emergent (ɪ'mɜ:dʒənt) *adj* **1** coming into being or notice: *an emergent political structure.* **2** (of a nation) recently independent. ◆ *n* **3** an aquatic plant with stem and leaves above the water. ▸ **e'mergently** *adv*

emergent evolution *n Philosophy.* the doctrine that, in the course of evolution, some entirely new properties, such as life and consciousness, appear at certain critical points, usually because of an unpredictable rearrangement of the already existing entities.

emerging market *n* a financial or consumer market in a newly developing country or former communist country.

emeritus (ɪ'mɛrɪtəs) *adj* (*usually postpositive*) retired or honourably discharged from full-time work, but retaining one's title on an honorary basis: *a professor emeritus.* [C19: from Latin, from *merēre* to deserve; see MERIT]

emersed (ɪ'mɜ:st) *adj* (of the leaves or stems of aquatic plants) protruding above the surface of the water.

emersion (ɪ'mɜ:ʃən) *n* **1** the act or an instance of emerging. **2** Also called: **egress.** *Astronomy.* the reappearance of a celestial body after an eclipse or occultation. [C17: from Latin *ēmersus,* from *ēmergere;* see EMERGE]

Emerson ('ɛməsᵊn) *n* **Ralph Waldo.** (rælf 'wɔ:ldəʊ). 1803–82, U.S. poet, essayist, and transcendentalist.

emery ('ɛmərɪ) *n* **a** a hard greyish-black mineral consisting of corundum with either magnetite or haematite: used as an abrasive and polishing agent, esp. as a coating on paper, cloth, etc. Formula: Al_2O_3. **b** (*as modifier*): *emery paper.* [C15: from Old French *esmeril,* ultimately from Greek *smuris* powder for rubbing]

emery board *n* a strip of cardboard or wood with a rough surface of crushed emery, for filing one's nails.

emery wheel *n* a grinding or polishing wheel the surface of which is coated with abrasive emery particles.

emesis ('ɛmɪsɪs) *n* the technical name for **vomiting.** [C19: via New Latin from Greek, from *emein* to vomit]

emetic (ɪ'mɛtɪk) *adj* **1** causing vomiting. ◆ *n* **2** an emetic agent or drug. [C17: from Late Latin *ēmeticus,* from Greek *emetikos,* from *emein* to vomit] ▸ **e'metically** *adv*

emetine ('ɛməˌti:n, -tɪn) *or* **emetin** ('ɛmətɪn) *n* a white bitter poisonous alkaloid obtained from ipecacuanha: the hydrochloride is used to treat amoebic infections. Formula: $C_{29}H_{40}O_4N_2$. [C19: from French *émétine;* see EMETIC, -INE[2]]

emf *or* **EMF** *abbrev. for* electromotive force.

-emia *n combining form.* a U.S. variant of **-aemia.**

emigrant ('ɛmɪgrənt) *n* **a** a person who leaves one place or country, esp. a native country, to settle in another. Compare **immigrant. b** (*as modifier*): *an emigrant worker.*

emigrate ('ɛmɪˌgreɪt) *vb* (*intr*) to leave one place or country, esp. one's native country, in order to settle in another. Compare **immigrate.** [C18: from Latin *ēmīgrāre,* from *mīgrāre* to depart, MIGRATE] ▸ **'emiˌgratory** *adj*

emigration (ˌɛmɪ'greɪʃən) *n* **1** the act or an instance of emigrating. **2** emigrants considered collectively.

émigré ('ɛmɪˌgreɪ; *French* emigre) *n* an emigrant, esp. one forced to leave his native country for political reasons. [C18: from French, from *émigrer* to EMIGRATE]

Emilia-Romagna (ɪ'mi:lɪərəʊ'mɑ:njə; *Italian* e'mi:lia-ro'maɲɲa) *n* a region of N central Italy, on the Adriatic: rises from the plains of the Po valley in the north to the Apennines in the south. Capital: Bologna. Pop.: 3 924 456 (1996 est.). Area: 22 123 sq. km (8628 sq. miles).

eminence ('ɛmɪnəns) *n, pl* **-nences. 1** a position of superiority, distinction, high rank, or fame. **2** a high or raised piece of ground. **3** *Anatomy.* a projection of an organ or part. ◆ Also: **eminency.** [C17: from French, from Latin *ēminentia* a standing out; see EMINENT]

Eminence ('ɛmɪnəns) *or* **Eminency** *n, pl* **-nences** *or* **-nencies.** (preceded by *Your* or *His*) a title used to address or refer to a cardinal.

éminence grise *French.* (eminɑ̃s griz) *n, pl* ***éminences grises*** (eminɑ̃s griz). a person who wields power and influence unofficially or behind the scenes. [C19: literally: grey eminence, originally applied to Père Joseph (François Le Clerc du Tremblay; died 1638), French monk, secretary of Cardinal Richelieu]

eminent ('ɛmɪnənt) *adj* **1** above others in rank, merit, or reputation; distinguished: *an eminent scientist.* **2** (*prenominal*) noteworthy, conspicuous, or outstanding: *eminent good sense.* **3** projecting or protruding; prominent. [C15: from Latin *ēminēre* to project, stand out, from *minēre* to stand] ▸ **'eminently** *adv*

eminent domain *n Law.* the right of a state to confiscate private property for public use, payment usually being made to the owners in compensation.

eminently ('ɛmɪnəntlɪ) *adv* extremely: *eminently sensible.*

emir (ɛ'mɪə) *n* (in the Islamic world) **1** an independent ruler or chieftain. **2** a military commander or governor. **3** a descendant of Mohammed. ◆ Also spelled: **amir.** [C17: via French from Spanish *emir,* from Arabic *'amīr* commander]

emirate (ɛ'mɪərɪt, 'ɛmɪrɪt) *n* **1** the rank or office of an emir. **2** the government, jurisdiction, or territory of an emir.

Emiscan (ˌɛmɪ'skæn) *n Trademark.* a computerized radiological technique for examining the soft tissues of the body, esp. the brain, to detect the presence of tumours, abscesses, etc.

emissary ('ɛmɪsərɪ, -ɪsrɪ) *n, pl* **-saries. 1a** an agent or messenger sent on a mission, esp. one who represents a government or head of state. **1b** (*as modifier*): *an emissary delegation.* **2** an agent sent on a secret mission, as a spy. ◆ *adj* **3** (of veins) draining blood from sinuses in the dura mater to veins outside the skull. [C17: from Latin *ēmissārius* emissary, spy, from *ēmittere* to send out; see EMIT]

emission (ɪ'mɪʃən) *n* **1** the act of emitting or sending forth. **2** energy, in the form of heat, light, radio waves, etc., emitted from a source. **3** a substance, fluid, etc., that is emitted; discharge. **4** a measure of the number of electrons emitted by a cathode or electron gun: *at 1000°C the emission is 3 mA.* See also **secondary emission, thermionic emission. 5** *Physiol.* any bodily discharge, esp. an involuntary release of semen during sleep. **6** an issue, as of currency. [C17: from Latin *ēmissiō,* from *ēmittere* to send forth, EMIT] ▸ **e'missive** *adj*

emission nebula *n* a type of nebula that emits radiation. See **nebula.**

emission spectrum *n* the continuous spectrum or pattern of bright lines or bands seen when the electromagnetic radiation emitted by a substance is passed into a spectrometer. The spectrum is characteristic of the emitting substance and the type of excitation to which it is subjected. Compare **absorption spectrum.**

emissivity (ˌɪmɪ'sɪvɪtɪ, ˌɛm-) *n* a measure of the ability of a surface to radiate energy; the ratio of the radiant flux emitted per unit area to that emitted by a black body at the same temperature. Symbol: ε

emit (ɪ'mɪt) *vb* **emits, emitting, emitted.** (*tr*) **1** to give or send forth; discharge: *the pipe emitted a stream of water.* **2** to give voice to; utter: *she emitted a shrill scream.* **3** *Physics.* to give off (radiation or particles). **4** to put (currency) into circulation. [C17: from Latin *ēmittere* to send out, from *mittere* to send]

emitter (ɪ'mɪtə) *n* **1** a person or thing that emits. **2** a radioactive substance that emits radiation: *a beta emitter.* **3** the region in a transistor in which the charge-carrying holes or electrons originate.

Emmanuel (ɪ'mænjʊəl) *n* a variant spelling of **Immanuel.**

Emmen ('ɛmən; *Dutch* 'ɛmə) *n* a city in the NE Netherlands, in Drenthe province: a new town developed since World War II. Pop.: 93 476 (1994).

emmenagogue (ɪ'mɛnəˌgɒg, -'miː-) *n* **1** a drug or agent that increases menstrual flow. ◆ *adj also* **emmenagogic** (ɪˌmɛnə'gɒdʒɪk). **2** inducing or increasing menstrual flow. [C18: from Greek *emmēna* menses, (from *mēn* month) + -AGOGUE]

Emmenthal, Emmental ('ɛmənˌtɑːl), *or* **Emmenthaler, Emmentaler** *n* a hard Swiss cheese with holes in it, similar to Gruyère. [C20: named after *Emmenthal,* a valley in Switzerland]

emmer ('ɛmə) *n* a variety of wheat, *Triticum dicoccum,* grown in mountainous parts of Europe as a cereal crop and for livestock food: thought to be an ancestor of many other varieties of wheat. [C20: from German; related to Old High German *amari* spelt]

emmet ('ɛmɪt) *n* **1** *Brit.* an archaic or dialect word for **ant. 2** *Cornish dialect.* a tourist or holiday-maker. [Old English *ǣmette* ANT; related to Old Norse *meita,* Old High German *āmeiza,* Gothic *maitan*]

Emmet ('ɛmɪt) *n* **Robert.** 1778–1803, Irish nationalist, executed for leading an uprising for Irish independence.

emmetropia (ˌɛmɪ'trəʊpɪə) *n* the normal condition of perfect vision, in which parallel light rays are focused on the retina without the need for accommodation. [C19: from New Latin, from Greek *emmetros* in due measure + -OPIA] ▸ **emmetropic** (ˌɛmɪ'trɒpɪk) *adj*

Emmy ('ɛmɪ) *n, pl* **-mys** *or* **-mies.** (in the U.S.) one of the gold-plated statuettes awarded annually for outstanding television performances and productions. [C20: alteration of *Immy,* short for *image orthicon tube*]

emollient (ɪ'mɒljənt) *adj* **1** softening or soothing, esp. to the skin. **2** helping to avoid confrontation; calming. ◆ *n* **3** any preparation or substance that has a softening or soothing effect, esp. when applied to the skin. [C17: from Latin *ēmollīre* to soften, from *mollis* soft] ▸ **e'mollience** *n*

emolument (ɪ'mɒljʊmənt) *n* the profit arising from an office or employment, usually in the form of fees or wages. [C15: from Latin *ēmolumentum* benefit; originally, fee paid to a miller, from *ēmolere,* from *molere* to grind]

emote (ɪ'məʊt) *vb* (*intr*) to display exaggerated emotion, as in acting; behave theatrically. [C20: back formation from EMOTION] ▸ **e'moter** *n*

emotion (ɪ'məʊʃən) *n* any strong feeling, as of joy, sorrow, or fear. [C16: from French, from Old French *esmovoir* to excite, from Latin *ēmovēre* to disturb, from *movēre* to MOVE] ▸ **e'motionless** *adj*

emotional (ɪ'məʊʃənᵊl) *adj* **1** of, characteristic of, or expressive of emotion. **2** readily or excessively affected by emotion. **3** appealing to or arousing emotion: *an emotional piece of music.* **4** caused, determined, or actuated by emotion rather than reason: *an emotional argument.* ▸ **eˌmotion'ality** *n* ▸ **e'motionally** *adv*

emotionalism (ɪ'məʊʃənəˌlɪzəm) *n* **1** emotional nature, character, or quality. **2** a tendency to yield readily to the emotions. **3** an appeal to the emotions, esp. an excessive appeal, as to an audience. **4** a doctrine stressing the value of deeply felt responses in ethics and the arts. ▸ **e'motionalist** *n* ▸ **eˌmotional'istic** *adj*

emotionalize *or* **emotionalise** (ɪ'məʊʃənəˌlaɪz) *vb* (*tr*) to make emotional; subject to emotional treatment. ▸ **eˌmotionali'zation** *or* **eˌmotionali'sation** *n*

emotive (ɪ'məʊtɪv) *adj* **1** tending or designed to arouse emotion. **2** of or characterized by emotion. ▸ **e'motively** *adv* ▸ **e'motiveness** *or* **ˌemo'tivity** *n*

USAGE *Emotional* is preferred to *emotive* when describing a display of emotion: *he was given an emotional* (not *emotive*) *welcome.*

emotivism (ɪ'məʊtɪˌvɪzəm) *n Ethics.* the theory that moral utterances do not have a truth value but express the feelings of the speaker, so that *murder is wrong* is equivalent to *down with murder.* Also called: **boo-hurrah theory.** Compare **prescriptivism, descriptivism.**

Emp. *abbrev. for:* **1** Emperor. **2** Empire. **3** Empress.

empale (ɪm'peɪl) *vb* a less common spelling of **impale.** ▸ **em'palement** *n* ▸ **em'paler** *n*

empanel *or* **impanel** (ɪm'pænᵊl) *vb* **-els, -elling, -elled** *or U.S.* **-els, -eling, -eled.** (*tr*) *Law.* **1** to enter on a list (names of persons to be summoned for jury service). **2** to select (a jury) from the names on such a list. ▸ **em'panelment** *or* **im'panelment** *n*

empathic (ɛm'pæθɪk) *or* **empathetic** (ˌɛmpə'θɛtɪk) *adj* of or relating to empathy. ▸ **em'pathically** *or* **ˌempa'thetically** *adv*

empathize *or* **empathise** ('ɛmpəˌθaɪz) *vb* (*intr*) to engage in or feel empathy.

empathy ('ɛmpəθɪ) *n* **1** the power of understanding and imaginatively entering into another person's feelings. See also **identification** (sense 3b.). **2** the attribution to an object, such as a work of art, of one's own emotional or intellectual feelings about it. [C20: from Greek *empatheia* affection, passion, intended as a rendering of German *Einfühlung,* literally: a feeling in; see EN-², -PATHY] ▸ **'empathist** *n*

Empedocles (ɛm'pɛdəˌkliːz) *n* ?490–430 B.C., Greek philosopher and scientist, who held that the world is composed of four elements, air, fire, earth, and water, which are governed by the opposing forces of love and discord.

empennage (ɛm'pɛnɪdʒ; *French* ɑ̃pɛnaʒ) *n* the rear part of an aircraft, comprising the fin, rudder, and tailplane. [C20: from French: feathering, from *empenner* to feather an arrow, from *penne* feather, from Latin *pinna*]

emperor ('ɛmpərə) *n* **1** a monarch who rules or reigns over an empire. **2** Also called: **emperor moth.** any of several large saturniid moths with eyelike markings on each wing, esp. *Saturnia pavonia* of Europe. See also **giant peacock moth. 3** See **purple emperor.** [C13: from Old French *empereor,* from Latin *imperātor* commander-in-chief, from *imperāre* to command, from IM- + *parāre* to make ready] ▸ **'emperorˌship** *n*

emperor penguin *n* an Antarctic penguin, *Aptenodytes forsteri,* with orange-yellow patches on the neck: the largest penguin, reaching a height of 1.3 m (4 ft.).

empery ('ɛmpərɪ) *n, pl* **-peries.** *Archaic.* dominion or power; empire. [C13 (in the sense: the status of an emperor): from Anglo-French *emperie,* from Latin *imperium*power; see EMPIRE]

emphasis ('ɛmfəsɪs) *n, pl* **-ses** (-siːz). **1** special importance or significance. **2** an object, idea, etc., that is given special importance or significance. **3** stress made to fall on a particular syllable, word, or phrase in speaking. **4** force or intensity of expression: *he spoke with special emphasis on the subject of civil rights.* **5** sharpness or clarity of form or outline: *the sunlight gave emphasis to the shape of the mountain.* [C16: via Latin from Greek: meaning, (in rhetoric) significant stress; see EMPHATIC]

emphasize *or* **emphasise** ('ɛmfəˌsaɪz) *vb* (*tr*) to give emphasis or prominence to; stress.

emphatic (ɪm'fætɪk) *adj* **1** expressed, spoken, or done with emphasis. **2** forceful and positive; definite; direct: *an emphatic personality.* **3** sharp or clear in form, contour, or outline. **4** important or significant; stressed: *the emphatic points in an argument.* **5** *Phonetics.* denoting certain dental consonants of Arabic that are pronounced with accompanying pharyngeal constriction. ◆ *n* **6** *Phonetics.* an emphatic consonant, as used in Arabic. [C18: from Greek *emphatikos* expressive, forceful, from *emphainein* to exhibit, display, from *phainein* to show] ▸ **em'phatically** *adv*

emphysema (ˌɛmfɪ'siːmə) *n Pathol.* **1** Also called: **pulmonary emphysema.** a condition in which the air sacs of the lungs are grossly enlarged, causing breathlessness and wheezing. **2** the abnormal presence of air in a tissue or part. [C17: from New Latin, from Greek *emphusēma,* a swelling up, from *emphusan* to inflate, from *phusan* to blow] ▸ **emphysematous** (ˌɛmfɪ'sɛmətəs, -'siː-) *adj*

empire ('ɛmpaɪə) *n* **1** an aggregate of peoples and territories, often of great extent, under the rule of a single person, oligarchy, or sovereign state. **2** any monarchy that for reasons of history, prestige, etc., has an emperor rather than a king as head of state. **3** the period during which a particular empire exists. **4** supreme power; sovereignty. Related adj: **imperial. 5** a large industrial organization with many ramifications, esp. a multinational corporation. [C13: from Old French, from Latin *imperium* rule, from *imperāre* to command, from *parāre* to prepare]

Empire ('ɛmpaɪə) *n* **the. 1** See **British Empire. 2** *French history.* **2a** the period of imperial rule in France from 1804 to 1815 under Napoleon Bonaparte. **2b** Also called: **Second Empire.** the period from 1852 to 1870 when Napoleon III ruled as emperor. ◆ *adj* **3** denoting, characteristic of, or relating to the British Empire. **4** denoting, characteristic of, or relating to either French Empire, esp. the first: in particular, denoting the neoclassical style of architecture and furniture and the high-waisted style of women's dresses characteristic of the period.

empire-builder *n Informal.* a person who seeks extra power for its own sake, esp. by increasing the number of his subordinates or staff. ▸ **'empire-ˌbuilding** *n, adj*

Empire Day *n* the former name of **Commonwealth Day.**

Empire State *n* nickname of **New York** (state).

empiric (ɛm'pɪrɪk) *n* **1** a person who relies on empirical methods. **2** a medical quack; charlatan. ◆ *adj* **3** a variant of **empirical.** [C16: from Latin *empīricus,* from Greek *empeirikos* practised, from *peiran* to attempt]

empirical (ɛm'pɪrɪkᵊl) *adj* **1** derived from or relating to experiment and observation rather than theory. **2** (of medical treatment) based on practical experience rather than scientific proof. **3** *Philosophy.* **3a** (of knowledge) derived from experience rather than by logic from first principles. Compare **a priori, a posteriori. 3b** (of a proposition) subject, at least theoretically, to verification. Compare **analytic** (sense 4), **synthetic** (sense 4). **4** of or relating to medical quackery. ◆ *n* **5** *Statistics.* the posterior probability of an event derived on the basis of its observed frequency in a sample. Compare **mathematical probability.** See also **posterior probability.** ▸ **em'pirically** *adv* ▸ **em'piricalness** *n*

empirical formula *n* **1** a chemical formula indicating the proportion of each element present in a molecule: *$C_6H_{12}O_6$ is the molecular formula of sucrose whereas CH_2O is its empirical formula.* Compare **molecular formula, structural formula. 2** a formula or expression obtained from experimental data rather than theory.

empiricism (ɛm'pɪrɪˌsɪzəm) *n* **1** *Philosophy.* the doctrine that all knowledge of matters of fact derives from experience and that the mind is not furnished with a set of concepts in advance of experience. Compare **intuitionism, rationalism. 2** the use of empirical methods. **3** medical quackery; charlatanism. ▸ **em'piricist** *n, adj*

emplace (ɪm'pleɪs) *vb* (*tr*) to put in place or position.

emplacement (ɪm'pleɪsmənt) *n* **1** a prepared position for the siting of a gun or other weapon. **2** the act of putting or state of being put in place. [C19: from French, from obsolete *emplacer* to put in position, from PLACE]

emplane (ɪm'pleɪn) *vb* to board or put on board an aeroplane.

employ (ɪm'plɔɪ) *vb* (*tr*) **1** to engage or make use of the services of (a person) in return for money; hire. **2** to provide work or occupation for; keep busy; occupy: *collecting stamps employs a lot of his time.* **3** to use as a means: *to employ secret measures to get one's ends.* ◆ *n* **4** the state of being employed (esp. in the phrase **in someone's employ**). [C15: from Old French *emploier,* from Latin *implicāre* to entangle, engage, from *plicāre* to fold] ► **em'ployable** *adj* ► **em,ploya'bility** *n*

employee (ɛm'plɔiː, ,ɛmplɔɪ'iː) *or U.S.* **employe** *n* a person who is hired to work for another or for a business, firm, etc., in return for payment. Also called (esp. formerly): **employé**.

employee association *n* an organization, other than a trade union, whose members comprise employees of a single employing organization. The aims of the association may be social, recreational, or professional.

employer (ɪm'plɔɪə) *n* **1** a person, business, firm, etc., that employs workers. **2** a person who employs; user.

employers' association *n* a body of employers, usually from the same sector of the economy, associated to further the interests of member companies by conducting negotiations with trade unions, providing advice, making representations to other bodies, etc.

employment (ɪm'plɔɪmənt) *n* **1** the act of employing or state of being employed. **2** the work or occupation in which a person is employed. **3** the purpose for which something is used.

employment agency *n* a private firm whose business is placing people in jobs.

employment exchange *n Brit.* a former name for **employment office**.

employment office *n Brit.* any of a number of government offices established to collect and supply to the unemployed information about job vacancies and to employers information about availability of prospective workers. Former names: **employment exchange, labour exchange**. See also **Jobcentre**.

empoison (ɪm'pɔɪzᵊn) *vb (tr)* **1** *Rare.* to embitter or corrupt. **2** an archaic word for **poison** (senses 6–9). ► **em'poisonment** *n*

empolder (ɪm'pəʊldə) *vb* a variant spelling of **impolder**.

emporium (ɛm'pɔːrɪəm) *n, pl* **-riums** *or* **-ria** (-rɪə). a large and often ostentatious retail shop offering for sale a wide variety of merchandise. [C16: from Latin, from Greek *emporion*, from *emporos* merchant, from *poros* a journey]

empoverish (ɪm'pɒvərɪʃ) *vb* an obsolete spelling of **impoverish**. ► **em'poverisher** *n* ► **em'poverishment** *n*

empower (ɪm'paʊə) *vb (tr)* **1** to give or delegate power or authority to; authorize. **2** to give ability to; enable or permit. ► **em'powerment** *n*

empress ('ɛmprɪs) *n* **1** the wife or widow of an emperor. **2** a woman who holds the rank of emperor in her own right. **3** a woman of great power and influence. [C12: from Old French *empereriz*, from Latin *imperātrix* feminine of *imperātor* EMPEROR]

emprise (ɛm'praɪz) *n Archaic.* **1** a chivalrous or daring enterprise; adventure. **2** chivalrous daring or prowess. [C13: from Old French, from *emprendre* to undertake; see ENTERPRISE]

Empson ('ɛmpsᵊn) *n* Sir **William**. 1906–84, English poet and critic; author of *Seven Types of Ambiguity* (1930).

empt (ɛmpt, ɛmt) *vb (tr) Dialect.* to empty. [from Old English *ǣmtian* to be without duties; compare EMPTY]

empty ('ɛmptɪ) *adj* **-tier, -tiest. 1** containing nothing. **2** without inhabitants; vacant or unoccupied. **3** carrying no load, passengers, etc. **4** without purpose, substance, or value: *an empty life*. **5** insincere or trivial: *empty words*. **6** not expressive or vital; vacant: *she has an empty look*. **7** *Informal.* hungry. **8** *(postpositive,* foll. by *of)* devoid; destitute: *a life empty of happiness*. **9** *Informal.* drained of energy or emotion: *after the violent argument he felt very empty*. **10** *Maths, logic.* (of a set or class) containing no members. **11** *Philosophy, logic.* (of a name or description) having no reference. ♦ *vb* **-ties, -tying, -tied. 12** to make or become empty. **13** (when *intr*, foll. by *into*) to discharge (contents). **14** *(tr;* often foll. by *of)* to unburden or rid (oneself): *to empty oneself of emotion*. ♦ *n, pl* **-ties. 15** an empty container, esp. a bottle. [Old English *ǣmtig*, from *ǣmetta* free time, from *ǣ-* without + *-metta*, from *mōtan* to be obliged to; see MUST[1]] ► **'emptiable** *adj* ► **'emptier** *n* ► **'emptily** *adv* ► **'emptiness** *n*

empty cow *n* a cow that does not produce calves during the breeding season.

empty-handed *adj* **1** carrying nothing in the hands. **2** having gained nothing: *they returned from the negotiations empty-handed*.

empty-headed *adj* lacking intelligence or sense; frivolous.

empty-nester *n Informal.* a married person whose children have grown up and left home.

Empty Quarter *n* another name for **Rub' al Khali**.

empyema (,ɛmpaɪ'iːmə) *n, pl* **-emata** (-'iːmətə) *or* **-emas**. a collection of pus in a body cavity, esp. in the chest. [C17: from Medieval Latin, from Greek *empuēma* abscess, from *empuein* to suppurate, from *puon* pus] ► **,empy'emic** *adj*

empyrean (,ɛmpaɪ'riːən) *n* **1** *Archaic.* the highest part of the (supposedly spherical) heavens, thought in ancient times to contain the pure element of fire and by early Christians to be the abode of God and the angels. **2** *Poetic.* the heavens or sky. ♦ *adj also* **empyreal**. **3** of or relating to the sky, the heavens, or the empyrean. **4** heavenly or sublime. **5** *Archaic.* composed of fire. [C17: from Medieval Latin *empyreus*, from Greek *empuros* fiery, from *pur* fire]

empyreuma (,ɛmpɪ'ruːmə) *n, pl* **-mata** (-mətə). the smell and taste associated with burning vegetable and animal matter. [C17: from Greek, from *empureuein* to set on fire]

Ems (ɛmz) *n* **1** a town in W Germany, in the Rhineland-Palatinate: famous for the **Ems Telegram** (1870), Bismarck's dispatch that led to the outbreak of the Franco-Prussian War. Pop.: 10 241 (latest est.). **2** a river in West Germany, rising in the Teutoburger Wald and flowing generally north to the North Sea. Length: about 370 km (230 miles).

EMS *abbrev. for* European Monetary System.

emu ('iːmjuː) *n* a large Australian flightless bird, *Dromaius novaehollandiae*, similar to the ostrich but with three-toed feet and grey or brown plumage: order *Casuariiformes*. See also **ratite**. [C17: changed from Portuguese *ema* ostrich, from Arabic *Na-'amah* ostrich]

EMU 1 *abbrev. for* European Monetary Union. **2** see **e.m.u.**

e.m.u. *or* **EMU** *abbrev. for* electromagnetic unit.

emu-bob *Austral. informal.* ♦ *vb* **-bobs, -bobbing, -bobbed. 1** *(intr)* to bend over to collect litter or small pieces of wood. ♦ *n* **2** Also called: **emu parade**. a parade of soldiers or schoolchildren for litter collection. ► **'emu-bobbing** *n*

emu bush *n* any of various Australian shrubs, esp. those of the genus *Eremophila* (family Myoporaceae), whose fruits are eaten by emus.

emulate ('ɛmjʊ,leɪt) *vb (tr)* **1** to attempt to equal or surpass, esp. by imitation. **2** to rival or compete with. **3** to make one computer behave like (another different type of computer) so that the imitating system can operate on the same data and execute the same programs as the imitated system. [C16: from Latin *aemulārī*, from *aemulus* competing with; probably related to *imitārī* to IMITATE] ► **'emulative** *adj* ► **'emulatively** *adv* ► **'emu,lator** *n*

emulation (,ɛmjʊ'leɪʃən) *n* **1** the act of emulating or imitating. **2** the effort or desire to equal or surpass another or others. **3** *Archaic.* jealous rivalry.

emulous ('ɛmjʊləs) *adj* **1** desiring or aiming to equal or surpass another; competitive. **2** characterized by or arising from emulation or imitation. **3** *Archaic.* envious or jealous. [C14: from Latin *aemulus* rivalling; see EMULATE] ► **'emulously** *adv* ► **'emulousness** *n*

emulsifier (ɪ'mʌlsɪ,faɪə) *n* an agent that forms or preserves an emulsion, esp. any food additive, such as lecithin, that prevents separation of sauces or other processed foods.

emulsify (ɪ'mʌlsɪ,faɪ) *vb* **-fies, -fying, -fied.** to make or form into an emulsion. ► **e,mulsi'fiable** *or* **e'mulsible** *adj* ► **e,mulsifi'cation** *n*

emulsion (ɪ'mʌlʃən) *n* **1** *Photog.* a light-sensitive coating on a base, such as paper or film, consisting of fine grains of silver bromide suspended in gelatine. **2** *Chem.* a colloid in which both phases are liquids: *an oil-in-water emulsion*. **3** Also called: **emulsion paint**. a type of paint in which the pigment is suspended in a vehicle, usually a synthetic resin, that is dispersed in water as an emulsion. It usually gives a mat finish. **4** *Pharmacol.* a mixture in which an oily medicine is dispersed in another liquid. **5** any liquid resembling milk. [C17: from New Latin *ēmulsiō*, from Latin *ēmulsus* milked out, from *ēmulgēre* to milk out, drain out, from *mulgēre* to milk] ► **e'mulsive** *adj*

emulsoid (ɪ'mʌlsɔɪd) *n Chem.* a sol with a liquid disperse phase.

emunctory (ɪ'mʌŋktərɪ) *adj* **1** of or relating to a bodily organ or duct having an excretory function. ♦ *n, pl* **-ries. 2** an excretory organ or duct, such as a skin pore. [C16: from New Latin *ēmunctōrium*, from Latin *ēmungere* to wipe clean, from *mungere* to wipe]

emu parade *n Austral.* an army exercise devoted to emu-bobbing.

emu-wren *n* any Australian wren of the genus *Stipiturus*, having long plumy tail feathers.

EMV *abbrev. for* expected monetary value: the product of the monetary outcome of a particular decision in a decision tree and the probability of this outcome happening.

en (ɛn) *n Printing.* a unit of measurement, half the width of an em. Also called: **nut**. See also **ennage**.

EN (in Britain) *abbrev. for* **1** enrolled nurse. **2** English Nature.

en-[1] *or* **em-** *prefix forming verbs.* **1** *(from nouns)* **1a** put in or on: *entomb; enthrone*. **1b** go on or into: *enplane*. **1c** surround or cover with: *enmesh*. **1d** furnish with: *empower*. **2** *(from adjectives and nouns)* cause to be in a certain condition: *enable; encourage; enrich; enslave*. [via Old French from Latin *in-* IN-[2]]

en-[2] *or* **em-** *prefix forming nouns and adjectives.* in; into; inside: *endemic*. [from Greek (often via Latin); compare IN-[1], IN-[2]]

-en[1] *suffix forming verbs from adjectives and nouns.* cause to be; become; cause to have: *blacken; heighten*. [Old English *-n-*, as in *fæst-n-ian* to fasten, of common Germanic origin; compare Icelandic *fastna*]

-en[2] *suffix forming adjectives from nouns.* of; made of; resembling: *ashen; earthen; wooden*. [Old English *-en*; related to Gothic *-eins*, Latin *-īnus* -INE[1]]

enable (ɪn'eɪbᵊl) *vb (tr)* **1** to provide (someone) with adequate power, means, opportunity, or authority (to do something). **2** to make possible. **3** to put (a digital electronic circuit element) into an operative condition by supplying a suitable input pulse. ► **en'ablement** *n* ► **en'abler** *n*

enabling act *n* a legislative act conferring certain specified powers on a person or organization.

enact (ɪn'ækt) *vb (tr)* **1** to make into an act or statute. **2** to establish by law; ordain or decree. **3** to represent or perform in or as if in a play; to act out. ► **en'actable** *adj* ► **en'active** *or* **en'actory** *adj* ► **en'actment** *or* **en'action** *n* ► **en'actor** *n*

enalapril (ɪ'næləprɪl) *n* an ACE inhibitor used to treat high blood pressure and congestive heart failure.

enamel (ɪ'næməl) *n* **1** a coloured glassy substance, translucent or opaque, fused to the surface of articles made of metal, glass, etc., for ornament or protection. **2** an article or articles ornamented with enamel. **3** an enamel-like paint or varnish. **4** any smooth glossy coating resembling enamel. **5** another word for **nail polish**. **6** the hard white calcified substance that covers the crown of each tooth. **7** *(modifier)* **7a** decorated or covered with enamel: *an enamel ring*. **7b** made with enamel: *enamel paste*. ♦ *vb* **-els, -elling, -elled** *or U.S.* **-els, -eling, -eled.** *(tr)* **8** to inlay, coat, or otherwise decorate with enamel. **9** to ornament with glossy variegated colours, as if with enamel. **10** to portray in enamel. [C15: from Old French *esmail*, of Germanic origin; compare Old High German *smalz* lard; see SMELT[1]] ► **e'nameller, e'namellist** *or U.S.* **e'nameler, e'namelist** *n* ► **e'namel,work** *n*

enamour *or U.S.* **enamor** (ɪn'æmə) *vb (tr; usually passive* and foll. by *of)* to inspire with love; captivate; charm. [C14: from Old French *enamourer,* from *amour* love, from Latin *amor*] ▸ **en'amoured** *or U.S.* **en'amored** *adj*

enantiomer (ɛn'æntɪəmə) *n Chem.* a molecule that exhibits stereoisomerism because of the presence of one or more chiral centres.

enantiomorph (ɛn'æntɪəˌmɔːf) *n* either of the two crystal forms of a substance that are mirror images of each other. [C19: from Greek *enantios* opposite + -MORPH] ▸ **enˌantio'morphic** *adj* ▸ **enˌantio'morphism** *n*

enarthrosis (ˌɛnɑː'θrəʊsɪs) *n, pl* **-ses** (-siːz). *Anatomy.* a ball-and-socket joint, such as that of the hip. [C17: via New Latin from Greek, from *arthrōsis,* from *arthron* a joint + -OSIS] ▸ **ˌenar'throdial** *adj*

enate ('iːneɪt) *adj also* **enatic** (iː'nætɪk). **1** *Biology.* growing out or outwards. **2** related on the side of the mother. ◆ *n* **3** a relative on the mother's side. [C17: from Latin *ēnātus,* from *ēnāscī* to be born from, from *nāscī* to be born]

en attendant *French.* (ɑ̃n atɑ̃dɑ̃) *adv* in the mean time; while waiting.

en bloc *French.* (ɑ̃ blɔk) *adv* in a lump or block; as a body or whole; all together.

en brochette *French.* (ɑ̃ brɔʃɛt) *adj, adv* (esp. of meat) roasted or grilled on a skewer. [literally: on a skewer]

en brosse *French.* (ɑ̃ brɔs) *adj, adv* (of the hair) cut very short so that the hair stands up stiffly. [literally: in the style of a brush]

enc. *abbrev. for:* **1** enclosed. **2** enclosure.

encaenia (ɛn'siːnɪə) *n Rare.* a festival of dedication or commemoration. [C14: via Late Latin from Greek *enkainia,* from *kainos* new]

encage (ɪn'keɪdʒ) *vb (tr)* to confine in or as in a cage.

encamp (ɪn'kæmp) *vb* to lodge or cause to lodge in a camp.

encampment (ɪn'kæmpmənt) *n* **1** the act of setting up a camp. **2** the place where a camp, esp. a military camp, is set up.

encapsulate *or* **incapsulate** (ɪn'kæpsjʊˌleɪt) *vb* **1** to enclose or be enclosed in or as if in a capsule. **2** *(tr)* to sum up in a short or concise form; condense; abridge. ▸ **enˌcapsu'lation** *or* **inˌcapsu'lation** *n*

encarnalize *or* **encarnalise** (ɪn'kɑːnəˌlaɪz) *vb (tr) Rare.* **1** to provide with a bodily form; incarnate. **2** to make carnal, gross, or sensual.

encase *or* **incase** (ɪn'keɪs) *vb (tr)* to place or enclose in or as if in a case. ▸ **en'casement** *or* **in'casement** *n*

encash (ɪn'kæʃ) *vb (tr) Brit., formal.* to exchange (a cheque) for cash. ▸ **en'cashable** *adj* ▸ **en'cashment** *n*

encastré (ɛn'kɑːstreɪ) *adj Civil engineering.* (of a beam) fixed at the ends; built into its supports. [C19: from French, past participle of *encastrer,* from Latin *incastrare* to cut in; see CASTRATE]

encaustic (ɪn'kɒstɪk) *Ceramics, etc.* ◆ *adj* **1** decorated by any process involving burning in colours, esp. by inlaying coloured clays and baking or by fusing wax colours to the surface. ◆ *n* **2** the process of burning in colours. **3** a product of such a process. [C17: from Latin *encausticus,* from Greek *enkaustikos,* from *enkaiein* to burn in, from *kaiein* to burn] ▸ **en'caustically** *adv*

-ence *or* **-ency** *suffix forming nouns.* indicating an action, state, condition, or quality: *benevolence; residence; patience.* [via Old French from Latin *-entia,* from *-ēns,* present participial ending]

enceinte[1] (ɒn'sænt; *French* ɑ̃sɛ̃t) *adj* another word for **pregnant.** [C17: from French, from Latin *inciēns* pregnant; related to Greek *enkuos,* from *kuein* to be pregnant]

enceinte[2] (ɒn'sænt; *French* ɑ̃sɛ̃t) *n* **1** a boundary wall enclosing a defended area. **2** the area enclosed. [C18: from French: enclosure, from *enceindre* to encompass, from Latin *incingere,* from *cingere* to gird]

Enceladus[1] (ɛn'sɛlədəs) *n Greek myth.* a giant who was punished for his rebellion against the gods by a fatal blow from a stone cast by Athena. He was believed to be buried under Mount Etna in Sicily.

Enceladus[2] *n* a very bright satellite of Saturn.

encephalalgia (ɛnˌsɛfə'lældʒɪə) *n Med.* pain in the head; headache.

encephalic (ˌɛnsɪ'fælɪk, ˌɛnkɪ-) *adj* of or relating to the brain.

encephalin (ɛn'sɛfəlɪn) *n* a variant of **enkephalin.**

encephalitis (ˌɛnsɛfə'laɪtɪs, ˌɛnkɛf-) *n* inflammation of the brain. ▸ **encephalitic** (ˌɛnsɛfə'lɪtɪk) *adj*

encephalitis lethargica (lɪ'θɑːdʒɪkə) *n Pathol.* a technical name for **sleeping sickness** (sense 2).

encephalo- *or before a vowel* **encephal-** *combining form.* indicating the brain: *encephalogram; encephalitis.* [from New Latin, from Greek *enkephalos,* from *en-* in + *kephalē* head]

encephalogram (ɛn'sɛfələˌɡræm) *n* **1** an X-ray photograph of the brain, esp. one (a **pneumoencephalogram**) taken after replacing some of the cerebrospinal fluid with air or oxygen so that the brain cavities show clearly. **2** short for **electroencephalogram.**

encephalograph (ɛn'sɛfələˌɡrɑːf, -ˌɡræf) *n* **1** short for **electroencephalograph. 2** any other apparatus used to produce an encephalogram.

encephalography (ˌɛnsɛfə'lɒɡrəfɪ) *n* **1** the branch of medical science concerned with taking and analysing X-ray photographs of the brain. **2** another name for **electroencephalography.** ▸ **encephalographic** (ɛnˌsɛfələ'ɡræfɪk) *adj* ▸ **enˌcephalo'graphically** *adv*

encephaloma (ˌɛnsɛfə'ləʊmə) *n, pl* **-mas** *or* **-mata** (-mətə). a brain tumour.

encephalomyelitis (ɛnˌsɛfələʊˌmaɪə'laɪtɪs) *n* acute inflammation of the brain and spinal cord. ▸ **encephalomyelitic** (ɛnˌsɛfələʊˌmaɪə'lɪtɪk) *adj*

encephalon (ɛn'sɛfəˌlɒn) *n, pl* **-la** (-lə). a technical name for **brain.** [C18: from New Latin, from Greek *enkephalos* brain (literally: that which is in the head), from EN-[2] + *kephalē* head] ▸ **en'cephalous** *adj*

encephalopathy (ɛnˌsɛfə'lɒpəθɪ) *n* any degenerative disease of the brain, often associated with toxic conditions. See also **BSE.**

enchain (ɪn'tʃeɪn) *vb (tr)* **1** to bind with chains. **2** to hold fast or captivate (the attention, etc.). ▸ **en'chainment** *n*

enchant (ɪn'tʃɑːnt) *vb (tr)* **1** to cast a spell on; bewitch. **2** to delight or captivate utterly; fascinate; charm. [C14: from Old French *enchanter,* from Latin *incantāre* to chant a spell, from *cantāre* to chant, from *canere* to sing] ▸ **en'chanted** *adj* ▸ **en'chanter** *n* ▸ **en'chantress** *fem n*

enchanter's nightshade *n* any of several onagraceous plants of the genus *Circaea,* esp. *C. lutetiana,* having small white flowers and bristly fruits.

enchanting (ɪn'tʃɑːntɪŋ) *adj* pleasant; delightful. ▸ **en'chantingly** *adv*

enchantment (ɪn'tʃɑːntmənt) *n* **1** the act of enchanting or state of being enchanted. **2** a magic spell or act of witchcraft. **3** great charm or fascination.

enchase (ɪn'tʃeɪs) *vb (tr)* a less common word for **chase**[3]. [C15: from Old French *enchasser* to enclose, set, from EN-[1] + *casse* CASE[2]] ▸ **en'chaser** *n*

enchilada (ˌɛntʃɪ'lɑːdə) *n* a Mexican dish consisting of a tortilla fried in hot fat, filled with meat, and served with a chilli sauce. [C19: American Spanish, feminine of *enchilado* seasoned with chilli, from *enchilar* to spice with chilli, from *chile* CHILLI]

enchiridion (ˌɛnkaɪ'rɪdɪən) *n, pl* **-ions** *or* **-ia** (-ɪə). *Rare.* a handbook or manual. [C16: from Late Latin, from Greek *enkheiridion,* from EN-[2] + *kheir* hand]

enchondroma (ˌɛnkən'drəʊmə) *n, pl* **-mas** *or* **-mata** (-mətə). *Pathol.* a benign cartilaginous tumour, most commonly in the bones of the hands or feet. [C19: New Latin from Greek, from EN-[2] + *khondros* cartilage] ▸ **ˌenchon'dromatous** *adj*

enchorial (ɛn'kɔːrɪəl) *or* **enchoric** *adj* of or used in a particular country: used esp. of the popular (demotic) writing of the ancient Egyptians. [C19: via Late Latin from Greek *enkhōrios,* from EN-[2] + *khōra* country]

-enchyma *combining form.* denoting cellular tissue: *aerenchyma.* [C20: abstracted from PARENCHYMA]

encipher (ɪn'saɪfə) *vb (tr)* to convert (a message, document, etc.) from plain text into code or cipher; encode. ▸ **en'cipherer** *n* ▸ **en'cipherment** *n*

encircle (ɪn'sɜːkᵊl) *vb (tr)* to form a circle around; enclose within a circle; surround. ▸ **en'circlement** *n* ▸ **en'circling** *adj*

Encke (*German* 'ɛŋkə) *n* **Johann Franz.** 1791–1865, German astronomer, who discovered **Encke's Division** in the outer ring of Saturn.

encl. *abbrev. for:* **1** enclosed. **2** enclosure.

en clair *French.* (ɑ̃ klɛr) *adv, adj* in ordinary language; not in cipher. [literally: in clear]

enclasp (ɪn'klɑːsp) *vb (tr)* to clasp; embrace.

enclave ('ɛnkleɪv) *n* a part of a country entirely surrounded by foreign territory: viewed from the position of the surrounding territories. Compare **exclave.** [C19: from French, from Old French *enclaver* to enclose, from Vulgar Latin *inclāvāre* (unattested) to lock up, from Latin IN-[2] + *clavis* key]

enclitic (ɪn'klɪtɪk) *adj* **1a** denoting or relating to a monosyllabic word or form that is treated as a suffix of the preceding word, as Latin *-que* in *populusque.* **1b** (in classical Greek) denoting or relating to a word that throws an accent back onto the preceding word. ◆ *n* **2** an enclitic word or linguistic form. ◆ Compare **proclitic.** [C17: from Late Latin *encliticus,* from Greek *enklitikos,* from *enklinein* to cause to lean, from EN-[2] + *klinein* to lean] ▸ **en'clitically** *adv*

enclose *or* **inclose** (ɪn'kləʊz) *vb (tr)* **1** to close; hem in; surround. **2** to surround (land) with or as if with a fence. **3** to put in an envelope or wrapper, esp. together with a letter. **4** to contain or hold. ▸ **en'closable** *or* **in'closable** *adj* ▸ **en'closer** *or* **in'closer** *n*

enclosed order *n* a Christian religious order that does not permit its members to go into the outside world.

enclosure *or* **inclosure** (ɪn'kləʊʒə) *n* **1** the act of enclosing or state of being enclosed. **2** a region or area enclosed by or as if by a fence. **3a** the act of appropriating land, esp. common land, by putting a hedge or other barrier around it. **3b** *History.* such acts as were carried out at various periods in England, esp. between the 12th and 14th centuries and finally in the 18th and 19th centuries. **4** a fence, wall, etc., that serves to enclose. **5** something, esp. a supporting document, enclosed within an envelope or wrapper, esp. together with a letter. **6** *Brit.* a section of a sports ground, racecourse, etc., allotted to certain spectators.

encode (ɪn'kəʊd) *vb (tr)* **1** to convert (a message) from plain text into code. **2** *Computing.* to convert (characters and symbols) into a digital form as a series of impulses. Compare **decode** (sense 2). **3** to convert (an electrical signal) into a form suitable for transmission. **4** to convert (a nerve signal) into a form that can be received by the brain. **5** to use (a word, phrase, etc., esp. of a foreign language) in the construction appropriate to it in that language. ▸ **en'codement** *n* ▸ **en'coder** *n*

encomiast (ɛn'kəʊmɪˌæst) *n* a person who speaks or writes an encomium. [C17: from Greek *enkōmiastēs,* from *enkōmiazein* to utter an ENCOMIUM] ▸ **enˌcomi'astic** *or* **enˌcomi'astical** *adj* ▸ **enˌcomi'astically** *adv*

encomium (ɛn'kəʊmɪəm) *n, pl* **-miums** *or* **-mia** (-mɪə). a formal expression of praise; eulogy; panegyric. [C16: from Latin, from Greek *enkōmion,* from EN-[2] + *kōmos* festivity]

encompass (ɪn'kʌmpəs) *vb (tr)* **1** to enclose within a circle; surround. **2** to bring about; cause to happen; contrive: *he encompassed the enemy's ruin.* **3** to include entirely or comprehensively: *this book encompasses the whole range of knowledge.* ▸ **en'compassment** *n*

encopresis (ˌɛnkəʊ'priːsɪs) *n* involuntary discharge of faeces, esp. when associated with psychiatric disturbance. [C20: from New Latin, from Greek EN-[2] + COPR(O)-, + *-esis* as in ENURESIS] ▸ **encopretic** (ˌɛnkəʊ'prɛtɪk) *adj*

encore ('ɒŋkɔː) *interj* **1** again; once more: used by an audience to demand an extra or repeated performance. ◆ *n* **2** an extra or repeated performance given in response to enthusiastic demand. ◆ *vb* **3** *(tr)* to demand an extra or repeated performance of (a work, piece of music, etc.) by (a performer). [C18: from French: still, again, perhaps from Latin *in hanc hōram* until this hour]

encounter (ɪn'kaʊntə) *vb* **1** to come upon or meet casually or unexpectedly. **2** to come into conflict with (an enemy, army, etc.) in battle or contest. **3** *(tr)* to be faced with; contend with: *he encounters many obstacles in his work.* ◆ *n* **4** a meeting with a person or thing, esp. when casual or unexpected. **5** a hostile meeting; contest or conflict. [C13: from Old French *encontrer,* from Vulgar

Latin *incontrāre* (unattested), from Latin IN-[2] + *contrā* against, opposite] ▸ en'counterer *n*

encounter group *n* a group of people who meet in order to develop self-awareness and mutual understanding by openly expressing their feelings, by confrontation, physical contact, etc.

encourage (ɪn'kʌrɪdʒ) *vb* (*tr*) **1** to inspire (someone) with the courage or confidence (to do something). **2** to stimulate (something or someone to do something) by approval or help; support. ▸ **en'couragement** *n* ▸ **en'courager** *n* ▸ **en'couraging** *adj* ▸ **en'couragingly** *adv*

encrinite ('ɛnkrɪ,naɪt) *n* a fossil crinoid, esp. one of the genus *Encrinus*. Sometimes shortened to **crinite**. [C19: from New Latin *encrinus* (from Greek EN-[2] + *krinon* lily) + -ITE[1]]

encroach (ɪn'krəʊtʃ) *vb* (*intr*) **1** (often foll. by *on* or *upon*) to intrude gradually, stealthily, or insidiously upon the rights, property, etc., of another. **2** to advance beyond the usual or proper limits. [C14: from Old French *encrochier* to seize, literally: fasten upon with hooks, from EN-[1] + *croc* hook, of Germanic origin; see CROOK] ▸ **en'croacher** *n* ▸ **en'croachingly** *adv* ▸ **en'croachment** *n*

encrust *or* **incrust** (ɪn'krʌst) *vb* **1** (*tr*) to cover or overlay with or as with a crust or hard coating. **2** to form or cause to form a crust or hard coating. **3** (*tr*) to decorate lavishly, as with jewels. ▸ **,encrus'tation** *or* **,incrus'tation** *n*

encrypt (ɪn'krɪpt) *vb* (*tr*) **1** to put (a message) into code. **2** to put (computer data) into a coded form. **3** to distort (a television or other signal) so that it cannot be understood without the appropriate decryption equipment. [C20: from EN-[1] + *crypt*, as in CRYPTO-] ▸ **en'crypted** *adj* ▸ **en'cryption** *n*

enculturation (ɛn,kʌltʃʊ'reɪʃən) *n* another word for **socialization**. ▸ **enculturative** (ɛn'kʌltʃʊrətɪv) *adj*

encumber *or* **incumber** (ɪn'kʌmbə) *vb* (*tr*) **1** to hinder or impede; make difficult; hamper: *encumbered with parcels after going shopping at Christmas; his stupidity encumbers his efforts to learn.* **2** to fill with superfluous or useless matter. **3** to burden with debts, obligations, etc. [C14: from Old French *encombrer*, from EN-[1] + *combre* a barrier, from Late Latin *combrus*, of uncertain origin] ▸ **en'cumberingly** *or* **in'cumberingly** *adv*

encumbrance *or* **incumbrance** (ɪn'kʌmbrəns) *n* **1** a thing that impedes or is burdensome; hindrance. **2** *Law.* a burden or charge upon property, such as a mortgage or lien. **3** *Rare.* a dependent person, esp. a child.

encumbrancer (ɪn'kʌmbrənsə) *n Law.* a person who holds an encumbrance on property belonging to another.

ency., encyc., *or* **encycl.** *abbrev. for* encyclopedia.

-ency *suffix forming nouns.* a variant of **-ence**: *fluency; permanency.*

encyclical (ɛn'sɪklɪkəl) *n* **1** a letter sent by the pope to all Roman Catholic bishops throughout the world. ◆ *adj also* **encyclic**. **2** (of letters) intended for general or wide circulation. [C17: from Late Latin *encyclicus*, from Greek *enkuklios* general, from *kuklos* circle]

encyclopedia *or* **encyclopaedia** (ɛn,saɪkləʊ'piːdɪə) *n* a book, often in many volumes, containing articles on various topics, often arranged in alphabetical order, dealing either with the whole range of human knowledge or with one particular subject: *a medical encyclopedia.* [C16: from New Latin *encyclopaedia*, erroneously for Greek *enkuklios paideia* general education, from *enkuklios* general (see ENCYCLICAL), + *paideia* education, from *pais* child]

encyclopedic *or* **encyclopaedic** (ɛn,saɪkləʊ'piːdɪk) *adj* **1** of, characteristic of, or relating to an encyclopedia. **2** covering a wide range of knowledge; comprehensive. ▸ **en,cyclo'pedically** *or* **en,cyclo'paedically** *adv*

encyclopedist *or* **encyclopaedist** (ɛn,saɪkləʊ'piːdɪst) *n* a person who compiles or contributes to an encyclopedia. ▸ **en,cyclo'pedism** *or* **en,cyclo'paedism** *n*

encyst (ɛn'sɪst) *vb Biology.* to enclose or become enclosed by a cyst, thick membrane, or shell. ▸ **en'cysted** *adj* ▸ **en'cystment** *or* **,encys'tation** *n*

end[1] (ɛnd) *n* **1** the extremity of the length of something, such as a road, line, etc. **2** the surface at either extremity of a three-dimensional object. **3** the extreme extent, limit, or degree of something. **4** the most distant place or time that can be imagined: *the ends of the earth.* **5** the time at which something is concluded. **6a** the last section or part. **6b** (*as modifier*): *the end office.* **7** a share or part: *his end of the bargain.* **8** (*often pl*) a remnant or fragment (esp. in the phrase **odds and ends**). **9** a final state, esp. death; destruction. **10** the purpose of an action or existence. **11** *Sport.* either of the two defended areas of a playing field, rink, etc. **12** *Bowls, etc.* a section of play from one side of the rink to the other. **13** *American and Canadian football.* a player at the extremity of the playing line; wing. **14 all ends up.** totally or completely. **15 a sticky end.** *Informal.* an unpleasant death. **16 at a loose end** *or* (*U.S. and Canadian*) **at loose ends.** without purpose or occupation. **17 at an end.** exhausted or completed. **18 at the end of the day.** See **day** (sense 10). **19 come to an end.** to become completed or exhausted. **20 end on. 20a** with the end pointing towards one. **20b** with the end adjacent to the end of another object. **21 go off the deep end.** *Informal.* to lose one's temper; react angrily. **22 in the end.** finally. **23 make (both) ends meet.** to spend no more than the money one has. **24 no end (of).** *Informal.* (intensifier): *I had no end of work.* **25 on end. 25a** upright. **25b** without pause or interruption. **26 the end.** *Informal.* **26a** the worst, esp. something that goes beyond the limits of endurance. **26b** *Chiefly U.S.* the best in quality. **27 the end of the road.** the point beyond which survival or continuation is impossible. **28 throw (someone) in at the deep end.** to put (someone) into a new situation, job, etc., without preparation or introduction. Related adjs: **final, terminal, ultimate.** ◆ *vb* **29** to bring or come to a finish; conclude. **30** to die or cause to die. **31** (*tr*) surpass; outdo: *a novel to end all novels.* **32 end it all.** *Informal.* to commit suicide. ◆ See also **end up.** [Old English *ende*; related to Old Norse *endir*, Gothic *andeis*, Old High German *endi*, Latin *antiae* forelocks, Sanskrit *antya* last] ▸ **'ender** *n*

end[2] (ɛnd) *vb* (*tr*) *Brit.* to put (hay or grain) into a barn or stack. [Old English *innian*; related to Old High German *innōn*; see INN]

end- *combining form.* a variant of **endo-** before a vowel.

-end *suffix forming nouns.* See **-and.**

end-all *n* short for **be-all and end-all.**

endamage (ɛn'dæmɪdʒ) *vb* (*tr*) to cause injury to; damage. ▸ **en'damagement** *n*

endamoeba *or U.S.* **endameba** (,ɛndə'miːbə) *n, pl* **-bae** (-biː) *or* **-bas.** variants of **entamoeba.**

endanger (ɪn'deɪndʒə) *vb* (*tr*) to put in danger or peril; imperil. ▸ **en'dangerment** *n*

endangered (ɪn'deɪndʒəd) *adj* in danger: used esp. of animals in danger of extinction: *the giant panda is an endangered species.*

endarch ('ɛnd,ɑːk) *adj Botany.* (of a xylem strand) having the first-formed xylem internal to that formed later. Compare **exarch**[2], **mesarch.** [C20: from ENDO- + Greek *arkhē* beginning]

en dash *or* **rule** *n Printing.* a dash (–) one en long.

end-blown *adj Music.* (of a recorder) held downwards and blown through one end.

endbrain ('ɛnd,breɪn) *n Anatomy.* another name for **telencephalon.**

endear (ɪn'dɪə) *vb* (*tr*) to cause to be beloved or esteemed. ▸ **en'dearing** *adj* ▸ **en'dearingly** *adv*

endearment (ɪn'dɪəmənt) *n* **1** something that endears, such as an affectionate utterance. **2** the act or process of endearing or the condition of being endeared.

endeavour *or U.S.* **endeavor** (ɪn'dɛvə) *vb* **1** to try (to do something). ◆ *n* **2** an effort to do or attain something. [C14: *endeveren*, from EN-[1] + *-deveren* from *dever* duty, from Old French *deveir*; see DEVOIRS] ▸ **en'deavourer** *or U.S.* **en'deavorer** *n*

endemic (ɛn'dɛmɪk) *adj also* **endemial** (ɛn'dɛmɪəl) *or* **endemical. 1** present within a localized area or peculiar to persons in such an area. ◆ *n* **2** an endemic disease or plant. [C18: from New Latin *endēmicus*, from Greek *endēmos* native, from EN-[2] + *dēmos* the people] ▸ **en'demically** *adv* ▸ **'endemism** *or* **,ende'micity** *n*

Enderby Land ('ɛndəbɪ) *n* part of the coastal region of Antarctica, between Kempland and Queen Maud Land: the westernmost part of the Australian Antarctic Territory; discovered in 1831.

endergonic (,ɛndə'gɒnɪk) *adj* (of a biochemical reaction) requiring energy to proceed. Compare **exergonic.** [C20: from END(O)- + Greek *ergon* work + -IC]

endermic (ɛn'dɜːmɪk) *adj* (of a medicine) acting by absorption through the skin. [C19: from EN-[2] + Greek *derma* skin]

Enders ('ɛndəz) *n* **John Franklin.** 1897–1985, U.S. microbiologist: shared the Nobel prize for physiology or medicine (1954) with Frederick Robbins and Thomas Weller for their work on viruses.

endgame ('ɛnd,geɪm) *n* **1** Also called: **ending.** the closing stage of a game of chess, in which only a few pieces are left on the board. **2** the closing stage of any of certain other games.

ending ('ɛndɪŋ) *n* **1** the act of bringing to or reaching an end. **2** the last part of something, as a book, film, etc. **3** the final part of a word, esp. a suffix. **4** *Chess.* another word for **endgame.**

endive ('ɛndaɪv) *n* a plant, *Cichorium endivia*, cultivated for its crisp curly leaves, which are used in salads: family *Compositae* (composites). Compare **chicory.** [C15: from Old French, from Medieval Latin *endīvia*, variant of Latin *intubus, entubus*, of uncertain origin]

endless ('ɛndlɪs) *adj* **1** having or seeming to have no end; eternal or infinite. **2** continuing too long or continually recurring. **3** formed with the ends joined: *an endless belt.* ▸ **'endlessly** *adv* ▸ **'endlessness** *n*

endlong ('ɛnd,lɒŋ) *adv Archaic.* lengthways or on end.

end matter *n* another name for **back matter.**

endmost ('ɛnd,məʊst) *adj* nearest the end; most distant.

endo- *or before a vowel* **end-** *combining form.* inside; within: *endocrine.* [from Greek, from *endon* within]

endobiotic (,ɛndəʊbaɪ'ɒtɪk) *adj* **1** (of a plant) growing within another plant. **2** formed within a host cell.

endoblast ('ɛndəʊ,blæst) *n* **1** *Embryol.* a less common name for **endoderm. 2** another name for **hypoblast** (sense 1). ▸ **,endo'blastic** *adj*

endocardial (,ɛndəʊ'kɑːdɪəl) *or* **endocardiac** *adj* **1** of or relating to the endocardium. **2** within the heart.

endocarditis (,ɛndəʊkɑː'daɪtɪs) *n* inflammation of the endocardium. ▸ **endocarditic** (,ɛndəʊkɑː'dɪtɪk) *adj*

endocardium (,ɛndəʊ'kɑːdɪəm) *n, pl* **-dia** (-dɪə). the membrane that lines the cavities of the heart and forms part of the valves. [C19: from New Latin, from ENDO- + Greek *kardia* heart]

endocarp ('ɛndə,kɑːp) *n* the inner, usually woody, layer of the pericarp of a fruit, such as the stone of a peach or cherry. ▸ **,endo'carpal** *or* **,endo'carpic** *adj*

endocentric (,ɛndəʊ'sɛntrɪk) *adj Grammar.* (of a construction) fulfilling the grammatical role of one of its constituents; as in *three blind mice*, where the whole noun phrase fulfills the same role as its head noun *mice*. Compare **exocentric.**

endocranial cast (,ɛndəʊ'kreɪnɪəl) *n* a cast made of the inside of a cranial cavity to show the size and shape of the brain: used esp. in anthropology. Sometimes shortened to **endocast.**

endocranium (,ɛndəʊ'kreɪnɪəm) *n, pl* **-nia** (-nɪə). *Anatomy.* the thick fibrous membrane that lines the cranial cavity and forms the outermost layer of the dura mater.

endocrine ('ɛndəʊ,kraɪn, -krɪn) *adj also* **endocrinal** (,ɛndəʊ'kraɪnəl), **endocrinic** (,ɛndəʊ'krɪnɪk), *or* **endocrinous** (ɛn'dɒkrɪnəs). **1** of or denoting endocrine glands or their secretions: *endocrine disorders.* ◆ *n* **2** an endocrine gland.

◆ Compare **exocrine.** [C20: from ENDO- + *-crine,* from Greek *krinein* to separate]

endocrine gland *n* any of the glands that secrete hormones directly into the bloodstream, including the pituitary, pineal, thyroid, parathyroid, adrenal, testes, ovaries, and the pancreatic islets of Langerhans. Also called: **ductless gland.**

endocrinology (ˌɛndəʊkraɪˈnɒlədʒɪ, -krɪ-) *n* the branch of medical science concerned with the endocrine glands and their secretions. ▸ **endocrinologic** (ˌɛndəʊˌkrɪnəˈlɒdʒɪk) *or* **ˌendoˌcrinoˈlogical** *adj* ▸ **ˌendocriˈnologist** *n*

endocrinopathy (ˌɛndəʊkrɪˈnɒpəθɪ) *n* any disease due to disorder of the endocrine system. ▸ **endocrinopathic** (ˌɛndəʊˌkrɪnəʊˈpæθɪk) *adj*

endocuticle (ˈɛndəʊˌkjuːtɪkᵊl) *n* the inner layer of the cuticle of an insect.

endocytosis (ˌɛndəʊsaɪˈtəʊsɪs) *n* the process by which a living cell takes up molecules bound to its surface.

endoderm (ˈɛndəʊˌdɜːm) *or* **entoderm** *n* the inner germ layer of an animal embryo, which gives rise to the lining of the digestive and respiratory tracts. See also **ectoderm** and **mesoderm.** ▸ **ˌendoˈdermal, ˌendoˈdermic** *or* **ˌentoˈdermal, ˌentoˈdermic** *adj*

endodermis (ˌɛndəʊˈdɜːmɪs) *n Botany.* the specialized innermost layer of cortex in roots and some stems, which controls the passage of water and dissolved substances between the cortex and stele. [C19: from New Latin, from ENDO- + Greek *derma* skin]

endodontics (ˌɛndəʊˈdɒntɪks) *n (functioning as sing)* the branch of dentistry concerned with diseases of the dental pulp. [C19: from New Latin *endodontia,* from ENDO- + Greek *odōn* tooth] ▸ **ˌendoˈdontal** *or* **ˌendoˈdontic** *adj* ▸ **ˌendoˈdontist** *n*

endoenzyme (ˌɛndəʊˈɛnzaɪm) *n* any of a group of enzymes, esp. endopeptidases, that act upon inner chemical bonds in a chain of molecules. Compare **exoenzyme** (sense 1).

endoergic (ˌɛndəʊˈɜːdʒɪk) *adj* (of a nuclear reaction) occurring with absorption of energy, as opposed to *exoergic.* Compare **endothermic.** [from ENDO- + *-ergic* from Greek *ergon* work]

end of steel *n Canadian.* **1** a point up to which railway tracks have been laid. **2** a town located at such a point.

endogamy (ɛnˈdɒgəmɪ) *n* **1** *Anthropol.* marriage within one's own tribe or similar unit. Compare **exogamy** (sense 1). **2** pollination between two flowers on the same plant. ▸ **enˈdogamous** *or* **endogamic** (ˌɛndəʊˈgæmɪk) *adj*

endogen (ˈɛndəʊˌdʒɛn) *n* a former name for **monocotyledon.**

endogenous (ɛnˈdɒdʒɪnəs) *adj* **1** *Biology.* developing or originating within an organism or part of an organism: *endogenous rhythms.* **2** having no apparent external cause: *endogenous depression.* ▸ **enˈdogenously** *adv* ▸ **enˈdogeny** *n*

endolithic (ˌɛndəʊˈlɪθɪk) *adj* (of organisms, such as algae) growing inside rock.

endolymph (ˈɛndəʊˌlɪmf) *n* the fluid that fills the membranous labyrinth of the internal ear. ▸ **endolymphatic** (ˌɛndəʊlɪmˈfætɪk) *adj*

endometriosis (ˌɛndəʊˌmiːtrɪˈəʊsɪs) *n Pathol.* the presence of endometrium in areas other than the lining of the uterus, as on the ovaries, resulting in premenstrual pain.

endometritis (ˌɛndəʊmɪˈtraɪtɪs) *n* inflammation of the endometrium, which is caused by infection, as by bacteria, foreign bodies, etc.

endometrium (ˌɛndəʊˈmiːtrɪəm) *n, pl* **-tria** (-trɪə). the mucous membrane that lines the uterus. [C19: New Latin, from ENDO- + Greek *mētra* uterus] ▸ **ˌendoˈmetrial** *adj*

endomitosis (ˌɛndəʊmaɪˈtəʊsɪs) *n Biology.* the division of chromosomes but not of the cell nucleus, resulting in a polyploid cell.

endomorph (ˈɛndəʊˌmɔːf) *n* **1** a person with a fat and heavy body build: said to be correlated with viscerotonia. Compare **ectomorph, mesomorph. 2** a mineral that naturally occurs enclosed within another mineral, as within quartz. ▸ **ˌendoˈmorphic** *adj* ▸ **ˈendoˌmorphy** *n*

endomorphism (ˌɛndəʊˈmɔːˌfɪzəm) *n Geology.* a type of metamorphism in which changes are induced in the cooling molten rock material by contact with the older rocks surrounding it.

endoneurium (ˌɛndəʊˈnjʊərɪəm) *n* the delicate connective tissue surrounding nerve fibres within a bundle. [New Latin, from ENDO- + NEURO- + -IUM]

endonuclease (ˌɛndəʊˈnjuːklɪˌeɪz) *n* an enzyme that is responsible for scission of a nucleic acid chain, the action of which is not confined to the terminal nucleotide. Compare **exonuclease.**

endoparasite (ˌɛndəʊˈpærəˌsaɪt) *n* a parasite, such as the tapeworm, that lives within the body of its host. ▸ **endoparasitic** (ˌɛndəʊˌpærəˈsɪtɪk) *adj*

endopeptidase (ˌɛndəʊˈpɛptɪˌdeɪz) *n* any proteolytic enzyme, such as pepsin, that splits a protein into smaller peptide fragments. Also called: **proteinase.** Compare **exopeptidase.**

endophyte (ˈɛndəʊˌfaɪt) *n* any plant, parasitic fungus, or alga that lives within a plant. ▸ **endophytic** (ˌɛndəʊˈfɪtɪk) *adj* ▸ **ˌendoˈphytically** *adv*

endoplasm (ˈɛndəʊˌplæzəm) *n Cytology.* the inner cytoplasm that in many cells is more granular and fluid than the outer cytoplasm (see **ectoplasm** (sense 1)). ▸ **ˌendoˈplasmic** *adj*

endoplasmic reticulum *n* an extensive intracellular membrane system in which certain proteins are synthesized by particles (ribosomes) attached to the membrane, for transport through or secretion from the cell.

end organ *n Anatomy.* the expanded end of a peripheral motor or sensory nerve.

endorphin (ɛnˈdɔːfɪn) *n* any of a class of polypeptides, including enkephalin, occurring naturally in the brain, that bind to pain receptors and so block pain sensation. [C20: from ENDO- + MORPHINE]

endorse *or* **indorse** (ɪnˈdɔːs) *vb (tr)* **1** to give approval or sanction to. **2** to sign (one's name) on the back of (a cheque, etc.) to specify oneself as payee. **3** *Commerce.* **3a** to sign the back of (a negotiable document) to transfer ownership of the rights to a specified payee. **3b** to specify (a designated sum) as transferable to another as payee. **4** to write (a qualifying comment, recommendation, etc.) on the back of a document. **5** to sign (a document), as when confirming receipt of payment. **6** *Chiefly Brit.* to record (a conviction) on (a driving licence). [C16: from Old French *endosser* to put on the back, from EN-[1] + *dos* back, from Latin *dorsum*] ▸ **enˈdorsable** *or* **inˈdorsable** *adj* ▸ **enˈdorser, enˈdorsor** *or* **inˈdorser, inˈdorsor** *n*

endorsee (ɪnˌdɔːˈsiː, ˌɛndɔː-) *or* **indorsee** *n* the person in whose favour a negotiable instrument is endorsed.

endorsement *or* **indorsement** (ɪnˈdɔːsmənt) *n* **1** the act or an instance of endorsing. **2** something that endorses, such as a signature or qualifying comment. **3** approval or support. **4** a record of a motoring offence on a driving licence. **5** *Insurance.* a clause in or amendment to an insurance policy allowing for alteration of coverage.

endoscope (ˈɛndəʊˌskəʊp) *n* a long slender medical instrument used for examining the interior of hollow organs including the lung, stomach, bladder and bowel. ▸ **endoscopic** (ˌɛndəʊˈskɒpɪk) *adj* ▸ **endoscopist** (ɛnˈdɒskəpɪst) *n* ▸ **enˈdoscopy** *n*

endoskeleton (ˌɛndəʊˈskɛlɪtᵊn) *n* the internal skeleton of an animal, esp. the bony or cartilaginous skeleton of vertebrates. Compare **exoskeleton.** ▸ **ˌendoˈskeletal** *adj*

endosmosis (ˌɛndɒsˈməʊsɪs, -dɒz-) *n Biology.* osmosis in which water enters a cell or organism from the surrounding solution. Compare **exosmosis.** ▸ **endosmotic** (ˌɛndɒsˈmɒtɪk, -dɒz-) *adj* ▸ **ˌendosˈmotically** *adv*

endosperm (ˈɛndəʊˌspɜːm) *n* the tissue within the seed of a flowering plant that surrounds and nourishes the developing embryo. ▸ **ˌendoˈspermic** *adj*

endospore (ˈɛndəʊˌspɔː) *n* **1** a small asexual spore produced by some bacteria and algae. **2** the innermost wall of a spore or pollen grain. ▸ **endosporous** (ɛnˈdɒspərəs, ˌɛndəʊˈspɔːrəs) *adj*

endosteum (ɛnˈdɒstɪəm) *n, pl* **-tea** (-tɪə). a highly vascular membrane lining the internal surface of long bones, such as the femur and humerus. [C19: New Latin, from ENDO- + Greek *osteon* bone] ▸ **enˈdosteal** *adj*

endostosis (ˌɛndɒsˈtəʊsɪs) *n, pl* **-ses** (-siːz). the conversion of cartilage into bone.

endosymbiosis (ˌɛndəʊˌsɪmbɪˈəʊsɪs) *n* a type of symbiosis in which one organism lives inside the other, the two typically behaving as a single organism.

endothecium (ˌɛndəʊˈθiːʃɪəm, -sɪəm) *n, pl* **-cia** (-ʃɪə, -sɪə). *Botany.* **1** the inner mass of cells of the developing capsule in mosses. **2** the fibrous tissue of the inner wall of an anther. [C19: New Latin, from ENDO- + Greek *thēkion* case; see THECA] ▸ **ˌendoˈthecial** *adj*

endothelioma (ˌɛndəʊˌθiːlɪˈəʊmə) *n, pl* **-mata** (-mətə). *Pathol.* a tumour originating in endothelial tissue, such as the lining of blood vessels.

endothelium (ˌɛndəʊˈθiːlɪəm) *n, pl* **-lia** (-lɪə). a tissue consisting of a single layer of cells that lines the blood and lymph vessels, heart, and some other cavities. [C19: New Latin, from ENDO- + *-thelium,* from Greek *thēlē* nipple] ▸ **ˌendoˈthelial** *adj* ▸ **ˌendoˈtheliˌoid** *adj*

endothermic (ˌɛndəʊˈθɜːmɪk) *or* **endothermal** *adj* (of a chemical reaction or compound) occurring or formed with the absorption of heat. Compare **exothermic, endoergic.** ▸ **ˌendoˈthermically** *adv* ▸ **ˌendoˈthermism** *n*

endotoxin (ˌɛndəʊˈtɒksɪn) *n* a toxin contained within the protoplasm of an organism, esp. a bacterium, and liberated only at death. ▸ **ˌendoˈtoxic** *adj*

endotrophic (ˌɛndəʊˈtrɒfɪk) *adj Botany.* denoting a type of mycorrhiza in which the fungus lives within the cells of the roots of the plant. Compare **ectotrophic.**

endow (ɪnˈdaʊ) *vb (tr)* **1** to provide with or bequeath a source of permanent income. **2** (usually foll. by *with*) to provide (with qualities, characteristics, etc.). **3** *Obsolete.* to provide with a dower. [C14: from Old French *endouer,* from EN-[1] + *douer,* from Latin *dōtāre,* from *dōs* dowry] ▸ **enˈdower** *n*

endowment (ɪnˈdaʊmənt) *n* **1a** the source of income with which an institution, etc., is endowed. **1b** the income itself. **2** the act or process of endowing. **3** *(usually pl)* natural talents or qualities.

endowment assurance *or* **insurance** *n* a form of life insurance that provides for the payment of a specified sum directly to the policyholder at a designated date or to his beneficiary should he die before this date.

endowment mortgage *n* an arrangement whereby a person takes out a mortgage and pays the capital repayment instalments into a life assurance policy and only the interest to the mortgagee during the term of the policy. The loan is repaid by the policy either when it matures or on the prior death of the policyholder.

endozoic (ˌɛndəʊˈzəʊɪk) *adj Botany.* **1** (of a plant) living within an animal. **2** denoting seed dispersal in which the seeds are swallowed by an animal and subsequently pass out in the faeces.

endpaper (ˈɛndˌpeɪpə) *n* either of two leaves at the front and back of a book pasted to the inside of the board covers and the first leaf of the book to secure the binding.

end pin *n Music.* the adjustable metal spike attached to the bottom of a cello, double bass, etc., that supports it while it is being played.

endplate (ˈɛndˌpleɪt) *n* **1** any usually flat platelike structure at the end of something. **2** *Physiol.* the flattened end of a motor nerve fibre, which transmits impulses to muscle.

endplay (ˈɛndˌpleɪ) *Bridge.* ◆ *n* **1** a way of playing the last few tricks in a hand so that an opponent is forced to make a particular lead. ◆ *vb (tr)* **2** to force (an opponent) to make a particular lead near the end of a hand: *declarer endplayed West for the jack of spades.*

end point *n* **1** *Chem.* the point at which a titration is complete, usually marked by a change in colour of an indicator. **2** the point at which anything is complete.

end product *n* the final result or outcome of a process, series, endeavour, etc., esp. in manufacturing.

end-stopped *adj* (of verse) having a pause at the end of each line.

endue *or* **indue** (ɪn'djuː) *vb* **-dues, -duing, -dued.** (*tr*) **1** (usually foll. by *with*) to invest or provide, as with some quality or trait. **2** *Rare.* (foll. by *with*) to clothe or dress (in). [C15: from Old French *enduire,* from Latin *indūcere,* from *dūcere* to lead]

end up *vb* (*adv*) **1** (*copula*) to become eventually; turn out to be: *he ended up a thief.* **2** (*intr*) to arrive, esp. by a circuitous or lengthy route or process: *to end up in prison.*

endurance (ɪn'djʊərəns) *n* **1** the capacity, state, or an instance of enduring. **2** something endured; a hardship, strain, or privation.

endure (ɪn'djʊə) *vb* **1** to undergo (hardship, strain, privation, etc.) without yielding; bear. **2** (*tr*) to permit or tolerate. **3** (*intr*) to last or continue to exist. [C14: from Old French *endurer,* from Latin *indūrāre* to harden, from *dūrus* hard] ▸ **en'durable** *adj* ▸ **en,dura'bility** *or* **en'durableness** *n* ▸ **en'durably** *adv*

enduring (ɪn'djʊərɪŋ) *adj* **1** permanent; lasting. **2** having forbearance; long-suffering. ▸ **en'duringly** *adv* ▸ **en'duringness** *n*

end user *n* **1a** (in international trading) the person, organization, or nation that will be the ultimate recipient of goods, esp. such as arms or advanced technology. **1b** (*as modifier*): *an end-user certificate.* **2** *Computing.* the ultimate destination, such as a program or operator, of information that is being transferred within a system.

endways ('ɛnd,weɪz) *or esp. U.S. and Canadian* **endwise** ('ɛnd,waɪz) *adv* **1** having the end forwards or upwards. ◆ *adj* **2** vertical or upright. **3** lengthways. **4** standing or lying end to end.

Endymion (ɛn'dɪmɪən) *n Greek myth.* a handsome youth who was visited every night by the moon goddess Selene, who loved him.

endysis (ɛn'daɪsɪs) *n Zoology.* the formation of new layers of integument after ecdysis.

end zone *n American football.* the area behind the goals at each end of the field that the ball must cross for a touchdown to be awarded.

ENE *symbol for* east-northeast.

-ene *n combining form.* (in chemistry) indicating an unsaturated compound containing double bonds: *benzene; ethylene.* [from Greek *-ēnē,* feminine patronymic suffix]

ENEA *abbrev. for* European Nuclear Energy Agency: the European body responsible for the development of nuclear-generated electric power.

enema ('ɛnɪmə) *n, pl* **-mas** *or* **-mata** (-mətə). *Med.* **1** the introduction of liquid into the rectum to evacuate the bowels, medicate, or nourish. **2** the liquid so introduced. [C15: from New Latin, from Greek: injection, from *enienai* to send in, from *hienai* to send]

enemy ('ɛnəmɪ) *n, pl* **-mies. 1** a person hostile or opposed to a policy, cause, person, or group, esp. one who actively tries to do damage; opponent. **2a** an armed adversary; opposing military force. **2b** (*as modifier*): *enemy aircraft.* **3a** a hostile nation or people. **3b** (*as modifier*): *an enemy alien.* **4** something that harms or opposes; adversary: *courage is the enemy of failure.* ◆ Related adj: **inimical.** [C13: from Old French *enemi,* from Latin *inimīcus* hostile, from IN-[1] + *amīcus* friend]

energetic (,ɛnə'dʒɛtɪk) *adj* having or showing much energy or force; vigorous. ▸ **,ener'getically** *adv*

energetics (,ɛnə'dʒɛtɪks) *n* (*functioning as sing*) the branch of science concerned with energy and its transformations.

energid ('ɛnədʒɪd) *n* a biological unit that consists of nucleus and cytoplasm but does not constitute a cell. [C19: adapted from German, from ENERGY + -ID[1]]

energize *or* **energise** ('ɛnə,dʒaɪz) *vb* **1** to have or cause to have energy; invigorate. **2** (*tr*) to apply a source of electric current or electromotive force to (a circuit, field winding, etc.). ▸ **'ener,gizer** *or* **'ener,giser** *n*

energumen (,ɛnə'gjuːmɛn) *n* **1** a person thought to be possessed by an evil spirit. **2** a fanatic or zealot. [C18: via Late Latin from Greek *energoumenos* having been worked on, from *energein* to be in action, from *energos* effective; see ENERGY]

energy ('ɛnədʒɪ) *n, pl* **-gies. 1** intensity or vitality of action or expression; forcefulness. **2** capacity or tendency for intense activity; vigour. **3** vigorous or intense action; exertion. **4** *Physics.* **4a** the capacity of a body or system to do work. **4b** a measure of this capacity, expressed as the work that it does in changing to some specified reference state. It is measured in joules (SI units). Symbol: *E* See also **kinetic energy, potential energy.** [C16: from Late Latin *energīa,* from Greek *energeia* activity, from *energos* effective, from EN-[2] + *ergon* work]

energy band *n Physics.* a range of energies associated with the quantum states of electrons in a crystalline solid. In a semiconductor or an insulator there is a **valence band** containing many states, most of which are occupied. Above this is a **forbidden band** with only a few isolated states caused by impurities. Above this is a **conduction band** containing many states most of which are empty. In a metal there is a continuous **valence-conduction band.** See also **energy gap.**

energy conversion *n* the process of changing one form of energy into another, such as nuclear energy into heat or solar energy into electrical energy.

energy gap *n Physics.* the difference of energy between the bottom of the conduction band and the top of the valence band of the electrons in a crystalline solid. For values below about 2eV the substance is considered to be a semiconductor whilst for higher values it is considered to be an insulator.

energy level *n Physics.* **1** a constant value of energy in the distribution of energies among a number of atomic particles. **2** the energy of a quantum state of a system. The terms **energy level** and **energy state** are often used loosely to mean **quantum state.** This is avoided in precise communication.

enervate *vb* ('ɛnə,veɪt). **1** (*tr*) to deprive of strength or vitality; weaken physically or mentally; debilitate. ◆ *adj* (ɪ'nɜːvɪt). **2** deprived of strength or vitality; weakened. [C17: from Latin *ēnervāre* to remove the nerves from, from *nervus* nerve, sinew] ▸ **'ener,vating** *adj* ▸ **,ener'vation** *n* ▸ **'ener,vative** *adj* ▸ **'ener,vator** *n*

Enesco (ɛ'nɛskəʊ) *n* **Georges** (ʒɔrʒ), original name *George Enescu.* 1881–1955, Romanian violinist and composer.

enface (ɪn'feɪs) *vb* (*tr*) to write, print, or stamp (something) on the face of (a document). ▸ **en'facement** *n*

en face *French.* (ɑ̃ fas) *adj* **1** facing forwards. **2** opposite; facing.

en famille *French.* (ɑ̃ famij) *adv* **1** with one's family; at home. **2** in a casual way; informally.

enfant terrible *French.* (ɑ̃fɑ̃ tɛriblə) *n, pl* ***enfants terribles*** (ɑ̃fɑ̃ tɛriblə). a person given to unconventional conduct or indiscreet remarks. [C19: literally: terrible child]

enfeeble (ɪn'fiːbᵊl) *vb* (*tr*) to make weak; deprive of strength. ▸ **en'feeblement** *n* ▸ **en'feebler** *n*

enfeoff (ɪn'fiːf) *vb* (*tr*) **1** *Property law.* to invest (a person) with possession of a freehold estate in land. **2** (in feudal society) to take (someone) into vassalage by giving a fee or fief in return for certain services. [C14: from Anglo-French *enfeoffer;* see FIEF] ▸ **en'feoffment** *n*

en fête *French.* (ɑ̃ fɛt) *adv* **1** dressed for a festivity. **2** engaged in a festivity. [C19: literally: in festival]

Enfield ('ɛnfiːld) *n* a borough of Greater London: a N residential suburb. Pop.: 259 800 (1994 est.). Area: 55 sq. km (31 sq. miles).

Enfield rifle *n* **1** a breech-loading bolt-action magazine rifle, usually .303 calibre, used by the British army until World War II and by other countries. **2** a nineteenth-century muzzle-loading musket used by the British army. [C19: from ENFIELD, where it was first made]

enfilade (,ɛnfɪ'leɪd) *Military.* ◆ *n* **1** a position or formation subject to fire from a flank along the length of its front. ◆ *vb* (*tr*) **2** to subject (a position or formation) to fire from a flank. **3** to position (troops or guns) so as to be able to fire at a flank. [C18: from French: suite, from *enfiler* to thread on string, from *fil* thread]

enfleurage *French.* (ɑ̃flœraʒ) *n* the process of exposing odourless oils to the scent of fresh flowers, used in perfume-making. [C19: literally: inflowering]

enfold *or* **infold** (ɪn'fəʊld) *vb* (*tr*) **1** to cover by enclosing. **2** to embrace. **3** to form with or as with folds. ▸ **en'folder** *or* **in'folder** *n* ▸ **en'foldment** *or* **in'foldment** *n*

enforce (ɪn'fɔːs) *vb* (*tr*) **1** to ensure observance of or obedience to (a law, decision, etc.). **2** to impose (obedience, loyalty, etc.) by or as by force. **3** to emphasize or reinforce (an argument, demand, etc.). ▸ **en'forceable** *adj* ▸ **en,forcea'bility** *n* ▸ **enforcedly** (ɪn'fɔːsɪdlɪ) *adv* ▸ **en'forcement** *n* ▸ **en'forcer** *n*

enfranchise (ɪn'fræntʃaɪz) *vb* (*tr*) **1** to grant the power of voting to, esp. as a right of citizenship. **2** to liberate, as from servitude. **3** (in England) to invest (a town, city, etc.) with the right to be represented in Parliament. **4** *English law.* (formerly) to convert (copyhold land) to freehold. ▸ **en'franchisement** *n* ▸ **en'franchiser** *n*

eng (ɛŋ) *n Phonetics.* another name for **agma.**

ENG *abbrev. for* electronic news gathering: TV news obtained at the point of action by means of modern video equipment.

eng. *abbrev. for:* **1** engine. **2** engineer. **3** engineering. **4** engraved. **5** engraver. **6** engraving.

Eng. *abbrev. for:* **1** England. **2** English.

Engadine ('ɛŋgə,diːn) *n* the upper part of the valley of the River Inn in Switzerland, in Graubünden canton: tourist and winter sports centre.

engage (ɪn'geɪdʒ) *vb* (*mainly tr*) **1** to secure the services of; employ. **2** to secure for use; reserve: *engage a room.* **3** to involve (a person or his attention) intensely; engross; occupy. **4** to attract (the affection) of (a person): *her innocence engaged him.* **5** to draw (somebody) into conversation. **6** (*intr*) to take part; participate: *he engages in many sports.* **7** to promise (to do something). **8** (*also intr*) *Military.* to begin an action with (an enemy). **9** to bring (a mechanism) into operation: *he engaged the clutch.* **10** (*also intr*) to undergo or cause to undergo interlocking, as of the components of a driving mechanism, such as a gear train. **11** *Machinery.* to locate (a locking device) in its operative position or to advance (a tool) into a workpiece to commence cutting. [C15: from Old French *engagier,* from EN-[1] + *gage* a pledge, see GAGE[1]] ▸ **en'gager** *n*

engagé *or* (*fem*) ***engagée*** *French.* (ɑ̃gaʒe) *adj* (of a writer or artist) morally or politically committed to some ideology.

engaged (ɪn'geɪdʒd) *adj* **1** pledged to be married; betrothed. **2** employed, occupied, or busy. **3** *Architect.* built against or attached to a wall or similar structure: *an engaged column.* **4** (of a telephone line) already in use. ▸ **engagedly** (ɪn'geɪdʒɪdlɪ) *adv*

engaged tone *n Brit.* a repeated single note heard on a telephone when the number called is already in use. U.S. and Canadian equivalent: **busy signal.** Compare **ringing tone, dialling tone.**

engagement (ɪn'geɪdʒmənt) *n* **1** a pledge of marriage; betrothal. **2** an appointment or arrangement, esp. for business or social purposes. **3** the act of engaging or condition of being engaged. **4** a promise, obligation, or other condition that binds. **5** a period of employment, esp. a limited period. **6** an action; battle. **7** (*pl*) financial obligations.

engagement ring *n* a ring given by a man to a woman as a token of their betrothal.

engaging (ɪn'geɪdʒɪŋ) *adj* pleasing, charming, or winning. ▸ **en'gagingly** *adv* ▸ **en'gagingness** *n*

en garde *French.* (ɑ̃ gard) *interj* **1** on guard; a call to a fencer to adopt a defensive stance in readiness for an attack or bout. ◆ *adj* **2** (of a fencer) in such a stance.

Engels (*German* 'ɛŋəls) *n* **Friedrich** ('fri:drɪç). 1820–95, German socialist leader and political philosopher, in England from 1849. He collaborated with Marx on *The Communist Manifesto* (1848) and his own works include *Condition of the Working Classes in England* (1844) and *The Origin of the Family, Private Property and the State* (1884).

engender (ɪn'dʒɛndə) *vb* **1** (*tr*) to bring about or give rise to; produce or cause. **2** to be born or cause to be born; bring or come into being. [C14: from Old French *engendrer,* from Latin *ingenerāre,* from *generāre* to beget] ▸ **en'genderer** *n* ▸ **en'genderment** *n*

engin. *abbrev. for* engineering.

engine ('ɛndʒɪn) *n* **1** any machine designed to convert energy, esp. thermal energy, into mechanical work: *a steam engine; a petrol engine.* **2a** a railway locomotive. **2b** (*as modifier*): *the engine cab.* **3** *Military.* any of various pieces of equipment formerly used in warfare, such as a battering ram or gun. **4** *Obsolete.* any instrument or device: *engines of torture.* [C13: from Old French *engin,* from Latin *ingenium* nature, talent, ingenious contrivance, from IN-[2] + *-genium,* related to *gignere* to beget, produce]

engine driver *n Chiefly Brit.* a man who drives a railway locomotive; train driver.

engineer (ˌɛndʒɪ'nɪə) *n* **1** a person trained in any branch of the profession of engineering. **2** the originator or manager of a situation, system, etc. **3** a mechanic; one who repairs or services machines. **4** *U.S. and Canadian.* the driver of a railway locomotive. **5** an officer responsible for a ship's engines. **6** Informal name: **sapper.** a member of the armed forces, esp. the army, trained in engineering and construction work. ◆ *vb* (*tr*) **7** to originate, cause, or plan in a clever or devious manner: *he engineered the minister's downfall.* **8** to design, plan, or construct as a professional engineer. [C14: *enginer,* from Old French *engigneor,* from *engignier* to contrive, ultimately from Latin *ingenium* skill, talent; see ENGINE]

engineering (ˌɛndʒɪ'nɪərɪŋ) *n* the profession of applying scientific principles to the design, construction, and maintenance of engines, cars, machines, etc. (**mechanical engineering**), buildings, bridges, roads, etc. (**civil engineering**), electrical machines and communication systems (**electrical engineering**), chemical plant and machinery (**chemical engineering**), or aircraft (**aeronautical engineering**). See also **military engineering.**

engineer officer *n* a ship's officer who is qualified to be in charge of the vessel's propulsion and other machinery.

engine pod *n Aeronautics.* an aircraft turbojet unit comprising the engine and its cowling suspended by a pylon, often below the wing.

engine room *n* a place where engines are housed, esp. on a ship.

enginery ('ɛndʒɪnrɪ) *n, pl* **-ries. 1** a collection or assembly of engines; machinery. **2** engines employed in warfare. **3** *Rare.* skilful manoeuvring or contrivance.

englacial (ɪn'gleɪsɪəl) *adj* embedded in, carried by, or running through a glacier: *englacial drift; an englacial river.* ▸ **en'glacially** *adv*

England ('ɪŋglənd) *n* the largest division of Great Britain, bordering on Scotland and Wales: unified in the mid-tenth century and conquered by the Normans in 1066; united with Wales in 1536 and Scotland in 1707; monarchy overthrown in 1649 but restored in 1660. Capital: London. Pop.: 47 055 200 (1991). Area: 130 439 sq. km (50 352 sq. miles). See **United Kingdom, Great Britain.**

Engler degrees ('ɛŋlə) *n* (*functioning as sing*) a scale of measurement of viscosity based on the ratio of the time taken by a particular liquid to flow through a standard orifice to the time taken by water to flow through the same orifice. [named after C. *Engler* (1842–1925), German chemist, who proposed it]

English ('ɪŋglɪʃ) *n* **1** the official language of Britain, the U.S., most parts of the Commonwealth, and certain other countries. It is the native language of over 280 million people and is acquired as a second language by many more. It is an Indo-European language belonging to the West Germanic branch. See also **Middle English, Old English, Modern English. 2 the English.** (*functioning as pl*) the natives or inhabitants of England or (loosely) of Britain collectively. **3** (formerly) a size of printer's type approximately equal to 14 point. **4** an old style of black-letter typeface. **5** (*often not cap.*) the usual U.S. and Canadian term for **side** (in billiards). ◆ *adj* **6** denoting, using, or relating to the English language. **7** relating to or characteristic of England or the English. ◆ *vb* (*tr*) **8** *Archaic.* to translate or adapt into English. ◆ Related prefix: **Anglo-.** ▸ **'Englishness** *n*

English bond *n* a bond used in brickwork that has a course of headers alternating with a course of stretchers.

English Canadian *n* a Canadian citizen whose first language is English, esp. one of English descent.

English Channel *n* an arm of the Atlantic Ocean between S England and N France, linked with the North Sea by the Strait of Dover. Length: about 560 km (350 miles). Width: between 32 km (20 miles) and 161 km (100 miles).

English flute *n Music.* another name for **recorder** (sense 4).

English Heritage *n* an organization, partly funded by government aid, that looks after ancient monuments and historic buildings in England. Official name: **The Historic Buildings and Monuments Commission for England.**

English horn *n Music.* another name for **cor anglais.**

Englishism ('ɪŋglɪˌʃɪzəm) *n Chiefly U.S.* **1** an English custom, practice, etc. **2** a word or expression not found in forms of English other than British English; Anglicism. **3** high regard for English customs, institutions, etc.

Englishman ('ɪŋglɪʃmən) *or* (*fem*) **Englishwoman** *n, pl* **-men** *or* **-women. 1** a native or inhabitant of England. **2** (loosely) a citizen of the United Kingdom.

Englishman's tie *or* **knot** *n* a type of knot for tying together heavy ropes.

Englishry ('ɪŋglɪʃrɪ) *n Now rare.* **1** people of English descent, esp. in Ireland. **2** the fact or condition of being an Englishman or Englishwoman, esp. by birth.

English setter *n* a breed of setter having a white coat speckled with liver, brown, or yellowish markings.

English springer spaniel *n* See **springer spaniel.**

englut (ɪn'glʌt) *vb* **-gluts, -glutting, -glutted.** (*tr*) *Literary.* **1** to devour ravenously; swallow eagerly. **2** to glut or sate (oneself); surfeit; satiate.

engorge (ɪn'gɔ:dʒ) *vb* (*tr*) **1** *Pathol.* to congest with blood. **2** to eat (food) ravenously or greedily. **3** to gorge (oneself); glut; satiate. ▸ **en'gorgement** *n*

engr *abbrev. for:* **1** engineer. **2** engraver.

engr. *abbrev. for* engraved.

engraft *or* **ingraft** (ɪn'grɑ:ft) *vb* (*tr*) **1** to graft (a shoot, bud, etc.) onto a stock. **2** to incorporate in a firm or permanent way; implant: *they engrafted their principles into the document.* ▸ **ˌengraf'tation, ˌingraf'tation** *or* **en'graftment, in'graftment** *n*

engrail (ɪn'greɪl) *vb* (*tr*) to decorate or mark (the edge of) (a coin) with small carved notches. [C14: from Old French *engresler,* from EN-[1] + *gresle* slim, from Latin *gracilis* slender, graceful] ▸ **en'grailment** *n*

engrain (ɪn'greɪn) *vb* a variant spelling of **ingrain.**

engram ('ɛngræm) *n Psychol.* the physical basis of an individual memory in the brain. See also **memory trace.** [C20: from German *Engramm,* from Greek *en-* IN + *gramma* letter] ▸ **en'grammic** *or* **ˌengram'matic** *adj*

engrave (ɪn'greɪv) *vb* (*tr*) **1** to inscribe (a design, writing, etc.) onto (a block, plate, or other surface used for printing) by carving, etching with acid, or other process. **2** to print (designs or characters) from a printing plate so made. **3** to fix deeply or permanently in the mind. [C16: from EN-[1] + GRAVE[3], on the model of French *engraver*] ▸ **en'graver** *n*

engraving (ɪn'greɪvɪŋ) *n* **1** the art of a person who engraves. **2** a block, plate, or other surface that has been engraved. **3** a print made from such a surface. Related adj: **glyptic.**

engross (ɪn'grəʊs) *vb* (*tr*) **1** to occupy one's attention completely; absorb. **2** to write or copy (manuscript) in large legible handwriting. **3** *Law.* to write or type out formally (a deed, agreement, or other document) preparatory to execution. **4** another word for **corner** (sense 21b). [C14 (in the sense: to buy up wholesale): from Old French *en gros* in quantity; C15 (in the sense: to write in large letters): probably from Medieval Latin *ingrossāre;* both from Latin *grossus* thick, GROSS] ▸ **en'grossed** *adj* ▸ **engrossedly** (ɪn'grəʊsɪdlɪ) *adv* ▸ **en'grosser** *n* ▸ **en'grossing** *adj*

engrossment (ɪn'grəʊsmənt) *n* **1** a deed or other document that has been engrossed. **2** the state of being engrossed.

engulf *or* **ingulf** (ɪn'gʌlf) *vb* (*tr*) **1** to immerse, plunge, bury, or swallow up. **2** (*often passive*) to overwhelm: *engulfed by debts.* ▸ **en'gulfment** *n*

enhance (ɪn'hɑ:ns) *vb* (*tr*) to intensify or increase in quality, value, power, etc.; improve; augment. [C14: from Old French *enhaucier,* from EN-[1] + *haucier* to raise, from Vulgar Latin *altiāre* (unattested), from Latin *altus* high] ▸ **en'hancement** *n* ▸ **en'hancer** *n* ▸ **en'hancive** *adj*

enhanced oil recovery *n* any of several techniques that make it possible to recover more oil than can be obtained by natural pressure, such as the injection of fluid or gases into an oilfield to force more oil to the surface.

enhanced radiation weapon *n* a technical name for **neutron bomb.**

enharmonic (ˌɛnhɑ:'mɒnɪk) *adj Music.* **1** denoting or relating to a small difference in pitch between two notes such as A flat and G sharp: not present in instruments of equal temperament such as the piano, but significant in the intonation of stringed and wind instruments. **2** denoting or relating to enharmonic modulation. [C17: from Latin *enharmonicus,* from Greek *enarmonios,* from EN-[2] + *harmonia;* see HARMONY] ▸ **ˌenhar'monically** *adv*

enharmonic modulation *n Music.* a change of key achieved by regarding a note in one key as an equivalent note in another. Thus E flat in the key of A flat could be regarded as D sharp in the key of B major.

Enid ('i:nɪd) *n* (in Arthurian legend) the faithful wife of Geraint.

enigma (ɪ'nɪgmə) *n* a person, thing, or situation that is mysterious, puzzling, or ambiguous. [C16: from Latin *aenigma,* from Greek *ainigma,* from *ainissesthai* to speak in riddles, from *ainos* fable, story] ▸ **enigmatic** (ˌɛnɪg'mætɪk) *or* **ˌenig'matical** *adj* ▸ **ˌenig'matically** *adv*

enigmatize *or* **enigmatise** (ɪ'nɪgməˌtaɪz) *vb* (*tr*) to make enigmatic.

enisle (ɪn'aɪl) *vb* (*tr*) *Poetic.* to put on or make into an island.

Eniwetok (ˌɛnə'wi:tɒk, ə'ni:wɪˌtɔ:k) *n* an atoll in the W Pacific Ocean, in the NW Marshall Islands: taken by the U.S. from Japan in 1944; became a naval base and later a testing ground for atomic weapons. Pop.: 715 (1988).

enjambment *or* **enjambement** (ɪn'dʒæmmənt; *French* ɑ̃ʒɑ̃bmɑ̃) *n Prosody.* the running over of a sentence from one line of verse into the next. [C19: from French, literally: a straddling, from *enjamber* to straddle, from EN-[1] + *jambe* leg; see JAMB] ▸ **en'jambed** *adj*

enjoin (ɪn'dʒɔɪn) *vb* (*tr*) **1** to order (someone) to do (something); urge strongly; command. **2** to impose or prescribe (a condition, mode of behaviour, etc.). **3** *Law.* to require (a person) to do or refrain from doing (some act), esp. by issuing an injunction. [C13: from Old French *enjoindre,* from Latin *injungere* to fasten to, from IN-[2] + *jungere* to JOIN] ▸ **en'joiner** *n* ▸ **en'joinment** *n*

enjoy (ɪn'dʒɔɪ) *vb* (*tr*) **1** to receive pleasure from; take joy in. **2** to have the benefit of; use with satisfaction. **3** to have as a condition; experience: *the land enjoyed a summer of rain.* **4** *Archaic.* to have sexual intercourse with. **5 enjoy oneself.** to have a good time. [C14: from Old French *enjoir,* from EN-[1] + *joir* to find pleasure in, from Latin *gaudēre* to rejoice] ▸ **en'joyable** *adj* ▸ **en'joyableness** *n* ▸ **en'joyably** *adv* ▸ **en'joyer** *n*

enjoyment (ɪn'dʒɔɪmənt) *n* **1** the act or condition of receiving pleasure from something. **2** the use or possession of something that is satisfying or beneficial. **3** something that provides joy or satisfaction. **4** the possession or exercise of a legal right.

enkephalin (ɛn'kɛfəlɪn) *or* **encephalin** (ɛn'sɛfəlɪn) *n* a chemical occurring in the brain, having effects similar to those of morphine. See also **endorphin.**

enkindle (ɪn'kɪndəl) *vb* (*tr*) **1** to set on fire; kindle. **2** to excite to activity or ardour; arouse. ▸ **en'kindler** *n*

enl. *abbrev. for:* **1** enlarge(d). **2** enlisted.

enlace (ɪn'leɪs) *vb* (*tr*) **1** to bind or encircle with or as with laces. **2** to entangle; intertwine. ▸ **en'lacement** *n*

enlarge (ɪn'lɑːdʒ) *vb* **1** to make or grow larger in size, scope, etc.; increase or expand. **2** (*tr*) to make (a photographic print) of a larger size than the negative. **3** (*intr; foll. by on or upon*) to speak or write (about) in greater detail; expatiate (on). ▸ **en'largeable** *adj*

enlargement (ɪn'lɑːdʒmənt) *n* **1** the act of enlarging or the condition of being enlarged. **2** something that enlarges or is intended to enlarge. **3** a photographic print that is larger than the negative from which it is made.

enlarger (ɪn'lɑːdʒə) *n* an optical instrument for making enlarged photographic prints in which a negative is brightly illuminated and its enlarged image is focused onto a sheet of sensitized paper.

enlighten (ɪn'laɪtən) *vb* (*tr*) **1** to give information or understanding to; instruct; edify. **2** to free from ignorance, prejudice, or superstition. **3** to give spiritual or religious revelation to. **4** *Poetic.* to shed light on. ▸ **en'lightener** *n* ▸ **en'lightening** *adj*

enlightened (ɪn'laɪtənd) *adj* **1** factually well-informed, tolerant of alternative opinions, and guided by rational thought: *an enlightened administration; enlightened self-interest.* **2** privy to or claiming a sense of spiritual or religious revelation of truth: *an enlightened spiritual master.*

enlightenment (ɪn'laɪtənmənt) *n* **1** the act or means of enlightening or the state of being enlightened. **2** *Buddhism.* the awakening to ultimate truth by which man is freed from the endless cycle of personal reincarnations to which all men are otherwise subject. **3** *Hinduism.* a state of transcendent divine experience represented by Vishnu: regarded as a goal of all religion.

Enlightenment (ɪn'laɪtənmənt) *n* **the.** an 18th-century philosophical movement stressing the importance of reason and the critical reappraisal of existing ideas and social institutions.

enlist (ɪn'lɪst) *vb* **1** to enter or persuade to enter into an engagement to serve in the armed forces. **2** (*tr*) to engage or secure (a person, his services, or his support) for a venture, cause, etc. **3** (*intr;* foll. by *in*) to enter into or join an enterprise, cause, etc. ▸ **en'lister** *n* ▸ **en'listment** *n*

enlisted man *n U.S.* a serviceman who holds neither a commission nor a warrant and is not under training for officer rank as a cadet or midshipman.

enliven (ɪn'laɪvən) *vb* (*tr*) **1** to make active, vivacious, or spirited; invigorate. **2** to make cheerful or bright; gladden or brighten. ▸ **en'livener** *n* ▸ **en'livening** *adj* ▸ **en'livenment** *n*

en masse (*French* ɑ̃ mas) *adv* in a group, body, or mass; as a whole; all together. **[**C19: from French**]**

enmesh, inmesh (ɪn'mɛʃ), *or* **immesh** *vb* (*tr*) to catch or involve in or as if in a net or snare; entangle. ▸ **en'meshment** *n*

enmity ('ɛnmɪtɪ) *n, pl* **-ties.** a feeling of hostility or ill will, as between enemies; antagonism. **[**C13: from Old French *enemistié,* from *enemi* ENEMY**]**

ennage ('ɛnɪdʒ) *n Printing.* the total number of ens in a piece of matter to be set in type.

ennead ('ɛnɪˌæd) *n* **1** a group or series of nine. **2** the sum of or number nine. **[**C17: from Greek *enneas,* from *ennea* nine**]** ▸ ˌ**enne'adic** *adj*

enneagon ('ɛnɪəgən) *n* another name for **nonagon.**

enneahedron (ˌɛnɪə'hiːdrən) *n, pl* **-drons** *or* **-dra** (-drə). a solid figure having nine plane faces. See also **polyhedron.** ▸ ˌ**ennea'hedral** *adj*

Ennerdale Water ('ɛnəˌdeɪl) *n* a lake in NW England, in Cumbria in the Lake District. Length: 4 km (2.5 miles).

Ennis ('ɛnɪs) *n* a town in the W Republic of Ireland, county town of Co. Clare. Pop.: 13 750 (1991).

Enniskillen (ˌɛnɪs'kɪlɪn) *or* (*formerly*) **Inniskilling** *n* a town in SW Northern Ireland, in Fermanagh, on an island in the River Erne: scene of the defeat of James II's forces in 1689. Pop.: 11 436 (1991).

Ennius ('ɛnɪəs) *n* **Quintus** ('kwɪntəs). 239–169 B.C., Roman epic poet and dramatist.

ennoble (ɪ'nəubəl) *vb* (*tr*) **1** to make noble, honourable, or excellent; dignify; exalt. **2** to raise to a noble rank; confer a title of nobility upon. ▸ **en'noblement** *n* ▸ **en'nobler** *n* ▸ **en'nobling** *adj*

ennui ('ɒnwiː; *French* ɑ̃nɥi) *n* a feeling of listlessness and general dissatisfaction resulting from lack of activity or excitement. **[**C18: from French: apathy, from Old French *enui* annoyance, vexation; see ANNOY**]**

ennuied, ennuyed ('ɒnwiːd) *or* **ennuyé** (*French* ɑ̃nɥije) *adj* affected with ennui; bored.

ENO *abbrev. for* English National Opera.

Enoch ('iːnɒk) *n Old Testament.* **1** the eldest son of Cain after whom the first city was named (Genesis 4:17). **2** the father of Methuselah: said to have walked with God and to have been taken by God at the end of his earthly life (Genesis 5:24).

enol ('iːnɒl) *n* any organic compound containing the group -CH:CO-, often existing in chemical equilibrium with the corresponding keto form. See **keto-enol tautomerism.** **[**C19: from -ENE + -OL[1]**]** ▸ **e'nolic** *adj*

enology (iː'nɒlədʒɪ) *n* the usual U.S. spelling of **oenology.**

enormity (ɪ'nɔːmɪtɪ) *n, pl* **-ties. 1** the quality or character of being outrageous; extreme wickedness. **2** an act of great wickedness; atrocity. **3** *Informal.* vastness of size or extent. **[**C15: from Old French *enormite,* from Late Latin *ēnormitās* hugeness; see ENORMOUS**]**

USAGE In modern English, it is common to talk about the *enormity* of something such as a task or a problem, but one should not talk about the *enormity* of an object or area: *distribution is a problem because of India's enormous size* (not *India's enormity*).

enormous (ɪ'nɔːməs) *adj* **1** unusually large in size, extent, or degree; immense; vast. **2** *Archaic.* extremely wicked; heinous. **[**C16: from Latin *ēnormis,* from *ē-* out of, away from + *norma* rule, pattern**]** ▸ **e'normously** *adv* ▸ **e'normousness** *n*

Enos ('iːnɒs) *n Old Testament.* a son of Seth (Genesis 4:26; 5:6).

enosis ('ɛnəusɪs) *n* the union of Greece and Cyprus: the aim of a group of Greek Cypriots. **[**C20: Modern Greek: from Greek *henoun* to unite, from *heis* one**]**

enough (ɪ'nʌf) *determiner* **1a** sufficient to answer a need, demand, supposition, or requirement; adequate: *enough cake.* **1b** (*as pronoun*): *enough is now known.* **2 that's enough!** that will do: used to put an end to an action, speech, performance, etc. ◆ *adv* **3** so as to be adequate or sufficient; as much as necessary: *you have worked hard enough.* **4** (*not used with a negative*) very or quite; rather: *she was pleased enough to see me.* **5** (intensifier): *oddly enough; surprisingly enough.* **6** just adequately; tolerably: *he did it well enough.* **[**Old English *genōh;* related to Old Norse *gnōgr,* Gothic *ganōhs,* Old High German *ginuog***]**

enounce (ɪ'nauns) *vb* (*tr*) *Formal.* **1** to enunciate. **2** to pronounce. **[**C19: from French *énoncer,* from Latin *ēnuntiāre* ENUNCIATE**]** ▸ **e'nouncement** *n*

enow (ɪ'nau) *adj, adv* an archaic word for **enough.**

en passant (ɒn pæ'sɑːnt; *French* ɑ̃ pasɑ̃) *adv* in passing: in chess, said of capturing a pawn that has made an initial move of two squares to its fourth rank, bypassing the square where an enemy pawn on its own fifth rank could capture it. The capture is made as if the captured pawn had moved one square instead of two. **[**C17: from French**]**

en pension *French.* (ɑ̃ pɑ̃sjɔ̃) *adv* in lodgings with all meals provided.

enphytotic (ˌɛnfaɪ'tɒtɪk) *adj* (of plant diseases) causing a constant amount of damage each year. **[**C20: from EN-[2] + -PHYTE + -OTIC**]**

enplane (ɛn'pleɪn) *vb* (*intr*) to board an aircraft.

en plein (*French* ɑ̃ plɛ̃) *adj* (*postpositive*), *adv* (of a gambling bet) placed entirely on a single number, etc. **[**from French: in full**]**

enprint ('ɛnprɪnt) *n* a standard photographic print (5 × 3.5 in.) produced from a negative.

en prise (*French* ɑ̃ priz) *adj* (*postpositive*), *adv* (of a chess piece) exposed to capture. **[**C19: from French; see PRIZE[1]**]**

enquire (ɪn'kwaɪə) *vb* a variant of **inquire.** ▸ **en'quirer** *n* ▸ **en'quiry** *n*

enrage (ɪn'reɪdʒ) *vb* (*tr*) to provoke to fury; put into a rage; anger. ▸ **en'raged** *adj* ▸ **enragedly** (ɪn'reɪdʒɪdlɪ) *adv* ▸ **en'ragement** *n*

en rapport *French.* (ɑ̃ rapɔr) *adj* (*postpositive*), *adv* in sympathy, harmony, or accord.

enrapture (ɪn'ræptʃə) *vb* (*tr*) to fill with delight; enchant.

enrich (ɪn'rɪtʃ) *vb* (*tr*) **1** to increase the wealth of. **2** to endow with fine or desirable qualities: *to enrich one's experience by travelling.* **3** to make more beautiful; adorn; decorate: *a robe enriched with jewels.* **4** to improve in quality, colour, flavour, etc. **5** to increase the food value of by adding nutrients: *to enrich dog biscuits with calcium.* **6** to make (soil) more productive, esp. by adding fertilizer. **7** *Physics.* to increase the concentration or abundance of one component or isotope in (a solution or mixture); concentrate: *to enrich a solution by evaporation; enrich a nuclear fuel.* ▸ **en'riched** *adj* ▸ **en'richer** *n* ▸ **en'richment** *n*

Enright ('ɛnraɪt) *n* **D(ennis) J(oseph).** born 1920, British poet, essayist, and editor.

enrobe (ɪn'rəub) *vb* (*tr*) to dress in or as if in a robe; attire. ▸ **en'rober** *n*

enrol *or U.S.* **enroll** (ɪn'rəul) *vb* **-rols** *or U.S.* **-rolls, -rolling -rolled.** (*mainly tr*) **1** to record or note in a roll or list. **2** (*also intr*) to become or cause to become a member; enlist; register. **3** to put on record; record. **4** *Rare.* to roll or wrap up. ▸ ˌ**enrol'lee** *n* ▸ **en'roller** *n*

enrolment *or U.S.* **enrollment** (ɪn'rəulmənt) *n* **1** the act of enrolling or state of being enrolled. **2** a list of people enrolled. **3** the total number of people enrolled.

enroot (ɪn'ruːt) *vb* (*tr; usually passive*) **1** to establish (plants) by fixing their roots in the earth. **2** to fix firmly, implant, or embed: *to enroot an idea in the mind.*

en route (ɒn 'ruːt; *French* ɑ̃ rut) *adv* on or along the way; on the road. **[**C18: from French**]**

ens (ɛnz) *n, pl* **entia** ('ɛnʃɪə). *Metaphysics.* **1** being or existence in the most general abstract sense. **2** a real thing, esp. as opposed to an attribute; entity. **[**C16: from Late Latin, literally: being, from Latin *esse* to be**]**

Ens. *abbrev. for* Ensign.

ENSA ('ɛnsə) *n acronym for* Entertainments National Service Association: a British organization providing entertainment for the armed forces during World War II.

ensample (ɛn'sɑːmpəl) *n* an archaic word for **example.**

ensanguine (ɪn'sæŋgwɪn) *vb* (*tr*) *Literary.* to cover or stain with or as with blood.

Enschede (*Dutch* 'ɛnsxədeː) *n* a city in the E Netherlands, in Overijssel province: a major centre of the Dutch cotton industry. Pop.: 147 924 (1995 est.).

ensconce (ɪn'skɒns) *vb* (*tr; often passive*) **1** to establish or settle firmly or comfortably: *ensconced in a chair.* **2** to place in safety; hide. **[**C16: see EN-[1], SCONCE[2]**]**

ensemble (ɒn'sɒmbəl; *French* ɑ̃sɑ̃blə) *n* **1** all the parts of something considered together and in relation to the whole. **2** a person's complete costume; outfit. **3a** the cast of a play other than the principals; supporting players. **3b** (*as modifier*): *an ensemble role.* **4** *Music.* **4a** a group of soloists singing or playing together. **4b** (*as modifier*): *an ensemble passage.* **5** *Music.* the degree of precision and unity exhibited by a group of instrumentalists or singers performing together: *the ensemble of the strings is good.* **6** the general or total effect of something made up of individual parts. 7 *Physics.* 7a a set of systems (such as a set of collections of atoms) that are identical in all respects apart from the motions of their constituents. 7b a single system (such as a collection of atoms) in which the properties are determined by the statistical behaviour of its constituents. ◆ *adv* 8 all together or at once. [C15: from French: together, from Latin *insimul,* from IN-[2] + *simul* at the same time]

enshrine *or* **inshrine** (ɪn'ʃraɪn) *vb (tr)* 1 to place or enclose in or as if in a shrine. 2 to hold as sacred; cherish; treasure. ► **en'shrinement** *n*

enshroud (ɪn'ʃraʊd) *vb (tr)* to cover or hide with or as if with a shroud: *the sky was enshrouded in mist.*

ensiform ('ɛnsɪˌfɔːm) *adj Biology.* shaped like a sword blade: *ensiform leaves.* [C16: from Latin *ensis* sword]

ensign ('ɛnsaɪn) *n* 1 (*also* 'ɛnsən). a flag flown by a ship, branch of the armed forces, etc., to indicate nationality, allegiance, etc. See also **Red Ensign, White Ensign.** 2 any flag, standard, or banner. 3 a standard-bearer. 4 a symbol, token, or emblem; sign. 5 (in the U.S. Navy) a commissioned officer of the lowest rank. 6 (in the British infantry) a colours bearer. 7 (formerly in the British infantry) a commissioned officer of the lowest rank. [C14: from Old French *enseigne,* from Latin INSIGNIA] ► **'ensign,ship** *or* **'ensigncy** *n*

ensilage ('ɛnsɪlɪdʒ) *n* 1 the process of ensiling green fodder. 2 a less common name for **silage.**

ensile (ɛn'saɪl, 'ɛnsaɪl) *vb (tr)* 1 to store and preserve (green fodder) in an enclosed pit or silo. 2 to turn (green fodder) into silage by causing it to ferment in a closed pit or silo. [C19: from French *ensiler,* from Spanish *ensilar,* from EN-[1] + *silo* SILO] ► **en,sila'bility** *n*

enslave (ɪn'sleɪv) *vb (tr)* to make a slave of; reduce to slavery; subjugate. ► **en'slavement** *n* ► **en'slaver** *n*

ensnare *or* **insnare** (ɪn'snɛə) *vb (tr)* 1 to catch or trap in a snare. 2 to trap or gain power over someone by dishonest or underhand means. ► **en'snarement** *n* ► **en'snarer** *n*

Ensor ('ɛnsɔː) *n* **James (Sydney).** 1860–1949, Belgian expressionist painter, noted for his macabre subjects.

ensoul *or* **insoul** (ɪn'səʊl) *vb (tr)* 1 to endow with a soul. 2 to cherish within the soul. ► **en'soulment** *or* **in'soulment** *n*

ensphere *or* **insphere** (ɪn'sfɪə) *vb (tr)* 1 to enclose in or as if in a sphere. 2 to make spherical in form.

enstatite ('ɛnstəˌtaɪt) *n* a grey, green, yellow, or brown pyroxene mineral consisting of magnesium silicate in orthorhombic crystalline form. Formula: $Mg_2Si_2O_6$. [C19: from Greek *enstatēs* adversary (referring to its refractory quality) + -ITE[1]]

ensue (ɪn'sjuː) *vb* **-sues, -suing, -sued.** 1 (*intr*) to follow subsequently or in order; come next or afterwards. 2 (*intr*) to follow or occur as a consequence; result. 3 (*tr*) *Obsolete.* to pursue. [C14: from Anglo-French *ensuer,* from Old French *ensuivre,* from EN-[1] + *suivre* to follow, from Latin *sequī*] ► **en'suing** *adj*

en suite *French.* (ɑ̃ sɥit) *adv* as part of a set; forming a unit: *a hotel room with bathroom en suite.* [C19: literally: in sequence]

ensure (ɛn'ʃʊə, -'ʃɔː) *or (esp. U.S.)* **insure** *vb (tr)* 1 (*may take a clause as object*) to make certain or sure; guarantee: *this victory will ensure his happiness.* 2 to make safe or secure; protect. ► **en'surer** *n*

enswathe (ɪn'sweɪð) *vb (tr)* to bind or wrap; swathe. ► **en'swathement** *n*

ENT *Med. abbrev. for* ear, nose, and throat.

-ent *suffix forming adjectives and nouns.* causing or performing an action or existing in a certain condition; the agent that performs an action: *astringent; dependent.* [from Latin *-ent-, -ens,* present participial ending]

entablature (ɛn'tæblətʃə) *n Architect.* 1 the part of a classical temple above the columns, having an architrave, a frieze, and a cornice. 2 any construction of similar form. [C17: from French, from Italian *intavolatura* something put on a table, hence, something laid flat, from *tavola* table, from Latin *tabula* TABLE]

entablement (ɪn'teɪbᵊlmənt) *n* the platform of a pedestal, above the dado, that supports a statue. [C17: from Old French]

entail (ɪn'teɪl) *vb (tr)* 1 to bring about or impose by necessity; have as a necessary consequence: *this task entails careful thought.* 2 *Property law.* to restrict (the descent of an estate) to a designated line of heirs. 3 *Logic.* to have as a necessary consequence. ◆ *n* 4 *Property law.* 4a the restriction imposed by entailing an estate. 4b an estate that has been entailed. [C14: *entaillen,* from EN-[1] + *taille* limitation, TAIL[2]] ► **en'tailer** *n*

entailment (ɪn'teɪlmənt) *n* 1 the act of entailing or the condition of being entailed. 2 *Philosophy, logic.* 2a a relationship between propositions such that one must be true if the others are. 2b a proposition whose truth depends on such a relationship. Usual symbol: —ɜ See **fish-hook** (sense 2).

entamoeba (ˌɛntə'miːbə), **endamoeba** *or U.S.* **entameba, endameba** *n, pl* **-bae** (-biː) *or* **-bas.** any parasitic amoeba of the genus *Entamoeba* (or *Endamoeba*), esp. *E. histolytica,* which lives in the intestines of man and causes amoebic dysentery.

entangle (ɪn'tæŋgᵊl) *vb (tr)* 1 to catch or involve in or as if in a tangle; ensnare or enmesh. 2 to make tangled or twisted; snarl. 3 to make complicated; confuse. 4 to involve in difficulties; entrap. ► **en'tangler** *n*

entanglement (ɪn'tæŋgᵊlmənt) *n* 1 something that entangles or is itself entangled. 2 a sexual relationship regarded as unfortunate, damaging, or compromising.

entasis ('ɛntəsɪs) *n, pl* **-ses** (-siːz). 1 a slightly convex curve given to the shaft of a column, pier, or similar structure, to correct the illusion of concavity produced by a straight shaft. 2 Also called: **entasia** (ɛn'teɪzɪə). *Physiol.* an involuntary or spasmodic muscular contraction. [C18: from Greek, from *enteinein* to stretch tight, from *teinein* to stretch]

Entebbe (ɛn'tɛbɪ) *n* a town in S Uganda, on Lake Victoria: British administrative centre of Uganda (1893–1958); international airport. Pop.: 41 638 (1991).

entelechy (ɛn'tɛlɪkɪ) *n, pl* **-chies.** *Metaphysics.* 1 (in the philosophy of Aristotle) actuality as opposed to potentiality. 2 (in the system of Leibnitz) the soul or principle of perfection of an object or person; a monad or basic constituent. 3 something that contains or realizes a final cause, esp. the vital force thought to direct the life of an organism. [C17: from Late Latin *entelechia,* from Greek *entelekheia,* from EN-[2] + *telos* goal, completion + *ekhein* to have]

entellus (ɛn'tɛləs) *n* an Old World monkey, *Presbytes entellus,* of S Asia. This langur is regarded as sacred in India. Also called: **hanuman.** [C19: New Latin, apparently from the name of the aged Sicilian character in Book V of Virgil's *Aeneid*]

entente (*French* ɑ̃tɑ̃t) *n* 1 short for **entente cordiale.** 2 the parties to an entente cordiale collectively. [C19: French: understanding]

entente cordiale (*French* ɑ̃tɑ̃t kɔrdjal) *n* 1 a friendly understanding between political powers: less formal than an alliance. 2 (*often caps.*) the understanding reached by France and Britain in April 1904, which settled outstanding colonial disputes. [C19: French: cordial understanding]

enter ('ɛntə) *vb* 1 to come or go into (a place, house, etc.). 2 to penetrate or pierce. 3 (*tr*) to introduce or insert. 4 to join (a party, organization, etc.). 5 (when *intr,* foll. by *into*) to become involved or take part (in): *to enter a game; to enter into an agreement.* 6 (*tr*) to record (an item such as a commercial transaction) in a journal, account, register, etc. 7 (*tr*) to record (a name, etc.) on a list. 8 (*tr*) to present or submit: *to enter a proposal.* 9 (*intr*) *Theatre.* to come on stage: used as a stage direction: *enter Juliet.* 10 (when *intr,* often foll. by *into, on,* or *upon*) to begin; start: *to enter upon a new career.* 11 (*intr;* often foll. by *upon*) to come into possession (of). 12 (*tr*) to place (evidence, a plea, etc.) before a court of law or upon the court records. 13 (*tr*) *Law.* 13a to go onto and occupy (land). 13b *Chiefly U.S.* to file a claim to (public lands). [C13: from Old French *entrer,* from Latin *intrāre* to go in, from *intrā* within] ► **'enterable** *adj* ► **'enterer** *n*

enterectomy (ˌɛntə'rɛktəmɪ) *n* surgical excision of part of the intestine.

enteric (ɛn'tɛrɪk) *or* **enteral** ('ɛntərəl) *adj* intestinal. [C19: from Greek *enterikos,* from *enteron* intestine] ► **'enterally** *adv*

enteric fever *n* another name for **typhoid fever.**

enter into *vb (intr, prep)* 1 to be considered as a necessary part of (one's plans, calculations, etc.). 2 to be in sympathy with: *he enters into his patient's problems.*

enteritis (ˌɛntə'raɪtɪs) *n* inflammation of the intestine.

entero- *or before a vowel* **enter-** *combining form.* indicating an intestine: *enterovirus; enteritis.* [from New Latin, from Greek *enteron* intestine]

enterobacterium (ˌɛntərəʊbæk'tɪərɪəm) *n* any of a class of Gram-negative rodlike bacteria that occur in the gut.

enterobiasis (ˌɛntərəʊ'baɪəsɪs) *n* a disease, common in children, caused by infestation of the large intestine with nematodes of the genus *Enterobius,* esp. the pinworm (*E. vermicularis*).

enterocolitis (ˌɛntərəʊkɒ'laɪtɪs) *n* inflammation of the small intestine and colon.

enterogastrone (ˌɛntərəʊ'gæstrəʊn) *n* a hormone liberated by the upper intestinal mucosa when stimulated by fat: reduces peristalsis and secretion in the stomach. [C20: from ENTERO- + GASTRO- + (HORM)ONE]

enterokinase (ˌɛntərəʊ'kaɪneɪz) *n* an enzyme in intestinal juice that converts trypsinogen to trypsin.

enteron ('ɛntəˌrɒn) *n, pl* **-tera** (-tərə). the alimentary canal, esp. of an embryo or a coelenterate. [C19: via New Latin from Greek: intestine; related to Latin *inter* between]

enterostomy (ˌɛntə'rɒstəmɪ) *n, pl* **-mies.** surgical formation of a permanent opening into the intestine through the abdominal wall, used as an artificial anus, for feeding, etc.

enterotomy (ˌɛntə'rɒtəmɪ) *n, pl* **-mies.** surgical incision into the intestine.

enterovirus (ˌɛntərəʊ'vaɪrəs) *n, pl* **-viruses.** any of a group of viruses that occur in and cause diseases of the gastrointestinal tract.

enterprise ('ɛntəˌpraɪz) *n* 1 a project or undertaking, esp. one that requires boldness or effort. 2 participation in such projects. 3 readiness to embark on new ventures; boldness and energy. 4a initiative in business. 4b (*as modifier*): *the enterprise culture.* 5 a business unit; a company or firm. [C15: from Old French *entreprise* (n), from *entreprendre* from *entre-* between (from Latin: INTER-) + *prendre* to take, from Latin *prehendere* to grasp] ► **'enter,priser** *n*

Enterprise Allowance Scheme *n* (in Britain) a scheme to provide a weekly allowance to an unemployed person who wishes to set up a business and is willing to invest a specified amount in it during its first year.

Enterprise Investment Scheme *n* (in Britain) a scheme to provide tax relief on investments in certain small companies: came into operation in 1994, when it replaced the Business Expansion Scheme.

enterprise zone *n* a designated zone in a depressed area, esp. an inner urban area, where firms are given tax concessions and various planning restrictions are lifted, in order to attract new industry and business to the area: first introduced in Britain in 1981.

enterprising ('ɛntəˌpraɪzɪŋ) *adj* ready to embark on new ventures; full of boldness and initiative. ► **'enter,prisingly** *adv*

entertain (ˌɛntə'teɪn) *vb* 1 to provide amusement for (a person or audience). 2 to show hospitality to (guests). 3 (*tr*) to hold in the mind: *to entertain an idea.* [C15: from Old French *entretenir,* from *entre-* mutually + *tenir* to hold, from Latin *tenēre*]

entertainer (ˌɛntə'teɪnə) *n* 1 a professional singer, comedian, or other performer who takes part in public entertainments. 2 any person who entertains.

entertaining (ˌɛntə'teɪnɪŋ) *adj* serving to entertain or give pleasure; diverting; amusing. ► **ˌenter'tainingly** *adv*

entertainment (ˌɛntə'teɪnmənt) *n* 1 the act or art of entertaining or state of being entertained. **2** an act, production, etc., that entertains; diversion; amusement.

enthalpy ('ɛnθælpɪ, ɛn'θæl-) *n* a thermodynamic property of a system equal to the sum of its internal energy and the product of its pressure and volume. Symbol: *H* Also called: **heat content, total heat.** [C20: from Greek *enthalpein* to warm in, from EN-[2] + *thalpein* to warm]

enthetic (ɛn'θɛtɪk) *adj* (esp. of infectious diseases) introduced into the body from without. [C19: from Greek *enthetikos,* from *entithenai* to put in]

enthral *or U.S.* **enthrall** (ɪn'θrɔːl) *vb* **-thrals** *or U.S.* **-thralls, -thralling, -thralled.** (*tr*) **1** to hold spellbound; enchant; captivate. **2** *Obsolete.* to hold as thrall; enslave. [C16: from EN-[1] + THRALL] ► **en'thraller** *n* ► **en'thralling** *adj* ► **en'thralment** *or U.S.* **en'thrallment** *n*

enthrone (ɛn'θrəʊn) *vb* (*tr*) **1** to place on a throne. **2** to honour or exalt. **3** to assign authority to. ► **en'thronement** *n*

enthuse (ɪn'θjuːz) *vb* to feel or show or cause to feel or show enthusiasm.

enthusiasm (ɪn'θjuːzɪˌæzəm) *n* **1** ardent and lively interest or eagerness. **2** an object of keen interest; passion. **3** *Archaic.* extravagant or unbalanced religious fervour. **4** *Obsolete.* possession or inspiration by a god. [C17: from Late Latin *enthūsiasmus,* from Greek *enthousiasmos,* from *enthousiazein* to be possessed by a god, from *entheos* inspired, from EN-[2] + *theos* god]

enthusiast (ɪn'θjuːzɪˌæst) *n* **1** a person filled with or motivated by enthusiasm; fanatic. **2** *Archaic.* a religious visionary, esp. one whose zeal for religion is extravagant or unbalanced. ► **enˌthusi'astic** *adj* ► **enˌthusi'astically** *adv*

enthymeme ('ɛnθɪˌmiːm) *n Logic.* **1** an incomplete syllogism, in which one or more premises are unexpressed as their truth is considered to be self-evident. **2** any argument some of whose premises are omitted as obvious. [C16: via Latin from Greek *enthumēma,* from *enthumeisthai* to infer (literally: to have in the mind), from EN-[2] + *thumos* mind] ► **ˌenthyme'matic** *or* **ˌenthyme'matical** *adj*

entice (ɪn'taɪs) *vb* (*tr*) to attract or draw towards oneself by exciting hope or desire; tempt; allure. [C13: from Old French *enticier,* from Vulgar Latin *intitiāre* (unattested) to incite, from Latin *titiō* firebrand] ► **en'ticement** *n* ► **en'ticer** *n* ► **en'ticing** *adj* ► **en'ticingly** *adv* ► **en'ticingness** *n*

entire (ɪn'taɪə) *adj* **1** (*prenominal*) whole; complete: *the entire project is going well.* **2** (*prenominal*) without reservation or exception; total: *you have my entire support.* **3** not broken or damaged; intact. **4** consisting of a single piece or section; undivided; continuous. **5** (of leaves, petals, etc.) having a smooth margin not broken up into teeth or lobes. **6** not castrated: *an entire horse.* **7** *Obsolete.* of one substance or kind; unmixed; pure. ◆ *n* **8** a less common word for **entirety. 9** an uncastrated horse. **10** *Philately.* **10a** a complete item consisting of an envelope, postcard, or wrapper with stamps affixed. **10b on entire.** (of a stamp) placed on an envelope, postcard, etc., and bearing postal directions. [C14: from Old French *entier,* from Latin *integer* whole, from IN-[1] + *tangere* to touch] ► **en'tireness** *n*

entirely (ɪn'taɪəlɪ) *adv* **1** without reservation or exception; wholly; completely. **2** solely or exclusively; only.

entirety (ɪn'taɪərɪtɪ) *n, pl* **-ties. 1** the state of being entire or whole; completeness. **2** a thing, sum, amount, etc., that is entire; whole; total.

entitle (ɪn'taɪtᵊl) *vb* (*tr*) **1** to give (a person) the right to do or have something; qualify; allow. **2** to give a name or title to. **3** to confer a title of rank or honour upon. [C14: from Old French *entituler,* from Late Latin *intitulāre,* from Latin *titulus* TITLE] ► **en'titlement** *n*

entity ('ɛntɪtɪ) *n, pl* **-ties. 1** something having real or distinct existence; a thing, esp. when considered as independent of other things. **2** existence or being. **3** the essence or real nature. [C16: from Medieval Latin *entitās,* from *ēns* being; see ENS] ► **entitative** ('ɛntɪtətɪv) *adj*

ento- *combining form.* inside; within: *entoderm.* [New Latin, from Greek *entos* within]

entoblast ('ɛntəʊˌblæst) *n* **1** *Embryol.* a less common name for **endoderm. 2** a less common name for **hypoblast.** ► **entoblastic** (ˌɛntəʊ'blæstɪk) *adj*

entoderm ('ɛntəʊˌdɜːm) *n Embryol.* another name for **endoderm.** ► **ˌento'dermal** *or* **ˌento'dermic** *adj*

entoil (ɪn'tɔɪl) *vb* (*tr*) an archaic word for **ensnare.** ► **en'toilment** *n*

entomb (ɪn'tuːm) *vb* (*tr*) **1** to place in or as if in a tomb; bury; inter. **2** to serve as a tomb for. ► **en'tombment** *n*

entomic (ɛn'tɒmɪk) *adj* denoting or relating to insects. [C19: from Greek *entomon* (see ENTOMO-) + -IC]

entomo- *combining form.* indicating an insect: *entomology.* [from Greek *entomon* insect (literally: creature cut into sections), from *en-* in + *-tomon,* from *temnein* to cut]

entomol. *or* **entom.** *abbrev. for* entomology.

entomologize *or* **entomologise** (ˌɛntə'mɒləˌdʒaɪz) *vb* (*intr*) to collect or study insects.

entomology (ˌɛntə'mɒlədʒɪ) *n* the branch of science concerned with the study of insects. ► **entomological** (ˌɛntəmə'lɒdʒɪkᵊl) *or* **ˌentomo'logic** *adj* ► **ˌentomo'logically** *adv* ► **ˌento'mologist** *n*

entomophagous (ˌɛntə'mɒfəgəs) *adj* feeding mainly on insects; insectivorous.

entomophilous (ˌɛntə'mɒfɪləs) *adj* (of flowering plants such as orchids) pollinated by insects. Compare **anemophilous.** ► **ˌento'mophily** *n*

entomostracan (ˌɛntə'mɒstrəkən) *n* **1** any small crustacean of the group (formerly subclass) *Entomostraca,* including the branchiopods, ostracods, and copepods. ◆ *adj* **2** of, relating to, or belonging to the *Entomostraca.* [C19: from New Latin ENTOMO- + Greek *ostrakon* shell; see OSTRACIZE] ► **ˌento'mostracous** *adj*

entophyte ('ɛntəʊˌfaɪt) *n Botany.* a variant of **endophyte.** ► **entophytic** (ˌɛntəʊ'fɪtɪk) *adj*

entopic (ɛn'tɒpɪk) *adj Anatomy.* situated in its normal place or position. See also **ectopia.** [from Greek *entopos* in a place, from *topos* place]

entoptic (ɛn'tɒptɪk) *adj* (of visual sensation) resulting from structures within the eye itself. [ENTO- + OPTIC]

entourage (ɒntʊ'rɑːʒ; *French* ɑ̃turaʒ) *n* **1** a group of attendants or retainers, esp. such as surround an important person; retinue. **2** surroundings or environment. [C19: from French, from *entourer* to surround, from *entour* around, from *tour* circuit; see TOUR, TURN]

entozoic (ˌɛntəʊ'zəʊɪk) *adj* **1** of or relating to an entozoon. **2** living inside an animal: *entozoic fungi.*

entozoon (ˌɛntəʊ'zəʊɒn) *or* **entozoan** *n, pl* **-zoa** (-'zəʊə). any animal, such as a tapeworm, that lives within another animal, usually as a parasite.

entr'acte (ɒn'trækt; *French* ɑ̃trakt) *n* **1** an interval between two acts of a play or opera. **2** (esp. formerly) an entertainment during an interval, such as dancing between acts of an opera. [C19: French, literally: between-act]

entrails ('ɛntreɪlz) *pl n* **1** the internal organs of a person or animal; intestines; guts. **2** the innermost parts of anything. [C13: from Old French *entrailles,* from Medieval Latin *intrālia,* changed from Latin *interānea* intestines, ultimately from *inter* between]

entrain[1] (ɪn'treɪn) *vb* to board or put aboard a train. ► **en'trainment** *n*

entrain[2] (ɪn'treɪn) *vb* (*tr*) **1** (of a liquid or gas) to carry along (drops of liquid, bubbles, etc.), as in certain distillations. **2** to disperse (air bubbles) through concrete in order to increase its resistance to frost. **3** *Zoology.* to adjust (an internal rhythm of an organism) so that it synchronizes with an external cycle, such as that of light and dark. ► **en'trainment** *n*

entrammel (ɪn'træməl) *vb* **-mels, -melling, -melled.** (*tr*) to hamper or obstruct by entangling.

entrance[1] ('ɛntrəns) *n* **1** the act or an instance of entering; entry. **2** a place for entering, such as a door or gate. **3a** the power, liberty, or right of entering; admission. **3b** (*as modifier*): *an entrance fee.* **4** the coming of an actor or other performer onto a stage. [C16: from French, from *entrer* to ENTER]

entrance[2] (ɪn'trɑːns) *vb* (*tr*) **1** to fill with wonder and delight; enchant. **2** to put into a trance; hypnotize. ► **en'trancement** *n* ► **en'trancing** *adj*

entrant ('ɛntrənt) *n* **1** a person who enters. **2** a new member of a group, society, or association. **3** a person who enters a competition or contest; competitor. [C17: from French, literally: entering, from *entrer* to ENTER]

entrap (ɪn'træp) *vb* **-traps, -trapping, -trapped.** (*tr*) **1** to catch or snare in or as if in a trap. **2** to lure or trick into danger, difficulty, or embarrassment. ► **en'trapper** *n*

entrapment (ɪn'træpmənt) *n* the luring, by a police officer, of a person into committing a crime so that he may be prosecuted for it.

entreat *or* **intreat** (ɪn'triːt) *vb* **1** to ask (a person) earnestly; beg or plead with; implore. **2** to make an earnest request or petition for (something). **3** an archaic word for **treat** (sense 4). [C15: from Old French *entraiter,* from EN-[1] + *traiter* to TREAT] ► **en'treatingly** *or* **in'treatingly** *adv* ► **en'treatment** *or* **in'treatment** *n*

entreaty (ɪn'triːtɪ) *n, pl* **-treaties.** an earnest request or petition; supplication; plea.

entrechat (*French* ɑ̃trəʃa) *n* a leap in ballet during which the dancer repeatedly crosses his feet or beats them together. [C18: from French, from earlier *entrechase,* changed by folk etymology from Italian (*capriola*) *intrecciata,* literally: entwined (caper), from *intrecciare* to interlace, from IN-[2] + *treccia* TRESS]

entrecôte (*French* ɑ̃trəkot) *n* a beefsteak cut from between the ribs. [C19: French *entrecôte,* from *entre-* INTER- + *côte* rib, from Latin *costa*]

Entre-Deux-Mers (*French* ɑ̃trədømɛr) *n* any wine produced in the area of the Gironde between the rivers Dordogne and Garonne in S France.

entrée ('ɒntreɪ) *n* **1** a dish served before a main course. **2** *Chiefly U.S.* the main course of a meal. **3** the power or right of entry. [C18: from French, from *entrer* to ENTER; in cookery, so called because formerly the course was served after an intermediate course called the *relevé* (remove)]

entremets (*French* ɑ̃trəmɛ) *n, pl* **-mets** (*French* -mɛ). **1** a dessert. **2** a light dish, formerly served at formal dinners between the main course and the dessert. [C18: from French, from Old French *entremes,* from *entre-* between, INTER- + *mes* dish, MESS]

entrench *or* **intrench** (ɪn'trɛntʃ) *vb* **1** (*tr*) to construct (a defensive position) by digging trenches around it. **2** (*tr*) to fix or establish firmly, esp. so as to prevent removal or change. **3** (*intr*; foll. by *on* or *upon*) to trespass or encroach; infringe. ► **en'trenched** *or* **in'trenched** *adj* ► **en'trencher** *or* **in'trencher** *n*

entrenchment *or* **intrenchment** (ɪn'trɛntʃmənt) *n* **1** the act of entrenching or state of being entrenched. **2** a position protected by trenches. **3** one of a series of deep trenches constructed as a shelter from gunfire.

entre nous (*French* ɑ̃trə nu) *adv* between ourselves; in confidence. [C17: from French]

entrepôt (*French* ɑ̃trəpo) *n* **1** a warehouse for commercial goods. **2a** a trading centre or port at a geographically convenient location, at which goods are imported and re-exported without incurring liability for duty. **2b** (*as modifier*): *an entrepôt trade.* [C18: French, from *entreposer* to put in, from *entre-* between, INTER- + *poser* to place (see POSE[1]); formed on the model of DEPOT]

entrepreneur (ˌɒntrəprə'nɜː; *French* ɑ̃trəprənœr) *n* **1** the owner or manager of a business enterprise who, by risk and initiative, attempts to make profits. **2** a middleman or commercial intermediary. [C19: from French, from *entreprendre* to undertake; see ENTERPRISE] ► **ˌentrepre'neurial** *adj* ► **ˌentrepre'neurship** *n*

entresol (ˌɒntrə'sɒl; *French* ɑ̃trəsɔl) *n* another name for **mezzanine** (sense 1). [C18: from French, literally: between floors, from *entre-* INTER- + *sol* floor, ground, from Latin *solum*]

entropy ('ɛntrəpɪ) *n, pl* **-pies. 1** a thermodynamic quantity that changes in a reversible process by an amount equal to the heat absorbed or emitted divided by the thermodynamic temperature. It is measured in joules per kelvin. Symbol: *S* See also **law of thermodynamics** (sense 1). **2** a statistical measure of the disorder of a closed system expressed by $S = k\log P + c$ where *P* is the probability that a particular state of the system exists, *k* is the Boltzmann constant, and *c* is another constant. **3** lack of pattern or organization; disorder. **4** a measure of the efficiency of a system, such as a code or language, in transmitting information. [C19: from EN-[2] + -TROPE]

entrust *or* **intrust** (ɪnˈtrʌst) *vb* (*tr*) **1** (usually foll. by *with*) to invest or charge (with a duty, responsibility, etc.). **2** (often foll. by *to*) to put into the care or protection of someone. ▸ **en'trustment** *or* **in'trustment** *n*

USAGE It is usually considered incorrect to talk about *entrusting* someone *to do* something: *the army cannot be trusted* (not *entrusted*) *to carry out orders.*

entry (ˈɛntrɪ) *n, pl* **-tries. 1** the act or an instance of entering; entrance. **2** a point or place for entering, such as a door, gate, etc. **3a** the right or liberty of entering; admission; access. **3b** (*as modifier*): *an entry permit.* **4** the act of recording an item, such as a commercial transaction, in a journal, account, register, etc. **5** an item recorded, as in a diary, dictionary, or account. **6a** a person, horse, car, etc., entering a competition or contest; competitor. **6b** (*as modifier*): *an entry fee.* **7** the competitors entering a contest considered collectively: *a good entry this year for the speed trials.* **8** the people admitted at one time to a school, college, or course of study, etc., considered collectively; intake. **9** the action of an actor in going on stage or his manner of doing this. **10** *Criminal law.* the act of unlawfully going onto the premises of another with the intention of committing a crime. **11** *Property law.* the act of going upon another person's land with the intention of asserting the right to possession. **12** any point in a piece of music, esp. a fugue, at which a performer commences or resumes playing or singing. **13** *Cards.* a card that enables one to transfer the lead from one's own hand to that of one's partner or to the dummy hand. **14** *English dialect.* a passage between the backs of two rows of terraced houses. [C13: from Old French *entree,* past participle of *entrer* to ENTER]

entryism (ˈɛntrɪɪzəm) *n* the policy or practice of members of a particular political group joining an existing political party with the intention of changing its principles and policies, instead of forming a new party. ▸ **'entryist** *n, adj*

entry-level *adj* **1** (of a job or worker) at the most elementary level in a career structure. **2** (of a product) characterized by being at the most appropriate level for use by a beginner: *an entry-level camera.*

entwine *or* **intwine** (ɪnˈtwaɪn) *vb* (of two or more things) to twine together or (of one or more things) to twine around (something else). ▸ **en'twinement** *or* **in'twinement** *n*

enucleate *vb* (ɪˈnjuːklɪˌeɪt). (*tr*) **1** *Biology.* to remove the nucleus from (a cell). **2** *Surgery.* to remove (a tumour or other structure) from its capsule without rupturing it. **3** *Archaic.* to explain or disclose. ◆ *adj* (ɪˈnjuːklɪɪt, -ˌeɪt). **4** (of cells) deprived of their nuclei. [C16: from Latin *ēnūcleāre* to remove the kernel, from *nūcleus* kernel] ▸ **eˌnucle'ation** *n*

Enugu (eˈnuːguː) *n* a city and state in S Nigeria, capital of Enugu state: capital of the former Eastern region and of the breakaway state of Biafra during the Civil War (1967–70): coal-mining. Pop.: 316 100 (1996 est.).

E number *n* any of a series of numbers with the prefix E indicating a specific food additive recognized by the European Union and used on labels of processed food.

enumerate (ɪˈnjuːməˌreɪt) *vb* **1** (*tr*) to mention separately or in order; name one by one; list. **2** (*tr*) to determine the number of; count. **3** *Canadian.* to compile or enter (a name or names) in a voting list for an area. [C17: from Latin *ēnumerāre,* from *numerāre* to count, reckon; see NUMBER] ▸ **e'numerable** *adj* ▸ **eˌnumer'ation** *n* ▸ **e'numerative** *adj*

enumerator (ɪˈnjuːməˌreɪtə) *n* **1** a person or thing that enumerates. **2** *Canadian.* a person who compiles the voting list for an area. **3** *Brit.* a person who issues and retrieves forms during a census of population.

enunciable (ɪˈnʌnsɪəbᵊl) *adj* capable of being enunciated.

enunciate (ɪˈnʌnsɪˌeɪt) *vb* **1** to articulate or pronounce (words), esp. clearly and distinctly. **2** (*tr*) to state precisely or formally. [C17: from Latin *ēnuntiāre* to declare, from *nuntiāre* to announce, from *nuntius* messenger] ▸ **eˌnunci'ation** *n* ▸ **e'nunciative** *or* **e'nunciatory** *adj* ▸ **e'nunciatively** *adv* ▸ **e'nunciˌator** *n*

enure (ɪˈnjʊə) *vb* a variant spelling of **inure.** ▸ **en'urement** *n*

enuresis (ˌɛnjʊˈriːsɪs) *n* involuntary discharge of urine, esp. during sleep. [C19: from New Latin, from Greek EN-[2] + *ourein* to urinate, from *ouron* urine] ▸ **enuretic** (ˌɛnjʊˈrɛtɪk) *adj*

envelop (ɪnˈvɛləp) *vb* (*tr*) **-lops, -loping, -loped. 1** to wrap or enclose in or as if in a covering. **2** to conceal or obscure, as from sight or understanding: *a plan enveloped in mystery.* **3** to surround or partially surround (an enemy force). [C14: from Old French *envoluper,* from EN-[1] + *voluper, voloper,* of obscure origin] ▸ **en'velopment** *n*

envelope (ˈɛnvəˌləʊp, ˈɒn-) *n* **1** a flat covering of paper, usually rectangular in shape and with a flap that can be folded over and sealed, used to enclose a letter, etc. **2** any covering or wrapper. **3** *Biology.* any enclosing structure, such as a membrane, shell, or skin. **4** the bag enclosing the gas in a balloon. **5** *Maths.* a curve or surface that is tangential to each one of a group of curves or surfaces. **6** *Electronics.* the sealed glass or metal housing of a valve, electric light, etc. **7** *Telecomm.* the outer shape of a modulated wave, formed by the peaks of successive cycles of the carrier wave. [C18: from French *enveloppe,* from *envelopper* to wrap around; see ENVELOP]

envenom (ɪnˈvɛnəm) *vb* (*tr*) **1** to fill or impregnate with venom; make poisonous. **2** to fill with bitterness or malice.

Enver Pasha (ˈɛnvə ˈpɑːʃə) *n* 1881–1922, Turkish soldier and leader of the Young Turks: minister of war (1914–18).

enviable (ˈɛnvɪəbᵊl) *adj* exciting envy; fortunate or privileged. ▸ **'enviableness** *n* ▸ **'enviably** *adv*

envious (ˈɛnvɪəs) *adj* feeling, showing, or resulting from envy. [C13: from Anglo-Norman, ultimately from Latin *invidiōsus* full of envy, INVIDIOUS; see ENVY] ▸ **'enviously** *adv* ▸ **'enviousness** *n*

environ (ɪnˈvaɪrən) *vb* (*tr*) to encircle or surround. [C14: from Old French *environner* to surround, from *environ* around, from EN-[1] + *viron* a circle, from *virer* to turn, VEER[1]]

environment (ɪnˈvaɪrənmənt) *n* **1** external conditions or surroundings, esp. those in which people live or work. **2** *Ecology.* the external surroundings in which a plant or animal lives, which tend to influence its development and behaviour. **3** the state of being environed; encirclement. **4** *Computing.* an operating system, program, or integrated suite of programs that provides all the facilities necessary for a particular application: *a word-processing environment.* ▸ **enˌviron'mental** *adj* ▸ **enˌviron'mentally** *adv*

environmental audit *n* the systematic examination of a business operation's interaction with the environment, to assess the success of its conservation or antipollution programme.

Environmental Health Officer *n* (in Britain) an employee of the Environmental Health Service. Former names: **public health inspector, sanitary inspector.**

Environmental Health Service *n* (in Britain) a service provided by a local authority, which deals with prevention of the spread of communicable diseases, food safety and hygiene, control of infestation by insects or rodents, etc.

environmentalism (ɪnˌvaɪrənˈmɛntəˌlɪzəm) *n Psychol.* the belief that a person's behaviour is affected chiefly by his environment. Compare **hereditarianism.**

environmentalist (ɪnˌvaɪrənˈmɛntəlɪst) *n* **1** an adherent of environmentalism. **2** a specialist in the maintenance of ecological balance and the conservation of the environment. **3** a person concerned with issues that affect the environment, such as pollution.

environs (ɪnˈvaɪrənz) *pl n* a surrounding area or region, esp. the suburbs or outskirts of a town or city; vicinity.

envisage (ɪnˈvɪzɪdʒ) *vb* (*tr*) **1** to form a mental image of; visualize; contemplate. **2** to conceive of as a possibility in the future; foresee. **3** *Archaic.* to look in the face of; confront. [C19: from French *envisager,* from EN-[1] + *visage* face, VISAGE] ▸ **en'visagement** *n*

USAGE It was formerly considered incorrect to use a clause after *envisage* as in *it is envisaged that the new centre will cost £40 million,* but this use is now acceptable.

envision (ɪnˈvɪʒən) *vb* (*tr*) to conceive of as a possibility, esp. in the future; foresee.

envoy[1] (ˈɛnvɔɪ) *n* **1** Formal name: **envoy extraordinary and minister plenipotentiary.** a diplomat of the second class, ranking between an ambassador and a minister resident. **2** an accredited messenger, agent, or representative. [C17: from French *envoyé,* literally: sent, from *envoyer* to send, from Vulgar Latin *inviāre* (unattested) to send on a journey, from IN-[2] + *via* road] ▸ **'envoyship** *n*

envoy[2] *or* **envoi** (ˈɛnvɔɪ) *n* **1** a brief dedicatory or explanatory stanza concluding certain forms of poetry, notably ballades. **2** a postscript in other forms of verse or prose. [C14: from Old French *envoye,* from *envoyer* to send; see ENVOY[1]]

envy (ˈɛnvɪ) *n, pl* **-vies. 1** a feeling of grudging or somewhat admiring discontent aroused by the possessions, achievements, or qualities of another. **2** the desire to have for oneself something possessed by another; covetousness. **3** an object of envy. ◆ *vb* **-vies, -vying, -vied. 4** to be envious of (a person or thing). [C13: via Old French from Latin *invidia,* from *invidēre* to eye maliciously, from IN-[2] + *vidēre* to see] ▸ **'envier** *n* ▸ **'envyingly** *adv*

enwind (ɪnˈwaɪnd) *vb* **-winds, -winding, -wound.** (*tr*) to wind or coil around; encircle.

enwomb (ɪnˈwuːm) *vb* (*tr; often passive*) to enclose in or as if in a womb.

enwrap *or* **inwrap** (ɪnˈræp) *vb* **-wraps, -wrapping, -wrapped.** (*tr*) **1** to wrap or cover up; envelop. **2** (*usually passive*) to engross or absorb: *enwrapped in thought.*

enwreath (ɪnˈriːð) *vb* (*tr*) to surround or encircle with or as with a wreath or wreaths.

Enzed (ˈɛnˈzɛd) *n Austral. and N.Z. informal.* **1** New Zealand. **2** Also called: **'En'zedder.** a New Zealander.

enzootic (ˌɛnzəʊˈɒtɪk) *adj* **1** (of diseases) affecting animals within a limited region. ◆ *n* **2** an enzootic disease. ◆ Compare **epizootic.** [C19: from EN-[2] + Greek *zōion* animal + -OTIC] ▸ **ˌenzo'otically** *adv*

enzyme (ˈɛnzaɪm) *n* any of a group of complex proteins or conjugated proteins that are produced by living cells and act as catalysts in specific biochemical reactions. [C19: from Medieval Greek *enzumos* leavened, from Greek EN-[2] + *zumē* leaven] ▸ **enzymatic** (ˌɛnzaɪˈmætɪk, -zɪ-) *or* **enzymic** (ɛnˈzaɪmɪk, -ˈzɪm-) *adj*

enzyme-linked immunosorbent assay (ˌɪmjʊnəʊˈsɔːbənt) *n* the full name for **ELISA.**

enzymology (ˌɛnzaɪˈmɒlədʒɪ) *n* the branch of science concerned with the study of enzymes. ▸ **enzymological** (ˌɛnzaɪməˈlɒdʒɪkᵊl) *adj* ▸ **ˌenzy'mologist** *n*

enzymolysis (ˌɛnzaɪˈmɒlɪsɪs) *n* a biochemical decomposition, such as a fermentation, that is catalysed by an enzyme. ▸ **enzymolytic** (ˌɛnzaɪməˈlɪtɪk) *adj*

e.o. *abbrev. for* ex officio.

eo- *combining form.* early or primeval: *Eocene; eohippus.* [from Greek, from *ēōs* dawn]

eobiont (ˌiːəʊˈbaɪənt) *n* a hypothetical chemical precursor of a living cell.

[C20: from EO- + Greek *biōnt* stem of present participle of *biōn* to live, from *bios* life]

EOC *abbrev. for* Equal Opportunities Commission.

Eocene ('iːəʊˌsiːn) *adj* **1** of, denoting, or formed in the second epoch of the Tertiary period, which lasted for 20 000 000 years, during which hooved mammals appeared. ◆ *n* **2 the.** the Eocene epoch or rock series. [C19: from EO- + -CENE]

Eogene ('iːəʊˌdʒiːn) *adj, n* another word for **Palaeogene.**

eohippus (ˌiːəʊ'hɪpəs) *n, pl* **-puses.** the earliest horse: an extinct Eocene dog-sized animal of the genus *Hyracotherium,* with four-toed forelegs, three-toed hindlegs, and teeth specialized for browsing. [C19: New Latin, from EO- + Greek *hippos* horse]

Eolian (iː'əʊlɪən) *adj, n* a variant spelling of **Aeolian.**

Eolic (iː'ɒlɪk, ɪ'əʊlɪk) *adj, n* a variant spelling of **Aeolic.**

eolipile (iː'ɒlɪˌpaɪl) *n* a variant spelling of **aeolipile.**

eolith ('iːəʊlɪθ) *n* a stone, usually crudely broken, used as a primitive tool in Eolithic times.

Eolithic (ˌiːəʊ'lɪθɪk) *adj* denoting, relating to, or characteristic of the early part of the Stone Age, characterized by the use of crude stone tools.

e.o.m. *Commerce. abbrev. for* end of the month.

eon ('iːən, 'iːɒn) *n* **1** the usual U.S. spelling of **aeon. 2** *Geology.* the longest division of geological time, comprising two or more eras.

eonian (iː'əʊnɪən) *adj* **1** the usual U.S. spelling of **aeonian. 2** *Geology.* of or relating to an **eon** (sense 2).

eonism ('iːəˌnɪzəm) *n Psychiatry.* the adoption of female dress and behaviour by a male. See also **transvestite.** [C19: named after Charles *Éon* de Beaumont (died 1810), French transvestite]

Eos ('iːɒs) *n Greek myth.* the winged goddess of the dawn, the daughter of Hyperion. Roman counterpart: **Aurora.**

eosin ('iːəʊsɪn) *or* **eosine** ('iːəʊsɪn, -ˌsiːn) *n* **1** Also called: **bromeosin.** a red crystalline water-insoluble derivative of fluorescein. Its soluble salts are used as dyes. Formula: $C_{20}H_8Br_4O_5$. **2** any of several similar dyes. [C19: from Greek *ēōs* dawn + -IN; referring to the colour it gives to silk] ▸ ˌ**eo'sinic** *adj* ▸ '**eosin-ˌlike** *adj*

eosinophil (ˌiːəʊ'sɪnəfɪl) *or* **eosinophile** (ˌiːəʊ'sɪnəˌfaɪl) *n* a leucocyte with a bilobed nucleus and coarse granular cytoplasm that stains readily with acidic dyes such as eosin. ▸ ˌ**eoˌsino'philic** *or* **eosinophilous** (ˌiːəʊsɪ'nɒfɪləs) *adj*

eosinophilia (ˌiːəʊˌsɪnə'fɪlɪə) *n* the presence of abnormally large numbers of eosinophils in the blood, occurring in various diseases and in response to certain drugs.

Eötvös ('ɜːtvɒs) *n* Baron **Roland von.** 1848–1919, Hungarian physicist noted for his studies of gravity and surface tension.

-eous *suffix of adjectives.* relating to or having the nature of: *gaseous.* Compare **-ious.** [from Latin *-eus*]

Eozoic (ˌiːəʊ'zəʊɪk) *adj* of or formed in the part of the Precambrian era during which life first appeared.

EP *n* an extended-play single, one of the formats in which music is sold, usually comprising four or five tracks.

Ep. *abbrev. for* Epistle.

e.p. *Chess. abbrev. for* en passant.

ep- *prefix* variant of **epi-** before a vowel: *epexegesis.*

EPA *abbrev. for* eicosapentaenoic acid: a fatty acid, found in certain fish oils, that can reduce blood cholesterol.

epact ('iːpækt) *n* **1** the difference in time, about 11 days, between the solar year and the lunar year. **2** the number of days between the beginning of the calendar year and the new moon immediately preceding this. **3** the difference in time between the calendar month and the synodic month. [C16: via Late Latin from Greek *epaktē,* from *epagein* to bring in, intercalate, from *agein* to lead]

Epaminondas (ɛˌpæmɪ'nɒndæs) *n* ?418–362 B.C., Greek Theban statesman and general: defeated the Spartans at Leuctra (371) and Mantinea (362) and restored power in Greece to Thebes.

epanalepsis (ɪˌpænə'lɛpsɪs) *n Rhetoric.* the repetition, after a more or less lengthy passage of subordinate or parenthetic text, of a word or clause that was used before. [C16: from Greek, from EPI- + ANA- + *lēpis* taking, from *lambanein* to take up] ▸ ˌ**epana'leptic** *adj*

epanaphora (ˌɛpə'næfərə) *n Rhetoric.* another word for **anaphora.** ▸ ˌ**ep-anaph'oral** *adj*

epanorthosis (ɪˌpænɔː'θəʊsɪs) *n Rhetoric.* the almost immediate replacement of a preceding word or phrase by a more correct or more emphatic one, as for example in *thousands, nay, millions.* [C16: from Greek: correction, from EPI- + ANA- + *orthos* straight] ▸ ˌ**epanor'thotic** *adj*

eparch ('ɛpɑːk) *n* **1** a bishop or metropolitan in charge of an eparchy (sense 1). **2** a government official in charge of an eparchy (senses 2 or 3). [C17: from Greek *eparkhos,* from *epi-* over, on + -ARCH]

eparchy ('ɛpɑːkɪ) *or* **eparchate** ('ɛpɑːkɪt) *n, pl* **-chies** *or* **-chates. 1** a diocese of the Eastern Christian Church. **2** (in ancient Greece) a province. **3** (in modern Greece) a subdivision of a province. ▸ **ep'archial** *adj*

épatant *French.* (epatɑ̃) *adj* startling or shocking, esp. through being unconventional. [C20: from present participle of *épater* to flabbergast]

epaulette *or U.S.* **epaulet** ('ɛpəˌlɛt, -lɪt) *n* a piece of ornamental material on the shoulder of a garment, esp. a military uniform. [C18: from French *épaulette,* from *épaule* shoulder, from Latin *spatula* shoulder blade; see SPATULA]

épée ('ɛpeɪ; *French* epe) *n* a sword similar to the foil but with a larger guard and a heavier blade of triangular cross section. [C19: from French: sword, from Latin *spatha,* from Greek *spathē* blade; see SPADE[1]]

épéeist ('ɛpeɪɪst) *n Fencing.* one who uses or specializes in using an épée.

epeiric (ɪ'paɪrɪk) *adj Geology.* in, of, or relating to a continent: *an epeiric sea.* [C20: from Greek *ēpeiros* continent + -IC]

epeirogeny (ˌɛpaɪ'rɒdʒɪnɪ) *or* **epeirogenesis** (ɪˌpaɪrəʊ'dʒɛnɪsɪs) *n* the formation and submergence of continents by broad relatively slow displacements of the earth's crust. Also called: **epirogeny.** [C19: from Greek *ēpeiros* continent + -GENY] ▸ **epeirogenic** (ɪˌpaɪrəʊ'dʒɛnɪk) *or* **epeirogenetic** (ɪˌpaɪrəʊdʒɪ'nɛtɪk) *adj*

epencephalon (ˌɛpɛn'sɛfəˌlɒn) *n, pl* **-la** (-lə). *Anatomy.* **1** the cerebellum and pons Varolii. **2** the part of the embryonic brain that develops into this; metencephalon. [C19: New Latin; see EPI-, ENCEPHALON] ▸ ˌ**epencephalic** (ˌɛpɛnsɪ'fælɪk) *adj*

ependyma (ɪ'pɛndɪmə) *n* the membrane lining the ventricles of the brain and the central canal of the spinal cord. ▸ **e'pendymal** *adj*

epenthesis (ɛ'pɛnθɪsɪs) *n, pl* **-ses** (-ˌsiːz). the insertion of a sound or letter into a word. [C17: via Late Latin from Greek, from *epentithenai* to insert, from EPI- + EN-[2] + *tithenai* to place] ▸ **epenthetic** (ˌɛpɛn'θɛtɪk) *adj*

epergne (ɪ'pɜːn) *n* an ornamental centrepiece for a table: a stand with holders for sweetmeats, fruit, flowers, etc. [C18: probably from French *épargne* a saving, from *épargner* to economize, of Germanic origin; compare SPARE]

epexegesis (ɛˌpɛksɪ'dʒiːsɪs) *n, pl* **-ses** (-ˌsiːz). *Rhetoric.* **1** the addition of a phrase, clause, or sentence to a text to provide further explanation. **2** the phrase, clause, or sentence added for this purpose. [C17: from Greek; see EPI-, EXEGESIS] ▸ **epexegetic** (ɛˌpɛksɪ'dʒɛtɪk) *or* **epˌexe'getical** *adj* ▸ **epˌex-e'getically** *adv*

Eph. *or* **Ephes.** *Bible. abbrev. for* Ephesians.

eph- *prefix* a variant of **epi-** before an aspirate: *ephedra; ephedrine.*

ephah *or* **epha** ('iːfə) *n* a Hebrew unit of dry measure equal to approximately one bushel or about 33 litres. [C16: from Hebrew *'ephāh,* of Egyptian origin]

ephebe (ɪ'fiːb, 'ɛfiːb) *n* (in ancient Greece) a youth about to enter full citizenship, esp. one undergoing military training. [C19: from Latin *ephēbus,* from Greek *ephēbos,* from *hēbē* young manhood] ▸ **e'phebic** *adj*

ephedra (ɪ'fɛdrə) *n* any gymnosperm shrub of the genus *Ephedra,* of warm regions of America and Eurasia: the source of ephedrine: family *Ephedraceae,* phylum *Gnetophyta.* [C18: New Latin, from Latin, from Greek *ephedros* a sitting upon, from EPI- + *hedra* seat]

ephedrine *or* **ephedrin** (ɪ'fɛdrɪn, 'ɛfɪˌdriːn, -drɪn) *n* a white crystalline alkaloid obtained from plants of the genus *Ephedra:* used for the treatment of asthma and hay fever; l-phenyl-2-methylaminopropanol. Formula: $C_6H_5CH(OH)CH(NHCH_3)CH_3$. [C19: from New Latin EPHEDRA + -INE[2]]

ephemera (ɪ'fɛmərə) *n, pl* **-eras** *or* **-erae** (-əˌriː). **1** a mayfly, esp. one of the genus *Ephemera.* **2** something transitory or short-lived. **3** (*functioning as pl*) a class of collectable items not originally intended to last for more than a short time, such as tickets, posters, postcards, or labels. **4** a plural of **ephemeron.** [C16; see EPHEMERAL]

ephemeral (ɪ'fɛmərəl) *adj* **1** lasting for only a short time; transitory; short-lived: *ephemeral pleasure.* ◆ *n* **2** a short-lived organism, such as the mayfly. [C16: from Greek *ephēmeros* lasting only a day, from *hēmera* day] ▸ **e'phemerally** *adv* ▸ **eˌphemer'ality** *or* **e'phemeralness** *n*

ephemerid (ɪ'fɛmərɪd) *n* any insect of the order *Ephemeroptera* (or *Ephemerida*), which comprises the mayflies. Also called: **ephemeropteran.** [C19: from New Latin *Ephēmerida,* from Greek *ephēmeros* short-lived + -ID[2]]

ephemeris (ɪ'fɛmərɪs) *n, pl* **ephemerides** (ˌɛfɪ'mɛrɪˌdiːz). **1** a table giving the future positions of a planet, comet, or satellite. **2** an annual publication giving the positions of the sun, moon, and planets during the course of a year, information concerning eclipses, astronomical constants, etc. **3** *Obsolete.* a diary or almanac. [C16: from Latin, from Greek: diary, journal; see EPHEMERAL]

ephemeris time *n* time that is based on the orbit of the earth around the sun rather than the axial rotation of the earth, one **ephemeris second** being 1/31 556 925.9747 of the tropical year 1900. It was used from 1960 to 1983 as an astronomical timescale but has been replaced by terrestrial dynamical time and barycentric dynamic time. See **TDT, TDB.**

ephemeron (ɪ'fɛməˌrɒn) *n, pl* **-era** (-ərə) *or* **-erons.** (*usually pl*). something transitory or short-lived. [C16: see EPHEMERAL]

ephemeropteran (iːˌfɛmə'rɒptərən) *n* **1** another word for **ephemerid.** ◆ *adj* **2** of or relating to the *Ephemeroptera.*

Ephesian (ɪ'fiːʒən) *adj* **1** of or relating to Ephesus. ◆ *n* **2** an inhabitant or native of Ephesus.

Ephesians (ɪ'fiːʒənz) *n* (*functioning as sing*) a book of the New Testament (in full **The Epistle of Paul the Apostle to the Ephesians**), containing an exposition of the divine plan for the world and the consummation of this in Christ.

Ephesus ('ɛfɪsəs) *n* (in ancient Greece) a major trading city on the W coast of Asia Minor: famous for its temple of Artemis (Diana); sacked by the Goths (262 A.D.).

ephod ('iːfɒd) *n Old Testament.* an embroidered vestment believed to resemble an apron with shoulder straps, worn by priests in ancient Israel. [C14: from Hebrew *ēphōdh*]

ephor ('ɛfɔː) *n, pl* **-ors** *or* **-ori** (-əˌraɪ). (in ancient Greece) one of a board of senior magistrates in any of several Dorian states, esp. the five Spartan ephors, who were elected by vote of all full citizens and who wielded effective power. [C16: from Greek *ephoros,* from *ephoran* to supervise, from EPI- + *horan* to look] ▸ '**ephoral** *adj* ▸ '**ephorate** *n*

Ephraim ('iːfreɪɪm) *n Old Testament.* **1a** the younger son of Joseph, who received the principal blessing of his grandfather Jacob (Genesis 48:8–22). **1b** the tribe descended from him. **1c** the territory of this tribe, west of the River Jordan. **2** the northern kingdom of Israel after the kingdom of Solomon had been divided into two.

Ephraimite ('iːfreɪˌmaɪt) *n* a member of the tribe of Ephraim.

epi-, eph-, *or before a vowel* **ep-** *prefix* **1** on; upon; above; over: *epidermis; epicentre.* **2** in addition to: *epiphenomenon.* **3** after: *epigenesis; epilogue.* **4** near; close to: *epicalyx.* [from Greek, from *epi* (prep)]

epibiosis (ˌɛpɪbaɪ'əʊsɪs) *n* any relationship between two organisms in which one grows on the other but is not parasitic on it. See also **epiphyte, epizoite.** ► **epibiotic** (ˌɛpɪbaɪˈɒtɪk) *adj*

epiblast (ˈɛpɪˌblæst) *n Embryol.* the outermost layer of an embryo, which becomes the ectoderm at gastrulation. Also called: **ectoblast.** ► ˌ**epiˈblastic** *adj*

epiblem (ˈɛpɪblɛm) *n Botany.* the outermost cell layer of a root; epidermis.

epiboly (ɪˈpɪbəlɪ) *n, pl* **-lies.** *Embryol.* a process that occurs during gastrulation in vertebrates, in which cells on one side of the blastula grow over and surround the remaining cells and yolk and eventually form the ectoderm. [C19: from Greek *epibolē* a laying on, from *epiballein* to throw on, from EPI- + *ballein* to throw] ► **epibolic** (ˌɛpɪˈbɒlɪk) *adj*

epic (ˈɛpɪk) *n* **1** a long narrative poem recounting in elevated style the deeds of a legendary hero, esp. one originating in oral folk tradition. **2** the genre of epic poetry. **3** any work of literature, film, etc., having heroic deeds for its subject matter or having other qualities associated with the epic: *a Hollywood epic.* **4** an episode in the lives of men in which heroic deeds are performed or attempted: *the epic of Scott's expedition to the South Pole.* ♦ *adj* **5** denoting, relating to, or characteristic of an epic or epics. **6** of heroic or impressive proportions: *an epic voyage.* [C16: from Latin *epicus,* from Greek *epikos,* from *epos* speech, word, song]

epicalyx (ˌɛpɪˈkeɪlɪks, -ˈkæl-) *n, pl* **-lyxes** *or* **-lyces** (-lɪˌsiːz). *Botany.* a series of small sepal-like bracts forming an outer calyx beneath the true calyx in some flowers.

epicanthus (ˌɛpɪˈkænθəs) *n, pl* **-thi** (-θaɪ). a fold of skin extending vertically over the inner angle of the eye: characteristic of Mongolian peoples and a congenital anomaly among other races. Also called: **epicanthic fold.** [C19: New Latin, from EPI- + Latin *canthus* corner of the eye, from Greek *kanthos*] ► ˌ**epiˈcanthic** *adj*

epicardium (ˌɛpɪˈkɑːdɪəm) *n, pl* **-dia** (-dɪə). *Anatomy.* the innermost layer of the pericardium, in direct contact with the heart. [C19: New Latin, from EPI- + Greek *kardia* heart] ► ˌ**epiˈcardiac** *or* ˌ**epiˈcardial** *adj*

epicarp (ˈɛpɪˌkɑːp) *or* **exocarp** *n* the outermost layer of the pericarp of fruits: forms the skin of a peach or grape. [C19: from French *épicarpe,* from EPI- + Greek *karpos* fruit]

epicedium (ˌɛpɪˈsiːdɪəm) *n, pl* **-dia** (-dɪə). *Rare.* a funeral ode. [C16: Latin, from Greek *epikēdeion,* from EPI- + *kēdos* care]

epicene (ˈɛpɪˌsiːn) *adj* **1** having the characteristics of both sexes; hermaphroditic. **2** of neither sex; sexless. **3** effeminate. **4** *Grammar.* **4a** denoting a noun that may refer to a male or a female, such as *teacher* as opposed to *businessman* or *shepherd.* **4b** (in Latin, Greek, etc.) denoting a noun that retains the same grammatical gender regardless of the sex of the referent. ♦ *n* **5** an epicene person or creature. **6** an epicene noun. [C15: from Latin *epicoenus* of both genders, from Greek *epikoinos* common to many, from *koinos* common] ► ˌ**epiˈcenism** *n*

epicentre *or U.S.* **epicenter** (ˈɛpɪˌsɛntə), *n, pl* **-tres** *or U.S.* **-ters.** the point on the earth's surface directly above the focus of an earthquake or underground nuclear explosion. Compare **focus** (sense 6). [C19: from New Latin *epicentrum,* from Greek *epikentros* over the centre, from EPI- + *kentron* needle; see CENTRE] ► ˌ**epiˈcentral** *adj*

epiclesis (ˌɛpɪˈkliːsɪs) *n, pl* **-ses** (-siːz). *Christianity.* the invocation of the Holy Spirit to consecrate the bread and wine of the Eucharist. [C19: from Greek, from EPI- + *klēsis* a prayer, from *kalein* to call]

epicontinental (ˌɛpɪˌkɒntɪˈnɛntᵊl) *adj* (esp. of a sea) situated on a continental shelf or continent.

epicotyl (ˌɛpɪˈkɒtɪl) *n* the part of an embryo plant stem above the cotyledons but beneath the terminal bud. [C19: from EPI- + Greek *kotulē*; see COTYLEDON]

epicrisis (ˈɛpɪˌkraɪsɪs) *n Pathol.* a secondary crisis occurring in the course of a disease. [C20: from EPI- + CRISIS]

epicritic (ˌɛpɪˈkrɪtɪk) *adj* (of certain nerve fibres of the skin) serving to perceive and distinguish fine variations of temperature or touch. [C20: from Greek *epikritikos* decisive, from *epikrinein* to decide, from EPI- + *krinein* to judge]

epic simile *n* an extended simile, as used in the epic poetry of Homer and other writers.

Epictetus (ˌɛpɪkˈtiːtəs) *n* ?50–?120 A.D., Greek Stoic philosopher, who stressed self-renunciation and the brotherhood of man.

epicure (ˈɛpɪˌkjʊə) *n* **1** a person who cultivates a discriminating palate for the enjoyment of good food and drink; gourmet. **2** a person devoted to sensual pleasures. [C16: from Medieval Latin *epicūrus,* after EPICURUS] ► ˈ**epicurˌism** *n*

epicurean (ˌɛpɪkjʊˈriːən) *adj* **1** devoted to sensual pleasures, esp. food and drink; hedonistic. **2** suitable for an epicure: *an epicurean feast.* ♦ *n* **3** an epicure; gourmet. ► ˌ**epicuˈreanism** *n*

Epicurean (ˌɛpɪkjʊˈriːən) *adj* **1** of or relating to the philosophy of Epicurus. ♦ *n* **2** a follower of the philosophy of Epicurus. ► ˌ**Epicuˈreanism** *n*

Epicurus (ˌɛpɪˈkjʊərəs) *n* 341–270 B.C., Greek philosopher, who held that the highest good is pleasure and that the world is a series of fortuitous combinations of atoms.

epicuticle (ˈɛpɪˌkjuːtɪkᵊl) *n* **1** *Botany.* a waxy layer on the surface of the cuticle. **2** *Zoology.* the outermost lipoprotein layer of the insect cuticle.

epicycle (ˈɛpɪˌsaɪkᵊl) *n* **1** *Astronomy.* (in the Ptolemaic system) a small circle, around which a planet was thought to revolve, whose centre describes a larger circle (the **deferent**) centred on the earth. **2** a circle that rolls around the inside or outside of another circle, so generating an epicycloid or hypocycloid. [C14: from Late Latin *epicyclus,* from Greek *epikuklos;* see EPI-, CYCLE] ► **epicyclic** (ˌɛpɪˈsaɪklɪk, -ˈsɪklɪk) *or* ˌ**epiˈcyclical** *adj*

epicyclic train *n* a cluster of gears consisting of a central gearwheel with external teeth (the sun), a coaxial gearwheel of greater diameter with internal teeth (the annulus), and one or more planetary gears engaging with both of them to provide a large gear ratio in a compact space.

epicycloid (ˌɛpɪˈsaɪklɔɪd) *n* the curve described by a point on the circumference of a circle as this circle rolls around the outside of another fixed circle, the two circles being coplanar. Compare **hypocycloid, cycloid** (sense 4). ► ˌ**epicyˈcloidal** *adj*

epicycloidal wheel *n* one of the planetary gears of an epicyclic train.

Epidaurus (ˌɛpɪˈdɔːrəs; *Greek* ɛpiˈðaurɔs) *n* an ancient port in Greece, in the NE Peloponnese, in Argolis on the Saronic Gulf.

epideictic (ˌɛpɪˈdaɪktɪk) *adj* designed to display something, esp. the skill of the speaker in rhetoric. Also: **epidictic** (ˌɛpɪˈdɪktɪk). [C18: from Greek *epideiktikos,* from *epideiknunai* to display, show off, from *deiknunai* to show]

epidemic (ˌɛpɪˈdɛmɪk) *adj* **1** (esp. of a disease) attacking or affecting many persons simultaneously in a community or area. ♦ *n* **2** a widespread occurrence of a disease: *an influenza epidemic.* **3** a rapid development, spread, or growth of something, esp. something unpleasant: *an epidemic of strikes.* [C17: from French *épidémique,* via Late Latin from Greek *epidēmia* literally: among the people, from EPI- + *dēmos* people] ► ˌ**epiˈdemically** *adv*

epidemic encephalitis *n Pathol.* a technical name for **sleeping sickness** (sense 2).

epidemic meningitis *n* another name for **cerebrospinal meningitis.**

epidemic parotitis *n* another name for **mumps.**

epidemiology (ˌɛpɪˌdiːmɪˈɒlədʒɪ) *n* the branch of medical science concerned with the occurrence, transmission, and control of epidemic diseases. ► **epidemiological** (ˌɛpɪˌdiːmɪəˈlɒdʒɪkᵊl) *adj* ► ˌ**epiˌdemioˈlogically** *adv* ► ˌ**epiˌdemiˈologist** *n*

epidermis (ˌɛpɪˈdɜːmɪs) *n* **1** Also called: **cuticle.** the thin protective outer layer of the skin, composed of stratified epithelial tissue. **2** the outer layer of cells of an invertebrate. **3** the outer protective layer of cells of a plant, which may be thickened by a cuticle. [C17: via Late Latin from Greek, from EPI- + *derma* skin] ► ˌ**epiˈdermal,** ˌ**epiˈdermic,** *or* ˌ**epiˈdermoid** *adj*

epidiascope (ˌɛpɪˈdaɪəˌskəʊp) *n* an optical device for projecting a magnified image onto a screen. See also **episcope.**

epididymis (ˌɛpɪˈdɪdɪmɪs) *n, pl* **-didymides** (-dɪˈdɪmɪˌdiːz). *Anatomy.* a convoluted tube situated along the posterior margin of each testis, in which spermatozoa are stored and conveyed to the vas deferens. [C17: from Greek *epididumis,* from EPI- + *didumos* twin, testicle; see DIDYMOUS] ► ˌ**epiˈdidymal** *adj*

epidote (ˈɛpɪˌdəʊt) *n* a green mineral consisting of hydrated calcium iron aluminium silicate in monoclinic crystalline form: common in metamorphic rocks. Formula: $Ca_2(Al,Fe)_3(SiO_4)_3(OH)$. [C19: from French *épidote,* ultimately from Greek *epididonai* to increase, from *didonai* to give; so called because two sides of its crystal are longer than the other two sides] ► **epidotic** (ˌɛpɪˈdɒtɪk) *adj*

epidural (ˌɛpɪˈdjʊərəl) *adj* **1** Also: **extradural.** upon or outside the dura mater. ♦ *n* **2** Also called: **epidural anaesthesia. 2a** injection of anaesthetic into the space outside the dura mater enveloping the spinal cord. **2b** anaesthesia induced by this method. [C19: from EPI- + DUR(A MATER) + -AL[1]]

epifocal (ˌɛpɪˈfəʊkᵊl) *adj Geology.* situated or occurring at an epicentre.

epigamic (ˌɛpɪˈgæmɪk) *adj Zoology.* attractive to the opposite sex: *epigamic coloration.*

epigastrium (ˌɛpɪˈgæstrɪəm) *n, pl* **-tria** (-trɪə). the upper middle part of the abdomen, above the navel and below the breast. [C17: from New Latin, from Greek EPI- + *gastrion,* from *gastēr* stomach] ► ˌ**epiˈgastric** *or* ˌ**epiˈgastrial** *adj*

epigeal (ˌɛpɪˈdʒiːəl), **epigean,** *or* **epigeous** *adj* **1** of or relating to seed germination in which the cotyledons appear above the ground because of the growth of the hypocotyl. **2** living or growing on or close to the surface of the ground. [C19: from Greek *epigeios* of the earth, from EPI- + *gē* earth]

epigene (ˈɛpɪˌdʒiːn) *adj* formed or taking place at the surface of the earth. Compare **hypogene.** [C19: from French *épigène,* ultimately from Greek *epigignesthai* to be born after, from *gignesthai* to be born]

epigenesis (ˌɛpɪˈdʒɛnɪsɪs) *n* **1** the widely accepted theory that an individual animal or plant develops by the gradual differentiation and elaboration of a fertilized egg cell. Compare **preformation** (sense 2). **2** the formation of ore deposits after the surrounding rock has been formed. **3** alteration of the mineral composition of a rock by external agents: a type of metamorphism. ► ˌ**epiˈgenesist** *or* **epigenist** (ɪˈpɪdʒɪnɪst) *n* ► **epigenetic** (ˌɛpɪdʒɪˈnɛtɪk) *adj* ► ˌ**epigeˈnetically** *adv*

epigenous (ɪˈpɪdʒɪnəs) *adj Biology.* growing on the surface, esp. the upper surface, of an organism or part: *an epigenous fungus.*

epigeous (ˌɛpɪˈdʒiːəs) *adj* a variant of **epigeal.**

epiglottis (ˌɛpɪˈglɒtɪs) *n, pl* **-tises** *or* **-tides** (-tɪˌdiːz). a thin cartilaginous flap that covers the entrance to the larynx during swallowing, preventing food from entering the trachea. ► ˌ**epiˈglottal** *or* ˌ**epiˈglottic** *adj*

epignathous (ˌɛpɪgˈneɪθəs) *adj Zoology.* having a protruding upper jaw.

epigone (ˈɛpɪˌgəʊn) *or* **epigon** (ˈɛpɪˌgɒn) *n Rare.* an inferior follower or imitator. [C19: from Greek *epigonos* one born after, from *epigignesthai;* see EPIGENE]

Epigoni (ɪˈpɪgəˌnaɪ) *pl n, sing* **-onus** (-ənəs). *Greek myth.* the descendants of the Seven against Thebes, who undertook a second expedition against the city and eventually captured and destroyed it. [C20: from Greek *epigonoi* those born after]

epigram (ˈɛpɪˌgræm) *n* **1** a witty, often paradoxical remark, concisely expressed. **2** a short, pungent, and often satirical poem, esp. one having a witty and ingenious ending. [C15: from Latin *epigramma,* from Greek: inscription, from *epigraphein* to write upon, from *graphein* to write] ► ˌ**epigramˈmatic** *adj* ► ˌ**epigramˈmatically** *adv*

epigrammatize *or* **epigrammatise** (ˌɛpɪˈɡræməˌtaɪz) *vb* to make an epigram or epigrams (about). ▸ ˌ**epiˈgrammatism** *n* ▸ ˌ**epiˈgrammatist** *n*

epigraph (ˈɛpɪˌɡrɑːf, -ˌɡræf) *n* **1** a quotation at the beginning of a book, chapter, etc., suggesting its theme. **2** an inscription on a monument or building. [C17: from Greek *epigraphē*; see EPIGRAM] ▸ **epigraphic** (ˌɛpɪˈɡræfɪk) or ˌ**epiˈgraphical** *adj* ▸ ˌ**epiˈgraphically** *adv*

epigraphy (ɪˈpɪɡrəfɪ) *n* **1** the study of ancient inscriptions. **2** epigraphs collectively. ▸ **eˈpigraphist** *or* **eˈpigrapher** *n*

epigynous (ɪˈpɪdʒɪnəs) *adj* (of flowers) having the receptacle enclosing and fused with the gynoecium so that the other floral parts arise above it. [C19: from EPI- + Greek *gunē* (female organ, pistil) + -OUS] ▸ **eˈpigyny** *n*

epilate (ˈɛpɪˌleɪt) *vb* (*tr*) *Rare.* to remove hair from. [C19: from French *épiler* (modelled on *dépiler* DEPILATE) + -ATE[1]] ▸ ˌ**epiˈlation** *n*

epilator (ˈɛpɪˌleɪtə) *n* an electrical appliance consisting of a metal spiral head that rotates at high speed, plucking unwanted hair.

epilepsy (ˈɛpɪˌlɛpsɪ) *n* a disorder of the central nervous system characterized by periodic loss of consciousness with or without convulsions. In some cases it is due to brain damage but in others the cause is unknown. See also **grand mal, petit mal.** [C16: from Late Latin *epilēpsia*, from Greek, from *epilambanein* to attack, seize, from *lambanein* to take]

epileptic (ˌɛpɪˈlɛptɪk) *adj* **1** of, relating to, or having epilepsy. ♦ *n* **2** a person who has epilepsy. ▸ ˌ**epiˈleptically** *adv*

epileptogenic (ˌɛpɪˌlɛptəʊˈdʒɛnɪk) *adj* causing an epileptic attack.

epileptoid (ˌɛpɪˈlɛptɔɪd) *or* **epileptiform** (ˌɛpɪˈlɛptɪˌfɔːm) *adj* resembling epilepsy.

epilimnion (ˌɛpɪˈlɪmnɪən) *n* the upper layer of water in a lake. [C20: from EPI- + Greek *limnion*, diminutive of *limnē* lake]

epilithic (ˌɛpɪˈlɪθɪk) *adj* (of plants) growing on the surface of rock.

epilogue (ˈɛpɪˌlɒɡ) *n* **1a** a speech, usually in verse, addressed to the audience by an actor at the end of a play. **1b** the actor speaking this. **2** a short postscript to any literary work, such as a brief description of the fates of the characters in a novel. **3** *Brit.* the concluding programme of the day on a radio or television station, often having a religious content. [C15: from Latin *epilogus*, from Greek *epilogos*, from *logos* word, speech] ▸ **epilogist** (ɪˈpɪlədʒɪst) *n*

epimere (ˈɛpɪˌmɪə) *n Embryol.* the dorsal part of the mesoderm of a vertebrate embryo, consisting of a series of segments (somites).

epimerism (ɪˈpɪməˌrɪzəm) *n* optical isomerism in which isomers (**epimers**) can form about asymmetric atoms within the molecule, esp. in carbohydrates. [C20: from German *Epimer* (see EPI-, -MER) + -ISM] ▸ **epimeric** (ˌɛpɪˈmɛrɪk) *adj*

epimorphosis (ˌɛpɪmɔːˈfəʊsɪs) *n* a type of development in animals, such as certain insect larvae, in which segmentation of the body is complete before hatching. ▸ ˌ**epiˈmorphic** *adj*

epimysium (ˌɛpɪˈmɪzɪəm) *n, pl* **-sia** (-zɪə). *Anatomy.* the sheath of connective tissue that encloses a skeletal muscle. [from New Latin, from EPI- + Greek *mus* mouse, MUSCLE]

epinasty (ˈɛpɪˌnæstɪ) *n, pl* **-ties.** increased growth of the upper surface of a plant part, such as a leaf, resulting in a downward bending of the part. Compare **hyponasty.** [C19: from EPI- + *-nasty*, from Greek *nastos* pressed down, from *nassein* to press] ▸ ˌ**epiˈnastic** *adj*

epinephrine (ˌɛpɪˈnɛfrɪn, -riːn) *or* **epinephrin** *n* a U.S. name for **adrenaline.** [C19: from EPI- + *nephro-* + -INE[2]]

epineurium (ˌɛpɪˈnjʊərɪəm) *n* a sheath of connective tissue around two or more bundles of nerve fibres. [C19: from New Latin, from EPI- + Greek *neuron* nerve + -IUM] ▸ ˌ**epiˈneurial** *adj*

epipelagic (ˌɛpɪpəˈlædʒɪk) *adj* of, relating to, or inhabiting the upper zone of the ocean from just below the surface to approximately 100 metres deep.

epipetalous (ˌɛpɪˈpɛtələs) *adj Botany.* (of stamens) attached to the petals.

Epiph. *abbrev. for* Epiphany.

epiphany (ɪˈpɪfənɪ) *n, pl* **-nies. 1** the manifestation of a supernatural or divine reality. **2** any moment of great or sudden revelation. [C17: via Church Latin from Greek *epiphaneia* an appearing, from EPI- + *phainein* to show] ▸ **epiphanic** (ˌɛpɪˈfænɪk) *adj*

Epiphany (ɪˈpɪfənɪ) *n, pl* **-nies.** a Christian festival held on Jan. 6, commemorating, in the Western Church, the manifestation of Christ to the Magi and, in the Eastern Church, the baptism of Christ.

epiphenomenalism (ˌɛpɪfɪˈnɒmɪnəˌlɪzəm) *n* the dualistic doctrine that consciousness is merely a by-product of physiological processes and has no power to affect them. Compare **interactionism, parallelism.** ▸ ˌ**epipheˈnomenalist** *n, adj*

epiphenomenon (ˌɛpɪfɪˈnɒmɪnən) *n, pl* **-na** (-nə). **1** a secondary or additional phenomenon; by-product. **2** *Pathol.* an unexpected or atypical symptom or occurrence during the course of a disease. ▸ ˌ**epipheˈnomenal** *adj* ▸ ˌ**epipheˈnomenally** *adv*

epiphragm (ˈɛpɪˌfræm) *n* a disc of calcium phosphate and mucilage secreted by snails over the aperture of their shells before hibernation. [C19: via New Latin from Greek *epiphragma* a lid, from *epiphrassein*, from EPI- + *phrassein* to place in an enclosure]

epiphyllous (ˌɛpɪˈfɪləs) *adj Botany.* (of plants) growing on, or attached to, the leaf of another plant.

epiphysis (ɪˈpɪfɪsɪs) *n, pl* **-ses** (-ˌsiːz). **1** the end of a long bone, initially separated from the shaft (diaphysis) by a section of cartilage that eventually ossifies so that the two portions fuse together. **2** Also called: **epiphysis cerebri** (ˈsɛrɪbraɪ). the technical name for **pineal gland.** [C17: via New Latin from Greek: a growth upon, from EPI- + *phusis* growth, from *phuein* to bring forth, produce] ▸ **epiphyseal** *or* **epiphysial** (ˌɛpɪˈfɪzɪəl) *adj*

epiphyte (ˈɛpɪˌfaɪt) *n* a plant, such as a moss, that grows on another plant but is not parasitic on it. ▸ **epiphytic** (ˌɛpɪˈfɪtɪk), ˌ**epiˈphytal**, *or* ˌ**epiˈphytical** *adj* ▸ ˌ**epiˈphytically** *adv*

epiphytotic (ˌɛpɪfaɪˈtɒtɪk) *adj* (of plant diseases and parasites) affecting plants over a wide geographical region. [from EPI- + -PHYTE + -OTIC]

epirogeny (ˌɛpaɪˈrɒdʒɪnɪ) *n* a variant spelling of **epeirogeny.** ▸ **epirogenic** (ɪˌpaɪrəʊˈdʒɛnɪk) *or* **epirogenetic** (ɪˌpaɪrəʊdʒɪˈnɛtɪk) *adj*

Epirus (ɪˈpaɪərəs) *n* **1** a region of NW Greece, part of ancient Epirus ceded to Greece after independence in 1830. **2** (in ancient Greece) a region between the Pindus mountains and the Ionian Sea, straddling the modern border with Albania.

Epis. *abbrev. for:* **1** Also: **Episc.** Episcopal or Episcopalian. **2** *Bible.* Also: **Epist.** Epistle.

episcopacy (ɪˈpɪskəpəsɪ) *n, pl* **-cies. 1** government of a Church by bishops. **2** another word for **episcopate.**

episcopal (ɪˈpɪskəp°l) *adj* of, denoting, governed by, or relating to a bishop or bishops. [C15: from Church Latin *episcopālis*, from *episcopus* BISHOP] ▸ **eˈpiscopally** *adv*

Episcopal (ɪˈpɪskəp°l) *adj* belonging to or denoting the Episcopal Church. ▸ **Eˈpiscopally** *adv*

Episcopal Church *n* an autonomous branch of the Anglican Communion in Scotland and the U.S.

episcopalian (ɪˌpɪskəˈpeɪlɪən) *adj also* **episcopal. 1** practising or advocating the principle of Church government by bishops. ♦ *n* **2** an advocate of such Church government. ▸ **eˌpiscoˈpalianism** *n*

Episcopalian (ɪˌpɪskəˈpeɪlɪən) *adj* **1** belonging to or denoting the Episcopal Church. ♦ *n* **2** a member or adherent of this Church.

episcopalism (ɪˈpɪskəpəˌlɪzəm) *n* the belief that a Church should be governed by bishops.

episcopate (ɪˈpɪskəpɪt, -ˌpeɪt) *n* **1** the office, status, or term of office of a bishop. **2** bishops collectively.

episcope (ˈɛpɪˌskəʊp) *n Brit.* an optical device that projects an enlarged image of an opaque object, such as a printed page or photographic print, onto a screen by means of reflected light. U.S. and Canadian name: **opaque projector.** See also **epidiascope.**

episematic (ˌɛpɪsɪˈmætɪk) *adj Zoology.* (esp. of coloration) aiding recognition between animals of the same species.

episiotomy (əˌpiːzɪˈɒtəmɪ) *n, pl* **-mies.** surgical incision into the perineum during the late stages of labour to prevent its laceration during childbirth. [C20: from *episio-*, from Greek *epision* pubic region + -TOMY]

episode (ˈɛpɪˌsəʊd) *n* **1** an incident, event, or series of events. **2** any one of the sections into which a serialized novel or radio or television programme is divided. **3** an incident, sequence, or scene that forms part of a narrative but may be a digression from the main story. **4** (in ancient Greek tragedy) a section between two choric songs. **5** *Music.* a contrasting section between statements of the subject, as in a fugue or rondo. [C17: from Greek *epeisodion* something added, from *epi-* (in addition) + *eisodios* coming in, from *eis-* in + *hodos* road]

episodic (ˌɛpɪˈsɒdɪk) *or* **episodical** *adj* **1** resembling or relating to an episode. **2** divided into or composed of episodes. **3** irregular, occasional, or sporadic. ▸ ˌ**epiˈsodically** *adv*

episome (ˈɛpɪˌsəʊm) *n* any of various genetic particles, esp. viruses, that occur in bacteria and replicate either independently or in association with the chromosome.

epispastic (ˌɛpɪˈspæstɪk) *Med.* ♦ *adj* **1** producing a serous discharge or a blister. ♦ *n* **2** an epispastic agent. [C17: from Greek *epispastikos*, from *epispan* to attract, from *span* to draw; alluding to the ancient belief that blisters consisted of humours drawn to the surface of the skin]

Epist. *or* **Epis.** *Bible. abbrev. for* Epistle.

epistasis (ɪˈpɪstəsɪs) *n* **1** scum on the surface of a liquid, esp. on an old specimen of urine. **2** *Med.* the arrest or checking of a bodily discharge, esp. bleeding. **3** Also called: **hypostasis.** *Genetics.* the suppression by a gene of the effect of another gene that is not its allele. [C19: from Greek: a stopping, from *ephistanai* to stop, from EPI- + *histanai* to put] ▸ **epistatic** (ˌɛpɪˈstætɪk) *adj*

epistaxis (ˌɛpɪˈstæksɪs) *n* the technical name for **nosebleed.** [C18: from Greek: a dropping, from *epistazein* to drop on, from *stazein* to drip]

epistemic (ˌɛpɪˈstiːmɪk) *adj* **1** of or relating to knowledge or epistemology. **2** denoting the branch of modal logic that deals with the formalization of certain epistemological concepts, such as knowledge, certainty, and ignorance. ♦ See also **doxastic.** [C20: from Greek *epistēmē* knowledge] ▸ ˌ**episˈtemically** *adv*

epistemics (ˌɛpɪˈstiːmɪks, -ˈstem-) *n* (*functioning as sing*) *Chiefly Brit.* the interdisciplinary study of knowledge and human information-processing, using the formal techniques of logic, linguistics, philosophy, and psychology. Compare **artificial intelligence.**

epistemological (ɪˌpɪstɪməˈlɒdʒɪk°l) *adj* **1** concerned with or arising from epistemology. **2** (of a philosophical problem) requiring an account of how knowledge of the given subject could be obtained. ▸ **eˌpistemoˈlogically** *adv*

epistemology (ɪˌpɪstɪˈmɒlədʒɪ) *n* the theory of knowledge, esp. the critical study of its validity, methods, and scope. [C19: from Greek *epistēmē* knowledge] ▸ **eˌpisteˈmologist** *n*

episternum (ˌɛpɪˈstɜːnəm) *n, pl* **-na** (-nə). **1** the manubrium of the sternum in mammals. **2** another name for **interclavicle.** ▸ ˌ**epiˈsternal** *adj*

epistle (ɪˈpɪs°l) *n* **1** a letter, esp. one that is long, formal, or didactic. **2** a literary work in letter form, esp. a dedicatory verse letter of a type originated by Horace. [Old English *epistol*, via Latin from Greek *epistolē*, from *epistellein* to send to, from *stellein* to prepare, send]

Epistle (ɪˈpɪs°l) *n* **1** *New Testament.* any of the apostolic letters of Saints Paul, Peter, James, Jude, or John. **2** a reading from one of the Epistles, forming part of the Eucharistic service in many Christian Churches.

epistler (ɪˈpɪslə, ɪˈpɪstlə) *or* **epistoler** (ɪˈpɪst°lə) *n* (*often cap.*) **1** a writer of an epistle or epistles. **2** the person who reads the Epistle in a Christian religious service.

epistolary (ɪ'pɪstələrɪ) *or* (*archaic*) **epistolatory** *adj* **1** relating to, denoting, conducted by, or contained in letters. **2** (of a novel or other work) constructed in the form of a series of letters.

epistrophe (ɪ'pɪstrəfɪ) *n Rhetoric.* repetition of a word at the end of successive clauses or sentences. [C17: New Latin, from Greek, from EPI- + *strophē* a turning]

epistyle ('ɛpɪˌstaɪl) *n* another name for **architrave** (sense 1). [C17: via Latin *epistȳlium* from Greek *epistulion,* from EPI- + *stulos* column, STYLE]

epitaph ('ɛpɪˌtɑːf, -ˌtæf) *n* **1** a commemorative inscription on a tombstone or monument. **2** a speech or written passage composed in commemoration of a dead person. **3** a final judgment on a person or thing. [C14: via Latin from Greek *epitaphion,* from *epitaphios* over a tomb, from EPI- + *taphos* tomb] ▸ **epitaphic** (ˌɛpɪ'tæfɪk) *adj* ▸ **'epiˌtaphist** *n*

epitasis (ɪ'pɪtəsɪs) *n* (in classical drama) the part of a play in which the main action develops. Compare **protasis** (sense 2), **catastrophe** (sense 2). [C16: from Greek: a stretching, intensification, from *teinein* to stretch]

epitaxial transistor (ˌɛpɪ'tæksɪəl) *n* a transistor made by depositing a thin pure layer of semiconductor material (**epitaxial layer**) onto a crystalline support by epitaxy. The layer acts as one of the electrode regions, usually the collector.

epitaxy ('ɛpɪˌtæksɪ) *or* **epitaxis** *n* the growth of a thin layer on the surface of a crystal so that the layer has the same structure as the underlying crystal. ▸ **epitaxial** (ˌɛpɪ'tæksɪəl) *adj*

epithalamium (ˌɛpɪθə'leɪmɪəm) *or* **epithalamion** *n, pl* **-mia** (-mɪə). a poem or song written to celebrate a marriage; nuptial ode. [C17: from Latin, from Greek *epithalamion* marriage song, from *thalamos* bridal chamber] ▸ **epithalamic** (ˌɛpɪθə'læmɪk) *adj*

epitheca (ˌɛpɪ'θiːkə) *n, pl* **-cae** (-siː). the outer and older layer of the cell wall of a diatom. Compare **hypotheca.** [C19: from EPI- + THECA]

epithelioma (ˌɛpɪˌθiːlɪ'əʊmə) *n, pl* **-mas** *or* **-mata** (-mətə). *Pathol.* a malignant tumour of epithelial tissue. ▸ **epitheliomatous** (ˌɛpɪˌθiːlɪ'ɒmətəs) *adj*

epithelium (ˌɛpɪ'θiːlɪəm) *n, pl* **-liums** *or* **-lia** (-lɪə). an animal tissue consisting of one or more layers of closely packed cells covering the external and internal surfaces of the body. The cells vary in structure according to their function, which may be protective, secretory, or absorptive. [C18: New Latin, from EPI- + Greek *thēlē* nipple] ▸ **ˌepi'thelial** *adj*

epithet ('ɛpɪˌθɛt) *n* a descriptive word or phrase added to or substituted for a person's name: *"Lackland" is an epithet for King John.* [C16: from Latin *epitheton,* from Greek, from *epitithenai* to add, from *tithenai* to put] ▸ **ˌepi'thetic** *or* **ˌepi'thetical** *adj*

epitome (ɪ'pɪtəmɪ) *n* **1** a typical example of a characteristic or class; embodiment; personification: *he is the epitome of sloth.* **2** a summary of a written work; abstract. [C16: via Latin from Greek *epitomē,* from *epitemnein* to abridge, from EPI- + *temnein* to cut] ▸ **epitomical** (ˌɛpɪ'tɒmɪk^{ə}l) *or* **ˌepi'tomic** *adj*

epitomize *or* **epitomise** (ɪ'pɪtəˌmaɪz) *vb* (*tr*) **1** to be a personification of; typify. **2** to make an epitome of. ▸ **e'pitomist** *n* ▸ **eˌpitomi'zation** *or* **eˌpitomi'sation** *n* ▸ **e'pitoˌmizer** *or* **e'pitoˌmiser** *n*

epizoic (ˌɛpɪ'zəʊɪk) *adj* **1** (of an animal or plant) growing or living on the exterior of a living animal. **2** (of plants) having seeds or fruit dispersed by animals. ▸ **ˌepi'zoism** *n*

epizoite (ˌɛpɪ'zəʊɪt) *n* an organism that lives on an animal but is not parasitic on it.

epizoon (ˌɛpɪ'zəʊɒn) *n, pl* **-zoa** (-'zəʊə). an animal, such as a parasite, that lives on the body of another animal. [C19: New Latin, from EPI- + Greek *zōion* animal] ▸ **ˌepi'zoan** *adj*

epizootic (ˌɛpɪzəʊ'ɒtɪk) *adj* **1** (of a disease) suddenly and temporarily affecting a large number of animals. ◆ *n* **2** an epizootic disease. Compare **enzootic.** ▸ **ˌepizo'otically** *adv*

e pluribus unum *Latin.* (eɪ 'plʊərɪbʊs 'uːnʊm) one out of many: the motto of the U.S.A.

EPNS *abbrev. for* electroplated nickel silver.

epoch ('iːpɒk) *n* **1** a point in time beginning a new or distinctive period: *the invention of nuclear weapons marked an epoch in the history of warfare.* **2** a long period of time marked by some predominant or typical characteristic; era. **3** *Astronomy.* a precise date to which information, such as coordinates, relating to a celestial body is referred. **4** *Geology.* a unit of geological time within a period during which a series of rocks is formed: *the Pleistocene epoch.* **5** *Physics.* the displacement of an oscillating or vibrating body at zero time. [C17: from New Latin *epocha,* from Greek *epokhē* cessation; related to *ekhein* to hold, have] ▸ **epochal** ('ɛpˌɒk^{ə}l) *adj* ▸ **'epˌochally** *adv*

epoch-making *adj* of great importance; momentous.

epode ('ɛpəʊd) *n Greek prosody.* **1** the part of a lyric ode that follows the strophe and the antistrophe. **2** a type of lyric poem composed of couplets in which a long line is followed by a shorter one, invented by Archilochus. [C16: via Latin from Greek *epōidos* a singing after, from *epaidein* to sing after, from *aidein* to sing]

eponym ('ɛpənɪm) *n* **1** a name, esp. a place name, derived from the name of a real or mythical person, as for example *Constantinople* from *Constantine I.* **2** the name of the person from which such a name is derived: *in the Middle Ages, "Brutus" was thought to be the eponym of "Britain."* [C19: from Greek *epōnumos* giving a significant name] ▸ **ˌepo'nymic** *adj*

eponymous (ɪ'pɒnɪməs) *adj* **1** (of a person) being the person after whom a literary work, film, etc., is named: *the eponymous heroine in the film of Jane Eyre.* **2** (of a literary work, film, etc.) named after its central character or creator: *The Stooges' eponymous debut album.* ▸ **e'ponymously** *adv*

eponymy (ɪ'pɒnɪmɪ) *n* the derivation of names of places, etc., from those of persons.

epopee ('ɛpəʊˌpiː; *French* epɔpe) *or* **epopoeia** (ˌɛpə'piːə) *n* **1** an epic poem. **2** epic poetry in general. [C17: from French *épopée,* from Greek *epopoiia,* from EPOS + *poiein* to make]

epos ('ɛpɒs) *n* **1** a body of poetry in which the tradition of a people is conveyed, esp. a group of poems concerned with a common epic theme. **2** another word for **epic** (sense 1). [C19: via Latin from Greek: speech, word, epic poem, song; related to Latin *vōx* VOICE]

EPOS ('iːpɒs) *acronym for* electronic point of sale.

epoxide (ɪ'pɒksaɪd) *n* **a** a compound containing an oxygen atom joined to two different groups that are themselves joined to other groups. **b** (*as modifier*): *epoxide resin.* [C20: from EPI- + OXIDE]

epoxy (ɪ'pɒksɪ) *adj Chem.* **1** of, consisting of, or containing an oxygen atom joined to two different groups that are themselves joined to other groups: *epoxy group.* **2** of, relating to, or consisting of an epoxy resin. ◆ *n, pl* **epoxies. 3** short for **epoxy resin.** [C20: from EPI- + OXY-[2]]

epoxy *or* **epoxide resin** *n* any of various tough resistant thermosetting synthetic resins containing epoxy groups: used in surface coatings, laminates, and adhesives.

EPP *abbrev. for* executive pension plan.

Epping ('ɛpɪŋ) *n* a town in E England, in Essex, on the edge of Epping Forest: a residential centre for London. Pop.: 9922 (1991).

Epping Forest ('ɛpɪŋ) *n* a forest in E England, northeast of London: formerly a royal hunting ground.

EPR *abbrev. for* electron paramagnetic resonance.

EPROM ('iːprɒm) *n Computing. acronym for* erasable programmable read only memory.

eps *abbrev. for* earnings per share.

epsilon ('ɛpsɪˌlɒn, ɛp'saɪlən) *n* the fifth letter of the Greek alphabet (Ε, ε), a short vowel, transliterated as *e.* [Greek *e psilon,* literally: simple *e*]

Epsilon ('ɛpsɪˌlɒn, ɛp'saɪlən) *n* (*foll. by the genitive case of a specified constellation*) the fifth brightest star in a constellation: *Epsilon Aurigae.*

Epsom ('ɛpsəm) *n* a town in SE England, in Surrey: famous for its mineral springs and for horse racing. Pop. (with Ewell): 64 405 (1991).

Epsom salts *n* (*functioning as sing or pl*) a medicinal preparation of hydrated magnesium sulphate, used as a purgative, to reduce inflammation, etc. [C18: named after EPSOM, where they occur naturally in the water]

Epstein ('ɛpstaɪn) *n* Sir **Jacob.** 1880–1959, British sculptor, born in the U.S. of Russo-Polish parents.

Epstein-Barr virus *n* a virus belonging to the herpes family that causes infectious mononucleosis; it is also implicated in the development of Burkitt lymphoma. Abbrev.: **EBV.** [C20: named after Sir M. A. *Epstein* (born 1921), and Yvonne M. *Barr* (born 1932), British pathologists who discovered the virus]

epyllion (ɪ'pɪlɪən) *n, pl* **-lia** (-lɪə). a miniature epic. [C19: from Greek, diminutive of EPOS]

eq. *abbrev. for:* **1** equal. **2** equation. **3** equivalent.

equable ('ɛkwəb^{ə}l) *adj* **1** even-tempered; placid. **2** unvarying; uniform: *an equable climate.* [C17: from Latin *aequābilis,* from *aequāre* to make equal] ▸ **ˌequa'bility** *or* **'equableness** *n* ▸ **'equably** *adv*

equal ('iːkwəl) *adj* **1** (often foll. by *to* or *with*) identical in size, quantity, degree, intensity, etc.; the same (as). **2** having identical privileges, rights, status, etc.: *all men are equal before the law.* **3** having uniform effect or application: *equal opportunities.* **4** evenly balanced or proportioned: *the game was equal between the teams.* **5** (usually foll. by *to*) having the necessary or adequate strength, ability, means, etc. (for): *to be equal to one's work.* **6** another word for **equivalent** (sense 3a). ◆ *n* **7** a person or thing equal to another, esp. in merit, ability, etc.: *he has no equal when it comes to boxing.* ◆ *vb* **equals, equalling, equalled** *or U.S.* **equals, equaling, equaled. 8** (*tr*) to be equal to; correspond to; match: *my offer equals his.* **9** (*intr;* usually foll. by *out*) to become equal or level. **10** (*tr*) to make, perform, or do something equal to: *to equal the world record.* **11** (*tr*) *Archaic.* to make equal. [C14: from Latin *aequālis,* from *aequus* level, of obscure origin] ▸ **'equally** *adv*

USAGE The use of *more equal* as in *from now on their relationship will be a more equal one* is acceptable in modern English usage. *Equally* is preferred to *equally as* in sentences such as *reassuring the victims is equally important. Just as* is preferred to *equally as* in sentences such as *their surprise was just as great as his.*

equal-area *n* (*modifier*) (of a map projection) showing area accurately and therefore distorting shape and direction. Also: **homolographic.**

equali (ɪ'kwɑːlɪ) *pl n Music.* pieces for a group of instruments of the same kind: *Beethoven's Equali for four trombones.* [Italian: old pl form of *uguale* equal]

equalitarian (ɪˌkwɒlɪ'tɛərɪən) *adj, n* a less common word for **egalitarian.** ▸ **eˌquali'tarianism** *n*

equality (ɪ'kwɒlɪtɪ) *n, pl* **-ties. 1** the state of being equal. **2** *Maths.* a statement, usually an equation, indicating that quantities or expressions on either side of an equal sign are equal in value.

equalize *or* **equalise** ('iːkwəˌlaɪz) *vb* **1** (*tr*) to make equal or uniform; regularize. **2** (*intr*) (in sports) to reach the same score as one's opponent or opponents. ▸ **ˌequali'zation** *or* **ˌequali'sation** *n*

equalizer *or* **equaliser** ('iːkwəˌlaɪzə) *n* **1** a person or thing that equalizes, esp. a device to counterbalance opposing forces. **2** an electronic network introduced into a transmission circuit to alter its response, esp. to reduce distortion by equalizing its response over a specified frequency range. **3** *Sport.* a goal, point, etc., that levels the score. **4** *U.S. slang.* a weapon, esp. a gun.

Equal Opportunities Commission *n* (in Britain) a body appointed by the Government to enforce the provisions of the Equal Pay Act 1970 and the Sex Discrimination Act 1975. Abbrev.: **EOC.**

equal opportunity *n* **a** the offering of employment, pay, or promotion equally to all, without discrimination as to sex, race, colour, disability, etc. **b** (*as modifier*): *our equal-opportunity policy; an equal-opportunities employer.*

equal pay *n* the right of a man or woman to receive the same pay as a person of the opposite sex doing the same or similar work for the same or a similar employer.

equal sign *or* **equals sign** *n* the symbol =, used to indicate a mathematical equality.

equanimity (ˌi:kwəˈnɪmɪtɪ, ˌɛkwə-) *n* calmness of mind or temper; composure. [C17: from Latin *aequanimitās,* from *aequus* even, EQUAL + *animus* mind, spirit] ▸ **equanimous** (ɪˈkwænɪməs) *adj* ▸ **eˈquanimously** *adv*

equate (ɪˈkweɪt) *vb* (*mainly tr*) **1** to make or regard as equivalent or similar, esp. in order to compare or balance. **2** *Maths.* to indicate the equality of; form an equation from. **3** (*intr*) to be equal; correspond. [C15: from Latin *aequāre* to make EQUAL] ▸ **eˈquatable** *adj* ▸ **eˌquataˈbility** *n*

equation (ɪˈkweɪʒən, -ʃən) *n* **1** a mathematical statement that two expressions are equal: it is either an **identity,** in which the variables can assume any value, or a **conditional equation,** in which the variables have only certain values (roots). **2** the act of regarding as equal; equating. **3** the act of making equal or balanced; equalization. **4** a situation, esp. one regarded as having a number of conflicting elements: *what you want doesn't come into the equation.* **5** the state of being equal, equivalent, or equally balanced. **6** a situation or problem in which a number of factors need to be considered. **7** See **chemical equation.** **8** *Astronomy.* See **personal equation.** ▸ **eˈquational** *adj* ▸ **eˈquationally** *adv*

equation of state *n* any equation that expresses the relationship between the temperature, pressure, and volume of a substance.

equation of time *n* the difference between apparent solar time and mean solar time, being at a maximum in February (over 14 minutes) and November (over 16 minutes).

equator (ɪˈkweɪtə) *n* **1** the great circle of the earth with a latitude of 0°, lying equidistant from the poles; dividing the N and S hemispheres. **2** a circle dividing a sphere or other surface into two equal symmetrical parts. **3** See **magnetic equator.** **4** *Astronomy.* See **celestial equator.** [C14: from Medieval Latin (*circulus*) *aequātor* (*diei et noctis*) (circle) that equalizes (the day and night), from Latin *aequāre* to make EQUAL]

equatorial (ˌɛkwəˈtɔ:rɪəl) *adj* **1** of, like, or existing at or near the equator. **2** *Astronautics.* lying in the plane of the equator: *an equatorial orbit.* **3** *Astronomy.* of or referring to the celestial equator: *equatorial coordinates.* ◆ *n* **4** an equatorial mounting. ▸ ˌ**equaˈtorially** *adv*

Equatorial Guinea *n* a republic of W Africa, consisting of Río Muni on the mainland and the island of Bioko in the Gulf of Guinea, with four smaller islands: ceded by Portugal to Spain in 1778; gained independence in 1968. Official languages: Spanish and French. Religion: Roman Catholic majority. Currency: franc. Capital: Malabo. Pop.: 454 000 (1998 est.). Area: 28 049 sq. km (10 830 sq. miles). Former name (until 1964): **Spanish Guinea.**

equatorial mounting *n* an astronomical telescope mounting that allows motion of the telescope about two mutually perpendicular axes, one of which is parallel to the earth's axis.

equerry (ˈɛkwərɪ; *at the British court* ɪˈkwɛrɪ) *n, pl* **-ries. 1** an officer attendant upon the British sovereign. **2** (formerly) an officer in a royal household responsible for the horses. [C16: alteration (through influence of Latin *equus* horse) of earlier *escuirie,* from Old French: stable, group of squires, from *escuyer* SQUIRE]

equestrian (ɪˈkwɛstrɪən) *adj* **1** of or relating to horses and riding. **2** on horseback; mounted. **3** depicting or representing a person on horseback: *an equestrian statue.* **4** of, relating to, or composed of Roman equites. **5** of, relating to, or composed of knights, esp. the imperial free knights of the Holy Roman Empire. ◆ *n* **6** a person skilled in riding and horsemanship. [C17: from Latin *equestris,* from *eques* horseman, knight, from *equus* horse] ▸ **eˈquestrianˌism** *n*

equestrienne (ɪˌkwɛstrɪˈɛn) *n* a female rider on horseback, esp. one in a circus who performs acrobatics.

equi- *combining form.* equal or equally: *equidistant; equilateral.*

equiangular (ˌi:kwɪˈæŋgjʊlə) *adj* having all angles equal.

equidistant (ˌi:kwɪˈdɪstənt) *adj* distant by equal amounts from two or more places. ▸ ˌ**equiˈdistance** *n* ▸ ˌ**equiˈdistantly** *adv*

equilateral (ˌi:kwɪˈlætərəl) *adj* **1** having all sides of equal length: *an equilateral triangle.* ◆ *n* **2** a geometric figure having all its sides of equal length. **3** a side that is equal in length to other sides. ▸ ˌ**equiˈlaterally** *adv*

equilibrant (ɪˈkwɪlɪbrənt) *n* a force capable of balancing another force and producing equilibrium.

equilibrate (ˌi:kwɪˈlaɪbreɪt, ɪˈkwɪlɪˌbreɪt) *vb* to bring to or be in equilibrium; balance. [C17: from Late Latin *aequilībrāre,* from *aequilībris* in balance; see EQUILIBRIUM] ▸ **equilibration** (ˌi:kwɪlaɪˈbreɪʃən, ɪˌkwɪlɪ-) *n* ▸ **equilibrator** (ɪˈkwɪlɪˌbreɪtə) *n*

equilibrist (ɪˈkwɪlɪbrɪst) *n* a person who performs balancing feats, esp. on a high wire. ▸ **eˌquiliˈbristic** *adj*

equilibrium (ˌi:kwɪˈlɪbrɪəm) *n, pl* **-riums** *or* **-ria** (-rɪə). **1** a stable condition in which forces cancel one another. **2** a state or feeling of mental balance; composure. **3** any unchanging condition or state of a body, system, etc., resulting from the balance or cancelling out of the influences or processes to which it is subjected. See **thermodynamic equilibrium.** **4** *Physics.* a state of rest or uniform motion in which there is no resultant force on a body. **5** *Chem.* the condition existing when a chemical reaction and its reverse reaction take place at equal rates. **6** *Physics.* the condition of a system that has its total energy distributed among its component parts in the statistically most probable manner. **7** *Physiol.* a state of bodily balance, maintained primarily by special receptors in the inner ear. **8** the economic condition in which there is neither excess demand nor excess supply in a market. [C17: from Latin *aequilībrium,* from *aequi-* EQUI- + *lībra* pound, balance]

equimolecular (ˌi:kwɪməˈlɛkjʊlə) *adj* (of substances, solutions, etc.) containing equal numbers of molecules.

equine (ˈɛkwaɪn) *adj* **1** of, relating to, or resembling a horse. **2** of, relating to, or belonging to the family *Equidae,* which comprises horses, zebras, and asses. [C18: from Latin *equīnus,* from *equus* horse] ▸ **ˈequinely** *adv*

equine distemper *n* another name for **strangles.**

equinoctial (ˌi:kwɪˈnɒkʃəl) *adj* **1** relating to or occurring at either or both equinoxes. **2** (of a plant) having flowers that open and close at specific regular times. **3** *Astronomy.* of or relating to the celestial equator. ◆ *n* **4** a storm or gale at or near an equinox. **5** another name for **celestial equator.** [C14: from Latin *aequinoctiālis* concerning the EQUINOX]

equinoctial circle *or* **line** *n* another name for **celestial equator.**

equinoctial point *n* either of the two points at which the celestial equator intersects the ecliptic.

equinox (ˈi:kwɪˌnɒks) *n* **1** either of the two occasions, six months apart, when day and night are of equal length. See **vernal equinox, autumnal equinox.** **2** another name for **equinoctial point.** [C14: from Medieval Latin *equinoxium,* changed from Latin *aequinoctium,* from *aequi-* EQUI- + *nox* night]

equinumerous (ˌi:kwɪˈnju:mərəs) *adj Logic.* having the same number of members.

equip (ɪˈkwɪp) *vb* **equips, equipping, equipped.** (*tr*) **1** to furnish with (necessary supplies, etc.). **2** (*usually passive*) to provide with abilities, understanding, etc.: *her son was never equipped to be a scholar.* **3** to dress out; attire. [C16: from Old French *eschiper* to embark, fit out (a ship), of Germanic origin; compare Old Norse *skipa* to put in order, *skip* SHIP] ▸ **eˈquipper** *n*

equipage (ˈɛkwɪpɪdʒ) *n* **1** a horse-drawn carriage, esp. one elegantly equipped and attended by liveried footmen. **2** (formerly) the stores and equipment of a military unit. **3** *Archaic.* **3a** a set of useful articles. **3b** a group of attendants; retinue.

equipartition (ˌɛkwɪpɑ:ˈtɪʃən) *n* the equal division of the energy of a system in thermal equilibrium between different degrees of freedom. This principle was assumed to be exact in classical physics, but quantum theory shows that it is true only in certain special cases.

équipe (eɪˈki:p) *n* (esp. in motor racing) a team. [French]

equipment (ɪˈkwɪpmənt) *n* **1** an act or instance of equipping. **2** the items so provided. **3** a set of tools, devices, kit, etc., assembled for a specific purpose, such as a soldier's kit and weapons.

equipoise (ˈɛkwɪˌpɔɪz) *n* **1** even balance of weight or other forces; equilibrium. **2** a counterbalance; counterpoise. ◆ *vb* **3** (*tr*) to offset or balance in weight or force; balance.

equipollent (ˌi:kwɪˈpɒlənt) *adj* **1** equal or equivalent in significance, power, or effect. **2** *Logic.* (of two propositions) logically deducible from each other; equivalent. **3** *Maths, logic.* (of two classes) having the same cardinality. ◆ *n* **4** something that is equipollent. [C15: from Latin *aequipollēns* of equal importance, from EQUI- + *pollēre* to be able, be strong] ▸ ˌ**equiˈpollence** *or* ˌ**equiˈpollency** *n* ▸ ˌ**equiˈpollently** *adv*

equiponderate (ˌi:kwɪˈpɒndəˌreɪt) *vb* (*tr*) to equal or balance in weight, power, force, etc.; offset; counterbalance. [C17: from Medieval Latin *aequiponderāre,* from Latin EQUI- + *ponderāre* to weigh] ▸ ˌ**equiˈponderance** *or* ˌ**equiˈponderancy** *n* ▸ ˌ**equiˈponderant** *adj*

equipotential (ˌi:kwɪpəˈtɛnʃəl) *adj* **1** having the same electric potential or uniform electric potential. **2** Also: **equipotent** (ˌi:kwɪˈpəʊtᵊnt). equivalent in power or effect. ◆ *n* **3** an equipotential line or surface. ▸ ˌ**equipoˌtentiˈality** *n*

equiprobable (ˌi:kwɪˈprɒbəᵊl) *adj* equally probable. ▸ ˌ**equiˌprobaˈbility** *n*

equisetum (ˌɛkwɪˈsi:təm) *n, pl* **-tums** *or* **-ta** (-tə). any tracheophyte plant of the genus *Equisetum,* which comprises the horsetails. [C19: New Latin, changed from Latin *equisaetum,* from *equus* horse + *saeta* bristle]

equitable (ˈɛkwɪtəbᵊl) *adj* **1** impartial or reasonable; fair; just: *an equitable decision.* **2** *Law.* relating to or valid in equity, as distinct from common law or statute law. **3** *Law.* (formerly) recognized in a court of equity only, as claims, rights, etc. [C17: from French *équitable,* from *équité* EQUITY] ▸ **ˈequitableness** *n* ▸ **ˈequitably** *adv*

equitant (ˈɛkwɪtᵊnt) *adj* (of a leaf) having the base folded around the stem so that it overlaps the leaf above and opposite. [C19: from Latin *equitāns* riding, from *equitāre* to ride, from *equus* horse]

equitation (ˌɛkwɪˈteɪʃən) *n* the study and practice of riding and horsemanship. [C16: from Latin *equitātiō,* from *equitāre* to ride, from *equus* horse]

equites (ˈɛkwɪˌti:z) *pl n* (in ancient Rome) **1** the cavalry. **2** members of a social order distinguished by wealth and ranking just below the senators. ◆ Also called: **knights.** [from Latin, plural of *eques* horseman, from *equus* horse]

equities (ˈɛkwɪtɪz) *pl n* another name for **ordinary shares.**

equity (ˈɛkwɪtɪ) *n, pl* **-ties. 1** the quality of being impartial or reasonable; fairness. **2** an impartial or fair act, decision, etc. **3** *Law.* a system of jurisprudence founded on principles of natural justice and fair conduct. It supplements the common law and mitigates its inflexibility, as by providing a remedy where none exists at law. **4** *Law.* an equitable right or claim: *equity of redemption.* **5** the interest of ordinary shareholders in a company. **6** the market value of a debtor's property in excess of all debts to which it is liable. [C14: from Old French *equite,* from Latin *aequitās,* from *aequus* level, EQUAL]

Equity (ˈɛkwɪtɪ) *n* the actors' trade union. Full name: **Actors' Equity Association.**

equity capital *n* the part of the share capital of a company owned by ordinary shareholders or in certain circumstances by other classes of shareholder.

equity-linked policy *n* an insurance or assurance policy in which premiums are invested partially or wholly in ordinary shares for the eventual benefit of the beneficiaries of the policy.

equity of redemption *n Property law.* the right that a mortgager has in equity to redeem his property on payment of the sum owing, even though the sum is overdue. See also **foreclose.**

equiv. *abbrev. for* equivalent.

equivalence (ɪˈkwɪvələns) *or* **equivalency** *n* **1** the state of being equivalent or interchangeable. **2** *Maths, logic.* **2a** the relationship between two statements each of which implies the other. **2b** the binary truth-function that takes the value *true* when both component sentences are true or when both are false, corresponding to English *if and only if.* Symbol: ≡ or ↔, as in $-(p \wedge q) \equiv -p \vee -q$ Also called: **biconditional.**

equivalence relation *n Logic, maths.* a relation that is reflexive, symmetric, and transitive: it imposes a partition on its domain of definition so that two elements belong to the same subset if and only if the relation holds between them.

equivalency (ˌɛkwɪˈveɪlənsɪ) *or* **equivalence** *n Chem.* the state of having equal valencies. ▸ **ˌequiˈvalent** *adj*

equivalent (ɪˈkwɪvələnt) *adj* **1** equal or interchangeable in value, quantity, significance, etc. **2** having the same or a similar effect or meaning. **3** *Maths.* **3a** (of two geometric figures) having a particular property in common; equal. **3b** (of two equations or inequalities) having the same set of solutions. **3c** (of two sets) having the same cardinal number. **4** *Maths, logic.* (of two propositions) having an equivalence between them. ◆ *n* **5** something that is equivalent. **6** short for **equivalent weight.** [C15: from Late Latin *aequivalēns,* from *aequivalēre* to be equally significant, from Latin *aequi-* EQUI- + *valēre* to be worth] ▸ **eˈquivalently** *adv*

equivalent air speed *n* the speed at sea level that would produce the same Pitot-static tube reading as that measured at altitude.

equivalent circuit *n* an arrangement of simple electrical components that is electrically equivalent to a complex circuit and is used to simplify circuit analysis.

equivalent focal length *n Optics.* the ratio of the size of an image of a small distant object near the optical axis to the angular distance of the object in radians.

equivalent weight *n* the weight of an element or compound that will combine with or displace 8 grams of oxygen or 1.007 97 grams of hydrogen. Also called: **gram equivalent.**

equivocal (ɪˈkwɪvəkˀl) *adj* **1** capable of varying interpretations; ambiguous. **2** deliberately misleading or vague; evasive. **3** of doubtful character or sincerity; dubious. [C17: from Late Latin *aequivocus,* from Latin EQUI- + *vōx* voice] ▸ **eˈquivocally** *adv* ▸ **eˌquivoˈcality** *or* **eˈquivocalness** *n*

equivocate (ɪˈkwɪvəˌkeɪt) *vb (intr)* to use vague or ambiguous language, esp. in order to avoid speaking directly or honestly; hedge. [C15: from Medieval Latin *aequivocāre,* from Late Latin *aequivocus* ambiguous, EQUIVOCAL] ▸ **eˈquivoˌcatingly** *adv* ▸ **eˈquivoˌcator** *n* ▸ **eˈquivocatory** *adj*

equivocation (ɪˌkwɪvəˈkeɪʃən) *n* **1** the act or an instance of equivocating. **2** *Logic.* a fallacy based on the use of the same term in different senses, esp. as the middle term of a syllogism, as *the badger lives in the bank, and the bank is in the High Street, so the badger lives in the High Street.*

equivoque *or* **equivoke** (ˈɛkwɪˌvəʊk) *n* **1** a play on words; pun. **2** an ambiguous phrase or expression. **3** double meaning; ambiguity. [C14: *equivoc* EQUIVOCAL]

Equuleus (ɛˈkwʊlɪəs) *n, Latin genitive* **Equulei** (ɛˈkwʊlɪˌaɪ). a small faint constellation in the N hemisphere between Pegasus and Aquarius. [from Latin: a young horse, from *equus* horse]

er (ə, ɜː) *interj* a sound made when hesitating in speech.

Er *the chemical symbol for* erbium.

ER *abbrev. for:* **1** Elizabeth Regina. [Latin: Queen Elizabeth] **2** Eduardus Rex. [Latin: King Edward]

-er[1] *suffix forming nouns.* **1** a person or thing that performs a specified action: *reader; decanter; lighter.* **2** a person engaged in a profession, occupation, etc.: *writer; baker; bootlegger.* **3** a native or inhabitant of: *islander; Londoner; villager.* **4** a person or thing having a certain characteristic: *newcomer; double-decker; fiver.* [Old English *-ere;* related to German *-er,* Latin *-ārius*]

-er[2] *suffix.* forming the comparative degree of adjectives (*deeper, freer, sunnier,* etc.) and adverbs (*faster, slower,* etc.). [Old English *-rd, -re* (adj), *-or* (adv)]

era (ˈɪərə) *n* **1** a period of time considered as being of a distinctive character; epoch. **2** an extended period of time the years of which are numbered from a fixed point or event: *the Christian era.* **3** a point in time, esp. one beginning a new or distinctive period: *the discovery of antibiotics marked an era in modern medicine.* **4** *Geology.* a major division of geological time, divided into several periods: *the Mesozoic era.* [C17: from Latin *aera* counters, plural of *aes* brass, pieces of brass money]

ERA (ˈiːrə) *n* (in Britain) *acronym for* Education Reform Act: the 1988 act which established the key elements of the National Curriculum and the Basic Curriculum.

eradiate (ɪˈreɪdɪˌeɪt) *vb* a less common word for **radiate.** Compare **irradiate.** ▸ **eˌradiˈation** *n*

eradicate (ɪˈrædɪˌkeɪt) *vb (tr)* **1** to obliterate; stamp out. **2** to pull or tear up by the roots. [C16: from Latin *ērādīcāre* to uproot, from EX-[1] + *rādīx* root] ▸ **eˈradicable** *adj* ▸ **eˈradicably** *adv* ▸ **eˌradiˈcation** *n* ▸ **eˈradicative** *adj* ▸ **eˈradiˌcator** *n*

erase (ɪˈreɪz) *vb* **1** to obliterate or rub out (something written, typed, etc.). **2** *(tr)* to destroy all traces of; remove completely: *time erases grief.* **3** to remove (a recording) from (magnetic tape). **4** *(tr) Computing.* to replace (data) on a storage device with characters representing an absence of data. [C17: from Latin *ērādere* to scrape off, from EX-[1] + *rādere* to scratch, scrape] ▸ **eˈrasable** *adj*

eraser (ɪˈreɪzə) *n* an object, such as a piece of rubber or felt, used for erasing something written, typed, etc.: *a pencil eraser.*

erasion (ɪˈreɪʒən) *n* **1** the act of erasing; erasure. **2** the surgical scraping away of tissue, esp. of bone.

Erasmus (ɪˈræzməs) *n* **Desiderius** (ˌdɛzɪˈdɪərɪəs), real name *Gerhard Gerhards.* ?1466–1536, Dutch humanist, the leading scholar of the Renaissance in northern Europe. He published the first Greek edition of the New Testament in 1516; his other works include the satirical *Encomium Moriae* (1509); *Colloquia* (1519), a series of dialogues; and an attack on the theology of Luther, *De Libero Arbitrio* (1524).

Erastianism (ɪˈræstɪəˌnɪzəm) *n* the theory that the state should have authority over the church in ecclesiastical matters. [C17: named after Thomas *Erastus* (1524–83), Swiss theologian to whom such views were attributed] ▸ **Eˈrastian** *n, adj*

erasure (ɪˈreɪʒə) *n* **1** the act or an instance of erasing. **2** the place or mark, as on a piece of paper, where something has been erased.

Erato (ˈɛrəˌtəʊ) *n Greek myth.* the Muse of love poetry.

Eratosthenes (ˌɛrəˈtɒsθɪˌniːz) *n* ?276–?194 B.C., Greek mathematician and astronomer, who calculated the circumference of the earth by observing the angle of the sun's rays at different places.

Erbil, Irbil (ˈɜːbɪl), *or* **Arbil** *n* a city in N Iraq: important in Assyrian times. Pop.: 485 968 (1987). Ancient name: **Arbela.**

erbium (ˈɜːbɪəm) *n* a soft malleable silvery-white element of the lanthanide series of metals: used in special alloys, room-temperature lasers, and as a pigment. Symbol: Er; atomic no.: 68; atomic wt.: 167.26; valency: 3; relative density: 9.006; melting pt.: 1529°C; boiling pt.: 2868°C. [C19: from New Latin, from *(Ytt)erb(y),* Sweden, where it was first found + -IUM]

Erciyas Daği (*Turkish* ˈɛrdʒijɑs dɑːˈi) *n* an extinct volcano in central Turkey. Height 3916 m (12 848 ft.).

ERCP *abbrev. for* endoscopic retrograde cholangiopancreatography.

ERDF *abbrev. for* European Regional Development Fund: a fund to provide money for specific projects for work on the infrastructure in countries of the European Union.

ere (ɛə) *conj, prep* a poetic word for **before.** [Old English *ǣr;* related to Old Norse *ār* early, Gothic *airis* earlier, Old High German *ēr* earlier, Greek *eri* early]

Erebus[1] (ˈɛrɪbəs) *n Greek myth.* **1** the god of darkness, son of Chaos and brother of Night. **2** the darkness below the earth, thought to be the abode of the dead or the region they pass through on their way to Hades.

Erebus[2] (ˈɛrɪbəs) *n* **Mount.** a volcano in Antarctica, on Ross Island: discovered by Sir James Ross in 1841 and named after his ship. Height: 3794 m (12 448 ft.).

Erechtheum (ɪˈrɛkθɪəm, ˌɛrəkˈθiːəm) *or* **Erechtheion** (ɪˈrɛkθɪən, ˌɛrəkˈθiːən) *n* a temple on the Acropolis at Athens, which has a porch of caryatids.

Erechtheus (ɛˈrɛkθjuːs, -θɪəs) *n Greek myth.* a king of Athens who sacrificed one of his daughters because the oracle at Delphi said this was the only way to win the war against the Eleusinians.

erect (ɪˈrɛkt) *adj* **1** upright in posture or position; not bent or leaning: *an erect stance.* **2** (of an optical image) having the same orientation as the object; not inverted. **3** *Physiol.* (of the penis, clitoris, or nipples) firm or rigid after swelling with blood, esp. as a result of sexual excitement. **4** (of plant parts) growing vertically or at right angles to the parts from which they arise. ◆ *vb (mainly tr)* **5** to put up; construct; build. **6** to raise to an upright position; lift up: *to erect a flagpole.* **7** to found or form; set up. **8** *(also intr) Physiol.* to become or cause to become firm or rigid by filling with blood. **9** to hold up as an ideal; exalt. **10** *Optics.* to change (an inverted image) to an upright position. **11** to draw or construct (a line, figure, etc.) on a given line or figure, esp. at right angles to it. [C14: from Latin *ērigere* to set up, from *regere* to control, govern] ▸ **eˈrectable** *adj* ▸ **eˈrectly** *adv* ▸ **eˈrectness** *n*

erectile (ɪˈrɛktaɪl) *adj* **1** *Physiol.* (of tissues or organs, such as the penis or clitoris) capable of becoming rigid or erect as the result of being filled with blood. **2** capable of being erected. ▸ **erectility** (ɪrɛkˈtɪlɪtɪ, ˌiːrɛk-) *n*

erection (ɪˈrɛkʃən) *n* **1** the act of erecting or the state of being erected. **2** something that has been erected; a building or construction. **3** *Physiol.* the enlarged state or condition of erectile tissues or organs, esp. the penis, when filled with blood. **4** an erect penis.

erector *or* **erecter** (ɪˈrɛktə) *n* **1** *Anatomy.* any muscle that raises a part or makes it erect. **2** a person or thing that erects.

E region *or* **layer** *n* a region of the ionosphere, extending from a height of 90 to about 150 kilometres. It reflects radio waves of medium wavelength. Also called: **Heaviside layer, Kennelly-Heaviside layer.** See also **ionosphere.**

erelong (ɛəˈlɒŋ) *adv Archaic or poetic.* before long; soon.

eremite (ˈɛrɪˌmaɪt) *n* a Christian hermit or recluse. Compare **coenobite.** [C13: see HERMIT] ▸ **eremitic** (ˌɛrɪˈmɪtɪk) or **ˌereˈmitical** *adj* ▸ **eremitism** (ˈɛrɪmaɪˌtɪzəm) *n*

Erenburg (ˈɛrənbɜːg; *Russian* ɛrɪnˈburk) *n* a variant spelling of (Ilya Grigorievich) **Ehrenburg.**

erepsin (ɪˈrɛpsɪn) *n* a mixture of proteolytic enzymes secreted by the small intestine. [C20: *er-,* from Latin *ēripere* to snatch (from *rapere* to seize) + (P)EPSIN]

erethism (ˈɛrɪˌθɪzəm) *n* **1** *Physiol.* an abnormally high degree of irritability or sensitivity in any part of the body. **2** *Psychiatry.* **2a** a personality disorder resulting from mercury poisoning. **2b** an abnormal tendency to become aroused quickly, esp. sexually, as the result of a verbal or psychic stimulus. [C18: from French *éréthisme,* from Greek *erethismos* irritation, from *erethizein* to excite, irritate] ▸ **ˌereˈthismic, ˌereˈthistic,** *or* **ˌereˈthitic** *adj*

Eretria (ɪˈrɛtrɪə) *n* an ancient city in Greece, on the S coast of Euboea: founded as an Ionian colony; destroyed by the Persians in 490 B.C. following which it never regained its former significance.

Eretz Yisrael *or* ***Eretz Israel*** *Hebrew.* (*Hebrew* ˈɛrɛts jisˈrɑɛl; *Yiddish* ˈɛrɛts jisrɑˈeɪl) *n Judaism.* **1** the Holy Land; Israel. **2** the concept, favoured by some extreme Zionists, of a Jewish state the territory of which matched the largest expanse of biblical Israel. [literally: Land of Israel]

erev ('ɛrɛv) *n* (*in combination*) *Judaism.* the day before; the eve of: *erev Shabbat* (the Sabbath eve, i.e., Friday); *erev Pesach* (the day before Passover). [from Hebrew]

Erevan (*Russian* jɪrɪ'van) *n* a variant spelling of **Yerevan.**

erewhile (ɛə'waɪl) *or* **erewhiles** *adv Archaic.* a short time ago; a little while before.

erf (ɜ:f) *n, pl* **erven** ('ɜ:vən). *S. African.* a plot of land, usually urban, marked off for building purposes. [Afrikaans]

Erf (ɜ:f) *abbrev. for* electrorheological fluid: a man-made liquid that thickens or solidifies when an electric current passes through it and returns to a liquid when the current ceases.

Erfurt (*German* 'ɛrfʊrt) *n* an industrial city in central Germany, the capital of Thuringia: university (1392). Pop.: 211 108 (1996 est.).

erg[1] (ɜ:g) *n* the cgs unit of work or energy. 1 erg is equivalent to 10^{-7} joule. [C19: from Greek *ergon* work]

erg[2] (ɜ:g) *n, pl* **ergs** *or* **areg.** an area of shifting sand dunes in a desert, esp. the Sahara. [C19: from Arabic *'irj*]

ergastoplasm (ɜ:'gæstəˌplæzəm) *n* a former name for **endoplasmic reticulum.**

ergative ('ɜ:gətɪv) *Linguistics.* ◆ *adj* **1** denoting a type of verb that takes the same noun as either direct object or as subject, with equivalent meaning. Thus, "fuse" is an ergative verb: "He fused the lights" and "The lights fused" have equivalent meaning. **2** denoting a case of nouns in certain languages, for example, Eskimo or Basque, marking a noun used interchangeably as either the direct object of a transitive verb or the subject of an intransitive verb. **3** denoting a language that has ergative verbs or ergative nouns. ◆ *n* **4** an ergative verb. **5** an ergative noun or case of nouns. [C20: from Greek *ergatēs* a workman + -IVE]

ergatocracy (ˌɜ:gə'tɒkrəsɪ) *n, pl* **-cies.** *Rare.* government by the workers. [C20: from Greek *ergatēs* a workman, from *ergon* work, deed + -CRACY]

ergo ('ɜ:gəʊ) *sentence connector.* therefore; hence. [C14: from Latin: therefore]

ergograph ('ɜ:gəˌgrɑ:f, -ˌgræf) *n* an instrument that measures and records the amount of work a muscle does during contraction, its rate of fatigue, etc.

ergometer (ɜ:'gɒmɪtə) *n* a dynamometer. [C20: from Greek *ergon* work + -METER]

ergonomic (ˌɜ:gə'nɒmɪk) *adj* **1** of or relating to ergonomics. **2** designed to minimize physical effort and discomfort, and hence maximize efficiency.

ergonomics (ˌɜ:gə'nɒmɪks) *n* (*functioning as sing*) the study of the relationship between workers and their environment, esp. the equipment they use. Also called: **biotechnology.** [C20: from Greek *ergon* work + (ECO)NOMICS] ▸ **ergonomist** (ɜ:'gɒnəmɪst) *n*

ergosterol (ɜ:'gɒstəˌrɒl) *n* a plant sterol that is converted into vitamin D by the action of ultraviolet radiation. Formula: $C_{28}H_{43}OH$.

ergot ('ɜ:gət, -gɒt) *n* **1** a disease of cereals and other grasses caused by ascomycete fungi of the genus *Claviceps,* esp. *C. purpurea,* in which the seeds or grain of the plants are replaced by the spore-containing bodies (sclerotia) of the fungus. **2** any fungus causing this disease. **3** the dried sclerotia of *C. purpurea,* used as the source of certain alkaloids used to treat haemorrhage, facilitate uterine contraction in childbirth, etc. [C17: from French: spur (of a cock), of unknown origin]

ergotism ('ɜ:gəˌtɪzəm) *n* ergot poisoning, producing either burning pains and eventually gangrene in the limbs or itching skin and convulsions. Also called: **Saint Anthony's fire.**

Erhard (*German* 'e:rhart) *n* **Ludwig** ('lu:tvɪç). 1897–1977, German statesman: chief architect of the *Wirtschaftswunder* ("economic miracle") of West Germany's recovery after World War II; chancellor (1963–66).

eric *or* **eriach** ('ɛrɪk) *n* (in old Irish law) a fine paid by a murderer to the family of his victim. Compare **wergild.** [C16: from Irish *eiric*]

Eric XIV ('ɛrɪk) *n* 1533–77, king of Sweden (1560–68). His attempts to dominate the Baltic led to war with Denmark (1563–70); deposed and imprisoned.

erica ('ɛrɪkə) *n* any shrub of the ericaceous genus *Erica,* including the heaths and some heathers. [C19: via Latin from Greek *ereikē* heath]

ericaceous (ˌɛrɪ'keɪʃəs) *adj* of, relating to, or belonging to the *Ericaceae,* a family of trees and shrubs with typically bell-shaped flowers: includes heather, rhododendron, azalea, and arbutus. [C19: from New Latin *Ericācaeae,* from Latin *erīca* heath, from Greek *ereikē*]

ericoid ('ɛrɪˌkɔɪd) *adj Botany.* (of leaves) small and tough, resembling those of heather.

Ericson *or* **Ericsson** ('ɛrɪksᵊn) *n* **Leif** (li:f). 10th–11th centuries A.D., Norse navigator, who discovered Vinland (?1000), variously identified as the coast of New England, Labrador, or Newfoundland; son of Eric the Red.

Eric the Red ('ɛrɪk) *n* ?940–?1010 A.D., Norse navigator: discovered and colonized Greenland; father of Leif Ericson.

Eridanus (ɛ'rɪdənəs) *n, Latin genitive* **Eridani** (ɛ'rɪdəˌnaɪ). a long twisting constellation in the S hemisphere extending from Orion to Hydrus and containing the first magnitude star Achernar. [from Greek *Eridanos* river in Italy (sometimes identified with the Po) into which, according to legend, Phaëthon fell]

Erie[1] ('ɪərɪ) *n* **1** (*pl* **Eries** *or* **Erie**) a member of a North American Indian people formerly living south of Lake Erie. **2** the language of this people, possibly belonging to the Iroquoian family.

Erie[2] ('ɪərɪ) *n* **1 Lake.** a lake between the U.S. and Canada: the southernmost and the shallowest of the Great Lakes; empties by the Niagara River into Lake Ontario. Area: 25 718 sq. km (9930 sq. miles). **2** a port in NW Pennsylvania, on Lake Erie. Pop.: 105 270 (1996 est.).

Erie Canal *n* a canal in New York State between Albany and Buffalo, linking the Hudson River with Lake Erie. Length: 579 km (360 miles).

Erigena (ˌɛrɪ'dʒi:nə) *n* **John Scotus.** ?800–?877 A.D., Irish Neo-Platonist philosopher.

erigeron (ɪ'rɪdʒərən, -'rɪg-) *n* any plant of the genus *Erigeron,* whose flowers resemble asters but have narrower rays: family *Compositae* (composites). See also **fleabane** (sense 1). [C17: via Latin from Greek, from *ēri* early + *gerōn* old man; from the white down characteristic of some species]

Erin ('ɪərɪn, 'ɛərɪn) *n* an archaic or poetic name for **Ireland**[1]. [from Irish Gaelic *Éirinn,* dative of Ireland]

erinaceous (ˌɛrɪ'neɪʃəs) *adj* of, relating to, or resembling hedgehogs. [C18: from Latin *ērināceus* hedgehog]

eringo (ɪ'rɪŋgəʊ) *n, pl* **-goes** *or* **-gos.** a variant spelling of **eryngo.**

erinus (ɪ'raɪnəs) *n* any plant of the scrophulariaceous genus *Erinus,* native to S Africa and S Europe, esp. *E. alpinus,* grown as a rock plant for its white, purple, or carmine flowers. [New Latin, from Greek *erinos,* an unidentified plant]

Erinyes (ɪ'rɪnɪˌi:z) *pl n, sing* **Erinys** (ɪ'rɪnɪs, ɪ'raɪ-). *Myth.* another name for the **Furies.**

Eris ('ɛrɪs) *n Greek myth.* the goddess of discord, sister of Ares.

eristic (ɛ'rɪstɪk) *adj also* **eristical. 1** of, relating to, or given to controversy or logical disputation, esp. for its own sake. ◆ *n* **2** a person who engages in logical disputes; a controversialist. **3** the art or practice of logical disputation, esp. if specious. [C17: from Greek *eristikos,* from *erizein* to wrangle, from *eris* discord]

Eritrea (ˌɛrɪ'treɪə) *n* a small country in NE Africa, on the Red Sea: became an Italian colony in 1890; federated with Ethiopia (1952–93); an independence movement was engaged in war with the Ethiopian government from 1961 until independence was gained in 1993; consists of hot and arid coastal lowlands, rising to the foothills of the Ethiopian highlands. Languages: Arabic, English, Afar, and others. Religions: Muslim and Christian. Currency: nakfa. Capital: Asmara. Pop.: 3 842 000 (1998 est.). Area: 117 400 sq. km (45 300 sq. miles). ▸ **ˌEri-'trean** *adj, n*

Erivan (*Russian* jɪrɪ'van) *n* a variant spelling of **Yerevan.**

erk (ɜ:k) *n Brit. slang.* an aircraftman or naval rating. [C20: perhaps a corruption of *AC* (aircraftman)]

erlang ('ɜ:læŋ) *n* a unit of traffic intensity in a telephone system equal to the intensity for a specific period when the average number of simultaneous calls is unity. Abbrev.: **e** [C20: named after A. K. *Erlang* (1878–1929), Danish mathematician]

Erlangen (*German* 'ɛrlaŋən) *n* a town in central Germany, in Bavaria: university (1743). Pop.: 101 406 (1996 est.).

Erlanger ('ɜ:læŋə) *n* **Joseph.** 1874–1965, U.S. physiologist. He shared a Nobel prize for physiology or medicine (1944) with Gasser for their work on the electrical signs of nervous activity.

Erlenmeyer flask ('ɜ:lənˌmaɪə) *n* a flask, for use in a laboratory, with a narrow neck, wide base, and conical shape; conical flask. [C19: named after Emil *Erlenmeyer* (1825–1909), German chemist]

erlking ('ɜ:lˌkɪŋ) *n German myth.* a malevolent spirit who carries children off to death. [C18: from German *Erlkönig,* literally: alder king, coined in 1778 by Herder, a mistranslation of Danish *ellerkonge* king of the elves]

ERM *abbrev. for* Exchange Rate Mechanism.

Ermanaric (ə'mænərɪk) *n* died ?375 A.D., king of the Ostrogoths: ruled an extensive empire in eastern Europe, which was overrun by the Huns in the 370s.

ermine ('ɜ:mɪn) *n, pl* **-mines** *or* **-mine. 1** the stoat in northern regions, where it has a white winter coat with a black-tipped tail. **2** the fur of this animal. **3** one of the two principal furs used on heraldic shields, conventionally represented by a white field flecked with black ermine tails. Compare **vair. 4** the dignity or office of a judge, noble, or king. **5** short for **ermine moth.** [C12: from Old French *hermine,* from Medieval Latin *Armenius* (*mūs*) Armenian (mouse)]

ermine moth *n* **1** Also called: **ermine.** an arctiid moth of the genus *Spilosoma,* characterized by dark spots on the light coloured wings, and producing woolly bear caterpillars. **2 small ermine.** an unrelated micro, *Yponomeuta padella.*

Ermite ('ɜ:maɪt) *n* a salty blue cheese made in Quebec, Canada. [via Canadian French from French *ermite* hermit, the cheese being made originally by monks]

erne *or* **ern** (ɜ:n) *n* another name for the (European) **sea eagle.** [Old English *earn;* related to Old Norse *örn* eagle, Old High German *aro* eagle, Greek *ornis* bird]

Erne (ɜ:n) *n* a river in N central Republic of Ireland, rising in County Cavan and flowing north across the border, through **Upper Lough Erne** and **Lower Lough Erne,** and then west to Donegal Bay. Length: about 96 km (60 miles).

Ernie ('ɜ:nɪ) *n* (in Britain) a machine that randomly selects winning numbers of Premium Bonds. [C20: acronym of Electronic Random Number Indicator Equipment]

Ernst (*German* ɛrnst) *n* **Max** (maks). 1891–1976, German painter, resident in France and the U.S., a prominent exponent of Dada and surrealism: developed the technique of collage.

ERO (in New Zealand) *abbrev. for* Education Review Office.

erode (ɪ'rəʊd) *vb* **1** to grind or wear down or away or become ground or worn down or away. **2** to deteriorate or cause to deteriorate: *jealousy eroded the relationship.* **3** (*tr; usually passive*) *Pathol.* to remove (tissue) by ulceration. [C17: from Latin *ērōdere,* from EX-[1] + *rōdere* to gnaw] ▸ **e'rodent** *adj, n* ▸ **e'rodible** *adj*

erogenous (ɪ'rɒdʒɪnəs) *or* **erogenic** (ˌɛrə'dʒɛnɪk) *adj* **1** sensitive to sexual stimulation: *erogenous zones of the body.* **2** arousing sexual desire or giving sexual pleasure. [C19: from Greek *erōs* love, desire + -GENOUS] ▸ **erogeneity** (ˌɛrədʒɪ'ni:ɪtɪ) *n*

Eros[1] ('ɪərɒs, 'ɛrɒs) *n* **1** *Greek myth.* the god of love, son of Aphrodite. Roman counterpart: **Cupid. 2** Also called: **life instinct.** (in Freudian theory) the group of instincts, esp. sexual, that govern acts of self-preservation and that tend towards uninhibited enjoyment of life. Compare **Thanatos.** [Greek: desire, sexual love]

Eros[2] (ˈɪərɒs, ˈɛrɒs) *n* an asteroid with a mean distance from the earth of 217 million kilometres, though it may come within 25 million kilometres.

erose (ɪˈrəʊs, -ˈrəʊz) *adj* jagged or uneven, as though gnawed or bitten: *erose leaves.* [C18: from Latin *ērōsus* eaten away, from *ērōdere* to ERODE] ▸ **eˈrosely** *adv*

erosion (ɪˈrəʊʒən) *n* **1** the wearing away of rocks and other deposits on the earth's surface by the action of water, ice, wind, etc. **2** the act or process of eroding or the state of being eroded. ▸ **eˈrosive** *or* **eˈrosional** *adj*

erotema (ˌɛrəʊˈtiːmə), **eroteme** (ˈɛrəʊˌtiːm), *or* **erotesis** (ˌɛrəʊˈtiːsɪs) *n Rhetoric.* a rhetorical question. [C16: New Latin, from Greek, from *erōtaein* to ask]

erotetic (ˌɛrəˈtɛtɪk) *adj* **1** *Rhetoric.* pertaining to a rhetorical question. **2** *Grammar, philosophy.* pertaining to questions; interrogative.

erotic (ɪˈrɒtɪk) *adj also* **erotical. 1** of, concerning, or arousing sexual desire or giving sexual pleasure. **2** marked by strong sexual desire or being especially sensitive to sexual stimulation. ◆ *n* **3** a person who has strong sexual desires or is especially responsive to sexual stimulation. [C17: from Greek *erōtikos* of love, from *erōs* love] ▸ **eˈrotically** *adv*

erotica (ɪˈrɒtɪkə) *pl n* explicitly sexual literature or art. [C19: from Greek *erōtika,* neuter plural of *erōtikos* EROTIC]

eroticism (ɪˈrɒtɪˌsɪzəm) *or* **erotism** (ˈɛrəˌtɪzəm) *n* **1** erotic quality or nature. **2** the use of sexually arousing or pleasing symbolism in literature or art. **3** sexual excitement or desire. **4** a tendency to exalt sex. **5** *Psychol.* an overt display of sexual behaviour.

eroticize *or* **eroticise** (ɪˈrɒtɪˌsaɪz) *vb* (*tr*) to regard or present in a sexual way. ▸ **eˌroticiˈzation** *or* **eˌroticiˈsation** *n*

eroto- *combining form.* denoting erotic desire, excitement, etc.: *erotogenic; erotology.* [from Greek *erōt-, erōs* love]

erotogenic (ɪˌrɒtəˈdʒɛnɪk) *adj* originating from or causing sexual stimulation; erogenous.

erotology (ˌɛrəˈtɒlədʒɪ) *n* **1** the study of erotic stimuli and sexual behaviour. **2** a description of such stimuli and behaviour. ▸ **erotological** (ˌɛrətəˈlɒdʒɪkᵊl) *adj* ▸ **ˌerotˈologist** *n*

erotomania (ɪˌrɒtəʊˈmeɪnɪə) *n* **1** abnormally strong sexual desire. **2** a condition in which a person is obsessed with another person and groundlessly believes that person to be in love with him or her. ▸ **eˌrotoˈmaniac** *n*

err (ɜː) *vb* (*intr*) **1** to make a mistake; be incorrect. **2** to stray from the right course or accepted standards; sin. **3** to act with bias, esp. favourable bias: *to err on the side of justice.* [C14: *erren* to wander, stray, from Old French *errer,* from Latin *errāre*]

errancy (ˈɛrənsɪ) *n, pl* **-cies. 1** the state or an instance of erring or a tendency to err. **2** *Christianity.* the holding of views at variance with accepted doctrine.

errand (ˈɛrənd) *n* **1** a short trip undertaken to perform a necessary task or commission (esp. in the phrase **run errands**). **2** the purpose or object of such a trip. [Old English *ǣrende;* related to *ār* messenger, Old Norse *erendi* message, Old High German *ārunti,* Swedish *ärende*]

errand boy *n* (in Britain, esp. formerly) a boy employed by a shopkeeper to deliver goods and run other errands.

errant (ˈɛrənt) *adj* (*often postpositive*) **1** *Archaic or literary.* wandering in search of adventure. **2** erring or straying from the right course or accepted standards. [C14: from Old French: journeying, from Vulgar Latin *iterāre* (unattested), from Latin *iter* journey; influenced by Latin *errāre* to ERR] ▸ **ˈerrantly** *adv*

errantry (ˈɛrəntrɪ) *n, pl* **-ries.** the way of life of a knight errant.

errata (ɪˈrɑːtə) *n* the plural of **erratum.**

erratic (ɪˈrætɪk) *adj* **1** irregular in performance, behaviour, or attitude; inconsistent and unpredictable. **2** having no fixed or regular course; wandering. ◆ *n* **3** a piece of rock that differs in composition, shape, etc., from the rock surrounding it, having been transported from its place of origin, esp. by glacial action. **4** an erratic person or thing. [C14: from Latin *errāticus,* from *errāre* to wander, ERR] ▸ **erˈratically** *adv*

erratum (ɪˈrɑːtəm) *n, pl* **-ta** (-tə). **1** an error in writing or printing. **2** another name for **corrigendum.** [C16: from Latin: mistake, from *errāre* to ERR]

errhine (ˈɛraɪn, ˈɛrɪn) *Med.* ◆ *adj* **1** causing nasal secretion. ◆ *n* **2** an errhine drug or agent. [C17: from Greek *errhinos,* from EN-[2] + *rhis* nose]

Er Rif (ɛə rɪf) *n* a mountainous region of N Morocco, near the Mediterranean coast.

erroneous (ɪˈrəʊnɪəs) *adj* based on or containing error; mistaken; incorrect. [C14: (in the sense: deviating from what is right), from Latin *errōneus,* from *errāre* to wander] ▸ **erˈroneously** *adv* ▸ **erˈroneousness** *n*

error (ˈɛrə) *n* **1** a mistake or inaccuracy, as in action or speech: *a typing error.* **2** an incorrect belief or wrong judgment. **3** the condition of deviating from accuracy or correctness, as in belief, action, or speech: *he was in error about the train times.* **4** deviation from a moral standard; wrongdoing: *he saw the error of his ways.* **5** *Maths, statistics.* a measure of the difference between some quantity and an approximation to or estimate of it, often expressed as a percentage: *an error of* $\pm 5\%$. **6** *Statistics.* see **type I error, type II error.** [C13: from Latin, from *errāre* to ERR] ▸ **ˈerror-ˌfree** *adj*

error correction *n Computing.* the automatic correction of errors in data that arise from missing or distorted digital pulses.

error message *n* a message displayed on a visual display unit, printout, etc., indicating that an incorrect instruction has been given to the computer.

error of closure *n Surveying.* the amount by which a computed, plotted, or observed quantity or position differs from the true or established one, esp. when plotting a closed traverse. Also called: **closing error.**

ERS *abbrev. for* earnings related supplement.

ersatz (ˈɛəzæts, ˈɜː-) *adj* **1** made in imitation of some natural or genuine product; artificial. ◆ *n* **2** an ersatz substance or article. [C20: German, from *ersetzen* to substitute]

Erse (ɜːs) *n* **1** another name for Irish **Gaelic.** ◆ *adj* **2** of or relating to the Irish Gaelic language. [C14: from Lowland Scots *Erisch* Irish; Irish being regarded as the literary form of Gaelic]

Ershad (ˈɜːʃæd) *n* **Hussain Mohammed.** born 1930, Bangladeshi soldier and statesman. He seized power in a coup in 1982, becoming president in 1983. He was deposed in 1990.

Erskine (ˈɜːskɪn) *n* **Thomas,** 1st Baron. 1750–1823, Scottish lawyer: noted as a defence advocate, esp. in cases involving civil liberties.

erst (ɜːst) *adv Archaic.* **1** long ago; formerly. **2** at first. [Old English *ǣrest* earliest, superlative of *ǣr* early; see ERE; related to Old High German *ērist,* Dutch *eerst*]

erstwhile (ˈɜːstˌwaɪl) *adj* **1** former; one-time: *my erstwhile companions.* ◆ *adv* **2** *Archaic.* long ago; formerly.

Erté (ɛrte) *n* real name *Romain de Tirtoff.* 1892–1990, French fashion illustrator and designer, born in Russia, noted for his extravagant costumes and tableaux for the Folies-Bergère in Paris.

erubescence (ˌɛrʊˈbɛsᵊns) *n* the process of growing red or a condition of redness. [C18: from Latin *ērubescentia* blushing, from *rubēscere* to grow red, from *ruber* red] ▸ **ˌeruˈbescent** *adj*

erucic acid (ɪˈruːsɪk) *n* a crystalline fatty acid derived from the oils of rapeseed, mustard seed, and wallflower seed.

eruct (ɪˈrʌkt) *or* **eructate** *vb* **1** to raise (gas and often a small quantity of acid) from the stomach; belch. **2** (of a volcano) to pour out (fumes or volcanic matter). [C17: from Latin *ēructāre,* from *ructāre* to belch] ▸ **eructation** (ɪˌrʌkˈteɪʃən, ˌiːrʌk-) *n* ▸ **eructative** (ɪˈrʌktətɪv) *adj*

erudite (ˈɛrʊˌdaɪt) *adj* having or showing extensive scholarship; learned. [C15: from Latin *ērudītus,* from *ērudīre* to polish, from EX-[1] + *rudis* unpolished, rough] ▸ **ˈeruˌditely** *adv* ▸ **erudition** (ˌɛrʊˈdɪʃən) *or* **ˈeruˌditeness** *n*

erumpent (ɪˈrʌmpənt) *adj* bursting out or (esp. of plant parts) developing as though bursting through an overlying structure. [C17: from Latin *ērumpere* to burst forth, from *rumpere* to shatter, burst]

erupt (ɪˈrʌpt) *vb* **1** to eject (steam, water, and volcanic material such as lava and ash) violently or (of volcanic material, etc.) to be so ejected. **2** (*intr*) (of a skin blemish) to appear on the skin; break out. **3** (*intr*) (of a tooth) to emerge through the gum and become visible during the normal process of tooth development. **4** (*intr*) to burst forth suddenly and violently, as from restraint: *to erupt in anger.* [C17: from Latin *ēruptus* having burst forth, from *ērumpere,* from *rumpere* to burst] ▸ **eˈruptible** *adj* ▸ **eˈruption** *n*

eruptive (ɪˈrʌptɪv) *adj* **1** erupting or tending to erupt. **2** resembling or of the nature of an eruption. **3** (of rocks) formed by solidification of magma; igneous. **4** (of a disease) characterized by skin eruptions. ▸ **eˈruptively** *adv* ▸ **eˌrupˈtivity** *or* **eˈruptiveness** *n*

eruv (ˈɛəruːv, ˈɛruːv) *n Judaism.* an area, circumscribed by a symbolic line, within which certain activities forbidden to Orthodox Jews on the Sabbath are permitted. [C20: from Hebrew, literally: mixture, mixing]

-ery *or* **-ry** *suffix forming nouns.* **1** indicating a place of business or some other activity: *bakery; brewery; refinery.* **2** indicating a class or collection of things: *cutlery; greenery.* **3** indicating qualities or actions collectively: *snobbery; trickery.* **4** indicating a practice or occupation: *husbandry.* **5** indicating a state or condition: *slavery.* [from Old French *-erie;* see -ER[1], -Y[3]]

Erymanthian boar (ˌɛrɪˈmænθɪən) *n Greek myth.* a wild boar that ravaged the district around Mount Erymanthus: captured by Hercules as his fourth labour.

Erymanthus (ˌɛrɪˈmænθəs) *n* **Mount.** a mountain in SW Greece, in the NW Peloponnese. Height: 2224 m (7297 ft.). Modern Greek name: **Erímanthos** (eˈrimanθɔs).

eryngium (ɪˈrɪndʒɪəm) *n* any plant of the temperate and sub-tropical perennial genus *Eryngium,* with distinctive spiny foliage, metallic blue flower heads, and bluish stems, several species of which are grown as garden plants: family *Umbelliferae.* See also **sea holly.** [New Latin, from Greek *ērynggion* a species of thistle]

eryngo (ɪˈrɪŋgəʊ) *n, pl* **-goes** *or* **-gos.** any umbelliferous plant of the genus *Eryngium,* such as the sea holly, having toothed or lobed leaves. Also called: **eringo.** [C16: from Latin *ēryngion* variety of thistle, from Greek *ērungion,* diminutive of *ērungos* thistle]

erysipelas (ˌɛrɪˈsɪpɪləs) *n* an acute streptococcal infectious disease of the skin, characterized by fever, headache, vomiting, and purplish raised lesions, esp. on the face. Also called: **Saint Anthony's fire.** [C16: from Latin, from Greek *erusipelas,* from Greek *erusi-* red + *-pelas* skin] ▸ **erysipelatous** (ˌɛrɪsɪˈpɛlətəs) *adj*

erysipeloid (ˌɛrɪˈsɪpɪˌlɔɪd) *n* an infective dermatitis mainly affecting the hands, characterized by inflammation and caused by the microorganism *Erysipelothrix rhusiopathiae* on contaminated meat, poultry, or fish: most prevalent among fishermen and butchers.

erythema (ˌɛrɪˈθiːmə) *n Pathol.* redness of the skin, usually occurring in patches, caused by irritation or injury to the tissue. [C18: from New Latin, from Greek *eruthēma,* from *eruthros* red] ▸ **erythematic** (ˌɛrɪθɪˈmætɪk), **erythematous** (ˌɛrɪˈθiːmətəs), *or* **ˌeryˈthemal** *adj*

erythraemia *or esp. U.S.* **erythremia** (ˌɛrɪˈθriːmɪə) *n Med.* another name for **polycythaemia vera** (see **polycythaemia**).

erythrism (ɪˈrɪθrɪzəm) *n* abnormal red coloration, as in plumage or hair. ▸ **erythrismal** (ˌɛrɪˈθrɪzməl) *adj*

erythrite (ɪˈrɪθraɪt) *n* **1** Also called: **cobalt bloom.** a pink to purple secondary mineral consisting of hydrated cobalt arsenate in monoclinic crystalline form. Formula: $Co_3(AsO_4)_2.8H_2O$. **2** another name for **erythritol.**

erythritol (ɪˈrɪθrɪˌtɒl) *or* **erythrite** *n* a sweet crystalline compound extracted from certain algae and lichens and used in medicine to dilate the blood vessels of the heart; 1,2,3,4-butanetetrol. Formula: $C_4H_{10}O_4$.

erythro- *or before a vowel* **erythr-** *combining form.* red: *erythrocyte.* [from Greek *eruthros* red]

erythroblast (ɪ'rɪθrəʊˌblæst) *n* a nucleated cell in bone marrow that develops into an erythrocyte. ▸ **eˌrythro'blastic** *adj*

erythroblastosis (ɪˌrɪθrəʊblæ'stəʊsɪs) *n* **1** the abnormal presence of erythroblasts in the circulating blood. **2** an anaemic blood disease of a fetus or newborn child, characterized by erythroblasts in the circulating blood: caused by a blood incompatibility between mother and fetus.

erythrocyte (ɪ'rɪθrəʊˌsaɪt) *n* a blood cell of vertebrates that transports oxygen and carbon dioxide, combined with the red pigment haemoglobin, to and from the tissues. Also called: **red blood cell.** ▸ **erythrocytic** (ɪˌrɪθrəʊ'sɪtɪk) *adj*

erythrocytometer (ɪˌrɪθrəʊsaɪ'tɒmɪtə) *n* an instrument for counting the number or measuring the size of red blood cells in a sample of blood. ▸ **eˌrythrocy'tometry** *n*

erythromycin (ɪˌrɪθrəʊ'maɪsɪn) *n* an antibiotic used in treating infections caused by Gram-positive bacteria. It is obtained from the bacterium *Streptomyces erythreus.* Formula: $C_{37}M_{67}NO_{13}$. [C20: from ERYTHRO- + Greek *mukēs* fungus + -IN]

erythronium (ˌɛrɪ'θrəʊnɪəm) *n* any plant of the bulbous genus *Erythronium,* with decoratively mottled leaves and cyclamen-like yellow, rose, purple, or white flowers: family *Liliaceae.* See also **dogtooth violet.** [New Latin, from Greek *erythros* red]

erythropenia (ɪˌrɪθrəʊ'piːnɪə) *n* the presence of decreased numbers of erythrocytes in the blood, as occurs in some forms of anaemia. [from ERYTHRO- + Greek *penia* poverty]

erythropoiesis (ɪˌrɪθrəʊpɔɪ'iːsɪs) *n Physiol.* the formation of red blood cells. [C19: from ERYTHRO- + Greek *poiēsis* a making, from *poiein* to make] ▸ **eˌrythropoi'etic** *adj*

erythropoietin (ɪˌrɪθrəʊpɔɪ'iːtɪn) *n* a hormone, secreted by the kidney in response to low levels of oxygen in the tissues, that increases the rate of erythropoiesis.

erythropsia (ˌɛrɪ'θrɒpsɪə) *n Med.* a defect of vision in which objects appear red.

Erzgebirge (*German* 'eːrtsgəbɪrgə) *pl n* a mountain range on the border between Germany and the Czech Republic: formerly rich in mineral resources. Highest peak: Mount Klínovec (Keilberg), 1244 m (4081 ft.). Czech name: **Krušné Hory.** Also called: **Ore Mountains.**

Erzurum ('ɛəzʊrʊm) *n* a city in E Turkey: a strategic centre; scene of two major battles against Russian forces (1877 and 1916); important military base and a closed city to unofficial visitors. Pop.: 247 585 (1995 est.).

Es *the chemical symbol for* einsteinium.

ES *international car registration for* El Salvador.

-es *suffix.* **1** a variant of **-s**[1] for nouns ending in *ch, s, sh, z,* postconsonantal *y,* for some nouns ending in a vowel, and nouns in *f* with *v* in the plural: *ashes; heroes; calves.* **2** a variant of **-s**[2] for verbs ending in *ch, s, sh, z,* postconsonantal *y,* or a vowel: *preaches; steadies; echoes.*

ESA *abbrev. for:* **1** Environmentally Sensitive Area: an area which contains a natural feature, such as the habitat of a rare species, and which is protected by government regulations. **2** European Space Agency.

Esaki diode (ɪ'sɑːkɪ) *n* another name for **tunnel diode.** [named after L. *Esaki* (born 1925), its Japanese designer]

Esau ('iːsɔː) *n Bible.* son of Isaac and Rebecca and twin brother of Jacob, to whom he sold his birthright (Genesis 25).

ESB *abbrev. for* electrical stimulation of the brain.

Esbjerg (*Danish* 'ɛsbjɛr) *n* a port in SW Denmark, in Jutland on the North Sea: Denmark's chief fishing port. Pop.: 82 579 (1995 est.).

escadrille (ˌɛskə'drɪl; *French* ɛskadrij) *n* **1** a French squadron of aircraft, esp. in World War I. **2** a small squadron of ships. [from French: flotilla, from Spanish *escuadrilla,* from *escuadra* SQUADRON]

escalade (ˌɛskə'leɪd) *n* **1** an assault by the use of ladders, esp. on a fortification. ◆ *vb* **2** to gain access to (a place) by the use of ladders. [C16: from French, from Italian *scalata,* from *scalare* to mount, SCALE[3]] ▸ **ˌesca'lader** *n*

escalate ('ɛskəˌleɪt) *vb* to increase or be increased in extent, intensity, or magnitude: *to escalate a war; prices escalated because of inflation.* [C20: back formation from ESCALATOR] ▸ **ˌesca'lation** *n*

escalator ('ɛskəˌleɪtə) *n* **1** a moving staircase consisting of stair treads fixed to a conveyor belt, for transporting passengers between levels, esp. between the floors of a building. **2** short for **escalator clause.** [C20: originally a trademark]

escalator clause *n* a clause in a contract stipulating an adjustment in wages, prices, etc., in the event of specified changes in conditions, such as a large rise in the cost of living or price of raw materials.

escallonia (ˌɛskə'ləʊnɪə) *n* any evergreen shrub of the South American saxifragaceous genus *Escallonia,* with white or red flowers: cultivated for ornament. [C19: from *Escallon,* 18th-century Spanish traveller who discovered it]

escallop (ɛ'skɒləp, ɛ'skæl-) *n, vb* another word for **scallop.**

escalope ('ɛskəˌlɒp) *n* a thin slice of meat, usually veal, coated with egg and breadcrumbs, fried, and served with a rich sauce. [C19: from Old French: shell]

escapade ('ɛskəˌpeɪd, ˌɛskə'peɪd) *n* **1** a wild or exciting adventure, esp. one that is mischievous or unlawful; scrape. **2** any lighthearted or carefree episode; prank; romp. [C17: from French, from Old Italian *scappata,* from Vulgar Latin *excappāre* (unattested) to ESCAPE]

escape (ɪ'skeɪp) *vb* **1** to get away or break free from (confinements, captors, etc.): *the lion escaped from the zoo.* **2** to manage to avoid (imminent danger, punishment, evil, etc.): *to escape death.* **3** (*intr;* usually foll. by *from*) (of gases, liquids, etc.) to issue gradually, as from a crack or fissure; seep; leak: *water was escaping from the dam.* **4** (*tr*) to elude; be forgotten by: *the actual figure escapes me.* **5** (*tr*) to be articulated inadvertently or involuntarily: *a roar escaped his lips.* **6** (*intr*) (of cultivated plants) to grow wild. ◆ *n* **7** the act of escaping or state of having escaped. **8** avoidance of injury, harm, etc.: *a narrow escape.* **9a** a means or way of escape. **9b** (*as modifier*): *an escape route.* **10** a means of distraction or relief, esp. from reality or boredom: *angling provides an escape for many city dwellers.* **11** a gradual outflow; leakage; seepage. **12** Also called: **escape valve, escape cock.** a valve that releases air, steam, etc., above a certain pressure; relief valve. **13** a plant that was originally cultivated but is now growing wild. [C14: from Old Northern French *escaper,* from Vulgar Latin *excappāre* (unattested) to escape (literally: to remove one's cloak, hence free oneself), from EX-[1] + Late Latin *cappa* cloak] ▸ **es'capable** *adj* ▸ **es'caper** *n*

escape clause *n* a clause in a contract freeing one of the parties from his obligations in certain circumstances.

escapee (ɪˌskeɪ'piː) *n* a person who has escaped, esp. an escaped prisoner.

escape hatch *n* a means of escape in an emergency, esp. from a submarine.

escape mechanism *n Psychol.* any emotional or mental mechanism that enables a person to avoid acknowledging unpleasant or threatening realities. See also **escapism.**

escapement (ɪ'skeɪpmənt) *n* **1** *Horology.* a mechanism consisting of an escape wheel and anchor, used in timepieces to provide periodic impulses to the pendulum or balance. **2** any similar mechanism that regulates movement, usually consisting of toothed wheels engaged by rocking levers. **3** (in a piano) the mechanism that allows the hammer to clear the string after striking, so that the string can vibrate. **4** an overflow channel. **5** *Rare.* an act or means of escaping.

escape pipe *n* a pipe for overflowing water, escaping steam, etc.

escape road *n* a road, usually ending in a pile of sand, provided on a hill for a driver to drive into if his brakes fail or on a bend if he loses control of the turn.

escape routine *n Computing.* a means of leaving a computer-program sequence before its end, in order to commence another sequence.

escape shaft *n* a shaft in a mine through which miners can escape if the regular shaft is blocked.

escape velocity *n* the minimum velocity that a body must have in order to escape from the gravitational field of the earth or other celestial body.

escape wheel *n Horology.* a toothed wheel that engages intermittently with a balance wheel or pendulum, causing the mechanism to oscillate and thereby moving the hands of a clock or watch. Also called: **scapewheel.**

escapism (ɪ'skeɪpɪzəm) *n* an inclination to or habit of retreating from unpleasant reality, as through diversion or fantasy. ▸ **es'capist** *n, adj*

escapologist (ˌɛskə'pɒlədʒɪst) *n* an entertainer who specializes in freeing himself from confinement. Also called: **escape artist.** ▸ **ˌesca'pology** *n*

escargot *French.* (ɛskargo) *n* a variety of edible snail, usually eaten with a sauce made of melted butter and garlic.

escarp (ɪ'skɑːp) *n* **1** *Fortifications.* the inner side of the ditch separating besiegers and besieged. Compare **counterscarp.** ◆ *vb* **2** a rare word for **scarp** (sense 3). [C17: from French *escarpe;* see SCARP]

escarpment (ɪ'skɑːpmənt) *n* **1a** the long continuous steep face of a ridge or plateau formed by erosion; scarp. **1b** any steep slope, such as one resulting from faulting. **2** a steep artificial slope immediately in front of the rampart of a fortified place.

Escaut (ɛsko) *n* the French name for the **Scheldt.**

-escent *suffix forming adjectives.* beginning to be, do, show, etc.: *convalescent; luminescent.* [via Old French from Latin *-ēscent-,* stem of present participial suffix of *-ēscere,* ending of inceptive verbs] ▸ **-escence** *suffix forming nouns.*

eschalot ('ɛʃəˌlɒt, ˌɛʃə'lɒt) *n* another name for a **shallot.** [C18: from Old French *eschalotte* a little SCALLION]

eschar ('ɛskɑː) *n* a dry scab or slough, esp. one following a burn or cauterization of the skin. [C16: from Late Latin *eschara* scab, from Greek *eskhara* hearth, pan of hot coals (which could inflict burns); see SCAR[1]]

escharotic (ˌɛskə'rɒtɪk) *Med.* ◆ *adj* **1** capable of producing an eschar. ◆ *n* **2** a caustic or corrosive agent.

eschatology (ˌɛskə'tɒlədʒɪ) *n* the branch of theology or biblical exegesis concerned with the end of the world. [C19: from Greek *eskhatos* last] ▸ **eschatological** (ˌɛskətə'lɒdʒɪkᵊl) *adj* ▸ **ˌeschato'logically** *adv* ▸ **ˌescha'tologist** *n*

escheat (ɪs'tʃiːt) *Law.* ◆ *n* **1** (in England before 1926) the reversion of property to the Crown in the absence of legal heirs. **2** (in feudal times) the reversion of property to the feudal lord in the absence of legal heirs or upon outlawry of the tenant. **3** the property so reverting. ◆ *vb* **4** to take (land) by escheat or (of land) to revert by escheat. [C14: from Old French *eschete,* from *escheoir* to fall to the lot of, from Late Latin *excadere* (unattested), from Latin *cadere* to fall] ▸ **es'cheatable** *adj* ▸ **es'cheatage** *n*

Escher figure ('ɛʃə) *n* another name for **impossible figure.** [named after M. C. *Escher* (1898–1970), Dutch graphic artist who produced many such drawings]

Escherichia (ˌɛʃə'rɪkɪə) *n* a genus of Gram-negative rodlike bacteria that form acid and gas in the presence of carbohydrates and are found in the intestines of man and many animals, esp. *E. coli,* which is sometimes pathogenic and is widely used in genetic research. [C19: named after Theodor *Escherich* (1857–1911), German paediatrician who first described *E. coli*]

eschew (ɪs'tʃuː) *vb* (*tr*) to keep clear of or abstain from (something disliked, injurious, etc.); shun; avoid. [C14: from Old French *eschiver,* of Germanic origin; compare Old High German *skiuhan* to frighten away; see SHY[1], SKEW] ▸ **es'chewal** *n* ▸ **es'chewer** *n*

eschscholtzia *or* **eschscholzia** (ɛ'ʃɒltsɪə) *n* See **California poppy.** [named after J. F. von *Eschscholtz* (1743–1831), German naturalist]

Escoffier (*French* ɛskɔfje) *n* (**Georges**) **Auguste** (ogyst). 1846–1935, French chef at the Savoy Hotel, London (1890–99).

escolar (ˌɛskəˈlɑː) *n, pl* **-lars** *or* **-lar.** any slender spiny-finned fish of the family *Gempylidae,* of warm and tropical seas: similar and closely related to the scombroid fishes. Also called: **snake mackerel.** [from Spanish: SCHOLAR; so called from the rings round its eyes, suggestive of spectacles]

Escorial (ˌɛskɒrɪˈɑːl, ɛˈskɔːrɪəl) *or* **Escurial** *n* a village in central Spain, northwest of Madrid: site of an architectural complex containing a monastery, palace, and college, built by Philip II between 1563 and 1584.

escort *n* (ˈɛskɔːt). **1** one or more persons, soldiers, vehicles, etc., accompanying another or others for protection, guidance, restraint, or as a mark of honour. **2** a man or youth who accompanies a woman or girl: *he was her escort for the evening.* **3a** a person, esp. a young woman, who may be hired to accompany another for entertainment, etc. **3b** (*as modifier*): *an escort agency.* ◆ *vb* (ɪsˈkɔːt). **4** (*tr*) to accompany or attend as an escort. [C16: from French *escorte,* from Italian *scorta,* from *scorgere* to guide, from Latin *corrigere* to straighten; see CORRECT]

escribe (ɪˈskraɪb) *vb* (*tr*) to draw (a circle) so that it is tangential to one side of a triangle and to the other two sides produced. [C16 (meaning: to write out): from EX-[1] + Latin *scrībere* to write]

escritoire (ˌɛskrɪˈtwɑː) *n* a writing desk with compartments and drawers, concealed by a hinged flap, on a chest of drawers or plain stand. [C18: from French, from Medieval Latin *scriptōrium* writing room in a monastery, from Latin *scrībere* to write]

escrow (ˈɛskrəʊ, ɛˈskrəʊ) *Law.* ◆ *n* **1** money, goods, or a written document, such as a contract bond, delivered to a third party and held by him pending fulfilment of some condition. **2** the state or condition of being an escrow (esp. in the phrase **in escrow**). ◆ *vb* (*tr*) **3** to place (money, a document, etc.) in escrow. [C16: from Old French *escroe,* of Germanic origin; see SCREED, SHRED, SCROLL]

escuage (ˈɛskjuɪdʒ) *n* (in medieval Europe) another word for **scutage.** [C16: from Old French, from *escu* shield, from Latin *scūtum*]

escudo (ɛˈskuːdəʊ; *Portuguese* ɪʃˈkuðu) *n, pl* **-dos** (-dəʊz; *Portuguese* -ðuʃ). **1** the standard monetary unit of Cape Verde and Portugal, divided into 100 centavos. **2** a former monetary unit of Chile, divided into 100 centesimos. **3** an old Spanish silver coin worth 10 reals. [C19: Spanish, literally: shield, from Latin *scūtum*]

esculent (ˈɛskjʊlənt) *n* **1** any edible substance. ◆ *adj* **2** edible. [C17: from Latin *ēsculentus* good to eat, from *ēsca* food, from *edere* to eat]

Escurial (ɛˌskjʊərɪˈɑːl, ɛˈskjʊərɪəl) *n* a variant of **Escorial.**

escutcheon (ɪˈskʌtʃən) *n* **1** a shield, esp. a heraldic one that displays a coat of arms. **2** Also called: **escutcheon plate.** a plate or shield that surrounds a keyhole, door handle, light switch, etc., esp. an ornamental one protecting a door or wall surface. **3** the place on the stern or transom of a vessel where the name is shown. **4 blot on one's escutcheon.** a stain on one's honour. [C15: from Old Northern French *escuchon,* ultimately from Latin *scūtum* shield] ▸ **es'cutcheoned** *adj*

Esd. *Bible. abbrev. for* Esdras.

ESDA *or* **Esda** (ˈɛzdə) *n acronym for* Electrostatic Deposition Analysis: a technique used to check the sequence in which a statement written in police custody was made. The chronology of the statement is arrived at by the examination of indentations on subsequent pages.

Esdraelon (ˌɛsdreɪˈiːlɒn) *n* a plain in N Israel, east of Mount Carmel. Also called: (Plain of) **Jezreel.**

Esdras (ˈɛzdræs) *n* **1** either of two books of the Apocrypha, **I** and **II Esdras,** called **III** and **IV Esdras** in the Douay Bible. **2** either of two books of the Douay Bible Old Testament, **I** and **II Esdras,** corresponding to the books of Ezra and Nehemiah in the Authorized Version.

ESE *symbol. for* east-southeast.

-ese *suffix forming adjectives and nouns.* indicating place of origin, language, or style: *Cantonese; Japanese; journalese.*

esemplastic (ˌɛsɛmˈplæstɪk) *adj Literature.* making into one; unifying. [C19 (first used by Samuel Taylor Coleridge): from Greek *es, eis* into + *em,* from *hen,* neuter of *heis* one + -PLASTIC]

Esenin (jeˈsenɪn) *or* **Yesenin** *n* **Sergey Aleksandrovich.** 1895–1925, Soviet poet, author of *Confessions of a Hooligan* (1924): married to Isadora Duncan.

eserine (ˈɛsəriːn, -rɪn) *n* another name for **physostigmine.** [C19: *eser-,* of African origin + -INE[2]]

Eşfahān (ˌɛʃfəˈhɑːn) *n* a variant of **Isfahan.**

ESG (in Britain) *abbrev. for* Educational Support Grant: a government grant given to a Local Education Authority to fund educational schemes dealing with important social issues, such as drug abuse.

Esher (ˈiːʃə) *n* a town in SE England, in NE Surrey near London: racecourse. Pop.: 46 599 (1991).

esker (ˈɛskə) *or* **eskar** (ˈɛskɑː, -kə) *n* a long winding ridge of gravel, sand, etc., originally deposited by a meltwater stream running under a glacier. Also called: **os.** [C19: from Old Irish *escir* ridge]

Eskilstuna (*Swedish* ˈeskilstuːna) *n* an industrial city in SE Sweden. Pop.: 89 761 (1994).

Eskimo (ˈɛskɪˌməʊ) *n* **1** (*pl* **-mos** *or* **-mo**) a member of a group of peoples inhabiting N Canada, Greenland, Alaska, and E Siberia, having a material culture adapted to an extremely cold climate. **2** the language of these peoples. **3** a family of languages that includes Eskimo and Aleut. ◆ *adj* **4** relating to, denoting, or characteristic of the Eskimos. ◆ Former spelling: **Esquimau.** See also **Inuit, Inuktitut.** [C18 *Esquimawes:* related to Abnaki *esquimantsic* eaters of raw flesh]

USAGE *Eskimo* is considered by many people to be offensive, and in North America the term *Inuit* is often used.

Eskimo dog *n* a large powerful breed of sled dog with a long thick coat and curled tail.

Eskişehir (*Turkish* ɛsˈkiʃɛˌhir) *n* an industrial city in NW Turkey: founded around hot springs in Byzantine times. Pop.: 455 285 (1995 est.).

Esky (ˈɛskɪ) *n, pl* **-kies.** (*sometimes not cap.*) *Austral. trademark.* a portable insulated container for keeping food and drink cool. [C20: from ESKIMO, alluding to the Eskimos' cold habitat]

ESL *abbrev. for* English as a second language.

ESN *abbrev. for* educationally subnormal; formerly used to designate a person of limited intelligence who needs special schooling.

esophagus (iːˈsɒfəgəs) *n, pl* **-gi** (-ˌdʒaɪ) *or* **-guses.** the U.S. spelling of **oesophagus.** ▸ **esophageal** (iːˌsɒfəˈdʒiːəl) *adj*

esoteric (ˌɛsəʊˈtɛrɪk) *adj* **1** restricted to or intended for an enlightened or initiated minority, esp. because of abstruseness or obscurity: *an esoteric cult.* Compare **exoteric. 2** difficult to understand; abstruse: *an esoteric statement.* **3** not openly admitted; private: *esoteric aims.* [C17: from Greek *esōterikos,* from *esōterō* inner] ▸ **ˌesoˈterically** *adv* ▸ **ˌesoˈteriˌcism** *n*

ESP *abbrev. for:* **1** English for specific (*or* Special) Purposes: the technique of teaching English to students who need it for a particular purpose, such as business dealings. **2** extrasensory perception.

esp. *abbrev. for* especially.

espadrille (ˌɛspəˈdrɪl) *n* a light shoe with a canvas upper, esp. with a braided cord sole. [C19: from French, from Provençal *espardilho,* diminutive of *espart* ESPARTO; so called from the use of esparto for the soles of such shoes]

espalier (ɪˈspæljə) *n* **1** an ornamental shrub or fruit tree that has been trained to grow flat, as against a wall. **2** the trellis, framework, or arrangement of stakes on which such plants are trained. **3** the method used to produce such plants. ◆ *vb* **4** (*tr*) to train (a plant) on an espalier. [C17: from French: trellis, from Old Italian: shoulder supports, from *spalla* shoulder, from Late Latin SPATULA]

España (esˈpaɲa) *n* the Spanish name for **Spain.**

esparto *or* **esparto grass** (ɛˈspɑːtəʊ) *n, pl* **-tos.** any of various grasses, esp. *Stipa tenacissima* of S Europe and N Africa, that yield a fibre used to make ropes, mats, etc. [C18: from Spanish, via Latin from Greek *sparton* rope made of rushes, from *spartos* a kind of rush]

especial (ɪˈspɛʃəl) *adj* (*prenominal*) **1** unusual; notable; exceptional: *he paid especial attention to her that evening.* **2** applying to one person or thing in particular; not general; specific; peculiar: *he had an especial dislike of relatives.* [C14: from Old French, from Latin *speciālis* individual; see SPECIAL] ▸ **es'pecially** *adv*

USAGE *Especial* and *especially* have a more limited use than *special* and *specially. Special* is always used in preference to *especial* when the sense is one of being out of the ordinary: *a special lesson; he has been specially trained. Special* is also used when something is referred to as being for a particular purpose: *the word was specially underlined for you.* Where an idea of preeminence or individuality is involved, either *especial* or *special* may be used: *he is my especial* (or *special*) *friend; he is especially* (or *specially*) *good at his job.* In informal English, however, *special* is usually preferred in all contexts.

esperance (ˈɛspərəns) *n Archaic.* hope or expectation. [C15: from Old French, from Vulgar Latin *sperantia* (unattested), from Latin *spērāre* to hope, from *spēs* hope]

Esperanto (ˌɛspəˈræntəʊ) *n* an international artificial language based on words common to the chief European languages, invented in 1887. [C19: literally: the one who hopes, pseudonym of Dr. L. L. Zamenhof (1859–1917), Polish philologist who invented it] ▸ **ˌEspeˈrantist** *n, adj*

espial (ɪˈspaɪəl) *n Archaic.* **1** the act or fact of being seen or discovered. **2** the act of noticing. **3** the act of spying upon; secret observation.

espionage (ˈɛspɪəˌnɑːʒ, ˌɛspɪəˈnɑːʒ, ˈɛspɪənɪdʒ) *n* **1** the systematic use of spies to obtain secret information, esp. by governments to discover military or political secrets. **2** the act or practice of spying. [C18: from French *espionnage,* from *espionner* to spy, from *espion* spy, from Old Italian *spione,* of Germanic origin; compare German *spähen* to SPY]

Espírito Santo (*Portuguese* ɪʃˈpiritu ˈsɐntu) *n* a state of E Brazil, on the Atlantic: swampy coastal plain with mountains in the west; heavily forested. Capital: Vitória. Pop.: 2 786 700 (1995 est.). Area: 45 597 sq. km (17 601 sq. miles).

Espíritu Santo (ɛsˈpɪrɪtu ˈsæntəʊ) *n* an island in the SW Pacific: the largest and westernmost of the Vanuatu islands. Pop.: 25 581 (1989). Area: 4856 sq. km (1875 sq. miles).

esplanade (ˌɛspləˈneɪd, -ˈnɑːd) *n* **1** a long open level stretch of ground for walking along, esp. beside the seashore. Compare **promenade** (sense 1). **2** an open area in front of a fortified place, in which attackers are exposed to the defenders' fire. [C17: from French, from Old Italian *spianata,* from *spianare* to make level, from Latin *explānāre;* see EXPLAIN]

Espoo (*Finnish* ˈespoː) *n* a city in S Finland. Pop.: 196 260 (1997 est.).

espousal (ɪˈspaʊzᵊl) *n* **1** adoption or support: *an espousal of new beliefs.* **2** (*sometimes pl*) *Archaic.* a marriage or betrothal ceremony.

espouse (ɪˈspaʊz) *vb* (*tr*) **1** to adopt or give support to (a cause, ideal, etc.): *to espouse socialism.* **2** *Archaic.* (esp. of a man) to take as spouse; marry. [C15: from Old French *espouser,* from Latin *spōnsāre* to affiance, espouse] ▸ **es'pouser** *n*

espressivo (ˌɛsprɛˈsiːvəʊ) *adj, adv Music.* (to be performed) in an expressive manner. [Italian]

espresso (ɛˈsprɛsəʊ) *n, pl* **-sos. 1** strong coffee made by forcing steam or boiling water through ground coffee beans. **2** an apparatus for making coffee in this way. [C20: Italian, short for *caffè espresso,* literally: pressed coffee]

esprit (ɛˈspriː) *n* spirit and liveliness, esp. in wit. [C16: from French, from Latin *spīritus* a breathing, SPIRIT[1]]

esprit de corps (ɛˈspriː də ˈkɔː; *French* ɛspri də kɔr) *n* consciousness of and pride in belonging to a particular group; the sense of shared purpose and fellowship.

espy (ɪ'spaɪ) *vb* **-pies, -pying, -pied.** (*tr*) to catch sight of or perceive (something distant or previously unnoticed); detect: *to espy a ship on the horizon.* [C14: from Old French *espier* to SPY, of Germanic origin] ▸ **es'pier** *n*

Esq. *abbrev. for* esquire: used esp. in correspondence.

-esque *suffix forming adjectives.* indicating a specified character, manner, style, or resemblance: *picturesque; Romanesque; statuesque; Chaplinesque.* [via French from Italian *-esco,* of Germanic origin; compare -ISH]

Esquiline ('ɛskwəˌlaɪn) *n* one of the seven hills on which ancient Rome was built.

Esquimau ('ɛskɪˌməʊ) *n, pl* **-maus** *or* **-mau,** *adj* a former spelling of **Eskimo.**

esquire (ɪ'skwaɪə) *n* **1** *Chiefly Brit.* a title of respect, usually abbreviated *Esq.,* placed after a man's name. **2** (in medieval times) the attendant and shield bearer of a knight, subsequently often knighted himself. **3** *Rare.* a male escort. [C15: from Old French *escuier,* from Late Latin *scūtārius* shield bearer, from Latin *scūtum* shield]

ESR *abbrev. for* electron spin resonance.

ESRC *abbrev. for* Economic and Social Research Council.

ESRO ('ezrəʊ) *n acronym for* European Space Research Organization.

-ess *suffix forming nouns.* indicating a female: *waitress; lioness.* [via Old French from Late Latin *-issa,* from Greek]

USAGE The suffix *-ess* in such words as *poetess, authoress* is now often regarded as disparaging; a sexually neutral term *poet, author* is preferred.

Essaouira (ˌɛsə'wɪərə) *n* a port in SW Morocco on the Atlantic. Pop.: 42 000 (1982). Former name (until 1956): **Mogador.**

essay *n* ('ɛseɪ; *senses 2,3 also* ɛ'seɪ). **1** a short literary composition dealing with a subject analytically or speculatively. **2** an attempt or endeavour; effort. **3** a test or trial. ◆ *vb* (ɛ'seɪ). (*tr*) **4** to attempt or endeavour; try. **5** to test or try out. [C15: from Old French *essaier* to attempt, from *essai* an attempt, from Late Latin *exagium* a weighing, from Latin *agere* to do, compel, influenced by *exigere* to investigate]

essayist ('ɛseɪɪst) *n* a person who writes essays.

esse ('ɛsɪ) *n Philosophy.* **1** existence. **2** essential nature; essence. [C17: from Latin: to be]

Essen (*German* 'ɛsən) *n* a city in W Germany, in North Rhine-Westphalia: the leading administrative centre of the Ruhr; university. Pop.: 614 861 (1996 est.).

essence ('ɛsᵊns) *n* **1** the characteristic or intrinsic feature of a thing, which determines its identity; fundamental nature. **2** the most distinctive element of a thing: *the essence of a problem.* **3** a perfect or complete form of something, esp. a person who typifies an abstract quality: *he was the essence of gentility.* **4** *Philosophy.* **4a** the unchanging and unchangeable nature of something which is necessary to its being the thing it is; its necessary properties. Compare **accident** (sense 4). **4b** the properties in virtue of which something is called by its name. **4c** the nature of something as distinct from, and logically prior to, its existence. **5** *Theol.* an immaterial or spiritual entity. **6a** the constituent of a plant, usually an oil, alkaloid, or glycoside, that determines its chemical or pharmacological properties. **6b** an alcoholic solution of such a substance. **7** a substance, usually a liquid, containing the properties of a plant or foodstuff in concentrated form: *vanilla essence.* **8** a rare word for **perfume. 9 in essence.** essentially; fundamentally. **10 of the essence.** indispensable; vitally important. [C14: from Medieval Latin *essentia,* from Latin: the being (of something), from *esse* to be]

Essene ('ɛsiːn, ɛ'siːn) *n Judaism.* a member of an ascetic sect that flourished in Palestine from the second century B.C. to the second century A.D., living in strictly organized communities. ▸ **Essenian** (ɛ'siːnɪən) *or* **Essenic** (ɛ'sɛnɪk) *adj*

essential (ɪ'sɛnʃəl) *adj* **1** vitally important; absolutely necessary. **2** basic; fundamental: *the essential feature.* **3** completely realized; absolute; perfect: *essential beauty.* **4** *Biochem.* (of an amino acid or a fatty acid) necessary for the normal growth of an organism but not synthesized by the organism and therefore required in the diet. **5** derived from or relating to an extract of a plant, drug, etc.: *an essential oil.* **6** *Logic.* (of a property) guaranteed by the identity of the subject; necessary. Thus, if having the atomic number 79 is an essential property of gold, nothing can be gold unless it has that atomic number. **7** *Music.* denoting or relating to a note that belongs to the fundamental harmony of a chord or piece. **8** *Pathol.* (of a disease) having no obvious external cause: *essential hypertension.* **9** *Geology.* (of a mineral constituent of a rock) necessary for defining the classification of a rock. Its absence alters the rock's name and classification. ◆ *n* **10** something fundamental or indispensable: *a sharp eye is an essential for a printer.* **11** *Music.* an essential note. ▸ **essentiality** (ɪˌsɛnʃɪ'ælɪtɪ) *or* **es'sentialness** *n* ▸ **es'sentially** *adv*

essential element *n Biochem.* any chemical element required by an organism for healthy growth. It may be required in large amounts (see **macronutrient**) or in very small amounts (see **trace element**).

essentialism (ɪ'sɛnʃəˌlɪzəm) *n* **1** *Philosophy.* one of a number of related doctrines which hold that there are necessary properties of things, that these are logically prior to the existence of the individuals which instantiate them, and that their classification depends upon their satisfaction of sets of necessary conditions. **2** the doctrine that education should concentrate on teaching basic skills and encouraging intellectual self-discipline. ▸ **es'sentialist** *n*

essential oil *n* any of various volatile organic oils present in plants, usually containing terpenes and esters and having the odour or flavour of the plant from which they are extracted: used in flavouring and perfumery. Compare **fixed oil.** See also **oleoresin.**

Essequibo (ˌɛsɪ'kwiːbəʊ) *n* a river in Guyana, rising near the Brazilian border and flowing north to the Atlantic: drains over half of Guyana. Length: 1014 km (630 miles).

Essex[1] ('ɛsɪks) *n* **1** a county of SE England, on the North Sea and the Thames estuary. Administrative centre: Chelmsford. Pop.: 1 569 900 (1994 est.). Area: 3672 sq. km (1417 sq. miles). **2** an Anglo-Saxon kingdom that in the early 7th century A.D. comprised the modern county of Essex and much of Hertfordshire and Surrey. By the late 8th century, Essex had become a dependency of the kingdom of Mercia.

Essex[2] ('ɛsɪks) *n* **2nd Earl of,** title of *Robert Devereux.* ?1566–1601, English soldier and favourite of Queen Elizabeth I; executed for treason.

Essex Man *n Informal, derogatory.* a working man, typically a Londoner who has moved out to Essex, who flaunts his new-found success and status.

Esslingen ('ɛsˌlɪŋən) *n* a town in SW Germany, on the River Neckar: Gothic church, medieval buildings: wines, light industry. Pop.: 91 685 (1991 est.).

essonite ('ɛsəˌnaɪt) *n* a variant spelling of **hessonite.**

Essonne (*French* ɛsɔn) *n* a department of N France, south of Paris in Île-de-France region: formed in 1964. Capital: Évry. Pop.: 1 145 900 (1995). Area: 1811 sq. km (706 sq. miles).

est (ɛst) *n* a treatment intended to help people towards psychological growth, in which they spend many hours in large groups, deprived of food and water and hectored by stewards. [*E*rhard *S*eminars *T*raining; after Werner Erhard, American businessman, who devised the system]

EST *abbrev. for:* **1** (in the U.S. and Canada) Eastern Standard Time. **2** electric-shock treatment.

est. *abbrev. for:* **1** Also: **estab.** established. **2** *Law.* estate. **3** estimate(d). **4** estuary.

-est[1] *suffix.* forming the superlative degree of adjectives and adverbs: *shortest; fastest.* [Old English *-est, -ost*]

-est[2] *or* **-st** *suffix.* forming the archaic second person singular present and past indicative tense of verbs: *thou goest; thou hadst.* [Old English *-est, -ast*]

establish (ɪ'stæblɪʃ) *vb* (*usually tr*) **1** to make secure or permanent in a certain place, condition, job, etc.: *to establish one's usefulness; to establish a house.* **2** to create or set up (an organization, etc.) on or as if on a permanent basis: *to establish a company.* **3** to prove correct or free from doubt; validate: *to establish a fact.* **4** to cause (a principle, theory, etc.) to be widely or permanently accepted: *to establish a precedent.* **5** to give (a Church) the status of a national institution. **6** (of a person) to become recognized and accepted: *he established himself as a reliable GP.* **7** (in works of imagination) to cause (a character, place, etc.) to be credible and recognized: *the first scene established the period.* **8** *Cards.* to make winners of (the remaining cards of a suit) by forcing out opponents' top cards. **9** (*also intr*) to cause (a plant) to grow or (of a plant) to grow in a new place: *the birch scrub has established over the past 25 years.* [C14: from Old French *establir,* from Latin *stabilīre* to make firm, from *stabilis* STABLE[2]] ▸ **es'tablisher** *n*

Established Church *n* a Church that is officially recognized as a national institution, esp. the Church of England.

establishment (ɪ'stæblɪʃmənt) *n* **1** the act of establishing or state of being established. **2a** a business organization or other large institution. **2b** the place where a business is carried on. **3** the staff and equipment of a commercial or other organization. **4** the approved size, composition, and equipment of a military unit, government department, business division, etc., as formally promulgated. **5** any large organization, institution, or system. **6** a household or place of residence. **7** a body of employees or servants. **8** (*modifier*) belonging to or characteristic of the Establishment; orthodox or conservative: *the establishment view of history.*

Establishment (ɪ'stæblɪʃmənt) *n* **the.** a group or class of people having institutional authority within a society, esp. those who control the civil service, the government, the armed forces, and the Church: usually identified with a conservative outlook.

establishmentarian (ɪˌstæblɪʃmən'tɛərɪən) *adj* **1** denoting or relating to an Established Church, esp. the Church of England. **2** denoting or relating to the principle of a Church being officially recognized as a national institution. ◆ *n* **3** an upholder of this principle, esp. as applied to the Church of England. ▸ **esˌtablishmen'tarianism** *n*

estaminet *French.* (ɛstaminɛ) *n* a small café, bar, or bistro, esp. a shabby one. [C19: from French, perhaps from Walloon dialect *staminet* manger]

estancia (ɪ'stænsɪə; *Spanish* es'tanθia) *n* (in Spanish America) a large estate or cattle ranch. [C18: from American Spanish, from Spanish: dwelling, from Vulgar Latin *stantia* (unattested) a remaining, from Latin *stāre* to stand]

estate (ɪ'steɪt) *n* **1** a large piece of landed property, esp. in the country. **2** *Chiefly Brit.* a large area of property development, esp. of new houses or (**trading estate**) of factories. **3** *Property law.* **3a** property or possessions. **3b** the nature of interest that a person has in land or other property, esp. in relation to the right of others. **3c** the total extent of the real and personal property of a deceased person or bankrupt. **4** Also called: **estate of the realm.** an order or class of persons in a political community, regarded collectively as a part of the body politic: usually regarded as being the lords temporal (peers), lords spiritual and commons. See also **States General, fourth estate. 5** state, period, or position in life, esp. with regard to wealth or social standing: *youth's estate; a poor man's estate.* [C13: from Old French *estat,* from Latin *status* condition, STATE]

estate agent *n* **1** *Brit.* an agent concerned with the valuation, management, lease, and sale of property. Usual U.S. and Canadian name: **real-estate agent. 2** the administrator of a large landed property, acting on behalf of its owner; estate manager.

estate car *n Brit.* a car with a comparatively long body containing a large carrying space, reached through a rear door: usually the back seats can be folded forward to increase the carrying space. Also called (esp. U.S., Canadian, Austral., and N.Z.): **station wagon.**

estate duty *n* another name for **death duty.**

Estates General *n* See **States General.**

Este ('ɛste) *n* a noble family of Italy founded by Alberto Azzo II (996–1097), who was invested with the town of Este in NE Italy as a fief of the Holy Roman Empire. The family governed Ferrara (13th–16th centuries), Modena, and Reggio (13th–18th centuries).

esteem (ɪ'sti:m) *vb (tr)* **1** to have great respect or high regard for: *to esteem a colleague.* **2** *Formal.* to judge or consider; deem: *to esteem an idea improper.* ◆ *n* **3** high regard or respect; good opinion. **4** *Archaic.* judgment; opinion. [C15: from Old French *estimer,* from Latin *aestimāre* ESTIMATE] ▸ **es'teemed** *adj*

ester ('ɛstə) *n Chem.* any of a class of compounds produced by reaction between acids and alcohols with the elimination of water. Esters with low molecular weights, such as ethyl acetate, are usually volatile fragrant liquids; fats are solid esters. [C19: from German, probably a contraction of *Essigäther* acetic ether, from *Essig* vinegar (ultimately from Latin *acētum*) + *Äther* ETHER]

esterase ('ɛstəˌreɪs, -ˌreɪz) *n* any of a group of enzymes that hydrolyse esters into alcohols and acids.

Esterházy ('ɛstəˌhɑ:zɪ) *n* a noble Hungarian family that produced many soldiers, diplomats, and patrons of the arts. Prince **Miklós József Esterházy** (1714–90) rebuilt the family castle of Esterháza and employed Haydn as his musical director (1766–90).

esterify (ɛ'stɛrəˌfaɪ) *vb* **-fies, -fying, -fied.** *Chem.* to change or cause to change into an ester. ▸ **esˌterifi'cation** *n*

Esth. *Bible. abbrev. for* Esther.

Esther ('ɛstə) *n Old Testament.* **1** a beautiful Jewess who became queen of Persia and saved her people from massacre. **2** the book in which this episode is recounted.

esthesia (i:s'θi:zɪə) *n* a U.S. spelling of **aesthesia.**

esthete ('i:sθi:t) *n* a U.S. spelling of **aesthete.** ▸ **esthetic** (ɛs'θɛtɪk) *or* **es'thetical** *adj* ▸ **es'thetically** *adv* ▸ **esthetician** (ˌi:sθɪ'tɪʃən) ▸ **es'thetiˌcism** *n* ▸ **es'thetics** *n*

Esthonia (ɛ'stəʊnɪə, ɛ'sθəʊ-) *n* See **Estonia.**

Estienne *or* **Étienne** (*French* etjɛn) *n* a family of French printers, scholars, and dealers in books, including **Henri** (ɑ̃ri), ?1460–1520, who founded the printing business in Paris, his son **Robert** (rɔbɛr), 1503–59, and his grandson **Henri,** 1528–98.

estimable ('ɛstɪməbᵊl) *adj* worthy of respect; deserving of admiration: *my estimable companion.* ▸ **'estimableness** *n* ▸ **'estimably** *adv*

estimate *vb* ('ɛstɪˌmeɪt). **1** to form an approximate idea of (distance, size, cost, etc.); calculate roughly; gauge. **2** (*tr; may take a clause as object*) to form an opinion about; judge: *to estimate one's chances.* **3** to submit (an approximate price) for (a job) to a prospective client. **4** (*tr*) *Statistics.* to assign a value (a **point estimate**) or range of values (an **interval estimate**) to a parameter of a population on the basis of sampling statistics. See **estimator.** ◆ *n* ('ɛstɪmɪt). **5** an approximate calculation. **6** a statement indicating the likely charge for or cost of certain work. **7** a judgment; appraisal; opinion. [C16: from Latin *aestimāre* to assess the worth of, of obscure origin] ▸ **'estimative** *adj*

estimation (ˌɛstɪ'meɪʃən) *n* **1** a considered opinion; judgment: *what is your estimation of the situation?* **2** esteem; respect. **3** the act of estimating.

estimator ('ɛstɪˌmeɪtə) *n* **1** a person or thing that estimates. **2** *Statistics.* a derived random variable that generates estimates of a parameter of a given distribution, such as $\bar{X}$, the mean of a number of identically distributed random variables X_i. If $\bar{X}$ is unbiased, $\bar{x}$, the observed value should be close to $E(X_i)$. See also **sampling statistic.**

estipulate (ɪ'stɪpjʊlɪt, -ˌleɪt) *adj* a variant of **exstipulate.**

estival (i:'staɪvᵊl, 'ɛstɪ-) *adj* the usual U.S. spelling of **aestival.**

estivate ('i:stɪˌveɪt, 'ɛs-) *vb (intr)* the usual U.S. spelling of **aestivate.** ▸ **'estiˌvator** *n*

estivation (ˌi:stɪ'veɪʃən, ˌɛs-) *n* the usual U.S. spelling of **aestivation.**

Estonia *or* **Esthonia** (ɛ'stəʊnɪə, ɛ'sθəʊ-) *n* a republic in NE Europe, on the Gulf of Finland and the Baltic: low-lying with many lakes and forests, it includes numerous islands in the Baltic Sea. It was under Scandinavian and Teutonic rule from the 13th century to 1721, when it passed to Russia: it was an independent republic from 1920 to 1940, when it was annexed by the Soviet Union; became independent in 1991. Official language: Estonian. Religion: believers are mostly Christian. Currency: kroon. Capital: Tallinn. Pop.: 1 447 000 (1998 est.). Area: 45 227 sq. km (17 462 sq. miles).

Estonian *or* **Esthonian** (ɛ'stəʊnɪən, ɛ'sθəʊ-) *adj* **1** of, relating to, or characteristic of Estonia, its people, or their language. ◆ *n* **2** the official language of Estonia: belongs to the Finno-Ugric family. **3** a native or inhabitant of Estonia.

estop (ɪ'stɒp) *vb* **-tops, -topping, -topped.** (*tr*) **1** *Law.* to preclude by estoppel. **2** *Archaic.* to stop. [C15: from Old French *estoper* to plug, ultimately from Latin *stuppa* tow; see STOP] ▸ **es'toppage** *n*

estoppel (ɪ'stɒpᵊl) *n Law.* a rule of evidence whereby a person is precluded from denying the truth of a statement of facts he has previously asserted. See also **conclusion.** [C16: from Old French *estoupail* plug, from *estoper* to stop up; see ESTOP]

Estoril ('ɛʃtɔ:ˌri:l) *n* a resort in W Portugal, near Lisbon, on the Atlantic Ocean: noted esp. for a famous avenue of palm trees leading to the seafront. Pop.: 24 850 (1991).

estovers (ɛ'stəʊvəz) *pl n Law.* necessaries allowed by law to tenants of land, esp. wood for fuel and repairs. [C15: from Anglo-French, plural of *estover,* n. use of Old French *estovoir* to be necessary, from Latin *est opus* there is need]

estrade (ɪs'trɑ:d) *n* a dais or raised platform. [C17: from French, from Spanish *estrado* carpeted floor, from Latin: STRATUM]

estradiol (ˌɛstrə'daɪɒl, ˌi:strə-) *n* the U.S. spelling of **oestradiol.**

estragon ('ɛstrəˌgɒn) *n* another name for **tarragon.**

estrange (ɪ'streɪndʒ) *vb (tr)* **1** (*usually passive;* often foll. by *from*) to separate and live apart from (one's spouse): *he is estranged from his wife.* **2** (*usually passive;* often foll. by *from*) to antagonize or lose the affection of (someone previously friendly); alienate. [C15: from Old French *estranger,* from Late Latin *extrāneāre* to treat as a stranger, from Latin *extrāneus* foreign; see STRANGE] ▸ **es'tranged** *adj* ▸ **es'trangement** *n*

estray (ɪ'streɪ) *n Law.* a stray domestic animal of unknown ownership. [C16: from Anglo-French, from Old French *estraier* to STRAY]

estreat (ɪ'stri:t) *Law.* ◆ *n* **1** a true copy of or extract from a court record. ◆ *vb* (*tr*) **2** to enforce (a recognizance that has been forfeited) by sending an extract of the court record to the proper authority. [C14: from Old French *estraite,* feminine of *estrait* extracted, from *estraire* to EXTRACT]

Estremadura (*Portuguese* ɪʃtrəmə'ðurə) *n* a region of W Spain: arid and sparsely populated except in the valleys of the Tagus and Guadiana Rivers. Area: 41 593 sq. km (16 059 sq. miles). Spanish name: **Extremadura.**

estrin ('ɛstrɪn, 'i:strɪn) *n* the U.S. spelling of **oestrin.**

estriol ('ɛstrɪˌɒl, 'i:strɪ-) *n* the usual U.S. spelling of **oestriol.**

estrogen ('ɛstrədʒən, 'i:strə-) *n* the usual U.S. spelling of **oestrogen.** ▸ **estrogenic** (ˌɛstrə'dʒɛnɪk, ˌi:strə-) *adj* ▸ **ˌestro'genically** *adv*

estrone ('ɛstrəʊn, 'i:strəʊn) *n* the usual U.S. spelling of **oestrone.**

estrus ('ɛstrəs, 'i:strəs) *n* the usual U.S. spelling of **oestrus.** ▸ **'estrous** *adj*

estuarine ('ɛstjʊəˌraɪn, -rɪn) *adj* **1** formed or deposited in an estuary: *estuarine muds.* **2** growing in, inhabiting, or found in an estuary: *an estuarine fauna.*

estuary ('ɛstjʊərɪ) *n, pl* **-aries. 1** the widening channel of a river where it nears the sea, with a mixing of fresh water and salt (tidal) water. **2** an inlet of the sea. [C16: from Latin *aestuārium* marsh, channel, from *aestus* tide, billowing movement, related to *aestās* summer] ▸ **estuarial** (ˌɛstjʊ'ɛərɪəl) *adj*

estuary English *n* a variety of standard British English in which the pronunciation reflects various features characteristic of London and the Southeast of England. [C20: from the area around the Thames ESTUARY where it originated]

e.s.u. *or* **ESU** *abbrev. for* electrostatic unit.

esurient (ɪ'sjʊərɪənt) *adj* greedy; voracious. [C17: from Latin *ēsurīre* to be hungry, from *edere* to eat] ▸ **e'surience** *or* **e'suriency** *n* ▸ **e'suriently** *adv*

E. Sussex *abbrev. for* East Sussex.

Et *the chemical symbol for* ethyl.

ET 1 *abbrev. for* Employment Training: a government scheme offering training in technological and business skills to unemployed people. **2** *international car registration for* Egypt.

-et *suffix of nouns.* small or lesser: *islet; baronet.* [from Old French *-et, -ete*]

eta[1] ('i:tə) *n* the seventh letter in the Greek alphabet (Η, η), a long vowel sound, transliterated as *e* or *ē.* [Greek, of Phoenician origin; compare Hebrew HETH]

eta[2] ('eɪtə) *n, pl* **eta** or **etas.** (in Japan, formerly) a member of a class of outcasts who did menial and dirty tasks. [C19: Japanese]

ETA[1] *abbrev. for* estimated time of arrival.

ETA[2] ('ɛtə) *n acronym for* Euzkadi ta Askatsuna: an organization of militant Basque nationalists attempting to gain independence for the Basques, esp. those ruled by Spain, until a cease-fire in 1998, by means of guerrilla warfare. [Basque, literally: Basque Nation and Liberty]

etaerio (ɛ'tɪərɪəʊ) *n* an aggregate fruit, as one consisting of drupes (raspberry) or achenes (traveller's joy). [C19: from French *etairion,* from Greek *hetaireia* association]

étagère *French.* (etaʒɛr) *n* a stand with open shelves for displaying ornaments, etc. [C19: from French, from *étage* shelf; see STAGE]

et al. *abbrev. for:* **1** et alibi. [Latin: and elsewhere] **2** et alii. [Latin: and others]

etalon ('ɛtəˌlɒn) *n Physics.* a device used in spectroscopy to measure wavelengths by interference effects produced by multiple reflections between parallel half-silvered glass or quartz plates. [C20: French *étalon* a fixed standard of weights and measures, from Old French *estalon;* see also STALLION]

etamine ('ɛtəˌmi:n) *or* **etamin** ('ɛtəmɪn) *n* a cotton or worsted fabric of loose weave, used for clothing, curtains, etc. [C18: from French, from Latin *stāminea,* from *stāmineus* made of threads, from *stamen* thread, warp]

etc. *abbrev. for* et cetera.

et cetera *or* **etcetera** (ɪt 'sɛtrə) **1** and the rest; and others; and so forth: used at the end of a list to indicate that other items of the same class or type should be considered or included. **2** or the like; or something else similar. ◆ Abbrevs.: **etc., &c.** ◆ See also **etceteras.** [from Latin, from *et* and + *cetera* the other (things)]

USAGE It is unnecessary to use *and* before *etc.* as *etc.* (*et cetera*) already means *and other things.* The repetition of *etc.,* as in *he brought paper, ink, notebooks, etc., etc.,* is avoided except in informal contexts.

etceteras (ɪt'sɛtrəz) *pl n* miscellaneous extra things or persons.

etch (ɛtʃ) *vb* **1** (*tr*) to wear away the surface of (a metal, glass, etc.) by chemical action, esp. the action of an acid. **2** to cut or corrode (a design, decoration, etc.) on (a metal or other plate to be used for printing) by using the action of acid on parts not covered by wax or other acid-resistant coating. **3** (*tr*) to cut with or as if with a sharp implement: *he etched his name on the table.* **4** (*tr; usually passive*) to imprint vividly: *the event was etched on her memory.* [C17: from Dutch *etsen,* from Old High German *azzen* to feed, bite] ▸ **'etcher** *n*

etchant ('ɛtʃənt) *n* any acid or corrosive used for etching.

etching ('ɛtʃɪŋ) *n* **1** the art, act, or process of preparing etched surfaces or of printing designs from them. **2** an etched plate. **3** an impression made from an etched plate.

ETD *abbrev. for* estimated time of departure.

Eteocles (ɪ'ti:əˌkli:z, 'ɛtrə-) *n Greek myth.* a son of Oedipus and Jocasta. He expelled his brother Polynices from Thebes; they killed each other in single combat when Polynices returned as leader of the Seven against Thebes.

eternal (ɪ'tɜ:nᵊl)) *adj* **1a** without beginning or end; lasting for ever: *eternal life.* **1b** (*as n*): *the eternal.* **2** (*often cap.*) denoting or relating to that which is without beginning and end, regarded as an attribute of God. **3** unchanged by time, esp. being true or valid for all time; immutable: *eternal truths.* **4** seemingly unceasing; occurring again and again: *eternal bickering.* [C14: from Late Latin *aeternālis,* from Latin *aeternus;* related to Latin *aevum* age] ▸ ˌ**eter'nality** *or* **e'ternalness** *n* ▸ **e'ternally** *adv*

Eternal City *n* **the.** Rome.

eternalize (ɪ'tɜːnəˌlaɪz), **eternize** (ɪ'tɜːnaɪz), *or* **eternalise, eternise** *vb* (*tr*) **1** to make eternal. **2** to make famous for ever; immortalize. ▸ **eˌternali'zation, eˌterni'zation** *or* **eˌternali'sation, eˌterni'sation** *n*

eternal triangle *n* an emotional relationship in which there are conflicts involving a man and two women or a woman and two men.

eterne (ɪ'tɜːn) *adj* an archaic or poetic word for **eternal.** [C14: from Old French, from Latin *aeternus*]

eternity (ɪ'tɜːnɪtɪ) *n, pl* **-ties. 1** endless or infinite time. **2** the quality, state, or condition of being eternal. **3** (*usually pl*) any of the aspects of life and thought that are considered to be timeless, esp. timeless and true. **4** *Theol.* the condition of timeless existence, believed by some to characterize the afterlife. **5** a seemingly endless period of time: *an eternity of waiting.*

eternity ring *n* a ring given as a token of lasting affection, esp. one set all around with stones to symbolize continuity.

etesian (ɪ'tiːʒɪən) *adj* (of NW winds) recurring annually in the summer in the E Mediterranean. [C17: from Latin *etēsius* yearly, from Greek *etēsios,* from *etos* year]

ETF *abbrev. for* electronic transfer of funds.

eth (ɛð, ɛθ) *n* a variant of **edh.**

ETH *international car registration for* Ethiopia.

Eth. *abbrev. for:* **1** Ethiopia(n). **2** Ethiopic.

-eth[1] *suffix.* forming the archaic third person singular present indicative tense of verbs: *goeth; taketh.* [Old English *-eth, -th*]

-eth[2] *or* **-th** *suffix forming ordinal numbers.* a variant of **-th**[2]: *twentieth.*

ethambutol (ɛ'θæmbjʊˌtɒl) *n* a compound used in the treatment of tuberculosis. [from ETH(YLENE) + AM(INE) + BUT(AN)OL]

ethanal ('ɛθəˌnæl, 'iːθə-) *n* the modern name for **acetaldehyde.**

ethane ('iːθeɪn, 'ɛθ-) *n* a colourless odourless flammable gaseous alkane obtained from natural gas and petroleum: used as a fuel and in the manufacture of organic chemicals. Formula: C_2H_6. [C19: from ETH(YL) + -ANE]

ethanedioic acid (ˌiːθeɪndaɪ'əʊɪk, ˌɛθ-) *n* the technical name for **oxalic acid.** [C20: from ETHANE + DI-[1] + -O- + -IC]

ethanediol ('iːθeɪnˌdaɪɒl, 'ɛθ-) *n* a clear colourless syrupy soluble liquid substance, used as an antifreeze and solvent. Formula: CH_2OHCH_2OH. Also called: **glycol, ethylene glycol.** [C20: from ETHANE + DI-[1] + -OL[1]]

ethanoic acid (ˌɛθə'nəʊɪk, ˌiːθə-) *n* the modern name for **acetic acid.**

ethanol ('ɛθəˌnɒl, 'iːθə-) *n* the technical name for **alcohol** (sense 1).

ethanoyl ('ɛθəˌnɔɪl) *n* (*modifier*) of, consisting of, or containing the monovalent group CH_3CO-: *ethanoyl group or radical.* [C20: from ETH(YL) + -OYL]

ethanoyl chloride *n* another name for **acetyl chloride.**

Ethelbert ('ɛθəlˌbɜːt) *or* **Æthelbert** ('æθəlˌbɜːt) *n* **Saint.** ?552–616 A.D., king of Kent (560–616): converted to Christianity by St Augustine; issued the earliest known code of English laws. Feast day: Feb. 24 or 25.

Ethelred I ('ɛθəlˌrɛd) *or* **Æthelred** ('æθəlˌrɛd) *n* died 871, king of Wessex (866–71). He led resistance to the Danish invasion of England; died following his victory at Ashdown.

Ethelred II *or* **Æthelred** *n* known as *Ethelred the Unready.* ?968–1016 A.D., king of England (978–1016). He was temporarily deposed by the Danish king Sweyn (1013) but was recalled on Sweyn's death (1014).

Ethelwulf ('ɛθəlˌwʊlf) *or* **Æthelwulf** ('æθəlˌwʊlf) *n* died 858 A.D., king of Wessex (839–858).

ethene ('ɛθiːn) *n* the technical name for **ethylene.**

ether ('iːθə) *n* **1** Also called: **diethyl ether, ethyl ether, ethoxyethane.** a colourless volatile highly flammable liquid with a characteristic sweetish odour, made by the reaction of sulphuric acid with ethanol: used as a solvent and anaesthetic. Formula: $C_2H_5OC_2H_5$. **2** any of a class of organic compounds with the general formula ROR′ where R and R′ are alkyl groups, as in diethyl ether $C_2H_5OC_2H_5$. **3 the ether.** the hypothetical medium formerly believed to fill all space and to support the propagation of electromagnetic waves. **4** *Greek myth.* the upper regions of the atmosphere; clear sky or heaven. **5** a rare word for **air.** ◆ Also (for senses 3–5): **aether.** [C17: from Latin *aether,* from Greek *aithēr,* from *aithein* to burn] ▸ **etheric** (iː'θɛrɪk) *adj*

ethereal (ɪ'θɪərɪəl) *adj* **1** extremely delicate or refined; exquisite. **2** almost as light as air; impalpable; airy. **3** celestial or spiritual. **4** of, containing, or dissolved in an ether, esp. diethyl ether: *an ethereal solution.* **5** of or relating to the ether. [C16: from Latin *aethereus,* from Greek *aitherios,* from *aithēr* ETHER] ▸ **eˌthere'ality** *or* **e'therealness** *n* ▸ **e'thereally** *adv*

etherealize *or* **etherealise** (ɪ'θɪərɪəˌlaɪz) *vb* (*tr*) **1** to make or regard as being ethereal. **2** to add ether to or make into ether or something resembling ether. ▸ **eˌthereali'zation** *or* **eˌthereali'sation** *n*

Etherege ('ɛθərɪdʒ) *n* Sir **George.** ?1635–?92, English Restoration dramatist; author of the comedies *The Comical Revenge* (1664), *She would if she could* (1668), and *The Man of Mode* (1676).

etherify ('iːθərɪˌfaɪ, iː'θɛrɪ-) *vb* **-fies, -fying, -fied.** (*tr*) to change (a compound, such as an alcohol) into an ether. ▸ **eˌtherifi'cation** *n*

etherize *or* **etherise** ('iːθəˌraɪz) *vb* (*tr*) *Obsolete.* to subject (a person) to the anaesthetic influence of ether fumes; anaesthetize. ▸ ˌ**etheri'zation** *or* ˌ**etheri'sation** *n* ▸ **'etherˌizer** *or* **'etherˌiser** *n*

Ethernet ('iːθəˌnɛt) *n Trademark. Computing.* a widely used type of local area network.

ethic ('ɛθɪk) *n* **1** a moral principle or set of moral values held by an individual or group: *the Puritan ethic.* ◆ *adj* **2** another word for **ethical.** ◆ See also **ethics.** [C15: from Latin *ēthicus,* from Greek *éthikos,* from *ēthos* custom; see ETHOS]

ethical ('ɛθɪk°l) *adj* **1** in accordance with principles of conduct that are considered correct, esp. those of a given profession or group. **2** of or relating to ethics. **3** (of a medicinal agent) available legally only with a doctor's prescription or consent. ▸ **'ethically** *adv* ▸ **'ethicalness** *or* ˌ**ethi'cality** *n*

ethical investment *n* an investment in a company whose activities or products are not considered by the investor to be unethical.

ethicize *or* **ethicise** ('ɛθɪˌsaɪz) *vb* (*tr*) to make or consider as ethical.

ethics ('ɛθɪks) *n* **1** (*functioning as sing*) the philosophical study of the moral value of human conduct and of the rules and principles that ought to govern it; moral philosophy. See also **meta-ethics. 2** (*functioning as pl*) a social, religious, or civil code of behaviour considered correct, esp. that of a particular group, profession, or individual. **3** (*functioning as pl*) the moral fitness of a decision, course of action, etc.: *he doubted the ethics of their verdict.* ▸ **'ethicist** *n*

Ethiop ('iːθɪˌɒp) *or* **Ethiope** ('iːθɪˌəʊp) *adj* archaic words for **Black**[1].

Ethiopia (ˌiːθɪ'əʊpɪə) *n* a state in NE Africa, on the Red Sea: consolidated as an empire under Menelik II (1889–1913); federated with Eritrea from 1952 until 1993; Emperor Haile Selassie was deposed by the military in 1974 and the monarchy was abolished in 1975; an independence movement in Eritrea was engaged in war with the government from 1961 until 1993. It lies along the Great Rift Valley and consists of deserts in the southeast and northeast and a high central plateau with many rivers (including the Blue Nile) and mountains rising over 4500 m (15 000 ft.); the main export is coffee. Language: Amharic. Religion: Christian majority. Currency: birr. Capital: Addis Ababa. Pop.: 58 390 000 (1998 est.). Area: 1 128 215 sq. km (435 614 sq. miles). Former name: **Abyssinia.**

Ethiopian (ˌiːθɪ'əʊpɪən) *adj* **1** of, relating to, or characteristic of Ethiopia, its people, or any of their languages. **2** of or denoting a zoogeographical region consisting of Africa south of the Sahara. **3** *Anthropol., obsolete.* of or belonging to a postulated racial group characterized by dark skin, an oval elongated face, and thin lips, living chiefly in Africa south of the Sahara. ◆ *n* **4** a native or inhabitant of Ethiopia. **5** any of the languages of Ethiopia, esp. Amharic. ◆ *n, adj* **6** an archaic word for **Black**[1].

Ethiopic (ˌiːθɪ'ɒpɪk, -'əʊpɪk) *n* **1** the ancient language of Ethiopia, belonging to the Semitic subfamily of the Afro-Asiatic family: a Christian liturgical language. See also **Ge'ez. 2** the group of languages developed from this language, including Amharic, Tigre, and Tigrinya. ◆ *adj* **3** denoting or relating to this language or group of languages. **4** a less common word for **Ethiopian.**

ethmoid ('ɛθmɔɪd) *Anatomy.* ◆ *adj also* **ethmoidal. 1** denoting or relating to a bone of the skull that forms part of the eye socket and the nasal cavity. ◆ *n* **2** the ethmoid bone. [C18: from Greek *ēthmoeidēs* like a sieve, from *ēthmos* sieve, from *ēthein* to sift]

ethnarch ('ɛθnɑːk) *n* the ruler of a people or province, as in parts of the Roman and Byzantine Empires. [C17: from Greek *ethnarkhēs,* from *ethnos* nation + *arkhein* to rule] ▸ **'ethnarchy** *n*

ethnic ('ɛθnɪk) *or* **ethnical** *adj* **1** relating to or characteristic of a human group having racial, religious, linguistic, and certain other traits in common. **2** relating to the classification of mankind into groups, esp. on the basis of racial characteristics. **3** denoting or deriving from the cultural traditions of a group of people: *the ethnic dances of Slovakia.* **4** characteristic of another culture, esp. a peasant culture: *the ethnic look; ethnic food.* ◆ *n* **5** *Chiefly U.S. and Austral.* a member of an ethnic group, esp. a minority group. [C14 (in the senses: heathen, Gentile): from Late Latin *ethnicus,* from Greek *ethnikos,* from *ethnos* race] ▸ **'ethnically** *adv* ▸ **ethnicity** (ɛθ'nɪsɪtɪ) *n*

ethnic cleansing *n Euphemistic.* the violent removal by one ethnic group of other ethnic groups from the population of a particular area: used esp. of the activities of Serbs against Croats and Muslims in the former Yugoslavia.

ethnic minority *n* an immigrant or racial group regarded by those claiming to speak for the cultural majority as distinct and unassimilated.

ethno- *combining form.* indicating race, people, or culture: *ethnology.* [via French from Greek *ethnos* race]

ethnobiology (ˌɛθnəʊbaɪ'ɒlədʒɪ) *n* the branch of biology involving the study of the traditional uses of plants and animals in various human societies.

ethnobotany (ˌɛθnəʊ'bɒtənɪ) *n* the branch of botany concerned with the use of plants in folklore, religion, etc. ▸ ˌ**ethno'botanist** *n*

ethnocentrism (ˌɛθnəʊ'sɛnˌtrɪzəm) *n* belief in the intrinsic superiority of the nation, culture, or group to which one belongs, often accompanied by feelings of dislike for other groups. ▸ ˌ**ethno'centric** *adj* ▸ ˌ**ethno'centrically** *adv* ▸ ˌ**ethnocen'tricity** *n*

ethnogeny (ɛθ'nɒdʒɪnɪ) *n* the branch of ethnology that deals with the origin of races or peoples. ▸ **ethnogenic** (ˌɛθnəʊ'dʒɛnɪk) *adj* ▸ **eth'nogenist** *n*

ethnography (ɛθ'nɒgrəfɪ) *n* the branch of anthropology that deals with the scientific description of individual human societies. ▸ ˌ**eth'nographer** *n* ▸ **ethnographic** (ˌɛθnəʊ'græfɪk) *or* ˌ**ethno'graphical** *adj* ▸ ˌ**ethno'graphically** *adv*

ethnol. *abbrev. for* ethnology.

ethnology (ɛθ'nɒlədʒɪ) *n* the branch of anthropology that deals with races and peoples, their relations to one another, their origins, and their distinctive characteristics. ▸ **ethnologic** (ˌɛθnə'lɒdʒɪk) *or* ˌ**ethno'logical** *adj* ▸ ˌ**ethno'logically** *adv* ▸ **eth'nologist** *n*

ethnomethodology (ˌɛθnəʊmɛθə'dɒlədʒɪ) *n* a method of studying linguistic communication that emphasizes common-sense views of conversation and the world. Compare **phenomenology.**

ethnomusicology (ˌɛθnəʊmjuːzɪ'kɒlədʒɪ) *n* the study of the music of different cultures. ▸ ˌ**ethnomusi'cologist** *n*

ethology (ɪ'θɒlədʒɪ) *n* the study of the behaviour of animals in their normal environment. [C17 (in the obsolete sense: mimicry): via Latin from Greek *ēthologia,* from *ēthos* character; current sense, C19] ▸ **ethological** (ˌɛθə'lɒdʒɪk°l) *adj* ▸ ˌ**etho'logically** *adv* ▸ **e'thologist** *n*

ethonone ('ɛθəˌnəʊn) *n* another name for **ketene.**

ethos ('iːθɒs) *n* the distinctive character, spirit, and attitudes of a people, culture, era, etc.: *the revolutionary ethos.* [C19: from Late Latin: habit, from Greek]

ethoxide (iːˈθɒksaɪd) *n* any of a class of saltlike compounds with the formula MOC_2H_5, where M is a metal atom. Also called: **ethylate.** [C20: from *ethox(yl)* (from ETH(YL) + OX(YGEN) + -YL) + -IDE]

ethoxyethane (ɛˌθɒksɪˈiːθeɪn) *n* the technical name for **ether** (sense 1). [C20: from ETH(YL) + OXY-[2] + ETHANE]

ethyl ('iːθaɪl, 'ɛθɪl) *n* (*modifier*) of, consisting of, or containing the monovalent group C_2H_5-: *ethyl group or radical.* [C19: from ETH(ER) + -YL] ▸ **ethylic** (ɪˈθɪlɪk) *adj*

ethyl acetate *n* a colourless volatile flammable fragrant liquid ester, made from acetic acid and ethanol: used in perfumes and flavourings and as a solvent for plastics, etc. Formula: $CH_3COOC_2H_5$.

ethyl alcohol *n* another name for **alcohol** (sense 1).

ethylate ('ɛθɪˌleɪt) *vb* **1** to undergo or cause to undergo a chemical reaction in which an ethyl group is introduced into a molecule. ◆ *n* **2** another name for an **ethoxide.** ▸ ˌ**ethylˈation** *n*

ethyl carbamate *n* a colourless odourless crystalline ester that is used in the manufacture of pesticides, fungicides, and pharmaceuticals. Formula: $CO(NH_2)OC_2H_5$. Also called: **urethane.**

ethylene ('ɛθɪˌliːn) *n* a colourless flammable gaseous alkene with a sweet odour, obtained from petroleum and natural gas and used in the manufacture of polythene and many other chemicals. Formula: $CH_2{:}CH_2$. Also called: **ethene.** ▸ ethylenic (ˌɛθɪˈliːnɪk) *adj*

ethylene glycol *n* another name for **ethanediol.**

ethylene group *or* **radical** *n Chem.* the divalent group, $-CH_2CH_2-$, derived from ethylene.

ethylene series *n Chem.* the homologous series of unsaturated hydrocarbons that contain one double bond and have the general formula, C_nH_{2n}; alkene series.

ethyl ether *n* a more formal name for **ether** (sense 1).

ethyne ('iːθaɪn, 'ɛθaɪn) *n* another name for **acetylene.** [C20: from ETHYL + -INE[2]]

Étienne (*French* etjɛn) *n* a variant spelling of **Estienne.**

etiolate ('iːtɪəʊˌleɪt) *vb* **1** *Botany.* to whiten (a green plant) through lack of sunlight. **2** to become or cause to become pale and weak, as from malnutrition. [C18: from French *étioler* to make pale, probably from Old French *estuble* straw, from Latin *stipula*] ▸ ˌ**etioˈlation** *n*

etiology (ˌiːtɪˈɒlədʒɪ) *n, pl* **-gies.** a variant spelling of **aetiology.** ▸ **etiological** (ˌiːtɪəˈlɒdʒɪkᵊl) *adj* ▸ ˌ**etioˈlogically** *adv* ▸ **etiˈologist** *n*

etiquette ('ɛtɪˌkɛt, ˌɛtɪˈkɛt) *n* **1** the customs or rules governing behaviour regarded as correct or acceptable in social or official life. **2** a conventional but unwritten code of practice followed by members of any of certain professions or groups: *medical etiquette.* [C18: from French, from Old French *estiquette* label, from *estiquier* to attach; see STICK[2]]

Etna ('ɛtnə) *n* **Mount.** an active volcano in E Sicily: the highest volcano in Europe and the highest peak in Italy south of the Alps. Height: 3323 m (10 902 ft.).

Eton ('iːtᵊn) *n* **1** a town in S England, in Berkshire near the River Thames: site of **Eton College,** a public school for boys founded in 1440. Pop.: 1974 (1991). **2** this college. ▸ **Etonian** (iːˈtəʊnɪən) *adj, n*

Eton collar *n* a broad stiff white collar worn outside an Eton jacket.

Eton crop *n* a short mannish hairstyle worn by women in the 1920s.

Eton jacket *n* a waist-length jacket with a V-shaped back, open in front, formerly worn by pupils of Eton College.

étrier (*French* etrije) *n Mountaineering.* a short portable ladder or set of webbing loops that can be attached to a karabiner or fifi hook. U.S. name: **stirrup.** [C20: from French: stirrup]

Etruria (ɪˈtrʊərɪə) *n* **1** an ancient country of central Italy, between the Rivers Arno and Tiber, roughly corresponding to present-day Tuscany and part of Umbria. **2** a factory established in Staffordshire by Josiah Wedgwood in 1769.

Etruscan (ɪˈtrʌskən) *or* **Etrurian** (ɪˈtrʊərɪən) *n* **1** a member of an ancient people of central Italy whose civilization influenced the Romans, who had suppressed them by about 200 B.C. **2** the non-Indo-European language of the ancient Etruscans, whose few surviving records have not been fully interpreted. ◆ *adj* **3** of, relating to, or characteristic of Etruria, the Etruscans, their culture, or their language.

et seq. *abbrev. for:* **1** et sequens [Latin: and the following] **2** Also: **et seqq.** et sequentia [Latin: and those that follow]

-ette *suffix of nouns.* **1** small: *cigarette; kitchenette.* **2** female: *majorette; suffragette.* **3** (esp. in trade names) imitation: *Leatherette.* [from French, feminine of -ET]

étude ('eɪtjuːd; *French* etyd) *n* a short musical composition for a solo instrument, esp. one designed as an exercise or exploiting technical virtuosity. [C19: from French: STUDY]

étui (ɛˈtwiː) *n, pl* **étuis.** a small usually ornamented case for holding needles, cosmetics, or other small articles. [C17: from French, from Old French *estuier* to enclose; see TWEEZERS]

ety., etym., *or* **etymol.** *abbrev. for:* **1** etymological. **2** etymology.

etymologize *or* **etymologise** (ˌɛtɪˈmɒləˌdʒaɪz) *vb* to trace, state, or suggest the etymology of (a word).

etymology (ˌɛtɪˈmɒlədʒɪ) *n, pl* **-gies. 1** the study of the sources and development of words and morphemes. **2** an account of the source and development of a word or morpheme. [C14: via Latin from Greek *etumologia;* see ETYMON, -LOGY] ▸ **etymological** (ˌɛtɪməˈlɒdʒɪkᵊl) *adj* ▸ ˌ**etymoˈlogically** *adv* ▸ ˌ**etyˈmologist** *n*

etymon ('ɛtɪˌmɒn) *n, pl* **-mons** *or* **-ma** (-mə). a form of a word or morpheme, usually the earliest recorded form or a reconstructed form, from which another word or morpheme is derived: *the etymon of English "ewe" is Indo-European "*owi".* [C16: via Latin, from Greek *etumon* basic meaning, from *etumos* true, actual]

Etzel ('ɛtsᵊl) *n German legend.* a great king who, according to the *Nibelungenlied,* was the second husband of Kriemhild after the death of Siegfried: identified with Attila the Hun. Compare **Atli.**

Eu *the chemical symbol for* europium.

EU *abbrev. for* European Union.

eu- *combining form.* well, pleasant, or good: *eupeptic; euphony.* [via Latin from Greek, from *eus* good]

eubacteria (ˌjuːbækˈtɪərɪə) *pl n, sing* **-rium** (-rɪəm). a large group of bacteria characterized by a rigid cell wall and, in motile types, flagella; the true bacteria. [C20: via New Latin from Greek, from EU- (in the sense: true) + BACTERIUM]

Euboea (juːˈbɪə) *n* an island in the W Aegean Sea: the largest island after Crete of the Greek archipelago; linked with the mainland by a bridge across the Euripus channel. Capital: Chalcis. Pop.: 188 410 (1981). Area: 3908 sq. km (1509 sq. miles). Modern Greek name: **Évvoia.** Former English name: **Negropont.** ▸ **Euˈboean** *adj, n*

eucaine (juːˈkeɪn) *n* a crystalline optically active substance formerly used as a local anaesthetic. Formula: $C_{15}H_{21}NO_2$.

eucalyptol (ˌjuːkəˈlɪptɒl) *or* **eucalyptole** (ˌjuːkəˈlɪptəʊl) *n* a colourless oily liquid with a camphor-like odour and a spicy taste, obtained from eucalyptus oil and used in perfumery and as a flavouring. Formula: $C_{10}H_{18}O$. Also called: **cineol.**

eucalyptus (ˌjuːkəˈlɪptəs) *or* **eucalypt** ('juːkəˌlɪpt) *n, pl* **-lyptuses, -lypti** (-ˈlɪptaɪ), *or* **-lypts.** any myrtaceous tree of the mostly Australian genus *Eucalyptus,* such as the blue gum and ironbark, widely cultivated for the medicinal oil in their leaves (**eucalyptus oil**), timber, and ornament. [C19: New Latin, from EU- + Greek *kaluptos* covered, from *kaluptein* to cover, hide]

eucaryote (juːˈkærɪɒt) *n* a variant spelling of **eukaryote.**

eucharis ('juːkərɪs) *n* any amaryllidaceous plant of the South American genus *Eucharis,* cultivated for their large white fragrant flowers. [C19: New Latin, from Late Latin: charming, from Greek *eukharis,* from EU- + *kharis* grace]

Eucharist ('juːkərɪst) *n* **1** the Christian sacrament in which Christ's Last Supper is commemorated by the consecration of bread and wine. **2** the consecrated elements of bread and wine offered in the sacrament. **3** Mass, esp. when regarded as the service where the sacrament of the Eucharist is administered. [C14: via Church Latin from Greek *eukharistia,* from *eukharistos* thankful, from EU- + *kharizesthai* to show favour, from *kharis* favour] ▸ ˌ**Euchaˈristic** *or* ˌ**Euchaˈristical** *adj* ▸ ˌ**Euchaˈristically** *adv*

euchlorine (juːˈklɔːriːn) *or* **euchlorin** (juːˈklɔːrɪn) *n* an explosive gaseous mixture of chlorine and chlorine dioxide.

euchre ('juːkə) *n* **1** a U.S. and Canadian card game similar to écarté for two to four players, using a poker pack with joker. **2** an instance of euchring another player, preventing him from making his contracted tricks. ◆ *vb* (*tr*) **3** to prevent (a player) from making his contracted tricks. **4** (usually foll. by *out*) *U.S., Canadian, Austral., and N.Z. informal.* to outwit or cheat. **5** *Austral. and N.Z. informal.* to ruin or exhaust. [C19: of unknown origin]

euchromatin (juːˈkrəʊmətɪn) *n* the part of a chromosome that constitutes the major genes and does not stain strongly with basic dyes when the cell is not dividing. Compare **heterochromatin.** ▸ **euchromatic** (ˌjuːkrəʊˈmætɪk) *adj*

Eucken (*German* ˈɔykən) *n* **Rudolph Christoph** ('ruːdɔlf ˈkrɪstɔf). 1846–1926, German idealist philosopher: Nobel prize for literature 1908.

Euclid ('juːklɪd) *n* **1** 3rd century B.C., Greek mathematician of Alexandria; author of *Elements,* which sets out the principles of geometry and remained a text until the 19th century at least. **2** the works of Euclid, esp. his system of geometry. ▸ **Euclidean** *or* **Euclidian** (juːˈklɪdɪən) *adj*

eucryphia (juːˈkrɪfɪə) *n* any tree or shrub of the mostly evergreen genus *Eucryphia,* native to Australia and S America, having leaves of a dark lustrous green and white flowers. [from Greek *eu* well + *kryphios* hidden, from *kryptein* to hide, referring to the sepals being joined at the top]

eudemon *or* **eudaemon** (juːˈdiːmən) *n* a benevolent spirit or demon. [C17: from Greek *eudaimōn,* from EU- + *daimōn* in-dwelling spirit; see DEMON]

eudemonia *or* **eudaemonia** (ˌjuːdɪˈməʊnɪə) *n* happiness, esp. (in the philosophy of Aristotle) that resulting from a rational active life.

eudemonics *or* **eudaemonics** (ˌjuːdɪˈmɒnɪks) *n* (*functioning as sing*) **1** the art or theory of happiness. **2** another word for **eudemonism.** ▸ ˌ**eudeˈmonic** *or* ˌ**eudaeˈmonic** *adj*

eudemonism *or* **eudaemonism** (juːˈdiːməˌnɪzəm) *n Philosophy.* an ethical doctrine holding that the value of moral action lies in its capacity to produce happiness. ▸ **euˈdemonist** *or* **euˈdaemonist** *n* ▸ **euˌdemonˈistic, euˌdaemonˈistic** *or* **euˌdemonˈistical, euˌdaemonˈistical** *adj* ▸ **euˌdemonˈistically** *or* **euˌdaemonˈistically** *adv*

eudiometer (ˌjuːdɪˈɒmɪtə) *n* a graduated glass tube used in the study and volumetric analysis of gas reactions. [C18: from Greek *eudios,* literally: clear skied (from EU- + *Dios,* genitive of *Zeus* god of the heavens) + -METER] ▸ **eudiometric** (ˌjuːdɪəˈmɛtrɪk) *or* ˌ**eudioˈmetrical** *adj* ▸ ˌ**eudioˈmetrically** *adv* ▸ ˌ**euˈdiˈometry** *n*

Eudoxus of Cnidus (juːˈdɒksəs; ˈnaɪdəs) *n* ?406–?355 B.C., Greek astronomer and mathematician; believed to have calculated the length of the solar year.

eugarie ('juːgərɪ) *n Queensland dialect.* another name for **pipi.**

Eugène (*French* øʒɛn) *n* **Prince,** title of *François Eugène de Savoie-Carignan.* 1663–1736, Austrian general, born in France: with Marlborough defeated the French at Blenheim (1704), Oudenaarde (1708), and Malplaquet (1709).

eugenics (juːˈdʒɛnɪks) *n* (*functioning as sing*) the study of methods of improving the quality of the human race, esp. by selective breeding. [C19: from

Greek *eugenēs* well-born, from EU- + *-genēs* born; see -GEN] ▸ **eu'genic** *adj* ▸ **eu'genically** *adv* ▸ **eu'genicist** *n* ▸ **eugenist** ('ju:dʒənɪst) *n, adj*

Eugénie (*French* øʒeni) *n* original name *Eugénia Maria de Montijo de Guzman, Comtesse de Téba.* 1826–1920, Empress of France (1853–71) as wife of Napoleon III.

eugenol ('ju:dʒɪˌnɒl) *n* a colourless or pale yellow oily liquid substance with a spicy taste and an odour of cloves, used in perfumery; 4-allyl-2-methoxyphenol. Formula: $C_{10}H_{12}O_2$. [C19: *eugen-*, from *Eugenia caryophyllata* kind of clove from which oil may be obtained + -OL[1]]

euglena (ju:'gli:nə) *n* any freshwater unicellular organism of the genus *Euglena,* moving by means of flagella and typically having holophytic nutrition. It has been variously regarded as an alga or a protozoan but is now usually classified as a protoctist (phylum *Euglenophyta*). [C19: from New Latin, from EU- + Greek *glēnē* eyeball, socket of a joint] ▸ **eu'glenoid** *adj, n*

euhemerism (ju:'hi:məˌrɪzəm) *n* **1** the theory that gods arose out of the deification of historical heroes. **2** any interpretation of myths that derives the gods from outstanding men and seeks the source of mythology in history. [C19: named after *Euhemerus* (?300 B.C.), Greek philosopher who propounded this theory] ▸ **eu'hemerist** *n* ▸ **euˌhemer'istic** *adj* ▸ **euˌhemer'istically** *adv*

euhemerize *or* **euhemerise** (ju:'hi:məˌraɪz) *vb* to deal with or explain (myths) by euhemerism.

eukaryote *or* **eucaryote** (ju:'kærɪɒt) *n* an organism having cells each with a distinct nucleus within which the genetic material is contained. All organisms except bacteria are eukaryotes. Compare **prokaryote.** [from EU- + KARYO- + *-ote* as in *zygote*] ▸ **eukaryotic** *or* **eucaryotic** (ˌju:kærɪ'ɒtɪk) *adj*

eulachon ('ju:ləˌkɒn) *or* **eulachan** *n, pl* **-chons, -chon** *or* **-chans, -chan.** another name for **candlefish.** [from Chinook Jargon *ulâkân*]

Eulenspiegel ('ɔɪlənˌʃpi:gᵊl) *n* See **Till Eulenspiegel.**

Euler (*German* 'ɔɪlər) *n* **1 Leonhard** ('le:ɔnhart). 1707–83, Swiss mathematician, noted esp. for his work on the calculus of variation: considered the founder of modern mathematical analysis. **2 Ulf (Svante) von** (ʊlf fɔn). 1905–83, Swedish physiologist: shared the Nobel prize (1970) for physiology or medicine with Julius Axelrod and Bernard Katz for their work on the catecholamines: son of Hans von Euler-Chelpin.

Euler-Chelpin (*German* 'ɔɪlər 'kɛlpi:n) *n* **Hans (Karl August) von.** 1873–1964, Swedish biochemist, born in Germany: shared the Nobel prize for chemistry (1929) with Sir Arthur Harden for their work on enzymes: father of Ulf von Euler.

Euler's circles *pl n Logic.* a diagram in which the terms of categorial statements are represented by circles whose inclusion in one another represents the inclusion of the extensions of the terms in one another. Compare **Venn diagram.** [named after L. EULER]

eulogia (ju:'ləʊdʒɪə) *n* **1** *Eastern Christian Church.* blessed bread distributed to members of the congregation after the liturgy, esp. to those who have not communed. **2** *Archaic.* a blessing or something blessed. [C18: from Greek: blessing; see EULOGY]

eulogize *or* **eulogise** ('ju:ləˌdʒaɪz) *vb* to praise (a person or thing) highly in speech or writing. ▸ **'eulogist, 'euloˌgizer,** *or* **'euloˌgiser** *n* ▸ **ˌeulo'gistic** *or* **ˌeulo'gistical** *adj* ▸ **ˌeulo'gistically** *adv*

eulogy ('ju:lədʒɪ) *n, pl* **-gies. 1** a formal speech or piece of writing praising a person or thing, esp. a person who has recently died. **2** high praise or commendation. ◆ Also called (archaic): **eulogium** (ju:'ləʊdʒɪəm). [C16: from Late Latin *eulogia,* from Greek: praise, from EU- + -LOGY; influenced by Latin *ēlogium* short saying, inscription]

USAGE Avoid confusion with **elegy.**

Eumenides (ju:'mɛnɪˌdi:z) *pl n* another name for the **Furies,** used by the Greeks as a euphemism. [from Greek, literally: the benevolent ones, from *eumenēs* benevolent, from EU- + *menos* spirit]

eunuch ('ju:nək) *n* **1** a man who has been castrated, esp. (formerly) for some office such as a guard in a harem. **2** *Informal.* an ineffective man: *a political eunuch.* [C15: via Latin from Greek *eunoukhos* attendant of the bedchamber, from *eunē* bed + *ekhein* to have, keep]

euonymus (ju:'ɒnɪməs) *or* **evonymus** *n* any tree or shrub of the N temperate genus *Euonymus,* such as the spindle tree, whose seeds are each enclosed in a fleshy, typically red, aril: family *Celastraceae.* [C18: from Latin: spindle tree, from Greek *euōnumos* fortunately named, from EU- + *onoma* NAME]

eupatorium (ˌju:pə'tɔ:rɪəm) *n* any plant of the genus *Eupatorium,* of tropical America and the Caribbean: cultivated for their ornamental clusters of purple, pink, or white flowers: family *Compositae* (composites). [C16: from New Latin, from Greek *eupatorion* hemp agrimony, from *Eupator* surname of Mithridates VI, king of Pontus and traditionally the first to have used it medicinally]

eupatrid (ju:'pætrɪd) *n, pl* **-patridae** (-'pætrɪˌdi:) *or* **-patrids.** (in ancient Greece) a hereditary noble or landowner. [C19: via Latin from Greek *eupatridēs,* literally: having a good father, from EU- + *patēr* father]

Eupen and Malmédy (*French* øpɛn; malmedi) *n* a region of Belgium in Liège province: ceded by Germany in 1919. Pop.: 27 675 (1995 est.).

eupepsia (ju:'pɛpsɪə) *or* **eupepsy** (ju:'pɛpsɪ) *n Physiol.* good digestion. [C18: from New Latin, from Greek, from EU- + *pepsis* digestion, from *peptein* to digest] ▸ **eupeptic** (ju:'pɛptɪk) *adj*

euphausiid (ju:'fɔ:zɪɪd) *n* any small pelagic shrimplike crustacean of the order *Euphausiacea:* an important constituent of krill. [C19: from New Latin *Euphausiacea,* perhaps from Greek EU- + *pha-* from *phainein* to reveal, show + *ousia* substance, stuff]

euphemism ('ju:fɪˌmɪzəm) *n* **1** an inoffensive word or phrase substituted for one considered offensive or hurtful, esp. one concerned with religion, sex, death, or excreta. Examples of euphemisms are: *sleep with* for *have sexual intercourse with; departed* for *dead; relieve oneself* for *urinate.* **2** the use of such inoffensive words or phrases. [C17: from Greek *euphēmismos,* from EU- + *phēmē* speech] ▸ **ˌeuphe'mistic** *adj* ▸ **ˌeuphe'mistically** *adv*

euphemize *or* **euphemise** ('ju:fɪˌmaɪz) *vb* to speak in euphemisms or refer to by means of a euphemism. ▸ **'eupheˌmizer** *or* **'eupheˌmiser** *n*

euphonic (ju:'fɒnɪk) *or* **euphonious** (ju:'fəʊnɪəs) *adj* **1** denoting or relating to euphony; pleasing to the ear. **2** (of speech sounds) altered for ease of pronunciation. ▸ **eu'phonically** *or* **eu'phoniously** *adv* ▸ **eu'phoniousness** *n*

euphonium (ju:'fəʊnɪəm) *n* a brass musical instrument with four valves; the tenor of the tuba family. It is used mainly in brass bands. [C19: New Latin, from EUPH(ONY + HARM)ONIUM]

euphonize *or* **euphonise** ('ju:fəˌnaɪz) *vb* **1** to make pleasant to hear; render euphonious. **2** to change (speech sounds) so as to facilitate pronunciation.

euphony ('ju:fənɪ) *n, pl* **-nies. 1** the alteration of speech sounds, esp. by assimilation, so as to make them easier to pronounce. **2** a pleasing sound, esp. in speech. [C17: from Late Latin *euphōnia,* from Greek, from EU- + *phōnē* voice]

euphorbia (ju:'fɔ:bɪə) *n* any plant of the genus *Euphorbia,* such as the spurges and poinsettia: family *Euphorbiaceae.* [C14 *euforbia:* from Latin *euphorbea* African plant named after *Euphorbus,* first-century A.D. Greek physician]

euphorbiaceous (ju:ˌfɔ:bɪ'eɪʃəs) *adj* of, relating to, or belonging to the *Euphorbiaceae,* a family of plants typically having capsular fruits: includes the spurges, the castor oil and cassava plants, cascarilla, and poinsettia.

euphoria (ju:'fɔ:rɪə) *n* a feeling of great elation, esp. when exaggerated. [C19: from Greek: good ability to endure, from EU- + *pherein* to bear] ▸ **euphoric** (ju:'fɒrɪk) *adj*

euphoriant (ju:'fɔ:rɪənt) *adj* **1** relating to or able to produce euphoria. ◆ *n* **2** a euphoriant drug or agent.

euphotic (ju:'fəʊtɪk, -'fɒt-) *adj Ecology.* denoting or relating to the uppermost part of a sea or lake down to about 100 metres depth, which receives enough light to enable photosynthesis to take place. [C20: from EU- + PHOTIC]

euphrasy ('ju:frəsɪ) *n, pl* **-sies.** another name for **eyebright.** [C15 *eufrasie:* from Medieval Latin *eufrasia,* from Greek *euphrasia* gladness, from *euphrainein* to make glad, from EU- + *phrēn* mind]

Euphrates (ju:'freɪti:z) *n* a river in SW Asia, rising in E Turkey and flowing south across Syria and Iraq to join the Tigris, forming the Shatt-al-Arab, which flows to the head of the Persian Gulf: important in ancient times for the extensive irrigation of its valley (in Mesopotamia). Length: 3598 km (2235 miles).

euphroe *or* **uphroe** ('ju:frəʊ, -vrəʊ) *n Nautical.* a wooden block with holes through which the lines of a crowfoot are rove. [C19: from Dutch *juffrouw* maiden, earlier *joncfrouwe* (from *jonc* YOUNG + *frouwe* woman)]

Euphrosyne (ju:'frɒzɪˌni:) *n Greek myth.* one of the three Graces. [from Greek: mirth, merriment]

euphuism ('ju:fju:ˌɪzəm) *n* **1** an artificial prose style of the Elizabethan period, marked by extreme use of antithesis, alliteration, and extended similes and allusions. **2** any stylish affectation in speech or writing, esp. a rhetorical device or expression. [C16: after *Euphues,* prose romance by John Lyly] ▸ **'euphuist** *n* ▸ **ˌeuphu'istic** *or* **ˌeuphu'istical** *adj* ▸ **ˌeuphu'istically** *adv*

euplastic (ju:'plæstɪk) *adj* healing quickly and well. [C19: from Greek *euplastos* readily moulded; see EU-, PLASTIC]

euploid ('ju:plɔɪd) *Biology.* ◆ *adj* **1** having chromosomes present in an exact multiple of the haploid number. ◆ *n* **2** a euploid cell or individual. ◆ Compare **aneuploid.** [C20: from EU- + *-ploid,* as in HAPLOID] ▸ **'euploidy** *n*

eupnoea *or U.S.* **eupnea** (ju:p'nɪə) *n Physiol.* normal relaxed breathing. Compare **dyspnoea.** [C18: from New Latin, from Greek *eupnoia,* from *eupnous* breathing easily, from EU- + *pnoē,* from *pnein* to breathe] ▸ **eup'noeic** *or U.S.* **eup'neic** *adj*

eur. *abbrev. for* Europe(an).

eur- *combining form.* a variant of **Euro-** before a vowel.

Eurasia (jʊə'reɪʃə, -ʒə) *n* the continents of Europe and Asia considered as a whole.

Eurasian (jʊə'reɪʃən, -ʒən) *adj* **1** of or relating to Eurasia. **2** of mixed European and Asian descent. ◆ *n* **3** a person of mixed European and Asian descent.

Euratom (jʊə'rætəm) *n* short for **European Atomic Energy Community;** an authority established by the European Economic Community (now the European Union) to develop peaceful uses of nuclear energy.

Eure (*French* œr) *n* a department of N France, in Haute-Normandie region. Capital: Évreux. Pop.: 535 400 (1995). Area: 6037 sq. km (2354 sq. miles).

Eure-et-Loir (*French* œrelwar) *n* a department of N central France, in Centre region. Capital: Chartres. Pop.: 410 100 (1995). Area: 5940 sq. km (2317 sq. miles).

eureka (jʊ'ri:kə) *interj* an exclamation of triumph on discovering or solving something. [C17: from Greek *heurēka* I have found (it), from *heuriskein* to find; traditionally the exclamation of Archimedes when he realized, during bathing, that the volume of an irregular solid could be calculated by measuring the water displaced when it was immersed]

Eureka Stockade *n* a violent incident in Ballarat, Australia, in 1854 between gold miners and the military, as a result of which the miners won their democratic rights in the state parliament.

eurhythmic (ju:'rɪðmɪk), **eurhythmical** *or esp. U.S.* **eurythmic, eurythmical** *adj* **1** having a pleasing and harmonious rhythm, order, or structure. **2** of or relating to eurhythmics.

eurhythmics *or esp. U.S.* **eurythmics** (ju:'rɪðmɪks) *n* (*functioning as sing*) **1** a system of training through physical movement to music, originally taught by Émile Jaques-Dalcroze, to develop grace and musical understanding. **2** dancing of this style, expressing the rhythm and spirit of the music through body movements.

eurhythmy *or esp. U.S. or* **eurythmy** (ju:'rɪðmɪ) *n* **1** rhythmic movement. **2**

harmonious structure. [C17: from Latin *eurythmia*, from Greek *eurhuthmia*, from EU- + *rhuthmos* proportion, RHYTHM]

Euripides (jʊˈrɪpɪˌdiːz) *n* ?480–406 B.C., Greek tragic dramatist. His plays, 18 of which are extant, include *Alcestis, Medea, Hippolytus, Hecuba, Trojan Women, Electra, Iphigeneia in Tauris, Iphigeneia in Aulis,* and *Bacchae.*

euripus (jʊˈraɪpəs) *n, pl* **-pi** (-paɪ). a strait or channel with a strong current or tide. [C17: from Latin, from Greek *Euripos* the strait between Boeotia and Euboea, from *ripē* force, rush]

euro (ˈjʊərəʊ) *n, pl* **-ros.** the official currency unit, divided into 100 cents, of the member countries of the European Union who have adopted European Monetary Union: these are Austria, Belgium, Finland, France, Germany, Ireland, Italy, Luxembourg, the Netherlands, Portugal, and Spain.

euro- (ˈjʊərəʊ-) *or before a vowel* **eur-** *combining form.* (*sometimes cap.*) Europe or European: *eurodollar.*

euro-ad (ˈjʊərəʊˌæd) *n* an advertisement designed to be suitable for all countries in the European Union.

Eurobeach (ˈjʊərəʊˌbiːtʃ) *n* a beach that has been designated as suitable for bathing from because it meets the limits set by European Union regulations for bacteria in bathing areas.

eurobond (ˈjʊərəʊˌbɒnd) *n* (*sometimes cap.*) a bond issued in a eurocurrency.

Eurocentric (ˌjʊərəʊˈsɛntrɪk) *adj* chiefly concerned with or concentrating on Europe and European culture: *the Eurocentric curriculum.*

eurocheque (ˈjʊərəʊˌtʃɛk) *n* (*sometimes cap.*) a cheque drawn on a European bank that can be cashed at any bank or bureau de change displaying the EC sign or that can be used to pay for goods or services at any outlet displaying this sign.

Euroclydon (jʊˈrɒklɪˌdɒn) *n* **1** a stormy wind from the north or northeast that occurs in the Levant, which caused the ship in which St Paul was travelling to be wrecked (Acts 27:14). **2** any stormy wind. [C17: from Greek *eurokludōn*, from *Euros* EURUS + Greek *akulōn* (unattested) north wind, from Latin *aquilō*]

euro-commercial paper (ˌjuːrəʊkəˈmɜːʃəl) *n* commercial paper issued in a eurocurrency.

Eurocommunism (ˌjʊərəʊˈkɒmjʊˌnɪzəm) *n* the policies, doctrines, and practices of Communist Parties in Western Europe in the 1970s and 1980s, esp. those rejecting democratic centralism and favouring nonalignment with the Soviet Union and China. ► **ˌEuroˈcommunist** *n, adj*

eurocrat (ˈjʊərəˌkræt) *n* (*sometimes cap.*) a member, esp. a senior member, of the administration of the European Union.

eurocurrency (ˈjʊərəʊˌkʌrənsɪ) *n* (*sometimes cap.*) **a** the currency of any country held on deposit in Europe outside its home market: used as a source of short- or medium-term finance, esp. in international trade, because of easy convertibility. **b** (*as modifier*): *the eurocurrency market.*

eurodeposit (ˌjʊərəʊdɪˈpɒzɪt) *n* (*sometimes cap.*) a deposit of the currency of any country in the eurocurrency market.

eurodollar (ˈjʊərəʊˌdɒlə) *n* (*sometimes cap.*) a U.S. dollar as part of a European holding. See **eurocurrency.**

Euroland (ˈjʊərəʊˌlænd) *n* the geographical area containing the countries that have joined the European single currency.

euromarket (ˈjʊərəʊˌmɑːkɪt) *n* **1** a market for financing international trade backed by the central banks and commercial banks of the European Union. **2** the European Union treated as one large market for the sale of goods and services.

Euro MP *n Informal.* a member of the European Parliament.

euronote (ˈjuːrəʊˌnəʊt) *n* a form of euro-commercial paper consisting of short-term negotiable bearer notes.

Europa[1] (jʊˈrəʊpə) *n Greek myth.* a Phoenician princess who had three children by Zeus in Crete, where he had taken her after assuming the guise of a white bull. Their offspring were Rhadamanthys, Minos, and Sarpedon.

Europa[2] (jʊˈrəʊpə) *n* the smallest of the four Galilean satellites of Jupiter. Diameter: 3140 km; orbital radius: 671 000 km.

Europe (ˈjʊərəp) *n* **1** the second smallest continent, forming the W extension of Eurasia: the border with Asia runs from the Urals to the Caspian and the Black Sea. The coastline is generally extremely indented and there are several peninsulas (notably Scandinavia, Italy, and Iberia) and offshore islands (including the British Isles and Iceland). It contains a series of great mountain systems in the south (Pyrenees, Alps, Apennines, Carpathians, Caucasus), a large central plain, and a N region of lakes and mountains in Scandinavia. Pop.: 729 370 000 (1996 est.). Area: about 10 400 000 sq. km (4 000 000 sq. miles). **2** *Brit.* the continent of Europe except for the British Isles: *we're going to Europe for our holiday.* **3** *Brit.* the European Union: *when did Britain go into Europe?*

European (ˌjʊərəˈpɪən) *adj* **1** of or relating to Europe or its inhabitants. **2** native to or derived from Europe. ◆ *n* **3** a native or inhabitant of Europe. **4** a person of European descent. **5** a supporter of the European Union or of political union of the countries of Europe or a part of it. ► **ˌEuroˈpean ˌism** *n*

European Central Bank *n* a European bank established in 1998 to oversee the Exchange Rate Mechanism that stabilizes the euro and other European Union currencies. Abbrev.: **ECB.**

European Commission *n* the executive body of the European Union formed in 1967, which initiates action in the EU and mediates between member governments. Former name (until 1993): **Commission of the European Communities.**

European Community *or* **Communities** *n* the former name (until 1993) of the **European Union.** Abbrev.: **EC.**

European Council *n* an executive body of the European Union, made up of the President of the European Commission and representatives of the Member states, including the foreign and other ministers. The Council acts at the request of the Commission.

European Currency Unit *n* See **ECU.**

European Economic Community *n* the former European common market set up by the six member states of the European Coal and Steel Community in 1957, which broadened into the European Community and was replaced in 1993 by the European Union. Also called: **Common Market.** Abbrev.: **EEC.**

European Free Trade Association *n* See **EFTA.**

Europeanize *or* **Europeanise** (ˌjʊərəˈpɪəˌnaɪz) *vb* (*tr*) **1** to make European in culture, dress, etc. **2** to integrate (a country, economy, etc.) into the European Union. ► **ˌEuroˌpeaniˈzation** *or* **ˌEuroˌpeaniˈsation** *n*

European Monetary Institute *n* an organization set up in 1991 to coordinate economic and monetary policy within the European Union.

European Monetary System *n* the system used in the European Union for stabilizing exchange rates between the currencies of member states participating in the Exchange Rate Mechanism and the balance-of-payments support mechanism. The original exchange rate mechanism was formed in 1979 but superseded in 1999 when the euro was adopted as official currency of 11 EU member states. A new exchange rate mechanism (ERM II) based on the euro will be used to regulate the currencies of EU member states that have not adopted the euro. Abbrev.: **EMS.**

European Parliament *n* the assembly of the European Union in Strasbourg. It consists of 626 directly elected members and its role is largely advisory.

European plan *n U.S.* a hotel rate of charging covering room and service but not meals. Compare **American plan.**

European Recovery Programme *n* the official name for the **Marshall Plan.**

European Union *n* an economic and political grouping that was formed (1993) to extend the European Community by adding common foreign and security policies to the single market. There are 15 members: the twelve members of the European Community and Austria, Finland, and Sweden, which joined in 1995. Abbrev.: **EU.**

Europhile (ˈjʊərəʊˌfaɪl) (*sometimes not cap.*) *n* **1** a person who admires Europe, Europeans, or the European Union. ◆ *adj* **2** marked by or possesing admiration for Europe, Europeans, or the European Union.

europium (jʊˈrəʊpɪəm) *n* a soft ductile reactive silvery-white element of the lanthanide series of metals: used as the red phosphor in colour television and in lasers. Symbol: Eu; atomic no.: 63; atomic wt.: 151.965; valency: 2 or 3; relative density: 5.244; melting pt.: 822°C; boiling pt.: 1527°C. [C20: named after EUROPE + -IUM]

Europoort (*Dutch* ˈøːroːpoːrt) *n* a port in the Netherlands near Rotterdam: developed in the 1960s; handles chiefly oil.

Euro-sceptic (ˈjʊərəʊˌskɛptɪk) (in Britain) *n* **1** a person who is opposed to closer links with the European Union. ◆ *adj* **2** opposing closer links with the European Union: *Euro-sceptic MPs.*

Eurosterling (ˈjʊərəʊˌstɜːlɪŋ) *n* sterling as part of a European holding. See **eurocurrency.**

Eurotunnel (ˈjʊərəʊˌtʌnəl) *n* another name for **Channel Tunnel.**

Eurovision (ˈjʊərəʊˌvɪʒən) *n* **a** the network of the European Broadcasting Union for the exchange of news and television programmes amongst its member organizations and for the relay of news and programmes from outside the network. **b** (*as modifier*): *the Eurovision song contest.*

Eurozone (ˈjʊərəʊˌzəʊn) *n* another name for **Euroland.**

Eurus (ˈjʊərəs) *n Greek myth.* the east or southeast wind personified. [Latin, from Greek *euros*]

eury- *combining form.* broad or wide: *eurythermal.* [New Latin, from Greek, from *eurus* wide]

Euryale (jʊˈraɪəlɪ) *n Greek myth.* one of the three Gorgons.

Eurydice (jʊˈrɪdɪsɪ) *n Greek myth.* a dryad married to Orpheus, who sought her in Hades after she died. She could have left Hades with him had he not broken his pact and looked back at her.

euryhaline (ˌjʊərɪˈheɪliːn, -laɪn) *adj* (of certain aquatic animals) able to tolerate a wide range of salinity. Compare **stenohaline.** [C20: from EURY- + *haline*, from Greek *hals* salt + -INE[1]]

eurypterid (jʊˈrɪptərɪd) *n* any large extinct scorpion-like aquatic arthropod of the group *Eurypterida*, of Palaeozoic times, thought to be related to the horseshoe crabs. [C19: from New Latin *Eurypterida*, from EURY- + Greek *pteron* wing, feather]

Eurystheus (jʊˈrɪsθjuːs, -θɪəs) *n Greek myth.* a grandson of Perseus, who, through the favour of Hera, inherited the kingship of Mycenae, which Zeus had intended for Hercules.

eurythermal (ˌjʊərɪˈθɜːməl), **eurythermic,** *or* **eurythermous** *adj* (of organisms) able to tolerate a wide range of temperatures in the environment. Compare **stenothermal.**

eurythmics (juːˈrɪðmɪks) *n* a variant spelling (esp. U.S.) of **eurhythmics.** ► **euˈrythmic** *or* **euˈrythmical** *adj* ► **euˈrythmy** *n*

eurytopic (ˌjʊərɪˈtɒpɪk) *adj Ecology.* (of a species) able to tolerate a wide range of environmental changes. Compare **stenotopic.** [C20: from EURY- + *top* from Greek *topos* place + -IC]

Eusebio (juːˈseɪbɪəʊ) *n* **Silva Ferreira da** (ˈsɪlvə fɛrˈeɪrə də). born 1942, Portuguese footballer.

Eusebius (juːˈsiːbɪəs) *n* ?265–?340 A.D., bishop of Caesarea: author of a history of the Christian Church to 324 A.D.

eusporangiate (ˌjuːspɔːˈrændʒɪɪt) *adj* (of ferns) having each sporangium developing from a group of cells rather than a single cell. [from New Latin *eusporangiātus* (unattested), from EU- + SPORANGIUM]

Eustachian tube (juːˈsteɪʃən) *n* a tube that connects the middle ear with the nasopharynx and equalizes the pressure between the two sides of the eardrum. [C18: named after Bartolomeo *Eustachio*, 16th-century Italian anatomist]

eustatic (juːˈstætɪk) *adj* denoting or relating to worldwide changes in sea level, caused by the melting of ice sheets, movements of the ocean floor, sedimentation, etc. [C20: from Greek, from EU- + STATIC] ► **eustasy** ('ju:stəsɪ) *n* ► **eu'statically** *adv*

eutaxia (ju:'tæksɪə) *n Engineering.* the condition of being easily melted.

eutectic (ju:'tɛktɪk) *adj* **1** (of a mixture of substances, esp. an alloy) having the lowest freezing point of all possible mixtures of the substances. **2** concerned with or suitable for the formation of eutectic mixtures. ◆ *n* **3** a eutectic mixture. **4** the temperature on a phase diagram at which a eutectic mixture forms. [C19: from Greek *eutēktos* melting readily, from EU- + *tēkein* to melt]

eutectoid (ju:'tɛktɔɪd) *n* **1** a mixture of substances similar to a eutectic, but forming two or three constituents from a solid instead of from a melt. ◆ *adj* **2** concerned with or suitable for eutectoid mixtures. [C20: from EUTECT(IC) + -OID]

Euterpe (ju:'tɜ:pɪ) *n Greek myth.* the Muse of lyric poetry and music. ► **Eu'terpean** *adj*

euthanasia (ˌju:θə'neɪzɪə) *n* the act of killing someone painlessly, esp. to relieve suffering from an incurable illness. Also called: **mercy killing.** [C17: via New Latin from Greek: easy death, from EU- + *thanatos* death]

euthenics (ju:'θɛnɪks) *n* (*functioning as sing*) the study of the control of the environment, esp. with a view to improving the health and living standards of the human race. [C20: from Greek *euthēnein* to thrive] ► **eu'thenist** *n*

eutherian (ju:'θɪərɪən) *adj* **1** of, relating to, or belonging to the *Eutheria,* a subclass of mammals all of which have a placenta and reach an advanced state of development before birth. The group includes all mammals except monotremes and marsupials. ◆ *n* **2** any eutherian mammal. ◆ Compare **metatherian, prototherian.** [C19: from New Latin *Euthēria,* from Greek EU- + *thēria,* plural of *thērion* beast]

euthymia (ju:'θɪmɪə) *n Psychol.* a pleasant state of mind. [EU- + -THYMIA]

eutrophic (ju:'trɒfɪk, -'trəʊ-) *adj* (of lakes and similar habitats) rich in organic and mineral nutrients and supporting an abundant plant life, which in the process of decaying depletes the oxygen supply for animal life. Compare **oligotrophic.** [C18: probably from *eutrophy,* from Greek *eutrophia* sound nutrition, from *eutrophos* well-fed, from EU- + *trephein* to nourish] ► **'eutrophy** *n*

eutrophication (ju:ˌtrɒfɪ'keɪʃən) *n* a process by which pollution from such sources as sewage effluent or leachate from fertilized fields causes a lake, pond, or fen to become overrich in organic and mineral nutrients, so that algae and cyanobacteria grow rapidly and deplete the oxygen supply.

euxenite ('ju:ksɪˌnaɪt) *n* a rare brownish-black mineral containing erbium, cerium, uranium, columbium, and yttrium. [C19: from Greek *euxenos* hospitable (literally: well-disposed to strangers), from EU- + *xenos* stranger; from its containing a number of rare elements]

Euxine Sea ('ju:ksaɪn) *n* another name for the **Black Sea.**

eV *abbrev. for* electronvolt.

EV *abbrev. for* English Version (of the Bible).

EVA *Astronautics. abbrev. for* extravehicular activity.

evacuant (ɪ'vækjʊənt) *adj* **1** serving to promote excretion, esp. of the bowels. ◆ *n* **2** an evacuant agent.

evacuate (ɪ'vækjʊˌeɪt) *vb* (*mainly tr*) **1** (*also intr*) to withdraw or cause to withdraw from (a place of danger) to a place of greater safety. **2** to make empty by removing the contents of. **3** (*also intr*) *Physiol.* **3a** to eliminate or excrete (faeces); defecate. **3b** to discharge (any waste product) from (a part of the body). **4** (*tr*) to create a vacuum in (a bulb, flask, reaction vessel, etc.). [C16: from Latin *ēvacuāre* to void, from *vacuus* empty] ► **eˌvacu'ation** *n* ► **e'vacuative** *adj* ► **e'vacuˌator** *n*

evacuee (ɪˌvækju'i:) *n* a person evacuated from a place of danger, esp. in wartime.

evade (ɪ'veɪd) *vb* (*mainly tr*) **1** to get away from or avoid (imprisonment, captors, etc.); escape. **2** to get around, shirk, or dodge (the law, a duty, etc.). **3** (*also intr*) to avoid answering (a question). [C16: from French *évader,* from Latin *ēvādere* to go forth, from *vādere* to go] ► **e'vadable** *adj* ► **e'vader** *n* ► **e'vadingly** *adv*

evaginate (ɪ'vædʒɪˌneɪt) *vb* (*tr*) *Med.* to turn (an organ or part) inside out; turn the outer surface (of an organ or part) back on itself. [C17: from Late Latin *ēvāgīnāre* to unsheathe, from *vāgīna* sheath] ► **eˌvagi'nation** *n*

evaluate (ɪ'væljʊˌeɪt) *vb* (*tr*) **1** to ascertain or set the amount or value of. **2** to judge or assess the worth of; appraise. **3** *Maths, logic.* to determine the unique member of the range of a function corresponding to a given member of its domain. [C19: back formation from *evaluation,* from French, from *evaluer* to evaluate; see VALUE] ► **eˌvalu'ation** *n* ► **e'valuˌator** *n*

evaluative (ɪ'væljʊətɪv) *adj* **1** of, denoting, or based on an act of evaluating. **2** *Philosophy.* expressing an attitude or value judgment; emotive.

evanesce (ˌɛvə'nɛs) *vb* (*intr*) (of smoke, mist, etc.) to fade gradually from sight; vanish. [C19: from Latin *ēvānēscere* to disappear; see VANISH]

evanescent (ˌɛvə'nɛsᵊnt) *adj* **1** passing out of sight; fading away; vanishing. **2** ephemeral or transitory. ► **ˌeva'nescence** *n* ► **ˌeva'nescently** *adv*

evang. *or* **evan.** (*often cap.*) *abbrev. for* evangelical.

evangel (ɪ'vændʒəl) *n* **1** *Archaic.* the gospel of Christianity. **2** (*often cap.*) any of the four Gospels of the New Testament. **3** any body of teachings regarded as central or basic. **4** *U.S.* an evangelist. [C14: from Church Latin *ēvangelium,* from Greek *evangelion* good news, from EU- + *angelos* messenger; see ANGEL]

evangelical (ˌi:væn'dʒɛlɪkᵊl) *Christianity.* ◆ *adj* **1** of, based upon, or following from the Gospels. **2** denoting or relating to any of certain Protestant sects or parties, which emphasize the importance of personal conversion and faith in atonement through the death of Christ as a means of salvation. **3** another word for **evangelistic.** ◆ *n* **4** an upholder of evangelical doctrines or a member of an evangelical sect or party, esp. the Low-Church party of the Church of England. ► **ˌevan'gelicalism** *n* ► **ˌevan'gelically** *adv*

evangelism (ɪ'vændʒɪˌlɪzəm) *n* **1** (in Protestant churches) the practice of spreading the Christian gospel. R.C. Church term: **evangelization** *or* **evangelisation. 2** ardent or missionary zeal for a cause. **3** the work, methods, or characteristic outlook of a revivalist or evangelist preacher. **4** a less common word for **evangelicalism.**

evangelist (ɪ'vændʒɪlɪst) *n* **1** an occasional preacher, sometimes itinerant and often preaching at meetings in the open air. **2** a preacher of the Christian gospel. **3** any zealous advocate of a cause. **4** another word for **revivalist** (sense 1).

Evangelist (ɪ'vændʒɪlɪst) *n* **1** any of the writers of the New Testament Gospels: Matthew, Mark, Luke, or John. **2** a senior official or dignitary of the Mormon Church.

evangelistic (ɪˌvændʒɪ'lɪstɪk) *adj* **1** denoting, resembling, or relating to evangelists or their methods and attitudes: *evangelistic zeal.* **2** zealously advocating a cause. **3** (*often cap.*) of or relating to all or any of the four Evangelists. ► **eˌvange'listically** *adv*

evangelize *or* **evangelise** (ɪ'vændʒɪˌlaɪz) *vb* **1** to preach the Christian gospel or a particular interpretation of it (to). **2** (*intr*) to advocate a cause with the object of making converts. ► **eˌvangeli'zation** *or* **eˌvangeli'sation** *n* ► **e'vangeˌlizer** *or* **e'vangeˌliser** *n*

evanish (ɪ'vænɪʃ) *vb* a poetic word for **vanish.** [C15: from Old French *esvanir,* from Latin *ēvānēscere* to VANISH] ► **e'vanishment** *n*

Evans ('ɛvənz) *n* **1** Sir **Arthur** (**John**). 1851–1941, British archaeologist, whose excavations of the palace of Knossos in Crete provided evidence for the existence of the Minoan civilization. **2** Dame **Edith** (**Mary Booth**). 1888–1976, British actress. **3** Sir **Geraint** (**Llewellyn**). 1922–92, Welsh operatic baritone. **4 Herbert McLean.** 1882–1971, U.S. anatomist and embryologist; discoverer of vitamin E (1922). **5 Mary Ann.** real name of (George) **Eliot. 6 Oliver.** 1755–1819, U.S. engineer: invented the continuous production line and a high-pressure steam engine. **7 Walker.** 1903–75, U.S. photographer, noted esp. for his studies of rural poverty in the Great Depression.

Evanston ('ɛvənstən) *n* a city in NE Illinois, on Lake Michigan north of Chicago: Northwestern University (1851). Pop.: 73 233 (1990).

Evansville ('ɛvənzˌvɪl) *n* a city in SW Indiana, on the Ohio River. Pop.: 123 456 (1996 est.).

evaporate (ɪ'væpəˌreɪt) *vb* **1** to change or cause to change from a liquid or solid state to a vapour. Compare **boil**[1] (sense 1). **2** to lose or cause to lose liquid by vaporization leaving a more concentrated residue. **3** to disappear or cause to disappear; fade away or cause to fade away: *all her doubts evaporated.* **4** (*tr*) to deposit (a film, metal, etc.) by vaporization of a liquid or solid and the subsequent condensation of its vapour. [C16: from Late Latin *ēvapōrāre,* from Latin *vapor* steam; see VAPOUR] ► **e'vaporable** *adj* ► **eˌvapora'bility** *n* ► **eˌvapo'ration** *n* ► **e'vaporative** *adj* ► **e'vapoˌrator** *n*

evaporated milk *n* thick unsweetened tinned milk from which some of the water has been evaporated.

evaporimeter (ɪˌvæpə'rɪmɪtə) *or* **evaporometer** (ɪˌvæpə'rɒmɪtə) *n* another name for **atmometer.**

evaporite (ɪ'væpəˌraɪt) *n* any sedimentary rock, such as rock salt, gypsum, or anhydrite, formed by evaporation of former seas or salt-water lakes. [C20: EVAPORATION + -ITE[1]]

evapotranspiration (ɪˌvæpəʊˌtrænspə'reɪʃən) *n* the return of water vapour to the atmosphere by evaporation from land and water surfaces and by the transpiration of vegetation.

evasion (ɪ'veɪʒən) *n* **1** the act of evading or escaping, esp. from a distasteful duty, responsibility, etc., by trickery, cunning, or illegal means: *tax evasion.* **2** trickery, cunning, or deception used to dodge a question, duty, etc.; means of evading. [C15: from Late Latin *ēvāsiō,* from Latin *ēvādere* to go forth; see EVADE]

evasive (ɪ'veɪsɪv) *adj* **1** tending or seeking to evade; avoiding the issue; not straightforward. **2** avoiding or seeking to avoid trouble or difficulties: *to take evasive action.* **3** hard to catch or obtain; elusive. ► **e'vasively** *adv* ► **e'vasiveness** *n*

Evatt ('ɛvæt) *n* **Herbert Vere.** 1894–1965, Australian jurist and Labor political leader, president of the General Assembly of the United Nations 1948–49.

eve (i:v) *n* **1a** the evening or day before some special event or festival. **1b** (*cap. when part of a name*): *New Year's Eve.* **2** the period immediately before an event: *on the eve of civil war.* **3** an archaic word for **evening.** [C13: variant of EVEN[2]]

Eve (i:v) *n Old Testament.* the first woman; mother of the human race, fashioned by God from the rib of Adam (Genesis 2:18-25).

evection (ɪ'vɛkʃən) *n* irregularity in the moon's motion caused by perturbations of the sun and planets. [C17: from Latin *ēvectiō* a going up, from *ēvehere* to lead forth, from *vehere* to carry] ► **e'vectional** *adj*

Evelyn ('i:vlɪn, 'ɛv-) *n* **John.** 1620–1706, English author, noted chiefly for his diary (1640–1706).

even[1] ('i:vᵊn) *adj* **1** level and regular; flat: *an even surface.* **2** (*postpositive;* foll. by *with*) on the same level or in the same plane (as): *one surface even with another.* **3** without variation or fluctuation; regular; constant: *an even rate of progress.* **4** not readily moved or excited; placid; calm: *an even temper.* **5** equally balanced between two sides: *an even game.* **6** equal or identical in number, quantity, etc.: *two even spoonfuls of sugar.* **7a** (of a number) divisible by two. **7b** characterized or indicated by such a number: *maps are on the even pages.* Compare **odd** (sense 4). **8** relating to or denoting two or either of two alternatives, events, etc., that have an equal probability: *an even chance of missing or catching a train.* **9** having no balance of debt; neither owing nor being owed. **10** just and impartial; fair: *an even division.* **11** exact in number, amount, or extent: *an even pound.* **12** equal, as in score; level: *now the teams are even.* **13** *Maths.* (of a function) unchanged in value when the sign of the independent variable is changed, as in $y = z^2$. Compare **odd** (sense 8). **14 even money. 14a** a bet in which the winnings are the same as the amount staked.

14b (*as modifier*): *the even-money favourite.* **15 get even (with).** *Informal.* to exact revenge (on); settle accounts (with). **16 of even date.** *Legal, formal, or obsolete.* of the same or today's date. ◆ *adv* **17** (intensifier; used to suggest that the content of a statement is unexpected or paradoxical): *even an idiot can do that.* **18** (intensifier; used with comparative forms): *this is even better.* **19** notwithstanding; in spite of: *even having started late she soon caught him up.* **20** used to introduce a more precise version of a word, phrase, or statement: *he is base, even depraved.* **21** used preceding a clause of supposition or hypothesis to emphasize the implication that whether or not the condition in it is fulfilled, the statement in the main clause remains valid: *even if she died he wouldn't care.* **22** *Archaic.* that is to say; namely (used for emphasis): *he, even he, hath spoken these things.* **23** *Archaic.* all the way; fully: *I love thee even unto death.* **24 even as.** (*conj*) at the very same moment or in the very same way that: *even as I spoke, it thundered.* **25 even so.** in spite of any assertion to the contrary: nevertheless. ◆ *vb* **26** to make or become even. ◆ See also **break even, even out, evens, even up.** [Old English *efen;* related to Old Norse *jafn* even, equal, Gothic *ibns,* Old High German *eban*] ▸ **'evener** *n* ▸ **'evenly** *adv* ▸ **'evenness** *n*

even[2] ('i:vən) *n* an archaic word for **eve** or **evening.** [Old English *ǣfen;* related to Old Frisian *ēvend,* Old High German *āband*]

evenfall ('i:vən,fɔ:l) *n Archaic.* early evening; dusk.

even-handed *adj* dealing fairly with all; impartial. ▸ **,even-'handedly** *adv* ▸ **,even-'handedness** *n*

evening ('i:vnɪŋ) *n* **1** the latter part of the day, esp. from late afternoon until nightfall. **2** the latter or concluding period: *the evening of one's life.* **3** the early part of the night spent in a specified way: *an evening at the theatre.* **4** an entertainment, meeting, or reception held in the early part of the night. **5** *Southern U.S. and Brit. dialect.* the period between noon and sunset. **6** (*modifier*) of, used, or occurring in the evening: *the evening papers.* ◆ See also **evenings.** [Old English *ǣfnung;* related to Old Frisian *ēvend,* Old High German *āband*]

evening class *n* a class held in the evenings at certain colleges, normally for adults.

evening dress *n* attire for wearing at a formal occasion during the evening, esp. (for men) a dinner jacket and black tie, or (less commonly, for women) a floor-length gown.

evening primrose *n* any onagraceous plant of the American genus *Oenothera,* esp. *O. biennis,* typically having yellow flowers that open in the evening.

evening primrose oil *n* an oil, obtained from the seeds of the evening primrose, that is claimed to stimulate the production of prostaglandins.

evenings ('i:vnɪŋz) *adv Informal.* in the evening, esp. regularly.

evening star *n* a planet, usually Venus, seen just after sunset during the time that the planet is east of the sun. Compare **morning star.**

Evenki (ə'vɛŋkɪ) *n* **1** (*pl* **Evenki**) a Tungus people of E Siberia. **2** the language of this people.

even out *vb* (*adv*) to make or become even, as by the removal of bumps, inequalities, etc.: *the land evens out beyond that rise.*

evens ('i:vənz) *adj, adv* **1** (of a bet) winning the same as the amount staked if successful. **2** (of a runner) offered at such odds.

evensong ('i:vən,sɒŋ) *n* **1** Also called: **Evening Prayer, vespers.** *Church of England.* the daily evening service of Bible readings and prayers prescribed in the Book of Common Prayer. **2** *Archaic.* another name for **vespers. 3** an archaic or poetic word for **evening.**

event (ɪ'vɛnt) *n* **1** anything that takes place or happens, esp. something important; happening; incident. **2** the actual or final outcome; result (esp. in the phrases **in the event, after the event**). **3** any one contest in a programme of sporting or other contests: *the high jump is his event.* **4** *Philosophy.* **4a** an occurrence regarded as a bare instant of space-time as contrasted with an object which fills space and has endurance. **4b** an occurrence regarded in isolation from, or contrasted with, human agency. Compare **act** (sense 8). **5 in any event** *or* **at all events.** regardless of circumstances; in any case. **6 in the event of.** in case of; if (such a thing) happens: *in the event of rain the race will be cancelled.* **7 in the event that.** if it should happen that. ◆ *vb* **8** to take part or ride (a horse) in eventing. [C16: from Latin *ēventus* a happening, from *ēvenīre* to come forth, happen, from *venīre* to come]

even-tempered *adj* not easily angered or excited; calm.

eventful (ɪ'vɛntfʊl) *adj* full of events or incidents: *an eventful day.* ▸ **e'ventfully** *adv* ▸ **e'ventfulness** *n*

event horizon *n Astronomy.* the spherical area around a black hole enclosing the space from which electromagnetic radiation cannot escape due to excessive gravitational attraction. The radius is proportional to the mass of the black hole.

eventide ('i:vən,taɪd) *n Archaic or poetic.* another word for **evening.**

eventide home ('i:vən,taɪd) *n Euphemistic.* an old people's home.

eventing (ɪ'vɛntɪŋ) *n* the sport of taking part in equestrian competitions (esp. **three-day events**), usually consisting of three sections: dressage, cross-country riding, and showjumping. ▸ **e'venter** *n*

eventration (,i:vɛn'treɪʃən) *n Pathol.* protrusion of the bowel through the abdomen.

eventual (ɪ'vɛntʃʊəl) *adj* (*prenominal*) happening in due course of time; ultimate: *the eventual outcome was his defeat.*

eventuality (ɪ,vɛntʃʊ'ælɪtɪ) *n, pl* **-ties.** a possible event, occurrence, or result; contingency.

eventually (ɪ'vɛntʃʊəlɪ) *adv* **1** at the very end; finally. **2** (*as sentence modifier*) after a long time or long delay: *eventually, he arrived.*

eventuate (ɪ'vɛntʃʊ,eɪt) *vb* (*intr*) **1** (often foll. by *in*) to result ultimately (in). **2** to come about as a result: *famine eventuated from the crop failure.* ▸ **e,ventu'ation** *n*

even up *vb* (*adv*) to make or become equal, esp. in respect of claims or debts; settle or balance.

ever ('ɛvə) *adv* **1** at any time: *have you ever seen it?* **2** by any chance; in any case: *how did you ever find out?* **3** at all times; always: *ever busy.* **4** in any possible way or manner: *come as fast as ever you can.* **5** *Informal, chiefly Brit.* (intensifier, in the phrases **ever so, ever such,** and **ever such a**): *ever so good; ever such bad luck; ever such a waste.* **6 ever and again** (*or* **anon**). *Archaic.* now and then; from time to time. **7 is he** *or* **she ever!** *U.S. and Canadian slang.* he or she displays the quality concerned in abundance. ◆ See also **forever.** [Old English *ǣfre,* of uncertain origin]

Everest ('ɛvərɪst) *n* **1 Mount.** a mountain in S Asia on the border between Nepal and Tibet, in the Himalayas: the highest mountain in the world; first climbed by a British expedition (1953). Height: 8848 m (29 028 ft.). **2** any high point of ambition or achievement. [C19: named after Sir G. *Everest* (1790–1866), Surveyor-General of India]

Everglades ('ɛvə,gleɪdz) *pl n* **the.** a subtropical marshy region of Florida, south of Lake Okeechobee: contains the **Everglades National Park,** established to preserve the flora and fauna of the swamps. Area: over 13 000 sq. km (5000 sq. miles).

evergreen ('ɛvə,gri:n) *adj* **1** (of certain trees and shrubs) bearing foliage throughout the year; continually shedding and replacing leaves. Compare **deciduous. 2** remaining fresh and vital. ◆ *n* **3** an evergreen tree or shrub.

evergreen fund *n* a fund that provides capital for new companies and makes regular injections of capital to support their development.

everlasting (,ɛvə'lɑ:stɪŋ) *adj* **1** never coming to an end; eternal. **2** lasting for an indefinitely long period. **3** lasting so long or occurring so often as to become tedious; incessant: *I cannot bear her everlasting complaints.* ◆ *n* **4** endless duration; eternity. **5** Also called: **everlasting flower.** another name for **immortelle.** See also **cat's-foot.** ▸ **,ever'lastingly** *adv* ▸ **,ever'lastingness** *n*

Everly Brothers ('ɛvəlɪ) *pl n* **the.** U.S. pop singing duo comprising Don Everly (born 1937) and Phil Everly (born 1939), noted for their close harmonies.

evermore (,ɛvə'mɔ:) *adv* (often preceded by *for*) all time to come.

evert (ɪ'vɜ:t) *vb* (*tr*) to turn (an eyelid, the intestines, or some other bodily part) outwards or inside out. [C16: from Latin *ēvertere* to overthrow, from *vertere* to turn] ▸ **e'versible** *adj* ▸ **e'version** *n*

Evert ('ɛvət) *n* **Chris(tine).** born 1954, U.S. tennis player: Wimbledon champion 1974, 1976, and 1981; U.S. champion 1975–78, 1980, and 1982.

evertor (ɪ'vɜ:tə) *n* any muscle that turns a part outwards.

every ('ɛvrɪ) *determiner* **1** each one (of the class specified), without exception: *every child knows it.* **2** (*not used with a negative*) the greatest or best possible: *every hope of success.* **3** each: used before a noun phrase to indicate the recurrent, intermittent, or serial nature of a thing: *every third day; every now and then; every so often.* **4 every bit.** (used in comparisons with *as*) quite; just; equally: *every bit as funny as the other show.* **5 every other.** each alternate; every second: *every other day.* **6 every which way. 6a** in all directions; everywhere: *I looked every which way for you.* **6b** *U.S. and Canadian.* from all sides: *stones coming at me every which way.* [C15 *everich,* from Old English *ǣfre ǣlc,* from *ǣfre* EVER + *ǣlc* EACH]

everybody ('ɛvrɪ,bɒdɪ) *pron* every person; everyone.

USAGE See at **everyone.**

everyday ('ɛvrɪ,deɪ) *adj* **1** happening each day; daily. **2** commonplace or usual; ordinary. **3** suitable for or used on ordinary days as distinct from Sundays or special days.

Everyman ('ɛvrɪ,mæn) *n* **1** a medieval English morality play in which the central figure represents mankind, whose earthly destiny is dramatized from the Christian viewpoint. **2** (*often not cap.*) the ordinary person; common man.

everyone ('ɛvrɪ,wʌn, -wən) *pron* every person; everybody.

USAGE *Everyone* and *everybody* are interchangeable, as are *no one* and *nobody,* and *someone* and *somebody.* Care should be taken to distinguish between *everyone* and *someone* as single words and *every one* and *some one* as two words, the latter form correctly being used to refer to each individual person or thing in a particular group: *every one of them is wrong.*

every one *pron* each person or thing in a group, without exception: *every one of the large cats is a fast runner.*

everyplace ('ɛvrɪ,pleɪs) *adv U.S.* an informal word for **everywhere.**

everything ('ɛvrɪ,θɪŋ) *pron* **1** the entirety of a specified or implied class: *she lost everything in the War.* **2** a great deal, esp. of something very important: *she means everything to me.*

everywhere ('ɛvrɪ,wɛə) *adv* to or in all parts or places.

Evesham ('i:vʃəm) *n* a town in W central England, in W Worcestershire, on the River Avon: scene of the Battle of Evesham in 1265 (Lord Edward's defeat of Simon de Montfort and the barons); centre of the **Vale of Evesham,** famous for market gardens and orchards. Pop.: 17 823 (1991).

Eve's pudding *n Brit.* a baked sponge pudding with a layer of apple at the bottom.

evict (ɪ'vɪkt) *vb* (*tr*) **1** to expel (a tenant) from property by process of law; turn out. **2** to recover (property or the title to property) by judicial process or by virtue of a superior title. [C15: from Late Latin *ēvincere,* from Latin: to vanquish utterly, from *vincere* to conquer] ▸ **e'viction** *n* ▸ **e'victor** *n*

evidence ('ɛvɪdəns) *n* **1** ground for belief or disbelief; data on which to base proof or to establish truth or falsehood. **2** a mark or sign that makes evident; indication: *his pallor was evidence of ill health.* **3** *Law.* matter produced before a court of law in an attempt to prove or disprove a point in issue, such as the statements of witnesses, documents, material objects, etc. See also **circumstantial evidence, direct evidence. 4 turn queen's (king's, state's) evidence.** (of an accomplice) to act as witness for the prosecution and testify against those associated with him in crime. **5 in evidence.** on display; apparent; conspicuous: *her engagement ring was in evidence.* ◆ *vb* (*tr*) **6** to make evident; show clearly. **7** to give proof of or evidence for.

evident ('ɛvɪdənt) *adj* easy to see or understand; readily apparent. [C14: from Latin *ēvidēns,* from *vidēre* to see]

evidential (ˌɛvɪ'dɛnʃəl) *adj* relating to, serving as, or based on evidence. ► **ˌevi'dentially** *adv*

evidently ('ɛvɪdəntlɪ) *adv* **1** without question; clearly; undoubtedly. **2** to all appearances; apparently: *they are evidently related.*

evil ('iːvᵊl) *adj* **1** morally wrong or bad; wicked: *an evil ruler.* **2** causing harm or injury; harmful: *an evil plan.* **3** marked or accompanied by misfortune; unlucky: *an evil fate.* **4** (of temper, disposition, etc.) characterized by anger or spite. **5** not in high esteem; infamous: *an evil reputation.* **6** offensive or unpleasant: *an evil smell.* ◆ *n* **7** the quality or an instance of being morally wrong; wickedness: *the evils of war.* **8** (*sometimes cap.*) a force or power that brings about wickedness or harm: *evil is strong in the world.* **9** *Archaic.* an illness or disease, esp. scrofula (the **king's evil**). ◆ *adv* **10** (*now usually in combination*) in an evil manner; badly: *evil-smelling.* [Old English *yfel,* of Germanic origin; compare Old Frisian *evel,* Old High German *ubil* evil, Old Irish *adbal* excessive] ► **'evilly** *adv* ► **'evilness** *n*

evildoer ('iːvᵊlˌduːə) *n* a person who does evil. ► **'evilˌdoing** *n*

evil eye *n* **the. 1** a look or glance superstitiously supposed to have the power of inflicting harm or injury. **2** the power to inflict harm, etc., by such a look. ► **ˌevil-'eyed** *adj*

evil-minded *adj* inclined to evil thoughts; wicked; malicious or spiteful. ► **ˌevil-'mindedly** *adv* ► **ˌevil-'mindedness** *n*

Evil One *n* **the.** the devil; Satan.

evince (ɪ'vɪns) *vb* (*tr*) to make evident; show (something, such as an emotion) clearly. [C17: from Latin *ēvincere* to overcome; see EVICT] ► **e'vincible** *adj* ► **e'vincive** *adj*

USAGE *Evince* is sometimes wrongly used where *evoke* is meant: *the proposal evoked* (not *evinced*) *a storm of protest.*

eviscerate (ɪ'vɪsəˌreɪt) *vb* **1** (*tr*) to remove the internal organs of; disembowel. **2** (*tr*) to deprive of meaning or significance. **3** (*tr*) *Surgery.* to remove the contents of (the eyeball or other organ). **4** (*intr*) *Surgery.* (of the viscera) to protrude through a weakened abdominal incision after an operation. ◆ *adj* **5** having been disembowelled. [C17: from Latin *ēviscerāre* to disembowel, from *viscera* entrails] ► **eˌviscer'ation** *n* ► **e'viscerˌator** *n*

evitable ('ɛvɪtəbᵊl) *adj Rare.* able to be avoided. [C16: from Latin *ēvītābilis,* from *ēvītāre,* from *vītāre* to avoid]

evite (ɪ'vaɪt) *vb* an archaic word for **avoid.**

evocation (ˌɛvə'keɪʃən) *n* **1** the act or an instance of evoking. **2** *French law.* the transference of a case from an inferior court for adjudication by a higher tribunal. **3** another word for **induction** (sense 6). [C17: from Latin *ēvocātiō* a calling forth, from *ēvocāre* to EVOKE]

evocative (ɪ'vɒkətɪv) *adj* tending or serving to evoke. ► **e'vocatively** *adv* ► **e'vocativeness** *n*

evocator ('ɛvəˌkeɪtə) *n* **1** a person or thing that evokes. **2** *Embryol.* a substance or tissue that induces morphogenesis.

evoke (ɪ'vəʊk) *vb* (*tr*) **1** to call or summon up (a memory, feeling, etc.), esp. from the past. **2** to call forth or provoke; produce; elicit: *his words evoked an angry reply.* **3** to cause (spirits) to appear; conjure up. [C17: from Latin *ēvocāre* to call forth, from *vocāre* to call] ► **evocable** ('ɛvəkəbᵊl) *adj* ► **e'voker** *n*

USAGE See at **evince** and **invoke.**

evolute ('ɛvəˌluːt) *n* **1** a geometric curve that describes the locus of the centres of curvature of another curve (the **involute**). The tangents to the evolute are at right angles to the involute. ◆ *adj* **2** *Biology.* having the margins rolled outwards. [C19: from Latin *ēvolūtus* unrolled, from *ēvolvere* to roll out, EVOLVE]

evolution (ˌiːvə'luːʃən) *n* **1** *Biology.* a gradual change in the characteristics of a population of animals or plants over successive generations: accounts for the origin of existing species from ancestors unlike them. See also **natural selection. 2** a gradual development, esp. to a more complex form: *the evolution of modern art.* **3** the act of throwing off, as heat, gas, vapour, etc. **4** a pattern formed by a series of movements or something similar. **5** an algebraic operation in which the root of a number, expression, etc., is extracted. Compare **involution** (sense 6). **6** *Military.* an exercise carried out in accordance with a set procedure or plan. [C17: from Latin *ēvolūtiō* an unrolling, from *ēvolvere* to EVOLVE] ► **ˌevo'lutionary** *or* **ˌevo'lutional** *adj*

evolutionist (ˌiːvə'luːʃənɪst) *n* **1** a person who believes in a theory of evolution, esp. Darwin's theory of the evolution of plant and animal species. ◆ *adj* **2** of or relating to a theory of evolution. ► **ˌevo'lutionism** *n* ► **ˌevolution'istic** *adj*

evolutive (iː'vɒljʊtɪv) *adj* relating to, tending to, or promoting evolution.

evolve (ɪ'vɒlv) *vb* **1** to develop or cause to develop gradually. **2** (of animal or plant species) to undergo evolution of (organs or parts). **3** (*tr*) to yield, emit, or give off (heat, gas, vapour, etc.). [C17: from Latin *ēvolvere* to unfold, from *volvere* to roll] ► **e'volvable** *adj* ► **e'volvement** *n* ► **e'volver** *n*

evonymus (e'vɒnɪməs) *n* a variant of **euonymus.**

Évora (*Portuguese* 'ɛvura) *n* a city in S central Portugal: ancient Roman settlement; occupied by the Moors from 712 to 1166; residence of the Portuguese court in 15th and 16th centuries. Pop.: 34 100 (latest est.). Ancient name: **Ebora** ('iːbərə).

Évreux (*French* evrø) *n* an industrial town in NW France: severely damaged in World War II; cathedral (12th–16th centuries). Pop.: 51 450 (1990).

Évros ('ɛvrɔs) *n* transliteration of the Modern Greek name for the **Maritsa.**

evulsion (ɪ'vʌlʃən) *n Rare.* the act of extracting by force. [C17: from Latin *ēvulsiō,* from *ēvellere,* from *vellere* to pluck]

Évvoia ('ɛvia) *n* transliteration of the Modern Greek name for **Euboea.**

evzone ('ɛvzəʊn) *n* a soldier in an elite Greek infantry regiment. [C19: from Modern Greek, from Greek *euzōnos* literally: well-girt, from EU- + *zōne* girdle]

EW *international car registration for* Estonia.

Ewart ('juːət) *n* **Gavin** (**Buchanan**). 1916–95, British poet, noted for his light satirical verse.

ewe (juː) *n* **a** a female sheep. **b** (*as modifier*): *a ewe lamb.* [Old English *ēowu;* related to Old Norse *ǣr* ewe, Old High German *ou,* Latin *ovis* sheep, Sanskrit *avi*]

Ewe ('ɛwe) *n* **1** (*pl* **Ewe** *or* **Ewes**) a member of a Negroid people of W Africa living chiefly in the forests of E Ghana, Togo, and Benin. **2** the language of this people, belonging to the Kwa branch of the Niger-Congo family.

ewe equivalent *n N.Z.* the basic measure for calculating stock unit: *one Jersey cow is equal to 6.5 ewe equivalents.*

ewe-neck *n* **1** a condition in horses in which the neck is straight and sagging rather than arched. **2** a horse or other animal with this condition. ► **'ewe-ˌnecked** *adj*

ewer ('juːə) *n* a large jug or pitcher with a wide mouth. [C14: from Old French *evier,* from Latin *aquārius* water carrier, from *aqua* water]

EWO *abbrev. for* Educational Welfare Officer.

ex[1] (ɛks) *prep* **1** *Finance.* not participating in; excluding; without: *ex bonus; ex dividend; ex rights.* **2** *Commerce.* without charge to the buyer until removed from: *ex quay; ex ship; ex works.* [C19: from Latin: out of, from]

ex[2] (ɛks) *n Informal.* (a person's) former wife, husband, etc.

ex. *abbrev. for:* **1** examination. **2** examined. **3** example. **4** except(ed). **5** exception. **6** exchange. **7** excursion. **8** executed. **9** executive. **10** express. **11** extra.

Ex. *Bible. abbrev. for* Exodus.

ex-[1] *prefix* **1** out of; outside of; from: *exclosure; exurbia.* **2** former: *ex-wife.* [from Latin, from *ex* (prep), identical in meaning and origin with Greek *ex, ek;* see EC-]

ex-[2] *combining form.* a variant of **exo-** before a vowel: *exergonic.*

exa- *prefix* denoting 10^{18}: *exametres.* Symbol: E

exacerbate (ɪg'zæsəˌbeɪt, ɪk'sæs-) *vb* (*tr*) **1** to make (pain, disease, emotion, etc.) more intense; aggravate. **2** to exasperate or irritate (a person). [C17: from Latin *exacerbāre* to irritate, from *acerbus* bitter] ► **exˌacer'bation** *n*

exact (ɪg'zækt) *adj* **1** correct in every detail; strictly accurate: *an exact copy.* **2** precise, as opposed to approximate; neither more nor less: *the exact sum.* **3** (*prenominal*) specific; particular: *this exact spot.* **4** operating with very great precision: *exact instruments.* **5** allowing no deviation from a standard; rigorous; strict: *an exact mind.* **6** based mainly on measurement and the formulation of laws, as opposed to description and classification: *physics is an exact science.* ◆ *vb* (*tr*) **7** to force or compel (payment or performance); extort: *to exact tribute.* **8** to demand as a right; insist upon: *to exact respect from one's employees.* **9** to call for or require: *this work exacts careful effort.* [C16: from Latin *exactus* driven out, from *exigere* to drive forth, from *agere* to drive] ► **ex'actable** *adj* ► **ex'actness** *n* ► **ex'actor** *or* **ex'acter** *n*

exacting (ɪg'zæktɪŋ) *adj* making rigorous or excessive demands: *an exacting job.* ► **ex'actingly** *adv* ► **ex'actingness** *n*

exaction (ɪg'zækʃən) *n* **1** the act or an instance of exacting, esp. money. **2** an excessive or harsh demand, esp. for money; extortion. **3** a sum or payment exacted.

exactitude (ɪg'zæktɪˌtjuːd) *n* the quality of being exact; precision; accuracy.

exactly (ɪg'zæktlɪ) *adv* **1** in an exact manner; accurately or precisely. **2** in every respect; just: *it is exactly what he wants.* ◆ *sentence substitute.* **3** just so! precisely! **4 not exactly.** *Ironical.* not at all; by no means.

exacum ('ɛksəkəm) *n* any plant of the annual or perennial tropical genus *Exacum;* some are grown as greenhouse biennials for their bluish-purple platter-shaped flowers: family *Gentianaceae.* [Latin, a name for centaury, from *ex* out + *agere* to drive]

exaggerate (ɪg'zædʒəˌreɪt) *vb* **1** to regard or represent as larger or greater, more important or more successful, etc., than is true. **2** (*tr*) to make greater, more noticeable, etc., than usual: *his new clothes exaggerated his awkwardness.* [C16: from Latin *exaggerāre* to magnify, from *aggerāre* to heap, from *agger* heap] ► **ex'aggerˌatingly** *adv* ► **exˌagger'ation** *n* ► **ex'aggerative** *or* **ex'aggeratory** *adj* ► **ex'aggerˌator** *n*

exaggerated (ɪg'zædʒəˌreɪtɪd) *adj* **1** unduly or excessively magnified; enlarged beyond truth or reasonableness. **2** *Pathol.* abnormally enlarged: *an exaggerated spleen.* ► **ex'aggerˌatedly** *adv*

ex all *adv Finance.* without the right to any benefits: *shares quoted ex all.*

exalt (ɪg'zɔːlt) *vb* (*tr*) **1** to raise or elevate in rank, position, dignity, etc. **2** to praise highly; glorify; extol. **3** to stimulate the mind or imagination of; excite. **4** to increase the intensity of (a colour, etc.). **5** to fill with joy or delight; elate. **6** *Obsolete.* to lift up physically. [C15: from Latin *exaltāre* to raise, from *altus* high] ► **ex'alter** *n*

USAGE *Exalt* is sometimes wrongly used where *exult* is meant: *he was exulting* (not *exalting*) *in his win earlier that day.*

exaltation (ˌɛgzɔːl'teɪʃən) *n* **1** the act of exalting or state of being exalted. **2** a feeling of intense well-being or exhilaration; elation; rapture. **3** a flock of larks.

exalted (ɪg'zɔːltɪd) *adj* **1** high or elevated in rank, position, dignity, etc. **2** elevated in character; noble; lofty: *an exalted ideal.* **3** *Informal.* excessively high; inflated: *he has an exalted opinion of himself.* **4** intensely excited; elated. ► **ex'altedly** *adv* ► **ex'altedness** *n*

exam (ɪg'zæm) *n* short for **examination.**

examen (ɪg'zeɪmɛn) *n R.C. Church.* an examination of conscience, usually made daily by Jesuits and others. [C17: from Latin: tongue of a balance, from *exigere* to thrust out, from *agere* to thrust]

examination (ɪgˌzæmɪ'neɪʃən) *n* **1** the act of examining or state of being examined. **2** *Education.* **2a** written exercises, oral questions, or practical tasks, set to test a candidate's knowledge and skill. **2b** (*as modifier*): *an examination paper.*

3 *Med.* **3a** physical inspection of a patient or parts of his body, in order to verify health or diagnose disease. **3b** laboratory study of secretory or excretory products, tissue samples, etc., esp. in order to diagnose disease. **4** *Law.* the formal interrogation of a person on oath, esp. of an accused or a witness. ▸ **ex,am-i'national** *adj*

examine (ɪg'zæmɪn) *vb* (*tr*) **1** to look at, inspect, or scrutinize carefully or in detail; investigate. **2** *Education.* to test the knowledge or skill of (a candidate) in (a subject or activity) by written or oral questions or by practical tests. **3** *Law.* to interrogate (a witness or accused person) formally on oath. **4** *Med.* to investigate the state of health of (a patient). [C14: from Old French *examiner,* from Latin *exāmināre* to weigh, from *exāmen* means of weighing; see EXAMEN] ▸ **ex'aminable** *adj* ▸ **ex'aminer** *n* ▸ **ex'amining** *adj*

examinee (ɪg,zæmɪ'niː) *n* a person who takes an examination.

examine-in-chief *vb* (*tr*) *Law.* to examine (one's own witness) in attempting to adduce a case. Compare **cross-examine.** ▸ **ex,ami'nation-in-chief** *n*

example (ɪg'zɑːmpᵊl) *n* **1** a specimen or instance that is typical of the group or set of which it forms part; sample. **2** a person, action, thing, etc., that is worthy of imitation; pattern: *you must set an example to the younger children.* **3** a precedent, illustration of a principle, or model: *an example in a maths book.* **4** a punishment or the recipient of a punishment serving or intended to serve as a warning: *the headmaster made an example of him.* **5 for example.** as an illustration; for instance. ◆ *vb* **6** (*tr; now usually passive*) to present an example of; exemplify. [C14: from Old French, from Latin *exemplum* pattern, from *eximere* to take out, from EX-[1] + *emere* to purchase]

exanimate (ɪg'zænɪmɪt, -,meɪt) *adj Rare.* lacking life; inanimate. [C16: from Latin *exanimāre* to deprive of air, kill, from *anima* breath, spirit] ▸ **ex,an-i'mation** *n*

exanthema (,ɛksæn'θiːmə) *or* **exanthem** (ɛk'sænθəm) *n, pl* **-themata** (-'θiːmətə), **-themas,** *or* **-thems.** a skin eruption or rash occurring as a symptom in a disease such as measles or scarlet fever. [C17: via Late Latin from Greek, from *exanthein* to burst forth, from *anthein* to blossom, from *anthos* flower] ▸ **exanthematous** (,ɛksæn'θɛmətəs) *or* **exanthematic** (ɛk,sæn-θɪ'mætɪk) *adj*

exarate ('ɛksə,reɪt) *adj* (of the pupa of such insects as ants and bees) having the legs, wings, antennae, etc., free and movable. [C19: from Latin *exarātus,* literally: ploughed up (apparently referring to the way this type of pupa throws off the larval skin), from *exarāre,* from *arā* plough]

exarch[1] ('ɛksɑːk) *n* **1** the head of certain autonomous Orthodox Christian Churches, such as that of Bulgaria and Cyprus. **2** any of certain Eastern Orthodox bishops, lower in rank than a patriarch but higher than a metropolitan. **3** the governor of a province in the Byzantine Empire. [C16: from Late Latin *exarchus* overseer, from Greek *exarkhos,* from *exarkhein* to take the lead, from *arkhein* to rule] ▸ **ex'archal** *adj*

exarch[2] ('ɛksɑːk) *adj Botany.* (of a xylem strand) having the first-formed xylem external to that formed later. Compare **endarch, mesarch.** [C19: from EX-[1] (outside) + Greek *arkhē* beginning, origin]

exarchate ('ɛksɑː,keɪt, ɛk'sɑːkeɪt) *or* **exarchy** ('ɛksɑːkɪ) *n, pl* **-chates** *or* **-chies.** the office, rank, or jurisdiction of an exarch.

exasperate (ɪg'zɑːspə,reɪt) *vb* (*tr*) **1** to cause great irritation or anger to; infuriate. **2** to cause (an unpleasant feeling, condition, etc.) to worsen; aggravate. ◆ *adj* **3** *Botany.* having a rough prickly surface because of the presence of hard projecting points. [C16: from Latin *exasperāre* to make rough, from *asper* rough] ▸ **ex'asper,atedly** *adv* ▸ **ex'asper,ater** *n* ▸ **ex'asper,ating** *adj* ▸ **ex'asper,atingly** *adv* ▸ **ex,asper'ation** *n*

exc. *abbrev. for:* **1** excellent. **2** except(ed). **3** exception. **4** excursion.

Exc. *abbrev. for* Excellency.

Excalibur (ɛk'skælɪbə) *n* (in Arthurian legend) the magic sword of King Arthur. [C14: from Old French *Escalibor,* from Medieval Latin *Caliburnus,* from Welsh *Caledvwlch,* perhaps related to Irish *Caladbolg* a legendary sword (literally: hard belly, hence, voracious)]

ex cathedra (ɛks kə'θiːdrə) *adj, adv* **1** with authority. **2** *R.C. Church.* (of doctrines of faith or morals) defined by the pope as infallibly true, to be accepted by all Catholics. [Latin, literally: from the chair]

excaudate (ɛks'kɔːdeɪt) *adj Zoology.* having no tail or tail-like process; tailless.

excavate ('ɛkskə,veɪt) *vb* **1** to remove (soil, earth, etc.) by digging; dig out. **2** to make (a hole, cavity, or tunnel) in (solid matter) by hollowing or removing the centre or inner part: *to excavate a tooth.* **3** to unearth (buried objects) methodically in an attempt to discover information about the past. [C16: from Latin *excavāre,* from *cavāre* to make hollow, from *cavus* hollow] ▸ **,exca'vation** *n*

excavator ('ɛkskə,veɪtə) *n* **1** a powered machine for digging earth, gravel, sand, etc., esp. a caterpillar tractor so equipped. **2** any person, animal, or thing that excavates.

exceed (ɪk'siːd) *vb* **1** to be superior to (a person or thing), esp. in size or quality; excel. **2** (*tr*) to go beyond the limit or bounds of: *to exceed one's income; exceed a speed limit.* **3** to be greater in degree or quantity than (a person or thing). [C14: from Latin *excēdere* to go beyond, from *cēdere* to go] ▸ **ex'ceedable** *adj* ▸ **ex'ceeder** *n*

exceeding (ɪk'siːdɪŋ) *adj* **1** very great; exceptional or excessive. ◆ *adv* **2** an archaic word for **exceedingly.**

exceedingly (ɪk'siːdɪŋlɪ) *adv* to a very great or unusual degree; extremely; exceptionally.

excel (ɪk'sɛl) *vb* **-cels, -celling, -celled. 1** to be superior to (another or others); surpass. **2** (*intr;* foll. by *in* or *at*) to be outstandingly good or proficient: *he excels at tennis.* [C15: from Latin *excellere* to rise up]

excellence ('ɛksələns) *n* **1** the state or quality of excelling or being exceptionally good; extreme merit; superiority. **2** an action, characteristic, feature, etc., in which a person excels. ▸ **'excellent** *adj* ▸ **'excellently** *adv*

Excellency ('ɛksələnsɪ) *or* **Excellence** *n, pl* **-lencies** *or* **-lences. 1** (usually preceded by *Your, His,* or *Her*) a title used to address or refer to a high-ranking official, such as an ambassador or governor. **2** *R.C. Church.* a title of bishops and archbishops in many non-English-speaking countries.

excelsior (ɪk'sɛlsɪ,ɔː) *interj, adv, n* **1** excellent: used as a motto and as a trademark for various products, esp. in the U.S. for fine wood shavings used for packing breakable objects. **2** upwards. [C19: from Latin: higher]

except (ɪk'sɛpt) *prep* **1** Also: **except for.** other than; apart from; with the exception of: *he likes everyone except you; except for this mistake, you did very well.* **2 except that.** (*conj*) but for the fact that; were it not true that. ◆ *conj* **3** an archaic word for **unless. 4** *Informal; not standard in the U.S.* except that; but for the fact that: *I would have arrived earlier, except I lost my way.* ◆ *vb* **5** (*tr*) to leave out; omit; exclude. **6** (*intr;* often foll. by *to*) *Rare.* to take exception; object. [C14: from Old French *excepter* to leave out, from Latin *exceptāre,* from *excipere* to take out, from *capere* to take]

excepting (ɪk'sɛptɪŋ) *prep* **1** excluding; except; except for (esp. in the phrase **not excepting**). ◆ *conj* **2** an archaic word for **unless.**

USAGE The use of *excepting* is considered by many people to be acceptable only after *not, only, always,* or *without.* Elsewhere *except* is preferred: *every country agreed to the proposal except* (not *excepting*) *Spain; he was well again except for* (not *excepting*) *a slight pain in his chest.*

exception (ɪk'sɛpʃən) *n* **1** the act of excepting or fact of being excepted; omission. **2** anything excluded from or not in conformance with a general rule, principle, class, etc. **3** criticism, esp. when it is adverse; objection. **4** *Law.* (formerly) a formal objection in the course of legal proceedings. **5** *Law.* a clause or term in a document that restricts the usual legal effect of the document. **6 take exception. 6a** (usually foll. by *to*) to make objections (to); demur (at). **6b** (often foll. by *at*) to be offended (by); be resentful (at).

exceptionable (ɪk'sɛpʃənəbᵊl) *adj* open to or subject to objection; objectionable. ▸ **ex'ceptionableness** *n* ▸ **ex'ceptionably** *adv*

exceptional (ɪk'sɛpʃənᵊl) *adj* **1** forming an exception; not ordinary. **2** having much more than average intelligence, ability, or skill. ▸ **ex'ceptionally** *adv*

exceptive (ɪk'sɛptɪv) *adj* relating to or forming an exception.

excerpt *n* ('ɛksɜːpt). **1** a part or passage taken from a book, speech, play, etc., and considered on its own; extract. ◆ *vb* (ɛk'sɜːpt). **2** (*tr*) to take (a part or passage) from a book, speech, play, etc. [C17: from Latin *excerptum,* literally: (something) picked out, from *excerpere* to select, from *carpere* to pluck] ▸ **ex'cerptor** *n* ▸ **ex'cerptible** *adj* ▸ **ex'cerption** *n*

excess *n* (ɪk'sɛs, 'ɛksɛs). **1** the state or act of going beyond normal, sufficient, or permitted limits. **2** an immoderate or abnormal amount, number, extent, or degree too much or too many: *an excess of tolerance.* **3** the amount, number, extent, or degree by which one thing exceeds another. **4** *Chem.* a quantity of a reagent that is greater than the quantity required to complete a reaction: *add an excess of acid.* **5** overindulgence or intemperance. **6** *Insurance, chiefly Brit.* a specified contribution towards the cost of a claim, stipulated on certain insurance policies as being payable by the policyholder. **7 in excess of.** of more than; over. **8 to excess.** to an inordinate extent; immoderately: *he drinks to excess.* ◆ *adj* ('ɛksɛs, ɪk'sɛs). (*usually prenominal*) **9** more than normal, necessary, or permitted; surplus: *excess weight.* **10** payable as a result of previous underpayment: *excess postage; an excess fare for a railway journey.* [C14: from Latin *excessus,* from *excēdere* to go beyond; see EXCEED]

excess demand *n Economics.* a situation in which the market demand for a commodity is greater than its market supply, thus causing its market price to rise.

excessive (ɪk'sɛsɪv) *adj* exceeding the normal or permitted extents or limits; immoderate; inordinate. ▸ **ex'cessively** *adv* ▸ **ex'cessiveness** *n*

excess luggage *or* **baggage** *n* luggage that is greater in weight or in number of pieces than an airline, etc., will carry free.

excess supply *n Economics.* a situation in which the market supply of a commodity is greater than the market demand for it, thus causing its market price to fall.

exch. *abbrev. for:* **1** exchange. **2** exchequer.

exchange (ɪks'tʃeɪndʒ) *vb* **1** (*tr*) to give up, part with, or transfer (one thing) for an equivalent: *to exchange gifts; to exchange francs for dollars.* **2** (*tr*) to give and receive (information, ideas, etc.); interchange. **3** (*tr*) to replace (one thing) with another, esp. to replace unsatisfactory goods. **4** to transfer or hand over (goods) in return for the equivalent value in kind rather than in money; barter; trade. **5** (*tr*) *Chess.* to capture and surrender (pieces, usually of the same value) in a single sequence of moves. ◆ *n* **6** the act or process of exchanging. **7a** anything given or received as an equivalent, replacement, or substitute for something else. **7b** (*as modifier*): *an exchange student.* **8** an argument or quarrel; altercation: *the two men had a bitter exchange.* **9** Also called: **telephone exchange.** a switching centre in which telephone lines are interconnected. **10a** a place where securities or commodities are sold, bought, or traded, esp. by brokers or merchants: *a stock exchange; a corn exchange.* **10b** (*as modifier*): *an exchange broker.* **11a** the system by which commercial debts between parties in different places are settled by commercial documents, esp. bills of exchange, instead of by direct payment of money. **11b** the percentage or fee charged for accepting payment in this manner. **12** a transfer or interchange of sums of money of equivalent value, as between different national currencies or different issues of the same currency. **13** (*often pl*) the cheques, drafts, bills, etc., exchanged or settled between banks in a clearing house. **14** *Chess.* the capture by both players of pieces of equal value, usually on consecutive moves. **15 win** (*or* **lose**) **the exchange.** *Chess.* to win (or lose) a rook in return for a bishop or knight. **16** *Med.* another word for **transfusion** (sense 2). **17** *Physics.* a process in which a particle is transferred between two nucleons, such as the transfer of a meson between two nucleons. ◆ See also **bill of exchange, exchange rate, foreign exchange, labour exchange.** [C14: from Anglo-French *eschaungier,* from Vulgar Latin *excambiāre* (unattested), from Latin *cambīre* to barter] ▸ **ex'changeable** *adj* ▸ **ex,changea'bility** *n* ▸ **ex'changeably** *adv* ▸ **ex'changer** *n*

exchange force *n Physics.* **1** a force between two elementary particles resulting from the exchange of a virtual particle. **2** the force causing the alignment of the magnetic dipole moments of atoms in ferromagnetic materials.

exchange rate *n* the rate at which the currency unit of one country may be exchanged for that of another.

Exchange Rate Mechanism *n* **1** the mechanism formerly used in the European Monetary System in which participating governments committed themselves to maintain the values of their currencies in relation to the ECU. Abbrev.: **ERM. 2** Also **Exchange Rate Mechanism II.** the mechanism used to stabilize the currencies of European Union states that have not adopted the euro but wish to participate in European Monetary Union. Abbrev.: **ERM II.**

exchequer (ɪks'tʃɛkə) *n* **1** (*often cap.*) *Government.* (in Britain and certain other countries) the accounting department of the Treasury, responsible for receiving and issuing funds. **2** *Informal.* personal funds; finances. [C13 (in the sense: chessboard, counting table): from Old French *eschequier*, from *eschec* CHECK]

Exchequer (ɪks'tʃɛkə) *n* See **Court of Exchequer.**

excide (ɪk'saɪd) *vb* (*tr*) *Rare.* to cut out; excise. [C18: from Latin *excīdere* to cut off, from *caedere* to cut]

excimer ('ɛk,saɪmə) *n Physics.* an excited dimer formed by the association of excited and unexcited molecules, which would remain dissociated in the ground state.

excipient (ɪk'sɪpɪənt) *n* an inert substance, such as sugar or gum, used to prepare drugs in a form suitable for oral administration. [C18: from Latin *excipiēns* excepting, from *excipere* to EXCEPT]

excisable (ɪk'saɪzəbᵊl) *adj* liable to an excise tax.

excise[1] *n* ('ɛksaɪz, ɛk'saɪz). **1** Also called: **excise tax.** a tax on goods, such as spirits, produced for the home market. **2** a tax paid for a licence to carry out various trades, sports, etc. **3** *Brit.* that section of the government service responsible for the collection of excise, now the Board of Customs and Excise. [C15: probably from Middle Dutch *excijs*, probably from Old French *assise* a sitting, assessment, from Latin *assidēre* to sit beside, assist in judging, from *sedēre* to sit] ▸ **ex'cisable** *adj*

excise[2] (ɪk'saɪz) *vb* (*tr*) **1** to delete (a passage, sentence, etc.); expunge. **2** to remove (an organ, structure, or part) surgically. [C16: from Latin *excīdere* to cut down; see EXCIDE] ▸ **excision** (ɪk'sɪʒən) *n*

exciseman ('ɛksaɪz,mæn) *n, pl* **-men.** *Brit.* (formerly) a government agent whose function was to collect excise and prevent smuggling.

excitable (ɪk'saɪtəbᵊl) *adj* **1** easily excited; volatile. **2** (esp. of a nerve) ready to respond to a stimulus. ▸ **ex,cita'bility** *or* **ex'citableness** *n* ▸ **ex'citably** *adv*

excitant (ɪk'saɪtᵊnt, 'ɛksɪtənt) *adj also* **excitative** (ɪk'saɪtətɪv) *or* **excitatory** (ɪk'saɪtətərɪ). **1** able to excite or stimulate. ◆ *n* **2** something, such as a drug or other agent, able to excite; stimulant.

excitation (,ɛksɪ'teɪʃən) *n* **1** the act or process of exciting or state of being excited. **2** a means of exciting or cause of excitement. **3a** the current in a field coil of a generator, motor, etc., or the magnetizing current in a transformer. **3b** (*as modifier*): *an excitation current.* **4** the action of a stimulus on an animal or plant organ, inducing it to respond.

excite (ɪk'saɪt) *vb* (*tr*) **1** to arouse (a person) to strong feeling, esp. to pleasurable anticipation or nervous agitation. **2** to arouse or elicit (an emotion, response, etc.); evoke: *her answers excited curiosity.* **3** to cause or bring about; stir up: *to excite a rebellion.* **4** to arouse sexually. **5** *Physiol.* to cause a response in or increase the activity of (an organ, tissue, or part); stimulate. **6** to raise (an atom, molecule, electron, nucleus, etc.) from the ground state to a higher energy level. **7** to supply electricity to (the coils of a generator or motor) in order to create a magnetic field. **8** to supply a signal to a stage of a valve or transistor circuit. [C14: from Latin *excitāre*, from *exciēre* to stimulate, from *ciēre* to set in motion, rouse]

excited (ɪk'saɪtɪd) *adj* **1** emotionally aroused, esp. to pleasure or agitation. **2** characterized by excitement: *an excited dance.* **3** sexually aroused. **4** (of an atom, molecule, etc.) having an energy level above the ground state. ▸ **ex'citedly** *adv* ▸ **ex'citedness** *n*

excitement (ɪk'saɪtmənt) *n* **1** the state of being excited. **2** a person or thing that excites; stimulation or thrill.

exciter (ɪk'saɪtə) *n* **1** a person or thing that excites. **2** a small generator that excites a larger machine. **3** an oscillator producing a transmitter's carrier wave.

exciting (ɪk'saɪtɪŋ) *adj* causing excitement; stirring; stimulating. ▸ **ex'citingly** *adv*

exciton ('ɛksaɪ,tɒn) *n* a mobile neutral entity in a crystalline solid consisting of an excited electron bound to the hole produced by its excitation. [C20: from EXCIT(ATION) + -ON]

excitor (ɪk'saɪtə) *n* **1** a nerve that, when stimulated, causes increased activity in the organ or part it supplies. **2** a variant spelling of **exciter.**

excl. *abbrev. for:* **1** exclamation. **2** excluding. **3** exclusive.

exclaim (ɪk'skleɪm) *vb* to cry out or speak suddenly or excitedly, as from surprise, delight, horror, etc. [C16: from Latin *exclāmāre*, from *clāmāre* to shout] ▸ **ex'claimer** *n*

exclamation (,ɛksklə'meɪʃən) *n* **1** an abrupt, emphatic, or excited cry or utterance; interjection; ejaculation. **2** the act of exclaiming. ▸ **,excla'mational** *adj*

exclamation mark *or U.S.* **point** *n* **1** the punctuation mark **!** used after exclamations and vehement commands. **2** this mark used for any other purpose, as to draw attention to an obvious mistake, in road warning signs, (in chess commentaries) beside the notation of a move considered a good one, (in mathematics) as a symbol of the factorial function, or (in logic) occurring with an existential quantifier.

exclamatory (ɪk'sklæmətərɪ, -trɪ) *adj* using, containing, or relating to exclamations. ▸ **ex'clamatorily** *adv*

exclaustration (,ɛksklɔː'streɪʃən) *n* the return of a monk or nun to the outside world after being released from his or her religious vows. [from EX-[1] + Latin *claustrum* cloister]

exclave ('ɛkskleɪv) *n* a part of a country entirely surrounded by foreign territory: viewed from the position of the home country. Compare **enclave.** [C20: from EX-[1] + *-clave*, on the model of ENCLAVE]

exclosure (ɪk'skləʊʒə) *n* an area of land, esp. in a forest, fenced round to keep out unwanted animals.

exclude (ɪk'skluːd) *vb* (*tr*) **1** to keep out; prevent from entering. **2** to reject or not consider; leave out. **3** to expel forcibly; eject. [C14: from Latin *exclūdere*, from *claudere* to shut] ▸ **ex'cludable** *or* **ex'cludible** *adj* ▸ **ex'cluder** *n*

excluded middle *n Logic.* the principle that every proposition is either true or false, so that there is no third truth-value and no statements lack truth-value.

excluding (ɪk'skluːdɪŋ) *prep* excepting.

exclusion (ɪk'skluːʒən) *n* the act or an instance of excluding or the state of being excluded. ▸ **ex'clusionary** *adj*

exclusionist (ɪk'skluːʒənɪst) *adj* **1** *Chiefly U.S.* denoting or relating to a policy of excluding various types of immigrants, imports, etc. ◆ *n* **2** a supporter of a policy of exclusion. ▸ **ex'clusion,ism** *n*

exclusion principle *n* See **Pauli exclusion principle.**

exclusive (ɪk'skluːsɪv) *adj* **1** excluding all else; rejecting other considerations, possibilities, events, etc.: *an exclusive preoccupation with money.* **2** belonging to a particular individual or group and to no other; not shared: *exclusive rights; an exclusive story.* **3** belonging to or catering for a privileged minority, esp. a fashionable clique: *an exclusive restaurant.* **4** (*postpositive;* foll. by *to*) limited (to); found only (in): *this model is exclusive to Harrods.* **5** single; unique; only: *the exclusive means of transport on the island was the bicycle.* **6** separate and incompatible: *mutually exclusive principles.* **7** (*immediately postpositive*) not including the numbers, dates, letters, etc., mentioned: *1980–84 exclusive.* **8** (*postpositive;* foll. by *of*) except (for); not taking account (of): *exclusive of bonus payments, you will earn this amount.* **9** *Commerce.* (of a contract, agreement, etc.) binding the parties to do business only with each other with respect to a class of goods or services. **10** *Logic.* (of a disjunction) true if only one rather than both of its component propositions is true. Compare **inclusive** (sense 4). ◆ *n* **11** an exclusive story; a story reported in only one newspaper. ▸ **ex'clusively** *adv* **exclusivity** (,ɛkskluː'sɪvɪtɪ) *or* ▸ **ex'clusiveness** *n*

Exclusive Brethren *pl n* one of the two main divisions of the Plymouth Brethren, which, in contrast to the Open Brethren, restricts its members' contacts with those outside the sect.

exclusive economic zone *n* the coastal water and sea bed around a country's shores, to which it claims exclusive rights for fishing, oil exploration, etc. Sometimes shortened to **economic zone.**

exclusive or *n Logic.* the connective that gives the value *true* to a disjunction if one or other, but not both, of the disjuncts are true. Also called: **exclusive disjunction.** Compare **inclusive or.**

exclusive OR circuit *or* **gate** *n Electronics.* a computer logic circuit having two or more input wires and one output wire and giving a high-voltage output signal if a low-voltage signal is fed to one or more, but not all, of the input wires. Compare **OR circuit.**

excogitate (ɛks'kɒdʒɪ,teɪt) *vb* (*tr*) **1** to devise, invent, or contrive. **2** to think out in detail. [C16: from Latin *excōgitāre*, from *cōgitāre* to ponder, COGITATE] ▸ **ex'cogitable** *adj* ▸ **ex,cogi'tation** *n* ▸ **ex'cogitative** *adj* ▸ **ex'cogi,tator** *n*

excommunicate *R.C. Church.* ◆ *vb* (,ɛkskə'mjuːnɪ,keɪt). **1** (*tr*) to sentence (a member of the Church) to exclusion from the communion of believers and from the privileges and public prayers of the Church. ◆ *adj* (,ɛkskə'mjuːnɪkɪt, -,keɪt). **2** having incurred such a sentence. ◆ *n* (,ɛkskə'mjuːnɪkɪt, -,keɪt). **3** an excommunicated person. [C15: from Late Latin *excommūnicāre*, literally: to exclude from the community, from Latin *commūnis* COMMON] ▸ **,excom'municable** *adj* ▸ **,excom,muni'cation** *n* ▸ **,excom'municative** *or* **,excom'municatory** *adj* ▸ **,excom'municator** *n*

excoriate (ɪk'skɔːrɪ,eɪt) *vb* (*tr*) **1** to strip (the skin) from (a person or animal); flay. **2** *Med.* to lose (a superficial area of skin), as by scratching, the application of chemicals, etc. **3** to denounce vehemently; censure severely. [C15: from Late Latin *excoriāre* to strip, flay, from Latin *corium* skin, hide] ▸ **ex,cori'ation** *n*

excrement ('ɛkskrɪmənt) *n* waste matter discharged from the body, esp. faeces; excreta. [C16: from Latin *excrēmentum*, from *excernere* to sift, EXCRETE] ▸ **excremental** (,ɛkskrɪ'mɛntᵊl) *or* **excrementitious** (,ɛkskrɪmɛn'tɪʃəs) *adj*

excrescence (ɪk'skrɛsᵊns) *n* a projection or protuberance, esp. an outgrowth from an organ or part of the body. ▸ **excrescential** (,ɛkskrɪ'sɛnʃəl) *adj*

excrescency (ɪk'skrɛsənsɪ) *n, pl* **-cies. 1** the state or condition of being excrescent. **2** another word for **excrescence.**

excrescent (ɪk'skrɛsᵊnt) *adj* **1** denoting, relating to, or resembling an abnormal outgrowth. **2** uselessly added; not essential; superfluous. **3** denoting or relating to a speech sound or letter inserted into a word without etymological justification, such as the *b* in *nimble.* [C17: from Latin *excrēscēns*, from *excrēscere*, from *crēscere* to grow] ▸ **ex'crescently** *adv*

excreta (ɪk'skriːtə) *pl n* waste matter, such as urine, faeces, or sweat, discharged from the body; excrement. [C19: New Latin, from Latin *excernere* to EXCRETE] ▸ **ex'cretal** *adj*

excrete (ɪk'skriːt) *vb* **1** to discharge (waste matter, such as urine, sweat, carbon dioxide, or faeces) from the body through the kidneys, skin, lungs, bowels, etc. **2** (of plants) to eliminate (waste matter, such as carbon dioxide and salts) through the leaves, roots, etc. [C17: from Latin *excernere* to separate, discharge, from *cernere* to sift] ▸ **ex'creter** *n* ▸ **ex'cretion** *n* ▸ **ex'cretive** *or* **ex'cretory** *adj*

excruciate (ɪk'skruːʃɪˌeɪt) *vb* (*tr*) **1** to inflict mental suffering on; torment. **2** *Obsolete*. to inflict physical pain on; torture. [C16: from Latin *excruciāre*, from *cruciāre* to crucify, from *crux* cross] ▸ **exˌcruci'ation** *n*

excruciating (ɪk'skruːʃɪˌeɪtɪŋ) *adj* **1** unbearably painful; agonizing. **2** intense; extreme: *he took excruciating pains to do it well*. **3** *Informal*. irritating; trying. **4** *Humorous*. very bad: *an excruciating pun*. ▸ **ex'cruciˌatingly** *adv*

exculpate ('ɛkskʌlˌpeɪt, ɪk'skʌlpeɪt) *vb* (*tr*) to free from blame or guilt; vindicate or exonerate. [C17: from Medieval Latin *exculpāre*, from Latin EX-[1] + *culpāre* to blame, from *culpa* fault, blame] ▸ **exculpable** (ɪk'skʌlpəbᵊl) *adj* ▸ **ˌexcul'pation** *n* ▸ **ex'culpatory** *adj*

excurrent (ɛk'skʌrənt) *adj* **1** *Zoology*. having an outward flow, as certain pores in sponges, ducts, etc. **2** *Botany*. **2a** (of veins) extending beyond the margin of the leaf. **2b** having an undivided main stem or trunk, as the spruce and other conifers. **3** flowing or running in an outward direction. [C19: from Latin *excurrere* to run forth; see EXCURSION]

excursion (ɪk'skɜːʃən, -ʒən) *n* **1** a short outward and return journey, esp. for relaxation, sightseeing, etc.; outing. **2** a group of people going on such a journey. **3** (*modifier*) of or relating to special reduced rates offered on certain journeys by rail: *an excursion ticket*. **4** a digression or deviation; diversion: *an excursion into politics*. **5** (formerly) a raid or attack. **6** *Physics*. **6a** a movement from an equilibrium position, as in an oscillation. **6b** the magnitude of this displacement. **7** the normal movement of a movable bodily organ or part from its resting position, such as the lateral movement of the lower jaw. **8** *Machinery*. the locus of a point on a moving part, esp. the deflection of a whirling shaft. [C16: from Latin *excursiō* an attack, from *excurrere* to run out, from *currere* to run]

excursionist (ɪk'skɜːʃənɪst, -ʒənɪst) *n* a person who goes on an excursion.

excursive (ɪk'skɜːsɪv) *adj* **1** tending to digress. **2** involving detours; rambling. [C17: from Latin *excursus*, from *excurrere* to run forth] ▸ **ex'cursively** *adv* ▸ **ex'cursiveness** *n*

excursus (ɛk'skɜːsəs) *n, pl* **-suses** *or* **-sus**. an incidental digression from the main topic under discussion or from the main story in a narrative. [C19: from Latin: a running forth, from *excurrere* to run out]

excusatory (ɪk'skjuːzətərɪ, -trɪ) *adj* tending to or intended to excuse; apologetic.

excuse *vb* (ɪk'skjuːz). (*tr*) **1** to pardon or forgive: *he always excuses her unpunctuality*. **2** to seek pardon or exemption for (a person, esp. oneself): *to excuse oneself for one's mistakes*. **3** to make allowances for; judge leniently: *to excuse someone's ignorance*. **4** to serve as an apology or explanation for; vindicate or justify: *her age excuses her behaviour*. **5** to exempt from a task, obligation, etc.: *you are excused making breakfast*. **6** to dismiss or allow to leave: *he asked them to excuse him*. **7** to seek permission for (someone, esp. oneself) to leave: *he excused himself and left*. **8** **be excused**. *Euphemistic*. to go to the lavatory. **9** **excuse me!** an expression used to catch someone's attention or to apologize for an interruption, disagreement, or social indiscretion. ◆ *n* (ɪk'skjuːs). **10** an explanation offered in defence of some fault or offensive behaviour or as a reason for not fulfilling an obligation, etc.: *he gave no excuse for his rudeness*. **11** *Informal*. an inferior example of something specified; makeshift substitute: *she is a poor excuse for a hostess*. **12** the act of excusing. [C13: from Latin *excusāre*, from EX-[1] + *-cūsare*, from *causa* cause, accusation] ▸ **ex'cusable** *adj* ▸ **ex'cusableness** *n* ▸ **ex'cusably** *adv*

excuse-me *n* a dance in which a person may take another's partner.

ex-directory *adj Chiefly Brit*. not listed in a telephone directory, by request, and not disclosed to inquirers. U.S. and Canadian term: **unlisted**.

ex div. *abbrev. for* ex dividend.

ex dividend *adv* without the right to the current dividend: *to quote shares ex dividend*. Compare **cum dividend**.

exeat ('ɛksɪət) *n Brit*. **1** leave of absence from school or some other institution. **2** a bishop's permission for a priest to leave his diocese in order to take up an appointment elsewhere. [C18: Latin, literally: he may go out, from *exīre*]

exec. *abbrev. for*: **1** executive. **2** executor.

execrable ('ɛksɪkrəbᵊl) *adj* **1** deserving to be execrated; abhorrent. **2** of very poor quality: *an execrable meal*. [C14: from Latin *exsecrābilis*, from *exsecrārī* to EXECRATE] ▸ **'execrableness** *n* ▸ **'execrably** *adv*

execrate ('ɛksɪˌkreɪt) *vb* **1** (*tr*) to loathe; detest; abhor. **2** (*tr*) to profess great abhorrence for; denounce; deplore. **3** to curse (a person or thing); damn. [C16: from Latin *exsecrārī* to curse, from EX-[1] + *-secrārī* from *sacer* SACRED] ▸ **ˌexe'cration** *n* ▸ **'exeˌcrative** *or* **'exeˌcratory** *adj* ▸ **'exeˌcratively** *adv*

executant (ɪg'zɛkjutənt) *n* a performer, esp. of musical works.

execute ('ɛksɪˌkjuːt) *vb* (*tr*) **1** to put (a condemned person) to death; inflict capital punishment upon. **2** to carry out; complete; perform; do: *to execute an order*. **3** to perform; accomplish; effect: *to execute a pirouette*. **4** to make or produce: *to execute a drawing*. **5** to carry into effect (a judicial sentence, the law, etc.); enforce. **6** *Law*. to comply with legal formalities in order to render (a deed, etc.) effective, as by signing, sealing, and delivering. **7** to sign (a will) in the presence of witnesses and in accordance with other legal formalities. **8** to carry out the terms of (a contract, will, etc.). [C14: from Old French *executer*, back formation from *executeur* EXECUTOR] ▸ **'exeˌcutable** *adj* ▸ **'exeˌcuter** *n*

execution (ˌɛksɪ'kjuːʃən) *n* **1** the act or process of executing. **2** the carrying out or undergoing of a sentence of death. **3** the style or manner in which something is accomplished or performed; technique: *as a pianist his execution is poor*. **4a** the enforcement of the judgment of a court of law. **4b** the writ ordering such enforcement.

executioner (ˌɛksɪ'kjuːʃənə) *n* **1** an official charged with carrying out the death sentence passed upon a condemned person. **2** an assassin, esp. one appointed by a political or criminal organization.

executive (ɪg'zɛkjutɪv) *n* **1a** a person or group responsible for the administration of a project, activity, or business. **1b** (*as modifier*): *executive duties; an executive position*. **2a** the branch of government responsible for carrying out laws, decrees, etc.; administration. **2b** any administration. Compare **judiciary**, **legislature**. ◆ *adj* **3** having the function or purpose of carrying plans, orders, laws, etc., into practical effect. **4** of, relating to, or designed for an executive: *the executive suite*. **5** *Informal*. of the most expensive or exclusive type: *executive housing; executive class*. ▸ **ex'ecutively** *adv*

Executive Council *n* (in Australia and New Zealand) a body consisting of ministers of the Crown presided over by the Governor or Governor-General that formally approves Cabinet decisions, etc.

executive director *n* a member of the board of directors of a company who is also an employee (usually full-time) of that company and who often has a specified area of responsibility, such as finance or production. Compare **non-executive director**.

executive officer *n* **1** the second-in-command of any of certain military units. **2** a specialist seaman officer, responsible under the captain for the routine efficient running of the ship in the U.S., British (formerly), and certain other navies.

executive session *n U.S. government*. a session of the Senate for the discussion of executive business, such as the ratification of treaties: formerly held in secret.

executor (ɪg'zɛkjutə) *n* **1** *Law*. a person appointed by a testator to carry out the wishes expressed in his will. **2** a person who executes. [C13: from Anglo-French *executour*, from Latin *execūtor*, from EX-[1] + *sequi* follow] ▸ **exˌecu'torial** *adj* ▸ **ex'ecutorˌship** *n*

executory (ɪg'zɛkjutərɪ, -trɪ) *adj* **1** (of a law, agreement, etc.) coming into operation at a future date; not yet effective: *an executory contract*. **2** executive; administrative.

executrix (ɪg'zɛkjutrɪks) *n, pl* **executrices** (ɪgˌzɛkju'traɪsiːz) *or* **executrixes**. *Law*. a female executor.

exedra ('ɛksɪdrə, ɛk'siː-) *n* **1** a building, room, portico, or apse containing a continuous bench, used in ancient Greece and Rome for holding discussions. **2** an outdoor bench in a recess. [C18: via Latin from Greek, from *hedra* seat]

exegesis (ˌɛksɪ'dʒiːsɪs) *n, pl* **-ses** (-siːz). explanation or critical interpretation of a text, esp. of the Bible. Compare **eisegesis**. [C17: from Greek, from *exēgeisthai* to interpret, from EX-[1] + *hēgeisthai* to guide]

exegete ('ɛksɪˌdʒiːt) *or* **exegetist** (ˌɛksɪ'dʒiːtɪst, -'dʒɛt-) *n* a person who practises exegesis. [C18: from Greek *exēgētēs*, from *exēgeisthai* to interpret; see EXEGESIS]

exegetic (ˌɛksɪ'dʒɛtɪk) *or* **exegetical** *adj* of or relating to exegesis; expository. ▸ **ˌexe'getically** *adv*

exegetics (ˌɛksɪ'dʒɛtɪks) *n* (*functioning as sing*) the scientific study of exegesis and exegetical methods.

exemplar (ɪg'zɛmplə, -plɑː) *n* **1** a person or thing to be copied or imitated; model. **2** a typical specimen or instance; example. **3** a copy of a book or text on which further printings have been based. [C14: from Latin *exemplarium* model, from *exemplum* EXAMPLE]

exemplary (ɪg'zɛmplərɪ) *adj* **1** fit for imitation; model: *an exemplary performance*. **2** serving as a warning; admonitory: *an exemplary jail sentence*. **3** representative; typical: *an action exemplary of his conduct*. ▸ **ex'emplarily** *adv* ▸ **ex'emplariness** *n*

exemplary damages *pl n Law*. damages awarded to a plaintiff above the value of actual loss sustained so that they serve also as a punishment to the defendant and a deterrent to others.

exemplify (ɪg'zɛmplɪˌfaɪ) *vb* **-fies, -fying, -fied**. (*tr*) **1** to show by example. **2** to serve as an example of. **3** *Law*. **3a** to make an official copy of (a document from public records) under seal. **3b** to transcribe (a legal document). [C15: via Old French from Medieval Latin *exemplificāre*, from Latin *exemplum* EXAMPLE + *facere* to make] ▸ **ex'empliˌfiable** *adj* ▸ **exˌemplifi'cation** *n* ▸ **ex'empliˌcative** *adj* ▸ **ex'empliˌfier** *n*

exempli gratia *Latin*. (ɪg'zɛmplaɪ 'grɑːtɪˌɑː) for the sake of example. Abbrevs.: **e.g., eg**.

exemplum (ɪg'zɛmpləm) *n, pl* **-pla** (-plə). **1** an anecdote that supports a moral point or sustains an argument, used esp. in medieval sermons. **2** an example or illustration. [from Latin: EXAMPLE]

exempt (ɪg'zɛmpt) *vb* **1** (*tr*) to release from an obligation, liability, tax, etc.; excuse: *to exempt a soldier from drill*. ◆ *adj* (*sometimes postpositive*) **2** freed from or not subject to an obligation, liability, tax, etc.; excused: *exempt gilts; tax-exempt bonus*. **3** *Obsolete*. set apart; remote. ◆ *n* **4** a person who is exempt from an obligation, tax, etc. [C14: from Latin *exemptus* removed, from *eximere* to take out, from *emere* to buy, obtain] ▸ **ex'emption** *n*

exenterate *vb* (ɪg'zɛntəˌreɪt). (*tr*) **1** *Surgery*. to remove (internal organs, an eyeball, etc.); eviscerate. **2** a rare word for **disembowel**. ◆ *adj* (ɪg'zɛntəˌreɪt, -rɪt). **3** *Rare*. having been disembowelled. [C17: from Latin *exenterāre*, from EX-[1] + Greek *enteron* intestine] ▸ **exˌenter'ation** *n*

exequatur (ˌɛksɪ'kweɪtə) *n* **1** an official authorization issued by a host country to a consular agent, permitting him to perform his official duties. **2** an act by which the civil governments of certain nations permit the laws of the Roman Catholic Church to take effect in their territories. [C18: from Latin, literally: let him perform, from *exequī* to perform, from EX-[1] + *sequī* to follow]

exequies ('ɛksɪkwɪz) *pl n, sing* **-quy**. the rites and ceremonies used at funerals. [C14: from Latin *exequiae* (plural) funeral procession, rites, from *exequī* to follow to the end, from *sequī* to follow]

exercise ('ɛksəˌsaɪz) *vb* (*mainly tr*) **1** to put into use; employ: *to exercise tact*. **2** (*intr*) to take exercise or perform exercises; exert one's muscles, etc., esp. in order to keep fit. **3** to practise using in order to develop or train: *to exercise one's voice.* **4** to perform or make proper use of: *to exercise one's rights.* **5** to bring to bear; exert: *to exercise one's influence.* **6** (*often passive*) to occupy the attentions of, esp. so as to worry or vex: *to be exercised about a decision.* **7** *Military.* to carry out or cause to carry out, manoeuvres, simulated combat operations, etc. ♦ *n* **8** physical exertion, esp. for the purpose of development, training, or keeping fit. **9** mental or other activity or practice, esp. in order to develop a skill. **10** a set of movements, questions, tasks, etc., designed to train, improve, or test one's ability in a particular field: *piano exercises.* **11** a performance or work of art done as practice or to demonstrate a technique. **12** the performance of a function; discharge: *the exercise of one's rights; the object of the exercise is to win.* **13** (*sometimes pl*) *Military.* a manoeuvre or simulated combat operation carried out for training and evaluation. **14** (*usually pl*) *U.S. and Canadian.* a ceremony or formal routine, esp. at a school or college: *opening exercises; graduation exercises.* **15** *Gymnastics.* a particular type of event, such as performing on the horizontal bar. [C14: from Old French *exercice,* from Latin *exercitium,* from *exercēre* to drill, from EX-[1] + *arcēre* to ward off] ► **'exer,cisable** *adj*

exercise bike *or* **cycle** *n* a stationary exercise machine that is pedalled like a bicycle as a method of increasing cardiovascular fitness.

exercise book *n* a notebook used by pupils and students.

exercise price *n Stock exchange.* the price at which the holder of a traded option may exercise his right to buy (or sell) a security.

exerciser ('ɛksə,saɪzə) *n* **1** a device with springs or elasticated cords for muscular exercise. **2** a person or thing that exercises.

exercitation (ɪg,zɜːsɪ'teɪʃən) *n* a rare word for **exercise.** [C14: from Latin *exercitātiō,* from *exercitāre* frequentative of *exercēre* to EXERCISE]

exergonic (,ɛksə'gɒnɪk) *adj* (of a biochemical reaction) producing energy and therefore occurring spontaneously. Compare **endergonic.** [C20: from EX(O)- + Greek *ergon* work + -IC]

exergue (ɛk'sɜːg) *n* a space on the reverse of a coin or medal below the central design, often containing the date, place of minting, etc. [C17: from French, from Medieval Latin *exergum,* from Greek *ex* outside + *ergon* work] ► **ex'ergual** *adj*

exert (ɪg'zɜːt) *vb* (*tr*) **1** to use (influence, authority, etc.) forcefully or effectively. **2** to apply (oneself) diligently; make a strenuous effort. [C17 (in the sense: push forth, emit): from Latin *exserere* to thrust out, from EX-[1] + *serere* to bind together, entwine] ► **ex'ertion** *n* ► **ex'ertive** *adj*

Exeter ('ɛksɪtə) *n* a city in SW England, administrative centre of Devon; university (1955). Pop.: 94 717 (1991).

exeunt ('ɛksɪ,ʌnt) *Latin.* they go out: used as a stage direction.

exeunt omnes ('ɛksɪ,ʌnt 'ɒmneɪz) *Latin.* they all go out: used as a stage direction.

exfoliate (ɛks'fəʊlɪ,eɪt) *vb* **1** (of bark, skin, etc.) to peel off in (layers, flakes, or scales). **2** (*intr*) (of rocks or minerals) to shed the thin outermost layer because of weathering or heating. **3** (of some minerals, esp. mica) to split or cause to split into thin flakes: *a factory to exfoliate vermiculite.* [C17: from Late Latin *exfoliāre* to strip off leaves, from Latin *folium* leaf] ► **ex,foli'ation** *n* ► **ex'foliative** *adj*

ex gratia ('greɪʃə) *adj* given as a favour or gratuitously where no legal obligation exists: *an ex gratia payment.* [New Latin, literally: out of kindness]

exhalant (ɛks'heɪlənt, ɪg'zeɪ-) *adj* **1** emitting a vapour or liquid; exhaling: *an exhalant siphon; exhalant duct.* ♦ *n* **2** an organ or vessel that emits a vapour or liquid.

exhale (ɛks'heɪl, ɪg'zeɪl) *vb* **1** to expel (breath, tobacco smoke, etc.) from the lungs; breathe out. **2** to give off (air, vapour, fumes, etc.) or (of air, vapour, etc.) to be given off; emanate. [C14: from Latin *exhālāre* to breathe out, from *hālāre* to breathe] ► **ex'halable** *adj* ► **,exha'lation** *n*

exhaust (ɪg'zɔːst) *vb* (*mainly tr*) **1** to drain the energy of; tire out: *to exhaust someone by constant questioning.* **2** to deprive of resources, etc.: *a nation exhausted by war.* **3** to deplete totally; expend; consume: *to exhaust food supplies.* **4** to empty (a container) by drawing off or pumping out (the contents). **5** to develop or discuss thoroughly so that no further interest remains: *to exhaust a topic of conversation.* **6** to remove gas from (a vessel, etc.) in order to reduce the pressure or create a vacuum; evacuate. **7** to remove or use up the active ingredients from (a drug, solution, etc.). **8** to destroy the fertility of (soil) by excessive cultivation. **9** (*intr*) (of steam or other gases) to be emitted or to escape from an engine after being expanded. ♦ *n* **10** gases ejected from an engine as waste products. **11a** the expulsion of expanded gas or steam from an engine. **11b** (*as modifier*): *exhaust stroke.* **12a** the parts of an engine through which the exhausted gases or steam pass. **12b** (*as modifier*): *exhaust valve; exhaust pipe.* [C16: from Latin *exhaustus* made empty, from *exhaurīre* to draw out, from *haurīre* to draw, drain] ► **ex'hausted** *adj* ► **ex'hauster** *n* ► **ex'haustible** *adj* ► **ex,hausti'bility** *n* ► **ex'hausting** *adj*

exhaustion (ɪg'zɔːstʃən) *n* **1** extreme tiredness; fatigue. **2** the condition of being used up; consumption: *exhaustion of the earth's resources.* **3** the act of exhausting or the state of being exhausted.

exhaustive (ɪg'zɔːstɪv) *adj* **1** comprehensive in scope; thorough: *an exhaustive survey.* **2** tending to exhaust. ► **ex'haustively** *adv* ► **ex'haustiveness** *n*

exhaust stroke *n* another name for **scavenge stroke.**

exhibit (ɪg'zɪbɪt) *vb* (*mainly tr*) **1** (*also intr*) to display (something) to the public for interest or instruction: *this artist exhibits all over the world.* **2** to manifest; display; show: *the child exhibited signs of distress.* **3** *Law.* to produce (a document or object) in court to serve as evidence. ♦ *n* **4** an object or collection exhibited to the public. **5** *Law.* a document or object produced in court and referred to or identified by a witness in giving evidence. [C15: from Latin *exhibēre* to hold forth, from *habēre* to have] ► **ex'hibitory** *adj*

exhibition (,ɛksɪ'bɪʃən) *n* **1** a public display of art, products, skills, activities, etc.: *a judo exhibition.* **2** the act of exhibiting or the state of being exhibited. **3 make an exhibition of oneself.** to behave so foolishly in public that one excites notice or ridicule. **4** *Brit.* an allowance or scholarship awarded to a student at a university or school.

exhibitioner (,ɛksɪ'bɪʃənə) *n Brit.* a student who has been awarded an exhibition.

exhibitionism (,ɛksɪ'bɪʃə,nɪzəm) *n* **1** a compulsive desire to attract attention to oneself, esp. by absurd or exaggerated behaviour or boasting. **2** *Psychiatry.* a compulsive desire to expose one's genital organs publicly. ► **,exhi'bitionist** *n, adj* ► **,exhi,bition'istic** *adj*

exhibitive (ɪg'zɪbɪtɪv) *adj* (*usually postpositive* and foll. by *of*) illustrative or demonstrative: *a masterpiece exhibitive of his talent.* ► **ex'hibitively** *adv*

exhibitor (ɪg'zɪbɪtə) *n* **1** a person or thing that exhibits. **2** an individual or company that shows films, esp. the manager or owner of a cinema.

exhilarant (ɪg'zɪlərənt) *adj* **1** exhilarating; invigorating. ♦ *n* **2** something that exhilarates.

exhilarate (ɪg'zɪlə,reɪt) *vb* (*tr*) to make lively and cheerful; gladden; elate. [C16: from Latin *exhilarāre,* from *hilarāre* to cheer; see HILARIOUS] ► **ex,hila'ration** *n* ► **ex'hilarative** *or* **ex'hilaratory** *adj*

exhilarating (ɪg'zɪlə,reɪtɪŋ) *adj* causing strong feelings of excitement and happiness: *an exhilarating helicopter trip.* ► **ex'hila,ratingly** *adv*

exhort (ɪg'zɔːt) *vb* to urge or persuade (someone) earnestly; advise strongly. [C14: from Latin *exhortārī,* from *hortārī* to urge] ► **exhortative** (ɪg'zɔːtətɪv) *or* **ex'hortatory** *adj* ► **ex'horter** *n*

exhortation (,ɛgzɔː'teɪʃən) *n* **1** the act or process of exhorting. **2** a speech or written passage intended to persuade, inspire, or encourage.

exhume (ɛks'hjuːm) *vb* (*tr*) **1** to dig up (something buried, esp. a corpse); disinter. **2** to reveal; disclose; unearth: *don't exhume that old argument.* [C18: from Medieval Latin *exhumāre,* from Latin EX-[1] + *humāre* to bury, from *humus* the ground] ► **exhumation** (,ɛkshju'meɪʃən) *n* ► **ex'humer** *n*

ex hypothesi (ɛks haɪ'pɒθəsɪ) *adv* in accordance with or following from the hypothesis stated. [C17: New Latin]

exigency ('ɛksɪdʒənsɪ, ɪg'zɪdʒənsɪ) *or* **exigence** ('ɛksɪdʒəns) *n, pl* **-gencies** *or* **-gences. 1** the state of being exigent; urgency. **2** (*often pl*) an urgent demand; pressing requirement. **3** an emergency.

exigent ('ɛksɪdʒənt) *adj* **1** urgent; pressing. **2** exacting; demanding. [C15: from Latin *exigere* to drive out, weigh out, from *agere* to drive, compel] ► **'exigently** *adv*

exigible ('ɛksɪdʒəb^əl) *adj* liable to be exacted or required: *part of the debt is exigible this month.* [C17: from French, from *exiger* to demand, from Latin *exigere;* see EXIGENT]

exiguous (ɪg'zɪgjʊəs, ɪk'sɪg-) *adj* scanty or slender; meagre: *an exiguous income.* [C17: from Latin *exiguus,* from *exigere* to weigh out; see EXIGENT] ► **exiguity** (,ɛksɪ'gjuːɪtɪ) *or* **ex'iguousness** *n* ► **ex'iguously** *adv*

exile ('ɛgzaɪl, 'ɛksaɪl) *n* **1** a prolonged, usually enforced absence from one's home or country; banishment. **2** the expulsion of a person from his native land by official decree. **3** a person banished or living away from his home or country; expatriate. ♦ *vb* **4** to expel from home or country, esp. by official decree as a punishment; banish. [C13: from Latin *exsilium* banishment, from *exsul* banished person; perhaps related to Greek *alasthai* to wander] ► **exilic** (ɛg'zɪlɪk, ɛk'sɪlɪk) *or* **ex'ilian** *adj*

Exile ('ɛgzaɪl, 'ɛksaɪl) *n* **the.** another name for the **Babylonian captivity** (of the Jews).

eximious (ɛg'zɪmɪəs) *adj Rare.* select and distinguished; eminent. [C16: from Latin *eximius,* from *eximere* to take out, from *emere* to purchase] ► **ex'imiously** *adv*

exine ('ɛksɪn, -aɪn) *n* another name for **extine.**

ex int. *Banking. abbrev. for* without [Latin *ex*] interest.

exist (ɪg'zɪst) *vb* (*intr*) **1** to have being or reality; to be. **2** to eke out a living; stay alive; survive: *he could barely exist on such a low wage.* **3** to be living; live. **4** to be present under specified conditions or in a specified place: *sharks exist in the Pacific.* **5** *Philosophy.* **5a** to be actual rather than merely possible. **5b** to be a member of the domain of some theory, an element of some possible world, etc. **5c** to have contingent being while free, responsible, and aware of one's situation. [C17: from Latin *exsistere* to step forth, from EX-[1] + *sistere* to stand] ► **ex'isting** *adj*

existence (ɪg'zɪstəns) *n* **1** the fact or state of existing; being. **2** the continuance or maintenance of life; living, esp. in adverse circumstances: *a struggle for existence; she has a wretched existence.* **3** something that exists; a being or entity. **4** everything that exists, esp. that is living.

existent (ɪg'zɪstənt) *adj* **1** in existence; extant; current. **2** having existence; living. ♦ *n* **3** a person or a thing that exists.

existential (,ɛgzɪ'stɛnʃəl) *adj* **1** of or relating to existence, esp. human existence. **2** *Philosophy.* pertaining to what exists, and is thus known by experience rather than reason; empirical as opposed to theoretical. **3** *Logic.* denoting or relating to a formula or proposition asserting the existence of at least one object fulfilling a given condition; containing an existential quantifier. **4** of or relating to existentialism. ♦ *n Logic.* **5a** an existential statement or formula. **5b** short for **existential quantifier.** ► **,exis'tentially** *adv*

existentialism (,ɛgzɪ'stɛnʃə,lɪzəm) *n* a modern philosophical movement stressing the importance of personal experience and responsibility and the demands that they make on the individual, who is seen as a free agent in a deterministic and seemingly meaningless universe. ► **,exis'tentialist** *adj, n*

existential quantifier *n Logic.* a formal device, for which the conventional symbol is $\exists$, which indicates that the open sentence that follows is true of at least one member of the relevant universe of interpretation, as $(\exists x)\ Fx$ meaning "something is (an) F," "something Fs," or "there are (some) Fs."

exit ('ɛgzɪt, 'ɛksɪt) *n* **1** a way out; door or gate by which people may leave. **2** the act or an instance of going out; departure. **3a** the act of leaving or right to leave a particular place. **3b** (*as modifier*): *an exit visa.* **4** departure from life; death. **5** *Theatre.* the act of going offstage. **6** (in Britain) a point at which vehicles may leave or join a motorway. **7** *Bridge, whist, etc.* **7a** the act of losing the lead deliberately. **7b** a card enabling one to do this. ◆ *vb* (*intr*) **8** to go away or out; depart; leave. **9** *Theatre.* to go offstage: used as a stage direction: *exit Hamlet.* **10** *Bridge, whist, etc.* to lose the lead deliberately. **11** (*sometimes tr*) *Computing.* to leave (a computer program or system). [C17: from Latin *exitus* a departure, from *exīre* to go out, from EX-[1] + *īre* to go]

Exit (ˈɛgzɪt, ˈɛksɪt) *n* (in Britain) a society that seeks to promote the legitimization of voluntary euthanasia.

exitance (ˈɛksɪtəns) *n* a measure of the ability of a surface to emit radiation. See **luminous exitance, radiant exitance.**

exit poll *n* a poll taken by an organization by asking people how they voted in an election as they leave a polling station.

ex lib. *abbrev. for* ex libris.

ex libris (ɛks ˈliːbrɪs) *adj* **1** from the collection or library of: frequently printed on bookplates. ◆ *n* **ex-libris. 2** a bookplate bearing the owner's name, coat of arms, etc. [C19: from Latin, literally: from the books (of)]

Exmoor (ˈɛksˌmʊə, -ˌmɔː) *n* **1** a high moorland in SW England, in W Somerset and N Devon: chiefly grazing ground for Exmoor ponies, sheep, and red deer. **2** a small stocky breed of pony with a fawn-coloured nose, originally from Exmoor.

Exmouth (ˈɛksməθ) *n* a town in SW England, in Devon, at the mouth of the River Exe: tourism, fishing. Pop.: 28 414 (1991).

ex new *adv, adj* (of shares, etc.) without the right to take up any scrip issue or rights issue. Compare **cum new.**

exo- *combining form.* external, outside, or beyond: *exobiology; exothermal.* [from Greek *exō* outside]

exobiology (ˌɛksəʊbaɪˈɒlədʒɪ) *n* another name for **astrobiology.** ▸ **ˌexobiˈologist** *n*

exocarp (ˈɛksəʊˌkɑːp) *n* another name for **epicarp.**

exocentric (ˌɛksəʊˈsɛntrɪk) *adj Grammar.* (of a construction) not fulfilling the grammatical role of any of its constituents; as in *until last Easter,* where the constituents are prepositional, adjectival, and nominal, while the whole construction is adverbial. Compare **endocentric.**

Exocet (ˈɛksəʊsɛt) *n Trademark.* a tactical missile with a high-explosive warhead, which is guided by computer and radar, travels at a very low altitude at high subsonic speed, and has a range of up to 70 km. It may be launched from a ship, aircraft, or submarine. [C20: from French, from New Latin *Exocoetus volitans* flying fish]

exocrine (ˈɛksəʊˌkraɪn, -krɪn) *adj* **1** of or relating to exocrine glands or their secretions. ◆ *n* **2** an exocrine gland. ◆ Compare **endocrine.** [C20: EXO- + *-crine* from Greek *krinein* to separate]

exocrine gland *n* any gland, such as a salivary or sweat gland, that secretes its products through a duct onto an epithelial surface.

exocuticle (ˈɛksəʊˌkjuːtɪkᵊl) *n* the layer of an insect's cuticle between the epicuticle and the endocuticle, which is often hard and dark in colour.

exocytosis (ˌɛksəʊsaɪˈtəʊsɪs) *n* a process by which material is exported from a biological cell.

Exod. *Bible. abbrev. for* Exodus.

exoderm (ˈɛksəʊˌdɜːm) *n Embryol.* another name for **ectoderm.**

exodontics (ˌɛksəʊˈdɒntɪks) *n* (*functioning as sing*) the branch of dental surgery concerned with the extraction of teeth. Also called: **exodontia** (ˌɛksəʊˈdɒnʃə). [C20: New Latin, from EX-[1] + *-odontia,* from Greek *odōn* tooth] ▸ **ˌexoˈdontist** *n*

exodus (ˈɛksədəs) *n* the act or an instance of going out. [C17: via Latin from Greek *exodos* from EX-[1] + *hodos* way]

Exodus (ˈɛksədəs) *n* **1 the.** the departure of the Israelites from Egypt led by Moses. **2** the second book of the Old Testament, recounting the events connected with this and the divine visitation of Moses at Mount Sinai.

exoenzyme (ˌɛksəʊˈɛnzaɪm) *n* **1** any enzyme, esp. an exopeptidase, that acts upon terminal chemical bonds in a chain of molecules. Compare **endoenzyme. 2** another name for **ectoenzyme.**

exoergic (ˌɛksəʊˈɜːdʒɪk) *adj* (of a nuclear reaction) occurring with evolution of energy. Compare **endoergic, exothermic.** [EXO- + *-ergic,* from Greek *ergon* work]

ex off. *abbrev. for* ex officio.

ex officio (ˈɛks əˈfɪʃɪəʊ, əˈfɪsɪəʊ) *adv, adj* by right of position or office. Abbrev.: **ex off.** [Latin]

exogamy (ɛkˈsɒgəmɪ) *n* **1** *Sociol., anthropol.* the custom or an act of marrying a person belonging to another tribe, clan, or similar social unit. Compare **endogamy. 2** *Biology.* fusion of gametes from parents that are not closely related. ▸ **exogamous** (ɛkˈsɒgəməs) *or* **exogamic** (ˌɛksəʊˈgæmɪk) *adj*

exogenous (ɛkˈsɒdʒɪnəs) *adj* **1** having an external origin. **2** *Biology.* **2a** developing or originating outside an organism or part of an organism. **2b** of or relating to external factors, such as light, that influence an organism. **3** *Psychiatry.* (of a mental illness) caused by external factors. ▸ **exˈogenously** *adv*

exon[1] (ˈɛksɒn) *n Brit.* one of the four officers who command the Yeomen of the Guard. [C17: a pronunciation spelling of French *exempt* EXEMPT]

exon[2] (ˈɛksɒn) *n* any segment of a discontinuous gene the segments of which are separated by introns. Compare **intron.** [C20: from EX-[1] + -ON] ▸ **exˈonic** *adj*

exonerate (ɪgˈzɒnəˌreɪt) *vb* (*tr*) **1** to clear or absolve from blame or a criminal charge. **2** to relieve from an obligation or task; exempt. [C16: from Latin *exonerāre* to free from a burden, from *onus* a burden] ▸ **exˌonerˈation** *n* ▸ **exˈonerative** *adj* ▸ **exˈonerˌator** *n*

exonuclease (ˌɛksəʊˈnjuːklɪˌeɪz) *n* an enzyme that is capable of detaching the terminal nucleotide from a nucleic acid chain. Compare **endonuclease.**

exonym (ˈɛksəˌnɪm) *n* a name given to a place by foreigners: *Londres is an exonym of London.* [C20: from Greek EX-[1] + -ONYM]

exoparasite (ˌɛksəʊˈpærəˌsaɪt) *n* another word for **ectoparasite.** ▸ **exoparasitic** (ˌɛksəʊˌpærəˈsɪtɪk) *adj*

exopeptidase (ˌɛksəʊˈpɛptɪˌdeɪz) *n* any proteolytic enzyme, such as erepsin, that acts on the terminal bonds in a peptide chain. Compare **endopeptidase.**

exophoric (ˌɛksəʊˈfɒrɪk) *adj Grammar.* denoting or relating to a pronoun such as "I" or "you", the meaning of which is determined by reference outside the discourse rather than by a preceding or following expression. Compare **anaphora.** [from EXO- + Greek *pherein* to carry]

exophthalmic goitre *n* a form of hyperthyroidism characterized by enlargement of the thyroid gland, protrusion of the eyeballs, increased basal metabolic rate, and weight loss. Also called: **Graves' disease.**

exophthalmos (ˌɛksɒfˈθælmɒs), **exophthalmus** (ˌɛksɒfˈθælməs), *or* **exophthalmia** (ˌɛksɒfˈθælmɪə) *n* abnormal protrusion of the eyeball, as caused by hyperthyroidism. Also called: **proptosis, ocular proptosis.** [C19: via New Latin from Greek, from EX-[1] + *ophthalmos* eye] ▸ **ˌexophˈthalmic** *adj*

exoplasm (ˈɛksəʊˌplæzəm) *n* another name for **ectoplasm.**

exor. (ˈɛksɔː) *Brit. abbrev. for* executor.

exorable (ˈɛksərəbᵊl) *adj* able to be persuaded or moved by pleading. [C16: from Latin *exōrābilis,* from *exōrāre* to persuade, from *ōrāre* to beseech] ▸ **ˌexoraˈbility** *n*

exorbitant (ɪgˈzɔːbɪtᵊnt) *adj* (of prices, demands, etc.) in excess of what is reasonable; excessive; extravagant; immoderate. [C15: from Late Latin *exorbitāre* to deviate, from Latin *orbita* track] ▸ **exˈorbitance** *n* ▸ **exˈorbitantly** *adv*

exorcize *or* **exorcise** (ˈɛksɔːˌsaɪz) *vb* (*tr*) to expel or attempt to expel (one or more evil spirits) from (a person or place believed to be possessed or haunted), by prayers, adjurations, and religious rites. [C15: from Late Latin *exorcizāre,* from Greek *exorkizein,* from EX-[1] + *horkizein* to adjure] ▸ **ˈexorˌcizer** *or* **ˈexorˌciser** *n* ▸ **ˈexorcism** *n* ▸ **ˈexorcist** *n*

exordium (ɛkˈsɔːdɪəm) *n, pl* **-diums** *or* **-dia** (-dɪə). an introductory part or beginning, esp. of an oration or discourse. [C16: from Latin, from *exōrdīrī* to begin, from *ōrdīrī* to begin] ▸ **exˈordial** *adj*

exoskeleton (ˌɛksəʊˈskɛlɪtᵊn) *n* the protective or supporting structure covering the outside of the body of many animals, such as the thick cuticle of arthropods. Compare **endoskeleton.** ▸ **ˌexoˈskeletal** *adj*

exosmosis (ˌɛksɒzˈməʊsɪs, -sɒs-) *n Biology.* osmosis in which water flows from a cell or organism into the surrounding solution. Compare **endosmosis.** ▸ **exosmotic** (ˌɛksɒzˈmɒtɪk, -sɒs-) *or* **exosmic** (ɛkˈsɒzmɪk, -ˈsɒs-) *adj*

exosphere (ˈɛksəʊˌsfɪə) *n* the outermost layer of the earth's atmosphere. It extends from about 400 kilometres above the earth's surface.

exospore (ˈɛksəʊˌspɔː) *n* the outer layer of the spores of some algae and fungi. ▸ **ˌexoˈsporous** *adj*

exostosis (ˌɛksɒˈstəʊsɪs) *n, pl* **-ses** (-siːz). an abnormal bony outgrowth from the surface of a bone. [C18: via New Latin from Greek, from EX-[1] + *osteon* bone]

exoteric (ˌɛksəʊˈtɛrɪk) *adj* **1** intelligible to or intended for more than a select or initiated minority: *an exoteric account of a philosophical doctrine.* **2** external; exterior. [C17: from Latin *exōtericus* external, from Greek *exōterikos,* from *exōterō* further outside; see EXO-] ▸ **ˌexoˈterically** *adv* ▸ **ˌexoˈteriˌcism** *n*

exothermic (ˌɛksəʊˈθɜːmɪk) *or* **exothermal** *adj* (of a chemical reaction or compound) occurring or formed with the evolution of heat. Compare **endothermic, exoergic.** ▸ **ˌexoˈthermically** *or* **ˌexoˈthermally** *adv*

exotic (ɪgˈzɒtɪk) *adj* **1** originating in a foreign country, esp. one in the tropics; not native: *an exotic plant.* **2** having a strange or bizarre allure, beauty, or quality. **3** *N.Z.* (of trees, esp. pine trees) native to the northern hemisphere but cultivated in New Zealand: *an exotic forest.* **4** of or relating to striptease. ◆ *n* **5** an exotic person or thing. [C16: from Latin *exōticus,* from Greek *exōtikos* foreign, from *exō* outside] ▸ **exˈotically** *adv* ▸ **exˈotiˌcism** *n* ▸ **exˈoticness** *n*

exotica (ɪgˈzɒtɪkə) *pl n* exotic objects, esp. when forming a collection. [C19: Latin, neuter plural of *exōticus;* see EXOTIC]

exotic dancer *n* a striptease dancer or belly dancer.

exotoxin (ˌɛksəʊˈtɒksɪn) *n* a toxin produced by a microorganism and secreted into the surrounding medium. ▸ **ˌexoˈtoxic** *adj*

exp *Maths. Symbol for* exponential (sense 2).

exp. *abbrev. for:* **1** expenses. **2** experiment(al). **3** expired. **4** export(ed). **5** exporter. **6** express.

expand (ɪkˈspænd) *vb* **1** to make or become greater in extent, volume, size, or scope; increase. **2** to spread out or be spread out; unfold; stretch out. **3** (*intr;* often foll. by *on*) to enlarge or expatiate on (a story, topic, etc.) in detail. **4** (*intr*) to become increasingly relaxed, friendly, or talkative. **5** *Maths.* to express (a function or expression) as the sum or product of terms. [C15: from Latin *expandere* to spread out, from *pandere* to spread, extend] ▸ **exˈpandable** *adj*

expanded (ɪkˈspændɪd) *adj* **1** Also: **extended.** (of printer's type) wider than usual for a particular height. Compare **condensed. 2** (of a plastic) having been foamed during manufacture by the introduction of a gas in order to make a light packaging material or heat insulator: *expanded polystyrene.* See also **expanded metal.**

expanded metal *n* an open mesh of metal produced by stamping out alternating slots in a metal sheet and stretching it into an open pattern. It is used for reinforcing brittle or friable materials and in fencing.

expander (ɪkˈspændə) *n* **1** a device for exercising and developing the muscles of the body: *a chest expander.* **2** an electronic device for increasing the variations in signal amplitude in a transmission system according to a specified law. Compare **compressor** (sense 5), **compander.**

expanding universe theory *n* the theory, developed from the observed red shifts of celestial bodies, that all the galaxies are receding from each other at velocities that increase as the distance from earth increases. See also **oscillating universe theory.**

expanse (ɪk'spæns) *n* **1** an uninterrupted surface of something that spreads or extends, esp. over a wide area; stretch: *an expanse of water.* **2** expansion or extension. [C17: from New Latin *expansum* the heavens, from Latin *expansus* spread out, from *expandere* to EXPAND]

expansible (ɪk'spænsəbᵊl) *adj* able to expand or be expanded. ▸ **ex,pansi'bility** *n*

expansile (ɪk'spænsaɪl) *adj* **1** able to expand or cause expansion. **2** of or relating to expansion.

expansion (ɪk'spænʃən) *n* **1** the act of expanding or the state of being expanded. **2** something expanded; an expanded surface or part. **3** the degree, extent, or amount by which something expands. **4** an increase, enlargement, or development, esp. in the activities of a company. **5** *Maths.* **5a** the form of an expression or function when it is written as the sum or product of its terms. **5b** the act or process of determining this expanded form. **6** the part of an engine cycle in which the working fluid does useful work by increasing in volume. **7** the increase in the dimensions of a body or substance when subjected to an increase in temperature, internal pressure, etc. ▸ **ex'pansionary** *adj*

expansion bend *n Engineering.* a loop in a pipe conveying hot fluid that provides flexibility which takes up thermal expansion and thus reduces temperature-induced stress in the pipe to an acceptable level.

expansion bolt *n* a bolt that expands on tightening, enabling it to be secured into an unthreaded hole.

expansionism (ɪk'spænʃə,nɪzəm) *n* the doctrine or practice of expanding the economy or territory of a country. ▸ **ex'pansionist** *n, adj* ▸ **ex,pansion'istic** *adj*

expansion joint *n Engineering.* a gap in steel or concrete to allow for thermal expansion.

expansion slot *n* a physical electronic interface provided in a computer system to enable extra facilities to be added at a later date.

expansive (ɪk'spænsɪv) *adj* **1** able or tending to expand or characterized by expansion. **2** wide; extensive. **3** friendly, open, or talkative: *an expansive person.* **4** grand or extravagant: *an expansive way of life.* **5** *Psychiatry.* lacking restraint in the expression of feelings, esp. in having delusions of grandeur or being inclined to overvalue oneself or one's work. ▸ **ex'pansively** *adv* ▸ **ex'pansiveness** *n*

expansivity (,ɛkspæn'sɪvɪtɪ) *n* **1** the quality of being expansive. **2** another name for **coefficient of expansion.**

ex parte (ɛks 'pɑːtɪ) *adj Law.* (of an application in a judicial proceeding) on behalf of one side or party only: *an ex parte injunction.* [Latin]

expat (,ɛks'pæt) *n, adj Informal.* short for **expatriate.**

expatiate (ɪk'speɪʃɪ,eɪt) *vb* (*intr*) **1** (foll. by *on* or *upon*) to enlarge (on a theme, topic, etc.) at length or in detail; elaborate (on). **2** *Rare.* to wander about. [C16: from Latin *exspatiārī* to digress, from *spatiārī* to walk about] ▸ **ex,pati'ation** *n* ▸ **ex'pati,ator** *n*

expatriate *adj* (ɛks'pætrɪɪt, -,eɪt). **1** resident in a foreign country. **2** exiled or banished from one's native country: *an expatriate American.* ◆ *n* (ɛks'pætrɪɪt, -,eɪt). **3** a person who lives in a foreign country. **4** an exile; expatriate person. ◆ *vb* (ɛks'pætrɪ,eɪt). (*tr*) **5** to exile (oneself) from one's native country or cause (another) to go into exile. **6** to deprive (oneself or another) of citizenship. [C18: from Medieval Latin *expatriāre,* from Latin EX-[1] + *patria* native land] ▸ **ex,patri'ation** *n*

expect (ɪk'spɛkt) *vb* (*tr; may take a clause as object or an infinitive*) **1** to regard as probable or likely; anticipate: *he expects to win.* **2** to look forward to or be waiting for: *we expect good news today.* **3** to decide that (something) is requisite or necessary; require: *the teacher expects us to work late today.* ◆ See also **expecting.** [C16: from Latin *exspectāre* to watch for, from *spectāre* to look at] ▸ **ex'pectable** *adj* ▸ **ex'pectably** *adv*

expectancy (ɪk'spɛktənsɪ) *or* **expectance** *n* **1** something expected, esp. on the basis of a norm or average: *his life expectancy was 30 years.* **2** anticipation; expectation. **3** the prospect of a future interest or possession, esp. in property: *an estate in expectancy.*

expectant (ɪk'spɛktənt) *adj* **1** expecting, anticipating, or hopeful: *an expectant glance.* **2** having expectations, esp. of possession of something or prosperity. **3** pregnant: *an expectant mother.* ◆ *n* **4** a person who expects something. **5** *Obsolete.* a candidate for office, esp. for ecclesiastical preferment. ▸ **ex'pectantly** *adv*

expectation (,ɛkspɛk'teɪʃən) *n* **1** the act or state of expecting or the state of being expected. **2** (*usually pl*) something looked forward to, whether feared or hoped for: *we have great expectations for his future; their worst expectations.* **3** an attitude of expectancy or hope; anticipation: *to regard something with expectation.* **4** *Statistics.* **4a** the numerical probability that an event will occur. **4b** another term for **expected value.** ▸ **expectative** (ɪk'spɛktətɪv) *adj*

expected frequency *n Statistics.* the number of occasions on which an event may be presumed to occur on average in a given number of trials.

expected utility *n Statistics.* the weighted average utility of the possible outcomes of a probabilistic situation; the sum or integral of the product of the probability distribution and the utility function.

expected value *n Statistics.* the sum or integral of all possible values of a random variable, or any given function of it, multiplied by the respective probabilities of the values of the variable. Symbol: $E(X)$. $E(X)$ is the mean of the distribution; $E(X-c) = E(X)-c$ where c is a constant. Also called: **mathematical expectation.**

expecting (ɪk'spɛktɪŋ) *adj Informal.* pregnant.

expectorant (ɪk'spɛktərənt) *Med.* ◆ *adj* **1** promoting the secretion, liquefaction, or expulsion of sputum from the respiratory passages. ◆ *n* **2** an expectorant drug or agent.

expectorate (ɪk'spɛktə,reɪt) *vb* to cough up and spit out (sputum from the respiratory passages). [C17: from Latin *expectorāre,* literally: to drive from the breast, expel, from *pectus* breast] ▸ **ex,pecto'ration** *n* ▸ **ex'pecto,rator** *n*

expediency (ɪk'spiːdɪənsɪ) *or* **expedience** *n, pl* **-encies** *or* **-ences. 1** appropriateness; suitability. **2** the use of or inclination towards methods that are advantageous rather than fair or just. **3** another word for **expedient** (sense 3).

expedient (ɪk'spiːdɪənt) *adj* **1** suitable to the circumstances; appropriate. **2** inclined towards methods or means that are advantageous rather than fair or just. ◆ *n also* **expediency. 3** something suitable or appropriate, esp. something used during an urgent situation. [C14: from Latin *expediēns* setting free; see EXPEDITE] ▸ **ex'pediently** *adv*

expediential (ɪk,spiːdɪ'ɛnʃəl) *adj* denoting, based on, or involving expediency. ▸ **ex,pedi'entially** *adv*

expedite ('ɛkspɪ,daɪt) *vb* (*tr*) **1** to hasten the progress of; hasten or assist. **2** to do or process (something, such as business matters) with speed and efficiency. **3** *Rare.* to dispatch (documents, messages, etc.). ◆ *adj Obsolete.* **4** unimpeded or prompt; expeditious. **5** alert or prepared. [C17: from Latin *expedīre,* literally: to free the feet (as from a snare), hence, liberate, from EX-[1] + *pēs* foot]

expediter *or* **expeditor** ('ɛkspɪ,daɪtə) *n* a person who expedites something, esp. a person employed in an industry to ensure that work on each job progresses efficiently.

expedition (,ɛkspɪ'dɪʃən) *n* **1** an organized journey or voyage for a specific purpose, esp. for exploration or for a scientific or military purpose. **2** the people and equipment comprising an expedition. **3** a pleasure trip; excursion. **4** promptness in acting; dispatch. [C15: from Latin *expedītiō,* from *expedīre* to prepare, EXPEDITE]

expeditionary (,ɛkspɪ'dɪʃənərɪ) *adj* relating to or constituting an expedition, esp. a military one: *an expeditionary force.*

expeditious (,ɛkspɪ'dɪʃəs) *adj* characterized by or done with speed and efficiency; prompt; quick. ▸ **,expe'ditiously** *adv* ▸ **,expe'ditiousness** *n*

expel (ɪk'spɛl) *vb* **-pels, -pelling, -pelled.** (*tr*) **1** to eject or drive out with force. **2** to deprive of participation in or membership of a school, club, etc. [C14: from Latin *expellere* to drive out, from *pellere* to thrust, drive] ▸ **ex'pellable** *adj* ▸ **expellee** (,ɛkspɛ'liː) *n* ▸ **ex'peller** *n*

expellant *or* **expellent** (ɪk'spɛlənt) *adj* **1** forcing out or having the capacity to force out. ◆ *n* **2** a medicine used to expel undesirable substances or organisms from the body, esp. worms from the digestive tract.

expellers (ɪk'spɛləz) *pl n* the residue remaining after an oilseed has been crushed to expel the oil, used for animal fodder: *groundnut expellers.* Compare **extractions.**

expend (ɪk'spɛnd) *vb* (*tr*) **1** to spend; disburse. **2** to consume or use up. [C15: from Latin *expendere,* from *pendere* to weigh] ▸ **ex'pender** *n*

expendable (ɪk'spɛndəbᵊl) *adj* **1** that may be expended or used up. **2** not essential; not worth preserving. **3** able to be sacrificed to achieve an objective, esp. a military one. ◆ *n* **4** something that is expendable. ▸ **ex,penda'bility** *n*

expenditure (ɪk'spɛndɪtʃə) *n* **1** something expended, such as time or money. **2** the act of expending.

expense (ɪk'spɛns) *n* **1** a particular payment of money; expenditure. **2** money needed for individual purchases; cost; charge. **3** (*pl*) incidental money spent in the performance of a job, commission, etc., usually reimbursed by an employer or allowable against tax. **4** something requiring money for its purchase or upkeep: *the car was more of an expense than he had expected.* **5 at the expense of.** to the detriment of: *he succeeded at the expense of his health.* ◆ *vb* **6** (*tr*) *U.S. and Canadian.* to treat as an expense for book-keeping or tax purposes. [C14: from Late Latin *expēnsa,* from Latin *expēnsus* weighed out; see EXPEND]

expense account *n* **1** an arrangement by which expenses incurred in the course of a person's work are refunded by his employer or deducted from his income for tax purposes. **2** a record of such expenses. **3** (*modifier*) *Informal.* paid for by an employer or by money allowable against tax: *an expense-account lunch.*

expensive (ɪk'spɛnsɪv) *adj* high-priced; costly; dear. ▸ **ex'pensively** *adv* ▸ **ex'pensiveness** *n*

experience (ɪk'spɪərɪəns) *n* **1** direct personal participation or observation; actual knowledge or contact: *experience of prison life.* **2** a particular incident, feeling, etc., that a person has undergone: *an experience to remember.* **3** accumulated knowledge, esp. of practical matters: *a man of experience.* **4a** the totality of characteristics, both past and present, that make up the particular quality of a person, place, or people. **4b** the impact made on an individual by the culture of a people, nation, etc.: *the American experience.* **5** *Philosophy.* **5a** the content of a perception regarded as independent of whether the apparent object actually exists. Compare **sense datum. 5b** the faculty by which a person acquires knowledge of contingent facts about the world, as contrasted with reason. **5c** the totality of a person's perceptions, feelings, and memories. ◆ *vb* (*tr*) **6** to participate in or undergo. **7** to be emotionally or aesthetically moved by; feel: *to experience beauty.* [C14: from Latin *experientia,* from *experīrī* to prove; related to Latin *perīculum* PERIL] ▸ **ex'perienceable** *adj*

experienced (ɪk'spɪərɪənst) *adj* having become skilful or knowledgeable from extensive contact or participation or observation.

experience table *n Insurance.* an actuarial table, esp. a mortality table based on past statistics.

experiential (ɪk,spɪərɪ'ɛnʃəl) *adj Philosophy.* relating to or derived from experience; empirical. ▸ **ex,peri'entially** *adv*

experiment *n* (ɪk'spɛrɪmənt). **1** a test or investigation, esp. one planned to provide evidence for or against a hypothesis: a *scientific experiment.* **2** the act of conducting such an investigation or test; experimentation; research. **3** an attempt at something new or different; an effort to be original: *a poetic experi-*

ment. 4 an obsolete word for **experience.** ◆ *vb* (ɪk'spɛrɪ,mɛnt). 5 (*intr*) to make an experiment or experiments. [C14: from Latin *experīmentum* proof, trial, from *experīrī* to test; see EXPERIENCE] ▸ **ex'peri,menter** *n*

experimental (ɪk,spɛrɪ'mɛntᵊl) *adj* 1 relating to, based on, or having the nature of experiment: *an experimental study.* 2 based on or derived from experience; empirical: *experimental evidence.* 3 tending to experiment: *an experimental artist.* 4 tentative or provisional: *an experimental rule in football.* ▸ **ex,peri'mentally** *adv*

experimental condition *n Statistics.* one of the distinct states of affairs or values of the independent variable for which the dependent variable is measured in order to carry out statistical tests or calculations. Also called: **condition.**

experimentalism (ɪk,spɛrɪ'mɛntə,lɪzəm) *n* employment of or reliance upon experiments; empiricism. ▸ **ex,peri'mentalist** *n*

experimentalize *or* **experimentalise** (ɪk,spɛrɪ'mɛntə,laɪz) *vb* (*intr*) to engage in experiments.

experimental psychology *n* the scientific study of the individual behaviour of man and other animals, esp. of perception, learning, memory, motor skills, and thinking.

experimentation (ɪk,spɛrɪmɛn'teɪʃən) *n* the act, process, or practice of experimenting.

experimenter effect *n Psychol.* the influence of an experimenter's expectations on his results.

expert ('ɛkspɜːt) *n* 1 a person who has extensive skill or knowledge in a particular field. ◆ *adj* 2 skilful or knowledgeable. 3 of, involving, or done by an expert: *an expert job.* [C14: from Latin *expertus* known by experience, from *experīrī* to test; see EXPERIENCE] ▸ **'expertly** *adv* ▸ **'expertness** *n*

expertise (,ɛkspɜː'tiːz) *n* special skill, knowledge, or judgment; expertness. [C19: from French: expert skill, from EXPERT]

expertize *or* **expertise** ('ɛkspɜː,taɪz) *vb U.S.* to act as an expert or give an expert opinion (on).

expert system *n* a computer program that can offer intelligent advice or make intelligent decisions using rule-based programs.

expiable ('ɛkspɪəbᵊl) *adj* capable of being expiated or atoned for.

expiate ('ɛkspɪ,eɪt) *vb* (*tr*) to atone for or redress (sin or wrongdoing); make amends for. [C16: from Latin *expiāre,* from *pius* dutiful; see PIOUS] ▸ **'expi,ator** *n*

expiation (,ɛkspɪ'eɪʃən) *n* the act, process, or a means of expiating; atonement.

expiatory ('ɛkspɪətərɪ, -trɪ) *adj* 1 capable of making expiation. 2 given or offered in expiation.

expiration (,ɛkspɪ'reɪʃən) *n* 1 the finish of something; ending; expiry. 2 the act, process, or sound of breathing out. 3 *Rare.* a last breath; death.

expiratory (ɪk'spaɪərətərɪ, -trɪ) *adj* relating to the expulsion of air from the lungs during respiration.

expire (ɪk'spaɪə) *vb* 1 (*intr*) to finish or run out; cease; come to an end. 2 to breathe out (air); exhale. 3 (*intr*) to die. [C15: from Old French *expirer,* from Latin *exspīrāre* to breathe out, from *spīrāre* to breathe] ▸ **ex'pirer** *n*

expiry (ɪk'spaɪərɪ) *n, pl* **-ries.** 1a a coming to an end, esp. of a contract period; termination: *expiry of a lease.* 1b (*as modifier*): *the expiry date.* 2 death.

explain (ɪk'spleɪn) *vb* 1 (when *tr, may take a clause as object*) to make (something) comprehensible, esp. by giving a clear and detailed account of the relevant structure, operation, surrounding circumstances, etc. 2 (*tr*) to justify or attempt to justify (oneself) by giving reasons for one's actions or words. [C15: from Latin *explānāre* to flatten, from *plānus* level] ▸ **ex'plainable** *adj* ▸ **ex'plainer** *n*

explain away *vb* (*tr, adv*) to offer excuses or reasons for (bad conduct, mistakes, etc.).

explanation (,ɛksplə'neɪʃən) *n* 1 the act or process of explaining. 2 a statement or occurrence that explains. 3 a clarification of disputed terms or points; reconciliation.

explanatory (ɪk'splænətərɪ, -trɪ) *or* **explanative** *adj* serving or intended to serve as an explanation. ▸ **ex'planatorily** *adv*

explant (ɛks'plɑːnt) *vb* 1 to transfer (living tissue) from its natural site to a culture medium. ◆ *n* 2 a piece of tissue treated in this way. ▸ **,explan'tation** *n*

expletive (ɪk'spliːtɪv) *n* 1 an exclamation or swearword; an oath or a sound expressing an emotional reaction rather than any particular meaning. 2 any syllable, word, or phrase conveying no independent meaning, esp. one inserted in a line of verse for the sake of the metre. ◆ *adj also* **expletory** (ɪk'spliːtərɪ). 3 expressing no particular meaning, esp. when filling out a line of verse. [C17: from Late Latin *explētīvus* for filling out, from *explēre,* from *plēre* to fill] ▸ **ex'pletively** *adv*

explicable ('ɛksplɪkəbᵊl, ɪk'splɪk-) *adj* capable of being explained.

explicate ('ɛksplɪ,keɪt) *vb* (*tr*) *Formal.* 1 to make clear or explicit; explain. 2 to formulate or develop (a theory, hypothesis, etc.). [C16: from Latin *explicāre* to unfold, from *plicāre* to fold] ▸ **explicative** (ɪk'splɪkətɪv) *or* **explicatory** (ɪk'splɪkətərɪ, -trɪ) *adj* ▸ **'expli,cator** *n*

explication (,ɛksplɪ'keɪʃən) *n* 1 the act or process of explicating. 2 analysis or interpretation, esp. of a literary passage or work or philosophical doctrine. 3 a comprehensive exposition or description.

explication de texte *French.* (ɛksplikasjɔ̃ də tɛkst) *n, pl* ***explications de texte*** (ɛksplikasjɔ̃ də tɛkst). a close textual analysis of a literary work. [literally: explanation of (the) text]

explicit[1] (ɪk'splɪsɪt) *adj* 1 precisely and clearly expressed, leaving nothing to implication; fully stated: *explicit instructions.* 2 graphically detailed, leaving little to the imagination: *sexually explicit scenes.* 3 openly expressed without reservations; unreserved. 4 *Maths.* (of a function) having an equation of the form $y=f(x)$, in which y is expressed directly in terms of x, as in $y=x^4+x+z$. Compare **implicit** (sense 4). [C17: from Latin *explicitus* unfolded, from *explicāre;* see EXPLICATE] ▸ **ex'plicitly** *adv* ▸ **ex'plicitness** *n*

explicit[2] (ɪk'splɪsɪt) the end; an indication, used esp. by medieval scribes, of the end of a book, part of a manuscript, etc. [Late Latin, probably short for *explicitus est liber* the book is unfolded (or complete); shortened by analogy with INCIPIT]

explode (ɪk'spləʊd) *vb* 1 to burst or cause to burst with great violence as a result of internal pressure, esp. through the detonation of an explosive; blow up. 2 to destroy or be destroyed in this manner: *to explode a bridge.* 3 (of a gas) to undergo or cause (a gas) to undergo a sudden violent expansion, accompanied by heat, light, a shock wave, and a loud noise, as a result of a fast uncontrolled exothermic chemical or nuclear reaction. 4 (*intr*) to react suddenly or violently with emotion, etc.: *to explode with anger.* 5 (*intr*) (esp. of a population) to increase rapidly. 6 (*tr*) to show (a theory, etc.) to be baseless; refute and make obsolete. 7 (*tr*) *Phonetics.* to pronounce (a stop) with audible plosion. ◆ Compare **implode.** [C16: from Latin *explōdere* to drive off by clapping, hiss (an actor) off, from EX-[1] + *plaudere* to clap] ▸ **ex'ploder** *n*

exploded view *n* a drawing or photograph of a complicated mechanism that shows the individual parts separately, usually indicating their relative positions.

exploding star *n* an irregular variable star, such as a nova, supernova, or flare star, in which rapid increases in luminosity occur, caused by some form of explosion.

exploit *n* ('ɛksplɔɪt). 1 a notable deed or feat, esp. one that is noble or heroic. ◆ *vb* (ɪk'splɔɪt). (*tr*) 2 to take advantage of (a person, situation, etc.), esp. unethically or unjustly for one's own ends. 3 to make the best use of: *to exploit natural resources.* [C14: from Old French: accomplishment, from Latin *explicitum* (something) unfolded, from *explicāre* to EXPLICATE] ▸ **ex'ploitable** *adj* ▸ **,exploi'tation** *n* ▸ **ex'ploitive** *or* **ex'ploitative** *adj*

exploration (,ɛksplə'reɪʃən) *n* 1 the act or process of exploring. 2 *Med.* examination of an organ or part for diagnostic purposes. 3 an organized trip into unfamiliar regions, esp. for scientific purposes; expedition. ▸ **exploratory** (ɪk'splɒrətərɪ, -trɪ) *or* **ex'plorative** *adj*

explore (ɪk'splɔː) *vb* 1 (*tr*) to examine or investigate, esp. systematically. 2 to travel to or into (unfamiliar or unknown regions), esp. for organized scientific purposes. 3 (*tr*) *Med.* to examine (an organ or part) for diagnostic purposes. 4 (*tr*) *Obsolete.* to search for or out. [C16: from Latin *explōrāre,* from EX-[1] + *plōrāre* to cry aloud; probably from the shouts of hunters sighting prey] ▸ **ex'plorer** *n*

Explorer[1] (ɪk'splɔːrə) *n U.S.* a member of the senior branch of the Scouts. Brit. equivalent: **Venture Scout.**

Explorer[2] (ɪk'splɔːrə) *n* any of the first series of U.S. satellites. **Explorer 1,** launched in 1958, confirmed the existence of intense radiation belts around the earth.

explosion (ɪk'spləʊʒən) *n* 1 the act or an instance of exploding. 2 a violent release of energy resulting from a rapid chemical or nuclear reaction, esp. one that produces a shock wave, loud noise, heat, and light. Compare **implosion** (sense 1). 3 a sudden or violent outburst of activity, noise, emotion, etc. 4 a rapid increase, esp. in a population. 5 *Phonetics.* another word for **plosion.** [C17: from Latin *explōsiō,* from *explōdere* to EXPLODE]

explosion welding *n Engineering.* the welding of two parts forced together by a controlled explosion.

explosive (ɪk'spləʊsɪv) *adj* 1 of, involving, or characterized by an explosion or explosions. 2 capable of exploding or tending to explode. 3 potentially violent or hazardous; dangerous: *an explosive situation.* 4 *Phonetics.* another word for **plosive.** ◆ *n* 5 a substance that decomposes rapidly under certain conditions with the production of gases, which expand by the heat of the reaction. The energy released is used in firearms, blasting, and rocket propulsion. 6 a plosive consonant; stop. ▸ **ex'plosively** *adv* ▸ **ex'plosiveness** *n*

explosive forming *n Engineering.* a rapid method of forming a metal object in which components are made by subjecting the metal to very high pressures generated by a controlled explosion.

expo ('ɛkspəʊ) *n, pl* **-pos.** short for **exposition** (sense 3).

exponent (ɪk'spəʊnənt) *n* 1 (usually foll. by *of*) a person or thing that acts as an advocate (of an idea, cause, etc.). 2 a person or thing that explains or interprets. 3 a performer or interpretive artist, esp. a musician. 4 Also called: **power, index.** *Maths.* a number or variable placed as a superscript to the right of another number or quantity indicating the number of times the number or quantity is to be multiplied by itself. ◆ *adj* 5 offering a declaration, explanation, or interpretation. [C16: from Latin *expōnere* to set out, expound, from *pōnere* to set, place]

exponential (,ɛkspəʊ'nɛnʃəl) *adj* 1 *Maths.* (of a function, curve, series, or equation) of, containing, or involving one or more numbers or quantities raised to an exponent, esp. e^x. 2 *Maths.* raised to the power of e, the base of natural logarithms. Symbol: exp 3 of or involving an exponent or exponents. 4 *Informal.* very rapid. ◆ *n* 5 *Maths.* an exponential function, etc. ▸ **,expo'nentially** *adv*

exponential distribution *n Statistics.* a continuous single-parameter distribution used esp. when making statements about the length of life of certain materials or waiting times between randomly occurring events. Its density function is $p(x) = \lambda e^{-\lambda x}$ for positive λ and nonnegative x, and it is a special case of the gamma distribution.

exponential horn *n* a horn for the radiation of acoustic or high-frequency electromagnetic waves, of which the cross-sectional area increases exponentially with the length.

export *n* ('ɛkspɔːt). 1 (*often pl*) 1a goods (**visible exports**) or services (**invisible exports**) sold to a foreign country or countries. 1b (*as modifier*): *an export licence; export finance.* ◆ *vb* (ɪk'spɔːt, 'ɛkspɔːt). 2 to sell (goods or services) or ship (goods) to a foreign country or countries. **3** (*tr*) to transmit or spread (an idea, social institution, etc.) abroad. ◆ Compare **import.** [C15: from Latin *exportāre* to carry away, from *portāre* to carry] ▸ **ex'portable** *adj* ▸ **ex,porta'bility** *n* ▸ **ex'porter** *n*

exportation (,ɛkspɔː'teɪʃən) *n* **1** the act, business, or process of exporting goods or services. **2** *Chiefly U.S.* an exported product or service.

export reject *n* an article that fails to meet a standard of quality required for export and that is sold on the home market.

expose (ɪk'spəʊz) *vb* (*tr*) **1** to display for viewing; exhibit. **2** to bring to public notice; disclose; reveal: *to expose the facts.* **3** to divulge the identity of; unmask. **4** (foll. by *to*) to make subject or susceptible (to attack, criticism, etc.). **5** to abandon (a child, animal, etc.) in the open to die. **6** (foll. by *to*) to introduce (to) or acquaint (with): *he was exposed to the classics at an early age.* **7** *Photog.* to subject (a photographic film or plate) to light, X-rays, or some other type of actinic radiation. **8** *R.C. Church.* to exhibit (the consecrated Eucharistic Host or a relic) for public veneration. **9 expose oneself.** to display one's sexual organs in public. [C15: from Old French *exposer,* from Latin *expōnere* to set out; see EXPONENT] ▸ **ex'posable** *adj* ▸ **ex'posal** *n* ▸ **ex'poser** *n*

exposé (ɛks'pəʊzeɪ) *n* **1** the act or an instance of bringing a scandal, crime, etc., to public notice. **2** an article, book, or statement that discloses a scandal, crime, etc.

exposed (ɪk'spəʊzd) *adj* **1** not concealed; displayed for viewing. **2** without shelter from the elements. **3** susceptible to attack or criticism; vulnerable. **4** *Mountaineering.* (of a climb, pitch, or move) performed on a high, sheer, and unsheltered rock face. ▸ **exposedness** (ɪk'spəʊzɪdnɪs) *n*

exposition (,ɛkspə'zɪʃən) *n* **1** a systematic, usually written statement about, commentary on, or explanation of a specific subject. **2** the act of expounding or setting forth information or a viewpoint. **3** a large public exhibition, esp. of industrial products or arts and crafts. **4** the act of exposing or the state of being exposed. **5** the part of a play, novel, etc., in which the theme and main characters are introduced. **6** *Music.* the first statement of the subjects or themes of a movement in sonata form or a fugue. **7** *R.C. Church.* the exhibiting of the consecrated Eucharistic Host or a relic for public veneration. [C14: from Latin *expositiō* a setting forth, from *expōnere* to display; see EXPONENT] ▸ **,expo'sitional** *adj*

expositor (ɪk'spɒzɪtə) *n* a person who expounds.

expository (ɪk'spɒzɪtərɪ, -trɪ) *or* **expositive** *adj* of, involving, or assisting in exposition; explanatory. ▸ **ex'positorily** *or* **ex'positively** *adv*

ex post facto (ɛks pəʊst 'fæktəʊ) *adj* having retrospective effect: *an ex post facto law.* [C17: from Latin *ex* from + *post* afterwards + *factus* done, from *facere* to do]

expostulate (ɪk'spɒstjʊ,leɪt) *vb* (*intr;* usually foll. by *with*) to argue or reason (with), esp. in order to dissuade from an action or intention. [C16: from Latin *expostulāre* to require, from *postulāre* to demand; see POSTULATE] ▸ **ex'postu,latingly** *adv* ▸ **ex,postu'lation** *n* ▸ **ex'postu,lator** *n* ▸ **ex'postulatory** *or* **ex'postulative** *adj*

exposure (ɪk'spəʊʒə) *n* **1** the act of exposing or the condition of being exposed. **2** the position or outlook of a house, building, etc.; aspect: *the bedroom has a southern exposure.* **3** lack of shelter from the weather, esp. the cold: *to die of exposure.* **4** a surface that is exposed: *an exposure of granite.* **5** *Mountaineering.* the degree to which a climb, etc. is exposed (see **exposed** (sense 4)). **6** *Photog.* **6a** the act of exposing a photographic film or plate to light, X-rays, etc. **6b** an area on a film or plate that has been exposed to light, etc. **6c** (*as modifier*): *exposure control.* **7** *Photog.* **7a** the intensity of light falling on a photographic film or plate multiplied by the time for which it is exposed. **7b** a combination of lens aperture and shutter speed used in taking a photograph: *he used the wrong exposure.* **8** appearance or presentation before the public, as in a theatre, on television, or in films. **9** See **indecent exposure.**

exposure meter *n Photog.* an instrument for measuring the intensity of light, usually by means of a photocell, so that the suitable camera settings of shutter speed and f-number (or lens aperture) can be determined. Also called: **light meter.**

expound (ɪk'spaʊnd) *vb* (when *intr,* foll. by *on* or *about*) to explain or set forth (an argument, theory, etc.) in detail: *to expound on one's theories; he expounded his reasoning.* [C13: from Old French *espondre,* from Latin *expōnere* to set forth, from *pōnere* to put] ▸ **ex'pounder** *n*

express (ɪk'sprɛs) *vb* (*tr*) **1** to transform (ideas) into words; utter; verbalize. **2** to show or reveal; indicate: *tears express grief.* **3** to communicate (emotion, etc.) without words, as through music, painting, etc. **4** to indicate through a symbol, formula, etc. **5** to force or squeeze out: *to express the juice from an orange.* **6** to send by rapid transport or special messenger. **7 express oneself.** to communicate one's thoughts or ideas. ◆ *adj* (*prenominal*) **8** clearly indicated or shown; explicitly stated: *an express wish.* **9** done or planned for a definite reason or goal; particular: *an express purpose.* **10** of, concerned with, or designed for rapid transportation of people, merchandise, mail, money, etc.: *express delivery; an express depot.* ◆ *n* **11a** a system for sending merchandise, mail, money, etc., rapidly. **11b** merchandise, mail, etc., conveyed by such a system. **11c** *Chiefly U.S. and Canadian.* an enterprise operating such a system. **12** Also called: **express train.** a fast train stopping at none or only a few of the intermediate stations between its two termini. **13** See **express rifle.** ◆ *adv* **14** by means of a special delivery or express delivery: *it went express.* [C14: from Latin *expressus,* literally: squeezed out, hence, prominent, from *exprimere* to force out, from EX-[1] + *premere* to press] ▸ **ex'presser** *n* ▸ **ex'pressible** *adj*

expressage (ɪk'sprɛsɪdʒ) *n* **1** the conveyance of merchandise by express. **2** the fee charged for such conveyance.

expression (ɪk'sprɛʃən) *n* **1** the act or an instance of transforming ideas into words. **2** a manifestation of an emotion, feeling, etc., without words: *tears are an expression of grief.* **3** communication of emotion through music, painting, etc. **4** a look on the face that indicates mood or emotion: *a joyful expression.* **5** the choice of words, phrases, syntax, intonation, etc., in communicating. **6** a particular phrase used conventionally to express something: *a dialect expression.* **7** the act or process of forcing or squeezing out a liquid. **8** *Maths.* a variable, function, or some combination of constants, variables, or functions. **9** *Genetics.* the effect of a particular gene on the phenotype. ▸ **ex'pressional** *adj* ▸ **ex'pressionless** *adj* ▸ **ex'pressionlessly** *adv*

expressionism (ɪk'sprɛʃə,nɪzəm) *n* (*sometimes cap.*) an artistic and literary movement originating in Germany at the beginning of the 20th century, which sought to express emotions rather than to represent external reality: characterized by the use of symbolism and of exaggeration and distortion. ▸ **ex'pressionist** *n, adj* ▸ **ex,pression'istic** *adj*

expression mark *n* one of a set of musical directions, usually in Italian, indicating how a piece or passage is to be performed.

expressive (ɪk'sprɛsɪv) *adj* **1** of, involving, or full of expression. **2** (*postpositive;* foll. by *of*) indicative or suggestive (of): *a look expressive of love.* **3** having a particular meaning, feeling, or force; significant. ▸ **ex'pressively** *adv* ▸ **ex'pressiveness** *n*

expressivity (,ɛksprɛ'sɪvɪtɪ) *n* **1** (esp. of a work of art) the quality of being expressive. **2** *Genetics.* the strength of the effect of a gene on the phenotype.

expressly (ɪk'sprɛslɪ) *adv* **1** for an express purpose; with specific intentions. **2** plainly, exactly, or unmistakably.

expresso (ɪk'sprɛsəʊ) *n* a variant of **espresso.**

express rifle *n* a high-velocity hunting rifle for big game shooting.

expressway (ɪk'sprɛs,weɪ) *n* a motorway.

expropriate (ɛks'prəʊprɪ,eɪt) *vb* (*tr*) to deprive (an owner) of (property), esp. by taking it for public use. See also **eminent domain.** [C17: from Medieval Latin *expropriāre* to deprive of possessions, from *proprius* own] ▸ **ex'propriable** *adj* ▸ **ex,propri'ation** *n* ▸ **ex'propri,ator** *n*

exptl *abbrev. for* experimental.

expulsion (ɪk'spʌlʃən) *n* the act of expelling or the fact or condition of being expelled. [C14: from Latin *expulsiō* a driving out, from *expellere* to EXPEL]

expulsive (ɪk'spʌlsɪv) *adj* tending or serving to expel.

expunge (ɪk'spʌndʒ) *vb* (*tr*) **1** to delete or erase; blot out; obliterate. **2** to wipe out or destroy. [C17: from Latin *expungere* to blot out, from *pungere* to prick] ▸ **expunction** (ɪk'spʌŋkʃən) *n* ▸ **ex'punger** *n*

expurgate ('ɛkspə,geɪt) *vb* (*tr*) to amend (a book, text, etc.) by removing (obscene or offensive sections). [C17: from Latin *expurgāre* to clean out, from *purgāre* to purify; see PURGE] ▸ **,expur'gation** *n* ▸ **'expur,gator** *n* ▸ **expurgatory** (ɛks'pɜːgətərɪ, -trɪ) *or* **expurgatorial** (ɛk,spɜːgə'tɔːrɪəl) *adj*

exquisite (ɪk'skwɪzɪt, 'ɛkskwɪzɪt) *adj* **1** possessing qualities of unusual delicacy and fine craftsmanship: *jewels in an exquisite setting.* **2** extremely beautiful and pleasing: *an exquisite face.* **3** outstanding or excellent: *an exquisite victory.* **4** sensitive; discriminating: *exquisite taste.* **5** fastidious and refined. **6** intense or sharp in feeling: *exquisite pleasure; exquisite pain.* ◆ *n* **7** *Obsolete.* a dandy. [C15: from Latin *exquīsītus* excellent, from *exquīrere* to search out, from *quaerere* to seek] ▸ **ex'quisitely** *adv* ▸ **ex'quisiteness** *n*

exr *abbrev. for* executor.

exsanguinate (ɪk'sæŋgwɪneɪt) *vb* (*tr*) *Rare.* to drain the blood from. [C19: from Latin *exsanguināre*] ▸ **ex,sanguin'ation** *n*

exsanguine (ɪk'sæŋgwɪn) *or* **exsanguinous** *adj* without blood; bloodless or anaemic. [C17: from Latin *exsanguis,* from *sanguis* blood] ▸ **,exsan'guinity** *n*

exscind (ɛk'sɪnd) *vb* (*tr*) to cut off or out; excise. [C17: *exscind,* from Latin *exscindere* to extirpate, destroy, from *scindere* to cut, tear, split]

exsect (ɛk'sɛkt) *vb* (*tr*) to cut out. [C17: *exsect,* from Latin *exsecāre* to cut away, from *secāre* to cut] ▸ **exsection** (ɛk'sɛkʃən) *n*

exsert (ɛk'sɜːt) *vb* **1** (*tr*) to thrust out; protrude. ◆ *adj also* **exserted. 2** protruded, stretched out, or (esp. of stamens) projecting beyond the corolla of a flower. [C19: from Latin *exserere* to thrust out; see EXERT] ▸ **ex'sertion** *n* ▸ **exsertile** (ɛk'sɜːtaɪl) *adj*

ex-service *adj* having formerly served in the armed forces.

ex-serviceman *or* (*fem*) **ex-servicewoman** *n, pl* **-men** *or* **-women.** a person who has served in the army, navy, or air force.

exsiccate ('ɛksɪ,keɪt) *vb* to dry up; desiccate. [C15: from Latin *exsiccāre,* from *siccus* dry] ▸ **,exsic'cation** *n* ▸ **'exsiccative** *adj* ▸ **'exsic,cator** *n*

ex silentio *Latin.* (ɛks sɪ'lɛnʃɪ,əʊ) *adv, adj* (of a theory, assumption, etc.) based on a lack of evidence to the contrary. [literally: from silence]

exstipulate (ɛk'stɪpjʊlɪt, -,leɪt) *or* **estipulate** *adj* (of a flowering plant) having no stipules.

exstrophy ('ɛkstrəfɪ) *n Med.* congenital eversion of a hollow organ, esp. the urinary bladder. [C19: from Greek EX-[1] + *strophein* to turn]

ext *abbrev. for:* **1** extinct. **2** extract.

ext. *abbrev. for:* **1** extension. **2** external(ly). **3** extra.

extant (ɛk'stænt, 'ɛkstənt) *adj* **1** still in existence; surviving. **2** *Archaic.* standing out; protruding. [C16: from Latin *exstāns* standing out, from *exstāre,* from *stāre* to stand]

USAGE *Extant* is sometimes wrongly used simply to say that something exists, without any connotation of survival: *plutonium is perhaps the deadliest element in existence* (not *the deadliest element extant*).

extemporaneous (ɪk,stɛmpə'reɪnɪəs) *or* **extemporary** (ɪk'stɛmpərərɪ, -prərɪ) *adj* **1** spoken, performed, etc., without planning or preparation; impromptu; extempore. **2** done in a temporary manner; improvised. ▸ **ex,tempo'raneously** *or* **ex'temporarily** *adv* ▸ **ex,tempo'raneousness** *or* **ex'temporariness** *n*

extempore (ɪk'stɛmpərɪ) *adv, adj* without planning or preparation; impromptu. [C16: from Latin *ex tempore* instantaneously, from EX-[1] out of + *tempus* time]

extemporize *or* **extemporise** (ɪk'stɛmpə,raɪz) *vb* **1** to perform, speak, or compose (an act, speech, piece of music, etc.) without planning or preparation. **2** to use (a temporary solution) for an immediate need; improvise. ▸ **ex,tempori'zation** *or* **ex,tempori'sation** *n* ▸ **ex'tempo,rizer** *or* **ex'tempo,riser** *n*

extend (ɪk'stɛnd) *vb* **1** to draw out or be drawn out; stretch. **2** to last for a certain time: *his schooling extended for three years.* **3** (*intr*) to reach a certain point in time or distance: *the land extends five miles.* **4** (*intr*) to exist or occur: *the trees extended throughout the area.* **5** (*tr*) to increase (a building, etc.) in size or area; add to or enlarge. **6** (*tr*) to broaden the meaning or scope of: *the law was extended.* **7** (*tr*) to put forth, present, or offer: *to extend greetings.* **8** to stretch forth (an arm, etc.). **9** (*tr*) to lay out (a body) at full length. **10** (*tr*) to strain or exert (a person or animal) to the maximum. **11** (*tr*) to prolong (the time originally set) for payment of (a debt or loan), completion of (a task), etc. **12** (*tr*) *Book-keeping.* **12a** to carry forward. **12b** to calculate the amount of (a total, balance, etc.). **13** (*tr*) *Law.* (formerly in England) to value or assess (land). [C14: from Latin *extendere* to stretch out, from *tendere* to stretch] ▸ **ex'tendible** *or* **ex'tendable** *adj* ▸ **ex,tendi'bility** *or* **ex,tenda'bility** *n*

extended (ɪk'stɛndɪd) *adj* **1** stretched out in time, space, influence, application, etc. **2** (of a horse's pace) free-moving and with long steps: *an extended trot.* **3** *Printing.* another word for **expanded** (sense 1). ▸ **ex'tendedly** *adv* ▸ **ex'tendedness** *n*

extended family *n Sociol., anthropol.* a social unit that contains the nuclear family together with blood relatives, often spanning three or more generations.

extended-play *adj* denoting an EP record.

extender (ɪk'stɛndə) *n* **1** a person or thing that extends. **2** a substance, such as French chalk or china clay, added to paints to give them body and decrease their rate of settlement. **3** a substance added to glues and resins to dilute them or to modify their viscosity. **4** a substance added to elastomers to assist the plasticizer. **5** *Printing.* the part of certain lower-case letters that extends either above (the ascender) or below (the descender) the body of the letter.

extensible (ɪk'stɛnsəbᵊl) *or* **extensile** (ɪk'stɛnsaɪl) *adj* capable of being extended. ▸ **ex,tensi'bility** *or* **ex'tensibleness** *n*

extension (ɪk'stɛnʃən) *n* **1** the act of extending or the condition of being extended. **2** something that can be extended or that extends another object. **3** the length, range, etc., over which something is extended; extent. **4** an additional telephone set connected to the same telephone line as another set or other sets. **5** a room or rooms added to an existing building. **6** a delay, esp. one agreed by all parties, in the date originally set for payment of a debt or completion of a contract. **7** the property of matter by which it occupies space; size. **8a** the act of straightening or extending an arm or leg. **8b** its position after being straightened or extended. **9** *Med.* a steady pull applied to a fractured or dislocated arm or leg to restore it to its normal position. See also **traction** (sense 3). **10a** a service by which some of the facilities of an educational establishment, library, etc., are offered to outsiders. **10b** (*as modifier*): *a university extension course.* **11** *Logic.* **11a** the class of entities to which a given word correctly applies: thus, the extension of *satellite of Mars* is the set containing only Deimos and Phobos. Compare **intension** (sense 1a). **11b conservative extension.** a formal theory that includes among its theorems all the theorems of a given theory. [C14: from Late Latin *extensiō* a stretching out; see EXTEND]

extensional (ɪk'stɛnʃənᵊl) *adj* **1** relating to or characterized by extension. **2** *Logic.* explicable solely in terms of extensions; ignoring differences of meaning that do not affect the extension. See also **extensionality, substitutivity, transparent context.** ▸ **ex'tensionally** *adv* ▸ **ex'tensionalism** *n*

extensionality (ɪk,stɛnʃə'nælɪtɪ) *n Logic.* the principle that sets are definable in terms of their elements alone, whatever way they may have been selected. Thus {a, b}={b, a}={first two letters of the alphabet}.

extension ring *or* **tube** *n Photog.* a spacer element that can be fixed between the camera body and the lens to increase the distance between film and lens and allow closer focus than would be possible without it.

extensity (ɪk'stɛnsɪtɪ) *n* **1** *Psychol.* that part of sensory perception relating to the spatial aspect of objects. **2** *Rare.* the condition of being extensive or extended.

extensive (ɪk'stɛnsɪv) *adj* **1** having a large extent, area, scope, degree, etc.; vast: *extensive deserts; an extensive inheritance.* **2** widespread: *extensive coverage in the press.* **3** *Agriculture.* involving or farmed with minimum expenditure of capital or labour, esp. depending on a large area of land. Compare **intensive** (sense 3). **4** *Physics.* of or relating to a property, measurement, etc., that is dependent on mass: *heat is an extensive property.* Compare **intensive** (sense 7). **5** *Logic.* **5a** of or relating to logical extension. **5b** (of a definition) in terms of the objects to which the term applies rather than its meaning. ▸ **ex'tensively** *adv* ▸ **ex'tensiveness** *n*

extensometer (,ɛkstɛn'sɒmɪtə) *or* **extensimeter** (,ɛkstɛn'sɪmɪtə) *n* an apparatus for studying small changes of length, as in the thermal expansion or mechanical compression of a solid.

extensor (ɪk'stɛnsə, -sɔː) *n* any muscle that stretches or extends an arm, leg, or other bodily part. Compare **flexor.** [C18: from New Latin, from Latin *extensus* stretched out]

extent (ɪk'stɛnt) *n* **1** the range over which something extends; scope: *the extent of the damage.* **2** an area or volume: *a vast extent of concrete.* **3** *U.S. law.* a writ authorizing a person to whom a debt is due to assume temporary possession of his debtor's lands. **4** *Logic.* another word for **extension** (sense 11). [C14: from Old French *extente,* from Latin *extentus* extensive, from *extendere* to EXTEND]

extenuate (ɪk'stɛnjʊ,eɪt) *vb* (*tr*) **1** to represent (an offence, a fault, etc.) as being less serious than it appears, as by showing mitigating circumstances. **2** to cause to be or appear less serious; mitigate. **3** to underestimate or make light of. **4** *Archaic.* **4a** to emaciate or weaken. **4b** to dilute or thin out. [C16: from Latin *extenuāre* to make thin, from *tenuis* thin, frail] ▸ **ex'tenu,ating** *adj* ▸ **ex,tenu'ation** *n* ▸ **ex'tenu,ator** *n* ▸ **ex'tenuatory** *adj*

exterior (ɪk'stɪərɪə) *n* **1** a part, surface, or region that is on the outside. **2** the observable outward behaviour or appearance of a person. **3** a film or scene shot outside a studio. ◆ *adj* **4** of, situated on, or suitable for the outside: *exterior cleaning.* **5** coming or acting from without; external: *exterior complications.* **6** of or involving foreign nations. [C16: from Latin, comparative of *exterus* on the outside, from *ex* out of] ▸ **ex'teriorly** *adv*

exterior angle *n* **1** an angle of a polygon contained between one side extended and the adjacent side. **2** any of the four angles made by a transversal that are outside the region between the two intersected lines.

exteriorize *or* **exteriorise** (ɪk'stɪərɪə,raɪz) *vb* (*tr*) **1** *Surgery.* to expose (an attached organ or part) outside a body cavity, esp. in order to remove it from an operating area. **2** another word for **externalize.** ▸ **ex,teriori'zation** *or* **ex,teriori'sation** *n*

exterminate (ɪk'stɜːmɪ,neɪt) *vb* (*tr*) to destroy (living things, esp. pests or vermin) completely; annihilate; eliminate. [C16: from Latin *extermināre* to drive away, from *terminus* boundary] ▸ **ex'terminable** *adj* ▸ **ex,termi'nation** *n* ▸ **ex'terminative** *or* **ex'terminatory** *adj* ▸ **ex'termi,nator** *n*

extern *or* **externe** ('ɛkstɜːn, ɪk'stɜːn) *n U.S.* a person, such as a physician at a hospital, who has an official connection with an institution but does not reside in it. [C16: from Latin *externus* EXTERNAL]

external (ɪk'stɜːnᵊl) *adj* **1** of, situated on, or suitable for the outside; outer. **2** coming or acting from without: *external evidence from an independent source.* **3** of or involving foreign nations; foreign. **4** of, relating to, or designating a medicine that is applied to the outside of the body. **5** *Anatomy.* situated on or near the outside of the body: *the external ear.* **6** *Education.* denoting assessment by examiners who are not employed at the candidate's place of study. **7** (of a student) studying a university subject extramurally. **8** *Philosophy.* (of objects, etc.) taken to exist independently of a perceiving mind. ◆ *n* **9** (*often pl*) an external circumstance or aspect, esp. one that is superficial or inessential. **10** *Austral. and N.Z.* a student taking an extramural subject. [C15: from Latin *externus* outward, from *exterus* on the outside, from *ex* out of] ▸ **ex'ternally** *adv*

external-combustion engine *n* a heat engine in which the working fluid is heated in an external boiler or heat exchanger and is thus isolated from the process of fuel combustion.

external ear *n* the part of the ear consisting of the auricle and the auditory canal.

externalism (ɪk'stɜːnə,lɪzəm) *n* **1** exaggerated emphasis on outward form, esp. in religious worship. **2** a philosophical doctrine holding that only objects that can be perceived by the senses are real; phenomenalism. ▸ **ex'ternalist** *n*

externality (,ɛkstɜː'nælɪtɪ) *n, pl* **-ties. 1** the state or condition of being external. **2** something external. **3** *Philosophy.* the quality of existing independently of a perceiving mind. **4** an economic effect that results from an economic choice but is not reflected in market prices.

externalize (ɪk'stɜːnə,laɪz), **exteriorize** (ɪk'stɪərɪə,raɪz) *or* **externalise, exteriorise** *vb* (*tr*) **1** to make external; give outward shape to. **2** *Psychol.* to attribute (one's own feelings) to one's surroundings. ▸ **ex,ternali'zation, ex,teriori'zation** *or* **ex,ternali'sation, ex,teriori'sation** *n*

exteroceptor ('ɛkstərəʊ,sɛptə) *n* any sensory organ or part of the body, such as the eye, able to receive stimuli from outside the body. Compare **interoceptor, proprioceptor.** [C20: *extero-,* from Latin *exterus* EXTERIOR + (RE)CEPTOR] ▸ **,extero'ceptive** *adj*

exterritorial (,ɛkstɛrɪ'tɔːrɪəl) *adj* a variant of **extraterritorial.** ▸ **ex,terri,tori'ality** *n* ▸ **,exterri'torially** *adv*

extinct (ɪk'stɪŋkt) *adj* **1** (of an animal or plant species) having no living representative; having died out. **2** quenched or extinguished. **3** (of a volcano) no longer liable to erupt; inactive. **4** void or obsolete: *an extinct political office.* [C15: from Latin *exstinctus* quenched, from *exstinguere* to EXTINGUISH]

extinction (ɪk'stɪŋkʃən) *n* **1** the act of making extinct or the state of being extinct. **2** the act of extinguishing or the state of being extinguished. **3** complete destruction; annihilation. **4** *Physics.* reduction of the intensity of radiation as a result of absorption or scattering by matter. **5** *Astronomy.* the dimming of light from a celestial body as it passes through an absorbing or scattering medium, such as the earth's atmosphere or interstellar dust. **6** *Psychol.* a process in which the frequency or intensity of a learned response is decreased as a result of reinforcement being withdrawn. Compare **habituation.**

extinctive (ɪk'stɪŋktɪv) *adj* tending or serving to extinguish or make extinct.

extine ('ɛkstɪn, -tiːn, -taɪn) *or* **exine** ('ɛksɪn, -aɪn) *n Botany.* the outermost coat of a pollen grain or a spore. Compare **intine.** [C19: from Latin *extimus* outermost + -INE¹]

extinguish (ɪk'stɪŋgwɪʃ) *vb* (*tr*) **1** to put out or quench (a light, flames, etc.). **2** to remove or destroy entirely; annihilate. **3** *Archaic.* to eclipse or obscure by or as if by superior brilliance. **4** *Law.* to discharge (a debt). [C16: from Latin *exstinguere,* from *stinguere* to quench] ▸ **ex'tinguishable** *adj* ▸ **ex'tinguisher** *n* ▸ **ex'tinguishment** *n*

extinguishant (ɪk'stɪŋgwɪʃənt) *n* a substance, such as a liquid, foam, powder, etc., used in extinguishing fires.

extirpate ('ɛkstə,peɪt) *vb* (*tr*) **1** to remove or destroy completely. **2** to pull up or out; uproot. **3** to remove (an organ or part) surgically. [C16: from Latin *exstirpāre* to root out, from *stirps* root, stock] ▸ **,extir'pation** *n* ▸ **'extir,pative** *adj* ▸ **'extir,pator** *n*

extol *or U.S.* **extoll** (ɪk'stəʊl) *vb* **-tols, -tolling, -tolled** *or U.S.* **-tolls, -tolling, -tolled.** (*tr*) to praise lavishly; exalt. [C15: from Latin *extollere* to elevate, from *tollere* to raise] ▸ **ex'toller** *n* ▸ **ex'tollingly** *adv* ▸ **ex'tolment** *n*

extort (ɪk'stɔːt) *vb* (*tr*) **1** to secure (money, favours, etc.) by intimidation, violence, or the misuse of influence or authority. **2** to obtain by importunate demands: *the children extorted a promise of a trip to the zoo.* **3** to overcharge for (something, esp. interest on a loan). [C16: from Latin *extortus* wrenched out, from *extorquēre* to wrest away, from *torquēre* to twist, wrench] ► **ex'tortion** *n* ► **ex'tortioner, ex'tortionist,** *or* **ex'torter** *n* ► **ex'tortive** *adj*

extortionate (ɪk'stɔːʃənɪt) *adj* **1** (of prices, etc.) excessive; exorbitant. **2** (of persons) using extortion. ► **ex'tortionately** *adv*

extra ('ɛkstrə) *adj* **1** being more than what is usual or expected; additional. ◆ *n* **2** a person or thing that is additional. **3** something for which an additional charge is made: *the new car had many extras.* **4** an additional edition of a newspaper, esp. to report a new development or crisis. **5** *Films.* an actor or person temporarily engaged, usually for crowd scenes. **6** *Cricket.* a run not scored from the bat, such as a wide, no-ball, bye, or leg bye. **7** *U.S.* something that is better than usual in quality. ◆ *adv* **8** unusually; exceptionally: *an extra fast car.* [C18: perhaps shortened from EXTRAORDINARY]

extra- *prefix* outside or beyond an area or scope: *extrasensory; extraterritorial.* [from Latin *extrā* outside, beyond, changed from *extera,* from *exterus* outward]

extracanonical (ˌɛkstrəkə'nɒnɪkᵊl) *adj Christianity.* not included in the canon of Scripture.

extracellular (ˌɛkstrə'sɛljʊlə) *adj Biology.* situated or occurring outside a cell or cells. ► ˌ**extra'cellularly** *adv*

extracorporeal (ˌɛkstrəkɔː'pɔːrɪəl) *adj* outside the body.

extra cover *n Cricket.* a fielding position between cover and mid-off.

extract *vb* (ɪk'strækt). (*tr*) **1** to withdraw, pull out, or uproot by force. **2** to remove or separate. **3** to derive (pleasure, information, etc.) from some source or situation. **4** to deduce or develop (a doctrine, policy, etc.). **5** *Informal.* to extort (money, etc.). **6** to obtain (a substance) from a mixture or material by a chemical or physical process, such as digestion, distillation, the action of a solvent, or mechanical separation. **7** to cut out or copy out (an article, passage, quotation, etc.) from a publication. **8** to determine the value of (the root of a number). ◆ *n* ('ɛkstrækt). **9** something extracted, such as a part or passage from a book, speech, etc. **10** a preparation containing the active principle or concentrated essence of a material: *beef extract; yeast extract.* **11** *Pharmacol.* a solution of plant or animal tissue containing the active principle. [C15: from Latin *extractus* drawn forth, from *extrahere,* from *trahere* to drag] ► **ex'tractable** *adj* ► **exˌtracta'bility** *n*

USAGE *Extract* is sometimes wrongly used where *extricate* would be better: *he will find it difficult extricating* (not *extracting*) *himself from this situation.*

extraction (ɪk'strækʃən) *n* **1** the act of extracting or the condition of being extracted. **2** something extracted; an extract. **3a** the act or an instance of extracting a tooth or teeth. **3b** a tooth or teeth extracted. **4** origin, descent, lineage, or ancestry: *of German extraction.*

extractions (ɪk'strækʃənz) *pl n* the residue remaining after an oilseed has had the oil extracted by a solvent. Used as a feed for animals: *groundnut extractions.* Compare **expellers.**

extractive (ɪk'stræktɪv) *adj* **1** tending or serving to extract. **2** of, involving, or capable of extraction. ◆ *n* **3** something extracted or capable of being extracted. **4** the part of an extract that is insoluble.

extractor (ɪk'stræktə) *n* **1** a person or thing that extracts. **2** an instrument for pulling something out or removing tight-fitting components. **3** a device for extracting liquid from a solid, esp. a centrifugal dryer. **4** short for **extractor fan. 5** a fitting in many firearms for removing spent cartridges from the chamber.

extractor fan *or* **extraction fan** *n* a fan used in kitchens, bathrooms, workshops, etc., to remove stale air or fumes.

extracurricular (ˌɛkstrəkə'rɪkjʊlə) *adj* **1** taking place outside the normal school timetable: *extracurricular activities.* **2** beyond the regular duties, schedule, etc.

extraditable ('ɛkstrəˌdaɪtəbᵊl) *adj* **1** (of a crime) rendering the offender liable to extradition: *an extraditable offence.* **2** (of a person) subject to extradition.

extradite ('ɛkstrəˌdaɪt) *vb* (*tr*) **1** to surrender (an alleged offender) for trial to a foreign state. **2** to procure the extradition of. [C19: back formation from EXTRADITION]

extradition (ˌɛkstrə'dɪʃən) *n* the surrender of an alleged offender or fugitive to the state in whose territory the alleged offence was committed. [C19: from French, from Latin *trāditiō* a handing over; see TRADITION]

extrados (ɛk'streɪdɒs) *n, pl* **-dos** (-dəʊz) *or* **-doses.** *Architect.* the outer curve or surface of an arch or vault. Compare **intrados.** [C18: from French, from EXTRA- + *dos* back, from Latin *dorsum*]

extradural (ˌɛkstrə'djʊərəl) *adj* another word for **epidural** (sense 1).

extragalactic (ˌɛkstrəgə'læktɪk) *adj* occurring or existing beyond the Galaxy.

extragalactic nebula *n* the former name for **galaxy.**

extrajudicial (ˌɛkstrədʒuː'dɪʃəl) *adj* **1** outside the ordinary course of legal proceedings: *extrajudicial evidence.* **2** beyond the jurisdiction or authority of the court: *an extrajudicial opinion.* ► ˌ**extraju'dicially** *adv*

extramarital (ˌɛkstrə'mærɪtᵊl) *adj* (esp. of sexual relations) occurring outside marriage.

extramundane (ˌɛkstrə'mʌndeɪn) *adj* not of the physical world or universe.

extramural (ˌɛkstrə'mjʊərəl) *adj* **1** connected with but outside the normal courses or programme of a university, college, etc.: *extramural studies.* **2** located beyond the boundaries or walls of a city, castle, etc. ► ˌ**extra'murally** *adv*

extraneous (ɪk'streɪnɪəs) *adj* **1** not essential. **2** not pertinent or applicable; irrelevant. **3** coming from without; of external origin. **4** not belonging; unrelated to that to which it is added or in which it is contained. [C17: from Latin *extrāneus* external, from *extrā* outside] ► **ex'traneously** *adv* ► **ex'traneousness** *n*

extranuclear (ˌɛkstrə'njuːklɪə) *adj Biology.* situated or occurring in part of a cell outside the nucleus.

extraordinary (ɪk'strɔːdᵊnrɪ, -dᵊnərɪ) *adj* **1** very unusual, remarkable, or surprising. **2** not in an established manner, course, or order. **3** employed for particular events or purposes. **4** (*usually postpositive*) (of an official, etc.) additional or subordinate to the usual one: *a minister extraordinary.* [C15: from Latin *extraordinārius* beyond what is usual; see ORDINARY] ► **ex'traordinarily** *adv* ► **ex'traordinariness** *n*

extraordinary general meeting *n* a meeting specially called to discuss a particular item of a company's business, usually one of some importance. The meeting may be called by a group of shareholders or by the directors. Abbrev.: **EGM.**

extraordinary ray *n Optics.* the plane-polarized ray of light that does not obey the laws of refraction in a doubly refracting crystal. See **double refraction.** Compare **ordinary ray.**

extrapolate (ɪk'stræpəˌleɪt) *vb* **1** *Maths.* to estimate (a value of a function or measurement) beyond the values already known, by the extension of a curve. Compare **interpolate** (sense 4). **2** to infer (something not known) by using but not strictly deducing from the known facts. [C19: EXTRA- + *-polate,* as in INTERPOLATE] ► **exˌtrapo'lation** *n* ► **ex'trapolative** *or* **ex'trapolatory** *adj* ► **ex'trapoˌlator** *n*

extraposition (ˌɛkstrəpə'zɪʃən) *n* **1** placement of something outside something else. **2** *Transformational grammar.* a rule that moves embedded clauses out to the end of the main clause, converting, for example, *A man who will help has just arrived* into *A man has just arrived who will help.*

extrasensory (ˌɛkstrə'sɛnsərɪ) *adj* of or relating to extrasensory perception.

extrasensory perception *n* the supposed ability of certain individuals to obtain information about the environment without the use of normal sensory channels. Also called: **cryptaesthesia.** See also **clairvoyance** (sense 1), **telepathy.** Abbrev.: **ESP.**

extraterrestrial (ˌɛkstrətɪ'rɛstrɪəl) *adj* **1** occurring or existing beyond the earth's atmosphere. ◆ *n* **2** (in science fiction) a being from beyond the earth's atmosphere.

extraterritorial (ˌɛkstrəˌtɛrɪ'tɔːrɪəl) *or* **exterritorial** *adj* **1** beyond the limits of a country's territory. **2** of, relating to, or possessing extraterritoriality. ► ˌ**extraˌterri'torially** *or* ˌ**exterri'torially** *adv*

extraterritoriality (ˌɛkstrəˌtɛrɪˌtɔːrɪ'ælɪtɪ) *n International law.* **1** the privilege granted to some aliens, esp. diplomats, of being exempt from the jurisdiction of the state in which they reside. **2** the right or privilege of a state to exercise authority in certain circumstances beyond the limits of its territory.

extra time *n Sport.* an additional period played at the end of a match, to compensate for time lost through injury or (in certain circumstances) to allow the teams to achieve a conclusive result.

extrauterine (ˌɛkstrə'juːtəˌraɪn) *adj* situated or developing outside the cavity of the uterus.

extravagance (ɪk'strævɪgəns) *n* **1** excessive outlay of money; wasteful spending. **2** immoderate or absurd speech or behaviour.

extravagant (ɪk'strævɪgənt) *adj* **1** spending money excessively or immoderately. **2** going beyond usual bounds; unrestrained: *extravagant praise.* **3** ostentatious; showy. **4** exorbitant in price; overpriced. [C14: from Medieval Latin *extravagāns,* from Latin EXTRA- + *vagārī* to wander] ► **ex'travagantly** *adv*

Extravagantes (ɪkˌstrævə'gæntiːz) *pl n R.C. Church.* decretals circulating outside some recognized collection of canon law. Those of John XXII and the so-called Extravagantes communes form part of the Corpus Juris Canonici. [Latin: wandering, circulating]

extravaganza (ɪkˌstrævə'gænzə) *n* **1** an elaborately staged and costumed light entertainment. **2** any lavish or fanciful display, literary or other composition, etc. [C18: from Italian: EXTRAVAGANCE]

extravagate (ɪk'strævəˌgeɪt) *vb* (*intr*) *Archaic.* **1** to exceed normal limits or propriety. **2** to roam at will. [C17: from Latin *extravagārī;* see EXTRAVAGANT] ► **exˌtrava'gation** *n*

extravasate (ɪk'strævəˌseɪt) *vb* **1** *Pathol.* to cause (blood or lymph) to escape or (of blood or lymph) to escape into the surrounding tissues from their proper vessels. **2** to exude (molten material, such as lava) or (of molten material) to be exuded. ◆ *n* **3** *Pathol.* the material extravasated. [C17: from Latin EXTRA- + *vās* vessel] ► **exˌtrava'sation** *n*

extravascular (ˌɛkstrə'væskjʊlə) *adj Anatomy.* situated or occurring outside a lymph or blood vessel.

extravehicular (ˌɛkstrəvɪ'hɪkjʊlə) *adj* occurring or used outside a spacecraft, either in space or on the surface of the moon or another planet: *extravehicular activity.*

extraversion (ˌɛkstrə'vɜːʃən) *n* a variant spelling of **extroversion.** ► ˌ**extra'versive** *adj*

extravert ('ɛkstrəˌvɜːt) *n, adj* a variant spelling of **extrovert.**

extra virgin *adj* (of olive oil) of the highest quality, extracted by cold pressing rather than chemical treatment.

Extremadura (estrema'ðura) *n* the Spanish name for **Estremadura.**

extremal (ɪk'striːmᵊl) *n Maths, logic.* the clause in a recursive definition that specifies that no items other than those generated by the stated rules fall within the definition, as in *1 is an integer, if n is an integer so is n+1, and nothing else is.*

extreme (ɪk'striːm) *adj* **1** being of a high or of the highest degree or intensity: *extreme cold; extreme difficulty.* **2** exceeding what is usual or reasonable; immoderate: *extreme behaviour.* **3** very strict, rigid, or severe; drastic: *an extreme measure.* **4** (*prenominal*) farthest or outermost in direction: *the extreme boundary.* **5** *Meteorol.* of, relating to, or characteristic of a **continental climate.** ◆ *n* **6** the highest or furthest degree (often in the phrases **in the extreme, go to extremes**). **7** (*often pl*) either of the two limits or ends of a scale or range of possibilities: *extremes of temperature.* **8** *Maths.* **8a** the first or last term of a series or a proportion. **8b** a maximum or minimum value of a function. **9** *Logic.* the subject or predicate of the conclusion of a syllogism. [C15:

from Latin *extrēmus* outermost, from *exterus* on the outside; see EXTERIOR] ► **ex'tremeness** *n*

extremely (ɪk'striːmlɪ) *adv* **1** to the extreme; exceedingly. **2** (intensifier): *she behaved extremely badly.*

USAGE See at **very.**

extremely high frequency *n* a radio frequency between 30 000 and 300 000 megahertz. Abbrev.: **EHF.**

extremely low frequency *n* a radio frequency or radio-frequency band below 3 kilohertz. Abbrev.: **ELF.**

extreme unction *n R.C. Church.* a former name for **anointing of the sick.**

extremist (ɪk'striːmɪst) *n* **1** a person who favours or resorts to immoderate, uncompromising, or fanatical methods or behaviour, esp. in being politically radical. ◆ *adj* **2** of, relating to, or characterized by immoderate or excessive actions, opinions, etc. ► **ex'tremism** *n*

extremity (ɪk'strɛmɪtɪ) *n, pl* **-ties. 1** the farthest or outermost point or section; termination. **2** the greatest or most intense degree. **3** an extreme condition or state, as of adversity or disease. **4** a limb, such as a leg, arm, or wing, or the part of such a limb farthest from the trunk. **5** (*usually pl*) *Archaic.* a drastic or severe measure.

extricate ('ɛkstrɪˌkeɪt) *vb* (*tr*) to remove or free from complication, hindrance, or difficulty; disentangle. [C17: from Latin *extrīcāre* to disentangle, from EX-[1] + *trīcae* trifles, vexations] ► **'extricable** *adj* ► **ˌextri'cation** *n*

USAGE See at **extract.**

extrinsic (ɛk'strɪnsɪk) *adj* **1** not contained or included within; extraneous. **2** originating or acting from outside; external. [C16: from Late Latin *extrinsecus* (adj) outward, from Latin (adv) from without, on the outward side, from *exter* outward + *secus* alongside, related to *sequī* to follow] ► **ex'trinsically** *adv*

extrorse (ɛk'strɔːs) *or* **extrorsal** *adj Botany.* turned or opening outwards or away from the axis: *extrorse anthers.* [C19: from Late Latin *extrorsus* in an outward direction, from Latin EXTRA- + *versus* turned towards]

extroversion *or* **extraversion** (ˌɛkstrə'vɜːʃən) *n* **1** *Psychol.* the directing of one's interest outwards, esp. towards social contacts. **2** *Pathol.* a turning inside out of an organ or part. ◆ Compare **introversion.** [C17: from *extro-* (variant of EXTRA-, contrasting with INTRO-) + *-version,* from Latin *vertere* to turn] ► **ˌextro'versive** *or* **ˌextra'versive** *adj* ► **ˌextro'versively** *or* **ˌextra'versively** *adv*

extrovert *or* **extravert** ('ɛkstrəˌvɜːt) *Psychol.* ◆ *n* **1** a person concerned more with external reality than inner feelings. ◆ *adj* **2** of or characterized by extroversion: *extrovert tendencies.* ◆ Compare **introvert.** [C20: from *extro-* (variant of EXTRA-, contrasting with INTRO-) + *-vert,* from Latin *vertere* to turn] ► **'extroˌverted** *or* **'extraˌverted** *adj*

extrude (ɪk'struːd) *vb* **1** (*tr*) to squeeze or force out. **2** (*tr*) to produce (moulded sections of plastic, metal, etc.) by ejection under pressure from a suitably shaped nozzle or die. **3** (*tr*) to chop up or pulverize (an item of food) and re-form it to look like a whole: *a factory-made rod of extruded egg.* **4** a less common word for **protrude.** [C16: from Latin *extrūdere* to thrust out, from *trūdere* to push, thrust] ► **ex'truded** *adj*

extrusion (ɪk'struːʒən) *n* **1** the act or process of extruding. **2a** the movement of magma through volcano craters and cracks in the earth's crust, forming igneous rock. **2b** any igneous rock formed in this way. **3** a component or material formed by the process of extruding. [C16: from Medieval Latin *extrūsiō,* from *extrūdere* to EXTRUDE] ► **ex'trusible** *adj*

extrusive (ɪk'struːsɪv) *adj* **1** tending to extrude. **2** (of igneous rocks) formed from magma issuing from volcanoes or cracks in the earth's crust; volcanic. Compare **intrusive** (sense 2).

exuberant (ɪg'zjuːbərənt) *adj* **1** abounding in vigour and high spirits; full of vitality. **2** lavish or effusive; excessively elaborate: *exuberant compliments.* **3** growing luxuriantly or in profusion. [C15: from Latin *exūberāns,* from *ūberāre* to be fruitful, from *ūber* fertile] ► **ex'uberance** *n* ► **ex'uberantly** *adv*

exuberate (ɪg'zjuːbəˌreɪt) *vb* (*intr*) *Rare.* **1** to be exuberant. **2** to abound or grow in profusion. [C15: from Latin *exūberāre* to be abundant; see EXUBERANT]

exudation (ˌɛksjʊ'deɪʃən) *n* **1** the act of exuding or oozing out. **2** Also called: **exudate** ('ɛksjʊˌdeɪt). an exuded substance, such as sweat or cellular debris. ► **exudative** (ɪg'zjuːdətɪv) *adj*

exude (ɪg'zjuːd) *vb* **1** to release or be released through pores, incisions, etc., as sweat from the body or sap from trees. **2** (*tr*) to make apparent by mood or behaviour: *he exuded confidence.* [C16: from Latin *exsūdāre,* from *sūdāre* to sweat]

exult (ɪg'zʌlt) *vb* (*intr*) **1** to be joyful or jubilant, esp. because of triumph or success; rejoice. **2** (often foll. by *over*) to triumph (over); show or take delight in the defeat or discomfiture (of). [C16: from Latin *exsultāre* to jump or leap for joy, from *saltāre* to leap] ► **exultation** (ˌɛgzʌl'teɪʃən) *n* ► **ex'ultingly** *adv*

USAGE See at **exalt.**

exultant (ɪg'zʌltənt) *adj* elated or jubilant, esp. because of triumph or success. ► **ex'ultance** *or* **ex'ultancy** *n* ► **ex'ultantly** *adv*

exurbia (ɛks'ɜːbɪə) *n Chiefly U.S.* the region outside the suburbs of a city, consisting of residential areas (**exurbs**) that are occupied predominantly by rich commuters (**exurbanites**). Compare **stockbroker belt.** [C20: from EX-[1] + Latin *urbs* city, on pattern of *suburbia*] ► **ex'urban** *adj*

exuviae (ɪg'zjuːvɪˌiː) *pl n* layers of skin or cuticle shed by animals during ecdysis. [C17: from Latin: something stripped off (the body), from *exuere* to strip off] ► **ex'uvial** *adj*

exuviate (ɪg'zjuːvɪˌeɪt) *vb* to shed (a skin or similar outer covering). ► **exˌuvi'ation** *n*

ex voto *Latin.* (ɛks 'vəʊtəʊ) *adv, adj* **1** in accordance with a vow. ◆ *n* **2** an offering made in fulfilment of a vow.

ex works *adv, adj* (**ex-works** *when prenominal*) *Brit.* (of a price, value, etc.) excluding the cost of delivery from the factory and sometimes excluding the commission or profit of the distributor or retailer: *the price is £500 ex works.*

-ey *suffix.* a variant of **-y**[1] and **-y**[2].

Eyam ('iːjəm) *n* a village in N central England, in Derbyshire. When plague reached the village in 1665 the inhabitants isolated themselves to prevent it spreading further: as a result, most of them died.

eyas ('aɪəs) *n* a nestling hawk or falcon, esp. one reared for training in falconry. [C15: mistaken division of earlier *a nyas,* from Old French *niais* nestling, from Latin *nīdus* nest]

Eyck (aɪk) *n* See (Jan) **van Eyck.**

eye[1] (aɪ) *n* **1** the organ of sight of animals, containing light-sensitive cells associated with nerve fibres, so that light entering the eye is converted to nervous impulses that reach the brain. In man and other vertebrates the iris controls the amount of light entering the eye and the lens focuses the light onto the retina. Related adjs.: **ocular, oculate, ophthalmic, optic. 2** (*often pl*) the ability to see; sense of vision: *weak eyes.* **3** the visible external part of an eye, often including the area around it: *heavy-lidded eyes; piercing eyes.* **4** a look, glance, expression, or gaze: *a stern eye.* **5** a sexually inviting or provocative look (esp. in the phrases **give (someone) the (glad) eye, make eyes at**). **6** attention or observation (often in the phrases **catch someone's eye, keep an eye on, cast an eye over**). **7** ability to recognize, judge, or appreciate: *an eye for antiques.* **8** (*often pl*) opinion, judgment, point of view, or authority: *in the eyes of the law.* **9** a structure or marking having the appearance of an eye, such as the bud on a twig or potato tuber or a spot on a butterfly wing. **10** a small loop or hole, as at one end of a needle. **11** a small area of low pressure and calm in the centre of a tornado. **12** See **photocell. 13** *Informal.* See **private eye. 14 all eyes.** *Informal.* acutely vigilant or observant: *the children were all eyes.* **15 (all) my eye.** *Informal.* rubbish; nonsense. **16 an eye for an eye.** retributive or vengeful justice; retaliation. **17 cut one's eye after, at,** *or* **on (someone).** *Caribbean.* to look rudely at (a person) and then turn one's face away sharply while closing one's eyes: a gesture of contempt. **18 eyes out.** *N.Z.* with every possible effort: *he went at the job eyes out.* **19 get one's eye in.** *Chiefly sports.* to become accustomed to the conditions, light, etc., with a consequent improvement in one's performance. **20 half an eye. 20a** a modicum of perceptiveness: *anyone with half an eye can see she's in love.* **20b** continuing unobtrusive observation or awareness: *the dog had half an eye on the sheep.* **21 have eyes for.** to be interested in: *she has eyes only for him.* **22 in one's mind's eye.** pictured within the mind; imagined or remembered vividly. **23 in the public eye.** exposed to public curiosity or publicity. **24 keep an eye open** *or* **out (for).** to watch with special attention (for). **25 keep one's eyes peeled** (or **skinned**). to watch vigilantly (for). **26 look (someone) in the eye.** to look openly and without shame or embarrassment at. **27 make (sheep's) eyes (at).** *Old-fashioned.* to ogle amorously. **28 more than meets the eye.** hidden motives, meaning, or facts. **29 pick the eyes out (of).** *Austral. and N.Z.* to select the best parts or pieces (of). **30 see eye to eye (with).** to agree (with). **31 set, lay,** *or* **clap eyes on.** (*usually used with a negative*) to see: *she had never laid eyes on him before.* **32 the eye of the wind.** *Nautical.* the direction from which the wind is blowing. **33 turn a blind eye to** *or* **close one's eyes to.** to pretend not to notice or ignore deliberately. **34 up to one's eyes (in).** extremely busy (with). **35 with a ... eye.** in a ... manner: *he regards our success with a jealous eye.* **36 with** *or* **having an eye to.** (*prep*) **36a** regarding; with reference to: *with an eye to one's own interests.* **36b** with the intention or purpose of: *with an eye to reaching agreement.* **37 with one's eyes open.** in the full knowledge of all relevant facts. **38 with one's eyes shut. 38a** with great ease, esp. as a result of thorough familiarity: *I could drive home with my eyes shut.* **38b** without being aware of all the facts. ◆ *vb* **eyes, eyeing** *or* **eying, eyed.** (*tr*) **39** to look at carefully or warily. **40** Also: **eye up.** to look at in a manner indicating sexual interest; ogle. ◆ See also **eyes.** [Old English *ēage;* related to Old Norse *auga,* Old High German *ouga,* Sanskrit *akṣi*] ► **'eyeless** *adj* ► **'eyeˌlike** *adj*

eye[2] (aɪ) *n* another word for **nye.**

eyeball ('aɪˌbɔːl) *n* **1** the entire ball-shaped part of the eye. **2 eyeball to eyeball.** in close confrontation.

eyebank ('aɪˌbæŋk) *n* a place in which corneas are stored for use in corneal grafts.

eyebath ('aɪˌbɑːθ) *n* a small vessel with a rim shaped to fit round the eye, used for applying medicated or cleansing solutions to the eyeball. Also called (U.S. and Canadian): **eyecup.**

eyeblack ('aɪˌblæk) *n* another name for **mascara.**

eyebolt ('aɪˌbəʊlt) *n* a threaded bolt, the head of which is formed into a ring or eye for lifting, pulling, or securing.

eyebright ('aɪˌbraɪt) *n* any scrophulariaceous annual plant of the genus *Euphrasia,* esp. *E. nemorosa,* having small white-and-purple two-lipped flowers: formerly used in the treatment of eye disorders. Also called: **euphrasy.**

eyebrow ('aɪˌbraʊ) *n* **1** the transverse bony ridge over each eye. **2** the arch of hair that covers this ridge. related adj: **superciliary. 3 raise an eyebrow.** See **raise** (sense 31).

eyebrow pencil *n* a cosmetic in pencil form for applying colour and shape to the eyebrows.

eye-catching *adj* tending to attract attention; striking. ► **'eye-ˌcatcher** *n*

eye contact *n* a direct look between two people; meeting of eyes: *he maintained eye contact with his interrogator.*

eyecup ('aɪˌkʌp) *n* a U.S. and Canadian name for an **eyebath.**

eyed (aɪd) *adj* **a** having an eye or eyes (as specified). **b** (*in combination*): *one-eyed; brown-eyed.*

eye dog *n N.Z.* a dog trained to control sheep by staring fixedly at them. Also called: **strong-eye dog.**

eyeful ('aɪfʊl) *n Informal.* **1** a view, glance, or gaze: *he got an eyeful of the secret before they blindfolded him.* **2** a very beautiful or attractive sight, esp. a woman.

eyeglass ('aɪˌglɑːs) *n* **1** a lens for aiding or correcting defective vision, esp. a monocle. **2** another word for **eyepiece.**

eyeglasses ('aɪˌglɑːsɪz) *pl n Now chiefly U.S.* another word for **spectacles.**

eyehole ('aɪˌhəʊl) *n* **1** a hole through which something, such as a rope, hook, or bar, is passed. **2** the cavity that contains the eyeball; eye socket. **3** another word for **peephole.**

eyehook ('aɪˌhʊk) *n* a hook attached to a ring at the extremity of a rope or chain.

eyelash ('aɪˌlæʃ) *n* **1** any one of the short curved hairs that grow from the edge of the eyelids. **2** a row or fringe of these hairs. Related adj: **ciliary.**

eyelet ('aɪlɪt) *n* **1** a small hole for a lace or cord to be passed through or for a hook to be inserted into. **2** a small metal ring or tube with flared ends bent back, reinforcing an eyehole in fabric. **3** a chink or small opening, such as a peephole in a wall. **4** *Embroidery.* **4a** a small hole with finely stitched edges, forming part of an ornamental pattern. **4b** Also called: **eyelet embroidery.** a piece of embroidery decorated with such work. **5** fabric decorated with such work produced by machine. **6** a small eye or eyelike marking. ◆ *vb* **7** (*tr*) to supply with an eyelet or eyelets. **[C14:** from Old French *oillet,* literally: a little eye, from *oill* eye, from Latin *oculus* eye; see EYE[1]**]**

eyeleteer (ˌaɪlɪ'tɪə) *n* a small bodkin or other pointed tool for making eyelet holes.

eyelevel ('aɪˌlevᵊl) *adj* level with a person's eyes when looking straight ahead: *an eyelevel grill.*

eyelid ('aɪˌlɪd) *n* **1** either of the two muscular folds of skin that can be moved to cover the exposed portion of the eyeball. Related adj: **palpebral. 2** Also called: **clamshell.** *Aeronautics.* a set of movable parts at the rear of a jet engine that redirect the exhaust flow to assist braking during landing.

eyeliner ('aɪˌlaɪnə) *n* a cosmetic used to outline the eyes.

eye of day *n Poetic.* the sun.

eye-opener *n Informal.* **1** something startling or revealing. **2** *U.S. and Canadian.* an alcoholic drink taken early in the morning.

eyepiece ('aɪˌpiːs) *n* the lens or combination of lenses in an optical instrument nearest the eye of the observer.

eye rhyme *n* a rhyme involving words that are similar in spelling but not in sound, such as *stone* and *none.*

eyes (aɪz) *pl n Nautical.* the part of the bows of a ship that are furthest forward at the level of the main deck.

eyes front *interj* **1** *Military.* a command to troops to look ahead. **2** a demand for attention.

eyeshade ('aɪˌʃeɪd) *n* an opaque or tinted translucent visor, worn on the head like a cap to protect the eyes from glare.

eye shadow *n* a coloured cosmetic put around the eyes so as to enhance their colour or shape.

eyeshot ('aɪˌʃɒt) *n* range of vision; view.

eyesight ('aɪˌsaɪt) *n* the ability to see; faculty of sight.

eyes left *interj Military.* a command to troops to look left, esp. as a salute when marching.

eye socket *n* the nontechnical name for **orbit** (sense 3).

eyesore ('aɪˌsɔː) *n* something very ugly.

eye splice *n* an eye formed in a rope by splicing the end into its standing part.

eyespot ('aɪˌspɒt) *n* **1** a small area of light-sensitive pigment in some protozoans and algae and in other simple organisms. **2** an eyelike marking, as on the wings of certain butterflies.

eyes right *interj Military.* a command to troops to look right, esp. as a salute when marching.

eyestalk ('aɪˌstɔːk) *n* a movable stalk bearing a compound eye at its tip: occurs in crustaceans and some molluscs.

eyestrain ('aɪˌstreɪn) *n* fatigue or irritation of the eyes, resulting from excessive use, as from prolonged reading of small print, or uncorrected defects of vision.

Eyetie ('aɪtaɪ) *n, adj Brit. slang, offensive.* Italian. **[C20:** based on a jocular mispronunciation of *Italian***]**

eyetooth (ˌaɪ'tuːθ) *n, pl* **-teeth. 1** either of the two canine teeth in the upper jaw. **2 give one's eyeteeth for.** to go to any lengths to achieve or obtain (something): *I'd give my eyeteeth for a radio as good as that.*

eyewash ('aɪˌwɒʃ) *n* **1** a mild solution for applying to the eyes for relief of irritation, etc. **2** *Informal.* nonsense; rubbish.

eyewitness ('aɪˌwɪtnɪs) *n* **a** a person present at an event who can describe what happened. **b** (*as modifier*): *an eyewitness account.*

eyot (aɪt) *n Brit., obsolete except in place names.* island. **[**variant of AIT**]**

eyra ('ɛərə, 'aɪərə) *n* a reddish-brown variety of the jaguarondi. **[C19:** from American Spanish, from Tupi *eirara***]**

eyre (ɛə) *n English legal history.* **1** any of the circuit courts held in each shire from 1176 until the late 13th century. **2 justices in eyre.** the justices travelling on circuit and presiding over such courts. **[C13:** from Old French *erre* journey, from *errer* to travel, from Latin *errāre* to wander**]**

Eyre[1] (ɛə) *n* **Lake.** a shallow salt lake in NE central South Australia, about 11 m (35 ft.) below sea level. Area: 9600 sq. km (3700 sq. miles). **[C19:** named after E. J. EYRE**]**

Eyre[2] (ɛə) *n* **1 Edward John.** 1815–1901, British explorer and colonial administrator. He was governor of Jamaica (1864–66) until his authorization of 400 executions to suppress an uprising led to his recall. **2 Richard.** born 1943, British theatre director: director of the Royal National Theatre (1988–97).

Eyre Peninsula *n* a peninsula of South Australia, between the Great Australian Bight and Spencer Gulf.

eyrie ('ɪərɪ, 'ɛərɪ, 'aɪərɪ) *or* **aerie** *n* **1** the nest of an eagle or other bird of prey, built in a high inaccessible place. **2** the brood of a bird of prey, esp. an eagle. **3** any high isolated position or place. **[C16:** from Medieval Latin *airea,* from Latin *ārea* open field, hence nest**]**

eyrir ('eɪrɪə) *n, pl* **aurar** ('ɔːrɑː). an Icelandic monetary unit worth one hundredth of a krona. **[**Old Norse: ounce (of silver), money; related to Latin *aureus* golden**]**

Eysenck ('aɪzeŋk) *n* **Hans Jürgen** (hænz 'jɜːgən). 1916–97, British psychologist, born in Germany, who developed a dimensional theory of personality that stressed the influence of heredity.

Ez. *or* **Ezr.** *Bible. abbrev. for* Ezra.

Ezek. *Bible. abbrev. for* Ezekiel.

Ezekiel (ɪ'ziːkɪəl) *n Old Testament.* **1** a Hebrew prophet of the 6th century B.C., exiled to Babylon in 597 B.C. **2** the book containing his oracles, which describe the downfall of Judah and Jerusalem and their subsequent restoration. Douay spelling: **Ezechiel.**

Ezra ('ɛzrə) *n Old Testament.* **1** a Jewish priest of the 5th century B.C., who was sent from Babylon by the Persian king Artaxerxes I to reconstitute observance of the Jewish law and worship in Jerusalem after the captivity. **2** the book recounting his efforts to perform this task.

Ff

f *or* **F** (ɛf) *n, pl* **f's, F's,** *or* **Fs. 1** the sixth letter and fourth consonant of the modern English alphabet. **2** a speech sound represented by this letter, usually a voiceless labio-dental fricative, as in *fat.*

f *symbol for:* **1** *Music.* forte: an instruction to play loudly. **2** *Physics.* frequency. **3** (in the Netherlands) guilder. [from Dutch: florin] **4** *Maths.* function (of). **5** *Physics.* femto-. **6** *Chess.* See **algebraic notation.**

f, f/, *or* **f:** *symbol for* f-number.

F *symbol for:* **1** *Music.* **1a** a note having a frequency of 349.23 hertz (**F above middle C**) or this value multiplied or divided by any power of 2; the fourth note of the scale of C major. **1b** a key, string, or pipe producing this note. **1c** the major or minor key having this note as its tonic. **2** Fahrenheit. **3** Fellow. **4** *Chem.* fluorine. **5** Helmholtz function. **6** *Physics.* force. **7** franc(s). **8** farad(s). **9** *Genetics.* a generation of filial offspring, F_1 being the first generation of offspring, F_2 being the second generation, etc. ◆ **10** *international car registration for* France.

f. *or* **F.** *abbrev. for:* **1** fathom(s). **2** female. **3** *Grammar.* feminine. **4** *Metallurgy.* fine. **5** filly. **6** (*pl* **ff.** *or* **FF.**) folio. **7** (*pl* **ff.**) following (page). **8** *Sport.* foul.

F- (of U.S. military aircraft) *abbrev. for* fighter: *F-106.*

fa (fɑː) *n Music.* a variant spelling of **fah.**

FA *abbrev. for:* **1** *Military.* field artillery. **2** (in Britain) Football Association. See also **FA Cup.**

f.a. *or* **FA** *abbrev. for:* **1** freight agent. **2** fanny adams.

faa *or* **fa'** (fɔː) *vb* a Scot. word for **fall.**

FAA *abbrev. for:* **1** Fleet Air Arm. **2** Fellow of the Australian Academy (of Science).

fab (fæb) *adj, interj Informal, chiefly Brit.* short for **fabulous:** an expression of approval or enthusiasm.

fabaceous (fəˈbeɪʃəs) *adj* a less common term for **leguminous.** [C18: from Late Latin *fabāceus* of beans, from Latin *faba* bean]

Fabergé (ˈfæbəˌʒeɪ) *n* **Peter Carl.** 1846–1920, Russian goldsmith and jeweller, known for the golden Easter eggs and other ornate and fanciful objects that he created for the Russian and other royal families.

Fabian (ˈfeɪbɪən) *adj* **1** of, relating to, or resembling the delaying tactics of Q. Fabius Maximus; cautious; circumspect. ◆ *n* **2** a member of or sympathizer with the Fabian Society. [C19: from Latin *Fabiānus* of Fabius]

Fabianism (ˈfeɪbɪəˌnɪzəm) *n* the beliefs, principles, or practices of the Fabian Society. ► **ˈFabianist** *n, adj*

Fabian Society *n* an association of British socialists advocating the establishment of democratic socialism by gradual reforms within the law: founded in 1884.

Fabius Maximus (ˈfeɪbɪəs ˈmæksɪməs) *n* full name *Quintus Fabius Maximus Verrucosus,* called *Cunctator* (the delayer). died 203 B.C., Roman general and statesman. As commander of the Roman army during the Second Punic War, he withstood Hannibal by his strategy of harassing the Carthaginians while avoiding a pitched battle.

fable (ˈfeɪbᵊl) *n* **1** a short moral story, esp. one with animals as characters. **2** a false, fictitious, or improbable account; fiction or lie. **3** a story or legend about supernatural or mythical characters or events. **4** legends or myths collectively. Related adj: **fabulous. 5** *Archaic.* the plot of a play or of an epic or dramatic poem. ◆ *vb* **6** to relate or tell (fables). **7** (*intr*) to speak untruthfully; tell lies. **8** (*tr*) to talk about or describe in the manner of a fable: *ghosts are fabled to appear at midnight.* [C13: from Latin *fābula* story, narrative, from *fārī* to speak, say] ► **ˈfabler** *n*

fabled (ˈfeɪbᵊld) *adj* **1** made famous in fable. **2** fictitious.

fabliau (ˈfæblɪˌəʊ; *French* fablijo) *n, pl* **fabliaux** (ˈfæblɪˌəʊz; *French* fablijo). a comic usually ribald verse tale, of a kind popular in France in the 12th and 13th centuries. [C19: from French: a little tale, from *fable* tale]

Fablon (ˈfæblən, -lɒn) *n Trademark.* a brand of adhesive-backed plastic material used to cover and decorate shelves, worktops, etc., and for handicraft purposes.

Fabre (*French* fabrə) *n* **Jean Henri** (ʒɑ̃ ɑ̃ri). 1823–1915, French entomologist; author of many works on insect life, remarkable for their vivid and minute observation, esp. *Souvenirs Entomologiques* (1879–1907). Nobel prize for literature 1910.

fabric (ˈfæbrɪk) *n* **1** any cloth made from yarn or fibres by weaving, knitting, felting, etc. **2** the texture of a cloth. **3** a structure or framework: *the fabric of society.* **4** a style or method of construction. **5** *Rare.* a building. **6** the texture, arrangement, and orientation of the constituents of a rock. [C15: from Latin *fabrica* workshop, from *faber* craftsman]

fabricant (ˈfæbrɪkənt) *n Archaic.* a manufacturer.

fabricate (ˈfæbrɪˌkeɪt) *vb* (*tr*) **1** to make, build, or construct. **2** to devise, invent, or concoct (a story, lie, etc.). **3** to fake or forge. [C15: from Latin *fabricāre* to build, make, from *fabrica* workshop; see FABRIC] ► **ˌfabriˈcation** *n* ► **ˈfabricative** *adj* ► **ˈfabriˌcator** *n*

Fabrikoid (ˈfæbrɪˌkɔɪd) *n Trademark.* a waterproof fabric made of cloth coated with pyroxylin.

Fabry (*French* fabri) *n* **Charles** (ʃarl). 1867–1945, French physicist: discovered ozone in the upper atmosphere.

fabulist (ˈfæbjʊlɪst) *n* **1** a person who invents or recounts fables. **2** a person who lies or falsifies.

fabulous (ˈfæbjʊləs) *adj* **1** almost unbelievable; astounding; legendary: *fabulous wealth.* **2** *Informal.* extremely good: *a fabulous time at the party.* **3** of, relating to, or based upon fable: *a fabulous beast.* [C15: from Latin *fābulōsus* celebrated in fable, from *fābula* FABLE] ► **ˈfabulously** *adv* ► **ˈfabulousness** *n*

fac. *abbrev. for:* **1** facsimile. **2** factor. **3** factory.

Fac. *abbrev. for* Faculty.

façade *or* **facade** (fəˈsɑːd, fæ-) *n* **1** the face of a building, esp. the main front. **2** a front or outer appearance, esp. a deceptive one. [C17: from French, from Italian *facciata,* from *faccia* FACE]

face (feɪs) *n* **1a** the front of the head from the forehead to the lower jaw; visage. **1b** (*as modifier*): *face flannel; face cream.* **2a** the expression of the countenance; look: *a sad face.* **2b** a distorted expression, esp. to indicate disgust; grimace: *she made a face.* **3** *Informal.* make-up (esp. in the phrase **put one's face on.**) **4** outward appearance: *the face of the countryside is changing.* **5** appearance or pretence (esp. in the phrases **put a bold, good, bad,** etc., **face on**). **6** worth in the eyes of others; dignity (esp. in the phrases **lose** or **save face**). **7** *Informal.* impudence or effrontery. **8** the main side of an object, building, etc., or the front: *the face of a palace; a cliff face.* **9** the marked surface of an instrument, esp. the dial of a timepiece. **10** the functional or working side of an object, as of a tool or playing card. **11a** the exposed area of a mine from which coal, ore, etc., may be mined. **11b** (*as modifier*): *face worker.* **12** the uppermost part or surface: *the face of the earth.* **13** Also called: **side.** any one of the plane surfaces of a crystal or other solid figure. **14** *Mountaineering.* a steep side of a mountain, bounded by ridges. **15** either of the surfaces of a coin, esp. the one that bears the head of a ruler. **16** *Brit. slang.* a well-known or important person. **17** Also called: **typeface.** *Printing.* **17a** the printing surface of any type character. **17b** the style, the design, or sometimes the size of any type fount. **17c** the print made from type. **18** *Nautical, aeronautics.* the aft or near side of a propeller blade. **19 fly in the face of.** to act in defiance of. **20 in one's face.** directly opposite or against one. **21 in (the) face of.** despite. **22 look (someone) in the face.** to look directly at a person without fear or shame. **23 on the face of it.** to all appearances. **24 set one's face against.** to oppose with determination. **25 show one's face.** to make an appearance. **26 shut one's face.** *Slang.* (*often imperative*) to be silent. **27 to someone's face.** in someone's presence; directly and openly: *I told him the truth to his face.* **28 until one is blue in the face.** *Informal.* to the utmost degree; indefinitely. ◆ *vb* **29** (when *intr,* often foll. by *to, towards,* or *on*) to look or be situated or placed (in a specified direction): *the house faces on the square.* **30** to be opposite: *facing page 9.* **31** (*tr*) to meet or be confronted by: *in his work he faces many problems.* **32** (*tr*) to provide with a surface of a different material: *the cuffs were faced with velvet.* **33** to dress the surface of (stone or other material). **34** (*tr*) to expose (a card) with the face uppermost. **35** *Military, chiefly U.S.* to order (a formation) to turn in a certain direction or (of a formation) to turn as required: *right face!* **36** *Ice hockey.* **36a** (of the referee) to drop (the puck) between two opposing players, as when starting or restarting play. See also **face-off. 36b** to start or restart play in this manner. **37 face the music.** *Informal.* to confront the consequences of one's actions. ◆ See also **face out, face up to.** [C13: from Old French, from Vulgar Latin *facia* (unattested), from Latin *faciēs* form, related to *facere* to make] ► **ˈfaceable** *adj*

FACE *abbrev. for* Fellow of the Australian College of Education.

face-ache *n* **1** neuralgia. **2** *Slang.* an ugly or miserable-looking person.

facebar (ˈfeɪsˌbɑː) *n* a wrestling hold in which a wrestler stretches the skin on his opponent's face backwards.

face card *n* the usual U.S. and Canadian term for **court card.**

face-centred *adj* (of a crystal) having a lattice point at the centre of each face of each unit cell as well as at the corners. Compare **body-centred.**

face cloth *or* **face flannel** *n Brit.* a small piece of cloth used to wash the face and hands. U.S. equivalent: **washcloth.**

face-harden *vb* (*tr*) to harden the surface of (steel or iron) by the addition of carbon at high temperature.

faceless (ˈfeɪslɪs) *adj* **1** without a face. **2** without identity; anonymous. ► **ˈfacelessness** *n*

face-lift *n* **1** a cosmetic surgical operation for tightening sagging skin and smoothing unwanted wrinkles on the face. **2** any improvement or renovation, as of a building, etc.

face-off *n* **1** *Ice hockey.* the method of starting a game, in which the referee drops the puck, etc. between two opposing players. **2** a confrontation. ◆ *vb* **face off.** (*adv*) **3** to start play by (a face-off).

face out *vb* (*tr, adv*) **1** to endure (trouble). **2** to defy or act boldly in spite of (criticism, blame, etc.). **3** Also (esp. U.S. and Canadian): **face down.** to cause to concede by a bold stare.

face pack *n* a cream treatment that cleanses and tones the skin.

faceplate (ˈfeɪsˌpleɪt) *n* **1** a perforated circular metal plate, attached to the headstock of a lathe, on which a workpiece can be mounted. **2** Also called: **surface plate.** a flat rigid plate used to check the flatness and squareness of the faces of a component. **3** the part of a cathode-ray tube carrying the phosphor screen.

face powder *n* a flesh-tinted cosmetic powder worn to make the face look less shiny, softer, etc.

facer ('feɪsə) *n* **1** a person or thing that faces. **2** a lathe tool used to turn a face perpendicular to the axis of rotation. **3** *Brit. informal.* a difficulty or problem.

face-saving *adj* maintaining dignity or prestige. ► **'face-ˌsaver** *n*

facet ('fæsɪt) *n* **1** any of the surfaces of a cut gemstone. **2** an aspect or phase, as of a subject or personality. **3** *Architect.* the raised surface between the flutes of a column. **4** any of the lenses that make up the compound eye of an insect or other arthropod. **5** *Anatomy.* any small smooth area on a hard surface, as on a bone. ◆ *vb* **-ets, -eting, -eted** *or* **-ets, -etting, -etted. 6** (*tr*) to cut facets in (a gemstone). [C17: from French *facette* a little FACE]

facetiae (fə'siːʃɪˌiː) *pl n* **1** humorous or witty sayings. **2** obscene or coarsely witty books. [C17: from Latin: jests, plural of *facētia* witticism, from *facētus* elegant]

facetious (fə'siːʃəs) *adj* **1** characterized by levity of attitude and love of joking: *a facetious person.* **2** jocular or amusing, esp. at inappropriate times: *facetious remarks.* [C16: from Old French *facetieux,* from *facetie* witty saying; see FACETIAE] ► **fa'cetiously** *adv* ► **fa'cetiousness** *n*

face to face *adv, adj* (**face-to-face** *as adj*) **1** opposite one another. **2** in confrontation.

face up to *vb* (*intr, adv + prep*) to accept (an unpleasant fact, reality, etc.).

face validity *n Psychol.* the extent to which a psychological test appears to measure what it is intended to measure.

face value *n* **1** the value written or stamped on the face of a commercial paper or coin. **2** apparent worth or value, as opposed to real worth.

facia ('feɪʃɪə) *n* a variant spelling of **fascia.** ► **'facial** *adj*

facial ('feɪʃəl) *adj* **1** of or relating to the face. ◆ *n* **2** a beauty treatment for the face, involving cleansing, massage, and cosmetic packs. ► **'facially** *adv*

facial angle *n* the angle formed between a line from the base of the nose to the opening of the ear and a line from the base of the nose to the most prominent part of the forehead: often used in comparative anthropology.

facial eczema *n* a disease of sheep and cattle, occurring in warm areas of North Island, New Zealand. It is caused by a fungus, *Pithomyces chartarum,* and causes impairment of liver function and reddening, itching, scab formation, and swelling of the skin, esp. on the face.

facial index *n* the ratio of the length of the face to the width of the face multiplied by 100: often used in comparative anthropology. Compare **cranial index.**

facial nerve *n* the seventh cranial nerve, supplying the muscles controlling facial expression, glands of the palate and nose, and the taste buds in the anterior two-thirds of the tongue.

-facient *suffix forming adjectives and nouns.* indicating a state or quality: *absorbefacient; rubefacient.* [from Latin *facient-, faciēns,* present participle of *facere* to do]

facies ('feɪʃɪˌiːz) *n, pl* **-cies. 1** the general form and appearance of an individual or a group of plants or animals. **2** the characteristics of a rock or series of rocks reflecting their appearance, composition, and conditions of formation. **3** *Med.* the general facial expression of a patient, esp. when typical of a specific disease or disorder. [C17: from Latin: appearance, FACE]

facile ('fæsaɪl) *adj* **1** easy to perform or achieve. **2** working or moving easily or smoothly. **3** without depth; superficial: *a facile solution.* **4** *Archaic.* relaxed in manner; easygoing. [C15: from Latin *facilis* easy, from *facere* to do] ► **'facilely** *adv* ► **'facileness** *n*

facile princeps *Latin.* ('fæsɪlɪ 'prɪnseps) *n* an obvious leader. [literally: easily first]

facilitate (fə'sɪlɪˌteɪt) *vb* (*tr*) to make easier; assist the progress of. ► **fa'cilitative** *adj* ► **fa'ciliˌtator** *n*

facilitation (fəˌsɪlɪ'teɪʃən) *n* **1** the act or process of facilitating. **2** *Physiol.* the increased ease of transmission of impulses in a nerve fibre, caused by prior excitation.

facility (fə'sɪlɪtɪ) *n, pl* **-ties. 1** ease of action or performance; freedom from difficulty. **2** ready skill or ease deriving from practice or familiarity. **3** (*often pl*) the means or equipment facilitating the performance of an action. **4** *Rare.* easy-going disposition. **5** *Military.* an organization or building offering supporting capability. **6** (*usually pl*) a euphemistic word for **lavatory.** [C15: from Latin *facilitās,* from *facilis* easy; see FACILE]

facing ('feɪsɪŋ) *n* **1** a piece of material used esp. to conceal the seam of a garment and prevent fraying. **2** (*usually pl*) a piece of additional cloth, esp. in a different colour, on the collar, cuffs, etc., of the jacket of a military uniform, formerly used to denote the regiment. **3** an outer layer or coat of material applied to the surface of a wall. **4** *Marketing.* an area of retail shelf space.

façonné *or* **faconne** ('fæsəˌneɪ) *adj* **1** denoting a fabric with the design woven in. ◆ *n* **2** such a fabric. [C19: French, from *façonner* to fashion]

facsimile (fæk'sɪmɪlɪ) *n* **1a** an exact copy or reproduction. **1b** (*as modifier*): *a facsimile publication.* **2** an image produced by facsimile transmission. ◆ *vb* **-les, -leing, -led. 3** (*tr*) to make an exact copy of. [C17: from Latin *fac simile!* make something like it!, from *facere* to make + *similis* similar, like]

facsimile machine *n* a machine which transmits and receives documents in facsimile transmission. Often shortened to **fax, fax machine.**

facsimile transmission *n* an international system of transmitting a written, printed, or pictorial document over the telephone system by scanning it photoelectrically and reproducing the image xerographically after transmission. Often shortened to **fax.**

fact (fækt) *n* **1** an event or thing known to have happened or existed. **2** a truth verifiable from experience or observation. **3** a piece of information: *get me all the facts of this case.* **4** *Law.* (*often pl*) an actual event, happening, etc., as distinguished from its legal consequences. Questions of fact are decided by the jury, questions of law by the court or judge. **5** *Philosophy.* a proposition that may be either true or false, as contrasted with an evaluative statement. **6 after** (*or* **before**) **the fact.** *Criminal law.* after (or before) the commission of the offence: *an accessory after the fact.* **7 as a matter of fact, in fact, in point of fact.** in reality or actuality. **8 fact of life.** an inescapable truth, esp. an unpleasant one. **9 the fact of the matter.** the truth. [C16: from Latin *factum* something done, from *factus* made, from *facere* to make] ► **'factful** *adj*

fact-finding *adj* having the purpose of ascertaining facts: *a fact-finding tour of the Northeast.*

factice ('fæktɪs) *n* a soft rubbery material made by reacting sulphur or sulphur chloride with vegetable oil. [C19: from Greek *faktis,* from Latin *factīcius* FACTITIOUS]

faction[1] ('fækʃən) *n* **1** a group of people forming a minority within a larger body, esp. a dissentious group. **2** strife or dissension within a group. [C16: from Latin *factiō* a making, from *facere* to make, do] ► **'factional** *adj* ► **'factionalˌism** *n* ► **'factionalist** *n*

faction[2] ('fækʃən) *n* a television programme, film, or literary work comprising a dramatized presentation of actual events. [C20: a blend of FACT and FICTION]

faction fight *n S. African.* a fight between rival Black groups, usually originating in tribal or clan feuds.

factious ('fækʃəs) *adj* given to, producing, or characterized by faction. ► **'factiously** *adv* ► **'factiousness** *n*

USAGE See at **fractious.**

factitious (fæk'tɪʃəs) *adj* **1** artificial rather than natural: *factitious demands created by the mass media.* **2** not genuine; sham: *factitious enthusiasm.* [C17: from Latin *factīcius,* from *facere* to make, do] ► **fac'titiously** *adv* ► **fac'titiousness** *n*

factitive ('fæktɪtɪv) *adj Grammar.* denoting a verb taking a direct object as well as a noun in apposition, as for example *elect* in *They elected John president,* where *John* is the direct object and *president* is the complement. [C19: from New Latin *factitīvus,* from Latin *factitāre* to do frequently, from *facere* to do] ► **'factitively** *adv*

factive ('fæktɪv) *adj Logic, linguistics, philosophy.* (of a linguistic context) giving rise to the presupposition that a sentence occurring in that context is true, as *John regrets that Mary did not attend.*

factoid ('fæktɔɪd) *n* a piece of unreliable information believed to be true because of the way it is presented or repeated in print. [C20: coined by Norman MAILER from FACT + -OID]

factor ('fæktə) *n* **1** an element or cause that contributes to a result. **2** *Maths.* **2a** one of two or more integers or polynomials whose product is a given integer or polynomial: *2 and 3 are factors of 6.* **2b** an integer or polynomial that can be exactly divided into another integer or polynomial: *1, 2, 3, and 6 are all factors of 6.* **3** (foll. by identifying numeral) *Med.* any of several substances that participate in the clotting of blood: *factor VIII.* **4** a person who acts on another's behalf, esp. one who transacts business for another. **5** *Commerce.* a business that makes loans in return for or on security of trade debts. **6** former name for a **gene. 7** *Commercial law.* a person to whom goods are consigned for sale and who is paid a factorage. **8** (in Scotland) the manager of an estate. ◆ *vb* **9** (*intr*) to engage in the business of a factor. ◆ See also **factor in.** [C15: from Latin: one who acts, from *facere* to do] ► **'factorable** *adj* ► **ˌfactora'bility** *n* ► **'factorˌship** *n*

USAGE *Factor* (sense 1) should only be used to refer to something which contributes to a result. It should not be used to refer to a part of something such as a plan or arrangement; instead a word such as *component* or *element* should be used.

factor VIII *n* a protein that participates in the clotting of blood. It is extracted from donated serum and used in the treatment of the commonest type of haemophilia, in which it is absent.

factorage ('fæktərɪdʒ) *n* the commission payable to a factor.

factor analysis *n Statistics.* any of several techniques for deriving from a number of given variables a smaller number of different, more useful, variables.

factor cost *n* (in social accounting) valuation of goods and services at their overall commercial cost, including markups but excluding indirect taxes and subsidies.

factorial (fæk'tɔːrɪəl) *Maths.* ◆ *n* **1** the product of all the positive integers from one up to and including a given integer. Factorial zero is assigned the value of one: *factorial four is* $1 \times 2 \times 3 \times 4$. Symbol: $n!$, $\underline{n|}$, where n is the given integer. ◆ *adj* **2** of or involving factorials or factors. ► **fac'torially** *adv*

factor in *vb* (*tr, adv*) *Chiefly U.S.* to take account of (something) when making a calculation.

factoring ('fæktərɪŋ) *n* **1** the business of a factor. **2** the business of purchasing debts from clients at a discount and making a profit from their collection.

factorize *or* **factorise** ('fæktəˌraɪz) *vb* (*tr*) *Maths.* to resolve (an integer or polynomial) into factors. ► **ˌfactori'zation** *or* **ˌfactori'sation** *n*

factor of production *n* a resource or input entering the production of wealth, such as land, labour, capital, etc. Also called: **agent of production.**

factor of safety *n* the ratio of the breaking stress of a material or structure to the calculated maximum stress when in use. Also called: **safety factor.**

factory ('fæktərɪ) *n, pl* **-ries. 1a** a building or group of buildings containing a plant assembly for the manufacture of goods. **1b** (*as modifier*): *a factory worker.* **2** *Rare.* a trading station maintained by factors in a foreign country. **3** *Canadian.* (formerly) a main trading station for the exchange and transshipment of furs. [C16: from Late Latin *factorium;* see FACTOR] ► **'factory-ˌlike** *adj*

factory farm *n* a farm in which animals are bred and fattened using modern industrial methods. ► **factory farming** *n*

factory ship *n* a fishing boat that processes the fish that are caught.

factotum (fæk'təʊtəm) *n* a person employed to do all kinds of work. [C16: from Medieval Latin, from Latin *fac!* do! + *tōtum,* from *tōtus* (adj) all]

facts and figures *pl n* details; precise information.

factsheet ('fækt,ʃi:t) *n* a printed sheet containing information relating to items covered in a television or radio programme.

facts of life *pl n* **the.** the details of sexual behaviour and reproduction, esp. as told to children.

factual ('fæktʃʊəl) *adj* **1** of, relating to, or characterized by facts. **2** of the nature of fact; real; actual. ▸ **'factualism** *n* ▸ **'factualist** *n* ▸ **,factual'istic** *adj* ▸ **'factually** *adv* ▸ **'factualness** *or* **,factu'ality** *n*

facture ('fæktʃə) *n Rare.* **1** construction. **2** workmanship; quality. [C15: from Old French, from Latin *factūra*]

facula ('fækjʊlə) *n, pl* **-lae** (-,li:). any of the bright areas on the sun's surface, usually appearing just before a sunspot and subject to the same 11-year cycle. [C18: from Latin: little torch, from *fax* torch] ▸ **'facular** *adj*

facultative ('fækəltətɪv) *adj* **1** empowering but not compelling the doing of an act. **2** *Philosophy.* that may or may not occur. **3** *Insurance.* denoting a form of reinsurance in which the reinsurer has no obligation to accept a particular risk nor the insurer to reinsure, terms and conditions being negotiated for each reinsurance. **4** *Biology.* able to exist under more than one set of environmental conditions: *a facultative parasite can exist as a parasite or a saprotroph.* Compare **obligate** (sense 4). **5** of or relating to a faculty. ▸ **'facultatively** *adv*

faculty ('fækəltɪ) *n, pl* **-ties. 1** one of the inherent powers of the mind or body, such as reason, memory, sight, or hearing. **2** any ability or power, whether acquired or inherent. **3** a conferred power or right. **4a** a department within a university or college devoted to a particular branch of knowledge. **4b** the staff of such a department. **4c** *Chiefly U.S. and Canadian.* all the teaching staff at a university, college, school, etc. **5** all members of a learned profession. **6** *Archaic.* occupation. [C14 (in the sense: department of learning): from Latin *facultās* capability; related to Latin *facilis* easy]

Faculty of Advocates *n Law.* the college or society of advocates in Scotland.

FA Cup *n Soccer.* (in England) **1** an annual knockout competition for a silver trophy, open to all member teams of the Football Association. **2** the trophy itself.

fad (fæd) *n Informal.* **1** an intense but short-lived fashion; craze. **2** a personal idiosyncrasy or whim. [C19: of uncertain origin] ▸ **'faddish** *or* **'faddy** *adj* ▸ **'faddishness** *n* ▸ **'faddism** *n* ▸ **'faddist** *n*

FAD *n Biochem.* flavin adenine dinucleotide: an ester of riboflavin with ADP that acts as the prosthetic group for many flavoproteins. See also **FMN.**

Fadden ('fædən) *n* Sir **Arthur William.** 1895–1973, Australian statesman; prime minister of Australia (1941).

fade (feɪd) *vb* **1** to lose or cause to lose brightness, colour, or clarity. **2** (*intr*) to lose freshness, vigour, or youth; wither. **3** (*intr;* usually foll. by *away* or *out*) to vanish slowly; die out. **4a** to decrease the brightness or volume of (a television or radio programme or film sequence) or (of a television programme, etc.) to decrease in this way. **4b** to decrease the volume of (a sound) in a recording system or (of a sound) to be so reduced in volume. **5** (*intr*) (of the brakes of a vehicle) to lose power. **6** to cause (a golf ball) to move with a controlled left-to-right trajectory or (of a golf ball) to veer gradually from left to right. ◆ *n* **7** the act or an instance of fading. [C14: from *fade* (adj) dull, from Old French, from Vulgar Latin *fatidus* (unattested), probably blend of Latin *vapidus* VAPID + Latin *fatuus* FATUOUS] ▸ **'fadable** *adj* ▸ **'fadedness** *n* ▸ **'fader** *n*

fade-in *n* **1** *Films.* an optical effect in which a shot appears gradually out of darkness. **2** a gradual increase in the volume in a radio or television broadcast. ◆ *vb* **fade in** (*adv*). **3** Also: **fade up.** to increase or cause to increase gradually, as vision or sound in a film or broadcast.

fadeless ('feɪdlɪs) *adj* not subject to fading.

fade-out *n* **1** *Films.* an optical effect in which a shot slowly disappears into darkness. **2** a gradual reduction in signal strength in a radio or television broadcast. **3** a gradual and temporary loss of a received radio or television signal due to atmospheric disturbances, magnetic storms, etc. **4** a slow or gradual disappearance. ◆ *vb* **fade out.** (*adv*) **5** to decrease or cause to decrease gradually, as vision or sound in a film or broadcast.

fadge (fædʒ) *vb* (*intr*) *Archaic or dialect.* **1** to agree. **2** to succeed. ◆ *n* **3** *N.Z.* a package of wool in a wool-bale that weighs less than 100 kilograms. [C16: of uncertain origin]

fading ('feɪdɪŋ) *n* a variation in the strength of received radio signals due to variations in the conditions of the transmission medium.

fado *Portuguese.* ('fa:du) *n* a type of melancholy Portuguese folk song. [literally: FATE]

fadometer (fə'dɒmɪtə) *n Chem.* an instrument used to determine the resistance to fading of a pigment or dye.

fae (feɪ) *prep* a Scot. word for **from.**

faecal *or esp. U.S.* **fecal** ('fi:kəl) *adj* of, relating to, or consisting of faeces.

faeces *or esp. U.S.* **feces** ('fi:si:z) *pl n* bodily waste matter derived from ingested food and the secretions of the intestines and discharged through the anus. [C15: from Latin *faecēs,* plural of *faex* sediment, dregs]

faena *Spanish.* (fa'ena) *n Bullfighting.* the matador's final series of passes with sword and cape before the kill. [literally: task, from obsolete Catalan (modern *feina*), from Latin *facienda* things to be done, from *facere* to do]

Faenza (*Italian* fa'ɛntsa) *n* a city in N Italy, in Emilia-Romagna: famous in the 15th and 16th centuries for its majolica earthenware, esp. faïence. Pop.: 54 050 (1990).

faerie *or* **faery** ('feɪərɪ, 'fɛərɪ) *n, pl* **-ries.** *Archaic or poetic.* **1** the land of fairies. **2** enchantment. ◆ *adj, n* **3** a variant of **fairy.**

Faeroes *or* **Faroes** ('fɛərəʊz) *pl n* a group of 21 basalt islands in the North Atlantic between Iceland and the Shetland Islands: a self-governing community within the kingdom of Denmark; fishing. Capital: Thorshavn. Pop.: 44 300 (1998 est.). Area: 1400 sq. km (540 sq. miles). Also called: **Faeroe Islands** or **Faroe Islands.**

Faeroese *or* **Faroese** (,fɛərəʊ'i:z) *adj* **1** of, relating to, or characteristic of the Faeroes, their inhabitants, or their language. ◆ *n* **2** the chief language of the Faeroes, closely related to Icelandic, although they are not mutually intelligible. **3** (*pl* **-ese**) a native or inhabitant of the Faeroes.

faff (fæf) *vb* (*intr;* often foll. by *about*) *Brit. informal.* to dither or fuss. [C19: of obscure origin]

Fafnir ('fæfnɪə, 'fæv-) *n Norse myth.* the son of Hreidmar, whom he killed to gain the cursed treasure of Andvari. He became a dragon and was slain by Sigurd while guarding the treasure.

fag[1] (fæg) *n* **1** *Informal.* a boring or wearisome task: *it's a fag having to walk all that way.* **2** *Brit.* (esp. formerly) a young public school boy who performs menial chores for an older boy or prefect. ◆ *vb* **fags, fagging, fagged. 3** (when *tr,* often foll. by *out*) *Informal.* to become or cause to become exhausted by hard toil or work. **4** (*usually intr*) *Brit.* to do or cause to do menial chores in a public school: *Brown fags for Lee.* [C18: of obscure origin]

fag[2] (fæg) *n* **1** *Brit.* a slang word for **cigarette. 2** a fag end, as of cloth. [C16 (in the sense: something hanging loose, flap): of obscure origin]

fag[3] (fæg) *n Slang, chiefly U.S. and Canadian.* short for **faggot**[2].

fagaceous (fə'geɪʃəs) *adj* of, relating to, or belonging to the *Fagaceae,* a family of trees, including beech, oak, and chestnut, whose fruit is partly or wholly enclosed in a husk (cupule). [C19: from New Latin *Fāgāceae,* from Latin *fāgus* beech]

fag end *n* **1** the last and worst part, esp. when it is of little use. **2** *Brit. informal.* the stub of a cigarette. [C17: see FAG[2]]

faggot[1] *or esp. U.S.* **fagot** ('fægət) *n* **1** a bundle of sticks or twigs, esp. when bound together and used as fuel. **2** a bundle of iron bars, esp. a box formed by four pieces of wrought iron and filled with scrap to be forged into wrought iron. **3** a ball of chopped meat, usually pork liver, bound with herbs and bread and eaten fried. **4** a bundle of anything. ◆ *vb* (*tr*) **5** to collect into a bundle or bundles. **6** *Needlework.* to do faggoting on (a garment, piece of cloth, etc.). [C14: from Old French, perhaps from Greek *phakelos* bundle]

faggot[2] ('fægət) *n Slang, chiefly U.S. and Canadian.* a male homosexual. Often shortened to **fag.** [C20: special use of FAGGOT[1]] ▸ **'faggoty** *adj*

faggoting *or esp. U.S.* **fagoting** ('fægətɪŋ) *n* **1** decorative needlework done by tying vertical threads together in bundles. **2** a decorative way of joining two hems by crisscross stitches.

faggot vote *n* (formerly) a vote created by the allotting of property to a person to give him the status of an elector. [C19: perhaps from the former use of FAGGOT[1] meaning a person spuriously entered on a military roll]

fag hag *n U.S. slang, usually derogatory.* a heterosexual woman who prefers the company of homosexual men.

fah *or* **fa** (fa:) *n Music.* **1** (in the fixed system of solmization) the note F. **2** (in tonic sol-fa) the fourth degree of any major scale; subdominant. [C14: see GAMUT]

Fah. *or* **Fahr.** *abbrev. for* Fahrenheit.

FAHA *abbrev. for* Fellow of the Australian Academy of the Humanities.

Fahd ibn Abdul Aziz (fa:d 'ɪbən 'æbdʊl ə'zi:z) *n* born 1923, king of Saudi Arabia from 1982.

fahlband ('fa:l,bænd) *n* a thin bed of schistose rock impregnated with metallic sulphides. [C19: from German: pale band]

Fahrenheit[1] ('færən,haɪt) *adj* of or measured according to the Fahrenheit scale of temperature. Symbol: F

Fahrenheit[2] (*German* 'fa:rənhait) *n* **Gabriel Daniel** ('ga:brie:l 'da:nie:l). 1686–1736, German physicist, who invented the mercury thermometer and devised the temperature scale that bears his name.

Fahrenheit scale ('færən,haɪt) *n* a scale of temperatures in which 32° represents the melting point of ice and 212° represents the boiling point of pure water under standard atmospheric pressure. Compare **Celsius scale.**

Fa-hsien ('fa:'sjen) *n* a variant transliteration of **Fa Xian.**

FAI *abbrev. for:* **1** Fédération aéronautique internationale. [French: International Aeronautical Federation] **2** Football Association of Ireland.

Faial *or* **Fayal** (*Portuguese* fə'ial) *n* an island in the central Azores archipelago. Chief town: Horta. Area: 171 sq. km (66 sq. miles).

Faidherbe (*French* fɛdɛrb) *n* **Louis** (**Léon César**). 1818–89, French soldier and governor of Senegal (1854–65); founder of Dakar.

faïence (faɪ'ɑ:ns, feɪ-) *n* **a** tin-glazed earthenware, usually that of French, German, Italian, or Scandinavian origin. **b** (*as modifier*): *a faïence cup.* [C18: from French, strictly: pottery from FAENZA]

fail[1] (feɪl) *vb* **1** to be unsuccessful in an attempt (at something or to do something). **2** (*intr*) to stop operating or working properly: *the steering failed suddenly.* **3** to judge or be judged as being below the officially accepted standard required for success in (a course, examination, etc.). **4** (*tr*) to prove disappointing, undependable, or useless to (someone). **5** (*tr*) to neglect or be unable (to do something). **6** (*intr*) to prove partly or completely insufficient in quantity, duration, or extent. **7** (*intr*) to weaken; fade away. **8** (*intr*) to go bankrupt or become insolvent. ◆ *n* **9** a failure to attain the required standard, as in an examination. **10 without fail.** definitely; with certainty. [C13: from Old French *faillir,* ultimately from Latin *fallere* to disappoint; probably related to Greek *phēlos* deceitful]

fail[2] (fel) *n Scot.* a turf; sod. [perhaps from Scottish Gaelic *fàl*]

failing ('feɪlɪŋ) *n* **1** a weak point; flaw. ◆ *prep* **2** (*used to express a condition*) in default of: *failing a solution this afternoon, the problem will have to wait until Monday.* ▸ **'failingly** *adv*

faille (feɪl; *French* faj) *n* a soft light ribbed fabric of silk, rayon, or taffeta. [C16: from French: head covering, hence, fabric used for this, of obscure origin]

fail-safe *adj* **1** designed to return to a safe condition in the event of a failure or malfunction. **2** (of a nuclear weapon) capable of being deactivated in the event of a failure or accident. **3** unlikely to fail; foolproof. ◆ *vb* **4** (*intr*) to return to a safe condition in the event of a failure or malfunction.

failure (ˈfeɪljə) *n* **1** the act or an instance of failing. **2** a person or thing that is unsuccessful or disappointing: *the evening was a failure.* **3** nonperformance of something required or expected: *failure to attend will be punished.* **4** cessation of normal operation; breakdown: *a power failure.* **5** an insufficiency or shortage: *a crop failure.* **6** a decline or loss, as in health or strength. **7** the fact of not reaching the required standard in an examination, test, course, etc. **8** the act or process of becoming bankrupt or the state of being bankrupt.

fain (feɪn) *adv* **1** (usually with *would*) *Archaic.* willingly; gladly: *she would fain be dead.* ◆ *adj* **2** *Obsolete.* **2a** willing or eager. **2b** compelled. [Old English *fægen;* related to Old Norse *fegiun* happy, Old High German *gifehan* to be glad, Gothic *fahehs* joy; see FAWN[2]]

fainéant (ˈfeɪnɪənt; *French* fɛneɑ̃) *n* **1** a lazy person; idler. ◆ *adj* **2** indolent. [C17: from French, modification of earlier *fait-nient* (he) does nothing, by folk etymology from Old French *faignant* shirker, from *faindre* to be lazy] ▶ **ˈfaineance** *or* **ˈfaineancy** *n*

fainites (ˈfeɪnaɪts) *or* **fains** (feɪnz) *interj Dialect.* a cry for truce or respite from the rules of a game. [C19: from *fains I* I decline, from *feine* feign, from Old French *se feindre* in the sense: back out, esp. of battle]

fáinne (ˈfaːɲə) *n Irish.* a small ring-shaped metal badge worn by advocates of the Irish language. [Irish Gaelic, literally: ring]

faint (feɪnt) *adj* **1** lacking clarity, brightness, volume, etc.: *a faint noise.* **2** lacking conviction or force; weak: *faint praise.* **3** feeling dizzy or weak as if about to lose consciousness. **4** without boldness or courage; timid (esp. in the combination **faint-hearted**). **5 not the faintest** (**idea** *or* **notion**). no idea whatsoever: *I haven't the faintest.* ◆ *vb* (*intr*) **6** to lose consciousness, esp. momentarily, as through weakness. **7** *Archaic or poetic.* to fail or become weak, esp. in hope or courage. ◆ *n* **8** a sudden spontaneous loss of consciousness, usually momentary, caused by an insufficient supply of blood to the brain. Technical name: **syncope.** [C13: from Old French, from *faindre* to be idle] ▶ **ˈfainter** *n* ▶ **ˈfaintingly** *adv* ▶ **ˈfaintish** *adj* ▶ **ˈfaintishness** *n* ▶ **ˈfaintly** *adv* ▶ **ˈfaintness** *n*

faints (feɪnts) *pl n* a variant spelling of **feints.**

fair[1] (fɛə) *adj* **1** free from discrimination, dishonesty, etc.; just; impartial. **2** in conformity with rules or standards; legitimate: *a fair fight.* **3** (of the hair or complexion) light in colour. **4** beautiful or lovely to look at. **5** moderately or quite good: *a fair piece of work.* **6** unblemished; untainted. **7** (of the tide or wind) favourable to the passage of a vessel. **8** sunny, fine, or cloudless. **9** (*prenominal*) *Informal.* thorough; real: *a fair battle to get to the counter.* **10** pleasant or courteous. **11** apparently good or valuable, but really false: *fair words.* **12** open or unobstructed: *a fair passage.* **13** (of handwriting) clear and legible. **14 a fair crack of the whip** *or* (*Austral.*) **a fair shake of the dice, fair go.** *Informal.* a fair opportunity; fair chance. **15 fair and square.** in a correct or just way. **16 fair do's. 16a** equal shares or treatment. **16b** an expression of appeal for equal shares or treatment. **17 fair enough!** an expression of agreement. **18 fair go!** *Austral. and N.Z. informal.* come off it!; I don't believe it! **19 fair to middling.** about average. ◆ *adv* **20** in a fair way; correctly: *act fair, now!* **21** absolutely or squarely; quite: *the question caught him fair off his guard.* **22** *Dialect.* really or very: *fair tired.* ◆ *vb* **23** (*intr*) *Dialect.* (of the weather) to become fine and mild. ◆ *n* **24** *Archaic.* a person or thing that is beautiful or valuable, esp. a woman. [Old English *fæger;* related to Old Norse *fagr,* Old Saxon, Old High German *fagar,* Gothic *fagrs* suitable] ▶ **ˈfairness** *n*

fair[2] (fɛə) *n* **1** a travelling entertainment with sideshows, rides, etc., esp. one that visits places at the same time each year. **2** a gathering of producers of and dealers in a given class of products to facilitate business: *a world fair.* **3** an event including amusements and the sale of goods, esp. for a charity; bazaar. **4** a regular assembly at a specific place for the sale of goods, esp. livestock. [C13: from Old French *feire,* from Late Latin *fēria* holiday, from Latin *fēriae* days of rest: related to *festus* FESTAL]

Fairbanks[1] (ˈfɛəˌbæŋks) *n* a city in central Alaska, at the terminus of the Alaska Highway. Pop.: 30 800 (1990).

Fairbanks[2] (ˈfɛəˌbæŋks) *n* **1 Douglas (Elton)**, real name *Julius Ullman.* 1883–1939, U.S. film actor and producer. **2** his son, **Douglas, Jnr.** born 1909, U.S. film actor.

fair copy *n* a clean copy of a document on which all corrections have been made.

fairfaced (ˈfɛəˌfeɪst) *adj* (of brickwork) having a neat smooth unplastered surface.

Fairfax (ˈfɛəfæks) *n* **Thomas,** 3rd Baron Fairfax. 1612–71, English general and statesman: commanded the Parliamentary army (1645–50), defeating Charles I at Naseby (1645). He was instrumental in restoring Charles II to the throne (1660).

fair game *n* **1** a legitimate object for ridicule or attack. **2** *Hunting, archaic.* quarry that may legitimately be pursued according to the rules of a particular sport.

fairground (ˈfɛəˌgraʊnd) *n* an open space used for a fair or exhibition.

fair-haired boy *n* the usual U.S. name for **blue-eyed boy.**

fairing[1] (ˈfɛərɪŋ) *n* an external metal structure fitted around parts of an aircraft, car, vessel, etc., to reduce drag. Also called: **fillet.** Compare **cowling.** [C20: FAIR[1] + -ING[1]]

fairing[2] (ˈfɛərɪŋ) *n* **1** *Archaic.* a present, esp. from a fair. **2** a sweet circular biscuit made with butter.

fairish (ˈfɛərɪʃ) *adj* **1** moderately good, well, etc. **2** (of the hair, complexion, etc.) moderately light in colour.

Fair Isle *n* an intricate multicoloured pattern knitted with Shetland wool into various garments, such as sweaters. [C19: named after one of the Shetland Islands where the pattern originated]

fairlead (ˈfɛəˌliːd) *or* **fairleader** *n Nautical.* a block or ring through which a line is rove to keep it clear of obstructions, prevent chafing, or maintain it at an angle.

fairly (ˈfɛəlɪ) *adv* **1** (*not used with a negative*) moderately. **2** as deserved; justly. **3** (*not used with a negative*) positively; absolutely: *the hall fairly rang with applause.* **4** *Archaic.* clearly. **5** *Obsolete.* courteously.

fair-minded *adj* just or impartial. ▶ **ˌfair-ˈmindedness** *n*

fair play *n* **1** an established standard of decency, honesty, etc. **2** abidance by this standard.

fair rent *n* (in Britain) the rent for a private tenancy, fixed and registered by a rent officer, and based on the size, condition, and usefulness of the property, but not its scarcity value.

fair sex *n* **the.** women collectively.

fair-spoken *adj* civil, courteous, or elegant in speech. ▶ **ˌfair-ˈspokenness** *n*

fairway (ˈfɛəˌweɪ) *n* **1** Also called: **fair green.** (on a golf course) the areas of shorter grass between the tees and greens, esp. the avenue approaching a green bordered by rough. **2** *Nautical.* **2a** the navigable part of a river, harbour, etc. **2b** the customary course followed by vessels.

fair-weather *adj* **1** suitable for use in fair weather only. **2** not reliable or present in situations of hardship or difficulty (esp. in the phrase **fair-weather friend**).

Fairweather (ˈfɛəˌwɛðə) *n* **Mount.** a mountain in W North America, on the border between Alaska and British Columbia. Height: 4663 m (15 300 ft.).

fairy (ˈfɛərɪ) *n, pl* **fairies. 1** an imaginary supernatural being, usually represented in diminutive human form and characterized as clever, playful, and having magical powers. **2** *Slang.* a male homosexual. ◆ *adj* (*prenominal*) **3** of or relating to a fairy or fairies. **4** resembling a fairy or fairies, esp. in being enchanted or delicate. [C14: from Old French *faerie* fairyland, from *feie* fairy, from Latin *Fāta* the Fates; see FATE, FAY[1]] ▶ **ˈfairy-ˌlike** *adj*

fairy cycle *n* a child's bicycle.

fairyfloss (ˈfɛərɪˌflɒs) *n* the Australian word for **candyfloss.**

fairy godmother *n* **1** a character in certain fairy stories who brings unexpected benefits to the hero or heroine. **2** any benefactress, esp. an unknown one.

fairyland (ˈfɛərɪˌlænd) *n* **1** the imaginary domain of the fairies; an enchanted or wonderful place. **2** a fantasy world, esp. one resulting from a person's wild imaginings.

fairy lights *pl n* small coloured electric bulbs strung together and used for decoration, esp. on a Christmas tree.

fairy penguin *n* a small penguin, *Eudyptula minor,* with a bluish head and back, found on the Australian coast. Also called: **little** or **blue penguin.**

fairy ring *n* **1** a ring of dark luxuriant vegetation in grassy ground corresponding to the outer edge of an underground fungal mycelium: popularly associated with the dancing of fairies: seasonally marked by a ring of mushrooms. **2** short for **fairy ring mushroom,** *Marasmius oreades,* a dainty buff-coloured edible basidiomycetous fungus, characteristically forming rings in grassland.

fairy shrimp *n* any small freshwater branchiopod crustacean of the genera *Chirocephalus, Artemia,* etc., having a transparent body with many appendages and habitually swimming on its back: order *Anostraca.*

fairy swallow *n* (*sometimes caps.*) a variety of domestic fancy pigeon having blue-and-white plumage and heavily muffed feet.

fairy tale *or* **story** *n* **1** a story about fairies or other mythical or magical beings, esp. one of traditional origin told to children. **2** a highly improbable account.

fairy-tale *adj* **1** of or relating to a fairy tale. **2** resembling a fairy tale, esp. in being extremely happy or fortunate: *a true story with a fairy-tale ending.* **3** highly improbable: *he came out with a fairy-tale account of his achievements.*

Faisal I *or* **Feisal I** (ˈfaɪsᵊl) *n* 1885–1933, king of Syria (1920) and first king of Iraq (1921–33): a leader of the Arab revolt against the Turks (1916–18).

Faisal II *or* **Feisal II** *n* 1935–58, last king of Iraq (1939–58).

Faisalabad (faɪˈʒɑːləˌbɑːd) *n* a city in NE Pakistan: commercial and manufacturing centre of a cotton- and wheat-growing region; university (1961). Pop.: 1 875 000 (1995 est.). Former name (until 1979): **Lyallpur.**

Faisal Ibn Abdul Aziz (ˈɪbᵊn æbˈdʊl æˈziːz) *n* 1905–75, king of Saudi Arabia (1964–75).

fait accompli *French.* (fɛt akɔ̃pli) *n, pl* ***faits accomplis*** (fɛz akɔ̃pli). something already done and beyond alteration. [literally: accomplished fact]

faites vos jeux *French.* (fɛt vo ʒø) place your bets! (a phrase used by croupiers in roulette and other casino gambling games).

faith (feɪθ) *n* **1** strong or unshakeable belief in something, esp. without proof or evidence. **2** a specific system of religious beliefs: *the Jewish faith.* **3** *Christianity.* trust in God and in his actions and promises. **4** a conviction of the truth of certain doctrines of religion, esp. when this is not based on reason. **5** complete confidence or trust in a person, remedy, etc. **6** any set of firmly held principles or beliefs. **7** allegiance or loyalty, as to a person or cause (esp. in the phrases **keep faith, break faith**). **8 bad faith.** insincerity or dishonesty. **9 good faith.** honesty or sincerity, as of intention in business (esp. in the phrase **in good faith**). ◆ *interj* **10** *Archaic.* indeed; really (also in the phrases **by my faith, in faith**). [C12: from Anglo-French *feid,* from Latin *fidēs* trust, confidence]

faither (ˈfeðər) *n* a Scot. word for **father.**

faithful (ˈfeɪθfʊl) *adj* **1** having faith; remaining true, constant, or loyal. **2** maintaining sexual loyalty to one's lover or spouse. **3** consistently reliable: *a faithful worker.* **4** reliable or truthful: *a faithful source.* **5** accurate in detail: *a faithful translation.* ◆ *n* **6 the faithful. 6a** the believers in and loyal adherents of a religious faith, esp. Christianity. **6b** any group of loyal and steadfast followers. ▶ **ˈfaithfully** *adv* ▶ **ˈfaithfulness** *n*

faith healing *n* treatment of a sick person throught the supposed power of religious faith. ▸ **'faith healer** *n*

faithless ('feɪθlɪs) *adj* **1** unreliable or treacherous. **2** dishonest or disloyal. **3** having no faith or trust. **4** lacking faith, esp. religious faith. ▸ **'faithlessly** *adv* ▸ **'faithlessness** *n*

faitour ('feɪtə) *n Obsolete.* an impostor. [C14: from Anglo-French: cheat, from Old French *faitor,* from Latin: FACTOR]

Faiyûm *or* **Fayum** (faɪ'ju:m) *n* See **El Faiyûm.**

fajitas (fə'hi:təz) *pl n* a Mexican dish of soft tortillas wrapped around fried strips of meat, vegetables, etc. [Mexican Spanish]

fake[1] (feɪk) *vb* **1** (*tr*) to cause (something inferior or not genuine) to appear more valuable, desirable, or real by fraud or pretence. **2** to pretend to have (an illness, emotion, etc.): *to fake a headache.* **3** to improvise (music, stage dialogue, etc.). ◆ *n* **4** an object, person, or act that is not genuine; sham, counterfeit, or forgery. ◆ *adj* **5** not genuine; spurious. [originally (C18) thieves' slang to mug or do someone; probably via Polari from Italian *facciare* to make or do] ▸ **'faker** *n* ▸ **'fakery** *n*

fake[2] (feɪk) *Nautical.* ◆ *vb* **1** (*tr;* usually foll. by *down*) to coil (a rope) on deck. ◆ *n* **2** one round of a coil of rope. [Middle English *faken,* perhaps via Lingua Franca from Italian *facciare* to make or do; see FAKE[1]]

fakir, faqir (fə'kɪə, 'feɪkə), *or* **fakeer** (fə'kɪə) *n* **1** a member of any religious order of Islam. **2** a Hindu ascetic mendicant or holy man. [C17: from Arabic *faqīr* poor]

fa-la *or* **fal la** (fɑ:'lɑ:) *n* (esp. in 16th-century songs) a refrain sung to the syllables *fa-la-la.*

falafel *or* **felafel** (fəl'ɑ:fəl) *n* a ball or cake of ground spiced chickpeas, deep-fried and often served with pitta bread. [C20: from Arabic *felāfil*]

Falange ('fælændʒ; *Spanish* fa'lanxe) *n* the Fascist movement founded in Spain in 1933; the one legal party in Spain under the Franco regime. [Spanish: PHALANX] ▸ **Fa'langist** *n, adj*

Falasha (fə'læʃə) *n, pl* **-sha** *or* **-shas.** a member of a tribe of Black Ethiopian Jews. [from Amharic, from *fālasi* stranger]

falbala ('fælbələ) *n* a gathered flounce, frill, or ruffle. [C18: from French, from (dialect) *ferbelà;* see FURBELOW]

falcate ('fælkeɪt) *or* **falciform** ('fælsɪˌfɔ:m) *adj Biology.* shaped like a sickle. [C19: from Latin *falcātus,* from *falx* sickle]

falchion ('fɔ:ltʃən, 'fɔ:lʃən) *n* **1** a short and slightly curved medieval sword broader towards the point. **2** an archaic word for **sword.** [C14: from Italian *falcione,* from *falce,* from Latin *falx* sickle]

falcon ('fɔ:lkən, 'fɔ:kən) *n* **1** any diurnal bird of prey of the family *Falconidae,* esp. any of the genus *Falco* (gyrfalcon, peregrine falcon, etc.), typically having pointed wings and a long tail. **2a** any of these or related birds, trained to hunt small game. **2b** the female of such a bird (compare **tercel**). Related adj: **falconine. 3** a light-medium cannon used from the 15th to 17th centuries. [C13: from Old French *faucon,* from Late Latin *falcō* hawk, probably of Germanic origin; perhaps related to Latin *falx* sickle]

falconer ('fɔ:lkənə, 'fɔ:kə-) *n* a person who breeds or trains hawks or who follows the sport of falconry.

falconet ('fɔ:lkəˌnɛt, 'fɔ:kə-) *n* **1** any of various small falcons, esp. any of the Asiatic genus *Microhierax.* **2** a small light cannon used from the 15th to 17th centuries.

falcon-gentle *or* **falcon-gentil** *n Falconry.* a female falcon, esp. a female peregrine falcon. [C14: from Old French *faucon-gentil* literally: noble falcon]

falconiform (fæl'kəʊnɪˌfɔ:m) *adj* of, relating to, or belonging to the order *Falconiformes,* which includes the vultures, hawks, eagles, buzzards, and falcons.

falconine ('fɔ:lkəˌnaɪn, 'fɔ:kə-) *adj* **1** of, relating to, or resembling a falcon. **2** of, relating to, or belonging to the family *Falconidae,* which includes the falcons.

falconry ('fɔ:lkənrɪ, 'fɔ:kən-) *n* **1** the art of keeping falcons and training them to return from flight to a lure or to hunt quarry. **2** the sport of causing falcons to return from flight to their trainer and to hunt quarry under his direction.

falcula ('fælkjʊlə) *n, pl* **-lae** (-li:). *Zoology.* a sharp curved claw, esp. of a bird. ▸ **'falculate** *adj*

falderal ('fældɪˌræl), **falderol** ('fældɪˌrɒl), *or* **folderol** ('fɒldɪˌrɒl) *n* **1** a showy but worthless trifle. **2** foolish nonsense. **3** a nonsensical refrain in old songs.

Faldo ('fældəʊ) *n* **Nick.** born 1957, British golfer: winner of the British Open Championship (1987, 1990, 1992) and the US Masters (1989, 1990, 1996).

faldstool ('fɔ:ldˌstu:l) *n* a backless seat, sometimes capable of being folded, used by bishops and certain other prelates. [C11 *fyldestol,* probably a translation of Medieval Latin *faldistolium* folding stool, of Germanic origin; compare Old High German *faldstuol*]

Falerii (fə'lɪərɪˌaɪ) *n* an ancient city of S Italy, in Latium: important in pre-Roman times.

Faliscan (fə'lɪskən) *n* an ancient language of Italy, spoken in the area north of the Tiber. It was closely related to Latin, which displaced it before 200 B.C.

Falkirk ('fɔ:lkɜ:k) *n* **1** a town in Scotland, the administrative centre of Falkirk council area: scene of Edward I's defeat of Wallace (1298) and Prince Charles Edward's defeat of General Hawley (1746); iron works. Pop.: 35 610 (1991). **2** a council area in central Scotland, on the Firth of Forth: created in 1996 from part of Central Region: largely agricultural, with heavy industry in Falkirk and Grangemouth. Administrative centre: Falkirk. Pop.: 142 610 (1996 est.). Area: 299 sq. km (115 sq. miles).

Falkland Islands ('fɔ:lklənd) *pl n* a group of over 100 islands in the S Atlantic: a UK Overseas Territory; invaded by Argentina, who had long laid claim to the islands, on 2 April 1982; recaptured by a British expeditionary force on 14 June 1982. Chief town: Stanley. Pop.: 2121 (1991). Area: about 12 200 sq. km (4700 sq. miles). Spanish name: **Islas Malvinas.**

Falkland Islands Dependencies *pl n* a group of almost uninhabited islands south of the Falkland Islands: consisting of the South Sandwich Islands and South Georgia. Area: 4090 sq. km (1580 sq. miles).

Falkner ('fɔ:knə) *n* a variant spelling of (William) **Faulkner.**

fall (fɔ:l) *vb* **falls, falling, fell** (fɛl), **fallen** ('fɔ:lən). (*mainly intr*) **1** to descend by the force of gravity from a higher to a lower place. **2** to drop suddenly from an erect position. **3** to collapse to the ground, esp. in pieces. **4** to become less or lower in number, quality, etc.: *prices fell in the summer.* **5** to become lower in pitch. **6** to extend downwards: *her hair fell to her waist.* **7** to be badly wounded or killed. **8** to slope in a downward direction. **9** *Christianity.* to yield to temptation or sin. **10** to diminish in status, estimation, etc. **11** to yield to attack: *the city fell under the assault.* **12** to lose power: *the government fell after the riots.* **13** to pass into or take on a specified condition: *to fall asleep; fall in love.* **14** to adopt a despondent expression: *her face fell.* **15** to be averted: *her gaze fell.* **16** to come by chance or presumption: *suspicion fell on the butler.* **17** to occur; take place: *night fell; Easter falls early this year.* **18** (of payments) to be due. **19** to be directed to a specific point. **20** (foll. by *back, behind,* etc.) to move in a specified direction. **21** to occur at a specified place: *the accent falls on the last syllable.* **22** (foll. by *to*) to return (to); be inherited (by): *the estate falls to the eldest son.* **23** (often foll. by *into, under,* etc.) to be classified or included: *the subject falls into two main areas.* **24** to issue forth: *a curse fell from her lips.* **25** (of animals, esp. lambs) to be born. **26** *Brit. dialect.* to become pregnant. **27** (*tr*) *Dialect, Austral., and N.Z.* to fell (trees). **28** *Cricket.* (of a batsman's wicket) to be taken by the bowling side: *the sixth wicket fell for 96.* **29** *Archaic.* to begin to do: *fall a-doing; fall to doing.* **30 fall flat.** to fail to achieve a desired effect. **31 fall foul of. 31a** to come into conflict with. **31b** *Nautical.* to come into collision with. **32 fall short. 32a** to prove inadequate. **32b** (often foll. by *of*) to fail to reach or measure up to (a standard). ◆ *n* **33** an act or instance of falling. **34** something that falls: *a fall of snow.* **35** *Chiefly U.S.* autumn. **36** the distance that something falls: *a hundred-foot fall.* **37** a sudden drop from an upright position. **38** (*often pl*) **38a** a waterfall or cataract. **38b** (*cap. when part of a name*): *Niagara Falls.* **39** a downward slope or decline. **40** a decrease in value, number, etc. **41** a decline in status or importance. **42** a moral lapse or failing. **43** a capture or overthrow: *the fall of the city.* **44** a long false hairpiece; switch. **45** a piece of loosely hanging material, such as a veil on a hat. **46** *Machinery, nautical.* the end of a tackle to which power is applied to hoist it. **47** *Nautical.* one of the lines of a davit for holding, lowering, or raising a boat. **48** Also called: **pinfall.** *Wrestling.* a scoring move, pinning both shoulders of one's opponent to the floor for a specified period. **49** *Hunting.* **49a** another word for **deadfall. 49b** (*as modifier*): *a fall trap.* **50a** the birth of an animal. **50b** the animals produced at a single birth. **51 take the fall.** *Slang, chiefly U.S.* to be blamed, punished, or imprisoned. ◆ See also **fall about, fall among, fall apart, fall away, fall back, fall behind, fall down, fall for, fall in, fall off, fall on, fallout, fall over, fall through, fall to.** [Old English *feallan;* related to Old Norse *falla,* Old Saxon, Old High German *fallan* to fall; see FELL[2]]

Fall (fɔ:l) *n* **the.** *Theol.* Adam's sin of disobedience and the state of innate sinfulness ensuing from this for himself and all mankind. See also **original sin.**

Falla (*Spanish* 'faʎa) *n* **Manuel de** (ma'nwɛl de). 1876–1946, Spanish composer and pianist, composer of the opera *La Vida Breve* (1905), the ballet *The Three-Cornered Hat* (1919), guitar and piano music, and songs.

fall about *vb* (*intr, adv*) to laugh in an uncontrolled manner: *we fell about when we saw him.*

fallacious (fə'leɪʃəs) *adj* **1** containing or involving a fallacy; illogical; erroneous. **2** tending to mislead. **3** delusive or disappointing: *a fallacious hope.* ▸ **fal'laciously** *adv* ▸ **fal'laciousness** *n*

fallacy ('fæləsɪ) *n, pl* **-cies. 1** an incorrect or misleading notion or opinion based on inaccurate facts or invalid reasoning. **2** unsound or invalid reasoning. **3** the tendency to mislead. **4** *Logic.* an error in reasoning that renders an argument logically invalid. [C15: from Latin *fallācia,* from *fallax* deceitful, from *fallere* to deceive]

fallacy of many questions *n Logic.* the rhetorical trick of asking a question that cannot be answered without admitting a presupposition that may be false, as *have you stopped beating your wife?*

fallal (fæl'læl) *n* a showy ornament, trinket, or article of dress. [C18: perhaps based on FALBALA] ▸ **fal'lalery** *n*

fall among *vb* (*intr, prep*) to enter the company of (a group of people), esp. by chance: *he fell among thieves.*

fall apart *vb* (*intr, adv*) **1** to break owing to long use or poor construction: *the chassis is falling apart.* **2** to become disorganized and ineffective: *since you resigned, the office has fallen apart.*

fall away *vb* (*intr, adv*) **1** (of friendship) to be withdrawn. **2** to slope down.

fall back *vb* (*intr, adv*) **1** to recede or retreat. **2** (foll. by *on* or *upon*) to have recourse (to). ◆ *n* **fall-back. 3** a retreat. **4** a reserve, esp. money, that can be called upon in need. **5a** anything to which one can have recourse as a second choice. **5b** (*as modifier*): *a fall-back position.*

fall behind *vb* (*intr, adv*) **1** to drop back; fail to keep up. **2** to be in arrears, as with a payment.

fall down *vb* (*intr, adv*) **1** to drop suddenly or collapse. **2** (often foll. by *on*) *Informal.* to prove unsuccessful; fail.

fallen ('fɔ:lən) *vb* **1** the past participle of **fall.** ◆ *adj* **2** having sunk in reputation or honour: *a fallen woman.* **3** killed in battle with glory: *our fallen heroes.* **4** defeated.

fallen arch *n* collapse of the arch formed by the instep of the foot, resulting in flat feet.

faller ('fɔ:lə) *n* **1** any device that falls or operates machinery by falling, as in a spinning machine. **2** one that falls, esp. a horse that falls at a fence in a steeplechase. **3** *U.S. and Canadian.* a person who fells trees.

fallfish ('fɔ:lˌfɪʃ) *n, pl* **-fish** *or* **-fishes.** a large North American freshwater cyprinid fish, *Semotilus corporalis,* resembling the chub.

fall for *vb (intr, prep)* **1** to become infatuated with (a person). **2** to allow oneself to be deceived by (a lie, trick, etc.).
fall guy *n Informal.* **1** a person who is the victim of a confidence trick. **2** a scapegoat.
fallible ('fælɪbᵊl) *adj* **1** capable of being mistaken; erring. **2** liable to mislead. [C15: from Medieval Latin *fallibilis*, from Latin *fallere* to deceive] ▸ **,falli'bility** *or* **'fallibleness** *n* ▸ **'fallibly** *adv*
fall in *vb (intr, adv)* **1** to collapse; no longer act as a support. **2** to adopt a military formation, esp. as a soldier taking his place in a line. **3** (of a lease) to expire. **4** (of land) to come into the owner's possession on the expiry of the lease. **5** (often foll. by *with*) **5a** to meet and join. **5b** to agree with or support a person, suggestion, etc. **6** *Austral. and N.Z.* to make a mistake or come to grief. **7** *N.Z.* to become pregnant. ◆ *sentence substitute.* **8** the order to adopt a military formation.
falling band *n* a man's large flat collar, often lace-trimmed, worn during the 17th century.
falling sickness *or* **evil** *n* a former name (nontechnical) for **epilepsy.**
falling star *n* an informal name for **meteor.**
fall line *n* **1** *Skiing.* the natural downward course between two points on a slope. **2** the edge of a plateau.
Fall Line *n* a natural junction, running parallel to the E coast of the U.S., between the hard rocks of the Appalachians and the softer coastal plain, along which rivers form falls and rapids.
fall off *vb (intr)* **1** to drop unintentionally to the ground from (a high object, bicycle, etc.), esp. after losing one's balance. **2** *(adv)* to diminish in size, intensity, etc.; decline or weaken: *business fell off after Christmas.* **3** *(adv) Nautical.* to allow or cause a vessel to sail downwind of her former heading. ◆ *n* **fall-off. 4** a decline or drop.
fall on *vb (intr, prep)* **1** Also: **fall upon.** to attack or snatch (an army, booty, etc.). **2 fall flat on one's face.** to fail, esp. in a ridiculous or humiliating manner. **3 fall on one's feet.** to emerge unexpectedly well from a difficult situation.
Fallopian tube (fə'ləʊpɪən) *n* either of a pair of slender tubes through which ova pass from the ovaries to the uterus in female mammals. See **oviduct.** Related adjs: **oviducal, oviductal.** [C18: named after Gabriello *Fallopio* (1523–62), Italian anatomist who first described the tubes]
fallout ('fɔːl,aʊt) *n* **1** the descent of solid material in the atmosphere onto the earth, esp. of radioactive material following a nuclear explosion. **2** any solid particles that so descend. **3** *Informal.* side-effects; secondary consequences. ◆ *vb* **fall out.** *(intr, adv)* **4** *Informal.* to quarrel or disagree. **5** *(intr)* to happen or occur. **6** *Military.* to leave a parade or disciplinary formation. ◆ *sentence substitute.* **7** *Military.* the order to leave a parade or disciplinary formation.
fall over *vb (intr, adv)* **1** to lose one's balance and collapse to the ground. **2** to fall from an upright position: *the vase fell over.* **3 fall over oneself.** to do everything within one's power: *he fell over himself to be as helpful as possible.*
fallow[1] ('fæləʊ) *adj* **1** (of land) left unseeded after being ploughed and harrowed to regain fertility for a crop. **2** (of an idea, state of mind, etc.) undeveloped or inactive, but potentially useful. ◆ *n* **3** land treated in this way. ◆ *vb* **4** *(tr)* to leave (land) unseeded after ploughing and harrowing it. [Old English *fealga;* related to Greek *polos* ploughed field] ▸ **'fallowness** *n*
fallow[2] ('fæləʊ) *adj* of a light yellowish-brown colour. [Old English *fealu;* related to Old Norse *fölr,* Old Saxon, Old High German *falo,* Latin *pallidus* Greek *polios* grey]
fallow deer *n* either of two deer, *Dama dama* or *D. mesopotamica,* native to the Mediterranean region and Persia respectively. The antlers are flattened and the summer coat is reddish with white spots.
fall through *vb (intr, adv)* to miscarry or fail.
fall to *vb (intr)* **1** *(adv)* to begin some activity, as eating, working, or fighting. **2** *(prep)* to devolve on (a person): *the task fell to me.* **3 fall to the ground.** (of a plan, theory, etc.) to be rendered invalid, esp. because of lack of necessary information.
Falmouth ('fælməθ) *n* a port and resort in SW England, in S Cornwall. Pop.: 20 297 (1991).
false (fɔːls) *adj* **1** not in accordance with the truth or facts. **2** irregular or invalid: *a false start.* **3** untruthful or lying: *a false account.* **4** not genuine, real, or natural; artificial; fake: *false eyelashes.* **5** being or intended to be misleading or deceptive: *a false rumour.* **6** disloyal or treacherous: *a false friend.* **7** based on mistaken or irrelevant ideas or facts: *false pride; a false argument.* **8** *(prenominal)* (esp. of plants) superficially resembling the species specified: *false hellebore.* **9** serving to supplement or replace, often temporarily: *a false keel.* **10** *Music.* **10a** (of a note, interval, etc.) out of tune. **10b** (of the interval of a perfect fourth or fifth) decreased by a semitone. **10c** (of a cadence) interrupted or imperfect. ◆ *adv* **11** in a false or dishonest manner (esp. in the phrase **play (someone) false**). [Old English *fals,* from Latin *falsus,* from *fallere* to deceive] ▸ **'falsely** *adv* ▸ **'falseness** *n*
false acacia *n* another name for the **locust tree** (see **locust** (sense 2)).
false alarm *n* **1** a needless alarm given in error or with intent to deceive. **2** an occasion on which danger is perceived but fails to materialize.
false ankylosis *n* a nontechnical name for **pseudoarthrosis.**
False Bay *n* a bay in SW South Africa, near the Cape of Good Hope.
false bedding *n* another name for **cross bedding.**
false-card ('fɔːls,kɑːd) *vb (intr) Bridge.* to play a misleading card, esp. a high loser, in order to deceive an opponent.
false cirrus *n* a type of thick cirrus cloud spreading from the top of a cumulonimbus cloud.
false colour *n* colour used in a computer or photographic display to help in interpreting the image, as in the use of red to show high temperatures and blue to show low temperatures in an infrared image converter.
false colours *pl n* **1** a flag to which one is not entitled, flown esp. in order to deceive: *the ship was sailing under false colours.* **2** an assumed or misleading name or guise: *to trade under false colours.*
false dawn *n* zodiacal light appearing just before sunrise.
false diamond *n* any of a number of semiprecious stones that resemble diamond, such as zircon and white topaz.
false fruit *n* another name for **pseudocarp.**
falsehood ('fɔːls,hʊd) *n* **1** the quality of being untrue. **2** an untrue statement; lie. **3** the act of deceiving or lying.
false imprisonment *n Law.* the restraint of a person's liberty without lawful authority.
false joint *n* a nontechnical name for **pseudoarthrosis.**
false keel *n* an extension to the keel of a vessel either for protecting the keel from damage or for reducing leeway.
false memory syndrome *n* an alleged condition in which a person undergoing psychotherapy erroneously believes in traumatic events in his or her childhood. See also **recovered memory.**
false negative *n* **1** a result in a medical test which wrongly indicates the absence of the condition being tested for. **2** a person from whom such a result is obtained.
false position *n* a situation in which a person is forced to act or seems to be acting against his principles or interests.
false positive *n* **1** a result in a medical test which wrongly indicates the presence of the condition being tested for. **2** a person from whom such a result is obtained.
false pregnancy *n* another name for **phantom pregnancy.**
false pretences *pl n* **1** *Criminal law.* a former name for **deception** (see **obtaining by deception**). **2** a similar misrepresentation used to obtain anything, such as trust or affection (esp. in the phrase **under false pretences**).
false relation *n Music.* a harmonic clash that occurs when a note in one part sounds simultaneously with or immediately before or after its chromatically altered (sharpened or flattened) equivalent appearing in another part. Also called (esp. U.S.): **cross relation.**
false ribs *pl n* any of the lower five pairs of ribs in man, attached behind to the thoracic vertebrae but in front not attached directly to the breastbone. See **floating rib.**
false scorpion *n* any small predatory arachnid of the order *Pseudoscorpionida,* which includes the **book scorpion** and is named from the claw-shaped palps, which are poison organs.
false step *n* **1** an unwise action. **2** a stumble; slip.
false teeth *pl n* a denture, esp. a removable complete set of artificial teeth for one or both jaws.
falsetto (fɔːl'sɛtəʊ) *n, pl* **-tos.** a form of vocal production used by male singers to extend their range upwards beyond its natural compass by limiting the vibration of the vocal cords. [C18: from Italian, from *falso* FALSE]
false vampire *n* any large insectivorous bat of of the family *Megadermatidae,* of Africa, S and SE Asia, and Australia. They eat insects and small vertebrates but do not feed on blood.
falsework ('fɔːls,wɜːk) *n* a framework supporting something under construction.
falsies ('fɔːlsɪz) *pl n Informal.* pads of soft material, such as foam rubber, worn to exaggerate the size of or simulate the appearance of a woman's breasts.
falsify ('fɔːlsɪ,faɪ) *vb* **-fies, -fying, -fied. 1** *(tr)* to make (a report, evidence, accounts, etc.) false or inaccurate by alteration, esp. in order to deceive. **2** *(tr)* to prove false; disprove. [C15: from Old French *falsifier,* from Late Latin *falsificāre,* from Latin *falsus* FALSE + *facere* to make] ▸ **'falsi,fiable** *adj* ▸ **falsification** (,fɔːlsɪfɪ'keɪʃən) *n* ▸ **'falsi,fier** *n*
falsity ('fɔːlsɪtɪ) *n, pl* **-ties. 1** the state of being false or untrue. **2** something false; a lie or deception.
Falstaffian (fɔːl'stɑːfɪən) *adj* jovial, plump, and dissolute. [C19: after *Sir John Falstaff,* a character in Shakespeare's *Henry IV, Parts I–II* (1597)]
Falster ('fɑːlstə) *n* an island in the Baltic Sea, part of SE Denmark. Chief town: Nykøbing. Pop.: 42 846 (1990 est.). Area: 513 sq. km (198 sq. miles).
faltboat ('fælt,bəʊt) *n* a collapsible boat made of waterproof material stretched over a light framework. [German *Faltboot,* from *falten* to FOLD[1] + *Boot* BOAT]
falter ('fɔːltə) *vb* **1** *(intr)* to be hesitant, weak, or unsure; waver. **2** *(intr)* to move unsteadily or hesitantly; stumble. **3** to utter haltingly or hesitantly; stammer. ◆ *n* **4** uncertainty or hesitancy in speech or action. **5** a quavering or irregular sound. [C14: probably of Scandinavian origin; compare Icelandic *faltrast*] ▸ **'falterer** *n* ▸ **'falteringly** *adv*
Falun (,fɑː'lʌn) *n* a city in central Sweden: iron and pyrites mines. Pop.: 55 014 (1994).
fam. *abbrev. for:* **1** familiar. **2** family.
F.A.M. *abbrev. for* Free and Accepted Masons. See **Freemason.**
Famagusta (,fæmə'gʊstə) *n* a port in E Cyprus, on **Famagusta Bay:** became one of the richest cities in Christendom in the 14th century. Pop.: 67 167 (1994).
fame (feɪm) *n* **1** the state of being widely known or recognized; renown; celebrity. **2** *Archaic.* rumour or public report. ◆ *vb* **3** *(tr; now usually passive)* to make known or famous; celebrate: *he was famed for his ruthlessness.* [C13: from Latin *fāma* report; related to *fārī* to say] ▸ **'famed** *adj*
familial (fə'mɪlɪəl) *adj* **1** of or relating to the family. **2** occurring in the members of a family: *a familial disease.*
familiar (fə'mɪlɪə) *adj* **1** well-known; easily recognized: *a familiar figure.* **2** frequent or customary: *a familiar excuse.* **3** *(postpositive;* foll. by *with)* acquainted. **4** friendly; informal. **5** close; intimate. **6** more intimate than is acceptable; presumptuous. **7** an archaic word for **familial.** ◆ *n* **8** Also called: **familiar spirit.** a supernatural spirit often assuming animal form, supposed to at-

tend and aid a witch, wizard, etc. **9** a person, attached to the household of the pope or a bishop, who renders service in return for support. **10** an officer of the Inquisition who arrested accused persons. **11** a friend or frequent companion. [C14: from Latin *familiāris* domestic, from *familia* FAMILY] ▸ **fa'miliarly** *adv* ▸ **fa'miliarness** *n*

familiarity (fə,mɪlɪ'ærɪtɪ) *n, pl* **-ties. 1** reasonable knowledge or acquaintance, as with a subject or place. **2** close acquaintanceship or intimacy. **3** undue intimacy. **4** (*sometimes pl*) an instance of unwarranted intimacy.

familiarize *or* **familiarise** (fə'mɪljə,raɪz) *vb* (*tr*) **1** to make (oneself or someone else) familiar, as with a particular subject. **2** to make (something) generally known or accepted. ▸ **fa,miliari'zation** *or* **fa,miliari'sation** *n* ▸ **fa'miliar,izer** *or* **fa'miliar,iser** *n*

Familist ('fæmɪlɪst) *n* a member of the Family of Love, a mystical Christian religious sect of the 16th and 17th centuries based upon love. ▸ **'Familism** *n*

famille *French.* (famij) *n* a type of Chinese porcelain characterized either by a design on a background of yellow (***famille jaune***) or black (***famille noire***) or by a design in which the predominant colour is pink (***famille rose***) or green (***famille verte***). [C19: literally: family]

family ('fæmɪlɪ, 'fæmlɪ) *n, pl* **-lies. 1a** a primary social group consisting of parents and their offspring, the principal function of which is provision for its members. **1b** (*as modifier*): *family quarrels; a family unit.* **2** one's wife or husband and one's children. **3** one's children, as distinguished from one's husband or wife. **4** a group of persons related by blood; a group descended from a common ancestor. Compare **extended family. 5** all the persons living together in one household. **6** any group of related things or beings, esp. when scientifically categorized. **7** *Biology.* any of the taxonomic groups into which an order is divided and which contains one or more genera. *Felidae* (cat family) and *Canidae* (dog family) are two families of the order *Carnivora.* **8** *Ecology.* a group of organisms of the same species living together in a community. **9** a group of historically related languages assumed to derive from one original language. **10** *Chiefly U.S.* an independent local group of the Mafia. **11** *Maths.* a group of curves or surfaces whose equations differ from a given equation only in the values assigned to one or more constants in each curve: *a family of concentric circles.* **12** *Physics.* the isotopes, collectively, that comprise a radioactive series. **13 in the family way.** *Informal.* pregnant. [C15: from Latin *familia* a household, servants of the house, from *famulus* servant]

family allowance *n* **1** (in Britain) a former name for **child benefit. 2** (*caps.*) the Canadian equivalent of **child benefit.**

family Bible *n* a large Bible used for family worship in which births, marriages, and deaths are recorded.

family circle *n* **1** members of a family regarded as a closed group. **2** *Chiefly U.S.* the cheap seating area in a theatre behind or above the dress circle.

Family Compact *n Canadian.* **1 the.** the ruling oligarchy in Upper Canada in the early 19th century. **2** (*often not cap.*) any influential clique.

family credit *n* (in Britain) a means-tested allowance paid to families who have at least one dependent child, and whose earnings from full-time work are low. It replaced Family Income Supplement.

Family Division *n Brit. law.* a division of the High Court of Justice dealing with divorce, the custody of and rights of access to children, etc.

family doctor *n* See **general practitioner.**

family grouping *n* a system, used usually in the infant school, of grouping children of various ages together, esp. for project work. Also called: **vertical grouping.**

Family Income Supplement *n* (in Britain) formerly a means-tested benefit for families who had at least one dependent child, and whose earnings from full-time work were low. Abbrev. **FIS.**

family man *n* a man who is married and has children, esp. one who is devoted to his family.

family name *n* **1** a surname, esp. when regarded as representing the family honour. **2** a first or middle name frequently used in a family, often originally a surname.

family planning *n* the control of the number of children in a family and of the intervals between them, esp. by the use of contraceptives. See also **birth control.**

family skeleton *n* a closely guarded family secret.

family support *n N.Z.* a means-tested allowance for families in need.

family therapy *n* a form of psychotherapy in which the members of a family participate, with the aim of improving communications between them and the ways in which they relate to each other.

family tree *n* a chart showing the genealogical relationships and lines of descent of a family. Also called: **genealogical tree.**

famine ('fæmɪn) *n* **1** a severe shortage of food, as through crop failure or overpopulation. **2** acute shortage of anything. **3** violent hunger. [C14: from Old French, via Vulgar Latin, from Latin *famēs* hunger]

famish ('fæmɪʃ) *vb* **1** (*now usually passive*) to be or make very hungry or weak. **2** *Archaic.* to die or cause to die from starvation. **3** *Irish.* to make very cold: *I was famished with the cold.* [C14: from Old French *afamer,* via Vulgar Latin, from Latin *famēs* FAMINE] ▸ **'famishment** *n*

famous ('feɪməs) *adj* **1** known to or recognized by many people; renowned. **2** *Informal.* excellent; splendid. **3** *Archaic.* of ill repute. [C14: from Latin *fāmōsus;* see FAME] ▸ **'famousness** *n*

famously ('feɪməslɪ) *adv* **1** well-known: *her famously relaxed manner.* **2** very well: *the two got on famously.*

famulus ('fæmjʊləs) *n, pl* **-li** (-,laɪ). (formerly) the attendant of a sorcerer or scholar. [C19: from Latin: servant]

fan[1] (fæn) *n* **1a** any device for creating a current of air by movement of a surface or number of surfaces, esp. a rotating device consisting of a number of blades attached to a central hub. **1b** a machine that rotates such a device. **2** any of various hand-agitated devices for cooling onself, esp. a collapsible semicircular series of flat segments of paper, ivory, etc. **3** something shaped like such a fan, such as the tail of certain birds. **4** *Agriculture.* **4a** a kind of basket formerly used for winnowing grain. **4b** a machine equipped with a fan for winnowing or cleaning grain. ◆ *vb* **fans, fanning, fanned.** (*mainly tr*) **5** to cause a current of air, esp. cool air, to blow upon, as by means of a fan: *to fan one's face.* **6** to agitate or move (air, smoke, etc.) with or as if with a fan. **7** to make fiercer, more ardent, etc.: *fan one's passion.* **8** (*also intr;* often foll. by *out*) to spread out or cause to spread out in the shape of a fan. **9a** to fire (an automatic gun) continuously by keeping the trigger depressed. **9b** to fire (a nonautomatic gun) several times by repeatedly chopping back the hammer with the palm. **10** to winnow (grain) by blowing the chaff away from it. [Old English *fann,* from Latin *vannus*] ▸ **'fanlike** *adj* ▸ **'fanner** *n*

fan[2] (fæn) *n* **1** an ardent admirer of a pop star, film actor, football team, etc. **2** a devotee of a sport, hobby, etc. [C17, re-formed C19: from FAN(ATIC)]

Fanagalo ('fænəgələʊ) *or* **Fanakalo** *n* (in South Africa) a Zulu-based pidgin with English and Afrikaans components, esp. associated with the mines. [C20: from Fanagalo *fana go lo,* literally: to be like this; compare Zulu *fand* to be like, *ka-lo* of this]

fanatic (fə'nætɪk) *n* **1** a person whose enthusiasm or zeal for something is extreme or beyond normal limits. **2** *Informal.* a person devoted to a particular hobby or pastime; fan: *a jazz fanatic.* ◆ *adj* **3** a variant of **fanatical.** [C16: from Latin *fānāticus* belonging to a temple, hence, inspired by a god, frenzied, from *fānum* temple]

fanatical (fə'nætɪkᵊl) *adj* surpassing what is normal or accepted in enthusiasm for or belief in something; excessively or unusually dedicated or devoted. ▸ **fa'natically** *adv*

fanaticism (fə'nætɪ,sɪzəm) *n* wildly excessive or irrational devotion, dedication, or enthusiasm.

fanaticize *or* **fanaticise** (fə'nætɪ,saɪz) *vb* to make or become fanatical.

fan belt *n* any belt that drives a fan, esp. the belt that drives a cooling fan together with a dynamo or alternator in a car engine.

fancied ('fænsɪd) *adj* **1** imaginary; unreal. **2** thought likely to win or succeed: *a fancied runner.*

fancier ('fænsɪə) *n* **1** a person with a special interest in something. **2** a person who breeds plants or animals, often as a pastime: *a bird fancier.*

fanciful ('fænsɪful) *adj* **1** not based on fact; dubious or imaginary: *fanciful notions.* **2** made or designed in a curious, intricate, or imaginative way. **3** indulging in or influenced by fancy; whimsical. ▸ **'fancifully** *adv* ▸ **'fancifulness** *n*

fan club *n* **1** an organized group of admirers of a particular pop singer, film star, etc. **2 be a member of someone's fan club.** *Informal.* to approve of someone strongly.

fancy ('fænsɪ) *adj* **-cier, -ciest. 1** not plain; ornamented or decorative: *a fancy cake; fancy clothes.* **2** requiring skill to perform; intricate: *a fancy dance routine.* **3** arising in the imagination; capricious or illusory. **4** (often used ironically) superior in quality or impressive: *a fancy course in business administration.* **5** higher than expected: *fancy prices.* **6** (of a domestic animal) bred for particular qualities. ◆ *n, pl* **-cies. 7** a sudden capricious idea; whim. **8** a sudden or irrational liking for a person or thing. **9** the power to conceive and represent decorative and novel imagery, esp. in poetry. Fancy was held by Coleridge to be more casual and superficial than imagination. See **imagination** (sense 4). **10** an idea or thing produced by this. **11** a mental image. **12** taste or judgment, as in art of dress. **13** Also called: **fantasy, fantasia.** *Music.* a composition for solo lute, keyboard, etc., current during the 16th and 17th centuries. **14 the fancy.** *Archaic.* those who follow a particular sport, esp. prize fighting. ◆ *vb* **-cies, -cying, -cied.** (*tr*) **15** to picture in the imagination. **16** to suppose; imagine: *I fancy it will rain.* **17** (*often used with a negative*) to like: *I don't fancy your chances!* **18** (*reflexive*) to have a high or ill-founded opinion of oneself: *he fancied himself as a doctor.* **19** *Informal.* to have a wish for; desire: *she fancied some chocolate.* **20** *Brit. informal.* to be physically attracted to (another person). **21** to breed (animals) for particular characteristics. ◆ *interj* **22** Also: **fancy that!** an exclamation of surprise or disbelief. [C15 *fantsy,* shortened from *fantasie;* see FANTASY] ▸ **'fancily** *adv* ▸ **'fanciness** *n*

fancy dress *n* a costume worn at masquerades, etc., usually representing a particular role, historical figure, etc. **b** (*as modifier*): *a fancy-dress ball.*

fancy-free *adj* having no commitments; carefree.

fancy goods *pl n* small decorative gifts; knick-knacks.

fancy man *n Slang.* **1** a woman's lover. **2** a pimp.

fancy woman *n Slang.* a mistress or prostitute.

fancywork ('fænsɪ,wɜːk) *n* any ornamental needlework, such as embroidery or crochet.

fan dance *n* a dance in which large fans are manipulated in front of the body, partially revealing or suggesting nakedness.

fandangle (fæn'dæŋgᵊl) *n Informal.* **1** elaborate ornament. **2** nonsense. [C19: perhaps from FANDANGO]

fandango (fæn'dæŋgəʊ) *n, pl* **-gos. 1** an old Spanish courtship dance in triple time between a couple who dance closely and provocatively. **2** a piece of music composed for or in the rhythm of this dance. [C18: from Spanish, of uncertain origin]

fane (feɪn) *n Archaic or poetic.* a temple or shrine. [C14: from Latin *fānum*]

fanfare ('fænfɛə) *n* **1** a flourish or short tune played on brass instruments, used as a military signal, at a ceremonial event, etc. **2** an ostentatious flourish or display. [C17: from French, back formation from *fanfarer* to play a flourish on trumpets; see FANFARONADE]

fanfaronade (,fænfærə'nɑːd) *n Rare.* boasting or flaunting behaviour; bluster. [C17: via French from Spanish *fanfaronada,* from *fanfarron* boaster, from Arabic *farfār* garrulous]

fang (fæŋ) *n* **1** the long pointed hollow or grooved tooth of a venomous snake through which venom is injected. **2** any large pointed tooth, esp. the canine or carnassial tooth of a carnivorous mammal. **3** the root of a tooth. **4** (*usually pl*) *Brit. informal.* tooth: *clean your fangs.* [Old English *fang* what is caught, prey; related to Old Norse *fang* a grip, German *Fang* booty] ▸ **fanged** *adj* ▸ **'fangless** *adj* ▸ **'fang,like** *adj*

Fang (fæŋ, fɑːŋ) *n* **1** (*pl* **Fangs** *or* **Fang**) a member of a Negroid people of W Africa, living chiefly in the rain forests of Gabon and Rio Muni: noted for their use of iron and copper money and for their sculpture. **2** the language of this people, belonging to the Bantu group of the Niger-Congo family.

Fangio (*Spanish* 'faŋxjo) *n* **Juan Manuel** (xwan ma'nwɛl). 1911–95, Argentinian racing driver who won the World Championship five times between 1951 and 1957.

fango ('fæŋgəʊ) *n* mud from thermal springs in Italy, used in the treatment of rheumatic disease. [from Italian]

Fa Ngum ('fɑː 'ŋʊm) *n* 1316–74, founder and first king of Lan Xang (1354–73), a kingdom that included the present-day republic of Laos; abdicated.

fan heater *n* a space heater consisting of an electrically heated element with an electrically driven fan to disperse the heat by forced convection.

fanion ('fænjən) *n* a small flag used by surveyors to mark stations. [C18: from French, from *fanon* maniple, of Germanic origin]

fanjet ('fæn,dʒɛt) *n* another name for **turbofan** (senses 1, 2).

fankle ('fæŋkᵊl) *Scot. dialect.* ◆ *vb* (*tr*) **1** to entangle. ◆ *n* **2** a tangle; confusion. [from *fank* a coil of rope, from *fang*, obsolete variant of VANG]

fanlight ('fæn,laɪt) *n* **1** a semicircular window over a door or window, often having sash bars like the ribs of a fan. **2** a small rectangular window over a door. U.S name: **transom. 3** another name for **skylight.**

fan mail *n* mail sent to a famous person, such as a pop musician or film star, by admirers.

fanny ('fænɪ) *n, pl* **-nies.** *Slang.* **1** *Taboo, Brit.* the female genitals. **2** *Chiefly U.S. and Canadian.* the buttocks. [C20: perhaps from *Fanny*, pet name from *Frances*]

fanny adams *n Brit. slang.* **1** (usually preceded by *sweet*) absolutely nothing at all. Often shortened to **f.a., FA** *or* **SFA. 2** *Chiefly nautical.* (formerly) tinned meat, esp. mutton. [C19: from the name of a young murder victim whose body was cut up into small pieces. For sense 1: a euphemism for *fuck all*]

fanon ('fænən) *n R.C. Church.* **1** a collar-shaped vestment worn by the pope when celebrating mass. **2** (formerly) various pieces of embroidered fabric used in the liturgy. [Middle English, of Germanic origin; related to Old High German *fano* cloth]

fan palm *n* any of various palm trees, such as the talipot and palmetto, that have fan-shaped leaves. Compare **feather palm.**

fantail ('fæn,teɪl) *n* **1** a breed of domestic pigeon having a large tail that can be opened like a fan. **2** any Old World flycatcher of the genus *Rhipidura*, of Australia, New Zealand, and SE Asia, having a broad fan-shaped tail. **3** a tail shaped like an outspread fan. **4** *Architect.* a part or structure having a number of components radiating from a common centre. **5** a burner that ejects fuel to produce a wide flat flame in a lamp or furnace. **6** a flat jet of air and coal dust projected into the air stream of a pulverized-coal furnace. **7** an auxiliary sail on the upper portion of a windmill that turns the mill to face the wind. **8** *U.S.* a curved part of the deck projecting aft of the sternpost of a ship. ▸ **'fan-,tailed** *adj*

fan-tan *n* **1** a Chinese gambling game in which a random number of counters are placed under a bowl and wagers laid on how many will remain after they have been divided by four. **2** a card game played in sequence, the winner being the first to use up all his cards. [C19: from Chinese (Cantonese) *fan t'an* repeated divisions, from *fan* times + *t'an* division]

fantasia (fæn'teɪzɪə, ,fæntə'zɪə) *n* **1** any musical composition of a free or improvisatory nature. **2** a potpourri of popular tunes woven freely into a loosely bound composition. **3** another word for **fancy** (sense 13). [C18: from Italian: fancy; see FANTASY]

fantasize *or* **fantasise** ('fæntə,saɪz) *vb* **1** (when *tr*, takes a clause as object) to conceive extravagant or whimsical ideas, images, etc. **2** (*intr*) to conceive pleasant or satisfying mental images.

fantasm ('fæntæzəm) *n* an archaic spelling of **phantasm.** ▸ **fan'tasmal** *or* **fan'tasmic** *adj* ▸ **fan'tasmally** *or* **fan'tasmically** *adv*

fantast ('fæntæst) *n* a dreamer or visionary. [C16: from German *Phantast*, from Greek *phantastēs* boaster; English word influenced in meaning by FANTASTIC]

fantastic (fæn'tæstɪk) *adj also* **fantastical. 1** strange, weird, or fanciful in appearance, conception, etc. **2** created in the mind; illusory. **3** extravagantly fanciful; unrealistic: *fantastic plans.* **4** incredible or preposterous; absurd: *a fantastic verdict.* **5** *Informal.* very large or extreme; great: *a fantastic fortune; he suffered fantastic pain.* **6** *Informal.* very good; excellent. **7** of, given to, or characterized by fantasy. **8** not constant; capricious; fitful: *given to fantastic moods.* ◆ *n* **9** *Archaic.* a person who dresses or behaves eccentrically. [C14 *fantastik* imaginary, via Late Latin from Greek *phantastikos* capable of imagining, from *phantazein* to make visible] ▸ **,fantasti'cality** *or* **fan'tasticalness** *n*

fantastically (fæn'tæstɪkəlɪ) *adv* **1** in a fantastic manner. **2** *Informal.* (intensifier): *it's fantastically cheap.*

fantasy *or* **phantasy** ('fæntəsɪ) *n, pl* **-sies. 1a** imagination unrestricted by reality. **1b** (*as modifier*): *a fantasy world.* **2** a creation of the imagination, esp. a weird or bizarre one. **3** *Psychol.* **3a** a series of pleasing mental images, usually serving to fulfil a need not gratified in reality. **3b** the activity of forming such images. **4** a whimsical or far-fetched notion. **5** an illusion, hallucination, or phantom. **6** a highly elaborate imaginative design or creation. **7** *Music.* another word for **fantasia** (senses 1, 2), **fancy** (sense 13), or (rare) **development** (sense 5). **8a** literature having a large fantasy content. **8b** a prose or dramatic composition of this type. ◆ *vb* **-sies, -sying, -sied. 9** a less common word for **fantasize.** [C14 *fantasie*, from Latin *phantasia*, from Greek *phantazein* to make visible]

Fanti ('fæntɪ) *n* **1** a language of Ghana: one of the two chief dialects of Akan. Compare **Twi. 2** (*pl* **-tis** *or* **-ti**) a member of a Negroid people who speak this language, inhabiting the rain forests of Ghana and the Ivory Coast.

Fantin-Latour (*French* fɑ̃tɛ̃latur) *n* (**Ignace**) **Henri** (**Joseph Théodore**) (ɑ̃ri). 1836–1904, French painter, noted for his still lifes and portrait groups.

fantoccini (,fæntə'tʃiːnɪ) *pl n* **1** marionettes. **2** puppet shows in which they are used. [C18: from Italian: little puppets, plural of *fantoccino*, from *fantoccio* puppet, from *fante* boy, from Latin *infāns* INFANT]

fantod ('fæntəd) *n* **1** crotchety or faddish behaviour. **2** (*pl*) a state of restlessness or unease. [C19: of uncertain origin]

fantom ('fæntəm) *n* an archaic spelling of **phantom.**

fantoosh (fæn'tuːʃ) *adj Scot.* pretentious; ostentatious. [of uncertain origin]

fan tracery *n Architect.* the carved ornamentation on fan vaulting.

fan vaulting *n Architect.* vaulting having ribs that radiate like those of a fan and spring from the top of a capital or corbel. Also called: **palm vaulting.**

fan worm *n* any tube-dwelling polychaete worm of the family *Sabellidae*, having long tentacles that spread into a fan when the worm emerges from its tube.

FANY ('fænɪ) *n* **1** *acronym for* First Aid Nursing Yeomanry. **2** Also called: **Fany, Fanny,** *pl* **FANYs, Fanys, Fannies.** a member of this organization.

fanzine ('fæn,ziːn) *n* a small-circulation magazine produced by amateurs for fans of a specific interest, pop group, etc. [C20: from FAN[2] + (MAGA)ZINE]

FAO *abbrev. for* **1** Food and Agriculture Organization (of the United Nations). **2** for the attention of.

f.a.q. *abbrev. for:* **1** *Commerce.* fair average quality. **2** free alongside quay.

faqir (fə'kɪə, 'feɪkə) *n* a variant spelling of **fakir.**

far (fɑː) *adv* **farther** *or* **further, farthest** *or* **furthest. 1** at, to, or from a great distance. **2** at or to a remote time: *far in the future.* **3** to a considerable degree; very much: *a far better plan.* **4 as far as. 4a** to the degree or extent that. **4b** to the distance or place of. **5 by far.** by a considerable margin. **6 far and away.** by a very great margin. **7 far and wide.** over great distances; everywhere. **8 far be it from me.** I would not presume; on no account: *far be it from me to tell you what to do.* **9 far gone. 9a** in an advanced state of deterioration. **9b** *Informal.* extremely drunk. **10 go far. 10a** to be successful; achieve much: *your son will go far.* **10b** to be sufficient or last long: *the wine didn't go far.* **11 go too far.** to exceed reasonable limits. **12 how far?** to what extent, distance, or degree? **13 in so far as.** to the degree or extent that. **14 so far. 14a** up to the present moment. **14b** up to a certain point, extent, degree, etc. **15 so far, so good.** an expression of satisfaction with progress made. ◆ *adj* (*prenominal*) **16** remote in space or time: *a far country; in the far past.* **17** extending a great distance; long. **18** more distant: *the far end of the room.* **19 a far cry. 19a** a long way. **19b** something very different. **20 far from.** in a degree, state, etc., remote from: *he is far from happy.* [Old English *feorr*; related to Old Frisian *fīr*, Old High German *ferro*, Latin *porro* forwards, Greek *pera* further] ▸ **'farness** *n*

farad ('færəd, -æd) *n Physics.* the derived SI unit of electric capacitance; the capacitance of a capacitor between the plates of which a potential of 1 volt is created by a charge of 1 coulomb. Symbol: F [C19: named after Michael FARADAY]

faraday ('færə,deɪ) *n* a quantity of electricity, used in electrochemical calculations, equivalent to unit amount of substance of electrons. It is equal to the product of the Avogadro number and the charge on the electron and has the value 96 487 coulombs per mole. Symbol: *F* [C20: named after Michael FARADAY]

Faraday ('færə,deɪ) *n* **Michael.** 1791–1867, English physicist and chemist who discovered electromagnetic induction, leading to the invention of the dynamo. He also carried out research into the principles of electrolysis.

Faraday cage *n* an earthed conducting cage or container used to protect electrical equipment against electric fields. [C20: named after Michael FARADAY]

faradic (fə'rædɪk) *or* **faradaic** (,færə'deɪɪk) *adj* of or concerned with an intermittent asymmetric alternating current such as that induced in the secondary winding of an induction coil. [C19: from French *faradique*, from Michael FARADAY]

faradism ('færə,dɪzəm) *n* the therapeutic use of faradic currents.

faradize *or* **faradise** ('færə,daɪz) *vb* (*tr*) to treat (an organ or part) with faradic currents. ▸ **,faradi'zation** *or* **,faradi'sation** *n* ▸ **'fara,dizer** *or* **'fara,diser** *n*

farandole ('færən,dəʊl; *French* farɑ̃dɔl) *n* **1** a lively dance in six-eight or four-four time from Provence. **2** a piece of music composed for or in the rhythm of this dance. [C19: from French, from Provençal *farandoulo*, of uncertain origin; compare Spanish *farándula* itinerant group of actors]

faraway ('fɑːrə,weɪ) *adj* (**far away** *when postpositive*). **1** very distant; remote. **2** dreamy or absent-minded.

farce (fɑːs) *n* **1** a broadly humorous play based on the exploitation of improbable situations. **2** the genre of comedy represented by works of this kind. **3** a ludicrous situation or action. **4** Also: **farcemeat.** another name for **forcemeat.** ◆ *vb* (*tr*) *Obsolete.* **5** to enliven (a speech, etc.) with jokes. **6** to stuff (meat, fowl, etc.) with forcemeat. [C14 (in the sense: stuffing): from Old French, from Latin *farcīre* to stuff, interpolate passages (in the mass, in religious plays, etc.)]

farceur (*French* farsœr) *n* **1** a writer of or performer in farces. **2** a joker. ▸ **far'ceuse** *fem n*

farci (fɑː'siː) *adj* (of food) stuffed. [French: stuffed; see FARCE]

farcical ('fɑːsɪkᵊl) *adj* **1** ludicrous; absurd. **2** of or relating to farce. ▸ **,farci'cality** *or* **'farcicalness** *n* ▸ **'farcically** *adv*

farcy ('fɑːsɪ) *n, pl* **-cies.** *Vet. science.* a form of glanders in which lymph vessels near the skin become thickened, with skin lesions and abscess-forming nodules. [C15: from Old French *farcin,* from Late Latin *farcīminum* glanders, from Latin *farcīmen* a sausage, from *farcīre* to stuff]

fard (fɑːd) *n Archaic.* paint for the face, esp. white paint. [C15: from Old French *farder* to use facial cosmetics, of Germanic origin]

fardel (ˈfɑːdᵊl) *n Archaic.* a bundle or burden. [C13: from Old French *farde,* ultimately from Arabic *fardah*]

fare (fɛə) *n* **1** the sum charged or paid for conveyance in a bus, train, aeroplane, etc. **2** a paying passenger, esp. when carried by taxi. **3** a range of food and drink; diet. ◆ *vb* (*intr*) **4** to get on (as specified); manage: *he fared well.* **5** (with *it* as a subject) to turn out or happen as specified: *it fared badly with him.* **6** *Archaic.* to eat: *we fared sumptuously.* **7** (often foll. by *forth*) *Archaic.* to go or travel. [Old English *faran;* related to Old Norse *fara* to travel, Old High German *faran* to go, Greek *poros* ford] ▸ **ˈfarer** *n*

Far East *n* **the.** the countries of E Asia, usually including China, Japan, North and South Korea, Indonesia, Malaysia, and the Philippines: sometimes extended to include all territories east of Afghanistan. ▸ **Far Eastern** *adj*

Fareham (ˈfɛərəm) *n* a market town in S England, in S Hampshire. Pop.: 54 866 (1991).

fare stage *n* **1** a section of a bus journey for which a set charge is made. **2** a bus stop marking the end of such a section.

fare-thee-well *or* **fare-you-well** *n Informal, chiefly U.S.* a state of perfection: *the steak was cooked to a fare-thee-well.*

farewell (ˌfɛəˈwɛl) *sentence substitute.* **1** goodbye; adieu. ◆ *n* **2** a parting salutation. **3** an act of departure; leave-taking. **4** (*modifier*) expressing leave-taking: *a farewell speech.* ◆ *vb* (*tr*) **5** *Austral. and N.Z.* to honour (a person) at his departure, retirement, etc.

far-fetched *adj* improbable in nature; unlikely.

far-flung *adj* **1** widely distributed. **2** far distant; remote.

Fargo (ˈfɑːɡəʊ) *n* **William.** 1818–81, U.S. businessman: founded (1852) with Henry Wells the express mail service Wells, Fargo and Company.

Faridabad (fæˈrɪdəbæd) *n* a city in NE India, in Haryana: industrial centre. Pop.: 617 717 (1991).

farina (fəˈriːnə) *n* **1** flour or meal made from any kind of cereal grain. **2** *Chiefly Brit.* starch, esp. prepared from potato flour. [C18: from Latin *fār* spelt, coarse meal]

farinaceous (ˌfærɪˈneɪʃəs) *adj* **1** consisting or made of starch, such as bread, macaroni, and potatoes. **2** having a mealy texture or appearance. **3** containing starch: *farinaceous seeds.*

farinose (ˈfærɪˌnəʊs, -ˌnəʊz) *adj* **1** similar to or yielding farina. **2** *Botany.* covered with very short hairs resembling a whitish mealy dust. ▸ **ˈfariˌnosely** *adv*

farl *or* **farle** (fɑːl) *n* a thin cake of oatmeal, often triangular in shape. [C18: from earlier *fardel* fourth part, from Old English *fēortha* fourth + Middle English *del* part]

farm (fɑːm) *n* **1a** a tract of land, usually with house and buildings, cultivated as a unit or used to rear livestock. **1b** (*as modifier*): *farm produce.* **1c** (*in combination*): *farmland.* **2** a unit of land or water devoted to the growing or rearing of some particular type of vegetable, fruit, animal, or fish: *a fish farm.* **3** an installation for storage. **4** a district of which one or more taxes are leased. **5** *History.* **5a** a fixed sum paid by an individual or group for the right of collecting and retaining taxes, rents, etc. **5b** a fixed sum paid regularly by a town, county, etc., in lieu of taxes. **5c** the leasing of a source of revenue to an individual or group. **5d** a fixed tax, rent, etc., paid regularly. ◆ *vb* **6** (*tr*) **6a** to cultivate (land). **6b** to rear (stock, etc.) on a farm. **7** (*intr*) to engage in agricultural work, esp. as a way of life. **8** (*tr*) to look after a child for a fixed sum. **9a** to collect the moneys due and retain the profits from (a tax district, business, etc.) for a specified period on payment of a sum or sums. **9b** to operate (a franchise) under similar conditions. ◆ See also **farm out.** [C13: from Old French *ferme* rented land, ultimately from Latin *firmāre* to settle] ▸ **ˈfarmable** *adj*

farm-bike *n N.Z.* a motorcycle built for off-road travel.

farmed (fɑːmd) *adj* (of fish and game) reared on a farm rather than caught in the wild.

farmer (ˈfɑːmə) *n* **1** a person who operates or manages a farm. **2** a person who obtains the right to collect and retain a tax, rent, etc., or operate a franchise for a specified period on payment of a fee. **3** a person who looks after a child for a fixed sum.

Farmer (ˈfɑːmə) *n* **John.** ?1565–1605, English madrigal composer and organist.

farmer-general *n, pl* **farmers-general.** (in France before 1789) a member of a group allowed to farm certain taxes. ▸ **ˈfarmer-ˈgeneralˌship** *n*

farmer's lung *n* inflammation of the alveoli of the lungs caused by an allergic response to fungal spores in hay.

farm-gate sale *n N.Z.* the sale of produce direct from the producer.

farm hand *n* a person who is hired to work on a farm.

farmhouse (ˈfɑːmˌhaʊs) *n* **1** a house attached to a farm, esp. the dwelling from which the farm is managed. **2** Also called: **farmhouse loaf.** *Brit.* a large white loaf, baked in a tin, with slightly curved sides and top.

farming (ˈfɑːmɪŋ) *n* **a** the business, art, or skill of agriculture. **b** (*as modifier*): *farming methods.*

farmland (ˈfɑːmˌlænd) *n* land used or suitable for farming.

farm out *vb* (*tr, adv*) **1** to send (work) to be done by another person, firm, etc.; subcontract. **2** to put (a child, etc.) into the care of a private individual; foster. **3** to lease to another for a rent or fee the right to operate (a business for profit, land, etc.) or the right to collect (taxes).

farmstead (ˈfɑːmˌstɛd) *n* a farm or the part of a farm comprising its main buildings together with adjacent grounds.

farm-toun (ˈfærmˌtun, ˈfɑːmˌtun) *n Scot.* a farmhouse together with its outbuildings.

farmyard (ˈfɑːmˌjɑːd) *n* **a** an area surrounded by or adjacent to farm buildings. **b** (*as modifier*): *farmyard animals.*

Farnborough (ˈfɑːnbərə, -brə) *n* a town in S England, in NE Hampshire: military base, with an aeronautical research centre. Pop.: 52 535 (1991).

Farnese (*Italian* farˈneːse) *n* **1 Alessandro** (alesˈsandro). original name of (Pope) **Paul III. 2 Alessandro,** duke of Parma and Piacenza. 1545–92, Italian general, statesman, and diplomat in the service of Philip II of Spain. As governor of the Netherlands (1578–92), he successfully suppressed revolts against Spanish rule.

farnesol (ˈfɑːnɪˌsɒl) *n* a colourless aromatic sesquiterpene alcohol found in many essential oils and used in the form of its derivatives in perfumery; 3,7,11-trimethyl-2,6,10-dodecatrienol. Formula: $C_{15}H_{26}O$. [C20: from New Latin (*Acacia*) *farnesiāna;* named after Odoardo *Farnese,* C17 Italian cardinal]

Farnham (ˈfɑːnəm) *n* a town in S England, in NW Surrey. Pop.: 36 178 (1991).

Far North *n* **the.** the Arctic and sub-Arctic regions of the world.

faro (ˈfɛərəʊ) *n* a gambling game in which players bet against the dealer on what cards he will turn up. [C18: probably spelling variant of *Pharoah*]

Faro (ˈfɑːrəʊ) *n* a port and resort in S Portugal: destroyed by earthquakes in 1722 and 1755. Pop.: 31 970 (1990).

Faroes (ˈfɛərəʊz) *n* a variant spelling of **Faeroes.** ▸ **Faroese** (ˌfɛərəʊˈiːz) *adj, n*

far-off *adj* (**far off** *when postpositive*). remote in space or time; distant.

farouche *French.* (faruʃ) *adj* **1** sullen or shy. **2** socially inept. [C18: from French, from Old French *faroche,* from Late Latin *forasticus* from without, from Latin *foras* out of doors]

Farouk I *or* **Faruk I** (fəˈruːk) *n* 1920–65, last king of Egypt (1936–52). He was forced to abdicate (1952).

far-out *Slang.* ◆ *adj* (**far out** *when postpositive*) **1** bizarre or avant-garde. **2** excellent; wonderful. ◆ *interj* **far out. 3** an expression of amazement or delight.

Farquhar (ˈfɑːkwə, -kə) *n* **George.** 1678–1707, Irish-born dramatist; author of comedies such as *The Recruiting Officer* (1706) and *The Beaux' Stratagem* (1707).

Farquhar Islands *pl n* an island group in the Indian Ocean: administratively part of the Seychelles.

farrago (fəˈrɑːɡəʊ) *n, pl* **-gos** *or* **-goes.** a hotchpotch. [C17: from Latin: mash for cattle (hence, a mixture), from *fār* spelt] ▸ **farraginous** (fəˈrædʒɪnəs) *adj*

far-reaching *adj* extensive in influence, effect, or range.

Farrell (ˈfærəl) *n* **1 J(ames) G(ordon).** 1935–79, British novelist: author of *Troubles* (1970), *The Siege of Krishnapur* (1973), and *The Singapore Grip* (1978). **2 James T(homas).** 1904–79, U.S. writer. His works include the trilogy *Young Lonigan* (1932), *The Young Manhood of Studs Lonigan* (1934), and *Judgment Day* (1935).

farrier (ˈfærɪə) *n Chiefly Brit.* **1** a person who shoes horses. **2** another name for **veterinary surgeon. 3** *Military.* a noncommissioned officer who looks after horses. [C16: from Old French *ferrier,* from Latin *ferrārius* smith, from *ferrum* iron]

farriery (ˈfærɪərɪ) *n, pl* **-eries.** *Chiefly Brit.* the art, work, or establishment of a farrier.

farrow[1] (ˈfærəʊ) *n* **1** a litter of piglets. ◆ *vb* **2** (of a sow) to give birth to (a litter). [Old English *fearh;* related to Old High German *farah* young pig, Latin *porcus* pig, Greek *porkos*]

farrow[2] (ˈfærəʊ) *adj* (of a cow) not calving in a given year. [C15: from Middle Dutch *verwe-* (unattested) cow that has ceased to bear; compare Old English *fearr* ox]

far-seeing *adj* having shrewd judgment; far-sighted.

Farsi (ˈfɑːsiː) *n* the Indo-European language of modern Iran. See also **Persian** (sense 4).

far-sighted *adj* **1** possessing prudence and foresight. **2** *Med.* of, relating to, or suffering from hyperopia. **3** another word for **long-sighted.** ▸ **ˌfar-ˈsightedly** *adv* ▸ **ˌfarˈsightedness** *n*

fart (fɑːt) *Taboo.* ◆ *n* **1** an emission of intestinal gas from the anus, esp. an audible one. **2** *Slang.* a contemptible person. ◆ *vb* (*intr*) **3** to expel intestinal gas from the anus; to break wind. **4 fart about** *or* **around.** *Slang.* **4a** to behave foolishly or aimlessly. **4b** to waste time. [Middle English *farten;* related to Old Norse *freta,* Old High German *ferzan* to break wind, Sanskrit *pardatē* he breaks wind]

farther (ˈfɑːðə) *adv* **1** to or at a greater distance in space or time. **2** in addition. ◆ *adj* **3** more distant or remote in space or time. **4** additional. [C13: see FAR, FURTHER]

USAGE *Farther, farthest, further,* and *furthest* can all be used to refer to literal distance, but *further* and *furthest* are regarded as more correct for figurative senses denoting greater or additional amount, time, etc.: *further to my letter. Further* and *furthest* are also preferred for figurative distance.

farthermost (ˈfɑːðəˌməʊst) *adj* most distant or remote.

farthest (ˈfɑːðɪst) *adv* **1** to or at the greatest distance in space or time. ◆ *adj* **2** most distant in space or time. **3** most extended. [C14 *ferthest,* from *ferther* FURTHER]

farthing (ˈfɑːðɪŋ) *n* **1** a former British bronze coin worth a quarter of an old penny that ceased to be legal tender in 1961. **2** something of negligible value; jot. [Old English *fēorthing* from *fēortha* FOURTH + -ING[1]]

farthingale (ˈfɑːðɪŋˌɡeɪl) *n* a hoop or framework worn under skirts, esp. in the Elizabethan period, to shape and spread them. [C16: from French *verdugale,* from Old Spanish *verdugado,* from *verdugo* rod]

fartlek (ˈfɑːtlɛk) *n Sport.* another name for **interval training.** [Swedish, literally: speed play]

Faruk I (fəˈruːk) *n* a variant spelling of **Farouk I.**

FAS *or* **f.a.s.** *abbrev. for* free alongside ship.

fasces (ˈfæsiːz) *pl n, sing* **-cis** (-sɪs). **1** (in ancient Rome) one or more bundles of rods containing an axe with its blade protruding; a symbol of a magistrate's power. **2** (in modern Italy) such an object used as the symbol of Fascism. [C16: from Latin, plural of *fascis* bundle]

fascia *or* **facia** ('feɪʃɪə) *n, pl* **-ciae** (-ʃɪˌiː). **1** the flat surface above a shop window. **2** *Architect.* a flat band or surface, esp. a part of an architrave or cornice. **3** ('fæʃɪə). fibrous connective tissue occurring in sheets beneath the surface of the skin and between muscles and groups of muscles. **4** *Biology.* a distinctive band of colour, as on an insect or plant. **5** *Brit.* a less common name for **dashboard** (sense 1). [C16: from Latin: band: related to *fascis* bundle; see FASCES] ▸ **'fascial** *or* **'facial** *adj*

fasciate ('fæʃɪˌeɪt) *or* **fasciated** *adj* **1** *Botany.* **1a** (of stems and branches) abnormally flattened due to coalescence. **1b** growing in a bundle. **2** (of birds, insects, etc.) marked by distinct bands of colour. [C17: probably from New Latin *fasciātus* (unattested) having bands; see FASCIA] ▸ **'fasciˌately** *adv*

fasciation (ˌfæʃɪ'eɪʃən) *n Botany.* an abnormal flattening of stems due to failure of the lateral branches to separate from the main stem.

fascicle ('fæsɪkᵊl) *n* **1** a bundle or cluster of branches, leaves, etc. **2** Also called: **fasciculus.** *Anatomy.* a small bundle of fibres, esp. nerve fibres. **3** *Printing.* another name for **fascicule. 4** any small bundle or cluster. [C15: from Latin *fasciculus* a small bundle, from *fascis* a bundle] ▸ **'fascicled** *adj* ▸ **fascicular** (fə'sɪkjulə) *or* **fasciculate** (fə'sɪkjuˌleɪt, -lɪt) *adj* ▸ **fas'ciculately** *adv* ▸ **fasˌcicu'lation** *n*

fascicule ('fæsɪˌkjuːl) *n* one part of a printed work that is published in instalments. Also called: **fascicle, fasciculus.**

fasciculus (fə'sɪkjuləs) *n, pl* **-li** (-ˌlaɪ). another name for **fascicle** (sense 2) or **fascicule.**

fascinate ('fæsɪˌneɪt) *vb* (*mainly tr*) **1** to attract and delight by arousing interest or curiosity: *his stories fascinated me for hours.* **2** to render motionless, as with a fixed stare or by arousing terror or awe. **3** *Archaic.* to put under a spell. [C16: from Latin *fascināre,* from *fascinum* a bewitching] ▸ **'fasciˌnatedly** *adv* ▸ **ˌfasci'nation** *n* ▸ **'fascinative** *adj*

USAGE A person can be fascinated *by* or *with* another person or thing. It is correct to speak of someone's fascination *with* a person or thing; one can also say a person or thing has a fascination *for* someone.

fascinating ('fæsɪˌneɪtɪŋ) *adj* **1** arousing great interest. **2** enchanting or alluring: *a fascinating woman.* ▸ **'fasciˌnatingly** *adv*

fascinator ('fæsɪˌneɪtə) *n Rare.* a lace or crocheted head covering for women.

fascine (fæ'siːn, fə-) *n* a bundle of long sticks used for filling in ditches and in the construction of embankments, roads, fortifications, etc. [C17: from French, from Latin *fascīna;* see FASCES]

fascism ('fæʃɪzəm) *n* (*sometimes cap.*) **1** any ideology or movement inspired by Italian Fascism, such as German National Socialism; any right-wing nationalist ideology or movement with an authoritarian and hierarchical structure that is fundamentally opposed to democracy and liberalism. **2** any ideology, movement, programme, tendency, etc., that may be characterized as right-wing, chauvinist, authoritarian, etc. [C20: from Italian *fascismo,* from *fascio* political group, from Latin *fascis* bundle; see FASCES]

Fascism ('fæʃɪzəm) *n* the political movement, doctrine, system, or regime of Benito Mussolini in Italy. Fascism encouraged militarism and nationalism, organizing the country along hierarchical authoritarian lines.

fascist ('fæʃɪst) (*sometimes cap.*) ◆ *n* **1** an adherent or practitioner of fascism. **2** any person regarded as having right-wing authoritarian views. ◆ *adj also* **fascistic** (fə'ʃɪstɪk). **3** characteristic of or relating to fascism. ▸ **fa'scistically** *adv*

Fascist ('fæʃɪst) *n* **1** a supporter or member of the Italian Fascist movement. ◆ *adj* **2** of or relating to Italian Fascism.

fash (fæʃ) *Scot.* ◆ *n* **1** worry; trouble; bother. ◆ *vb* **2** to trouble; bother; annoy. [C16: from obsolete French *fascher* to annoy, ultimately from Latin *fastīdium* disgust, aversion]

fashion ('fæʃən) *n* **1a** style in clothes, cosmetics, behaviour, etc., esp. the latest or most admired style. **1b** (*as modifier*): *a fashion magazine.* **2** (*modifier*) (esp. of accessories) designed to be in the current fashion, but not necessarily to last. **3a** manner of performance; mode; way: *in a striking fashion.* **3b** (*in combination*): *crab-fashion.* **4** a way of life that revolves around the activities, dress, interests, etc., that are most fashionable. **5** shape, appearance, or form. **6** sort; kind; type. **7 after** *or* **in a fashion. 7a** in some manner, but not very well: *I mended it, after a fashion.* **7b** of a low order; of a sort: *he is a poet, after a fashion.* **8 after the fashion of.** like; similar to. **9 of fashion.** of high social standing. ◆ *vb* (*tr*) **10** to give a particular form to. **11** to make suitable or fitting. **12** *Obsolete.* to contrive; manage. [C13 *facioun* form, manner, from Old French *faceon,* from Latin *factiō* a making, from *facere* to make] ▸ **'fashioner** *n*

fashionable ('fæʃənəbᵊl) *adj* **1** conforming to fashion; in vogue. **2** of, characteristic of, or patronized by people of fashion: *a fashionable café.* **3** (usually foll. by *with*) patronized (by); popular (with). ▸ **'fashionableness** *n* ▸ **'fashionably** *adv*

fashion house *n* an establishment in which fashionable clothes are designed, made, and sold.

fashion plate *n* **1** an illustration of the latest fashion in dress. **2** a fashionably dressed person.

fashion victim *n Informal.* a person who slavishly follows fashion.

Fashoda (fə'ʃəudə) *n* a small town in SE Sudan: scene of a diplomatic incident (1898) in which French occupation of the fort at Fashoda caused a crisis between France and Great Britain. Modern name: **Kodok.**

FASSA *abbrev. for* Fellow of the Academy of Social Sciences in Australia.

Fassbinder (*German* 'fasbɪndər) *n* **Rainer Werner** ('raɪnər 'vɛrnər). 1946–82, West German film director. His films include *The Bitter Tears of Petra von Kant* (1972), *Fear Eats the Soul* (1974), and *The Marriage of Maria Braun* (1978).

fast[1] (fɑːst) *adj* **1** acting or moving or capable of acting or moving quickly; swift. **2** accomplished in or lasting a short time: *fast work; a fast visit.* **3** (*prenominal*) adapted to or facilitating rapid movement: *the fast lane of a motorway.* **4** requiring rapidity of action or movement: *a fast sport.* **5** (of a clock, etc.) indicating a time in advance of the correct time. **6** given to an active dissipated life. **7** of or characteristic of such activity: *a fast life.* **8** not easily moved; firmly fixed; secure. **9** firmly fastened, secured, or shut. **10** steadfast; constant (esp. in the phrase **fast friends**). **11** *Sport.* (of a playing surface, running track, etc.) conducive to rapid speed, as of a ball used on it or of competitors playing or racing on it. **12** that will not fade or change colour readily: *a fast dye.* **13a** proof against fading: *the colour is fast to sunlight.* **13b** (*in combination*): *washfast.* **14** *Photog.* **14a** requiring a relatively short time of exposure to produce a given density: *a fast film.* **14b** permitting a short exposure time: *a fast shutter.* **15** *Cricket.* (of a bowler) characteristically delivering the ball rapidly. **16** *Informal.* glib or unreliable; deceptive: *a fast talker.* **17** *Archaic.* sound; deep: *a fast sleep.* **18 a fast one.** *Informal.* a deceptive or unscrupulous trick (esp. in the phrase **pull a fast one**). **19 fast worker.** a person who achieves results quickly, esp. in seductions. ◆ *adv* **20** quickly; rapidly. **21** soundly; deeply: *fast asleep.* **22** firmly; tightly. **23** in quick succession. **24** in advance of the correct time: *my watch is running fast.* **25** in a reckless or dissipated way. **26 fast by** *or* **beside.** *Archaic.* close or hard by; very near. **27 play fast and loose.** *Informal.* to behave in an insincere or unreliable manner. ◆ *interj* **28** *Archery.* (said by the Field Captain to archers) stop shooting! [Old English *fæst* strong, tight; related to Old High German *festi* firm, Old Norse *fastr*]

fast[2] (fɑːst) *vb* **1** (*intr*) to abstain from eating all or certain foods or meals, esp. as a religious observance. ◆ *n* **2** an act or period of fasting. [Old English *fæstan;* related to Old High German *fastēn* to fast, Gothic *fastan*] ▸ **'faster** *n*

fastback ('fɑːstˌbæk) *n* **1** a car having a back that forms one continuous slope from roof to rear. **2** *Brit.* a type of pig developed from the landrace or large white and bred for lean meat.

fast-breeder reactor *n* a nuclear reactor that uses little or no moderator and produces more fissionable material than it consumes. See also **breeder reactor, fast reactor.**

fasten ('fɑːsᵊn) *vb* **1** to make or become fast or secure. **2** to make or become attached or joined. **3** to close or become closed by fixing firmly in place, locking, etc. **4** (*tr;* foll. by *in* or *up*) to enclose or imprison. **5** (*tr;* usually foll. by *on*) to cause (blame, a nickname, etc.) to be attached (to); place (on) or impute (to). **6** (usually foll. by *on* or *upon*) to direct or be directed in a concentrated way; fix: *he fastened his gaze on the girl.* **7** (*intr;* usually foll. by *on*) take firm hold (of). [Old English *fæstnian;* related to Old Norse *fastna* to pledge, Old High German *fastinōn* to make fast; see FAST[1]] ▸ **'fastener** *n*

fastening ('fɑːsᵊnɪŋ) *n* something that fastens, such as a clasp or lock.

fast food *n* **1** food that requires little preparation before being served. ◆ *adj* **fast-food. 2** (of a restaurant, café, etc.) serving such food.

fast-forward *vb* (*intr*) to move rapidly. [C20: from the fast-forward wind control in a tape deck]

fastidious (fæ'stɪdɪəs) *adj* **1** very critical; hard to please. **2** excessively particular about details. **3** exceedingly delicate; easily disgusted. [C15: from Latin *fastīdiōsus* scornful, from *fastīdium* loathing, from *fastus* pride + *taedium* weariness] ▸ **fas'tidiously** *adv* ▸ **fas'tidiousness** *n*

fastigiate (fæ'stɪdʒɪɪt, -ˌeɪt) *or* **fastigiated** *adj Biology.* **1** (of plants) having erect branches, often appearing to form a single column with the stem. **2** (of parts or organs) united in a tapering group. [C17: from Medieval Latin *fastīgiātus* lofty, from Latin *fastīgium* height]

fast lane *n* **1** the outside lane on a motorway or dual carriageway for vehicles overtaking or travelling at high speed. **2** *Informal.* the quickest but most competitive route to success.

fast motion *n Films.* action that appears to have occurred at a faster speed than that at which it was filmed. Compare **slow motion** (sense 1).

fastness ('fɑːstnɪs) *n* **1** a stronghold; fortress. **2** the state or quality of being firm or secure. **3** the ability of a dye to remain permanent and not run or fade. **4** *Archaic.* swiftness. [Old English *fæstnes;* see FAST[1]]

fast neutron *n Physics.* **a** a neutron produced by nuclear fission that has lost little energy by collision; a neutron with a kinetic energy in excess of 0.1 MeV. **b** a neutron with a kinetic energy in excess of 1.5 MeV, the fission threshold of uranium-238.

fast reactor *n* a nuclear reactor using little or no moderator, fission being caused by fast neutrons.

fast talk *Slang.* ◆ *n* **1** fervent, deceptive patter. ◆ *vb* **fast-talk. 2** to influence (a person) by means of such patter.

fast-track *adj* taking the quickest and often most competitive route to success or personal advancement: *fast-track executives.*

fat (fæt) *n* **1** any of a class of naturally occurring soft greasy solids that are esters of glycerol and certain fatty acids. They are present in some plants and in the adipose tissue of animals, forming a reserve energy source, and are used in making soap and paint and in the food industry. See also **oil** (sense 1). **2** vegetable or animal tissue containing fat. Related adjs: **adipose, lipoid, stearic. 3** corpulence, obesity, or plumpness. **4** the best or richest part of something. **5** a part in a play that gives an actor a good opportunity to show his talents. **6 chew the fat.** *Slang.* **6a** to argue over a point. **6b** to talk idly; gossip. **7 the fat is in the fire.** an irrevocable action has been taken, esp. one from which dire consequences are expected. **8 the fat of the land.** the best that is obtainable. ◆ *adj* **fatter, fattest. 9** having much or too much flesh or fat. **10** consisting of or containing fat; greasy: *fat pork.* **11** profitable; lucrative: *a fat year.* **12** affording great opportunities: *a fat part in the play.* **13** fertile or productive: *a fat land.* **14** thick, broad, or extended: *a fat log of wood.* **15** having a high content of a particular material or ingredient, such as resin in wood or oil in paint. **16** plentifully supplied: *a fat larder.* **17** *Slang.* empty; stupid: *get this into your fat head.* **18** *Slang.* very little or none; minimal (in phrases such as **a fat chance, a fat lot of good,** etc.). ◆ *vb* **fats, fatting, fatted. 19** to make or become fat;

fatten. [Old English *fætt,* past participle of *fætan* to cram; related to Old Norse *feita,* Old High German *feizen* to fatten; compare Gothic *fētjan* to adorn] ▸ **'fatless** *adj* ▸ **'fat,like** *adj* ▸ **'fatly** *adv* ▸ **'fatness** *n* ▸ **'fattish** *adj*

Fatah ('fætə) *n* **Al.** a Palestinian terrorist organization, founded in 1956, with the aim of destroying the state of Israel: it has splintered into rival factions since 1988.

fatal ('feɪtᵊl) *adj* **1** resulting in or capable of causing death: *a fatal accident.* **2** bringing ruin; disastrous. **3** decisively important; fateful. **4** decreed by fate; destined; inevitable. [C14: from Old French *fatal* or Latin *fātālis,* from *fātum,* see FATE]

fatalism ('feɪtə,lɪzəm) *n* **1** the philosophical doctrine that all events are predetermined so that man is powerless to alter his destiny. **2** the acceptance of and submission to this doctrine. **3** a lack of effort or action in the face of difficulty. ▸ **'fatalist** *n* ▸ **,fatal'istic** *adj* ▸ **,fatal'istically** *adv*

fatality (fə'tælɪtɪ) *n, pl* **-ties. 1** an accident or disaster resulting in death. **2** a person killed in an accident or disaster. **3** the power of causing death or disaster; deadliness. **4** the quality or condition of being fated. **5** something caused or dictated by fate.

fatally ('feɪtəlɪ) *adv* **1** resulting in death or disaster. **2** as decreed by fate; inevitably.

Fata Morgana ('fɑːtə mɔː'gɑːnə; *Italian* 'faːta mɔr'gaːna) *n* a mirage, esp. one in the Strait of Messina attributed to the sorcery of Morgan le Fay. [C19: from Italian: MORGAN LE FAY]

fatback ('fæt,bæk) *n* the fat, usually salted, from the upper part of a side of pork.

fat body *n Zoology.* **1** a mass of fatty tissue in insects, used as an energy source during hibernation and metamorphosis. **2** a similar tissue mass in amphibians and reptiles.

fat cat *n Slang.* **a** a very wealthy or influential person. **b** (*as modifier*): *a fat-cat industrialist.*

fate (feɪt) *n* **1** the ultimate agency that predetermines the course of events. **2** the inevitable fortune that befalls a person or thing; destiny. **3** the end or final result. **4** a calamitous or unfavourable outcome or result; death, destruction, or downfall. ◆ *vb* **5** (*tr; usually passive*) to predetermine; doom: *he was fated to lose the game.* [C14: from Latin *fātum* oracular utterance, from *fārī* to speak]

fated ('feɪtɪd) *adj* **1** destined. **2** doomed to death or destruction.

fateful ('feɪtfʊl) *adj* **1** having important consequences; decisively important. **2** bringing death or disaster. **3** controlled by or as if by fate. **4** prophetic. ▸ **'fatefully** *adv* ▸ **'fatefulness** *n*

Fates (feɪts) *pl n* **1** *Greek myth.* the three goddesses who control the destinies of the lives of man, which are likened to skeins of thread that they spin, measure out, and at last cut. See **Atropos, Clotho, Lachesis. 2** *Norse myth.* another name for the **Norns** (see Norn[1]).

fath. *abbrev. for* fathom.

fathead ('fæt,hɛd) *n Informal.* a stupid person; fool. ▸ **'fat,headed** *adj*

fat hen *n* a common plant, *Chenopodium album,* with small green flowers and whitish scales on the stem and leaves: family *Chenopodiaceae* (chenopods). Also called (U.S.): **pigweed, lamb's-quarters.**

father ('fɑːðə) *n* **1** a male parent. **2** a person who founds a line or family; forefather. **3** any male acting in a paternal capacity. Related adj: **paternal. 4** (*often cap.*) a respectful term of address for an old man. **5** a male who originates something: *the father of modern psychology.* **6** a leader of an association, council, etc.; elder: *a city father.* **7** *Brit.* the eldest or most senior member in a society, profession, etc.: *father of the House.* **8** (*often pl*) a senator or patrician in ancient Rome. **9 the father of.** *Informal.* a very large, severe, etc., example of a specified kind: *the father of a whipping.* ◆ *vb* (*tr*) **10** to procreate or generate (offspring); beget. **11** to create, found, originate, etc. **12** to act as a father to. **13** to acknowledge oneself as father or originator of. **14** (foll. by *on* or *upon*) to impose or place without a just reason. [Old English *fæder;* related to Old Norse *fathir,* Old Frisian *feder,* Old High German *fater,* Latin *pater,* Greek *patēr,* Sanskrit *pitṛ*] ▸ **'fathering** *n*

Father ('fɑːðə) *n* **1** God, esp. when considered as the first person of the Christian Trinity. **2** Also called: **Church Father.** any of the writers on Christian doctrine of the pre-Scholastic period. **3** a title used for Christian priests.

Father Christmas *n* another name for **Santa Claus.**

father confessor *n* **1** *Christianity.* a priest who hears confessions and advises on religious or moral matters. **2** any person to whom one tells private matters.

fatherhood ('fɑːðə,hʊd) *n* the state or responsibility of being a father.

father-in-law *n, pl* **fathers-in-law.** the father of one's wife or husband.

fatherland ('fɑːðə,lænd) *n* **1** a person's native country. **2** the country of a person's ancestors.

father lasher *n* a large sea scorpion, *Myoxocephalus scorpius,* occurring in British and European coastal waters. Also called: **short-spined sea scorpion.**

fatherless ('fɑːðəlɪs) *adj* having no father.

fatherly ('fɑːðəlɪ) *adj* of, resembling, or suitable to a father. ▸ **'fatherliness** *n*

father of the chapel *n* (in British trade unions in the publishing and printing industries) a shop steward. Abbrev.: **FoC.**

Father's Day *n* a day observed as a day in honour of fathers; in Britain the third Sunday in June.

Father Time *n* time personified as an old bearded man, usually carrying a scythe and an hourglass.

fathom ('fæðəm) *n* **1** a unit of length equal to six feet (1.829 metres), used to measure depths of water. **2** *Mining.* a unit of volume usually equal to six cubic feet, used in measuring ore bodies. **3** *Forestry.* a unit of volume equal to six cubic feet, used for measuring timber. ◆ *vb* (*tr*) **4** to measure the depth of, esp. with a sounding line; sound. **5** to penetrate (a mystery, problem, etc.); discover the meaning of. [Old English *fæthm;* related to Old Frisian *fethem* outstretched arms, Old Norse *fathmr* embrace, Old High German *fadum* cubit, Latin *patēre* to gape] ▸ **'fathomable** *adj* ▸ **'fathomer** *n*

Fathometer (fə'ðɒmɪtə) *n Trademark.* a type of echo sounder used for measuring the depth of water.

fathomless ('fæðəmlɪs) *adj* another word for **unfathomable.** ▸ **'fathomlessly** *adv* ▸ **'fathomlessness** *n*

fatidic (feɪ'tɪdɪk) *or* **fatidical** *adj Rare.* prophetic. [C17: from Latin *fātidicus,* from *fātum* FATE + *dīcere* to say] ▸ **fa'tidically** *adv*

fatigue (fə'tiːg) *n* **1** physical or mental exhaustion due to exertion. **2** a tiring activity or effort. **3** *Physiol.* the temporary inability of an organ or part to respond to a stimulus because of overactivity. **4** the weakening of a material subjected to alternating stresses, esp. vibrations. **5** the temporary inability to respond to a situation or perform a function, because of overexposure or overactivity: *compassion fatigue.* **6a** any of the mainly domestic duties performed by military personnel, esp. as a punishment. **6b** (*as modifier*): *fatigue duties.* **7** (*pl*) special clothing worn by military personnel to carry out such duties. ◆ *vb* **-tigues, -tiguing, -tigued. 8** to make or become weary or exhausted. **9** to weaken or break (a material or part) by inducing fluctuating stresses in it, or (of a metal or part) to become weakened or fail as a result of fluctuating stresses. [C17: from French, from *fatiguer* to tire, from Latin *fatīgāre*] ▸ **fatigable** ('fætɪgəbᵊl) *adj* ▸ **fa'tigueless** *adj*

Fatima ('fætɪmə) *n* ?606–632 A.D., daughter of Mohammed; wife of Ali.

Fátima (*Portuguese* 'fatimə) *n* a village in central Portugal: Roman Catholic shrine and pilgrimage centre.

Fatimid ('fætɪmɪd) *n* **1** a member of the Moslem dynasty, descended from Fatima and Ali, that ruled over North Africa and parts of Egypt and Syria (909–1171). **2** Also called: **Fatimite** ('fætɪ,maɪt). a descendant of Fatima and Ali.

fat lamb *n Austral. and N.Z.* a lamb bred for its tender meat, esp. for export trade.

fatling ('fætlɪŋ) *n* a young farm animal fattened for killing.

fat mouse *n* any nocturnal African mouse of the genus *Steatomys,* of dry regions: eaten as a delicacy by Africans because of their high fat content: family *Muridae.*

Fatshan ('fɑːt'ʃɑːn) *n* a variant transliteration of the Chinese name for **Foshan.**

fatshedera (fæts'hɛdərə) *n* an evergreen garden shrub with shiny green leaves and umbels of pale green flowers; a bigeneric hybrid between *Fatsia japonica moseri* and *Hedera hibernica:* family *Araliaceae.*

fatsia ('fætsɪə) *n* any shrub of the araliaceous genus *Fatsia,* esp. *F. japonica,* with large deeply palmate leaves and umbels of white flowers. [New Latin, from the Japanese name]

fatso ('fætsəʊ) *n, pl* **-sos** *or* **-soes.** *Slang.* a fat person: used as an insulting or disparaging term of address.

fat-soluble *adj* soluble in nonpolar substances, such as ether, chloroform, and oils. Fat-soluble compounds are often insoluble in water.

fat stock *n* livestock fattened and ready for market.

fatten ('fætᵊn) *vb* **1** to grow or cause to grow fat or fatter. **2** (*tr*) to cause (an animal or fowl) to become fat by feeding it. **3** (*tr*) to make fuller or richer. **4** (*tr*) to enrich (soil) by adding fertilizing agents. ▸ **'fattenable** *adj* ▸ **'fattener** *n* ▸ **'fattening** *adj*

fatty ('fætɪ) *adj* **-tier, -tiest. 1** containing, consisting of, or derived from fat. **2** having the properties of fat; greasy; oily. **3** (esp. of tissues, organs, etc.) characterized by the excessive accumulation of fat. ◆ *n, pl* **-ties. 4** *Informal.* a fat person. ▸ **'fattily** *adv* ▸ **'fattiness** *n*

fatty acid *n* **1** any of a class of aliphatic carboxylic acids, such as palmitic acid, stearic acid, and oleic acid, that form part of a lipid molecule. **2** another name for **carboxylic acid,** esp. a naturally occurring one.

fatty degeneration *n Pathol.* the abnormal formation of tiny globules of fat within the cytoplasm of a cell.

fatty oil *n* another name for **fixed oil.**

fatuity (fə'tjuːɪtɪ) *n, pl* **-ties. 1** complacent foolishness; inanity. **2** a fatuous remark, act, sentiment, etc. **3** *Archaic.* idiocy. ▸ **fa'tuitous** *adj*

fatuous ('fætjʊəs) *adj* complacently or inanely foolish. [C17: from Latin *fatuus;* related to *fatiscere* to gape] ▸ **'fatuously** *adv* ▸ **'fatuousness** *n*

fatwa *or* **fatwah** ('fætwə) *n* a religious decree issued by a Muslim leader. [Arabic]

faubourg ('fəʊbʊəg; *French* fobur) *n* a suburb or quarter, esp. of a French city. [C15: from French *fauxbourg,* perhaps a modification through folk etymology of Old French *forsborc,* from Latin *foris* outside + Old French *borc* BURG]

faucal ('fɔːkᵊl) *or* **faucial** ('fɔːʃəl) *adj* **1** *Anatomy.* of or relating to the fauces. **2** *Phonetics.* articulated in that part of the vocal tract between the back of the mouth and the larynx; pharyngeal.

fauces ('fɔːsiːz) *n, pl* **-ces.** *Anatomy.* the area between the cavity of the mouth and the pharynx, including the surrounding tissues. [C16: from Latin: throat]

faucet ('fɔːsɪt) *n* **1** a tap fitted to a barrel. **2** the U.S. and Canadian name for a **tap**[2]. [C14: from Old French *fausset,* from Provençal *falset,* from *falsar* to bore]

faugh (fɔː) *interj* an exclamation of disgust, scorn, etc.

Faulkner *or* **Falkner** ('fɔːknə) *n* **William.** 1897–1962, U.S. novelist and short-story writer. Most of his works portray the problems of the southern U.S., esp. the novels set in the imaginary county of Yoknapatawpha in Mississippi. Other novels include *The Sound and the Fury* (1929) and *Light in August* (1932): Nobel prize for literature 1949.

fault (fɔːlt) *n* **1** an imperfection; failing or defect; flaw. **2** a mistake or error. **3** an offence; misdeed. **4** responsibility for a mistake or misdeed; culpability. **5** *Electronics.* a defect in a circuit, component, or line, such as a short circuit. **6** *Geology.* a fracture in the earth's crust resulting in the relative displacement and loss of continuity of the rocks on either side of it. **7** *Tennis, squash, etc.* an invalid serve, such as one that lands outside a prescribed area. **8** (in showjumping) a penalty mark given for failing to clear or refusing a fence, exceeding a time limit, etc. **9** *Hunting.* an instance of the hounds losing the scent. **10** deficiency; lack; want. **11 at fault. 11a** guilty of error; culpable. **11b** perplexed. **11c** (of hounds) having temporarily lost the scent. **12 find fault (with).** to seek out minor imperfections or errors (in); carp (at). **13 to a fault.** excessively. ◆ *vb* **14** *Geology.* to undergo or cause to undergo a fault. **15** (*tr*) to find a fault in, criticize, or blame. **16** (*intr*) to commit a fault. [C13: from Old French *faute,* from Vulgar Latin *fallita* (unattested), ultimately from Latin *fallere* to fail]

fault-finding *n* **1** continual and usually trivial criticism. **2** the systematic investigation of malfunctions in electronic apparatus. ◆ *adj* **3** given to finding fault. ▸ **ˈfault-ˌfinder** *n*

faultless (ˈfɔːltlɪs) *adj* without fault; perfect or blameless. ▸ **ˈfaultlessly** *adv* ▸ **ˈfaultlessness** *n*

fault line *n* **1** Also called: **fault plane.** *Geology.* the surface of a fault fracture along which the rocks have been displaced. **2** a potentially disruptive division or area of contention: *Europe remains the main fault line in the Tory Party.*

fault tree *n* a diagram providing a model of the interactions between the components of a system when a failure occurs.

faulty (ˈfɔːltɪ) *adj* **faultier, faultiest. 1** defective or imperfect. **2** *Archaic.* culpable. ▸ **ˈfaultily** *adv* ▸ **ˈfaultiness** *n*

faun (fɔːn) *n* (in Roman legend) a rural deity represented as a man with a goat's ears, horns, tail, and hind legs. [C14: back formation from *Faunes* (plural), from Latin FAUNUS] ▸ **ˈfaunˌlike** *adj*

fauna (ˈfɔːnə) *n, pl* **-nas** *or* **-nae** (-niː). **1** all the animal life of a given place or time, esp. when distinguished from the plant life (flora). **2** a descriptive list of such animals. [C18: from New Latin, from Late Latin *Fauna* a goddess, sister of FAUNUS] ▸ **ˈfaunal** *adj* ▸ **ˈfaunally** *adv*

faunula (ˈfɔːnjʊlə) *or* **faunule** (ˈfɔːnjuːl) *n, pl* **-ulae** (-jʊliː) *or* **-ules. 1** the fauna of a small single environment. **2** fossil fauna found in a single stratum or in several thin adjacent strata. [C20: from FAUNA + -ULE]

Faunus (ˈfɔːnəs) *n* an ancient Italian deity of pastures and forests, later identified with the Greek Pan.

faur (fɔːr) *adj* a Scot. word for **far.**

Fauré (ˈfɔːreɪ; *French* fore) *n* **Gabriel** (**Urbain**) (gabriɛl). 1845–1924, French composer and teacher, noted particularly for his song settings of French poems, esp. those of Verlaine, his piano music, and his *Messe de Requiem* (1887).

Faust (faust) *or* **Faustus** (ˈfaustəs) *n German legend.* a magician and alchemist who sells his soul to the devil in exchange for knowledge and power. ▸ **ˈFaustian** *adj*

faut (fɔːt) *n, vb* a Scot. word for **fault.**

faute de mieux *French.* (fot də mjø; *English* fəut də mjɜː) for lack of anything better.

fauteuil (ˈfəutɜːɪ; *French* fotœj) *n* an armchair, the sides of which are not upholstered. [C18: from French, from Old French *faudestuel,* folding chair, of Germanic origin; see FALDSTOOL]

Fauve (*French* fov) *n* **1** one of a group of French painters prominent from 1905, including Matisse, Vlaminck, and Derain, characterized by the use of bright colours and simplified forms. ◆ *adj* **2** (*often not cap.*) of this group or its style. [C20: from French, literally: wild beast, alluding to the violence of colours, etc.] ▸ **ˈFauvism** *n* ▸ **ˈFauvist** *n, adj*

faux-naïf (*French* fonaif) *adj* **1** appearing or seeking to appear simple and unsophisticated: *a faux-naïf narration.* ◆ *n* **2** a person who pretends to be naïve. [French: false naïve]

faux pas (fəʊ pɑː; *French* fo pɑ) *n, pl* **faux pas** (fəʊ pɑːz; *French* fo pɑ). a social blunder or indiscretion. [C17: from French: false step]

favela (fɑːˈvelə) *n* (in Brazil) a shanty or shantytown. [C20: from Portuguese]

faveolate (fəˈviːəˌleɪt) *or* **favose** (ˈfævəus) *adj* pitted with cell-like cavities. [C19: from New Latin *faveolus* a little honeycomb, blend of Latin *favus* honeycomb + *alveolus* a small hollow]

favonian (fəˈvəunɪən) *adj* **1** of or relating to the west wind. **2** *Poetic.* favourable. [C17: from Latin *Favōniānus*]

favorite son *n* (in the U.S.) a politician popular in his home state but little admired beyond it.

favour *or U.S.* **favor** (ˈfeɪvə) *n* **1** an approving attitude; good will. **2** an act performed out of good will, generosity, or mercy. **3** prejudice and partiality; favouritism. **4** a condition of being regarded with approval or good will (esp. in the phrases **in favour, out of favour**). **5** *Archaic.* leave; permission. **6** a token of love, goodwill, etc. **7** a small gift or toy given to a guest at a party. **8** *History.* a badge or ribbon worn or given to indicate loyalty, often bestowed on a knight by a lady. **9** *Obsolete, chiefly Brit.* a communication, esp. a business letter. **10** *Archaic.* appearance. **11 find favour with.** to be approved of by someone. **12 in favour of. 12a** approving. **12b** to the benefit of. **12c** (of a cheque, etc.) made out to. **12d** in order to show preference for: *I rejected him in favour of George.* ◆ *vb* (*tr*) **13** to regard with especial kindness or approval. **14** to treat with partiality or favouritism. **15** to support; advocate. **16** to perform a favour for; oblige. **17** to help; facilitate. **18** *Informal.* to resemble: *he favours his father.* **19** to wear habitually: *she favours red.* **20** to treat gingerly or with tenderness; spare: *a footballer favouring an injured leg.* ◆ See also **favours.** [C14: from Latin, from *favēre* to protect] ▸ **ˈfavourer** *or U.S.* **ˈfavorer** *n* ▸ **ˈfavouringly** *or U.S.* **ˈfavoringly** *adv*

favourable *or U.S.* **favorable** (ˈfeɪvərəbəl, ˈfeɪvrə-) *adj* **1** advantageous, encouraging, or promising. **2** giving consent. ▸ **ˈfavourableness** *or U.S.* **ˈfavorableness** *n* ▸ **ˈfavourably** *or U.S.* **ˈfavorably** *adv*

favourable pressure gradient *n Engineering.* a decrease of pressure in the direction of flow.

-favoured *adj* (*in combination*) having an appearance (as specified): *ill-favoured.*

favourite *or U.S.* **favorite** (ˈfeɪvərɪt, ˈfeɪvrɪt) *adj* **1** (*prenominal*) most liked; preferred above all others. ◆ *n* **2a** a person or thing regarded with especial preference or liking. **2b** (*as modifier*): *a favourite book.* **3** *Sport.* a competitor thought likely to win. [C16: from Italian *favorito,* from *favorire* to favour, from Latin *favēre*]

favouritism *or U.S.* **favoritism** (ˈfeɪvərɪˌtɪzəm, ˈfeɪvrɪ-) *n* **1** the practice of giving special treatment to a person or group. **2** the state of being treated as a favourite.

favours *or U.S.* **favors** (ˈfeɪvəz) *pl n* sexual intimacy, as when consented to by a woman.

Favrile glass (fəˈvriːl) *n* a type of iridescent glass developed by L.C. Tiffany.

favus (ˈfeɪvəs) *n* an infectious fungal skin disease of man and some domestic animals, characterized by formation of a honeycomb-like mass of roundish dry cup-shaped crusts. [C19: from New Latin, from Latin: honeycomb]

Fawcett (ˈfɔːsɪt) *n* Dame **Millicent Garrett.** 1847–1929, British suffragette.

Fawkes (fɔːks) *n* **Guy.** 1570–1606, English conspirator, executed for his part in the Gunpowder Plot to blow up King James I and the Houses of Parliament (1605). Effigies of him (guys) are burnt in Britain on Guy Fawkes Day (Nov. 5).

fawn[1] (fɔːn) *n* **1** a young deer of either sex aged under one year. **2a** a light greyish-brown colour. **2b** (*as adj*): *a fawn raincoat.* **3 in fawn.** (of deer) pregnant. ◆ *vb* **4** (of deer) to bear (young). [C14: from Old French *faon,* from Latin *fētus* offspring; see FETUS] ▸ **ˈfawnˌlike** *adj*

fawn[2] (fɔːn) *vb* (*intr; often foll. by on or upon*) **1** to seek attention and admiration (from) by cringing and flattering. **2** (of animals, esp. dogs) to try to please by a show of extreme friendliness and fondness (towards). [Old English *fægnian* to be glad, from *fægen* glad; see FAIN] ▸ **ˈfawner** *n* ▸ **ˈfawningly** *adv* ▸ **ˈfawningness** *n*

fawn lily *n* another name for **dogtooth violet.**

fax (fæks) *n* **1** Also **fax machine.** short for **facsimile machine. 2** short for **facsimile transmission. 3** a message or document sent by fax. ◆ *vb* **4** (*tr*) to send (a message, document, etc.) by fax.

Fa Xian (ˈfɑː ˈʃjɑːn) *or* **Fa-hsien** *n* original name *Sehi.* 5th century A.D., Chinese Buddhist monk: his pilgrimage to India (399–414) began relations between China and India.

fay[1] (feɪ) *n* **1** a fairy or sprite. ◆ *adj* **2** of or resembling a fay. **3** *Informal.* pretentious or precious. [C14: from Old French *feie,* ultimately from Latin *fātum* FATE]

fay[2] (feɪ) *vb* to fit or be fitted closely or tightly. [Old English *fēgan* to join; related to Old High German *fuogen,* Latin *pangere* to fasten]

fay[3] (feɪ) *n* an obsolete word for **faith.** [C13: from Anglo-French *feid;* see FAITH]

Fayal (*Portuguese* fəˈial) *n* a variant spelling of **Faial.**

fayalite (ˈfeɪəˌlaɪt, faɪˈɑːlaɪt) *n* a rare brown or black mineral of the olivine group, consisting of iron silicate. Formula: Fe_2SiO_4. [C19: named after FAYAL]

Fayum (faɪˈjuːm) *n* See **El Faiyûm.**

faze (feɪz) *vb* (*tr*) to disconcert; worry; disturb. [C19: variant of FEEZE]

FBA *abbrev. for* Fellow of the British Academy.

FBI (in the U.S.) *abbrev. for* Federal Bureau of Investigation; an agency of the Justice Department responsible for investigating violations of Federal laws.

FBW *Aeronautics. abbrev. for* fly-by-wire.

fc *Printing. abbrev. for* follow copy.

FC (in Britain) *abbrev. for* Football Club.

FCA (in Britain) *abbrev. for* Fellow of the Institute of Chartered Accountants.

fcap *abbrev. for* foolscap.

FCC (in the U.S.) *abbrev. for* Federal Communications Commission.

FCCA (in Britain) *abbrev. for* Fellow of the Chartered Association of Certified Accountants.

FCII (in Britain) *abbrev. for* Fellow of the Chartered Insurance Institute.

F clef *n* another name for **bass clef.**

FCO *abbrev. for* Foreign and Commonwealth Office.

FD *abbrev. for* Fidei Defensor. [Latin: Defender of the Faith]

F distribution *n Statistics.* a continuous distribution obtained from the ratio of two chi-square distributions and used esp. to test the equality of the variances of two normally distributed variances.

fdm *abbrev. for* frequency-division multiplex. See **multiplex.**

FDP *abbrev. for* Freie Demokratische Partei. [German: Free Democratic Party]

FDR *abbrev. for* Franklin Delano Roosevelt.

Fe *the chemical symbol for* iron. [from New Latin *ferrum*]

feal (fiːl) *adj* an archaic word for **faithful.** [C16: from Old French *feeil,* from Latin *fidēlis*]

fealty (ˈfiːəltɪ) *n, pl* **-ties.** (in feudal society) the loyalty sworn to one's lord on becoming his vassal. See **homage** (sense 2). [C14: from Old French *fealte,* from Latin *fidēlitās* FIDELITY]

fear (fɪə) *n* **1** a feeling of distress, apprehension, or alarm caused by impending danger, pain, etc. **2** a cause of this feeling. **3** awe; reverence: *fear of God.* **4** concern; anxiety. **5** possibility; chance: *there is no fear of that happening.* **6 for fear of, that** *or* **lest.** to forestall or avoid. **7 no fear.** certainly not. **8 put the fear of God into.** to frighten. ◆ *vb* **9** to be afraid (to do something) or of (a person or thing); dread. **10** (*tr*) to revere; respect. **11** (*tr; takes a clause as object*) to be sorry: used to lessen the effect of an unpleasant statement: *I fear that you have not won.* **12** (*intr;* foll. by *for*) to feel anxiety about something. **13** an archaic word for **frighten.** [Old English *fǣr;* related to Old High German *fāra,* Old Norse *fār* hostility, Latin *perīculum* danger] ▸ **ˈfearer** *n* ▸ **ˈfearless** *adj* ▸ **ˈfearlessly** *adv* ▸ **ˈfearlessness** *n*

fearful (ˈfɪəfʊl) *adj* **1** having fear; afraid. **2** causing fear; frightening. **3** *Informal.* very unpleasant or annoying: *a fearful cold.* ▸ **ˈfearfulness** *n*

fearfully (ˈfɪəfʊlɪ) *adv* **1** in a fearful manner. **2** (intensifier): *you're fearfully kind.*

fearnought *or* **fearnaught** (ˈfɪəˌnɔːt) *n* **1** a heavy woollen fabric. **2** a coat made of such fabric.

fearsome ('fɪəsəm) *adj* **1** frightening. **2** timorous; afraid. ▸ **'fearsomely** *adv* ▸ **'fearsomeness** *n*

feasibility study *n* a study designed to determine the practicability of a system or plan.

feasible ('fi:zəbᵊl) *adj* **1** able to be done or put into effect; possible. **2** likely; probable: *a feasible excuse.* [C15: from Anglo-French *faisable,* from *faire* to do, from Latin *facere*] ▸ **,feasi'bility** *or* **'feasibleness** *n* ▸ **'feasibly** *adv*

feast (fi:st) *n* **1** a large and sumptuous meal, usually given as an entertainment for several people. **2** a periodic religious celebration. **3** something extremely pleasing or sumptuous: *a feast for the eyes.* **4 movable feast.** a festival or other event of variable date. ◆ *vb* **5** (*intr*) **5a** to eat a feast. **5b** (usually foll. by *on*) to enjoy the eating (of), as if feasting: *to feast on cakes.* **6** (*tr*) to give a feast to. **7** (*intr;* foll. by *on*) to take great delight (in): *to feast on beautiful paintings.* **8** (*tr*) to regale or delight: *to feast one's mind or one's eyes.* [C13: from Old French *feste,* from Latin *festa,* neuter plural (later assumed to be feminine singular) of *festus* joyful; related to Latin *fānum* temple, *fēriae* festivals] ▸ **'feaster** *n*

Feast of Dedication *n Judaism.* a literal translation of **Chanukah.**

Feast of Lanterns *n* **1** *Hinduism.* another name for **Diwali. 2** Also called: **Festival of Lanterns.** *Japanese Buddhism.* another name for **Bon**[1].

Feast of Lights *n Judaism.* an English name for **Chanukah.**

Feast of Tabernacles *n Judaism.* a literal translation of **Sukkoth.**

Feast of Weeks *n Judaism.* a literal translation of **Shavuot.**

feat[1] (fi:t) *n* a remarkable, skilful, or daring action; exploit; achievement: *feats of strength.* [C14: from Anglo-French *fait,* from Latin *factum* deed; see FACT]

feat[2] (fi:t) *adj Archaic.* **1** another word for **skilful. 2** another word for **neat**[1] or **suitable.** [C14: from Old French *fet,* from Latin *factus* made, from *facere* to make] ▸ **'featly** *adv*

feather ('fɛðə) *n* **1** any of the flat light waterproof epidermal structures forming the plumage of birds, each consisting of a hollow shaft having a vane of barbs on either side. They are essential for flight and help maintain body temperature. **2** something resembling a feather, such as a tuft of hair or grass. **3** *Archery.* **3a** a bird's feather or artificial substitute fitted to an arrow to direct its flight. **3b** the feathered end of an arrow, opposite the head. **4** a strip, spline, or tongue of wood fitted into a groove. **5** the wake created on the surface of the water by the raised periscope of a submarine. **6** *Rowing.* the position of an oar turned parallel to the water between strokes. Compare **square** (sense 8). **7** a step in ballroom dancing in which a couple maintain the conventional hold but dance side by side. **8** condition of spirits; fettle: *in fine feather.* **9** something of negligible value; jot: *I don't care a feather.* **10 birds of a feather.** people of the same type, character, or interests. **11 feather in one's cap.** a cause for pleasure at one's achievements: *your promotion is a feather in your cap.* **12 not take** *or* **knock a feather out of (someone).** *Irish.* to fail to upset or injure (someone): *it didn't take a feather out of him.* ◆ *vb* **13** (*tr*) to fit, cover, or supply with feathers. **14** *Rowing.* to turn (an oar) parallel to the water during recovery between strokes, principally in order to lessen wind resistance. Compare **square** (sense 41). **15** (in canoeing) to turn (a paddle) parallel to the direction of the canoe between strokes, while keeping it in the water, principally in order to move silently. **16** to change the pitch of (an aircraft propeller) so that the chord lines of the blades are in line with the airflow. **17** (*tr*) to join (two boards) by means of a tongue-and-groove joint. **18** (*intr*) (of a bird) to grow feathers. **19** (*intr*) to move or grow like feathers. **20 feather one's nest.** to provide oneself with comforts, esp. financial. ◆ See also **feathers.** [Old English *fether;* related to Old Frisian *fethere,* Old Norse *fjöthr* feather, Old High German *fedara* wing, Greek *petesthai* to fly, Sanskrit *patati* he flies] ▸ **'featherless** *adj* ▸ **'feather-,like** *adj* ▸ **'feathery** *adj*

feather bed *n* **1** a mattress filled with feathers or down. ◆ *vb* **featherbed, -beds, -bedding, -bedded. 2** (*tr*) to pamper; spoil. **3** (*intr*) *U.S.* to be subject to or engage in featherbedding.

featherbedding ('fɛðə,bɛdɪŋ) *n* the practice of limiting production, duplicating work, or overmanning, esp. in accordance with a union contract, in order to prevent redundancies or create jobs.

featherbrain ('fɛðə,breɪn) *or* **featherhead** *n* a frivolous or forgetful person. ▸ **'feather,brained** *or* **'feather,headed** *adj*

featheredge ('fɛðər,ɛdʒ) *n* a board or plank that tapers to a thin edge at one side. ▸ **'feather,edged** *adj*

feather grass *n* a perennial grass, *Stipa pennata,* native to the steppes of Europe and N Asia, cultivated as an ornament for its feathery inflorescence.

feathering ('fɛðərɪŋ) *n* **1** the plumage of a bird; feathers. **2** another word for **feathers** (sense 2). **3** *Printing.* **3a** an imperfection in print caused by the spreading of ink. **3b** the use of additional space between lines in typesetting in order to fill the page.

feather palm *n* any of various palm trees, such as the wax palm and date palm, that have pinnate or feather-like leaves. Compare **fan palm.**

feathers ('fɛðəz) *pl n* **1** the plumage of a bird. **2** Also called: **feathering.** the long hair on the legs or tail of certain breeds of horses and dogs. **3** *Informal.* dress; attire: *her best feathers.* **4 ruffle feathers.** to cause upset or offence.

feather star *n* any free-swimming crinoid echinoderm of the genus *Antedon* and related genera, living on muddy sea bottoms and having ten feathery arms radiating from a small central disc.

featherstitch ('fɛðə,stɪtʃ) *n* **1** a zigzag embroidery stitch. ◆ *vb* **2** to decorate (cloth) with featherstitch.

feather-veined *adj* (of a leaf) having a network of veins branching from the midrib to the margin.

featherweight ('fɛðə,weɪt) *n* **1a** something very light or of little importance. **1b** (*as modifier*): *featherweight considerations.* **2a** a professional boxer weighing 118–126 pounds (53.5–57 kg). **2b** an amateur boxer weighing 54–57 kg (119–126 pounds). **2c** (*as modifier*): *the featherweight challenger.* **3** a wrestler in a similar weight category (usually 126–139 pounds (57–63 kg)).

featly ('fi:tlɪ) *adv Archaic.* **1** neatly. **2** fitly. ▸ **'featliness** *n*

feature ('fi:tʃə) *n* **1** any one of the parts of the face, such as the nose, chin, or mouth. **2** a prominent or distinctive part or aspect, as of a landscape, building, book, etc. **3** the principal film in a programme at a cinema. **4** an item or article appearing regularly in a newspaper, magazine, etc.: *a gardening feature.* **5** Also called: **feature story.** a prominent story in a newspaper, etc.: *a feature on prison reform.* **6** a programme given special prominence on radio or television as indicated by attendant publicity. **7** an article offered for sale as a special attraction, as in a large retail establishment. **8** *Archaic.* general form or make-up. **9** *Linguistics.* a quality of a linguistic unit at some level of description: *grammatical feature; semantic feature.* ◆ *vb* **10** (*tr*) to have as a feature or make a feature of. **11** to give prominence to (an actor, famous event, etc.) in a film or (of an actor, etc.) to have prominence in a film. **12** (*tr*) *U.S. informal.* to imagine; consider: *I can't feature that happening.* [C14: from Anglo-French *feture,* from Latin *factūra* a making, from *facere* to make]

-featured *adj* (*in combination*) having features as specified: *heavy-featured.*

feature-length *adj* (of a film or programme) similar in extent to a feature although not classed as such.

featureless ('fi:tʃəlɪs) *adj* without distinctive points or qualities; undistinguished. ▸ **'featurelessness** *n*

feaze[1] (fi:z) *vb Nautical.* to make or become unravelled or frayed. [C16: perhaps from obsolete Dutch *vese* fringe, from Middle Dutch *vese, veze* fringe; related to Old English *fæs*]

feaze[2] (fi:z) *vb, n* a variant of **feeze** or **faze.**

Feb. *abbrev. for* February.

febri- *combining form.* indicating fever: *febrifuge.* [from Latin *febris* fever]

febricity (fɪ'brɪsɪtɪ) *n Rare.* the condition of having a fever. [C19: from Medieval Latin *febricitās,* from Latin *febris* fever]

febrifacient (,fɛbrɪ'feɪʃənt) *adj* **1** producing fever. ◆ *n* **2** something that produces fever.

febrific (fɪ'brɪfɪk) *or* **febriferous** *adj* causing or having a fever.

febrifuge ('fɛbrɪ,fju:dʒ) *n* **1** any drug or agent for reducing fever. ◆ *adj* **2** serving to reduce fever. [C17: from Medieval Latin *febrifugia* feverfew; see FEBRI-, -FUGE] ▸ **febrifugal** (fɪ'brɪfjʊgᵊl, ,fɛbrɪ'fju:gᵊl) *adj*

febrile ('fi:braɪl) *adj* of or relating to fever; feverish. [C17: from medical Latin *febrīlis,* from Latin *febris* fever] ▸ **febrility** (fɪ'brɪlɪtɪ) *n*

February ('fɛbrʊərɪ) *n, pl* **-aries.** the second month of the year, consisting of 28 or (in a leap year) 29 days. [C13: from Latin *Februārius mēnsis* month of expiation, from *februa* Roman festival of purification held on February 15, from plural of *februum* a purgation]

February Revolution *n* another name for the **Russian Revolution** (sense 1).

fec. *abbrev. for* fecit.

fecal ('fi:kᵊl) *adj* the usual U.S. spelling of **faecal.**

feces ('fi:si:z) *pl n* the usual U.S. spelling of **faeces.**

Fechner (*German* 'fɛçnər) *n* **Gustav Theodor** ('gʊstaf 'te:odo:r). 1801–87, German physicist, philosopher, and psychologist, noted particularly for his work on psychophysics, *Elemente der Psychophysik* (1860).

fecht (fɛxt) *vb, n* a Scot. word for **fight.** ▸ **'fechter** *n*

fecit *Latin.* ('feɪkɪt) (he or she) made it: used formerly on works of art next to the artist's name. Abbrev.: **fec.**

feck (fɛk) *n Scot. obsolete.* **a** worth; value. **b** amount; quantity. **c** the greater part; the majority. [C15 (Scottish dialect) *fek,* short for EFFECT]

feckless ('fɛklɪs) *adj* feeble; weak; ineffectual; irresponsible. [C16: from obsolete *feck* value, effect + -LESS] ▸ **'fecklessly** *adv* ▸ **'fecklessness** *n*

fecula ('fɛkjʊlə) *n, pl* **-lae** (-,li:). **1** starch obtained by washing the crushed parts of plants, such as the potato. **2** faecal material, esp. of insects. [C17: from Latin: burnt tartar, appearing as a crust in wine, from *faex* sediment]

feculent ('fɛkjʊlənt) *adj* **1** filthy, scummy, muddy, or foul. **2** of the nature of or containing waste matter. [C15: from Latin *faeculentus;* see FAECES] ▸ **'feculence** *n*

fecund ('fi:kənd, 'fɛk-) *adj* **1** greatly productive; fertile. **2** intellectually productive; prolific. [C14: from Latin *fēcundus;* related to Latin *fētus* offspring]

fecundate ('fi:kən,deɪt, 'fɛk-) *vb* (*tr*) **1** to make fruitful. **2** to fertilize; impregnate. [C17: from Latin *fēcundāre* to fertilize] ▸ **,fecun'dation** *n* ▸ **'fecun,dator** *n* ▸ **fecundatory** (fɪ'kʌndətərɪ, -trɪ) *adj*

fecundity (fɪ'kʌndɪtɪ) *n* **1** fertility; fruitfulness. **2** intellectual fruitfulness; creativity.

fed[1] (fɛd) *vb* **1** the past tense and past participle of **feed. 2 fed to death** *or* **fed (up) to the (back) teeth.** *Informal.* bored or annoyed.

fed[2] (fɛd) *n U.S. slang.* an agent of the FBI.

Fed. *or* **fed.** *abbrev. for:* **1** Federal. **2** Federation. **3** Federated.

fedayee (fə'dɑ:ji:) *n, pl* **-yeen** (-ji:n). (*sometimes cap.*) (in Arab states) a commando, esp. one fighting against Israel. [from Arabic *fidā'i* one who risks his life in a cause, from *fidā'* redemption]

federal ('fɛdərəl) *adj* **1** of or relating to a form of government or a country in which power is divided between one central and several regional governments. **2** of or relating to a treaty between provinces, states, etc., that establishes a political unit in which power is so divided. **3** of or relating to the central government of a federation. **4** of or relating to any union or association of parties or groups that retain some autonomy. **5** (of a university) comprised of relatively independent colleges. ◆ *n* **6** a supporter of federal union or federation. [C17: from Latin *foedus* league] ▸ **'federally** *adv*

Federal ('fɛdərəl) *adj* **1a** of or relating to the Federalist party or Federalism. **1b** characteristic of or supporting the Union government during the American Civil War. ◆ *n* **2a** a supporter of the Union government during the American Civil War. **2b** a Federalist.

Federal Bureau of Investigation *n* See **FBI.**

federal district *or* **territory** *n* an area used as the seat of central government in a federal system.

Federal Government *n* the national government of a federated state, such as that of Australia located in Canberra.

federalism ('fɛdərəˌlɪzəm) *n* **1** the principle or a system of federal union. **2** advocacy of federal union. ▸ **'federalist** *n, adj* ▸ **ˌfederal'istic** *adj*

Federalism ('fɛdərəˌlɪzəm) *n U.S. history.* the principles and policies of the Federalist party.

Federalist ('fɛdərəlɪst) *U.S. history.* ◆ *n* **1** a supporter or member of the Federalist party. ◆ *adj also* ˌ**Federal'istic. 2** characteristic of the Federalists.

Federalist Party *or* **Federal Party** *n* the American political party founded in 1787 and led initially by Alexander Hamilton. It took an active part in the shaping of the U.S. Constitution and thereafter favoured strong centralized government and business interests.

federalize *or* **federalise** ('fɛdərəˌlaɪz) *vb* (*tr*) **1** to unite in a federation or federal union; federate. **2** to subject to federal control. ▸ **ˌfederali'zation** *or* **ˌfederali'sation** *n*

Federal Republic of Germany *n* the official name of **Germany**, formerly of West Germany.

Federal Reserve note *n* a bank note issued by the Federal Reserve Banks and now serving as the prevailing paper currency in circulation in the U.S.

Federal Reserve System *n* (in the U.S.) a banking system consisting of twelve **Federal Reserve Districts**, each containing member banks regulated and served by a **Federal Reserve Bank**. It operates under the supervision of the **Federal Reserve Board** and performs functions similar to those of the Bank of England.

federate *vb* ('fɛdəˌreɪt). **1** to unite or cause to unite in a federal union. ◆ *adj* ('fɛdərɪt). **2** federal; federated. ▸ **'federative** *adj*

Federated Malay States *pl n* See **Malay States.**

federation (ˌfɛdə'reɪʃən) *n* **1** the act of federating. **2** the union of several provinces, states, etc., to form a federal union. **3** a political unit formed in such a way. **4** any league, alliance, or confederacy. **5** a union of several parties, groups, etc. **6** any association or union for common action.

Federation (ˌfɛdə'reɪʃən) *n Austral.* **1 the.** the federation of the Australian colonies in 1901. **2** a style of domestic architecture of that period, characterized by red brick, terracotta roof tiles, sinuous curves, and heavy window frames.

Federation of Rhodesia and Nyasaland *n* a federation (1953–63) of Northern Rhodesia, Southern Rhodesia, and Nyasaland.

Federation wheat *n Austral.* an early-maturing drought-resistant variety of wheat developed by William Farrar in 1902.

fedora (fɪ'dɔːrə) *n* a soft felt or velvet medium-brimmed hat, usually with a band. [C19: allegedly named after *Fédora* (1882), play by Victorien Sardou (1831–1908)]

fed up *adj* (*usually postpositive*) *Informal.* annoyed, discontented, or bored: *I'm fed up with your conduct.*

fee (fiː) *n* **1** a payment asked by professional people or public servants for their services: *a doctor's fee; school fees.* **2** a charge made for a privilege: *an entrance fee.* **3** *Property law.* **3a** an interest in land capable of being inherited. See **fee simple, fee tail. 3b** the land held in fee. **4** (in feudal Europe) the land granted by a lord to his vassal. **5** an obsolete word for a **gratuity. 6 in fee. 6a** *Law.* (of land) in absolute ownership. **6b** *Archaic.* in complete subjection. ◆ *vb* **fees, feeing, feed. 7** *Rare.* to give a fee to. **8** *Chiefly Scot.* to hire for a fee. [**C14:** from Old French *fie*, of Germanic origin; see FIEF] ▸ **'feeless** *adj*

feeble ('fiːbəl) *adj* **1** lacking in physical or mental strength; frail; weak. **2** inadequate; unconvincing: *feeble excuses.* **3** easily influenced or indecisive. [**C12:** from Old French *feble, fleible*, from Latin *flēbilis* to be lamented, from *flēre* to weep] ▸ **'feebleness** *n* ▸ **'feebly** *adv*

feeble-minded *adj* **1** lacking in intelligence; stupid. **2** mentally defective. **3** lacking decision; irresolute. ▸ **ˌfeeble-'mindedly** *adv* ▸ **ˌfeeble-'mindedness** *n*

feed (fiːd) *vb* **feeds, feeding, fed** (fɛd). (*mainly tr*) **1** to give food to: *to feed the cat.* **2** to give as food: *to feed meat to the cat.* **3** (*intr*) to eat food: *the horses feed at noon.* **4** to provide food for: *these supplies can feed 10 million people.* **5** to provide what is necessary for the existence or development of: *to feed one's imagination.* **6** to gratify; satisfy: *to feed one's eyes on a beautiful sight.* **7** (*also intr*) to supply (a machine, furnace, etc.) with (the necessary materials or fuel) for its operation, or (of such materials) to flow or move forwards into a machine, etc. **8** to use (land) as grazing. **9** *Theatre, informal.* to cue (an actor, esp. a comedian) with lines or actions. **10** *Sport.* to pass a ball to (a teammate). **11** *Electronics.* to introduce (electrical energy) into a circuit, esp. by means of a feeder. **12** (*also intr*; foll. by *on* or *upon*) to eat or cause to eat. ◆ *n* **13** the act or an instance of feeding. **14** food, esp. that of animals or babies. **15** the process of supplying a machine or furnace with a material or fuel. **16** the quantity of material or fuel so supplied. **17** the rate of advance of a cutting tool in a lathe, drill, etc. **18** a mechanism that supplies material or fuel or controls the rate of advance of a cutting tool. **19** *Theatre, informal.* a performer, esp. a straight man, who provides cues. **20** an informal word for **meal**[1]. [Old English *fēdan*; related to Old Norse *fœtha* to feed, Old High German *fuotan*, Gothic *fōthjan*; see FOOD, FODDER] ▸ **'feedable** *adj*

feedback ('fiːdˌbæk) *n* **1a** the return of part of the output of an electronic circuit, device, or mechanical system to its input, so modifying its characteristics. In **negative feedback** a rise in output energy reduces the input energy; in **positive feedback** an increase in output energy reinforces the input energy. **1b** that part of the output signal fed back into the input. **2** the return of part of the sound output by a loudspeaker to the microphone or pick-up so that a high-pitched whistle is produced. **3** the whistling noise so produced. **4a** the effect of a product or action in a cyclic biological reaction on another stage in the same reaction. **4b** the substance or reaction causing such an effect, such as the release of a hormone in a biochemical pathway. **5** information in response to an inquiry, experiment, etc.: *there was little feedback from our questionnaire.* ◆ *vb* **feed back.** (*adv*) **6** (*tr*) to return (part of the output of a system) to its input. **7** to offer or suggest (information, ideas, etc.) in reaction to an inquiry, experiment, etc.

feedbag ('fiːdˌbæg) *n* **1** any bag in which feed for livestock is sacked. **2** the usual U.S. and Canadian name for **nosebag.**

feeder ('fiːdə) *n* **1** a person or thing that feeds or is fed. **2** a child's feeding bottle or bib. **3** *Agriculture, chiefly U.S. and Canadian.* a head of livestock being fattened for slaughter. **4** a person or device that feeds the working material into a system or machine. **5** a tributary channel. **6a** a road, service, etc., that links secondary areas to the main traffic network. **6b** (*as modifier*): *a feeder bus.* **7a** a transmission line connecting an aerial to a transmitter or receiver. **7b** a power line for transmitting electrical power from a generating station to a distribution network.

feeding bottle *n* a bottle fitted with a rubber teat from which infants or young animals suck liquids. Also called: **nursing bottle.**

feeding frenzy *n* **1** a phenomenon in which fish, esp. sharks, become so excited when eating that they attack each other. **2** a period of intense excitement over or interest in a person or thing: *the media erupt into a feeding frenzy.*

feedlot ('fiːdˌlɒt) *n* an area or building where livestock are fattened rapidly for market.

feedstock ('fiːdˌstɒk) *n* the main raw material used in the manufacture of a product.

feedthrough ('fiːdˌθruː) *n Electronics.* a conductor used to connect two sides of a part, such as a printed circuit board.

feedwater ('fiːdˌwɔːtə) *n* water, previously purified to prevent scale deposit or corrosion, that is fed to boilers for steam generation.

feel (fiːl) *vb* **feels, feeling, felt** (fɛlt). **1** to perceive (something) by touching. **2** to have a physical or emotional sensation of (something): *to feel heat; to feel anger.* **3** (*tr*) to examine (something) by touch. **4** (*tr*) to find (one's way) by testing or cautious exploration. **5** (*copula*) to seem or appear in respect of the sensation given: *I feel tired; it feels warm.* **6** to have an indistinct, esp. emotional conviction; sense (esp. in the phrase **feel in one's bones**). **7** (*intr*; foll. by *for*) to show sympathy or compassion (towards): *I feel for you in your sorrow.* **8** to believe, think, or be of the opinion (that): *he feels he must resign.* **9** (*tr; often foll. by up*) *Slang.* to pass one's hands over the sexual organs of. **10 feel like.** to have an inclination (for something or doing something): *I don't feel like going to the pictures.* **11 feel (quite) oneself.** to be fit and sure of oneself. **12 feel up to.** (*usually used with a negative or in a question*) to be fit enough for (something or doing something): *I don't feel up to going out tonight.* ◆ *n* **13** the act or an instance of feeling, esp. by touching. **14** the quality of or an impression from something perceived through feeling: *the house has a homely feel about it.* **15** the sense of touch: *the fabric is rough to the feel.* **16** an instinctive aptitude; knack: *she's got a feel for this sort of work.* [Old English *fēlan*; related to Old High German *fuolen*, Old Norse *fālma* to grope, Latin *palma* PALM[1]]

feeler ('fiːlə) *n* **1** a person or thing that feels. **2** an organ in certain animals, such as an antenna or tentacle, that is sensitive to touch. **3** a remark designed to probe the reactions or intentions of other people.

feeler gauge *n* a thin metal strip of known thickness used to measure a narrow gap or to set a gap between two parts.

feel-good *adj* causing or characterized by a feeling of self-satisfaction: *feel-good factor.*

feeling ('fiːlɪŋ) *n* **1** the sense of touch. **2a** the ability to experience physical sensations, such as heat, pain, etc. **2b** the sensation so experienced. **3** a state of mind. **4** a physical or mental impression: *a feeling of warmth.* **5** fondness; sympathy: *to have a great deal of feeling for someone.* **6** an ability to feel deeply: *a person of feeling.* **7** a sentiment: *a feeling that the project is feasible.* **8** an impression or mood; atmosphere: *the feeling of a foreign city.* **9** an emotional disturbance, esp. anger or dislike: *a lot of bad feeling about the increase in taxes.* **10** intuitive appreciation and understanding: *a feeling for words.* **11** sensibility in the performance of something. **12** (*pl*) emotional or moral sensitivity, as in relation to principles or personal dignity (esp. in the phrase **hurt** or **injure the feelings of**). ◆ *adj* **13** sentient; sensitive. **14** expressing or containing emotion. **15** warm-hearted; sympathetic. ▸ **'feelingly** *adv*

fee simple *n Property law.* an absolute interest in land over which the holder has complete freedom of disposition during his life. Compare **fee tail.** [**C15:** from Anglo-French: fee (or fief) simple]

feet (fiːt) *n* **1** the plural of **foot. 2 at (someone's) feet.** as someone's disciple. **3 be run** *or* **rushed off one's feet.** to be very busy. **4 carry** *or* **sweep off one's feet.** to fill with enthusiasm. **5 feet of clay.** a weakness that is not widely known. **6 get one's feet wet.** to begin to participate in something. **7 have** (*or* **keep**) **one's feet on the ground.** to be practical and reliable. **8 on one's** *or* **its feet. 8a** standing up. **8b** in good health. **8c** (of a business, company, etc.) thriving. **9 put one's feet up.** to rest. **10 stand on one's own feet.** to be independent. ▸ **'feetless** *adj*

fee tail *n Property law.* **a** a freehold interest in land restricted to a particular line of heirs. **b** an estate in land subject to such restriction. Compare **fee simple.** [**C15:** from Anglo-French *fee tailé* fee (or fief) determined, from *taillier* to cut]

feeze *or* **feaze** (fiːz) *Dialect.* ◆ *vb* **1** (*tr*) to beat. **2** to drive off. **3** *Chiefly U.S.* to disconcert; worry. ◆ *n* **4** a rush. **5** *Chiefly U.S.* a state of agitation. [Old English *fēsian*]

feign (feɪn) *vb* **1** to put on a show of (a quality or emotion); pretend: *to feign innocence.* **2** (*tr*) to make up; invent: *to feign an excuse.* **3** (*tr*) to copy; imitate: *to feign someone's laugh.* [**C13:** from Old French *feindre* to pretend, from Latin *fingere* to form, shape, invent] ▸ **'feigner** *n* ▸ **'feigningly** *adv*

feijoa (fiː'dʒəʊə) *n* **1** an evergreen shrub, *Feijoa sellowiana*, of South America. **2**

the fruit of this shrub. [C19: from New Latin, named after J. da Silva *Feijo,* 19th-century Spanish botanist]

Feininger ('faɪnɪŋə) *n* **Lyonel.** 1871–1956, U.S. artist, who worked at the Bauhaus, noted for his use of superimposed translucent planes of colour.

feint[1] (feɪnt) *n* **1** a mock attack or movement designed to distract an adversary, as in a military manoeuvre or in boxing, fencing, etc. **2** a misleading action or appearance. ◆ *vb* **3** (*intr*) to make a feint. [C17: from French *feinte,* from *feint* pretended, from Old French *feindre* to FEIGN]

feint[2] (feɪnt) *n Printing.* the narrowest rule used in the production of ruled paper. [C19: variant of FAINT]

feints *or* **faints** (feɪnts) *pl n* the leavings of the second distillation of Scotch malt whisky.

Feisal ('faɪsᵊl) *n* a variant spelling of **Faisal.**

feisty ('faɪstɪ) *adj* **feistier, feistiest.** *Informal.* **1** lively, resilient, and self-reliant. **2** *U.S. and Canadian.* frisky. **3** *U.S. and Canadian.* irritable. [C19: from dialect *feist, fist* small dog; related to Old English *fīsting* breaking wind]

felafel (fəl'ɑːfəl) *n* a variant spelling of **falafel.**

feldsher, feldscher, *or* **feldschar** ('fɛldʃə) *n* (in Russia) a medical doctor's assistant. [C19: Russian, from German *Feldscher* a field surgeon, from *Feld* field + *Scherer* surgeon, from *scheren* to shear]

feldspar ('fɛldˌspɑː, 'fɛlˌspɑː) *or* **felspar** *n* any of a group of hard rock-forming minerals consisting of aluminium silicates of potassium, sodium, calcium, or barium: the principal constituents of igneous rocks. The group includes orthoclase, microcline, and the plagioclase minerals. [C18: from German *feldspat(h),* from *feld* field + *spat(h)* SPAR[3]] ▸ **feldspathic** (fɛld'spæθɪk, fɛl'spæθ-), **'feldspathˌose** *or* **fel'spathic, 'felspathˌose** *adj*

feldspathoid ('fɛldspəˌθɔɪd) *n* any of a group of rock-forming minerals, such as leucite and sodalite, that are similar to feldspars but contain less silica.

felicific (ˌfiːlɪ'sɪfɪk) *adj* making or tending to make happy. [C19: from Latin *fēlix* happy + *facere* to make]

felicitate (fɪ'lɪsɪˌteɪt) *vb* to wish joy to; congratulate. ▸ **fe'liciˌtator** *n*

felicitation (fɪˌlɪsɪ'teɪʃən) *n* a less common word for **congratulation.**

felicitous (fɪ'lɪsɪtəs) *adj* **1** well-chosen; apt. **2** possessing an agreeable style. **3** producing or marked by happiness. ▸ **fe'licitously** *adv* ▸ **fe'licitousness** *n*

felicity (fɪ'lɪsɪtɪ) *n, pl* **-ties. 1** happiness; joy. **2** a cause of happiness. **3** an appropriate expression or style. **4** the quality or display of such expressions or style. **5** *Philosophy.* appropriateness (of a speech act). The performative *I appoint you ambassador* can only possess felicity if uttered by one in whom the authority for such appointments is vested. [C14: from Latin *fēlīcitās* happiness, from *fēlix* happy]

feline ('fiːlaɪn) *adj* **1** of, relating to, or belonging to the *Felidae,* a family of predatory mammals, including cats, lions, leopards, and cheetahs, typically having a round head and retractile claws: order *Carnivora* (carnivores). **2** resembling or suggestive of a cat, esp. in stealth or grace. ◆ *n also* **felid** ('fiːlɪd). **3** any animal belonging to the family *Felidae;* a cat. [C17: from Latin *fēlīnus,* from *fēlēs* cat] ▸ **'felinely** *adv* ▸ **'felineness** *or* **felinity** (fɪ'lɪnɪtɪ) *n*

Felixstowe ('fiːlɪkˌstəʊ) *n* a port and resort in E England, in Suffolk: ferry connections to Rotterdam and Zeebrugge. Pop.: 28 606 (1991).

fell[1] (fɛl) *vb* the past tense of **fall.**

fell[2] (fɛl) *vb* (*tr*) **1** to cut or knock down: *to fell a tree; to fell an opponent.* **2** *Needlework.* to fold under and sew flat (the edges of a seam). ◆ *n* **3** *U.S. and Canadian.* the timber felled in one season. **4** a seam finished by felling. [Old English *fellan;* related to Old Norse *fella,* Old High German *fellen;* see FALL] ▸ **'fellable** *adj*

fell[3] (fɛl) *adj* **1** *Archaic.* cruel or fierce; terrible. **2** *Archaic.* destructive or deadly: *a fell disease.* **3 one fell swoop.** a single hasty action or occurrence. [C13 *fel,* from Old French: cruel, from Medieval Latin *fellō* villain; see FELON[1]] ▸ **'fellness** *n*

fell[4] (fɛl) *n* an animal skin or hide. [Old English; related to Old High German *fel* skin, Old Norse *berfjall* bearskin, Latin *pellis* skin; see PEEL[1]]

fell[5] (fɛl) *n* (*often pl*) *Northern English and Scot.* **a** a mountain, hill, or tract of upland moor. **b** (*in combination*): *fell-walking.* [C13: from Old Norse *fjall;* related to Old High German *felis* rock]

fella ('fɛlə) *n* a nonstandard variant of **fellow.**

fellah ('fɛlə) *n, pl* **fellahs, fellahin,** *or* **fellaheen** (ˌfɛlə'hiːn). a peasant in Arab countries. [C18: from Arabic, dialect variant of *fallāh,* from *falaha* to cultivate]

fellate (fɛ'leɪt, fɪ-) *vb* (*tr*) to perform fellatio on (a person). [C20: back formation from FELLATIO]

fellatio (fɪ'leɪʃɪəʊ, fɛ-) *or* **fellation** *n* a sexual activity in which the penis is stimulated by the partner's mouth. Compare **cunnilingus.** [C19: New Latin, from Latin *fellāre* to suck] ▸ **fel'lator** *n* ▸ **fel'latrix** *fem n*

feller[1] ('fɛlə) *n* **1** a person or thing that fells. **2** an attachment on a sewing machine for felling seams.

feller[2] ('fɛlə) *n* a nonstandard variant of **fellow.**

Felling ('fɛlɪŋ) *n* a town in NE England, in Gateshead unitary authority, Tyne and Wear; formerly noted for coal mining. Pop.: 35 053 (1991).

Fellini (*Italian* fel'liːni) *n* **Federico** (fede'riko). 1920–93, Italian film director. His films include *La Dolce Vita* (1959), *8½* (1963), *Satyricon* (1969), *Intervista* (1987), and *The Voice of the Moon* (1990).

fellmonger ('fɛlˌmʌŋgə) *n* a person who deals in animal skins or hides. ▸ **'fellˌmongering** *or* **'fellˌmongery** *n*

felloe ('fɛləʊ) *or* **felly** ('fɛlɪ) *n, pl* **-loes** *or* **-lies.** a segment or the whole rim of a wooden wheel to which the spokes are attached and onto which a metal tyre is usually shrunk. [Old English *felge;* related to Old High German *felga,* Middle Dutch *velge,* of unknown origin]

fellow ('fɛləʊ) *n* **1** a man or boy. **2** an informal word for **boyfriend. 3** *Informal.* one or oneself: *a fellow has to eat.* **4** a person considered to be of little importance or worth. **5a** (*often pl*) a companion; comrade; associate. **5b** (*as modifier*): *fellow travellers.* **6** (at Oxford and Cambridge universities) a member of the governing body of a college, who is usually a member of the teaching staff. **7** a member of the governing body or established teaching staff at any of various universities or colleges. **8** a postgraduate student employed, esp. for a fixed period, to undertake research and, often, to do some teaching. **9a** a person in the same group, class, or condition: *the surgeon asked his fellows.* **9b** (*as modifier*): *fellow students; a fellow sufferer.* **10** one of a pair; counterpart; mate: *looking for the glove's fellow.* [Old English *fēolaga,* from Old Norse *fēlagi,* one who lays down money, from *fē* money + *lag* a laying down]

Fellow ('fɛləʊ) *n* a member of any of various learned societies: *Fellow of the British Academy.*

fellow feeling *n* **1** mutual sympathy or friendship. **2** an opinion held in common.

fellowship ('fɛləʊˌʃɪp) *n* **1** the state of sharing mutual interests, experiences, activities, etc. **2** a society of people sharing mutual interests, experiences, activities, etc.; club. **3** companionship; friendship. **4** the state or relationship of being a fellow. **5a** mutual trust and charitableness between Christians. **5b** a Church or religious association. **6** *Education.* **6a** a financed research post providing study facilities, privileges, etc., often in return for teaching services. **6b** a foundation endowed to support a postgraduate research student. **6c** an honorary title carrying certain privileges awarded to a postgraduate student. **7** (*often cap.*) the body of fellows in a college, university, etc.

fellow traveller *n* **1** a companion on a journey. **2** a non-Communist who sympathizes with Communism.

felo de se ('fiːləʊ dɪ 'siː, 'fɛləʊ) *n, pl* **felones de se** ('fiːləʊˌniːz dɪ 'siː, 'fɛl-) *or* **felos de se.** *Law.* **a** suicide. **b** a person who commits suicide. [C17: from Anglo-Latin, from *felō* felon + Latin *dē* of + *sē* oneself]

felon[1] ('fɛlən) *n* **1** *Criminal law.* (formerly) a person who has committed a felony. **2** *Obsolete.* a wicked person. ◆ *adj* **3** *Archaic or poetic.* evil; cruel. [C13: from Old French: villain, from Medieval Latin *fellō,* of uncertain origin]

felon[2] ('fɛlən) *n* a purulent inflammation of the end joint of a finger, sometimes affecting the bone. [C12: from Medieval Latin *fellō* sore, perhaps from Latin *fel* poison]

felonious (fɪ'ləʊnɪəs) *adj* **1** *Criminal law.* of, involving, or constituting a felony. **2** *Obsolete.* wicked; base. ▸ **fe'loniously** *adv* ▸ **fe'loniousness** *n*

felonry ('fɛlənrɪ) *n, pl* **-ries. 1** felons collectively. **2** (formerly) the convict population of a penal colony, esp. in Australia.

felony ('fɛlənɪ) *n, pl* **-nies.** *Criminal law.* (formerly) a serious crime, such as murder or arson. All distinctions between felony and misdemeanour were abolished in England and Wales in 1967.

felsite ('fɛlsaɪt) *or* **felstone** ('fɛlˌstəʊn) *n* any fine-grained igneous rock consisting essentially of quartz and feldspar. [C18: FELS(PAR) + -ITE[1]] ▸ **felsitic** (fɛl'sɪtɪk) *adj*

felspar ('fɛlˌspɑː) *n* a variant (esp. Brit.) of **feldspar.** ▸ **felspathic** (fɛl'spæθɪk) *or* **'felspathˌose** *adj*

felt[1] (fɛlt) *vb* the past tense and past participle of **feel.**

felt[2] (fɛlt) *n* **1a** a matted fabric of wool, hair, etc., made by working the fibres together under pressure or by heat or chemical action. **1b** (*as modifier*): *a felt hat.* **2** any material, such as asbestos, made by a similar process of matting. ◆ *vb* **3** (*tr*) to make into or cover with felt. **4** (*intr*) to become matted. [Old English; related to Old Saxon *filt,* Old High German *filz* felt, Latin *pellere* to beat, Greek *pelas* close; see ANVIL, FILTER]

felting ('fɛltɪŋ) *n* **1** felted material; felt. **2** the process of making felt. **3** materials for making felt.

felt-tip pen *n* a pen having a writing point made from pressed fibres. Also called: **fibre-tip pen.**

felucca (fɛ'lʌkə) *n* a narrow lateen-rigged vessel of the Mediterranean. [C17: from Italian *felucca,* probably from obsolete Spanish *faluca,* probably from Arabic *fulūk* ships, from Greek *epholkion* small boat, from *ephelkein* to tow]

felwort ('fɛlˌwɜːt) *n* a biennial gentianaceous plant, *Gentianella amarella,* of Europe and SW China, having purple flowers and rosettes of leaves. [Old English *feldwyrt;* see FIELD, WORT]

fem. *abbrev. for:* **1** female. **2** feminine.

female ('fiːmeɪl) *adj* **1** of, relating to, or designating the sex producing gametes (ova) that can be fertilized by male gametes (spermatozoa). **2** of, relating to, or characteristic of a woman: *female charm.* **3** for or composed of women or girls: *female suffrage; a female choir.* **4** (of reproductive organs such as the ovary and carpel) capable of producing female gametes. **5** (of gametes such as the ovum) capable of being fertilized by a male gamete in sexual reproduction. **6** (of flowers) lacking, or having nonfunctional, stamens. **7** having an internal cavity into which a projecting male counterpart can be fitted: *a female thread.* ◆ *n* **8a** a female animal or plant. **8b** *Mildly offensive.* a woman or girl. [C14: from earlier *femelle* (influenced by *male*), from Latin *fēmella* a young woman, from *fēmina* a woman] ▸ **'femaleness** *n*

female impersonator *n* a male theatrical performer who acts as a woman.

female suffrage *n Chiefly U.S.* another name for **women's suffrage.**

feme (fɛm) *n Law.* a woman or wife. [C16: from Anglo-French, ultimately from Latin *fēmina* woman]

feme covert *n Law.* a married woman. [C16: from Anglo-French: a covered woman, one protected by marriage]

feme sole *n Law.* **1** a single woman, whether spinster, widow, or divorcee. **2** a woman separated from her husband, or otherwise independent of him, as by owning her own property. [C16: from Anglo-French: a woman alone]

femineity (ˌfɛmɪ'niːɪtɪ) *n* the quality of being feminine; womanliness.

feminine ('fɛmɪnɪn) *adj* **1** suitable to or characteristic of a woman: *a feminine fashion.* **2** possessing qualities or characteristics considered typical of or appropriate to a woman. **3** effeminate; womanish. **4** *Grammar.* **4a** denoting or belonging to a gender of nouns, occurring in many inflected languages, that includes all kinds of referents as well as some female animate referents. **4b** (*as n*): *German* Zeit *"time" and* Ehe *"marriage" are feminines.* [**C14**: from Latin *fēminīnus,* from *fēmina* woman] ► **'femininely** *adv* ► **'feminineness** *n*

feminine ending *n Prosody.* an unstressed syllable at the end of a line of verse.

feminine rhyme *n Prosody.* a rhyme between words in which one, two, or more unstressed syllables follow a stressed one, as in *elation, nation* or *merrily, verily.* Compare **masculine rhyme.**

femininity (ˌfɛmɪˈnɪnɪtɪ) *n* **1** the quality of being feminine. **2** womanhood.

feminism (ˈfɛmɪˌnɪzəm) *n* a doctrine or movement that advocates equal rights for women. ► **'feminist** *n, adj*

feminize *or* **feminise** (ˈfɛmɪˌnaɪz) *vb* **1** to make or become feminine. **2** to cause (a male animal) to develop female characteristics. ► **ˌfemini'zation** *or* **ˌfemini'sation** *n*

femme *French.* (fam; *English* fɛm) *n* a woman or wife.

femme de chambre *French.* (fam də ʃɑ̃brə) *n, pl* ***femmes de chambre*** (fam də ʃɑ̃brə). **1** a chambermaid. **2** *Rare.* a personal maid. [**C18**: woman of the bedroom]

femme fatale *French.* (fam fatal; *English* ˈfɛm fəˈtæl, -ˈtɑːl) *n, pl* ***femmes fatales*** (fam fatal; *English* ˈfɛm fəˈtælz, -ˈtɑːlz). an alluring or seductive woman, esp. one who causes men to love her to their own distress. [fatal woman]

femoral (ˈfɛmərəl) *adj* of or relating to the thigh or femur.

femto- *prefix* denoting 10^{-15}: *femtometer.* Symbol: f [from Danish or Norwegian *femten* fifteen]

femur (ˈfiːmə) *n, pl* **femurs** *or* **femora** (ˈfɛmərə). **1** the longest thickest bone of the human skeleton, articulating with the pelvis above and the knee below. Nontechnical name: **thighbone. 2** the corresponding bone in other vertebrates. **3** the segment of an insect's leg nearest to the body. [**C18**: from Latin: thigh]

fen[1] (fɛn) *n* low-lying flat land that is marshy or artificially drained. [Old English *fenn;* related to Old High German *fenna,* Old Norse *fen,* Gothic *fani* clay, Sanskrit *panka* mud]

fen[2] (fɛn) *n, pl* **fen.** a monetary unit of the People's Republic of China worth one hundredth of a yuan. [from Mandarin Chinese]

fence (fɛns) *n* **1** a structure that serves to enclose an area such as a garden or field, usually made of posts of timber, concrete, or metal connected by wire, netting, rails, or boards. **2** *Slang.* a dealer in stolen property. **3** an obstacle for a horse to jump in steeplechasing or showjumping. **4** *Machinery.* a guard or guide, esp. in a circular saw or plane. **5** a projection usually fitted to the top surface of a sweptback aircraft wing to prevent movement of the airflow towards the wing tips. **6 mend one's fences. 6a** *Chiefly U.S. and Canadian.* to restore a position or reputation that has been damaged, esp. in politics. **6b** to re-establish friendly relations (with someone). **7** (**sit**) **on the fence.** (to be) unable or unwilling to commit oneself. **8 over the fence.** *Austral. and N.Z. informal.* unreasonable, unfair, or unjust. ◆ *vb* **9** (*tr*) to construct a fence on or around (a piece of land, etc.). **10** (*tr;* foll. by *in* or *off*) to close (in) or separate (off) with or as if with a fence: *he fenced in the livestock.* **11** (*intr*) to fight using swords or foils. **12** (*intr*) to evade a question or argument, esp. by quibbling over minor points. **13** (*intr*) to engage in skilful or witty debate, repartee, etc. **14** (*intr*) *Slang.* to receive stolen property. **15** (*tr*) *Archaic.* to ward off or keep out. [**C14** *fens,* shortened from *defens* DEFENCE] ► **'fenceless** *adj* ► **'fenceˌlike** *adj*

fencer (ˈfɛnsə) *n* **1** a person who fights with a sword, esp. one who practises the art of fencing. **2** *Chiefly Austral. and N.Z.* a person who erects and repairs fences.

fencible (ˈfɛnsəbᵊl) *adj* **1** a Scot. word for **defensible.** ◆ *n* **2** (formerly) a person who undertook military service in immediate defence of his homeland only.

fencing (ˈfɛnsɪŋ) *n* **1** the practice, art, or sport of fighting with swords, esp. the sport of using foils, épées, or sabres under a set of rules to score points. **2a** wire, stakes, etc., used as fences. **2b** fences collectively. **3** skilful or witty debate. **4** the avoidance of direct answers; evasiveness. **5** *Slang.* the business of buying and selling stolen property.

fencing wire *n* a heavy-gauge galvanized wire used for farm fences.

fend (fɛnd) *vb* **1** (*intr;* foll. by *for*) to give support (to someone, esp. oneself); provide (for). **2** (*tr;* usually foll. by *off*) to ward off or turn aside (blows, questions, attackers, etc.). **3** (*tr*) *Archaic.* to defend or resist. **4** (*intr*) *Scot. and northern English dialect.* to struggle; strive. ◆ *n* **5** *Scot. and northern English dialect.* a shift or effort. [**C13** *fenden,* shortened from *defenden* to DEFEND]

fender (ˈfɛndə) *n* **1** a low metal frame which confines falling coals to the hearth. **2** *Chiefly U.S.* a metal frame fitted to the front of locomotives to absorb shock, clear the track, etc. **3** a cushion-like device, such as a car tyre hung over the side of a vessel to reduce damage resulting from accidental contact or collision. **4** the U.S. and Canadian name for **wing** (sense 10) or **mudguard.** ► **'fendered** *adj*

Fender (ˈfɛndə) *n Trademark.* a type of solid-body electric guitar. [**C20**: named after Leo *Fender,* its U.S. inventor (1951)]

fender pile *n* an upright pile driven into the sea bed or a riverbed beside a berth to protect the dock wall or wharf from the impact of vessels.

Fénelon (*French* fenlɔ̃) *n* **François de Salignac de La Mothe** (frɑ̃swa də saliɲak də la mɔt). 1651–1715, French theologian and writer; author of *Maximes des saints* (1697), a defence of quietism, and *Les aventures de Télémaque* (1699), which was construed as criticizing the government of Louis XIV.

fenestella (ˌfɛnɪˈstɛlə) *n, pl* **-lae** (-liː). **1** *R.C. Church.* a small aperture in the front of an altar, containing relics. **2** *Ecclesiast.* a niche in the side wall of a chancel, in which the credence or piscina are set. **3** *Architect.* a small window or an opening in a wall. [**C18**: from Latin: a little window, from *fenestra* window]

fenestra (fɪˈnɛstrə) *n, pl* **-trae** (-triː). **1** *Biology.* a small opening, esp. either of two openings between the middle and inner ears. **2** *Zoology.* a transparent marking or spot, as on the wings of moths. **3** *Architect.* a window or window-like opening in the outside wall of a building. [**C19**: via New Latin from Latin: wall opening, window] ► **fe'nestral** *adj*

fenestrated (fɪˈnɛsˌtreɪtɪd, ˈfɛnɪˌstreɪtɪd) *or* **fenestrate** *adj* **1** *Architect.* having windows or window-like openings. **2** *Biology.* perforated or having fenestrae.

fenestration (ˌfɛnɪˈstreɪʃən) *n* **1** the arrangement and design of windows in a building. **2** a surgical operation to restore hearing by making an artificial opening into the labyrinth of the ear.

F Eng *abbrev. for* Fellow of the Fellowship of Engineering.

feng shui (ˈfʌŋ ˈʃweɪ) *n* the Chinese art of determining the most propitious design and placement of a grave, building, room, etc., so that the maximum harmony is achieved between the flow of chi of the environment and that of the user, believed to bring good fortune. [**C20**: from Chinese *feng* wind + *shui* water]

Fenian (ˈfiːnɪən) *n* **1** (formerly) a member of an Irish revolutionary organization founded in the U.S. in the 19th century to fight for an independent Ireland. **2** *Irish myth.* one of the **Fianna. 3** *Derogatory, offensive.* an Irish Catholic or a person of Irish Catholic descent. ◆ *adj* **4** of or relating to the Fenians. [**C19**: from Irish Gaelic *féinne,* plural of *fian* band of warriors] ► **'Fenianism** *n*

fennec (ˈfɛnɛk) *n* a very small nocturnal fox, *Fennecus zerda,* inhabiting deserts of N Africa and Arabia, having pale fur and enormous ears. [**C18**: from Arabic *fenek* fox]

fennel (ˈfɛnᵊl) *n* **1** a strong-smelling yellow-flowered umbelliferous plant, *Foeniculum vulgare,* whose seeds and feathery leaves are used to season and flavour food. See also **finocchio. 2 dog fennel.** another name for **mayweed.** [Old English *fenol,* from Latin *faeniculum* fennel, diminutive of *faenum* hay]

fennelflower (ˈfɛnᵊlˌflaʊə) *n* any of various Mediterranean ranunculaceous plants of the genus *Nigella,* having finely divided leaves and white, blue, or yellow flowers. See also **love-in-a-mist.**

fenny (ˈfɛnɪ) *adj* **1** boggy or marshy: *fenny country.* **2** found in, characteristic of, or growing in fens.

Fenrir (ˈfɛnrɪə), **Fenris** (ˈfɛnrɪs), *or* **Fenriswolf** (ˈfɛnrɪsˌwʊlf) *n Norse myth.* an enormous wolf, fathered by Loki, which killed Odin.

Fens (fɛnz) *pl n* **the.** a flat low-lying area of E England, west and south of the Wash: consisted of marshes until reclaimed in the 17th to 19th centuries.

fentanyl (ˈfɛntəˌnaɪl) *n* a narcotic drug used in medicine to relieve pain.

Fenton (ˈfɛntən) *n* **James** (**Martin**). born 1949, British poet, journalist, and critic. His poetry includes the collections *A German Requiem* (1980) and *Out of Danger* (1993).

fenugreek (ˈfɛnjʊˌgriːk) *n* an annual heavily scented Mediterranean leguminous plant, *Trigonella foenum-graecum,* with hairy stems and white flowers: cultivated for forage and for its medicinal seeds. [Old English *fēnogrēcum,* from Latin *fēnum Graecum* literally: Greek hay]

feoff (fiːf) *Medieval history.* ◆ *n* **1** a variant spelling of **fief.** ◆ *vb* **2** (*tr*) to invest with a benefice or fief. [**C13**: from Anglo-French *feoffer,* from *feoff* a FIEF] ► **'feoffor** *or* **'feoffer** *n*

feoffee (fɛˈfiː, fiːˈfiː) *n* (in feudal society) a vassal granted a fief by his lord.

feoffment (ˈfiːfmənt) *n* (in medieval Europe) a lord's act of granting a fief to his man.

-fer *n combining form.* indicating a person or thing that bears something specified: *crucifer; conifer.* [from Latin, from *ferre* to bear]

feral[1] (ˈfɪərəl, ˈfɛr-) *or* **ferine** *adj* **1** (of animals and plants) existing in a wild or uncultivated state, esp. after being domestic or cultivated. **2** savage; brutal. [**C17**: from Medieval Latin *ferālis,* from Latin *fera* a wild beast, from *ferus* savage] ► **ferity** (ˈfɛrɪtɪ) *n*

feral[2] (ˈfɪərəl, ˈfɛr-) *adj Archaic.* **1** *Astrology.* associated with death. **2** gloomy; funereal. [**C17**: from Latin *fērālis* relating to corpses; perhaps related to *ferre* to carry]

ferbam (ˈfɜːbæm) *n* a black slightly water-soluble fluffy powder used as a fungicide. Formula: $[(CH_3)_2NCSS]_3Fe$. [**C20**: from *fer(ric dimethyldithiocar)bam(ate)*]

fer-de-lance (ˌfɛədəˈlɑːns) *n* a large highly venomous tropical American snake, *Trimeresurus* (or *Bothops*) *atrox,* with a greyish-brown mottled coloration: family *Crotalidae* (pit vipers). [**C19**: from French, literally: iron (head) of a lance]

Ferdinand (ˈfɜːdɪˌnænd; *German* ˈfɛrdinant) *n* See **Franz Ferdinand.**

Ferdinand I (ˈfɜːdɪˌnænd) *n* **1** known as *Ferdinand the Great.* ?1016–65, king of Castile (1035–65) and León (1037–65): achieved control of the Moorish kings of Saragossa, Seville, and Toledo. **2** 1503–64, king of Hungary and Bohemia (1526–64); Holy Roman Emperor (1558–64), bringing years of religious warfare to an end. **3** 1751–1825, king of the Two Sicilies (1816–25); king of Naples (1759–1806; 1815–25), as Ferdinand IV, being dispossessed by Napoleon (1806–15). **4** 1793–1875, king of Hungary (1830–48) and emperor of Austria (1835–48); abdicated after the Revolution of 1848 in favour of his nephew, Franz Josef I. **5** 1861–1948, ruling prince of Bulgaria (1887–1908) and tsar from 1908 until his abdication in 1918. **6** 1865–1927, king of Romania (1914–27); sided with the Allies in World War I.

Ferdinand II *n* **1** 1578–1637, Holy Roman Emperor (1619–37); king of Bohemia (1617–19; 1620–37) and of Hungary (1617–37). His anti-Protestant policies led to the Thirty Years' War. **2** title as king of Aragon and Sicily of **Ferdinand V.**

Ferdinand III *n* **1** 1608–57, Holy Roman Emperor (1637–57) and king of Hungary (1625–57); son of Ferdinand II. **2** title as king of Naples of **Ferdinand V.**

Ferdinand V *n* known as *Ferdinand the Catholic.* 1452–1516, king of Castile (1474–1504); as Ferdinand II, king of Aragon (1479–1516) and Sicily

(1468–1516); as Ferdinand III, king of Naples (1504–16). His marriage to Isabella I of Castile (1469) led to the union of Aragon and Castile and his reconquest of Granada from the Moors (1492) completed the unification of Spain. He introduced the Inquisition (1478), expelled the Jews from Spain (1492), and financed Columbus' voyage to the New World.

Ferdinand VII *n* 1784–1833, king of Spain (1808; 1814–33). He precipitated the Carlist Wars by excluding his brother Don Carlos as his successor.

fere (fɪə; *Scot.* fiːr) *n Archaic or Scot.* **1** a companion. **2** Also: **fier.** a husband or wife. [Old English *gefēra,* from *fēran* to travel; see FARE]

feretory ('fɛrɪtərɪ, -trɪ) *n, pl* **-ries.** *Chiefly R.C. Church.* **1** a shrine, usually portable, for a saint's relics. **2** the chapel in which a shrine is kept. [C14: from Middle French *fiertre,* from Latin *feretrum* a bier, from Greek *pheretron,* from *pherein* to bear]

Fergana *or* **Ferghana** (fə'gɑːnə) *n* **1** a region of W central Asia, surrounded by high mountains and accessible only from the west; mainly in Uzbekistan and partly in Tajikistan and Kyrgyzstan. **2** the chief city of this region, in E Uzbekistan. Pop.: 191 000 (1993 est.).

Fergus ('fɜːgəs) *n* (in Irish legend) a warrior king of Ulster, who was supplanted by Conchobar.

Ferguson ('fɜːgəsən) *n* Sir **Alex(ander) Chapman.** born 1941, Scottish footballer and manager; manager of Manchester United from 1986.

feria ('fɪərɪə) *n, pl* **-rias** *or* **-riae** (-rɪˌiː). *R.C. Church.* a weekday, other than Saturday, on which no feast occurs. [C19: from Late Latin: day of the week (as in *prīma fēria* Sunday), singular of Latin *fēriae* festivals]

ferial ('fɪərɪəl) *adj* **1** of or relating to a feria. **2** *Rare.* of or relating to a holiday.

ferine ('fɪəraɪn) *adj* another word for **feral**[1]. [C17: from Latin *ferīnus* of wild animals, from *fera* wild beast]

ferity ('fɛrɪtɪ) *n, pl* **-ties.** *Rare.* **1** the state of being wild or uncultivated. **2** savagery; ferocity. [C16: from Latin *feritās,* from *ferus* savage, untamed]

Ferlinghetti (fɜːlɪŋ'gɛtɪ) *n* **Lawrence.** born 1920, U.S. poet of the Beat Generation. His poetry includes the collections *Pictures of the Gone World* (1955) and *When I Look at Pictures* (1990).

ferly ('fɛrlɪ) *Scot.* ◆ *adj* **1** wonderful; strange. ◆ *n, pl* **-lies. 2** a wonder; something strange or marvellous. ◆ *vb (intr)* **-lies, -lying, -lied. 3** to wonder; be surprised. [Old English *færlic* sudden]

Fermanagh (fə'mænə) *n* a district and historical county of SW Northern Ireland: contains the Upper and Lower Lough Erne. Pop.: 54 033 (1991). Area (excluding water): 1700 sq. km (656 sq. miles).

Fermat (fɜː'mæt; *French* fɛrma) *n* **Pierre de** (pjɛr də). 1601–65, French mathematician, regarded as the founder of the modern theory of numbers. He studied the properties of whole numbers and, with Pascal, investigated the theory of probability.

fermata (fə'mɑːtə) *n, pl* **-tas** *or* **-te** (-tɪ). *Music.* another word for **pause** (sense 5). [from Italian, from *fermare* to stop, from Latin *firmāre* to establish; see FIRM[1]]

Fermat's last theorem *n* (in number theory) the hypothesis that the equation $x^n + y^n = z^n$ has no integral solutions for *n* greater than two.

Fermat's principle *n Physics.* the principle that a ray of light passes from one point to another in such a way that the time taken is a minimum.

ferment *n* ('fɜːmɛnt). **1** any agent or substance, such as a bacterium, mould, yeast, or enzyme, that causes fermentation. **2** another word for **fermentation. 3** commotion; unrest. ◆ *vb* (fə'mɛnt). **4** to undergo or cause to undergo fermentation. **5** to stir up or seethe with excitement. [C15: from Latin *fermentum* yeast, from *fervēre* to seethe] ▸ **fer'mentable** *adj* ▸ **fer,menta'bility** *n* ▸ **fer'menter** *n*

USAGE See at **foment.**

fermentation (ˌfɜːmɛn'teɪʃən) *n* a chemical reaction in which a ferment causes an organic molecule to split into simpler substances, esp. the anaerobic conversion of sugar to ethyl alcohol by yeast. Also called: **ferment.** Related adj: **zymotic.** ▸ **fer'mentative** *adj* ▸ **fer'mentatively** *adv* ▸ **fer'mentativeness** *n*

fermentation lock *n* a valve placed on the top of bottles of fermenting wine to allow bubbles to escape.

fermi ('fɜːmɪ) *n* a unit of length used in nuclear physics equal to 10^{-15} metre.

Fermi ('fɜːmɪ; *Italian* 'fɛrmi) *n* **Enrico** (en'riːko). 1901–54, Italian nuclear physicist, in the U.S. from 1939. He was awarded a Nobel prize for physics in 1938 for his work on radioactive substances and nuclear bombardment and headed the group that produced the first controlled nuclear reaction (1942).

Fermi-Dirac statistics *n Physics.* the branch of quantum statistics used to calculate the permitted energy arrangements of the particles in a system in terms of the exclusion principle. Compare **Bose-Einstein statistics.** [C20: named after Enrico FERMI and Paul DIRAC]

Fermi energy *or* **level** *n* the level in the distribution of electron energies in a solid at which a quantum state is equally likely to be occupied or empty. [C20: named after Enrico FERMI]

fermion ('fɜːmɪˌɒn) *n* any of a group of elementary particles, such as a nucleon, that has half-integral spin and obeys Fermi-Dirac statistics. Compare **boson.** [C20: named after Enrico FERMI; see -ON]

fermium ('fɜːmɪəm) *n* a transuranic element artificially produced by neutron bombardment of plutonium. Symbol: Fm; atomic no.: 100; half-life of most stable isotope, ^{257}Fm: 80 days (approx.). [C20: named after Enrico FERMI]

Fermor ('fɜːmɔː) *n* **Patrick (Michael) Leigh.** born 1915, British traveller and author, noted esp. for the travel books *A Time of Gifts* (1977) and *Between the Woods and the Water* (1986).

fern (fɜːn) *n* **1** any tracheophyte plant of the phylum *Filicinophyta,* having roots, stems, and fronds and reproducing by spores formed in structures (sori) on the fronds. See also **tree fern. 2** any of certain similar but unrelated plants, such as the sweet fern. [Old English *fearn;* related to Old High German *farn,* Sanskrit *parná* leaf] ▸ **'fern,like** *adj* ▸ **'ferny** *adj*

Fernandel (*French* fɛrnɑ̃dɛl) *n* real name *Fernand Joseph Désiré Contandin.* 1903–71, French comic film actor.

Fernando de Noronha (*Portuguese* fer'nəndu di no'roɲa) *n* a volcanic island in the S Atlantic northeast of Cape São Roque: constitutes a federal territory of Brazil; a penal colony since the 18th century; inhabited by military personnel. Area: 26 sq. km (10 sq. miles).

Fernando Po (fə'nændəʊ pəʊ) *n* a former name (until 1973) of **Bioko.**

fernbird ('fɜːnˌbɜːd) *n* a small brown and white New Zealand swamp bird, *Bowdleria punctata,* with a fernlike tail.

fernery ('fɜːnərɪ) *n, pl* **-eries. 1** a place where ferns are grown. **2** a collection of ferns grown in such a place.

fern seed *n* the minute particles by which ferns reproduce themselves, formerly thought to be invisible. Possession of them was thought to make a person invisible.

ferocious (fə'rəʊʃəs) *adj* savagely fierce or cruel: *a ferocious tiger; a ferocious argument.* [C17: from Latin *ferox* fierce, untamable, warlike] ▸ **fe'rociously** *adv* ▸ **ferocity** (fə'rɒsɪtɪ) *or* **fe'rociousness** *n*

-ferous *adj combining form.* bearing or producing: *coniferous; crystalliferous.* Compare **-gerous.** [from -FER + -OUS]

Ferrar ('fɛrə) *n* **Nicholas.** 1592–1637, English mystic. He founded (1625) an Anglican religious community at Little Gidding, Huntingdonshire.

Ferrara (fə'rɑːrə; *Italian* fer'rara) *n* a city in N Italy, in Emilia-Romagna: a centre of the Renaissance under the House of Este; university (1391). Pop.: 135 135 (1996 est.).

Ferrari (*Italian* fɛr'raːrɪ) *n* **Enzo** ('ɛntso). 1898–1988, Italian designer and manufacturer of racing cars.

ferrate ('fɛreɪt) *n* a salt containing the divalent ion, FeO_4^{2-}. Ferrates are derivatives of the hypothetical acid H_2FeO_4. [C19: from Latin *ferrum* iron]

ferredoxin (ˌfɛrɪ'dɒksɪn) *n* any of certain iron-containing proteins, found in plants and some bacteria, that are involved in photosynthesis and nitrogen fixation.

ferreous ('fɛrɪəs) *adj* containing or resembling iron: *a ferreous alloy; a ferreous substance.* [C17: from Latin *ferreus* made of iron, from *ferrum* iron]

ferret[1] ('fɛrɪt) *n* **1** a domesticated albino variety of the polecat *Mustela putorius,* bred for hunting rats, rabbits, etc. **2 black-footed ferret.** a musteline mammal, *Mustela nigripes,* of W North America, closely related to the weasels. ◆ *vb* **-rets, -reting, -reted. 3** to hunt (rabbits, rats, etc.) with ferrets. **4** *(tr;* usually foll. by *out)* to drive from hiding: *to ferret out snipers.* **5** *(tr;* usually foll. by *out)* to find by persistent investigation. **6** *(intr)* to search around. [C14: from Old French *furet,* from Latin *fur* thief] ▸ **'ferreter** *n* ▸ **'ferrety** *adj*

ferret[2] ('fɛrɪt) *or* **ferreting** *n* silk binding tape. [C16: from Italian *fioretti* floss silk, plural of *fioretto:* a little flower, from *fiore* flower, from Latin *flōs*]

ferret badger *n* any small badger of the genus *Melogale,* of SE Asia, resembling a ferret in appearance and smell.

ferri- *combining form.* indicating the presence of iron, esp. in the trivalent state: *ferricyanide; ferriferous.* Compare **ferro-.** [from Latin *ferrum* iron]

ferriage ('fɛrɪɪdʒ) *n* **1** transportation by ferry. **2** the fee charged for passage on a ferry.

ferric ('fɛrɪk) *adj* of or containing iron in the trivalent state: *ferric oxide;* designating an iron(III) compound. [C18: from Latin *ferrum* iron]

ferric oxide *n* a red crystalline insoluble oxide of iron that occurs as haematite and rust and is made by heating ferrous sulphate: used as a pigment and metal polish (**jeweller's rouge**), and as a sensitive coating on magnetic tape. Formula: Fe_2O_3. Systematic name: **iron(III) oxide.**

ferricyanic acid (ˌfɛrɪsaɪ'ænɪk) *n* a brown soluble unstable solid tribasic acid, usually known in the form of ferricyanide salts. Formula: $H_3Fe(CN)_6$.

ferricyanide (ˌfɛrɪ'saɪəˌnaɪd) *n* any salt of ferricyanic acid.

Ferrier ('fɛrɪə) *n* **Kathleen.** 1912–53, British contralto; noted for her expressive voice.

ferriferous (fe'rɪfərəs) *adj* producing or yielding iron; iron-bearing: *a ferriferous rock.*

ferrimagnetism (ˌfɛrɪ'mægnɪˌtɪzəm) *n* a phenomenon exhibited by certain substances, such as ferrites, in which the magnetic moments of neighbouring ions are antiparallel and unequal in magnitude. The substances behave like ferromagnetic materials. See also **antiferromagnetism.** ▸ **ferrimagnetic** (ˌfɛrɪmæg'nɛtɪk) *adj*

Ferris wheel ('fɛrɪs) *n* a fairground wheel having seats freely suspended from its rim; the seats remain horizontal throughout its rotation. [C19: named after G.W.G. *Ferris* (1859–96), American engineer]

ferrite ('fɛraɪt) *n* **1** any of a group of ferromagnetic highly resistive ceramic compounds with the formula MFe_2O_4, where M is usually a metal such as cobalt or zinc. **2** any of the body-centred cubic allotropes of iron, such as alpha iron, occurring in steel, cast iron, etc. **3** any of various microscopic grains, probably composed of iron compounds, in certain igneous rocks. [C19: from FERRI- + -ITE[1]]

ferrite-rod aerial *n* a type of aerial, normally used in radio reception, consisting of a small coil of wire mounted on a ferrite core, the coil serving as a tuning inductance.

ferritin ('fɛrɪtɪn) *n Biochem.* a protein that contains iron and plays a part in the storage of iron in the body. It occurs in the liver and spleen. [C20: from FERRITE + -IN]

ferro- *combining form.* **1** indicating a property of iron or the presence of iron: *ferromagnetism; ferromanganese.* **2** indicating the presence of iron in the divalent state: *ferrocyanide.* Compare **ferri-.** [from Latin *ferrum* iron]

ferrocene ('fɛrəʊˌsiːn) *n* a reddish-orange insoluble crystalline compound. Its molecules have an iron atom sandwiched between two cyclopentadiene rings. Formula: $Fe(C_5H_5)_2$. [C20: from FERRO- + C(YCLOPENTADI)ENE]

ferrochromium (ˌfɛrəʊˈkrəʊmɪəm) *or* **ferrochrome** *n* an alloy of iron and chromium (60–72 per cent), used in the production of very hard steel.

ferroconcrete (ˌfɛrəʊˈkɒŋkriːt) *n* another name for **reinforced concrete.**

ferrocyanic acid (ˌfɛrəʊsaɪˈænɪk) *n* a white volatile unstable solid tetrabasic acid, usually known in the form of ferrocyanide salts. Formula: $H_4Fe(CN)_6$.

ferrocyanide (ˌfɛrəʊˈsaɪəˌnaɪd) *n* any salt of ferrocyanic acid, such as potassium ferrocyanide, $K_4Fe(CN)_6$.

ferroelectric (ˌfɛrəʊɪˈlɛktrɪk) *adj* **1** (of a substance) exhibiting spontaneous polarization that can be reversed by the application of a suitable electric field. **2** of or relating to ferroelectric substances. ◆ *n* **3** a ferroelectric substance. ► ˌ**ferroeˈlectrically** *adv* ► **ferroelectricity** (ˌfɛrəʊɪlɛkˈtrɪsɪtɪ, -ˌiːlɛk-) *n*

Ferrol (*Spanish* fɛˈrrɔl) *n* See **El Ferrol.**

ferromagnesian (ˌfɛrəʊmægˈniːʒən) *adj* (of minerals such as biotite) containing a high proportion of iron and magnesium.

ferromagnetism (ˌfɛrəʊˈmægnɪˌtɪzəm) *n* the phenomenon exhibited by substances, such as iron, that have relative permeabilities much greater than unity and increasing magnetization with applied magnetizing field. Certain of these substances retain their magnetization in the absence of the applied field. The effect is caused by the alignment of electron spin in regions called domains. Compare **diamagnetism, paramagnetism.** See also **magnet, Curie-Weiss law.** ► ferromagnetic (ˌfɛrəʊmægˈnɛtɪk) *adj*

ferromanganese (ˌfɛrəʊˈmæŋgəˌniːz) *n* an alloy of iron and manganese, used in making additions of manganese to cast iron and steel.

ferromolybdenum (ˌfɛrəʊmɒˈlɪbdɪnəm) *n* an alloy of iron and molybdenum used in making alloy steels.

ferronickel (ˌfɛrəʊˈnɪkᵊl) *n* an alloy of iron and nickel used in making nickel steels.

ferrosilicon (ˌfɛrəʊˈsɪlɪkən) *n* an alloy of iron and silicon, used in making cast iron and steel.

ferrotype (ˈfɛrəʊˌtaɪp) *n* **1** a photographic print produced directly in a camera by exposing a sheet of iron or tin coated with a sensitized enamel. **2** the process by which such a print is produced. ◆ Also called: **tintype.**

ferrous (ˈfɛrəs) *adj* of or containing iron in the divalent state; designating an iron(II) compound. [C19: from FERRI- + -OUS]

ferrous sulphate *n* an iron salt with a saline taste, usually obtained as greenish crystals of the heptahydrate, which are converted to the white monohydrate above 100°C: used in inks, tanning, water purification, and in the treatment of anaemia. Formula: $FeSO_4$. Systematic name: **iron(II) sulphate.** Also called: **copperas, green vitriol.**

ferruginous (fɛˈruːdʒɪnəs) *adj* **1** (of minerals, rocks, etc.) containing iron: *a ferruginous clay.* **2** rust-coloured. [C17: from Latin *ferrūgineus* of a rusty colour, from *ferrūgō* iron rust, from *ferrum* iron]

ferruginous duck *n* a common European duck, *Aythyra nyroca,* having reddish-brown plumage with white wing bars.

ferrule *or* **ferule** (ˈfɛruːl, -rəl) *n* **1** a metal ring, tube, or cap placed over the end of a stick, handle, or post for added strength or to increase wear. **2** a side opening in a pipe that gives access for inspection or cleaning. **3** a bush, gland, small length of tube, etc., esp. one used for making a joint. ◆ *vb* **4** (*tr*) to equip (a stick, etc.,) with a ferrule. [C17: from Middle English *virole,* from Old French *virol,* from Latin *viriola* a little bracelet, from *viria* bracelet; influenced by Latin *ferrum* iron]

ferry (ˈfɛrɪ) *n, pl* **-ries. 1** Also called: **ˈferryˌboat.** a vessel for transporting passengers and usually vehicles across a body of water, esp. as a regular service. **2a** such a service. **2b** (*in combination*): *a ferryman.* **3** a legal right to charge for transporting passengers by boat. **4** the act or method of delivering aircraft by flying them to their destination. ◆ *vb* **-ries, -rying, -ried. 5** to transport or go by ferry. **6** to deliver (an aircraft) by flying it to its destination. **7** (*tr*) to convey (passengers, goods, etc.): *the guests were ferried to the church in taxis.* [Old English *ferian* to carry, bring; related to Old Norse *ferja* to transport, Gothic *farjan;* see FARE]

fertile (ˈfɜːtaɪl) *adj* **1** capable of producing offspring. **2a** (of land) having nutrients capable of sustaining an abundant growth of plants. **2b** (of farm animals) capable of breeding stock. **3** *Biology.* **3a** capable of undergoing growth and development: *fertile seeds; fertile eggs.* **3b** (of plants) capable of producing gametes, spores, seeds, or fruits. **4** producing many offspring; prolific. **5** highly productive; rich; abundant: *a fertile brain.* **6** *Physics.* (of a substance) able to be transformed into fissile or fissionable material, esp. in a nuclear reactor. **7** conducive to productiveness: *fertile rain.* [C15: from Latin *fertilis,* from *ferre* to bear] ► **ˈfertilely** *adv* ► **ˈfertileness** *n*

Fertile Crescent *n* an area of fertile land in the Middle East, extending around the Rivers Tigris and Euphrates in a semicircle from Israel to the Persian Gulf, where the Sumerian, Babylonian, Assyrian, Phoenician, and Hebrew civilizations flourished.

fertility (fɜːˈtɪlɪtɪ) *n* **1** the ability to produce offspring, esp. abundantly. **2** the state or quality of being fertile.

fertility cult *n* the practice in some settled agricultural communities of performing religious or magical rites to ensure good weather and crops and the perpetuity of the tribe.

fertility symbol *n* an object, esp. a phallic symbol, used in fertility-cult ceremonies to symbolize regeneration.

fertilization *or* **fertilisation** (ˌfɜːtɪlaɪˈzeɪʃən) *n* **1** the union of male and female gametes, during sexual reproduction, to form a zygote. **2** the act or process of fertilizing. **3** the state of being fertilized.

fertilize *or* **fertilise** (ˈfɜːtɪˌlaɪz) *vb* (*tr*) **1** to provide (an animal, plant, or egg cell) with sperm or pollen to bring about fertilization. **2** to supply (soil or water) with mineral and organic nutrients to aid the growth of plants. **3** to make fertile or productive. ► **ˈfertiˌlizable** *or* **ˈfertiˌlisable** *adj*

fertilizer *or* **fertiliser** (ˈfɜːtɪˌlaɪzə) *n* **1** any substance, such as manure or a mixture of nitrates, added to soil or water to increase its productivity. **2** an object or organism such as an insect that fertilizes an animal or plant.

ferula (ˈfɛrʊlə, ˈfɛrjʊ-) *n, pl* **-las** *or* **-lae** (-ˌliː). **1** any large umbelliferous plant of the Mediterranean genus *Ferula,* having thick stems and dissected leaves: cultivated as the source of several strongly scented gum resins, such as galbanum. **2** a rare word for **ferule**[1]. [C14: from Latin: giant fennel] ► **ferulaceous** (ˌfɛruːˈleɪʃəs, ˌfɛrjuː-) *adj*

ferule[1] (ˈfɛruːl, -rəl) *n* **1** a flat piece of wood, such as a ruler, used in some schools to cane children on the hand. ◆ *vb* **2** (*tr*) *Rare.* to punish with a ferule. [C16: from Latin *ferula* giant fennel, whip, rod; the stalk of the plant was used for punishment]

ferule[2] (ˈfɛruːl, -rəl) *n* a variant spelling of **ferrule.**

fervency (ˈfɜːvənsɪ) *n, pl* **-cies.** another word for **fervour.**

fervent (ˈfɜːvənt) *or* **fervid** (ˈfɜːvɪd) *adj* **1** intensely passionate; ardent: *a fervent desire to change society.* **2** *Archaic or poetic.* boiling, burning, or glowing: *fervent heat.* [C14: from Latin *fervēre* to boil, glow] ► **ˈfervently** *or* **ˈfervidly** *adv* ► **ˈferventness** *or* **ˈfervidness** *n*

Fervidor *French.* (fɛrvidɔr) *n* another name for **Thermidor.** [probably from *ferveur* heat + THERMIDOR]

fervour *or U.S.* **fervor** (ˈfɜːvə) *n* **1** great intensity of feeling or belief; ardour; zeal. **2** *Rare.* intense heat. [C14: from Latin *fervor* heat, from *fervēre* to glow, boil]

Fès (fɛs) *or* **Fez** *n* a city in N central Morocco, traditional capital of the north: became an independent kingdom in the 11th century, at its height in the 14th century; religious centre; university (850). Pop.: 263 828 (1994).

Fescennine (ˈfɛsɪˌnaɪn) *adj Rare.* scurrilous or obscene. [C17: from Latin *Fescennīnus* of *Fescennia,* a city in Etruria noted for the production of mocking or obscene verse]

fescue (ˈfɛskjuː) *or* **fescue grass** *n* any grass of the genus *Festuca:* widely cultivated as pasture and lawn grasses, having stiff narrow leaves. See also **meadow fescue, sheep's fescue.** [C14: from Old French *festu,* ultimately from Latin *festūca* stem, straw]

fesse *or* **fess** (fɛs) *n Heraldry.* an ordinary consisting of a horizontal band across a shield, conventionally occupying a third of its length and being wider than a bar. [C15: from Anglo-French *fesse,* from Latin *fascia* band, fillet]

fesse point *n Heraldry.* the midpoint of a shield.

fest (fɛst) *n* **a** a meeting or event at which the emphasis is on a particular activity: *a fashion fest.* **b** (*in combination*): *schmaltz-fest; lovefest.* [C19: from German *Fest* festival]

festal (ˈfɛstᵊl) *adj* another word for **festive.** [C15: from Latin *festum* holiday, banquet; see FEAST] ► **ˈfestally** *adv*

fester (ˈfɛstə) *vb* **1** to form or cause to form pus. **2** (*intr*) to become rotten; decay. **3** to become or cause to become bitter, irritated, etc., esp. over a long period of time; rankle: *resentment festered his imagination.* **4** (*intr*) *Informal, chiefly Brit.* to be idle or inactive. ◆ *n* **5** a small ulcer or sore containing pus. [C13: from Old French *festre* suppurating sore, from Latin: FISTULA]

festina lente *Latin.* (fɛsˈtiːnə ˈlɛntɪ) hasten slowly.

festination (ˌfɛstɪˈneɪʃən) *n* an involuntary quickening of gait, as in some persons with Parkinson's disease. [C16: from Latin *festīnātiō,* from *festīnāre* to hasten]

festival (ˈfɛstɪvᵊl) *n* **1** a day or period set aside for celebration or feasting, esp. one of religious significance. **2** any occasion for celebration, esp. one which commemorates an anniversary or other significant event. **3** an organized series of special events and performances, usually in one place: *a festival of drama.* **4** *Archaic.* a time of revelry; merrymaking. **5** (*modifier*) relating to or characteristic of a festival. [C14: from Church Latin *fēstivālis* of a feast, from Latin *festīvus* FESTIVE]

Festival Hall *n* a concert hall in London, on the South Bank of the Thames: constructed for the 1951 Festival of Britain; completed 1964–65. Official name: **Royal Festival Hall.**

festive (ˈfɛstɪv) *adj* appropriate to or characteristic of a holiday, etc.; merry. [C17: from Latin *festīvus* joyful, from *festus* of a FEAST] ► **ˈfestively** *adv* ► **ˈfestiveness** *n*

festivity (fɛsˈtɪvɪtɪ) *n, pl* **-ties. 1** merriment characteristic of a festival, party, etc. **2** any festival or other celebration. **3** (*pl*) festive proceedings; celebrations.

festoon (fɛˈstuːn) *n* **1** a decorative chain of flowers, ribbons, etc., suspended in loops; garland. **2** a carved or painted representation of this, as in architecture, furniture, or pottery. **3a** the scalloped appearance of the gums where they meet the teeth. **3b** a design carved on the base material of a denture to simulate this. **4a** either of two *Zerynthia* species of white pierid butterfly of southern Europe, typically mottled red, yellow, and brown. **4b** an ochreous brown moth, *Apoda avellana,* the unusual sluglike larvae of which feed on oak leaves. ◆ *vb* (*tr*) **5** to decorate or join together with festoons. **6** to form into festoons. [C17: from French *feston,* from Italian *festone* ornament for a feast, from *festa* FEAST]

festoon blind *n* a window blind consisting of vertical rows of horizontally gathered fabric that may be drawn up to form a series of ruches.

festoonery (fɛˈstuːnərɪ) *n* an arrangement of festoons.

festschrift (ˈfɛstˌʃrɪft) *n, pl* **-schriften** (-ˌʃrɪftən) *or* **-schrifts.** a collection of essays or learned papers contributed by a number of people to honour an eminent scholar, esp. a colleague. [German, from *Fest* celebration, FEAST + *Schrift* writing]

FET *abbrev. for* field-effect transistor.

feta (ˈfɛtə) *n* a white sheep or goat cheese popular in Greece. [Modern Greek, from the phrase *turi pheta,* from *turi* cheese + *pheta,* from Italian *fetta* a slice]

fetal *or* **foetal** (ˈfiːtᵊl) *adj* of, relating to, or resembling a fetus.

fetal alcohol syndrome *n* a condition in newborn babies caused by excessive intake of alcohol by the mother during pregnancy: characterized by various defects including mental retardation.

fetal diagnosis *n* prenatal determination of genetic or chemical abnormalities in a fetus, esp. by amniocentesis.

fetal position *n* a bodily position similar to that of a fetus in the womb, with the knees up towards the chest and the head bent forward.

fetation *or* **foetation** (fiːˈteɪʃən) *n* **1** the state of pregnancy. **2** the process of development of a fetus.

fetch[1] (fɛtʃ) *vb* (*mainly tr*) **1** to go after and bring back; get: *to fetch help.* **2** to cause to come; bring or draw forth: *the noise fetched him from the cellar.* **3** (*also intr*) to cost or sell for (a certain price): *the table fetched six hundred pounds.* **4** to utter (a sigh, groan, etc.). **5** *Informal.* to deal (a blow, slap, etc.). **6** (*also intr*) *Nautical.* to arrive at or proceed by sailing. **7** *Informal.* to attract: *to be fetched by an idea.* **8** (used esp. as a command to dogs) to retrieve (shot game, an object thrown, etc.). **9** *Rare.* to draw in (a breath, gasp, etc.), esp. with difficulty. **10 fetch and carry.** to perform menial tasks or run errands. ◆ *n* **11** the reach, stretch, etc., of a mechanism. **12** a trick or stratagem. **13** the distance in the direction of the prevailing wind that waves can travel continuously without obstruction before reaching the nearest coast. [Old English *feccan*; related to Old Norse *feta* to step, Old High German *sih fazzōn* to climb] ▸ **ˈfetcher** *n*

fetch[2] (fɛtʃ) *n* the ghost or apparition of a living person. [C18: of unknown origin]

fetching (ˈfɛtʃɪŋ) *adj Informal.* **1** attractively befitting: *a fetching hat.* **2** charming: *a fetching personality.* ▸ **ˈfetchingly** *adv*

fetch up *vb* (*adv*) **1** (*intr*; usually foll. by *at* or *in*) *Informal.* to arrive (at) or end up (in): *to fetch up in New York.* **2** (*intr*) *Nautical.* to stop suddenly, as from running aground: *to fetch up on a rock.* **3** *Slang.* to vomit (food, etc.). **4** (*tr*) *Brit. dialect.* to rear (children, animals, etc.).

fête *or* **fete** (feɪt) *n* **1** a gala, bazaar, or similar entertainment, esp. one held outdoors in aid of charity. **2** a feast day or holiday, esp. one of religious significance. **3** *Caribbean informal.* an organized group entertainment, esp. a party or a dance. ◆ *vb* **4** (*tr*) to honour or entertain with or as if with a fête: *the author was fêted by his publishers.* **5** (*intr*) *Caribbean informal.* to join in a fête. [C18: from French: FEAST]

fête champêtre *French.* (fɛt ʃɑ̃pɛtrə) *n, pl* ***fêtes champêtres*** (fɛt ʃɑ̃pɛtrə). **1** a garden party, picnic, or similar outdoor entertainment. **2** Also called: ***fête galante*** (fɛt galɑ̃t). *Arts.* **2a** a genre of painting popular in France from the early 18th century, characterized by the depiction of figures in pastoral settings. Watteau was its most famous exponent. **2b** a painting in this genre. [C18: from French, literally: country festival]

fetial (ˈfiːʃəl) *n, pl* **fetiales** (ˌfiːʃɪˈeɪliːz). **1** (in ancient Rome) any of the 20 priestly heralds involved in declarations of war and in peace negotiations. ◆ *adj* **2** of or relating to the fetiales. **3** a less common word for **heraldic.** [C16: from Latin *fētiālis*, probably from Old Latin *fētis* treaty]

feticide *or* **foeticide** (ˈfiːtɪˌsaɪd) *n* the destruction of a fetus in the uterus; aborticide. ▸ **ˌfetiˈcidal** *or* **ˌfoetiˈcidal** *adj*

fetid *or* **foetid** (ˈfɛtɪd, ˈfiː-) *adj* having a stale nauseating smell, as of decay. [C16: from Latin *fētidus*, from *fētēre* to stink; related to *fūmus* smoke] ▸ **ˈfetidly** *or* **ˈfoetidly** *adv* ▸ **ˈfetidness** *or* **ˈfoetidness** *n*

fetiparous *or* **foetiparous** (fɪˈtɪpərəs) *adj* (of marsupials, such as the kangaroo) giving birth to incompletely developed offspring. [C19: from FETUS + -PAROUS]

fetish *or* **fetich** (ˈfɛtɪʃ, ˈfiːtɪʃ) *n* **1** something, esp. an inanimate object, that is believed in certain cultures to be the embodiment or habitation of a spirit or magical powers. **2a** a form of behaviour involving fetishism. **2b** any object that is involved in fetishism. **3** any object, activity, etc., to which one is excessively or irrationally devoted: *to make a fetish of cleanliness.* [C17: from French *fétiche*, from Portuguese *feitiço* (n) sorcery, from adj: artificial, from Latin *factīcius* made by art, FACTITIOUS] ▸ **ˈfetish-ˌlike** *or* **ˈfetich-ˌlike** *adj*

fetishism *or* **fetichism** (ˈfɛtɪˌʃɪzəm, ˈfiː-) *n* **1** a condition in which the handling of an inanimate object or a specific part of the body other than the sexual organs is a source of sexual satisfaction. **2** belief in or recourse to a fetish for magical purposes. **3** excessive attention or attachment to something. ▸ **ˈfetishist** *or* **ˈfetichist** *n* ▸ **ˌfetishˈistic** *or* **ˌfetichˈistic** *adj*

fetlock (ˈfɛtˌlɒk) *or* **fetterlock** *n* **1** a projection behind and above a horse's hoof: the part of the leg between the cannon bone and the pastern. **2** Also called: **fetlock joint.** the joint at this part of the leg. **3** the tuft of hair growing from this part. [C14 *fetlak*; related to Middle High German *vizzeloch* fetlock, from *vizzel* pastern + *-och*; see FOOT]

fetor *or* **foetor** (ˈfiːtə, -tɔː) *n* an offensive stale or putrid odour; stench. [C15: from Latin, from *fētēre* to stink]

fetoscope (ˈfiːtəʊˌskəʊp) *n* a fibreoptic instrument that can be passed through the abdomen of a pregnant woman to enable examination of the fetus and withdrawal of blood for sampling in prenatal diagnosis. ▸ **fetoscopy** (fiːˈtɒskəpɪ) *n*

fetter (ˈfɛtə) *n* **1** (*often pl*) a chain or bond fastened round the ankle; shackle. **2** (*usually pl*) a check or restraint: *in fetters.* ◆ *vb* (*tr*) **3** to restrict or confine. **4** to bind in fetters. [Old English *fetor*; related to Old Norse *fjötur* fetter, Old High German *fezzera*, Latin *pedica* fetter, *impedīre* to hinder] ▸ **ˈfetterer** *n* ▸ **ˈfetterless** *adj*

fetter bone *n* another name for **pastern** (sense 2).

fetterlock (ˈfɛtəˌlɒk) *n* another name for **fetlock.**

fettle (ˈfɛtᵊl) *vb* (*tr*) **1** to remove (excess moulding material and casting irregularities) from a cast component. **2** to line or repair (the walls of a furnace). **3** *Brit. dialect.* **3a** to prepare or arrange (a thing, oneself, etc.), esp. to put a finishing touch to. **3b** to repair or mend (something). ◆ *n* **4** state of health, spirits, etc. (esp. in the phrase **in fine fettle**). **5** another name for **fettling.** [C14 (in the sense: to put in order): back formation from *fetled* girded up, from Old English *fetel* belt]

fettler (ˈfɛtlə) *n Austral.* a person employed to maintain railway tracks.

fettling (ˈfɛtlɪŋ) *n* a refractory material used to line the hearth of puddling furnaces. Also called: **fettle.**

fettucine, fettuccine, *or* **fettucini** (ˌfɛtuːˈtʃiːnɪ) *n* a type of pasta in the form of narrow ribbons. [Italian *fettuccine*, plural of *fettuccina*, diminutive of *fetta* slice]

fetus *or* **foetus** (ˈfiːtəs) *n, pl* **-tuses.** the embryo of a mammal in the later stages of development, when it shows all the main recognizable features of the mature animal, esp. a human embryo from the end of the second month of pregnancy until birth. Compare **embryo** (sense 2). [C14: from Latin: offspring, brood]

feu (fjuː) *n* **1** *Scot. legal history.* **1a** a feudal tenure of land for which rent was paid in money or grain instead of by the performance of military service. **1b** the land so held. **2** *Scots Law.* a right to the use of land in return for a fixed annual payment (**feu duty**). [C15: from Old French; see FEE]

feuar (ˈfjuə) *n Scot.* the tenant of a feu.

Feuchtwanger (*German* ˈfɔɪçtvaŋər) *n* **Lion** (ˈliːɔn). 1884–1958, German novelist and dramatist, lived in the U.S. (1940–58): noted for his historical novels, including *Die hässliche Herzogin* (1923) and *Jud Süss* (1925).

feud[1] (fjuːd) *n* **1** long and bitter hostility between two families, clans, or individuals; vendetta. **2** a quarrel or dispute. ◆ *vb* **3** (*intr*) to take part in or carry on a feud. [C13 *fede*, from Old French *feide*, from Old High German *fēhida*; related to Old English *fæhth* hostility; see FOE]

feud[2] *or* **feod** (fjuːd) *n Feudal law.* land held in return for service. [C17: from Medieval Latin *feodum*, of Germanic origin; see FEE]

feudal[1] (ˈfjuːdᵊl) *adj* **1** of, resembling, relating to, or characteristic of feudalism or its institutions. **2** of, characteristic of, or relating to a fief. Compare **allodial. 3** *Disparaging.* old-fashioned, reactionary, etc. [C17: from Medieval Latin *feudālis*, from *feudum* FEUD[2]]

feudal[2] (ˈfjuːdᵊl) *adj* of or relating to a feud or quarrel.

feudalism (ˈfjuːdəˌlɪzəm) *n* **1** Also called: **feudal system.** the legal and social system that evolved in W Europe in the 8th and 9th centuries, in which vassals were protected and maintained by their lords, usually through the granting of fiefs, and were required to serve under them in war. See also **vassalage, fief. 2** any social system or society, such as medieval Japan or Ptolemaic Egypt, that resembles medieval European feudalism. ▸ **ˈfeudalist** *n* ▸ **ˌfeudalˈistic** *adj*

feudality (fjuːˈdælɪtɪ) *n, pl* **-ties. 1** the state or quality of being feudal. **2** a fief or fee.

feudalize *or* **feudalise** (ˈfjuːdəˌlaɪz) *vb* (*tr*) to make feudal; create feudal institutions in (a society). ▸ **ˌfeudaliˈzation** *or* **ˌfeudaliˈsation** *n*

feudatory (ˈfjuːdətərɪ, -trɪ) (in feudal Europe) ◆ *n* **1** a person holding a fief; vassal. ◆ *adj* **2** relating to or characteristic of the relationship between lord and vassal. **3** (esp. of a kingdom) under the overlordship of another sovereign. [C16: from Medieval Latin *feudātor*]

feu de joie (fø də ʒwa) *n, pl* ***feux de joie*** (fø). a salute of musketry fired successively by each man in turn along a line and back. [C18: from French, literally: fire of joy]

feudist (ˈfjuːdɪst) *n U.S.* a person who takes part in a feud or quarrel.

Feuerbach (*German* ˈfɔɪərbax) *n* **Ludwig Andreas** (ˈluːtvɪç anˈdreːas). 1804–72, German materialist philosopher: in *The Essence of Christianity* (1841), translated into English by George Eliot (1853), he maintained that God is merely an outward projection of man's inner self.

Feuillant *French.* (fœjɑ̃) *n French history.* a member of a club formed in 1791 by Lafayette advocating a limited constitutional monarchy: forced to disband in 1792 as the revolution became more violent and antimonarchical. [from the convent of Notre Dame des *Feuillants*, where meetings were held]

feuilleton (ˈfɜɪˌtɒn; *French* fœjtɔ̃) *n* **1** the part of a European newspaper carrying reviews, serialized fiction, etc. **2** such a review or article. [C19: from French, from *feuillet* sheet of paper, diminutive of *feuille* leaf, from Latin *folium*] ▸ **ˈfeuilletonism** *n* ▸ **ˈfeuilletonist** *n* ▸ **ˌfeuilletonˈistic** *adj*

fever (ˈfiːvə) *n* **1** an abnormally high body temperature, accompanied by a fast pulse rate, dry skin, etc. Related adjs: **febrile, pyretic. 2** any of various diseases, such as yellow fever or scarlet fever, characterized by a high temperature. **3** intense nervous excitement or agitation: *she was in a fever about her party.* ◆ *vb* **4** (*tr*) to affect with or as if with fever. [Old English *fēfor*, from Latin *febris*] ▸ **ˈfevered** *adj* ▸ **ˈfeverless** *adj*

fever blister *or* **sore** *n* another name for **cold sore.**

feverfew (ˈfiːvəˌfjuː) *n* a bushy European strong-scented perennial plant, *Chrysanthemum parthenium*, with white flower heads, formerly used medicinally: family *Compositae* (composites). [Old English *feferfuge*, from Late Latin *febrifugia*, from Latin *febris* fever + *fugāre* to put to flight]

feverish (ˈfiːvərɪʃ) *or* **feverous** *adj* **1** suffering from fever, esp. a slight fever. **2** in a state of restless excitement. **3** of, relating to, caused by, or causing fever. ▸ **ˈfeverishly** *or* **ˈfeverously** *adv* ▸ **ˈfeverishness** *n*

fever pitch *n* a state of intense excitement: *things were at fever pitch with the election coming up.*

fever therapy *n* a former method of treating disease by raising the body temperature. Compare **cryotherapy.**

fever tree *n U.S.* **1** any of several trees that produce a febrifuge or tonic, esp. *Pinckneya pubens*, a rubiaceous tree of SE North America. **2** a tall mimosaceous swamp tree, *Acacia xanthophloea*, of southern Africa, with fragrant yellow flowers.

feverwort (ˈfiːvəˌwɜːt) *n U.S.* any of several plants considered to have medicinal properties, such as horse gentian and boneset.

few (fjuː) *determiner* **1a** a small number of; hardly any: *few men are so cruel.* **1b** (*as pronoun; functioning as pl*): *many are called but few are chosen.* **2** (preceded by *a*) **2a** a small number of: *a few drinks.* **2b** (*as pronoun; functioning as* *pl): a few of you.* **3 a good few.** *Informal.* several. **4 few and far between. 4a** at great intervals; widely spaced. **4b** not abundant; scarce. **5 have a few (too many).** to consume several (*or* too many) alcoholic drinks. **6 not *or* quite a few.** *Informal.* several. ◆ *n* **7 the few.** a small number of people considered as a class: *the few who fell at Thermopylae.* Compare **many** (sense 4). [Old English *fēawa;* related to Old High German *fao* little, Old Norse *fār* little, silent] ▸ **'fewness** *n*

USAGE See at **less.**

fey (feɪ) *adj* **1** interested in or believing in the supernatural. **2** attuned to the supernatural; clairvoyant; visionary. **3** *Chiefly Scot.* fated to die; doomed. **4** *Chiefly Scot.* in a state of high spirits or unusual excitement, formerly believed to presage death. [Old English *fæge* marked out for death; related to Old Norse *feigr* doomed, Old High German *feigi*] ▸ **'feyness** *n*

Feydeau (*French* fɛdo) *n* **Georges** (ʒɔrʒ). 1862–1921, French dramatist, noted for his farces, esp. *La Dame de chez Maxim* (1899) and *Occupe-toi d'Amélie* (1908).

Feynman ('faɪnmən) *n* **Richard.** 1918–88, U.S. physicist, noted for his research on quantum electrodynamics; shared the Nobel prize for physics in 1965.

Feynman diagram *n Physics.* a graphical representation of the interactions between elementary particles.

fez (fɛz) *n, pl* **fezzes.** an originally Turkish brimless felt or wool cap, shaped like a truncated cone, usually red and with a tassel. [C19: via French from Turkish, from FEZ] ▸ **fezzed** *adj*

Fez (fɛz) *n* a variant of **Fès.**

Fezzan (fɛ'zɑːn) *n* a region of SW Libya, in the Sahara: a former province (until 1963).

ff *symbol for:* **1** Also: **ff.** folios. **2** Also: **ff.** following (pages, lines, etc.). **3** *Music.* fortissimo: an instruction to play very loudly.

ffa *Commerce. abbrev. for* free from alongside (ship).

Ffestiniog (fɛs'tɪnjɒg) *n* a town in N Wales, in Gwynedd: tourist attractions include former slate quarries and a narrow-gauge railway at nearby Blaenau Ffestiniog. Pop.: 800 (latest est.).

FI *abbrev. for* Falkland Islands.

FIA (in Britain) *abbrev. for* Fellow of the Institute of Actuaries.

fiacre (fɪ'ɑːkrə) *n* a small four-wheeled horse-drawn carriage, usually with a folding roof. [C17: named after the Hotel de St *Fiacre,* Paris, where these vehicles were first hired out]

fiancé *or (fem)* **fiancée** (fɪ'ɒnseɪ) *n* a person who is engaged to be married. [C19: from French, from Old French *fiancier* to promise, betroth, from *fiance* a vow, from *fier* to trust, from Latin *fidere*]

fianchetto (ˌfɪən'tʃɛtəʊ, -'kɛtəʊ) *Chess.* ◆ *n, pl* **-tos, -ti** (-tiː). **1** the development of a bishop on the second rank of the neighbouring knight's file or the third rank of the nearer rook's file. ◆ *vb* **-toes, -toing, -toed. 2** to develop (a bishop) thus. [C19: from Italian diminutive of *fianco* FLANK]

Fianna ('fiːənə) *pl n* a legendary band of Irish warriors noted for their heroic exploits, attributed to the 2nd and 3rd centuries A.D. Also called: **Fenians.**

Fianna Fáil ('fɪənə 'fɑːl) *n* one of the major Irish political parties, founded by de Valera in 1926 as a republican party. [from Irish Gaelic *Fianna* warriors + *Fáil* of Ireland, from *Fál* an ancient and poetic name for Ireland]

fiasco (fɪ'æskəʊ) *n, pl* **-cos** *or* **-coes.** a complete failure, esp. one that is ignominious or humiliating. [C19: from Italian, literally: FLASK; sense development obscure]

fiat ('faɪət, -æt) *n* **1** official sanction; authoritative permission. **2** an arbitrary order or decree. **3** *Chiefly literary.* any command, decision, or act of will that brings something about. [C17: from Latin, literally: let it be done, from *fierī* to become]

fiat money *n Chiefly U.S.* money declared by a government to be legal tender though it is not convertible into standard specie.

fib (fɪb) *n* **1** a trivial and harmless lie. ◆ *vb* **fibs, fibbing, fibbed. 2** (*intr*) to tell such a lie. [C17: perhaps from *fibble-fable* an unlikely story; see FABLE] ▸ **'fibber** *n*

fiber ('faɪbə) *n* the usual U.S. spelling of **fibre.**

Fibiger (*Danish* 'fibigər) *n* **Johannes Andreas Grib** (jo'hanəs an'dreːas grɪb). 1867–1928, Danish physician: Nobel prize for physiology or medicine (1926) for his work in cancer research.

Fibonacci (*Italian* fibo'nattʃi) *n* **Leonardo** (leo'nardo), also called *Leonardo of Pisa.* ?1170–?1250, Italian mathematician: popularized the decimal system in Europe.

Fibonacci sequence *or* **series** (ˌfɪbə'nɑːtʃɪ) *n* the infinite sequence of numbers, 0, 1, 1, 2, 3, 5, 8, etc., in which each member (**Fibonacci number**) is the sum of the previous two. [named after Leonardo FIBONACCI]

fibre *or U.S.* **fiber** ('faɪbə) *n* **1** a natural or synthetic filament that may be spun into yarn, such as cotton or nylon. **2** cloth or other material made from such yarn. **3** a long fine continuous thread or filament. **4** the structure of any material or substance made of or as if of fibres; texture. **5** essential substance or nature: *all the fibres of his being were stirred.* **6** strength of character (esp. in the phrase **moral fibre**). **7** See **dietary fibre. 8** *Botany.* **8a** a narrow elongated thick-walled cell: a constituent of sclerenchyma tissue. **8b** such tissue extracted from flax, hemp, etc., used to make linen, rope, etc. **8c** a very small root or twig. **9** *Anatomy.* any thread-shaped structure, such as a nerve fibre. [C14: from Latin *fibra* filament, entrails] ▸ **'fibred** *or U.S.* **'fibered** *adj* ▸ **'fibreless** *or U.S.* **'fiberless** *adj*

fibreboard *or U.S.* **fiberboard** ('faɪbəˌbɔːd) *n* a building material made of compressed wood or other plant fibres, esp. one in the form of a thin semirigid sheet.

fibrefill *or U.S.* **fiberfill** ('faɪbəˌfɪl) *n* a synthetic fibre used as a filling for pillows, quilted materials, etc.

fibreglass *or U.S.* **fiberglass** ('faɪbəˌglɑːs) *n* **1** material consisting of matted fine glass fibres, used as insulation in buildings, in fireproof fabrics, etc. **2** a fabric woven from this material or a light strong material made by bonding fibreglass with a synthetic resin; used for car bodies, boat hulls, etc. Also called: **glass fibre.**

fibre optics *n* (*functioning as sing*) the transmission of information modulated on light carried down very thin flexible fibres of glass. See also **optical fibre.** ▸ **ˌfibre'optic** *adj*

fibrescope *or U.S.* **fiberscope** ('faɪbəˌskəʊp) *n* an endoscope that transmits images of the interior of a hollow organ by fibre optics.

fibriform ('faɪbrɪˌfɔːm, 'fɪb-) *adj* having the form of a fibre or fibres.

fibril ('faɪbrɪl) *or* **fibrilla** (faɪ'brɪlə, fɪ-) *n, pl* **-brils** *or* **-brillae** (-'brɪliː). **1** a small fibre or part of a fibre. **2** *Biology.* a threadlike structure, such as a root hair or a thread of muscle tissue. [C17: from New Latin *fibrilla* a little FIBRE] ▸ **'fibrilar, fi'brillar,** *or* **fi'brillose** *adj* ▸ **fi'brilliˌform** *adj*

fibrillation (ˌfaɪbrɪ'leɪʃən, ˌfɪb-) *n* **1** a local and uncontrollable twitching of muscle fibres, not affecting the entire muscle. **2** irregular twitchings of the muscular wall of the heart, often interfering with the normal rhythmic contractions.

fibrin ('fɪbrɪn) *n* a white insoluble elastic protein formed from fibrinogen when blood clots: forms a network that traps red cells and platelets.

fibrinogen (fɪ'brɪnədʒən) *n* a soluble protein, a globulin, in blood plasma, converted to fibrin by the action of the enzyme thrombin when blood clots. ▸ **fibrinogenic** (ˌfaɪbrɪnəʊ'dʒɛnɪk) *or* **fibrinogenous** (ˌfaɪbrɪ'nɒdʒənəs) *adj*

fibrinolysis (ˌfɪbrɪ'nɒlɪsɪs) *n* the breakdown of fibrin in blood clots, esp. by enzymes. ▸ **fibrinolytic** (ˌfaɪbrɪnəʊ'lɪtɪk) *adj*

fibrinous ('fɪbrɪnəs) *adj* of, containing, or resembling fibrin.

fibro ('faɪbrəʊ) *n Austral. informal.* **1a** short for **fibrocement. 1b** (*as modifier*): *a fibro shack.* **2** a house built of fibrocement.

fibro- *combining form.* **1** indicating fibrous tissue: *fibroin; fibrosis.* **2** indicating fibre: *fibrocement.* [from Latin *fibra* FIBRE]

fibroblast ('faɪbrəʊˌblæst) *n* a cell in connective tissue that synthesizes collagen. ▸ **ˌfibro'blastic** *adj*

fibrocement (ˌfaɪbrəʊsɪ'mɛnt) *n* (formerly) cement combined with asbestos fibre, used esp. in sheets for building.

fibroid ('faɪbrɔɪd) *adj* **1** *Anatomy.* (of structures or tissues) containing or resembling fibres. ◆ *n* **2** a benign tumour, composed of fibrous and muscular tissue, occurring in the wall of the uterus and often causing heavy menstruation.

fibroin ('faɪbrəʊɪn) *n* a tough elastic protein that is the principal component of spiders' webs and raw silk.

Fibrolite ('faɪbrəlaɪt) *n N.Z. trademark.* a type of building board containing asbestos and cement.

fibroma (faɪ'brəʊmə) *n, pl* **-mata** (-mətə) *or* **-mas.** a benign tumour derived from fibrous connective tissue. ▸ **fibromatous** (faɪ'brɒmətəs) *adj*

fibromyalgia (ˌfaɪbrəʊmaɪ'ældʒɪə) *n* a rheumatoid disorder characterized by muscle pain and headaches: may be due to a disorder of deep sleep.

fibrosis (faɪ'brəʊsɪs) *n* the formation of an abnormal amount of fibrous tissue in an organ or part as the result of inflammation, irritation, or healing. ▸ **fibrotic** (faɪ'brɒtɪk) *adj*

fibrositis (ˌfaɪbrə'saɪtɪs) *n* inflammation of white fibrous tissue, esp. that of muscle sheaths.

fibrous ('faɪbrəs) *adj* consisting of, containing, or resembling fibres: *fibrous tissue.* ▸ **'fibrously** *adv* ▸ **'fibrousness** *n*

fibrovascular (ˌfaɪbrəʊ'væskjʊlə) *adj Botany.* (of a vascular bundle) surrounded by sclerenchyma or within sclerenchymatous tissue.

fibula ('fɪbjʊlə) *n, pl* **-lae** (-ˌliː) *or* **-las. 1** the outer and thinner of the two bones between the knee and ankle of the human leg. Compare **tibia. 2** the corresponding bone in other vertebrates. **3** a metal brooch resembling a safety pin, often highly decorated, common in Europe after 1300 B.C. [C17: from Latin: clasp, probably from *figere* to fasten] ▸ **'fibular** *adj*

-fic *suffix forming adjectives.* causing, making, or producing: *honorific.* [from Latin *-ficus,* from *facere* to do, make]

fiche (fiːʃ) *n* See **microfiche, ultrafiche.**

Fichte (*German* 'fɪçtə) *n* **Johann Gottlieb** (jo'han 'gɔtliːp). 1762–1814, German philosopher: expounded ethical idealism.

fichu ('fiːʃuː) *n* a woman's shawl or scarf of some light material, worn esp. in the 18th century. [C19: from French: small shawl, from *ficher* to fix with a pin, from Latin *figere* to fasten, FIX]

Ficino (*Italian* fi'tʃiːno) *n* **Marsilio** (mar'siːlio). 1433–99, Italian Neoplatonist philosopher: attempted to integrate Platonism with Christianity.

fickle ('fɪkᵊl) *adj* changeable in purpose, affections, etc.; capricious. [Old English *ficol* deceitful; related to *fician* to wheedle, *befician* to deceive] ▸ **'fickleness** *n*

fico ('fiːkəʊ) *n, pl* **-coes.** *Archaic.* **1** a worthless trifle. **2** another word for **fig**[1] (sense 7). [C16: from Italian: FIG[1]]

fictile ('fɪktaɪl) *adj* **1** moulded or capable of being moulded from clay; plastic. **2** made of clay by a potter. **3** relating to the craft of pottery. [C17: from Latin *fictilis* that can be moulded, hence, made of clay, from *fingere* to shape]

fiction ('fɪkʃən) *n* **1** literary works invented by the imagination, such as novels or short stories. **2** an invented story or explanation; lie. **3** the act of inventing a story or explanation. **4** *Law.* something assumed to be true for the sake of convenience, though probably false. [C14: from Latin *fictiō* a fashioning, hence something imaginary, from *fingere* to shape] ▸ **'fictional** *adj* ▸ **'fictionally** *adv* ▸ **ˌfictio'neer** *or* **'fictionist** *n*

fictionalize *or* **fictionalise** ('fɪkʃənəˌlaɪz) *vb* (*tr*) to make into fiction or give a fictional aspect to. ▸ **ˌfictionali'zation** *or* **ˌfictionali'sation** *n*

fictitious (fɪk'tɪʃəs) *adj* **1** not genuine or authentic; assumed; false: *to give a fic-*

titious address. **2** of, related to, or characteristic of fiction; created by the imagination. ▸ **fic'titiously** *adv* ▸ **fic'titiousness** *n*

fictive ('fɪktɪv) *adj* **1** *Rare.* of, relating to, or able to create fiction. **2** a rare word for **fictitious.** ▸ **'fictively** *adv*

ficus ('fi:kəs) *n* any plant of the genus *Ficus,* which includes the edible fig and several greenhouse and house plants. See **rubber plant, weeping ivy.**

fid (fɪd) *n Nautical.* **1** a spike for separating strands of rope in splicing. **2** a wooden or metal bar for supporting the heel of a topmast. [C17: of unknown origin]

-fid *adj combining form.* divided into parts or lobes: *bifid; pinnatifid.* [from Latin *-fidus,* from *findere* to split]

Fid. Def. *or* **FID DEF** *abbrev. for* Fidei Defensor.

fiddle ('fɪdᵊl) *n* **1** *Informal or sometimes when used of a classical violin disparaging.* any instrument of the viol or violin family, esp. the violin. **2** a violin played as a folk instrument. **3** time-wasting or trifling behaviour; nonsense; triviality. **4** *Nautical.* a small railing around the top of a table to prevent objects from falling off it in bad weather. **5** *Brit. informal.* an illegal or fraudulent transaction or arrangement. **6** *Brit. informal.* a manually delicate or tricky operation. **7 at** *or* **on the fiddle.** *Informal.* engaged in an illegal or fraudulent undertaking. **8 face as long as a fiddle.** *Informal.* a dismal or gloomy facial expression. **9 fit as a fiddle.** *Informal.* in very good health. **10 play second fiddle.** *Informal.* to be subordinate; play a minor part. ◆ *vb* **11** to play (a tune) on the fiddle. **12** (*intr; often foll. by with*) to make restless or aimless movements with the hands. **13** (when *intr,* often foll. by *about* or *around*) *Informal.* to spend (time) or act in a careless or inconsequential manner; waste (time). **14** (often foll. by *with*) *Informal.* to tamper or interfere (with). **15** *Informal.* to contrive to do (something) by illicit means or deception: *he fiddled his way into a position of trust.* **16** (*tr*) *Informal.* to falsify (accounts, etc.); swindle. [Old English *fithele,* probably from Medieval Latin *vītula,* from Latin *vītulārī* to celebrate; compare Old High German *fidula* fiddle; see VIOLA[1]]

fiddle-back *n* **1** a chair with a fiddle-shaped back. **2** a chasuble with a fiddle-shaped front.

fiddle-de-dee, fiddlededee, *or* **fiddledeedee** (ˌfɪdᵊldɪ'di:) *interj Rare.* an exclamation of impatience, disbelief, or disagreement.

fiddle-faddle ('fɪdᵊlˌfædᵊl) *n, interj* **1** trivial matter; nonsense. ◆ *vb* **2** (*intr*) to fuss or waste time, esp. over trivial matters. [C16: reduplication of FIDDLE] ▸ **'fiddle-ˌfaddler** *n*

fiddlehead ('fɪdᵊlˌhɛd) *or* **fiddleneck** *n* **1** *Nautical.* an ornamental carving, in the shape of the scroll at the head end of a fiddle, fitted to the top of the stem or cutwater. **2** *U.S. and Canadian.* the edible coiled tip of a young fern frond.

fiddle pattern *n* the style of a spoon or fork with a violin-shaped handle.

fiddler ('fɪdlə) *n* **1** a person who plays the fiddle, esp. in folk music. **2** See **fiddler crab. 3** a person who wastes time or acts aimlessly. **4** *Informal.* a cheat or petty rogue.

fiddler crab *n* any of various burrowing crabs of the genus *Uca* of American coastal regions, the males of which have one of their anterior pincer-like claws very much enlarged. [C19: referring to the rapid fiddling movement of the enlarged anterior claw of the males, used to attract females]

fiddlestick ('fɪdᵊlˌstɪk) *n* **1** *Informal.* a violin bow. **2** any meaningless or inconsequential thing; trifle. **3 fiddlesticks!** an expression of annoyance or disagreement.

fiddlewood ('fɪdᵊlˌwʊd) *n* **1** any of various tropical American verbenaceous trees of the genus *Citharexylum* and related genera. **2** the hard durable wood of any of these trees.

fiddling ('fɪdlɪŋ) *adj* trifling or insignificant; petty.

fiddly ('fɪdlɪ) *adj* **-dlier, -dliest.** small and awkward to do or handle.

FIDE *abbrev. for* Fédération Internationale des Echecs: International Chess Federation.

fideicommissary (ˌfɪdɪaɪ'kɒmɪsərɪ) *Civil law.* ◆ *n, pl* **-saries. 1** a person who receives a fideicommissum. ◆ *adj* **2** of, relating to, or resembling a fideicommissum.

fideicommissum (ˌfɪdɪaɪkə'mɪsəm) *n, pl* **-sa** (-sə). *Civil law.* a gift of property, usually by will, to be held on behalf of another who cannot receive the gift directly. [C18: from Late Latin: (something) bequeathed in trust, from Latin *fidēs* trust, faith + *committere* to entrust]

Fidei Defensor *Latin.* ('faɪdɪˌaɪ dɪ'fɛnsɔ:) *n* defender of the faith; a title given to Henry VIII by Pope Leo X, and appearing on Brit. coins as FID DEF or FD.

fideism ('fi:deɪˌɪzəm) *n* the theological doctrine that religious truth is a matter of faith and cannot be established by reason. Compare **natural theology.** [C19: from Latin *fidēs* faith] ▸ **'fideist** *n* ▸ **ˌfide'istic** *adj*

Fidelism (fi:'dɛlɪzəm) *n* belief in, adherence to, or advocacy of the principles of Fidel Castro. Also called: **Castroism.** ▸ **Fi'delist** *n*

fidelity (fɪ'dɛlɪtɪ) *n, pl* **-ties. 1** devotion to duties, obligations, etc.; faithfulness. **2** loyalty or devotion, as to a person or cause. **3** faithfulness to one's spouse, lover, etc. **4** adherence to truth; accuracy in reporting detail. **5** *Electronics.* the degree to which the output of a system, such as an amplifier or radio, accurately reproduces the characteristics of the input signal. See also **high fidelity.** [C15: from Latin *fidēlitās,* from *fidēlis* faithful, from *fidēs* faith, loyalty]

fidge (fɪdʒ) *vb* (*intr*) an obsolete word for **fidget.** [C18: probably variant of dialect *fitch* to FIDGET]

fidget ('fɪdʒɪt) *vb* **1** (*intr*) to move about restlessly. **2** (*intr; often foll. by with*) to make restless or uneasy movements (with something); fiddle: *he fidgeted with his pen.* **3** (*tr*) to cause to fidget. **4** (*tr*) to cause to worry; make uneasy. ◆ *n* **5** (*often pl*) a state of restlessness or unease, esp. as expressed in continual motion: *he's got the fidgets.* **6** a person who fidgets. [C17: from earlier *fidge,* probably from Old Norse *fīkjast* to desire eagerly] ▸ **'fidgetingly** *adv* ▸ **'fidgety** *adj*

fiducial (fɪ'dju:ʃɪəl) *adj* **1** *Physics.* used as a standard of reference or measurement: *a fiducial point.* **2** of or based on trust or faith. **3** *Law.* a less common word for **fiduciary.** [C17: from Late Latin *fīdūciālis,* from Latin *fīdūcia* confidence, reliance, from *fīdere* to trust] ▸ **fi'ducially** *adv*

fiduciary (fɪ'du:ʃɪərɪ) *Law.* ◆ *n* **1** a person bound to act for another's benefit, as a trustee in relation to his beneficiary. ◆ *adj* **2a** having the nature of a trust. **2b** of or relating to a trust or trustee. [C17: from Latin *fīdūciārius* relating to something held in trust, from *fīdūcia* trust; see FIDUCIAL] ▸ **fi'duciarily** *adv*

fiduciary issue *n* an issue of banknotes not backed by gold.

fidus Achates ('faɪdəs ə'keɪti:z) *n* a faithful friend or companion. [Latin, literally: faithful Achates, the name of the faithful companion of Aeneas in Virgil's *Aeneid*]

fie (faɪ) *interj Obsolete or facetious.* an exclamation of distaste or mock dismay. [C13: from Old French *fi,* from Latin *fī,* exclamation of disgust]

fief *or* **feoff** (fi:f) *n* (in feudal Europe) the property or fee granted to a vassal for his maintenance by his lord in return for service. [C17: from Old French *fie,* of Germanic origin; compare Old English *fēo* cattle, money, Latin *pecus* cattle, *pecūnia* money, Greek *pokos* fleece]

fiefdom ('fi:fdəm) *n* **1** (in feudal Europe) the property owned by a lord. **2** an area over which a person or organization exerts authority or influence.

field (fi:ld) *n* **1** an open tract of uncultivated grassland; meadow. Related adj: **campestral. 2** a piece of land cleared of trees and undergrowth, usually enclosed with a fence or hedge and used for pasture or growing crops: *a field of barley.* **3** a limited or marked off area, usually of mown grass, on which any of various sports, athletic competitions, etc., are held: *a soccer field.* **4** an area that is rich in minerals or other natural resources: *a coalfield.* **5** short for **battlefield** and **airfield. 6** the mounted followers that hunt with a pack of hounds. **7a** all the runners in a particular race or competitors in a competition. **7b** the runners in a race or competitors in a competition excluding the favourite. **8** *Cricket.* the fielders collectively, esp. with regard to their positions. **9** a wide or open expanse: *a field of snow.* **10a** an area of human activity: *the field of human knowledge.* **10b** a sphere or division of knowledge, interest, etc.: *his field is physics.* **11a** a place away from the laboratory, office, library, etc., usually out of doors, where practical work is done or original material or data collected. **11b** (*as modifier*): *a field course.* **12** the surface or background, as of a flag, coin, or heraldic shield, on which a design is displayed. **13** Also called: **field of view.** the area within which an object may be observed with a telescope, microscope, etc. **14** *Physics.* **14a** See **field of force. 14b** a region of space that is a vector field. **14c** a region of space under the influence of some scalar quantity, such as temperature. **15** *Maths.* a set of entities subject to two binary operations, addition and multiplication, such that the set is a commutative group under addition and the set, minus the zero, is a commutative group under multiplication. **16** *Maths, logic.* the set of elements that are either arguments or values of a function; the union of its domain and range. **17** *Computing.* **17a** a set of one or more characters comprising a unit of information. **17b** a predetermined section of a record. **18** *Television.* one of two or more sets of scanning lines which when interlaced form the complete picture. **19** *Obsolete.* the open country: *beasts of the field.* **20 hold** *or* **keep the field.** to maintain one's position in the face of opposition. **21 in the field. 21a** *Military.* in an area in which operations are in progress. **21b** actively or closely involved with or working on something (rather than being in a more remote or administrative position). **22 lead the field.** to be in the leading or most pre-eminent position. **23 leave the field.** *Informal.* to back out of a competition, contest, etc. **24 take the field.** to begin or carry on activity, esp. in sport or military operations. **25 play the field.** *Informal.* to disperse one's interests or attentions among a number of activities, people, or objects. **26** (*modifier*) *Military.* of or relating to equipment, personnel, etc., specifically designed or trained for operations in the field: *a field gun; a field army.* ◆ *vb* **27** (*tr*) *Sport.* to stop, catch, or return (the ball) as a fielder. **28** (*tr*) *Sport.* to send (a player or team) onto the field to play. **29** (*intr*) *Sport.* (of a player or team) to act or take turn as a fielder or fielders. **30** (*tr*) *Military.* to put (an army, a unit, etc.) in the field. **31** (*tr*) to enter (a person) in a competition: *each party fielded a candidate.* **32** (*tr*) *Informal.* to deal with or handle, esp. adequately and by making a reciprocal gesture: *to field a question.* [Old English *feld;* related to Old Saxon, Old High German *feld,* Old English *fold* earth, Greek *platus* broad]

Field (fi:ld) *n* **John.** 1782–1837, Irish composer and pianist, lived in Russia from 1803: invented the nocturne.

field ambulance *n Military.* a mobile medical unit that accepts casualties from forward units, treating the lightly wounded and stabilizing the condition of the seriously wounded before evacuating them to a hospital.

field army *n Military.* the largest formation of a land force, usually consisting of two or more corps with supporting arms and services.

field artillery *n* artillery capable of deployment in support of front-line troops, due mainly to its mobility.

field battery *n* a small unit of usually four field guns.

field boot *n* a close-fitting knee-length boot.

field captain *n* the senior official at an archery meeting, responsible for safety.

field centre *n* a centre equipped for field studies, usually situated in or near an area where field studies are carried out.

field corn *n U.S.* any variety of corn that is grown as a feed for livestock.

field cornet *n S. African.* a commander of burgher troops called up in time of war or in an emergency, esp. during the 19th century. Often shortened to **cornet.**

fieldcraft ('fi:ldˌkrɑ:ft) *n* ability and experience in matters concerned with living out-of-doors, esp. in a wild area.

field day *n* **1** a day spent in some special outdoor activity, such as nature study or sport. **2** a day-long competition between amateur radio operators using battery or generator power, the aim being to make the most contacts with other operators around the world. **3** *Military.* a day devoted to manoeuvres or exercises, esp. before an audience. **4** *Informal.* a day or time of exciting or successful activity: *the children had a field day with their new toys.* **5** *Austral.* **5a** a day or series of days devoted to the demonstration of farm machinery in country centres. **5b** a combined open day and sale on a stud property.

field drain *or* **tile** *n* an underground earthenware pipe used for draining fields.

field-effect transistor *n* a unipolar transistor consisting of three or more electrode regions, the source, one or more gates, and the drain. A current flowing in a channel between the highly doped source and drain is controlled by the electric field arising from a voltage applied between source and gate. Abbrev.: **FET.** See also **JFET, IGFET.**

field emission *n* the emission of electrons from a solid or liquid subjected to a high electric field.

fielder ('fi:ldə) *n Cricket, baseball, etc.* **a** a player in the field. **b** a member of the fielding rather than the batting side.

field event *n* a competition, such as the discus, high jump, etc., that takes place on a field or similar area as opposed to those on the running track.

fieldfare ('fi:ld,fɛə) *n* a large Old World thrush, *Turdus pilaris,* having a pale grey head and rump, brown wings and back, and a blackish tail. [Old English *feldefare;* see FIELD, FARE]

field glass *n* **1** a small telescope often incorporating a prism and held in one hand. **2** a former name for **field glasses.**

field glasses *pl n or* (*formerly*) **field glass** *n* another name for **binoculars.**

field goal *n* **1** *Basketball.* a goal scored while the ball is in normal play rather than from a free throw. **2** *American and Canadian football.* a score of three points made by kicking the ball through the opponent's goalposts above the crossbar.

field guidance *n* a method of guiding a missile to a point within a gravitational or radio field by means of the properties of the field.

field gun *n* a gun specially designed for service in direct support of front-line troops.

field hockey *n U.S. and Canadian.* hockey played on a field, as distinguished from ice hockey.

field-holler *n* a cry employing falsetto, portamento, and sudden changes of pitch, used in African-American work songs, later integrated into the techniques of the blues.

field hospital *n* a temporary hospital set up near a battlefield equipped to provide remedial surgery and post-operative care.

Fielding ('fi:ldɪŋ) *n* **Henry.** 1707–54, English novelist and dramatist, noted particularly for his picaresque novel *Tom Jones* (1749) and for *Joseph Andrews* (1742), which starts as a parody of Richardson's *Pamela:* also noted as an enlightened magistrate and a founder of the Bow Street runners (1749).

field layer *n* See **layer** (sense 2).

field magnet *n* a permanent magnet or an electromagnet that produces the magnetic field in a generator, electric motor, or similar device.

field marshal *n* an officer holding the highest rank in the British and certain other armies.

fieldmouse ('fi:ld,maʊs) *n, pl* **-mice. 1** any nocturnal mouse of the genus *Apodemus,* inhabiting woods, fields, and gardens of the Old World: family *Muridae.* They have yellowish-brown fur and feed on fruit, vegetables, seeds, etc. **2** a former name for **vole**[1].

field officer *n* an officer holding **field rank,** namely that of major, lieutenant colonel, or colonel.

field of fire *n* the area that a weapon or group of weapons can cover with fire from a given position.

field of force *n* the region of space surrounding a body, such as a charged particle or a magnet, within which it can exert a force on another similar body not in contact with it. See also **electric field, magnetic field, gravitational field.**

field of honour *n* the place or scene of a battle or duel, esp. of jousting tournaments in medieval times.

fieldpiece ('fi:ld,pi:s) *n* a former name for **field gun.**

field poppy *n* another name for **corn poppy.**

field post office *n* a place to which mail intended for military units in the field is sent to be sorted and forwarded. Abbrev.: **FPO.**

Fields (fi:ldz) *n* **1** Dame **Gracie.** real name *Grace Stansfield.* 1898–1979, English popular singer and entertainer. **2 W. C.** real name *William Claude Dukenfield.* 1880–1946, U.S. film actor, noted for his portrayal of comic roles.

fieldsman ('fi:ldzmən) *n, pl* **-men.** *Cricket.* another name for **fielder.**

field spaniel *n* a robust, low-slung breed of spaniel developed by crossing the cocker spaniel with the Sussex spaniel.

field sports *pl n* sports carried on in the open countryside, such as hunting, shooting, or fishing.

fieldstone ('fi:ld,stəʊn) *n* building stone found in fields.

field strength *n* **1** *Radio, television.* the intensity of an electromagnetic wave at any point in the area covered by a radio or television transmitter. **2** *Physics.* the intensity of an electric or magnetic field. See **intensity.**

field study *n* (*often pl*) a research project carried out in the field. See **field** (sense 11).

field tile *n Brit. and N.Z.* an earthenware drain used in farm drainage.

field trial *n* **1** *Hunting.* a test of or contest between gun dogs to determine their proficiency and standard of training in retrieving or pointing. **2** (*often pl*) a test to display performance, efficiency, or durability, as of a vehicle or invention.

field trip *n* an expedition, as by a group of students or research workers, to study something at first hand.

field winding ('waɪndɪŋ) *n* the insulated current-carrying coils on a field magnet that produce the magnetic field intensity required to set up the electrical excitation in a generator or motor.

fieldwork ('fi:ld,wɜ:k) *n Military.* a temporary structure used in defending or fortifying a place or position.

field work *n* an investigation or search for material, data, etc., made in the field as opposed to the classroom, laboratory, or official headquarters. ▸ **field worker** *n*

fiend (fi:nd) *n* **1** an evil spirit; demon; devil. **2** a person who is extremely wicked, esp. in being very cruel or brutal. **3** *Informal.* **3a** a person who is intensely interested in or fond of something: *a fresh-air fiend; he is a fiend for cards.* **3b** an addict: *a drug fiend.* **4** *Informal.* a mischievous or spiteful person, esp. a child. [Old English *fēond;* related to Old Norse *fjāndi* enemy, Gothic *fijands,* Old High German *fiant*] ▸ **'fiend,like** *adj*

Fiend (fi:nd) *n* **the.** the devil; Satan.

fiendish ('fi:ndɪʃ) *adj* **1** of or like a fiend. **2** diabolically wicked or cruel. **3** *Informal.* extremely difficult or unpleasant: *a fiendish problem.* ▸ **'fiendishly** *adv* ▸ **'fiendishness** *n*

fier *or* **fiere** (fi:r) *n Scot.* variant spellings of **fere.**

fierce (fɪəs) *adj* **1** having a violent and unrestrained nature; savage: *a fierce dog.* **2** wild or turbulent in force, action, or intensity: *a fierce storm.* **3** vehement, intense, or strong: *fierce competition.* **4** *Informal.* very disagreeable or unpleasant. [C13: from Old French *fiers,* from Latin *ferus*] ▸ **'fiercely** *adv* ▸ **'fierceness** *n*

fieri facias ('faɪə,raɪ 'feɪʃɪəs) *n Law.* a writ ordering a levy on the belongings of an adjudged debtor to satisfy the debt. [C15: from Latin, literally: cause (it) to be done]

fiery ('faɪərɪ) *adj* **fierier, fieriest. 1** of, containing, or composed of fire. **2** resembling fire in heat, colour, ardour, etc.: *a fiery desert wind; a fiery speaker.* **3** easily angered or aroused: *a fiery temper.* **4** (of food) producing a burning sensation: *a fiery curry.* **5** (of the skin or a sore) inflamed. **6** flammable or containing flammable gas. **7** (of a cricket pitch) making the ball bounce dangerously high. ▸ **'fierily** *adv* ▸ **'fieriness** *n*

fiery cross *n* **1** a burning cross, used as a symbol by the Ku Klux Klan. **2** a wooden cross with ends charred or dipped in blood formerly used by Scottish Highlanders to summon the clans to battle.

Fiesole[1] (*Italian* 'fie:zole) *n* a town in central Italy, in Tuscany near Florence: Etruscan and Roman remains. Pop.: 4 000 (1987 est.). Ancient name: **Faesulae** ('fi:sjʊli:).

Fiesole[2] (*Italian* 'fie:zole) *n* **Giovanni da** (dʒo'vanni da). the monastic name of (Fra) **Angelico.**

fiesta (fɪ'estə; *Spanish* 'fjesta) *n* (esp. in Spain and Latin America) **1** a religious festival or celebration, esp. on a saint's day. **2** a holiday or carnival. [Spanish, from Latin *festa,* plural of *festum* festival; see FEAST]

FIFA ('fi:fə) *n acronym for* Fédération Internationale de Football Association. [from French]

fife (faɪf) *n* **1** a small high-pitched flute similar to the piccolo and usually having no keys, used esp. in military bands. ◆ *vb* **2** to play (music) on a fife. [C16: from Old High German *pfīfa;* see PIPE[1]] ▸ **'fifer** *n*

Fife[1] (faɪf) *n* a council area and historical county of E central Scotland, bordering on the North Sea between the Firths of Tay and Forth: coastal lowlands in the north and east, with several ranges of hills; mainly agricultural. Administrative centre: Glenrothes. Pop.: 351 200 (1996 est.). Area: 1323 sq. km (511 sq. miles).

Fife[2] (faɪf) *n* **Duncan.** See (Duncan) **Phyfe, Duncan Phyfe.**

fife rail *n Nautical.* a rail at the base of a mast of a sailing vessel, fitted with pins for belaying running rigging. Compare **pin rail.** [C18: of unknown origin]

fifi hook ('fi:fi:) *n Mountaineering.* a metal hook at the top of an étrier for attaching it to a peg and also connected by a cord to the climber's harness to pull the étrier up and prevent it being dropped. [C20: of unknown origin]

FIFO ('faɪfəʊ) *acronym for* first in, first out (as an accounting principle in costing stock). Compare **LIFO.**

fifteen ('fɪf'ti:n) *n* **1** the cardinal number that is the sum of ten and five. **2** a numeral, 15, XV, etc., representing this number. **3** something represented by, representing, or consisting of 15 units. **4** a rugby football team. ◆ *determiner* **5a** amounting to fifteen: *fifteen jokes.* **5b** (*as pronoun*): *fifteen of us danced.* [Old English *fīftēne*]

Fifteen ('fɪf'ti:n) *n* **the.** *British history.* the Jacobite rising of 1715.

fifteenth ('fɪf'ti:nθ) *adj* **1a** coming after the fourteenth in order, position, time, etc. Often written 15th. **1b** (*as n*): *the fifteenth of the month.* ◆ *n* **2a** one of 15 equal or nearly equal parts of something. **2b** (*as modifier*): *a fifteenth part.* **3** the fraction equal to one divided by 15 (1/15). **4a** an interval of two octaves. **4b** one of two notes constituting such an interval in relation to the other, esp. the one higher in pitch. **4c** an organ stop of diapason quality sounding a note two octaves higher than that normally produced by the key depressed; a two-foot stop.

fifth (fɪfθ) *adj* (*usually prenominal*) **1a** coming after the fourth in order, position, time, etc. Often written 5th. **1b** (*as n*): *he came on the fifth.* ◆ *n* **2a** one of five equal or nearly equal parts of an object, quantity, measurement, etc. **2b** (*as modifier*): *a fifth part.* **3** the fraction equal to one divided by five (1/5). **4** *Music.* **4a** the interval between one note and another five notes away from it counting inclusively along the diatonic scale. **4b** one of two notes constituting such an interval in relation to the other. See also **perfect** (sense 9), **diminished** (sense 2), **interval** (sense 5). **5** an additional high gear fitted to some vehicles, esp. certain sports cars. ◆ *adv* **6** Also: **fifthly.** after the fourth person, position, event, etc. ◆ *sentence connector.* **7** Also: **fifthly.** as the fifth point: linking what follows with the previous statements, as in a speech or argument. [Old English *fīfta*]

Fifth Amendment *n* **1** an amendment to the U.S. Constitution stating that no person may be compelled to testify against himself and that no person may be tried for a second time on a charge for which he has already been acquitted. **2 take the fifth (amendment).** *U.S.* to refuse to answer a question on the grounds that it might incriminate oneself.

fifth column *n* **1** (originally) a group of Falangist sympathizers in Madrid during the Spanish Civil War who were prepared to join the four columns of insurgents marching on the city. **2** any group of hostile or subversive infiltrators; an enemy in one's midst. ► **fifth columnist** *n*

fifth disease *n* a mild infectious disease of childhood, caused by a virus, characterized by fever and a red rash spreading from the cheeks to the limbs and trunk. Also called: **slapped-cheek disease**. Technical name: **erythema infectiosum**. [C20: from its being among the five most common childhood infections]

fifth force *n* a hypothetical non-Newtonian repulsive component of the force of gravity, postulated as an addition to the four known fundamental forces (gravitational, electromagnetic, strong, and weak).

fifth-generation *adj* denoting developments in computer design to produce machines with artifical intelligence.

Fifth Republic *n* the French republic established in 1958 as the successor to the Fourth Republic. Its constitution is characterized by the strong position of the president.

fifth wheel *n* **1** a spare wheel for a four-wheeled vehicle. **2** a steering bearing that enables the front axle of a horse-drawn vehicle to rotate relative to the body. **3** a superfluous or unnecessary person or thing.

fiftieth ('fɪftɪɪθ) *adj* **1a** being the ordinal number of *fifty* in order, position, time, etc. Often written 50th. **1b** (*as n*): *the fiftieth in the series.* ♦ *n* **2a** one of 50 equal or approximately equal parts of something. **2b** (*as modifier*): *a fiftieth part.* **3** the fraction equal to one divided by 50 (1/50).

fifty ('fɪftɪ) *n, pl* **-ties. 1** the cardinal number that is the product of ten and five. **2** a numeral, 50, L, etc., representing this number. **3** something represented by, representing, or consisting of 50 units. ♦ *determiner* **4a** amounting to fifty: *fifty people.* **4b** (*as pronoun*): *fifty should be sufficient.* [Old English *fīftig*]

fifty-fifty *adj, adv Informal.* shared or sharing equally; in equal parts.

fig[1] (fɪg) *n* **1** any moraceous tree or shrub of the tropical and subtropical genus *Ficus*, in which the flowers are borne inside a pear-shaped receptacle. **2** the fruit of any of these trees, esp. of *F. carica*, which develops from the receptacle and has sweet flesh containing numerous seedlike structures. **3** any of various plants or trees having a fruit similar to this. **4 Hottentot** *or* **sour fig.** a succulent plant, *Mesembryanthemum edule*, of southern Africa, having a capsular fruit containing edible pulp: family *Aizoaceae*. **5** (*used with a negative*) something of negligible value; jot: *I don't care a fig for your opinion.* **6** Also: **feg.** *Dialect.* a piece or segment from an orange. **7** Also called: **fico.** an insulting gesture made with the thumb between the first two fingers or under the upper teeth. [C13: from Old French *figue*, from Old Provençal *figa*, from Latin *fīcus* fig tree]

fig[2] (fɪg) *Slang.* ♦ *vb* **figs, figging, figged.** (*tr*) **1** (foll. by *out* or *up*) to dress (up) or rig (out). **2** to administer stimulating drugs to (a horse). ♦ *n* **3** dress, appearance, or array (esp. in the phrase **in full fig**). **4** physical condition or form: *in bad fig.* [C17 *feague*, of uncertain origin]

fig. *abbrev. for:* **1** figurative(ly). **2** figure.

fig-bird *n* any Australian oriole of the genus *Sphecotheres*, feeding on figs and other fruit.

fight (faɪt) *vb* **fights, fighting, fought. 1** to oppose or struggle against (an enemy) in battle. **2** to oppose or struggle against (a person, thing, cause, etc.) in any manner. **3** (*tr*) to engage in or carry on (a battle, contest, etc.). **4** (when *intr*, often foll. by *for*) to uphold or maintain (a cause, ideal, etc.) by fighting or struggling: *to fight for freedom.* **5** (*tr*) to make or achieve (a way) by fighting. **6** (*intr*) *Boxing.* **6a** to box, as for a living. **6b** to use aggressive rough tactics. **7** to engage (another or others) in combat. **8 fight it out.** to contend or struggle until a decisive result is obtained. **9 fight shy of.** to keep aloof from. ♦ *n* **10** a battle, struggle, or physical combat. **11** a quarrel, dispute, or contest. **12** resistance (esp. in the phrase **to put up a fight**). **13** the desire to take part in physical combat (esp. in the phrase **to show fight**). **14** a boxing match. ♦ See also **fight back, fight off.** [Old English *feohtan*; related to Old Frisian *fiuchta*, Old Saxon, Old High German *fehtan* to fight] ► '**fighting** *n, adj*

fight back *vb* (*adv*) **1** (*intr*) to resist an attack. **2** (*intr*) to counterattack. **3** (*tr*) to struggle to repress: *she tried to fight back her tears.* ♦ *n* **fightback. 4** an act or campaign of resistance. **5** a counterattack.

fighter ('faɪtə) *n* **1** a person who fights, esp. a professional boxer. **2** a person who has determination. **3** *Military.* an armed aircraft designed for destroying other aircraft.

fighter-bomber *n* a high-performance aircraft that combines the roles of fighter and bomber.

fighting chance *n* a slight chance of success dependent on a struggle.

fighting cock *n* **1** another name for **gamecock. 2** a pugnacious person.

fighting fish *n* any of various labyrinth fishes of the genus *Betta*, esp. the Siamese fighting fish.

fighting top *n* one of the gun platforms on the lower masts of sailing men-of-war, used in attacking the crew of an enemy ship with swivel guns and muskets.

fight off *vb* (*tr, adv*) **1** to repulse; repel. **2** to struggle to avoid or repress: *to fight off a cold.*

fight-or-flight *n* (*modifier*) involving or relating to an involuntary response to stress in which the hormone adrenaline is secreted into the blood in readiness for physical action, such as fighting or running away.

fig leaf *n* **1** a leaf from a fig tree. **2** a representation of a leaf, usually a vine leaf rather than an actual fig leaf, used in painting or sculpture to cover the genitals of nude figures. **3** a device intended to conceal something regarded as shameful or indecent.

fig marigold *n* an erect species of mesembryanthemum, *M. tricolor*, grown as a garden annual for its red-orange flowers with yellow centres.

figment ('fɪgmənt) *n* a fantastic notion, invention, or fabrication: *a figment of the imagination.* [C15: from Late Latin *figmentum* a fiction, from Latin *fingere* to shape]

figuline ('fɪgjʊˌlaɪn) *Rare.* ♦ *adj* **1** of or resembling clay. ♦ *n* **2** an article made of clay. [C17: from Latin *figulīnus* of a potter, from *figulus* a potter, from *fingere* to mould]

figural ('fɪgərəl) *adj* composed of or relating to human or animal figures.

figurant ('fɪgjʊrənt) *n* **1** a ballet dancer who does group work but no solo roles. **2** *Theatre.* a minor character, esp. one who does not speak. [C18: from French, from *figurer* to represent, appear, FIGURE] ► **figurante** (ˌfɪgjʊ'rɒnt) *fem n*

figurate ('fɪgjʊrɪt) *adj* **1** *Music.* exhibiting or produced by figuration; florid or decorative. **2** having a definite or particular shape or figure. [C15: from Latin *figūrāre* to shape] ► '**figurately** *adv*

figuration (ˌfɪgə'reɪʃən) *n* **1** *Music.* **1a** the employment of characteristic patterns of notes, esp. in variations on a theme. **1b** decoration or florid ornamentation in general. **2** the act or an instance of representing figuratively, as by means of allegory or emblem. **3** a figurative or emblematic representation. **4** the act of decorating with a design.

figurative ('fɪgərətɪv) *adj* **1** of the nature of, resembling, or involving a figure of speech; not literal; metaphorical. **2** using or filled with figures of speech. **3** representing by means of an emblem, likeness, figure, etc. **4** (in painting, sculpture, etc.) of, relating to, or characterized by the naturalistic representation of the external world. ► '**figuratively** *adv* ► '**figurativeness** *n*

figure ('fɪgə; *U.S.* 'fɪgjər) *n* **1** any written symbol other than a letter, esp. a whole number. **2** another name for **digit** (sense 2). **3** an amount expressed numerically: *a figure of 1800 was suggested.* **4** (*pl*) calculations with numbers: *he's good at figures.* **5** visible shape or form; outline. **6** the human form, esp. as regards size or shape: *a girl with a slender figure.* **7** a slim bodily shape (esp. in the phrases **keep** *or* **lose one's figure**). **8** a character or personage, esp. a prominent or notable one; personality: *a figure in politics.* **9** the impression created by a person through behaviour (esp. in the phrase **to cut a fine, bold, etc., figure**). **10a** a person as impressed on the mind: *the figure of Napoleon.* **10b** (*in combination*): *father-figure.* **11** a representation in painting or sculpture, esp. of the human form. **12** an illustration or explanatory diagram in a text. **13** a representative object or symbol; emblem. **14** a pattern or design, as on fabric or in wood. **15** a predetermined set of movements in dancing or skating. **16** *Geometry.* any combination of points, lines, curves, or planes. A **plane figure,** such as a circle, encloses an area; a **solid figure,** such as a sphere, encloses a volume. **17** *Rhetoric.* See **figure of speech. 18** *Logic.* one of the four possible arrangements of the three terms in the premises of a syllogism. Compare **mood**[2] (sense 2). **19** *Music.* **19a** a numeral written above or below a note in a part. See **figured bass, thorough bass. 19b** a characteristic short pattern of notes. ♦ *vb* **20** (when *tr*, often foll. by *up*) to calculate or compute (sums, amounts, etc.). **21** (*tr; usually takes a clause as object*) *Informal, chiefly U.S., Canadian, and N.Z.* to think or conclude; consider. **22** (*tr*) to represent by a diagram or illustration. **23** (*tr*) to pattern or mark with a design. **24** (*tr*) to depict or portray in a painting, etc. **25** (*tr*) *Rhetoric.* to express by means of a figure of speech. **26** (*tr*) to imagine. **27** (*tr*) *Music.* **27a** to decorate (a melody line or part) with ornamentation. **27b** to provide figures above or below (a bass part) as an indication of the accompanying harmonies required. See **figured bass, thorough bass. 28** (*intr;* usually foll. by *in*) to be included: *his name figures in the article.* **29** (*intr*) *Informal.* to accord with expectation; be logical: *it figures that he wouldn't come.* ♦ See also **figure on, figure out.** [C13: from Latin *figūra* a shape, from *fingere* to mould] ► '**figureless** *adj* ► '**figurer** *n*

figured ('fɪgəd) *adj* **1** depicted as a figure in graphic art, painting, or sculpture. **2** decorated or patterned with a design. **3** having a form. **4** *Music.* **4a** ornamental. **4b** (of a bass part) provided with numerals indicating accompanying harmonies.

figured bass (beɪs) *n* a shorthand method of indicating a thorough-bass part in which each bass note is accompanied by figures indicating the intervals to be played in the chord above it in the realization.

figure-ground phenomenon *n* the division of the perceptual field into background and objects that appear to stand out against it. The concept was evolved by the Gestalt psychologists, who invented *ambiguous* figures in which the same part could be seen either as figure or ground.

figurehead ('fɪgəˌhɛd) *n* **1** a person nominally having a prominent position, but no real authority. **2** a carved bust or full-length figure at the upper end of the stems of some sailing vessels.

figure of eight *or* **figure eight** *n* **1** an outline of the number 8 traced on ice by a skater. **2** a flight manoeuvre by an aircraft outlining a figure 8. **3a** a knot in the shape of a figure 8 made to prevent the unreeving of a rope. **3b** a climber's knot in the shape of a figure 8 made with a doubled rope to provide a secure loop. **3c** an angler's knot sometimes used to attach a fly to a leader or dropper.

figure of merit *n* **1** *Aeronautics.* a measure of the efficiency of a helicopter in hover. **2** *Electrical engineering.* a measure of the efficiency of a component, such as a circuit.

figure of speech *n* an expression of language, such as simile, metaphor, or personification, by which the usual or literal meaning of a word is not employed.

figure on *or* **upon** *vb* (*intr, prep*) *Informal, chiefly U.S. and Canadian.* **1** to depend on (support or help.) **2** to take into consideration.

figure out *vb* (*tr, adv; may take a clause as object*) *Informal.* **1** to calculate or reckon. **2** to understand.

figure skating *n* ice skating in which the skater traces outlines of selected patterns. ► **figure skater** *n*

figurine (ˌfɪgə'riːn) *n* a small carved or moulded figure; statuette. [C19: from French, from Italian *figurina* a little FIGURE]

figwort ('fɪgˌwɜːt) *n* any scrophulariaceous plant of the N temperate genus *Scrophularia*, having square stems and small greenish flowers.

Fiji ('fiːdʒiː, fiː'dʒiː) *n* **1** an independent republic, consisting of 844 islands (chiefly Viti Levu and Vanua Levu) in the SW Pacific: a British colony (1874–1970); a member of the Commonwealth (1970–87 and from 1997); the large islands are of volcanic origin, surrounded by coral reefs; smaller ones are of coral. Official language: English. Religion: Christian and Hindu. Currency: dollar. Capital: Suva. Pop.: 793 000 (1998 est.). Area: 18 272 sq. km (7055 sq. miles). ◆ *n, adj* 2 another word for **Fijian.**

Fijian (fiːˈdʒiːən) *n* **1** a member of the indigenous people of mixed Melanesian and Polynesian descent inhabiting Fiji. **2** the language of this people, belonging to the Malayo-Polynesian family. ◆ *adj* **3** of, relating to, or characteristic of Fiji or its inhabitants. ◆ Also: **Fiji.**

filagree (ˈfɪlə,griː) *n, adj, vb* a less common variant of **filigree.**

filament (ˈfɪləmənt) *n* **1** the thin wire, usually tungsten, inside a light bulb that emits light when heated to incandescence by an electric current. **2** *Electronics.* a high-resistance wire or ribbon, forming the cathode in some valves. **3** a single strand of a natural or synthetic fibre; fibril. **4** *Botany.* **4a** the stalk of a stamen. **4b** any of the long slender chains of cells into which some algae and fungi are divided. **5** *Ornithol.* the barb of a down feather. **6** *Anatomy.* any slender structure or part, such as the tail of a spermatozoon; filum. [C16: from New Latin *fīlāmentum,* from Medieval Latin *fīlāre* to spin, from Latin *fīlum* thread] ▸ **filamentary** (,fɪləˈmentərɪ, -trɪ) *or* ,**filaˈmentous** *adj*

filar (ˈfaɪlə) *adj* **1** of thread. **2** (of an optical instrument) having fine threads across the eyepiece forming a reticle or set of cross wires. [C19: from Latin *fīlum* thread]

filaria (fɪˈlɛərɪə) *n, pl* **-iae** (-ɪ,iː). any parasitic nematode worm of the family *Filariidae,* living in the blood and tissues of vertebrates and transmitted by insects: the cause of filariasis. [C19: New Latin (former name of genus), from Latin *fīlum* thread] ▸ **fiˈlarial** *or* **fiˈlarian** *adj*

filariasis (,fɪləˈraɪəsɪs, fɪ,lɛərɪˈeɪsɪs) *n* a disease common in tropical and subtropical countries resulting from infestation of the lymphatic system with the nematode worms *Wuchereria bancrofti* or *Brugia malayi,* transmitted by mosquitoes: characterized by inflammation and obstruction of the lymphatic vessels. See also **elephantiasis.** [C19: from New Latin; see FILARIA]

filature (ˈfɪlətʃə) *n* **1** the act or process of spinning silk, etc., into threads. **2** the reel used for this. **3** a place where such spinning or reeling is done. [C18: from Medieval Latin *fīlātūra* the art of spinning, from *fīlāre* to spin thread; see FILAMENT]

filbert (ˈfɪlbət) *n* **1** any of several N temperate shrubs of the genus *Corylus,* esp. *C. maxima,* that have edible rounded brown nuts: family *Corylaceae.* **2** Also called: **hazelnut, cobnut.** the nut of any of these shrubs. ◆ See also **hazel** (senses 1, 3). [C14: named after St *Philbert,* 7th-century Frankish abbot, because the nuts are ripe around his feast day, Aug. 22]

filch (fɪltʃ) *vb (tr)* to steal or take surreptitiously in small amounts; pilfer. [C16 *filchen* to steal, attack, perhaps from Old English *gefylce* band of men] ▸ **ˈfilcher** *n*

file[1] (faɪl) *n* **1** a folder, box, etc., used to keep documents or other items in order. **2** the documents, etc., kept in this way. **3** documents or information about a specific subject, person, etc.: *we have a file on every known thief.* **4** an orderly line or row. **5** a line of people in marching formation, one behind another. Compare **rank**[1] (sense 6). **6** any of the eight vertical rows of squares on a chessboard. **7** *Computing.* a named collection of information, in the form of text, programs, graphics, etc., held on a permanent storage device such as a magnetic disk. **8** *Obsolete.* a list or catalogue. **9 on file.** recorded or catalogued for reference, as in a file. ◆ *vb* **10** to place (a document, letter, etc.) in a file. **11** *(tr)* to put on record, esp. to place (a legal document) on public or official record; register. **12** *(tr)* to bring (a suit, esp. a divorce suit) in a court of law. **13** *(tr)* to submit (copy) to a newspaper or news agency. **14** *(intr)* to march or walk in a file or files: *the ants filed down the hill.* [C16 (in the sense: string on which documents are hung): from Old French *filer,* from Medieval Latin *fīlāre;* see FILAMENT] ▸ **ˈfiler** *n*

file[2] (faɪl) *n* **1** a hand tool consisting essentially of a steel blade with small cutting teeth on some or all of its faces. It is used for shaping or smoothing metal, wood, etc. **2** *Rare, Brit. slang.* a cunning or deceitful person. ◆ *vb* **3** *(tr)* to shape or smooth (a surface) with a file. [Old English *fīl;* related to Old Saxon *fīla,* Old High German *fīhala* file, Greek *pikros* bitter, sharp] ▸ **ˈfiler** *n*

file[3] (faɪl) *vb (tr) Obsolete.* to pollute or defile. [Old English *fȳlan;* related to Middle Low German *vülen;* see DEFILE[1], FILTH, FOUL]

filecard (ˈfaɪl,kɑːd) *n* a type of brush with sharp steel bristles, used for cleaning the teeth of a file.

filefish (ˈfaɪl,fɪʃ) *n, pl* **-fish** *or* **-fishes.** any tropical triggerfish, such as *Alutera scripta,* having a narrow compressed body and a very long dorsal spine. [C18: referring to its file-like scales]

filename (ˈfaɪl,neɪm) *n* an arrangement of characters that enables a computer system to permit the user to have access to a particular file.

file server *n Computing.* the central unit of a local area network that controls its operation and provides access to separately stored data files.

filet (ˈfɪlɪt, ˈfɪleɪ; *French* filɛ) *n* a variant spelling of **fillet** (senses 1-3). [C20: from French: net, from Old Provençal *filat,* from *fil* thread, from Latin *fīlum*]

filet mignon (ˈfɪleɪ ˈmiːnjɒn) *n* a small tender boneless cut of beef from the inside of the loin. [from French, literally: dainty fillet]

filial (ˈfɪljəl) *adj* **1** of, resembling, or suitable to a son or daughter: *filial affection.* **2** *Genetics.* designating any of the generations following the parental generation. Abbrev.: **F**; F_1 indicates the first filial generation, F_2 the second, etc. [C15: from Late Latin *fīliālis,* from Latin *fīlius* son] ▸ **ˈfilially** *adv* ▸ **ˈfilialness** *n*

filiate (ˈfɪlɪ,eɪt) *vb (tr)* **1** *Law.* to fix judicially the paternity of (a child, esp. one born out of wedlock). **2** *Law.* a less common word for **affiliate. 3** *Archaic.* to affiliate or associate. [C18: from Medieval Latin *fīliātus* acknowledged as a son, from Latin *fīlius* son]

filiation (,fɪlɪˈeɪʃən) *n* **1** line of descent; lineage; derivation. **2** the fact of being the child of certain parents. **3** *Law.* the act or process of filiating. **4** *Law.* a less common word for **affiliation order. 5** the set of rules governing the attachment of children to their parents and its social consequences.

filibeg, fillibeg, *or* **philibeg** (ˈfɪlɪ,bɛg) *n* the kilt worn by Scottish Highlanders. [C18: from Scottish Gaelic *fēileadhbeag,* from *fēileadh* kilt + *beag* small]

filibuster (ˈfɪlɪ,bʌstə) *n* **1** the process or an instance of obstructing legislation by means of long speeches and other delaying tactics. **2** Also called: **filibusterer.** a legislator who engages in such obstruction. **3** a buccaneer, freebooter, or irregular military adventurer, esp. a revolutionary in a foreign country. ◆ *vb* **4** to obstruct (legislation) with delaying tactics. **5** *(intr)* to engage in unlawful and private military action. [C16: from Spanish *filibustero,* from French *flibustier,* probably from Dutch *vrijbuiter* pirate, literally: one plundering freely; see FREEBOOTER] ▸ **ˈfili,busterer** *n* ▸ **ˈfili,busterism** *n*

filicide (ˈfɪlɪ,saɪd) *n* **1** the act of killing one's own son or daughter. **2** a person who does this. [C17: from Latin *fīlius* son or *fīlia* daughter + -CIDE] ▸ ,**filiˈcidal** *adj*

filiform (ˈfɪlɪ,fɔːm, ˈfaɪ-) *adj Biology.* having the form of a thread. [C18: from Latin *fīlum* thread]

filigree (ˈfɪlɪ,griː), **filagree,** *or* **fillagree** *n* **1** delicate ornamental work of twisted gold, silver, or other wire. **2** any fanciful delicate ornamentation. ◆ *adj* **3** made of or as if with filigree. ◆ *vb* **-grees, -greeing, -greed. 4** *(tr)* to decorate with or as if with filigree. [C17: from earlier *filigreen,* from French *filigrane,* from Latin *fīlum* thread + *grānum* GRAIN]

filing clerk *n* an employee who maintains office files.

filings (ˈfaɪlɪŋz) *pl n* shavings or particles removed by a file: *iron filings.*

Filipino (,fɪlɪˈpiːnəʊ) *n* **1** *(pl* **-nos)** Also (fem): **Filipina.** a native or inhabitant of the Philippines. **2** another name for **Tagalog.** ◆ *adj* **3** of or relating to the Philippines or their inhabitants.

fill (fɪl) *vb (mainly tr;* often foll. by *up)* **1** *(also intr)* to make or become full: *to fill up a bottle; the bath fills in two minutes.* **2** to occupy the whole of: *the party filled two floors of the house.* **3** to plug (a gap, crevice, cavity, etc.). **4** to meet (a requirement or need) satisfactorily. **5** to cover (a page or blank space) with writing, drawing, etc. **6** to hold and perform the duties of (an office or position). **7** to appoint or elect an occupant to (an office or position). **8** *Building trades.* to build up (ground) with fill. **9** *(also intr)* to swell or cause to swell with wind, as in manoeuvring the sails of a sailing vessel. **10** to increase the bulk of by adding an inferior substance. **11** *Poker.* to complete (a full house, etc.) by drawing the cards needed. **12** *Chiefly U.S. and Canadian.* to put together the necessary materials for (a prescription or order). **13 fill the bill.** *Informal.* to serve or perform adequately. ◆ *n* **14** material such as gravel, stones, etc., used to bring an area of ground up to a required level. **15 one's fill.** the quantity needed to satisfy one: *to eat your fill.* ◆ See also **fill away, fill in, fill out, fill up.** [Old English *fyllan;* related to Old Frisian *fella,* Old Norse *fylla,* Gothic *fulljan,* Old High German *fullen;* see FULL[1], FULFIL]

fillagree (ˈfɪlə,griː) *n, adj, vb* a less common variant of **filigree.**

fill away *vb (intr, adv) Nautical.* to cause a vessel's sails to fill, either by steering it off the wind or by bracing the yards.

fille de joie *French.* (fij də ʒwa) *n, pl* ***filles de joie*** (fij də ʒwa). a prostitute. [girl of pleasure]

filled gold *n* another name (esp. U.S.) for **rolled gold.**

filler (ˈfɪlə) *n* **1** a person or thing that fills. **2** an object or substance used to add weight or size to something or to fill in a gap. **3** a paste, used for filling in cracks, holes, etc., in a surface before painting. **4** *Architect.* a small joist inserted between and supported by two beams. **5a** the inner portion of a cigar. **5b** the cut tobacco for making cigarettes. **6** *Journalism.* articles, photographs, etc., to fill space between more important articles in the layout of a newspaper or magazine. **7** *Informal.* something, such as a musical selection, to fill time in a broadcast or stage presentation. **8** a small radio or television transmitter used to fill a gap in coverage.

filler cap *n* a device sealing the filling pipe to the petrol tank in a motor vehicle.

filler metal *n* metal supplied in the form of a welding rod, sometimes flux coated, melted by an arc or a flame into a joint between components to be joined.

fillet (ˈfɪlɪt) *n* **1a** Also called: **fillet steak.** a strip of boneless meat, esp. the undercut of a sirloin of beef. **1b** the boned side of a fish. **1c** the white meat of breast and wing of a chicken. **2** a narrow strip of any material. **3** a thin strip of ribbon, lace, etc., worn in the hair or around the neck. **4** a narrow flat moulding, esp. one between other mouldings. **5** a narrow band between two adjacent flutings on the shaft of a column. **6** Also called: **fillet weld.** a narrow strip of welded metal used to join steel members at right angles. **7** *Heraldry.* a horizontal division of a shield, one quarter of the depth of the chief. **8** Also called: **listel, list.** the top member of a cornice. **9** *Anatomy.* a band of sensory nerve fibres in the brain connected to the thalamus. Technical name: **lemniscus. 10a** a narrow decorative line, impressed on the cover of a book. **10b** a wheel tool used to impress such lines. **11** another name for **fairing**[1]. ◆ *vb (tr)* **-lets, -leting, -leted. 12** to cut or prepare (meat or fish) as a fillet. **13** to cut fillets from (meat or fish). **14** to bind or decorate with or as if with a fillet. ◆ Also (for senses 1-3): **filet.** [C14: from Old French *filet,* from *fil* thread, from Latin *fīlum*]

fill in *vb (adv)* **1** *(tr)* to complete (a form, drawing, etc.). **2** *(intr)* to act as a substitute: *a girl is filling in while the typist is away.* **3** *(tr)* to put material into (a hole or cavity), esp. so as to make it level with a surface. **4** *(tr) Informal.* to inform with facts or news. **5** *(tr) Brit. slang.* to attack and injure severely. ◆ *n* **fill-in. 6** a substitute. **7** *U.S. informal.* a briefing to complete one's understanding.

filling (ˈfɪlɪŋ) *n* **1** the substance or thing used to fill a space or container: *pie filling.* **2** *Dentistry.* **2a** any of various substances (metal, plastic, etc.) for inserting into the prepared cavity of a tooth. **2b** the cavity of a tooth so filled. **3** *Textiles.* another term for **weft.** ◆ *adj* **4** (of food or a meal) substantial and satisfying.

filling station *n* a place where petrol and other supplies for motorists are sold.

fillip ('fɪlɪp) *n* **1** something that adds stimulation or enjoyment. **2** the action of holding a finger towards the palm with the thumb and suddenly releasing it outwards to produce a snapping sound. **3** a quick blow or tap made by a finger snapped in this way. ◆ *vb* **4** (*tr*) to stimulate or excite. **5** (*tr*) to strike or project sharply with a fillip. **6** (*intr*) to make a fillip. **[C15** *philippe,* of imitative origin**]**

fillister, filister, *or* **fillester** ('fɪlɪstə) *n* **1** Also called: **fillister plane.** an adjustable plane for cutting rabbets, grooves, etc. **2** Also called: **sash fillister.** a rabbet or groove, esp. one in a window sash bar for a pane of glass. **[C19:** of unknown origin**]**

fill light *n Photog.* a light that supplements the key light without changing its character, used esp. to lighten shadows.

Fillmore ('fɪlmɔː) *n* **Millard.** 1800–74, 13th president of the U.S. (1850-53); a leader of the Whig Party.

fill out *vb* (*adv*) **1** to make or become fuller, thicker, or rounder: *her figure has filled out since her marriage.* **2** to make more substantial: *the writers were asked to fill their stories out.* **3** (*tr*) to complete (a form, application, etc.).

fill up *vb* (*adv*) **1** (*tr*) to complete (a form, application, etc.). **2** to make or become completely full. ◆ *n* **fill-up. 3** the act of filling something completely, esp. the petrol tank of a car.

filly ('fɪlɪ) *n, pl* **-lies. 1** a female horse or pony under the age of four. **2** *Informal, rare.* a spirited girl or young woman. **[C15:** from Old Norse *fylja;* related to Old High German *fulihha;* see FOAL**]**

film (fɪlm) *n* **1a** a sequence of images of moving objects photographed by a camera and providing the optical illusion of continuous movement when projected onto a screen. **1b** a form of entertainment, information, etc., composed of such a sequence of images and shown in a cinema, etc. **1c** (*as modifier*): *film techniques.* **2** a thin flexible strip of cellulose coated with a photographic emulsion, used to make negatives and transparencies. **3** a thin coating or layer. **4** a thin sheet of any material, as of plastic for packaging. **5** a fine haze, mist, or blur. **6** a gauzy web of filaments or fine threads. **7** *Pathol.* an abnormally opaque tissue, such as the cornea in some eye diseases. ◆ *vb* **8a** to photograph with a cine camera. **8b** to make a film of (a screenplay, event, etc.). **9** (often foll. by *over*) to cover or become covered or coated with a film. **[**Old English *filmen* membrane; related to Old Frisian *filmene,* Greek *pelma* sole of the foot; see FELL[4]**]**

film colour *n Physiol.* a misty appearance produced when no lines or edges are present in the visual field.

filmic ('fɪlmɪk) *adj* **1** of or relating to films or the cinema. **2** having characteristics that are suggestive of films or the cinema. ► **'filmically** *adv*

film library *n* a collection of films as archives or for loan or hire.

film noir (nwɑː) *n* a gangster thriller, made esp. in the 1940s in Hollywood characterized by contrasty lighting and often somewhat impenetrable plots. **[C20:** French, literally: black film**]**

filmography (fɪl'mɒgrəfɪ) *n* **1** a list of the films made by a particular director, actor, etc. **2** any writing that deals with films or the cinema.

film pack *n* a box containing several sheets of film for use in a plate camera.

film set *n* the scenery and props as arranged for shooting a film.

filmset ('fɪlm,sɛt) *vb* **-sets, -setting, -set.** (*tr*) to set (type matter) by filmsetting. ► **'film,setter** *n*

filmsetting ('fɪlm,sɛtɪŋ) *n Printing.* typesetting by exposing type characters onto photographic film from which printing plates are made.

film speed *n* **1** the sensitivity to light of a photographic film, specified in terms of the film's ISO rating. **2** the rate at which the film passes through a motion picture camera or projector.

film star *n* a popular film actor or actress.

film strip *n* a strip of film composed of different images projected separately as slides.

filmy ('fɪlmɪ) *adj* **filmier, filmiest. 1** composed of or resembling film; transparent or gauzy. **2** covered with or as if with a film; hazy; blurred. ► **'filmily** *adv* ► **'filminess** *n*

filmy fern *n* any fern of the family *Hymenophyllaceae,* growing in humid regions and having thin translucent leaves.

filo ('fiːləʊ) *n* a type of Greek flaky pastry in very thin sheets. **[C20:** Modern Greek *phullon* leaf**]**

Filofax ('faɪləʊ,fæks) *n Trademark.* a type of loose-leaf ring binder with sets of different-coloured paper, used as a portable personal filing system, including appointments, addresses, etc.

filoplume ('fɪlə,pluːm, 'faɪ-) *n Ornithol.* any of the hairlike feathers that lack vanes and occur between the contour feathers. **[C19:** from New Latin *filoplūma,* from Latin *fīlum* thread + *plūma* feather**]**

filose ('faɪləʊs, -ləʊz) *adj Biology.* resembling or possessing a thread or threadlike process: *filose pseudopodia.* **[C19:** from Latin *fīlum* thread**]**

filoselle (,fɪləʊ'sɛl) *n* soft silk thread, used esp. for embroidery. **[C17:** from French: silk, silkworm, from Italian *filosello,* perhaps from Latin *folliculus* little bag**]**

fils[1] *French.* (fis) an addition to a French surname to specify the son rather than the father of the same name: *a book by Dumas fils.* Compare **père. [**French: son**]**

fils[2] (fɪls) *or* **fil** (fɪl) *n, pl* **fils. a** a fractional monetary unit of Bahrain, Iraq, Jordan, and Kuwait, worth one thousandth of a dinar. **b** a fractional monetary unit of the United Arab Emirates, worth one hundredth of a dirham. **c** a fractional monetary unit of Yemen, worth one hundredth of a riyal. **[**from Arabic**]**

filter ('fɪltə) *n* **1** a porous substance, such as paper or sand, that allows fluid to pass but retains suspended solid particles: used to clean fluids or collect solid particles. **2** any device containing such a porous substance for separating suspensions from fluids. **3** any of various porous substances built into the mouth end of a cigarette or cigar for absorbing impurities such as tar. **4** any electronic, optical, or acoustic device that blocks signals or radiations of certain frequencies while allowing others to pass. See also **band-pass filter. 5** any transparent disc of gelatine or glass used to eliminate or reduce the intensity of given frequencies from the light leaving a lamp, entering a camera, etc. **6** *Brit.* a traffic signal at a road junction consisting of a green arrow which when illuminated permits vehicles to turn either left or right when the main signals are red. ◆ *vb* **7** (often foll. by *out*) to remove or separate (suspended particles, wavelengths of radiation, etc.) from (a liquid, gas, radiation, etc.) by the action of a filter. **8** (*tr*) to obtain by filtering. **9** (*intr;* foll. by *through*) to pass (through a filter or something like a filter): *dust filtered through the screen.* **10** (*intr*) to flow slowly; trickle. **[C16** *filtre,* from Medieval Latin *filtrum* piece of felt used as a filter, of Germanic origin; see FELT[2]**]**

filterable ('fɪltərəbᵊl) *or* **filtrable** ('fɪltrəbᵊl) *adj* **1** capable of being filtered. **2** (of most viruses and certain bacteria) capable of passing through the pores of a fine filter. ► **,filtera'bility** *or* **'filterableness** *n*

filter bed *n* **1** a layer of sand or gravel in a tank or reservoir through which a liquid is passed so as to purify it. Compare **bacteria bed. 2** any layer of material through which a liquid is passed so as to filter it.

filter cake *n Chem.* the solid material accumulated by a filter press.

filter feeding *n Zoology.* a method of feeding occurring in some aquatic animals, such as planktonic invertebrates and whalebone whales, in which minute food particles are filtered from the surrounding water. ► **filter feeder** *n*

filter out *or* **through** *vb* (*intr, adv*) to become known gradually; leak: *rumours filtered out about the divorce.*

filter paper *n* a porous paper used for filtering liquids.

filter press *n* an apparatus used for filtration consisting of a set of frames covered with filter cloth on both sides, between which the liquid to be filtered is pumped.

filter pump *n* a vacuum pump used to assist laboratory filtrations in which a jet of water inside a glass tube entrains air molecules from the system to be evacuated.

filter tip *n* **1** an attachment to the mouth end of a cigarette for trapping impurities such as tar during smoking. It consists of any of various dense porous substances, such as cotton. **2** a cigarette having such an attachment. ► **'filter-,tipped** *adj*

filth (fɪlθ) *n* **1** foul or disgusting dirt; refuse. **2** extreme physical or moral uncleanliness; pollution. **3** vulgarity or obscenity, as in language. **4** *Derogatory slang.* **the.** the police. **[**Old English *fȳlth;* related to Old Saxon, Old High German *fūlitha;* see FOUL, DEFILE**]**

filthy ('fɪlθɪ) *adj* **filthier, filthiest. 1** characterized by or full of filth; very dirty or obscene. **2** offensive or vicious: *that was a filthy trick to play.* **3** *Informal, chiefly Brit.* extremely unpleasant: *filthy weather.* ◆ *adv* **4** extremely; disgustingly: *filthy rich.* ► **'filthily** *adv* ► **'filthiness** *n*

filtrate ('fɪltreɪt) *n* **1** a liquid or gas that has been filtered. ◆ *vb* **2** another name for **filter** (sense 7). **[C17:** from Medieval Latin *filtrāre* to FILTER**]** ► **'filtratable** *adj*

filtration (fɪl'treɪʃən) *n* the act or process of filtering.

filum ('faɪləm) *n, pl* **-la** (-lə). *Anatomy.* any threadlike structure or part. **[**Latin: thread, cord, fibre**]**

fimble ('fɪmbᵊl) *n* the male plant of the hemp, which matures before the female plant. **[C15:** from Middle Dutch *femeel,* from Old French *chanvre femelle* female hemp, from *chanvre* hemp + *femelle* FEMALE**]**

fimbria ('fɪmbrɪə) *n, pl* **-briae** (-brɪ,iː). *Anatomy.* a fringe or fringelike margin or border, esp. at the opening of the Fallopian tubes. **[C18:** from Late Latin, from Latin *fimbriae* threads, shreds**]** ► **'fimbrial** *adj*

fimbriate ('fɪmbrɪɪt, -,eɪt), **fimbriated,** *or* **fimbrillate** ('fɪmbrɪlɪt, -,leɪt) *adj* having a fringed margin, as some petals, antennae, etc. ► **,fimbri'ation** *n*

fimicolous (fɪ'mɪkələs) *adj Biology.* (esp. of fungi) growing in or on dung. **[C19:** from Latin *fimus* dung + *colere* to inhabit**]**

fin[1] (fɪn) *n* **1** any of the firm appendages that are the organs of locomotion and balance in fishes and some other aquatic animals. Most fishes have paired and unpaired fins, the former corresponding to the limbs of higher vertebrates. **2** a part or appendage that resembles a fin. **3a** *Brit.* a vertical surface to which the rudder is attached, usually placed at the rear of an aeroplane to give stability about the vertical axis. U.S. name: **vertical stabilizer. 3b** a tail surface fixed to a rocket or missile to give stability. **4** *Nautical.* a fixed or adjustable blade projecting under water from the hull of a vessel to give it stability or control. **5** a projecting rib to dissipate heat from the surface of an engine cylinder, motor casing, or radiator. **6** (*often pl*) another name for **flipper** (sense 2). ◆ *vb* **fins, finning, finned. 7** (*tr*) to provide with fins. **8** (*tr*) to remove the fins from (a dead fish). **9** (*intr*) (esp. of a whale) to agitate the fins violently in the water. **[**Old English *finn;* related to Middle Dutch *vinne,* Old Swedish *fina,* Latin *pinna* wing**]** ► **'finless** *adj*

fin[2] (fɪn) *n U.S. slang.* a five-dollar bill. **[**from Yiddish *finf* five, ultimately from Old High German *funf, finf***]**

FIN *international car registration for* Finland.

fin. *abbrev. for:* **1** finance. **2** financial. **3** finish.

Fin. *abbrev. for:* **1** Finland. **2** Finnish.

finable *or* **fineable** ('faɪnəbᵊl) *adj* liable to a fine. ► **'finableness** *or* **'fineableness** *n*

finagle (fɪ'neɪgᵊl) *vb Informal.* **1** (*tr*) to get or achieve by trickery, craftiness, or persuasion; wangle. **2** to use trickery or craftiness on (a person). **[C20:** probably changed from dialect *fainaigue***]** ► **fi'nagler** *n*

final ('faɪnᵊl) *adj* **1** of or occurring at the end; concluding; ultimate; last. **2** having no possibility for further discussion, action, or change; conclusive; decisive: *a final decree of judgment.* **3** relating to or constituting an end or purpose: *a final clause may be introduced by "in order to".* **4** *Phonetics.* at the end of a word: *"cat" has a final "t".* Compare **medial** (sense 1), **initial** (sense 1). **5** *Music.* another word for **perfect** (sense 9b). ◆ *n* **6** a terminal or last thing; end. **7** a deciding contest between the winners of previous rounds in a competition. **8** *Music.* the tonic note of a church mode. ◆ See also **finals.** **[C14:** from Latin *fīnālis,* from *fīnis* limit, boundary**]**

final cause *n Philosophy.* the end or purpose of a thing or process, as opposed to its efficient cause. See **cause** (sense 7).

finale (fɪˈnɑːlɪ) *n* **1** the concluding part of any performance or presentation. **2** the closing section or movement of a musical composition. **[C18:** from Italian, n use of adj *finale, from* Latin *fīnālis* FINAL**]**

finalism (ˈfaɪnəˌlɪzəm) *n Philosophy.* the doctrine that final causes determine the course of all events. ► **ˌfinaˈlistic** *adj*

finalist (ˈfaɪnəlɪst) *n* a contestant who has reached the last and decisive stage of a sports or other competition.

finality (faɪˈnælɪtɪ) *n, pl* **-ties. 1** the condition or quality of being final or settled; conclusiveness: *the finality of death.* **2** a final or conclusive act. **3** *Metaphysics.* the doctrine of the efficacy of final causes. Compare **teleology.**

finalize *or* **finalise** (ˈfaɪnəˌlaɪz) *vb* **1** *(tr)* to put into final form; settle: *to finalize plans for the merger.* **2** *(intr)* to complete arrangements or negotiations; reach agreement on a transaction. ► **ˌfinaliˈzation** *or* **ˌfinaliˈsation** *n*

USAGE Although *finalize* has been in widespread use for some time, many speakers and writers still prefer to use *complete, conclude,* or *make final,* esp. in formal contexts.

finally (ˈfaɪnəlɪ) *adv* **1** after a long delay; at last; eventually. **2** at the end or final point; lastly. **3** completely; conclusively; irrevocably. ◆ *sentence connector.* **4** in the end; lastly: *finally, he put his tie on.* **5** as the last or final point: linking what follows with the previous statements, as in a speech or argument.

finals (ˈfaɪnᵊlz) *pl n* **1** the deciding part or parts of a sports or other competition. **2** *Education.* the last examination series in an academic or professional course.

finance (fɪˈnæns, ˈfaɪnæns) *n* **1** the system of money, credit, etc., esp. with respect to government revenues and expenditures. **2** funds or the provision of funds. **3** *(pl)* funds; financial condition. ◆ *vb* **4** *(tr)* to provide or obtain funds, capital, or credit for. **5** *(intr)* to manage or secure financial resources. **[C14:** from Old French, from *finer* to end, settle by payment**]**

finance bill *n* a legislative bill providing money for the public treasury.

finance company *or* **house** *n* an enterprise engaged in the loan of money against collateral or speculatively to manufacturers and retailers, esp. one specializing in the financing of hire-purchase contracts.

financial (fɪˈnænʃəl, faɪ-) *adj* **1** of or relating to finance or finances. **2** of or relating to persons who manage money, capital, or credit. **3** *Austral. and N.Z. informal.* having money; in funds. **4** *Austral. and N.Z.* (of a club member) fully paid-up. ► **fiˈnancially** *adv*

financial futures *pl n* futures in a stock-exchange index, currency exchange rate, or interest rate enabling banks, building societies, brokers, and speculators to hedge their involvement in these markets.

Financial Ombudsman *n* any of five British ombudsmen: the **Banking Ombudsman,** set up in 1986 to investigate complaints from bank customers; the **Building Society Ombudsman,** set up in 1987 to investigate complaints from building society customers; the **Insurance Ombudsman,** set up in 1981 to investigate complaints by policyholders (since 1988 this ombudsman has also operated a **Unit Trust Ombudsman** scheme); the **Investment Ombudsman,** set up in 1989 to investigate complaints by investors (the **Personal Investment Authority Ombudsman** is responsible for investigating complaints by personal investors); and the **Pensions Ombudsman,** set up in 1993 to investigate complaints regarding pension schemes.

Financial Services Authority *n* (in the UK) a regulatory body that oversees London's financial markets, each of which has its own self-regulatory organization: it succeeded the Securities and Investments Board. Abbrev.: **FSA.**

Financial Times Industrial Ordinary Share Index *n* an index of share prices produced by the *Financial Times,* designed to reflect general price trends: based on the average price of thirty British shares.

Financial Times Stock Exchange 100 Index *n* an index of share prices produced by the *Financial Times* based on an average of 100 securities and giving the best indication of daily movements. Abbrev.: **FTSE 100 Index.** Informal name: **Footsie.**

financial year *n Brit.* **1** any annual period at the end of which a firm's accounts are made up. **2** the annual period ending April 5, over which Budget estimates are made by the British Government and which functions as the income-tax year. U.S. and Canadian equivalent: **fiscal year.**

financier (fɪˈnænsɪə, faɪ-) *n* a person who is engaged or skilled in large-scale financial operations.

financing gap *n* the difference between a country's requirements for foreign exchange to finance its debts and imports and its income from overseas.

finback (ˈfɪnˌbæk) *n* another name for **rorqual.**

finch (fɪntʃ) *n* **1** any songbird of the family *Fringillidae,* having a short stout bill for feeding on seeds and, in most species, a bright plumage in the male. Common examples are the goldfinch, bullfinch, chaffinch, siskin, and canary. **2** any of various similar or related birds. Related adj: **fringilline. [**Old English *finc;* related to Old High German *finko,* Middle Dutch *vinker,* Greek *spingos***]**

Finchley (ˈfɪntʃlɪ) *n* a residential district of N London, part of the Greater London borough of Barnet from 1965.

find (faɪnd) *vb* **finds, finding, found** (faʊnd). *(mainly tr)* **1** to meet with or discover by chance. **2** to discover or obtain, esp. by search or effort: *to find happiness.* **3** *(may take a clause as object)* to become aware of; realize: *he found that nobody knew.* **4** *(may take a clause as object)* to regard as being; consider: *I find this wine a little sour.* **5** to look for and point out (something to be criticized): *to find fault.* **6** *(also intr) Law.* to determine an issue after judicial inquiry and pronounce a verdict (upon): *the court found the accused guilty.* **7** to regain (something lost or not functioning): *to find one's tongue.* **8** to reach (a target): *the bullet found its mark.* **9** to provide, esp. with difficulty: *we'll find room for you too.* **10** to be able to pay: *I can't find that amount of money.* **11 find oneself.** to realize and accept one's real character; discover one's true vocation. **12 find one's feet.** to become capable or confident, as in a new job. ◆ *n* **13** a person, thing, etc., that is found, esp. a valuable or fortunate discovery. **[**Old English *findan;* related to Old Norse *finna,* Gothic *finthan,* Old High German *fintan* to find**]** ► **ˈfindable** *adj*

finder (ˈfaɪndə) *n* **1** a person or thing that finds. **2** *Physics.* a small low-power wide-angle telescope fitted to a more powerful larger telescope, used to locate celestial objects to be studied by the larger instrument. **3** *Photog.* short for **viewfinder. 4 finders keepers.** *Informal.* whoever finds something has the right to keep it.

fin de siècle *French.* (fɛ̃ də sjɛklə) *n* **1** the end of the 19th century, when traditional social, moral, and artistic values were in transition. ◆ *adj* ***fin-de-siècle.*** **2** of or relating to the close of the 19th century. **3** decadent, esp. in artistic tastes.

finding (ˈfaɪndɪŋ) *n* **1** a thing that is found or discovered. **2** *Law.* the conclusion reached after a judicial inquiry; verdict. **3** *(pl) U.S.* the tools and equipment of an artisan.

find out *vb (adv)* **1** to gain knowledge of (something); learn: *he found out what he wanted.* **2** to detect the crime, deception, etc., of (someone).

find the lady *n* another name for **three-card trick.**

fine[1] (faɪn) *adj* **1** excellent or choice in quality; very good of its kind: *a fine speech.* **2** superior in skill, ability, or accomplishment: *a fine violinist.* **3** (of weather) clear and dry. **4** enjoyable or satisfying: *a fine time.* **5** *(postpositive) Informal.* quite well; in satisfactory health: *I feel fine.* **6** satisfactory; acceptable: *that's fine by me.* **7** of delicate composition or careful workmanship: *fine crystal.* **8** (of precious metals) pure or having a high or specified degree of purity: *fine silver; gold 98 per cent fine.* **9** subtle in perception; discriminating: *a fine eye for antique brasses.* **10** abstruse or subtle: *a fine point in argument.* **11** very thin or slender: *fine hair.* **12** very small: *fine dust; fine print.* **13** (of edges, blades, etc.) sharp; keen. **14** ornate, showy, or smart. **15** good-looking; handsome: *a fine young woman.* **16** polished, elegant, or refined: *a fine gentleman.* **17** morally upright and commendable: *a fine man.* **18** *Cricket.* (of a fielding position) oblique to and behind the wicket: *fine leg.* **19** *(prenominal) Informal.* disappointing or terrible: *a fine mess.* ◆ *adv* **20** *Informal.* quite well; all right: *that suits me fine.* **21** a nonstandard word for **finely. 22** *Billiards, etc.* (of a stroke on the cue ball) so as to merely brush the object ball. **23 cut it fine.** to allow little margin of time, space, etc. ◆ *vb* **24** to make or become finer; refine. **25** (often foll. by *down* or *away*) to make or become smaller. **26** *(tr)* to clarify (wine, etc.) by adding finings. **27** *(tr) Billiards.* to hit (a cue ball) fine. **28** *(intr;* foll by *up) Austral. and N.Z. informal.* (of the weather) to become fine. **[C13:** from Old French *fin,* from Latin *fīnis* end, boundary, as in *fīnis honōrum* the highest degree of honour**]**

fine[2] (faɪn) *n* **1** a certain amount of money exacted as a penalty: *a parking fine.* **2** a payment made by a tenant at the start of his tenancy to reduce his subsequent rent; premium. **3** *Feudal law.* a sum of money paid by a man to his lord, esp. for a privilege. **4** a method of transferring land in England by bringing a fictitious law suit: abolished 1833. **5 in fine. 5a** in short; briefly. **5b** in conclusion; finally. ◆ *vb* **6** *(tr)* to impose a fine on. **[C12** (in the sense: conclusion, settlement): from Old French *fin;* see FINE[1]**]**

fine[3] (ˈfiːneɪ) *n Music.* **1** the point at which a piece is to end, usually after a *da capo* or *dal segno.* **2** an ending or finale. **[**Italian, from Latin *fīnis* end**]**

fine[4] *French.* (fin) *n* brandy of ordinary quality. **[**literally: fine**]**

fineable (ˈfaɪnəbᵊl) *adj* a variant spelling of **finable.** ► **ˈfineableness** *n*

fine art *n* **1** art produced chiefly for its aesthetic value, as opposed to applied art. **2** *(often pl)* Also called: **beaux arts.** any of the fields in which such art is produced, such as painting, sculpture, and engraving.

fine-cut *adj* (of tobacco) finely cut or shredded.

fine-draw *vb* **-draws, -drawing, -drew, -drawn.** *(tr)* **1** to sew together so finely that the join is scarcely noticeable. **2** to carry out the last drawing-out operation on (wire, tube, etc.) to reduce its diameter.

fine-drawn *adj* **1** (of arguments, distinctions, etc.) precise or subtle. **2** (of wire) drawn out until very fine; attenuated. **3** (of features) delicate or refined.

Fine Gael (ˈfɪnə ˈgeːl) *n* one of the major political parties in the Republic of Ireland formed in 1933. **[**from Irish Gaelic *fine* tribe, race + *Gael* of the Gaels**]**

fine-grain *adj Photog.* having or producing an image with grain of inconspicuous size: *a fine-grain image; a fine-grain developer.*

fine-grained *adj* (of wood, leather, etc.) having a fine smooth even grain.

fine leg *n Cricket.* **a** a fielding position between long leg and square leg. **b** a fielder in this position.

finely (ˈfaɪnlɪ) *adv* **1** into small pieces; minutely. **2** precisely or subtly. **3** splendidly or delicately.

fineness (ˈfaɪnnɪs) *n* **1** the state or quality of being fine. **2** a measurement of the purity of precious metal, expressed as the number of parts per thousand that is precious metal.

fine print *n* matter set in small type, as in a contract, esp. considered as containing unfavourable conditions that the signer might overlook. Also called: **small print.**

finery[1] (ˈfaɪnərɪ) *n* elaborate or showy decoration, esp. clothing and jewellery.

finery[2] (ˈfaɪnərɪ) *n, pl* **-eries.** a hearth for converting cast iron into wrought iron. **[C17:** from Old French *finerie,* from *finer* to refine; see FINE[1]**]**

fines herbes *(French* finz ɛrb) *pl n* a mixture of finely chopped herbs, used to flavour omelettes, salads, etc.

finespun ('faɪn'spʌn) *adj* **1** spun or drawn out to a fine thread. **2** excessively subtle or refined; not practical.

finesse (fɪ'nɛs) *n* **1** elegant skill in style or performance. **2** subtlety and tact in handling difficult situations. **3** *Bridge, whist.* an attempt to win a trick when opponents hold a high card in the suit led by playing a lower card, hoping the opponent who has already played holds the missing card. **4** a trick, artifice, or strategy. ◆ *vb* **5** to manage or bring about with finesse. **6** to play (a card) as a finesse. [C15: from Old French, from *fin* fine, delicate; see FINE[1]]

fine structure *n* the splitting of a spectral line into two or more closely spaced components as a result of interaction between the spin and orbital angular momenta of the atomic electrons. Compare **hyperfine structure.**

fine-tooth comb *or* **fine-toothed comb** *n* **1** a comb with fine teeth set closely together. **2 go over** (*or* **through**) **with a fine-tooth(ed) comb.** to examine very thoroughly.

fine-tune *vb* (*tr*) to make fine adjustments to (something) in order to obtain optimum performance.

finfoot ('fɪn,fʊt) *n, pl* **-foots.** any aquatic bird of the tropical and subtropical family *Heliornithidae,* having broadly lobed toes, a long slender head and neck, and pale brown plumage: order *Gruiformes* (cranes, rails etc.). Also called: **sungrebe.**

Fingal's Cave ('fɪŋg[ə]lz) *n* a cave in W Scotland, on Staffa Island in the Inner Hebrides: basaltic pillars. Length: 69 m (227 ft.). Height: 36 m (117 ft.).

finger ('fɪŋgə) *n* **1a** any of the digits of the hand, often excluding the thumb. Technical name: **digitus manus. 1b** (*as modifier*): *a finger bowl.* **1c** (*in combination*): *a fingernail.* Related adj: **digital. 2** the part of a glove made to cover a finger. **3** something that resembles a finger in shape or function: *a finger of land.* **4** Also called: **digit.** the length or width of a finger used as a unit of measurement. **5** a quantity of liquid in a glass, etc., as deep as a finger is wide; tot. **6** a projecting machine part, esp. one serving as an indicator. **7 burn one's fingers.** to suffer from having meddled or been rash. **8 get** *or* **pull one's finger out.** *Brit. informal.* to begin or speed up activity, esp. after initial delay or slackness. **9 have a** (*or* **one's**) **finger in the pie. 9a** to have an interest in or take part in some activity. **9b** to meddle or interfere. **10 lay a finger on.** (*usually negative*) to harm. **11 lay** *or* **put one's finger on.** to indicate, identify, or locate accurately. **12 not lift** (*or* **raise**) **a finger.** (*foll. by an infinitive*) not to make any effort (to do something). **13 let slip through one's fingers.** to allow to escape; miss narrowly. **14 point the finger at.** to accuse or blame. **15 twist** *or* **wrap around one's little finger.** to have easy and complete control or influence over. **16 put the finger on.** *Informal.* **16a** to inform on or identify, esp. for the police. **16b** to choose (the victim or location of an intended crime). ◆ *vb* **17** (*tr*) to touch or manipulate with the fingers; handle. **18** (*tr*) *Informal, chiefly U.S.* to identify as a criminal or suspect. **19** (*intr*) to extend like a finger. **20** to use one's fingers in playing (an instrument, such as a piano or clarinet). **21** to indicate on (a composition or part) the fingering required by a pianist, harpsichordist, etc. **22** (*tr; usually passive*) to arrange the keys of (a clarinet, flute, etc.) for playing in a certain way. [Old English; related to Old Norse *fingr,* Gothic *figgrs,* Old High German *fingar;* see FIVE, FIST] ▸ **'fingerer** *n* ▸ **'fingerless** *adj*

fingerboard ('fɪŋgə,bɔːd) *n* the long strip of hard wood on a violin, guitar, or related stringed instrument upon which the strings are stopped by the fingers.

finger bowl *n* a small bowl filled with water for rinsing the fingers at the table after a meal.

fingerbreadth ('fɪŋgə,brɛdθ, -,brɛtθ) *or* **finger's breadth** *n* the width of a finger, used as an indication of length.

finger buffet ('bʊfeɪ) *n* a buffet meal at which food that may be picked up with the fingers (**finger food**), such as canapés or vol-au-vents, is served.

fingered ('fɪŋgəd) *adj* **1** marked or dirtied by handling. **2a** having a finger or fingers. **2b** (*in combination*): *nine-fingered; red-fingered.* **3** (of a musical part) having numerals indicating the necessary fingering.

fingering[1] ('fɪŋgərɪŋ) *n* **1** the technique or art of using one's fingers in playing a musical instrument, esp. the piano. **2** the numerals in a musical part indicating this.

fingering[2] ('fɪŋgərɪŋ) *n* fine wool for knitting. [C17: from earlier *fingram,* perhaps from Old French *fin grain* fine grain]

fingerling ('fɪŋgəlɪŋ) *n* **1** a very young fish, esp. the parr of salmon or trout. **2** a diminutive creature or object.

fingermark ('fɪŋgə,mɑːk) *n* a mark left by dirty or greasy fingers on paintwork, walls, etc.

fingernail ('fɪŋgə,neɪl) *n* a thin horny translucent plate covering part of the dorsal surface of the end joint of each finger. Related adjs: **ungual, ungular.**

finger painting *n* **1** the process or art of painting with **finger paints** of starch, glycerine, and pigments, using the fingers, hand, or arm. **2** a painting made in this way.

finger post *n* a signpost showing a pointing finger or hand.

fingerprint ('fɪŋgə,prɪnt) *n* **1** an impression of the pattern of ridges on the palmar surface of the end joint of each finger and thumb. **2** any identifying characteristic. **3** *Biochem.* the pattern of fragments obtained when a protein is digested by a proteolytic enzyme, usually observed following two-dimensional separation by chromatography and electrophoresis. ◆ *vb* **4** (*tr*) to take an inked impression of the fingerprints of (a person). **5** to take a sample of (a person's) DNA.

fingerstall ('fɪŋgə,stɔːl) *n* a protective covering for a finger. Also called: **cot, fingertip.**

finger tight *adj* made as tight as possible by hand.

fingertip ('fɪŋgə,tɪp) *n* **1** the end joint or tip of a finger. **2** another term for **fingerstall. 3 at one's fingertips.** readily available and within one's mental grasp.

finger trouble *n Computing.* trouble caused by operator error, such as striking the wrong key.

finger wave *n Hairdressing.* a wave set in wet hair by using fingers and comb only.

Fingo ('fɪŋgəʊ) *n, pl* **-go** *or* **-gos.** a member of a Xhosa-speaking people settled in southern Africa in the Ciskei and Transkei: originally refugees from the Zulu wars of conquest.

finial ('faɪnɪəl) *n* **1** an ornament on top of a spire, gable, etc., esp. in the form of a foliated fleur-de-lys. **2** an ornament at the top of a piece of furniture, etc. [C14: from *finial* (adj), variant of FINAL] ▸ **'finialed** *adj*

finical ('fɪnɪk[ə]l) *adj* another word for **finicky.** [C16: probably from slang FINE[1] + -ICAL] ▸ **,fini'cality** *n* ▸ **'finically** *adv* ▸ **'finicalness** *n*

finicky ('fɪnɪkɪ) *or* **finicking** *adj* **1** excessively particular, as in tastes or standards; fussy. **2** full of trivial detail; overelaborate. [C19: from FINICAL]

fining ('faɪnɪŋ) *n* **1** the process of removing undissolved gas bubbles from molten glass. **2** the process of clarifying liquors by the addition of a coagulant. **3** (*pl*) a substance, such as isinglass, added to wine, beer, etc., to clarify it. [C17: from FINE[1] (in the sense: to clarify, refine)]

finis ('fɪnɪs) *n* the end; finish: used at the end of books, films, etc. [C15: from Latin]

finish ('fɪnɪʃ) *vb* (*mainly tr*) **1** to bring to an end; complete, conclude, or stop. **2** (*intr;* sometimes foll. by *up*) to be at or come to the end; use up. **3** to bring to a desired or complete condition. **4** to put a particular surface texture on (wood, cloth, etc.). **5** (often foll. by *off*) to destroy or defeat completely. **6** to train (a person) in social graces and talents. **7** (*intr;* foll. by *with*). **7a** to end a relationship or association. **7b** to stop punishing a person: *I haven't finished with you yet!* ◆ *n* **8** the final or last stage or part; end. **9a** the death, destruction, or absolute defeat of a person or one side in a conflict: *a fight to the finish.* **9b** the person, event, or thing that brings this about. **10a** the surface texture or appearance of wood, cloth, etc.: *a rough finish.* **10b** a preparation, such as varnish, used to produce such a texture. **11** a thing, event, etc., that completes. **12** completeness and high quality of workmanship. **13** refinement in social graces. **14** *Sport.* ability to sprint at the end of a race: *he has a good finish.* [C14: from Old French *finir,* from Latin *fīnīre* see FINE[1]]

finished ('fɪnɪʃt) *adj* **1** perfected. **2** (*predicative*) at the end of a task, activity, etc.: *they were finished by four.* **3** (*predicative*) without further hope of success or continuation: *she was finished as a prima ballerina.*

finisher ('fɪnɪʃə) *n* **1** a craftsman who carries out the final tasks in a manufacturing process. **2** *Boxing.* a knockout blow.

finishing ('fɪnɪʃɪŋ) *n Football.* the act or skill of goal scoring: *his finishing is deadly.*

finishing school *n* a private school for girls that prepares them for society by teaching social graces and accomplishments.

Finistère (,fɪnɪ'stɛə; *French* finistɛr) *n* a department of NW France, at the tip of the Breton peninsula. Capital: Quimper. Pop.: 840 600 (1995). Area: 7029 sq. km (2741 sq. miles).

Finisterre (,fɪnɪ'stɛə) *n* **1 Cape.** a headland in NW Spain: the westernmost point of the Spanish mainland. **2** an English name for **Finistère.**

finite ('faɪnaɪt) *adj* **1** bounded in magnitude or spatial or temporal extent: *a finite difference.* **2** *Maths, logic.* having a countable number of elements; capable of being put into one-to-one correspondence with an initial segment of the natural numbers. Compare **denumerable, infinite** (sense 4). **3a** limited or restricted in nature: *human existence is finite.* **3b** (*as n*): *the finite.* **4** denoting any form or occurrence of a verb inflected for grammatical features such as person, number, and tense. [C15: from Latin *fīnītus* limited, from *fīnīre* to limit, end] ▸ **'finitely** *adv* ▸ **'finiteness** *n*

finitism ('faɪnaɪt,ɪzəm) *n Philosophy, logic.* the view that only those entities may be admitted to mathematics that can be constructed in a finite number of steps, and only those propositions entertained whose truth can be proved in a finite number of steps. Compare **intuitionism.**

fink (fɪŋk) *Slang, chiefly U.S. and Canadian.* ◆ *n* **1** a strikebreaker; blackleg. **2** an informer, such as one working for the police; spy. **3** an unpleasant, disappointing, or contemptible person. ◆ *vb* **4** (*intr;* often foll. by *on*) to inform (on someone), as to the police. [C20: of uncertain origin]

fin keel *n* a projection from the keel of a vessel to give it additional stability.

fink out *vb* (*intr, adv*) *Slang, chiefly U.S.* to fail to carry something out or through; give up.

Finland ('fɪnlənd) *n* **1** a republic in N Europe, on the Baltic Sea: ceded to Russia by Sweden in 1809; gained independence in 1917; Soviet invasion successfully withstood in 1939–40, with the loss of Karelia; a member of the European Union. It is generally low-lying, with about 50 000 lakes, extensive forests, and peat bogs. Official languages: Finnish and Swedish. Religion: Christian, Lutheran majority. Currency: euro and markka. Capital: Helsinki. Pop.: 5 154 000 (1998 est.). Area: 337 000 sq. km (130 120 sq. miles). Finnish name: **Suomi. 2 Gulf of.** an arm of the Baltic Sea between Finland, Estonia, and Russia.

Finlandization *or* **Finlandisation** (,fɪnləndaɪ'zeɪʃən) *n* neutralization of a small country by a superpower, using conciliation, as the former Soviet Union did in relation to Finland.

Finlay ('fɪnlɪ) *n* **Carlos Juan** ('karlos xwan). 1833–1915, Cuban physician: discovered that the mosquito was the vector of yellow fever.

Finn[1] (fɪn) *n* **1** a native, inhabitant, or citizen of Finland. **2** a speaker of a Finnic language, esp. one of the original inhabitants of Russia, who were pushed northwards during the Slav migrations. [Old English *Finnas* (plural); related to Old Norse *Finnr* Finn, Latin *Fennī* the Finns, Greek *Phinnoi*]

Finn[2] (fɪn) *n* known as *Finn MacCool.* (in Irish legend) chief of the Fianna, father of the heroic poet Ossian.

finnan haddock ('fɪnən) *or* **haddie** ('hædɪ) *n* smoked haddock. [C18: *finnan* after *Findon,* a village in Scotland south of Aberdeen + HADDOCK]

finned (fɪnd) *adj* having one or more fins or finlike parts.

finner ('fɪnə) *n* another name for **rorqual.** [C18: from FIN[1] + -ER[1]]

Finney ('fɪnɪ) *n* **1 Albert.** born 1936, British stage and film actor. **2 Tom.** born 1922, English footballer: won 76 international caps as a winger.

Finnic ('fɪnɪk) *n* **1** one of the two branches of the Finno-Ugric family of languages, including Finnish and several languages of NE Europe. Compare **Ugric.** ◆ *adj* **2** of or relating to this group of languages or to the Finns.

Finnish ('fɪnɪʃ) *adj* **1** of, relating to, or characteristic of Finland, the Finns, or their language. ◆ *n* **2** the official language of Finland, also spoken in Estonia and NW Russia, belonging to the Finno-Ugric family.

Finnmark ('fɪn,mɑːk) *n* a county of N Norway: the largest, northernmost, and least populated county; mostly a barren plateau. Capital: Vadsø. Pop.: 76 502 (1996 est.). Area: 48 649 sq. km (18 779 sq. miles).

finnock ('fɪnək) *n* a young sea trout on its first return to fresh water. [originally Scot.: from Gaelic *fionnag,* from *fionn* white]

Finno-Ugric ('fɪnəʊ'uːgrɪk, -'juː-) *or* **Finno-Ugrian** *n* **1** a family of languages spoken in Scandinavia, Hungary, and NE Europe, including Finnish, Estonian, Hungarian, Ostyak, and Vogul: generally regarded as a subfamily of Uralic. See also **Ural-Altaic.** ◆ *adj* **2** of, relating to, speaking, or belonging to this family of languages.

finny ('fɪnɪ) *adj* **-nier, -niest. 1** *Poetic.* relating to or containing many fishes. **2** having or resembling a fin or fins.

fino ('fiːnəʊ) *n* a very dry sherry. [from Spanish: FINE[1]]

finocchio *or* **finochio** (fɪ'nɒkɪ,əʊ) *n* a variety of fennel, *Foeniculum vulgare dulce,* with thickened stalks that resemble celery and are eaten as a vegetable, esp. in S Europe. Also called: **Florence fennel.** [C18: from Italian: FENNEL]

Finsen (*Danish* 'fensən) *n* **Niels Ryberg** (neːls 'ryber). 1860–1904, Danish physician; founder of phototherapy: Nobel prize for physiology or medicine 1903.

Finsteraarhorn (*German* ,fɪnstər'aːrhɔrn) *n* a mountain in S central Switzerland: highest peak in the Bernese Alps. Height: 4274 m (14 022 ft.).

Finzi ('fɪnzɪ) *n* **Gerald.** 1901–56, British composer. His works include the cantata *Dies Natalis* (1940).

fiord (fjɔːd) *n* a variant spelling of **fjord.**

fiorin ('faɪərɪn) *n* a temperate perennial grass, *Agrostis stolonifera.* Also called: **creeping bent grass.** See **bent grass.** [C19: from Irish Gaelic *fiorthann* wheat grass]

fioritura (,fjɔːrɪ'tʊərə, ,fiːərɪ-) *n, pl* **-ture** (-'tʊəreɪ). *Music.* embellishment, esp. ornamentation added by the performer. [Italian: a blossoming]

fipple ('fɪpᵊl) *n* **1** a wooden plug forming a flue in the end of a pipe, as the mouthpiece of a recorder. **2** a similar device in an organ pipe with a flutelike tone. [C17: of unknown origin]

fipple flute *n* an end-blown flute provided with a fipple, such as the recorder or flageolet.

fir (fɜː) *n* **1** any pyramidal coniferous tree of the N temperate genus *Abies,* having single needle-like leaves and erect cones: family *Pinaceae.* See also **red fir, silver fir, balsam fir. 2** any of various other trees of the family *Pinaceae,* such as the Douglas fir. **3** the wood of any of these trees. [Old English *furh;* related to Old Norse *fura,* Old High German *foraha* fir, Latin *quercus* oak]

Firbank ('fɜːbæŋk) *n* **(Arthur Annesley) Ronald.** 1886–1926, English novelist, whose works include *Valmouth* (1919), *The Flower beneath the Foot* (1923), and *Concerning the Eccentricities of Cardinal Pirelli* (1926).

Firdausi (fɪə'daʊsɪ) *or* **Firdusi** (fɪə'duːsɪ) *n* pen name of *Abul Qasim Mansur.* ?935–1020 A.D., Persian epic poet; author of *Shah Nama* (*The Book of Kings*), a chronicle of the legends and history of Persia.

fire (faɪə) *n* **1** the state of combustion in which inflammable material burns, producing heat, flames, and often smoke. **2a** a mass of burning coal, wood, etc., used esp. in a hearth to heat a room. **2b** (*in combination*): *firewood; firelighter.* **3** a destructive conflagration, as of a forest, building, etc. **4** a device for heating a room, etc. **5** something resembling a fire in light or brilliance: *a diamond's fire.* **6** a flash or spark of or as if of fire. **7a** the act of discharging weapons, artillery, etc. **7b** the shells, etc., fired. **8** a burst or rapid volley: *a fire of questions.* **9** intense passion; ardour. **10** liveliness, as of imagination, thought, etc. **11** a burning sensation sometimes produced by drinking strong alcoholic liquor. **12** fever and inflammation. **13** a severe trial or torment (esp. in the phrase **go through fire and water**). **14 catch fire.** to ignite. **15 draw someone's fire.** to attract the criticism or censure of someone. **16 hang fire. 16a** to delay firing. **16b** to delay or be delayed. **17 no smoke without fire.** the evidence strongly suggests something has indeed happened. **18 on fire. 18a** in a state of ignition. **18b** ardent or eager. **19 open fire.** to start firing a gun, artillery, etc. **20 play with fire.** to be involved in something risky. **21 set fire to** *or* **set on fire. 21a** to ignite. **21b** to arouse or excite. **22 set the world** *or* (*Brit.*) **the Thames** *or* (*Scot.*) **the heather on fire.** *Informal.* to cause a great sensation. **23 under fire.** being attacked, as by weapons or by harsh criticism. **24** (*modifier*) *Astrology.* of or relating to a group of three signs of the zodiac, Aries, Leo, and Sagittarius. Compare **earth** (sense 10), **air** (sense 19), **water** (sense 12). ◆ *vb* **25** to discharge (a firearm or projectile) or (of a firearm, etc.) to be discharged. **26** to detonate (an explosive charge or device) or (of such a charge or device) to be detonated. **27** (*tr*) *Informal.* to dismiss from employment. **28** (*tr*) *Ceramics.* to bake in a kiln to harden the clay, fix the glaze, etc. **29** to kindle or be kindled; ignite. **30** (*tr*) to provide with fuel: *oil fires the heating system.* **31** (*intr*) to tend a fire. **32** (*tr*) to subject to heat. **33** (*tr*) to heat slowly so as to dry. **34** (*tr*) to arouse to strong emotion. **35** to glow or cause to glow. **36** (*intr*) (of an internal-combustion engine) to ignite. **37** (*intr*) (of grain) to become blotchy or yellow before maturity. **38** *Vet. science.* another word for **cauterize. 39** (*intr*) *Austral. informal.* (of a sportsman, etc.) to play well or with enthusiasm. ◆ *sentence substitute.* **40** a cry to warn others of a fire. **41** the order to begin firing a gun, artillery, etc. [Old English *fȳr;* related to Old Saxon *fiur,* Old Norse *fūrr,* Old High German *fūir,* Greek *pur*] ► **'fireable** *adj* ► **'fireless** *adj* ► **'firer** *n*

fire alarm *n* **1** a device to give warning of fire, esp. a bell, siren, or hooter. **2** a shout to warn that a fire has broken out.

fire-and-brimstone *adj* (of a sermon, preacher, etc.) zealous, esp. in threatening eternal damnation.

fire ant *n* any mound-building predatory ant of the genus *Solenopsis,* of tropical and subtropical America, that can inflict a painful sting.

firearm ('faɪər,ɑːm) *n* a weapon, esp. a portable gun or pistol, from which a projectile can be discharged by an explosion caused by igniting gunpowder, etc.

fire away *vb* (*intr, adv; often imperative*) *Informal.* to begin to speak or to ask questions.

fireback ('faɪə,bæk) *n* **1** Also called: **reredos.** an ornamental iron slab against the back wall of a hearth. **2** any pheasant of the genus *Lophura,* of SE Asia.

fireball ('faɪə,bɔːl) *n* **1** a ball-shaped discharge of lightning. **2** the bright spherical region of hot ionized gas at the centre of a nuclear explosion. **3** *Astronomy.* another name for **bolide. 4** *Slang.* an energetic person.

firebird ('faɪə,bɜːd) *n Chiefly U.S.* any of various songbirds having a bright red plumage, esp. the Baltimore oriole.

fire blight *n* a disease of apples, pears, and similar fruit trees, caused by the bacterium *Erwinia amylovora* and characterized by blackening of the blossoms and leaves, and cankers on the branches.

fireboat ('faɪə,bəʊt) *n* a motor vessel with fire-fighting apparatus.

firebomb ('faɪə,bɒm) *n* another name for **incendiary** (sense 6).

firebox ('faɪə,bɒks) *n* **1** the furnace chamber of a boiler in a steam locomotive. **2** an obsolete word for **tinderbox.**

firebrand ('faɪə,brænd) *n* **1** a piece of burning or glowing wood or other material. **2** a person who causes unrest or is very energetic.

firebrat ('faɪə,bræt) *n* a small primitive wingless insect, *Thermobia domestica,* that occurs in warm buildings, feeding on starchy food scraps, fabric, etc.: order *Thysanura* (bristletails).

firebreak ('faɪə,breɪk), **fireguard** ('faɪə,gɑːd), *or* **fire line** *n* a strip of open land in forest or prairie, to arrest the advance of a fire.

firebrick ('faɪə,brɪk) *n* a refractory brick made of fire clay, used for lining furnaces, flues, etc.

fire brigade *n Chiefly Brit.* an organized body of firefighters.

firebug ('faɪə,bʌg) *n Informal.* a person who deliberately sets fire to property.

fire clay *n* a heat-resistant clay used in the making of firebricks, furnace linings, etc.

fire company *n* **1** an insurance company selling policies relating to fire risk. **2** *U.S.* an organized body of firemen.

fire control *n Military.* the procedures by which weapons are brought to engage a target.

firecracker ('faɪə,krækə) *n* a small cardboard container filled with explosive powder and lit by a fuse.

firecrest ('faɪə,krest) *n* a small European warbler, *Regulus ignicapillus,* having a crown striped with yellow, black, and white.

fire-cure *vb* (*tr*) to cure (tobacco) by exposure to the smoke and heat of an open fire.

firedamp ('faɪə,dæmp) *n* a mixture of hydrocarbons, chiefly methane, formed in coal mines. It forms explosive mixtures with air. See also **afterdamp.**

fire department *n U.S. and Canadian.* the department of a local authority responsible for the prevention and extinguishing of fires.

firedog ('faɪə,dɒg) *n* either of a pair of decorative metal stands used to support logs in an open fire.

fire door *n* **1** a door made of noncombustible material, the purpose of which is to prevent a fire from spreading within a building. **2** a similar door, leading to the outside of a building, that can be easily opened from inside; emergency exit.

firedrake ('faɪə,dreɪk) *or* **firedragon** ('faɪə,drægən) *n Myth.* a fire-breathing dragon.

fire drill *n* a rehearsal of duties or escape procedures to be followed in case of fire.

fire-eater *n* **1** a performer who simulates the swallowing of fire. **2** a belligerent person. ► **'fire-,eating** *n, adj*

fire engine *n* a heavy road vehicle that carries firemen and fire-fighting equipment to a fire.

fire escape *n* a means of evacuating persons from a building in the event of fire, esp. a metal staircase outside the building.

fire-extinguisher *n* a portable device for extinguishing fires, usually consisting of a canister with a directional nozzle used to direct a spray of water, chemically generated foam, inert gas, or fine powder onto the fire.

firefight ('faɪə,faɪt) *n* a brief small-scale engagement between opposing military ground forces using short-range light weapons.

firefighter ('faɪə,faɪtə) *n* a person who fights fires, usually a public employee or trained volunteer.

firefly ('faɪə,flaɪ) *n, pl* **-flies. 1** any nocturnal beetle of the family *Lampyridae,* common in warm and tropical regions, having luminescent abdominal organs. See also **glow-worm. 2** any tropical American click beetle of the genus *Pyrophorus,* esp. *P. noctiluca,* that have luminescent thoracic organs.

fireguard ('faɪə,gɑːd) *n* **1** Also called: **fire screen.** a metal panel or meshed frame put before an open fire to protect against falling logs, sparks, etc. **2** a less common word for **firebreak.**

fire hydrant *n* a hydrant for use as an emergency supply for fighting fires, esp. one in a street. Also called (esp. U.S. and N.Z.): **fireplug.**

fire insurance *n* insurance covering damage or loss caused by fire or lightning.

fire irons *pl n* metal fireside implements, such as poker, shovel, and tongs.

fireless cooker *n* an insulated container that retains enough heat to cook food or keep it warm.

firelock ('faɪə,lɒk) *n* **1** an obsolete type of gunlock with a priming mechanism ignited by sparks. **2** a gun or musket having such a lock.

fireman ('faɪəmən) *n, pl* **-men. 1** a man who fights fires, usually a public employee or trained volunteer. **2a** (on steam locomotives) the man who stokes the fire and controls the injectors feeding water to the boiler. **2b** (on diesel and electric locomotives) the driver's assistant. **3** a man who tends furnaces; stoker. **4** Also called: **deputy.** a mine official responsible for safety precautions. U.S. equivalent: **fire boss. 5** *U.S. Navy.* a junior rating who works on marine engineering equipment.

fire marshal *n U.S.* **1** a public official responsible for investigating the causes of fires, enforcing fire prevention laws, etc. **2** the head of a fire prevention organization.

Firenze (fi'rɛntse) *n* the Italian name for **Florence.**

fire opal *n* an orange-red translucent variety of opal, valued as a gemstone.

firepan ('faɪə,pæn) *n* a metal container for a fire in a room.

fireplace ('faɪə,pleɪs) *n* **1** an open recess in a wall of a room, at the base of a chimney, etc., for a fire; hearth. **2** *Austral.* an authorized place or installation for outside cooking, esp. by a roadside.

fireplug ('faɪə,plʌg) *n* another name (esp. U.S. and N.Z.) for **fire hydrant.**

fire power *n Military.* **1** the amount of fire that may be delivered by a unit or weapon. **2** the capability of delivering fire.

fireproof ('faɪə,pruːf) *adj* **1** capable of resisting damage by fire. ◆ *vb* **2** (*tr*) to make resistant to fire.

fire raiser *n* a person who deliberately sets fire to property. ▸ **fire raising** *n*

fire screen *n* **1** a decorative screen placed in the hearth when there is no fire. **2** a screen placed before a fire to protect the face from intense heat.

fire ship *n* a vessel loaded with explosives and used, esp. formerly, as a bomb by igniting it and directing it to drift among an enemy's warships.

fireside ('faɪə,saɪd) *n* **1** the hearth. **2** family life; the home.

fire station *n* a building where fire-fighting vehicles and equipment are stationed and where firefighters on duty wait. Also called (U.S.): **'fire,house, station house.**

firestone ('faɪə,stəʊn) *n* a sandstone that withstands intense heat, esp. one used for lining kilns, furnaces, etc.

firestorm ('faɪə,stɔːm) *n* an uncontrollable blaze sustained by violent winds that are drawn into the column of rising hot air over the burning area: often the result of heavy bombing.

firethorn ('faɪə,θɔːn) *n* any rosaceous evergreen spiny shrub of the genus *Pyracantha,* of SE Europe and Asia, having bright red or orange fruits: cultivated for ornament.

fire trail *n Austral.* a permanent track cleared through the bush to provide access for fire-fighting.

firetrap ('faɪə,træp) *n* a building that would burn easily or one without fire escapes.

fire walking *n* a religious rite in which people walk barefoot over white-hot ashes, stones, etc.

firewall *n* **1** a fireproof wall or partition used to impede the progress of a fire, as from one room or compartment to another. **2** *Computing.* a computer system that isolates another computer from the Internet in order to prevent unauthorized access.

firewarden ('faɪə,wɔːdᵊn) *n U.S. and Canadian.* an officer responsible for fire prevention and control in an area, esp. in a forest.

fire watcher *n* a person who watches for fires, esp. those caused by aerial bombardment.

firewater ('faɪə,wɔːtə) *n* any strong spirit, esp. whisky.

fireweed ('faɪə,wiːd) *n* **1** any of various plants that appear as first vegetation in burnt-over areas. **2** Also called: **pilewort.** a weedy North American plant, *Erechtites hieracifolia,* having small white or greenish flowers: family *Compositae* (composites). **3** another name for **rosebay willowherb.** See **rosebay** (sense 2).

firework ('faɪə,wɜːk) *n* a device, such as a Catherine wheel, Roman candle, or rocket, in which combustible materials are ignited and produce coloured flames, sparks, and smoke, sometimes accompanied by bangs.

fireworks ('faɪə,wɜːks) *pl n* **1** a show in which large numbers of fireworks are let off simultaneously. **2** *Informal.* an exciting or spectacular exhibition, as of musical virtuosity or wit. **3** *Informal.* a burst of temper.

firing ('faɪərɪŋ) *n* **1** the process of baking ceramics, etc., in a kiln or furnace: *a second firing.* **2** the act of stoking a fire or furnace. **3** a discharge of a firearm. **4** something used as fuel, such as coal or wood. **5** *U.S.* a scorching of plants, as a result of disease, drought, or heat.

firing line *n* **1** *Military.* **1a** the positions from which fire is delivered. **1b** the soldiers occupying these positions. **2** the leading or most advanced position in an activity.

firing order *n* the sequence of ignition in the cylinders of an internal-combustion engine.

firing party *n* **1** a military detachment detailed to fire a salute at a funeral. **2** another name for **firing squad.**

firing pin *n* the part of the firing mechanism of a firearm that ignites the charge by striking the primer.

firing squad *n* a small military detachment formed to implement a death sentence by shooting.

firkin ('fɜːkɪn) *n* **1** a small wooden barrel or similar container. **2** *Brit.* a unit of capacity equal to nine gallons. [C14 *fir,* from Middle Dutch *vierde* FOURTH + -KIN]

firm[1] (fɜːm) *adj* **1** not soft or yielding to a touch or pressure; rigid; solid. **2** securely in position; stable or stationary. **3** definitely established; decided; settled. **4** enduring or steady; constant. **5** having determination or strength; resolute. **6** (of prices, markets, etc.) tending to rise. ◆ *adv* **7** in a secure, stable, or unyielding manner: *he stood firm over his obligation to pay.* ◆ *vb* **8** (sometimes foll. by *up*) to make or become firm. **9** (*intr*) *Austral. horse racing.* (of a horse) to shorten in odds. [C14: from Latin *firmus*] ▸ **'firmly** *adv* ▸ **'firmness** *n*

firm[2] (fɜːm) *n* **1** a business partnership. **2** any commercial enterprise. **3** a team of doctors and their assistants. **4** *Brit. slang.* **4a** a gang of criminals. **4b** a gang of football hooligans. [C16 (in the sense: signature): from Spanish *firma* signature, title of a partnership or business concern, from *firmar* to sign, from Latin *firmāre* to confirm, from *firmus* firm]

firmament ('fɜːməmənt) *n* the expanse of the sky; heavens. [C13: from Late Latin *firmāmentum* sky (considered as fixed above the earth), from Latin: prop, support, from *firmāre*to make FIRM[1]] ▸ **firmamental** (,fɜːmə'mɛntᵊl) *adj*

firman (fɜː'mɑːn, 'fɜː-) *n* **1** an edict of an Oriental sovereign. **2** any authoritative grant of permission. [C17: from Persian *fermān*]

firmer chisel ('fɜːmə) *n* a chisel or gouge with a thin blade, used on wood. Sometimes shortened to **firmer.**

firmware ('fɜːm,wɛə) *n Computing.* a fixed form of software programmed into a read-only memory.

firn (fɪən) *n* another name for **névé** (sense 1). [C19: from German (Swiss dialect) *firn* of the previous year, from Old High German *firni* old]

firn line *n* **1** Also called: **firn limit.** the zone of a glacier between the lower region of solid ice and the upper region of névé, above which ablation occurs. **2** the snow line on a glacier.

firry ('fɜːrɪ) *adj* **1** of, relating to, or made from fir trees. **2** abounding in or dominated by firs.

first (fɜːst) *adj* (*usually prenominal*) **1a** coming before all others; earliest, best, or foremost. **1b** (*as n*)*: I was the first to arrive.* **2** preceding all others in numbering or counting order; the ordinal number of *one.* Often written: 1st. **3** rated, graded, or ranked above all other levels. **4** denoting the lowest forward ratio of a gearbox in a motor vehicle. **5** *Music.* **5a** denoting the highest part assigned to one of the voice parts in a chorus or one of the sections of an orchestra: *first soprano; the first violins.* **5b** denoting the principal player in a specific orchestral section: *he plays first horn.* **6 first thing.** as the first action of the day: *I'll see you first thing tomorrow.* **7 first things first.** things must be done in order of priority. **8 the first thing, idea, etc.** (*in negative constructions*) even one thing, etc.: *he doesn't know the first thing about me.* ◆ *n* **9** the beginning; outset: *I knew you were a rogue from the first; I couldn't see at first because of the mist.* **10** *Education, chiefly Brit.* an honours degree of the highest class. Full term: **first-class honours degree. 11** the lowest forward ratio of a gearbox in a motor vehicle; low gear. **12** *Music.* **12a** the highest part in a particular section of a chorus or orchestra. **12b** the instrument or voice taking such a part. **12c** the chief or leading player in a section of an orchestra; principal. **13** *Music.* a rare word for **prime** (sense 11). ◆ *adv* **14** before anything else in order, time, preference, importance, etc.: *do this first; first, remove the head and tail of the fish.* **15 first and last.** on the whole; overall. **16 from first to last.** throughout. **17** for the first time: *I've loved you since I first saw you.* **18** (*sentence modifier*) in the first place or beginning of a series of actions: *first I want to talk about criminality.* ◆ See also **firsts.** [Old English *fyrest;* related to Old Saxon *furist,* Old Norse *fyrstr,* German *Fürst* prince, one who is first in rank]

first aid *n* **1a** immediate medical assistance given in an emergency. **1b** (*as modifier*)*: first-aid box.* **2** (in Barbados) a small shop that sells domestic items after hours.

first base *n* **1** *Baseball.* **1a** the base that a runner must reach safely to score a hit, and the first of the three bases he must reach safely on the way to home plate in order to score a run. **1b** the fielding position nearest this base. **2 get to first base.** *Informal, chiefly U.S. and Canadian.* to accomplish the first step of an undertaking.

first-born *adj* **1** eldest of the children in a family. ◆ *n* **2** the eldest child in a family.

first cause *n* **1** a source or cause of something. **2** (*often caps.*) (esp. in philosophy) God considered as the uncaused creator of all beings apart from himself.

first class *n* **1** the class or grade of the best or highest value, quality, etc. ◆ *adj* (**first-class** *when prenominal*). **2** of the best or highest class or grade: *a first-class citizen.* **3** excellent; first-rate. **4** of or denoting the most comfortable and expensive class of accommodation in a hotel, aircraft, train, etc. **5a** (in Britain) of or relating to mail that is processed most quickly. **5b** (in the U.S. and Canada) of or relating to mail that consists mainly of written letters, cards, etc. **6** *Education.* See **first** (sense 10). ◆ *adv* **first-class. 7** by first-class mail, means of transportation, etc.

first-day cover *n Philately.* a cover, usually an envelope, postmarked on the first day of the issue of its stamps.

first-degree burn *n Pathol.* See **burn**[1] (sense 22).

First Empire *n* the period of imperial rule in France (1804–14) under Napoleon Bonaparte.

first estate *n* the first of the three estates of the realm, such as the Lords Spiritual in England or the clergy in France until the revolution.

First Fleet *n Austral.* the fleet of convict ships that arrived at Port Jackson in 1788. ▸ **First Fleeter** *n*

first floor *n* **1** *Brit.* the floor or storey of a building immediately above the ground floor. U.S. and Canadian term: **second floor. 2** *U.S. and Canadian.* another term for **ground floor.**

first-foot *Chiefly Scot.* ◆ *n also* **first-footer. 1** the first person to enter a household in the New Year. By Hogmanay tradition a dark-haired man who crosses the threshold at midnight brings good luck. ◆ *vb* **2** to enter (a house) as first-foot. ▸ **'first-'footing** *n*

first four ships *pl n N.Z.* **1** the earliest settlers' ships to arrive in the Canterbury Province. **2 come with the first four ships.** to be a founder member of Canterbury.

first fruits *pl n* **1** the first results, products, or profits of an undertaking. **2** fruit that ripens first.

first-hand *adj, adv* **1** from the original source; direct or directly: *first-hand news; he got the news first-hand.* **2 at first hand.** from the original source; directly.

First International *n* an association of socialists and labour leaders founded in London in 1864 and dissolved in Philadelphia in 1876. Official name: **International Workingmen's Association.**

first lady *n* (*often caps.*) **1** (in the U.S.) the wife or official hostess of a chief executive, esp. of a state governor or a president. **2** a woman considered to be at the top of her profession or art: *the first lady of jazz.*

first language *n* a person's native language.

first lieutenant *n* **1** the officer responsible for the upkeep and maintenance of a warship, esp. the executive officer of a smaller ship in the Royal Navy. **2** an officer holding commissioned rank in the U.S. Army, Air Force, Marine Corps, or in certain other forces, senior to a second lieutenant and junior to a captain.

first light *n* the time when light first appears in the morning; dawn.

firstling ('fɜ:stlɪŋ) *n* the first, esp. the first offspring.

first-loss policy *n* an insurance policy for goods in which a total loss is extremely unlikely and the insurer agrees to provide cover for a sum less than the total value of the property.

firstly ('fɜ:stlɪ) *adv* coming before other points, questions, etc.

first mate *n* an officer second in command to the captain of a merchant ship. Also called: **first officer.**

First Minister *n* **1** the chief minister of the Northern Ireland Assembly. **2** the chief minister of the Scottish Parliament.

first mortgage *n* a mortgage that has priority over other mortgages on the same property, except for taxation and other statutory liabilities.

First Mover *n* the Aristotelian conception of God as the unmoved mover of everything else.

first name *n* a name given to a person at birth, as opposed to a surname. Also called: **Christian name, forename, given name.**

First Nation *n Canadian.* another name for **band**[1] (sense 5).

first night *n* **a** the first public performance of a play or other production. **b** (*as modifier*): *first-night nerves.*

first-nighter *n* a member of an opening night audience, esp. one who habitually attends first nights.

first offender *n* a person convicted of any criminal offence for the first time.

first officer *n* **1** another name for **first mate. 2** the member of an aircraft crew who is second in command to the captain.

first-order *adj Logic.* quantifying only over individuals and not over predicates or clauses: **first-order predicate calculus** studies the logical properties of such quantification.

first-past-the-post *n* (*modifier*) of or relating to a voting system in which a candidate may be elected by a simple majority rather than an absolute majority. Compare **proportional representation.**

first person *n* a grammatical category of pronouns and verbs used by the speaker to refer to or talk about himself, either alone (**first person singular**) or together with others (**first person plural**).

first post *n Brit.* the first of two military bugle calls ordering or giving notice of the time to retire for the night. The second is called **last post.**

first principle *n* (*usually pl*) **1** one of the fundamental assumptions on which a particular theory or procedure is thought to be based. **2** an axiom of a mathematical or scientific theory.

first quarter *n* one of the four principal phases of the moon, occurring between new moon and full moon, when half of the lighted surface is visible from earth. Compare **last quarter.**

first-rate *adj* **1** of the best or highest rated class or quality. **2** *Informal.* very good; excellent. ◆ *adv* **3** *Not standard.* very well; excellently.

first reading *n* the introduction of a bill in a legislative assembly.

first refusal *n* the chance of buying a house, merchandise, etc., before the offer is made to other potential buyers.

First Republic *n* the republic in France, which lasted from the abolition of the monarchy in 1792 until Napoleon Bonaparte proclaimed himself emperor in 1804.

firsts (fɜ:sts) *pl n* saleable goods of the highest quality.

first school *n Brit.* a school for children aged between 5 and 8 or 9. Compare **middle school.**

first-strike *adj* (of a nuclear missile) intended for use in an opening attack calculated to destroy the enemy's nuclear weapons.

first string *n* **1** the top player of a team in an individual sport, such as squash. ◆ *adj* **first-string. 2** being a regular member of a team rather than a substitute or reserve. **3** being the top player of a team in an individual sport. **4** of high rating; first-class.

first water *n* **1** the finest quality of diamond or other precious stone. **2** the highest grade or best quality. **3** the most extreme kind: *a fool of the first water.*

First World War *n* another name for **World War I.**

firth (fɜ:θ) *or* **frith** *n* a relatively narrow inlet of the sea, esp. in Scotland. [C15: from Old Norse *fjörthr* FIORD]

fisc (fɪsk) *n Rare.* a state or royal treasury. [C16: from Latin *fiscus* treasury, originally money-bag]

fiscal ('fɪsk[ə]l) *adj* **1** of or relating to government finances, esp. tax revenues. **2** of or involving financial matters. ◆ *n* **3a** (in some countries) a public prosecutor. **3b** *Scot.* short for **procurator fiscal. 4** a postage or other stamp signifying payment of a tax. [C16: from Latin *fiscālis* concerning the state treasury, from *fiscus* public money; see FISC] ▸ **'fiscally** *adv*

fiscal drag *n Economics.* the process by which, during inflation, rising incomes draw people into higher tax brackets, so that their real incomes may fall; this acts as a restraint on the expansion of the economy.

fiscal year *n* the U.S. and Canadian term for **financial year.**

Fischer ('fɪʃər) *n* **1 Emil Hermann** ('e:mi:l 'hɛrman). 1852–1919, German chemist, noted particularly for his work on synthetic sugars and the purine group: Nobel prize for chemistry 1902. **2 Ernst Otto.** 1918–94, German chemist: shared the Nobel prize for chemistry in 1973 with Geoffrey Wilkinson for his work on inorganic complexes. **3 Hans** (hans). 1881–1945, German chemist, noted particularly for his work on chlorophyll, haemin, and the porphyrins: Nobel prize for chemistry 1930. **4 Robert James,** known as *Bobby.* born 1943, U.S. chess player; world champion 1972–75.

Fischer-Dieskau (*German* -'di:skau) *n* **Dietrich** ('di:trɪç). born 1925, German baritone, noted particularly for his interpretation of Schubert's song cycles.

Fischer von Erlach (*German* 'fɪʃər fɔn 'ɛrlax) *n* **Johann Bernhard** (jo'han 'bɛrnhart). 1656–1723, Austrian architect: a leading exponent of the German baroque.

fish (fɪʃ) *n, pl* **fish** *or* **fishes. 1a** any of a large group of cold-blooded aquatic vertebrates having jaws, gills, and usually fins and a skin covered in scales: includes the sharks and rays (class *Chondrichthyes:* **cartilaginous fishes**) and the teleosts, lungfish, etc. (class *Osteichthyes:* **bony fishes**). **1b** (*in combination*): *fishpond.* Related adjs: **ichthyic, ichthyoid, piscine. 2** any of various similar but jawless vertebrates, such as the hagfish and lamprey. **3** (*not in technical use*) any of various aquatic invertebrates, such as the cuttlefish, jellyfish, and crayfish. **4** the flesh of fish used as food. **5** *Informal.* a person of little emotion or intelligence: *a poor fish.* **6** short for **fishplate. 7** Also called: **tin fish.** an informal word for **torpedo** (sense 1). **8 a fine kettle of fish.** an awkward situation; mess. **9 drink like a fish.** to drink (esp. alcohol) to excess. **10 have other fish to fry.** to have other activities to do, esp. more important ones. **11 like a fish out of water.** out of one's usual place. **12 neither fish, flesh, nor fowl.** neither this nor that. **13 make fish of one and flesh of another.** *Irish.* to discriminate unfairly between people. ◆ *vb* **14** (*intr*) to attempt to catch fish, as with a line and hook or with nets, traps, etc. **15** (*tr*) to fish in (a particular area of water). **16** to search (a body of water) for something or to search for something, esp. in a body of water. **17** (*intr;* foll. by *for*) to seek something indirectly: *to fish for compliments.* ◆ See also **fish out.** [Old English *fisc;* related to Old Norse *fiskr,* Gothic *fiscs,* Russian *piskar,* Latin *piscis*] ▸ **'fishable** *adj* ▸ **'fish,like** *adj*

fish and chips *n* fish fillets coated with batter and deep-fried, eaten with potato chips.

fish-and-chip shop *n* (esp. in Britain) a place where fish and chips are cooked and sold.

fishbolt ('fɪʃ,bəult) *n* a bolt used for fastening a fishplate to a rail.

fishbowl ('fɪʃ,bəul) *n* another name for **goldfish bowl.**

fish cake *n* a fried ball of flaked fish mixed with mashed potatoes.

fish eagle *n* another name for the **osprey.**

fisher ('fɪʃə) *n* **1** a person who fishes; fisherman. **2** Also called: **pekan. 2a** a large North American marten, *Martes pennanti,* having thick dark brown fur. **2b** the fur of this animal. **3 fisher of men.** an evangelist.

Fisher ('fɪʃə) *n* **1 Andrew.** 1862–1928, Australian statesman, born in Scotland: prime minister of Australia (1908–09; 1910–13; 1914–15). **2 Saint John.** ?1469–1535, English prelate and scholar: executed for refusing to acknowledge Henry VIII as supreme head of the church. Feast day: June 22. **3 John Arbuthnot,** 1st Baron Fisher of Kilverstone. 1841–1920, British admiral; First Sea Lord (1904–10; 1914–15); introduced the dreadnought.

fisherman ('fɪʃəmən) *n, pl* **-men. 1** a person who fishes as a profession or for sport. **2** a vessel used for fishing.

fisherman's bend *n* a knot used to fasten a rope to an anchor, ring, or spar.

fisherman's knot *n* a knot for joining two ropes of equal thickness consisting of an overhand knot or double overhand knot by each rope round the other, so that the two knots jam when pulled tight.

fishery ('fɪʃərɪ) *n, pl* **-eries. 1a** the industry of catching, processing, and selling fish. **1b** a place where this is carried on. **2** a place where fish are reared. **3** a fishing ground. **4** another word for **piscary** (sense 2).

Fishes ('fɪʃɪz) *n* **the.** the constellation Pisces, the twelfth sign of the zodiac.

fisheye lens ('fɪʃ,aɪ) *n Photog.* a lens of small focal length, having a highly curved protruding front element, that covers an angle of view of almost 180°. It yields a circular image having considerable linear distortion.

fishfinger ('fɪʃ'fɪŋgə) *or U.S. and Canadian* **fish stick** *n* an oblong piece of filleted or minced fish coated in breadcrumbs.

fish flake *n Canadian.* a platform on which fish are dried.

fishgig ('fɪʃ,gɪg) *n* a pole with barbed prongs for impaling fish. Also: **fizgig.** [C17: of uncertain origin; perhaps altered from Spanish *fisga* harpoon]

Fishguard ('fɪʃ,gɑ:d) *n* a port and resort in SW Wales, in Pembrokeshire: ferry connections to Cork and Rosslare. Pop.: 2679 (1991).

fish hawk *n* another name for the **osprey.**

fish-hook *n* **1** a sharp hook used in angling, esp. one with a barb. **2** *Logic.* a symbol (—ɜ) for entailment.

fishing ('fɪʃɪŋ) *n* **1a** the occupation of catching fish. **1b** (*as modifier*): *a fishing match.* **2** another word for **piscary** (sense 2). Related adj: **piscatorial.**

fishing ground *n* an area of water that is good for fishing.

fishing rod *n* a long tapered flexible pole, often in jointed sections, for use with a fishing line and, usually, a reel.

fishing tackle *n* all the equipment, such as rods, lines, bait, etc., used in angling.

fish joint *n* a connection formed by fishplates at the meeting point of two rails, beams, etc., as on a railway.
fish ladder *n* a row of ascending pools or weirs connected by short falls to allow fish to pass barrages or dams.
fish louse *n* any small flat rounded crustacean of the subclass *Branchiura,* having sucking mouth parts: parasites of fish.
fishmeal ('fɪʃˌmiːl) *n* ground dried fish used as feed for farm animals, as a fertilizer, etc.
fishmonger ('fɪʃˌmʌŋɡə) *n Chiefly Brit.* a retailer of fish.
fishnet ('fɪʃˌnet) *n* **1** *Chiefly U.S. and Canadian.* a net for catching fish. **2a** an open mesh fabric resembling netting. **2b** *(as modifier): fishnet tights.*
fish out *vb (tr, adv)* to find or extract (something): *to fish keys out of a pocket.*
fishplate ('fɪʃˌpleɪt) *n* a flat piece of metal joining one rail or beam to the next, esp. on railway tracks.
fishskin disease ('fɪʃˌskɪn) *n Pathol.* a nontechnical name for **ichthyosis.**
fishtail ('fɪʃˌteɪl) *n* **1** an aeroplane manoeuvre in which the tail is moved from side to side to reduce speed. **2** a nozzle having a long narrow slot at the top, placed over a Bunsen burner to produce a thin fanlike flame. ♦ *vb* **3** *(intr)* to slow an aeroplane by moving the tail from side to side.
fish tail *n* a step in ballroom dancing in which the feet are quickly crossed.
fishway ('fɪʃˌweɪ) *n U.S. and Canadian.* another name for **fish ladder.**
fishwife ('fɪʃˌwaɪf) *n, pl* **-wives. 1** a woman who sells fish. **2** a coarse scolding woman.
fishy ('fɪʃɪ) *adj* **fishier, fishiest. 1** of, involving, or suggestive of fish. **2** abounding in fish. **3** *Informal.* suspicious, doubtful, or questionable: *their leaving at the same time looked fishy.* **4** dull and lifeless: *a fishy look.* ▸ **'fishily** *adv* ▸ **'fishiness** *n*
fissi- *combining form.* indicating a splitting or cleft: *fissirostral.* [from Latin *fissus,* past participle of *findere* to split]
fissile ('fɪsaɪl) *adj* **1** *Brit.* capable of undergoing nuclear fission as a result of the impact of slow neutrons. **2** another word (esp. U.S. and Canadian) for **fissionable. 3** tending to split or capable of being split. [C17: from Latin *fissilis,* from *fissus* split; see FISSI-] ▸ **fissility** (fɪ'sɪlɪtɪ) *n*
fission ('fɪʃən) *n* **1** the act or process of splitting or breaking into parts. **2** *Biology.* a form of asexual reproduction in single-celled animals and plants involving a division into two or more equal parts that develop into new cells. **3** short for **nuclear fission.** [C19: from Latin *fissiō* a cleaving]
fissionable ('fɪʃənəbᵊl) *adj* capable of undergoing nuclear fission as a result of any process. Compare **fissile** (sense 1). ▸ **ˌfissiona'bility** *n*
fission bomb *n* a bomb in which the energy is supplied by nuclear fission. See **atomic bomb.**
fission-fusion bomb *n* another name for **fusion bomb.**
fission product *n* a nuclide produced either directly by nuclear fission or by the radioactive decay of such a nuclide.
fission reactor *n* a nuclear reactor in which a fission reaction takes place.
fission-track dating *n* the dating of samples of minerals by comparing the tracks in them by fission fragments of the uranium nuclei they contain, before and after irradiation by neutrons.
fissipalmate (ˌfɪsɪ'pælmeɪt) *adj* (of some birds' feet) partially webbed, having lobes and fringes on separate toes.
fissiparous (fɪ'sɪpərəs) *adj Biology.* reproducing by fission. ▸ **fis'siparously** *adv* ▸ **fis'siparousness** *n*
fissiped ('fɪsɪˌpɛd) *adj also* **fissipedal** (fɪ'sɪpɪdᵊl, ˌfɪsɪ'piːdᵊl). **1** having toes that are separated from one another, as dogs, cats, bears, and similar carnivores. ♦ *n* **2** a fissiped animal. ♦ Compare **pinniped.**
fissirostral (ˌfɪsɪ'rɒstrəl) *adj* **1** (of the beaks of some birds) broad and deeply cleft. **2** having such a beak, as swifts and swallows.
fissure ('fɪʃə) *n* **1** any long narrow cleft or crack, esp. in a rock. **2** a weakness or flaw indicating impending disruption or discord: *fissures in a decaying empire.* **3** *Anatomy.* a narrow split or groove that divides an organ such as the brain, lung, or liver into lobes. See also **sulcus. 4** a small unnatural crack in the skin or mucous membrane, as between the toes or at the anus. **5** a minute crack in the surface of a tooth, caused by imperfect joining of enamel during development. ♦ *vb* **6** to crack or split apart. [C14: from medical Latin *fissūra,* from Latin *fissus* split]
fissure eruption *n* the emergence of lava from a fissure in the ground rather than from a volcanic cone or vent.
fissure of Rolando (rəʊ'lændəʊ) *n* another name for **central sulcus.** [C19: named after L. *Rolando* (died 1831), Italian anatomist]
fissure of Sylvius ('sɪlvɪəs) *n* a deep horizontal cleft in each cerebral hemisphere: marks the separation of the temporal lobe from the frontal and parietal lobes. [named after Franciscus *Sylvius* (died 1652), German anatomist]
fist (fɪst) *n* **1** a hand with the fingers clenched into the palm, as for hitting. **2** Also called: **fistful.** the quantity that can be held in a fist or hand. **3** an informal word for **hand** or **index** (sense 9). ♦ *vb* **4** *(tr)* to hit with the fist. [Old English *fȳst;* related to Old Frisian *fest,* Old Saxon, Old High German *fūst;* see FIVE]
fistic ('fɪstɪk) *adj* of or relating to fisticuffs or boxing.
fisticuffs ('fɪstɪˌkʌfs) *pl n* combat with the fists. [C17: probably from *fisty* with the fist + CUFF²]
fistmele ('fɪstˌmiːl) *n Archery.* a measure of the width of a hand and the extended thumb, used to calculate the approximate height of the string of a braced bow. [C17: from FIST + *mele,* variant of obsolete *meal* measure]
fistula ('fɪstjʊlə) *n, pl* **-las** *or* **-lae** (-ˌliː). **1** *Pathol.* an abnormal opening between one hollow organ and another or between a hollow organ and the surface of the skin, caused by ulceration, congenital malformation, etc. **2** *Obsolete.* any musical wind instrument; a pipe. [C14: from Latin: pipe, tube, hollow reed, ulcer]
fistulous ('fɪstjʊləs), **fistular** ('fɪstjʊlə), *or* **fistulate** ('fɪstjʊlɪt) *adj* **1** *Pathol.* containing, relating to, or resembling a fistula. **2** hollow, esp. slender and hollow; reedlike or tubular. **3** containing tubes or tubelike parts.
fit¹ (fɪt) *vb* **fits, fitting, fitted** *or U.S.* **fit. 1** to be appropriate or suitable for (a situation, etc.). **2** to be of the correct size or shape for (a connection, container, etc.). **3** *(tr)* to adjust in order to render appropriate: *they had to fit the idea to their philosophy.* **4** *(tr)* to supply with that which is needed. **5** *(tr)* to try clothes on (someone) in order to make adjustments if necessary. **6** *(tr)* to make competent or ready: *the experience helped to fit him for the task.* **7** *(tr)* to locate with care. **8** *(intr)* to correspond with the facts or circumstances. ♦ *adj* **fitter, fittest. 9** suitable to a purpose or design; appropriate. **10** having the right qualifications; qualifying. **11** in good health. **12** worthy or deserving: *a book fit to be read.* **13** *(foll. by an infinitive)* in such an extreme condition that a specified consequence is likely: *she was fit to scream; you look fit to drop.* ♦ *n* **14** the manner in which something fits. **15** the act or process of fitting. **16** *Statistics.* the correspondence between observed and predicted characteristics of a distribution or model. See **goodness of fit.** ♦ See also **fit in, fit out, fit up.** [C14: probably from Middle Dutch *vitten;* related to Old Norse *fitja* to knit] ▸ **'fittable** *adj*
fit² (fɪt) *n* **1** *Pathol.* a sudden attack or convulsion, such as an epileptic seizure. **2** a sudden spell of emotion: *a fit of anger.* **3** an impulsive period of activity or lack of activity; mood: *a fit of laziness.* **4 give (a person) a fit.** to surprise (a person) in an outrageous manner. **5 have** *or* **throw a fit.** *Informal.* to become very angry or excited. **6 in** *or* **by fits and starts.** in spasmodic spells; irregularly. [Old English *fitt* conflict; see FIT³]
fit³ (fɪt) *n Archaic.* a story or song or a section of a story or song. [Old English *fitt;* related to Old Norse *fit* hem, Old High German *fizza* yarn]
fitch (fɪtʃ) *or* **fitchet** ('fɪtʃɪt) *n* **1** another name for **polecat** (sense 1). **2** the fur of the polecat or ferret. [C16: probably from *ficheux* FITCHEW]
fitchew ('fɪtʃuː) *n* an archaic name for **polecat.** [C14 *ficheux,* from Old French *ficheau,* from Middle Dutch *vitsau,* of obscure origin]
fitful ('fɪtfʊl) *adj* characterized by or occurring in irregular spells: *fitful sleep.* ▸ **'fitfully** *adv* ▸ **'fitfulness** *n*
fit in *vb* **1** *(tr)* to give a place or time to: *if my schedule allows it, I'll fit you in.* **2** *(intr, adv)* to belong or conform, esp. after adjustment: *he didn't fit in with their plans.*
fitly ('fɪtlɪ) *adv* in a proper manner or place or at a proper time.
fitment ('fɪtmənt) *n* **1** *Machinery.* an accessory attached to an assembly of parts. **2** *Chiefly Brit.* a detachable part of the furnishings of a room.
fitness ('fɪtnɪs) *n* **1** the state of being fit. **2** *Biology.* **2a** the degree of adaptation of an organism to its environment, determined by its genetic constitution. **2b** the ability of an organism to produce viable offspring capable of surviving to the next generation.
fit out *vb (tr, adv)* to equip; supply with necessary or new equipment, clothes, etc.
fitted ('fɪtɪd) *adj* **1** designed for excellent fit: *a fitted suit.* **2** (of a carpet) cut, sewn, or otherwise adapted to cover a floor completely. **3a** (of furniture) built to fit a particular space: *a fitted cupboard.* **3b** (of a room) equipped with fitted furniture: *a fitted kitchen.* **4** (of sheets) having ends that are elasticated and shaped to fit tightly over a mattress. **5** having accessory parts.
fitter ('fɪtə) *n* **1** a person who fits a garment, esp. when it is made for a particular person. **2** a person who is skilled in the assembly and adjustment of machinery, esp. of a specified sort: *an electrical fitter.* **3** a person who supplies something for an expedition, activity, etc.
fitting ('fɪtɪŋ) *adj* **1** appropriate or proper; suitable. ♦ *n* **2** an accessory or part: *an electrical fitting.* **3** *(pl)* furnishings or accessories in a building. **4** work carried out by a fitter. **5** the act of trying on clothes so that they can be adjusted to fit. **6** *Brit.* size in clothes or shoes: *a narrow fitting.* ▸ **'fittingly** *adv* ▸ **'fittingness** *n*
Fittipaldi (ˌfɪtɪ'pældɪ) *n* **Emerson.** born 1946, Brazilian motor-racing driver: world champion in 1972 and 1974.
fit up *vb (tr, adv)* **1** (often foll. by *with*) to equip or provide: *the optician will soon fit you up with a new pair of glasses.* **2** *Brit. slang.* to incriminate (someone) on a false charge; frame: *he was fitted up for the bank job.* ♦ *n* **fit-up. 3** *Theatre slang.* a stage and accessories that can be erected quickly for plays. **4** *Brit. slang.* a frame-up.
Fitzgerald (fɪts'dʒɛrəld) *n* **1 Edward.** 1809–83, English poet, noted particularly for his free translation of the *Rubáiyát of Omar Khayyám* (1859). **2 Ella.** 1918–96, U.S. jazz singer, noted esp. for her vocal range and scat singing. **3 F(rancis) Scott (Key).** 1896–1940, U.S. novelist and short-story writer, noted particularly for his portrayal of the 1920s in *The Great Gatsby* (1925) and *Tender is the Night* (1934). **4 Garret.** born 1926, Irish politician; leader of Fine Gael Party (1977–87); prime minister of the Republic of Ireland (1981–82; and 1982–87).
Fitzgerald-Lorentz contraction (fɪts'dʒɛrəldlɔː'rents) *n Physics.* the contraction that a moving body exhibits when its velocity approaches that of light. [C19: named after G. F. *Fitzgerald* (1851–1901), Irish physicist and H. A. LORENTZ]
Fitzrovia (fɪts'rəʊvɪə) *n Informal.* the district north of Oxford Street, London, around Fitzroy Square and its pubs, noted in the 1930s and 40s as a haunt of poets.
Fitzsimmons (ˌfɪt'sɪmənz) *n* **Bob.** 1862–1917, New Zealand boxer, born in England: world middleweight (1891–97), heavyweight (1897–99), and light-heavyweight (1903–05) champion.
Fitzwilliam Museum (ˌfɪtz'wɪljəm) *n* a museum, attached to Cambridge University and founded in 1816, noted esp. for its paintings and collections devoted to the applied arts. [C19: named after the 7th Viscount *Fitzwilliam* of Merrion, who donated the first collection]
Fiume ('fiuːme) *n* the Italian name for **Rijeka.**

five (faɪv) *n* **1** the cardinal number that is the sum of four and one. **2** a numeral, 5, V, etc., representing this number. **3** the amount or quantity that is one greater than four. **4** something representing, represented by, or consisting of five units, such as a playing card with five symbols on it. ◆ *determiner* **5a** amounting to five: *five minutes; five nights.* **5b** (*as pronoun*): *choose any five you like.* ◆ Related prefixes: **penta-, quinque-.** ◆ See also **fives.** [Old English *fīf;* related to Old Norse *fimm,* Gothic *fimf,* Old High German *finf,* Latin *quinque,* Greek *pente,* Sanskrit *pañca*]

five-a-side *n* **a** a version of soccer with five players on each side. **b** (*as modifier*): *a five-a-side tournament.*

five-eighth *n Austral., N.Z.* a rugby player positioned between the halfbacks and three-quarters.

five-faced bishop *n Brit.* another name for **moschatel.**

five-finger *n* any of various plants having five-petalled flowers or five lobed leaves, such as cinquefoil and Virginia creeper.

fivefold ('faɪvˌfəʊld) *adj* **1** equal to or having five times as many or as much. **2** composed of five parts. ◆ *adv* **3** by or up to five times as many or as much.

five hundred *n* a card game for three players, with 500 points for game.

five Ks *pl n* **the.** items traditionally worn or carried by Sikhs, each possessing a symbolic importance. See **Kachera, Kangha, Kara, Kesh, Kirpan.** [translation of Punjabi *panch kakke*]

Five Nations *pl n* (formerly) a confederacy of North American Indian peoples living mainly in and around present-day New York state, consisting of the Cayugas, Mohawks, Oneidas, Onondagas, and Senecas. Also called: **Iroquois.** See also **Six Nations.**

five-o'clock shadow *n* beard growth visible late in the day on a man's shaven face.

fivepenny ('faɪfpənɪ) *adj* (*prenominal*) *U.S.* (of a nail) one and three-quarters of an inch in length.

fivepins ('faɪvˌpɪnz) *n* (*functioning as sing*) a bowling game using five pins, played esp. in Canada. ▸ **'fiveˌpin** *adj*

fiver ('faɪvə) *n Informal.* **1** (in Britain) a five-pound note. **2** (in the U.S.) a five-dollar bill.

fives (faɪvz) *n* (*functioning as sing*) a ball game similar to squash but played with bats or the hands.

five-spot *n* (in the U.S.) a five-dollar bill.

five-star *adj* (of a hotel) first-class, top-quality, or offering exceptional luxury.

five stones *n* the game of jacks played with five stones.

Five Towns *n* **the.** the name given in his fiction by Arnold Bennett to the Potteries towns (actually six in number) of Burslem, Fenton, Hanley, Longton, Stoke-upon-Trent, and Tunstall, now part of the city of Stoke-on-Trent.

Five-Year Plan *n* (in socialist economies) a government plan for economic development over a period of five years.

fix (fɪks) *vb* (*mainly tr*) **1** (*also intr*) to make or become firm, stable, or secure. **2** to attach or place permanently: *fix the mirror to the wall.* **3** (often foll. by *up*) to settle definitely; decide: *let us fix a date.* **4** to hold or direct (eyes, attention, etc.) steadily: *he fixed his gaze on the woman.* **5** to call to attention or rivet. **6** to make rigid: *to fix one's jaw.* **7** to place or ascribe: *to fix the blame on someone.* **8** to mend or repair. **9** *Informal.* to provide with: *how are you fixed for supplies?* **10** *Informal.* to influence (a person, outcome of a contest, etc.) unfairly, as by bribery. **11** *Slang.* to take revenge on; get even with, esp. by killing. **12** *Informal.* to give (someone) his just deserts: *that'll fix him.* **13** *Informal.* to arrange or put in order: *to fix one's hair.* **14** *Informal.* to prepare: *to fix a meal.* **15** *Dialect or informal.* to spay or castrate (an animal). **16** *U.S. dialect or informal.* to prepare oneself: *I'm fixing to go out.* **17** *Photog.* to treat (a film, plate, or paper) with fixer to make permanent the image rendered visible by developer. **18** *Cytology.* to kill, preserve, and harden (tissue, cells, etc.) for subsequent microscopic study. **19** to convert (atmospheric nitrogen) into nitrogen compounds, as in the manufacture of fertilizers or the action of bacteria in the soil. **20** to reduce (a substance) to a solid or condensed state or a less volatile state. **21** (*intr*) *Slang.* to inject a drug. ◆ *n* **22** *Informal.* a predicament; dilemma. **23** the ascertaining of the navigational position, as of a ship, by radar, observation, etc. **24** *Slang.* an intravenous injection of a drug, esp. heroin. **25** *Informal.* an act or instance of bribery. ◆ See also **fix up.** [C15: from Medieval Latin *fixāre,* from Latin *fixus* fixed, from Latin *figere*] ▸ **'fixable** *adj*

fixate ('fɪkseɪt) *vb* **1** to become or cause to become fixed. **2** to direct the eye or eyes at a point in space so that the image of the point falls on the centre (fovea) of the eye or eyes. **3** *Psychol.* to engage in fixation. **4** (*tr; usually passive*) *Informal.* to obsess or preoccupy. [C19: from Latin *fixus* fixed + -ATE[1]]

fixation (fɪk'seɪʃən) *n* **1** the act of fixing or the state of being fixed. **2** a preoccupation or obsession. **3** *Psychol.* **3a** the act of fixating. **3b** (in psychoanalytical schools) a strong attachment of a person to another person or an object in early life. **4** *Chem.* **4a** the conversion of nitrogen in the air into a compound, esp. a fertilizer. **4b** the conversion of a free element into one of its compounds. **5** the reduction of a substance from a volatile or fluid form to a nonvolatile or solid form.

fixative ('fɪksətɪv) *adj* **1** serving or tending to fix. ◆ *n* **2** a fluid usually consisting of a transparent resin, such as shellac, dissolved in alcohol and sprayed over drawings to prevent smudging. **3** *Cytology.* a fluid, such as formaldehyde or ethanol, that fixes tissues and cells for microscopic study. **4** a substance added to a liquid, such as a perfume, to make it less volatile.

fixed (fɪkst) *adj* **1** attached or placed so as to be immovable. **2** not subject to change; stable: *fixed prices.* **3** steadily directed: *a fixed expression.* **4** established as to relative position: *a fixed point.* **5** not fluctuating; always at the same time: *a fixed holiday.* **6** (of ideas, notions, etc.) firmly maintained. **7** (of an element) held in chemical combination: *fixed nitrogen.* **8** (of a substance) nonvolatile. **9** arranged. **10** *Astrology.* of, relating to, or belonging to the group consisting of the four signs of the zodiac Taurus, Leo, Scorpio, and Aquarius, which are associated with stability. Compare **cardinal** (sense 9), **mutable** (sense 2). **11** *Informal.* equipped or provided for, as with money, possessions, etc. **12** *Informal.* illegally arranged: *a fixed trial.* ▸ **fixedly** ('fɪksɪdlɪ) *adv* ▸ **'fixedness** *n*

fixed assets *pl n* nontrading business assets of a relatively permanent nature, such as plant, fixtures, or goodwill. Also called: **capital assets.** Compare **current assets.**

fixed charge *n* **1** an invariable expense usually at regular intervals, such as rent. **2** a legal charge on specific assets or property, as of a company.

fixed costs *pl n* **1** another name for **overheads. 2** costs that do not vary with output.

fixed-head coupé *n* another name (esp. Brit.) for **coupé** (sense 1).

fixed idea *n* an idea, esp. one of an obsessional nature, that is persistently maintained and not subject to change. Also called: ***idée fixe.***

fixed oil *n* a natural animal or vegetable oil that is not volatile: a mixture of esters of fatty acids, usually triglycerides. Also called: **fatty oil.** Compare **essential oil.**

fixed point *n* **1** *Physics.* a reproducible invariant temperature; the boiling point, freezing point, or triple point of a substance, such as water, that is used to calibrate a thermometer or define a temperature scale. **2** *Maths.* a point that is not moved by a given transformation.

fixed-point representation *n Computing.* the representation of numbers by a single set of digits such that the radix point has a predetermined location, the value of the number depending on the position of each digit relative to the radix point. Compare **floating-point representation.**

fixed satellite *n* a satellite revolving in a stationary orbit so that it appears to remain over a fixed point on the earth's surface.

fixed star *n* **1** any of the stars in the Ptolemaic system, all of which were thought to be attached to an outer crystal sphere thus explaining their apparent lack of movement. **2** an extremely distant star whose position appears to be almost stationary over a long period of time.

fixer ('fɪksə) *n* **1** a person or thing that fixes. **2** *Photog.* a solution containing one or more chemical compounds that is used, in fixing, to dissolve unexposed silver halides. It sometimes has an additive to stop the action of developer. **3** *Slang.* a person who makes arrangements, esp. by underhand or illegal means.

fixing ('fɪksɪŋ) *n* a means of attaching one thing to another, as a pipe to a wall, slate to a roof, etc.

fixings ('fɪksɪŋz) *pl n Chiefly U.S. and Canadian.* **1** apparatus or equipment. **2** accompaniments for a dish; trimmings.

fixity ('fɪksɪtɪ) *n, pl* **-ties. 1** the state or quality of being fixed; stability. **2** something that is fixed; a fixture.

fixture ('fɪkstʃə) *n* **1** an object firmly fixed in place, esp. a household appliance. **2** a person or thing regarded as fixed in a particular place or position. **3** *Property law.* an article attached to land and regarded as part of it. **4** a device to secure a workpiece in a machine tool. **5** *Chiefly Brit.* **5a** a sports match or social occasion. **5b** the date of such an event. **6** *Rare.* the act of fixing. [C17: from Late Latin *fixūra* a fastening (with *-t-* by analogy with *mixture*)] ▸ **'fixtureless** *adj*

fix up *vb* (*tr, adv*) **1** to arrange: *let's fix up a date.* **2** (often foll. by *with*) to provide: *I'm sure we can fix you up with a room.* **3** *Informal.* to repair or rearrange: *to fix up one's house.*

fizgig ('fɪzˌgɪg) *n* **1** a frivolous or flirtatious girl. **2** a firework or whirling top that fizzes as it moves. **3** a variant of **fishgig.** [C16: probably from obsolete *fise* a breaking of wind + *gig* girl]

fizz (fɪz) *vb* (*intr*) **1** to make a hissing or bubbling sound. **2** (of a drink) to produce bubbles of carbon dioxide, either through fermentation or aeration. ◆ *n* **3** a hissing or bubbling sound. **4** the bubbly quality of a drink; effervescence. **5** any effervescent drink. [C17: of imitative origin] ▸ **'fizzy** *adj* ▸ **'fizziness** *n*

fizzer ('fɪzə) *n* **1** anything that fizzes. **2** *Austral. slang.* a person or thing that disappoints, fails to succeed, etc.: *the horse proved to be a fizzer.*

fizzle ('fɪzᵊl) *vb* (*intr*) **1** to make a hissing or bubbling sound. **2** (often foll. by *out*) *Informal.* to fail or die out, esp. after a promising start. ◆ *n* **3** a hissing or bubbling sound; fizz. **4** *Informal.* an outright failure; fiasco. [C16: probably from obsolete *fist* to break wind]

fjeld *or* **field** (fjɛld) *n* a high rocky plateau with little vegetation in Scandinavian countries. [C19: Norwegian; related to Old Norse *fjall* mountain; see FELL[5]]

FJI *international car registration for* Fiji.

fjord *or* **fiord** (fjɔːd) *n* a long narrow inlet of the sea between high steep cliffs. It is common in Norway and was probably formed by glacial action. [C17: from Norwegian, from Old Norse *fjörthr;* see FIRTH, FORD]

FL *abbrev. for:* **1** Flight Lieutenant. **2** Florida. ◆ **3** *international car registration for* Liechtenstein. [from German *Fürstentum Liechtenstein* Principality of Liechtenstein]

fl. *abbrev. for:* **1** floor. **2** floruit. **3** fluid. **4** (in the Netherlands) *symbol for* guilder.

Fl. *abbrev. for:* **1** Flanders. **2** Flemish.

Fla. *abbrev. for* Florida.

flab (flæb) *n* unsightly or unwanted fat on the body; flabbiness. [C20: back formation from FLABBY]

flabbergast ('flæbəˌgɑːst) *vb* (*tr; usually passive*) *Informal.* to overcome with astonishment; amaze utterly; astound. [C18: of uncertain origin] ▸ **'flabberˌgasted** *adj*

flabby ('flæbɪ) *adj* **-bier, -biest. 1** lacking firmness; loose or yielding: *flabby muscles.* **2** having flabby flesh, esp. through being overweight. **3** lacking vitality; weak; ineffectual. [C17: alteration of *flappy,* from FLAP + -Y[1]; compare Dutch *flabbe* drooping lip] ▸ **'flabbily** *adv* ▸ **'flabbiness** *n*

flabellate (flə'bɛlɪt, -eɪt) *or* **flabelliform** (flə'bɛlɪˌfɔːm) *adj Biology.* shaped like a fan.

flabellum (flə'bɛləm) *n, pl* **-la** (-lə). **1** a fan-shaped organ or part, such as the tip of the proboscis of a honeybee. **2** *R.C. Church.* a large ceremonial fan. [C19: from Latin: small fan, from *flābra* breezes, from *flāre* to blow]

flaccid ('flæksɪd, 'flæs-) *adj* lacking firmness; soft and limp; flabby. [C17: from Latin *flaccidus,* from *flaccus*] ▸ **flac'cidity** *or* **'flaccidness** *n* ▸ **'flaccidly** *adv*

flack[1] (flæk) *n Chiefly U.S. and Canadian.* a press or publicity agent. [C20: of unknown origin]

flack[2] (flæk) *n* a variant spelling of **flak.**

flacon (*French* flakõ) *n* a small stoppered bottle or flask, such as one used for perfume. [C19: from French; see FLAGON]

flag[1] (flæg) *n* **1** a piece of cloth, esp. bunting, often attached to a pole or staff, decorated with a design and used as an emblem, symbol, or standard or as a means of signalling. **2** a small paper flag, emblem, or sticker sold on flag days. **3** an indicator, that may be set or unset, used to indicate a condition or to stimulate a particular reaction in the execution of a computer program. **4** *Informal.* short for **flag officer** and **flagship. 5** *Journalism.* another name for **masthead** (sense 2). **6** the fringe of long hair, tapering towards the tip, on the underside of the tail of certain breeds of dog, such as setters. **7** the conspicuously marked tail of a deer. **8** a less common name for **bookmark. 9** *Austral. and N.Z.* the part of a taximeter that is raised when a taxi is for hire. **10 the.** (in Victoria, Australia) the Australian Rules premiership. **11 fly the flag.** to represent or show support for one's country, an organization, etc. **12 show the flag. 12a** to assert a claim, as to a territory or stretch of water, by military presence. **12b** *Informal.* to be present; make an appearance. **13 strike** (*or* **lower**) **the flag. 13a** to relinquish command, esp. of a ship. **13b** to submit or surrender. ◆ *vb* **flags, flagging, flagged.** (*tr*) **14** to decorate or mark with a flag or flags. **15** (often foll. by *down*) to warn or signal (a vehicle) to stop. **16** to send or communicate (messages, information, etc.) by flag. **17** to decoy (game or wild animals) by waving a flag or similar object so as to attract their attention. **18** to mark (a page in a book, card, etc.) for attention by attaching a small tab or flag. **19** (foll. by *away* or *by*) *N.Z.* to consider unimportant; brush aside. ◆ See also **flags.** [C16: of uncertain origin] ▸ **'flagger** *n* ▸ **'flagless** *adj*

flag[2] (flæg) *n* **1** any of various plants that have long swordlike leaves, esp. the iris *Iris pseudacorus* (**yellow flag**). **2** the leaf of any such plant. ◆ See also **sweet flag.** [C14: probably of Scandinavian origin; compare Dutch *flag,* Danish *flæg* yellow iris]

flag[3] (flæg) *vb* **flags, flagging, flagged.** (*intr*) **1** to hang down; become limp; droop. **2** to decline in strength or vigour; become weak or tired. [C16: of unknown origin]

flag[4] (flæg) *n* **1** short for **flagstone.** ◆ *vb* **flags, flagging, flagged. 2** (*tr*) to furnish (a floor) with flagstones.

flag captain *n* the captain of a flagship.

flag day *n Brit.* a day on which money is collected by a charity and small flags, emblems, or stickers are given to contributors.

Flag Day *n* June 14, the annual holiday in the U.S. to celebrate the adoption in 1777 of the Stars and Stripes.

flagellant ('flædʒɪlənt, flə'dʒɛlənt) *or* **flagellator** ('flædʒɪˌleɪtə) *n* **1** a person who whips himself or others either as part of a religious penance or for sexual gratification. **2** (*often cap.*) (in medieval Europe) a member of a religious sect who whipped themselves in public. [C16: from Latin *flagellāre* to whip, from FLAGELLUM] ▸ **'flagellantˌism** *n*

flagellate *vb* ('flædʒɪˌleɪt). **1** (*tr*) to whip; scourge; flog. ◆ *adj* ('flædʒɪlɪt, -ˌleɪt), *also* **flagellated. 2** possessing one or more flagella. **3** resembling a flagellum; whiplike. ◆ *n* ('flædʒɪlɪt, -ˌleɪt). **4** a flagellate organism, esp. any protozoan of the phylum *Zoomastigina.* ▸ **ˌflagel'lation** *n*

flagelliform (flə'dʒɛlɪˌfɔːm) *adj* slender, tapering, and whiplike, as the antennae of certain insects.

flagellin (flə'dʒɛlɪn) *n* the structural protein of bacterial flagella.

flagellum (flə'dʒɛləm) *n, pl* **-la** (-lə) *or* **-lums. 1** *Biology.* a long whiplike outgrowth from a cell that acts as an organ of locomotion: occurs in some protozoans, gametes, spores, etc. **2** *Botany.* a long thin supple shoot or runner. **3** *Zoology.* the terminal whiplike part of an arthropod's appendage, esp. of the antenna of many insects. [C19: from Latin: a little whip, from *flagrum* a whip, lash] ▸ **fla'gellar** *adj*

flageolet (ˌflædʒə'lɛt) *n* a high-pitched musical instrument of the recorder family having six or eight finger holes. [C17: from French, modification of Old French *flajolet* a little flute, from *flajol* flute, from Vulgar Latin *flabeolum* (unattested), from Latin *flāre* to blow]

flag fall *n Austral.* the minimum charge for hiring a taxi, to which the rate per kilometre is added.

flagging ('flægɪŋ) *n* flagstones or a flagged area.

flaggy[1] ('flægɪ) *adj* **-gier, -giest.** drooping; limp.

flaggy[2] ('flægɪ) *adj* made of or similar to flagstone.

flagitious (flə'dʒɪʃəs) *adj* atrociously wicked; vicious; outrageous. [C14: from Latin *flāgitiōsus* infamous, from *flāgitium* a shameful act; related to Latin *flagrum* whip] ▸ **fla'gitiously** *adv* ▸ **fla'gitiousness** *n*

flag lieutenant *n* an admiral's ADC.

flagman ('flægmən) *n, pl* **-men.** a person who has charge of, carries, or signals with a flag, esp. a railway employee.

flag of convenience *n* a national flag flown by a ship registered in that country to gain financial or legal advantage.

flag officer *n* an officer in certain navies of the rank of rear admiral or above and entitled to fly its flag.

flag of truce *n* a white flag indicating the peaceful intent of its bearer or an invitation to an enemy to negotiate.

flagon ('flægən) *n* **1** a large bottle of wine, cider, etc. **2** a vessel having a handle, spout, and narrow neck. [C15: from Old French *flascon,* from Late Latin *flascō,* probably of Germanic origin; see FLASK]

flagpole ('flægˌpəʊl) *or* **flagstaff** ('flægˌstɑːf) *n, pl* **-poles, -staffs,** *or* **-staves** (-ˌsteɪvz). a pole or staff on which a flag is hoisted and displayed.

flag rank *n* the rank of a flag officer.

flagrant ('fleɪgrənt) *adj* **1** openly outrageous. **2** *Obsolete.* burning or blazing. [C15: from Latin *flagrāre* to blaze, burn] ▸ **'flagrancy, 'flagrance,** *or* **'flagrantness** *n* ▸ **'flagrantly** *adv*

flagrante delicto (flə'græntɪ dɪ'lɪktəʊ) *adv* See **in flagrante delicto.**

flags (flægz) *pl n Rare.* the long feathers on the leg of a hawk or falcon.

flagship ('flægˌʃɪp) *n* **1** a ship, esp. in a fleet, aboard which the commander of the fleet is quartered. **2** the most important ship belonging to a shipping company. **3** a single item from a related group considered as the most important, often in establishing a public image: *the nine o'clock news is the flagship of the BBC.*

Flagstad ('flægstæd; *Norwegian* 'flaksta) *n* **Kirsten** ('çirstən). 1895–1962, Norwegian operatic soprano, noted particularly for her interpretations of Wagner.

flagstone ('flægˌstəʊn) *or* **flag** *n* **1** a hard fine-textured rock, such as a sandstone or shale, that can be split up into slabs for paving. **2** a slab of such a rock. [C15 *flag* (in the sense: sod, turf), from Old Norse *flaga* slab; compare Old English *flæcg*plaster, poultice]

flag-waving *n Informal.* **a** an emotional appeal or display intended to arouse patriotic or nationalistic feeling. **b** (*as modifier*): *a flag-waving speech.* ▸ **'flag-ˌwaver** *n*

Flaherty ('flæhətɪ) *n* **Robert (Joseph).** 1884–1951, U.S. film director, a pioneer of documentary film; his work includes *Nanook of the North* (1922) and *Elephant Boy* (1935).

flail (fleɪl) *n* **1** an implement used for threshing grain, consisting of a wooden handle with a free-swinging metal or wooden bar attached to it. **2** a weapon so shaped used in the Middle Ages. ◆ *vb* **3** (*tr*) to beat or thrash with or as if with a flail. **4** to move or be moved like a flail; thresh about: *with arms flailing.* [C12 *fleil,* ultimately from Late Latin *flagellum* flail, from Latin: whip]

flair[1] (flɛə) *n* **1** natural ability; talent; aptitude. **2** instinctive discernment; perceptiveness. **3** stylishness or elegance; dash: *to dress with flair.* **4** *Hunting, rare.* **4a** the scent left by quarry. **4b** the sense of smell of a hound. [C19: from French, literally: sense of smell, from Old French: scent, from *flairier* to give off a smell, ultimately from Latin *frāgrāre* to smell sweet; see FRAGRANT]

flair[2] (fler) *n* a Scot. word for **floor.**

flak *or* **flack** (flæk) *n* **1** anti-aircraft fire or artillery. **2** *Informal.* a great deal of adverse criticism. [C20: from German *Fl(ieger)a(bwehr)k(anone),* literally: aircraft defence gun]

flake[1] (fleɪk) *n* **1** a small thin piece or layer chipped off or detached from an object or substance; scale. **2** a small piece or particle: *a flake of snow.* **3** a thin layer or stratum. **4** *Archaeol.* **4a** a fragment removed by chipping or hammering from a larger stone used as a tool or weapon. See also **blade. 4b** (*as modifier*): *flake tool.* **5** *Slang, chiefly U.S.* an eccentric, crazy, or unreliable person. ◆ *vb* **6** to peel or cause to peel off in flakes; chip. **7** to cover or become covered with or as with flakes. **8** (*tr*) to form into flakes. [C14: of Scandinavian origin; compare Norwegian *flak* disc, Middle Dutch *vlacken* to flutter] ▸ **'flaker** *n*

flake[2] (fleɪk) *n* a rack or platform for drying fish or other produce. [C14: from Old Norse *flaki;* related to Dutch *vlaak* hurdle]

flake[3] (fleɪk) *vb Nautical.* another word for **fake**[2].

flake[4] (fleɪk) *n* (in Australia) the commercial name for the meat of the gummy shark.

flake out *vb* (*intr, adv*) *Informal.* to collapse or fall asleep as through extreme exhaustion.

flake white *n* a pigment made from flakes of white lead.

flak jacket *n* a reinforced sleeveless jacket for protection against gunfire or shrapnel worn by soldiers, policemen, etc.

flaky ('fleɪkɪ) *adj* **flakier, flakiest. 1** like or made of flakes. **2** tending to peel off or break easily into flakes. **3** Also: **flakey.** *U.S. slang.* eccentric; crazy. ▸ **'flakily** *adv* ▸ **'flakiness** *n*

flaky pastry *n* a rich pastry in the form of very thin layers, used for making pies, small cakes, etc.

flam[1] (flæm) *Now chiefly dialect.* ◆ *n* **1** a falsehood, deception, or sham. **2** nonsense; drivel. ◆ *vb* **flams, flamming, flammed. 3** (*tr*) to cheat or deceive. [C16: probably short for FLIMFLAM]

flam[2] (flæm) *n* a drumbeat in which both sticks strike the head almost simultaneously but are heard to do so separately. [C18: probably imitative of the sound]

flambé *or* **flambée** ('flɑːmbeɪ, 'flæm-; *French* flɑ̃be) *adj* **1** (of food, such as steak or pancakes) served in flaming brandy. ◆ *vb* **-béeing, -béed. 2** (*tr*) to pour brandy over (food) and ignite it. [French, past participle of *flamber* to FLAME]

flambeau ('flæmbəʊ) *n, pl* **-beaux** (-bəʊ, -bəʊz) *or* **-beaus. 1** a burning torch, as used in night processions. **2** a large ornamental candlestick. [C17: from Old French: torch, literally: a little flame, from *flambe* FLAME]

Flamborough Head ('flæmbərə, -brə) *n* a chalk promontory in NE England, on the coast of the East Riding of Yorkshire.

flamboyant (flæm'bɔɪənt) *adj* **1** elaborate or extravagant; florid; showy. **2** rich or brilliant in colour; resplendent. **3** of, denoting, or relating to the French Gothic style of architecture characterized by flamelike tracery and elaborate carving. ◆ *n* **4** another name for **royal poinciana.** [C19: from French: flaming, from *flamboyer* to FLAME] ▸ **flam'boyance** *or* **flam'boyancy** *n* ▸ **flam'boyantly** *adv*

flame (fleɪm) *n* **1** a hot usually luminous body of burning gas often containing small incandescent particles, typically emanating in flickering streams from burning material or produced by a jet of ignited gas. **2** (*often pl*) the state or condition of burning with flames: *to burst into flames*. **3** a brilliant light; fiery glow. **4a** a strong reddish-orange colour. **4b** (*as adj*): *a flame carpet*. **5** intense passion or ardour; burning emotion. **6** *Informal*. a lover or sweetheart (esp. in the phrase **an old flame**). **7** *Informal*. an abusive message sent by electronic mail, esp. to express anger or criticism of an Internet user by sending them large numbers of messages. ♦ *vb* **8** to burn or cause to burn brightly; give off or cause to give off flame. **9** (*intr*) to burn or glow as if with fire; become red or fiery: *his face flamed with anger*. **10** (*intr*) to show great emotion; become angry or excited. **11** (*tr*) to apply a flame to (something). **12** (*tr*) *Archaic*. to set on fire, either physically or with emotion. **13** *Informal*. to send an abusive message by electronic mail. ♦ See also **flameout**. [C14: from Anglo-French *flaume*, from Old French *flambe*, modification of *flamble*, from Latin *flammula* a little flame, from *flamma* flame] ▸ **'flamer** *n* ▸ **'flameless** *adj* ▸ **'flamelet** *n* ▸ **'flame,like** *adj* ▸ **'flamy** *adj*

flame-arc light *n Electrical engineering*. an arc light that uses flame carbons to colour the arc.

flame carbon *n Electrical engineering*. a carbon electrode containing metallic salts that colour the arc in a flame-arc light.

flame cell *n* an organ of excretion in flatworms: a hollow cup-shaped cell containing a bunch of cilia, whose movement draws in waste products and wafts them to the outside through a connecting tubule.

flame cutting *n Engineering*. a method of cutting ferrous metals in which the metal is heated by a torch to about 800°C and is oxidized by a stream of oxygen from the torch.

flame gun *n* a type of flame-thrower for destroying garden weeds.

flame hardening *n Engineering*. the surface hardening of ferrous metals by heating the metal with an oxyacetylene flame followed by rapid cooling.

flame lamp *n Electrical engineering*. a filament lamp in which the bulb resembles the shape of a flame.

flamen ('fleɪmen) *n, pl* **flamens** *or* **flamines** ('flæmɪ,ni:z). (in ancient Rome) any of 15 priests who each served a particular deity. [C14: from Latin; probably related to Old English *blōtan* to sacrifice, Gothic *blotan* to worship]

flamenco (flə'meŋkəʊ) *n, pl* **-cos**. **1** a type of dance music for vocal soloist and guitar, characterized by elaborate melody and sad mood. **2** the dance performed to such music. [from Spanish: like a gipsy, literally: Fleming, from Middle Dutch *Vlaminc* Fleming]

flame-of-the-forest *n* **1** (esp. in Malaysia) another name for **royal poinciana**. **2** a papilionaceous tree, *Butea frondosa*, native to E India and Myanmar, having hanging clusters of scarlet flowers.

flameout ('fleɪm,aʊt) *n* **1** the failure of an aircraft jet engine in flight due to extinction of the flame. ♦ *vb* **flame out**. (*adv*) **2** (of a jet engine) to fail in flight or to cause (a jet engine) to fail in flight.

flameproof ('fleɪm,pru:f) *adj* **1** not liable to catch fire or be damaged by fire. **2** (of electrical apparatus) designed so that an internal explosion will not ignite external flammable gas.

flame retarder *n* a material that, while not incombustible, does not itself maintain combustion without an external heat source and therefore retards the spread of fire.

flame test *n* a test for detecting the presence of certain metals in compounds by the coloration they give to a flame. Sodium, for example, turns a flame yellow.

flame-thrower *n* a weapon that ejects a stream or spray of burning fluid.

flame tree *n* any of various tropical trees with red or orange flowers, such as flame-of-the-forest.

flaming ('fleɪmɪŋ) *adj* **1** burning with or emitting flames. **2** glowing brightly; brilliant. **3** intense or ardent; vehement; passionate: *a flaming temper*. **4** *Informal*. (intensifier): *you flaming idiot*. **5** an obsolete word for **flagrant**. ▸ **'flamingly** *adv*

flamingo (flə'mɪŋgəʊ) *n, pl* **-gos** *or* **-goes**. **1** any large wading bird of the family *Phoenicopteridae*, having a pink-and-red plumage and downward-bent bill and inhabiting brackish lakes: order *Ciconiiformes*. **2a** a reddish-orange colour. **2b** (*as adj*): *flamingo gloves*. [C16: from Portuguese *flamengo*, from Provençal *flamenc*, from Latin *flamma* flame + Germanic suffix *-ing* denoting descent from or membership of; compare -ING[3]]

Flaminian Way (flə'mɪnɪən) *n* an ancient road in Italy, extending north from Rome to Rimini: constructed in 220 B.C. by Gaius Flaminius. Length: over 322 km (200 miles). Latin name: **Via Flaminia**.

Flamininus (,flæmɪ'naɪnəs) *n* **Titus Quinctius** ('taɪtəs 'kwɪŋktɪəs). ?230–?174 B.C., Roman general and statesman: defeated Macedonia (197) and proclaimed the independence of the Greek states (196).

Flaminius (flə'mɪnɪəs) *n* **Gaius** ('gaɪəs). died 217 B.C., Roman statesman and general: built the Flaminian Way; defeated by Hannibal at Trasimene (217).

flammable ('flæməb[ə]l) *adj* liable to catch fire; readily combustible; inflammable. ▸ **,flamma'bility** *n*

USAGE *Flammable* and *inflammable* are interchangeable when used of the properties of materials. *Flammable* is, however, often preferred for warning labels as there is less likelihood of misunderstanding (*inflammable* being sometimes taken to mean *not flammable*). *Inflammable* is preferred in figurative contexts: *this could prove to be an inflammable situation*.

Flamsteed ('flæm,sti:d) *n* **John**. 1646–1719, English astronomer: the first Astronomer Royal and first director of the Royal Observatory, Greenwich (1675). He increased the accuracy of existing stellar catalogues, greatly aiding navigation.

flan (flæn) *n* **1** an open pastry or sponge tart filled with fruit or a savoury mixture. **2** a piece of metal ready to receive the die or stamp in the production of coins; shaped blank; planchet. [C19: from French, from Old French *flaon*, from Late Latin *fladō* flat cake, of Germanic origin]

flanch (flæntʃ) *n* a variant of **flaunch**.

Flanders ('flɑ:ndəz) *n* a powerful medieval principality in the SW part of the Low Countries, now in the Belgian provinces of East and West Flanders, the Netherlands province of Zeeland, and the French department of the Nord; scene of battles in many wars.

Flanders poppy *n* another name for **corn poppy**.

flânerie *French*. (flɑnri) *n* aimless strolling or lounging; idleness. [C19: from *flâner* to stroll, dawdle, ultimately from Old Norse *flana* to wander about]

flâneur *French*. (flɑnœr) *n* an idler or loafer. [C19: see FLÂNERIE]

flange (flændʒ) *n* **1** a radially projecting collar or rim on an object for locating or strengthening it or for attaching it to another object. **2** a flat outer face of a rolled-steel joist, esp. of an I- or H-beam. **3** a tool for forming a flange. ♦ *vb* **4** (*tr*) to attach or provide (a component) with a flange. **5** (*intr*) to take the form of a flange. [C17: probably changed from earlier *flaunche* curved segment at side of a heraldic field, from French *flanc* FLANK] ▸ **flanged** *adj* ▸ **'flangeless** *adj* ▸ **'flanger** *n*

flange coupling *n Engineering*. a driving coupling between rotating shafts that consists of flanges (or **half couplings**) one of which is fixed at the end of each shaft, the two flanges being bolted together with a ring of bolts to complete the drive.

flanged rail *n* another name for **flat-bottomed rail**.

flank (flæŋk) *n* **1** the side of a man or animal between the ribs and the hip. **2** (loosely) the outer part of the human thigh. **3** a cut of beef from the flank. **4** the side of anything, such as a mountain or building. **5** the side of a naval or military formation. ♦ *vb* **6** (when *intr*, often foll. by *on* or *upon*) to be located at the side of (an object, building, etc.). **7** *Military*. to position or guard on or beside the flank of (a formation, etc.). **8** *Military*. to move past or go round (a flank). [C12: from Old French *flanc*, of Germanic origin]

flanker ('flæŋkə) *n* **1** one of a detachment of soldiers detailed to guard the flanks, esp. of a formation. **2** a projecting fortification, used esp. to protect or threaten a flank.

flannel ('flæn[ə]l) *n* **1** a soft light woollen fabric with a slight nap, used for clothing. **2** (*pl*) trousers or other garments made of flannel. **3** See **cotton flannel**. **4** *Brit*. a small piece of cloth used to wash the face and hands; face cloth. U.S. and Canadian equivalent: **washcloth**. **5** *Brit. informal*. indirect or evasive talk; deceiving flattery. ♦ *vb* **-nels, -nelling, -nelled** *or U.S.* **-nels, -neling, -neled**. (*tr*) **6** to cover or wrap with flannel. **7** to rub, clean, or polish with flannel. **8** *Brit. informal*. to talk evasively to; flatter in order to mislead. [C14: probably variant of *flanen* sackcloth, from Welsh *gwlanen* woollen fabric, from *gwlân* wool] ▸ **'flannelly** *adj*

flannelboard ('flæn[ə]l,bɔ:d) *or* **flannelgraph** ('flæn[ə]l,grɑ:f, -,græf) *n* a visual aid used in teaching consisting of a board covered with flannel to which pictures, diagrams, etc. will stick when pressed on.

flannelette (,flæn[ə]'lɛt) *n* a cotton imitation of flannel.

flannel flower *n* any Australian plant of the umbelliferous genus *Actinotus* having white flannel-like bracts beneath the flowers.

flap (flæp) *vb* **flaps, flapping, flapped**. **1** to move (wings or arms) up and down, esp. in or as if in flying, or (of wings or arms) to move in this way. **2** to move or cause to move noisily back and forth or up and down: *the curtains flapped in the breeze*. **3** (*intr*) *Informal*. to become agitated or flustered; panic. **4** to deal (a person or thing) a blow with a broad flexible object. **5** (*tr*; sometimes foll. by *down*) to toss, fling, slam, etc., abruptly or noisily. **6** (*tr*) *Phonetics*. to pronounce (an (r) sound) by allowing the tongue to give a single light tap against the alveolar ridge or uvula. ♦ *n* **7** the action, motion, or noise made by flapping: *with one flap of its wings the bird was off*. **8** a piece of material, etc., attached at one edge and usually used to cover an opening, as on a tent, envelope, or pocket. **9** a blow dealt with a flat object; slap. **10** a movable surface fixed to the trailing edge of an aircraft wing that increases lift during takeoff and drag during landing. **11** *Surgery*. a piece of tissue partially connected to the body, either following an amputation or to be used as a graft. **12** *Informal*. a state of panic, distress, or agitation. **13** *Phonetics*. an (r) produced by allowing the tongue to give a single light tap against the alveolar ridge or uvula. [C14: probably of imitative origin]

flapdoodle ('flæp,du:d[ə]l) *n Slang*. foolish talk; nonsense. [C19: of unknown origin]

flapjack ('flæp,dʒæk) *n* **1** a chewy biscuit made with rolled oats. **2** *Chiefly U.S. and Canadian*. another word for **pancake**. [C17: from FLAP (in the sense: toss) + JACK[1]]

flapper ('flæpə) *n* **1** a person or thing that flaps. **2** (in the 1920s) a young woman, esp. one flaunting her unconventional dress and behaviour.

flare (flɛə) *vb* **1** to burn or cause to burn with an unsteady or sudden bright flame. **2** to spread or cause to spread outwards from a narrow to a wider shape. **3** (*tr*) to make a conspicuous display of. **4** to increase the temperature of (a molten metal or alloy) until a gaseous constituent of the melt burns with a characteristic flame or (of a molten metal or alloy) to show such a flame. **5** (*tr*; sometimes foll. by *off*) (in the oil industry) to burn off (unwanted gas) at an oil well. ♦ *n* **6** an unsteady flame. **7** a sudden burst of flame. **8a** a blaze of light or fire used to illuminate, identify, alert, signal distress, etc. **8b** the device producing such a blaze. **9** a spreading shape or anything with a spreading shape: *a skirt with a flare*. **10** a sudden outburst, as of emotion. **11** *Optics*. **11a** the unwanted light reaching the image region of an optical device by reflections inside the instrument, etc. **11b** the fogged area formed on a negative by such reflections. **12** *Astronomy*. short for **solar flare**. **13** *Aeronautics*. the final transition phase of an aircraft landing, from the steady descent path to touchdown. **14** an open flame used to burn off unwanted gas at an oil well. [C16 (to spread out): of unknown origin] ▸ **flared** *adj*

flare path *n* an airstrip illuminated for use at night or in bad weather.

flares (flɛəz) *pl n Informal*. trousers with legs that widen below the knee.

flare star *n* a red dwarf star in which outbursts, thought to be analogous to solar flares, occur, increasing the luminosity by several magnitudes in a few minutes.

flare-up *n* **1** a sudden burst of fire or light. **2** *Informal.* a sudden burst of emotion or violence. ◆ *vb* **flare up.** (*intr, adv*). **3** to burst suddenly into fire or light. **4** *Informal.* to burst into anger.

flash (flæʃ) *n* **1** a sudden short blaze of intense light or flame: *a flash of sunlight.* **2** a sudden occurrence or display, esp. one suggestive of brilliance: *a flash of understanding.* **3** a very brief space of time: *over in a flash.* **4** an ostentatious display: *a flash of her diamonds.* **5** Also called: **newsflash.** a short news announcement concerning a new event. **6** Also called: **patch.** *Chiefly Brit.* an insignia or emblem worn on a uniform, vehicle, etc., to identify its military formation. **7** a patch of bright colour on a dark background, such as light marking on an animal. **8** a volatile mixture of inorganic salts used to produce a glaze on bricks or tiles. **9a** a sudden rush of water down a river or watercourse. **9b** a device, such as a sluice, for producing such a rush. **10** *Photog., informal.* short for **flashlight** (sense 2) or **flash photography. 11** a ridge of thin metal or plastic formed on a moulded object by the extrusion of excess material between dies. **12** *Yorkshire and Lancashire dialect.* a pond, esp. one produced as a consequence of subsidence. **13** (*modifier*) involving, using, or produced by a flash of heat, light, etc.: *flash blindness; flash distillation.* **14 flash in the pan.** a project, person, etc., that enjoys only short-lived success, notoriety, etc. ◆ *adj* **15** *Informal.* ostentatious or vulgar. **16** *Informal.* of or relating to gamblers and followers of boxing and racing. **17** sham or counterfeit. **18** *Informal.* relating to or characteristic of the criminal underworld. **19** brief and rapid: *flash freezing.* ◆ *vb* **20** to burst or cause to burst suddenly or intermittently into flame. **21** to emit or reflect or cause to emit or reflect light suddenly or intermittently. **22** (*intr*) to move very fast: *he flashed by on his bicycle.* **23** (*intr*) to come rapidly (into the mind or vision). **24** (*intr;* foll. by *out* or *up*) to appear like a sudden light: *his anger really flashes out at times.* **25a** to signal or communicate very fast: *to flash a message.* **25b** to signal by use of a light, such as car headlights. **26** (*tr*) *Informal.* to display ostentatiously: *to flash money around.* **27** (*tr*) *Informal.* to show suddenly and briefly. **28** (*intr*) *Brit. slang.* to expose oneself indecently. **29** (*tr*) to cover (a roof) with flashing. **30** to send a sudden rush of water down (a river, etc.), or to carry (a vessel) down by this method. **31** (in the making of glass) to coat (glass) with a thin layer of glass of a different colour. **32** (*tr*) to subject to a brief pulse of heat or radiation. **33** (*tr*) to change (a liquid) to a gas by causing it to hit a hot surface. **34** *Obsolete.* to splash or dash (water). [C14 (in the sense: to rush, as of water): of unknown origin]

flashback ('flæʃ,bæk) *n* **1** a transition in a novel, film, etc., to an earlier scene or event. ◆ *vb* **flash back. 2** (*intr, adv*) to return in a novel, film, etc., to a past event.

flashboard ('flæʃ,bɔːd) *n* a board or boarding that is placed along the top of a dam to increase its height and capacity.

flashbulb ('flæʃ,bʌlb) *n Photog.* a small expendable glass light bulb formerly used to produce a bright flash of light. Also called **photoflash.** Compare **electronic flash.**

flashbulb memory *n Psychol.* the clear recollections that a person may have of the circumstances associated with a dramatic event.

flash burn *n Pathol.* a burn caused by momentary exposure to intense radiant heat.

flash card *n* a card on which are written or printed words for children to look at briefly, used as an aid to learning.

flash eliminator *or* **suppressor** *n* a device fitted to the muzzle of a firearm to reduce the flash made by the ignited propellant gases.

flasher ('flæʃə) *n* **1** something that flashes, such as a direction indicator on a vehicle. **2** *Brit. slang.* a person who indecently exposes himself.

flash flood *n* a sudden short-lived torrent, usually caused by a heavy storm, esp. in desert regions.

flash gun *n* a type of electronic flash, attachable to or sometimes incorporated in a camera, that emits a very brief flash of light when the shutter is open.

flashing ('flæʃɪŋ) *n* a weatherproof material, esp. thin sheet metal, used to cover the valleys between the slopes of a roof, the junction between a chimney and a roof, etc.

flashlight ('flæʃ,laɪt) *n* **1** another word (esp. U.S. and Canadian) for **torch. 2** *Photog.* the brief bright light emitted by an electronic flash unit. Sometimes shortened to **flash. 3** *Chiefly U.S. and Canadian.* a light that flashes, used for signalling, in a lighthouse, etc.

flashover ('flæʃ,əʊvə) *n* an electric discharge over or around the surface of an insulator.

flash photography *n* photography in which a flashbulb or electronic flash is used to provide momentary illumination of a dark or insufficiently lit subject.

flash photolysis *n Physics.* a technique for producing and investigating free radicals. A low-pressure gas is subjected to a flash of radiation to produce the radicals, subsequent flashes being used to identify them and assess their lifetimes by absorption spectroscopy.

flash point *or* **flashing point** *n* **1** the lowest temperature at which the vapour above a liquid can be ignited in air. **2** a critical moment beyond which a situation will inevitably erupt into violence: *the political mood has reached flash point.*

flash set *n Civil engineering.* undesirably rapid setting of cement in concrete.

flash smelting *n* a smelting process for sulphur-containing ores in which the dried and powdered ore, mixed with oxygen, is ignited on discharge from a nozzle, melts, and drops to the bottom of a settling chamber. Sulphur is released mainly in its solid form, thus reducing atmospheric pollution.

flashy ('flæʃɪ) *adj* **flashier, flashiest. 1** brilliant and dazzling, esp. for a short time or in a superficial way. **2** cheap and ostentatious. ▸ **'flashily** *adv* ▸ **'flashiness** *n*

flask (flɑːsk) *n* **1** a bottle with a narrow neck, esp. used in a laboratory or for wine, oil, etc. **2** Also called: **hip flask.** a small flattened container of glass or metal designed to be carried in a pocket, esp. for liquor. **3** See **powder flask. 4** a container packed with sand to form a mould in a foundry. **5** See **vacuum flask. 6** Also called: **cask, coffin.** *Engineering.* a container used for transporting irradiated nuclear fuel. [C14: from Old French *flasque, flaske,* from Medieval Latin *flasca, flasco,* perhaps of Germanic origin; compare Old English *flasce, flaxe*]

flasket ('flɑːskɪt) *n* **1** a long shallow basket. **2** a small flask. [C15: from Old French *flasquet* a little FLASK]

flat[1] (flæt) *adj* **flatter, flattest. 1** horizontal; level: *flat ground; a flat roof.* **2** even or smooth, without projections or depressions: *a flat surface.* **3** lying stretched out at full length; prostrate: *he lay flat on the ground.* **4** having little depth or thickness; shallow: *a flat dish.* **5** (*postpositive;* often foll. by *against*) having a surface or side in complete contact with another surface: *flat against the wall.* **6** spread out, unrolled, or levelled. **7** (of a tyre) deflated, either partially or completely. **8** (of shoes) having an unraised or only slightly raised heel. **9** *Chiefly Brit.* **9a** (of races, racetracks, or racecourses) not having obstacles to be jumped. **9b** of, relating to, or connected with flat racing as opposed to steeplechasing and hurdling: *flat jockeys earn more.* **10** without qualification; total: *a flat denial.* **11** without possibility of change; fixed: *a flat rate.* **12** (*prenominal or immediately postpositive*) neither more nor less; exact: *he did the journey in thirty minutes flat; a flat thirty minutes.* **13** unexciting or lacking point or interest: *a flat joke.* **14** without variation or resonance; monotonous: *a flat voice.* **15** (of food) stale or tasteless. **16** (of beer, sparkling wines, etc.) having lost effervescence, as by exposure to air. **17** (of trade, business, a market, etc.) commercially inactive; sluggish. **18** (of a battery) fully discharged; dead. **19** (of a print, photograph, or painting) lacking contrast or shading between tones. **20** (of paint) without gloss or lustre; matt. **21** (of a painting) lacking perspective. **22** (of lighting) diffuse. **23** *Music.* **23a** (*immediately postpositive*) denoting a note of a given letter name (or the sound it represents) that has been lowered in pitch by one chromatic semitone: *B flat.* **23b** (of an instrument, voice, etc.) out of tune by being too low in pitch. Compare **sharp** (sense 12). **24** *Phonetics.* another word for **lenis. 25** *Phonetics.* **flat a.** the vowel sound of *a* as in the usual U.S. or S Brit. pronunciation of *hand, cat,* usually represented by the symbol (æ). ◆ *adv* **26** in or into a prostrate, level, or flat state or position: *he held his hand out flat.* **27** completely or utterly; absolutely: *he went flat against the rules.* **28** exactly; precisely: *in three minutes flat.* **29** *Music.* **29a** lower than a standard pitch. **29b** too low in pitch: *she sings flat.* Compare **sharp** (sense 18). **30 fall flat.** to fail to achieve a desired effect, etc. **31 flat out.** *Informal.* **31a** with the maximum speed or effort. **31b** totally exhausted. ◆ *n* **32** a flat object, surface, or part. **33** (*often pl*) a low-lying tract of land, esp. a marsh or swamp. **34** (*often pl*) a mud bank exposed at low tide. **35** *Music.* **35a** an accidental that lowers the pitch of the following note by one chromatic semitone. Usual symbol: ♭ **35b** a note affected by this accidental. Compare **sharp** (sense 19). **36** *Theatre.* a rectangular wooden frame covered with painted canvas, etc., used to form part of a stage setting. **37** a punctured car tyre. **38** (*often cap.;* preceded by *the*) *Chiefly Brit.* **38a** flat racing, esp. as opposed to steeplechasing and hurdling. **38b** the season of flat racing. **39** *Nautical.* a flatboat or lighter. **40** *U.S. and Canadian.* a shallow box or container, used for holding plants, growing seedlings, etc. ◆ *vb* **flats, flatting, flatted. 41** to make or become flat. **42** *Music.* the usual U.S. word for **flatten** (sense 3). ◆ See also **flats.** [C14: from Old Norse *flatr;* related to Old High German *flaz* flat, Greek *platus* flat, broad] ▸ **'flatly** *adv* ▸ **'flatness** *n*

flat[2] (flæt) *n* **1** a set of rooms comprising a residence entirely on one floor of a building. Usual U.S. and Canadian name: **apartment. 2** *Brit. and N.Z.* a portion of a house used as separate living quarters. **3** *N.Z.* a house shared with people who are not members of one's own family. ◆ *vb* (*intr*) **4** *Austral. informal. and N.Z.* to live in a flat (with someone). [Old English *flett* floor, hall, house; related to FLAT[1]]

flat-bed lorry ('flæt,bɛd) *n* a lorry with a flat platform for its body.

flat-bed press *n* a printing machine on which the type forme is carried on a flat bed under a revolving paper-bearing cylinder. Also called: **cylinder press.**

flat-bed scanner *n* a computer-controlled device which electronically scans images placed on its flat plate, allowing them to be manipulated and stored for later use such as in desktop publishing.

flatboat ('flæt,bəʊt) *n* any boat with a flat bottom, usually for transporting goods on a canal or river.

flat-bottomed rail *n Railways.* a rail having a cross section like an inverted T, with the top extremity enlarged slightly to form the head. Also called: **flanged rail.**

flat cap *n* **1** another name for **cloth cap** (sense 1). **2** an Elizabethan man's hat with a narrow down-turned brim.

flatette (,flæt'ɛt) *n Austral.* a very small flat.

flatfish ('flæt,fɪʃ) *n, pl* **-fish** *or* **-fishes.** any marine spiny-finned fish of the order *Heterosomata,* including the halibut, plaice, turbot, and sole, all of which (when adult) swim along the sea floor on one side of the body, which is highly compressed and has both eyes on the uppermost side.

flatfoot ('flæt,fʊt) *n* **1** Also called: **splayfoot.** a condition in which the entire sole of the foot is able to touch the ground because of flattening of the instep arch. **2** (*pl* **-foots** *or* **-feet**) a slang word (usually derogatory) for a **policeman.**

flat-footed (,flæt'fʊtɪd) *adj* **1** having flatfoot. **2** *Brit. informal.* **2a** clumsy or awkward. **2b** downright and uncompromising. **3** *Informal.* off guard or unawares (often in the phrase **catch flat-footed**). ▸ **,flat-'footedly** *adv* ▸ **,flat-'footedness** *n*

flathead ('flæt,hɛd) *n, pl* **-head** *or* **-heads.** any Pacific scorpaenoid food fish of the family *Platycephalidae,* which resemble gurnards.

flatiron ('flæt,aɪən) *n* (formerly) an iron for pressing clothes that was heated by being placed on a stove, etc.

flat knot *n* another name for **reef knot.**

flatlet ('flætlɪt) *n* a flat having only a few rooms.

flatling ('flætlɪŋ) *Archaic or dialect.* ◆ *adv* **1** in a flat or prostrate position. ◆ *adj, adv* **2** with the flat side, as of a sword. ◆ Also (for adv): **'flatlings.**

flatmate ('flæt,meɪt) *n Brit.* a person with whom one shares a flat.

flat racing *n* **a** the racing of horses on racecourses without jumps. **b** (*as modifier*): *the flat-racing season.*

flats (flæts) *or* **flatties** ('flætɪz) *pl n* shoes with flat heels or no heels.

flat spin *n* **1** an aircraft spin in which the longitudinal axis is more nearly horizontal than vertical. **2** *Informal.* a state of confusion; dither.

flat spot *n* **1** *Engineering.* a region of poor acceleration over a narrow range of throttle openings, caused by a weak mixture in the carburettor. **2** any narrow region of poor performance in a mechanical device.

flatten ('flæt^ən) *vb* **1** (sometimes foll. by *out*) to make or become flat or flatter. **2** (*tr*) *Informal.* **2a** to knock down or injure; prostrate. **2b** to crush or subdue: *failure will flatten his self-esteem.* **3** (*tr*) *Music.* to lower the pitch of (a note) by one chromatic semitone. Usual U.S. word: **flat. 4** (*intr;* foll. by *out*) to manoeuvre an aircraft into horizontal flight, esp. after a dive. ► **'flattener** *n*

flatter[1] ('flætə) *vb* **1** to praise insincerely, esp. in order to win favour or reward. **2** to show to advantage: *that dress flatters her.* **3** (*tr*) to make to appear more attractive, etc., than in reality. **4** to play upon or gratify the vanity of (a person): *it flatters her to be remembered.* **5** (*tr*) to beguile with hope; encourage, esp. falsely: *this success flattered him into believing himself a champion.* **6** (*tr*) to congratulate or deceive (oneself): *I flatter myself that I am the best.* [C13: probably from Old French *flater* to lick, fawn upon, of Frankish origin] ► **'flatterable** *adj* ► **'flatterer** *n* ► **'flatteringly** *adv*

flatter[2] ('flætə) *n* **1** a blacksmith's tool, resembling a flat-faced hammer, that is placed on forged work and struck to smooth the surface of the forging. **2** a die with a narrow rectangular orifice for drawing flat sections.

flattery ('flætərɪ) *n, pl* **-teries. 1** the act of flattering. **2** excessive or insincere praise.

flattie ('flætɪ) *n N.Z. informal.* a flounder or other flatfish.

flatties ('flætɪz) *pl n* another word for **flats.**

flatting ('flætɪŋ) *n* **1** *Metallurgy.* the process of flattening metal into a sheet by rolling. **2** *N.Z.* the practice of sharing a house with people who are not members of one's own family. **3 go flatting.** *N.Z.* to leave the parental home and live independently in a flat, usually with people of the same age group.

flattish ('flætɪʃ) *adj* somewhat flat.

flattop ('flæt,tɒp) *n U.S.* an informal name for **aircraft carrier.**

flat top *n* a style of haircut in which the hair is cut shortest on the top of the head so that it stands up from the scalp and appears flat from the crown to the forehead.

flat tuning *n* the condition of a radio receiver that does not discriminate sharply between signals on different frequencies.

flatulent ('flætjʊlənt) *adj* **1** suffering from or caused by an excessive amount of gas in the alimentary canal, producing uncomfortable distension. **2** generating excessive gas in the alimentary canal. **3** pretentious or windy in style. [C16: from New Latin *flātulentus,* from Latin: FLATUS] ► **'flatulence** *or* **'flatulency** *n* ► **'flatulently** *adv*

flatus ('fleɪtəs) *n, pl* **-tuses.** gas generated in the alimentary canal. [C17: from Latin: a blowing, snorting, from *flāre* to breathe, blow]

flatware ('flæt,wɛə) *n U.S. and Canadian* **1** cutlery. **2** any relatively flat tableware such as plates, saucers, etc. Compare **hollowware.**

flatways ('flæt,weɪz) *or U.S.* **flatwise** *adv* with the flat or broad side down or in contact with another surface.

flatworm ('flæt,wɜːm) *n* any parasitic or free-living invertebrate of the phylum *Platyhelminthes,* including planarians, flukes, and tapeworms, having a flattened body with no circulatory system and only one opening to the intestine.

flat-woven *adj* (of a carpet) woven without pile.

Flaubert ('fləʊbɛə; *French* flobɛr) *n* **Gustave** (gystav). 1821–80, French novelist and short-story writer, regarded as a leader of the 19th-century naturalist school. His most famous novel, *Madame Bovary* (1857), for which he was prosecuted (and acquitted) on charges of immorality, and *L'Éducation sentimentale* (1869) deal with the conflict of romantic attitudes and bourgeois society. His other major works include *Salammbô* (1862), *La Tentation de Saint Antoine* (1874), and *Trois contes* (1877).

flaunch (flɔːntʃ) *n* a cement or mortar slope around a chimney top, manhole, etc., to throw off water. Also called: **flaunching.** [C18: variant of FLANGE]

flaunt (flɔːnt) *vb* **1** to display (possessions, oneself, etc.) ostentatiously; show off. **2** to wave or cause to wave freely; flutter. ◆ *n* **3** the act of flaunting. [C16: perhaps of Scandinavian origin; compare Norwegian dialect *flanta* to wander about] ► **'flaunter** *n* ► **'flauntingly** *adv*

USAGE *Flaunt* is sometimes wrongly used where *flout* is meant: *they must be prevented from flouting* (not *flaunting*) *the law.*

flaunty ('flɔːntɪ) *adj* **flauntier, flauntiest.** *Chiefly U.S.* characterized by or inclined to ostentatious display or flaunting. ► **'flauntily** *adv* ► **'flauntiness** *n*

flautist ('flɔːtɪst) *or U.S. and Canadian* **flutist** ('fluːtɪst) *n* a player of the flute. [C19: from Italian *flautista,* from *flauto* FLUTE]

flavescent (flə'vɛs^ənt) *adj* turning yellow; yellowish. [C19: from Latin *flāvēscere* to become yellow, from *flāvēre* to be yellow, from *flāvus* yellow]

flavin *or* **flavine** ('fleɪvɪn) *n* **1** a heterocyclic ketone that forms the nucleus of certain natural yellow pigments, such as riboflavin. Formula: $C_{10}H_6N_4O_2$. See **flavoprotein. 2** any yellow pigment based on flavin. **3** another name for **quercetin.** [C19: from Latin *flāvus* yellow]

flavine ('fleɪvɪn) *n* **1** another name for **acriflavine hydrochloride. 2** a variant spelling of **flavin.**

flavone ('fleɪvəʊn) *n* **1** a crystalline compound occurring in plants. Formula: $C_{15}H_{10}O_2$. **2** any of a class of yellow plant pigments derived from flavone. [C19: from German *Flavon,* from Latin *flāvus* yellow + -ONE]

flavonoid ('fleɪvə,nɔɪd) *n* any of a group of organic compounds that occur as pigments in fruit and flowers. [C20: from FLAVONE + -OID]

flavoprotein (,fleɪvəʊ'prəʊtiːn) *n* any of a group of enzymes that contain a derivative of riboflavin linked to a protein and catalyse oxidation in cells. Also called: **cytochrome reductase.** See also **FMN, FAD.** [C20: from FLAVIN + PROTEIN]

flavopurpurin (,fleɪvəʊ'pɜːpjʊrɪn) *n* a yellow crystalline dye derived from anthraquinone. Formula: $C_{14}H_5O_2(OH)_3$. [C20: from Latin *flāvus* yellow + PURPURIN]

flavorous ('fleɪvərəs) *adj* having flavour; tasty.

flavour *or U.S.* **flavor** ('fleɪvə) *n* **1** taste perceived in food or liquid in the mouth. **2** a substance added to food, etc., to impart a specific taste. **3** a distinctive quality or atmosphere; suggestion: *a poem with a Shakespearean flavour.* **4** *Physics.* a property of quarks that enables them to be differentiated into six types: up, down, strange, charm, bottom (or beauty), and top (or truth). **5 flavour of the month.** a person or thing that is the most popular at a certain time. ◆ *vb* **6** (*tr*) to impart a flavour, taste, or quality to. [C14: from Old French *flaour,* from Late Latin *flātor* (unattested) bad smell, breath, from Latin *flāre* to blow] ► **'flavourer** *or U.S.* **'flavorer** *n* ► **'flavourless** *or U.S.* **'flavorless** *adj* ► **'flavoursome** *or U.S.* **'flavorsome** *adj*

flavour enhancer *n* another term for **monosodium glutamate.**

flavourful *or U.S.* **flavorful** ('fleɪvəfʊl) *adj* having a full pleasant taste or flavour. ► **'flavourfully** *or U.S.* **'flavorfully** *adv*

flavouring *or U.S.* **flavoring** ('fleɪvərɪŋ) *n* a substance used to impart a particular flavour to food: *rum flavouring.*

flaw[1] (flɔː) *n* **1** an imperfection, defect, or blemish. **2** a crack, breach, or rift. **3** *Law.* an invalidating fault or defect in a document or proceeding. ◆ *vb* **4** to make or become blemished, defective, or imperfect. [C14: probably from Old Norse *flaga* stone slab; related to Swedish *flaga* chip, flake, flaw] ► **'flawless** *adj* ► **'flawlessly** *adv* ► **'flawlessness** *n*

flaw[2] (flɔː) *n* **1a** a sudden short gust of wind; squall. **1b** a spell of bad, esp. windy, weather. **2** *Obsolete.* an outburst of strong feeling. [C16: of Scandinavian origin; related to Norwegian *flaga* squall, gust, Middle Dutch *vlāghe*] ► **'flawy** *adj*

flax (flæks) *n* **1** any herbaceous plant or shrub of the genus *Linum,* esp. *L. usitatissimum,* which has blue flowers and is cultivated for its seeds (flaxseed) and for the fibres of its stems: family *Linaceae.* **2** the fibre of this plant, made into thread and woven into linen fabrics. **3** any of various similar plants. **4** *N.Z.* a swamp plant producing a fibre that is used by Maoris for decorative work, baskets, etc. [Old English *fleax;* related to Old Frisian *flax,* Old High German *flahs* flax, Greek *plekein* to plait]

flaxen ('flæksən) *or* **flaxy** *adj* **1** of, relating to, or resembling flax. **2** of a soft yellow colour: *flaxen hair.*

flax kit *n N.Z.* a basket woven from flax fibres.

Flaxman ('flæksmən) *n* **John.** 1755–1826, English neoclassical sculptor and draughtsman, noted particularly for his monuments and his engraved illustrations for the *Iliad,* the *Odyssey,* and works by Dante and Aeschylus.

flaxseed ('flæks,siːd) *n* the seed of the flax plant, which yields linseed oil. Also called: **linseed.**

flay (fleɪ) *vb* (*tr*) **1** to strip off the skin or outer covering of, esp. by whipping; skin. **2** to attack with savage criticism. **3** to strip of money or goods, esp. by cheating or extortion. [Old English *flēan;* related to Old Norse *flā* to peel, Lithuanian *plěšti* to tear] ► **'flayer** *n*

fld *abbrev. for* field.

fl. dr. *abbrev. for* fluid dram.

flea (fliː) *n* **1** any small wingless parasitic blood-sucking insect of the order *Siphonaptera,* living on the skin of mammals and birds and noted for its power of leaping. **2** any of various invertebrates that resemble fleas, such as the water flea and flea beetle. **3 flea in one's ear.** *Informal.* a sharp rebuke. [Old English *flēah;* related to Old Norse *flō,* Old High German *flōh*]

fleabag ('fliː,bæg) *n Slang.* **1** *Brit.* a dirty or unkempt person, esp. a woman. **2** *U.S.* a cheap or dirty hotel.

fleabane ('fliː,beɪn) *n* **1** any of several plants of the genus *Erigeron,* such as *E. acer,* having purplish tubular flower heads with orange centres: family *Compositae* (composites). **2** any of several plants of the related genus *Pulicaria,* esp. the Eurasian *P. dysenterica,* which has yellow daisy-like flower heads. **3 Canadian fleabane.** a related plant, *Conyza* (or *Erigeron*) *canadensis,* with small white tubular flower heads. U.S. name: **horseweed. 4** any of various other plants reputed to ward off fleas.

flea beetle *n* any small common beetle of the genera *Phyllotreta, Chalcoides,* etc., having enlarged hind legs and capable of jumping: family *Chrysomelidae.* The larvae of many species are very destructive to turnips and other cruciferous vegetables.

fleabite ('fliː,baɪt) *n* **1** the bite of a flea. **2** a slight or trifling annoyance or discomfort.

flea-bitten *adj* **1** bitten by or infested with fleas. **2** *Informal.* shabby or decrepit; mean. **3** (of the coat of a horse) having reddish-brown spots on a lighter background.

fleam (fliːm) *n* a lancet used for letting blood. [C16: from Old French *flieme,* alteration of Late Latin *phlebotomus* lancet (literally: vein cutter); see PHLEBOTOMY]

flea market *n* an open-air market selling cheap and often second-hand goods.

fleapit ('fliː,pɪt) *n Informal.* a shabby cinema or theatre.

fleawort ('fliː,wɜːt) *n* **1** any of various plants of the genus *Senecio,* esp. *S. integrifolius,* a European species with yellow daisy-like flowers and rosettes of downy leaves: family *Compositae* (composites). **2** a Eurasian plantain, *Plan-*

tago psyllium (or *P. indica*), whose seeds resemble fleas and were formerly used as a flea repellent. **3** another name for **ploughman's spikenard.**

flèche (fleɪʃ, flɛʃ) *n* **1** Also called: **spirelet.** a slender spire, esp. over the intersection of the nave and transept ridges of a church roof. **2** a pointed part of a fortification directed towards the attackers. **3** *Fencing.* a short running attack. [C18: from French: spire (literally: arrow), probably of Germanic origin; related to Middle Low German *flieke* long arrow]

fléchette (fleɪˈʃɛt) *n* a steel dart or missile dropped from an aircraft, as in World War I. [from French; see FLÈCHE]

fleck (flɛk) *n* **1** a small marking or streak; speckle. **2** a small particle; speck: *a fleck of dust.* ◆ *vb* **3** (*tr*) Also: **ˈflecker.** to mark or cover with flecks; speckle. [C16: probably from Old Norse *flekkr* stain, spot; related to Old High German *flec* spot, plot of land]

Flecker (ˈflɛkə) *n* **James Elroy.** 1884–1915, English poet and dramatist; author of *Hassan* (1922).

flection (ˈflɛkʃən) *n* **1** the act of bending or the state of being bent. **2** something bent; bend. **3** *Grammar.* a less common word for **inflection.** ◆ See also **flexion.** [C17: from Latin *flexiō* a bending, from *flectere* to curve, bow] ▸ **ˈflectional** *adj* ▸ **ˈflectionless** *adj*

fled (flɛd) *vb* the past tense and past participle of **flee**[1].

fledge (flɛdʒ) *vb* **1** (*tr*) to feed and care for (a young bird) until it is able to fly. **2** (*tr*) Also called: **fletch.** to fit (something, esp. an arrow) with a feather or feathers. **3** (*intr*) (of a young bird) to grow feathers. **4** (*tr*) to cover or adorn with or as if with feathers. [Old English *-flycge,* as in *unflycge* unfledged; related to Old High German *flucki* able to fly; see FLY[1]]

fledgling *or* **fledgeling** (ˈflɛdʒlɪŋ) *n* **1** a young bird that has just fledged. **2** a young and inexperienced person.

fledgy (ˈflɛdʒɪ) *adj* **fledgier, fledgiest.** *Rare.* feathery or feathered.

flee[1] (fliː) *vb* **flees, fleeing, fled. 1** to run away from (a place, danger, etc.); fly: *to flee the country.* **2** (*intr*) to run or move quickly; rush; speed: *she fled to the door.* [Old English *flēon;* related to Old Frisian *fliā,* Old High German *fliohan,* Gothic *thliuhan*] ▸ **ˈfleer** *n*

flee[2] (fliː) *vb* **1** a Scot. word for **fly**[1]. ◆ *n* **2** a Scot. word for **fly**[2].

fleece (fliːs) *n* **1** the coat of wool that covers the body of a sheep or similar animal and consists of a mass of crinkly hairs. **2** the wool removed from a single sheep. **3** something resembling a fleece in texture or warmth. **4** sheepskin or a fabric with soft pile, used as a lining for coats, etc. ◆ *vb* (*tr*) **5** to defraud or charge exorbitantly; swindle. **6** another term for **shear** (sense 1). [Old English *flēos;* related to Middle High German *vlius,* Dutch *vlies* fleece, Latin *plūma* feather, down]

fleecie (ˈfliːsɪ) *n N.Z.* a person who collects fleeces after shearing and prepares them for baling. Also called: **fleece-oh.**

fleecy (ˈfliːsɪ) *adj* **fleecier, fleeciest.** of or resembling fleece; woolly. ▸ **ˈfleecily** *adv* ▸ **ˈfleeciness** *n*

fleein' (ˈfliːɪn) *adj Scot. dialect.* drunk. [literally: flying, from FLEE[2]]

fleer (flɪə) *Archaic.* ◆ *vb* **1** to grin or laugh at; scoff; sneer. ◆ *n* **2** a derisory glance or grin. [C14: of Scandinavian origin; compare Norwegian *flire* to snigger] ▸ **ˈfleeringly** *adv*

fleet[1] (fliːt) *n* **1** a number of warships organized as a tactical unit. **2** all the warships of a nation. **3** a number of aircraft, ships, buses, etc., operating together or under the same ownership. [Old English *flēot* ship, flowing water, from *flēotan* to FLOAT]

fleet[2] (fliːt) *adj* **1** rapid in movement; swift. **2** *Poetic.* fleeting; transient. ◆ *vb* **3** (*intr*) to move rapidly. **4** (*intr*) *Archaic.* to fade away smoothly; glide. **5** (*tr*) *Nautical.* **5a** to change the position of (a hawser). **5b** to pass (a messenger or lead) to a hawser from a winch for hauling in. **5c** to spread apart (the blocks of a tackle). **6** (*intr*) *Obsolete.* to float or swim. **7** (*tr*) *Obsolete.* to cause (time) to pass rapidly. [probably Old English *flēotan* to float, glide rapidly; related to Old High German *fliozzan* to flow, Latin *pluere* to rain] ▸ **ˈfleetly** *adv* ▸ **ˈfleetness** *n*

fleet[3] (fliːt) *n Chiefly southeastern Brit.* a small coastal inlet; creek. [Old English *flēot* flowing water; see FLEET[1]]

Fleet (fliːt) *n* **the. 1** a stream that formerly ran into the Thames between Ludgate Hill and Fleet Street and is now a covered sewer. **2** Also called: **Fleet Prison** (formerly) a London prison, esp. used for holding debtors.

fleet admiral *n* an officer holding the most senior commissioned rank in the U.S. and certain other navies.

Fleet Air Arm *n* the aviation branch of the Royal Navy. Abbrev.: **FAA.**

fleet chief petty officer *n* a noncommissioned officer in the Royal Navy comparable in rank to a warrant officer in the British Army or Royal Air Force.

fleeting (ˈfliːtɪŋ) *adj* rapid and transient: *a fleeting glimpse of the sea.* ▸ **ˈfleetingly** *adv* ▸ **ˈfleetingness** *n*

fleet rate *or* **fleet rating** *n* a reduced rate quoted by an insurance company to underwrite the risks to a fleet of vehicles, aircraft, etc.

Fleet Street *n* **1** a street in central London in which many newspaper offices were formerly situated. **2** British journalism or journalists collectively.

Fleetwood (ˈfliːtˌwʊd) *n* a fishing port in NW England, in Lancashire. Pop.: 27 227 (1991).

fleishik *or* **fleishig** (ˈfleɪʃɪk, ˈflaɪ-) *adj Judaism.* (of food) containing or derived from meat or meat products and therefore to be prepared and eaten separately from dairy foods. Also: **meaty.** Compare **milchik.** See also **kashruth.**

Flem. *abbrev. for* Flemish.

Flémalle (*French* flemal) *n* **Master of.** See (Robert) **Campin.**

Fleming[1] (ˈflɛmɪŋ) *n* a native or inhabitant of Flanders or a Flemish-speaking Belgian. Compare **Walloon.** [C14: from Middle Dutch *Vlaminc*]

Fleming[2] (ˈflɛmɪŋ) *n* **1** Sir **Alexander.** 1881–1955, Scottish bacteriologist: discovered lysozyme (1922) and penicillin (1928): shared the Nobel prize for physiology or medicine in 1945. **2 Ian (Lancaster).** 1908–64, English author of spy novels; creator of the secret agent James Bond. **3** Sir **John Ambrose.** 1849–1945, English electrical engineer: invented the thermionic valve (1904).

Fleming's rules *pl n Physics.* two rules used as mnemonics for the relationship between the directions of current flow, motion, and magnetic field in electromagnetic induction. The hand is held with the thumb, first, and second fingers at right angles, respectively indicating the directions of motion, field, and electric current. The left hand is used for electric motors and the right hand for dynamos. [C19: named after Sir John Ambrose FLEMING, who devised them]

Flemish (ˈflɛmɪʃ) *n* **1** one of the two official languages of Belgium, almost identical in form with Dutch. **2 the.** (*functioning as pl*) the Flemings collectively. ◆ *adj* **3** of, relating to, or characteristic of Flanders, the Flemings, or their language.

Flemish bond *n* a bond used in brickwork that has alternating stretchers and headers in each course, each header being placed centrally over a stretcher.

Flemish Brabant *n* a province of central Belgium, formed in 1995 from the N part of Brabant province: densely populated and intensively farmed, with large industrial centres. Pop.: 999 186 (1996 est.). Area: 2106 sq. km (813 sq. miles).

Flensburg (*German* ˈflɛnsbʊrk) *n* a port in N Germany, in Schleswig-Holstein: taken from Denmark by Prussia in 1864; voted to remain German in 1920. Pop.: 87 240 (1991).

flense (flɛns), **flench** (flɛntʃ), *or* **flinch** (flɪntʃ) *vb* (*tr*) to strip (a whale, seal, etc.) of (its blubber or skin). [C19: from Danish *flense;* related to Dutch *flensen*] ▸ **ˈflenser, ˈflencher,** *or* **ˈflincher** *n*

flesh (flɛʃ) *n* **1** the soft part of the body of an animal or human, esp. muscular tissue, as distinct from bone and viscera. Related adj: **sarcoid. 2** *Informal.* excess weight; fat. **3** *Archaic.* the edible tissue of animals as opposed to that of fish or, sometimes, fowl; meat. **4** the thick usually soft part of a fruit or vegetable, as distinct from the skin, core, stone, etc. **5** the human body and its physical or sensual nature as opposed to the soul or spirit. Related adj: **carnal. 6** mankind in general. **7** animate creatures in general. **8** one's own family; kin (esp. in the phrase **one's own flesh and blood**). **9** a yellowish-pink to greyish-yellow colour. **10** *Christian Science.* belief on the physical plane which is considered erroneous, esp. the belief that matter has sensation. **11** (*modifier*) *Tanning.* of or relating to the inner or under layer of a skin or hide: *a flesh split.* **12 in the flesh.** in person; actually present. **13 make one's flesh creep.** (esp. of something ghostly) to frighten and horrify one. **14 press the flesh.** *Informal.* to shake hands, usually with large numbers of people, esp. in political campaigning. ◆ *vb* **15** (*tr*) *Hunting.* to stimulate the hunting instinct of (hounds or falcons) by giving them small quantities of raw flesh. **16** to wound the flesh of with a weapon. **17** *Archaic or poetic.* to accustom or incite to bloodshed or battle by initial experience. **18** *Tanning.* to remove the flesh layer of (a hide or skin). **19** to fatten; fill out. [Old English *flǣsc;* related to Old Norse *flesk* ham, Old High German *fleisk* meat, flesh]

flesher (ˈflɛʃə) *n* **1** a person or machine that fleshes hides or skins. **2** *Scot.* a person who sells meat; butcher.

flesh fly *n* any dipterous fly of the genus *Sarcophaga,* esp. *S. carnaria,* whose larvae feed on carrion or the tissues of living animals: family *Calliphoridae.*

fleshings (ˈflɛʃɪŋz) *pl n* **1** flesh-coloured tights. **2** bits of flesh scraped from the hides or skins of animals.

fleshly (ˈflɛʃlɪ) *adj* **-lier, -liest. 1** relating to the body, esp. its sensual nature; carnal: *fleshly desire.* **2** worldly as opposed to spiritual. **3** fleshy; fat. ▸ **ˈfleshliness** *n*

flesh out *vb* (*adv*) **1** (*tr*) to give substance to (an argument, description, etc.). **2** (*intr*) to expand or become more substantial.

fleshpots (ˈflɛʃˌpɒts) *pl n Often facetious.* **1** luxurious or self-indulgent living. **2** places, such as striptease clubs, where bodily desires are gratified or titillated. [C16: from the Biblical use as applied to Egypt (Exodus 16:3)]

flesh wound (wuːnd) *n* a wound affecting superficial tissues.

fleshy (ˈflɛʃɪ) *adj* **fleshier, fleshiest. 1** fat; plump. **2** related to or resembling flesh. **3** *Botany.* (of some fruits, leaves, etc.) thick and pulpy. ▸ **ˈfleshiness** *n*

fletch (flɛtʃ) *vb* another word for **fledge** (sense 2). [C17: probably back formation from FLETCHER]

fletcher (ˈflɛtʃə) *n* a person who makes arrows. [C14: from Old French *flechier,* from *fleche* arrow; see FLÈCHE]

Fletcher (ˈflɛtʃə) *n* **John.** 1579–1625, English Jacobean dramatist, noted for his romantic tragicomedies written in collaboration with Francis Beaumont, esp. *Philaster* (1610) and *The Maid's Tragedy* (1611).

Fletcherism (ˈflɛtʃəˌrɪzəm) *n* the practice of chewing food thoroughly and drinking liquids in small sips to aid digestion. [C20: named after Horace *Fletcher* (1849–1919), American nutritionist]

fletchings (ˈflɛtʃɪŋz) *pl n* arrow feathers. [plural of *fletching,* from FLETCH]

fleur-de-lys *or* **fleur-de-lis** (ˌflɜːdəˈliː) *n, pl* **fleurs-de-lys** *or* **fleurs-de-lis** (ˌflɜːdəˈliːz). **1** *Heraldry.* a charge representing a lily with three distinct petals. **2** another name for **iris** (sense 2). [C19: from Old French *flor de lis,* literally: lily flower]

fleurette *or* **fleuret** (flʊəˈrɛt, flɜː-) *n* an ornament resembling a flower. [C19: French, literally: a small flower, from *fleur* flower]

fleuron (ˈflʊərɒn, -rən, ˈflɜː-) *n* **1** another name for **flower** (sense 8). **2** *Cookery.* a decorative piece of pastry. [C14: from French, from Old French *floron,* from *flor* FLOWER]

Fleury (*French* flœri) *n* **André Hercule de** (ɑ̃dre ɛrkyl də). 1653–1743, French cardinal and statesman: Louis XV's chief adviser and virtual ruler of France (1726–43).

flew[1] (fluː) *vb* the past tense of **fly**[1].

flew[2] (fluː) *n* a variant spelling of **flue**[3].

flews (fluːz) *pl n* the fleshy hanging upper lip of a bloodhound or similar dog. [C16: of unknown origin]

flex (flɛks) *n* **1** *Brit.* a flexible insulated electric cable, used esp. to connect appliances to mains. U.S. and Canadian name: **cord.** **2** *Informal.* flexibility or pliability. ◆ *vb* **3** to bend or be bent: *he flexed his arm; his arm flexed.* **4** to contract (a muscle) or (of a muscle) to contract. **5** (*intr*) to work according to flexitime. **6 flex one's muscles.** to test or display one's authority or strength. [C16: from Latin *flexus* bent, winding, from *flectere* to bend, bow]

flexible ('flɛksɪbᵊl) *adj* **1** Also: **flexile** ('flɛksaɪl). able to be bent easily without breaking; pliable. **2** adaptable or variable: *flexible working hours.* **3** able to be persuaded easily; tractable. ▸ ˌ**flexi'bility** *or* '**flexibleness** *n* ▸ '**flexibly** *adv*

flexible disk *n* another name for **floppy disk.**

flexion ('flɛkʃən) *n* **1** the act of bending a joint or limb. **2** the condition of the joint or limb so bent. **3** a variant spelling of **flection.** ▸ '**flexional** *adj* ▸ '**flexionless** *adj*

flexitime ('flɛksɪˌtaɪm) *or* **flextime** ('flɛksˌtaɪm) *n* a system permitting flexibility of working hours at the beginning or end of the day, provided an agreed period of each day (**core time**) is spent at work.

flexo ('flɛksəʊ) *n, adj, adv* short for **flexography, flexographic,** or **flexographically.**

flexography (flɛk'sɒgrəfɪ) *n* **1** a method of rotary letterpress printing using a resilient printing plate and solvent-based ink: used characteristically for printing on metal foil or plastic. **2** matter printed by this method. ◆ Abbrev.: **flexo.** ▸ flexographic (ˌflɛksə'græfɪk) *adj* ▸ ˌ**flexo'graphically** *adv*

flexor ('flɛksə) *n* any muscle whose contraction serves to bend a joint or limb. Compare **extensor.** [C17: New Latin; see FLEX]

flexuous ('flɛksjʊəs) *or* **flexuose** ('flɛksjʊˌəʊs) *adj* **1** full of bends or curves; winding. **2** variable; unsteady. [C17: from Latin *flexuōsus* full of bends, tortuous, from *flexus* a bending; see FLEX] ▸ '**flexuously** *adv*

flexure ('flɛkʃə) *n* **1** the act of flexing or the state of being flexed. **2** a bend, turn, or fold. ▸ '**flexural** *adj*

flex-wing *n Aeronautics.* a collapsible fabric delta wing, as used with hang-gliders.

fley *or* **flay** (fleɪ) *vb Scot. and northern English dialect.* **1** to be afraid or cause to be afraid. **2** (*tr*) to frighten away; scare. [Old English *āflēgan* to put to flight; related to Old Norse *fleygja*]

flibbertigibbet ('flɪbətɪˌdʒɪbɪt) *n* an irresponsible, silly, or gossipy person. [C15: of uncertain origin]

flick[1] (flɪk) *vb* **1** (*tr*) to touch with or as if with the finger or hand in a quick jerky movement. **2** (*tr*) to propel or remove by a quick jerky movement, usually of the fingers or hand: *to flick a piece of paper at someone.* **3** to move or cause to move quickly or jerkily. **4** (intr; foll. by *through*) to read or look at (a book, newspaper, etc.) quickly or idly. **5** to snap or click (the fingers) to produce a sharp sound. ◆ *n* **6** a tap or quick stroke with the fingers, a whip, etc. **7** the sound made by such a stroke. **8** a fleck, streak, or particle. [C15: of imitative origin; compare French *flicflac*]

flick[2] (flɪk) *n Slang.* **1** a cinema film. **2** (*pl*) **the.** the cinema: *what's on at the flicks tonight?*

flicker[1] ('flɪkə) *vb* **1** (*intr*) to shine with an unsteady or intermittent light: *a candle flickers.* **2** (*intr*) to move quickly to and fro; quiver, flutter, or vibrate. **3** (*tr*) to cause to flicker. ◆ *n* **4** an unsteady or brief light or flame. **5** a swift quivering or fluttering movement. **6** a visual sensation, often seen in a television image, produced by periodic fluctuations in the brightness of light at a frequency below that covered by the persistence of vision. [Old English *flicorian;* related to Dutch *flikkeren,* Old Norse *flökra* to flutter] ▸ '**flickeringly** *adv* ▸ '**flickery** *adj*

flicker[2] ('flɪkə) *n* any North American woodpecker of the genus *Colaptes,* esp. *C. auratus* (**yellow-shafted flicker**), which has a yellow undersurface to the wings and tail. [C19: perhaps imitative of the bird's call]

flick knife *n* a knife with a retractable blade that springs out when a button is pressed. U.S. and Canadian word: **switchblade.**

flier ('flaɪə) *n* a variant spelling of **flyer.**

flight[1] (flaɪt) *n* **1** the act, skill, or manner of flying. **2** a journey made by a flying animal or object. **3a** a scheduled airline journey. **3b** an aircraft flying on such a journey. **4** a group of flying birds or aircraft: *a flight of swallows.* **5** the basic tactical unit of a military air force. **6** a journey through space, esp. of a spacecraft. **7** rapid movement or progress. **8** a soaring mental journey above or beyond the normal everyday world: *a flight of fancy.* **9a** a single line of hurdles across a track in a race. **9b** a series of such hurdles. **10** a bird's wing or tail feather; flight feather. **11** a feather or plastic attachment fitted to an arrow or dart to give it stability in flight. **12** See **flight arrow.** **13** the distance covered by a flight arrow. **14** *Sport, esp. cricket.* **14a** a flighted movement imparted to a ball, dart, etc. **14b** the ability to flight a ball. **15** *Angling.* a device on a spinning lure that revolves rapidly. **16** a set of steps or stairs between one landing or floor and the next. **17** a large enclosed area attached to an aviary or pigeon loft where the birds may fly but not escape. ◆ *vb* **18** (*tr*) *Sport.* to cause (a ball, dart, etc.) to float slowly or deceptively towards its target. **19** (*intr*) (of wild fowl) to fly in groups. **20** (*tr*) to shoot (a bird) in flight. **21** (*tr*) to fledge (an arrow or a dart). [Old English *flyht;* related to Middle Dutch *vlucht,* Old Saxon *fluht*]

flight[2] (flaɪt) *n* **1** the act of fleeing or running away, as from danger. **2 put to flight.** to cause to run away; rout. **3 take (to) flight.** to run away or withdraw hastily; flee. [Old English *flyht* (unattested); related to Old Frisian *flecht,* Old High German *fluht,* Old Norse *flōtti*]

flight arrow *n* a long thin arrow used for shooting long distances. Often shortened to **flight.**

flight attendant *n* a person who attends to the needs of passengers on a commercial flight.

flight capital *n* funds transferred abroad in order to avoid high taxes or to provide for a person's needs if flight from the country becomes necessary.

flight deck *n* **1** the crew compartment in an airliner. Compare **cockpit** (sense 1). **2** the upper deck of an aircraft carrier from which aircraft take off and on which they land.

flight engineer *n* the member of an aircraft crew who is responsible for the operation of the aircraft's systems, including the engines, during flight.

flight feather *n* any of the large stiff feathers that cover the wings and tail of a bird and are adapted for flying.

flight formation *n* two or more aircraft flying together in a set pattern.

flightless ('flaɪtlɪs) *adj* (of certain birds and insects) unable to fly. See also **ratite.**

flight level *n Aeronautics.* a specified height at which an aircraft is allowed to fly.

flight lieutenant *n* an officer holding a commissioned rank senior to a flying officer and junior to a squadron leader in the RAF and certain other air forces.

flight line *n* an area of an airfield or airport on which aircraft, esp. military aircraft, are parked and serviced.

flight management systems *pl n* a suite of computer programs in a computer on board an aircraft used to calculate the most economical flying speeds and altitudes during a flight and to identify possible choices in emergencies.

flight path *n* the course through the air of an aircraft, rocket, or projectile. Compare **approach** (sense 10), **glide path.**

flight plan *n* a written statement of the details of a proposed aircraft flight.

flight recorder *n* an electronic device fitted to an aircraft for storing information concerning its performance in flight. It is often used to determine the cause of a crash. Also called: **black box.**

flight sergeant *n* a noncommissioned officer in the Royal Air Force junior in rank to a master aircrew.

flight simulator *n* a ground-training device that reproduces exactly the conditions experienced on the flight deck of an aircraft. Compare **Link trainer.**

flight strip *n* **1** a strip of cleared land used as an emergency runway for aircraft. **2** another name for **runway** (sense 1). **3** a strip of continuous aerial photographs.

flight surgeon *n* a medical officer specializing in aviation medicine in the U.S. and certain other air forces.

flighty ('flaɪtɪ) *adj* **flightier, flightiest. 1** frivolous and irresponsible; capricious; volatile. **2** mentally erratic, unstable, or wandering. **3** flirtatious; coquettish. ▸ '**flightily** *adv* ▸ '**flightiness** *n*

flimflam ('flɪmˌflæm) *Informal.* ◆ *n* **1a** nonsense; foolishness. **1b** (*as modifier*): *flimflam arguments.* **2** a deception; swindle. ◆ *vb* **-flams, -flamming, -flammed. 3** (*tr*) to deceive; trick; swindle; cheat. [C16: probably of Scandinavian origin; compare Old Norse *flīm* mockery, Norwegian *flire* to giggle] ▸ '**flimˌflammer** *n*

flimsy ('flɪmzɪ) *adj* **-sier, -siest. 1** not strong or substantial; fragile: *a flimsy building.* **2** light and thin: *a flimsy dress.* **3** unconvincing or inadequate; weak: *a flimsy excuse.* ◆ *n* **4** thin paper used for making carbon copies of a letter, etc. **5** a copy made on such paper. **6** a slang word for **banknote.** [C17: of uncertain origin] ▸ '**flimsily** *adv* ▸ '**flimsiness** *n*

flinch[1] (flɪntʃ) *vb* (*intr*) **1** to draw back suddenly, as from pain, shock, etc.; wince: *he flinched as the cold water struck him.* **2** (often foll. by *from*) to avoid contact (with); shy away: *he never flinched from his duty.* ◆ *n* **3** the act or an instance of drawing back. **4** a card game in which players build sequences. [C16: from Old French *flenchir;* related to Middle High German *lenken* to bend, direct] ▸ '**flincher** *n* ▸ '**flinchingly** *adv*

flinch[2] (flɪntʃ) *vb* a variant of **flense.**

flinders ('flɪndəz) *pl n Rare.* small fragments or splinters (esp. in the phrase **fly into flinders**). [C15: probably of Scandinavian origin; compare Norwegian *flindra* thin piece of stone]

Flinders bar ('flɪndəz) *n Navigation.* a bar of soft iron mounted on a binnacle to compensate for local magnetism causing error to the compass. [C19: named after Matthew *Flinders* (died 1814), English navigator]

Flinders Island *n* an island off the coast of NE Tasmania: the largest of the Furneaux Islands. Pop.: 1100 (latest est.). Area: 2077 sq. km (802 sq. miles).

Flinders Range *n* a mountain range in E South Australia, between Lake Torrens and Lake Frome. Highest peak: 1188 m (3898 ft.).

fling (flɪŋ) *vb* **flings, flinging, flung** (flʌŋ). (*mainly tr*) **1** to throw, esp. with force or abandon; hurl or toss. **2** to put or send without warning or preparation: *to fling someone into jail.* **3** (*also intr*) to move (oneself or a part of the body) with abandon or speed: *he flung himself into a chair.* **4** (usually foll. by *into*) to apply (oneself) diligently and with vigour (to). **5** to cast aside; disregard: *she flung away her scruples.* **6** to utter violently or offensively. **7** *Poetic.* to give out; emit. ◆ *n* **8** the act or an instance of flinging; toss; throw. **9** a period or occasion of unrestrained, impulsive, or extravagant behaviour: *to have a fling.* **10** any of various vigorous Scottish reels full of leaps and turns, such as the Highland fling. **11** a trial; try: *to have a fling at something different.* [C13: of Scandinavian origin; related to Old Norse *flengja* to flog, Swedish *flänga,* Danish *flänge*] ▸ '**flinger** *n*

flint (flɪnt) *n* **1** an impure opaque microcrystalline greyish-black form of quartz that occurs in chalk. It produces sparks when struck with steel and is used in the manufacture of pottery, flint glass, and road-construction materials. Formula: SiO_2. **2** any piece of flint, esp. one used as a primitive tool or for striking fire. **3** a small cylindrical piece of an iron alloy, used in cigarette lighters. **4** Also called: **flint glass, white flint.** colourless glass other than plate glass. **5** See **optical flint.** ◆ *vb* **6** (*tr*) to fit or provide with a flint. [Old English; related to Old High German *flins,* Old Swedish *flinta* splinter of stone, Latin *splendēre* to shine]

Flint (flɪnt) *n* **1** a town in NE Wales, in Flintshire, on the Dee estuary. Pop.: 11 737 (1991). **2** a city in SE Michigan: closure of the car production plants led to a high level of unemployment. Pop.: 134 881 (1996 est.).

flint glass *n* another name for **optical flint, flint** (sense 4).

flintlock ('flɪnt,lɒk) *n* **1** an obsolete gunlock in which the charge is ignited by a spark produced by a flint in the hammer. **2** a firearm having such a lock.

Flintshire ('flɪntʃɪə, -ʃə) *n* a county of NE Wales, on the Irish Sea and the Dee estuary: became part of Clwyd in 1974, reinstated with reduced borders in 1996: includes the industrialized Deeside region in the E and the Clwydian Hills in the SW. Administrative centre: Mold. Pop.: 145 000 (1996 est.). Area: 437 sq. km (169 sq. miles).

flinty ('flɪntɪ) *adj* **flintier, flintiest. 1** of, relating to, or resembling flint. **2** hard or cruel; obdurate; unyielding. ▸ **'flintily** *adv* ▸ **'flintiness** *n*

flip (flɪp) *vb* **flips, flipping, flipped. 1** to throw (something light or small) carelessly or briskly; toss: *he flipped me an envelope.* **2** to throw or flick (an object such as a coin) so that it turns or spins in the air. **3** to propel by a sudden movement of the finger; flick: *to flip a crumb across the room.* **4** (foll. by *through*) to read or look at (a book, newspaper, etc.) quickly, idly, or incompletely. **5** (*intr*) (of small objects) to move or bounce jerkily. **6** (*intr*) to make a snapping movement or noise with the finger and thumb. **7** (*intr*) *Slang.* to fly into a rage or an emotional outburst (also in the phrases **flip one's lid, flip one's top**). **8** (*intr*) *Slang.* to become ecstatic or very excited: *he flipped over the jazz group.* ◆ *n* **9** a snap or tap, usually with the fingers. **10** a rapid jerk. **11** a somersault, esp. one performed in the air, as in a dive, rather than from a standing position. **12** same as **nog**[1] (sense 1). ◆ *adj* **13** *Informal.* impertinent, flippant, or pert. [C16: probably of imitative origin; see FILLIP]

flip chart *n* a pad, containing large sheets of paper that can be easily turned over, mounted on a stand and used to present reports, data, etc.

flip-flop *n* **1** a backward handspring. **2** Also called: **bistable.** an electronic device or circuit that can assume either of two stable states by the application of a suitable pulse. **3** a complete change of opinion, policy, etc. **4** a repeated flapping or banging noise. **5** Also called (U.S., Canadian, Austral., and N.Z.): **thong.** a rubber-soled sandal attached to the foot by a thong between the big toe and the next toe. ◆ *vb* **-flops, -flopping, -flopped. 6** (*intr*) to move with repeated flaps. ◆ *adv* **7** with repeated flappings: *to go flip-flop.* [C16: reduplication of FLIP]

flippant ('flɪpənt) *adj* **1** marked by inappropriate levity; frivolous or offhand. **2** impertinent; saucy. **3** *Obsolete.* talkative or nimble. [C17: perhaps from FLIP] ▸ **'flippancy** *n* ▸ **'flippantly** *adv*

flipper ('flɪpə) *n* **1** the flat broad limb of seals, whales, penguins, and other aquatic animals, specialized for swimming. **2** (*often pl*) Also called: **fin.** either of a pair of rubber paddle-like devices worn on the feet as an aid in swimming, esp. underwater. **3** *Cricket.* a ball bowled with topspin imparted by the action of the bowler's wrist.

flipping ('flɪpɪŋ) *adj, adv Brit. slang.* (intensifier): *a flipping idiot; it's flipping cold.* [C19: perhaps a euphemism for FUCKING]

flip side *n* **1** another term for **B-side. 2** another, less familiar aspect of a person or thing: *the flip side of John Lennon.*

flirt (flɜːt) *vb* **1** (*intr*) to behave or act amorously without emotional commitment; toy or play with another's affections; dally. **2** (*intr;* usually foll. by *with*) to deal playfully or carelessly (with something dangerous or serious); trifle: *the motorcyclist flirted with death.* **3** (*intr;* usually foll. by *with*) to think casually (about); toy (with): *to flirt with the idea of leaving.* **4** (*intr*) to move jerkily; dart; flit. **5** (*tr*) to subject to a sudden swift motion; flick or toss. ◆ *n* **6** a person who acts flirtatiously. [C16: of uncertain origin] ▸ **'flirter** *n* ▸ **'flirty** *adj* ▸ **'flirtingly** *adv*

flirtation (flɜː'teɪʃən) *n* **1** behaviour intended to arouse sexual feelings or advances without emotional commitment; coquetry. **2** any casual involvement without commitment: *a flirtation with journalism.*

flirtatious (flɜː'teɪʃəs) *adj* **1** given to flirtation. **2** expressive of playful sexual invitation: *a flirtatious glance.* ▸ **flir'tatiously** *adv* ▸ **flir'tatiousness** *n*

flit (flɪt) *vb* **flits, flitting, flitted.** (*intr*) **1** to move along rapidly and lightly; skim or dart. **2** to fly rapidly and lightly; flutter. **3** to pass quickly; fleet: *a memory flitted into his mind.* **4** *Scot. and northern English dialect.* to move house. **5** *Brit. informal.* to depart hurriedly and stealthily in order to avoid obligations. **6** an informal word for **elope.** ◆ *n* **7** the act or an instance of flitting. **8** *Slang, chiefly U.S.* a male homosexual. **9** *Brit. informal.* a hurried and stealthy departure in order to avoid obligations (esp. in the phrase **do a flit**). **10** See **moonlight flit.** [C12: from Old Norse *flytja* to carry] ▸ **'flitter** *n*

flitch (flɪtʃ) *n* **1** a side of pork salted and cured. **2** a steak cut from the side of certain fishes, esp. halibut. **3** a piece of timber cut lengthways from a tree trunk, esp. one that is larger than 4 by 12 inches. ◆ *vb* **4** (*tr*) to cut (a tree trunk) into flitches. [Old English *flicce;* related to Old Norse *flikki,* Middle Low German *vlicke,* Norwegian *flika;* see FLESH]

flite *or* **flyte** (flaɪt; *Scot.* fləɪt) *Scot. and northern English dialect.* ◆ *vb* **1** (*tr*) to scold or rail at. ◆ *n* **2** a dispute or scolding. [Old English *flītan* to wrangle, of Germanic origin; related to Old Frisian *flīt* strife, Old High German *flīz* strife]

flitter ('flɪtə) *vb* a less common word for **flutter.**

flittermouse ('flɪtə,maus) *n, pl* **-mice.** a dialect name for **bat**[2] (the animal). [C16: translation of German *Fledermaus;* see FLITTER, MOUSE]

flivver ('flɪvə) *n* an old, cheap, or battered car. [C20: of unknown origin]

float (fləut) *vb* **1** to rest or cause to rest on the surface of a fluid or in a fluid or space without sinking; be buoyant or cause to exhibit buoyancy: *oil floats on water; to float a ship.* **2** to move or cause to move buoyantly, lightly, or freely across a surface or through air, water, etc.; drift: *fog floated across the road.* **3** to move about aimlessly, esp. in the mind: *thoughts floated before him.* **4** to suspend or be suspended without falling; hang: *lights floated above them.* **5** (*tr*) **5a** to launch or establish (a commercial enterprise, etc.). **5b** to offer for sale (stock or bond issues, etc.) on the stock market. **6** (*tr*) *Finance.* to allow (a currency) to fluctuate against other currencies in accordance with market forces. **7** (*tr*) to flood, inundate, or irrigate (land), either artificially or naturally. **8** (*tr*) to spread, smooth, or level (a surface of plaster, rendering, etc.). ◆ *n* **9** something that floats. **10** *Angling.* an indicator attached to a baited line that sits on the water and moves when a fish bites. **11** a small hand tool with a rectangular blade used for floating plaster, etc. **12** *Chiefly U.S.* any buoyant object, such as a platform or inflated tube, used offshore by swimmers or, when moored alongside a pier, as a dock by vessels. **13** Also called: **paddle.** a blade of a paddle wheel. **14** *Brit.* a buoyant garment or device to aid a person in staying afloat. **15** a hollow watertight structure fitted to the underside of an aircraft to allow it to land on water. **16** another name for **air bladder** (sense 2). **17** an exhibit carried in a parade, esp. a religious parade. **18** a motor vehicle used to carry a tableau or exhibit in a parade, esp. a civic parade. **19** a small delivery vehicle, esp. one powered by batteries: *a milk float.* **20** *Austral. and N.Z.* a vehicle for transporting horses. **21** *Banking, chiefly U.S.* the total value of uncollected cheques and other commercial papers. **22** *Chiefly U.S. and Canadian.* a sum to be applied to minor expenses; petty cash. **23** a sum of money used by shopkeepers to provide change at the start of the day's business, this sum being subtracted from the total at the end of the day when calculating the day's takings. **24** the hollow floating ball of a ballcock. **25** *Engineering.* a hollow cylindrical structure in a carburettor that actuates the fuel valve. **26** *Chiefly U.S. and Canadian.* a carbonated soft drink with a scoop of ice cream in it. **27** (in textiles) a single thread brought to or above the surface of a woven fabric, esp. to form a pattern. **28** *Forestry.* a measure of timber equal to eighteen loads. ◆ See also **floats.** [Old English *flotian;* related to Old Norse *flota,* Old Saxon *flotōn;* see FLEET[2]] ▸ **'floatable** *adj* ▸ **,floata'bility** *n*

floatage ('fləutɪdʒ) *n* a variant spelling of **flotage.**

floatation (fləu'teɪʃən) *n* a variant spelling of **flotation.**

float chamber *n* a chamber in a carburettor in which a floating valve controls the entry and level of petrol.

floatcut file ('fləut,kʌt) *n Engineering.* a file having rows of parallel teeth.

floatel (fləu'tɛl) *n* a variant spelling of **flotel.**

floater ('fləutə) *n* **1** a person or thing that floats. **2** any of a number of dark spots that appear in one's vision as a result of dead cells or fragments in the lens or vitreous humour of the eye. **3** *U.S. and Canadian.* **3a** a person of no fixed political opinion. **3b** a person who votes illegally in more than one district at one election. **3c** a voter who can be bribed. **4** Also called: **floating policy.** *Insurance, U.S. and Canadian.* a policy covering loss or theft of or damage to movable property, such as jewels or furs, regardless of its location. **5** *U.S. informal.* a person who often changes employment, residence, etc.; drifter. **6** *Austral.* a loose gold- or opal-bearing rock. **7** *Austral.* (esp. in Adelaide) a meat pie in a plate of pea soup.

float-feed *adj* (of a fuel system) controlled by a float operating a needle valve.

float glass *n* a type of flat polished transparent glass made by allowing the molten glass to harden as it floats on liquid of higher density.

floating ('fləutɪŋ) *adj* **1** having little or no attachment. **2** (of an organ or part) displaced from the normal position or abnormally movable: *a floating kidney.* **3** not definitely attached to one place or policy; uncommitted or unfixed: *the floating vote.* **4** *Finance.* **4a** (of capital) not allocated or invested; available for current use. **4b** (of debt) short-term and unfunded, usually raised by a government or company to meet current expenses. **4c** (of a currency) free to fluctuate against other currencies in accordance with market forces. **5** *Machinery.* operating smoothly through being free from external constraints. **6** (of an electronic circuit or device) not connected to a source of voltage. ▸ **'floatingly** *adv*

floating assets *pl n* another term for **current assets.**

floating charge *n Chiefly Brit.* an unsecured charge on the assets of an enterprise that allows such assets to be used commercially until the enterprise ceases to operate or the creditor intervenes to demand collateral.

floating debt *n* short-term government borrowing, esp. by the issue of three-month Treasury bills.

floating dock *n* a large boxlike structure that can be submerged to allow a vessel to enter it and then floated to raise the vessel out of the water for maintenance or repair. Also called: **floating dry dock.**

floating heart *n* any perennial aquatic freshwater plant of the genus *Nymphoides,* esp. *N. lacunosum,* having floating heart-shaped leaves: family *Menyanthaceae.*

floating island *n* a floating mass of soil held together by vegetation.

floating-point representation *n Computing.* the representation of numbers by two sets of digits (a, b), the set a indicating the significant digits, the set b giving the position of the radix point. The number is the product ar^b, where r is the base of the number system used. Compare **fixed-point representation.**

floating policy *n* **1** (in marine insurance) a policy covering loss of or damage to specified goods irrespective of the ship in which they are consigned. **2** another term for **floater** (sense 4).

floating-rate note *n* a eurobond, often issued as a negotiable bearer bond, that has a floating rate of interest.

floating rib *n* any rib of the lower two pairs of ribs in man, which are not attached to the breastbone.

floating voter *n* a person who does not vote consistently for any single political party.

floats (fləuts) *pl n Theatre.* another word for **footlights.**

floaty ('fləutɪ) *adj* **floatier, floatiest. 1** filmy and light: *floaty material.* **2** capable of floating; buoyant. **3** (of a vessel) riding high in the water; of shallow draught.

floc (flɒk) *n* another word for **floccule.** [C20: from Latin *floccus* a tuft of wool, FLOCK[2]]

floccose ('flɒkəus) *adj* consisting of or covered with woolly tufts or hairs: *floccose growths of bacteria.* [C18: from Latin *floccōsus* full of flocks of wool]

flocculant ('flɒkjulənt) *n* a substance added to a suspension to enhance aggregation of the suspended particles.

flocculate ('flɒkjʊˌleɪt) *vb* to form or be formed into an aggregated flocculent mass. ▸ **ˌfloccuˈlation** *n*

floccule ('flɒkjuːl), **flocculus, flock,** *or* **floc** *n* **1** a small aggregate of flocculent material. **2** something resembling a tuft of wool. [C19: from Late Latin *flocculus* a little tuft; see FLOCK[2]]

flocculent ('flɒkjʊlənt) *adj* **1** like wool; fleecy. **2** *Chem.* aggregated in woolly cloudlike masses: *a flocculent precipitate.* **3** *Biology.* covered with tufts or flakes of a waxy or wool-like substance. ▸ **'flocculence** *or* **'flocculency** *n* ▸ **'flocculently** *adv*

flocculus ('flɒkjʊləs) *n, pl* **-li** (-ˌlaɪ). **1** a marking on the sun's surface or in its atmosphere, as seen on a spectroheliogram. It consists of calcium when lighter than the surroundings and of hydrogen when darker. **2** *Anatomy.* a tiny ovoid prominence on each side of the cerebellum. **3** another word for **floccule.**

floccus ('flɒkəs) *n, pl* **flocci** ('flɒksaɪ). **1** a downy or woolly covering, as on the young of certain birds. **2** a small woolly tuft of hair. ◆ *adj* **3** (of a cloud) having the appearance of woolly tufts at odd intervals in its structure. [C19: from Latin: tuft of hair or wool, FLOCK[2]]

flock[1] (flɒk) *n* (*sometimes functioning as pl*) **1** a group of animals of one kind, esp. sheep or birds. **2** a large number of people; crowd. **3** a body of Christians regarded as the pastoral charge of a priest, a bishop, the pope, etc. **4** *Rare.* a band of people; group. ◆ *vb* (*intr*) **5** to gather together or move in a flock. **6** to go in large numbers: *people flocked to the church.* [Old English *flocc;* related to Old Norse *flokkr* crowd, Middle Low German *vlocke*]

flock[2] (flɒk) *n* **1** a tuft, as of wool, hair, cotton, etc. **2a** waste from fabrics such as cotton, wool, or other cloth used for stuffing mattresses, upholstered chairs, etc. **2b** (*as modifier*): *flock mattress.* **3** very small tufts of wool applied to fabrics, wallpaper, etc., to give a raised pattern. **4** another word for **floccule.** ◆ *vb* **5** (*tr*) to fill, cover, or ornament with flock. [C13: from Old French *floc,* from Latin *floccus;* probably related to Old High German *floccho* down, Norwegian *flugsa* snowflake] ▸ **'flocky** *adj*

flock paper *n* a type of wallpaper with a raised pattern. See also **flock**[2] (sense 3).

Flodden ('flɒdᵊn) *n* a hill in Northumberland where invading Scots were defeated by the English in 1513 and James IV of Scotland was killed. Also called: **Flodden Field.**

floe (fləʊ) *n* See **ice floe.** [C19: probably from Norwegian *flo* slab, layer, from Old Norse; see FLAW[1]]

flog (flɒg) *vb* **flogs, flogging, flogged.** **1** (*tr*) to beat harshly, esp. with a whip, strap, etc. **2** *Brit. slang.* to sell. **3** (*intr*) (of a sail) to flap noisily in the wind. **4** (*intr*) to make progress by painful work. **5** *N.Z.* to steal. **6 flog** *or* **beat a dead horse.** *Chiefly Brit.* **6a** to harp on some long discarded subject. **6b** to pursue the solution of a problem long realized to be insoluble. **7 flog to death.** to persuade a person so persistently of the value of (an idea or venture) that he loses interest in it. [C17: probably from Latin *flagellāre;* see FLAGELLANT] ▸ **'flogger** *n* ▸ **'flogging** *n*

flokati (flə'kɑːtɪ) *n* a Greek hand-woven shaggy woollen rug. [C20: from Modern Greek *phlokatē* a peasant's blanket]

flong (flɒŋ) *n* **1** *Printing.* a material, usually pulped paper or cardboard, used for making moulds in stereotyping. **2** *Journalism, slang.* material that is not urgently topical. [C20: variant of FLAN]

flood (flʌd) *n* **1a** the inundation of land that is normally dry through the overflowing of a body of water, esp. a river. **1b** the state of a river that is at an abnormally high level (esp. in the phrase **in flood**). Related adj: **diluvial.** **2** a great outpouring or flow: *a flood of words.* **3a** the rising of the tide from low to high water. **3b** (*as modifier*): *the flood tide.* Compare **ebb** (sense 3). **4** *Theatre.* short for **floodlight.** **5** *Archaic.* a large body of water, as the sea or a river. ◆ *vb* **6** (of water) to inundate or submerge (land) or (of land) to be inundated or submerged. **7** to fill or be filled to overflowing, as with a flood: *the children's home was flooded with gifts.* **8** (*intr*) to flow; surge: *relief flooded through him.* **9** to supply an excessive quantity of petrol to (a carburettor or petrol engine) or (of a carburettor, etc.) to be supplied with such an excess. **10** (*intr*) to rise to a flood; overflow. **11** (*intr*) **11a** to bleed profusely from the uterus, as following childbirth. **11b** to have an abnormally heavy flow of blood during a menstrual period. [Old English *flōd;* related to Old Norse *flōth,* Gothic *flōdus,* Old High German *fluot* flood, Greek *plōtos* navigable; see FLOW, FLOAT] ▸ **'floodable** *adj* ▸ **'flooder** *n* ▸ **'floodless** *adj*

Flood[1] (flʌd) *n Old Testament.* **the.** the flood extending over all the earth from which Noah and his family and livestock were saved in the ark. (Genesis 7–8); the Deluge.

Flood[2] (flʌd) *n* **Henry.** 1732–91, Anglo-Irish politician: leader of the parliamentary opposition to English rule.

flood basalt *n* a very extensive lava flow that has issued from a fissure, often to be found as part of a series of such flows one on top of another, forming a plateau. See **fissure eruption.**

flood control *n* the technique or practice of preventing or controlling floods with dams, artificial channels, etc.

flooded gum *n* any of various eucalyptus trees of Australia, esp. *Eucalyptus saligna* (the Sydney blue gum), that grow in damp soil.

floodgate ('flʌdˌgeɪt) *n* **1** Also called: **head gate, water gate.** a gate in a sluice that is used to control the flow of water. See also **sluicegate.** **2** (*often pl*) a control or barrier against an outpouring or flow: *to open the floodgates to immigration.*

flooding ('flʌdɪŋ) *n* **1** the submerging of land under water, esp. due to heavy rain, a lake or river overflowing, etc. **2** *Psychol.* a method of eliminating anxiety in a given situation, by exposing a person to the situation until the anxiety subsides.

floodlight ('flʌdˌlaɪt) *n* **1** a broad intense beam of artificial light, esp. as used in the theatre or to illuminate the exterior of buildings. **2** the lamp or source producing such light. ◆ *vb* **-lights, -lighting, -lit.** **3** (*tr*) to illuminate by or as if by a floodlight.

flood plain *n* the flat area bordering a river, composed of sediment deposited during flooding.

floor (flɔː) *n* **1** Also called: **flooring.** the inner lower surface of a room. **2** a storey of a building: *the second floor.* **3** a flat bottom surface in or on any structure: *the floor of a lift; a dance floor.* **4** the bottom surface of a tunnel, cave, river, sea, etc. **5** *Mining.* an underlying stratum. **6** *Nautical.* the bottom, or the lowermost framing members at the bottom, of a vessel. **7** that part of a legislative hall in which debate and other business is conducted. **8** the right to speak in a legislative or deliberative body (esp. in the phrases **get, have,** or **be given the floor**). **9** the room in a stock exchange where trading takes place. **10** the earth; ground. **11** a minimum price charged or paid: *a wage floor.* **12 take the floor.** to begin dancing on a dance floor. ◆ *vb* **13** to cover with or construct a floor. **14** (*tr*) to knock to the floor or ground. **15** (*tr*) *Informal.* to disconcert, confound, or defeat: *to be floored by a problem.* [Old English *flōr;* related to Old Norse *flōrr,* Middle Low German *vlōr* floor, Latin *plānus* level, Greek *planan* to cause to wander]

floorage ('flɔːrɪdʒ) *n* an area of floor; floor space.

floorboard ('flɔːˌbɔːd) *n* one of the boards forming a floor.

flooring ('flɔːrɪŋ) *n* **1** the material used in making a floor, esp. the surface material. **2** another word for **floor** (sense 1).

flooring saw *n* a type of saw curved at the end for cutting through floorboards.

floor leader *n U.S. government.* a member of a legislative body who organizes his party's activities.

floor manager *n* **1** the stage manager employed in the production of a television programme. **2** a person in overall charge of one floor of a large shop or department store.

floor plan *n* a drawing to scale of the arrangement of rooms on one floor of a building. Compare **elevation** (sense 5).

floor show *n* a series of entertainments, such as singing, dancing, and comedy acts, performed in a nightclub.

floor trading *n* trading by personal contact on the floor of a market or exchange. Compare **screen trading.**

floorwalker ('flɔːˌwɔːkə) *n* the U.S. name for **shopwalker.**

floozy, floozie, *or* **floosie** ('fluːzɪ) *n, pl* **-zies** *or* **-sies.** *Slang.* a disreputable woman. [C20: of unknown origin]

flop (flɒp) *vb* **flops, flopping, flopped.** **1** (*intr*) to bend, fall, or collapse loosely or carelessly: *his head flopped backwards.* **2** (when *intr,* often foll. by *into, onto,* etc.) to fall, cause to fall, or move with a sudden noise: *the books flopped onto the floor.* **3** (*intr*) *Informal.* to fail; be unsuccessful: *the scheme flopped.* **4** (*intr*) to fall flat onto the surface of water, hitting it with the front of the body. **5** (*intr;* often foll. by *out*) *Slang.* to go to sleep. ◆ *n* **6** the act of flopping. **7** *Informal.* a complete failure. **8** *U.S. and Canadian slang.* a place to sleep. **9** *Athletics.* See **Fosbury flop.** [C17: variant of FLAP]

flophouse ('flɒpˌhaʊs) *n Slang.* the U.S. and Canadian word for **dosshouse.**

floppy ('flɒpɪ) *adj* **-pier, -piest.** **1** limp or hanging loosely: *a dog with floppy ears.* ◆ *n* **2** short for **floppy disk.** ▸ **'floppily** *adv* ▸ **'floppiness** *n*

floppy disk *n* a flexible magnetic disk that stores information and can be used to store data for use in a microprocessor. Also called: **diskette, flexible disk.**

flops *or* **FLOPS** *abbrev. for* floating-point operations per second: used as a measure of computer processing power (in combination with a prefix): *megaflops; gigaflops.*

flor. *abbrev. for* floruit.

flora ('flɔːrə) *n, pl* **-ras** *or* **-rae** (-riː). **1** all the plant life of a given place or time. **2** a descriptive list of such plants, often including a key for identification. **3** short for **intestinal flora.** [C18: from New Latin, from Latin *Flōra* goddess of flowers, from *flōs* FLOWER]

Flora ('flɔːrə) *n* the Roman goddess of flowers. [C16: from Latin, from *flōs* flower]

floral ('flɔːrəl) *adj* **1** decorated with or consisting of flowers or patterns of flowers. **2** of, relating to, or associated with flowers: *floral leaves.* ▸ **'florally** *adv*

floral envelope *n* the part of a flower that surrounds the stamens and pistil: the calyx and corolla (considered together) or the perianth.

Floréal *French.* (flɔreal) *n* the month of flowers: the eighth month of the French revolutionary calendar, extending from April 21 to May 20. [C19: ultimately from Latin *flōreus* of flowers, from *flōs* a flower]

floreat *Latin.* ('flɒrɪæt) *vb* (*intr*), *pl* ***floreant.*** may (a person, institution, etc.) flourish: *floreat Oxonia!*

floreated ('flɔːrɪˌeɪtɪd) *adj* a variant spelling of **floriated.**

Florence ('flɒrəns) *n* a city in central Italy, on the River Arno in Tuscany: became an independent republic in the 14th century; under Austrian and other rule intermittently from 1737 to 1859; capital of Italy 1865–70. It was the major cultural and artistic centre of the Renaissance and is still one of the world's chief art centres. Pop.: 383 594 (1996 est.). Ancient name: **Florentia** (flɒ'rɛntsɪə, -rɛntɪə). Italian name: **Firenze.**

Florence fennel *n* another name for **finocchio.**

Florence flask *n* a round flat-bottomed glass flask with a long neck, used in chemical experiments.

Florentine ('flɒrənˌtaɪn) *adj* **1** of or relating to Florence. **2** (*usually postpositive*) (of food) served or prepared with spinach. ◆ *n* **3** a native or inhabitant of Florence. **4** a biscuit containing nuts and dried fruit and coated with chocolate. **5** a type of domestic fancy pigeon somewhat resembling the Modena.

Flores ('flɔːres) *n* **1** an island in Indonesia, one of the Lesser Sunda Islands, between the Flores Sea and the Savu Sea: mountainous, with active volcanoes and unexplored forests. Chief town: Ende. Area: 17 150 sq. km (6622 sq. miles). **2** (*also Portuguese* 'florɪʃ). an island in the Atlantic, the westernmost of the Azores. Chief town: Santa Cruz. Area: 142 sq. km (55 sq. miles).

florescence (flɔː'rɛsəns) *n* the process, state, or period of flowering. [C18: from New Latin *flōrēscentia,* from Latin *flōrēscere* to come into flower]

Flores Sea *n* a part of the Pacific Ocean in Indonesia between Celebes and the Lesser Sunda Islands.

floret ('flɔːrɪt) *n* a small flower, esp. one of many making up the head of a composite flower. [C17: from Old French *florete* a little flower, from *flor* FLOWER]

Florey ('flɔːrɪ) *n* **Howard Walter,** Baron Florey. 1898–1968, British pathologist: shared the Nobel prize for physiology or medicine (1945) with E. B. Chain and Alexander Fleming for their work on penicillin.

Florianópolis (*Portuguese* floriə'nɔpulis) *n* a port in S Brazil, capital of Santa Caterina state, on the W coast of Santa Caterina Island. Pop.: 191 664 (1991).

floriated *or* **floreated** ('flɔːrɪˌeɪtɪd) *adj Architect.* having ornamentation based on flowers and leaves. [C19: from Latin *flōs* FLOWER]

floribunda (ˌflɔːrɪ'bʌndə) *n* any of several varieties of cultivated hybrid roses whose flowers grow in large sprays. [C19: from New Latin, feminine of *flōribundus* flowering freely]

floriculture ('flɔːrɪˌkʌltʃə) *n* the cultivation of flowering plants. ▸ ˌ**flori'cultural** *adj* ▸ ˌ**flori'culturist** *n*

florid ('flɒrɪd) *adj* **1** having a red or flushed complexion. **2** excessively ornate; flowery: *florid architecture.* **3** an archaic word for **flowery.** [C17: from Latin *flōridus* blooming] ▸ **flo'ridity** *or* **'floridness** *n* ▸ **'floridly** *adv*

Florida ('flɒrɪdə) *n* **1** a state of the southeastern U.S., between the Atlantic and the Gulf of Mexico: consists mostly of a low-lying peninsula ending in the **Florida Keys,** a chain of small islands off the coast of S Florida, extending southwest for over 160 km (100 miles). Capital: Tallahassee. Pop.: 14 653 945 (1997 est.). Area: 143 900 sq. km (55 560 sq. miles). Abbrevs.: **Fla.** or (with zip code) **FL** **2 Straits of.** a sea passage between the Florida Keys and Cuba, linking the Atlantic with the Gulf of Mexico. ▸ **Flo'ridian** *adj*

floriferous (flɔː'rɪfərəs) *adj* bearing or capable of bearing many flowers.

florigen ('flɒrɪdʒən) *n* the hypothetical plant hormone that induces flowering, thought to be synthesized in the leaves as a photoperiodic response and transmitted to the flower buds. [C20: from Latin *flōr-, flōs* FLOWER + -GEN]

florilegium (ˌflɔːrɪ'liːdʒɪəm) *n, pl* **-gia** (-dʒɪə). **1** (formerly) a lavishly illustrated book on flowers. **2** *Rare.* an anthology. [C17: Modern Latin, from Latin *florilegus* flower-collecting, from *flōs* flower + *legere* to collect]

florin ('flɒrɪn) *n* **1** a former British coin, originally silver and later cupronickel, equivalent to ten (new) pence. **2** (formerly) another name for **guilder** (sense 1). **3** any of various gold coins of Florence, Britain, or Austria. [C14: from French, from Old Italian *fiorino* Florentine coin, from *fiore* flower, from Latin *flōs*]

Florio ('flɔːrɪˌəʊ) *n* **John.** ?1553–?1625, English lexicographer, noted for his translation of Montaigne's *Essays* (1603).

florist ('flɒrɪst) *n* a person who grows or deals in flowers.

floristic (flɒ'rɪstɪk) *adj* of or relating to flowers or a flora. ▸ **flo'ristically** *adv*

floristics (flɒ'rɪstɪks) *n* (*functioning as sing*) the branch of botany concerned with the types, numbers, and distribution of plant species in a particular area.

-florous *adj combining form.* indicating number or type of flowers: *tubuliflorous.*

floruit *Latin.* ('flɒruːɪt) *vb* (he or she) flourished: used to indicate the period when a historical figure, whose birth and death dates are unknown, was most active. Abbrevs.: **fl., flor.**

florula ('flɒrjʊlə) *or* **florule** ('flɒrjuːl) *n, pl* **-ulae** (-juliː) *or* **ules. 1** the flora of a small single environment. **2** a fossil flower found in a single stratum or in several thin adjacent strata. [C19: FLORA + -ULE]

flory ('flɔːrɪ) *or* **fleury** ('flʊərɪ, 'flɜːrɪ) *adj* (*usually postpositive*) *Heraldry.* containing a fleur-de-lys. [C15: from Old French *floré,* from *flor* FLOWER]

flos ferri ('flɒs 'fɛrɪ) *n* a variety of aragonite that is deposited from hot springs in the form of a white branching mass. [C18: from New Latin, literally: flower of iron]

floss (flɒs) *n* **1** the mass of fine silky fibres obtained from cotton and similar plants. **2** any similar fine silky material, such as the hairlike styles and stigmas of maize or the fibres prepared from silkworm cocoons. **3** untwisted silk thread used in embroidery, etc. **4** See **dental floss.** ◆ *vb* **5** (*tr*) to clean (between one's teeth) with dental floss. [C18: perhaps from Old French *flosche* down]

flossy ('flɒsɪ) *adj* **flossier, flossiest. 1** consisting of or resembling floss. **2** *U.S. and Canadian slang.* (esp. of dress) showy.

flotage *or* **floatage** ('fləʊtɪdʒ) *n* **1** the act or state of floating; flotation. **2** buoyancy; power or ability to float. **3** objects or material that float on the surface of the water; flotsam.

flotation *or* **floatation** (fləʊ'teɪʃən) *n* **1a** the launching or financing of a commercial enterprise by bond or share issues. **1b** the raising of a loan or new capital by bond or share issues. **2** power or ability to float; buoyancy. **3** Also called: **froth flotation.** a process to concentrate the valuable ore in low-grade ores. The ore is ground to a powder, mixed with water containing surface-active chemicals, and vigorously aerated. The bubbles formed trap the required ore fragments and carry them to the surface froth, which is then skimmed off.

flotation bags *pl n* bags inflated to keep a spacecraft or helicopter afloat and upright when it lands in the sea.

flotation tank *or* **chamber** *n* an enclosed ventilated tank filled with a saline solution at body temperature, in which a person floats in darkness in order to relax or meditate.

flote grass (fləʊt) *n* an aquatic perennial grass, *Glyceria fluitans,* whose metre-long stems and pale green leaves are often seen floating in still or sluggish water. The related **sweet grass** (*G. plicata*) has broader, darker leaves and owes its name to the fact that cattle like to eat it. [C16: *flote* obsolete spelling of FLOAT]

flotel *or* **floatel** (fləʊ'tel) *n* (in the oil industry) an oil rig or boat used as accommodation for workers in off-shore oil fields. [C20: from *float* + *hotel*]

flotilla (flə'tɪlə) *n* a small fleet or a fleet of small vessels. [C18: from Spanish *flota* fleet, from French *flotte,* ultimately from Old Norse *floti*]

Flotow (*German* 'floːto) *n* **Friedrich von** ('friːdrɪç fɔn). 1812–83, German composer of operas, esp. *Martha* (1847).

flotsam ('flɒtsəm) *n* **1** wreckage from a ship found floating. Compare **jetsam** (sense 1), **lagan. 2** useless or discarded objects; odds and ends (esp. in the phrase **flotsam and jetsam**). **3** vagrants. [C16: from Anglo-French *floteson,* from *floter* to FLOAT]

flounce[1] (flaʊns) *vb* **1** (*intr;* often foll. by *about, away, out,* etc.) to move or go with emphatic or impatient movements. ◆ *n* **2** the act of flouncing. [C16: of Scandinavian origin; compare Norwegian *flunsa* to hurry, Swedish *flunsa* to splash]

flounce[2] (flaʊns) *n* an ornamental gathered ruffle sewn to a garment by its top edge. [C18: from Old French *fronce* wrinkle, from *froncir* to wrinkle, of Germanic origin]

flouncing ('flaʊnsɪŋ) *n* material, such as lace or embroidered fabric, used for making flounces.

flounder[1] ('flaʊndə) *vb* (*intr*) **1** to struggle; to move with difficulty, as in mud. **2** to behave awkwardly; make mistakes. ◆ *n* **3** the act of floundering. [C16: probably a blend of FOUNDER[2] + BLUNDER; perhaps influenced by FLOUNDER[2]]

USAGE *Flounder* is sometimes wrongly used where *founder* is meant: *the project foundered* (not *floundered*) *because of a lack of funds.*

flounder[2] ('flaʊndə) *n, pl* **-der** *or* **-ders. 1** Also called: **fluke.** a European flatfish, *Platichthys flesus,* having a greyish-brown body covered with prickly scales: family *Pleuronectidae:* an important food fish. **2** *U.S. and Canadian.* any flatfish of the families *Bothidae* (turbot, etc.) and *Pleuronectidae* (plaice, halibut, sand dab, etc.). [C14: probably of Scandinavian origin; compare Old Norse *flythra,* Norwegian *flundra*]

flour ('flaʊə) *n* **1** a powder, which may be either fine or coarse, prepared by sifting and grinding the meal of a grass, esp. wheat. **2** any finely powdered substance. ◆ *vb* **3** (*tr*) to make (grain) into flour. **4** (*tr*) to dredge or sprinkle (food or cooking utensils) with flour. **5** (of mercury) to break into fine particles on the surface of a metal rather than amalgamating, or to produce such an effect on (a metal). The effect is caused by impurities, esp. sulphur. [C13 *flur* finer portion of meal, FLOWER] ▸ **'floury** *adj*

flourish ('flʌrɪʃ) *vb* **1** (*intr*) to thrive; prosper. **2** (*intr*) to be at the peak of condition. **3** (*intr*) to be healthy: *plants flourish in the light.* **4** to wave or cause to wave in the air with sweeping strokes. **5** to display or make a display. **6** to play (a fanfare, etc.) on a musical instrument. **7** (*intr*) to embellish writing, characters, etc., with ornamental strokes. **8** to add decorations or embellishments to (speech or writing). **9** (*intr*) an obsolete word for **blossom.** ◆ *n* **10** the act of waving or brandishing. **11** a showy gesture: *he entered with a flourish.* **12** an ornamental embellishment in writing. **13** a display of ornamental language or speech. **14** a grandiose passage of music. **15** an ostentatious display or parade. **16** *Obsolete.* **16a** the state of flourishing. **16b** the state of flowering. [C13: from Old French *florir,* ultimately from Latin *flōrēre* to flower, from *flōs* a flower] ▸ **'flourisher** *n*

flour mite *n* any of several mites that infest flour and other stored organic materials and may be a serious pest; some may cause itching in persons handling infected material.

flour moth *n* a pyralid moth, *Ephestia Kuehniella,* the larvae of which are an important pest of flour mills and granaries.

flout (flaʊt) *vb* (when *intr,* usually foll. by *at*) to show contempt (for); scoff or jeer (at). [C16: perhaps from Middle English *flouten* to play the flute, from Old French *flauter;* compare Dutch *fluiten;* see FLUTE] ▸ **'flouter** *n* ▸ **'floutingly** *adv*

USAGE See at **flaunt.**

flow (fləʊ) *vb* (*mainly intr*) **1** (of liquids) to move or be conveyed as in a stream. **2** (of blood) to circulate around the body. **3** to move or progress freely as if in a stream: *the crowd flowed into the building.* **4** to proceed or be produced continuously and effortlessly: *ideas flowed from her pen.* **5** to show or be marked by smooth or easy movement. **6** to hang freely or loosely: *her hair flowed down her back.* **7** to be present in abundance: *wine flows at their parties.* **8** an informal word for **menstruate. 9** (of tide water) to advance or rise. Compare **ebb** (sense 1). **10** (*tr*) to cover or swamp with liquid; flood. **11** (of rocks such as slate) to yield to pressure without breaking so that the structure and arrangement of the constituent minerals are altered. ◆ *n* **12** the act, rate, or manner of flowing: *a fast flow.* **13** a continuous stream or discharge. **14** continuous progression. **15** the advancing of the tide. **16** a stream of molten or solidified lava. **17** the amount of liquid that flows in a given time. **18** an informal word for **menstruation. 19** *Scot.* **19a** a marsh or swamp. **19b** an inlet or basin of the sea. **19c** (cap. when part of a name): *Scapa Flow.* **20 flow of spirits.** natural happiness. [Old English *flōwan;* related to Old Norse *flōa,* Middle Low German *vlōien,* Greek *plein* to float, Sanskrit *plavate* he swims]

flowage ('fləʊɪdʒ) *n* **1** the act of flowing or overflowing or the state of having overflowed. **2** the liquid that flows or overflows. **3** a gradual deformation or motion of certain solids, such as asphalt, which flow without fracture.

flow chart *or* **sheet** *n* a diagrammatic representation of the sequence of operations or equipment in an industrial process, computer program, etc.

Flow Country *n* an area of moorland and peat bogs in northern Scotland known for its wildlife, now partly afforested.

flower ('flaʊə) *n* **1a** a bloom or blossom on a plant. **1b** a plant that bears blooms or blossoms. **2** the reproductive structure of angiosperm plants, consisting of stamens and carpels surrounded by petals and sepals all borne on the receptacle. In some plants it is conspicuous and brightly coloured and attracts insects for pollination. Related adj: **floral.** Related prefix: **antho-. 3** any similar reproductive structure in other plants. **4** the prime; peak: *in the flower of his youth.* **5** the choice or finest product, part, or representative: *the flower of the young* *men.* **6** a decoration or embellishment. **7** *Printing.* a type ornament, used with others in borders, chapter headings, etc. **8** Also called: **fleuron.** an embellishment or ornamental symbol depicting a flower. **9** (*pl*) fine powder, usually produced by sublimation: *flowers of sulphur.* ◆ *vb* **10** (*intr*) to produce flowers; bloom. **11** (*intr*) to reach full growth or maturity. **12** (*tr*) to deck or decorate with flowers or floral designs. [C13: from Old French *flor,* from Latin *flōs;* see BLOW[3]] ▸ **'flower-ˌlike** *adj*

flowerage ('flaʊərɪdʒ) *n* **1** a mass of flowers. **2** *Now rare.* the process or act of flowering.

flowerbed ('flaʊəˌbɛd) *n* a plot of ground in which flowers are grown in a garden, park, etc.

flower bug *n* any of a number of bugs of the family *Cimicidae,* related to the debris bugs but frequenting flowers and feeding on the small insects found there.

flower-de-luce ('flaʊədə'lu:s) *n, pl* **flowers-de-luce.** an archaic name for the **iris** (sense 2) and **lily** (sense 1). [C16: anglicized variant of French *fleur de lis*]

flowered ('flaʊəd) *adj* **1** having or abounding in flowers. **2** decorated with flowers or a floral design.

flowerer ('flaʊərə) *n* a plant that flowers at a specified time or in a specified way: *a late flowerer.*

floweret ('flaʊərɪt) *n* another name for **floret.**

flower girl *n* **1** a girl or woman who sells flowers in the street. **2** *U.S. and Scot.* a young girl who carries flowers in a procession, esp. at weddings.

flower head *n* an inflorescence in which stalkless florets are crowded together at the tip of the stem.

flowering ('flaʊərɪŋ) *adj* (of certain species of plants) capable of producing conspicuous flowers: *a flowering ash.*

flowering currant *n* an ornamental shrub, *Ribes sanguineum,* growing to 2 to 3 metres (6 to 9ft.) in height, with red, crimson, yellow, or white flowers: family *Saxifragaceae.*

flowering maple *n* any tropical shrub of the malvaceous genus *Abutilon,* esp. *A. hybridum,* having lobed leaves like those of the maple and brightly coloured flowers.

flowerless ('flaʊəlɪs) *adj* designating any plant that does not produce seeds. See **cryptogam.**

flower-of-an-hour *n* a malvaceous Old World herbaceous plant, *Hibiscus trionum,* having pale yellow flowers with a bladder-like calyx. Also called: **bladder ketmia.**

flower-pecker *n* any small songbird of the family *Dicaeidae,* of SE Asia and Australasia, typically feeding on nectar, berries, and insects.

flowerpot ('flaʊəˌpɒt) *n* a pot in which plants are grown.

flower power *n Informal.* a youth cult of the late 1960s advocating peace and love, using the flower as a symbol; associated with drug-taking. Its adherents were known as **flower children** or **flower people.**

flowers of sulphur *pl n* minute crystals of sulphur obtained by condensing sulphur vapour on a cold surface.

flowery ('flaʊərɪ) *adj* **1** abounding in flowers. **2** decorated with flowers or floral patterns. **3** like or suggestive of flowers: *a flowery scent.* **4** (of language or style) elaborate; ornate. ▸ **'floweriness** *n*

flowmeter ('fləʊˌmi:tə) *n* an instrument that measures the rate of flow of a liquid or gas within a pipe or tube.

flown[1] (fləʊn) *vb* the past participle of **fly**[1].

flown[2] (fləʊn) *adj* relating to coloured (usually blue) decoration on porcelain that, during firing, has melted into the surrounding glaze giving a halo-like effect. [probably from the obsolete past participle of FLOW]

flow-on *n Austral. and N.Z.* a wage or salary increase granted to one group of workers as a consequence of a similar increase granted to another group.

flow sheet *n* another name for **flow chart.**

fl. oz. *abbrev. for* fluid ounce.

flu (flu:) *n Informal.* **1** (often preceded by *the*) short for **influenza. 2** any of various viral infections, esp. a respiratory or intestinal infection.

fluctuant ('flʌktjʊənt) *adj* inclined to vary or fluctuate; unstable.

fluctuate ('flʌktjʊˌeɪt) *vb* **1** to change or cause to change position constantly; be or make unstable; waver or vary. **2** (*intr*) to rise and fall like a wave; undulate. [C17: from Latin *fluctuāre,* from *fluctus* a wave, from *fluere* to flow]

fluctuation (ˌflʌktjʊ'eɪʃən) *n* **1** constant change; vacillation; instability. **2** undulation. **3** a variation in an animal or plant that is determined by environment rather than heredity.

flue[1] (flu:) *n* **1** a shaft, tube, or pipe, esp. as used in a chimney, to carry off smoke, gas, etc. **2** *Music.* the passage in an organ pipe or flute within which a vibrating air column is set up. See also **flue pipe.** [C16: of unknown origin]

flue[2] (flu:) *n* loose fluffy matter; down. [C16: from Flemish *vluwe,* from Old French *velu* shaggy] ▸ **'fluey** *adj*

flue[3] *or* **flew** (flu:) *n* a type of fishing net. [Middle English, from Middle Dutch *vlūwe*]

flue[4] (flu:) *n* another word for **fluke**[1] (senses 1, 3). ▸ **flued** *adj*

flue-cure *vb* (*tr*) to cure (tobacco) by means of radiant heat from pipes or flues connected to a furnace.

flue gas *n* the smoke in the uptake of a boiler fire: it consists mainly of carbon dioxide, carbon monoxide, and nitrogen.

fluellin *or* **fluellen** (flʊ'ɛlən) *n* **1** either of two weedy scrophulariaceous annuals related to the toadflaxes, **round-leaved fluellin** (*Kickxia spuria*) and **sharp-leaved fluellin** (*K. elatine*). **2** *Obsolete.* any of several speedwells, especially *Veronica officinalis.* [C16: shortened from Welsh *llysiau Llewelyn* Llewelyn's flower]

fluency ('flu:ənsɪ) *n* the quality of being fluent, esp. facility in speech or writing.

fluent ('flu:ənt) *adj* **1** able to speak or write a specified foreign language with facility. **2** spoken or written with facility: *his French is fluent.* **3** easy and graceful in motion or shape. **4** flowing or able to flow freely. [C16: from Latin: flowing, from *fluere* to flow] ▸ **'fluently** *adv*

flue pipe *or* **flue** *n* an organ pipe or tubular instrument of the flute family whose sound is produced by the passage of air across a sharp-edged fissure in the side. This sets in motion a vibrating air column within the pipe or instrument.

flue stop *n* an organ stop controlling a set of flue pipes.

fluff (flʌf) *n* **1** soft light particles, such as the down or nap of cotton or wool. **2** any light downy substance. **3** an object, matter, etc., of little importance; trifle. **4** *Informal.* a mistake, esp. in speaking or reading lines or performing music. **5** *Informal.* a young woman (esp. in the phrase **a bit of fluff**). ◆ *vb* **6** to make or become soft and puffy by shaking or patting; puff up. **7** *Informal.* to make a mistake in performing (an action, dramatic speech, music, etc.). [C18: perhaps from FLUE[2]]

fluffy ('flʌfɪ) *adj* **fluffier, fluffiest. 1** of, resembling, or covered with fluff. **2** soft and light: *fluffy hair.* ▸ **'fluffily** *adv* ▸ **'fluffiness** *n*

flugelhorn ('flu:gəlˌhɔ:n) *n* a type of valved brass instrument consisting of a tube of conical bore with a cup-shaped mouthpiece, used esp. in brass bands. It is a transposing instrument in B flat or C, and has the same range as the cornet in B flat. [German *Flügelhorn,* from *Flügel* wing + *Horn* HORN]

fluid ('flu:ɪd) *n* **1** a substance, such as a liquid or gas, that can flow, has no fixed shape, and offers little resistance to an external stress. ◆ *adj* **2** capable of flowing and easily changing shape. **3** of, concerned with, or using a fluid or fluids. **4** constantly changing or apt to change. **5** smooth in shape or movement; flowing. [C15: from Latin *fluidus,* from *fluere* to flow] ▸ **'fluidal** *adj* ▸ **'fluidness** *n* ▸ **'fluidly** *or* **'fluidally** *adv*

fluid dram *n* another name for **drachm.**

fluid drive *n* a type of coupling for transmitting power from the engine of a motor vehicle to the transmission, using a torque converter. Also called: **fluid coupling, fluid clutch, fluid flywheel.**

fluidextract ('flu:ɪd'ɛkstrækt) *n* an alcoholic solution of a vegetable drug, one millilitre of which has an equivalent activity to one gram of the powdered drug.

fluidics (flu:'ɪdɪks) *n* (*functioning as sing*) the study and use of systems in which the flow of fluids in tubes simulates the flow of electricity in conductors. Such systems are used in place of electronics in certain applications, such as the control of apparatus. ▸ **flu'idic** *adj*

fluidity (flu:'ɪdɪtɪ) *n* **1** the state of being fluid. **2** *Physics.* the reciprocal of viscosity.

fluidize *or* **fluidise** ('flu:ɪˌdaɪz) *vb* (*tr*) to make fluid, esp. to make (solids) fluid by pulverizing them so that they can be transported in a stream of gas as if they were liquids: *fluidized coal.* ▸ **ˌfluidi'zation** *or* **ˌfluidi'sation** *n* ▸ **'fluidˌizer** *or* **'fluidˌiser** *n*

fluidized bed *n Chemical engineering.* a bed of fluidized solids used as a heat exchanger medium.

fluid lubrication *n Engineering.* lubrication in which bearing surfaces are separated by an oil film sustained by the motion of the parts.

fluid mechanics *n* (*functioning as sing*) the study of the mechanical and flow properties of fluids, esp. as they apply to practical engineering. Also called: **hydraulics.** See also **hydrodynamics, hydrostatics, hydrokinetics.**

fluid ounce *n* a unit of capacity equal to the volume of one avoirdupois ounce of distilled water at 62°F: there are twenty fluid ounces in an Imperial pint and sixteen in a U.S. pint.

fluid pressure *n* the pressure exerted by a fluid at any point inside it. The difference of pressure between two levels is determined by the product of the difference of height, the density, and the acceleration of free fall.

fluke[1] (flu:k) *n* **1** Also called: **flue.** a flat bladelike projection at the end of the arm of an anchor. **2** either of the two lobes of the tail of a whale or related animal. **3** Also called: **flue.** the barb or barbed head of a harpoon, arrow, etc. [C16: perhaps a special use of FLUKE[3] (in the sense: a flounder)]

fluke[2] (flu:k) *n* **1** an accidental stroke of luck. **2** any chance happening. ◆ *vb* **3** (*tr*) to gain, make, or hit by a fluke. [C19: of unknown origin]

fluke[3] (flu:k) *n* **1** any parasitic flatworm, such as the blood fluke and liver fluke, of the classes *Monogenea* and *Digenea* (formerly united in a single class *Trematoda*). **2** another name for **flounder**[2] (sense 1). [Old English *flōc;* related to Old Norse *flōki* flounder, Old Saxon *flaka* sole, Old High German *flah* smooth]

fluky *or* **flukey** ('flu:kɪ) *adj* **flukier, flukiest.** *Informal.* **1** done or gained by an accident, esp. a lucky one. **2** variable; uncertain: *fluky weather.* ▸ **'flukiness** *n*

flume (flu:m) *n* **1** a ravine through which a stream flows. **2** a narrow artificial channel made for providing water for power, floating logs, etc. **3** a slide in the form of a long and winding tube with a stream of water running through it that descends into a purpose-built pool. ◆ *vb* **4** (*tr*) to transport (logs) in a flume. [C12: from Old French *flum,* ultimately from Latin *flūmen* stream, from *fluere* to flow]

flummery ('flʌmərɪ) *n, pl* **-meries. 1** *Informal.* meaningless flattery; nonsense. **2** *Chiefly Brit.* a cold pudding of oatmeal, etc. [C17: from Welsh *llymru*]

flummox ('flʌməks) *vb* (*tr*) to perplex or bewilder. [C19: of unknown origin]

flung (flʌŋ) *vb* the past tense and past participle of **fling.**

flunk (flʌŋk) *Informal, chiefly U.S., Canadian, and N.Z.* ◆ *vb* **1** to fail or cause to fail to reach the required standard in (an examination, course, etc.). **2** (*intr;* foll. by *out*) to be dismissed from a school or college through failure in examinations. ◆ *n* **3** a low grade below the pass standard. [C19: perhaps from FLINCH[1] + FUNK[1]]

flunky *or* **flunkey** ('flʌŋkɪ) *n, pl* **flunkies** *or* **flunkeys. 1** a servile or fawning person. **2** a person who performs menial tasks. **3** *Usually derogatory.* a man-servant in livery. **[C18:** of unknown origin**]**

Fluon ('flu:ɒn) *n* a trademark for **polytetrafluoroethylene.**

fluor ('flu:ɔ:) *n* another name for **fluorspar. [C17:** from Latin: a flowing; so called from its use as a metallurgical flux**]**

fluor- *combining form.* a variant of **fluoro-** before a vowel: *fluorene; fluorine.*

fluorapatite (ˌflʊəˈræpətaɪt) *n* a mineral consisting of calcium fluorophosphate; the most common form of apatite.

fluorene ('flʊəri:n) *n* a white insoluble crystalline solid used in making dyes. Formula: $(C_6H_4)_2CH_2$.

fluoresce (ˌflʊəˈrɛs) *vb (intr)* to exhibit fluorescence. **[C19:** back formation from FLUORESCENCE**]**

fluorescein *or* **fluoresceine** (ˌflʊəˈrɛsɪɪn) *n* an orange-red crystalline compound that in aqueous solution exhibits a greenish-yellow fluorescence in reflected light and is reddish-orange in transmitted light: used as a marker in sea water and as an indicator. Formula: $C_{20}H_{12}O_5$.

fluorescence (ˌflʊəˈrɛsəns) *n* **1** *Physics.* **1a** the emission of light or other radiation from atoms or molecules that are bombarded by particles, such as electrons, or by radiation from a separate source. The bombarding radiation produces excited atoms, molecules, or ions and these emit photons as they fall back to the ground state. **1b** such an emission of photons that ceases as soon as the bombarding radiation is discontinued. **1c** such an emission of photons for which the average lifetime of the excited atoms and molecules is less than about 10^{-8} seconds. **2** the radiation emitted as a result of fluorescence. Compare **phosphorescence. [C19:** FLUOR + *-escence* (as in *opalescence*)**]**

fluorescent (ˌflʊəˈrɛsᵊnt) *adj* exhibiting or having the property of fluorescence.

fluorescent lamp *n* **1** a type of lamp in which an electrical gas discharge is maintained in a tube with a thin layer of phosphor on its inside surface. The gas, which is often mercury vapour, emits ultraviolet radiation causing the phosphor to fluoresce. **2** a type of lamp in which an electrical discharge is maintained in a tube containing a gas such as neon, mercury vapour, or sodium vapour at low pressure. Gas atoms in the discharge are struck by electrons and fluoresce.

fluorescent screen *n* a transparent screen coated on one side with a phosphor that fluoresces when exposed to X-rays or cathode rays.

fluoric (flu:ˈɔ:rɪk) *adj* of, concerned with, or produced from fluorine or fluorspar.

fluoridate ('flʊərɪˌdeɪt) *vb* to subject (water) to fluoridation.

fluoridation (ˌflʊərɪˈdeɪʃən) *n* the addition of about one part per million of fluorides to the public water supply as a protection against tooth decay.

fluoride ('flʊəˌraɪd) *n* **1** any salt of hydrofluoric acid, containing the fluoride ion, F^-. **2** any compound containing fluorine, such as methyl fluoride.

fluorinate ('flʊərɪˌneɪt) *vb* to treat or combine with fluorine. ▸ **ˌfluoriˈnation** *n*

fluorine ('flʊəri:n) *or* **fluorin** ('flʊərɪn) *n* a toxic pungent pale yellow gas of the halogen group that is the most electronegative and reactive of all the elements, occurring principally in fluorspar and cryolite: used in the production of uranium, fluorocarbons, and other chemicals. Symbol: F; atomic no.: 9; atomic wt.: 18.9984032; valency: 1; density: 1.696 kg/m³; relative density: 1.108; freezing pt.: –219.62°C; boiling pt.: –188.13°C.

fluorite ('flʊəraɪt) *n* the U.S. and Canadian name for **fluorspar.**

fluoro- *or before a vowel* **fluor-** *combining form.* **1** indicating the presence of fluorine: *fluorocarbon.* **2** indicating fluorescence: *fluoroscope.*

fluorocarbon (ˌflʊərəʊˈkɑ:bᵊn) *n* any compound derived by replacing all or some of the hydrogen atoms in hydrocarbons by fluorine atoms. Many of them are used as lubricants, solvents, and coatings. See also **Freon, polytetrafluoroethylene, CFC.**

fluorochrome ('flʊərəʊˌkrəʊm) *n* a chemical entity, such as a molecule or group, that exhibits fluorescence.

fluorography (flʊəˈrɒgrəfɪ) *n* the photographic recording of fluoroscopic images.

fluorometer (ˌflʊəˈrɒmɪtə) *or* **fluorimeter** (ˌflʊəˈrɪmɪtə) *n* **1** an instrument for inducing fluorescence by irradiation and for examination of the emission spectrum of the resulting fluorescent light. **2** a device for detecting and measuring ultraviolet radiation by determining the amount of fluorescence that it produces from a phosphor. ▸ **fluorometric** (ˌflʊərəʊˈmɛtrɪk) *or* **fluorimetric** (ˌflʊərɪˈmɛtrɪk) *adj* ▸ **ˌfluoˈrometry** *or* **ˌfluoˈrimetry** *n*

fluorophore ('flʊərəʊˌfɔ:) *n* a chemical group responsible for fluorescence.

fluoroscope ('flʊərəˌskəʊp) *n* a device consisting of a fluorescent screen and an X-ray source that enables an X-ray image of an object, person, or part to be observed directly. ▸ **fluoroscopic** (ˌflʊərəˈskɒpɪk) *adj* ▸ **ˌfluoroˈscopically** *adv*

fluoroscopy (flʊəˈrɒskəpɪ) *n* examination of a person or object by means of a fluoroscope.

fluorosis (flʊəˈrəʊsɪs) *n* fluoride poisoning, due to ingestion of too much fluoride in drinking water over a long period or to ingestion of pesticides containing fluoride salts. Chronic fluorosis results in mottling of the teeth of children.

fluorspar ('flʊəˌspɑ:), **fluor,** *or U.S. and Canadian* **fluorite** *n* a white or colourless mineral sometimes fluorescent and often tinted by impurities, found in veins and as deposits from hot gases. It is used in the manufacture of glass, enamel, and jewellery, and is the chief ore of fluorine. Composition: calcium fluoride. Formula: CaF_2. Crystal structure: cubic.

flurry ('flʌrɪ) *n, pl* **-ries. 1** a sudden commotion or burst of activity. **2** a light gust of wind or rain or fall of snow. **3** *Stock Exchange.* a sudden brief increase in trading or fluctuation in stock prices. **4** the death spasms of a harpooned whale. ◆ *vb* **-ries, -rying, -ried. 5** to confuse or bewilder or be confused or bewildered. **[C17:** from obsolete *flurr* to scatter, perhaps formed on analogy with HURRY**]**

flush[1] (flʌʃ) *vb* **1** to blush or cause to blush. **2** to flow or flood or cause to flow or flood with or as if with water. **3** to glow or shine or cause to glow or shine with a rosy colour. **4** to send a volume of water quickly through (a pipe, channel, etc.) or into (a toilet) for the purpose of cleansing, emptying, etc. **5** to cause (soluble substances in the soil) to be washed towards the surface, as by the action of underground springs, or (of such substances) to be washed towards the soil surface. **6** *(tr; usually passive)* to excite or elate. ◆ *n* **7** a rosy colour, esp. in the cheeks; blush. **8** a sudden flow or gush, as of water. **9** a feeling of excitement or elation: *the flush of success.* **10** early bloom; freshness: *the flush of youth.* **11** redness of the skin, esp. of the face, as from the effects of a fever, alcohol, etc. **12** *Ecology.* an area of boggy land fed by ground water. ◆ *adj* **13** having a ruddy or heightened colour. **[C16** (in the sense: to gush forth): perhaps from FLUSH[3]**]** ▸ **ˈflusher** *n*

flush[2] (flʌʃ) *adj (usually postpositive)* **1** level or even with another surface. **2** directly adjacent; continuous. **3** *Informal.* having plenty of money. **4** *Informal.* abundant or plentiful, as money. **5** full of vigour. **6** full to the brim or to the point of overflowing. **7** *Printing.* having an even margin, right or left, with no indentations. **8** (of a blow) accurately delivered. **9** (of a vessel) having no superstructure built above the flat level of the deck. ◆ *adv* **10** so as to be level or even. **11** directly or squarely. ◆ *vb (tr)* **12** to cause (surfaces) to be on the same level or in the same plane. **13** to enrich the diet of (a ewe) during the breeding season. ◆ *n* **14** a period of fresh growth of leaves, shoots, etc. **[C18:** probably from FLUSH[1] (in the sense: spring out)**]** ▸ **ˈflushness** *n*

flush[3] (flʌʃ) *vb (tr)* to rouse (game, wild creatures, etc.) and put to flight. **[C13** *flusshen,* perhaps of imitative origin**]**

flush[4] (flʌʃ) *n* (in poker and similar games) a hand containing only one suit. **[C16:** from Old French *flus,* from Latin *fluxus* FLUX**]**

flushing ('flʌʃɪŋ) *n* an extra feeding given to ewes before mating to increase the lambing percentage.

Flushing ('flʌʃɪŋ) *n* a port in the SW Netherlands, in Zeeland province, on Walcheren Island, at the mouth of the West Scheldt river: the first Dutch city to throw off Spanish rule (1572). Pop.: 43 947 (1989). Dutch name: **Vlissingen.**

flushwork ('flʌʃˌwɜ:k) *n Architect.* decorative treatment of the surface of an outside wall with flints split to show their smooth black surface, combined with dressed stone to form patterns such as tracery or initials.

fluster ('flʌstə) *vb* **1** to make or become confused, nervous, or upset. ◆ *n* **2** a state of confusion or agitation. **[C15:** probably of Scandinavian origin; compare Icelandic *flaustr* to hurry, *flaustra* to bustle**]**

flute (flu:t) *n* **1** a wind instrument consisting of an open cylindrical tube of wood or metal having holes in the side stopped either by the fingers or by pads controlled by keys. The breath is directed across a mouth hole cut in the side, causing the air in the tube to vibrate. Range: about three octaves upwards from middle C. **2** any pipe blown directly on the principle of a flue pipe, either by means of a mouth hole or through a fipple. **3** *Architect.* a rounded shallow concave groove on the shaft of a column, pilaster, etc. **4** a groove or furrow in cloth, etc. **5** a tall narrow wineglass. **6** anything shaped like a flute. ◆ *vb* **7** to produce or utter (sounds) in the manner or tone of a flute. **8** *(tr)* to make grooves or furrows in. **[C14:** from Old French *flahute,* via Old Provençal, from Vulgar Latin *flabeolum* (unattested); perhaps also influenced by Old Provençal *laut* lute; see FLAGEOLET**]** ▸ **ˈfluteˌlike** *adj* ▸ **ˈfluty** *adj*

fluted ('flu:tɪd) *adj* **1** (esp. of the shaft of a column) having flutes. **2** sounding like a flute.

fluter ('flu:tə) *n* **1** a craftsman who makes flutes or fluting. **2** a tool used to make flutes or fluting. **3** a less common word, used esp. in folk music, for **flautist.**

fluting ('flu:tɪŋ) *n* **1** a design or decoration of flutes on a column, pilaster, etc. **2** grooves or furrows, as in cloth.

flutist ('flu:tɪst) *n Now chiefly U.S. and Canadian.* a variant of **flautist.**

flutter ('flʌtə) *vb* **1** to wave or cause to wave rapidly; flap. **2** *(intr)* (of birds, butterflies, etc.) to flap the wings. **3** *(intr)* to move, esp. downwards, with an irregular motion. **4** *(intr) Pathol.* (of the auricles of the heart) to beat abnormally rapidly, esp. in a regular rhythm. **5** to be or make nervous or restless. **6** *(intr)* to move about restlessly. **7** *Swimming.* to cause (the legs) to move up and down in a flutter kick or (of the legs) to move in this way. **8** *(tr) Brit. informal.* to wager or gamble (a small amount of money). ◆ *n* **9** a quick flapping or vibrating motion. **10** a state of nervous excitement or confusion. **11** excited interest; sensation; stir. **12** *Brit. informal.* a modest bet or wager. **13** *Pathol.* an abnormally rapid beating of the auricles of the heart (200 to 400 beats per minute), esp. in a regular rhythm, sometimes resulting in heart block. **14** *Electronics.* a slow variation in pitch in a sound-reproducing system, similar to wow but occurring at higher frequencies. **15** a potentially dangerous oscillation of an aircraft, or part of an aircraft, caused by the interaction of aerodynamic forces, structural elastic reactions, and inertia. **16** *Swimming.* See **flutter kick. 17** Also called: **flutter tonguing.** *Music.* a method of sounding a wind instrument, esp. the flute, with a rolling movement of the tongue. **[**Old English *floterian* to float to and fro; related to German *flattern;* see FLOAT**]** ▸ **ˈflutterer** *n* ▸ **ˈflutteringly** *adv* ▸ **ˈfluttery** *adj*

flutterboard ('flʌtəˌbɔ:d) *n U.S. and Canadian.* an oblong board or piece of polystyrene plastic used by swimmers in training or practice. Brit. word: **float.**

flutter kick *n* a type of kick used in certain swimming strokes, such as the crawl, in which the legs are held straight and alternately moved up and down rapidly in the water.

fluvial ('flu:vɪəl) *or* **fluviatile** ('flu:vɪəˌtaɪl, -tɪl) *adj* of, relating to, or occurring in a river: *fluvial deposits.* **[C14:** from Latin *fluviālis,* from *fluvius* river, from *fluere* to flow**]**

fluviomarine (ˌflu:vɪˌəʊməˈri:n) *adj* **1** (of deposits) formed by joint action of the sea and a river or stream. **2** (esp. of fish) able to live in both rivers and the sea. **[C19:** *fluvio-,* from Latin *fluvius* river + MARINE**]**

fluvioterrestrial (ˌfluːvɪəʊtəˈrestrɪəl) *adj* (of animals) able to live in rivers and on land.

fluvoxamine (fluːˈvɒksəmiːn) *n* an antidepressant drug that acts by preventing the uptake of serotonin in the brain, thereby prolonging its action. See **SSRI**.

flux (flʌks) *n* **1** a flow or discharge. **2** continuous change; instability. **3** a substance, such as borax or salt, that gives a low melting-point mixture with a metal oxide. It is used for cleaning metal surfaces during soldering, etc., and for protecting the surfaces of liquid metals. **4** *Metallurgy.* a chemical used to increase the fluidity of refining slags in order to promote the rate of chemical reaction. **5** a similar substance used in the making of glass. **6** *Physics.* **6a** the rate of flow of particles, energy, or a fluid, such as that of neutrons (**neutron flux**) or of light energy (**luminous flux**). **6b** the strength of a field in a given area expressed as the product of the area and the component of the field strength at right angles to the area: *magnetic flux; electric flux.* **7** *Pathol.* an excessive discharge of fluid from the body, such as watery faeces in diarrhoea. **8** the act or process of melting; fusion. **9** (in the philosophy of Heraclitus) the state of constant change in which all things exist. ◆ *vb* **10** to make or become fluid. **11** (*tr*) to apply flux to (a metal, soldered joint, etc.). **12** (*tr*) an obsolete word for **purge.** [C14: from Latin *fluxus* a flow, from *fluere* to flow]

flux density *n Physics.* the amount of flux per unit of cross-sectional area.

fluxion (ˈflʌkʃən) *n* **1** *Maths, obsolete.* the rate of change of a function, especially the instantaneous velocity of a moving body; derivative. **2** a less common word for **flux** (senses 1, 2). [C16: from Late Latin *fluxiō* a flowing] ► **ˈfluxional** *or* **ˈfluxionary** *adj* ► **ˈfluxionally** *adv*

fluxmeter (ˈflʌksˌmiːtə) *n* any instrument for measuring magnetic flux, usually by measuring the charge that flows through a coil when the flux changes.

fly[1] (flaɪ) *vb* **flies, flying, flew, flown. 1** (*intr*) (of birds, aircraft, etc.) to move through the air in a controlled manner using aerodynamic forces. **2** to travel over (an area of land or sea) in an aircraft. **3** to operate (an aircraft or spacecraft). **4** to float, flutter, or be displayed in the air or cause to float, etc., in this way: *to fly a kite; they flew the flag.* **5** to transport or be transported by or through the air by aircraft, wind, etc. **6** (*intr*) to move or be moved very quickly, forcibly, or suddenly: *she came flying towards me; the door flew open.* **7** (*intr*) to pass swiftly: *time flies.* **8** to escape from (an enemy, place, etc.); flee: *he flew the country.* **9** (*intr;* may be foll. by *at* or *upon*) to attack a person. **10** (*intr*) to have a sudden outburst: *he flew into a rage again.* **11** (*intr*) (of money, etc.) to vanish rapidly. **12** (*tr*) *Falconry.* (of hawks) to fly at (quarry) in attack: *peregrines fly rooks.* **13** (*tr*) *Theatre.* to suspend (scenery) above the stage so that it may be lowered into view. **14 fly a kite. 14a** to procure money by an accommodation bill. **14b** to release information or take a step in order to test public opinion. **15 fly high.** *Informal.* **15a** to have a high aim. **15b** to prosper or flourish. **16 fly in the face of.** See **face** (sense 19). **17 fly off the handle.** *Informal.* to lose one's temper. **18 fly the coop.** *U.S. and Canadian informal.* to leave suddenly. **19 go fly a kite.** *U.S. and Canadian informal.* go away. **20 let fly.** *Informal.* **20a** to lose one's temper (with a person): *she really let fly at him.* **20b** to shoot or throw (an object). ◆ *n, pl* **flies. 21** (*often pl*) Also called: **fly front.** a closure that conceals a zip, buttons, or other fastening, by having one side overlapping, as on trousers. **22** Also called: **fly sheet. 22a** a flap forming the entrance to a tent. **22b** a piece of canvas drawn over the ridgepole of a tent to form an outer roof. **23** short for **flywheel. 24** the horizontal weighted arm of a fly press. **25a** the outer edge of a flag. **25b** the distance from the outer edge of a flag to the staff. Compare **hoist** (sense 9). **26** *Brit.* a light one-horse covered carriage formerly let out on hire. **27** *Austral. and N.Z.* an attempt: *I'll give it a fly.* **28** *Printing.* **28a** a device for transferring printed sheets from the press to a flat pile. **28b** Also called: **flyhand.** a person who collects and stacks printed matter from a printing press. **28c** a piece of paper folded once to make four pages, with printing only on the first page. **29** (*pl*) *Theatre.* the space above the stage out of view of the audience, used for storing scenery, etc. **30** *Rare.* the act of flying. [Old English *flēogan;* related to Old Frisian *fliāga,* Old High German *fliogan,* Old Norse *fljūga*] ► **ˈflyable** *adj*

fly[2] (flaɪ) *n, pl* **flies. 1** any dipterous insect, esp. the housefly, characterized by active flight. See also **horsefly, blowfly, tsetse fly, crane fly. 2** any of various similar but unrelated insects, such as the caddis fly, firefly, dragonfly, and chalcid fly. **3** *Angling.* a lure made from a fish-hook dressed with feathers, tinsel, etc., to resemble any of various flies or nymphs: used in fly-fishing. See also **dry fly, wet fly. 4** (in southern Africa) an area that is infested with the tsetse fly. **5 drink with the flies.** *Austral. slang.* to drink alone. **6 fly in amber.** See **amber** (sense 2). **7 fly in the ointment.** *Informal.* a slight flaw that detracts from value, completeness, or enjoyment. **8 fly on the wall.** a person who watches others, while not being noticed himself. **9 there are no flies on him, her,** etc. *Informal.* he, she, etc., is no fool. [Old English *flēoge;* related to Old Norse *fluga,* Old High German *flioga;* see FLY[1]] ► **ˈflyless** *adj*

fly[3] (flaɪ) *adj* **1** *Slang, chiefly Brit.* knowing and sharp; smart. **2** *Slang, chiefly Scot.* furtive or sneaky. **3 on the fly.** *Slang, chiefly Scot.* in secret; sneakily. [C19: of uncertain origin]

fly agaric *n* a saprotrophic agaricaceous woodland fungus, *Amanita muscaria,* having a scarlet cap with white warts and white gills: poisonous but rarely fatal. See also **amanita.** [so named from its use as a poison on flypaper]

fly ash *n* fine solid particles of ash carried into the air during combustion, esp. the combustion of pulverized fuel in power stations.

flyaway (ˈflaɪəˌweɪ) *adj* **1** (of hair or clothing) loose and fluttering. **2** frivolous or flighty; giddy. ◆ *n* **3** a person who is frivolous or flighty.

flyback (ˈflaɪˌbæk) *n* the fast return of the spot on a cathode-ray tube after completion of each trace.

flyblow (ˈflaɪˌbləʊ) *vb* **blows, blowing, blew, blown. 1** (*tr*) to contaminate, esp. with the eggs or larvae of the blowfly; taint. ◆ *n* **2** (*usually pl*) the egg or young larva of a blowfly, deposited on meat, paper, etc.

flyblown (ˈflaɪˌbləʊn) *adj* **1** covered with flyblows. **2** contaminated; tainted.

flyboat (ˈflaɪˌbəʊt) *n* any small swift boat.

flybook (ˈflaɪˌbʊk) *n* a small case or wallet used by anglers for storing artificial flies.

flyby (ˈflaɪˌbaɪ) *n, pl* **-bys.** a flight past a particular position or target, esp. the close approach of a spacecraft to a planet or satellite for investigation of conditions.

fly-by-light *n* aircraft control through systems operated by optical fibres rather than mechanical rods. Abbrev.: **FBL.**

fly-by-night *Informal.* ◆ *adj* **1** unreliable or untrustworthy, esp. in finance. **2** brief; impermanent. ◆ *n* Also called: **fly-by-nighter. 3** an untrustworthy person, esp. one who departs secretly or by night to avoid paying debts. **4** a person who goes out at night to places of entertainment.

fly-by-wire *n* aircraft control through systems operated by electronic circuits rather than mechanical rods. Abbrev.: **FBW.**

flycatcher (ˈflaɪˌkætʃə) *n* **1** any small insectivorous songbird of the Old World subfamily *Muscicapinae,* having small slender bills fringed with bristles: family *Muscicapidae.* See also **spotted flycatcher. 2** any American passerine bird of the family *Tyrannidae.*

flyer *or* **flier** (ˈflaɪə) *n* **1** a person or thing that flies or moves very fast. **2** an aviator or pilot. **3** *Informal.* a long flying leap; bound. **4** a fast-moving machine part, esp. one having periodic motion. **5** a rectangular step in a straight flight of stairs. Compare **winder** (sense 5). **6** *Athletics.* an informal word for **flying start. 7** *Chiefly U.S.* a speculative business transaction. **8** a small handbill.

fly-fish *vb* (*intr*) *Angling.* to fish using artificial flies as lures. See **dry fly, wet fly.** ► **ˈfly-ˌfisher** *n* ► **ˈfly-ˌfishing** *n*

fly half *n Rugby.* another name for **stand-off half.**

flying (ˈflaɪɪŋ) *adj* **1** (*prenominal*) hurried; fleeting: *a flying visit.* **2** (*prenominal*) designed for fast action. **3** (*prenominal*) moving or passing quickly on or as if on wings: *a flying leap; the flying hours.* **4** hanging, waving, or floating freely: *flying hair.* **5** *Nautical.* (of a sail) not hauled in tight against the wind. ◆ *n* **6** the act of piloting, navigating, or travelling in an aircraft. **7** (*modifier*) relating to, capable of, accustomed to, or adapted for flight: *a flying machine. Related adj:* **volar.** ◆ *adv* **8** *Nautical.* freely flapping in the wind.

flying boat *n* a seaplane in which the fuselage consists of a hull that provides buoyancy in the water.

flying bomb *n* another name for the **V-1.**

flying bridge *n* an auxiliary bridge of a vessel, usually built above or far outboard of the main bridge.

flying buttress *n* a buttress supporting a wall or other structure by an arch or part of an arch that transmits the thrust outwards and downwards. Also called: **arc-boutant.**

flying circus *n* **1** an exhibition of aircraft aerobatics. **2** the aircraft and men who take part in such exhibitions.

flying colours *pl n* conspicuous success; triumph: *he passed his test with flying colours.*

flying doctor *n* (in areas of sparse or scattered population) a doctor who visits patients by aircraft.

Flying Dutchman *n Legend.* **1** a phantom ship sighted in bad weather, esp. off the Cape of Good Hope. **2** the captain of this ship.

flying field *n* a small airport; an airfield.

flying fish *n* any marine teleost fish of the family *Exocoetidae,* common in warm and tropical seas, having enlarged winglike pectoral fins used for gliding above the surface of the water.

flying fox *n* **1** any large fruit bat, esp. any of the genus *Pteropus* of tropical Africa and Asia: family *Pteropodidae.* **2** *Austral. and N.Z.* a cable mechanism used for transportation across a river, gorge, etc.

flying frog *n* any of several tropical frogs of the family *Rhacophoridae,* esp. *Rhacophorus reinwardtii* of Malaya, that glide between trees by means of long webbed digits.

flying gurnard *n* any marine spiny-finned gurnard-like fish of the mostly tropical family *Dactylopteridae,* having enlarged fan-shaped pectoral fins used to glide above the surface of the sea.

flying jib *n* the jib set furthest forward or outboard on a vessel with two or more jibs.

flying lemur *n* either of the two arboreal mammals of the genus *Cynocephalus,* family *Cynocephalidae,* and order *Dermoptera,* of S and SE Asia. They resemble lemurs but have a fold of skin between the limbs enabling movement by gliding leaps. Also called: **colugo.**

flying lizard *or* **dragon** *n* any lizard of the genus *Draco,* of S and SE Asia, having an extensible fold of skin on each side of the body, used to make gliding leaps: family *Agamidae* (agamas).

flying mare *n* a wrestling throw in which a wrestler seizes his opponent's arm or head (**flying head mare**) and turns to throw him over his shoulder.

flying officer *n* an officer holding commissioned rank senior to a pilot officer but junior to a flight lieutenant in the British and certain other air forces.

flying phalanger *n* any nocturnal arboreal phalanger of the genus *Petaurus,* of E Australia and New Guinea, having black-striped greyish fur and moving with gliding leaps using folds of skin between the hind limbs and forelimbs. Also called: **glider.**

flying picket *n* (in industrial disputes) a member of a group of pickets organized to be able to move quickly from place to place.

flying saucer *n* any unidentified disc-shaped flying object alleged to come from outer space.

flying-spot *adj* denoting an electronic system in which a rapidly moving spot of light is used to encode or decode data, for example to obtain a television signal by scanning a photographic film or slide.

flying squad *n* a small group of police, soldiers, etc., ready to move into action quickly.

flying squirrel *n* any nocturnal sciurine rodent of the subfamily *Petauristinae,* of Asia and North America. Furry folds of skin between the forelegs and hind legs enable these animals to move by gliding leaps.

flying start *n* **1** Also called (informal): **flyer.** (in sprinting) a start by a competitor anticipating the starting signal. **2** a start to a race or time trial in which the competitor is already travelling at speed as he passes the starting line. **3** any promising beginning. **4** an initial advantage over others.

flying wing *n* **1** an aircraft consisting mainly of one large wing and no fuselage or tailplane. **2** (in Canadian football) the twelfth player, who has a variable position behind the scrimmage line.

flyleaf ('flaɪˌliːf) *n, pl* **-leaves.** the inner leaf of the endpaper of a book, pasted to the first leaf.

flyman ('flaɪmən) *n, pl* **-men.** *Theatre.* a stagehand who operates the scenery, curtains, etc., in the flies.

Flynn (flɪn) *n* **1 Errol.** 1909–59, Australian actor, who was noted for his swashbuckling roles; his films included *Captain Blood* (1935), *The Adventures of Robin Hood* (1938), and *Too Much Too Soon* (1958). **2** Rev. **John.** 1880–1951, founder of the Australian flying doctor service.

fly orchid *n* a European orchid, *Ophrys insectifera,* whose flowers resemble and attract certain wasps: found in wood margins and scrub on chalk soils.

flyover ('flaɪˌəʊvə) *n* **1** Also called: **overpass.** *Brit.* **1a** an intersection of two roads at which one is carried over the other by a bridge. **1b** such a bridge. **2** the U.S. name for a **fly-past.**

flypaper ('flaɪˌpeɪpə) *n* paper with a sticky and poisonous coating, usually hung from the ceiling to trap flies.

fly-past *n* a ceremonial flight of aircraft over a given area. Also called (esp. U.S.): **flyover.**

flyposting ('flaɪˌpəʊstɪŋ) *n* the posting of advertising or political bills, posters, etc. in unauthorized places.

fly press *n* a hand-operated press in which a horizontal beam with heavy steel balls attached to the ends gives additional momentum to the descending member.

Fly River *n* a river in W Papua New Guinea, flowing southeast to the Gulf of Papua. Length: about 1300 km (800 miles).

fly rod *n* a light flexible rod, now usually made of fibreglass or split cane, used in fly-fishing.

Flysch (flɪʃ) *n* (*sometimes not cap.*) *n* a sequence of sediments or sedimentary rocks comprising sandstones, conglomerates, marls, shales and clays that were formed by erosion during a period of mountain building and subsequently deformed as the mountain building continued. The phenomenon was first observed in the Alps. [Swiss German]

flyscreen ('flaɪˌskriːn) *n* a wire-mesh screen over a window to prevent flies from entering a room.

fly sheet *n* **1** another name for **fly** (sense 22). **2** a short handbill or circular.

flyspeck ('flaɪˌspɛk) *n* **1** the small speck of the excrement of a fly. **2** a small spot or speck. ◆ *vb* **3** (*tr*) to mark with flyspecks.

fly spray *n* a liquid used to destroy flies and other insects, sprayed from an aerosol.

flystrike ('flaɪstraɪk) *n Austral. and N.Z.* the infestation of wounded sheep by blowflies or maggots.

flyte (flaɪt; *Scot.* fləɪt) *vb* a variant spelling of **flite.**

fly-tipping *n* the deliberate dumping of rubbish in an unauthorized place.

flytrap ('flaɪˌtræp) *n* **1** any of various insectivorous plants, esp. Venus's flytrap. **2** a device for catching flies.

fly way *n* the usual route used by birds when migrating.

flyweight ('flaɪˌweɪt) *n* **1a** a professional boxer weighing not more than 112 pounds (51 kg). **1b** an amateur boxer weighing 48–51 kg (106–112 pounds). **1c** (*as modifier*): *a flyweight contest.* **2** (in Olympic wrestling) a wrestler weighing not more than 115 pounds (52 kg).

flywheel ('flaɪˌwiːl) *n* a heavy wheel that stores kinetic energy and smooths the operation of a reciprocating engine by maintaining a constant speed of rotation over the whole cycle.

fm *abbrev. for:* **1** Also: **fm.** fathom. **2** from.

Fm *the chemical symbol for* fermium.

FM *abbrev. for:* **1** frequency modulation. **2** Field Marshal. **3** *Aeronautics.* figure of merit.

FMCG *abbrev. for* fast-moving consumer goods.

FMN *n Biochem.* flavin mononucleotide; a phosphoric ester of riboflavin that acts as the prosthetic group for many flavoproteins. See also **FAD.**

FMS *Aeronautics abbrev. for* flight management systems.

f-number *or* **f number** *n Photog.* the numerical value of the relative aperture. If the relative aperture is f8, 8 is the f-number and indicates that the focal length of the lens is 8 times the size of the lens aperture. See also **T-number.**

Fo (fəʊ) *n* **Dario** ('dærɪəʊ). born 1926, Italian playwright and actor. His plays include *The Accidental Death of an Anarchist* (1970), *Trumpets and Raspberries* (1984), and *The Tricks of the Trade* (1991). Nobel prize for literature 1997.

FO *abbrev. for:* **1** *Army.* Field Officer. **2** *Air Force.* Flying Officer. **3** Foreign Office.

fo. *abbrev. for* folio.

foal (fəʊl) *n* **1** the young of a horse or related animal. ◆ *vb* **2** to give birth to (a foal). [Old English *fola;* related to Old Frisian *fola,* Old High German *folo* foal, Latin *pullus* young creature, Greek *pōlos* foal]

foam (fəʊm) *n* **1** a mass of small bubbles of gas formed on the surface of a liquid, such as the froth produced by agitating a solution of soap or detergent in water. **2** frothy saliva sometimes formed in and expelled from the mouth, as in rabies. **3** the frothy sweat of a horse or similar animal. **4a** any of a number of light cellular solids made by creating bubbles of gas in the liquid material and solidifying it: used as insulators and in packaging. **4b** (*as modifier*): *foam rubber; foam plastic.* **5** a colloid consisting of a gas suspended in a liquid. **6** a mixture of chemicals sprayed from a fire extinguisher onto a burning substance to create a stable layer of bubbles which smothers the flames. **7** a poetic word for the **sea.** ◆ *vb* **8** to produce or cause to produce foam; froth. **9** (*intr*) to be very angry (esp. in the phrase **foam at the mouth**). [Old English *fām;* related to Old High German *feim,* Latin *spūma,* Sanskrit *phena*] ► **'foamless** *adj* ► **'foamˌlike** *adj*

foamflower ('fəʊmˌflaʊə) *n* a perennial saxifragaceous plant, *Tiarella cordifolia,* of North America and Asia, having spring-blooming white flowers.

foamy ('fəʊmɪ) *adj* **foamier, foamiest.** of, resembling, consisting of, or covered with foam. ► **'foamily** *adv* ► **'foaminess** *n*

fob[1] (fɒb) *n* **1** a chain or ribbon by which a pocket watch is attached to a waistcoat. **2** any ornament hung on such a chain. **3** a small pocket in a man's waistcoat, for holding a watch. **4** a metal or plastic tab on a key ring. [C17: probably of Germanic origin; compare German dialect *Fuppe* pocket]

fob[2] (fɒb) *vb* **fobs, fobbing, fobbed.** an archaic word for **cheat.** [C15: probably from German *foppen* to trick]

f.o.b. *or* **FOB** *Commerce. abbrev. for* free on board.

fob off *vb* (*tr, adv*) **1** to appease or trick (a person) with lies or excuses. **2** to dispose of (goods) by trickery.

FoC *abbrev. for* father of the chapel.

focaccia (fə'kætʃə) *n* a flat Italian bread made with olive oil and yeast. [from Italian]

focal ('fəʊkᵊl) *adj* **1** of or relating to a focus. **2** situated at, passing through, or measured from the focus. ► **'focally** *adv*

focal infection *n* a bacterial infection limited to a specific part of the body, such as the tonsils or a gland.

focalize *or* **focalise** ('fəʊkəˌlaɪz) *vb* a less common word for **focus.** ► **ˌfocali'zation** *or* **ˌfocali'sation** *n*

focal length *or* **distance** *n* the distance from the focal point of a lens or mirror to the reflecting surface of the mirror or the centre point of the lens.

focal plane *n* **1** the plane that is perpendicular to the axis of a lens or mirror and passes through the focal point. **2** the plane in a telescope, camera, or other optical instrument in which a real image is in focus.

focal point *n* **1** Also called: **principal focus, focus.** the point on the axis of a lens or mirror to which parallel rays of light converge or from which they appear to diverge after refraction or reflection. **2** a central point of attention or interest.

focal ratio *n Photog.* another name for **f-number.**

Foch (*French* fɔʃ) *n* **Ferdinand** (fɛrdinɑ̃). 1851–1929, marshal of France; commander in chief of Allied armies on the Western front in World War I (1918).

focometer (fəʊ'kɒmɪtə) *n* an instrument for measuring the focal length of a lens.

fo'c's'le *or* **fo'c'sle** ('fəʊksᵊl) *n* a variant spelling of **forecastle.**

focus ('fəʊkəs) *n, pl* **-cuses** *or* **-ci** (-saɪ, -kaɪ, -kiː). **1** a point of convergence of light or other electromagnetic radiation, particles, sound waves, etc., or a point from which they appear to diverge. **2** another name for **focal point** (sense 1) or **focal length. 3** *Optics.* the state of an optical image when it is distinct and clearly defined or the state of an instrument producing this image: *the picture is in focus; the telescope is out of focus.* **4** a point upon which attention, activity, etc., is directed or concentrated. **5** *Geometry.* a fixed reference point on the concave side of a conic section, used when defining its eccentricity. **6** the point beneath the earth's surface at which an earthquake or underground nuclear explosion originates. Compare **epicentre. 7** *Pathol.* the main site of an infection or a localized region of diseased tissue. ◆ *vb* **-cuses, -cusing, -cused** *or* **-cusses, -cussing, -cussed. 8** to bring or come to a focus or into focus. **9** (*tr; often foll. by on*) to fix attention (on); concentrate. [C17: via New Latin from Latin: hearth, fireplace] ► **'focusable** *adj* ► **'focuser** *n*

focused strategy *n* a business strategy in which an organization divests itself of all but its core activities, using the funds raised to enhance the distinctive abilities that give it an advantage over its rivals.

focus group *n* a group of people brought together to give their opinions on a particular issue or product, often for the purpose of market research.

focus puller *n Films.* the member of a camera crew who adjusts the focus of the lens as the camera is tracked in or out.

fodder ('fɒdə) *n* **1** bulk feed for livestock, esp. hay, straw, etc. **2** raw experience or material: *fodder for the imagination.* ◆ *vb* **3** (*tr*) to supply (livestock) with fodder. [Old English *fōdor;* related to Old Norse *fōthr,* Old High German *fuotar;* see FOOD, FORAGE]

foe (fəʊ) *n Formal or literary.* another word for **enemy.** [Old English *fāh* hostile; related to Old High German *fēhan* to hate, Old Norse *feikn* dreadful; see FEUD[1]]

FoE *or* **FOE** *abbrev. for* Friends of the Earth.

foehn (fɜːn; *German* føːn) *n Meteorol.* a variant spelling of **föhn.**

foeman ('fəʊmən) *n, pl* **-men.** *Archaic or poetic.* an enemy in war; foe.

foetal ('fiːtᵊl) *adj* a variant spelling of **fetal.**

foetation (fiː'teɪʃən) *n* a variant spelling of **fetation.**

foeticide ('fiːtɪˌsaɪd) *n* a variant spelling of **feticide.** ► **ˌfoeti'cidal** *adj*

foetid ('fɛtɪd, 'fiː-) *adj* a variant spelling of **fetid.** ► **'foetidly** *adv* ► **'foetidness** *n*

foetor ('fiːtə) *n* a variant spelling of **fetor.**

foetus ('fiːtəs) *n, pl* **-tuses.** a variant spelling of **fetus.**

fog[1] (fɒg) *n* **1** a mass of droplets of condensed water vapour suspended in the air, often greatly reducing visibility, corresponding to a cloud but at a lower level. **2** a cloud of any substance in the atmosphere reducing visibility. **3** a state of mental uncertainty or obscurity. **4** *Photog.* a blurred or discoloured area on a developed negative, print, or transparency caused by the action of extraneous light, incorrect development, etc. **5** a colloid or suspension consisting of liquid particles dispersed in a gas. ◆ *vb* **fogs, fogging, fogged. 6** to envelop or become enveloped with or as if with fog. **7** to confuse or become confused: *to fog an issue.* **8** *Photog.* to produce fog on (a negative, print, or transparency) or (of a negative, print, or transparency) to be affected by fog. [C16: perhaps back formation from *foggy* damp, boggy, from FOG[2]]

fog[2] (fɒg) *n* **a** a second growth of grass after the first mowing. **b** grass left to grow long in winter. [C14: probably of Scandinavian origin; compare Norwegian *fogg* rank grass]

fog bank *n* a distinct mass of fog, esp. at sea.

fogbound ('fɒg,baʊnd) *adj* **1** prevented from operation by fog: *the airport was fogbound.* **2** obscured by or enveloped in fog: *the skyscraper was fogbound.*

fogbow ('fɒg,bəʊ) *n* a faint arc of light sometimes seen in a fog bank. Also called: **seadog, white rainbow.**

fogdog ('fɒg,dɒg) *n* a whitish spot sometimes seen in fog near the horizon. Also called: **seadog.**

fogey *or* **fogy** ('fəʊgɪ) *n, pl* **-geys** *or* **-gies.** an extremely fussy, old-fashioned, or conservative person (esp. in the phrase **old fogey**). [C18: of unknown origin] ► **'fogeyish** *or* **'fogyish** *adj* ► **'fogeyism** *or* **'fogyism** *n*

fogged (fɒgd) *or* **foggy** *adj Photog.* affected or obscured by fog.

Foggia (*Italian* 'fɔddʒa) *n* a city in SE Italy, in Apulia: seat of Emperor Frederick II; centre for Carbonari revolutionary societies in the revolts of 1820, 1848, and 1860. Pop.: 156 032 (1996 est.).

foggy ('fɒgɪ) *adj* **-gier, -giest. 1** thick with fog. **2** obscure or confused. **3** another word for **fogged. 4 not the foggiest** (**idea** *or* **notion**). no idea whatsoever: *I haven't the foggiest.* ► **'foggily** *adv* ► **'fogginess** *n*

foghorn ('fɒg,hɔːn) *n* **1** a mechanical instrument sounded at intervals to serve as a warning to vessels in fog. **2** *Informal.* a loud deep resounding voice.

fog level *n* the density produced by the development of photographic materials that have not been exposed to light or other actinic radiation. It forms part of the characteristic curve of a particular material.

fog signal *n* a signal used to warn railway engine drivers in fog, consisting of a detonator placed on the line.

föhn *or* **foehn** (fɜːn; *German* føːn) *n* a warm dry wind blowing down the northern slopes of the Alps. It originates as moist air blowing from the Mediterranean, rising on reaching the Alps and cooling at the saturated adiabatic lapse rate, and descending on the leeward side, warming at the dry adiabatic lapse rate, thus gaining heat. See also **lapse rate.** [German, from Old High German *phōnno,* from Latin *favōnius;* related to *fovēre* to warm]

foible ('fɔɪbᵊl) *n* **1** a slight peculiarity or minor weakness; idiosyncrasy. **2** the most vulnerable part of a sword's blade, from the middle to the tip. Compare **forte**[1] (sense 2). [C17: from obsolete French, from obsolete adj: FEEBLE]

foie gras (*French* fwagrɑ) *n* See **pâté de foie gras.**

foil[1] (fɔɪl) *vb* (*tr*) **1** to baffle or frustrate (a person, attempt, etc.). **2** *Hunting.* (of hounds, hunters, etc.) to obliterate the scent left by a hunted animal or (of a hunted animal) to run back over its own trail. **3** *Archaic.* to repulse or defeat (an attack or assailant). ◆ *n* **4** *Hunting.* any scent that obscures the trail left by a hunted animal. **5** *Archaic.* a setback or defeat. [C13 *foilen* to trample, from Old French *fouler,* from Old French *fuler* tread down, FULL[2]] ► **'foilable** *adj*

foil[2] (fɔɪl) *n* **1** metal in the form of very thin sheets: *gold foil; tin foil.* **2** the thin metallic sheet forming the backing of a mirror. **3** a thin leaf of shiny metal set under a gemstone to add brightness or colour. **4** a person or thing that gives contrast to another. **5** *Architect.* a small arc between cusps, esp. as used in Gothic window tracery. **6** short for **aerofoil** or **hydrofoil.** ◆ *vb* (*tr*) **7** to back or cover with foil. **8** Also: **foliate.** *Architect.* to ornament (windows) with foils. [C14: from Old French *foille,* from Latin *folia* leaves, plural of *folium*]

foil[3] (fɔɪl) *n* a light slender flexible sword tipped by a button and usually having a bell-shaped guard. [C16: of unknown origin]

foilsman ('fɔɪlzmən) *n, pl* **-men.** *Fencing.* a person who uses or specializes in using a foil.

foin (fɔɪn) *Archaic.* ◆ *n* **1** a thrust or lunge with a weapon. ◆ *vb* **2** to thrust with a weapon. [C14: probably from Old French *foine,* from Latin *fuscina* trident]

Foism ('fəʊ,ɪzəm) *n* Chinese Buddhism, the version introduced from India from the 4th century A.D. onwards and essentially belonging to the Mahayana school. [from Mandarin Chinese *fo* BUDDHA] ► **'Foist** *n, adj*

foison ('fɔɪzᵊn) *n Archaic or poetic.* a plentiful supply or yield. [C13: from Old French, from Latin *fūsiō* a pouring out, from *fundere* to pour; see FUSION]

foist (fɔɪst) *vb* (*tr*) **1** (often foll. by *off* or *on*) to sell or pass off (something, esp. an inferior article) as genuine, valuable, etc. **2** (usually foll. by *in* or *into*) to insert surreptitiously or wrongfully. [C16: probably from obsolete Dutch *vuisten* to enclose in one's hand, from Middle Dutch *vuist* fist]

Fokine (*Russian* 'fɔkin; *French* fɔkin) *n* **Michel** (miʃɛl). 1880–1942, U.S. choreographer, born in Russia, regarded as the creator of modern ballet. He worked with Diaghilev as director of the Ballet Russe (1909–15), producing works such as *Les Sylphides* and *Petrushka.*

Fokker ('fɒkə; *Dutch* 'fɔkər) *n* **Anthony Herman Gerard** (ɑn'toːniː 'hɛrman 'xeːrɑrt). 1890–1939, Dutch designer and builder of aircraft, born in Java.

FOL (in New Zealand) *abbrev. for* Federation of Labour.

fol. *abbrev. for:* **1** folio. **2** followed. **3** following.

folacin ('fɒləsɪn) *n* another name for **folic acid.** [C20: from FOL(IC) AC(ID) + -IN]

fold[1] (fəʊld) *vb* **1** to bend or be bent double so that one part covers another: *to fold a sheet of paper.* **2** (*tr*) to bring together and intertwine (the arms, legs, etc.): *she folded her hands.* **3** (*tr*) (of birds, insects, etc.) to close (the wings) together from an extended position. **4** (*tr;* often foll. by *up* or *in*) to enclose in or as if in a surrounding material. **5** (*tr;* foll. by *in*) to clasp (a person) in the arms. **6** (*tr;* usually foll. by *round, about,* etc.) to wind (around); entwine. **7** (*tr*) *Poetic.* to cover completely: *night folded the earth.* **8** Also: **fold in.** (*tr*) to mix (a whisked mixture) with other ingredients by gently turning one part over the other with a spoon. **9** to produce a bend (in stratified rock) or (of stratified rock) to display a bend. **10** (*intr;* often foll. by *up*) *Informal.* to collapse; fail: *the business folded.* ◆ *n* **11** a piece or section that has been folded: *a fold of cloth.* **12** a mark, crease, or hollow made by folding. **13** a hollow in undulating terrain. **14** a bend in stratified rocks that results from movements within the earth's crust and produces such structures as anticlines and synclines. **15** *Anatomy.* another word for **plica** (sense 1). **16** a coil, as in a rope, etc. **17** an act of folding. ◆ See also **fold up.** [Old English *fealdan;* related to Old Norse *falda,* Old High German *faldan,* Latin *duplus* double, Greek *haploos* simple] ► **'foldable** *adj*

fold[2] (fəʊld) *n* **1a** a small enclosure or pen for sheep or other livestock, where they can be gathered. **1b** the sheep or other livestock gathered in such an enclosure. **1c** a flock of sheep. **2** a church or the members of it. **3** any group or community sharing a way of life or holding the same values. ◆ *vb* **4** (*tr*) to gather or confine (sheep or other livestock) in a fold. [Old English *falod;* related to Old Saxon *faled,* Middle Dutch *vaelt*]

-fold *suffix forming adjectives and adverbs.* having so many parts, being so many times as much or as many, or multiplied by so much or so many: *threefold; three-hundredfold.* [Old English *-fald, -feald*]

fold-and-thrust belt *n Geology.* a linear or arcuate region of the earth's surface that has been subjected to severe folding and thrust faulting.

foldaway ('fəʊldə,weɪ) *adj* (*prenominal*) (of a bed) able to be folded and put away when not in use.

foldback ('fəʊld,bæk) *n* (in multitrack recording) a process for returning a signal to a performer instantly. Also called: **cueing.**

foldboat ('fəʊld,bəʊt) *n* another name for **faltboat.**

folded dipole *n* a type of aerial, widely used with television and VHF radio receivers, consisting of two parallel dipoles connected together at their outer ends and fed at the centre of one of them. The length is usually half the operating wavelength.

folder ('fəʊldə) *n* **1** a binder or file for holding loose papers, etc. **2** a folded circular. **3** a machine for folding printed sheets. **4** a person or thing that folds. **5** *Computing.* another name for **directory** (sense 5).

folderol ('fɒldə,rɒl) *n* a variant of **falderal.**

folding door *n* a door in the form of two or more vertical hinged leaves that can be folded one against another.

folding money *n Informal.* paper money.

folding press *n* a fall in wrestling won by folding one's opponent's legs up to his head and pressing his shoulders to the floor.

foldout ('fəʊld,aʊt) *n Printing.* another name for **gatefold.**

fold up *vb* (*adv*) **1** (*tr*) to make smaller or more compact. **2** (*intr*) to collapse, as with laughter or pain.

foley *or* **foley artist** ('fəʊlɪ) *n Films.* the U.S. name for **footsteps editor.** [C20: named after the inventor of the technique]

folia ('fəʊlɪə) *n* the plural of **folium.**

foliaceous (,fəʊlɪ'eɪʃəs) *adj* **1** having the appearance of the leaf of a plant. **2** bearing leaves or leaflike structures. **3** *Geology.* (of certain rocks, esp. schists) consisting of thin layers. [C17: from Latin *foliāceus*]

foliage ('fəʊlɪɪdʒ) *n* **1** the green leaves of a plant. **2** sprays of leaves used for decoration. **3** an ornamental leaflike design. [C15: from Old French *fuellage,* from *fuelle* leaf; influenced in form by Latin *folium*] ► **'foliaged** *adj*

foliar ('fəʊlɪə) *adj* of or relating to a leaf or leaves. [C19: from French *foliaire,* from Latin *folium* leaf]

foliate *adj* ('fəʊlɪɪt, -,eɪt). **1a** relating to, possessing, or resembling leaves. **1b** (*in combination*): *trifoliate.* **2** (of certain metamorphic rocks, esp. schists) having the constituent minerals arranged in thin leaflike layers. ◆ *vb* ('fəʊlɪ,eɪt). **3** (*tr*) to ornament with foliage or with leaf forms such as foils. **4** to hammer or cut (metal) into thin plates or foil. **5** (*tr*) to coat or back (glass, etc.) with metal foil. **6** (*tr*) to number the leaves of (a book, manuscript, etc.). Compare **paginate. 7** (*intr*) (of plants) to grow leaves. [C17: from Latin *foliātus* leaved, leafy]

foliated ('fəʊlɪ,eɪtɪd) *adj* **1** *Architect.* ornamented with or made up of foliage or foils. **2** (of rocks and minerals, esp. schists) composed of thin easily separable layers. **3** (esp. of parts of animals or plants) resembling a leaf.

foliation (,fəʊlɪ'eɪʃən) *n* **1** *Botany.* **1a** the process of producing leaves. **1b** the state of being in leaf. **1c** the arrangement of leaves in a leaf bud; vernation. **2** *Architect.* **2a** ornamentation consisting of foliage. **2b** ornamentation consisting of cusps and foils. **3** any decoration with foliage. **4** the consecutive numbering of the leaves of a book. **5** *Geology.* the arrangement of the constituents of a rock in leaflike layers, as in schists.

folic acid ('fəʊlɪk, 'fɒl-) *n* any of a group of vitamins of the B complex, including pteroylglutamic acid and its derivatives: used in the treatment of megaloblastic anaemia. Also called: **folacin.** [C20: from Latin *folium* leaf; so called because it may be obtained from green leaves]

folie à deux ('fɒlɪ æ 'dɜː) *n Psychiatry.* mental illness occurring simultaneously in two intimately related persons who share some of the elements of the illness, such as delusions. [French: madness involving two (people)]

folie de grandeur *French.* (fɔli də grɑ̃dœr) *n* delusions of grandeur. [literally: madness of grandeur]

folio ('fəʊlɪəʊ) *n, pl* **-lios. 1** a sheet of paper folded in half to make two leaves for a book or manuscript. **2** a book or manuscript of the largest common size made up of such sheets. **3** a leaf of paper or parchment numbered on the front side only. **4** a page number in a book. **5** *Law.* a unit of measurement of the length of legal documents, determined by the number of words, generally 72 or 90 in Britain and 100 in the U.S. ◆ *adj* **6** relating to or having the format of a folio: *a folio edition.* ◆ *vb* **-lios, -lioing, -lioed. 7** (*tr*) to number the leaves of (a book) consecutively. [C16: from Latin phrase *in foliō* in a leaf, from *folium* leaf]

foliolate ('fəʊlɪə,leɪt; fəʊ'lɪəlɪt, -,leɪt) *adj Botany.* possessing or relating to leaflets. [C19: from Late Latin *foliolum* little leaf, from Latin *folium* leaf]

foliose ('fəʊlɪˌəʊs, -ˌəʊz) *adj* another word for **foliaceous** (senses 1, 2). **[**C18: from Latin *foliōsus* full of leaves**]**

folium ('fəʊlɪəm) *n, pl* **-lia** (-lɪə). **1** a plane geometrical curve consisting of a loop whose two ends, intersecting at a node, are asymptotic to the same line. Standard equation: $x^3 + y^3 = 3axy$ where $x = y + a$ is the equation of the line. **2** any thin leaflike layer, esp. of some metamorphic rocks. **[**C19: from Latin, literally: leaf**]**

folk (fəʊk) *n, pl* **folk** *or* **folks. 1** (*functioning as pl; often pl in form*) people in general, esp. those of a particular group or class: *country folk.* **2** (*functioning as pl; usually pl in form*) *Informal.* members of a family. **3** (*functioning as sing*) *Informal.* short for **folk music. 4** a people or tribe. **5** (*modifier*) relating to, originating from, or traditional to the common people of a country: *a folk song.* **[**Old English *folc;* related to Old Saxon, Old Norse, Old High German *folk***]** ▸ **'folkish** *adj* ▸ **'folkishness** *n*

folk dance *n* **1** any of various traditional rustic dances often originating from festivals or rituals. **2** a piece of music composed for such a dance. ◆ *vb* **folk-dance.** (*intr*) **3** to perform a folk dance. ▸ **folk dancing** *n*

Folkestone ('fəʊkstən) *n* a port and resort in SE England, in E Kent. Pop.: 45 587 (1991).

Folketing ('fəʊlkətɪŋ; *Danish* 'fɔlgətɛŋ) *n* the unicameral Danish parliament. **[**Danish, from *folk* the people, FOLK + Old Norse *thing* assembly**]**

folk etymology *n* **1** the gradual change in the form of a word through the influence of a more familiar word or phrase with which it becomes associated, as for example *sparrow-grass* for *asparagus.* **2** a popular but erroneous conception of the origin of a word.

folkie *or* **folky** ('fəʊkɪ) *n, pl* **-ies.** *Informal.* a devotee of folk music.

folklore ('fəʊkˌlɔː) *n* **1** the unwritten literature of a people as expressed in folk tales, proverbs, riddles, songs, etc. **2** the body of stories and legends attached to a particular place, group, activity, etc.: *Hollywood folklore; rugby folklore.* **3** the anthropological discipline concerned with the study of folkloric materials. ▸ **'folkˌloric** *adj* ▸ **'folkˌlorist** *n, adj* ▸ **ˌfolklor'istic** *adj*

folk medicine *n* the traditional art of medicine as practised among rustic communities and primitive peoples, consisting typically of the use of herbal remedies, fruits and vegetables thought to have healing power, etc.

folk memory *n* the memory of past events as preserved in a community.

folkmoot ('fəʊkˌmuːt), **folkmote,** *or* **folkmot** ('fəʊkˌməʊt) *n* (in early medieval England) an assembly of the people of a district, town, or shire. **[**Old English *folcmōt,* from *folc* FOLK + *mōt* from *mǣtan* to MEET[1]**]**

folk music *n* **1** music that is passed on from generation to generation by oral tradition. Compare **art music. 2** any music composed in the idiom of this oral tradition.

folk-rock *n* a style of rock music influenced by folk, including traditional material arranged for electric instruments.

folk singer *n* a person who sings folk songs or other songs in the folk idiom. ▸ **folk singing** *n*

folk song *n* **1** a song of which the music and text have been handed down by oral tradition among the common people. **2** a modern song which employs or reflects the folk idiom.

folksy ('fəʊksɪ) *adj* **-sier, -siest. 1** of or like ordinary people; sometimes used derogatorily to describe affected simplicity. **2** *Informal, chiefly U.S. and Canadian.* friendly; affable. **3** of or relating to folk art. ▸ **'folksiness** *n*

folk tale *or* **story** *n* a tale or legend originating among a people and typically becoming part of an oral tradition.

folkways ('fəʊkˌweɪz) *pl n Sociol.* traditional and customary ways of living.

folk weave *n* a type of fabric with a loose weave.

foll. *abbrev. for:* **1** followed. **2** following.

follicle ('fɒlɪk[ə]l) *n* **1** any small sac or cavity in the body having an excretory, secretory, or protective function: *a hair follicle.* **2** *Botany.* a dry fruit, formed from a single carpel, that splits along one side only to release its seeds: occurs in larkspur and columbine. **[**C17: from Latin *folliculus* small bag, from *follis* pair of bellows, leather money-bag**]** ▸ **follicular** (fɒ'lɪkjʊlə), **folliculate** (fɒ'lɪkjʊˌleɪt), *or* **fol'licuˌlated** *adj*

follicle-stimulating hormone *n* a gonadotrophic hormone secreted by the pituitary gland that stimulates maturation of ovarian follicles in female mammals and growth of seminiferous tubules in males. Abbrev.: **FSH.** See also **luteinizing hormone, prolactin.**

folliculin (fɒ'lɪkjʊlɪn) *n* another name for **oestrone.**

follow ('fɒləʊ) *vb* **1** to go or come after in the same direction: *he followed his friend home.* **2** (*tr*) to accompany; attend: *she followed her sister everywhere.* **3** to come after as a logical or natural consequence. **4** (*tr*) to keep to the course or track of: *she followed the towpath.* **5** (*tr*) to act in accordance with; obey: *to follow instructions.* **6** (*tr*) to accept the ideas or beliefs of (a previous authority, etc.): *he followed Donne in most of his teachings.* **7** to understand (an explanation, argument, etc.): *the lesson was difficult to follow.* **8** to watch closely or continuously: *she followed his progress carefully.* **9** (*tr*) to have a keen interest in: *to follow athletics.* **10** (*tr*) to help in the cause of or accept the leadership of: *the men who followed Napoleon.* **11** (*tr*) *Rare.* to earn a living at or in: *to follow the Navy.* **12 follow suit. 12a** *Cards.* to play a card of the same suit as the card played immediately before it. **12b** to do the same as someone else. ◆ *n* **13** *Billiards, etc.* **13a** a forward spin imparted to a cue ball causing it to roll after the object ball. **13b** a shot made in this way. ◆ *See also* **follow-on, follow out, follow through, follow up. [**Old English *folgian;* related to Old Frisian *folgia,* Old Saxon *folgōn,* Old High German *folgēn***]** ▸ **'followable** *adj*

follower ('fɒləʊə) *n* **1** a person who accepts the teachings of another; disciple; adherent: *a follower of Marx.* **2** an attendant or henchman. **3** an enthusiast or supporter, as of a sport or team. **4** (esp. formerly) a male admirer. **5** *Rare.* a pursuer. **6** a machine part that derives its motion by following the motion of another part.

following ('fɒləʊɪŋ) *adj* **1a** (*prenominal*) about to be mentioned, specified, etc.: *the following items.* **1b** (*as n*): *will the following please raise their hands?* **2** (of winds, currents, etc.) moving in the same direction as the course of a vessel. ◆ *n* **3** a group of supporters or enthusiasts: *he attracted a large following wherever he played.* ◆ *prep* **4** as a result of: *he was arrested following a tip-off.*

USAGE The use of *following* to mean *as a result of* is very common in journalism, but should be avoided in other kinds of writing.

follow-my-leader *n* a game in which the players must repeat the actions of the leader. U.S., Canadian, and Irish name: **follow-the-leader.**

follow-on *Cricket.* ◆ *n* **1** an immediate second innings forced on a team scoring a prescribed number of runs fewer than its opponents in the first innings. ◆ *vb* **follow on. 2** (*intr, adv*) (of a team) to play a follow-on.

follow out *vb* (*tr, adv*) to implement (an idea or action) to a conclusion.

follow through *vb* (*adv*) **1** *Sport.* to complete (a stroke or shot) by continuing the movement to the end of its arc. **2** (*tr*) to pursue (an aim) to a conclusion. ◆ *n* **follow-through. 3** *Sport.* **3a** the act of following through. **3b** the part of the stroke after the ball has been hit. **4** the completion of a procedure, esp. after a first action.

follow up *vb* (*tr, adv*) **1** to pursue or investigate (a person, evidence, etc.) closely. **2** to continue (action) after a beginning, esp. to increase its effect. ◆ *n* **follow-up. 3a** something done to reinforce an initial action. **3b** (*as modifier*): *a follow-up letter.* **4** *Med.* a routine examination of a patient at various intervals after medical or surgical treatment.

folly ('fɒlɪ) *n, pl* **-lies. 1** the state or quality of being foolish; stupidity; rashness. **2** a foolish action, mistake, idea, etc. **3** a building in the form of a castle, temple, etc., built to satisfy a fancy or conceit, often of an eccentric kind. **4** (*pl*) *Theatre.* an elaborately costumed revue. **5** *Archaic.* **5a** evil; wickedness. **5b** lewdness; wantonness. **[**C13: from Old French *folie* madness, from *fou* mad; see FOOL[1]**]**

Folsom man ('fɒlsəm) *n* a type of early man from a North American culture of the Pleistocene period, thought to have used flint tools and to have subsisted mainly by hunting bison. **[**C20: named after *Folsom,* a settlement in New Mexico, where archaeological evidence was found**]**

Fomalhaut ('fəʊməˌləʊt) *n* the brightest star in the constellation Piscis Austrinus. Distance: 24 light years. **[**C16: from Arabic *fum'l-hūt* mouth of the fish, referring to its position in the constellation**]**

foment (fə'mɛnt) *vb* (*tr*) **1** to encourage or instigate (trouble, discord, etc.); stir up. **2** *Med.* to apply heat and moisture to (a part of the body) to relieve pain and inflammation. **[**C15: from Late Latin *fōmentāre,* from Latin *fōmentum* a poultice, ultimately from *fovēre* to foster**]** ▸ **fomentation** (ˌfəʊmɛn'teɪʃən) *n* ▸ **fo'menter** *n*

USAGE Both *foment* and *ferment* can be used to talk about stirring up trouble: *he was accused of fomenting/fermenting unrest.* Only *ferment* can be used intransitively or as a noun: *his anger continued to ferment* (not *foment*)*; rural areas were unaffected by the ferment in the cities.*

fomes ('fəʊmiːz) *n, pl* **-mites** (-mɪtiːz). *Med.* any material, such as bedding or clothing, that may harbour pathogens and therefore convey disease. **[**C18: from Latin *fōmes* tinder**]**

fond[1] (fɒnd) *adj* **1** (*postpositive;* foll. by *of*) predisposed (to); having a liking (for). **2** loving; tender: *a fond embrace.* **3** indulgent; doting: *a fond mother.* **4** (of hopes, wishes, etc.) cherished but unlikely to be realized: *he had fond hopes of starting his own business.* **5** *Archaic or dialect.* **5a** foolish. **5b** credulous. **[**C14 *fonned,* from *fonnen* to be foolish, from *fonne* a fool**]** ▸ **'fondly** *adv* ▸ **'fondness** *n*

fond[2] (fɒnd; *French* fɔ̃) *n* **1** the background of a design, as in lace. **2** *Obsolete.* fund; stock. **[**C17: from French, from Latin *fundus* bottom; see FUND**]**

Fonda ('fɒndə) *n* **1 Henry.** 1905–82, U.S. film actor. His many films include *Young Mr Lincoln* (1939), *The Grapes of Wrath* (1940), *Twelve Angry Men* (1957), and *On Golden Pond* (1981) for which he won an Oscar. **2** his daughter **Jane.** born 1937, U.S. film actress. Her films include *Klute* (1971) for which she won an Oscar, *Julia* (1977), *The China Syndrome* (1979), *On Golden Pond* (1981), and *The Old Gringo* (1989). **3** her brother, **Peter.** born 1939, U.S. film actor, who made his name in *Easy Rider* (1969).

fondant ('fɒndənt) *n* **1** a thick flavoured paste of sugar and water, used in sweets and icings. **2** a sweet made of this mixture. ◆ *adj* **3** (of a colour) soft; pastel. **[**C19: from French, literally: melting, from *fondre* to melt, from Latin *fundere;* see FOUND[3]**]**

fondle ('fɒnd[ə]l) *vb* **1** (*tr*) to touch or stroke tenderly; caress. **2** (*intr*) *Archaic.* to act in a loving manner. **[**C17: from (obsolete) vb *fond* to fondle; see FOND[1]**]** ▸ **'fondler** *n* ▸ **'fondlingly** *adv*

fondue ('fɒndjuː; *French* fɔ̃dy) *n* a Swiss dish, consisting of cheese melted in white wine or cider, into which small pieces of bread are dipped and then eaten. **[**C19: from French, feminine of *fondu* melted, from *fondre* to melt; see FONDANT**]**

fondue Bourguignonne ('bʊəgɪˌnjɒn; *French* burgiɲɔn) *n* a dish consisting of pieces of steak impaled on forks, cooked in oil at the table and dipped in sauces. **[**French: Burgundy fondue**]**

Fonseca (*Spanish* fɔn'seka) *n* **Gulf of.** an inlet of the Pacific Ocean in W Central America.

fons et origo *Latin.* (fɒnz ɛt 'ɒrɪgəʊ) *n* the source and origin.

font[1] (fɒnt) *n* **1a** a large bowl for baptismal water, usually mounted on a pedestal. **1b** a receptacle for holy water. **2** the reservoir for oil in an oil lamp. **3** *Archaic or poetic.* a fountain or well. **[**Old English, from Church Latin *fons,* from Latin: fountain**]** ▸ **'fontal** *adj*

font[2] (fɒnt) *n Printing.* another name (esp. U.S. and Canadian) for **fount**[2]**.**

Fontainebleau ('fɒntɪnˌbləʊ; *French* fɔ̃tɛnblo) *n* a town in N France, in the **Forest of Fontainebleau:** famous for its palace (now a museum), one of the largest royal residences in France, built largely by Francis I (16th century). Pop.: 18 753 (1982).

Fontane (*German* fɔn'taːnə) *n* **Theodor** ('teodoːr). 1819–98, German novelist and journalist; his novels include *Vor dem Sturm* (1878) and *Effi Briest* (1898).

fontanelle *or chiefly U.S.* **fontanel** (ˌfɒntə'nel) *n Anatomy.* any of several soft membranous gaps between the bones of the skull in a fetus or infant. [C16 (in the sense: hollow between muscles): from Old French *fontanele,* literally: a little spring, from *fontaine* FOUNTAIN]

Fontenelle (*French* fɔ̃tənɛl) *n* **Bernard le Bovier de** (bɛrnar lə bɔvje də). 1657–1757, French philosopher. His writings include *Digressions sur les anciens et les modernes* (1688) and *Éléments de la géométrie de l'infini* (1727).

Fonteyn (fɒn'teɪn) *n* Dame **Margot.** real name *Margaret Hookham.* 1919–91, English classical ballerina.

Fonthill Abbey ('fɒnthɪl) *n* a ruined Gothic Revival mansion in Wiltshire: rebuilt (1790–1810) for William Beckford by James Wyatt; the main tower collapsed in 1800 and, after rebuilding, again in 1827.

Foochow ('fuː'tʃaʊ) *n* a variant transliteration of the Chinese name for **Fuzhou.**

food (fuːd) *n* **1** any substance containing nutrients, such as carbohydrates, proteins, and fats, that can be ingested by a living organism and metabolized into energy and body tissue. Related adj: **alimentary. 2** nourishment in more or less solid form as opposed to liquid form: *food and drink.* **3** anything that provides mental nourishment or stimulus: *food for thought.* [Old English *fōda;* related to Old Frisian *fōdia* to nourish, feed, Old Norse *fœthi,* Gothic *fōdeins* food; see FEED, FODDER] ▸ **'foodless** *adj*

food additive *n* any of various natural or synthetic substances, such as salt, monosodium glutamate, or citric acid, used in the commercial processing of food as preservatives, antioxidants, emulsifiers, etc., in order to preserve or add flavour, colour, or texture to processed food.

food body *n Botany.* a mass of nutrients attached to a seed coat, which attracts ants and thus aids dispersal of the seed.

food chain *n Ecology.* a series of organisms in a community, each member of which feeds on another in the chain and is eaten in turn by another member.

foodie *or* **foody** ('fuːdɪ) *n, pl* **-ies.** *Informal.* a person having an enthusiastic interest in the preparation and consumption of good food.

food poisoning *n* an acute illness typically characterized by gastrointestinal inflammation, vomiting, and diarrhoea, caused by food that is either naturally poisonous or contaminated by pathogenic bacteria (esp. *Salmonella*).

food pollen *n* infertile pollen produced by some plants that attracts insects and thus aids pollination.

food processor *n Cookery.* an electric domestic appliance designed to speed the preparation and mixing of ingredients by automatic chopping, grating, blending, etc.

foodstuff ('fuːdˌstʌf) *n* any material, substance, etc., that can be used as food.

food vacuole *n Biology.* a cavity surrounding ingested food particles in some protozoans.

fool[1] (fuːl) *n* **1** a person who lacks sense or judgement. **2** a person who is made to appear ridiculous. **3** (formerly) a professional jester living in a royal or noble household. **4** *Obsolete.* an idiot or imbecile: *the village fool.* **5 form the fool.** *Caribbean.* to play the fool or behave irritatingly. **6 no fool.** a wise or sensible person. **7 play** *or* **act the fool.** to deliberately act foolishly; indulge in buffoonery. ◆ *vb* **8** (*tr*) to deceive (someone), esp. in order to make him look ridiculous. **9** (*intr;* foll. by *with, around with,* or *about with*) *Informal.* to act or play (with) irresponsibly or aimlessly: *to fool around with a woman.* **10** (*intr*) to speak or act in a playful, teasing, or jesting manner. **11** (*tr;* foll. by *away*) to squander; fritter: *he fooled away a fortune.* **12 fool along.** *U.S.* to move or proceed in a leisurely way. ◆ *adj* **13** *Informal.* short for **foolish.** [C13: from Old French *fol* mad person, from Late Latin *follis* empty-headed fellow, from Latin: bellows; related to Latin *flāre* to blow]

fool[2] (fuːl) *n Chiefly Brit.* a dessert made from a purée of fruit with cream or custard: *gooseberry fool.* [C16: perhaps from FOOL[1]]

foolery ('fuːlərɪ) *n, pl* **-eries. 1** foolish behaviour. **2** an instance of this, esp. a prank or trick.

foolhardy ('fuːlˌhɑːdɪ) *adj* **-hardier, -hardiest.** heedlessly rash or adventurous. [C13: from Old French *fol hardi,* from *fol* foolish + *hardi* bold] ▸ **'foolˌhardily** *adv* ▸ **'foolˌhardiness** *n*

foolish ('fuːlɪʃ) *adj* **1** unwise; silly. **2** resulting from folly or stupidity. **3** ridiculous or absurd; not worthy of consideration. **4** weak-minded; simple. **5** an archaic word for **insignificant.** ▸ **'foolishly** *adv* ▸ **'foolishness** *n*

foolproof ('fuːlˌpruːf) *adj* **1** proof against failure; infallible: *a foolproof idea.* **2** (esp. of machines) proof against human misuse, error, etc.

foolscap ('fuːlzˌkæp) *n* **1** *Chiefly Brit.* a size of writing or printing paper, 13½ by 17 inches or 13¼ by 16½ inches. **2** a book size, 4¼ by 6¾ inches (**foolscap octavo**) or (chiefly Brit.) 6¾ by 8½ inches (**foolscap quarto**). **3** a variant spelling of **fool's cap.** [C17: see FOOL[1], CAP; so called from the watermark formerly used on this kind of paper]

fool's cap *n* **1** a hood or cap with bells or tassels, worn by court jesters. **2** a dunce's cap.

fool's errand *n* a fruitless undertaking.

fool's gold *n* any of various yellow minerals, esp. pyrite or chalcopyrite, that can be mistaken for gold.

fool's mate *n Chess.* a checkmate achieved by Black's second move: the quickest possible mate.

fool's paradise *n* illusory happiness.

fool's-parsley *n* an evil-smelling Eurasian umbelliferous plant, *Aethusa cynapium,* with small white flowers: contains the poison coniine.

foot (fʊt) *n, pl* **feet** (fiːt). **1** the part of the vertebrate leg below the ankle joint that is in contact with the ground during standing and walking. Related adj: **pedal. 2** any of various organs of locomotion or attachment in invertebrates, including molluscs. **3** *Botany.* the lower part of some plants or plant structures, as of developing moss or fern sporophytes. **4a** a unit of length equal to one third of a yard or 12 inches. 1 Imperial foot is equivalent to 0.3048 metre. Abbrev.: **ft. 4b** any of various units of length used at different times and places, typically about 10 per cent greater than the Imperial foot. **5** any part resembling a foot in form or function: *the foot of a chair.* **6** the lower part of something; base; bottom: *the foot of the page; the foot of a hill.* **7** the end of a series or group: *the foot of the list.* **8** manner of walking or moving; tread; step: *a heavy foot.* **9a** infantry, esp. in the British army. **9b** (*as modifier*): *a foot soldier.* **10** any of various attachments on a sewing machine that hold the fabric in position, such as a presser foot for ordinary sewing and a zipper foot. **11** *Music.* **11a** a unit used in classifying organ pipes according to their pitch, in terms of the length of an equivalent column of air. **11b** this unit applied to stops and registers on other instruments. **12** *Printing.* **12a** the margin at the bottom of a page. **12b** the undersurface of a piece of type. **13** *Prosody.* a group of two or more syllables in which one syllable has the major stress, forming the basic unit of poetic rhythm. **14 a foot in the door.** an action, appointment, etc., that provides an initial step towards a desired goal, esp. one that is not easily attainable. **15 kick with the wrong foot.** *Scot. and Irish.* to be of the opposite religion to that which is regarded as acceptable or to that of the person who is speaking. **16 my foot!** an expression of disbelief, often of the speaker's own preceding statement: *he didn't know, my foot! Of course he did!* **17 of foot.** *Archaic.* in manner of movement: *fleet of foot.* **18 on foot. 18a** walking or running. **18b** in progress; astir; afoot. **19 one foot in the grave.** *Informal.* near to death. **20 on the wrong** (*or* **right**) **foot.** *Informal.* in an inauspicious (or auspicious) manner. **21 put a foot wrong.** to make a mistake. **22 put one's best foot forward. 22a** to try to do one's best. **22b** to hurry. **23 put one's foot down.** *Informal.* **23a** to act firmly. **23b** to increase speed (in a motor vehicle) by pressing down on the accelerator. **24 put one's foot in it.** *Informal.* to blunder. **25 set on foot.** to initiate or start (something). **26 tread under foot.** to oppress. **27 under foot.** on the ground; beneath one's feet. ◆ *vb* **28** to dance to music (esp. in the phrase **foot it**). **29** (*tr*) to walk over or set foot on; traverse (esp. in the phrase **foot it**). **30** (*tr*) to pay the entire cost of (esp. in the phrase **foot the bill**). **31** (usually foll. by *up*) *Archaic or dialect.* to add up. ◆ See also **feet, foots.** [Old English *fōt;* related to Old Norse *fōtr,* Gothic *fōtus,* Old High German *fuoz,* Latin *pēs,* Greek *pous,* Sanskrit *pad*] ▸ **'footless** *adj*

USAGE In front of another noun, the plural for the unit of length is *foot: a 20-foot putt; his 70-foot ketch. Foot* can also be used instead of *feet* when mentioning a quantity and in front of words like *tall: four foot of snow; he is at least six foot tall.*

Foot (fʊt) *n* **Michael** (**Mackintosh**). born 1913, British Labour politician and journalist; secretary of state for employment (1974–76); leader of the House of Commons (1976–79); leader of the Labour Party (1980–83).

footage ('fʊtɪdʒ) *n* **1** a length or distance measured in feet. **2a** the extent of film material shot and exposed. **2b** the sequences of filmed material. **3a** payment, by the linear foot of work done. **3b** the amount paid.

foot-and-mouth disease *n* an acute highly infectious viral disease of cattle, pigs, sheep, and goats, characterized by the formation of vesicular eruptions in the mouth and on the feet, esp. around the hoofs. Also called: **hoof-and-mouth disease.**

football ('fʊtˌbɔːl) *n* **1a** any of various games played with a round or oval ball and usually based on two teams competing to kick, head, carry, or otherwise propel the ball into each other's goal, territory, etc. See **association football, rugby, Australian Rules, American football, Gaelic football. 1b** (*as modifier*): *a football ground; a football supporter.* **2** the ball used in any of these games or their variants. **3** a problem, issue, etc., that is continually passed from one group or person to another and treated as a pretext for argument instead of being resolved: *he accused the government of using the strike as a political football.* ▸ **'footˌballer** *n*

footboard ('fʊtˌbɔːd) *n* **1** a treadle or foot-operated lever on a machine. **2** a vertical board at the foot of a bed.

footboy ('fʊtˌbɔɪ) *n* a boy servant; page.

foot brake *n* a brake operated by applying pressure to a foot pedal. Also called: **pedal brake.**

footbridge ('fʊtˌbrɪdʒ) *n* a narrow bridge for the use of pedestrians.

foot-candle *n* a former unit of illumination, equal to one lumen per square foot or 10.764 lux.

footcloth ('fʊtˌklɒθ) *n* an obsolete word for **caparison** (sense 1).

-footed *adj* **1** having a foot or feet as specified: *four-footed.* **2** having a tread as specified: *heavy-footed.*

footer[1] ('fʊtə) *n* **1** *Archaic.* a person who goes on foot; walker. **2** (*in combination*) a person or thing of a specified length or height in feet: *a six-footer.*

footer[2] ('fʊtə) *n Brit. informal.* short for **football** (the game).

footer[3] *or* **fouter** ('fuːtər, 'fuːtə) *Scot.* ◆ *vb* (*intr*) **1** to potter; occupy oneself trivially or to little effect. ◆ *n* **2** a person who footers. [perhaps from French *foutre;* see FOOTLE]

footfall ('fʊtˌfɔːl) *n* the sound of a footstep.

foot fault *n Tennis.* a fault that occurs when the server fails to keep both feet behind the baseline until he has served.

footgear ('fʊtˌɡɪə) *n* another name for **footwear.**

foothill ('fʊtˌhɪl) *n* (*often pl*) a lower slope of a mountain or a relatively low hill at the foot of a mountain.

foothold ('fʊtˌhəʊld) *n* **1** a ledge, hollow, or other place affording a secure grip for the foot, as during climbing. **2** a secure position from which further progress may be made: *a foothold for a successful career.*

footie ('fʊtɪ) *n* a variant spelling of **footy.**

footing ('fʊtɪŋ) *n* **1** the basis or foundation on which something is established:

the business was on a secure footing. **2** the relationship or status existing between two persons, groups, etc.: *the two countries were on a friendly footing.* **3** a secure grip by or for the feet. **4** the lower part of a foundation of a column, wall, building, etc. **5** *Chiefly U.S.* **5a** the act of adding a column of figures. **5b** the total obtained. **6** *Rare.* a fee paid upon entrance into a craft, society, etc., or such an entrance itself.

foot-lambert *n* a former unit of luminance equal to the luminance of a surface emitting or reflecting 1 lumen per square foot. A completely reflecting surface illuminated by 1 foot-candle has a luminance of 1 foot-lambert. Symbol: **ft-L**.

footle ('fu:tᵊl) *Informal.* ◆ *vb* **1** (*intr;* often foll. by *around* or *about*) to loiter aimlessly; potter. **2** (*intr*) to talk nonsense. ◆ *n* **3** *Rare.* foolishness. [C19: probably from French *foutre* to copulate with, from Latin *futuere*]

footlights ('fʊt,laɪts) *pl n Theatre.* **1** lights set in a row along the front of the stage floor and shielded on the audience side. **2** *Informal.* the acting profession; the stage.

footling ('fu:tlɪŋ) *adj Informal.* silly, trivial, or petty.

footloose ('fʊt,lu:s) *adj* **1** free to go or do as one wishes. **2** eager to travel; restless: *to feel footloose.*

footman ('fʊtmən) *n, pl* **-men. 1** a male servant, esp. one in livery. **2** a low four-legged metal stand used in a fireplace for utensils, etc. **3** (formerly) a foot soldier. **4** any of several arctiid moths related to the tiger moths, esp. the **common footman** (*Eilema lurideola*), with yellowish hind wings and brown forewings with a yellow front stripe; they produce woolly bear larvae.

footmark ('fʊt,mɑ:k) *n* a mark or trace of mud, wetness, etc., left by a person's foot on a surface.

footnote ('fʊt,nəʊt) *n* **1** a note printed at the bottom of a page, to which attention is drawn by means of a reference mark in the body of the text. **2** an additional comment, as to a main statement. ◆ *vb* **3** (*tr*) to supply (a page, book, etc.) with footnotes.

footpace ('fʊt,peɪs) *n* **1** a normal or walking pace. **2** Also called (in the Roman Catholic Church): **predella**. the platform immediately before an altar at the top of the altar steps.

footpad ('fʊt,pæd) *n Archaic.* a robber or highwayman, on foot rather than horseback.

footpath ('fʊt,pɑ:θ) *n* **1** a narrow path for walkers only. **2** *Chiefly Austral. and N.Z.* another word for **pavement**.

footplate ('fʊt,pleɪt) *n Chiefly Brit.* **a** a platform in the cab of a locomotive on which the crew stand to operate the controls. **b** (*as modifier*): *a footplate man.*

foot-pound *n* an fps unit of work or energy equal to the work done when a force of 1 pound moves through a distance of 1 foot. Abbrev.: **ft-lb**.

foot-poundal *n* a unit of work or energy equal to the work done when a force of one poundal moves through a distance of one foot: it is equal to 0.042 14 joule.

foot-pound-second *n* See **fps units**.

footprint ('fʊt,prɪnt) *n* **1** an indentation or outline of the foot of a person or animal on a surface. **2** an identifying characteristic on land or water, such as the area in which an aircraft's sonic boom can be heard or the area covered by the down-blast of a hovercraft. **3** the area in which the signal from a direct broadcasting satellite is receivable.

footrest ('fʊt,rɛst) *n* something that provides a support for the feet, such as a low stool, rail, etc.

footrope ('fʊt,rəʊp) *n Nautical.* **1** the part of a boltrope to which the foot of a sail is stitched. **2** a rope fixed so as to hang below a yard to serve as a foothold.

foot rot *n Vet. science.* See **rot**[1] (sense 11).

foot rule *n* a rigid measure, one foot in length.

foots (fʊts) *pl n* (*sometimes sing*) the sediment that accumulates at the bottom of a vessel containing any of certain liquids, such as vegetable oil or varnish; dregs.

footsie ('fʊtsɪ) *n Informal.* flirtation involving the touching together of feet, knees, etc. (esp. in the phrase **play footsie**).

Footsie ('fʊtsɪ) *n* an informal name for **Financial Times Stock Exchange 100 Index.**

footslog ('fʊt,slɒg) *vb* **-slogs, -slogging, -slogged.** (*intr*) to march; tramp. ▸ **'foot,slogger** *n*

foot soldier *n* an infantryman.

footsore ('fʊt,sɔ:) *adj* having sore or tired feet, esp. from much walking. ▸ **'foot,soreness** *n*

footstalk ('fʊt,stɔ:k) *n* a small supporting stalk in animals and plants; a pedicel, peduncle, or pedicle.

footstall ('fʊt,stɔ:l) *n* **1** the pedestal, plinth, or base of a column, pier, or statue. **2** the stirrup on a sidesaddle.

footstep ('fʊt,stɛp) *n* **1** the action of taking a step in walking. **2** the sound made by stepping or walking. **3** the distance covered with a step; pace. **4** a footmark. **5** a single stair; step. **6 follow in someone's footsteps.** to continue the tradition or example of another.

footsteps editor *n Brit. films.* the technician who adds sound effects, such as doors closing, rain falling, etc., during the postproduction sound-dubbing process. U.S. name: **foley** *or* **foley artist.**

footstock ('fʊt,stɒk) *n* another name for **tailstock**.

footstool ('fʊt,stu:l) *n* a low stool used for supporting or resting the feet of a seated person.

foot-ton *n* a unit of work or energy equal to 2240 foot-pounds.

foot valve *n* **1** another name for **suction valve. 2** a nonreturn valve at the inlet end of a pipe.

footwall ('fʊt,wɔ:l) *n* the rocks on the lower side of an inclined fault plane or mineral vein. Compare **hanging wall.**

footway ('fʊt,weɪ) *n* a way or path for pedestrians, such as a raised walk along the edge of a bridge.

footwear ('fʊt,wɛə) *n* anything worn to cover the feet.

footwork ('fʊt,wɜ:k) *n* skilful use of the feet, as in sports, dancing, etc.

footworn ('fʊt,wɔ:n) *adj* **1** Also: **'foot,weary.** footsore. **2** worn away by the feet: *a footworn staircase.*

footy *or* **footie** ('fʊtɪ) *n Informal.* **a** football. **b** (*as modifier*): *footy boots.*

foo yong ('fu: 'jɒŋ), **foo yoong** ('fu: 'jʊŋ), **foo yung,** *or* **fu yung** ('fu: 'jʌŋ) *n* a Chinese dish made of eggs mixed with chicken, crab meat, etc., and cooked like an omelette. [from Chinese *fu yung* hibiscus]

foozle ('fu:zᵊl) *Chiefly golf.* ◆ *vb* **1** to bungle (a shot). ◆ *n* **2** a bungled shot. [C19: perhaps from German dialect *fuseln* to do slipshod work] ▸ **'foozler** *n*

fop (fɒp) *n* a man who is excessively concerned with fashion and elegance. [C15: related to German *foppen* to trick; see FOB[2]] ▸ **'foppish** *adj* ▸ **'foppishly** *adv* ▸ **'foppishness** *n*

foppery ('fɒpərɪ) *n, pl* **-peries.** the clothes, affectations, obsessions, etc., of or befitting a fop.

for (fɔ:; *unstressed* fə) *prep* **1** intended to reach; directed or belonging to: *there's a phone call for you.* **2** to the advantage of: *I only did it for you.* **3** in the direction of: *heading for the border.* **4** over a span of (time or distance): *working for six days; the river ran for six miles.* **5** in favour of; in support of: *those for the proposal; vote for me.* **6** in order to get or achieve: *I do it for money; he does it for pleasure; what did you do that for?* **7** appropriate to; designed to meet the needs of; meant to be used in: *these kennels are for puppies.* **8** in exchange for; at a cost of; to the amount of: *I got it for hardly any money.* **9** such as explains or results in: *his reason for changing his job was not given.* **10** in place of: *a substitute for the injured player.* **11** because of; through: *she wept for pure relief.* **12** with regard or consideration to the usual characteristics of: *he's short for a man; it's cool for this time of year.* **13** concerning; as regards: *desire for money.* **14** as being: *we took him for the owner; I know that for a fact.* **15** at a specified time: *a date for the next evening.* **16** to do or partake of: *an appointment for supper.* **17** in the duty or task of: *that's for him to say.* **18** to allow of: *too big a job for us to handle.* **19** despite; notwithstanding: *she's a good wife, for all her nagging.* **20** in order to preserve, retain, etc.: *to fight for survival.* **21** as a direct equivalent to: *word for word; weight for weight.* **22** in order to become or enter: *to go for a soldier; to train for the priesthood.* **23** in recompense for: *I paid for it last week; he took the punishment for his crime.* **24 for it.** *Brit. informal.* liable for punishment or blame: *you'll be for it if she catches you.* **25 nothing for it.** no choice; no other course. ◆ *conj* **26** (*coordinating*) for the following reason; because; seeing that: *I couldn't stay, for the area was violent.* [Old English; related to Old Norse *fyr* for, Old High German *fora* before, Latin *per* through, *prō* before, Greek *pro* before, in front]

for. *abbrev. for:* **1** foreign. **2** forestry.

f.o.r. *or* **FOR** *Commerce. abbrev. for* free on rail.

for- *prefix* **1** indicating rejection or prohibition: *forbear; forbid.* **2** indicating falsity or wrongness: *forswear.* **3** used to give intensive force: *forgive; forlorn.* [Old English *for-;* related to German *ver-*, Latin *per-*, Greek *peri-*]

forage ('fɒrɪdʒ) *n* **1** food for horses or cattle, esp. hay or straw. **2** the act of searching for food or provisions. **3** *Military.* a raid or incursion. ◆ *vb* **4** to search (the countryside or a town) for food, provisions, etc. **5** (*intr*) *Military.* to carry out a raid. **6** (*tr*) to obtain by searching about. **7** (*tr*) to give food or other provisions to. **8** (*tr*) to feed (cattle or horses) with such food. [C14: from Old French *fourrage,* probably of Germanic origin; see FOOD, FODDER] ▸ **'forager** *n*

forage cap *n* a soldier's undress cap.

forage mite *n* a mite normally occurring in forage but sometimes infesting the skin of mammals, esp. horses, and birds.

foramen (fɒ'reɪmɛn) *n, pl* **-ramina** (-'ræmɪnə) *or* **-ramens.** a natural hole, esp. one in a bone through which nerves and blood vessels pass. [C17: from Latin, from *forāre* to bore, pierce] ▸ **foraminal** (fɒ'ræmɪnᵊl) *adj*

foramen magnum *n* the large opening at the base of the skull through which the spinal cord passes. [New Latin: large hole]

foraminifer (,fɒrə'mɪnɪfə) *n* any marine protozoan of the phylum *Foraminifera,* having a shell with numerous openings through which cytoplasmic processes protrude. Often shortened to **foram**. See also **globigerina, nummulite.** [C19: from New Latin, from FORAMEN + -FER] ▸ **foraminiferal** (fɒ,ræmɪ'nɪfərəl) *or* **fo,rami'niferous** *adj*

forasmuch as (fərəz'mʌtʃ) *conj* (*subordinating*) *Archaic or legal.* seeing that; since.

foray ('fɒreɪ) *n* **1** a short raid or incursion. **2** a first attempt or new undertaking. ◆ *vb* **3** to raid or ravage (a town, district, etc.). [C14: from *forrayen* to pillage, from Old French *forreier,* from *forrier* forager, from *fuerre* fodder; see FORAGE] ▸ **'forayer** *n*

forb (fɔ:b) *n* any herbaceous plant that is not a grass. [C20: from Greek *phorbē* food, from *pherbein* to graze]

forbade (fə'bæd, -'beɪd) *or* **forbad** (fə'bæd) *vb* the past tense of **forbid.**

forbear[1] (fɔ:'bɛə) *vb* **-bears, -bearing, -bore, -borne. 1** (when *intr,* often foll. by *from* or an infinitive) to cease or refrain (from doing something). **2** *Archaic.* to tolerate or endure (misbehaviour, mistakes, etc.). [Old English *forberan;* related to Gothic *frabairan* to endure] ▸ **for'bearer** *n* ▸ **for'bearingly** *adv*

forbear[2] ('fɔ:,bɛə) *n* a variant spelling of **forebear.**

forbearance (fɔ:'bɛərəns) *n* **1** the act of forbearing. **2** self-control; patience. **3** *Law.* abstention from or postponement of the enforcement of a legal right, esp. by a creditor allowing his debtor time to pay.

Forbes (fɔ:bz) *n* **George William.** 1869–1947, New Zealand statesman; prime minister of New Zealand (1930–35).

forbid (fə'bɪd) *vb* **-bids, -bidding, -bade** *or* **-bad, -bidden** *or* **-bid.** (*tr*) **1** to prohibit (a person) in a forceful or authoritative manner (from doing something or having something). **2** to make impossible; hinder. **3** to shut out or exclude. **4 God forbid!** may it not happen. [Old English *forbēodan;* related to

Old High German *farbiotan,* Gothic *faurbiudan;* see FOR-, BID] ▶ **for'biddance** *n* ▶ **for'bidder** *n*

USAGE It was formerly considered incorrect to talk of *forbidding* someone *from* doing something, but in modern usage either *from* or *to* can be used: *he was forbidden from entering/to enter the building.*

forbidden (fə'bɪdᵊn) *adj* **1** not permitted by order or law. **2** *Physics.* involving a change in quantum numbers that is not permitted by certain rules derived from quantum mechanics, esp. rules for changes in the electrical dipole moment of the system.

forbidden band *n* See **energy band.**

Forbidden City *n* **the. 1** Lhasa, Tibet: once famed for its inaccessibility and hostility to strangers. **2** a walled section of Beijing, China, enclosing the Imperial Palace and associated buildings of the former Chinese Empire.

forbidden fruit *n* any pleasure or enjoyment regarded as illicit, esp. sexual indulgence.

forbidden transition *n Physics.* an electronic transition in a molecule, etc., that has a very low probability of occurring.

forbidding (fə'bɪdɪŋ) *adj* **1** hostile or unfriendly. **2** dangerous or ominous. ▶ **for'biddingly** *adv* ▶ **for'biddingness** *n*

forbore (fɔː'bɔː) *vb* the past tense of **forbear**[1].

forborne (fɔː'bɔːn) *vb* the past participle of **forbear**[1].

forby *or* **forbye** (fɔː'baɪ; *Scot.* fər'baɪ) *prep, adv Scot.* **1** besides; in addition (to). **2** *Obsolete.* near; nearby.

force[1] (fɔːs) *n* **1** strength or energy; might; power: *the force of the blow; a gale of great force.* **2** exertion or the use of exertion against a person or thing that resists; coercion. **3** *Physics.* **3a** a dynamic influence that changes a body from a state of rest to one of motion or changes its rate of motion. The magnitude of the force is equal to the product of the mass of the body and its acceleration. **3b** a static influence that produces an elastic strain in a body or system or bears weight. Symbol: F **4** *Physics.* any operating influence that produces or tends to produce a change in a physical quantity: *electromotive force; coercive force.* **5a** intellectual, social, political, or moral influence or strength: *the force of his argument; the forces of evil.* **5b** a person or thing with such influence: *he was a force in the land.* **6** vehemence or intensity: *he spoke with great force.* **7** a group of persons organized for military or police functions: *armed forces.* **8** (*sometimes cap.;* preceded by *the*) *Informal.* the police force. **9** a group of persons organized for particular duties or tasks: *a workforce.* **10** *Criminal law.* violence unlawfully committed or threatened. **11** *Philosophy, logic.* that which an expression is normally used to achieve. See **speech act, illocution, perlocution. 12 in force. 12a** (of a law) having legal validity or binding effect. **12b** in great strength or numbers. **13 join forces.** to combine strengths, efforts, etc. ◆ *vb* (*tr*) **14** to compel or cause (a person, group, etc.) to do something through effort, superior strength, etc.; coerce. **15** to acquire, secure, or produce through effort, superior strength, etc.: *to force a confession.* **16** to propel or drive despite resistance: *to force a nail into wood.* **17** to break down or open (a lock, safe, door, etc.). **18** to impose or inflict: *he forced his views on them.* **19** to cause (plants or farm animals) to grow or fatten artificially at an increased rate. **20** to strain or exert to the utmost: *to force the voice.* **21** to rape; ravish. **22** *Cards.* **22a** to compel (a player) to trump in order to take a trick. **22b** to compel a player by the lead of a particular suit to play (a certain card). **22c** (in bridge) to induce (a bid) from one's partner by bidding in a certain way. **23 force down.** to compel an aircraft to land. **24 force a smile.** to make oneself smile. **25 force the pace.** to adopt a high speed or rate of procedure. [C13: from Old French, from Vulgar Latin *fortia* (unattested), from Latin *fortis* strong] ▶ **'forceable** *adj* ▶ **'forceless** *adj* ▶ **'forcer** *n* ▶ **'forcingly** *adv*

force[2] (fɔːs) *n* (in northern England) a waterfall. [C17: from Old Norse *fors*]

forced (fɔːst) *adj* **1** done because of force; compulsory: *forced labour.* **2** false or unnatural: *a forced smile.* **3** due to an emergency or necessity: *a forced landing.* **4** *Physics.* caused by an external agency: *a forced vibration; a forced draught.* ▶ **forcedly** ('fɔːsɪdlɪ) *adv* ▶ **'forcedness** *n*

forced development *n* the processing of underexposed photographic film to increase the image density.

force de frappe (fɔːs də fræp) *n* a military strike force, esp. the independent nuclear strike force of France. [C20: French, literally: striking force]

forced march *n Military.* a march in which normal needs are subordinated to the need for speed.

force-feed *vb* **-feeds, -feeding, -fed.** (*tr*) **1** to force (a person or animal) to eat or swallow food. **2** to force (someone) to receive opinions, propaganda, etc. ◆ *n* **force feed. 3** a method of lubrication in which a pump forces oil into the bearings of an engine, etc.

force-field analysis *n* a decision-making technique, often presented graphically, that identifies all the positive and negative forces impinging on a problem.

forceful ('fɔːsfʊl) *adj* **1** powerful. **2** persuasive or effective. ▶ **'forcefully** *adv* ▶ **'forcefulness** *n*

force majeure ('fɔːs mæ'ʒɜː, -'dʒʊə) *n Law.* irresistible force or compulsion such as will excuse a party from performing his part of a contract. [from French: superior force]

forcemeat ('fɔːsˌmiːt) *n* a mixture of chopped or minced ingredients used for stuffing. Also called: **farce, farcemeat.** [C17: from *force* (see FARCE) + MEAT]

forceps ('fɔːsɪps) *n, pl* **-ceps** *or* **-cipes** (-sɪˌpiːz). **1a** a surgical instrument in the form of a pair of pincers, used esp. in the delivery of babies. **1b** (*as modifier*): *a forceps baby.* **2** any pincer-like instrument. **3** any part or structure of an organism shaped like a forceps. [C17: from Latin, from *formus* hot + *capere* to seize] ▶ **'forceps-ˌlike** *adj*

force pump *n* a pump that ejects fluid under pressure. Compare **lift pump.**

force-ripe *Caribbean.* ◆ *adj* **1** (of fruit) prematurely picked and ripened by squeezing or warm storage. **2** precocious, esp. sexually. ◆ *vb* **3** (*tr*) to ripen (prematurely picked fruit) by squeezing or warm storage.

Forces ('fɔːsɪz) *pl n* (usually preceded by *the*) the armed services of a nation.

forcible ('fɔːsəbᵊl) *adj* **1** done by, involving, or having force. **2** convincing or effective: *a forcible argument.* ▶ **'forcibleness** *or* ˌ**forci'bility** *n* ▶ **'forcibly** *adv*

forcing bid *n Contract bridge.* a bid, often at a higher level than is required, that is understood to oblige the bidder's partner to reply.

forcing frequency *n Physics.* the frequency of an oscillating force applied to a system. Compare **natural frequency.**

forcing house *n* a place where growth or maturity (as of fruit, animals, etc.) is artificially hastened.

ford (fɔːd) *n* **1** a shallow area in a river that can be crossed by car, horseback, etc. ◆ *vb* **2** (*tr*) to cross (a river, brook, etc.) over a shallow area. [Old English; related to Old Frisian *forda,* Old High German *furt* ford, Latin *porta* door, *portus* PORT[1]] ▶ **'fordable** *adj*

Ford (fɔːd) *n* **1 Ford Madox** ('mædəks), original name *Ford Madox Hueffer.* 1873–1939, English novelist, editor, and critic; works include *The Good Soldier* (1915) and the war tetralogy *Parade's End* (1924–28). **2 Gerald R(udolph).** born 1913, U.S. politician; 38th president of the U.S. (1974–77). **3 Harrison.** born 1942, U.S. film actor. His films include *Star Wars* (1977) and its sequels, *Raiders of the Lost Ark* (1981) and its sequels, *Bladerunner* (1982), *Clear and Present Danger* (1994), and *Air Force One* (1997). **4 Henry.** 1863–1947, U.S. car manufacturer, who pioneered mass production. **5 John.** 1586–?1639, English dramatist; author of revenge tragedies such as *'Tis Pity She's a Whore* (1633). **6 John,** real name *Sean O'Feeney.* 1895–1973, U.S. film director, esp. of Westerns such as *Stagecoach* (1939) and *She Wore a Yellow Ribbon* (1949).

fordo *or* **foredo** (fɔː'duː) *vb* **-does, -doing, -did, -done.** (*tr*) *Archaic.* **1** to destroy. **2** to exhaust. [Old English *fordōn;* related to Old Saxon *fardōn,* Old High German *fartuon,* Dutch *verdoen;* see FOR-, DO[1]]

fore[1] (fɔː) *adj* **1** (*usually in combination*) located at, in, or towards the front: *the forelegs of a horse.* ◆ *n* **2** the front part. **3** something located at, in, or towards the front. **4** short for **foremast. 5 fore and aft.** located at or directed towards both ends of a vessel: *a fore-and-aft rig.* **6 to the fore. 6a** to or into the front or conspicuous position. **6b** *Scot. and Irish.* alive or active: *is your grandfather still to the fore?* ◆ *adv* **7** at or towards a ship's bow. **8** *Obsolete.* before. ◆ *prep, conj* **9** a less common word for **before.** [Old English; related to Old Saxon, Old High German *fora,* Gothic *faura,* Greek *para,* Sanskrit *pura*]

fore[2] (fɔː) *interj* (in golf) a warning shout made by a player about to make a shot. [C19: probably short for BEFORE]

fore- *prefix* **1** before in time or rank: *foresight; forefather; foreman.* **2** at or near the front; before in place: *forehead; forecourt.* [Old English, from *fore* (adv)]

fore-and-after *n Nautical.* **1** any vessel with a fore-and-aft rig. **2** a double-ended vessel.

forearm[1] ('fɔːrˌɑːm) *n* the part of the arm from the elbow to the wrist. Related adjs.: **cubital, radial.** [C18: from FORE- + ARM[1]]

forearm[2] (fɔːr'ɑːm) *vb* (*tr*) to prepare or arm (someone, esp. oneself) in advance. [C16: from FORE- + ARM[2]]

forearm smash ('fɔːrˌɑːm) *n* a blow like a punch delivered with the forearm in certain types of wrestling.

forebear *or* **forbear** ('fɔːˌbɛə) *n* an ancestor; forefather.

forebode (fɔː'bəʊd) *vb* **1** to warn of or indicate (an event, result, etc.) in advance. **2** to have an intuition or premonition of (an event). ▶ **fore'boder** *n*

foreboding (fɔː'bəʊdɪŋ) *n* **1** a feeling of impending evil, disaster, etc. **2** an omen or portent. ◆ *adj* **3** presaging something. ▶ **fore'bodingly** *adv* ▶ **fore'bodingness** *n*

forebrain ('fɔːˌbreɪn) *n* the nontechnical name for **prosencephalon.**

forecast ('fɔːˌkɑːst) *vb* **-casts, -casting, -cast** *or* **-casted. 1** to predict or calculate (weather, events, etc.), in advance. **2** (*tr*) to serve as an early indication of. **3** (*tr*) to plan in advance. ◆ *n* **4** a statement of probable future weather conditions calculated from meteorological data. **5** a prophecy or prediction. **6** the practice or power of forecasting. ▶ **'foreˌcaster** *n*

forecastle, fo'c's'le, *or* **fo'c'sle** ('fəʊksᵊl) *n* the part of a vessel at the bow where the crew is quartered and stores, machines, etc., may be stowed.

foreclose (fɔː'kləʊz) *vb* **1** *Law.* to deprive (a mortgagor, etc.) of the right to redeem (a mortgage or pledge). **2** (*tr*) to shut out; bar. **3** (*tr*) to prevent or hinder. **4** (*tr*) to answer or settle (an obligation, promise, etc.) in advance. **5** (*tr*) to make an exclusive claim to. [C15: from Old French *forclore,* from *for-* out + *clore* to close, from Latin *claudere*] ▶ **fore'closable** *adj* ▶ **foreclosure** (fɔː'kləʊʒə) *n*

forecourse ('fɔːˌkɔːs) *n Nautical.* the lowest foresail on a square-rigged vessel.

forecourt ('fɔːˌkɔːt) *n* **1** a courtyard in front of a building, as one in a filling station. **2** Also called: **front court.** the front section of the court in tennis, badminton, etc., esp. the area between the service line and the net.

foredeck ('fɔːˌdɛk) *n Nautical.* the deck between the bridge and the forecastle.

foredo (fɔː'duː) *vb* **-does, -doing, -did, -done.** (*tr*) a variant spelling of **fordo.**

foredoom (fɔː'duːm) *vb* (*tr*) to doom or condemn beforehand.

fore-edge *n* the outer edge of the pages of a book.

forefather ('fɔːˌfɑːðə) *n* an ancestor, esp. a male. ▶ **'foreˌfatherly** *adj*

forefend (fɔː'fɛnd) *vb* (*tr*) a variant spelling of **forfend.**

forefinger ('fɔːˌfɪŋgə) *n* the finger next to the thumb. Also called: **index finger.**

forefoot ('fɔːˌfʊt) *n, pl* **-feet. 1** either of the front feet of a quadruped. **2** *Nautical.* the forward end of the keel.

forefront ('fɔːˌfrʌnt) *n* **1** the extreme front. **2** the position of most prominence, responsibility, or action.

foregather *or* **forgather** (fɔː'gæðə) *vb* (*intr*) **1** to gather together; assemble. **2** *Rare.* to meet, esp. unexpectedly. **3** (foll. by *with*) to socialize.

forego[1] (fɔːˈgəʊ) *vb* **-goes, -going, -went, -gone.** to precede in time, place, etc. [Old English *foregān*] ▸ **foreˈgoer** *n*

forego[2] (fɔːˈgəʊ) *vb* **-goes, -going, -went, -gone.** (*tr*) a variant spelling of **forgo.** ▸ **foreˈgoer** *n*

foregoing (fɔːˈgəʊɪŋ) *adj* (*prenominal*) (esp. of writing or speech) going before; preceding.

foregone (fɔːˈgɒn, ˈfɔːˌgɒn) *adj* gone or completed; past. ▸ **foreˈgoneness** *n*

foregone conclusion *n* an inevitable result or conclusion.

foreground (ˈfɔːˌgraʊnd) *n* **1** the part of a scene situated towards the front or nearest to the viewer. **2** the area of space in a perspective picture, depicted as nearest the viewer. **3** a conspicuous or active position. ◆ *vb* **4** (*tr*) to emphasize (an issue, idea, or word).

foreground processing *n Computing.* the ability of a system to handle two or more processes virtually simultaneously so that it appears to be editing one text while printing another in the background.

foregut (ˈfɔːˌgʌt) *n* **1** the anterior part of the digestive tract of vertebrates, between the buccal cavity and the bile duct. **2** the anterior part of the digestive tract of arthropods. ◆ See also **midgut, hindgut.**

forehand (ˈfɔːˌhænd) *adj* (*prenominal*) **1** *Tennis, squash, etc.* **1a** (of a stroke) made with the racket held so that the wrist is facing the direction of the stroke. **1b** of or relating to the right side of a right-handed player or the left side of a left-handed player. **2** foremost or paramount. **3** done or given beforehand. ◆ *n* **4** *Tennis, squash, etc.* **4a** a forehand stroke. **4b** the side on which such strokes are made. **5** the part of a horse in front of the saddle. **6** a frontal position. ◆ *adv* **7** *Tennis, squash, etc.* with a forehand stroke. ◆ *vb* **8** to play (a shot) forehand.

forehanded (ˌfɔːˈhændɪd) *adj* **1** *U.S.* **1a** thrifty. **1b** well-off. ◆ *adv, adj* **2** *Tennis, squash, etc.* a less common word for **forehand.** ▸ **ˌforeˈhandedly** *adv* ▸ **ˌforeˈhandedness** *n*

forehead (ˈfɒrɪd, ˈfɔːˌhɛd) *n* the part of the face between the natural hairline and the eyes, formed skeletally by the frontal bone of the skull; brow. Related adj: **frontal.** [Old English *forhēafod;* related to Old Frisian *forhāfd,* Middle Low German *vorhōved*]

forehock (ˈfɔːˌhɒk) *n* a foreleg cut of bacon or pork.

foreign (ˈfɒrɪn) *adj* **1** of, involving, located in, or coming from another country, area, people, etc.: *a foreign resident.* **2** dealing or concerned with another country, area, people, etc.: *a foreign office.* **3** not pertinent or related: *a matter foreign to the discussion.* **4** not familiar: strange. **5** in an abnormal place or position: *foreign matter.* **6** *Law.* outside the jurisdiction of a particular state; alien. [C13: from Old French *forain,* from Vulgar Latin *forānus* (unattested) situated on the outside, from Latin *foris* outside] ▸ **ˈforeignly** *adv* ▸ **ˈforeignness** *n*

foreign affairs *pl n* **1** matters abroad that involve the homeland, such as relations with another country. **2** matters that do not involve the homeland.

foreign aid *n* economic and other assistance given by one country to another.

foreign bill *or* **draft** *n* a bill of exchange that is drawn in one country and made payable in another: used extensively in foreign trade. Compare **inland bill.**

foreign correspondent *n Journalism.* a reporter who visits or resides in a foreign country in order to report on its affairs.

foreigner (ˈfɒrɪnə) *n* **1** a person from a foreign country; alien. **2** an outsider or interloper. **3** something from a foreign country, such as a ship or product.

foreign exchange *n* **1** the system by which one currency is converted into another, enabling international transactions to take place without the physical transportation of gold. **2** foreign bills and currencies.

foreignism (ˈfɒrɪˌnɪzəm) *n* **1** a custom, mannerism, idiom, etc., that is foreign. **2** imitation of something foreign.

foreign legion *n* a body of foreign volunteers serving in an army, esp. that of France.

foreign minister *or* **secretary** *n* (*often caps.*) a cabinet minister who is responsible for a country's dealings with other countries. U.S. equivalent: **secretary of state.** ▸ **foreign ministry** *n*

foreign mission *n* **1** a body of persons sent to a non-Christian country in order to propagate Christianity. **2** a diplomatic or other mission sent by one country to another.

foreign office *n* the ministry of a country or state that is concerned with dealings with other states. U.S. equivalent: **State Department.** Canadian equivalent: **(department of) external affairs.**

foreign service *n Chiefly U.S.* the diplomatic and usually consular personnel of a foreign affairs ministry or foreign office collectively who represent their country abroad, deal with foreign diplomats at home, etc.

forejudge[1] (fɔːˈdʒʌdʒ) *vb* to judge (someone or an event, circumstance, etc.) before the facts are known; prejudge.

forejudge[2] (fɔːˈdʒʌdʒ) *vb Law.* a variant spelling of **forjudge.** ▸ **foreˈjudgment** *n*

foreknow (fɔːˈnəʊ) *vb* **-knows, -knowing, -knew, -known.** (*tr*) to know in advance. ▸ **foreˈknowable** *adj* ▸ **foreˈknowledge** *n* ▸ **foreˈknowingly** *adv*

foreland (ˈfɔːlənd) *n* **1** a headland, cape, or promontory. **2** land lying in front of something, such as water.

Foreland (ˈfɔːlənd) *n* either of two headlands (**North Foreland** and **South Foreland**) in SE England, on the coast of Kent.

foreleg (ˈfɔːˌlɛg) *n* either of the front legs of a horse, sheep, or other quadruped.

forelimb (ˈfɔːˌlɪm) *n* either of the front or anterior limbs of a four-limbed vertebrate: a foreleg, flipper, or wing.

forelock[1] (ˈfɔːˌlɒk) *n* **1** a lock of hair growing or falling over the forehead. **2** a lock of a horse's mane that grows forwards between the ears.

forelock[2] (ˈfɔːˌlɒk) *n* **1** a wedge or peg passed through the tip of a bolt to prevent withdrawal. ◆ *vb* **2** (*tr*) to secure (a bolt) by means of a forelock.

foreman (ˈfɔːmən) *n, pl* **-men. 1** a person, often experienced, who supervises other workmen. Female equivalent: **forewoman. 2** *Law.* the principal juror, who presides at the deliberations of a jury. ▸ **ˈforemanˌship** *n*

Foreman (ˈfɔːmən) *n* **George.** born 1949, U.S. boxer: WBA world heavyweight champion (1973–74); he regained the title in 1994 but refused to fight the WBA's top-ranked challenger and was stripped of the title in 1995; recognized as WBU champion until 1997.

foremast (ˈfɔːˌmɑːst; *Nautical* ˈfɔːməst) *n* the mast nearest the bow on vessels with two or more masts.

foremilk (ˈfɔːˌmɪlk) *n* **1** another word for **colostrum. 2** the first milk drawn from a cow's udder prior to milking.

foremost (ˈfɔːˌməʊst) *adj, adv* first in time, place, rank, etc. [Old English *formest,* from *forma* first; related to Old Saxon *formo* first, Old High German *fruma* advantage]

forename (ˈfɔːˌneɪm) *n* a first or Christian name.

forenamed (ˈfɔːˌneɪmd) *adj* (*prenominal*) named or mentioned previously; aforesaid.

forenoon (ˈfɔːˌnuːn) *n* **a** the daylight hours before or just before noon. **b** (*as modifier*): *a forenoon conference.*

forensic (fəˈrɛnsɪk) *adj* relating to, used in, or connected with a court of law: *forensic science.* [C17: from Latin *forēnsis* public, from FORUM] ▸ **forensicality** (fəˌrɛnsɪˈkælɪtɪ) *n* ▸ **foˈrensically** *adv*

forensic medicine *n* the applied use of medical knowledge or practice, esp. pathology, to the purposes of the law, as in determining the cause of death. Also called: **medical jurisprudence, legal medicine.**

forensics (fəˈrɛnsɪks) *n* (*functioning as sing or pl*) the art or study of formal debating.

foreordain (ˌfɔːrɔːˈdeɪn) *vb* (*tr; may take a clause as object*) to determine (events, results, etc.) in the future. ▸ **ˌforeorˈdainment** *or* **foreordination** (ˌfɔːrɔːdɪˈneɪʃən) *n*

forepart (ˈfɔːˌpɑːt) *n* the first or front part in place, order, or time.

forepaw (ˈfɔːˌpɔː) *n* either of the front feet of most land mammals that do not have hoofs.

forepeak (ˈfɔːˌpiːk) *n Nautical.* the interior part of a vessel that is furthest forward.

foreplay (ˈfɔːˌpleɪ) *n* mutual sexual stimulation preceding sexual intercourse.

forequarter (ˈfɔːˌkwɔːtə) *n* the front portion, including the leg, of half of a carcass, as of beef or lamb.

forequarters (ˈfɔːˌkwɔːtəz) *pl n* the part of the body of a horse or similar quadruped that consists of the forelegs, shoulders, and adjoining parts.

forereach (fɔːˈriːtʃ) *vb* **1** (*intr*) *Nautical.* to keep moving under momentum without engine or sails. **2** (*tr*) to surpass or outdo.

forerun (fɔːˈrʌn) *vb* **-runs, -running, -ran, -run.** (*tr*) **1** to serve as a herald for. **2** to go before; precede. **3** to prevent or forestall.

forerunner (ˈfɔːˌrʌnə) *n* **1** a person or thing that precedes another; precursor. **2** a person or thing coming in advance to herald the arrival of someone or something; harbinger. **3** an indication beforehand of something to follow; omen; portent.

foresaid (ˈfɔːˌsɛd) *adj* a less common word for **aforesaid.**

foresail (ˈfɔːˌseɪl; *Nautical* ˈfɔːsəl) *n Nautical.* **1** the aftermost headsail of a fore-and-aft rigged vessel. **2** the lowest sail set on the foremast of a square-rigged vessel.

foresee (fɔːˈsiː) *vb* **-sees, -seeing, -saw, -seen.** (*tr; may take a clause as object*) to see or know beforehand: *he did not foresee that.* ▸ **foreˈseeable** *adj* ▸ **foreˈseer** *n*

foreshadow (fɔːˈʃædəʊ) *vb* (*tr*) to show, indicate, or suggest in advance; presage. ▸ **foreˈshadower** *n*

foreshank (ˈfɔːˌʃæŋk) *n* **1** the top of the front leg of an animal. **2** a cut of meat from this part.

foresheet (ˈfɔːˌʃiːt) *n* **1** the sheet of a foresail. **2** (*pl*) the part forward of the foremost thwart of a boat.

foreshock (ˈfɔːˌʃɒk) *n* a relatively small earthquake heralding the arrival of a much larger one. Some large earthquakes are preceded by a series of foreshocks. Compare **aftershock.**

foreshore (ˈfɔːˌʃɔː) *n* **1** the part of the shore that lies between the limits for high and low tides. **2** the part of the shore that lies just above the high-water mark.

foreshorten (fɔːˈʃɔːtən) *vb* (*tr*) **1** to represent (a line, form, object, etc.) as shorter than actual length in order to give an illusion of recession or projection, in accordance with the laws of linear perspective. **2** to make shorter or more condensed; reduce or abridge.

foreshow (fɔːˈʃəʊ) *vb* **-shows, -showing, -showed, -shown.** (*tr*) *Archaic.* to indicate in advance; foreshadow.

foreside (ˈfɔːˌsaɪd) *n* **1** the front or upper side or part. **2** *U.S.* land extending along the sea.

foresight (ˈfɔːˌsaɪt) *n* **1** provision for or insight into future problems, needs, etc. **2** the act or ability of foreseeing. **3** the act of looking forward. **4** *Surveying.* a reading taken looking forwards to a new station, esp. in levelling from a point of known elevation to a point the elevation of which is to be determined. Compare **backsight. 5** the front sight on a firearm. ▸ **ˌforeˈsighted** *adj* ▸ **ˌforeˈsightedly** *adv* ▸ **ˌforeˈsightedness** *n*

foreskin (ˈfɔːˌskɪn) *n Anatomy.* the nontechnical name for **prepuce** (sense 1). Related adj: **preputial.**

forespeak (fɔːˈspiːk) *vb* **-speaks, -speaking, -spoke, -spoken.** (*tr*) *Rare.* **1** to predict; foresee. **2** to arrange or speak of in advance.

forespent (fɔːˈspɛnt) *adj* a variant spelling of **forspent.**

forest (ˈfɒrɪst) *n* **1** a large wooded area having a thick growth of trees and plants. **2** the trees of such an area. **3** *N.Z.* an area planted with exotic pines or similar trees. Compare **bush**[1] (sense 4). **4** something resembling a large wooded area, esp. in density: *a forest of telegraph poles.* **5** *Law.* (formerly) an area of woodland, esp. one owned by the sovereign and set apart as a hunting ground with its own laws and officers. Compare **park** (sense 5). **6** (*modifier*) of, involving, or living in a forest or forests: *a forest glade.* ◆ *vb* **7** (*tr*) to create a forest (in); plant with trees. [**C13**: from Old French, from Medieval Latin *forestis* unfenced woodland, from Latin *foris* outside] ▸ **'forestal** *or* **foresteal** (fə'rɛstɪəl) *adj* ▸ **'forested** *adj* ▸ **'forestless** *adj* ▸ **'forest-,like** *adj*

forestall (fɔː'stɔːl) *vb* (*tr*) **1** to delay, stop, or guard against beforehand. **2** to anticipate. **3a** to prevent or hinder sales at (a market, etc.) by buying up merchandise in advance, etc. **3b** to buy up (merchandise) for profitable resale. Compare **corner** (sense 21). [**C14** *forestallen* to waylay, from Old English *foresteall* an ambush, from *fore-* in front of + *steall* place] ▸ **fore'staller** *n* ▸ **fore'stalment** *or esp. U.S.* **fore'stallment** *n*

forestation (,fɒrɪ'steɪʃən) *n* the planting of trees over a wide area.

forestay ('fɔː,steɪ) *n Nautical.* an adjustable stay leading from the truck of the foremast to the deck, stem, or bowsprit, for controlling the motion or bending of the mast.

forestaysail (fɔː'steɪ,seɪl; *Nautical* fɔː'steɪsəl) *n Nautical.* the triangular headsail set aftermost on a vessel.

forester ('fɒrɪstə) *n* **1** a person skilled in forestry or in charge of a forest. **2** any of various Old World moths of the genus *Ino,* characterized by brilliant metallic green wings: family *Zygaenidae.* **3** a person or animal that lives in a forest. **4** (*cap.*) a member of the Ancient Order of Foresters, a friendly society.

Forester ('fɒrɪstə) *n* **C(ecil) S(cott).** 1899–1966, English novelist; creator of Captain Horatio Hornblower in a series of novels on the Napoleonic Wars.

forest park *n N.Z.* a recreational reserve which may include bush and exotic trees.

forest ranger *n Chiefly U.S. and Canadian.* a government official who patrols and protects forests, wildlife, etc.

forestry ('fɒrɪstrɪ) *n* **1** the science of planting and caring for trees. **2** the planting and management of forests. **3** *Rare.* forest land.

foretaste *n* ('fɔː,teɪst). **1** an early but limited experience or awareness of something to come. ◆ *vb* (fɔː'teɪst). **2** (*tr*) to have a foretaste of.

foretell (fɔː'tɛl) *vb* **-tells, -telling, -told.** (*tr; may take a clause as object*) to tell or indicate (an event, a result, etc.) beforehand; predict. ▸ **fore'teller** *n*

forethought ('fɔː,θɔːt) *n* **1** advance consideration or deliberation. **2** thoughtful anticipation of future events. ▸ **fore'thoughtful** *adj* ▸ **fore'thoughtfully** *adv* ▸ **fore'thoughtfulness** *n*

foretime ('fɔː,taɪm) *n* time already gone; the past.

foretoken *n* ('fɔː,təʊkən). **1** a sign of a future event. ◆ *vb* (fɔː'təʊkən). **2** (*tr*) to foreshadow.

foretooth ('fɔː,tuːθ) *n, pl* **-teeth** (-,tiːθ). *Dentistry.* another word for an **incisor.**

foretop ('fɔː,tɒp; *Nautical* 'fɔːtəp) *n Nautical.* a platform at the top of the foremast.

fore-topgallant (,fɔːtɒp'gælənt; *Nautical* ,fɔːtə'gælənt) *adj Nautical.* of, relating to, or being the topmost portion of a foremast, above the topmast: *the fore-topgallant mast.*

fore-topmast (fɔː'tɒp,mɑːst; *Nautical* fɔː'tɒpməst) *n Nautical.* a mast stepped above a foremast.

fore-topsail (fɔː'tɒp,seɪl; *Nautical* fɔː'tɒpsəl) *n Nautical.* a sail set on a fore-topmast.

foretriangle ('fɔːtraɪ,æŋgəl) *n* the triangular area formed by the deck, foremast, and headstay of a sailing vessel.

forever (fɔː'rɛvə, fə-) *adv* **1** Also: **for ever.** without end; everlastingly; eternally. **2** at all times; incessantly. **3** *Informal.* for a very long time: *he went on speaking forever.* ◆ *n* **4** (*as object*) *Informal.* a very long time: *it took him forever to reply.* **5 ... forever!** an exclamation expressing support or loyalty: *Scotland forever!*

USAGE *Forever* and *for ever* can both be used to say that something is without end. For all other meanings, *forever* is the preferred form.

for evermore *or* **forevermore** (fɔː,rɛvə'mɔː, fə-) *adv* a more emphatic or emotive term for **forever.**

forewarn (fɔː'wɔːn) *vb* (*tr*) to warn beforehand. ▸ **fore'warner** *n* ▸ **fore'warningly** *adv*

forewent (fɔː'wɛnt) *vb* the past tense of **forego.**

forewind ('fɔː,wɪnd) *n Nautical.* a favourable wind.

forewing ('fɔː,wɪŋ) *n* either wing of the anterior pair of an insect's two pairs of wings.

foreword ('fɔː,wɜːd) *n* an introductory statement to a book. [**C19**: literal translation of German *Vorwort*]

foreworn (fɔː'wɔːn) *adj* a variant spelling of **forworn.**

forex ('fɒreks) *n* short for **foreign exchange.**

foreyard ('fɔː,jɑːd) *n Nautical.* a yard for supporting the foresail of a square-rigger.

forfaiting ('fɔː,feitɪŋ) *n* the financial service of discounting, without recourse, a promissory note, bill of exchange, letter of credit, etc., received from an overseas buyer by an exporter; a form of debt discounting. [**C20**: from French *forfaire* to forfeit or surrender]

Forfar ('fɔːfər, -fɑː) *n* a market town in E Scotland, the administrative centre of Angus: site of a castle, residence of Scottish kings between the 11th and 14th centuries. Pop.: 12 961 (1991).

forfeit ('fɔːfɪt) *n* **1** something lost or given up as a penalty for a fault, mistake, etc. **2** the act of losing or surrendering something in this manner. **3** *Law.* something confiscated as a penalty for an offence, breach of contract, etc. **4** (*sometimes pl*) **4a** a game in which a player has to give up an object, perform a specified action, etc., if he commits a fault. **4b** an object so given up. ◆ *vb* **5** (*tr*) to lose or be liable to lose in consequence of a mistake, fault, etc. **6** (*tr*) *Law.* **6a** to confiscate as punishment. **6b** to surrender (something exacted as a penalty). ◆ *adj* **7** surrendered or liable to be surrendered as a penalty. [**C13**: from Old French *forfet* offence, from *forfaire* to commit a crime, from Medieval Latin *foris facere* to act outside (what is lawful), from Latin *foris* outside + *facere* to do] ▸ **'forfeitable** *adj* ▸ **'forfeiter** *n*

forfeiture ('fɔːfɪtʃə) *n* **1** something forfeited. **2** the act of forfeiting or paying a penalty.

forfend *or* **forefend** (fɔː'fɛnd) *vb* (*tr*) **1** *U.S.* to protect or secure. **2** *Obsolete.* to prohibit or prevent.

forfex ('fɔːfɛks) *n Entomol.* a pair of pincers, esp. the paired terminal appendages of an earwig. [**C18**: Latin: a pair of scissors]

forficate ('fɔːfɪkɪt, -,keɪt) *adj* (esp. of the tails of certain birds) deeply forked. [**C19**: from Latin *forfex* scissors]

forfochen (fər'foxən) *adj Scot.* exhausted. [a variant of earlier *forfoughten* worn out by fighting]

forgat (fə'gæt) *vb Archaic.* a past tense of **forget.**

forgather (fɔː'gæðə) *vb* a variant spelling of **foregather.**

forgave (fə'geɪv) *vb* the past tense of **forgive.**

forge[1] (fɔːdʒ) *n* **1** a place in which metal is worked by heating and hammering; smithy. **2** a hearth or furnace used for heating metal. **3** a machine used to shape metals by hammering. ◆ *vb* **4** (*tr*) to shape (metal) by heating and hammering. **5** (*tr*) to form, shape, make, or fashion (objects, articles, etc.). **6** (*tr*) to invent or devise (an agreement, understanding, etc.). **7** to make or produce a fraudulent imitation of (a signature, banknote, etc.) or to commit forgery. [**C14**: from Old French *forgier* to construct, from Latin *fabricāre,* from *faber* craftsman] ▸ **'forgeable** *adj* ▸ **'forger** *n*

forge[2] (fɔːdʒ) *vb* (*intr*) **1** to move at a steady and persevering pace. **2 forge ahead.** to increase speed; spurt. [**C17**: of unknown origin]

forgery ('fɔːdʒərɪ) *n, pl* **-geries. 1** the act of reproducing something for a deceitful or fraudulent purpose. **2** something forged, such as a work of art or an antique. **3** *Criminal law.* **3a** the false making or altering of any document, such as a cheque or character reference (and including a postage stamp), or any tape or disc on which information is stored, intending that anyone shall accept it as genuine and so act to his or another's prejudice. **3b** something forged. **4** *Criminal law.* the counterfeiting of a seal or die with intention to defraud.

forget (fə'gɛt) *vb* **-gets, -getting, -got, -gotten** *or* (*Archaic or dialect*) **-got. 1** (when *tr, may take a clause as object or an infinitive*) to fail to recall (someone or something once known); be unable to remember. **2** (*tr; may take a clause as object or an infinitive*) to neglect, usually as the result of an unintentional error. **3** (*tr*) to leave behind by mistake. **4** (*tr*) to disregard intentionally. **5** (when *tr, may take a clause as object*) to fail to mention. **6 forget oneself. 6a** to act in an improper manner. **6b** to be unselfish. **6c** to be deep in thought. **7 forget it!** an exclamation of annoyed or forgiving dismissal of a matter or topic. [Old English *forgietan;* related to Old Frisian *forgeta,* Old Saxon *fargetan,* Old High German *firgezzan*] ▸ **for'gettable** *adj* ▸ **for'getter** *n*

forgetful (fə'gɛtfʊl) *adj* **1** tending to forget. **2** (*often postpositive;* foll. by *of*) inattentive (to) or neglectful (of). **3** *Poetic.* causing loss of memory. ▸ **for'getfully** *adv* ▸ **for'getfulness** *n*

forget-me-not *n* any temperate low-growing plants of the mainly European boraginaceous genus *Myosotis,* esp. *M. scorpioides,* having clusters of small typically blue flowers. Also called: **scorpion grass.**

forging ('fɔːdʒɪŋ) *n* **1** the process of producing a metal component by hammering. **2** the act of a forger. **3** a metal component produced by this process. **4** the collision of a horse's hind shoe and fore shoe.

forgive (fə'gɪv) *vb* **-gives, -giving, -gave, -given. 1** to cease to blame or hold resentment against (someone or something). **2** to grant pardon for (a mistake, wrongdoing, etc.). **3** (*tr*) to free or pardon (someone) from penalty. **4** (*tr*) to free from the obligation of (a debt, payment, etc.). [Old English *forgiefan;* see FOR-, GIVE] ▸ **for'givable** *adj* ▸ **for'givably** *adv* ▸ **for'giver** *n*

forgiveness (fə'gɪvnɪs) *n* **1** the act of forgiving or the state of being forgiven. **2** willingness to forgive.

forgiving (fə'gɪvɪŋ) *adj* willing to forgive; merciful. ▸ **for'givingly** *adv* ▸ **for'givingness** *n*

forgo *or* **forego** (fɔː'gəʊ) *vb* **-goes, -going, -went, -gone.** (*tr*) **1** to give up or do without. **2** *Archaic.* to leave. [Old English *forgān;* see FOR-, GO[1]] ▸ **for'goer** *or* **fore'goer** *n*

forgot (fə'gɒt) *vb* **1** the past tense of **forget. 2** *Archaic or dialect.* a past participle of **forget.**

forgotten (fə'gɒtən) *vb* a past participle of **forget.**

forint (*Hungarian* 'forint) *n* the standard monetary unit of Hungary, divided into 100 fillér. [from Hungarian, from Italian *fiorino* FLORIN]

forjudge *or* **forejudge** (fɔː'dʒʌdʒ) *vb* (*tr*) *Law.* **1** to deprive of a right by the judgment of a court. **2** *Chiefly U.S.* to expel (an officer or attorney) from court for misconduct. ▸ **for'judgment** *or* **fore'judgment** *n*

fork (fɔːk) *n* **1** a small usually metal implement consisting of two, three, or four long thin prongs on the end of a handle, used for lifting food to the mouth or turning it in cooking, etc. **2** an agricultural tool consisting of a handle and three or four metal prongs, used for lifting, digging, etc. **3** a pronged part of any machine, device, etc. **4** (of a road, river, etc.) **4a** a division into two or more branches. **4b** the point where the division begins. **4c** such a branch. **5** *Chiefly U.S.* the main tributary of a river. **6** *Chess.* a position in which two pieces are forked. ◆ *vb* **7** (*tr*) to pick up, dig, etc., with a fork. **8** (*tr*) *Chess.* to place (two enemy pieces) under attack with one of one's own pieces, esp. a knight. **9** (*tr*) to make into the shape of a fork. **10** (*intr*) to be divided into two or more branches. **11** to take one or other branch at a fork in a road, river, etc. [Old English *forca,* from Latin *furca*] ▸ **'forkful** *n*

forked (fɔːkt, 'fɔːkɪd) *adj* **1a** having a fork or forklike parts. **1b** (*in combination*): *two-forked.* **2** having sharp angles; zigzag. **3** insincere or equivocal (esp. in the phrase **forked tongue**). ▸ **forkedly** ('fɔːkɪdlɪ) *adv* ▸ **'forkedness** *n*

forked lightning *n* a zigzag form of lightning. Also called: **chain lightning.**

fork-lift truck *n* a vehicle having two power-operated horizontal prongs that can be raised and lowered for loading, transporting, and unloading goods, esp. goods that are stacked on wooden pallets. Sometimes shortened to **forklift.**

fork out, over, *or* **up** *vb* (*adv*) *Slang.* to pay (money, goods, etc.), esp. with reluctance.

Forlì (*Italian* for'li) *n* a city in N Italy, in Emilia-Romagna. Pop.: 108 017 (1996 est.). Ancient name: **Forum Livii** ('lɪvɪaɪ).

forlorn (fə'lɔ:n) *adj* **1** miserable, wretched, or cheerless; desolate. **2** deserted; forsaken. **3** (*postpositive;* foll. by *of*) destitute; bereft: *forlorn of hope.* **4** desperate: *the last forlorn attempt.* [Old English *forloren* lost, from *forlēosan* to lose; related to Old Saxon *farliosan,* Gothic *fraliusan,* Greek *luein* to release] ▸ **for'lornly** *adv* ▸ **for'lornness** *n*

forlorn hope *n* **1** a hopeless or desperate enterprise. **2** a faint hope. **3** *Obsolete.* a group of soldiers assigned to an extremely dangerous duty. [C16 (in the obsolete sense): changed (by folk etymology) from Dutch *verloren hoop* lost troop, from *verloren,*past participle of *verliezen* to lose + *hoop* troop (literally: heap)]

form (fɔ:m) *n* **1** the shape or configuration of something as distinct from its colour, texture, etc. **2** the particular mode, appearance, etc., in which a thing or person manifests itself: *water in the form of ice; in the form of a bat.* **3** a type or kind: *imprisonment is a form of punishment.* **4a** a printed document, esp. one with spaces in which to insert facts or answers: *an application form.* **4b** (*as modifier*): *a form letter.* **5** physical or mental condition, esp. good condition, with reference to ability to perform: *off form.* **6** the previous record of a horse, athlete, etc., esp. with regard to fitness. **7** *Brit. slang.* a criminal record. **8** style, arrangement, or design in the arts, as opposed to content. **9** a fixed mode of artistic expression or representation in literary, musical, or other artistic works: *sonata form; sonnet form.* **10** a mould, frame, etc., that gives shape to something. **11** organized structure or order, as in an artistic work. **12** *Education, chiefly Brit.* a group of children who are taught together; class. **13** manner, method, or style of doing something, esp. with regard to recognized standards. **14** behaviour or procedure, esp. as governed by custom or etiquette: *good form.* **15** formality or ceremony. **16** a prescribed set or order of words, terms, etc., as in a religious ceremony or legal document. **17** *Philosophy.* **17a** the structure of anything as opposed to its constitution or content. **17b** essence as opposed to matter. **17c** (*often cap.*) (in the philosophy of Plato) the ideal universal that exists independently of the particulars which fall under it. See also **Form. 17d** (in the philosophy of Aristotle) the constitution of matter to form a substance; by virtue of this its nature can be understood. **18** See **logical form. 19** *Brit.* a bench, esp. one that is long, low, and backless. **20** the nest or hollow in which a hare lives. **21** a group of organisms within a species that differ from similar groups by trivial differences, as of colour. **22** *Linguistics.* **22a** the phonological or orthographic shape or appearance of a linguistic element, such as a word. **22b** a linguistic element considered from the point of view of its shape or sound rather than, for example, its meaning. **23** *Crystallog.* See **crystal form. 24** *Taxonomy.* a group distinguished from other groups by a single characteristic: ranked below a variety. ◆ *vb* **25** to give shape or form to or to take shape or form, esp. a specified or particular shape. **26** to come or bring into existence: *a scum formed on the surface.* **27** to make, produce, or construct or be made, produced, or constructed. **28** to construct or develop in the mind: *to form an opinion.* **29** (*tr*) to train, develop, or mould by instruction, discipline, or example. **30** (*tr*) to acquire, contract, or develop: *to form a habit.* **31** (*tr*) to be an element of, serve as, or constitute: *this plank will form a bridge.* **32** (*tr*) to draw up; organize: *to form a club.* [C13: from Old French *forme,* from Latin *forma* shape, model] ▸ **'formable** *adj*

Form (fɔ:m) *n* (in the philosophy of Plato) an ideal archetype existing independently of those individuals which fall under it, supposedly explaining their common properties and serving as the only objects of true knowledge as opposed to the mere opinion obtainable of matters of fact. Also called: **Idea.**

-form *adj combining form.* having the shape or form of or resembling: *cruciform; vermiform.* [from New Latin *-formis,* from Latin, from *fōrma* FORM]

formal[1] ('fɔ:məl) *adj* **1** of, according to, or following established or prescribed forms, conventions, etc.: *a formal document.* **2** characterized by observation of conventional forms of ceremony, behaviour, dress, etc.: *a formal dinner.* **3** methodical, precise, or stiff. **4** suitable for occasions organized according to conventional ceremony: *formal dress.* **5** denoting or characterized by idiom, vocabulary, etc., used by educated speakers and writers of a language. **6** acquired by study in academic institutions: *a formal education.* **7** regular or symmetrical in form: *a formal garden.* **8** of or relating to the appearance, form, etc., of something as distinguished from its substance. **9** logically deductive: *formal proof.* **10** *Philosophy.* **10a** of or relating to form as opposed to matter or content. **10b** pertaining to the essence or nature of something: *formal cause.* **10c** (in the writings of Descartes) pertaining to the correspondence between an image or idea and its object. **10d** being in the formal mode. **11** denoting a second-person pronoun in some languages used when the addressee is a stranger, social superior, etc.: *in French the pronoun "vous" is formal, while "tu" is informal.* [C14: from Latin *formālis*] ▸ **'formally** *adv* ▸ **'formalness** *n*

formal[2] ('fɔ:mæl) *n* another name for **methylal.** [C19: from FORM(IC) + -AL[3]]

formaldehyde (fɔ:'mældɪ,haɪd) *n* a colourless poisonous irritating gas with a pungent characteristic odour, made by the oxidation of methanol and used as formalin and in the manufacture of synthetic resins. Formula: HCHO. Systematic name: **methanal.** [C19: FORM(IC) + ALDEHYDE; on the model of German *Formaldehyd*]

formal equivalence *n Logic.* the relation that holds between two open sentences when their universal closures are materially equivalent.

formalin ('fɔ:məlɪn) *or* **formol** ('fɔ:mɒl) *n* a 40 per cent solution of formaldehyde in water, used as a disinfectant, preservative for biological specimens, etc.

formalism ('fɔ:mə,lɪzəm) *n* **1** scrupulous or excessive adherence to outward form at the expense of inner reality or content. **2a** the mathematical or logical structure of a scientific argument as distinguished from its subject matter. **2b** the notation, and its structure, in which information is expressed. **3** *Theatre.* a stylized mode of production. **4** (in Marxist criticism) excessive concern with artistic technique at the expense of social values, etc. **5** the philosophical theory that a mathematical statement has no meaning but that its symbols, regarded as physical objects, exhibit a structure that has useful applications. Compare **logicism, intuitionism.** ▸ **'formalist** *n* ▸ **,formal'istic** *adj* ▸ **,formal'istically** *adv*

formality (fɔ:'mælɪtɪ) *n, pl* **-ties. 1** a requirement of rule, custom, etiquette, etc. **2** the condition or quality of being formal or conventional. **3** strict or excessive observance of form, ceremony, etc. **4** an established, proper, or conventional method, act, or procedure.

formalize *or* **formalise** ('fɔ:mə,laɪz) *vb* **1** to be or make formal. **2** (*tr*) to make official or valid. **3** (*tr*) to give a definite shape or form to. **4** *Logic.* to extract the logical form of (an expression), to express in the symbols of some formal system. ▸ **,formali'zation** *or* **,formali'sation** *n* ▸ **'formal,izer** *or* **'formal,iser** *n*

formal language *n* **1** a language designed for use in situations in which natural language is unsuitable, as for example in mathematics, logic, or computer programming. The symbols and formulas of such languages stand in precisely specified syntactic and semantic relations to one another. **2** *Logic.* a logistic system for which an interpretation is provided: distinguished from formal calculus in that the semantics enable it to be regarded as *about* some subject matter.

formal logic *n* **1** the study of systems of deductive argument in which symbols are used to represent precisely defined categories of expressions. Also called: **symbolic logic.** Compare **philosophical logic. 2** a specific formal system that can be interpreted as representing a fragment of natural argument.

formal mode *n Philosophy.* the style in which words are explicitly mentioned rather than used of their subject matter. *"Fido" is a dog's name* is in the formal mode, while *"Fido is a dog"* is in the material mode. See also **mention** (sense 7).

formal system *n Logic.* an uninterpreted symbolic system whose syntax is precisely defined, and on which a relation of deducibility is defined in purely syntactic terms; a logistic system. Also called: **formal theory, formal calculus.** Compare **formal language.**

Forman ('fɔ:mən) *n* **Miloš** ('mi:ləuʃ). born 1932, Czech film director working in the U.S.A. since 1968. His films include *One Flew over the Cuckoo's Nest* (1976), *Amadeus* (1985), and *The People vs Larry Flynt* (1996).

formant ('fɔ:mənt) *n Acoustics, phonetics.* any of several frequency ranges within which the partials of a sound, esp. a vowel sound, are at their strongest, thus imparting to the sound its own special quality, tone colour, or timbre.

format ('fɔ:mæt) *n* **1** the general appearance of a publication, including type style, paper, binding, etc. **2** an approximate indication of the size of a publication as determined by the number of times the original sheet of paper is folded to make a leaf. See also **duodecimo, quarto. 3** style, plan, or arrangement, as of a television programme. **4** *Computing.* **4a** the defined arrangement of data encoded in a file or for example on magnetic disk or CD-ROM, essential for the correct recording and recovery of data on different devices. **4b** the arrangement of text on printed output or a display screen, or a coded description of such an arrangement. ◆ *vb* **-mats, -matting, -matted.** (*tr*) **5** to arrange (a book, page, etc.) into a specified format. [C19: via French from German, from Latin *liber formātus* volume formed]

formate ('fɔ:meɪt) *n* any salt or ester of formic acid containing the ion $HCOO^-$ or the group HCOO-. [C19: from FORM(IC) + -ATE[1]]

formation (fɔ:'meɪʃən) *n* **1** the act of giving or taking form, shape, or existence. **2** something that is formed. **3** the manner in which something is formed or arranged. **4** a formal arrangement of a number of persons or things acting as a unit, such as a troop of soldiers, aircraft in flight, or a football team. **5** a series of rocks with certain characteristics in common. **6** *Ecology.* a community of plants, such as a tropical rain forest, extending over a very large area. ▸ **for'mational** *adj*

formation dance *n* any dance in which a number of couples form a certain arrangement, such as two facing lines or a circle, and perform a series of figures within or based on that arrangement. ▸ **formation dancing** *n*

formation rules *pl n Logic.* the set of rules that specify the syntax of a formal system; the algorithm that generates the well-formed formulae.

formative ('fɔ:mətɪv) *adj* **1** of or relating to formation, development, or growth: *formative years.* **2** shaping; moulding: *a formative experience.* **3** (of tissues and cells in certain parts of an organism) capable of growth and differentiation. **4** functioning in the formation of derived, inflected, or compound words. ◆ *n* **5** an inflectional or derivational affix. **6** (in generative grammar) any of the minimum units of a sentence that have syntactic function. ▸ **'formatively** *adv* ▸ **'formativeness** *n*

formative assessment *n* ongoing assessment of a pupil's educational development within a particular subject area. Compare **summative assessment.**

Formby ('fɔ:mbɪ) *n* **George.** Real name *George Booth.* 1904–61, British comedian. He made many musical films in the 1930s, accompanying his songs on the ukulele.

form class *n* **1** another term for **part of speech. 2** a group of words distinguished by common inflections, such as the weak verbs of English.

form criticism *n* literary criticism concerned esp. with analysing the Bible in terms of the literary forms used, such as proverbs, songs, or stories, and relating them to their historical forms and background. ▸ **form critic** *n* ▸ **form critical** *adj*

form drag *n* the drag on a body moving through a fluid as a result of the shape of the body. It can be reduced by streamlining.

forme *or U.S.* **form** (fɔːm) *n Printing.* type matter, blocks, etc., assembled in a chase and ready for printing. **[C15:** from French: FORM**]**

former[1] (ˈfɔːmə) *adj (prenominal)* **1** belonging to or occurring in an earlier time: *former glory.* **2** having been at a previous time: *a former colleague.* **3** denoting the first or first mentioned of two: *in the former case.* **4** near the beginning. ◆ *n* **5 the former.** the first or first mentioned of two: distinguished from *latter.*

former[2] (ˈfɔːmə) *n* **1** a person or thing that forms or shapes. **2** *Electrical engineering.* a tool for giving a coil or winding the required shape, sometimes consisting of a frame on which the wire can be wound, the frame then being removed.

formerly (ˈfɔːməlɪ) *adv* **1** at or in a former time; in the past. **2** *Obsolete.* in the immediate past; just now.

form genus *n* a group of species (**form species**) that have similar structural characteristics but are not closely related.

formic (ˈfɔːmɪk) *adj* **1** of, relating to, or derived from ants. **2** of, containing, or derived from formic acid. **[C18:** from Latin *formīca* ant; the acid occurs naturally in ants**]**

Formica (fɔːˈmaɪkə) *n Trademark.* any of various laminated plastic sheets, containing melamine, used esp. for heat-resistant surfaces that can be easily cleaned.

formic acid *n* a colourless corrosive liquid carboxylic acid found in some insects, esp. ants, and many plants: used in dyeing textiles and the manufacture of insecticides and refrigerants. Formula: HCOOH. Systematic name: **methanoic acid.**

formicary (ˈfɔːmɪkərɪ) *or* **formicarium** (ˌfɔːmɪˈkɛərɪəm) *n, pl* **-caries** *or* **-caria** (-ˈkɛərɪə). less common names for **ant hill.** **[C19:** from Medieval Latin *formīcārium;* see FORMIC**]**

formicate (ˈfɔːmɪˌkeɪt) *vb (intr) Now rare.* **1** to crawl around like ants. **2** to swarm with ants or other crawling things. **[C17:** from Latin *formīcāre,* from *formīca* ant**]**

formication (ˌfɔːmɪˈkeɪʃən) *n* a sensation of insects crawling on the skin; symptom of a nerve disorder.

formidable (ˈfɔːmɪdəbᵊl) *adj* **1** arousing or likely to inspire fear or dread. **2** extremely difficult to defeat, overcome, manage, etc.: *a formidable problem.* **3** tending to inspire awe or admiration because of great size, strength, excellence, etc. **[C15:** from Latin *formīdābilis,* from *formīdāre* to dread, from *formīdō* fear**]** ► **ˌformidaˈbility** *or* **ˈformidableness** *n* ► **ˈformidably** *adv*

formless (ˈfɔːmlɪs) *adj* without a definite shape or form; amorphous. ► **ˈformlessly** *adv* ► **ˈformlessness** *n*

form letter *n* a single copy of a letter that has been mechanically reproduced in large numbers for circulation.

Formosa (fɔːˈməʊsə) *n* the former name of **Taiwan.**

Formosa Strait *n* an arm of the Pacific between Taiwan and mainland China, linking the East and South China Seas. Also called: **Taiwan Strait.**

formula (ˈfɔːmjʊlə) *n, pl* **-las** *or* **-lae** (-ˌliː). **1** an established form or set of words, as used in religious ceremonies, legal proceedings, etc. **2** *Maths, physics.* a general relationship, principle, or rule stated, often as an equation, in the form of symbols. **3** *Chem.* a representation of molecules, radicals, ions, etc., expressed in the symbols of the atoms of their constituent elements. See **molecular formula, empirical formula, structural formula. 4a** a method, pattern, or rule for doing or producing something, often one proved to be successful. **4b** (*as modifier*): *formula fiction.* **5a** a prescription for making up a medicine, baby's food, etc. **5b** a substance prepared according to such a prescription. **6** *Motor racing.* the specific category in which a particular type of car competes, judged according to engine size, weight, and fuel capacity. **[C17:** from Latin: diminutive of *forma* FORM**]** ► **formulaic** (ˌfɔːmjʊˈleɪɪk) *adj*

Formula One *n* **1** the top class of professional motor racing. **2** the most important world championship in motor racing.

formularize *or* **formularise** (ˈfɔːmjʊləˌraɪz) *vb* a less common word for **formulate** (sense 1). ► **ˌformulariˈzation** *or* **ˌformulariˈsation** *n* ► **ˈformularˌizer** *or* **ˈformularˌiser** *n*

formulary (ˈfɔːmjʊlərɪ) *n, pl* **-laries. 1** a book or system of prescribed formulas, esp. relating to religious procedure or doctrine. **2** a formula. **3** *Pharmacol.* a book containing a list of pharmaceutical products with their formulas and means of preparation. ◆ *adj* **4** of, relating to, or of the nature of a formula.

formulate (ˈfɔːmjʊˌleɪt) *vb (tr)* **1** to put into or express in systematic terms; express in or as if in a formula. **2** to devise. ► **ˌformuˈlation** *n* ► **ˈformuˌlator** *n*

formulism (ˈfɔːmjʊˌlɪzəm) *n* adherence to or belief in formulas. ► **ˈformulist** *n, adj* ► **ˌformuˈlistic** *adj*

formwork (ˈfɔːmˌwɜːk) *n* an arrangement of wooden boards, bolts, etc., used to shape reinforced concrete while it is setting. Also called (esp. Brit.): **shuttering.**

formyl (ˈfɔːmaɪl) *n* (*modifier*) of, consisting of, or containing the monovalent group HCO-: *a formyl group or radical.* **[C19:** from FORM(IC) + -YL**]**

Fornax (ˈfɔːnæks) *n, Latin genitive* **Fornacis** (fɔːˈneɪsɪs, -ˈnæs-). a faint constellation in the S hemisphere lying between Cetus and Phoenix. **[**Latin: oven, kiln**]**

fornenst (fɔːˈnenst) *prep Scot. and northeast English dialect.* situated against or facing towards. **[**from Scottish, from FORE[1] + *anenst* a variant of archaic ANENT**]**

fornicate[1] (ˈfɔːnɪˌkeɪt) *vb (intr)* to indulge in or commit fornication. **[C16:** from Late Latin *fornicārī,* from Latin *fornix* vault, brothel situated therein**]** ► **ˈforniˌcator** *n*

fornicate[2] (ˈfɔːnɪkɪt, -ˌkeɪt) *or* **fornicated** *adj Biology.* arched or hoodlike in form. **[C19:** from Latin *fornicātus* arched, from *fornix* vault**]**

fornication (ˌfɔːnɪˈkeɪʃən) *n* **1** voluntary sexual intercourse outside marriage. **2** *Law.* voluntary sexual intercourse between two persons of the opposite sex, where one is or both are unmarried. **3** *Bible.* sexual immorality in general, esp. adultery.

fornix (ˈfɔːnɪks) *n, pl* **-nices** (-nɪˌsiːz). *Anatomy.* any archlike structure, esp. the arched band of white fibres at the base of the brain. **[C17:** from Latin; see FORNICATE[2]**]** ► **ˈfornical** *adj*

Forrest (ˈfɒrɪst) *n* **John,** 1st Baron Forrest. 1847–1918, Australian statesman and explorer; first premier of Western Australia (1890–1901).

forsake (fəˈseɪk) *vb* **-sakes, -saking, -sook** (-ˈsʊk), **-saken** (-ˈseɪkən). *(tr)* **1** to abandon. **2** to give up (something valued or enjoyed). **[**Old English *forsacan***]** ► **forˈsaker** *n*

forsaken (fəˈseɪkən) *vb* **1** the past participle of **forsake.** ◆ *adj* **2** completely deserted or helpless; abandoned. ► **forˈsakenly** *adv* ► **forˈsakenness** *n*

forsook (fəˈsʊk) *vb* the past tense of **forsake.**

forsooth (fəˈsuːθ) *adv Archaic.* in truth; indeed. **[**Old English *forsōth***]**

forspeak (fɔːˈspiːk) *vb* **-speaks, -speaking, -spoke, -spoken.** *(tr) Scot. archaic.* to bewitch.

forspent *or* **forespent** (fɔːˈspent) *adj Archaic.* tired out; exhausted.

Forster (ˈfɔːstə) *n* **E(dward) M(organ).** 1879–1970, English novelist, short-story writer, and essayist. His best-known novels are *A Room with a View* (1908), *Howard's End* (1910), and *A Passage to India* (1924), in all of which he stresses the need for sincerity and sensitivity in human relationships and criticizes English middle-class values.

forsterite (ˈfɔːstəˌraɪt) *n* a white, yellow, or green mineral of the olivine group consisting of magnesium silicate. Formula: Mg_2SiO_4. **[C19:** named after J. R. *Forster* (1729–98), German naturalist**]**

forswear (fɔːˈswɛə) *vb* **-swears, -swearing, -swore, -sworn. 1** *(tr)* to reject or renounce with determination or as upon oath. **2** *(tr)* to deny or disavow absolutely or upon oath: *he forswore any knowledge of the crime.* **3** to perjure (oneself). **[**Old English *forswearian***]** ► **forˈswearer** *n*

forsworn (fɔːˈswɔːn) *vb* the past participle of **forswear.** ► **forˈswornness** *n*

Forsyth (ˈfɔːsaɪθ) *n* **1 Bill.** born 1947, Scottish writer and director. His films include *Gregory's Girl* (1981), *Local Hero* (1983), and *Rebecca's Daughters* (1992). **2 Frederick.** born 1938, British thriller writer. His books include *The Day of the Jackal* (1970), *The Odessa File* (1972), and *The Fourth Protocol* (1984).

forsythia (fɔːˈsaɪθɪə) *n* any oleaceous shrub of the genus *Forsythia,* native to China, Japan, and SE Europe but widely cultivated for its showy yellow bell-shaped flowers, which appear in spring before the foliage. **[C19:** New Latin, named after William *Forsyth* (1737–1804), English botanist**]**

fort (fɔːt) *n* **1** a fortified enclosure, building, or position able to be defended against an enemy. **2 hold the fort.** *Informal.* to maintain or guard something temporarily. **[C15:** from Old French, from *fort* (adj) strong, from Latin *fortis***]**

fort. *abbrev. for:* **1** fortification. **2** fortified.

Fortaleza (*Portuguese* fortaˈleza) *n* a port in NE Brazil, capital of Ceará state. Pop.: 2 660 000 (1995). Also called: **Ceará.**

fortalice (ˈfɔːtəlɪs) *n* a small fort or outwork of a fortification. **[C15:** from Medieval Latin *fortalitia,* from Latin *fortis* strong; see FORTRESS**]**

Fort-de-France (*French* fɔrdəfrɑ̃s) *n* the capital of Martinique, a port on the W coast: commercial centre of the French Antilles. Pop.: 104 000 (1995 est.).

forte[1] (fɔːt, ˈfɔːteɪ) *n* **1** something at which a person excels; strong point: *cooking is my forte.* **2** *Fencing.* the stronger section of a sword blade, between the hilt and the middle. Compare **foible. [C17:** from French *fort,* from *fort* (adj) strong, from Latin *fortis***]**

forte[2] (ˈfɔːtɪ) *Music.* ◆ *adj, adv* **1** loud or loudly. Symbol: f ◆ *n* **2** a loud passage in music. **[C18:** from Italian, from Latin *fortis* strong**]**

fortepiano (ˌfɔːtɪpɪˈænəʊ) *n* an early type of piano popular in the late 18th century. **[**from Italian, loud-soft**]**

forte-piano (ˌfɔːtɪˈpjɑːnəʊ) *Music.* ◆ *adj, adv* **1** loud and then immediately soft. Symbol: fp ◆ *n* **2** a note played in this way.

forth (fɔːθ) *adv* **1** forward in place, time, order, or degree. **2** out, as from concealment, seclusion, or inaction. **3** away, as from a place or country. **4 and so forth.** and so on; et cetera. ◆ *prep* **5** *Archaic.* out of; away from. **[**Old English; related to Middle High German *vort;* see FOR, FURTHER**]**

Forth (fɔːθ) *n* **1 Firth of.** an inlet of the North Sea in SE Scotland: spanned by a cantilever railway bridge 1600 m (almost exactly 1 mile) long (1889), and by a road bridge (1964). **2** a river in S Scotland, flowing generally east to the Firth of Forth. Length: about 104 km (65 miles).

forthcoming (ˌfɔːθˈkʌmɪŋ) *adj* **1** approaching in time: *the forthcoming debate.* **2** about to appear: *his forthcoming book.* **3** available or ready: *the money wasn't forthcoming.* **4** open or sociable. ► **ˌforthˈcomingness** *n*

forthright *adj* (ˈfɔːθˌraɪt). **1** direct and outspoken. ◆ *adv* (ˌfɔːθˈraɪt, ˈfɔːθˌraɪt), *also* **forthrightly. 2** in a direct manner; frankly. **3** at once. ► **ˈforthˌrightness** *n*

forthwith (ˌfɔːθˈwɪθ, -ˈwɪð) *adv* at once; immediately.

fortieth (ˈfɔːtɪɪθ) *adj* **1a** being the ordinal number of *forty* in numbering or counting order, position, time, etc.: often written 40th. **1b** (*as n*)*: he was the fortieth.* ◆ *n* **2a** one of 40 approximately equal parts of something. **2b** (*as modifier*)*: a fortieth part.* **3** the fraction equal to one divided by 40 (1/40). **[**Old English *fēowertigotha***]**

fortification (ˌfɔːtɪfɪˈkeɪʃən) *n* **1** the act, art, or science of fortifying or strengthening. **2a** a wall, mound, etc., used to fortify a place. **2b** such works collectively. **3** any place that can be militarily defended.

fortified pa *n N.Z. history.* a Maori hilltop dwelling with trenches and palisades for defensive occupation.

fortified wine *n* wine treated by the addition of brandy or alcohol, such as port, marsala, and sherry.

fortify (ˈfɔːtɪˌfaɪ) *vb* **-fies, -fying, -fied.** (*mainly tr*) **1** (*also intr*) to make (a place) defensible, as by building walls, digging trenches, etc. **2** to strengthen physically, mentally, or morally. **3** to strengthen, support, or reinforce (a garment, structure, etc.). **4** to add spirits or alcohol to (wine), in order to produce sherry, port, etc. **5** to increase the nutritious value of (a food), as by adding vitamins and minerals. **6** to support or confirm: *to fortify an argument with facts.* [**C15**: from Old French *fortifier,* from Late Latin *fortificāre,* from Latin *fortis* strong + *facere* to make] ▸ **'forti,fiable** *adj* ▸ **'forti,fier** *n* ▸ **'forti,fyingly** *adv*

fortis ('fɔ:tɪs) *Phonetics.* ♦ *adj* **1** (of a consonant) articulated with considerable muscular tension of the speech organs or with a great deal of breath pressure or plosion. ♦ *n, pl* **-tes** (-ti:z). **2** a consonant, such as English *p* or *f,* pronounced with considerable muscular force or breath pressure. ♦ Compare **lenis.** [Latin: strong]

fortissimo (fɔ:'tɪsɪ,məʊ) *Music.* ♦ *adj, adv* **1** very loud. Symbol: ff ♦ *n* **2** a very loud passage in music. [**C18**: from Italian, from Latin *fortissimus,* from *fortis* strong]

fortitude ('fɔ:tɪ,tju:d) *n* strength and firmness of mind; resolute endurance. [**C15**: from Latin *fortitūdō* courage] ▸ **,forti'tudinous** *adj*

Fort Knox (nɒks) *n* a military reservation in N Kentucky: site of the U.S. Gold Bullion Depository. Pop.: 38 277 (1989 est.).

Fort Lamy ('fɔ:t 'lɑ:mɪ; *French* fɔr lami) *n* the former name (until 1973) of **Ndjamena.**

Fort Lauderdale ('lɔ:də,deɪl) *n* a city in SE Florida, on the Atlantic. Pop.: 151 805 (1996 est.).

fortnight ('fɔ:t,naɪt) *n* a period of 14 consecutive days; two weeks. [Old English *fēowertīene niht* fourteen nights]

fortnightly ('fɔ:t,naɪtlɪ) *Chiefly Brit.* ♦ *adj* **1** occurring or appearing once each fortnight. ♦ *adv* **2** once a fortnight. ♦ *n, pl* **-lies. 3** a publication issued at intervals of two weeks.

FORTRAN *or* **Fortran** ('fɔ:træn) *n* a high-level computer programming language for mathematical and scientific purposes, designed to facilitate and speed up the solving of complex problems. [**C20**: from *for(mula) tran(slation)*]

fortress ('fɔ:trɪs) *n* **1** a large fort or fortified town. **2** a place or source of refuge or support. ♦ *vb* **3** (*tr*) to protect with or as if with a fortress. [**C13**: from Old French *forteresse,* from Medieval Latin *fortalitia,* from Latin *fortis* strong]

Fort Sumter ('sʌmtə) *n* a fort in SE South Carolina, guarding Charleston Harbour. Its capture by Confederate forces (1861) was the first action of the Civil War.

fortuitism (fɔ:'tju:ɪ,tɪzəm) *n Philosophy.* the doctrine that evolutionary adaptations are the result of chance. Compare **tychism.** ▸ **for'tuitist** *n, adj*

fortuitous (fɔ:'tju:ɪtəs) *adj* happening by chance, esp. by a lucky chance; unplanned; accidental. [**C17**: from Latin *fortuitus* happening by chance, from *forte* by chance, from *fors* chance, luck] ▸ **for'tuitously** *adv* ▸ **for'tuitousness** *n*

fortuity (fɔ:'tju:ɪtɪ) *n, pl* **-ties. 1** a chance or accidental occurrence. **2** fortuitousness. **3** chance or accident.

Fortuna (fɔ:'tju:nə) *n* the Roman goddess of fortune and good luck. Greek counterpart: **Tyche.**

fortunate ('fɔ:tʃənɪt) *adj* **1** having good luck; lucky. **2** occurring by or bringing good fortune or luck; auspicious. ▸ **'fortunately** *adv* ▸ **'fortunateness** *n*

fortune ('fɔ:tʃən) *n* **1** an amount of wealth or material prosperity, esp., when unqualified, a great amount. **2 small fortune.** a large sum of money. **3** a power or force, often personalized, regarded as being responsible for human affairs; chance. **4** luck, esp. when favourable. **5** (*often pl*) a person's lot or destiny. ♦ *vb* **6** *Archaic.* **6a** (*tr*) to endow with great wealth. **6b** (*intr*) to happen by chance. [**C13**: from Old French, from Latin *fortūna,* from *fors* chance] ▸ **'fortuneless** *adj*

fortune-hunter *n* a person who seeks to secure a fortune, esp. through marriage. ▸ **'fortune-,hunting** *adj, n*

fortune-teller *n* a person who makes predictions about the future as by looking into a crystal ball, reading palms, etc. ▸ **'fortune-,telling** *adj, n*

Fort Wayne (weɪn) *n* a city in NE Indiana. Pop.: 184 783 (1996 est.).

Fort William *n* a town in W Scotland, in Highland at the head of Loch Linnhe: tourist centre; the fort itself, built in 1655 and renamed after William III in 1690, was demolished in 1866. Pop.: 10 391 (1991).

Fort Worth (wɜ:θ) *n* a city in N Texas, at the junction of the Clear and West forks of the Trinity River: aircraft works, electronics. Pop.: 479 716 (1996 est.).

forty ('fɔ:tɪ) *n, pl* **-ties. 1** the cardinal number that is the product of ten and four. See also **number** (sense 1). **2** a numeral, 40, XL, etc., representing this number. **3** something representing, represented by, or consisting of 40 units. ♦ *determiner* **4a** amounting to forty: *forty thieves.* **4b** (*as pronoun*): *there were forty in the herd.* [Old English *fēowertig*]

forty-five *n* **1** a gramophone record played at 45 revolutions per minute. **2** *U.S. and Canadian.* a pistol having .45 calibre.

Forty-Five *n* **the.** *British history.* another name for the **Jacobite Rebellion** (sense 2).

forty-niner *n* (*sometimes cap.*) *U.S. history.* a prospector who took part in the California gold rush of 1849.

forty winks *n* (*functioning as sing or pl*) *Informal.* a short light sleep; nap.

forum ('fɔ:rəm) *n, pl* **-rums** *or* **-ra** (-rə). **1** a meeting or assembly for the open discussion of subjects of public interest. **2** a medium for open discussion, such as a magazine. **3** a public meeting place for open discussion. **4** a court; tribunal. **5** (in ancient Italy) an open space, usually rectangular in shape, serving as a city's marketplace and centre of public business. [**C15**: from Latin: public place; related to Latin *foris* outside]

Forum *or* **Forum Romanum** (rəʊ'mɑ:nəm) *n* **the.** the main forum of ancient Rome, situated between the Capitoline and the Palatine Hills.

forward ('fɔ:wəd) *adj* **1** directed or moving ahead. **2** lying or situated in or near the front part of something. **3** presumptuous, pert, or impudent: *a forward remark.* **4** well developed or advanced, esp. in physical, material, or intellectual growth or development: *forward ideas.* **5** *Archaic.* (*often postpositive*) ready, eager, or willing. **6a** of or relating to the future or favouring change; progressive. **6b** (*in combination*): *forward-looking.* **7** *N.Z.* (of an animal) in good condition. ♦ *n* **8a** an attacking player in any of various sports, such as soccer, hockey, or basketball. **8b** (in American football) a lineman. ♦ *adv* **9** a variant of **forwards. 10** ('fɔ:wəd; *Nautical* 'fɒrəd). towards the front or bow of an aircraft or ship. **11** into prominence or a position of being subject to public scrutiny; out; forth: *the witness came forward.* ♦ *vb* (*tr*) **12** to send forward or pass on to an ultimate destination: *the letter was forwarded from a previous address.* **13** to advance, help, or promote: *to forward one's career.* **14** *Bookbinding.* to prepare (a book) for the finisher. [Old English *foreweard*] ▸ **'forwardly** *adv*

forward bias *or* **voltage** *n* a voltage applied to a circuit or device, esp. a semiconductor device, in the direction that produces the larger current.

forward delivery *n* (in commerce) delivery at a future date.

forwarder ('fɔ:wədə) *n* **1** a person or thing that forwards. **2** a person engaged in the bookbinding process of forwarding. **3** See **forwarding agent.**

forwarding ('fɔ:wədɪŋ) *n* all the processes involved in the binding of a book subsequent to cutting and up to the fitting of its cover.

forwarding agent *n* a person, agency, or enterprise engaged in the collection, shipment, and delivery of goods.

forward market *n* a market in which contracts are made to buy or sell currencies, commodities, etc., at some future date at a price fixed at the date of the contract. Compare **spot market.**

forwardness ('fɔ:wədnɪs) *n* **1** lack of modesty; presumption; boldness. **2** willing readiness; eagerness. **3** a state or condition of advanced progress or development.

forward pass *n Rugby.* an illegal pass towards the opponent's dead-ball line. Also called: **throw-forward.**

forward quotation *n* (in commerce) the price quoted for goods sent on forward delivery.

forward roll *n* a gymnastic movement in which the body is turned heels over head with the back of the neck resting on the ground.

forwards ('fɔ:wədz) *or* **forward** *adv* **1** towards or at a place ahead or in advance, esp. in space but also in time. **2** towards the front.

forwent (fɔ:'went) *vb* the past tense of **forgo.**

forwhy (fɔ:'waɪ) *Archaic.* ♦ *adv* **1** for what reason; why. ♦ *conj* **2** (*subordinating*) because. [Old English *for hwī*]

forworn *or* **foreworn** (fɔ:'wɔ:n) *adj Archaic.* weary. [**C16**: past participle of obsolete *forwear* to wear out, from Middle English *forweren* to hollow out]

forza ('fɔ:tsə) *n Music.* force. [**C19**: Italian, literally: force]

forzando (fɔ:'tsændəʊ) *adj, adv, n* another word for **sforzando.**

Fosbury flop ('fɒzbərɪ, -brɪ) *n Athletics.* a modern high-jumping technique whereby the jumper clears the bar headfirst and backwards. [**C20**: named after Dick *Fosbury,* U.S. winner of men's high jump at Mexico Olympics in 1968, who perfected the technique]

Foscolo (*Italian* 'fɔskolo) *n* **Ugo** ('u:go), real name *Niccolò Foscolo.* 1778–1827, Italian poet and writer; his patriotic verse includes *Dei sepolcri* (1807).

Foshan ('fɔ:'ʃɑ:n) *or* **Fatshan** *n* a city in SE China, in W Guangdong province. Pop.: 303 160 (1990 est.). Also called: **Namhoi.**

fossa[1] ('fɒsə) *n, pl* **-sae** (-si:). an anatomical depression, trench, or hollow area. [**C19**: from Latin: ditch, from *fossus* dug up, from *fodere* to dig up]

fossa[2] ('fɒsə) *n* a large primitive catlike viverrine mammal, *Cryptoprocta ferox,* inhabiting the forests of Madagascar: order *Carnivora* (carnivores). It has thick reddish-brown fur and preys on lemurs, poultry, etc. [from Malagasy]

fosse *or* **foss** (fɒs) *n* a ditch or moat, esp. one dug as a fortification. [**C14**: from Old French, from Latin *fossa;* see FOSSA[1]]

fossette (fɒ'sɛt) *n* **1** *Anatomy.* a small depression or fossa, as in a bone. **2** *Pathol.* a small deep ulcer of the cornea. [**C19**: from French: dimple, from *fosse* ditch]

Fosse Way (fɒs) *n* a Roman road in Britain between Lincoln and Exeter, with a fosse on each side.

fossick ('fɒsɪk) *vb Austral. and N.Z.* **1** (*intr*) to search for gold or precious stones in abandoned workings, rivers, etc. **2** to rummage or search for (something). [**C19**: Australian, probably from English dialect *fussock* to bustle about, from FUSS] ▸ **'fossicker** *n*

fossil ('fɒsᵊl) *n* **1a** a relic, remnant, or representation of a plant or animal that existed in a past geological age, occurring in the form of mineralized bones, shells, etc., as casts, impressions, and moulds, and as frozen perfectly preserved organisms. **1b** (*as modifier*): *fossil insects.* **2** *Informal, derogatory.* **2a** a person, idea, thing, etc., that is outdated or incapable of change. **2b** (*as modifier*): *fossil politicians.* **3** *Linguistics.* a form once current but now appearing only in one or two special contexts, as for example *stead,* which is found now only in *instead* (*of*) and in phrases like *in his stead.* **4** *Obsolete.* any rock or mineral dug out of the earth. [**C17**: from Latin *fossilis* dug up, from *fodere* to dig]

fossil energy *n* heat energy released by burning fossil fuel.

fossil fuel *n* any naturally occurring carbon or hydrocarbon fuel, such as coal, petroleum, peat, and natural gas, formed by the decomposition of prehistoric organisms.

fossiliferous (,fɒsɪ'lɪfərəs) *adj* (of sedimentary rocks) containing fossils.

fossilize *or* **fossilise** ('fɒsɪ,laɪz) *vb* **1** to convert or be converted into a fossil. **2** to become or cause to become antiquated or inflexible. ▸ **'fossil,izable** *or* **'fossil,isable** *adj* ▸ **,fossili'zation** *or* **,fossili'sation** *n*

fossorial (fɒ'sɔ:rɪəl) *adj* **1** (of the forelimbs and skeleton of burrowing animals) adapted for digging. **2** (of burrowing animals, such as the mole and armadillo) having limbs of this type. [C19: from Medieval Latin *fossōrius* from Latin *fossor* digger, from *fodere* to dig]

foster ('fɒstə) *vb* (*tr*) **1** to promote the growth or development of. **2** to bring up (a child, etc.); rear. **3** to cherish (a plan, hope, etc.) in one's mind. **4** *Chiefly Brit.* **4a** to place (a child) in the care of foster parents. **4b** to bring up under fosterage. ◆ *adj* **5** (*in combination*) of or involved in the rearing of a child by persons other than his natural or adopted parents: *foster parents; foster home.* [Old English *fōstrian* to feed, from *fōstor* FOOD] ▸ **'fosterer** *n* ▸ **'fosteringly** *adv*

Foster ('fɒstə) *n* **1 Jodie.** born 1962, U.S. film actress: her films include *Taxi Driver* (1976), *The Accused* (1988), *The Silence of the Lambs* (1990), *Little Man Tate* (1991; also directed), and *Contact* (1997). **2 Norman**, Baron. born 1935, British architect. His works include the Willis Faber building (1978) in Ipswich, Stansted Airport, Essex (1991), Chek Lap Kok Airport, Hong Kong (1998), and the renovation of the Reichstag, Berlin (1999). **3 Stephen Collins.** 1826–64, U.S. composer of songs such as *The Old Folks at Home* and *Oh Susanna.*

fosterage ('fɒstərɪdʒ) *n* **1** the act of caring for or bringing up a foster child. **2** the condition or state of being a foster child. **3** the act of encouraging or promoting.

foster child *n* a child looked after temporarily or brought up by people other than its natural or adoptive parents.

foster father *n* a man who looks after or brings up a child or children as a father, in place of the natural or adoptive father.

fosterling ('fɒstəlɪŋ) *n* a less common word for **foster child.**

foster mother *n* a woman who looks after or brings up a child or children as a mother, in place of the natural or adoptive mother.

Fotheringhay ('fɒðərɪŋ,geɪ) *n* a village in E England, in NE Northamptonshire: ruined castle, scene of the imprisonment and execution of Mary Queen of Scots (1587).

fou (fuː) *adj Scot.* **1** full. **2** drunk. [perhaps a Scot. variant of *full*]

Foucault (*French* fuko) *n* **1 Jean Bernard Léon** (ʒɑ̃ bɛrnar leɔ̃). 1819–68, French physicist. He determined the velocity of light and proved that light travels more slowly in water than in air (1850). He demonstrated by means of the pendulum named after him the rotation of the earth on its axis (1851) and invented the gyroscope (1852). **2 Michel.** 1926–84, French philosopher. His publications include *Histoire de la folie* (1961) and *Les Mots et les choses* (1966).

Foucault current *n* another name for **eddy current.**

Foucquet (*French* fukɛ) *n* a variant spelling of (Nicolas) **Fouquet.**

foudroyant (fuː'drɔɪənt) *adj* **1** (of a disease) occurring suddenly and with great severity. **2** *Rare.* stunning, dazzling, or overwhelming. [C19: from French, from *foudroyer* to strike with lightning, from Old French *foudre* lightning, from Latin *fulgur*]

fouetté *French.* (fwete) *n* a step in ballet in which the dancer stands on one foot and makes a whiplike movement with the other. [C19: French, past participle of *fouetter* to whip, from *fouet* a whip]

fought (fɔːt) *vb* the past tense and past participle of **fight.**

foul (faʊl) *adj* **1** offensive to the senses; revolting. **2** offensive in odour; stinking. **3** charged with or full of dirt or offensive matter; filthy. **4** (of food) putrid; rotten. **5** morally or spiritually offensive; wicked; vile. **6** obscene; vulgar: *foul language.* **7** not in accordance with accepted standards or established rules; unfair: *to resort to foul means.* **8** (esp. of weather) unpleasant or adverse. **9** blocked or obstructed with dirt or foreign matter: *a foul drain.* **10** entangled or impeded: *a foul anchor.* **11** (of the bottom of a vessel) covered with barnacles and other growth that slow forward motion. **12** *Informal.* unsatisfactory or uninteresting; bad: *a foul book.* **13** *Archaic.* ugly. ◆ *n* **14** *Sport.* **14a** a violation of the rules. **14b** (*as modifier*): *a foul shot; a foul blow.* **15** something foul. **16** an entanglement or collision, esp. in sailing or fishing. ◆ *vb* **17** to make or become dirty or polluted. **18** to become or cause to become entangled or snarled. **19** (*tr*) to disgrace or dishonour. **20** to become or cause to become clogged or choked. **21** (*tr*) *Nautical.* (of underwater growth) to cling to (the bottom of a vessel) so as to slow its motion. **22** (*tr*) *Sport.* to commit a foul against (an opponent). **23** (*tr*) *Baseball.* to hit (a ball) in an illegal manner. **24** (*intr*) *Sport.* to infringe the rules. **25** to collide with (a boat, etc.). ◆ *adv* **26** in a foul or unfair manner. **27 fall foul of. 27a** to come into conflict with. **27b** *Nautical.* to come into collision with. ◆ See also **foul up.** [Old English *fūl;* related to Old Norse *fūll,* Gothic *fūls* smelling offensively, Latin *pūs* PUS, Greek *puol* pus] ▸ **'foully** *adv*

foulard (fuː'lɑːd, 'fuːlɑː) *n* **1** a soft light fabric of plain-weave or twill-weave silk or rayon, usually with a printed design. **2** something made of this fabric, esp. a scarf or handkerchief. [C19: from French, of unknown origin]

foul marten *n* another name for the **polecat** (sense 1). See also **sweet marten.**

foul-mouthed *adj* given to using obscene, abusive, or blasphemous language.

foulness ('faʊlnɪs) *n* **1** the state or quality of being foul. **2** obscenity; vulgarity. **3** viciousness or inhumanity. **4** foul matter; filth.

Foulness (faʊl'nɛs) *n* a flat marshy island in SE England, in Essex north of the Thames estuary.

foul play *n* **1** unfair or treacherous conduct esp. with violence. **2** a violation of the rules in a game or sport.

foul shot *n Basketball.* another term (esp. U.S. and Canadian) for **free throw.**

foul up *vb* (*adv*) **1** (*tr*) to bungle; mismanage. **2** (*tr*) to make dirty; contaminate. **3** to be or cause to be blocked, choked, or entangled. ◆ *n* **foul-up. 4** a state of confusion or muddle caused by bungling.

foumart ('fuːmɑːt, -mət) *n* a former name for the **polecat** (sense 1). [C15 *folmarde:* from Old English *fūl* foul + *mearth* a marten]

found[1] (faʊnd) *vb* **1** the past tense and past participle of **find.** ◆ *adj* **2** furnished, or fitted out: *the boat is well found.* **3** *Brit.* with meals, heating, bed linen, etc., provided without extra charge (esp. in the phrase **all found**).

found[2] (faʊnd) *vb* **1** (*tr*) to bring into being, set up, or establish (something, such as an institution, society, etc.). **2** (*tr*) to build or establish the foundation or basis of. **3** (*also intr;* foll. by *on* or *upon*) to have a basis (in); depend (on). [C13: from Old French *fonder,* from Latin *fundāre,* from *fundus* bottom]

found[3] (faʊnd) *vb* (*tr*) **1** to cast (a material, such as metal or glass) by melting and pouring into a mould. **2** to shape or make (articles) in this way; cast. [C14: from Old French *fondre,* from Latin *fundere* to melt]

foundation (faʊn'deɪʃən) *n* **1** that on which something is founded; basis. **2** (*often pl*) a construction below the ground that distributes the load of a building, wall, etc. **3** the base on which something stands. **4** the act of founding or establishing or the state of being founded or established. **5a** an endowment or legacy for the perpetual support of an institution such as a school or hospital. **5b on the foundation.** entitled to benefit from the funds of a foundation. **6** an institution supported by an endowment, often one that provides funds for charities, research, etc. **7** the charter incorporating or establishing a society or institution and the statutes or rules governing its affairs. **8** a cosmetic in cream or cake form used as a base for make-up. **9** See **foundation garment. 10** *Cards.* a card on which a sequence may be built. ▸ **foun'dational** *adj* ▸ **foun'dationally** *adv* ▸ **foun'dationary** *adj*

foundation garment *n* a woman's undergarment worn to shape and support the figure; brassiere or corset.

foundation stone *n* a stone laid at a ceremony to mark the foundation of a new building.

foundation subjects *pl n Brit. Education.* the subjects studied as part of the National Curriculum, including the compulsory core subjects.

founder[1] ('faʊndə) *n* a person who establishes an institution, company, society, etc. [C14: see FOUND[2]]

founder[2] ('faʊndə) *vb* (*intr*) **1** (of a ship) to sink. **2** to break down or fail: *the project foundered.* **3** to sink into or become stuck in soft ground. **4** to fall in or give way; collapse. **5** (of a horse) to stumble or go lame. **6** (of animals, esp. livestock) to become ill from overeating. ◆ *n* **7** *Vet. science.* another name for **laminitis.** [C13: from Old French *fondrer* to submerge, from Latin *fundus* bottom; see FOUND[2]]

USAGE *Founder* is sometimes wrongly used where *flounder* is meant: *this unexpected turn of events left him floundering* (not *foundering*).

founder[3] ('faʊndə) *n* **a** a person who makes metal castings. **b** (*in combination*): *an iron founder.* [C15: see FOUND[3]]

founders' shares *pl n* shares awarded to the founders of a company and often granting special privileges.

founder's type *n Printing.* special type cast by a type founder for hand composition, as opposed to type cast in a mechanical composing machine.

founding father *n* (*often caps.*) a person who founds or establishes an important institution, esp. a member of the U.S. Constitutional Convention (1787).

foundling ('faʊndlɪŋ) *n* an abandoned infant whose parents are not known. [C13: *foundeling;* see FIND]

found object *n* another name for ***objet trouvé.***

foundry ('faʊndrɪ) *n, pl* **-ries. 1** a place in which metal castings are produced. **2** the science or practice of casting metal. **3** cast-metal articles collectively. [C17: from Old French *fonderie,* from *fondre;* see FOUND[3]]

foundry proof *n Printing.* a proof taken from a forme before duplicate plates are made from it.

foundry sand *n* silica-based sand mixed with clay, oil, etc., to improve its cohesive strength, used in moulding.

fount[1] (faʊnt) *n* **1** *Poetic.* a spring or fountain. **2** source or origin. [C16: back formation from FOUNTAIN]

fount[2] (faʊnt, fɒnt) *n Printing.* a complete set of type of one style and size. Also called (esp. U.S. and Canadian): **font.** [C16: from Old French *fonte* a founding, casting, from Vulgar Latin *funditus* (unattested) a casting, from Latin *fundere* to melt; see FOUND[3]]

fountain ('faʊntɪn) *n* **1** a jet or spray of water or some other liquid. **2** a structure from which such a jet or a number of such jets spurt, often incorporating figures, basins, etc. **3** a natural spring of water, esp. the source of a stream. **4** a stream, jet, or cascade of sparks, lava, etc. **5** a principal source or origin. **6** a reservoir or supply chamber, as for oil in a lamp. **7** short for **drinking fountain** or **soda fountain.** [C15: from Old French *fontaine,* from Late Latin *fontāna,* from Latin *fons* spring, source] ▸ **'fountained** *adj* ▸ **'fountainless** *adj* ▸ **'fountain-,like** *adj*

fountainhead ('faʊntɪn,hɛd) *n* **1** a spring that is the source of a stream. **2** a principal or original source.

fountain pen *n* a pen the nib of which is supplied with ink from a cartridge or a reservoir in its barrel.

Fountains Abbey ('faʊntɪns) *n* a ruined Cistercian abbey near Ripon in Yorkshire: founded 1132, dissolved 1539; landscaped 1720.

Fouqué (*German* fu'keː) *n* **Friedrich Heinrich Karl** ('friːdrɪç 'hainrɪç karl), Baron de la Motte. 1777–1843, German romantic writer; author of *Undine* (1811).

Fouquet (*French* fukɛ) *n* **1 Jean** (ʒɑ̃). ?1420–?80, French painter and miniaturist. **2** Also: **Foucquet. Nicolas** (nikɔla), *Marquis de Belle-Isle.* 1615–80, French statesman; superintendent of finance (1653–61) under Louis XIV. He was imprisoned for embezzlement, having been denounced by Colbert.

Fouquier-Tinville (*French* fukjetɛ̃vil) *n* **Antoine Quentin** (ɑ̃twan kɑ̃tɛ̃). 1746–95, French revolutionary; as public prosecutor (1793–94) during the Reign of Terror, he sanctioned the guillotining of Desmoulins, Danton, and Robespierre.

four (fɔː) *n* **1** the cardinal number that is the sum of three and one. **2** a numeral, 4, IV, etc., representing this number. **3** something representing, represented by, or consisting of four units, such as a playing card with four symbols on it. **4** Also called: **four o'clock.** four hours after noon or midnight. **5** *Cricket.* **5a** a shot that crosses the boundary after hitting the ground. **5b** the four runs scored for such a shot. **6** *Rowing.* **6a** a racing shell propelled by four oarsmen pulling one oar each, with or without a cox. **6b** the crew of such a shell. ◆ *determiner* **7a** amounting to four: *four thousand eggs; four times.* **7b** (*as pronoun*): *four are ready.* ◆ Related prefixes: **quadri-, tetra-.** [Old English *fēower;* related to Old Frisian *fiūwer,* Old Norse *fjōrir,* Old High German *fior,* Latin *quattuor,* Greek *tessares,* Sanskrit *catur*]

four-ball *n Golf.* a match for two pairs in which each player uses his own ball, the better score of each pair being counted at every hole. Compare **foursome** (sense 2), **greensome.**

four-by-four *n* a vehicle equipped with four-wheel drive.

four-by-two *n Austral. and N.Z.* a piece of timber with a cross section that measures 4 inches by 2 inches.

fourchette (fʊəˈʃɛt) *n* **1** *Anatomy.* the bandlike fold of skin, about one inch from the anus, forming the posterior margin of the vulva. **2** a less common name for **furcula** or **frog**[3]. [C18: from French: a little fork, from Old French *forche,* from Latin *furca* FORK]

four-colour *n* (*modifier*) (of a print or photographic process) using the principle in which four colours (magenta, cyan, yellow, and black) are used in combination to produce almost any other colour.

four-cycle *adj* the U.S. and Canadian word for **four-stroke.**

four-deal bridge *n* a version of bridge in which four hands only are played, the players then cutting for new partners.

four-dimensional *adj* having or specified by four dimensions, esp. the three spatial dimensions and the dimension of time: *a four-dimensional continuum.*

Fourdrinier (fʊəˈdrɪnɪə) *n* a particular type of paper-making machine that forms the paper in a continuous web. [C19: named after Henry (died 1854) and Sealy (died 1847) *Fourdrinier,* English paper makers]

four-eyed fish *n* either of two viviparous tropical American freshwater cyprinodont fishes, *Anableps anableps* or *A. microlepis,* that swim at the surface of the water and have half of each eye specialized for seeing in air, the other half for seeing in water.

four-eyes *n* a disparaging term of address for a person wearing spectacles. ▸ **ˈfour-ˌeyed** *adj*

four flush *n* **1** a useless poker hand, containing four of a suit and one odd card. ◆ *vb* **four-flush.** (*intr*) **2** to bid confidently on a poor hand such as a four flush. **3** *U.S. and Canadian.* a slang word for **bluff**[1].

four-flusher (ˈfɔːˌflʌʃə) *n U.S. and Canadian slang.* a person who bluffs or attempts to deceive.

fourfold (ˈfɔːˌfəʊld) *adj* **1** equal to or having four times as many or as much. **2** composed of four parts. ◆ *adv* **3** by or up to four times as many or as much.

four-four time *n Music.* a form of simple quadruple time in which there are four crotchets to the bar, indicated by the time signature $\frac{4}{4}$. Often shortened to **four-four.** Also called: **common time.**

fourgon *French.* (furgɔ̃) *n* a long covered wagon, used mainly for carrying baggage, supplies, etc. [C19: from French: from Old French *forgon* poker, from *furgier* to search, ultimately from Latin *fūr* thief]

four-handed *adj* **1** (of a card game) arranged for four players. **2** (of a musical composition) written for two performers at the same piano. ▸ **ˌfour-ˈhandedly** *adv*

Four Hundred *n* **the.** *U.S.* the most exclusive or affluent social clique in a particular place.

Fourier (ˈfʊərɪˌeɪ; *French* furje) *n* **1** (**François Marie**) **Charles** (ʃarl). 1772–1837, French social reformer: propounded a system of cooperatives known as Fourierism, esp. in his work *Le Nouveau monde industriel* (1829–30). **2 Jean Baptiste Joseph** (ʒɑ̃ batist ʒozɛf). 1768–1830, French mathematician, Egyptologist, and administrator, noted particularly for his research on the theory of heat and the method of analysis named after him.

Fourier analysis *n* the analysis of a periodic function into its simple sinusoidal or harmonic components, whose sum forms a Fourier series.

Fourierism (ˈfʊərɪəˌrɪzəm) *n* the system of Charles Fourier under which society was to be organized into self-sufficient cooperatives. ▸ **ˈFourierist** *or* **Fourierite** (ˈfʊərɪəˌraɪt) *n, adj* ▸ **ˌFourierˈistic** *adj*

Fourier series *n* an infinite trigonometric series of the form $\frac{1}{2}a_0 + a_1\cos x + b_1\sin x + a_2\cos 2x + b_2\sin 2x + \dots$, where a_0, a_1, b_1, a_2, b_2 ... are the **Fourier coefficients.** It is used, esp. in mathematics and physics, to represent or approximate any single-valued periodic function by assigning suitable values to the coefficients. [C19: named after Baron Jean Baptiste Joseph FOURIER]

Fourier transform *n* an integral transform, used in many branches of science, of the form $F(x) = [1/\sqrt{(2\pi)}]\int e^{ixy}f(y)dy$, where the limits of integration are from $-\infty$ to $+\infty$ and the function F is the transform of the function f.

four-in-hand *n* **1** Also called: **tally-ho.** a road vehicle drawn by four horses and driven by one driver. **2** a four-horse team in a coach or carriage. **3** a long narrow tie formerly worn tied in a flat slipknot with the ends dangling.

four-leaf clover *or* **four-leaved clover** *n* **1** a clover with four leaves rather than three, supposed to bring good luck. **2** another name for **cloverleaf** (sense 1).

four-letter word *n* any of several short English words referring to sex or excrement: often used as swearwords and regarded generally as offensive or obscene.

Fournier (*French* furnje) *n* See **Alain-Fournier.**

four-o'clock *n* **1** Also called: **marvel-of-Peru.** a tropical American nyctaginaceous plant, *Mirabilis jalapa,* cultivated for its tubular yellow, red, or white flowers that open in late afternoon. **2** an Australian name for **friarbird,** esp. the noisy friarbird (*Philemon corniculatus*): so called because of its cry.

four-part *adj Music.* arranged for four voices or instruments.

fourpence (ˈfɔːpəns) *n* a former English silver coin then worth four pennies.

fourpenny (ˈfɔːpənɪ) *adj* **fourpenny one.** *Brit. slang.* a blow, esp. with the fist.

four-poster *n* a bed with posts at each corner supporting a canopy and curtains. Also called: **four-poster bed.**

fourragère (ˈfʊərəˌʒɛə; *French* furaʒɛr) *n* an ornamental cord worn on the shoulder of a uniform for identification or as an award, esp. in the U.S. and French Armies. [French, feminine adj of *fourrager* relating to forage, from *fourrage* FORAGE]

fourscore (ˌfɔːˈskɔː) *determiner* an archaic word for **eighty.**

foursome (ˈfɔːsəm) *n* **1** a set or company of four. **2** *Sport.* a game between two pairs of players, esp. a form of golf in which each partner in a pair takes alternate strokes at the same ball. Compare **four-ball, greensome. 3** (*modifier*) of or performed by a company of four: *a foursome competition.*

foursquare (ˌfɔːˈskwɛə) *adv* **1** squarely; firmly. ◆ *adj* **2** solid and strong. **3** forthright; honest. **4** a rare word for **square.** ▸ **ˌfourˈsquarely** *adv* ▸ **ˌfourˈsquareness** *n*

four-stroke *adj* relating to or designating an internal-combustion engine in which the piston makes four strokes for every explosion. U.S. and Canadian name: **four-cycle.** Compare **two-stroke.**

fourteen (ˈfɔːˈtiːn) *n* **1** the cardinal number that is the sum of ten and four. **2** a numeral, 14, XIV, etc., representing this number. **3** something represented by, representing, or consisting of 14 units. ◆ *determiner* **4a** amounting to fourteen: *fourteen cats.* **4b** (*as pronoun*): *the fourteen who remained.* [Old English *fēowertīene*]

Fourteen Points *pl n* the principles expounded by President Wilson in 1918 as war aims of the U.S.

fourteenth (ˈfɔːˈtiːnθ) *adj* **1a** coming after the thirteenth in order, position, time etc. Often written: 14th. **1b** (*as n*): *the fourteenth in succession.* ◆ *n* **2a** one of 14 equal or nearly equal parts of something. **2b** (*as modifier*): *a fourteenth part.* **3** the fraction equal to one divided by 14 (1/14).

fourth (fɔːθ) *adj* (*usually prenominal*) **1a** coming after the third in order, position, time, etc. Often written: 4th. **1b** (*as n*): *the fourth in succession.* **2** denoting the highest forward ratio of a gearbox in most motor vehicles. ◆ *n* **3** *Music.* **3a** the interval between one note and another four notes away from it counting inclusively along the diatonic scale. **3b** one of two notes constituting such an interval in relation to the other. See also **perfect** (sense 9), **interval** (sense 5), **diminished** (sense 2). **4** the fourth forward ratio of a gearbox in a motor vehicle, usually the highest gear in cars; top gear: *he changed into fourth as soon as he had passed me.* **5** a less common word for **quarter** (sense 2). ◆ *adv also:* **fourthly. 6** after the third person, position, event, etc. ◆ *sentence connector. also:* **fourthly. 7** as the fourth point: linking what follows with the previous statements, as in a speech or argument.

fourth-class *U.S.* ◆ *adj* **1** of or relating to mail that is carried at the lowest rate. ◆ *adv* **2** by fourth-class mail.

fourth dimension *n* **1** the dimension of time, which is necessary in addition to three spatial dimensions to specify fully the position and behaviour of a point or particle. **2** the concept in science fiction of a dimension in addition to three spatial dimensions, used to explain supranatural phenomena, events, etc. ▸ **ˌfourth-diˈmensional** *adj*

fourth estate *n* (*sometimes caps.*) journalists or their profession; the press. See **estate** (sense 4).

Fourth International *n* another name for any of the **Trotskyist Internationals.**

Fourth of July *n* (preceded by *the*) a holiday in the United States, traditionally celebrated with fireworks: the day of the adoption of the Declaration of Independence in 1776. Official name: **Independence Day.**

Fourth Republic *n* the fourth period of republican government in France or the republic itself (1945–58).

Fourth World *n* **1** the poorest countries in the most undeveloped parts of the world in Africa, Asia, and Latin America. **2** the poorest people in developed countries.

four-way *adj* (*usually prenominal*) **1** giving passage in four directions. **2** made up of four elements.

four-wheel drive *n* a system used in motor vehicles in which all four wheels are connected to the source of power.

fovea (ˈfəʊvɪə) *n, pl* **-veae** (-vɪˌiː). **1** *Anatomy.* any small pit or depression in the surface of a bodily organ or part. **2** See **fovea centralis.** [C19: from Latin: a small pit] ▸ **ˈfoveal** *adj* ▸ **ˈfoveate** *or* **ˈfoveˌated** *adj*

fovea centralis (sɛnˈtrɑːlɪs) *n* a small depression in the back of the retina, in the centre, that contains only cone cells and is therefore the area of sharpest vision. [C19: from New Latin: central fovea]

foveola (fəʊˈviːələ) *n, pl* **-lae** (-ˌliː). *Biology.* a small fovea. [C19: from New Latin, diminutive of FOVEA] ▸ **foˈveolar** *adj* ▸ **foveolate** (ˈfəʊvɪəˌleɪt) *or* **ˈfoveoˌlated** *adj*

Fowey (fɔɪ) *n* a resort and fishing village in SW England, in Cornwall, linked administratively with St Austell in 1968. Pop.: 1939 (1991).

fowl (faʊl) *n* **1** See **domestic fowl. 2** any other bird, esp. any gallinaceous bird, that is used as food or hunted as game. See also **waterfowl, wildfowl. 3** the flesh or meat of fowl, esp. of chicken. **4** an archaic word for any **bird.** ◆ *vb* **5** (*intr*) to hunt or snare wildfowl. [Old English *fugol;* related to Old Frisian *fugel,* Old Norse *fogl,* Gothic *fugls,* Old High German *fogal*]

Fowler (ˈfaʊlə) *n* **Henry Watson.** 1858–1933, English lexicographer and grammarian; compiler of *Modern English Usage* (1926).

Fowles (faʊlz) *n* **John** (**Martin**). born 1926, British novelist. His books include *The Collector* (1963), *The Magus* (1966), *The French Lieutenant's Woman* (1969), and *The Tree* (1991).

Fowliang *or* **Fou-liang** (ˈfuːˈljæŋ) *n* a variant transliteration of the Chinese name for **Jingdezhen.**

fowling ('faʊlɪŋ) *n* the shooting or trapping of birds for sport or as a livelihood. ▸ **'fowler** *n*

fowl mite *n* any of various mites parasitic in birds, usually bloodsucking and including the **red fowl mite** (*Dermanyssus gallinae*) and the **northern fowl mite** (*Ornithonyssus sylviarum*), both pests of poultry.

fowl pest *n* **1** an acute and usually fatal viral disease of domestic fowl, characterized by refusal to eat, high temperature, and discoloration of the comb and wattles. **2** another name for **Newcastle disease.**

fox (fɒks) *n, pl* **foxes** *or* **fox. 1** any canine mammal of the genus *Vulpes* and related genera. They are mostly predators that do not hunt in packs and typically have large pointed ears, a pointed muzzle, and a bushy tail. Related adj: **vulpine. 2** the fur of any of these animals, usually reddish-brown or grey in colour. **3** a person who is cunning and sly. **4** *Slang, chiefly U.S.* a sexually attractive woman. **5** *Bible.* **5a** a jackal. **5b** an image of a false prophet. **6** *Nautical.* small stuff made from yarns twisted together and then tarred. ◆ *vb* **7** (*tr*) *Informal.* to perplex or confound: *to fox a person with a problem.* **8** to cause (paper, wood, etc.) to become discoloured with spots, or (of paper, etc.) to become discoloured, as through mildew. **9** (*tr*) to trick; deceive. **10** (*intr*) to act deceitfully or craftily. **11** (*tr*) *Austral. informal.* to pursue stealthily; tail. **12** (*tr*) *Austral. informal.* to chase and retrieve (a ball). **13** (*tr*) *Obsolete.* to befuddle with alcoholic drink. [Old English; related to Old High German *fuhs*, Old Norse *fōa* fox, Sanskrit *puccha* tail; see VIXEN] ▸ **'fox,like** *adj*

Fox[1] (fɒks) *n* **1** (*pl* **Fox** *or* **Foxes**) a member of a North American Indian people formerly living west of Lake Michigan along the Fox River. **2** the language of this people, belonging to the Algonquian family.

Fox[2] (fɒks) *n* **1 Charles James.** 1749–1806, British Whig statesman and orator. He opposed North over taxation of the American colonies and Pitt over British intervention against the French Revolution. He advocated parliamentary reform and the abolition of the slave trade. **2 George.** 1624–91, English religious leader; founder (1647) of the Society of Friends (Quakers). **3** Sir **William.** 1812–93, New Zealand statesman, born in England: prime minister of New Zealand (1856; 1861–62; 1869–72; 1873).

Foxe (fɒks) *n* **John.** 1516–87, English Protestant clergyman; author of *History of the Acts and Monuments of the Church* (1563), popularly known as the *Book of Martyrs.*

Foxe Basin *n* an arm of the Atlantic in NE Canada, between Melville Peninsula and Baffin Island.

foxfire ('fɒks,faɪə) *n* a luminescent glow emitted by certain fungi on rotting wood. See also **bioluminescence.**

foxglove ('fɒks,glʌv) *n* any Eurasian scrophulariaceous plant of the genus *Digitalis,* esp. *D. purpurea,* having spikes of purple or white thimble-like flowers. The soft wrinkled leaves are a source of digitalis.

fox grape *n* a common wild grape, *Vitis labrusca* of the northern U.S., having purplish-black fruit and woolly leaves: the source of many cultivated grapes, including the catawba.

foxhole ('fɒks,həʊl) *n Military.* a small pit dug during an action to provide individual shelter against hostile fire.

foxhound ('fɒks,haʊnd) *n* either of two breeds (the English and the American) of dog having a short smooth coat and pendent ears. Though not large (height about 60 cm or 23 in.) they have great stamina and are usually kept for hunting foxes.

fox hunt *n* **1a** the hunting of foxes with hounds. **1b** an instance of this. **2** an organization for fox-hunting within a particular area.

fox-hunting *n* a sport in which hunters follow a pack of hounds in pursuit of a fox. ▸ **'fox-,hunter** *n*

foxie ('fɒksɪ) *n Austral.* an informal name for **fox terrier.**

foxing ('fɒksɪŋ) *n* a piece of leather used to reinforce or trim part of the upper of a shoe.

fox moth *n* a coppery-brown European eggar moth, *Macrothylacia rubi,* whose black-and-yellow woolly larvae are commonly found on heather and bramble.

fox squirrel *n* a large squirrel, *Sciurus niger,* occurring in E North America.

foxtail ('fɒks,teɪl) *n* **1** any grass of the genus *Alopecurus,* esp. *A. pratensis,* of Europe, Asia, and South America, having soft cylindrical spikes of flowers: cultivated as a pasture grass. **2** any of various similar and related grasses, esp. any of the genus *Setaria.*

Fox Talbot ('tɔːlbət) *n* **William Henry.** 1800–77, English physicist; a pioneer of photography.

fox terrier *n* either of two breeds of small terrier, the wire-haired and the smooth, having a white coat with markings of black or tan or both.

foxtrot ('fɒks,trɒt) *n* **1** a ballroom dance in quadruple time, combining short and long steps in various sequences. ◆ *vb* **-trots, -trotting, -trotted. 2** (*intr*) to perform this dance.

Foxtrot ('fɒks,trɒt) *n Communications.* a code word for the letter *f.*

foxy ('fɒksɪ) *adj* **foxier, foxiest. 1** of or resembling a fox, esp. in craftiness. **2** smelling strongly like a fox. **3** of a reddish-brown colour. **4** (of paper, wood, etc.) spotted, esp. by mildew. **5** (of wine) having the flavour of fox grapes. **6** *Slang.* sexy; sexually attractive. ▸ **'foxily** *adv* ▸ **'foxiness** *n*

foyboat ('fɔɪ,bəʊt) *n Tyneside dialect.* **a** a small rowing boat. **b** (*in combination*): *a foyboatman.* [C19: from *foy* to provide aid for ships, esp. those in distress]

foyer ('fɔɪeɪ, 'fɔɪə) *n* a hall, lobby, or anteroom, used for reception and as a meeting place, as in a hotel, theatre, cinema, etc. [C19: from French: fireplace, from Medieval Latin *focārius,* from Latin *focus* fire]

fp 1 *abbrev. for* fine point. **2** *Music. symbol for* fortepiano.

FP *or* **fp** *abbrev. for:* **1** freezing point. **2** fully paid.

FPA *abbrev. for* Family Planning Association.

FPO *abbrev. for* field post office.

fps *abbrev. for:* **1** feet per second. **2** foot-pound-second. **3** *Photog.* frames per second.

fps units *pl n* an Imperial system of units based on the foot, pound, and second as the units of length, mass, and time. For scientific and most technical purposes these units have been replaced by SI units.

Fr 1 *Christianity. abbrev. for* **1a** Frater. [Latin: brother] **1b** Father. **2** *the chemical symbol for* francium.

FR *international car registration for* Faeroes.

fr. *abbrev. for:* **1** fragment. **2** franc. **3** from.

Fr. *abbrev. for:* **1** *Christianity.* Father. **2** France. **3** French. **4** the German equivalent of **Mrs.** [from German *Frau*]

Fra (frɑː) *n* brother: a title given to an Italian monk or friar. [Italian, short for *frate* brother (in either natural or religious sense), from Latin *frāter* BROTHER]

fracas ('frækɑː) *n* a noisy quarrel; brawl. [C18: from French, from *fracasser* to shatter, from Latin *frangere* to break, influenced by *quassāre* to shatter]

FRACP *abbrev. for* Fellow of the Royal Australasian College of Physicians.

FRACS *abbrev. for* Fellow of the Royal Australasian College of Surgeons.

fractal ('fræktəl) *Maths.*◆ n. **1** a figure or surface generated by successive subdivisions of a simpler polygon or polyhedron, according to some iterative process. ◆ *adj.* **2** of, relating to, or involving such a process: *fractal geometry; fractal curve.* [C20: from Latin *frāctus* past participle of *frangere* to break]

fraction ('frækʃən) *n* **1** *Maths.* **1a** a ratio of two expressions or numbers other than zero. **1b** any rational number that can be expressed as the ratio of two integers, *a*/*b*, where *b* does not equal *a*, 1, or 0, and *a* does not equal 0. **2** any part or subdivision: *a substantial fraction of the nation.* **3** a small piece; fragment. **4** *Chem.* a component of a mixture separated by a fractional process, such as fractional distillation. **5** *Christianity.* the formal breaking of the bread in Communion. **6** the act of breaking. ◆ *vb* **7** (*tr*) to divide. [C14: from Late Latin *fractiō* a breaking into pieces, from Latin *fractus* broken, from *frangere* to break]

fractional ('frækʃənᵊl) *adj* **1** relating to, containing, or constituting one or more fractions. **2** of or denoting a process in which components of a mixture are separated by exploiting differences in their physical properties, such as boiling points, solubility, etc.: *fractional distillation; fractional crystallization.* **3** very small or insignificant. **4** broken up; fragmented. ◆ Also called: **fractionary** ('frækʃənərɪ). ▸ **'fractionally** *adv*

fractional crystallization *n Chem.* the process of separating the components of a solution on the basis of their different solubilities, by means of evaporating the solution until the least soluble component crystallizes out.

fractional currency *n* paper or metal money of smaller denomination than the standard monetary unit.

fractional distillation *n* **1** the process of separating the constituents of a liquid mixture by heating it and condensing separately the components according to their different boiling points. **2** a distillation in which the vapour is brought into contact with a countercurrent of condensed liquid to increase the purity of the final products. ◆ Sometimes shortened to **distillation.**

fractionate ('frækʃə,neɪt) *vb* **1** to separate or cause to separate into constituents or into fractions containing concentrated constituents. **2** (*tr*) *Chem.* to obtain (a constituent of a mixture) by a fractional process. ▸ **,fraction'ation** *n* ▸ **'fraction,ator** *n*

fractionating column *n Chem.* a long vertical cylinder used in fractional distillation, in which internal reflux enables separation of high and low boiling fractions to take place.

fractionize *or* **fractionise** ('frækʃə,naɪz) *vb* to divide (a number or quantity) into fractions. ▸ **,fractioni'zation** *or* **,fractioni'sation** *n*

fractious ('frækʃəs) *adj* **1** irritable. **2** unruly. [C18: from (obsolete) *fraction* discord + -OUS] ▸ **'fractiously** *adv* ▸ **'fractiousness** *n*

USAGE *Fractious* is sometimes wrongly used where *factious* is meant: *this factious* (not *fractious*) *dispute has split the party still further.*

fractocumulus (,fræktəʊ'kjuːmjʊləs) *n, pl* **-li** (-,laɪ). low ragged slightly bulbous cloud, often appearing below nimbostratus clouds during rain. Also called: **fractocumulus cloud.** [C19: from Latin *fractus* broken + CUMULUS]

fractostratus (,fræktəʊ'strɑːtəs, -'stræt-) *n, pl* **-ti** (-taɪ). low ragged layered cloud often appearing below nimbostratus clouds during rain. [C19: from Latin *fractus* broken + STRATUS]

fracture ('fræktʃə) *n* **1** the act of breaking or the state of being broken. **2a** the breaking or cracking of a bone or the tearing of a cartilage. **2b** the resulting condition. See also **Colles' fracture, comminuted fracture, compound fracture, greenstick fracture, impacted** (sense 2), **simple fracture. 3** a division, split, or breach. **4** *Mineralogy.* **4a** the characteristic appearance of the surface of a freshly broken mineral or rock. **4b** the way in which a mineral or rock naturally breaks. ◆ *vb* **5** to break or cause to break; split. **6** to break or crack (a bone) or (of a bone) to become broken or cracked. **7** to tear (a cartilage) or (of a cartilage) to become torn. [C15: from Old French, from Latin *fractūra,* from *frangere* to break] ▸ **'fracturable** *adj* ▸ **'fractural** *adj*

frae (freɪ) *prep* a Scot. word for **from.**

fraenum *or* **frenum** ('friːnəm) *n, pl* **-na** (-nə). a fold of membrane or skin, such as the fold beneath the tongue, that supports an organ. [C18: from Latin: bridle]

frag (fræg) *vb* **frags, fragging, fragged.** (*tr*) *U.S. military slang.* to kill or wound (a fellow soldier or superior officer) deliberately with an explosive device. [C20: short for *fragmentation grenade,* as used in Vietnam] ▸ **'fragging** *n*

fragile ('frædʒaɪl) *adj* **1** able to be broken easily. **2** in a weakened physical state. **3** delicate; light: *a fragile touch.* **4** slight; tenuous: *a fragile link with the past.* [C17: from Latin *fragilis,* from *frangere* to break] ▸ **'fragilely** *adv* ▸ **fragility** (frə'dʒɪlɪtɪ) *or* **'fragileness** *n*

fragile-X syndrome *n* an inherited condition characterized by mental subnormality: affected individuals have an X-chromosome that is easily damaged under certain conditions.

fragment *n* ('frægmənt). **1** a piece broken off or detached: *fragments of rock.* **2** an incomplete piece; portion: *fragments of a novel.* **3** a scrap; morsel; bit. ◆ *vb* (fræg'mɛnt), *also U.S.* **fragmentize** ('frægmən,taɪz). **4** to break or cause to break into fragments. [C15: from Latin *fragmentum,* from *frangere* to break]

fragmental (fræg'mɛntᵊl) *adj* **1** (of rocks or deposits) composed of fragments of pre-existing rocks and minerals. **2** another word for **fragmentary.** ▸ **frag'mentally** *adv*

fragmentary ('frægməntərɪ, -trɪ) *adj* made up of fragments; disconnected; incomplete. Also: **fragmental.** ▸ **'fragmentarily** *adv* ▸ **'fragmentariness** *n*

fragmentation (,frægmɛn'teɪʃən) *n* **1** the act of fragmenting or the state of being fragmented. **2** the disintegration of norms regulating behaviour, thought, and social relationships. **3** the steel particles of an exploded projectile. **4** (*modifier*) of or relating to a weapon designed to explode into many small pieces, esp. as an antipersonnel weapon: *a fragmentation bomb.*

Fragonard (*French* fragɔnar) *n* **Jean-Honoré** (ʒɑ̃ ɔnɔre). 1732–1806, French artist, noted for richly coloured paintings typifying the frivolity of 18th-century French court life.

fragrance ('freɪgrəns) *or* **fragrancy** *n, pl* **-grances** *or* **-grancies. 1** a pleasant or sweet odour; scent; perfume. **2** the state of being fragrant.

fragrant ('freɪgrənt) *adj* having a pleasant or sweet smell. [C15: from Latin *frāgrāns,* from *frāgrāre* to emit a smell] ▸ **'fragrantly** *adv*

fragrant orchid *n* another name for **scented orchid.**

frail[1] (freɪl) *adj* **1** physically weak and delicate. **2** fragile: *a frail craft.* **3** easily corrupted or tempted. [C13: from Old French *frele,* from Latin *fragilis,* FRAGILE] ▸ **'frailly** *adv* ▸ **'frailness** *n*

frail[2] (freɪl) *n* **1** a rush basket for figs or raisins. **2** a quantity of raisins or figs equal to between 50 and 75 pounds. [C13: from Old French *fraiel,* of uncertain origin]

frailty ('freɪltɪ) *n, pl* **-ties. 1** physical or moral weakness. **2** (*often pl*) a fault symptomatic of moral weakness.

fraise (freɪz) *n* **1** a neck ruff worn during the 16th century. **2** a sloping or horizontal rampart of pointed stakes. **3a** a tool for enlarging a drill hole. **3b** a tool for cutting teeth on watch wheels. [C18: from French: mesentery of a calf, from Old French *fraiser* to remove a shell, from Latin *frendere* to crush]

Fraktur (*German* frak'tuːr) *n* a style of typeface, formerly used in German typesetting for many printed works. [German, from Latin *fractūra* a breaking, FRACTURE; from the curlicues that seem to interrupt the continuous line of a word]

framboesia *or U.S.* **frambesia** (fræm'biːzɪə) *n Pathol.* another name for **yaws.** [C19: from New Latin, from French *framboise* raspberry; see FRAMBOISE; so called because of its raspberry-like excrescences]

framboise *French.* (frɑ̃bwaz) *n* a brandy distilled from raspberries in the Alsace-Lorraine region. [C16: from Old French: raspberry, probably of Germanic origin]

frame (freɪm) *n* **1** an open structure that gives shape and support to something, such as the transverse stiffening ribs of a ship's hull or an aircraft's fuselage or the skeletal beams and uprights of a building. **2** an enclosing case or border into which something is fitted: *the frame of a picture.* **3** the system around which something is built up: *the frame of government.* **4** the structure of the human body. **5** a condition; state (esp. in the phrase **frame of mind**). **6a** one of a series of individual exposures on a strip of film used in making motion pictures. **6b** an individual exposure on a film used in still photography. **6c** an individual picture in a comic strip. **7a** a television picture scanned by one or more electron beams at a particular frequency. **7b** the area of the picture so formed. **8** *Snooker, etc.* **8a** the wooden triangle used to set up the balls. **8b** the balls when set up. **8c** a single game finished when all the balls have been potted. U.S. and Canadian equivalent (for **a** and **b**): **rack. 9** short for **cold frame. 10** one of the sections of which a beehive is composed, esp. one designed to hold a honeycomb. **11** a machine or part of a machine over which yarn is stretched in the production of textiles. **12** (in language teaching, etc.) a syntactic construction with a gap in it, used for assigning words to syntactic classes by seeing which words may fill the gap. **13** *Statistics.* an enumeration of a population for the purposes of sampling, esp. as the basis of a stratified sample. **14** (in telecommunications, computers, etc.) one cycle of a regularly recurring number of pulses in a pulse train. **15** *Slang.* another word for **frame-up. 16** *Obsolete.* shape; form. **17 in the frame.** likely to be awarded or to achieve: *I'm in the frame for the top job.* ◆ *vb* (*mainly tr*) **18** to construct by fitting parts together. **19** to draw up the plans or basic details for; outline: *to frame a policy.* **20** to compose, contrive, or conceive: *to frame a reply.* **21** to provide, support, or enclose with a frame: *to frame a picture.* **22** to form (words) with the lips, esp. silently. **23** *Slang.* to conspire to incriminate (someone) on a false charge. **24** *Slang.* to contrive the dishonest outcome of (a contest, match, etc.); rig. **25** (*intr*) *Yorkshire and northeastern English dialect.* **25a** (*usually imperative or dependent imperative*) to make an effort. **25b** to have ability. [Old English *framiae* to avail; related to Old Frisian *framia* to carry out, Old Norse *frama*] ▸ **'framable** *or* **'frameable** *adj* ▸ **'frameless** *adj* ▸ **'framer** *n*

Frame (freɪm) *n* **Janet.** born 1924, and New Zealand writer: author of the novels *Owls Do Cry* (1957) and *Faces in the Water* (1961), the collection of verse *The Pocket Mirror* (1967), and volumes of autobiography including *An Angel at My Table* (1984), which was made into a film in 1990.

frame aerial *n* another name for **loop aerial.**

frame house *n* a house that has a timber framework and cladding.

frame line *n Films.* a black horizontal bar appearing between successive picture images.

frame of reference *n* **1** a set of basic assumptions or standards that determines and sanctions behaviour. **2** any set of planes or curves, such as the three coordinate axes, used to locate or measure movement of a point in space.

frame saw *n* a saw with a thin blade held in a specially shaped frame. Also called: **span saw.**

frame-up *n Slang.* **1** a conspiracy to incriminate someone on a false charge. **2** a plot to bring about a dishonest result, as in a contest.

framework ('freɪm,wɜːk) *n* **1** a structural plan or basis of a project. **2** a structure or frame supporting or containing something. **3** frames collectively. **4** work such as embroidery or weaving done in or on a frame.

framing ('freɪmɪŋ) *n* **1** a frame, framework, or system of frames. **2** the way in which something is framed. **3** adjustment of the longitudinal position of the film in a projector gate to secure proper vertical positioning of the picture on the screen.

franc (fræŋk; *French* frɑ̃) *n* **1** the standard monetary unit of France, French dependencies, and Monaco, divided into 100 centimes. Also called: **French franc. 2** the standard monetary and currency unit of Belgium, divided into 100 centimes, also legal tender in Luxembourg. Also called: **Belgian franc. 3** the standard monetary and currency unit of Switzerland and Liechtenstein, divided into 100 centimes. Also called: **Swiss franc. 4** the standard monetary and currency unit, comprising 100 centimes, of the following countries: Benin, Burkina-Faso, Cameroon, the Central African Republic, Chad, Congo, Côte d'Ivoire, Equatorial Guinea, Gabon, Mali, Niger, Senegal, and Togo. Also called: **franc CFA, CFA franc, franc of the African financial community. 5** the standard monetary and currency unit of Burundi (**Burundi franc**), Comoros (**Comorian franc**), Democratic Republic of the Congo (formerly Zaïre; **Congolese franc**), Djibouti (**Djibouti franc**), Guinea (**Guinea franc**), Luxembourg (**Luxembourg franc**), Madagascar (**franc malgache**), and Rwanda (**Rwanda franc**). **6** a Moroccan monetary unit worth one hundredth of a dirham. [C14: from Old French; from the Latin phrase *Rex Francōrum* King of the Franks, inscribed on 14th-century francs]

France[1] (frɑːns) *n* a republic in W Europe, between the English Channel, the Mediterranean, and the Atlantic: the largest country wholly in Europe; became a republic in 1793 after the French Revolution and an empire in 1804 under Napoleon; reverted to a monarchy (1815–48), followed by the Second Republic (1848–52), the Second Empire (1852–70), the Third Republic (1870–1940), and the Fourth and Fifth Republics (1946 and 1958); a member of the European Union. It is generally flat or undulating in the north and west and mountainous in the south and east. Official language: French. Religion: Roman Catholic majority. Currency: euro and franc. Capital: Paris. Pop.: 58 841 000 (1998 est.). Area: (including Corsica) 551 600 sq. km (212 973 sq. miles). Related adjs.: **French, Gallic.**

France[2] (*French* frɑ̃s) *n* **Anatole** (anatɔl), real name *Anatole François Thibault.* 1844–1924, French novelist, short-story writer, and critic. His works include *Le Crime de Sylvestre Bonnard* (1881), *L'Île des Pingouins* (1908), and *La Révolte des anges* (1914): Nobel prize for literature 1921.

Francesca (*Italian* fran'tʃeska) *n* See **Piero Della Francesca.**

Franche-Comté (*French* frɑ̃ʃkɔ̃te) *n* a region of E France, covering the Jura and the low country east of the Saône: part of the Kingdom of Burgundy (6th cent. A.D.–1137); autonomous as the Free County of Burgundy (1137–1384); under Burgundian rule again (1384–1477) and Hapsburg rule (1493–1674); annexed by France (1678).

franchise ('fræntʃaɪz) *n* **1** (usually preceded by *the*) the right to vote, esp. for representatives in a legislative body; suffrage. **2** any exemption, privilege, or right granted to an individual or group by a public authority, such as the right to use public property for a business. **3** *Commerce.* authorization granted by a manufacturing enterprise to a distributor to market the manufacturer's products. **4** the full rights of citizenship. **5** (in marine insurance) a sum or percentage stated in a policy, below which the insurer disclaims all liability. ◆ *vb* **6** (*tr*) *Commerce, chiefly U.S. and Canadian.* to grant (a person, firm, etc.) a franchise. **7** an obsolete word for **enfranchise.** [C13: from Old French, from *franchir* to set free, from *franc* free; see FRANK] ▸ **franchisement** ('fræntʃɪzmənt) *n*

Francis ('frɑːnsɪs) *n* **1 Dick,** full name *Richard Stanley Francis.* born 1920, British thriller writer, formerly a champion jockey. His books include *Dead Cert* (1962), *The Edge* (1988), and *Come to Grief* (1995). **2** Sir **Philip.** 1740–1818, British politician; probable author of the *Letters of Junius* (1769–72). He played an important part in the impeachment of Warren Hastings (1788–95).

Francis I *n* **1** 1494–1547, king of France (1515–47). His reign was dominated by his rivalry with Emperor Charles V for the control of Italy. He was a noted patron of the arts and learning. **2** 1708–65, duke of Lorraine (1729–37), grand duke of Tuscany (1737–65), and Holy Roman Emperor (1745–65). His marriage (1736) to Maria Theresa led to the War of the Austrian Succession (1740–48). **3** title as emperor of Austria of **Francis II.**

Francis II *n* **1** 1544–60, king of France (1559–60); son of Henry II and Catherine de' Medici; first husband of Mary, Queen of Scots. **2** 1768–1835, last Holy Roman Emperor (1792–1806) and, as Francis I, first emperor of Austria (1804–35). The Holy Roman Empire was dissolved (1806) following his defeat by Napoleon at Austerlitz.

Franciscan (fræn'sɪskən) *n* **a** a member of any of several Christian religious orders of mendicant friars or nuns tracing their origins back to Saint Francis of Assisi; a Grey Friar. **b** (*as modifier*): *a Franciscan friar.*

Francis of Assisi *n* **Saint.** original name *Giovanni di Bernardone.* ?1181–1226, Italian monk; founder of the Franciscan order of friars. He is remembered for his humility and love for all creation and was the first person to exhibit stigmata (1224). Feast day: Oct. 4.

Francis of Sales (seɪlz; *French* sal) *n* **Saint.** 1567–1622, French ecclesiastic and theologian; bishop of Geneva (1602–22) and an opponent of Calvinism; author of *Introduction to a Devout Life* (1609) and founder of the Order of the Visitation (1610). Feast day: Jan. 24.

Francis turbine *n* a water turbine designed to produce high flow from a low head of pressure: used esp. in hydroelectric power generation. [named after J. B. *Francis* (1815–92), English-born hydraulic engineer, who invented it]

Francis Xavier ('zeɪvɪə) *n* **Saint.** See (Saint Francis) **Xavier.**

francium ('frænsɪəm) *n* an unstable radioactive element of the alkali-metal group, occurring in minute amounts in uranium ores. Symbol: Fr; atomic no.: 87; half-life of most stable isotope, ^{223}Fr: 22 minutes; valency: 1; melting pt.: 27°C; boiling pt.: 677°C. [C20: from New Latin, from FRANCE + -IUM; so-called because first found in France]

Franck *n* **1** (*French* frɑ̃k). **César** (**Auguste**) (sezar). 1822–90, French composer, organist, and teacher, born in Belgium. His works, some of which make use of cyclic form, include a violin sonata, a string quartet, the *Symphony in D Minor* (1888), and much organ music. **2** (fræŋk). **James.** 1882–1964, U.S. physicist, born in Germany: shared a Nobel prize for physics with Gustav Hertz (1925) for work on the quantum theory, particularly the effects of bombarding atoms with electrons.

Franco ('fræŋkəʊ; *Spanish* 'franko) *n* **Francisco** (fran'θisko), called *el Caudillo.* 1892–1975, Spanish general and statesman; head of state (1939–1975). He was commander-in-chief of the Falangists in the Spanish Civil War (1936–39), defeating the republican government and establishing a dictatorship (1939). He kept Spain neutral in World War II.

Franco- ('fræŋkəʊ-) *combining form.* indicating France or French: *Franco-Prussian.* [from Medieval Latin *Francus,* from Late Latin: FRANK]

francolin ('fræŋkəʊlɪn) *n* any African or Asian partridge of the genus *Francolinus.* [C17: from French, from Old Italian *francolino,* of unknown origin]

Franconia (fræŋ'kəʊnɪə) *n* a medieval duchy of Germany, inhabited by the Franks from the 7th century, now chiefly in Bavaria, Hesse, and Baden-Württemberg.

Franconian (fræŋ'kəʊnɪən) *n* **1** a group of medieval Germanic dialects spoken by the Franks in an area from N Bavaria and Alsace to the mouth of the Rhine. **Low Franconian** developed into Dutch, while **Upper Franconian** contributed to High German, of which it remains a recognizable dialect. See also **Old Low German, Old High German, Frankish.** ◆ *adj* **2** of or relating to Franconia, the Franks, or their languages.

Francophile ('fræŋkəʊ,faɪl) *or* **Francophil** ('fræŋkəʊfɪl) (*sometimes not cap.*) ◆ *n* **1** a person who admires France and the French. ◆ *adj* **2** marked by or possessing admiration of France and the French.

Francophobe ('fræŋkəʊ,fəʊb) *n* (*sometimes not cap.*) **1** a person who hates or despises France or its people. **2** *Canadian.* a person who hates or fears Canadian Francophones.

Francophone ('fræŋkəʊ,fəʊn) (*often not cap.*) ◆ *n* **1** a person who speaks French, esp. a native speaker. ◆ *adj* **2** speaking French as a native language. **3** using French as a lingua franca. ◆ Compare **Anglophone.**

Franco-Prussian War *n* the war of 1870–71 between France and Prussia culminating in the fall of the French Second Empire and the founding of the German empire.

franc-tireur *French.* (frɑ̃tirœr) *n* **1** a sniper. **2** a guerrilla or irregular soldier. [C19: from *franc* free + *tireur* shooter, from *tirer* to shoot, of unknown origin]

franger ('fræŋə) *n Austral. slang.* a condom. [C20: perhaps related to FRENCH LETTER]

frangible ('frændʒɪbᵊl) *adj* breakable or fragile. [C15: from Old French, ultimately from Latin *frangere* to break] ▸ ,**frangi'bility** *or* '**frangibleness** *n*

frangipane ('frændʒɪ,peɪn) *n* **1a** a pastry filled with cream and flavoured with almonds. **1b** a rich cake mixture containing ground almonds. **2** a variant of **frangipani** (the perfume).

frangipani (,frændʒɪ'pɑːnɪ) *n, pl* **-panis** *or* **-pani. 1** any tropical American apocynaceous shrub of the genus *Plumeria,* esp. *P. rubra,* cultivated for its waxy typically white or pink flowers, which have a sweet overpowering scent. **2** a perfume prepared from this plant or resembling the odour of its flowers. **3 native frangipani.** *Austral.* an Australian evergreen tree, *Hymenosporum flavum,* with large fragrant yellow flowers: family *Pittosporaceae.* [C17: via French from Italian: perfume for scenting gloves, named after the Marquis Muzio *Frangipani,* 16th-century Roman nobleman who invented it]

Franglais (*French* frɑ̃glɛ) *n* informal French containing a high proportion of words of English origin. [C20: from French *français* French + *anglais* English]

frank (fræŋk) *adj* **1** honest and straightforward in speech or attitude: *a frank person.* **2** outspoken or blunt. **3** open and avowed; undisguised: *frank interest.* **4** an obsolete word for **free** or **generous.** ◆ *vb* (*tr*) **5** *Chiefly Brit.* to put a mark on (a letter, parcel, etc.), either cancelling the postage stamp or in place of a stamp, ensuring free carriage. See also **postmark. 6** to mark (a letter, parcel, etc.) with an official mark or signature, indicating the right of free delivery. **7** to facilitate or assist (a person) to come and go, pass, or enter easily. **8** to obtain immunity for or exempt (a person). ◆ *n* **9** an official mark or signature affixed to a letter, parcel, etc., ensuring free delivery or delivery without stamps. **10** the privilege, issued to certain people and establishments, entitling them to delivery without postage stamps. [C13: from Old French *franc,* from Medieval Latin *francus* free; identical with FRANK[1] (in Frankish Gaul only members of this people enjoyed full freedom)] ▸ '**frankable** *adj* ▸ '**franker** *n* ▸ '**frankness** *n*

Frank[1] (fræŋk) *n* a member of a group of West Germanic peoples who spread from the east bank of the middle Rhine into the Roman Empire in the late 4th century A.D., gradually conquering most of Gaul and Germany. The Franks achieved their greatest power under Charlemagne. [Old English *Franca;* related to Old High German *Franko;* perhaps from the name of a typical Frankish weapon (compare Old English *franca* javelin)]

Frank[2] (*Dutch* fraŋk) *n* **1 Anne.** 1929–45, German Jewess, whose *Diary* (1947) recorded the experiences of her family while in hiding from the Nazis in Amsterdam (1942–44). They were betrayed and she died in a concentration camp. **2 Robert.** born 1924, U.S. photographer and film maker, born in Switzerland; best known for his photographic book *The Americans* (1959).

frankalmoign ('fræŋkᵊl,mɔɪn) *n English legal history.* a form of tenure by which religious bodies held lands, esp. on condition of praying for the soul of the donor. [C16: from Anglo-French *fraunke almoigne,* from *fraunke* FRANK + *almoign* church treasury, alms chest]

franked investment income *n* dividends from one UK company received by another on which the paying company has paid corporation tax so that the receiving company has no corporation tax to pay; the tax credit included in the dividend can be set against the receiving company's advance corporation tax on its own dividends.

Frankenstein ('fræŋkɪn,staɪn) *n* **1** a person who creates something that brings about his ruin. **2** Also called: **Frankenstein's monster.** a thing that destroys its creator. [C19: after Baron *Frankenstein,* who created a destructive monster from parts of corpses in the novel by Mary Shelley (1818)] ▸ ,**Franken'steinian** *adj*

Frankfort ('fræŋkfət) *n* **1** a city in N Kentucky: the state capital. Pop.: 25 535 (1990). **2** *Now rare.* an English spelling of **Frankfurt.**

Frankfurt (**am Main**) (*German* 'fraŋkfurt (am 'main)) *n* a city in central Germany, in Hesse on the Main River: a Roman settlement in the 1st century; a free imperial city (1372–1806); seat of the federal assembly (1815–66); university (1914); trade fairs since the 13th century. Pop.: 650 055 (1996 est.).

Frankfurt (**an der Oder**) (*German* 'fraŋkfurt (an der 'oːdər)) *n* a city in E Germany on the Polish border: member of the Hanseatic League (1368–1450). Pop.: 85 360 (1991).

frankfurter ('fræŋk,fɜːtə) *n* a light brown smoked sausage, made of finely minced pork or beef, often served in a bread roll. [C20: short for German *Frankfurter Wurst* sausage from FRANKFURT (AM MAIN)]

Frankfurter ('fræŋk,fɜːtə) *n* an inhabitant or native of Frankfurt.

Frankfurt School *n Philosophy.* a school of thought, founded at the University of Frankfurt in 1923 by Theodor Adorno, Herbert Marcuse and others, derived from Marxist, Freudian, and Hegelian theory.

frankincense ('fræŋkɪn,sens) *n* an aromatic gum resin obtained from trees of the burseraceous genus *Boswellia,* which occur in Asia and Africa. Also called: **olibanum.** [C14: from Old French *franc* free, pure + *encens* INCENSE[1]; see FRANK]

Frankish ('fræŋkɪʃ) *n* **1** the ancient West Germanic language of the Franks, esp. the dialect that contributed to the vocabulary of modern French. See also **Franconian, Old High German.** ◆ *adj* **2** of or relating to the Franks or their language.

franklin ('fræŋklɪn) *n* (in 14th- and 15th-century England) a substantial landholder of free but not noble birth. [C13: from Anglo-French *fraunclein,* from Old French *franc* free, on the model of CHAMBERLAIN]

Franklin ('fræŋklɪn) *n* **1 Aretha** (ə'riːθə). born 1942, U.S. soul, pop, and gospel singer. **2 Benjamin.** 1706–90, American statesman, scientist, and author. He helped draw up the Declaration of Independence (1776) and, as ambassador to France (1776–85), he negotiated an alliance with France and a peace settlement with Britain. As a scientist, he is noted particularly for his researches in electricity, esp. his invention of the lightning conductor. **3** Sir **John.** 1786–1847, English explorer of the Arctic: lieutenant-governor of Van Diemen's Land (now Tasmania) (1836–43): died while on a voyage to discover the Northwest Passage. **4 Rosalind.** 1920–58, British x-ray crystallographer. She contributed to the discovery of the structure of DNA, before her premature death from cancer.

franklinite ('fræŋklɪ,naɪt) *n* a black mineral consisting of an oxide of iron, manganese, and zinc: a source of iron and zinc. Formula: $(Fe,Mn,Zn)(Fe,Mn)_2O_4$. [C19: from *Franklin,* New Jersey, where it is found, + -ITE[1]]

frankly ('fræŋklɪ) *adv* **1** (*sentence modifier*) in truth; to be honest: *frankly, I can't bear him.* **2** in a frank manner.

frankpledge ('fræŋk,plɛdʒ) *n* (in medieval England) **1** the corporate responsibility of members of a tithing for the good behaviour of each other. **2** a member of a tithing. **3** a tithing itself. [C15: via Anglo-French from Old French *franc* free (see FRANK) + *plege* PLEDGE]

frantic ('fræntɪk) *adj* **1** distracted with fear, pain, joy, etc. **2** marked by or showing frenzy: *frantic efforts.* **3** *Archaic.* insane. [C14: from Old French *frenetique,* from Latin *phrenēticus* mad, FRENETIC] ▸ '**frantically** *or* '**franticly** *adv* ▸ '**franticness** *n*

Franz Ferdinand (*German* frants 'fɛrdinant) *n* English name *Francis Ferdinand.* 1863–1914, archduke of Austria; heir apparent of Franz Josef I. His assassination contributed to the outbreak of World War I.

Franz Josef I (*German* frants 'joːzɛf) *n* English name *Francis Joseph I.* 1830–1916, emperor of Austria (1848–1916) and king of Hungary (1867–1916).

Franz Josef Land *n* an archipelago of over 100 islands in the Arctic Ocean, administratively part of Russia. Area: about 21 000 sq. km (8000 sq. miles). Russian name: **Zemlya Frantsa Iosifa** (zji'mlja 'frantsə 'jɔsifə).

frap (fræp) *vb* **fraps, frapping, frapped.** (*tr*) *Nautical.* to lash down or together. [C14: from Old French *fraper* to hit, probably of imitative origin]

frappé ('fræpeɪ; *French* frape) *n* **1** a drink consisting of a liqueur, etc., poured over crushed ice. ◆ *adj* **2** (*postpositive*) (esp. of drinks) chilled; iced. [C19: from French, from *frapper* to strike, hence, chill; see FRAP]

Frascati (fræ'skɑːtɪ) *n* a dry or semisweet white wine from the Lazio region of Italy.

Fraser[1] ('freɪzə) *n* a river in SW Canada, in S central British Columbia, flowing northwest, south, and west through spectacular canyons in the Coast Mountains to the Strait of Georgia. Length: 1370 km (850 miles).

Fraser[2] ('freɪzə) *n* **1** (**John**) **Malcolm.** born 1930, Australian statesman; prime minister of Australia (1975–83). **2 Peter.** 1884–1950, New Zealand statesman, born in Scotland; prime minister (1940–49).

frass (fræs) *n* excrement or other refuse left by insects and insect larvae. [C19: from German, from *fressen* to devour]

frat (fræt) *n U.S. slang.* **a** a member of a fraternity. **b** (*as modifier*): *the frat kid.*

fratchy ('frætʃɪ) *adj* **fratchier, fratchiest.** *Informal.* quarrelsome; irritable. [C19: from obsolete *fratch* to make a harsh noise; perhaps of imitative origin]

frater[1] ('freɪtə) *n* a mendicant friar or a lay brother in a monastery or priory. [C16: from Latin: BROTHER]

frater[2] ('freɪtə) *n Archaic.* a refectory. [C13: from Old French *fraiteur,* aphetic variant of *refreitor,* from Late Latin *rēfectōrium* REFECTORY]

fraternal (frə'tɜːnᵊl) *adj* **1** of or suitable to a brother; brotherly. **2** of or relating to a fraternity. **3** designating either or both of a pair of twins of the same or opposite sex that developed from two separate fertilized ova. Compare **identical** (sense 3). [C15: from Latin *frāternus,* from *frāter* brother] ▸ **fra'ternalism** *n* ▸ **fra'ternally** *adv*

fraternity (frə'tɜːnɪtɪ) *n, pl* **-ties. 1** a body of people united in interests, aims, etc.: *the teaching fraternity.* **2** brotherhood. **3** *U.S. and Canadian.* a secret society joined by male students, usually functioning as a social club.

fraternize *or* **fraternise** ('frætəˌnaɪz) *vb* (*intr;* often foll. by *with*) to associate on friendly terms. ▸ **ˌfraterni'zation** *or* **ˌfraterni'sation** *n* ▸ **'frater,nizer** *or* **'frater,niser** *n*

fratricide ('frætrɪˌsaɪd, 'freɪ-) *n* **1** the act of killing one's brother. **2** a person who kills his brother. **3** *Military.* the destruction of or interference with a nuclear missile before it can strike its target caused by the earlier explosion of a warhead at a nearby target. [C15: from Latin *frātricīda;* see FRATER[1], -CIDE] ▸ **ˌfratri'cidal** *adj*

Frau (fraʊ) *n, pl* **Frauen** ('fraʊən) *or* **Fraus.** a married German woman: usually used as a title equivalent to *Mrs* and sometimes extended to older unmarried women. [from Old High German *frouwa;* related to Dutch *vrouw*]

fraud (frɔːd) *n* **1** deliberate deception, trickery, or cheating intended to gain an advantage. **2** an act or instance of such deception. **3** something false or spurious: *his explanation was a fraud.* **4** *Informal.* a person who acts in a false or deceitful way. [C14: from Old French *fraude,* from Latin *fraus* deception]

Fraud Squad *n* (in Britain) the department of a police force that is concerned with criminal fraud.

fraudster ('frɔːdstə) *n* a swindler.

fraudulent ('frɔːdjʊlənt) *adj* **1** acting with or having the intent to deceive. **2** relating to or proceeding from fraud or dishonest action. [C15: from Latin *fraudulentus* deceitful] ▸ **'fraudulence** *or* **'fraudulency** *n* ▸ **'fraudulently** *adv*

Frauenfeld (*German* 'frauənfɛlt) *n* a town in NE Switzerland, capital of Thurgau canton. Pop.: 19 402 (1990).

fraughan ('frɒhən) *n* an Irish word for **whortleberry** (senses 1, 2). [from Irish Gaelic fraochán, diminutive of *fraoch* heather]

fraught (frɔːt) *adj* **1** (*usually postpositive* and foll. by *with*) filled or charged; attended: *a venture fraught with peril.* **2** *Informal.* showing or producing tension or anxiety: *she looks rather fraught; a fraught situation.* **3** *Archaic.* (*usually postpositive* and foll. by *with*) freighted. ◆ *n* **4** an obsolete word for **freight.** [C14: from Middle Dutch *vrachten,* from *vracht* FREIGHT]

Fräulein (*German* 'frɔylain; *English* 'frɔːlaɪn, 'fraʊ-) *n, pl* **-lein** *or English* **-leins.** an unmarried German woman: formerly used as a title equivalent to *Miss.* Abbrev.: **Frl.** [from Middle High German *vrouwelīn,* diminutive of *vrouwe* lady]

Fraunhofer (*German* 'fraunhoːfər) *n* **Joseph von** ('joːzɛf fɔn). 1787–1826, German physicist and optician, who investigated spectra of the sun, planets, and fixed stars, and improved telescopes and other optical instruments.

Fraunhofer lines *pl n* a set of dark lines appearing in the continuous emission spectrum of the sun. It is caused by the absorption of light of certain wavelengths coming from the hotter region of the sun by elements in the cooler outer atmosphere.

fraxinella (ˌfræksɪ'nɛlə) *n* another name for **gas plant.** [C17: from New Latin: a little ash tree, from Latin *frāxinus* ash]

fray[1] (freɪ) *n* **1** a noisy quarrel. **2** a fight or brawl. **3** an archaic word for **fright.** ◆ *vb Archaic.* **4** (*tr*) to frighten. [C14: short for AFFRAY]

fray[2] (freɪ) *vb* **1** to wear or cause to wear away into tatters or loose threads, esp. at an edge or end. **2** to make or become strained or irritated. **3** to rub or chafe (another object) or (of two objects) to rub against one another. ◆ *n* **4** a frayed place, as in cloth. [C14: from French *frayer* to rub, from Latin *fricāre;* see FRICTION, FRIABLE]

Fray Bentos (ˌfreɪ 'bɛntɒs) *n* a port in W Uruguay, on the River Uruguay: noted for meat-packing. Pop.: 21 400 (1995 est.).

Frayn (freɪn) *n* **Michael.** born 1933, British playwright, novelist, and translator; his plays include *The Two of Us* (1970), *Noises Off* (1982), *Look, Look* (1990), and *A Landing on the Sun* (1991).

Frazer ('freɪzə) *n* Sir **James George.** 1854–1941, Scottish anthropologist; author of many works on primitive religion, and magic, esp. *The Golden Bough* (1890).

Frazier ('freɪʒə) *n* **Joe.** born 1944, U.S. boxer: won the world heavyweight title in 1970 and was the first to beat Muhammad Ali professionally (1971).

frazil ('freɪzɪl) *n* small pieces of ice that form in water moving turbulently enough to prevent the formation of a sheet of ice. [C19: from Canadian French *frasil,* from French *fraisil* cinders, ultimately from Latin *fax* torch]

frazzle ('fræzᵊl) *vb* **1** *Informal.* to make or become exhausted or weary; tire out. **2** a less common word for **fray**[2] (sense 1). ◆ *n* **3** *Informal.* the state of being frazzled or exhausted. **4** a frayed end or remnant. **5 to a frazzle.** *Informal.* absolutely; completely (esp. in the phrase **burnt to a frazzle**). [C19: probably from Middle English *faselen* to fray, from *fasel* fringe; influenced by FRAY[2]]

FRCM (in Britain) *abbrev. for* Fellow of the Royal College of Music.

FRCO (in Britain) *abbrev. for* Fellow of the Royal College of Organists.

FRCP (in Britain) *abbrev. for* Fellow of the Royal College of Physicians.

FRCS (in Britain) *abbrev. for* Fellow of the Royal College of Surgeons.

FRCVS (in Britain) *abbrev. for* Fellow of the Royal College of Veterinary Surgeons.

freak[1] (friːk) *n* **1** a person, animal, or plant that is abnormal or deformed; monstrosity. **2a** an object, event, etc., that is abnormal or extremely unusual. **2b** (*as modifier*): *a freak storm.* **3** a personal whim or caprice. **4** *Informal.* a person who acts or dresses in a markedly unconventional or strange way. **5** *Informal.* a person who is obsessed with something specified: *a jazz freak.* ◆ *vb* **6** See **freak out.** [C16: of obscure origin]

freak[2] (friːk) *Rare.* ◆ *n* **1** a fleck or streak of colour. ◆ *vb* **2** (*tr*) to streak with colour; variegate. [C17: from earlier *freaked,* probably coined by Milton, based on STREAK[1] + obsolete *freckt* freckled; see FRECKLE]

freakish ('friːkɪʃ) *adj* **1** of, related to, or characteristic of a freak; abnormal or unusual. **2** unpredictable or changeable: *freakish weather.* ▸ **'freakishly** *adv* ▸ **'freakishness** *n*

freak out *vb* (*adv*) *Informal.* to be or cause to be in a heightened emotional state, such as that of fear, anger, or excitement.

freaky ('friːkɪ) *adj* **freakier, freakiest. 1** *Slang.* strange; unconventional; bizarre. **2** another word for **freakish.** ▸ **'freakily** *adv* ▸ **'freakiness** *n*

freckle ('frɛkᵊl) *n* **1** a small brownish spot on the skin: a localized deposit of the pigment melanin, developed by exposure to sunlight. Technical name: **lentigo. 2** any small area of discoloration; a spot. **3** *Austral. slang.* the anus. ◆ *vb* **4** to mark or become marked with freckles or spots. [C14: from Old Norse *freknur* freckles; related to Swedish *fräkne,* Danish *fregne*] ▸ **'freckled** *or* **'freckly** *adj*

Fredericia (*Danish* freðə'redsja) *n* a port in Denmark, in E Jutland at the N end of the Little Belt. Pop.: 28 000 (1990).

Frederick I ('frɛdrɪk) *n* **1** See **Frederick Barbarossa. 2** 1657–1713, first king of Prussia (1701–13); son of Frederick William.

Frederick II *n* **1** 1194–1250, Holy Roman Emperor (1220–50), king of Germany (1212–50), and king of Sicily (1198–1250). **2** See **Frederick the Great.**

Frederick III *n* **1** 1415–93, Holy Roman Emperor (1452–93) and, as Frederick IV, king of Germany (1440–93). **2** called *the Wise.* 1463–1525, elector of Saxony (1486–1525). He protected Martin Luther in Wartburg Castle after the Diet of Worms (1521).

Frederick IV *n* See **Frederick III** (sense 1).

Frederick V *n* called *the Winter King.* 1596–1632, elector of the Palatinate (1610–23) and king of Bohemia (1619–20). He led the revolt of Bohemian Protestants at the beginning of the Thirty Years' War.

Frederick IX *n* 1899–1972, king of Denmark (1947–72).

Frederick Barbarossa (ˌbɑːbə'rɒsə) *n* official title *Frederick I.* ?1123–90, Holy Roman Emperor (1155–90), king of Germany (1152–90). His attempt to assert imperial rights in Italy ended in his defeat at Legnano (1176) and the independence of the Lombard cities (1183).

Frederick Henry *n* 1584–1647, prince of Orange and count of Nassau; son of William (I) the Silent.

Frederick the Great *n* official title *Frederick II.* 1712–86, king of Prussia (1740–86); son of Frederick William I. He gained Silesia during the War of Austrian Succession (1740–48) and his military genius during the Seven Years' War (1756–63) established Prussia as a European power. He was also a noted patron of the arts.

Frederick William *n* called *the Great Elector.* 1620–88, elector of Brandenburg (1640–88).

Frederick William I *n* 1688–1740, king of Prussia (1713–40); son of Frederick I: reformed the Prussian army.

Frederick William II *n* 1744–97, king of Prussia (1786–97).

Frederick William III *n* 1770–1840, king of Prussia (1797–1840).

Frederick William IV *n* 1795–1861, king of Prussia (1840–61). He submitted to the 1848 Revolution but refused the imperial crown offered by the Frankfurt Parliament (1849). In 1857 he became insane and his brother, William I, became regent (1858–61).

Fredericton ('frɛdrɪktən) *n* a city in SE Canada, capital of New Brunswick, on the St John River. Pop.: 45 364 (1991).

Frederiksberg (*Danish* freðregs'bɛr) *n* a city in E Denmark, within the area of greater Copenhagen: founded in 1651 by King Frederick III. Pop.: 88 002 (1995 est.).

Fredrikstad (*Norwegian* 'frɛdrikstad) *n* a port in SE Norway at the entrance to Oslo Fjord. Pop.: 26 546 (1990).

free (friː) *adj* **freer, freest. 1** able to act at will; not under compulsion or restraint. **2a** having personal rights or liberty; not enslaved or confined. **2b** (*as n*): *land of the free.* **3** (*often postpositive* and foll. by *from*) not subject (to) or restricted (by some regulation, constraint, etc.); exempt: *a free market; free from pain.* **4** (of a country, etc.) autonomous or independent. **5** exempt from external direction or restriction; not forced or induced: *free will.* **6** not subject to conventional constraints: *free verse.* **7** (of jazz) totally improvised, with no preset melodic, harmonic, or rhythmic basis. **8** not exact or literal: *a free translation.* **9** costing nothing; provided without charge: *free entertainment.* **10** *Law.* (of property) **10a** not subject to payment of rent or performance of services; freehold. **10b** not subject to any burden or charge, such as a mortgage or lien; unencumbered. **11** (*postpositive;* often foll. by *of* or *with*) ready or generous in using or giving; liberal; lavish: *free with advice.* **12** unrestrained by propriety or good manners; licentious. **13** not occupied or in use; available: *a free cubicle.* **14** not occupied or busy; without previous engagements: *I'm not free until Wednesday.* **15** open or available to all; public. **16** without charge to the subscriber or user: *freepost; freephone.* **17** not fixed or joined; loose: *the free end of a chain.* **18** without obstruction or impediment: *free passage.* **19** *Chem.* chemically uncombined: *free nitrogen.* **20** *Phonetics.* denoting a vowel that can occur in an open syllable, such as the vowel in *see* as opposed to the vowel in *cat.* **21** *Grammar.* denoting a morpheme that can occur as a separate word. Compare **bound**[1] (sense 8a). **22** *Logic.* denoting an occurrence of a variable not bound by a quantifier. Compare **bound**[1] (sense 9). **23** (of some materials, such as certain kinds of stone) easily worked. **24** *Nautical.* (of the wind) blowing from the quarter. **25 free and easy.** casual or tolerant; easy-going. **26 for free.** *Nonstandard.* without charge or cost. **27 feel free.** (usually imperative) to regard oneself as having permission to perform a specified action. **28 make free with.** to take liberties with; behave too familiarly towards. ◆ *adv* **29** in a free manner; freely. **30** without charge or cost. **31** *Nautical.* with the wind blowing from the quarter: *a yacht sailing free.* ◆ *vb* **frees, freeing, freed.** (*tr*) **32** (sometimes foll. by *up*) to set at liberty; release. **33** to remove obstructions, attachments, or impediments from; disengage. **34** (often foll. by *of* or *from*) to relieve or rid (of obstacles, pain, etc.). [Old English *frēo;* related to Old Saxon, Old High German *frī,* Gothic *freis* free, Sanskrit *priya* dear] ▸ **'freer** *n* ▸ **'freely** *adv* ▸ **'freeness** *n*

-free *adj combining form.* free from: *trouble-free; lead-free petrol.*

free agent *n* a person whose actions are not constrained by others.

free alongside ship *adj* (of a shipment of goods) delivered to the dock without charge to the buyer, but excluding the cost of loading onto the vessel. Compare **free on board.** Abbrevs.: **FAS, f.a.s.** Also: **free alongside vessel.**

free association *n* **1** *Psychoanal.* a method of exploring a person's unconscious by eliciting words and thoughts that are associated with key words provided by a psychoanalyst. **2** a spontaneous mental process whereby ideas, words, or images suggest other ideas, etc., in a nonlogical chain reaction.

freebase ('friːˌbeɪs) *vb Slang.* to refine (cocaine) for smoking.

freebie ('friːbɪ) *Slang.* ◆ *n* **1** something provided without charge. ◆ *adj* **2** without charge; free.

freeboard ('friːˌbɔːd) *n* the space or distance between the deck of a vessel and the waterline.

freeboot ('friːˌbuːt) *vb* (*intr*) to act as a freebooter; pillage.

freebooter ('friːˌbuːtə) *n* **1** a person, such as a pirate, living from plunder. **2** *Informal.* a person, esp. an itinerant, who seeks pleasure, wealth, etc., without responsibility. [C16: from Dutch *vrijbuiter,* from *vrijbuit* booty; see FILIBUSTER]

freeborn ('friːˌbɔːn) *adj* **1** not born in slavery. **2** of, relating to, or suitable for people not born in slavery.

Free Church *n Chiefly Brit.* **a** any Protestant Church, esp. the Presbyterian, other than the Established Church. **b** (*as modifier*): *Free-Church attitudes.*

free city *n* a sovereign or autonomous city; city-state.

free climbing *n Mountaineering.* climbing without using pitons, étriers, etc., as direct aids to ascent, but using ropes, belays, etc., at discretion for security. Compare **aid climbing.**

free coinage *n U.S.* coinage of bullion brought to the mint by any individual.

free companion *n* (in medieval Europe) a member of a company of mercenary soldiers.

free company *n European history.* a band of mercenary soldiers during the Middle Ages.

freedman ('friːdˌmæn) *n, pl* **-men.** a man who has been freed from slavery. ▸ **'freedˌwoman** *fem n*

freedom ('friːdəm) *n* **1** personal liberty, as from slavery, bondage, serfdom, etc. **2** liberation or deliverance, as from confinement or bondage. **3** the quality or state of being free, esp. to enjoy political and civil liberties. **4** (usually foll. by *from*) the state of being without something unpleasant or bad; exemption or immunity: *freedom from taxation.* **5** the right or privilege of unrestricted use or access: *the freedom of a city.* **6** autonomy, self-government, or independence. **7** the power or liberty to order one's own actions. **8** *Philosophy.* the quality, esp. of the will or the individual, of not being totally constrained; able to choose between alternative actions in identical circumstances. **9** ease or frankness of manner; candour: *she talked with complete freedom.* **10** excessive familiarity of manner; boldness. **11** ease and grace, as of movement; lack of effort. [Old English *frēodōm*]

freedom fighter *n* a militant revolutionary.

Freedomites ('friːdəˌmaɪts) *pl n* another name for **Sons of Freedom.**

freedom of the seas *n International law.* **1** the right of ships of all nations to sail the high seas in peacetime. **2** (in wartime) the immunity accorded to neutral ships from attack. **3** the exclusive jurisdiction possessed by a state over its own ships sailing the high seas in peacetime.

freedom rider *n U.S.* a person who participated, esp. in the 1960s, in an organized tour, usually by public transport in the South, in order to protest against racism and put federal laws on integration to the test.

free electron *n* any electron that is not attached to an ion, atom, or molecule and is free to move under the influence of an applied electric or magnetic field.

free energy *n* a thermodynamic property that expresses the capacity of a system to perform work under certain conditions. See **Gibbs function, Helmholtz function.**

free enterprise *n* an economic system in which commercial organizations compete for profit with little state control.

free fall *n* **1** free descent of a body in which the gravitational force is the only force acting on it. **2** the part of a parachute descent before the parachute opens.

free flight *n* the flight of a rocket, missile, etc., when its engine has ceased to produce thrust.

free-floating *adj* unattached or uncommitted, as to a cause, a party, etc. ▸ **ˌfree-'floater** *n*

free-floating anxiety *n Psychiatry.* chronic anxiety occurring for no identifiable cause.

Freefone ('friːˌfəʊn) *n Brit. trademark.* a system of telephone use in which the cost of calls in response to an advertisement is borne by the advertiser.

free-for-all *n Informal.* a disorganized brawl or argument, usually involving all those present.

free form *Arts.* ◆ *n* **1** an irregular flowing shape, often used in industrial or fabric design. ◆ *adj* **free-form. 2** freely flowing, spontaneous.

free gift *n* something given away, esp. as an incentive to a purchaser.

free gold *n* **1** gold, uncombined with other minerals, found in a pure state. **2** *U.S.* the excess of gold held by the Federal Reserve Banks over the legal reserve.

free hand *n* **1** unrestricted freedom to act (esp. in the phrase **give (someone) a free hand**). ◆ *adj, adv* **freehand. 2** (done) by hand without the use of guiding instruments: *a freehand drawing.*

free-handed *adj* generous or liberal; unstinting. ▸ **ˌfree-'handedly** *adv* ▸ **ˌfree-'handedness** *n*

free-hearted *adj* frank and spontaneous; open; generous. ▸ **ˌfree-'heartedly** *adv* ▸ **ˌfree-'heartedness** *n*

freehold ('friːˌhəʊld) *Property law.* *n* **1a** tenure by which land is held in fee simple, fee tail, or for life. **1b** an estate held by such tenure. ◆ *adj* **2** relating to or having the nature of freehold.

freeholder ('friːˌhəʊldə) *n Property law.* a person in possession of a freehold building or estate in land.

free house *n Brit.* a public house not bound to sell only one brewer's products.

free kick *n Soccer.* a place kick awarded for a foul or infringement, either direct, from which a goal may be scored, or indirect, from which the ball must be touched by at least one other player for a goal to be allowed.

free labour *n* **1** the labour of workers who are not members of trade unions. **2** such workers collectively.

freelance ('friːˌlɑːns) *n* **1a** Also called: **'freeˌlancer.** a self-employed person, esp. a writer or artist, who is not employed continuously but hired to do specific assignments. **1b** (*as modifier*): *a freelance journalist.* **2** a person, esp. a politician, who supports several causes or parties without total commitment to any one. **3** (in medieval Europe) a mercenary soldier or adventurer. ◆ *vb* **4** to work as a freelance on (an assignment, etc.). ◆ *adv* **5** as a freelance. [C19 (in sense 3): later applied to politicians, writers, etc.]

free list *n* **1** *Commerce, chiefly U.S.* a list of commodities not subject to tariffs. **2** a list of people admitted free.

free-living *adj* **1** given to ready indulgence of the appetites. **2** (of animals and plants) not parasitic; existing independently. ▸ **ˌfree-'liver** *n*

freeload ('friːˌləʊd) *vb* (*intr*) *Slang.* to act as a freeloader; sponge.

freeloader ('friːˌləʊdə) *n Slang.* a person who habitually depends on the charity of others for food, shelter, etc. ▸ **'freeˌloading** *n*

free love *n* the practice of sexual relationships without fidelity to a single partner or without formal or legal ties.

freeman ('friːmən) *n, pl* **-men. 1** a person who is not a slave or in bondage. **2** a person who enjoys political and civil liberties; citizen. **3** a person who enjoys a privilege or franchise, such as the freedom of a city.

free market *n* **a** an economic system that allows supply and demand to regulate prices, wages, etc., rather than government policy. **b** (*as modifier*): *a free-market economy.*

freemartin ('friːˌmɑːtɪn) *n* the female of a pair of twin calves of unlike sex that is imperfectly developed and sterile, probably due to the influence of the male hormones of its twin during development in the uterus. [C17: of uncertain origin]

freemason ('friːˌmeɪsᵊn) *n Medieval history.* a member of a guild of itinerant skilled stonemasons, who had a system of secret signs and passwords with which they recognized each other. ▸ **freemasonic** (ˌfriːmə'sɒnɪk) *adj*

Freemason ('friːˌmeɪsᵊn) *n* a member of the widespread secret order, constituted in London in 1717, of **Free and Accepted Masons,** pledged to brotherly love, faith, and charity. Sometimes shortened to **Mason.** ▸ **Freemasonic** (ˌfriːmə'sɒnɪk) *adj*

freemasonry ('friːˌmeɪsᵊnrɪ) *n* natural or tacit sympathy and understanding.

Freemasonry ('friːˌmeɪsᵊnrɪ) *n* **1** the institutions, rites, practices, etc., of Freemasons. **2** Freemasons collectively.

free on board *adj* (of a shipment of goods) delivered on board ship or other carrier without charge to the buyer. Compare **free alongside ship.** Abbrevs.: **FOB, f.o.b.**

free on rail *adj* (of a consignment of goods) delivered to a railway station and loaded onto a train without charge to the buyer. Abbrevs.: **FOR, f.o.r.**

freephone ('friːˌfəʊn) *n* a common spelling of **Freefone** (*Trademark*).

free port *n* **1** a port open to all commercial vessels on equal terms. **2** Also called: **free zone.** a zone adjoining a port that permits the duty-free entry of foreign goods intended for re-export.

Freepost ('friːˌpəʊst) *n Brit. trademark.* a method of postage by which the cost of replies to an advertisement is borne by the advertiser.

free radical *n* an atom or group of atoms containing at least one unpaired electron and existing for a brief period of time before reacting to produce a stable molecule. Sometimes shortened to **radical.** Compare **group** (sense 10).

free-range *adj Chiefly Brit.* kept or produced in natural nonintensive conditions: *free-range hens; free-range eggs.*

free recall *n Psychol.* the recollection of the members of a list of items without regard to their serial order.

free-running *adj* **1** (of a mechanism, material, etc.) moving smoothly and uninterruptedly. **2** *Electronics.* of or relating to a periodic signal that is not synchronized to a timing source: *free-running interference produces moving patterns on a television screen.*

free-select *vb* (*tr*) *Austral. history.* to select (areas of crown land) and acquire the freehold by a series of annual payments. ▸ **ˌfree-se'lection** *n* ▸ **ˌfree-se'lector** *n*

freesheet ('friːˌʃiːt) *n* a newspaper that is distributed free, paid for by its advertisers. Also called: **giveaway.**

freesia ('friːzɪə, 'friːʒə) *n* any iridaceous plant of the genus *Freesia,* of southern

Africa, cultivated for their white, yellow, or pink tubular fragrant flowers. [C19: New Latin, named after F. H. T. *Freese* (died 1876), German physician]

free silver *n* the unlimited minting of silver coins, esp. when at a fixed ratio to gold.

free skating *n* either the short programme of specified movements or the long programme chosen by a skater in a figure-skating competition.

Free Soil Party *n* a former U.S. political party opposing slavery from 1848 until 1854 when it merged with the Republican party.

free space *n* a region that has no gravitational and electromagnetic fields: used as an absolute standard. Also called (no longer in technical usage): **vacuum.**

free speech *n* the right to express one's opinions publicly.

free-spoken *adj* speaking frankly or without restraint. ► ˌ**free-ˈspokenly** *adv* ► ˌ**free-ˈspokenness** *n*

freestanding (ˌfriːˈstændɪŋ) *adj* **1** standing apart; not attached to or supported by another object. **2** (in systemic grammar) denoting a clause that can stand alone as a sentence; denoting or being a main clause. Compare **bound**[1] (sense 8b).

Free State *n* **1** a province of central South Africa; replaced the former province of Orange Free State in 1994: gold and uranium mining. Capital: Bloemfontein. Pop.: 2 782 500 (1995 est.). Area: 129 480 sq. km (49 992 sq. miles). **2** *U.S. history.* (before the Civil War). any state prohibiting slavery. **3** short for the **Irish Free State.**

freestone (ˈfriːˌstəʊn) *n* **1a** any fine-grained stone, esp. sandstone or limestone, that can be cut and worked in any direction without breaking. **1b** (*as modifier*): *a freestone house.* **2** *Botany.* **2a** a fruit, such as a peach, in which the flesh separates readily from the stone. **2b** (*as modifier*): *a freestone peach.* Compare **clingstone.**

freestyle (ˈfriːˌstaɪl) *n* **1** a competition or race, as in swimming, in which each participant may use a style of his or her choice instead of a specified style. **2a International freestyle.** an amateur style of wrestling with an agreed set of rules. **2b** Also called: **all-in wrestling.** a style of professional wrestling with no internationally agreed set of rules. **3** a series of acrobatics performed in skiing, etc. **4** (*as modifier*): *a freestyle event.*

free-swimming *adj* (of aquatic animals or larvae) not sessile or attached to any object and therefore able to swim freely in the water. ► ˌ**free-ˈswimmer** *n*

freethinker (ˌfriːˈθɪŋkə) *n* a person who forms his ideas and opinions independently of authority or accepted views, esp. in matters of religion. ► ˌ**freeˈthinking** *n, adj*

free thought *n* thought unrestrained and uninfluenced by dogma or authority, esp. in religious matters.

free throw *n Basketball.* an unimpeded shot at the basket from the **free-throw line,** given for a technical fault (one free shot) or a foul (two free shots).

Freetown (ˈfriːˌtaʊn) *n* the capital and chief port of Sierra Leone: founded in 1787 for slaves freed and destitute in England. Pop.: 669 000 (1990 est.).

free trade *n* **1** international trade that is free of such government interference as import quotas, export subsidies, protective tariffs, etc. Compare **protection** (sense 3). **2** *Archaic.* illicit trade; smuggling.

free-trader *n* **1** a person who supports or advocates free trade. **2** *Archaic.* a smuggler or smuggling vessel.

free verse *n* unrhymed verse without a metrical pattern.

free vote *n Chiefly Brit.* a parliamentary division in which members are not constrained by a party whip.

freeware (ˈfriːˌwɛə) *n* computer software that may be distributed and used without payment.

freeway (ˈfriːˌweɪ) *n U.S.* **1** another name for **expressway. 2** a major road that can be used without paying a toll.

freewheel (ˌfriːˈwiːl) *n* **1** a ratchet device in the rear hub of a bicycle wheel that permits the wheel to rotate freely while the pedals are stationary. **2** a device in the transmission of some vehicles that automatically disengages the drive shaft when it rotates more rapidly than the engine shaft, so that the drive shaft can turn freely. ♦ *vb* **3** (*intr*) to coast in a vehicle or on a bicycle using the freewheel.

freewheeling (ˌfriːˈwiːlɪŋ) *adj* **1** relating to, operating as, or having a freewheel; coasting. **2** *Informal.* free of restraints; carefree or uninhibited.

free will *n* **1a** the apparent human ability to make choices that are not externally determined. **1b** the doctrine that such human freedom of choice is not illusory. Compare **determinism. 1c** (*as modifier*): *a free-will decision.* **2** the ability to make a choice without coercion: *he left of his own free will: I did not influence him.*

Free World *n* **the.** the non-Communist countries collectively, esp. those that are actively anti-Communist.

freeze (friːz) *vb* **freezes, freezing, froze** (frəʊz), **frozen** (ˈfrəʊzᵊn). **1** to change (a liquid) into a solid as a result of a reduction in temperature, or (of a liquid) to solidify in this way, esp. to convert or be converted into ice. **2** (when *intr,* sometimes foll. by *over* or *up*) to cover, clog, or harden with ice, or become so covered, clogged, or hardened: *the lake froze over last week.* **3** to fix fast or become fixed (to something) because of the action of frost. **4** (*tr*) to preserve (food) by subjection to extreme cold, as in a freezer. **5** to feel or cause to feel the sensation or effects of extreme cold. **6** to die or cause to die of frost or extreme cold. **7** to become or cause to become paralysed, fixed, or motionless, esp. through fear, shock, etc.: *he froze in his tracks.* **8** (*tr*) to cause (moving film) to stop at a particular frame. **9** to decrease or cause to decrease in animation or vigour. **10** to make or become formal, haughty, etc., in manner. **11** (*tr*) to fix (prices, incomes, etc.) at a particular level, usually by government direction. **12** (*tr*) to forbid by law the exchange, liquidation, or collection of (loans, assets, etc.). **13** (*tr*) to prohibit the manufacture, sale, or use of (something specified). **14** (*tr*) to stop (a process) at a particular stage of development. **15** (*tr*) *Informal.* to render (tissue or a part of the body) insensitive, as by the application or injection of a local anaesthetic. **16** (*intr;* foll. by *onto*) *Informal, chiefly U.S.* to cling. ♦ *n* **17** the act of freezing or state of being frozen. **18** *Meteorol.* a spell of temperatures below freezing point, usually over a wide area. **19** the fixing of incomes, prices, etc., by legislation. **20** another word for **frost.** ♦ *sentence substitute.* **21** *Chiefly U.S.* a command to stop still instantly or risk being shot. [Old English *frēosan;* related to Old Norse *frjōsa,* Old High German *friosan,* Latin *prūrīre* to itch; see FROST] ► ˈ**freezable** *adj*

freeze-dry *vb* **-dries, -drying, -dried.** (*tr*) to preserve (a substance) by rapid freezing and subsequently drying in a vacuum.

freeze-frame *n* **1** *Films, television.* a single frame of a film repeated to give an effect like a still photograph. **2** *Video.* a single frame of a video recording viewed as a still by stopping the tape.

freeze out *vb* (*tr, adv*) *Informal.* to force out or exclude, as by unfriendly behaviour, boycotting, etc.

freezer (ˈfriːzə) *n* **1** Also called: **deepfreeze.** a device that freezes or chills, esp. an insulated cold-storage cabinet for long-term storage of perishable foodstuffs. **2** a former name for a **refrigerator.**

freeze-up *n Informal.* **1** a period of freezing or extremely cold weather. **2** *U.S., Canadian.* **2a** the freezing of lakes, rivers, and topsoil in autumn or early winter. **2b** the time of year when this occurs.

freezing (ˈfriːzɪŋ) *adj Informal.* extremely cold.

freezing mixture *n* a mixture of two substances, usually salt and ice, to give a temperature below 0°C.

freezing point *n* the temperature below which a liquid turns into a solid. It is equal to the melting point.

freezing works *n Austral. and N.Z.* a slaughterhouse at which animal carcasses are frozen for export. See also **chamber** (sense 10).

free zone *n* an area at a port where certain customs restrictions are not implemented. See also **free port.**

Frege (*German* ˈfreːgə) *n* **Gottlob.** 1848–1925, German logician and philosopher, who laid the foundations of modern formal logic and semantics in his *Begriffsschrift* (1879).

F region *n* the highest region of the ionosphere, extending from a height of about 150 kilometres to about 1000 kilometres. It contains the highest proportion of free electrons and is the most useful region for long-range radio transmission. Also called: **Appleton layer.** See also **ionosphere.**

Freiburg (*German* ˈfraibʊrk) *n* **1** a city in SW Germany, in SW Baden-Württemberg: under Austrian rule (1368–1805); university (1457). Pop.: 199 273 (1996 est.). Official name: **Freiburg im Breisgau** (ɪm ˈbraisgau). **2** the German name for **Fribourg.**

freight (freɪt) *n* **1a** commercial transport that is slower and cheaper than express. **1b** the price charged for such transport. **1c** goods transported by this means. **1d** (*as modifier*): *freight transport.* **2** *Chiefly Brit.* a ship's cargo or part of it. ♦ *vb* (*tr*) **3** to load with goods for transport. **4** *Chiefly U.S. and Canadian.* to convey commercially as or by freight. **5** to load or burden; charge. [C16: from Middle Dutch *vrecht;* related to French *fret,* Spanish *flete,* Portuguese *frete*] ► ˈ**freightless** *adj*

freightage (ˈfreɪtɪdʒ) *n* **1** the commercial conveyance of goods. **2** the goods so transported. **3** the price charged for such conveyance.

freighter (ˈfreɪtə) *n* **1** a ship or aircraft designed for transporting cargo. **2** a person concerned with the loading or chartering of a ship.

freightliner (ˈfreɪtˌlaɪnə) *n* **1** *Trademark.* a goods train carrying containers that can be transferred onto lorries or ships. **2** (in Britain) (*cap.*) *Trademark.* a containerized transportation service involving both rail and road.

freight ton *n* the full name for **ton**[1] (sense 4).

Fremantle (ˈfriːˌmæntᵊl) *n* a port in SW Western Australia, on the Indian Ocean. Pop.: 24 010 (1986).

fremd (frɛmd, freɪmd) *adj Archaic.* alien or strange. [Old English *fremde;* related to Old High German *fremidi*]

fremitus (ˈfrɛmɪtəs) *n, pl* **-tus.** *Med.* a vibration felt by the hand when placed on a part of the body, esp. the chest, when the patient is speaking or coughing. [C19: from Latin: a roaring sound, a humming, from *fremere* to make a low roaring, murmur]

French[1] (frɛntʃ) *n* **1** the official language of France: also an official language of Switzerland, Belgium, Canada, and certain other countries. It is the native language of approximately 70 million people; also used for diplomacy. Historically, French is an Indo-European language belonging to the Romance group. See also **Old French, Anglo-French. 2 the French.** (*functioning as pl*) the natives, citizens, or inhabitants of France collectively. **3** See **French vermouth.** ♦ *adj* **4** relating to, denoting, or characteristic of France, the French, or their language. ♦ Related prefixes: **Franco-, Gallo-. 5** (in Canada) of or relating to French Canadians. [Old English *Frencisc* French, Frankish; see FRANK[1]] ► ˈ**Frenchness** *n*

French[2] (frɛntʃ) *n* Sir **John Denton Pinkstone,** 1st Earl of Ypres. 1852–1925, British field marshal in World War I: commanded the British Expeditionary Force in France and Belgium (1914–15); Lord Lieutenant of Ireland (1918–21).

French Academy *n* an association of 40 French scholars and writers, founded by Cardinal Richelieu in 1635, devoted chiefly to preserving the purity of the French language.

French and Indian War *n* the war (1755–60) between the French and British, each aided by different Indian tribes, that formed part of the North American Seven Years' War.

French bean *n* **1** a small twining bushy or annual bean plant, *Phaseolus vulgaris,* with white or lilac flowers and slender green edible pods. **2** the pod of this plant. See also **haricot.** ♦ Also called: **dwarf bean, kidney bean.**

French bread *n* white bread in a long slender loaf that is made from a water dough and has a crisp brown crust.

French bulldog *n* a small stocky breed of dog with a sleek coat, usually brindled or pied, a large square head, and large erect rounded ears.

French Cameroons *pl n* the part of Cameroon formerly administered by France (1919–60).

French Canada *n* the areas of Canada, esp. in the province of Quebec, where French Canadians predominate.

French Canadian *n* **1** a Canadian citizen whose native language is French. ♦ *adj* **French-Canadian. 2** of or relating to French Canadians or their language.

French chalk *n* a compact variety of talc used to mark cloth or remove grease stains from materials.

French Community *n* an international association consisting of France and a number of former French colonies: founded in 1958 as a successor to the French Union.

French cricket *n* a child's game resembling cricket, in which the batsman's legs are used as the wicket.

French cuff *n* a double cuff formed by a backward fold of the material.

French curve *n* a thin plastic sheet with profiles of several curves, used by draughtsmen for drawing curves.

French doors *pl n* the U.S. and Canadian name for **French windows.**

French dressing *n* a salad dressing made from oil and vinegar with seasonings; vinaigrette.

French Equatorial Africa *n* the former French overseas territories of Chad, Gabon, Middle Congo, and Ubangi-Shari (1910–58).

French fact *n* (in Canada) the presence of French Canada as a distinct cultural force within Confederation.

French Foreign Legion *n* a unit of the French Army serving outside France, esp. formerly in French North African colonies. It is largely recruited from foreigners.

French fried potatoes *pl n* a more formal name for **chips.** Also called (U.S. and Canadian): **French fries.**

French Guiana *n* a French overseas region in NE South America, on the Atlantic: colonized by the French in about 1637; tropical forests. Capital: Cayenne. Pop.: 169 000 (1998 est.). Area: about 91 000 sq. km (23 000 sq. miles). ▸ **French Guianese** *or* **Guianan** *adj, n*

French Guinea *n* a former French territory of French West Africa: became independent as Guinea in 1958.

French heel *n* a fairly high and narrow-waisted heel on women's shoes. ▸ **ˌFrench-ˈheeled** *adj*

French horn *n Music.* a valved brass instrument with a funnel-shaped mouthpiece and a tube of conical bore coiled into a spiral. It is a transposing instrument in F. Range: about three and a half octaves upwards from B on the second leger line below the bass staff. See **horn.**

Frenchify (ˈfrɛntʃɪˌfaɪ) *vb* **-fies, -fying, -fied.** *Informal.* to make or become French in appearance, behaviour, etc. ▸ **ˌFrenchifiˈcation** *n*

French India *n* a former French overseas territory in India, including Chandernagore and Pondicherry: restored to India between 1949 and 1954.

French Indochina *n* the territories of SE Asia that were colonized by France and held mostly until 1954: included Cochin China, Annam, and Tonkin (now largely Vietnam), Cambodia, Laos, and Kuang-Chou Wan (returned to China in 1945, now Zhanjiang).

French kiss *n* a kiss involving insertion of the tongue into the partner's mouth.

French knickers *pl n* women's wide-legged underpants.

French knot *n* an ornamental stitch made by looping the thread three or four times around the needle before putting it into the fabric.

French leave *n* an unauthorized or unannounced absence or departure. **[C18:** alluding to a custom in France of leaving without saying goodbye to one's host or hostess**]**

French letter *n Brit.* a slang term for **condom.**

French lilac *n* another name for **goat's-rue** (sense 1).

Frenchman (ˈfrɛntʃmən) *n, pl* **-men.** a native, citizen, or inhabitant of France. ▸ **ˈFrenchˌwoman** *fem n*

French Morocco *n* a former French protectorate in NW Africa, united in 1956 with Spanish Morocco and Tangier to form the kingdom of Morocco.

French mustard *n* a mild mustard paste made with vinegar rather than water.

French navy *n* **a** a dark dull navy blue. **b** (*as adj*): *a French-navy dress.*

French North Africa *n* the former French possessions of Algeria, French Morocco, and Tunisia.

French Oceania *n* a former name (until 1958) of **French Polynesia.**

French pastry *n* a rich pastry made esp. from puff pastry and filled with cream, fruit, etc.

French pleat *or* **roll** *n* a woman's hair style with the hair gathered at the back into a cylindrical roll.

French polish *n* **1** a varnish for wood consisting of shellac dissolved in alcohol. **2** the gloss finish produced by repeated applications of this polish.

French-polish *vb* to treat with French polish or give a French polish (to).

French Polynesia *n* a French Overseas Territory in the S Pacific Ocean, including the Society Islands, the Tuamotu group, the Gambier group, the Tubuai Islands, and the Marquesas Islands. Capital: Papeete, on Tahiti. Pop.: 228 000 (1998 est.). Area: about 4000 sq. km (1500 sq. miles). Former name (until 1958): **French Oceania.**

French Revolution *n* the anticlerical and republican revolution in France from 1789 until 1799, when Napoleon seized power.

French Revolutionary calendar *n* the full name for the **Revolutionary calendar.**

French seam *n* a seam in which the edges are not visible.

French sixth *n* (in musical harmony) an augmented sixth chord having a major third and an augmented fourth between the root and the augmented sixth.

French Somaliland *n* a former name (until 1967) of **Djibouti.**

French Southern and Antarctic Territories *pl n* a French overseas territory, comprising Adélie Land in Antarctica and the islands of Amsterdam and St Paul and the Kerguelen and Crozet archipelagos in the S Indian Ocean.

French stick *n Brit.* a long straight notched stick loaf. Also called: **French stick loaf.**

French Sudan *n* a former name (1898–1959) of **Mali.**

French toast *n* **1** *Brit.* toast cooked on one side only. **2** bread dipped in beaten egg and lightly fried.

French Togoland *n* a former United Nations Trust Territory in W Africa, administered by France (1946–60), now the independent republic of Togo.

French Union *n* a union of France with its dependencies (1946–58): replaced by the French Community.

French vermouth *n* a dry aromatic white wine. Also called: **French.**

French West Africa *n* a former group (1895–1958) of French Overseas Territories: consisted of Senegal, Mauritania, French Sudan, Burkina-Faso, Niger, French Guinea, the Ivory Coast, and Dahomey.

French West Indies *pl n* **the.** a group of islands in the Lesser Antilles, administered by France. Pop.: 632 754 (latest est.). Area: 2792 sq. km (1077 sq. miles).

French windows *pl n* (*sometimes sing*) *Brit.* a pair of casement windows extending to floor level and opening onto a balcony, garden, etc. U.S. and Canadian name: **French doors.**

Frenchy (ˈfrɛntʃɪ) *adj* **1** *Informal.* characteristic of or resembling the French. ♦ *n, pl* **-ies. 2** an informal name for a French person.

Freneau (ˈfrɛnəʊ) *n* **Philip.** 1752–1832, U.S. poet, journalist, and patriot; editor of the *National Gazette* (1791–93).

frenetic (frɪˈnɛtɪk) *adj* distracted or frantic; frenzied. **[C14:** via Old French *frenetique* from Latin *phrenēticus,* from Greek *phrenētikos,* from *phrenitis* insanity, from *phrēn* mind**]** ▸ **freˈnetically** *adv* ▸ **freˈneticness** *n*

Frenkel defect (ˈfrɛnkᵊl) *n Physics.* a crystal defect in which a lattice ion has moved to an interstitial position leaving a vacant lattice site. **[C20:** named after I. I. *Frenkel* (1894–1952), Russian physicist**]**

frenulum (ˈfrɛnjʊləm) *n, pl* **-la** (-lə). **1** a strong bristle or group of bristles on the hind wing of some moths and other insects, by which the forewing and hind wing are united during flight. **2** a small fraenum. **[C18:** New Latin, diminutive of Latin *frēnum* bridle**]**

frenum (ˈfriːnəm) *n, pl* **-na** (-nə). a variant spelling (esp. U.S.) of **fraenum.**

frenzied (ˈfrɛnzɪd) *adj* filled with or as if with frenzy; wild; frantic. ▸ **ˈfrenziedly** *adv*

frenzy (ˈfrɛnzɪ) *n, pl* **-zies. 1** violent mental derangement. **2** wild excitement or agitation; distraction. **3** a bout of wild or agitated activity: *a frenzy of preparations.* ♦ *vb* **-zies, -zying, -zied. 4** (*tr*) to make frantic; drive into a frenzy. **[C14:** from Old French *frenesie,* from Late Latin *phrenēsis* madness, delirium, from Late Greek, ultimately from Greek *phrēn* mind; compare FRENETIC**]**

Freon (ˈfriːɒn) *n Trademark.* any of a group of chemically unreactive chlorofluorocarbons used as aerosol propellants, refrigerants, and solvents.

freq. *abbrev. for:* **1** frequent(ly). **2** frequentative.

frequency (ˈfriːkwənsɪ) *n, pl* **-cies. 1** the state of being frequent; frequent occurrence. **2** the number of times that an event occurs within a given period; rate of recurrence. **3** *Physics.* the number of times that a periodic function or vibration repeats itself in a specified time, often 1 second. It is usually measured in hertz. Symbol: ν or *f* **4** *Statistics.* **4a** the number of individuals in a class (**absolute frequency**). **4b** the ratio of this number to the total number of individuals under survey (**relative frequency**). **5** *Ecology.* **5a** the number of individuals of a species within a given area. **5b** the percentage of quadrats that contains individuals of a species. ♦ Also called (for senses 1, 2): **frequence. [C16:** from Latin *frequentia* a large gathering, from *frequēns* numerous, crowded**]**

frequency band *n* a continuous range of frequencies, esp. in the radio spectrum, between two limiting frequencies.

frequency distribution *n Statistics.* the function of the distribution of a sample corresponding to the probability density function of the underlying population and tending to it as the sample size increases, the set of relative frequencies of sample points falling within given intervals of the range of the random variable.

frequency-division multiplex *n* See **multiplex** (sense 1).

frequency modulation *n* a method of transmitting information using a radio-frequency carrier wave. The frequency of the carrier wave is varied in accordance with the amplitude and polarity of the input signal, the amplitude of the carrier remaining unchanged. Abbrev.: **FM.** Compare **amplitude modulation.**

frequent *adj* (ˈfriːkwənt). **1** recurring at short intervals. **2** constant or habitual. ♦ *vb* (frɪˈkwɛnt). **3** (*tr*) to visit repeatedly or habitually. **[C16:** from Latin *frequēns* numerous; perhaps related to Latin *farcīre* to stuff**]** ▸ **freˈquentable** *adj* ▸ **freˈquenter** *n* ▸ **ˈfrequently** *adv* ▸ **ˈfrequentness** *n*

frequentation (ˌfriːkwɛnˈteɪʃən) *n* the act or practice of frequenting or visiting often.

frequentative (frɪˈkwɛntətɪv) *Grammar.* ♦ *adj* **1** denoting an aspect of verbs in some languages used to express repeated or habitual action. **2** (in English) denoting a verb or an affix having meaning that involves repeated or habitual action, such as the verb *wrestle,* from *wrest.* ♦ *n* **3a** a frequentative verb or affix. **3b** the frequentative aspect of verbs.

fresco (ˈfrɛskəʊ) *n, pl* **-coes** *or* **-cos. 1** a very durable method of wall-painting using watercolours on wet plaster or, less properly, dry plaster (**fresco secco**), with a less durable result. **2** a painting done in this way. **[C16:** from Italian: fresh plaster, coolness, from *fresco* (adj) fresh, cool, of Germanic origin**]**

Frescobaldi (*Italian* fresko'baldi) *n* **Girolamo** (dʒi'rɔ:lamo). 1583–1643, Italian organist and composer, noted esp. for his organ and harpsichord music.

fresh (frɛʃ) *adj* **1** not stale or deteriorated; newly made, harvested, etc.: *fresh bread; fresh strawberries.* **2** newly acquired, created, found, etc.: *fresh publications.* **3** novel; original: *a fresh outlook.* **4** latest; most recent: *fresh developments.* **5** further; additional; more: *fresh supplies.* **6** not canned, frozen, or otherwise preserved: *fresh fruit.* **7** (of water) not salt. **8** bright or clear: *a fresh morning.* **9** chilly or invigorating: *a fresh breeze.* **10** not tired; alert; refreshed. **11** not worn or faded: *fresh colours.* **12** having a healthy or ruddy appearance. **13** newly or just arrived; straight: *fresh from the presses.* **14** youthful or inexperienced. **15** *Chiefly U.S.* designating a female farm animal, esp. a cow, that has recently given birth. **16** *Informal.* presumptuous or disrespectful; forward. **17** *Northern English dialect.* partially intoxicated; tipsy. ◆ *n* **18** the fresh part or time of something. **19** another name for **freshet.** ◆ *vb* **20** *Obsolete.* to make or become fresh; freshen. ◆ *adv* **21** in a fresh manner; freshly. **22 fresh out of.** *Informal.* having just run out of supplies of. [Old English *fersc* fresh, unsalted; related to Old High German *frisc,* Old French *freis,* Old Norse *ferskr*] ▸ **'freshly** *adv* ▸ **'freshness** *n*

fresh breeze *n* a fairly strong breeze of force five on the Beaufort scale.

freshen ('frɛʃən) *vb* **1** to make or become fresh or fresher. **2** (often foll. by *up*) to refresh (oneself), esp. by washing. **3** (*intr*) (of the wind) to increase. **4** to lose or cause to lose saltiness. **5** (*intr*) *Chiefly U.S.* **5a** (of farm animals) to give birth. **5b** (of cows) to commence giving milk after calving. ▸ **'freshener** *n*

fresher ('frɛʃə) *or* **freshman** ('frɛʃmən) *n, pl* **-ers** *or* **-men.** a first-year student at college or university.

freshet ('frɛʃɪt) *n* **1** the sudden overflowing of a river caused by heavy rain or melting snow. **2** a stream of fresh water emptying into the sea.

fresh gale *n* a gale of force eight on the Beaufort scale.

fresh-run *adj* (of fish) newly migrated upstream from the sea, esp. to spawn.

freshwater ('frɛʃ,wɔ:tə) *n* (*modifier*) **1** of, relating to, or living in fresh water. **2** (esp. of a sailor who has not sailed on the sea) unskilled or inexperienced. **3** *U.S.* small and little known: *a freshwater school.*

fresnel ('freɪnɛl; *French* frɛnɛl) *n* a unit of frequency equivalent to 10^{12} hertz. [C20: named after A. J. FRESNEL]

Fresnel (*French* frɛnɛl) *n* **Augustin Jean** (ogystɛ̃ ʒɑ̃). 1788–1827, French physicist: worked on the interference of light, contributing to the wave theory of light.

Fresnel lens *n* a lens consisting of a number of smaller lenses arranged to give a flat surface of short focal length. [C20: named after A. J. FRESNEL]

Fresno ('frɛznəʊ) *n* a city in central California, in the San Joaquin Valley. Pop.: 396 011 (1996 est.).

fret[1] (frɛt) *vb* **frets, fretting, fretted. 1** to distress or be distressed; worry. **2** to rub or wear away. **3** to irritate or be irritated; feel or give annoyance or vexation. **4** to eat away or be eaten away by chemical action; corrode. **5** (*intr*) (of a road surface) to become loose so that potholes develop; scab. **6** to agitate (water) or (of water) to be agitated. **7** (*tr*) to make by wearing away; erode. ◆ *n* **8** a state of irritation or anxiety. **9** the result of fretting; corrosion. **10** a hole or channel caused by fretting. [Old English *fretan* to EAT; related to Old High German *frezzan,* Gothic *fraitan,* Latin *peredere*]

fret[2] (frɛt) *n* **1** a repetitive geometrical figure, esp. one used as an ornamental border. **2** such a pattern made in relief and with numerous small openings; fretwork. **3** *Heraldry.* a charge on a shield consisting of a mascle crossed by a saltire. ◆ *vb* **frets, fretting, fretted. 4** (*tr*) to ornament with fret or fretwork. [C14: from Old French *frete* interlaced design used on a shield, probably of Germanic origin] ▸ **'fretless** *adj*

fret[3] (frɛt) *n* any of several small metal bars set across the fingerboard of a musical instrument of the lute, guitar, or viol family at various points along its length so as to produce the desired notes when the strings are stopped by the fingers. [C16: of unknown origin] ▸ **'fretless** *adj*

fret[4] (frɛt) *n* short for **sea fret.**

fretboard ('frɛtbɔ:d) *n* a fingerboard with frets on a stringed musical instrument.

fretful ('frɛtfʊl) *adj* peevish, irritable, or upset. ▸ **'fretfully** *adv* ▸ **'fretfulness** *n*

fret saw *n* a fine-toothed saw with a long thin narrow blade, used for cutting designs in thin wood or metal.

fretted ('frɛtɪd) *adj* **1** ornamented with angular designs or frets. **2** decorated with fretwork.

fretwork ('frɛt,wɜ:k) *n* **1** decorative geometrical carving or openwork. **2** any similar pattern of light and dark. **3** ornamental work of three-dimensional frets.

Freud (frɔɪd) *n* **1 Anna.** 1895–1982, Austrian psychiatrist: daughter of Sigmund Freud and pioneer of child psychoanalysis. **2 Lucian.** born 1922, British painter, esp. of nudes and portraits; grandson of Sigmund Freud. **3 Sigmund** ('zi:kmʊnt). 1856–1939, Austrian psychiatrist; originator of psychoanalysis, based on free association of ideas and analysis of dreams. He stressed the importance of infantile sexuality in later development, evolving the concept of the Oedipus complex. His works include *The Interpretation of Dreams* (1900) and *The Ego and the Id* (1923).

Freudian ('frɔɪdɪən) *adj* **1** of or relating to Sigmund Freud or his ideas. ◆ *n* **2** a person who follows or believes in the basic ideas of Sigmund Freud. ▸ **'Freudian,ism** *n*

Freudian slip *n* any action, such as a slip of the tongue, that may reveal an unconscious thought.

Frey (freɪ) *or* **Freyr** (freɪə) *n Norse myth.* the god of earth's fertility and dispenser of prosperity.

Freya *or* **Freyja** ('freɪə) *n Norse myth.* the goddess of love and fecundity, sister of Frey.

Freytag (*German* 'fraita:k) *n* **Gustav** ('gustaf). 1816–95, German novelist and dramatist; author of the comedy *Die Journalisten* (1853) and *Soll und Haben* (1855), a novel about German commercial life.

FRG *abbrev. for* Federal Republic of Germany.

FRGS (in Britain) *abbrev. for* Fellow of the Royal Geographical Society.

Fri. *abbrev. for* Friday.

friable ('fraɪəbᵊl) *adj* easily broken up; crumbly. [C16: from Latin *friābilis,* from *friāre* to crumble; related to Latin *fricāre* to rub down] ▸ **,fria'bility** *or* **'friableness** *n*

friar ('fraɪə) *n* a member of any of various chiefly mendicant religious orders of the Roman Catholic Church, the main orders being the **Black Friars** (Dominicans), **Grey Friars** (Franciscans), **White Friars** (Carmelites), and **Austin Friars** (Augustinians). [C13 *frere,* from Old French: brother, from Latin *frāter* BROTHER] ▸ **'friarly** *adj*

friarbird ('fraɪə,bɜ:d) *n* any of various Australian honeyeaters of the genus *Philemon,* having a naked head.

Friar Minor *n, pl* **Friars Minor.** *Christianity.* a member of either of two of the three orders into which the order founded by St Francis of Assisi came to be divided, namely the **Order of Friars Minor** and the **Order of Friars Minor Conventual.** Compare **Capuchin.**

friar's balsam *n* a compound containing benzoin, mixed with hot water and used as an inhalant to relieve colds and sore throats.

friar's lantern *n* another name for **will-o'-the-wisp.**

Friar Tuck *n English legend.* a jolly friar who joined Robin Hood's band and aided their exploits.

friary ('fraɪərɪ) *n, pl* **-aries.** *Christianity.* a convent or house of friars.

frib (frɪb) *n Austral. and N.Z.* a short heavy-conditioned piece of wool removed from a fleece during classing. [of unknown origin]

fribble ('frɪbᵊl) *vb* **1** (*tr*) to fritter away; waste. **2** (*intr*) to act frivolously; trifle. ◆ *n* **3** a wasteful or frivolous person or action. ◆ *adj* **4** frivolous; trifling. [C17: of unknown origin] ▸ **'fribbler** *n*

Fribourg (*French* fribur) *n* **1** a canton in W Switzerland. Capital: Fribourg. Pop.: 224 552 (1996 est.). Area: 1676 sq. km (645 sq. miles). **2** a town in W Switzerland, capital of Fribourg canton: university (1889). Pop.: 35 000 (1989). German name: **Freiburg.**

fricandeau *or* **fricando** ('frɪkən,dəʊ) *n, pl* **-deaus, -deaux,** *or* **-does** (-,dəʊz). a larded and braised veal fillet. [C18: from Old French, probably based on FRICASSEE]

fricassee (,frɪkə'si:, 'frɪkəsɪ, 'frɪkə,seɪ) *n* **1** stewed meat, esp. chicken or veal, and vegetables, served in a thick white sauce. ◆ *vb* **-sees, -seeing, -seed. 2** (*tr*) to prepare (meat) as a fricassee. [C16: from Old French, from *fricasser* to fricassee; probably related to *frire* to FRY[1]]

fricative ('frɪkətɪv) *n* **1** a continuant consonant produced by partial occlusion of the airstream, such as (f) or (z). ◆ *adj* **2** relating to or denoting a fricative. [C19: from New Latin *fricātivus,* from Latin *fricāre* to rub]

FRICS (in Britain) *abbrev. for* Fellow of the Royal Institution of Chartered Surveyors.

friction ('frɪkʃən) *n* **1** a resistance encountered when one body moves relative to another body with which it is in contact. **2** the act, effect, or an instance of rubbing one object against another. **3** disagreement or conflict; discord. **4** *Phonetics.* the hissing element of a speech sound, such as a fricative. **5** perfumed alcohol used on the hair to stimulate the scalp. [C16: from French, from Latin *frictiō* a rubbing, from *fricāre* to rub, rub down; related to Latin *friāre* to crumble] ▸ **'frictional** *adj* ▸ **'frictionless** *adj*

frictional soil *n* another term for **cohesionless soil.**

frictional unemployment *n* those people who are in the process of moving from one job to another and who therefore appear in the unemployment statistics collected at any given time.

friction clutch *n* a mechanical clutch in which the drive is transmitted by the friction between surfaces, lined with cork, asbestos, or other fibrous materials, attached to the driving and driven shafts.

friction layer *n* the atmospheric layer extending up to about 600 m, in which the aerodynamic effects of surface friction are appreciable.

friction match *n* a match that ignites as a result of the heat produced by friction when it is struck on a rough surface. See also **safety match.**

friction rub *or* **murmur** *n Med.* the sound, heard through a stethoscope, made by the rubbing together of the two inflamed layers of pericardium in patients with pericarditis.

friction tape *n* the U.S. and Canadian name for **insulating tape.**

friction welding *n* a form of welding in which the welding heat is generated by pressure and relative movement at the interface in the area of the weld.

Friday ('fraɪdɪ) *n* **1** the sixth day of the week; fifth day of the working week. **2** See **girl Friday, man Friday.** [Old English *Frīgedæg,* literally: Freya's day; related to Old Frisian *frīadei,* Old High German *frīatag*]

fridge (frɪdʒ) *n Informal.* short for **refrigerator.**

fried (fraɪd) *vb* the past tense and past participle of **fry**[1].

Friedan ('fri:dən) *n* **Betty.** born 1921, U.S. feminist, founder and first president (1966–70) of the National Organization for Women. Her books include *The Feminine Mystique* (1963), *The Second Stage* (1982), and *The Fountain of Life* (1993).

Friedman ('fri:dmən) *n* **Milton.** born 1912. U.S. economist, particularly associated with monetarism; a forceful advocate of free market capitalism. ▸ **'Friedman,ite** *n, adj*

Friedrich (*German* 'fri:drɪç) *n* **Caspar David** ('kaspar 'da:fɪt). 1774–1840, German romantic landscape painter, noted for his skill in rendering changing effects of light.

friend (frɛnd) *n* **1** a person known well to another and regarded with liking, affection, and loyalty; an intimate. **2** an acquaintance or associate. **3** an ally in a fight or cause; supporter. **4** a fellow member of a party, society, etc. **5** a patron or supporter: *a friend of the opera.* **6 be friends (with).** to be friendly (with). **7 make friends (with).** to become friendly (with). ◆ *vb* **8** (*tr*) an archaic word for **befriend.** [Old English *frēond;* related to Old Saxon *friund,* Old Norse *frǣndi,* Gothic *frijōnds,* Old High German *friunt*] ▸ **'friendless** *adj* ▸ **'friendlessness** *n* ▸ **'friendship** *n*

Friend[1] (frend) *n* a member of the Religious Society of Friends; Quaker.

Friend[2] (frend) *n Mountaineering, trademark.* a device consisting of a shaft with double-headed spring-loaded cams that can be wedged in a crack to provide an anchor point.

friend at court *n* an influential acquaintance who can promote one's interests.

friendly ('frendlɪ) *adj* **-lier, -liest. 1** showing or expressing liking, goodwill, or trust: *a friendly smile.* **2** on the same side; not hostile. **3** tending or disposed to help or support; favourable: *a friendly breeze helped them escape.* ◆ *n, pl* **-lies. 4** Also called: **friendly match.** *Sport.* a match played for its own sake, and not as part of a competition, etc. ▸ **'friendlily** *adv* ▸ **'friendliness** *n*

-friendly *adj combining form.* helpful, easy, or good for the person or thing specified: *ozone-friendly.*

friendly fire *n Military.* firing by one's own side, esp. when it harms one's own personnel.

Friendly Islands *pl n* another name for **Tonga**[2].

friendly society *n Brit.* an association of people who pay regular dues or other sums in return for old-age pensions, sickness benefits, etc. U.S. term: **benefit society.**

Friends of the Earth *n* (*functioning as sing or pl*) an organization of environmentalists and conservationists whose aim is to promote the rational and sustainable use of the earth's resources. Abbrevs.: **FoE, FOE.**

frier ('fraɪə) *n* a variant spelling of **fryer.**

fries (fraɪz) *pl n* another name for **French fried potatoes.**

Friese-Greene (ˌfriːz'griːn) *n* **William.** 1855–1921, British photographer. He invented (with Mortimer Evans) the first practicable motion-picture camera.

Friesian[1] ('friːʒən) *n Brit.* any of several breeds of black-and-white dairy cattle having a high milk yield. Usual U.S. and Canadian name: **Holstein.**

Friesian[2] ('friːʒən) *n, adj* a variant of **Frisian.**

Friesland ('friːzlənd; *Dutch* 'friːslɑnt) *n* **1** a province of the N Netherlands, on the IJsselmeer and the North Sea: includes four of the West Frisian Islands; flat, with sand dunes and fens (under reclamation), canals, and lakes. Capital: Leeuwarden. Pop.: 612 000 (1996 est.). Area: 3319 sq. km (1294 sq. miles). Official and Frisian name: **Fryslân. 2** an area comprising the province of Friesland in the Netherlands along with the regions of **East Friesland** and **North Friesland** in Germany.

frieze[1] (friːz) *n* **1** *Architect.* **1a** the horizontal band between the architrave and cornice of a classical entablature, esp. one that is decorated with sculpture. **1b** the upper part of the wall of a room, below the cornice, esp. one that is decorated. **2** any ornamental band or strip on a wall. [C16: from French *frise,* perhaps from Medieval Latin *frisium,* changed from Latin *Phrygium* Phrygian (work), from *Phrygia* Phrygia, famous for embroidery in gold]

frieze[2] (friːz) *n* a heavy woollen fabric with a long nap, used for coats, etc. [C15: from Old French *frise,* from Middle Dutch *friese, vriese,* perhaps from *Vriese* Frisian]

frig (frɪg) *vb* **frigs, frigging, frigged.** *Taboo slang.* **1** to have sexual intercourse with. **2** to masturbate. **3** (*intr;* foll. by *around, about,* etc.) to behave foolishly or aimlessly. [C15 (in the sense: to wriggle): of uncertain origin; perhaps related to obsolete *frike* strong, or to Old English *frīgan* to love]

frigate ('frɪgɪt) *n* **1** a medium-sized square-rigged warship of the 18th and 19th centuries. **2a** *Brit.* a warship larger than a corvette and smaller than a destroyer. **2b** *U.S.* (formerly) a warship larger than a destroyer and smaller than a cruiser. **2c** *U.S.* a small escort vessel. [C16: from French *frégate,* from Italian *fregata,* of unknown origin]

frigate bird *n* any bird of the genus *Fregata* and family *Fregatidae,* of tropical and subtropical seas, having a long bill with a downturned tip, a wide wingspan, and a forked tail: order *Pelecaniformes* (pelicans, cormorants, etc.). Also called: **man-of-war bird.**

Frigg (frɪg) *or* **Frigga** ('frɪgə) *n Norse myth.* the wife of Odin; goddess of the heavens and married love.

frigging ('frɪgɪŋ) *adj Taboo slang.* (intensifier, used as a milder word for *fucking*): *you frigging idiot.*

fright (fraɪt) *n* **1** sudden intense fear or alarm. **2** a sudden alarming shock. **3** *Informal.* a horrifying, grotesque, or ludicrous person or thing: *she looks a fright in that hat.* **4 take fright.** to become frightened. ◆ *vb* **5** a poetic word for **frighten.** [Old English *fryhto;* related to Gothic *faurhtei,* Old Frisian *fruchte,* Old High German *forhta*]

frighten ('fraɪtᵊn) *vb* (*tr*) **1** to cause fear in; terrify; scare. **2** to drive or force to go (away, off, out, in, etc.) by making afraid. ▸ **'frightenable** *adj* ▸ **'frightener** *n* ▸ **'frighteningly** *adv*

frightful ('fraɪtfʊl) *adj* **1** very alarming, distressing, or horrifying. **2** unpleasant, annoying, or extreme: *a frightful hurry.* ▸ **'frightfulness** *n*

frightfully ('fraɪtfəlɪ) *adv* (intensifier): *I'm frightfully glad.*

frigid ('frɪdʒɪd) *adj* **1** formal or stiff in behaviour or temperament; lacking in affection or warmth. **2** (esp. of women) **2a** lacking sexual responsiveness. **2b** averse to sexual intercourse or unable to achieve orgasm during intercourse. **3** characterized by physical coldness: *a frigid zone.* [C15: from Latin *frigidus* cold, from *frīgēre* to be cold, freeze; related to Latin *frīgus* frost] ▸ **fri'gidity** *or* **'frigidness** *n* ▸ **'frigidly** *adv*

Frigid Zone *n* the cold region inside the Arctic or Antarctic Circle where the sun's rays are very oblique.

frigorific (ˌfrɪgə'rɪfɪk) *adj Obsolete.* causing cold or freezing. [C17: from French *frigorifique,* from Latin *frīgorificus,* from *frīgus* cold, coldness + *facere* to make]

frijol ('friːhəʊl; *Spanish* fri'xol) *n, pl* **-joles** (-həʊlz; *Spanish* -'xoles). a variety of bean, esp. of the French bean, extensively cultivated for food in Mexico. [C16: from Spanish, ultimately from Latin *phaseolus,* diminutive of *phasēlus,* from Greek *phasēlos* bean with edible pod]

frill (frɪl) *n* **1** a gathered, ruched, or pleated strip of cloth sewn on at one edge only, as on garments, as ornament, or to give extra body. **2** a ruff of hair or feathers around the neck of a dog or bird or a fold of skin around the neck of a reptile or amphibian. **3** Full name: **oriental frill.** (*often cap.*) a variety of domestic fancy pigeon having a ruff of curled feathers on the chest and crop. **4** *Photog.* a wrinkling or loosening of the emulsion at the edges of a negative or print. **5** (*often pl*) *Informal.* a superfluous or pretentious thing or manner; affectation: *he made a plain speech with no frills.* ◆ *vb* **6** (*tr*) to adorn or fit with a frill or frills. **7** to form into a frill or frills. **8** (*intr*) *Photog.* (of an emulsion) to develop a frill. [C14: perhaps of Flemish origin] ▸ **'frilliness** *n* ▸ **'frilly** *adj*

frilled lizard *n* a large arboreal insectivorous Australian lizard, *Chlamydosaurus kingi,* having an erectile fold of skin around the neck: family *Agamidae* (agamas).

Frimaire *French.* (frimɛr) *n* the frosty month: the third month of the French Revolutionary calendar, extending from Nov. 22 to Dec. 21. [C19: from French, from *frimas* hoarfrost, from Old French *frim,* of Germanic origin; related to Old Norse *hrīm* RIME[1]]

fringe (frɪndʒ) *n* **1** an edging consisting of hanging threads, tassels, etc. **2a** an outer edge; periphery. **2b** (*as modifier*): *fringe dwellers; a fringe area.* **3** (*modifier*) unofficial; not conventional in form: *fringe theatre.* **4** *Chiefly Brit.* a section of the front hair cut short over the forehead. **5** an ornamental border or margin. **6** *Physics.* any of the light and dark or coloured bands produced by diffraction or interference of light. ◆ *vb* (*tr*) **7** to adorn or fit with a fringe or fringes. **8** to be a fringe for: *fur fringes the satin.* [C14: from Old French *frenge,* ultimately from Latin *fimbria* fringe, border; see FIMBRIA] ▸ **'fringeless** *adj*

fringe benefit *n* an incidental or additional advantage, esp. a benefit provided by an employer to supplement an employee's regular pay, such as a pension, company car, luncheon vouchers, etc.

fringed orchis *n* any orchid of the genus *Habenaria,* having yellow, white, purple, or greenish flowers with fringed petals. See also **purple-fringed orchid.**

fringe tree *n* either of two ornamental oleaceous shrubs or small trees of the genus *Chionanthus,* of North America and China, having clusters of white narrow-petalled flowers.

fringilline (frɪn'dʒɪlaɪn, -ɪn) *or* **fringillid** (frɪn'dʒɪlɪd) *adj* of, relating to, or belonging to the *Fringillidae,* a family of songbirds that includes the finches. [C19: from New Latin *Fringilla* type genus, from Latin *fringilla* a small bird, perhaps a chaffinch]

fringing reef *n* a coral reef close to the shore to which it is attached, having a steep seaward edge.

Frink (frɪŋk) *n* Dame **Elisabeth.** 1930–93, British sculptor.

frippery ('frɪpərɪ) *n, pl* **-peries. 1** ornate or showy clothing or adornment. **2** showiness; ostentation. **3** unimportant considerations; trifles; trivia. [C16: from Old French *freperie,* from *frepe* frill, rag, old garment, from Medieval Latin *faluppa* a straw, splinter, of obscure origin]

frippet ('frɪpɪt) *n Brit. informal; old-fashioned.* a frivolous or flamboyant young woman.

Fris. *abbrev. for* Frisian.

Frisbee ('frɪzbiː) *n Trademark.* a light plastic disc, usually 20–25 centimetres in diameter, thrown with a spinning motion for recreation or in competition.

Frisch (frɪʃ) *n* **1 Karl von.** 1886–1982, Austrian zoologist; studied animal behaviour, esp. of bees; shared the Nobel prize for physiology or medicine 1973. **2 Max** (maks). 1911–91, Swiss dramatist and novelist. His works are predominantly satirical and include the plays *Biedermann und die Brandstifter* (1953) and *Andorra* (1961), and the novel *Stiller* (1954). **3 Otto.** 1904–79, British nuclear physicist, born in Austria, who contributed to the development of the first atomic bomb. **4 Ragnar** (**Anton Kittil**). 1895–1973, Norwegian economist, who pioneered the study of econometrics and greatly influenced the management of the Norwegian economy from 1945: shared the first Nobel prize for economics (1969) with Jan Tinbergen.

Frisches Haff ('frɪʃəs 'haf) *n* the German name for **Vistula** (sense 2).

frisé ('friːzeɪ) *n* a fabric with a long normally uncut nap used for upholstery and rugs. [from French, literally: curled]

frisette *or* **frizette** (frɪ'zet) *n* a curly or frizzed fringe, often an artificial hairpiece, worn by women on the forehead. [C19: from French, literally: little curl, from *friser* to curl, shrivel up, probably from *frire* to FRY[1]]

friseur *French.* (frizœr) *n* a hairdresser. [C18: literally: one who curls (hair); see FRISETTE]

Frisian ('frɪʒən) *or* **Friesian** *n* **1** a language spoken in the NW Netherlands, parts of N Germany, and adjacent islands, belonging to the West Germanic branch of the Indo-European family: the nearest relative of the English language; it has three main dialects. **2** a native or inhabitant of Friesland or a speaker of the Frisian language. ◆ *adj* **3a** of or relating to the Frisian language or its speakers. **3b** of or relating to Friesland or its peoples and culture. [C16: from Latin *Frīsiī* people of northern Germany]

Frisian Islands *pl n* a chain of islands in the North Sea along the coasts of the Netherlands, Germany, and Denmark: separated from the mainland by shallows.

frisk (frɪsk) *vb* **1** (*intr*) to leap, move about, or act in a playful manner; frolic. **2** (*tr*) (esp. of animals) to whisk or wave briskly: *the dog frisked its tail.* **3** (*tr*) *In-*

formal. **3a** to search (someone) by feeling for concealed weapons, etc. **3b** to rob by searching in this way. ♦ *n* **4** a playful antic or movement; frolic. **5** *Informal.* the act or an instance of frisking a person. [C16: from Old French *frisque,* of Germanic origin; related to Old High German *frisc* lively, FRESH] ► **'frisker** *n* ► **'friskingly** *adv*

frisket ('frɪskɪt) *n Printing.* a light rectangular frame, attached to the tympan of a hand printing press, that carries a parchment sheet to protect the nonprinting areas. [C17: from French *frisquette,* of obscure origin]

frisky ('frɪskɪ) *adj* **friskier, friskiest.** lively, high-spirited, or playful. ► **'friskily** *adv* ► **'friskiness** *n*

frisson *French.* (frisɔ̃) *n* a shudder or shiver; thrill. [C18 (but in common use only from C20): literally: shiver]

frit *or* **fritt** (frɪt) *n* **1a** the basic materials, partially or wholly fused, for making glass, glazes for pottery, enamel, etc. **1b** a glassy substance used in some soft-paste porcelain. **2** the material used for making the glaze for artificial teeth. ♦ *vb* **frits** *or* **fritts, fritting, fritted. 3** (*tr*) to fuse (materials) in making frit. [C17: from Italian *fritta,* literally: fried, from *friggere* to fry, from Latin *frīgere*]

frit fly *n* a small black dipterous fly, *Oscinella frit,* whose larvae are destructive to barley, wheat, rye, oats, etc.: family *Chloropidae.*

frith (frɪθ) *n* a variant of **firth.**

fritillary (frɪ'tɪlərɪ) *n, pl* **-laries. 1** any N temperate liliaceous plant of the genus *Fritillaria,* having purple or white drooping bell-shaped flowers, typically marked in a chequered pattern. See also **snake's head. 2** any of various nymphalid butterflies of the genera *Argynnis, Boloria,* etc., having brownish wings chequered with black and silver. [C17: from New Latin *fritillāria,* from Latin *fritillus* dice box; probably with reference to the spotted markings]

fritter[1] ('frɪtə) *vb* (*tr*) **1** (usually foll. by *away*) to waste or squander: *to fritter away time.* **2** to break or tear into small pieces; shred. ♦ *n* **3** a small piece; shred. [C18: probably from obsolete *fitter* to break into small pieces, ultimately from Old English *fitt* a piece] ► **'fritterer** *n*

fritter[2] ('frɪtə) *n* a piece of food, such as apple or clam, that is dipped in batter and fried in deep fat. [C14: from Old French *friture,* from Latin *frictus* fried, roasted, from *frīgere* to fry, parch]

Friuli (*Italian* fri'u:li) *n* a historic region of SW Europe, between the Carnic Alps and the Gulf of Venice: the W part (**Venetian Friuli**) was ceded by Austria to Italy in 1866 and **Eastern Friuli** in 1919; in 1947 Eastern Friuli (except Gorizia) was ceded to Yugoslavia.

Friulian (frɪ'u:lɪən) *n* **1** the Rhaetian dialect spoken in parts of Friuli. See also **Ladin, Romansch. 2** an inhabitant of Friuli or a speaker of Friulian. ♦ *adj* **3** of or relating to Friuli, its inhabitants, or their language.

Friuli-Venezia Giulia (*Italian* 'dʒu:lja) *n* a region of NE Italy, formed in 1947 from **Venetian Friuli** and part of **Eastern Friuli.** Capital: Trieste. Pop.: 1 188 897 (1996 est.). Area: 7851 sq. km (3031 sq. miles).

frivol ('frɪvᵊl) *vb* **-ols, -olling, -olled** *or U.S.* **-ols, -oling, -oled.** *Informal.* **1** (*intr*) to behave frivolously; trifle. **2** (*tr;* often foll. by *away*) to waste on frivolous pursuits. [C19: back formation from FRIVOLOUS] ► **'frivoller** *or U.S.* **'frivoler** *n*

frivolous ('frɪvələs) *adj* **1** not serious or sensible in content, attitude, or behaviour; silly: *a frivolous remark.* **2** unworthy of serious or sensible treatment; unimportant: *frivolous details.* [C15: from Latin *frīvolus* silly, worthless] ► **'frivolously** *adv* ► **'frivolousness** *or* **frivolity** (frɪ'vɒlɪtɪ) *n*

frizette (frɪ'zɛt) *n* a variant spelling of **frisette.**

frizz (frɪz) *vb* **1** (of the hair, nap, etc.) to form or cause (the hair, etc.) to form tight wiry curls or crisp tufts. ♦ *n* **2** hair that has been frizzed. **3** the state of being frizzed. [C19: from French *friser* to curl, shrivel up (see FRISETTE): influenced by FRIZZLE[1]] ► **'frizzer** *n*

frizzante (frɪ'zæntɪ; *Italian* frid'dzante) *adj* (of wine) slightly effervescent. [Italian, from *frizzare* to sparkle]

frizzle[1] ('frɪzᵊl) *vb* **1** to form (the hair) into tight crisp curls; frizz. ♦ *n* **2** a tight crisp curl. [C16: probably related to Old English *frīs* curly, Old Frisian *frēsle* curl, ringlet] ► **'frizzler** *n* ► **'frizzly** *adj*

frizzle[2] ('frɪzᵊl) *vb* **1** to scorch or be scorched, esp. with a sizzling noise. **2** (*tr*) to fry (bacon, etc.) until crisp. [C16: probably blend of FRY[1] + SIZZLE]

frizzy ('frɪzɪ) *or* **frizzly** ('frɪzlɪ) *adj* **-zier, -ziest** *or* **-zlier, -zliest.** (of the hair) in tight crisp wiry curls. ► **'frizzily** *adv* ► **'frizziness** *or* **'frizzliness** *n*

Frl. *abbrev. for* Fräulein. [German: Miss]

fro (frəʊ) *adv* back or from. See **to and fro.** [C12: from Old Norse *frā;* related to Old English *fram* FROM]

Frobisher ('frəʊbɪʃə) *n* Sir **Martin.** ?1535–94, English navigator and explorer: made three unsuccessful voyages in search of the Northwest Passage (1576; 1577; 1578), visiting Labrador and Baffin Island.

Frobisher Bay *n* **1** an inlet of the Atlantic in NE Canada, in the SE coast of Baffin Island. **2** the former name of **Iqaluit.**

frock (frɒk) *n* **1** a girl's or woman's dress. **2** a loose garment of several types, such as a peasant's smock. **3** a coarse wide-sleeved outer garment worn by members of some religious orders. ♦ *vb* **4** (*tr*) to invest (a person) with the office or status of a cleric. [C14: from Old French *froc;* related to Old Saxon, Old High German *hroc* coat]

frock coat *n* a man's single- or double-breasted skirted coat, as worn in the 19th century.

frocking ('frɒkɪŋ) *n* coarse material suitable for making frocks or work clothes.

Fröding (*Swedish* 'frø:dɪŋ) *n* **Gustaf** ('gustav). 1860–1911, Swedish poet. His popular lyric verse includes the collections *Guitar and Concertina* (1891), *New Poems* (1894), and *Splashes and Rags* (1896).

froe *or* **frow** (frəʊ) *n* a cutting tool with handle and blade at right angles, used for stripping young trees, etc. [C16: from *frower,* from *froward* (in the sense: turned away)]

Froebel *or* **Fröbel** (*German* 'frø:bəl) *n* **1 Friedrich** (**Wilhelm August**) ('fri:drɪç). 1782–1852, German educator: founded the first kindergarten (1840). ♦ *adj* **2** of, denoting, or relating to a system of kindergarten education developed by him or to the training and qualification of teachers to use this system.

frog[1] (frɒg) *n* **1** any insectivorous anuran amphibian of the family *Ranidae,* such as *Rana temporaria* of Europe, having a short squat tailless body with a moist smooth skin and very long hind legs specialized for hopping. **2** any of various similar amphibians of related families, such as the tree frog. Related adj: **batrachian. 3** any spiked or perforated object used to support plant stems in a flower arrangement. **4** a recess in a brick to reduce its weight. **5 a frog in one's throat.** phlegm on the vocal cords that affects one's speech. ♦ *vb* **frogs, frogging, frogged. 6** (*intr*) to hunt or catch frogs. [Old English *frogga;* related to Old Norse *froskr,* Old High German *forsk*] ► **'froggy** *adj*

frog[2] (frɒg) *n* **1** (*often pl*) a decorative fastening of looped braid or cord, as on the front of a 19th-century military uniform. **2** a loop or other attachment on a belt to hold the scabbard of a sword, etc. **3** *Music.* another name (esp. U.S. and Canadian) for **nut** (sense 11). [C18: perhaps ultimately from Latin *floccus* tuft of hair, FLOCK[2]]

frog[3] (frɒg) *n* a tough elastic horny material in the centre of the sole of a horse's foot. [C17: of uncertain origin]

frog[4] (frɒg) *n* a grooved plate of iron or steel placed to guide train wheels over an intersection of railway lines. [C19: of uncertain origin; perhaps a special use of FROG[1]]

Frog (frɒg) *or* **Froggy** ('frɒgɪ) *n, pl* **Frogs** *or* **Froggies.** *Brit. slang.* a derogatory word for a French person.

frog-bit *n* a floating aquatic Eurasian plant, *Hydrocharis morsus-ranae,* with heart-shaped leaves and white flowers: family *Hydrocharitaceae.*

frogfish ('frɒg,fɪʃ) *n, pl* **-fish** *or* **-fishes.** any angler (fish) of the family *Antennariidae,* in which the body is covered with fleshy processes, including a fleshy lure on top of the head.

frogged (frɒgd) *adj* (of a coat) fitted with ornamental frogs.

frogging ('frɒgɪŋ) *n* the ornamental frogs on a coat collectively.

froghopper ('frɒg,hɒpə) *n* any small leaping herbivorous homopterous insect of the family *Cercopidae,* whose larvae secrete a protective spittle-like substance around themselves. Also called: **spittle insect, spittlebug.**

frog kick *n* a type of kick used in swimming, as in the breast stroke, in which the legs are simultaneously drawn towards the body and bent at the knees with the feet together, straightened out with the legs apart, and then brought together again quickly.

frogman ('frɒgmən) *n, pl* **-men.** a swimmer equipped with a rubber suit, flippers, and breathing equipment for working underwater.

frogmarch ('frɒg,mɑ:tʃ) *Chiefly Brit.* *n* **1** a method of carrying a resisting person in which each limb is held by one person and the victim is carried horizontally and face downwards. **2** any method of making a resisting person move forward against his will. ♦ *vb* **3** (*tr*) to carry in a frogmarch or cause to move forward unwillingly.

frogmouth ('frɒg,maʊθ) *n* any nocturnal insectivorous bird of the genera *Podargus* and *Batrachostomus,* of SE Asia and Australia, similar to the nightjars: family *Podargidae,* order *Caprimulgiformes.*

frog orchid *n* any of several orchids having greenish flowers thought to resemble small frogs, esp. *Coeloglossum viride* of calcareous turf.

frogspawn ('frɒg,spɔ:n) *n* a mass of fertilized frogs' eggs or developing tadpoles, each egg being surrounded by a protective nutrient jelly.

frog spit *or* **spittle** *n* **1** another name for **cuckoo spit. 2** a foamy mass of threadlike green algae floating on ponds.

Froissart (*French* frwasar) *n* **Jean** (ʒɑ̃). ?1333–?1400, French chronicler and poet, noted for his *Chronique,* a vivid history of Europe from 1325 to 1400.

frolic ('frɒlɪk) *n* **1** a light-hearted entertainment or occasion. **2** light-hearted activity; gaiety; merriment. ♦ *vb* **-ics, -icking, -icked. 3** (*intr*) to caper about; act or behave playfully. ♦ *adj* **4** *Archaic or literary.* full of merriment or fun. [C16: from Dutch *vrolijk,* from Middle Dutch *vro* happy, glad; related to Old High German *frō* happy] ► **'frolicker** *n*

frolicsome ('frɒlɪksəm) *or* **frolicky** *adj* given to frolicking; merry and playful. ► **'frolicsomely** *adv* ► **'frolicsomeness** *n*

from (frɒm; *unstressed* frəm) *prep* **1** used to indicate the original location, situation, etc.: *from Paris to Rome; from behind the bushes; from childhood to adulthood.* **2** in a period of time starting at: *he lived from 1910 to 1970.* **3** used to indicate the distance between two things or places: *a hundred miles from here.* **4** used to indicate a lower amount: *from five to fifty pounds.* **5** showing the model of: *painted from life.* **6** used with the gerund to mark prohibition, restraint, etc.: *nothing prevents him from leaving.* **7** because of: *exhausted from his walk.* [Old English *fram;* related to Old Norse *frā,* Old Saxon, Old High German, Gothic *fram* from, Greek *promos* foremost]

fromage frais ('frɒmɑ:ʒ 'freɪ) *n* a low-fat soft cheese with a smooth light texture. [French, literally: fresh cheese]

Frome (frəʊm) *n* **Lake.** a shallow salt lake in NE South Australia: intermittently filled with water. Length: 100 km (60 miles). Width: 48 km (30 miles).

fromenty ('frəʊməntɪ) *n* a variant of **frumenty.**

Fromm (frɒm) *n* **Erich** ('ɛrɪk). 1900–80, U.S. psychologist and philosopher, born in Germany. His works include *The Art of Loving* (1956) and *To Have and To Be* (1976).

frond (frɒnd) *n* **1** the compound leaf of a fern. **2** the leaf of a palm or a cycad. **3** the thallus of a seaweed or a lichen. [C18: from Latin *frōns*] ► **'fronded** *adj* ► **'frondless** *adj*

Fronde (frɒnd; *French* frɔ̃d) *n French history.* either of two rebellious movements against the ministry of Cardinal Mazarin in the reign of Louis XIV, the first led by the parlement of Paris (1648–49) and the second by the princes (1650–53). [C18: from French, literally: sling, the insurgent parliamentarians being likened to naughty schoolboys using slings]

frondescence (frɒn'desəns) *n* **1** the process or state of producing leaves. **2** a less common name for **foliage.** [C19: from New Latin *frondēscentia,* from Latin *frondēscere* to put forth leaves, from *frōns* foliage; see FROND] ▸ **fron'descent, 'frondose,** *or* **'frondous** *adj*

Frondeur (frɒn'dɜː; *French* frɔ̃dœr) *n* **1** *French history.* a member of the Fronde. **2** any malcontent or troublemaker.

frons (frɒnz) *n, pl* **frontes** ('frɒntiːz). an anterior cuticular plate on the head of some insects, in front of the clypeus. [C19: from Latin: forehead, brow, FRONT]

front (frʌnt) *n* **1** that part or side that is forward, prominent, or most often seen or used. **2** a position or place directly before or ahead: *a fountain stood at the front of the building.* **3** the beginning, opening, or first part: *the front of the book.* **4** the position of leadership; forefront; vanguard: *in the front of scientific knowledge.* **5** land bordering a lake, street, etc. **6** land along a seashore or large lake, esp. a promenade. **7** *Military.* **7a** the total area in which opposing armies face each other. **7b** the lateral space in which a military unit or formation is operating: *to advance on a broad front.* **7c** the direction in which troops are facing when in a formed line. **8** *Meteorol.* the dividing line or plane between two air masses of different origins and having different characteristics. See also **warm front, cold front. 9** outward aspect or bearing, as when dealing with a situation: *a bold front.* **10** assurance, overconfidence, or effrontery. **11** *Informal.* a business or other activity serving as a respectable cover for another, usually criminal, organization. **12** *Chiefly U.S.* a nominal leader of an organization, etc., who lacks real power or authority; figurehead. **13** *Informal.* outward appearance of rank or wealth. **14** a particular field of activity involving some kind of struggle: *on the wages front.* **15** a group of people with a common goal: *a national liberation front.* **16** a false shirt front; a dicky. **17** *Archaic.* the forehead or the face. ◆ *adj (prenominal)* **18** of, at, or in the front: *a front seat.* **19** *Phonetics.* of, relating to, or denoting a vowel articulated with the blade of the tongue brought forward and raised towards the hard palate, as for the sound of *ee* in English *see* or *a* in English *hat.* ◆ *vb* **20** (when *intr,* foll. by *on* or *onto*) to be opposite (to); face (onto): *this house fronts the river.* **21** (*tr*) to be a front of or for. **22** (*tr*) *Informal.* to appear as a presenter in (a television show). **23** (*tr*) to be the lead singer or player in (a band). **24** (*tr*) to confront, esp. in hostility or opposition. **25** (*tr*) to supply a front for. **26** (*intr;* often foll. by *up*) *Austral.* and *N.Z. informal.* to appear (at): *to front up at the police station.* [C13 (in the sense: forehead, face): from Latin *frōns* forehead, foremost part] ▸ **'frontless** *adj*

front. *abbrev. for* frontispiece.

frontage ('frʌntɪdʒ) *n* **1** the façade of a building or the front of a plot of ground. **2** the extent of the front of a shop, plot of land, etc., esp. along a street, river, etc. **3** the direction in which a building faces: *a frontage on the river.*

frontal ('frʌntᵊl) *adj* **1** of, at, or in the front. **2** of or relating to the forehead: *frontal artery.* **3** *Meteorol.* of, relating to, or resulting from a front or its passage: *frontal rainfall.* ◆ *n* **4** a decorative hanging for the front of an altar. **5** See **frontal lobe, frontal bone. 6** another name for **frontlet** (sense 1). [C14 (in the sense: adornment for forehead, altar cloth): via Old French *frontel,*from Latin *frontālia* (pl) ornament worn on forehead, *frontellum*altar cloth, both from *frōns* forehead, FRONT] ▸ **'frontally** *adv*

frontal bone *n* the bone that forms the front part of the skull.

frontality (frən'tælɪtɪ) *n Fine arts.* a frontal view, as in a painting or other work of art.

frontal lobe *n Anatomy.* the anterior portion of each cerebral hemisphere, situated in front of the central sulcus.

front bench *n Brit.* **a** the foremost bench of either the Government or Opposition in the House of Commons. **b** the leadership (**frontbenchers**) of either group, who occupy this bench. **c** (*as modifier*): *a front-bench decision.*

front door *n* **1** the main entrance to a house. **2** an open legitimate means of obtaining a job, position, etc.: *to get in by the front door.*

Frontenac (et Palluau) (*French* frɔ̃tnak (e palyo)) *n* **Comte de** (kɔ̃t də). title of *Louis de Buade.* 1620–98, governor of New France (1672–82; 1689–98).

front-end *adj* (of money, costs, etc.) required or incurred in advance of a project in order to get it under way.

front-end load *n* commission and other expenses paid for as a large proportion of the early payments made by an investor in an insurance policy or a long-term investment plan. ▸ **front-end loading** *n*

front-end processor *n* a small computer that receives data from input devices and performs some initial processing tasks on it before passing it to a more powerful computer for final processing.

frontier ('frʌntɪə, frʌn'tɪə) *n* **1a** the region of a country bordering on another or a line, barrier, etc., marking such a boundary. **1b** (*as modifier*): *a frontier post.* **2** *U.S. and Canadian.* **2a** the edge of the settled area of a country. **2b** (*as modifier*): *the frontier spirit.* **3** (*often pl*) the limit of knowledge in a particular field: *the frontiers of physics have been pushed back.* **4** *Maths.* the part of the closure of a topological set that lies outside its interior. [C14: from Old French *frontiere,* from *front* (in the sense: part which is opposite); see FRONT]

frontiersman ('frʌntɪəzmən, frʌn'tɪəz-) *or* (*fem*) **frontierswoman** *n, pl* **-men** *or* **-women.** (formerly) a person living on a frontier, esp. in a newly pioneered territory of the U.S.

frontispiece ('frʌntɪs,piːs) *n* **1** an illustration facing the title page of a book. **2** the principal façade of a building; front. **3** a pediment, esp. an ornamented one, over a door, window, etc. [C16 *frontispice,* from French, from Late Latin *frontispicium* façade, inspection of the forehead, from Latin *frōns* forehead + *specere* to look at; influenced by PIECE]

frontlet ('frʌntlɪt) *n* **1** Also called: **frontal.** a small decorative loop worn on a woman's forehead, projecting from under her headdress, in the 15th century. **2** the forehead of an animal, esp. of a bird when it is a different colour from the rest of the head. **3** the decorated border of an altar frontal. **4** *Judaism.* a phylactery worn on the forehead. See also **tefillah.** [C15: from Old French *frontelet* a little FRONTAL]

front line *n* **1** *Military.* the most advanced military units or elements in a battle. **2** the most advanced, exposed, or conspicuous element in any activity or situation. **3** (*modifier*) **3a** of, relating to, or suitable for the front line of a military formation: *frontline troops.* **3b** to the fore; advanced, conspicuous, etc.: *frontline news.* **3c** of or relating to a country bordering on or close to a hostile country or scene of armed conflict: *leaders of the frontline states attended the summit.*

front loader *n* a washing machine with a door at the front which opens one side of the drum into which washing is placed.

front man *n Informal.* **1** a nominal leader of an organization, etc., who lacks real power or authority, esp. one who lends respectability to some nefarious activity. **2** the leader or visual focus of a group of musicians, usually the singer. ◆ Also called: **front person.**

front matter *n* another name for **prelims** (sense 1).

front of house *n* the areas of a theatre, opera house, etc., used by the audience.

frontogenesis (,frʌntəʊ'dʒenɪsɪs) *n Meteorol.* the formation or development of a front through the meeting of air masses from different origins. ▸ **frontogenetic** (,frʌntəʊdʒə'netɪk) *adj* ▸ **,frontoge'netically** *adv*

frontolysis (frʌn'tɒlɪsɪs) *n Meteorol.* the weakening or dissipation of a front.

fronton ('frɒntɒn, frɒn'tɒn) *n* a wall against which pelota or jai alai is played. [C17: from Spanish *frontón,* from *frente* forehead, from Latin *frōns*]

front-page *n* (*modifier*) important or newsworthy enough to be put on the front page of a newspaper.

frontrunner ('frʌnt,rʌnə) *n Informal.* the leader or a favoured contestant in a race, election, etc.

frontrunning ('frʌnt,rʌnɪŋ) *n Stock Exchange.* the practice by market makers of using advance information provided by their own investment analysts before it has been given to clients.

frontwards ('frʌntwədz) *or* **frontward** *adv* towards the front.

frore (frɔː) *adj Archaic.* very cold or frosty. [C13 *froren,* past participle of Old English *frēosan* to FREEZE]

frost (frɒst) *n* **1** a white deposit of ice particles, esp. one formed on objects out of doors at night. See also **hoarfrost. 2** an atmospheric temperature of below freezing point, characterized by the production of this deposit. **3 degrees of frost.** degrees below freezing point: eight degrees of frost indicates a temperature of either −8°C or 24°F. **4** *Informal.* something given a cold reception; failure. **5** *Informal.* coolness of manner. **6** the act of freezing. ◆ *vb* **7** to cover or be covered with frost. **8** (*tr*) to give a frostlike appearance to (glass, etc.), as by means of a fine-grained surface. **9** (*tr*) *Chiefly U.S. and Canadian.* to decorate (cakes, etc.) with icing or frosting. **10** (*tr*) to kill or damage (crops, etc.) with frost. [Old English *frost;* related to Old Norse, Old Saxon, Old High German *frost;* see FREEZE] ▸ **'frost,like** *adj*

Frost (frɒst) *n* **Robert (Lee).** 1874–1963, U.S. poet, noted for his lyrical verse on country life in New England. His books include *A Boy's Will* (1913), *North of Boston* (1914), and *New Hampshire* (1923).

frostbite ('frɒst,baɪt) *n* **1** destruction of tissues, esp. those of the fingers, ears, toes, and nose, by freezing, characterized by tingling, blister formation, and gangrene. **2** *N.Z.* a type of small sailing dinghy.

frostbitten ('frɒst,bɪtᵊn) *adj* of or affected with frostbite.

frosted ('frɒstɪd) *adj* **1** covered or injured by frost. **2** covered with icing, as a cake. **3** (of glass, etc.) having a surface roughened, as if covered with frost, to prevent clear vision through it.

frost heave *n* the upthrust and cracking of a ground surface through the freezing and expansion of water underneath. Also called: **frost heaving.**

frost hollow *n* a depression in a hilly area in which cold air collects, becoming very cold at night.

frosting ('frɒstɪŋ) *n* **1** a soft icing based on sugar and egg whites. **2** another word (esp. U.S. and Canadian) for **icing. 3** a rough or matt finish on glass, silver, etc.

frost line *n* **1** the deepest point in the ground to which frost will penetrate. **2** the limit towards the equator beyond which frosts do not occur.

frostwork ('frɒst,wɜːk) *n* **1** the patterns made by frost on glass, metal, etc. **2** similar artificial ornamentation.

frosty ('frɒstɪ) *adj* **frostier, frostiest. 1** characterized by frost: *a frosty night.* **2** covered by or decorated with frost. **3** lacking warmth or enthusiasm: *the new plan had a frosty reception.* **4** like frost in appearance or colour; hoary. ▸ **'frostily** *adv* ▸ **'frostiness** *n*

froth (frɒθ) *n* **1** a mass of small bubbles of air or a gas in a liquid, produced by fermentation, detergent, etc. **2** a mixture of saliva and air bubbles formed at the lips in certain diseases, such as rabies. **3** trivial ideas, talk, or entertainment. ◆ *vb* **4** to produce or cause to produce froth. **5** (*tr*) to give out in the form of froth. **6** (*tr*) to cover with froth. [C14: from Old Norse *frotha* or *frauth;* related to Old English *āfrēothan* to foam, Sanskrit *prothati* he snorts] ▸ **'frothy** *adj* ▸ **'frothily** *adv* ▸ **'frothiness** *n*

froth flotation *n* another name for **flotation** (in metallurgy).

frottage ('frɒtɑːʒ; *French* frɔtaʒ) *n* **1** the act or process of taking a rubbing from a rough surface, such as wood, for a work of art. **2** sexual excitement obtained by rubbing against another person's clothed body. [French, from *frotter* to rub]

Froude (fruːd) *n* **1 James Anthony.** 1818–94, English historian; author of a controversial biography (1882–84) of Carlyle. **2** his brother **William.** 1810–79, English civil engineer.

Froude number (fraud) *n* a dimensionless number used in hydrodynamics for model simulation of actual conditions. [named after W. FROUDE]

froufrou ('fruː,fruː) *n* **1** a swishing sound, as made by a long silk dress. **2** elaborate dress or ornamentation, esp. worn by women. [C19: from French, of imitative origin]

frow (frau) *n* a variant spelling of **froe**.

froward ('frəuəd) *adj Archaic.* obstinate; contrary. [C14: see FRO, -WARD] ▸ **'frowardly** *adv* ▸ **'frowardness** *n*

frown (fraun) *vb* **1** (*intr*) to draw the brows together and wrinkle the forehead, esp. in worry, anger, or concentration. **2** (*intr;* foll. by *on* or *upon*) to have a dislike (of); look disapprovingly (upon): *the club frowned upon political activity by its members.* **3** (*tr*) to express (worry, etc.) by frowning. **4** (*tr;* often foll. by *down*) to force, silence, etc., by a frowning look. ◆ *n* **5** the act of frowning. **6** a show of dislike or displeasure. [C14: from Old French *froigner,* of Celtic origin; compare Welsh *ffroen* nostril, Middle Breton *froan*] ▸ **'frowner** *n* ▸ **'frowningly** *adv*

frowst (fraust) *n Brit. informal.* a hot and stale atmosphere; fug. [C19: back formation from *frowsty* musty, stuffy, variant of FROWZY]

frowsty ('fraustɪ) *adj* ill-smelling; stale; musty. ▸ **'frowstiness** *n*

frowzy, frouzy, *or* **frowsy** ('frauzɪ) *adj* **frowzier, frowziest; frouzier, frouziest;** *or* **frowsier, frowsiest. 1** untidy or unkempt in appearance; shabby. **2** ill-smelling; frowsty. [C17: of unknown origin] ▸ **'frowziness, 'frouziness,** *or* **'frowsiness** *n*

froze (frəuz) *vb* the past tense of **freeze.**

frozen ('frəuzᵊn) *vb* **1** the past participle of **freeze.** ◆ *adj* **2** turned into or covered with ice. **3** obstructed or blocked by ice. **4** killed, injured, or stiffened by extreme cold. **5** (of a region or climate) icy or snowy. **6** (of food) preserved by a freezing process. **7a** (of prices, wages, etc.) arbitrarily pegged at a certain level. **7b** (of business assets) not convertible into cash, as by government direction or business conditions. **8** frigid, unfeeling, or disdainful in manner. **9** motionless or unyielding: *he was frozen with horror.* ▸ **'frozenly** *adv* ▸ **'frozenness** *n*

frozen shoulder *n Pathol.* a painful stiffness in a shoulder joint.

FRPS (in Britain) *abbrev. for* Fellow of the Royal Photographic Society.

FRS (in Britain) *abbrev. for* Fellow of the Royal Society.

Frs. *abbrev. for* Frisian.

FRSC (in Britain) *abbrev. for* Fellow of the Royal Society of Chemistry.

FRSNZ *abbrev. for* Fellow of the Royal Society of New Zealand.

frt *abbrev. for* freight.

fructan ('frʌktən) *n* a type of polymer of fructose, present in certain fruits.

Fructidor *French.* (fryktidɔr) *n* the month of fruit: the twelfth month of the French Revolutionary calendar, extending from Aug. 19 to Sept. 22. [C18: from Latin *frūctus* fruit + Greek *dōron* gift]

fructiferous (frʌk'tɪfərəs, fruk-) *adj* (of plants or trees) bearing or yielding fruit. ▸ **fruc'tiferously** *adv*

fructification (ˌfrʌktɪfɪ'keɪʃən, ˌfruk-) *n* **1** the act or state of fructifying. **2** the fruit of a seed-bearing plant. **3** any spore-bearing structure in ferns, mosses, fungi, etc.

fructify ('frʌktɪˌfaɪ, 'fruk-) *vb* **-fies, -fying, -fied. 1** to bear or cause to bear fruit. **2** to make or become productive or fruitful. [C14: from Old French *fructifier,* from Late Latin *frūctificāre* to bear fruit, from Latin *frūctus* fruit + *facere* to make, produce] ▸ **'fructiˌfier** *n*

fructose ('frʌktəus, -təuz, 'fruk-) *n* a white crystalline water-soluble sugar occurring in honey and many fruits. Formula: $C_6H_{12}O_6$. Also called: **laevulose, fruit sugar.** [C19: from Latin *frūctus* fruit + -OSE²]

fructuous ('frʌktjuəs, 'fruk-) *adj* productive or fruitful; fertile. [C14: from Latin *frūctuōsus,* from *frūctus* fruit + -OUS] ▸ **'fructuously** *adv* ▸ **'fructuousness** *n*

frugal ('fru:gᵊl) *adj* **1** practising economy; living without waste; thrifty. **2** not costly; meagre. [C16: from Latin *frūgālis,* from *frūgī* useful, temperate, from *frux* fruit] ▸ **fru'gality** *or* **'frugalness** *n* ▸ **'frugally** *adv*

frugivorous (fru:'dʒɪvərəs) *adj* feeding on fruit; fruit-eating. [C18: from *frugi-* (as in FRUGAL) + -VOROUS]

fruit (fru:t) *n* **1** *Botany.* the ripened ovary of a flowering plant, containing one or more seeds. It may be dry, as in the poppy, or fleshy, as in the peach. **2** any fleshy part of a plant, other than the above structure, that supports the seeds and is edible, such as the strawberry. **3** the spore-producing structure of plants that do not bear seeds. **4** any plant product useful to man, including grain, vegetables, etc. **5** (*often pl*) the result or consequence of an action or effort. **6** *Brit. slang, old-fashioned.* chap; fellow: used as a term of address. **7** *Slang, chiefly Brit.* a person considered to be eccentric or insane. **8** *Slang, chiefly U.S. and Canadian.* a male homosexual. **9** *Archaic.* offspring of man or animals; progeny. ◆ *vb* **10** to bear or cause to bear fruit. [C12: from Old French, from Latin *frūctus* enjoyment, profit, fruit, from *frūī* to enjoy] ▸ **'fruitˌlike** *adj*

fruitage ('fru:tɪdʒ) *n* **1** the process, state, or season of producing fruit. **2** fruit collectively.

fruitarian (fru:'teərɪən) *n* **1** a person who eats only fruit. ◆ *adj* **2** of or relating to a fruitarian: *a fruitarian diet.* ▸ **frui'tarianˌism** *n*

fruit bat *n* any large Old World bat of the suborder *Megachiroptera,* occurring in tropical and subtropical regions and feeding on fruit. Compare **insectivorous bat.**

fruit body *n* a variant of **fruiting body.**

fruitcake ('fru:tˌkeɪk) *n* **1** a rich cake containing mixed dried fruit, lemon peel, nuts, etc. **2** *Slang, chiefly Brit.* a person considered to be eccentric or insane.

fruit cocktail *n* fruit salad consisting of small or diced fruits.

fruit cup *n* a variety of fruits served in a cup or glass as an appetizer or dessert.

fruit drop *n* **1** the premature shedding of fruit from a tree before fully ripe. **2** a boiled sweet with a fruity flavour.

fruiter ('fru:tə) *n* **1** a fruit grower. **2** any tree that bears fruit, esp. edible fruit.

fruiterer ('fru:tərə) *n Chiefly Brit.* a fruit dealer or seller.

fruit fly *n* **1** any small dipterous fly of the family *Trypetidae,* which feed on and lay their eggs in plant tissues. See also **gallfly. 2** any dipterous fly of the genus *Drosophila.* See **drosophila.**

fruitful ('fru:tful) *adj* **1** bearing fruit in abundance. **2** productive or prolific, esp. in bearing offspring. **3** causing or assisting prolific growth. **4** producing results or profits: *a fruitful discussion.* ▸ **'fruitfully** *adv* ▸ **'fruitfulness** *n*

fruiting body *n* the part of a fungus in which the spores are produced. Also: **fruit body.**

fruition (fru:'ɪʃən) *n* **1** the attainment or realization of something worked for or desired; fulfilment. **2** enjoyment of this. **3** the act or condition of bearing fruit. [C15: from Late Latin *fruitiō* enjoyment, from Latin *fruī* to enjoy]

fruit knife *n* a small stainless knife for cutting fruit.

fruitless ('fru:tlɪs) *adj* **1** yielding nothing or nothing of value; unproductive; ineffectual. **2** without fruit. ▸ **'fruitlessly** *adv* ▸ **'fruitlessness** *n*

fruit machine *n Brit.* a gambling machine that pays out when certain combinations of diagrams, usually of fruit, appear on a dial.

fruit salad *n* a dish consisting of sweet fruits cut up and served in a syrup: often sold canned.

fruit sugar *n* another name for **fructose.**

fruit tree *n* any tree that bears edible fruit.

fruity ('fru:tɪ) *adj* **fruitier, fruitiest. 1** of or resembling fruit. **2** (of a voice) mellow or rich. **3** ingratiating or unctuous. **4** *Informal, chiefly Brit.* erotically stimulating; salacious. **5** *Slang.* eccentric or insane. **6** *Chiefly U.S. and Canadian.* a slang word for **homosexual.** ▸ **'fruitiness** *n* ▸ **'fruitily** *adv*

frumentaceous (ˌfru:men'teɪʃəs) *adj* resembling or made of wheat or similar grain. [C17: from Late Latin *frūmentāceus,* from Latin *frūmentum* corn, grain]

frumenty ('fru:məntɪ), **fromenty, furmenty,** *or* **furmity** *n Brit.* a kind of porridge made from hulled wheat boiled with milk, sweetened, and spiced. [C14: from Old French *frumentee,* from *frument* grain, from Latin *frūmentum*]

frump (frʌmp) *n* a woman who is dowdy, drab, or unattractive. [C16 (in the sense: to be sullen; C19: dowdy woman): from Middle Dutch *verrompelen* to wrinkle, RUMPLE] ▸ **'frumpy** *or* **'frumpish** *adj* ▸ **'frumpily** *or* **'frumpishly** *adv* ▸ **'frumpiness** *or* **'frumpishness** *n*

Frunze (*Russian* 'frunzɪ) *n* the former name (until 1991) of **Bishkek.**

frusemide ('frʌsəˌmaɪd) *n* a diuretic used to treat hypertension and to relieve oedema due to heart or kidney disease.

frustrate (frʌ'streɪt) *vb* (*tr*) **1** to hinder or prevent (the efforts, plans, or desires) of; thwart. **2** to upset, agitate, or tire: *her constant complaints began to frustrate him.* ◆ *adj* **3** *Archaic.* frustrated or thwarted; baffled. [C15: from Latin *frustrāre* to cheat, from *frustrā* in error] ▸ **frus'trater** *n*

frustrated (frʌ'streɪtɪd) *adj* having feelings of dissatisfaction or lack of fulfilment.

frustration (frʌ'streɪʃən) *n* **1** the condition of being frustrated. **2** something that frustrates. **3** *Psychol.* **3a** the prevention or hindering of a potentially satisfying activity. **3b** the emotional reaction to such prevention that may involve aggression.

frustule ('frʌstju:l) *n Botany.* the hard siliceous cell wall of a diatom. [C19: from French, from Late Latin *frustulum* a small piece, from *frustum* a bit]

frustum ('frʌstəm) *n, pl* **-tums** *or* **-ta** (-tə). **1** *Geometry.* **1a** the part of a solid, such as a cone or pyramid, contained between the base and a plane parallel to the base that intersects the solid. **1b** the part of such a solid contained between two parallel planes intersecting the solid. **2** *Architect.* a single drum of a column or a single stone used to construct a pier. [C17: from Latin: piece; probably related to Old English *brȳsan* to crush, BRUISE]

frutescent (fru:'tesᵊnt) *or* **fruticose** ('fru:tɪˌkəus, -ˌkəuz) *adj* having the appearance or habit of a shrub; shrubby. [C18: from Latin *frutex* shrub, bush] ▸ **fru'tescence** *n*

fry¹ (fraɪ) *vb* **fries, frying, fried. 1** (when *tr,* sometimes foll. by *up*) to cook or be cooked in fat, oil, etc., usually over direct heat. **2** (*intr*) *Informal.* to be excessively hot. **3** *Slang, chiefly U.S.* to kill or be killed by electrocution, esp. in the electric chair. ◆ *n, pl* **fries. 4** a dish of something fried, esp. the offal of a specified animal: *pig's fry.* **5** *U.S. and Canadian.* a social occasion, often outdoors, at which the chief food is fried. **6 fry-up.** *Brit. informal.* the act of preparing a mixed fried dish or the dish itself. [C13: from Old French *frire,* from Latin *frīgere* to roast, fry]

fry² (fraɪ) *pl n* **1** the young of various species of fish. **2** the young of certain other animals, such as frogs. **3** young children. ◆ See also **small fry.** [C14 (in the sense: young, offspring): perhaps via Norman French from Old French *freier* to spawn, rub, from Latin *fricāre* to rub]

Fry (fraɪ) *n* **1 Christopher.** born 1907, English dramatist; author of the verse dramas *A Phoenix Too Frequent* (1946), *The Lady's Not For Burning* (1948), *Venus Observed* (1950), and *One Thing More* (1986). **2 Elizabeth.** 1780–1845, English prison reformer and Quaker. **3 Roger Eliot.** 1866–1934, English art critic and painter who helped to introduce the postimpressionists to Britain. His books include *Vision and Design* (1920) and *Cézanne* (1927).

fryer *or* **frier** ('fraɪə) *n* **1** a person or thing that fries. **2** a young chicken suitable for frying.

frying pan *or esp. U.S.* **fry-pan** *n* **1** a long-handled shallow pan used for frying. **2 out of the frying pan into the fire.** from a bad situation to a worse one.

f.s. *abbrev. for* foot-second.

FSA *abbrev. for:* **1** Fellow of the Society of Antiquaries. **2** Financial Services Authority.

FSH *abbrev. for* follicle-stimulating hormone.

FSK *Computing. abbrev. for* Frequency Shift Keying.

f-stop *n* any of the settings for the f-number of a camera.

ft *abbrev. for* fort.

FT (in Britain) *abbrev. for* Financial Times.

ft. *abbrev. for:* **1** foot *or* feet. **2** fortification.

fth. *or* **fthm.** *abbrev. for* fathom.

ft-lb *abbrev. for* foot-pound.

FTP *or* **ftp** *abbrev. for* file transfer protocol. *n* **1** the standard mechanism used to transfer files across the Internet, or a similar network, between computer systems. **2** the program implementing this. ◆ *vb* (*tr*) **3** to transfer (a file) in this way.

FT-SE 100 Index *abbrev. for* Financial Times Stock Exchange 100 Index.

FT Share Indexes *pl n* any of a number of share indexes published by the *Financial Times* to reflect various aspects of stock exchange prices. See **Financial Times Industrial Ordinary Share Index; Financial Times Stock Exchange 100 Index.**

Fuad I (fuː'ɑːd) *n* original name *Ahmed Fuad Pasha.* 1868–1936, sultan of Egypt (1917–22) and king (1922–36).

fubsy ('fʌbzɪ) *adj* **-sier, -siest.** *Archaic or dialect.* short and stout; squat. **[C18:** from obsolete *fubs* plump person**]**

Fu-chou ('fuː'tʃau) *n* a variant transliteration of the Chinese name for **Fuzhou.**

Fuchs (fʊks, fuːks) *n* **1 Klaus Emil** (klaus 'eːmiːl). 1911–88, East German physicist. He was born in Germany, became a British citizen (1942), and was imprisoned (1950–59) for giving secret atomic research information to the Soviet Union. **2** Sir **Vivian Ernest.** born 1908, English explorer and geologist: led the Commonwealth Trans-Antarctic Expedition (1955–58).

fuchsia ('fjuːʃə) *n* **1** any onagraceous shrub of the mostly tropical genus *Fuchsia,* widely cultivated for their showy drooping purple, red, or white flowers. **2** Also called: **California fuchsia.** a North American onagraceous plant, *Zauschneria californica,* with tubular scarlet flowers. **3a** a reddish-purple to purplish-pink colour. **3b** (*as adj*): *a fuchsia dress.* **[C18:** from New Latin, named after Leonhard *Fuchs* (1501–66), German botanist**]**

fuchsin ('fuːksɪn) *or* **fuchsine** ('fuːksiːn, -sɪn) *n* a greenish crystalline substance, the quaternary chloride of rosaniline, forming a red solution in water: used as a textile dye and a biological stain. Formula: $C_{20}H_{19}N_3HCl$. Also called: **magenta. [C19:** from FUCHS(IA) + -IN; from its similarity in colour to the flower**]**

fucivorous (fjuː'sɪvərəs) *adj Zoology.* feeding on seaweed. **[C19:** from Greek *phukos* seaweed + -VOROUS**]**

fuck (fʌk) *Taboo. vb* **1** to have sexual intercourse with (someone). ◆ *n* **2** an act of sexual intercourse. **3** *Slang.* a partner in sexual intercourse, esp. one of specified competence or experience: *she was a good fuck.* **4 not care** *or* **give a fuck.** not to care at all. ◆ *interj* **5** *Offensive.* an expression of strong disgust or anger (often in exclamatory phrases such as **fuck you! fuck it!** etc.). **[C16:** of Germanic origin; related to Middle Dutch *fokken* to strike**]**

fuck about *or* **around** *vb* (*adv*) *Offensive taboo slang.* **1** (*intr*) to act in a stupid or aimless manner. **2** (*tr*) to treat (someone) in an inconsiderate or selfish way.

fucker ('fʌkə) *n Taboo.* **1** *Slang.* a despicable or obnoxious person. **2** *Slang.* a person; fellow. **3** a person who fucks.

fucking ('fʌkɪŋ) *adj* (*prenominal*), *adv Taboo slang.* (intensifier): *a fucking good time.*

fuck off *Offensive taboo slang.* ◆ *interj* **1** a forceful expression of dismissal or contempt. ◆ *vb* **2** (*intr, adv*) to go away.

fuck up *Offensive taboo slang.* ◆ *vb* (*tr, adv*) **1** to damage or bungle: *to fuck up a machine.* **2** to make confused. ◆ *n* **fuck-up. 3** an act or an instance of bungling.

fuckwit ('fʌkwɪt) *n Taboo slang.* a fool or idiot.

fucoid ('fjuːkɔɪd) *adj also* **fucoidal** *or* **fucous** ('fjuːkəs). **1** of, relating to, or resembling seaweeds of the genus *Fucus.* ◆ *n* **2** any seaweed of the genus *Fucus.*

fucoxanthin (ˌfjuːkəʊ'zænθɪn) *n* a carotenoid pigment that gives brown algae and diatoms their colour: functions in photosynthesis. Formula: $C_{40}H_{56}O_6$ or $C_{40}H_{60}O_6$.

fucus ('fjuːkəs) *n, pl* **-ci** (-saɪ) *or* **-cuses.** any seaweed of the genus *Fucus,* common in the intertidal regions of many shores and typically having greenish-brown slimy fronds. See also **wrack**[2] (sense 2). **[C16:** from Latin: rock lichen, from Greek *phukos* seaweed, dye, of Semitic origin**]**

fuddle ('fʌdᵊl) *vb* **1** (*tr; often passive*) to cause to be confused or intoxicated. **2** (*intr*) to drink excessively; tipple. ◆ *n* **3** a muddled or confused state. **[C16:** of unknown origin**]**

fuddy-duddy ('fʌdɪˌdʌdɪ) *n, pl* **-dies.** *Informal.* a person, esp. an elderly one, who is extremely conservative or dull. **[C20:** of uncertain origin**]**

fudge[1] (fʌdʒ) *n* a soft variously flavoured sweet made from sugar, butter, cream, etc. **[C19:** of unknown origin**]**

fudge[2] (fʌdʒ) *n* **1** foolishness; nonsense. ◆ *interj* **2** a mild exclamation of annoyance. ◆ *vb* **3** (*intr*) to talk foolishly or emptily. **[C18:** of uncertain origin**]**

fudge[3] (fʌdʒ) *n* **1** a small section of type matter in a box in a newspaper allowing late news to be included without the whole page having to be remade. **2** the box in which such type matter is placed. **3** the late news so inserted. **4** a machine attached to a newspaper press for printing this. **5** an unsatisfactory compromise reached to evade a difficult problem or controversial issue. ◆ *vb* **6** (*tr*) to make or adjust in a false or clumsy way. **7** (*tr*) to misrepresent; falsify. **8** to evade (a problem, issue, etc.); dodge; avoid. **[C19:** see FADGE**]**

Fuegian (fjuː'iːdʒɪən, 'fweɪdʒ-) *adj* **1** of or relating to Tierra del Fuego or its indigenous Indians. ◆ *n* **2** an Indian of Tierra del Fuego.

fuel (fjʊəl) *n* **1** any substance burned as a source of heat or power, such as coal or petrol. **2** the material, containing a fissile substance such as uranium-235, that produces energy in a nuclear reactor. **3** something that nourishes or builds up emotion, action, etc. ◆ *vb* **fuels, fuelling, fuelled** *or U.S.* **fuels, fueling, fueled. 4** to supply with or receive fuel. **[C14:** from Old French *feuaile,* from *feu* fire, ultimately from Latin *focus* fireplace, hearth**]** ▸ **'fueller** *or U.S.* **'fueler** *n*

fuel cell *n* a cell in which the energy produced by oxidation of a fuel is converted directly into electrical energy.

fuel element *n* a can containing nuclear fuel for use in a reactor.

fuel injection *n* a system for introducing atomized liquid fuel under pressure directly into the combustion chambers of an internal-combustion engine without the use of a carburettor.

fuel oil *n* a liquid petroleum product having a flash point above 37.8°C: used as a substitute for coal in industrial furnaces, domestic heaters, ships, and locomotives.

fuel rod *n* a long tube, often made of a zirconium alloy and containing uranium-oxide pellets, that is stacked in bundles of about 200 to provide the fuel in certain types of nuclear reactor.

Fuentes ('fwɛnteɪs) *n* **Carlos.** born 1928, Mexican novelist and writer. His novels include *A Change of Skin* (1967), *Terra Nostra* (1975), and *Cristóbal Nonato* (1987).

fug (fʌg) *n Chiefly Brit.* a hot, stale, or suffocating atmosphere. **[C19:** perhaps variant of FOG[1]**]** ▸ **'fuggy** *adj*

fugacious (fjuː'geɪʃəs) *adj* **1** passing quickly away; transitory; fleeting. **2** *Botany.* lasting for only a short time: *fugacious petals.* **[C17:** from Latin *fugax* inclined to flee, swift, from *fugere* to flee; see FUGITIVE**]** ▸ **fu'gaciously** *adv* ▸ **fu'gaciousness** *n*

fugacity (fjuː'gæsɪtɪ) *n* **1** Also called: **escaping tendency.** *Thermodynamics.* a property of a gas that expresses its tendency to escape or expand, given by $d(\log_e f) = d\mu/RT$, where μ is the chemical potential, R the gas constant, and T the thermodynamic temperature. Symbol: f **2** the state or quality of being fugacious.

fugal ('fjuːgᵊl) *adj* of, relating to, or in the style of a fugue. ▸ **'fugally** *adv*

Fugard ('fuːgɑːd) *n* **Athol** ('æθəl). born 1932, South African dramatist and theatre director. His plays include *The Blood-Knot* (1961), *Sizwe Bansi is Dead* (1972), *Statements after an Arrest under the Immorality Act* (1974), and *Sign of Hope* (1992).

fugato (fjʊ'gɑːtəʊ) *Music.* ◆ *adv, adj* **1** in the manner or style of a fugue. ◆ *n* **2** a movement, section, or piece in this style. **[C19:** from Italian, from *fugare* to compose in the style of a FUGUE**]**

-fuge *n combining form.* indicating an agent or substance that expels or drives away: *vermifuge.* **[**from Latin *fugāre* to expel, put to flight**]** ▸ **-fugal** *adj combining form.*

Fugger (*German* 'fʊgər) *n* a German family of merchants and bankers, prominent in 15th- and 16th-century Europe.

fugio ('fjuːdʒɪəʊ) *n, pl* **-gios.** a former U.S. copper coin worth one dollar, the first authorized by Congress (1787). **[C18:** Latin: I flee; one of the words inscribed on the coin**]**

fugitive ('fjuːdʒɪtɪv) *n* **1** a person who flees. **2** a thing that is elusive or fleeting. ◆ *adj* **3** fleeing, esp. from arrest or pursuit. **4** not permanent; fleeting; transient. **5** moving or roving about. **[C14:** from Latin *fugitīvus* fleeing away, from *fugere* to take flight, run away**]** ▸ **'fugitively** *adv* ▸ **'fugitiveness** *n*

fugitometer (ˌfjuːdʒɪ'tɒmɪtə) *n* an instrument used for measuring the fastness to light of dyed materials.

fugleman ('fjuːgᵊlmən) *n, pl* **-men. 1** (formerly) a soldier used as an example for those learning drill. **2** any person who acts as a leader or example. **[C19:** from German *Flügelmann,* from *Flügel* wing, flank + *Mann* MAN**]**

fugue (fjuːg) *n* **1** a musical form consisting essentially of a theme repeated a fifth above or a fourth below the continuing first statement. **2** *Psychiatry.* a dream-like altered state of consciousness, lasting from a few hours to several days, during which a person loses his memory for his previous life and often wanders away from home. **[C16:** from French, from Italian *fuga,* from Latin: a running away, flight**]** ▸ **'fugueˌlike** *adj*

fuguist ('fjuːgɪst) *n* a composer of fugues.

Führer *or* ***Fuehrer*** *German.* ('fyːrər; *English* 'fjʊərə) *n* a leader: applied esp. to Adolf Hitler (***der Führer***) while he was Chancellor. **[**German, from *führen* to lead**]**

Fuji ('fuːdʒɪ) *n* **Mount.** an extinct volcano in central Japan, in S central Honshu: the highest mountain in Japan, famous for its symmetrical snow-capped cone. Height: 3776 m (12 388 ft.). Also called: **Fujiyama, Fuji-san.**

Fujian *or* **Fukien** ('fuː'kjen) *n* **1** a province of SE China: mountainous and forested, drained chiefly by the Min River; noted for the production of flower-scented teas. Capital: Fuzhou. Pop.: 32 370 000 (1996 est.). Area: 123 000 sq. km (47 970 sq. miles). **2** any of the Chinese dialects of this province. See also **Min.**

Fukuoka (ˌfuːkuː'əʊkə) *n* an industrial city and port in SW Japan, in N Kyushu: an important port in ancient times; site of Kyushu university. Pop.: 1 284 741 (1995).

Fukushima (ˌfuːkuː'ʃiːmə) *n* a city in Japan, in N Honshu: noted for production of silk. Pop.: 285 745 (1995).

Fukuyama (ˌfuːkuː'jɑːmə) *n* a city in Japan, in SW Honshu: industrial and commercial centre. Pop.: 374 510 (1995).

-ful *suffix.* **1** (*forming adjectives*) full of or characterized by: *painful; spiteful; restful.* **2** (*forming adjectives*) able or tending to: *helpful; useful.* **3** (*forming nouns*) indicating as much as will fill the thing specified: *mouthful; spoonful.* **[**Old English *-ful, -full,* from FULL[1]**]**

USAGE Where the amount held by a spoon, etc., is used as a rough unit of measurement, the correct form is *spoonful,* etc.: *take a spoonful of this medicine every day. Spoon full* is used in a sentence such as *he held out a spoon full of dark liquid,* where *full of* describes the spoon. A plural form such as *spoonfuls* is preferred by many speakers and writers to *spoonsful.*

Fula ('fuːlə) *or* **Fulah** ('fuːlɑː) *n* **1** (*pl* **-la, -las** *or* **-lah, -lahs**) a member of a pastoral nomadic people of W and central Africa, living chiefly in the sub-Sahara region from Senegal to N Cameroon: a racial mixture of light-skinned Berber peoples of the North and darker-skinned W Africans. **2** the language of this people; Fulani.

Fulani (fuːˈlɑːnɪ, ˈfuːlənɪ) *n* **1** the language of the Fula, belonging to the West Atlantic branch of the Niger-Congo family, widely used as a trade pidgin in W Africa. **2** (*pl* **-nis, -ni**) another name for **Fula** (the people). **3** (*pl* **-nis, -ni**) a humped breed of cattle from W Africa. ◆ *adj* **4** of or relating to the Fula or their language.

fulcrum (ˈfulkrəm, ˈfʌl-) *n, pl* **-crums** *or* **-cra** (-krə). **1** the pivot about which a lever turns. **2** something that supports or sustains; prop. **3** a spinelike scale occurring in rows along the anterior edge of the fins in primitive bony fishes such as the sturgeon. [C17: from Latin: foot of a couch, bedpost, from *fulcire* to prop up]

fulfil *or U.S.* **fulfill** (fulˈfɪl) *vb* **-fils** *or U.S.* **-fills, -filling, -filled.** (*tr*) **1** to bring about the completion or achievement of (a desire, promise, etc.). **2** to carry out or execute (a request, etc.). **3** to conform with or satisfy (regulations, demands, etc.). **4** to finish or reach the end of: *he fulfilled his prison sentence.* **5 fulfil oneself.** to achieve one's potential or desires. [Old English *fulfyllan*] ▸ **fulˈfiller** *n* ▸ **fulˈfilment** *or U.S.* **fulˈfillment** *n*

fulgent (ˈfʌldʒənt) *or* **fulgid** (ˈfʌldʒɪd) *adj Poetic.* shining brilliantly; resplendent; gleaming. [C15: from Latin *fulgēre* to shine, flash] ▸ **ˈfulgently** *adv*

fulgurate (ˈfʌlgjuˌreɪt) *vb* (*intr*) *Rare.* to flash like lightning. [C17: from Latin *fulgurāre*, from *fulgur* lightning] ▸ **fulgurant** (ˈfʌlgjurənt) *adj*

fulgurating (ˈfʌlgjuˌreɪtɪŋ) *adj* **1** *Pathol.* (of pain) sudden and sharp; piercing. **2** *Surgery.* of or relating to fulguration.

fulguration (ˌfʌlgjuˈreɪʃən) *n Surgery.* destruction of tissue by means of high-frequency (more than 10 000 per second) electric sparks.

fulgurite (ˈfʌlgjuˌraɪt) *n* a tube of glassy mineral matter found in sand and rock, formed by the action of lightning. [C19: from Latin *fulgur* lightning]

fulgurous (ˈfʌlgjurəs) *adj Rare.* flashing like or resembling lightning; fulgurant. [C17: from Latin *fulgur* lightning]

Fulham (ˈfuləm) *n* a district of the Greater London borough of Hammersmith and Fulham (since 1965): contains **Fulham Palace** (16th century), residence of the Bishop of London.

fuliginous (fjuːˈlɪdʒɪnəs) *adj* **1** sooty or smoky. **2** of the colour of soot; dull greyish-black or brown. [C16: from Late Latin *fūlīginōsus* full of soot, from Latin *fūlīgō* soot] ▸ **fuˈliginously** *adv* ▸ **fuˈliginousness** *n*

full[1] (ful) *adj* **1** holding or containing as much as possible; filled to capacity or near capacity. **2** abundant in supply, quantity, number, etc.: *full of energy.* **3** having consumed enough food or drink. **4** (esp. of the face or figure) rounded or plump; not thin. **5** (*prenominal*) with no part lacking; complete: *a full dozen.* **6** (*prenominal*) with all privileges, rights, etc.; not restricted: *a full member.* **7** (*prenominal*) of, relating to, or designating a relationship established by descent from the same parents: *full brother.* **8** filled with emotion or sentiment: *a full heart.* **9** (*postpositive;* foll. by *of*) occupied or engrossed (with): *full of his own projects.* **10** *Music.* **10a** powerful or rich in volume and sound. **10b** completing a piece or section; concluding: *a full close.* **11** (of a garment, esp. a skirt) containing a large amount of fabric; of ample cut. **12** (of sails, etc.) distended by wind. **13** (of wine, such as a burgundy) having a heavy body. **14** (of a colour) containing a large quantity of pure hue as opposed to white or grey; rich; saturated. **15** *Informal.* drunk. **16 full and by.** *Nautical.* another term for **close-hauled. 17 full of oneself.** full of pride or conceit; egoistic. **18 full up.** filled to capacity: *the cinema was full up.* **19 in full cry.** (esp. of a pack of hounds) in hot pursuit of quarry. **20 in full swing.** at the height of activity: *the party was in full swing.* ◆ *adv* **21a** completely; entirely. **21b** (*in combination*): *full-grown; full-fledged.* **22** exactly; directly; right: *he hit him full in the stomach.* **23** very; extremely (esp. in the phrase **full well**). **24 full out.** with maximum effort or speed. ◆ *n* **25** the greatest degree, extent, etc. **26** *Brit.* a ridge of sand or shingle along a seashore. **27 in full.** without omitting, decreasing, or shortening: *we paid in full for our mistake.* **28 to the full.** to the greatest extent; thoroughly; fully. ◆ *vb* **29** (*tr*) *Needlework.* to gather or tuck. **30** (*intr*) (of the moon) to be fully illuminated. [Old English; related to Old Norse *fullr,* Old High German *foll,* Latin *plēnus,* Greek *plērēs;* see FILL] ▸ **ˈfullness** *or esp. U.S.* **ˈfulness** *n*

full[2] (ful) *vb* (of cloth, yarn, etc.) to become or to make (cloth, yarn, etc.) heavier and more compact during manufacture through shrinking and beating or pressing. [C14: from Old French *fouler,* ultimately from Latin *fullō* a FULLER[1]]

fullback (ˈfulˌbæk) *n* **1** *Soccer, hockey.* one of two defensive players positioned in front of the goalkeeper. **2** *Rugby.* a defensive player positioned close to his own line. **3** the position held by any of these players.

full blood *n* **1** an individual, esp. a horse or similar domestic animal, of unmixed race or breed. **2** the relationship between individuals having the same parents.

full-blooded *adj* **1** (esp. of horses) of unmixed ancestry; thoroughbred. **2** having great vigour or health; hearty; virile. ▸ **ˌfull-ˈbloodedness** *n*

full-blown *adj* **1** characterized by the fullest, strongest, or best development. **2** in full bloom.

full board *n* **a** the provision by a hotel of a bed and all meals. **b** (*as modifier*): *full board accommodation.*

full-bodied *adj* having a full rich flavour or quality.

full-bottomed *adj* (of a wig) long at the back.

full-court press *n Basketball.* the tactic of harrying the opposing team in all areas of the court, as opposed to the more usual practice of trying to defend one's own basket.

full-cream *adj* denoting or made with whole unskimmed milk.

full dress *n* **a** a formal or ceremonial style of dress, such as white tie and tails for a man and a full-length evening dress for a woman. **b** (*as modifier*): *full-dress uniform.*

full employment *n* a state in which the labour force and other economic resources of a country are utilized to their maximum.

fuller[1] (ˈfulə) *n* a person who fulls cloth for his living. [Old English *fullere,* from Latin *fullō*]

fuller[2] (ˈfulə) *n* **1** Also called: **fullering tool.** a tool for forging a groove. **2** a tool for caulking a riveted joint. ◆ *vb* **3** (*tr*) to forge (a groove) or caulk (a riveted joint) with a fuller. [C19: perhaps from the name *Fuller*]

Fuller (ˈfulə) *n* **1** (**Richard**) **Buckminster.** 1895–1983, U.S. architect and engineer: developed the geodesic dome. **2 Roy** (**Broadbent**). 1912–91, British poet and writer, whose collections include *The Middle of a War* (1942) and *A Lost Season* (1944), both of which are concerned with World War II, *Epitaphs and Occasions* (1949), and *Available for Dreams* (1989). **3 Thomas.** 1608–61, English clergyman and antiquarian; author of *The Worthies of England* (1662).

fullerene (ˈfuləˌriːn) *n* **1** short for **buckminsterfullerene. 2** any of various carbon molecules with a polyhedral structure similar to that of buckminsterfullerene, such as C_{70}, C_{76}, and C_{84}.

fulleride (ˈfuləˌraɪd) *n* a compound of a fullerene in which atoms are trapped inside the cage of carbon atoms.

fullerite (ˈfuləˌraɪt) *n* a crystalline form of a fullerene.

fuller's earth *n* a natural absorbent clay used, after heating, for decolorizing oils and fats, fulling cloth, etc.

fuller's teasel *n* **1** a Eurasian teasel plant, *Dipsacus fullonum,* whose prickly flower heads are used for raising the nap on woollen cloth. **2** a similar and related plant, *Dipsacus sativum.*

full-faced *adj* **1** having a round full face. **2** Also: **full face.** facing towards the viewer, with the entire face visible. **3** another name for **bold face.** ▸ **ˈfullˈface** *n, adv*

full-fledged *adj* See **fully fledged.**

full-frontal *adj* **1** *Informal.* (of a nude person or a photograph of a nude person) exposing the genitals to full view. **2** all-out; unrestrained. ◆ *n* **full frontal. 3** a full-frontal photograph.

full house *n* **1** *Poker.* a hand with three cards of the same value and another pair. **2** a theatre, etc., filled to capacity. **3** (in bingo, etc.) the set of numbers needed to win.

full-length *n* (*modifier*) **1** extending to or showing the complete length: *a full-length mirror.* **2** of the original length; not abridged.

full monty (ˈmɒntɪ) *n* **the.** *Informal.* something in its entirety. [of unknown origin]

full moon *n* **1** one of the four phases of the moon, occurring when the earth lies between the sun and the moon so that the moon is visible as a fully illuminated disc. **2** the moon in this phase. **3** the time at which this occurs.

full-mouthed *adj* **1** (of livestock) having a full adult set of teeth. **2** uttered loudly: *a full-mouthed oath.*

full nelson *n* a wrestling hold, illegal in amateur wrestling, in which a wrestler places both arms under his opponent's arms from behind and exerts pressure with both palms on the back of the neck. Compare **half-nelson.**

full-on *adj Informal.* complete; unrestrained: *full-on military intervention; full-on hard rock.*

full pitch *n Cricket.* another term for **full toss.**

full professor *n U.S. and Canadian.* a university teacher of the highest academic rank.

full radiator *n Physics.* another name for **black body.**

full-rigged *adj* (of a sailing vessel) having three or more masts rigged square.

full sail *adv* **1** at top speed. ◆ *adj* (*postpositive*), *adv* **2** with all sails set. ▸ **ˌfull-ˈsailed** *adj*

full-scale *n* (*modifier*) **1** (of a plan, etc.) of actual size; having the same dimensions as the original. **2** done with thoroughness or urgency; using all resources; all-out.

full score *n* the entire score of a musical composition, showing each part separately.

full stop *or* **full point** *n* the punctuation mark (.) used at the end of a sentence that is not a question or exclamation, after abbreviations, etc. Also called (esp. U.S. and Canadian): **period.**

full time *n* the end of a football or other match. Compare **half-time.**

full-time *adj* **1** for the entire time appropriate to an activity: *a full-time job; a full-time student.* ◆ *adv* **full time. 2** on a full-time basis: *he works full time.* ◆ Compare **part-time.** ▸ **ˌfull-ˈtimer** *n*

full toss *or* **full pitch** *n Cricket.* a bowled ball that reaches the batsman without bouncing.

full-wave rectifier *n* an electronic circuit in which both half-cycles of incoming alternating current furnish the direct current output.

fully (ˈfulɪ) *adv* **1** to the greatest degree or extent; totally; entirely. **2** amply; sufficiently; adequately: *they were fully fed.* **3** at least: *it was fully an hour before she came.*

fully fashioned *adj* (of stockings, knitwear, etc.) shaped and seamed so as to fit closely.

fully fledged *or* **full-fledged** *adj* **1** (of a young bird) having acquired its adult feathers and thus able to fly. **2** developed or matured to the fullest degree. **3** of full rank or status.

fulmar (ˈfulmə) *n* any heavily built short-tailed oceanic bird of the genus *Fulmarus* and related genera, of polar regions: family *Procellariidae,* order *Procellariiformes* (petrels). [C17: of Scandinavian origin; related to Old Norse *fūlmār,* from *fūll* foul + *mār* gull]

fulminant (ˈfʌlmɪnənt, ˈful-) *adj* **1** sudden and violent; fulminating. **2** *Pathol.* (of pain) sudden and sharp; piercing. [C17: from Latin *fulmināre* to cause lightning, from *fulmen* lightning that strikes]

fulminate (ˈfʌlmɪˌneɪt, ˈful-) *vb* **1** (*intr;* often foll. by *against*) to make criticisms or denunciations; rail. **2** to explode with noise and violence. **3** (*intr*) *Ar-*

chaic. to thunder and lighten. ◆ *n* **4** any salt or ester of fulminic acid, esp. the mercury salt, which is used as a detonator. [C15: from Medieval Latin *fulmināre;* see FULMINANT] ▸ ˌ**fulmiˈnation** *n* ▸ ˈ**fulmiˌnator** *n* ▸ ˈ**fulmiˌnatory** *adj*

fulminating powder *n* powder that detonates by percussion.

fulminic acid (fʌlˈmɪnɪk, fʊl-) *n* an unstable volatile acid known only in solution and in the form of its salts and esters. Formula: HONC. Compare **cyanic acid.** [C19: from Latin *fulmen* lightning]

fulminous (ˈfʌlmɪnəs, ˈfʊl-) *adj Rare.* **1** harshly critical. **2** of, involving, or resembling thunder and lightning.

fulsome (ˈfʊlsəm) *adj* **1** excessive or insincere, esp. in an offensive or distasteful way: *fulsome compliments.* **2** *Not standard.* extremely complimentary. **3** *Archaic.* disgusting; loathsome. ▸ ˈ**fulsomely** *adv* ▸ ˈ**fulsomeness** *n*

Fulton (ˈfʊltᵊn) *n* **Robert.** 1765–1815, U.S. engineer: designed the first successful steamboat (1807) and steam warship (1814).

fulvous (ˈfʌlvəs, ˈfʊl-) *adj* of a dull brownish-yellow colour; tawny. [C17: from Latin *fulvus* reddish yellow, gold-coloured, tawny; probably related to *fulgēre* to shine]

fumaric acid (fjuːˈmærɪk) *n* a colourless crystalline acid with a fruity taste, found in some plants and manufactured from benzene; *trans*-butenedioic acid: used esp. in synthetic resins. Formula: HCOOCH:CHCOOH. [C19: from New Latin *Fumāria* name of genus, from Late Latin: fumitory, from Latin *fūmus* smoke]

fumarole (ˈfjuːməˌrəʊl) *n* a vent in or near a volcano from which hot gases, esp. steam, are emitted. [C19: from French *fumerolle,* from Late Latin *fūmāriolum* smoke hole, from Latin *fūmus* smoke] ▸ **fumarolic** (ˌfjuːməˈrɒlɪk) *adj*

fumatorium (ˌfjuːməˈtɔːrɪəm) *n, pl* **-riums** *or* **-ria** (-rɪə). an airtight chamber in which insects and fungi on organic matter or plants are destroyed by fumigation. Also called: **fumatory.** [New Latin, from Latin *fūmāre* to smoke]

fumatory (ˈfjuːmətərɪ, -trɪ) *adj* **1** of or relating to smoking or fumigation. ◆ *n, pl* **-ries. 2** another name for a **fumatorium.**

fumble (ˈfʌmbᵊl) *vb* **1** (*intr;* often foll. by *for* or *with*) to grope about clumsily or blindly, esp. in searching: *he was fumbling in the dark for the money he had dropped.* **2** (*intr;* foll. by *at* or *with*) to finger or play with, esp. in an absent-minded way. **3** to say or do hesitantly or awkwardly: *he fumbled the introduction badly.* **4** to fail to catch or grasp (a ball, etc.) cleanly. ◆ *n* **5** the act of fumbling. [C16: probably of Scandinavian origin; related to Swedish *fumla*] ▸ ˈ**fumbler** *n* ▸ ˈ**fumblingly** *adv* ▸ ˈ**fumblingness** *n*

fume (fjuːm) *vb* **1** (*intr*) to be overcome with anger or fury; rage. **2** to give off (fumes) or (of fumes) to be given off, esp. during a chemical reaction. **3** (*tr*) to subject to or treat with fumes; fumigate. ◆ *n* **4** (*often pl*) a pungent or toxic vapour. **5** a sharp or pungent odour. **6** a condition of anger. [C14: from Old French *fum,* from Latin *fūmus* smoke, vapour] ▸ ˈ**fumeless** *adj* ▸ ˈ**fumeˌlike** *adj* ▸ ˈ**fumer** *n* ▸ ˈ**fumingly** *adv* ▸ ˈ**fumy** *adj*

fume cupboard *n* a ventilated enclosure for storing or experimenting with chemicals with harmful vapours.

fumed (fjuːmd) *adj* (of wood, esp. oak) having a dark colour and distinctive grain from exposure to ammonia fumes.

fumet[1] (fjuːˈmeɪ) *n* a strong-flavoured liquor from cooking fish, meat, or game: used to flavour sauces. [French, literally: aroma]

fumet[2] (ˈfjuːmət) *n* (*often pl*) *Archaic.* the dropping of a deer. [C16 *fewmet:* probably via Old French from Latin *fimāre* to spread dung on, from *fimus* dung]

fumigant (ˈfjuːmɪgənt) *n* a substance used for fumigating.

fumigate (ˈfjuːmɪˌgeɪt) *vb* to treat (something contaminated or infected) with fumes or smoke. [C16: from Latin *fūmigāre* to smoke, steam, from *fūmus* smoke + *agere* to drive, produce] ▸ ˌ**fumiˈgation** *n* ▸ ˈ**fumiˌgator** *n*

fuming sulphuric acid *n* a mixture of pyrosulphuric acid, $H_2S_2O_7$, and other condensed acids, made by dissolving sulphur trioxide in concentrated sulphuric acid. Also called: **oleum, Nordhausen acid** (ˈnɔːdhaʊzᵊn).

fumitory (ˈfjuːmɪtərɪ, -trɪ) *n, pl* **-ries.** any plant of the chiefly European genus *Fumaria,* esp. *F. officinalis,* having spurred flowers and formerly used medicinally: family *Fumariaceae.* [C14: from Old French *fumetere,* from Medieval Latin *fūmus terrae,* literally: smoke of the earth; see FUME]

fun (fʌn) *n* **1** a source of enjoyment, amusement, diversion, etc. **2** pleasure, gaiety, or merriment. **3** jest or sport (esp. in the phrases **in** or **for fun**). **4 fun and games.** *Ironic or facetious.* gay amusement; frivolous activity. **5 like fun.** *Informal.* **5a** (*adv*) quickly; vigorously. **5b** (*interj*) not at all! certainly not! **6 make fun of** *or* **poke fun at.** to ridicule or deride. **7** (*modifier*) full of amusement, diversion, gaiety, etc.: *a fun sport.* ◆ *vb* **funs, funning, funned. 8** (*intr*) *Informal.* to act in a joking or sporting manner. [C17: perhaps from obsolete *fon* to make a fool of; see FOND[1]]

funambulist (fjuːˈnæmbjʊlɪst) *n* a tightrope walker. [C18: from Latin *fūnambulus* rope dancer, from *fūnis* rope + *ambulāre* to walk] ▸ **fuˈnambulism** *n*

Funchal (*Portuguese* fũˈʃal) *n* the capital and chief port of the Madeira Islands, on the S coast of Madeira. Pop.: 44 111 (1987).

function (ˈfʌŋkʃən) *n* **1** the natural action or intended purpose of a person or thing in a specific role: *the function of a hammer is to hit nails into wood.* **2** an official or formal social gathering or ceremony. **3** a factor dependent upon another or other factors: *the length of the flight is a function of the weather.* **4** Also called: **map, mapping.** *Maths, logic.* a relation between two sets that associates a unique element (the value) of the second (the range) with each element (the argument) of the first (the domain): a many-one relation. Symbol: f(x) The value of f(x) for x = 2 is f(2). ◆ *vb* (*intr*) **5** to operate or perform as specified; work properly. **6** (foll. by *as*) to perform the action or role (of something or someone else): *a coin may function as a screwdriver.* [C16: from Latin *functiō,* from *fungī* to perform, discharge] ▸ ˈ**functionless** *adj*

functional (ˈfʌŋkʃənᵊl) *adj* **1** of, involving, or containing a function or functions. **2** practical rather than decorative; utilitarian: *functional architecture.* **3** capable of functioning; working. **4** *Psychol.* **4a** relating to the purpose or context of a behaviour. **4b** denoting a psychosis such as schizophrenia assumed not to have a direct organic cause, like deterioration or poisoning of the brain. ◆ *n* **5** *Maths.* a function whose domain is a set of functions and whose range is another set of functions that can be a set of numbers. ▸ ˈ**functionally** *adv*

functional calculus *n* **1** another name for **predicate calculus. 2** the branch of mathematics that studies the properties of functions and operations upon functions.

functional disease *n* a disease in which there is no observable change in the structure of an organ or part. Compare **organic disease.**

functional group *n Chem.* the group of atoms in a compound, such as the hydroxyl group in an alcohol, that determines the chemical behaviour of the compound.

functional illiterate *n* a person whose literacy is insufficient for most work and normal daily situations. ▸ **functional illiteracy** *n*

functionalism (ˈfʌŋkʃənəˌlɪzəm) *n* **1** the theory of design that the form of a thing should be determined by its use. **2** any doctrine that stresses utility or purpose. **3** *Psychol.* a system of thought based on the premise that all mental processes derive from their usefulness to the organism in adapting to the environment. ▸ ˈ**functionalist** *n, adj*

functionary (ˈfʌŋkʃənərɪ) *n, pl* **-aries. 1** a person acting in an official capacity, as for a government; an official. ◆ *adj* **2** a less common word for **functional** or **official.**

function key *n Computing.* a key on the keyboard of a microcomputer, etc. that gives special commands to the computer.

function shift *or* **change** *n* **1** *Grammar.* a change in the syntactic function of a word, as when the noun *mushroom* is used as an intransitive verb. **2** *Linguistics.* sound change involving a realignment of the phonemic system of a language.

function word *n Grammar.* a word, such as *the,* with a particular grammatical role but little identifiable meaning. Compare **content word, grammatical meaning.**

fund (fʌnd) *n* **1** a reserve of money, etc., set aside for a certain purpose. **2** a supply or store of something; stock: *it exhausted his fund of wisdom.* ◆ *vb* (*tr*) **3** to furnish money to in the form of a fund. **4** to place or store up in a fund. **5** to convert (short-term floating debt) into long-term debt bearing fixed interest and represented by bonds. **6** to provide a fund for the redemption of principal or payment of interest of. **7** to accumulate a fund for the discharge of (a recurrent liability): *to fund a pension plan.* **8** to invest (money) in government securities. ◆ See also **funds.** [C17: from Latin *fundus* the bottom, piece of land, estate; compare FOND[2]] ▸ ˈ**funder** *n*

fundament (ˈfʌndəmənt) *n* **1** *Euphemistic or facetious.* the buttocks. **2** the natural features of the earth's surface, unaltered by man. **3** a base or foundation, esp. of a building. **4** a theory, principle, or underlying basis. [C13: from Latin *fundāmentum* foundation, from *fundāre* to FOUND[2]]

fundamental (ˌfʌndəˈmentᵊl) *adj* **1** of, involving, or comprising a foundation; basic. **2** of, involving, or comprising a source; primary. **3** *Music.* denoting or relating to the principal or lowest note of a harmonic series. **4** of or concerned with the component of lowest frequency in a complex vibration. ◆ *n* **5** a principle, law, etc., that serves as the basis of an idea or system. **6a** the principal or lowest note of a harmonic series. **6b** the bass note of a chord in root position. **7** Also called: **fundamental frequency, first harmonic.** *Physics.* **7a** the component of lowest frequency in a complex vibration. **7b** the frequency of this component. ▸ ˌ**fundamenˈtality** *or* ˌ**fundaˈmentalness** *n* ▸ ˌ**fundaˈmentally** *adv*

fundamental constant *n* a physical constant, such as the gravitational constant or speed of light, that plays a fundamental role in physics and chemistry and usually has an accurately known value.

fundamental interaction *n* any of the four basic interactions that occur in nature: the gravitational, electromagnetic, strong, and weak interactions.

fundamentalism (ˌfʌndəˈmentəˌlɪzəm) *n* **1** *Christianity.* (esp. among certain Protestant sects) the belief that every word of the Bible is divinely inspired and therefore true. **2** *Islam.* a movement favouring strict observance of the teachings of the Koran and Islamic law. **3** strict adherence to the fundamental principles of any set of beliefs. ▸ ˌ**fundaˈmentalist** *n, adj* ▸ ˌ**fundaˌmentalˈistic** *adj*

fundamental law *n* the law determining the constitution of the government of a state; organic law.

fundamental particle *n* another name for **elementary particle.**

fundamental unit *n* one of a set of unrelated units that form the basis of a system of units. For example, the metre, kilogram, and second are fundamental units of the SI system.

funded debt *n* the part of the national debt, consisting mostly of consols, that the government has no obligation to repay by a specified date.

fundholding (ˈfʌndˌhəʊldɪŋ) *n* (formerly, in the National Health Service in Britain) the system enabling general practitioners to receive a fixed budget from which to pay for primary care, drugs, and nonurgent hospital treatment for patients. ▸ ˈ**fundˌholder** *n*

fundi[1] (ˈfundiː) *n E. African.* a person skilled in repairing or maintaining machinery; mechanic. [C20: from Swahili]

fundi[2] (ˈfundiː) *n S. African.* an expert. [C20: from Nguni *umfindisi* a teacher]

funding operations *pl n Finance.* the conversion of government floating stock or short-term debt into holdings of long-term bonds.

fund manager *n* an employee of an insurance company, pension fund, investment trust, etc., who manages its fund of investments.

fundraiser (ˈfʌndˌreɪzə) *n* **1** a person who raises money for a cause. **2** an event held to raise money for a cause.

funds (fʌndz) *pl n* **1** money that is readily available. **2** British government securities representing national debt.

fundus ('fʌndəs) *n, pl* **-di** (-daɪ). *Anatomy.* the base of an organ or the part farthest away from its opening. [C18: from Latin, literally: the bottom, a farm, estate] ▸ **'fundic** *adj*

Fundy ('fʌndɪ) *n* **Bay of.** an inlet of the Atlantic in SE Canada, between S New Brunswick and W Nova Scotia: remarkable for its swift tides of up to 21 m (70 ft.).

Funen ('fuːnən) *n* the second largest island of Denmark, between the Jutland peninsula and the island of Sjælland. Pop.: 605 868 (1995 est.). Area: 3481 sq. km (1344 sq. miles). Danish name: **Fyn.** German name: **Fünen.**

funeral ('fjuːnərəl) *n* **1a** a ceremony at which a dead person is buried or cremated. **1b** (*as modifier*): *a funeral service.* **2** a procession of people escorting a corpse to burial. **3** *Informal.* worry; concern; affair: *that's your funeral.* [C14: from Medieval Latin *fūnerālia,* from Late Latin *fūnerālis* (adj), from Latin *fūnus* funeral]

funeral director *n* an undertaker.

funeral parlour *n* a place where the dead are prepared for burial or cremation. Usual U.S. name: **funeral home.**

funerary ('fjuːnərərɪ) *adj* of, relating to, or for a funeral.

funereal (fjuː'nɪərɪəl) *adj* suggestive of a funeral; gloomy or mournful. Also: **funebrial** (fjuː'niːbrɪəl). [C18: from Latin *fūnereus*] ▸ **fu'nereally** *adv*

funfair ('fʌnˌfɛə) *n Brit.* an amusement park or fairground.

fun fur *n* a relatively inexpensive synthetic fur garment.

fungal ('fʌŋgᵊl) *adj* of, derived from, or caused by a fungus or fungi: *fungal spores; a fungal disease.*

fungi ('fʌŋgaɪ, 'fʌndʒaɪ, 'fʌndʒɪ) *n* a plural of **fungus.**

fungi- *or before a vowel* **fung-** *combining form.* fungus: *fungicide; fungoid.*

fungible ('fʌndʒɪbᵊl) *Law.* ◆ *n* **1** (*often pl*) moveable perishable goods of a sort that may be estimated by number or weight, such as grain, wine, etc. ◆ *adj* **2** having the nature or quality of fungibles. [C18: from Medieval Latin *fungibilis,* from Latin *fungī* to perform; see FUNCTION] ▸ **ˌfungi'bility** *n*

fungible issue *n Finance.* a bond issued by a company on the same terms as a bond previously issued by that company, although the redemption yield will probably be different.

fungicide ('fʌndʒɪˌsaɪd) *n* a substance or agent that destroys or is capable of destroying fungi. ▸ **ˌfungi'cidal** *adj*

fungiform ('fʌndʒɪˌfɔːm) *adj* shaped like a mushroom or similar fungus: *the fungiform papillae of the tongue.*

fungistat ('fʌndʒɪˌstæt) *n* a substance that inhibits the growth of fungi. ▸ **ˌfungi'static** *adj*

fungoid ('fʌŋgɔɪd) *adj* resembling a fungus or fungi: *a fungoid growth.*

fungous ('fʌŋgəs) *adj* **1** appearing suddenly and spreading quickly like a fungus, but not lasting. **2** a less common word for **fungal.**

fungus ('fʌŋgəs) *n, pl* **fungi** ('fʌŋgaɪ, 'fʌndʒaɪ, 'fʌndʒɪ) *or* **funguses. 1** any member of a kingdom of organisms (Fungi) that lack chlorophyll, leaves, true stems, and roots, reproduce by spores, and live as saprotrophs or parasites. The group includes moulds, mildews, rusts, yeasts, and mushrooms. **2** something resembling a fungus, esp. in suddenly growing and spreading rapidly. **3** *Pathol.* any soft tumorous growth. [C16: from Latin: mushroom, fungus; probably related to Greek *spongos* SPONGE] ▸ **fungic** ('fʌndʒɪk) *adj* ▸ **'fungus-ˌlike** *adj*

funicle ('fjuːnɪkᵊl) *n Botany.* the stalk that attaches an ovule or seed to the wall of the ovary. Also called: **funiculus.** [C17: from Latin *fūniculus* a thin rope, from *fūnis* rope] ▸ **funiculate** (fjʊ'nɪkjʊlɪt, -ˌleɪt) *adj*

funicular (fjuː'nɪkjʊlə) *n* **1** Also called: **funicular railway.** a railway up the side of a mountain, consisting of two counterbalanced cars at either end of a cable passing round a driving wheel at the summit. ◆ *adj* **2** relating to or operated by a rope, cable, etc. **3** of or relating to a funicle.

funiculus (fjuː'nɪkjʊləs) *n, pl* **-li** (-ˌlaɪ). **1** *Anatomy.* a cordlike part or structure, esp. a small bundle of nerve fibres in the spinal cord. **2** a variant of **funicle.** [C17: from Latin; see FUNICLE]

funk[1] (fʌŋk) *Informal, chiefly Brit.* ◆ *n* **1** Also called: **blue funk.** a state of nervousness, fear, or depression (esp. in the phrase **in a funk**). **2** a coward. ◆ *vb* **3** to flinch from (responsibility) through fear. **4** (*tr; usually passive*) to make afraid. [C18: university slang, perhaps related to FUNK[2]] ▸ **'funker** *n*

funk[2] (fʌŋk) *n U.S. slang.* a strong foul odour. [C17 (in the sense: tobacco smoke): from *funk* (vb) to smoke (tobacco), probably of French dialect origin; compare Old French *funkier* to smoke, from Latin *fūmigāre*]

funk[3] (fʌŋk) *n Informal.* a type of polyrhythmic Black dance music with heavy syncopation. [C20: back formation from FUNKY[1]]

Funk (fʌŋk) *n* **Casimir** ('kæzɪˌmɪə). 1884–1967, U.S. biochemist, born in Poland: studied and named vitamins.

funk hole *n Informal.* **1** *Military.* a dugout. **2** a job that affords exemption from military service.

funky[1] ('fʌŋkɪ) *adj* **funkier, funkiest.** *Informal.* **1** (of music) passionate, soulful; of or pertaining to funk. **2** authentic; earthy. [C20: from FUNK[2], perhaps alluding to music that was smelly, that is, earthy (like the early blues)]

funky[2] ('fʌŋkɪ) *adj* **funkier, funkiest.** *Slang, chiefly U.S.* evil-smelling; foul. [C18: from FUNK[2]]

funnel ('fʌnᵊl) *n* **1** a hollow utensil with a wide mouth tapering to a small hole, used for pouring liquids, powders, etc., into a narrow-necked vessel. **2** something resembling this in shape or function. **3** a smokestack for smoke and exhaust gases, as on a steamship or steam locomotive. **4** a shaft or tube, as in a building, for ventilation. ◆ *vb* **-nels, -nelling, -nelled** *or U.S.* **-nels, -neling, -neled. 5** to move or cause to move or pour through or as if through a funnel. **6** to concentrate or focus or be concentrated or focused in a particular direction: *they funnelled their attention on the problem.* **7** (*intr*) to take on a funnel-like shape. [C15: from Old Provençal *fonilh,* ultimately from Latin *infundibulum* funnel, hopper (in a mill), from *infundere* to pour in] ▸ **'funnel-ˌlike** *adj*

funnel cap *n* any of various basidiomycetous fungi of the genus *Clitocybe,* characterized by the funnel-shaped caps and, usually, markedly decurrent gills.

funnel cloud *n* a whirling column of cloud extending downwards from the base of a cumulonimbus cloud: part of a waterspout or tornado.

funnel-web *n Austral.* any large poisonous black spider of the family *Dipluridae,* constructing funnel-shaped webs.

funnies ('fʌnɪz) *pl n U.S. and Canadian informal.* comic strips in a newspaper.

funny ('fʌnɪ) *adj* **-nier, -niest. 1** causing amusement or laughter; humorous; comical. **2** peculiar; odd. **3** suspicious or dubious (esp. in the phrase **funny business**). **4** *Informal.* faint or ill: *to feel funny.* ◆ *n, pl* **-nies. 5** *Informal.* a joke or witticism. ▸ **'funnily** *adv* ▸ **'funniness** *n*

funny bone *n* the area near the elbow where the ulnar nerve is close to the surface of the skin: when it is struck, a sharp tingling sensation is experienced along the forearm and hand. Also called (U.S.): **crazy bone.**

funny farm *n Facetious.* a mental institution.

funny paper *n U.S. and Canadian.* a section or separate supplement of a newspaper, etc., containing comic strips.

fun run *n* a long run or part-marathon run for exercise and pleasure, often by large numbers of people.

fur (fɜː) *n* **1** the dense coat of fine silky hairs on such mammals as the cat, seal, and mink. **2a** the dressed skin of certain fur-bearing animals, with the hair left on. **2b** (*as modifier*): *a fur coat.* **3** a garment made of fur, such as a coat or stole. **4a** a pile fabric made in imitation of animal fur. **4b** a garment made from such a fabric. **5** *Heraldry.* any of various stylized representations of animal pelts or their tinctures, esp. ermine or vair, used in coats of arms. **6 make the fur fly.** to cause a scene or disturbance. **7** *Informal.* a whitish coating of cellular debris on the tongue, caused by excessive smoking, an upset stomach, etc. **8** *Brit.* a whitish-grey deposit consisting chiefly of calcium carbonate precipitated from hard water onto the insides of pipes, boilers, and kettles. ◆ *vb* **furs, furring, furred. 9** (*tr*) to line or trim a garment, etc., with fur. **10** (often foll. by *up*) to cover or become covered with a furlike lining or deposit. **11** (*tr*) to clothe (a person) in a fur garment or garments. [C14: from Old French *forrer* to line a garment, from *fuerre* sheath, of Germanic origin; related to Old English *fōdder* case, Old Frisian *fōder* coat lining] ▸ **'furless** *adj*

fur. *abbrev. for* furlong.

furaldehyde (fjʊə'rældəˌhaɪd) *n* either of two aldehydes derived from furan, esp. **2-furaldehyde** (see **furfuraldehyde**). [C20: shortened from *furfuraldehyde,* from *furfurol* (see FURFUR, -OL[1]) + ALDEHYDE]

furan ('fjʊəræn, fjʊə'ræn) *n* a colourless flammable toxic liquid heterocyclic compound, used in the manufacture of cotton textiles and in the synthesis of nylon. Formula: C_4H_4O. Also called: **furfuran.** [C19: shortened form of *furfuran,* from FURFUR]

furbelow ('fɜːbɪˌləʊ) *n* **1** a flounce, ruffle, or other ornamental trim. **2** (*often pl*) showy ornamentation. ◆ *vb* **3** (*tr*) to put a furbelow on (a garment). [C18: by folk etymology from French dialect *farbella;* see FALBALA]

furbish ('fɜːbɪʃ) *vb* (*tr*) **1** to make bright by polishing; burnish. **2** (often foll. by *up*) to improve the appearance or condition of; renovate; restore. [C14: from Old French *fourbir* to polish, of Germanic origin] ▸ **'furbisher** *n*

fur brigade *n Canadian.* (formerly) a convoy of canoes, horses, or dog sleighs that transported furs and other goods between trading posts and towns or factories.

furca ('fɜːkə) *n, pl* **-cae** (-kiː). *Zoology.* any forklike structure, esp. in insects. [Latin: fork] ▸ **'furcal** *adj*

furcate *vb* ('fɜːkeɪt). **1** to divide into two parts; fork. ◆ *adj* ('fɜːkeɪt, -kɪt) *or* **furcated. 2** forked; divided: *furcate branches.* [C19: from Late Latin *furcātus* forked, from Latin *furca* a fork] ▸ **fur'cation** *n*

furcula ('fɜːkjʊlə) *or* **furculum** ('fɜːkjʊləm) *n, pl* **-lae** (-ˌliː) *or* **-la** (-lə). any forklike part or organ, esp. the fused clavicles (wishbone) of birds. [C19: from Latin: a forked support for a wall, diminutive of *furca* fork]

furfur ('fɜːfə) *n, pl* **furfures** ('fɜːfjʊˌriːz, -fəˌriːz). **1** a scaling of the skin; dandruff. **2** any scale of the epidermis. [C17: from Latin: bran, scurf]

furfuraceous (ˌfɜːfjʊ'reɪʃəs, -fə'reɪ-) *adj* **1** relating to or resembling bran. **2** *Med.* resembling dandruff; scaly. ▸ **ˌfurfu'raceously** *adv*

furfuraldehyde (ˌfɜːfjə'rældəˌhaɪd) *n* a colourless flammable soluble mobile liquid with a penetrating odour, present in oat and rice hulls; 2-furaldehyde: used as a solvent and in the manufacture of resins. Formula: $C_5H_4O_2$. Also called: **furfural.**

furfuran ('fɜːfəˌræn, 'fɜːfjʊ-) *n* another name for **furan.**

Furies ('fjʊərɪz) *pl n, sing* **Fury.** *Classical myth.* the snake-haired goddesses of vengeance, usually three in number, who pursued unpunished criminals. Also called: **Erinyes, Eumenides.**

furioso (ˌfjʊərɪ'əʊsəʊ) *Music.* ◆ *adj, adv* **1** in a frantically rushing manner. ◆ *n* **2** a passage or piece to be performed in this way. [C19: Italian, literally: furious; see FURY]

furious ('fjʊərɪəs) *adj* **1** extremely angry or annoyed; raging. **2** violent, wild, or unrestrained, as in speed, vigour, energy, etc. ▸ **'furiously** *adv* ▸ **'furiousness** *n*

furl (fɜːl) *vb* **1** to roll up (an umbrella, a flag, etc.) neatly and securely or (of an umbrella, flag, etc.) to be rolled up in this way. **2** (*tr*) *Nautical.* to gather in (a square sail). ◆ *n* **3** the act or an instance of furling. **4** a single rolled-up section. [C16: from Old French *ferlier* to bind tightly, from *ferm* tight (from Latin *firmus* FIRM[1]) + *lier* to tie, bind, from Latin *ligāre*] ▸ **'furlable** *adj* ▸ **'furler** *n*

furlong ('fɜːˌlɒŋ) *n* a unit of length equal to 220 yards (201.168 metres). [Old English *furlang,* from *furh* FURROW + *lang* LONG[1]]

furlough ('fɜːləʊ) *n* **1** leave of absence from military duty. **2** *U.S.* a temporary laying-off of employees, usually because there is insufficient work to occupy them. ◆ *vb (tr)* **3** to grant a furlough to. **4** *U.S.* to lay off (staff) temporarily. [C17: from Dutch *verlof,* from *ver-* FOR- + *lof* leave, permission; related to Swedish *förlof*]

furmenty ('fɜːməntɪ) *or* **furmity** ('fɜːmɪtɪ) *n* variants of **frumenty.**

furnace ('fɜːnɪs) *n* **1** an enclosed chamber in which heat is produced to generate steam, destroy refuse, smelt or refine ores, etc. **2** a very hot or stifling place. [C13: from Old French *fornais,* from Latin *fornax* oven, furnace; related to Latin *formus* warm] ▸ **'furnace-,like** *adj*

Furness ('fɜːnɪs) *n* a region in NW England in Cumbria, forming a peninsula between the Irish Sea and Morecambe Bay.

furnish ('fɜːnɪʃ) *vb (tr)* **1** to provide (a house, room, etc.) with furniture, carpets, etc. **2** to equip with what is necessary; fit out. **3** to give; supply: *the records furnished the information required.* [C15: from Old French *fournir,* of Germanic origin; related to Old High German *frummen* to carry out] ▸ **'furnisher** *n*

furnishings ('fɜːnɪʃɪŋz) *pl n* **1** furniture and accessories, including carpets and curtains, with which a room, house, etc., is furnished. **2** *U.S. and Canadian.* articles of dress and accessories.

furniture ('fɜːnɪtʃə) *n* **1** the movable, generally functional, articles that equip a room, house, etc. **2** the equipment necessary for a ship, factory, etc. **3** *Printing.* lengths of wood, plastic, or metal, used in assembling formes to create the blank areas and to surround the type. **4** *Obsolete.* the full armour, trappings, etc., for a man and horse. **5** See **door furniture** and **street furniture.** [C16: from French *fourniture,* from *fournir* to equip, FURNISH]

furniture beetle *n* See **anobiid.**

Furnivall ('fɜːnɪvᵊl) *n* **Frederick James.** 1825–1910, English philologist: founder of the Early English Text Society and one of the founders of the *Oxford English Dictionary.*

furore (fjʊ'rɔːrɪ) *or esp. U.S.* **furor** ('fjʊərɔː) *n* **1** a public outburst, esp. of protest; uproar. **2** a sudden widespread enthusiasm for something; craze. **3** frenzy; rage; madness. [C15: from Latin: frenzy, rage, from *furere* to rave]

furphy ('fɜːfɪ) *n, pl* **-phies.** *Austral. slang.* a rumour or fictitious story. [C20: from *Furphy* carts (used for water or sewage in World War I), made at a foundry established by the Furphy family]

Furphy ('fɜːfɪ) *n* **Joseph,** pen name *Tom Collins.* 1843–1912, Australian author. His works include the classic Australian novel *Such is Life* (1903) and *The Buln-Buln and the Brolga* (1948).

furred (fɜːd) *adj* **1** made of, lined with, or covered in fur. **2** wearing fur. **3** (of animals) having fur. **4** another word for **furry** (sense 4). **5** Also: **furry.** provided with furring strips. **6** (of a pipe, kettle, etc.) lined with hard lime or other salts deposited from water.

furrier ('fʌrɪə) *n* a person whose occupation is selling, making, dressing, or repairing fur garments. [C14: *furour,* from Old French *fourrer* to trim or line with FUR]

furriery ('fʌrɪərɪ) *n, pl* **-eries. 1** the occupation of a furrier. **2** furs worn as a garment or trim collectively.

furring ('fɜːrɪŋ) *n* **1a** short for **furring strip. 1b** the fixing of furring strips. **1c** furring strips collectively. **2** the formation of fur on the tongue. **3** trimming of animal fur, as on a coat or other garment, or furs collectively.

furring strip *n* a strip of wood or metal fixed to a wall, floor, or ceiling to provide a surface for the fixing of plasterboard, floorboards, etc. Sometimes shortened to **furring.**

furrow ('fʌrəʊ) *n* **1** a long narrow trench made in the ground by a plough or a trench resembling this. **2** any long deep groove, esp. a deep wrinkle on the forehead. ◆ *vb* **3** to develop or cause to develop furrows or wrinkles. **4** to make a furrow or furrows in (land). [Old English *furh;* related to Old Frisian *furch,* Old Norse *for,* Old High German *furuh* furrow, Latin *porca* ridge between furrows] ▸ **'furrower** *n* ▸ **'furrowless** *adj* ▸ **'furrow-,like** *or* **'furrowy** *adj*

furry ('fɜːrɪ) *adj* **-rier, -riest. 1** covered with fur or something furlike. **2** of, relating to, or resembling fur. **3** another word for **furred** (sense 5). **4** Also: **furred.** (of the tongue) coated with whitish cellular debris. ▸ **'furrily** *adv* ▸ **'furriness** *n*

fur seal *n* any of various eared seals, esp. of the genus *Arctocephalus,* that have a fine dense underfur and are hunted as a source of sealskin.

Fur Seal Islands *pl n* another name for the **Pribilof Islands.**

furth (fʌrθ) *adv Scot.* out; outside; to the outside. [a Scot. variant of FORTH]

Fürth (*German* fyːrt) *n* a city in S central Germany, in Bavaria northwest of Nuremberg: Pop.: 108 418 (1996 est.).

further ('fɜːðə) *adv* **1** in addition; furthermore. **2** to a greater degree or extent. **3** to or at a more advanced point. **4** to or at a greater distance in time or space; farther. ◆ *adj* **5** additional; more. **6** more distant or remote in time or space; farther. ◆ *vb* **7** *(tr)* to assist the progress of; promote. ◆ See also **far, furthest.** [Old English *furthor;* related to Old Frisian *further,* Old Saxon *furthor,* Old High German *furdar;* see FORTH] ▸ **'furtherer** *n*

USAGE See at **farther.**

furtherance ('fɜːðərəns) *n* **1** the act of furthering; advancement. **2** something that furthers or advances.

further education *n* (in Britain) formal education beyond school other than at a university or polytechnic.

furthermore ('fɜːðə,mɔː) *adv* in addition; moreover.

furthermost ('fɜːðə,məʊst) *adj* most distant; furthest.

furthest ('fɜːðɪst) *adv* **1** to the greatest degree or extent. **2** to or at the greatest distance in time or space; farthest. ◆ *adj* **3** most distant or remote in time or space; farthest.

furtive ('fɜːtɪv) *adj* characterized by stealth; sly and secretive. [C15: from Latin *furtīvus* stolen, clandestine, from *furtum* a theft, from *fūr* a thief; related to Greek *phōr* thief] ▸ **'furtively** *adv* ▸ **'furtiveness** *n*

Furtwängler (*German* 'furtvɛŋlər) *n* **Wilhelm** ('vɪlhɛlm). 1886–1954, German conductor, noted for his interpretations of Wagner.

furuncle ('fjʊərʌŋkᵊl) *n Pathol.* the technical name for **boil**[2]. [C17: from Latin *fūrunculus* pilferer, petty thief, sore on the body, from *fūr* thief] ▸ **furuncular** (fjʊ'rʌŋkjʊlə) *or* **fu'runculous** *adj*

furunculosis (fjʊ,rʌŋkjʊ'ləʊsɪs) *n* **1** a skin condition characterized by the presence of multiple boils. **2** an infectious ulcerative disease of salmon and trout caused by the bacterium *Aeromonas salmonicida.*

fury ('fjʊərɪ) *n, pl* **-ries. 1** violent or uncontrolled anger; wild rage. **2** an outburst of such anger. **3** uncontrolled violence: *the fury of the storm.* **4** a person, esp. a woman, with a violent temper. **5** See **Furies. 6 like fury.** *Informal.* violently; furiously: *they rode like fury.* [C14: from Latin *furia* rage, from *furere* to be furious]

furze (fɜːz) *n* another name for **gorse.** [Old English *fyrs*] ▸ **'furzy** *adj*

fusain (fjuː'zeɪn; *French* fyzɛ̃) *n* **1** a fine charcoal pencil or stick made from the spindle tree. **2** a drawing done with such a pencil. **3** a dull black brittle form of carbon resembling charcoal, found in certain coals. [C19: from French: spindle tree or charcoal made from it, from Vulgar Latin *fūsāgō* (unattested) a spindle (generally made from the spindle tree), from Latin *fūsus*]

fuscous ('fʌskəs) *adj* of a brownish-grey colour. [C17: from Latin *fuscus* dark, swarthy, tawny]

fuse[1] *or U.S.* **fuze** (fjuːz) *n* **1** a lead of combustible black powder in a waterproof covering (**safety fuse**), or a lead containing an explosive (**detonating fuse**), used to fire an explosive charge. **2** any device by which an explosive charge is ignited. **3 blow a fuse.** See **blow**[1] (sense 12). ◆ *vb* **4** *(tr)* to provide or equip with such a fuse. [C17: from Italian *fuso* spindle, from Latin *fūsus*] ▸ **'fuseless** *adj*

fuse[2] (fjuːz) *vb* **1** to unite or become united by melting, esp. by the action of heat: *to fuse borax and copper sulphate at a high temperature.* **2** to become or cause to become liquid, esp. by the action of heat; melt. **3** to join or become combined; integrate. **4** *(tr)* to equip (an electric circuit, plug, etc.) with a fuse. **5** *Brit.* to fail or cause to fail as a result of the blowing of a fuse: *the lights fused.* ◆ *n* **6** a protective device for safeguarding electric circuits, etc., containing a wire that melts and breaks the circuit when the current exceeds a certain value. [C17: from Latin *fūsus* melted, cast, poured out, from *fundere* to pour out, shed; sense 5 influenced by FUSE[1]]

fuse box *n* a housing for electric fuses.

fusee *or* **fuzee** (fjuː'ziː) *n* **1** (in early clocks and watches) a spirally grooved spindle, functioning as an equalizing force on the unwinding of the mainspring. **2** a friction match with a large head, capable of remaining alight in a wind. **3** an explosive fuse. [C16: from French *fusée* spindleful of thread, from Old French *fus* spindle, from Latin *fūsus*]

fuselage ('fjuːzɪ,lɑːʒ) *n* the main body of an aircraft, excluding the wings, tailplane, and fin. [C20: from French, from *fuseler* to shape like a spindle, from Old French *fusel* spindle; see FUSEE]

Fuseli ('fjuːzəlɪ) *n* **Henry.** original name *Johann Heinrich Füssli.* 1741–1825, British painter, born in Switzerland. His paintings include *Nightmare* (1782).

fusel oil *or* **fusel** ('fjuːzᵊl) *n* a mixture of amyl alcohols, propanol, and butanol: a by-product in the distillation of fermented liquors used as a source of amyl alcohols. [C19: from German *Fusel* bad spirits]

Fushih *or* **Fu-shih** ('fuː'ʃiː) *n* another name for **Yanan.**

Fushun ('fuː'ʃʌn) *n* a city in NE China, in central Liaoning province near Shenyang: situated on one of the richest coalfields in the world; site of the largest thermal power plant in NE Asia. Pop.: 1 350 000 (1991 est.).

fusible ('fjuːzəbᵊl) *adj* capable of being fused or melted. ▸ **,fusi'bility** *or* **'fusibleness** *n* ▸ **'fusibly** *adv*

fusible metal *or* **alloy** *n* any of various alloys with low melting points that contain bismuth, lead, and tin. They are used as solders and in safety devices.

fusiform ('fjuːzɪ,fɔːm) *adj* elongated and tapering at both ends; spindle-shaped. [C18: from Latin *fūsus* spindle]

fusil[1] ('fjuːzɪl) *n* a light flintlock musket. [C16 (in the sense: steel for a tinderbox): from Old French *fuisil,* from Vulgar Latin *focīlis* (unattested), from Latin *focus* fire]

fusil[2] ('fjuːzɪl) *n Heraldry.* a charge shaped like a lengthened lozenge. [C15: from Old French *fusel,* ultimately from Latin *fūsus* spindle, FUSE[1] (the heraldic lozenge originally represented a spindle covered with tow for spinning)]

fusile ('fjuːzaɪl) *or* **fusil** *adj* **1** easily melted; fusible. **2** formed by casting or melting; founded. [C14: from Latin *fūsilis* molten, from *fundere* to pour out, melt]

fusilier (,fjuːzɪ'lɪə) *n* **1** (formerly) an infantryman armed with a light musket. **2** Also: **,fusi'leer. 2a** a soldier, esp. a private, serving in any of certain British or other infantry regiments. **2b** (*pl; cap. when part of a name*): *the Royal Welch Fusiliers.* [C17: from French; see FUSIL[1]]

fusillade (,fjuːzɪ'leɪd, -'lɑːd) *n* **1** a simultaneous or rapid continual discharge of firearms. **2** a sudden outburst, as of criticism. ◆ *vb* **3** *(tr)* to attack with a fusillade. [C19: from French, from *fusiller* to shoot; see FUSIL[1]]

fusion ('fjuːʒən) *n* **1** the act or process of fusing or melting together; union. **2** the state of being fused. **3** something produced by fusing. **4** See **nuclear fusion. 5** the merging of juxtaposed speech sounds, morphemes, or words. **6** a coalition of political parties or other groups, esp. to support common candidates at an election. **7** a kind of popular music that is a blend of two or more styles, such as jazz and funk. **8** *Psychol.* the processing by the mind of elements falling on the two eyes so that they yield a single percept. [C16: from Latin *fūsiō* a pouring out, melting, casting, from *fundere* to pour out, FOUND[3]]

fusion bomb *n* a type of bomb in which most of the energy is provided by nuclear fusion, esp. the fusion of hydrogen isotopes. Also called: **thermonuclear bomb, fission-fusion bomb.** See also **hydrogen bomb.**

fusionism ('fjuːʒəˌnɪzəm) *n* the favouring of coalitions among political groups. ▸ **'fusionist** *n, adj*

fusion reactor *n* a nuclear reactor in which a thermonuclear fusion reaction takes place.

fuss (fʌs) *n* **1** nervous activity or agitation, esp. when disproportionate or unnecessary. **2** complaint or objection: *he made a fuss over the bill.* **3** an exhibition of affection or admiration, esp. if excessive: *they made a great fuss over the new baby.* **4** a quarrel; dispute. ◆ *vb* **5** (*intr*) to worry unnecessarily. **6** (*intr*) to be excessively concerned over trifles. **7** (when *intr*, usually foll. by *over*) to show great or excessive concern, affection, etc. (for). **8** (*intr;* foll. by *with*) *Jamaican.* to quarrel violently. **9** (*tr*) to bother (a person). [C18: of uncertain origin] ▸ **'fusser** *n*

fusspot ('fʌsˌpɒt) *n Brit. informal.* a person who fusses unnecessarily. Also called (U.S.): **fuss-budget.**

fussy ('fʌsɪ) *adj* **fussier, fussiest. 1** inclined to fuss over minor points. **2** very particular about detail. **3** characterized by overelaborate detail: *the furniture was too fussy to be elegant.* ▸ **'fussily** *adv* ▸ **'fussiness** *n*

fustanella (ˌfʌstə'nɛlə) *or* **fustanelle** *n* a white knee-length pleated skirt worn by men in Greece and Albania. [C19: from Italian, from Modern Greek *phoustani,* probably from Italian *fustagno* FUSTIAN]

fustian ('fʌstɪən) *n* **1a** a hard-wearing fabric of cotton mixed with flax or wool with a slight nap. **1b** (*as modifier*): *a fustian jacket.* **2** pompous or pretentious talk or writing. ◆ *adj* **3** cheap; worthless. **4** pompous; bombastic. [C12: from Old French *fustaigne,* from Medieval Latin *fustāneum,* from Latin *fustis* cudgel]

fustic ('fʌstɪk) *n* **1** Also called: **old fustic.** a large tropical American moraceous tree, *Chlorophora tinctoria.* **2** the yellow dye obtained from the wood of this tree. **3** any of various trees or shrubs that yield a similar dye, esp. *Rhus cotinus* (**young fustic**), a European sumach. [C15: from French *fustoc,* from Spanish, from Arabic *fustuq,* from Greek *pistakē* pistachio tree]

fustigate ('fʌstɪˌgeɪt) *vb* (*tr*) *Archaic.* to beat; cudgel. [C17: from Late Latin *fūstīgāre* to cudgel to death, from Latin *fūstis* cudgel] ▸ **ˌfusti'gation** *n* ▸ **'fustiˌgator** *n* ▸ **ˌfusti'gatory** *adj*

fusty ('fʌstɪ) *adj* **-tier, -tiest. 1** smelling of damp or mould; musty. **2** old-fashioned in attitude. [C14: from *fust* wine cask, from Old French: cask, tree trunk, from Latin *fūstis* cudgel, club] ▸ **'fustily** *adv* ▸ **'fustiness** *n*

fut. *abbrev. for* future.

futhark, futharc ('fuːθɑːk) *or* **futhorc, futhork** ('fuːθɔːk) *n* a phonetic alphabet consisting of runes. [C19: from the first six letters: *f, u, th, a, r, k;* compare ALPHABET]

futile ('fjuːtaɪl) *adj* **1** having no effective result; unsuccessful. **2** pointless; unimportant; trifling. **3** inane or foolish: *don't be so futile!* [C16: from Latin *futtilis* pouring out easily, worthless, from *fundere* to pour out] ▸ **'futilely** *adv* ▸ **'futileness** *n*

futilitarian (fjuːˌtɪlɪ'tɛərɪən) *adj* **1** of or relating to the belief that human endeavour can serve no useful purpose. ◆ *n* **2** one who holds this belief. [C19: facetious coinage from FUTILE + UTILITARIAN] ▸ **fuˌtili'tarianˌism** *n*

futility (fjuː'tɪlɪtɪ) *n, pl* **-ties. 1** lack of effectiveness or success. **2** lack of purpose or meaning. **3** something futile.

futon (ˌfuː'tɒn) *n* a Japanese padded quilt, laid on the floor for use as a bed. [C19: from Japanese]

futtock ('fʌtək) *n Nautical.* one of the ribs in the frame of a wooden vessel. [C13: perhaps variant of *foothook*]

futtock plate *n Nautical.* a horizontal metal disc fixed at the top of a lower mast for holding the futtock shrouds.

futtock shroud *n Nautical.* any of several metal rods serving as a brace between the futtock plate on a lower mast and the topmast.

future ('fjuːtʃə) *n* **1** the time yet to come. **2** undetermined events that will occur in that time. **3** the condition of a person or thing at a later date: *the future of the school is undecided.* **4** likelihood of later improvement or advancement: *he has a future as a singer.* **5** *Grammar.* **5a** a tense of verbs used when the action or event described is to occur after the time of utterance. **5b** a verb in this tense. **6** **in future.** from now on; henceforth. ◆ *adj* **7** that is yet to come or be. **8** of or expressing time yet to come. **9** (*prenominal*) destined to become: *a future president.* **10** *Grammar.* in or denoting the future as a tense of verbs. ◆ See also **futures.** [C14: from Latin *fūtūrus* about to be, from *esse* to be] ▸ **'futureless** *adj*

future life *n* a life after death; afterlife.

future perfect *Grammar.* ◆ *adj* **1** denoting a tense of verbs describing an action that will have been performed by a certain time. In English this is formed with *will have* or *shall have* plus the past participle. ◆ *n* **2a** the future perfect tense. **2b** a verb in this tense.

futures ('fjuːtʃəz) *pl n* **a** commodities or other financial products bought or sold at an agreed price for delivery at a specified future date. See also **financial futures. b** (*as modifier*): *futures contract; futures market.*

future value *n* the value that a sum of money invested at compound interest will have after a specified period.

futurism ('fjuːtʃəˌrɪzəm) *n* an artistic movement that arose in Italy in 1909 to replace traditional aesthetic values with the characteristics of the machine age. ▸ **'futurist** *n, adj*

futuristic (ˌfjuːtʃə'rɪstɪk) *adj* **1** denoting or relating to design, technology, etc., that is thought likely to be current or fashionable at some future time; ultramodern. **2** of or relating to futurism. ▸ **ˌfutur'istically** *adv*

futurity (fjuː'tjʊərɪtɪ) *n, pl* **-ties. 1** a less common word for **future. 2** the quality of being in the future. **3** a future event.

futurology (ˌfjuːtʃə'rɒlədʒɪ) *n* the study or prediction of the future of mankind. ▸ **ˌfutur'ologist** *n*

fuze (fjuːz) *n Chiefly U.S.* a variant spelling of **fuse**[1].

fuzee (fjuː'ziː) *n* a variant spelling of **fusee.**

Fuzhou ('fuː'dʒəʊ), **Foochow,** *or* **Fuchou** *n* a port in SE China, capital of Fujian province on the Min Jiang: one of the original five treaty ports (1842). Pop.: 874 809 (1990 est.).

fuzz[1] (fʌz) *n* **1** a mass or covering of fine or curly hairs, fibres, etc. **2** a blur. ◆ *vb* **3** to make or become fuzzy. **4** to make or become indistinct; blur. [C17: perhaps from Low German *fussig* loose]

fuzz[2] (fʌz) *n* a slang word for **police** or **policeman.** [C20: of uncertain origin]

fuzz box *n Music.* an electronic device that breaks up the sound passing through it, used esp. by guitarists.

fuzzy ('fʌzɪ) *adj* **fuzzier, fuzziest. 1** of, resembling, or covered with fuzz. **2** indistinct; unclear or distorted. **3** not clearly thought out or expressed. **4** (of the hair) tightly curled or very wavy. **5** *Maths.* of or relating to a form of set theory in which set membership depends on a likelihood function: *fuzzy set; fuzzy logic.* **6** (of a computer program or system) designed to operate according to the principles of fuzzy logic, so as to be able to deal with data which is imprecise or has uncertain boundaries. ▸ **'fuzzily** *adv* ▸ **'fuzziness** *n*

fuzzy logic *n* a branch of logic designed to allow degrees of imprecision in reasoning and knowledge, typified by terms such as 'very', 'quite possibly', and 'unlikely', to be represented in such a way that the information can be processed by computer.

fuzzy-wuzzy ('fʌzɪˌwʌzɪ) *n, pl* **-ies** *or* **-y.** *Archaic, offensive slang.* a Black fuzzy-haired native of any of various countries.

fuzzy wuzzy angel *n Austral. informal.* any native of Papua New Guinea who assisted as a stretcher-bearer in World War II.

fv *abbrev. for* folio verso. [Latin: on the reverse (that is left-hand) page]

fwd *abbrev. for* forward.

f.w.d. *abbrev. for:* **1** four-wheel drive. **2** front-wheel drive.

f-word *n* **the** (*sometimes cap.*) a euphemistic way of referring to the word **fuck.** [from F(UCK) + WORD]

FX *Films, informal.* short for **special effects.** [C20: a phonetic respelling of EFFECTS]

-fy *suffix forming verbs.* to make or become: *beautify; simplify; liquefy.* [from Old French *-fier,* from Latin *-ficāre,* verbal ending formed from *-ficus* -FIC]

fyke (faɪk) *n U.S.* a fish trap consisting of a net suspended over a series of hoops, laid horizontally in the water. [C19: from Middle Dutch *fuycke*]

Fylde (faɪld) *n* a region in NW England in Lancashire between the Wyre and Ribble estuaries.

fylfot ('faɪlfɒt) *n* a rare word for **swastika.** [C16 (apparently meaning: a sign or device for the lower part or foot of a painted window): from *fillen* to FILL + *fot* FOOT]

Fyn (*Danish* fyːn) *n* the Danish name for **Funen.**

fyrd (fɪəd, faɪəd) *n History.* the local militia of an Anglo-Saxon shire, in which all freemen had to serve.

FYROM *abbrev. for* Former Yugoslav Republic of Macedonia.

FZS *abbrev. for* Fellow of the Zoological Society.

Gg

g *or* **G** (dʒiː) *n, pl* **g's, G's,** *or* **Gs. 1** the seventh letter and fifth consonant of the modern English alphabet. **2** a speech sound represented by this letter, in English usually either a voiced velar stop, as in *grass,* or a voiced palato-alveolar affricate, as in *page.*

g *symbol for:* **1** gallon(s). **2** gram(s). **3** acceleration of free fall (due to gravity). **4** grav. **5** *Chess.* See **algebraic notation.**

G *symbol for:* **1** *Music.* **1a** a note having a frequency of 392 hertz (**G above middle C**) or this value multiplied or divided by any power of 2; the fifth note of the scale of C major. **1b** a key, string, or pipe producing this note. **1c** the major or minor key having this note as its tonic. **2** gauss. **3** gravitational constant. **4** *Physics.* conductance. **5** *Biochem.* guanine. **6** German. **7** Gibbs function. **8** giga. **9** good. **10** *Slang, chiefly U.S.* grand (a thousand dollars or pounds). **11** (in Australia) **11a** general exhibition (used to describe a category of film certified as suitable for viewing by anyone). **11b** (*as modifier*): *a G film.*

G. *or* **g.** *abbrev. for:* **1** gauges. **2** gelding. **3** Gulf. **4** guilder(s). **5** guinea(s).

G3 *abbrev. for* Group of Three.

G5 *abbrev. for* Group of Five.

G7 *abbrev. for* Group of Seven.

G10 *abbrev. for* Group of Ten.

G24 *abbrev. for* Group of Twenty-Four.

G77 *abbrev. for* Group of Seventy-Seven.

Ga[1] *the chemical symbol for* gallium.

Ga[2] *or* **Gã** (gɑː) *n* **1** (*pl* **Ga, Gas** *or* **Gã, Gãs**) a member of a Negroid people of W Africa living chiefly in S Ghana. **2** the language of this people, belonging to the Kwa branch of the Niger-Congo family.

GA *abbrev. for:* **1** General Assembly (of the United Nations). **2** general average. **3** Georgia.

Ga. *abbrev. for* Georgia.

GAA (in Ireland) *abbrev. for* Gaelic Athletic Association.

gab[1] (gæb) *Informal.* ◆ *vb* **gabs, gabbing, gabbed. 1** (*intr*) to talk excessively or idly, esp. about trivial matters; gossip; chatter. ◆ *n* **2** idle or trivial talk. **3 gift of the gab.** ability to speak effortlessly, glibly, or persuasively. [C18: variant of Northern dialect *gob* mouth, probably from Irish Gaelic *gob* beak, mouth] ▸ **'gabber** *n*

gab[2] (gæb) *n* **1** a hook or open notch in a rod or lever that drops over the spindle of a valve to form a temporary connection for operating the valve. **2** a pointed tool used in masonry. [C18: probably from Flemish *gabbe* notch, gash]

GABA ('gæbə) *n acronym for* gamma-aminobutyric acid: a biologically active substance found in plants and in brain and other animal tissues; it is a neurotransmitter that inhibits activation of neurones.

Gabar ('gɑːbə), **Gheber,** *or* **Ghebre** *n* **1** a member of an Iranian religious sect practising a modern version of Zoroastrianism. ◆ *adj* **2** of, relating to, or characterizing the Gabar sect or its beliefs.

gabardine *or* **gaberdine** ('gæbəˌdiːn, ˌgæbə'diːn) *n* **1** a twill-weave worsted, cotton, or spun-rayon fabric. **2** an ankle-length loose coat or frock worn by men, esp. by Jews, in the Middle Ages. **3** any of various other garments made of gabardine, esp. a child's raincoat. [C16: from Old French *gauvardine* pilgrim's garment, from Middle High German *wallewart* pilgrimage; related to Spanish *gabardina*]

gabble ('gæb^{ə}l) *vb* **1** to utter (words, etc.) rapidly and indistinctly; jabber. **2** (*intr*) (of geese and some other birds or animals) to utter rapid cackling noises. ◆ *n* **3** rapid and indistinct speech or noises. [C17: from Middle Dutch *gabbelen,* of imitative origin] ▸ **'gabbler** *n*

gabbro ('gæbrəʊ) *n, pl* **-bros.** a dark coarse-grained basic plutonic igneous rock consisting of plagioclase feldspar, pyroxene, and often olivine. [C19: from Italian, probably from Latin *glaber* smooth, bald] ▸ **gab'broic** *or* **ˌgabbro'itic** *adj*

gabby ('gæbɪ) *adj* **-bier, -biest.** *Informal.* inclined to chatter; talkative.

gabelle (gæ'bɛl) *n French history.* a salt tax levied until 1790. [C15: from Old Italian *gabella,* from Arabic *qabālah* tribute, from *qabala* he received] ▸ **ga'belled** *adj*

gaberdine ('gæbəˌdiːn, ˌgæbə'diːn) *n* a variant spelling of **gabardine.**

gaberlunzie (ˌgæbə'lʌnzɪ, -'luːnjɪ) *n Scot. archaic or literary.* a wandering beggar. Also called: **gaberlunzie-man.** [C16: variant of earlier *gaberlungy*]

Gaberones (ˌgæbə'rəʊnɛs) *n* the former name for **Gaborone.**

Gabès ('gɑːbɛs; *French* gabɛs) *n* **1** a port in E Tunisia. Pop.: 98 800 (1994). **2 Gulf of.** an inlet of the Mediterranean on the E coast of Tunisia. Ancient name: **Syrtis Minor.** Arabic name: **Qabis.**

gabfest ('gæbfɛst) *n Informal, chiefly U.S. and Canadian.* **1** prolonged gossiping or conversation. **2** an informal gathering for conversation. [C19: from GAB[1] + FEST]

gabion ('geɪbɪən) *n* **1** a cylindrical metal container filled with stones, used in the construction of underwater foundations. **2** a wickerwork basket filled with stones or earth, used (esp. formerly) as part of a fortification. [C16: from French: basket, from Italian *gabbione,* from *gabbia* cage, from Latin *cavea;* see CAGE]

gabionade *or* **gabionnade** (ˌgeɪbɪə'neɪd) *n* **1** a row of gabions submerged in a waterway, stream, river, etc., to control the flow of water. **2** a fortification constructed of gabions. [C18: from French; see GABION]

gable ('geɪb^{ə}l) *n* **1** the triangular upper part of a wall between the sloping ends of a pitched roof (**gable roof**). **2** a triangular ornamental feature in the form of a gable, esp. as used over a door or window. **3** the triangular wall on both ends of a gambrel roof. [C14: Old French *gable,* probably from Old Norse *gafl;* related to Old English *geafol* fork, Old High German *gibil* gable] ▸ **'gabled** *adj* ▸ **'gable-ˌlike** *adj*

Gable ('geɪb^{ə}l) *n* **(William) Clark.** 1901–60, U.S. film actor. His films include *It Happened One Night* (1934), *San Francisco* (1936), *Gone with the Wind* (1939), *Mogambo* (1953), and *The Misfits* (1960).

gable end *n* the end wall of a building on the side which is topped by a gable.

gablet ('geɪblɪt) *n* a small gable.

gable window *n* a window positioned in a gable or having a small gable over it.

Gabo ('gɑːbəʊ, -bə) *n* **Naum** (naʊm), original name *Naum Neemia Pevsner.* 1890–1977, U.S. sculptor, born in Russia: a leading constructivist.

Gabon (gə'bɒn; *French* gabɔ̃) *n* a republic in W central Africa, on the Atlantic: settled by the French in 1839; made part of the French Congo in 1888; became independent in 1960; almost wholly forested. Official language: French. Religion: Christian majority; significant animist minority. Currency: franc. Capital: Libreville. Pop.: 1 208 000 (1998 est.). Area: 267 675 sq. km (103 350 sq. miles). ▸ **Gabonese** (ˌgæbə'niːz) *adj, n*

gaboon (gə'buːn) *n* the dark mahogany-like wood from a western and central African burseraceous tree, *Aucoumea klaineana,* used in plywood, for furniture, and as a veneer. [C20: altered from GABON]

gaboon viper *n* a large venomous viper, *Bitis gabonica,* that occurs in African rainforests. It has brown and purple markings and hornlike projections on its snout.

Gabor (gə'bɔː) *n* **Dennis.** 1900–79, British electrical engineer, born in Hungary. He invented holography: Nobel prize for physics 1971.

Gaborone (ˌgæbə'rəʊnɪ) *n* the capital of Botswana (since 1964), in the extreme southeast. Pop.: 182 000 (1995 est.). Former name: **Gaberones.**

Gabriel[1] ('geɪbrɪəl) *n Bible.* one of the archangels, the messenger of good news (Daniel 8:16–26; Luke 1:11–20, 26–38).

Gabriel[2] (*French* gabriɛl) *n* **Jacques-Ange** (ʒakɑ̃ʒ). 1698–1782, French architect: designed the Petit Trianon at Versailles.

Gabrieli (*Italian* gabrɪ'ɛli) *or* **Gabrielli** *n* **1 Andrea** (an'drɛːa). 1520–86, Italian organist and composer; chief organist of St Mark's, Venice. **2** his nephew, **Giovanni** (dʒo'vanni). 1558–1612, Italian organist and composer.

gaby ('geɪbɪ) *n, pl* **-bies.** *Archaic or dialect.* a simpleton. [C18: of unknown origin]

gad[1] (gæd) *vb* **gads, gadding, gadded. 1** (*intr;* often foll. by *about* or *around*) to go out in search of pleasure, esp. in an aimless manner; gallivant. ◆ *n* **2** carefree adventure (esp. in the phrase **on** *or* **upon the gad**). [C15: back formation from obsolete *gadling* companion, from Old English, from *gæd* fellowship; related to Old High German *gatuling*] ▸ **'gadder** *n*

gad[2] (gæd) *n* **1** *Mining.* a short chisel-like instrument for breaking rock or coal from the face. **2** a goad for driving cattle. **3** a western U.S. word for **spur** (sense 1). ◆ *vb* **gads, gadding, gadded. 4** (*tr*) *Mining.* to break up or loosen with a gad. [C13: from Old Norse *gaddr* spike; related to Old High German *gart,* Gothic *gazds* spike]

Gad[1] (gæd) *n, interj* an archaic euphemism for **God:** used as or in an oath.

Gad[2] (gæd) *n Old Testament.* **1a** Jacob's sixth son, whose mother was Zilpah, Leah's maid. **1b** the Israelite tribe descended from him. **1c** the territory of this tribe, lying to the east of the Jordan and extending southwards from the Sea of Galilee. **2** a prophet and admonisher of David (I Samuel 22; II Samuel 24).

gadabout ('gædəˌbaʊt) *n Informal.* a person who restlessly seeks amusement.

Gadarene ('gædəˌriːn) *adj* relating to or engaged in a headlong rush. [C19: via Late Latin from Greek *Gadarēnos,* of Gadara (Palestine), alluding to the Biblical Gadarene swine (Matthew 8:28ff.)]

Gaddafi *or* **Qaddafi** (gə'dɑːfɪ) *n* **Mu'ammar Muhammad al-** ('məʊəˌmɑː æl). born 1942, Libyan army officer and statesman; head of state from 1969.

gadfly ('gædˌflaɪ) *n, pl* **-flies. 1** any of various large dipterous flies, esp. the horsefly, that annoy livestock by sucking their blood. **2** a constantly irritating or harassing person. [C16: from GAD[2] (sting) + FLY[2]]

gadget ('gædʒɪt) *n* **1** a small mechanical device or appliance. **2** any object that is interesting for its ingenuity or novelty rather than for its practical use. [C19: perhaps from French *gâchette* lock catch, trigger, diminutive of *gâche* staple] ▸ **'gadgety** *adj*

gadgeteer (ˌgædʒɪ'tɪə) *n* a person who delights in gadgetry.

gadgetry ('gædʒɪtrɪ) *n* **1** gadgets collectively. **2** use of or preoccupation with gadgets and their design.

Gadhelic (gæd'hɛlɪk) *n, adj* another term for **Goidelic.** [C19: from Old Irish *Gaídelc, Goídelc* the Gaelic language]

gadid ('geɪdɪd) *n* **1** any marine teleost fish of the family *Gadidae,* which includes the cod, haddock, whiting, and pollack. ◆ *adj* **2** of, relating to, or belonging to the *Gadidae.* [C19: see GADOID]

gadoid ('geɪdɔɪd) *adj* **1** of, relating to, or belonging to the *Anacanthini,* an order of marine soft-finned fishes typically having the pectoral and pelvic fins close together and small cycloid scales. The group includes gadid fishes and hake. ◆ *n* **2** any gadoid fish. **[C19:** from New Latin *Gadidae,* from *gadus* cod; see -OID**]**

gadolinite ('gædəlɪˌnaɪt) *n* a rare brown or black mineral consisting of a silicate of iron, beryllium, and yttrium in monoclinic crystalline form. Formula: $2BeO.FeO.Y_2O_3.2SiO_2$. Also called: **ytterbite. [C19:** named after Johan *Gadolin* (1760–1852), Finnish mineralogist**]**

gadolinium (ˌgædə'lɪnɪəm) *n* a ductile malleable silvery-white ferromagnetic element of the lanthanide series of metals: occurs principally in monazite and bastnaesite. Symbol: Gd; atomic no.: 64; atomic wt.: 157.25; valency: 3; relative density: 7.901; melting pt.: 1313±°C; boiling pt.: 3273°C (approx.). **[C19:** New Latin, from GADOLINITE**]** ► ˌ**gado'linic** *adj*

gadroon *or* **godroon** (gə'druːn) *n* **1** a moulding composed of a series of convex flutes and curves joined to form a decorative pattern, used esp. as an edge to silver articles. **2** *Architect.* a carved ornamental moulding having a convex cross section. **[C18:** from French *godron,* perhaps from Old French *godet* cup, goblet, drinking vessel**]** ► **ga'drooned** *or* **go'drooned** *adj*

Gadsden Purchase ('gædzdən) *n* an area of about 77 000 sq. km (30 000 sq. miles) in present-day Arizona and New Mexico, bought by the U.S. from Mexico for 10 million dollars in 1853. The purchase was negotiated by James Gadsden (1788–1858), U.S. diplomat.

gadwall ('gædˌwɔːl) *n, pl* **-walls** *or* **-wall.** a duck, *Anas strepera,* related to the mallard. The male has a grey body and black tail. **[C17:** of unknown origin**]**

gadzooks (gæd'zuːks) *interj Archaic.* a mild oath. **[C17:** perhaps from *God's hooks* (the nails of the cross); see GAD[1]**]**

gae (ge) *vb* **gaes, gaun, gaed, gane.** a Scot. word for **go**[1].

Gaea ('dʒiːə), **Gaia,** *or* **Ge** *n Greek myth.* the goddess of the earth, who bore Uranus and by him Oceanus, Cronus and the Titans. **[**from Greek *gaia* earth**]**

Gaekwar *or* **Gaikwar** ('gaɪkwɑː) *n History.* the title of the ruler of the former native state of Baroda in India. **[C19:** from Marathi *Gaekvād,* literally: Guardian of the Cows, from Sanskrit *gauh* cow + *-vad* guardian**]**

Gael (geɪl) *n* a person who speaks a Gaelic language, esp. a Highland Scot or an Irishman. **[C19:** from Gaelic *Gaidheal;* related to Old Irish *goidel,* Old Welsh *gwyddel* Irishman**]** ► **'Gaeldom** *n*

Gaelic ('geɪlɪk, 'gæl-) *n* **1** any of the closely related languages of the Celts in Ireland, Scotland, or (formerly) the Isle of Man. Compare **Goidelic.** ◆ *adj* **2** of, denoting, or relating to the Celtic people of Ireland, Scotland, or the Isle of Man or their language or customs.

Gaelic coffee *n* another name for **Irish coffee.**

Gaelic football *n* an Irish game played with 15 men on each side and goals resembling rugby posts with a net on the bottom part. Players are allowed to kick, punch, and bounce the ball and attempt to get it over the bar or in the net.

Gaeltacht ('geːltəxt) *or* **Gaedhealtacht** ('geɪlˌtæxt, 'gæl-) *n* any of the regions in Ireland in which Irish Gaelic is the vernacular speech. The form *Gaeltacht* is sometimes also used to mean the region of Scotland in which Scottish Gaelic is spoken. See also **Gaidhealtachd. [C20:** from Irish Gaelic**]**

gaff[1] (gæf) *n* **1** *Angling.* a stiff pole with a stout prong or hook attached for landing large fish. **2** *Nautical.* a boom hoisted aft of a mast to support a gaffsail. **3** a metal spur fixed to the leg of a gamecock. ◆ *vb* **4** *(tr) Angling.* to hook or land (a fish) with a gaff. **5** *(tr) Slang.* to cheat; hoax. **[C13:** from French *gaffe,* from Provençal *gaf* boathook**]**

gaff[2] (gæf) *n* **1** *Slang.* foolish talk; nonsense. **2 blow the gaff.** *Brit. slang.* to divulge a secret. **3 stand the gaff.** *Slang, chiefly U.S. and Canadian.* to endure ridicule, difficulties, etc. **[C19:** of unknown origin**]**

gaff[3] (gæf) *n Brit. slang, archaic.* **1** a person's home, esp. a flat. **2** Also called: **penny-gaff.** a cheap or low-class place of entertainment, esp. a cheap theatre or music hall in Victorian England. **[C18:** of unknown origin**]**

gaffe (gæf) *n* a social blunder, esp. a tactless remark. **[C19:** from French**]**

gaffer ('gæfə) *n* **1** an old man, esp. one living in the country: often used affectionately or patronizingly. Compare **gammer. 2** *Informal, chiefly Brit.* a boss, foreman, or owner of a factory, mine, etc. **3** the senior electrician on a television or film set. **[C16:** alteration of GODFATHER**]**

gaffer tape *n Brit.* strong adhesive tape used in electrical repairs.

gaff-rigged *adj* (of a sailing vessel) rigged with one or more gaffsails.

gaffsail ('gæfˌseɪl, -səl) *n* a quadrilateral fore-and-aft sail on a sailing vessel.

gaff-topsail *n* a sail set above a gaffsail.

gag[1] (gæg) *vb* **gags, gagging, gagged. 1** *(tr)* to stop up (a person's mouth), esp. with a piece of cloth, etc., to prevent him from speaking or crying out. **2** *(tr)* to suppress or censor (free expression, information, etc.). **3** to retch or cause to retch. **4** *(intr)* to struggle for breath; choke. **5** *(tr)* to hold (the jaws) of (a person or animal) apart with a surgical gag. **6** *(tr)* to apply a gag-bit to (a horse). ◆ *n* **7** a piece of cloth, rope, etc., stuffed into or tied across the mouth. **8** any restraint on or suppression of information, free speech, etc. **9** a surgical device for keeping the jaws apart, as during a tonsillectomy. **10** *Parliamentary procedure.* another word for **closure** (sense 4). **[C15** *gaggen;* perhaps imitative of a gasping sound**]**

gag[2] (gæg) *Informal.* ◆ *n* **1** a joke or humorous story, esp. one told by a professional comedian. **2** a hoax, practical joke, etc.: *he did it for a gag.* ◆ *vb* **gags, gagging, gagged. 3** *(intr)* to tell jokes or funny stories, as comedians in nightclubs, etc. **4** (often foll. by *up*) *Theatre.* **4a** to interpolate lines or business not in the actor's stage part, usually comic and improvised. **4b** to perform a stage jest, either spoken or based on movement. **[C19:** perhaps special use of GAG[1]**]**

gaga ('gɑːgɑː) *adj Informal.* **1** senile; doting. **2** slightly crazy. **[C20:** from French, of imitative origin**]**

Gagarin (*Russian* ga'garin) *n* **Yuri** ('jurɪ). 1934–68, Soviet cosmonaut: made the first manned space flight (1961).

Gagauzi (gə'gɔːzɪ) *n* a language spoken chiefly in the Ukraine, on the NW coast of the Black Sea, belonging to the Turkic branch of the Altaic family.

gag-bit *n* a powerful type of bit used in breaking horses.

gage[1] (geɪdʒ) *n* **1** something deposited as security against the fulfilment of an obligation; pledge. **2** (formerly) a glove or other object thrown down to indicate a challenge to combat. ◆ *vb* **3** *(tr) Archaic.* to stake, pledge, or wager. **[C14:** from Old French *gage,* of Germanic origin; compare Gothic *wadi* pledge**]**

gage[2] (geɪdʒ) *n* short for **greengage.**

gage[3] (geɪdʒ) *n U.S. dated slang.* marijuana. **[C20:** of uncertain origin; compare GANJA**]**

gage[4] (geɪdʒ) *n, vb U.S.* a variant spelling (esp. in technical senses) of **gauge.**

Gage (geɪdʒ) *n* **Thomas.** 1721–87, British general and governor in America; commander in chief of British forces at Bunker Hill (1775).

gager ('geɪdʒə) *n* a variant spelling of **gauger.**

gagger ('gægə) *n* **1** a person or thing that gags. **2** a wedge for a core in a casting mould.

gaggle ('gæg^əl) *vb* **1** *(intr)* (of geese) to cackle. ◆ *n* **2** a flock of geese. **3** *Informal.* a disorderly group of people. **4** a gabbling or cackling sound. **[C14:** of Germanic origin; compare Old Norse *gagl* gosling, Dutch *gaggelen* to cackle, all of imitative origin**]**

gag rule *or* **resolution** *n U.S.* any closure regulation adopted by a deliberative body.

gahnite ('gɑːnaɪt) *n* a dark green mineral of the spinel group consisting of zinc aluminium oxide. Formula: $ZnAl_2O_4$. **[C19:** named after J. G. *Gahn* (1745–1818), Swedish chemist; see -ITE[1]**]**

Gaia ('geɪə) *n* a variant of **Gaea.**

Gaia hypothesis *or* **theory** ('gaɪə) *n* the theory that the earth and everything on it constitutes a single self-regulating living entity. **[C20:** from *Gaia,* variant of GAEA**]**

Gaidhealtachd ('geɪlˌtæxt, 'gælˌtaxg) *n* **1** the area of Scotland in which Scottish Gaelic is the vernacular speech. See also **Gaeltacht. 2** the culture and traditions of the Scottish Gaels. **[**Scottish Gaelic**]**

gaiety ('geɪətɪ) *n, pl* **-ties. 1** the state or condition of being merry, bright, or lively. **2** festivity; merrymaking. ◆ Also (esp. U.S.): **gayety.**

USAGE See at **gay.**

Gaikwar ('gaɪkwɑː) *n* a variant spelling of **Gaekwar.**

Gaillard Cut (gɪl'jɑːd, 'geɪlɑːd) *n* the SE section of the Panama Canal, cut through Culebra Mountain. Length: about 13 km (8 miles). Former name: **Culebra Cut. [C19:** named after David Du Bose *Gaillard* (1859–1913), U.S. army engineer in charge of the work**]**

gaillardia (geɪ'lɑːdɪə) *n* any plant of the North American genus *Gaillardia,* having ornamental flower heads with yellow or red rays and purple discs: family *Compositae* (composites). **[C19:** from New Latin, named after *Gaillard* de Marentonneau, 18th-century French amateur botanist**]**

gaily ('geɪlɪ) *adv* **1** in a lively manner; cheerfully. **2** with bright colours; showily.

gain[1] (geɪn) *vb* **1** *(tr)* to acquire (something desirable); obtain. **2** *(tr)* to win in competition: *to gain the victory.* **3** to increase, improve, or advance: *the car gained speed; the shares gained in value.* **4** *(tr)* to earn (a wage, living, etc.). **5** *(intr;* usually foll. by *on* or *upon)* **5a** to get nearer (to) or catch up (on). **5b** to get farther away (from). **6** *(tr)* (esp. of ships) to get to; reach: *the steamer gained port.* **7** (of a timepiece) to operate too fast, so as to indicate a time ahead of the true time or to run fast by a specified amount: *this watch gains; it gains ten minutes a day.* **8 gain ground.** to make progress or obtain an advantage. **9 gain time. 9a** to obtain extra time by a delay or postponement. **9b** (of a timepiece) to operate too fast. ◆ *n* **10** something won, acquired, earned, etc.; profit; advantage. **11** an increase in size, amount, etc. **12** the act of gaining; attainment; acquisition. **13** Also called: **amplification.** *Electronics.* the ratio of the output signal of an amplifier to the input signal, usually measured in decibels. ◆ See also **gains. [C15:** from Old French *gaaignier,* of Germanic origin; related to Old High German *weidenen* to forage, hunt**]** ► **'gainable** *adj*

gain[2] (geɪn) *n* **1** a notch, mortise, or groove, esp. one cut to take the flap of a butt hinge. ◆ *vb* **2** *(tr)* to cut a gain or gains in. **[C17:** of obscure origin**]**

GAIN (geɪn) *n* (in Canada) *abbrev. or acronym for* Guaranteed Annual Income.

gainer ('geɪnə) *n* **1** a person or thing that gains. **2** Also called: **full gainer.** a type of dive in which the diver leaves the board facing forward and completes a full backward somersault to enter the water feet first with his back to the diving board. Compare **half gainer.**

gainful ('geɪnfʊl) *adj* profitable; lucrative: *gainful employment.* ► **'gainfully** *adv* ► **'gainfulness** *n*

gainings ('geɪnɪŋz) *pl n* profits or earnings.

gainly ('geɪnlɪ) *Obsolete or dialect.* ◆ *adj* **1** graceful or well-formed; shapely. ◆ *adv* **2** conveniently or suitably. ► **'gainliness** *n*

gains (geɪnz) *pl n* profits or winnings: *ill-gotten gains.*

gainsay (geɪn'seɪ) *vb* **-says, -saying, -said.** *(tr) Archaic or literary.* to deny (an allegation, a statement, etc.); contradict. **[C13** *gainsaien,* from *gain-* AGAINST + *saien* to SAY[1]**]** ► **gain'sayer** *n*

Gainsborough ('geɪnzbərə, -brə) *n* **Thomas.** 1727–88, English painter, noted particularly for his informal portraits and for his naturalistic landscapes.

'gainst *or* **gainst** (genst, geɪnst) *prep Poetic.* short for **against.**

Gaiseric ('gaɪzərɪk) *n* a variant of **Genseric.**

gait (geɪt) *n* **1** manner of walking or running; bearing. **2** (used esp. of horses and dogs) the pattern of footsteps at various speeds, as the walk, trot, canter, etc., each pattern being distinguished by a particular rhythm and footfall. ◆ *vb* **3** *(tr)* to teach (a horse) a particular gait. **[C16:** variant of GATE[1]**]**

-gaited ('geɪtɪd) *adj (in combination)* having a gait as specified: *slow-gaited.*

gaiter ('geɪtə) *n (often pl)* **1** a cloth or leather covering for the leg or ankle buttoned on one side and usually strapped under the foot. **2** Also called: **spat.** a similar covering extending from the ankle to the instep. **3** a waterproof covering for the ankle worn by climbers and walkers to prevent snow, mud, or gravel entering over the top of the boot. **[C18:** from French *guêtre,* probably of Germanic origin and related to WRIST**]** ▸ **'gaiterless** *adj*

Gaitskell ('geɪtskɪl) *n* **Hugh (Todd Naylor).** 1906–63, British politician; leader of the Labour Party (1955–63).

Gaius ('gaɪəs) *or* **Caius** *n* **1** ?110–?180 A.D., Roman jurist. His *Institutes* were later used as the basis for those of Justinian. **2 Gaius Caesar.** See **Caligula.**

gal[1] (gæl) *n Slang.* a girl.

gal[2] (gæl) *n* a unit of acceleration equal to 1 centimetre per second per second. **[C20:** named after GALILEO**]**

gal. *or* **gall.** *abbrev. for* gallon.

Gal. *Bible. abbrev. for* Galatians.

gala ('gɑːlə, 'geɪlə) *n* **1a** a celebration; festive occasion. **1b** (*as modifier*)*: a gala occasion.* **2** *Chiefly Brit.* a sporting occasion involving competitions in several events: *a swimming gala.* **[C17:** from French or Italian, from Old French *gale* pleasure, from Old French *galer* to make merry, probably of Germanic origin; compare GALLANT**]**

galactagogue (gə'læktəˌgɒg) *adj* **1** inducing milk secretion. ◆ *n* **2** a galactagogue agent. **[C19:** from Greek *gala, galaktos,* milk + -AGOGUE**]**

galactic (gə'læktɪk) *adj* **1** *Astronomy.* of or relating to a galaxy, esp. the Galaxy: *the galactic plane.* **2** *Med.* of or relating to milk. **[C19:** from Greek *galaktikos;* see GALAXY**]**

galactic equator *or* **circle** *n* the great circle on the celestial sphere containing the galactic plane.

galactic halo *n Astronomy.* a spheroidal aggregation of globular clusters, individual stars, dust, and gas that surrounds the Galaxy.

galactic plane *n* the plane passing through the spiral arms of the Galaxy.

galactic poles *pl n* the two points on the celestial sphere, diametrically opposite each other, that can be joined by an imaginary line perpendicular to the galactic plane.

galacto- *or before a vowel* **galact-** *combining form.* milk or milky: *galactometer.* **[**from Greek *galakt-, gala***]**

galactometer (ˌgæləkˈtɒmɪtə) *n* an instrument, similar to a hydrometer, for measuring the relative density of milk. It is used to determine the fat content. ▸ **ˌgalac'tometry** *n*

galactopoietic (gəˌlæktəʊpɔɪ'ɛtɪk) *adj* **1** inducing or increasing the secretion of milk. ◆ *n* **2** a galactopoietic agent. ▸ **galactopoiesis** (gəˌlæktəʊpɔɪ'iːsɪs) *n*

galactose (gə'læktəʊz, -əʊs) *n* a white water-soluble monosaccharide found in lactose. Formula: $C_6H_{12}O_6$.

galago (gə'lɑːgəʊ) *n, pl* **-gos.** another name for **bushbaby. [C19:** from New Latin, perhaps from Wolof *golokh* monkey**]**

galah (gə'lɑː) *n* **1** an Australian cockatoo, *Kakatoe roseicapilla,* having grey wings, back, and crest and a pink body. **2** *Austral. slang.* a fool or simpleton. **[C19:** from a native Australian language**]**

Galahad ('gæləˌhæd) *n* **1 Sir.** (in Arthurian legend) the most virtuous knight of the Round Table, destined to regain the Holy Grail; son of Lancelot and Elaine. **2** a pure or noble man.

galangal (gə'læŋgᵊl) *n* **1** another name for **galingale. 2** a zingiberaceous plant, *Alpinia officinarum,* of China and the East Indies. **3** the pungent aromatic root of this plant, dried and used as a seasoning and in medicine.

galant (gə'lɑːnt) *n* an 18th-century style of music characterized by homophony and elaborate ornamentation. **[C17:** from Old French *galant,* from *galer* to make merry, from *gale* enjoyment, pleasure**]**

galantine ('gælənˌtiːn) *n* a cold dish of meat or poultry, which is boned, cooked, stuffed, then pressed into a neat shape and glazed. **[C14:** from Old French, from Medieval Latin *galatina,* probably from Latin *gelātus* frozen, set; see GELATINE**]**

galanty show (gə'læntɪ) *n* (formerly) a pantomime shadow play, esp. one in miniature using figures cut from paper. **[C19:** perhaps from Italian *galante* GALLANT**]**

Galápagos Islands (gə'læpəgəs; *Spanish* ga'lapaɣos) *pl n* a group of 15 islands in the Pacific west of Ecuador, of which they form a province: discovered (1535) by the Spanish; main settlement on San Cristóbal. Pop.: 13 976 (1996 est.). Area: 7844 sq. km (3028 sq. miles). Official Spanish name: **Archipiélago de Colón.**

Galashiels (ˌgælə'ʃiːlz) *n* a town in SE Scotland, in central Scottish Borders. Pop.: 13 753 (1997).

Galata ('gælətə) *n* a port in NW Turkey, a suburb and the chief business section of Istanbul.

galatea (ˌgælə'tɪə) *n* a strong twill-weave cotton fabric, striped or plain, for clothing. **[C19:** named after the man-of-war H.M.S. *Galatea* (the fabric was at one time in demand for children's sailor suits)**]**

Galatea (ˌgælə'tɪə) *n Greek myth.* a statue of a maiden brought to life by Aphrodite in response to the prayers of the sculptor Pygmalion, who had fallen in love with his creation.

Galaţi (*Romanian* ga'latsj) *n* an inland port in SE Romania, on the River Danube. Pop.: 326 728 (1994 est.).

Galatia (gə'leɪʃə, -ʃɪə) *n* an ancient region in central Asia Minor, conquered by Gauls 278–277 B.C.: later a Roman province. ▸ **Ga'latian** *adj, n*

Galatians (gə'leɪʃənz, -ʃɪənz) *n* (*functioning as sing*) a book of the New Testament (in full **The Epistle of Paul the Apostle to the Galatians**).

galaxy ('gæləksɪ) *n, pl* **-axies. 1** any of a vast number of star systems held together by gravitational attraction in an asymmetric shape (an **irregular galaxy**) or, more usually, in a symmetrical shape (a **regular galaxy**), which is either a spiral or an ellipse. Former names: **island universe, extragalactic nebula. 2** a splendid gathering, esp. one of famous or distinguished people. Related adj: **galactic. [C14** (in the sense: the Milky Way), from Medieval Latin *galaxia,* from Latin *galaxias,* from Greek, from *gala* milk; related to Latin *lac* milk**]**

Galaxy ('gæləksɪ) *n* **the.** the spiral galaxy, approximately 100 000 light years in diameter, that contains the solar system about three fifths of the distance from its centre. Also called: the **Milky Way System.** See also **Magellanic Cloud.**

Galba ('gælbə) *n* **Servius Sulpicius** ('sɜːvɪəs sʌl'pɪʃəs). ?3 B.C.–69 A.D., Roman emperor (68–69) after the assassination of Nero.

galbanum ('gælbənəm) *n* a bitter aromatic gum resin extracted from any of several Asian umbelliferous plants of the genus *Ferula,* esp. *F. galbaniflua,* and used in incense and medicinally as a counterirritant. **[C14:** from Latin, from Greek *khalbanē,* from Hebrew *helbenāh***]**

Galbraith (gæl'breɪθ) *n* **John Kenneth.** born 1908, U.S. economist and diplomat born in Canada; author of *The Affluent Society* (1958) and *The New Industrial State* (1967). ▸ **Gal'braithian** *adj*

gale[1] (geɪl) *n* **1** a strong wind, specifically one of force seven to ten on the Beaufort scale or from 45 to 90 kilometres per hour. **2** (*often pl*) a loud outburst, esp. of laughter. **3** *Archaic and poetic.* a gentle breeze. **[C16:** of unknown origin**]**

gale[2] (geɪl) *n* short for **sweet gale. [**Old English *gagel;* related to Middle Low German *gagel***]**

galea ('geɪlɪə) *n, pl* **-leae** (-lɪˌiː). a part or organ shaped like a helmet or hood, such as the petals of certain flowers. **[C18:** from Latin: helmet**]** ▸ **'galeˌate** *or* **'galeˌated** *adj* ▸ **'galeiˌform** *adj*

Galen ('geɪlən) *n* Latin name *Claudius Galenus.* ?130–?200 A.D., Greek physician, anatomist, and physiologist. He codified existing medical knowledge and his authority continued until the Renaissance.

galena (gə'liːnə) *or* **galenite** (gə'liːnaɪt) *n* a grey mineral, found in hydrothermal veins. It is the chief source of lead. Composition: lead sulphide. Formula: PbS. Crystal structure: cubic. **[C17:** from Latin: lead ore, dross left after melting lead**]**

Galenic (geɪ'lɛnɪk, gə-) *adj* of or relating to Galen or his teachings or methods.

galenical (geɪ'lɛnɪkᵊl, gə-) *Pharmacol.* ◆ *n* **1** any drug obtained from plant or animal tissue, esp. vegetables, rather than being chemically synthesized. ◆ *adj* **2** denoting or belonging to this group of drugs. **[C17:** after GALEN**]**

Galenism ('geɪlɪˌnɪzəm) *n* a system of medicine based on the 84 surviving technical treatises of Galen, including the theory of the four bodily humours. ▸ **'Galenist** *adj, n*

galère *French.* (galɛr) *n* **1** a group of people having a common interest, esp. a coterie of undesirable people. **2** an unpleasant situation. **[C18:** literally: a galley**]**

Galerius (gə'lɛərɪəs) *n* full name *Gaius Galerius Valerius Maximianus.* ?250–311 A.D., Eastern Roman Emperor (305–311): noted for his persecution of Christians.

Galibi (gɑː'liːbɪ) *n* **1** (*pl* **-bi** *or* **-bis**) a member of an American Indian people of French Guiana. **2** the language of this people, belonging to the Carib family.

Galicia *n* **1** (gə'lɪʃɪə, -'lɪʃə). a region of E central Europe on the N side of the Carpathians, now in SE Poland and the Ukraine. **2** (*Spanish* ga'liθja). an autonomous region and former kingdom of NW Spain, on the Bay of Biscay and the Atlantic. Pop.: 2 742 622 (1996 est.)

Galician (gə'lɪʃɪən, -ʃən) *adj* **1** of or relating to Galicia in E central Europe. **2** of or relating to Galicia in NW Spain. ◆ *n* **3** a native or inhabitant of either Galicia. **4** the Romance language or dialect of Spanish Galicia, sometimes regarded as a dialect of Spanish, although historically it is more closely related to Portuguese.

Galilean[1] (ˌgælɪ'liːən) *n* **1** a native or inhabitant of Galilee. **2a the.** an epithet of Jesus Christ. **2b** (*often pl*) a Christian. ◆ *adj* **3** of Galilee.

Galilean[2] (ˌgælɪ'leɪən) *adj* of or relating to Galileo.

Galilean satellite *n* any of the four large satellites of the planet Jupiter – Io, Europa, Ganymede, or Callisto – discovered in 1610 by Galileo.

Galilean telescope (ˌgælɪ'leɪən) *n* a type of telescope with a convex objective lens and a concave eyepiece; it produces an erect image and is suitable for terrestrial use.

galilee ('gælɪˌliː) *n* a porch or chapel at the entrance to some medieval churches and cathedrals in England.

Galilee ('gælɪˌliː) *n* **1 Sea of.** Also called: Lake **Tiberias,** Lake **Kinneret.** a lake in NE Israel, 209 m (686 ft.) below sea level, through which the River Jordan flows. Area: 165 sq. km (64 sq. miles). **2** a northern region of Israel: scene of Christ's early ministry.

Galileo[1] (ˌgælɪ'leɪəʊ) *n* full name *Galileo Galilei.* 1564–1642, Italian mathematician, astronomer, and physicist. He discovered the isochronism of the pendulum and demonstrated that falling bodies of different weights descend at the same rate. He perfected the refracting telescope, which led to his discovery of Jupiter's satellites, sunspots, and craters on the moon. He was forced by the Inquisition to recant his support of the Copernican system.

Galileo[2] (ˌgælɪ'leɪəʊ) *n* a US spacecraft, launched 1989, that entered orbit around Jupiter in late 1995 to study the planet and its major satellites.

galimatias (ˌgælɪ'meɪʃɪəs, -'mætɪəs) *n Rare.* confused talk; gibberish. **[C17:** from French, of unknown origin**]**

galingale ('gælɪŋˌgeɪl) *or* **galangal** *n* a European cyperaceous plant, *Cyperus longus,* with rough-edged leaves, reddish spikelets of flowers, and aromatic roots. **[C13:** from Old French *galingal,* from Arabic *khalanjān,* from Chinese *kaoliang-chiang,* from *Kaoliang* district in Guangdong province + *chiang* ginger**]**

galiot *or* **galliot** ('gælɪət) *n* **1** a small swift galley formerly sailed on the Mediterranean. **2** a shallow-draught ketch formerly used along the coasts of Germany and the Netherlands. **[C14:** from Old French *galiote,* from Italian *galeotta,* from Medieval Latin *galea* GALLEY**]**

galipot *or* **gallipot** ('gælɪˌpɒt) *n* a resin obtained from several species of pine, esp. from the S European *Pinus pinaster*. [C18: from French, of unknown origin]

gall[1] (gɔːl) *n* **1** *Informal.* impudence. **2** bitterness; rancour. **3** something bitter or disagreeable. **4** *Physiol.* an obsolete term for **bile**. **5** an obsolete term for **gall bladder**. [from Old Norse, replacing Old English *gealla;* related to Old High German *galla,* Greek *kholē*]

gall[2] (gɔːl) *n* **1** a sore on the skin caused by chafing. **2** something that causes vexation or annoyance: *a gall to the spirits.* **3** irritation; exasperation. ◆ *vb* **4** *Pathol.* to abrade (the skin, etc.) as by rubbing. **5** (*tr*) to irritate or annoy; vex. [C14: of Germanic origin; related to Old English *gealla* sore on a horse, and perhaps to GALL[1]]

gall[3] (gɔːl) *n* an abnormal outgrowth in plant tissue caused by certain parasitic insects, fungi, bacteria, or mechanical injury. [C14: from Old French *galle,* from Latin *galla*]

gall. *or* **gal.** *abbrev. for* gallon.

Galla (ˈgælə) *n* **1** (*pl* **-las** *or* **-la**) a member of a tall dark-skinned people inhabiting Somalia and SE Ethiopia. **2** the language of this people, belonging to the Cushitic subfamily of the Afro-Asiatic family of languages.

gallant *adj* (ˈgælənt). **1** brave and high-spirited; courageous and honourable; dashing: *a gallant warrior.* **2** (gəˈlænt, ˈgælənt). (of a man) attentive to women; chivalrous. **3** imposing; dignified; stately: *a gallant ship.* **4** *Archaic.* showy in dress. ◆ *n* (ˈgælənt, gəˈlænt). *Archaic.* **5** a woman's lover or suitor. **6** a dashing or fashionable young man, esp. one who pursues women. **7** a brave, high-spirited, or adventurous man. ◆ *vb* (gəˈlænt, ˈgælənt). *Rare.* **8** (when *intr*, usually foll. by *with*) to court or flirt (with). **9** (*tr*) to attend or escort (a woman). [C15: from Old French *galant,* from *galer* to make merry, from *gale* enjoyment, pleasure, of Germanic origin; related to Old English *wela* WEAL[2]] ▶ **ˈgallantly** *adv* ▶ **ˈgallantness** *n*

gallantry (ˈgæləntrɪ) *n, pl* **-ries**. **1** conspicuous courage, esp. in war: *the gallantry of the troops.* **2** polite attentiveness to women. **3** a gallant action, speech, etc.

gallant soldier *n* a South American plant, *Galinsoga parviflora,* widely distributed as a weed, having small daisy-like flowers surrounded by silvery scales: family *Compositae* (composites). Also called: **Joey Hooker**. [C20: by folk etymology from New Latin *Galinsoga*]

gall bladder *n* a muscular sac, attached to the right lobe of the liver, that stores bile and ejects it into the duodenum.

Galle (ˈgɑːlə) *n* a port in SW Sri Lanka. Pop.: 84 000 (1990). Former name: **Point de Galle**.

galleass *or* **galliass** (ˈgælɪˌæs) *n Nautical.* a three-masted lateen-rigged galley used as a warship in the Mediterranean from the 15th to the 18th centuries. [C16: from French *galleasse,* from Italian *galeazza,* from *galea* GALLEY]

galleon (ˈgælɪən) *n Nautical.* a large sailing ship having three or more masts, lateen-rigged on the after masts and square-rigged on the foremast and mainmast, used as a warship or trader from the 15th to the 18th centuries. [C16: from Spanish *galeón,* from French *galion,* from Old French *galie* GALLEY]

galleria (ˌgæləˈriːə) *n* a central court through several storeys of a shopping centre or department store onto which shops or departments open at each level. [C20: from Italian; see GALLERY]

gallery (ˈgælərɪ) *n, pl* **-leries**. **1** a room or building for exhibiting works of art. **2** a covered passageway open on one side or on both sides. See also **colonnade** (sense 1). **3a** a balcony running along or around the inside wall of a church, hall, etc. **3b** a covered balcony, sometimes with columns on the outside. **4** *Theatre.* **4a** an upper floor that projects from the rear over the main floor and contains the cheapest seats. **4b** the seats there. **4c** the audience seated there. **5** a long narrow room, esp. one used for a specific purpose: *a shooting gallery.* **6** *Chiefly U.S.* a building or room where articles are sold at auction. **7** an underground passage, as in a mine, the burrow of an animal, etc. **8** *Theatre.* a narrow raised platform at the side or along the back of the stage for the use of technicians and stagehands. **9** (in a TV studio) a glass-fronted soundproof room high up to one side of the studio looking into it. One gallery is used by the director and an assistant and one is for lighting, etc. **10** *Nautical.* a balcony or platform at the quarter or stern of a ship, sometimes used as a gun emplacement. **11** a small ornamental metal or wooden balustrade or railing on a piece of furniture, esp. one surrounding the top of a desk, table, etc. **12** any group of spectators, as at a golf match. **13 play to the gallery.** to try to gain popular favour, esp. by crude appeals. [C15: from Old French *galerie,* from Medieval Latin *galeria,* probably from *galilea* GALILEE] ▶ **ˈgalleried** *adj*

gallery forest *n* a stretch of forest along a river in an area of otherwise open country.

gallery tray *n* a tray usually of silver with a raised rim, used for serving drinks.

galley (ˈgælɪ) *n* **1** any of various kinds of ship propelled by oars or sails used in ancient or medieval times as a warship or as a trader. **2** the kitchen of a ship, boat, or aircraft. **3** any of various long rowing boats. **4** *Printing.* **4a** (in hot-metal composition) a tray open at one end for holding composed type. **4b** short for **galley proof**. [C13: from Old French *galie,* from Medieval Latin *galea,* from Greek *galaia,* of unknown origin; the sense development apparently is due to the association of a galley or slave ship with a ship's kitchen and hence with a hot furnace, trough, printer's tray, etc.]

galley proof *n* a printer's proof, esp. one taken on a long strip of paper from type in a galley, used to make corrections before the matter has been split into pages. Often shortened to **galley**.

galley slave *n* **1** a criminal or slave condemned to row in a galley. **2** *Informal.* a drudge.

galley-west *adv Slang, chiefly U.S.* into confusion, inaction, or unconsciousness (esp. in the phrase **knock** (**someone** *or* **something**) **galley-west**). [C19: from English dialect *colly-west* awry, perhaps from *Collyweston,* a village in Northamptonshire]

gallfly (ˈgɔːlˌflaɪ) *n, pl* **-flies**. any of several small insects that produce galls in plant tissues, such as the gall wasp and gall midge.

Gallia (ˈgælɪə) *n* the Latin name of **Gaul**.

galliambic (ˌgælɪˈæmbɪk) *Prosody.* ◆ *adj* **1** of or relating to a metre consisting of four lesser Ionics, used by Callimachus and Catullus and imitated by Tennyson in *Boadicea.* ◆ *n* **2** a verse in this metre. [C19: from Latin *galliambus* song of the *Galli* (priests of Cybele)]

galliard (ˈgæljəd) *n* **1** a spirited dance in triple time for two persons, popular in the 16th and 17th centuries. **2** a piece of music composed for this dance. ◆ *adj* **3** *Archaic.* lively; spirited. [C14: from Old French *gaillard* valiant, perhaps of Celtic origin]

gallic[1] (ˈgælɪk) *adj* of or containing gallium in the trivalent state. [C18: from GALL(IUM) + -IC]

gallic[2] (ˈgælɪk) *adj* of, relating to, or derived from plant galls. [C18: from French *gallique;* see GALL[3]]

Gallic (ˈgælɪk) *adj* **1** of or relating to France. **2** of or relating to ancient Gaul or the Gauls.

gallic acid *n* a colourless crystalline compound obtained from tannin: used as a tanning agent and in making inks, paper, and pyrogallol; 3,4,5-trihydroxybenzoic acid. Formula: $C_6H_2(OH)_3COOH$.

Gallican (ˈgælɪkən) *adj* **1** of or relating to Gallicanism. ◆ *n* **2** an upholder of Gallicanism.

Gallicanism (ˈgælɪkəˌnɪzəm) *n* a movement among French Roman Catholic clergy that favoured the restriction of papal control and greater autonomy for the French church. Compare **ultramontanism**.

Gallice (ˈgælɪsɪ) *adv* in French. [C19: from Latin]

Gallicism (ˈgælɪˌsɪzəm) *n* a word or idiom borrowed from French.

Gallicize *or* **Gallicise** (ˈgælɪˌsaɪz) *vb* to make or become French in attitude, language, etc. ▶ **ˌGalliciˈzation** *or* **ˌGalliciˈsation** *n* ▶ **ˈGalliˌcizer** *or* **ˈGalliˌciser** *n*

galligaskins *or* **gallygaskins** (ˌgælɪˈgæskɪnz) *pl n* **1** loose wide breeches or hose, esp. as worn by men in the 17th century. **2** leather leggings, as worn in the 19th century. [C16: from obsolete French *garguesques,* from Italian *grechesco* Greek, from Latin *Graecus*]

gallimaufry (ˌgælɪˈmɔːfrɪ) *n, pl* **-fries**. a jumble; hotchpotch. [C16: from French *galimafrée* ragout, hash, of unknown origin]

gallinacean (ˌgælɪˈneɪʃən) *n* any gallinaceous bird.

gallinaceous (ˌgælɪˈneɪʃəs) *adj* **1** of, relating to, or belonging to the *Galliformes,* an order of birds, including domestic fowl, pheasants, grouse, etc., having a heavy rounded body, short bill, and strong legs. **2** of, relating to, or resembling the domestic fowl. [C18: from Latin *gallīnāceus,* from *gallīna* hen]

Gallinas Point (gɑːˈjiːnəs) *n* a cape in NE Colombia: the northernmost point of South America. Spanish name: **Punta Gallinas** (ˈpunta gaˈʎinas).

galling (ˈgɔːlɪŋ) *adj* **1** irritating, exasperating, or bitterly humiliating. **2** *Obsolete.* rubbing painfully; chafing. ▶ **ˈgallingly** *adv*

gallinule (ˈgælɪˌnjuːl) *n* **1** any of various aquatic birds of the genera *Porphyrio* and *Porphyrula,* typically having a dark plumage, red bill, and a red shield above the bill: family *Rallidae* (rails). **2 common gallinule.** the U.S. name for **moorhen** (sense 1). [C18: from New Latin *Gallīnula* genus name, from Late Latin: pullet, chicken, from Latin *gallīna* hen]

galliot (ˈgælɪət) *n* a variant spelling of **galiot**.

Gallipoli (gəˈlɪpəlɪ) *n* **1** a peninsula in NW Turkey, between the Dardanelles and the Gulf of Saros: scene of a costly but unsuccessful Allied campaign in 1915. **2** a port in NW Turkey, at the entrance to the Sea of Marmara: historically important for its strategic position. Pop.: 16 751 (1985 est.). Turkish name: **Gelibolu**.

gallipot[1] (ˈgælɪˌpɒt) *n* a small earthenware pot used by pharmacists as a container for ointments, etc. [C16: probably from GALLEY + POT[1]; so called because imported in galleys]

gallipot[2] (ˈgælɪˌpɒt) *n* a variant spelling of **galipot**.

gallium (ˈgælɪəm) *n* a silvery metallic element that is liquid for a wide temperature range. It occurs in trace amounts in some ores and is used in high-temperature thermometers and low-melting alloys. **Gallium arsenide** is a semiconductor. Symbol: Ga; atomic no.: 31; atomic wt.: 69.723; valency: 2 or 3; relative density: 5.904; melting pt.: 29.77°C; boiling pt.: 2205°C. [C19: from New Latin, from Latin *gallus* cock, translation of French *coq* in the name of its discoverer, *Lecoq* de Boisbaudran, 19th-century French chemist]

gallivant, galivant, *or* **galavant** (ˈgælɪˌvænt) *vb* (*intr*) to go about in search of pleasure; gad about. [C19: perhaps whimsical modification of GALLANT]

Gällivare (*Swedish* ˈjelivɑːrə) *n* a town in N Sweden, within the Arctic Circle: iron mines. Pop.: 22 400 (1990).

galliwasp (ˈgælɪˌwɒsp) *n* any lizard of the Central American genus *Diploglossus,* esp. *D. monotropis* of the Caribbean: family *Anguidae.* [C18: of unknown origin]

gall midge *n* any of various small fragile mosquito-like dipterous flies constituting the widely distributed family *Cecidomyidae,* many of which have larvae that produce galls on plants. Also called: **gallfly, gall gnat**. See also **Hessian fly**.

gall mite *n* any of various plant-feeding mites of the family *Phytoptidae* that cause galls or blisters on buds, leaves, or fruit.

gallnut (ˈgɔːlˌnʌt) *or* **gall-apple** *n* a type of plant gall that resembles a nut.

Gallo- (ˈgæləʊ) *combining form.* denoting Gaul or France: *Gallo-Roman.* [from Latin *Gallus* a Gaul]

galloglass *or* **gallowglass** (ˈgæləʊˌglɑːs) *n* a heavily armed mercenary soldier, originally Hebridean (Gaelic-Norse), maintained by Irish and some other Celtic chiefs from about 1235 to the 16th century. [C16: from Irish Gaelic *gallóglach,* from *gall* foreigner + *óglach,* young warrior-servant, from *og* young + *-lach* a noun suffix]

gallon (ˈgælən) *n* **1** Also called: **imperial gallon**. *Brit.* a unit of capacity equal to 277.42 cubic inches. 1 Brit. gallon is equivalent to 1.20 U.S. gallons or 4.55 litres. **2** *U.S.* a unit of capacity equal to 231 cubic inches. 1 U.S. gallon is equivalent to 0.83 imperial gallon or 3.79 litres. **[**C13: from Old Northern French *galon* (Old French *jalon*), perhaps of Celtic origin**]**

gallonage ('gælənɪdʒ) *n* **1** a capacity measured in gallons. **2** the rate of pumping, transmission, or consumption of a fluid in gallons per unit of time.

galloon (gə'luːn) *n* a narrow band of cord, embroidery, silver or gold braid, etc., used on clothes and furniture. **[**C17: from French *galon,* from Old French *galonner* to trim with braid, of unknown origin**]** ► **gal'looned** *adj*

galloot (gə'luːt) *n* a variant spelling of **galoot.**

gallop ('gæləp) *vb* **-lops, -loping, -loped. 1** (*intr*) (of a horse or other quadruped) to run fast with a two-beat stride in which all four legs are off the ground at once. **2** to ride (a horse, etc.) at a gallop. **3** (*intr*) to move, read, talk, etc., rapidly; hurry. ◆ *n* **4** the fast two-beat gait of horses and other quadrupeds. **5** an instance of galloping. **[**C16: from Old French *galoper,* of uncertain origin**]** ► **'galloper** *n*

gallopade *or* **galopade** (ˌgælə'peɪd) *n* another word for **galop.**

galloping ('gæləpɪŋ) *adj* (*prenominal*) progressing at or as if at a gallop: *galloping consumption.*

Gallo-Romance *or* **Gallo-Roman** *n* **1** the vernacular language or group of dialects, of which few records survive, spoken in France between about 600 A.D. and 900 A.D.; the intermediate stage between Vulgar Latin and Old French. ◆ *adj* **2** denoting or relating to this language or the period during which it was spoken.

gallous ('gæləs) *adj* of or containing gallium in the divalent state.

Gallovidian (ˌgæləʊ'vɪdɪən) *n* **1** a native or inhabitant of Galloway. ◆ *adj* **2** of or relating to Galloway. ◆ Also: **Galwegian.**

Galloway ('gæləˌweɪ) *n* **1** an area of SW Scotland, on the Solway Firth: consists of the former counties of Kirkcudbright and Wigtown, now part of Dumfries and Galloway; in the west is a large peninsula, the **Rhinns of Galloway,** with the **Mull of Galloway,** a promontory, at the south end of it (the southernmost point of Scotland). Related adjs.: **Gallovidian, Galwegian. 2** a breed of hardy cattle, usually black, originally bred in Galloway.

gallows ('gæləʊz) *n, pl* **-lowses** *or* **-lows. 1** a wooden structure usually consisting of two upright posts with a crossbeam from which a rope is suspended, used for hanging criminals. **2** any timber structure resembling this, such as (in Australia and New Zealand) a frame for hoisting up the bodies of slaughtered cattle. **3 the gallows.** execution by hanging. **[**C13: from Old Norse *galgi,* replacing Old English *gealga;* related to Old High German *galgo***]**

gallows bird *n Informal.* a person considered deserving of hanging.

gallows humour *n* sinister and ironic humour.

gallows tree *or* **gallow tree** *n* another name for **gallows** (sense 1).

gallsickness ('gɔːlˌsɪknɪs) *n* a disease of cattle and sheep, caused by infection with rickettsiae of the genus *Anaplasma,* resulting in anaemia and jaundice. Also called: **anaplasmosis.**

gallstone ('gɔːlˌstəʊn) *n Pathol.* a small hard concretion of cholesterol, bile pigments, and lime salts, formed in the gall bladder or its ducts. Also called: **bilestone.**

Gallup ('gæləp) *n* **George Horace.** 1901–84, U.S. statistician: devised the Gallup Poll; founded the American Institute of Public Opinion (1935) and its British counterpart (1936).

Gallup Poll ('gæləp) *n* a sampling by the American Institute of Public Opinion or its British counterpart of the views of a representative cross section of the population, used esp. as a means of forecasting voting.

gallus ('gæləs) *adj Scot.* bold; daring; reckless. **[**a variant of *gallows* used as an adjective, meaning fit for the gallows**]**

galluses ('gæləsɪz) *pl n Dialect.* braces for trousers. **[**C18: variant spelling of *gallowses,* from GALLOWS (in the obsolete sense: braces)**]**

gall wasp *n* any small solitary wasp of the family *Cynipidae* and related families that produces galls in plant tissue, which provide shelter and food for the larvae.

Galois theory ('gælwɑː) *n Maths.* the theory applying group theory to solving algebraic equations. **[**C19: named after Évariste *Galois* (1811–32), French mathematician**]**

galoot *or* **galloot** (gə'luːt) *n Slang, chiefly U.S.* a clumsy or uncouth person. **[**C19: of unknown origin**]**

galop ('gæləp) *n* **1** a 19th-century couple dance in quick duple time. **2** a piece of music composed for this dance. ◆ Also called: **gallopade. [**C19: from French; see GALLOP**]**

galore (gə'lɔː) *determiner* (*immediately postpositive*) in great numbers or quantity: *there were daffodils galore in the park.* **[**C17: from Irish Gaelic *go leór* to sufficiency**]**

galoshes *or* **goloshes** (gə'lɒʃɪz) *pl n* (*sometimes sing*) a pair of waterproof overshoes. **[**C14 (in the sense: wooden shoe): from Old French *galoche,* from Late Latin *gallicula* Gallic shoe**]**

Galsworthy ('gɔːlzˌwɜːðɪ) *n* **John.** 1867–1933, English novelist and dramatist, noted for *The Forsyte Saga* (1906–28): Nobel prize for literature 1932.

Galt (gɔːlt) *n* **John.** 1779–1839, Scottish novelist, noted for his ironic humour, esp. in *Annals of the Parish* (1821), *The Provost* (1822), and *The Entail* (1823).

Galton ('gɔːltən) *n* Sir **Francis.** 1822–1911, English explorer and scientist, a cousin of Charles Darwin, noted for his researches in heredity, meteorology, and statistics. He founded the study of eugenics and the theory of anticyclones.

galtonia (gɔːl'təʊnɪə) *n* any plant of the bulbous genus *Galtonia,* esp. *G. candicans,* with lanceolate leaves, drooping racemes of waxy white flowers, and a fragrant scent: family *Liliaceae.* **[**named after Sir Francis GALTON**]**

galumph (gə'lʌmpf, -'lʌmf) *vb* (*intr*) *Informal.* to leap or move about clumsily or joyfully. **[**C19 (coined by Lewis Carroll): probably a blend of GALLOP + TRIUMPH**]**

galv. *abbrev. for:* **1** galvanic. **2** galvanism.

Galvani (*Italian* gal'vaːni) *n* **Luigi** (lu'iːdʒi). 1737–98, Italian physiologist: observed that muscles contracted on contact with dissimilar metals. This led to the galvanic cell and the electrical theory of muscle control by nerves.

galvanic (gæl'vænɪk) *or* **galvanical** *adj* **1** Also: **voltaic.** of, producing, or concerned with an electric current, esp. a direct current produced chemically: *a galvanic cell.* **2** *Informal.* resembling the effect of an electric shock; convulsive, startling, or energetic: *galvanic reflexes.* ► **gal'vanically** *adv*

galvanic pile *n* another name for **voltaic pile.**

galvanic skin response *n* a change in the electrical resistance of the skin occurring in moments of strong emotion; measurements of this change are used in lie detector tests. Abbrev.: **GSR.**

galvanism ('gælvəˌnɪzəm) *n* **1** *Obsolete.* electricity, esp. when produced by chemical means as in a cell or battery. **2** *Med.* treatment involving the application of electric currents to tissues. **[**C18: via French from Italian *galvanismo,* after GALVANI**]**

galvanize *or* **galvanise** ('gælvəˌnaɪz) *vb* (*tr*) **1** to stimulate to action; excite; startle. **2** to cover (iron, steel, etc.) with a protective zinc coating by dipping into molten zinc or by electrodeposition. **3** to stimulate by application of an electric current. ◆ *n* **4** *Caribbean.* galvanized iron, usually in the form of corrugated sheets as used in roofing. ► **ˌgalvani'zation** *or* **ˌgalvani'sation** *n* ► **'galvaˌnizer** *or* **'galvaˌniser** *n*

galvanized iron *or* **galvanised iron** *n Building trades.* iron, esp. a sheet of corrugated iron, covered with a protective coating of zinc.

galvano- *combining form.* indicating a galvanic current: *galvanometer.*

galvanometer (ˌgælvə'nɒmɪtə) *n* any sensitive instrument for detecting or measuring small electric currents. ► **galvanometric** (ˌgælvənəʊ'metrɪk, gælˌvænə-) *or* **ˌgalvano'metrical** *adj* ► **ˌgalvano'metrically** *adv* ► **ˌgalva'nometry** *n*

galvanoscope ('gælvənəˌskəʊp, gæl'vænə-) *n* a galvanometer that depends for its action on the deflection of a magnetic needle in a magnetic field produced by the electric current that is to be detected. ► **galvanoscopic** (ˌgælvənə'skɒpɪk, gælˌvænə-) *adj* ► **ˌgalva'noscopy** *n*

galvanotropism (ˌgælvə'nɒtrəˌpɪzəm) *n* the directional growth of an organism, esp. a plant, in response to an electrical stimulus. ► **galvanotropic** (ˌgælvənəʊ'trɒpɪk, gælˌvænəʊ-) *adj*

Galveston plan ('gælvɪstən) *n* another term for **commission plan.**

galvo ('gælvəʊ) *n, pl* **-vos.** an informal name for a **galvanometer.**

Galway ('gɔːlweɪ) *n* **1** a county of W Republic of Ireland, in S Connacht, on **Galway Bay** and the Atlantic: it has a deeply indented coastline and many offshore islands, including the Aran Islands. County town: Galway. Pop.: 189 000 (1996). Area: 5939 sq. km (2293 sq. miles). **2** a port in W Republic of Ireland, county town of Co. Galway, on Galway Bay: important fisheries (esp. for salmon). Pop.: 50 853 (1991).

Galwegian (gæl'wiːdʒən) *n* **1** another word for **Gallovidian** (sense 1). **2** a native or inhabitant of the town or county of Galway in W Republic of Ireland. ◆ *adj* **3** another word for **Gallovidian** (sense 2). **[**C18: influenced by *Norway, Norwegian***]**

galyak *or* **galyac** ('gæljæk, gæl'jæk) *n* a smooth glossy fur obtained from the skins of newborn or premature lambs and kids. **[**from Russian (Uzbek dialect)**]**

gam[1] (gæm) *n* **1** a school of whales. **2** *Nautical.* an informal visit between crew members of whalers. **3** *N.Z.* a flock of large sea birds. ◆ *vb* **gams, gamming, gammed. 4** (*intr*) (of whales) to form a school. **5** *Nautical.* (of members of the crews of whalers) to visit (each other) informally. **6** (*tr*) *U.S.* to visit or exchange visits with. **[**C19: perhaps dialect variant of GAME[1]**]**

gam[2] (gæm) *n Slang.* a leg, esp. a woman's shapely leg. **[**C18: probably from Old Northern French *gambe* or Lingua Franca *gambe;* see JAMB**]**

Gama ('gɑːmə) *n* **Vasco da** ('væskəʊ də). ?1469–1524, Portuguese navigator, who discovered the sea route from Portugal to India around the Cape of Good Hope (1498).

gama grass ('gɑːmə) *n* a tall perennial grass, *Tripsacum dactyloides,* of SE North America: cultivated for fodder. **[**C19: *gama,* probably changed from GRAMA**]**

gamahuche ('gæməˌhuːʃ) *or* **gamaruche** ('gæməˌruːʃ) *Taboo.* ◆ *vb* (*tr*) **1** to practise cunnilingus or fellatio on. ◆ *n* **2** cunnilingus or fellatio. **[**C19: from French *gamahucher***]**

gamba ('gæmbə) *n* short for **viola da gamba.**

gambado[1] (gæm'beɪdəʊ) *n, pl* **-dos** *or* **-does. 1** either of two leather holders for the feet attached to a horse's saddle like stirrups. **2** either of a pair of leggings. **[**C17: from Italian *gamba* leg, from Late Latin: leg, hoof; see JAMB**]**

gambado[2] (gæm'beɪdəʊ) *or* **gambade** (gæm'beɪd, -'bɑːd) *n, pl* **-bados, -badoes,** *or* **-bades. 1** *Dressage.* another word for **curvet. 2** a leap or gambol; caper. **[**C19: from French *gambade* spring (of a horse), ultimately from Spanish or Italian *gamba* leg**]**

gamba stop *n* an organ stop with a tone resembling that of stringed instruments.

gambeson ('gæmbɪsᵊn) *n* a quilted and padded or stuffed leather or cloth garment worn under chain mail in the Middle Ages and later as a doublet by men and women. **[**C13: from Old French, of Germanic origin; related to Old High German *wamba* belly; see WOMB**]**

Gambetta (gæm'betə; *French* gɑ̃bɛta) *n* **Léon** (leɔ̃). 1838–82, French statesman; prime minister (1881–82). He organized resistance during the Franco-Prussian War (1870–71) and was a founder of the Third Republic (1871).

Gambia ('gæmbɪə) *n* **The.** a republic in W Africa, entirely surrounded by Senegal except for an outlet to the Atlantic: sold to English merchants by the Portuguese in 1588; became a British colony in 1843; gained independence and became a member of the Commonwealth in 1965; joined with Senegal in 1982 to form the Confederation of Senegambia; consists of a strip of land about 16 km (10 miles) wide, on both banks of the **Gambia River**, extending inland for about 480 km (300 miles). Official language: English. Religion: Muslim majority. Currency: dalasi. Capital: Banjul. Pop.: 1 292 000 (1998 est.). Area: 11 295 sq. km (4361 sq. miles). ► **'Gambian** *adj, n*

gambier *or* **gambir** ('gæmbɪə) *n* an astringent resinous substance obtained from a rubiaceous tropical Asian woody climbing plant, *Uncaria gambir* (or *U. gambier*): used as an astringent and tonic and in tanning. **[C19**: from Malay**]**

Gambier Islands ('gæmbɪə) *pl n* a group of islands in the S Pacific Ocean, in French Polynesia. Chief settlement: Rikitéa. Pop.: 582 (1988). Area: 30 sq. km (11 sq. miles).

gambit ('gæmbɪt) *n* **1** *Chess.* an opening move in which a chessman, usually a pawn, is sacrificed to secure an advantageous position. **2** an opening comment, manoeuvre, etc., intended to secure an advantage or promote a point of view. **[C17**: from French, from Italian *gambetto* a tripping up, from *gamba* leg**]**

gamble ('gæmbᵊl) *vb* **1** (*intr*) to play games of chance to win money. **2** to risk or bet (money) on the outcome of an event, sport, etc. **3** (*intr;* often foll. by *on*) to act with the expectation of: *to gamble on its being a sunny day.* **4** (often foll. by *away*) to lose by or as if by betting; squander. ◆ *n* **5** a risky act or venture. **6** a bet, wager, or other risk or chance taken for possible monetary gain. **[C18**: probably variant of GAME[1]**]** ► **'gambler** *n* ► **'gambling** *n*

gamblers' fallacy *n Psychol.* the fallacy that in a series of chance events the probability of one event occurring increases with the number of times another event has occurred in succession.

gamboge (gæm'bəʊdʒ, -'buːʒ) *n* **1a** a gum resin used as the source of a yellow pigment and as a purgative. **1b** the pigment made from this resin. **2 gamboge tree.** any of several tropical Asian trees of the genus *Garcinia,* esp. *G. hanburyi,* that yield this resin: family *Guttiferae.* **3** a strong yellow colour. ◆ Also called (for senses 1, 2): **cambogia. [C18**: from New Latin *gambaugium,* from CAMBODIA**]** ► **gam'bogian** *adj*

gambol ('gæmbᵊl) *vb* **-bols, -bolling, -bolled** *or U.S.* **-bols, -boling, -boled. 1** (*intr*) to skip or jump about in a playful manner; frolic. ◆ *n* **2** a playful antic; frolic. **[C16**: from French *gambade;* see GAMBADO[2], JAMB**]**

gambrel ('gæmbrəl) *n* **1** the hock of a horse or similar animal. **2** a frame of wood or metal shaped like a horse's hind leg, used by butchers for suspending carcasses of meat. **3** short for **gambrel roof. [C16**: from Old Northern French *gamberel,* from *gambe* leg**]**

gambrel roof *n* **1** *Chiefly Brit.* a hipped roof having a small gable at both ends. **2** *Chiefly U.S. and Canadian.* a roof having two slopes on both sides, the lower slopes being steeper than the upper. Compare **mansard** (sense 1). ◆ Sometimes shortened to **gambrel.** ► **'gambrel-ˌroofed** *adj*

Gambrinus (gæm'braɪnəs) *n* a legendary Flemish king who was said to have invented beer.

game[1] (geɪm) *n* **1** an amusement or pastime; diversion. **2** a contest with rules, the result being determined by skill, strength, or chance. **3** a single period of play in such a contest, sport, etc. **4** the score needed to win a contest. **5** a single contest in a series; match. **6** (*pl; often cap.*) an event consisting of various sporting contests, esp. in athletics: *Olympic Games; Highland Games.* **7** equipment needed for playing certain games. **8** short for **computer game. 9** style or ability in playing a game: *he is a keen player but his game is not good.* **10** a scheme, proceeding, etc., practised like a game: *the game of politics.* **11** an activity undertaken in a spirit of levity; joke: *marriage is just a game to him.* **12a** wild animals, including birds and fish, hunted for sport, food, or profit. **12b** (*as modifier*): *game laws.* **13** the flesh of such animals, used as food: generally taken not to include fish. **14** an object of pursuit; quarry; prey (esp. in the phrase **fair game**). **15** *Informal.* work or occupation. **16** *Informal.* a trick, strategy, or device: *I can see through your little game.* **17** *Obsolete.* pluck or courage; bravery. **18** *Slang, chiefly Brit.* prostitution (esp. in the phrase **on the game**). **19 give the game away.** to reveal one's intentions or a secret. **20 make (a) game of.** to make fun of; ridicule; mock. **21 on** (*or* **off**) **one's game.** playing well (or badly). **22 play the game.** to behave fairly or in accordance with rules. **23 the game is up.** there is no longer a chance of success. ◆ *adj* **24** *Informal.* full of fighting spirit; plucky; brave. **25 (as) game as Ned Kelly.** *Austral. informal.* extremely brave; indomitable. **26** (usually foll. by *for*) *Informal.* prepared or ready; willing: *I'm game for a try.* ◆ *vb* **27** (*intr*) to play games of chance for money, stakes, etc.; gamble. **[**Old English *gamen;* related to Old Norse *gaman,* Old High German *gaman* amusement**]** ► **'gameˌlike** *adj*

game[2] (geɪm) *adj* a less common word for **lame**[1] (esp. in the phrase **game leg**). **[C18**: probably from Irish *cam* crooked**]**

game-ball *adj Irish.* **1** (of a person) in perfect health. **2** (of an arrangement, plan, etc.) excellent.

game bird *n* a bird of any species hunted as game.

game chips *pl n* round thin potato chips served with game.

gamecock ('geɪmˌkɒk) *n* a cock bred and trained for fighting. Also called: **fighting cock.**

game fish *n* any fish providing sport for the angler.

game fowl *n* any of several breeds of domestic fowl reared for cockfighting.

gamekeeper ('geɪmˌkiːpə) *n* a person employed to take care of game and wildlife, as on an estate. ► **'gameˌkeeping** *n*

gamelan ('gæmɪˌlæn) *n* a type of percussion orchestra common in the East Indies. **[**from Javanese**]**

game laws *pl n* laws governing the hunting and preservation of game.

gamely ('geɪmlɪ) *adv* in a brave or sporting manner.

gameness ('geɪmnɪs) *n* courage or bravery; pluck.

game park *n* (esp. in Africa) a large area of country set aside as a reserve for wild animals.

game plan *n* **1** a strategy. **2** a plan of campaign, esp. in politics.

game point *n Tennis, etc.* a stage at which winning one further point would enable one player or side to win a game.

gamesmanship ('geɪmzmənˌʃɪp) *n Informal.* the art of winning games or defeating opponents by clever or cunning practices without actually cheating. ► **'gamesman** *n*

gamesome ('geɪmsəm) *adj* full of merriment; sportive. ► **'gamesomely** *adv* ► **'gamesomeness** *n*

gamester ('geɪmstə) *n* a person who habitually plays games for money; gambler.

gametangium (ˌgæmɪ'tændʒɪəm) *n, pl* **-gia** (-dʒɪə). *Biology.* an organ or cell in which gametes are produced, esp. in algae and fungi. **[C19**: New Latin, from GAMETO- + Greek *angeion* vessel**]** ► **ˌgame'tangial** *adj*

gamete ('gæmiːt, gə'miːt) *n* a haploid germ cell, such as a spermatozoon or ovum, that fuses with another germ cell during fertilization. **[C19**: from New Latin, from Greek *gametē* wife, from *gamos* marriage**]** ► **ga'metal** *or* **gametic** (gə'mɛtɪk) *adj*

gamete intrafallopian transfer (ˌɪntrəfə'ləʊpɪən) *n* the full name for **GIFT.**

game theory *n* mathematical theory concerned with the optimum choice of strategy in situations involving a conflict of interest. Also called: **theory of games.** ► **ˌgame-ˌtheo'retic** *adj*

gameto- *or sometimes before a vowel* **gamet-** *combining form.* gamete: *gametocyte.*

gametocyte (gə'miːtəʊˌsaɪt) *n* an animal or plant cell that develops into gametes by meiosis. See also **oocyte, spermatocyte.**

gametogenesis (ˌgæmɪtəʊ'dʒɛnɪsɪs) *or* **gametogeny** (ˌgæmɪ'tɒdʒɪnɪ) *n* the formation and maturation of gametes. See also **spermatogenesis, oogenesis.** ► **ˌgameto'genic** *or* **ˌgame'togenous** *adj*

gametophore (gə'miːtəʊˌfɔː) *n* the part of a plant that bears the reproductive organs. ► **gaˌmeto'phoric** *adj*

gametophyte (gə'miːtəʊˌfaɪt) *n* the plant body, in species showing alternation of generations, that produces the gametes. Compare **sporophyte.** ► **gametophytic** (ˌgæmɪtəʊ'fɪtɪk) *adj*

game warden *n* a person who looks after game, as in a game reserve.

gamey *or* **gamy** ('geɪmɪ) *adj* **gamier, gamiest. 1** having the smell or flavour of game, esp. high game. **2** *Informal.* spirited; plucky; brave. ► **'gamily** *adv* ► **'gaminess** *n*

gamic ('gæmɪk) *adj* (esp. of reproduction) requiring the fusion of gametes; sexual. **[C19**: from Greek *gamikos* of marriage; see GAMETE**]**

gamin ('gæmɪn; *French* gamɛ̃) *n* a street urchin; waif. **[**from French**]**

gamine ('gæmiːn; *French* gamin) *n* **a** a slim and boyish girl or young woman; an elfish tomboy. **b** (*as modifier*): *a gamine style of haircut.* **[**from French**]**

gaming ('geɪmɪŋ) *n* **a** gambling on games of chance. **b** (*as modifier*): *gaming house; gaming losses.*

gamma ('gæmə) *n* **1** the third letter in the Greek alphabet (Γ, γ), a consonant, transliterated as *g.* When double, it is transcribed and pronounced as *ng.* **2** the third highest grade or mark, as in an examination. **3** a unit of magnetic field strength equal to 10^{-5} oersted. 1 gamma is equivalent to $0.795\,775 \times 10^{-3}$ ampere per metre. **4** *Photog., television.* the numerical value of the slope of the characteristic curve of a photographic emulsion or television camera; a measure of the contrast reproduced in a photographic or television image. **5** (*modifier*) **5a** involving or relating to photons of very high energy: *a gamma detector.* **5b** relating to one of two or more allotropes or crystal structures of a solid: *gamma iron.* **5c** relating to one of two or more isomeric forms of a chemical compound, esp. one in which a group is attached to the carbon atom next but one to the atom to which the principal group is attached. **[C14**: from Greek; related to Hebrew *gīmel* third letter of the Hebrew alphabet (probably: camel)**]**

Gamma ('gæmə) *n* (*foll. by the genitive case of a specified constellation*) the third brightest star in a constellation: *Gamma Leonis.*

gamma-aminobutyric acid (ˌgæməəˌmiːnəʊbjʊ'tɪrɪk) *n* the full name for **GABA.**

gamma camera *n* a medical apparatus that detects gamma rays emitted from a person's body after the administration of a radioactive drug and so produces images of the organ being investigated.

gammadion (gæ'meɪdɪən) *n, pl* **-dia** (-dɪə). a decorative figure composed of a number of Greek capital gammas, esp. radiating from a centre, as in a swastika. **[C19**: from Late Greek, literally: little GAMMA**]**

gamma distribution *n Statistics.* a continuous two-parameter distribution from which the chi-square and exponential distributions are derived, written $Ga(2,v)$, and defined in terms of the gamma function.

gamma function *n Maths.* a function defined by $\Gamma(x) = \int_0^\infty t^{x-1}e^{-t}dx$, where x is real and greater than zero.

gamma globulin *n* any of a group of proteins in blood plasma that includes most known antibodies.

gamma iron *n* an allotrope of iron that is nonmagnetic and exists between 910°C and 1400°C.

gamma radiation *n* **1** electromagnetic radiation emitted by atomic nuclei; the wavelength is generally in the range 1×10^{-10} to 2×10^{-13} metres. **2** electromagnetic radiation of very short wavelength emitted by any source, esp. the portion of the electromagnetic spectrum with a wavelength less than about 1×10^{-11} metres.

gamma-ray astronomy *n* the investigation of cosmic gamma rays, such as those from quasars.

gamma rays *pl n* streams of gamma radiation.

gamma stock *n* any of the third rank of active securities on the London Stock Exchange. Prices displayed by market makers are given as an indication rather than an offer to buy or sell.

gammat (xamat) *n S. African derogatory.* a reference to the accent of Cape Coloured people. **[C20**: corruption of *Achmet,* a common Arabic name**]**

gammer ('gæmə) *n Rare, chiefly Brit.* a dialect word for an old woman: now chiefly humorous or contemptuous. Compare **gaffer** (sense 1). [C16: probably alteration of GODMOTHER or GRANDMOTHER]

gammon[1] ('gæmən) *n* **1** a cured or smoked ham. **2** the hindquarter of a side of bacon, cooked either whole or cut into large rashers. [C15: from Old Northern French *gambon,* from *gambe* leg; see GAMBREL]

gammon[2] ('gæmən) *n* **1** a double victory in backgammon in which one player throws off all his pieces before his opponent throws any. **2** *Archaic.* the game of backgammon. ◆ *vb* **3** (*tr*) to score a gammon over. [C18: probably special use of Middle English *gamen* GAME[1]]

gammon[3] ('gæmən) *Brit. informal.* ◆ *n* **1** deceitful nonsense; humbug. ◆ *vb* **2** to deceive (a person). [C18: perhaps special use of GAMMON[2]] ▸ **'gammoner** *n*

gammon[4] ('gæmən) *vb* (*tr*) *Nautical.* to fix (a bowsprit) to the stemhead of a vessel. [C18: perhaps related to GAMMON[1], with reference to the tying up of a ham]

gammy ('gæmɪ) *adj* **-mier, -miest.** *Brit. slang.* (esp. of the leg) malfunctioning, injured, or lame; game. U.S. equivalent: **gimpy.** [C19: from Shelta *gyamyath* bad, altered form of Irish *cam* crooked; see GAME[2]]

gamo- *or before a vowel* **gam-** *combining form.* **1** indicating sexual union or reproduction: *gamogenesis.* **2** united or fused: *gamopetalous.* [from Greek *gamos* marriage]

gamogenesis (ˌgæməʊ'dʒɛnɪsɪs) *n* another name for **sexual reproduction.** ▸ **gamogenetic** (ˌgæməʊdʒɪ'nɛtɪk) *or* **ˌgamoge'netical** *adj* ▸ **ˌgamoge'netically** *adv*

gamone ('gæməʊn) *n Botany.* a chemical substance secreted by a gamete that attracts another gamete during sexual reproduction.

gamopetalous (ˌgæməʊ'pɛtələs) *adj* (of flowers) having petals that are united or partly united, as the primrose. Also: **sympetalous.** Compare **polypetalous.**

gamophyllous (ˌgæməʊ'fɪləs) *adj* (of flowers) having united leaves or perianth segments.

gamosepalous (ˌgæməʊ'sɛpələs) *adj* (of flowers) having united or partly united sepals, as the primrose. Compare **polysepalous.**

-gamous *adj combining form.* denoting marrying or uniting sexually: *monogamous.* [from Greek *gamos;* see -GAMY]

gamp (gæmp) *n Brit. informal.* an umbrella. [C19: after Mrs Sarah *Gamp,* a nurse in Dickens' *Martin Chuzzlewit,* who carried a faded cotton umbrella]

gamut ('gæmət) *n* **1** entire range or scale, as of emotions. **2** *Music.* **2a** a scale, esp. (in medieval theory) one starting on the G on the bottom line of the bass staff. **2b** the whole range of notes. **3** *Physics.* the range of chromaticities that can be obtained by mixing three colours. [C15: from Medieval Latin, changed from *gamma ut,* from *gamma,* the lowest note of the hexachord as established by Guido d'Arezzo + *ut* (now, *doh*), the first of the notes of the scale *ut, re, mi, fa, sol, la, si,* derived from a Latin hymn to St John: *Ut* queant laxis *re*sonare fibris, *Mi*ra gestorum *fa*muli tuorum, *Sol*ve polluti *la*bi reatum, Sancte *I*ohannes]

-gamy *n combining form.* denoting marriage or sexual union: *bigamy.* [from Greek *-gamia,* from *gamos* marriage]

gan[1] (gæn) *vb Archaic or poetic.* the past tense of **gin**[3].

gan[2] (gæn) *vb* **gans, ganning, ganned.** (*intr*) *Northeast English dialect.* to go. [from Old English *gangan;* related to Old Norse *ganga.* See GANG[1]]

Gäncä ('ganʒə) *n* a variant transliteration of the Azerbaijani name for **Gandzha.**

Gance (*French* gɑ̃s) *n* **Abel** (abɛl). 1889–1981, French film director, whose works include *J'accuse* (1919, 1937) and *Napoléon* (1927), which introduced the split-screen technique.

Gand (gɑ̃) *n* the French name for **Ghent.**

Ganda ('gændə) *n* **1** (*pl* **-das** *or* **-da**) a member of the Buganda people of Uganda, whose kingdom was formerly the largest in E Africa. See also **Luganda. 2** the Luganda language of this people.

gander ('gændə) *n* **1** a male goose. **2** *Informal.* a quick look (esp. in the phrase **take** (*or* **have**) **a gander**). **3** *Informal.* a simpleton. [Old English *gandra, ganra;* related to Low German and Dutch *gander* and to GANNET]

Gandhi ('gændɪ) *n* **1** Mrs **Indira** (**Priyadarshini**) (ɪn'dɪərə, 'ɪndərə), daughter of Jawaharlal Nehru. 1917–84, Indian stateswoman; prime minister of India (1966–77; 1980–84); assassinated. **2 Mohandas Karamchand** (ˌməʊhən'dʌs ˌkʌrəm'tʃʌnd), known as *Mahatma Gandhi.* 1869–1948, Indian political and spiritual leader and social reformer. He played a major part in India's struggle for home rule and was frequently imprisoned by the British for organizing acts of civil disobedience. He advocated passive resistance and hunger strikes as means of achieving reform, campaigned for the untouchables, and attempted to unite Muslims and Hindus. He was assassinated by a Hindu extremist. **3 Rajiv** (ræ'dʒiːv), son of Indira Gandhi. 1944–91, Indian statesman; prime minister of India (1984–89); assassinated.

Gandhian ('gændɪən) *adj* **1** of or relating to Mahatma Gandhi or his ideas. ◆ *n* **2** a follower of Gandhi or his ideas.

Gandhi cap *n* a cap made of white hand-woven cloth worn by some men in India.

Gandhiism ('gændɪˌɪzəm) *or* **Gandhism** ('gænˌdɪzəm) *n* the political principles of M. K. Gandhi, esp. civil disobedience and passive resistance as means of achieving reform.

G & S *abbrev. for* Gilbert and Sullivan.

gandy dancer ('gændɪ) *n Slang.* a railway track maintenance worker. [C20: of uncertain origin]

Gandzha (*Russian* gan'dʒa) *or* **Gäncä** *n* a city in NW Azerbaijan: annexed by the Russians in 1804; centre of a cotton-growing region. Pop.: 292 200 (1995 est.). Former names: **Yelisavetpol** (1813–1920), **Kirovabad** (1936–91).

gane (gen) *vb* the past participle of **gae.**

ganef, ganev, ganof ('gɑːnəf), **gonif,** *or* **gonof** *n U.S. slang.* an unscrupulous opportunist who stoops to sharp practice. [from Yiddish, from Hebrew *gannābh* thief, from *gānnabh* he stole]

Ganesa (gæ'niːsə) *n* the Hindu god of prophecy, represented as having an elephant's head.

gang[1] (gæŋ) *n* **1** a group of people who associate together or act as an organized body, esp. for criminal or illegal purposes. **2** an organized group of workmen. **3** a herd of buffaloes or elks or a pack of wild dogs. **4** *N.Z.* a group of shearers who travel to different shearing sheds, shearing, classing, and baling wool. **5a** a series of similar tools arranged to work simultaneously in parallel. **5b** (*as modifier*)*: a gang saw.* ◆ *vb* **6** to form into, become part of, or act as a gang. **7** (*tr*) *Electronics.* to mount (two or more components, such as variable capacitors) on the same shaft, permitting adjustment by a single control. ◆ See also **gang up.** [Old English *gang* journey; related to Old Norse *gangr,* Old High German *gang,* Sanskrit *jangha* foot] ▸ **ganged** *adj*

gang[2] (gæŋ) *vb Scot.* to go. [Old English *gangan* to GO[1]]

gang[3] (gæŋ) *n* a variant spelling of **gangue.**

Ganga jal ('gʌŋgɑː dʒʌl) *n* sacred water from the River Ganges in India. [Hindi, from *Ganga* GANGES + *jal* water]

gangbang ('gæŋˌbæŋ) *Taboo slang.* ◆ *n* **1** an instance of sexual intercourse between one woman and several men one after the other, esp. against her will. ◆ *vb* **2** (*tr*) to force (a woman) to take part in a gangbang. **3** (*intr*) to take part in a gangbang. ◆ Also called: **gangshag** ('gæŋˌʃæg).

gang-banger *n U.S. slang.* a member of a street gang. ▸ **'gang-ˌbanging** *n*

ganger ('gæŋə) *n Chiefly Brit.* the foreman of a gang of labourers.

Ganges ('gændʒiːz) *n* the great river of N India and central Bangladesh: rises in two headstreams in the Himalayas and flows southeast to Allahabad, where it is joined by the Jumna; continues southeast into Bangladesh, where it enters the Bay of Bengal in a great delta; the most sacred river to Hindus, with many places of pilgrimage, esp. Varanasi. Length: 2507 km (1557 miles). Hindi name: **Ganga** ('gʌŋgə, 'gɑːŋ-). ▸ **Gangetic** (gæn'dʒɛtɪk) *adj*

gang-gang ('gæŋˌgæŋ) *n* a small black cockatoo, *Callocephalon fimbriatum,* of SE Australia, the male of which has a scarlet head. [C19: from a native Australian language]

gangland ('gæŋˌlænd, -lənd) *n* the criminal underworld.

gangling ('gæŋglɪŋ) *or* **gangly** ('gæŋglɪ) *adj* tall, lanky, and awkward in movement. [perhaps related to GANGREL; see GANG[2]]

ganglion ('gæŋglɪən) *n, pl* **-glia** (-glɪə) *or* **-glions. 1** an encapsulated collection of nerve-cell bodies, usually located outside the brain and spinal cord. **2** any concentration of energy, activity, or strength. **3** a cystic tumour on a tendon sheath or joint capsule. [C17: from Late Latin: swelling, from Greek: cystic tumour] ▸ **'ganglial** *or* **'gangliar** *adj* ▸ **ˌgangli'onic** *or* **'gangliˌated** *adj*

Gangnail ('gæŋˌneɪl) *n Trademark.* a particular arrangement of nails on a metal plate, used as a connecting piece in strong timber joints.

Gang of Four *n* **the.** a radical faction within the Chinese Communist Party that emerged as a political force in the spring of 1976 and was suppressed later that year. Its members, Zhang Chunqiao, Wang Hongwen, Yao Wenyuan, and Jiang Qing, were tried and imprisoned (1981).

gangplank ('gæŋˌplæŋk) *or* **gangway** *n Nautical.* a portable bridge for boarding and leaving a vessel at dockside.

gang plough *n* a plough having two or more shares, coulters, and mouldboards designed to work simultaneously.

gangrel ('gæŋgrəl, 'gæŋrəl) *n Scot. archaic or literary.* **1** a wandering beggar. **2** a child just able to walk; toddler. [C16: from Old English *gangan* to GO[1]]

gangrene ('gæŋgriːn) *n* **1** death and decay of tissue as the result of interrupted blood supply, disease, or injury. **2** moral decay or corruption. ◆ *vb* **3** to become or cause to become affected with gangrene. [C16: from Latin *gangraena,* from Greek *gangraina* an eating sore; related to Greek *gran* to gnaw] ▸ **gangrenous** ('gæŋgrɪnəs) *adj*

gang saw *n* a saw having several parallel blades making simultaneous cuts. ▸ **gang sawyer** *n*

gangsta rap ('gæŋstə) *n* a style of rap music, usually characterized by lyrics about Black street gangs in the U.S., often with violent, nihilistic, and misogynistic themes. [C20: phonetic rendering of GANGSTER] ▸ **gangsta rapper** *n*

gangster ('gæŋstə) *n* a member of an organized gang of criminals, esp. one who resorts to violence. ▸ **'gangsterism** *n*

Gangtok ('gʌŋtɒk) *n* a city in NE India: capital of Sikkim state. Pop.: 24 970 (1991).

gangue *or* **gang** (gæŋ) *n* valueless and undesirable material, such as quartz in small quantities, in an ore. [C19: from French *gangue,* from German *Gang* vein of metal, course; see GANG[1]]

gang up *vb* (often foll. by *on* or *against*) *Informal.* to combine in a group (against).

gangway ('gæŋˌweɪ) *n* **1** an opening in a ship's side to take a gangplank. **2** another word for **gangplank. 3** *Brit.* an aisle between rows of seats. **4** Also called: **logway.** *Chiefly U.S.* a ramp for logs leading into a sawmill. **5** a main passage in a mine. **6** temporary planks over mud or earth, as on a building site. ◆ *sentence substitute.* **7** clear a path!

ganister *or* **gannister** ('gænɪstə) *n* **1** a highly refractory siliceous sedimentary rock occurring beneath coal seams: used for lining furnaces. **2** a similar material synthesized from ground quartz and fireclay. [C19: of unknown origin]

ganja ('gɑːndʒə) *n* a highly potent form of cannabis, usually used for smoking. [from Hindi *gājā,* from Sanskrit *grñja*]

gannet ('gænɪt) *n* **1** any of several heavily built marine birds of the genus *Morus* (or *Sula*), having a long stout bill and typically white plumage with dark markings: family *Sulidae,* order *Pelecaniformes* (pelicans, cormorants, etc.). See also **booby** (sense 3). **2** *Slang.* a gluttonous or greedy person. [Old English *ganot;* related to Old High German *gannazzo* gander]

ganof ('gɑːnəf) *n* a variant spelling of **ganef.**

ganoid ('gænɔɪd) *adj* **1** (of the scales of certain fishes) consisting of an inner bony layer and an outer layer of an enamel-like substance (ganoin). **2** denoting fishes, including the sturgeon and bowfin, having such scales. ◆ *n* **3** a ganoid fish. [C19: from French *ganoïde,* from Greek *ganos* brightness + -OID]

gansey ('gænzɪ) *n Dialect.* a jersey or pullover. [from the island of GUERNSEY]

Gansu ('gæn'su:) *or* **Kansu** *n* a province of NW China, between Tibet and Inner Mongolia: mountainous, with desert regions; forms a corridor, the Old Silk Road, much used in early and medieval times for trade with Turkestan, India, and Persia. Capital: Lanzhou. Pop.: 24 380 000 (1996 est.). Area: 366 500 sq. km (141 500 sq. miles).

gantlet[1] ('gæntlɪt, 'gɔ:nt-) *n* **1** a section of a railway where two tracks overlap. **2** *U.S.* a variant spelling of **gauntlet**[2]. [C17 *gantlope* (modern spelling influenced by GAUNTLET[1]), from Swedish *gatlopp,* literally: passageway, from *gata* way (related to GATE[3]) + *lop* course]

gantlet[2] ('gæntlɪt, 'gɔ:nt-) *n* a variant of **gauntlet**[1].

gantline ('gænt,laɪn, -lɪn) *n Nautical.* a line rove through a sheave for hoisting men or gear. [C19: variant of *girtline;* see GIRT[1], LINE]

gantry ('gæntrɪ) *or* **gauntry** *n, pl* **-tries. 1** a bridgelike framework used to support a travelling crane, signals over a railway track, etc. **2** Also called: **gantry scaffold.** the framework tower used to attend to a large rocket on its launching pad. **3** a supporting framework for a barrel or cask. **4a** the area behind a bar where bottles, esp. spirit bottles mounted in optics, are kept for use or display. **4b** the range or quality of the spirits on view: *this pub's got a good gantry.* [C16 (in the sense: wooden platform for barrels): from Old French *chantier,* from Medieval Latin *cantārius,* changed from Latin *canthērius* supporting frame, pack ass; related to Greek *kanthēlios* pack ass]

Gantt chart (gænt) *n* a chart showing, in horizontal lines, activity planned to take place during specified periods, which are indicated in vertical bands. [C20: named after Henry L. *Gantt* (1861–1919), U.S. management consultant]

Ganymede[1] ('gænɪ,mi:d) *n Classical myth.* a beautiful Trojan youth who was abducted by Zeus to Olympus and made the cupbearer of the gods.

Ganymede[2] ('gænɪ,mi:d) *n* the brightest and largest of the four Galilean satellites of Jupiter, and the largest in the solar system. Diameter: 5260 km; orbital radius: 1 070 000 km.

Gao ('gɑ:əʊ, gaʊ) *n* a town in E Mali, on the River Niger: a small river port. Pop.: 54 874 (1987).

gaol (dʒeɪl) *n, vb Brit.* a variant spelling of **jail.** ▸ **'gaoler** *n*

Gaoxiong (,jaʊə'ʃɒŋ) *n* a variant transliteration of the Chinese name for **Kaohsiung.**

gap (gæp) *n* **1** a break or opening in a wall, fence, etc. **2** a break in continuity; interruption; hiatus: *there is a serious gap in the accounts.* **3** a break in a line of hills or mountains affording a route through. **4** *Chiefly U.S.* a gorge or ravine. **5** a divergence or difference; disparity: *there is a gap between his version of the event and hers; the generation gap.* **6** *Electronics.* **6a** a break in a magnetic circuit that increases the inductance and saturation point of the circuit. **6b** See **spark gap. 7 bridge, close, fill,** *or* **stop a gap.** to remedy a deficiency. ◆ *vb* **gaps, gapping, gapped. 8** *(tr)* to make a breach or opening in. [C14: from Old Norse *gap* chasm; related to *gapa* to GAPE, Swedish *gap,* Danish *gab* open mouth, opening] ▸ **'gapless** *adj* ▸ **'gappy** *adj*

gape (geɪp) *vb (intr)* **1** to stare in wonder or amazement, esp. with the mouth open. **2** to open the mouth wide, esp. involuntarily, as in yawning or hunger. **3** to be or become wide open: *the crater gaped under his feet.* ◆ *n* **4** the act of gaping. **5** a wide opening; breach. **6** the width of the widely opened mouth of a vertebrate. **7** a stare or expression of astonishment. ◆ See also **gapes.** [C13: from Old Norse *gapa;* related to Middle Dutch *gapen,* Danish *gabe*] ▸ **'gaping** *adj* ▸ **'gapingly** *adv*

gaper ('geɪpə) *n* **1** a person or thing that gapes. **2** any of various large marine bivalve molluscs of the genera *Mya* and *Lutraria* that burrow in muddy sand. *M. arenaria* is the American soft-shelled clam and the two species of *Lutraria* are the otter shells. The valves have a permanent gap at the hind end.

gapes (geɪps) *n (functioning as sing)* **1** a disease of young domestic fowl, characterized by gaping or gasping for breath and caused by gapeworms. **2** *Informal.* a fit of yawning. ▸ **'gapy** *adj*

gapeworm ('geɪp,wɜ:m) *n* a parasitic nematode worm, *Syngamus trachea,* that lives in the trachea of birds and causes gapes in domestic fowl: family *Syngamidae.*

gapped scale *n Music.* a scale, such as a pentatonic scale, containing fewer than seven notes.

gapping ('gæpɪŋ) *n* (in transformational grammar) a rule that deletes repetitions of a verb, as in the sentence *Bill voted for Smith, Sam for McKay, and Dave for Harris.*

gap-toothed *adj* having wide spaces between the teeth.

gap year *n* a year's break taken by a student between leaving school and starting further education.

gar[1] (gɑ:) *n, pl* **gar** *or* **gars.** short for **garpike** (sense 1).

gar[2] (gɑ:r) *vb (tr) Scot.* to cause or compel. [from Old Norse]

garage ('gærɑ:ʒ, -rɪdʒ) *n* **1** a building or part of a building used to house a motor vehicle. **2** a commercial establishment in which motor vehicles are repaired, serviced, bought, and sold, and which usually also sells motor fuels. **3a** a rough-and-ready style of rock music. **3b** a type of disco music based on soul. ◆ *vb* **4** *(tr)* to put into, keep in, or take to a garage. [C20: from French, from *garer* to dock (a ship), from Old French: to protect, from Old High German *warōn;* see BEWARE]

garage band *n* a rough-and-ready amateurish rock group. [perhaps from the practice of such bands rehearsing in a garage]

garage sale *n* a sale of personal belongings or household effects held at a person's home, usually in the garage.

garaging ('gærədʒɪŋ) *n* accommodation for housing a motor vehicle: *there is garaging for two cars.*

garam masala ('gɑ:rəm mɑ:'sɑ:lə) *n* an aromatic mixture of spices, extensively used in curries. [from Hindi]

Garamond ('gærəmɒnd) *n* a typeface, designed by Claude Garamond (?1480–1561), French type founder.

Garand rifle ('gærənd, gə'rænd) *n* another name for **M-1 rifle.** [C20: named after John C. *Garand* (1888–1974), U.S. gun designer]

garb (gɑ:b) *n* **1** clothes, esp. the distinctive attire of an occupation or profession: *clerical garb.* **2** style of dress; fashion. **3** external appearance, covering, or attire. ◆ *vb* **4** *(tr)* to clothe or cover; attire. [C16: from Old French *garbe* graceful contour, from Old Italian *garbo* grace, probably of Germanic origin] ▸ **'garbless** *adj*

garbage ('gɑ:bɪdʒ) *n* **1** worthless, useless, or unwanted matter. **2** another word (esp. U.S. and Canadian) for **rubbish. 3** *Computing.* invalid data. **4** *Informal.* nonsense. [C15: probably from Anglo-French *garbelage* removal of discarded matter, of uncertain origin; compare Old Italian *garbuglio* confusion]

garbage can *n* a U.S. and Canadian name for **dustbin.** Also called: **ash bin, ash can, trash can.**

garbage collection *n Computing.* a systems routine for eliminating invalid or out-of-date data and releasing storage locations.

garbage truck *n* a U.S. and Canadian name for **dustcart.**

garbanzo (gɑ:'bænzəʊ) *n, pl* **-zos.** another name for **chickpea.** [C18: from Spanish, from *arvanço,* probably of Germanic origin; compare Old High German *araweiz* pea]

garble ('gɑ:bᵊl) *vb (tr)* **1** to jumble (a story, quotation, etc.), esp. unintentionally. **2** to distort the meaning of (an account, text, etc.), as by making misleading omissions; corrupt. **3** *Rare.* to select the best part of. ◆ *n* **4a** the act of garbling. **4b** garbled matter. [C15: from Old Italian *garbellare* to strain, sift, from Arabic *gharbala,* from *ghirbāl* sieve, from Late Latin *crībellum* small sieve, from *crībrum* sieve] ▸ **'garbled** *adj* ▸ **'garbler** *n*

garbo ('gɑ:bəʊ) *n, pl* **garbos.** *Austral. informal.* a dustman. [C20: from GARBAGE]

Garbo ('gɑ:bəʊ) *n* **Greta** ('grɛtə), real name *Greta Lovisa Gustafson.* 1905–90, U.S. film actress, born in Sweden. Her films include *Grand Hotel* (1932), *Queen Christina* (1933), *Anna Karenina* (1935), *Camille* (1936), and *Ninotchka* (1939).

garboard ('gɑ:,bɔ:d) *n Nautical.* the bottommost plank of a vessel's hull. Also called: **garboard plank, garboard strake.** [C17: from Dutch *gaarboord,* probably from Middle Dutch *gaderen* to GATHER + *boord* BOARD]

garboil ('gɑ:bɔɪl) *n Archaic.* confusion or disturbance; uproar. [C16: from Old French *garbouil,* from Old Italian *garbuglio,* ultimately from Latin *bullīre* to boil, hence, seethe with indignation]

garbology (gɑ:'bɒlədʒɪ) *n* the study of the contents of domestic dustbins to analyse the consumption patterns of households. [C20: from GARB(AGE) + OLOGY] ▸ **gar'bologist** *n*

García Lorca (*Spanish* gar'θia 'lɔrka) *n* See (Federico García) **Lorca.**

García Márquez (*Spanish* gar'sia 'markes) *n* **Gabriel.** born 1928, Colombian novelist and short-story writer. His novels include *One Hundred Years of Solitude* (1967), *The Autumn of the Patriarch* (1977), *Love in the Time of Cholera* (1984), and *News of a Kidnapping* (1996). Nobel prize for literature 1982.

garçon (*French* garsɔ̃) *n* a waiter or male servant, esp. if French. [C19: from Old French *gars* lad, probably of Germanic origin]

Gard (*French* gar) *n* a department of S France, in Languedoc-Roussillon region. Capital: Nîmes. Pop.: 607 100 (1995). Area: 5881 sq. km (2294 sq. miles).

garda ('gɑ:rdə) *n, pl* **gardaí** ('gɑ:rdi:). a member of the **Garda Síochána.**

Garda ('gɑ:də) *n* **Lake.** a lake in N Italy: the largest lake in the country. Area: 370 sq. km (143 sq. miles).

gardant ('gɑ:dᵊnt) *adj* a less common spelling of **guardant.**

Garda Síochána ('gɑ:rdə ,ʃɪə'xɑ:nə) *n* the police force of the Republic of Ireland. [C20: from Irish Gaelic *garda* guard + *síochána* of the peace, from *síocháin* peace]

garden ('gɑ:dᵊn) *n* **1** *Brit.* **1a** an area of land, usually planted with grass, trees, flowerbeds, etc., adjoining a house. U.S. and Canadian word: **yard. 1b** *(as modifier): a garden chair.* **2a** an area of land used for the cultivation of ornamental plants, herbs, fruit, vegetables, trees, etc. **2b** *(as modifier): garden tools.* Related adj: **horticultural. 3** *(often pl)* such an area of land that is open to the public, sometimes part of a park: *botanical gardens.* **4a** a fertile and beautiful region. **4b** *(as modifier): a garden paradise.* **5** *(modifier)* provided with or surrounded by a garden or gardens: *a garden flat.* **6 lead (a person) up the garden path.** *Informal.* to mislead or deceive (a person). ◆ *adj* **7 common or garden.** *Informal.* ordinary; unexceptional. ◆ *vb* **8** to work in, cultivate, or take care of (a garden, plot of land, etc.). [C14: from Old French *gardin,* of Germanic origin; compare Old High German *gart* enclosure; see YARD[2] (sense 1)] ▸ **'gardenless** *adj* ▸ **'garden-,like** *adj*

garden centre *n* a place where gardening tools and equipment, plants, seeds, etc., are sold.

garden city *n Brit.* a planned town of limited size with broad streets and spacious layout, containing trees and open spaces and surrounded by a rural belt. See also **garden suburb.**

garden cress *n* a pungent-tasting cruciferous plant, *Lepidium sativum,* with white or reddish flowers: cultivated for salads, as a garnish, etc.

gardener ('gɑ:dnə) *n* **1** a person who works in or takes care of a garden as an occupation or pastime. **2** any bowerbird of the genus *Amblyornis.*

garden flat *n* a flat with direct access to a garden: typically, a garden flat consists of basement accommodation in prewar property, but some are in purpose-built blocks in urban areas.

garden frame *n* another name for a **cold frame.**

gardenia (gɑːˈdiːnɪə) *n* **1** any evergreen shrub or tree of the Old World tropical rubiaceous genus *Gardenia,* cultivated for their large fragrant waxlike typically white flowers. **2** the flower of any of these shrubs. [C18: New Latin, named after Dr Alexander *Garden* (1730–91), American botanist]

gardening (ˈgɑːdᵊnɪŋ) *n* **a** the planning and cultivation of a garden. **b** (*as modifier*): *gardening gloves.*

Garden of Eden *n* the full name for **Eden.**

garden party *n* a social gathering held in the grounds of a house, school, etc., usually with light refreshments.

garden snail *n* any of several land snails common in gardens, where they may become pests, esp. *Helix aspersa,* and sometimes including *Cepaea nemoralis,* common in woods and hedgerows.

garden suburb *n Brit.* a suburb of a large established town or city, planned along the lines of a garden city.

garden warbler *n* any of several small brownish-grey European songbirds of the genus *Sylvia* (warblers), esp. *S. borin,* common in woods and hedges: in some parts of Europe they are esteemed as a delicacy.

garderobe (ˈgɑːdˌrəʊb) *n Archaic.* **1** a wardrobe or the contents of a wardrobe. **2** a bedroom or private room. **3** a privy. [C14: from French, from *garder* to keep + *robe* dress, clothing; see WARDROBE]

Gardiner (ˈgɑːdnə) *n* **Stephen.** ?1483–1555, English bishop and statesman; lord chancellor (1553–55). He opposed Protestantism, supporting the anti-Reformation policies of Mary I.

Gardner (ˈgɑːdnə) *n* **Ava.** 1922–90, U.S. film actress. Her films include *The Killers* (1946), *The Sun also Rises* (1957), and *The Night of the Iguana* (1964).

Garfield (ˈgɑːˌfiːld) *n* **James Abram.** 1831–81, 20th president of the U.S. (1881); assassinated in office.

garfish (ˈgɑːˌfɪʃ) *n, pl* **-fish** *or* **-fishes. 1** another name for **garpike** (sense 1). **2** an elongated European marine teleost fish, *Belone belone,* with long toothed jaws: related to the flying fishes. [Old English *gār* spear + FISH]

garganey (ˈgɑːgənɪ) *n* a small Eurasian duck, *Anas querquedula,* closely related to the mallard. The male has a white stripe over each eye. [C17: from Italian dialect *garganei,* of imitative origin]

Gargantua (gɑːˈgæntjʊə) *n* a gigantic king noted for his great capacity for food and drink, in Rabelais' satire *Gargantua and Pantagruel* (1534).

gargantuan (gɑːˈgæntjʊən) *adj* (*sometimes cap.*) huge; enormous.

USAGE Some people think that *gargantuan* should only be used to describe things connected with food: *a gargantuan meal; his gargantuan appetite.*

garget (ˈgɑːgɪt) *n* inflammation of the mammary gland of domestic animals, esp. cattle. [C16 (in the sense: throat): from Old French *gargate,* perhaps from Latin *gurges* gulf] ▸ **ˈgargety** *adj*

gargle (ˈgɑːgᵊl) *vb* **1** to rinse (the mouth and throat) with a liquid, esp. a medicinal fluid by slowly breathing out through the liquid. **2** to utter (words, sounds, etc.) with the throaty bubbling noise of gargling. ◆ *n* **3** the liquid used for gargling. **4** the sound produced by gargling. [C16: from Old French *gargouiller* to gargle, make a gurgling sound, from *gargouille* throat, perhaps of imitative origin] ▸ **ˈgargler** *n*

gargoyle (ˈgɑːgɔɪl) *n* **1** a waterspout carved in the form of a grotesque face or creature and projecting from a roof gutter, esp. of a Gothic church. **2** any grotesque ornament or projection, esp. on a building. **3** a person with a grotesque appearance. [C15: from Old French *gargouille* gargoyle, throat; see GARGLE] ▸ **ˈgargoyled** *adj*

garibaldi (ˌgærɪˈbɔːldɪ) *n* **1** a woman's loose blouse with long sleeves popular in the 1860s, copied from the red flannel shirt worn by Garibaldi's soldiers. **2** *Brit.* a type of biscuit having a layer of currants in the centre.

Garibaldi (ˌgærɪˈbɔːldɪ) *n* **Giuseppe** (dʒuˈzeppe). 1807–82, Italian patriot; a leader of the Risorgimento. He fought against the Austrians and French in Italy (1848–49; 1859) and, with 1000 volunteers, conquered Sicily and Naples for the emerging kingdom of Italy (1860).

garish (ˈgeərɪʃ) *adj* gay or colourful in a crude or vulgar manner; gaudy. [C16: from earlier *gaure* to stare + -ISH] ▸ **ˈgarishly** *adv* ▸ **ˈgarishness** *n*

garland (ˈgɑːlənd) *n* **1** a wreath or festoon of flowers, leaves, etc., worn round the head or neck or hung up. **2** a representation of such a wreath, as in painting, sculpture, etc. **3** a collection of short literary pieces, such as ballads or poems; miscellany or anthology. **4** *Nautical.* a ring or grommet of rope. ◆ *vb* **5** (*tr*) to deck or adorn with a garland or garlands. [C14: from Old French *garlande,* perhaps of Germanic origin]

Garland (ˈgɑːlənd) *n* **Judy,** real name *Frances Gumm.* 1922–69, U.S. singer and film actress. Already a child star, she achieved international fame with *The Wizard of Oz* (1939). Later films included *Meet Me in St Louis* (1944) and *A Star is Born* (1954).

garlic (ˈgɑːlɪk) *n* **1** a hardy widely cultivated Asian alliaceous plant, *Allium sativum,* having a stem bearing whitish flowers and bulbils. **2a** the bulb of this plant, made up of small segments (cloves) that have a strong odour and pungent taste and are used in cooking. **2b** (*as modifier*): *a garlic taste.* **3** any of various other plants of the genus *Allium.* [Old English *gārlēac,* from *gār* spear + *lēac* LEEK]

garlicky (ˈgɑːlɪkɪ) *adj* containing or resembling the taste or odour of garlic.

garlic mustard *n* a cruciferous plant, *Alliaria petiolata,* of N temperate regions, with small white flowers and an odour of garlic. Also called: **jack-by-the-hedge, hedge garlic.** Compare **garlic.**

garment (ˈgɑːmənt) *n* **1** (*often pl*) an article of clothing. **2** outer covering. ◆ *vb* **3** (*tr; usually passive*) to cover or clothe. [C14: from Old French *garniment,* from *garnir* to equip; see GARNISH] ▸ **ˈgarmentless** *adj*

garner (ˈgɑːnə) *vb* (*tr*) **1** to gather or store in or as if in a granary. ◆ *n* **2** an archaic word for **granary. 3** *Archaic.* a place for storage or safekeeping. [C12: from Old French *gernier* granary, from Latin *grānārium,* from *grānum* grain]

Garner (ˈgɑːnə) *n* **Erroll.** 1921–77, U.S. jazz pianist and composer.

garnet[1] (ˈgɑːnɪt) *n* any of a group of hard glassy red, yellow, or green minerals consisting of the silicates of calcium, iron, manganese, chromium, magnesium, and aluminium in cubic crystalline form: used as a gemstone and abrasive. Formula: $A_3B_2(SiO_4)_3$ where A is a divalent metal and B is a trivalent metal. [C13: from Old French *grenat,* from *grenat* (adj) red, from *pome grenate* POMEGRANATE] ▸ **ˈgarnet-ˌlike** *adj*

garnet[2] (ˈgɑːnɪt) *n Nautical.* a tackle used for lifting cargo. [C15: probably from Middle Dutch *garnaat*]

garnet paper *n* sandpaper having powdered garnet as the abrasive.

Garnett (ˈgɑːnɪt) *n* **1 Constance.** 1862–1946, British translator of Russian novels. **2** her son, **David.** 1892–1981, British novelist and editor. His novels include *Lady Into Fox* (1922) and *Aspects of Love* (1955).

garnierite (ˈgɑːnɪəˌraɪt) *n* a green amorphous mineral consisting of hydrated nickel magnesium silicate: a source of nickel. [C19: named after Jules *Garnier* (died 1904), French geologist]

garnish (ˈgɑːnɪʃ) *vb* (*tr*) **1** to decorate; trim. **2** to add something to (food) in order to improve its appearance or flavour. **3** *Law.* **3a** to serve with notice of proceedings; warn. **3b** *Obsolete.* to summon to proceedings already in progress. **3c** to attach (a debt). **4** *Slang.* to extort money from. ◆ *n* **5** a decoration; trimming. **6** something, such as parsley, added to a dish for its flavour or decorative effect. **7** *Obsolete slang.* a payment illegally extorted, as from a prisoner by his jailer. [C14: from Old French *garnir* to adorn, equip, of Germanic origin; compare Old High German *warnōn* to pay heed] ▸ **ˈgarnisher** *n*

garnishee (ˌgɑːnɪˈʃiː) *Law.* ◆ *n* **1** a person upon whom a garnishment has been served. ◆ *vb* **-nishees, -nisheeing, -nisheed.** (*tr*) **2** to attach (a debt or other property) by garnishment. **3** to serve (a person) with a garnishment.

garnishment (ˈgɑːnɪʃmənt) *n* **1** the act of garnishing. **2** decoration or embellishment; garnish. **3** *Law.* **3a** a notice or warning. **3b** *Obsolete.* a summons to court proceedings already in progress. **3c** a notice warning a person holding money or property belonging to a debtor whose debt has been attached to hold such property until directed by the court to apply it.

garniture (ˈgɑːnɪtʃə) *n* decoration or embellishment. [C16: from French, from *garnir* to GARNISH]

Garonne (*French* garɔn) *n* a river in SW France, rising in the central Pyrenees in Spain and flowing northeast then northwest into the Gironde estuary. Length: 580 km (360 miles).

garotte (gəˈrɒt) *n, vb* a variant spelling of **garrotte.** ▸ **gaˈrotter** *n*

garpike (ˈgɑːˌpaɪk) *n* **1** Also called: **garfish, gar.** any primitive freshwater elongated bony fish of the genus *Lepisosteus,* of North and Central America, having very long toothed jaws and a body covering of thick scales. **2** another name for **garfish** (sense 2).

garret (ˈgærɪt) *n* another word for **attic** (sense 1). [C14: from Old French *garite,* watchtower, from *garir* to protect, of Germanic origin; see WARY]

garret window *n* a skylight that lies along the slope of the roof.

Garrick (ˈgærɪk) *n* **David.** 1717–79, English actor and theatre manager.

garrigue *French.* (garig) *n* another name for **maquis** (sense 1).

garrison (ˈgærɪsᵊn) *n* **1** the troops who maintain and guard a base or fortified place. **2a** the place itself. **2b** (*as modifier*): *garrison town.* ◆ *vb* **3** (*tr*) to station (troops) in (a fort). [C13: from Old French *garison,* from *garir* to defend, of Germanic origin; compare Old Norse *verja* to defend, Old English, Old High German *werian*]

garron (ˈgærən) *n* a small sturdy pony bred and used chiefly in Scotland and Ireland. [C16: from Gaelic *gearran*]

garrotte, garrote, *or* **garotte** (gəˈrɒt) *n* **1** a Spanish method of execution by strangulation or by breaking the neck. **2** the device, usually an iron collar, used in such executions. **3** *Obsolete.* strangulation of one's victim while committing robbery. ◆ *vb* (*tr*) **4** to execute by means of the garrotte. **5** to strangle, esp. in order to commit robbery. [C17: from Spanish *garrote,* perhaps from Old French *garrot* cudgel; of obscure origin] ▸ **garˈrotter, garˈroter,** *or* **gaˈrotter** *n*

garrulous (ˈgærʊləs) *adj* **1** given to constant and frivolous chatter; loquacious; talkative. **2** wordy or diffuse; prolix. [C17: from Latin *garrulus,* from *garrīre* to chatter] ▸ **ˈgarrulously** *adv* ▸ **ˈgarrulousness** *or* **garrulity** (gæˈruːlɪtɪ) *n*

garrya (ˈgærɪə) *n* any ornamental catkin-bearing evergreen shrub of the North American genus *Garrya:* family *Garryaceae.* [C19: named after Nicholas *Garry* (1781–1856), an officer of the Hudson's Bay Company]

garryowen (ˌgærɪˈəʊɪn) *n* (in rugby union) another term for **up-and-under.** [C20: named after *Garryowen* RFC, Ireland]

garter (ˈgɑːtə) *n* **1** a band, usually of elastic, worn round the arm or leg to hold up a shirtsleeve, sock, or stocking. **2** the U.S. and Canadian word for **suspender.** ◆ *vb* **3** (*tr*) to fasten, support, or secure with or as if with a garter. [C14: from Old Northern French *gartier,* from *garet* bend of the knee, probably of Celtic origin]

Garter (ˈgɑːtə) *n* **the. 1** See **Order of the Garter. 2** (*sometimes not cap.*) **2a** the badge of this Order. **2b** membership of this Order.

garter snake *n* any nonvenomous North American colubrid snake of the genus *Thamnophis,* typically marked with longitudinal stripes.

garter stitch *n* knitting in which all the rows are knitted in plain stitch instead of alternating with purl rows.

garth[1] (gɑːθ) *n* **1** a courtyard surrounded by a cloister. **2** *Archaic.* a yard or garden. [C14: from Old Norse *garthr;* related to Old English *geard* YARD[2]]

garth[2] (gɑːθ) *n Northern English dialect.* a child's hoop, often the rim of a bicycle wheel. [dialect variant of GIRTH]

Garvey (ˈgɑːvɪ) *n* **Marcus.** 1887–1940, Jamaican Black nationalist leader, active in the U.S. He founded (1914) the Universal Negro Improvement Association and led the Back-to-Africa movement: gaoled for fraud (1925–27).

Gary (ˈgærɪ) *n* a port in NW Indiana, on Lake Michigan: a major world steel producer. Pop.: 110 975 (1996 est.).

gas (gæs) *n, pl* **gases** *or* **gasses. 1** a substance in a physical state in which it does not resist change of shape and will expand indefinitely to fill any container. If very high pressure is applied a gas may become liquid or solid, otherwise its density tends towards that of the condensed phase. Compare **liquid** (sense 1), **solid** (sense 1). **2** any substance that is gaseous at room temperature and atmospheric pressure. **3** any gaseous substance that is above its critical temperature and therefore not liquefiable by pressure alone. Compare **vapour** (sense 2). **4a** a fossil fuel in the form of a gas, used as a source of domestic and industrial heat. See also **coal gas, natural gas. 4b** (*as modifier*): *a gas cooker; gas fire.* **5** a gaseous anaesthetic, such as nitrous oxide. **6** *Mining.* firedamp or the explosive mixture of firedamp and air. **7** the usual U.S., Canadian, and New Zealand word for **petrol**, a shortened form of **gasoline. 8 step on the gas.** *Informal.* **8a** to increase the speed of a motor vehicle; accelerate. **8b** to hurry. **9** a toxic or suffocating substance in suspension in air used against an enemy. **10** *Informal.* idle talk or boasting. **11** *Slang.* a delightful or successful person or thing: *his latest record is a gas.* **12** *U.S.* an informal name for **flatus.** ♦ *vb* **gases** *or* **gasses, gassing, gassed. 13** (*tr*) to provide or fill with gas. **14** (*tr*) to subject to gas fumes, esp. so as to asphyxiate or render unconscious. **15** (*intr*) to give off gas, as in the charging of a battery. **16** (*tr*) (in textiles) to singe (fabric) with a flame from a gas burner to remove unwanted fibres. **17** (*intr;* foll. by *to*) *Informal.* to talk in an idle or boastful way (to a person). **18** (*tr*) *Slang, chiefly U.S. and Canadian.* to thrill or delight. [C17 (coined by J. B. van Helmont (1577–1644), Flemish chemist): modification of Greek *khaos* atmosphere] ▶ **'gasless** *adj*

gasbag ('gæs,bæg) *Informal.* ♦ *n* **1** a person who talks in a voluble way, esp. about unimportant matters. ♦ *vb* **-bags, -bagging, -bagged. 2** (*intr.*) *Irish.* to talk in a voluble way, esp. about unimportant matters.

gas black *n* finely powdered carbon produced by burning natural gas. It is used as a pigment in paints, etc.

gas burner *n* **1** Also called: **gas jet.** a jet or nozzle from which a combustible gas issues in order to form a stable flame. **2** an assembly of such jets or nozzles, used esp. in cooking.

gas chamber *or* **oven** *n* an airtight room into which poison gas is introduced to kill people or animals.

gas chromatography *n* a technique for analysing a mixture of volatile substances in which the mixture is carried by an inert gas through a column packed with a selective adsorbent and a detector records on a moving strip the conductivity of the gas leaving the tube. Peaks on the resulting graph indicate the presence of a particular component. Also called: **gas-liquid chromatography.**

gas coal *n* coal that is rich in volatile hydrocarbons, making it a suitable source of domestic gas.

Gascoigne ('gæscɔɪn) *n* **Paul**, known as *Gazza.* born 1967, English footballer.

gascon ('gæskən) *n Rare.* a boaster; braggart. [C14: from Old French *gascoun;* compare Latin *Vascōnēs* Basque]

Gascon ('gæskən) *n* **1** a native or inhabitant of Gascony. **2** the dialect of French spoken in Gascony. ♦ *adj* **3** of or relating to Gascony, its inhabitants, or their dialect of French.

gasconade (,gæskə'neɪd) *Rare.* ♦ *n* **1** boastful talk, bragging, or bluster. ♦ *vb* **2** (*intr*) to boast, brag, or bluster. [C18: from French *gasconnade,* from *gasconner* to chatter, boast like a GASCON] ▶ **,gascon'ader** *n*

gas constant *n* the constant in the gas equation. It is equal to 8.3143 joules per kelvin per mole. Symbol: *R* Also called: **universal gas constant.**

Gascony ('gæskənɪ) *n* a former province of SW France. French name: **Gascogne** (gaskɔɲ).

gas-cooled reactor *n* a nuclear reactor using a gas as the coolant. In the Mark I type the coolant is carbon dioxide, the moderator is graphite, and the fuel is uranium cased in magnox. See also **advanced gas-cooled reactor.**

gas-discharge tube *n Electronics.* any tube in which an electric discharge takes place through a gas.

gaselier (,gæsə'lɪə) *n* a variant spelling of **gasolier.**

gas engine *n* a type of internal-combustion engine using a flammable gas, such as coal gas or natural gas, as fuel.

gaseous ('gæsɪəs, -ʃəs, -ʃɪəs, 'geɪ-) *adj* of, concerned with, or having the characteristics of a gas. ▶ **'gaseousness** *n*

gas equation *n* an equation that equates the product of the pressure and the volume of one mole of a gas to the product of its thermodynamic temperature and the **gas constant.** The equation is exact for an ideal gas and is a good approximation for real gases at low pressures. Also called: **ideal gas equation** *or* **law.**

gas gangrene *n* gangrene resulting from infection of a wound by anaerobic bacteria (esp. *Clostridium welchii*) that cause gas bubbles and swelling in the surrounding tissues.

gash[1] (gæʃ) *vb* **1** (*tr*) to make a long deep cut or wound in; slash. ♦ *n* **2** a long deep cut or wound. [C16: from Old French *garser* to scratch, wound, from Vulgar Latin *charissāre* (unattested), from Greek *kharassein* to scratch]

gash[2] (gæʃ) *adj Slang.* surplus to requirements; unnecessary, extra, or spare. [C20: of unknown origin]

gasholder ('gæs,həʊldə) *n* **1** Also called: **gasometer.** a large tank for storing coal gas or natural gas prior to distribution to users. **2** any vessel for storing or measuring a gas.

gasiform ('gæsɪ,fɔːm) *adj* in a gaseous form.

gasify ('gæsɪ,faɪ) *vb* **-fies, -fying, -fied. 1** to make into or become a gas. **2** to subject (coal, etc.) to destructive distillation to produce gas, esp. for use as a fuel. ▶ **'gasi,fiable** *adj* ▶ **,gasifi'cation** *n* ▶ **'gasi,fier** *n*

Gaskell ('gæskəl) *n* **Mrs.** married name of *Elizabeth Cleghorn Stevenson.* 1810–65, English novelist. Her novels include *Mary Barton* (1848), an account of industrial life in Manchester, and *Cranford* (1853), a social study of a country village.

gasket ('gæskɪt) *n* **1** a compressible packing piece of paper, rubber, asbestos, etc., sandwiched between the faces of a metal joint to provide a seal. **2** *Nautical.* a piece of line used as a sail stop. **3 blow a gasket.** *Slang.* to burst out in anger. [C17 (in the sense: rope lashing a furled sail): probably from French *garcette* rope's end, literally: little girl, from Old French *garce* girl, feminine of *gars* boy, servant]

gaskin ('gæskɪn) *n* the lower part of a horse's thigh, between the hock and the stifle. [C16: perhaps shortened from GALLIGASKINS]

gas laws *pl n* the physical laws obeyed by gases, esp. Boyle's law and Charles' law. See also **gas equation.**

gaslight ('gæs,laɪt) *n* **1** a type of lamp in which the illumination is produced by an incandescent mantle heated by a jet of gas. **2** the light produced by such a lamp.

gas lighter *n* **1** a device for igniting a jet of gas. **2** a cigarette lighter using a gas as fuel.

gas-liquid chromatography *n* another name for **gas chromatography.**

gas main *n* a large pipeline in which gas is carried for distribution through smaller pipes to consumers.

gasman ('gæs,mæn) *n, pl* **-men.** a man employed to read household gas meters, supervise gas fittings, etc.

gas mantle *n* a mantle for use in a gaslight. See **mantle** (sense 4).

gas mask *n* a mask fitted with a chemical filter to enable the wearer to breathe air free of poisonous or corrosive gases: used for military or industrial purposes. Also called (in Britain): **respirator.**

gas meter *n* an apparatus for measuring and recording the amount of gas passed through it.

gasohol ('gæsə,hɒl) *n* a mixture of 80% or 90% petrol with 20% or 10% ethyl alcohol, for use as a fuel in internal-combustion engines.

gas oil *n* a fuel oil obtained in the distillation of petroleum, intermediate in viscosity and boiling point between paraffin and lubricating oils. It boils above about 250°C.

gasolier *or* **gaselier** (,gæsə'lɪə) *n* a branched hanging fitting for gaslights. [C19: from GAS + (CHAND)ELIER]

gasoline *or* **gasolene** ('gæsə,liːn) *n* a U.S. and Canadian name for **petrol.** ▶ **gasolinic** (,gæsə'lɪnɪk) *adj*

gasometer (gæs'ɒmɪtə) *n* a nontechnical name for **gasholder.**

gasometry (gæs'ɒmɪtrɪ) *n* the measurement of quantities of gases. ▶ **gasometric** (,gæsə'metrɪk) *or* **,gaso'metrical** *adj*

gas oven *n* **1** a domestic oven heated by gas. **2** a gas-fuelled cremation chamber. **3** another name for **gas chamber.**

gasp (gɑːsp) *vb* **1** (*intr*) to draw in the breath sharply, convulsively, or with effort, esp. in expressing awe, horror, etc. **2** (*intr;* foll. by *after* or *for*) to crave. **3** (*tr;* often foll. by *out*) to utter or emit breathlessly. ♦ *n* **4** a short convulsive intake of breath. **5** a short convulsive burst of speech. **6 at the last gasp. 6a** at the point of death. **6b** at the last moment. [C14: from Old Norse *geispa* to yawn; related to Swedish dialect *gispa,* Danish *gispe*] ▶ **'gaspingly** *adv*

Gaspar ('gæspə, 'gæspɑː) *n* a variant of **Caspar.**

Gaspé Peninsula (gæ'speɪ; *French* gaspe) *n* a peninsula in E Canada, in SE Quebec between the St Lawrence River and New Brunswick: mountainous and wooded with many lakes and rivers. Area: about 29 500 sq. km (11 400 sq. miles). Also called: **the Gaspé.**

gasper ('gɑːspə) *n* **1** a person who gasps. **2** *Brit. dated slang.* a cheap cigarette.

gas-permeable lens *n* a contact lens made of rigid plastic that is more permeable to air than a standard hard lens. Abbrev.: **GP.** Compare **hard lens, soft lens.**

gas plant *n* an aromatic white-flowered Eurasian rutaceous plant, *Dictamnus albus,* that emits a vapour capable of being ignited. Also called: **burning bush, dittany, fraxinella.**

gas poker *n* a long tubular gas burner used to kindle a fire.

gas ring *n* a circular assembly of gas jets, used esp. for cooking.

gassed (gæst) *adj Slang.* drunk.

Gassendi (*French* gasɛ̃dɪ) *n* **Pierre.** 1592–1655, French physicist and philosopher, who promoted an atomic theory of matter.

gasser ('gæsə) *n* a drilling or well that yields natural gas.

Gasser ('gæsə) *n* **Herbert Spencer.** 1888–1963, U.S. physiologist: shared a Nobel prize for physiology or medicine (1944) with Erlanger for work on electrical signs of nervous activity.

gassing ('gæsɪŋ) *n* **1** the act or process of supplying or treating with gas. **2** the affecting or poisoning of persons with gas or fumes. **3** the evolution of a gas, esp. in electrolysis.

gas station *n Chiefly U.S. and Canadian.* another term for **filling station.**

gassy ('gæsɪ) *adj* **-sier, -siest. 1** filled with, containing, or resembling gas. **2** *Informal.* full of idle or vapid talk. ▶ **'gassiness** *n*

gasteropod ('gæstərə,pɒd) *n, adj* a variant of **gastropod.**

gas thermometer *n* a device for measuring temperature by observing the pressure of gas at a constant volume or the volume of a gas kept at a constant pressure.

gastight ('gæs,taɪt) *adj* not allowing gas to enter or escape.

gastralgia (gæs'trældʒɪə) *n* pain in the stomach. ▶ **gas'tralgic** *adj*

gastrectomy (gæs'trɛktəmɪ) *n, pl* **-mies.** surgical removal of all or part of the stomach.

gastric ('gæstrɪk) *adj* of, relating to, near, or involving the stomach: *gastric pains.*

gastric juice *n* a digestive fluid secreted by the stomach, containing hydrochloric acid, pepsin, rennin, etc.

gastric ulcer *n* an ulcer of the mucous membrane lining the stomach. Compare **peptic ulcer.**

gastrin ('gæstrɪn) *n* a polypeptide hormone secreted by the stomach: stimulates secretion of gastric juice.

gastritis (gæs'traɪtɪs) *n* inflammation of the stomach. ▸ **gastritic** (gæs'trɪtɪk) *adj*
gastro- *or often before a vowel* **gastr-** *combining form.* stomach: *gastroenteritis; gastritis.* [from Greek *gastēr*]
gastrocolic (ˌgæstrəʊ'kɒlɪk) *adj* of or relating to the stomach and colon: *gastrocolic reflex.*
gastroduodenostomy (ˌgæstrəʊˌdjuːəʊdiː'nɒstəmɪ) *n* a surgical operation in which the duodenum is joined to a new opening in the stomach, esp. to bypass an obstruction.
gastroenteric (ˌgæstrəʊɛn'tɛrɪk) *adj* another word for **gastrointestinal.**
gastroenteritis (ˌgæstrəʊˌɛntə'raɪtɪs) *n* inflammation of the stomach and intestines. ▸ **gastroenteritic** (ˌgæstrəʊˌɛntə'rɪtɪk) *adj*
gastroenterology (ˌgæstrəʊˌɛntə'rɒlədʒɪ) *n* the branch of medical science concerned with diseases of the stomach and intestines. ▸ **ˌgastroˌenter'ologist** *n*
gastroenterostomy (ˌgæstrəʊˌɛntə'rɒstəmɪ) *n, pl* **-mies.** surgical formation of an artificial opening between the stomach and the small intestine.
gastrointestinal (ˌgæstrəʊɪn'tɛstɪnᵊl) *adj* of or relating to the stomach and intestinal tract.
gastrolith ('gæstrəlɪθ) *n Pathol.* a stone in the stomach; gastric calculus.
gastrology (gæs'trɒlədʒɪ) *n* another name for **gastroenterology.** ▸ **gastrological** (ˌgæstrə'lɒdʒɪkᵊl) *adj* ▸ **gas'trologist** *n*
gastronome ('gæstrəˌnəʊm), **gastronomer** (gæs'trɒnəmə), *or* **gastronomist** *n* less common words for **gourmet.**
gastronomy (gæs'trɒnəmɪ) *n* **1** the art of good eating. **2** the type of cookery of a particular region: *the gastronomy of Provence.* [C19: from French *gastronomie,* from Greek *gastronomia,* from *gastēr* stomach; see -NOMY] ▸ **gastronomic** (ˌgæstrə'nɒmɪk) *or* **ˌgastro'nomical** *adj* ▸ **ˌgastro'nomically** *adv*
gastropod ('gæstrəˌpɒd) *or* **gasteropod** *n* **1** any mollusc of the class *Gastropoda,* typically having a flattened muscular foot for locomotion and a head that bears stalked eyes. The class includes the snails, whelks, limpets, and slugs. ◆ *adj* **2** of, relating to, or belonging to the *Gastropoda.* ▸ **gastropodan** (gæs'trɒpədᵊn) *adj, n* ▸ **gas'tropodous** *adj*
gastroscope ('gæstrəˌskəʊp) *n* a medical instrument for examining the interior of the stomach. ▸ **gastroscopic** (ˌgæstrə'skɒpɪk) *adj* ▸ **gastroscopist** (gæs'trɒskəpɪst) *n* ▸ **gas'troscopy** *n*
gastrostomy (gæs'trɒstəmɪ) *n, pl* **-mies.** surgical formation of an artificial opening into the stomach from the skin surface: used for feeding.
gastrotomy (gæs'trɒtəmɪ) *n, pl* **-mies.** surgical incision into the stomach.
gastrotrich ('gæstrətrɪk) *n* any minute aquatic multicellular animal of the phylum *Gastrotricha,* having a wormlike body covered with cilia and bristles. [from New Latin *gastrotricha,* from GASTRO- + Greek *-trichos* -haired: see TRICHO-]
gastrovascular (ˌgæstrəʊ'væskjʊlə) *adj* (esp. of the body cavities of coelenterates) functioning in digestion and circulation.
gastrula ('gæstrʊlə) *n, pl* **-las** *or* **-lae** (-ˌliː). a saclike animal embryo consisting of three layers of cells (see **ectoderm, mesoderm,** and **endoderm**) surrounding a central cavity (archenteron) with a small opening (blastopore) to the exterior. [C19: New Latin: little stomach, from Greek *gastēr* belly] ▸ **'gastrular** *adj*
gastrulation (ˌgæstrʊ'leɪʃən) *n Embryol.* the process in which a gastrula is formed from a blastula by the inward migration of cells.
gas turbine *n* an internal-combustion engine in which the expanding gases emerging from one or more combustion chambers drive a turbine. A rotary compressor driven by the turbine compresses the air used for combustion, power being taken either as torque from the turbine or thrust from the expanding gases.
gas vacuole *n Biology.* a gas-filled structure that provides buoyancy in some aquatic bacteria.
gas welding *n* a method of welding in which a combination of gases, usually oxyacetylene, is used to provide a hot flame.
gas well *n* a well for obtaining natural gas.
gasworks ('gæsˌwɜːks) *n* (*functioning as sing*) a plant in which gas, esp. coal gas, is made.
gat[1] (gæt) *vb Archaic.* a past tense of **get.**
gat[2] (gæt) *n Slang, chiefly U.S.* a pistol or revolver. [C20: shortened from GATLING GUN]
gat[3] (gæt) *n* a narrow channel of water. [C18: probably from Old Norse *gat* passage; related to GATE[1]]
gate[1] (geɪt) *n* **1** a movable barrier, usually hinged, for closing an opening in a wall, fence, etc. **2** an opening to allow passage into or out of an enclosed place. **3** any means of entrance or access. **4** a mountain pass or gap, esp. one providing entry into another country or region. **5a** the number of people admitted to a sporting event or entertainment. **5b** the total entrance money received from them. **6** (in a large airport) any of the numbered exits leading to the airfield or aircraft: *passengers for Paris should proceed to gate 14.* **7** *Horse racing.* short for **starting gate. 8** *Electronics.* **8a** a logic circuit having one or more input terminals and one output terminal, the output being switched between two voltage levels determined by the combination of input signals. **8b** a circuit used in radar that allows only a fraction of the input signal to pass. **9** the electrode region or regions in a field-effect transistor that is biased to control the conductivity of the channel between the source and drain. **10** a component in a motion-picture camera or projector that holds each frame flat and momentarily stationary behind the lens. **11** a slotted metal frame that controls the positions of the gear lever in a motor vehicle. **12** *Rowing.* a hinged clasp to prevent the oar from jumping out of a rowlock. **13** a frame surrounding the blade or blades of a saw. ◆ *vb* (*tr*) **14** to provide with a gate or gates. **15** *Brit.* to restrict (a student) to the school or college grounds as a punishment. **16** to select (part of a waveform) in terms of amplitude or time. [Old English *geat;* related to Old Frisian *jet* opening, Old Norse *gat* opening, passage] ▸ **'gateless** *adj* ▸ **'gateˌlike** *adj*
gate[2] (geɪt) *n Dialect.* **1** the channels by which molten metal is poured into a mould. **2** the metal that solidifies in such channels. [C17: probably related to Old English *gyte* a pouring out, *geotan* to pour]
gate[3] (geɪt) *n Scot. and northern English dialect.* **1** a way, road, street, or path. **2** a way or method of doing something. [C13: from Old Norse *gata* path; related to Old High German *gazza* road, street]
-gate *n combining form.* indicating a person or thing that has been the cause of, or is associated with, a public scandal. [C20: on the analogy of WATERGATE]
gateau *or* **gâteau** ('gætəʊ) *n, pl* **-teaux** (-təʊz). any of various elaborate cakes, usually layered with cream and richly decorated. [French: cake]
gate-crash *vb* to gain entry to (a party, concert, etc.) without invitation or payment. ▸ **'gate-ˌcrasher** *n*
gatefold ('geɪtˌfəʊld) *n* an oversize page in a book or magazine that is folded in. Also called: **foldout.**
gatefold sleeve *n* a record sleeve that opens out like a book.
gatehouse ('geɪtˌhaʊs) *n* **1** a building above or beside an entrance gate to a city, university, etc., often housing a porter or guard, or (formerly) used as a fortification. **2** a small house at the entrance to the grounds of a country mansion. **3** a structure that houses the controls operating lock gates or dam sluices.
gatekeeper ('geɪtˌkiːpə) *n* **1** a person who has charge of a gate and controls who may pass through it. **2** any of several Eurasian butterflies of the genus *Pyronia,* esp. *P. tithonus,* having brown-bordered orange wings with a black-and-white eyespot on each forewing: family *Satyridae.* **3** a manager in a large organization who controls the flow of information, esp. to parent and subsidiary companies.
gate-leg table *or* **gate-legged table** *n* a table with one or two drop leaves that are supported when in use by a hinged leg swung out from the frame.
gate money *n* the total receipts taken for admission to a sporting event or other entertainment.
gatepost ('geɪtˌpəʊst) *n* **1a** the post on which a gate is hung. **1b** the post to which a gate is fastened when closed. **2 between you, me, and the gatepost.** confidentially. **3** *Logic.* another name for **turnstile** (sense 3).
Gates (geɪts) *n* **1 Bill,** full name *William Henry Gates.* born 1955, U.S. computer-software executive; founder (1976) of Microsoft Corporation. **2 Horatio.** ?1728–1806, American Revolutionary general: defeated the British at Saratoga (1777).
Gateshead ('geɪtsˌhɛd) *n* **1** a port in NE England, in Gateshead unitary authority, Tyne and Wear: engineering works. Pop.: 83 159 (1991). **2** a unitary authority in NE England, in Tyne and Wear. Pop.: 200 968 (1996 est.). Area: 142 sq. km (55 sq. miles).
gate valve *n* a valve in a pipe or channel having a sliding plate that controls the flow.
gateway ('geɪtˌweɪ) *n* **1** an entrance that may be closed by or as by a gate. **2** a means of entry or access: *Bombay, gateway to India.* **3** *Computing.* hardware and software that connect incompatible computer networks, allowing information to be passed from one to another.
Gath (gæθ) *n Old Testament.* one of the five cities of the Philistines, from which Goliath came (I Samuel 17:4) and near which Saul fell in battle (II Samuel 1:20). Douay spelling: **Geth** (gɛθ).
Gatha ('gɑːtə) *n Zoroastrianism.* any of a number of versified sermons in the Avesta that are in a more ancient dialect than the rest. [from Avestan *gāthā-;* related to Sanskrit *gāthā* song]
gather ('gæðə) *vb* **1** to assemble or cause to assemble. **2** to collect or be collected gradually; muster. **3** (*tr*) to learn from information given; conclude or assume. **4** (*tr*) to pick or harvest (flowers, fruit, etc.). **5** (*tr;* foll. by *to* or *into*) to clasp or embrace: *the mother gathered the child into her arms.* **6** (*tr*) to bring close (to) or wrap (around): *she gathered her shawl about her shoulders.* **7** to increase or cause to increase gradually, as in force, speed, intensity, etc. **8** to contract (the brow) or (of the brow) to become contracted into wrinkles; knit. **9** (*tr*) to assemble (sections of a book) in the correct sequence for binding. **10** (*tr*) to collect by making a selection. **11** (*tr*) to prepare or make ready: *to gather one's wits.* **12** to draw (material) into a series of small tucks or folds by passing a thread through it and then pulling it tight. **13** (*intr*) (of a boil or other sore) to come to a head; form pus. ◆ *n* **14a** the act of gathering. **14b** the amount gathered. **15** a small fold in material, as made by a tightly pulled stitch; tuck. **16** *Printing.* an informal name for **section** (sense 17). [Old English *gadrian;* related to Old Frisian *gaderia,* Middle Low German *gaderen*] ▸ **'gatherable** *adj* ▸ **'gatherer** *n*
gathering ('gæðərɪŋ) *n* **1** a group of people, things, etc., that are gathered together; assembly. **2** *Sewing.* a gather or series of gathers in material. **3a** the formation of pus in a boil. **3b** the pus so formed. **4** *Printing.* an informal name for **section** (sense 17).
Gatling gun ('gætlɪŋ) *n* a hand-cranked automatic machine gun equipped with a rotating cluster of barrels that are fired in succession using brass cartridges. [C19: named after R. J. *Gatling* (1818–1903), its U.S. inventor]
GATT (gæt) *n acronym for* General Agreement on Tariffs and Trade: a multilateral international treaty signed in 1947 to promote trade, esp. by means of the reduction and elimination of tariffs and import quotas; replaced in 1995 by the World Trade Organization.
Gatún Lake (*Spanish* ga'tun) *n* a lake in Panama, part of the Panama Canal: formed in 1912 on the completion of the **Gatún Dam** across the Chagres River. Area: 424 sq. km (164 sq. miles).
gauche (gəʊʃ) *adj* lacking ease of manner; tactless. [C18: French: awkward, left, from Old French *gauchir* to swerve, ultimately of Germanic origin; related to Old High German *wankōn* to stagger] ▸ **'gauchely** *adv* ▸ **'gaucheness** *n*

gaucherie (ˌgəʊʃəˈriː, ˈgəʊʃərɪ; *French* goʃri) *n* **1** the quality of being gauche. **2** a gauche act.

gaucho (ˈgaʊtʃəʊ) *n, pl* **-chos.** a cowboy of the South American pampas, usually one of mixed Spanish and Indian descent. [C19: from American Spanish, probably from Quechuan *wáhcha* orphan, vagabond]

gaud (gɔːd) *n* an article of cheap finery; trinket; bauble. [C14: probably from Old French *gaudir* to be joyful, from Latin *gaudēre*]

gaudeamus igitur (ˌgaʊdɪˈɑːmʊs ˈɪgɪˌtʊə, ˌgɔːdɪˈeɪməs ˈɪdʒɪtə) *interj* let us therefore rejoice. [Latin, from a medieval student song]

gaudery (ˈgɔːdərɪ) *n, pl* **-eries.** cheap finery or display.

Gaudí (ˈgaʊdɪ; *Spanish* gauˈði) *n* **Antonio** (anˈtonjo). 1852–1926, Spanish architect, regarded as one of the most original exponents of Art Nouveau in Europe and noted esp. for the church of the Sagrada familia, Barcelona.

Gaudier-Brzeska (*French* godjebʒɛska) *n* **Henri** (ɑ̃ri), original name *Henri Gaudier.* 1891–1915, French vorticist sculptor.

gaudy[1] (ˈgɔːdɪ) *adj* **gaudier, gaudiest.** gay, bright, or colourful in a crude or vulgar manner; garish. [C16: from GAUD] ▸ **ˈgaudily** *adv* ▸ **ˈgaudiness** *n*

gaudy[2] (ˈgɔːdɪ) *n, pl* **gaudies.** *Brit.* a celebratory festival or feast held at some schools and colleges. [C16: from Latin *gaudium* joy, from *gaudēre* to rejoice]

gauffer (ˈgəʊfə) *n, vb* a less common spelling of **goffer.**

gauge *or* **gage** (geɪdʒ) *vb* (*tr*) **1** to measure or determine the amount, quantity, size, condition, etc., of. **2** to estimate or appraise; judge. **3** to check for conformity or bring into conformity with a standard measurement, dimension, etc. ◆ *n* **4** a standard measurement, dimension, capacity, or quantity. **5** any of various instruments for measuring a quantity: *a pressure gauge.* **6** any of various devices used to check for conformity with a standard measurement. **7** a standard or means for assessing; test; criterion. **8** scope, capacity, or extent. **9** the diameter of the barrel of a gun, esp. a shotgun. **10** the thickness of sheet metal or the diameter of wire. **11** the distance between the rails of a railway track: in Britain 4 ft. 8½ in. (1.435 m). **12** the distance between two wheels on the same axle of a vehicle, truck, etc. **13** *Nautical.* the position of a vessel in relation to the wind and another vessel. One vessel may be windward (**weather gauge**) or leeward (**lee gauge**) of the other. **14** the proportion of plaster of Paris added to mortar to accelerate its setting. **15** the distance between the nails securing the slates, tiles, etc., of a roof. **16** a measure of the fineness of woven or knitted fabric, usually expressed as the number of needles used per inch. **17** the width of motion-picture film or magnetic tape. ◆ *adj* **18** (of a pressure measurement) measured on a pressure gauge that registers zero at atmospheric pressure; above or below atmospheric pressure: *5 bar gauge.* See also **absolute** (sense 10). [C15: from Old Northern French, probably of Germanic origin] ▸ **ˈgaugeable** *or* **ˈgageable** *adj* ▸ **ˈgaugeably** *or* **ˈgageably** *adv*

gauge boson *n Physics.* a boson that mediates the interaction between elementary particles. There are four types: photons for electromagnetic interactions, gluons for strong interactions, intermediate vector bosons for weak interactions, and gravitons for gravitational interactions.

gauger *or* **gager** (ˈgeɪdʒə) *n* **1** a person or thing that gauges. **2** *Chiefly Brit.* a customs officer who inspects bulk merchandise, esp. liquor casks, for excise duty purposes. **3** a collector of excise taxes.

gauge theory *n Physics.* a type of theory of elementary particles designed to explain the strong, weak, and electromagnetic interactions in terms of exchange of virtual particles.

Gauguin (*French* gogɛ̃) *n* **Paul** (pɔl). 1848–1903, French postimpressionist painter, who worked in the South Pacific from 1891. Inspired by primitive art, his work is characterized by flat contrasting areas of pure colours.

Gauhati (gaʊˈhɑːtɪ) *n* a city in NE India, in Assam on the River Brahmaputra: centre of British administration in Assam (1826–74). Pop.: 584 342 (1991).

Gaul (gɔːl) *n* **1** an ancient region of W Europe corresponding to N Italy, France, Belgium, part of Germany, and the S Netherlands: divided into Cisalpine Gaul, which became a Roman province before 100 B.C., and Transalpine Gaul, which was conquered by Julius Caesar (58–51 B.C.). Latin name: **Gallia. 2** a native of ancient Gaul. **3** a Frenchman.

Gauleiter (ˈgaʊˌlaɪtə) *n* **1** a provincial governor in Germany under Hitler. **2** (*sometimes not cap.*) *Informal.* a person in a position of petty or local authority who behaves in an overbearing authoritarian manner. [from German, from *Gau* district + *Leiter* LEADER]

Gaulish (ˈgɔːlɪʃ) *n* **1** the extinct language of the pre-Roman Gauls, belonging to the Celtic branch of the Indo-European family. ◆ *adj* **2** of or relating to ancient Gaul, the Gauls, or their language.

Gaulle (gəʊl, gɔːl; *French* gol) *n* **Charles de.** See (Charles) **de Gaulle.**

Gaullism (ˈgəʊlɪzəm, ˈgɔː-) *n* **1** the conservative French nationalist policies and principles associated with General de Gaulle. **2** a political movement founded on and supporting General de Gaulle's principles and policies.

Gaullist (ˈgəʊlɪst, ˈgɔː-) *n* **1** a supporter of Gaullism. ◆ *adj* **2** of, characteristic of, supporting, or relating to Gaullism.

gault (gɔːlt) *n* a stiff compact clay or thick heavy clayey soil. [C16: of obscure origin]

Gault (gɔːlt) *n* **the.** the Lower Cretaceous clay formation in eastern England.

gaultheria (gɔːlˈθɪərɪə) *n* any aromatic evergreen shrub of the ericaceous genus *Gaultheria,* of America, Asia, Australia, and New Zealand, esp. the wintergreen. [C19: New Latin, after Jean-François *Gaultier,* 18th-century Canadian physician and botanist]

Gaultier (*French* gotje) *n* **Jean-Paul** (ʒɑ̃pɔl). born 1952, French fashion designer.

gaumless ((ˈgɔːmlɪs) *adj* a variant spelling of **gormless.**

gaun (gɔːn) *vb* the present participle of **gae.**

gaunt (gɔːnt) *adj* **1** bony and emaciated in appearance. **2** (of places) bleak or desolate. [C15: perhaps of Scandinavian origin; compare Norwegian dialect *gand* tall lean person] ▸ **ˈgauntly** *adv* ▸ **ˈgauntness** *n*

gauntlet[1] (ˈgɔːntlɪt) *or* **gantlet** *n* **1** a medieval armoured leather glove. **2** a heavy glove with a long cuff. **3 take up** (*or* **throw down**) **the gauntlet.** to accept (or offer) a challenge. [C15: from Old French *gantelet,* diminutive of *gant* glove, of Germanic origin]

gauntlet[2] (ˈgɔːntlɪt) *n* **1** a punishment in which the victim is forced to run between two rows of men who strike at him as he passes: formerly a military punishment. **2 run the gauntlet. 2a** to suffer this punishment. **2b** to endure an onslaught or ordeal, as of criticism. **3** a testing ordeal; trial. **4** a variant spelling of **gantlet**[1] (sense 1). [C15: changed (through influence of GAUNTLET[1]) from earlier *gantlope;* see GANTLET[1]]

gauntry (ˈgɔːntrɪ) *n, pl* **-tries.** a variant of **gantry.**

gaup (gɔːp) *vb* a variant spelling of **gawp.**

gaur (gaʊə) *n* a large wild member of the cattle tribe, *Bos gaurus,* inhabiting mountainous regions of S Asia. [C19: from Hindi, from Sanskrit *gāura*]

Gause's principle (ˈgaʊzəz) *n Ecology.* the principle that similar species cannot coexist for long in the same ecological niche. [named after G. F. *Gause,* 20th-century Soviet biologist]

gauss (gaʊs) *n, pl* **gauss.** the cgs unit of magnetic flux density; the flux density that will induce an emf of 1 abvolt (10^{-8} volt) per centimetre in a wire moving across the field at a velocity of 1 centimetre per second. 1 gauss is equivalent to 10^{-4} tesla. [after K.F. GAUSS]

Gauss (*German* gaus) *n* **Karl Friedrich** (karl ˈfriːdrɪç). 1777–1855, German mathematician: developed the theory of numbers and applied mathematics to astronomy, electricity and magnetism, and geodesy. ▸ **Gaussian** (ˈgaʊsɪən) *adj*

Gaussian distribution *n* another name for **normal distribution.**

gaussmeter (ˈgaʊsˌmiːtə) *n* an instrument for measuring the intensity of a magnetic field.

Gautama (ˈgaʊtəmə) *n* the Sanskrit form of the family name of Siddhartha, the historical Buddha.

Gauteng (xaʊˈtɛŋ) *n* a province of N South Africa; formed in 1994 from part of the former province of Transvaal: service industries, mining, and manufacturing. Capital: Johannesburg. Pop.: 7 048 300 (1995 est.). Area: 18 810 sq. km (7262 sq. miles).

Gautier (*French* gotje) *n* **Théophile** (teɔfil). 1811–72, French poet, novelist, and critic. His early extravagant romanticism gave way to a preoccupation with poetic form and expression that anticipated the Parnassians.

gauze (gɔːz) *n* **1a** a transparent cloth of loose plain or leno weave. **1b** (*as modifier*): *a gauze veil.* **2** a surgical dressing of muslin or similar material. **3** any thin openwork material, such as wire. **4** a fine mist or haze. [C16: from French *gaze,* perhaps from GAZA, where it was believed to originate]

gauzy (ˈgɔːzɪ) *adj* **gauzier, gauziest.** resembling gauze; thin and transparent. ▸ **ˈgauzily** *adv* ▸ **ˈgauziness** *n*

gavage (ˈgævɑːʒ) *n* forced feeding by means of a tube inserted into the stomach through the mouth. [C19: from French, from *gaver,* from Old French (dialect) *gave* throat]

Gavaskar (gæˈvæskɑː) *n* **Sunil Manohar** (ˈsʊnɪl ˈmænəohɑː). born 1949, Indian cricketer. He captained India 1978–83 and 1984–85.

gave (geɪv) *vb* the past tense of **give.**

gavel (ˈgævᵊl) *n* **1** a small hammer used by a chairman, auctioneer, etc., to call for order or attention. **2** a hammer used by masons to trim rough edges off stones. [C19: of unknown origin]

gavelkind (ˈgævᵊlˌkaɪnd) *n* **1** a former system of land tenure peculiar to Kent based on the payment of rent to the lord instead of the performance of services by the tenant. **2** the land subject to such tenure. **3** *English law.* (formerly) land held under this system. [C13: from Old English *gafol* tribute + *gecynd* KIND[2]]

gavial (ˈgeɪvɪəl), **gharial,** *or* **garial** (ˈgærɪəl) *n* **1** a large fish-eating Indian crocodilian, *Gavialis gangeticus,* with a very long slender snout: family *Gavialidae.* **2 false gavial.** a SE Asian crocodile, *Tomistoma schlegeli,* similar to but smaller than the gavial. [C19: from French, from Hindi *ghariyāl*]

Gävle (*Swedish* ˈjɛːvlə) *n* a port in E Sweden, on an inlet of the Gulf of Bothnia. Pop.: 90 270 (1994).

gavotte *or* **gavot** (gəˈvɒt) *n* **1** an old formal dance in quadruple time. **2** a piece of music composed for or in the rhythm of this dance. [C17: from French, from Provençal *gavoto,* from *gavot* mountaineer, dweller in the Alps (where the dance originated), from *gava* goitre (widespread in the Alps), from Old Latin *gaba* (unattested) throat]

gawk (gɔːk) *n* **1** a clumsy stupid person; lout. ◆ *vb* **2** (*intr*) to stare in a stupid way; gape. [C18: from Old Danish *gaukr;* probably related to GAPE]

gawky (ˈgɔːkɪ) *or* **gawkish** *adj* **gawkier, gawkiest. 1** clumsy or ungainly; awkward. **2** *West Yorkshire dialect.* left-handed. ▸ **ˈgawkily** *or* **ˈgawkishly** *adv* ▸ **ˈgawkiness** *or* **ˈgawkishness** *n*

gawp *or* **gaup** (gɔːp) *vb* (*intr;* often foll. by *at*) *Brit. slang.* to stare stupidly; gape. [C14 *galpen;* probably related to Old English *gielpan* to boast, YELP. Compare Dutch *galpen* to yelp] ▸ **ˈgawper** *n*

gay (geɪ) *adj* **1a** homosexual. **1b** (*as n*): *a group of gays.* **2a** carefree and merry: *a gay temperament.* **2b** brightly coloured; brilliant: *a gay hat.* **2c** given to pleasure, esp. in social entertainment: *a gay life.* [C13: from Old French *gai,* from Old Provençal, of Germanic origin] ▸ **ˈgayness** *n*

USAGE *Gayness* is the state of being homosexual. The noun which refers to the state of being carefree and merry is *gaiety.*

Gay (geɪ) *n* **John.** 1685–1732, English poet and dramatist; author of *The Beggar's Opera* (1728).

Gaya (ˈgɑːjə, ˈgaɪə) *n* a city in NE India, in central Bihar: Hindu place of pilgrimage and one of the holiest sites of Buddhism. Pop.: 291 675 (1991).

gayal (gəˈjæl) *n, pl* **gayal** *or* **gayals.** an ox of India and Myanmar, *Bibos frontalis,* possibly a semidomesticated variety of gaur, black or brown with white stockings. [C19: from Bengali *gayāl,* from Sanskrit *gāura;* compare GAUR]

Gay Gordons ('gɔ:dᵊnz) *n* (*functioning as sing*) *Brit.* an energetic old-time dance.

Gay-Lussac ('geɪ'lu:sæk; *French* gelysak) *n* **Joseph Louis** (ʒozef lwi). 1778–1850, French physicist and chemist: discovered the law named after him (1808), investigated the effects of terrestrial magnetism, isolated boron and cyanogen, and discovered methods of manufacturing sulphuric and oxalic acids.

Gay-Lussac's law *n* **1** the principle that gases react together in volumes (measured at the same temperature and pressure) that bear a simple ratio to each other and to the gaseous products. **2** another name for **Charles' law.**

Gayomart (gɑ:'jəumɑ:t) *n Zoroastrianism.* the first man, whose seed was buried in the earth for 40 years and then produced the first human couple.

gaz. *abbrev. for:* **1** gazette. **2** gazetteer.

Gaza ('gɑ:zə) *n* a city in the Gaza Strip: a Philistine city in biblical times. It was under Egyptian administration from 1949 until occupied by Israel (1967). Pop.: 293 000 (1990 est.). Arabic name: **Ghazzah.**

gazania (gə'zeɪnɪə) *n* any plant of the S. African genus *Gazania,* grown for their rayed flowers in variegated colours; the flowers close in the afternoon: family *Compositae.* Also called: **treasure flower.** [named after Theodore of *Gaza,* 1398–1478, translator of the botanical treatises of Theophrastus]

Gazankulu (ˌgazaŋ'ku:lu:) *n* (formerly) a Bantu homeland in South Africa; abolished in 1993. Capital: Giyani.

Gaza Strip *n* a coastal region on the SE corner of the Mediterranean: administered by Egypt from 1949; occupied by Israel from 1967; granted autonomy in 1993 and administered by the Palestinian National Authority from 1994. Pop.: 1 082 000 (1998 est.).

gaze (geɪz) *vb* **1** (*intr*) to look long and fixedly, esp. in wonder or admiration. ♦ *n* **2** a fixed look; stare. [C14: from Swedish dialect *gasa* to gape at] ▸ **'gazer** *n*

gazebo (gə'zi:bəu) *n, pl* **-bos** *or* **-boes.** a summerhouse, garden pavilion, or belvedere, sited to command a view. [C18: perhaps a pseudo-Latin coinage based on GAZE]

gazehound ('geɪzˌhaʊnd) *n* a hound such as a greyhound that hunts by sight rather than by scent.

gazelle (gə'zɛl) *n, pl* **-zelles** *or* **-zelle.** any small graceful usually fawn-coloured antelope of the genera *Gazella* and *Procapra,* of Africa and Asia, such as *G. thomsoni* (**Thomson's gazelle**). [C17: from Old French, from Arabic *ghazāl*] ▸ **ga'zelle-ˌlike** *adj*

gazette (gə'zɛt) *n* **1a** a newspaper or official journal. **1b** (*cap. when part of the name of a newspaper*): *the Thame Gazette.* **2** *Brit.* an official document containing public notices, appointments, etc. Abbrev.: **gaz.** ♦ *vb* **3** (*tr*) *Brit.* to announce or report (facts or an event) in a gazette. [C17: from French, from Italian *gazzetta,* from Venetian dialect *gazeta* news-sheet costing one *gazet,* small copper coin, perhaps from *gaza* magpie, from Latin *gaia, gaius* jay]

gazetted officer *n* (in India) a senior official whose appointment is published in the government gazette.

gazetteer (ˌgæzɪ'tɪə) *n* **1** a book or section of a book that lists and describes places. Abbrev.: **gaz.** **2** *Archaic.* a writer for a gazette or newspaper; journalist.

Gaziantep (ˌgɑ:zi:ɑ:n'tɛp) *n* a city in S Turkey: base for Ibrahim Pasha's campaign against the Turks (1839) and centre of Turkish resistance to French forces (1921). Pop.: 730 435 (1995 est.). Former name (until 1921): **Aintab.**

gazpacho (gəz'pɑ:tʃəu, gæs-) *n* a Spanish soup made from tomatoes, peppers, etc., and served cold. [from Spanish]

gazump (gə'zʌmp) *Brit.* ♦ *vb* **1** to raise the price of something, esp. a house, after agreeing a price verbally with (an intending buyer). **2** (*tr*) to swindle or overcharge. ♦ *n* **3** the act or an instance of gazumping. [C20: of uncertain origin] ▸ **ga'zumper** *n*

gazunder (gə'zʌndə) *Brit.* ♦ *vb* **1** to reduce an offer on a property immediately before exchanging contracts, having previously agreed a higher price with (the seller). ♦ *n* **2** an act or instance of gazundering. [C20: modelled on GAZUMP] ▸ **ga'zunderer** *n*

Gb **1** *symbol for* gilbert. **2** Also **GB.** *abbrev. for* gigabyte.

GB *abbrev. for* **1** Great Britain. **2** Also **Gb.** gigabyte. ♦ **3** *international car registration for* Great Britain.

GBA *international car registration for* Alderney.

GBE *abbrev. for* (Knight or Dame) Grand Cross of the British Empire (a Brit. title).

GBG *international car registration for* Guernsey.

GBH *abbrev. for* grievous bodily harm.

GBJ *international car registration for* Jersey.

GBM *international car registration for* Isle of Man.

GBS *abbrev. for* George Bernard Shaw.

GBZ *international car registration for* Gibraltar.

GC *abbrev. for* George Cross (a Brit. award for bravery).

GCA **1** *Aeronautics. abbrev. for* ground control approach. ♦ **2** *international car registration for* Guatemala.

GCB *abbrev. for* (Knight) Grand Cross of the Bath (a Brit. title).

GCE (in Britain) *abbrev. for* General Certificate of Education: a public examination in specified subjects taken as qualifying examinations for entry into a university, college, etc. The GCSE has replaced it at O level. See also **A level, S level.**

GCF *or* **gcf** *abbrev. for* greatest common factor.

GCHQ (in Britain) *abbrev. for* Government Communications Headquarters.

G clef *n* another name for **treble clef.**

GCM *or* **gcm** *abbrev. for* greatest common measure.

GCMG *abbrev. for* (Knight or Dame) Grand Cross of the Order of St Michael and St George (a Brit. title).

G-cramp *n* another name for **cramp**[2] (sense 2).

GCSE (in Britain) *abbrev. for* General Certificate of Secondary Education: a public examination in specified subjects for 16-year-old schoolchildren. It replaced the GCE O-level and CSE.

GCVO *abbrev. for* (Knight or Dame) Grand Cross of the Royal Victorian Order (a Brit. title).

Gd *the chemical symbol for* gadolinium.

Gdańsk (*Polish* gdajinsk) *n* **1** the chief port of Poland, on the Baltic: a member of the Hanseatic league; under Prussian rule (1793–1807 and 1814–1919); a free city under the League of Nations from 1919 until annexed by Germany in 1939; returned to Poland in 1945. Pop.: 462 800 (1996 est.). German name: **Danzig.** **2 Bay of.** a wide inlet of the Baltic Sea on the N coast of Poland.

g'day *or* **gidday** (gə'daɪ) *sentence substitute.* an Australian and N.Z. informal variant of **good day.**

Gdns *abbrev. for* Gardens.

GDP *or* **gdp** *abbrev. for* gross domestic product.

GDR *abbrev. for* German Democratic Republic (East Germany; DDR).

gds *abbrev. for* goods.

Gdynia (*Polish* 'gdɪnja) *n* a port in N Poland, near Gdańsk: developed 1924–39 as the outlet for trade through the Polish Corridor; naval base. Pop.: 251 400 (1996 est.).

Ge[1] (dʒi:) *n* another name for **Gaea.**

Ge[2] *the chemical symbol for* germanium.

gean (gi:n) *n* **1** Also called: **wild cherry.** a white-flowered rosaceous tree, *Prunus avium,* of Europe, W Asia, and N Africa, the ancestor of the cultivated sweet cherries. **2** see **sweet cherry** (sense 1).

geanticline (dʒi:'æntɪˌklaɪn) *n* a gently sloping anticline covering a large area. [C19: from Greek *gē* earth, land + ANTICLINE] ▸ **geˌanti'clinal** *adj*

gear (gɪə) *n* **1** a toothed wheel that engages with another toothed wheel or with a rack in order to change the speed or direction of transmitted motion. **2** a mechanism for transmitting motion by gears, esp. for a specific purpose: *the steering gear of a boat.* **3** the engagement or specific ratio of a system of gears: *in gear; high gear.* **4** personal equipment and accoutrements; belongings. **5** equipment and supplies for a particular operation, sport, etc.: *fishing gear.* **6** *Nautical.* all equipment or appurtenances belonging to a certain vessel, sailor, etc. **7** short for **landing gear. 8** *Informal.* up-to-date clothes and accessories, esp. those bought by young people. **9** *Slang.* **9a** stolen goods. **9b** illegal drugs. **10** a less common word for **harness** (sense 1). **11 in gear.** working or performing effectively or properly. **12 out of gear.** out of order; not functioning properly. ♦ *vb* **13** (*tr*) to adjust or adapt (one thing) so as to fit in or work with another: *to gear our output to current demand.* **14** (*tr*) to equip with or connect by gears. **15** (*intr*) to be in or come into gear. **16** (*tr*) to equip with harness. [C13: from Old Norse *gervi;* related to Old High German *garawī* equipment, Old English *gearwe*] ▸ **'gearless** *adj*

gearbox ('gɪəˌbɒks) *n* **1** the metal casing within which a train of gears is sealed. **2** this metal casing and its contents, esp. in a motor vehicle.

gear cluster *n Engineering.* an assembly of gears permanently attached to a shaft.

gear down *vb* (*tr, adv*) to adapt to a new situation by decreasing output, intensity of operations, etc.

gearing ('gɪərɪŋ) *n* **1** an assembly of gears designed to transmit motion. **2** the act or technique of providing gears to transmit motion. **3** Also called: **capital gearing.** *Accounting, Brit.* the ratio of a company's debt capital to its equity capital. U.S. word: **leverage.**

gear lever *or U.S. and Canadian* **gearshift** ('gɪəˌʃɪft) *n* a lever used to move gearwheels relative to each other, esp. in a motor vehicle.

gear train *n Engineering.* a system of gears that transmits power from one shaft to another.

gear up *vb* (*adv*) **1** (*tr*) to equip with gears. **2** to prepare, esp. for greater efficiency: *is our industry geared up for the new millennium?*

gearwheel ('gɪəˌwi:l) *n* another name for **gear** (sense 1).

Geber ('dʒi:bə) *n* Latinized form of Jabir, assumed in honour of Jabir ibn Hayyan by a 14th-century alchemist, probably Spanish: he described the preparation of nitric and sulphuric acids.

gecko ('gɛkəu) *n, pl* **-os** *or* **-oes.** any small insectivorous terrestrial lizard of the family *Gekkonidae,* of warm regions. The digits have adhesive pads, which enable these animals to climb on smooth surfaces. [C18: from Malay *ge'kok,* of imitative origin]

gedact (gə'dɑ:kt, -'dækt) *or* **gedeckt** (gə'dɛkt) *n Music.* a flutelike stopped metal diapason organ pipe. [(*gedeckt*) from German: covered, from *decken* to cover]

gee[1] (dʒi:) *interj* **1** Also: **gee up!** an exclamation, as to a horse or draught animal, to encourage it to turn to the right, go on, or go faster. ♦ *vb* **gees, geeing, geed. 2** (usually foll. by *up*) to move (an animal, esp. a horse) ahead; urge on. ♦ *n* **3** *Slang.* See **gee-gee.** [C17: origin uncertain]

gee[2] (dʒi:) *interj U.S. and Canadian informal.* a mild exclamation of surprise, admiration, etc. Also: **gee whizz.** [C20: euphemism for JESUS]

Gee (dʒi:) *n* **Maurice.** born 1931, New Zealand novelist.

geebung ('dʒi:bʌŋ) *n* **1** any of various trees and shrubs of the genus *Persoonia* of Australia having an edible but tasteless fruit. **2** the fruit of these trees. **3** (in the 19th century) an uncultivated Australian from the country districts. [from a native Australian language]

gee-gee ('dʒi:ˌdʒi:) *n Slang.* a horse. [C19: reduplication of GEE[1]]

geek (gi:k) *n Slang.* **1** a boring and unattractive social misfit. **2** a degenerate. [C19: probably variant of Scottish *geck* fool, from Middle Low German *geck*] ▸ **'geeky** *adj*

geelbek ('xɪəlˌbɛk) *n S. African.* a yellow-jawed edible marine fish. [from Afrikaans *geel* yellow + *bek* mouth]

Geelong (dʒə'lɒŋ) *n* a port in SE Australia, in S Victoria on Port Phillip Bay. Pop.: 152 600 (1995 est.).

geepound ('dʒiː,paʊnd) *n* another name for **slug**[2] (sense 1). [C20: from *gee*, representing G(RAVITY) + POUND[2]]

geese (giːs) *n* the plural of **goose**.

geest (giːst) *n* an area of sandy heathland in N Germany and adjacent areas. [C19: Low German *Geest* dry soil]

Ge'ez ('giːɛz) *n* the classical form of the ancient Ethiopic language, having an extensive Christian literature and still used in Ethiopia as a liturgical language.

geezer ('giːzə) *n Informal.* a man. [C19: probably from dialect pronunciation of *guiser*, from GUISE + -ER[1]]

gefilte fish *or* **gefüllte fish** (gə'fɪltə) *n Jewish cookery.* a dish consisting of fish and matzo meal rolled into balls and poached, formerly served stuffed into the skin of a fish. [Yiddish, literally: filled fish]

gegenschein ('geɪgən,ʃaɪn) *n* a faint glow in the sky, just visible at a position opposite to that of the sun and having a similar origin to zodiacal light. Also called: **counterglow**. [German, from *gegen* against, opposite + *Schein* light; see SHINE]

Gehenna (gɪ'hɛnə) *n* **1** *Old Testament.* the valley below Jerusalem, where children were sacrificed and where idolatry was practised (II Kings 23:10; Jeremiah 19:6) and where later offal and refuse were slowly burned. **2** *New Testament, Judaism.* a place where the wicked are punished after death. **3** a place or state of pain and torment. [C16: from Late Latin, from Greek *Geena*, from Hebrew *Gê' Hinnōm*, literally: valley of Hinnom, symbolic of hell]

gehlenite ('geɪlə,naɪt) *n* a green mineral consisting of calcium aluminium silicate in tetragonal crystalline form. Formula: $Ca_2Al_2SiO_7$. [named after A. F. *Gehlen* (1775–1815), German chemist; see -ITE[1]]

Geiger ('gaɪgə) *n* **Hans** (hans). 1882–1945, German physicist: developed the Geiger counter.

Geiger counter *or* **Geiger-Müller counter** ('gaɪgə'mʊlə) *n* an instrument for detecting and measuring the intensity of ionizing radiation. It consists of a gas-filled tube containing a fine wire anode along the axis of a cylindrical cathode with a potential difference of several hundred volts. Any particle or photon which ionizes any number of gas molecules in the tube causes a discharge which is registered by electronic equipment. The magnitude of the discharge does not depend upon the nature or the energy of the ionizing particle. Compare **proportional counter**. [C20: named after Hans GEIGER and W. *Müller*, 20th-century German physicist]

Geikie ('giːkɪ) *n* Sir **Archibald**. 1835–1924, Scottish geologist noted for his study of British volcanic rocks.

geisha ('geɪʃə) *n, pl* **-sha** *or* **-shas**. a professional female companion for men in Japan, trained in music, dancing, and the art of conversation. [C19: from Japanese, from *gei* art + *sha* person, from Ancient Chinese *ngi* and *che*]

Geissler tube ('gaɪslə) *n* a glass or quartz vessel, usually having two bulbs containing electrodes separated by a capillary tube, for maintaining an electric discharge in a low-pressure gas as a source of visible or ultraviolet light for spectroscopy. [C19: named after Heinrich *Geissler* (1814–79), German mechanic]

geitonogamy (,gaɪtə'nɒgəmɪ) *n Botany.* the transfer of pollen to a stigma of a different flower on the same plant. [C19: from Greek *geitōn* neighbour + -GAMY]

gel (dʒɛl) *n* **1** a semirigid jelly-like colloid in which a liquid is dispersed in a solid: *nondrip paint is a gel.* **2** See **hair gel**. **3** *Theatre, informal.* See **gelatine** (sense 4). ◆ *vb* **gels, gelling, gelled. 4** to become or cause to become a gel. **5** a variant spelling of **jell**. [C19: by shortening from GELATINE]

gelada ('dʒɛlədə, 'gel-; dʒɪ'lɑːdə, gɪ-) *n* a NE African baboon, *Theropithecus gelada*, with dark brown hair forming a mane over the shoulders, a bare red chest, and a ridge muzzle: family *Cercopithecidae*. Also called: **gelada baboon**. [probably from Arabic *qilādah* mane]

Geländesprung (gə'lɛndə,ʃprʊŋ) *or* **gelände jump** (gə'lɛndə) *n Skiing.* a jump made in downhill skiing, usually over an obstacle. [German, from *Gelände* terrain + *Sprung* jump]

gelatine ('dʒɛlə,tiːn) *or* **gelatin** ('dʒɛlətɪn) *n* **1** a colourless or yellowish water-soluble protein prepared by boiling animal hides and bones: used in foods, glue, photographic emulsions, etc. **2** an edible jelly made of this substance, sweetened and flavoured. **3** any of various substances that resemble gelatine. **4** Also called (informal): **gel**. a translucent substance used for colour effects in theatrical lighting. [C19: from French *gélatine*, from Medieval Latin *gelātina*, from Latin *gelāre* to freeze]

gelatinize *or* **gelatinise** (dʒɪ'lætɪ,naɪz) *vb* **1** to make or become gelatinous. **2** (*tr*) *Photog.* to coat (glass, paper, etc.) with gelatine. ▸ **ge,latini'zation** *or* **ge,latini'sation** *n* ▸ **ge'lati,nizer** *or* **ge'lati,niser** *n*

gelatinoid (dʒɪ'lætɪ,nɔɪd) *adj* **1** resembling gelatine. ◆ *n* **2** a gelatinoid substance, such as collagen.

gelatinous (dʒɪ'lætɪnəs) *adj* **1** consisting of or resembling jelly; viscous. **2** of, containing, or resembling gelatine. ▸ **ge'latinously** *adv* ▸ **ge'latinousness** *n*

gelation[1] (dʒɪ'leɪʃən) *n* the act or process of freezing a liquid. [C19: from Latin *gelātiō* a freezing; see GELATINE]

gelation[2] (dʒɪ'leɪʃən) *n* the act or process of forming into a gel. [C20: from GEL]

geld[1] (gɛld) *vb* **gelds, gelding, gelded** *or* **gelt.** (*tr*) **1** to castrate (a horse or other animal). **2** to deprive of virility or vitality; emasculate; weaken. [C13: from Old Norse *gelda*, from *geldr* barren] ▸ **'gelder** *n*

geld[2] (gɛld) *n* a tax on land levied in late Anglo-Saxon and Norman England. [Old English *gield* service, tax; related to Old Norse *gjald* tribute, Old Frisian *jeld*, Old High German *gelt* retribution, income]

Gelderland *or* **Guelderland** ('gɛldə,lænd; *Dutch* 'xɛldərlɑnt) *n* a province of the E Netherlands: formerly a duchy, belonging successively to several different European powers. Capital: Arnhem. Pop.: 1 876 300 (1996 est.). Area: 5014 sq. km (1955 sq. miles). Also called: **Guelders**.

gelding ('gɛldɪŋ) *n* a castrated male horse. [C14: from Old Norse *geldingr*; see GELD[1], -ING[1]]

Geldof ('gɛldɒf) *n* **Bob**. Full name *Robert Frederick Zenon Geldof*. born 1954, Irish rock singer and philanthropist: formerly lead vocalist with the Boomtown Rats (1977–86): organizer of the Band Aid charity for famine relief in Africa. He received an honorary Knighthood in 1986.

Gelée (*French* ʒəle) *n* **Claude** (klod). the original name of **Claude Lorrain**.

Gelibolu (gɛ'libɔlu) *n* the Turkish name for **Gallipoli**.

gelid ('dʒɛlɪd) *adj* very cold, icy, or frosty. [C17: from Latin *gelidus* icy cold, from *gelu* frost] ▸ **ge'lidity** *or* **'gelidness** *n* ▸ **'gelidly** *adv*

gelignite ('dʒɛlɪg,naɪt) *n* a type of dynamite in which the nitrogelatine is absorbed in a base of wood pulp and potassium or sodium nitrate. Also called (informal): **gelly** ('dʒɛlɪ). [C19: from GEL(ATINE) + Latin *ignis* fire + -ITE[1]]

Gelligaer (*Welsh* ,gɛhli:'gaɪr) *n* a town in S Wales, in Caerphilly county borough. Pop.: 15 906 (1991).

Gell-Mann ('gel'mæn) *n* **Murray**. born 1929, U.S. physicist, noted for his research on the interaction and classification of elementary particles: Nobel prize for physics in 1969.

gelsemium (dʒɛl'siːmɪəm) *n, pl* **-miums** *or* **-mia** (-mɪə). **1** any climbing shrub of the loganiaceous genus *Gelsemium*, of SE Asia and North America, esp. the yellow jasmine, having fragrant yellow flowers. **2** the powdered root of the yellow jasmine, formerly used as a sedative. [C19: New Latin, from Italian *gelsomino* JASMINE]

Gelsenkirchen (*German* gelzən'kɪrçən) *n* an industrial city in W Germany, in North Rhine-Westphalia. Pop.: 291 164 (1996 est.).

gelt[1] (gelt) *vb Archaic or dialect.* a past tense and past participle of **geld**[1].

gelt[2] (gelt) *n Slang, chiefly U.S.* cash or funds; money. [C19: from Yiddish, from Old High German *gelt* reward]

gem (dʒɛm) *n* **1** a precious or semiprecious stone used in jewellery as a decoration; jewel. **2** a person or thing held to be a perfect example; treasure. **3** a size of printer's type, approximately equal to 4 point. **4** *N.Z.* a type of small sweet cake. ◆ *vb* **gems, gemming, gemmed. 5** (*tr*) to set or ornament with gems. [C14: from Old French *gemme*, from Latin *gemma* bud, precious stone] ▸ **'gem,like** *adj* ▸ **'gemmy** *adj*

Gemara (ge'mɔrə; *Hebrew* gema'ra) *n Judaism.* the main body of the Talmud, consisting of a record of ancient rabbinical debates about the interpretation of the Mishna and constituting the primary source of Jewish religious law. See also **Talmud**. [C17: from Aramaic *gemārā* completion, from *gemār* to complete] ▸ **Ge'maric** *adj* ▸ **Ge'marist** *n*

gemeinschaft (*German* gə'mainʃaft) *n, pl* **-schaften** (*German* -ʃaftən). (*often cap.*) a social group united by common beliefs, family ties, etc. Compare **gesellschaft**. [German, literally: community]

gemfibrozil (dʒɛm'faɪbrəʊzɪl) *n* a drug that lowers the level of low-density lipoproteins in the blood and is therefore used to treat patients with hypercholesterolaemia.

gemfish ('dʒɛm,fɪʃ) *n, pl* **-fish** *or* **-fishes**. a food fish, *Rexea solandri* of Australia, having a delicate flavour.

geminate *adj* ('dʒɛmɪnɪt, -,neɪt) *also* **geminated. 1** combined in pairs; doubled: *a geminate leaf; a geminate consonant.* ◆ *vb* ('dʒɛmɪ,neɪt). **2** to arrange or be arranged in pairs: *the "t"s in "fitted" are geminated.* [C17: from Latin *gemināre* to double, from *geminus* born at the same time, twin] ▸ **'geminately** *adv*

gemination (,dʒɛmɪ'neɪʃən) *n* **1** the act or state of being doubled or paired. **2** the doubling of a consonant. **3** the immediate repetition of a word, phrase, or clause for rhetorical effect.

Gemini ('dʒɛmɪ,naɪ, -,niː) *n, Latin genitive* **Geminorum** (,dʒɛmɪ'nɔːrəm). **1** *Astronomy.* a zodiacal constellation in the N hemisphere lying between Taurus and Cancer on the ecliptic and containing the stars Castor and Pollux. **2** *Classical myth.* another name for **Castor and Pollux**. **3** *Astronautics.* any of a series of manned U.S. spacecraft launched between the Mercury and Apollo projects to improve orbital rendezvous and docking techniques. **4** *Astrology.* **4a** Also called: **the Twins**. the third sign of the zodiac, symbol ♊, having a mutable air classification and ruled by the planet Mercury. The sun is in this sign between about May 21 and June 20. **4b** a person born when the sun is in this sign. ◆ *adj* **5** *Astrology.* born under or characteristic of Gemini. ◆ Also (for senses 4b, 5): **Geminian** (,dʒɛmɪ'naɪən).

Geminid ('dʒɛmɪ,nɪd) *n* a member of a shower of meteors (the *Geminids*) occurring annually around December 13.

gem iron *n N.Z.* a heavy, usually cast-iron oven dish used for baking small cakes (gems).

gemma ('dʒɛmə) *n, pl* **-mae** (-miː). **1** a small asexual reproductive structure in liverworts, mosses, etc., that becomes detached from the parent and develops into a new individual. **2** *Zoology.* another name for **gemmule** (sense 1). [C18: from Latin: bud, GEM] ▸ **gemmaceous** (dʒɛ'meɪʃəs) *adj*

gemmate ('dʒɛmeɪt) *adj* **1** (of some plants and animals) having or reproducing by gemmae. ◆ *vb* **2** (*intr*) to produce or reproduce by gemmae. ▸ **gem'mation** *n*

gemmiparous (dʒɛ'mɪpərəs) *adj* (of plants and animals) reproducing by gemmae or buds. Also: **gemmiferous** (dʒɛ'mɪfərəs). ▸ **gem'miparously** *adv*

gemmulation (,dʒɛmjʊ'leɪʃən) *n* the process of reproducing by or bearing gemmules.

gemmule ('dʒɛmjuːl) *n* **1** *Zoology.* a cell or mass of cells produced asexually by sponges and developing into a new individual; bud. **2** *Botany.* a small gemma. **3** a small hereditary particle postulated by Darwin in his theory of pangenesis. [C19: from French, from Latin *gemmula* a little bud; see GEM]

gemology *or* **gemmology** (dʒɛ'mɒlədʒɪ) *n* the branch of mineralogy that is concerned with gems and gemstones. ▸ **gemological** *or* **gemmological** (ˌdʒɛməˈlɒdʒɪkᵊl) *adj* ▸ **gemˈologist** *or* **gemˈmologist** *n*

gemot *or* **gemote** (gɪˈməʊt) *n* (in Anglo-Saxon England) a legal or administrative assembly of a community, such as a shire or hundred. [Old English *gemōt* MOOT]

gemsbok *or* **gemsbuck** (ˈgɛmzˌbʌk) *n, pl* **-bok, -boks** *or* **-buck, -bucks.** *S. African.* another word for **oryx.** [C18: from Afrikaans, from German *Gemsbock,* from *Gemse* chamois + *Bock* BUCK[1]]

gemstone (ˈdʒɛmˌstəʊn) *n* a precious or semiprecious stone, esp. one cut and polished for setting in jewellery. Related adj: **lapidary.**

gemütlich *German.* (gəˈmyːtlɪç) *adj* having a feeling or atmosphere of warmth and friendliness; cosy.

gen (dʒɛn) *n Informal.* information: *give me the gen on your latest project.* See also **gen up.** [C20: from *gen(eral information)*]

gen. *abbrev. for:* **1** gender. **2** general(ly). **3** generic. **4** genitive. **5** genus.

Gen. *abbrev. for:* **1** General. **2** *Bible.* Genesis.

-gen *suffix forming nouns.* **1** producing or that which produces: *hydrogen.* **2** something produced: *carcinogen.* [via French *-gène,* from Greek *-genēs* born]

genappe (dʒəˈnæp) *n* a smooth worsted yarn used for braid, etc. [C19: from *Genappe,* Belgium, where originally manufactured]

Genck (*Flemish* xɛŋk) *n* a variant spelling of **Genk.**

gendarme (ˈʒɒndɑːm; *French* ʒɑ̃darm) *n* **1** a member of the police force in France or in countries formerly influenced or controlled by France. **2** a slang word for a **policeman. 3** a sharp pinnacle of rock on a mountain ridge, esp. in the Alps. [C16: from French, from *gens d'armes* people of arms]

gendarmerie *or* **gendarmery** (ʒɒnˈdɑːmərɪ; *French* ʒɑ̃darməri) *n* **1** the whole corps of gendarmes. **2** the headquarters or barracks of a body of gendarmes.

gender (ˈdʒɛndə) *n* **1** a set of two or more grammatical categories into which the nouns of certain languages are divided, sometimes but not necessarily corresponding to the sex of the referent when animate. See also **natural gender. 2** any of the categories, such as masculine, feminine, neuter, or common, within such a set. **3** *Informal.* the state of being male, female, or neuter. **4** *Informal.* all the members of one sex: *the female gender.* [C14: from Old French *gendre,* from Latin *genus* kind] ▸ **ˈgenderless** *adj*

gender-bender *n Informal.* a person who adopts an androgynous style of dress, hair, make-up, etc.

gene (dʒiːn) *n* a unit of heredity composed of DNA occupying a fixed position on a chromosome. A gene may determine a characteristic of an individual by specifying a polypeptide chain that forms a protein or part of a protein (**structural gene**); or regulate the operation of other genes (**operator genes**); or repress such operation (**repressor gene**). See also **operon.** [C20: from German *Gen,* shortened from *Pangen;* see PAN-, -GEN]

-gene *suffix forming nouns.* a variant of **-gen.**

geneal. *abbrev. for* genealogy.

genealogical tree *n* another name for a **family tree.**

genealogy (ˌdʒiːnɪˈælədʒɪ) *n, pl* **-gies. 1** the direct descent of an individual or group from an ancestor. **2** the study of the evolutionary development of animals and plants from earlier forms. **3** a chart showing the relationships and descent of an individual, group, etc. [C13: from Old French *genealogie,* from Late Latin *geneālogia,* from Greek, from *genea* race] ▸ **genealogical** (ˌdʒiːnɪəˈlɒdʒɪkᵊl) *or* ˌ**geneaˈlogic** *adj* ▸ ˌ**geneaˈlogically** *adv* ▸ ˌ**geneˈalogist** *n*

gene bank *n Botany.* **1** a collection of seeds, plants, tissue cultures, etc., of potentially useful species, esp. species containing genes of significance to the breeding of crops. **2** another name for **gene library.**

gene clone *n* See **clone** (sense 2).

genecology (ˌdʒɛnɪˈkɒlədʒɪ) *n* the study of the gene frequency of a species in relation to its population distribution within a particular environment.

gene flow *n* the movement and exchange of genes between interbreeding populations.

gene frequency *n* the frequency of occurrence of a particular gene in a population in relation to the frequency of its alleles.

gene library *n* a collection of gene clones that represents the genetic material of an organism: used in genetic engineering. Also called: **gene bank.**

gene pool *n* the sum of all the genes in an interbreeding population.

genera (ˈdʒɛnərə) *n* a plural of **genus.**

generable (ˈdʒɛnərəbᵊl) *adj* able to be generated. [C15: from Late Latin *generābilis,* from Latin *generāre* to beget]

general (ˈdʒɛnərəl, ˈdʒɛnrəl) *adj* **1** common; widespread: *a general feeling of horror at the crime.* **2** of, including, applying to, or participated in by all or most of the members of a group, category, or community. **3** relating to various branches of an activity, profession, etc.; not specialized: *general office work.* **4** including various or miscellaneous items: *general knowledge; a general store.* **5** not specific as to detail; overall: *a general description of the merchandise.* **6** not definite; vague: *give me a general idea of when you will finish.* **7** applicable or true in most cases; usual. **8** (*prenominal or immediately postpositive*) having superior or extended authority or rank: *general manager; consul general.* **9** Also: **pass.** designating a degree awarded at some universities, studied at a lower academic standard than an honours degree. See **honours** (sense 2). **10** *Med.* relating to or involving the entire body or many of its parts; systemic. **11** *Logic.* (of a statement) not specifying an individual subject but quantifying over a domain. ◆ *n* **12** an officer of a rank senior to lieutenant general, esp. one who commands a large military formation. **13** any person acting as a leader and applying strategy or tactics. **14** a general condition or principle: opposed to *particular.* **15** a title for the head of a religious order, congregation, etc. **16** *Med.* short for **general anaesthetic. 17** *Archaic.* the people; public. **18 in general.** generally; mostly or usually. [C13: from Latin *generālis* of a particular kind, from *genus* kind] ▸ **ˈgeneralness** *n*

general anaesthetic *n* a drug producing anaesthesia of the entire body, with loss of consciousness.

General Assembly *n* **1** the deliberative assembly of the United Nations. Abbrev.: **GA. 2** the former name for the parliament of New Zealand. **3** the supreme governing body of certain religious denominations, esp. of the Presbyterian Church.

general average *n Insurance.* loss or damage to a ship or its cargo that is shared among the shipowners and all the cargo owners. Abbrev.: **GA.** Compare **particular average.**

General Certificate of Education *n* See **GCE.**

General Certificate of Secondary Education *n* See **GCSE.**

general delivery *n* the U.S. and Canadian equivalent of **poste restante.**

general election *n* **1** an election in which representatives are chosen in all constituencies of a state. **2** *U.S.* a final election from which successful candidates are sent to a legislative body. Compare **primary. 3** *U.S. and Canadian.* (in the U.S.) a national or state election or (in Canada) a federal or provincial election in contrast to a local election.

general hospital *n* a hospital not specializing in the treatment of particular illnesses or of patients of a particular sex or age group.

generalissimo (ˌdʒɛnərəˈlɪsɪˌməʊ, ˌdʒɛnrə-) *n, pl* **-mos.** a supreme commander of combined military, naval, and air forces, esp. one who wields political as well as military power. [C17: from Italian, superlative of *generale* GENERAL]

generalist (ˈdʒɛnərəlɪst, ˈdʒɛnrə-) *n* **1a** a person who is knowledgeable in many fields of study. **1b** (*as modifier*): *a generalist profession.* **2** *Ecology.* an organism able to utilize many food sources and therefore able to flourish in many habitats. Compare **specialist** (sense 3).

generality (ˌdʒɛnəˈrælɪtɪ) *n, pl* **-ties. 1** a principle or observation having general application, esp. when imprecise or unable to be proved. **2** the state or quality of being general. **3** *Archaic.* the majority.

generalization *or* **generalisation** (ˌdʒɛnrəlaɪˈzeɪʃən) *n* **1** a principle, theory, etc., with general application. **2** the act or an instance of generalizing. **3** *Psychol.* the evoking of a response learned to one stimulus by a different but similar stimulus. See also **conditioning. 4** *Logic.* the derivation of a general statement from a particular one, formally by prefixing a quantifier and replacing a subject term by a bound variable. If the quantifier is universal (**universal generalization**) the argument is not in general valid; if it is existential (**existential generalization**) it is valid. **5** *Logic.* any statement ascribing a property to every member of a class (**universal generalization**) or to one or more members (**existential generalization**).

generalize *or* **generalise** (ˈdʒɛnrəˌlaɪz) *vb* **1** to form (general principles or conclusions) from (detailed facts, experience, etc.); infer. **2** (*intr*) to think or speak in generalities, esp. in a prejudiced way. **3** (*tr; usually passive*) to cause to become widely used or known. **4** (*intr*) (of a disease) **4a** to spread throughout the body. **4b** to change from a localized infection or condition to a systemic one. ▸ **ˈgeneralˌizer** *or* **ˈgeneralˌiser** *n*

generalized other *n Psychol.* an individual's concept of other people.

generally (ˈdʒɛnrəlɪ) *adv* **1** usually; as a rule. **2** commonly or widely. **3** without reference to specific details or facts; broadly.

general officer *n* an officer holding a commission of brigadier's rank or above in the army, air force, or marine corps.

general paralysis of the insane *n* a disease of the central nervous system: a late manifestation of syphilis, often occurring up to 15 years after the original infection, characterized by mental deterioration, speech defects, and progressive paralysis. Abbrev.: **GPI.** Also called: **general paresis, dementia paralytica.**

General Post Office *n* **1** (in Britain until 1969) the department of the central Government that provided postal and telephone services. **2** the main post office in a locality.

general practitioner *n* a physician who does not specialize but has a medical practice (**general practice**) in which he treats all illnesses. Informal name: **family doctor.** Abbrev.: **GP.**

general-purpose *adj* having a range of uses or applications; not restricted to one function.

general semantics *n* (*functioning as sing*) a school of thought, founded by Alfred Korzybski, that stresses the arbitrary nature of language and other symbols and the problems that result from misunderstanding their nature.

generalship (ˈdʒɛnrəlˌʃɪp) *n* **1** the art or duties of exercising command of a major military formation or formations. **2** tactical or administrative skill.

general staff *n* officers assigned to advise commanders in the planning and execution of military operations.

general strike *n* a strike by all or most of the workers of a country, province, city, etc., esp. (*caps.*) such a strike that took place in Britain in 1926.

General Synod *n* the governing body, under Parliament, of the Church of England, made up of the bishops and elected clerical and lay representatives.

general theory of relativity *n* the theory of gravitation, developed by Einstein in 1916, extending the special theory of relativity to include acceleration and leading to the conclusion that gravitational forces are equivalent to forces caused by acceleration.

general will *n* (in the philosophy of Rousseau) the source of legitimate authority residing in the collective will as contrasted with individual interests.

generate (ˈdʒɛnəˌreɪt) *vb* (*mainly tr*) **1** to produce or bring into being; create. **2** (*also intr*) to produce (electricity), esp. in a power station. **3** to produce (a substance) by a chemical process. **4** *Maths, linguistics.* to provide a precise criterion or specification for membership in (a set): *these rules will generate all the noun phrases in English.* **5** *Geometry.* to trace or form by moving a point, line, or plane in a specific way: *circular motion of a line generates a cylinder.* [C16: from Latin *generāre* to beget, from *genus* kind]

generation (ˌdʒenəˈreɪʃən) *n* **1** the act or process of bringing into being; production or reproduction, esp. of offspring. **2** a successive stage in natural descent of people or animals or the individuals produced at each stage. **3** the normal or average time between two such generations of a species: about 35 years for humans. **4** a phase or form in the life cycle of a plant or animal characterized by a particular type of reproduction: *the gametophyte generation.* **5** all the people of approximately the same age, esp. when considered as sharing certain attitudes, etc. **6** production of electricity, heat, etc. **7** *Physics.* a set of nuclei formed directly from a preceding set in a chain reaction. **8** (*modifier, in combination*) **8a** belonging to a generation specified as having been born in or as having parents, grandparents, etc., born in a given country: *a third-generation American.* **8b** belonging to a specified stage of development in manufacture, usually implying improvement: *a second-generation computer.* ▸ **ˌgenerˈational** *adj*

generation gap *n* the years separating one generation from the generation that precedes or follows it, esp. when regarded as representing the difference in outlook and the lack of understanding between them.

Generation X *n* members of the generation of people born between the mid-1960s and the mid-1970s who are highly educated and underemployed, reject consumer culture, and have little hope for the future. [C20: from the novel *Generation X: Tales for an Accelerated Culture* by Douglas Coupland]

generative (ˈdʒenərətɪv) *adj* **1** of or relating to the production of offspring, parts, etc.: *a generative cell.* **2** capable of producing or originating.

generative grammar *n* a description of a language in terms of explicit rules that ideally generate all and only the grammatical sentences of the language. Compare **transformational grammar.**

generative semantics *n* (*functioning as sing*) a school of semantic theory based on the doctrine that syntactic and semantic structure are of the same formal nature and that there is a single system of rules that relates surface structure to meaning. Compare **interpretive semantics.**

generator (ˈdʒenəˌreɪtə) *n* **1** *Physics.* **1a** any device for converting mechanical energy into electrical energy by electromagnetic induction, esp. a large one as in a power station. **1b** a device for producing a voltage electrostatically. **1c** any device that converts one form of energy into another form: *an acoustic generator.* **2** an apparatus for producing a gas. **3** a person or thing that generates.

generatrix (ˈdʒenəˌreɪtrɪks) *n, pl* **generatrices** (ˈdʒenəˌreɪtrɪˌsiːz). a point, line, or plane that is moved in a specific way to produce a geometric figure.

generic (dʒɪˈnerɪk) *or* **generical** *adj* **1** applicable or referring to a whole class or group; general. **2** *Biology.* of, relating to, or belonging to a genus: *the generic name.* **3** (of a drug, food product, etc.) not having a trademark. [C17: from French; see GENUS] ▸ **geˈnerically** *adv*

generosity (ˌdʒenəˈrɒsɪtɪ) *n, pl* **-ties. 1** willingness and liberality in giving away one's money, time, etc.; magnanimity. **2** freedom from pettiness in character and mind. **3** a generous act. **4** abundance; plenty.

generous (ˈdʒenərəs, ˈdʒenrəs) *adj* **1** willing and liberal in giving away one's money, time, etc.; munificent. **2** free from pettiness in character and mind. **3** full or plentiful: *a generous portion.* **4** (of wine) rich in alcohol. **5** (of a soil type) fertile. [C16: via Old French from Latin *generōsus* nobly born, from *genus* race; see GENUS] ▸ **ˈgenerously** *adv* ▸ **ˈgenerousness** *n*

genesis (ˈdʒenɪsɪs) *n, pl* **-ses** (-ˌsiːz). a beginning or origin of anything. [Old English: via Latin from Greek; related to Greek *gignesthai* to be born]

Genesis (ˈdʒenɪsɪs) *n* the first book of the Old Testament recounting the events from the Creation of the world to the sojourning of the Israelites in Egypt.

-genesis *n combining form.* indicating genesis, development, or generation: *biogenesis; parthenogenesis.* [New Latin, from Latin: GENESIS] ▸ **-genetic** *or* **-genic** *adj combining form.*

genet[1] (ˈdʒenɪt) *or* **genette** (dʒɪˈnet) *n* **1** any agile catlike viverrine mammal of the genus *Genetta,* inhabiting wooded regions of Africa and S Europe, having an elongated head, thick spotted or blotched fur, and a very long tail. **2** the fur of such an animal. [C15: from Old French *genette,* from Arabic *jarnayt*]

genet[2] (ˈdʒenɪt) *n* an obsolete spelling of **jennet.**

Genet (*French* ʒənɛ) *n* **Jean** (ʒɑ̃). 1910–86, French dramatist and novelist; his novels include *Notre-Dame des Fleurs* (1944) and his plays *Les Bonnes* (1947) and *Le Balcon* (1956).

gene therapy *n* the replacement or alteration of defective genes in order to prevent the occurrence of such inherited diseases as haemophilia. Effected by genetic engineering techniques, it is still at the experimental stage.

genetic (dʒɪˈnetɪk) *or* **genetical** *adj* of or relating to genetics, genes, or the origin of something. [C19: from GENESIS] ▸ **geˈnetically** *adv*

genetic code *n Biochem.* the order in which the nitrogenous bases of DNA are arranged in the molecule, which determines the type and amount of protein synthesized in the cell. The four bases are arranged in groups of three in a specific order, each group acting as a unit (codon), which specifies a particular amino acid. See also **messenger RNA, transfer RNA.**

genetic counselling *n* the provision of advice for couples with a history of inherited disorders who wish to have children, including the likelihood of having affected children, the course and management of the disorder, etc.

genetic engineering *n* alteration of the DNA of a cell for purposes of research, as a means of manufacturing animal proteins, correcting genetic defects, or making improvements to plants and animals bred by man.

genetic fingerprint *n* the pattern of DNA unique to each individual that can be analysed in a sample of blood, saliva, or tissue: used as a means of identification.

geneticist (dʒɪˈnetɪsɪst) *n* a person who studies or specializes in genetics.

genetic map *n* a graphic representation of the order of genes within chromosomes by means of detailed analysis of the DNA. See also **chromosome map.** ▸ **genetic mapping** *n*

genetics (dʒɪˈnetɪks) *n* **1** (*functioning as sing*) the study of heredity and variation in organisms. **2** the genetic features and constitution of a single organism, species, or group.

Geneva (dʒɪˈniːvə) *n* **1** a city in SW Switzerland, in the Rhône valley on Lake Geneva: centre of Calvinism; headquarters of the International Red Cross (1864), the International Labour Office (1925), the League of Nations (1929–46), the World Health Organization, and the European office of the United Nations; banking centre. Pop.: 172 737 (1995 est.). **2** a canton in SW Switzerland. Capital: Geneva. Pop.: 395 466 (1996 est.). Area: 282 sq. km (109 sq. miles). **3 Lake.** a lake between SW Switzerland and E France: fed and drained by the River Rhône, it is the largest of the Alpine lakes; the surface is subject to considerable changes of level. Area: 580 sq. km (224 sq. miles). French name: **Lac Léman.** German name: **Genfersee.** ◆ (for senses 1 and 2) French name: **Genève;** German name: **Genf.**

Geneva bands *pl n* a pair of white lawn or linen strips hanging from the front of the neck or collar of some ecclesiastical and academic robes. [C19: named after GENEVA, where originally worn by Swiss Calvinist clergy]

Geneva Convention *n* the international agreement, first formulated in 1864 at Geneva, establishing a code for wartime treatment of the sick or wounded: revised and extended on several occasions to cover maritime warfare and prisoners of war.

Geneva gown *n* a long loose black gown with very wide sleeves worn by academics or Protestant clerics. [C19: named after GENEVA; see GENEVA BANDS]

Genevan (dʒɪˈniːvᵊn) *or* **Genevese** (ˌdʒenɪˈviːz) *adj* **1** of, relating to, or characteristic of Geneva. **2** of, adhering to, or relating to the teachings of Calvin or the Calvinists. ◆ *n, pl* **-vans** *or* **-vese. 3** a native or inhabitant of Geneva. **4** a less common name for a **Calvinist.**

Geneva protocol *n* the agreement in 1925 to ban the use of asphyxiating, poisonous, or other gases in war. It does not ban the development or manufacture of such gases.

Genève (ʒənev) *n* the French name for **Geneva.**

Geneviève (ˈdʒenɪˌviːv; *French* ʒənvjev) *n* **Saint.** ?422–?512 A.D., French nun; patron saint of Paris. Feast day: Jan. 3.

Genf (gɛnf) *n* the German name for **Geneva** (senses 1, 2).

Genfersee (ˈgɛnfərzeː) *n* the German name for (Lake) **Geneva.**

Genghis Khan (ˈdʒeŋgɪs kɑːn) *n* original name *Temuchin* or *Temujin.* ?1162–1227, Mongol ruler, whose empire stretched from the Black Sea to the Pacific. Also called: **Jinghis Khan, Jenghis Khan.**

genial[1] (ˈdʒiːnjəl, -nɪəl) *adj* **1** cheerful, easy-going, and warm in manner or behaviour. **2** pleasantly warm, so as to give life, growth, or health: *the genial sunshine.* [C16: from Latin *geniālis* relating to birth or marriage, from *genius* tutelary deity; see GENIUS] ▸ **geniality** (ˌdʒiːnɪˈælɪtɪ) *or* **ˈgenialness** *n* ▸ **ˈgenially** *adv*

genial[2] (dʒɪˈniːəl) *adj Anatomy.* of or relating to the chin. [C19: from Greek *geneion,* from *genus* jaw]

genic (ˈdʒenɪk) *adj* of or relating to a gene or genes.

-genic *adj combining form.* **1** relating to production or generation: *carcinogenic.* **2** well suited to or suitable for: *photogenic.* [from -GEN + -IC]

genicular (dʒɪˈnɪkjʊlə) *adj Anatomy.* of or relating to the knee: *genicular artery.* [C19: from Latin *genu* knee]

geniculate (dʒɪˈnɪkjʊlɪt, -ˌleɪt) *adj* **1** *Biology.* bent at a sharp angle: *geniculate antennae.* **2** having a joint or joints capable of bending sharply. [C17: from Latin *geniculātus* jointed, from *geniculum* a little knee, small joint, from *genu* knee] ▸ **geˈniculately** *adv* ▸ **geˌnicuˈlation** *n*

genie (ˈdʒiːnɪ) *n* **1** (in fairy tales and stories) a servant who appears by magic and fulfils a person's wishes. **2** another word for **jinni.** [C18: from French *génie,* from Arabic *jinni* demon, influenced by Latin *genius* attendant spirit; see GENIUS]

genii (ˈdʒiːnɪˌaɪ) *n* the plural of **genius** (senses 5, 6).

genip (ˈdʒenɪp) *n* another word for **genipap.** [C18: from Spanish *genipa,* from French, from Guarani]

genipap (ˈdʒenɪˌpæp) *or* **genip** *n* **1** an evergreen Caribbean rubiaceous tree, *Genipa americana,* with reddish-brown edible orange-like fruits. **2** the fruit of this tree. [C17: from Portuguese *genipapo,* from Tupi]

genit. *abbrev. for* genitive.

genital (ˈdʒenɪtᵊl) *adj* **1** of or relating to the sexual organs or to reproduction. **2** *Psychoanal.* relating to the mature stage of psychosexual development in which an affectionate relationship with one's sex partner is established. Compare **anal** (sense 2), **oral** (sense 7), **phallic** (sense 2). [C14: from Latin *genitālis* concerning birth, from *gignere* to beget]

genital herpes *n* a sexually transmitted disease caused by a variety of the herpes simplex virus in which painful blisters occur in the genital region.

genitals (ˈdʒenɪtᵊlz) *or* **genitalia** (ˌdʒenɪˈteɪlɪə, -ˈteɪljə) *pl n* the sexual organs; the testicles and penis of a male or the labia, clitoris, and vagina of a female. Related adj: **venereal.** ▸ **genitalic** (ˌdʒenɪˈtælɪk) *adj*

genitive (ˈdʒenɪtɪv) *Grammar.* ◆ *adj* **1** denoting a case of nouns, pronouns, and adjectives in inflected languages used to indicate a relation of ownership or association, usually translated by English *of.* ◆ *n* **2a** the genitive case. **2b** a word or speech element in this case. [C14: from Latin *genetīvus* relating to birth, from *gignere* to produce] ▸ **genitival** (ˌdʒenɪˈtaɪvᵊl) *adj* ▸ **ˌgeniˈtivally** *adv*

genitor (ˈdʒenɪtə, -tɔː) *n* the biological father as distinguished from the pater or legal father. [C15: from Latin, from *gignere* to beget]

genitourinary (ˌdʒenɪtəʊˈjʊərɪnərɪ) *adj* of or relating to both the reproductive and excretory organs; urogenital.

genitourinary medicine *n* the branch of medical science concerned with the study and treatment of diseases of the genital and urinary organs, esp. sexually transmitted diseases.

genius ('dʒiːnɪəs, -njəs) *n, pl* **-uses** *or* (for senses 5, 6) **genii** ('dʒiːnɪˌaɪ). **1** a person with exceptional ability, esp. of a highly original kind. **2** such ability or capacity: *Mozart's musical genius.* **3** the distinctive spirit or creative nature of a nation, era, language, etc. **4** a person considered as exerting great influence of a certain sort: *an evil genius.* **5** *Roman myth.* **5a** the guiding spirit who attends a person from birth to death. **5b** the guardian spirit of a place, group of people, or institution. **6** *Arabic myth.* (*usually pl*) a demon; jinn. [C16: from Latin, from *gignere* to beget]

genius loci *Latin.* ('dʒiːnɪəs 'ləʊsaɪ) *n* **1** the guardian spirit of a place. **2** the special atmosphere of a particular place. [genius of the place]

genizah (ge'niːzə) *n Judaism.* a repository (usually in a synagogue) for books and other sacred objects which can no longer be used but which may not be destroyed. [C19: from Hebrew, literally: a hiding place, from *gānaz* to hide, set aside]

Genk *or* **Genck** (*Flemish* xɛŋk) *n* a town in NE Belgium, in Limburg province: coal-mining. Pop.: 61 996 (1995 est.).

Genl *or* **genl** *abbrev. for* General *or* general.

genoa ('dʒɛnəʊə) *n Yachting.* a large triangular jib sail, often with a foot that extends as far aft as the clew of the mainsail. Also called: **genoa jib.** Sometimes shortened to **genny, jenny.**

Genoa ('dʒɛnəʊə) *n* a port in NW Italy, capital of Liguria, on the **Gulf of Genoa:** Italy's main port; an independent commercial city with many colonies in the Middle Ages; university (1243); heavy industries. Pop.: 659 116 (1996 est.). Italian name: **Genova.**

Genoa cake *n* a rich fruit cake, usually decorated with almonds.

genocide ('dʒɛnəʊˌsaɪd) *n* the policy of deliberately killing a nationality or ethnic group. [C20: from *geno-*, from Greek *genos* race + -CIDE] ► **ˌgeno'cidal** *adj*

Genoese (ˌdʒɛnəʊ'iːz) *or* **Genovese** (ˌdʒɛnə'viːz) *n, pl* **-ese** *or* **-vese. 1** a native or inhabitant of Genoa. ◆ *adj* **2** of or relating to Genoa or its inhabitants.

genome *or* **genom** ('dʒiːnəʊm) *n* the complement of haploid chromosomes contained in a single gamete or nucleus. [C20: from German *Genom,* from *Gen* GENE + (CHROMOS)OME]

genotype ('dʒɛnəʊˌtaɪp) *n* **1** the genetic constitution of an organism. **2** a group of organisms with the same genetic constitution. ◆ Compare **phenotype.** ► **genotypic** (ˌdʒɛnəʊ'tɪpɪk) *or* ˌ**geno'typical** *adj* ► ˌ**geno'typically** *adv* ► **genotypicity** (ˌdʒɛnəʊtɪ'pɪsɪtɪ) *n*

-genous *adj combining form.* **1** yielding or generating: *androgenous; erogenous.* **2** generated by or issuing from: *endogenous.* [from -GEN + -OUS]

Genova ('dʒɛːnova) *n* the Italian name for **Genoa.**

genre ('ʒɑːnrə) *n* **1a** kind, category, or sort, esp. of literary or artistic work. **1b** (*as modifier*): *genre fiction.* **2** a category of painting in which domestic scenes or incidents from everyday life are depicted. [C19: from French, from Old French *gendre;* see GENDER]

genro ('gɛn'rəʊ) *n* **1** (*functioning as sing or pl*) a group of highly respected elder statesmen in late 19th- and early 20th-century Japan. **2** a member of this group. [C20: from Japanese, from Ancient Chinese *nguan lao,* from *nguan* first + *lao* elder]

gens (dʒɛnz) *n, pl* **gentes** ('dʒɛntiːz). **1** (in ancient Rome) any of a group of aristocratic families, having a common name and claiming descent from a common ancestor in the male line. **2** *Anthropol.* a group based on descent in the male line. [C19: from Latin: race; compare GENUS, GENDER]

Genseric ('gensərɪk, 'dʒɛn-) *or* **Gaiseric** *n* ?390–477 A.D., king of the Vandals (428–77). He seized Roman lands, esp. extensive parts of N Africa, and sacked Rome (455).

gent (dʒɛnt) *n Informal.* short for **gentleman.**

Gent (xɛnt) *n* the Flemish name for **Ghent.**

genteel (dʒɛn'tiːl) *adj* **1** affectedly proper or refined; excessively polite. **2** respectable, polite, and well-bred: *a genteel old lady.* **3** appropriate to polite or fashionable society: *genteel behaviour.* [C16: from French *gentil* well-born; see GENTLE] ► **gen'teelly** *adv* ► **gen'teelness** *n*

genteelism (dʒɛn'tiːlɪzəm) *n* a word or phrase used in place of a less genteel one.

gentian ('dʒɛnʃən) *n* **1** any gentianaceous plant of the genus *Gentiana,* having blue, yellow, white, or red showy flowers. **2** the bitter-tasting dried rhizome and roots of *Gentiana lutea* (**European** or **yellow gentian**), which can be used as a tonic. **3** any of several similar plants, such as the horse gentian. [C14: from Latin *gentiāna;* perhaps named after *Gentius,* a second-century B.C. Illyrian king, reputedly the first to use it medicinally]

gentianaceous (ˌdʒɛnʃɪə'neɪʃəs) *adj* of, relating to, or belonging to the *Gentianaceae,* a family of flowering plants that includes centaury, felwort, and gentian.

gentian blue *n* **a** a purplish-blue colour. **b** (*as adj*): *gentian-blue shoes.*

gentianella (ˌdʒɛnʃə'nɛlə, -ʃɪə-) *n* any of various gentianaceous plants, esp. the alpine species *Gentiana acaulis,* which has showy blue flowers. [C17: from New Latin, literally: a little GENTIAN]

gentian violet *n* a greenish crystalline substance, obtained from rosaniline, that forms a violet solution in water, used as an indicator, antiseptic, and in the treatment of burns. Also called: **crystal violet.**

gentile ('dʒɛntaɪl) *adj* **1** denoting an adjective or proper noun used to designate a place or the inhabitants of a place, as *Spanish* and *Spaniard.* **2** of or relating to a tribe or people. [C14: from Late Latin *gentīlis,* from Latin: one belonging to the same tribe or family; see GENS]

Gentile[1] ('dʒɛntaɪl) *n* **1** a person who is not a Jew. **2** a Christian, as contrasted with a Jew. **3** a person who is not a member of one's own church: used esp. by Mormons. **4** a heathen or pagan. ◆ *adj* **5** of or relating to a race or religion that is not Jewish. **6** Christian, as contrasted with Jewish. **7** not being a member of one's own church: used esp. by Mormons. **8** pagan or heathen.

Gentile[2] (*Italian* dʒɛn'tiːle) *n* **Giovanni** (dʒo'vanni). 1875–1944, Italian Idealist philosopher and Fascist politician: minister of education (1922–24).

Gentile da Fabriano (*Italian* dʒɛn'tiːle da fabri'ɑːno) *n* original name *Niccolo di Giovanni di Massio.* ?1370–1427, Italian painter. His works, in the International Gothic style, include the *Adoration of the Magi* (1423).

gentilesse ('dʒɛntᵊˌlɛs) *n Archaic.* politeness or good breeding. [C14: from Old French *gentillesse;* see GENTEEL]

gentility (dʒɛn'tɪlɪtɪ) *n, pl* **-ties. 1** respectability and polite good breeding. **2** affected politeness. **3** noble birth or ancestry. **4** people of noble birth. [C14: from Old French *gentilite,* from Latin *gentīlitās* relationship of those belonging to the same tribe or family; see GENS]

gentle ('dʒɛntᵊl) *adj* **1** having a mild or kindly nature or character. **2** soft or temperate; mild; moderate: *a gentle scolding.* **3** gradual: *a gentle slope.* **4** easily controlled; tame: *a gentle horse.* **5** *Archaic.* of good breeding; noble: *gentle blood.* **6** *Archaic.* gallant; chivalrous. ◆ *vb* (*tr*) **7** to tame or subdue (a horse). **8** to appease or mollify. **9** *Obsolete.* to ennoble or dignify. ◆ *n* **10** a maggot, esp. when used as bait in fishing. **11** *Archaic.* a person who is of good breeding. [C13: from Old French *gentil* noble, from Latin *gentīlis* belonging to the same family; see GENS] ► **'gently** *adv*

gentle breeze *n Meteorol.* a light breeze of force three on the Beaufort scale, blowing at 8–12 mph.

gentlefolk ('dʒɛntᵊlˌfəʊk) *or* **gentlefolks** *pl n* persons regarded as being of good breeding.

gentleman ('dʒɛntᵊlmən) *n, pl* **-men. 1** a man regarded as having qualities of refinement associated with a good family. **2** a man who is cultured, courteous, and well-educated. **3** a polite name for a man. **4** the personal servant of a gentleman (esp. in the phrase **gentleman's gentleman**). **5** *British history.* a man of gentle birth, who was entitled to bear arms, ranking above a yeoman in social position. **6** (formerly) a euphemistic word for a **smuggler.** ► **'gentlemanly** *adj* ► **'gentlemanliness** *n*

gentleman-at-arms *n, pl* **gentlemen-at-arms.** a member of the guard who attend the British sovereign on ceremonial and state occasions.

gentleman-farmer *n, pl* **gentlemen-farmers. 1** a person who engages in farming but does not depend on it for his living. **2** a person who owns farmland but does not farm it personally.

gentlemen's agreement *or* **gentleman's agreement** *n* a personal understanding or arrangement based on honour and not legally binding.

gentleness ('dʒɛntᵊlnɪs) *n* **1** the quality of being gentle. **2** *Physics.* a property of elementary particles, conserved in certain strong interactions. See also **charm** (sense 7).

gentlewoman ('dʒɛntᵊlˌwʊmən) *n, pl* **-women. 1** *Archaic.* a woman regarded as being of good family or breeding; lady. **2** *Rare.* a woman who is cultured, courteous, and well-educated. **3** *History.* a woman in personal attendance on a high-ranking lady. ► **'gentleˌwomanly** *adj* ► **'gentleˌwomanliness** *n*

Gentoo ('dʒɛntuː) *n, pl* **-toos.** (*sometimes not cap.*) *Archaic.* a Hindu, esp. as distinguished from a Muslim. [C17: from Portuguese *gentio* pagan (literally: GENTILE[1])]

gentrification (ˌdʒɛntrɪfɪ'keɪʃən) *n Brit.* a process by which middle-class people take up residence in a traditionally working-class area of a city, changing the character of the area. [C20: from *gentrify* (to become GENTRY)] ► **'gentriˌfier** *n*

gentry ('dʒɛntrɪ) *n* **1** persons of high birth or social standing; aristocracy. **2** *Brit.* persons just below the nobility in social rank. **3** *Informal, often derogatory.* people, esp. of a particular group or kind. [C14: from Old French *genterie,* from *gentil* GENTLE]

gents (dʒɛnts) *n* (*functioning as sing*) *Brit. informal.* a men's public lavatory.

genu ('dʒɛnjuː) *n, pl* **genua** ('dʒɛnjʊə). *Anatomy.* **1** the technical name for the **knee. 2** any kneelike bend in a structure or part. [Latin: knee]

genuflect ('dʒɛnjʊˌflɛkt) *vb* (*intr*) **1** to act in a servile or deferential manner. **2** *R.C. Church.* to bend one or both knees as a sign of reverence, esp. when passing before the Blessed Sacrament. [C17: from Medieval Latin *genūflectere,* from Latin *genu* knee + *flectere* to bend] ► ˌ**genu'flection** *or* (*esp. Brit.*) ˌ**genu'flexion** *n* ► **'genuˌflector** *n*

genuine ('dʒɛnjʊɪn) *adj* **1** not fake or counterfeit; original; real; authentic. **2** not pretending; frank; sincere. **3** being of authentic or original stock. [C16: from Latin *genuīnus* inborn, hence (in Late Latin) authentic, from *gignere* to produce] ► **'genuinely** *adv* ► **'genuineness** *n*

gen up *vb* **gens up, genning up, genned up.** (*adv; often passive;* when *intr,* usually foll. by *on*) *Brit. informal.* to brief (someone) or study (something) in detail; make or become fully conversant with: *I can only take over this job if I am properly genned up.*

genus ('dʒiːnəs) *n, pl* **genera** ('dʒɛnərə) *or* **genuses. 1** *Biology.* any of the taxonomic groups into which a family is divided and which contains one or more species. For example, *Vulpes* (foxes) is a genus of the dog family (*Canidae*). **2** *Logic.* a class of objects or individuals that can be divided into two or more groups or species. **3** a class, group, etc., with common characteristics. [C16: from Latin: race]

-geny *n combining form.* indicating origin or manner of development: *phylogeny.* [from Greek *-geneia,* from *-genēs* born] ► **-genic** *adj combining form.*

geo *or* **gio** ('dʒiːəʊ) *n, pl* **geos** *or* **gios.** (esp. in Shetland) a small fjord or gully. [C18: from Old Norse *gjā* ravine; related to Old English *gionian* to YAWN]

geo- *combining form.* indicating earth: *geomorphology.* [from Greek, from *gē* earth]

geocarpy ('dʒiːəʊˌkɑːpɪ) *n Botany.* the ripening of fruits below ground, as occurs in the peanut.

geocentric (ˌdʒiːəʊˈsɛntrɪk) *adj* **1** having the earth at its centre: *the Ptolemaic system postulated a geocentric universe.* **2** measured from or relating to the centre of the earth. ► ˌ**geoˈcentrically** *adv*

geocentric parallax *n* See **parallax** (sense 2).

geochemistry (ˌdʒiːəʊˈkɛmɪstrɪ) *n* the chemistry of the earth's crust. ► **geochemical** (ˌdʒiːəʊˈkɛmɪkᵊl) *adj* ► ˌ**geoˈchemist** *n*

geochronology (ˌdʒiːəʊkrəˈnɒlədʒɪ) *n* the branch of geology concerned with ordering and dating of events in the earth's history, including the origin of the earth itself. ► **geochronological** (ˌdʒiːəʊˌkrɒnᵊˈlɒdʒɪkᵊl) *adj*

geod. *abbrev. for:* **1** geodesy. **2** geodetic.

geode (ˈdʒiːəʊd) *n* a cavity, usually lined with crystals, within a rock mass or nodule. [C17: from Latin *geōdēs* a precious stone, from Greek: earthlike; see GEO-, -ODE[1]] ► **geodic** (dʒɪˈɒdɪk) *adj*

geodemographics (ˌdʒiːəʊdɛməˈgræfɪks) *pl n* (*functioning as sing*) the study and grouping of the people in a geographical area according to socioeconomic criteria, esp. for market research.

geodesic (ˌdʒiːəʊˈdɛsɪk, -ˈdiː-) *adj* **1** Also: **geodetic, geodesical.** relating to or involving the geometry of curved surfaces. ◆ *n* **2** Also called: **geodesic line.** the shortest line between two points on a curved or plane surface.

geodesic dome *n* a light structural framework arranged as a set of polygons in the form of a shell and covered with sheeting made of plastic, plywood, metal, etc.; developed by Buckminster Fuller.

geodesy (dʒɪˈɒdɪsɪ) *or* **geodetics** (ˌdʒiːəʊˈdɛtɪks) *n* the branch of science concerned with determining the exact position of geographical points and the shape and size of the earth. [C16: from French *géodésie*, from Greek *geōdaisia*, from GEO- + *daiein* to divide] ► **geˈodesist** *n*

geodetic (ˌdʒiːəʊˈdɛtɪk) *adj* **1** of or relating to geodesy. **2** another word for **geodesic.** ► ˌ**geoˈdetically** *adv*

geodetic surveying *n* the surveying of the earth's surface, making allowance for its curvature and giving an accurate framework for smaller-scale surveys.

geodynamics (ˌdʒiːəʊdaɪˈnæmɪks) *n* (*functioning as sing*) the branch of geology concerned with the forces and processes, esp. large-scale, of the earth's interior, particularly as regards their effects on the crust or lithosphere. ► ˌ**geodyˈnamic** *adj* ► ˌ**geodyˈnamicist** *n*

Geoffrey of Monmouth (ˈdʒɛfrɪ) *n* ?1100–54, Welsh bishop and chronicler; author of *Historia Regum Britanniae,* the chief source of Arthurian legends.

geog. *abbrev. for:* **1** geographer. **2** geographic(al). **3** geography.

geognosy (dʒɪˈɒgnəsɪ) *n* the study of the origin and distribution of minerals and rocks in the earth's crust: superseded generally by the term **geology.** [C18: from French *géognosie,* from GEO- + Greek *gnōsis* a seeking to know, knowledge] ► **geognostic** (ˌdʒiːɒgˈnɒstɪk) *adj*

geographical determinism *n Sociol.* the theory that human activity is determined by geographical conditions.

geographical mile *n* a former name for **nautical mile.**

geographic north *n* another name for **true north.**

geography (dʒɪˈɒgrəfɪ) *n, pl* **-phies. 1** the study of the natural features of the earth's surface, including topography, climate, soil, vegetation, etc., and man's response to them. **2** the natural features of a region. **3** an arrangement of constituent parts; plan; layout. ► **geˈographer** *n* ► **geographical** (ˌdʒɪəˈgræfɪkᵊl) *or* ˌ**geoˈgraphic** *adj* ► ˌ**geoˈgraphically** *adv*

geoid (ˈdʒiːɔɪd) *n* **1** a hypothetical surface that corresponds to mean sea level and extends at the same level under the continents. **2** the shape of the earth.

geol. *abbrev. for:* **1** geologic(al). **2** geologist. **3** geology.

geological cycle *n* the series of events in which a rock of one type is converted to one or more other types and then back to the original type.

Geological Survey *n* a government-sponsored organization working in the field of geology, such as the U.S. Geological Survey, the Geological Survey of India, or the Institute of Geological Sciences (U.K.).

geological timescale *n* any division of geological time into chronological units, whether relative (with units in the correct temporal sequence) or absolute (with numerical ages attached).

geologize *or* **geologise** (dʒɪˈɒləˌdʒaɪz) *vb* to study the geological features of (an area).

geology (dʒɪˈɒlədʒɪ) *n* **1** the scientific study of the origin, history, structure, and composition of the earth. **2** the geological features of a district or country. ► **geological** (ˌdʒɪəˈlɒdʒɪkᵊl) *or* ˌ**geoˈlogic** *adj* ► ˌ**geoˈlogically** *adv* ► **geˈologist** *or* **geˈologer** *n*

geom. *abbrev. for:* **1** geometric(al). **2** geometry.

geomagnetism (ˌdʒiːəʊˈmægnɪˌtɪzəm) *n* **1** the magnetic field of the earth. **2** the branch of physics concerned with this. ► **geomagnetic** (ˌdʒiːəʊmægˈnɛtɪk) *adj*

geomancy (ˈdʒiːəʊˌmænsɪ) *n* prophecy from the pattern made when a handful of earth is cast down or dots are drawn at random and connected with lines. ► ˈ**geoˌmancer** *n* ► ˌ**geoˈmantic** *adj*

geomechanics (ˌdʒiːəʊmɪˈkænɪks) *n* (*functioning as sing*) the study and application of rock and soil mechanics.

geometer (dʒɪˈɒmɪtə) *or* **geometrician** (dʒɪˌɒmɪˈtrɪʃən, ˌdʒiːəʊmɪ-) *n* a person who is practised in or who studies geometry.

geometric (ˌdʒɪəˈmɛtrɪk) *or* **geometrical** *adj* **1** of, relating to, or following the methods and principles of geometry. **2** consisting of, formed by, or characterized by points, lines, curves, or surfaces: *a geometric figure.* **3** (of design or ornamentation) composed predominantly of simple geometric forms, such as circles, rectangles, triangles, etc. ► ˌ**geoˈmetrically** *adv*

geometric distribution *n Statistics.* the distribution of the number, *x*, of independent trials required to obtain a first success: where the probability in each is *p*, the probability that $x = r$ is $p(1-p)^{r-1}$, with mean $1/p$. See also **Bernoulli trial.**

geometric mean *n* the average value of a set of *n* integers, terms, or quantities, expressed as the *n*th root of their product. Compare **arithmetic mean.**

geometric pace *n* a modern form of a Roman pace, a measure of length taken as 5 feet.

geometric progression *n* a sequence of numbers, each of which differs from the succeeding one by a constant ratio, as 1, 2, 4, 8, ... Compare **arithmetic progression.**

geometric series *n* a geometric progression written as a sum, as in 1 + 2 + 4 + 8.

geometrid (dʒɪˈɒmɪtrɪd) *n* **1** any moth of the family *Geometridae,* the larvae of which are called measuring worms, inchworms, or loopers. ◆ *adj* **2** of, relating to, or belonging to the *Geometridae.* [C19: from New Latin *Geōmetridae,* from Latin, from Greek *geometrēs:* land measurer, from the looping gait of the larvae]

geometrize *or* **geometrise** (dʒɪˈɒmɪˌtraɪz) *vb* **1** to use or apply geometric methods or principles (to). **2** (*tr*) to represent in geometric form.

geometry (dʒɪˈɒmɪtrɪ) *n* **1** the branch of mathematics concerned with the properties, relationships, and measurement of points, lines, curves, and surfaces. See also **analytical geometry, non-Euclidean geometry. 2a** any branch of geometry using a particular notation or set of assumptions: *analytical geometry.* **2b** any branch of geometry referring to a particular set of objects: *solid geometry.* **3** a shape, configuration, or arrangement. **4** *Arts.* the shape of a solid or a surface. [C14: from Latin *geōmetria,* from Greek, from *geōmetrein* to measure the land]

geomorphic (ˌdʒiːəʊˈmɔːfɪk) *adj* of, relating to, or resembling the earth's surface.

geomorphology (ˌdʒiːəʊmɔːˈfɒlədʒɪ) *or* **geomorphogeny** (ˌdʒiːəʊmɔːˈfɒdʒənɪ) *n* the branch of geology that is concerned with the structure, origin, and development of the topographical features of the earth's crust. ► **geomorphological** (ˌdʒiːəʊˌmɔːfəˈlɒdʒɪkᵊl) *or* ˌ**geoˌmorphoˈlogic** *adj* ► ˌ**geoˌmorphoˈlogically** *adv*

geophagy (dʒɪˈɒfədʒɪ), **geophagia** (ˌdʒɪəˈfeɪdʒə, -dʒɪə), *or* **geophagism** (dʒɪˈɒfədʒɪzəm) *n* **1** the practice of eating earth, clay, chalk, etc., found in some primitive tribes. **2** *Zoology.* the habit of some animals, esp. earthworms, of eating soil. ► **geˈophagist** *n* ► **geophagous** (dʒɪˈɒfəgəs) *adj*

geophysics (ˌdʒiːəʊˈfɪzɪks) *n* (*functioning as sing*) the study of the earth's physical properties and of the physical processes acting upon, above, and within the earth. It includes seismology, geomagnetism, meteorology, and oceanography. ► ˌ**geoˈphysical** *adj* ► ˌ**geoˈphysicist** *n*

geophyte (ˈdʒiːəʊˌfaɪt) *n* a perennial plant that propagates by means of buds below the soil surface. ► **geophytic** (ˌdʒiːəʊˈfɪtɪk) *adj*

geopolitics (ˌdʒiːəʊˈpɒlɪtɪks) *n* **1** (*functioning as sing*) the study of the effect of geographical factors on politics, esp. international politics; political geography. **2** (*functioning as pl*) the combination of geographical and political factors affecting a country or area. ► **geopolitical** (ˌdʒiːəʊpəˈlɪtɪkᵊl) *adj* ► ˌ**geoˌpoliˈtician** *n*

geoponic (ˌdʒiːəʊˈpɒnɪk) *adj* **1** of or relating to agriculture, esp. as a science. **2** rural; rustic. [C17: from Greek *geōponikos* concerning land cultivation, from *geōponein* to till the soil, from GEO- + *ponein* to labour]

geoponics (ˌdʒiːəʊˈpɒnɪks) *n* (*functioning as sing*) the science of agriculture.

Geordie (ˈdʒɔːdɪ) *Brit.* ◆ *n* **1** a person who comes from or lives in Tyneside. **2** the dialect spoken by these people. ◆ *adj* **3** of or relating to these people or their dialect. [C19: a diminutive of *George*]

George[1] (dʒɔːdʒ) *n* **1 David Lloyd.** See **Lloyd George. 2 Henry.** 1839–97, U.S. economist: advocated a single tax on land values, esp. in *Progress and Poverty* (1879). **3 Saint.** died ?303 A.D., Christian martyr, the patron saint of England; the hero of a legend in which he slew a dragon. Feast day: April 23. **4** (*German* geˈɔrgə). **Stefan (Anton)** (ˈʃtefan). 1868–1933, German poet and aesthete. Influenced by the French Symbolists, esp. Mallarmé and later by Nietzsche, he sought for an idealized purity of form in his verse. He refused Nazi honours and went into exile in 1933.

George[2] (dʒɔːdʒ) *n Brit. informal.* the automatic pilot in an aircraft. [C20: originally a slang name for an airman]

George I *n* 1660–1727, first Hanoverian king of Great Britain and Ireland (1714–27) and elector of Hanover (1698–1727). His dependence in domestic affairs on his ministers led to the emergence of Walpole as the first prime minister.

George II *n* **1** 1683–1760, king of Great Britain and Ireland and elector of Hanover (1727–60); son of George I. His victory over the French at Dettingen (1743) in the War of the Austrian Succession was the last appearance on a battlefield by a British king. **2** 1890–1947, king of Greece (1922–24; 1935–47). He was overthrown by the republicans (1924) and exiled during the German occupation of Greece (1941–45).

George III *n* 1738–1820, king of Great Britain and Ireland (1760–1820) and of Hanover (1814–20). During his reign the American colonies were lost. He became insane in 1811, and his son acted as regent for the rest of the reign.

George IV *n* 1762–1830, king of Great Britain and Ireland and also of Hanover (1820–30); regent (1811–20). His father (George III) disapproved of his profligate ways, which undermined the prestige of the crown, and of his association with the Whig opposition.

George V *n* 1865–1936, king of Great Britain and Northern Ireland and emperor of India (1910–36).

George VI *n* 1895–1952, king of Great Britain and Northern Ireland (1936–52) and emperor of India (1936–47). The second son of George V, he succeeded to the throne after the abdication of his brother, Edward VIII.

George Cross *n* a British award for bravery, esp. of civilians: instituted 1940. Abbrev.: **GC.**

Georgetown (ˈdʒɔːdʒˌtaʊn) *n* **1** the capital and chief port of Guyana, at the mouth of the Demerara River: became capital of the Dutch colonies of Essequibo and Demerara in 1784; seat of the University of Guyana. Pop.: 254 000 (1995 est.). Former name (until 1812): **Stabroek. 2** the capital of the Cayman Islands: a port on Grand Cayman Island. Pop.: 16 600 (1995 est.).

George Town *n* a port in NW Malaysia, capital of Penang state, in NE Penang Island: the first chartered city of the Malayan federation. Pop.: 219 376 (1991). Also called: **Penang.**

georgette *or* **georgette crepe** (dʒɔːˈdʒɛt) *n* **a** a thin silk or cotton crepe fabric with a mat finish. **b** (*as modifier*): *a georgette blouse.* [C20: from the name Mme *Georgette,* a French modiste]

Georgia (ˈdʒɔːdʒjə) *n* **1** a republic in NW Asia, on the Black Sea: an independent kingdom during the middle ages, it was divided by Turkey and Persia in 1555; became part of Russia in 1918 and a separate Soviet republic in 1936; its independence was recognized internationally in 1992. It is rich in minerals and has hydroelectric resources. Official language: Georgian. Religion: believers are mainly Christian or Muslim. Currency: lari. Capital Tbilisi. Pop.: 5 431 000 (1998 est.). Area: 69 493 sq. km (26 831 sq. miles). **2** a state of the southeastern U.S., on the Atlantic: consists of coastal plains with forests and swamps, rising to the Cumberland Plateau and the Appalachians in the northwest. Capital: Atlanta. Pop.: 7 486 242 (1997 est.). Area: 152 489 sq. km (58 876 sq. miles). Abbrevs.: **Ga.** or (with zip code) **GA**

Georgian (ˈdʒɔːdʒjən) *adj* **1** of, characteristic of, or relating to any or all of the four kings who ruled Great Britain and Ireland from 1714 to 1830, or to their reigns. **2** of or relating to George V of Great Britain and Northern Ireland or his reign (1910–36): *the Georgian poets.* **3** of or relating to the republic of Georgia, its people, or their language. **4** of or relating to the American State of Georgia or its inhabitants. **5** in or imitative of the style prevalent in England during the 18th century (reigns of George I, II, and III); in architecture, dominated by the ideas of Palladio, and in furniture represented typically by the designs of Sheraton. ◆ *n* **6** the official language of Georgia, belonging to the South Caucasian family. **7** a native or inhabitant of Georgia. **8** an aboriginal inhabitant of the Caucasus. **9** a native or inhabitant of the American State of Georgia. **10** a person belonging to or imitating the styles of either of the Georgian periods in England.

Georgian Bay *n* a bay in S central Canada, in Ontario, containing many small islands: the NE part of Lake Huron. Area: 15 000 sq. km (5800 sq. miles).

georgic (ˈdʒɔːdʒɪk) *adj* **1** *Literary.* agricultural. ◆ *n* **2** a poem about rural or agricultural life. [C16: from Latin *geōrgicus,* from Greek *geōrgikos,* from *geōrgos* farmer, from *gē* land, earth + *-ourgos,* from *ergon* work]

geoscience (ˌdʒiːəʊˈsaɪəns) *n* **1** any science, such as geology, geophysics, geochemistry, or geodesy, concerned with the earth; an earth science. **2** these sciences collectively.

geosphere (ˈdʒiːəʊˌsfɪə) *n* another name for **lithosphere.**

geostatic (ˌdʒiːəʊˈstætɪk) *adj* **1** denoting or relating to the pressure exerted by a mass of rock or a similar substance. **2** (of a construction) able to resist the pressure of a mass of earth or similar material.

geostatics (ˌdʒiːəʊˈstætɪks) *n* (*functioning as sing*) the branch of physics concerned with the statics of rigid bodies, esp. the balance of forces within the earth.

geostationary (ˌdʒiːəʊˈsteɪʃənərɪ) *adj* (of a satellite) in a circular equatorial orbit in which it circles the earth once in 24 hours so that it appears stationary in relation to the earth's surface.

geostrategy (ˌdʒiːəʊˈstrætədʒɪ) *n* the study of geopolitics and strategics, esp. as they affect the analysis of a region.

geostrophic (ˌdʒiːəʊˈstrɒfɪk) *adj* of, relating to, or caused by the force produced by the rotation of the earth: *geostrophic wind.*

geosynchronous (ˌdʒiːəʊˈsɪŋkrənəs) *adj* (of a satellite) in an orbit in which it circles the earth once in 24 hours.

geosyncline (ˌdʒiːəʊˈsɪŋklaɪn) *n* a broad elongated depression in the earth's crust containing great thicknesses of sediment. ▸ **ˌgeosynˈclinal** *adj*

geotaxis (ˌdʒiːəʊˈtæksɪs) *n* movement of an organism in response to the stimulus of gravity. ▸ **ˌgeoˈtactic** *adj* ▸ **ˌgeoˈtactically** *adv*

geotectonic (ˌdʒiːəʊtɛkˈtɒnɪk) *adj* of or relating to the formation, arrangement, and structure of the rocks of the earth's crust.

geotextile (ˌdʒiːəʊˈtɛkstaɪl) *n* any strong synthetic fabric used in civil engineering, as to retain an embankment.

geotherm (ˈdʒiːəʊˌθɜːm) *n* **1** a line or surface within or on the earth connecting points of equal temperature. **2** the representation of such a line or surface on a map or diagram.

geothermal (ˌdʒiːəʊˈθɜːməl) *or* **geothermic** *adj* of or relating to the heat in the interior of the earth.

geothermal power *n* power generated using steam produced by heat emanating from the molten core of the earth.

geotropism (dʒɪˈɒtrəˌpɪzəm) *n* the response of a plant part to the stimulus of gravity. Plant stems, which grow upwards irrespective of the position in which they are placed, show **negative geotropism.** ▸ **geotropic** (ˌdʒiːəʊˈtrɒpɪk) *adj* ▸ **ˌgeoˈtropically** *adv*

ger. *abbrev. for:* **1** gerund. **2** gerundive.

Ger. *abbrev. for:* **1** German. **2** Germany.

Gera (*German* ˈgeːra) *n* an industrial city in E central Germany, in Thuringia. Pop.: 123 555 (1996 est.).

gerah (ˈgɪərə) *n* **1** an ancient Hebrew unit of weight. **2** an ancient Hebrew coin equal to one twentieth of a shekel. [C16: from Hebrew *gērāh* bean]

geraniaceous (dʒɪˌreɪnɪˈeɪʃəs) *adj* of, relating to, or belonging to the *Geraniaceae,* a family of plants with typically hairy stems and beaklike fruits: includes the geranium, pelargonium, storksbill, and cranesbill. [C19: from New Latin *Geraniāceae;* see GERANIUM]

geranial (dʒɪˈreɪnɪəl) *n* the *cis-* isomer of citral. [C19: from GERANI(UM) + AL(DEHYDE)]

geraniol (dʒɪˈreɪnɪˌɒl, dʒɪˈrɑː-) *n* a colourless or pale yellow terpine alcohol with an odour of roses, found in many essential oils: used in perfumery. Formula: $C_{10}H_{18}O$. [C19: from GERANI(UM + ALCOH)OL]

geranium (dʒɪˈreɪnɪəm) *n* **1** any cultivated geraniaceous plant of the genus *Pelargonium,* having scarlet, pink, or white showy flowers. See also **pelargonium, rose geranium, lemon geranium. 2** any geraniaceous plant of the genus *Geranium,* such as cranesbill and herb Robert, having divided leaves and pink or purplish flowers. **3** a strong red to a moderate or strong pink colour. [C16: from Latin: cranesbill, from Greek *geranion,* from *geranos* CRANE]

Gérard (*French* ʒerar) *n* **François** (**Pascal Simon**), Baron. 1770–1837, French painter, court painter to Napoleon I and Louis XVIII.

geratology (ˌdʒɛrəˈtɒlədʒɪ) *n* the branch of medicine concerned with the elderly and the phenomena associated with ageing; geriatrics and gerontology. [C19: from *gerato-,* from Greek *gēras* old age + -LOGY] ▸ **geratologic** (ˌdʒɛrətəˈlɒdʒɪk) *adj*

gerbera (ˈdʒɜːbərə) *n* any plant of the perennial genus *Gerbera,* esp. the Barberton daisy from S. Africa, *G. jamesonii,* grown, usually as a greenhouse plant, for its large brightly coloured daisy-like flowers: family *Compositae.* [named after Traugott *Gerber* (died 1743), German naturalist]

gerbil *or* **gerbille** (ˈdʒɜːbɪl) *n* any burrowing rodent of the subfamily *Gerbillinae,* inhabiting hot dry regions of Asia and Africa and having soft pale fur: family *Cricetidae.* [C19: from French *gerbille,* from New Latin *gerbillus* a little JERBOA]

gerent (ˈdʒɛrənt) *n Rare.* a person who rules or manages. [C16: from Latin *gerēns* managing, from *gerere* to bear]

gerenuk (ˈgɛrɪˌnʊk) *n* a slender E African antelope, *Litocranius walleri,* with a long thin neck and backward-curving horns. [from Somali *garanug*]

gerfalcon (ˈdʒɜːˌfɔːlkən, -ˌfɔːkən) *n* a variant spelling of **gyrfalcon.**

geriatric (ˌdʒɛrɪˈætrɪk) *adj* **1** of or relating to geriatrics or to elderly people. **2** *Facetious, derogatory, or offensive.* (of people or machines) old, obsolescent, worn out, or useless. ◆ *n* **3** an elderly person. **4** *Derogatory.* an older person considered as one who may be disregarded as senile or irresponsible. ◆ See also **psychogeriatric.** [C20: from Greek *gēras* old age + IATRIC]

geriatrician (ˌdʒɛrɪəˈtrɪʃən) *or* **geriatrist** (ˌdʒɛrɪˈætrɪst) *n* a physician who specializes in geriatrics.

geriatrics (ˌdʒɛrɪˈætrɪks) *n* (*functioning as sing*) the branch of medical science concerned with the diagnosis and treatment of diseases affecting elderly people. Compare **gerontology.**

Géricault (*French* ʒeriko) *n* (**Jean Louis André**) **Théodore** (teɔdɔr). 1791–1824, French romantic painter, noted for his skill in capturing movement, esp. of horses.

Gerlachovka (*Czech* ˈgɛrlaxɔfka) *n* a mountain in N Slovakia, in the Tatra Mountains: the highest peak of the Carpathian Mountains. Height: 2663 m (8737 ft.).

germ (dʒɜːm) *n* **1** a microorganism, esp. one that produces disease in animals or plants. **2** (*often pl*) the rudimentary or initial form of something: *the germs of revolution.* **3** a simple structure, such as a fertilized egg, that is capable of developing into a complete organism. [C17: from French *germe,* from Latin *germen* sprig, bud, sprout, seed]

german[1] (ˈdʒɜːmən) *n U.S.* a dance consisting of complicated figures and changes of partners. [C19: shortened from *German cotillion*]

german[2] (ˈdʒɜːmən) *adj* **1** (used in combination) **1a** having the same parents as oneself: *a brother-german.* **1b** having a parent that is a brother or sister of either of one's own parents: *cousin-german.* **2** a less common word for **germane.** [C14: via Old French *germain,* from Latin *germānus* of the same race, from *germen* sprout, offshoot]

German (ˈdʒɜːmən) *n* **1** the official language of Germany and Austria and one of the official languages of Switzerland; the native language of approximately 100 million people. It is an Indo-European language belonging to the West Germanic branch, closely related to English and Dutch. There is considerable diversity of dialects; modern standard German is a development of Old High German, influenced by Martin Luther's translation of the Bible. See also **High German, Low German. 2** a native, inhabitant, or citizen of Germany. **3** a person whose native language is German: *Swiss Germans; Volga Germans.* ◆ *adj* **4** denoting, relating to, or using the German language. **5** relating to, denoting, or characteristic of any German state or its people. ◆ Related prefixes: **Germano-, Teuto-.**

German Baptist Brethren *pl n* a Protestant sect founded in 1708 in Germany but who migrated to the U.S. in 1719–29, the members of which (Dunkers) insist on adult baptism by total immersion. Also called: **Church of the Brethren.**

German cockroach *n* a small cockroach, *Blattella germanica:* a common household pest. Also called (U.S.): **Croton bug.**

German Democratic Republic *n* (formerly) the official name of **East Germany.** Abbrevs.: **GDR, DDR.**

germander (dʒɜːˈmændə) *n* any of several plants of the genus *Teucrium,* esp. *T. chamaedrys* (**wall germander**) of Europe, having two-lipped flowers with a very small upper lip: family *Labiatae* (labiates). [C15: from Medieval Latin *germandrea,* from Late Greek *khamandrua,* from Greek *khamaidrus,* from *khamai* on the ground + *drus* oak tree]

germander speedwell *n* a creeping scrophulariaceous Eurasian plant, *Veronica chamaedrys,* naturalized in North America, having small bright blue flowers with white centres. Usual U.S. name: **bird's-eye speedwell.**

germane (dʒɜːˈmeɪn) *adj* (*postpositive;* usually foll. by *to*) related (to the topic being considered); akin; relevant: *an idea germane to the conversation.* [variant of GERMAN[2]] ▸ **gerˈmanely** *adv* ▸ **gerˈmaneness** *n*

German East Africa *n* a former German territory in E Africa, consisting of Tanganyika and Ruanda-Urundi: divided in 1919 between Great Britain and Belgium; now in Tanzania, Rwanda, and Burundi.

germanic (dʒɜːˈmænɪk) *adj* of or containing germanium in the tetravalent state.

Germanic (dʒɜːˈmænɪk) *n* **1** a branch of the Indo-European family of languages that includes English, Dutch, German, the Scandinavian languages, and Gothic. See **East Germanic, West Germanic, North Germanic.** Abbrev.: **Gmc. 2** the unrecorded language from which all of these languages developed; Proto-Germanic. ♦ *adj* **3** of, denoting, or relating to this group of languages. **4** of, relating to, or characteristic of Germany, the German language, or any people that speaks a Germanic language.

Germanicus Caesar (dʒɜːˈmænɪkəs) *n* 15 B.C.–19 A.D., Roman general; nephew of the emperor Tiberius; waged decisive campaigns against the Germans (14–16).

Germanism (ˈdʒɜːməˌnɪzəm) *n* **1** a word or idiom borrowed from or modelled on German. **2** a German custom, trait, practice, etc. **3** attachment to or high regard for German customs, institutions, etc.

germanite (ˈdʒɜːməˌnaɪt) *n* a mineral consisting of a complex copper arsenic sulphide containing germanium, gallium, iron, zinc, and lead: an ore of germanium and gallium. **[**from GERMANIUM + -ITE[1]**]**

germanium (dʒɜːˈmeɪnɪəm) *n* a brittle crystalline grey element that is a semiconducting metalloid, occurring principally in zinc ores and argyrodite: used in transistors, as a catalyst, and to strengthen and harden alloys. Symbol: Ge; atomic no.: 32; atomic wt.: 72.61; valency: 2 or 4; relative density: 5.323; melting pt.: 938.35°C; boiling pt.: 2834°C. **[C19:** New Latin, named after GERMANY**]**

Germanize *or* **Germanise** (ˈdʒɜːməˌnaɪz) *vb* to adopt or cause to adopt German customs, speech, institutions, etc. ▸ **ˌGermaniˈzation** *or* **ˌGermaniˈsation** *n* ▸ **ˈGermanˌizer** *or* **ˈGermanˌiser** *n*

German measles *n* (*functioning as sing*) a nontechnical name for **rubella.**

German Ocean *n* a former name for the **North Sea.**

Germanophile (dʒɜːˈmænəˌfaɪl) *or* **Germanophil** *n* a person having admiration for or devotion to Germany and the Germans. ▸ **Germanophilia** (dʒɜːˌmænəˈfɪlɪə) *n*

Germanophobe (dʒɜːˈmænəˌfəʊb) *n* a person who hates Germany or its people. ▸ **Gerˌmanoˈphobia** *n*

germanous (dʒɜːˈmænəs) *adj* of or containing germanium in the divalent state.

German shepherd *or* **German shepherd dog** *n* another name for **Alsatian** (sense 1).

German silver *n* another name for **nickel silver.**

German sixth *n* (in musical harmony) an augmented sixth chord having a major third and a perfect fifth between the root and the augmented sixth. Compare **Italian sixth, French sixth.**

Germany (ˈdʒɜːmənɪ) *n* a country in central Europe: in the Middle Ages the centre of the Holy Roman Empire; dissolved into numerous principalities; united under the leadership of Prussia in 1871 after the Franco-Prussian War; became a republic with reduced size in 1919 after being defeated in World War I; under the dictatorship of Hitler from 1933 to 1945; defeated in World War II and divided by the Allied Powers into four zones, which became established as East and West Germany in the late 1940s; reunified in 1990: a member of the European Union. It is flat and low-lying in the north with plateaus and uplands (including the Black Forest and the Bavarian Alps) in the centre and south. Official language: German. Religion: Christianity, Protestant majority. Currency: euro and Deutschmark. Capital: Berlin, with Bonn as the current seat of government. Pop.: 82 148 000 (1998 est.). Area: 357 041 sq. km (137 825 sq. miles). German name: **Deutschland.** Official name: **Federal Republic of Germany.** See also **East Germany, West Germany.** Related adj: **Teutonic.**

germ cell *n* a sexual reproductive cell; gamete. Compare **somatic cell.**

germen (ˈdʒɜːmən) *n, pl* **-mens** *or* **-mina** (-mɪnə). *Biology.* the mass of undifferentiated cells that gives rise to the germ cells. **[C17:** from Latin; see GERM**]**

germicide (ˈdʒɜːmɪˌsaɪd) *n* any substance that kills germs or other microorganisms. ▸ **ˌgermiˈcidal** *adj*

germinal (ˈdʒɜːmɪnᵊl) *adj* **1** of, relating to, or like germs or a germ cell. **2** of, or in the earliest stage of development; embryonic. **[C19:** from New Latin *germinālis,* from Latin *germen* bud; see GERM**]** ▸ **ˈgerminally** *adv*

Germinal *French.* (ʒerminal) *n* the month of buds: the seventh month of the French revolutionary calendar, from March 22 to April 20.

germinal vesicle *n Biology.* the large nucleus of an oocyte before it develops into an ovum.

germinant (ˈdʒɜːmɪnənt) *adj* in the process of germinating; sprouting.

germinate (ˈdʒɜːmɪˌneɪt) *vb* **1** to cause (seeds or spores) to sprout or (of seeds or spores) to sprout or form new tissue following increased metabolism. **2** to grow or cause to grow; develop. **3** to come or bring into existence; originate: *the idea germinated with me.* **[C17:** from Latin *germināre* to sprout; see GERM**]** ▸ **ˈgerminable** *or* **ˈgerminative** *adj* ▸ **ˌgermiˈnation** *n* ▸ **ˈgermiˌnator** *n*

Germiston (ˈdʒɜːmɪstən) *n* a city in South Africa, southeast of Johannesburg: industrial centre, with the world's largest gold refinery, serving the Witwatersrand mines. Pop.: 134 005 (1991).

germ layer *n Embryol.* any of the three layers of cells formed during gastrulation. See **ectoderm, mesoderm, endoderm.**

germ line *n* the lineage of cells culminating in the germ cells.

germ plasm *n* **a** the part of a germ cell that contains hereditary material; the chromosomes and genes. **b** the germ cells collectively. Compare **somatoplasm.**

germ theory *n* **1** the theory that all infectious diseases are caused by microorganisms. **2** the theory that living organisms develop from other living organisms by the growth and differentiation of germ cells.

germ tube *n Botany.* a tube produced by a germinating spore, such as the pollen tube produced by a pollen grain.

germ warfare *n* the military use of disease-spreading bacteria against an enemy. Also called: **bacteriological warfare.**

Gerona (*Spanish* xeˈrona) *n* a city in NE Spain: city walls and 14th-century cathedral; often besieged, in particular by the French (1809). Pop.: 67 578 (1986). Ancient name: **Gerunda** (dʒəˈruːndə).

Geronimo (dʒəˈrɒnɪˌməʊ) *n* **1** 1829–1909, Apache Indian chieftain: led a campaign against the White settlers until his final capture in 1886. **2** *U.S.* a shout given by paratroopers as they jump into battle.

gerontic (dʒɛˈrɒntɪk) *adj Biology.* of or relating to the senescence of an organism.

geronto- *or before a vowel* **geront-** *combining form.* indicating old age: *gerontology; gerontophilia.* **[**from Greek *gerōn, geront-* old man**]**

gerontocracy (ˌdʒɛrɒnˈtɒkrəsɪ) *n, pl* **-cies. 1** government by old people. **2** a governing body of old people. ▸ **gerontocratic** (dʒəˌrɒntəˈkrætɪk) *adj* ▸ **geˈrontoˌcrat** *n*

gerontology (ˌdʒɛrɒnˈtɒlədʒɪ) *n* the scientific study of ageing and the problems associated with elderly people. Compare **geriatrics.** ▸ **gerontological** (ˌdʒɛrɒntəˈlɒdʒɪkᵊl) *adj* ▸ **ˌgeronˈtologist** *n*

-gerous *adj combining form.* bearing or producing: *armigerous.* Compare **-ferous. [**from Latin *-ger* bearing + -OUS**]**

gerrymander (ˈdʒɛrɪˌmændə) *vb* **1** to divide the constituencies of (a voting area) so as to give one party an unfair advantage. **2** to manipulate or adapt to one's advantage. ♦ *n* **3** an act or result of gerrymandering. **[C19:** from Elbridge *Gerry,* U.S. politician + (SALA)MANDER; from the salamander-like outline of an electoral district reshaped (1812) for political purposes while Gerry was governor of Massachusetts**]** ▸ **ˌgerryˈmandering** *n*

Gers (*French* ʒɛr) *n* a department of SW France, in Midi-Pyrénées region. Capital: Auch. Pop.: 172 300 (1995). Area: 6291 sq. km (2453 sq. miles).

Gershwin (ˈgɜːʃwɪn) *n* **1 George,** original name *Jacob Gershvin.* 1898–1937, U.S. composer: incorporated jazz into works such as *Rhapsody in Blue* (1924) for piano and jazz band and the opera *Porgy and Bess* (1935). **2** his brother, **Ira,** original name *Israel Gershvin.* 1896–1983, U.S. song lyricist, noted esp. for his collaboration with George Gershwin.

gerund (ˈdʒɛrənd) *n* a noun formed from a verb, denoting an action or state. In English, the gerund, like the present participle, is formed in *-ing: the living is easy.* **[C16:** from Late Latin *gerundium,* from Latin *gerundum* something to be carried on, from *gerere* to wage**]** ▸ **gerundial** (dʒɪˈrʌndɪəl) *adj*

gerundive (dʒɪˈrʌndɪv) *n* **1** (in Latin grammar) an adjective formed from a verb, expressing the desirability of the activity denoted by the verb. ♦ *adj* **2** of or relating to the gerund or gerundive. **[C17:** from Late Latin *gerundīvus,* from *gerundium* GERUND**]** ▸ **gerundival** (ˌdʒɛrənˈdaɪvᵊl) *adj* ▸ **geˈrundively** *adv*

Geryon (ˈgɛrɪən) *n Greek myth.* a winged monster with three bodies joined at the waist, killed by Hercules, who stole the monster's cattle as his tenth labour.

gesellschaft (*German* gəˈzɛlʃaft) *n, pl* **-schaften** (*German* -ʃaftən). (*often cap.*) a social group held together by practical concerns, formal and impersonal relationships, etc. Compare **gemeinschaft. [**German, literally: society**]**

gesneria (gɛsˈnɪərɪə) *n* any plant of the mostly tuberous-rooted S. American genus *Gesneria,* grown as a greenhouse plant for its large leaves and showy tubular flowers in a range of bright colours: family *Gesneriaceae.* **[**named after Conrad *Gesner,* 1516–65, Swiss naturalist**]**

gesso (ˈdʒɛsəʊ) *n* **1** a white ground of plaster and size, used esp. in the Middle Ages and Renaissance to prepare panels or canvas for painting or gilding. **2** any white substance, esp. plaster of Paris, that forms a ground when mixed with water. **[C16:** from Italian: chalk, GYPSUM**]**

gest *or* **geste** (dʒɛst) *n Archaic.* **1** a notable deed or exploit. **2** a tale of adventure or romance, esp. in verse. See also **chanson de geste. [C14:** from Old French, from Latin *gesta* deeds, from *gerere* to carry out**]**

GEST (dʒɛst) *n* (in Britain) *acronym for* Grants for Education, Support and Training: money allocated to Local Education Authorities by the central government.

Gestalt (gəˈʃtælt) *n, pl* **-stalts** *or* **-stalten** (-ˈʃtæltən). (*sometimes not cap.*) a perceptual pattern or structure possessing qualities as a whole that cannot be described merely as a sum of its parts. See also **Gestalt psychology. [C20:** German: form, from Old High German *stellen* to shape**]**

Gestalt psychology *n* a system of thought, derived from experiments carried out by German psychologists, that regards all mental phenomena as being arranged in gestalts.

Gestalt psychotherapy *n* a therapy devised in the U.S. in the 1960s in which patients are encouraged to concentrate on the immediate present and to express their true feelings.

Gestapo (gɛˈstɑːpəʊ; *German* geˈʃtaːpo) *n* the secret state police in Nazi Germany, noted for its brutal methods of interrogation. **[**from German *Ge(heime) Sta(ats)po(lizei),* literally: secret state police**]**

Gesta Romanorum (ˈdʒɛstə ˌrəʊməˈnɔːrəm) *n* a popular collection of tales in Latin with moral applications, compiled in the late 13th century as a manual for preachers. **[**Latin: deeds of the Romans**]**

gestate (ˈdʒɛsteɪt) *vb* **1** (*tr*) to carry (developing young) in the uterus during pregnancy. **2** (*tr*) to develop (a plan or idea) in the mind. **3** (*intr*) to be in the process of gestating. **[C19:** back formation from GESTATION**]**

gestation (dʒɛˈsteɪʃən) *n* **1a** the development of the embryo of a viviparous mammal, between conception and birth: about 266 days in humans, 624 days in elephants, and 63 days in cats. **1b** (*as modifier*): *gestation period.* **2** the development of an idea or plan in the mind. **3** the period of such a development.

[C16: from Latin *gestātiō* a bearing, from *gestāre* to bear, frequentative of *gerere* to carry] ▸ **ges'tational** *or* **gestative** ('dʒɛstətɪv, dʒɛ'steɪ-) *adj* ▸ **'gestatory** *adj*

gestatorial chair (ˌdʒɛstə'tɔːrɪəl) *n* a ceremonial chair on which the pope is carried.

gesticulate (dʒɛ'stɪkjuˌleɪt) *vb* to express by or make gestures. [C17: from Latin *gesticulārī*, from Latin *gesticulus* (unattested except in Late Latin) gesture, diminutive of *gestus* gesture, from *gerere* to bear, conduct] ▸ **ges'ticulative** *adj* ▸ **ges'ticuˌlator** *n*

gesticulation (dʒɛˌstɪkju'leɪʃən) *n* **1** the act of gesticulating. **2** an animated or expressive gesture. ▸ **ges'ticulatory** *adj*

gesture ('dʒɛstʃə) *n* **1** a motion of the hands, head, or body to emphasize an idea or emotion, esp. while speaking. **2** something said or done as a formality or as an indication of intention: *a political gesture.* **3** *Obsolete.* the manner in which a person bears himself; posture. ◆ *vb* **4** to express by or make gestures; gesticulate. [C15: from Medieval Latin *gestūra* bearing, from Latin *gestus*, past participle of *gerere* to bear] ▸ **'gestural** *adj* ▸ **'gesturer** *n*

Gesualdo (*Italian* dʒezu'aldo) *n* **Carlo** ('karlo), Prince of Venosa. ?1560–1613, Italian composer, esp. of madrigals.

gesundheit (*German* gə'zʊnthaɪt) *sentence substitute.* an expression used to wish good health to someone who has just sneezed. [from *gesund* healthy + *-heit* -HOOD; see SOUND[2]]

get (gɛt) *vb* **gets, getting, got** (gɒt). (*mainly tr*) **1** to come into possession of; receive or earn. **2** to bring or fetch. **3** to contract or be affected by: *he got a chill at the picnic.* **4** to capture or seize: *the police finally got him.* **5** (*also intr*) to become or cause to become or act as specified: *to get a window open; get one's hair cut; get wet.* **6** (*intr;* foll. by a preposition or adverbial particle) to succeed in going, coming, leaving, etc.: *get off the bus.* **7** (*takes an infinitive*) to manage or contrive: *how did you get to be captain?* **8** to make ready or prepare: *to get a meal.* **9** to hear, notice, or understand: *I didn't get your meaning.* **10** *U.S. and Canadian informal.* to learn or master by study. **11** (*intr;* often foll. by *to*) to come (to) or arrive (at): *we got home safely; to get to London.* **12** to catch or enter: *to get a train.* **13** to induce or persuade: *get him to leave at once.* **14** to reach by calculation: *add 2 and 2 and you will get 4.* **15** to receive (a broadcast signal). **16** to communicate with (a person or place), as by telephone. **17** (*also intr;* foll. by *to*) *Informal.* to have an emotional effect (on): *that music really gets me.* **18** *Informal.* to annoy or irritate: *her high voice gets me.* **19** *Informal.* to bring a person into a difficult position from which he cannot escape. **20** *Informal.* to puzzle; baffle. **21** *Informal.* to hit: *the blow got him in the back.* **22** *Informal.* to be revenged on, esp. by killing. **23** *U.S. slang.* **23a** (foll. by *to*) to gain access (to a person) with the purpose of bribing him. **23b** (often foll. by *to*) to obtain access (to someone) and kill or silence him. **24** *Informal.* to have the better of: *your extravagant habits will get you in the end.* **25** (*intr;* foll. by present participle) *Informal.* to begin: *get moving.* **26** (used as a command) *Informal.* go! leave now! **27** *Archaic.* to beget or conceive. **28 get even with.** See **even**[1] (sense 15). **29 get it (in the neck).** *Informal.* to be reprimanded or punished severely. **30 get with it.** *Slang.* to allow oneself to respond to new ideas, styles, etc. **31 get with child.** *Archaic.* to make pregnant. ◆ *n* **32** *Rare.* the act of begetting. **33** *Rare.* something begotten; offspring. **34** *Brit. slang.* a variant of **git. 35** *Informal.* (in tennis) a successful return of a shot that was difficult to reach. ◆ See also **get about, get across, get ahead, get along, get at, get away, get back, get by, get down, get in, get into, get off, get on, get onto, get out, get over, get round, get through, get-together, get up, got, gotten.** [Old English *gietan;* related to Old Norse *geta* to get, learn, Old High German *bigezzan* to obtain] ▸ **'getable** *or* **'gettable** *adj*

USAGE The use of *off* after *get* as in *I got this chair off an antique dealer* is acceptable in conversation, but should not be used in formal writing.

get about *or* **around** *vb* (*intr, adv*) **1** to move around, as when recovering from an illness. **2** to be socially active. **3** (of news, rumour, etc.) to become known; spread.

get across *vb* **1** to cross or cause or help to cross. **2** (*adv*) to be or cause to be readily understood. **3** (*intr, prep*) *Informal.* to annoy: *her constant interference really got across him.*

get ahead *vb* (*intr, adv*) **1** to be successful; prosper. **2** (foll. by *of*) to surpass or excel.

get along *vb* (*intr, adv*) **1** (often foll. by *with*) to be friendly or compatible: *my brother gets along well with everybody.* **2** to manage, cope, or fare: *how are you getting along in your job?* **3** (*also prep; often imperative*) to go or move away; leave. ◆ *interj* **4** *Brit. informal.* an exclamation indicating mild disbelief.

get around *vb* See **get about, get round.**

get at *vb* (*intr, prep*) **1** to gain access to: *the dog could not get at the meat on the high shelf.* **2** to mean or intend: *what are you getting at when you look at me like that?* **3** to irritate or annoy persistently; criticize: *she is always getting at him.* **4** to influence or seek to influence, esp. illegally by bribery, intimidation, etc.: *someone had got at the witness before the trial.*

get-at-able *adj Informal.* accessible.

get away *vb* (*adv, mainly intr*) **1** to make an escape; leave. **2** to make a start. **3 get away with. 3a** to steal and escape (with money, goods, etc.). **3b** to do (something wrong, illegal, etc.) without being discovered or punished or with only a minor punishment. ◆ *interj* **4** an exclamation indicating mild disbelief. ◆ *n* **getaway. 5** the act of escaping, esp. by criminals. **6** a start or acceleration. **7** (*modifier*) used for escaping: *a getaway car.*

get back *vb* (*adv*) **1** (*tr*) to recover or retrieve. **2** (*intr;* often foll. by *to*) to return, esp. to a former position or activity: *let's get back to the original question.* **3** (*intr;* foll. by *at*) to retaliate (against); wreak vengeance (on). **4 get one's own back.** *Informal.* to obtain one's revenge.

get by *vb* **1** to pass; go past or overtake. **2** (*intr, adv*) *Informal.* to manage, esp. in spite of difficulties: *I can get by with little money.* **3** (*intr*) to be accepted or permitted: *that book will never get by the authorities.*

get down *vb* (*mainly adv*) **1** (*intr; also prep*) to dismount or descend. **2** (*tr; also prep*) to bring down: *we could not get the wardrobe down the stairs.* **3** (*tr*) to write down. **4** (*tr*) to make depressed: *your nagging gets me down.* **5** (*tr*) to swallow: *he couldn't get the meal down.* **6** (*intr;* foll. by *to*) to attend seriously (to); concentrate (on) (esp. in the phrases **get down to business** *or* **brass tacks**). **7** (*intr*) *Informal, chiefly U.S.* to enjoy oneself uninhibitedly, esp. by dancing.

Gethsemane (gɛθ'sɛmənɪ) *n New Testament.* the garden in Jerusalem where Christ was betrayed on the night before his Crucifixion (Matthew 26:36–56).

get in *vb* (*mainly adv*) **1** (*intr*) to enter a car, train, etc. **2** (*intr*) to arrive, esp. at one's home or place of work: *I got in at midnight.* **3** (*tr*) to bring in or inside: *get the milk in.* **4** (*tr*) to insert or slip in: *he got his suggestion in before anyone else.* **5** (*tr*) to gather or collect (crops, debts, etc.). **6** (*tr*) to ask (a person, esp. a specialist) to give a service: *shall I get the doctor in?* **7** to be elected or cause to be elected: *he got in by 400 votes.* **8** (*tr*) to succeed in doing (something), esp. during a specified period: *I doubt if I can get this task in today.* **9** (*intr*) to obtain a place at university, college, etc. **10** (foll. by *on*) to join or cause to join (an activity or organization). **11 get in with.** to be or cause to be on friendly terms with (a person). **12** (*prep*) See **get into.** ◆ *n* **get-in. 13** *Theatre.* the process of moving into a theatre the scenery, props, and costumes for a production.

get into *vb* (*prep*) **1** (*intr*) to enter. **2** (*intr*) to reach (a destination): *the train got into London at noon.* **3** to get dressed in (clothes). **4** (*intr*) to preoccupy or obsess (a person's emotions or thoughts): *what's got into him tonight?* **5** to assume or cause to assume (a specified condition, habit, etc.): *to get into debt; get a person into a mess.* **6** to be elected to or cause to be elected to: *to get into Parliament.* **7** (*usually intr*) *Informal.* to become or cause to become familiar with (a skill): *once you get into driving you'll enjoy it.* **8** (*usually intr*) *Informal.* to develop or cause to develop an absorbing interest in (a hobby, subject, or book).

get off *vb* **1** (*intr, adv*) to escape the consequences of an action: *he got off very lightly in the accident.* **2** (*adv*) to be or cause to be acquitted: *a good lawyer got him off.* **3** (*adv*) to depart or cause to depart: *to get the children off to school.* **4** (*intr*) to descend (from a bus, train, etc.); dismount: *she got off at the terminus.* **5** to move or cause to move to a distance (from): *get off the field.* **6** (*tr, adv*) to remove; take off: *get your coat off.* **7** (*adv*) to go or send to sleep. **8** (*adv*) to send (letters) or (of letters) to be sent. **9** (*intr, adv*) *Slang.* to become high on or as on heroin or some other drug. **10 get off with.** *Brit. informal.* to establish an amorous or sexual relationship with. **11 tell (someone) where to get off.** *Informal.* to rebuke or criticize harshly.

get on *vb* (*mainly adv*) **1** Also (when *prep*): **get onto.** to board or cause or help to board (a bus, train, etc.). **2** (*tr*) to dress in (clothes as specified). **3** (*intr*) to grow late or (of time) to elapse: *it's getting on and I must go.* **4** (*intr*) (of a person) to grow old. **5** (*intr;* foll. by *for*) to approach (a time, age, amount, etc.): *she is getting on for seventy.* **6** (*intr*) to make progress, manage, or fare: *how did you get on in your exam?* **7** (*intr;* often foll. by *with*) to establish a friendly relationship: *he gets on well with other people.* **8** (*intr;* foll. by *with*) to continue to do: *get on with your homework!* ◆ *interj* **9** I don't believe you!

get onto *vb* (*prep*) **1** Also: **get on.** to board or cause or help to board (a bus, train, etc.). **2** (*intr*) to make contact with; communicate with. **3** (*intr*) to become aware of (something illicit or secret): *the boss will get onto their pilfering unless they're careful.* **4** (*intr*) to deliver a demand, request, or rebuke to: *I'll get onto the manufacturers to replace these damaged goods.* See usage note at **onto.**

get out *vb* (*adv*) **1** to leave or escape or cause to leave or escape: used in the imperative when dismissing a person. **2** to make or become known; publish or be published. **3** (*tr*) to express with difficulty. **4** (*tr;* often foll. by *of*) to extract (information or money) (from a person): *to get a confession out of a criminal.* **5** (*tr*) to gain or receive something, esp. something of significance or value: *you get out of life what you put into it.* **6** (foll. by *of*) to avoid or cause to avoid: *she always gets out of swimming.* **7** (*tr*) to solve (a puzzle or problem) successfully. **8** *Cricket.* to dismiss or be dismissed. ◆ *n* **get-out. 9** an escape, as from a difficult situation. **10** *Theatre.* the process of moving out of a theatre the scenery, props, and costumes after a production.

get over *vb* **1** to cross or surmount (something): *get the children over the fence.* **2** (*intr, prep*) to recover from (an illness, shock, etc.). **3** (*intr, prep*) to overcome or master (a problem): *you'll soon get over your shyness.* **4** (*intr, prep*) to appreciate fully: *I just can't get over seeing you again.* **5** (*tr, adv*) to communicate effectively: *he had difficulty getting the message over.* **6** (*tr, adv;* sometimes foll. by *with*) to bring (something necessary but unpleasant) to an end: *let's get this job over with quickly.*

get round *or* **around** *vb* (*intr*) **1** (*prep*) to circumvent or overcome: *he got round the problem by an ingenious trick.* **2** (*prep*) *Informal.* to have one's way with; cajole: *that girl can get round anyone.* **3** (*prep*) to evade (a law or rules). **4** (*adv;* foll. by *to*) to reach or come to at length: *I'll get round to that job in an hour.*

getter ('gɛtə) *n* **1** a person or thing that gets. **2** a substance, usually a metal such as titanium, evaporated onto the walls of a vacuum tube, vessel, etc., to adsorb the residual gas and lower the pressure. ◆ *vb* **3** (*tr*) to remove (a gas) by the action of a getter.

get through *vb* **1** to succeed or cause or help to succeed in an examination, test, etc. **2** to bring or come to a destination, esp. after overcoming problems: *we got through the blizzards to the survivors.* **3** (*intr, adv*) to contact, as by telephone. **4** (*intr, prep*) to use, spend, or consume (money, supplies, etc.). **5** to complete or cause to complete (a task, process, etc.): *to get a bill through Parliament.* **6** (*adv;* foll. by *to*) to reach the awareness and understanding (of a person): *I just can't get the message through to him.* **7** (*intr, adv*) *U.S. slang.* to obtain drugs.

get-together *n* **1** *Informal.* a small informal meeting or social gathering. ◆ *vb* **get together.** (*adv*) **2** (*tr*) to gather or collect. **3** (*intr*) (of people) to meet socially. **4** (*intr*) to discuss, esp. in order to reach an agreement. **5 get it together.** *Informal.* **5a** to achieve one's full potential, either generally as a person or in a particular field of activity. **5b** to achieve a harmonious frame of mind.

Getty ('gɛtɪ) *n* **J(ean) Paul.** 1892–1976, U.S. oil executive, millionaire, and art collector.

Gettysburg ('getɪz,bɜ:g) *n* a small town in S Pennsylvania, southwest of Harrisburg: scene of a crucial battle (1863) during the American Civil War, in which Meade's Union forces defeated Lee's Confederate army; site of the national cemetery dedicated by President Lincoln. Pop.: 7194 (1980).

Gettysburg Address *n U.S. history.* the speech made by President Lincoln at the dedication of the national cemetery on the Civil War battlefield at Gettysburg in Nov. 1863.

get up *vb* (*mainly adv*) **1** to wake and rise from one's bed or cause to wake and rise from bed. **2** (*intr*) to rise to one's feet; stand up. **3** (*also prep*) to ascend or cause to ascend: *the old van couldn't get up the hill.* **4** to mount or help to mount (a bicycle, horse, etc.). **5** to increase or cause to increase in strength: *the wind got up at noon.* **6** (*tr*) *Informal.* to dress (oneself) in a particular way, esp. showily or elaborately. **7** (*tr*) *Informal.* to devise or create: *to get up an entertainment for Christmas.* **8** (*tr*) *Informal.* to study or improve one's knowledge of: *I must get up my history.* **9** (*intr; foll. by to*) *Informal.* to be involved in: *he's always getting up to mischief.* **10** (*intr*) *Austral. informal.* to win, esp. in a sporting event. ◆ *n* **get-up. 11** *Informal.* a costume or outfit, esp. one that is striking or bizarre. **12** *Informal.* the arrangement or production of a book, etc.

get-up-and-go *n Informal.* energy, drive, or ambition.

Getz (gets) *n* **Stanley,** known as *Stan.* 1927–91, U.S. jazz saxophonist: leader of his own group from 1949.

geum ('dʒi:əm) *n* any herbaceous plant of the rosaceous genus *Geum,* having compound leaves and red, orange, or white flowers. See also **avens.** [C19: New Latin, from Latin: herb bennet, avens]

GeV *abbrev. for* giga-electronvolts (10^9 electronvolts). Sometimes written (esp. U.S. and Canadian) **BeV** (billion electronvolts).

gewgaw ('gju:gɔ:, 'gu:-) *n* **1** a showy but valueless trinket. ◆ *adj* **2** showy and valueless; gaudy. [C15: of unknown origin]

Gewürztraminer (gə'vʊətstrə,mi:nə; *German* gə'vyrtstra,mi:nər) *n* **1** a white grape grown in Alsace, Germany, and elsewhere, used for making wine. **2** any of various fragrant white wines made from this grape. [German, from *Gewürz* spice, seasoning + *Traminer* a variety of grape first grown in the *Tramin* area of the South Tyrol]

gey (gaɪ; *Scot.* gəɪ) *adv Scot. and Northumberland dialect.* (intensifier): *it's gey cold.* [variant of GAY]

geyser ('gi:zə; *U.S.* 'gaɪzər) *n* **1** a spring that discharges steam and hot water. **2** *Brit.* a domestic gas water heater. [C18: from Icelandic *Geysir,* from Old Norse *geysa* to gush]

geyserite ('gi:zə,raɪt) *n* a mineral form of hydrated silica resembling opal, deposited from the waters of geysers and hot springs. Formula: $SiO_2.nH_2O$.

Gezira (dʒə'zɪərə) *n* a region of the E central Sudan between the Blue and White Niles: site of a large-scale irrigation system.

G-force *n* the force of gravity.

GG *abbrev. for:* **1** Girl Guides. **2** Governor General.

GH *international car registration for* Ghana.

Ghan (gæn) *n Austral.* **1** short for **Afghan** (sense 3). **2 the.** the train connecting Adelaide and Alice Springs. [from the number of Afghan camelmen at the Oodnadatta railhead]

Ghana ('gɑ:nə) *n* a republic in W Africa, on the Gulf of Guinea: a powerful empire from the 4th to the 13th centuries; a major source of gold and slaves for Europeans after 1471; British colony of the Gold Coast established in 1874; united with British Togoland in 1957 and became a republic and a member of the Commonwealth in 1960. Official language: English. Religions: Christian, Muslim, and animist. Currency: cedi. Capital: Accra. Pop.: 18 497 000 (1998 est.). Area: 238 539 sq. km (92 100 sq. miles). ▸ **Ghanaian** (gɑ:'neɪən) *or* **'Ghanian** *adj, n*

gharial ('gærɪəl) *n* another name for for **gavial.**

gharry *or* **gharri** ('gærɪ) *n, pl* **-ries.** (in India) a horse-drawn vehicle available for hire. [C19: from Hindi *gāṛī*]

ghastly ('gɑ:stlɪ) *adj* **-lier, -liest. 1** *Informal.* very bad or unpleasant. **2** deathly pale; wan. **3** *Informal.* extremely unwell; ill: *they felt ghastly after the party.* **4** terrifying; horrible. ◆ *adv* **5** unhealthily; sickly: *ghastly pale.* **6** *Archaic.* in a horrible or hideous manner. [Old English *gāstlīc* spiritual; see GHOSTLY] ▸ **'ghastliness** *n*

ghat (gɔ:t) *n* (in India) **1** stairs or a passage leading down to a river. **2** a mountain pass or mountain range. **3** a place of cremation. [C17: from Hindi *ghāt,* from Sanskrit *ghatta*]

Ghats (gɔ:ts) *pl n* See **Eastern Ghats** and **Western Ghats.**

ghaut (gʌt) *n Caribbean.* a small cleft in a hill through which a rivulet runs down to the sea. [C17 *gaot,* a mountain pass, from Hindi: GHAT]

Ghazali ('gɑ:z,ɑ:lɪ) *n* **al-.** 1058–1111, Muslim theologian, philosopher, and mystic.

ghazi ('gɑ:zɪ) *n, pl* **-zis. 1** a Muslim fighter against infidels. **2** (*often cap.*) a Turkish warrior of high rank. [C18: from Arabic, from *ghazā* he made war]

Ghazzah ('gɑ:zə, 'gʌzə) *n* transliteration of the Arabic name for **Gaza.**

Gheber *or* **Ghebre** ('geɪbə, 'gi:-) *n* other words for **Gabar.**

ghee (gi:) *n* butter, clarified by boiling, used in Indian cookery. [C17: from Hindi *ghī,* from Sanskrit *ghri* sprinkle]

Ghent (gent) *n* an industrial city and port in NW Belgium, capital of East Flanders province, at the confluence of the Rivers Lys and Scheldt: formerly famous for its cloth industry; university (1816). Pop.: 226 464 (1996 est.). Flemish name: **Gent.** French name: **Gand.**

gherao (gɛ'raʊ) *n* a form of industrial action in India in which workers imprison their employers on the premises until their demands are met. [from Hindi *gherna* to besiege]

gherkin ('gɜ:kɪn) *n* **1** the immature fruit of any of various cucumbers, used for pickling. **2a** a tropical American cucurbitaceous climbing plant, *Cucumis anguria.* **2b** the small edible fruit of this plant. [C17: from early modern Dutch *agurkkijn,* diminutive of *gurk,* from Slavonic, ultimately from Greek *angourion*]

ghetto ('getəʊ) *n, pl* **-tos** *or* **-toes. 1** *Sociol.* a densely populated slum area of a city inhabited by a socially and economically deprived minority. **2** an area in a European city in which Jews were formerly required to live. **3** a group or class of people that is segregated in some way. [C17: from Italian, perhaps shortened from *borghetto,* diminutive of *borgo* settlement outside a walled city; or from the Venetian *ghetto* the medieval iron-founding district, largely inhabited by Jews]

ghetto blaster *n Informal.* a large portable cassette recorder or CD player with built-in speakers.

ghettoize *or* **ghettoise** ('getəʊ,aɪz) *vb* (*tr*) to confine or restrict to a particular area, activity, or category: *to ghettoize women as housewives.* ▸ **,ghettoi'zation** *or* **,ghettoi'sation** *n*

Ghibelline ('gɪbɪ,laɪn, -,li:n) *n* **1** a member of the political faction in medieval Italy originally based on support for the German emperor. **2** (*modifier*) of or relating to the Ghibellines. Compare **Guelph**[1]. [C16: from Italian *Ghibellino,* probably from Middle High German *Waiblingen,* a Hohenstaufen estate] ▸ **'Ghibel,linism** *n*

Ghiberti (*Italian* gi'bɛrti) *n* **Lorenzo** (lo'rɛntso). 1378–1455, Italian sculptor, painter, and goldsmith of the quattrocento: noted esp. for the bronze doors of the baptistry of Florence Cathedral.

ghibli *or* **gibli** ('gɪblɪ) *n* a fiercely hot wind of North Africa. [C20: from Arabic *gibliy* south wind]

ghillie ('gɪlɪ) *n* **1** a type of tongueless shoe with lacing up the instep, originally worn by the Scots. **2** a variant spelling of **gillie.** [from Scottish Gaelic *gille* boy]

Ghirlandaio *or* **Ghirlandajo** (*Italian* girlan'da:jo) *n* **Domenico** (do'me:niko). original name *Domenico Bigordi.* 1449–94, Italian painter of frescoes.

ghost (gəʊst) *n* **1** the disembodied spirit of a dead person, supposed to haunt the living as a pale or shadowy vision; phantom. Related adj: **spectral. 2** a haunting memory: *the ghost of his former life rose up before him.* **3** a faint trace or possibility of something; glimmer: *a ghost of a smile.* **4** the spirit; soul (archaic, except in the phrase **the Holy Ghost**). **5** *Physics.* **5a** a faint secondary image produced by an optical system. **5b** a similar image on a television screen, formed by reflection of the transmitting waves or by a defect in the receiver. **6** See **ghost word. 7** Also called: **ghost edition.** an entry recorded in a bibliography of which no actual proof exists. **8** See **ghostwriter. 9** (*modifier*) falsely recorded as doing a particular job or fulfilling a particular function in order that some benefit, esp. money, may be obtained: *a ghost worker.* **10 give up the ghost. 10a** to die. **10b** (of a machine) to stop working. ◆ *vb* **11** See **ghostwrite. 12** (*tr*) to haunt. [Old English *gāst;* related to Old Frisian *jēst,* Old High German *geist* spirit, Sanskrit *hēḍa* fury, anger] ▸ **'ghost,like** *adj*

ghost dance *n* a religious dance of certain North American Indians, connected with a political movement (from about 1888) that looked to reunion with the dead and a return to an idealized state of affairs before Europeans came.

ghost gum *n Austral.* a eucalyptus tree with white trunk and branches.

ghostly ('gəʊstlɪ) *adj* **-lier, -liest. 1** of or resembling a ghost; spectral: *a ghostly face appeared at the window.* **2** suggesting the presence of ghosts; eerie. **3** *Archaic.* of or relating to the soul or spirit. ▸ **'ghostliness** *n*

ghost moth *n* any of various large pale moths of the family *Hepialidae* that are active at dusk.

ghost town *n* a deserted town, esp. one in the western U.S. that was formerly a boom town.

ghost word *n* a word that has entered the language through the perpetuation, in dictionaries, etc., of an error.

ghostwrite ('gəʊst,raɪt) *vb* **-writes, -writing, -wrote, -written.** to write (an autobiographical or other article) on behalf of a person who is then credited as author. Often shortened to **ghost.** ▸ **'ghost,writer** *n*

ghoul (gu:l) *n* **1** a malevolent spirit or ghost. **2** a person interested in morbid or disgusting things. **3** a person who robs graves. **4** (in Muslim legend) an evil demon thought to eat human bodies, either stolen corpses or children. [C18: from Arabic *ghūl,* from *ghāla* he seized] ▸ **'ghoulish** *adj* ▸ **'ghoulishly** *adv* ▸ **'ghoulishness** *n*

GHQ *Military. abbrev. for* General Headquarters.

ghyll (gɪl) *n* a variant spelling of **gill**[3].

gi (gi:) *n* a loose-fitting white suit worn in judo, karate, and other martial arts: *a karate gi.* [from Japanese *-gi* costume, from *ki* to wear]

Gi *Electronics. abbrev. for* gilbert.

GI[1] *n U.S. informal.* **1** (*pl* **GIs** *or* **GI's**). a soldier in the U.S. Army, esp. an enlisted man. ◆ *adj* **2** conforming to U.S. Army regulations; of standard government issue. [C20: abbrev. of *government issue*]

GI[2] *or* **g.i.** *abbrev. for* gastrointestinal.

gi. *abbrev. for* gill (unit of measure).

Giacometti (*Italian* dʒako'metti) *n* **Alberto** (al'bɛrto). 1901–66, Swiss sculptor and painter, noted particularly for his long skeletal statues of isolated figures.

Giambologna (*Italian* dʒambo'lɔɲa) *n*, original name *Giovanni da Bologna* or *Jean de Boulogne.* 1529–1608, Italian mannerist sculptor, born in Flanders: noted for his fountains and such works as *Samson Slaying a Philistine* (1565).

giant ('dʒaɪənt) *n* **1** Also (fem): **giantess** ('dʒaɪəntɪs). a mythical figure of superhuman size and strength, esp. in folklore or fairy tales. **2** a person or thing of exceptional size, reputation, etc.: *a giant in nuclear physics.* **3** *Greek myth.* any of the large and powerful offspring of Uranus (sky) and Gaea (earth) who rebelled against the Olympian gods but were defeated in battle. **4** *Pathol.* a person suffering from gigantism. **5** *Astronomy.* See **giant star. 6** *Mining.* another word for **monitor** (sense 7). ◆ *adj* **7** remarkably or supernaturally large. **8** *Architect.* another word for **colossal.** **[C13:** from Old French *geant,* from Vulgar Latin *gagās* (unattested), from Latin *gigant-, gigās,* from Greek**]** ▸ **'giant,like** *adj*

giant cell *n Histology.* an exceptionally large cell, often possessing several nuclei, such as an osteoclast.

giant hogweed *n* an umbelliferous garden escape, *Heracleum mantegazzianum,* a tall species of cow parsley that grows up to 3½ metres (10 ft.) and whose irritant hairs and sap can cause a severe reaction if handled. Also called: **cartwheel flower.**

giantism ('dʒaɪən,tɪzəm) *n* another term for **gigantism.**

giant killer *n* a person, sports team, etc., that defeats an apparently superior opponent.

giant panda *n* See **panda** (sense 1).

giant peacock moth *n* the largest European moth, an emperor, *Saturnia pyri,* reaching 15 cm (6 in.) in wingspan. It is mottled brown with a prominent ocellus on each wing and being night-flying can be mistaken for a bat.

giant planet *n* any of the planets Jupiter, Saturn, Uranus, and Neptune, characterized by enormous mass, low density, and an extensive atmosphere.

giant powder *n* dynamite composed of trinitroglycerine absorbed in kieselguhr.

Giant's Causeway *n* a promontory of columnar basalt on the N coast of Northern Ireland, in Antrim: consists of several thousand pillars, mostly hexagonal, that were formed by the rapid cooling of lava and the inward contraction of the lava flow.

giant slalom *n Skiing.* a type of slalom in which the course is longer and the obstacles are further apart than in a standard slalom.

giant star *n* any of a class of stars, such as Capella and Arcturus, that have swelled and brightened considerably as they approach the end of their life, their energy supply having changed. Sometimes shortened to **giant.** Compare **supergiant.**

giant tortoise *n* any of various very large tortoises of the genus *Testudo,* of the Galápagos, Seychelles, and certain other islands, weighing up to 225 kilograms (495 lbs.).

giaour ('dʒaʊə) *n* a derogatory term for a non-Muslim, esp. a Christian, used esp. by the Turks. **[C16:** from Turkish *giaur* unbeliever, from Persian *gaur,* variant of *gäbr***]**

giardiasis (,dʒaɪɑː'daɪəsɪs) *n* infection with the parasitic protozoan *Giardia lamblia,* which may cause severe diarrhoea, nausea, etc.

gib[1] (gɪb) *n* **1** a metal wedge, pad, or thrust bearing, esp. a brass plate let into a steam engine crosshead. ◆ *vb* **gibs, gibbing, gibbed. 2** (*tr*) to fasten or supply with a gib. **[C18:** of unknown origin**]**

gib[2] (gɪb) *n* a male cat, esp. a castrated one. **[C14:** probably a shortening and alteration of the proper name *Gilbert***]**

Gib (dʒɪb) *n* an informal name for **Gibraltar.**

gibber[1] ('dʒɪbə) *vb* **1** to utter rapidly and unintelligibly; prattle. **2** (*intr*) (of monkeys and related animals) to make characteristic chattering sounds. ◆ *n* **3** a less common word for **gibberish.** **[C17:** of imitative origin**]**

gibber[2] ('gɪbə) *n Austral.* **1** a stone or boulder. **2** (*modifier*) of or relating to a dry flat area of land covered with wind-polished stones: *gibber plains.* **[C19:** from a native Australian language**]**

Gibberd ('gɪbəd) *n* Sir **Frederick.** 1908–84, British architect and town planner. His buildings include the Liverpool Roman Catholic cathedral (1960–67) and the Regent's Park Mosque in London (1977). Harlow in the U.K. and Santa Teresa in Venezuela were built to his plans.

gibberellic acid (,dʒɪbə'rɛlɪk) *n* a slightly soluble crystalline plant hormone first isolated from the fungus *Gibberella fujikuroi*: a giberellin. Formula: $C_{19}H_{22}O_6$. **[C20:** from New Latin *Gibberella,* literally: a little hump, from Latin *gibber* hump + -IC**]**

gibberellin (,dʒɪbə'rɛlɪn) *n* any of several plant hormones, including gibberellic acid, whose main action is to cause elongation of the stem: used in promoting the growth of plants, in the malting of barley, etc.

gibberish ('dʒɪbərɪʃ) *n* **1** rapid chatter like that of monkeys. **2** incomprehensible talk; nonsense.

gibbet ('dʒɪbɪt) *n* **1a** a wooden structure resembling a gallows, from which the bodies of executed criminals were formerly hung to public view. **1b** a gallows. ◆ *vb* (*tr*) **2** to put to death by hanging on a gibbet. **3** to hang (a corpse) on a gibbet. **4** to expose to public ridicule. **[C13:** from Old French *gibet* gallows, literally: little cudgel, from *gibe* cudgel; of uncertain origin**]**

Gib board *n N.Z. informal.* short for **Gibraltar board.**

gibbon ('gɪbᵊn) *n* any small agile arboreal anthropoid ape of the genus *Hylobates,* inhabiting forests in S Asia. **[C18:** from French, probably from an Indian dialect word**]**

Gibbon ('gɪbᵊn) *n* **1 Edward.** 1737–94, English historian; author of *The History of the Decline and Fall of the Roman Empire* (1776–88), controversial in its historical criticism of Christianity. **2 Lewis Grassic** ('græsɪk), real name *James Leslie Mitchell.* 1901–35, Scottish writer: best known for his trilogy of novels *Scots Quair* (1932–34).

Gibbons ('gɪbᵊnz) *n* **1 Grinling.** 1648–1721, English sculptor and woodcarver, noted for his delicate carvings of fruit, flowers, birds, etc. **2 Orlando.** 1583–1625, English organist and composer, esp. of anthems, motets, and madrigals.

gibbosity (gɪ'bɒsɪtɪ) *n, pl* **-ties.** *Rare.* **1** the state of being gibbous. **2** *Biology.* a bulge or protuberance.

gibbous ('gɪbəs) *or* **gibbose** ('gɪbəʊs) *adj* **1** (of the moon or a planet) more than half but less than fully illuminated. **2** having a hunchback; hunchbacked. **3** bulging. **[C17:** from Late Latin *gibbōsus* humpbacked, from Latin *gibba* hump**]** ▸ **'gibbously** *adv* ▸ **'gibbousness** *n*

Gibbs (gɪbz) *n* **1 James.** 1682–1754, British architect; his buildings include St Martin's-in-the-Fields, London (1722–26), and the Radcliffe Camera, Oxford (1737–49). **2 Josiah Willard.** 1839–1903, U.S. physicist and mathematician: founder of chemical thermodynamics.

Gibbs function (gɪbz) *n* a thermodynamic property of a system equal to the difference between its enthalpy and the product of its temperature and its entropy. It is usually measured in joules. Symbol: *G* or (esp. U.S.) *F* Also called: **Gibbs free energy, free enthalpy.** Compare **Helmholtz function.** **[C19:** named after J. W. GIBBS**]**

gibbsite ('gɪbzaɪt) *n* a mineral consisting of hydrated aluminium oxide: a constituent of bauxite and a source of alumina. Formula: $Al(OH)_3$. **[C19:** named after George *Gibbs* (died 1833), American mineralogist**]**

gibe[1] *or* **jibe** (dʒaɪb) *vb* **1** to make jeering or scoffing remarks (at); taunt. ◆ *n* **2** a derisive or provoking remark. **[C16:** perhaps from Old French *giber* to treat roughly, of uncertain origin**]** ▸ **'giber** *or* **'jiber** *n* ▸ **'gibingly** *or* **'jibingly** *adv*

gibe[2] (dʒaɪb) *vb, n Nautical.* a variant spelling of **gybe.**

Gibeon ('gɪbɪən) *n* an ancient town of Palestine: the excavated site thought to be its remains lies about 9 kilometres (6 miles) northwest of Jerusalem.

Gibeonite ('gɪbɪə,naɪt) *n Old Testament.* one of the inhabitants of the town of Gibeon, who were compelled by Joshua to serve the Hebrews (Joshua 9).

giblets ('dʒɪblɪts) *pl n* (*sometimes sing*) the gizzard, liver, heart, and neck of a fowl. **[C14:** from Old French *gibelet* stew of game birds, probably from *gibier* game, of Germanic origin**]**

gibli ('gɪblɪ) *n* a variant spelling of **ghibli.**

Gibraltar (dʒɪ'brɔːltə) *n* **1 City of.** a city on the **Rock of Gibraltar,** a limestone promontory at the tip of S Spain: settled by Moors in 711 and taken by Spain in 1462; ceded to Britain in 1713; a British crown colony (1830–1969), still politically associated with Britain; a naval and air base of strategic importance. Pop.: 27 100 (1998 est.). Area: 6.5 sq. km (2.5 sq. miles). Ancient name: **Calpe. 2 Strait of.** a narrow strait between the S tip of Spain and the NW tip of Africa, linking the Mediterranean with the Atlantic. ▸ **Gibraltarian** (,dʒɪbrɔːl'tɛərɪən) *adj, n*

Gibraltar board *n N.Z. trademark.* a type of lining board with a cardboard surface and a gypsum core.

Gibran (dʒɪ'brɑːn) *n* **Kahlil** ('kɑːliːl). 1883–1931, Syro-Lebanese poet, mystic, and painter, resident in the U.S. after 1910; author of *The Prophet* (1923).

Gibson[1] ('gɪbsᵊn) *n Chiefly U.S.* a cocktail consisting of four or more parts dry gin and one part dry vermouth, iced and served with a pickled pearl onion.

Gibson[2] ('gɪbsᵊn) *n* **Mel.** born 1956, Australian film actor: his films include *Mad Max* (1979), *Hamlet* (1990), and *Braveheart* (1996; also directed).

Gibson Desert *n* a desert in W central Australia, between the Great Sandy Desert and the Victoria Desert: salt marshes, salt lakes, and scrub. Area: about 220 000 sq. km (85 000 sq. miles).

Gibson girl *n* the ideal fashionable American girl of the late 1890s and early 1900s, as portrayed in the drawings of Charles Dana Gibson, 1867–1944, U.S. illustrator.

gibus ('dʒaɪbəs) *n* another name for **opera hat.** **[C19:** named after *Gibus,* 19th-century Frenchman who invented it**]**

gid (gɪd) *n* a disease of sheep characterized by an unsteady gait and staggering, caused by infestation of the brain with tapeworms (*Taenia caenuris*). **[C17:** back formation from GIDDY**]**

giddap (gɪ'dæp) *or* **giddy-up** (,gɪdɪ'ʌp) *interj* an exclamation used to make a horse go faster. **[C20:** colloquial form of *get up***]**

giddy ('gɪdɪ) *adj* **-dier, -diest. 1** affected with a reeling sensation and feeling as if about to fall; dizzy. **2** causing or tending to cause vertigo. **3** impulsive; scatterbrained. **4 my giddy aunt.** an exclamation of surprise. ◆ *vb* **-dies, -dying, -died. 5** to make or become giddy. **[**Old English *gydig* mad, frenzied, possessed by God; related to GOD**]** ▸ **'giddily** *adv* ▸ **'giddiness** *n*

Gide (*French* ʒid) *n* **André** (ɑ̃dre). 1869–1951, French novelist, dramatist, critic, diarist, and translator, noted particularly for his exploration of the conflict between self-fulfilment and conventional morality. His novels include *L'Immoraliste* (1902), *La Porte étroite* (1909), and *Les Faux-Monnayeurs* (1926): Nobel prize for literature 1947.

Gideon ('gɪdɪən) *n Old Testament.* a Hebrew judge who led the Israelites to victory over their Midianite oppressors (Judges 6:11–8:35).

Gideon Bible *n* a Bible purchased by members of a Christian organization (**Gideons**) and placed in a hotel room, hospital ward, etc.

gidgee *or* **gidjee** ('gɪdʒiː) *n Austral.* a small acacia tree, *Acacia cambagei,* yielding useful timber. **[C19:** from a native Australian language**]**

gie (giː) *vb* a Scot. word for **give.**

Gielgud ('giːlgʊd) *n* Sir **John.** born 1904, English stage, film, and television actor and director.

Giessen (*German* 'giːsən) *n* a city in central Germany, in Hesse: university (1607). Pop.: 71 750 (1989 est.).

gift (gɪft) *n* **1** something given; a present. **2** a special aptitude, ability, or power; talent. **3** the power or right to give or bestow (esp. in the phrases **in the gift of, in (someone's) gift**). **4** the act or process of giving. **5 look a gift-horse in the mouth.** (*usually negative*) to find fault with a free gift or chance benefit. ◆ *vb* (*tr*) **6** to present (something) as a gift to (a person). **7** *Rare.* to endow with; bestow. **[**Old English *gift* payment for a wife, dowry; related to Old Norse *gipt,*

Old High German *gift,* Gothic *fragifts* endowment, engagement; see GIVE] ▸ 'giftless *adj*

GIFT (gɪft) *n acronym for* gamete intrafallopian transfer: a technique, similar to in vitro fertilization, that enables some women who are unable to conceive to bear children. Egg cells are removed from the woman's ovary, mixed with sperm, and introduced into one of her Fallopian tubes.

gifted ('gɪftɪd) *adj* having or showing natural talent or aptitude: *a gifted musician; a gifted performance.* ▸ **'giftedly** *adv* ▸ **'giftedness** *n*

gift of tongues *n* an utterance, partly or wholly unintelligible, produced under the influence of ecstatic religious emotion and conceived to be a manifestation of the Holy Ghost: practised in certain Christian churches, usually called Pentecostal. Also called: **glossolalia.**

gift tax *n* another name for **capital transfer tax.**

giftwrap ('gɪft,ræp) *vb* **-wraps, -wrapping, -wrapped.** to wrap (an article intended as a gift) attractively.

Gifu ('giːfuː) *n* a city in Japan, on central Honshu: hot springs, textile and paper lantern manufacturing. Pop.: 407 145 (1995).

gig[1] (gɪg) *n* **1** a light two-wheeled one-horse carriage without a hood. **2** *Nautical.* a light tender for a vessel, often for the personal use of the captain. **3** a long light rowing boat, used esp. for racing. **4** a machine for raising the nap of a fabric. ◆ *vb* **gigs, gigging, gigged. 5** (*intr*) to travel in a gig. **6** (*tr*). to raise the nap of (fabric). [C13 (in the sense: flighty girl, spinning top): perhaps of Scandinavian origin; compare Danish *gig* top, Norwegian *giga* to shake about]

gig[2] (gɪg) *n* **1** a cluster of barbless hooks drawn through a shoal of fish to try to impale them. **2** short for **fishgig.** ◆ *vb* **gigs, gigging, gigged. 3** to catch (fish) with a gig. [C18: shortened from FISHGIG]

gig[3] (gɪg) *Informal.* ◆ *n* **1** a job, esp. a single booking for jazz or pop musicians to play at a concert or club. **2** the performance itself. ◆ *vb* **gigs, gigging, gigged.** (*intr*) **3** to perform at a gig or gigs. [C20: of unknown origin]

gig[4] (gɪg) *n Informal.* short for **gigabyte.**

giga- *combining form.* **1** denoting 10^9: *gigavolt.* Symbol: G **2** (in computer technology) denoting 2^{30}: *gigabyte.* [from Greek *gigas* GIANT]

gigabyte ('gaɪgə,baɪt) *n Computing.* one thousand and twenty-four megabytes. See also **giga-** (sense 2).

gigaflop ('gaɪgə,flɒp) *n Computing.* a measure of processing speed, consisting of a thousand million floating-point operations a second. [C20: from GIGA- + *flo(ating) p(oint)*]

gigahertz ('gaɪgə,hɜːts, 'dʒɪg-) *n, pl* **-hertz.** a unit of frequency equal to 10^9 hertz. Symbol: GHz

gigantic (dʒaɪ'gæntɪk) *adj* **1** very large; enormous: *a gigantic error.* **2** Also: **gigantesque** (,dʒaɪgæn'tɛsk). of or suitable for giants. [C17: from Greek *gigantikos,* from *gigas* GIANT] ▸ **gi'gantically** *adv* ▸ **gi'ganticness** *n*

gigantism ('dʒaɪgæn,tɪzəm, dʒaɪ'gæntɪzəm) *n* **1** Also called: **giantism.** excessive growth of the entire body, caused by over-production of growth hormone by the pituitary gland during childhood or adolescence. Compare **acromegaly. 2** the state or quality of being gigantic.

gigantomachy (,dʒaɪgæn'tɒməkɪ) *or* **gigantomachia** (dʒaɪ,gæntəʊ'meɪkɪə) *n, pl* **-chies** or **-chias. 1** *Greek myth.* the war fought between the gods of Olympus and the rebelling giants. See **giant** (sense 3). **2** any battle fought between or as if between giants. [C17: from Greek *gigantomakhia,* from *gigas* giant + *makhē* battle]

giggle ('gɪgᵊl) *vb* **1** (*intr*) to laugh nervously or foolishly. ◆ *n* **2** such a laugh. **3** *Informal.* something or someone that provokes amusement. **4 the giggles.** a fit of prolonged and uncontrollable giggling. **5 for a giggle.** *Informal.* as a joke or prank; not seriously. [C16: of imitative origin] ▸ **'giggler** *n* ▸ **'giggling** *n, adj* ▸ **'gigglingly** *adv* ▸ **'giggly** *adj*

gig-lamps *pl n* an old-fashioned slang term for **spectacles.**

Gigli (*Italian* 'dʒiʎʎi) *n* **Beniamino** (benja'miːno). 1890–1957, Italian operatic tenor.

GIGO ('gaɪgəʊ) *n Slang. Computing. acronym for* garbage in, garbage out.

gigolo ('ʒɪgə,ləʊ) *n, pl* **-los. 1** a man who is kept by a woman, esp. an older woman. **2** a man who is paid to dance with or escort women. [C20: from French, back formation from *gigolette* girl for hire as a dancing partner, prostitute, from *giguer* to dance, from *gigue* a fiddle; compare GIGOT, GIGUE, JIG]

gigot ('ʒiːgəʊ, 'dʒɪgət) *n* **1** a leg of lamb or mutton. **2** a leg-of-mutton sleeve. [C16: from Old French: leg, a small fiddle, from *gigue* a fiddle, of Germanic origin]

gigue (ʒiːg) *n* **1** a piece of music, usually in six-eight time and often fugal, incorporated into the classical suite. **2** a formal couple dance of the 16th and 17th centuries, derived from the jig. [C17: from French, from Italian *giga,* literally: a fiddle; see GIGOT]

GI Joe *n U.S. informal.* a U.S. enlisted soldier; a GI.

Gijón (giː'hɔːn; *Spanish* xi'xɔn) *n* a port in NW Spain, on the Bay of Biscay: capital of the kingdom of Asturias until 791. Pop.: 270 867 (1995 est.). Ancient name: **Gigia.**

Gila monster ('hiːlə) *n* a large venomous brightly coloured lizard, *Heloderma suspectum,* inhabiting deserts of the southwestern U.S. and Mexico and feeding mostly on eggs and small mammals: family *Helodermatidae.* [C19: after the *Gila,* a river in New Mexico and Arizona]

gilbert ('gɪlbət) *n* a unit of magnetomotive force; the magnetomotive force resulting from the passage of 4π abamperes through one turn of a coil. 1 gilbert is equivalent to $10/4\pi = 0.795\ 775$ ampere-turn. Symbols: Gb or Gi [C19: named after William GILBERT]

Gilbert ('gɪlbət) *n* **1 Grove Karl.** 1843–1918, U.S. geologist who pioneered the study of river development and valley erosion. **2** Sir **Humphrey.** ?1539–83, English navigator: founded the colony at St John's, Newfoundland (1583). **3 William.** 1540–1603, English physician and physicist, noted for his study of terrestrial magnetism in *De Magnete* (1600). **4** Sir **W(illiam) S(chwenck).** 1836–1911, English dramatist, humorist, and librettist. He collaborated (1871–96) with Arthur Sullivan on the famous series of comic operettas, including *The Pirates of Penzance* (1879), *Iolanthe* (1882), and *The Mikado* (1885).

Gilbert and George *n* a team of artists, **Gilbert Proesch,** Italian, born 1942, and **George Passmore,** British, born 1943: noted esp. for their photomontages and performance works.

Gilbertian (gɪl'bɜːtɪən) *adj* characteristic of or resembling the style or whimsical humour of Sir W. S. Gilbert.

Gilbertine ('gɪlbətaɪn, -tɪn) *n* **1** a member of a Christian order founded in approximately 1135 by St Gilbert of Sempringham, composed of nuns who followed the Cistercian rule and Augustinian canons who ministered to them. It was the only religious order of English origin and never spread to Europe. ◆ *adj* **2** of, relating to, or belonging to this order.

Gilbert Islands *pl n* a group of islands in the W Pacific: with Banaba, the Phoenix Islands, and three of the Line Islands they constitute the independent state of Kiribati; until 1975 they formed part of the British colony of **Gilbert and Ellice Islands;** achieved full independence in 1979. Pop.: 67 508 (1990). Area: 295 sq. km (114 sq. miles).

gild[1] (gɪld) *vb* **gilds, gilding, gilded** *or* **gilt** (gɪlt). (*tr*) **1** to cover with or as if with gold. **2 gild the lily. 2a** to adorn unnecessarily something already beautiful. **2b** to praise someone inordinately. **3** to give a falsely attractive or valuable appearance to. **4** *Archaic.* to smear with blood. [Old English *gyldan,* from *gold* GOLD; related to Old Norse *gylla,* Middle High German *vergülden*] ▸ **'gilder** *n*

gild[2] (gɪld) *n* a variant spelling of **guild** (sense 2). ▸ **'gildsman** *n*

gilder ('gɪldə) *n* a variant spelling of **guilder.**

gilding ('gɪldɪŋ) *n* **1** the act or art of applying gilt to a surface. **2** the surface so produced. **3** another word for **gilt**[1] (sense 2).

Gilead[1] ('gɪlɪ,æd) *n* a historic mountainous region east of the River Jordan, rising over 1200 m (4000 ft.).

Gilead[2] ('gɪlɪ,æd) *n Old Testament.* a grandson of Manasseh; ancestor of the Coileadites (Numbers 26: 29–30).

Gileadite ('gɪlɪə,daɪt) *n* **1** an inhabitant of the region of Gilead. **2** a descendant of Gilead (the man).

Giles (dʒaɪlz) *n* **1 Saint.** 7th century A.D., Greek hermit in France; patron saint of cripples, beggars, and lepers. Feast day: Sept. 1. **2 William Ernest Powell.** 1835–97, Australian explorer, born in England. He was noted esp. for his exploration of the western desert (1875–76).

gilet (dʒɪ'leɪ) *n* **1** a waist- or hip-length garment, usually sleeveless, fastening up the front; sometimes made from a quilted fabric, and designed to be worn over a blouse, shirt, etc. **2** a bodice resembling a waistcoat in a woman's dress. **3** such a bodice as part of a ballet dancer's costume. [C19: French, literally: waistcoat]

gilgai ('gɪlgaɪ) *n Austral.* a natural water hole. [C19: from a native Australian language]

Gilgamesh ('gɪlgə,mɛʃ) *n* a legendary Sumerian king.

gill[1] (gɪl) *n* **1** the respiratory organ in many aquatic animals, consisting of a membrane or outgrowth well supplied with blood vessels. **External gills** occur in tadpoles, some molluscs, etc.; **internal gills,** within gill slits, occur in most fishes. Related adj: **branchial. 2** any of the radiating leaflike spore-producing structures on the undersurface of the cap of a mushroom. ◆ *vb* **3** to catch (fish) or (of fish) to be caught in a gill net. **4** (*tr*) to gut (fish). ◆ See also **gills.** [C14: of Scandinavian origin; compare Swedish *gäl,* Danish *gjælle,* Greek *khelunē* lip] ▸ **gilled** *adj* ▸ **'gill-less** *adj* ▸ **'gill-,like** *adj*

gill[2] (dʒɪl) *n* **1** a unit of liquid measure equal to one quarter of a pint. **2** *Northern Brit. dialect.* half a pint, esp. of beer. [C14: from Old French *gille* vat, tub, from Late Latin *gillō* cooling vessel for liquids, of obscure origin]

gill[3] *or* **ghyll** (gɪl) *n Dialect.* **1** a narrow stream; rivulet. **2** a wooded ravine. **3** (*cap. when part of place name*) a deep natural hole in rock; pothole: *Gaping Gill.* [C11: from Old Norse *gil* steep-sided valley]

gill[4] (dʒɪl) *n* **1** *Archaic.* a girl or sweetheart. **2** *Dialect.* Also spelt: **jill.** a female ferret. **3** an archaic or dialect name for **ground ivy.** [C15: special use of *Gill,* short for *Gillian,* girl's name]

Gill (gɪl) *n* **(Arthur) Eric (Rowton).** 1882–1940, British sculptor, engraver, and typographer: his sculptures include the *Stations of the Cross* in Westminster Cathedral, London.

Gilles de la Tourette syndrome (dʒiːl də læ tʊə'rɛt) *n* another name for **Tourette syndrome.**

Gillespie (gɪ'lɛspɪ) *n* **Dizzy,** nickname of *John Birks Gillespie.* 1917–93, U.S. jazz trumpeter.

gill fungus (gɪl) *n* any fungus of the basidiomycetous family *Agaricaceae,* in which the spores are produced on gills underneath a cap. See also **agaric.**

gillie, ghillie, *or* **gilly** ('gɪlɪ) *n, pl* **-lies.** *Scot.* **1** an attendant or guide for hunting or fishing. **2** (formerly) a Highland chieftain's male attendant or personal servant. [C17: from Scottish Gaelic *gille* boy, servant]

Gillingham ('dʒɪlɪŋəm) *n* a town in SE England, in N Kent on the Medway estuary: former dockyards. Pop.: 94 923 (1991).

gillion ('dʒɪljən) *n Brit.* (no longer in technical use) one thousand million. U.S. and Canadian equivalent: **billion.** [C20: from G(IGA-) + (M)ILLION]

gill net (gɪl) *n Fishing.* a net suspended vertically in the water to trap fish by their gills in its meshes.

gill pouch (gɪl) *n* any of a series of paired linear pouches in chordate embryos, arising as outgrowths of the wall of the pharynx. In fish and some amphibians they become the gill slits.

Gillray ('gɪlreɪ) *n* **James.** 1757–1815, English caricaturist.

gills (gɪlz) *pl n* **1** (*sometimes sing*) the wattle of birds such as domestic fowl. **2 green around** *or* **about the gills.** *Informal.* looking or feeling nauseated.

gill slit (gɪl) *n* any of a series of paired linear openings to the exterior from the sides of the pharynx in fishes and some amphibians. They contain the gills.

gillyflower *or* **gilliflower** ('dʒɪlɪˌflaʊə) *n* **1** any of several plants having fragrant flowers, such as the stock and wallflower. **2** an archaic name for **carnation.** [C14: changed (through influence of *flower*) from *gilofre,* from Old French *girofle,*from Medieval Latin, from Greek *karuophullon* clove tree, from*karuon* nut + *phullon* leaf]

Gilolo (dʒaɪ'ləʊləʊ, dʒɪ-) *n* See **Halmahera.**

Gilsonite ('gɪlsəˌnaɪt) *n Trademark.* a very pure form of asphalt found in Utah and Colorado; used for making paints, varnishes, and linoleum. [C19: named after S. H. *Gilson* of Salt Lake City, Utah, who discovered it]

gilt[1] (gɪlt) *vb* **1** a past tense and past participle of **gild**[1]. ◆ *n* **2** gold or a substance simulating it, applied in gilding. **3** another word for **gilding** (senses 1, 2). **4** superficial or false appearance of excellence; glamour. **5** a gilt-edged security. **6 take the gilt off the gingerbread.** to destroy the part of something that gives it its appeal. ◆ *adj* **7** covered with or as if with gold or gilt; gilded.

gilt[2] (gɪlt) *n* a young female pig, esp. one that has not had a litter. [C15: from Old Norse *gyltr;* related to Old English *gelte,* Old High German *gelza,* Middle Low German *gelte*]

gilt-edged *adj* **1** *Stock Exchange.* denoting government securities on which interest payments will certainly be met and that will certainly be repaid at par on the due date. **2** of the highest quality: *the last track on the album is a gilt-edged classic.* **3** (of books, papers, etc.) having gilded edges.

gilthead ('gɪltˌhɛd) *n* **1** a sparid fish, *Sparus aurata,* of Mediterranean and European Atlantic waters, having a gold-coloured band between the eyes. **2** any similar or related fish.

gimbals ('dʒɪmbᵊlz, 'gɪm-) *pl n* a device, consisting of two or three pivoted rings at right angles to each other, that provides free suspension in all planes for an object such as a gyroscope, compass, chronometer, etc. Also called: **gimbal ring.** [C16: variant of earlier *gimmal* finger ring, from Old French *gemel,* from Latin *gemellus,* diminutive of *geminus* twin]

gimcrack ('dʒɪmˌkræk) *adj* **1** cheap; shoddy. ◆ *n* **2** a cheap showy trifle or gadget. [C18: changed from C14 *gibecrake* little ornament, of unknown origin] ▸ **'gimˌcrackery** *n*

gimel ('gɪməl; *Hebrew* 'giːmɛl) *n* the third letter of the Hebrew alphabet (ג) transliterated as *g* or, when final, *gh.* [literally: camel]

gimlet ('gɪmlɪt) *n* **1** a small hand tool consisting of a pointed spiral tip attached at right angles to a handle, used for boring small holes in wood. **2** *U.S.* a cocktail consisting of half gin or vodka and half lime juice. **3** a eucalyptus of W Australia having a twisted bole. ◆ *vb* **4** (*tr*) to make holes in (wood) using a gimlet. ◆ *adj* **5** penetrating; piercing (esp. in the phrase **gimlet-eyed**). [C15: from Old French *guimbelet,* of Germanic origin, see WIMBLE]

gimme ('gɪmiː) *interj Slang.* give me!

gimmick ('gɪmɪk) *n* **1** something designed to attract extra attention, interest, or publicity. **2** any clever device, gadget, or stratagem, esp. one used to deceive. **3** *Chiefly U.S.* a device or trick of legerdemain that enables a magician to deceive the audience. [C20: originally U.S. slang, of unknown origin] ▸ **'gimmickry** *n* ▸ **'gimmicky** *adj*

gimp *or* **guimpe** (gɪmp) *n* a tapelike trimming of silk, wool, or cotton, often stiffened with wire. [C17: probably from Dutch *gimp,* of unknown origin]

gimpy ('gɪmpɪ) *adj* the U.S. equivalent of **gammy.**

gin[1] (dʒɪn) *n* **1** an alcoholic drink obtained by distillation and rectification of the grain of malted barley, rye, or maize, flavoured with juniper berries. **2** any of various grain spirits flavoured with other fruit or aromatic essences: *sloe gin.* **3** an alcoholic drink made from any rectified spirit. [C18: shortened from Dutch *genever* juniper, via Old French from Latin *jūniperus* JUNIPER]

gin[2] (dʒɪn) *n* **1** a primitive engine in which a vertical shaft is turned by horses driving a horizontal beam or yoke in a circle. **2** Also called: **cotton gin.** a machine of this type used for separating seeds from raw cotton. **3** a trap for catching small mammals, consisting of a noose of thin strong wire. **4** a hand-operated hoist that consists of a drum winder turned by a crank. ◆ *vb* **gins, ginning, ginned.** (*tr*) **5** to free (cotton) of seeds with a gin. **6** to trap or snare (game) with a gin. [C13 *gyn,* shortened from ENGINE] ▸ **'ginner** *n*

gin[3] (gɪn) *vb* **gins, ginning, gan, gun.** an archaic word for **begin.**

gin[4] (gɪn) *conj Scot.* if. [perhaps related to *gif,* an earlier form of *if*]

gin[5] (dʒɪn) *n Austral. offensive slang.* an Aboriginal woman. [C19: from a native Australian language]

ging (gɪŋ) *n Austral. slang.* a child's catapult. [of unknown origin]

ginger ('dʒɪndʒə) *n* **1** any of several zingiberaceous plants of the genus *Zingiber,* esp. *Z. officinale* of the East Indies, cultivated throughout the tropics for its spicy hot-tasting underground stem. See also **galangal.** Compare **wild ginger. 2** the underground stem of this plant, which is used fresh or powdered as a flavouring or crystallized as a sweetmeat. **3** any of certain related plants. **4a** a reddish-brown or yellowish-brown colour. **4b** (*as adj*): *ginger hair.* **5** *Informal.* liveliness; vigour. ◆ *vb* **6** (*tr*) to add the spice ginger to (a dish). ◆ See also **ginger up.** [C13: from Old French *gingivre,* from Medieval Latin *gingiber,* from Latin *zinziberi,* from Greek *zingiberis,* probably from Sanskrit *śṛṅgaveram,* from *śṛṅga-* horn + *vera-* body, referring to its shape]

ginger ale *n* a sweetened effervescent nonalcoholic drink flavoured with ginger extract.

ginger beer *n* a slightly alcoholic drink made by fermenting a mixture of syrup and root ginger.

gingerbread ('dʒɪndʒəˌbrɛd) *n* **1** a moist brown cake, flavoured with ginger and treacle or syrup. **2a** a rolled biscuit, similarly flavoured, cut into various shapes and sometimes covered with icing. **2b** (*as modifier*): *gingerbread man.* **3a** an elaborate but unsubstantial ornamentation. **3b** (*as modifier*): *gingerbread style of architecture.*

gingerbread tree *n* a W African rosaceous tree, *Parinarium macrophyllum,* with large mealy edible fruits (**gingerbread plums**): family *Chrysobalanaceae.*

ginger group *n Chiefly Brit.* a group within a party, association, etc., that enlivens or radicalizes its parent body.

gingerly ('dʒɪndʒəlɪ) *adv* **1** in a cautious, reluctant, or timid manner. ◆ *adj* **2** cautious, reluctant, or timid. [C16: perhaps from Old French *gensor* dainty, from *gent* of noble birth; see GENTLE] ▸ **'gingerliness** *n*

ginger nut *or* **snap** *n* a crisp biscuit flavoured with ginger.

ginger up *vb* (*tr, adv*) to enliven (an activity, group, etc.).

ginger wine *n* an alcoholic drink made from fermented bruised ginger, sugar, and water.

gingery ('dʒɪndʒərɪ) *adj* **1** like or tasting of ginger. **2** of or like the colour ginger. **3** full of vigour; high-spirited. **4** pointed; biting: *a gingery remark.*

gingham ('gɪŋəm) *n Textiles.* **a** a cotton fabric, usually woven of two coloured yarns in a checked or striped design. **b** (*as modifier*): *a gingham dress.* [C17: from French *guingan,* from Malay *ginggang* striped cloth]

gingili, gingelli, *or* **gingelly** ('dʒɪndʒɪlɪ) *n* **1** the oil obtained from sesame seeds. **2** another name for **sesame.** [C18: from Hindi *jingalī*]

gingiva ('dʒɪndʒɪvə, dʒɪn'dʒaɪvə) *n, pl* **-givae** (-dʒɪˌviː, -'dʒaɪviː). *Anatomy.* the technical name for the **gum**[2]. [from Latin] ▸ **'gingival** *adj*

gingivitis (ˌdʒɪndʒɪ'vaɪtɪs) *n* inflammation of the gums.

ginglymus ('dʒɪŋglɪməs, 'gɪŋ-) *n, pl* **-mi** (-ˌmaɪ). *Anatomy.* a hinge joint. See **hinge** (sense 2). [C17: New Latin, from Greek *ginglumos* hinge]

gink (gɪŋk) *n Slang.* a man or boy, esp. one considered to be odd. [C20: of unknown origin]

ginkgo ('gɪŋkgəʊ) *or* **gingko** ('gɪŋkəʊ) *n, pl* **-goes** *or* **-koes.** a widely planted ornamental Chinese gymnosperm tree, *Ginkgo biloba,* with fan-shaped deciduous leaves and fleshy yellow fruit: phylum *Ginkgophyta.* Also called: **maidenhair tree.** [C18: from Japanese *ginkyō,* from Ancient Chinese *yin* silver + *hang* apricot]

ginnel ('gɪnᵊl, 'dʒɪn-) *n Northern English dialect.* a narrow passageway between buildings. [C17: perhaps a corruption of CHANNEL[1]]

ginormous (dʒaɪ'nɔːməs) *adj Informal.* very large. [C20: blend of *giant* or *gigantic* and *enormous*]

gin palace (dʒɪn) *n* (formerly) a gaudy drinking house.

gin rummy (dʒɪn) *n* a version of rummy in which a player may go out if the odd cards outside his sequences total less than ten points. Often shortened to **gin.** [C20: from GIN[1] + RUMMY[1], apparently from a humorous allusion to gin and rum]

Ginsberg ('gɪnzbɜːg) *n* **Allen.** 1926–97, U.S. poet of the Beat Generation. His poetry includes *Howl* (1956) and *Kaddish* (1960).

ginseng ('dʒɪnsɛŋ) *n* **1** either of two araliaceous plants, *Panax schinseng* of China or *P. quinquefolius* of North America, whose forked aromatic roots are used medicinally. **2** the root of either of these plants or a substance obtained from the roots, believed to possess stimulant, tonic, and energy-giving properties. [C17: from Mandarin Chinese *jen shen,* from *jen* man (from a resemblance of the roots to human legs) + *shen* ginseng]

gin sling (dʒɪn) *n* an iced drink made from gin and water, sweetened, and flavoured with lemon or lime juice.

Ginzburg (*Italian* 'gindzburg) *n* **Natalia** (nata'liːa). 1916–91, Italian writer and dramatist. Her books include *The Road to the City* (1942), *Voices in the Evening* (1961), and *Family Sayings* (1963).

gio ('dʒiːəʊ) *n* a variant spelling of **geo.**

Gioconda (*Italian* dʒo'konda) *n* **La.** See **Mona Lisa.** [Italian: the smiling (lady)]

Giorgione (*Italian* dʒor'dʒoːne) *n* **Il.** original name *Giorgio Barbarelli.* ?1478–1511, Italian painter of the Venetian school, who introduced a new unity between figures and landscape.

Giorgi system ('dʒɔːdʒɪ) *n* a system of units based on the metre, kilogram, second, and ampere, in which the magnetic constant has the value $4\pi \times 10^{-7}$ henries per metre. It was used as a basis for SI units. Also called: **MKSA system.** [C20: named after Giovanni *Giorgi* (1871–1950), Italian physicist]

Giotto[1] (*Italian* 'dʒɔtto) *n* also known as *Giotto di Bondone.* ?1267–1337, Florentine painter, who broke away from the stiff linear design of the Byzantine tradition and developed the more dramatic and naturalistic style characteristic of the Renaissance: his work includes cycles of frescoes in Assisi, the Arena Chapel in Padua, and the Church of Santa Croce, Florence.

Giotto[2] ('dʒɒtəʊ) *n* a European spacecraft that intercepted the path of Halley's comet in March 1986, gathering data and recording images, esp. of the comet's nucleus.

gip (dʒɪp) *vb* **gips, gipping, gipped. 1** a variant spelling of **gyp**[1]. ◆ *n* **2** a variant spelling of **gyp**[2].

gipon (dʒɪ'pɒn, 'dʒɪpɒn) *n* another word for **jupon.**

Gippsland ('gɪpsˌlænd) *n* a fertile region of SE Australia, in SE Victoria, extending east along the coast from Melbourne to the New South Wales border. Area: 35 200 sq. km (13 600 sq. miles).

gippy ('dʒɪpɪ) *Slang.* ◆ *n, pl* **-pies. 1** an Egyptian person or thing. **2** Also called: **gippo,** *pl* **-poes.** a Gypsy. ◆ *adj* **3** Egyptian. **4 gippy tummy.** diarrhoea, esp. as experienced by visitors to hot climates. [C19: from GYPSY and EGYPTIAN]

Gipsy ('dʒɪpsɪ) *n, pl* **-sies.** (*sometimes not cap.*) a variant spelling of **Gypsy.** ▸ **'Gipsyish** *adj* ▸ **'Gipsydom** *n* ▸ **'Gipsyˌhood** *n* ▸ **'Gipsy-ˌlike** *adj*

gipsy moth *n* a European moth, *Lymantria dispar,* introduced into North America, where it is a serious pest of shade trees: family *Lymantriidae* (or *Liparidae*). See also **tussock moth.**

gipsywort ('dʒɪpsɪˌwɜːt) *n* a hairy Eurasian plant, *Lycopus europaeus,* having two-lipped white flowers with purple dots on the lower lip: family *Labiatae* (labiates). See also **bugleweed** (sense 1).

giraffe (dʒɪ'rɑːf, -'ræf) *n, pl* **-raffes** *or* **-raffe.** a large ruminant mammal,

Giraffa camelopardalis, inhabiting savannas of tropical Africa: the tallest mammal, with very long legs and neck and a colouring of regular reddish-brown patches on a beige ground: family *Giraffidae.* [C17: from Italian *giraffa,* from Arabic *zarāfah,* probably of African origin]

Giraldus Cambrensis (dʒɪ'rældəs kæm'brɛnsɪs) *n* literary name of *Gerald de Barri.* ?1146–?1223, Welsh chronicler and churchman, noted for his accounts of his travels in Ireland and Wales.

girandole ('dʒɪrən,dəʊl) *or* **girandola** (dʒɪ'rændələ) *n* **1** an ornamental branched wall candleholder, usually incorporating a mirror. **2** an earring or pendant having a central gem surrounded by smaller ones. **3** a kind of revolving firework. **4** *Artillery.* a group of connected mines. [C17: from French, from Italian *girandola,* from *girare* to revolve, from Latin *gȳrāre* to GYRATE]

girasol, girosol, *or* **girasole** ('dʒɪrə,sɒl, -,səʊl) *n* a type of opal that has a red or pink glow in bright light; fire opal. [C16: from Italian, from *girare* to revolve (see GYRATE) + *sole* the sun, from Latin *sōl*]

Giraud (*French* ʒiro) *n* **Henri Honoré** (ɑ̃ri ɔnɔre). 1879–1949, French general, who commanded French forces in North Africa (1942–43).

Giraudoux (*French* ʒirodu) *n* **(Hyppolyte) Jean** (ʒɑ̃). 1882–1944, French dramatist. His works include the novel *Suzanne et le Pacifique* (1921) and the plays *Amphitryon 38* (1929) and *La Guerre de Troie n'aura pas lieu* (1935).

gird[1] (gɜːd) *vb* **girds, girding, girded** *or* **girt.** (*tr*) **1** to put a belt, girdle, etc., around (the waist or hips). **2** to bind or secure with or as if with a belt: *to gird on one's armour.* **3** to surround; encircle. **4** to prepare (oneself) for action (esp. in the phrase **gird (up) one's loins**). **5** to endow with a rank, attribute, etc., esp. knighthood. [Old English *gyrdan,* of Germanic origin; related to Old Norse *gyrtha,* Old High German *gurten*]

gird[2] (gɜːd) *Northern English dialect.* ◆ *vb* **1** (when *intr,* foll. by *at*) to jeer (at someone); mock. **2** (*tr*) to strike (a blow at someone). **3** (*intr*) to move at high speed. ◆ *n* **4a** a blow or stroke. **4b** a taunt; gibe. **5** a display of bad temper or anger (esp. in the phrases **in a gird; throw a gird**). [C13 *girden* to strike, cut, of unknown origin]

gird[3] (gɪrd) *n Scot.* a hoop, esp. a child's hoop. Also: **girr.** [a Scot. variant of GIRTH]

girder ('gɜːdə) *n* **1** a large beam, esp. one made of steel, used in the construction of bridges, buildings, etc. **2** *Botany.* the structure composed of tissue providing mechanical support for a stem or leaf.

girdle[1] ('gɜːdᵊl) *n* **1** a woman's elastic corset covering the waist to the thigh. **2** anything that surrounds or encircles. **3** a belt or sash. **4** *Jewellery.* the outer edge of a gem. **5** *Anatomy.* any encircling structure or part. See **pectoral girdle, pelvic girdle.** **6** the mark left on a tree trunk after the removal of a ring of bark. ◆ *vb* (*tr*) **7** to put a girdle on or around. **8** to surround or encircle. **9** to remove a ring of bark from (a tree or branch), thus causing it to die. [Old English *gyrdel,* of Germanic origin; related to Old Norse *gyrthill,* Old Frisian *gerdel,* Old High German *gurtila;* see GIRD[1]] ▸ **'girdle-,like** *adj*

girdle[2] ('gɜːdᵊl) *n Scot. and northern English dialect.* another word for **griddle.**

girdler ('gɜːdlə) *n* **1** a person or thing that girdles. **2** a maker of girdles. **3** any insect, such as the twig girdler, that bores circular grooves around the stems or twigs in which it lays its eggs.

girdlescone ('gɜːdᵊl,skəʊn, -,skɒn), **girdle scone,** *or* **girdlecake** ('gɜːdᵊl,keɪk) *n* less common names for **drop scone.**

girdle traverse *n Mountaineering.* a climb that consists of a complete traverse of a face or crag.

Girgenti (*Italian* dʒir'dʒɛnti) *n* a former name (until 1927) of **Agrigento.**

girl (gɜːl) *n* **1** a female child from birth to young womanhood. **2** a young unmarried woman; lass; maid. **3** *Informal.* a sweetheart or girlfriend. **4** *Informal.* a woman of any age. **5** an informal word for **daughter.** **6** a female employee, esp. a female servant. **7** *S. African derogatory.* a Black female servant of any age. **8** (*usually pl* and preceded by *the*) *Informal.* a group of women, esp. acquaintances. [C13: of uncertain origin; perhaps related to Low German *Göre* boy, girl]

girl Friday *n* a female employee who has a wide range of duties, usually including secretarial and clerical work. [C20: coined on the pattern of MAN FRIDAY]

girlfriend ('gɜːl,frɛnd) *n* **1** a female friend with whom a man or boy is romantically or sexually involved; sweetheart. **2** any female friend.

Girl Guide *n* See **Guide.**

girlhood ('gɜːl,hʊd) *n* the state or time of being a girl.

girlie ('gɜːlɪ) *n* **1** a little girl. ◆ *adj* **2** (*modifier*) displaying or featuring nude or scantily dressed women: *a girlie magazine.* **3** suited to or designed to appeal to young women: *a girlie night out.*

girlish ('gɜːlɪʃ) *adj* of or like a girl in looks, behaviour, innocence, etc. ▸ **'girlishly** *adv* ▸ **'girlishness** *n*

Girls' Brigade *n* (in Britain) an organization for girls, founded in 1893, with the aim of promoting self-discipline and self-respect.

Girl Scout *n U.S.* a member of the equivalent organization for girls to the Scouts. Brit. equivalent: **Guide.**

girn (gərn, gɜːn) *vb* (*intr*) *Scot. and northern English dialect.* **1** to snarl. **2** to grimace; pull grotesque faces. **3** to complain fretfully or peevishly. [C14: a variant of GRIN]

giro ('dʒaɪrəʊ) *n, pl* **-ros.** **1** a system of transferring money within the financial institutions of a country, such as banks and post offices, by which bills, etc. may be paid by filling in a giro form authorizing the debit of a specified sum from one's own account to the credit of the payee's account. **2** *Brit. informal.* an unemployment or income support payment by giro cheque, posted fortnightly. [C20: ultimately from Greek *guros* circuit]

giron *or* **gyron** ('dʒaɪrɒn) *n Heraldry.* a charge consisting of the lower half of a diagonally divided quarter, usually in the top left corner of the shield. [C16: from Old French *giron* a triangular piece of material, of Germanic origin; related to Old High German *gēro* triangular object; compare GORE[3]]

Gironde (*French* ʒirɔ̃d) *n* **1** a department of SW France, in Aquitaine region. Capital: Bordeaux. Pop.: 1 263 500 (1995). Area: 10 726 sq. km (4183 sq. miles). **2** an estuary in SW France, formed by the confluence of the Rivers Garonne and Dordogne. Length: 72 km (45 miles).

Girondist (dʒɪ'rɒndɪst) *n* **1** a member of a party of moderate republicans during the French Revolution, many of whom came from Gironde: overthrown (1793) by their rivals the Jacobins. See also **Jacobin** (sense 1). ◆ *adj* **2** of or relating to the Girondists or their principles. ▸ **Gi'rondism** *n*

gironny *or* **gyronny** (dʒaɪ'rɒnɪ) *adj* (*usually postpositive*) *Heraldry.* divided into segments from the fesse point.

girosol ('dʒɪrə,sɒl, -,səʊl) *n* a variant spelling of **girasol.**

girr (gɪr) *n Scot.* a variant of **gird**[3].

girt[1] (gɜːt) *vb* **1** a past tense and past participle of **gird**[1]. ◆ *adj* **2** *Nautical.* moored securely to prevent swinging.

girt[2] (gɜːt) *vb* **1** (*tr*) to bind or encircle; gird. **2** to measure the girth of (something).

girth (gɜːθ) *n* **1** the distance around something; circumference. **2** size or bulk: *a man of great girth.* **3** a band around a horse's belly to keep the saddle in position. ◆ *vb* **4** (usually foll. by *up*) to fasten a girth on (a horse). **5** (*tr*) to encircle or surround. [C14: from Old Norse *gjörth* belt; related to Gothic *gairda* GIRDLE[1]; see GIRD[1]]

gisarme (gɪ'zɑːm) *n* a long-shafted battle-axe with a sharp point on the back of the axe head. [C13: from Old French *guisarme,* probably from Old High German *getīsarn* weeding tool, from *getan* to weed + *īsarn* IRON]

Gisborne ('gɪzbən) *n* a port in N New Zealand, on E North Island on Poverty Bay. Pop.: 31 700 (1994).

Giscard d'Estaing (*French* ʒiskardɛstɛ̃) *n* **Valéry** (valeri). born 1926, French politician; minister of finance and economic affairs (1962–66; 1969–74); president (1974–81).

Gish (gɪʃ) *n* **1 Dorothy.** 1898–1968, U.S. film actress, chiefly in silent films. **2** her sister, **Lillian.** 1896–1993, U.S. film and stage actress, noted esp. for her roles in such silent films as *The Birth of a Nation* (1915) and *Intolerance* (1916).

Gissing ('gɪsɪŋ) *n* **George (Robert).** 1857–1903, English novelist, noted for his depiction of middle-class poverty. His works include *Demos* (1886) and *New Grub Street* (1891).

gist (dʒɪst) *n* **1** the point or substance of an argument, speech, etc. **2** *Law.* the essential point of an action. [C18: from Anglo-French, as in *cest action gist en* this action consists in, literally: lies in, from Old French *gésir* to lie, from Latin *jacēre,* from *jacere* to throw]

git (gɪt) *n Brit. slang.* **1** a contemptible person, often a fool. **2** a bastard. [C20: from GET (in the sense: *to beget,* hence a bastard, fool)]

gîte (ʒiːt) *n* a self-catering holiday cottage for let in France. [C20: French]

gittarone (,gɪtə'rəʊnɪ) *n Music.* an acoustic bass guitar.

gittern ('gɪtɜːn) *n Music.* an obsolete medieval stringed instrument resembling the guitar. Compare **cittern.** [C14: from Old French *guiterne,* ultimately from Old Spanish *guitarra* GUITAR; see CITTERN]

Giulini (*Italian* dʒu'liːni) *n* **Carlo Maria** ('karlo ma'riːa). born 1914, Italian orchestral conductor, esp. of opera.

Giulio Romano (*Italian* 'dʒuːljo ro'maːno) *n* ?1499–1546, Italian architect and painter; a founder of mannerism.

giusto ('dʒuːstəʊ) *adv Music.* (of a tempo marking) **a** to be observed strictly. **b** to be observed appropriately: *allegro giusto.* [Italian: just, proper]

give (gɪv) *vb* **gives, giving, gave** (geɪv), **given** ('gɪvᵊn). (*mainly tr*) **1** (*also intr*) to present or deliver voluntarily (something that is one's own) to the permanent possession of another or others. **2** (often foll. by *for*) to transfer (something that is one's own, esp. money) to the possession of another as part of an exchange: *to give fifty pounds for a painting.* **3** to place in the temporary possession of another: *I gave him my watch while I went swimming.* **4** (when *intr,* foll. by *of*) to grant, provide, or bestow: *give me some advice.* **5** to administer: *to give a reprimand.* **6** to award or attribute: *to give blame, praise,* etc. **7** to be a source of: *he gives no trouble.* **8** to impart or communicate: *to give news; give a person a cold.* **9** to utter or emit: *to give a shout.* **10** to perform, make, or do: *the car gave a jolt and stopped.* **11** to sacrifice or devote: *he gave his life for his country.* **12** to surrender: *to give place to others.* **13** to concede or yield: *I will give you this game.* **14** (*intr*) *Informal.* to happen: *what gives?* **15** (often foll. by *to*) to cause; lead: *she gave me to believe that she would come.* **16** (foll. by *for*) to value (something) at: *I don't give anything for his promises.* **17** to perform or present as an entertainment: *to give a play.* **18** to propose as a toast: *I give you the Queen.* **19** (*intr*) to yield or break under force or pressure: *this surface will give if you sit on it; his courage will never give.* **20 give as good as one gets.** to respond to verbal or bodily blows to at least an equal extent as those received. **21 give battle.** to commence fighting. **22 give birth.** (often foll. by *to*) **22a** to bear (offspring). **22b** to produce, originate, or create (an idea, plan, etc.). **23 give (a person) five** *or* **some skin.** *Slang.* to greet or congratulate (someone) by slapping raised hands. **24 give ground.** to draw back or retreat. **25 give (someone) one.** *Brit. taboo slang.* to have sex with someone. **26 give rise to.** to be the cause of. **27 give me.** *Informal.* I prefer: *give me hot weather any day!* **28 give or take.** plus or minus: *three thousand people came, give or take a few hundred.* **29 give way.** See **way** (sense 24). **30 give (a person) what for.** *Informal.* to punish or reprimand (a person) severely. ◆ *n* **31** a tendency to yield under pressure; resilience: *there's bound to be some give in a long plank; there is no give in his moral views.* ◆ See also **give away, give in, give off, give onto, give out, give over, give up.** [Old English *giefan;* related to Old Norse *gefa,* Gothic *giban,* Old High German *geban,* Swedish *giva*] ▸ **'givable** *or* **'giveable** *adj* ▸ **'giver** *n*

give-and-take *n* **1** mutual concessions, shared benefits, and cooperation. **2** a smoothly flowing exchange of ideas and talk. ◆ *vb* **give and take.** (*intr*) **3** to make mutual concessions.

give away *vb* (*tr, adv*) **1** to donate or bestow as a gift, prize, etc. **2** to sell very cheaply. **3** to reveal or betray (esp. in the phrases **give the game** *or* **show away**). **4** to fail to use (an opportunity) through folly or neglect. **5** to present (a bride) formally to her husband in a marriage ceremony. **6** *Austral. and N.Z. informal.* to give up or abandon (something). ◆ *n* **giveaway. 7** a betrayal or disclosure of information, esp. when unintentional. **8** *Chiefly U.S. and Canadian.* something given, esp. with articles on sale, at little or no charge to increase sales, attract publicity, etc. **9** *Journalism.* another name for **freesheet. 10** *Chiefly U.S. and Canadian.* a radio or television programme characterized by the award of money and prizes. **11** (*modifier*) **11a** very cheap (esp. in the phrase **giveaway prices**). **11b** free of charge: *a giveaway property magazine.*

give in *vb* (*adv*) **1** (*intr*) to yield; admit defeat. **2** (*tr*) to submit or deliver (a document).

given ('gɪvᵊn) *vb* **1** the past participle of **give.** ◆ *adj* **2** (*postpositive;* foll. by *to*) tending (to); inclined or addicted (to). **3** specific or previously stated. **4** assumed as a premise. **5** *Maths.* known or determined independently: *a given volume.* **6** (on official documents) issued or executed, as on a stated date. ◆ *n* **7** an assumed fact. **8** *Philosophy.* the supposed raw data of experience. See also **sense datum.**

given name *n* another term for **first name.**

give off *vb* (*tr, adv*) to emit or discharge: *the mothballs gave off an acrid odour.*

give onto *vb* (*intr; prep*) to afford a view or prospect of: *their new house gives onto the sea.*

give out *vb* (*adv*) **1** (*tr*) to emit or discharge. **2** (*tr*) to publish or make known: *the chairman gave out that he would resign.* **3** (*tr*) to hand out or distribute: *they gave out free chewing gum on the street.* **4** (*intr*) to become exhausted; fail: *the supply of candles gave out.* **5** (*intr;* foll. by *to*) *Irish informal.* to reprimand (someone) at length. **6** (*tr*) *Cricket.* (of an umpire) to declare (a batsman) dismissed.

give over *vb* (*adv*) **1** (*tr*) to transfer, esp. to the care or custody of another. **2** (*tr*) to assign or resign to a specific purpose or function: *the day was given over to pleasure.* **3** *Informal.* to cease (an activity): *give over fighting, will you!*

give up *vb* (*adv*) **1** to abandon hope (for). **2** (*tr*) to renounce (an activity, belief, etc.): *I have given up smoking.* **3** (*tr*) to relinquish or resign from: *he gave up the presidency.* **4** (*tr; usually reflexive*) to surrender: *the escaped convict gave himself up.* **5** (*tr*) to reveal or disclose (information). **6** (*intr*) to admit one's defeat or inability to do something. **7** (*tr; often passive or reflexive*) to devote completely (to): *she gave herself up to caring for the sick.*

Gîza ('giːzə) *n* See **El Gîza.**

gizmo *or* **gismo** ('gɪzməʊ) *n, pl* **-mos.** *Slang.* a device; gadget. [C20: of unknown origin]

gizzard ('gɪzəd) *n* **1** the thick-walled part of a bird's stomach, in which hard food is broken up by muscular action and contact with grit and small stones. **2** a similar structure in many invertebrates. **3** *Informal.* the stomach and entrails generally. [C14: from Old North French *guisier* fowl's liver, alteration of Latin *gigēria* entrails of poultry when cooked, of uncertain origin]

Gk *abbrev. for* Greek.

gl. *abbrev. for:* **1** glass. **2** gloss.

glabella (glə'bɛlə) *n, pl* **-lae** (-liː). *Anatomy.* a smooth elevation of the frontal bone just above the bridge of the nose: a reference point in physical anthropology or craniometry. [C19: New Latin, from Latin *glabellus* smooth, from *glaber* bald, smooth] ▸ **gla'bellar** *adj*

glabrescent (gleɪ'brɛsənt) *adj Botany.* **1** becoming hairless at maturity: *glabrescent stems.* **2** nearly hairless. [C19: from Latin *glabrescere* to become smooth]

glabrous ('gleɪbrəs) *or* **glabrate** ('gleɪbreɪt, -brɪt) *adj Biology.* without hair or a similar growth; smooth: *a glabrous stem.* [C17 *glabrous,* from Latin *glaber*] ▸ **'glabrousness** *n*

glacé ('glæseɪ) *adj* **1** crystallized or candied: *glacé cherries.* **2** covered in icing. **3** (of leather, silk, etc.) having a glossy finish. **4** *Chiefly U.S.* frozen or iced. ◆ *vb* **-cés, -céing, -céed. 5** (*tr*) to ice or candy (cakes, fruits, etc.). [C19: from French *glacé,* literally: iced, from *glacer* to freeze, from *glace* ice, from Latin *glaciēs*]

glacial ('gleɪsɪəl, -ʃəl) *adj* **1** characterized by the presence of masses of ice. **2** relating to, caused by, or deposited by a glacier. **3** extremely cold; icy. **4** cold or hostile in manner: *a glacial look.* **5** (of a chemical compound) of or tending to form crystals that resemble ice: *glacial acetic acid.* **6** very slow in progress: *a glacial pace.* ▸ **'glacially** *adv*

glacial acetic acid *n* pure acetic acid (more than 99.8 per cent).

glacialist ('gleɪsɪəlɪst, -ʃəl-) *n* a person who studies ice and its effects on the earth's surface.

glacial period *n* **1** any period of time during which a large part of the earth's surface was covered with ice, due to the advance of glaciers, as in the late Carboniferous period, and during most of the Pleistocene; glaciation. **2** (*often caps.*) the Pleistocene epoch. ◆ Also called: **glacial epoch, ice age.**

glaciate ('gleɪsɪˌeɪt) *vb* **1** to cover or become covered with glaciers or masses of ice. **2** (*tr*) to subject to the effects of glaciers, such as denudation and erosion. ▸ **ˌglaci'ation** *n*

glacier ('glæsɪə, 'gleɪs-) *n* a slowly moving mass of ice originating from an accumulation of snow. It can either spread out from a central mass (**continental glacier**) or descend from a high valley (**alpine glacier**). [C18: from French (Savoy dialect), from Old French *glace* ice, from Late Latin *glacia,* from Latin *glaciēs* ice]

glacier cream *n Mountaineering.* a barrier cream, esp. against ultraviolet radiation, used when climbing above the snow line.

glacier milk *n* water flowing in a stream from the snout of a glacier and containing particles of rock.

glacier table *n* a rock sitting on a pillar of ice on top of a glacier, as a result of the ice immediately beneath the rock being protected from the heat of the sun and not melting.

glaciology (ˌglæsɪ'ɒlədʒɪ, ˌgleɪ-) *n* the study of the distribution, character, and effects of glaciers. ▸ **glaciological** (ˌglæsɪə'lɒdʒɪkᵊl, ˌgleɪ-) *or* **ˌglacio'logic** *adj* ▸ **ˌglaci'ologist** *or* **'glacialist** *n*

glacis ('glæsɪs, 'glæsɪ, 'gleɪ-) *n, pl* **-ises** *or* **-is** (-iːz, -ɪz). **1** a slight incline; slope. **2** an open slope in front of a fortified place. **3** short for **glacis plate.** [C17: from French, from Old French *glacier* to freeze, slip, from Latin *glaciāre,* from *glaciēs* ice]

glacis plate *n* **1** the frontal plate armour on a tank. **2** a section of armour plate shielding an opening on a naval vessel.

glad[1] (glæd) *adj* **gladder, gladdest. 1** happy and pleased; contented. **2** causing happiness or contentment. **3** (*postpositive;* foll. by *to*) very willing: *he was glad to help.* **4** (*postpositive;* foll. by *of*) happy or pleased to have: *glad of her help.* ◆ *vb* **glads, gladding, gladded. 5** an archaic word for **gladden.** [Old English *glæd;* related to Old Norse *glathr,* Old High German *glat* smooth, shining, Latin *glaber* smooth, Lithuanian *glodùs* fitting closely] ▸ **'gladly** *adv* ▸ **'gladness** *n*

glad[2] (glæd) *n Informal.* short for **gladiolus.** Also called (Austral.): **gladdie** ('glædɪ).

Gladbeck (*German* 'glatbɛk) *n* a city in NW Germany, in North Rhine-Westphalia. Pop.: 79 190 (1989 est.).

gladden ('glædᵊn) *vb* to make or become glad and joyful. ▸ **'gladdener** *n*

gladdon ('glædᵊn) *n* another name for the **stinking iris.** [Old English, of uncertain origin]

glade (gleɪd) *n* an open place in a forest; clearing. [C16: of uncertain origin; perhaps related to GLAD[1] (in obsolete sense: bright); see GLEAM] ▸ **'gladeˌlike** *adj*

glad eye *n Informal.* an inviting or seductive glance (esp. in the phrase **give** (**someone**) **the glad eye**).

glad hand *n* **1a** a welcoming hand. **1b** a welcome. ◆ *vb* **glad-hand. 2** (*tr*) to welcome by or as if by offering a hand.

gladiate ('glædɪɪt, -ˌeɪt, 'gleɪ-) *adj Botany.* shaped like a sword: *gladiate leaves.* [C18: from Latin *gladius* sword]

gladiator ('glædɪˌeɪtə) *n* **1** (in ancient Rome and Etruria) a man trained to fight in arenas to provide entertainment. **2** a person who supports and fights publicly for a cause. [C16: from Latin: swordsman, from *gladius* sword]

gladiatorial (ˌglædɪə'tɔːrɪəl) *adj* of, characteristic of, or relating to gladiators, combat, etc.

gladiolus (ˌglædɪ'əʊləs) *n, pl* **-lus, -li** (-laɪ), *or* **-luses. 1** Also called: **sword lily, gladiola.** any iridaceous plant of the widely cultivated genus *Gladiolus,* having sword-shaped leaves and spikes of funnel-shaped brightly coloured flowers. **2** *Anatomy.* the large central part of the breastbone. [C16: from Latin: a small sword, sword lily, from *gladius* a sword]

glad rags *pl n Informal.* best clothes or clothes used on special occasions.

gladsome ('glædsəm) *adj* an archaic word for **glad**[1]. ▸ **'gladsomely** *adv* ▸ **'gladsomeness** *n*

Gladstone[1] ('glædstən) *n* a light four-wheeled horse-drawn vehicle. [C19: named after W. E. GLADSTONE]

Gladstone[2] ('glædstən) *n* **William Ewart.** 1809–98, British statesman. He became leader of the Liberal Party in 1867 and was four times prime minister (1868–74; 1880–85; 1886; 1892–94). In his first ministry he disestablished the Irish Church (1869) and introduced educational reform (1870) and the secret ballot (1872). He succeeded in carrying the Reform Act of 1884 but failed to gain support for a Home Rule Bill for Ireland, to which he devoted much of the latter part of his career.

Gladstone bag *n* a piece of hand luggage consisting of two equal-sized hinged compartments. [C19: named after W. E. GLADSTONE]

Glagolitic (ˌglægə'lɪtɪk) *adj* of, relating to, or denoting a Slavic alphabet whose invention is attributed to Saint Cyril, preserved only in certain Roman Catholic liturgical books found in Dalmatia. [C19: from New Latin *glagoliticus,* from Serbo-Croat *glagolica* the Glagolitic alphabet; related to Old Church Slavonic *glagolŭ* word]

glaikit *or* **glaiket** ('gleɪkɪt) *adj Scot.* foolish; silly; thoughtless. [C15: of obscure origin] ▸ **'glaikitness** *or* **'glaiketness** *n*

glair (glɛə) *n* **1** white of egg, esp. when used as a size, glaze, or adhesive, usually in bookbinding. **2** any substance resembling this. ◆ *vb* **3** (*tr*) to apply glair to (something). [C14: from Old French *glaire,* from Vulgar Latin *clāria* (unattested) CLEAR, from Latin *clārus*] ▸ **'glairy** *or* **'glaireous** *adj* ▸ **'glairiness** *n*

glaive (gleɪv) *n* an archaic word for **sword.** [C13: from Old French: javelin, from Latin *gladius* sword] ▸ **glaived** *adj*

glam (glæm) *adj Slang.* short for **glamorous.**

Glamis Castle (glɑːmz) *n* a castle near Glamis in Angus, Scotland: ancestral seat of the Lyons family, forebears of Elizabeth, the Queen Mother; famous for its legend of a secret chamber.

Glamorgan (glə'mɔːgən) *or* **Glamorganshire** (glə'mɔːgənˌʃɪə, -ʃə) *n* a former county of SE Wales: divided into West Glamorgan, Mid Glamorgan, and South Glamorgan in 1974; since 1996 administered by the county of Swansea and the county boroughs of Neath Port Talbot, Bridgend, Rhondda Cynon Taff, Vale of Glamorgan, Merthyr Tydfil, and part of Caerphilly.

glamorize, glamorise, *or U.S.* (*sometimes*) **glamourize** ('glæməˌraɪz) *vb* (*tr*) to cause to be or seem glamorous; romanticize or beautify. ▸ **ˌglamori'zation** *or* **ˌglamori'sation** *n* ▸ **'glamorˌizer** *or* **'glamorˌiser** *n*

glamorous *or* **glamourous** ('glæmərəs) *adj* **1** possessing glamour; alluring and fascinating: *a glamorous career.* **2** beautiful and smart, esp. in a showy way: *a glamorous woman.* ▸ **'glamorously** *or* **'glamourously** *adv* ▸ **'glamorousness** *or* **'glamourousness** *n*

glamour *or U.S. (sometimes)* **glamor** ('glæmə) *n* **1** charm and allure; fascination. **2a** fascinating or voluptuous beauty, often dependent on artifice. **2b** *(as modifier): a glamour girl.* **3** *Archaic.* a magic spell; charm. [C18: Scottish variant of GRAMMAR (hence a magic spell, because occult practices were popularly associated with learning)]

glam rock *n* a style of rock music of the early 1970s, characterized by the glittery flamboyance and androgynous image of its performers.

glance[1] (glɑːns) *vb* **1** *(intr)* to look hastily or briefly. **2** *(intr; foll. by over, through, etc.)* to look over briefly: *to glance through a report.* **3** *(intr)* to reflect, glint, or gleam: *the sun glanced on the water.* **4** *(intr; usually foll. by off)* to depart (from an object struck) at an oblique angle: *the arrow glanced off the tree.* **5** *(tr)* to strike at an oblique angle: *the arrow glanced the tree.* ◆ *n* **6** a hasty or brief look; peep. **7 at a glance.** from one's first look; immediately. **8** a flash or glint of light; gleam. **9** the act or an instance of an object glancing or glancing off another. **10** a brief allusion or reference. **11** *Cricket.* a stroke in which the ball is deflected off the bat to the leg side; glide. [C15: modification of *glacen* to strike obliquely, from Old French *glacier* to slide (see GLACIS); compare Middle English *glenten* to make a rapid sideways movement, GLINT] ▸ **'glancingly** *adv*

USAGE *Glance* is sometimes wrongly used where *glimpse* is meant: *he caught a glimpse* (not *glance*) *of her making her way through the crowd.*

glance[2] (glɑːns) *n* any mineral having a metallic lustre, esp. a simple sulphide: *copper glance.* [C19: from German *Glanz* brightness, lustre]

gland[1] (glænd) *n* **1** a cell or organ in man and other animals that synthesizes chemical substances and secretes them for the body to use or eliminate, either through a duct (see **exocrine gland**) or directly into the bloodstream (see **endocrine gland**). **2** a structure, such as a lymph node, that resembles a gland in form. **3** a cell or organ in plants that synthesizes and secretes a particular substance. Related adj: **adenoid.** [C17: from Latin *glāns* acorn] ▸ **'gland,like** *adj*

gland[2] (glænd) *n* a device that prevents leakage of fluid along a rotating shaft or reciprocating rod passing through a boundary between areas of high and low pressure. It often consists of a flanged metal sleeve bedding into a stuffing box. [C19: of unknown origin]

glanders ('glændəz) *n (functioning as sing)* a highly infectious bacterial disease of horses, sometimes communicated to man, caused by *Actinobacillus mallei* and characterized by inflammation and ulceration of the mucous membranes of the air passages, skin and lymph glands. [C16: from Old French *glandres* enlarged glands, from Latin *glandulae,* literally: little acorns, from *glāns* acorn; see GLAND[1]] ▸ **'glandered** *adj* ▸ **'glanderous** *adj*

glandular ('glændjʊlə) *or* **glandulous** ('glændjʊləs) *adj* of, relating to, containing, functioning as, or affecting a gland: *glandular tissue.* [C18: from Latin *glandula,* literally: a little acorn; see GLANDERS] ▸ **'glandularly** *or* **'glandulously** *adv*

glandular fever *n* another name for **infectious mononucleosis.**

glandule ('glændjuːl) *n* a small gland.

glans (glænz) *n, pl* **glandes** ('glændiːz). *Anatomy.* any small rounded body or glandlike mass, such as the head of the penis (**glans penis**). [C17: from Latin: acorn; see GLAND[1]]

glare[1] (glɛə) *vb* **1** *(intr)* to stare angrily; glower. **2** *(tr)* to express by glowering. **3** *(intr)* (of light, colour, etc.) to be very bright and intense. **4** *(intr)* to be dazzlingly ornamented or garish. ◆ *n* **5** an angry stare. **6** a dazzling light or brilliance. **7** garish ornamentation or appearance; gaudiness. [C13: probably from Middle Low German, Middle Dutch *glaren* to gleam; probably related to Old English *glæren* glassy; see GLASS] ▸ **'glareless** *adj* ▸ **'glary** *adj*

glare[2] (glɛə) *adj Chiefly U.S. and Canadian.* smooth and glassy: *glare ice.* [C16: special use of GLARE[1]]

glaring ('glɛərɪŋ) *adj* **1** conspicuous: *a glaring omission.* **2** dazzling or garish. ▸ **'glaringly** *adv* ▸ **'glaringness** *n*

Glarus *(German* 'glaːrʊs) *n* **1** an Alpine canton of E central Switzerland. Capital: Glarus. Pop.: 39 410 (1996 est.). Area 684 sq. km (264 sq. miles). **2** a town in E central Switzerland, the capital of Glarus canton. Pop.: 5541 (1990). ◆ French name: **Glaris** (glari).

Glaser ('gleɪzə) *n* **Donald Arthur.** born 1926, U.S. physicist: invented the bubble chamber; Nobel prize for physics 1960.

Glasgow ('glɑːzgəʊ, 'glæz-) *n* **1** a city in W central Scotland, in City of Glasgow council area on the River Clyde: the largest city in Scotland; centre of a major industrial region, formerly an important port; universities (1451, 1964). Pop.: 662 954 (1991). Related adj: **Glaswegian. 2 City of.** a council area in W central Scotland. Pop.: 623 850 (1996 est.). Area: 175 sq. km (68 sq. miles).

glasnost ('glæs,nɒst) *n* the policy of public frankness and accountability developed in the former Soviet Union under the leadership of Mikhail Gorbachov. [C20: Russian, literally: openness]

glass (glɑːs) *n* **1a** a hard brittle transparent or translucent noncrystalline solid, consisting of metal silicates or similar compounds. It is made from a fused mixture of oxides, such as lime, silicon dioxide, etc., and is used for making windows, mirrors, bottles, etc. **1b** *(as modifier): a glass bottle.* Related adjs.: **vitreous, vitric. 2** any compound that has solidified from a molten state into a noncrystalline form. **3** something made of glass, esp. a drinking vessel, a barometer, or a mirror. **4** Also called: **glassful.** the amount contained in a drinking glass. **5** glassware collectively. **6** See **volcanic glass. 7** See **fibreglass.** ◆ *vb (tr)* **8** to cover with, enclose in, or fit with glass. **9** *Informal.* to hit (someone) in the face with a glass or a bottle. [Old English *glæs;* related to Old Norse *gler,* Old High German *glas,* Middle High German *glast* brightness; see GLARE[1]] ▸ **'glassless** *adj* ▸ **'glass,like** *adj*

Glass (glɑːs) *n* **Philip.** born 1937, U.S. avant-garde composer noted for his minimalist style: his works include *Music in Fifths* (1970), *Akhnaten* (1984), *The Voyage* (1992), and *Monsters of Grace* (1998).

glass-blowing *n* the process of shaping a mass of molten or softened glass into a vessel, shape, etc., by blowing air into it through a tube. ▸ **'glass-,blower** *n*

glass ceiling *n* a situation in which progress, esp. promotion, appears to be possible but restrictions or discrimination create a barrier that prevents it.

glasses ('glɑːsɪz) *pl n* a pair of lenses for correcting faulty vision, in a frame that rests on the bridge of the nose and hooks behind the ears. Also called: **spectacles, eyeglasses.**

glass eye *n* an artificial eye made of glass.

glass fibre *n* another name for **fibreglass.**

glass harmonica *n* a musical instrument of the 18th century consisting of a set of glass bowls of graduated pitches, played by rubbing the fingers over the moistened rims or by a keyboard mechanism. Sometimes shortened to **harmonica.** Also called: **musical glasses.**

glasshouse ('glɑːs,haʊs) *n* **1** *Brit.* a glass building, esp. a greenhouse, used for growing plants in protected or controlled conditions. **2** *Informal, chiefly Brit.* a military detention centre. **3** *U.S.* another word for **glassworks.**

glassine (glæ'siːn) *n* a glazed translucent paper used for book jackets.

glass jaw *n Boxing, informal.* a jaw that is excessively fragile or susceptible to punches.

glass-maker *n* a person who makes glass or glass objects. ▸ **'glass-,making** *n*

glassman ('glɑːsmən) *n, pl* **-men. 1** a man whose work is making or selling glassware. **2** a less common word for **glazier.**

glasspaper ('glɑːs,peɪpə) *n* **1** strong paper coated with powdered glass or other abrasive material for smoothing and polishing. ◆ *vb* **2** to smooth or polish with glasspaper.

glass snake *n* any snakelike lizard of the genus *Ophisaurus,* of Europe, Asia, and North America, with vestigial hind limbs and a tail that breaks off easily: family *Anguidae.*

glass string *n* (in Malaysia) the string of a kite used in kite fighting that has an abrasive coating of glue and crushed glass.

glassware ('glɑːs,wɛə) *n* articles made of glass.

glass wool *n* fine spun glass massed into a wool-like bulk, used in insulation, filtering, etc.

glasswork ('glɑːs,wɜːk) *n* **1** the production of glassware. **2** the fitting of glass. **3** articles of glass. ▸ **'glass-,worker** *n*

glassworks ('glɑːs,wɜːks) *n (functioning as sing)* a factory for the moulding of glass.

glasswort ('glɑːs,wɜːt) *n* **1** Also called: **marsh samphire.** any plant of the chenopodiaceous genus *Salicornia,* of salt marshes, having fleshy stems and scalelike leaves: formerly used as a source of soda for glass-making. **2** another name for **saltwort** (sense 1).

glassy ('glɑːsɪ) *adj* **glassier, glassiest. 1** resembling glass, esp. in smoothness, slipperiness, or transparency. **2** void of expression, life, or warmth: *a glassy stare.* ▸ **'glassily** *adv* ▸ **'glassiness** *n*

Glastonbury ('glæstənbərɪ, -brɪ) *n* a town in SW England, in Somerset: remains of prehistoric lake villages; the reputed burial place of King Arthur; site of a ruined Benedictine abbey, probably the oldest in England. Pop.: 7747 (1991).

Glaswegian (glæz'wiːdʒən) *adj* **1** of or relating to Glasgow or its inhabitants. ◆ *n* **2** a native or inhabitant of Glasgow. [C19: influenced by *Norway, Norwegian*]

Glauber's salt ('glaʊbəz) *or* **Glauber salt** ('glaʊbə) *n* the crystalline decahydrate of sodium sulphate. [C18: named after J. R. *Glauber* (1604–68), German chemist]

Glauce ('glɔːsɪ) *n Greek myth.* **1** the second bride of Jason, murdered on her wedding day by Medea, whom Jason had deserted. **2** a sea nymph, one of the Nereids.

glaucoma (glɔː'kəʊmə) *n* a disease of the eye in which pressure within the eyeball damages the optic disc, impairing vision, sometimes progressing to blindness. [C17: from Latin, from Greek *glaukōma,* from *glaukos;* see GLAUCOUS] ▸ **glau'comatous** *adj*

glauconite ('glɔːkə,naɪt) *n* a green mineral consisting of the hydrated silicate of iron, potassium, aluminium, and magnesium: found in greensand and other similar rocks. Formula: $K_2(Mg,Fe)_2Al_6(Si_4O_{10})_3(OH)_{12}$. [C19: from Greek *glaukon,* neuter of *glaukos* bluish-green + -ITE[1]; see GLAUCOUS] ▸ **glauconitic** (,glɔːkə'nɪtɪk) *adj*

glaucous ('glɔːkəs) *adj* **1** *Botany.* covered with a waxy or powdery bloom. **2** bluish-green. [C17: from Latin *glaucus* silvery, bluish-green, from Greek *glaukos*] ▸ **'glaucously** *adv*

glaucous gull *n* a gull, *Larus hyperboreus,* of northern and arctic regions, with a white head and tail and pale grey back and wings.

glaur (glɔːr) *n Scot.* mud or mire. [C16: of unknown origin] ▸ **'glaury** *adj*

glaze (gleɪz) *vb* **1** *(tr)* to fit or cover with glass. **2** *(tr) Ceramics.* to cover with a vitreous solution, rendering impervious to liquid and smooth to the touch. **3** *(tr)* to cover (a painting) with a layer of semitransparent colour to modify the tones. **4** *(tr)* to cover (foods) with a shiny coating by applying beaten egg, sugar, etc. **5** *(tr)* to make glossy or shiny. **6** (when *intr,* often foll. by *over*) to become or cause to become glassy: *his eyes were glazing over.* ◆ *n* **7** *Ceramics.* **7a** a vitreous or glossy coating. **7b** the substance used to produce such a coating. **8** a semitransparent coating applied to a painting to modify the tones. **9** a smooth lustrous finish on a fabric produced by applying various chemicals. **10** something used to give a glossy surface to foods: *a syrup glaze.* [C14 *glasen,* from *glas* GLASS] ▸ **glazed** *adj* ▸ **'glazer** *n* ▸ **'glazy** *adj*

glaze ice *or* **glazed frost** *n Brit.* a thin clear layer of ice caused by the freezing of rain or water droplets in the air on impact with a cool surface or by refreezing after a thaw. Also called: **silver frost.** U.S. term: **glaze.**

glazier ('gleɪzɪə) *n* a person who glazes windows, etc. ▸ **'glaziery** *n*

glazing ('gleɪzɪŋ) *n* **1** the surface of a glazed object. **2** glass fitted, or to be fitted, in a door, frame, etc.

glazing-bar *n* a supporting or strengthening bar for a glass window, door, etc. Usual U.S. word: **muntin.**

Glazunov ('glæzʊnɒf; *Russian* gləzu'nɔf) *n* **Aleksandr Konstantinovich** (alɪk'sandr kənstan'tinəvitʃ). 1865–1936, Russian composer, in France from 1928. A pupil of Rimsky-Korsakov, he wrote eight symphonies and concertos for piano and for violin among other works.

GLC *abbrev. for* Greater London Council, abolished 1986.

gld *abbrev. for* guilder.

gleam (gliːm) *n* **1** a small beam or glow of light, esp. reflected light. **2** a brief or dim indication: *a gleam of hope.* ◆ *vb* (*intr*) **3** to send forth or reflect a beam of light. **4** to appear, esp. briefly: *intelligence gleamed in his eyes.* [Old English *glǣm;* related to Old Norse *gljā* to flicker, Old High German *gleimo* glow-worm, *glīmo* brightness, Old Irish *glē* bright] ▸ **'gleaming** *adj* ▸ **'gleamy** *adj*

glean (gliːn) *vb* **1** to gather (something) slowly and carefully in small pieces: *to glean information from the newspapers.* **2** to gather (the useful remnants of a crop) from the field after harvesting. [C14: from Old French *glener,* from Late Latin *glennāre,* probably of Celtic origin] ▸ **'gleanable** *adj* ▸ **'gleaner** *n*

gleanings ('gliːnɪŋz) *pl n* the useful remnants of a crop that can be gathered from the field after harvesting.

glebe (gliːb) *n* **1** *Brit.* land granted to a clergyman as part of his benefice. **2** *Poetic.* land, esp. when regarded as the source of growing things. [C14: from Latin *glaeba*]

glede (gliːd) *or* **gled** (glɛd) *n* a former Brit. name for the **red kite.** See **kite** (sense 4). [Old English *glida;* related to Old Norse *gletha,* Middle Low German *glede*]

glee (gliː) *n* **1** great merriment or delight, often caused by someone else's misfortune. **2** a type of song originating in 18th-century England, sung by three or more unaccompanied voices. Compare **madrigal** (sense 1). [Old English *glēo;* related to Old Norse *glȳ*]

glee club *n Now chiefly U.S. and Canadian.* a club or society organized for the singing of choral music.

gleeful ('gliːfʊl) *adj* full of glee; merry. ▸ **'gleefully** *adv* ▸ **'gleefulness** *n*

gleeman ('gliːmən) *n, pl* **-men.** *Obsolete.* a minstrel.

gleet (gliːt) *n* **1** inflammation of the urethra with a slight discharge of thin pus and mucus: a stage of chronic gonorrhoea. **2** the pus and mucus discharged. [C14: from Old French *glette* slime, from Latin *glittus* sticky] ▸ **'gleety** *adj*

Gleichschaltung ('glaɪk,ʃæltʊŋ) *n* the enforcement of standardization and the elimination of all opposition within the political, economic, and cultural institutions of a state. [C20: German]

Gleiwitz ('glaɪvɪts) *n* the German name for **Gliwice.**

glen (glɛn) *n* a narrow and deep mountain valley, esp. in Scotland or Ireland. [C15: from Scottish Gaelic *gleann,* from Old Irish *glend*] ▸ **'glen,like** *adj*

Glen Albyn ('ælbɪn, 'ɔːl-) *n* another name for the **Great Glen.**

Glencoe (glɛn'kəʊ) *n* a glen in W Scotland, in S Highland: site of a massacre of Macdonalds by Campbells and English troops (1692).

Glendower (glɛn'daʊə) *n* **Owen,** Welsh name *Owain Glyndŵr.* ?1350–?1416, Welsh chieftain, who led a revolt against Henry IV's rule in Wales (1400–15).

glengarry (glɛn'gærɪ) *n, pl* **-ries.** a brimless Scottish woollen cap with a crease down the crown, often with ribbons dangling at the back. Also called: **glengarry bonnet.** [C19: after *Glengarry,* Scotland]

Glen More (mɔː) *n* another name for the **Great Glen.**

Glenn (glɛn) *n* **John.** born 1921, U.S. astronaut and politician. The first American to orbit the earth (Feb., 1962), he later became a senator.

glenoid ('gliːnɔɪd) *adj Anatomy.* **1** resembling or having a shallow cavity. **2** denoting the cavity in the shoulder blade into which the head of the upper arm bone fits. [C18: from Greek *glēnoeidēs,* from *glēnē* socket of a joint]

Glenrothes (glɛn'rɒθɪs) *n* a new town in E central Scotland, the administrative centre of Fife: founded in 1948. Pop.: 38 650 (1991).

gley *or* **glei** (gleɪ) *n* a bluish-grey compact sticky soil occurring in certain humid regions. [C20: from Russian *glei* clay]

glia ('gliːə) *n* the delicate web of connective tissue that surrounds and supports nerve cells. Also called: **neuroglia.** ▸ **'glial** *adj*

gliadin ('glaɪədɪn) *or* **gliadine** ('glaɪə,diːn, -dɪn) *n* a protein of cereals, esp. wheat, with a high proline content: forms a sticky mass with water that binds flour into dough. Compare **glutelin.** [C19: from Italian *gliadina,* from Greek *glia* glue]

glib (glɪb) *adj* **glibber, glibbest.** fluent and easy, often in an insincere or deceptive way. [C16: probably from Middle Low German *glibberich* slippery] ▸ **'glibly** *adv* ▸ **'glibness** *n*

glide (glaɪd) *vb* **1** to move or cause to move easily without jerks or hesitations: *to glide in a boat down the river.* **2** (*intr*) to pass slowly or without perceptible change: *to glide into sleep.* **3** to cause (an aircraft) to come into land without engine power, or (of an aircraft) to land in this way. **4** (*intr*) to fly a glider. **5** (*intr*) *Music.* to execute a portamento from one note to another. **6** (*intr*) *Phonetics.* to produce a glide. ◆ *n* **7** a smooth easy movement. **8a** any of various dances featuring gliding steps. **8b** a step in such a dance. **9** a manoeuvre in which an aircraft makes a gentle descent without engine power. See also **glide path.** **10** the act or process of gliding. **11** *Music.* **11a** a long portion of tubing slipped in and out of a trombone to increase its length for the production of lower harmonic series. See also **valve** (sense 5). **11b** a portamento or slur. **12** *Phonetics.* **12a** a transitional sound as the speech organs pass from the articulatory position of one speech sound to that of the next, as the (w) sound in some pronunciations of the word *doing.* **12b** another word for **semivowel.** **13** *Crystallog.* another name for **slip**[1] (sense 33). **14** *Cricket.* another word for **glance**[1] (sense 11). [Old English *glīdan;* related to Old High German *glītan*] ▸ **'glidingly** *adv*

glide path *n* the approach path of an aircraft when landing, usually defined by a radar beam.

glider ('glaɪdə) *n* **1** an aircraft capable of gliding and soaring in air currents without the use of an engine. See also **sailplane.** **2** a person or thing that glides. **3** another name for **flying phalanger.**

glide time *n* the New Zealand term for **flexitime.**

gliding ('glaɪdɪŋ) *n* the sport of flying in a glider.

glim (glɪm) *n Slang.* **1** a light or lamp. **2** an eye. [C17: probably short for GLIMMER; compare GLIMPSE]

glimmer ('glɪmə) *vb* (*intr*) **1** (of a light, candle, etc.) to glow faintly or flickeringly. **2** to be indicated faintly: *hope glimmered in his face.* ◆ *n* **3** a glow or twinkle of light. **4** a faint indication. [C14: compare Middle High German *glimmern,* Swedish *glimra,* Danish *glimre*] ▸ **'glimmeringly** *adv*

glimpse (glɪmps) *n* **1** a brief or incomplete view: *to catch a glimpse of the sea.* **2** a vague indication: *he had a glimpse of what the lecturer meant.* **3** *Archaic.* a glimmer of light. ◆ *vb* **4** (*tr*) to catch sight of briefly or momentarily. **5** (*intr;* usually foll. by *at*) *Chiefly U.S.* to look (at) briefly or cursorily; glance (at). **6** (*intr*) *Archaic.* to shine faintly; glimmer. [C14: of Germanic origin; compare Middle High German *glimsen* to glimmer] ▸ **'glimpser** *n*

USAGE *Glimpse* is sometimes wrongly used where *glance* is meant: *he gave a quick glance* (not *glimpse*) *at his watch.*

Glinka (*Russian* 'glinkə) *n* **Mikhail Ivanovich** (mixa'il i'vanəvitʃ). 1803–57, Russian composer who pioneered the Russian national school of music. His works include the operas *A Life for the Tsar* (1836) and *Russlan and Ludmilla* (1842).

glint (glɪnt) *vb* **1** to gleam or cause to gleam brightly. ◆ *n* **2** a bright gleam or flash. **3** brightness or gloss. **4** a brief indication. [C15: probably of Scandinavian origin; compare Swedish dialect *glänta, glinta* to gleam]

glioma (glaɪ'əʊmə) *n, pl* **-mata** (-mətə) *or* **-mas.** a tumour of the brain and spinal cord, composed of neuroglia cells and fibres. [C19: from New Latin, from Greek *glia* glue + -OMA] ▸ **gli'omatous** *adj*

glissade (glɪ'sɑːd, -'seɪd) *n* **1** a gliding step in ballet, in which one foot slides forwards, sideways, or backwards. **2** a controlled slide down a snow slope. ◆ *vb* **3** (*intr*) to perform a glissade. [C19: from French, from *glisser* to slip, from Old French *glicier,* of Frankish origin; compare Old High German *glītan* to GLIDE] ▸ **glis'sader** *n*

glissando (glɪ'sændəʊ) *n, pl* **-di** (-diː) *or* **-dos.** **1** a rapidly executed series of notes on the harp or piano, each note of which is discretely audible. **2** a portamento, esp. as executed on the violin, viola, etc. [C19: probably Italianized variant of GLISSADE]

glisten ('glɪsᵊn) *vb* (*intr*) **1** (of a wet or glossy surface) to gleam by reflecting light: *wet leaves glisten in the sunlight.* **2** (of light) to reflect with brightness: *the sunlight glistens on wet leaves.* ◆ *n* **3** *Rare.* a gleam or gloss. [Old English *glisnian;* related to *glisian* to glitter, Middle High German *glistern*] ▸ **'glisteningly** *adv*

glister ('glɪstə) *vb, n* an archaic word for **glitter.** [C14: probably from Middle Dutch *glisteren*] ▸ **'glisteringly** *adv*

glitch (glɪtʃ) *n* **1** a sudden instance of malfunctioning or irregularity in an electronic system. **2** a change in the rotation rate of a pulsar. [C20: of unknown origin]

glitter ('glɪtə) *vb* (*intr*) **1** (of a hard, wet, or polished surface) to reflect light in bright flashes. **2** (of light) to be reflected in bright flashes. **3** (usually foll. by *with*) to be decorated or enhanced by the glamour (of): *the show glitters with famous actors.* ◆ *n* **4** sparkle or brilliance. **5** show and glamour. **6** tiny pieces of shiny decorative material used for ornamentation, as on the skin. **7** *Canadian.* Also called: **silver thaw.** ice formed from freezing rain. [C14: from Old Norse *glitra;* related to Old High German *glīzan* to shine] ▸ **'glitteringly** *adv* ▸ **'glittery** *adj*

glitterati (,glɪtə'rɑːtiː) *pl n Informal.* the leaders of society, esp. the rich and beautiful; fashionable celebrities. [C20: from GLITTER + *-ati* as in LITERATI]

glitz (glɪts) *n Slang.* ostentatious showiness; gaudiness or glitter. [C20: back formation from GLITZY]

glitzy ('glɪtsɪ) *adj* **glitzier, glitziest.** *Slang.* showily attractive; flashy or glittery. [C20: originally U.S., probably via Yiddish from German *glitzern* to glitter]

Gliwice (*Polish* gli'vitsɛ) *n* an industrial city in S Poland. Pop.: 214 000 (1996 est.). German name: **Gleiwitz.**

gloaming ('gləʊmɪŋ) *n Scot. or poetic.* twilight or dusk. [Old English *glōmung,* from *glōm;* related to Old Norse *glāmr* moon]

gloat (gləʊt) *vb* **1** (*intr;* often foll. by *over*) to dwell (on) with malevolent smugness or exultation. ◆ *n* **2** the act of gloating. [C16: probably of Scandinavian origin; compare Old Norse *glotta* to grin, Middle High German *glotzen* to stare] ▸ **'gloater** *n* ▸ **'gloatingly** *adv*

glob (glɒb) *n Informal.* a rounded mass of some thick fluid or pliable substance: *a glob of cream.* [C20: probably from GLOBE, influenced by BLOB]

global ('gləʊbᵊl) *adj* **1** covering, influencing, or relating to the whole world. **2** comprehensive. ▸ **'globally** *adv*

globalization *or* **globalisation** (,gləʊbᵊlaɪ'zeɪʃən) *n* **1** the process enabling financial and investment markets to operate internationally, largely as a result of deregulation and improved communications. **2** the process by which a company, etc., expands to operate internationally.

globalize *or* **globalise** ('gləʊbᵊ,laɪz) *vb* (*tr*) to put into effect or spread worldwide.

global positioning system *n* a system of earth-orbiting satellites, transmitting signals continuously towards the earth, that enables the position of a receiving device on or near the earth's surface to be accurately estimated from the difference in arrival times of the signals. Abbrev.: **GPS.**

global product *n* a commercial product, such as Coca Cola, that is marketed throughout the world under the same brand name.

global rule *n* (in transformational grammar) a rule that makes reference to nonconsecutive stages of a derivation.
global search *n Word processing.* an operation in which a complete computer file or set of files is searched for every occurrence of a particular word or other sequence of characters.
global village *n* the whole world considered as being closely connected by modern telecommunications and as being interdependent economically, socially, and politically. [C20: coined by Marshal MCLUHAN]
global warming *n* an increase in the average temperature worldwide believed to be caused by the greenhouse effect.
globate ('gləʊbeɪt) *or* **globated** *adj* shaped like a globe.
globe (gləʊb) *n* **1** a sphere on which a map of the world or the heavens is drawn or represented. **2 the.** the world; the earth. **3** a planet or some other astronomical body. **4** an object shaped like a sphere, such as a glass lampshade or fishbowl. **5** *Austral., N.Z., and S. African.* an electric light bulb. **6** an orb, usually of gold, symbolic of authority or sovereignty. ◆ *vb* **7** to form or cause to form into a globe. [C16: from Old French, from Latin *globus*] ▸ **'globe,like** *adj*
globe artichoke *n* See **artichoke** (senses 1, 2).
globefish ('gləʊb,fɪʃ) *n, pl* **-fish** *or* **-fishes.** another name for **puffer** (sense 2) or **porcupine fish.**
globeflower ('gləʊb,flaʊə) *n* any ranunculaceous plant of the genus *Trollius,* having pale yellow, white, or orange globe-shaped flowers.
globetrotter ('gləʊb,trɒtə) *n* a habitual worldwide traveller, esp. a tourist or businessman. ▸ **'globe,trotting** *n, adj*
globigerina (gləʊ,bɪdʒə'raɪnə) *n, pl* **-nas** *or* **-nae** (-niː). **1** any marine protozoan of the genus *Globigerina,* having a rounded shell with spiny processes: phylum *Foraminifera* (foraminifers). **2 globigerina ooze.** a deposit on the ocean floor consisting of the shells of these protozoans. [C19: from New Latin, from Latin *globus* GLOBE + *gerere* to carry, bear]
globin ('gləʊbɪn) *n Biochem.* the protein component of the pigments myoglobin and haemoglobin. [C19: from Latin *globus* ball, sphere + -IN]
globoid ('gləʊbɔɪd) *adj* **1** shaped approximately like a globe. ◆ *n* **2** a globoid body, such as any of those occurring in certain plant granules.
globose ('gləʊbəʊs, gləʊ'bəʊs) *or* **globous** ('gləʊbəs) *adj* spherical or approximately spherical. [C15: from Latin *globōsus;* see GLOBE] ▸ **'globosely** *adv* ▸ **globosity** (gləʊ'bɒsɪtɪ) *or* **'globoseness** *n*
globular ('glɒbjʊlə) *or* **globulous** *adj* **1** shaped like a globe or globule. **2** having or consisting of globules. ▸ **globularity** (,glɒbjʊ'lærɪtɪ) *or* **'globularness** *n* ▸ **'globularly** *adv*
globular cluster *n Astronomy.* a densely populated spheroidal star cluster with the highest concentration of stars near its centre, found in the galactic halo.
globule ('glɒbjuːl) *n* **1** a small globe, esp. a drop of liquid. **2** *Astronomy.* a small dark nebula thought to be a site of star formation. [C17: from Latin *globulus,* diminutive of *globus* GLOBE]
globuliferous (,glɒbjʊ'lɪfərəs) *adj* producing, containing, or having globules.
globulin ('glɒbjʊlɪn) *n* any of a group of simple proteins, including gamma globulin, that are generally insoluble in water but soluble in salt solutions and coagulated by heat. [C19: from GLOBULE + -IN]
globus ('gləʊbəs) *n Anatomy.* any spherelike structure.
globus hystericus (hɪ'stɛrɪkəs) *n* the technical name for a **lump in the throat.** See **lump** (sense 8).
glochidium (gləʊ'kɪdɪəm) *n, pl* **-chidia** (-'kɪdɪə). **1** any of the barbed hairs among the spore masses of some ferns and on certain other plants. **2** a parasitic larva of certain freshwater mussels that attaches itself to the fins or gills of fish by hooks or suckers. [C19: from New Latin, from Greek *glōkhis* projecting point] ▸ **glo'chidiate** *adj*
glockenspiel ('glɒkən,spiːl, -,ʃpiːl) *n* a percussion instrument consisting of a set of tuned metal plates played with a pair of small hammers. [C19: German, from *Glocken* bells + *Spiel* play]
glogg (glɒg) *n* a hot alcoholic mixed drink, originally from Sweden, consisting of sweetened brandy, red wine, bitters or other flavourings, and blanched almonds. [from Swedish *glögg,* from *glödga* to burn]
glomerate ('glɒmərɪt) *adj* **1** gathered into a compact rounded mass. **2** wound up like a ball of thread. **3** *Anatomy.* (esp. of glands) conglomerate in structure. [C18: from Latin *glomerāre* to wind into a ball, from *glomus* ball]
glomeration (,glɒmə'reɪʃən) *n* a conglomeration or cluster.
glomerule ('glɒmə,ruːl) *n Botany.* **1** a cymose inflorescence in the form of a ball-like cluster of flowers. **2** a ball-like cluster of spores. [C18: from New Latin GLOMERULUS] ▸ **glomerulate** (glɒ'mɛrʊlɪt, -,leɪt) *adj*
glomerulonephritis (glɒ,mɛrʊləʊnɪ'fraɪtɪs) *n* any of various kidney diseases in which the glomeruli are affected.
glomerulus (glɒ'mɛrʊləs) *n, pl* **-li** (-,laɪ). **1** a knot of blood vessels in the kidney projecting into the capsular end of a urine-secreting tubule. **2** any cluster or coil of blood vessels, nerve fibres, etc., in the body. [C18: from New Latin, diminutive of *glomus* ball] ▸ **glo'merular** *adj*
Glomma (*Norwegian* 'glɔma) *n* a river in SE Norway, rising near the border with Sweden and flowing generally south to the Skagerrak: the largest river in Scandinavia; important for hydroelectric power and floating timber. Length: 588 km (365 miles).
gloom (gluːm) *n* **1** partial or total darkness. **2** a state of depression or melancholy. **3** an appearance or expression of despondency or melancholy. **4** *Poetic.* a dim or dark place. ◆ *vb* **5** (*intr*) to look sullen or depressed. **6** to make or become dark or gloomy. [C14 *gloumben* to look sullen; related to Norwegian dialect *glome* to eye suspiciously] ▸ **'gloomful** *adj* ▸ **'gloomfully** *adv* ▸ **'gloomless** *adj*
gloomy ('gluːmɪ) *adj* **gloomier, gloomiest. 1** dark or dismal. **2** causing depression, dejection, or gloom: *gloomy news.* **3** despairing; sad. ▸ **'gloomily** *adv* ▸ **'gloominess** *n*
gloria ('glɔːrɪə) *n* **1** a silk, wool, cotton, or nylon fabric used esp. for umbrellas. **2** a halo or nimbus, esp. as represented in art. [C16: from Latin: GLORY]
Gloria ('glɔːrɪə, -,ɑː) *n* **1** any of several doxologies beginning with the word *Gloria,* esp. the Greater and the Lesser Doxologies. **2** a musical setting of one of these.
Gloria in Excelsis Deo ('glɔːrɪə ɪn ɛk'sɛlsɪs'deɪəʊ, 'glɔːrɪ,ɑː, ɛks'tʃɛlsɪs) *n* **1** the Greater Doxology (see **doxology**), beginning in Latin with these words. **2** a musical setting of this, usually incorporated into the Ordinary of the Mass. Often shortened to **Gloria.** [literally: glory to God in the highest]
Gloria Patri ('glɔːrɪə 'pɑːtrɪ, 'glɔːrɪ,ɑː,'pæt-) *n* **1** the Lesser Doxology (see **doxology**), beginning in Latin with these words. **2** a musical setting of this. [literally: glory to the father]
glorification (,glɔːrɪfɪ'keɪʃən) *n* **1** the act of glorifying or state of being glorified. **2** *Informal.* an enhanced or favourably exaggerated version or account. **3** *Brit. informal.* a celebration.
glorify ('glɔːrɪ,faɪ) *vb* **-fies, -fying, -fied.** (*tr*) **1** to make glorious. **2** to make more splendid; adorn. **3** to worship, exalt, or adore. **4** to extol. **5** to cause to seem more splendid or imposing than reality. ▸ **'glori,fiable** *adj* ▸ **'glori,fier** *n*
gloriole ('glɔːrɪ,əʊl) *n* another name for a **halo** or **nimbus** (senses 2, 3). [C19: from Latin *glōriola,* literally: a small GLORY]
gloriosa (,glɔːrɪ'əʊsə) *n* any plant of the bulbous tropical African genus *Gloriosa,* some species of which are grown as ornamental greenhouse climbers for their showy flowers of yellow, orange, and red: family *Liliaceae.* Also called: **glory lily.** [New Latin, from Latin *gloriosus* glorious]
glorious ('glɔːrɪəs) *adj* **1** having or full of glory; illustrious. **2** conferring glory or renown: *a glorious victory.* **3** brilliantly beautiful. **4** delightful or enjoyable. **5** *Informal.* drunk. ▸ **'gloriously** *adv* ▸ **'gloriousness** *n*
Glorious Revolution *n* the events of 1688–89 in England that resulted in the ousting of James II and the establishment of William III and Mary II as joint monarchs. Also called: **Bloodless Revolution.**
glory ('glɔːrɪ) *n, pl* **-ries. 1** exaltation, praise, or honour, as that accorded by general consent: *the glory for the exploit went to the captain.* **2** something that brings or is worthy of praise (esp. in the phrase **crowning glory**). **3** thanksgiving, adoration, or worship: *glory be to God.* **4** pomp; splendour: *the glory of the king's reign.* **5** radiant beauty; resplendence: *the glory of the sunset.* **6** the beauty and bliss of heaven. **7** a state of extreme happiness or prosperity. **8** another word for **halo** or **nimbus.** ◆ *vb* **-ries, -rying, -ried. 9** (*intr;* often foll. by *in*) to triumph or exult. **10** (*intr*) *Obsolete.* to brag. ◆ *interj* **11** *Informal.* a mild interjection to express pleasure or surprise (often in the exclamatory phrase **glory be!**). [C13: from Old French *glorie,* from Latin *glōria,* of obscure origin]
glory box *n Austral. and N.Z. informal.* a box in which a young woman stores clothes, etc., in preparation for marriage.
glory hole *n* **1** *Informal.* a room, cupboard, or other storage space that contains an untidy and miscellaneous collection of objects. **2** *Nautical.* another term for **lazaretto** (sense 1).
glory-of-the-snow *n* a small W Asian liliaceous plant, *Chionodoxa luciliae,* cultivated for its early-blooming blue flowers.
Glos *abbrev. for* Gloucestershire.
gloss[1] (glɒs) *n* **1** lustre or sheen, as of a smooth surface. **2** a superficially attractive appearance. **3** See **gloss paint. 4** a cosmetic preparation applied to the skin to give it a faint sheen: *lip gloss.* ◆ *vb* **5** to give a gloss to or obtain a gloss. ◆ See also **gloss over.** [C16: probably of Scandinavian origin; compare Icelandic *glossi* flame, Middle High German *glosen* to glow] ▸ **'glosser** *n* ▸ **'glossless** *adj*
gloss[2] (glɒs) *n* **1** a short or expanded explanation or interpretation of a word, expression, or foreign phrase in the margin or text of a manuscript, etc. **2** an intentionally misleading explanation or interpretation. **3** short for **glossary.** ◆ *vb* (*tr*) **4** to add glosses to. [C16: from Latin *glōssa* unusual word requiring explanatory note, from Ionic Greek] ▸ **'glosser** *n* ▸ **'glossingly** *adv*
gloss. *abbrev. for* glossary.
glossa ('glɒsə) *n, pl* **-sae** (-siː) *or* **-sas. 1** *Anatomy.* a technical word for the **tongue. 2** a paired tonguelike lobe in the labium of an insect. ▸ **'glossal** *adj*
glossary ('glɒsərɪ) *n, pl* **-ries.** an alphabetical list of terms peculiar to a field of knowledge with definitions or explanations. Sometimes called: **gloss.** [C14: from Late Latin *glossārium;* see GLOSS[2]] ▸ **glossarial** (glɒ'sɛərɪəl) *adj* ▸ **glos'sarially** *adv* ▸ **'glossarist** *n*
glossator (glɒ'seɪtə) *n* **1** Also called: **glossarist, glossist, glossographer.** a writer of glosses and commentaries, esp. (in the Middle Ages) an interpreter of Roman and Canon Law. **2** a compiler of a glossary.
glossectomy (glɒ'sɛktəmɪ) *n, pl* **-mies.** surgical removal of all or part of the tongue.
glosseme ('glɒsiːm) *n* the smallest meaningful unit of a language, such as stress, form, etc. [C20: from Greek *glōssēma;* see GLOSS[2], -EME]
glossitis (glɒ'saɪtɪs) *n* inflammation of the tongue. ▸ **glossitic** (glɒ'sɪtɪk) *adj*
glosso- *or before a vowel* **gloss-** *combining form.* indicating a tongue or language: *glossolaryngeal.* [from Greek *glossa* tongue]
glossography (glɒ'sɒgrəfɪ) *n* the art of writing textual glosses or commentaries. ▸ **glos'sographer** *n*
glossolalia (,glɒsə'leɪlɪə) *n* **1** another term for **gift of tongues. 2** *Psychol.* babbling in a nonexistent language. [C19: New Latin, from GLOSSO- + Greek *lalein* to babble]
glossology (glɒ'sɒlədʒɪ) *n* an obsolete term for **linguistics.** ▸ **glossological** (,glɒsə'lɒdʒɪk'l) *adj* ▸ **glos'sologist** *n*
glossopharyngeal nerve (,glɒsəʊ,færɪn'dʒiːəl) *n* the ninth cranial nerve,

which supplies the muscles of the pharynx, the tongue, the middle ear, and the parotid gland.

gloss over *vb* (*tr, adv*) **1** to hide under a deceptively attractive surface or appearance. **2** to deal with (unpleasant facts) rapidly and cursorily, or to omit them altogether from an account of something.

gloss paint *n* a type of paint composed of pigments ground up in a varnish medium, which produces a hard, shiny, and usually durable finish. Also called: **gloss.**

glossy ('glɒsɪ) *adj* **glossier, glossiest. 1** smooth and shiny; lustrous. **2** superficially attractive; plausible. **3** (of a magazine) lavishly produced on shiny paper and usually with many colour photographs. ◆ *n, pl* **glossies. 4** Also called (U.S.): **slick.** an expensively produced magazine, typically a sophisticated fashion or glamour magazine, printed on shiny paper and containing high quality colour photography. Compare **pulp** (sense 3). **5** a photograph printed on paper that has a smooth shiny surface. ▸ **'glossily** *adv* ▸ **'glossiness** *n*

glottal ('glɒtᵊl) *adj* **1** of or relating to the glottis. **2** *Phonetics.* articulated or pronounced at or with the glottis.

glottal stop *n* a plosive speech sound produced as the sudden onset of a vowel in several languages, such as German, by first tightly closing the glottis and then allowing the air pressure to build up in the trachea before opening the glottis, causing the air to escape with force.

glottic ('glɒtɪk) *adj* of or relating to the tongue or the glottis.

glottis ('glɒtɪs) *n, pl* **-tises** *or* **-tides** (-tɪˌdiːz). the vocal apparatus of the larynx, consisting of the two true vocal cords and the opening between them. **[C16:** from New Latin, from Greek *glōttis,* from *glōtta,* Attic form of Ionic *glōssa* tongue; see GLOSS[2]**]** ▸ **glottidean** (glɒ'tɪdɪən) *adj*

glottochronology (ˌglɒtəʊkrə'nɒlədʒɪ) *n* the use of lexicostatistics to establish that languages are historically related. **[C20** *glotto-,* from Greek *glōtta* tongue**]**

Gloucester[1] ('glɒstə) *n* a city in SW England, administrative centre of Gloucestershire, on the River Severn; cathedral (founded 1100). Pop.: 104 800 (1993 est.). Latin name: **Glevum** ('gliːvʊm).

Gloucester[2] ('glɒstə) *n* **1 Humphrey,** Duke of. 1391–1447, English soldier and statesman; son of Henry IV. He acted as protector during Henry VI's minority (1422–29) and was noted for his patronage of humanists. **2 Duke of.** See **Richard III. 3 Duke of.** See **Thomas of Woodstock.**

Gloucester Old Spot *n* a hardy breed of pig, white with a few black markings, that originally lived off windfalls in orchards in the Severn valley.

Gloucestershire ('glɒstəˌʃɪə, -ʃə) *n* a county of SW England, situated around the lower Severn valley: contains the Forest of Dean and the main part of the Cotswold Hills: the geographical and ceremonial county includes the unitary authority of South Gloucestershire (part of Avon county from 1974 to 1996). Administrative centre: Gloucester. Pop. (including South Gloucestershire): 769 500 (1996 est.). Area (including South Gloucestershire): 3153 sq. km (1217 sq. miles). Abbrev.: **Glos.**

glove (glʌv) *n* **1** (*often pl*) a shaped covering for the hand with individual sheaths for the fingers and thumb, made of leather, fabric, etc. See also **gauntlet**[1] (sense 2). **2** any of various large protective hand covers worn in sports, such as a boxing glove. **3 hand in glove.** *Informal.* in an intimate relationship or close association. **4 handle with kid gloves.** *Informal.* to treat with extreme care. **5 with the gloves off.** *Informal.* (of a dispute, argument, etc.) conducted mercilessly and in earnest, with no reservations. ◆ *vb* **6** (*tr; usually passive*) to cover or provide with or as if with gloves. **[**Old English *glōfe;* related to Old Norse *glōfi***]** ▸ **'gloved** *adj* ▸ **'gloveless** *adj*

glove box *n* a closed box in which toxic or radioactive substances can be handled by an operator who places his hands through protective gloves sealed to the box.

glove compartment *n* a small compartment in a car dashboard for the storage of miscellaneous articles.

glove puppet *n* a small figure of a person or animal that fits over and is manipulated by the hand.

glover ('glʌvə) *n* a person who makes or sells gloves.

glow (gləʊ) *n* **1** light emitted by a substance or object at a high temperature. **2** a steady even light without flames. **3** brilliance or vividness of colour. **4** brightness or ruddiness of complexion. **5** a feeling of wellbeing or satisfaction. **6** intensity of emotion; ardour. ◆ *vb* (*intr*) **7** to emit a steady even light without flames. **8** to shine intensely, as if from great heat. **9** to be exuberant or high-spirited, as from excellent health or intense emotion. **10** to experience a feeling of wellbeing or satisfaction: *to glow with pride.* **11** (esp. of the complexion) to show a strong bright colour, esp. a shade of red. **12** to be very hot. **[**Old English *glōwan;* related to Old Norse *glōa,* Old High German *gluoen,* Icelandic *glōra* to sparkle**]**

glow discharge *n* a silent luminous discharge of electricity through a low-pressure gas.

glower ('glaʊə) *vb* **1** (*intr*) to stare hard and angrily. ◆ *n* **2** a sullen or angry stare. **[C16:** probably of Scandinavian origin; related to Middle Low German *glūren* to watch**]** ▸ **'gloweringly** *adv*

glowing ('gləʊɪŋ) *adj* **1** emitting a steady bright light without flames: *glowing embers.* **2** warm and rich in colour: *the room was decorated in glowing shades of gold and orange.* **3** flushed and rosy, as from exercise or excitement: *glowing cheeks.* **4** displaying or indicative of extreme satisfaction, pride, or emotion: *he gave a glowing account of his son's achievements.* ▸ **'glowingly** *adv*

glow lamp *n* a small light consisting of two or more electrodes in an inert gas, such as neon, at low pressure, across which an electrical discharge occurs when the voltage applied to the electrodes exceeds the ionization potential.

glow plug *n* one of usually four plugs fitted to the cylinder block of a diesel engine that warms the engine chamber to facilitate starting in cold weather. Also called: **heater plug.**

glow-worm *n* **1** a European beetle, *Lampyris noctiluca,* the females and larvae of which bear luminescent organs producing a greenish light: family *Lampyridae.* **2** any of various other beetles or larvae of the family *Lampyridae.* ◆ See also **firefly** (sense 1).

gloxinia (glɒk'sɪnɪə) *n* any of several tropical plants of the genus *Sinningia,* esp. the South American *S. speciosa,* cultivated for its large white, red, or purple bell-shaped flowers: family *Gesneriaceae.* **[C19:** named after Benjamin P. *Gloxin,* 18th-century German physician and botanist who first described it**]**

gloze (gləʊz) *Archaic.* ◆ *vb* **1** (*tr; often foll. by over*) to explain away; minimize the effect or importance of. **2** to make explanatory notes or glosses on (a text). **3** to use flattery (on). ◆ *n* **4** flattery or deceit. **5** an explanatory note or gloss. **6** specious or deceptive talk or action. **[C13:** from Old French *glosser* to comment; see GLOSS[2]**]**

glucagon ('gluːkəˌgɒn, -gən) *n* a polypeptide hormone, produced in the pancreas by the islets of Langerhans, that stimulates the release of glucose into the blood. Compare **insulin. [C20:** from GLUC(OSE) + *-agon,* perhaps from Greek *agein* to lead**]**

glucan ('gluːˌkæn) *n* any polysaccharide consisting of a polymer of glucose, such as cellulose or starch.

glucinum (gluː'saɪnəm) *or* **glucinium** (gluː'sɪnɪəm) *n* a former name for **beryllium. [C19:** New Latin *glucina* beryllium oxide, from Greek *glukus* sweet + -IN; alluding to the sweet taste of some of the salts**]**

Gluck (*German* glʊk) *n* **Christoph Willibald von** ('krɪstɔf 'vɪlibalt fɔn). 1714–87, German composer, esp. of operas, including *Orfeo ed Euridice* (1762) and *Alceste* (1767).

glucocorticoid (ˌgluːkəʊ'kɔːtɪˌkɔɪd) *n* any of a class of corticosteroids that control carbohydrate, protein, and fat metabolism and have anti-inflammatory activity.

gluconeogenesis (ˌgluːkəʊˌniːəʊ'dʒenɪsɪs) *n Biochem.* the sequence of metabolic reactions by which glucose is synthesized, esp. in the liver, from noncarbohydrate sources, such as amino acids, pyruvic acid, or glycerol. Also called: **glyconeogenesis.**

glucophore ('gluːkəʊˌfɔː) *n* a chemical group responsible for sweetness of taste.

glucoprotein (ˌgluːkəʊ'prəʊtiːn) *n* another name for **glycoprotein.**

glucose ('gluːkəʊz, -kəʊs) *n* **1** a white crystalline monosaccharide sugar that has several optically active forms, the most abundant being dextrose: a major energy source in metabolism. Formula: $C_6H_{12}O_6$. **2** a yellowish syrup (or, after desiccation, a solid) containing dextrose, maltose, and dextrin, obtained by incomplete hydrolysis of starch: used in confectionery, fermentation, etc. **[C19:** from French, from Greek *gleukos* sweet wine; related to Greek *glukus* sweet**]** ▸ **glucosic** (gluː'kɒsɪk) *adj*

glucoside ('gluːkəʊˌsaɪd) *n Biochem.* any of a large group of glycosides that yield glucose on hydrolysis. ▸ **ˌgluco'sidal** *or* **glucosidic** (ˌgluːkəʊ'sɪdɪk) *adj*

glucosuria (ˌgluːkəʊ'sjʊərɪə) *n Pathol.* a less common word for **glycosuria.** ▸ **ˌgluco'suric** *adj*

glue (gluː) *n* **1** any natural or synthetic adhesive, esp. a sticky gelatinous substance prepared by boiling animal products such as bones, skin, and horns. **2** any other sticky or adhesive substance. ◆ *vb* **glues, gluing** *or* **glueing, glued. 3** (*tr*) to join or stick together with or as if with glue. **[C14:** from Old French *glu,* from Late Latin *glūs;* compare Greek *gloios***]** ▸ **'glueˌlike** *adj* ▸ **'gluer** *n* ▸ **'gluey** *adj*

glue ear *n* accumulation of fluid in the middle ear in children, caused by infection and sometimes resulting in deafness.

glue-sniffing *n* the practice of inhaling the fumes of certain types of glue to produce intoxicating or hallucinatory effects. ▸ **'glue-ˌsniffer** *n*

glug (glʌg) *n* a word representing a gurgling sound, as of liquid being poured from a bottle or swallowed. **[C19:** of imitative origin**]**

gluhwein ('gluːˌvaɪn) *n* mulled wine. **[**German**]**

glum (glʌm) *adj* **glummer, glummest.** silent or sullen, as from gloom. **[C16:** variant of GLOOM**]** ▸ **'glumly** *adv* ▸ **'glumness** *n*

glume (gluːm) *n Botany.* one of a pair of dry membranous bracts at the base of the inflorescence, esp. the spikelet, of grasses. **[C18:** from Latin *glūma* husk of corn; related to Latin *glūbere* to remove the bark from**]** ▸ **glu'maceous** *adj* ▸ **'glumeˌlike** *adj*

gluon ('gluːɒn) *n* a hypothetical particle believed to be exchanged between quarks in order to bind them together to form particles. **[C20:** from GLUE + -ON**]**

glut (glʌt) *n* **1** an excessive amount, as in the production of a crop, often leading to a fall in price. **2** the act of glutting or state of being glutted. ◆ *vb* **gluts, glutting, glutted.** (*tr*) **3** to feed or supply beyond capacity. **4** to supply (a market) with a commodity in excess of the demand for it. **5** to cram full or choke up: *to glut a passage.* **[C14:** probably from Old French *gloutir,* from Latin *gluttīre;* see GLUTTON[1]**]** ▸ **'gluttingly** *adv*

glutamate ('gluːtəˌmeɪt) *n* any salt of glutamic acid, esp. its sodium salt (see **monosodium glutamate**). **[C19:** from GLUTAM(IC) ACID + -ATE[1]**]**

glutamic acid (gluː'tæmɪk) *or* **glutaminic acid** (ˌgluːtə'mɪnɪk) *n* a nonessential amino acid, occurring in proteins, that acts as a neurotransmitter and plays a part in nitrogen metabolism.

glutamine ('gluːtəˌmiːn, -mɪn) *n* a nonessential amino acid occurring in proteins: plays an important role in protein metabolism. **[C19:** from GLUT(EN) + -AMINE**]**

glutaraldehyde (ˌgluːtə'ældɪˌhaɪd) *n* a water-soluble oil used as a disinfectant, tanning agent, and in resins. Formula: $C_5H_8O_2$.

glutathione (ˌgluːtə'θaɪəʊn, -θaɪ'əʊn) *n Biochem.* a tripeptide consisting of glutamic acid, cysteine, and glycine: important in biological oxidations and the activation of some enzymes. Formula: $C_{10}H_{17}N_3O_6S$. **[C20:** from GLUTA(MIC ACID) + THI- + -ONE**]**

glutelin ('gluːtɪlɪn) *n* any of a group of water-insoluble plant proteins found in cereals. They are precipitated by alcohol and are not coagulated by heat. Compare **gliadin.** [C20: See GLUTEN, -IN]

gluten ('gluːtᵊn) *n* a protein consisting of a mixture of glutelin and gliadin, present in cereal grains, esp. wheat. A gluten-free diet is necessary in cases of coeliac disease. [C16: from Latin: GLUE] ▸ **'glutenous** *adj*

gluten bread *n* bread made from flour containing a high proportion of gluten.

gluteus *or* **glutaeus** (gluˈtiːəs) *n, pl* **-tei** *or* **-taei** (-ˈtiːaɪ). any one of the three large muscles that form the human buttock and move the thigh, esp. the **gluteus maximus.** [C17: from New Latin, from Greek *gloutos* buttock, rump] ▸ **gluˈteal** *or* **gluˈtaeal** *adj*

glutinous ('gluːtɪnəs) *adj* resembling glue in texture; sticky. ▸ **'glutinously** *adv* ▸ **'glutinousness** *or* **glutinosity** (ˌgluːtɪˈnɒsɪtɪ) *n*

glutton[1] ('glʌtᵊn) *n* **1** a person devoted to eating and drinking to excess; greedy person. **2** *Often ironical.* a person who has or appears to have a voracious appetite for something: *a glutton for punishment.* [C13: from Old French *glouton,* from Latin *glutto,* from *gluttīre* to swallow] ▸ **'gluttonous** *adj* ▸ **'gluttonously** *adv*

glutton[2] ('glʌtᵊn) *n* another name for **wolverine.** [C17: from GLUTTON[1], apparently translating German *Vielfrass* great eater]

gluttony ('glʌtənɪ) *n* the act or practice of eating to excess.

glyceric (glɪˈsɛrɪk) *adj* of, containing, or derived from glycerol.

glyceric acid *n* a viscous liquid carboxylic acid produced by the oxidation of glycerol; 2,3-dihydroxypropanoic acid. Formula: $C_3H_6O_4$.

glyceride ('glɪsəˌraɪd) *n* any fatty-acid ester of glycerol.

glycerine ('glɪsərɪn, ˌglɪsəˈriːn) *or* **glycerin** ('glɪsərɪn) *n* another name (not in technical usage) for **glycerol.** [C19: from French *glycérine,* from Greek *glukeros* sweet + *-ine* -IN; related to Greek *glukus* sweet]

glycerol ('glɪsəˌrɒl) *n* a colourless or pale yellow odourless sweet-tasting syrupy liquid; 1,2,3-propanetriol: a by-product of soap manufacture, used as a solvent, antifreeze, plasticizer, and sweetener (**E422**). Formula: $C_3H_8O_3$. Also called (not in technical usage): **glycerine, glycerin.** [C19: from GLYCER(INE) + -OL[1]]

glyceryl ('glɪsərɪl) *n* (*modifier*) derived from glycerol by replacing or removing one or more of its hydroxyl groups: *a glyceryl group or radical.*

glyceryl trinitrate *n* another name for **nitroglycerine.**

glycine ('glaɪsiːn, glaɪˈsiːn) *n* a nonessential amino acid occurring in most proteins that acts as a neurotransmitter; aminoacetic acid. [C19: GLYCO- + -INE[2]]

glyco- *or before a vowel* **glyc-** *combining form.* indicating sugar: *glycogen.* [from Greek *glukus* sweet]

glycogen ('glaɪkəʊdʒən, -dʒɛn) *n* a polysaccharide consisting of glucose units: the form in which carbohydrate is stored in the liver and muscles in man and animals. It can easily be hydrolysed to glucose. Also called: **animal starch.** ▸ **glycogenic** (ˌglaɪkəʊˈdʒɛnɪk) *adj*

glycogenesis (ˌglaɪkəʊˈdʒɛnɪsɪs) *n* the formation of sugar, esp. (in animals) from glycogen. ▸ **glycogenetic** (ˌglaɪkəʊdʒɪˈnɛtɪk) *adj*

glycol ('glaɪkɒl) *n* another name (not in technical usage) for **ethanediol** or a **diol.** ▸ **glycolic** *or* **glycollic** (glaɪˈkɒlɪk) *adj*

glycolic acid *n* a colourless crystalline soluble hygroscopic compound found in sugar cane and sugar beet: used in tanning and in the manufacture of pharmaceuticals, pesticides, adhesives, and plasticizers; hydroxyacetic acid. Formula: $CH_2(OH)COOH$.

glycolipid (ˌglaɪkəʊˈlɪpɪd) *n* any of a group of lipids containing a carbohydrate group, commonly glucose or galactose.

glycolysis (glaɪˈkɒlɪsɪs) *n Biochem.* the breakdown of glucose by enzymes into pyruvic and lactic acids with the liberation of energy.

glyconeogenesis (ˌglaɪkəʊˌniːəʊˈdʒɛnɪsɪs) *n* another name for **gluconeogenesis.**

glycophyte ('glaɪkəʊˌfaɪt) *n* any plant that will only grow healthily in soils with a low content of sodium salts. ▸ **glycophytic** (ˌglaɪkəʊˈfɪtɪk) *adj*

glycoprotein (ˌglaɪkəʊˈprəʊtiːn), **glucoprotein,** *or* **glycopeptide** (ˌglaɪkəʊˈpɛptaɪd) *n* any of a group of conjugated proteins containing small amounts of carbohydrates as prosthetic groups. See also **mucoprotein.**

glycose ('glaɪkəʊz, -kəʊs) *n* **1** an older word for **glucose. 2** any of various monosaccharides.

glycoside ('glaɪkəʊˌsaɪd) *n* any of a group of substances, such as digitoxin, derived from monosaccharides by replacing the hydroxyl group by another group. Many are important medicinal drugs. See also **glucoside.** ▸ **glycosidic** (ˌglaɪkəʊˈsɪdɪk) *adj*

glycosuria (ˌglaɪkəʊˈsjʊərɪə) *or* **glucosuria** *n* the presence of excess sugar in the urine, as in diabetes. [C19: from New Latin, from French *glycose* GLUCOSE + -URIA] ▸ **ˌglycoˈsuric** *or* **ˌglucoˈsuric** *adj*

glycosylation (ˌglaɪkəʊsəˈleɪʃən) *n* the process by which sugars are chemically attached to proteins to form glycoproteins. [from *glycosyl* radical derived from *glycose* + -ATION]

Glyndebourne ('glaɪndˌbɔːn) *n* an estate in SE England, in East Sussex: site of a famous annual festival of opera founded in 1934 by John Christie.

glyoxaline (glaɪˈɒksəlɪn) *n* another name (not in technical usage) for **imidazole.**

glyph (glɪf) *n* **1** a carved channel or groove, esp. a vertical one as used on a Doric frieze. **2** *Now rare.* another word for **hieroglyphic.** [C18: from French *glyphe,* from Greek *gluphē* carving, from *gluphein* to carve] ▸ **'glyphic** *adj*

glyphography (glɪˈfɒgrəfɪ) *n* a plate-making process in which an electrotype is made from an engraved copper plate. [C19: from Greek *gluphē* carving + -GRAPHY] ▸ **glyphograph** ('glɪfəˌgrɑːf, -ˌgræf) *n* ▸ **glyˈphographer** *n* ▸ **glyphographic** (ˌglɪfəˈgræfɪk) *or* **ˌglyphoˈgraphical** *adj*

glyptal ('glɪptəl) *n* an alkyd resin obtained from polyhydric alcohols and polybasic organic acids or their anhydrides; used for surface coatings. [C20: a trademark, perhaps from GLY(CEROL) + P(H)T(H)AL(IC)]

glyptic ('glɪptɪk) *adj* of or relating to engraving or carving, esp. on precious stones. [C19: from French *glyptique,* from Greek *gluptikos,* from *gluptos,* from *gluphein* to carve]

glyptics ('glɪptɪks) *n* (*functioning as sing*) the art of engraving precious stones.

glyptodont ('glɪptəˌdɒnt) *n* any extinct late Cenozoic edentate mammal of the genus *Glyptodon* and related genera, of South America, which resembled giant armadillos. [C19: from Greek *gluptos* carved + -ODONT]

glyptography (glɪpˈtɒgrəfɪ) *n* the art of carving or engraving upon gemstones. ▸ **glypˈtographer** *n* ▸ **glyptographic** (ˌglɪptəˈgræfɪk) *or* **ˌglyptoˈgraphical** *adj*

GM *abbrev. for:* **1** general manager. **2** genetically modified. **3** (in Britain) George Medal. **4** Grand Master. **5** grant-maintained.

G-man *n, pl* **G-men. 1** *U.S. slang.* an FBI agent. **2** *Irish.* a political detective.

GMB *abbrev. for:* **1** Grand Master Bowman; the highest standard of archer. **2** General, Municipal, and Boilermakers (trades union).

GmbH (in Germany) *abbrev. for* Gesellschaft mit beschränkter Haftung; a limited company. [German: company with limited liabilities]

Gmc *abbrev. for* Germanic.

GMC *abbrev. for:* **1** general management committee. **2** General Medical Council.

GMO *abbrev. for* genetically modified organism.

GMT *abbrev. for* Greenwich Mean Time.

GMWU (in Britain) *abbrev. for* National Union of General and Municipal Workers.

gnamma hole ('næmə) *n* a variant spelling of **namma hole.**

gnarl[1] (nɑːl) *n* **1** any knotty protuberance or swelling on a tree. ◆ *vb* **2** (*tr*) to knot or cause to knot. [C19: back formation from *gnarled,* probably variant of *knurled;* see KNURL]

gnarl[2] (nɑːl) *or* **gnar** (nɑː) *vb* (*intr*) *Obsolete.* to growl or snarl. [C16: of imitative origin]

gnarled (nɑːld) *or* **gnarly** ('nɑːlɪ) *adj* **1** having gnarls. **2** (esp. of hands) rough, twisted, and weather-beaten in appearance. **3** perverse or ill-tempered.

gnash (næʃ) *vb* **1** to grind (the teeth) together, as in pain or anger. **2** (*tr*) to bite or chew as by grinding the teeth. ◆ *n* **3** the act of gnashing the teeth. [C15: probably of Scandinavian origin; compare Old Norse *gnastan* gnashing of teeth, *gnesta* to clatter] ▸ **'gnashingly** *adv*

gnashers ('næʃəz) *pl n Slang.* teeth, esp. false ones.

gnat (næt) *n* any of various small fragile biting dipterous insects of the suborder *Nematocera,* esp. *Culex pipiens* (**common gnat**), which abounds near stagnant water. [Old English *gnætt;* related to Middle High German *gnaz* scurf, German dialect *Gnitze* gnat] ▸ **'gnatˌlike** *adj*

gnatcatcher ('nætˌkætʃə) *n* any of various small American songbirds of the genus *Polioptila* and related genera, typically having a long tail and a pale bluish-grey plumage: family *Muscicapidae* (Old World flycatchers, etc.).

gnathic ('næθɪk) *or* **gnathal** *adj Anatomy.* of or relating to the jaw. [C19: from Greek *gnathos* jaw]

gnathion ('neɪθɪˌɒn, 'næθ-) *n* the lowest point of the midline of the lower jaw: a reference point in craniometry. [C19: from New Latin, from Greek *gnathos* jaw]

gnathite ('neɪθaɪt, 'næθ-) *n Zoology.* an appendage of an arthropod that is specialized for grasping or chewing; mouthpart. [C19: from Greek *gnathos* jaw]

gnathonic (næˈθɒnɪk) *adj Literary.* deceitfully flattering; sycophantic. [C17: from Latin *gnathōnicus,* from *Gnathō,* such a character in the *Eunuchus,* Roman comedy by Terence] ▸ **gnaˈthonically** *adv*

gnathostome ('neɪθəʊˌstəʊm) *n* any vertebrate of the superclass *Gnathostomata,* having a mouth with jaws, including all vertebrates except the agnathans. [from New Latin *Gnathostomata,* from Greek *gnathos* jaw + *stoma* mouth] ▸ **ˌgnathoˈstomatous** *adj*

-gnathous *adj combining form.* indicating or having a jaw of a specified kind: *prognathous.* [from New Latin *-gnathus,* from Greek *gnathos* jaw]

gnaw (nɔː) *vb* **gnaws, gnawing, gnawed; gnawed** *or* **gnawn** (nɔːn). **1** (when *intr,* often foll. by *at* or *upon*) to bite (at) or chew (upon) constantly so as to wear away little by little. **2** (*tr*) to form by gnawing: *to gnaw a hole.* **3** to cause erosion of (something). **4** (when *intr,* often foll. by *at*) to cause constant distress or anxiety (to). ◆ *n* **5** the act or an instance of gnawing. [Old English *gnagan;* related to Old Norse *gnaga,* Old High German *gnagan*] ▸ **'gnawable** *adj* ▸ **'gnawer** *n* ▸ **'gnawing** *adj, n* ▸ **'gnawingly** *adv*

GNC (in Britain) *abbrev. for* General Nursing Council.

gneiss (naɪs) *n* any coarse-grained metamorphic rock that is banded or foliated: represents the last stage in the metamorphism of rocks before melting. [C18: from German *Gneis,* probably from Middle High German *ganeist* spark; related to Old Norse *gneista* to give off sparks] ▸ **'gneissic, 'gneissoid,** *or* **'gneissose** *adj*

gnocchi ('nɒkɪ, gəˈnɒkɪ, 'gnɒkɪ) *pl n* dumplings made of pieces of semolina pasta, or sometimes potato, used to garnish soup or served alone with sauce. [Italian, plural of *gnocco* lump, probably of Germanic origin; compare Middle High German *knoche* bone]

gnome[1] (nəʊm) *n* **1** one of a species of legendary creatures, usually resembling small misshapen old men, said to live in the depths of the earth and guard buried treasure. **2** the statue of a gnome, esp. in a garden. **3** a very small or ugly person. **4** *Facetious or derogatory.* an international banker or financier (esp. in the phrase **gnomes of Zürich**). [C18: from French, from New Latin *gnomus,* coined by Paracelsus, of obscure origin] ▸ **'gnomish** *adj*

gnome[2] (nəʊm) *n* a short pithy saying or maxim expressing a general truth or principle. [C16: from Greek *gnōmē,* from *gignōskein* to know]

gnomic ('nəʊmɪk, 'nɒm-) *or* **gnomical** *adj* **1** consisting of, containing, or relating to gnomes or aphorisms. **2** of or relating to a writer of such sayings. ▸ **'gnomically** *adv*

gnomon ('nəʊmɒn) *n* **1** the stationary arm that projects the shadow on a sundial. **2** a geometric figure remaining after a parallelogram has been removed from one corner of a larger parallelogram. [C16: from Latin, from Greek: interpreter, from *gignōskein* to know] ▶ **gno'monic** *adj* ▶ **gno'monically** *adv*

gnosis ('nəʊsɪs) *n, pl* **-ses** (-siːz). supposedly revealed knowledge of various spiritual truths, esp. that said to have been possessed by ancient Gnostics. [C18: ultimately from Greek: knowledge, from *gignōskein* to know]

-gnosis *n combining form.* (esp. in medicine) recognition or knowledge: *prognosis; diagnosis.* [via Latin from Greek: GNOSIS] ▶ **-gnostic** *adj combining form.*

gnostic ('nɒstɪk) *or* **gnostical** *adj* of, relating to, or possessing knowledge, esp. esoteric spiritual knowledge. ▶ **'gnostically** *adv*

Gnostic ('nɒstɪk) *n* **1** an adherent of Gnosticism. ◆ *adj* **2** of or relating to Gnostics or to Gnosticism. [C16: from Late Latin *Gnosticī* the Gnostics, from Greek *gnōstikos* relating to knowledge, from *gnōstos* known, from *gignōskein* to know]

Gnosticism ('nɒstɪˌsɪzəm) *n* a religious movement characterized by a belief in gnosis, through which the spiritual element in man could be released from its bondage in matter: regarded as a heresy by the Christian Church.

Gnosticize *or* **Gnosticise** ('nɒstɪˌsaɪz) *vb* **1** (*intr*) to maintain or profess Gnostic views. **2** to put a Gnostic interpretation upon (something). ▶ **'Gnostiˌcizer** *or* **'Gnostiˌciser** *n*

gnotobiotics (ˌnəʊtəʊbaɪ'ɒtɪks) *n* (*functioning as sing*) the study of organisms living in germ-free conditions or when inoculated with known microorganisms. [C20: from Greek, from *gnōtos,* from *gignōskein* to know + *bios* known life] ▶ **ˌgnotobi'otic** *adj* ▶ **ˌgnotobi'otically** *adv*

gnow (naʊ) *n W Austral.* another name for **mallee fowl.**

GNP *abbrev. for* gross national product.

gnr. *abbrev. for* gunner.

GnRH *Biochem. abbrev. for* gonadotrophin-releasing hormone: a peptide that is released from the brain and stimulates the pituitary gland to secrete gonadotrophic hormones that act in turn on the sex glands.

gns. *abbrev. for* guineas.

gnu (nuː) *n, pl* **gnus** *or* **gnu.** either of two sturdy antelopes, *Connochaetes taurinus* (**brindled gnu**) or the much rarer *C. gnou* (**white-tailed gnu**), inhabiting the savannas of Africa, having an oxlike head and a long tufted tail. Also called: **wildebeest.** [C18: from Xhosa *nqu*]

GNVQ (in Britain) *abbrev. for* general national vocational qualification: a qualification which rewards the development of skills which are likely to be of use to employers.

go[1] (gəʊ) *vb* **goes, going, went, gone.** (*mainly intr*) **1** to move or proceed, esp. to or from a point or in a certain direction: *to go to London; to go home.* **2** (*tr; takes an infinitive,* often with *to* omitted or replaced by *and*) to proceed towards a particular person or place with some specified intention or purpose: *I must go and get that book.* **3** to depart: *we'll have to go at eleven.* **4** to start, as in a race: often used in commands. **5** to make regular journeys: *this train service goes to the east coast.* **6** to operate or function effectively: *the radio won't go.* **7** (*copula*) to become: *his face went red with embarrassment.* **8** to make a noise as specified: *the gun went bang.* **9** to enter into a specified state or condition: *to go into hysterics; to go into action.* **10** to be or continue to be in a specified state or condition: *to go in rags; to go in poverty.* **11** to lead, extend, or afford access: *this route goes to the north.* **12** to proceed towards an activity: *to go to supper; to go to sleep.* **13** (*tr; takes an infinitive*) to serve or contribute: *this letter goes to prove my point.* **14** to follow a course as specified; fare: *the lecture went badly.* **15** to be applied or allotted to a particular purpose or recipient: *her wealth went to her son; his money went on drink.* **16** to be sold or otherwise transferred to a recipient: *the necklace went for three thousand pounds.* **17** to be ranked; compare: *this meal is good as my meals go.* **18** to blend or harmonize: *these chairs won't go with the rest of your furniture.* **19** (foll. by *by* or *under*) to be known (by a name or disguise). **20** to fit or extend: *that skirt won't go round your waist.* **21** to have a usual or proper place: *those books go on this shelf.* **22** (of music, poetry, etc.) to be sounded; expressed, etc.: *how does that song go?* **23** to fail or give way: *my eyesight is going.* **24** to break down or collapse abruptly: *the ladder went at the critical moment.* **25** to die: *the old man went at 2 a.m.* **26** (often foll. by *by*) **26a** (of time) to elapse: *the hours go by so slowly at the office.* **26b** to travel past: *the train goes by her house at four.* **26c** to be guided (by). **27** to occur: *happiness does not always go with riches.* **28** to be eliminated, abolished, or given up: *this entry must go to save space.* **29** to be spent or finished: *all his money has gone.* **30** to circulate or be transmitted: *the infection went around the whole community.* **31** to attend: *go to school; go to church.* **32** to join a stated profession: *go to the bar; go on the stage.* **33** (foll. by *to*) to have recourse (to); turn: *to go to arbitration.* **34** (foll. by *to*) to subject or put oneself (to): *she goes to great pains to please him.* **35** to proceed, esp. up to or beyond certain limits: *you will go too far one day and then you will be punished.* **36** to be acceptable or tolerated: *anything goes in this place.* **37** to carry the weight of final authority: *what the boss says goes.* **38** (foll. by *into*) to be contained in: *four goes into twelve three times.* **39** (often foll. by *for*) to endure or last out: *we can't go for much longer without water in this heat.* **40** (*tr*) *Cards.* to bet or bid: *I go two hearts.* **41** (*tr*) *Informal, chiefly U.S.* to have as one's weight: *I went 112 pounds a year ago.* **42** *U.S. and Canadian.* (*usually used in commands;* takes an infinitive without *to*) **42a** to start to act so as to: *go shut the door.* **42b** to leave so as to: *go blow your brains out.* **43** *Informal.* to perform well; be successful: *that group can really go.* **44** (*tr*) *Nonstandard.* to say: widely used, esp. in the historic present, in reporting dialogue: *Then she goes, "Give it to me!" and she just snatched it.* **45 go and.** *Informal.* to be so foolish or unlucky as to: *then she had to go and lose her hat.* **46 be going.** to intend or be about to start (to do or be doing something): often used as an alternative future construction: *what's going to happen to us?* **47 go ape.** *Slang.* to become crazy, enraged, or out of control. **48 go ape over.** *Slang.* to become crazy or extremely enthusiastic about. **49 go astray.** to be mislaid; go missing. **50 go bail.** to act as surety. **51 go bush.** See **bush** (sense 13). **52 go halves.** See **half** (sense 15). **53 go hard.** (often foll. by *with*) to cause trouble or unhappiness (to). **54 go it.** *Slang.* to do something or move energetically. **55 go it alone.** *Informal.* to act or proceed without allies or help. **56 go much on.** *Informal.* to approve of or be in agreement with (something): usually used in the negative: *I don't go much on the idea.* **57 go one better.** *Informal.* to surpass or outdo (someone). **58 go the whole hog.** *Informal.* See **hog** (sense 9). **59 let go. 59a** to relax one's hold (on); release. **59b** *Euphemistic.* to dismiss (from employment). **59c** to discuss or consider no further. **60 let oneself go. 60a** to act in an uninhibited manner. **60b** to lose interest in one's appearance, manners, etc. **61 to go. 61a** remaining. **61b** *U.S. and Canadian informal.* (of food served by a restaurant) for taking away. ◆ *n, pl* **goes. 62** the act of going. **63** *Informal.* **63a** an attempt or try: *he had a go at the stamp business.* **63b** an attempt at stopping a person suspected of a crime: *the police are not always in favour of the public having a go.* **63c** an attack, esp. verbal: *she had a real go at them.* **64** a turn: *it's my go next.* **65** *Informal.* the quality of being active and energetic: *she has much more go than I.* **66** *Informal.* hard or energetic work: *it's all go.* **67** *Informal.* a successful venture or achievement: *he made a go of it.* **68** *Informal.* a bout or attack (of an illness): *he had a bad go of flu last winter.* **69** *Informal.* an unforeseen, usually embarrassing or awkward, turn of events: *here's a rum go.* **70** *Informal.* a bargain or agreement. **71 all the go.** *Informal.* very popular; in fashion. **72 from the word go.** *Informal.* from the very beginning. **73** See **get-up-and-go. 74 no go.** *Informal.* impossible; abortive or futile: *it's no go, I'm afraid.* **75 on the go.** *Informal.* active and energetic. ◆ *adj* **76** (*postpositive*) *Informal.* functioning properly and ready for action: esp. used in astronautics: *all systems are go.* ◆ See also **go about, go against, go ahead, go along, go around, go at, go away, go back, go by, go down, go for, go forth, go in, going, go into, gone, go off, go on, go out, go over, go through, go to, go together, go under, go up, go with, go without.** [Old English *gān;* related to Old High German *gēn,* Greek *kikhanein* to reach, Sanskrit *jahāti* he forsakes]

go[2] (gəʊ) *or* **I-go** *n* a game for two players in which stones are placed on a board marked with a grid, the object being to capture territory on the board. [from Japanese]

GO *Military. abbrev. for* general order.

goa ('gəʊə) *n* a gazelle, *Procapra picticaudata,* inhabiting the plains of the Tibetan plateau, having a brownish-grey coat and backward-curving horns. [C19: from Tibetan *dgoba*]

Goa ('gəʊə) *n* a state on the W coast of India: a Portuguese overseas territory from 1510 until annexed by India in 1961. Area: 3702 sq. km (1430 sq. miles). Pop.: 1 235 000 (1994 est.).

go about *vb* (*intr*) **1** (*adv*) to move from place to place. **2** (*prep*) to busy oneself with: *to go about one's duties.* **3** (*prep*) to tackle (a problem or task). **4** (*prep*) to be actively and constantly engaged in (doing something): *he went about doing good.* **5** to circulate (in): *there's a lot of flu going about.* **6** (*adv*) (of a sailing ship) to change from one tack to another.

goad (gəʊd) *n* **1** a sharp pointed stick for urging on cattle, etc. **2** anything that acts as a spur or incitement. ◆ *vb* **3** (*tr*) to drive with or as if with a goad; spur; incite. [Old English *gād,* of Germanic origin, related to Old English *gār,* Old Norse *geirr* spear] ▶ **'goadˌlike** *adj*

Goa, Daman, and Diu *n* a former Union Territory of India consisting of the widely separated districts of Goa and Daman and the island of Diu. Capital: Panaji. Area: 3814 sq. km (1472 sq. miles).

go against *vb* (*intr, prep*) **1** to be contrary to (principles or beliefs). **2** to be unfavourable to (a person): *the case went against him.*

go ahead *vb* **1** (*intr, adv*) to start or continue, often after obtaining permission. ◆ *n* **go-ahead. 2** (usually preceded by *the*) *Informal.* permission to proceed. ◆ *adj* **go-ahead. 3** enterprising or ambitious.

goal (gəʊl) *n* **1** the aim or object towards which an endeavour is directed. **2** the terminal point of a journey or race. **3** (in various sports) the net, basket, etc. into or over which players try to propel the ball, puck, etc., to score. **4** *Sport.* **4a** a successful attempt at scoring. **4b** the score so made. **5** (in soccer, hockey, etc.) the position of goalkeeper. [C16: perhaps related to Middle English *gol* boundary, Old English *gǣlan* to hinder, impede] ▶ **'goalless** *adj*

goal area *n Soccer.* a rectangular area to the sides and front of the goal, measuring 20 × 6 yards on a full-sized pitch, from which goal kicks are taken. Also called: **six-yard area.**

goalball ('gəʊlˌbɔːl) *n* **1** a game played by two teams who compete to score goals by throwing a ball that emits audible sound when in motion. Players, who may be blind or sighted, are blindfolded during play. **2** the ball used in this game.

goalie ('gəʊlɪ) *n Informal.* short for **goalkeeper.**

goalkeeper ('gəʊlˌkiːpə) *n Sport.* a player in the goal whose duty is to prevent the ball, puck, etc., from entering or crossing it. ▶ **'goalˌkeeping** *n*

goal kick *n Soccer.* a kick taken from the six-yard line by the defending team after the ball has been put out of play by an opposing player.

goal line *n Sport.* the line marking each end of the pitch, on which the goals stand.

goalmouth ('gəʊlˌmaʊθ) *n Soccer, hockey, etc.* the area in front of the goal.

go along *vb* (*intr, adv;* often foll. by *with*) to refrain from disagreement; assent.

goalpost ('gəʊlˌpəʊst) *n* **1** either of two upright posts supporting the crossbar of a goal. **2 move the goalposts.** to change the aims of an activity to ensure the desired results.

goanna (gəʊ'ænə) *n* any of various Australian monitor lizards. [C19: changed from IGUANA]

Goa powder *n* another name for **araroba** (sense 2).

go around *or* **round** *vb* (*intr*) **1** (*adv*) to move about. **2** (*adv;* foll. by *with*) to frequent the society (of a person or group of people): *she went around with* *older men.* **3** (*adv*) to be sufficient: *are there enough sweets to go round?* **4** to circulate (in): *measles is going round the school.* **5** (*prep*) to be actively and constantly engaged in (doing something): *she went around caring for the sick.* **6** to be long enough to encircle: *will that belt go round you?*

goat (gəʊt) *n* **1** any sure-footed agile bovid mammal of the genus *Capra,* naturally inhabiting rough stony ground in Europe, Asia, and N Africa, typically having a brown-grey colouring and a beard. Domesticated varieties (*C. hircus*) are reared for milk, meat, and wool. Related adjs: **caprine, hircine. 2** short for **Rocky Mountain goat. 3** *Informal.* a lecherous man. **4** a bad or inferior member of any group (esp. in the phrase **separate the sheep from the goats**). **5** short for **scapegoat. 6 act** (*or* **play**) **the** (**giddy**) **goat.** to fool around. **7 get** (**someone's**) **goat.** *Slang.* to cause annoyance to (someone). [Old English *gāt;* related to Old Norse *geit,* Old High German *geiz,* Latin *haedus* kid] ▸ **'goat,like** *adj*

Goat (gəʊt) *n* **the.** the constellation Capricorn, the tenth sign of the zodiac.

go at *vb* (*intr, prep*) **1** to make an energetic attempt at (something). **2** to attack vehemently.

goat antelope *n* any bovid mammal of the tribe *Rupicaprini,* including the chamois, goral, serow, and Rocky Mountain goat, having characteristics of both goats and antelopes.

goatee (gəʊ'tiː) *n* a pointed tuftlike beard on the chin. [C19: from GOAT + *-ee* (see -Y[2])] ▸ **goat'eed** *adj*

goatfish ('gəʊt,fɪʃ) *n, pl* **-fish** *or* **-fishes.** the U.S. name for the **red mullet.**

goatherd ('gəʊt,hɜːd) *n* a person employed to tend or herd goats.

goatish ('gəʊtɪʃ) *adj* **1** of, like, or relating to a goat. **2** *Archaic or literary.* lustful or lecherous. ▸ **'goatishly** *adv* ▸ **'goatishness** *n*

goat moth *n* a large European moth, *Cossus cossus,* with pale brownish-grey variably marked wings: family *Cossidae.*

goatsbeard *or* **goat's-beard** ('gəʊts,bɪəd) *n* **1** Also called: **Jack-go-to-bed-at-noon.** a Eurasian plant, *Tragopogon pratensis,* with woolly stems and large heads of yellow rayed flowers surrounded by large green bracts: family *Compositae* (composites). **2** an American rosaceous plant, *Aruncus sylvester,* with long spikes of small white flowers.

goatskin ('gəʊt,skɪn) *n* **1** the hide of a goat. **2a** something made from the hide of a goat, such as leather or a container for wine. **2b** (*as modifier*): *a goatskin rug.*

goat's-rue *n* **1** Also called: **French lilac.** a Eurasian leguminous plant, *Galega officinalis,* cultivated for its white, mauve, or pinkish flowers: formerly used medicinally. **2** a North American leguminous plant, *Tephrosia virginiana,* with pink-and-yellow flowers.

goatsucker ('gəʊt,sʌkə) *n* the U.S. and Canadian name for **nightjar.**

go away *vb* (*intr, adv*) to leave, as when starting from home on holiday.

go-away bird *n S. African.* a common name for a grey-plumaged **lourie** of the genus *Corythaixoides.* [C19: imitative of its call]

gob[1] (gɒb) *n* **1** a lump or chunk, esp. of a soft substance. **2** (*often pl*) *Informal.* a great quantity or amount. **3** *Mining.* **3a** waste material such as clay, shale, etc. **3b** a worked-out area in a mine often packed with this. **4** a lump of molten glass used to make a piece of glassware. **5** *Informal.* a globule of spittle or saliva. ◆ *vb* **gobs, gobbing, gobbed. 6** (*intr*) *Brit. informal.* to spit. [C14: from Old French *gobe* lump, from *gober* to gulp down; see GOBBET]

gob[2] (gɒb) *n U.S. slang.* an enlisted ordinary seaman in the U.S. Navy. [C20: of unknown origin]

gob[3] (gɒb) *n* a slang word (esp. Brit.) for the **mouth.** [C16: perhaps from Gaelic *gob*]

go back *vb* (*intr, adv*) **1** to return. **2** (often foll. by *to*) to originate (in): *the links with France go back to the Norman Conquest.* **3** (foll. by *on*) to change one's mind about; repudiate (esp. in the phrase **go back on one's word**). **4** (of clocks and watches) to be set to an earlier time, as during British Summer Time: *when do the clocks go back this year?*

gobbet ('gɒbɪt) *n* a chunk, lump, or fragment, esp. of raw meat. [C14: from Old French *gobet, from gober* to gulp down]

Gobbi (*Italian* 'gɔbbi) *n* **Tito** ('tiːto). 1915–84, Italian operatic baritone.

gobble[1] ('gɒbᵊl) *vb* **1** (when *tr,* often foll. by *up*) to eat or swallow (food) hastily and in large mouthfuls. **2** (*tr;* often foll. by *up*) *Informal.* to snatch. [C17: probably from GOB[1]]

gobble[2] ('gɒbᵊl) *n* **1** the loud rapid gurgling sound made by male turkeys. ◆ *interj* **2** an imitation of this sound. ◆ *vb* **3** (*intr*) (of a turkey) to make this sound. [C17: probably of imitative origin]

gobbledegook *or* **gobbledygook** ('gɒbᵊldɪ,guːk) *n* pretentious or unintelligible jargon, such as that used by officials. [C20: whimsical formation from GOBBLE[2]]

gobbler ('gɒblə) *n Informal.* a male turkey.

Gobelin ('gəʊbəlɪn; *French* gɔblɛ̃) *adj* **1** of or resembling tapestry made at the Gobelins' factory in Paris, having vivid pictorial scenes. ◆ *n* **2** a tapestry of this kind. [C19: from the *Gobelin* family, who founded the factory]

go-between *n* a person who acts as agent or intermediary for two people or groups in a transaction or dealing.

Gobi ('gəʊbɪ) *n* a desert in E Asia, mostly in Mongolia and the Inner Mongolian Autonomous Region of China: sometimes considered to include all the arid regions east of the Pamirs and north of the plateau of Tibet and the Great Wall of China: one of the largest deserts in the world. Length: about 1600 km (1000 miles). Width: about 1000 km (625 miles). Average height: 900 m (3000 ft.). Chinese name: **Shamo.** ▸ **'Gobian** *adj*

Gobind Singh ('gəʊbɪnd sɪŋ) *or* **Govind Singh** *n* 1666–1708, tenth and last guru of the Sikhs (1675–1708): assassinated.

gobioid ('gəʊbɪ,ɔɪd) *adj* **1** of or relating to the *Gobioidea,* a suborder of spiny-finned teleost fishes that includes gobies and mudskippers (family *Gobiidae*) and sleepers (family *Eleotridae*). ◆ *n* **2** any gobioid fish. [C19: from New Latin *Gobioidea,* from Latin *gōbius* gudgeon]

goblet ('gɒblɪt) *n* **1** a vessel for drinking, usually of glass or metal, with a base and stem but without handles. **2** *Archaic.* a large drinking cup shaped like a bowl. [C14: from Old French *gobelet* a little cup, from *gobel* ultimately of Celtic origin]

goblin ('gɒblɪn) *n* (in folklore) a small grotesque supernatural creature, regarded as malevolent towards human beings. [C14: from Old French, from Middle High German *kobolt;* compare COBALT]

gobo ('gəʊbəʊ) *n, pl* **-bos** *or* **-boes. 1** a shield placed around a microphone to exclude unwanted sounds. **2** a black screen placed around a camera lens, television lens, etc., to reduce the incident light. [C20: of unknown origin]

gobshite ('gɒb,ʃaɪt) *n Taboo slang.* a stupid person. [C20: from GOB[3] + *shite* excrement; see SHIT]

gobsmacked ('gɒb,smækt) *adj Brit. slang.* astounded; astonished. [C20: from GOB[3] + SMACK[2]]

gobstopper ('gɒb,stɒpə) *n Brit.* a large hard sweet consisting of different coloured concentric layers that are revealed as it is sucked.

goby ('gəʊbɪ) *n, pl* **-by** *or* **-bies. 1** any small spiny-finned fish of the family *Gobiidae,* of coastal or brackish waters, having a large head, an elongated tapering body, and the ventral fins modified as a sucker. **2** any other gobioid fish. [C18: from Latin *gōbius* gudgeon, fish of little value, from Greek *kōbios*]

go-by *n Slang.* a deliberate snub or slight (esp. in the phrase **give** (**a person**) **the go-by**).

go by *vb* (*intr*) **1** to pass: *the cars went by; as the years go by we all get older; don't let those opportunities go by!* **2** (*prep*) to be guided by: *in the darkness we could only go by the stars.* **3** (*prep*) to use as a basis for forming an opinion or judgment: *it's wise not to go only by appearances.*

go-cart *n* **1** *Chiefly U.S. and Canadian.* a small wagon for young children to ride in or pull. **2** *Chiefly U.S. and Canadian.* a light frame on casters or wheels that supports a baby while learning to walk. Brit. word: **baby-walker. 3** *Motor racing.* See **kart. 4** another word for **handcart.**

GOC(-in-C) *abbrev. for* General Officer Commanding(-in-Chief).

god (gɒd) *n* **1** a supernatural being, who is worshipped as the controller of some part of the universe or some aspect of life in the world or is the personification of some force. Related adj: **divine. 2** an image, idol, or symbolic representation of such a deity. **3** any person or thing to which excessive attention is given: *money was his god.* **4** a man who has qualities regarded as making him superior to other men. **5** (*in pl*) the gallery of a theatre. [Old English *god;* related to Old Norse *goth,* Old High German *got,* Old Irish *guth* voice]

God (gɒd) *n* **1** *Theol.* the sole Supreme Being, eternal, spiritual, and transcendent, who is the Creator and ruler of all and is infinite in all attributes; the object of worship in monotheistic religions. **2 play God.** to behave in an imperious or superior manner. ◆ *interj* **3** an oath or exclamation used to indicate surprise, annoyance, etc. (and in such expressions as **My God!** or **God Almighty!**).

Godard (*French* gɔdar) *n* **Jean-Luc** (ʒɑ̃lyk). born 1930, French film director and writer. Influenced by surrealism, his early works explored the political and documentary use of film. His works include *À bout de souffle* (1960), *Weekend* (1967), *Pravda* (1969), and *Hélas pour moi* (1993).

Godavari (gəʊ'dɑːvərɪ) *n* a river in central India, rising in the Western Ghats and flowing southeast to the Bay of Bengal: extensive delta, linked by canal with the Krishna delta; a sacred river to Hindus. Length: about 1500 km (900 miles).

godchild ('gɒd,tʃaɪld) *n, pl* **-children** (-,tʃɪldrən). a person, usually an infant, who is sponsored by adults at baptism.

goddamn ('gɒd'dæm) *Informal, chiefly U.S. and Canadian.* ◆ *interj also* **God damn. 1** an oath expressing anger, surprise, etc. ◆ *adv also* **goddam,** *adj also* **goddam** *or* **goddamned. 2** (intensifier): *a goddamn fool.*

Goddard ('gɒdɑːd) *n* **Robert Hutchings.** 1882–1945, U.S. physicist. He made the first workable liquid-fuelled rocket.

goddaughter ('gɒd,dɔːtə) *n* a female godchild.

goddess ('gɒdɪs) *n* **1** a female divinity. **2** a woman who is adored or idealized, esp. by a man. ▸ **'goddess,hood** *or* **'goddess-,ship** *n*

Godefroy de Bouillon (*French* gɔdfrwa də bujɔ̃) *n* ?1060–1100, French leader of the First Crusade (1096–99), becoming first ruler of the Latin kingdom of Jerusalem.

Gödel ('gɜːdᵊl) *n* **Kurt** (kʊrt). 1906–78, U.S. logician and mathematician, born in Austria-Hungary. He showed (**Gödel's proof**) that in a formal axiomatic system, such as logic or mathematics, it is impossible to prove consistency without using methods from outside the system.

Goderich ('gəʊdrɪtʃ) *n* **Viscount,** title of *Frederick John Robinson,* 1st Earl of Ripon. 1782–1859, British statesman; prime minister (1827–28).

Godesberg (*German* 'goːdəsbɛrk) *n* a town and spa in W Germany, in North Rhine-Westphalia on the Rhine: a SE suburb of Bonn. Official name: **Bad Godesberg.**

godet ('gəʊdeɪ, gəʊ'det) *n* a triangular piece of material inserted into a garment, such as into a skirt to create a flare. [C19: from French]

godetia (gə'diːʃə) *n* any plant of the American onagraceous genus *Godetia,* esp. one grown as a showy-flowered annual garden plant. [C19: named after C. H. *Godet* (died 1879), Swiss botanist]

godfather ('gɒd,fɑːðə) *n* **1** a male godparent. **2** the head of a Mafia family or other organized criminal ring. **3** an originator or leading exponent: *the godfather of South African pop.*

godfather offer *n Informal.* a takeover bid pitched so high that the management of the target company is unable to dissuade shareholders from accepting it. [C20: from the 1972 film *The Godfather,* in which a character was made an offer he could not refuse]

God-fearing *adj* pious; devout: *a God-fearing people.*
godforsaken ('gɒdfə,seɪkən, ,gɒdfə'seɪkən) *adj* (*sometimes cap.*) **1** (*usually prenominal*) desolate; dreary; forlorn. **2** wicked.
Godhead ('gɒd,hɛd) *n* (*sometimes not cap.*) **1** the essential nature and condition of being God. **2 the Godhead.** God.
godhood ('gɒd,hʊd) *n* the state of being divine.
Godiva (gə'daɪvə) *n* **Lady.** ?1040–1080, wife of Leofric, Earl of Mercia. According to legend, she rode naked through Coventry in order to obtain remission for the townspeople from the heavy taxes imposed by her husband.
godless ('gɒdlɪs) *adj* **1** wicked or unprincipled. **2** lacking a god. **3** refusing to acknowledge God. ▸ **'godlessly** *adv* ▸ **'godlessness** *n*
godlike ('gɒd,laɪk) *adj* resembling or befitting a god or God; divine.
godly ('gɒdlɪ) *adj* **-lier, -liest.** having a religious character; pious; devout: *a godly man.* ▸ **'godliness** *n*
godmother ('gɒd,mʌðə) *n* a female godparent.
Godolphin (gə'dɒlfɪn) *n* **Sidney.** 1st Earl of Godolphin. 1645–1712, English statesman; as Lord Treasurer, he managed the financing of Marlborough's campaigns in the War of the Spanish Succession.
godown ('gəʊ,daʊn) *n* (in the East, esp. in India and Malaya) a warehouse. **[**C16: from Malay *godong***]**
go down *vb* (*intr, mainly adv*) **1** (*also prep*) to move or lead to or as if to a lower place or level; sink, decline, decrease, etc.: *the ship went down this morning; prices are going down; the path goes down to the sea.* **2** to be defeated; lose. **3** to be remembered or recorded (esp. in the phrase **go down in history**). **4** to be received: *his speech went down well.* **5** (of food) to be swallowed. **6** *Bridge.* to fail to make the number of tricks previously contracted for. **7** *Brit.* to leave a college or university at the end of a term or the academic year. **8** (usually foll. by *with*) to fall ill; be infected. **9** (of a celestial body) to sink or set: *the sun went down before we arrived.* **10** *Brit. slang.* to go to prison, esp. for a specified period: *he went down for six months.* **11** *Slang, chiefly U.S..* to happen.
Godoy (*Spanish* go'ðoɪ) *n* **Manuel de.** 1767–1851, Spanish statesman: Charles IV's unpopular chief minister (1792–97; 1801–08).
godparent ('gɒd,pɛərənt) *n* a person who stands sponsor to another at baptism.
godroon (gə'dru:n) *n* a variant spelling of **gadroon.** ▸ **go'drooned** *adj*
God's acre *n Literary.* a churchyard or burial ground. **[**C17: translation of German *Gottesacker***]**
godsend ('gɒd,sɛnd) *n* a person or thing that comes unexpectedly but is particularly welcome. **[**C19: changed from C17 *God's send,* alteration of *goddes sand* God's message, from Old English *sand;* see SEND[1]**]**
godslot ('gɒd,slɒt) *n Informal.* a time in a television or radio schedule traditionally reserved for religious broadcasts.
godson ('gɒd,sʌn) *n* a male godchild.
Godspeed ('gɒd'spi:d) *interj, n* an expression of one's good wishes for a person's success and safety. **[**C15: from *God spede* may God prosper (you)**]**
godsquad ('gɒd,skwɒd) *n Informal, derogatory.* any group of evangelical Christians, members of which are regarded as intrusive and exuberantly pious.
Godthaab (*Danish* 'gɔdhɔ:b) *n* the former name for **Nuuk.**
Godunov ('gɒdə,nɒf, 'gʊd-; *Russian* gəduˈnɔf) *n* **Boris Fyodorovich** (ba'ris 'fjɔdərəvitʃ). ?1551–1605, Russian regent (1584–98) and tsar (1598–1605).
Godwin ('gɒdwɪn) *n* **1** died 1053, Earl of Wessex. He was chief adviser to Canute and Edward the Confessor. His son succeeded Edward to the throne as Harold II. **2 Mary.** See (Mary) **Wollstonecraft. 3 William.** 1756–1836, British political philospher and novelist. In *An Enquiry concerning Political Justice* (1793), he rejected government and social institutions, including marriage. His views greatly influenced English romantic writers.
Godwin Austen *n* another name for **K2.**
godwit ('gɒdwɪt) *n* any large shore bird of the genus *Limosa,* of northern and arctic regions, having long legs and a long upturned bill: family *Scolopacidae* (sandpipers, etc.), order *Charadriiformes.* **[**C16: of unknown origin**]**
Goebbels (*German* 'gœbəls) *n* **Paul Joseph** (paul 'jo:zɛf). 1897–1945, German Nazi politician; minister of propaganda (1933–45).
goer ('gəʊə) *n* **1a** a person who attends something regularly. **1b** (*in combination*): *filmgoer.* **2** an energetic person. **3** *Informal.* an acceptable or feasible idea, proposal, etc. **4** *Austral. and N.Z. informal.* a person trying to succeed.
Goering (*German* 'gø:rɪŋ) *n* See (Hermann Wilhelm) **Göring.**
Goes (gu:s) *n* **Hugo van der.** ?1440–82, Flemish painter: works include the *Pontinari Altarpiece* and *The Death of a Virgin.*
Goethe (*German* 'gø:tə) *n* **Johann Wolfgang von** (jo'han 'vɔlfgaŋ fɔn). 1749–1832, German poet, novelist, and dramatist, who settled in Weimar in 1775. His early works of the *Sturm und Drang* period include the play *Götz von Berlichingen* (1773) and the novel *The Sorrows of Young Werther* (1774). After a journey to Italy (1786–88) his writings, such as the epic play *Iphigenie auf Tauris* (1787) and the epic idyll *Hermann und Dorothea* (1797), showed the influence of classicism. Other works include the *Wilhelm Meister* novels (1796–1829) and his greatest masterpiece *Faust* (1808; 1832).
goethite *or* **göthite** ('gəʊθaɪt; *German* 'gø:ti:t) *n* a black, brown, or yellow mineral consisting of hydrated iron oxide in the form of orthorhombic crystals or fibrous masses. Formula: FeO(OH). **[**C19: named after GOETHE**]**
go-faster stripe *n Informal.* a decorative line, often suggestive of high speed, on the bodywork of a car.
gofer ('gəʊfə) *n Slang, chiefly U.S. and Canadian.* an employee or assistant whose duties include menial tasks such as running errands. **[**C20: originally U.S.: alteration of *go for***]**
goffer *or* **gauffer** ('gəʊfə) *vb* **1** (*tr*) to press pleats into (a frill). **2** (*tr*) to decorate (the gilt edges of a book) with a repeating pattern. ◆ *n* **3** an ornamental frill made by pressing pleats. **4** the decoration formed by goffering books. **5** the iron or tool used in making goffers. **[**C18: from French *gaufrer* to impress a pattern, from *gaufre,* from Middle Low German *wāfel;* see WAFFLE[1], WAFER**]**
go for *vb* (*intr, prep*) **1** to go somewhere in order to have or fetch: *he went for a drink; shall I go for a doctor?* **2** to seek to obtain: *I'd go for that job if I were you.* **3** to apply to: *what I told him goes for you too.* **4** to prefer or choose; like: *I really go for that new idea of yours.* **5** to be to the advantage of: *you'll have great things going for you in the New Year.* **6** to make a physical or verbal attack on. **7** to be considered to be of a stated importance or value: *his twenty years went for nothing when he was made redundant.* **8 go for it.** *Informal.* to make the maximum effort to achieve a particular goal.
go forth *vb* (*intr, adv*) *Archaic or formal.* **1** to be issued: *the command went forth that taxes should be collected.* **2** to go out: *the army went forth to battle.*
Gog and Magog (gɒg; 'meɪgɒg) *n* **1** *Old Testament.* a hostile prince and the land from which he comes to attack Israel (Ezekiel 38). **2** *New Testament.* two kings, who are to attack the Church in a climactic battle, but are then to be destroyed by God (Revelation 20:8–10). **3** *British folklore.* two giants, the only survivors of a race of giants destroyed by Brutus, the legendary founder of Britain.
go-getter *n Informal.* an ambitious enterprising person. ▸ **'go-,getting** *adj*
gogga ('xɒxə) *n S. African informal.* any small animal that crawls or flies, esp. an insect. **[**C20: from Khoikhoi *xoxon* insects collectively**]**
goggle ('gɒgᵊl) *vb* **1** (*intr*) to stare stupidly or fixedly, as in astonishment. **2** to cause (the eyes) to roll or bulge or (of the eyes) to roll or bulge. ◆ *n* **3** a fixed or bulging stare. **4** (*pl*) spectacles, often of coloured glass or covered with gauze: used to protect the eyes. **[**C14: from *gogelen* to look aside, of uncertain origin; see AGOG**]** ▸ **'goggly** *adj*
gogglebox ('gɒgᵊl,bɒks) *n Brit. slang.* a television set.
goggle-eyed *adj* (*often postpositive*) with a surprised, staring, or fixed expression.
Gogh (gɒx; *Dutch* xɔx) *n* See (Vincent) **van Gogh.**
goglet ('gɒglɪt) *or* **gurglet** *n* a long-necked water-cooling vessel of porous earthenware, used esp. in India. Also called: **guglet** ('gʌglɪt). **[**C17: from Portuguese *gorgoleta* a little throat, from *gorja* throat; related to French *gargoule;* see GARGLE**]**
go-go *adj Informal, chiefly U.S. and Canadian.* **1** of or relating to discos or the lively music and dancing performed in them. **2** dynamic or forceful. **[**C20: altered from French *à-gogo* aplenty, ad lib: sense influenced by English verb *go***]**
go-go dancer *n* a dancer, usually scantily dressed, who performs rhythmic and often erotic modern dance routines, esp. in a nightclub or disco.
Gogol ('gəʊgɒl; *Russian* 'gɔgəlj) *n* **Nikolai Vasilievich** (nika'laj va'siljɪvitʃ). 1809–52, Russian novelist, dramatist, and short-story writer. His best-known works are *The Government Inspector* (1836), a comedy satirizing bureaucracy, and the novel *Dead Souls* (1842).
Gogra ('gɒgrə) *n* a river in N India, rising in Tibet, in the Himalayas, and flowing southeast through Nepal as the Karnali, then through Uttar Pradesh to join the Ganges. Length: about 1000 km (600 miles).
Goiânia (gɔɪ'ɑ:nɪə; *Portuguese* go'jənja) *n* a city in central Brazil, capital of Goiás state: planned in 1933 to replace the old capital, Goiás; two universities. Pop.: 1 033 000 (1995).
Goiás (*Portuguese* gɔ'jas) *n* a state of central Brazil, in the Brazilian Highlands: contains Brasília, the capital of Brazil. Capital: Goiânia. Pop.: 4 308 400 (1995 est.). Area: 341 289 sq. km (131 772 sq. miles).
Goidel ('gɔɪdᵊl) *n* a Celt who speaks a Goidelic language; Gael. Compare **Brython.**
Goidelic, Goidhelic (gɔɪ'dɛlɪk), *or* **Gadhelic** *n* **1** the N group of Celtic languages, consisting of Irish Gaelic, Scottish Gaelic, and Manx. Compare **Brythonic.** ◆ *adj* **2** of, relating to, or characteristic of this group of languages. **[**C19: from Old Irish *Goidel* a Celt, from Old Welsh *gwyddel,* from *gwydd* savage**]**
go in *vb* (*intr, mainly adv*) **1** to enter. **2** (*prep*) See **go into. 3** (of the sun) to become hidden behind a cloud. **4** to be assimilated or grasped: *nothing much goes in if I try to read in the evenings.* **5** *Cricket.* to begin an innings. **6 go in for. 6a** to enter as a competitor or contestant. **6b** to adopt as an activity, interest, or guiding principle: *she went in for nursing; some men go in for football in a big way.*
going ('gəʊɪŋ) *n* **1** a departure or farewell. **2** the condition of a surface such as a road or field with regard to walking, riding, etc.: *muddy going.* **3** *Informal.* speed, progress, etc.: *we made good going on the trip.* ◆ *adj* **4** thriving (esp. in the phrase **a going concern**). **5** current or accepted, as from past negotiations or commercial operation: *the going rate for electricians; the going value of the firm.* **6** (*postpositive*) available: *the best going.* **7 going, going, gone!** a statement by an auctioneer that the bidding has almost finished.
going-over *n, pl* **goings-over.** *Informal.* **1** a check, examination, or investigation. **2** a castigation or thrashing.
goings-on *pl n Informal.* **1** actions or conduct, esp. when regarded with disapproval. **2** happenings or events, esp. when mysterious or suspicious: *there were strange goings-on up at the Hall.*
go into *vb* (*intr, prep*) **1** to enter. **2** to start a career in: *to go into publishing.* **3** to investigate or examine: *to go into the problem of price increases.* **4** to discuss: *we won't go into that now.* **5** to dress oneself differently in: *to go into mourning.* **6** to hit: *the car had gone into a lamppost.* **7** to go to live in or be admitted to, esp. temporarily: *she went into hospital on Tuesday.* **8** to enter a specified state: *she went into fits of laughter.*
goitre *or U.S.* **goiter** ('gɔɪtə) *n Pathol.* a swelling of the thyroid gland, in some cases nearly doubling the size of the neck, usually caused by under- or overproduction of hormone by the gland. **[**C17: from French *goitre,* from Old French *goitron* ultimately from Latin *guttur* throat**]** ▸ **'goitred** *or U.S.* **'goitered** *adj* ▸ **'goitrous** *adj*
go-kart *or* **go-cart** *n* See **kart.**

Golan Heights ('gəʊ,læn) *pl n* a range of hills in the Middle East, possession of which is disputed between Israel and Syria: under Syrian control until 1967 when they were stormed by Israeli forces; Jewish settlements have since been established. Highest peak: 2224 m (7297 ft.).

Golconda (gɒl'kɒndə) *n* **1** a ruined town and fortress in S central India, in W Andhra Pradesh near Hyderabad city: capital of one of the five Muslim kingdoms of the Deccan from 1512 to 1687, then annexed to the Mogul empire; renowned for its diamonds. **2** (*sometimes not cap.*) a source of wealth or riches, esp. a mine.

gold (gəʊld) *n* **1a** a dense inert bright yellow element that is the most malleable and ductile metal, occurring in rocks and alluvial deposits: used as a monetary standard and in jewellery, dentistry, and plating. The radioisotope gold-198 (**radiogold**), with a half-life of 2.69 days, is used in radiotherapy. Symbol: Au; atomic no.: 79; atomic wt.: 196.96654; valency: 1 or 3; relative density: 19.3; melting pt.: 1064.43°C; boiling pt.: 2857°C. Related adjs: **aurous, auric. 1b** (*as modifier*): *a gold mine.* **2** a coin or coins made of this metal. **3** money; wealth. **4** something precious, beautiful, etc., such as a noble nature (esp. in the phrase **heart of gold**). **5a** a deep yellow colour, sometimes with a brownish tinge. **5b** (*as adj*): *a gold carpet.* **6** *Archery.* the bull's eye of a target, scoring nine points. **7** short for **gold medal. [**Old English *gold;* related to Old Norse *gull,* Gothic *gulth,* Old High German *gold***]**

Gold (gəʊld) *n* **Thomas.** born 1920, Austrian-born astronomer, working in England and the U.S.: with Bondi and Hoyle he proposed the steady-state theory of the universe.

goldarn (gɒl'dɑ:n) *interj, adv U.S. and Canadian slang.* a euphemistic variant of **goddamn.**

Goldbach's conjecture ('gəʊld,bɑ:xs) *n* the hypothesis that every even number greater than two is the sum of two prime numbers. **[**named after C. *Goldbach* (1690–1764), German mathematician**]**

gold basis *n* the gold standard as a criterion for the determination of prices.

goldbeater's skin ('gəʊld,bi:təz) *n* animal membrane used to separate sheets of gold that are being hammered into gold leaf.

gold-beating *n* the act, process, or skill of hammering sheets of gold into gold leaf. ► **'gold-,beater** *n*

gold beetle *or* **goldbug** ('gəʊld,bʌg) *n* any American beetle of the family *Chrysomelidae* having a bright metallic lustre.

gold brick *n* **1** something with only a superficial appearance of value. **2** *U.S. slang.* an idler or shirker.

gold card *n* a credit card issued by credit-card companies to favoured clients, entitling them to high unsecured overdrafts, some insurance cover, etc.

gold certificate *n* (in the U.S.) **1** a currency note issued exclusively to the Federal Reserve Banks by the U.S. Treasury. It forms a claim on gold reserves deposited by the Federal Reserve Banks at the Treasury and is used to transfer interbank balances within the Federal Reserve System. **2** Also called: **gold note.** (formerly) a banknote issued by the U.S. Treasury to the public and redeemable in gold.

Gold Coast *n* **1** the former name (until 1957) of **Ghana. 2** a line of resort towns and beaches in E Australia, extending for over 30 km (20 miles) along the SE coast of Queensland and the NE coast of New South Wales.

goldcrest ('gəʊld,krest) *n* a small Old World warbler, *Regulus regulus,* having a greenish plumage and a bright yellow-and-black crown.

gold-digger *n* **1** a person who prospects or digs for gold. **2** *Informal.* a woman who uses her sexual attractions to accumulate gifts and wealth or advance her social position. ► **'gold-,digging** *n*

gold disc *n* **a** (in Britain) an LP record certified to have sold 250 000 copies or a single certified to have sold 500 000 copies. **b** (in the U.S.) an LP record certified to have sold 1 000 000 copies or a single certified to have sold 500 000 copies. Compare **silver disc, platinum disc.**

gold dust *n* **1** gold in the form of small particles or powder, as found in placer-mining. **2** a valuable or rare thing: *tickets for this match are gold dust.*

golden ('gəʊldən) *adj* **1** of the yellowish or brownish-yellow metallic colour of gold: *golden hair.* **2** made from or largely consisting of gold: *a golden statue.* **3** happy or prosperous: *golden days.* **4** (*sometimes cap.*) (of anniversaries) the 50th in a series: *Golden Jubilee; golden wedding.* **5** *Informal.* very successful or destined for success: *the golden girl of tennis.* **6** extremely valuable or advantageous: *a golden opportunity.* ► **'goldenly** *adv* ► **'goldenness** *n*

golden age *n* **1** *Classical myth.* the first and best age of mankind, when existence was happy, prosperous, and innocent. **2** the most flourishing and outstanding period, esp. in the history of an art or nation: *the golden age of poetry.* **3** the great classical period of Latin literature, occupying approximately the 1st century B.C. and represented by such writers as Cicero and Virgil.

golden aster *n* any North American plant of the genus *Chrysopsis,* esp. *C. mariana* of the eastern U.S., having yellow rayed flowers: family *Compositae* (composites).

golden calf *n* **1** *Old Testament.* **1a** an idol made by Aaron and set up for the Israelites to worship (Exodus 32). **1b** either of two similar idols set up by Jeroboam I at Dan and Bethel in the northern kingdom (I Kings 12:28–30). **2** *Informal.* the pursuit or idolization of material wealth.

golden chain *n* another name for **laburnum.**

Golden Delicious *n* a variety of eating apple having sweet flesh and greenish-yellow skin.

golden eagle *n* a large eagle, *Aquila chrysaetos,* of mountainous regions of the N hemisphere, having a plumage that is golden brown on the back and brown elsewhere.

goldeneye ('gəʊldən,aɪ) *n, pl* **-eyes** *or* **-eye. 1** either of two black-and-white diving ducks, *Bucephala clangula* or *B. islandica,* of northern regions. **2** any lacewing of the family *Chrysopidae* that has a greenish body and eyes of a metallic lustre.

Golden Fleece *n Greek myth.* the fleece of a winged ram that rescued Phrixus and brought him to Colchis, where he sacrificed it to Zeus. Phrixus gave the fleece to King Aeëtes who kept it in a sacred grove, whence Jason and the Argonauts stole it with the help of Aeëtes' daughter. See also **Phrixus.**

Golden Gate *n* a strait between the Pacific and San Francisco Bay: crossed by the **Golden Gate Bridge,** with a central span of 1280 m (4200 ft.).

golden goose *n* a goose in folklore that laid a golden egg a day until its greedy owner killed it in an attempt to get all the gold at once.

golden handcuffs *pl n Informal.* payments deferred over a number of years that induce a person to stay with a particular company or in a particular job.

golden handshake *n Informal.* a sum of money, usually large, given to an employee, either on retirement in recognition of long or excellent service or as compensation for loss of employment.

golden hello *n Informal.* a payment made to a sought-after recruit on signing a contract of employment with a company.

Golden Horde *n* the Mongol horde that devastated E Europe in the early 13th century. It established the westernmost Mongol khanate, which at its height ruled most of European Russia. Defeated by the power of Muscovy (1380), the realm split into four smaller khanates in 1405.

Golden Horn *n* an inlet of the Bosporus in NW Turkey, forming the harbour of Istanbul. Turkish name: **Haliç.**

golden hour *n* the first hour after a serious accident, when it is crucial that the victim receives medical treatment in order to have a chance of surviving.

golden mean *n* **1** the middle course between extremes. **2** another term for **golden section.**

golden number *n* a number between 1 and 19, used to indicate the position of any year in the Metonic cycle, calculated as the remainder when 1 is added to the given year and the sum is divided by 19. If the remainder is zero the number is 19: *the golden number of 1984 is 9.*

golden oldie *n* something old or long-established, esp. a hit record or song that has remained popular or is enjoying a revival. Also called: **oldie.**

golden oriole *n* a European oriole, *Oriolus oriolus,* the male of which has a bright yellow head and body with black wings and tail.

golden parachute *n Informal.* a clause in the employment contract of a senior executive providing for special benefits if the executive's employment is terminated as a result of a takeover.

golden perch *n* another name for **callop.**

golden pheasant *n* a brightly coloured pheasant, *Chrysolophus pictus,* of the mountainous regions of W and central Asia, the males of which have a crest and ruff.

golden plover *n* any of several plovers of the genus *Pluvialis,* such as *P. apricaria* of Europe and Asia, that have golden brown back, head, and wings.

golden ratio *n* the ratio of two lengths, equal in value to 1.618 033 988..., and given by $b/a = (b + a)/b$; it is the reciprocal of the **golden section** and also equal to (1 + golden section). Symbol: Φ

golden retriever *n* a compact medium-sized breed of dog having a silky coat of flat or wavy hair of a gold or dark-cream colour, well-feathered on the legs and tail.

goldenrod (,gəʊldən'rɒd) *n* **1** any plant of the genus *Solidago,* of North America, Europe, and Asia, having spikes of small yellow flowers: family *Compositae* (composites). See also **yellowweed. 2** any of various similar related plants, such as *Brachychaeta sphacelata* (**false goldenrod**) of the southern U.S.

golden rule *n* **1** any of a number of rules of fair conduct, such as *Whatsoever ye would that men should do to you, do ye even so to them* (Matthew 7:12) or *thou shalt love thy neighbour as thyself* (Leviticus 19:28). **2** any important principle: *a golden rule of sailing is to wear a life jacket.* **3** another name for **rule of three.**

goldenseal (,gəʊldən'si:l) *n* a ranunculaceous woodland plant, *Hydrastis canadensis,* of E North America, whose thick yellow rootstock contains such alkaloids as berberine and hydrastine and was formerly used medicinally.

golden section *or* **mean** *n* the proportion of the two divisions of a straight line or the two dimensions of a plane figure such that the smaller is to the larger as the larger is to the sum of the two. If the sides of a rectangle are in this proportion and a square is constructed internally on the shorter side, the rectangle that remains will also have sides in the same proportion. Compare: **golden ratio.**

golden share *n* a share in a company that controls at least 51% of the voting rights, esp. one retained by the UK government in some privatization issues.

Golden Starfish *n* an award given to a bathing beach that meets EU standards of cleanliness.

golden syrup *n Brit.* a light golden-coloured treacle produced by the evaporation of cane sugar juice, used to sweeten and flavour cakes, puddings, etc.

golden triangle *n* **the.** an opium-producing area of SE Asia, comprising parts of Myanmar, Laos, and Thailand.

golden wattle *n* **1** an Australian yellow-flowered mimosaceous plant, *Acacia pycnantha,* that yields a useful gum and bark. **2** any of several similar and related plants, esp. *Acacia longifolia* of Australia.

gold-exchange standard *n* a monetary system by which one country's currency, which is not itself based on the gold standard, is kept at a par with another currency that is based on the gold standard.

goldeye ('gəʊld,aɪ) *n, pl* **-eyes** *or* **-eye.** a North American clupeoid fish, *Hiodon alosoides,* with yellowish eyes, silvery sides, and a dark blue back: family *Hiodontidae* (mooneyes).

goldfinch ('gəʊld,fɪntʃ) *n* **1** a common European finch, *Carduelis carduelis,* the adult of which has a red-and-white face and yellow-and-black wings. **2** any of several North American finches of the genus *Spinus,* esp. the yellow-and-black species *S. tristis.*

goldfinny ('gəʊld,fɪnɪ) *n, pl* **-nies.** another name for **goldsinny.**

goldfish ('gəʊld,fɪʃ) *n, pl* **-fish** *or* **-fishes. 1** a freshwater cyprinid fish, *Carassius auratus,* of E Europe and Asia, esp. China, widely introduced as a pond or aquarium fish. It resembles the carp and has a typically golden or orange-red coloration. **2** any of certain similar ornamental fishes, esp. the golden orfe (see **orfe**).

goldfish bowl *n* **1** Also called: **fishbowl.** a glass bowl, typically spherical, in which fish are kept as pets. **2** a place or situation open to observation by onlookers.

gold foil *n* thin gold sheet that is thicker than gold leaf.

goldilocks ('gəʊldɪ,lɒks) *n (functioning as sing)* **1** a Eurasian plant, *Aster linosyris* (or *Linosyris vulgaris*), with clusters of small yellow flowers: family *Compositae* (composites). **2** a Eurasian ranunculaceous woodland plant, *Ranunculus auricomus,* with yellow flowers. See also **buttercup. 3** (*sometimes cap.*) a person, esp. a girl, with light blond hair.

Golding ('gəʊldɪŋ) *n* Sir **William** (**Gerald**). 1911–93, English novelist noted for his allegories of man's proclivity for evil. His novels include *Lord of the Flies* (1954), *Darkness Visible* (1979), *Rites of Passage* (1980), *Close Quarters* (1987), and *Fire Down Below* (1989). Nobel prize for literature 1983.

gold leaf *n* very thin gold sheet with a thickness between about 0.076 and 0.127 micrometre, produced by rolling or hammering gold and used for gilding woodwork, etc.

gold medal *n* a medal of gold, awarded to the winner of a competition or race. Compare **silver medal, bronze medal.**

gold mine *n* **1** a place where gold ore is mined. **2** a source of great wealth, profit, etc. ▸ **'gold-,miner** *n* ▸ **'gold-,mining** *n*

gold note *n* (in the U.S.) another name for **gold certificate.**

gold-of-pleasure *n* a yellow-flowered Eurasian cruciferous plant, *Camelina sativa,* widespread as a weed, esp. in flax fields: formerly cultivated for its oil-rich seeds.

Goldoni (*Italian* gol'do:ni) *n* **Carlo** ('karlo). 1707–93, Italian dramatist; author of over 250 plays in Italian or French, including *La Locandiera* (1753). His work introduced realistic Italian comedy, superseding the commedia dell'arte.

gold-plate *vb (tr)* to coat (other metal) with gold, usually by electroplating.

gold plate *n* **1** a thin coating of gold, usually produced by electroplating. **2** vessels or utensils made of gold.

gold point *n Finance.* either of two exchange rates (the **gold export point** and the **gold import point**) at which it is as cheap to settle international accounts by exporting or importing gold bullion as by selling or buying bills of exchange. Also called: **specie point.**

gold record *n* a former name for **gold disc.**

gold reserve *n* the gold reserved by a central bank to support domestic credit expansion, to cover balance of payments deficits, and to protect currency.

gold rush *n* a large-scale migration of people to a territory where gold has been found.

Goldschmidt ('gəʊld,ʃmɪt) *n* **Richard Benedikt.** 1878–1958, U.S. geneticist, born in Germany. He advanced the theory that heredity is determined by the chemical configuration of the chromosome molecule rather than by the qualities of the individual genes.

goldsinny ('gəʊld,sɪnɪ) *n, pl* **-nies.** any of various small European wrasses, esp. the brightly coloured *Ctenolabrus rupestris.* Also called: **goldfinny.** [origin obscure, but probably has reference to the colour of the fins and tail]

goldsmith ('gəʊld,smɪθ) *n* **1a** a dealer in articles made of gold. **1b** an artisan who makes such articles. **2** (formerly) a dealer or manufacturer of gold articles who also engaged in banking or other financial business. **3** (in Malaysia) a Chinese jeweller.

Goldsmith ('gəʊld,smɪθ) *n* **Oliver.** ?1730–74, Irish poet, dramatist, and novelist. His works include the novel *The Vicar of Wakefield* (1766), the poem *The Deserted Village* (1770), and the comedy *She Stoops to Conquer* (1773).

goldsmith beetle *n* any of various scarabaeid beetles that have a metallic golden lustre, esp. the rose chafer.

gold standard *n* a monetary system in which the unit of currency is defined with reference to gold.

Gold Stick *n* (*sometimes not caps.*) **1** a gilt rod carried by the colonel of the Life Guards or the captain of the gentlemen-at-arms. **2** the bearer of this rod.

goldstone ('gəʊld,stəʊn) *n* another name for **aventurine** (senses 2, 3).

goldtail moth ('gəʊld,teɪl) *n* a European moth, *Euproctis chrysorrhoea* (or *similis*), having white wings and a soft white furry body with a yellow tail tuft: its hairy caterpillars are known as palmer worms: family *Lymantriidae.* Also called: **yellowtail, yellowtail moth.**

goldthread ('gəʊld,θrɛd) *n* **1** a North American woodland ranunculaceous plant, *Coptis trifolia* (or *C. groenlandica*), with slender yellow roots. **2** the root of this plant, which yields a medicinal tonic and a dye.

gold tranche *n* former name for **reserve tranche.**

golem ('gəʊlɛm) *n* (in Jewish legend) an artificially created human being brought to life by supernatural means. [from Yiddish *goylem,* from Hebrew *gōlem* formless thing]

golf (gɒlf) *n* **1a** a game played on a large open course, the object of which is to hit a ball using clubs, with as few strokes as possible, into each of usually 18 holes. **1b** (*as modifier*): *a golf bag.* ◆ *vb* **2** (*intr*) to play golf. [C15: perhaps from Middle Dutch *colf* CLUB]

Golf (gɒlf) *n Communications.* a code word for the letter *g.*

golf ball *n* **1** a small resilient, usually white, ball of either two-piece or three-piece construction, the former consisting of a solid inner core with a thick covering of toughened material, the latter consisting of a liquid centre, rubber-wound core, and a thin layer of balata. **2** (in some electric typewriters) a small detachable metal sphere, around the surface of which type characters are arranged.

golf cart *n* **1** a small motorized vehicle for transporting golfers and their equipment round a golf course. **2** a two-wheeled trolley with a long handle used for carrying golf clubs.

golf club *n* **1** any of various long-shafted clubs with wood or metal heads used to strike a golf ball. **2a** an association of golf players, usually having its own course and facilities. **2b** the premises of such an association.

golf course *n* a general term for an area of ground, either inland or beside the sea, laid out for the playing of golf.

golfer ('gɒlfə) *n* **1** a person who plays golf. **2** a type of cardigan.

golf links *pl n* a large open undulating stretch of land beside the sea laid out for the playing of golf. See also **links.**

Golgi (*Italian* 'gɔldʒi) *n* **Camillo** (ka'millo). 1844–1926, Italian neurologist and histologist, noted for his work on the central nervous system and his discovery in animal cells of the bodies known by his name: shared the Nobel prize for physiology or medicine 1906.

Golgi body, apparatus, *or* **complex** *n* a membranous complex of vesicles, vacuoles, and flattened sacs in the cytoplasm of most cells: involved in intracellular secretion and transport. [C20: named after C. GOLGI]

Golgotha ('gɒlgəθə) *n* **1** another name for **Calvary. 2** (*sometimes not cap.*) *Now rare.* a place of burial. [C17: from Late Latin, from Greek, from Aramaic, based on Hebrew *gulgōleth* skull]

goliard ('gəʊljəd) *n* one of a number of wandering scholars in 12th- and 13th-century Europe famed for their riotous behaviour, intemperance, and composition of satirical and ribald Latin verse. [C15: from Old French *goliart* glutton, from Latin *gula* gluttony] ▸ **goliardic** (gəʊl'jɑ:dɪk) *adj*

goliardery (gəʊl'jɑ:dərɪ) *n* the poems of the goliards.

Goliath (gə'laɪəθ) *n Old Testament.* a Philistine giant from Gath who terrorized the Hebrews until he was killed by David with a stone from his sling (I Samuel 17).

goliath beetle *n* any very large tropical scarabaeid beetle of the genus *Goliathus,* esp. *G. giganteus* of Africa, which may grow to a length of 20 centimetres.

goliath frog *n* the largest living frog, *Rana goliath,* which occurs in the Congo region of Africa and can grow to a length of 30 centimetres.

golliwog *or* **golliwogg** ('gɒlɪ,wɒg) *n* a soft doll with a black face, usually made of cloth or rags. [C19: from the name of a doll character in children's books by Bertha Upton (died 1912), U.S. writer, and Florence Upton (died 1922), U.S. illustrator]

gollop ('gɒləp) *vb* to eat or drink (something) quickly or greedily. [dialect variant of GULP] ▸ **'golloper** *n*

golly[1] ('gɒlɪ) *interj* an exclamation of mild surprise or wonder. [C19: originally a euphemism for GOD]

golly[2] ('gɒlɪ) *n, pl* **-lies.** *Brit. informal.* short for **golliwog:** used chiefly by children.

golly[3] ('gɒlɪ) *Austral. slang.* ◆ *vb* **-lies, -lying, -lied. 1** to spit. ◆ *n, pl* **-lies. 2** a gob of spit. [C20: altered from *gollion* a gob of phlegm, probably of imitative origin]

goloshes (gə'lɒʃɪz) *pl n* a less common spelling of **galoshes.**

GOM *abbrev. for* Grand Old Man: used to describe an old and respected person or institution.

gombeenism ('gɒmbi:nɪzəm) *n Irish.* the practice of usury. [C19: from Irish Gaelic *gaimbín* interest on a loan, from Middle English *cambie* exchange, barter, from Latin *cambium*]

gombeen-man ('gɒmbi:n,mæn) *n Irish.* a shopkeeper who practises usury.

Gomberg ('gɒmbɜ:g) *n* **Moses.** 1866–1947, U.S. chemist, born in Russia, noted for his work on free radicals.

gombroon (gɒm'bru:n) *n* Persian and Chinese pottery and porcelain wares. [C17: named after *Gombroon,* Iran, from which it was originally exported]

Gomel (*Russian* 'gɔmɪlj) *n* an industrial city in SE Belarus, on the River Sozh; an industrial centre. Pop.: 512 000 (1996 est.).

gomeril ('gɒmərɪl) *n Scot.* a slow-witted or stupid person. [C19: of uncertain origin]

Gomorrah *or* **Gomorrha** (gə'mɒrə) *n* **1** *Old Testament.* one of two ancient cities near the Dead Sea, the other being Sodom, that were destroyed by God as a punishment for the wickedness of their inhabitants (Genesis 19:24). **2** any place notorious for vice and depravity. ▸ **Go'morrean** *or* **Go'morrhean** *adj*

Gompers ('gɒmpəz) *n* **Samuel.** 1850–1924, U.S. labour leader, born in England; a founder of the American Federation of Labor and its president (1886–94; 1896–1924).

gomphosis (gɒm'fəʊsɪs) *n, pl* **-ses** (-si:z). *Anatomy.* a form of immovable articulation in which a peglike part fits into a cavity, as in the setting of a tooth in its socket. [C16: from New Latin, from Greek *gomphoein* to bolt together, from *gomphos* tooth, peg]

Gomulka (gə'mʊlkə) *n* **Władysław** (vwa'diswaf). 1905–82, Polish statesman; first secretary of the Polish Communist Party (1956–70).

gomuti *or* **gomuti palm** (gə'mu:tɪ) *n, pl* **gomutis** *or* **gomuti palms. 1** an East Indian feather palm, *Arenga pinnata,* whose sweet sap is a source of sugar. **2** a black wiry fibre obtained from the leafstalks of this plant, used for making rope, etc. **3** a Malaysian sago palm, *Metroxylon sagu.* [from Malay *gĕmuti*]

gon- *combining form.* a variant of **gono-** before a vowel: *gonidium.*

-gon *n combining form.* indicating a figure having a specified number of angles: *pentagon.* [from Greek *-gōnon,* from *gōnia* angle]

gonad ('gɒnæd) *n* an animal organ in which gametes are produced, such as a testis or an ovary. [C19: from New Latin *gonas,* from Greek *gonos* seed] ▸ **'gonadal, gonadial** (gɒ'neɪdɪəl), *or* **go'nadic** *adj*

gonadotrophin (,gɒnədəʊ'trəʊfɪn) *or* **gonadotropin** (,gɒnədəʊ'trəʊpɪn) *n* any of several glycoprotein hormones secreted by the pituitary gland and placenta that stimulate the gonads and control reproductive activity. See **chorionic gonadotrophin, follicle-stimulating hormone, luteinizing hormone, prolactin.** ▸ **,gonado'trophic** *or* **,gonado'tropic** *adj*

Gonaïves (*French* gɔnaiv) *n* a port in W Haiti, on the **Gulf of Gonaïves;** scene of the proclamation of Haiti's independence (1804). Pop.: 63 291 (1992).

Goncharov (ˌgʌntʃəˈrɒf) *n* **Ivan Aleksandrovich** (ɪˈvan alɛksanˈdrɒvɪtʃ). 1812–91, Russian novelist: his best-known work is *Oblomov* (1859).

Goncourt (*French* gɔ̃kur) *n* **Edmond Louis Antoine Huot de** (ɛdmɔ̃ lwi ɑ̃twan yo də), 1822–96, and his brother, **Jules Alfred Huot de** (ʒyl alfrɛd), 1830–70, French writers, noted for their collaboration, esp. on their *Journal,* and for the Académie Goncourt founded by Edmond's will.

Gond (gɒnd) *n* a member of a formerly tribal people now living in scattered enclaves throughout S central India.

Gondar (ˈgɒndɑː) *n* a city in NW Ethiopia: capital of Ethiopia from the 17th century until 1868. Pop.: 166 593 (1994 est.).

Gondi (ˈgɒndɪ) *n* the language or group of languages spoken by the Gonds, belonging to the Dravidian family of languages.

gondola (ˈgɒndələ) *n* **1** a long narrow flat-bottomed boat with a high ornamented stem and a platform at the stern where an oarsman stands and propels the boat by sculling or punting: traditionally used on the canals of Venice. **2a** a car or cabin suspended from an airship or balloon. **2b** a moving cabin suspended from a cable across a valley, etc. **3** a flat-bottomed barge used on canals and rivers of the U.S. as far west as the Mississippi. **4** *U.S. and Canadian.* a low open flat-bottomed railway goods wagon. **5** a set of island shelves in a self-service shop: used for displaying goods. **6** *Canadian.* a broadcasting booth built close to the roof over an ice-hockey arena, used by commentators. [**C16**: from Italian (Venetian dialect), from Medieval Latin *gondula,* perhaps ultimately from Greek *kondu* drinking vessel]

gondolier (ˌgɒndəˈlɪə) *n* a man who propels a gondola.

Gondwanaland (gɒndˈwɑːnəˌlænd) *or* **Gondwana** *n* one of the two ancient supercontinents produced by the first split of the even larger supercontinent Pangaea about 200 million years ago, comprising chiefly what are now Africa, South America, Australia, Antarctica, and the Indian subcontinent. [**C19**: from *Gondwana* region in central north India, where the rock series was originally found]

gone (gɒn) *vb* **1** the past participle of **go**[1]. ◆ *adj* (*usually postpositive*) **2** ended; past. **3** lost; ruined (esp. in the phrases **gone goose** *or* **gosling**). **4** dead or near to death. **5** spent; consumed; used up. **6** *Informal.* faint or weak. **7** *Informal.* having been pregnant (for a specified time): *six months gone.* **8** (usually foll. by *on*) *Slang.* in love (with). **9** *Slang.* in an exhilarated state, as through music or the use of drugs. **10 gone out.** *Informal.* blankly and without comprehension, as if stupefied in surprise. ◆ *adv* **11** past: *it's gone midnight.*

goner (ˈgɒnə) *n Slang.* a person or thing beyond help or recovery, esp. a person who is dead or about to die.

gonfalon (ˈgɒnfələn) *or* **gonfanon** (ˈgɒnfənən) *n* **1** a banner hanging from a crossbar, used esp. by certain medieval Italian republics or in ecclesiastical processions. **2** a battle flag suspended crosswise on a staff, usually having a serrated edge to give the appearance of streamers. [**C16**: from Old Italian *gonfalone,* from Old French *gonfalon,* of Germanic origin; compare Old English *gūthfana* war banner, Old Norse *gunnfani*]

gonfalonier (ˌgɒnfələˈnɪə) *n* the chief magistrate or other official of a medieval Italian republic, esp. the bearer of the republic's gonfalon.

gong (gɒŋ) *n* **1** Also called: **tam-tam.** a percussion instrument of indefinite pitch, consisting of a metal platelike disc struck with a soft-headed drumstick. **2** a rimmed metal disc, hollow metal hemisphere, or metal strip, tube, or wire that produces a note when struck. It may be used to give alarm signals when operated electromagnetically. **3** a fixed saucer-shaped bell, as on an alarm clock, struck by a mechanically operated hammer. **4** *Brit. slang.* a medal, esp. a military one. ◆ *vb* **5** (*intr*) to sound a gong. **6** (*tr*) (of traffic police) to summon (a driver) to stop by sounding a gong. [**C17**: from Malay, of imitative origin] ▸ **ˈgongˌlike** *adj*

Góngora y Argote (*Spanish* ˈgɔngora i arˈɣote) *n* **Luis de** (lwis de). 1561–1627, Spanish lyric poet, noted for the exaggerated pedantic style of works such as *Las Soledades.*

Gongorism (ˈgɒŋgəˌrɪzəm) *n* **1** an affected literary style characterized by intricate language and obscurity. **2** an example of this. [**C19**: from Spanish *gongorismo;* see GÓNGORA Y ARGOTE] ▸ **ˈGongorist** *n* ▸ **ˌGongoˈristic** *adj*

goniatite (ˈgəʊnɪəˌtaɪt) *n* any extinct cephalopod mollusc of the genus *Goniatites* and related genera, similar to ammonites: a common fossil of Devonian and Carboniferous rocks. [**C19**: from Greek *gōnia* angle, referring to the angular sutures in some species + -ITE[1]]

gonidium (gəˈnɪdɪəm) *n, pl* **-ia** (-ɪə). **1** a green algal cell in the thallus of a lichen. **2** an asexual reproductive cell in some colonial algae. [**C19**: from New Latin, diminutive from GONO-] ▸ **goˈnidial** *or* **goˈnidic** *adj*

goniometer (ˌgəʊnɪˈɒmɪtə) *n* **1** an instrument for measuring the angles between the faces of a crystal. **2** an instrument consisting of a transformer circuit connected to two directional aerials, used to determine the bearing of a distant radio station. [**C18**: via French from Greek *gōnia* angle] ▸ **goniometric** (ˌgəʊnɪəˈmɛtrɪk) *or* **ˌgonioˈmetrical** *adj* ▸ **ˌgonioˈmetrically** *adv* ▸ **ˌgoniˈometry** *n*

gonion (ˈgəʊnɪən) *n, pl* **-nia** (-nɪə). *Anatomy.* the point or apex of the angle of the lower jaw. [**C19**: from New Latin, from Greek *gōnia* angle]

gonioscope (ˈgəʊnɪəʊˌskəʊp) *n* an instrument used for examining the structures of the eye between the cornea and the lens that are not directly visible.

-gonium *n combining form.* indicating a seed or reproductive cell: *archegonium.* [from New Latin *gonium,* from Greek *gonos* seed]

gonna (ˈgɒnə) *vb Slang. contraction of* going to.

gono- *or before a vowel* **gon-** *combining form.* sexual or reproductive: *gonorrhoea.* [New Latin, from Greek *gonos* seed]

gonococcus (ˌgɒnəʊˈkɒkəs) *n, pl* **-cocci** (-ˈkɒksaɪ). a spherical Gram-negative bacterium, *Neisseria gonorrhoeae,* that causes gonorrhoea: family *Neisseriaceae.* ▸ **ˌgonoˈcoccal** *or* **ˌgonoˈcoccic** *adj* ▸ **ˌgonoˈcoccoid** *adj*

gonocyte (ˈgɒnəʊˌsaɪt) *n* an oocyte or spermatocyte.

gonoduct (ˈgɒnəʊˌdʌkt) *n Zoology.* a duct leading from a gonad to the exterior, through which gametes pass.

gonof *or* **gonif** (ˈgɒnəf) *n* a variant of **ganef.**

gonophore (ˈgɒnəʊˌfɔː) *n* **1** *Zoology.* a polyp in certain coelenterates that bears gonads. **2** *Botany.* an elongated structure in certain flowers that bears the stamens and pistil above the level of the other flower parts. ▸ **gonophoric** (ˌgɒnəʊˈfɒrɪk) *or* **gonophorous** (gəʊˈnɒfərəs) *adj*

gonopod (ˈgɒnəʊˌpɒd) *n Zoology.* either member of a pair of appendages that are the external reproductive organs of insects and some other arthropods.

gonopore (ˈgɒnəˌpɔː) *n* an external pore in insects, earthworms, etc., through which the gametes are extruded.

gonorrhoea *or esp. U.S.* **gonorrhea** (ˌgɒnəˈrɪə) *n* an infectious venereal disease caused by a gonococcus, characterized by a burning sensation when urinating and a mucopurulent discharge from the urethra or vagina. [**C16**: from Late Latin, from Greek, from *gonos* seed + *rhoia* flux, flow] ▸ **ˌgonorˈrhoeal, ˌgonorˈrhoeic** *or esp. U.S.* **ˌgonorˈrheal, ˌgonorˈrheic** *adj*

gonosome (ˈgɒnəʊˌsəʊm) *n Zoology.* the individuals, collectively, in a colonial animal that are involved with reproduction.

-gony *n combining form.* genesis, origin, or production: *cosmogony.* [from Latin *-gonia,* from Greek, *-goneia,* from *gonos* seed, procreation]

González (*Spanish* gɔnˈθaleθ) *n* **Julio** (ˈxuljo). 1876–1942, Spanish sculptor: one of the first to create abstract geometric forms with soldered iron.

González Márquez (*Spanish* gɔnˈθaleθ ˈmarkeθ) *n* **Felipe** (feˈlipe). born 1942, Spanish statesman; prime minister of Spain (1982–96).

gonzo (ˈgɒnzəʊ) *adj Slang.* **1** wild or crazy. **2** (of journalism) explicitly including the writer's feelings at the time of witnessing the events or undergoing the experiences written about. [**C20**: perhaps from Italian, literally: fool, or Spanish *ganso* idiot, bumpkin (literally: goose)]

goo (guː) *n Informal.* **1** a sticky or viscous substance. **2** coy or sentimental language or ideas. [**C20**: of uncertain origin]

goober *or* **goober pea** (ˈguːbə) *n* another name for **peanut.** [**C19**: of African (Angolan) origin; related to Kongo *nguba*]

gooby (ˈguːbɪ) *n, pl* **goobies.** *N.Z. informal.* spittle.

Gooch (guːtʃ) *n* **Graham (Alan).** born 1953, English cricketer; captain of England (1988, 1989–93).

good (gʊd) *adj* **better, best. 1** having admirable, pleasing, superior, or positive qualities; not negative, bad or mediocre: *a good idea; a good teacher.* **2a** morally excellent or admirable; virtuous; righteous: *a good man.* **2b** (*as collective n;* preceded by *the*): *the good.* **3** suitable or efficient for a purpose: *a good secretary; a good winter coat.* **4** beneficial or advantageous: *vegetables are good for you.* **5** not ruined or decayed; sound or whole: *the meat is still good.* **6** kindly, generous, or approving: *you are good to him.* **7** right or acceptable: *your qualifications are good for the job.* **8** rich and fertile: *good land.* **9** valid or genuine: *I would not do this without good reason.* **10** honourable or held in high esteem: *a good family.* **11** commercially or financially secure, sound, or safe: *good securities; a good investment.* **12** (of a draft) drawn for a stated sum. **13** (of debts) expected to be fully paid. **14** clever, competent, or talented: *he's good at science.* **15** obedient or well-behaved: *a good dog.* **16** reliable, safe, or recommended: *a good make of clothes.* **17** affording material pleasure or indulgence: *the good things in life; the good life.* **18** having a well-proportioned, beautiful, or generally fine appearance: *a good figure; a good complexion.* **19** complete; full: *I took a good look round the house.* **20** propitious; opportune: *a good time to ask the manager for a rise.* **21** satisfying or gratifying: *a good rest.* **22** comfortable: *did you have a good night?* **23** newest or of the best quality: *to keep the good plates for important guests.* **24** fairly large, extensive, or long: *a good distance away.* **25** sufficient; ample: *we have a good supply of food.* **26** *U.S.* (of meat) of the third government grade, above *standard* and below *choice.* **27** serious or intellectual: *good music.* **28** used in a traditional description: *the good ship "America".* **29** used in polite or patronizing phrases or to express anger (often intended ironically): *how is your good lady?; look here, my good man!* **30 a good one. 30a** an unbelievable assertion. **30b** a very funny joke. **31 as good as.** virtually; practically: *it's as good as finished.* **32 as good as gold.** excellent; very good indeed. **33 be as** *or* **so good as to.** would you please. **34 come good.** to recover and perform well after a bad start or setback. **35 good and.** *Informal.* (intensifier): *good and mad.* **36** (intensifier; used in mild oaths): *good grief! good heavens!* ◆ *interj* **37** an exclamation of approval, agreement, pleasure, etc. ◆ *n* **38** moral or material advantage or use; benefit or profit: *for the good of our workers; what is the good of worrying?* **39** positive moral qualities; goodness; virtue; righteousness; piety. **40** (*sometimes cap.*) moral qualities seen as a single abstract entity: *we must pursue the Good.* **41** a good thing. **42** *Economics.* a commodity or service that satisfies a human need. **43 for good (and all).** forever; permanently: *I have left them for good.* **44 make good. 44a** to recompense or repair damage or injury. **44b** to be successful. **44c** to demonstrate or prove the truth of (a statement or accusation). **44d** to secure and retain (a position). **44e** to effect or fulfil (something intended or promised). **45 good on** *or* **for you (him,** etc.) well done, well said, etc.: a term of congratulation. **46 get any** (*or* **some**) **good of.** *Irish.* **46a** to handle to good effect: *I never got any good of this machine.* **46b** to understand properly: *I could never get any good of him.* **46c** to receive cooperation from. ◆ See also **goods.** [Old English *gōd;* related to Old Norse *gōthr,* Old High German *guot* good] ▸ **ˈgoodish** *adj*

good afternoon *sentence substitute.* a conventional expression of greeting or farewell used in the afternoon.

Good Book *n* a name for the **Bible.** Also called: **the Book.**

goodbye (ˌgʊdˈbaɪ) *sentence substitute.* **1** farewell: a conventional expression used at leave-taking or parting with people and at the loss or rejection of things or ideas. ◆ *n* 2 a leave-taking; parting: *they prolonged their goodbyes for a few more minutes.* 3 a farewell: *they said goodbyes to each other.* [C16: contraction of *God be with ye*]

good day *sentence substitute.* a conventional expression of greeting or farewell used during the day.

good evening *sentence substitute.* a conventional expression of greeting or farewell used in the evening.

good-for-nothing *n* 1 an irresponsible or worthless person. ◆ *adj* 2 irresponsible; worthless.

Good Friday *n* the Friday before Easter, observed as a commemoration of the Crucifixion of Jesus.

good hair *n Caribbean.* hair showing evidence of some European strain in a person's blood.

Good Hope *n* **Cape of.** See **Cape of Good Hope.**

good-humoured *adj* being in or expressing a pleasant, tolerant, and kindly state of mind. ► ˌ**good-'humouredly** *adv* ► ˌ**good-'humouredness** *n*

goodies ('gʊdɪz) *pl n* any objects, rewards, prizes, etc., considered particularly desirable, attractive, or pleasurable.

Good King Henry *n* a weedy chenopodiaceous plant, *Chenopodium bonus-henricus,* of N Europe, W Asia, and North America, having arrow-shaped leaves and clusters of small green flowers.

good-looker *n* a handsome or pretty person.

good-looking *adj* handsome or pretty.

good looks *pl n* personal attractiveness or beauty.

goodly ('gʊdlɪ) *adj* **-lier, -liest. 1** considerable: *a goodly amount of money.* **2** *Obsolete.* attractive, pleasing, or fine: *a goodly man.* ► **'goodliness** *n*

goodman ('gʊdmən) *n, pl* **-men.** *Archaic.* **1** a husband. **2** a man not of gentle birth: used as a title. **3** a master of a household.

Goodman ('gʊdmən) *n* **Benny,** full name *Benjamin David Goodman.* 1909–86, U.S. jazz clarinetist and bandleader, whose treatment of popular songs created the jazz idiom known as swing.

good morning *sentence substitute.* a conventional expression of greeting or farewell used in the morning.

good-natured *adj* of a tolerant and kindly disposition. ► ˌ**good-'naturedly** *adv* ► ˌ**good-'naturedness** *n*

goodness ('gʊdnɪs) *n* **1** the state or quality of being good. **2** generosity; kindness. **3** moral excellence; piety; virtue. ◆ *interj* **4** a euphemism for **God:** used as an exclamation of surprise (often in phrases such as **goodness knows!, thank goodness!**).

goodness of fit *n Statistics.* the extent to which observed sample values of a variable approximate to values derived from a theoretical density, often measured by a chi-square test.

good night *sentence substitute.* a conventional expression of farewell, or, rarely, of greeting, used in the late afternoon, the evening, or at night, esp. when departing to bed.

good-oh *or* **good-o** ('gʊd'əʊ) *Informal.* ◆ *interj* **1** *Brit. and Austral.* an exclamation of pleasure, agreement, approval, etc. ◆ *adj, adv* **2** *Austral.* all right: *it was good-oh; I was getting on good-oh.*

good oil *n* (usually preceded by *the*) *Austral. slang.* true or reliable facts, information, etc.

good people *pl n* **the.** *Folklore.* fairies.

good question *n* a question that is hard to answer immediately.

goods (gʊdz) *pl n* **1** possessions and personal property. **2** (*sometimes sing*) *Economics.* commodities that are tangible, usually movable, and generally not consumed at the same time as they are produced. Compare **services. 3** articles of commerce; merchandise. **4** *Chiefly Brit.* **4a** merchandise when transported, esp. by rail; freight. **4b** (*as modifier*): *a goods train.* **5 the goods. 5a** *Informal.* that which is expected or promised: *to deliver the goods.* **5b** *Slang.* the real thing. **5c** *U.S. and Canadian slang.* incriminating evidence (esp. in the phrase **have the goods on someone**). **6 a piece of goods.** *Slang.* a person, esp. a woman.

Good Samaritan *n* **1** *New Testament.* a figure in one of Christ's parables (Luke 10:30–37) who is an example of compassion towards those in distress. **2** a kindly person who helps another in difficulty or distress.

goods and chattels *pl n* any property that is not freehold, usually limited to include only moveable property.

Good Shepherd *n New Testament.* a title given to Jesus Christ in John 10:11–12.

good-sized *adj* quite large.

good sort *n Informal.* **1** a person of a kindly and likable disposition. **2** *Austral.* an agreeable or attractive woman.

good-tempered *adj* of a kindly and generous disposition.

good-time *adj* (of a person) wildly seeking pleasure.

good turn *n* a helpful and friendly act; good deed; favour.

goodwife ('gʊdˌwaɪf) *n, pl* **-wives.** *Archaic.* **1** the mistress of a household. **2** a woman not of gentle birth: used as a title.

goodwill (ˌgʊd'wɪl) *n* **1** a feeling of benevolence, approval, and kindly interest. **2** (*modifier*) resulting from, showing, or designed to show goodwill: *the government sent a goodwill mission to Moscow.* **3** willingness or acquiescence. **4** *Accounting.* an intangible asset taken into account in assessing the value of an enterprise and reflecting its commercial reputation, customer connections, etc.

Goodwin Sands ('gʊdwɪn) *pl n* a dangerous stretch of shoals at the entrance to the Strait of Dover: separated from the E coast of Kent by the Downs roadstead.

Goodwood ('gʊdˌwʊd) *n* an area in SE England, in Sussex: site of a famous racecourse and of **Goodwood House,** built 1780–1800.

goody[1] ('gʊdɪ) *interj* **1** a child's exclamation of pleasure and approval. ◆ *n, pl* **goodies. 2** short for **goody-goody. 3** *Informal.* the hero in a film, book, etc. **4** something particularly pleasant to have or (often) to eat. See also **goodies.**

goody[2] ('gʊdɪ) *n, pl* **goodies.** *Archaic or literary.* a married woman of low rank: used as a title: *Goody Two-Shoes.* [C16: shortened from GOODWIFE]

Goodyear ('gʊdˌjɪə) *n* **Charles.** 1800–60, U.S. inventor of vulcanized rubber.

goody-goody *n, pl* **-goodies. 1** *Informal.* a smugly virtuous or sanctimonious person. ◆ *adj* **2** smug and sanctimonious.

gooey ('guːɪ) *adj* **gooier, gooiest.** *Informal.* **1** sticky, soft, and often sweet. **2** oversweet and sentimental. ► **'gooily** *adv*

goof (guːf) *Informal.* ◆ *n* **1** a foolish error or mistake. **2** a stupid person. ◆ *vb* **3** to bungle (something); botch. **4** (*intr;* often foll. by *about* or *around*) to fool (around); mess (about). **5** (*tr*) to dope with drugs. **6** (*intr;* often foll. by *off*) *U.S. and Canadian.* to waste time; idle. [C20: probably from (dialect) *goff* simpleton, from Old French *goffe* clumsy, from Italian *goffo,* of obscure origin]

goofball ('guːfˌbɔːl) *n U.S. and Canadian slang.* **1** a barbiturate sleeping pill. **2** a fool.

go off *vb* (*intr*) **1** (*adv*) (of power, a water supply, etc.) to cease to be available, running, or functioning: *the lights suddenly went off.* **2** (*adv*) to be discharged or activated; explode. **3** (*adv*) to occur as specified: *the meeting went off well.* **4** to leave (a place): *the actors went off stage.* **5** (*adv*) (of a sensation) to gradually cease to be felt or perceived. **6** (*adv*) to fall asleep. **7** (*adv*) to enter a specified state or condition: *she went off into hysterics.* **8** (*adv;* foll. by *with*) to abscond (with). **9** (*adv*) (of concrete, mortar, etc.) to harden. **10** (*adv*) *Brit. informal.* (of food, milk, etc.) to become stale or rotten. **11** (*prep*) *Brit. informal.* to cease to like: *she went off him after their marriage.* **12** (*adv*) *Taboo slang.* to have an orgasm. **13** (*adv*) *Austral. slang.* (of premises) to be raided by the police. **14** (*adv*) *Austral. slang.* (of a racehorse) to win a fixed race. **15** (*adv*) *Austral. slang.* to be stolen.

goofy ('guːfɪ) *adj* **goofier, goofiest.** *Informal.* **1** foolish; silly; stupid. **2** *Brit.* (of teeth) sticking out; protruding. ► **'goofily** *adv* ► **'goofiness** *n*

goofy-footer *n Austral. informal.* a surfboard rider who stands with his right foot forward instead of his left foot forward.

goog (gʊg) *n Austral. informal.* **1** an egg. **2 full as a goog.** drunk.

googly ('guːglɪ) *n, pl* **-lies.** *Cricket.* an off break bowled with a leg break action. [C20: Australian, of unknown origin]

googol ('guːgɒl, -gəl) *n* the number represented as one followed by 100 zeros (10^{100}). [C20: coined by E. Kasner (1878–1955), American mathematician]

googolplex ('guːgɒlˌplɛks, -gəl-) *n* the number represented as one followed by a googol (10^{100}) of zeros. [C20: from GOOGOL + (DU)PLEX]

gook (gʊk, guːk) *n U.S.* **1** *Slang.* a derogatory word for a person from a Far Eastern country. **2** *Informal.* a messy sticky substance; muck. [C20: of uncertain origin]

Goolagong ('guːləˌgɒŋ) *n* **Evonne.** See (Evonne) **Cawley.**

Goole (guːl) *n* an inland port in NE England, in the East Riding of Yorkshire at the confluence of the Ouse and Don Rivers, 75 km (47 miles) from the North Sea. Pop.: 19 410 (1991).

goolie *or* **gooly** ('guːlɪ) *n, pl* **-lies. 1** (*usually pl*) *Taboo slang.* a testicle. **2** *Austral. slang.* a stone or pebble. [from Hindustani *goli* a ball, bullet]

goon (guːn) *n* **1** a stupid or deliberately foolish person. **2** *U.S. informal.* a thug hired to commit acts of violence or intimidation, esp. in an industrial dispute. [C20: partly from dialect *gooney* fool, partly after the character Alice the *Goon,* created by E. C. Segar (1894–1938), American cartoonist]

go on *vb* (*intr, mostly adv*) **1** to continue or proceed. **2** to happen or take place: *there's something peculiar going on here.* **3** (of power, water supply, etc.) to start running or functioning. **4** (*prep*) to mount or board and ride on, esp. as a treat: *children love to go on donkeys at the seaside.* **5** *Theatre.* to make an entrance on stage. **6** to act or behave: *he goes on as though he's rich.* **7** to talk excessively; chatter. **8** to continue talking, esp. after a short pause: *"When I am Prime Minister," he went on, "we shall abolish taxes."* **9** (foll. by *at*) to criticize or nag: *stop going on at me all the time!* **10** (*prep*) to use as a basis for further thought or action: *the police had no evidence at all to go on in the murder case.* **11** (foll. by *for*) *Brit.* to approach (a time, age, amount, etc.): *he's going on for his hundredth birthday.* **12** *Cricket.* to start to bowl. **13** to take one's turn. **14** (of clothes) to be capable of being put on. **15 go much on.** (*used with a negative*) *Brit.* to care for; like. **16 something to go on** *or* **to be going on with.** something that is adequate for the present time. ◆ *interj* **17** I don't believe what you're saying.

gooney bird ('guːnɪ) *n* an informal name for **albatross,** esp. the black-footed albatross (*Diomedea nigripes*). [C19 *gony* (originally sailors' slang), probably from dialect *gooney* fool, of obscure origin; compare GOON]

goop (guːp) *n U.S. and Canadian slang.* **1** a rude or ill-mannered person. **2** any sticky or semiliquid substance. [C20: coined by G. Burgess (1866–1951), American humorist] ► **'goopy** *adj*

goorie *or* **goory** ('guːrɪ) *n, pl* **-ries.** *N.Z. informal.* See **kuri.**

goosander (guː'sændə) *n* a common merganser (a duck), *Mergus merganser,* of Europe and North America, having a dark head and white body in the male. [C17: probably from GOOSE[1] + Old Norse *önd* (genitive *andar*) duck]

goose[1] (guːs) *n, pl* **geese** (giːs). **1** any of various web-footed long-necked birds of the family *Anatidae:* order *Anseriformes.* They are typically larger and less aquatic than ducks and are gregarious and migratory. Related adj: **anserine.** See also **brent goose, barnacle goose, greylag, snow goose. 2** the female of such a bird, as opposed to the male (gander). **3** *Informal.* a silly person. **4** (*pl* **gooses**). a pressing iron with a long curving handle, used esp. by tailors. **5** the flesh of the goose, used as food. **6 all his geese are swans.** he constantly exaggerates the importance of a person or thing. **7 cook someone's goose.** *Informal.* **7a** to spoil someone's plans. **7b** to bring about someone's ruin, downfall, etc. **8 kill the goose that lays the golden eggs.** to sacrifice future benefits for the sake of momentary present needs. See also **golden goose.** [Old English *gōs;* related to Old Norse *gās,* Old High German *gans,* Old Irish *gēiss* swan, Greek *khēn,* Sanskrit *hainsas*]

goose[2] (gu:s) *Slang.* ◆ *vb* **1** (*tr*) to prod (a person) playfully in the behind. ◆ *n, pl* **gooses. 2** a playful prod in the behind. [C19: from GOOSE[1], probably from a comparison with the jabbing of a goose's bill]

goose barnacle *n* any barnacle of the genus *Lepas,* living attached by a stalk to pieces of wood, having long feathery appendages (cirri) and flattened shells.

gooseberry ('gʊzbərɪ, -brɪ) *n, pl* **-ries. 1** a Eurasian shrub, *Ribes uva-crispa* (or *R. grossularia*), having greenish, purple-tinged flowers and ovoid yellow-green or red-purple berries: family *Grossulariaceae.* See also **currant** (sense 2). **2a** the berry of this plant. **2b** (*as modifier*): *gooseberry jam.* **3** *Brit. informal.* an unwanted single person in a group of couples, esp. a third person with a couple (often in the phrase **play gooseberry**). **4 Cape gooseberry.** a tropical American solanaceous plant, *Physalis peruviana,* naturalized in southern Africa, having yellow flowers and edible yellow berries. See also **ground cherry.**

gooseberry bush *n* **1** See **gooseberry** (sense 1). **2 under a gooseberry bush.** used humorously in answering children's questions regarding their birth.

gooseberry stone *n* another name for **grossularite.**

goosefish ('gu:s,fɪʃ) *n, pl* **-fish** *or* **-fishes.** *U.S.* another name for **monkfish** (sense 1).

goose flesh *n* the bumpy condition of the skin induced by cold, fear, etc., caused by contraction of the muscles at the base of the hair follicles with consequent erection of papillae: so called because of the resemblance to the skin of a freshly-plucked fowl. Also called: **goose bumps, goose pimples, goose skin.**

goosefoot ('gu:s,fʊt) *n, pl* **-foots.** any typically weedy chenopodiaceous plant of the genus *Chenopodium,* having small greenish flowers and leaves shaped like a goose's foot. See also **Good King Henry, fat hen.**

goosegog ('gʊzgɒg) *or* **goosegob** *n Brit.* a dialect or informal word for **gooseberry.** [from *goose* in GOOSEBERRY + *gog,* variant of GOB[1]]

goosegrass ('gu:s,grɑ:s) *n* another name for **cleavers.**

gooseneck ('gu:s,nɛk) *n* **1** *Nautical.* a pivot between the forward end of a boom and a mast, to allow the boom to swing freely. **2** something in the form of a neck of a goose. ▸ **'goose,necked** *adj*

goose step *n* **1** a military march step in which the leg is swung rigidly to an exaggerated height, esp. as in the German army in the Third Reich. ◆ *vb* **goose-step, -steps, -stepping, -stepped. 2** (*intr*) to march in goose step.

Goossens ('gu:sənz) *n* **1** Sir **Eugene.** 1893–1962, British composer and conductor, born in Belgium. **2** his brother, **Leon.** 1896–1988, British oboist.

goosy *or* **goosey** ('gu:sɪ) *adj* **goosier, goosiest. 1** of or like a goose. **2** having goose flesh. **3** silly and foolish. ▸ **'goosiness** *n*

go out *vb* (*intr, adv*) **1** to depart from a room, house, country, etc. **2** to cease to illuminate, burn, or function: *the fire has gone out.* **3** to cease to be fashionable or popular: *that style went out ages ago!* **4** to become unconscious or fall asleep: *she went out like a light.* **5** (of a broadcast) to be transmitted. **6** to go to entertainments, social functions, etc. **7** (usually foll. by *with* or *together*) to associate (with a person of the opposite sex) regularly; date. **8** (of workers) to begin to strike. **9** (foll. by *to*) to be extended (to): *our sympathy went out to her on the death of her sister.* **10** *Card games, etc.* to get rid of the last card, token, etc., in one's hand. **11 go all out.** to make a great effort to achieve or obtain something: *he went all out to pass the exam.*

go over *vb* (*intr*) **1** to be received in a specified manner: *the concert went over very well.* **2** (*prep*) Also: **go through.** to examine and revise as necessary: *he went over the accounts.* **3** (*prep*) Also: **go through.** to clean: *she went over the room before her mother came.* **4** (*prep*) to check and repair: *can you go over my car please?* **5** (*prep*) Also: **go through.** to rehearse: *I'll go over my lines before the play.* **6** (*adv;* foll. by *to*) **6a** to change (to a different practice or system): *will Britain ever go over to driving on the right?* **6b** to change one's allegiances. **7** (*prep*) *Slang.* to do physical violence to: *they went over him with an iron bar.*

GOP (in the U.S.) *abbrev. for* Grand Old Party.

gopak ('gəʊ,pæk) *n* a spectacular high-leaping Russian peasant dance for men. [from Russian, from Ukrainian *hopak,* from *hop!* a cry in the dance, from German *hopp!*]

gopher ('gəʊfə) *n* **1** Also called: **pocket gopher.** any burrowing rodent of the family *Geomyidae,* of North and Central America, having a thickset body, short legs, and cheek pouches. **2** another name for **ground squirrel. 3** any burrowing tortoise of the genus *Gopherus,* of SE North America. **4 gopher snake.** another name for **bull snake.** [C19: shortened from earlier *megopher* or *magopher,* of obscure origin]

gopherwood ('gəʊfə,wʊd) *n U.S.* another name for **yellowwood** (sense 1).

gopher wood *n* the wood used in the construction of Noah's ark, thought to be a type of cypress (Genesis 6:14). [from Hebrew *gōpher*]

Gorakhpur ('gɔ:rək,pʊə) *n* a city in N India, in SE Uttar Pradesh: formerly an important Muslim garrison. Pop.: 505 566 (1991).

goral ('gɔ:rəl) *n* a small goat antelope, *Naemorhedus goral,* inhabiting mountainous regions of S Asia. It has a yellowish-grey and black coat and small conical horns. [C19: from Hindi, probably of Sanskrit origin]

Gorbachov *or* **Gorbachev** (gərba'tʃɒf) *n* **Mikhail Sergeevich** (mixa'il sir'gjejivitʃ). born 1931, Soviet statesman; general secretary of the Soviet Communist Party (1985–91): president (1988–91). Nobel peace prize 1990. His reforms ended the Communist monopoly of power and led to the break-up of the Soviet Union.

Gorbals ('gɔ:bəlz) *n* **the.** a district of Glasgow, formerly known for its slums.

gorblimey (gɔ:'blaɪmɪ) *interj* a variant of **cor blimey.**

gorcock ('gɔ:,kɒk) *n* the male of the red grouse. [C17: *gor-* (of unknown origin) + COCK[1]]

Gordian knot ('gɔ:dɪən) *n* **1** (in Greek legend) a complicated knot, tied by King Gordius of Phrygia, that Alexander the Great cut with a sword. **2** a complicated and intricate problem (esp. in the phrase **cut the Gordian knot**).

Gordimer ('gɔ:dɪmə) *n* **Nadine.** born 1923, South African novelist. Her books include *The Lying Days* (1952), *July's People* (1981), *The Conservationist* (1974), which won the Booker prize, *None to Accompany Me* (1994), and *The House Gun* (1998). Her works were banned in South Africa for their condemnation of apartheid. Nobel prize for literature 1991.

Gordon ('gɔ:dən) *n* **1 Adam Lindsay.** 1833–70, Australian poet and horseman, born in the Azores, who developed the bush ballad as a literary form, esp. in *Bush Ballads and Galloping Rhymes* (1870). **2 Charles George,** known as *Chinese Gordon.* 1833–85, British general and administrator. He helped to crush the Taiping rebellion (1863–64), and was governor of the Sudan (1877–80), returning in 1884 to aid Egyptian forces against the Mahdi. He was killed in the siege of Khartoum. **3** Lord **George.** 1751–93, English religious agitator. He led the Protestant opposition to legislation relieving Roman Catholics of certain disabilities, which culminated in the Gordon riots (1780). **4 George Hamilton.** See (4th Earl of) **Aberdeen.**

Gordon setter *n* a breed of setter originating in Scotland, with a black-and-tan coat. [C19: named after Alexander *Gordon* (1743–1827), Scottish nobleman who promoted this breed]

gore[1] (gɔ:) *n* **1** blood shed from a wound, esp. when coagulated. **2** *Informal.* killing, fighting, etc. [Old English *gor* dirt; related to Old Norse *gor* half-digested food, Middle Low German *göre,* Dutch *goor*]

gore[2] (gɔ:) *vb* (*tr*) (of an animal, such as a bull) to pierce or stab (a person or another animal) with a horn or tusk. [C16: probably from Old English *gār* spear]

gore[3] (gɔ:) *n* **1** a tapering or triangular piece of material used in making a shaped skirt, umbrella, etc. **2** a similarly shaped piece, esp. of land. ◆ *vb* **3** (*tr*) to make into or with a gore or gores. [Old English *gāra;* related to Old Norse *geiri* gore, Old High German *gēro*] ▸ **gored** *adj*

Gore (gɔ:) *n* **Al(bert) Jr.** born 1948, U.S. Democrat politician; vice president of the U.S. from 1993.

Gore-Tex ('gɔ:,tɛks) *n Trademark.* a type of synthetic fabric which is waterproof yet allows the wearer's skin to breathe, used for sportswear.

gorge (gɔ:dʒ) *n* **1** a deep ravine, esp. one through which a river runs. **2** the contents of the stomach. **3** feelings of disgust or resentment (esp. in the phrase **one's gorge rises**). **4** an obstructing mass: *an ice gorge.* **5** *Fortifications.* **5a** a narrow rear entrance to a work. **5b** the narrow part of a bastion or outwork. **6** *Archaic.* the throat or gullet. ◆ *vb also* **engorge. 7** (*intr*) *Falconry.* (of hawks) to eat until the crop is completely full. **8** to swallow (food) ravenously. **9** (*tr*) to stuff (oneself) with food. [C14: from Old French *gorger* to stuff, from *gorge* throat, from Late Latin *gurga,* modification of Latin *gurges* whirlpool] ▸ **'gorgeable** *adj* ▸ **'gorger** *n*

gorgeous ('gɔ:dʒəs) *adj* **1** strikingly beautiful or magnificent: *gorgeous array; a gorgeous girl.* **2** *Informal.* extremely pleasing, fine, or good: *gorgeous weather.* [C15: from Old French *gorgias* elegant, from *gorgias* wimple, from *gorge;* see GORGE] ▸ **'gorgeously** *adv* ▸ **'gorgeousness** *n*

gorgerin ('gɔ:dʒərɪn) *n Architect.* another name for **necking.** [C17: from French, from *gorge* throat; see GORGE]

gorget ('gɔ:dʒɪt) *n* **1** a collar-like piece of armour worn to protect the throat. **2** a part of a wimple worn by women to cover the throat and chest, esp. in the 14th century. **3** a band of distinctive colour on the throat of an animal, esp. a bird. [C15: from Old French, from *gorge;* see GORGE] ▸ **'gorgeted** *adj*

Gorgias ('gɔ:dʒɪəs) *n* ?485–?380 B.C., Greek sophist and rhetorician, subject of a dialogue by Plato.

Gorgio ('gɔ:dʒəʊ, -dʒɪəʊ) *n, pl* **-gios.** (*sometimes not cap.*) a word used by Gypsies for a non-Gypsy. [from Romany]

Gorgon ('gɔ:gən) *n* **1** *Greek myth.* any of three winged monstrous sisters, Stheno, Euryale, and Medusa, who had live snakes for hair, huge teeth, and brazen claws. **2** (*often not cap.*) *Informal.* a fierce or unpleasant woman. [via Latin *Gorgō* from Greek, from *gorgos* terrible]

gorgoneion (,gɔ:gə'ni:ɒn) *n, pl* **-neia** (-'ni:ə). a representation of a Gorgon's head, esp. Medusa's. [C19: from Greek, from *gorgoneios* of a GORGON]

gorgonian (gɔ:'gəʊnɪən) *n* **1** any coral of the order *Gorgonacea,* having a horny or calcareous branching skeleton: includes the sea fans and red corals. ◆ *adj* **2** of, relating to, or belonging to the *Gorgonacea.*

Gorgonian (gɔ:'gəʊnɪən) *adj* of or resembling a Gorgon.

Gorgonzola *or* **Gorgonzola cheese** (,gɔ:gən'zəʊlə) *n* a semihard blue-veined cheese of sharp flavour, made from pressed milk. [C19: named after *Gorgonzola,* Italian town where it originated]

Gorica ('gɔritsa) *n* the Serbo-Croat name for **Gorizia.**

gorilla (gə'rɪlə) *n* **1** the largest anthropoid ape, *Gorilla gorilla,* inhabiting the forests of central W Africa. It is stocky and massive, with a short muzzle and coarse dark hair. **2** *Informal.* a large, strong, and brutal-looking man. [C19: New Latin, from Greek *Gorillai,* an African tribe renowned for their hirsute appearance] ▸ **go'rilla-,like** *adj* ▸ **go'rillian** *or* **gorilline** (gə'rɪlaɪn) *adj* ▸ **go'rilloid** *adj*

Göring *or* **Goering** (*German* 'gø:rɪŋ) *n* **Hermann Wilhelm** ('hɛrman 'vɪlhɛlm). 1893–1946, German Nazi leader and field marshal. He commanded Hitler's storm troops (1923) and as Prussian prime minister and German commissioner for aviation (1933–45) he founded the Gestapo and mobilized Germany for war. Sentenced to death at Nuremberg, he committed suicide.

Gorizia (*Italian* go'rittsja) *n* a city in NE Italy, in Friuli-Venezia Giulia, on the Isonzo River: cultural centre under the Hapsburgs. Pop.: 39 230 (1990). German name: **Görz.** Serbo-Croat name: **Gorica.**

Gorki[1] *or* **Gorky** (*Russian* 'gɔrjkij) *n* the former name (until 1991) of **Nizhni Novgorod.**

Gorki[2] *or* **Gorky** (*Russian* 'gɔrjkij) *n* **Maxim** (mak'sim), pen name of *Aleksey Maximovich Peshkov.* 1868–1936, Russian novelist, dramatist, and short-story writer, noted for his depiction of the outcasts of society. His works include the play *The Lower Depths* (1902), the novel *Mother* (1907), and an autobiographical trilogy (1913–23).

Gorky ('gɔːkɪ) *n* **Arshile** ('ɑːʃɪl). 1904–48, U.S. abstract expressionist painter, born in Armenia. Influenced by Picasso and Miró, his style is characterized by fluid lines and resonant colours.

Görlitz (*German* 'gœrlɪts) *n* a city in E Germany, in Saxony on the Neisse River: divided in 1945, the area on the E bank of the river becoming the Polish town of **Zgorzelec.** Pop.: 70 450 (1991).

Gorlovka (*Russian* 'gɔrləfkə) *n* a city in the SE Ukraine in the centre of the Donets Basin: a major coal-mining centre. Pop.: 322 000 (1996 est.).

gormand ('gɔːmənd) *n* a less common variant of **gourmand.**

gormandize *or* **gormandise** *vb* ('gɔːmən,daɪz). **1** to eat (food) greedily and voraciously. ◆ *n* ('gɔːmən,diːz). **2** a less common variant of **gourmandise.** ▸ **'gormand,izer** *or* **'gormand,iser** *n*

gormless ('gɔːmlɪs) *adj Brit. informal.* stupid; dull. [C19: variant of C18 *gaumless,* from dialect *gome,* from Old English *gom, gome,* from Old Norse *gaumr* heed]

Gorno-Altai Republic ('gɔːnəuæl'taɪ, -'æltaɪ) *n* a constituent republic of S Russia: mountainous, rising over 4350 m (14 500 ft.) in the Altai Mountains of the south. Capital: Gorno-Altaisk. Pop.: 200 000 (1995 est.). Area: 92 600 sq. km (35 740 sq. miles). Also called: **Altai Republic.**

Gorno-Badakhshan Autonomous Republic (-bə'dækʃɑːn) *n* an administrative division of Tajikistan: generally mountainous and inaccessible. Capital: Khorog. Pop.: 167 000 (1991 est.). Area: 63 700 sq. km (24 590 sq. miles). Also called: **Badakhshan.**

gorse (gɔːs) *n* any evergreen shrub of the papilionaceous genus *Ulex,* esp. the European species *U. europeaus,* which has yellow flowers and thick green spines instead of leaves. Also called: **furze, whin.** [Old English *gors;* related to Old Irish *garb* rough, Latin *horrēre* to bristle, Old High German *gersta* barley, Greek *khēr* hedgehog] ▸ **'gorsy** *adj*

Gorsedd ('gɔːseð) *n* (in Wales) the bardic institution associated with the eisteddfod, esp. a meeting of bards and druids held daily before the eisteddfod. [from Welsh, literally: throne]

Gorton ('gɔːtᵊn) *n* Sir **John Grey.** born 1911, Australian statesman; prime minister (1968–71).

gory ('gɔːrɪ) *adj* **gorier, goriest. 1** horrific or bloodthirsty: *a gory story.* **2** involving bloodshed and killing: *a gory battle.* **3** covered in gore. ▸ **'gorily** *adv* ▸ **'goriness** *n*

Görz (gœrts) *n* the German name for **Gorizia.**

gosh (gɒʃ) *interj* an exclamation of mild surprise or wonder. [C18: euphemistic for *God,* as in *by gosh!*]

goshawk ('gɒs,hɔːk) *n* a large hawk, *Accipiter gentilis,* of Europe, Asia, and North America, having a bluish-grey back and wings and paler underparts: used in falconry. [Old English *gōshafoc;* see GOOSE[1], HAWK[1]]

Goshen ('gəuʃən) *n* **1** a region of ancient Egypt, east of the Nile delta: granted to Jacob and his descendants by the king of Egypt and inhabited by them until the Exodus (Genesis 45:10). **2** a place of comfort and plenty.

Goslar ('gɒslɑː) *n* a city in N central Germany, in Lower Saxony: imperial palace and other medieval buildings, silver mines. Pop.: 46 000 (1989).

gosling ('gɒzlɪŋ) *n* **1** a young goose. **2** an inexperienced or youthful person. [C15: from Old Norse *gæslingr;* related to Danish *gäsling;* see GOOSE[1], -LING[1]]

go-slow *n* **1** *Brit.* **1a** a deliberate slackening of the rate of production by organized labour as a tactic in industrial conflict. **1b** (*as modifier*): *go-slow tactics.* U.S. and Canadian equivalent: **slowdown.** ◆ *vb* **go slow. 2** (*intr*) to work deliberately slowly as a tactic in industrial conflict.

gospel ('gɒspᵊl) *n* **1** Also called: **gospel truth.** an unquestionable truth: *to take someone's word as gospel.* **2** a doctrine maintained to be of great importance. **3** Black religious music originating in the churches of the Southern states of the United States. **4** the message or doctrine of a religious teacher. **5a** the story of Christ's life and teachings as narrated in the Gospels. **5b** the good news of salvation in Jesus Christ. **5c** (*as modifier*): *the gospel story.* [Old English *gōdspell,* from *gōd* GOOD + *spell* message; see SPELL[2]; compare Old Norse *guthspjall,* Old High German *guotspell*]

Gospel ('gɒspᵊl) *n* **1** any of the first four books of the New Testament, namely Matthew, Mark, Luke, and John. **2** a reading from one of these in a religious service.

gospeller ('gɒspələ) *n* **1** a person who reads or chants the Gospel in a religious service. **2** a person who professes to preach a gospel held exclusively by him and others of a like mind.

gospel oath *n* an oath sworn on the Gospels.

Gosplan ('gɒs,plæn) *n* the state planning commission of the former Soviet Union or any of its constituent republics: it was responsible for coordination and development of the economy, social services, etc. [C20: from Russian *Gos(udarstvennaya) Plan(ovaya Comissiya)* State Planning Committee]

gospodin *Russian.* (gəspa'din) *n, pl* **-poda** (-pa'da). a Russian title of address, often indicating respect, equivalent to *sir* when used alone or to *Mr* when before a name. [literally: lord]

Gosport ('gɒs,pɔːt) *n* a town in S England, in Hampshire on Portsmouth harbour: naval base since the 16th century. Pop.: 67 802 (1991).

gossamer ('gɒsəmə) *n* **1** a gauze or silk fabric of the very finest texture. **2** a filmy cobweb often seen on foliage or floating in the air. **3** anything resembling gossamer in fineness or filminess. **4** (*modifier*) made of or resembling gossamer: *gossamer wings.* [C14 (in the sense: a filmy cobweb): probably from *gos* GOOSE[1] + *somer* SUMMER[1]; the phrase refers to *St Martin's summer,* a period in November when goose was traditionally eaten; from the prevalence of the cobweb in the autumn; compare German *Gänsemonat,* literally: goosemonth, used for November] ▸ **'gossamery** *adj*

Gosse (gɒs) *n* Sir **Edmund William.** 1849–1928, English critic and poet, noted particularly for his autobiographical work *Father and Son* (1907).

gossip ('gɒsɪp) *n* **1** casual and idle chat: *to have a gossip with a friend.* **2** a conversation involving malicious chatter or rumours about other people: *a gossip about the neighbours.* **3** Also called: **gossipmonger.** a person who habitually talks about others, esp. maliciously. **4** light easy communication: *to write a letter full of gossip.* **5** *Archaic.* a close woman friend. ◆ *vb* **-sips, -siping, -siped. 6** (*intr;* often foll. by *about*) to talk casually or maliciously (about other people). [Old English *godsibb* godparent, from GOD + SIB; the term came to be applied to familiar friends, esp. a woman's female friends at the birth of a child, hence a person, esp. a woman, fond of light talk] ▸ **'gossiper** *n* ▸ **'gossiping** *n, adj* ▸ **'gossipingly** *adv* ▸ **'gossipy** *adj*

gossipmonger ('gɒsɪp,mʌŋgə) *n* another word for **gossip** (sense 3).

gossoon (gɒ'suːn) *n Irish.* a boy, esp. a servant boy. [C17: from Old French *garçon*]

gossypol ('gɒsɪ,pɒl) *n* a toxic crystalline pigment that is a constituent of cottonseed oil. [C19: from Modern Latin *gossypium* cotton plant + -OL[1]]

goster ('gɒstə) *vb* (*intr*) *Northern English dialect.* to laugh uncontrollably. [C18: from earlier *gauster,* from Middle English *galstre,* of obscure origin]

got (gɒt) *vb* **1** the past tense and past participle of **get. 2 have got. 2a** to possess: *he has got three apples.* **2b** (*takes an infinitive*) used as an auxiliary to express compulsion felt to be imposed by or upon the speaker: *I've got to get a new coat.* **3 have got it bad** *or* **badly.** *Informal.* to be infatuated.

Göta (*Swedish* 'jøːta) *n* a river in S Sweden, draining Lake Vänern and flowing south-southwest to the Kattegat: forms part of the **Göta Canal,** which links Göteborg in the west with Stockholm in the east. Length: 93 km (58 miles).

Gotama ('gəutəmə) *n* the Pali form of the name **Gautama.**

Göteborg (*Swedish* jœtə'bɔrj) *or* **Gothenburg** *n* a port in SW Sweden, at the mouth of the Göta River: the largest port and second largest city in the country; developed through the Swedish East India Company and grew through Napoleon's continental blockade and with the opening of the Göta Canal (1832); university (1891). Pop.: 454 016 (1997 est.).

Goth (gɒθ) *n* **1** a member of an East Germanic people from Scandinavia who settled south of the Baltic early in the first millennium A.D. They moved on to the Ukrainian steppes and raided and later invaded many parts of the Roman Empire from the 3rd to the 5th century. See also **Ostrogoth, Visigoth. 2** a rude or barbaric person. **3** (*sometimes not cap.*) Also called: **Gothic.** an aficionado of Goth music and fashion.◆ *adj* **4** (*sometimes not cap.*) Also: **Gothic. 4a** (of music) in a style of guitar-based rock with some similarities to heavy metal and punk and usually characterized by depressing or mournful lyrics. **4b** (of fashion) characterized by black clothes and heavy make-up, often creating a ghostly appearance.

Goth. *abbrev. for* Gothic.

Gotha ('gəuθə; *German* 'goːta) *n* a town in central Germany, in Thuringia on the N edge of the Thuringian forest: capital of Saxe-Coburg-Gotha (1826–1918); noted for the *Almanach de Gotha* (a record of the royal and noble houses of Europe, first published in 1764). Pop.: 57 360 (1989 est.).

Gothenburg ('gɒθən,bɜːg) *n* the English name for **Göteborg.**

Gothic ('gɒθɪk) *adj* **1** denoting, relating to, or resembling the style of architecture that was used in W Europe from the 12th to the 16th centuries, characterized by the lancet arch, the ribbed vault, and the flying buttress. See also **Gothic Revival. 2** of or relating to the style of sculpture, painting, or other arts as practised in W Europe from the 12th to the 16th centuries. **3** (*sometimes not cap.*) of or relating to a literary style characterized by gloom, the grotesque, and the supernatural, popular esp. in the late 18th century: when used of modern literature, films, etc., sometimes spelt: **Gothick. 4** of, relating to, or characteristic of the Goths or their language. **5** (*sometimes not cap.*) primitive and barbarous in style, behaviour, etc. **6** of or relating to the Middle Ages. **7** another word for **Goth** (sense 4). ◆ *n* **8** Gothic architecture or art. **9** the extinct language of the ancient Goths, known mainly from fragments of a translation of the Bible made in the 4th century by Bishop Wulfila. See also **East Germanic. 10** Also called (esp. Brit): **black letter.** the family of heavy script typefaces. **11** another word for **Goth** (sense 3). ▸ **'Gothically** *adv*

Gothic arch *n* another name for **lancet arch.**

Gothicism ('gɒθɪ,sɪzəm) *n* **1** conformity to, use of, or imitation of the Gothic style, esp. in architecture. **2** crudeness of manner or style.

Gothicize *or* **Gothicise** ('gɒθɪ,saɪz) *vb* (*tr*) to make Gothic in style. ▸ **'Gothi,cizer** *or* **'Gothi,ciser** *n*

Gothic Revival *n* a Gothic style of architecture popular between the late 18th and late 19th centuries, exemplified by the Houses of Parliament in London (1840). Also called: **neogothic.**

go through *vb* (*intr*) **1** (*adv*) to be approved or accepted: *the amendment went through.* **2** (*prep*) to consume; exhaust: *we went through our supplies in a day; some men go through a pair of socks in no time.* **3** (*prep*) Also: **go over.** to examine and revise as necessary: *he went through the figures.* **4** (*prep*) to suffer: *she went through tremendous pain.* **5** (*prep*) Also: **go over.** to rehearse: *let's just go through the details again.* **6** (*prep*) Also: **go over.** to clean: *she went through the cupboards in the spring-cleaning.* **7** (*prep*) to participate in: *she went through the degree ceremony without getting too nervous.* **8** (*adv;* foll. by *with*) to bring to a successful conclusion, often by persistence. **9** (*prep*) (of a book) to be published in: *that book has gone through three printings this year alone.*

Gotland ('gɒtlənd; *Swedish* 'gɔtlant), **Gothland** ('gɒθlənd), *or* **Gottland** ('gɒtlənd) *n* an island in the Baltic Sea, off the SE coast of Sweden: important trading centre since the Bronze Age; long disputed between Sweden and Denmark, finally becoming Swedish in 1645; tourism and agriculture now important. Capital: Visby. Pop.: (including associated islands) 58 237 (1994 est.). Area: 3140 sq. km (1212 sq. miles).

go to *vb (intr, prep)* **1** to be awarded to: *the Nobel prize last year went to a Scot.* **2 go to it.** to tackle a task vigorously. ◆ *interj* **3** *Archaic.* an exclamation expressing surprise, encouragement, etc.

go together *vb (intr, adv)* **1** to be mutually suited; harmonize: *the colours go well together.* **2** *Informal.* (of two people) to have a romantic or sexual relationship: *they had been going together for two years.*

gotta ('gɒtə) *vb Slang. contraction of* got to.

gotten ('gɒtᵊn) *vb U.S.* **1** a past participle of **get. 2 have gotten.** (*not usually in the infinitive*) **2a** to have obtained: *he had gotten a car for his 21st birthday.* **2b** to have become: *I've gotten sick of your constant bickering.*

Götterdämmerung (ˌgɒtə'dɛməˌrʊŋ; *German* gœtər'dɛmərʊŋ) *n German myth.* the twilight of the gods; their ultimate destruction in a battle with the forces of evil. Norse equivalent: **Ragnarök.**

Gottfried von Strassburg (*German* 'gɔtfriːt fɔn 'ʃtraːsbʊrk) *n* early 13th-century German poet; author of the incomplete epic *Tristan and Isolde,* the version of the legend that served as the basis of Wagner's opera.

Göttingen ('gœtɪŋən) *n* a city in central Germany, in Lower Saxony: important member of the Hanseatic League (14th century); university, founded in 1734 by George II of England. Pop.: 126 253 (1996 est.).

Gottsched (*German* 'gɔtʃɛd) *n* **Johann Christoph.** 1700–66, German critic, dramatist, and translator.

Götz von Berlichingen (*German* gœts fɔn 'bɛrlɪçɪŋən). See **Berlichingen.**

gouache (gʊ'ɑːʃ) *n* **1** Also called: **body colour.** a painting technique using opaque watercolour paint in which the pigments are bound with glue and the lighter tones contain white. **2** the paint used in this technique. **3** a painting done by this method. [C19: from French, from Italian *guazzo* puddle, from Latin *aquātiō* a watering place, from *aqua* water]

Gouda ('gaʊdə; *Dutch* 'xɔudaː) *n* **1** a town in the W Netherlands, in South Holland province: important medieval cloth trade; famous for its cheese. Pop.: 69 917 (1994). **2** a large round Dutch cheese, mild and similar in taste to Edam.

gouge (gaʊdʒ) *vb (mainly tr)* **1** (usually foll. by *out*) to scoop or force (something) out of its position, esp. with the fingers or a pointed instrument. **2** (sometimes foll. by *out*) to cut (a hole or groove) in (something) with a sharp instrument or tool. **3** *U.S. and Canadian informal.* to extort from. **4** (*also intr*) *Austral.* to dig for (opal). ◆ *n* **5** a type of chisel with a blade that has a concavo-convex section. **6** a mark or groove made with, or as if with, a gouge. **7** *Geology.* a fine deposit of rock fragments, esp. clay, occurring between the walls of a fault or mineral vein. **8** *U.S. and Canadian informal.* extortion; swindling. [C15: from French, from Late Latin *gulbia* a chisel, of Celtic origin]

gouger ('gaʊdʒə) *n* **1** a person or tool that gouges. **2** *Irish dialect.* a low-class city lout.

goujon ('guːʒɒn) *n* a small strip of fish or chicken, coated in breadcrumbs and deep-fried. [French, literally: gudgeon]

goulash ('guːlæʃ) *n* **1** Also called: **Hungarian goulash.** a rich stew, originating in Hungary, made of beef, lamb, or veal highly seasoned with paprika. **2** *Bridge.* a method of dealing in threes and fours without first shuffling the cards, to produce freak hands. [C19: from Hungarian *gulyás hus* herdsman's meat, from *gulya* herd]

Gould (guːld) *n* **1 Benjamin Apthorp.** 1824–96, U.S. astronomer: the first to use the telegraph to determine longitudes; founded the *Astronomical Journal* (1849). **2 Glenn.** 1932–82, Canadian pianist.

go under *vb (intr, mainly adv)* **1** (*also prep*) to sink below (a surface). **2** to founder or drown. **3** to be conquered or overwhelmed: *the firm went under in the economic crisis.*

Gounod ('guːnəʊ; *French* guno) *n* **Charles François** (ʃarl frɑ̃swa). 1818–93, French composer of the operas *Faust* (1859) and *Romeo and Juliet* (1867).

go up *vb (intr, mainly adv)* **1** (*also prep*) to move or lead to or as if to a higher place or level; rise; increase: *prices are always going up; the curtain goes up at eight o'clock; new buildings are going up all around us.* **2** to be destroyed: *the house went up in flames.* **3** *Brit.* to go or return (to college or university) at the beginning of a term or academic year.

gourami ('gʊərəmɪ) *n, pl* **-mi** *or* **-mis. 1** a large SE Asian labyrinth fish, *Osphronemus goramy,* used for food and (when young) as an aquarium fish. **2** any of various other labyrinth fishes, such as *Helostoma temmincki* (**kissing gourami**), many of which are brightly coloured and popular aquarium fishes. [from Malay *gurami*]

gourd (gʊəd) *n* **1** the fruit of any of various cucurbitaceous or similar plants, esp. the bottle gourd and some squashes, whose dried shells are used for ornament, drinking cups, etc. **2** any plant that bears this fruit. See also **sour gourd, dishcloth gourd, calabash. 3** a bottle or flask made from the dried shell of the bottle gourd. **4** a small bottle shaped like a gourd. [C14: from Old French *gourde,* ultimately from Latin *cucurbita*] ▸ **'gourdˌlike** *adj* ▸ **'gourd-ˌshaped** *adj*

gourde (gʊəd) *n* the standard monetary unit of Haiti, divided into 100 centimes. [C19: from French, feminine of *gourd* heavy, from Latin *gurdus* a stupid person]

gourmand ('gʊəmənd; *French* gurmɑ̃) *or* **gormand** *n* a person devoted to eating and drinking, esp. to excess. [C15: from Old French *gourmant,* of uncertain origin] ▸ **'gourmandˌism** *n*

gourmandise (ˌgʊəmən'diːz) *or* **gormandize** *n* a love of and taste for good food.

gourmet ('gʊəmeɪ; *French* gurmɛ) *n* a person who cultivates a discriminating palate for the enjoyment of good food and drink. [C19: from French, from Old French *gromet* serving boy]

Gourmont (*French* gurmɔ̃) *n* **Remy de** (rəmi də). 1858–1915, French symbolist critic and novelist.

gout (gaʊt) *n* **1** a metabolic disease characterized by painful inflammation of certain joints, esp. of the big toe and foot, caused by deposits of sodium urate in them. **2** *Archaic.* a drop or splash, esp. of blood. [C13: from Old French *goute* gout (thought to result from drops of humours), from Latin *gutta* a drop] ▸ **'gouty** *adj* ▸ **'goutily** *adv* ▸ **'goutiness** *n*

goût *French.* (gu) *n* taste or good taste.

goutweed ('gaʊtˌwiːd) *n* a widely naturalized Eurasian umbelliferous plant, *Aegopodium podagraria,* with white flowers and creeping underground stems. Also called: **bishop's weed, ground elder, herb Gerard.**

Gov. *or* **gov.** *abbrev. for:* **1** government. **2** governor.

govern ('gʌvᵊn) *vb (mainly tr)* **1** (*also intr*) to direct and control the actions, affairs, policies, functions, etc., of (a political unit, organization, nation, etc.); rule. **2** to exercise restraint over; regulate or direct: *to govern one's temper.* **3** to be a predominant influence on (something); decide or determine (something): *his injury governed his decision to avoid sports.* **4** to control the speed of (an engine, machine, etc.) using a governor. **5** to control the rate of flow of (a fluid) by using an automatic valve. **6** (of a word) to determine the inflection of (another word): *Latin nouns govern adjectives that modify them.* [C13: from Old French *gouverner,* from Latin *gubernāre* to steer, from Greek *kubernan*] ▸ **'governable** *adj* ▸ **ˌgoverna'bility** *or* **'governableness** *n*

governance ('gʌvənəns) *n* **1** government, control, or authority. **2** the action, manner, or system of governing.

governess ('gʌvənɪs) *n* a woman teacher employed in a private household to teach and train the children.

government ('gʌvənmənt, 'gʌvəmənt) *n* **1** the exercise of political authority over the actions, affairs, etc., of a political unit, people, etc., as well as the performance of certain functions for this unit or body; the action of governing; political rule and administration. **2** the system or form by which a community, etc., is ruled: *tyrannical government.* **3a** the executive policy-making body of a political unit, community, etc.; ministry or administration: *yesterday we got a new government.* **3b** (*cap. when of a specific country*): *the British Government.* **4a** the state and its administration: *blame it on the government.* **4b** (*as modifier*): *a government agency.* **5** regulation; direction. **6** *Grammar.* the determination of the form of one word by another word. ▸ **governmental** (ˌgʌvən'mɛntᵊl, ˌgʌvə'mɛntᵊl) *adj* ▸ **ˌgovern'mentally** *adv*

government issue *adj* supplied by a government or government agency.

government man *n Austral.* (in the 19th century) a convict.

governor ('gʌvənə) *n* **1** a person who governs. **2** the ruler or chief magistrate of a colony, province, etc. **3** the representative of the Crown in a British colony. **4** *Brit.* the senior administrator or head of a society, prison, etc. **5** the chief executive of any state in the U.S. **6** a device that controls the speed of an engine, esp. by regulating the supply of fuel, etc., either to limit the maximum speed or to maintain a constant speed. **7** *Grammar.* Also called: **head. 7a** a word in a phrase or clause that is the principal item and gives the function of the whole, as *hat* in *the big red hat.* **7b** (*as modifier*): *a governor noun.* **8** *Brit. informal.* a name or title of respect for a father, employer, etc. ◆ Related adj: **gubernatorial.**

governor general *n, pl* **governors general** *or* **governor generals. 1** the representative of the Crown in a dominion of the Commonwealth or a British colony; vicegerent. **2** *Brit.* a governor with jurisdiction or precedence over other governors. ▸ **ˌgovernor-'generalˌship** *n*

governorship ('gʌvənəˌʃɪp) *n* the office, jurisdiction, or term of a governor.

Govind Singh ('gəʊvɪnd sɪŋ) *n* See **Gobind Singh.**

Govt *or* **govt** *abbrev. for* government.

gowan ('gaʊən) *n Scot.* any of various yellow or white flowers growing in fields, esp. the common daisy. [C16: variant of *gollan,* probably of Scandinavian origin; compare Old Norse *gullin* golden] ▸ **'gowaned** *adj* ▸ **'gowany** *adj*

Gower[1] ('gaʊə) *n* **the.** a peninsula in S Wales, in Swansea county in the Bristol Channel: mainly agricultural with several resorts.

Gower[2] ('gaʊə) *n* **1 David** (**Ivon**). born 1957, English cricketer. **2 John.** ?1330–1408, English poet, noted particularly for his tales of love, the *Confessio Amantis.*

go with *vb (intr, prep)* **1** to accompany. **2** to blend or harmonize: *that new wallpaper goes well with the furniture.* **3** to be a normal part of: *three acres of land go with the house.* **4** to be of the same opinion as: *I'm sorry I can't go with you on your new plan.* **5** (of two people) to associate frequently with (each other).

go without *vb (intr)* **1** *Chiefly Brit.* to be denied or deprived of (something, esp. food): *if you don't like your tea you can go without.* **2 that goes without saying.** that is obvious or self-evident.

gowk (gaʊk) *n Scot. and northern English dialect.* **1** a stupid person; fool. **2** a cuckoo. [from Old Norse *gaukr* cuckoo; related to Old High German *gouh*]

gown (gaʊn) *n* **1** any of various outer garments, such as a woman's elegant or formal dress, a dressing robe, or a protective garment, esp. one worn by surgeons during operations. **2** a loose wide garment indicating status, such as worn by academics. **3** the members of a university as opposed to the other residents of the university town. Compare **town** (sense 7). ◆ *vb* **4** (*tr*) to supply with or dress in a gown. [C14: from Old French *goune,* from Late Latin *gunna* garment made of leather or fur, of Celtic origin]

goy (gɔɪ) *n, pl* **goyim** ('gɔɪɪm) *or* **goys.** a Jewish word for a gentile. [from Yiddish, from Hebrew *goi* people] ▸ **'goyish** *adj*

Goya ('gɔɪə; *Spanish* 'goja) *n* **Francisco de** (fran'θisko de), full name *Francisco José de Goya y Lucientes.* 1746–1828, Spanish painter and etcher; well known for his portraits, he became court painter to Charles IV of Spain (1799). He recorded the French invasion of Spain in a series of etchings *The Disasters of War* (1810–14) and two paintings *2 May 1808* and *3 May 1808* (1814).

Goyen ('gɔɪən) *n* **Jan Josephszoon van** (dʒæn 'dʒəʊzɪfsˌzʊn væn). 1596–1656, Dutch landscape painter and etcher.

GP *abbrev. for:* **1** general practitioner. **2** Gallup Poll. **3** (in Britain) graduated pension. **4** Grand Prix. **5** gas-permeable (contact lens). **6** *Music.* general pause.
GPI *abbrev. for* general paralysis of the insane (general paresis).
GPMU (in Britain) *abbrev. for* Graphical, Paper and Media Union.
GPO *abbrev. for* general post office.
GPS *abbrev. for:* **1** global positioning system. **2** (in Australia) Great Public Schools; used of a group of mainly nonstate schools, and of sporting competitions between them.
GPU *abbrev. for* State Political Administration; the Soviet police and secret police from 1922 to 1923. **[**from Russian *Gosudarstvennoye politicheskoye upravlenie***]**
GQ *Military. abbrev. for* general quarters.
GR *international car registration for* Greece.
gr. *abbrev. for:* **1** grade. **2** grain. **3** gross. **4** gram.
Gr. *abbrev. for:* **1** Grecian. **2** Greece. **3** Greek.
Graafian follicle ('grɑːfɪən) *n* a fluid-filled vesicle in the mammalian ovary containing a developing egg cell. **[C17:** named after R. de *Graaf* (1641–73), Dutch anatomist**]**
grab (græb) *vb* **grabs, grabbing, grabbed. 1** to seize hold of (something). **2** (*tr*) to seize illegally or unscrupulously. **3** (*tr*) to arrest; catch. **4** (*intr*) (of a brake or clutch in a vehicle) to grip and release intermittently causing juddering. **5** (*tr*) *Informal.* to catch the attention or interest of; impress. ◆ *n* **6** the act or an instance of grabbing. **7** a mechanical device for gripping objects, esp. the hinged jaws of a mechanical excavator. **8** something that is grabbed. **9 up for grabs.** *Informal.* available to be bought, claimed, or won. **[C16:** probably from Middle Low German or Middle Dutch *grabben;* related to Swedish *grabba,* Sanskrit *grbhnāti* he seizes**]** ▸ **'grabber** *n*
grab bag *n* **1** a collection of miscellaneous things. **2** *U.S., Canadian, and Austral.* a bag or other container from which gifts are drawn at random.
grabble ('græbᵊl) *vb* **1** (*intr*) to scratch or feel about with the hands. **2** (*intr*) to fall to the ground; sprawl. **3** (*tr*) *Caribbean.* to seize rashly. **[C16:** probably from Dutch *grabbelen,* from *grabben* to GRAB**]** ▸ **'grabbler** *n*
graben ('grɑːbᵊn) *n* an elongated trough of land produced by subsidence of the earth's crust between two faults. **[C19:** from German, from Old High German *graban* to dig**]**
Gracchus ('grækəs) *n* **Tiberius Sempronius** (taɪ'bɪərɪəs sɛm'prəʊnɪəs). ?163–133 B.C., and his younger brother, **Gaius Sempronius** ('gaɪəs), 153–121 B.C., known as *the Gracchi.* Roman tribunes and reformers. Tiberius attempted to redistribute public land among the poor but was murdered in the ensuing riot. Violence again occurred when the reform was revived by Gaius, and he too was killed.
grace (greɪs) *n* **1** elegance and beauty of movement, form, expression, or proportion. **2** a pleasing or charming quality. **3** goodwill or favour. **4** the granting of a favour or the manifestation of goodwill, esp. by a superior. **5** a sense of propriety and consideration for others. **6** (*pl*) **6a** affectation of manner (esp. in the phrase **airs and graces**). **6b in (someone's) good graces.** regarded favourably and with kindness by (someone). **7** mercy; clemency. **8** *Christianity.* **8a** the free and unmerited favour of God shown towards man. **8b** the divine assistance and power given to man in spiritual rebirth and sanctification. **8c** the condition of being favoured or sanctified by God. **8d** an unmerited gift, favour, etc., granted by God. **9** a short prayer recited before or after a meal to invoke a blessing upon the food or give thanks for it. **10** *Music.* a melodic ornament or decoration. **11** See **days of grace. 12 with (a) bad grace.** unwillingly or grudgingly. **13 with (a) good grace.** willingly or cheerfully. ◆ *vb* **14** (*tr*) to add elegance and beauty to: *flowers graced the room.* **15** (*tr*) to honour or favour: *to grace a party with one's presence.* **16** to ornament or decorate (a melody, part, etc.) with nonessential notes. **[C12:** from Old French, from Latin *grātia,* from *grātus* pleasing**]**
Grace[1] (greɪs) *n* (preceded by *your, his,* or *her*) a title used to address or refer to a duke, duchess, or archbishop.
Grace[2] (greɪs) *n* **W(illiam) G(ilbert).** 1848–1915, English cricketer.
grace-and-favour *n* (*modifier*) *Brit.* (of a house, flat, etc.) owned by the sovereign and granted free of rent to a person to whom the sovereign wishes to express gratitude.
grace cup *n* a cup, as of wine, passed around at the end of the meal for the final toast.
graceful ('greɪsfʊl) *adj* characterized by beauty of movement, style, form, etc. ▸ **'gracefully** *adv* ▸ **'gracefulness** *n*
graceless ('greɪslɪs) *adj* **1** lacking any sense of right and wrong; depraved. **2** lacking grace or excellence. ▸ **'gracelessly** *adv* ▸ **'gracelessness** *n*
grace note *n Music.* a note printed in small type to indicate that it is melodically and harmonically nonessential.
Graces ('greɪsɪz) *pl n Greek myth.* three sisters, the goddesses Aglaia, Euphrosyne, and Thalia, givers of charm and beauty.
gracile ('græsaɪl) *adj* **1** gracefully thin or slender. **2** a less common word for **graceful. [C17:** from Latin *gracilis* slender**]** ▸ **gracility** (græ'sɪlɪtɪ) *or* **'gracileness** *n*
gracioso (ˌgræsɪ'əʊsəʊ; *Spanish* gra'θjoso) *n, pl* **-sos.** a clown in Spanish comedy. **[C17:** from Spanish: GRACIOUS**]**
gracious ('greɪʃəs) *adj* **1** characterized by or showing kindness and courtesy. **2** condescendingly courteous, benevolent, or indulgent. **3** characterized by or suitable for a life of elegance, ease, and indulgence: *gracious living; gracious furnishings.* **4** merciful or compassionate. **5** *Obsolete.* fortunate, prosperous, or happy. ◆ *interj* **6** an expression of mild surprise or wonder (often in exclamatory phrases such as **good gracious!, gracious me!**). ▸ **'graciously** *adv* ▸ **'graciousness** *n*
grackle ('grækᵊl) *n* **1** Also called: **crow blackbird.** any American songbird of the genera *Quiscalus* and *Cassidix,* having a dark iridescent plumage: family *Icteridae* (American orioles). **2** any of various starlings of the genus *Gracula,* such as *G. religiosa* (**Indian grackle** or **hill mynah**). **[C18:** from New Latin *Grācula,* from Latin *grāculus* jackdaw**]**
grad (græd) *n Informal.* a graduate.
grad. *abbrev. for:* **1** *Maths.* gradient. **2** *Education.* graduate(d).
gradable ('greɪdəbᵊl) *adj* **1** capable of being graded. **2** *Linguistics.* denoting or relating to a word in whose meaning there is some implicit relationship to a standard: *"big" and "small" are gradable adjectives.* ◆ *n* **3** *Linguistics.* a word of this kind. ▸ **ˌgrada'bility** *or* **'gradableness** *n*
gradate (grə'deɪt) *vb* **1** to change or cause to change imperceptibly, as from one colour, tone, or degree to another. **2** (*tr*) to arrange in grades or ranks.
gradation (grə'deɪʃən) *n* **1** a series of systematic stages; gradual progression. **2** (*often pl*) a stage or degree in such a series or progression. **3** the act or process of arranging or forming in stages, grades, etc., or of progressing evenly. **4** (in painting, drawing, or sculpture) transition from one colour, tone, or surface to another through a series of very slight changes. **5** *Linguistics.* any change in the quality or length of a vowel within a word indicating certain distinctions, such as inflectional or tense differentiations. See **ablaut. 6** *Geology.* the natural levelling of land as a result of the building up or wearing down of pre-existing formations. ▸ **gra'dational** *adj* ▸ **gra'dationally** *adv*
grade (greɪd) *n* **1** a position or degree in a scale, as of quality, rank, size, or progression: *small-grade eggs; high-grade timber.* **2** a group of people or things of the same category. **3** *Chiefly U.S.* a military or other rank. **4** a stage in a course of progression. **5** a mark or rating indicating achievement or the worth of work done, as at school. **6** *U.S. and Canadian.* a unit of pupils of similar age or ability taught together at school. **7** another word (esp. U.S. and Canadian) for **gradient** (senses 1, 2). **8** a unit of angle equal to one hundredth of a right angle or 0.9 degree. **9** *Stockbreeding.* **9a** an animal with one purebred parent and one of unknown or unimproved breeding. **9b** (*as modifier*): *a grade sheep.* Compare **crossbred** (sense 2), **purebred** (sense 2). **10** *Linguistics.* one of the forms of the vowel in a morpheme when this vowel varies because of gradation. **11 at grade. 11a** on the same level. **11b** (of a river profile or land surface) at an equilibrium level and slope, because there is a balance between erosion and deposition. **12 make the grade.** *Informal.* **12a** to reach the required standard. **12b** to succeed. ◆ *vb* **13** (*tr*) to arrange according to quality, rank, etc. **14** (*tr*) to determine the grade of or assign a grade to. **15** (*intr*) to achieve or deserve a grade or rank. **16** to change or blend (something) gradually; merge. **17** (*tr*) to level (ground, a road, etc.) to a suitable gradient. **18** (*tr*) *Stockbreeding.* to cross (one animal) with another to produce a grade animal. **[C16:** from French, from Latin *gradus* step, from *gradī* to step**]**
-grade *adj combining form.* indicating a kind or manner of movement or progression: *plantigrade; retrograde.* **[**via French from Latin *-gradus,* from *gradus* a step, from *gradī* to walk**]**
grade cricket *n Austral.* competitive cricket, in which cricket club teams are arranged in grades.
grade crossing *n* the U.S. and Canadian name for **level crossing.**
graded post *n Brit.* a position in a school having special responsibility for which additional payment is given.
gradely ('greɪdlɪ) *adj* **-lier, -liest.** *Midland English dialect.* fine; excellent. **[C13** *greithlic, greithli,* from Old Norse *greidhligr,* from *greidhr* ready**]**
grader ('greɪdə) *n* **1** a person or thing that grades. **2** a machine, either self-powered or towed by a tractor, that levels earth, rubble, etc., as in road construction.
grade school *n U.S.* another name for **elementary school.**
gradient ('greɪdɪənt) *n* **1** Also called (esp. U.S.): **grade.** a part of a railway, road, etc., that slopes upwards or downwards; inclination. **2** Also called (esp. U.S. and Canadian): **grade.** a measure of such a slope, esp. the ratio of the vertical distance between two points on the slope to the horizontal distance between them. **3** *Physics.* a measure of the change of some physical quantity, such as temperature or electric potential, over a specified distance. **4** *Maths.* **4a** (of a curve) the slope of the tangent at any point on a curve with respect to the horizontal axis. **4b** (of a function, $f(x, y, z)$) the vector whose components along the axes are the partial derivatives of the function with respect to each variable, and whose direction is that in which the derivative of the function has its maximum value. Usually written: grad **f**, ∇f or $\nabla \mathbf{f}$. Compare **curl** (sense 11), **divergence** (sense 4). ◆ *adj* **5** sloping uniformly. **[C19:** from Latin *gradiēns* stepping, from *gradī* to go**]**
gradient post *n* a small white post beside a railway line at a point where the gradient changes having arms set at angles representing the gradients.
gradin ('greɪdɪn) *or* **gradine** (grə'diːn) *n* **1** a ledge above or behind an altar on which candles, a cross, or other ornaments stand. **2** one of a set of steps or seats arranged on a slope, as in an amphitheatre. **[C19:** from French, from Italian *gradino,* a little step, from *grado* step; see GRADE**]**
gradiometer (ˌgrædɪ'ɒmɪtə) *n* **1** *Physics.* an instrument for measuring the gradient of a magnetic field. **2** *Surveying.* an instrument used to ensure that a long gradient remains constant.
gradual ('grædjʊəl) *adj* **1** occurring, developing, moving, etc., in small stages: *a gradual improvement in health.* **2** not steep or abrupt: *a gradual slope.* ◆ *n* **3** (*often cap.*) *Christianity.* **3a** an antiphon or group of several antiphons, usually from the Psalms, sung or recited immediately after the epistle at Mass. **3b** a book of plainsong containing the words and music of the parts of the Mass that are sung by the cantors and choir. **[C16:** from Medieval Latin *graduālis* relating to steps, from Latin *gradus* a step**]** ▸ **'gradually** *adv* ▸ **'gradualness** *n*
gradualism ('grædjʊəˌlɪzəm) *n* **1** the policy of seeking to change something or achieve a goal gradually rather than quickly or violently, esp. in politics. **2** the theory that explains major changes in rock strata, fossils, etc. in terms of gradual evolutionary processes rather than sudden violent catastrophes. Compare **catastrophism.** ▸ **'gradualist** *n, adj* ▸ **ˌgradual'istic** *adj*

graduand ('grædjuˌænd) *n Chiefly Brit.* a person who is about to graduate. [C19: from Medieval Latin *graduandus,* gerundive of *graduārī* to GRADUATE]

graduate *n* ('grædjuɪt). **1a** a person who has been awarded a first degree from a university or college. **1b** *(as modifier): a graduate profession.* **2** *U.S. and Canadian.* a student who has completed a course of studies at a high school and received a diploma. **3** *U.S.* a container, such as a flask, marked to indicate its capacity. ◆ *vb* ('grædjuˌeɪt). **4** to receive or cause to receive a degree or diploma. **5** *(tr) Chiefly U.S. and Canadian.* to confer a degree, diploma, etc. upon. **6** *(tr)* to mark (a thermometer, flask, etc.) with units of measurement; calibrate. **7** *(tr)* to arrange or sort into groups according to type, quality, etc. **8** *(intr; often foll. by to)* to change by degrees (from something to something else). [C15: from Medieval Latin *graduārī* to take a degree, from Latin *gradus* a step] ▶ **'graduˌator** *n*

graduation (ˌgrædju'eɪʃən) *n* **1** the act of graduating or the state of being graduated. **2** the ceremony at which school or college degrees and diplomas are conferred. **3** a mark or division or all the marks or divisions that indicate measure on an instrument or vessel.

gradus ('greɪdəs) *n, pl* **-duses. 1** a book of études or other musical exercises arranged in order of increasing difficulty. **2** *Prosody.* a dictionary or textbook of prosody for use in writing Latin or Greek verse. [C18: shortened from Latin *Gradus ad Parnassum* a step towards Parnassus, a dictionary of prosody used in the 18th and 19th centuries]

Graeae ('griːiː) *or* **Graiae** *pl n Greek myth.* three aged sea deities, having only one eye and one tooth among them, guardians of their sisters, the Gorgons.

Graecism *or esp. U.S.* **Grecism** ('griːsɪzəm) *n* **1** Greek characteristics or style. **2** admiration for or imitation of these, as in sculpture or architecture. **3** a form of words characteristic or imitative of the idiom of the Greek language.

Graecize, Graecise, *or esp. U.S.* **Grecize** ('griːsaɪz) *vb* another word for **Hellenize.** [C17: from Latin *graecizāre* to imitate the Greeks, from Greek *graikizein*]

Graeco- *or esp. U.S.* **Greco-** ('griːkəʊ, 'grɛkəʊ) *combining form.* Greek: *Graeco-Roman.*

Graeco-Roman *or esp. U.S.* **Greco-Roman** *adj* **1** of, characteristic of, or relating to Greek and Roman influences, as found in Roman sculpture. **2** denoting a style of wrestling in which the legs may not be used to obtain a fall and no hold may be applied below the waist.

Graf (græf) *n* **Steffi.** born 1969, German tennis player: Wimbledon champion 1988, 1989, 1991, 1992, 1993, 1995, and 1996.

Graf *German.* (graːf) *n, pl* ***Grafen*** ('graːfən). a German count: often used as a title. [German, from Old High German *grāvo*]

graffiti (græ'fiːtiː) *pl n sing* **-to** (-təʊ). **1** *(sometimes with sing vb)* drawings, messages, etc., often obscene, scribbled on the walls of public lavatories, advertising posters, etc. **2** *Archaeol.* inscriptions or drawings scratched or carved onto a surface, esp. rock or pottery. [C19: *graffito* from Italian: a little scratch, from *graffio,* from Latin *graphium* stylus, from Greek *grapheion;* see GRAFT[1]] ▶ **graf'fitist** *n*

graft[1] (grɑːft) *n* **1** *Horticulture.* **1a** a small piece of plant tissue (the scion) that is made to unite with an established plant (the stock), which supports and nourishes it. **1b** the plant resulting from the union of scion and stock. **1c** the point of union between the scion and the stock. **2** *Surgery.* a piece of tissue or an organ transplanted from a donor or from the patient's own body to an area of the body in need of the tissue. **3** the act of joining one thing to another by or as if by grafting. ◆ *vb* **4** *Horticulture.* **4a** to induce (a plant or part of a plant) to unite with another part or (of a plant or part of a plant) to unite in this way. **4b** to produce (fruit, flowers, etc.) by this means or (of fruit, flowers, etc.) to grow by this means. **5** to transplant (tissue) or (of tissue) to be transplanted. **6** to attach or incorporate or become attached or incorporated: *to graft a happy ending onto a sad tale.* [C15: from Old French *graffe,* from Medieval Latin *graphium,* from Latin: stylus, from Greek *grapheion,* from *graphein* to write] ▶ **'grafter** *n* ▶ **'grafting** *n*

graft[2] (grɑːft) *Informal.* ◆ *n* **1** work. (esp. in the phrase **hard graft**). **2a** the acquisition of money, power, etc., by dishonest or unfair means, esp. by taking advantage of a position of trust. **2b** something gained in this way, such as profit from government business. **2c** a payment made to a person profiting by such a practice. ◆ *vb* **3** *(intr)* to work. **4** to acquire by or practise graft. [C19: of uncertain origin] ▶ **'grafter** *n*

graft hybrid *n* a plant produced by grafting a scion and stock from dissimilar plants; chimera.

graham ('greɪəm) *n (modifier) Chiefly U.S. and Canadian.* made of graham flour: *graham crackers.* [C19: named after S. *Graham* (1794–1851), American dietetic reformer]

Graham ('greɪəm) *n* **1 Martha.** 1893–1991, U.S. dancer and choreographer. **2 Thomas.** 1805–69, British physicist: proposed **Graham's law** (1831) of gaseous diffusion and coined the terms osmosis, crystalloids, and colloids. **3 William Franklin,** known as *Billy Graham.* born 1918, U.S. evangelist.

Grahame ('greɪəm) *n* **Kenneth.** 1859–1932, Scottish author, noted for the children's classic *The Wind in the Willows* (1908).

graham flour *n Chiefly U.S. and Canadian.* unbolted wheat flour ground from whole-wheat grain, similar to whole-wheat flour.

Graham Land *n* the N part of the Antarctic Peninsula: became part of the British Antarctic Territory in 1962 (formerly part of the Falkland Islands Dependencies).

Graiae ('greɪiː, 'graɪiː) *pl n* a variant of **Graeae.**

Graian Alps ('greɪən, 'graɪ-) *pl n* the N part of the Western Alps, in France and NW Piedmont, Italy. Highest peak: Gran Paradiso, 4061 m (13 323 ft.).

Grail (greɪl) *n* See **Holy Grail.**

grain (greɪn) *n* **1** the small hard seedlike fruit of a grass, esp. a cereal plant. **2** a mass of such fruits, esp. when gathered for food. **3** the plants, collectively, from which such fruits are harvested. **4** a small hard particle: *a grain of sand.* **5a** the general direction or arrangement of the fibrous elements in paper or wood: *to saw across the grain.* **5b** the pattern or texture of wood resulting from such an arrangement: *the attractive grain of the table.* **6** the relative size of the particles of a substance: *sugar of fine grain.* **7a** the granular texture of a rock, mineral, etc. **7b** the appearance of a rock, mineral, etc., determined by the size and arrangement of its constituents. **8a** the outer (hair-side) layer of a hide or skin from which the hair or wool has been removed. **8b** the pattern on the outer surface of such a hide or skin. **9** a surface artificially imitating the grain of wood, leather, stone, etc.; graining. **10** the smallest unit of weight in the avoirdupois, Troy, and apothecaries' systems, based on the average weight of a grain of wheat: in the avoirdupois system it equals 1/7000 of a pound, and in the Troy and apothecaries' systems it equals 1/5760 of a pound. 1 grain is equal to 0.0648 gram. Abbrev.: **gr. 11** Also called: **metric grain.** a metric unit of weight used for pearls or diamonds, equal to 50 milligrams or one quarter of a carat. **12** the threads or direction of threads in a woven fabric. **13** *Photog.* any of a large number of particles in a photographic emulsion, the size of which limit the extent to which an image can be enlarged without serious loss of definition. **14** *Television.* a granular effect in a television picture caused by electrical noise. **15** cleavage lines in crystalline material, parallel to growth planes. **16** *Chem.* any of a large number of small crystals forming a polycrystalline solid, each having a regular array of atoms that differs in orientation from that of the surrounding crystallites. **17** a state of crystallization: *to boil syrup to the grain.* **18** a very small amount: *a grain of truth.* **19** natural disposition, inclination, or character (esp. in the phrase **go against the grain**). **20** *Astronautics.* a homogenous mass of solid propellant in a form designed to give the required combustion characteristics for a particular rocket. **21** *(not in technical usage)* kermes or a red dye made from this insect. **22** *Dyeing.* an obsolete word for **colour. 23 with a grain** *or* **pinch of salt.** without wholly believing: sceptically. ◆ *vb (mainly tr)* **24** *(also intr)* to form grains or cause to form into grains; granulate; crystallize. **25** to give a granular or roughened appearance or texture to. **26** to paint, stain, etc., in imitation of the grain of wood or leather. **27a** to remove the hair or wool from (a hide or skin) before tanning. **27b** to raise the grain pattern on (leather). [C13: from Old French, from Latin *grānum*] ▶ **'grainer** *n* ▶ **'grainless** *adj*

grain alcohol *n* ethanol containing about 10 per cent of water, made by the fermentation of grain.

grain elevator *n* a machine for raising grain to a higher level, esp. one having an endless belt fitted with scoops.

Grainger ('greɪndʒə) *n* **Percy Aldridge.** 1882–1961, Australian pianist, composer, and collector of folk music on which many of his works are based.

graining ('greɪnɪŋ) *n* **1** the pattern or texture of the grain of wood, leather, etc. **2** the process of painting, printing, staining, etc., a surface in imitation of a grain. **3** a surface produced by such a process.

grains of paradise *pl n* the peppery seeds of either of two African zingiberaceous plants, *Aframomum melegueta* or *A. granum-paradisi* used as stimulants, diuretics, etc. Also called: **guinea grains.**

grainy ('greɪnɪ) *adj* **grainier, grainiest. 1** resembling, full of, or composed of grain; granular. **2** resembling the grain of wood, leather, etc. **3** *Photog.* having poor definition because of large grain size. ▶ **'graininess** *n*

grallatorial (ˌgrælə'tɔːrɪəl) *adj* of or relating to long-legged wading birds, such as cranes, herons, and storks. [C19: from New Latin *grallātōrius,* from Latin *grallātor* one who walks on stilts, from *grallae* stilts]

gralloch ('grælək; *Scot.* 'grælɒx) *Brit.* ◆ *n* **1** the entrails of a deer. **2** the act or an instance of disembowelling a deer killed in a hunt. ◆ *vb (tr)* **3** to disembowel (a deer killed in a hunt). [C19: from Scottish Gaelic *grealach* intestines]

gram[1] (græm) *n* a metric unit of mass equal to one thousandth of a kilogram. It is equivalent to 15.432 grains or 0.002 205 pounds. Symbol: g [C18: from French *gramme,* from Late Latin *gramma,* from Greek: small weight, from *graphein* to write]

gram[2] (græm) *n* **1** any of several leguminous plants, such as the beans *Phaseolus mungo* (**black gram** or **urd**) and *P. aureus* (**green gram**), whose seeds are used as food in India. **2** the seed of any of these plants. [C18: from Portuguese *gram* (modern spelling: *grão*), from Latin *grānum* GRAIN]

gram[3] (grɑːm) *n* (in India) a village. [Hindi]

gram. *abbrev. for:* **1** grammar. **2** grammatical.

-gram *n combining form.* indicating a drawing or something written or recorded: *hexagram; telegram.* [from Latin *-gramma,* from Greek, from *gramma* letter and *grammē* line]

grama *or* **grama grass** ('grɑːmə) *n* any of various grasses of the genus *Bouteloua,* of W North America and South America: often used as pasture grasses. [C19: from Spanish, ultimately from Latin *grāmen* grass]

gramarye *or* **gramary** ('græmərɪ) *n Archaic.* magic, necromancy, or occult learning. [C14: from Old French *gramaire* GRAMMAR]

gram atom *or* **gram-atomic weight** *n* an amount of an element equal to its atomic weight expressed in grams: now replaced by the mole. See **mole**[3].

gram calorie *n* another name for **calorie.**

gram equivalent *or* **gram-equivalent weight** *n* an amount of a substance equal to its equivalent weight expressed in grams.

gramercy (grə'mɜːsɪ) *interj Archaic.* **1** many thanks. **2** an expression of surprise, wonder, etc. [C13: from Old French *grand merci* great thanks]

gramicidin *or* **gramicidin D** (ˌgræmɪ'saɪdɪn) *n* an antibiotic used in treating local Gram-positive bacterial infections: obtained from the soil bacterium *Bacillus brevis.* [C20: from GRAM(-POSITIVE) + -CID(E) + -IN]

gramineous (grə'mɪnɪəs) *adj* **1** of, relating to, or belonging to the grass family, *Gramineae.* **2** resembling a grass; grasslike. ◆ Also: **graminaceous** (ˌgræmɪ'neɪʃəs). [C17: from Latin *grāmineus* of grass, grassy, from *grāmen* grass]

graminicolous (ˌɡræmɪˈnɪkələs) *adj* (esp. of parasitic fungi) living on grass.

graminivorous (ˌɡræmɪˈnɪvərəs) *adj* (of animals) feeding on grass. **[C18:** from Latin *grāmen* grass + -VOROUS**]**

grammage (ˈɡræmɪdʒ) *n* the weight of paper expressed as grams per square metre.

grammar (ˈɡræmə) *n* **1** the branch of linguistics that deals with syntax and morphology, sometimes also phonology and semantics. **2** the abstract system of rules in terms of which a person's mastery of his native language can be explained. **3** a systematic description of the grammatical facts of a language. **4** a book containing an account of the grammatical facts of a language or recommendations as to rules for the proper use of a language. **5a** the use of language with regard to its correctness or social propriety, esp. in syntax: *the teacher told him to watch his grammar.* **5b** (*as modifier*): *a grammar book.* **6** the elementary principles of a science or art: *the grammar of drawing.* **[C14:** from Old French *gramaire,* from Latin *grammatica,* from Greek *grammatikē* (*tekhnē*) the grammatical (art), from *grammatikos* concerning letters, from *gramma* letter**]** ▸ **ˈgrammarless** *adj*

grammarian (ɡrəˈmɛərɪən) *n* **1** a person whose occupation is the study of grammar. **2** the author of a grammar.

grammar school *n* **1** *Brit.* (esp. formerly) a state-maintained secondary school providing an education with an academic bias for children who are selected by the eleven-plus examination, teachers' reports, or other means. Compare **secondary modern school, comprehensive school. 2** *U.S.* another term for **elementary school. 3** *N.Z.* a secondary school forming part of the public education system.

grammatical (ɡrəˈmætɪkᵊl) *adj* **1** of or relating to grammar. **2** (of a sentence) well formed; regarded as correct and acceptable by native speakers of the language. ▸ **gramˈmatically** *adv* ▸ **gramˈmaticalness** *n*

grammatical meaning *n* the meaning of a word by reference to its function within a sentence rather than to a world outside the sentence. Compare **lexical meaning, function word.**

grammatology (ˌɡræməˈtɒlədʒɪ) *n* the scientific study of writing systems. ▸ **ˌgrammaˈtologist** *n*

gram molecule *or* **gram-molecular weight** *n* an amount of a compound equal to its molecular weight expressed in grams: now replaced by the mole. See **mole**[3]. ▸ **ˌgram-moˈlecular** *or* **gram-molar** (ˌɡræmˈməʊlə) *adj*

Grammy (ˈɡræmɪ) *n, pl* **-mys** *or* **-mies.** (in the U.S.) one of the gold-plated discs awarded annually for outstanding achievement in the record industry. **[C20:** from GRAM(OPHONE) + *my* as in EMMY**]**

Gram-negative *adj* designating bacteria that fail to retain the violet stain in Gram's method.

gramophone (ˈɡræməˌfəʊn) *n* **1a** Also called: **acoustic gramophone.** a device for reproducing the sounds stored on a record: now usually applied to the nearly obsolete type that uses a clockwork motor and acoustic horn. U.S. and Canadian name: **phonograph. 1b** (*as modifier*): *a gramophone record.* **2** the technique and practice of recording sound on disc: *the gramophone has made music widely available.* **[C19:** originally a trademark, perhaps based on an inversion of *phonogram;* see PHONO-, -GRAM**]** ▸ **gramophonic** (ˌɡræməˈfɒnɪk) *adj*

Grampian Mountains (ˈɡræmpɪən) *pl n* **1** a mountain system of central Scotland, extending from the southwest to the northeast and separating the Highlands from the Lowlands. Highest peak: Ben Nevis, 1343 m (4406 ft.). **2** a mountain range in SE Australia, in W Victoria. ◆ Also called: **the Grampians.**

Grampian Region *n* a former local government region in NE Scotland, formed in 1975 from Aberdeenshire, Kincardineshire, and most of Banffshire and Morayshire; replaced in 1996 by the council areas of Aberdeenshire, City of Aberdeen, and Moray.

Gram-positive *adj* designating bacteria that retain the violet stain in Gram's method.

grampus (ˈɡræmpəs) *n, pl* **-puses. 1** a widely distributed slaty-grey dolphin, *Grampus griseus,* with a blunt snout. **2** another name for **killer whale. [C16:** from Old French *graspois,* from *gras* fat (from Latin *crassus*) + *pois* fish (from Latin *piscis*)**]**

Gramsci (*Italian* ˈɡramʃɪ) *n* **Antonio.** 1891–1937, Italian politician and Marxist theorist: founder (1921) of the Italian Communist party. His important works were written during his imprisonment (1926–37) by the Fascists.

Gram's method *n Bacteriol.* a staining technique used to classify bacteria, based on their ability to retain or lose a violet colour, produced by crystal violet and iodine, after treatment with a decolorizing agent. See also **Gram-negative, Gram-positive. [C19:** named after Hans Christian Joachim *Gram* (1853–1938), Danish physician**]**

gran (ɡræn) *n* an informal word for **grandmother.**

Granada (ɡrəˈnɑːdə) *n* **1** a former kingdom of S Spain, in Andalusia: founded in the 13th century and divided in 1833 into the present-day provinces of Granada, Almería, and Málaga, in Andalusia. **2** a city in S Spain, in Andalusia: capital of the Moorish kingdom of Granada from 1238 to 1492 and a great commercial and cultural centre, containing the Alhambra palace (13th and 14th centuries); university (1531). Pop.: 272 738 (1995 est.). **3** a city in SW Nicaragua, on the NW shore of Lake Nicaragua: the oldest city in the country, founded in 1523 by Córdoba; attacked frequently by pirates in the 17th century. Pop.: 74 396 (1995 est.).

granadilla (ˌɡrænəˈdɪlə) *n* **1** any of various passionflowers, such as *Passiflora quadrangularis* (**giant granadilla**), that have edible egg-shaped fleshy fruit. **2** Also called: **passion fruit.** the fruit of such a plant. **[C18:** from Spanish, diminutive of *granada* pomegranate, from Late Latin *grānātum***]**

Granados (*Spanish* ɡraˈnaðɔs) *n* **Enrique** (enˈrrike), full name *Enrique Granados y Campina.* 1867–1916, Spanish composer, noted for the *Goyescas* (1911) for piano, which formed the basis for an opera of the same name.

granary (ˈɡrænərɪ; *U.S.* ˈɡreɪnərɪ) *n, pl* **-ries. 1** a building or store room for storing threshed grain, farm feed, etc. **2** a region that produces a large amount of grain. ◆ *adj* **3** (*cap.*) *Trademark.* (of bread, flour, etc.) containing malted wheat grain. **[C16:** from Latin *grānārium,* from *grānum* GRAIN**]**

Gran Canaria (ɡraŋ kaˈnarja) *n* the Spanish name for **Grand Canary.**

gran cassa (*Italian* ɡran ˈkassa) *n Music.* another name for **bass drum. [**Italian: great drum**]**

Gran Chaco (*Spanish* ɡran ˈtʃako) *n* a plain of S central South America, between the Andes and the Paraguay River in SE Bolivia, E Paraguay, and N Argentina: huge swamps and scrub forest. Area: about 780 000 sq. km (300 000 sq. miles). Often shortened to: **Chaco.**

grand (ɡrænd) *adj* **1** large or impressive in size, extent, or consequence: *grand mountain scenery.* **2** characterized by or attended with magnificence or display; sumptuous: *a grand feast.* **3** of great distinction or pretension; dignified or haughty. **4** designed to impress: *he punctuated his story with grand gestures.* **5** very good; wonderful. **6** comprehensive; complete: *a grand total.* **7** worthy of respect; fine: *a grand old man.* **8** large or impressive in conception or execution: *grand ideas.* **9** most important; chief: *the grand arena.* ◆ *n* **10** short for **grand piano. 11** (*pl* **grand**) *Slang.* a thousand pounds or dollars. **[C16:** from Old French, from Latin *grandis***]** ▸ **ˈgrandly** *adv* ▸ **ˈgrandness** *n*

grand- *prefix* (in designations of kinship) one generation removed in ascent or descent: *grandson; grandfather.* **[**from French *grand-,* on the model of Latin *magnus* in such phrases as *avunculus magnus* great-uncle**]**

grandad, granddad (ˈɡrænˌdæd), **grandaddy,** *or* **granddaddy** (ˈɡrænˌdædɪ) *n, pl* **-dads** *or* **-daddies.** informal words for **grandfather.**

grandad shirt *n* a long-sleeved collarless shirt.

grandam (ˈɡrændəm, -dæm) *or* **grandame** (ˈɡrændeɪm, -dəm) *n* an archaic word for **grandmother. [C13:** from Anglo-French *grandame,* from Old French GRAND- + *dame* lady, mother**]**

grandaunt (ˈɡrændˌɑːnt) *n* another name for **great-aunt.**

Grand Bahama *n* an island in the Atlantic, in the W Bahamas. Pop.: 40 898 (1990). Area: 1114 sq. km (430 sq. miles).

Grand Banks *pl n* a part of the continental shelf in the Atlantic, extending for about 560 km (350 miles) off the SE coast of Newfoundland: meeting place of the cold Labrador Current and the warm Gulf Stream, producing frequent fogs and rich fishing grounds.

Grand Canal *n* **1** a canal in E China, extending north from Hangzhou to Tianjin: the longest canal in China, now partly silted up; central section, linking the Yangtze and Yellow Rivers, finished in 486 B.C.; north section finished by Kublai Khan between 1282 and 1292. Length: about 1600 km (1000 miles). Chinese name: **Da Yunhe. 2** a canal in Venice, forming the main water thoroughfare: noted for its bridges, the Rialto, and the fine palaces along its banks.

Grand Canary *n* an island in the Atlantic, in the Canary Islands: part of the Spanish province of Las Palmas. Capital: Las Palmas. Pop.: 631 000 (latest est.). Area: 1533 sq. km (592 sq. miles). Spanish name: **Gran Canaria.**

Grand Canyon *n* a gorge of the Colorado River in N Arizona, extending from its junction with the Little Colorado River to Lake Mead; cut by vertical river erosion through the multicoloured strata of a high plateau; partly contained in the **Grand Canyon National Park,** covering 2610 sq. km (1008 sq. miles). Length: 451 km (280 miles). Width: 6 km (4 miles) to 29 km (18 miles). Greatest depth: over 1.5 km (1 mile).

grand chain *n* a figure in formation dances, such as the lancers and Scottish reels, in which couples split up and move around in a circle in opposite directions, passing all other dancers until reaching their original partners.

grandchild (ˈɡrænˌtʃaɪld) *n, pl* **-children** (-ˌtʃɪldrən). the son or daughter of one's child.

Grand Coulee (ˈkuːlɪ) *n* a canyon in central Washington State, over 120 m (400 ft.) deep, at the N end of which is situated the **Grand Coulee Dam,** on the Columbia River. Height of dam: 168 m (550 ft.). Length of dam: 1310 m (4300 ft.).

granddaughter (ˈɡrænˌdɔːtə) *n* a daughter of one's son or daughter.

grand duchess *n* **1** the wife or a widow of a grand duke. **2** a woman who holds the rank of grand duke in her own right.

grand duchy *n* the territory, state, or principality of a grand duke or grand duchess.

grand duke *n* **1** a prince or nobleman who rules a territory, state, or principality. **2** a son or a male descendant in the male line of a Russian tsar. **3** a medieval Russian prince who ruled over other princes.

grande dame *French.* (ɡrɑ̃d dam) *n* a woman regarded as the most experienced, prominent, or venerable member of her profession, etc.: *the* grande dame *of fashion.*

grandee (ɡrænˈdiː) *n* **1** a Spanish or Portuguese prince or nobleman of the highest rank. **2** a man of great rank or eminence. **[C16:** from Spanish *grande***]** ▸ **granˈdeeship** *n*

Grande-Terre (*French* ɡrɑ̃dtɛr) *n* a French island in the Caribbean, in the Lesser Antilles: one of the two main islands which constitute Guadeloupe. Chief town: Pointe-à-Pitre.

grandeur (ˈɡrændʒə) *n* **1** personal greatness, esp. when based on dignity, character, or accomplishments. **2** magnificence; splendour. **3** pretentious or bombastic behaviour.

Grand Falls *pl n* the former name (until 1965) of **Churchill Falls.**

grandfather (ˈɡrænˌfɑːðə, ˈɡrænd-) *n* **1** the father of one's father or mother. **2** (*often pl*) a male ancestor. **3** (*often cap.*) a familiar term of address for an old man. **4** *Dialect.* a caterpillar or woodlouse.

grandfather clause *n* **1** *U.S. history.* a clause in the constitutions of several Southern states that waived electoral literacy requirements for lineal descendants of people voting before 1867, thus ensuring the franchise for illiterate

Whites: declared unconstitutional in 1915. **2** a clause in legislation that forbids or regulates an activity so that those engaged in it are exempted from the ban.

grandfather clock *n* any of various types of long-pendulum clocks in tall standing wooden cases, usually between six and eight feet tall. Also called: **longcase clock.**

grandfatherly ('græn,fɑːðəlɪ, 'grænd-) *adj* of, resembling, or suitable to a grandfather, esp. in being kindly.

grand final *n Austral.* the final game of the season in any of various sports, esp. football.

Grand Guignol *French.* (grɑ̃ giɲɔl) *n* **a** a brief sensational play intended to horrify. **b** (*modifier*) of, relating to, or like plays of this kind. [C20: after *Le Grand Guignol,* a small theatre in Montmartre, Paris]

grandiloquent (græn'dɪləkwənt) *adj* inflated, pompous, or bombastic in style or expression. [C16: from Latin *grandiloquus,* from *grandis* great + *loquī* to speak] ► **gran'diloquence** *n* ► **gran'diloquently** *adv*

grandiose ('grændɪ,əʊs) *adj* **1** pretentiously grand or stately. **2** imposing in conception or execution. [C19: from French, from Italian *grandioso,* from *grande* great; see GRAND] ► **'grandi,osely** *adv* ► **grandiosity** (,grændɪ'ɒsɪtɪ) *n*

grandioso (,grændɪ'əʊsəʊ) *adj, adv Music.* (to be played) in a grand manner.

grand jury *n Law.* (esp. in the U.S. and, now rarely, in Canada) a jury of between 12 and 23 persons summoned to inquire into accusations of crime and ascertain whether the evidence is adequate to found an indictment. Abolished in Britain in 1948. Compare **petit jury.**

Grand Lama *n* either of two high priests of Lamaism, the Dalai Lama or the Panchen Lama.

grand larceny *n* **1** (formerly in England) the theft of property valued at over 12 pence. Abolished in 1827. **2** (in some states of the U.S.) the theft of property of which the value is above a specified figure, varying from state to state but usually being between $25 and $60. Compare **petit larceny.**

grandma ('græn,mɑː, 'grænd-, 'græm-), **grandmama,** *or* **grandmamma** ('grænmə,mɑː, 'grænd-) *n* informal words for **grandmother.**

grand mal (grɒn mæl; *French* grɑ̃ mal) *n* a form of epilepsy characterized by loss of consciousness for up to five minutes and violent convulsions. Compare **petit mal.** [French: great illness]

Grandma Moses *n* the nickname of (Anna Mary Robertson) **Moses.**

Grand Manan (mə'næn) *n* a Canadian island, off the SW coast of New Brunswick: separated from the coast of Maine by the **Grand Manan Channel.** Area: 147 sq. km (57 sq. miles).

Grand Marnier ('grɒn 'mɑːnɪ,eɪ; *French* grɑ̃ marnje) *n Trademark.* a French cognac-based liqueur with an orange flavour.

grandmaster ('grænd,mɑːstə) *n* **1** *Chess.* **1a** one of the top chess players of a particular country. **1b** (*cap. as part of title*): *Grandmaster of the USSR.* **2** *Chess.* Also called: **International Grandmaster.** a player who has been awarded the highest title by the Fédération Internationale des Échecs. **3** a leading exponent of any of various arts.

Grand Master *n* the title borne by the head of any of various societies, orders, and other organizations, such as the Templars or Freemasons, or the various martial arts.

grandmother ('græn,mʌðə, 'grænd-) *n* **1** the mother of one's father or mother. **2** (*often pl*) a female ancestor. **3** (*often cap.*) a familiar term of address for an old woman. **4 teach one's grandmother to suck eggs.** See **egg**[1] (sense 8).

grandmother clock *n* a longcase clock with a pendulum, about two thirds the size of a grandfather clock.

grandmotherly ('græn,mʌðəlɪ, 'grænd-) *adj* of, resembling, or suitable to a grandmother, esp. in being protective, indulgent, or solicitous.

Grand Mufti *n* **1** the titular head of the Muslim community in Jerusalem and formerly the chief constitutional administrator there. **2** (in Turkey) the former official head of the state religion.

Grand National *n* **the.** an annual steeplechase run at Aintree, Liverpool, since 1839.

grandnephew ('græn,nɛvjuː, -,nɛfjuː, 'grænd-) *n* another name for **great-nephew.**

grandniece ('græn,niːs, 'grænd-) *n* another name for **great-niece.**

Grand Old Party *n* (in the U.S.) a nickname for the Republican Party since 1880. Abbrev.: **GOP.**

grand opera *n* an opera that has a serious plot and is entirely in musical form, with no spoken dialogue.

grandpa ('græn,pɑː, 'grænd-, 'græm-) *or* **grandpapa** ('grænpə,pɑː, 'grænd-) *n* informal words for **grandfather.**

grandparent ('græn,pɛərənt, 'grænd-) *n* the father or mother of either of one's parents.

grand piano *n* a form of piano in which the strings are arranged horizontally. Grand pianos exist in three sizes (see **baby grand, boudoir grand, concert grand**). Compare **upright piano.**

Grand Pré (grɒn preɪ; *French* grɑ̃ pre) *n* a village in SE Canada, in W Nova Scotia: setting of Longfellow's *Evangeline.*

Grand Prix (*French* grɑ̃ pri) *n* **1a** any of a series of formula motor races held to determine the annual Drivers' World Championship. **1b** (*as modifier*): *a Grand Prix car.* **2** *Horse racing.* a race for three-year-old horses run at Maisons Lafitte near Paris. **3** a very important competitive event in various other sports, such as athletics, snooker, or powerboating. [French: great prize]

Grand Rapids *n* (*functioning as sing*) a city in SW Michigan: electronics, car parts. Pop.: 188 242 (1996 est.).

Grand Remonstrance *n* **the.** *English history.* the document prepared by the Long Parliament in 1640 listing the evils of the king's government, the abuses already rectified, and the reforms Parliament advocated.

grand seigneur *French.* (grɑ̃ sɛɲœr) *n, pl* ***grands seigneurs*** (grɑ̃ sɛɲœr). *Often ironic.* a dignified or aristocratic man. [literally: great lord]

grand siècle *French.* (grɑ̃ sjɛklə) *n, pl* ***grands siècles*** (grɑ̃ sjɛklə). the 17th century in French art and literature, esp. the classical period of Louis XIV. [literally: great century]

grandsire[1] ('græn,saɪə, 'grænd-) *n* an archaic word for **grandfather.**

grandsire[2] ('grændsə, -,saɪə) *n Bell-ringing.* a well-established method used in change-ringing. See **method** (sense 4).

grand slam *n* **1** *Bridge, etc.* the winning of 13 tricks by one player or side or the contract to do so. **2** the winning of all major competitions in a season, esp. in tennis and golf. **3** (*often cap.*) *Rugby union.* the winning of all four games in the annual Five Nations Championship involving Scotland, England, Wales, Ireland, and France. Compare **triple crown** (sense 3).

grandson ('grænsʌn, 'grænd-) *n* a son of one's son or daughter.

grandstand ('græn,stænd, 'grænd-) *n* **1a** a terraced block of seats, usually under a roof, commanding the best view at racecourses, football pitches, etc. **1b** (*as modifier*): *grandstand tickets.* **2** the spectators in a grandstand. **3** (*modifier*) as if from a grandstand; unimpeded (esp. in the phrase **grandstand view**). ◆ *vb* **4** (*intr*) *Informal, chiefly U.S. and Canadian.* to behave ostentatiously in an attempt to impress onlookers. ► **'grand,stander** *n*

grand tour *n* **1** (formerly) an extended tour through the major cities of Europe, esp. one undertaken by a rich or aristocratic Englishman to complete his education. **2** *Informal.* an extended sightseeing trip, tour of inspection, etc.

granduncle ('grænd,ʌŋkᵊl) *n* another name for **great-uncle.**

grand unified theory *n Physics.* any of a number of theories of elementary particles and fundamental interactions designed to explain the electromagnetic, strong, and weak interactions in terms of a single mathematical formalism. Abbrev.: **GUT.**

Grand Union Canal *n* a canal in S England linking London and the Midlands: opened in 1801.

grand vizier *n* (formerly) the chief officer or minister of state in the Ottoman Empire and other Muslim countries.

grange (greɪndʒ) *n* **1** *Chiefly Brit.* a farm, esp. a farmhouse or country house with its various outbuildings. **2** *History.* an outlying farmhouse in which a religious establishment or feudal lord stored crops and tithes in kind. **3** *Archaic.* a granary or barn. [C13: from Anglo-French *graunge,* from Medieval Latin *grānica,* from Latin *grānum* GRAIN]

Grange (greɪndʒ) *n* (in the U.S.) **1 the.** an association of farmers that strongly influenced state legislatures in the late 19th century. **2** a lodge of this association.

Grangemouth ('greɪndʒmaʊθ, -məθ) *n* a port in Scotland, in Falkirk council area: now Scotland's second port, with oil refineries, shipyards, and chemical industries. Pop.: 18 739 (1991).

grangerize *or* **grangerise** ('greɪndʒə,raɪz) *vb* (*tr*) **1** to illustrate (a book) by inserting prints, drawings, etc., taken from other works. **2** to raid (books) to acquire material for illustrating another book. [C19: named after Joseph *Granger,* 18th-century English writer, whose *Biographical History of England* (1769) included blank pages for illustrations to be supplied by the reader] ► **'grangerism** *n* ► **,grangeri'zation** *or* **,grangeri'sation** *n* ► **'granger,izer** *or* **'granger,iser** *n*

grani- *combining form.* indicating grain: *graniform.* [from Latin, from *grānum* GRAIN]

Granicus (grə'naɪkəs) *n* an ancient river in NW Asia Minor where Alexander the Great won his first major battle against the Persians (334 B.C.).

granite ('grænɪt) *n* **1** a light-coloured coarse-grained acid plutonic igneous rock consisting of quartz, feldspars, and such ferromagnesian minerals as biotite or hornblende: widely used for building. **2** great hardness, endurance, or resolution. **3** another name for a **stone** (sense 9). [C17: from Italian *granito* grained, from *granire* to grain, from *grano* grain, from Latin *grānum*] ► **'granite-,like** *adj* ► **granitic** (grə'nɪtɪk) *or* **'granit,oid** *adj*

graniteware ('grænɪt,wɛə) *n* **1** iron vessels coated with enamel of a granite-like appearance. **2** a type of very durable white semivitreous pottery. **3** a type of pottery with a speckled glaze.

granitite ('grænɪ,taɪt) *n* any granite with a high content of biotite.

granitization *or* **granitisation** (,grænɪtaɪ'zeɪʃən) *n* the metamorphic conversion of a rock into granite.

granivorous (græ'nɪvərəs) *adj* (of animals) feeding on seeds and grain. ► **granivore** ('grænɪ,vɔː) *n*

grannies ('grænɪz) *pl n N.Z. informal.* Granny Smith apples.

grannom ('grænəm) *n* a widespread caddis fly, *Brachycentrus subnubilus,* the larvae of which attach their cases to vegetation under running water and are esteemed as a bait by anglers. [C18: altered from *green tail*]

granny *or* **grannie** ('grænɪ) *n, pl* **-nies. 1** informal words for **grandmother. 2** *Informal.* an irritatingly fussy person. **3** a revolving cap on a chimneypot that keeps out rain, etc. **4** *Southern U.S.* a midwife or nurse. **5** See **granny knot.**

granny bond *n* (in Britain) an informal name for **retirement issue certificate,** an index-linked savings certificate, originally available only to people over retirement age.

granny flat *n* self-contained accommodation within or built onto a house, suitable for an elderly parent. Also called: **granny annexe.**

granny knot *or* **granny's knot** *n* a reef knot with the ends crossed the wrong way, making it liable to slip or jam.

Granny Smith *n* a variety of hard green-skinned apple eaten raw or cooked. [C19: named after Maria Ann Smith, known as *Granny Smith* (died 1870), who first produced them at Eastwood, Sydney]

grano- *combining form.* of or resembling granite: *granolith.* [from German, from *Granit* GRANITE]

granodiorite (,grænəʊ'daɪə,raɪt) *n* a coarse-grained acid igneous rock containing almost twice as much plagioclase as orthoclase: intermediate in structure between granite and diorite. [C19: from *grano* + DIORITE]

granolith ('grænəʊ,lɪθ) *n* a paving material consisting of a mixture of cement and crushed granite or granite chippings. ▶ ,**grano'lithic** *adj, n*

granophyre ('grænəʊ,faɪə) *n* a fine-grained granitic rock in which irregular crystals of intergrown quartz and feldspar are embedded in a groundmass of these minerals. [C19: from GRAN(ITE) + *-phyre* after *porphyry*] ▶ **granophyric** (,grænəʊ'fɪrɪk) *adj*

Gran Paradiso (*Italian* gram para'di:zo) *n* a mountain in NW Italy, in NW Piedmont: the highest peak of the Graian Alps. Height: 4061 m (13 323 ft.).

grant (grɑ:nt) *vb* (*tr*) **1** to consent to perform or fulfil: *to grant a wish.* **2** (*may take a clause as object*) to permit as a favour, indulgence, etc.: *to grant an interview.* **3** (*may take a clause as object*) to acknowledge the validity of; concede: *I grant what you say is true.* **4** to bestow, esp. in a formal manner. **5** to transfer (property) to another, esp. by deed; convey. **6 take for granted. 6a** to accept or assume without question: *one takes certain amenities for granted.* **6b** to fail to appreciate the value, merit, etc., of (a person). ◆ *n* **7** a sum of money provided by a government, local authority, or public fund to finance educational study, overseas aid, building repairs, etc. **8** a privilege, right, etc., that has been granted. **9** the act of granting. **10** a transfer of property by deed or other written instrument; conveyance. **11** *U.S.* a territorial unit in Maine, New Hampshire, and Vermont, originally granted to an individual or organization. [C13: from Old French *graunter*, from Vulgar Latin *credentāre* (unattested), from Latin *crēdere* to believe] ▶ **'grantable** *adj* ▶ **'granter** *n*

Grant (grɑ:nt) *n* **1 Cary**, real name *Alexander Archibald Leach.* 1904–86, U.S. film actor, born in England. His many films include *Bringing up Baby* (1938), *The Philadelphia Story* (1940), *Arsenic and Old Lace* (1944), and *Mr Blandings Builds his Dream House* (1948). **2 Duncan (James Corrowr).** 1885–1978, British painter and designer. **3 Ulysses S(impson)**, real name *Hiram Ulysses Grant.* 1822–85, 18th president of the U.S. (1869–77); commander in chief of Union forces in the American Civil War (1864–65).

Granta ('græntə, 'grɑ:ntə) *n* the original name, still in use locally, for the River Cam.

grantee (grɑ:n'ti:) *n Law.* a person to whom a grant is made.

Granthi ('grʌn,ti:) *n* the caretaker of a gurdwara and the reader of the Guru Granth, who officiates at Sikh ceremonies. [from Punjabi: keeper of the (GURU) GRANTH]

Grantham ('grænθəm) *n* a town in E England, in Lincolnshire: birthplace of Sir Isaac Newton and Margaret Thatcher. Pop.: 33 243 (1991).

grant-in-aid *n, pl* **grants-in-aid. 1** a sum of money granted by one government to a lower level of government or to a dependency for a programme, etc. **2** *Education.* a grant provided by the central government or local education authority to ensure consistent standards in buildings and other facilities.

grant-maintained *adj* (**grant maintained** *when postpostive*). (of schools or educational institutions) funded directly by central government.

grant of probate *n Law.* an instrument authorizing an executor to control and dispose of a deceased person's estate if a will has been made.

grantor (grɑ:n'tɔ:, 'grɑ:ntə) *n Law.* a person who makes a grant.

gran turismo ('græn tʊə'rɪzməʊ) *n, pl* **gran turismos.** the full form of **GT.** [C20: Italian, literally: great touring (i.e., touring on a grand scale)]

granular ('grænjʊlə) *adj* **1** of, like, containing, or resembling a granule or granules. **2** having a grainy or granulated surface. ▶ **granularity** (,grænjʊ'lærɪtɪ) *n* ▶ **'granularly** *adv*

granulate ('grænjʊ,leɪt) *vb* **1** (*tr*) to make into grains. **2** to make or become roughened in surface texture. **3** (*intr*) (of a wound, ulcer, etc.) to form granulation tissue. ▶ **'granulative** *adj* ▶ **'granu,lator** *or* **'granu,later** *n*

granulated sugar *n* a coarsely ground white sugar.

granulation (,grænjʊ'leɪʃən) *n* **1** the act or process of granulating. **2** a granulated texture or surface. **3** a single bump or grain in such a surface. **4** See **granulation tissue. 5** Also called: **granule.** *Astronomy.* any of numerous bright regions (approximate diameter 900 km) having a fine granular structure that can appear briefly on any part of the sun's surface.

granulation tissue *n* a mass of new connective tissue and capillaries formed on the surface of a healing ulcer or wound, usually leaving a scar. Nontechnical name: **proud flesh.**

granule ('grænju:l) *n* **1** a small grain. **2** *Geology.* a single rock fragment in gravel, smaller than a pebble but larger than a sand grain. **3** *Astronomy.* another name for **granulation** (sense 5). [C17: from Late Latin *grānulum* a small GRAIN]

granulite ('grænjʊ,laɪt) *n* a granular foliated metamorphic rock in which the minerals form a mosaic of equal-sized granules. ▶ **granulitic** (,grænjʊ'lɪtɪk) *adj*

granulocyte ('grænjʊlə,saɪt) *n* any of a group of phagocytic leucocytes having cytoplasmic granules that take up various dyes. See also **eosinophil, neutrophil** (sense 1), **basophil** (sense 2). ▶ **granulocytic** (,grænjʊlə'sɪtɪk) *adj*

granulocytopenia (,grænjʊləʊ,saɪtəʊ'pi:nɪə) *n* a diminished number of granulocytes in the blood, which occurs in certain forms of anaemia.

granuloma (,grænjʊ'ləʊmə) *n, pl* **-mas** *or* **-mata** (-mətə). a tumour composed of granulation tissue. ▶ **granulomatous** (,grænjʊ'lɒmətəs) *adj*

granulose ('grænjʊ,ləʊs, -,ləʊz) *adj* a less common word for **granular.**

Granville ('grænvɪl) *n* **1 1st Earl**, title of *John Carteret.* 1690–1763, British statesman: secretary of state (1742–44); a leading opponent of Walpole. **2 2nd Earl**, title of *Granville George Leveson-Gower.* 1815–91, British Liberal politician: Gladstone's foreign secretary (1870–74; 1880–85) and a supporter of Irish Home Rule.

Granville-Barker ('grænvɪl'bɑ:kə) *n* **Harley.** 1877–1946, English dramatist, theatre director, and critic, noted particularly for his *Prefaces to Shakespeare* (1927–47).

grape (greɪp) *n* **1** the fruit of the grapevine, which has a purple or green skin and sweet flesh: eaten raw, dried to make raisins, currants, or sultanas, or used for making wine. **2** any of various plants that bear grapelike fruit, such as the Oregon grape. **3** See **grapevine** (sense 1). **4 the.** an informal term for **wine. 5** See **grapeshot.** [C13: from Old French *grape* bunch of grapes, of Germanic origin; compare Old High German *krāpfo;* related to CRAMP[2], GRAPPLE] ▶ **'grapeless** *adj* ▶ **'grape,like** *adj* ▶ **'grapey** *or* **'grapy** *adj*

grapefruit ('greɪp,fru:t) *n, pl* **-fruit** *or* **-fruits. 1** a tropical or subtropical evergreen rutaceous tree, *Citrus paradisi.* **2** the large round edible fruit of this tree, which has yellow rind and juicy slightly bitter pulp.

grape hyacinth *n* any of various Eurasian liliaceous plants of the genus *Muscari*, esp. *M. botryoides,* with clusters of rounded blue flowers resembling tiny grapes.

grape ivy *n* See **rhoicissus.**

grapes (greɪps) *n* (*functioning as sing*) *Vet. science.* an abnormal growth, resembling a bunch of grapes, on the fetlock of a horse.

grapeshot ('greɪp,ʃɒt) *n* ammunition for cannons consisting of a canvas tube containing a cluster of small iron balls that scatter after firing.

grape sugar *n* another name for **dextrose.**

grapevine ('greɪp,vaɪn) *n* **1** any of several vitaceous vines of the genus *Vitis,* esp. *V. vinifera* of E Asia, widely cultivated for its fruit (grapes): family *Vitaceae.* **2** *Informal.* an unofficial means of relaying information, esp. from person to person. **3** a wrestling hold in which a wrestler entwines his own leg around his opponent's and exerts pressure against various joints.

graph (grɑ:f, græf) *n* **1** Also called: **chart.** a drawing depicting the relation between certain sets of numbers or quantities by means of a series of dots, lines, etc., plotted with reference to a set of axes. See also **bar graph. 2** *Maths.* a drawing depicting a functional relation between two or three variables by means of a curve or surface containing only those points whose coordinates satisfy the relation. **3** *Linguistics.* a symbol in a writing system not further subdivisible into other such symbols. ◆ *vb* **4** (*tr*) to draw or represent in a graph. [C19: short for *graphic formula*]

-graph *n combining form.* **1** an instrument that writes or records: *telegraph.* **2** a writing, record, or drawing: *autograph; lithograph.* [via Latin from Greek *-graphos,* from *graphein* to write] ▶ **-graphic** *or* **-graphical** *adj combining form.* ▶ **-graphically** *adv combining form.*

grapheme ('græfi:m) *n Linguistics.* one of a set of orthographic symbols (letters or combinations of letters) in a given language that serve to distinguish one word from another and usually correspond to or represent phonemes, e.g. the *f* in *fun,* the *ph* in *phantom,* and the *gh* in *laugh.* [C20: from Greek *graphēma* a letter] ▶ **gra'phemically** *adv*

-grapher *n combining form.* **1** indicating a person who writes about or is skilled in a subject: *geographer; photographer.* **2** indicating a person who writes, records, or draws in a specified way: *stenographer; lithographer.*

graphic ('græfɪk) *or* **graphical** *adj* **1** vividly or clearly described: *a graphic account of the disaster.* **2** of or relating to writing or other inscribed representations: *graphic symbols.* **3** *Maths.* using, relating to, or determined by a graph: *a graphic representation of the figures.* **4** of or relating to the graphic arts. **5** *Geology.* having or denoting a texture formed by intergrowth of the crystals to resemble writing: *graphic granite.* [C17: from Latin *graphicus,* from Greek *graphikos,* from *graphein* to write; see CARVE] ▶ **'graphically** *or* **'graphicly** *adv* ▶ **'graphicalness** *or* **'graphicness** *n*

graphicacy ('græfɪkəsɪ) *n* the ability to understand and use maps, plans, symbols, etc. [C20: formed on the model of *literacy*]

graphical user interface *n* an interface between a user and a computer system that involves the use of a mouse-controlled screen cursor to select options from menus, make choices with buttons, start programs by clicking icons, etc. Abbrev.: **GUI.**

graphic arts *pl n* any of the fine or applied visual arts based on drawing or the use of line, as opposed to colour or relief, on a plane surface, esp. illustration and printmaking of all kinds.

graphic equalizer *n* an electronic device for cutting or boosting selected frequencies, using small linear faders. Compare **parametric equalizer.**

graphic novel *n* a novel in the form of a comic strip.

graphics ('græfɪks) *n* **1** (*functioning as sing*) the process or art of drawing in accordance with mathematical principles. **2** (*functioning as sing*) the study of writing systems. **3** (*functioning as pl*) the drawings, photographs, etc., in the layout of a magazine or book, or in a television or film production. **4** (*functioning as pl*) the information displayed on a visual display unit or on a computer printout in the form of diagrams, graphs, pictures, and symbols.

graphite ('græfaɪt) *n* a blackish soft allotropic form of carbon in hexagonal crystalline form: used in pencils, crucibles, and electrodes, as a lubricant, as a moderator in nuclear reactors, and, in a carbon fibre form, as a tough lightweight material for sporting equipment. Also called: **plumbago.** [C18: from German *Graphit;* from Greek *graphein* to write + -ITE[1]] ▶ **graphitic** (grə'fɪtɪk) *adj*

graphitize *or* **graphitise** ('græfɪ,taɪz) *vb* (*tr*) **1** to convert (a substance) into graphite, usually by heating. **2** to coat or impregnate with graphite. ▶ ,**graphiti'zation** *or* ,**graphiti'sation** *n*

graphology (græ'fɒlədʒɪ) *n* **1** the study of handwriting, esp. to analyse the writer's character. **2** *Linguistics.* the study of writing systems. ▶ **graphologic** (,græfə'lɒdʒɪk) *or* ,**grapho'logical** *adj* ▶ **gra'phologist** *n*

graphomotor ('græfə,məʊtə) *adj* of or relating to the muscular movements used or required in writing.

graph paper *n* paper printed with intersecting lines, usually horizontal and vertical and equally spaced, for drawing graphs, diagrams, etc.

-graphy *n combining form.* **1** indicating a form or process of writing, representing, etc.: *calligraphy; photography.* **2** indicating an art or descriptive science:

choreography; oceanography. [via Latin from Greek *-graphia,* from *graphein* to write]

grapnel ('græpnᵊl) *n* **1** a device with a multiple hook at one end and attached to a rope, which is thrown or hooked over a firm mooring to secure an object attached to the other end of the rope. **2** a light anchor for small boats. [C14: from Old French *grapin* a little hook, from *grape* a hook; see GRAPE]

grappa ('græpə) *n* a spirit distilled from the fermented remains of grapes after pressing. [Italian: grape stalk, of Germanic origin; see GRAPE]

Grappelli *or* **Grappelly** (grə'pɛlɪ) *n* **Stéphane** ('stɛfᵊn). 1908–97, French jazz violinist: with Django Reinhardt, he led the Quintet of the Hot Club of France between 1934 and 1939.

grapple ('græpᵊl) *vb* **1** to come to grips with (one or more persons), esp. to struggle in hand-to-hand combat. **2** (*intr;* foll. by *with*) to cope or contend: *to grapple with a financial problem.* **3** (*tr*) to secure with a grapple. ◆ *n* **4** any form of hook or metal instrument by which something is secured, such as a grapnel. **5a** the act of gripping or seizing, as in wrestling. **5b** a grip or hold. **6** a contest of grappling, esp. a wrestling match. [C16: from Old French *grappelle* a little hook, from *grape* hook; see GRAPNEL] ▸ **'grappler** *n*

grapple plant *n* a herbaceous plant, *Harpagophytum procumbens,* of southern Africa, whose fruits are covered with large woody barbed hooks: family *Pedaliaceae.* Also called: **wait-a-bit.**

grappling ('græplɪŋ) *n* **1** the act of gripping or seizing, as in wrestling. **2** a hook used for securing something.

grappling iron *or* **hook** *n* a grapnel, esp. one used for securing ships.

graptolite ('græptə,laɪt) *n* any extinct Palaeozoic colonial animal of the class *Graptolithina,* usually regarded as related to the coelenterates: a common fossil. [C19: from Greek *graptos* written, from *graphein* to write + -LITE]

Grasmere ('grɑːs,mɪə) *n* a village in NW England, in Cumbria at the head of **Lake Grasmere**: home of William Wordsworth and of Thomas de Quincey.

grasp (grɑːsp) *vb* **1** to grip (something) firmly with or as if with the hands. **2** (when *intr,* often foll. by *at*) to struggle, snatch, or grope (for). **3** (*tr*) to understand, esp. with effort. ◆ *n* **4** the act of grasping. **5** a grip or clasp, as of a hand. **6** the capacity to accomplish (esp. in the phrase **within one's grasp**). **7** total rule or possession. **8** understanding; comprehension. [C14: from Low German *grapsen;* related to Old English *græppian* to seize, Old Norse *grāpa* to steal] ▸ **'graspable** *adj* ▸ **'grasper** *n*

grasping ('grɑːspɪŋ) *adj* greedy; avaricious; rapacious. ▸ **'graspingly** *adv*

grass (grɑːs) *n* **1** any monocotyledonous plant of the family *Gramineae,* having jointed stems sheathed by long narrow leaves, flowers in spikes, and seedlike fruits. The family includes cereals, bamboo, etc. **2** such plants collectively, in a lawn, meadow, etc. Related adjs: **gramineous, verdant. 3** any similar plant, such as knotgrass, deergrass, or scurvy grass. **4** ground on which such plants grow; a lawn, field, etc. **5** ground on which animals are grazed; pasture. **6** a slang word for **marijuana.** **7** *Brit. slang.* a person who informs, esp. on criminals. **8** short for **sparrowgrass. 9 let the grass grow under one's feet.** to squander time or opportunity. **10 put out to grass. 10a** to retire (a racehorse). **10b** *Informal.* to retire (a person). ◆ *vb* **11** to cover or become covered with grass. **12** to feed or be fed with grass. **13** (*tr*) to spread (cloth) out on grass for drying or bleaching in the sun. **14** (*tr*) *Sport.* to knock or bring down (an opponent). **15** (*tr*) to shoot down (a bird). **16** (*tr*) to land (a fish) on a river bank. **17** (*intr;* usually foll. by *on*) *Brit. slang.* to inform, esp. to the police. ◆ See also **grass up.** [Old English *græs;* related to Old Norse, Gothic, Old High German *gras,* Middle High German *gruose* sap] ▸ **'grassless** *adj* ▸ **'grass,like** *adj*

Grass (*German* gras) *n* **Günter (Wilhelm)** ('gyntər). born 1927, German novelist, dramatist, and poet, his novels include *The Tin Drum* (1959), *Dog Years* (1963), *The Rat* (1986), and *Toad Croaks* (1992). Nobel prize for literature 1999.

grass box *n* a container attached to a lawn mower that receives grass after it has been cut.

grass cloth *n* a cloth made from plant fibres, such as jute or hemp.

grass court *n* a tennis court covered with grass. See also **hard court.**

grassfinch ('grɑːs,fɪntʃ) *n* any Australian weaverbird of the genus *Poephila* and related genera, many of which are brightly coloured and kept as cagebirds.

grass hockey *n Canadian.* field hockey, as contrasted with ice hockey.

grasshook ('grɑːs,hʊk) *n* another name for **sickle.**

grasshopper ('grɑːs,hɒpə) *n* **1** any orthopterous insect of the families *Acrididae* (**short-horned grasshoppers**) and *Tettigoniidae* (**long-horned grasshoppers**), typically terrestrial, feeding on plants, and producing a ticking sound by rubbing the hind legs against the leathery forewings. See also **locust** (sense 1), **katydid. 2 knee-high to a grasshopper.** *Informal.* very young or very small. **3** an iced cocktail of equal parts of crème de menthe, crème de cacao, and cream. **4** (*modifier*) unable to concentrate on any one subject for long: *a grasshopper mind.*

grassland ('grɑːs,lænd) *n* **1** land, such as a prairie, on which grass predominates. **2** land reserved for natural grass pasture.

grass moth *n* any of a large subfamily of small night-flying pyralid moths, esp. *Crambus pratellus,* that during the day cling to grass stems.

grass-of-Parnassus *n* a herbaceous perennial N temperate marsh plant, *Parnassia palustris,* with solitary whitish flowers: family *Parnassiaceae.*

grassquit ('grɑːs,kwɪt) *n* any tropical American finch of the genus *Tiaris* and related genera, such as *T. olivacea* (**yellow-faced grassquit**). [from GRASS + *quit,* a bird name in Jamaica]

grass roots *pl n* **1a** the ordinary people as distinct from the active leadership of a party or organization: used esp. of the rank-and-file members of a political party, or of the voters themselves. **1b** (*as modifier*): *the newly elected MP expressed a wish for greater contact with people at grass-roots level.* **2** the origin or essentials. [C20: sense 1 originally U.S., with reference to rural areas in contrast to the towns]

grass snake *n* **1** a harmless nonvenomous European colubrid snake, *Natrix natrix,* having a brownish-green body with variable markings. **2** any of several similar related European snakes, such as *Natrix maura* (**viperine grass snake**).

grass tree *n* **1** Also called: **blackboy.** any liliaceous plant of the Australian genus *Xanthorrhoea,* having a woody stem, stiff grasslike leaves, and a spike of small white flowers. Some species produce fragrant resins. See also **acaroid gum. 2** any of several similar Australasian plants.

grass up *vb* (*tr, adv*) *Slang.* to inform on (someone), esp. to the police.

grass widow *or* (*masc*) **grass widower** *n* **1** a person divorced, separated, or living away from his or her spouse. **2** a person whose spouse is regularly away for a short period. [C16, meaning a discarded mistress: perhaps an allusion to a grass bed as representing an illicit relationship; compare BASTARD; C19 in the modern sense]

grassy ('grɑːsɪ) *adj* **grassier, grassiest.** covered with, containing, or resembling grass. ▸ **'grassiness** *n*

grate[1] (greɪt) *vb* **1** (*tr*) to reduce to small shreds by rubbing against a rough or sharp perforated surface: *to grate carrots.* **2** to scrape (an object) against something or (objects) together, producing a harsh rasping sound, or (of objects) to scrape with such a sound. **3** (*intr;* foll. by *on* or *upon*) to annoy. ◆ *n* **4** a harsh rasping sound. [C15: from Old French *grater* to scrape, of Germanic origin; compare Old High German *krazzōn*]

grate[2] (greɪt) *n* **1** a framework of metal bars for holding fuel in a fireplace, stove, or furnace. **2** a less common word for **fireplace. 3** another name for **grating**[1] (sense 1). **4** *Mining.* a perforated metal screen for grading crushed ore. ◆ *vb* **5** (*tr*) to provide with a grate or grates. [C14: from Old French *grate,* from Latin *crātis* hurdle]

grateful ('greɪtfʊl) *adj* **1** thankful for gifts, favours, etc.; appreciative. **2** showing gratitude: *a grateful letter.* **3** favourable or pleasant: *a grateful rest.* [C16: from obsolete *grate,* from Latin *grātus* + -FUL] ▸ **'gratefully** *adv* ▸ **'gratefulness** *n*

grater ('greɪtə) *n* **1** a kitchen utensil with sharp-edged perforations for grating carrots, cheese, etc. **2** a person or thing that grates.

Gratian ('greɪʃɪən) *n* Latin name *Flavius Gratianus.* 359–383 A.D., Roman emperor (367–383): ruled with his father Valentinian I (367–375); ruled the Western Roman Empire with his brother Valentinian II (375-83); appointed Theodosius I emperor of the Eastern Roman Empire (379).

graticule ('grætɪ,kjuːl) *n* **1** the grid of intersecting lines of latitude and longitude on which a map is drawn. **2** another name for **reticle. 3** a transparent scale in front of a cathode-ray oscilloscope or other measuring instrument. [C19: from French, from Latin *crāticula,* from *crātis* wickerwork]

gratification (,grætɪfɪ'keɪʃən) *n* **1** the act of gratifying or the state of being gratified. **2** something that gratifies. **3** an obsolete word for **gratuity.**

gratify ('grætɪ,faɪ) *vb* **-fies, -fying, -fied.** (*tr*) **1** to satisfy or please. **2** to yield to or indulge (a desire, whim, etc.). **3** *Obsolete.* to reward. [C16: from Latin *grātificārī* to do a favour to, from *grātus* grateful + *facere* to make] ▸ **'grati,fier** *n* ▸ **'grati,fying** *adj* ▸ **'grati,fyingly** *adv*

gratin (*French* gratɛ̃) See **au gratin.**

grating[1] ('greɪtɪŋ) *n* **1** Also called: **grate.** a framework of metal bars in the form of a grille set into a wall, pavement, etc., serving as a cover or guard but admitting air and sometimes light. **2** short for **diffraction grating.**

grating[2] ('greɪtɪŋ) *adj* **1** (of sounds) harsh and rasping. **2** annoying; irritating. ◆ *n* **3** (*often pl*) something produced by grating. ▸ **'gratingly** *adv*

gratis ('greɪtɪs, 'grætɪs, 'grɑːtɪs) *adv, adj* (*postpositive*) without payment; free of charge. [C15: from Latin: out of kindness, from *grātiīs,* ablative pl of *grātia* favour]

gratitude ('grætɪ,tjuːd) *n* a feeling of thankfulness or appreciation, as for gifts or favours. [C16: from Medieval Latin *grātitūdō,* from Latin *grātus* GRATEFUL]

Grattan ('grætᵊn) *n* **Henry.** 1746–1820, Irish statesman and orator: led the movement that secured legislative independence for Ireland (1782), opposed union with England (1800), and campaigned for Catholic emancipation.

gratuitous (grə'tjuːɪtəs) *adj* **1** given or received without payment or obligation. **2** without cause; unjustified. **3** *Law.* given or made without receiving any value in return: *a gratuitous contract.* [C17: from Latin *grātuītus,* from *grātia* favour] ▸ **gra'tuitously** *adv* ▸ **gra'tuitousness** *n*

gratuity (grə'tjuːɪtɪ) *n, pl* **-ties. 1** a gift or reward, usually of money, for services rendered; tip. **2** something given without claim or obligation. **3** *Military.* a financial award granted for long or meritorious service.

gratulate ('grætjʊ,leɪt) *vb* (*tr*) *Archaic.* **1** to greet joyously. **2** to congratulate. [C16: from Latin *grātulārī,* from *grātus* pleasing] ▸ **'gratulant** *adj* ▸ **,gratu'lation** *n* ▸ **'gratulatory** *adj*

Graubünden (*German* grau'byndən) *n* an Alpine canton of E Switzerland: the largest of the cantons, but sparsely populated. Capital: Chur. Pop.: 185 063 (1996 est.). Area: 7109 sq. km (2773 sq. miles). Italian name: **Grigioni.** Romansch name: **Grishun.** French name: **Grisons.**

graunch (grɔːntʃ) *vb* (*tr*) *English dialect and N.Z.* to crush or destroy. [C19: of imitative origin]

graupel ('graupᵊl) *n* soft hail or snow pellets. [German, from *Graupe,* probably from Serbo-Croat *krupa;* related to Russian *krupá* peeled grain]

grav (græv) *n* a unit of acceleration equal to the standard acceleration of free fall. 1 grav is equivalent to 9.806 65 metres per second per second. Symbol: g

gravadlax ('grævəd,læks) *n* another name for **gravlax.**

gravamen (grə'veɪmɛn) *n, pl* **-vamina** (-'væmɪnə). **1** *Law.* that part of an accusation weighing most heavily against an accused. **2** *Law.* the substance or material grounds of a complaint. **3** a rare word for **grievance.** [C17: from Late Latin: trouble, from Latin *gravāre* to load, from *gravis* heavy; see GRAVE[2]]

grave[1] (greɪv) *n* **1** a place for the burial of a corpse, esp. beneath the ground and usually marked by a tombstone. Related adj: **sepulchral. 2** something resembling a grave or resting place: *the ship went to its grave.* **3** (often preceded by *the*) a poetic term for **death. 4 have one foot in the grave.** *Informal.* to be near death. **5 to make (someone) turn (over) in his grave.** to do something that would have shocked or distressed (someone now dead): *many modern dictionaries would make Dr Johnson turn in his grave.* [Old English *græf;* related to Old Frisian *gref,* Old High German *grab,* Old Slavonic *grobŭ;* see GRAVE[3]]

grave[2] (greɪv) *adj* **1** serious and solemn: *a grave look.* **2** full of or suggesting danger: *a grave situation.* **3** important; crucial: *grave matters of state.* **4** (of colours) sober or dull. **5** (*also* grɑːv). *Phonetics.* **5a** (of a vowel or syllable in some languages with a pitch accent, such as ancient Greek) spoken on a lower or falling musical pitch relative to neighbouring syllables or vowels. **5b** of or relating to an accent (`) over vowels, denoting a pronunciation with lower or falling musical pitch (as in ancient Greek), with certain special quality (as in French), or in a manner that gives the vowel status as a syllable nucleus not usually possessed by it in that position (as in English *agèd*). Compare **acute** (sense 8), **circumflex.** ◆ *n* **6** (*also* grɑːv) a grave accent. [C16: from Old French, from Latin *gravis;* related to Greek *barus* heavy; see GRAVAMEN] ► **'gravely** *adv* ► **'graveness** *n*

grave[3] (greɪv) *vb* **graves, graving, graved; graved** *or* **graven.** (*tr*) *Archaic.* **1** to cut, carve, sculpt, or engrave. **2** to fix firmly in the mind. [Old English *grafan;* related to Old Norse *grafa,* Old High German *graban* to dig]

grave[4] (greɪv) *vb* (*tr*) *Nautical.* to clean and apply a coating of pitch to (the bottom of a vessel). [C15: perhaps from Old French *grave* GRAVEL]

grave[5] ('grɑːvɪ) *adj, adv Music.* to be performed in a solemn manner. [C17: from Italian: heavy, from Latin *gravis*]

grave clothes *pl n* the wrappings in which a dead body is interred.

gravel ('grævᵊl) *n* **1** a mixture of rock fragments that is coarser than sand. **2** *Geology.* a mixture of rock fragments with diameters in the range 2-4 mm. **3** *Pathol.* small rough calculi in the kidneys or bladder. ◆ *vb* **-els, -elling, -elled** *or U.S.* **-els, -eling, -eled.** (*tr*) **4** to cover with gravel. **5** to confound or confuse. **6** *U.S. informal.* to annoy or disturb. [C13: from Old French *gravele,* diminutive of *grave* gravel, perhaps of Celtic origin] ► **'gravelish** *adj*

gravel-blind *adj Literary.* almost entirely blind. [C16: from GRAVEL + BLIND, formed on the model of SAND-BLIND]

gravelly ('grævəlɪ) *adj* **1** consisting of or abounding in gravel. **2** of or like gravel. **3** (esp. of a voice) harsh and grating.

gravel-voiced *adj* speaking in a rough and rasping tone.

graven ('greɪvᵊn) *vb* **1** a past participle of **grave**[3]. ◆ *adj* **2** strongly fixed.

Gravenhage (xraːvən'haːxə) *n* **'s.** a Dutch name for (The) **Hague.**

graven image *n Chiefly Bible.* a carved image used as an idol.

graveolent ('grævɪələnt) *adj* (of plants) having a strong fetid smell. [C17: from Latin *gravis* heavy + *olēre* to smell]

graver ('greɪvə) *n* any of various engraving, chasing, or sculpting tools, such as a burin.

Graves[1] (grɑːv) *n* (*sometimes not cap.*) a white or red wine from the district around Bordeaux, France.

Graves[2] (greɪvz) *n* **Robert** (**Ranke**). 1895–1985, English poet, novelist, and critic, whose works include his World War I autobiography, *Goodbye to All That* (1929), and the historical novels *I, Claudius* (1934) and *Claudius the God* (1934).

Graves' disease (greɪvz) *n* another name for **exophthalmic goitre.** [C19: named after R. J. *Graves* (1796–1853), Irish physician]

Gravesend (ˌgreɪvz'end) *n* a river port in SE England, in NW Kent on the Thames. Pop.: 51 435 (1991).

gravestone ('greɪvˌstəʊn) *n* a stone marking a grave and usually inscribed with the name and dates of the person buried.

Gravettian (grə'vetɪən) *adj* of, referring to, or characteristic of an Upper Palaeolithic culture, characterized esp. by small pointed blades with blunt backs. [C20: from *La Gravette* on the Dordogne, France]

grave-wax *n* the nontechnical name for **adipocere.**

graveyard ('greɪvˌjɑːd) *n* a place for graves; a burial ground, esp. a small one or one in a churchyard.

graveyard orbit *n* another name for **dump orbit.**

graveyard shift *n U.S.* the working shift between midnight and morning.

graveyard slot *n Television.* the hours from late night until early morning when the number of people watching television is at its lowest.

gravid ('grævɪd) *adj* the technical word for **pregnant.** [C16: from Latin *gravidus,* from *gravis* heavy] ► **gra'vidity** *or* **'gravidness** *n* ► **'gravidly** *adv*

gravimeter (grə'vɪmɪtə) *n* **1** an instrument for measuring the earth's gravitational field at points on its surface. **2** an instrument for measuring relative density. [C18: from French *gravimètre,* from Latin *gravis* heavy] ► **gra'vimetry** *n*

gravimetric (ˌgrævɪ'metrɪk) *or* **gravimetrical** *adj* of, concerned with, or using measurement by weight. Compare **volumetric.** ► **ˌgravi'metrically** *adv*

gravimetric analysis *n Chem.* quantitative analysis by weight, usually involving the precipitation, filtration, drying, and weighing of the precipitate. Compare **volumetric analysis.**

graving dock *n* another term for **dry dock.**

graviperception (ˌgrævɪpə'sepʃən) *n* the perception of gravity by plants.

gravitas ('grævɪˌtæs) *n* seriousness, solemnity, or importance. [C20: from Latin *gravitās* weight, from *gravis* heavy]

gravitate ('grævɪˌteɪt) *vb* (*intr*) **1** *Physics.* to move under the influence of gravity. **2** (usually foll. by *to* or *towards*) to be influenced or drawn, as by strong impulses. **3** to sink or settle. ► **'graviˌtater** *n*

gravitation (ˌgrævɪ'teɪʃən) *n* **1** the force of attraction that bodies exert on one another as a result of their mass. **2** any process or result caused by this interaction, such as the fall of a body to the surface of the earth. ◆ Also called: **gravity.** See also **Newton's law of gravitation.** ► **ˌgravi'tational** *adj* ► **ˌgravi'tationally** *adv*

gravitational constant *n* the factor relating force to mass and distance in Newton's law of gravitation. It is a universal constant with the value 6.670×10^{-11} N m^2 kg^{-2}. Symbol: *G*

gravitational field *n* the field of force surrounding a body of finite mass in which another body would experience an attractive force that is proportional to the product of the masses and inversely proportional to the square of the distance between them.

gravitational interaction *or* **force** *n* an interaction between particles or bodies resulting from their mass. It is very weak and occurs at all distances. See **interaction** (sense 2).

gravitational mass *n* the mass of a body determined by its response to the force of gravity. Compare **inertial mass.**

gravitational wave *n Physics.* another name for **gravity wave.**

gravitative ('grævɪˌteɪtɪv) *adj* **1** of, involving, or produced by gravitation. **2** tending or causing to gravitate.

graviton ('grævɪˌtɒn) *n* a postulated quantum of gravitational energy, usually considered to be a particle with zero charge and rest mass and a spin of 2. Compare **photon.**

gravity ('grævɪtɪ) *n, pl* **-ties. 1** the force of attraction that moves or tends to move bodies towards the centre of a celestial body, such as the earth or moon. **2** the property of being heavy or having weight. See also **specific gravity, centre of gravity. 3** another name for **gravitation. 4** seriousness or importance, esp. as a consequence of an action or opinion. **5** manner or conduct that is solemn or dignified. **6** lowness in pitch. **7** (*modifier*) of or relating to gravity or gravitation or their effects: *gravity wave; gravity feed.* [C16: from Latin *gravitās* weight, from *gravis* heavy]

gravity cell *n* an electrolytic cell in which the electrodes lie in two different electrolytes, which are separated into two layers by the difference in their relative densities.

gravity dam *n* a dam whose weight alone is great enough to prevent it from tipping over.

gravity fault *n* a fault in which the rocks on the upper side of an inclined fault plane have been displaced downwards; normal fault.

gravity platform *n* (in the oil industry) a drilling platform that rests directly on the sea bed and is kept in position by its own weight; it is usually made of reinforced concrete.

gravity scale *n* See **API gravity scale.**

gravity wave *n Physics.* **1** a wave propagated in a gravitational field, predicted to occur as a result of an accelerating mass. **2** a surface wave on water or other liquid propagated because of the weight of liquid in the crests. ◆ Also called: **gravitational wave.**

gravlax ('grævˌlæks) *or* **gravadlax** *n* dry-cured salmon, marinated in salt, sugar, and spices, as served in Scandinavia. [C20: from Norwegian, from *grav* grave (because the salmon is left to ferment) + *laks* or Swedish *lax* salmon]

gravure (grə'vjʊə) *n* **1** a method of intaglio printing using a plate with many small etched recesses. See also **rotogravure. 2** See **photogravure. 3** matter printed by this process. [C19: from French, from *graver* to engrave, of Germanic origin; see GRAVE[3]]

gravy ('greɪvɪ) *n, pl* **-vies. 1a** the juices that exude from meat during cooking. **1b** the sauce made by thickening and flavouring such juices. **2** *Slang.* money or gain acquired with little effort, esp. above that needed for ordinary living. [C14: from Old French *gravé,* of uncertain origin]

gravy boat *n* a small often boat-shaped vessel for serving gravy or other sauces.

gravy train *n Slang.* a job requiring comparatively little work for good pay, benefits, etc.

gray[1] (greɪ) *adj, n, vb* a variant spelling (now esp. U.S.) of **grey.** ► **'grayish** *adj* ► **'grayly** *adv* ► **'grayness** *n*

gray[2] (greɪ) *n* the derived SI unit of absorbed ionizing radiation dose or kerma equivalent to an absorption per unit mass of one joule per kilogram of irradiated material. Symbol: Gy 1 gray is equivalent to 100 rads. [C20: named after Louis Harold *Gray* (1905–65), English physicist]

Gray (greɪ) *n* **1 Simon** (**James Holiday**). born 1936, British writer: his plays include *Butley* (1971), *The Common Pursuit* (1988), and *Hidden Laughter* (1990). **2 Thomas.** 1716–71, English poet, best known for his *Elegy written in a Country Churchyard* (1751).

Gray code *n* a modification of a number system, esp. a binary code, in which any adjacent pair of numbers, in counting order, differ in their digits at one position only, the absolute difference being the value 1. [named after Frank *Gray,* 20th-century American physicist]

grayling ('greɪlɪŋ) *n, pl* **-ling** *or* **-lings. 1** any freshwater salmonoid food fish of the genus *Thymallus* and family *Thymallidae,* of the N hemisphere, having a long spiny dorsal fin, a silvery back, and greyish-green sides. **2** any butterfly of the satyrid genus *Hipparchia* and related genera, esp. *H. semele* of Europe, having grey or greyish-brown wings.

Gray's Inn *n* (in England) one of the four legal societies in London that together form the Inns of Court.

Graz (*German* graːts) *n* an industrial city in SE Austria, capital of Styria province: the second largest city in the country. Pop.: 237 810 (1991).

graze[1] (greɪz) *vb* **1** to allow (animals) to consume the vegetation on (an area of land), or (of animals, esp. cows and sheep) to feed thus. **2** (*tr*) to tend (livestock) while at pasture. **3** *Informal.* to eat snacks throughout the day rather than formal meals. **4** *U.S.* to pilfer and eat sweets, vegetables, etc., from supermarket shelves while shopping. [Old English *grasian,* from *græs* GRASS; related to Old High German *grasōn,* Dutch *grazen,* Norwegian *grasa*]

graze[2] (greɪz) *vb* **1** (when *intr,* often foll. by *against* or *along*) to brush or scrape (against) gently, esp. in passing. **2** (*tr*) to break the skin of (a part of the body) by scraping. ◆ *n* 3 the act of grazing. 4 a scrape or abrasion made by grazing. [C17: probably special use of GRAZE[1]; related to Swedish *gräsa*] ▸ **'grazer** *n* ▸ **'grazingly** *adv*

grazier ('greɪzɪə) *n* a rancher or farmer who rears or fattens cattle or sheep on grazing land.

grazing ('greɪzɪŋ) *n* 1 the vegetation on pastures that is available for livestock to feed upon. 2 the land on which this is growing.

grease *n* (gri:s, gri:z). 1 animal fat in a soft or melted condition. 2 any thick fatty oil, esp. one used as a lubricant for machinery, etc. 3 Also called: **grease wool.** shorn fleece before it has been cleaned. 4 *Vet. science.* inflammation of the skin of horses around the fetlocks, usually covered with an oily secretion. ◆ *vb* (gri:z, gri:s). (*tr*) 5 to soil, coat, or lubricate with grease. 6 to ease the course of: *his education greased his path to success.* 7 **grease the palm** (*or* **hand**) **of.** *Slang.* to bribe; influence by giving money to. [C13: from Old French *craisse,* from Latin *crassus* thick] ▸ **'greaseless** *adj*

grease cup *n* a container that stores grease and feeds it through a small hole into a bearing.

grease gun *n* a device for forcing grease through nipples into bearings, usually consisting of a cylinder with a plunger and nozzle fitted to it.

grease monkey *n Informal.* a mechanic, esp. one who works on cars or aircraft.

grease nipple *n* a metal nipple designed to engage with a grease gun for injecting grease into a bearing, etc.

greasepaint ('gri:sˌpeɪnt) *n* 1 a waxy or greasy substance used as make-up by actors. 2 theatrical make-up.

greaseproof paper ('gri:sˌpru:f) *n* any paper that is resistant to penetration by greases and oils.

greaser ('gri:zə, 'gri:sə) *n Brit. slang.* 1 a mechanic, esp. of motor vehicles. 2 a semiskilled engine attendant aboard a merchant ship. 3 a young long-haired motorcyclist, usually one of a gang. 4 an unpleasant person, esp. one who ingratiates himself with superiors.

greasewood ('gri:sˌwʊd) *or* **greasebush** ('gri:sˌbʊʃ) *n* 1 Also called: **chico.** a spiny chenopodiaceous shrub, *Sarcobatus vermiculatus* of W North America, that yields an oil used as a fuel. 2 any of various similar or related plants, such as the creosote bush.

greasy ('gri:zɪ, -sɪ) *adj* **greasier, greasiest.** 1 coated or soiled with or as if with grease. 2 composed of or full of grease. 3 resembling grease. 4 unctuous or oily in manner. ◆ *n, pl* **greasies.** *Austral. slang.* 5 a shearer. 6 an outback cook, esp. cooking for a number of men. ▸ **'greasily** *adv* ▸ **'greasiness** *n*

greasy spoon *n Slang.* a small, cheap, and often unsanitary restaurant, usually specializing in fried foods.

greasy wool *n* untreated wool, still retaining the lanolin, which is used for waterproof clothing.

great (greɪt) *adj* 1 relatively large in size or extent; big. 2 relatively large in number; having many parts or members: *a great assembly.* 3 of relatively long duration: *a great wait.* 4 of larger size or more importance than others of its kind: *the great auk.* 5 extreme or more than usual: *great worry.* 6 of significant importance or consequence: *a great decision.* 7a of exceptional talents or achievements; remarkable: *a great writer.* 7b (*as n*): *the great; one of the greats.* 8 arising from or possessing idealism in thought, action, etc.; heroic: *great deeds.* 9 illustrious or eminent: *a great history.* 10 impressive or striking: *a great show of wealth.* 11 much in use; favoured: *poetry was a great convention of the Romantic era.* 12 active or enthusiastic: *a great walker.* 13 doing or exemplifying (a characteristic or pursuit) on a large scale: *what a great buffoon; he's not a great one for reading.* 14 (often foll. by *at*) skilful or adroit: *a great carpenter; you are great at singing.* 15 *Informal.* excellent; fantastic. 16 *Brit. informal.* (intensifier): *a dirty great smack in the face.* 17 (*postpositive;* foll. by *with*) *Archaic.* 17a pregnant: *great with child.* 17b full (of): *great with hope.* 18 (intensifier, used in mild oaths): *Great Scott!* 19 **be great on.** *Informal.* 19a to be informed about. 19b to be enthusiastic about or for. ◆ *adv* 20 *Informal.* very well; excellently: *it was working great.* ◆ *n* 21 Also called: **great organ.** the principal manual on an organ. Compare **choir** (sense 4), **swell** (sense 16). [Old English *grēat;* related to Old Frisian *grāt,* Old High German *grōz;* see GRIT, GROAT] ▸ **'greatly** *adv* ▸ **'greatness** *n*

great- *prefix* 1 being the parent of a person's grandparent (in the combinations **great-grandfather, great-grandmother, great-grandparent**). 2 being the child of a person's grandchild (in the combinations **great-grandson, great-granddaughter, great-grandchild**).

great ape *n* any of the larger anthropoid apes, such as the chimpanzee, orang-utan, or gorilla.

Great Attractor *n Astron.* a large mass, possibly a gigantic cluster of galaxies, postulated to explain the fact that many galaxies appear to be moving towards a particular point in the sky.

great auk *n* a large flightless auk, *Pinguinus impennis,* extinct since the middle of the 19th century.

great-aunt *or* **grandaunt** *n* an aunt of one's father or mother; sister of one's grandfather or grandmother.

Great Australian Bight *n* a wide bay of the Indian Ocean, in S Australia, extending from Cape Pasley to the Eyre Peninsula: notorious for storms.

Great Barrier Reef *n* a coral reef in the Coral Sea, off the NE coast of Australia, extending for about 2000 km (1250 miles) from the Torres Strait along the coast of Queensland; the largest coral reef in the world.

Great Basin *n* a semiarid region of the western U.S., between the Wasatch and the Sierra Nevada Mountains, having no drainage to the ocean: includes Nevada, W Utah, and parts of E California, S Oregon, and Idaho. Area: about 490 000 sq. km (189 000 sq. miles).

Great Bear *n* **the.** the English name for **Ursa Major.**

Great Bear Lake *n* a lake in NW Canada, in the Northwest Territories: the largest freshwater lake entirely in Canada; drained by the **Great Bear River,** which flows to the Mackenzie River. Area: 31 792 sq. km (12 275 sq. miles).

Great Belt *n* a strait in Denmark, between Zealand and Funen islands, linking the Kattegat with the Baltic. Danish name: **Store Bælt.**

Great Britain *n* England, Wales, and Scotland including those adjacent islands governed from the mainland (i.e. excluding the Isle of Man and the Channel Islands). The United Kingdom of Great Britain was formed by the Act of Union (1707), although the term Great Britain had been in use since 1603, when James VI of Scotland became James I of England (including Wales). Later unions created the United Kingdom of Great Britain and Ireland (1801) and the United Kingdom of Great Britain and Northern Ireland (1922). Pop.: 56 388 200 (1992 est.). Area: 229 523 sq. km (88 619 sq. miles). See also **United Kingdom.**

great circle *n* a circular section of a sphere that has a radius equal to that of the sphere. Compare **small circle.**

greatcoat ('greɪtˌkəʊt) *n* a heavy overcoat, now worn esp. by men in the armed forces. ▸ **'greatˌcoated** *adj*

great council *n* (in medieval England) an assembly of the great nobles and prelates to advise the king.

great crested grebe *n* a European grebe, *Podiceps cristatus,* having blackish ear tufts and, in the breeding season, a dark brown frill around the head.

Great Dane *n* one of a very large powerful yet graceful breed of dog with a short smooth coat.

Great Divide *n* another name for the **continental divide.**

Great Dividing Range *pl n* a series of mountain ranges and plateaus roughly parallel to the E coast of Australia, in Queensland, New South Wales, and Victoria; the highest range is the Australian Alps, in the south.

Great Dog *n* **the.** the English name for **Canis Major.**

greaten ('greɪt[ə]n) *vb Archaic.* to make or become great.

Greater ('greɪtə) *adj* (of a city) considered with the inclusion of the outer suburbs: *Greater London.*

Greater Antilles *pl n* **the.** a group of islands in the Caribbean, including Cuba, Jamaica, Hispaniola, and Puerto Rico.

greater celandine *n* a Eurasian papaveraceous plant, *Chelidonium majus,* with yellow flowers and deeply divided leaves. Also called: **swallowwort.** Compare **lesser celandine.**

Greater London *n* See **London**[1] (sense 2).

Greater Manchester *n* a metropolitan county of NW England, administered since 1986 by the unitary authorities of Wigan, Bolton, Bury, Rochdale, Salford, Manchester, Oldham, Trafford, Stockport, and Tameside. Area: 1286 sq. km (496 sq. miles).

Greater Sunda Islands *pl n* a group of islands in the W Malay Archipelago, forming the larger part of the Sunda Islands: consists of Borneo, Sumatra, Java, and Sulawesi.

greatest ('greɪtɪst) *adj* 1 the superlative of **great.** ◆ *n* 2 **the greatest.** *Slang.* an exceptional person.

greatest common divisor *n* another name for **highest common factor.**

greatest happiness principle *n* the ethical principle that an action is right in so far as it promotes the greatest happiness of the greatest number of those affected. See **utilitarianism.**

Great Glen *n* **the.** a fault valley across the whole of Scotland, extending southwest from the Moray Firth in the east to Loch Linnhe and containing Loch Ness and Loch Lochy. Also called: **Glen More, Glen Albyn.**

great gross *n* a unit of quantity equal to one dozen gross (or 1728).

great-hearted *adj* benevolent or noble; magnanimous. ▸ **ˌgreat-'heartedness** *n*

Great Indian Desert *n* another name for the **Thar Desert.**

Great Lakes *pl n* a group of five lakes in central North America with connecting waterways: the largest group of lakes in the world: consists of Lakes Superior, Huron, Erie, and Ontario, which are divided by the border between the U.S. and Canada and Lake Michigan, which is wholly in the U.S.; constitutes the most important system of inland waterways in the world, discharging through the St Lawrence into the Atlantic. Total length: 3767 km (2340 miles). Area: 246 490 sq. km (95 170 sq. miles).

Great Leap Forward *n* **the.** the attempt by the People's Republic of China in 1959–60 to solve the country's economic problems by labour-intensive industrialization.

Great Mogul *n* any of the Muslim emperors of India (1526–1857).

great mountain buttercup *n N.Z.* See **Mount Cook lily.**

great-nephew *or* **grandnephew** *n* a son of one's nephew or niece; grandson of one's brother or sister.

great-niece *or* **grandniece** *n* a daughter of one's nephew or niece; granddaughter of one's brother or sister.

great northern diver *n* a large northern bird, *Gavia immer,* with a black-and-white chequered back and a black head and neck in summer: family *Gaviidae* (divers).

great organ *n* the full name for **great** (sense 21).

Great Ouse *n* See **Ouse** (sense 1).

Great Plains *pl n* a vast region of North America east of the Rocky Mountains, extending from the lowlands of the Mackenzie River (Canada), south to the Big Bend of the Rio Grande.

Great Power *n* a nation that has exceptional political influence, resources, and military strength.

great primer *n* (formerly) a size of printer's type approximately equal to 18 point.

Great Rebellion *n* **the.** another name for the English **Civil War.**

Great Red Spot *n* a large long-lived oval feature, south of Jupiter's equator, that is an anticyclonic disturbance in the atmosphere.

Great Rift Valley *n* the most extensive rift in the earth's surface, extending from the Jordan valley in Syria to Mozambique; marked by a chain of steep-sided lakes, volcanoes, and escarpments.

Great Russian *n* **1** *Linguistics.* the technical name for **Russian.** Compare **Belarussian, Ukrainian. 2** a member of the chief East Slavonic people of Russia. ◆ *adj* **3** of or relating to this people or their language.

Greats (greɪts) *pl n* (at Oxford University) **1** the Honour School of Literae Humaniores, involving the study of Greek and Roman history and literature and philosophy. **2** the final examinations at the end of this course.

Great Salt Lake *n* a shallow salt lake in NW Utah, in the Great Basin at an altitude of 1260 m (4200 ft.): the area has fluctuated from less than 2500 sq. km (1000 sq. miles) to over 5000 sq. km (2000 sq. miles).

Great Sandy Desert *n* **1** a desert in NW Australia. Area: about 415 000 sq. km (160 000 sq. miles). **2** the English name for the **Rub' al Khali.**

Great Schism *n* **1** the breach between the Eastern and Western churches, usually dated from 1054. **2** the division within the Roman Catholic Church from 1378 to 1429, during which rival popes reigned at Rome and Avignon.

great seal *n* (*often caps.*) the principal seal of a nation, sovereign, etc., used to authenticate signatures and documents of the highest importance.

Great Slave Lake *n* a lake in NW Canada, in the Northwest Territories: drained by the Mackenzie River into the Arctic Ocean. Area: 28 440 sq. km (10 980 sq. miles).

Great Slave River *n* another name for the **Slave River.**

Great Smoky Mountains *or* **Great Smokies** *pl n* the W part of the Appalachians, in W North Carolina and E Tennessee. Highest peak: Clingman's Dome, 2024 m (6642 ft.).

Great St Bernard Pass *n* a pass over the W Alps, between SW central Switzerland and N Italy: noted for the hospice at the summit, founded in the 11th century. Height: 2469 m (8100 ft.).

Great Stour *n* another name for **Stour** (sense 1).

great tit *n* a large common Eurasian tit, *Parus major,* with yellow-and-black underparts and a black-and-white head.

Great Trek *n* **the.** *South African history.* the migration of Boer farmers from the Cape Colony to the north and east from about 1836 to 1845 to escape British authority.

great-uncle *or* **granduncle** *n* an uncle of one's father or mother; brother of one's grandfather or grandmother.

Great Victoria Desert *n* a desert in S Australia, in SE Western Australia and W South Australia. Area: 323 750 sq. km (125 000 sq. miles).

Great Vowel Shift *n Linguistics.* a phonetic change that took place during the transition from Middle to Modern English, whereby the long vowels were raised (eː became iː, oː became uː, etc.). The vowels (iː) and (uː) underwent breaking and became the diphthongs (aɪ) and (aʊ).

Great Wall *n Astron.* a vast sheet of many thousands of gravitationally associated galaxies detected in the universe.

Great Wall of China *n* a defensive wall in N China, extending from W Gansu to the Gulf of Liaodong: constructed in the 3rd century B.C. as a defence against the Mongols; substantially rebuilt in the 15th century. Length: over 2400 km (1500 miles). Average height: 6 m (20 ft.). Average width: 6 m (20 ft.).

Great War *n* another name for **World War I.**

Great Week *n Eastern Church.* the week preceding Easter, the equivalent of Holy Week in the Western Church.

great white heron *n* **1** a large white heron, *Ardea occidentalis,* of S North America. **2** a widely distributed white egret, *Egretta* (or *Casmerodius*) *albus.*

Great White Way *n* the theatre district on Broadway in New York City.

Great Yarmouth (ˈjɑːməθ) *n* a port and resort in E England, in E Norfolk. Pop.: 56 190 (1991).

great year *n* one complete cycle of the precession of the equinoxes; about 25 800 years.

greave (griːv) *n* (*often pl*) a piece of armour worn to protect the shin from the ankle to the knee. **[C14:** from Old French *greve,* perhaps from *graver* to part the hair, of Germanic origin**]** ▸ **greaved** *adj*

greaves (griːvz) *pl n* the residue left after the rendering of tallow. **[C17:** from Low German *greven;* related to Old High German *griubo***]**

Greaves (griːvz) *n* **Jimmy.** born 1940, English footballer and television commentator on the sport.

grebe (griːb) *n* any aquatic bird, such as *Podiceps cristatus* (**great crested grebe**), of the order *Podicipediformes,* similar to the divers but with lobate rather than webbed toes and a vestigial tail. **[C18:** from French *grèbe,* of unknown origin**]**

Grecian (ˈgriːʃən) *adj* **1** (esp. of beauty or architecture) conforming to Greek ideals, esp. in being classically simple. ◆ *n* **2** a scholar of or expert in the Greek language or literature. ◆ *adj, n* **3** another word for **Greek.**

Grecism (ˈgriːˌsɪzəm) *n* a variant spelling (esp. U.S.) of **Graecism.**

Grecize (ˈgriːsaɪz) *vb* a variant spelling (esp. U.S.) of **Graecize.**

Greco (ˈgrɛkəʊ) *n* **El.** See **El Greco.**

Greco- (ˈgriːkəʊ, ˈgrɛkəʊ) *combining form.* a variant (esp. U.S.) of **Graeco-.**

gree[1] (griː) *n Scot. archaic.* **1** superiority or victory. **2** the prize for a victory. **[C14:** from Old French *gré,* from Latin *gradus* step**]**

gree[2] (griː) *n Obsolete.* **1** goodwill; favour. **2** satisfaction for an insult or injury. **[C14:** from Old French *gré,* from Latin *grātum* what is pleasing; see GRATEFUL**]**

gree[3] (griː) *vb* **grees, greeing, greed.** *Archaic or dialect.* to come or cause to come to agreement or harmony. **[C14:** variant of AGREE**]**

Greece (griːs) *n* a republic in SE Europe, occupying the S part of the Balkan Peninsula and many islands in the Ionian and Aegean Seas; site of two of Europe's earliest civilizations (the Minoan and Mycenaean); in the classical era divided into many small independent city-states, the most important being Athens and Sparta; part of the Roman and Byzantine Empires; passed under Turkish rule in the late Middle Ages; became an independent kingdom in 1827; taken over by a military junta (1967–74); the monarchy was abolished in 1973; became a republic in 1975; a member of the European Union. Official language: Greek. Official religion: Eastern (Greek) Orthodox. Currency: drachma. Capital: Athens. Pop.: 10 543 000 (1998 est.). Area: 131 944 sq. km (50 944 sq. miles). Modern Greek name: **Ellás.** Related adj: **Hellenic.**

greed (griːd) *n* **1** excessive consumption of or desire for food; gluttony. **2** excessive desire, as for wealth or power. **[C17:** back formation from GREEDY**]** ▸ **ˈgreedless** *adj*

greedy (ˈgriːdɪ) *adj* **greedier, greediest. 1** excessively desirous of food or wealth, esp. in large amounts; voracious. **2** (*postpositive;* foll. by *for*) eager (for): *a man greedy for success.* **[**Old English *grǣdig;* related to Old Norse *grāthugr,* Gothic *grēdags* hungry, Old High German *grātac***]** ▸ **ˈgreedily** *adv* ▸ **ˈgreediness** *n*

greedy guts *n* (*functioning as sing*) *Slang.* a glutton.

greegree (ˈgriːgriː) *n* a variant spelling of **grigri.**

Greek (griːk) *n* **1** the official language of Greece, constituting the Hellenic branch of the Indo-European family of languages. See **Ancient Greek, Late Greek, Medieval Greek, Modern Greek. 2** a native or inhabitant of Greece or a descendant of such a native. **3** a member of the Greek Orthodox Church. **4** *Informal.* anything incomprehensible (esp. in the phrase **it's (all) Greek to me**). **5 Greek meets Greek.** equals meet. ◆ *adj* **6** denoting, relating to, or characteristic of Greece, the Greeks, or the Greek language; Hellenic. **7** of, relating to, or designating the Greek Orthodox Church. **[**from Old English *Grēcas* (plural), or Latin *Graecus,* from Greek *Graikos***]** ▸ **ˈGreekness** *n*

Greek Catholic *n* **1** a member of an Eastern Church in communion with the Greek patriarchal see of Constantinople. **2** a member of one of the Uniat Greek Churches, which acknowledge the Pope's authority while retaining their own institutions, discipline, and liturgy.

Greek Church *n* another name for the **Greek Orthodox Church.**

Greek cross *n* a cross with each of the four arms of the same length.

greeked text (griːkt) *n Computing.* words which appear on screen as grey lines when the type size is too small for actual letters to be shown.

Greek fire *n* **1** a Byzantine weapon employed in naval warfare from 670 A.D. It consisted of an unknown mixture that, when wetted, exploded and was projected, burning, from tubes. **2** any of several other inflammable mixtures used in warfare up to the 19th century.

Greek gift *n* a gift given with the intention of tricking and causing harm to the recipient. **[C19:** in allusion to Virgil's *Aeneid* ii 49; see also TROJAN HORSE**]**

Greek mallow *n* See **sidalcea.**

Greek Orthodox Church *n* **1** Also called: **Greek Church.** the established Church of Greece, governed by the holy synod of Greece, in which the Metropolitan of Athens has primacy of honour. **2** another name for **Orthodox Church.**

Greek Revival *n* (*modifier*) denoting, relating to, or having the style of architecture used in Western Europe in the late 18th and early 19th centuries, based upon ancient Greek classical examples. ▸ **Greek Revivalism** *n* ▸ **Greek Revivalist** *adj, n*

Greeley (ˈgriːlɪ) *n* **Horace.** 1811–72, U.S. journalist and political leader: founder (1841) and editor of the *New York Tribune,* which championed the abolition of slavery.

green (griːn) *n* **1** any of a group of colours, such as that of fresh grass, that lie between yellow and blue in the visible spectrum in the wavelength range 575–500 nanometres. Green is the complementary colour of magenta and with red and blue forms a set of primary colours. Related adj: **verdant. 2** a dye or pigment of or producing these colours. **3** something of the colour green. **4** a small area of grassland, esp. in the centre of a village. **5** an area of ground used for a purpose: *a putting green.* **6** (*pl*) **6a** the edible leaves and stems of certain plants, eaten as a vegetable. **6b** freshly cut branches of ornamental trees, shrubs, etc., used as a decoration. **7** (*sometimes cap.*) a person, esp. a politician, who supports environmentalist issues (see sense 14). **8** *Slang.* money. **9** *Slang.* marijuana of low quality. **10** (*pl*) *Slang.* sexual intercourse. ◆ *adj* **11** of the colour green. **12** greenish in colour or having parts or marks that are greenish: *a green monkey.* **13** (*sometimes cap.*) concerned with or relating to conservation of the world's natural resources and improvement of the environment: *green policies; the green consumer.* **14** vigorous; not faded: *a green old age.* **15** envious or jealous. **16** immature, unsophisticated, or gullible. **17** characterized by foliage or green plants: *a green wood; a green salad.* **18** fresh, raw, or unripe: *green bananas.* **19** unhealthily pale in appearance: *he was green after his boat trip.* **20** denoting a unit of account that is adjusted in accordance with fluctuations between the currencies of the EU nations and is used to make payments to agricultural producers within the EU: *green pound; green franc.* **21** (of pottery) not fired. **22** (of meat) not smoked or cured; unprocessed: *green bacon.* **23** *Metallurgy.* (of a product, such as a sand mould or cermet) compacted but not yet fired; ready for firing. **24** (of timber) freshly felled; not dried or seasoned. **25** (of concrete) not having matured to design strength. ◆ *vb* **26** to make or become green. **[**Old English *grēne;* related to Old High German *gruoni;* see GROW**]** ▸ **ˈgreenish** *adj* ▸ **ˈgreenly** *adv* ▸ **ˈgreenness** *n* ▸ **ˈgreeny** *adj*

Green (griːn) *n* **1 Henry,** real name *Henry Vincent Yorke.* 1905–73, British novelist: author of *Living* (1929), *Loving* (1945), and *Back* (1946). **2 John Richard.** 1837–83, British historian; author of *A Short History of the English People* (1874). **3 T(homas) H(ill).** 1836–82, British idealist philosopher. His chief work, *Prolegomena to Ethics,* was unfinished at his death.

green algae *pl n* the algae of the phylum *Chlorophyta,* which possess the green pigment chlorophyll. The group includes sea lettuce and spirogyra.

Greenaway (ˈgriːnəˌweɪ) *n* **1 Kate.** 1846–1901, English painter, noted as an illustrator of children's books. **2 Peter.** born 1942, British film director; noted for such cerebral films as *The Draughtsman's Contract* (1982), *Prospero's Books* (1990), and *Eight and a Half Women* (1999).

greenback ('gri:n,bæk) *n* **1** *U.S. informal.* an inconvertible legal-tender U.S. currency note originally issued during the Civil War in 1862. **2** *U.S. slang.* a dollar bill.

Greenback Party *n U.S. history.* a political party formed after the Civil War advocating the use of fiat money and opposing the reduction of paper currency. ▸ **'Green,backer** *n* ▸ **'Green,backism** *n*

green ban *n Austral.* a trade union ban on any development that might be considered harmful to the environment.

green bean *n* any bean plant, such as the French bean, having narrow green edible pods when unripe.

green belt *n* a zone of farmland, parks, and open country surrounding a town or city: usually officially designated as such and preserved from urban development.

Green Beret *n* an informal name for a British or U.S. commando.

greenbone ('gri:n,bəʊn) *n N.Z.* another name for **butterfish** (sense 2).

greenbottle ('gri:n,bɒtᵊl) *n* a common dipterous fly, *Lucilia caesar,* that has a dark greenish body with a metallic lustre and lays its eggs in carrion: family *Calliphoridae.*

greenbrier ('gri:n,braɪə) *n* any of several prickly climbing plants of the liliaceous genus *Smilax,* esp. *S. rotundifolia* of the eastern U.S., which has small green flowers and blackish berries. Also called: **cat brier.**

green card *n* **1** an official permit allowing the holder permanent residence and employment, issued to foreign nationals in the U.S. **2** an insurance document covering motorists against accidents abroad. **3** *Social welfare.* (in Britain) an identification card issued by the Manpower Services Commission to a disabled person, to show registration for employment purposes and eligibility for special services. See also **handicap register, registered disabled.**

green corn *n* another name for **sweet corn** (sense 1).

Green Cross Code *n* (in Britain) a code for children giving rules for road safety: first issued in 1971.

green dragon *n* a North American aroid plant, *Arisaema dracontium,* with a long slender spadix projecting from a green or white long narrow spathe. Also called: **dragonroot.**

Greene (gri:n) *n* **1 Graham.** 1904–91, English novelist and dramatist; his works include the novels *Brighton Rock* (1938), *The Power and the Glory* (1940), and *The Captain and the Enemy* (1988), and the film script *The Third Man* (1949). **2 Robert.** ?1558–92, English poet, dramatist, and prose writer, noted for his autobiographical tract *A Groatsworth of Wit bought with a Million of Repentance* (1592), which contains an attack on Shakespeare.

greenery ('gri:nərɪ) *n* green foliage or vegetation, esp. when used for decoration.

green-eyed *adj* **1** jealous or envious. **2 the green-eyed monster.** jealousy or envy.

greenfield ('gri:n,fi:ld) *n (modifier).* denoting or located in a rural area which has not previously been built on: *new factories were erected on greenfield sites.*

greenfinch ('gri:n,fɪntʃ) *n* a common European finch, *Carduelis chloris,* the male of which has a dull green plumage with yellow patches on the wings and tail.

green fingers *pl n* considerable talent or ability to grow plants. U.S. and Canadian equivalent: **green thumb.**

green flash *n Astronomy.* a flash of bright green light sometimes seen as the sun passes below the horizon, caused by the dispersion of blue light.

greenfly ('gri:n,flaɪ) *n, pl* **-flies.** a greenish aphid commonly occurring as a pest on garden and crop plants.

greengage ('gri:n,geɪdʒ) *n* **1** a cultivated variety of plum tree, *Prunus domestica italica,* with edible green plumlike fruits. **2** the fruit of this tree. [C18: GREEN + *-gage,* after Sir W. *Gage* (1777–1864), English botanist who brought it from France]

green gland *n* one of a pair of excretory organs in some crustaceans that open at the base of each antenna.

green glass *n* glass in its natural colour, usually greenish as a result of metallic substances in the raw materials.

greengrocer ('gri:n,grəʊsə) *n Chiefly Brit.* a retail trader in fruit and vegetables. ▸ **'green,grocery** *n*

Greenham Common ('gri:nəm) *n* a village in Berkshire, near Newbury; site of a U.S. cruise missile base, and, since 1981, a camp of women protesters against nuclear weapons; although the base had closed by 1991 a small number of women still live at the site.

greenhead ('gri:n,hed) *n* a male mallard.

greenheart ('gri:n,hɑ:t) *n* **1** Also called: **bebeeru.** a tropical American lauraceous tree, *Ocotea* (or *Nectandra*) *rodiaei,* that has dark green durable wood and bark that yields the alkaloid bebeerine. **2** any of various similar trees. **3** the wood of any of these trees.

green heron *n* a small heron, *Butorides virescens,* of subtropical North America, with dark greenish wings and back.

greenhorn ('gri:n,hɔ:n) *n* **1** an inexperienced person, esp. one who is extremely gullible. **2** *Chiefly U.S.* a newcomer or immigrant. [C17: originally an animal with *green* (that is, young) horns]

greenhouse ('gri:n,haʊs) *n* **1** a building with transparent walls and roof, usually of glass, for the cultivation and exhibition of plants under controlled conditions. ◆ *adj* **2** relating to or contributing to the greenhouse effect: *greenhouse gases such as carbon dioxide.*

greenhouse effect *n* **1** an effect occurring in greenhouses, etc., in which radiant heat from the sun passes through the glass warming the contents, the radiant heat from inside being trapped by the glass. **2** the application of this effect to a planet's atmosphere; carbon dioxide and some other gases in the planet's atmosphere can absorb the infrared radiation emitted by the planet's surface as a result of exposure to solar ultraviolet radiation, thus increasing the mean temperature of the planet.

greenie ('gri:nɪ) *n Austral. informal.* a conservationist.

greening ('gri:nɪŋ) *n* the process of making or becoming more aware of environmental considerations. [C20: from GREEN (sense 13)]

green keeper *n* a person in charge of a golf course or bowling green.

Greenland ('gri:nlənd) *n* a large island, lying mostly within the Arctic Circle off the NE coast of North America: first settled by Icelanders in 986; resettled by Danes from 1721 onwards; integral part of Denmark (1953–79); granted internal autonomy 1979; mostly covered by an icecap up to 3300 m (11 000 ft.) thick, with ice-free coastal strips and coastal mountains; the population is largely Eskimo, with a European minority; fishing, hunting, and mining. Capital: Nuuk. Pop.: 56 200 (1998 est.). Area: 2 175 600 sq. km (840 000 sq. miles). Danish name: **Grønland.** Greenlandic name: **Kalaallit Nunaat.** ▸ **'Greenlander** *n*

Greenlandic (gri:n'lændɪk) *adj* **1** of, relating to, or characteristic of Greenland, the Greenlanders, or the Inuit dialect spoken in Greenland. ◆ *n* **2** the dialect of Inuit Eskimo spoken in Greenland.

Greenland Sea *n* the S part of the Arctic Ocean, off the NE coast of Greenland.

Greenland whale *n* an arctic right whale, *Balaena mysticetus,* that is black with a cream-coloured throat.

green leek *n* any of several Australian parrots with a green or mostly green plumage.

greenlet ('gri:nlɪt) *n* a vireo, esp. one of the genus *Hylophilus.*

green light *n* **1** a signal to go, esp. a green traffic light. **2** permission to proceed with a project. ◆ *vb* **greenlight, -lights, -lighting, -lighted.** *(tr)* **3** to permit (a project, etc.) to proceed.

greenling ('gri:nlɪŋ) *n* any scorpaenoid food fish of the family *Hexagrammidae* of the North Pacific Ocean.

greenmail ('gri:n,meɪl) *n* (esp. in the U.S.) the practice of a company buying sufficient shares in another company to threaten takeover and making a quick profit as a result of the threatened company buying back its shares at a higher price.

green manure *n* **1** a growing crop that is ploughed under to enrich the soil. **2** manure that has not yet decomposed.

green monkey *n* a W African variety of a common guenon monkey, *Cercopithecus aethiops,* having greenish-brown fur and a dark face. Compare **grivet, vervet.**

green monkey disease *n* another name for **Marburg disease.**

green mould *n* another name for **blue mould** (sense 1).

Green Mountain Boys *pl n* the members of the armed bands of Vermont organized in 1770 to oppose New York's territorial claims. Under Ethan Allen they won fame in the War of American Independence.

Green Mountains *pl n* a mountain range in E North America, extending from Canada through Vermont into W Massachusetts: part of the Appalachian system. Highest peak: Mount Mansfield, 1338 m (4393 ft.).

Greenock ('gri:nək) *n* a port in SW Scotland, in Inverclyde on the Firth of Clyde: shipbuilding and other marine industries. Pop.: 50 013 (1991).

greenockite ('gri:nə,kaɪt) *n* a rare yellowish mineral consisting of cadmium sulphide in hexagonal crystalline form: the only ore of cadmium. Formula: CdS. [C19: named after Lord C. C. *Greenock,* 19th-century English soldier]

Greenough ('gri:nəʊ) *n* **George Bellas.** 1778–1855, English geologist, founder of the Geological Society of London.

green paper *n (often caps.)* (in Britain) a command paper containing policy proposals to be discussed, esp. by Parliament.

Green Party *n* a political party whose policies are based on concern for the environment.

Greenpeace ('gri:n,pi:s) *n* an organization founded in 1971 that stresses the need to maintain a balance between human progress and environmental conservation. Members take active but nonviolent measures against what are regarded as threats to environmental safety, such as the dumping of nuclear waste in the sea.

green pepper *n* **1** the green unripe fruit of the sweet pepper, eaten raw or cooked. **2** the unripe fruit of various other pepper plants, eaten as a green vegetable.

green plover *n* another name for **lapwing.**

green pound *n* a unit of account used in calculating Britain's contributions to and payments from the Community Agricultural Fund of the EU.

green revolution *n* the introduction of high-yielding seeds and modern agricultural techniques in developing countries.

Green River *n* a river in the western U.S., rising in W central Wyoming and flowing south into Utah, east through NW Colorado, re-entering Utah before joining the Colorado River. Length: 1175 km (730 miles).

greenroom ('gri:n,ru:m, -,rʊm) *n* (esp. formerly) a backstage room in a theatre where performers may rest or receive visitors. [C18: probably from its original colour]

green run *n Skiing.* a very easy run, suitable for complete beginners.

greensand ('gri:n,sænd) *n* an olive-green sandstone consisting mainly of quartz and glauconite.

Greensboro ('gri:nzbərə, -brə) *n* a city in N central North Carolina. Pop.: 195 426 (1996 est.).

greenshank ('gri:n,ʃæŋk) *n* a large European sandpiper, *Tringa nebularia,* with greenish legs and a slightly upturned bill.

greensickness ('gri:n,sɪknɪs) *n* another name for **chlorosis.** ▸ **'green,sick** *adj*

green soap *n Med.* a soft or liquid alkaline soap made from vegetable oils, used in treating certain chronic skin diseases. Also called: **soft soap.**

greensome ('gri:nsəm) *n Golf.* a match for two pairs in which each of the four players tees off and after selecting the better drive the partners of each pair play that ball alternately. Compare **four-ball, foursome** (sense 2).

greenstick fracture ('gri:n,stɪk) *n* a fracture in children in which the bone is partly bent and splinters only on the convex side of the bend. [C20: alluding to the similar way in which a green stick splinters]

greenstone ('gri:n,stəʊn) *n* **1** any basic igneous rock that is dark green because of the presence of chlorite or epidote. **2** a variety of jade used in New Zealand for ornaments and tools.

greenstuff ('gri:n,stʌf) *n* green vegetables, such as cabbage or lettuce.

greensward ('gri:n,swɔ:d) *n Archaic or literary.* fresh green turf or an area of such turf.

green tea *n* a sharp tea made from tea leaves that have been steamed and dried quickly without fermenting.

green thumb *n* the U.S. and Canadian term for **green fingers.**

green turtle *n* a mainly tropical edible turtle, *Chelonia mydas,* with greenish flesh used to prepare turtle soup: family *Chelonidae.*

green vitriol *n* another name for **ferrous sulphate.**

green-wellie *n* (*modifier*) characterizing or belonging to the upper-class set devoted to hunting, shooting, and fishing: *the green-wellie brigade.*

Greenwich ('grɪnɪdʒ, -ɪtʃ, 'grɛn-) *n* a Greater London borough on the Thames: site of a Royal Naval College and of the original Royal Observatory designed by Christopher Wren (1675), accepted internationally as the prime meridian of longitude since 1884, and the basis of Greenwich Mean Time; also site of the Millennium Dome. Pop.: 212 200 (1994 est.). Area: 46 sq. km (18 sq. miles).

Greenwich Mean Time *or* **Greenwich Time** *n* mean solar time on the 0° meridian passing through Greenwich, England, measured from midnight: formerly a standard time in Britain and a basis for calculating times throughout most of the world, it has been replaced by an atomic timescale. See **universal time.** Abbrev.: **GMT.**

USAGE The name **Greenwich mean time** is ambiguous, having been measured from mean midday in astronomy up to 1925, and is not used for scientific purposes. It is generally and incorrectly used in the sense of **coordinated universal time**, an atomic timescale available since 1972 from broadcast signals, in addition to the earliest sense of **universal time**, adopted internationally in 1928 as the name for GMT measured from midnight.

Greenwich Village ('grɛnɪtʃ, 'grɪn-) *n* a part of New York City in the lower west side of Manhattan; traditionally the home of many artists and writers.

greenwood ('gri:n,wʊd) *n* a forest or wood when the leaves are green: the traditional setting of stories about English outlaws, esp. Robin Hood.

green woodpecker *n* a European woodpecker, *Picus viridis,* with a dull green back and wings and a red crown.

Greer ('grɪə) *n* **Germaine.** born 1939, Australian writer and feminist. Her books include *The Female Eunuch* (1970), *Sex and Destiny* (1984), and *The Whole Woman* (1998).

greet[1] (gri:t) *vb* (*tr*) **1** to meet or receive with expressions of gladness or welcome. **2** to send a message of friendship to. **3** to receive in a specified manner: *her remarks were greeted by silence.* **4** to become apparent to: *the smell of bread greeted him.* [Old English *grētan;* related to Old High German *gruozzen* to address] ▸ **'greeter** *n*

greet[2] (gri:t) *Scot. or archaic.* ♦ *vb* **1** (*intr*) to weep; lament. ♦ *n* **2** weeping; lamentation. [from Old English *grētan,* northern dialect variant of *grǣtan;* compare Old Norse *grāta,* Middle High German *grazen*]

greeting ('gri:tɪŋ) *n* **1** the act or an instance of welcoming or saluting on meeting. **2** (*often pl*) **2a** an expression of friendly salutation. **2b** (*as modifier*): *a greetings card.*

gregarine ('grɛgə,ri:n, -rɪn) *n* **1** any parasitic protozoan of the order *Gregarinida,* typically occurring in the digestive tract and body cavity of other invertebrates: phylum *Apicomplexa* (sporozoans). ♦ *adj also* **gregarinian** (,grɛgə'rɪnɪən). **2** of, relating to, or belonging to the *Gregarinida.* [C19: from New Latin *Gregarīna* genus name, from Latin *gregārius;* see GREGARIOUS]

gregarious (grɪ'gɛərɪəs) *adj* **1** enjoying the company of others. **2** (of animals) living together in herds or flocks. Compare **solitary** (sense 6). **3** (of plants) growing close together but not in dense clusters. **4** of, relating to, or characteristic of crowds or communities. [C17: from Latin *gregārius* belonging to a flock, from *grex* flock] ▸ **gre'gariously** *adv* ▸ **gre'gariousness** *n*

Gregorian (grɪ'gɔ:rɪən) *adj* relating to, associated with, or introduced by any of the popes named Gregory, esp. Gregory I or Gregory XIII.

Gregorian calendar *n* the revision of the Julian calendar introduced in 1582 by Pope Gregory XIII and still in force, whereby the ordinary year is made to consist of 365 days and a leap year occurs in every year whose number is divisible by four, except those centenary years, such as 1900, whose numbers are not divisible by 400.

Gregorian chant *n* another name for **plainsong.**

Gregorian telescope *n* a form of reflecting astronomical telescope with a concave secondary mirror and the eyepiece set in the centre of the parabolic primary mirror. [C18: named after J. *Gregory* (died 1675), Scottish mathematician who invented it]

Gregorian tone *n* a plainsong melody. See **tone** (sense 6).

Gregory ('grɛgərɪ) *n* Lady (**Isabella**) **Augusta** (**Persse**). 1852–1932, Irish dramatist; a founder and director of the Abbey Theatre, Dublin.

Gregory I *n* **Saint,** known as *Gregory the Great.* ?540–604 A.D., pope (590–604), who greatly influenced the medieval Church. He strengthened papal authority by centralizing administration, tightened discipline, and revised the liturgy. He appointed Saint Augustine missionary to England. Feast day: March 12 or Sept. 3.

Gregory VII *n* **Saint,** monastic name *Hildebrand.* ?1020–85, pope (1073–85), who did much to reform abuses in the Church. His assertion of papal supremacy and his prohibition (1075) of lay investiture was opposed by the Holy Roman Emperor Henry IV, whom he excommunicated (1076). He was driven into exile when Henry captured Rome (1084). Feast day: May 25.

Gregory IX *n* original name *Ugolino of Segni.* ?1148–1241, pope (1227–41). He excommunicated and waged war against Emperor Frederick II.

Gregory XIII *n* 1502–85, pope (1572–85). He promoted the Counter-Reformation and founded seminaries. His reformed (Gregorian) calendar was issued in 1582.

Gregory of Nazianzus (,næzɪ'ænzəs) *n* **Saint.** ?329–89 A.D., Cappadocian theologian: bishop of Caesarea (370–79). Feast days: Jan. 2, 25, and 30.

Gregory of Nyssa ('nɪsə) *n* **Saint.** ?335–394 A.D., Cappadocian theologian and brother of St Basil: bishop of Nyssa. Feast day: March 9.

Gregory of Tours *n* **Saint.** ?538–?594 A.D., Frankish bishop and historian. His *Historia Francorum* is the chief source of knowledge of 6th-century Gaul. Feast day: Nov. 17.

Gregory's powder *n* a compound of rhubarb powder used as a laxative or purgative. [C19: named after Dr James *Gregory* (1753–1821), who first made it]

greige (greɪʒ) *Chiefly U.S.* ♦ *adj* **1** (of a fabric or material) not yet dyed. ♦ *n* **2** an unbleached or undyed cloth or yarn. [C20: from French *grège* raw]

greisen ('graɪzᵊn) *n* a light-coloured metamorphic rock consisting mainly of quartz and white mica, formed by the pneumatolysis of granite. [C19: from German, from *greissen* to split]

gremial ('gri:mɪəl) *n R.C. Church.* a cloth spread upon the lap of a bishop when seated during Mass. [C17: from Latin *gremium* lap]

gremlin ('grɛmlɪn) *n* **1** an imaginary imp jokingly said to be responsible for malfunctions in machinery. **2** any mischievous troublemaker. [C20: of unknown origin]

Grenada (grɛ'neɪdə) *n* an island state in the Caribbean, in the Windward Islands: formerly a British colony (1783–1967); since 1974 an independent state within the Commonwealth; occupied by U.S. troops (1983–85); mainly agricultural. Official language: English. Religion: Christian majority. Currency: East Caribbean dollar. Capital: St George's. Pop.: 100 000 (1998 est.). Area: 344 sq. km (133 sq. miles). ▸ **Gre'nadian** *n, adj*

grenade (grɪ'neɪd) *n* **1** a small container filled with explosive thrown by hand or fired from a rifle. **2** a sealed glass vessel that is thrown and shatters to release chemicals, such as tear gas or a fire extinguishing agent. [C16: from French, from Spanish *granada* pomegranate, from Late Latin *grānāta,* from Latin *grānātus* seedy; see GRAIN]

grenadier (,grɛnə'dɪə) *n* **1** *Military.* **1a** (in the British Army) a member of the senior regiment of infantry in the Household Brigade. **1b** (formerly) a member of a special formation, usually selected for strength and height. **1c** (formerly) a soldier trained to throw grenades. **2** Also called: **rat-tail.** any deep-sea gadoid fish of the family *Macrouridae,* typically having a large head and trunk and a long tapering tail. **3** any of various African weaverbirds of the genus *Estrilda.* See **waxbill.** [C17: from French; see GRENADE]

grenadine[1] (,grɛnə'di:n) *n* a light thin leno-weave fabric of silk, wool, rayon, or nylon, used esp. for dresses. [C19: from French, from earlier *grenade* silk with a grained texture, from *grenu* grained; see GRAIN]

grenadine[2] (,grɛnə'di:n, 'grɛnə,di:n) *n* **1** a syrup made from pomegranate juice, used as a sweetening and colouring agent in various drinks. **2a** a moderate reddish-orange colour. **2b** (*as adj*): *a grenadine coat.* [C19: from French: a little pomegranate, from *grenade* pomegranate; see GRENADE]

Grenadines (,grɛnə'di:nz, 'grɛnə,di:nz) *pl n* **the.** a chain of about 600 islets in the Caribbean, part of the Windward Islands, extending for about 100 km (60 miles) between St Vincent and Grenada and divided administratively between the two states. Largest island: Carriacou.

Grendel ('grɛndᵊl) *n* (in Old English legend) a man-eating monster defeated by the hero Beowulf.

Grenfell ('grɛnfəl) *n* **Joyce,** real name *Joyce Irene Phipps.* 1910–79, British comedy actress and writer.

Grenoble (grə'nəʊbᵊl; *French* grənɔblə) *n* a city in SE France, on the Isère River: university (1339). Pop.: 153 973 (1990).

Grenville ('grɛnvɪl) *n* **1 George.** 1712–70, British statesman; prime minister (1763–65). His policy of taxing the American colonies precipitated the War of Independence. **2** Sir **Richard.** ?1541–91, English naval commander. He was fatally wounded aboard his ship, the *Revenge,* during a lone battle with a fleet of Spanish treasure ships. **3 William Wyndham,** Baron Grenville, son of George Grenville. 1759–1834, British statesman; prime minister (1806–07) of the coalition government known as the "ministry of all the talents".

grenz rays (grɛnz) *n Physics.* X-rays of long wavelength produced in a device when electrons are accelerated through 25 kilovolts or less. [C20: from *grenz* from German *Grenze* boundary]

Gresham ('grɛʃəm) *n* Sir **Thomas.** ?1519–79, English financier, who founded the Royal Exchange in London (1568).

Gresham's law *or* **theorem** *n* the economic hypothesis that bad money drives good money out of circulation; the superior currency will tend to be hoarded and the inferior will thus dominate the circulation. [C16: named after Sir T. GRESHAM]

gressorial (grɛ'sɔ:rɪəl) *or* **gressorious** *adj* **1** (of the feet of certain birds) specialized for walking. **2** (of birds, such as the ostrich) having such feet. [C19: from New Latin *gressōrius,* from *gressus* having walked, from *gradī* to step]

Gretna Green ('grɛtnə) *n* a village in S Scotland, in Dumfries and Galloway on the border with England: famous smithy where eloping couples were married by the blacksmith from 1754 until 1940, when such marriages became illegal. Pop.: 3149 (1991).

Greuze (*French* grøz) *n* **Jean Baptiste** (ʒɑ̃ batist). 1725–1805, French genre and portrait painter.

Greville ('grɛvɪl) *n* **Fulke** (fʊlk), 1st Baron Brooke. 1554–1628, English poet, writer, politician, and diplomat: Chancellor of the Exchequer (1614–22); author of *The Life of the Renowned Sir Philip Sidney* (1652).

grevillea (grəˈvɪljə) *n* any of a large variety of evergreen trees and shrubs that comprise the genus *Grevillea,* native to Australia, Tasmania, and New Caledonia. [named after C. F. *Greville* (1749–1809), a founder of the Royal Horticultural Society]

grew (gruː) *vb* the past tense of **grow.**

grewsome (ˈgruːsəm) *adj* an archaic or U.S. spelling of **gruesome.**

grey *or now esp. U.S.* **gray** (greɪ) *adj* **1** of a neutral tone, intermediate between black and white, that has no hue and reflects and transmits only a little light. **2** greyish in colour or having parts or marks that are greyish. **3** dismal or dark, esp. from lack of light; gloomy. **4** neutral or dull, esp. in character or opinion. **5** having grey hair. **6** of or relating to people of middle age or above: *grey power.* **7** ancient; venerable. **8** (of textiles) natural, unbleached, undyed, and untreated. ◆ *n* **9** any of a group of grey tones. **10** grey cloth or clothing: *dressed in grey.* **11** an animal, esp. a horse, that is grey or whitish. ◆ *vb* **12** to become or make grey. [Old English *grǣg;* related to Old High German *grão,* Old Norse *grar*] ▸ **ˈgreyish** *or now esp. U.S.* **ˈgrayish** *adj* ▸ **ˈgreyly** *or now esp. U.S.* **ˈgrayly** *adv* ▸ **ˈgreyness** *or now esp. U.S.* **ˈgrayness** *n*

Grey (greɪ) *n* **1 Charles,** 2nd Earl Grey. 1764–1845, British statesman. As Whig prime minister (1830–34), he carried the Reform Bill of 1832 and the bill for the abolition of slavery throughout the British Empire (1833). **2** Sir **Edward,** 1st Viscount Grey of Fallodon. 1862–1933, British statesman; foreign secretary (1905–16). **3** Sir **George.** 1812–98, British statesman and colonial administrator; prime minister of New Zealand (1877–79). **4** Lady **Jane.** 1537–54, queen of England (July 9–19, 1553); great-granddaughter of Henry VII. Her father-in-law, the Duke of Northumberland, persuaded Edward VI to alter the succession in her favour, but after ten days as queen she was imprisoned and later executed. **5 Zane.** 1875–1939, U.S. author of Westerns, including *Riders of the Purple Sage* (1912).

grey area *n* **1** (in Britain) a region in which unemployment is relatively high. **2** an area or part of something existing between two extremes and having mixed characteristics of both. **3** an area, situation, etc., lacking clearly defined characteristics.

greyback *or U.S.* **grayback** (ˈgreɪˌbæk) *n* any of various animals having a grey back, such as the grey whale and the hooded crow.

greybeard *or U.S.* **graybeard** (ˈgreɪˌbɪəd) *n* **1** an old man, esp. a sage. **2** a large stoneware or earthenware jar or jug for spirits. ▸ **ˈgreyˌbearded** *or U.S.* **ˈgrayˌbearded** *adj*

grey body *n Physics.* a body that emits radiation in constant proportion to the corresponding black-body radiation.

grey eminence *n* the English equivalent of **éminence grise.**

grey fox *n* **1** a greyish American fox, *Urocyon cinereoargenteus,* inhabiting arid and woody regions from S North America to N South America. **2 island grey fox.** a similar and related animal, *U. littoralis,* inhabiting islands off North America.

Grey Friar *n* a Franciscan friar.

greyhen (ˈgreɪˌhɛn) *n* the female of the black grouse. Compare **blackcock.**

grey heron *n* a large European heron, *Ardea cinerea,* with grey wings and back and a long black drooping crest.

greyhound (ˈgreɪˌhaʊnd) *n* a tall slender fast-moving dog of an ancient breed originally used for coursing.

greyhound racing *n* a sport in which a mechanically propelled dummy hare is pursued by greyhounds around a race track.

grey knight *n Informal.* an ambiguous intervener in a takeover battle, who makes a counterbid for the shares of the target company without having made his intentions clear. Compare **black knight, white knight.**

greylag *or* **greylag goose** (ˈgreɪˌlæg) *n* a large grey Eurasian goose, *Anser anser:* the ancestor of many domestic breeds of goose. U.S. spelling: **graylag.** [C18: from GREY + LAG[1], from its migrating later than other species]

grey market *n* **1** a system involving the secret but not illegal sale of goods at excessive prices. Compare **black market. 2** *Stock Exchange.* a market in the shares of a new issue, in which market makers deal with investors who have applied for shares but not yet received an allotment.

grey matter *n* **1** the greyish tissue of the brain and spinal cord, containing nerve cell bodies, dendrites, and bare (unmyelinated) axons. Technical name: **substantia grisea.** Compare **white matter. 2** *Informal.* brains or intellect.

grey mullet *n* any teleost food fish of the family *Mugilidae,* mostly occurring in coastal regions, having a spindle-shaped body and a broad fleshy mouth. U.S. name: **mullet.** Compare **red mullet.**

Greys *pl n* **the.** another name for (the) **Royal Scots Greys.**

grey sedge *n Brit.* an angler's name for a greyish caddis fly, *Odontocerum albicorne,* that frequents running water, in which its larvae make cases from grains of sand.

grey squirrel *n* a grey-furred squirrel, *Sciurus carolinensis,* native to E North America but now widely established.

grey-state *n* (*modifier*) (of a fabric or material) not yet dyed.

greywacke *or U.S.* **graywacke** (ˈgreɪˌwækə) *n* any dark sandstone or grit having a matrix of clay minerals. [C19: partial translation of German *Grauwacke;* see WACKE]

grey warbler *n N.Z.* a small bush bird that hatches the eggs of the shining cuckoo. Also called: **riroriro.**

grey water *n* water that has been used for one purpose but can be used again without repurification, e.g. bathwater, which can be used to water plants.

grey-wave *adj Informal.* denoting a company or an investment that is potentially profitable but is unlikely to fulfil expectations before the investor has grey hair.

greywether (ˈgreɪˌwɛðə) *n Geology.* another name for **sarsen.** [from its resemblance to a grey sheep; see WETHER]

grey whale *n* a large N Pacific whalebone whale, *Eschrichtius glaucus,* that is grey or black with white spots and patches: family *Eschrichtidae.*

grey wolf *n* another name for **timber wolf.**

GRF *Biochem. abbrev. for* growth hormone-releasing factor: a peptide that is released from the brain and stimulates the pituitary gland to secrete growth hormone.

gribble (ˈgrɪbᵊl) *n* any small marine isopod crustacean of the genus *Limnoria,* which bores into and damages wharves and other submerged wooden structures. [C19: perhaps related to GRUB]

grice (ˈgraɪs) *vb* **1** (*intr*) (of a railway enthusiast) to collect objects or visit places connected with trains and railways. ◆ *n* **2** an object collected or place visited by a railway enthusiast. [C20: origin obscure] ▸ **ˈgricer** *n* ▸ **ˈgricing** *n*

grid (grɪd) *n* **1** See **gridiron. 2** a network of horizontal and vertical lines superimposed over a map, building plan, etc., for locating points. **3** a grating consisting of parallel bars. **4 the grid.** the national network of transmission lines, pipes, etc., by which electricity, gas, or water is distributed. **5** *N.Z.* short for **national grid. 6** Also called: **control grid.** *Electronics.* **6a** an electrode situated between the cathode and anode of a valve usually consisting of a cylindrical mesh of wires, that controls the flow of electrons between cathode and anode. See also **screen grid, suppressor grid. 6b** (*as modifier*): *the grid bias.* **7** See **starting grid. 8** a plate in an accumulator that carries the active substance. **9** any interconnecting system of links: *the bus service formed a grid across the country.* [C19: back formation from GRIDIRON] ▸ **ˈgridded** *adj*

grid bias *n* the fixed voltage applied between the control grid and cathode of a valve.

grid declination *n* the angular difference between true north and grid north on a map.

griddle (ˈgrɪdᵊl) *n* **1** Also called: **girdle.** *Brit.* a thick round iron plate with a half hoop handle over the top, for making scones, etc. **2** any flat heated surface, esp. on the top of a stove, for cooking food. ◆ *vb* **3** (*tr*) to cook (food) on a griddle. [C13: from Old French *gridil,* from Late Latin *crātīculum* (unattested) fine wickerwork; see GRILL[1]]

griddlebread (ˈgrɪdᵊlˌbrɛd) *or* **griddlecake** (ˈgrɪdᵊlˌkeɪk) *n* bread or cake made on a griddle.

gride (graɪd) *vb* **1** (*intr*) *Literary.* to grate or scrape harshly. **2** *Obsolete.* to pierce or wound. ◆ *n* **3** *Literary.* a harsh or piercing sound. [C14: variant of *girde* GIRD[2]]

gridiron (ˈgrɪdˌaɪən) *n* **1** a utensil of parallel metal bars, used to grill meat, fish, etc. **2** any framework resembling this utensil. **3** a framework above the stage in a theatre from which suspended scenery, lights, etc., are manipulated. **4a** the field of play in American football. **4b** an informal name for American football. **4c** (*as modifier*): *a gridiron hero.* ◆ Often shortened to **grid.** [C13 *gredire,* perhaps variant (through influence of *ire* IRON) of *gredile* GRIDDLE]

gridlock (ˈgrɪdˌlɒk) *Chiefly U.S.* ◆ *n* **1** obstruction of urban traffic caused by queues of vehicles forming across junctions and causing further queues to form in the intersecting streets. **2** a point in a dispute at which no agreement can be reached; deadlock: *political gridlock.* ◆ *vb* **3** (*tr*) (of traffic) to block or obstruct (an area).

grid reference *n* a method of locating a point on a map or plan by a number referring to the lines of a grid drawn upon the map or plan and to subdivisions of the space between the lines.

grid variation *n Navigation.* the angle between grid north and magnetic north at a point on a map or chart. Also called: **grivation.**

grief (griːf) *n* **1** deep or intense sorrow or distress, esp. at the death of someone. **2** something that causes keen distress or suffering. **3** *Informal.* trouble or annoyance: *people were giving me grief for leaving ten minutes early.* **4 come to grief.** *Informal.* to end unsuccessfully or disastrously. [C13: from Anglo-French *gref,* from *grever* to GRIEVE[1]] ▸ **ˈgriefless** *adj*

grief-stricken *adj* deeply affected by sorrow or distress.

Grieg (griːg) *n* **Edvard (Hagerup)** (ˈɛdvard). 1843–1907, Norwegian composer. His works, often inspired by Norwegian folk music, include the incidental music for *Peer Gynt* (1876), a piano concerto, and many songs.

Grierson (ˈgrɪəsᵊn) *n* **John.** 1898–1972, Scottish film director. He coined the noun *documentary,* of which genre his *Industrial Britain* (1931) and *Song of Ceylon* (1934) are notable examples.

grievance (ˈgriːvᵊns) *n* **1** a real or imaginary wrong causing resentment and regarded as grounds for complaint. **2** a feeling of resentment or injustice at having been unfairly treated. **3** *Obsolete.* affliction or hardship. [C15 *grevance,* from Old French, from *grever* to GRIEVE[1]]

grieve[1] (griːv) *vb* **1** to feel or cause to feel great sorrow or distress, esp. at the death of someone. **2** (*tr*) *Obsolete.* to inflict injury, hardship, or sorrow on. [C13: from Old French *grever,* from Latin *gravāre* to burden, from *gravis* heavy] ▸ **ˈgriever** *n* ▸ **ˈgrieving** *n, adj* ▸ **ˈgrievingly** *adv*

grieve[2] (griːv) *n Scot.* a farm manager or overseer. [C15: from Old English (Northumbrian) *grǣfa* reeve]

grievous (ˈgriːvəs) *adj* **1** very severe or painful: *a grievous injury.* **2** very serious; heinous: *a grievous sin.* **3** showing or marked by grief: *a grievous cry.* **4** causing great pain or suffering: *a grievous attack.* ▸ **ˈgrievously** *adv* ▸ **ˈgrievousness** *n*

grievous bodily harm *n Criminal law.* really serious injury caused by one person to another. Abbrev.: **GBH.**

griff (grɪf) *n Slang.* information; news. [C20: from GRIFFIN[2]]

griffe (grɪf) *n Architect.* a carved ornament at the base of a column, often in the form of a claw. [C19: from French: claw, of Germanic origin]

griffin[1] (ˈgrɪfɪn), **griffon,** *or* **gryphon** *n* a winged monster with an eagle-like head and the body of a lion. [C14: from Old French *grifon,* from Latin *grȳphus,* from Greek *grups,* from *grupos* hooked]

griffin[2] (ˈgrɪfɪn) *n* a newcomer to the Orient, esp. one from W Europe. [C18: of unknown origin]

Griffith (ˈgrɪfɪθ) *n* **1 Arthur.** 1872–1922, Irish journalist and nationalist: founder of Sinn Féin (1905); president of the Irish Free State (1922). **2 D(avid Lewelyn) W(ark).** 1875–1948, U.S. film director and producer. He introduced several cinematic techniques, including the flashback and the fade-out, in his masterpiece *The Birth of a Nation* (1915).

Griffith-Joyner (ˌgrɪfɪθˈdʒɔɪnə) *n* **Florence,** known as *Flojo.* 1959–98, U.S. sprinter, winner of two gold medals at the 1988 Olympic Games.

griffon[1] (ˈgrɪfᵊn) *n* **1** any of various small wire-haired breeds of dog, originally from Belgium. **2** any large vulture of the genus *Gyps,* of Africa, S Europe, and SW Asia, having a pale plumage with black wings: family *Accipitridae* (hawks). [C19: from French: GRIFFIN[1]]

griffon[2] (ˈgrɪfᵊn) *n* a variant of **griffin**[1].

grig (grɪg) *n Dialect.* **1** a lively person. **2** a short-legged hen. **3** a young eel. [C14: dwarf, perhaps of Scandinavian origin; compare Swedish *krik* a little creature]

Grigioni (griˈdʒoːni) *n* the Italian name for **Graubünden.**

Grignard reagent (ˈgriːnjɑː; *French* griɲar) *n Chem.* any of a class of organometallic reagents, having the general formula RMgX, where R is an organic group and X is a halogen atom: used in the synthesis of organic compounds. [C20: named after Victor *Grignard* (1871–1934), French chemist]

grigri, gris-gris, *or* **greegree** (ˈgriːgriː) *n, pl* **-gris** (-griːz) *or* **-grees.** an African talisman, amulet, or charm. [of African origin]

grike *or* **gryke** (graɪk) *n* a solution fissure, a vertical crack about 0.5 m wide formed by the dissolving of limestone by water, that divides an exposed limestone surface into sections or clints. [C20 in geological sense: from northern dialect]

Grikwa (ˈgriːkwə, ˈgrɪk-) *n, pl* **-kwa** *or* **-kwas.** a variant spelling of **Griqua.**

grill[1] (grɪl) *vb* **1** to cook (meat, fish, etc.) by direct heat, as under a grill or over a hot fire, or (of meat, fish, etc.) to be cooked in this way. Usual U.S. and Canadian word: **broil. 2** (*tr; usually passive*) to torment with or as if with extreme heat: *the travellers were grilled by the scorching sun.* **3** (*tr*) *Informal.* to subject to insistent or prolonged questioning. ◆ *n* **4** a device with parallel bars of thin metal on which meat, fish, etc., may be cooked by a fire; gridiron. **5** a device on a cooker that radiates heat downwards for grilling meat, fish, etc. **6** food cooked by grilling. **7** See **grillroom.** [C17: from French *gril* gridiron, from Latin *crātīcula* fine wickerwork; see GRILLE] ▸ **ˈgriller** *n*

grill[2] (grɪl) *n* a variant spelling of **grille.** [C17: see GRILLE]

grillage (ˈgrɪlɪdʒ) *n* an arrangement of beams and crossbeams used as a foundation on soft ground. [C18: from French, from *griller* to furnish with a grille]

grille *or* **grill** (grɪl) *n* **1** Also called: **ˈgrillˌwork.** a framework, esp. of metal bars arranged to form an ornamental pattern, used as a screen or partition. **2** Also called: **radiator grille.** a grating, often chromium-plated, that admits cooling air to the radiator of a motor vehicle. **3** a metal or wooden openwork grating used as a screen or divider. **4** a protective screen, usually plastic or metal, in front of the loudspeaker in a radio, record player, etc. **5** *Real Tennis.* the opening in one corner of the receiver's end of the court. **6** a group of small pyramidal marks impressed in parallel rows into a stamp to prevent reuse. [C17: from Old French, from Latin *crātīcula* fine hurdlework, from *crātis* a hurdle]

grilled (grɪld) *adj* **1** cooked on a grill or gridiron. **2** having a grille.

Grillparzer (*German* ˈgrɪlpartsər) *n* **Franz** (frants). 1791–1872, Austrian dramatist and poet, noted for his historical and classical tragedies, which include *Sappho* (1818), the trilogy *The Golden Fleece* (1819–22), and *The Jewess of Toledo* (1872).

grillroom (ˈgrɪlˌruːm, -ˌrʊm) *n* a restaurant or room in a restaurant, etc., where grilled steaks and other meat are served.

grilse (grɪls) *n, pl* **grilses** *or* **grilse.** a young salmon that returns to fresh water after one winter in the sea. [C15 *grilles* (plural), of uncertain origin]

grim (grɪm) *adj* **grimmer, grimmest. 1** stern; resolute: *grim determination.* **2** harsh or formidable in manner or appearance. **3** harshly ironic or sinister: *grim laughter.* **4** cruel, severe, or ghastly: *a grim accident.* **5** *Archaic or poetic.* fierce: *a grim warrior.* **6** *Informal.* unpleasant; disagreeable. **7 hold on like grim death.** to hold very firmly or resolutely. [Old English *grimm;* related to Old Norse *grimmr,* Old High German *grimm* savage, Greek *khremizein* to neigh] ▸ **ˈgrimly** *adv* ▸ **ˈgrimness** *n*

grimace (grɪˈmeɪs) *n* **1** an ugly or distorted facial expression, as of wry humour, disgust, etc. ◆ *vb* **2** (*intr*) to contort the face. [C17: from French *grimace,* of Germanic origin; related to Spanish *grimazo* caricature; see GRIM] ▸ **griˈmacer** *n* ▸ **griˈmacingly** *adv*

Grimaldi[1] (grɪˈmɔːldɪ) *n* a large crater in the SE quadrant of the moon, about 190 kilometres in diameter, which is conspicuous because of its dark floor. [named after Francesco Maria *Grimaldi* (1618–63), Italian physicist]

Grimaldi[2] (grɪˈmɔːldɪ) *n* **Joseph.** 1779–1837, English actor, noted as a clown in pantomime.

Grimaldi man *n Anthropol.* a type of Aurignacian man having a negroid appearance, thought to be a race of Cro-Magnon man. [C20: named after the *Grimaldi* caves, Italy, where skeletons of this type were found]

grimalkin (grɪˈmælkɪn, -ˈmɔːl-) *n* **1** an old cat, esp. an old female cat. **2** a crotchety or shrewish old woman. [C17: from GREY + MALKIN]

grim dig *n N.Z. informal, obsolete.* an obdurate soldier.

grime (graɪm) *n* **1** dirt, soot, or filth, esp. when thickly accumulated or ingrained. ◆ *vb* **2** (*tr*) to make dirty or coat with filth. [C15: from Middle Dutch *grime;* compare Flemish *grijm,* Old English *grīma* mask] ▸ **ˈgrimy** *adj* ▸ **ˈgriminess** *n*

Grimm (grɪm) *n* **Jakob Ludwig Karl** (ˈjaːkɔp ˈluːtvɪç karl), 1785–1863, and his brother, **Wilhelm Karl** (ˈvɪlhɛlm karl), 1786–1859, German philologists and folklorists, who collaborated on *Grimm's Fairy Tales* (1812–22) and began a German dictionary. Jakob is noted also for his philological work *Deutsche Grammatik* (1819–37), in which he formulated the law named after him.

Grimm's law *n* the rules accounting for systematic correspondences between consonants in the Germanic languages and consonants in other Indo-European languages; it states that Proto-Indo-European voiced aspirated stops, voiced unaspirated stops, and voiceless stops became voiced unaspirated stops, voiceless stops, and voiceless fricatives respectively. [formulated by J. GRIMM]

grimoire (griːmˈwɑː) *n* a textbook of sorcery and magic. [C19: from French, altered from *grammaire* GRAMMAR; compare GLAMOUR]

Grimsby (ˈgrɪmzbɪ) *n* a port in E England, in North East Lincolnshire unitary authority, Lincolnshire, formerly important for fishing. Pop.: 90 703 (1991).

grin (grɪn) *vb* **grins, grinning, grinned. 1** to smile with the lips drawn back revealing the teeth or express (something) by such a smile: *to grin a welcome.* **2** (*intr*) to draw back the lips revealing the teeth, as in a snarl or grimace. **3 grin and bear it.** *Informal.* to suffer trouble or hardship without complaint. ◆ *n* **4** a broad smile. **5** a snarl or grimace. [Old English *grennian;* related to Old High German *grennen* to snarl, Old Norse *grenja* to howl; see GRUNT] ▸ **ˈgrinner** *n* ▸ **ˈgrinning** *adj, n*

grind (graɪnd) *vb* **grinds, grinding, ground. 1** to reduce or be reduced to small particles by pounding or abrading: *to grind corn; to grind flour.* **2** (*tr*) to smooth, sharpen, or polish by friction or abrasion: *to grind a knife.* **3** to scrape or grate together (two things, esp. the teeth) with a harsh rasping sound or (of such objects) to be scraped together. **4** (*tr; foll. by out*) to speak or say (something) in a rough voice. **5** (*tr; often foll. by down*) to hold down; oppress; tyrannize. **6** (*tr*) to operate (a machine) by turning a handle. **7** (*tr; foll. by out*) to produce in a routine or uninspired manner: *he ground out his weekly article for the paper.* **8** (*tr;* foll. by *out*) to continue to play in a dull or insipid manner: *the band only ground out old tunes all evening.* **9** (*tr;* often foll. by *into*) to instil (facts, information, etc.) by persistent effort: *they ground into the recruits the need for vigilance.* **10** (*intr*) *Informal.* to study or work laboriously. **11** (*intr*) *Chiefly U.S.* to dance erotically by rotating the pelvis (esp. in the phrase **bump and grind**). ◆ *n* **12** *Informal.* laborious or routine work or study. **13** *Slang, chiefly U.S.* a person, esp. a student, who works excessively hard. **14** a specific grade of pulverization, as of coffee beans: *coarse grind.* **15** *Brit. slang.* the act of sexual intercourse. **16** *Chiefly U.S.* a dance movement involving an erotic rotation of the pelvis. **17** the act or sound of grinding. ◆ See also **grind on.** [Old English *grindan;* related to Latin *frendere,* Lithuanian *gréndu* I rub, Low German *grand* sand] ▸ **ˈgrindingly** *adv*

grindelia (grɪnˈdiːlɪə) *n* **1** any coarse plant of the American genus *Grindelia,* having yellow daisy-like flower heads: family *Compositae* (composites). See also **gum plant. 2** the dried leaves and tops of certain species of these plants, used in tonics and sedatives. [C19: named after David Hieronymus *Grindel* (1777–1836), Russian botanist]

Grindelwald (*German* ˈgrɪndəlvalt) *n* a valley and resort in central Switzerland, in the Bernese Oberland: mountaineering centre, with the Wetterhorn and the Eiger nearby.

grinder (ˈgraɪndə) *n* **1** a person who grinds, esp. one who grinds cutting tools. **2** a machine for grinding. **3** a molar tooth.

grindery (ˈgraɪndərɪ) *n, pl* **-eries. 1** a place in which tools and cutlery are sharpened. **2** the equipment of a shoemaker.

grind in *vb* (*tr, adv*) *Engineering.* to make (a conical valve) fit its seating by grinding them together in the presence of an abrasive paste.

grinding wheel *n* an abrasive wheel, usually a composite of hard particles in a resin filler, used for grinding.

grind on *vb* (*intr, adv*) to move further relentlessly: *the enemy's invasion ground slowly on.*

grindstone (ˈgraɪndˌstəʊn) *n* **1a** a machine having a circular block of stone or composite abrasive rotated for sharpening tools or grinding metal. **1b** the stone used in this machine. **1c** any stone used for sharpening; whetstone. **2** another name for **millstone. 3 keep** *or* **have one's nose to the grindstone.** to work hard and perseveringly.

gringo (ˈgrɪŋgəʊ) *n, pl* **-gos.** a person from an English-speaking country: used as a derogatory term by Latin Americans. [C19: from Spanish: foreigner, probably from *griego* Greek, hence an alien]

griot (ˈgriːəʊ, griːˈɒt) *n* (in Western Africa) a member of a caste responsible for maintaining an oral record of tribal history in the form of music, poetry, and storytelling. [C20: from French *guirot,* perhaps from Portuguese *criado* domestic servant]

grip[1] (grɪp) *n* **1** the act or an instance of grasping and holding firmly: *he lost his grip on the slope.* **2** Also called: **handgrip.** the strength or pressure of such a grasp, as in a handshake: *a feeble grip.* **3** the style or manner of grasping an object, such as a tennis racket. **4** understanding, control, or mastery of a subject, problem, etc. (esp. in such phrases as **get** *or* **have a grip on**). **5** Also called: **handgrip.** a part by which an object is grasped; handle. **6** Also called: **handgrip.** a travelling bag or holdall. **7** See **hairgrip. 8** any device that holds by friction, such as certain types of brake. **9** a method of clasping or shaking hands used by members of secret societies to greet or identify one another. **10** a spasm of pain: *a grip in one's stomach.* **11** a worker in a camera crew or a stagehand who shifts sets and props, etc. **12** a small drainage channel cut above an excavation to conduct surface water away from the excavation. **13 get** *or* **come to grips.** (often foll. by *with*) **13a** to deal with (a problem or subject). **13b** to tackle (an assailant). ◆ *vb* **grips, gripping, gripped. 14** to take hold of firmly or tightly, as by a clutch. **15** to hold the interest or attention of: *to grip an audience.* [Old English *gripe* grasp; related to Old Norse *gripr* property, Old High German *grif*] ▸ **ˈgripper** *n* ▸ **ˈgrippingly** *adv*

grip[2] (grɪp) *n Med.* a variant spelling of **grippe.**

gripe (graɪp) *vb* **1** (*intr*) *Informal.* to complain, esp. in a persistent nagging manner. **2** to cause sudden intense pain in the intestines of (a person) or (of a person) to experience this pain. **3** (*intr*) *Nautical.* (of a ship) to tend to come up into the wind in spite of the helm. **4** *Archaic.* to clutch; grasp. **5** (*tr*) *Archaic.* to afflict. ◆ *n* **6** (*usually pl*) a sudden intense pain in the intestines; colic. **7** *Informal.* a complaint or grievance. **8** *Now rare.* **8a** the act of gripping. **8b** a firm grip. **8c** a device that grips. **9** (*in pl*) *Nautical.* the lashings that secure a boat. [Old English *grīpan;* related to Gothic *greipan,* Old High German *grīfan* to seize, Lithuanian *greibiu*] ▸ **'griper** *n* ▸ **'gripingly** *adv*

gripe water *n Brit.* a solution given to infants to relieve colic.

grippe *or* **grip** (grɪp) *n* a former name for **influenza.** [C18: from French *grippe,* from *gripper* to seize, of Germanic origin; see GRIP[1]]

grip tape *n* a rough tape for sticking to a surface to provide a greater grip.

Griqua *or* **Grikwa** ('griːkwə, 'grɪk-) *n* **1** (*pl* **-qua, -quas** *or* **-kwa, -kwas**) a member of a people of mixed European and Khoikhoi ancestry, living chiefly in Griqualand. **2** the language or dialect of Khoikhoi spoken by this people, belonging to the Khoisan family.

Griqualand East ('griːkwəˌlænd, 'grɪk-) *n* an area of central South Africa: settled in 1861 by Griquas led by Adam Kok III; annexed to the Cape Colony in 1879; part of the Transkei in 1903–94. Chief town: Kokstad. Area: 17 100 sq. km (6602 sq. miles).

Griqualand West *n* an area of N South Africa, north of the Orange river: settled after 1803 by the Griquas; annexed by the British in 1871 following a dispute with the Orange Free State; became part of the Cape Colony in 1880. Chief town: Kimberley. Area: 39 360 sq. km (15 197 sq. miles).

Gris (*Spanish* gris) *n* **Juan** (xwan). 1887–1927, Spanish cubist painter, resident in France from 1906.

grisaille (grɪ'zeɪl; *French* grizɑj) *n* **1** a technique of monochrome painting in shades of grey, as in an oil painting or a wall decoration, imitating the effect of relief. **2** a painting, stained glass window, etc., in this manner. [C19: from French, from *gris* grey]

griseofulvin (ˌgrɪzɪəʊ'fʊlvɪn) *n* an antibiotic used to treat fungal infections. [C20: from New Latin, from *Penicillium griseofulvum dierckx* (fungus from which it was isolated), from Medieval Latin *griseus* grey + Latin *fulvus* reddish yellow]

griseous ('grɪsɪəs, 'grɪz-) *adj* streaked or mixed with grey; somewhat grey. [C19: from Medieval Latin *griseus,* of Germanic origin]

grisette (grɪ'zɛt) *n* **1** (esp. formerly) a French working-class girl, esp. a pretty or flirtatious one. **2** an edible toadstool of the genus *Amanita* of broad-leaved and birch woods. [C18: from French, from *grisette* grey fabric used for dresses, from *gris* grey]

gris-gris ('griːgriː) *n, pl* **-gris** (-griːz). a variant spelling of **grigri.**

Grishun (griː'ʃʊn) *n* the Romansch name for **Graubünden.**

griskin ('grɪskɪn) *n Brit.* the lean part of a loin of pork. [C17: probably from dialect *gris* pig, from Old Norse *griss*]

grisly[1] ('grɪzlɪ) *adj* **-lier, -liest.** causing horror or dread; gruesome. [Old English *grislic;* related to Old Frisian *grislik,* Old High German *grīsenlīh*] ▸ **'grisliness** *n*

USAGE See at **grizzly.**

grisly[2] ('grɪzlɪ) *n, pl* **-lies.** *Obsolete.* a variant spelling of **grizzly.**

grison ('graɪs^ən, 'grɪz^ən) *n* either of two musteline mammals, *Grison* (or *Galictis*) *cuja* or *G. vittata,* of Central and South America, having a greyish back and black face and underparts. [C18: from French, from *grison* grey animal, from Old French *gris* grey]

Grisons (grizɔ̃) *n* the French name for **Graubünden.**

grist (grɪst) *n* **1a** grain intended to be or that has been ground. **1b** the quantity of such grain processed in one grinding. **2** *Brewing.* malt grains that have been cleaned and cracked. **3 grist to** (*or* **for**) **the** (*or* **one's**) **mill.** anything that can be turned to profit or advantage. [Old English *grīst;* related to Old Saxon *grist-grimmo* gnashing of teeth, Old High German *grist-grimmōn*]

gristle ('grɪs^əl) *n* cartilage, esp. when in meat. [Old English *gristle;* related to Old Frisian, Middle Low German *gristel*] ▸ **'gristly** *adj* ▸ **'gristliness** *n*

gristmill ('grɪstˌmɪl) *n* a mill, esp. one equipped with large grinding stones for grinding grain.

grit (grɪt) *n* **1** small hard particles of sand, earth, stone, etc. **2** Also called: **gritstone.** any coarse sandstone that can be used as a grindstone or millstone. **3** the texture or grain of stone. **4** indomitable courage, toughness, or resolution. **5** *Engineering.* an arbitrary measure of the size of abrasive particles used in a grinding wheel or other abrasive process. ◆ *vb* **grits, gritting, gritted. 6** to clench or grind together (two objects, esp. the teeth). **7** to cover (a surface, such as icy roads) with grit. [Old English *grēot;* related to Old Norse *grjōt* pebble, Old High German *grioz;* see GREAT, GROATS, GRUEL] ▸ **'gritless** *adj*

Grit (grɪt) *n, adj Canadian.* an informal word for **Liberal.**

grith (grɪθ) *n* **1** *English legal history.* security, peace, or protection, guaranteed either in a certain place, such as a church, or for a period of time. **2** a place of safety or protection. [Old English *grith;* related to Old Norse *grith* home]

grits (grɪts) *pl n* **1** hulled and coarsely ground grain. **2** *U.S.* See **hominy grits.** [Old English *grytt;* related to Old High German *gruzzi;* see GREAT, GRIT]

gritter ('grɪtə) *n Brit.* a vehicle which spreads grit on roads during icy weather, or when icy conditions are expected.

gritting ('grɪtɪŋ) *n Brit.* **a** the spreading of grit on road surfaces to render them less slippery for vehicles during icy weather. **b** (*as modifier*): *gritting lorries.*

gritty ('grɪtɪ) *adj* **-tier, -tiest. 1** courageous; hardy; resolute. **2** of, like, or containing grit. ▸ **'grittily** *adv* ▸ **'grittiness** *n*

grivation (grɪ'veɪʃən) *n Navigation.* short for **grid variation.**

grivet ('grɪvɪt) *n* an E African variety of a common guenon monkey, *Cercopithecus aethiops,* having long white tufts of hair on either side of the face. Compare **green monkey, vervet.** [C19: from French, of unknown origin]

grizzle[1] ('grɪz^əl) *vb* **1** to make or become grey. ◆ *n* **2** a grey colour. **3** grey or partly grey hair. **4** a grey wig. [C15: from Old French *grisel,* from *gris,* of Germanic origin; compare Middle High German *grīs* grey]

grizzle[2] ('grɪz^əl) *vb* (*intr*) *Informal, chiefly Brit.* **1** (esp. of a child) to fret; whine. **2** to sulk or grumble. [C18: of Germanic origin; compare Old High German *grist-grimmōn* gnashing of teeth, German *Griesgram* unpleasant person] ▸ **'grizzler** *n*

grizzled ('grɪz^əld) *adj* **1** streaked or mixed with grey; grizzly; griseous. **2** having grey or partly grey hair.

grizzly ('grɪzlɪ) *adj* **-zlier, -zliest. 1** somewhat grey; grizzled. ◆ *n, pl* **-zlies. 2** See **grizzly bear.**

USAGE *Grizzly* is sometimes wrongly used where *grisly* is meant: *a grisly* (not *grizzly*) *murder.*

grizzly bear *n* a variety of the brown bear, *Ursus arctos horribilis,* formerly widespread in W North America; its brown fur has cream or white hair tips on the back, giving a grizzled appearance. Often shortened to **grizzly.**

gro. *abbrev. for* gross (unit of quantity).

groan (grəʊn) *n* **1** a prolonged stressed dull cry expressive of agony, pain, or disapproval. **2** a loud harsh creaking sound, as of a tree bending in the wind. **3** *Informal.* a grumble or complaint, esp. a persistent one. ◆ *vb* **4** to utter (low inarticulate sounds) expressive of pain, grief, disapproval, etc.: *they all groaned at Larry's puns.* **5** (*intr*) to make a sound like a groan. **6** (*intr,* usually foll. by *beneath* or *under*) to be weighed down (by) or suffer greatly (under): *the country groaned under the dictator's rule.* **7** (*intr*) *Informal.* to complain or grumble. [Old English *grānian;* related to Old Norse *grīna,* Old High German *grīnan;* see GRIN] ▸ **'groaner** *n* ▸ **'groaning** *n, adj* ▸ **'groaningly** *adv*

groat (grəʊt) *n* an English silver coin worth four pennies, taken out of circulation in the 17th century. [C14: from Middle Dutch *groot,* from Middle Low German *gros,* from Medieval Latin (*denarius*) *grossus* thick (coin); see GROSCHEN]

groats (grəʊts) *pl n* **1** the hulled and crushed grain of oats, wheat, or certain other cereals. **2** the parts of oat kernels used as food. [Old English *grot* particle; related to *grota* fragment, as in *meregrota* pearl; see GRIT, GROUT]

grocer ('grəʊsə) *n* a dealer in foodstuffs and other household supplies. [C15: from Old French *grossier,* from *gros* large; see GROSS]

groceries ('grəʊsərɪz) *pl n* merchandise, esp. foodstuffs, sold by a grocer.

grocery ('grəʊsərɪ) *n, pl* **-ceries.** the business or premises of a grocer.

grockle ('grɒk^əl) *n Southwest English dialect.* a tourist, esp. one from the Midlands or the North of England. [C20: of unknown origin]

Grodno (*Russian* 'grɔdnə) *n* a city in W Belarus on the Neman River: part of Poland (1921–39); an industrial centre. Pop.: 301 000 (1996 est.).

grog (grɒg) *n* **1** diluted spirit, usually rum, as an alcoholic drink. **2** *Informal, chiefly Austral. and N.Z.* alcoholic drink in general, esp. spirits. [C18: from Old *Grog,* nickname of Edward Vernon (1684–1757), British admiral, who in 1740 issued naval rum diluted with water; his nickname arose from his grogram cloak]

groggy ('grɒgɪ) *adj* **-gier, -giest.** *Informal.* **1** dazed or staggering, as from exhaustion, blows, or drunkenness. **2** faint or weak. ▸ **'groggily** *adv* ▸ **'grogginess** *n*

grogram ('grɒgrəm) *n* a coarse fabric of silk, wool, or silk mixed with wool or mohair, often stiffened with gum, formerly used for clothing. [C16: from French *gros grain* coarse grain; see GROSGRAIN]

grogshop ('grɒgˌʃɒp) *n* **1** *Rare.* a drinking place, esp. one of disreputable character. **2** *Austral. and N.Z. informal.* a shop where liquor can be bought for drinking off the premises.

groin (grɔɪn) *n* **1** the depression or fold where the legs join the abdomen. Related adj: **inguinal. 2** *Euphemistic.* the genitals, esp. the testicles. **3** a variant spelling (esp. U.S.) of **groyne. 4** *Architect.* a curved arris formed where two intersecting vaults meet. ◆ *vb* **5** (*tr*) *Architect.* to provide or construct with groins. [C15: perhaps from English *grynde* abyss; related to GROUND[1]]

Grolier ('grəʊlɪə; *French* grɔlje) *adj* relating to or denoting a decorative style of bookbinding using interlaced leather straps, gilded ornamental scrolls, etc. [C19: named after Jean *Grolier de Servières* (1479–1565), French bibliophile]

grommet ('grɒmɪt) *or* **grummet** *n* **1** a ring of rubber or plastic or a metal eyelet designed to line a hole to prevent a cable or pipe passed through it from chafing. **2** a ring of rope hemp used to stuff the gland of a pipe joint. **3** *Medical.* a small tube inserted into the eardrum in cases of glue ear in order to allow air to enter the middle ear. [C15: from obsolete French *gourmette* chain linking the ends of a bit, from *gourmer* bridle, of unknown origin]

gromwell ('grɒmwəl) *n* any of various hairy plants of the boraginaceous genus *Lithospermum,* esp. *L. officinale,* having small greenish-white, yellow, or blue flowers, and smooth nutlike fruits. See also **puccoon** (sense 1). [C13: from Old French *gromil,* from *gres* sandstone + *mil* millet, from Latin *milium*]

Gromyko (*Russian* gra'mikə) *n* **Andrei Andreyevich** (an'drjej an'drjejɪvitʃ). 1909–89, Soviet statesman and diplomat; foreign minister (1957–85); president (1985–88).

Groningen ('grəʊnɪŋən; *Dutch* 'xroːnɪŋə) *n* **1** a province in the NE Netherlands: mainly agricultural. Capital: Groningen. Pop.: 558 100 (1996 est.). Area: 2336 sq. km (902 sq. miles). **2** a city in the NE Netherlands, capital of Groningen province. Pop.: 170 748 (1995 est.).

Grønland ('grœnlan) *n* the Danish name for **Greenland.**

groom (gruːm, grʊm) *n* **1** a person employed to clean and look after horses. **2** See **bridegroom. 3** any of various officers of a royal or noble household. **4** *Archaic.* a male servant or attendant. **5** *Archaic and poetic.* a young man. ◆ *vb* (*tr*) **6** to make or keep (clothes, appearance, etc.) clean and tidy. **7** to rub down, clean, and smarten (a horse, dog, etc.). **8** to train or prepare for a particular task, occupation, etc.: *to groom someone for the Presidency.* [C13 *grom* manservant; perhaps related to Old English *grōwan* to GROW] ▸ **'groomer** *n* ▸ **'grooming** *n*

groomsman ('gru:mzmən, 'grʊmz-) *n, pl* **-men.** a man who attends the bridegroom at a wedding, usually the best man.

groove (gru:v) *n* **1** a long narrow channel or furrow, esp. one cut into wood by a tool. **2** the spiral channel, usually V-shaped, in a gramophone record. See also **microgroove. 3** one of the spiral cuts in the bore of a gun. **4** *Anatomy.* any furrow or channel on a bodily structure or part; sulcus. **5** *Mountaineering.* a shallow fissure in a rock face or between two rock faces, forming an angle of more than 120°. **6** a settled existence, routine, etc., to which one is suited or accustomed, esp. one from which it is difficult to escape. **7** *Slang.* an experience, event, etc., that is groovy. **8 in the groove. 8a** *Jazz.* playing well and apparently effortlessly, with a good beat, etc. **8b** *U.S.* fashionable. ◆ *vb* **9** (*tr*) to form or cut a groove in. **10** (*intr*) *Dated slang.* to enjoy oneself or feel in rapport with one's surroundings. **11** (*intr*) *Jazz.* to play well, with a good beat, etc. [C15: from obsolete Dutch *groeve,* of Germanic origin; compare Old High German *gruoba* pit, Old Norse *grof*] ▸ **'grooveless** *adj* ▸ **'groove,like** *adj*

grooving saw *n* a circular saw used for making grooves.

groovy ('gru:vɪ) *adj* **groovier, grooviest.** *Slang, often jocular.* attractive, fashionable, or exciting.

grope (grəʊp) *vb* **1** (*intr;* usually foll. by *for*) to feel or search about uncertainly (for something) with the hands. **2** (*intr;* usually foll. by *for* or *after*) to search uncertainly or with difficulty (for a solution, answer, etc.). **3** (*tr*) to find or make (one's way) by groping. **4** (*tr*) *Slang.* to feel or fondle the body of (someone) for sexual gratification. ◆ *n* **5** the act of groping. [Old English *grāpian;* related to Old High German *greifōn,* Norwegian *greipa;* compare GRIPE] ▸ **'gropingly** *adv*

groper ('grəʊpə) *or* **grouper** *n, pl* **-er** *or* **-ers.** any large marine serranid fish of the genus *Epinephelus* and related genera, of warm and tropical seas. [C17: from Portuguese *garupa,* probably from a South American Indian word]

Gropius ('grəʊpɪəs) *n* **Walter.** 1883–1969, U.S. architect, designer, and teacher, born in Germany. He founded (1919) and directed (1919–28) the Bauhaus in Germany. His influence stemmed from his adaptation of architecture to modern social needs and his pioneering use of industrial materials, such as concrete and steel. His buildings include the Fagus factory at Alfeld (1911) and the Bauhaus at Dessau (1926).

Gros (*French* gro) *n* Baron **Antoine Jean** (ɑ̃twan ʒɑ̃). 1771–1835, French painter, noted for his battle scenes.

grosbeak ('grəʊs,bi:k, 'grɒs-) *n* **1** any of various finches, such as *Pinicola enucleator* (**pine grosbeak**), that have a massive powerful bill. **2 cardinal grosbeak.** any of various mostly tropical American buntings, such as the cardinal and pyrrhuloxia, the males of which have brightly coloured plumage. [C17: from French *grosbec,* from Old French *gros* large, thick + *bec* BEAK[1]]

groschen ('grəʊʃən; *German* 'grɔʃən) *n, pl* **-schen. 1** an Austrian monetary unit worth one hundredth of a schilling. **2** a German coin worth ten pfennigs. **3** a former German silver coin. [C17: from German: Bohemian dialect alteration of Middle High German *grosse,* from Medieval Latin (*denarius*) *grossus* thick (penny); see GROSS, GROAT]

gros de Londres *French.* (gro də lɔ̃drə) *n* a lightweight shiny ribbed silk fabric, the ribs alternating between wide and narrow between different colours or between different textures of yarn. [literally: heavy (fabric) from London]

grosgrain ('grəʊ,greɪn) *n* a heavy ribbed silk or rayon fabric or tape for trimming clothes, etc. [C19: from French *gros grain* coarse grain; see GROSS, GRAIN]

gros point ('grəʊ 'pɔɪnt; *French* gro pwɛ̃) *n* **1** a needlepoint stitch covering two horizontal and two vertical threads. **2** work done in this stitch. ◆ Compare **petit point.**

gross (grəʊs) *adj* **1** repellently or excessively fat or bulky. **2** with no deductions for expenses, tax, etc.; total: *gross sales; gross income.* Compare **net**[2] (sense 1). **3** (of personal qualities, tastes, etc.) conspicuously coarse or vulgar. **4** obviously or exceptionally culpable or wrong; flagrant: *gross inefficiency.* **5** lacking in perception, sensitivity, or discrimination: *gross judgments.* **6** (esp. of vegetation) dense; thick; luxuriant. **7** *Obsolete.* coarse in texture or quality. **8** *Rare.* rude; uneducated; ignorant. ◆ *interj Slang.* **9** an exclamation indicating disgust. ◆ *n* **10** *pl* **gross.** a unit of quantity equal to 12 dozen. **11** *pl* **grosses. 11a** the entire amount. **11b** the great majority. ◆ *vb* (*tr*) **12** to earn as total revenue, before deductions for expenses, tax, etc. ◆ See also **gross out, gross up.** [C14: from Old French *gros* large, from Late Latin *grossus* thick] ▸ **'grossly** *adv* ▸ **'grossness** *n*

gross domestic product *n* the total value of all goods and services produced domestically by a nation during a year. It is equivalent to gross national product minus net investment incomes from foreign nations. Abbrev.: **GDP.**

Grosseteste ('grəʊs,tɛst) *n* **Robert.** ?1175–1253, English prelate and scholar; bishop of Lincoln (1235–53). He attacked ecclesiastical abuses and wrote commentaries on Aristotle and treatises on theology, philosophy, and science.

gross national product *n* the total value of all final goods and services produced annually by a nation. Abbrev.: **GNP.**

gross out *U.S. slang.* ◆ *vb* (*tr, adv*) **1** to cause (a person) to feel distaste or strong dislike for (something). ◆ *n* **gross-out. 2** a person or thing regarded as disgusting or objectionable. ◆ *adj* **gross-out. 3** disgusting, boring, or objectionable.

gross profit *n Accounting.* the difference between total revenue from sales and the total cost of purchases or materials, with an adjustment for stock.

gross ton *n* another name for **long ton:** see **ton**[1] (sense 1).

grossularite ('grɒsjʊlə,raɪt) *n* a green or greenish-grey garnet, used as a gemstone. Formula: $Ca_3Al_2(SiO_4)_3$. Also called: **gooseberry stone.** [C19: from New Latin *grossulāria* gooseberry, from Old French *groselle* + -ITE[1]]

gross up *vb* (*tr, adv*) to increase (net income) to its pretax value.

Grosswardein (gro:svar'dain) *n* the German name for **Oradea.**

gross weight *n* total weight of an article inclusive of the weight of the container and packaging.

grosz (grɔ:ʃ) *n, pl* **groszy** ('grɔ:ʃɪ). a Polish monetary unit worth one hundredth of a zloty. [from Polish, from Czech *grosh;* see GROSCHEN]

Grosz (grəʊs; *German* grɔs) *n* **George.** 1893–1959, German painter, in the U.S. from 1932, whose works satirized German militarism and bourgeois society.

grot[1] (grɒt) *n Slang.* rubbish; dirt. [C20: from GROTTY]

grot[2] (grɒt) *n* a poetic word for **grotto.** [C16: from French *grotte,* from Old Italian *grotta;* see GROTTO]

Grote (grəʊt) *n* **George.** 1794–1871, English historian, noted particularly for his *History of Greece* (1846–56).

grotesque (grəʊ'tɛsk) *adj* **1** strangely or fantastically distorted; bizarre: *a grotesque reflection in the mirror.* **2** of or characteristic of the grotesque in art. **3** absurdly incongruous; in a ludicrous context: *a grotesque turn of phrase.* ◆ *n* **4** a 16th-century decorative style in which parts of human, animal, and plant forms are distorted and mixed. **5** a decorative device, as in painting or sculpture, in this style. **6** *Printing.* the family of 19th-century sans serif display types. **7** any grotesque person or thing. [C16: from French, from Old Italian (*pittura*) *grottesca* cave painting, from *grottesco* of a cave, from *grotta* cave; see GROTTO] ▸ **gro'tesquely** *adv* ▸ **gro'tesqueness** *n*

grotesquery *or* **grotesquerie** (grəʊ'tɛskərɪ) *n, pl* **-queries. 1** the state of being grotesque. **2** something that is grotesque, esp. an object such as a sculpture.

Grotius ('grəʊtɪəs) *n* **Hugo,** original name *Huig de Groot.* 1583–1645, Dutch jurist and statesman, whose *De Jure Belli ac Pacis* (1625) is regarded as the foundation of modern international law. ▸ **'Grotian** *adj* ▸ **'Grotianism** *n*

grotto ('grɒtəʊ) *n, pl* **-toes** *or* **-tos. 1** a small cave, esp. one with attractive features. **2** a construction in the form of a cave, esp. as in landscaped gardens during the 18th century. [C17: from Old Italian *grotta,* from Late Latin *crypta* vault; see CRYPT]

grotty ('grɒtɪ) *adj* **-tier, -tiest.** *Brit. slang.* **1** unpleasant, nasty, or unattractive. **2** of poor quality or in bad condition; unsatisfactory or useless. [C20: from GROTESQUE]

grouch (graʊtʃ) *Informal.* ◆ *vb* (*intr*) **1** to complain; grumble. ◆ *n* **2** a complaint, esp. a persistent one. **3** a person who is always grumbling. [C20: from obsolete *grutch,* from Old French *grouchier* to complain; see GRUDGE] ▸ **'grouchy** *adj* ▸ **'grouchily** *adv* ▸ **'grouchiness** *n*

grough (grʌf) *n Mountaineering.* a natural channel or fissure in a peat moor; a peat hag. [C20: possibly the same as *grough,* an obsolete variant of GRUFF in the obsolete sense: "rough" (of terrain)]

ground[1] (graʊnd) *n* **1** the land surface. **2** earth or soil: *he dug into the ground outside his house.* **3** (*pl*) the land around a dwelling house or other building. **4** (*sometimes pl*) an area of land given over to a purpose: *football ground; burial grounds.* **5** land having a particular characteristic: *level ground; high ground.* **6** matter for consideration or debate; field of research or inquiry: *the lecture was familiar ground to him; the report covered a lot of ground.* **7** a position or viewpoint, as in an argument or controversy (esp. in the phrases **give ground, hold, stand,** *or* **shift one's ground**). **8** position or advantage, as in a subject or competition (esp. in the phrases **gain ground, lose ground,** etc.). **9** (*often pl*) reason; justification: *grounds for complaint.* **10** *Arts.* **10a** the prepared surface applied to the support of a painting, such as a wall, canvas, etc., to prevent it reacting with or absorbing the paint. **10b** the support of a painting. **10c** the background of a painting or main surface against which the other parts of a work of art appear superimposed. **11a** the first coat of paint applied to a surface. **11b** (*as modifier*): *ground colour.* **12** the bottom of a river or the sea. **13** (*pl*) sediment or dregs, esp. from coffee. **14** *Chiefly Brit.* the floor of a room. **15** *Cricket.* **15a** the area from the popping crease back past the stumps, in which a batsman may legally stand. **15b** ground staff. **16** See **ground bass. 17** a mesh or network supporting the main pattern of a piece of lace. **18** *Electrical.* the usual U.S. and Canadian word for **earth** (sense 8). **19 above ground.** alive. **20 below ground.** dead and buried. **21 break new ground.** to do something that has not been done before. **22 cut the ground from under someone's feet.** to anticipate someone's action or argument and thus make it irrelevant or meaningless. **23** (**down**) **to the ground.** *Brit. informal.* completely; absolutely: *it suited him down to the ground.* **24 get off the ground.** *Informal.* to make a beginning, esp. one that is successful. **25 go to ground.** to go into hiding. **26 into the ground.** beyond what is requisite or can be endured; to exhaustion. **27 meet someone on his own ground.** to meet someone according to terms he has laid down himself. **28 the** (**moral**) **high ground.** a position of moral or ethical superiority in a dispute. **29 touch ground. 29a** (of a ship) to strike the sea bed. **29b** to arrive at something solid or stable after discussing or dealing with topics that are abstract or inconclusive. **30** (*modifier*) situated on, living on, or used on the ground: *ground frost; ground forces.* **31** (*modifier*) concerned with or operating on the ground, esp. as distinct from in the air: *ground crew; ground hostess.* **32** (*modifier*) (used in names of plants) low-growing and often trailing or spreading. ◆ *vb* **33** (*tr*) to put or place on the ground. **34** (*tr*) to instruct in fundamentals. **35** (*tr*) to provide a basis or foundation for; establish. **36** (*tr*) to confine (an aircraft, pilot, etc.) to the ground. **37** (*tr*) *Informal.* to confine (a child) to the house as a punishment. **38** the usual U.S. word for **earth** (sense 16). **39** (*tr*) *Nautical.* to run (a vessel) aground. **40** (*tr*) to cover (a surface) with a preparatory coat of paint. **41** (*intr*) to hit or reach the ground. [Old English *grund;* related to Old Norse *grunn* shallow, *grunnr, grund* plain, Old High German *grunt*]

ground[2] (graʊnd) *vb* **1** the past tense and past participle of **grind.** ◆ *adj* **2** having the surface finished, thickness reduced, or an edge sharpened by grinding. **3** reduced to fine particles by grinding.

groundage ('graʊndɪdʒ) *n Brit.* a fee levied on a vessel entering a port or anchored off a shore.

groundbait ('graʊnd,beɪt) *Angling.* ◆ *n* **1** bait, such as scraps of bread, maggots, etc., thrown into an area of water to attract fish. See **chum**[2]. ◆ *vb (tr)* **2** to prepare (an area of water) with groundbait.

ground bass *or* **ground** (beɪs) *n Music.* a short melodic bass line that is repeated over and over again.

ground beetle *n* **1** any beetle of the family *Carabidae,* often found under logs, stones, etc., having long legs and a dark coloration. **2** any beetle of the family *Tenebrionidae,* feeding on plants and plant products. **3** any of various other beetles that live close to or beneath the ground.

ground-breaking *adj* innovative: *a ground-breaking novel.*

ground bug *n* any member of a family (*Lygaeidae*) of hemipterous plant-eating insects, having generally dark bodies, sometimes marked with red, and lighter, yellowish wings.

ground cherry *n* any of various American solanaceous plants of the genus *Physalis,* esp. *P. pubescens,* having round fleshy fruit enclosed in a bladder-like husk. See also **winter cherry, gooseberry** (sense 4).

ground control *n* **1** the personnel, radar, computers, etc., on the ground that monitor the progress of aircraft or spacecraft. **2** a system for feeding continuous radio messages to an aircraft pilot to enable him to make a blind landing.

ground cover *n* **a** dense low herbaceous plants and shrubs that grow over the surface of the ground, esp., in a forest, preventing soil erosion or, in a garden, stifling weeds. **b** *(as modifier)*: *ground-cover plants.*

ground elder *n* another name for **goutweed.**

ground engineer *n* an engineer qualified and licensed to certify the airworthiness of an aircraft. Official name: **licensed aircraft engineer.**

ground floor *n* **1** the floor of a building level or almost level with the ground. **2 get in on** (*or* **start from**) **the ground floor.** *Informal.* **2a** to enter a business, organization, etc., at the lowest level. **2b** to be in a project, undertaking, etc., from its inception.

ground frost *n* the condition resulting from a temperature reading of 0°C or below on a thermometer in contact with a grass surface.

ground game *n Brit.* game animals, such as hares or deer, found on the earth's surface: distinguished from game birds.

ground glass *n* **1** glass that has a rough surface produced by grinding, used for diffusing light. **2** glass in the form of fine particles produced by grinding, used as an abrasive.

groundhog ('graʊnd,hɒg) *n* another name for **woodchuck.**

Groundhog Day *n* (in the U.S. and Canada) February 2nd, when, according to tradition, the groundhog emerges from hibernation; if it sees its shadow, it returns to its burrow for six weeks as a sunny day indicates a late spring, while a cloudy day would mean an early spring.

ground ice *n* ice formed below the surface of a body of water, either on the ground or on a submerged object.

grounding ('graʊndɪŋ) *n* a basic knowledge of or training in a subject.

ground ivy *n* a creeping or trailing Eurasian aromatic herbaceous plant, *Glechoma* (or *Nepeta*) *hederacea,* with scalloped leaves and purplish-blue flowers: family *Labiatae* (labiates).

ground layer *n* See **layer** (sense 2).

groundless ('graʊndlɪs) *adj* without reason or justification: *his suspicions were groundless.* ► **'groundlessly** *adv* ► **'groundlessness** *n*

groundling ('graʊndlɪŋ) *n* **1** any animal or plant that lives close to the ground or at the bottom of a lake, river, etc. **2a** (in Elizabethan theatre) a spectator standing in the yard in front of the stage and paying least. **2b** a spectator in the cheapest section of any theatre. **3** a person on the ground as distinguished from one in an aircraft.

ground loop *n* a sudden uncontrolled turn by an aircraft on the ground, while moving under its own power.

groundmass ('graʊnd,mæs) *n* the matrix of igneous rocks, such as porphyry, in which larger crystals (phenocrysts) are embedded.

groundnut ('graʊnd,nʌt) *n* **1** a North American climbing leguminous plant, *Apios tuberosa,* with fragrant brown flowers and small edible underground tubers. **2** the tuber of this plant. **3** any of several other plants having underground nutlike parts. **4** *Brit.* another name for **peanut.**

ground pine *n* **1** a hairy plant, *Ajuga chamaepitys,* of Europe and N Africa, having two-lipped yellow flowers marked with red spots: family *Labiatae* (labiates). It smells of pine when crushed. See also **bugle**[2]. **2** any of certain North American club mosses, esp. *Lycopodium obscurum.*

ground plan *n* **1** a drawing of the ground floor of a building, esp. one to scale. See also **plan** (sense 3). Compare **elevation** (sense 5). **2** a preliminary or basic outline.

ground-plane aerial *n Electronics.* a quarter-wave vertical dipole aerial in which the electrical image forming the other quarter-wave section is formed by reflection in a system of radially disposed metal rods or in a conductive sheet.

ground plate *n* a joist forming the lowest member of a timber frame. Also called: **groundsill, soleplate.**

ground plum *n* **1** a North American leguminous plant, *Astragalus caryocarpus,* with purple or white flowers and green thick-walled plumlike edible pods. **2** the pod of this plant.

ground provisions *pl n Caribbean.* starchy vegetables, esp. root crops and plantains.

ground rent *n Law.* the rent reserved by a lessor on granting a lease, esp. one for a long period of years to enable the lessee to develop the land.

ground rule *n* a procedural rule or principle.

ground run *n* the distance taken by an aircraft to brake from its landing speed to its taxiing speed or a stop.

groundsel ('graʊnsəl) *n* **1** any of certain plants of the genus *Senecio,* esp. *S. vulgaris,* a Eurasian weed with heads of small yellow flowers: family *Compositae* (composites). See also **ragwort. 2 groundsel tree.** a shrub, *Baccharis halimifolia,* of E North America, with white plumelike fruits: family *Compositae.* [Old English *grundeswelge,* changed from *gundeswilge,* from *gund* pus + *swelgan* to swallow; after its use in poultices on abscesses]

groundsheet ('graʊnd,ʃiːt) *or* **ground cloth** *n* **1** a waterproof rubber, plastic, or polythene sheet placed on the ground in a tent, etc., to keep out damp. **2** a similar sheet put over a sports field to protect it against rain.

groundsill ('graʊnd,sɪl) *n* another name for **ground plate.**

groundsman ('graʊndzmən) *n, pl* **-men.** a person employed to maintain a sports ground, park, etc.

groundspeed ('graʊnd,spiːd) *n* the speed of an aircraft relative to the ground. Compare **airspeed.**

ground squirrel *n* any burrowing sciurine rodent of the genus *Citellus* and related genera, resembling chipmunks and occurring in North America, E Europe, and Asia. Also called: **gopher.**

ground state *or* **level** *n* the lowest energy state of an atom, molecule, particle, etc. Compare **excited** (sense 4).

ground stroke *n Tennis.* any return made to a ball that has touched the ground, as opposed to a volley.

groundswell ('graʊnd,swɛl) *n* **1** a considerable swell of the sea, often caused by a distant storm or earthquake or by the passage of waves into shallow water. **2** a strong public feeling or opinion that is detectable even though not openly expressed: *a groundswell of discontent.*

ground water *n* underground water that has come mainly from the seepage of surface water and is held in the soil and in pervious rocks.

ground wave *or* **ray** *n* a radio wave that travels directly between a transmitting and a receiving aerial. Compare **sky wave.**

groundwork ('graʊnd,wɜːk) *n* **1** preliminary work as a foundation or basis. **2** the ground or background of a painting, etc.

ground zero *n* a point on the surface of land or water at or directly above or below the centre of a nuclear explosion.

group (gruːp) *n* **1** a number of persons or things considered as a collective unit. **2a** a number of persons bound together by common social standards, interests, etc. **2b** *(as modifier)*: *group behaviour.* **3** a small band of players or singers, esp. of pop music. **4** a number of animals or plants considered as a unit because of common characteristics, habits, etc. **5** *Grammar.* another word, esp. in systemic grammar, for **phrase** (sense 1). **6** an association of companies under a single ownership and control, consisting of a holding company, subsidiary companies, and sometimes associated companies. **7** two or more figures or objects forming a design or unit in a design, in a painting or sculpture. **8** a military formation comprising complementary arms and services, usually for a purpose: *a brigade group.* **9** an air force organization of higher level than a squadron. **10** Also called: **radical.** *Chem.* two or more atoms that are bound together in a molecule and behave as a single unit: *a methyl group* $-CH_3$. Compare **free radical. 11** a vertical column of elements in the periodic table that all have similar electronic structures, properties, and valencies. Compare **period** (sense 8). **12** *Geology.* any stratigraphical unit, esp. the unit for two or more formations. **13** *Maths.* a set under an operation involving any two members of the set such that the set is closed, associative, and contains both an identity and the inverse of each member. **14** See **blood group.** ◆ *vb* **15** to arrange or place (things, people, etc.) in or into a group or (of things, etc.) to form into a group. [C17: from French *groupe,* of Germanic origin; compare Italian *gruppo;* see CROP]

group captain *n* an officer holding commissioned rank senior to a wing commander but junior to an air commodore in the British RAF and certain other air forces.

group dynamics *n (functioning as sing) Psychol.* a field of social psychology concerned with the nature of human groups, their development, and their interactions with individuals, other groups, and larger organizations.

grouper ('gruːpə) *n* a variant of **groper.**

groupie ('gruːpɪ) *n Slang.* an ardent fan of a celebrity, esp. a pop star: originally, often a girl who followed the members of a pop group on tour in order to have sexual relations with them.

grouping ('gruːpɪŋ) *n* a planned arrangement of things, people, etc., within a group.

group insurance *n Chiefly U.S. and Canadian.* insurance relating to life, health, or accident and covering several persons, esp. the employees of a firm, under a single contract at reduced premiums.

group marriage *n* an arrangement in which several males live together with several females, forming a conjugal unit.

Group of Five *n* France, Japan, UK, U.S., and Germany acting as a group to stabilize their currency exchange rates. Abbrev.: **G5.**

Group of Seven *n* the seven leading industrial nations excepting the USSR, i.e. Canada, France, Italy, Japan, UK, U.S., and Germany (formerly West Germany), whose heads of state and finance ministers meet regularly to coordinate economic policy. Abbrev.: **G7.**

Group of Seventy Seven *n* the developing countries of the world. Abbrev.: **G77.**

Group of Ten *n* the ten nations who met in Paris in 1961 to arrange the special drawing rights of the IMF; Belgium, Canada, France, Italy, Japan, Netherlands, Sweden, UK, U.S., and West Germany. Abbrev.: **G10.**

Group of Three *n* Japan, U.S., and Germany (formerly West Germany), regarded as the largest western industrialized nations.

Group of Twenty-Four *n* the twenty-four richest and most industrialized countries of the world. Abbrev.: **G24.**

group practice *n* a medical practice undertaken by a group of associated doctors who work together as partners or as specialists in different areas.

group speed *or* **velocity** *n Physics.* the speed at which energy is propagated in a wave. This is the quantity determined when one measures the distance which the radiation travels in a given time. In a medium in which the speed increases with wavelength the group speed is less than the phase speed, and vice versa.

group therapy *n Psychol.* the simultaneous treatment of a number of individuals who are members of a natural group or who are brought together to share their problems in group discussion.

groupthink ('gru:pˌθɪŋk) *n* a tendency within organizations or society to promote or establish the view of the predominant group.

groupuscule ('gru:pəˌskju:l) *n Usually derogatory.* a small group within a political party or movement. [C20: from French: small group]

groupware ('gru:pˌwɛə) *n* software that enables computers within a group or organization to work together, allowing users to exchange electronic-mail messages, access shared files and databases, use video conferencing, etc.

grouse[1] (graʊs) *n, pl* **grouse** *or* **grouses. 1** any gallinaceous bird of the family *Tetraonidae,* occurring mainly in the N hemisphere, having a stocky body and feathered legs and feet. They are popular game birds. See also **black grouse, red grouse.** ◆ *adj* **2** *Austral. and N.Z. slang.* excellent. [C16: of unknown origin] ▸ **'grouseˌlike** *adj*

grouse[2] (graʊs) *vb* **1** (*intr*) to grumble; complain. ◆ *n* **2** a persistent complaint. [C19: of unknown origin] ▸ **'grouser** *n*

grout (graʊt) *n* **1** a thin mortar for filling joints between tiles, masonry, etc. **2** a fine plaster used as a finishing coat. **3** coarse meal or porridge. ◆ *vb* **4** (*tr*) to fill (joints) or finish (walls, etc.) with grout. [Old English *grūt;* related to Old Frisian *grēt* sand, Middle High German *grūz,* Middle Dutch *grūte* coarse meal; see GRIT, GROATS] ▸ **'grouter** *n*

grouts (graʊts) *pl n* **1** *Chiefly Brit.* sediment or grounds, as from making coffee. **2** a variant of **groats.**

grove (grəʊv) *n* **1** a small wooded area or plantation. **2a** a road lined with houses and often trees, esp. in a suburban area. **2b** (*cap. as part of a street name*): *Ladbroke Grove.* [Old English *grāf;* related to *grǣfa* thicket, GREAVE, Norwegian *greivla* to intertwine]

grovel ('grɒvᵊl) *vb* **-els, -elling, -elled** *or U.S.* **-els, -eling, -eled.** (*intr*) **1** to humble or abase oneself, as in making apologies or showing respect. **2** to lie or crawl face downwards, as in fear or humility. **3** (often foll. by *in*) to indulge or take pleasure (in sensuality or vice). [C16: back formation from obsolete *groveling* (adv), from Middle English *on grufe* on the face, of Scandinavian origin; compare Old Norse *ā grūfu,* from *grūfa* prone position; see -LING[2]] ▸ **'groveller** *n* ▸ **'grovelling** *n, adj* ▸ **'grovellingly** *adv*

Groves (grəʊvz) *n* Sir **Charles.** 1915–92, English orchestral conductor.

grovet ('grɒvət) *n* a wrestling hold in which a wrestler in a kneeling position grips the head of his kneeling opponent with one arm and forces his shoulders down with the other.

grow (grəʊ) *vb* **grows, growing, grew** (gru:), **grown** (grəʊn). **1** (of an organism or part of an organism) to increase in size or develop (hair, leaves, or other structures). **2** (*intr;* usually foll. by *out of* or *from*) to originate, as from an initial cause or source: *the federation grew out of the Empire.* **3** (*intr*) to increase in size, number, degree, etc.: *the population is growing rapidly.* **4** (*intr*) to change in length or amount in a specified direction: *some plants grow downwards; profits over the years grew downwards.* **5** (*copula; may take an infinitive*) (esp. of emotions, physical states, etc.) to develop or come into existence or being gradually: *to grow cold; to grow morose; he grew to like her.* **6** (*intr;* usually foll. by *up*) to come into existence: *a close friendship grew up between them.* **7** (*intr;* foll. by *together*) to be joined gradually by or as by growth: *the branches on the tree grew together.* **8** (*intr;* foll. by *away, together,* etc.) to develop a specified state of friendship: *the lovers grew together gradually; many friends grow apart over the years.* **9** (when *intr,* foll. by *with*) to become covered with a growth: *the path grew with weeds.* **10** to produce (plants) by controlling or encouraging their growth, esp. for home consumption or on a commercial basis. ◆ See also **grow into, grow on, grow out of, grow up.** [Old English *grōwan;* related to Old Norse *grōa,* Old Frisian *grōia,* Old High German *gruoen;* see GREEN, GRASS]

grow bag *n* a plastic bag containing a sufficient amount of a sterile growing medium and nutrients to enable a plant, such as a tomato or pepper, to be grown to full size in it, usually for one season only. [C20: from *Gro-bag,* trademark for the first ones marketed]

grower ('grəʊə) *n* **1** a person who grows plants: *a vegetable grower.* **2** a plant that grows in a specified way: *a fast grower.*

growing pains *pl n* **1** pains in muscles or joints sometimes experienced by children during a period of unusually rapid growth. **2** difficulties besetting a new enterprise in its early stages.

grow into *vb* (*intr, prep*) to become big or mature enough for: *his clothes were always big enough for him to grow into.*

growl (graʊl) *vb* **1** (of animals, esp. when hostile) to utter (sounds) in a low inarticulate manner: *the dog growled at us.* **2** to utter (words) in a gruff or angry manner: *he growled an apology.* **3** (*intr*) to make sounds suggestive of an animal growling: *the thunder growled around the lake.* ◆ *n* **4** the act or sound of growling. **5** *Jazz.* an effect resembling a growl, produced at the back of the throat when playing a wind instrument. [C18: from earlier *grolle,* from Old French *grouller* to grumble] ▸ **'growlingly** *adv*

growler ('graʊlə) *n* **1** a person, animal, or thing that growls. **2** *Brit. slang, obsolete.* a four-wheeled hansom cab. **3** *Canadian.* a small iceberg that has broken off from a larger iceberg or from a glacier, often hazardous to shipping. **4** *U.S. slang.* any container, such as a can, for draught beer.

grown (grəʊn) *adj* **a** developed or advanced: *fully grown.* **b** (*in combination*): *half-grown.*

grown-up *adj* **1** having reached maturity; adult. **2** suitable for or characteristic of an adult. ◆ *n* **3** an adult.

grow on *vb* (*intr, prep*) to become progressively more acceptable or pleasant to: *I don't think much of your new record, but I suppose it will grow on me.*

grow out of *vb* (*intr, adv + prep*) to become too big or mature for: *she soon grew out of her girlish ways.*

growth (grəʊθ) *n* **1** the process or act of growing, esp. in organisms following assimilation of food. **2** an increase in size, number, significance, etc. **3** something grown or growing: *a new growth of hair.* **4** a stage of development. **5** any abnormal tissue, such as a tumour. **6** (*modifier*) of, relating to, causing or characterized by growth: *a growth industry; growth hormone.*

growth curve *n* a curve on a graph in which a variable is plotted against time to illustrate the growth of the variable.

growth factor *n* any of several substances present in serum that induce growth of cells. Excessive amounts of growth factor may be associated with the production of cancer cells.

growth hormone *n* a hormone synthesized in and secreted by the anterior lobe of the pituitary gland that promotes growth of the long bones in the limbs and increases the synthesis of protein essential for growth. Also called: **somatotrophin.**

growth ring *n* another name for **annual ring.**

growth shares *pl n Finance.* ordinary shares with good prospects of appreciation in yield and value.

growth substance *n Botany.* any substance, produced naturally by a plant or manufactured commercially, that, in very low concentrations, affects plant growth; a plant hormone.

grow up *vb* (*intr, adv*) **1** to reach maturity; become adult. **2** to come into existence; develop.

groyne *or esp. U.S.* **groin** (grɔɪn) *n* a wall or jetty built out from a riverbank or seashore to control erosion. Also called: **spur, breakwater.** [C16: origin uncertain: perhaps altered from GROIN]

grozing iron ('grəʊzɪŋ) *n* an iron for smoothing joints between lead pipes. [C17: part translation of Dutch *gruisijzer,* from *gruizen* to crush, from *gruis* gravel + *yzer* iron]

Grozny (*Russian* 'grɔznij) *n* a city in S Russia, capital of the Chechen Republic: a major oil centre: it was badly damaged during fighting between separatists and Russian troops (1994–95); plans to rename it Dzhokar-Ghala were announced in 1997. Pop.: 364 000 (1993 est.).

GRU *abbrev.* (formerly) the Soviet military intelligence service; the military counterpart of the **KGB.** [from Russian *Glavnoye Razvedyvatelnoye Upravleniye* Main Intelligence Directorate]

grub (grʌb) *vb* **grubs, grubbing, grubbed. 1** (when *tr,* often foll. by *up* or *out*) to search for and pull up (roots, stumps, etc.) by digging in the ground. **2** to dig up the surface of (ground, soil, etc.), esp. to clear away roots, stumps, etc. **3** (*intr;* often foll. by *in* or *among*) to search carefully. **4** (*intr*) to work unceasingly, esp. at a dull task or research. **5** *Slang.* to provide (a person) with food or (of a person) to take food. **6** (*tr*) *Slang, chiefly U.S.* to scrounge: *to grub a cigarette.* ◆ *n* **7** the short legless larva of certain insects, esp. beetles. **8** *Slang.* food; victuals. **9** a person who works hard, esp. in a dull plodding way. **10** *Brit. informal.* a dirty child. [C13: of Germanic origin; compare Old High German *grubilōn* to dig, German *grübeln* to rack one's brain, Middle Dutch *grobben* to scrape together; see GRAVE[3], GROOVE]

grubber ('grʌbə) *n* **1** a person who grubs. **2** another name for **grub hoe.**

grubby ('grʌbɪ) *adj* **-bier, -biest. 1** dirty; slovenly. **2** mean; beggarly. **3** infested with grubs. ▸ **'grubbily** *adv* ▸ **'grubbiness** *n*

grub hoe *or* **grubbing hoe** *n* a heavy hoe for grubbing up roots. Also called: **grubber.**

grub screw *n* a small headless screw having a slot cut for a screwdriver or a socket for a hexagon key and used to secure a sliding component in a determined position.

grubstake ('grʌbˌsteɪk) *n* **1** *U.S. and Canadian. informal.* supplies provided for a prospector on the condition that the donor has a stake in any finds. ◆ *vb* (*tr*) **2** *U.S. informal.* to furnish with such supplies. **3** *Chiefly U.S. and Canadian.* to supply (a person) with a stake in a gambling game. ▸ **'grubˌstaker** *n*

Grub Street *n* **1** a former street in London frequented by literary hacks and needy authors. **2** the world or class of literary hacks, etc. ◆ *adj also* **'Grubˌstreet. 3** (*sometimes not cap.*) relating to or characteristic of hack literature.

grudge (grʌdʒ) *n* **1** a persistent feeling of resentment, esp. one due to some cause, such as an insult or injury. **2** (*modifier*) planned or carried out in order to settle a grudge: *a grudge fight.* ◆ *vb* **3** (*tr*) to give or allow unwillingly. **4** to feel resentful or envious about (someone else's success, possessions, etc.). [C15: from Old French *grouchier* to grumble, probably of Germanic origin; compare Old High German *grunnizōn* to grunt] ▸ **'grudgeless** *adj* ▸ **'grudger** *n* ▸ **'grudging** *adj* ▸ **'grudgingly** *adv*

grue (gru:) *Scot.* ◆ *n* **1** a shiver or shudder; a creeping of the flesh. ◆ *vb* (*intr*) **2** to shiver or shudder. **3** to feel strong aversion. [C14: of Scandinavian origin; compare Old Swedish *grua,* Old Danish *grue;* related to German *graven,* Dutch *gruwen* to abhor]

gruel ('gru:əl) *n* a drink or thin porridge, made by boiling meal, esp. oatmeal, in water or milk. [C14: from Old French, of Germanic origin; see GROUT]

gruelling *or U.S.* **grueling** ('gru:əlɪŋ) *adj* **1** severe or tiring: *a gruelling interview.* ◆ *n* **2** *Informal.* a severe experience, esp. punishment. [C19: from now obsolete vb *gruel* to exhaust, punish]

gruesome ('gru:səm) *adj* inspiring repugnance and horror; ghastly. [C16: originally Northern English and Scottish; see GRUE, -SOME[1]] ▸ **'gruesomely** *adv* ▸ **'gruesomeness** *n*

gruff (grʌf) *adj* **1** rough or surly in manner, speech, etc.: *a gruff reply.* **2** (of a voice, bark, etc.) low and throaty. [C16: originally Scottish, from Dutch *grof,* of Germanic origin; compare Old High German *girob;* related to Old English *hrēof,* Lithuanian *kraupùs*] ▸ **'gruffish** *adj* ▸ **'gruffly** *adv* ▸ **'gruffness** *n*

grugru ('gru:gru:) *n* **1** any of several tropical American palms, esp. *Acrocomia sclerocarpa,* which has a spiny trunk and leaves and edible nuts. **2** the large edible wormlike larva of a weevil, *Rhynchophorus palmarum,* that infests this palm. [C18: from American Spanish (Puerto Rican dialect) *grugrú,* of Cariban origin]

grumble ('grʌmbᵊl) *vb* **1** to utter (complaints) in a nagging or discontented way. **2** (*intr*) to make low dull rumbling sounds. ◆ *n* **3** a complaint; grouse. **4** a low rumbling sound. [C16: from Middle Low German *grommelen,* of Germanic origin; see GRIM] ► '**grumbler** *n* ► '**grumblingly** *adv* ► '**grumbly** *adj*

grumbling appendix *n Informal.* a condition in which the appendix causes intermittent pain but appendicitis has not developed.

grummet ('grʌmɪt) *n* another word for **grommet.**

grumous ('gru:məs) *or* **grumose** ('gru:məʊs) *adj* (esp. of plant parts) consisting of granular tissue. [C17: from *grume* a clot of blood, from Latin *grumus* a little heap; related to CRUMB]

grump (grʌmp) *Informal.* ◆ *n* **1** a surly or bad-tempered person. **2** (*pl*) a sulky or morose mood (esp. in the phrase **have the grumps**). ◆ *vb* **3** (*intr*) to complain or grumble. [C18: dialect *grump* surly remark, probably of imitative origin]

grumpy ('grʌmpɪ) *or* **grumpish** ('grʌmpɪʃ) *adj* **grumpier, grumpiest.** peevish; sulky. [C18: from GRUMP + -Y[1]] ► '**grumpily** *or* '**grumpishly** *adv* ► '**grumpiness** *or* '**grumpishness** *n*

Grundy ('grʌndɪ) *n* a narrow-minded person who keeps critical watch on the propriety of others. [C18: named after Mrs *Grundy,* the character in T. Morton's play *Speed the Plough* (1798)] ► '**Grundy,ism** *n* ► '**Grundyist** *or* '**Grundyite** *n*

Grünewald (*German* 'gry:nəvalt) *n* **Matthias** (ma'ti:as), original name *Mathis Gothardt.* ?1470–1528, German painter, the greatest exponent of late Gothic art in Germany. The *Isenheim Altarpiece* is regarded as his masterpiece.

grunge (grʌndʒ) *n* **1** *U.S. slang.* dirt or rubbish. **2** a style of rock music originating in the U.S. in the late 1980s, featuring a distorted guitar sound. **3** a deliberately untidy and uncoordinated fashion style. [C20: possibly a coinage imitating GRIME + SLUDGE]

grungy ('grʌndʒɪ) *adj* **-gier, -giest.** *Slang.* **1** *Chiefly U.S. and Canadian.* squalid or seedy. **2** (of pop music) characterized by a loud fuzzy guitar sound.

grunion ('grʌnjən) *n* a Californian marine teleost fish, *Leuresthes tenuis,* that spawns on beaches: family *Atherinidae* (silversides). [C20: probably from Spanish *gruñón* a grunter]

grunt (grʌnt) *vb* **1** (*intr*) (esp. of pigs and some other animals) to emit a low short gruff noise. **2** (when *tr, may take a clause as object*) to express something gruffly: *he grunted his answer.* ◆ *n* **3** the characteristic low short gruff noise of pigs, etc., or a similar sound, as of disgust. **4** any of various mainly tropical marine sciaenid fishes, such as *Haemulon macrostomum* (**Spanish grunt**), that utter a grunting sound when caught. **5** *U.S. slang.* an infantry soldier or U.S. marine, esp. in the Vietnam War. [Old English *grunnettan,* probably of imitative origin; compare Old High German *grunnizōn, grunni* moaning, Latin *grunnīre*] ► '**gruntingly** *adv*

grunter ('grʌntə) *n* **1** a person or animal that grunts, esp. a pig. **2** another name for **grunt** (sense 4).

gruntled ('grʌntᵊld) *adj Informal.* happy or contented; satisfied. [C20: back formation from DISGRUNTLED]

gruppetto (grʊ'petəʊ) *n, pl* **-ti** (-ti:). *Music.* a turn. [C19: from Italian, diminutive of *gruppo* a group, a turn]

Grus (grʊs) *n, Latin genitive* **Gruis** ('gru:ɪs). a constellation in the S hemisphere lying near Phoenix and Piscis Austrinus and containing two second magnitude stars. [via New Latin from Latin: crane]

Gruyère *or* **Gruyère cheese** ('gru:jɛə; *French* gryjɛr) *n* a hard flat whole-milk cheese, pale yellow in colour and with holes. [C19: after *Gruyère,* Switzerland where it originated]

gr. wt. *abbrev. for* gross weight.

gryke (graɪk) *n* a variant spelling of **grike.**

gryphon ('grɪfᵊn) *n* a variant of **griffin**[1].

grysbok ('graɪs,bɒk) *n* either of two small antelopes, *Raphicerus melanotis* or *R. sharpei,* of central and southern Africa, having small straight horns. [C18: Afrikaans, from Dutch *grijs* grey + *bok* BUCK[1]]

GS *abbrev. for:* **1** General Secretary. **2** General Staff.

gs. *abbrev. for* guineas.

gsm *abbrev. for* grams per square metre: the term used to specify the weight of paper.

G-spot *n* an area in the front wall of the vagina which is alleged to produce an extremely intense orgasm when stimulated. [C20: short for *Gräfenberg spot,* named after Ernst *Gräfenberg* (1881–1957), German gynaecologist]

GSR *abbrev. for* galvanic skin response.

GST (in Australia and New Zealand) *abbrev. for* goods and services tax.

G-string *n* **1** a piece of cloth attached to a narrow waistband covering the pubic area, worn esp. by strippers. **2** a strip of cloth attached to the front and back of a waistband and covering the loins. **3** *Music.* a string tuned to G, such as the lowest string of a violin.

G-suit *n* a close-fitting garment covering the legs and abdomen that is worn by the crew of high-speed aircraft and can be pressurized to prevent blackout during certain manoeuvres. Also called: **anti-G suit.** [C20: from *g(ravity) suit*]

GSVQ (in Britain) *abbrev. for* General Scottish Vocational Qualification. Compare: **GNVQ.**

GT *abbrev. for* **gran turismo,** a high-performance luxury sports car with a hard fixed roof, designed for covering long distances.

gt. *pl* **gtt.** *Pharmacy. abbrev. for* gutta.

GTC *abbrev. for:* **1** Also: **gtc.** (on a commercial order for goods) good till cancelled (*or* countermanded). **2** (in Scotland) General Teaching Council.

gtd *abbrev. for* guaranteed.

g.u. *or* **GU** *abbrev. for* genitourinary.

guacamole *or* **guachamole** (,gwɑ:kə'məʊlɪ) *n* **1** a spread of mashed avocado, tomato pulp, mayonnaise, and seasoning. **2** any of various Mexican or South American salads containing avocado. [from American Spanish, from Nahuatl *ahuacamolli,* from *ahuacatl* avocado + *molli* sauce]

guacharo ('gwɑ:tʃə,rəʊ) *n, pl* **-ros.** another name for **oilbird.** [C19: from Spanish *guácharo*]

guaco ('gwɑ:kəʊ) *n, pl* **-cos. 1** any of several tropical American plants whose leaves are used as an antidote to snakebite, esp. the climbers *Mikania guaco,* family *Compositae* (composites), or *Aristolochia maxima* (*A. serpentina*), family *Aristolochiaceae.* **2** the leaves of any of these plants. [C19: from American Spanish]

Guadalajara (,gwɑ:dᵊlə'hɑ:rə; *Spanish* gwaðala'xara) *n* **1** a city in W Mexico, capital of Jalisco state: the second largest city of Mexico: centre of the Indian slave trade until its abolition, declared here in 1810; two universities (1792 and 1935). Pop.: 1 650 042 (1990). **2** a city in central Spain, in New Castile. Pop.: 67 200 (1991).

Guadalcanal (,gwɑ:dᵊlkə'næl; *Spanish* gwaðalka'nal) *n* a mountainous island in the SW Pacific, the largest of the Solomon Islands: under British protection until 1978; occupied by the Japanese (1942–43). Pop.: 59 064 (1996 est.). Area: 6475 sq. km (2500 sq. miles).

Guadalquivir (,gwɑ:dᵊlkwɪ'vɪə; *Spanish* gwaðalki'βir) *n* the chief river of S Spain, rising in the Sierra de Segura and flowing west and southwest to the Gulf of Cádiz: navigable by ocean-going vessels to Seville. Length: 560 km (348 miles).

Guadalupe Hidalgo (,gwɑ:dᵊ'lu:p hɪ'dælgəʊ; *Spanish* gwaða'lupe i'ðalɣo) *n* a city in central Mexico, northwest of Mexico City: became a pilgrimage centre after an Indian convert had a vision of the Virgin Mary here in 1531. Pop.: 535 332 (1990). Former name (1931–71): **Gustavo A. Madero.**

Guadeloupe (,gwɑ:dᵊ'lu:p) *n* an overseas region of France in the E Caribbean, in the Leeward Islands, formed by the islands of Basse Terre and Grande Terre and their five dependencies. Capital: Basse-Terre. Pop.: 434 000 (1998 est.). Area: 1780 sq. km (687 sq. miles).

Guadiana (*Spanish* gwa'ðjana; *Portuguese* gwə'ðjənə) *n* a river in SW Europe, rising in S central Spain and flowing west, then south as part of the border between Spain and Portugal, to the Gulf of Cádiz. Length: 578 km (359 miles).

guaiacol ('gwaɪə,kɒl) *n* a yellowish oily creosote-like liquid extracted from guaiacum resin and hardwood tar, used medicinally as an expectorant. Formula: $C_7H_8O_2$. [from GUAIAC(UM) + -OL[2]]

guaiacum *or* **guaiocum** ('gwaɪəkəm) *n* **1** any tropical American evergreen tree of the zygophyllaceous genus *Guaiacum,* such as the lignum vitae. **2** the hard heavy wood of any of these trees. **3** Also called: **guaiac** ('gwaɪæk). a brownish resin obtained from the lignum vitae, used medicinally and in making varnishes. [C16: New Latin, from Spanish *guayaco,* of Taino origin]

Guam (gwɑ:m) *n* an island in the N Pacific, the largest and southernmost of the Marianas: belonged to Spain from the 17th century until 1898, when it was ceded to the U.S.; site of naval and air force bases. Capital: Agaña. Pop.: 148 000 (1998 est.). Area: 541 sq. km (209 sq. miles). ► **Guamanian** (gwɑ:'meɪnɪən) *n, adj*

guan (gwɑ:n) *n* any gallinaceous bird of the genera *Penelope, Pipile,* etc., of Central and South America: family *Cracidae* (curassows). [C18: from American Spanish]

Guanabara (*Portuguese* gwəna'bara) *n* (until 1975) a state of SE Brazil, on the Atlantic and **Guanabara Bay,** now amalgamated with the state of Rio de Janeiro.

guanaco (gwɑ:'nɑ:kəʊ) *n, pl* **-cos.** a cud-chewing South American artiodactyl mammal, *Lama guanicoe,* closely related to the domesticated llama: family *Camelidae.* [C17: from Spanish, from Quechuan *huanacu*]

Guanajuato (*Spanish* gwana'xwato) *n* **1** a state of central Mexico, on the great central plateau: mountainous in the north, with fertile plains in the south; important mineral resources. Capital: Guanajuato. Pop.: 4 393 160 (1995 est.). Area: 30 588 sq. km (11 810 sq. miles). **2** a city in central Mexico, capital of Guanajuato state: founded in 1554, it became one of the world's richest silver-mining centres. Pop.: 113 580 (1990).

guanase ('gwɑ:neɪz) *n* an enzyme that converts guanine to xanthine by removal of an amino group. [C20: from GUAN(INE) + -ASE]

Guangdong ('gwæŋ'dʊŋ) *or* **Kwangtung** *n* a province of SE China, on the South China Sea: includes the Leizhou Peninsula, with densely populated river valleys, Macao and Hong Kong; the only true tropical climate in China. Capital: Canton. Pop.: 68 680 000 (1996 est.). Area: 197 100 sq. km (76 100 sq. miles).

Guangxi Zhuang Autonomous Region ('gwæŋ'si: 'dʒwæŋ) *or* **Kwangsi-Chuang Autonomous Region** *n* an administrative division of S China. Capital: Nanning. Pop.: 45 430 000 (1996 est.). Area: 220 400 sq. km (85 100 sq. miles).

Guangzhou ('gwæŋ'dzəʊ) *n* the Pinyin transliteration of the Chinese name for **Canton.**

guanidine ('gwɑ:nɪ,di:n, -dɪn, 'gwænɪ-) *or* **guanidin** ('gwɑ:nɪdɪn, 'gwænɪ-) *n* a strongly alkaline crystalline substance, soluble in water and found in plant and animal tissues. It is used in organic synthesis. Formula: $HNC(NH_2)_2$. Also called: **carbamidine, iminourea.** [C19: from GUANO + -ID[3] + -INE[2]]

guanine ('gwɑ:ni:n, 'gu:ə,ni:n) *n* a white almost insoluble compound: one of the purine bases in nucleic acids. Formula: $C_5H_5N_5O$. [C19: from GUANO + -INE[2]]

guano ('gwɑ:nəʊ) *n, pl* **-nos. 1** the dried excrement of fish-eating sea birds, deposited in rocky coastal regions of South America: contains the urates, oxalates, and phosphates of ammonium and calcium; used as a fertilizer. **2** any similar but artificial fertilizer. [C17: from Spanish, from Quechuan *huano* dung]

guanosine ('gwɑːnəˌsiːn, -ˌziːn) *n Biochem.* a nucleoside consisting of guanine and ribose.

Guantánamo (*Spanish* gwan'tanamo) *n* a city in SE Cuba, on **Guantánamo Bay**: site of a U.S. naval base. Pop.: 207 796 (1994 est.).

guanylic acid (gwə'nɪlɪk) *n* a nucleotide consisting of guanine, ribose or deoxyribose, and a phosphate group. It is a constituent of DNA or RNA. Also called: **guanosine monophosphate.**

Guaporé (*Portuguese* gwapo'rɛ) *n* **1** a river in W central South America, rising in SW Brazil and flowing northwest as part of the border between Brazil and Bolivia, to join the Mamoré River. Length: 1750 km (1087 miles). Spanish name: **Iténez. 2** the former name (until 1956) of **Rondônia.**

guar (gwɑː) *n* **1** a leguminous Indian plant, *Cyamopsis tetragonolobus*, grown as a fodder crop and for the gum obtained from its seeds. **2** Also called: **guar gum.** a gum obtained from the seeds of this plant, used as a stabilizer and thickening agent in food (E412) and as sizing for paper. [C19: from Hindi]

guaraní ('gwɑːrənɪ) *n, pl* **-ní** *or* **-nís.** the standard monetary unit of Paraguay, divided into 100 céntimos.

Guarani (ˌgwɑːrə'niː) *n* **1** (*pl* **-ni** *or* **-nis**) a member of a South American Indian people of Paraguay, S Brazil, and Bolivia. **2** the language of this people, belonging to the Tupi-Guarani family; one of the official languages of Paraguay, along with Spanish.

guarantee (ˌgærən'tiː) *n* **1** a formal assurance, esp. in writing, that a product, service, etc., will meet certain standards or specifications. **2** *Law.* a promise, esp. a collateral agreement, to answer for the debt, default, or miscarriage of another. **3a** a person, company, etc., to whom a guarantee is made. **3b** a person, company, etc., who gives a guarantee. **4** a person who acts as a guarantor. **5** something that makes a specified condition or outcome certain. **6** a variant spelling of **guaranty.** ◆ *vb* **-tees, -teeing, -teed.** (*mainly tr*) **7** (*also intr*) to take responsibility for (someone else's debts, obligations, etc.). **8** to serve as a guarantee for. **9** to secure or furnish security for: *a small deposit will guarantee any dress.* **10** (usually foll. by *from* or *against*) to undertake to protect or keep secure, as against injury, loss, etc. **11** to ensure: *good planning will guarantee success.* **12** (*may take a clause as object or an infinitive*) to promise or make certain. [C17: perhaps from Spanish *garante* or French *garant,* of Germanic origin; compare WARRANT]

guarantor (ˌgærən'tɔː) *n* a person who gives or is bound by a guarantee or guaranty; surety.

guaranty ('gærəntɪ) *n, pl* **-ties. 1** a pledge of responsibility for fulfilling another person's obligations in case of that person's default. **2** a thing given or taken as security for a guaranty. **3** the act of providing security. **4** a person who acts as a guarantor. ◆ *vb* **-ties, -tying, -tied. 5** a variant of **guarantee.** [C16: from Old French *garantie,* variant of *warantie,* of Germanic origin; see WARRANTY]

guard (gɑːd) *vb* **1** to watch over or shield (a person or thing) from danger or harm; protect. **2** to keep watch over (a prisoner or other potentially dangerous person or thing), as to prevent escape. **3** (*tr*) to control: *to guard one's tongue.* **4** (*intr;* usually foll. by *against*) to take precautions. **5** to control entrance and exit through (a gate, door, etc.). **6** (*tr*) to provide (machinery, etc.) with a device to protect the operator. **7** (*tr*) **7a** *Chess, cards.* to protect or cover (a chess man or card) with another. **7b** *Curling, bowling.* to protect or cover (a stone or bowl) by placing one's own stone or bowl between it and another player. **8** (*tr*) *Archaic.* to accompany as a guard. ◆ *n* **9** a person or group who keeps a protecting, supervising, or restraining watch or control over people, such as prisoners, things, etc. Related adj: **custodial. 10** a person or group of people, such as soldiers, who form a ceremonial escort: *guard of honour.* **11** *Brit.* the official in charge of a train. **12a** the act or duty of protecting, restraining, or supervising. **12b** (*as modifier*): *guard duty.* **13** *Irish.* another word for **garda. 14** a device, part, or attachment on an object, such as a weapon or machine tool, designed to protect the user against injury, as on the hilt of a sword or the trigger of a firearm. **15** anything that provides or is intended to provide protection: *a guard against infection.* **16a** another name for **safety chain. 16b** a long neck chain often holding a chatelaine. **17** See **guard ring. 18** *Sport.* an article of light tough material worn to protect any of various parts of the body. **19** *Basketball.* **19a** the position of the two players in a team who play furthest from the basket. **19b** a player in this position. **20** the posture of defence or readiness in fencing, boxing, cricket, etc. **21 take guard.** *Cricket.* (of a batsman) to choose a position in front of the wicket to receive the bowling, esp. by requesting the umpire to indicate his position relative to the stumps. **22 give guard.** *Cricket.* (of an umpire) to indicate such a position to a batsman. **23 off (one's) guard.** having one's defences down; unprepared. **24 on (one's) guard.** prepared to face danger, difficulties, etc. **25 stand guard.** (of a military sentry, etc.) to keep watch. **26 mount guard. 26a** (of a sentry) to begin to keep watch. **26b** (with *over*) to take up a protective or defensive stance (over something). [C15: from Old French *garde,* from *garder* to protect, of Germanic origin; compare Spanish *guardar;* see WARD] ► **'guardable** *adj* ► **'guarder** *n* ► **'guardless** *adj* ► **'guardˌlike** *adj*

Guardafui (ˌgwɑːdə'fuːɪ) *n* **Cape.** a cape at the NE tip of Somalia, extending into the Indian Ocean.

guardant *or* **gardant** ('gɑːdᵊnt) *adj* (*usually postpositive*) *Heraldry.* (of a beast) shown full face. [C16: from French *gardant* guarding, from *garder* to GUARD]

guard band *n* a space left vacant between two radio frequency bands, or between two tracks on a magnetic tape recording, to avoid mutual interference.

guard cell *n Botany.* one of a pair of crescent-shaped cells that surround a pore (stoma) in the epidermis. Changes in the turgidity of the cells cause the opening and closing of the stoma.

guarded ('gɑːdɪd) *adj* **1** protected or kept under surveillance. **2** prudent, restrained, or noncommittal: *a guarded reply.* ► **'guardedly** *adv* ► **'guardedness** *n*

guardee (ˌgɑː'diː) *n Brit. informal.* a guardsman, esp. considered as representing smartness and dash.

guard hair *n* any of the coarse hairs that form the outer fur in certain mammals, rising above the underfur.

guardhouse ('gɑːdˌhaʊs) *n Military.* a building serving as the headquarters or a post for military police and in which military prisoners are detained.

Guardi (*Italian* 'gwardi) *n* **Francesco** (fran'tʃesko). 1712–93, Venetian landscape painter.

guardian ('gɑːdɪən) *n* **1** one who looks after, protects, or defends: *the guardian of public morals.* **2a** *Law.* someone legally appointed to manage the affairs of a person incapable of acting for himself, as a minor or person of unsound mind. **2b** *Social welfare.* (in England) a local authority, or person accepted by it, named under the Mental Health Act 1983 as having the powers to require a mentally disordered person to live at a specified place, attend for treatment, and be accessible to a doctor or social worker. **3** (*often cap.*) (in England) another word for **custos.** ◆ *adj* **4** protecting or safeguarding. ► **'guardianˌship** *n*

Guardian Angels *pl n* vigilante volunteers who patrol the underground railway in New York, London, and elsewhere, wearing red berets, to deter violent crime.

guardrail ('gɑːdˌreɪl) *n* **1** a railing at the side of a staircase, road, etc., as a safety barrier. **2** Also called (Brit.): **checkrail.** *Railways.* a short metal rail fitted to the inside of the main rail to provide additional support in keeping a train's wheels on the track.

guard ring *n* **1** Also called: **guard, keeper ring.** *Jewellery.* an extra ring worn to prevent another from slipping off the finger. **2** an electrode used to counteract distortion of the electric fields at the edges of other electrodes in a capacitor or electron lens.

guardroom ('gɑːdˌruːm, -ˌrʊm) *n* **1** a room used by guards. **2** a room in which prisoners are confined under guard.

Guards (gɑːdz) *pl n* **a** (esp. in European armies) any of various regiments responsible for ceremonial duties and, formerly, the protection of the head of state: *the Life Guards; the Grenadier Guards.* **b** (*as modifier*): *a Guards regiment.*

guardsman ('gɑːdzmən) *n, pl* **-men. 1** (in Britain) a member of a Guards battalion or regiment. **2** (in the U.S.) a member of the National Guard. **3** a guard.

guard's van *n Railways, Brit. and N.Z.* the van in which the guard travels, usually attached to the rear of a train. U.S. and Canadian equivalent: **caboose.**

Guarneri (gwɑː'nɪərɪ; *Italian* gwar'nɛːri), **Guarnieri** (*Italian* gwar'njɛːri), *or* **Guarnerius** (gwɑː'nɛərɪəs) *n, pl* **Guarneris, Guarnieris,** *or* **Guarneriuses. 1** an Italian family of 17th- and 18th-century violin-makers. **2** any violin made by a member of this family.

Guat. *abbrev. for* Guatemala.

Guatemala (ˌgwɑːtə'mɑːlə) *n* a republic in Central America: original Maya Indians conquered by the Spanish in 1523; became the centre of Spanish administration in Central America; gained independence and was annexed to Mexico in 1821, becoming an independent republic in 1839. Official language: Spanish. Religion: Roman Catholic majority. Currency: quetzal. Capital: Guatemala City. Pop.: 10 802 000 (1998 est.). Area: 108 889 sq. km (42 042 sq. miles). ► **ˌGuate'malan** *adj, n*

Guatemala City *n* the capital of Guatemala, in the southeast: founded in 1776 to replace the former capital, Antigua Guatemala, after an earthquake; university (1676). Pop.: 1 167 495 (1995).

guava ('gwɑːvə) *n* **1** any of various tropical American trees of the myrtaceous genus *Psidium,* esp. *P. guajava,* grown in tropical regions for their edible fruit. **2** the fruit of such a tree, having yellow skin and pink pulp: used to make jellies, jams, etc. [C16: from Spanish *guayaba,* from a South American Indian word]

Guayaquil (*Spanish* gwaja'kil) *n* a port in W Ecuador: the largest city in the country and its chief port; university (1867). Pop.: 1 973 880 (1997 est.).

guayule (gwə'juːlɪ) *n* **1** a bushy shrub, *Parthenium argentatum,* of the southwestern U.S.: family *Compositae* (composites). **2** rubber derived from the sap of this plant. [from American Spanish, from Nahuatl *cuauhuli,* from *cuahuitl* tree + *uli* gum]

gubbins ('gʌbɪnz) *n Informal.* **1** an object of little or no value. **2** a small device or gadget. **3** odds and ends; litter or rubbish. **4** a silly person. [C16 (meaning: fragments): from obsolete *gobbon,* probably related to GOBBET]

gubernatorial (ˌgjuːbənə'tɔːrɪəl, ˌguː-) *adj Chiefly U.S.* of or relating to a governor. [C18: from Latin *gubernātor* governor]

guberniya *Russian.* (gu'bjɛrnɪjə) *n* **1** a territorial division of imperial Russia. **2** a territorial and administrative subdivision in the former Soviet Union. [from Russian: government, ultimately from Latin *gubernāre* to GOVERN]

guck (gʌk, gʊk) *n* slimy matter; gunk. [C20: perhaps a blend of GOO and MUCK]

guddle ('gʌdᵊl) *Scot.* ◆ *vb* **1** to catch (fish) by groping with the hands under the banks or stones of a stream. ◆ *n* **2** a muddle; confusion. [C19: of unknown origin]

gudgeon[1] ('gʌdʒən) *n* **1** a small slender European freshwater cyprinid fish, *Gobio gobio,* with a barbel on each side of the mouth: used as bait by anglers. **2** any of various other fishes, such as the goby. **3** bait or enticement. **4** *Slang.* a person who is easy to trick or cheat. ◆ *vb* **5** (*tr*) *Slang.* to trick or cheat. [C15: from Old French *gougon,* probably from Latin *gōbius;* see GOBY]

gudgeon[2] ('gʌdʒən) *n* **1** the female or socket portion of a pinned hinge. **2** *Nautical.* one of two or more looplike sockets, fixed to the transom of a boat, into which the pintles of a rudder are fitted. [C14: from Old French *goujon,* perhaps from Late Latin *gulbia* chisel]

gudgeon pin *n Brit.* the pin through the skirt of a piston in an internal-combustion engine, to which the little end of the connecting rod is attached. U.S. and Canadian name: **wrist pin.**

Gudrun ('gudru:n), **Guthrun** ('guðru:n), *or* **Kudrun** ('kudru:n) *n Norse myth.* the wife of Sigurd and, after his death, of Atli, whom she slew for his murder of her brother Gunnar. She corresponds to Kriemhild in the *Nibelungenlied.*

guelder-rose ('gɛldə,rəuz) *n* a Eurasian caprifoliaceous shrub, *Viburnum opulus,* with clusters of white flowers and small red fruits. [C16: from Dutch *geldersche roos,* from *Gelderland* or *Gelders,* province of Holland]

Guelders ('gɛldəz) *n* another name for **Gelderland.**

Guelph[1] *or* **Guelf** (gwɛlf) *n* **1** a member of the political faction in medieval Italy that supported the power of the pope against the German emperors. Compare **Ghibelline. 2** a member of a secret society in 19th-century Italy opposed to foreign rule. ▸ **'Guelphic** *or* **'Guelfic** *adj* ▸ **'Guelphism** *or* **'Guelfism** *n*

Guelph[2] (gwɛlf) *n* a city in Canada, in SE Ontario. Pop.: 87 976 (1991).

guenon (gə'nɒn) *n* any slender agile Old World monkey of the genus *Cercopithecus,* inhabiting wooded regions of Africa and having long hind limbs and tail and long hair surrounding the face. [C19: from French, of unknown origin]

guerdon ('gɜ:dᵊn) *Poetic.* ◆ *n* **1** a reward or payment. ◆ *vb* **2** *(tr)* to give a guerdon to. [C14: from Old French *gueredon,* of Germanic origin; compare Old High German *widarlōn,* Old English *witherlēan;* final element influenced by Latin *dōnum* gift] ▸ **'guerdoner** *n*

guereza (gə'rɛzə) *n* a handsome colobus monkey of the mountain forests of Ethiopia. [C19: its native name]

Guericke (*German* 'ge:rikə) *n* **Otto von.** 1602–86, German physicist: invented the air pump (1650) and demonstrated the power of a vacuum with the Magdeburg hemispheres.

Guernica (gɜ:'ni:kə, 'gɜ:nɪkə; *Spanish* gɛr'nika) *n* a town in N Spain: formerly the seat of a Basque parliament; destroyed in 1937 by German bombers during the Spanish Civil War, an event depicted in one of Picasso's most famous paintings. Pop.: 16 378 (1989).

Guernsey ('gɜ:nzɪ) *n* **1** an island in the English Channel: the second largest of the Channel Islands, which, with Alderney and Sark, Herm, Jethou, and some islets, forms the bailiwick of Guernsey; finance, market gardening, dairy farming, and tourism. Capital: St Peter Port. Pop.: 61 700 (1998 est.). Area: 63 sq. km (24.5 sq. miles). **2** a breed of dairy cattle producing rich creamy milk, originating from the island of Guernsey. **3** *(sometimes not cap.)* a seaman's knitted woollen sweater. **4** *(not cap.) Austral.* a sleeveless woollen shirt or jumper worn by a football player. **5 get a guernsey.** *Austral.* to be selected or gain recognition for something.

Guernsey lily *n* See **nerine.**

Guerrero (*Spanish* ge'rrero) *n* a mountainous state of S Mexico, on the Pacific: rich mineral resources. Capital: Chilpancingo. Pop.: 2 915 497 (1995 est.). Area: 63 794 sq. km (24 631 sq. miles).

guerrilla *or* **guerilla** (gə'rɪlə) *n* **a** a member of an irregular usually politically motivated armed force that combats stronger regular forces, such as the army or police. **b** *(as modifier): guerrilla warfare.* [C19: from Spanish, diminutive of *guerra* WAR] ▸ **guer'rillaism** *or* **gue'rillaism** *n*

Guesclin (*French* geklɛ̃) *n* **Bertrand du** ?1320–80, French commander during the Hundred Years' War.

guess (gɛs) *vb* (when *tr, may take a clause as object*) **1** (when *intr,* often foll. by *at* or *about*) to form or express an uncertain estimate or conclusion (about something), based on insufficient information: *guess what we're having for dinner.* **2** to arrive at a correct estimate of (something) by guessing: *he guessed my age.* **3** *Informal, chiefly U.S. and Canadian.* to believe, think, or suppose (something): *I guess I'll go now.* **4 keep a person guessing.** to let a person remain in a state of uncertainty. ◆ *n* **5** an estimate or conclusion arrived at by guessing: *a bad guess.* **6** the act of guessing. **7 anyone's guess.** something difficult to predict. [C13: probably of Scandinavian origin; compare Old Swedish *gissa,* Old Danish *gitse,* Middle Dutch *gissen;* see GET] ▸ **'guessable** *adj* ▸ **'guesser** *n* ▸ **'guessingly** *adv*

guesstimate *or* **guestimate** *Informal.* ◆ *n* ('gɛstɪmɪt). **1** an estimate calculated mainly or only by guesswork. ◆ *vb* ('gɛstɪ,meɪt). **2** to form a guesstimate of.

guesswork ('gɛs,wɜ:k) *n* **1** a set of conclusions, estimates, etc., arrived at by guessing. **2** the process of making guesses.

guest (gɛst) *n* **1** a person who is entertained, taken out to eat, etc., and paid for by another. **2a** a person who receives hospitality at the home of another: *a weekend guest.* **2b** *(as modifier): the guest room.* **3a** a person who receives the hospitality of a government, establishment, or organization. **3b** *(as modifier): a guest speaker.* **4a** an actor, contestant, entertainer, etc., taking part as a visitor in a programme in which there are also regular participants. **4b** *(as modifier): a guest appearance.* **5** a patron of a hotel, boarding house, restaurant, etc. **6** *Zoology.* a nontechnical name for **inquiline. 7 be my guest.** *Informal.* do as you like. ◆ *vb* **8** *(intr)* (in theatre and broadcasting) to be a guest: *to guest on a show.* [Old English *giest* guest, stranger, enemy; related to Old Norse *gestr,* Gothic *gasts,* Old High German *gast,* Old Slavonic *gostĭ,* Latin *hostis* enemy]

guest beer *n* a draught beer stocked by a bar, often for a limited period, in addition to its usual range.

guesthouse ('gɛst,haus) *n* a private home or boarding house offering accommodation, esp. to travellers.

guest rope *n Nautical.* any line sent or trailed over the side of a vessel as a convenience for boats drawing alongside, as an aid in warping or towing, etc.

Guevara (gə'vɑ:rə; *Spanish* ge'βara) *n* **Ernesto** (ɛr'nesto), known as *Che Guevara.* 1928–67, Latin American politician and soldier, born in Argentina. He developed guerrilla warfare as a tool for revolution and was instrumental in Castro's victory in Cuba (1959), where he held government posts until 1965. He was killed while training guerrillas in Bolivia.

guff (gʌf) *n Slang.* ridiculous or insolent talk. [C19: imitative of empty talk; compare dialect Norwegian *gufs* puff of wind]

guffaw (gʌ'fɔ:) *n* **1** a crude and boisterous laugh. ◆ *vb* **2** to laugh crudely and boisterously or express (something) in this way. [C18: of imitative origin]

Guggenheim Museum ('gugən,haɪm) *n* a museum of modern art in New York: designed by Frank Lloyd Wright (1956–59).

GUI ('gu:i:) *acronym for* graphical user interface.

Guiana (gaɪ'ænə, gɪ'ɑ:nə) *or* **The Guianas** *n* a region of NE South America, including Guyana, Surinam, French Guiana, and the **Guiana Highlands** (largely in SE Venezuela and partly in N Brazil). Area: about 1 787 000 sq. km (690 000 sq. miles). ▸ **Guianese** (,gaɪə'ni:z, ,gɪə-) *or* **Guianan** (gaɪ'ænən, gɪ'ɑ:nən) *adj, n*

guichet ('gi:ʃeɪ) *n* a grating, hatch, or small opening in a wall, esp. a ticket-office window. [C19: from French]

guid (gyd, gɪd) *adj* a Scot. word for **good.**

guidance ('gaɪdᵊns) *n* **1** leadership, instruction, or direction. **2a** counselling or advice on educational, vocational, or psychological matters. **2b** *(as modifier): the marriage-guidance counsellor.* **3** something that guides. **4** any process by which the flight path of a missile is controlled in flight. See also **guided missile.**

guide (gaɪd) *vb* **1** to lead the way for (a person). **2** to control the movement or course of (an animal, vehicle, etc.) by physical action; steer. **3** to supervise or instruct (a person). **4** *(tr)* to direct the affairs of (a person, company, nation, etc.): *he guided the country through the war.* **5** *(tr)* to advise or influence (a person) in his standards or opinions: *let truth guide you always.* ◆ *n* **6a** a person, animal, or thing that guides. **6b** *(as modifier): a guide dog.* **7** a person, usually paid, who conducts tour expeditions, etc. **8** a model or criterion, as in moral standards or accuracy. **9** See **guidebook. 10** a book that instructs or explains the fundamentals of a subject or skill: *a guide to better living.* **11** any device that directs the motion of a tool or machine part. **12a** a mark, sign, etc., that points the way. **12b** *(in combination): guidepost.* **13** *Spiritualism.* a spirit believed to influence a medium so as to direct what he utters and convey messages through him. **14a** *Naval.* a ship in a formation used as a reference for manoeuvres, esp. with relation to maintaining the correct formation and disposition. **14b** *Military.* a soldier stationed to one side of a column or line to regulate alignment, show the way, etc. [C14: from (Old) French *guider,* of Germanic origin; compare Old English *wītan* to observe] ▸ **'guidable** *adj* ▸ **'guideless** *adj* ▸ **'guider** *n* ▸ **'guiding** *adj, n*

Guide (gaɪd) *n (sometimes not cap.)* a member of an organization for girls equivalent to the Scouts. U.S. equivalent: **Girl Scout.**

guidebook ('gaɪd,buk) *n* a handbook with information for visitors to a place, as a historic building, museum, or foreign country. Also called: **guide.**

guided missile *n* a missile, esp. one that is rocket-propelled, having a flight path controlled during flight either by radio signals or by internal preset or self-actuating homing devices. See also **command guidance, field guidance, homing guidance, inertial guidance, terrestrial guidance.**

guide dog *n* a dog that has been specially trained to live with and accompany someone who is blind, enabling the blind person to move about safely.

guideline ('gaɪd,laɪn) *n* a principle put forward to set standards or determine a course of action.

guidepost ('gaɪd,pəust) *n* **1** a sign on a post by a road indicating directions. **2** a principle or guideline.

Guider ('gaɪdə) *n (sometimes not cap.)* **1** in full: **Guide Guider.** a woman leader of a company of Guides. **2 Brownie Guider.** a woman leader of a pack of Brownie Guides.

guide rope *n* **1** a stay or rope attached to another rope that is lifting a load, either to steady the load or guide the rope. **2** another name for **dragrope** (sense 2).

guide vanes *pl n* fixed aerofoils that direct air, gas, or water into the moving blades of a turbine or into or around bends in ducts with minimum loss of energy.

Guido d'Arezzo (*Italian* 'gwi:do da'rettso) *n* ?995–?1050 A.D., Italian Benedictine monk and musical theorist: reputed inventor of solmization.

guidon ('gaɪdᵊn) *n* **1** a small pennant, used as a marker or standard, esp. by cavalry regiments. **2** the man or vehicle that carries this. [C16: from French, from Old Provençal *guidoo,* from *guida* GUIDE]

Guienne *or* **Guyenne** (*French* gɥijɛn) *n* a former province of SW France: formed, with Gascony, the duchy of Aquitaine during the 12th century.

guild *or* **gild** (gɪld) *n* **1** an organization, club, or fellowship. **2** (esp. in medieval Europe) an association of men sharing the same interests, such as merchants or artisans: formed for mutual aid and protection and to maintain craft standards or pursue some other purpose such as communal worship. **3** *Ecology.* a group of plants, such as a group of epiphytes, that share certain habits or characteristics. [C14: of Scandinavian origin; compare Old Norse *gjald* payment, *gildi* guild; related to Old English *gield* offering, Old High German *gelt* money]

guilder, gilder, ('gɪldə) *or* **gulden** *n, pl* **-ders, -der** *or* **-dens, -den. 1** the standard monetary unit of the Netherlands, divided into 100 cents. Also called: **florin. 2** the standard monetary unit of the Netherlands Antilles and Surinam, divided into 100 cents. **3** any of various former gold or silver coins of Germany, Austria, or the Netherlands. [C15: changed from Middle Dutch *gulden,* literally: GOLDEN]

Guildford ('gɪlfəd) *n* a city in S England, the administrative centre of Surrey: cathedral (1936–68); seat of the University of Surrey (1966). Pop.: 65 998 (1991).

guildhall ('gɪld,hɔ:l) *n* **1** *Brit.* **1a** the hall of a guild or corporation. **1b** a town hall. **2** Also: **gildhall.** the meeting place of a medieval guild.

guildsman, gildsman ('gɪldzmən) *or* (*fem*) **guildswoman, gildswoman** *n, pl* **-men** *or* **-women.** a member of a guild.

guild socialism *n* a form of socialism advocated in Britain in the early 20th century. Industry was to be owned by the state but managed and controlled by worker-controlled guilds. ▸ **guild socialist** *n*

guile (gaɪl) *n* clever or crafty character or behaviour. [C18: from Old French *guile,* of Germanic origin; see WILE] ▸ **'guileful** *adj* ▸ **'guilefully** *adv* ▸ **'guilefulness** *n*

guileless ('gaɪllɪs) *adj* free from guile; ingenuous. ▸ **'guilelessly** *adv* ▸ **'guilelessness** *n*

Guilin ('gweɪ'lɪn), **Kweilin,** *or* **Kuei-lin** *n* a city in S China, in Guangxi Zhuang AR on the Li River: noted for the unusual caves and formations of the surrounding karst scenery; trade and manufacturing centre. Pop.: 364 130 (1990 est.).

Guillaume de Lorris (*French* gijom də lɔris) *n* 13th century, French poet who wrote the first 4058 lines of the allegorical romance, the *Roman de la rose,* continued by Jean de Meung.

guillemet ('gɪlɪˌmɛt) *n Printing.* another name for **duckfoot quote.**

guillemot ('gɪlɪˌmɒt) *n* any northern oceanic diving bird of the genera *Uria* and *Cepphus,* having a black-and-white plumage and long narrow bill: family *Alcidae* (auks, etc.), order *Charadriiformes.* [C17: from French, diminutive of *Guillaume* William]

guilloche (gɪ'lɒʃ) *n* an ornamental band or border with a repeating pattern of two or more interwoven wavy lines, as in architecture. [C19: from French: tool used in ornamental work, perhaps from *Guillaume* William]

guillotine *n* ('gɪləˌtiːn). **1a** a device for beheading persons, consisting of a weighted blade set between two upright posts. **1b the guillotine.** execution by this instrument. **2** a device for cutting or trimming sheet material, such as paper or sheet metal, consisting of a blade inclined at a small angle that descends onto the sheet. **3** a surgical instrument for removing tonsils, growths in the throat, etc. **4** Also called: **closure by compartment.** (in Parliament, etc.) a form of closure under which a bill is divided into compartments, groups of which must be completely dealt with each day. ◆ *vb* (ˌgɪlə'tiːn). (*tr*) **5** to behead (a person) by guillotine. **6** (in Parliament, etc.) to limit debate on (a bill, motion, etc.) by the guillotine. [C18: from French, named after Joseph Ignace *Guillotin* (1738–1814), French physician, who advocated its use in 1789] ▸ **ˌguillo'tiner** *n*

guilt (gɪlt) *n* **1** the fact or state of having done wrong or committed an offence. **2** responsibility for a criminal or moral offence deserving punishment or a penalty. **3** remorse or self-reproach caused by feeling that one is responsible for a wrong or offence. **4** *Archaic.* sin or crime. [Old English *gylt,* of obscure origin]

guiltless ('gɪltlɪs) *adj* free of all responsibility for wrongdoing or crime; innocent. ▸ **'guiltlessly** *adv* ▸ **'guiltlessness** *n*

guilty ('gɪltɪ) *adj* **guiltier, guiltiest. 1** responsible for an offence or misdeed. **2** *Law.* having committed an offence or adjudged to have done so: *the accused was found guilty.* **3 plead guilty.** *Law.* (of a person charged with an offence) to admit responsibility; confess. **4** of, showing, or characterized by guilt. ▸ **'guiltily** *adv* ▸ **'guiltiness** *n*

guimpe (gɪmp, gæmp) *n* **1** a short blouse with sleeves worn under a pinafore dress. **2** a fill-in for a low-cut dress. **3** a piece of starched cloth covering the chest and shoulders of a nun's habit. **4** a variant spelling of **gimp.** [C19: variant of GIMP]

Guin. *abbrev. for* Guinea.

guinea ('gɪnɪ) *n* **1a** a British gold coin taken out of circulation in 1813, worth 21 shillings. **1b** the sum of 21 shillings (£1.05), still used in some contexts, as in quoting professional fees. **2** See **guinea fowl. 3** *U.S. slang, derogatory.* an Italian or a person of Italian descent. [C16: the coin was originally made of gold from Guinea]

Guinea ('gɪnɪ) *n* **1** a republic in West Africa, on the Atlantic: established as the colony of French Guinea in 1890 and became an independent republic in 1958. Official language: French. Religion: Muslim majority and animist. Currency: franc. Capital: Conakry. Pop.: 7 477 000 (1998 est.). Area: 245 855 sq. km (94 925 sq. miles). **2** (formerly) the coastal region of West Africa, between Cape Verde and Namibe (formerly Moçâmedes; Angola): divided by a line of volcanic peaks into **Upper Guinea** (between The Gambia and Cameroon) and **Lower Guinea** (between Cameroon and S Angola). **3 Gulf of.** a large inlet of the S Atlantic on the W coast of Africa, extending from Cape Palmas, Liberia, to Cape Lopez, Gabon: contains two large bays, the Bight of Biafra and the Bight of Benin, separated by the Niger delta. ▸ **'Guinean** *adj, n*

Guinea-Bissau *n* a republic in West Africa, on the Atlantic: first discovered by the Portuguese in 1446 and of subsequent importance in the slave trade; made a colony in 1879; became an independent republic in 1974. Official languages: Portuguese; Cape Verde creole is widely spoken. Religion: animist majority and Muslim. Currency: peso. Capital: Bissau. Pop.: 1 206 000 (1998 est.). Area: 36 125 sq. km (13 948 sq. miles). Former name (until 1974): **Portuguese Guinea.**

Guinea corn *n* another name for **durra.**

guinea fowl *or* **guinea** *n* any gallinaceous bird, esp. *Numida meleagris,* of the family *Numididae* of Africa and SW Asia, having a dark plumage mottled with white, a naked head and neck, and a heavy rounded body.

guinea grains *pl n* another name for **grains of paradise.**

guinea hen *n* a guinea fowl, esp. a female.

Guinea pepper *n* a variety of the pepper plant *Capsicum frutescens,* from which cayenne pepper is obtained.

guinea pig *n* **1** a domesticated cavy, probably descended from *Cavia porcellus,* commonly kept as a pet and used in scientific experiments. **2** a person or thing used for experimentation. [C17: origin uncertain: perhaps from old use of the name *Guinea* to mean any remote unknown land]

Guinea worm *n* a parasitic nematode worm, *Dracunculus medinensis,* that lives beneath the skin in man and other vertebrates and is common in India and Africa.

Guinevere ('gwɪnɪˌvɪə), **Guenevere** ('gwɛnɪˌvɪə), *or* **Guinever** ('gwɪnɪvə) *n* (in Arthurian legend) the wife of King Arthur and paramour of Lancelot.

Guinness ('gɪnɪs) *n* Sir **Alec.** born 1914, British stage and film actor. His films include *The Bridge on the River Kwai* (1957), for which he won an Oscar, and *Star Wars* (1977); TV roles include Le Carré's George Smiley.

guipure (gɪ'pjʊə) *n* **1** Also called: **guipure lace.** any of many types of heavy lace that have their pattern connected by brides, rather than supported on a net mesh. **2** a heavy corded trimming; gimp. [C19: from Old French *guipure,* from *guiper* to cover with cloth, of Germanic origin; see WIPE, WHIP]

Guiscard (*French* giskar) *n* **Robert** (rɔbɛr). ?1015–85, Norman conqueror in S Italy.

guise (gaɪz) *n* **1** semblance or pretence: *under the guise of friendship.* **2** external appearance in general. **3** *Archaic.* manner or style of dress. **4** *Obsolete.* customary behaviour or manner. ◆ *vb* **5** *Dialect.* to disguise or be disguised in fancy dress. **6** (*tr*) *Archaic.* to dress or dress up. [C13: from Old French *guise,* of Germanic origin; see WISE[2]]

guiser ('gaɪzə) *n* a mummer, esp. at Christmas or Halloween revels.

guitar (gɪ'tɑː) *n Music.* a plucked stringed instrument originating in Spain, usually having six strings, a flat sounding board with a circular sound hole in the centre, a flat back, and a fretted fingerboard. Range: more than three octaves upwards from E on the first leger line below the bass staff. See also **electric guitar, bass guitar, Hawaiian guitar.** [C17: from Spanish *guitarra,* from Arabic *qītār,* from Greek *kithara* CITHARA] ▸ **gui'tarist** *n* ▸ **gui'tar-ˌlike** *adj*

guitarfish (gɪ'tɑːˌfɪʃ) *n, pl* **-fish** *or* **-fishes.** any marine sharklike ray of the family *Rhinobatidae,* having a guitar-shaped body with a stout tail and occurring at the bottom of the sea.

Guitry (*French* gitri) *n* **Sacha** (saʃa). 1885–1957, French actor, dramatist, and film director, born in Russia: plays include *Nono* (1905).

Guiyang ('gweɪ'jæŋ), **Kweiyang,** *or* **Kuei-yang** *n* a city in S China, capital of Guizhou province: reached by rail in 1959, with subsequent industrial growth. Pop.: 1 530 000 (1991 est.).

Guizhou ('gweɪ'dʒəʊ), **Kweichow,** *or* **Kueichou** *n* a province of SW China, between the Yangtze and Xi Rivers: a high plateau. Capital: Guiyang. Pop.: 35 080 000 (1996 est.). Area: 174 000 sq. km (69 278 sq. miles).

Guizot (*French* gizo) *n* **François Pierre Guillaume** (frɑ̃swa pjɛr gijom). 1787–1874, French statesman and historian. As chief minister (1840–48), his reactionary policies contributed to the outbreak of the revolution of 1848.

Gujarat *or* **Gujerat** (ˌgudʒə'rɑːt) *n* **1** a state of W India: formed in 1960 from the N and W parts of Bombay State; one of India's most industrialized states. Capital: Gandhinagar. Pop.: 44 235 000 (1994 est.). Area: 196 024 sq. km (75 268 sq. miles). **2** a region of W India, north of the Narmada River: generally includes the areas north of Bombay city where Gujarati is spoken.

Gujarati *or* **Gujerati** (ˌgudʒə'rɑːtɪ) *n* **1** (*pl* **-ti**) a member of a people of India living chiefly in Gujarat. **2** the state language of Gujarat, belonging to the Indic branch of the Indo-European family. ◆ *adj* **3** of or relating to Gujarat, its people, or their language.

Gujranwala (guːdʒ'rɑːnˌwʌlə) *n* a city in NE Pakistan: textile manufacturing. Pop.: 1 663 000 (1995 est.).

Gulag ('guːlæg) *n* (formerly) the central administrative department of the Soviet security service, established in 1930, responsible for maintaining prisons and forced labour camps. [C20: from Russian *G(lavnoye) U(pravleniye Ispravitelno-Trudovykh) Lag(erei)* Main Administration for Corrective Labour Camps]

gular ('guːlə, 'gjuː-) *adj Anatomy.* of, relating to, or situated in the throat or oesophagus. [C19: from Latin *gula* throat]

Gulbenkian (gul'bɛŋkɪən) *n* **1 Calouste Sarkis** (kæ'luːst 'sɑːkɪz). 1869–1955, British industrialist, born in Turkey. He endowed the international Gulbenkian Foundation for the advancement of the arts, science, and education. **2** his son, **Nubar Sarkis** ('nuːbɑː 'sɑːkɪz). 1896–1972, British industrialist, diplomat, and philanthropist.

gulch (gʌltʃ) *n U.S. and Canadian.* a narrow ravine cut by a fast stream. [C19: of obscure origin]

gulden ('guldᵊn) *n, pl* **-dens** *or* **-den.** a variant of **guilder.**

Gülek Bogaz (guː'lɛk bəʊ'gɑːz) *n* the Turkish name for the **Cilician Gates.**

gules (gjuːlz) *adj* (*usually postpositive*), *n Heraldry.* red. [C14: from Old French *gueules* red fur worn around the neck, from *gole* throat, from Latin *gula* GULLET]

gulf (gʌlf) *n* **1** a large deep bay. **2** a deep chasm. **3** something that divides or separates, such as a lack of understanding. **4** something that engulfs, such as a whirlpool. ◆ *vb* **5** (*tr*) to swallow up; engulf. [C14: from Old French *golfe,* from Italian *golfo,* from Greek *kolpos*] ▸ **'gulfˌlike** *adj* ▸ **'gulfy** *adj*

Gulf (gʌlf) *n* **the. 1** the Persian Gulf. **2** *Austral.* **2a** the Gulf of Carpentaria. **2b** (*modifier*) of, relating to, or adjoining the Gulf: *Gulf country.* **3** *N.Z.* the Hauraki Gulf.

Gulf States *pl n* **the. 1** the oil-producing states around the Persian Gulf: Iran, Iraq, Kuwait, Saudi Arabia, Bahrain, Qatar, the United Arab Emirates, and Oman. **2** the states of the U.S. that border on the Gulf of Mexico: Alabama, Florida, Louisiana, Mississippi, and Texas.

Gulf Stream *n* **1** a relatively warm ocean current flowing northeastwards off the Atlantic coast of the U.S. from the Gulf of Mexico. **2** another name for **North Atlantic Drift.**

Gulf War *n* **1** the war (1991) between U.S.-led UN forces and Iraq, following Iraq's invasion of Kuwait. **2** See **Iran-Iraq War.**

Gulf War syndrome *n* a group of various debilitating symptoms experienced by many soldiers who served in the Gulf War of 1991. It is claimed to be associated with damage to the central nervous system, caused by exposure to pesticides containing organophosphates.

gulfweed ('gʌlf,wiːd) *n* any brown seaweed of the genus *Sargassum*, esp. *S. bacciferum*, having air bladders and forming dense floating masses in tropical Atlantic waters, esp. the Gulf Stream. Also called: **sargasso, sargasso weed.**

gull[1] (gʌl) *n* any aquatic bird of the genus *Larus* and related genera, such as *L. canus* (**common gull** or **mew**) having long pointed wings, short legs, and a mostly white plumage: family *Laridae*, order *Charadriiformes*. Related adj: **larine.** [C15: of Celtic origin; compare Welsh *gwylan*] ▸ **'gull-,like** *adj*

gull[2] (gʌl) *Archaic.* ♦ *n* **1** a person who is easily fooled or cheated. ♦ *vb* **2** (*tr*) to fool, cheat, or hoax. [C16: perhaps from dialect *gull* unfledged bird, probably from *gul*, from Old Norse *gulr* yellow]

Gullah ('gʌlə) *n* **1** (*pl* **-lahs** *or* **-lah**) a member of a Negroid people living on the Sea Islands or in the coastal regions of South Carolina, Georgia, and NE Florida. **2** the creolized English spoken by these people.

gullet ('gʌlɪt) *n* **1** a less formal name for the **oesophagus.** Related adj: **oesophageal. 2** the throat or pharynx. **3** *Mining, quarrying.* a preliminary cut in excavating, wide enough to take the vehicle that removes the earth. [C14: from Old French *goulet*, diminutive of *goule* throat, from Latin *gula* throat]

gullible ('gʌləbᵊl) *adj* easily taken in or tricked. ▸ **,gulli'bility** *n* ▸ **'gullibly** *adv*

gull-wing ('gʌl,wɪŋ) *adj* **1** (of a car door) opening upwards. **2** (of an aircraft wing) having a short upward-sloping inner section and a longer horizontal outer section.

gully[1] *or* **gulley** ('gʌlɪ) *n, pl* **-lies** *or* **-leys. 1** a channel or small valley, esp. one cut by heavy rainwater. **2** *N.Z.* a small bush-clad valley. **3** a deep, wide fissure between two buttresses in a mountain face, sometimes containing a stream or scree. **4** *Cricket.* **4a** a fielding position between the slips and point. **4b** a fielder in this position. **5** either of the two channels at the side of a tenpin bowling lane. ♦ *vb* **-lies, -lying, -lied. 6** (*tr*) to make (channels) in (the ground, sand, etc.). [C16: from French *goulet* neck of a bottle; see GULLET]

gully[2] ('gʌlɪ) *n, pl* **-lies.** *Scot.* a large knife, such as a butcher's knife. [C16: of obscure origin]

gulosity (gju'lɒsɪtɪ) *n Archaic.* greed or gluttony. [C16: from Late Latin *gulōsitās*, from Latin *gulōsus* gluttonous, from *gula* gullet]

gulp (gʌlp) *vb* **1** (*tr*; often foll. by *down*) to swallow rapidly, esp. in large mouthfuls: *to gulp down food.* **2** (*tr*; often foll. by *back*) to stifle or choke: *to gulp back sobs.* **3** (*intr*) to swallow air convulsively, as while drinking, because of nervousness, surprise, etc. **4** (*intr*) to make a noise, as when swallowing too quickly. ♦ *n* **5** the act of gulping. **6** the quantity taken in a gulp. [C15: from Middle Dutch *gulpen*, of imitative origin] ▸ **'gulper** *n* ▸ **'gulpingly** *adv* ▸ **'gulpy** *adj*

gulper eel *or* **fish** *n* any deep-sea eel-like fish of the genera *Eurypharynx* and *Saccopharynx* and order *Lyomeri*, having the ability to swallow large prey.

gum[1] (gʌm) *n* **1** any of various sticky substances that exude from certain plants, hardening on exposure to air and dissolving or forming viscous masses in water. **2** any of various products, such as adhesives, that are made from such exudates. **3** any sticky substance used as an adhesive; mucilage; glue. **4** *N.Z.* short for **kauri gum. 5** See **chewing gum, bubble gum,** and **gumtree. 6** *Chiefly Brit.* a gumdrop. ♦ *vb* **gums, gumming, gummed. 7** to cover or become covered, clogged, or stiffened with or as if with gum. **8** (*tr*) to stick together or in place with gum. **9** (*intr*) to emit or form gum. ♦ See also **gum up.** [C14: from Old French *gomme*, from Latin *gummi*, from Greek *kommi*, from Egyptian *kemai*] ▸ **'gumless** *adj* ▸ **'gum,like** *adj*

gum[2] (gʌm) *n* the fleshy tissue that covers the jawbones around the bases of the teeth. Technical name: **gingiva.** Related adj: **gingival.** [Old English *gōma* jaw; related to Old Norse *gōmr*, Middle High German *gūme*, Lithuanian *gomurỹs*]

gum[3] (gʌm) *n* used in the mild oath *by gum!* [C19: euphemism for GOD]

gum accroides (ə'krɔɪdiːz) *n* another name for **acaroid gum.**

gum ammoniac *n* another name for **ammoniac**[2].

gum arabic *n* a gum exuded by certain acacia trees, esp. *Acacia senegal:* used in the manufacture of ink, food thickeners, pills, emulsifiers, etc. Also called: **acacia, gum acacia.**

gum benzoin *n* another name for **benzoin.**

gumbo *or* **gombo** ('gʌmbəʊ) *n, pl* **-bos.** *U.S. and Canadian.* **1** the mucilaginous pods of okra. **2** another name for **okra. 3** a soup or stew thickened with okra pods. **4** a fine soil in the W prairies that becomes muddy when wet. [C19: from Louisiana French *gombo*, of Bantu origin]

Gumbo ('gʌmbəʊ) *n* (*sometimes not cap.*) a French patois spoken by Creoles in Louisiana and the Caribbean. [see GUMBO]

gumboil ('gʌm,bɔɪl) *n* an abscess on the gums, often at the root of a decayed tooth. Also called: **parulis.**

gumboots ('gʌm,buːts) *pl n* another name for **Wellington boots** (sense 1).

gumbotil ('gʌmbətɪl) *n* a sticky clay formed by the weathering of glacial drift. [C20: from GUMBO + TIL(L)[4]]

gum digger *n N.Z.* a person who digs for fossilized kauri gum in a gum field.

gum digger's spear *n N.Z.* a long steel probe used by gum diggers digging for kauri gum.

gumdrop ('gʌm,drɒp) *n* a small jelly-like sweet containing gum arabic and various colourings and flavourings. Also called (esp. Brit.): **gum.**

gum elastic *n* another name for **rubber**[1] (sense 1).

gum elemi *n* another name for **elemi.**

gum field *n N.Z.* an area of land containing buried fossilized kauri gum.

gumlands ('gʌm,lændz) *pl n N.Z.* infertile land from which the original kauri bush has been removed or burnt producing only kauri gum.

gumma ('gʌmə) *n, pl* **-mas** *or* **-mata** (-mətə). *Pathol.* a rubbery tumour characteristic of advanced syphilis, occurring esp. on the skin, liver, brain or heart. [C18: from New Latin, from Latin *gummi* GUM[1]] ▸ **'gummatous** *adj*

gummite ('gʌmaɪt) *n* an orange or yellowish amorphous secondary mineral consisting of hydrated uranium oxides.

gummosis (gʌ'məʊsɪs) *n* the abnormal production of excessive gum in certain trees, esp. fruit trees, as a result of wounding, infection, adverse weather conditions, severe pruning, etc. [C19: from New Latin; see GUMMA]

gummous ('gʌməs) *or* **gummose** ('gʌməʊs) *adj Rare.* resembling or consisting of gum.

gummy[1] ('gʌmɪ) *adj* **-mier, -miest. 1** sticky or tacky. **2** consisting of, coated with, or clogged by gum or a similar substance. **3** producing gum. [C14: from GUM[1] + -Y[1]] ▸ **'gumminess** *n*

gummy[2] ('gʌmɪ) *adj* **-mier, -miest. 1** toothless; not showing one's teeth. ♦ *n, pl* **-mies. 2** *Austral.* a small crustacean-eating shark, *Mustelus antarcticus*, with bony ridges resembling gums in its mouth. **3** *N.Z.* an old ewe that has lost its incisor teeth. [C20: from GUM[2] + -Y[1]] ▸ **'gummily** *adv*

gum nut *n Austral.* the hardened seed container of the gum tree *Eucalyptus gummifera.*

gum plant *or* **gumweed** ('gʌm,wiːd) *n* any of several American yellow-flowered plants of the genus *Grindelia*, esp. *G. robusta*, that have sticky flower heads: family *Compositae* (composites).

gumption ('gʌmpʃən) *n Informal.* **1** *Brit.* common sense or resourcefulness. **2** initiative or courage: *you haven't the gumption to try.* [C18: originally Scottish, of unknown origin]

gum resin *n* a mixture of resin and gum obtained from various plants and trees. See also **bdellium, gamboge.**

gumshield ('gʌm,ʃiːld) *n* a plate or strip of soft waxy substance used by boxers to protect the teeth and gums. Also called: **mouthpiece.**

gumshoe ('gʌm,ʃuː) *n* **1** a waterproof overshoe. **2** *U.S. and Canadian.* a rubber-soled shoe. **3** *U.S. and Canadian slang.* a detective or one who moves about stealthily. **4** *U.S. and Canadian slang.* a stealthy action or movement. ♦ *vb* **-shoes, -shoeing, -shoed. 5** (*intr*) *U.S. and Canadian slang.* to act stealthily.

gumsucker ('gʌm,sʌkə) *n Austral. informal.* (in the 19th century) **a** a native-born Australian. **b** a native of Victoria.

gumtree ('gʌm,triː) *n* **1** any of various trees that yield gum, such as the eucalyptus, sweet gum, and sour gum. Sometimes shortened to **gum. 2** Also called: **gumwood.** the wood of the eucalyptus tree. **3 up a gumtree.** *Informal.* in a very awkward position; in difficulties.

gum up *vb* (*tr, adv*) **1** to cover, dab, or stiffen with gum. **2** *Informal.* to make a mess of; bungle (often in the phrase **gum up the works**).

gun (gʌn) *n* **1a** a weapon with a metallic tube or barrel from which a missile is discharged, usually by force of an explosion. It may be portable or mounted. In a military context the term applies specifically to a flat-trajectory artillery piece. **1b** (*as modifier*): *a gun barrel.* **2** the firing of a gun as a salute or signal, as in military ceremonial. **3** a member of or a place in a shooting party or syndicate. **4** any device used to project something under pressure: *a grease gun; a spray gun.* **5** *U.S. slang.* an armed criminal; gunman. **6** *Austral. and N.Z. slang.* **6a** an expert. **6b** (*as modifier*): *a gun shearer; a gun batsman.* **7 go great guns.** *Slang.* to act or function with great speed, intensity, etc. **8 jump** *or* **beat the gun. 8a** (of a runner, etc.) to set off before the starting signal is given. **8b** *Informal.* to act prematurely. **9 spike someone's guns.** See **spike**[1] (sense 15). **10 stick to one's guns.** *Informal.* to maintain one's opinions or intentions in spite of opposition. ♦ *vb* **guns, gunning, gunned. 11** (when *tr*, often foll. by *down*) to shoot (someone) with a gun. **12** (*tr*) to press hard on the accelerator of (an engine): *to gun the engine of a car.* **13** (*intr*) to hunt with a gun. ♦ See also **gun for.** [C14: probably from a female pet name shortened from the Scandinavian name *Gunnhildr* (from Old Norse *gunnr* war + *hildr* war)]

gunboat ('gʌn,bəʊt) *n* a small shallow-draft vessel carrying mounted guns and used by coastal patrols, etc.

gunboat diplomacy *n* diplomacy conducted by threats of military intervention, esp. by a major power against a militarily weak state.

gun carriage *n* a mechanical frame on which a gun is mounted for adjustment and firing or for transportation.

guncotton ('gʌn,kɒtᵊn) *n* cellulose nitrate containing a relatively large amount of nitrogen: used as an explosive.

gun dog *n* **1** a dog trained to work with a hunter or gamekeeper, esp. in retrieving, pointing at, or flushing game. **2** a dog belonging to any breed adapted to these activities.

gunfight ('gʌn,faɪt) *n Chiefly U.S.* a fight between persons using firearms. ▸ **'gun,fighter** *n* ▸ **'gun,fighting** *n*

gunfire ('gʌn,faɪə) *n* **1** the firing of one or more guns, esp. when done repeatedly. **2** the use of firearms, as contrasted with other military tactics.

gunflint ('gʌn,flɪnt) *n* a piece of flint in a flintlock's hammer used to strike the spark that ignites the charge.

gun for *vb* (*intr, prep*) **1** to search for in order to reprimand, punish, or kill. **2** to try earnestly for: *he was gunning for promotion.*

gunge (gʌndʒ) *Informal.* ♦ *n* **1** sticky, rubbery, or congealed matter. ♦ *vb* **2** (*tr; usually passive;* foll. by *up*) to block or encrust with gunge; clog. [C20: of imitative origin, perhaps influenced by GOO and SPONGE] ▸ **'gungy** *adj*

gung ho (gʌŋ həʊ) *adj* **1** extremely enthusiastic and enterprising, sometimes to excess. **2** extremely keen to participate in military combat. [C20: pidgin English, from Mandarin Chinese *kung* work + *ho* together]

gunite ('gʌn,aɪt) *n Civil engineering.* a cement-sand mortar that is sprayed onto formwork, walls, or rock by a compressed air ejector giving a very dense strong concrete layer: used to repair reinforced concrete, to line tunnel walls or mine airways, etc. [C20: from GUN + -ITE[1]]

gunk (gʌŋk) *n Informal.* slimy, oily, or filthy matter. [C20: perhaps of imitative origin]

gunlock ('gʌn,lɒk) *n* the mechanism in some firearms that causes the charge to be exploded.

gunman ('gʌnmən) *n, pl* **-men. 1** a man who is armed with a gun, esp. unlawfully. **2** a man who is skilled with a gun. **3** *U.S.* a person who makes, repairs, or has expert knowledge of guns. ▸ **'gunman,ship** *n*

gunmetal ('gʌn,metᵊl) *n* **1** a type of bronze containing copper (88 per cent), tin (8–10 per cent), and zinc (2–4 per cent): used for parts that are subject to wear or to corrosion, esp. by sea water. **2** any of various dark grey metals used for toys, belt buckles, etc. **3** a dark grey colour with a purplish or bluish tinge.

gun moll *n Slang.* a female criminal or a woman who associates with criminals.

Gunn (gʌn) *n* **Thom(son William)**. born 1929, British poet resident in the U.S.A. His works include *Fighting Terms* (1954), *My Sad Captains* (1961), *Jack Straw's Castle* (1976), and *The Man with Night Sweats* (1992).

Gunnar ('gunɑː) *n Norse myth.* brother of Gudrun and husband of Brynhild, won for him by Sigurd. He corresponds to Gunther in the *Nibelungenlied.*

gunned (gʌnd) *adj* **a** having a gun or guns as specified: *heavily gunned.* **b** (*in combination*): *three-gunned.*

Gunn effect (gʌn) *n* a phenomenon observed in some semiconductors in which a steady electric field of magnitude greater than a threshold value generates electrical oscillations with microwave frequencies. [C20: named after John Battiscombe *Gunn* (born 1928), British physicist]

gunnel[1] ('gʌnᵊl) *n* any eel-like blennioid fish of the family *Pholidae,* occurring in coastal regions of northern seas. See also **butterfish.** [C17: of unknown origin]

gunnel[2] ('gʌnᵊl) *n* a variant spelling of **gunwale.**

Gunnell ('gʌnᵊl) *n* **Sally.** born 1966, British athlete: Olympic 400-metre hurdles gold medallist (1992).

gunner ('gʌnə) *n* **1** a serviceman who works with, uses, or specializes in guns. **2** *Naval.* (formerly) a warrant officer responsible for the training of gun crews, their performance in action, and accounting for ammunition. **3** (in the British Army) an artilleryman, esp. a private. Abbrev.: **gnr. 4** a person who hunts with a rifle or shotgun. ▸ **'gunner,ship** *n*

gunnera ('gʌnərə) *n* any herbaceous perennial plant of the genus *Gunnera,* found throughout the S hemisphere and cultivated for its large leaves. [C18: named after J. E. *Gunnerus* (1718–73), Norwegian bishop and botanist]

gunnery ('gʌnərɪ) *n* **1** the art and science of the efficient design and use of ordnance, esp. artillery. **2** guns collectively. **3** the use and firing of guns. **4** (*modifier*) of, relating to, or concerned with heavy guns, as in warfare: *a gunnery officer.*

gunning ('gʌnɪŋ) *n* **1** the act or an instance of shooting with guns. **2** the art, practice, or act of hunting game with guns.

gunny ('gʌnɪ) *n, pl* **-nies.** *Chiefly U.S.* **1** a coarse hard-wearing fabric usually made from jute and used for sacks, etc. **2** Also called: **gunny sack.** a sack made from this fabric. [C18: from Hindi *gōnī,* from Sanskrit *gonī* sack, probably of Dravidian origin]

gunpaper ('gʌn,peɪpə) *n* a cellulose nitrate explosive made by treating paper with nitric acid.

gunplay ('gʌn,pleɪ) *n Chiefly U.S.* the use of firearms, as by criminals.

gunpoint ('gʌn,pɔɪnt) *n* **1** the muzzle of a gun. **2 at gunpoint.** being under or using the threat of being shot.

gunpowder ('gʌn,paʊdə) *n* an explosive mixture of potassium nitrate, charcoal, and sulphur (typical proportions are 75:15:10): used in time fuses, blasting, and fireworks. Also called: **black powder.** ▸ **'gun,powdery** *adj*

Gunpowder Plot *n* the unsuccessful conspiracy to blow up James I and Parliament at Westminster on Nov. 5, 1605. See also **Guy Fawkes Day.**

gunpowder tea *n* a fine variety of green tea, each leaf of which is rolled into a pellet.

gun room *n* **1** (esp. in the Royal Navy) the mess allocated to subordinate or junior officers. **2** a room where guns are stored.

gunrunning ('gʌn,rʌnɪŋ) *n* the smuggling of guns and ammunition or other weapons of war into a country. ▸ **'gun,runner** *n*

gunsel ('gʌnsᵊl) *n U.S. slang.* **1** a catamite. **2** a stupid or inexperienced person, esp. a youth. **3** a criminal who carries a gun. [C20: probably from Yiddish *genzel;* compare German *ganslein* gosling, from *gans* GOOSE[1]]

gunshot ('gʌn,ʃɒt) *n* **1a** shot fired from a gun. **1b** (*as modifier*): *gunshot wounds.* **2** the range of a gun. **3** the shooting of a gun.

gun-shy *adj* afraid of a gun or the sound it makes: *a gun-shy dog is useless for shooting.*

gunslinger ('gʌn,slɪŋə) *n Slang.* a gunfighter or gunman, esp. in the Old West. ▸ **'gun,slinging** *n*

gunsmith ('gʌn,smɪθ) *n* a person who manufactures or repairs firearms, esp. portable guns. ▸ **'gun,smithing** *n*

gunstock ('gʌn,stɒk) *n* the wooden or metallic handle or support to which is attached the barrel of a rifle.

Gunter ('gʌntə) *n* **Edmund.** 1581–1626, English mathematician and astronomer, who invented various measuring instruments, including Gunter's chain.

gunter rig ('gʌntə) *n Nautical.* a type of gaffing in which the gaff is hoisted parallel to the mast. [C18: named after E. GUNTER] ▸ **'gunter-,rigged** *adj*

Gunter's chain *n Surveying.* a measuring chain 22 yards in length, or this length as a unit. See **chain** (sense 7). [C17: named after E. GUNTER]

Gunther ('guntə) *n* (in the *Nibelungenlied*) a king of Burgundy, allied with Siegfried, who won for him his wife Brunhild. He corresponds to Gunnar in Norse mythology.

Guntur (gun'tuə) *n* a city in E India, in central Andhra Pradesh: founded by the French in the 18th century; ceded to Britain in 1788. Pop.: 471 051 (1991).

gunwale *or* **gunnel** ('gʌnᵊl) *n* **1** *Nautical.* the top of the side of a boat or the topmost plank of a wooden vessel. **2 full to the gunwales.** completely full; full to overflowing.

gunyah ('gʌnjə) *n Austral.* a bush hut or shelter. [C19: from a native Australian language]

Günz (gunts) *n* the first major Pleistocene glaciation of the Alps. See also **Mindel, Riss, Würm.** [named after the river *Günz* in Germany]

guppy ('gʌpɪ) *n, pl* **-pies.** a small brightly coloured freshwater viviparous cyprinodont fish, *Lebistes reticulatus,* of N South America and the Caribbean: a popular aquarium fish. [C20: named after R. J. L. *Guppy,* 19th-century clergyman of Trinidad who first presented specimens to the British Museum]

Gupta ('gʌptə) *n* the dynasty ruling northern India from the early 4th century to the late 6th century A.D.: the period is famous for achievements in art, science, and mathematics.

Gur (guə) *n* a small group of languages of W Africa, spoken chiefly in Burkina-Faso and Ghana, forming a branch of the Niger-Congo family. Also called: **Voltaic.**

Gurdjieff ('gɛːdjef) *n* **Georgei Ivanovitch** ('dʒɔːdʒɪ ɪ'vanəˌvitʃ). ?1877–1949, Russian mystic: founded a teaching centre in Paris (1922).

gurdwara ('gɜːdwɑːrə) *n* a Sikh place of worship. [C20: from Punjabi *gurduārā,* from Sanskrit *guru* teacher + *dvārā* DOOR]

gurgitation (,gɜːdʒɪ'teɪʃən) *n* surging or swirling motion, esp. of water. [C16: from Late Latin *gurgitātus* engulfed, from *gurgitāre* to engulf, from Latin *gurges* whirlpool]

gurgle ('gɜːgᵊl) *vb* (*intr*) **1** (of liquids, esp. of rivers, streams, etc.) to make low bubbling noises when flowing. **2** to utter low throaty bubbling noises, esp. as a sign of contentment: *the baby gurgled with delight.* ◆ *n* **3** the act or sound of gurgling. [C16: perhaps from Vulgar Latin *gurgulāre,* from Latin *gurguliō* gullet] ▸ **'gurgling** *adj*

gurglet ('gɜːglɪt) *n* another word for **goglet.**

Gurindji (gʊ'rɪndʒɪ) *n* **1** an Aboriginal people of N central Australia. **2** the language of this people.

gurjun ('gɜːdʒən) *n* **1** any of several S or SE Asian dipterocarpaceous trees of the genus *Dipterocarpus* that yield a resin. **2** Also called: **gurjun balsam.** the resin from any of these trees, used as a varnish. [C19: from Bengali *garjon*]

Gurkha ('guəkɑː, 'gɜːkə) *n, pl* **-khas** *or* **-kha. 1** a member of a Hindu people, descended from Brahmins and Rajputs, living chiefly in Nepal, where they achieved dominance after being driven from India by the Muslims. **2** a member of this people serving as a soldier in the Indian or British army.

Gurkhali (,guə'kɑːlɪ, ,gɜː-) *n* the language of the Gurkhas, belonging to the Indic branch of the Indo-European family.

Gurmukhi ('guəmʊkɪ) *n* the script used for writing the Punjabi language. [Sanskrit, from *guru* teacher + *mukh* mouth]

gurn (gərn, gɜːn) *vb* (*intr*) a variant spelling of **girn.**

gurnard ('gɜːnəd) *or* **gurnet** ('gɜːnɪt) *n, pl* **-nard, -nards** *or* **-net, -nets.** any European marine scorpaenoid fish of the family *Triglidae,* such as *Trigla lucerna* (**tub** or **yellow gurnard**), having a heavily armoured head and finger-like pectoral fins. [C14: from Old French *gornard* grunter, from *grognier* to grunt, from Latin *grunnīre*]

gurney ('gɜːnɪ) *n U.S.* a wheeled stretcher for transporting hospital patients. [C20: of unknown origin]

Gurney ('gɜːnɪ) *n* **Ivor (Bertie).** 1890–1937, British poet and composer, noted esp. for his songs and his poems of World War I.

gurrier ('gʌrɪər) *n Dublin dialect.* a low-class tough ill-mannered person. [perhaps from CURRIER]

guru ('gʊruː, 'guːruː) *n* **1** a Hindu or Sikh religious teacher or leader, giving personal spiritual guidance to his disciples. **2** *Often derogatory.* a leader or chief theoretician of a movement, esp. a spiritual or religious cult. **3** *Often facetious.* a leading authority in a particular field: *a cricketing guru.* [C17: from Hindi *gurū,* from Sanskrit *guruh* weighty] ▸ **'guru,ship** *n*

Guru Granth *or* **Guru Granth Sahib** (grʌnt) *n* the sacred scripture of the Sikhs, believed by them to be the embodiment of the gurus. Also called: **Adi Granth.** [from Punjabi, from Sanskrit *grantha* a book]

Guru Nanak ('nɑː,nʌk) *n* 1469–1539, Indian religious leader and founder of Sikhism. Born near Lahore in India, he spent many years as a missionary before returning to the Punjab, where he gained many followers. See also **Ten Gurus.**

gush (gʌʃ) *vb* **1** to pour out or cause to pour out suddenly and profusely, usually with a rushing sound. **2** to act or utter in an overeffusive, affected, or sentimental manner. ◆ *n* **3** a sudden copious flow or emission, esp. of liquid. **4** something that flows out or is emitted. **5** an extravagant and insincere expression of admiration, sentiment, etc. [C14: probably of imitative origin; compare Old Norse *gjósa,* Icelandic *gusa*] ▸ **'gushing** *adj* ▸ **'gushingly** *adv*

gusher ('gʌʃə) *n* **1** a person who gushes, as in being unusually effusive or sentimental. **2** something, such as a spurting oil well, that gushes.

gushy ('gʌʃɪ) *adj* **gushier, gushiest.** *Informal.* displaying excessive admiration or sentimentality. ▸ **'gushily** *adv* ▸ **'gushiness** *n*

gusset ('gʌsɪt) *n* **1** an inset piece of material used esp. to strengthen or enlarge a garment. **2** a triangular metal plate for strengthening a corner joist between two structural members. **3** a piece of mail fitted between armour plates or into the leather or cloth underclothes worn with armour, to give added protection. ◆ *vb* **4** (*tr*) to put a gusset in (a garment). [C15: from Old French *gousset* a piece of mail, a diminutive of *gousse* pod, of unknown origin] ▸ **'gusseted** *adj*

gussy up ('gʌsɪ) *vb* (*tr, adv*) **-sies, -sying, -sied.** *Slang, chiefly U.S.* to give (a person or thing) a smarter or more interesting appearance. [C20: probably from the name *Gussie,* diminutive of *Augusta*]

gust (gʌst) *n* **1** a sudden blast of wind. **2** a sudden rush of smoke, sound, etc. **3** an outburst of emotion. ◆ *vb* (*intr*) **4** to blow in gusts: *the wind was gusting to more than 50 mph.* [C16: from Old Norse *gustr;* related to *gjósa* to GUSH; see GEYSER]

gustation (gʌ'steɪʃən) *n* the act of tasting or the faculty of taste. [C16: from Latin *gustātiō,* from *gustāre* to taste] ▸ **gustatory** ('gʌstətərɪ, -trɪ) *or* **'gustative** *adj*

Gustavo A. Madero (*Spanish* gus'taβo a ma'ðero) *n* the former name (1931–71) of **Guadalupe Hidalgo.**

Gustavus I (gʊ'stɑːvəs) *n* called *Gustavus Vasa.* ?1496–1560, king of Sweden (1523–60). He was elected king after driving the Danes from Sweden (1520–23).

Gustavus II *n* See **Gustavus Adolphus.**

Gustavus VI *n* title of *Gustaf Adolf.* 1882–1973, king of Sweden (1950–73).

Gustavus Adolphus (ə'dɒlfəs) *or* **Gustavus II** *n* 1594–1632, king of Sweden (1611–32). A brilliant general, he waged successful wars with Denmark, Russia, and Poland and in the Thirty Years' War led a Protestant army against the Catholic League and the Holy Roman Empire (1630–32). He defeated Tilly at Leipzig (1631) and Lech (1632) but was killed at the battle of Lützen.

gusto ('gʌstəʊ) *n* vigorous enjoyment, zest, or relish, esp. in the performance of an action: *the aria was sung with great gusto.* [C17: from Spanish: taste, from Latin *gustus* a tasting; see GUSTATION]

gusty ('gʌstɪ) *adj* **gustier, gustiest. 1** blowing or occurring in gusts or characterized by blustery weather: *a gusty wind.* **2** given to sudden outbursts, as of emotion or temperament. ▸ **'gustily** *adv* ▸ **'gustiness** *n*

gut (gʌt) *n* **1a** the lower part of the alimentary canal; intestine. **1b** the entire alimentary canal. Related adj: **visceral. 2** (*often pl*) the bowels or entrails, esp. of an animal. **3** *Slang.* the belly; paunch. **4** See **catgut. 5** a silky fibrous substance extracted from silkworms, used in the manufacture of fishing tackle. **6** a narrow channel or passage. **7** (*pl*) *Informal.* courage, willpower, or daring; forcefulness. **8** (*pl*) *Informal.* the essential part: *the guts of a problem.* **9 hate a person's guts.** *Informal.* to dislike a person very strongly. **10 sweat** *or* **work one's guts out.** *Informal.* to work very hard. ◆ *vb* **guts, gutting, gutted.** (*tr*) **11** to remove the entrails from (fish, etc.). **12** (esp. of fire) to destroy the inside of (a building). **13** to plunder; despoil: *the raiders gutted the city.* **14** to take out the central points of (an article), esp. in summary form. ◆ *adj* **15** *Informal.* arising from or characterized by what is basic, essential, or natural: *a gut problem; a gut reaction.* [Old English *gutt;* related to *gēotan* to flow; see FUSION] ▸ **'gut,like** *adj*

GUT (gʌt) *n acronym for* grand unified theory.

gutbucket ('gʌt,bʌkɪt) *n* a highly emotional style of jazz playing. [C20: from U.S. *gutbucket* a cheap gambling saloon where musicians could play for handouts]

Gutenberg ('guːtᵊn,bɜːg; *German* 'guːtənbɛrk) *n* **Johann** (jo'han), original name *Johannes Gensfleisch.* ?1398–1468, German printer; inventor of printing by movable type.

Gütersloh (*German* 'gyːtərsloː) *n* a town in NW Germany, in North Rhine-Westphalia. Pop.: 83 400 (1989 est.).

Guthrie ('gʌθrɪ) *n* **1 Samuel.** 1782–1848, U.S. chemist: invented percussion priming powder and a punch lock for exploding it, and discovered chloroform (1831). **2** Sir **(William) Tyrone.** 1900–71, English theatrical director. **3 Woody,** full name *Woodrow Wilson Guthrie.* 1912–67, U.S. folk singer and songwriter. His songs include "So Long, it's been Good to Know you" (1940) and "This Land is your Land" (1944).

Guthrun ('gʊðruːn) *n* a variant of **Gudrun.**

gutless ('gʌtlɪs) *adj Informal.* lacking courage or determination.

gut reaction *n* a reaction to a situation derived from a person's instinct and experience.

gutser ('gʌtsə) *n* **come a gutser.** *Austral. and N.Z. slang.* **1** to fall heavily to the ground. **2** to fail through error or misfortune. [C20: from *guts* + -ER[1]]

gutsy ('gʌtsɪ) *adj* **gutsier, gutsiest.** *Slang.* **1** gluttonous; greedy. **2** full of courage, determination, or boldness.

gutta ('gʌtə) *n, pl* **-tae** (-tiː). **1** *Architect.* one of a set of small droplike ornaments, esp. as used on the architrave of a Doric entablature. **2** *Med.* (formerly used in writing prescriptions) a technical name for **drop.** Abbrev.: **gt.** [C16: from Latin: a drop]

gutta-percha ('gʌtə'pɜːtʃə) *n* **1** any of several tropical trees of the sapotaceous genera *Palaquium* and *Payena,* esp. *Palaquium gutta.* **2** a whitish rubber substance derived from the coagulated milky latex of any of these trees: used in electrical insulation and dentistry. [C19: from Malay *getah* gum + *percha* name of a tree that produces it]

guttate ('gʌteɪt) *or* **guttated** *adj Biology.* **1** (esp. of plants) covered with small drops or droplike markings, esp. oil glands. **2** resembling a drop or drops. [C19: from Latin *guttātus* dappled, from *gutta* a drop] ▸ **gut'tation** *n*

gutted ('gʌtɪd) *adj Informal.* disappointed and upset.

gutter ('gʌtə) *n* **1** a channel along the eaves or on the roof of a building, used to collect and carry away rainwater. **2** a channel running along the kerb or the centre of a road to collect and carry away rainwater. **3** either of the two channels running parallel to a tenpin bowling lane. **4** *Printing.* **4a** the space between two pages in a forme. **4b** the white space between the facing pages of an open book. **c** the space between two columns of type. **5** the space left between stamps on a sheet in order to separate them. **6** *Surfing.* a dangerous deep channel formed by currents and waves. **7** *Austral.* (in gold-mining) the channel of a former watercourse that is now a vein of gold. **8 the gutter.** a poverty-stricken, degraded, or criminal environment. ◆ *vb* **9** (*tr*) to make gutters in. **10** (*intr*) to flow in a stream or rivulet. **11** (*intr*) (of a candle) to melt away by the wax forming channels and running down in drops. **12** (*intr*) (of a flame) to flicker and be about to go out. [C13: from Anglo-French *goutiere,* from Old French *goute* a drop, from Latin *gutta*] ▸ **'gutter-,like** *adj*

guttering ('gʌtərɪŋ) *n* **1** the gutters, downpipes, etc., that make up the rainwater disposal system on the outside of a building. **2** the materials used in this system.

gutter press *n* the section of the popular press that seeks sensationalism in its coverage.

guttersnipe ('gʌtə,snaɪp) *n* **1** a child who spends most of his time in the streets, esp. in a slum area. **2** a person regarded as having the behaviour, morals, etc., of one brought up in squalor. [C19: originally a name applied to the common snipe (the bird), then to a person who gathered refuse from gutters in city streets] ▸ **'gutter,snipish** *adj*

guttural ('gʌtərəl) *adj* **1** *Anatomy.* of or relating to the throat. **2** *Phonetics.* pronounced in the throat or the back of the mouth; velar or uvular. **3** raucous. ◆ *n* **4** *Phonetics.* a guttural consonant. [C16: from New Latin *gutturālis* concerning the throat, from Latin *guttur* gullet] ▸ **'gutturally** *adv* ▸ **'gutturalness, ,guttur'ality** *or* **'gutturalism** *n*

gutturalize *or* **gutturalise** ('gʌtərə,laɪz) *vb* **1** (*tr*) *Phonetics.* to change into a guttural speech sound or pronounce with guttural articulation or pharyngeal constriction. **2** to speak or utter in harsh raucous tones. ▸ **,gutturali'zation** *or* **,gutturali'sation** *n*

gutty ('gʌtɪ) *n, pl* **-ties.** *Irish dialect.* **1** an urchin or delinquent. **2** a low-class person. [probably from GUTTER, perhaps from the compound GUTTERSNIPE]

guv (gʌv) *or* **guv'nor** ('gʌvnə) *n Brit.* an informal name for **governor.**

guy[1] (gaɪ) *n* **1** *Informal.* a man or youth. **2** *Brit.* a crude effigy of Guy Fawkes, usually made of old clothes stuffed with straw or rags, that is burnt on top of a bonfire on Guy Fawkes Day. **3** *Brit.* a person in shabby or ludicrously odd clothes. **4** (*pl*) *Informal.* persons of either sex. ◆ *vb* **5** (*tr*) to make fun of; ridicule. [C19: short for Guy FAWKES]

guy[2] (gaɪ) *n* **1** a rope, chain, wire, etc., for anchoring an object, such as a radio mast, in position or for steadying or guiding it while being hoisted or lowered. ◆ *vb* **2** (*tr*) to anchor, steady, or guide with a guy or guys. [C14: probably from Low German; compare Dutch *gei* brail, *geiblok* pulley, Old French *guie* guide, from *guier* to GUIDE]

GUY *international car registration for* Guyana.

Guyana (gaɪ'ænə) *n* a republic in NE South America, on the Atlantic: colonized chiefly by the Dutch in the 17th and 18th centuries; became a British colony in 1831 and an independent republic within the Commonwealth in 1966. Official language: English. Religions: Christian and Hindu. Currency: dollar. Capital: Georgetown. Pop.: 782 000 (1998 est.). Area: about 215 000 sq. km (83 000 sq. miles). Former name (until 1966): **British Guiana.** ▸ **Guyanese** (,gaɪə'niːz) *or* **Guy'anan** *adj, n*

Guyenne (*French* gɥijɛn) *n* a variant spelling of **Guienne.**

Guy Fawkes Day *n* the anniversary of the discovery of the Gunpowder Plot, celebrated on Nov. 5 in Britain with fireworks and bonfires.

guyot ('giː,əʊ) *n* a flat-topped submarine mountain, common in the Pacific Ocean, thought to be an extinct volcano whose summit has been worn down by the erosive action of seawater. Compare **seamount.** [C20: named after A. H. *Guyot* (1807–84), Swiss geographer and geologist]

Guzmán Blanco (*Spanish* guð'man 'blaŋko) *n* **Antonio** (an'tonjo). 1829–99, Venezuelan statesman; president (1873–77; 1879–84; 1886–87). He was virtual dictator of Venezuela from 1870 until his overthrow (1889).

guzzle ('gʌzᵊl) *vb* to consume (food or drink) excessively or greedily. [C16: of unknown origin] ▸ **'guzzler** *n*

gv *abbrev. for* gravimetric volume.

Gwalior ('gwɑːlɪ,ɔː) *n* **1** a city in N central India, in Madhya Pradesh: built around the fort, which dates from before 525; industrial and commercial centre. Pop.: 690 765 (1991). **2** a former princely state of central India, established in the 18th century: merged with Madhya Bharat in 1948, which in turn merged with Madhya Pradesh in 1956.

Gwent (gwɛnt) *n* a former county of SE Wales: formed in 1974 from most of Monmouthshire and part of Breconshire; replaced in 1996 by Monmouthshire and the county boroughs of Newport, Torfaen, Blaenau Gwent, and part of Caerphilly.

Gweru ('gweɪruː) *n* a city in central Zimbabwe. Pop.: 124 735 (1992). Former name (until 1982): **Gwelo** ('gwiːləʊ).

Gwyn (gwɪn) *n* **Nell,** original name *Eleanor Gwynne.* 1650–87, English actress; mistress of Charles II.

Gwynedd ('gwɪneð) *n* a county of NW Wales, formed in 1974 from Anglesey, Caernarvonshire, part of Denbighshire, and most of Merionethshire; lost Anglesey and part of the NE in 1996: generally mountainous with many lakes, much of it lying in the Snowdonia National Park. Administrative centre: Caernarfon. Pop.: 118 005 (1996 est.). Area: 2550 sq. km (869 sq. miles).

gwyniad ('gwɪnɪ,æd) *n* a freshwater white fish, *Coregonus pennantii,* occurring in Lake Bala in Wales: related to the powan. [C17: Welsh, from *gwyn* white, related to Scottish Gaelic *fionn:* see FINNOCK]

Gyani ('gjɑːnɪ) *n* (in India) a title placed before the name of a Punjabi scholar. [Hindi, from Sanskrit *gyan* knowledge]

gybe *or* **jibe** (dʒaɪb) *Nautical.* ◆ *vb* **1** (*intr*) (of a fore-and-aft sail) to shift suddenly from one side of the vessel to the other when running before the wind, as the result of allowing the wind to catch the leech. **2** to cause (a sailing vessel) to gybe or (of a sailing vessel) to undergo gybing. ◆ *n* **3** an instance of gybing. [C17: from obsolete Dutch *gijben* (now *gijpen*), of obscure origin]

gym (dʒɪm) *n, adj* short for **gymnasium, gymnastics, gymnastic.**

gymkhana (dʒɪm'kɑːnə) *n* **1** *Chiefly Brit.* an event in which horses and riders display skill and aptitude in various races and contests. **2** (esp. in Anglo-India) a place providing sporting and athletic facilities. [C19: from Hindi *gend-khānā,* literally: ball house, from *khāna* house; influenced by GYMNASIUM]

gymnasiarch (dʒɪm'neɪzɪ,ɑːk) *n* **1** (in ancient Greece) an official who supervised athletic schools and contests. **2** *Obsolete.* the governor or chief tutor of an academy or college. [C17: from Latin, from Greek *gymnasiarchos,* from *gymnasion* gymnasium + *-archos* ruling]

gymnasiast (dʒɪm'neɪzɪ,æst) *n* a student in a gymnasium.

gymnasium (dʒɪm'neɪzɪəm) *n, pl* **-siums** *or* **-sia** (-zɪə). **1** a large room or hall equipped with bars, weights, ropes, etc., for games or physical training. **2** (in various European countries) a secondary school that prepares pupils for university. [C16: from Latin: school for gymnastics, from Greek *gumnasion,* from *gumnazein* to exercise naked, from *gumnos* naked]

gymnast ('dʒɪmnæst) *n* a person who is skilled or trained in gymnastics.

gymnastic (dʒɪm'næstɪk) *adj* of, relating to, like, or involving gymnastics. ▸ **gym'nastically** *adv*

gymnastics (dʒɪm'næstɪks) *n* **1** (*functioning as sing*) practice or training in exercises that develop physical strength and agility or mental capacity. **2** (*functioning as pl*) gymnastic exercises.

gymno- *combining form.* naked, bare, or exposed: *gymnosperm.* [from Greek *gumnos* naked]

gymnosophist (dʒɪm'nɒsəfɪst) *n* one of a sect of naked Indian ascetics who regarded food or clothing as detrimental to purity of thought. [C16: from Latin *gymnosophistae,* from Greek *gumnosophistai* naked philosophers] ▸ **gym'nosophy** *n*

gymnosperm ('dʒɪmnəʊˌspɜːm, 'gɪm-) *n* any seed-bearing plant in which the ovules are borne naked on the surface of the megasporophylls, which are often arranged in cones; any conifer or related plant. Gymnosperms are traditionally classified in the division *Gymnospermae* but in modern classifications are split into separate phyla. Compare **angiosperm.** ▸ **ˌgymno'spermous** *adj*

gympie ('gɪmpɪ) *n Austral.* **1** a tall tree with stinging hairs on its leaves. **2** a hammer. [C19: from a native Australian language]

gym shoe *n* another name for **plimsoll.**

gymslip ('dʒɪmˌslɪp) *n* a tunic or pinafore dress worn by schoolgirls, often part of a school uniform.

gyn. *abbrev. for:* **1** gynaecological. **2** gynaecology.

gyn- *combining form.* variant of **gyno-** before a vowel.

gynaeceum (ˌdʒaɪnɪ'siːəm) *n, pl* **-cea** (-'siːə). **1** (in ancient Greece and Rome) the inner section of a house, used as women's quarters. **2** (dʒaɪ'niːsɪəm, gaɪ-). a variant spelling of **gynoecium.** [C17: from Latin: women's apartments, from Greek *gunaikeion,* from *gunē* a woman]

gynaeco- *or U.S.* **gyneco-** *combining form.* relating to women; female: *gynaecology.* [from Greek, from *gunē, gunaik-* woman, female]

gynaecocracy *or U.S.* **gynecocracy** (ˌdʒaɪnɪ'kɒkrəsɪ, ˌgaɪ-) *n, pl* **-cies.** government by women or by a single woman. Also called: **gynarchy.** ▸ **gynaecocratic** *or U.S.* **gynecocratic** (dʒaɪˌniːkə'krætɪk, gaɪ-) *adj*

gynaecoid *or U.S.* **gynecoid** ('dʒaɪnɪˌkɔɪd, 'gaɪ-) *adj* resembling, relating to, or like a woman.

gynaecol. *abbrev. for:* **1** gynaecological. **2** gynaecology.

gynaecology *or U.S.* **gynecology** (ˌgaɪnɪ'kɒlədʒɪ) *n* the branch of medicine concerned with diseases in women, esp. those of the genitourinary tract. ▸ **gynaecological** (ˌgaɪnɪkə'lɒdʒɪkᵊl), **ˌgynaeco'logic** *or U.S.* **ˌgyneco'logical, ˌgyneco'logic** *adj* ▸ **ˌgynae'cologist** *or U.S.* **ˌgyne'cologist** *n*

gynaecomastia *or U.S.* **gynecomastia** (ˌgaɪnɪkəʊ'mæstɪə) *n* abnormal overdevelopment of the breasts in a man. [C19: from GYNAECO- + Greek *mastos* breast]

gynandromorph (dʒɪ'nændrəʊˌmɔːf, gaɪ-, dʒaɪ-) *n* an abnormal organism, esp. an insect, that has both male and female physical characteristics. Compare **hermaphrodite** (sense 1). ▸ **gyˌnandro'morphic** *or* **gyˌnandro'morphous** *adj* ▸ **gyˌnandro'morphism** *or* **gy'nandroˌmorphy** *n*

gynandrous (dʒaɪ'nændrəs, dʒɪ-, gaɪ-) *adj* **1** (of flowers such as the orchid) having the stamens and styles united in a column. **2** hermaphroditic. [C19: from Greek *gunandros* of uncertain sex, from *gunē* woman + *anēr* man] ▸ **gy'nandry** *or* **gy'nandrism** *n*

gynarchy ('dʒaɪˌnɑːkɪ, 'gaɪ-) *n, pl* **-chies.** another word for **gynaecocracy.**

gynecium (dʒaɪ'niːsɪəm, gaɪ-) *n, pl* **-cia** (-sɪə). a variant spelling (esp. U.S.) of **gynoecium.**

gyneco- *combining form.* a variant (esp. U.S.) of **gynaeco-.**

gyniatrics (ˌdʒaɪnɪ'ætrɪks, ˌgaɪ-) *or* **gyniatry** (dʒaɪ'naɪətrɪ, gaɪ-) *n Med.* less common words for **gynaecology.**

gyno- *or before a vowel* **gyn-** *combining form.* **1** relating to women; female: *gynarchy.* **2** denoting a female reproductive organ: *gynophore.* [from Greek, from *gunē* woman]

gynodioecious (ˌgaɪnəʊdaɪ'iːʃəs) *adj* (of a plant species) having some individuals bearing female flowers only and others bearing hermaphrodite flowers only.

gynoecium, gynaeceum, gynaecium, *or esp. U.S.* **gynecium** (dʒaɪ'niːsɪəm, gaɪ-) *n, pl* **-cia** *or* **-cea** (-sɪə). the carpels of a flowering plant collectively. [C18: New Latin, from Greek *gunaikeion* women's quarters, from *gunaik-, gunē* woman + *-eion,* suffix indicating place]

gynomonoecious (ˌgaɪnəʊmɔː'niːʃəs) *adj* (of a plant species) having each individual bearing both female and hermaphrodite flowers.

gynophore ('dʒaɪnəʊˌfɔː, 'gaɪ-) *n* a stalk in some plants that bears the gynoecium above the level of the other flower parts. ▸ **gynophoric** (ˌdʒaɪnəʊ'fɒrɪk, ˌgaɪ-) *adj*

-gynous *adj combining form.* **1** of or relating to women or females: *androgynous; misogynous.* **2** relating to female organs: *epigynous.* [from New Latin *-gynus,* from Greek *-gunos,* from *gunē* woman] ▸ **-gyny** *n combining form.*

Györ (*Hungarian* djøːr) *n* an industrial town in NW Hungary: medieval Benedictine abbey. Pop.: 127 000 (1997 est.).

gyp[1] *or* **gip** (dʒɪp) *Slang.* ◆ *vb* **gyps, gypping, gypped** *or* **gips, gipping, gipped. 1** (*tr*) to swindle, cheat, or defraud. ◆ *n* **2** an act of cheating. **3** a person who gyps. [C18: back formation from GYPSY]

gyp[2] (dʒɪp) *n Brit. and N.Z. slang.* severe pain; torture: *his arthritis gave him gyp.* [C19: probably a contraction of *gee up!;* see GEE[1]]

gyp[3] (dʒɪp) *n* a college servant at the universities of Cambridge and Durham. Compare **scout**[1] (sense 5). [C18: perhaps from GYPSY, or from obsolete *gippo* a scullion]

gypsophila (dʒɪp'sɒfɪlə) *n* any caryophyllaceous plant of the Mediterranean genus *Gypsophila,* such as baby's-breath, having small white or pink flowers. [C18: New Latin, from Greek *gupsos* chalk + *philos* loving]

gypsum ('dʒɪpsəm) *n* a colourless or white mineral sometimes tinted by impurities, found in beds as an evaporite. It is used in the manufacture of plaster of Paris, cement, paint, school chalk, glass, and fertilizer. Composition: hydrated calcium sulphate. Formula: $CaSO_4.2H_2O$. Crystal structure: monoclinic. [C17: from Latin, from Greek *gupsos* chalk, plaster, cement, of Semitic origin] ▸ **gypseous** ('dʒɪpsɪəs) *adj* ▸ **gypsiferous** (dʒɪp'sɪfərəs) *adj*

Gypsy *or* **Gipsy** ('dʒɪpsɪ) *n, pl* **-sies.** (*sometimes not cap.*) **1a** a member of a people scattered throughout Europe and North America, who maintain a nomadic way of life in industrialized societies. They migrated from NW India from about the 9th century onwards. **1b** (*as modifier*): *a Gypsy fortune-teller.* **2** the language of the Gypsies; Romany. **3** a person who looks or behaves like a Gypsy. [C16: from EGYPTIAN, since they were thought to have come originally from Egypt] ▸ **'Gypsydom** *or* **'Gipsydom** *n* ▸ **'Gypsyˌhood** *or* **'Gipsyˌhood** *n* ▸ **'Gypsyish** *or* **'Gipsyish** *adj* ▸ **'Gypsy-ˌlike** *or* **'Gipsy-ˌlike** *adj*

gypsy moth *n* a variant spelling of **gipsy moth.**

gyral ('dʒaɪrəl) *adj* **1** having a circular, spiral, or rotating motion; gyratory. **2** *Anatomy.* of or relating to a convolution (gyrus) of the brain. ▸ **'gyrally** *adv*

gyrate *vb* (dʒɪ'reɪt, dʒaɪ-). **1** (*intr*) to rotate or spiral, esp. about a fixed point or axis. ◆ *adj* ('dʒaɪrɪt, -reɪt). **2** *Biology.* curved or coiled into a circle; circinate. [C19: from Late Latin *gȳrāre,* from Latin *gȳrus* circle, from Greek *guros*] ▸ **gyratory** ('dʒaɪrətərɪ, -trɪ; dʒaɪ'reɪtərɪ) *adj*

gyration (dʒaɪ'reɪʃən) *n* **1** the act or process of gyrating; rotation. **2** any one of the whorls of a spiral-shaped shell.

gyrator (dʒaɪ'reɪtə) *n* an electronic circuit that inverts the impedance.

gyre (dʒaɪə) *Chiefly literary.* ◆ *n* **1** a circular or spiral movement or path. **2** a ring, circle, or spiral. ◆ *vb* **3** (*intr*) to whirl. [C16: from Latin *gȳrus* circle, from Greek *guros*]

gyrfalcon *or* **gerfalcon** ('dʒɜːˌfɔːlkən, -ˌfɔːkən) *n* a very large rare falcon, *Falco rusticolus,* of northern and arctic regions: often used for hunting. [C14: from Old French *gerfaucon,* perhaps from Old Norse *geirfalki,* from *geirr* spear + *falki* falcon]

gyro ('dʒaɪrəʊ) *n, pl* **-ros. 1** See **gyrocompass. 2** See **gyroscope.**

gyro- *or before a vowel* **gyr-** *combining form.* **1** indicating rotating or gyrating motion: *gyroscope.* **2** indicating a spiral. **3** indicating a gyroscope: *gyrocompass.* [via Latin from Greek *guro-,* from *guros* circle]

gyrocompass ('dʒaɪrəʊˌkʌmpəs) *n Navigation.* a nonmagnetic compass that uses a motor-driven gyroscope to indicate true north. Sometimes shortened to **gyro.**

gyrodyne ('dʒaɪrəʊˌdaɪn) *n* an aircraft that uses a powered rotor to take off and manoeuvre, but uses autorotation when cruising.

gyro horizon *n* another name for **artificial horizon** (sense 1).

gyromagnetic (ˌdʒaɪrəʊmæg'nɛtɪk) *adj* of or caused by magnetic properties resulting from the spin of a charged particle, such as an electron.

gyromagnetic ratio *n Physics.* the ratio of the magnetic moment of a rotating charged particle, such as an electron, to its angular momentum.

gyron ('dʒaɪrɒn) *n* a variant spelling of **giron.**

gyronny (dʒaɪ'rɒnɪ) *adj* a variant spelling of **gironny.**

gyroplane ('dʒaɪrəˌpleɪn) *n* another name for **autogiro.**

gyroscope ('dʒaɪrəˌskəʊp) *or* **gyrostat** *n* a device containing a disc rotating on an axis that can turn freely in any direction so that the disc resists the action of an applied couple and tends to maintain the same orientation in space irrespective of the movement of the surrounding structure. Sometimes shortened to **gyro.** ▸ **gyroscopic** (ˌdʒaɪrə'skɒpɪk) *adj* ▸ **ˌgyro'scopically** *adv* ▸ **ˌgyro'scopics** *n*

gyrose ('dʒaɪrəʊz) *adj Botany.* marked with sinuous lines.

gyrostabilizer *or* **gyrostabiliser** (ˌdʒaɪrəʊ'steɪbɪˌlaɪzə) *n* a gyroscopic device used to stabilize the rolling motion of a ship.

gyrostatic (ˌdʒaɪrəʊ'stætɪk) *adj* of or concerned with the gyroscope or with gyrostatics. ▸ **ˌgyro'statically** *adv*

gyrostatics (ˌdʒaɪrəʊ'stætɪks) *n* (*functioning as sing*) the science of rotating bodies.

gyrus ('dʒaɪrəs) *n, pl* **gyri** ('dʒaɪraɪ). another name for **convolution** (sense 3). [C19: from Latin; see GYRE]

gyve (dʒaɪv) *Archaic.* ◆ *vb* **1** (*tr*) to shackle or fetter. ◆ *n* **2** (*usually pl*) fetters. [C13: of unknown origin]

Hh

h *or* **H** (eɪtʃ) *n, pl* **h's, H's,** *or* **Hs. 1** the eighth letter and sixth consonant of the modern English alphabet. **2** a speech sound represented by this letter, in English usually a voiceless glottal fricative, as in *hat.* **3a** something shaped like an H. **3b** (*in combination*): *an H-beam.*

h *symbol for:* **1** *Physics.* Planck constant. **2** hecto-. **3** *Chess.* See **algebraic notation.**

H *symbol for:* **1** *Chem.* hydrogen. **2** *Physics.* **2a** magnetic field strength. **2b** Hamiltonian. **3** *Electronics.* henry or henries. **4** *Thermodynamics.* enthalpy. **5** (on Brit. pencils, signifying degree of hardness of lead) hard: *H; 2H; 3H.* Compare **B** (sense 9). **6** *Slang.* heroin. **7** *international car registration for* Hungary.

h. *or* **H.** *abbrev. for:* **1** harbour. **2** hard(ness). **3** height. **4** high. **5** *Music.* horn. **6** hour. **7** hundred. **8** husband.

ha[1] *or* **hah** (hɑː) *interj* **1** an exclamation expressing derision, triumph, surprise, etc., according to the intonation of the speaker. **2** (*reiterated*) a representation of the sound of laughter.

ha[2] *Symbol for* hectare.

h.a. *abbrev. for* hoc anno. [Latin: in this year]

HAA *abbrev. for* hepatitis-associated antigen; an antigen that occurs in the blood serum of some people, esp. those with serum hepatitis.

haaf (hɑːf) *n* a deep-sea fishing ground off the Shetland and Orkney Islands. [Old English *hæf* sea; related to Old Norse *haf;* see HEAVE]

Haakon IV ('hɑːkɒn) *n* surnamed *Haakonsson.* 1204–63, king of Norway (1217–63). He strengthened the monarchy and extended Norwegian territory to include Iceland and Greenland.

Haakon VII *n* 1872–1957, king of Norway (1905–57). During the Nazi occupation of Norway (1940–45) he led Norwegian resistance from England.

haar (hɑː) *n Eastern Brit.* a cold sea mist or fog off the North Sea. [C17: related to Dutch dialect *harig* damp]

Haarlem (*Dutch* 'haːrlɛm) *n* a city in the W Netherlands, capital of North Holland province. Pop.: 148 947 (1995 est.).

Hab. *Bible. abbrev. for* Habakkuk.

Habakkuk ('hæbəkək) *n Old Testament.* **1** a Hebrew prophet. **2** the book containing his oracles and canticle. Douay spelling: **Habacuc.**

Habana (a'βana) *n* the Spanish name for **Havana.**

habanera (ˌhæbə'nɛərə) *n* **1** a slow Cuban dance in duple time. **2** a piece of music composed for or in the rhythm of this dance. [from Spanish *danza habanera* dance from Havana]

Habanero (*Spanish* aβa'nero) *n, pl* **-ros** (-ros). a native or inhabitant of Havana.

habeas corpus ('heɪbɪəs 'kɔːpəs) *n Law.* a writ ordering a person to be brought before a court or judge, esp. so that the court may ascertain whether his detention is lawful. [C15: from the opening of the Latin writ, literally: you may have the body]

haberdasher ('hæbəˌdæʃə) *n* **1** *Brit.* a dealer in small articles for sewing, such as buttons, zips, and ribbons. **2** *U.S.* a men's outfitter. [C14: from Anglo-French *hapertas* small items of merchandise, of obscure origin]

haberdashery ('hæbəˌdæʃərɪ) *n, pl* **-eries.** the goods or business kept by a haberdasher.

habergeon ('hæbədʒən) *or* **haubergeon** *n* a light sleeveless coat of mail worn in the 14th century under the plated hauberk. [C14: from Old French *haubergeon* a little HAUBERK]

Habermas ('hɑːbərmas) *n* **Jürgen** ('jyrgən). born 1929, German social theorist: his chief works are *Theory and Practice* (1963) and *Knowledge and Human Interests* (1968).

Haber process ('hɑːbə) *n* an industrial process for producing ammonia by reacting atmospheric nitrogen with hydrogen at about 200 atmospheres (2×10^7 pascals) and 500°C in the presence of a catalyst, usually iron. [named after Fritz *Haber* (1868–1934), German chemist]

habile ('hæbiːl) *adj* **1** *Rare.* skilful. **2** *Obsolete.* fit. [C14: from Latin *habilis,* from *habēre* to have; see ABLE]

habiliment (hə'bɪlɪmənt) *n* (*often pl*) dress or attire. [C15: from Old French *habillement,* from *habiller* to dress, from *bille* log; see BILLET[2]]

habilitate (hə'bɪlɪˌteɪt) *vb* **1** (*tr*) *U.S., chiefly Western.* to equip and finance (a mine). **2** (*intr*) to qualify for office. **3** (*tr*) *Archaic.* to clothe. [C17: from Medieval Latin *habilitāre* to make fit, from Latin *habilitās* aptness, readiness; see ABILITY] ▸ **haˌbiliˈtation** *n* ▸ **haˈbiliˌtator** *n*

habit ('hæbɪt) *n* **1** a tendency or disposition to act in a particular way. **2** established custom, usual practice, etc. **3** *Psychol.* a learned behavioural response that has become associated with a particular situation, esp. one frequently repeated. **4** mental disposition or attitude: *a good working habit of mind.* **5a** a practice or substance to which a person is addicted: *drink has become a habit with him.* **5b** the state of being dependent on something, esp. a drug. **6** *Botany, zoology.* the method of growth, type of existence, or general appearance of a plant or animal: *a climbing habit; a burrowing habit.* **7** the customary apparel of a particular occupation, rank, etc., now esp. the costume of a nun or monk. **8** Also called: **riding habit.** a woman's riding dress. **9** *Crystallog.* short for **crystal habit.** ◆ *vb* (*tr*) **10** to clothe. **11** an archaic word for **inhabit** or **habituate.** [C13: from Latin *habitus* custom, from *habēre* to have]

habitable ('hæbɪtəbᵊl) *adj* able to be lived in. ▸ **ˌhabitaˈbility** *or* **ˈhabitableness** *n* ▸ **ˈhabitably** *adv*

habitant ('hæbɪtᵊnt) *n* **1** a less common word for **inhabitant. 2** ('hæbɪtᵊnt; *French* abitã). **2a** an early French settler in Canada or Louisiana, esp. a small farmer. **2b** a descendant of these settlers, esp. a farmer.

habitat ('hæbɪˌtæt) *n* **1** the natural home of an animal or plant. **2** the place in which a person, group, class, etc., is normally found. [C18: from Latin: it inhabits, from *habitāre* to dwell, from *habēre* to have]

habitation (ˌhæbɪ'teɪʃən) *n* **1** a dwelling place. **2** occupation of a dwelling place. ▸ **ˌhabiˈtational** *adj*

habited ('hæbɪtɪd) *adj* **1** dressed in a habit. **2** clothed.

habit-forming *adj* (of an activity, indulgence, etc.) tending to become a habit or addiction.

habitual (hə'bɪtjʊəl) *adj* **1** (*usually prenominal*) done or experienced regularly and repeatedly: *the habitual Sunday walk.* **2** (*usually prenominal*) by habit: *a habitual drinker.* **3** customary; usual: *his habitual comment.* ▸ **haˈbitually** *adv* ▸ **haˈbitualness** *n*

habituate (hə'bɪtjʊˌeɪt) *vb* **1** to accustom; make used (to). **2** *U.S. and Canadian archaic.* to frequent.

habituation (həˌbɪtjʊ'eɪʃən) *n* **1** the act or process of habituating. **2** *Psychol.* the temporary waning of an innate response that occurs when it is elicited many times in succession. Compare **extinction** (sense 6).

habitude ('hæbɪˌtjuːd) *n Rare.* habit or tendency. ▸ **ˌhabiˈtudinal** *adj*

habitué (hə'bɪtjʊˌeɪ) *n* a frequent visitor to a place. [C19: from French, from *habituer* to frequent]

habitus ('hæbɪtəs) *n, pl* **-tus. 1** *Med.* general physical state, esp. with regard to susceptibility to disease. **2** tendency or inclination, esp. of plant or animal growth; habit. [C19: from Latin: state, HABIT]

Habsburg ('hæpsbɜːk) *n* the German name for **Hapsburg.**

habu ('hɑːbuː) *n* a large venomous snake, *Trimeresurus flavoviridis,* of Okinawa and other Ryukyu Islands: family *Crotalidae* (pit vipers). [from the native name originally used in the Ryukyu Islands]

HAC *abbrev. for* Honourable Artillery Company.

háček ('hɑːtʃɛk) *n* a diacritic mark (ˇ) placed over certain letters in order to modify their sounds, esp. used in Slavonic languages to indicate various forms of palatal articulation, as in the affricate *č* and the fricative trill *ř* used in Czech. [from Czech]

hachure (hæ'ʃjʊə) *n* **1** another word for **hatching** (see **hatch**[3]). **2** shading of short lines drawn on a relief map to indicate gradients. ◆ *vb* **3** (*tr*) to mark or show by hachures. [C19: from French, from *hacher* to chop up, HATCH[3]]

hacienda (ˌhæsɪ'ɛndə) *n* (in Spain or Spanish-speaking countries) **1a** a ranch or large estate. **1b** any substantial stock-raising, mining, or manufacturing establishment in the country. **2** the main house on such a ranch or plantation. [C18: from Spanish, from Latin *facienda* things to be done, from *facere* to do]

hack[1] (hæk) *vb* **1** (when *intr,* usually foll. by *at* or *away*) to cut or chop (at) irregularly, roughly, or violently. **2** to cut and clear (a way, path, etc.), as through undergrowth. **3** (in sport, esp. rugby) to foul (an opposing player) by kicking or striking his shins. **4** *Basketball.* to commit the foul of striking (an opposing player) on the arm. **5** (*intr*) to cough in short dry spasmodic bursts. **6** (*tr*) to reduce or cut (a story, article, etc.) in a damaging way. **7** to manipulate a computer program skilfully, esp., to gain unauthorized access to another computer system. **8** (*tr*) *Slang.* to tolerate; cope with: *I joined the army but I couldn't hack it.* **9 hack to bits.** to damage severely: *his reputation was hacked to bits.* ◆ *n* **10** a cut, chop, notch, or gash, esp. as made by a knife or axe. **11** any tool used for shallow digging, such as a mattock or pick. **12** a chopping blow. **13** a dry spasmodic cough. **14** a kick on the shins, as in rugby. **15** a wound from a sharp kick. [Old English *haccian;* related to Old Frisian *hackia,* Middle High German *hacken*]

hack[2] (hæk) *n* **1** a horse kept for riding or (more rarely) for driving. **2** an old, ill-bred, or overworked horse. **3** a horse kept for hire. **4** *Brit.* a country ride on horseback. **5** a drudge. **6** a person who produces mediocre literary or journalistic work. **7** Also called: **hackney.** *U.S.* a coach or carriage that is for hire. **8** Also called: **hackie.** *U.S. informal.* **8a** a cab driver. **8b** a taxi. ◆ *vb* **9** *Brit.* to ride (a horse) cross-country for pleasure. **10** (*tr*) to let (a horse) out for hire. **11** (*tr*) *Informal.* to write (an article) as or in the manner of a hack. **12** (*intr*) *U.S. informal.* to drive a taxi. ◆ *adj* **13** (*prenominal*) banal, mediocre, or unoriginal: *hack writing.* [C17: short for HACKNEY]

hack[3] (hæk) *n* **1** a rack used for fodder for livestock. **2** a board on which meat is placed for a hawk. **3** a pile or row of unfired bricks stacked to dry. ◆ *vb* (*tr*) **4** to place (fodder) in a hack. **5** to place (bricks) in a hack. [C16: variant of HATCH[2]]

hackamore ('hækəˌmɔː) *n U.S. and N.Z.* a rope or rawhide halter used for unbroken foals. [C19: by folk etymology from Spanish *jáquima* headstall, from Old Spanish *xaquima,* from Arabic *shaqīmah*]

hackberry ('hækˌbɛrɪ) *n, pl* **-ries. 1** any American tree or shrub of the ulmaceous genus *Celtis,* having edible cherry-like fruits. **2** the fruit or soft yellowish wood of such a tree. [C18: variant of C16 *hagberry,* of Scandinavian origin; compare Old Norse *heggr* hackberry]

hackbut ('hækbʌt) *or* **hagbut** *n* another word for **arquebus.** ▸ ,**hack-but'eer, 'hackbutter,** *or* ,**hagbut'eer, 'hagbutter** *n*

hacker ('hækə) *n* **1** a person that hacks. **2** *Slang.* a computer fanatic, esp. one who through a personal computer breaks into the computer system of a company, government, etc.

hackery ('hækərɪ) *n* **1** *Ironic.* journalism; hackwork. **2** *Informal.* the practice of gaining illegal access to a computer system.

hack hammer *n* an adzelike tool, used for dressing stone.

hacking ('hækɪŋ) *adj* (of a cough) harsh, dry, and spasmodic.

hacking jacket *or* **coat** *n Chiefly Brit.* a riding jacket with side or back vents and slanting pockets.

hackle ('hæk^əl) *n* **1** any of the long slender feathers on the necks of poultry and other birds. **2** *Angling.* **2a** parts of an artificial fly made from hackle feathers, representing the legs and sometimes the wings of a real fly. **2b** short for **hackle fly. 3** a feathered ornament worn in the headdress of some British regiments. **4** a steel flax comb. ◆ *vb* (*tr*) **5** to comb (flax) using a hackle. ◆ See also **hackles.** [C15 *hakell,* probably from Old English; variant of HECKLE; see HATCHEL] ▸ **'hackler** *n*

hackle fly *n Angling.* an artificial fly in which the legs and wings are represented by hackle feathers.

hackles ('hæk^əlz) *pl n* **1** the hairs on the back of the neck and the back of a dog, cat, etc., which rise when the animal is angry or afraid. **2** anger or resentment (esp. in the phrases **get one's hackles up, make one's hackles rise**).

hackney ('hæknɪ) *n* **1** a compact breed of harness horse with a high-stepping trot. **2a** a coach or carriage that is for hire. **2b** (*as modifier*): *a hackney carriage.* **3** a popular term for **hack**[2] (sense 1). ◆ *vb* **4** (*tr; usually passive*) to make commonplace and banal by too frequent use. [C14: probably after HACKNEY, where horses were formerly raised; sense 4 meaning derives from the allusion to a weakened hired horse] ▸ **'hackneyism** *n*

Hackney ('hæknɪ) *n* a borough of NE Greater London: formed in 1965 from the former boroughs of Shoreditch, Stoke Newington, and Hackney; nearby are **Hackney Marshes,** the largest recreation ground in London. Pop.: 192 500 (1994 est.). Area: 19 sq. km (8 sq. miles).

hackneyed ('hæknɪd) *adj* (of phrases, fashions, etc.) used so often as to be trite, dull, and stereotyped.

hacksaw ('hæk,sɔː) *n* **1** a handsaw for cutting metal, with a hard-steel blade in a frame under tension. ◆ *vb* **-saws, -sawing, -sawed, -sawed** *or* **-sawn** (-,sɔːn). **2** (*tr*) to cut with a hacksaw.

hackwork ('hæk,wɜːk) *n* undistinguished literary work produced to order.

had (hæd) *vb* the past tense and past participle of **have.**

hadal ('heɪd^əl) *adj* of, relating to, or constituting the zones of the oceans deeper than **abyssal:** below about 6000 metres (18 000 ft.). [C20: from French, from *Hadès* HADES]

hadaway (,hædə'weɪ) *sentence substitute. Northeastern English dialect.* an exclamation urging the hearer to refrain from delay in the execution of a task. [perhaps from HOLD[1] + AWAY]

haddock ('hædək) *n, pl* **-docks** *or* **-dock.** a North Atlantic gadoid food fish, *Melanogrammus aeglefinus:* similar to but smaller than the cod. [C14: of uncertain origin]

hade (heɪd) *Geology* ◆ *n* **1** the angle made to the vertical by the plane of a fault or vein. ◆ *vb* **2** (*intr*) (of faults or veins) to incline from the vertical. [C18: of unknown origin]

hadedah ('hɑːdɪ,dɑː) *n S. African.* a large greyish-green ibis, *Hagedeshia hagedash,* having a greenish metallic sheen on the wing coverts and shoulders. [probably imitative of the bird's call]

Hades ('heɪdiːz) *n* **1** *Greek myth.* **1a** the underworld abode of the souls of the dead. **1b** Pluto, the god of the underworld, brother of Zeus and husband of Persephone. **2** *New Testament.* the abode or state of the dead. **3** (*often not cap.*) *Informal.* hell. ▸ **Hadean** (heɪ'diːən, 'heɪdɪən) *adj*

Hadhramaut *or* **Hadramaut** (,hɑːdrə'mɔːt) *n* a plateau region of the S Arabian Peninsula, in SE Yemen on the Indian Ocean; formerly in South Yemen: corresponds roughly to the former East Aden Protectorate. Area: about 151 500 sq. km (58 500 sq. miles).

Hadith ('hædɪθ, hɑː'diːθ) *n* the body of tradition and legend about Mohammed and his followers, used as a basis of Islamic law. [Arabic]

hadj (hædʒ) *n, pl* **hadjes.** a variant spelling of **hajj.**

hadji ('hædʒɪ) *n, pl* **hadjis.** a variant spelling of **hajji.**

Hadlee ('hædlɪ) *n* Sir **Richard (John).** born 1951, New Zealand cricketer.

hadn't ('hæd^ənt) *vb contraction of* had not.

Hadrian ('heɪdrɪən) *or* **Adrian** *n* Latin name *Publius Aelius Hadrianus.* 76–138 A.D., Roman emperor (117–138); adopted son and successor of Trajan. He travelled throughout the Roman Empire, strengthening its frontiers and encouraging learning and architecture, and in Rome he reorganized the army and codified Roman law.

Hadrian's Wall *n* a fortified Roman wall, of which substantial parts remain, extending across N England from the Solway Firth in the west to the mouth of the River Tyne in the east. It was built in 120–123 A.D. on the orders of the emperor Hadrian as a defence against the N British tribes.

hadron ('hædrɒn) *n* any elementary particle capable of taking part in a strong nuclear interaction and therefore excluding leptons and photons. [C20: from Greek *hadros* heavy, from *hadēn* enough + -ON] ▸ **had'ronic** *adj*

hadrosaur ('hædrə,sɔː) *or* **hadrosaurus** (,hædrə'sɔːrəs) *n* any bipedal Upper Cretaceous dinosaur of the genus *Anatosaurus* and related genera: partly aquatic, with a duck-billed skull and webbed feet. [C19: from Greek *hadros* thick, fat + -SAUR]

hadst (hædst) *vb Archaic or dialect.* (used with the pronoun *thou*) a singular form of the past tense (indicative mood) of **have.**

hae (heɪ, hæ) *vb* a Scottish variant of **have.**

haecceity (hɛk'siːɪtɪ, hiːk-) *n, pl* **-ties.** *Philosophy.* the property that uniquely identifies an object. Compare **quiddity.** [C17: from Medieval Latin *haecceitas,* literally: thisness, from *haec,* feminine of *hic* this]

Haeckel (*German* 'hɛkəl) *n* **Ernst Heinrich** (ɛrnst 'hainrɪç). 1834–1919, German biologist and philosopher. He formulated the recapitulation theory of evolution and was an exponent of the philosophy of materialistic monism. ▸ **Haeckelian** (hɛ'kiːlɪən) *adj*

haem *or U.S.* **heme** (hiːm) *n Biochem.* a complex red organic pigment containing ferrous iron, present in haemoglobin. [C20: shortened from HAEMATIN]

haem- *combining form.* a variant of **haemo-** before a vowel. Also (U.S.): **hem-.**

haema- *combining form.* a variant of **haemo-.** Also (U.S.): **hema-.**

haemachrome *or U.S.* **hemachrome** ('hiːmə,krəʊm, 'hɛm-) *n* variants of **haemochrome.**

haemacytometer *or U.S.* **hemacytometer** (,hiːməsaɪ'tɒmɪtə) *n Med.* variants of **haemocytometer.**

haemagglutinate *or U.S.* **hemagglutinate** (,hiːmə'gluːtɪ,neɪt, ,hɛm-) *vb* (*tr*) to cause the clumping of red blood cells in (a blood sample).

haemagglutinin *or U.S.* **hemagglutinin** (,hiːmə'gluːtɪnɪn, ,hɛm-) *n* an antibody that causes the clumping of red blood cells.

haemagogue *or U.S.* **hemagogue, hemagog** ('hiːmə,gɒg) *adj* **1** promoting the flow of blood. ◆ *n* **2** a drug or agent that promotes the flow of blood, esp. the menstrual flow. [C18: from HAEMO- + Greek *agōgos* leading]

haemal *or U.S.* **hemal** ('hiːməl) *adj* **1** of or relating to the blood or the blood vessels. **2** denoting or relating to the region of the body containing the heart.

haemangioma *or esp. U.S.* **hemangioma** (hɪ,mændʒɪ'əʊmə) *n, pl* **-mas** *or* **-mata** (-mətə). a nonmalignant tumour of blood vessels, esp. affecting those of the skin. See **strawberry mark.** [from HAEM(O)- + ANGI(O)- + -OMA]

haematein *or U.S.* **hematein** (,hiːmə'tiːɪn, ,hɛm-) *n* a dark purple water-insoluble crystalline substance obtained from logwood and used as an indicator and biological stain. Formula: $C_{16}H_{12}O_6$.

haematemesis *or U.S.* **hematemesis** (,hiːmə'tɛmɪsɪs, ,hɛm-) *n* vomiting of blood, esp. as the result of a bleeding ulcer. Compare **haemoptysis.** [C19: from HAEMATO- + Greek *emesis* vomiting]

haematic *or U.S.* **hematic** (hiː'mætɪk) *adj* **1** Also: **haemic.** relating to, acting on, having the colour of, or containing blood. ◆ *n* **2** *Med.* another name for a **haematinic.**

haematin *or U.S.* **hematin** ('hɛmətɪn, 'hiː-) *n Biochem.* a dark bluish or brownish pigment containing iron in the ferric state, obtained by the oxidation of haem.

haematinic *or U.S.* **hematinic** (,hɛmə'tɪnɪk, ,hiː-) *n* **1** Also called: **haematic.** an agent that stimulates the production of red blood cells or increases the amount of haemoglobin in the blood. ◆ *adj* **2** having the effect of enriching the blood.

haematite ('hiːmə,taɪt, 'hɛm-) *n* a variant spelling of **hematite.** ▸ **haematitic** (,hiːmə'tɪtɪk, ,hɛm-) *adj*

haemato- *or before a vowel* **haemat-** *combining form.* indicating blood: *haematolysis.* Also: **haemo-** or (U.S.) **hemato-, hemat-.** [from Greek *haima, haimat-* blood]

haematoblast *or U.S.* **hematoblast** (hiː'mætəʊ,blæst) *n* any of the undifferentiated cells in the bone marrow that develop into blood cells. ▸ **hae,mato'blastic** *or U.S.* **he,mato'blastic** *adj*

haematocele *or U.S.* **hematocele** ('hɛmətəʊ,siːl, 'hiː-) *n Pathol.* a collection of blood in a body cavity, as in the space surrounding the testis; blood cyst.

haematocrit *or U.S.* **hematocrit** ('hɛmətəʊkrɪt, 'hiː-) *n* **1** a centrifuge for separating blood cells from plasma. **2** Also called: **packed cell volume.** the ratio of the volume occupied by these cells, esp. the red cells, to the total volume of blood, expressed as a percentage. [C20: from HAEMATO- + Greek *kritēs* judge, from *krinein* to separate]

haematocryal *or U.S.* **hematocryal** (,hɛmətəʊ'kraɪəl, ,hiː-) *adj Zoology.* another word for **poikilothermic.**

haematogenesis *or U.S.* **hematogenesis** (,hɛmətəʊ'dʒɛnɪsɪs, ,hiː-) *n* another name for **haematopoiesis.** ▸ ,**haemato'genic, haematogenetic** (,hɛmətəʊdʒɪ'nɛtɪk, ,hiː-) *or U.S.* ,**hemato'genic,** ,**hematoge'netic** *adj*

haematogenous *or U.S.* **hematogenous** (,hɛmə'tɒdʒɪnəs, ,hiː-) *adj* **1** producing blood. **2** produced by, derived from, or originating in the blood. **3** (of bacteria, cancer cells, etc.) borne by or distributed by the blood.

haematoid ('hiːmə,tɔɪd, 'hɛm-), **haemoid** *or U.S.* **hematoid, hemoid** *adj* resembling blood.

haematology *or U.S.* **hematology** (,hiːmə'tɒlədʒɪ) *n* the branch of medical science concerned with diseases of the blood and blood-forming tissues. ▸ **haematologic** (,hiːmətə'lɒdʒɪk), ,**haemato'logical** *or U.S.* ,**hemato'logic,** ,**hemato'logical** *adj* ▸ ,**haema'tologist** *or U.S.* ,**hema'tologist** *n*

haematolysis *or U.S.* **hematolysis** (,hiːmə'tɒlɪsɪs) *n, pl* **-ses** (-,siːz). another name for **haemolysis.**

haematoma *or U.S.* **hematoma** (,hiːmə'təʊmə, ,hɛm-) *n, pl* **-mas** *or* **-mata** (-mətə). *Pathol.* a tumour of clotted or partially clotted blood.

haematophagous *or U.S.* **hematophagous** (,hiːmə'tɒfəgəs) *adj* (of certain animals) feeding on blood.

haematopoiesis (,hɛmətəʊpɔɪ'iːsɪs, ,hiː-), **haemopoiesis** *or U.S.* **hematopoiesis, hemopoiesis** *n Physiol.* the formation of blood. Also called: **haematosis, haematogenesis.** ▸ **haematopoietic** (,hɛmətəʊpɔɪ'ɛtɪk, ,hiː-), **haemopoietic** (,hiːməpɔɪ'ɛtɪk, ,hɛm-) *or U.S.* ,**hematopoi'etic,** ,**hemopoi'etic** *adj*

haematosis *or U.S.* **hematosis** (,hiːmə'təʊsɪs, ,hɛm-) *n Physiol.* **1** another word for **haematopoiesis. 2** the oxygenation of venous blood in the lungs.

haematothermal *or U.S.* **hematothermal** (,hɛmətəʊ'θɜːməl, ,hiː-) *adj Zoology.* another word for **homoiothermic.**

haematoxylin *or U.S.* **hematoxylin** (,hiːmə'tɒksɪlɪn, ,hɛm-) *n* **1** a colourless or yellowish crystalline compound that turns red on exposure to light: obtained from logwood and used in dyes and as a biological stain. Formula: $C_{16}H_{14}O_6.3H_2O$. **2** a variant spelling of **haematoxylon.** **[C19:** from New Latin *Haematoxylon* genus name of logwood, from HAEMATO- + Greek *xulon* wood + -IN**]**

haematoxylon (ˌhiːməˈtɒksɪlɒn) *or* **haematoxylin** *n* any thorny leguminous tree of the genus *Haematoxylon,* esp. the logwood, of tropical America and SW Africa. The heartwood yields the dye haematoxylin. **[C19:** see HAEMATOXYLIN**]** ▸ **haematoxylic** (ˌhiːmətɒkˈsɪlɪk) *adj*

haematozoon *or U.S.* **hematozoon** (ˌhiːmətəʊˈzəʊɒn, ˌhɛm-) *n, pl* **-zoa** (-ˈzəʊə). any microorganism, esp. a protozoan, that is parasitic in the blood.

haematuria *or U.S.* **hematuria** (ˌhiːməˈtjʊərɪə, ˌhɛm-) *n Pathol.* the presence of blood or red blood cells in the urine. ▸ **ˌhaemaˈturic** *or U.S.* **ˌhemaˈturic** *adj*

-haemia *or esp. U.S.* **-hemia** *n combining form.* variants of **-aemia.**

haemic *or U.S.* **hemic** (ˈhiːmɪk, ˈhɛm-) *adj* another word for **haematic.**

haemin *or U.S.* **hemin** (ˈhiːmɪn) *n Biochem.* haematin chloride; insoluble reddish-brown crystals formed by the action of hydrochloric acid on haematin in a test for the presence of blood. **[C20:** from HAEMO- + -IN**]**

haemo-, haema-, *or before a vowel* **haem-** *combining form.* denoting blood: *haemophobia.* Also: **haemato-** or (U.S.) **hemo-, hema-** or **hem-.** **[**from Greek *haima* blood**]**

haemochrome *or U.S.* **hemochrome** (ˈhiːməˌkrəʊm, ˈhɛm-) *n* a blood pigment, such as haemoglobin, that carries oxygen.

haemocoel *or U.S.* **hemocoel** (ˈhiːməˌsiːl) *n* the body cavity of many invertebrates, including arthropods and molluscs, developed from part of the blood system. **[C19:** from HAEMO- + New Latin *coel,* from Greek *koilos* hollow**]**

haemocyanin *or U.S.* **hemocyanin** (ˌhiːməʊˈsaɪənɪn) *n* a blue copper-containing respiratory pigment in crustaceans and molluscs that functions as haemoglobin.

haemocyte *or U.S.* **hemocyte** (ˈhiːməʊˌsaɪt, ˈhɛm-) *n* any blood cell, esp. a red blood cell.

haemocytometer (ˌhiːməʊsaɪˈtɒmɪtə), **haemacytometer** *or U.S.* **hemocytometer, hemacytometer** *n Med.* an apparatus for counting the number of cells in a quantity of blood, typically consisting of a graduated pipette for drawing and diluting the blood and a ruled glass slide on which the cells are counted under a microscope.

haemodialysis *or U.S.* **hemodialysis** (ˌhiːməʊdaɪˈælɪsɪs) *n, pl* **-ses** (-ˌsiːz). *Med.* the filtering of circulating blood through a semipermeable membrane in an apparatus (**haemodialyser** or **artificial kidney**) to remove waste products: performed in cases of kidney failure. Also called: **extracorporeal dialysis.** See also **dialysis.** **[C20:** from HAEMO- + DIALYSIS**]**

haemoflagellate *or U.S.* **hemoflagellate** (ˌhiːməˈflædʒəˌleɪt, ˌhɛm-) *n* a flagellate protozoan, such as a trypanosome, that is parasitic in the blood.

haemoglobin *or U.S.* **hemoglobin** (ˌhiːməʊˈgləʊbɪn, ˌhɛm-) *n* a conjugated protein, consisting of haem and the protein globin, that gives red blood cells their characteristic colour. It combines reversibly with oxygen and is thus very important in the transportation of oxygen to tissues. See also **oxyhaemoglobin.** **[C19:** shortened from *haematoglobulin,* from HAEMATIN + GLOBULIN the two components**]**

haemoglobinometer *or U.S.* **hemoglobinometer** (ˌhiːməʊgləʊbɪˈnɒmɪtə) *n* an instrument used to determine the haemoglobin content of blood.

haemoglobinopathy *or U.S.* **hemoglobinopathy** (ˌhiːməʊgləʊbɪˈnɒpəθɪ) *n* any of various inherited diseases, including sickle-cell anaemia and thalassaemia, characterized by abnormal haemoglobin.

haemoglobinuria *or U.S.* **hemoglobinuria** (ˌhiːməʊgləʊbɪˈnjʊərɪə, ˌhɛm-) *n Pathol.* the presence of haemoglobin in the urine.

haemoid *or U.S.* **hemoid** (ˈhiːmɔɪd) *adj* another word for **haematoid.**

haemolysin *or U.S.* **hemolysin** (ˌhiːməʊˈlaɪsɪn, ˌhɛməʊ-; hɪˈmɒlɪsɪn) *n Biochem.* any substance, esp. an antibody, that causes the breakdown of red blood cells.

haemolysis (hɪˈmɒlɪsɪs), **haematolysis** *or U.S.* **hemolysis, hematolysis** *n, pl* **-ses** (-ˌsiːz). the disintegration of red blood cells, with the release of haemoglobin, occurring in the living organism or in a blood sample. ▸ **haemolytic** *or U.S.* **hemolytic** (ˌhiːməʊˈlɪtɪk, ˌhɛm-) *adj*

haemophile *or U.S.* **hemophile** (ˈhiːməʊˌfaɪl, ˈhɛm-) *n* **1** another name for **haemophiliac. 2** a haemophilic bacterium.

haemophilia *or U.S.* **hemophilia** (ˌhiːməʊˈfɪlɪə, ˌhɛm-) *n* an inheritable disease, usually affecting only males but transmitted by women to their male children, characterized by loss or impairment of the normal clotting ability of blood so that a minor wound may result in fatal bleeding. ▸ **ˌhaemoˈphiliˌoid** *or U.S.* **ˌhemoˈphiliˌoid** *adj*

haemophiliac *or U.S.* **hemophiliac** (ˌhiːməʊˈfɪlɪˌæk, ˌhɛm-) *n* a person having haemophilia. Nontechnical name: **bleeder.** Also called: **haemophile.**

haemophilic *or U.S.* **hemophilic** (ˌhiːməʊˈfɪlɪk, ˌhɛm-) *adj* **1** of, relating to, or affected by haemophilia. **2** (of bacteria) growing well in a culture medium containing blood.

haemopoiesis *or U.S.* **hemopoiesis** (ˌhiːməʊpɔɪˈiːsɪs, ˌhɛm-) *n Physiol.* another name for **haematopoiesis.** ▸ **haemopoietic** *or U.S.* **hemopoietic** (ˌhiːməʊpɔɪˈɛtɪk, ˌhɛm-) *adj*

haemoptysis *or U.S.* **hemoptysis** (hɪˈmɒptɪsɪs) *n, pl* **-ses** (-ˌsiːz). spitting or coughing up of blood or blood-streaked mucus, as in tuberculosis. Compare **haematemesis.** **[C17:** from HAEMO- + *-ptysis,* from Greek *ptyein* to spit**]**

haemorrhage *or U.S.* **hemorrhage** (ˈhɛmərɪdʒ) *n* **1** profuse bleeding from ruptured blood vessels. **2** a steady or severe loss or depletion of resources, staff, etc. ◆ *vb* **3** (*intr*) to bleed profusely. **[C17:** from Latin *haemorrhagia;* see HAEMO-, -RRHAGIA**]** ▸ **haemorrhagic** *or U.S.* **hemorrhagic** (ˌhɛməˈrædʒɪk) *adj*

haemorrhoidectomy *or U.S.* **hemorrhoidectomy** (ˌhɛmərɔɪˈdɛktəmɪ) *n, pl* **-mies.** surgical removal of haemorrhoids.

haemorrhoids *or U.S.* **hemorrhoids** (ˈhɛməˌrɔɪdz) *pl n Pathol.* swollen and twisted veins in the region of the anus and lower rectum, often painful and bleeding. Nontechnical name: **piles.** **[C14:** from Latin *haemorrhoidae* (plural), from Greek, from *haimorrhoos* discharging blood, from *haimo-* HAEMO- + *rhein* to flow**]** ▸ **ˌhaemorˈrhoidal** *or U.S.* **ˌhemorˈrhoidal** *adj*

haemostasis (ˌhiːməʊˈsteɪsɪs, ˌhɛm-), **haemostasia** (ˌhiːməʊˈsteɪʒɪə, -ʒə, ˌhɛm-) *or U.S.* **hemostasis, hemostasia** *n* **1** the stopping of bleeding or arrest of blood circulation in an organ or part, as during a surgical operation. **2** stagnation of the blood. **[C18:** from New Latin, from HAEMO- + Greek *stasis* a standing still**]**

haemostat *or U.S.* **hemostat** (ˈhiːməʊˌstæt, ˈhɛm-) *n* **1** a surgical instrument that stops bleeding by compression of a blood vessel. **2** a chemical agent that retards or stops bleeding.

haemostatic *or U.S.* **hemostatic** (ˌhiːməʊˈstætɪk, ˌhɛm-) *adj* **1** retarding or stopping the flow of blood within the blood vessels. **2** retarding or stopping bleeding. ◆ *n* **3** a drug or agent that retards or stops bleeding.

haeremai (ˈhaɪrəˌmaɪ) *interj N.Z.* a Maori expression of welcome. **[C18:** Maori, literally: come hither**]**

haeres (ˈhɪəriːz) *n pl* **haeredes** (hɪˈriːdiːz). a variant spelling of **heres.**

Ha-erh-pin (ˈhɑːˈɛəˈpɪn) *n* transliteration of the Chinese name for **Harbin.**

haet (het) *n Scot.* a whit; iota; the least amount. **[C16:** originally in the phrase *deil hae' it* devil have it**]**

hafiz (ˈhɑːfɪz) *n Islam.* a title for a person who knows the Koran by heart. **[**from Persian, from Arabic *hāfiz,* from *hafiza* to guard**]**

Hafiz (ˈhɑːfɪz) *n* **Shams al-Din Muhammad** (ˌʃæmz ælˌdɪn məʊˈhæmɪd). ?1326–90, Persian lyric poet, best known for his many short poems about love and wine, often treated as religious symbols.

hafnium (ˈhæfnɪəm) *n* a bright metallic element found in zirconium ores: used in tungsten filaments and as a neutron absorber in nuclear reactors. Symbol: Hf; atomic no.: 72; atomic wt.: 178.49; valency: 4; relative density: 13.31; melting pt.: 2231±20°C; boiling pt.: 4603°C. **[C20:** New Latin, named after *Hafnia,* Latin name of Copenhagen + -IUM**]**

haft (hɑːft) *n* **1** the handle of an axe, knife, etc. ◆ *vb* **2** (*tr*) to provide with a haft. **[**Old English *hæft;* related to Old Norse *hapt,* Old High German *haft* fetter, *hefti* handle**]** ▸ **ˈhafter** *n*

Haftarah *or* **Haphtarah** (hɑːfˈtəʊrə; *Hebrew* haftaˈraː) *n, pl* **-taroth** (-ˈtəʊrəʊt; *Hebrew* -taˈroːt) *Judaism.* a short reading from the Prophets which follows the reading from the Torah on Sabbaths and festivals, and relates either to the theme of the Torah reading or to the observances of the day. See also **maftir.**

hag[1] (hæg) *n* **1** an unpleasant or ugly old woman. **2** a witch. **3** short for **hagfish. 4** *Obsolete.* a female demon. **[**Old English *hægtesse* witch; related to Old High German *hagazussa,* Middle Dutch *haghetisse***]** ▸ **ˈhaggish** *adj* ▸ **ˈhaggishly** *adv* ▸ **ˈhaggishness** *n* ▸ **ˈhagˌlike** *adj*

hag[2] (hæg, hɑːg) *n Scot. and northern English dialect.* **1** a firm spot in a bog. **2** a soft place in a moor. **[C13:** of Scandinavian origin; compare Old Norse *högg* gap; see HEW**]**

Hag. *Bible. abbrev. for* Haggai.

Hagar (ˈheɪgɑː, -gə) *n Old Testament.* an Egyptian maid of Sarah, who bore Ishmael to Abraham, Sarah's husband.

hagbut (ˈhægbʌt) *n* another word for **arquebus.** ▸ **ˌhagbutˈeer** *or* **ˈhagbutter** *n*

Hagen[1] (ˈhɑːgən) *n* (in the *Nibelungenlied*) Siegfried's killer, who in turn is killed by Siegfried's wife, Kriemhild.

Hagen[2] (*German* ˈhaːgən) *n* an industrial city in NW Germany, in North Rhine-Westphalia. Pop.: 212 003 (1996 est.).

Hagen[3] (ˈheɪgən) *n* **Walter.** 1892–1969, U.S. golfer.

hagfish (ˈhægˌfɪʃ) *n, pl* **-fish** *or* **-fishes.** any eel-like marine cyclostome vertebrate of the family *Myxinidae,* having a round sucking mouth and feeding on the tissues of other animals and on dead organic material. Often shortened to **hag.**

Haggadah *or* **Haggodoh** (həˈgɑːdə; *Hebrew* hagaˈdaː, -gɔˈdɔ) *n, pl* **-dahs, -das** *or* **-doth** (*Hebrew*-ˈdoːt). *Judaism.* **1a** a book containing the order of service of the traditional Passover meal. **1b** the narrative of the Exodus from Egypt that constitutes the main part of that service. ◆ See also **Seder. 2** another word for **Aggadah.** **[C19:** from Hebrew *haggādāh* a story, from *hagged* to tell**]** ▸ **haggadic** (həˈgædɪk, -ˈgɑː-) *or* **hagˈgadical** *adj*

haggadist (həˈgɑːdɪst) *n Judaism.* **1** a writer of Aggadoth. **2** an expert in or a student of haggadic literature. ▸ **haggadistic** (ˌhægəˈdɪstɪk) *adj*

Haggai (ˈhægeɪˌaɪ) *n Old Testament.* **1** a Hebrew prophet, whose oracles are usually dated between August and December of 520 B.C. **2** the book in which these oracles are contained, chiefly concerned with the rebuilding of the Temple after the Exile. Douay spelling: **Aggeus** (əˈdʒiːəs).

haggard[1] (ˈhægəd) *adj* **1** careworn or gaunt, as from lack of sleep, anxiety, or starvation. **2** wild or unruly. **3** (of a hawk) having reached maturity in the wild before being caught. ◆ *n* **4** *Falconry.* a hawk that has reached maturity before being caught. Compare **eyas, passage hawk.** **[C16:** from Old French *hagard* wild; perhaps related to HEDGE**]** ▸ **ˈhaggardly** *adv* ▸ **ˈhaggardness** *n*

haggard[2] (ˈhægərd) *n* (in Ireland and the Isle of Man) an enclosure beside a farmhouse in which crops are stored. **[C16:** related to Old Norse *heygarthr,* from *hey* hay + *garthr* yard**]**

Haggard (ˈhægəd) *n* Sir (**Henry**) **Rider.** 1856–1925, British author of romantic adventure stories, including *King Solomon's Mines* (1885).

haggis (ˈhægɪs) *n* a Scottish dish made from sheep's or calf's offal, oatmeal, suet, and seasonings boiled in a skin made from the animal's stomach. **[C15:** perhaps from *haggen* to HACK[1]**]**

haggle ('hæg^{ə}l) *vb* **1** (*intr;* often foll. by *over*) to bargain or wrangle (over a price, terms of an agreement, etc.); barter. **2** (*tr*) *Rare.* to hack. [C16: of Scandinavian origin; compare Old Norse *haggva* to HEW] ▸ **'haggler** *n*

hagiarchy ('hægɪˌɑːkɪ) *n, pl* **-archies. 1** government by saints, holy men, or men in holy orders. **2** an order of saints.

hagio- *or before a vowel* **hagi-** *combining form.* indicating a saint, saints, or holiness: *hagiography.* [via Late Latin from Greek, from *hagios* holy]

hagiocracy (ˌhægɪ'ɒkrəsɪ) *n, pl* **-cies. 1** government by holy men. **2** a state, community, etc., governed by holy men.

Hagiographa (ˌhægɪ'ɒgrəfə) *n* the third of the three main parts into which the books of the Old Testament are divided in Jewish tradition (the other two parts being the Law and the Prophets), comprising Psalms, Proverbs, Job, the Song of Solomon, Ruth, Lamentations, Ecclesiastes, Esther, Daniel, Ezra, Nehemiah, and Chronicles. Also called: **Writings.**

hagiographer (ˌhægɪ'ɒgrəfə) *or* **hagiographist** *n* **1** a person who writes about the lives of the saints. **2** one of the writers of the Hagiographa.

hagiography (ˌhægɪ'ɒgrəfɪ) *n, pl* **-phies. 1** the writing of the lives of the saints. **2** biography of the saints. **3** any biography that idealizes or idolizes its subject. ▸ **hagiographic** (ˌhægɪə'græfɪk) *or* **ˌhagio'graphical** *adj*

hagiolatry (ˌhægɪ'ɒlətrɪ) *n* worship or veneration of saints. ▸ **ˌhagi'olater** *n* ▸ **ˌhagi'olatrous** *adj*

hagiology (ˌhægɪ'ɒlədʒɪ) *n, pl* **-gies. 1** literature concerned with the lives and legends of saints. **2a** a biography of a saint. **2b** a collection of such biographies. **3** an authoritative canon of saints. **4** a history of sacred writings. ▸ **hagiologic** (ˌhægɪə'lɒdʒɪk) *or* **ˌhagio'logical** *adj* ▸ **ˌhagi'ologist** *n*

hagioscope ('hægɪəˌskəʊp) *n Architect.* another name for **squint** (sense 6). ▸ **hagioscopic** (ˌhægɪə'skɒpɪk) *adj*

hag-ridden *adj* **1** tormented or worried, as if by a witch. **2** *Facetious.* (of a man) harassed by women.

Hague[1] (heɪg) *n* **The.** the seat of government of the Netherlands and capital of South Holland province, situated about 3 km (2 miles) from the North Sea. Pop.: 442 105 (1995). Dutch names: **'s Gravenhage, Den Haag.**

Hague[2] (heɪg) *n* **William Jefferson.** born 1961, British politician; leader of the Conservative party from 1997.

Hague Tribunal *n* a tribunal of judges at The Hague, founded in 1899 to provide a panel of arbitrators for international disputes. It also chooses nominees for election by the United Nations to the International Court of Justice. Official name: **Permanent Court of Arbitration.**

hah (hɑː) *interj* a variant spelling of **ha**[1].

ha-ha[1] ('hɑː 'hɑː) *or* **haw-haw** *interj* **1** a representation of the sound of laughter. **2** an exclamation expressing derision, mockery, surprise, etc.

ha-ha[2] ('hɑː hɑː) *or* **haw-haw** *n* a wall or other boundary marker that is set in a ditch so as not to interrupt the landscape. [C18: from French *haha,* probably based on *ha!* ejaculation denoting surprise]

Hahn (*German* haːn) *n* **1 Kurt.** 1886–1974, German educationalist. During the Nazi era he escaped to Britain, where he founded Gordonstoun School (1935) and helped to establish the Duke of Edinburgh's award scheme. **2 Otto** ('ɔto). 1879–1968, German physicist: discovered the radioactive element protactinium with Meitner (1917); with Strassmann, demonstrated the nuclear fission of uranium, when it is bombarded with neutrons: Nobel prize for chemistry 1944.

Hahnemann (*German* 'haːnəman) *n* **(Christian Friedrich) Samuel** ('zaːmueːl). 1755–1843, German physician; founder of homeopathy.

hahnium ('hɑːnɪəm) *n* a transuranic element artificially produced from californium. Symbol: Ha; atomic no.: 105; half-life of most stable isotope, ^{262}Ha: 40 seconds. [C20: named after Otto HAHN]

Haida ('haɪdə) *n* **1** (*pl* **-das** *or* **-da**) a member of a seafaring group of North American Indian peoples inhabiting the coast of British Columbia and SW Alaska. **2** the language of these peoples, belonging to the Na-Dene phylum. ▸ **'Haidan** *adj*

Haidar Ali ('haɪdər 'ɑːlɪ) *n* a variant spelling of **Hyder Ali.**

Haiduk, Heyduck, *or* **Heiduc** ('haɪdʊk) *n* a rural brigand in the European part of the Ottoman Empire. [C17: from Hungarian *hajdúk* brigands]

Haifa ('haɪfə) *n* a port in NW Israel, near Mount Carmel, on the Bay of Acre: Israel's chief port, with an oil refinery and other heavy industry. Pop.: 255 300 (1997 est.).

Haig (heɪg) *n* **Douglas,** 1st Earl Haig. 1861–1928, British field marshal; commander in chief of the British forces in France and Flanders (1915–18).

haik *or* **haick** (haɪk, heɪk) *n* an Arab's outer garment of cotton, wool, or silk, for the head and body. [C18: from Arabic *hā'ik*]

haiku ('haɪkuː) *or* **hokku** *n, pl* **-ku.** an epigrammatic Japanese verse form in 17 syllables. [from Japanese, from *hai* amusement + *ku* verse]

hail[1] (heɪl) *n* **1** small pellets of ice falling from cumulonimbus clouds when there are very strong rising air currents. **2** a shower or storm of such pellets. **3** words, ideas, etc., directed with force and in great quantity: *a hail of abuse.* **4** a collection of objects, esp. bullets, spears, etc., directed at someone with violent force. ◆ *vb* **5** (*intr;* with *it* as subject) to be the case that hail is falling. **6** (often with *it* as subject) to fall or cause to fall as or like hail: *to hail criticism; bad language hailed about him.* [Old English *hægl;* related to Old Frisian *heil,* Old High German *hagal* hail, Greek *kakhlēx* pebble]

hail[2] (heɪl) *vb* (*mainly tr*) **1** to greet, esp. enthusiastically: *the crowd hailed the actress with joy.* **2** to acclaim or acknowledge: *they hailed him as their hero.* **3** to attract the attention of by shouting or gesturing: *to hail a taxi; to hail a passing ship.* **4** (*intr;* foll. by *from*) to be a native (of); originate (in): *she hails from India.* ◆ *n* **5** the act or an instance of hailing. **6** a shout or greeting. **7** distance across which one can attract attention (esp. in the phrase **within hail**). ◆ *sentence substitute.* **8** *Poetic.* an exclamation of greeting. [C12: from Old Norse *heill* WHOLE; see HALE[1], WASSAIL] ▸ **'hailer** *n*

Haile Selassie ('haɪlɪ sə'læsɪ) *n* title of *Ras Tafari Makonnen.* 1892–1975, emperor of Ethiopia (1930–36; 1941–74). During the Italian occupation of Ethiopia (1936–41), he lived in exile in England. He was a prominent figure in the Pan-African movement: deposed 1974.

hail-fellow-well-met *adj* genial and familiar, esp. in an offensive or ingratiating way: *a hail-fellow-well-met slap on the back.*

Hail Mary *n* **1** *R.C. Church.* a prayer to the Virgin Mary, based on the salutations of the angel Gabriel (Luke 1:28) and Elizabeth (Luke 1:42) to her. Also called: **Ave Maria. 2** *American football. Slang.* a very long high pass into the end zone, made in the final seconds of a half or of a game.

Hailsham of St Marylebone ('heɪlʃəm) *n* Baron, title of **Quintin (McGarel) Hogg** ('kwɪntɪn). born 1907, British Conservative politician; Lord Chancellor (1970–74; 1979–87). He renounced his viscountcy in 1963 when he made an unsuccessful bid for the Conservative Party leadership; he became a life peer in 1970.

hailstone ('heɪlˌstəʊn) *n* a pellet of hail.

hailstorm ('heɪlˌstɔːm) *n* a storm during which hail falls.

Hailwood ('heɪlwʊd) *n* **Mike,** full name *Stanley Michael Bailey Hailwood.* 1940–81, English racing motorcyclist: world champion (250 cc.) 1961 and 1966–67; (350 cc.) 1966–67; and (500 cc.) 1962–65.

Hainan ('haɪ'næn) *or* **Hainan Tao** (taʊ) *n* an island and province in the South China Sea, separated from the mainland of S China by **Hainan Strait:** part of Guangdong province until 1988; China's second largest offshore island. Pop.: 7 240 000 (1996 est.). Area: 33 572 sq. km (12 962 sq. miles).

Hainaut *or* **Hainault** (*French* ɛno) *n* a province of SW Belgium: stretches from the Flanders Plain in the north to the Ardennes in the south. Capital: Mons. Pop.: 1 284 761 (1996 est.). Area: 3797 sq. km (1466 sq. miles).

hain't (heɪnt) *Archaic or dialect. contraction of* has not, have not, *or* is not.

Haiphong ('haɪ'fɒŋ) *n* a port in N Vietnam, on the Red River delta: a major industrial centre. Pop.: 783 133 (1992 est.).

hair (hɛə) *n* **1** any of the threadlike pigmented structures that grow from follicles beneath the skin of mammals and consist of layers of dead keratinized cells. **2** a growth of such structures, as on the human head or animal body, which helps prevent heat loss from the body. **3** *Botany.* any threadlike outgrowth from the epidermis, such as a root hair. **4a** a fabric or material made from the hair of some animals. **4b** (*as modifier*)*: a hair carpet; a hair shirt.* **5** another word for **hair's-breadth:** *to lose by a hair.* **6 get in someone's hair.** *Informal.* to annoy someone persistently. **7 hair of the dog (that bit one).** an alcoholic drink taken as an antidote to a hangover. **8 keep your hair on!** *Brit. informal.* keep calm. **9 let one's hair down.** to behave without reserve. **10 not turn a hair.** to show no surprise, anger, fear, etc. **11 split hairs.** to make petty and unnecessary distinctions. [Old English *hær;* related to Old Norse *hār,* Old High German *hār* hair, Norwegian *herren* stiff, hard, Lettish *sari* bristles, Latin *crescere* to grow] ▸ **'hairˌlike** *adj*

hairball ('hɛəˌbɔːl) *n* a compact mass of hair that forms in the stomach of cats, calves, etc., as a result of licking and swallowing the fur, and causes indigestion and convulsions.

hairbrush ('hɛəˌbrʌʃ) *n* a brush for grooming the hair.

haircloth ('hɛəˌklɒθ) *n* a cloth woven from horsehair, used in upholstery.

haircut ('hɛəˌkʌt) *n* **1** the act or an instance of cutting the hair. **2** the style in which hair has been cut.

hairdo ('hɛəˌduː) *n, pl* **-dos.** the arrangement of a person's hair, esp. after styling and setting.

hairdresser ('hɛəˌdrɛsə) *n* **1** a person whose business is cutting, curling, colouring and arranging hair, esp. that of women. **2** a hairdresser's establishment. ◆ Related adj: **tonsorial.** ▸ **'hairˌdressing** *n*

hairdryer *or* **hairdrier** ('hɛəˌdraɪə) *n* **1** a hand-held electric device that blows out hot air and is used to dry and, sometimes, assist in styling the hair, as in blow-drying. **2** a device for drying the hair in which hot air is blown into a hood that surrounds the head of a seated person.

-haired *adj* having hair as specified: *long-haired.*

hair follicle *n* a narrow tubular cavity that contains the root of a hair, formed by an infolding of the epidermis and corium of the skin.

hair gel *n* a jelly-like substance applied to the hair before styling in order to retain the shape of the style.

hair grass *n* any grass of the genera *Aira, Deschampsia,* etc., having very narrow stems and leaves.

hairgrip ('hɛəˌgrɪp) *n Chiefly Brit.* a small tightly bent metal hair clip. Also called (esp. U.S., Canadian, and N.Z.): **bobby pin.**

hairif ('hɛərɪf) *n* another name for **cleavers.**

hair lacquer *n* another name for **hairspray.**

hairless ('hɛəlɪs) *adj* **1** having little or no hair. **2** *Brit. slang.* very angry; raging.

hairline ('hɛəˌlaɪn) *n* **1** the natural margin formed by hair on the head. **2a** a very narrow line. **2b** (*as modifier*)*: a hairline crack.* **3** *Printing.* **3a** a thin stroke in a typeface. **3b** any typeface consisting of such strokes. **3c** thin lines beside a character, produced by worn or poorly cast type. **4** a rope or line of hair.

hairline fracture *n* a very fine crack in a bone.

hairnet ('hɛəˌnɛt) *n* any of several kinds of light netting worn over the hair to keep it in place.

hairpiece ('hɛəˌpiːs) *n* **1** a wig or toupee. **2** Also called: **postiche.** a section of extra hair attached to a woman's real hair to give it greater bulk or length.

hairpin ('hɛəˌpɪn) *n* **1** a thin double-pronged pin used by women to fasten the hair. **2** (*modifier*) (esp. of a bend in a road) curving very sharply.

hair-raising *adj* inspiring horror; terrifying: *a hair-raising drop of 600 feet.* ▸ **'hair-ˌraiser** *n*

hair restorer *n* a lotion claimed to promote hair growth.

hair's-breadth *n* **a** a very short or imperceptible margin or distance. **b** (*as modifier*)*: a hair's-breadth escape.*

hair seal *n* any earless seal, esp. the harbour seal, having a coat of stiff hair with no underfur.

hair sheep *n* any variety of sheep growing hair instead of wool, yielding hides with a finer and tougher grain than those of wool sheep.

hair shirt *n* **1** a shirt made of haircloth worn next to the skin as a penance. **2** a secret trouble or affliction.

hair slide *n* a hinged clip with a tortoiseshell, bone, or similar back, used to fasten the hair.

hair space *n Printing.* the thinnest of the metal spaces used in setting type to separate letters or words.

hairsplitting ('hɛəˌsplɪtɪŋ) *n* **1** the making of petty distinctions. ♦ *adj* **2** occupied with or based on petty distinctions. ▸ **'hairˌsplitter** *n*

hairspray ('hɛəˌspreɪ) *n* a fixative solution sprayed onto the hair to keep a hairstyle in shape. Also called: **hair lacquer.**

hairspring ('hɛəˌsprɪŋ) *n Horology.* a very fine spiral spring in some timepieces, which, in combination with the balance wheel, controls the timekeeping.

hairstreak ('hɛəˌstriːk) *n* any small butterfly of the genus *Callophrys* and related genera, having fringed wings marked with narrow white streaks: family *Lycaenidae.*

hair stroke *n* a very fine line in a written character.

hairstyle ('hɛəˌstaɪl) *n* a particular mode of arranging, cutting, or setting the hair. ▸ **'hairˌstylist** *n*

hairtail ('hɛəˌteɪl) *n* any marine spiny-finned fish of the family *Trichiuridae,* most common in warm seas, having a long whiplike scaleless body and long sharp teeth. Usual U.S. name: **cutlass fish.**

hair trigger *n* **1** a trigger of a firearm that responds to very slight pressure. **2** *Informal.* **2a** any mechanism, reaction, etc., set in operation by slight provocation. **2b** *(as modifier): a hair-trigger temper.*

hairweaving ('hɛəˌwiːvɪŋ) *n* the interweaving of false hair with the hair on a balding person's head.

hairworm ('hɛəˌwɜːm) *n* **1** any hairlike nematode worm of the family *Trichostrongylidae,* such as the stomach worm, parasitic in the intestines of vertebrates. **2** Also called: **horsehair worm.** any very thin long worm of the phylum (or class) *Nematomorpha,* the larvae of which are parasitic in arthropods.

hairy ('hɛərɪ) *adj* **hairier, hairiest. 1** having or covered with hair. **2** *Slang.* **2a** difficult or problematic. **2b** scaring, dangerous, or exciting. ▸ **'hairiness** *n*

hairyback ('hɛərɪbæk) *n S. African slang.* an offensive word for an Afrikaner.

hairy frog *n* a W African frog, *Astylosternus robustus,* the males of which have glandular hairlike processes on the flanks.

hairy willowherb *n* another name for **codlins-and-cream.**

Haiti ('heɪtɪ, hɑː'iːtɪ) *n* **1** a republic occupying the W part of the island of Hispaniola in the Caribbean, the E part consisting of the Dominican Republic: ceded by Spain to France in 1697 and became one of the richest colonial possessions in the world, with numerous plantations; slaves rebelled under Toussaint L'Ouverture in 1793 and defeated the French; taken over by the U.S. (1915–41) after long political and economic chaos; under the authoritarian regimes of François Duvalier (1957–71) and his son Jean-Claude Duvalier (1971–86); returned to civilian rule in 1990, but another coup in 1991 brought military rule, which was ended in 1994 with U.S. intervention. Official languages: French and Haitian creole. Religions: Roman Catholic and voodoo. Currency: gourde. Capital: Port-au-Prince. Pop.: 6 781 000 (1998 est.). Area: 27 749 sq. km (10 714 sq. miles). **2** a former name for **Hispaniola.**

Haitian *or* **Haytian** ('heɪʃɪən, hɑː'iːʃən) *adj* **1** relating to or characteristic of Haiti, its inhabitants, or their language. ♦ *n* **2** a native, citizen, or inhabitant of Haiti. **3** the creolized French spoken in Haiti.

Haitink ('haɪˌtɪŋk) *n* **Bernard.** born 1929, Dutch orchestral conductor; received an honorary knighthood in 1977.

hajj *or* **hadj** (hædʒ) *n, pl* **hajjes** *or* **hadjes.** the pilgrimage to Mecca that every Muslim is required to make at least once in his life, provided he has enough money and the health to do so. [from Arabic *hajj* pilgrimage]

hajji, hadji, *or* **haji** ('hædʒɪ) *n, pl* **hajjis, hadjis,** *or* **hajis. 1** a Muslim who has made a pilgrimage to Mecca: also used as a title. **2** a Christian of the Greek Orthodox or Armenian Churches who has visited Jerusalem. ▸ **'hajjah** ('hædʒə) *fem n*

haka ('hɑkə) *n N.Z.* **1** a Maori war chant accompanied by gestures. **2** a similar performance by a rugby team. [Maori]

hake[1] (heɪk) *n, pl* **hake** *or* **hakes. 1** any gadoid food fish of the genus *Merluccius,* such as *M. merluccius* (European hake), of the N hemisphere, having an elongated body with a large head and two dorsal fins. **2** any North American fish of the genus *Urophycis,* similar and related to *Merluccius* species. **3** *Austral.* another name for **barracouta.** [C15: perhaps from Old Norse *haki* hook; compare Old English *hacod* pike; see HOOK]

hake[2] (heɪk) *n* a wooden frame for drying cheese or fish. [C18: variant of HECK[2]]

hakea ('hɑːkɪə, 'heɪkɪə) *n* any shrub or tree of the Australian genus *Hakea,* having a hard woody fruit and often yielding a useful wood: family *Proteaceae.* [C19: New Latin, named after C. L. von *Hake* (died 1818), German botanist]

Hakenkreuz *German* ('hɑːkənˌkrɔɪts) *n* the swastika. [literally: hooked cross]

hakim *or* **hakeem** (hɑː'kiːm, 'hɑːkiːm) *n* **1** a Muslim judge, ruler, or administrator. **2** a Muslim physician. [C17: from Arabic, from *hakama* to rule]

Hakluyt ('hækluːt) *n* **Richard.** ?1552–1616, English geographer, who compiled *The Principal Navigations, Voyages, and Discoveries of the English Nation* (1589).

Hakodate (ˌhɑːkəʊ'dɑːteɪ) *n* a port in N Japan, on S Hokkaido: fishing industry and shipbuilding. Pop.: 298 868 (1995).

hal- *combining form.* a variant of **halo-** before a vowel.

Halacha, Halaka, *or* ***Halakha*** (*Hebrew* hɑlɑ'xɑː; *Yiddish* hɑ'lochə) *n* **1a** Jewish religious law. **1b** a ruling on some specific matter. **2a** that part of the Talmud which is concerned with legal matters as distinct from homiletics. **2b** Jewish legal literature in general. ♦ Compare **Aggadah** (sense 1). [from Hebrew *hălākhāh* way]

Halafian (hə'lɑːfɪən) *adj* of or relating to the Neolithic culture extending from Iran to the Mediterranean.

halal *or* **hallal** (hɑː'lɑːl) *n* **1** meat from animals that have been killed according to Muslim law. ♦ *adj* **2** of or relating to such meat: *a halal butcher.* ♦ *vb* **-als, -alling, -alled** *(tr)* **3** to kill (animals) in this way. [from Arabic: lawful]

halation (hə'leɪʃən) *n Photog.* fogging usually seen as a bright ring surrounding a source of light: caused by reflection from the back of the film. [C19: from HALO + -ATION]

halberd ('hælbəd) *or* **halbert** ('hælbət) *n* a weapon consisting of a long shaft with an axe blade and a pick, topped by a spearhead: used in 15th- and 16th-century warfare. [C15: from Old French *hallebarde,* from Middle High German *helm* handle, HELM[1] + *barde* axe, from Old High German *bart* BEARD] ▸ ˌ**halber'dier** *n*

Halberstadt ('hælbəˌstæt) *n* a town in central Germany, in Saxony-Anhalt: industrial centre noted for its historic buildings. Pop.: 47 500 (1989 est.).

halcyon ('hælsɪən) *adj also* **halcyonian** (ˌhælsɪ'əʊnɪən) *or* **halcyonic** (ˌhælsɪ'ɒnɪk). **1** peaceful, gentle, and calm. **2** happy and carefree. ♦ *n* **3** *Greek myth.* a fabulous bird associated with the winter solstice. **4** a poetic name for the **kingfisher. 5 halcyon days. 5a** a fortnight of calm weather during the winter solstice. **5b** a period of peace and happiness. [C14: from Latin *alcyon,* from Greek *alkuōn* kingfisher, of uncertain origin]

Halcyone (hæl'saɪənɪ) *n* a variant of **Alcyone**[1].

Haldane ('hɔːldeɪn) *n* **1 J**(ohn) **B**(urdon) **S**(anderson). 1892–1964, Scottish biochemist, geneticist, and writer on science. **2** his father, **John Scott.** 1860–1936, Scottish physiologist, noted particularly for his research into industrial diseases. **3** his brother, **Richard Burdon,** 1st Viscount Haldane of Cloan. 1856–1928, British statesman and jurist. As secretary of state for war (1905–12) he reorganized the army and set up the territorial reserve.

hale[1] (heɪl) *adj* **1** healthy and robust (esp. in the phrase **hale and hearty**). **2** *Scot. and northern English dialect.* whole. [Old English *hæl* WHOLE] ▸ **'haleness** *n*

hale[2] (heɪl) *vb (tr)* to pull or drag; haul. [C13: from Old French *haler,* of Germanic origin; compare Old High German *halōn* to fetch, Old English *geholian* to acquire] ▸ **'haler** *n*

Hale (heɪl) *n* **1 George Ellery.** 1868–1938, U.S. astronomer: undertook research into sunspots and invented the spectroheliograph. **2** Sir **Matthew.** 1609–76, English judge and scholar; Lord Chief Justice (1671–76).

Haleakala (ˌhɑːliːˌɑːkɑː'lɑː) *n* a volcano in Hawaii, on E Mani Island. Height: 3057 m (10 032 ft.). Area of crater: 49 sq. km (19 sq. miles). Depth of crater: 829 m (2720 ft.).

haler ('hɑːlə) *n, pl* **-lers** *or* **-leru** (-ləˌruː). a monetary unit of the Czech Republic worth one hundredth of a koruna. Also called: **heller.** [Czech, from Middle High German *haller* a silver coin, after *Hall,* Swabian town where the coins were minted]

Halesowen (heɪlz'əʊɪn) *n* a town in W central England, in Dudley unitary authority, West Midlands. Pop.: 57 918 (1991).

Halévy (*French* alevi) *n* **1** (**Jacques François**) **Fromental** (fromɛ̃tal), original name *Elias Levy.* 1799–1862, French composer, noted for his operas, which include *La Juive* (1835). **2** his nephew, **Ludovic** (lydɔvik). 1834–1908, French dramatist and novelist, who collaborated with Meilhac on opera libretti.

Haley ('heɪlɪ) *n* **Bill,** full name *William John Clifton Haley.* 1925–81, U.S. rock and roll singer, best known for his recording of "Rock Around the Clock" (1955).

half (hɑːf) *n, pl* **halves** (hɑːvz). **1a** either of two equal or corresponding parts that together comprise a whole. **1b** a quantity equalling such a part: *half a dozen.* **2** half a pint, esp. of beer. **3** *Scot.* a small drink of spirits, esp. whisky. **4** *Football, hockey, etc.* the half of the pitch regarded as belonging to one team. **5** *Golf.* an equal score on a hole or round with an opponent. **6** (in various games) either of two periods of play separated by an interval (the **first half** and **second half**). **7** a half-price ticket on a bus, train, etc. **8** short for **half-hour. 9** short for **halfpenny** (sense 1). **10** *Sport.* short for **halfback. 11** *Obsolete.* a half-year period. **12 better half.** *Humorous.* a person's wife or husband. **13 by half.** by an excessive amount or to an excessive degree: *he's too arrogant by half.* **14 by halves.** *(used with a negative)* without being thorough or exhaustive: *we don't do things by halves.* **15 go halves.** (often foll. by *on, in,* etc.) **15a** to share the expenses (of something with one other person). **15b** to share the whole amount (of something with another person): *to go halves on an orange.* ♦ *determiner* **16a** being a half or approximately a half: *half the kingdom.* **16b** *(as pronoun; functioning as sing or pl): half of them came.* ♦ *adj* **17** not perfect or complete; partial: *he only did a half job on it.* ♦ *adv* **18** to the amount or extent of a half. **19** to a great amount or extent. **20** partially; to an extent. **21 half two, etc.** *Informal.* 30 minutes after two o'clock. **22 have half a mind to.** to have the intention of. **23 not half.** *Informal.* **23a** not in any way: *he's not half clever enough.* **23b** *Brit.* really; very; indeed: *he isn't half stupid.* **23c** certainly; yes, indeed. ♦ Related prefixes: **bi-, demi-, hemi-, semi-.** [Old English *healf;* related to Old Norse *halfr,* Old High German *halb,* Dutch *half*]

half-a-crown *n* another name for a **half-crown.**

half-a-dollar *n Brit. slang.* another name for a **half-crown.**

half-and-half *n* **1** a mixture of half one thing and half another thing. **2** a drink consisting of equal parts of beer and stout, or equal parts of bitter and mild. ♦ *adj* **3** of half one thing and half another thing. ♦ *adv* **4** in two equal parts.

half-assed *adj U.S. and Canadian slang.* **1** incompetent; inept. **2** lacking efficiency or organization.

halfback ('hɑːfˌbæk) *n* **1** *Rugby.* either the scrum half or the stand-off half. **2** *Soccer, old-fashioned.* any of three players positioned behind the line of for-

wards and in front of the fullbacks. **3** any of certain similar players in other team sports. **4** the position of a player who is halfback.
half-baked *adj* **1** insufficiently baked. **2** *Informal.* foolish; stupid. **3** *Informal.* poorly planned or conceived.
half-ball *n* **a** a contact in billiards, etc., in which the player aims through the centre of the cue ball to the edge of the object ball, so that half the object ball is covered. **b** (*as modifier*): *a half-ball stroke.*
halfbeak ('hɑːfˌbiːk) *n* any marine and freshwater teleost fish of the tropical and subtropical family *Hemiramphidae,* having an elongated body with a short upper jaw and a long protruding lower jaw.
half-binding *n* a type of hardback bookbinding in which the spine and corners are bound in one material, such as leather, and the sides in another, such as cloth.
half-blood *n* **1a** the relationship between individuals having only one parent in common. **1b** an individual having such a relationship. **2** a less common name for a **half-breed. 3** a half-blooded domestic animal.
half-blooded *adj* **1** being related to another individual through only one parent. **2** having parents of different races. **3** (of a domestic animal) having only one parent of known pedigree.
half-blue *n* (at Oxford and Cambridge universities) a sportsman who substitutes for a full blue or who represents the university in a minor sport. Compare **blue** (sense 4).
half board *n* **a** the daily provision by a hotel of bed, breakfast, and one main meal. **b** (*as modifier*): *half-board accommodation.* ◆ Also called: **demi-pension.**
half-board *n* a manoeuvre by a sailing ship enabling it to gain distance to windward by luffing up into the wind.
half-boot *n* a boot reaching to the midcalf.
half-bound *adj* (of a book) having a half-binding.
half-breed *n* **1** *Often offensive.* a person whose parents are of different races, esp. the offspring of a White person and an American Indian. ◆ *adj also* **half-bred. 2** of, relating to, or designating offspring of people or animals of different races or breeds.
half-brother *n* the son of either of one's parents by another partner.
half-butt *n* a snooker cue longer than an ordinary cue.
half-caste *n* **1** a person having parents of different races, esp. the offspring of a European and an Indian. ◆ *adj* **2** of, relating to, or designating such a person.
half-cock *n* **1** on a single-action firearm, a halfway position in which the hammer can be set for safety; in this position the trigger is cocked by the hammer which cannot reach the primer to fire the weapon. **2 go off at half-cock** *or* **half-cocked. 2a** to fail as a result of inadequate preparation or premature starting. **2b** to act or function prematurely.
half-cocked *adj* (of a firearm) at half-cock.
half-crown *n* a British silver or cupronickel coin worth two shillings and sixpence (now equivalent to 12½p), taken out of circulation in 1970. Also called: **half-a-crown.**
half-day *n* a day when one works only in the morning or only in the afternoon.
half-dead *adj Brit. informal.* very tired.
half-dollar *n* (in the U.S.) a 50-cent piece.
half eagle *n* a former U.S. gold coin worth five dollars.
half-forward *n Australian Rules football.* any of three forwards positioned between the centre line and the forward line.
half frame *n* **a** a photograph taking up half the normal area of a frame on a particular film, taken esp. on 35-millimetre film. **b** (*as modifier*): *a half-frame camera.*
half gainer *n* a type of dive in which the diver completes a half backward somersault to enter the water headfirst facing the diving board. Compare **gainer.**
half-hardy *adj* (of a cultivated plant) able to survive out of doors except during severe frost.
half-hearted *adj* without enthusiasm or determination. ▸ **ˌhalf-'heartedly** *adv* ▸ **ˌhalf-'heartedness** *n*
half-hitch *n* a knot made by passing the end of a piece of rope around itself and through the loop thus made.
half holiday *n* a day of which either the morning or the afternoon is a holiday.
half-hour *n* **1a** a period of 30 minutes. **1b** (*as modifier*): *a half-hour stint.* **2a** the point of time 30 minutes after the beginning of an hour. **2b** (*as modifier*): *a half-hour chime.* ▸ **ˌhalf-'hourly** *adv, adj*
half-hunter *n* a watch with a hinged lid in which a small circular opening or crystal allows the approximate time to be read. See **hunter** (sense 5).
half-inch *n* **1** a measure of length approximately equivalent to 13 millimetres. ◆ *vb* **2** *Slang, old-fashioned.* to steal. [sense 2: from rhyming slang for *pinch*]
half-jack *n S. African informal.* a flat pocket-sized bottle of alcohol. [C20 *jack,* probably from C16 *jack* a leather-covered vessel, from Old French *jaque,* of uncertain origin]
half landing *n* a landing halfway up a flight of stairs.
half-leather *n* a type of half-binding in which the backs and corners of a book are bound in leather.
half-length *adj* **1** (of a portrait) showing only the body from the waist up and including the hands. **2** of half the entire or original length. ◆ *n* **3** a half-length portrait.
half-life *n* **1** the time taken for half of the atoms in a radioactive material to undergo decay. Symbol: τ **2** the time required for half of a quantity of radioactive material absorbed by a living tissue or organism to be naturally eliminated (**biological half-life**) or removed by both elimination and decay (**effective half-life**).
half-light *n* a dim light, as at dawn or dusk.
half-marathon *n* a race on foot of 13 miles 352 yards (21.243 kilometres).
half-mast *n* **1** the lower than normal position to which a flag is lowered on a mast as a sign of mourning or distress. ◆ *vb* **2** (*tr*) to put (a flag) in this position.
half measure *n* (*often pl*) an inadequate measure.
half-miler *n* a runner who specializes in running races over half a mile.
half-moon *n* **1** the moon at first or last quarter when half its face is illuminated. **2** the time at which a half-moon occurs. **3a** something shaped like a half-moon. **3b** (*as modifier*): *half-moon spectacles.* **4** *Anatomy.* a nontechnical name for **lunula.**
half-mourning *n* dark grey clothes worn by some during a period after full formal mourning.
half-nelson *n* a wrestling hold in which a wrestler places an arm under one of his opponent's arms from behind and exerts pressure with his palm on the back of his opponent's neck. Compare **full nelson.**
half-note *n* the usual U.S. and Canadian name for **minim** (sense 2).
half-open *adj Chess.* (of a file) having a pawn or pawns of only one colour on it.
half-p *n, pl* **-ps.** an informal name for a **halfpenny** (sense 1).
half-pedalling *n* a technique of piano playing in which the sustaining pedal is raised and immediately depressed thus allowing the lower strings to continue sounding.
halfpenny *or* **ha'penny** ('heɪpnɪ, for sense 1 'hɑːfˌpenɪ) *n* **1** (*pl* **-pennies**) Also called: **half.** a small British coin worth half a new penny, withdrawn from circulation in 1985. **2** (*pl* **-pennies**) an old British coin worth half an old penny. **3** (*pl* **-pence**) the sum represented by half a penny. **4** (*pl* **-pence**) something of negligible value. **5** (*modifier*) having the value or price of a halfpenny. **6** (*modifier*) of negligible value.
halfpennyworth *or* **ha'p'orth** ('heɪpəθ) *n* **1** an amount that may be bought for a halfpenny. **2** a trifling or very small amount.
half-pie *adj* the N.Z. term for **half-baked** (sense 3). [from Maori *pai* good]
half-plate *n Photography.* a size of plate measuring 6½ × 4¼ inches.
half-price *adj, adv* for half the normal price: *children go half-price.*
half-quartern *n Brit.* a loaf having a weight, when baked, of 800 g.
half-rhyme *n* a rhyme in which the vowel sounds are not identical, such as *years* and *yours.* See **consonance** (sense 2).
half-round chisel *n* a cold chisel with a semicircular cutting edge used for making narrow channels.
half-round file *n Engineering.* a file having a semicircular cross-section.
half seas over *adj Brit. informal.* drunk.
half-section *n Engineering.* a scale drawing of a section through a symmetrical object that shows only half the object.
half-silvered *adj* (of a mirror) having an incomplete reflective coating, so that half the incident light is reflected and half transmitted: used in optical instruments and two-way mirrors.
half-sister *n* the daughter of either of one's parents by another partner.
half-size *n* any size, esp. in clothing, that is halfway between two sizes.
half-slip *n* a woman's topless slip that hangs from the waist. Also called: **waist-slip.**
half-sole *n* **1** a sole from the shank of a shoe to the toe. ◆ *vb* **2** (*tr*) to replace the half-sole of (a shoe).
half-step *n Music, U.S. and Canadian.* another word for **semitone.**
half term *n Brit. education.* **a** a short holiday midway through an academic term. **b** (*as modifier*): *a half-term holiday.*
half-tide *n* the state of the tide between flood and ebb.
half-timbered *or* **half-timber** *adj* (of a building, wall, etc.) having an ex-

ˌhalf-a'fraid *adj*
ˌhalf-a'sleep *adj*
ˌhalf-a'wake *adj*
ˌhalf-'blind *adj*
ˌhalf-'bottle *n*
ˌhalf-'buried *adj*
ˌhalf-'century *n, pl* **-ies.**
ˌhalf-'circle *n*
ˌhalf-'closed *adj*
ˌhalf-com'pleted *adj*
ˌhalf-con'cealed *adj*
ˌhalf-'conscious *adj*
ˌhalf-con'vinced *adj*
ˌhalf-'cooked *adj*
ˌhalf-'covered *adj*
ˌhalf-'crazy *adj*
ˌhalf-'cut *adj*
ˌhalf-de'serted *adj*
ˌhalf-di'gested *adj*
ˌhalf-'done *adj*
ˌhalf-'dozen *n*
ˌhalf-'dressed *adj*
ˌhalf-'drowned *adj*
ˌhalf-'drunk *adj*
ˌhalf-'eaten *adj*
ˌhalf-'eduˌcated *adj*
ˌhalf-'empty *adj*
ˌhalf-'English *adj*
ˌhalf-'filled *adj*
ˌhalf-'finished *adj*
ˌhalf-for'gotten *adj*
ˌhalf-'formed *adj*
ˌhalf-'frozen *adj*
ˌhalf-'full *adj*
ˌhalf-'grown *adj*
ˌhalf-'heard *adj*
ˌhalf-'hoping *adj*
ˌhalf-'human *adj*
ˌhalf-in'clined *adj*
ˌhalf-'joking *adj*
ˌhalf-'jokingly *adv*
ˌhalf-'mad *adj*
ˌhalf-'mile *n*
ˌhalf-'minute *n*
ˌhalf-'naked *adj*
ˌhalf-'pay *n*
ˌhalf-'raw *adj*
ˌhalf-re'membered *adj*
ˌhalf-'right *adj*
ˌhalf-'rotten *adj*
ˌhalf-'ruined *adj*
ˌhalf-'second *n*
ˌhalf-'serious *adj*
ˌhalf-'seriously *adv*
ˌhalf-'shut *adj*
ˌhalf-'smile *n*
ˌhalf-'starved *adj*
ˌhalf-sub'merged *adj*

posed timber framework filled with brick, stone, or plastered laths, as in Tudor architecture. ▸ ˌ**half-ˈtimbering** *n*

half-time *n Sport.* **a** a rest period between the two halves of a game. **b** (*as modifier*): *the half-time score.*

half-title *n* **1** the short title of a book as printed on the right-hand page preceding the title page. **2** a title on a separate page preceding a section of a book.

halftone (ˈhɑːfˌtəʊn) *n* **1a** a process used to reproduce an illustration by photographing it through a fine screen to break it up into dots. **1b** the etched plate thus obtained. **1c** the print obtained from such a plate. **2** *Art.* a tonal value midway between highlight and dark shading. ◆ *adj* **3** relating to, used in, or made by halftone.

half-track *n* a vehicle with caterpillar tracks on the wheels that supply motive power only. ▸ ˈ**half-ˌtracked** *adj*

half-truth *n* a partially true statement intended to mislead. ▸ ˈ**half-ˈtrue** *adj*

half volley *Sport.* ◆ *n* **1** a stroke or shot in which the ball is hit immediately after it bounces. ◆ *vb* **half-volley. 2** to hit or kick (a ball) immediately after it bounces.

halfway (ˌhɑːfˈweɪ) *adv, adj* **1** at or to half the distance; at or to the middle. **2** in or of an incomplete manner or nature. **3 meet halfway.** to compromise with.

halfway house *n* **1** a place to rest midway on a journey. **2** the halfway point in any progression. **3** a centre or hostel designed to facilitate the readjustment to private life of released prisoners, mental patients, etc. **4** *Brit.* a compromise: *a halfway house between fixed and floating exchange rates.*

halfwit (ˈhɑːfˌwɪt) *n* **1** a feeble-minded person. **2** a foolish or inane person. ▸ ˌ**halfˈwitted** *adj* ▸ ˌ**halfˈwittedly** *adv* ▸ ˌ**halfˈwittedness** *n*

hali- *combining form.* a variant of **halo-.**

halibut (ˈhælɪbət) *or* **holibut** (ˈhɒlɪbət) *n, pl* **-buts** *or* **-but. 1** the largest flatfish: a dark green North Atlantic species, *Hippoglossus hippoglossus,* that is a very important food fish: family *Pleuronectidae.* **2** any of several similar and related flatfishes, such as *Reinhardtius hippoglossoides* (**Greenland halibut**). [C15: from *hali* HOLY (because it was eaten on holy days) + *butte* flat fish, from Middle Dutch *butte*]

Haliç (haˈliːtʃ) *n* the Turkish name for the **Golden Horn.**

Halicarnassus (ˌhælɪkɑːˈnæsəs) *n* a Greek colony on the SW coast of Asia Minor: one of the major Hellenistic cities. ▸ ˌ**Halicarˈnassian** *adj*

halide (ˈhælaɪd) *or* **halid** (ˈhælɪd) *n* **1** a binary compound containing a halogen atom or ion in combination with a more electropositive element. **2** any organic compound containing halogen atoms in its molecules.

halidom (ˈhælɪdəm) *n Archaic.* a holy place or thing. [Old English *hāligdōm;* see HOLY, -DOM]

Halifax[1] (ˈhælɪˌfæks) *n* **1** a port in SE Canada, capital of Nova Scotia, on the Atlantic: founded in 1749 as a British stronghold. Pop.: 114 455 (1991). **2** a town in N England, in Calderdale unitary authority, West Yorkshire: textiles. Pop.: 91 069 (1991).

Halifax[2] (ˈhælɪˌfæks) *n* **1 Charles Montagu,** Earl of Halifax. 1661–1715, British statesman; founder of the National Debt (1692) and the Bank of England (1694). **2 Edward Frederick Lindley Wood,** Earl of Halifax. 1881–1959, British Conservative statesman. He was viceroy of India (1926–31), foreign secretary (1938–40), and ambassador to the U.S. (1941–46). **3 George Savile,** 1st Marquess of Halifax, known as *the Trimmer.* 1633–95, British politician, noted for his wavering opinions. He opposed the exclusion of the Catholic James II from the throne but later supported the Glorious Revolution.

haliplankton (ˈhælɪˌplæŋktən) *n* plankton living in sea water.

halite (ˈhælaɪt) *n* a colourless or white mineral sometimes tinted by impurities, found in beds as an evaporite. It is used to produce common salt and chlorine. Composition: sodium chloride. Formula: NaCl. Crystal structure: cubic. Also called: **rock salt.** [C19: from New Latin *halītes;* see HALO-, -ITE[2]]

halitosis (ˌhælɪˈtəʊsɪs) *n* the state or condition of having bad breath. [C19: New Latin, from Latin *hālitus* breath, from *hālāre* to breathe]

hall (hɔːl) *n* **1** a room serving as an entry area within a house or building. **2** (*sometimes cap.*) a building for public meetings. **3** (*often cap.*) the great house of an estate; manor. **4** a large building or room used for assemblies, worship, concerts, dances, etc. **5** a residential building, esp. in a university; hall of residence. **6a** a large room, esp. for dining, in a college or university. **6b** a meal eaten in this room. **7** the large room of a house, castle, etc. **8** *U.S. and Canadian.* a passage or corridor into which rooms open. **9** (*often pl*) *Informal.* short for **music hall.** [Old English *heall;* related to Old Norse *höll,* Old High German *halla* hall, Latin *cela* CELL[1], Old Irish *cuile* cellar, Sanskrit *śālā* hut; see HELL]

Hall (hɔːl) *n* **1 Charles Martin.** 1863–1914, U.S. chemist: discovered the electrolytic process for producing aluminium. **2** Sir **John.** 1824–1907, New Zealand statesman, born in England: prime minister of New Zealand (1879–82). **3** Sir **Peter.** born 1930, English stage director: director of the Royal Shakespeare Company (1960–73) and of the National Theatre (1973–88). **4** (**Marguerite**) **Radclyffe.** 1883–1943, British novelist and poet. Her frank treatment of a lesbian theme in the novel *The Well of Loneliness* (1928) led to an obscenity trial.

hallah (ˈhɑːlə; *Hebrew* xaˈla) *n, pl* **-lahs** *or* **-lot** (*Hebrew* -ˈlɔt). a variant spelling of **challah.**

Halle (*German* ˈhalə) *n* a city in E central Germany, in Saxony-Anhalt, on the River Saale: early saltworks; a Hanseatic city in the late Middle Ages; university (1694). Pop.: 282 784 (1996 est.). Official name: **Halle an der Saale** (an der ˈzaːlə).

Hallé (ˈhæleɪ) *n* Sir **Charles,** original name *Karl Hallé.* 1819–95, German conductor and pianist, in Britain from 1848. In 1857 he founded the Hallé Orchestra in Manchester.

Hall effect *n* the production of a potential difference across a conductor carrying an electric current when a magnetic field is applied in a direction perpendicular to that of the current flow. [named after Edwin Herbert *Hall* (1855–1938), American physicist who discovered it]

Hallel (*Hebrew* haˈlel; *Yiddish* hɑːˈleɪl) *n Judaism.* a section of the liturgy consisting of Psalms 113–18, read during the morning service on festivals, Chanukah, and Rosh Chodesh. [C18: from Hebrew *hallēl,* from *hellēl* to praise]

hallelujah, halleluiah (ˌhælɪˈluːjə), *or* **alleluia** (ˌælɪˈluːjə) *interj* **1** an exclamation of praise to God. **2** an expression of relief or a similar emotion. ◆ *n* **3** an exclamation of "Hallelujah". **4** a musical composition that uses the word *Hallelujah* as its text. [C16: from Hebrew *hallelūyāh* praise the Lord, from *hellēl* to praise + *yāh* the Lord, YAHWEH]

Haller (*German* ˈhalər) *n* **Albrecht von** (ˈalbrɛçt fɔn). 1708–77, Swiss biologist: founder of experimental physiology.

Halley (ˈhælɪ) *n* **Edmund.** 1656–1742, English astronomer and mathematician. He predicted the return of the comet now known as **Halley's comet,** constructed charts of magnetic declination, and produced the first wind maps.

Halley's Comet *n* a comet revolving around the sun in a period of about 76 years and last seen in 1985–86.

halliard (ˈhæljəd) *n* a variant spelling of **halyard.**

Hall-Jones (ˈhɔːlˈdʒəʊnz) *n* Sir **William.** 1851–1936, New Zealand statesman, born in England: prime minister of New Zealand (1906).

hallmark (ˈhɔːlˌmɑːk) *n* **1** *Brit.* an official series of marks stamped by the London Guild of Goldsmiths on gold, silver, or platinum articles to guarantee purity, date of manufacture, etc. **2** a mark or sign of authenticity or excellence. **3** an outstanding or distinguishing feature. ◆ *vb* **4** (*tr*) to stamp with or as if with a hallmark. ◆ Also (for senses 1 and 4): **platemark.** [C18: named after Goldsmiths' *Hall* in London, where items were graded and stamped]

hallo (həˈləʊ) *sentence substitute, n* **1** a variant spelling of **hello.** ◆ *sentence substitute, n, vb* **2** a variant spelling of **halloo.**

Hall of Fame *n Chiefly U.S. and Canadian.* (*sometimes not caps.*) **1** a building containing plaques or busts honouring famous people. **2** a group of famous people.

hall of residence *n* a residential block in or attached to a university, college, etc.

halloo (həˈluː), **hallo,** *or* **halloa** (həˈləʊ) *sentence substitute.* **1** a shout to attract attention, esp. to call hounds at a hunt. ◆ *n, pl* **-loos, -los,** *or* **-loas. 2** a shout of "halloo". ◆ *vb* **-loos, -looing, -looed; -los, -loing, -loed,** *or* **-loas, -loaing, -loaed. 3** to shout (something) to (someone). **4** (*tr*) to urge on or incite (dogs) with shouts. [C16: perhaps variant of *hallow* to encourage hounds by shouting]

hallow (ˈhæləʊ) *vb* (*tr*) **1** to consecrate or set apart as being holy. **2** to venerate as being holy. [Old English *hālgian,* from *hālig* HOLY] ▸ ˈ**hallower** *n*

hallowed (ˈhæləʊd; *liturgical* ˈhæləʊɪd) *adj* **1** set apart as sacred. **2** consecrated or holy. ▸ ˈ**hallowedness** *n*

Halloween *or* **Hallowe'en** (ˌhæləʊˈiːn) *n* the eve of All Saints' Day celebrated on Oct. 31 by masquerading; Allhallows Eve. [C18: see ALLHALLOWS, EVEN[2]]

Hallowmas *or* **Hallowmass** (ˈhæləʊˌmæs) *n Archaic.* the feast celebrating All Saints' Day. [C14: see ALLHALLOWS, MASS]

hall stand *or esp. U.S.* **hall tree** *n* a piece of furniture on which are hung coats, hats, etc.

Hallstatt (ˈhælstæt) *or* **Hallstattian** (hælˈstætɪən) *adj* of or relating to a late Bronze Age culture extending from central Europe to Britain and lasting from the 9th to the 5th century B.C., characterized by distinctive burial customs, bronze and iron tools, etc. [C19: named after *Hallstatt,* Austrian village where remains were found]

hallucinate (həˈluːsɪˌneɪt) *vb* (*intr*) to experience hallucinations. [C17: from Latin *ālūcinārī* to wander in mind; compare Greek *aluein* to be distraught] ▸ **halˈluciˌnator** *n*

hallucination (həˌluːsɪˈneɪʃən) *n* the alleged perception of an object when no object is present, occurring under hypnosis, in some mental disorders, etc. ▸ **halˌluciˈnational, halˈlucinative** *or* **halˈlucinatory** *adj*

hallucinogen (həˈluːsɪnəˌdʒɛn) *n* any drug, such as LSD or mescaline, that induces hallucinations. ▸ **hallucinogenic** (həˌluːsɪnəʊˈdʒɛnɪk) *adj*

hallucinosis (həˌluːsɪˈnəʊsɪs) *n Psychiatry.* a mental disorder the symptom of which is hallucinations, commonly associated with the ingestion of alcohol or other drugs.

hallux (ˈhæləks) *n* the first digit on the hind foot of a mammal, bird, reptile, or amphibian; the big toe of man. [C19: New Latin, from Late Latin *allex* big toe]

hallux valgus *n* an abnormal bending or deviation of the big toe towards the other toes of the same foot.

hallway (ˈhɔːlˌweɪ) *n* a hall or corridor.

halm (hɔːm) *n* a variant spelling of **haulm.**

halma (ˈhælmə) *n* a board game in which players attempt to transfer their pieces from their own to their opponents' bases. [C19: from Greek *halma* leap, from *hallesthai* to leap]

Halmahera (ˌhælməˈhɪərə) *n* an island in NE Indonesia, the largest of the Moluccas: consists of four peninsulas enclosing three bays; mountainous and forested. Area: 17 780 sq. km (6865 sq. miles). Dutch name: **Djailolo, Gilolo,** or **Jilolo.**

Halmstad (*Swedish* ˈhalmstɑːd) *n* a port in SW Sweden, on the Kattegat. Pop.: 83 080 (1994).

halo (ˈheɪləʊ) *n, pl* **-loes** *or* **-los. 1** a disc or ring of light around the head of an

ˌ**half-ˌunderˈstood** *adj*	ˌ**half-ˈused** *adj*	ˌ**half-ˈwild** *adj*	ˌ**half-ˈyear** *n*

angel, saint, etc., as in painting or sculpture. **2** the aura surrounding an idealized, famous, or admired person, thing, or event. **3** a circle of light around the sun or moon, caused by the refraction of light by particles of ice. **4** *Astronomy.* a spherical cloud of stars surrounding the Galaxy and other spiral galaxies. ◆ *vb* **-loes** *or* **-los, -loing, -loed. 5** to surround with or form a halo. [C16: from Medieval Latin, from Latin *halōs* circular threshing floor, from Greek] ▸ **'halo-,like** *adj*

halo-, hali-, *or before a vowel* **hal-** *combining form.* **1** indicating salt or the sea: *halophyte.* **2** relating to or containing a halogen: *halothane.* [from Greek *hals, hal-* sea, salt]

halobiont (ˌhæləʊ'baɪɒnt) *n* a plant or animal that lives in a salty environment such as the sea. [C20: from HALO- + *-biont* from Greek *bios* life] ▸ **ˌhalobi'ontic** *adj*

halo effect *n* See **horns and halo effect.**

halogen ('hæləˌdʒɛn) *n* any of the chemical elements fluorine, chlorine, bromine, iodine, and astatine. They are all monovalent and readily form negative ions. [C19: from Swedish; see HALO-, -GEN] ▸ **'halogenˌoid** *adj* ▸ **halogenous** (hə'lɒdʒɪnəs) *adj*

halogenate ('hælədʒəˌneɪt) *vb Chem.* to treat or combine with a halogen. ▸ **ˌhalogen'ation** *n*

haloid ('hælɔɪd) *Chem.* ◆ *adj* **1** resembling or derived from a halogen: *a haloid salt.* ◆ *n* **2** a compound containing halogen atoms in its molecules; halide.

halon ('hælɒn) *n* any of a class of chemical compounds derived from hydrocarbons by replacing one or more hydrogen atoms by bromine atoms and other hydrogen atoms by other halogen atoms (chlorine, fluorine, or iodine). Halons are stable compounds that are used in fire extinguishers, although they may contribute to depletion of the ozone layer.

halophile ('hæləʊˌfaɪl) *n* an organism that thrives in media of very high salt concentration, such as in the Dead Sea. ▸ **ˌhalo'philic** *adj*

halophyte ('hæləʊˌfaɪt) *n* a plant that grows in very salty soil, as in a salt marsh. ▸ **halophytic** (ˌhælə'fɪtɪk) *adj* ▸ **'haloˌphytism** *n*

halosere ('hæləʊˌsɪə) *n Ecology.* a plant community that originates and develops in conditions of high salinity.

halothane ('hæləʊˌθeɪn) *n* a colourless volatile slightly soluble liquid with an odour resembling that of chloroform; 2-bromo-2-chloro-1,1,1-trifluoroethane: a general anaesthetic. Formula: $CF_3CHBrCl$. [C20: from HALO- + *-thane,* as in METHANE]

Hals (*Dutch* hɑls) *n* **Frans** (frɑns). ?1580–1666, Dutch portrait and genre painter: his works include *The Laughing Cavalier* (1624).

Hälsingborg (*Swedish* hɛlsiŋ'bɔrj) *n* the former name (until 1971) of **Helsingborg.**

halt[1] (hɔːlt) *n* **1** an interruption or end to activity, movement, or progress. **2** *Chiefly Brit.* a minor railway station, without permanent buildings. **3 call a halt (to).** to put an end (to something); stop. ◆ *n, sentence substitute.* **4** a command to halt, esp. as an order when marching. ◆ *vb* **5** to come or bring to a halt. [C17: from the phrase *to make halt,* translation of German *halt machen,* from *halten* to HOLD[1], stop]

halt[2] (hɔːlt) *vb (intr)* **1** (esp. of logic or verse) to falter or be defective. **2** to waver or be unsure. **3** *Archaic.* to be lame. ◆ *adj* **4** *Archaic.* **4a** lame. **4b** (*as collective n;* preceded by *the*): *the halt.* ◆ *n* **5** *Archaic.* lameness. [Old English *healt* lame; related to Old Norse *haltr,* Old High German *halz* lame, Greek *kólos* maimed, Old Slavonic *kladivo* hammer]

halter ('hɔːltə) *n* **1** a rope or canvas headgear for a horse, usually with a rope for leading. **2** Also called: **halterneck.** a style of woman's top fastened behind the neck and waist, leaving the back and arms bare. **3** a rope having a noose for hanging a person. **4** death by hanging. ◆ *vb (tr)* **5** to secure with a halter or put a halter on. **6** to hang (someone). [Old English *hælfter;* related to Old High German *halftra,* Middle Dutch *heliftra*]

haltere ('hæltɪə) *or* **halter** ('hæltə) *n, pl* **halteres** (hæl'tɪəriːz). one of a pair of short projections in dipterous insects that are modified hind wings, used for maintaining equilibrium during flight. Also called: **balancer.** [C18: from Greek *haltēres* (plural) hand-held weights used as balancers or to give impetus in leaping, from *hallesthai* to leap]

halting ('hɔːltɪŋ) *adj* **1** hesitant: *halting speech.* **2** lame. ▸ **'haltingly** *adv* ▸ **'haltingness** *n*

Halton ('hɔːltən) *n* a unitary authority in NW England, in Greater Manchester. Pop.: 123 000 (1996 est.). Area: 75 sq. km (29 sq. miles).

halutz *Hebrew.* (xa'lʊts; *English* hɑː'lʊts) *n* a variant spelling of **chalutz.**

halvah, halva ('hælvɑː), *or* **halavah** ('hæləvɑː) *n* an Eastern Mediterranean, Middle Eastern, or Indian sweetmeat made of honey and containing sesame seeds, nuts, rose water, saffron, etc. [from Yiddish *halva,* from Romanian, from Turkish *helve,* from Arabic *halwā* sweetmeat]

halve (hɑːv) *vb (tr)* **1** to divide into two approximately equal parts. **2** to share equally. **3** to reduce by half, as by cutting. **4** *Golf.* to take the same number of strokes on (a hole or round) as one's opponent. [Old English *hielfan;* related to Middle High German *helben;* see HALF]

halyard *or* **halliard** ('hæljəd) *n Nautical.* a line for hoisting or lowering a sail, flag, or spar. [C14 *halier,* influenced by YARD[1]; see HALE[2]]

ham[1] (hæm) *n* **1** the part of the hindquarters of a pig or similar animal between the hock and the hip. **2** the meat of this part, esp. when salted or smoked. **3** *Informal.* **3a** the back of the leg above the knee. **3b** the space or area behind the knee. **4** *Needlework.* a cushion used for moulding curves. [Old English *hamm;* related to Old High German *hamma* haunch, Old Irish *cnāim* bone, *camm* bent, Latin *camur* bent]

ham[2] (hæm) *n* **1** *Theatre, informal.* **1a** an actor who overacts or relies on stock gestures or mannerisms. **1b** overacting or clumsy acting. **1c** (*as modifier*): *a ham actor.* **2** *Informal.* **2a** a licensed amateur radio operator. **2b** (*as modifier*): *a ham licence.* ◆ *vb* **hams, hamming, hammed. 3** *Informal.* to overact. [C19: special use of HAM[1]; in some senses probably influenced by AMATEUR]

Hama ('hɑːmɑː) *n* a city in W Syria, on the Orontes River: an early Hittite settlement; famous for its huge water wheels, used for irrigation since the Middle Ages. Pop.: 229 000 (1992 est.). Biblical name: **Hamath.**

Hamadān *or* **Hamedān** ('hæməˌdæn) *n* city in W central Iran, at an altitude of over 1830 m (6000 ft.): changed hands several times from the 17th century between Iraq, Persia, and Turkey; trading centre. Pop.: 406 070 (1994 est.).

hamadryad (ˌhæmə'draɪəd, -æd) *n* **1** *Classical myth.* one of a class of nymphs, each of which inhabits a tree and dies with it. **2** another name for **king cobra.** [C14: from Latin *Hamādryas,* from Greek *Hamadruas,* from *hama* together with + *drus* tree; see DRYAD]

hamadryas (ˌhæmə'draɪəs) *n* a baboon, *Papio* (or *Comopithecus*) *hamadryas,* of Arabia and NE Africa, having long silvery hair on the head, neck, and chest: regarded as sacred by the ancient Egyptians: family *Cercopithecidae.* Also called: **hamadryas baboon, sacred baboon.** [C19: via New Latin from Latin; see HAMADRYAD]

hamal, hammal, *or* **hamaul** (hə'mɑːl) *n* (in the Orient) a porter, bearer, or servant. [from Arabic *hamala* to carry]

Hamamatsu (ˌhæmə'mætsuː) *n* a city in central Japan, in S central Honshu: cotton textiles and musical instruments. Pop.: 561 568 (1995).

hamamelidaceous (ˌhæməˌmiːlɪ'deɪʃəs, -ˌmelɪ-) *adj* of, relating to, or belonging to the *Hamamelidaceae,* a chiefly subtropical family of trees and shrubs that includes the witch hazel. [C19: from New Latin *Hamamelis* type genus, from Greek: medlar, from *hama* together with + *mēlon* fruit]

hamartia (hə'mɑːtɪə) *n Literature.* the flaw in character which leads to the downfall of the protagonist in a tragedy. [C19: from Greek]

hamartiology (həˌmɑːtɪ'ɒlədʒɪ) *n* the doctrine of sin in Christian theology. [C19: from Greek *hamartia* sin + -LOGY]

Hamas ('hæmæs) *n* an organization founded in 1987 with the aim of establishing an Islamic state in Palestine. [C20: Arabic: zeal; also an acronym for *haraka musallaha islamya* Islamic Armed Movement]

hamate ('heɪmeɪt) *adj Rare.* hook-shaped. [C18: from Latin *hāmātus,* from *hāmus* hook]

hamba ('hæmbə) *interj S. African, usually offensive.* go away; be off. [from Nguni *ukuttamba* to go]

Hambletonian (ˌhæmbᵊl'təʊnɪən) *n* one of a breed of trotting horses descended from a stallion of that name.

Hamburg ('hæmbɜːg) *n* a city-state and port in NW Germany, on the River Elbe: the largest port in Germany; a founder member of the Hanseatic League; became a free imperial city in 1510 and a state of the German empire in 1871; university (1919); extensive shipyards. Pop.: 1 707 901 (1996 est.).

hamburger ('hæmˌbɜːgə) *or* **hamburg** *n* a flat fried cake of minced beef, often served in a bread roll. Also called: **Hamburger steak, beefburger.** [C20: shortened from *Hamburger steak* (that is, steak in the fashion of HAMBURG)]

hame[1] (heɪm) *n* either of the two curved bars holding the traces of the harness, attached to the collar of a draught animal. [C14: from Middle Dutch *hame;* related to Middle High German *hame* fishing rod]

hame[2] (hem) *n, adv* a Scot. word for **home.**

Hameln (*German* 'haːməln) *n* an industrial town in N Germany, in Lower Saxony on the Weser River: famous for the legend of the Pied Piper (supposedly took place in 1284). Pop.: 57 640 (1989 est.). English name: **Hamelin** ('hæməlɪn, 'hæmlɪn).

Hamersley Range ('hæməzlɪ) *n* a mountain range in N Western Australia: iron-ore deposits. Highest peak: 1236 m (4056 ft.).

hames (heɪmz) *n* **make a hames of.** *Irish informal.* to spoil through clumsiness or ineptitude. [of unknown origin]

ham-fisted *or* **ham-handed** *adj Informal.* lacking dexterity or elegance; clumsy.

Hamhung *or* **Hamheung** ('hɑːm'hʊŋ) *n* an industrial city in central North Korea: commercial and governmental centre of NE Korea during the Yi dynasty (1392–1910). Pop.: 701 000 (1987 est.).

Hamilcar Barca (hæ'mɪlkɑː 'bɑːkə, 'hæmɪlˌkɑː) *n* died ?228 B.C., Carthaginian general; father of Hannibal. He held command (247–41) during the first Punic War and established Carthaginian influence in Spain (237–?228).

Hamilton[1] ('hæməltən) *n* **1** a port in central Canada, in S Ontario on Lake Ontario: iron and steel industry. Pop.: 318 499 (1991). **2** a city in New Zealand, on central North Island. Pop.: 156 500 (1995 est.). **3** a town in S Scotland, in South Lanarkshire near Glasgow. Pop.: 49 991 (1991). **4** the capital and chief port of Bermuda. Pop.: 1100 (1995 est.). **5** the former name of the **Churchill** River in Labrador.

Hamilton[2] ('hæməltən) *n* **1 Alexander.** ?1757–1804, American statesman. He was a leader of the Federalists and as first secretary of the Treasury (1789–95) established a federal bank. **2** Lady **Emma.** ?1765–1815, mistress of Nelson. **3 James,** 1st Duke of Hamilton. 1606–49, Scottish supporter of Charles I in the English Civil War: defeated by Cromwell at the Battle of Preston and executed. **4 Richard.** born 1922, British artist: a pioneer of the pop art style. **5** Sir **William Rowan.** 1805–65, Irish mathematician: founded Hamiltonian mechanics and formulated the theory of quaternions.

Hamiltonian (ˌhæməl'təʊnɪən) *Physics, maths.* ◆ *n* **1** a mathematical function of the coordinates and momenta of a system of particles used to express their equations of motion. **2** a mathematical operator that generates such a function. Symbol: **H** ◆ *adj* **3** denoting or relating to Sir William Rowan Hamilton, or the theory of mechanics or mathematical operator devised by him.

Hamite ('hæmaɪt) *n* a member of a group of peoples of N Africa supposedly descended from Noah's son Ham (Genesis 5:32, 10:6), including the ancient Egyptians, the Berbers, etc.

Hamitic (hæ'mɪtɪk, hə-) *n* **1** a group of N African languages related to Semitic. They are now classified in four separate subfamilies of the Afro-Asiatic family: Egyptian, Berber, Cushitic, and Chadic. ◆ *adj* **2** denoting, relating to, or belonging to this group of languages. **3** denoting, belonging to, or characteristic of the Hamites.

Hamito-Semitic *n* **1** a former name for the **Afro-Asiatic** family of languages. ◆ *adj* **2** denoting or belonging to this family of languages.

hamlet ('hæmlɪt) *n* **1** a small village or group of houses. **2** (in Britain) a village without its own church. [C14: from Old French *hamelet,* diminutive of *hamel,* from *ham,* of Germanic origin; compare Old English *hamm* plot of pasture, Low German *hamm* enclosed land; see HOME]

Hamlisch ('hæmlɪʃ) *n* **Marvin.** born 1944, U.S. composer, best known for the musical *A Chorus Line* (1975).

Hamlyn ('hæmlɪn) *n* Baron **Paul.** born 1926, British businessman and publisher.

Hamm (*German* ham) *n* an industrial city in NW Germany, in North Rhine-Westphalia: a Hanse town from 1417; severely damaged in World War II. Pop.: 183 408 (1996 est.).

Hammarskjöld ('hæmə,ʃuld; *Swedish* 'hamarʃœld) *n* **Dag** (**Hjalmar Agne Carl**) (dɑːg). 1905–61, Swedish statesman; secretary-general of the United Nations (1953–61): Nobel peace prize 1961.

hammer ('hæmə) *n* **1** a hand tool consisting of a heavy usually steel head held transversely on the end of a handle, used for driving in nails, beating metal, etc. **2** any tool or device with a similar function, such as the moving part of a door knocker, the striking head on a bell, etc. **3** a power-driven striking tool, esp. one used in forging. A **pneumatic hammer** delivers a repeated blow from a pneumatic ram, a **drop hammer** uses the energy of a falling weight. **4** a part of a gunlock that rotates about a fulcrum to strike the primer or percussion cap, either directly or via a firing pin. **5** *Athletics.* **5a** a heavy metal ball attached to a flexible wire: thrown in competitions. **5b** the event or sport of throwing the hammer. **6** an auctioneer's gavel. **7** a device on a piano that is made to strike a string or group of strings causing them to vibrate. **8** *Anatomy.* the nontechnical name for **malleus. 9 go** (*or* **come**) **under the hammer.** to be offered for sale by an auctioneer. **10 hammer and tongs.** with great effort or energy: *fighting hammer and tongs.* **11 on someone's hammer.** *Austral. and N.Z. slang.* **11a** persistently demanding and critical of someone. **11b** in hot pursuit of someone. ◆ *vb* **12** to strike or beat (a nail, wood, etc.) with or as if with a hammer. **13** (*tr*) to shape or fashion with or as if with a hammer. **14** (*tr;* foll. by *in* or *into*) to impress or force (facts, ideas, etc.) into (someone) through constant repetition. **15** (*intr*) to feel or sound like hammering: *his pulse was hammering.* **16** (*intr;* often foll. by *away*) to work at constantly. **17** (*tr*) *Brit.* **17a** to question in a relentless manner. **17b** to criticize severely. **18** *Informal.* to inflict a defeat on. **19** (*tr*) *Slang.* to beat, punish, or chastise. **20** (*tr*) *Stock Exchange.* **20a** to announce the default of (a member). **20b** to cause prices of (securities, the market, etc.) to fall by bearish selling. ◆ See also **hammer out.** [Old English *hamor;* related to Old Norse *hamarr* crag, Old High German *hamar* hammer, Old Slavonic *kamy* stone] ▸ **'hammerer** *n* ▸ **'hammer-,like** *adj*

hammer and sickle *n* **1** the emblem on the flag of the former Soviet Union, representing the industrial workers and the peasants respectively. **2** a symbolic representation of the former Soviet Union or of Communism in general.

hammer beam *n* either of a pair of short horizontal beams that project from opposite walls to support arched braces and struts.

hammer drill *n* **1** a rock drill operated by compressed air in which the boring bit is not attached to the reciprocating piston. **2** an electric hand drill providing hammering in addition to rotating action.

Hammerfest (*Norwegian* 'hamərfɛst) *n* a port in N Norway, on the W coast of Kvalöy Island: the northernmost town in Europe, with uninterrupted daylight from May 17 to July 29 and no sun between Nov. 21 and Jan. 21; fishing and tourist centre. Pop.: 6900 (1991).

hammerhead ('hæmə,hɛd) *n* **1** any shark of the genus *Sphyrna* and family *Sphyrnidae,* having a flattened hammer-shaped head. **2** a heavily built tropical African wading bird, *Scopus umbretta,* related to the herons, having a dark plumage and a long backward-pointing crest: family *Scopidae,* order *Ciconiiformes.* **3** a large African fruit bat, *Hypsignathus monstrosus,* with a large square head and hammer-shaped muzzle. ▸ **'hammer,headed** *adj*

hammerless ('hæməlɪs) *adj* (of a firearm) having the hammer enclosed so that it is not visible.

hammerlock ('hæmə,lɒk) *n* a wrestling hold in which a wrestler twists his opponent's arm upwards behind his back.

hammer out *vb* (*tr, adv*) **1** to shape or remove with or as if with a hammer. **2** to form or produce (an agreement, plan, etc.) after much discussion or dispute.

hammer price *n* the price offered as the winning bid in a public auction.

Hammersmith and Fulham ('hæmə,smɪθ) *n* a borough of Greater London on the River Thames: established in 1965 by the amalgamation of Fulham and Hammersmith. Pop.: 156 600 (1994 est.). Area: 16 sq. km (6 sq. miles).

Hammerstein II ('hæmə,staɪn) *n* **Oscar.** 1895–1960, U.S. librettist and songwriter: collaborated with the composer Richard Rodgers in musicals such as *South Pacific* (1949) and *The Sound of Music* (1959).

hammerstone ('hæmə,stəʊn) *n* a stone used as a hammer in the production of tools during the Acheulian period.

hammertoe ('hæmə,təʊ) *n* **1** a deformity of the bones of a toe causing the toe to be bent in a clawlike arch. **2** such a toe.

Hammett ('hæmət) *n* **Dashiell.** 1894–1961, U.S. writer of detective novels. His books include *The Maltese Falcon* (1930) and *The Thin Man* (1932).

hammock[1] ('hæmək) *n* a length of canvas, net, etc., suspended at the ends and used as a bed. [C16: from Spanish *hamaca,* of Taino origin] ▸ **'hammock-,like** *adj*

hammock[2] ('hæmək) *n* a variant of **hummock** (sense 3).

Hammond[1] ('hæmənd) *n* a city in NW Indiana, adjacent to Chicago. Pop.: 80 081 (1996 est.).

Hammond[2] ('hæmənd) *n* **1** Dame **Joan.** 1912–96, Australian operatic singer, born in New Zealand. **2 Walter Reginald,** known as *Wally.* 1903–65, English cricketer. An all-rounder, he played for England 85 times between 1928 and 1946.

Hammond organ *n Trademark.* an electric organ with two keyboards, electronic tone generation, and a wide variety of tone colours: invented in 1934. [C20: named after Laurens *Hammond* (1895–1973), U.S. mechanical engineer]

Hammurabi (,hæmʊ'rɑːbɪ) *or* **Hammurapi** *n* ?18th century B.C., king of Babylonia; promulgator of one of the earliest known codes of law.

hammy ('hæmɪ) *adj* **-mier, -miest.** *Informal.* **1** (of an actor) overacting or tending to overact. **2** (of a play, performance, etc.) overacted or exaggerated.

Hampden ('hæmpdən, 'hæmdən) *n* **John.** 1594–1643, English statesman; one of the leaders of the Parliamentary opposition to Charles I.

hamper[1] ('hæmpə) *vb* **1** (*tr*) to prevent the progress or free movement of. ◆ *n* **2** *Nautical.* gear aboard a vessel that, though essential, is often in the way. [C14: of obscure origin; perhaps related to Old English *hamm* enclosure, *hemm* HEM[1]] ▸ **'hamperedness** *n* ▸ **'hamperer** *n*

hamper[2] ('hæmpə) *n* **1** a large basket, usually with a cover. **2** *Brit.* such a basket and its contents, usually food. **3** *U.S.* a laundry basket. [C14: variant of HANAPER]

Hampshire[1] ('hæmp,ʃɪə, -ʃə) *n* a county of S England, on the English Channel: crossed by the **Hampshire Downs** and the South Downs, with the New Forest in the southwest and many prehistoric and Roman remains: the geographical and ceremonial county includes Portsmouth and Southampton, which became independent unitary authorities in 1997. Administrative centre: Winchester. Pop. (including unitary authorities): 1 605 700 (1994 est.). Area (including unitary authorities): 3777 sq. km (1458 sq. miles). Abbrev.: **Hants.**

Hampshire[2] ('hæmpʃə) *n* Sir **Stuart.** born 1914, British philosopher: his publications include *Thought and Action* (1959), *Two Theories of Morality* (1977), and *Innocence and Experience* (1989).

Hampstead ('hæmpstɪd) *n* a residential district in N London: part of the Greater London borough of Camden since 1965; nearby is **Hampstead Heath,** a popular recreation area.

Hampton[1] ('hæmptən) *n* **1** a city in SE Virginia, on the harbour of **Hampton Roads** on Chesapeake Bay. Pop.: 138 757 (1996 est.). **2** a district of the Greater London borough of Richmond-upon-Thames, on the River Thames: famous for **Hampton Court Palace** (built in 1515 by Cardinal Wolsey).

Hampton[2] ('hæmptən) *n* **1 Christopher James.** born 1946, British playwright: his works include *When Did You Last See My Mother?* (1964) and the screenplays for the films *Dangerous Liaisons* (1988) and *Carrington* (1995). **2 Lionel.** 1913–96, U.S. jazz-band leader and vibraphone player.

hamshackle ('hæmʃæk[ə]l) *vb* (*tr*) to hobble (a cow, horse, etc.) by tying a rope around the head and one of the legs.

hamster ('hæmstə) *n* any Eurasian burrowing rodent of the tribe *Cricetini,* such as *Mesocricetus auratus* (**golden hamster**), having a stocky body, short tail, and cheek pouches: family *Cricetidae.* They are popular pets. [C17: from German, from Old High German *hamustro,* of Slavic origin]

hamstring ('hæm,strɪŋ) *n* **1** *Anatomy.* one of the tendons at the back of the knee. Related adj: **popliteal. 2** the large tendon at the back of the hock in the hind leg of a horse, etc. ◆ *vb* **-strings, -stringing, -strung** (*tr*) **3** to cripple by cutting the hamstring of. **4** to ruin or thwart. [C16: HAM[1] + STRING]

Hamsun (*Norwegian* 'hamsun) *n* **Knut** (knuːt), pen name of *Knut Pedersen.* 1859–1952, Norwegian novelist, whose works include *The Growth of the Soil* (1917): Nobel prize for literature 1920.

hamulus ('hæmjʊləs) *n, pl* **-li** (-,laɪ). *Biology.* a hook or hooklike process at the end of some bones or between the fore and hind wings of a bee or similar insect. [C18: from Latin: a little hook, from *hāmus* hook] ▸ **'hamular, 'hamu,late, 'hamu,lose,** *or* **'hamulous** *adj*

hamza *or* **hamzah** ('hɑːmzɑː, -zə) *n* the sign used in Arabic to represent the glottal stop. [from Arabic *hamzah,* literally: a compression]

Han[1] (hæn) *n* **1** the imperial dynasty that ruled China for most of the time from 206 B.C. to 221 A.D., expanding its territory and developing its bureaucracy. **2** the Chinese people as contrasted to Mongols, Manchus, etc.

Han[2] (hæn) *n* a river in E central China, rising in S Shaanxi and flowing southeast through Hubei to the Yangtze River at Wuhan. Length: about 1450 km (900 miles).

hanaper ('hænəpə) *n* a small wickerwork basket, often used to hold official papers. [C15: from Old French *hanapier,* from *hanap* cup, of Germanic origin; compare Old High German *hnapf* bowl, Old English *hnæp*]

Hanau (*German* 'haːnau) *n* a city in central Germany, in Hesse east of Frankfurt am Main: a centre of the jewellery industry. Pop.: 84 420 (1989 est.).

hance (hæns) *n* a variant of **haunch** (sense 3).

Han Cities *pl n* a group of three cities in E central China, in SE Hubei at the confluence of the Han and Yangtze Rivers: Hanyang, Hankow, and Wuchang; united in 1950 to form the conurbation of Wuhan, the capital of Hubei province.

Hancock ('hænkɒk) *n* **1 Anthony John,** known as *Tony.* 1924–68, British comedian, noted for his radio series *Hancock's Half Hour.* **2 John.** 1737–93, American statesman; first signatory of the Declaration of Independence.

hand (hænd) *n* **1a** the prehensile part of the body at the end of the arm, consisting of a thumb, four fingers, and a palm. **1b** the bones of this part. Related adj: **manual. 2** the corresponding or similar part in animals. **3** something resembling this in shape or function. **4a** the cards dealt to one or all players in one round of a card game. **4b** a player holding such cards. **4c** one round of a card game. **5** agency or influence: *the hand of God.* **6** a part in something done: *he had a hand in the victory.* **7** assistance: *to give someone a hand with his work.* **8** a pointer on a dial, indicator, or gauge, esp. on a clock: *the minute hand.* **9**

acceptance or pledge of partnership, as in marriage: *he asked for her hand; he gave me his hand on the merger.* **10** a position or direction indicated by its location to the side of an object or the observer: *on the right hand; on every hand.* **11** a contrastive aspect, condition, etc. (in the phrases **on the one hand, on the other hand**). **12** (preceded by an ordinal number) source or origin: *a story heard at third hand.* **13** a person, esp. one who creates something: *a good hand at painting.* **14** a labourer or manual worker: *we've just taken on a new hand at the farm.* **15** a member of a ship's crew: *all hands on deck.* **16** *Printing.* another name for **index** (sense 9). **17** a person's handwriting: *the letter was in his own hand.* **18** a round of applause: *give him a hand.* **19** ability or skill: *a hand for woodwork.* **20** a manner or characteristic way of doing something: *the hand of a master.* **21** a unit of length measurement equalling four inches, used for measuring the height of horses, usually from the front hoof to the withers. **22** a cluster or bundle, esp. of bananas. **23** a shoulder of pork. **24** one of the two possible mirror-image forms of an asymmetric object, such as the direction of the helix in a screw thread. **25 a free hand.** freedom to do as desired. **26 a hand's turn.** (*usually used with a negative*) a small amount of work: *he hasn't done a hand's turn.* **27 a heavy hand.** tyranny, persecution, or oppression: *he ruled with a heavy hand.* **28 a high hand.** an oppressive or dictatorial manner. **29** (**near**) **at hand.** very near or close, esp. in time. **30 at someone's hand**(**s**). from: *the acts of kindness received at their hands.* **31 by hand. 31a** by manual rather than mechanical means. **31b** by messenger or personally: *the letter was delivered by hand.* **32 come to hand.** to become available; be received. **33 force someone's hand.** to force someone to act. **34 from hand to hand.** from one person to another. **35 from hand to mouth. 35a** in poverty: *living from hand to mouth.* **35b** without preparation or planning. **36 hand and foot.** in all ways possible; completely: *they waited on him hand and foot.* **37 hand in glove.** in an intimate relationship or close association. **38 hand in hand. 38a** together; jointly. **38b** clasping each other's hands. **39 hand over fist.** steadily and quickly; with rapid progress: *he makes money hand over fist.* **40 hold one's hand.** to stop or postpone a planned action or punishment. **41 hold someone's hand.** to support, help, or guide someone, esp. by giving sympathy or moral support. **42 in hand. 42a** in possession. **42b** under control. **42c** receiving attention or being acted on. **42d** available for use; in reserve. **42e** with deferred payment: *he works a week in hand.* **43 keep one's hand in.** to continue or practise. **44 lend a hand.** to help. **45 on hand.** close by; present: *I'll be on hand to help you.* **46 out of hand. 46a** beyond control. **46b** without reservation or deeper examination: *he condemned him out of hand.* **47 set one's hand to. 47a** to sign (a document). **47b** to start (a task or undertaking). **48 show one's hand.** to reveal one's stand, opinion, or plans. **49 take in hand.** to discipline; control. **50 throw one's hand in.** See **throw in** (sense 3). **51 to hand.** accessible. **52 try one's hand.** to attempt to do something. **53** (*modifier*) **53a** of or involving the hand: *a hand grenade.* **53b** made to be carried in or worn on the hand: *hand luggage.* **53c** operated by hand: *a hand drill.* **54** (*in combination*) made by hand rather than by a machine: *hand-sewn.* ◆ *vb* (*tr*) **55** to transmit or offer by the hand or hands. **56** to help or lead with the hand. **57** *Nautical.* to furl (a sail). **58 hand it to someone.** to give credit to someone. ◆ See also **hand down, hand in, hand-off, hand on, hand-out, hand over, hands.** [Old English *hand;* related to Old Norse *hönd,* Gothic *handus,* Old High German *hant*] ▸ **'handless** *adj* ▸ **'hand,like** *adj*

handbag ('hænd,bæg) *n* **1** Also called: **bag, purse** (U.S. and Canadian), **pocketbook** (chiefly U.S.). a woman's small bag carried to contain personal articles. **2** a small suitcase that can be carried by hand. **3** a commercial style of House music. [(for sense 3) C20: humorous allusion to the trend for groups of women to dance round their handbags in discos, nightclubs, etc.]

handball ('hænd,bɔːl) *n* **1** a game in which two teams of seven players try to throw a ball into their opponent's goal. **2** a game in which two or four people strike a ball against a wall or walls with the hand, usually gloved. **3** the small hard rubber ball used in this game. **4** *Soccer.* the offence committed when a player other than a goalkeeper in his own penalty area touches the ball with a hand. ◆ *vb* **5** *Australian Rules football.* to pass (the ball) with a blow of the fist. ▸ **'hand,baller** *n*

handbarrow ('hænd,bærəu) *n* a flat tray for transporting loads, usually carried by two men.

handbell ('hænd,bɛl) *n* a bell rung by hand, esp. one of a tuned set used in musical performance.

handbill ('hænd,bɪl) *n* a small printed notice for distribution by hand.

handbook ('hænd,buk) *n* a reference book listing brief facts on a subject or place or directions for maintenance or repair, as of a car: *a tourists' handbook.*

handbrake ('hænd,breɪk) *n* **1** a brake operated by a hand lever. **2** the lever that operates the handbrake.

handbrake turn *n* a turn sharply reversing the direction of a vehicle by speedily applying the handbrake while turning the steering wheel.

handbreadth ('hænd,brɛtθ, -,brɛdθ) *or* **hand's-breadth** *n* the width of a hand used as an indication of length.

h and c *abbrev. for* hot and cold (water).

handcart ('hænd,kɑːt) *n* a simple cart, usually with one or two wheels, pushed or drawn by hand.

handclasp ('hænd,klɑːsp) *n U.S.* another word for **handshake.**

handcraft ('hænd,krɑːft) *n* **1** another word for **handicraft.** ◆ *vb* **2** (*tr*) to make by handicraft. ▸ **'hand,crafted** *adj*

handcuff ('hænd,kʌf) *vb* **1** (*tr*) to put handcuffs on (a person); manacle. ◆ *n* **2** (*pl*) a pair of locking metal rings joined by a short bar or chain for securing prisoners, etc.

hand down *vb* (*tr, adv*) **1** to leave to a later period or generation; bequeath. **2** to pass (an outgrown garment) on from one member of a family to a younger one. **3** *U.S. and Canadian law.* to announce or deliver (a verdict).

-handed *adj* **1** having a hand or hands as specified: *broad-handed; a four-handed game of cards.* **2** made as specified for either left- or right-hand operation or positioning.

handedness ('hændɪdnɪs) *n* **1** the tendency to use one hand more skilfully or in preference to the other. **2** the property of some chemical substances of rotating the plane of polarized light in one direction rather than another. See also **dextrorotation, laevorotation. 3** the relation between the vectors of spin and momentum of neutrinos and certain other elementary particles.

Handel ('hændᵊl) *n* **George Frederick.** German name *Georg Friedrich Händel.* 1685–1759, German composer, resident in England, noted particularly for his oratorios, including the *Messiah* (1741) and *Samson* (1743). Other works include over 40 operas, 12 concerti grossi, organ concertos, chamber and orchestral music, esp. *Water Music* (1717).

handfast ('hænd,fɑːst) *Archaic.* ◆ *n* **1** an agreement, esp. of marriage, confirmed by a handshake. **2** a firm grip. ◆ *vb* (*tr*) **3** to betroth or marry (two persons or another person) by joining the hands. **4** to grip with the hand.

handfasting ('hænd,fɑːstɪŋ) *n* **1** an archaic word for **betrothal. 2** (formerly) a kind of trial marriage marked by the formal joining of hands.

handfeed ('hænd,fiːd) *vb* **-feeds, -feeding, -fed** (-,fɛd). (*tr*) **1** to feed (a person or an animal) by hand. **2** *Agriculture.* to give food to (poultry or livestock) in fixed amounts and at fixed times, rather than use a self-feeding system.

handful ('hændful) *n, pl* **-fuls. 1** the amount or number that can be held in the hand. **2** a small number or quantity. **3** *Informal.* a person or thing difficult to manage or control.

hand glass *n* **1** a magnifying glass with a handle. **2** a small mirror with a handle. **3** a small glazed frame for seedlings or plants.

hand grenade *n* a small metal or plastic canister containing explosives, usually activated by a short fuse and used in close combat.

handgrip ('hænd,grɪp) *n* **1** another word for **grip**[1] (senses 2, 5, and 6). **2** *Tennis, golf, etc.* a covering, usually of towelling or rubber, that makes the handle of a racket or club easier to hold.

handgun ('hænd,gʌn) *n* a firearm that can be held, carried, and fired with one hand, such as a pistol.

hand-held *adj* **1** held in position by the hand **2** (of a film camera) held rather than mounted, as in close-up action shots. **3** (of a computer) able to be held in the hand and not requiring connection to a fixed power source.

handhold ('hænd,həuld) *n* **1** an object, crevice, etc., that can be used as a grip or support, as in climbing. **2** a grip or secure hold with the hand or hands.

handicap ('hændɪ,kæp) *n* **1** something that hampers or hinders. **2a** a contest, esp. a race, in which competitors are given advantages or disadvantages of weight, distance, time, etc., in an attempt to equalize their chances of winning. **2b** the advantage or disadvantage prescribed. **3** *Golf.* the number of strokes by which a player's averaged score exceeds the standard scratch score for the particular course: used as the basis for handicapping in competitive play. **4** any physical disability or disadvantage resulting from physical, mental, or social impairment or abnormality. ◆ *vb* **-caps, -capping, -capped.** (*tr*) **5** to be a hindrance or disadvantage to. **6** to assign a handicap or handicaps to. **7** to organize (a contest) by handicapping. **8** *U.S. and Canadian.* **8a** to attempt to forecast the winner of (a contest, esp. a horse race). **8b** to assign odds for or against (a contestant). [C17: probably from *hand in cap,* a lottery game in which players drew forfeits from a cap or deposited money in it] ▸ **'handi,capper** *n*

handicapped ('hændɪ,kæpt) *adj* **1** physically disabled. **2** *Psychol.* denoting a person whose social behaviour or emotional reactions are in some way impaired. **3** (of a competitor) assigned a handicap.

handicapper ('hændɪ,kæpə) *n* **1** an official appointed to assign handicaps to competitors in such sports as golf and horse racing. **2** a newspaper columnist employed to estimate the chances that horses have of winning races.

handicap register *n Social welfare.* (in Britain) **1** a list of the handicapped people in its area that a local authority has a duty to compile under the Chronically Sick and Disabled Persons Act 1970. Eligibility for certain welfare benefits may depend on registration. **2** a different list of handicapped people, kept by the Manpower Services Commission for employment purposes. See also **green card, registered disabled.**

handicraft ('hændɪ,krɑːft) *n* **1** skill or dexterity in working with the hands. **2** a particular skill or art performed with the hands, such as weaving, pottery, etc. **3** the work produced by such a skill or art: *local handicraft is on sale.* ◆ Also called: **handcraft.** [C15: changed from HANDCRAFT through the influence of HANDIWORK, which was analysed as if HANDY + WORK] ▸ **'handi,craftsman** *n*

handily ('hændɪlɪ) *adv* **1** in a handy way or manner. **2** conveniently or suitably: *handily nearby.* **3** *U.S. and Canadian.* easily: *the horse won handily.*

hand in *vb* (*tr, adv*) to return or submit (something, such as an examination paper).

handiwork ('hændɪ,wɜːk) *n* **1** work performed or produced by hand, such as embroidery or pottery. **2** the result of the action or endeavours of a person or thing. [Old English *handgeweorc,* from HAND + *geweorc,* from *ge-* (collective prefix) + *weorc* WORK]

handkerchief ('hæŋkətʃɪf, -tʃiːf) *n* a small square of soft absorbent material, such as linen, silk, or soft paper, carried and used to wipe the nose, etc.

hand-knit *adj also* **hand-knitted. 1** knitted by hand, not on a machine. ◆ *vb* **-knits, -knitting, -knitted** *or* **-knit. 2** to knit (garments) by hand.

handle ('hændᵊl) *n* **1** the part of a utensil, drawer, etc., designed to be held in order to move, use, or pick up the object. **2** *N.Z.* a glass beer mug with a handle. **3** *Slang.* a person's name or title. **4** *CB radio.* a slang name for **call sign. 5** an opportunity, reason, or excuse for doing something: *his background served as a handle for their mockery.* **6** the quality, as of textiles, perceived by touching or feeling. **7** the total amount of a bet on a horse race or similar event. **8 fly off the handle.** *Informal.* to become suddenly extremely angry. ◆ *vb* (*mainly tr*) **9** to pick up and hold, move, or touch with the hands. **10** to operate or employ using the hands: *the boy handled the reins well.* **11** to have power or control over: *my wife handles my investments.* **12** to manage successfully: *a secretary must be able to handle clients.* **13** to discuss (a theme, subject, etc.). **14** to deal with or treat in a specified way: *I was handled with great tact.* **15** to trade or deal in (specified merchandise). **16** (*intr*) to react or respond in a specified way to operation or control: *the car handles well on bends.* [Old English; related to Old Saxon *handlon* (vb), Old High German *hantilla* towel] ▸ **'handleable** *adj* ▸ **'handled** *adj* ▸ **'handleless** *adj*

handlebar moustache ('hænd^{ə}l,bɑː) *n* a bushy extended moustache with curled ends that resembles handlebars.

handlebars ('hænd^{ə}l,bɑːz) *pl n* (*sometimes sing*) a metal tube having its ends curved to form handles, used for steering a bicycle, motorcycle, etc.

handler ('hændlə) *n* **1** a person, esp. a police officer, in charge of a specially trained dog. **2** a person who handles some specified thing: *a baggage handler.* **3** a person who holds or incites a dog, gamecock, etc., esp. in a race or contest. **4** the trainer or second of a boxer.

Handley Page *n* Sir **Frederick.** See (Sir Frederick Handley) **Page.**

handling ('hændlɪŋ) *n* **1** the act or an instance of picking up, turning over, or touching something. **2** treatment, as of a theme in literature. **3a** the process by which a commodity is packaged, transported, etc. **3b** (*as modifier*): *handling charges.* **4** *Law.* the act of receiving property that one knows or believes to be stolen.

hand-loomed *adj* (of a garment) made on a hand loom.

handmade (ˌhænd'meɪd) *adj* made by hand, not by machine, esp. with care or craftsmanship.

handmaiden ('hænd,meɪd^{ə}n) *or* **handmaid** *n* **1** a person or thing that serves a useful but subordinate purpose: *logic is the handmaid of philosophy.* **2** *Archaic.* a female servant or attendant.

hand-me-down *n Informal.* **1a** something, esp. an outgrown garment, passed down from one person to another. **1b** (*as modifier*): *a hand-me-down dress.* **2a** anything that has already been used by another. **2b** (*as modifier*): *hand-me-down ideas.*

hand-off *Rugby.* ◆ *n* **1** the act of warding off an opposing player with the open hand. ◆ *vb* **hand off. 2** (*tr, adv*) to ward off (an opponent) using a hand-off.

hand on *vb* (*tr, adv*) to pass to the next in a succession.

hand organ *n* another name for **barrel organ.**

hand-out *n, pl* **hand-outs. 1** clothing, food, or money given to a needy person. **2** a leaflet, free sample, etc., given out to publicize something. **3** a statement or other document distributed to the press or an audience to confirm, supplement, or replace an oral presentation. ◆ *vb* **hand out.** (*tr, adv*) **4** to distribute.

hand over *vb* (*tr, adv*) **1** to surrender possession of; transfer. ◆ *n* **handover. 2** a transfer, surrender.

hand-pick *vb* (*tr*) to choose or select with great care, as for a special job or purpose. ▸ **ˌhand-'picked** *adj*

hand-piece *n Austral. and N.Z.* hand-held, power-operated shears used by a shearer. See also **comb** (sense 3).

handrail ('hænd,reɪl) *n* a rail alongside a stairway, etc., at a convenient height to be grasped to provide support.

hands (hændz) *pl n* **1** power or keeping: *your welfare is in his hands.* **2** Also called: **handling.** *Soccer.* the infringement of touching the ball with any part of the hand or arm. **3 change hands.** to pass from the possession of one person or group to another. **4 clean hands.** freedom from guilt. **5 hands down.** without effort; easily. **6 hands off.** do not touch or interfere. **7 hands up!** raise the hands above the level of the shoulders, an order usually given by an armed robber to a victim, etc. **8 have one's hands full. 8a** to be completely occupied. **8b** to be beset with problems. **9 have one's hands tied.** to be wholly unable to act. **10 in good hands.** in protective care. **11 join hands.** See **join** (sense 12). **12 lay hands on** *or* **upon. 12a** to seize or get possession of. **12b** to beat up; assault. **12c** to find: *I just can't lay my hands on it anywhere.* **12d** *Christianity.* to confirm or ordain by the imposition of hands. **13 off one's hands.** for which one is no longer responsible. **14 on one's hands. 14a** for which one is responsible: *I've got too much on my hands to help.* **14b** to spare: *time on my hands.* **15 out of one's hands.** no longer one's responsibility. **16 throw up one's hands.** to give up in despair. **17 wash one's hands of.** to have nothing more to do with.

Hands (hænz) *n* **Terence David,** known as *Terry.* born 1941, British theatre director: chief executive and artistic director (1986–91) of the Royal Shakespeare Company.

handsaw ('hænd,sɔː) *n* any saw for use in one hand only.

hand's-breadth *n* another name for **handbreadth.**

handsel *or* **hansel** ('hæns^{ə}l) *Archaic or dialect.* ◆ *n* **1** a gift for good luck at the beginning of a new year, new venture, etc. ◆ *vb* **-sels, -selling, -selled** *or U.S.* **-sels, -seling, -seled.** (*tr*) **2** to give a handsel to (a person). **3** to begin (a venture) with ceremony; inaugurate. [Old English *handselen* delivery into the hand; related to Old Norse *handsal* promise sealed with a handshake, Swedish *handsöl* gratuity; see HAND, SELL]

handset ('hænd,set) *n* a telephone mouthpiece and earpiece mounted so that they can be held simultaneously to mouth and ear.

hand setting *n Printing.* text matter composed in metal type by hand, rather than by machine.

handshake ('hænd,ʃeɪk) *n* the act of grasping and shaking a person's hand, as when being introduced or agreeing on a deal.

handshaking ('hænd,ʃeɪkɪŋ) *n Computing.* communication between a computer system and an external device, by which each tells the other that data is ready to be transferred, and that the receiver is ready to accept it.

hands-off *adj* (of a machine, device, etc.) without need of manual operation.

handsome ('hændsəm) *adj* **1** (of a man) good-looking, esp. in having regular, pleasing, and well-defined features. **2** (of a woman) fine-looking in a dignified way. **3** well-proportioned, stately, or comely: *a handsome room.* **4** liberal or ample: *a handsome allowance.* **5** gracious or generous: *a handsome action.* [C15 *handsom* easily handled; compare Dutch *handzaam;* see HAND, -SOME[1]] ▸ **'handsomely** *adv* ▸ **'handsomeness** *n*

hands-on *adj* involving practical experience of equipment, etc.: *hands-on training in the use of computers.*

handspike ('hænd,spaɪk) *n* a bar or length of pipe used as a lever.

handspring ('hænd,sprɪŋ) *n* a gymnastic feat in which a person starts from a standing position and leaps forwards or backwards into a handstand and then onto his feet.

handstand ('hænd,stænd) *n* the act or instance of supporting the body on the hands alone in an upside down position.

handstroke ('hænd,strəuk) *n Bell-ringing.* the downward movement of the bell rope as the bell swings around allowing the ringer to grasp and pull it. Compare **backstroke** (sense 4).

hand-to-hand *adj, adv* at close quarters: *they fought hand-to-hand.*

hand-to-mouth *adj, adv* with barely enough money or food to satisfy immediate needs: *a hand-to-mouth existence.*

handwork ('hænd,wɜːk) *n* work done by hand rather than by machine. ▸ **'hand,worked** *adj*

handwriting ('hænd,raɪtɪŋ) *n* **1** writing by hand rather than by typing or printing. **2** a person's characteristic writing style: *that signature is in my handwriting.*

handwritten ('hænd,rɪt^{ə}n) *adj* written by hand; not printed or typed.

handy ('hændɪ) *adj* **handier, handiest. 1** conveniently or easily within reach. **2** easy to manoeuvre, handle, or use: *a handy tool.* **3** skilful with one's hands. ▸ **'handiness** *n*

Handy ('hændɪ) *n* **W(illiam) C(hristopher).** 1873–1958, U.S. blues musician and songwriter, esp. noted for the song "St Louis Blues".

handyman ('hændɪ,mæn) *n, pl* **-men. 1** a man employed to do various tasks. **2** a man skilled in odd jobs, etc.

hanepoot ('hɑːnə,puət) *n S. African.* a variety of muscat grape used as a dessert fruit and in making wine. [from Afrikaans *hane* cock + *poot* claw]

Han Fei Zu ('hæn 'feɪ 'tʃuː) *n* died 233 B.C., Chinese diplomat and philosopher of law.

hang (hæŋ) *vb* **hangs, hanging, hung** (hʌŋ). **1** to fasten or be fastened from above, esp. by a cord, chain, etc.; suspend: *the picture hung on the wall; to hang laundry.* **2** to place or be placed in position as by a hinge so as to allow free movement around or at the place of suspension: *to hang a door.* **3** (*intr;* sometimes foll. by *over*) to be suspended or poised; hover: *a pall of smoke hung over the city.* **4** (*intr;* sometimes foll. by *over*) to be imminent; threaten. **5** (*intr*) to be or remain doubtful or unresolved (esp. in the phrase **hang in the balance**). **6** (*past tense and past participle* **hanged**) to suspend or be suspended by the neck until dead. **7** (*tr*) to fasten, fix, or attach in position or at an appropriate angle: *to hang a scythe to its handle.* **8** (*tr*) to decorate, furnish, or cover with something suspended or fastened: *to hang a wall with tapestry.* **9** (*tr*) to fasten to or suspend from a wall: *to hang wallpaper.* **10** to exhibit (a picture or pictures) by (a particular painter, printmaker, etc.) or (of a picture or a painter, etc.) to be exhibited in an art gallery, etc. **11** to fall or droop or allow to fall or droop: *to hang one's head in shame.* **12** (of cloth, clothing, etc.) to drape, fall, or flow, esp. in a specified manner: *her skirt hangs well.* **13** (*tr*) to suspend (game such as pheasant) so that it becomes slightly decomposed and therefore more tender and tasty. **14** (of a jury) to prevent or be prevented from reaching a verdict. **15** (*past tense and past participle* **hanged**) *Slang.* to damn or be damned: used in mild curses or interjections: *I'll be hanged before I'll go out in that storm.* **16** (*intr*) to pass slowly (esp. in the phrase **time hangs heavily**). **17 hang fire. 17a** to be delayed. **17b** to procrastinate. See also **fire** (sense 16). ◆ *n* **18** the way in which something hangs. **19** (*usually used with a negative*) *Slang.* a damn: *I don't care a hang for what you say.* **20 get the hang of.** *Informal.* **20a** to understand the technique of doing something. **20b** to perceive the meaning or significance of. ◆ See also **hang about, hang back, hang behind, hang in, hang on, hang out, hang together, hang up, hang with.** [Old English *hangian;* related to Old Norse *hanga,* Old High German *hangēn*]

hang about *or* **around** *vb* (*intr*) **1** to waste time; loiter. **2** (*adv;* foll. by *with*) to frequent the company (of someone). ◆ *interj* **3** wait a moment! stop!

hangar ('hæŋə) *n* a large workshop or building for storing and maintaining aircraft. [C19: from French: shed, perhaps from Medieval Latin *angārium* shed used as a smithy, of obscure origin]

hang back *vb* (*intr, adv;* often foll. by *from*) to be reluctant to go forward or carry on (with some activity).

hang behind *vb* (*intr, adv*) to remain in a place after others have left; linger.

hangbird ('hæŋ,bɜːd) *n U.S. and Canadian.* any bird, esp. the Baltimore oriole, that builds a hanging nest.

Hangchow *n* a variant transliteration of the Chinese name for **Hangzhou.**

hangdog ('hæŋ,dɒg) *adj* **1** downcast, furtive, or guilty in appearance or manner. ◆ *n* **2** a furtive or sneaky person.

hanger ('hæŋə) *n* **1a** any support, such as a hook, strap, peg, or loop, on or by which something may be hung. **1b** See **coat hanger. 2a** a person who hangs something. **2b** (*in combination*): *paperhanger.* **3** a bracket designed to attach one part of a mechanical structure to another, such as the one that attaches the spring shackle of a motor car to the chassis. **4** a wood on a steep hillside, characteristically beech growing on chalk in southern England. **5a** a loop or strap on a sword belt from which a short sword or dagger was hung. **5b** the weapon itself.

hanger-on *n, pl* **hangers-on.** a sycophantic follower or dependant, esp. one hoping for personal gain.

hang-glider *n* an unpowered aircraft consisting of a large cloth wing stretched over a light framework from which the pilot hangs in a harness, using a horizontal bar to control the flight. ▸ **'hang-gliding** *n*

hangi ('hʌŋiː) *n N.Z.* **1** an open-air cooking pit. **2** the food cooked in it. **3** the social gathering at the resultant meal. [Maori]
hang in *vb* (*intr, prep*) *Informal.* to persist: *just hang in there for a bit longer.*
hanging ('hæŋɪŋ) *n* **1a** the putting of a person to death by suspending the body by the neck from a noose. **1b** (*as modifier*): *a hanging offence.* **2** (*often pl*) a decorative textile such as a tapestry or drapery hung on a wall or over a window. **3** the act of a person or thing that hangs. ◆ *adj* **4** not supported from below; suspended. **5** undecided; still under discussion. **6** inclining or projecting downwards; overhanging. **7** situated on a steep slope or in a high place. **8** (*prenominal*) given to issuing harsh sentences, esp. death sentences: *a hanging judge.* **9** *Chess.* See **hanging pawn.**
Hanging Gardens of Babylon *n* (in ancient Babylon) gardens, probably planted on terraces of a ziggurat: one of the Seven Wonders of the World.
hanging glacier *n* a glacier situated on a shelf above a valley or another glacier; it may be joined to the lower level by an icefall or separate from it.
hanging indentation *n Printing.* a style of text-setting in which the first line of a paragraph is set to the full measure and subsequent lines are indented at the left-hand side.
hanging pawn *n Chess.* one of two or more adjacent pawns on central half-open files with no pawns of the same colour on the files immediately to left and right of them.
hanging valley *n Geography.* a tributary valley entering a main valley at a much higher level because of overdeepening of the main valley, esp. by glacial erosion.
hanging wall *n* the rocks on the upper side of an inclined fault plane or mineral vein. Compare **footwall.**
hangman ('hæŋmən) *n, pl* **-men.** an official who carries out a sentence of hanging on condemned criminals.
hangnail ('hæŋˌneɪl) *n* a piece of skin torn away from, but still attached to, the base or side of a fingernail. [C17: from Old English *angnægl,* from *enge* tight + *nægl* NAIL; influenced by HANG]
hang on *vb* (*intr*) **1** (*adv*) to continue or persist in an activity, esp. with effort or difficulty: *hang on at your present job until you can get another.* **2** (*adv*) to cling, grasp, or hold: *she hangs on to her mother's arm.* **3** (*prep*) to be conditioned or contingent on; depend on: *everything hangs on this business deal.* **4** (*prep*) Also: **hang onto, hang upon.** to listen attentively to: *she hung on his every word.* **5** (*adv*) *Informal.* to wait or remain: *hang on for a few minutes.*
hang out *vb* (*adv*) **1** to suspend, be suspended, or lean, esp. from an opening, as for display or airing: *to hang out the washing.* **2** (*intr*) *Informal.* to live at or frequent a place: *the police know where the thieves hang out.* **3** (*intr; foll. by with*) *Informal.* to frequent the company (of someone). **4** *Slang.* to relax completely in an unassuming way (esp. in the phrase **let it all hang out**). **5** (*intr*) *U.S. informal.* to act or speak freely, in an open, cooperative, or indiscreet manner. ◆ *n* **hang-out. 6** *Informal.* a place where one lives or that one frequently visits.
hangover ('hæŋˌəʊvə) *n* **1** the delayed aftereffects of drinking too much alcohol in a relatively short period of time, characterized by headache and sometimes nausea and dizziness. **2** a person or thing left over from or influenced by a past age.
Hang Seng Index (hæŋ sɛŋ) *n* an index of share prices based on an average of 33 stocks quoted on the Hong Kong Stock Exchange. [name of a Hong Kong bank]
hang together *vb* (*intr, adv*) **1** to be cohesive or united. **2** to be consistent: *your statements don't quite hang together.*
Hanguk ('hæn'gʊk) *n* the Korean name for **South Korea.**
hang up *vb* (*adv*) **1** (*tr*) to put on a hook, hanger, etc.: *please hang up your coat.* **2** to replace (a telephone receiver) on its cradle at the end of a conversation, often breaking a conversation off abruptly. **3** (*tr; usually passive;* usually foll. by *on*) *Informal.* to cause to have an emotional or psychological preoccupation or problem: *he's really hung up on his mother.* ◆ *n* **hang-up.** *Informal.* **4** an emotional or psychological preoccupation or problem. **5** a persistent cause of annoyance.
hang with *vb* (*intr, prep*) *U.S. informal.* to frequent the company of (someone).
Hangzhou ('hæŋ'dʒəʊ) *or* **Hangchow** *n* a port in E China, capital of Zhejiang province, on **Hangzhou Bay** (an inlet of the East China Sea), at the foot of the Eye of Heaven Mountains: regarded by Marco Polo as the finest city in the world; seat of two universities (1927, 1959). Pop.: 1 340 000 (1991 est.).
hank (hæŋk) *n* **1** a loop, coil, or skein, as of rope, wool, or yarn. **2** *Nautical.* a ringlike fitting that can be opened to admit a stay for attaching the luff of a sail. **3** a unit of measurement of cloth, yarn, etc., such as a length of 840 yards (767 m) of cotton or 560 yards (512 m) of worsted yarn. ◆ *vb* **4** (*tr*) *Nautical.* to attach (a sail) to a stay by hanks. [C13: of Scandinavian origin; compare Old Norse *hanka* to coil, Swedish *hank* string]
hanker ('hæŋkə) *vb* (foll. by *for, after,* or an infinitive) to have a yearning (for something or to do something). [C17: probably from Dutch dialect *hankeren*] ► **'hankering** *n*
Hankow *or* **Han-k'ou** ('hæn'kaʊ) *n* a former city in SE China, in SE Hubei at the confluence of the Han and Yangtze Rivers: one of the Han Cities; merged with Hanyang and Wuchang in 1950 to form the conurbation of Wuhan.
Hanks (hæŋks) *n* **Tom.** born 1956, U.S. film actor: his films include *Splash* (1984), *Philadelphia* (1993), *Forrest Gump* (1994), and *Saving Private Ryan* (1998).
hanky *or* **hankie** ('hæŋkɪ) *n, pl* **hankies.** *Informal.* short for **handkerchief.**
hanky-panky ('hæŋkɪ'pæŋkɪ) *n Informal.* **1** dubious or suspicious behaviour. **2** foolish behaviour or talk. **3** illicit sexual relations. [C19: variant of HOCUS-POCUS]
Hannah ('hænə) *n Old Testament.* the woman who gave birth to Samuel (I Samuel 1–2).
Hannibal ('hænɪbᵊl) *n* 247–182 B.C., Carthaginian general; son of Hamilcar Barca. He commanded the Carthaginian army in the Second Punic War (218–201). After capturing Sagunto in Spain, he invaded Italy (218), crossing the Alps with an army of about 40 000 men and defeating the Romans at Trasimene (217) and Cannae (216). In 203 he was recalled to defend Carthage and was defeated by Scipio at Zama (202). He was later forced into exile and committed suicide to avoid capture.
Hannover (*German* ha'noːfər) *n* a city in N Germany, capital of Lower Saxony: capital of the kingdom of Hannover (1815–66); situated on the Mittelland canal. Pop.: 523 147 (1996 est.). English spelling: **Hanover.**
Hanoi (hæ'nɔɪ) *n* the capital of Vietnam, on the Red River: became capital of Tonkin in 1802, of French Indochina in 1887, of Vietnam in 1945, and of North Vietnam (1954–75); university (1917); industrial centre. Pop.: 2 154 900 (1993 est.).
Hanover[1] ('hænəʊvə) *n* the English spelling of **Hannover.**
Hanover[2] ('hænəʊvə) *n* **1** a princely house of Germany (1692–1815), the head of which succeeded to the British throne as George I in 1714. **2** the royal house of Britain (1714–1901).
Hanoverian (ˌhænə'vɪərɪən) *adj* **1** of, relating to, or situated in Hannover. **2** of or relating to the princely house of Hanover or to the monarchs of England or their reigns from 1714 to 1901. ◆ *n* **3** a member or supporter of the house of Hanover.
Hanratty (hæn'rætɪ) *n* **James.** 1936–62, Englishman executed, despite conflicting evidence, for a murder on the A6 road. Subsequent public concern played a major part in the abolition of capital punishment in Britain.
Hansard ('hænsɑːd) *n* **1** the official report of the proceedings of the British Parliament. **2** a similar report kept by other legislative bodies. [C19: named after T.C. *Hansard* (1752–1828) and his son, who compiled the reports until 1889]
Hanse (hæns) *or* **Hansa** ('hænsə, -zə) *n* **1** a medieval guild of merchants. **2** a fee paid by the new members of a medieval trading guild. **3a** another name for the **Hanseatic League. 3b** (*as modifier*): *a Hanse town.* [C12: of Germanic origin; compare Old High German *hansa,* Old English *hōs* troop]
Hanseatic (ˌhænsɪ'ætɪk) *adj* **1** of or relating to the Hanseatic League. ◆ *n* **2** a member of the Hanseatic League.
Hanseatic League *n* a commercial association of towns in N Germany formed in the mid-14th century to protect and control trade. It was at its most powerful in the 15th century. Also called: **Hansa, Hanse.**
hansel ('hænsᵊl) *n, vb* a variant spelling of **handsel.**
Hansen's disease ('hænsənz) *n Pathol.* another name for **leprosy.** [C20: named after G. H. *Hansen* (1841–1912), Norwegian physician]
hansom ('hænsəm) *n* (*sometimes cap.*) a two-wheeled one-horse carriage with a fixed hood. The driver sits on a high outside seat at the rear. Also called: **hansom cab.** [C19: short for *hansom cab,* named after its designer J. A. *Hansom* (1803–82)]
hantavirus ('hæntəˌvaɪrəs) *n* any one of a group of viruses that are transmitted to humans by rodents and cause disease of varying severity, ranging from a mild form of influenza to respiratory or kidney failure. [C20: from *Hanta(an),* river in North and South Korea where the disease was first reported + VIRUS]
Hants (hænts) *abbrev. for* Hampshire.
hanukiah *or* **chanukiah** ('hɑːnukɪə, ˌhɑːnəkiːə; *Hebrew* xanu'kiːa) *n* a candelabrum having nine branches that is lit during the festival of Hanukkah. [from Hebrew]
Hanukkah, Hanukah, *or* **Chanukah** ('hɑːnəkə, -nʊˌkɑː; *Hebrew* xanu'ka) *n* the eight-day Jewish festival of lights beginning on the 25th of Kislev and commemorating the rededication of the temple by Judas Maccabaeus in 165 B.C. Also called: **Feast of Dedication, Feast of Lights.** [from Hebrew, literally: a dedication]
Hanuman (ˌhʌnʊ'mɑːn) *n* **1** another word for **entellus** (the monkey). **2** the monkey chief of Hindu mythology and devoted helper of Rama. [from Hindi *Hanumān,* from Sanskrit *hanumant* having (conspicuous) jaws, from *hanu* jaw]
Hanyang *or* **Han-yang** ('hæn'jæŋ) *n* a former city in SE China, in SE Hubei at the confluence of the Han and Yangtze Rivers: one of the Han Cities; merged with Hankow and Wuchang in 1950 to form the conurbation of Wuhan.
hap[1] (hæp) *n Archaic.* **1** luck; chance. **2** an occurrence. ◆ *vb* **haps, happing, happed. 3** (*intr*) an archaic word for **happen.** [C13: from Old Norse *happ* good luck; related to Old English *gehæplic* convenient, Old Slavonic *kobǔ* fate]
hap[2] (hæp) *Scot. and eastern English dialect.* ◆ *vb* (*tr*) **1** to cover up; wrap up warmly. ◆ *n* **2** a covering of any kind. [C14: perhaps of Norse origin]
hapaxanthic (ˌhæpə'zænθɪk) *or* **hapaxanthous** (ˌhæpə'zænθəs) *adj Botany.* another word for **monocarpic.** [from Greek: fruiting only once]
hapax legomenon ('hæpæks lə'gɒmɪˌnɒn) *n, pl* **hapax legomena** (lə'gɒmɪnə). another term for **nonce word.** [Greek: thing said only once]
ha'penny ('heɪpnɪ) *n, pl* **-nies.** *Brit.* a variant spelling of **halfpenny.**
haphazard (hæp'hæzəd) *adv, adj* **1** at random. ◆ *adj* **2** careless; slipshod. ◆ *n* **3** *Rare.* chance. ► **hap'hazardly** *adv* ► **hap'hazardness** *n*
Haphtarah (hɑːf'təʊrə; *Hebrew* hafta'raː) *n, pl* **-taroth** (-'təʊrəʊt; *Hebrew* -ta'roːt) *or* **-tarahs.** a variant spelling of **Haftarah.**
hapless ('hæplɪs) *adj* unfortunate; wretched. ► **'haplessly** *adv* ► **'haplessness** *n*
haplite ('hæplaɪt) *n* a variant of **aplite.** ► haplitic (hæp'lɪtɪk) *adj*
haplo- *or before a vowel* **hapl-** *combining form.* single or simple: *haplology; haplosis.* [from Greek *haplous* simple]
haplobiont (ˌhæpləʊ'baɪɒnt) *n Biology.* an organism, esp. a plant, that exists in either the diploid form or the haploid form (but never alternates between these forms) during its life cycle. ► ˌ**haplobi'ontic** *adj*
haplography (hæp'lɒgrəfɪ) *n, pl* **-phies.** the accidental writing of only one let-

ter or syllable where there should be two similar letters or syllables, as in spelling *endodontics* as *endontics*. [C19: from Greek, from *haplous* single + -GRAPHY]

haploid ('hæplɔɪd) *Biology*. ◆ *adj also* **haploidic**. 1 (esp. of gametes) having a single set of unpaired chromosomes. ◆ *n* 2 a haploid cell or organism. Compare **diploid**. [C20: from Greek *haploeidēs* single, from *haplous* single] ▸ **'haploidy** *n*

haplology (hæp'lɒlədʒɪ) *n* omission of a repeated occurrence of a sound or syllable in fluent speech, as for example in the pronunciation of *library* as ('laɪbrɪ). ▸ **haplologic** (ˌhæplə'lɒdʒɪk) *adj*

haplont ('hæplɒnt) *n Biology*. an organism, esp. a plant, that has the haploid number of chromosomes in its somatic cells. ▸ **ha'plontic** *adj*

haplosis (hæp'ləʊsɪs) *n Biology*. the production of a haploid number of chromosomes during meiosis.

haplostemonous (ˌhæpləʊ'stiːmənəs, -'stem-) *adj* (of plants) having the stamens arranged in a single whorl. [C19: from New Latin, from HAPLO- + *-stemonus* relating to a STAMEN]

haply ('hæplɪ) *adv* (*sentence modifier*) an archaic word for **perhaps**.

ha'p'orth ('heɪpəθ) *n Brit*. 1 a variant spelling of **halfpennyworth**. 2 *Informal*. a person considered as specified: *daft ha'p'orth*.

happen ('hæpᵊn) *vb* 1 (*intr*) (of an event in time) to come about or take place; occur. 2 (*intr*; foll. by *to*) (of some unforeseen circumstance or event, esp. death), to fall to the lot (of); be a source of good or bad fortune (to): *if anything happens to me it'll be your fault*. 3 (*tr*) to chance (to be or do something): *I happen to know him*. 4 (*tr*; *takes a clause as object*) to be the case, esp. if by chance, that: *it happens that I know him*. ◆ *adv, sentence substitute*. 5 *Northern English dialect*. 5a another word for **perhaps**. 5b (*as sentence modifier*): *happen I'll see thee tomorrow*. [C14: see HAP[1], -EN[1]]

USAGE See at **occur**.

happen by, past, along, *or* **in** *vb* (*intr, adv*) *Informal, chiefly U.S.* to appear, arrive, or come casually or by chance.

happening ('hæpənɪŋ, 'hæpnɪŋ) *n* 1 an occurrence; event. 2 an improvised or spontaneous display or performance consisting of bizarre and haphazard events. ◆ *adj* 3 *Informal*. fashionable and up-to-the-minute.

happen on *or* **upon** *vb* (*intr, prep*) to find by chance: *I happened upon a five-pound note lying in the street*.

happenstance ('hæpənˌstæns) *n* 1 chance. 2 a chance occurrence.

happy ('hæpɪ) *adj* **-pier, -piest**. 1 feeling, showing, or expressing joy; pleased. 2 willing: *I'd be happy to show you around*. 3 causing joy or gladness. 4 fortunate; lucky: *the happy position of not having to work*. 5 aptly expressed; appropriate: *a happy turn of phrase*. 6 (*postpositive*) *Informal*. slightly intoxicated. ◆ *interj* 7 (*in combination*): *happy birthday; happy Christmas*. ◆ See also **trigger-happy**. [C14: see HAP[1], -Y[1]] ▸ **'happily** *adv* ▸ **'happiness** *n*

happy camper *n Informal*. a happy, satisifed person (esp. in the phrase **not a happy camper**).

happy-clappy ('hæpɪ'klæpɪ) *Derogatory*. ◆ *adj* 1 of or denoting a form of evangelical Christianity in which members of the congregation sing and clap enthusiastically during acts of worship. ◆ *n, pl* **-pies**. 2 Also called: **happy clapper**. an enthusiastic evangelical Christian.

happy event *n Informal*. the birth of a child.

happy-go-lucky *adj* carefree or easy-going.

happy hour *n* a time, usually in the early evening, when some pubs or bars sell drinks at reduced prices.

happy hunting ground *n* 1 (in American Indian legend) the paradise to which a person passes after death. 2 a productive or profitable area for a person with a particular interest or requirement: *jumble sales proved happy hunting grounds in her search for old stone jars*.

happy medium *n* a course or state that avoids extremes.

happy release *n* liberation, esp. by death, from an unpleasant condition.

Hapsburg ('hæpsˌbɜːg) *n* a German princely family founded by Albert, count of Hapsburg (1153). From 1440 to 1806, the Hapsburgs wore the imperial crown of the Holy Roman Empire almost uninterruptedly. They also provided rulers for Austria, Spain, Hungary, Bohemia, etc. The line continued as the royal house of **Hapsburg-Lorraine**, ruling in Austria (1806–48) and Austria-Hungary (1848–1918). German name: **Habsburg**.

hapten ('hæptən) *or* **haptene** ('hæptiːn) *n Immunol*. an incomplete antigen that can stimulate antibody production only in combination with a particular protein. [C20: from German, from Greek *haptein* to fasten]

hapteron ('hæptərɒn) *n* a cell or group of cells that occurs in certain plants, esp. seaweeds, and attaches the plant to its substratum. [C20: from Greek *haptein* to make fast]

haptic ('hæptɪk) *adj* relating to or based on the sense of touch. [C19: from Greek, from *haptein* to touch]

haptotropism (ˌhæptəʊ'trəʊpɪzəm) *n* another name for **thigmotropism**.

hapu ('hɑːpuː) *n N.Z.* a subtribe. [Maori]

hapuka *or* **hapuku** (hə'puːkə, 'hɑːpukə) *n N.Z.* another name for **groper**. [Maori]

hara-kiri (ˌhærə'kɪrɪ) *or* **hari-kari** (ˌhærɪ'kɑːrɪ) *n* (formerly, in Japan) ritual suicide by disembowelment with a sword when disgraced or under sentence of death. Also called: **seppuku**. [C19: from Japanese taboo slang, from *hara* belly + *kiri* cutting]

Harald I ('hærəld) *n* called *Harald Fairhair*. ?850–933, first king of Norway: his rule caused emigration to the British Isles.

Harald III *n* surname *Hardraade*. 1015–66, king of Norway (1047–66); invaded England (1066) and died at the battle of Stamford Bridge.

haram ('hɑːˌrɑːm) *n* anything that is forbidden by Islamic law. [from Arabic, literally: forbidden]

harambee (ˌhɑːrɑːm'beɪ) *n* 1 a work chant used on the E African coast. 2 a rallying cry used in Kenya. ◆ *interj* 3 a cry of harambee. [Swahili: pull together]

harangue (hə'ræŋ) *vb* 1 to address (a person or crowd) in an angry, vehement, or forcefully persuasive way. ◆ *n* 2 a loud, forceful, or angry speech. [C15: from Old French, from Old Italian *aringa* public speech, probably of Germanic origin; related to Medieval Latin *harenga*; see HARRY, RING[1]] ▸ **ha'ranguer** *n*

Harappa (hə'ræpə) *n* an ancient city in the Punjab in NW Pakistan: one of the centres of the Indus civilization that flourished from 2500 to 1700 B.C.; probably destroyed by Indo-European invaders. ▸ **Ha'rappan** *adj, n*

Harar *or* **Harrer** ('hɑːrə) *n* a city in E Ethiopia: former capital of the Muslim state of Adal. Pop.: 122 932 (1994 est.).

Harare (hə'rɑːrɪ) *n* the capital of Zimbabwe, in the northeast: University of Zimbabwe (1957); industrial and commercial centre. Pop.: 1 184 169 (1992). Former name (until 1982): **Salisbury**.

harass ('hærəs, hə'ræs) *vb* (*tr*) to trouble, torment, or confuse by continual persistent attacks, questions, etc. [C17: from French *harasser*, variant of Old French *harer* to set a dog on, of Germanic origin; compare Old High German *harēn* to cry out] ▸ **'harassed** *adj* ▸ **'harassing** *adj, n* ▸ **'harassment** *n*

Harbin (hɑː'biːn, -'bɪn) *n* a city in NE China, capital of Heilongjiang province on the Songhua River: founded by the Russians in 1897; centre of tsarist activities after the October Revolution in Russia (1917). Pop.: 2 830 000 (1991 est.). Also called: **Ha-erh-pin**.

harbinger ('hɑːbɪndʒə) *n* 1 a person or thing that announces or indicates the approach of something; forerunner. 2 *Obsolete*. a person sent in advance of a royal party or army to obtain lodgings for them. ◆ *vb* 3 (*tr*) to announce the approach or arrival of. [C12: from Old French *herbergere*, from *herberge* lodging, from Old Saxon *heriberga*; compare Old High German *heriberga* army shelter; see HARRY, BOROUGH]

harbour *or U.S.* **harbor** ('hɑːbə) *n* 1 a sheltered port. 2 a place of refuge or safety. ◆ *vb* 3 (*tr*) to give shelter to: *to harbour a criminal*. 4 (*tr*) to maintain secretly: *to harbour a grudge*. 5 to shelter (a vessel) in a harbour or (of a vessel) to seek shelter. [Old English *herebeorg*, from *here* troop, army + *beorg* shelter; related to Old High German *heriberga* hostelry, Old Norse *herbergi*] ▸ **'harbourer** *or U.S.* **'harborer** *n* ▸ **'harbourless** *or U.S.* **'harborless** *adj*

harbourage *or U.S.* **harborage** ('hɑːbərɪdʒ) *n* shelter or refuge, as for a ship, or a place providing shelter.

harbour master *n* an official in charge of a harbour.

harbour seal *n* a common earless seal, *Phoca vitulina*, that is greyish-black with paler markings: occurs off the coasts of North America, N Europe, and NE Asia.

hard (hɑːd) *adj* 1 firm or rigid; not easily dented, crushed, or pierced. 2 toughened by or as if by physical labour; not soft or smooth: *hard hands*. 3 difficult to do or accomplish; arduous: *a hard task*. 4 difficult to understand or perceive: *a hard question*. 5 showing or requiring considerable physical or mental energy, effort, or application: *hard work; a hard drinker*. 6 stern, cold, or intractable: *a hard judge*. 7 exacting; demanding: *a hard master*. 8 harsh; cruel: *a hard fate*. 9 inflicting pain, sorrow, distress, or hardship: *hard times*. 10 tough or adamant: *a hard man*. 11 forceful or violent: *a hard knock*. 12 cool or uncompromising: *we took a long hard look at our profit factor*. 13 indisputable; real: *hard facts*. 14 *Chem*. (of water) impairing the formation of a lather by soap. See **hardness** (sense 3). 15 practical, shrewd, or calculating: *he is a hard man in business*. 16 too harsh to be pleasant: *hard light*. 17a (of cash, money, etc.) in coin and paper rather than cheques. 17b (of currency) in strong demand, esp. as a result of a good balance of payments situation. 17c (of credit) difficult to obtain; tight. 18 (of alcoholic drink) being a spirit rather than a wine, beer, etc.: *the hard stuff*. 19 (of a drug such as heroin, morphine, or cocaine) highly addictive. Compare **soft** (sense 20). 20 *Physics*. (of radiation, such as gamma rays and X-rays) having high energy and the ability to penetrate solids. 21 *Physics*. (of a vacuum) almost complete. 22 *Chiefly U.S.* (of goods) durable. 23 short for **hard-core**. 24 *Phonetics*. 24a an older word for **fortis**. 24b (not in modern technical usage) denoting the consonants *c* and *g* in English when they are pronounced as velar stops (k, g). 24c (of consonants in the Slavonic languages) not palatalized. 25a being heavily fortified and protected. 25b (of nuclear missiles) located underground in massively reinforced silos. 26 politically extreme: *the hard left*. 27 *Brit. and N.Z. informal*. incorrigible or disreputable (esp. in the phrase **a hard case**). 28 (of bread, etc.) stale and old. 29 **a hard nut to crack**. 29a a person not easily persuaded or won over. 29b a thing not easily understood. 30 **hard by**. near; close by. 31 **hard doer**. *N.Z.* a tough worker at anything. 32 **hard done by**. unfairly or badly treated. 33 **hard up**. *Informal*. 33a in need of money; poor. 33b (foll. by *for*) in great need (of): *hard up for suggestions*. 34 **put the hard word on**. *Austral. and N.Z. informal*. to ask or demand something from. ◆ *adv* 35 with great energy, force, or vigour: *the team always played hard*. 36 as far as possible; all the way: *hard left*. 37 with application; earnestly or intently: *she thought hard about the formula*. 38 with great intensity, force, or violence: *his son's death hit him hard*. 39 (foll. by *on, upon, by*, or *after*) close; near: *hard on his heels*. 40 (foll. by *at*) assiduously; devotedly. 41a with effort or difficulty: *their victory was hard won*. 41b (*in combination*): *hard-earned*. 42 slowly and reluctantly: *prejudice dies hard*. 43 **go hard with**. to cause pain or difficulty to (someone): *it will go hard with you if you don't tell the truth*. 44 **hard at it**. working hard. 45 **hard put** (**to it**). scarcely having the capacity (to do something): *he's hard put to get to work by 9:30*. ◆ *n* 46 any colorant that produces a harsh coarse appearance. 47 *Brit*. a roadway across a foreshore. 48 *Slang*. hard labour. 49 *Taboo slang*. an erection of the penis (esp. in the phrase **get** or **have a hard on**). [Old English *heard*; related to Old Norse *harthr*, Old Frisian *herd*, Old High German *herti*, Gothic *hardus* hard, Greek *kratus* strong]

hard and fast *adj* (**hard-and-fast** *when prenominal*) (esp. of rules) invariable or strict.

hardback ('hɑːdˌbæk) *n* 1 a book or edition with covers of cloth, cardboard, or leather. Compare **paperback.** ◆ *adj* **2** Also: **casebound, hardbound** ('hɑːd,baʊnd), **hardcover** ('hɑːd,kʌvə). of or denoting a hardback or the publication of hardbacks.

hardbake ('hɑːd,beɪk) *n* almond toffee.

hardball ('hɑːdbɔːl) *n* **1** *U.S. and Canadian.* baseball as distinct from softball. **2 play hardball.** *Informal, chiefly U.S. and Canadian.* to act in a ruthless or uncompromising way.

hard-bitten *adj* tough and realistic.

hardboard ('hɑːd,bɔːd) *n* a thin stiff sheet made of compressed sawdust and wood pulp bound together with plastic adhesive or resin under heat and pressure.

hard-boiled *adj* **1** (of an egg) boiled until the yolk and white are solid. **2** *Informal.* **2a** tough, realistic. **2b** cynical.

hard bop *n* a form of jazz originating in the late 1950s that is rhythmically less complex than bop.

hard card *n* a hard disk, mounted on a card, that can be added to a personal computer.

hard cash *n* money or payment in the form of coins or notes rather than cheques or credit.

hard cheese *sentence substitute, n Brit. slang.* bad luck.

hard cider *n U.S. and Canadian.* fermented apple juice. Compare **sweet cider.**

hard coal *n* another name for **anthracite.** Compare **soft coal.**

hard copy *n* computer output printed on paper, as contrasted with machine-readable output such as magnetic tape.

hardcore ('hɑːd,kɔː) *n* **1** a style of rock music characterized by short fast numbers with minimal melody and aggressive delivery. **2** a type of dance music with a very fast beat.

hard core *n* **1** the members of a group or movement who form an intransigent nucleus resisting change. **2** material, such as broken bricks, stones, etc., used to form a foundation for a road, paving, building, etc. ◆ *adj* **hard-core. 3** (of pornography) describing or depicting sexual acts in explicit detail. **4** extremely committed or fanatical: *a hard-core Communist.*

hard court *n* a tennis court made of asphalt, concrete, etc. See also **grass court.**

hard disk *n* a disk of rigid magnetizable material that is used to store data for computers: it is permanently mounted in its disk drive and usually has a storage capacity of a few gigabytes.

Hardecanute ('hɑːdɪkə,njuːt) *n* a variant of **Harthacanute.**

hard-edge *adj* of, relating to, or denoting a style of painting in which vividly coloured subjects are clearly delineated.

harden[1] ('hɑːdᵊn) *vb* **1** to make or become hard or harder; freeze, stiffen, or set. **2** to make or become more hardy, tough, or unfeeling. **3** to make or become stronger or firmer: *they hardened defences.* **4** to make or become more resolute or set: *hardened in his resolve.* **5** (*intr*) *Commerce.* **5a** (of prices, a market, etc.) to cease to fluctuate. **5b** (of price) to rise higher. ◆ See also **harden off, harden up.**

harden[2] ('hɑːdᵊn) *n* a rough fabric made from hards.

Hardenberg (*German* 'hardənbɛrk) *n* **Friedrich von** ('friːdrɪç fɔn). the original name of **Novalis.**

Hardenburg ('hɑːdᵊn,bɜːg) *n* **Fürst Karl** (**August**) **von.** 1750–1822, Prussian statesman: foreign minister (1804–06): prime minister (1807; 1810–22). His reforms enabled Prussia to break away from Napoleonic control in 1813.

hardened ('hɑːdᵊnd) *adj* **1** rigidly set, as in a mode of behaviour. **2** toughened, as by custom; seasoned. **3** (of a nuclear missile site) constructed to withstand a nuclear attack.

hardener ('hɑːdᵊnə) *n* **1** a person or thing that hardens. **2** a substance added to paint or varnish to increase durability. **3** an ingredient of certain adhesives and synthetic resins that accelerates or promotes setting.

hardening ('hɑːdᵊnɪŋ) *n* **1** the act or process of becoming or making hard. **2** a substance added to another substance or material to make it harder.

hardening of the arteries *n* a nontechnical name for **arteriosclerosis.**

harden off *vb* (*adv*) to accustom (a cultivated plant) or (of such a plant) to become accustomed to outdoor conditions by repeated exposure.

harden up *vb* (*intr*) *Nautical.* to tighten the sheets of a sailing vessel so as to prevent luffing.

hard feeling *n* (*often pl; often used with a negative*) resentment; ill will: *no hard feelings?*

hard fern *n* a common tufted erect fern of the polypody family, *Blechnum spicant,* having dark-green lanceolate leaves: it prefers acid soils, and in the U.S. is sometimes grown as deer feed. U.S. name: **deer fern.**

hardhack ('hɑːd,hæk) *n* a woody North American rosaceous plant, *Spiraea tomentosa,* with downy leaves and tapering clusters of small pink or white flowers. Also called: **steeplebush.**

hard hat *n* **1** a hat made of a hard material for protection, worn esp. by construction workers, equestrians, etc. **2** *Informal, chiefly U.S. and Canadian.* a construction worker. ◆ *adj* **hard-hat. 3** *Informal, chiefly U.S.* characteristic of the presumed conservative attitudes and prejudices typified by construction workers.

hard-headed *adj* **1** tough, realistic, or shrewd; not moved by sentiment. **2** *Chiefly U.S. and Canadian.* stubborn; obstinate. ► **,hard-'headedly** *adv* ► **,hard-'headedness** *n*

hardheads ('hɑːd,hɛdz) *n* (*functioning as sing*) a thistle-like plant, *Centaurea nigra,* native to Europe and introduced into North America and New Zealand, that has reddish-purple flower heads: family *Compositae* (composites). Also called: **knapweed.** See also **centaury** (sense 2).

hardhearted (,hɑːd'hɑːtɪd) *adj* unkind or intolerant. ► **,hard'heartedly** *adv* ► **,hard'heartedness** *n*

hard-hit *adj* seriously affected or hurt: *hard-hit by taxation.*

hard hitter *n N.Z. informal.* a bowler hat.

hard-hitting *adj* uncompromising; tough: *a hard-hitting report on urban deprivation.*

Hardicanute ('hɑːdɪkə,njuːt) *n* a variant of **Harthacanute.**

Hardie ('hɑːdɪ) *n* (**James**) **Keir** (kɪə). 1856–1915, British Labour leader and politician, born in Scotland; the first parliamentary leader of the Labour Party.

hardihood ('hɑːdɪ,hʊd) *n* courage, daring, or audacity.

hardily ('hɑːdɪlɪ) *adv* in a hardy manner; toughly or boldly.

hardiness ('hɑːdɪnɪs) *n* the condition or quality of being hardy, robust, or bold.

Harding ('hɑːdɪŋ) *n* **Warren G**(**amaliel**). 1865–1923, 29th president of the U.S. (1921–23).

Hardinge ('hɑːdɪŋ) *n* **Henry,** 1st Viscount Hardinge of Lahore. 1785–1856, British politician, soldier, and colonial administrator; governor general of India (1844–48).

hard labour *n Criminal law.* (formerly) the penalty of compulsory physical labour imposed in addition to a sentence of imprisonment: abolished in England in 1948.

hard landing *n* **1** a landing by a rocket or spacecraft in which the vehicle is destroyed on impact. **2** a solution to a problem, esp. an economic problem, that involves hardship. Compare **soft landing.**

hard lens *n* a rigid plastic lens which floats on the layer of tears in front of the cornea, worn to correct defects of vision. Compare **gas-permeable lens, soft lens.**

hard line *n* **a** an uncompromising course or policy. **b hardline.** (*as modifier*): *a hardline policy.* ► **,hard'liner** *n*

hard lines *sentence substitute, n Brit. informal.* bad luck. Also: **hard cheese.**

hardly ('hɑːdlɪ) *adv* **1** scarcely; barely: *we hardly knew the family.* **2** just; only just: *he could hardly hold the cup.* **3** *Often used ironically.* almost or probably not or not at all: *he will hardly incriminate himself.* **4** with difficulty or effort. **5** *Rare.* harshly or cruelly.

USAGE Since *hardly, scarcely,* and *barely* already have negative force, it is redundant to use another negative in the same clause: *he had hardly had* (not *he hadn't hardly had*) *time to think; there was scarcely any* (not *scarcely no*) *bread left.*

hard-mouthed *adj* **1** (of a horse) not responding satisfactorily to a pull on the bit. **2** stubborn; obstinate.

hard neck *n Irish informal.* audacity; nerve.

hardness ('hɑːdnɪs) *n* **1** the quality or condition of being hard. **2** one of several measures of resistance to indentation, deformation, or abrasion. See **Mohs scale, Brinell number. 3** the quality of water that causes it to impair the lathering of soap: caused by the presence of certain calcium salts. **Temporary hardness** can be removed by boiling whereas **permanent hardness** cannot.

hard-nosed *adj Informal.* tough, shrewd, and practical.

hard of hearing *adj* **a** deaf or partly deaf. **b** (*as collective n; preceded by the*): *the hard of hearing.*

Hardouin Mansart (*French* ardwɛ̃ mɑ̃saːr) *n* See (Jules Hardouin) **Mansart.**

hard pad *n* (in dogs) an abnormal increase in the thickness of the foot pads: one of the clinical signs of canine distemper. See **distemper**[1] (sense 1).

hard palate *n* the anterior bony portion of the roof of the mouth, extending backwards to the soft palate.

hardpan ('hɑːd,pæn) *n* a hard impervious layer of clay below the soil, resistant to drainage and root growth.

hard paste *n* **a** porcelain made with kaolin and petuntse, of Chinese origin and made in Europe from the early 18th century. **b** (*as modifier*): *hard-paste porcelain.*

hard-pressed *adj* **1** in difficulties: *the swimmer was hard-pressed.* **2** subject to severe competition. **3** subject to severe attack. **4** closely pursued.

hardrock ('hɑːd,rɒk) *Canadian.* ◆ *adj* **1** (of mining) concerned with extracting minerals other than coal, usually from solid rock. ◆ *n* **2** *Slang.* a tough uncompromising man.

hard rock *n Music.* a rhythmically simple and usually highly amplified style of rock and roll.

hard rubber *n* a hard fairly inelastic material made by vulcanizing natural rubber. See **vulcanite.**

hards (hɑːdz) *or* **hurds** *pl n* coarse fibres and other refuse from flax and hemp. [Old English *heordan* (plural); related to Middle Dutch *hēde,* Greek *keskeon* tow]

hard sauce *n* another name for **brandy butter.**

hard science *n* **a** one of the natural or physical sciences, such as physics, chemistry, biology, geology, or astronomy. **b** (*as modifier*): *a hard-science lecture.* ► **hard scientist** *n*

hardscrabble ('hɑːd,skræbᵊl) *n U.S. informal.* **1** (*modifier*) (of a place) difficult to make a living in; barren. **2** great effort made in the face of difficulties.

hard sell *n* an aggressive insistent technique of selling or advertising. Compare **soft sell.**

hard-shell *adj also* **hard-shelled. 1** *Zoology.* having a shell or carapace that is thick, heavy, or hard. **2** *U.S.* strictly orthodox. ◆ *n* **3** another name for the **quahog.**

hard-shell clam *n* another name for the **quahog.**

hard-shell crab *n* a crab, esp. of the edible species *Cancer pagurus,* that has not recently moulted and therefore has a hard shell. Compare **soft-shell crab.**

hardship ('hɑːdʃɪp) *n* **1** conditions of life difficult to endure. **2** something that causes suffering or privation.

hard shoulder *n Brit.* a surfaced verge running along the edge of a motorway for emergency stops.

hard-spun *adj* (of yarn) spun with a firm close twist.

hard standing *n* a hard surface on which vehicles, such as cars or aircraft, may be parked.

hardtack ('hɑːdˌtæk) *n* a kind of hard saltless biscuit, formerly eaten esp. by sailors as a staple aboard ship. Also called: **pilot biscuit, ship's biscuit, sea biscuit.**
hard tack *n Irish informal.* whisky.
hardtop ('hɑːdˌtɒp) *n* **1** a car equipped with a metal or plastic roof that is sometimes detachable. **2** the detachable hard roof of some sports cars.
hardware ('hɑːdˌwɛə) *n* **1** metal tools, implements, etc., esp. cutlery or cooking utensils. **2** *Computing.* the physical equipment used in a computer system, such as the central processing unit, peripheral devices, and memory. Compare **software. 3** mechanical equipment, components, etc. **4** heavy military equipment, such as tanks and missiles or their parts. **5** *Informal.* a gun or guns collectively.
hard-wearing *adj* resilient, durable, and tough.
hard wheat *n* a type of wheat with hard kernels, yielding a strong flour and used for bread, macaroni, etc.
Hardwick Hall ('hɑːdwɪk) *n* an Elizabethan mansion near Chesterfield in Derbyshire: built 1591–97 for Elizabeth, Countess of Shrewsbury (Bess of Hardwick).
hard-wired *adj* (of a circuit or instruction) permanently wired into a computer, replacing separate software.
hardwood ('hɑːdˌwʊd) *n* **1** the wood of any of numerous broad-leaved dicotyledonous trees, such as oak, beech, ash, etc., as distinguished from the wood of a conifer. **2** any tree from which this wood is obtained. ◆ Compare **softwood.**
hard-working *adj* (of a person) industrious; diligent.
hardy[1] ('hɑːdɪ) *adj* **-dier, -diest. 1** having or demanding a tough constitution; robust. **2** bold; courageous. **3** foolhardy; rash. **4** (of plants) able to live out of doors throughout the winter. **[**C13: from Old French *hardi* bold, past participle of *hardir* to become bold, of Germanic origin; compare Old English *hierdan* to HARDEN[1], Old Norse *hertha,* Old High German *herten***]**
hardy[2] ('hɑːdɪ) *n, pl* **-dies.** any blacksmith's tool made with a square shank so that it can be lodged in a square hole in an anvil. **[**C19: probably from HARD**]**
Hardy ('hɑːdɪ) *n* **1 Oliver.** See **Laurel and Hardy. 2 Thomas.** 1840–1928, British novelist and poet. Most of his novels are set in his native Dorset (part of his fictional Wessex) and include *Far from the Madding Crowd* (1874), *The Return of the Native* (1878), *The Mayor of Casterbridge* (1886), *Tess of the d'Urbervilles* (1891), and *Jude the Obscure* (1895), after which his work consisted chiefly of verse. **3** Sir **Thomas Masterman.** 1769–1839, British naval officer, flag captain under Nelson (1799–1805): 1st Sea Lord (1830).
hare (hɛə) *n, pl* **hares** *or* **hare. 1** any solitary leporid mammal of the genus *Lepus,* such as *L. europaeus* (**European hare**). Hares are larger than rabbits, having longer ears and legs, and live in shallow nests (forms). Related adj: **leporine. 2 run with the hare and hunt with the hounds.** to be on good terms with both sides. **3 make a hare of (someone).** *Irish informal.* to defeat (someone) completely. ◆ *vb* **4** (*intr;* often foll. by *off, after,* etc.) *Brit. informal.* to go or run fast or wildly. **[**Old English *hara;* related to Old Norse *heri,* Old High German *haso,* Swedish *hare,* Sanskrit *śaśā***]** ▸ **'hareˌlike** *adj*
Hare (hɛə) *n* **1** Sir **David.** born 1947, British dramatist and theatre director: his plays include *Plenty* (1978), *Pravda* (with Howard Brenton, 1985), *The Secret Rapture* (1989), *Racing Demon* (1990), and *The Judas Kiss* (1998). **2 William.** 19th century, Irish murderer and bodysnatcher: associate of William Burke.
hare and hounds *n* (*functioning as sing*) a game in which certain players (**hares**) run across country scattering pieces of paper that the other players (**hounds**) follow in an attempt to catch the hares.
harebell ('hɛəˌbel) *n* a N temperate campanulaceous plant, *Campanula rotundifolia,* having slender stems and leaves, and bell-shaped blue flowers. Also called (in Scotland): **bluebell.**
harebrained *or* **hairbrained** ('hɛəˌbreɪnd) *adj* rash, foolish, or badly thought out: *harebrained schemes.*
Hare Krishna ('hɑːrɪ 'krɪʃnə) *n* **1** a Hindu sect devoted to a form of Hinduism (**Krishna Consciousness**) based on the worship of the god Krishna. **2** (*pl* **Hare Krishnas**) a member or follower of this sect. **[**C20: from Hindi, literally: Lord Krishna (vocative): the opening words of a sacred verse often chanted in public by adherents of the movement**]**
harelip ('hɛəˌlɪp) *n* a congenital cleft or fissure in the midline of the upper lip, resembling the cleft upper lip of a hare, often occurring with cleft palate. ▸ **'hareˌlipped** *adj*
harem ('hɛərəm, hɑː'riːm) *or* **hareem** (hɑː'riːm) *n* **1** the part of an Oriental house reserved strictly for wives, concubines, etc. **2** a Muslim's wives and concubines collectively. **3** a group of female animals of the same species that are the mates of a single male. **[**C17: from Arabic *harīm* forbidden (place)**]**
hare's-foot *n* a papilionaceous annual plant, *Trifolium arvense,* that grows on sandy soils in Europe and NW Asia and has downy heads of white or pink flowers. Also called: **hare's-foot clover.**
harestail ('hɛəsˌteɪl) *n* a species of cotton grass, *Eriophorum vaginatum,* more tussocky than common cotton grass and having only a single flower head.
Harewood House ('hɛəwʊd) *n* a mansion near Harrogate in Yorkshire: built 1759–71 by John Carr for the Lascelles family; interior decoration by Robert Adam.
Harfleur ('hɑːflɜːr; *French* arflœr) *n* a port in N France, in the Seine-Maritime department: important centre in the Middle Ages. Pop.: 9700 (latest est.).
Hargeisa (hɑː'geɪsə) *n* a city in NW Somalia: former capital of British Somaliland (1941–60); trading centre for nomadic herders. Pop.: 400 000 (1987 est.).
Hargreaves ('hɑːgriːvz) *n* **James.** died 1778, English inventor of the spinning jenny.
haricot ('hærɪkəʊ) *n* **1** a variety of French bean with light-coloured edible seeds, which can be dried and stored. **2** another name for **French bean. 3** the seed or pod of any of these plants, eaten as a vegetable. **[**C17: from French, perhaps from Nahuatl *ayecotli***]**
Harijan ('hʌrɪdʒən) *n* a member of certain classes in India, formerly considered inferior and untouchable. See **scheduled castes. [**Hindi, literally: man of God (so called by Mahatma Gandhi), from *Hari* god + *jan* man**]**
hari-kari (ˌhærɪ'kɑːrɪ) *n* a non-Japanese variant of **hara-kiri.**
Haringey ('hærɪŋˌgeɪ) *n* a borough of N Greater London. Pop.: 212 300 (1994 est.). Area: 30 sq. km (12 sq. miles).
Harishchandra (ˌhærɪʃ'tʃændrə) *n* also known as *Bharatendu.* 1850–85, Indian poet, dramatist, and essayist, who established Hindi as a literary language.
hark (hɑːk) *vb* (*intr; usually imperative*) to listen; pay attention. **[**Old English *heorcnian* to HEARKEN; related to Old Frisian *herkia,* Old High German *hōrechen;* see HEAR**]**
hark back *vb* (*intr, adv*) to return to an earlier subject, point, or position, as in speech or thought.
harken ('hɑːkən) *vb* a variant spelling (esp. U.S.) of **hearken.** ▸ **'harkener** *n*
harl[1] (hærl, hɑːl) *Scot.* ◆ *vb* **1** (*tr*) to drag (something) along the ground. **2** (*intr*) to drag oneself; trail along. **3** (*tr*) to cover (a building) with a mixture of lime and gravel; roughcast. **4** (*intr*) to troll for fish. ◆ *n* **5** the act of harling or dragging. **6** a small quantity; a scraping. **7** a mixture of lime and gravel; roughcast. **[**C18: of unknown origin**]** ▸ **'harling** *n*
harl[2] (hɑːl) *n Angling.* a variant of **herl.**
Harlech ('hɑːˌlɪk) *n* a town in N Wales, in Gwynedd: noted for its ruined 13th-century castle overlooking Cardigan Bay: tourism. Pop.: 1233 (1991).
Harlem ('hɑːləm) *n* a district of New York City, in NE Manhattan: now largely a Black ghetto.
Harlem Globetrotters *pl n* a U.S. basketball team founded in 1927 by Abraham Saperstein, famous for their exhibition matches and clownish antics.
harlequin ('hɑːlɪkwɪn) *n* **1** (*sometimes cap.*) *Theatre.* a stock comic character originating in the commedia dell'arte; the foppish lover of Columbine in the English harlequinade. He is usually represented in diamond-patterned multi-coloured tights, wearing a black mask. **2** a clown or buffoon. ◆ *adj* **3** varied in colour or decoration. **4** (of certain animals) having a white coat with irregular patches of black or other dark colour: *harlequin Great Dane.* **5** comic, ludicrous, etc. **[**C16: from Old French *Herlequin, Hellequin* leader of band of demon horsemen, perhaps from Middle English *Herle king* (unattested) King Herle, mythical being identified with Woden**]**
harlequinade (ˌhɑːlɪkwɪ'neɪd) *n* **1** (*sometimes cap.*) *Theatre.* a play or part of a pantomime in which harlequin has a leading role. **2** buffoonery.
harlequin bug *n* a brightly coloured heteropterous insect, *Murgantia histrionica,* of the U.S. and Central America: a pest of cabbages and related plants: family *Pentatomidae.*
harlequin duck *n* a northern sea duck, *Histrionicus histrionicus,* the male of which has a blue and red plumage with black and white markings.
Harley ('hɑːlɪ) *n* **Robert,** 1st Earl of Oxford. 1661–1724, British statesman; head of the government (1710–14), negotiated the treaty of Utrecht (1713).
Harley Street *n* a street in central London famous for its large number of medical specialists' consulting rooms.
harlot ('hɑːlət) *n* **1** a prostitute or promiscuous woman. ◆ *adj* **2** *Archaic.* of or like a harlot. **[**C13: from Old French *herlot* rascal, of obscure origin**]** ▸ **'harlotry** *n*
Harlow[1] ('hɑːləʊ) *n* a town in SE England, in W Essex: designated a new town in 1947, with a planned population of 80 000. Pop.: 74 629 (1991).
Harlow[2] ('hɑːləʊ) *n* **Jean,** real name *Harlean Carpentier.* 1911–37, U.S. film actress, whose films include *Hell's Angels* (1930), *Red Dust* (1932), and *Bombshell* (1933).
harm (hɑːm) *n* **1** physical or mental injury or damage. **2** moral evil or wrongdoing. ◆ *vb* **3** (*tr*) to injure physically, morally, or mentally. **[**Old English *hearm;* related to Old Norse *harmr* grief, Old High German *harm* injury, Old Slavonic *sramŭ* disgrace**]** ▸ **'harmer** *n*
harmattan (hɑː'mætᵊn) *n* a dry dusty wind from the Sahara blowing towards the W African coast, esp. from November to March. **[**C17: from Twi *haramata,* perhaps from Arabic *harām* forbidden thing; see HAREM**]**
harmful ('hɑːmfʊl) *adj* causing or tending to cause harm; injurious. ▸ **'harmfully** *adv* ▸ **'harmfulness** *n*
harmless ('hɑːmlɪs) *adj* **1** not causing any physical or mental damage or injury. **2** unlikely to annoy or worry people: *a harmless sort of man.* ▸ **'harmlessly** *adv* ▸ **'harmlessness** *n*
harmolodics (ˌhɑːmə'lɒdɪks) *n* (*functioning as sing*) *Jazz.* the technique of each musician in a group simultaneously improvising around the melodic and rhythmic patterns in a tune, rather than one musician improvising on its underlying harmonic pattern while the others play an accompaniment. **[**C20: of unknown origin**]** ▸ **ˌharmo'lodic** *adj*
harmonic (hɑː'mɒnɪk) *adj* **1** of, involving, producing, or characterized by harmony; harmonious. **2** *Music.* of, relating to, or belonging to harmony. **3** *Maths.* **3a** capable of expression in the form of sine and cosine functions. **3b** of or relating to numbers whose reciprocals form an arithmetic progression. **4** *Physics.* of or concerned with an oscillation that has a frequency that is an integral multiple of a fundamental frequency. **5** *Physics.* of or concerned with harmonics. ◆ *n* **6** *Physics, music.* a component of a periodic quantity, such as a musical tone, with a frequency that is an integral multiple of the fundamental frequency. The **first harmonic** is the fundamental, the **second harmonic** (twice the fundamental frequency) is the **first overtone,** the **third harmonic** (three times the fundamental frequency) is the **second overtone,** etc. **7** *Music.* (not in technical use) overtone: in this case, the first overtone is the first harmonic, etc. ◆ See also **harmonics. [**C16: from Latin *harmonicus* relating to HARMONY**]** ▸ **har'monically** *adv*
harmonica (hɑː'mɒnɪkə) *n* **1** a small wind instrument of the reed organ family in which reeds of graduated lengths set into a metal plate enclosed in a narrow oblong box are made to vibrate by blowing and sucking. Also called: **mouth**

organ. **2** See **glass harmonica.** [C18: from Latin *harmonicus* relating to HARMONY]

harmonic analysis *n* **1** the representation of a periodic function by means of the summation and integration of simple trigonometric functions. **2** the study of this means of representation.

harmonic distortion *n Electronics.* distortion caused by nonlinear characteristics of electronic apparatus, esp. of audio amplifiers, that generate unwanted harmonics of the input frequencies.

harmonic mean *n* the reciprocal of the arithmetic mean of the reciprocals of a set of specified numbers: the harmonic mean of 2, 3, and 4 is $3(\frac{1}{2} + \frac{1}{3} + \frac{1}{4})^{-1}$ = 36/13.

harmonic minor scale *n Music.* a minor scale modified from the state of being natural by the sharpening of the seventh degree. See **minor.** Compare **melodic minor scale.**

harmonic motion *n* a periodic motion in which the displacement is symmetrical about a point or a periodic motion that is composed of such motions. See also **simple harmonic motion.**

harmonic progression *n* a sequence of numbers whose reciprocals form an arithmetic progression, as 1, ½, ⅓, ...

harmonics (hɑː'mɒnɪks) *n* **1** (*functioning as sing*) the science of musical sounds and their acoustic properties. **2** (*functioning as pl*) the overtones of a fundamental note, as produced by lightly touching the string of a stringed instrument at one of its node points while playing. See **harmonic** (sense 6).

harmonic series *n* **1** *Maths.* a series whose terms are in harmonic progression, as in 1 + ½ + ⅓ +.... **2** *Acoustics.* the series of tones with frequencies strictly related to one another and to the fundamental tone, as obtained by touching lightly the node points of a string while playing it. Its most important application is in the playing of brass instruments.

harmonious (hɑː'məʊnɪəs) *adj* **1** (esp. of colours or sounds) fitting together well. **2** having agreement or consensus. **3** tuneful, consonant, or melodious. ▸ **har'moniously** *adv*

harmonist ('hɑːmənɪst) *n* **1** a person skilled in the art and techniques of harmony. **2** a person who combines and collates parallel narratives. ▸ **,harmo'nistic** *adj* ▸ **,harmo'nistically** *adv*

harmonium (hɑː'məʊnɪəm) *n* a musical keyboard instrument of the reed organ family, in which air from pedal-operated bellows causes the reeds to vibrate. [C19: from French, from *harmonie* HARMONY]

harmonization *or* **harmonisation** (,hɑːmənaɪ'zeɪʃən) *n* **1** the act of harmonizing. **2** a system, particularly used in the EU, whereby the blue-collar workers and the white-collar workers in an organization have similar status and any former differences in terms and conditions of employment are levelled up.

harmonize *or* **harmonise** ('hɑːmə,naɪz) *vb* **1** to make or become harmonious. **2** (*tr*) *Music.* to provide a harmony for (a melody, tune, etc.). **3** (*intr*) to sing in harmony, as with other singers. **4** to collate parallel narratives. ▸ **'harmo,nizable** *or* **'harmo,nisable** *adj*

harmonizer *or* **harmoniser** ('hɑːmə,naɪzə) *n Music.* **1** a person skilled in the theory of composition of harmony. **2** a device that electronically duplicates a signal at a different pitch or different pitches.

harmony ('hɑːmənɪ) *n, pl* **-nies. 1** agreement in action, opinion, feeling, etc.; accord. **2** order or congruity of parts to their whole or to one another. **3** agreeable sounds. **4** *Music.* **4a** any combination of notes sounded simultaneously. **4b** the vertically represented structure of a piece of music. Compare **melody** (sense 1b), **rhythm** (sense 1). **4c** the art or science concerned with the structure and combinations of chords. **5** a collation of the material of parallel narratives, esp. of the four Gospels. [C14: from Latin *harmonia* concord of sounds, from Greek: harmony, from *harmos* a joint]

harmotome ('hɑːmə,təʊm) *n* a mineral of the zeolite group consisting of hydrated aluminium barium silicate in the form of monoclinic twinned crystals. [C19: from French, from Greek *harmos* a joint + *tomē* a slice, from *temnein* to cut]

Harmsworth ('hɑːmzwɜːθ) *n* **1 Alfred Charles William.** See (Viscount) **Northcliffe. 2 Harold Sydney.** See (1st Viscount) **Rothermere.**

Harnack (*German* 'harnak) *n* **Adolf von.** 1851–1930, German Protestant theologian, author of the influential *History of Dogma* (1886–90).

harness ('hɑːnɪs) *n* **1** an arrangement of leather straps buckled or looped together, fitted to a draught animal in order that the animal can be attached to and pull a cart. **2** something resembling this, esp. for attaching something to the body: *a parachute harness.* **3** *Mountaineering.* an arrangement of webbing straps that enables a climber to attach himself to the rope so that the impact of a fall is minimized. **4** the total system of electrical leads for a vehicle or aircraft. **5** *Weaving.* the part of a loom that raises and lowers the warp threads, creating the shed. **6** *Archaic.* armour collectively. **7 in harness.** at one's routine work. ◆ *vb* (*tr*) **8** to put harness on (a horse). **9** (usually foll. by *to*) to attach (a draught animal) by means of harness to (a cart, etc.). **10** to control so as to employ the energy or potential power of: *to harness the atom.* **11** to equip or clothe with armour. [C13: from Old French *harneis* baggage, probably from Old Norse *hernest* (unattested) provisions, from *herr* army + *nest* provisions] ▸ **'harnesser** *n* ▸ **'harnessless** *adj* ▸ **'harness-,like** *adj*

harnessed antelope *n* any of various antelopes with vertical white stripes on the back, esp. the bushbuck.

harness hitch *n* a knot forming a loop with no free ends.

harness race *n Horse racing.* a trotting or pacing race for standardbred horses driven in sulkies and harnessed in a special way to cause them to use the correct gait.

Harney Peak ('hɑːnɪ) *n* a mountain in SW South Dakota: the highest peak in the Black Hills. Height: 2207 m (7242 ft.).

Harold I ('hærəld) *n* surname *Harefoot.* died 1040, king of England (1037–40); son of Canute.

Harold II *n* ?1022–66, king of England (1066); son of Earl Godwin and successor of Edward the Confessor. His claim to the throne was disputed by William the Conqueror, who defeated him at the Battle of Hastings (1066).

harp (hɑːp) *n* **1** a large triangular plucked stringed instrument consisting of a soundboard connected to an upright pillar by means of a curved crossbar from which the strings extend downwards. The strings are tuned diatonically and may be raised in pitch either one or two semitones by the use of pedals (**double-action harp**). Basic key: B major; range: nearly seven octaves. **2** something resembling this, esp. in shape. **3** an informal name (esp. in pop music) for **harmonica.** ◆ *vb* **4** (*intr*) to play the harp. **5** (*tr*) *Archaic.* to speak; utter; express. **6** (*intr;* foll. by *on* or *upon*) to speak or write in a persistent and tedious manner. [Old English *hearpe;* related to Old Norse *harpa,* Old High German *harfa,* Latin *corbis* basket, Russian *korobit* to warp] ▸ **'harper** *or* **'harpist** *n*

Harper's Ferry ('hɑːpəz) *n* a village in NE West Virginia, at the confluence of the Potomac and Shenandoah Rivers: site of an arsenal seized by John Brown (1859). Pop.: 308 (1990).

harpings ('hɑːpɪŋz) *or* **harpins** ('hɑːpɪnz) *pl n* **1** *Nautical.* wooden members used for strengthening the bow of a vessel. **2** *Shipbuilding.* wooden supports used in construction. [C17: perhaps related to French *harpe* cramp iron]

harpoon (hɑː'puːn) *n* **1a** a barbed missile attached to a long cord and hurled or fired from a gun when hunting whales, etc. **1b** (*as modifier*): *a harpoon gun.* ◆ *vb* **2** (*tr*) to spear with or as if with a harpoon. [C17: probably from Dutch *harpoen,* from Old French *harpon* clasp, from *harper* to seize, perhaps of Scandinavian origin] ▸ **har'pooner** *or* **,harpoon'eer** *n* ▸ **har'poon-,like** *adj*

harp seal *n* a brownish-grey earless seal, *Pagophilus groenlandicus,* of the North Atlantic and Arctic Oceans.

harpsichord ('hɑːpsɪ,kɔːd) *n* a horizontally strung stringed keyboard instrument, triangular in shape, consisting usually of two manuals controlling various sets of strings plucked by pivoted plectrums mounted on jacks. Some harpsichords have a pedal keyboard and stops by which the tone colour may be varied. [C17: from New Latin *harpichordium,* from Late Latin *harpa* HARP + Latin *chorda* CHORD[1]] ▸ **'harpsi,chordist** *n*

harpy ('hɑːpɪ) *n, pl* **-pies.** a cruel grasping woman. [C16: from Latin *Harpyia,* from Greek *Harpuiai* the Harpies, literally: snatchers, from *harpazein* to seize]

Harpy ('hɑːpɪ) *n, pl* **-pies.** *Greek myth.* a ravenous creature with a woman's head and trunk and a bird's wings and claws.

harpy eagle *n* a very large tropical American eagle, *Harpia harpyja,* with a black-and-white plumage and a head crest.

harquebus ('hɑːkwɪbəs) *n, pl* **-buses.** a variant of **arquebus.**

harquebusier (,hɑːkwɪbə'sɪə) *n* (formerly) a soldier armed with an arquebus. Also called: **arquebusier.**

Harrer ('hɑːrə) *n* a variant spelling of **Harar.**

harridan ('hærɪdᵊn) *n* a scolding old woman; nag. [C17: of uncertain origin; perhaps related to French *haridelle,* literally: broken-down horse; of obscure origin]

harrier[1] ('hærɪə) *n* **1** a person or thing that harries. **2** any diurnal bird of prey of the genus *Circus,* having broad wings and long legs and tail and typically preying on small terrestrial animals: family *Accipitridae* (hawks, etc.). See also **marsh harrier, Montagu's harrier.**

harrier[2] ('hærɪə) *n* **1** a smallish breed of hound used originally for hare-hunting. **2** a cross-country runner. [C16: from HARE + -ER[1]; influenced by HARRIER[1]]

Harrier ('hærɪə) *n* a British subsonic multipurpose military jet plane capable of vertical takeoff and landing by means of vectoring the engine thrust.

Harriman ('hærɪmən) *n* **W(illiam) Averell.** 1891–1986, U.S. diplomat: negotiated the Nuclear Test Ban Treaty with the Soviet Union (1963); governor of New York (1955–58).

Harrington ('hærɪŋtən) *n* **James.** 1611–77, English republican and writer. He described his ideal form of government in *Oceana* (1656).

Harris[1] ('hærɪs) *n* the S part of the island of Lewis with Harris, in the Outer Hebrides. Pop.: (including Lewis) 23 390 (1981). Area: 500 sq. km (193 sq. miles).

Harris[2] ('hærɪs) *n* **1** Sir **Arthur Travers,** known as *Bomber Harris.* 1892–1984, British air marshal. He was commander-in-chief of Bomber Command of the RAF (1942–45). **2 Frank.** 1856–1931, British writer and journalist; his books include his autobiography *My Life and Loves* (1923–27) and *Contemporary Portraits* (1915–30). **3 Joel Chandler.** 1848–1908, U.S. writer; creator of Uncle Remus. **4 Roy.** 1898–1979, U.S. composer, esp. of orchestral and choral music incorporating American folk tunes.

Harrisburg ('hærɪs,bɜːg) *n* a city in S Pennsylvania, on the Susquehanna River: the state capital. Pop.: 53 430 (1992 est.).

Harrison ('hærɪsᵊn) *n* **1 Benjamin.** 1833–1901, 23rd president of the U.S. (1889–93). **2 George.** born 1943, British rock singer, guitarist, and songwriter: a member of the Beatles (1962–70). His solo recordings include *All Things Must Pass* (1970) and *Cloud Nine* (1987). **3 Rex** (**Carey**). 1908–90, British actor. His many films include *Major Barbara* (1940), *Blithe Spirit* (1945), and *My Fair Lady* (1964). **4 Tony.** born 1937, British poet, dramatist, and translator: best known for his long poem *v.* (1985) and his translations for the stage. **5** grandfather of Benjamin, **William Henry.** 1773–1841, 9th president of the U.S. (1841).

Harris Tweed *n Trademark.* a loose-woven tweed made in the Outer Hebrides, esp. Lewis and Harris.

Harrogate ('hærəgɪt) *n* a town in N England, in North Yorkshire: a spa. Pop.: 66 178 (1991).

Harrovian (hə'rəʊvɪən) *n* **1** a person educated at Harrow School. ◆ *adj* **2** of or concerning Harrow. [C19: from New Latin *Harrŏvia* HARROW + -AN]

harrow[1] ('hærəʊ) *n* **1** any of various implements used to level the ground, stir the soil, break up clods, destroy weeds, etc., in soil. ◆ *vb* **2** (*tr*) to draw a harrow over (land). **3** (*intr*) (of soil) to become broken up through harrowing. **4** (*tr*) to distress; vex. **[C13:** of Scandinavian origin; compare Danish *harv,* Swedish *harf;* related to Middle Dutch *harke* rake**]** ► **ˈharrower** *n* ► **ˈharrowing** *adj, n*

harrow[2] (ˈhærəʊ) *vb (tr) Archaic.* **1** to plunder or ravish. **2** (of Christ) to descend into (hell) to rescue righteous souls. **[C13:** variant of Old English *hergian* to HARRY**]** ► **ˈharrowment** *n*

Harrow (ˈhærəʊ) *n* a borough of NW Greater London; site of an English boys' public school founded in 1571 at **Harrow-on-the-Hill,** a part of this borough. Pop.: 210 300 (1994 est.). Area: 51 sq. km (20 sq. miles).

harrumph (həˈrʌmf) *vb (intr)* to clear or make the noise of clearing the throat.

harry (ˈhærɪ) *vb* **-ries, -rying, -ried. 1** *(tr)* to harass; worry. **2** to ravage (a town, etc.), esp. in war. **[**Old English *hergian;* related to *here* army, Old Norse *herja* to lay waste, Old High German *heriōn***]**

harsh (hɑːʃ) *adj* **1** rough or grating to the senses. **2** stern, severe, or cruel. **[C16:** probably of Scandinavian origin; compare Middle Low German *harsch,* Norwegian *harsk* rancid**]** ► **ˈharshly** *adv* ► **ˈharshness** *n*

harslet (ˈhɑːzlɪt, ˈhɑːs-) *n* a variant of **haslet.**

hart (hɑːt) *n, pl* **harts** *or* **hart.** the male of the deer, esp. the red deer aged five years or more. **[**Old English *heorot;* related to Old Norse *hjörtr,* Old High German *hiruz* hart, Latin *cervus* stag, Lithuanian *kárve* cow; see HORN**]**

Hart (hɑːt) *n* **1 Lorenz.** 1895–1943, U.S. lyricist: collaborated with Richard Rodgers in writing musicals. **2 Moss.** 1904–61, U.S. dramatist: collaborated with George Kaufman on Broadway comedies and wrote libretti for musicals.

hartal (hɑːˈtɑːl) *n* (in India) the act of closing shops or suspending work, esp. in political protest. **[C20:** from Hindi *hartāl,* from *hāt* shop (from Sanskrit *hatta*) + *tālā* bolt for a door (from Sanskrit: latch)**]**

Harte (hɑːt) *n* **(Francis) Bret.** 1836–1902, U.S. poet and short-story writer, noted for his sketches of Californian gold miners, such as *The Luck of Roaring Camp* (1870).

hartebeest (ˈhɑːtɪˌbiːst) *or* **hartbeest** (ˈhɑːtˌbiːst) *n* **1** either of two large African antelopes, *Alcelaphus buselaphus* or *A. lichtensteini,* having an elongated muzzle, lyre-shaped horns, and a fawn-coloured coat. **2** any similar and related animal, such as *Damaliscus hunteri* (**Hunter's hartebeest**). **[C18:** via Afrikaans from Dutch; see HART, BEAST**]**

Hartford (ˈhɑːtfəd) *n* a port in central Connecticut, on the Connecticut River: the state capital. Pop.: 133 086 (1996 est.).

Harthacanute (ˈhɑːθəkəˌnjuːt), **Hardecanute,** *or* **Hardicanute** *n* ?1019–42, king of Denmark (1035–42) and of England (1040–42); son of Canute.

Hartington (ˈhɑːtɪŋtən) *n* **Lord.** See (8th Duke of) **Devonshire.**

Hartlepool (ˈhɑːtlɪˌpuːl) *n* **1** a port in NE England, in Hartlepool unitary authority, Co. Durham, on the North Sea: greatly enlarged in 1967 by its amalgamation with West Hartlepool; engineering, clothing, food processing. Pop.: 87 310 (1991). **2** a unitary authority in NE England, in Co. Durham: formerly (1974–96) part of the county of Cleveland. Pop.: 90 409 (1994 est.). Area: 93 sq. km (36 sq. miles).

Hartley (ˈhɑːtlɪ) *n* **1 David.** 1705–57, English philosopher and physician. In *Observations of Man* (1749) he introduced the theory of psychological associationism. **2 L(eslie) P(oles).** 1895–1972, British novelist. His novels include the trilogy *The Shrimp and the Anemone* (1944), *The Sixth Heaven* (1946), and *Eustace and Hilda* (1947) as well as *The Go-Between* (1953).

Hartnell (ˈhɑːtnᵊl) *n* Sir **Norman.** 1901–79, English couturier.

hartshorn (ˈhɑːtsˌhɔːn) *n* an obsolete name for **sal volatile** (sense 2). **[**Old English *heortes horn* hart's horn (formerly a chief source of ammonia)**]**

hart's-tongue *n* an evergreen Eurasian fern, *Phyllitis scolopendrium,* with narrow undivided fronds bearing rows of sori: family *Polypodiaceae.*

harum-scarum (ˈhɛərəmˈskɛərəm) *adj, adv* **1** in a reckless way or of a reckless nature. ◆ *n* **2** a person who is impetuous or rash. **[C17:** perhaps from *hare* (in obsolete sense: harass) + *scare,* variant of STARE[1]; compare HELTER-SKELTER**]**

Harun al-Rashid (hæˈruːn ˈælræˈʃiːd) *n* ?763–809 A.D., Abbasid caliph of Islam (786–809), whose court at Baghdad was idealized in the *Arabian Nights.*

haruspex (həˈrʌspɛks) *n, pl* **haruspices** (həˈrʌspɪˌsiːz). (in ancient Rome) a priest who practised divination, esp. by examining the entrails of animals. **[C16:** from Latin, probably from *hīra* gut + *specere* to look**]** ► **haruspical** (həˈrʌspɪkᵊl) *adj* ► **haruspicy** (həˈrʌspɪsɪ) *n*

Harvard classification (ˈhɑːvəd) *n* a classification of stars based on the characteristic spectral absorption lines and bands of the chemical elements present. See **spectral type. [C20:** named after the observatory at *Harvard,* Massachusetts, where it was prepared and published as part of *The Henry Draper Catalogue* (1924)**]**

harvest (ˈhɑːvɪst) *n* **1** the gathering of a ripened crop. **2** the crop itself or the yield from it in a single growing season. **3** the season for gathering crops. **4** the product of an effort, action, etc.: *a harvest of love.* ◆ *vb* **5** to gather or reap (a ripened crop) from (the place where it has been growing). **6** *(tr)* to receive or reap (benefits, consequences, etc.). **7** *(tr) Chiefly U.S.* to remove (an organ) from the body for transplantation. **[**Old English *hærfest;* related to Old Norse *harfr* harrow, Old High German *herbist* autumn, Latin *carpere* to pluck, Greek *karpos* fruit, Sanskrit *krpāna* shears**]** ► **ˈharvesting** *n* ► **ˈharvestless** *adj*

harvester (ˈhɑːvɪstə) *n* **1** a person who harvests. **2** a harvesting machine, esp. a combine harvester.

harvest home *n* **1** the bringing in of the harvest. **2** *Chiefly Brit.* a harvest supper.

harvestman (ˈhɑːvɪstmən) *n, pl* **-men. 1** a person engaged in harvesting. **2** Also called (U.S. and Canadian): **daddy-longlegs.** any arachnid of the order *Opiliones* (or *Phalangida*), having a small rounded body and very long thin legs.

harvest mite *or* **tick** *n* the bright red parasitic larva of any of various free-living mites of the genus *Trombicula* and related genera, which causes intense itching of human skin.

harvest moon *n* the full moon occurring nearest to the autumnal equinox.

harvest mouse *n* **1** a very small reddish-brown Eurasian mouse, *Micromys minutus,* inhabiting cornfields, hedgerows, etc., and feeding on grain and seeds: family *Muridae.* **2 American harvest mouse.** any small greyish mouse of the American genus *Reithrodontomys:* family *Cricetidae.*

Harvey (ˈhɑːvɪ) *n* **William.** 1578–1657, English physician who discovered the mechanism of blood circulation, expounded in *On the motion of the heart* (1628).

Harwell (ˈhɑːˌwɛl) *n* a village in S England, in Oxfordshire: atomic research station (1947).

Harwich (ˈhærɪtʃ) *n* a port in SE England, in NE Essex on the North Sea. Pop.: 18 436 (1991).

Haryana (hərˈjɑːnə) *n* a state of NE India, formed in 1966 from the Hindi-speaking parts of the state of Punjab. Capital: Chandigarh (shared with Punjab). Pop.: 17 925 000 (1994 est.). Area: 44 506 sq. km (17 182 sq. miles).

Harz *or* **Harz Mountains** (hɑːts) *pl n* a range of wooded hills in central Germany, between the Rivers Weser and Elbe: source of many legends. Highest peak: Brocken, 1142 m (3746 ft.).

has (hæz) *vb* (used with *he, she, it,* or a singular noun) a form of the present tense (indicative mood) of **have.**

Hasan al-Basri (hæˈsæn æl ˈbæzrɪ) *n* **al.** died 728 A.D., Muslim religious thinker.

has-been *n Informal.* a person or thing that is no longer popular, successful, effective, etc.

Hasdrubal (ˈhæzdrʊbᵊl) *n* died 207 B.C., Carthaginian general: commanded the Carthaginian army in Spain (218–211); joined his brother Hannibal in Italy and was killed at the Metaurus.

Hašek (*Czech* ˈhaʃɛk) *n* **Jaroslav** (ˈjarɔslaf). 1883–1923, Czech novelist and short-story writer; author of *The Good Soldier Schweik* (1923).

hash[1] (hæʃ) *n* **1** a dish of diced cooked meat, vegetables, etc., reheated in a sauce. **2** something mixed up. **3** a reuse or rework of old material. **4 make a hash of.** *Informal.* **4a** to mix or mess up. **4b** to defeat or destroy. **5 settle** (*or* **fix**) **someone's hash.** *Informal.* to subdue or silence someone. ◆ *vb (tr)* **6** to chop into small pieces. **7** to mix or mess up. **[C17:** from Old French *hacher* to chop up, from *hache* HATCHET**]**

hash[2] (hæʃ) *n Slang.* short for **hashish.**

hash[3] (hæʃ) *or* **hash mark** *n* **1** the character (#) used to precede a number. **2** this sign used in printing or writing to indicate that a space should be inserted.

hash browns *pl n* diced boiled potatoes mixed with chopped onion, shaped and fried until brown.

HaShem (haˈʃɛm) *Judaism.* a periphrastic way of referring to God in contexts other than prayer, scriptural reading, etc. because the name itself is considered too holy for such use. **[**from Hebrew, literally: The Name**]**

Hashemite Kingdom of Jordan (ˈhæʃɪˌmaɪt) *n* the official name of **Jordan.**

hash house *n U.S. slang.* a cheap café or restaurant.

hashish (ˈhæʃiːʃ, -ɪʃ) *or* **hasheesh** (ˈhæʃiːʃ) *n* **1** a purified resinous extract of the dried flower tops of the female hemp plant, used as a hallucinogenic. See also **cannabis. 2** any hallucinogenic substance prepared from this resin. **[C16:** from Arabic *hashīsh* hemp, dried herbage**]**

haslet (ˈhæzlɪt) *or* **harslet** *n* a loaf of cooked minced pig's offal, eaten cold. **[C14:** from Old French *hastelet* piece of spit roasted meat, from *haste* spit, of Germanic origin; compare Old High German *harsta* frying pan**]**

hasn't (ˈhæzᵊnt) *vb contraction of* has not.

hasp (hɑːsp) *n* **1** a metal fastening consisting of a hinged strap with a slot that fits over a staple and is secured by a pin, bolt, or padlock. ◆ *vb* **2** *(tr)* to secure (a door, window, etc.) with a hasp. **[**Old English *hæpse;* related to Old Norse *hespa,* Old High German *haspa* hasp, Dutch *haspel* reel, Sanskrit *capa* bow**]**

Hassan II (hæˈsɑːn, ˈhæsᵊn) *n* 1929–99, king of Morocco (1961–99).

Hasselt (*Flemish* ˈhɑsəlt; *French* asɛlt) *n* a market town in E Belgium, capital of Limbourg province. Pop.: 67 486 (1995 est.).

Hassid *or* **Hasid** (ˈhæsɪd; *Hebrew* xaˈsid) *n* variant spellings of **Chassid.**

hassium (ˈhæsɪəm) *n* a synthetic element produced in small quantities by high-energy ion bombardment. Symbol: Hs; atomic no. 108. **[C20:** from Latin, from HESSE[1], German state where it was discovered**]**

hassle (ˈhæsᵊl) *Informal.* ◆ *n* **1** a prolonged argument; wrangle. **2** a great deal of trouble; difficulty; nuisance. ◆ *vb* **3** *(intr)* to quarrel or wrangle. **4** *(tr)* to cause annoyance or trouble to (someone); harass. **[C20:** of unknown origin**]**

hassock (ˈhæsək) *n* **1** a firm upholstered cushion used for kneeling on, esp. in church. **2** a thick clump of grass. **[**Old English *hassuc* matted grass**]**

hast (hæst) *vb Archaic or dialect.* (used with the pronoun *thou* or its relative equivalent) a singular form of the present tense (indicative mood) of **have.**

hastate (ˈhæsteɪt) *adj* (of a leaf) having a pointed tip and two outward-pointing lobes at the base. **[C18:** from Latin *hastātus* with a spear, from *hasta* spear**]**

haste (heɪst) *n* **1** speed, esp. in an action; swiftness; rapidity. **2** the act of hurrying in a careless or rash manner. **3** a necessity for hurrying; urgency. **4 make haste.** to hurry; rush. ◆ *vb* **5** a poetic word for **hasten. [C14:** from Old French *haste,* of Germanic origin; compare Old Norse *heifst* hate, Old English *hǣst* strife, Old High German *heisti* powerful**]** ► **ˈhasteful** *adj* ► **ˈhastefully** *adv*

hasten (ˈheɪsᵊn) *vb* **1** *(may take an infinitive)* to hurry or cause to hurry; rush. **2** *(tr)* to be anxious (to say something): *I hasten to add that we are just good friends.* ► **ˈhastener** *n*

Hastings[1] (ˈheɪstɪŋz) *n* **1** a port in SE England, in East Sussex on the English Channel: near the site of the **Battle of Hastings** (1066), in which William the Conqueror defeated King Harold; chief of the Cinque Ports. Pop.: 81 139

(1991). **2** a town in New Zealand, on E North Island: centre of a rich agricultural and fruit-growing region. Pop. (urban area): 58 700 (1995 est.).

Hastings[2] ('heɪstɪŋz) *n* **Warren.** 1732–1818, British administrator in India; governor general of Bengal (1773–85). He implemented important reforms but was impeached by parliament (1788) on charges of corruption; acquitted in 1795.

hasty ('heɪstɪ) *adj* **-tier, -tiest. 1** rapid; swift; quick. **2** excessively or rashly quick. **3** short-tempered. **4** showing irritation or anger: *hasty words.* ► **'hastily** *adv* ► **'hastiness** *n*

hasty pudding *n* **1** *Brit.* a simple pudding made from milk thickened with tapioca, semolina, etc., and sweetened. **2** *U.S.* a mush of cornmeal, served with treacle sugar.

hat (hæt) *n* **1a** any of various head coverings, esp. one with a brim and a shaped crown. **1b** (*in combination*): *hatrack.* **2** *Informal.* a role or capacity. **3 at the drop of a hat.** without hesitation or delay. **4 I'll eat my hat.** *Informal.* I will be greatly surprised if (something that proves me wrong) happens: *I'll eat my hat if this book comes out late.* **5 hat in hand.** humbly or servilely. **6 keep (something) under one's hat.** to keep (something) secret. **7 my hat.** (*interj*) *Brit. informal.* **7a** my word! my goodness! **7b** nonsense! **8 old hat.** something stale or old-fashioned. **9 out of a hat. 9a** as if by magic. **9b** at random. **10 pass (***or* **send) the hat round.** to collect money, as for a cause. **11 take off one's hat to.** to admire or congratulate. **12 talk through one's hat. 12a** to talk foolishly. **12b** to deceive or bluff. **13 throw one's hat at (it).** *Irish.* to give up all hope of getting or achieving (something): *you can throw your hat at it now.* **14 throw (***or* **toss) one's hat in the ring.** to announce one's intentions to be a candidate or contestant. ◆ *vb* **hats, hatting, hatted. 15** (*tr*) to supply (a person, etc.) with a hat or put a hat on (someone). **[**Old English *hætt;* related to Old Norse *höttr* cap, Latin *cassis* helmet; see HOOD[1]**]** ► **'hatless** *adj* ► **'hat,like** *adj*

hatband ('hæt,bænd) *n* a band or ribbon around the base of the crown of a hat.

hatbox ('hæt,bɒks) *n* a box or case for a hat or hats.

hatch[1] (hætʃ) *vb* **1** to cause (the young of various animals, esp. birds) to emerge from the egg or (of young birds, etc.) to emerge from the egg. **2** to cause (eggs) to break and release the fully developed young or (of eggs) to break and release the young animal within. **3** (*tr*) to contrive or devise (a scheme, plot, etc.). ◆ *n* **4** the act or process of hatching. **5** a group of newly hatched animals. **[C13:** of Germanic origin; compare Middle High German *hecken* to mate (used of birds), Swedish *häcka* to hatch, Danish *hække***]** ► **'hatchable** *adj* ► **'hatcher** *n*

hatch[2] (hætʃ) *n* **1** a covering for a hatchway. **2** short for **hatchway. 3** Also called: **serving hatch.** an opening in a wall between a kitchen and a dining area. **4** the lower half of a divided door. **5** a sluice or sliding gate in a dam, dyke, or weir. **6 down the hatch.** *Slang.* (used as a toast) drink up! **7 under hatches. 7a** below decks. **7b** out of sight. **7c** brought low; dead. **[**Old English *hæcc;* related to Middle High German *heck,* Dutch *hek* gate**]**

hatch[3] (hætʃ) *vb Drawing, engraving, etc.* to mark (a figure, shade, etc.) with fine parallel or crossed lines to indicate shading. Compare **hachure. [C15:** from Old French *hacher* to chop, from *hache* HATCHET**]** ► **'hatching** *n*

hatch[4] (hætʃ) *n Informal.* short for **hatchback.**

hatchback ('hætʃ,bæk) *n* **1a** a sloping rear end of a car having a single door that is lifted to open. **1b** (*as modifier*): *a hatchback model.* **2** a car having such a rear end.

hatchel ('hætʃəl) *vb* **-els, -elling, -elled** *or U.S.* **-els, -eling, -eled,** *n* another word for **heckle** (senses 2, 3). **[C13** *hechele,* of Germanic origin; related to Old High German *hāko* hook, Middle Dutch *hekele* HACKLE**]** ► **'hatcheller** *n*

hatchery ('hætʃərɪ) *n, pl* **-eries.** a place where eggs are hatched under artificial conditions.

hatchet ('hætʃɪt) *n* **1** a short axe used for chopping wood, etc. **2** a tomahawk. **3** (*modifier*) of narrow dimensions and sharp features: *a hatchet face.* **4 bury the hatchet.** to cease hostilities and become reconciled. **[C14:** from Old French *hachette,* from *hache* axe, of Germanic origin; compare Old High German *happa* knife**]** ► **'hatchet-,like** *adj*

hatchet job *n Informal.* a malicious or devastating verbal or written attack.

hatchet man *n Informal.* **1** a person carrying out unpleasant assignments for an employer or superior. **2** *U.S. and Canadian.* a hired murderer. **3** a severe or malicious critic.

hatchling ('hætʃlɪŋ) *n* a young animal that has newly emerged from an egg. **[C19:** from HATCH[1] + -LING[1]**]**

hatchment ('hætʃmənt) *n Heraldry.* a diamond-shaped tablet displaying the coat of arms of a dead person. Also called: **achievement. [C16:** changed from ACHIEVEMENT**]**

hatchway ('hætʃ,weɪ) *n* **1** an opening in the deck of a vessel to provide access below. **2** a similar opening in a wall, floor, ceiling, or roof, usually fitted with a lid or door. ◆ Often shortened to **hatch.**

hate (heɪt) *vb* **1** to dislike (something) intensely; detest. **2** (*intr*) to be unwilling (to be or do something). ◆ *n* **3** intense dislike. **4** *Informal.* a person or thing that is hated (esp. in the phrase **pet hate**). **5** (*modifier*) expressing or arousing feelings of hatred: *hate mail.* **[**Old English *hatian;* related to Old Norse *hata,* Old Saxon *hatōn,* Old High German *hazzēn***]** ► **'hateable** *or* **'hatable** *adj*

hateful ('heɪtfʊl) *adj* **1** causing or deserving hate; loathsome; detestable. **2** full of or showing hate. ► **'hatefully** *adv* ► **'hatefulness** *n*

Hatfield ('hæt,fiːld) *n* a market town in S central England, in Hertfordshire, with a new town of the same name built on the outskirts: site of **Hatfield House** (1607–11), the seat of the Cecil family. Pop.: 31 104 (1991).

hath (hæθ) *vb Archaic or dialect.* (used with the pronouns *he, she,* or *it* or a singular noun) a form of the present tense (indicative mood) of **have.**

Hathaway ('hæθə,weɪ) *n* **Anne.** ?1557–1623, wife of William Shakespeare.

hatha yoga ('hʌtə, 'hæθə) *n* (*sometimes caps.*) a form of yoga concerned chiefly with the regulation of breathing by exercises consisting of various postures designed to maintain healthy functioning of the body and to induce mental calm. Compare **raja yoga. [C20:** from Sanskrit *hatha* force + YOGA**]**

Hathor ('hæθɔː) *n* (in ancient Egyptian religion) the mother of Horus and goddess of creation. ► **Hathoric** (hæ'θɔːrɪk, -'θɒr-) *adj*

hatpin ('hæt,pɪn) *n* a sturdy pin used to secure a woman's hat to her hair, often having a decorative head.

hatred ('heɪtrɪd) *n* a feeling of intense dislike; enmity.

Hatshepsut (hæt'ʃepsuːt) *or* **Hatshepset** *n* queen of Egypt of the 18th dynasty (?1512–1482 B.C.). She built a great mortuary temple at Deir el Bahri near Thebes.

hat stand *or esp. U.S.* **hat tree** *n* a frame or pole equipped with hooks or arms for hanging up hats, coats, etc.

hatter ('hætə) *n* **1** a person who makes and sells hats. **2 mad as a hatter.** crazily eccentric.

Hatteras ('hætərəs) *n* **Cape.** a promontory off the E coast of North Carolina, on **Hatteras Island,** which is situated between Pamlico Sound and the Atlantic: known as the "Graveyard of the Atlantic" for its danger to shipping.

Hattersley ('hætəzlɪ) *n* **Roy (Sydney George),** Baron Hattersley of Sparkbrook. born 1932, British Labour politician; deputy leader of the Labour Party (1983–92); shadow home secretary (1980–83; 1987–92).

hat trick *n* **1** *Cricket.* the achievement of a bowler in taking three wickets with three successive balls. **2** any achievement of three successive points, victories, etc.

haubergeon ('hɔːbədʒən) *n* a variant of **habergeon.**

hauberk ('hɔːbɜːk) *n* a long coat of mail, often sleeveless. **[C13:** from Old French *hauberc,* of Germanic origin; compare Old High German *halsberc,* Old English *healsbeorg,* from *heals* neck + *beorg* protection, shelter**]**

haud (hɔːd, hʌd) *vb, n* a Scot. word for **hold**[1].

hauf (hɔːf) *n, determiner, adj, adv* a Scot. word for **half.**

haugh (hɑːk, hɑːf; *Scot.* hɒx) *n Northern English dialect and Scot.* a low-lying often alluvial riverside meadow. **[**Old English *healh* corner of land; see HOLLOW**]**

Haughey ('hɔːxɪ; *Irish* 'hʌhiː) *n* **Charles James.** born 1925, Irish politician; leader of the Fianna Fáil party; prime minister of the Republic of Ireland (1979–81; 1982; 1987–92).

haughty ('hɔːtɪ) *adj* **-tier, -tiest. 1** having or showing arrogance. **2** *Archaic.* noble or exalted. **[C16:** from Old French *haut,* literally: lofty, from Latin *altus* high**]** ► **'haughtily** *adv* ► **'haughtiness** *n*

Hauhau ('haʊhaʊ) *n N.Z. history.* a 19th-century Maori religious sect. **[**Maori**]**

haul (hɔːl) *vb* **1** to drag or draw (something) with effort. **2** (*tr*) to transport, as in a lorry. **3** *Nautical.* to alter the course of (a vessel), esp. so as to sail closer to the wind. **4** (*tr*) *Nautical.* to draw or hoist (a vessel) out of the water onto land or a dock for repair, storage, etc. **5** (*intr*) *Nautical.* (of the wind) to blow from a direction nearer the bow. Compare **veer**[1] (sense 3b). **6** (*intr*) to change one's opinion or action. ◆ *n* **7** the act of dragging with effort. **8** (esp. of fish) the amount caught at a single time. **9** something that is hauled. **10** the goods obtained from a robbery. **11** a distance of hauling: *a three-mile haul.* **12** the amount of a contraband seizure: *arms haul, drugs haul.* **13 in (***or* **over) the long haul. 13a** in a future time. **13b** over a lengthy period of time. **[C16:** from Old French *haler,* of Germanic origin; see HALE[2]**]**

haulage ('hɔːlɪdʒ) *n* **1** the act or labour of hauling. **2** a rate or charge levied for the transportation of goods, esp. by rail.

haulier ('hɔːljə) *or U.S.* **hauler** ('hɔːlə) *n* **1** a person or firm that transports goods by lorry; one engaged in road haulage. **2** a person that hauls, esp. a mine worker who conveys coal from the workings to the foot of the shaft.

haulm *or* **halm** (hɔːm) *n* **1** the stems or stalks of beans, peas, potatoes, grasses, etc., collectively, as used for thatching, bedding, etc. **2** a single stem of such a plant. **[**Old English *healm;* related to Old Norse *halmr,* Old High German *halm* stem, straw, Latin *culmus* stalk, Greek *kalamos* reed, Old Slavonic *slama* straw**]**

haul off *vb* (*intr, adv*) **1** (foll. by *and*) *U.S. and Canadian informal.* to draw back in preparation (esp. to strike or fight): *I hauled off and slugged him.* **2** *Nautical.* to alter the course of a vessel so as to avoid an obstruction, shallow waters, etc.

haul up *vb* (*adv*) **1** (*tr*) *Informal.* to call to account or criticize. **2** *Nautical.* to sail (a vessel) closer to the wind.

haunch (hɔːntʃ) *n* **1** the human hip or fleshy hindquarter of an animal, esp. a horse or similar quadruped. **2** the leg and loin of an animal, used for food: *a haunch of venison.* **3** Also called: **hance.** *Architect.* the part of an arch between the impost and the apex. **[C13:** from Old French *hanche;* related to Spanish, Italian *anca,* of Germanic origin; compare Low German *hanke***]** ► **haunched** *adj*

haunch bone *n* a nontechnical name for the **ilium** or **hipbone.**

haunt (hɔːnt) *vb* **1** to visit (a person or place) in the form of a ghost. **2** (*tr*) to intrude upon or recur to (the memory, thoughts, etc.): *he was haunted by the fear of insanity.* **3** to visit (a place) frequently. **4** to associate with (someone) frequently. ◆ *n* **5** (*often pl*) a place visited frequently: *an old haunt of hers.* **6** a place to which animals habitually resort for food, drink, shelter, etc. **[C13:** from Old French *hanter,* of Germanic origin; compare Old Norse *heimta* to bring home, Old English *hāmettan* to give a home to; see HOME**]** ► **'haunter** *n*

haunted ('hɔːntɪd) *adj* **1** frequented or visited by ghosts. **2** (*postpositive*) obsessed or worried.

haunting ('hɔːntɪŋ) *adj* **1** (of memories) poignant or persistent. **2** poignantly sentimental; enchantingly or eerily evocative. ► **'hauntingly** *adv*

Hauptmann (*German* 'hauptman) *n* **Gerhart** ('geːrhart). 1862–1946, German naturalist, dramatist, novelist, and poet. His works include the historical drama *The Weavers* (1892): Nobel prize for literature 1912.

Hauraki Gulf (hau'rækɪ) *n* an inlet of the Pacific in New Zealand, on the N coast of North Island.

Hausa ('hausə) *n* **1** (*pl* **-sas** *or* **-sa**) a member of a Negroid people of W Africa, living chiefly in N Nigeria. **2** the language of this people: the chief member of the Chadic subfamily of the Afro-Asiatic family of languages. It is widely used as a trading language throughout W Africa and the S Sahara.

hausfrau ('haus,frau) *n* a German housewife. [German, from *Haus* HOUSE + *Frau* woman, wife]

Haussmann (*French* əsmən) *n* **Georges-Eugène,** Baron. 1809–91, French town planner, noted for his major rebuilding of Paris in the reign of Napoleon III.

haustellum (hɔː'stɛləm) *n, pl* **-la** (-lə). the tip of the proboscis of a housefly or similar insect, specialized for sucking food. [C19: New Latin, diminutive of Latin *haustrum* device for drawing water, from *haurīre* to draw up; see EXHAUST] ▸ **haus'tellate** *adj*

haustorium (hɔː'stɔːrɪəm) *n, pl* **-ria** (-rɪə). the organ of a parasitic plant that penetrates the host tissues and absorbs food and water from them. [C19: from New Latin, from Late Latin *haustor* a water-drawer; see HAUSTELLUM] ▸ **haus'torial** *adj*

hautboy ('əubɔɪ) *n* **1** Also called: **hautbois strawberry, haubois** ('əubɔɪ). a strawberry, *Fragaria moschata,* of central Europe and Asia, with large fruit. **2** an archaic word for **oboe.** [C16: from French *hautbois,* from *haut* high + *bois* wood, of Germanic origin; see BUSH[1]]

haute couture *French.* (ot kutyr) *n* high fashion. [literally: high dressmaking]

haute cuisine *French.* (ot kwizin) *n* high-class cooking. [literally: high cookery]

haute école *French.* (ot ekɔl) *n* the classical art of riding. [literally: high school]

Haute-Garonne (*French* otgarɔn) *n* a department of SW France, in Midi-Pyrénées region. Capital: Toulouse. Pop.: 990 700 (1995). Area: 6367 sq. km (2483 sq. miles).

Haute-Loire (*French* otlwar) *n* a department of S central France, in Auvergne region. Capital: Le Puy. Pop.: 206 600 (1995). Area: 5001 sq. km (1950 sq. miles).

Haute-Marne (*French* otmarn) *n* a department of NE France, in Champagne-Ardenne region. Capital: Chaumont. Pop.: 200 100 (1995). Area: 6257 sq. km (2440 sq. miles).

Haute-Normandie (*French* otnɔrmɑ̃di) *n* a region of NW France, on the English Channel: generally fertile and flat.

Hautes-Alpes (*French* otzalp) *n* a department of SE France in Provence-Alpes-Côte d'Azur region. Capital: Gap. Pop.: 118 800 (1995). Area: 5643 sq. km (2201 sq. miles).

Haute-Saône (*French* otson) *n* a department of E France, in Franche-Comté region. Capital: Vesoul. Pop.: 229 900 (1995). Area: 5375 sq. km (2096 sq. miles).

Haute-Savoie (*French* otsavwa) *n* a department of E France, in Rhône-Alpes region. Capital: Annecy. Pop.: 617 300 (1995). Area: 4958 sq. km (1934 sq. miles).

Hautes-Pyrénées (*French* otpirene) *n* a department of SW France, in Midi-Pyrénées region. Capital: Tarbes. Pop.: 224 000 (1995). Area: 4534 sq. km (1768 sq. miles).

hauteur (əu'tɜː) *n* pride; haughtiness. [C17: from French, from *haut* high; see HAUGHTY]

Haute-Vienne (*French* otvjɛn) *n* a department of W central France, in Limousin region. Capital: Limoges. Pop.: 355 500 (1995). Area: 5555 sq. km (2166 sq. miles).

haut monde *French.* (o mɔ̃d) *n* high society. [literally: high world]

Haut-Rhin (*French* orɛ̃) *n* a department of E France in Alsace region. Capital: Colmar. Pop.: 695 700 (1995). Area: 3566 sq. km (1377 sq. miles).

Hauts-de-Seine (*French* odəsɛn) *n* a department of N central France, in Île-de-France region just west of Paris: formed in 1964. Capital: Nanterre. Pop.: 1 405 300 (1995). Area: 175 sq. km (68 sq. miles).

Havana (hə'vænə) *n* the capital of Cuba, a port in the northwest on the Gulf of Mexico: the largest city in the Caribbean; founded in 1514 as San Cristóbal de la Habana by Diego Velásquez. Pop.: 2 241 000 (1995 est.). Spanish name: **Habana.** Related adj: **Habanero.**

Havana cigar *n* any of various cigars manufactured in Cuba, known esp. for their high quality. Also called: **Havana.**

Havant ('hæv[ə]nt) *n* a market town in S England, in SE Hampshire. Pop.: 46 510 (1991).

havdalah *or* ***havdoloh*** *Hebrew.* (*Hebrew* havda'la; *Yiddish* hav'dɔlə) *n Judaism.* the ceremony marking the end of the sabbath or of a festival, including the blessings over wine, candles, and spices. [literally: separation]

have (hæv) *vb* **has, having, had.** (*mainly tr*) **1** to be in material possession of; own: *he has two cars.* **2** to possess as a characteristic quality or attribute: *he has dark hair.* **3** to receive, take, or obtain: *she had a present from him; have a look.* **4** to hold or entertain in the mind: *to have an idea.* **5** to possess a knowledge or understanding of: *I have no German.* **6** to experience or undergo: *to have a shock.* **7** to be infected with or suffer from: *to have a cold.* **8** to gain control of or advantage over: *you have me on that point.* **9** (*usually passive*) *Slang.* to cheat or outwit: *he was had by that dishonest salesman.* **10** (foll. by *on*) to exhibit (mercy, compassion, etc., towards): *have mercy on us, Lord.* **11** to engage or take part in: *to have a conversation.* **12** to arrange, carry out, or hold: *to have a party.* **13** to cause, compel, or require to (be, do, or be done): *have my shoes mended.* **14** (takes an infinitive with *to*) used as an auxiliary to express compulsion or necessity: *I had to run quickly to escape him.* **15** to eat, drink, or partake of: *to have a good meal.* **16** *Taboo slang.* to have sexual intercourse with: *he had her on the sofa.* **17** (*used with a negative*) to tolerate or allow: *I won't have all this noise.* **18** to declare, state, or assert: *rumour has it that they will marry.* **19** to put or place: *I'll have the sofa in this room.* **20** to receive as a guest: *to have three people to stay.* **21** to beget or bear (offspring): *she had three children.* **22** (*takes a past participle*) used as an auxiliary to form compound tenses expressing completed action: *I have gone; I shall have gone; I would have gone; I had gone.* **23 had better** *or* **best.** ought to: used to express compulsion, obligation, etc.: *you had better go.* **24 had rather** *or* **sooner.** to consider or find preferable that: *I had rather you left at once.* **25 have done.** See **done** (sense 3). **26 have had it.** *Informal.* **26a** to be exhausted, defeated, or killed. **26b** to have lost one's last chance. **26c** to become unfashionable. **27 have it.** to win a victory. **28 have it away** (*or* **off**). *Taboo, Brit. slang.* to have sexual intercourse. **29 have it coming.** *Informal.* to be about to receive or to merit punishment or retribution. **30 have it in for.** *Informal.* to wish or intend harm towards. **31 have it so good.** to have so many benefits, esp. material benefits. **32 have to do with. 32a** to have dealings or associate with: *I have nothing to do with her.* **32b** to be of relevance to: *this has nothing to do with you.* **33 I have it.** *Informal.* I know the answer. **34 let (someone) have it.** *Slang.* to launch or deliver an attack on, esp. to discharge a firearm at (someone). **35 not having any.** (foll. by *of*) *Informal.* refusing to take part or be involved (in). ◆ *n* **36** (*usually pl*) a person or group of people in possession of wealth, security, etc.: *the haves and the have-nots.* ◆ See also **have at, have in, have on, have out, have up.** [Old English *habban;* related to Old Norse *hafa,* Old Saxon *hebbian,* Old High German *habēn,* Latin *habēre*]

have-a-go *adj Informal.* (of people attempting arduous or dangerous tasks) brave or spirited: *a have-a-go pensioner.*

have at *vb* (*intr, prep*) *Archaic.* to make an opening attack on, esp. in fencing.

have in *vb* (*tr, adv*) **1** to ask (a person) to give a service: *we must have the electrician in to mend the fire.* **2** to invite to one's home.

Havel[1] (*German* 'haːfəl) *n* a river in E Germany, flowing south to Berlin, then west and north to join the River Elbe. Length: about 362 km (225 miles).

Havel[2] (*Czech* 'havɛl) *n* **Václav** ('vʌtslav). born 1936, Czech dramatist and statesman: founder of the Civil Forum movement for political change: president of Czechoslovakia (1989–92); president of the Czech Republic from 1993. His plays include *The Garden Party* (1963) and *Redevelopment* (1989).

havelock ('hævlɒk) *n* a light-coloured cover for a service cap with a flap extending over the back of the neck to protect the head and neck from the sun. [C19: named after Sir H. *Havelock* (1795–1857), English general in India]

haven ('heɪv[ə]n) *n* **1** a port, harbour, or other sheltered place for shipping. **2** a place of safety or sanctuary; shelter. ◆ *vb* **3** (*tr*) to secure or shelter in or as if in a haven. [Old English *hæfen,* from Old Norse *höfn;* related to Middle Dutch *havene,* Old Irish *cuan* to bend] ▸ **'havenless** *adj*

have-not *n* (*usually pl*) a person or group of people in possession of relatively little material wealth.

haven't ('hæv[ə]nt) *vb contraction of* have not.

have on *vb* (*tr*) **1** (*usually adv*) to wear. **2** (*usually adv*) to have (a meeting or engagement) arranged as a commitment: *what does your boss have on this afternoon?* **3** (*adv*) *Informal.* to trick or tease (a person). **4** (*prep*) to have available (information or evidence, esp. when incriminating) about (a person): *the police had nothing on him, so they let him go.*

have out *vb* (*tr, adv*) **1** to settle (a matter) or come to (a final decision), esp. by fighting or by frank discussion (often in the phrase **have it out**). **2** to have extracted or removed: *I had a tooth out.*

haver ('heɪvə) *vb* (*intr*) *Brit.* **1** to dither. **2** *Scot. and Northern English dialect.* to talk nonsense; babble. ◆ *n* **3** (*usually pl*) *Scot.* nonsense. [C18: of unknown origin]

Havering ('heɪvərɪŋ) *n* a borough of NE Greater London, formed in 1965 from Romford and Hornchurch (both previously in Essex). Pop.: 231 700 (1994 est.). Area: 120 sq. km (46 sq. miles).

haversack ('hævə,sæk) *n* a canvas bag for provisions or equipment, carried on the back or shoulder. [C18: from French *havresac,* from German *Habersack* oat bag, from Old High German *habaro* oats + *Sack* SACK[1]]

Haversian canal (hæ'vɜːʃən) *n Histology.* any of the channels that form a network in bone and contain blood vessels and nerves. [C19: named after C. *Havers* (died 1702), English anatomist who discovered them]

haversine ('hævə,saɪn) *n* half the value of the versed sine. [C19: combination of *half* + *versed* + SINE[1]]

have up *vb* (*tr, adv; usually passive*) to cause to appear for trial: *he was had up for breaking and entering.*

havildar ('hævɪl,dɑː) *n* a noncommissioned officer in the Indian army, equivalent in rank to sergeant. [C17: from Hindi, from Persian *hawāldār* one in charge]

havoc ('hævək) *n* **1** destruction; devastation; ruin. **2** *Informal.* confusion; chaos. **3 cry havoc.** *Archaic.* to give the signal for pillage and destruction. **4 play havoc.** (often foll. by *with*) to cause a great deal of damage, distress, or confusion (to). ◆ *vb* **-ocs, -ocking, -ocked. 5** (*tr*) *Archaic.* to lay waste. [C15: from Old French *havot* pillage, probably of Germanic origin] ▸ **'havocker** *n*

Havre ('hɑːvrə; *French* ɑvrə) *n* See **Le Havre.**

haw[1] (hɔː) *n* **1** the round or oval fruit (a pome) of the hawthorn, usually red or yellow, containing one to five seeds. **2** another name for **hawthorn.** [Old English *haga,* identical with *haga* HEDGE; related to Old Norse *hagi* pasture]

haw[2] (hɔː) *n, interj* **1** an inarticulate utterance, as of hesitation, embarrassment, etc.; hem. ◆ *vb* **2** (*intr*) to make this sound. **3 hem** (*or* **hum**) **and haw.** See **hem**[2] (sense 3). [C17: of imitative origin]

haw[3] (hɔː) *n Archaic.* a yard or close. [of unknown origin]

haw[4] (hɔː) *n* the nictitating membrane of a horse or other domestic animal. [C15: of unknown origin]

Hawaii (hə'waɪɪ) *n* a state of the U.S. in the central Pacific, consisting of over 20 volcanic islands and atolls, including Hawaii, Maui, Oahu, Kauai, and Molokai: discovered by Captain Cook in 1778; annexed by the U.S. in 1898; naval base at

Pearl Harbor attacked by the Japanese in 1941, a major cause of U.S. entry into World War II; became a state in 1959. Capital: Honolulu. Pop.: 1 186 602 (1997 est.). Area: 16 640 sq. km (6425 sq. miles). Former name: **Sandwich Islands.** Abbrevs.: **Ha.** or (with zip code) **HI**

Hawaiian (hə'waɪən) *adj* **1** of or relating to Hawaii, its people, or their language. ◆ *n* **2** a native or inhabitant of Hawaii, esp. one descended from Melanesian or Tahitian immigrants. **3** a language of Hawaii belonging to the Malayo-Polynesian family.

Hawaiian guitar *n* a lap-held steel-strung guitar with a wood or metal body, tuned to an open chord and played with a slide. Compare **Dobro, pedal steel guitar.**

Hawaiki ('hɑːwaɪkiː) *n N.Z.* a legendary Pacific island from which the Maoris migrated to New Zealand by canoe. [Maori]

Hawes Water (hɔːz) *n* a lake in NW England, in the Lake District: provides part of Manchester's water supply; extended by damming from 4 km (2.5 miles) to 6 km (4 miles).

hawfinch ('hɔːˌfɪntʃ) *n* an uncommon European finch, *Coccothraustes coccothraustes,* having a very stout bill and brown plumage with black-and-white wings.

haw-haw[1] ('hɔː'hɔː) *interj* a variant of **ha-ha**[1].

haw-haw[2] ('hɔːhɔː) *n* a variant of **ha-ha**[2].

Haw-Haw ('hɔːˌhɔː) *n* **Lord.** See (William) **Joyce.**

Hawick ('hɔːɪk) *n* a town in SE Scotland, in S central Scottish Borders: knitwear industry. Pop.: 15 812 (1991).

hawk[1] (hɔːk) *n* **1** any of various diurnal birds of prey of the family *Accipitridae,* such as the goshawk and Cooper's hawk, typically having short rounded wings and a long tail. Related adj: **accipitrine. 2** *U.S. and Canadian.* any of various other falconiform birds, including the falcons but not the eagles or vultures. **3** a person who advocates or supports war or warlike policies. Compare **dove**[1] (sense 2). **4** a ruthless or rapacious person. **5 know a hawk from a handsaw.** to be able to judge things; be discerning. [from Shakespeare (*Hamlet* II:2:375); *handsaw* is probably a corruption of dialect *heronshaw* heron] ◆ *vb* **6** (*intr*) to hunt with falcons, hawks, etc. **7** (*intr*) (of falcons or hawks) to fly in quest of prey. **8** to pursue or attack on the wing, as a hawk. [Old English *hafoc;* related to Old Norse *haukr,* Old Frisian *havek,* Old High German *habuh,* Polish *kobuz*] *adj* ► **'hawk,like** *adj*

hawk[2] (hɔːk) *vb* **1** to offer (goods) for sale, as in the street. **2** (*tr;* often foll. by *about*) to spread (news, gossip, etc.). [C16: back formation from HAWKER[1]]

hawk[3] (hɔːk) *vb* **1** (*intr*) to clear the throat noisily. **2** (*tr*) to force (phlegm) up from the throat. **3** *Brit.* a slang word for **spit**[1]. ◆ *n* **4** a noisy clearing of the throat. [C16: of imitative origin; see HAW[2]]

hawk[4] (hɔːk) *n* a small square board with a handle underneath, used for carrying wet plaster or mortar. Also called: **mortar board.** [of unknown origin]

hawkbill ('hɔːkˌbɪl) *n* another name for **hawksbill turtle.**

hawkbit ('hɔːkˌbɪt) *n* any of three composite perennial plants of the genus *Leontodon,* with yellow dandelion-like flowers and lobed leaves in a rosette, erect or prostrate: found in grassland. [C18: from HAWK(WEED) + (DEVIL'S) BIT]

Hawke (hɔːk) *n* **1 Edward,** 1st Baron. 1705–81, British admiral. He destroyed the French fleet in Quiberon Bay (1759), preventing a French invasion of England. **2 Robert** (**James Lee**), known as *Bob.* born 1929, Australian statesman; prime minister of Australia (1983–91).

hawker[1] ('hɔːkə) *n* a person who travels from place to place selling goods. [C16: probably from Middle Low German *hōker,* from *hōken* to peddle; see HUCKSTER]

hawker[2] ('hɔːkə) *n* a person who hunts with hawks, falcons, etc. [Old English *hafecere;* see HAWK[1], -ER[1]]

hawk-eyed *adj* **1** having extremely keen sight. **2** vigilant, watchful, or observant.

hawking ('hɔːkɪŋ) *n* another name for **falconry.**

Hawking ('hɔːkɪŋ) *n* **Stephen William.** born 1942, British physicist. Stricken with a progressive nervous disease since the 1960s, he has nevertheless been a leader in cosmological theory. His *A Brief History of Time* (1987) was a bestseller.

Hawkins ('hɔːkɪnz) *n* **1 Coleman.** 1904–69, U.S. pioneer of the tenor saxophone for jazz. **2** Sir **John.** 1532–95, English naval commander and slave trader, treasurer of the navy (1577–89); commander of a squadron in the fleet that defeated the Spanish Armada (1588).

hawkish ('hɔːkɪʃ) *adj* favouring the use or display of force rather than diplomacy to achieve foreign policy goals.

hawk moth *n* any of various moths of the family *Sphingidae,* having long narrow wings and powerful flight, with the ability to hover over flowers when feeding from the nectar. Also called: **sphinx moth, hummingbird moth.** See also **death's-head moth.**

hawk owl *n* a hawklike northern owl, *Surnia ulula,* with a long slender tail and brownish speckled plumage.

Hawks (hɔːks) *n* **Howard** (**Winchester**). 1896–1977, U.S. film director. His films include *Sergeant York* (1941) and *The Big Sleep* (1946).

hawk's-beard *n* any plant of the genus *Crepis,* having a ring of fine hairs surrounding the fruit and clusters of small dandelion-like flowers: family *Compositae* (composites).

hawksbill turtle *or* **hawksbill** ('hɔːksˌbɪl) *n* a small tropical turtle, *Eretmochelys imbricata,* with a hooked beaklike mouth: a source of tortoiseshell: family *Chelonidae.* Also called: **hawkbill, tortoiseshell turtle.**

hawk's-eye *n* a dark blue variety of the mineral crocidolite: a semiprecious gemstone.

Hawksmoor ('hɔːksˌmɔː) *n* **Nicholas.** 1661–1736, English architect. His designs include All Souls', Oxford, and a number of London churches, notably St Anne's, Limehouse.

hawkweed ('hɔːkˌwiːd) *n* any typically hairy plant of the genus *Hieracium,* with clusters of dandelion-like flowers: family *Compositae* (composites).

Haworth[1] ('hauəθ) *n* a village in N England, in Bradford unitary authority, West Yorkshire: home of Charlotte, Emily, and Anne Brontë. Pop.: 4956 (1991).

Haworth[2] ('hauəθ) *n* Sir **Walter Norman.** 1883–1950, British biochemist, who shared the Nobel prize for chemistry (1937) for being the first to synthesize ascorbic acid (vitamin C).

hawse (hɔːz) *Nautical.* ◆ *n* **1** the part of the bows of a vessel where the hawseholes are. **2** short for **hawsehole** or **hawsepipe. 3** the distance from the bow of an anchored vessel to the anchor. **4** the arrangement of port and starboard anchor ropes when a vessel is riding on both anchors. ◆ *vb* **5** (*intr*) (of a vessel) to pitch violently when at anchor. [C14: from earlier *halse,* probably from Old Norse *háls;* related to Old English *heals* neck]

hawsehole ('hɔːzˌhəul) *n Nautical.* one of the holes in the upper part of the bows of a vessel through which the anchor ropes pass. Often shortened to **hawse.**

hawsepipe ('hɔːzˌpaɪp) *n Nautical.* a strong metal pipe through which an anchor rope passes. Often shortened to **hawse.**

hawser ('hɔːzə) *n Nautical.* a large heavy rope. [C14: from Anglo-French *hauceour,* from Old French *haucier* to hoist, ultimately from Latin *altus* high]

hawser bend *n* a knot for tying two ropes together.

hawser-laid *adj* (of a rope) made up of three strands, the fibres (or yarns) of which have been twisted together in a left-handed direction. These three strands are then twisted together in a right-handed direction to make the rope.

hawthorn ('hɔːˌθɔːn) *n* any of various thorny trees or shrubs of the N temperate rosaceous genus *Crataegus,* esp. *C. oxyacantha,* having white or pink flowers and reddish fruits (haws). Also called (in Britain): **may, may tree, mayflower.** [Old English *haguthorn* from *haga* hedge + *thorn* thorn; related to Old Norse *hagthorn,* Middle High German *hagendorn,* Dutch *haagdoorn*]

Hawthorne ('hɔːˌθɔːn) *n* **Nathaniel.** 1804–64, U.S. novelist and short-story writer: his works include the novels *The Scarlet Letter* (1850) and *The House of the Seven Gables* (1851) and the children's stories *Tanglewood Tales* (1853).

Hawthorne effect *n* improvement in the performance of employees, students, etc., brought about by making changes in working methods, resulting from research into means of improving performance. Compare **iatrogenic, placebo effect.** [from the Western Electric Company's *Hawthorne* works in Chicago, U.S.A., where it was discovered during experiments in the 1920s]

hay[1] (heɪ) *n* **1a** grass, clover, etc., cut and dried as fodder. **1b** (*in combination*)*: a hayfield; a hayloft.* **2 hit the hay.** *Slang.* to go to bed. **3 make hay of.** to throw into confusion. **4 make hay while the sun shines.** to take full advantage of an opportunity. **5 roll in the hay.** *Informal.* sexual intercourse or heavy petting. ◆ *vb* **6** to cut, dry, and store (grass, clover, etc.) as fodder. **7** (*tr*) to feed with hay. [Old English *hieg;* related to Old Norse *hey,* Gothic *hawi,* Old Frisian *hē,* Old High German *houwi;* see HEW]

hay[2] *or* **hey** (heɪ) *n* **1** a circular figure in country dancing. **2** a former country dance in which the dancers wove in and out of a circle. [C16: of uncertain origin]

Hay (heɪ) *n* **Will.** 1888–1949, British music-hall comedian, who later starred in films, such as *Oh, Mr Porter!* (1937).

haybox ('heɪˌbɒks) *n* an airtight box full of hay or other insulating material used to keep partially cooked food warm and allow cooking by retained heat.

haycock ('heɪˌkɒk) *n* a small cone-shaped pile of hay left in the field until dry enough to carry to the rick or barn.

Haydn ('haɪdᵊn) *n* **1** (**Franz**) **Joseph** ('jɔːzɛf). 1732–1809, Austrian composer, who played a major part in establishing the classical forms of the symphony and the string quartet. His other works include the oratorios *The Creation* (1796–98) and *The Seasons* (1798–1801). **2** his brother, **Johann Michael** (*German* jo'han 'mɪçaeːl). 1737–1806, Austrian composer, esp. of Church music.

Haydon ('heɪdᵊn) *n* **Benjamin** (**Robert**). 1786–1846, British historical painter and art critic, best known for his *Autobiography and Journals* (1853).

Hayek ('haɪjək) *n* **Friedrich August von.** 1899–1992, British economist and political philosopher, born in Austria: noted for his advocacy of free-market ideas; shared the Nobel prize for economics 1974.

Hayes (heɪz) *n* **Rutherford B**(**irchard**). 1822–93, 19th president of the U.S. (1877–81).

hay fever *n* an allergic reaction to pollen, dust, etc., characterized by sneezing, runny nose, and watery eyes due to inflammation of the mucous membranes of the eyes and nose. Technical name: **pollinosis.**

hayfork ('heɪˌfɔːk) *n* a long-handled fork with two long curved prongs, used for moving or turning hay; pitchfork.

haymaker ('heɪˌmeɪkə) *n* **1** a person who helps to cut, turn, toss, spread, or carry hay. **2** Also called: **hay conditioner.** either of two machines, one designed to crush stems of hay, the other to break and bend them, in order to cause more rapid and even drying. **3** *Boxing slang.* a wild swinging punch. ► **'hay,making** *adj, n*

haymow ('heɪˌmau) *n* **1** a part of a barn where hay is stored. **2** a quantity of hay stored in a barn or loft.

hayrack ('heɪˌræk) *n* **1** a rack for holding hay for feeding to animals. **2** a rack fixed to a cart or wagon to increase the quantity of hay or straw that it can carry.

hayseed ('heɪˌsiːd) *n* **1** seeds or fragments of grass or straw. **2** *U.S. and Canadian informal, derogatory.* a yokel.

haystack ('heɪˌstæk) *or* **hayrick** ('heɪˌrɪk) *n* a large pile of hay, esp. one built in the open air and covered with thatch.

hayward ('heɪˌwɔːd) *n Brit. obsolete.* a parish officer in charge of enclosures and fences.

haywire (ˈheɪˌwaɪə) *adj* (*postpositive*) *Informal.* **1** (of things) not functioning properly; disorganized (esp. in the phrase **go haywire**). **2** (of people) erratic or crazy. [C20: alluding to the disorderly tangle of wire removed from bales of hay]

hazan *or* ***hazzan*** *Hebrew.* (xaˈzan; *English* ˈhɑːzᵊn) *n* variant spellings of **chazan.**

hazard (ˈhæzəd) *n* **1** exposure or vulnerability to injury, loss, evil, etc. **2 at hazard.** at risk; in danger. **3** a thing likely to cause injury, etc. **4** *Golf.* an obstacle such as a bunker, a road, rough, water, etc. **5** chance; accident (esp. in the phrase **by hazard**). **6** a gambling game played with two dice. **7** *Real Tennis.* **7a** the receiver's side of the court. **7b** one of the winning openings. **8** *Billiards.* a scoring stroke made either when a ball other than the striker's is pocketed (**winning hazard**) or the striker's cue ball itself (**losing hazard**). ◆ *vb* (*tr*) **9** to chance or risk. **10** to venture (an opinion, guess, etc.). **11** to expose to danger. [C13: from Old French *hasard,* from Arabic *az-zahr* the die] ▸ **ˈhazardable** *adj* ▸ **ˈhazard-ˌfree** *adj*

hazard lights *pl n* the indicator lights of a motor vehicle when flashing simultaneously to indicate that the vehicle is stationary and temporarily obstructing the traffic. Also called: **hazard warning lights, hazards.**

hazardous (ˈhæzədəs) *adj* **1** involving great risk. **2** depending on chance. ▸ **ˈhazardously** *adv* ▸ **ˈhazardousness** *n*

hazard warning device *n* an appliance fitted to a motor vehicle that operates the hazard lights.

haze[1] (heɪz) *n* **1** *Meteorol.* **1a** reduced visibility in the air as a result of condensed water vapour, dust, etc., in the atmosphere. **1b** the moisture or dust causing this. **2** obscurity of perception, feeling, etc. ◆ *vb* **3** (when *intr,* often foll. by *over*) to make or become hazy. [C18: back formation from HAZY]

haze[2] (heɪz) *vb* (*tr*) **1** *Chiefly U.S. and Canadian.* to subject (fellow students) to ridicule or abuse. **2** *Nautical.* to harass with humiliating tasks. [C17: of uncertain origin] ▸ **ˈhazer** *n*

hazel (ˈheɪzᵊl) *n* **1** Also called: **cob.** any of several shrubs of the N temperate genus *Corylus,* esp. *C. avellana,* having oval serrated leaves and edible rounded brown nuts: family *Corylaceae.* **2** the wood of any of these trees. **3** short for **hazelnut. 4a** a light yellowish-brown colour. **4b** (*as adj*): *hazel eyes.* [Old English *hæsel;* related to Old Norse *hasl,* Old High German *hasala,* Latin *corylus,* Old Irish *coll*]

hazelhen (ˈheɪzᵊlˌhɛn) *n* a European woodland gallinaceous bird, *Tetrastes bonasia,* with a speckled brown plumage and slightly crested crown: family *Tetraonidae* (grouse).

hazelnut (ˈheɪzᵊlˌnʌt) *n* the nut of a hazel shrub, having a smooth shiny hard shell. Also called: **filbert,** (Brit.) **cobnut, cob.**

Hazlitt (ˈhæzlɪt) *n* **William.** 1778–1830, English critic and essayist: works include *Characters of Shakespeare's Plays* (1817), *Table Talk* (1821), and *The Plain Speaker* (1826).

hazy (ˈheɪzɪ) *adj* **-zier, -ziest. 1** characterized by reduced visibility; misty. **2** indistinct; vague. [C17: of unknown origin] ▸ **ˈhazily** *adv* ▸ **ˈhaziness** *n*

hazzan *Hebrew.* (xaˈzan; *English* ˈhɑːzᵊn) *n* a variant spelling of **chazan.**

Hb *symbol for* haemoglobin.

HB (on Brit. pencils) *symbol for* hard-black: denoting a medium-hard lead. Compare **H** (sense 5), **B** (sense 9).

H-beam *n* a rolled steel joist or girder with a cross section in the form of a capital letter *H.* Compare **I-beam.**

HBM (in Britain) *abbrev. for* His (*or* Her) Britannic Majesty.

H-bomb *n* short for **hydrogen bomb.**

HC *abbrev. for:* **1** Holy Communion. **2** (in Britain) House of Commons.

HCF *or* **hcf** *abbrev. for* highest common factor.

HCG *abbrev. for* human chorionic gonadotrophin. See **gonadotrophin.**

hcp *abbrev. for* handicap.

hd *abbrev. for:* **1** hand. **2** head.

hdbk *abbrev. for* handbook.

HDL *abbrev. for* high-density lipoprotein.

hdqrs *abbrev. for* headquarters: replaced in military use by **HQ.**

HDR energy *n* hot dry rock energy; energy extracted from hot rocks below the earth's surface by pumping water around a circuit in the hot region and back to the surface.

HDTV *abbrev. for* high definition television.

he[1] (hiː; *unstressed* iː) *pron* (*subjective*) **1** refers to a male person or animal: *he looks interesting; he's a fine stallion.* **2** refers to an indefinite antecedent such as *one, whoever,* or *anybody: everybody can do as he likes in this country.* **3** refers to a person or animal of unknown or unspecified sex: *a member of the party may vote as he sees fit.* ◆ *n* **4a** a male person or animal. **4b** (*in combination*): *he-goat.* **5a** a children's game in which one player chases the others in an attempt to touch one of them, who then becomes the chaser. Compare **tag**[2]. **5b** the person chasing. Compare **it** (sense 7). [Old English *hē;* related to Old Saxon *hie,* Old High German *her* he, Old Slavonic *sĭ* this, Latin *cis* on this side]

he[2] (heɪ; *Hebrew* he) *n* the fifth letter of the Hebrew alphabet (ה), transliterated as *h.* [from Hebrew]

he[3] (hiː, heɪ) *interj* an expression of amusement or derision. Also: **he-he!** or **hee-hee!**

He *the chemical symbol for* helium.

HE *abbrev. for:* **1** high explosive. **2** His Eminence. **3** His (*or* Her) Excellency.

head (hɛd) *n* **1** the upper or front part of the body in vertebrates, including man, that contains and protects the brain, eyes, mouth, and nose and ears when present. Related adj: **cephalic. 2** the corresponding part of an invertebrate animal. **3** something resembling a head in form or function, such as the top of a tool. **4a** the person commanding most authority within a group, organization, etc. **4b** (*as modifier*): *head buyer.* **4c** (*in combination*): *headmaster.* **5** the position of leadership or command: *at the head of his class.* **6a** the most forward part of a thing; a part that juts out; front: *the head of a queue.* **6b** (*as modifier*): *head point.* **7** the highest part of a thing; upper end: *the head of the pass.* **8** the froth on the top of a glass of beer. **9** aptitude, intelligence, and emotions (esp. in the phrases **above** or **over one's head, have a head for, keep one's head, lose one's head,** etc.): *she has a good head for figures; a wise old head.* **10** (*pl* **head**) a person or animal considered as a unit: *the show was two pounds per head; six hundred head of cattle.* **11** the head considered as a measure of length or height: *he's a head taller than his mother.* **12** *Botany.* **12a** a dense inflorescence such as that of the daisy and other composite plants. **12b** any other compact terminal part of a plant, such as the leaves of a cabbage or lettuce. **13** a culmination or crisis (esp. in the phrase **bring** or **come to a head**). **14** the pus-filled tip or central part of a pimple, boil, etc. **15** the head considered as the part of the body on which hair grows densely: *a fine head of hair.* **16** the source or origin of a river or stream. **17** (*cap. when part of name*) a headland or promontory, esp. a high one. **18** the obverse of a coin, usually bearing a portrait of the head or a full figure of a monarch, deity, etc. Compare **tail**[1]. **19** a main point or division of an argument, discourse, etc. **20** (*often pl*) the headline at the top of a newspaper article or the heading of a section within an article. **21** *Nautical.* **21a** the front part of a ship or boat. **21b** (in sailing ships) the upper corner or edge of a sail. **21c** the top of any spar or derrick. **21d** any vertical timber cut to shape. **21e** (*often pl*) a slang word for **lavatory. 22** *Grammar.* another word for **governor** (sense 7). **23** the taut membrane of a drum, tambourine, etc. **24a** the height of the surface of liquid above a specific point, esp. when considered or used as a measure of the pressure at that point: *a head of four feet.* **24b** pressure of water, caused by height or velocity, measured in terms of a vertical column of water. **24c** any pressure: *a head of steam in the boiler.* **25** *Slang.* **25a** a person who regularly takes drugs, esp. LSD or cannabis. **25b** (*in combination*): *an acidhead.* **26** *Mining.* a road driven into the coal face. **27a** the terminal point of a route. **27b** (*in combination*): *railhead.* **28** a device on a turning or boring machine, such as a lathe, that is equipped with one or more cutting tools held to the work by this device. **29** See **cylinder head. 30** an electromagnet that can read, write, or erase information on a magnetic medium such as a magnetic tape, disk, or drum, used in computers, tape recorders, etc. **31** *Informal.* short for **headmaster** *or* **headmistress. 32a** the head of a horse considered as a narrow margin in the outcome of a race (in the phrase **win by a head**). **32b** any narrow margin of victory (in the phrase (**win**) **by a head**). **33** *Informal.* short for **headache. 34** *Curling.* the stones lying in the house after all 16 have been played. **35 against the head.** *Rugby.* from the opposing side's put-in to the scrum. **36 bite** *or* **snap someone's head off.** to speak sharply and angrily to someone. **37 bring** *or* **come to a head. 37a** to bring or be brought to a crisis: *matters came to a head.* **37b** (of a boil) to cause to be or be about to burst. **38 get it into one's head.** to come to believe (an idea, esp. a whimsical one): *he got it into his head that the earth was flat.* **39 give head.** *Slang, taboo.* to perform fellatio. **40 give someone** (*or* **something**) **his** (*or* **its**) **head. 40a** to allow a person greater freedom or responsibility. **40b** to allow a horse to gallop by lengthening the reins. **41 go to one's head. 41a** to make one dizzy or confused, as might an alcoholic drink. **41b** to make one conceited: *his success has gone to his head.* **42 head and shoulders above.** greatly superior to. **43 head over heels. 43a** turning a complete somersault. **43b** completely; utterly (esp. in the phrase **head over heels in love**). **44 hold up one's head.** to be unashamed. **45 keep one's head.** to remain calm. **46 keep one's head above water.** to manage to survive a difficult experience. **47 make head.** to make progress. **48 make head or tail of.** (*used with a negative*). to attempt to understand (a problem, etc.): *he couldn't make head or tail of the case.* **49 off** (*or* **out of**) **one's head.** *Slang.* insane or delirious. **50 off the top of one's head.** without previous thought; impromptu. **51 on one's** (**own**) **head.** at one's (own) risk or responsibility. **52 one's head off.** *Slang.* loudly or excessively: *the baby cried its head off.* **53 over someone's head. 53a** without a person in the obvious position being considered, esp. for promotion: *the graduate was promoted over the heads of several of his seniors.* **53b** without consulting a person in the obvious position but referring to a higher authority: *in making his complaint he went straight to the director, over the head of his immediate boss.* **53c** beyond a person's comprehension. **54 put** (**our, their,** *etc.*) **heads together.** *Informal.* to consult together. **55 take it into one's head.** to conceive a notion, desire, or wish (to do something). **56 turn heads.** to be so beautiful, unusual, or impressive as to attract a lot of attention. **57 turn** *or* **stand** (**something**) **on its head.** to treat or present (something) in a completely new and different way: *health care which has turned orthodox medicine on its head.* **58 turn someone's head.** to make someone vain, conceited, etc. ◆ *vb* **59** (*tr*) to be at the front or top of: *to head the field.* **60** (*tr;* often foll. by *up*) to be in the commanding or most important position. **61** (often foll. by *for*) to go or cause to go (towards): *where are you heading?* **62** to turn or steer (a vessel) as specified: *to head into the wind.* **63** *Soccer.* to propel (the ball) by striking it with the head. **64** (*tr*) to provide with or be a head or heading: *to head a letter; the quotation which heads chapter 6.* **65** (*tr*) to cut the top branches or shoots off (a tree or plant). **66** (*intr*) to form a head, as a boil or plant. **67** (*intr;* often foll. by *in*) (of streams, rivers, etc.) to originate or rise in. **68 head them.** *Austral.* to toss the coins in a game of two-up. ◆ See also **head for, head off, heads.** [Old English *hēafod;* related to Old Norse *haufuth,* Old Frisian *hāved,* Old Saxon *hōbid,* Old High German *houbit*] ▸ **ˈheadˌlike** *adj*

Head (hɛd) *n* **Edith.** 1907–81, U.S. dress designer: won many Oscars for her Hollywood film costume designs.

-head *combining form.* indicating a person having a preoccupation as specified: *breadhead.*

headache (ˈhɛdˌeɪk) *n* **1** pain in the head, caused by dilation of cerebral arteries, muscle contraction, insufficient oxygen in the cerebral blood, reaction to drugs, etc. Technical name: **cephalalgia. 2** *Informal.* any cause of worry, difficulty, or annoyance. ▸ **ˈheadˌachy** *adj*

head arrangement *n Jazz.* a spontaneous orchestration.
headband ('hɛd,bænd) *n* **1** a ribbon or band worn around the head. **2** a narrow cloth band attached to the top of the spine of a book for protection or decoration.
headbang ('hɛd,bæŋ) *vb* (*intr*) *Slang.* to nod one's head violently to the beat of loud rock music.
head-banger *n Slang.* **1** a heavy-metal rock fan. **2** a crazy or stupid person.
headboard ('hɛd,bɔːd) *n* a vertical board or terminal at the head of a bed.
head-butt *vb* (*tr*) **1** to deliberately strike (someone) with the head. ♦ *n* **head butt. 2** an act or an instance of deliberately striking someone with the head.
headcase ('hɛd,keɪs) *n Informal.* an insane person.
headcheese ('hɛd,tʃiːz) *n* the U.S. and Canadian name for **brawn** (sense 3).
head collar *n* the part of a bridle that fits round a horse's head. Also called (esp. U.S.): **headstall.**
headdress ('hɛd,drɛs) *n* any head covering, esp. an ornate one or one denoting a rank or occupation.
headed ('hɛdɪd) *adj* **1a** having a head or heads. **1b** (*in combination*): *two-headed; bullet-headed.* **2** having a heading: *headed notepaper.* **3** (*in combination*) having a mind or intellect as specified: *thickheaded.*
header ('hɛdə) *n* **1** a machine that trims the heads from castings, forgings, etc., or one that forms heads, as in wire, to make nails. **2** a person who operates such a machine. **3** Also called: **header tank.** a reservoir, tank, or hopper that maintains a gravity feed or a static fluid pressure in an apparatus. **4** a brick or stone laid across a wall so that its end is flush with the outer surface. Compare **stretcher** (sense 5). **5** the action of striking a ball with the head. **6** *Informal.* a headlong fall or dive. **7** *Computing.* **7a** the first element of various information storage systems that contains information relevant to the main contents. **7b** (*as modifier*): *header card; header label.* **8** *Dialect.* a mentally unbalanced person.
headfast ('hɛdfɑːst) *n* a mooring rope at the bows of a ship. [C16: from HEAD (in the sense: front) + *fast* a mooring rope, from Middle English *fest,* from Old Norse *festr;* related to FAST[1]]
headfirst ('hɛd'fɜːst) *adj, adv* **1** with the head foremost; headlong: *he fell headfirst.* ♦ *adv* **2** rashly or carelessly.
head for *vb* (*prep*) **1** to go or cause to go (towards). **2** to be destined for: *to head for trouble.*
head gate *n* **1** a gate that is used to control the flow of water at the upper end of a lock. Compare **tail gate. 2** another name for **floodgate** (sense 1).
headgear ('hɛd,gɪə) *n* **1** any head covering, esp. a hat. **2** any part of a horse's harness that is worn on the head. **3** the hoisting mechanism at the pithead of a mine.
head-hunting *n* **1** the practice among certain peoples of removing the heads of slain enemies and preserving them as trophies. **2** the recruitment, esp. through an agency, of executives from one company to another, often rival, company. **3** *U.S. slang.* the destruction or neutralization of political opponents. ▸ **'head-,hunter** *n*
heading ('hɛdɪŋ) *n* **1** a title for a page, paragraph, chapter, etc. **2** a main division, as of a lecture, speech, essay, etc. **3** *Mining.* **3a** a horizontal tunnel. **3b** the end of such a tunnel. **4** the angle between the direction of an aircraft and a specified meridian, often due north. **5** the compass direction parallel to the keel of a vessel. **6** the act of heading. **7** anything that serves as a head.
heading dog *n N.Z.* a dog that heads off a flock of sheep or a single sheep.
headland *n* **1** ('hɛdlənd). a narrow area of land jutting out into a sea, lake, etc. **2** ('hɛd,lænd). a strip of land along the edge of an arable field left unploughed to allow space for machines.
headless ('hɛdlɪs) *adj* **1** without a head. **2** without a leader. **3** foolish or stupid. **4** *Prosody.* another word for **catalectic.**
headlight ('hɛd,laɪt) *or* **headlamp** *n* a powerful light, equipped with a reflector and attached to the front of a motor vehicle, locomotive, etc. See also **quartz-iodine lamp.**
headline ('hɛd,laɪn) *n* **1** Also called: **head, heading. 1a** a phrase at the top of a newspaper or magazine article indicating the subject of the article, usually in larger and heavier type. **1b** a line at the top of a page indicating the title, page number, etc. **2** (*usually pl*) the main points of a television or radio news broadcast, read out before the full broadcast and summarized at the end. **3 hit the headlines.** to become prominent in the news. ♦ *vb* **4** (*tr*) to furnish (a story or page) with a headline. **5** to have top billing (in).
headliner ('hɛd,laɪnə) *n U.S.* a performer given prominent billing; star.
headline rate *n* a basic rate of inflation, taxation, etc., before distorting factors have been removed: *the headline rate of inflation.*
head-load *African.* ♦ *n* **1** baggage or goods arranged so as to be carried on the heads of African porters. ♦ *vb* **2** (*tr*) to convey or carry (goods) on the head.
headlock ('hɛd,lɒk) *n* a wrestling hold in which a wrestler locks his opponent's head between the crook of his elbow and the side of his body.
headlong ('hɛd,lɒŋ) *adv, adj* **1** with the head foremost; headfirst. **2** with great haste. ♦ *adj* **3** *Archaic.* (of slopes, etc.) very steep; precipitous.
headman ('hɛdmən) *n, pl* **-men. 1** *Anthropol.* a chief or leader. **2** a foreman or overseer.
headmaster (,hɛd'mɑːstə) *or* (*fem*) **headmistress** *n* the principal of a school. ▸ **,head'master,ship** *or* (*fem*) **,head'mistress,ship** *n*
headmasterly (,hɛd'mæstəlɪ) *or* (*fem*) **headmistressy** (,hɛd'mɪstrɪsɪ) *adj* relating to or typical of the duties and behaviour of a principal of a school.
head money *n* **1** a reward paid for the capture or slaying of a fugitive, outlaw, etc. **2** an archaic term for **poll tax.**
headmost ('hɛd,məʊst) *adj* a less common word for **foremost.**
head off *vb* (*tr, adv*) **1** to intercept and force to change direction: *to head off the stampede.* **2** to prevent or forestall (something that is likely to happen). **3** to depart or set out: *to head off to school.*
head of the river *n* **a** any of various annual rowing regattas held on particular rivers. **b** the boat or team winning such a regatta: *Eton are head of the river again this year.*
head-on *adv, adj* **1** with the front or fronts foremost: *a head-on collision.* **2** with directness or without compromise: *in his usual head-on fashion.*
headphones ('hɛd,fəʊnz) *pl n* an electrical device consisting of two earphones held in position by a flexible metallic strap passing over the head. Informal name: **cans.**
headpiece ('hɛd,piːs) *n* **1** *Printing.* a decorative band at the top of a page, chapter, etc. **2** any covering for the head, esp. a helmet. **3** *Archaic.* the intellect. **4** a less common word for **crownpiece** (sense 2).
headpin ('hɛd,pɪn) *n Tenpin bowling.* another word for **kingpin.**
headquarter (,hɛd'kwɔːtə) *vb Informal, chiefly U.S.* to place in or establish as headquarters.
headquarters (,hɛd'kwɔːtəz) *pl n* (*sometimes functioning as sing*) **1** any centre or building from which operations are directed, as in the military, the police, etc. **2** a military formation comprising the commander, his staff, and supporting echelons. ♦ Abbrevs.: **HQ, h.q.**
headrace ('hɛd,reɪs) *n* a channel that carries water to a water wheel, turbine, etc. Compare **tailrace.**
headrail ('hɛd,reɪl) *n Billiards, etc.* the end of the table from which play is started, nearest the baulkline.
headreach ('hɛd,riːtʃ) *Nautical.* ♦ *n* **1** the distance made to windward while tacking. ♦ *vb* **2** (*tr*) to gain distance over (another boat) when tacking.
headrest ('hɛd,rɛst) *n* a support for the head, as on a dentist's chair or car seat.
head restraint *n* an adjustable support for the head, attached to a car seat, to prevent the neck from being jolted backwards sharply in the event of a crash or sudden stop.
headroom ('hɛd,rʊm, -,ruːm) *or* **headway** *n* the height of a bridge, room, etc.; clearance.
heads (hɛdz) *interj, adv* **1** with the obverse side of a coin uppermost, esp. if it has a head on it: used as a call before tossing a coin. Compare **tails. 2 the.** *Austral. informal.* people in authority.
headsail ('hɛd,seɪl; *Nautical* 'hɛdsəl) *n* any sail set forward of the foremast.
headscarf ('hɛd,skɑːf) *n, pl* **-scarves** (-,skɑːvz). a scarf for the head, often worn tied under the chin.
head sea *n* a sea in which the waves run directly against the course of a ship.
headset ('hɛd,sɛt) *n* a pair of headphones, esp. with a microphone attached.
headship ('hɛdʃɪp) *n* **1** the position or state of being a leader; command; leadership. **2** *Education, Brit.* the position of headmaster or headmistress of a school.
headshrinker ('hɛd,ʃrɪŋkə) *n* **1** a slang name for **psychiatrist.** Often shortened to **shrink. 2** a head-hunter who shrinks the heads of his victims.
headsman ('hɛdzmən) *n, pl* **-men.** (formerly) an executioner who beheaded condemned persons.
headspring ('hɛd,sprɪŋ) *n* **1** a spring that is the source of a stream. **2** a spring using the head as a lever from a position lying on the ground. **3** *Rare.* a source.
headsquare ('hɛd,skwɛə) *n* a scarf worn on the head.
headstall ('hɛd,stɔːl) *n* another word (esp. U.S.) for **head collar.**
headstand ('hɛd,stænd) *n* the act or an instance of balancing on the head, usually with the hands as support.
head start *n* an initial advantage in a competitive situation. [originally referring to a horse's having its head in front of others at the start of a race]
head station *n Austral.* the main buildings on a large sheep or cattle farm.
headstock ('hɛd,stɒk) *n* **1** the part of a machine that supports and transmits the drive to the chuck. Compare **tailstock. 2** the wooden or metal block on which a church bell is hung.
headstone ('hɛd,stəʊn) *n* **1** a memorial stone at the head of a grave. **2** *Architect.* another name for **keystone.**
headstream ('hɛd,striːm) *n* a stream that is the source or a source of a river.
headstrong ('hɛd,strɒŋ) *adj* **1** self-willed; obstinate. **2** (of an action) heedless; rash. ▸ **'head,strongly** *adv* ▸ **'head,strongness** *n*
head teacher *n* a headmaster or headmistress.
head-to-head *Informal.* ♦ *adj* **1** in direct competition. ♦ *n* **2** a competition involving two people, teams, etc.
head-up display *n* the projection of readings from instruments onto a windscreen, enabling an aircraft pilot or car driver to see them without looking down.
head voice *or* **register** *n* the high register of the human voice, in which the vibrations of sung notes are felt in the head.
head waiter *n* a waiter who supervises the activities of other waiters and arranges the seating of guests.
headward ('hɛdwəd) *adj* **1** (of river erosion) cutting backwards or upstream above the original source, which recedes. ♦ *adv* **2** a variant of **headwards.**
headwards ('hɛdwədz) *or* **headward** *adv* backwards beyond the original source: *a river erodes headwards.*
headwaters ('hɛd,wɔːtəz) *pl n* the tributary streams of a river in the area in which it rises; headstreams.
headway ('hɛd,weɪ) *n* **1** motion in a forward direction: *the vessel made no headway.* **2** progress or rate of progress: *he made no headway with the problem.* **3** another name for **headroom. 4** the distance or time between consecutive trains, buses, etc., on the same route.
headwind ('hɛd,wɪnd) *n* a wind blowing directly against the course of an aircraft or ship. Compare **tailwind.**
headword ('hɛd,wɜːd) *n* a key word placed at the beginning of a line, paragraph, etc., as in a dictionary entry.
headwork ('hɛd,wɜːk) *n* **1** mental work. **2** the ornamentation of the keystone of an arch. ▸ **'head,worker** *n*
heady ('hɛdɪ) *adj* **headier, headiest. 1** (of alcoholic drink) intoxicating. **2**

strongly affecting the mind or senses; extremely exciting. **3** rash; impetuous. ▸ **'headily** *adv* ▸ **'headiness** *n*

heal (hi:l) *vb* **1** to restore or be restored to health. **2** (*intr;* often foll. by *over* or *up*) (of a wound, burn, etc.) to repair by natural processes, as by scar formation. **3** (*tr*) **3a** to treat (a wound, etc.) by assisting in its natural repair. **3b** to cure (a disease or disorder). **4** to restore or be restored to friendly relations, harmony, etc. [Old English *hǣlan;* related to Old Norse *heila,* Gothic *hailjan,* Old High German *heilen;* see HALE[1], WHOLE] ▸ **'healable** *adj* ▸ **'healer** *n* ▸ **'healing** *n, adj*

heal-all *n* another name for **selfheal.**

Healey ('hi:lɪ) *n* **Denis (Winston)**, Baron Healey. born 1917, British Labour politician; Chancellor of the Exchequer (1974–79); deputy leader of the Labour Party (1980–83).

health (hɛlθ) *n* **1** the state of being bodily and mentally vigorous and free from disease. **2** the general condition of body and mind: *in poor health.* **3** the condition of any unit, society, etc.: *the economic health of a nation.* **4** a toast to a person, wishing him or her good health, happiness, etc. **5** (*modifier*) of or relating to food or other goods reputed to be beneficial to the health: *health food; a health store.* **6** (*modifier*) of or relating to health, esp. to the administration of health: *a health committee; health resort; health service.* ◆ *interj* **7** an exclamation wishing someone good health as part of a toast (in the phrases **your health, good health,** etc.). [Old English *hǣlth;* related to *hāl* HALE[1]]

health camp *n N.Z.* a camp, usually at the seaside, for children requiring health care.

health centre *n* (in Britain) premises, owned by a local authority, providing health care for the local community and usually housing a group practice, nursing staff, a child-health clinic, X-ray facilities, etc.

health farm *n* a residential establishment, often in the country, visited by those who wish to improve their health by losing weight, eating health foods, taking exercise, etc.

health food *n* **a** vegetarian food organically grown and with no additives, eaten for its dietary value and benefit to health. **b** (*as modifier*): *a health-food shop.*

healthful ('hɛlθfʊl) *adj* a less common word for **healthy** (senses 1–3). ▸ **'healthfully** *adv* ▸ **'healthfulness** *n*

health physics *n* (*functioning as sing*) the branch of physics concerned with the health and safety of people in medical, scientific, and industrial work, esp. with protection from the biological effects of ionizing radiation.

health salts *pl n* magnesium sulphate or similar salts taken as a mild laxative.

Health Service Commissioner *n* (in Britain) the official name for an ombudsman who investigates personal complaints of injustice or hardship resulting from the failure, absence, or maladministration of a service for which a Regional or District Health Authority or Family Practitioner Committee is responsible, after other attempts to obtain redress have failed. See also **Commissioner for Local Administration, Parliamentary Commissioner.**

health stamp *n N.Z.* a postage stamp with a surcharge that is used to support a health camp.

health visitor *n* (in Britain) a nurse employed by a district health authority to visit people in their homes and give help and advice on health and social welfare, esp. to mothers of preschool children, to the handicapped, and to elderly people.

healthy ('hɛlθɪ) *adj* **healthier, healthiest. 1** enjoying good health. **2** functioning well or being sound: *the company's finances are not very healthy.* **3** conducive to health; salutary. **4** indicating soundness of body or mind: *a healthy appetite.* **5** *Informal.* considerable in size or amount: *a healthy sum.* ▸ **'healthily** *adv* ▸ **'healthiness** *n*

Healy ('hi:lɪ) *n* **Ian.** born 1964, Australian cricketer.

Heaney ('hi:nɪ) *n* **Seamus (Justin)** ('ʃeɪməs). born 1939, Irish poet and critic, born in Northern Ireland. His collections include *Death of a Naturalist* (1966), *North* (1975), *The Haw Lantern* (1987), *Seeing Things* (1991), and *The Spirit Level* (1996). Nobel prize for literature 1995.

heap (hi:p) *n* **1** a collection of articles or mass of material gathered together in one place. **2** (*often pl;* usually foll. by *of*) *Informal.* a large number or quantity. **3 give them heaps.** *Austral. slang.* to contend strenuously with an opposing sporting team. **4** *Informal.* a place or thing that is very old, untidy, unreliable, etc.: *the car was a heap.* ◆ *adv* **5 heaps.** (intensifier): *he said he was feeling heaps better.* ◆ *vb* **6** (often foll. by *up* or *together*) to collect or be collected into or as if into a heap or pile: *to heap up wealth.* **7** (*tr;* often foll. by *with, on,* or *upon*) to load or supply (with) abundantly: *to heap with riches.* [Old English *héap;* related to Old Frisian *hāp,* Old Saxon *hōp,* Old High German *houf*] ▸ **'heaper** *n*

heaping ('hi:pɪŋ) *adj U.S. and Canadian.* (of a spoonful) heaped.

hear (hɪə) *vb* **hears, hearing, heard** (hɜ:d). **1** (*tr*) to perceive (a sound) with the sense of hearing. **2** (*tr; may take a clause as object*) to listen to: *did you hear what I said?* **3** (when *intr,* sometimes foll. by *of* or *about;* when *tr, may take a clause as object*) to be informed (of); receive information (about): *to hear of his success; have you heard?* **4** *Law.* to give a hearing to (a case). **5** (when *intr,* usually foll. by *of* and used with a negative) to listen (to) with favour, assent, etc.: *she wouldn't hear of it.* **6** (*intr;* foll. by *from*) to receive a letter, news, etc. (from). **7 hear! hear!** an exclamation used to show approval of something said. **8 hear tell (of).** *Dialect.* to be told (about); learn (of). [Old English *hieran;* related to Old Norse *heyra,* Gothic *hausjan,* Old High German *hōren,* Greek *akouein*] ▸ **'hearable** *adj* ▸ **'hearer** *n*

Heard and McDonald Islands (hɜ:d, mək'dɒnəld) *pl n* a group of islands in the S Indian Ocean: an external territory of Australia from 1947. Area: 412 sq. km (159 sq. miles).

hearing ('hɪərɪŋ) *n* **1** the faculty or sense by which sound is perceived. Related adj: **audio. 2** an opportunity to be listened to. **3** the range within which sound can be heard; earshot. **4** the investigation of a matter by a court of law, esp. the preliminary inquiry into an indictable crime by magistrates. **5** a formal or official trial of an action or lawsuit.

hearing aid *n* a device for assisting the hearing of partially deaf people, typically consisting of a small battery-powered electronic amplifier with microphone and earphone, worn by a deaf person in or behind the ear. Also called: **deaf aid.**

hearing dog *n* a dog that has been specially trained to help deaf or partially deaf people by alerting them to sounds such as a ringing doorbell, an alarm, etc.

hearing loss *n* an increase in the threshold of audibility caused by age, infirmity, or prolonged exposure to intense noise.

hearken *or U.S.* (*sometimes*) **harken** ('hɑ:kən) *vb Archaic.* to listen to (something). [Old English *heorcnian;* see HARK] ▸ **'hearkener** *n*

hear out *vb* (*tr, adv*) to listen in regard to every detail and give a proper or full hearing to.

hearsay ('hɪəˌseɪ) *n* gossip; rumour.

hearsay evidence *n Law.* evidence based on what has been reported to a witness by others rather than what he has himself observed or experienced (not generally admissible as evidence).

hearse (hɜ:s) *n* a vehicle, such as a car or carriage, used to carry a coffin to the grave. [**C14**: from Old French *herce,* from Latin *hirpex* harrow]

Hearst (hɜ:st) *n* **William Randolph.** 1863–1951, U.S. newspaper publisher, whose newspapers were noted for their sensationalism.

heart (hɑ:t) *n* **1** the hollow muscular organ in vertebrates whose contractions propel the blood through the circulatory system. In mammals it consists of a right and left atrium and a right and left ventricle. Related adj: **cardiac. 2** the corresponding organ or part in invertebrates. **3** this organ considered as the seat of life and emotions, esp. love. **4** emotional mood or disposition: *a happy heart; a change of heart.* **5** tenderness or pity: *you have no heart.* **6** courage or spirit; bravery. **7** the inmost or most central part of a thing: *the heart of the city.* **8** the most important or vital part: *the heart of the matter.* **9** (of vegetables such as cabbage) the inner compact part. **10** the core of a tree. **11** the part nearest the heart of a person; breast: *she held him to her heart.* **12** a dearly loved person: usually used as a term of address: *dearest heart.* **13** a conventionalized representation of the heart, having two rounded lobes at the top meeting in a point at the bottom. **14a** a red heart-shaped symbol on a playing card. **14b** a card with one or more of these symbols or (*when pl*) the suit of cards so marked. **15** a fertile condition in land, conducive to vigorous growth in crops or herbage (esp. in the phrase **in good heart**). **16 after one's own heart.** appealing to one's own disposition, taste, or tendencies. **17 at heart.** in reality or fundamentally. **18 break one's** (*or* **someone's**) **heart.** to grieve (or cause to grieve) very deeply, esp. through love. **19 by heart.** by committing to memory. **20 cross my heart (and hope to die)!** I promise! **21 eat one's heart out.** to brood or pine with grief or longing. **22 from (the bottom of) one's heart.** very sincerely or deeply. **23 have a heart!** be kind or merciful. **24 have one's heart in it.** (*usually used with a negative*) to have enthusiasm for something. **25 have one's heart in one's boots.** to be depressed or down-hearted. **26 have one's heart in one's mouth** (*or* **throat**). to be full of apprehension, excitement, or fear. **27 have one's heart in the right place. 27a** to be kind, thoughtful, or generous. **27b** to mean well. **28 have the heart.** (*usually used with a negative*) to have the necessary will, callousness, etc., (to do something): *I didn't have the heart to tell him.* **29 heart and soul.** absolutely; completely. **30 heart of hearts.** the depths of one's conscience or emotions. **31 heart of oak.** a brave person. **32 in one's heart.** secretly; fundamentally. **33 lose heart.** to become despondent or disillusioned (over something). **34 lose one's heart to.** to fall in love with. **35 near** *or* **close to one's heart.** cherished or important. **36 set one's heart on.** to have as one's ambition to obtain; covet. **37 take heart.** to become encouraged. **38 take to heart.** to take seriously or be upset about. **39 to one's heart's content.** as much as one wishes. **40 wear one's heart on one's sleeve.** to show one's feelings openly. **41 with all one's** (*or* **one's whole**) **heart.** very willingly. ◆ *vb* **42** (*intr*) (of vegetables) to form a heart. **43** an archaic word for **hearten.** ◆ See also **hearts.** [Old English *heorte;* related to Old Norse *hjarta,* Gothic *hairtō,* Old High German *herza,* Latin *cor,* Greek *kardia,* Old Irish *cride*]

heartache ('hɑ:tˌeɪk) *n* intense anguish or mental suffering.

heart attack *n* any sudden severe instance of abnormal heart functioning, esp. coronary thrombosis.

heartbeat ('hɑ:tˌbi:t) *n* one complete pulsation of the heart. See **diastole, systole.**

heart block *n* impaired conduction or blocking of the impulse that regulates the heartbeat, resulting in a lack of coordination between the beating of the atria and the ventricles. Also called: **Adams-Stokes syndrome, atrioventricular block.**

heartbreak ('hɑ:tˌbreɪk) *n* intense and overwhelming grief, esp. through disappointment in love. ▸ **'heartˌbreaker** *n*

heartbreaking ('hɑ:tˌbreɪkɪŋ) *adj* extremely sad, disappointing, or pitiful. ▸ **'heartˌbreakingly** *adv*

heartbroken ('hɑ:tˌbrəʊkən) *adj* suffering from intense grief. ▸ **'heartˌbrokenly** *adv* ▸ **'heartˌbrokenness** *n*

heartburn ('hɑ:tˌbɜ:n) *n* a burning sensation beneath the breastbone caused by irritation of the oesophagus, as from regurgitation of the contents of the stomach. Technical names: **cardialgia, pyrosis.**

heart cherry *n* a heart-shaped variety of sweet cherry.

-hearted *adj* having a heart or disposition as specified: *good-hearted; cold-hearted; great-hearted; heavy-hearted.*

hearten ('hɑ:tᵊn) *vb* to make or become cheerful. ▸ **'heartening** *adj*

heart failure *n* **1** a condition in which the heart is unable to pump an adequate amount of blood to the tissues, usually resulting in breathlessness, swollen ankles, etc. **2** sudden and permanent cessation of the heartbeat, resulting in death.

heartfelt ('hɑːtˌfɛlt) *adj* sincerely and strongly felt.

hearth (hɑːθ) *n* **1a** the floor of a fireplace, esp. one that extends outwards into the room. **1b** (*as modifier*): *hearth rug.* **2** this part of a fireplace as a symbol of the home, etc. **3** the bottom part of a metallurgical furnace in which the molten metal is produced or contained. [Old English *heorth;* related to Old High German *herd* hearth, Latin *carbō* charcoal]

hearthstone ('hɑːθˌstəʊn) *n* **1** a stone that forms a hearth. **2** a less common word for **hearth** (sense 1). **3** soft stone used to clean and whiten floors, steps, etc.

heartily ('hɑːtɪlɪ) *adv* **1** thoroughly or vigorously: *to eat heartily.* **2** in a sincere manner: *he congratulated me heartily.*

heartland ('hɑːtˌlænd) *n* **1** the central region of a country or continent. **2** the core or most vital area: *the industrial heartland of England.*

heartless ('hɑːtlɪs) *adj* unkind or cruel; hard-hearted. ▸ **'heartlessly** *adv* ▸ **'heartlessness** *n*

heart-lung machine *n* a machine used to maintain the circulation and oxygenation of the blood during heart surgery.

heart murmur *n* an abnormal sound heard through a stethoscope over the region of the heart.

heart-rending *adj* causing great mental pain and sorrow. ▸ **'heart-ˌrendingly** *adv*

hearts (hɑːts) *n* (*functioning as sing*) a card game in which players must avoid winning tricks containing hearts or the queen of spades. Also called: **Black Maria.**

heart-searching *n* examination of one's feelings or conscience.

heartsease *or* **heart's-ease** ('hɑːtsˌiːz) *n* **1** another name for the **wild pansy. 2** peace of mind.

heartsick ('hɑːtˌsɪk) *adj* deeply dejected or despondent. ▸ **'heartˌsickness** *n*

heartsome ('hɑːtsəm) *adj Chiefly Scot.* **1** cheering or encouraging: *heartsome news.* **2** gay; cheerful. ▸ **'heartsomely** *adv* ▸ **'heartsomeness** *n*

heart starter *n Austral. slang.* the first drink of the day.

heartstrings ('hɑːtˌstrɪŋz) *pl n Often facetious.* deep emotions or feelings. [C15: originally referring to the tendons supposed to support the heart]

heart-throb *n* **1** an object of infatuation. **2** a heart beat.

heart-to-heart *adj* **1** (esp. of a conversation or discussion) concerned with personal problems or intimate feelings. ◆ *n* **2** an intimate conversation or discussion.

heart urchin *n* any echinoderm of the genus *Echinocardium,* having a heart-shaped body enclosed in a rigid spiny test: class *Echinoidea* (sea urchins).

heart-warming *adj* **1** pleasing; gratifying. **2** emotionally moving.

heart-whole *adj Rare.* **1** not in love. **2** sincere. **3** stout-hearted. ▸ **ˌheart-'wholeness** *n*

heartwood ('hɑːtˌwʊd) *n* the central core of dark hard wood in tree trunks, consisting of nonfunctioning xylem tissue that has become blocked with resins, tannins, and oils. Compare **sapwood.**

heartworm ('hɑːtˌwɜːm) *n* a parasitic nematode worm, *Dirofilaria immitis,* that lives in the heart and bloodstream of vertebrates.

hearty ('hɑːtɪ) *adj* **heartier, heartiest. 1** warm and unreserved in manner or behaviour. **2** vigorous and enthusiastic: *a hearty slap on the back.* **3** sincere and heartfelt: *hearty dislike.* **4** healthy and strong (esp. in the phrase **hale and hearty**). **5** substantial and nourishing. ◆ *n Informal.* **6** a comrade, esp. a sailor. **7** a vigorous sporting man: *a rugby hearty.* ▸ **'heartiness** *n*

heat (hiːt) *n* **1** the energy transferred as a result of a difference in temperature. Related adjs.: **thermal, calorific. 2** the sensation caused in the body by heat energy; warmth. **3** the state or quality of being hot. **4** hot weather: *the heat of summer.* **5** intensity of feeling; passion: *the heat of rage.* **6** pressure: *the political heat on the government over the economy.* **7** the most intense or active part: *the heat of the battle.* **8** a period or condition of sexual excitement in female mammals that occurs at oestrus. **9** *Sport.* **9a** a preliminary eliminating contest in a competition. **9b** a single section of a contest. **10** *Slang.* police activity after a crime: *the heat is off.* **11** *Chiefly U.S. slang.* criticism or abuse: *he took a lot of heat for that mistake.* **12 in the heat of the moment.** without pausing to think. **13 on** *or* **in heat. 13a** Also: **in season.** (of some female mammals) sexually receptive. **13b** in a state of sexual excitement. **14 the heat.** *Slang.* the police. **15 turn up** *or* **on the heat.** *Informal.* to increase the intensity of activity, coercion, etc. ◆ *vb* **16** to make or become hot or warm. **17** to make or become excited or intense. [Old English *hǣtu;* related to *hāt* HOT, Old Frisian *hēte* heat, Old High German *heizī*] ▸ **'heatless** *adj*

heat barrier *n* another name for **thermal barrier.**

heat capacity *n* the heat required to raise the temperature of a substance by unit temperature interval under specified conditions. Symbol: C_p (for constant pressure) or C_v (for constant volume).

heat content *n* another name for **enthalpy.**

heat death *n Thermodynamics.* the condition of any closed system when its total entropy is a maximum and it has no available energy. If the universe is a closed system it should eventually reach this state.

heated ('hiːtɪd) *adj* **1** made hot; warmed. **2** impassioned or highly emotional. ▸ **'heatedly** *adv* ▸ **'heatedness** *n*

heat engine *n* an engine that converts heat energy into mechanical energy.

heater ('hiːtə) *n* **1** any device for supplying heat, such as a hot-air blower, radiator, convector, etc. **2** *U.S. slang.* a pistol. **3** *Electronics.* a conductor carrying a current that indirectly heats the cathode in some types of valve.

heat exchanger *n* a device for transferring heat from one fluid to another without allowing them to mix.

heat exhaustion *n* a condition resulting from exposure to intense heat, characterized by dizziness, abdominal cramp, and prostration. Also called: **heat prostration.** Compare **heatstroke.**

heath (hiːθ) *n* **1** *Brit.* a large open area, usually with sandy soil and scrubby vegetation, esp. heather. **2** Also called: **heather.** any low-growing evergreen ericaceous shrub of the Old World genus *Erica* and related genera, having small bell-shaped typically pink or purple flowers. **3** any of several nonericaceous heathlike plants, such as sea heath. **4** *Austral.* any of various heathlike plants of the genus *Epacris.* **5** any of various small brown satyrid butterflies of the genus *Coenonympha,* with coppery-brown wings, esp. the **large heath** (*C. tullia*). [Old English *hǣth;* related to Old Norse *heithr* field, Old High German *heida* heather] ▸ **'heathˌlike** *adj* ▸ **'heathy** *adj*

Heath (hiːθ) *n* **Edward** (**Richard George**). born 1916, British statesman; leader of the Conservative Party (1965–75); prime minister 1970–74.

heathberry ('hiːθˌbɛrɪ) *n, pl* **-ries.** any of various plants that have berry-like fruits and grow on heaths, such as the bilberry and crowberry.

heath cock *n* another name for **blackcock.**

heathen ('hiːðən) *n, pl* **-thens** *or* **-then. 1** a person who does not acknowledge the God of Christianity, Judaism, or Islam; pagan. **2** an uncivilized or barbaric person. **3 the heathen.** (*functioning as pl*) heathens collectively. ◆ *adj* **4** irreligious; pagan. **5** unenlightened; uncivilized; barbaric. **6** of or relating to heathen peoples or their religious, moral, and other customs, practices, and beliefs. [Old English *hǣthen;* related to Old Norse *heithinn,* Old Frisian *hēthin,* Old High German *heidan*] ▸ **'heathenism** *or* **'heathenry** *n* ▸ **'heathenness** *n*

heathendom ('hiːðəndəm) *n* heathen lands, peoples, or beliefs.

heathenish ('hiːðənɪʃ) *adj* of, relating to, or resembling a heathen or heathen culture. ▸ **'heathenishly** *adv* ▸ **'heathenishness** *n*

heathenize *or* **heathenise** ('hiːðəˌnaɪz) *vb* **1** to render or become heathen, or bring or come under heathen influence. **2** (*intr*) to engage in heathen practices.

heather ('hɛðə) *n* **1** Also called: **ling, heath.** a low-growing evergreen Eurasian ericaceous shrub, *Calluna vulgaris,* that grows in dense masses on open ground and has clusters of small bell-shaped typically pinkish-purple flowers. **2** any of certain similar plants. **3** a purplish-red to pinkish-purple colour. ◆ *adj* **4** of a heather colour. **5** of or relating to interwoven yarns of mixed colours: *heather mixture.* [C14: originally Scottish and Northern English, probably from HEATH] ▸ **'heathered** *adj* ▸ **'heathery** *adj*

heathfowl ('hiːθˌfaʊl) *n* (in British game laws) an archaic name for the **black grouse.** Compare **moorfowl.**

heath grass *or* **heather grass** *n* a perennial European grass, *Sieglingia decumbens,* with flat hairless leaves.

heath hen *n* **1** another name for **greyhen. 2** a recently extinct variety of the prairie chicken.

Heath Robinson (rɒbɪnsᵊn) *adj* (of a mechanical device) absurdly complicated in design and having a simple function. [C20: named after William *Heath Robinson* (1872–1944), British cartoonist]

heath wren *n* either of two ground-nesting warblers of southern Australia, *Hylacola pyrrhopygia* or *H. cauta,* noted for their song and their powers of mimicry.

heating ('hiːtɪŋ) *n* **1** a device or system for supplying heat, esp. central heating, to a building. **2** the heat supplied.

heating element *n* a coil or other arrangement of wire in which heat is produced by an electric current.

heat-island *n Meteorol.* the mass of air over a large city, characteristically having a slightly higher average temperature than that of the surrounding air.

heat lightning *n* flashes of light seen near the horizon, esp. on hot evenings: reflections of more distant lightning.

heat of combustion *n Chem.* the heat evolved when one mole of a substance is burnt in oxygen at constant volume.

heat of formation *n Chem.* the heat evolved or absorbed when one mole of a compound is formed from its constituent atoms.

heat of reaction *n Chem.* the heat evolved or absorbed when one mole of a product is formed at constant pressure.

heat of solution *n Chem.* the heat evolved or absorbed when one mole of a substance dissolves completely in a large volume of solvent.

heat prostration *n* another name for **heat exhaustion.**

heat pump *n* a device, as used in a refrigerator, for extracting heat from a source and delivering it elsewhere at a much higher temperature.

heat rash *n* a nontechnical name for **miliaria.**

heat-seeking *adj* **1** (of a detecting device) able to detect sources of infrared radiation: *a heat-seeking camera.* **2** (of a missile) able to detect and follow a source of heat, as from an aircraft engine: *a heat-seeking missile.* ▸ **heat seeker** *n*

heat shield *n* a coating or barrier for shielding from excessive heat, such as that experienced by a spacecraft on re-entry into the earth's atmosphere.

heat sink *n* **1** a metal plate specially designed to conduct and radiate heat from an electrical component, such as a rectifier. **2** a layer of material placed within the outer skin of high-speed aircraft to absorb heat.

heatstroke ('hiːtˌstrəʊk) *n* a condition resulting from prolonged exposure to intense heat, characterized by high fever and in severe cases convulsions and coma. See **sunstroke.**

heat-treat *vb* (*tr*) to apply heat to (a metal or alloy) in one or more temperature cycles to give it desirable properties. ▸ **heat treatment** *n*

heat wave *n* **1** a continuous spell of abnormally hot weather. **2** an extensive slow-moving air mass at a relatively high temperature.

heaume (həʊm) *n* (in the 12th and 13th centuries) a large helmet reaching and supported by the shoulders. [C16: from Old French *helme;* see HELMET]

heave (hiːv) *vb* **heaves, heaving, heaved** *or* (*chiefly nautical*) **hove. 1** (*tr*) to lift or move with a great effort. **2** (*tr*) to throw (something heavy) with effort. **3**

to utter (sounds, sighs, etc.) or breathe noisily or unhappily: *to heave a sigh.* **4** to rise and fall or cause to rise and fall heavily. **5** (*past tense and past participle* **hove**) *Nautical.* **5a** to move or cause to move in a specified way, direction, or position: *to heave in sight.* **5b** (*intr*) (of a vessel) to pitch or roll. **6** (*tr*) to displace (rock strata, mineral veins, etc.) in a horizontal direction. **7** (*intr*) to retch. ◆ *n* **8** the act or an instance of heaving. **9** a fling. **10** a horizontal displacement of rock strata at a fault. ◆ See also **heave down, heaves, heave to.** [Old English *hebban;* related to Old Norse *hefja,* Old Saxon *hebbian,* Old High German *heffen* to raise, Latin *capere* to take, Sanskrit *kapatī* two hands full] ▸ **'heaver** *n*

heave down *vb* (*intr, adv*) *Naut.* to turn a vessel on its side for cleaning.

heave-ho *sentence substitute.* **1** a sailors' cry, as when hoisting anchor. ◆ *n* **2** *Informal.* dismissal, as from employment.

heaven ('hɛvᵊn) *n* **1** (*sometimes cap.*) *Christianity.* **1a** the abode of God and the angels. **1b** a place or state of communion with God after death. Compare **hell. 2** (*usually pl*) the sky, firmament or space surrounding the earth. **3** (in any of various mythologies) a place, such as Elysium or Valhalla, to which those who have died in the gods' favour are brought to dwell in happiness. **4** a place or state of joy and happiness. **5** (*sing* or *pl; sometimes cap.*) God or the gods, used in exclamatory phrases of surprise, exasperation, etc.: *for heaven's sake; heavens above.* **6 in seventh heaven.** ecstatically happy. **7 move heaven and earth.** to do everything possible (to achieve something). [Old English *heofon;* related to Old Saxon *heban*]

heavenly ('hɛvᵊnlɪ) *adj* **1** *Informal.* alluring, wonderful, or sublime. **2** of or occurring in space: *a heavenly body.* **3** divine; holy. ▸ **'heavenliness** *n*

heaven-sent *adj* providential; fortunate: *a heaven-sent opportunity.*

heavenward ('hɛvᵊnwəd) *adj* **1** directed towards heaven or the sky. ◆ *adv* **2** a variant of **heavenwards.**

heavenwards ('hɛvᵊnwədz) *or* **heavenward** *adv* towards heaven or the sky.

heaves (hiːvz) *n* (*functioning as sing or pl*) **1** Also called: **broken wind.** a chronic respiratory disorder of animals of the horse family, of unknown cause. **2 the heaves.** *Slang.* an attack of vomiting or retching.

heave to *vb* (*adv*) to stop (a vessel) or (of a vessel) to stop, as by trimming the sails, etc. Also: **lay to.**

heavier-than-air *adj* **1** having a density greater than that of air. **2** of or relating to an aircraft that does not depend on buoyancy for support but gains lift from aerodynamic forces.

Heaviside ('hɛvɪˌsaɪd) *n* **Oliver.** 1850–1925, English physicist. Independently of Kennelly, he predicted (1902) the existence of an ionized gaseous layer in the upper atmosphere (the **Heaviside layer**); he also contributed to telegraphy.

Heaviside layer *n* another name for **E region** (of the ionosphere). [C20: named after O. HEAVISIDE]

heavy ('hɛvɪ) *adj* **heavier, heaviest. 1** of comparatively great weight: *a heavy stone.* **2** having a relatively high density: *lead is a heavy metal.* **3** great in yield, quality, or quantity: *heavy rain; heavy traffic.* **4** great or considerable: *heavy emphasis.* **5** hard to bear, accomplish, or fulfil: *heavy demands.* **6** sad or dejected in spirit or mood: *heavy at heart.* **7** coarse or broad: *a heavy line; heavy features.* **8** (of soil) having a high clay content; cloggy. **9** solid or fat: *heavy legs.* **10** (of an industry) engaged in the large-scale complex manufacture of capital goods or extraction of raw materials. Compare **light**² (sense 19). **11** serious; grave. **12** *Military.* **12a** armed or equipped with large weapons, armour, etc. **12b** (of guns, etc.) of a large and powerful type. **13** (of a syllable) having stress or accentuation. Compare **light**² (sense 24). **14** dull and uninteresting: *a heavy style.* **15** prodigious: *a heavy drinker.* **16** (of cakes, bread, etc.) insufficiently leavened. **17** deep and loud: *a heavy thud.* **18** (of music, literature, etc.). **18a** dramatic and powerful; grandiose. **18b** not immediately comprehensible or appealing. **19** *Slang.* **19a** unpleasant or tedious. **19b** wonderful. **19c** (of rock music) having a powerful beat; hard. **20** weighted; burdened: *heavy with child.* **21** clumsy and slow: *heavy going.* **22** permeating: *a heavy smell.* **23** cloudy or overcast, esp. threatening rain: *heavy skies.* **24** not easily digestible: *a heavy meal.* **25** (of an element or compound) being or containing an isotope with greater atomic weight than that of the naturally occurring element: *heavy hydrogen; heavy water.* **26** *Horse racing.* (of the going on a racecourse) soft and muddy. **27** *Slang.* using, or prepared to use, violence or brutality: *the heavy mob.* **28 heavy on.** *Informal.* using large quantities of: *this car is heavy on petrol.* ◆ *n, pl* **heavies. 29a** a villainous role. **29b** an actor who plays such a part. **30** *Military.* **30a** a large fleet unit, esp. an aircraft carrier or battleship. **30b** a large calibre or weighty piece of artillery. **31** *Informal.* (*usually pl,* often preceded by *the*) a serious newspaper: *the Sunday heavies.* **32** *Informal.* a heavyweight boxer, wrestler, etc. **33** *Slang.* a man hired to threaten violence or deter others by his presence. **34** *Scot.* strong bitter beer. ◆ *adv* **35a** in a heavy manner; heavily: *time hangs heavy.* **35b** (*in combination*): *heavy-laden.* [Old English *hefig;* related to *hebban* to HEAVE, Old High German *hebīg*] ▸ **'heavily** *adv* ▸ **'heaviness** *n*

heavy breather *n* **1** a person who breathes stertorously or with difficulty. **2** an anonymous telephone caller who imitates such sounds, as being suggestive of sexual excitement.

heavy chain *n Immunol.* a type of polypeptide chain present in an immunoglobulin molecule.

heavy-duty *n* (*modifier*) **1** made to withstand hard wear, bad weather, etc.: *heavy-duty uniforms.* **2** subject to high import or export taxes.

heavy earth *n* another name for **barium oxide.**

heavy-footed *adj* having a heavy or clumsy tread.

heavy-handed *adj* **1** clumsy. **2** harsh and oppressive. ▸ **ˌheavy-'handedly** *adv* ▸ **ˌheavy-'handedness** *n*

heavy-hearted *adj* sad; melancholy.

heavy hydrogen *n* another name for **deuterium.**

heavy metal *n* **1a** a type of rock music characterized by a strong beat and amplified instrumental effects, often with violent, nihilistic, and misogynistic lyrics. **1b** (*as modifier*): *a heavy-metal band.* **2** a metal with a high specific gravity. **3** *Military.* large guns or shot.

heavy oil *n* a hydrocarbon mixture, heavier than water, distilled from coal tar.

heavy spar *n* another name for **barytes.**

heavy water *n* water that has been electrolytically decomposed to enrich it in the deuterium isotope in the form HDO or D_2O.

heavy-water reactor *n* a nuclear reactor that uses heavy water as moderator.

heavyweight ('hɛvɪˌweɪt) *n* **1** a person or thing that is heavier than average. **2a** a professional boxer weighing more than 175 pounds (79 kg). **2b** an amateur boxer weighing more than 81 kg (179 pounds). **2c** (*as modifier*): *the world heavyweight championship.* **3** a wrestler in a similar weight category (usually over 214 pounds (97 kg)). **4** *Informal.* an important or highly influential person.

Heb. *or* **Hebr.** *abbrev. for:* **1** Hebrew (language). **2** *Bible.* Hebrews.

Hebbel (*German* 'hɛbəl) *n* **Christian Friedrich** ('krɪstian 'friːdrɪç). 1813–63, German dramatist and lyric poet, whose historical works were influenced by Hegel; his major plays are *Maria Magdalena* (1844), *Herodes und Marianne* (1850), and the trilogy *Die Nibelungen* (1862).

hebdomad ('hɛbdəˌmæd) *n* **1** *Obsolete.* the number seven or a group of seven. **2** a rare word for **week.** [C16: from Greek, from *hebdomos* seventh, from *heptas* seven]

hebdomadal (hɛb'dɒmədᵊl) *or* **hebdomadary** (hɛb'dɒmədərɪ, -drɪ) *adj* a rare word for **weekly.** ▸ **heb'domadally** *adv*

Hebdomadal Council *n* the governing council or senate of Oxford University.

Hebe ('hiːbɪ) *n Greek myth.* the goddess of youth and spring, daughter of Zeus and Hera and wife of Hercules.

Hebei ('hʌ'beɪ), **Hopeh,** *or* **Hopei** *n* a province of NE China, on the Gulf of Chihli: important for the production of winter wheat, cotton, and coal. Capital: Shijiazhuang. Pop.: 64 370 000 (1996 est.). Area: 202 700 sq. km (79 053 sq. miles).

hebephrenia (ˌhiːbɪ'friːnɪə) *n* a form of pubertal schizophrenia, characterized by hallucinations, delusions, foolish behaviour, and senseless laughter. [C20: New Latin, from Greek *hēbē* youth + *-phrenia* mental disorder, from *phrēn* mind] ▸ **hebephrenic** (ˌhiːbɪ'frɛnɪk) *adj*

Hébert (*French* ebɛr) *n* **Jacques René** (ʒak rəne). 1755–94, French journalist and revolutionary: a leader of the sans-culottes during the French Revolution. He was guillotined under Robespierre.

hebetate ('hɛbɪˌteɪt) *adj* **1** (of plant parts) having a blunt or soft point. ◆ *vb* **2** *Rare.* to make or become blunted. [C16: from Latin *hebetāre* to make blunt, from *hebes* blunt] ▸ **ˌhebe'tation** *n* ▸ **'hebeˌtative** *adj*

hebetic (hɪ'bɛtɪk) *adj* of or relating to puberty. [C19: from Greek *hēbētikos* youth, from *hēbē* youth]

hebetude ('hɛbɪˌtjuːd) *n Rare.* mental dullness or lethargy. [C17: from Late Latin *hebetūdō,* from Latin *hebes* blunt] ▸ **ˌhebe'tudinous** *adj*

Hebraic (hɪ'breɪɪk), **Hebraical,** *or* **Hebrew** *adj* of, relating to, or characteristic of the Hebrews or their language or culture. ▸ **He'braically** *adv*

Hebraism ('hiːbreɪˌɪzəm) *n* a linguistic usage, custom, or other feature borrowed from or particular to the Hebrew language, or to the Jewish people or their culture.

Hebraist ('hiːbreɪɪst) *n* a person who studies the Hebrew language and culture. ▸ **ˌHebra'istic** *or* **ˌHebra'istical** *adj* ▸ **ˌHebra'istically** *adv*

Hebraize *or* **Hebraise** ('hiːbreɪˌaɪz) *vb* to become or cause to become Hebrew or Hebraic. ▸ **ˌHebrai'zation** *or* **ˌHebrai'sation** *n* ▸ **'HebraˌIzer** *or* **'HebraˌIser** *n*

Hebrew ('hiːbruː) *n* **1** the ancient language of the Hebrews, revived as the official language of Israel. It belongs to the Canaanitic branch of the Semitic subfamily of the Afro-Asiatic family of languages. **2** a member of an ancient Semitic people claiming descent from Abraham; an Israelite. **3** *Archaic or offensive.* a Jew. ◆ *adj* **4** of or relating to the Hebrews or their language. **5** *Archaic or offensive.* Jewish. [C13: from Old French *Ebreu,* from Latin *Hebraeus,* from Greek *Hebraios,* from Aramaic *ʿibhray,* from Hebrew *ʿibhrī* one from beyond (the river)]

Hebrew calendar *n* another term for the **Jewish calendar.**

Hebrews ('hiːbruːz) *n* (*functioning as sing*) a book of the New Testament.

Hebrides ('hɛbrɪˌdiːz) *pl n* **the.** a group of over 500 islands off the W coast of Scotland: separated by the North Minch, Little Minch, and the Sea of the Hebrides: the chief islands are Skye, Raasay, Rhum, Eigg, Coll, Tiree, Mull, Jura, Colonsay, and Islay (**Inner Hebrides**), and Lewis with Harris, North Uist, Benbecula, South Uist, and Barra (**Outer Hebrides**). Also called: **Western Isles.** ▸ **ˌHebri'dean** *or* **Hebridian** (hɛ'brɪdɪən) *adj, n*

Hebron ('hɛbrɒn, 'hiː-) *n* a city in the West Bank: famous for the Haram, which includes the cenotaphs of Abraham and Sarah, Isaac and Rebecca, and Jacob and Leah. Pop.: 80 000 (1990 est.). Arabic name: **El Khalil.**

Hecate *or* **Hekate** ('hɛkətɪ) *n Greek myth.* a goddess of the underworld.

hecatomb ('hɛkəˌtəʊm, -ˌtuːm) *n* **1** (in ancient Greece or Rome) any great public sacrifice and feast, originally one in which 100 oxen were sacrificed. **2** a great sacrifice. [C16: from Latin *hecatombē,* from Greek *hekatombē,* from *hekaton* hundred + *bous* ox]

heck¹ (hɛk) *interj* a mild exclamation of surprise, irritation, etc. [C19: euphemistic for *hell*]

heck² (hɛk) *n Northern English dialect.* a frame for obstructing the passage of fish in a river. [C14: variant of HATCH²]

heckelphone ('hɛkəlˌfəʊn) *n Music.* a type of bass oboe. [C20: named after W. *Heckel* (1856–1909), German inventor]

heckle ('hɛkᵊl) *vb* **1** to interrupt (a public speaker, performer, etc.) by comments, questions, or taunts. **2** (*tr*) Also: **hackle, hatchel.** to comb (hemp or flax). ◆ *n* **3** an instrument for combing flax or hemp. [C15: Northern and East Anglian form of HACKLE] ▸ **'heckler** *n*

hectare ('hɛktɑː) *n* one hundred ares. 1 hectare is equivalent to 10 000 square metres or 2.471 acres. Symbol: ha [C19: from French; see HECTO-, ARE[2]]

hectic ('hɛktɪk) *adj* **1** characterized by extreme activity or excitement. **2** associated with, peculiar to, or symptomatic of tuberculosis (esp. in the phrases **hectic fever, hectic flush**). ◆ *n* **3** a hectic fever or flush. **4** *Rare.* a person who is consumptive or who experiences a hectic fever or flush. [C14: from Late Latin *hecticus,* from Greek *hektikos* habitual, from *hexis* state, from *ekhein* to have] ▸ **'hectically** *adv*

hecto- *or before a vowel* **hect-** *prefix* denoting 100: *hectogram.* Symbol: h [via French from Greek *hekaton* hundred]

hectocotylus (ˌhɛktəʊ'kɒtɪləs) *n, pl* **-li** (-ˌlaɪ). a tentacle in certain male cephalopod molluscs, such as the octopus, that is specialized for transferring spermatozoa to the female. [C19: New Latin, from HECTO- + Greek *kotulē* cup]

hectogram *or* **hectogramme** ('hɛktəʊˌɡræm) *n* one hundred grams. 1 hectogram is equivalent to 3.527 ounces. Symbol: hg

hectograph ('hɛktəʊˌɡrɑːf, -ˌɡræf) *n* **1** Also called: **copygraph.** a process for copying type or manuscript from a glycerine-coated gelatine master to which the original has been transferred. **2** a machine using this process. ▸ **hectographic** (ˌhɛktəʊ'ɡræfɪk) *adj* ▸ ˌ**hecto'graphically** *adv* ▸ **hectography** (hɛk'tɒɡrəfɪ) *n*

hectolitre *or U.S.* **hectoliter** ('hɛktəʊˌliːtə) *n* one hundred litres. A measure of capacity equivalent to 3.531 cubic feet. Symbol: hl

hectometre *or U.S.* **hectometer** ('hɛktəʊˌmiːtə) *n* one hundred metres: 1 hectometre is equivalent to 328.089 feet. Symbol: hm

hector ('hɛktə) *vb* **1** to bully or torment. ◆ *n* **2** a blustering bully. [C17: after HECTOR (the son of Priam), in the sense: a bully]

Hector ('hɛktə) *n Classical myth.* a son of King Priam of Troy, who was killed by Achilles.

Hecuba ('hɛkjʊbə) *n Classical myth.* the wife of King Priam of Troy, and mother of Hector and Paris.

he'd (hiːd; *unstressed* iːd, hɪd, ɪd) *contraction of* he had *or* he would.

heddle ('hɛdᵊl) *n* one of a set of frames of vertical wires on a loom, each wire having an eye through which a warp thread can be passed. [Old English *hefeld* chain; related to Old Norse *hafald,* Middle Low German *hevelte*]

heder *Hebrew.* ('xɛdɛr; *English* 'heɪdə) *n, pl* **hadarim** (xada'riːm). a variant spelling of **cheder.**

hedera ('hɛdərə) *n* See **ivy** (sense 1). [Latin: ivy]

hedge (hɛdʒ) *n* **1** a row of shrubs or bushes forming a boundary to a field, garden, etc. **2** a barrier or protection against something. **3** the act or a method of reducing the risk of financial loss on an investment, bet, etc. **4** a cautious or evasive statement. **5** (*modifier; often in combination*) low, inferior, or illiterate: *a hedge lawyer.* ◆ *vb* **6** (*tr*) to enclose or separate with or as if with a hedge. **7** (*intr*) to make or maintain a hedge, as by cutting and laying. **8** (*tr;* often foll. by *in, about,* or *around*) to hinder, obstruct, or restrict. **9** (*intr*) to evade decision or action, esp. by making noncommittal statements. **10** (*tr*) to guard against the risk of loss in (a bet, the paying out of a win, etc.), esp. by laying bets with other bookmakers. **11** (*intr*) to protect against financial loss through future price fluctuations, as by investing in futures. [Old English *hecg;* related to Old High German *heckia,* Middle Dutch *hegge;* see HAW[1]] ▸ **'hedger** *n* ▸ **'hedging** *n* ▸ **'hedgy** *adj*

hedge garlic *n* another name for **garlic mustard.**

hedgehog ('hɛdʒˌhɒɡ) *n* **1** any small nocturnal Old World mammal of the genus *Erinaceus,* such as *E. europaeus,* and related genera, having a protective covering of spines on the back: family *Erinaceidae,* order *Insectivora* (insectivores). Related adj: **erinaceous. 2** any other insectivores of the family *Erinaceidae,* such as the moon rat. **3** *U.S.* any of various other spiny animals, esp. the porcupine.

hedgehop ('hɛdʒˌhɒp) *vb* **-hops, -hopping, -hopped.** (*intr*) (of an aircraft) to fly close to the ground, as in crop spraying. ▸ **'hedgeˌhopper** *n* ▸ **'hedgeˌhopping** *n, adj*

hedge hyssop *n* any of several North American scrophulariaceous plants of the genus *Gratiola,* esp. *G. aurea,* having small yellow or white flowers.

hedge laying *n* the art or practice of making or maintaining a hedge by cutting branches partway through, laying them horizontally, and pegging them in position in order to create a strong thick hedge.

hedgerow ('hɛdʒˌrəʊ) *n* a hedge of shrubs or low trees growing along a bank, esp. one bordering a field or lane.

hedge-school *n Irish history.* a school held out of doors in favourable weather, indoors in winter. ▸ **'hedge-schoolˌmaster** *n*

hedge sparrow *n* a small brownish European songbird, *Prunella modularis:* family *Prunellidae* (accentors). Also called: **dunnock.**

Hedjaz (hiː'dʒæz) *n* a variant spelling of **Hejaz.**

hedonics (hiː'dɒnɪks) *n* (*functioning as sing*) **1** the branch of psychology concerned with the study of pleasant and unpleasant sensations. **2** (in philosophy) the study of pleasure, esp. in its relation to duty.

hedonism ('hiːdᵊˌnɪzəm, 'hɛd-) *n* **1** *Ethics.* **1a** the doctrine that moral value can be defined in terms of pleasure. See **utilitarianism. 1b** the doctrine that the pursuit of pleasure is the highest good. **2** the pursuit of pleasure as a matter of principle. **3** indulgence in sensual pleasures. [C19: from Greek *hēdonē* pleasure] ▸ **he'donic** *or* ˌ**hedon'istic** *adj* ▸ **'hedonist** *n*

-hedron *n combining form.* indicating a geometric solid having a specified number of faces or surfaces: *tetrahedron.* [from Greek *-edron* -sided, from *hedra* seat, base] ▸ **-hedral** *adj combining form.*

heebie-jeebies ('hiːbɪ'dʒiːbɪz) *pl n* **the.** *Slang.* apprehension and nervousness. [C20: coined by W. De Beck (1890–1942), American cartoonist]

heed (hiːd) *n* **1** close and careful attention; notice (often in the phrases **give, pay,** *or* **take heed**). ◆ *vb* **2** to pay close attention to (someone or something). [Old English *hēdan;* related to Old Saxon *hōdian,* Old High German *huoten*] ▸ **'heeder** *n* ▸ **'heedful** *adj* ▸ **'heedfully** *adv* ▸ **'heedfulness** *n*

heedless ('hiːdlɪs) *adj* taking little or no notice; careless or thoughtless. ▸ **'heedlessly** *adv* ▸ **'heedlessness** *n*

heehaw (ˌhiː'hɔː) *interj* an imitation or representation of the braying sound of a donkey.

heel[1] (hiːl) *n* **1** the back part of the human foot from the instep to the lower part of the ankle. Compare **calcaneus. 2** the corresponding part in other vertebrates. **3** the part of a shoe, stocking, etc., designed to fit the heel. **4** the outer part of a shoe underneath the heel. **5** the part of the palm of a glove nearest the wrist. **6** the lower, end, or back section of something: *the heel of a loaf.* **7** *Horticulture.* the small part of the parent plant that remains attached to a young shoot cut for propagation and that ensures more successful rooting. **8** *Nautical.* **8a** the bottom of a mast. **8b** the after end of a ship's keel. **9** the back part of a golf club head where it bends to join the shaft. **10** *Rugby.* possession of the ball as obtained from a scrum (esp. in the phrase **get the heel**). **11** *Slang.* a contemptible person. **12 at** (*or* **on**) **one's heels.** just behind or following closely. **13 dig one's heels in.** See **dig in** (sense 5). **14 down at heel. 14a** shabby or worn. **14b** slovenly or careless. **15 kick** (*or* **cool**) **one's heels.** to wait or be kept waiting. **16 rock back on one's heels.** to astonish or be astonished. **17 show a clean pair of heels.** to run off. **18 take to one's heels.** to run off. **19 to heel.** disciplined or under control, as a dog walking by a person's heel. ◆ *vb* **20** (*tr*) to repair or replace the heel of (shoes, boots, etc.). **21** to perform (a dance) with the heels. **22** (*tr*) *Golf.* to strike (the ball) with the heel of the club. **23** *Rugby.* to kick (the ball) backwards using the sole and heel of the boot. **24** to follow at the heels of (a person). **25** (*tr*) to arm (a gamecock) with spurs. **26** (*tr*) *N.Z.* (of a cattle dog) to drive (cattle) by biting their heels. [Old English *hēla;* related to Old Norse *hǣll,* Old Frisian *hêl*] ▸ **'heelless** *adj*

heel[2] (hiːl) *vb* **1** (of a vessel) to lean over; list. ◆ *n* **2** inclined position from the vertical: *the boat is at ten degrees of heel.* [Old English *hieldan;* related to Old Norse *hallr* inclined, Old High German *helden* to bow]

heel-and-toe *adj* **1** of or denoting a style of walking in which the heel of the front foot touches the ground before the toes of the rear one leave it. ◆ *vb* **2** (*intr*) (esp. in motor racing) to use the heel and toe of the same foot to operate the brake and accelerator.

heelball ('hiːlˌbɔːl) *n* **a** a black waxy substance used by shoemakers to blacken the edges of heels and soles. **b** a similar substance used to take rubbings, esp. brass rubbings.

heel bar *n* a small shop or a counter in a department store where shoes are mended while the customer waits.

heel bone *n* the nontechnical name for **calcaneus.**

heeled (hiːld) *adj* **1a** having a heel or heels. **1b** (*in combination*): *high-heeled.* **2 well-heeled.** wealthy.

heeler ('hiːlə) *n* **1** *U.S.* See **ward heeler. 2** a person or thing that heels. **3** *Austral. and N.Z.* a dog that herds cattle by biting at their heels.

heel in *or* (*Dialect*) **hele in** *vb* (*tr, adv*) to insert (cuttings, shoots, etc.) into the soil before planting to keep them moist.

heelpiece ('hiːlˌpiːs) *n* the piece of a shoe, stocking, etc., designed to fit the heel.

heelpost ('hiːlˌpəʊst) *n* a post for carrying the hinges of a door or gate.

heeltap ('hiːlˌtæp) *n* **1** Also called: **lift.** a layer of leather, etc., in the heel of a shoe. **2** a small amount of alcoholic drink left at the bottom of a glass after drinking.

Heerlen ('hɪələn; *Dutch* 'heːrlə) *n* a city in the SE Netherlands, in Limburg province: industrial centre of a coal-mining region. Pop.: 95 794 (1994).

Hefei ('hʌ'feɪ) *or* **Hofei** *n* a city in SE China, capital of Anhui province: administrative and commercial centre in a rice- and cotton-growing region. Pop.: 1 000 000 (1991 est.).

heft (hɛft) *vb* (*tr*) *Brit. dialect and U.S. informal.* **1** to assess the weight of (something) by lifting. **2** to lift. ◆ *n* **3** weight. **4** *U.S.* the main part. [C19: probably from HEAVE, by analogy with *thieve, theft, cleave, cleft*] ▸ **'hefter** *n*

hefty ('hɛftɪ) *adj* **heftier, heftiest.** *Informal.* **1** big and strong. **2** characterized by vigour or force: *a hefty blow.* **3** large, bulky, or heavy. **4** sizable; involving a large amount of money: *a hefty bill; a hefty wage.* ▸ **'heftily** *adv* ▸ **'heftiness** *n*

Hegel ('heɪɡᵊl) *n* **Georg Wilhelm Friedrich** (ɡe'ɔrk 'vɪlhɛlm 'friːdrɪç). 1770–1831, German philosopher, who created a fundamentally influential system of thought. His view of man's mind as the highest expression of the Absolute is expounded in *The Phenomenology of Mind* (1807). He developed his concept of dialectic, in which the contradiction between a proposition (thesis) and its antithesis is resolved at a higher level of truth (synthesis), in *Science of Logic* (1812–16). ▸ **Hegelian** (hɪ'ɡeɪlɪən, heɪ'ɡiː-) *adj* ▸ **He'gelianˌism** *n*

Hegelian dialectic *n Philosophy.* an interpretive method in which the contradiction between a proposition (thesis) and its antithesis is resolved at a higher level of truth (synthesis).

hegemony (hɪ'ɡɛmənɪ) *n, pl* **-nies.** ascendancy or domination of one power or state within a league, confederation, etc., or of one social class over others. [C16: from Greek *hēgemonia* authority, from *hēgemōn* leader, from *hēgeisthai* to lead] ▸ **hegemonic** (ˌhɛɡə'mɒnɪk) *adj*

Hegira *or* **Hejira** ('hɛdʒɪrə) *n* **1** the departure of Mohammed from Mecca to Medina in 622 A.D.; the starting point of the Muslim era. **2** the Muslim era itself. See also **AH. 3** (*often not cap.*) an emigration escape or flight. ◆ Also called: **Hijrah.** [C16: from Medieval Latin, from Arabic *hijrah* emigration or flight]

hegumen (hɪ'ɡjuːmɛn) *or* **hegumenos** (hɪ'ɡjuːmɪˌnəʊs) *n* the head of a monastery of the Eastern Church. [C16: from Medieval Latin *hēgūmenus,* from Late Greek *hēgoumenos* leader, from Greek *hēgeisthai* to lead]

heh (heɪ) *interj* an exclamation of surprise or inquiry.

heid (hi:d) *n* a Scot. word for **head.**

Heidegger (*German* 'haidɛgər) *n* **Martin** ('marti:n). 1889–1976, German existentialist philosopher: he expounded his ontological system in *Being and Time* (1927).

Heidelberg ('haɪdᵊl,bɜ:g; *German* 'haidəlbɛrk) *n* a city in SW Germany, in NW Baden-Württemberg on the River Neckar: capital of the Palatinate from the 13th century until 1719; famous castle (begun in the 12th century) and university (1386), the oldest in Germany. Pop.: 138 781 (1996 est.).

Heidelberg man *n* a type of primitive man, *Homo heidelbergensis,* occurring in Europe in the middle Palaeolithic age, known only from a single fossil lower jaw. [C20: referring to the site where remains were found, at Mauer, near *Heidelberg,* Germany (1907)]

Heiduc ('haɪdʊk) *n* a variant spelling of **Haiduk.**

heifer ('hɛfə) *n* a young cow. [Old English *heahfore;* related to Greek *poris* calf; see HIGH]

Heifetz ('haɪfɪts) *n* **Jascha** ('jæʃə). 1901–87, U.S. violinist, born in Russia.

heigh-ho ('heɪ'həʊ) *interj* an exclamation of weariness, disappointment, surprise, or happiness.

height (haɪt) *n* **1** the vertical distance from the bottom or lowest part of something to the top or apex. **2** the vertical distance of an object or place above the ground or above sea level; altitude. **3** relatively great altitude or distance from the bottom to the top. **4** the topmost point; summit. **5** *Astronomy.* the angular distance of a celestial body above the horizon. **6** the period of greatest activity or intensity: *the height of the battle.* **7** an extreme example of its kind: *the height of rudeness.* **8** (*often pl*) an area of high ground. **9** (*often pl*) the state of being far above the ground: *I don't like heights.* **10** (*often pl*) a position of influence, fame, or power. [Old English *hīehthu;* related to Old Norse *hǣthe,* Gothic *hauhitha,* Old High German *hōhida;* see HIGH]

heighten ('haɪtᵊn) *vb* **1** to make or become high or higher. **2** to make or become more extreme or intense. ► **'heightened** *adj* ► **'heightener** *n*

height of land *n U.S. and Canadian.* a watershed.

height-to-paper *n* the overall height of printing plates and type, standardized as 0.9175 inch (Brit.) and 0.9186 inch (U.S.).

Heilbronn (*German* hail'brɔn) *n* a city in SW Germany, in N Baden-Württemberg on the River Neckar. Pop.: 121 509 (1996 est.).

Heilongjiang ('heɪ'lʊŋdʒaɪ'æŋ) *or* **Heilungkiang** ('heɪ'lʊŋ'kjæŋ, -kaɪ'æŋ) *n* a province of NE China, in Manchuria: coal-mining, with placer gold in some rivers. Capital: Harbin. Pop.: 37 010 000 (1996 est.). Area: 464 000 sq. km (179 000 sq. miles).

Heilong Jiang ('heɪ'lʊŋ 'dʒaɪ'æŋ) *n* the Pinyin transliteration of the Chinese name for the **Amur.**

Heimdall, Heimdal ('heɪm,dɑ:l), *or* **Heimdallr** ('heɪm,dɑ:lə) *n Norse myth.* the god of light and the dawn, and the guardian of the rainbow bridge Bifrost.

Heimlich manoeuvre ('haɪmlɪk) *n* a technique in first aid to dislodge a foreign body in a person's windpipe by applying sudden upward pressure on the upper abdomen. Also called: **abdominal thrust.** [C20: named after Henry J. *Heimlich* (born 1920), American surgeon]

Heine (*German* 'hainə) *n* **Heinrich** ('hainrɪç). 1797–1856, German poet and essayist, whose chief poetic work is *Das Buch der Lieder* (1827). Many of his poems have been set to music, notably by Schubert and Schumann.

Heinkel (*German* 'hainkᵊl) *n* **Ernst Heinrich** (ɛrnst 'hainrɪç). 1888–1958, German aircraft designer. His company provided many military aircraft in World Wars I and II, including the first jet-powered plane.

heinous ('heɪnəs, 'hi:-) *adj* evil; atrocious. [C14: from Old French *haineus,* from *haine* hatred, from *hair* to hate, of Germanic origin; see HATE] ► **'heinously** *adv* ► **'heinousness** *n*

heir (ɛə) *n* **1** *Civil law.* the person legally succeeding to all property of a deceased person, irrespective of whether such person died testate or intestate, and upon whom devolves as well as the rights the duties and liabilities attached to the estate. **2** any person or thing that carries on some tradition, circumstance, etc., from a forerunner. **3** an archaic word for **offspring.** [C13: from Old French, from Latin *hērēs;* related to Greek *khēros* bereaved] ► **'heirless** *adj*

heir apparent *n, pl* **heirs apparent.** *Property law.* a person whose right to succeed to certain property cannot be defeated, provided such person survives his ancestor. Compare **heir presumptive.**

heir-at-law *n, pl* **heirs-at-law.** *Property law.* the person entitled to succeed to the real property of a person who dies intestate.

heirdom ('ɛədəm) *n Property law.* succession by right of blood; inheritance.

heiress ('ɛərɪs) *n* **1** a woman who inherits or expects to inherit great wealth. **2** *Property law.* a female heir.

heirloom ('ɛə,lu:m) *n* **1** an object that has been in a family for generations. **2** *Property law.* an item of personal property inherited by special custom or in accordance with the terms of a will. [C15: from HEIR + *lome* tool; see LOOM¹]

heir presumptive *n Property law.* a person who expects to succeed to an estate but whose right may be defeated by the birth of one nearer in blood to the ancestor. Compare **heir apparent.**

heirship ('ɛəʃɪp) *n Law.* **1** the state or condition of being an heir. **2** the right to inherit; inheritance.

Heisenberg ('haɪzᵊn,bɜ:g; *German* 'haizənbɛrk) *n* **Werner Karl** ('vɛrnər karl). 1901–76, German physicist. He contributed to quantum mechanics and formulated the uncertainty principle (1927): Nobel prize for physics 1932.

Heisenberg uncertainty principle *n* a more formal name for **uncertainty principle.**

heist (haɪst) *Slang, chiefly U.S. and Canadian.* ◆ *n* **1** a robbery. ◆ *vb* **2** (*tr*) to steal or burgle. [variant of HOIST] ► **'heister** *n*

heitiki (heɪ'ti:ki:) *n N.Z.* a Maori neck ornament of greenstone. [C19: from Maori, from *hei* to hang + TIKI]

Heitler (*German* 'haitlər) *n* **Walter** ('valtər). 1904–81, German physicist, noted for his work on chemical bonds.

hejab (hɛ'dʒɑ:b) *n* a variant of **hijab.**

Hejaz, Hedjaz, *or* **Hijaz** (hi:'dʒæz) *n* a region of W Saudi Arabia, along the Red Sea and the Gulf of Aqaba: formerly an independent kingdom; united with Nejd in 1932 to form Saudi Arabia. Area: about 348 600 sq. km (134 600 sq. miles).

Hejira ('hɛdʒɪrə) *n* a variant spelling of **Hegira.**

Hekate ('hɛkətɪ) *n* a variant spelling of **Hecate.**

Hekla ('hɛklə) *n* a volcano in SW Iceland: several craters, with the last eruption in 1970. Height: 1491 m (4892 ft.).

Hel (hɛl) *or* **Hela** ('hɛlɑ:) *n Norse myth.* **1** the goddess of the dead. **2** the underworld realm of the dead.

held (hɛld) *vb* the past tense and past participle of **hold¹.**

Heldentenor *German.* ('hɛldəntenoːr) *n, pl* ***-tenöre*** (-te'nøːrə). a tenor with a powerful voice suited to singing heroic roles, esp. in Wagner. [literally: hero tenor]

hele in *vb* (*tr, adv*) a dialect variant of **heel in.** [Old English *helian* hide]

Helen ('hɛlɪn) *n Greek myth.* the beautiful daughter of Zeus and Leda, whose abduction by Paris from her husband Menelaus caused the Trojan War.

Helena¹ ('hɛlənə) *n* a city in W Montana: the state capital. Pop.: 24 569 (1990).

Helena² (hɛlənə) *n* **Saint.** ?248–?328 A.D., Roman empress, mother of Constantine I. After converting to Christianity (313) she made a pilgrimage to the Holy Land (?1326) where she supposedly discovered the cross on which Christ died. Feast day: May 21.

helenium (hə'li:nɪəm) *n* any plant of the American genus *Helenium,* up to 1.6 m (5 ft.) tall, some species of which are grown as border plants for their daisy-like yellow or variegated flowers: family *Compositae.* [New Latin, from Greek *helenion,* a plant name]

Helgoland ('hɛlgolant) *n* the German name for **Heligoland.**

heli- *combining form.* helicopter: *helipad.* [C20: shortened from HELICOPTER]

heliacal rising (hɪ'laɪəkᵊl) *n* **1** the rising of a celestial object at the same time as the rising of the sun. **2** the date at which such a celestial object first becomes visible in the dawn sky. [C17: from Late Latin *hēliacus* relating to the sun, from Greek *hēliakos,* from *hēlios* the sun]

helianthemum (hi:lɪ'ænθəməm) *n* any plant of the dwarf evergreen genus *Helianthemum,* some species of which are grown as rock-garden plants for their numerous papery yellow or orange flowers; related to the rockrose, which they resemble: family *Cistaceae.* Also called: **Cape primrose.** [New Latin, from Greek *hēlios* sun + *anthemon* flower]

helianthus (,hi:lɪ'ænθəs) *n, pl* **-thuses.** any plant of the genus *Helianthus,* such as the sunflower and Jerusalem artichoke, typically having large yellow daisy-like flowers with yellow, brown, or purple centres: family *Compositae* (composites). [C18: New Latin, from Greek *hēlios* sun + *anthos* flower]

helical ('hɛlɪkᵊl) *adj* of or shaped like a helix; spiral. ► **'helically** *adv*

helical gear *n* a gearwheel having the tooth form generated on a helical path about the axis of the wheel.

helical scan *n* (*modifier*) denoting a recording technique used with video tapes in which the recorded tracks on the tape are segments of a helix: *a helical-scan tape.*

helices ('hɛlɪ,si:z) *n* a plural of **helix.**

helichrysum (,hɛlɪ'kraɪzəm) *n* any plant of the widely cultivated genus *Helichrysum,* whose flowers retain their shape and colour when dried: family *Compositae* (composites). [C16: from Latin, from Greek *helikhrusos,* from *helix* spiral + *khrusos* gold]

helicity (hɪ'lɪsɪtɪ) *n, pl* **-ties.** *Physics.* the projection of the spin of an elementary particle on the direction of propagation. [C20: from HELIX + -ITY]

helicline ('hɛlɪ,klaɪn) *n Architect.* a spiral-shaped ramp. [from HELICO- + -CLINE]

helico- *or before a vowel* **helic-** *combining form.* spiral or helical: *helicograph.* [from Latin, from Greek *helix* spiral]

helicograph ('hɛlɪkəʊ,grɑ:f, -,græf) *n* an instrument for drawing spiral curves.

helicoid ('hɛlɪ,kɔɪd) *adj also* **helicoidal. 1** *Biology.* shaped like a spiral: *a helicoid shell.* ◆ *n* **2** *Geometry.* any surface resembling that of a screw thread. ► **,heli'coidally** *adv*

helicon ('hɛlɪkən) *n* a bass tuba made to coil over the shoulder of a band musician. [C19: probably from HELICON, associated with Greek *helix* spiral]

Helicon ('hɛlɪkən) *n* a mountain in Greece, in Boeotia: location of the springs of Hippocrene and Aganippe, believed by the Ancient Greeks to be the source of poetic inspiration and the home of the Muses. Height: 1749 m (5738 ft.). Modern Greek name: **Elikón.**

helicopter ('hɛlɪ,kɒptə) *n* **1** an aircraft capable of hover, vertical flight, and horizontal flight in any direction. Most get all of their lift and propulsion from the rotation of overhead blades. See also **autogiro.** ◆ *vb* **2** to transport (people or things) or (of people or things) to be transported by helicopter. [C19: from French *hélicoptère,* from HELICO- + Greek *pteron* wing]

helicopter gunship *n* a large heavily armed helicopter used for ground attack.

helideck ('hɛlɪ,dɛk) *n* a landing deck for helicopters on ships, oil platforms, etc. [C20: from HELI- + DECK]

Heligoland ('hɛlɪgəʊ,lænd) *n* a small island in the North Sea, one of the North Frisian Islands, separated from the coast of NW Germany by **Heligoland Bight:** administratively part of the German state of Schleswig-Holstein: a large island in early medieval times, now eroded to an area of about 150 hectares (380 acres); ceded by Britain to Germany in 1890 in exchange for Zanzibar. German name: **Helgoland.**

helio- *or before a vowel* **heli-** *combining form.* indicating the sun: *heliocentric; heliolithic.* [from Greek, from *hēlios* sun]

heliocentric (ˌhiːlɪəʊˈsɛntrɪk) *adj* **1** having the sun at its centre. **2** measured from or in relation to the centre of the sun. ▸ **ˌhelioˈcentrically** *adv* ▸ **heliocentricity** (ˌhiːlɪəʊsɛnˈtrɪsɪtɪ) *or* **heliocentricism** (ˌhiːlɪəʊˈsɛntrɪˌsɪzəm) *n*

heliocentric parallax *n* See **parallax** (sense 2).

Heliochrome (ˈhiːlɪəʊˌkrəʊm) *n Trademark.* a photograph that reproduces the natural colours of the subject. ▸ **ˌhelioˈchromic** *adj*

heliodor (ˈhiːlɪəʊˌdɔː) *n* a clear yellow form of beryl used as a gemstone.

Heliogabalus (ˌhiːlɪəʊˈgæbələs) *or* **Elagabalus** *n* original name *Varius Avitus Bassianus.* ?204–222 A.D., Roman emperor (218–222). His reign was notorious for debauchery and extravagance.

heliograph (ˈhiːlɪəʊˌgrɑːf, -ˌgræf) *n* **1** an instrument with mirrors and a shutter used for sending messages in Morse code by reflecting the sun's rays. **2** a device used to photograph the sun. ▸ **heliographer** (ˌhiːlɪˈɒgrəfə) *n* ▸ **heliographic** (ˌhiːlɪəʊˈgræfɪk) *or* **ˌhelioˈgraphical** *adj* ▸ **ˌheliˈography** *n*

heliolatry (ˌhiːlɪˈɒlətrɪ) *n* worship of the sun. ▸ **ˌheliˈolater** *n* ▸ **ˌheliˈolatrous** *adj*

heliolithic (ˌhiːlɪəʊˈlɪθɪk) *adj* of or relating to a civilization characterized by sun worship and megaliths.

heliometer (ˌhiːlɪˈɒmɪtə) *n* a refracting telescope having a split objective lens that is used to determine very small angular distances between celestial bodies. ▸ **heliometric** (ˌhiːlɪəʊˈmɛtrɪk) *or* **ˌhelioˈmetrical** *adj* ▸ **ˌhelioˈmetrically** *adv* ▸ **ˌheliˈometry** *n*

heliopause (ˈhiːlɪəʊˌpɔːz) *n* the region of space beyond the sun's magnetic field.

heliophyte (ˈhiːlɪəʊˌfaɪt) *n* any plant that grows best in direct sunlight.

Heliopolis (ˌhiːlɪˈɒpəlɪs) *n* **1** (in ancient Egypt) a city near the apex of the Nile delta: a centre of sun worship. Ancient Egyptian name: **On. 2** the Ancient Greek name for **Baalbek.**

Helios (ˈhiːlɪˌɒs) *n Greek myth.* the god of the sun, who drove his chariot daily across the sky. Roman counterpart: **Sol.**

heliosphere (ˈhiːlɪəʊˌsfɪə) *n* the region around the sun taken to be the boundary outside which the sun's influence is negligible and interstellar space begins.

heliostat (ˈhiːlɪəʊˌstæt) *n* an astronomical instrument used to reflect the light of the sun in a constant direction. ▸ **ˌhelioˈstatic** *adj*

heliotaxis (ˌhiːlɪəʊˈtæksɪs) *n* movement of an entire organism in response to the stimulus of sunlight. ▸ **heliotactic** (ˌhiːlɪəʊˈtæktɪk) *adj*

heliotherapy (ˌhiːlɪəʊˈθɛrəpɪ) *n* the therapeutic use of sunlight.

heliotrope (ˈhiːlɪəˌtrəʊp, ˈhɛljə-) *n* **1** any boraginaceous plant of the genus *Heliotropium,* esp. the South American *H. arborescens,* cultivated for its small fragrant purple flowers. **2 garden heliotrope.** a widely cultivated valerian, *Valeriana officinalis,* with clusters of small pink, purple, or white flowers. **3** any of various plants that turn towards the sun. **4a** a bluish-violet to purple colour. **4b** (*as adj*): *a heliotrope dress.* **5** an instrument used in geodetic surveying employing the sun's rays reflected by a mirror as a signal for the sighting of stations over long distances. **6** another name for **bloodstone.** [C17: from Latin *hēliotropium,* from Greek *hēliotropion,* from *hēlios* sun + *trepein* to turn]

heliotropin (ˌhiːlɪˈɒtrəpɪn) *n* another term for **piperonal.**

heliotropism (ˌhiːlɪˈɒtrəˌpɪzəm) *n* the growth of a plant in response to the stimulus of sunlight. ▸ **heliotropic** (ˌhiːlɪəʊˈtrɒpɪk) *adj* ▸ **ˌhelioˈtropically** *adv*

heliotype (ˈhiːlɪəʊˌtaɪp) *n* **1** a printing process in which an impression is taken in ink from a gelatine surface that has been exposed under a negative and prepared for printing. Also called: **heliotypy. 2** the gelatine plate produced by such a process. **3** a print produced from such a plate. ▸ **heliotypic** (ˌhiːlɪəʊˈtɪpɪk) *adj*

heliozoan (ˌhiːlɪəʊˈzəʊən) *n* any protozoan of the mostly freshwater group *Heliozoa,* typically having a siliceous shell and stiff radiating cytoplasmic projections: phylum *Actinopoda* (actinopods).

helipad (ˈhɛlɪˌpæd) *n* a place for helicopters to land and take off. [C20: from HELI- + PAD[1]]

heliport (ˈhɛlɪˌpɔːt) *n* an airport for helicopters. [C20: from HELI- + PORT[1]]

helium (ˈhiːlɪəm) *n* a very light nonflammable colourless odourless element that is an inert gas, occurring in certain natural gases: used in balloons and in cryogenic research. Symbol: He; atomic no.: 2; atomic wt.: 4.002602; density: 0.1785 kg/m^3; at normal pressures it is liquid down to absolute zero; melting pt.: below –272.2°C; boiling pt.: –268.90°C. See also **alpha particle.** [C19: New Latin, from HELIO- + -IUM; named from its having first been detected in the solar spectrum]

helix (ˈhiːlɪks) *n, pl* **helices** (ˈhɛlɪˌsiːz) *or* **helixes. 1** a curve that lies on a cylinder or cone, at a constant angle to the line segments making up the surface; spiral. **2** a spiral shape or form. **3** the incurving fold that forms the margin of the external ear. **4** another name for **volute** (sense 2). **5** any terrestrial gastropod mollusc of the genus *Helix,* which includes the garden snail (*H. aspersa*). [C16: from Latin, from Greek: spiral; probably related to Greek *helissein* to twist]

hell (hɛl) *n* **1** *Christianity.* (*sometimes cap.*) **1a** the place or state of eternal punishment of the wicked after death, with Satan as its ruler. **1b** forces of evil regarded as residing there. **2** (*sometimes cap.*) (in various religions and cultures) the abode of the spirits of the dead. See also **Hel, Hades, Sheol. 3** pain, extreme difficulty, etc. **4** *Informal.* a cause of such difficulty or suffering: *war is hell.* **5** *U.S. and Canadian.* high spirits or mischievousness: *there's hell in that boy.* **6** a box used by a tailor for discarded material. **7** *Now rare.* a gambling house, booth, etc. **8 as hell.** (intensifier): *tired as hell.* **9 for the hell of it.** *Informal.* for the fun of it. **10 from hell.** *Informal.* denoting a person or thing that is particularly bad or alarming: *neighbour from hell; hangover from hell.* **11 give someone hell.** *Informal.* **11a** to give someone a severe reprimand or punishment. **11b** to be a source of annoyance or torment to someone. **12 hell of a** *or* **helluva.** *Informal.* (intensifier): *a hell of a good performance.* **13 hell for leather.** at great speed. **14 (come) hell or high water.** *Informal.* whatever difficulties may arise. **15 hell to pay.** *Informal.* serious consequences, as of a foolish action. **16 like hell.** *Informal.* **16a** (*adv*) (intensifier): *he works like hell.* **16b** an expression of strong disagreement with a previous statement, request, order, etc. **17 play (merry) hell with.** *Informal.* to throw into confusion and disorder; disrupt. **18 raise hell. 18a** to create a noisy disturbance, as in fun. **18b** to react strongly and unfavourably. **19 the hell.** *Informal.* **19a** (intensifier): used in such phrases as **what the hell, who the hell,** etc. **19b** an expression of strong disagreement or disfavour: *the hell I will.* See **like hell.** ♦ *interj* **20** *Informal.* an exclamation of anger, annoyance, surprise, etc. (Also in exclamations such as **hell's bells, hell's teeth,** etc.). [Old English *hell;* related to *helan* to cover, Old Norse *hel,* Gothic *halja* hell, Old High German *hella*]

he'll (hiːl; *unstressed* iːl, hɪl, ɪl) *contraction of* he will *or* he shall.

hellacious (hɛˈleɪʃəs) *adj U.S. slang.* **1** remarkable; horrifying. **2** wonderful; excellent. [C20: from HELL + *-acious* as in AUDACIOUS]

Helladic (hɛˈlædɪk) *adj* of, characteristic of, or related to the Bronze Age civilization that flourished about 2900 to 1100 B.C. on the Greek mainland and islands.

Hellas (ˈhɛləs) *n* transliteration of the Ancient Greek name for **Greece.**

hellbender (ˈhɛlˌbɛndə) *n* a very large dark grey aquatic salamander, *Cryptobranchus alleganiensis,* with internal gills: inhabits rivers in E and central U.S.: family *Cryptobranchidae.*

hellbent (ˌhɛlˈbɛnt) *adj* (*postpositive* and foll. by *on*) *Informal.* strongly or rashly intent.

hellcat (ˈhɛlˌkæt) *n* a spiteful fierce-tempered woman.

helldiver (ˈhɛlˌdaɪvə) *n U.S. informal.* a small greyish-brown North American grebe, *Podilymbus podiceps,* with a small bill. Also called: **pied-billed grebe, dabchick.**

Helle (ˈhɛlɪ) *n Greek myth.* a daughter of King Athamas, who was borne away with her brother Phrixus on the golden winged ram. She fell from its back and was drowned in the Hellespont. See also **Phrixus, Golden Fleece.**

hellebore (ˈhɛlɪˌbɔː) *n* **1** any plant of the Eurasian ranunculaceous genus *Helleborus,* esp. *H. niger* (black hellebore), typically having showy flowers and poisonous parts. See also **Christmas rose. 2** any of various liliaceous plants of the N temperate genus *Veratrum,* esp. *V. album,* that have greenish flowers and yield alkaloids used in the treatment of heart disease. [C14: from Greek *helleboros,* of uncertain origin]

helleborine (ˌhɛlɪˈbɔːriːn) *n* any of various N temperate orchids of the genera *Cephalanthera* and *Epipactis.* [C16: ultimately from Greek *helleborinē* a plant resembling hellebore]

Hellen (ˈhɛlɪn) *n* (in Greek legend) a Thessalian king and eponymous ancestor of the Hellenes.

Hellene (ˈhɛliːn) *or* **Hellenian** (hɛˈliːnɪən) *n* another name for a **Greek.**

Hellenic (hɛˈlɛnɪk, -ˈliː-) *adj* **1** of or relating to the ancient or modern Greeks or their language. **2** of or relating to ancient Greece or the Greeks of the classical period (776–323 B.C.). Compare **Hellenistic. 3** another word for **Greek.** ♦ *n* **4** a branch of the Indo-European family of languages consisting of Greek in its various ancient and modern dialects. ▸ **Helˈlenically** *adv*

Hellenism (ˈhɛlɪˌnɪzəm) *n* **1** the principles, ideals, and pursuits associated with classical Greek civilization. **2** the spirit or national character of the Greeks. **3** conformity to, imitation of, or devotion to the culture of ancient Greece. **4** the cosmopolitan civilization of the Hellenistic world.

Hellenist (ˈhɛlɪnɪst) *n* **1** Also called: **Hellenizer.** (in the Hellenistic world) a non-Greek, esp. a Jew, who adopted Greek culture. **2** a student of the Greek civilization or language.

Hellenistic (ˌhɛlɪˈnɪstɪk) *or* **Hellenistical** *adj* **1** characteristic of or relating to Greek civilization in the Mediterranean world, esp. from the death of Alexander the Great (323 B.C.) to the defeat of Antony and Cleopatra (30 B.C.). **2** of or relating to the Greeks or to Hellenism. ▸ **ˌHellenˈistically** *adv*

Hellenize *or* **Hellenise** (ˈhɛlɪˌnaɪz) *vb* to make or become like the ancient Greeks. ▸ **ˌHelleniˈzation** *or* **ˌHelleniˈsation** *n* ▸ **ˈHellenˌizer** *or* **ˈHellenˌiser** *n*

heller[1] (ˈhɛlə) *n, pl* **-ler. 1** any of various old German or Austrian coins of low denomination. **2** another word for **haler.** [from German, after *Hall,* town in Swabia where the coins were minted]

heller[2] (ˈhɛlə) *n* another word for **hellion.**

Heller (ˈhɛlə) *n* **Joseph.** born 1923, U.S. novelist. His works include *Catch 22* (1961), *God Knows* (1984), *Picture This* (1988), and *Closing Time* (1994).

hellery (ˈhɛlərɪ) *n Canadian slang, rare.* wild or mischievous behaviour.

Helles (ˈhɛlɪs) *n* **Cape.** a cape in NW Turkey, at the S end of the Gallipoli Peninsula.

Hellespont (ˈhɛlɪˌspɒnt) *n* the ancient name for the **Dardanelles.**

hellfire (ˈhɛlˌfaɪə) *n* **1** the torment and punishment of hell, envisaged as eternal fire. **2** (*modifier*) characterizing sermons or preachers that emphasize this aspect of Christian belief.

hellgrammite (ˈhɛlgrəˌmaɪt) *n U.S.* the larva of the dobsonfly, about 10 cm long with biting mouthparts: used as bait for bass. Also called: **dobson.** [C19: of unknown origin]

hellhole (ˈhɛlˌhəʊl) *n* an unpleasant or evil place.

hellhound (ˈhɛlˌhaʊnd) *n* **1** a hound of hell. **2** a fiend.

hellion (ˈhɛljən) *n U.S. informal.* a rough or rowdy person, esp. a child; troublemaker. Also called: **heller.** [C19: probably from dialect *hallion* rogue, of unknown origin]

hellish (ˈhɛlɪʃ) *adj* **1** of or resembling hell. **2** wicked; cruel. **3** *Informal.* very difficult or unpleasant. ♦ *adv* **4** *Brit. informal.* (intensifier): *a hellish good idea.* ▸ **ˈhellishly** *adv* ▸ **ˈhellishness** *n*

Hellman (ˈhɛlmən) *n* **Lillian.** 1905–84, U.S. dramatist. Her works include the plays *The Little Foxes* (1939), *The Searching Wind* (1944), and the autobiographical *Scoundrel Time* (1976).

hello, hallo, *or* **hullo** (hɛˈləʊ, hə-; ˈhɛləʊ) *sentence substitute.* **1** an expression of greeting used on meeting a person or at the start of a telephone call. **2** a call used to attract attention. **3** an expression of surprise. ◆ *n, pl* **-los. 4** the act of saying or calling "hello". **[**C19: see HALLO**]**

Hell's Angel *n* a member of a motorcycle gang of a kind originating in the U.S. in the 1950s, who typically dress in denim and Nazi-style paraphernalia and are noted for their initiation rites, lawless behaviour, etc.

helluva (ˈhɛləvə) *adv, adj Informal.* (intensifier): *a helluva difficult job; he's a helluva guy.*

helm[1] (hɛlm) *n* **1** *Nautical.* **1a** the wheel, tiller, or entire apparatus by which a vessel is steered. **1b** the position of the helm: that is, on the side of the keel opposite from that of the rudder. **2** a position of leadership or control (esp. in the phrase **at the helm**). ◆ *vb* **3** (*tr*) to direct or steer. **[**Old English *helma;* related to Old Norse *hjalm* rudder, Old High German *halmo***]** ► **ˈhelmless** *adj*

helm[2] (hɛlm) *n* **1** an archaic or poetic word for **helmet.** ◆ *vb* **2** (*tr*) *Archaic or poetic.* to supply with a helmet. **[**Old English *helm;* related to *helan* to cover, Old Norse *hjalmr,* Gothic *hilms,* Old High German *helm* helmet, Sanskrit *śárman* protection**]**

Helmand (ˈhɛlmənd) *n* a river in S Asia, rising in E Afghanistan and flowing generally southwest to a marshy lake, Hamun Helmand, on the border with Iran. Length: 1400 km (870 miles).

helmet (ˈhɛlmɪt) *n* **1** a piece of protective or defensive armour for the head worn by soldiers, policemen, firemen, divers, etc. **2** *Biol.* a part or structure resembling a helmet, esp. the upper part of the calyx of certain flowers. **[**C15: from Old French, diminutive of *helme,* of Germanic origin**]** ► **ˈhelmeted** *adj*

Helmholtz (*German* ˈhɛlmhɔlts) *n* Baron **Hermann Ludwig Ferdinand von** (ˈhɛrman ˈluːtvɪç ˈfɛrdinant fɔn). 1821–94, German physiologist, physicist, and mathematician: helped to found the theory of the conservation of energy; invented the ophthalmoscope (1850); and investigated the mechanics of sight and sound.

Helmholtz function *n* a thermodynamic property of a system equal to the difference between its internal energy and the product of its temperature and its entropy. Symbol: *A* or *F* Also called: **Helmholtz free energy. [**C20: named after Baron Hermann Ludwig Ferdinand von HELMHOLTZ**]**

helminth (ˈhɛlmɪnθ) *n* any parasitic worm, esp. a nematode or fluke. **[**C19: from Greek *helmins* parasitic worm**]** ► **helminthoid** (ˈhɛlmɪnˌθɔɪd, hɛlˈmɪnθɔɪd) *adj*

helminthiasis (ˌhɛlmɪnˈθaɪəsɪs) *n* infestation of the body with parasitic worms. **[**C19: from New Latin, from Greek *helminthian* to be infested with worms**]**

helminthic (hɛlˈmɪnθɪk) *adj* **1** of, relating to, or caused by parasitic worms. ◆ *n, adj* **2** another word for **vermifuge.**

helminthology (ˌhɛlmɪnˈθɒlədʒɪ) *n* the study of parasitic worms. ► **helminthological** (ˌhɛlmɪnθəˈlɒdʒɪkˀl) *adj* ► **ˌhelminˈthologist** *n*

Helmont (*Flemish* ˈhɛlmɔnt) *n* **Jean Baptiste van** (ʒɑ̃ batist vɑn). 1577–1644, Flemish chemist and physician. He was the first to distinguish gases and claimed to have coined the word *gas.*

helmsman (ˈhɛlmzmən) *n, pl* **-men.** the person at the helm who steers the ship; steersman.

Héloïse (ˈɛləʊˌiːz; *French* elɔiz) *n* ?1101–64, pupil, mistress, and wife of Abelard.

helophyte (ˈhɛləfaɪt) *n* any perennial marsh plant that bears its overwintering buds in the mud below the surface. **[**C20: from Modern Greek *helos* marsh + -PHYTE**]**

Helot (ˈhɛlət, ˈhiː-) *n* **1** (in ancient Greece, esp. Sparta) a member of the class of unfree men above slaves owned by the state. **2** (*usually not cap.*) a serf or slave. **[**C16: from Latin *Hēlotēs,* from Greek *Heilōtes,* alleged to have meant originally: inhabitants of Helos, who, after its conquest, were serfs of the Spartans**]**

helotism (ˈhɛləˌtɪzəm, ˈhiː-) *n* **1** the condition or quality of being a Helot. **2** a sociopolitical system in which a class, minority, nation, etc., is held in a state of subjection. **3** *Zoology.* another name for **dulosis.** ◆ Also called (for senses 1, 2): **helotage.**

helotry (ˈhɛlətrɪ, ˈhiː-) *n* **1** serfdom or slavery. **2** serfs or slaves as a class.

help (hɛlp) *vb* **1** to assist or aid (someone to do something), esp. by sharing the work, cost, or burden of something: *he helped his friend to escape; she helped him climb out of the boat.* **2** to alleviate the burden of (someone else) by giving assistance. **3** (*tr*) to assist (a person) to go in a specified direction: *help the old lady up from the chair.* **4** to promote or contribute to: *to help the relief operations.* **5** to cause improvement in (a situation, person, etc.): *crying won't help.* **6** (*tr;* preceded by *can, could,* etc.; *usually used with a negative*) **6a** to avoid or refrain from: *we can't help wondering who he is.* **6b** (usually foll. by *it*) to prevent or be responsible for: *I can't help it if it rains.* **7** to alleviate (an illness, etc.). **8** (*tr*) to serve (a customer): *can I help you, madam?* **9** (*tr;* foll. by *to*) **9a** to serve (someone with food, etc.) (usually in the phrase **help oneself**): *may I help you to some more vegetables? help yourself to peas.* **9b** to provide (oneself with) without permission: *he's been helping himself to money out of the petty cash.* **10 cannot help but.** to be unable to do anything else except: *I cannot help but laugh.* **11 help a person on** *or* **off with.** to assist a person in the putting on or removal of (clothes). **12 so help me. 12a** on my honour. **12b** no matter what: *so help me, I'll get revenge.* ◆ *n* **13** the act of helping, or being helped, or a person or thing that helps: *she's a great help.* **14** a helping. **15a** a person hired for a job; employee, esp. a farm worker or domestic servant. **15b** (*functioning as sing*) several employees collectively. **16** a means of remedy: *there's no help for it.* ◆ *interj* **17** used to ask for assistance. ◆ See also **help out. [**Old English *helpan;* related to Old Norse *hjalpa,* Gothic *hilpan,* Old High German *helfan***]** ► **ˈhelpable** *adj* ► **ˈhelper** *n*

helpful (ˈhɛlpful) *adj* serving a useful function; giving help. ► **ˈhelpfully** *adv* ► **ˈhelpfulness** *n*

helping (ˈhɛlpɪŋ) *n* a single portion of food taken at a meal.

helping hand *n* assistance: *many people lent a helping hand in making arrangements for the party.*

helpless (ˈhɛlplɪs) *adj* **1** unable to manage independently. **2** made powerless or weak: *they were helpless from so much giggling.* **3** without help. ► **ˈhelplessly** *adv* ► **ˈhelplessness** *n*

helpline (ˈhɛlpˌlaɪn) *n* **1** a telephone line operated by a charitable organization for people in distress. **2** a telephone line operated by a commercial organization to provide information.

Helpmann (ˈhɛlpmən) *n* Sir **Robert.** 1909–86, Australian ballet dancer and choreographer: his ballets include *Miracle in the Gorbals* (1944), *Display* (1965), and *Yugen* (1965).

helpmate (ˈhɛlpˌmeɪt) *n* a companion and helper, esp. a wife.

helpmeet (ˈhɛlpˌmiːt) *n* a less common word for **helpmate. [**C17: from the phrase *an helpe meet* (suitable) *for him* Genesis 2:18**]**

help out *vb* (*adv*) **1** to assist or aid (someone), esp. by sharing the burden. **2** to share the burden or cost of something with (another person).

help screens *pl n* computer instructions displayed on a visual display unit.

Helsingborg (*Swedish* hɛlsiŋˈbɔrj) *n* a port in SW Sweden, on the Sound opposite Helsingør, Denmark: changed hands several times between Denmark and Sweden, finally becoming Swedish in 1710; shipbuilding. Pop.: 114 866 (1997 est.). Former name (until 1971): **Hälsingborg.**

Helsingør (*Danish* hɛlseŋˈøːr) *n* a port in NE Denmark, in NE Zealand: site of Kronborg Castle (16th century), famous as the scene of Shakespeare's *Hamlet.* Pop.: 56 855 (1995). English name: **Elsinore.**

Helsinki (ˈhɛlsɪŋkɪ, hɛlˈsɪŋ-) *n* the capital of Finland, a port in the south on the Gulf of Finland: founded by Gustavus I of Sweden in 1550; replaced Turku as capital in 1812, while under Russian rule; university. Pop.: 532 053 (1997 est.). Swedish name: **Helsingfors** (hɛlsɪŋˈfɔrs).

helter-skelter (ˈhɛltəˈskɛltə) *adj* **1** haphazard or carelessly hurried. ◆ *adv* **2** in a helter-skelter manner. ◆ *n* **3** *Brit.* a high spiral slide, as at a fairground. **4** disorder or haste. **[**C16: probably of imitative origin**]**

helve (hɛlv) *n* **1** the handle of a hand tool such as an axe or pick. ◆ *vb* **2** (*tr*) to fit a helve to (a tool). **[**Old English *hielfe;* related to Old Saxon *hèlvi,* Old High German *halb,* Lithuanian *kìlpa* stirrup; see HALTER**]**

Helvellyn (hɛlˈvɛlɪn) *n* a mountain in NW England, in the Lake District. Height: 950 m (3118 ft.).

Helvetia (hɛlˈviːʃə) *n* **1** the Latin name for Switzerland. **2** a Roman province in central Europe (1st century B.C. to the 5th century A.D.), corresponding to part of S Germany and parts of W and N Switzerland.

Helvetian (hɛlˈviːʃən) *adj* **1** of or relating to the Helvetii. **2** another word for **Swiss.** ◆ *n* **3** a native or citizen of Switzerland. **4** a member of the Helvetii.

Helvetic (hɛlˈvɛtɪk) *adj* **1** Helvetian or Swiss. **2** of or relating to the Helvetic Confessions or to Swiss Protestantism. ◆ *n* **3** a Swiss Protestant or reformed Calvinist who subscribes to one of the two **Helvetic Confessions** (of faith) formulated in 1536 and 1566.

Helvetii (hɛlˈviːʃɪˌaɪ) *pl n* a Celtic tribe from SW Germany who settled in Helvetia from about 200 B.C.

Helvétius (hɛlˈviːʃɪəs; *French* ɛlvesjys) *n* **Claude Adrien** (klod adriɛ̃). 1715–71, French philosopher. In his chief work *De l'Esprit* (1758), he asserted that the mainspring of human action is self-interest and that differences in human intellects are due only to differences in education.

hem[1] (hɛm) *n* **1** an edge to a piece of cloth, made by folding the raw edge under and stitching it down. **2** short for **hemline.** ◆ *vb* **hems, hemming, hemmed.** (*tr*) **3** to provide with a hem. **4** (usually foll. by *in, around,* or *about*) to enclose or confine. **[**Old English *hemm;* related to Old Frisian *hemme* enclosed land**]**

hem[2] (hɛm) *n, interj* **1** a representation of the sound of clearing the throat, used to gain attention, express hesitation, etc. ◆ *vb* **hems, hemming, hemmed. 2** (*intr*) to utter this sound. **3 hem** (*or* **hum**) **and haw.** to hesitate in speaking or in making a decision.

hem- *combining form.* a U.S. variant of **haemo-** before a vowel.

hema- *combining form.* a U.S. variant of **haemo-.**

he-man *n, pl* **-men.** *Informal.* a strongly built muscular man.

hematite (ˈhɛmətaɪt) *or* **haematite** (ˈhɛmətaɪt, ˈhiːm-) *n* a red, grey, or black mineral, found as massive beds and in veins and igneous rocks. It is the chief source of iron. Composition: iron (ferric) oxide. Formula: Fe_2O_3. Crystal structure: hexagonal (rhombohedral). **[**C16: via Latin from Greek *haimatitēs* resembling blood, from *haima* blood**]** ► **hematitic** *or* **haematitic** (ˌhɛməˈtɪtɪk, ˌhiː-) *adj*

hemato- *or before a vowel* **hemat-** *combining form.* U.S. variants of **haemato-.**

Hemel Hempstead (ˈhɛməl ˈhɛmstɪd) *n* a town in SE England, in W Hertfordshire: designated a new town in 1947. Pop.: 79 235 (1991).

hemelytron (hɛˈmɛlɪˌtrɒn) *or* **hemielytron** *n, pl* **-tra** (-trə). the forewing of plant bugs and related insects, having a thickened base and a membranous apex. **[**C19: from New Latin *hemielytron,* from HEMI- + Greek *elutron* a covering**]** ► **hemˈelytral** *or* **ˌhemiˈelytral** *adj*

hemeralopia (ˌhɛmərəˈləʊpɪə) *n* inability to see clearly in bright light. Nontechnical name: **day blindness.** Compare **nyctalopia. [**C18: New Latin, from Greek *hēmeralōps,* from *hēmera* day + *alaos* blind + *ōps* eye**]** ► **hemeralopic** (ˌhɛmərəˈlɒpɪk) *adj*

hemerocallis (ˌhɛmərəʊˈkælɪs) *n* See **day lily. [**from Greek *hemera* day + *kallos* beautiful**]**

hemi- *prefix* half: *hemicycle; hemisphere.* Compare **demi-** (sense 1), **semi-** (sense 1). **[**from Latin, from Greek *hēmi-***]**

-hemia *n combining form.* U.S. variant of **-aemia.**

hemialgia (ˌhɛmɪˈældʒɪə) *n* pain limited to one side of the body.

hemianopia (ˌhɛmɪænˈəʊpɪə) *n* loss of vision in either the whole left or the whole right half of the field of vision. Also called: **hemianopsia** (ˌhɛmɪænˈɒpsɪə). [C19: from HEMI- + AN- + Greek *opsis* sight]

hemicellulose (ˌhɛmɪˈsɛljʊˌləʊz) *n* any of a group of plant polysaccharides that occur chiefly in the cell wall.

hemichordate (ˌhɛmɪˈkɔːˌdeɪt) *n* **1** any small wormlike marine animal of the subphylum *Hemichordata* (or *Hemichorda*), having numerous gill slits in the pharynx: phylum *Chordata* (chordates). ◆ *adj* **2** of, relating to, or belonging to the subphylum *Hemichordata*. ◆ See also **acorn worm.**

hemicryptophyte (ˌhɛmɪˈkrɪptəfaɪt) *n* any perennial plant that bears its overwintering buds at soil level, where they are often partly covered by surface debris. [C20: HEMI- + CRYPTOPHYTE]

hemicrystalline (ˌhɛmɪˈkrɪstəˌlaɪn) *adj* (of igneous rocks) having both glass and crystalline components. Also: **hypocrystalline.** Compare **holocrystalline.**

hemicycle (ˈhɛmɪˌsaɪkᵊl) *n* **1** a semicircular structure, room, arena, wall, etc. **2** a rare word for **semicircle.** ▶ **hemicyclic** (ˌhɛmɪˈsaɪklɪk, -ˈsɪk-) *adj*

hemidemisemiquaver (ˌhɛmɪˌdɛmɪˈsɛmɪˌkweɪvə) *n Music.* a note having the time value of one sixty-fourth of a semibreve. Usual U.S. and Canadian name: **sixty-fourth note.**

hemielytron (ˌhɛmɪˈɛlɪˌtrɒn) *n, pl* **-tra** (-trə). a variant of **hemelytron.** ▶ ˌ**hemiˈelytral** *adj*

hemihedral (ˌhɛmɪˈhiːdrəl) *adj* (of a crystal) exhibiting only half the number of planes necessary for complete symmetry.

hemihydrate (ˌhɛmɪˈhaɪdreɪt) *n Chem.* a hydrate in which there are two molecules of substance to every molecule of water. ▶ ˌ**hemiˈhydrated** *adj*

hemimorphic (ˌhɛmɪˈmɔːfɪk) *adj* (of a crystal) having different forms at each end of an axis. ▶ ˌ**hemiˈmorphism** *or* ˈ**hemiˌmorphy** *n*

hemimorphite (ˌhɛmɪˈmɔːfaɪt) *n* a white mineral consisting of hydrated zinc silicate in orthorhombic crystalline form: a common ore of zinc. Formula: $Zn_4Si_2O_7(OH)_2.H_2O$.

Hemingway (ˈhɛmɪŋˌweɪ) *n* **Ernest.** 1899–1961, U.S. novelist and short-story writer. His novels include *The Sun Also Rises* (1926), *A Farewell to Arms* (1929), *For Whom the Bell Tolls* (1940), and *The Old Man and the Sea* (1952): Nobel prize for literature 1954.

hemiola (ˌhɛmɪˈəʊlə) *or* **hemiolia** *n Music.* a rhythmic device involving the superimposition of, for example, two notes in the time of three. Also called: **sesquialtera.** [New Latin, from Greek *hēmiolia* ratio of one to one and a half, from HEMI- + (*h*)*olos* whole] ▶ **hemiolic** (ˌhɛmɪˈɒlɪk) *adj*

hemiparasite (ˌhɛmɪˈpærɪˌsaɪt) *or* **semiparasite** *n* **1** a parasitic plant, such as mistletoe, that carries out photosynthesis but also obtains food from its host. **2** an organism that can live independently or parasitically.

hemiplegia (ˌhɛmɪˈpliːdʒɪə) *n* paralysis of one side of the body, usually as the result of injury to the brain. Compare **paraplegia, quadriplegia.** ▶ ˌ**hemiˈplegic** *adj*

hemipode (ˈhɛmɪˌpəʊd) *or* **hemipod** (ˈhɛmɪˌpɒd) *n* other names for **button quail.**

hemipteran (hɪˈmɪptərən) *n* **1** Also called: **hemipteron** (hɪˈmɪptəˌrɒn) any hemipterous insect. ◆ *adj* **2** another word for **hemipterous.** [C19: from HEMI- + Greek *pteron* wing]

hemipterous (hɪˈmɪptərəs) *or* **hemipteran** *adj* of, relating to, or belonging to the *Hemiptera*, a large order of insects having sucking or piercing mouthparts specialized as a beak (rostrum). The group is divided into the suborders *Homoptera* (aphids, cicadas, etc.) and *Heteroptera* (water bugs, bedbugs, etc.).

hemisphere (ˈhɛmɪˌsfɪə) *n* **1** one half of a sphere. **2a** half of the terrestrial globe, divided into **northern** and **southern hemispheres** by the equator or into **eastern** and **western hemispheres** by some meridians, usually 0° and 180°. **2b** a map or projection of one of the hemispheres. **3** either of the two halves of the celestial sphere that lie north or south of the celestial equator. **4** *Anatomy.* short for **cerebral hemisphere.** ▶ **hemispheric** (ˌhɛmɪˈsfɛrɪk) *or* ˌ**hemiˈspherical** *adj*

hemispheroid (ˌhɛmɪˈsfɪərɔɪd) *n* half of a spheroid. ▶ ˌ**hemispherˈoidal** *adj*

hemistich (ˈhɛmɪˌstɪk) *n Prosody.* a half line of verse.

hemiterpene (ˌhɛmɪˈtɜːpiːn) *n* any of a class of simple unsaturated hydrocarbons, such as isoprene, having the formula C_5H_8.

hemitrope (ˈhɛmɪˌtrəʊp) *n Chem.* another name for **twin** (sense 3). ▶ **hemitropic** (ˌhɛmɪˈtrɒpɪk) *adj* ▶ ˌ**hemiˈtropism** *or* **hemitropy** (hiːˈmɪtrəpɪ) *n*

hemizygous (ˌhɛmɪˈzaɪgəs) *adj Genetics.* (of a chromosome or gene) not having a homologue; not paired in a diploid cell.

hemline (ˈhɛmˌlaɪn) *n* the level to which the hem of a skirt or dress hangs; hem: *knee-length hemlines.*

hemlock (ˈhɛmˌlɒk) *n* **1** an umbelliferous poisonous Eurasian plant, *Conium maculatum*, having finely divided leaves, spotted stems, and small white flowers. U.S. name: **poison hemlock.** See also **water hemlock. 2** a poisonous drug derived from this plant. **3** Also called: **hemlock spruce.** any coniferous tree of the genus *Tsuga*, of North America and E Asia, having short flat needles: family *Pinaceae*. See also **western hemlock. 4** the wood of any of these trees, used for lumber and as a source of wood pulp. [Old English *hymlic;* perhaps related to *hymele* hop plant, Middle Low German *homele*, Old Norwegian *humli*, Old Slavonic *chŭmeli*]

hemmer (ˈhɛmə) *n* an attachment on a sewing machine for hemming.

hemo- *combining form.* a U.S. variant of **haemo-.**

hemp (hɛmp) *n* **1** Also called: **cannabis, marijuana.** an annual strong-smelling Asian moraceous plant, *Cannabis sativa*, having tough fibres, deeply lobed leaves, and small greenish flowers. See also **Indian hemp. 2** the fibre of this plant, used to make canvas, rope, etc. **3** any of several narcotic drugs obtained from some varieties of this plant, esp. from Indian hemp. See **bhang, cannabis, hashish, marijuana.** ◆ See also **bowstring hemp.** [Old English *hænep;* related to Old Norse *hampr*, Old High German *hanaf*, Greek *kannabis*, Dutch *hennep*] ▶ ˈ**hempen** *or* ˈ**hempˌlike** *adj*

hemp agrimony *n* a Eurasian plant, *Eupatorium cannabinum*, with small clusters of reddish flowers: family *Compositae* (composites).

hemp nettle *n* **1** a hairy weedy plant, *Galeopsis tetrahit*, of northern regions, having helmet-shaped pink, purple, and white flowers and toothed leaves: family *Labiatae* (labiates). **2** any of various other plants of the genus *Galeopsis*.

hemstitch (ˈhɛmˌstɪtʃ) *n* **1** a decorative edging stitch, usually for a hem, in which the cross threads are stitched in groups. ◆ *vb* **2** to decorate (a hem, etc.) with hemstitches. ▶ ˈ**hemˌstitcher** *n*

hen (hɛn) *n* **1** the female of any bird, esp. the adult female of the domestic fowl. **2** the female of certain other animals, such as the lobster. **3** *Informal.* a woman regarded as gossipy or foolish. **4** *Scot. dialect.* a term of address (often affectionate), used to women and girls. **5 scarce as a hen's teeth.** extremely rare. [Old English *henn;* related to Old High German *henna*, Old Frisian *henne*]

Henan (ˈhʌˈnæn) *or* **Honan** *n* a province of N central China: the chief centre of early Chinese culture; mainly agricultural (the largest wheat-producing province in China). Capital: Zhengzhou. Pop.: 91 000 000 (1996 est.).

hen-and-chickens *n, pl* **hens-and-chickens.** (*functioning as sing or pl*) any of several plants, such as the houseleek and ground ivy, that produce many offsets or runners.

henbane (ˈhɛnˌbeɪn) *n* a poisonous solanaceous Mediterranean plant, *Hyoscyamus niger*, with sticky hairy leaves and funnel-shaped greenish flowers: yields the drug hyoscyamine.

henbit (ˈhɛnˌbɪt) *n* a plant, *Lamium amplexicaule*, that is native to Europe and has toothed opposite leaves and small dark red flowers: family *Labiatae* (labiates).

hence (hɛns) *sentence connector.* **1** for this reason; following from this; therefore. ◆ *adv* **2** from this time: *a year hence.* **3** *Archaic.* **3a** from here or from this world; away. **3b** from this origin or source. ◆ *interj* **4** *Archaic.* begone! away! [Old English *hionane;* related to Old High German *hinana* away from here, Old Irish *cen* on this side]

henceforth (ˈhɛnsˈfɔːθ), **henceforwards,** *or* **henceforward** *adv* from this time forward; from now on.

henchman (ˈhɛntʃmən) *n, pl* **-men. 1** a faithful attendant or supporter. **2** *Archaic.* a squire; page. [C14 *hengestman*, from Old English *hengest* stallion + MAN; related to Old Norse *hestr* horse, Old High German *hengist* gelding]

hencoop (ˈhɛnˌkuːp) *n* a cage for poultry.

hendeca- *combining form.* eleven: *hendecagon; hendecahedron; hendecasyllable.* [from Greek *hendeka*, from *hen*, neuter of *heis* one + *deka* ten]

hendecagon (hɛnˈdɛkəgən) *n* a polygon having 11 sides. ▶ **hendecagonal** (ˌhɛndɪˈkægənᵊl) *adj*

hendecahedron (ˌhɛndɛkəˈhɛdrən, -ˈhiːdrən) *n, pl* **-drons** *or* **-dra** (-drə). a solid figure having 11 plane faces. See also **polyhedron.**

hendecasyllable (ˈhɛndɛkəˌsɪləbᵊl) *n Prosody.* a verse line of 11 syllables. [C18: via Latin from Greek *hendekasullabos*] ▶ **hendecasyllabic** (hɛnˌdɛkəsɪˈlæbɪk) *adj*

Henderson (ˈhɛndəsən) *n* **Arthur.** 1863–1935, British Labour politician. As foreign secretary (1929–31) he supported the League of Nations and international disarmament; Nobel peace prize 1934.

hendiadys (hɛnˈdaɪədɪs) *n* a rhetorical device by which two nouns joined by a conjunction, usually *and*, are used instead of a noun and a modifier, as in *to run with fear and haste* instead of *to run with fearful haste.* [C16: from Medieval Latin, changed from Greek phrase *hen dia duoin*, literally: one through two]

Hendrix (ˈhɛndrɪks) *n* **Jimi,** full name *James Marshall Hendrix.* 1942–70, U.S. rock guitarist, singer, and songwriter, noted for his innovative guitar technique. His recordings include "Purple Haze" (1967) and *Are you Experienced?* (1967).

Hendry (ˈhɛndrɪ) *n* **Stephen.** born 1969, British snooker player: world champion 1990, 1992, 1996, and 1999.

henequen, henequin, *or* **heniquen** (ˈhɛnɪkɪn) *n* **1** an agave plant, *Agave fourcroydes*, that is native to Yucatán. **2** the fibre of this plant, used in making rope, twine, and coarse fabrics. [C19: from American Spanish *henequén*, probably of Taino origin]

henge (hɛndʒ) *n* a circular area, often containing a circle of stones or sometimes wooden posts, dating from the Neolithic and Bronze Ages. [back formation from STONEHENGE]

Hengelo (*Dutch* ˈhɛŋəloː) *n* a city in the E Netherlands, in Overijssel province on the Twente Canal: industrial centre, esp. for textiles. Pop.: 77 514 (1994).

Hengist (ˈhɛŋgɪst) *n* died ?488 A.D., a leader, with his brother Horsa, of the first Jutish settlers in Britain; he is thought to have conquered Kent (?455).

Hengyang (ˈhɛŋˈjæŋ) *n* a city in SE central China, in Hunan province on the Xiang River. Pop.: 487 148 (1990 est.).

hen harrier *n* a common harrier, *Circus cyaneus*, that flies over fields and marshes and nests in marshes and open land. U.S. and Canadian names: **marsh hawk, marsh harrier.**

henhouse (ˈhɛnˌhaʊs) *n* a coop for hens.

Henie (ˈhɛnɪ) *n* **Sonja** (ˈsɒnjə). 1912–69, Norwegian figure-skater.

Henle's loop (ˈhɛnlɪz) *n Anatomy.* See **loop**[1] (sense 10b). [C19: named after F. G. J. *Henle* (1809–85), German anatomist]

Henley-on-Thames (ˈhɛnlɪ-) *n* a town in S England, in SE Oxfordshire on the River Thames: a riverside resort with an annual regatta. Pop.: 10 558 (1991). Often shortened to **Henley.**

henna (ˈhɛnə) *n* **1** a lythraceous shrub or tree, *Lawsonia inermis*, of Asia and N Africa, with white or reddish fragrant flowers. **2** a reddish dye obtained from the powdered leaves of this plant, used as a cosmetic and industrial dye. **3** a reddish-brown or brown colour. ◆ *vb* **4** (*tr*) to dye with henna. ◆ Archaic name (for senses 1, 2): **camphire.** **[**C16: from Arabic *hinnā'; see* ALKANET**]**

hennery ('hɛnərɪ) *n, pl* **-neries.** a place or farm for keeping poultry.

hen night *n Informal.* a party for women only, esp. held for a woman shortly before she is married. Compare **hen party, stag night.**

henotheism ('hɛnəuθiː,ɪzəm) *n* the worship of one deity (of several) as the special god of one's family, clan, or tribe. **[**C19: from Greek *heis* one + *theos* god**]** ▸ **'henotheist** *n* ▸ **,henothe'istic** *adj*

hen party *n Informal.* a party at which only women are present. Compare **hen night, stag night.**

henpeck ('hɛn,pɛk) *vb* (*tr*) (of a woman) to harass or torment (a man, esp. her husband) by persistent nagging. ▸ **'hen,pecked** *adj*

Henrietta Maria (,hɛnrɪ'ɛtə mə'riːə) *n* 1609–69, queen of England (1625–49), the wife of Charles I; daughter of Henry IV of France. Her Roman Catholicism contributed to the unpopularity of the crown in the period leading to the Civil War.

hen run *n* an enclosure for hens, esp. one made of chicken wire.

henry ('hɛnrɪ) *n, pl* **-ry, -ries,** *or* **-rys.** the derived SI unit of electric inductance; the inductance of a closed circuit in which an emf of 1 volt is produced when the current varies uniformly at the rate of 1 ampere per second. Symbol: H **[**C19: named after Joseph HENRY**]**

Henry ('hɛnrɪ) *n* **1 Joseph.** 1797–1878, U.S. physicist. He discovered the principle of electromagnetic induction independently of Faraday and constructed the first electromagnetic motor (1829). He also discovered self-induction and the oscillatory nature of electric discharges (1842). **2 O.** See **O. Henry. 3 Patrick.** 1736–99, American statesman and orator, a leading opponent of British rule during the War of American Independence. **4 Prince.** born 1984, second son of Charles, Prince of Wales, and Diana, Princess of Wales.

Henry I *n* **1** known as *Henry the Fowler.* ?876–936 A.D., duke of Saxony (912–36) and king of Germany (919–36): founder of the Saxon dynasty (918–1024). **2** 1068–1135, king of England (1100–35) and duke of Normandy (1106–35); son of William the Conqueror: crowned in the absence of his elder brother, Robert II, duke of Normandy; conquered Normandy (1106).

Henry II *n* **1** known as *Henry the Saint.* 973–1024, king of Germany and Holy Roman Emperor (1014–24): canonized in 1145. **2** 1133–89, first Plantagenet king of England (1154–89): extended his Anglo-French domains and instituted judicial and financial reforms. His attempts to control the church were opposed by Becket. **3** 1519–59, king of France (1547–59); husband of Catherine de' Medici. He recovered Calais from the English (1558) and suppressed the Huguenots.

Henry III *n* **1** 1017–56, king of Germany and Holy Roman Emperor (1046–56). He increased the power of the Empire but his religious policy led to rebellions. **2** 1207–72, king of England (1216–72); son of John. His incompetent rule provoked the Barons' War (1264–67), during which he was captured by Simon de Montfort. **3** 1551–89, king of France (1574–89). He plotted the massacre of Huguenots on St. Bartholomew's Day (1572) with his mother Catherine de' Medici, thus exacerbating the religious wars in France.

Henry IV *n* **1** 1050–1106, Holy Roman Emperor (1084–1105) and king of Germany (1056–1105). He was excommunicated by Pope Gregory VII, whom he deposed (1084). **2** surnamed *Bolingbroke.* 1367–1413, first Lancastrian king of England (1399–1413); son of John of Gaunt: deposed Richard II (1399) and suppressed rebellions led by Owen Glendower and the Earl of Northumberland. **3** known as *Henry of Navarre.* 1553–1610, first Bourbon king of France (1589–1610). He obtained toleration for the Huguenots with the Edict of Nantes (1598) and restored prosperity to France following the religious wars (1562–98).

Henry V *n* **1** 1081–1125, king of Germany (1089–1125) and Holy Roman Emperor (1111–25). **2** 1387–1422, king of England (1413–22); son of Henry IV. He defeated the French at the Battle of Agincourt (1415), conquered Normandy (1419), and was recognized as heir to the French throne (1420).

Henry VI *n* **1** 1165–97, king of Germany (1169–97) and Holy Roman Emperor (1190–97): added Sicily to the Empire. **2** 1421–71, last Lancastrian king of England (1422–61; 1470–71); son of Henry V. His weak rule was blamed for the loss by 1453 of all his possessions in France except Calais; from 1454 he suffered periods of insanity which contributed to the outbreak of the Wars of the Roses (1455–85). He was deposed by Edward IV (1461) but was briefly restored to the throne (1470).

Henry VII *n* **1** ?1275–1313, Holy Roman Emperor (1312–13) and, as Henry VI, count of Luxembourg (1288–1313). He became king of the Lombards in 1313. **2** 1457–1509, first Tudor king of England (1485–1509). He came to the throne (1485) after defeating Richard III at the Battle of Bosworth Field, ending the Wars of the Roses. Royal power and the prosperity of the country greatly increased during his reign.

Henry VIII *n* 1491–1547, king of England (1509–47); second son of Henry VII. The declaration that his marriage to Catherine of Aragon was invalid and his marriage to Anne Boleyn (1533) precipitated the Act of Supremacy, making Henry supreme head of the Church in England. Anne Boleyn was executed (1536) and Henry subsequently married Jane Seymour, Anne of Cleves, Catherine Howard, and Catherine Parr. His reign is also noted for the fame of his succession of advisers, Cardinal Wolsey, Sir Thomas More, and Thomas Cromwell.

Henry's law *n Chem.* the principle that the amount of a gas dissolved at equilibrium in a given quantity of a liquid is proportional to the pressure of the gas in contact with the liquid. **[**C19: named after William *Henry* (1774–1836), English chemist**]**

Henryson ('hɛnrɪsᵊn) *n* **Robert.** ?1430–?1506, Scottish poet. His works include *Testament of Cresseid* (1593), a sequel to Chaucer's *Troilus and Cressida,* the 13 *Moral Fables of Esope the Phrygian,* and the pastoral dialogue *Robene and Makyne.*

Henry the Lion *n* ?1129–95, duke of Saxony (1142–81). His ambitions led to conflict with the Holy Roman Emperors, notably Frederick Barbarossa.

Henry the Navigator *n* 1394–1460, prince of Portugal, noted for his patronage of Portuguese voyages of exploration of the W coast of Africa.

Henslowe ('hɛnzləu) *n* **Philip.** died 1616, English theatre manager, noted also for his diary.

hent (hɛnt) *Archaic.* ◆ *vb* **1** (*tr*) to seize; grasp. ◆ *n* **2** anything that has been grasped, esp. by the mind. **[**Old English *hentan* to pursue; related to *huntian* to HUNT**]**

Henze (*German* 'hɛntsə) *n* **Hans Werner** (hans'vɛrnər). born 1926, German composer, whose works, in many styles, include the operas *The Stag King* (1956), *The Bassarids* (1965), *The English Cat* (1983), and *Das verratene Meer* (1990) and the oratorio *The Raft of the Medusa* (1968).

hep (hɛp) *adj* **hepper, heppest.** *Slang.* an earlier word for **hip**[4].

heparin ('hɛpərɪn) *n* a polysaccharide, containing sulphate groups, present in most body tissues: an anticoagulant used in the treatment of thrombosis. **[**C20: from Greek *hēpar* the liver + -IN**]** ▸ **'heparin,oid** *adj*

hepatic (hɪ'pætɪk) *adj* **1** of or relating to the liver. **2** *Botany.* of or relating to the liverworts. **3** having the colour of liver. ◆ *n* **4** any of various drugs for use in treating diseases of the liver. **5** a less common name for a **liverwort. [**C15: from Latin *hēpaticus,* from Greek *hēpar* liver**]**

hepatica (hɪ'pætɪkə) *n* any ranunculaceous woodland plant of the N temperate genus *Hepatica,* having three-lobed leaves and white, mauve, or pink flowers. **[**C16: from Medieval Latin: liverwort, from Latin *hēpaticus* of the liver**]**

hepatitis (,hɛpə'taɪtɪs) *n* inflammation of the liver, characterized by fever, jaundice, and weakness. See **hepatitis A, hepatitis B, hepatitis C.**

hepatitis A *n* a form of hepatitis caused by a virus transmitted in contaminated food or drink.

hepatitis B *n* a form of hepatitis caused by a virus transmitted by infected blood (as in transfusions), contaminated hypodermic needles, sexual contact, or by contact with any other body fluid. Former name: **serum hepatitis.**

hepatitis C *n* a form of hepatitis caused by a virus that is transmitted in the same ways as that responsible for hepatitis B. Former name: **non-A, non-B hepatitis.**

hepato- *or before a vowel* **hepat-** *combining form.* denoting the liver: *hepatitis.* **[**from Greek *hēpat-, hēpar***]**

hepatogenous (,hɛpə'tɒdʒɪnəs) *adj* originating in the liver.

hepatomegaly (,hɛpətəu'mɛgəlɪ) *n* an abnormal enlargement of the liver, caused by congestion, inflammation, or a tumour. **[**C20: from HEPATO- + New Latin *megalia,* from Greek *megas* great**]**

Hepburn ('hɛp,bɜːn) *n* **1 Audrey.** 1929–93, U.S. actress, born in Belgium. Her films include *Roman Holiday* (1955), *Funny Face* (1957), and *My Fair Lady* (1964). **2 Katharine.** born 1909, U.S. film actress, whose films include *The Philadelphia Story* (1940), *Adam's Rib* (1949), *The African Queen* (1951), *The Lion in Winter* (1968) for which she won an Oscar, and *On Golden Pond* (1981).

hepcat ('hɛp,kæt) *n Obsolete slang.* a person who is hep, esp. a player or admirer of jazz and swing in the 1940s.

Hephaestus (hɪ'fiːstəs) *or* **Hephaistos** (hɪ'faɪstɒs) *n Greek myth.* the lame god of fire and metal-working. Roman counterpart: **Vulcan.**

Hepplewhite ('hɛpᵊl,waɪt) *adj* of, denoting, or made in a style of ornamental and carved 18th-century English furniture, of which oval or shield-shaped open chairbacks are characteristic. **[**C18: named after George *Hepplewhite* (1727–86), English cabinetmaker**]**

hepta- *or before a vowel* **hept-** *combining form.* seven: *heptameter.* **[**from Greek**]**

heptad ('hɛptæd) *n* **1** a group or series of seven. **2** the number or sum of seven. **3** an atom or element with a valency of seven. **[**C17: from Greek *heptas* seven**]**

heptadecanoic acid (,hɛptə,dɛkə'nəuɪk) *n* a colourless crystalline water-insoluble carboxylic acid used in organic synthesis. Formula: $CH_3(CH_2)_{15}COOH$. Also called: **margaric acid.**

heptagon ('hɛptəgən) *n* a polygon having seven sides. ▸ **heptagonal** (hɛp'tægənᵊl) *adj*

heptahedron (,hɛptə'hiːdrən) *n* a solid figure having seven plane faces. See also **polyhedron.** ▸ **,hepta'hedral** *adj*

heptamerous (hɛp'tæmərəs) *adj* (esp. of plant parts such as petals or sepals) arranged in groups of seven.

heptameter (hɛp'tæmɪtə) *n Prosody.* a verse line of seven metrical feet. ▸ **heptametrical** (,hɛptə'mɛtrɪkᵊl) *adj*

heptane ('hɛpteɪn) *n* an alkane existing in nine isomeric forms, esp. the isomer with a straight chain of carbon atoms (*n*-heptane), which is found in petroleum and used as an anaesthetic. Formula: C_7H_{16}. **[**C19: from HEPTA- + -ANE, so called because it has seven carbon atoms**]**

heptangular (hɛp'tæŋgjulə) *adj* having seven angles.

heptarchy ('hɛptɑːkɪ) *n, pl* **-chies. 1** government by seven rulers. **2** a state divided into seven regions each under its own ruler. **3a** the seven kingdoms into which Anglo-Saxon England is thought to have been divided from about the 7th to the 9th centuries A.D.: Kent, East Anglia, Essex, Sussex, Wessex, Mercia, and Northumbria. **3b** the period when this grouping existed. ▸ **'heptarch** *n* ▸ **hep'tarchic** *or* **hep'tarchal** *adj*

heptastich ('hɛptə,stɪk) *n Prosody.* a poem, strophe, or stanza that consists of seven lines.

Heptateuch ('hɛptə,tjuːk) *n* the first seven books of the Old Testament. **[**C17: from Late Latin *Heptateuchos,* from Greek HEPTA- + *teukhos* book**]**

heptathlon (hɛp'tæθlɒn) *n* an athletic contest for women in which each athlete competes in seven different events. [C20: from HEPTA- + Greek *athlon* contest] ► **hep'tathlete** *n*

heptavalent (hɛp'tævələnt, ˌhɛptə'veɪlənt) *adj Chem.* having a valency of seven. Also: **septivalent.**

heptose ('hɛptəʊs, -təʊz) *n* any monosaccharide that has seven carbon atoms per molecule.

Hepworth ('hɛpwəθ) *n* Dame **Barbara.** 1903–75, British sculptress of abstract works.

her (hɜː; *unstressed* hə, ə) *pron (objective)* **1** refers to a female person or animal: *he loves her; they sold her a bag; something odd about her; lucky her!* **2** refers to things personified as feminine or traditionally to ships and nations. **3** *Chiefly U.S.* a dialect word for **herself** when used as an indirect object: *she needs to get her a better job.* ◆ *determiner* **4** of, belonging to, or associated with her: *her silly ideas; her hair; her smoking annoys me.* [Old English *hire,* genitive and dative of *hēo* SHE, feminine of *hē* HE[1]; related to Old High German *ira,* Gothic *izōs,* Middle Dutch *hare*]

USAGE See at **me**[1].

her. *abbrev. for:* **1** heraldic. **2** heraldry.

Hera *or* **Here** ('hɪərə) *n Greek myth.* the queen of the Olympian gods and sister and wife of Zeus. Roman counterpart: **Juno.**

Heraclea (ˌhɛrə'kliːə) *n* any of several ancient Greek colonies. The most famous is the S Italian site where Pyrrhus of Epirus defeated the Romans (280 B.C.).

Heracleides *or* **Heraclides of Pontus** (ˌhɛrə'klaɪdiːz, 'pɒntəs) *n* ?390 B.C.–?322 B.C., Greek astronomer and philosopher: the first to state that the earth rotates on its axis.

Heracles *or* **Herakles** ('hɛrəˌkliːz) *n* the usual name (in Greek) for **Hercules.** ► ˌ**Hera'clean** *or* ˌ**Hera'klean** *adj*

Heraclid *or* **Heraklid** ('hɛrəklɪd) *n, pl* **Heraclidae** *or* **Heraklidae** (ˌhɛrə'klaɪdiː). any person claiming descent from Hercules, esp. one of the Dorian aristocrats of Sparta. ► **Heraclidan** *or* **Heraklidan** (ˌhɛrə'klaɪdᵊn) *adj*

Heraclitus (ˌhɛrə'klaɪtəs) *n* ?535–?475 B.C., Greek philosopher, who held that fire is the primordial substance of the universe and that all things are in perpetual flux.

Heraclius (hɛ'ræklɪəs) *n* ?575–641 A.D., Byzantine emperor, who restored the Holy Cross to Jerusalem (629).

Herakleion *or* **Heraklion** (*Greek* he'raːkliɔn) *n* variants of **Iráklion.**

herald ('hɛrəld) *n* **1a** a person who announces important news. **1b** (*as modifier*): *herald angels.* **2** *Often literary.* a forerunner; harbinger. **3** the intermediate rank of heraldic officer, between king-of-arms and pursuivant. **4** (in the Middle Ages) an official at a tournament. ◆ *vb (tr)* **5** to announce publicly. **6** to precede or usher in. [C14: from Old French *herault,* of Germanic origin; compare Old English *here* war; see WIELD]

heraldic (hɛ'rældɪk) *adj* **1** of or relating to heraldry. **2** of or relating to heralds. ► **he'raldically** *adv*

herald moth *n* a noctuid moth, *Scoliopteryx libatrix,* having brownish cryptically mottled forewings and plain dull hind wings. The adult hibernates and has a prolonged life.

heraldry ('hɛrəldrɪ) *n, pl* **-ries. 1** the occupation or study concerned with the classification of armorial bearings, the allocation of rights to bear arms, the tracing of genealogies, etc. **2** the duties and pursuit of a herald. **3** armorial bearings, insignia, devices, etc. **4** heraldic symbols or symbolism. **5** the show and ceremony of heraldry. ► **'heraldist** *n*

heralds' college *n* another name for **college of arms.**

Herat (hɛ'ræt) *n* a city in NW Afghanistan, on the Hari Rud River: on the site of several ancient cities; at its height as a cultural centre in the 15th century. Pop.: 186 800 (1990 est.).

Hérault (*French* ero) *n* a department of S France, in Languedoc-Roussillon region. Capital: Montpellier. Pop.: 859 900 (1995). Area: 6224 sq. km (2427 sq. miles).

herb (hɜːb; *U.S.* ɜːrb) *n* **1** a seed-bearing plant whose aerial parts do not persist above ground at the end of the growing season; herbaceous plant. **2a** any of various usually aromatic plants, such as parsley, rue, and rosemary, that are used in cookery and medicine. **2b** (*as modifier*): *a herb garden.* **3** *Caribbean.* a slang term for **marijuana.** [C13: from Old French *herbe,* from Latin *herba* grass, green plants] ► **'herbˌlike** *adj*

herbaceous (hɜː'beɪʃəs) *adj* **1** designating or relating to plants or plant parts that are fleshy as opposed to woody: *a herbaceous plant.* **2** (of petals and sepals) green and leaflike. **3** of or relating to herbs. ► **her'baceously** *adv*

herbaceous border *n* a flower bed that primarily contains perennials rather than annuals.

herbage ('hɜːbɪdʒ) *n* **1** herbaceous plants collectively, esp. the edible parts on which cattle, sheep, etc., graze. **2** the vegetation of pasture land; pasturage.

herbal ('hɜːbᵊl) *adj* **1** of or relating to herbs. ◆ *n* **2** a book describing and listing the properties of plants.

herbalist ('hɜːbᵊlɪst) *n* **1** a person who grows, collects, sells, or specializes in the use of herbs, esp. medicinal herbs. **2** (formerly) a descriptive botanist.

herbarium (hɜː'bɛərɪəm) *n, pl* **-iums** *or* **-ia** (-ɪə). **1** a collection of dried plants that are mounted and classified systematically. **2** a building, room, etc., in which such a collection is kept. ► **her'barial** *adj*

herb bennet *n* a Eurasian and N African rosaceous plant, *Geum urbanum,* with yellow flowers. Also called: **wood avens, bennet.** [C13 *herbe beneit,* from Old French *herbe benoite,* literally: blessed herb, from Medieval Latin *herba benedicta*]

herb Christopher *n, pl* **herbs Christopher.** another name for **baneberry.** [C16: named after St *Christopher*]

Herbert ('hɜːbət) *n* **1 Edward,** 1st Baron Herbert of Cherbury. 1583–1648, English philosopher and poet, noted for his deistic views. **2** his brother, **George.** 1593–1633, English Metaphysical poet. His chief work is *The Temple: Sacred Poems and Private Ejaculations* (1633). **3 Zbigniew** (ᵊz'bɪgnɪəf), 1924–98, Polish poet and dramatist, noted esp. for his dramatic monologues.

herb Gerard ('dʒɛˌrɑːd) *n, pl* **herbs Gerard.** another name for **goutweed.** [C16: named after St *Gerard* (feast day April 23), who was invoked by those suffering from gout]

herbicide ('hɜːbɪˌsaɪd) *n* a chemical that destroys plants, esp. one used to control weeds. ► ˌ**herbi'cidal** *adj*

herbivore ('hɜːbɪˌvɔː) *n* **1** an animal that feeds on grass and other plants. **2** *Informal.* a liberal, idealistic, or nonmaterialistic person. [C19: from New Latin *herbivora* grass-eaters]

herbivorous (hɜː'bɪvərəs) *adj* **1** (of animals) feeding on grass and other plants. **2** *Informal.* liberal, idealistic, or nonmaterialistic. ► **her'bivorously** *adv* ► **her'bivorousness** *n*

herb layer *n* See **layer** (sense 2).

herb of grace *n* an archaic name for **rue** (the plant).

herb Paris *n, pl* **herbs Paris.** a Eurasian woodland plant, *Paris quadrifolia,* with a whorl of four leaves and a solitary yellow flower: formerly used medicinally: family *Trilliaceae.* [C16: from Medieval Latin *herba paris,* literally: herb of a pair: so called because the four leaves on the stalk look like a true lovers' knot; associated in folk etymology with *Paris,* France]

herb Robert *n, pl* **herbs Robert.** a low-growing N temperate geraniaceous plant, *Geranium robertianum,* with strongly scented divided leaves and small purplish flowers. [C13: from Medieval Latin *herba Roberti* herb of Robert, probably named after St *Robert,* 11th-century French ecclesiastic]

herby ('hɜːbɪ) *adj* **herbier, herbiest. 1** abounding in herbs. **2** of or relating to medicinal or culinary herbs.

Hercegovina (*Serbo-Croat* 'hɛrtsɛgɔvina) *n* a variant of **Herzegovina.**

Herculaneum (ˌhɜːkjʊ'leɪnɪəm) *n* an ancient city in SW Italy, of marked Greek character, on the S slope of Vesuvius: buried along with Pompeii by an eruption of the volcano (79 A.D.). Excavation has uncovered well preserved streets, houses, etc.

herculean (ˌhɜːkjʊ'liːən) *adj* **1** requiring tremendous effort, strength, etc.: *a herculean task.* **2** (*sometimes cap.*) resembling Hercules in strength, courage, etc.

Hercules[1] ('hɜːkjʊˌliːz), **Heracles,** *or* **Herakles** *n* **1** Also called: **Alcides.** *Classical myth.* a hero noted for his great strength, courage, and for the performance of twelve immense labours. **2** a man of outstanding strength or size. ► ˌ**Hercu'lean,** ˌ**Hera'clean,** *or* ˌ**Hera'klean** *adj*

Hercules[2] ('hɜːkjʊˌliːz) *n, Latin genitive* **Herculeis** (ˌhɜːkjʊ'liːɪs) **1** a large constellation in the N hemisphere lying between Lyra and Corona Borealis. **2** a conspicuous crater in the NW quadrant of the moon, about 70 kilometres in diameter.

hercules beetle *n* a very large tropical American scarabaeid beetle, *Dynastes hercules:* the male has two large anterior curved horns.

Hercules'-club *n* **1** a prickly North American araliaceous shrub, *Aralia spinosa,* with medicinal bark and leaves. **2** a prickly North American rutaceous tree, *Zanthoxylum clava-herculis,* with medicinal bark and berries.

Hercynian (hɜː'sɪnɪən) *adj* denoting a period of mountain building in Europe in the late Palaeozoic. [C16: from Latin *Hercynia silva* the Hercynian forest (i.e., the wooded mountains of central Germany, esp. the Erzgebirge)]

herd[1] (hɜːd) *n* **1** a large group of mammals living and feeding together, esp. a group of cattle, sheep, etc. **2** *Often disparaging.* a large group of people. **3 the.** *Derogatory.* the large mass of ordinary people. ◆ *vb* **4** to collect or be collected into or as if into a herd. [Old English *heord;* related to Old Norse *hjörth,* Gothic *hairda,* Old High German *herta,* Greek *kórthus* troop]

herd[2] (hɜːd) *n* **1a** *Archaic or dialect.* a man or boy who tends livestock; herdsman. **1b** (*in combination*): *goatherd, swineherd.* ◆ *vb (tr)* **2** to drive forwards in a large group. **3** to look after (livestock). [Old English *hirde;* related to Old Norse *hirthir,* Gothic *hairdeis,* Old High German *hirti,* Old Saxon *hirdi, herdi;* see HERD[1]]

herd-book *n* a book containing the pedigrees of breeds of pigs, cattle, etc.

herder ('hɜːdə) *n Chiefly U.S.* a person who cares for or drives herds of cattle or flocks of sheep, esp. on an open range. Brit. equivalent: **herdsman.**

Herder (*German* 'hɛrdər) *n* **Johann Gottfried von** (jo'han 'gɔtfriːt fɔn). 1744–1803, German philosopher, critic, and poet, the leading figure in the *Sturm und Drang* movement in German literature. His chief work is *Outlines of a Philosophy of the History of Man* (1784–91).

herdic ('hɜːdɪk) *n U.S.* a small horse-drawn carriage with a rear entrance and side seats. [C19: named after P. *Herdic,* 19th-century American inventor]

herd instinct *n Psychol.* the inborn tendency to associate with others and follow the group's behaviour.

herdsman ('hɜːdzmən) *n, pl* **-men.** *Chiefly Brit.* a person who breeds, rears, or cares for cattle or (rarely) other livestock in the herd. U.S. equivalent: **herder.**

herd tester *n N.Z.* a technician trained to test the health and production of milk and butterfat of dairy cows. ► **herd testing** *n*

Herdwick ('hɜːdwɪk) *n* a hardy breed of coarse-woolled sheep from NW England. [C19: from obsolete *herdwick* pasture, sheep farm (see HERD[2] (sense 1), WICK[2]); the breed is thought to have originated on the herdwicks of Furness Abbey]

here (hɪə) *adv* **1** in, at, or to this place, point, case, or respect: *we come here every summer; here, the policemen do not usually carry guns; here comes Roy.* **2 here and there.** at several places in or throughout an area. **3 here goes.** an exclamation indicating that the speaker is about to perform an action. **4 here's to.** a formula used in proposing a toast to someone or something. **5 here today, gone tomorrow.** short-lived; transitory. **6 here we go again.** an event or process is about to repeat itself. **7 neither here nor there.** of no relevance or importance. **8 this here.** See **this** (senses 1–3). ◆ *n* **9** this place: *they* *leave here tonight.* **10** (**the**) **here and now.** the present time. [Old English *hēr;* related to Old Norse *hēr,* Old High German *hiar,* Old Saxon *hīr*]

hereabouts (ˌhɪərəˌbaʊts) *or* **hereabout** *adv* in this region or neighbourhood; near this place.

hereafter (ˌhɪərˈɑːftə) *adv* **1** *Formal or law.* in a subsequent part of this document, matter, case, etc. **2** a less common word for **henceforth. 3** at some time in the future. **4** in a future life after death. ◆ *n* (usually preceded by *the*) **5** life after death. **6** the future.

hereat (ˌhɪərˈæt) *adv Archaic.* because of this.

hereby (ˌhɪəˈbaɪ) *adv* **1** (used in official statements, proclamations, etc.) by means of or as a result of this. **2** *Archaic.* nearby.

heredes (hɪˈriːdiːz) *n* the plural of **heres.**

hereditable (hɪˈrɛdɪtəbᵊl) *adj* a less common word for **heritable.** ▸ **heˌreditaˈbility** *n* ▸ **heˈreditably** *adv*

hereditament (ˌhɛrɪˈdɪtəmənt) *n Property law.* **1** any kind of property capable of being inherited. **2** property that before 1926 passed to an heir if not otherwise disposed of by will.

hereditarianism (həˌrɛdɪˈtɛərɪəˌnɪzəm) *n Psychol.* a school of thought that emphasizes the influence of heredity in the determination of human behaviour. Compare **environmentalism.**

hereditary (hɪˈrɛdɪtərɪ, -trɪ) *adj* **1** of, relating to, or denoting factors that can be transmitted genetically from one generation to another. **2** *Law.* **2a** descending or capable of descending to succeeding generations by inheritance. **2b** transmitted or transmissible according to established rules of descent. **3** derived from one's ancestors; traditional: *hereditary feuds.* **4** *Maths, logic.* **4a** (of a set) containing all those elements which have a given relation to any element of the set. **4b** (of a property) transferred by the given relation, so that if *x* has the property *R* and *xRy,* then *y* also has the property. ▸ **heˈreditarily** *adv* ▸ **heˈreditariness** *n*

hereditist (həˈrɛdɪtɪst) *n* any person who places the role of heredity above that of the environment as the determining factor in human or animal behaviour.

heredity (hɪˈrɛdɪtɪ) *n, pl* **-ties. 1** the transmission from one generation to another of genetic factors that determine individual characteristics: responsible for the resemblances between parents and offspring. **2** the sum total of the inherited factors or their characteristics in an organism. [C16: from Old French *heredite,* from Latin *hērēditās* inheritance; see HEIR]

heredo-familial (həˌrɛdəʊfəˈmɪlɪəl) *adj* denoting a condition or disease that may be passed from generation to generation and to several members of one family.

Hereford (ˈhɛrɪfəd) *n* **1** a city in W England, in Herefordshire county on the River Wye: trading centre for agricultural produce; cathedral (begun 1079). Pop.: 54 326 (1991). **2** a hardy breed of beef cattle characterized by a red body, red and white head, and white markings.

Hereford and Worcester *n* a historical county of the W Midlands of England, formed in 1974 from the two former separate counties minus a small area of NW Worcestershire: replaced administratively in 1998 when Herefordshire became an independent unitary authority.

Herefordshire (ˈhɛrɪfədˌʃɪə, -ʃə) *n* a county of W England, from 1974 to 1998 part of Hereford and Worcester: drained chiefly by the Rivers Wye and Severn; agricultural (esp. fruit and cattle). Administrative centre: Hereford. Pop.: 166 750 (1998 est.). Area: 2180 sq. km (842 sq. miles).

herein (ˌhɪərˈɪn) *adv* **1** *Formal or law.* in or into this place, thing, document, etc. **2** *Rare.* in this respect, circumstance, etc.

hereinafter (ˌhɪərɪnˈɑːftə) *adv Formal or law.* in a subsequent part or from this point on in this document, statement, etc.

hereinbefore (ˌhɪərɪnbɪˈfɔː) *adv Formal or law.* in a previous part of or previously in this document, statement, etc.

hereinto (ˌhɪərˈɪntuː) *adv Formal or law.* into this place, circumstance, etc.

hereof (ˌhɪərˈɒv) *adv Formal or law.* of or concerning this.

hereon (ˌhɪərˈɒn) *adv* an archaic word for **hereupon.**

Herero (həˈrɛərəʊ, ˈhɛərəˌrəʊ) *n* **1** (*pl* **-ro** *or* **-ros**) a member of a formerly rich cattle-keeping Negroid people of southern Africa, living chiefly in central Namibia. **2** the language of this people, belonging to the Bantu group of the Niger-Congo family.

heres *or* **haeres** (ˈhɪəriːz) *n, pl* **heredes** *or* **haeredes** (hɪˈriːdiːz). *Civil law.* an heir. [from Latin]

heresiarch (hɪˈriːzɪˌɑːk) *n* the leader or originator of a heretical movement or sect.

heresy (ˈhɛrəsɪ) *n, pl* **-sies. 1a** an opinion or doctrine contrary to the orthodox tenets of a religious body or church. **1b** the act of maintaining such an opinion or doctrine. **2** any opinion or belief that is or is thought to be contrary to official or established theory. **3** belief in or adherence to unorthodox opinion. [C13: from Old French *eresie,* from Late Latin *haeresis,* from Latin: sect, from Greek *hairesis* a choosing, from *hairein* to choose]

heretic (ˈhɛrətɪk) *n* **1** *Now chiefly R.C. Church.* a person who maintains beliefs contrary to the established teachings of the Church. **2** a person who holds unorthodox opinions in any field. ▸ **heretical** (hɪˈrɛtɪkᵊl) *adj* ▸ **heˈretically** *adv*

hereto (ˌhɪəˈtuː) *adv* **1** *Formal or law.* to this place, thing, matter, document, etc. **2** an obsolete word for **hitherto.**

heretofore (ˌhɪətʊˈfɔː) *adv* **1** *Formal or law.* until now; before this time. ◆ *adj* **2** *Obsolete.* previous; former. ◆ *n* **3** (preceded by *the*) *Archaic.* the past.

hereunder (ˌhɪərˈʌndə) *adv Formal or law.* **1** (in documents, etc.) below this; subsequently; hereafter. **2** under the terms or authority of this.

hereunto (ˌhɪərʌnˈtuː) *adv* an archaic word for **hereto** (sense 1).

hereupon (ˌhɪərəˈpɒn) *adv* **1** following immediately after this; at this stage. **2** *Formal or law.* upon this thing, point, subject, etc.

Hereward (ˈhɛrɪwəd) *n* called *Hereward the Wake.* 11th-century Anglo-Saxon rebel, who defended the Isle of Ely against William the Conqueror (1070–71): a subject of many legends.

herewith (ˌhɪəˈwɪð, -ˈwɪθ) *adv* **1** *Formal.* together with this: *we send you herewith your statement of account.* **2** a less common word for **hereby** (sense 1).

Hering (ˈherɪŋ) *n* **Ewald** (ˈɛvalt). 1834–1918, German physiologist and experimental psychologist who studied vision and propounded the doctrine of nativism, the policy of favouring the natives of a country over the immigrants.

heriot (ˈhɛrɪət) *n* (in medieval England) a death duty paid by villeins and free tenants to their lord, often consisting of the dead man's best beast or chattel. [Old English *heregeatwa,* from *here* army + *geatwa* equipment]

Herisau (*German* ˈheːrizau) *n* a town in NE Switzerland, capital of Appenzell Outer Rhodes demicanton. Pop.: 14 955 (1987).

heritable (ˈhɛrɪtəbᵊl) *adj* **1** capable of being inherited; inheritable. **2** *Chiefly law.* capable of inheriting. [C14: from Old French, from *heriter* to INHERIT] ▸ **ˌheritaˈbility** *n* ▸ **ˈheritably** *adv*

heritage (ˈhɛrɪtɪdʒ) *n* **1** something inherited at birth, such as personal characteristics, status, and possessions. **2** anything that has been transmitted from the past or handed down by tradition. **3a** the evidence of the past, such as historical sites, buildings, and the unspoilt natural environment, considered collectively as the inheritance of present-day society. **3b** (*as modifier; cap. as part of name*): *Bannockburn Heritage Centre.* **4** something that is reserved for a particular person or group or the outcome of an action, way of life, etc.: *the sea was their heritage; the heritage of violence.* **5** *Law.* any property, esp. land, that by law has descended or may descend to an heir. **6** *Bible.* **6a** the Israelites regarded as belonging inalienably to God. **6b** the land of Canaan regarded as God's gift to the Israelites. [C13: from Old French; see HEIR]

heritor (ˈhɛrɪtə) *n Archaic or law.* a person who inherits; inheritor. ▸ **heritress** (ˈhɛrɪtrɪs) *or* **ˈheritrix** *fem n*

herl (hɜːl) *or* **harl** *n Angling.* **1** the barb or barbs of a feather, used to dress fishing flies. **2** an artificial fly dressed with such barbs. [C15: from Middle Low German *herle,* of obscure origin]

herm (hɜːm) *or* **herma** (ˈhɜːmə) *n, pl* **herms, hermae** (ˈhɜːmiː), *or* **hermai** (ˈhɜːmaɪ) (in ancient Greece) a stone head of Hermes surmounting a square stone pillar. [C16: from Latin *herma,* from Greek *hermēs* HERMES[1]]

Hermann (ˈhɜːmən; *German* ˈherman) *n* another name for **Arminius** (sense 1).

Hermannstadt (ˈhermanʃtat) *n* the German name for **Sibiu.**

hermaphrodite (hɜːˈmæfrəˌdaɪt) *n* **1** *Biology.* an individual animal or flower that has both male and female reproductive organs. **2** a person having both male and female sexual characteristics and genital tissues. **3** a person or thing in which two opposite forces or qualities are combined. ◆ *adj* **4** having the characteristics of a hermaphrodite. [C15: from Latin *hermaphrodītus,* from Greek, after HERMAPHRODITUS] ▸ **herˌmaphroˈditic** *or* **herˌmaphroˈditical** *adj* ▸ **herˌmaphroˈditically** *adv* ▸ **herˈmaphroditˌism** *n*

hermaphrodite brig *n* a sailing vessel with two masts, rigged square on the foremast and fore-and-aft on the aftermast. Also called: **brigantine.**

Hermaphroditus (hɜːˌmæfrəˈdaɪtəs) *n Greek myth.* a son of Hermes and Aphrodite who merged with the nymph Salmacis to form one body.

hermeneutic (ˌhɜːmɪˈnjuːtɪk) *or* **hermeneutical** *adj* **1** of or relating to the interpretation of Scripture; using or relating to hermeneutics. **2** interpretive. ▸ **ˌhermeˈneutically** *adv* ▸ **ˌhermeˈneutist** *n*

hermeneutics (ˌhɜːmɪˈnjuːtɪks) *n* (*functioning as sing*) **1** the science of interpretation, esp. of Scripture. **2** the branch of theology that deals with the principles and methodology of exegesis. **3** *Philosophy.* **3a** the study and interpretation of human behaviour and social institutions. **3b** (in existentialist thought) discussion of the purpose of life. [C18: from Greek *hermēneutikos* expert in interpretation, from *hermēneuein* to interpret, from *hermēneus* interpreter, of uncertain origin]

Hermes[1] (ˈhɜːmiːz) *n Greek myth.* the messenger and herald of the gods; the divinity of commerce, cunning, theft, travellers, and rascals. He was represented as wearing winged sandals. Roman counterpart: **Mercury.**

Hermes[2] (ˈhɜːmiːz) *n* a small asteroid that passes within 353 000 kilometres of the earth.

Hermes Trismegistus (ˌtrɪsməˈdʒɪstəs) *n* a Greek name for the Egyptian god Thoth, credited with various works on mysticism and magic. [Greek: Hermes thrice-greatest]

hermetic (hɜːˈmɛtɪk) *or* **hermetical** *adj* sealed so as to be airtight. [C17: from Medieval Latin *hermēticus* belonging to HERMES TRISMEGISTUS, traditionally the inventor of a magic seal] ▸ **herˈmetically** *adv*

Hermetic (hɜːˈmɛtɪk) *adj* **1** of or relating to Hermes Trismegistus or the writings and teachings ascribed to him. **2** of or relating to ancient science, esp. alchemy.

hermit (ˈhɜːmɪt) *n* **1** one of the early Christian recluses. **2** any person living in solitude. [C13: from Old French *hermite,* from Late Latin *erēmīta,* from Greek *erēmitēs* living in the desert, from *erēmia* desert, from *erēmos* lonely] ▸ **herˈmitic** *or* **herˈmitical** *adj* ▸ **herˈmitically** *adv* ▸ **ˈhermit-ˌlike** *adj*

hermitage (ˈhɜːmɪtɪdʒ) *n* **1** the abode of a hermit. **2** any place where a person may live in seclusion; retreat.

Hermitage[1] (ˈhɜːmɪtɪdʒ) *n* **the.** an art museum in Leningrad, originally a palace built by Catherine the Great.

Hermitage[2] (ˈhɜːmɪtɪdʒ) *n* a full-bodied red or white wine from the Rhône valley at Tain-l'Ermitage, in SE France.

hermit crab *n* any small soft-bodied decapod crustacean of the genus *Pagurus* and related genera, living in and carrying about the empty shells of whelks or similar molluscs.

Hermitian conjugate (hɜːˈmɪtɪən) *n Maths.* a matrix that is the transpose of the matrix of the complex conjugates of the entries of a given matrix. Also called: **adjoint.** [C19: named after Charles *Hermite* (1822–1901), French mathematician]

Hermitian matrix *n Maths.* a matrix whose transpose is equal to the matrix of the complex conjugates of its entries. [C20: named after Charles *Hermite* (1822–1901), French mathematician]

Hermon ('hɜːmən) *n* **Mount.** a mountain on the border between Lebanon and SW Syria, in the Anti-Lebanon Range: represented the NE limits of Israeli conquests under Moses and Joshua. Height: 2814 m (9232 ft.).

Hermosillo (*Spanish* ɛrmo'siʎo) *n* a city in NW Mexico, capital of Sonora state, on the Sonora River: university (1938); winter resort and commercial centre for an agricultural and mining region. Pop.: 406 417 (1990).

Hermoupolis (hɜː'muːpəlɪs) *n* a port in Greece, capital of Cyclades department, on the E coast of Syros Island. Pop.: 14 115 (1981).

hern (hɜːn) *n* an archaic or dialect word for **heron.**

Herne (*German* 'hɛrnə) *n* an industrial city in W Germany, in North Rhine-Westphalia, in the Ruhr on the Rhine-Herne Canal. Pop.: 179 897 (1996 est.).

hernia ('hɜːnɪə) *n, pl* **-nias** *or* **-niae** (-nɪˌiː). the projection of an organ or part through the lining of the cavity in which it is normally situated, esp. the protrusion of intestine through the front wall of the abdominal cavity. It is caused by muscular strain, injury, etc. Also called: **rupture.** [C14: from Latin] ► **'hernial** *adj* ► **'herniˌated** *adj*

herniorrhaphy (ˌhɜːnɪ'ɒrəfɪ) *n, pl* **-phies.** surgical repair of a hernia by means of a suturing operation.

hero ('hɪərəʊ) *n, pl* **-roes. 1** a man distinguished by exceptional courage, nobility, fortitude, etc. **2** a man who is idealized for possessing superior qualities in any field. **3** *Classical myth.* a being of extraordinary strength and courage, often the offspring of a mortal and a god, who is celebrated for his exploits. **4** the principal male character in a novel, play, etc. [C14: from Latin *hērōs,* from Greek]

Hero[1] ('hɪərəʊ) *n Greek myth.* a priestess of Aphrodite, who killed herself when her lover Leander drowned while swimming the Hellespont to visit her.

Hero[2] ('hɪərəʊ) *or* **Heron** *n* 1st century A.D., Greek mathematician and inventor.

Herod ('hɛrəd) *n* called *the Great.* ?73–4 B.C., king of Judaea (37–4). The latter part of his reign was notable for his cruelty: according to the New Testament he ordered the Massacre of the Innocents.

Herod Agrippa I *n* 10 B.C.–44 A.D., king of Judaea (41–44), grandson of Herod (the Great). A friend of Caligula and Claudius, he imprisoned Saint Peter and executed Saint James.

Herod Agrippa II *n* died ?93 A.D., king of territories in N Palestine (50–?93 A.D.). He presided (60) at the trial of Saint Paul and sided with the Roman authorities in the Jewish rebellion of 66.

Herod Antipas ('æntɪˌpæs) *n* died ?40 A.D., tetrarch of Galilee and Peraea (4 B.C.–40 A.D.); son of Herod the Great. At the instigation of his wife Herodias, he ordered the execution of John the Baptist.

Herodias (hɛ'rəʊdɪˌæs) *n* ?14 B.C.–?40 A.D., niece and wife of Herod Antipas and mother of Salome, whom she persuaded to ask for the head of John the Baptist. Her ambition led to the banishment of her husband.

Herodotus (hɪ'rɒdətəs) *n* called *the Father of History.* ?485–?425 B.C., Greek historian, famous for his *History* dealing with the causes and events of the wars between the Greeks and the Persians (490–479).

heroic (hɪ'rəʊɪk) *or* **heroical** *adj* **1** of, like, or befitting a hero. **2** courageous but desperate. **3** relating to or treating of heroes and their deeds. **4** of, relating to, or resembling the heroes of classical mythology. **5** (of language, manner, etc.) extravagant. **6** *Prosody.* of, relating to, or resembling heroic verse. **7** (of the arts, esp. sculpture) larger than life-size; smaller than colossal. ◆ See also **heroics.** ► **he'roically** *adv* ► **he'roicalness** *or* **he'roicness** *n*

heroic age *n* the period in an ancient culture, when legendary heroes are said to have lived.

heroic couplet *n Prosody.* a verse form consisting of two rhyming lines in iambic pentameter.

heroics (hɪ'rəʊɪks) *pl n* **1** *Prosody.* short for **heroic verse. 2** extravagant or melodramatic language, behaviour, etc.

heroic stanza *n Poetry.* a quatrain having the rhyme scheme a b a b.

heroic tenor *n* a tenor with a dramatic voice.

heroic verse *n Prosody.* a type of verse suitable for epic or heroic subjects, such as the classical hexameter, the French Alexandrine, or the English iambic pentameter.

heroin ('hɛrəʊɪn) *n* a white odourless bitter-tasting crystalline powder derived from morphine: a highly addictive narcotic. Formula: $C_{17}H_{17}NO(C_2H_3O_2)_2$. Technical name: **diamorphine.** [C19: coined in German as a trademark, probably from HERO, referring to its aggrandizing effect on the personality]

heroine ('hɛrəʊɪn) *n* **1** a woman possessing heroic qualities. **2** a woman idealized for possessing superior qualities. **3** the main female character in a novel, play, film, etc.

heroism ('hɛrəʊˌɪzəm) *n* the state or quality of being a hero.

heron ('hɛrən) *n* any of various wading birds of the genera *Butorides, Ardea,* etc., having a long neck, slim body, and a plumage that is commonly grey or white: family *Ardeidae,* order *Ciconiiformes.* [C14: from Old French *hairon,* of Germanic origin; compare Old High German *heigaro,* Old Norse *hegri*]

Heron ('hɪərɒn) *n* a variant of **Hero**[2].

heronry ('hɛrənrɪ) *n, pl* **-ries.** a colony of breeding herons.

Herophilus (hɪə'rɒfɪləs) *n* died ?280 B.C., Greek anatomist in Alexandria. He was the first to distinguish sensory from motor nerves.

hero worship *n* **1** admiration for heroes or idealized persons. **2** worship by the ancient Greeks and Romans of heroes. ◆ *vb* **hero-worship, -ships, -shipping, -shipped** *or U.S.* **-ships, -shiping, -shiped. 3** (*tr*) to feel admiration or adulation for. ► **'hero-ˌworshipper** *n*

herp., herpet., *or* **herpetol.** *abbrev. for* herpetology.

herpes ('hɜːpiːz) *n* any of several inflammatory diseases of the skin, esp. herpes simplex, characterized by the formation of small watery blisters. See also **genital herpes.** [C17: via Latin from Greek: a creeping, from *herpein* to creep]

herpes labialis (ˌleɪbɪ'ælɪs) *n* a technical name for **cold sore.** [New Latin: herpes of the lip]

herpes simplex ('sɪmplɛks) *n* an acute viral disease characterized by formation of clusters of watery blisters, esp. on the margins of the lips and nostrils or on the genitals. It can be sexually transmitted and may recur fitfully. [New Latin: simple herpes]

herpesvirus ('hɜːpiːzˌvaɪrəs) *n* any one of a family of viruses that includes the agents causing herpes, the Epstein-Barr virus, and the cytomegalovirus.

herpes zoster ('zɒstə) *n* a technical name for **shingles.** [New Latin: girdle herpes, from HERPES + Greek *zōstēr* girdle]

herpetic (hɜː'pɛtɪk) *adj* **1** of or relating to any of the herpes diseases. ◆ *n* **2** a person suffering from any of the herpes diseases.

herpetology (ˌhɜːpɪ'tɒlədʒɪ) *n* the study of reptiles and amphibians. [C19: from Greek *herpeton* creeping animal, from *herpein* to creep] ► **herpetologic** (ˌhɜːpɪtə'lɒdʒɪk) *or* **ˌherpeto'logical** *adj* ► **ˌherpeto'logically** *adv* ► **ˌherpe'tologist** *n*

herptile ('hɜːpˌtaɪl) *adj Chiefly U.S.* denoting, relating to, or characterizing both reptiles and amphibians. [from Greek *herp(eton)* (see HERPETOLOGY) + (REP)TILE]

Herr (*German* hɛr) *n, pl* **Herren** ('hɛrən). a German man: used before a name as a title equivalent to *Mr.* [German, from Old High German *herro* lord]

Herrenvolk *German.* ('hɛrənfɔlk) *n* See **master race.**

Herrick ('hɛrɪk) *n* **Robert.** 1591–1674, English poet. His chief work is the *Hesperides* (1648), a collection of short, delicate, sacred, and pastoral lyrics.

herring ('hɛrɪŋ) *n, pl* **-rings** *or* **-ring.** any marine soft-finned teleost fish of the family *Clupeidae,* esp. *Clupea harengus,* an important food fish of northern seas, having an elongated body covered, except in the head region, with large fragile silvery scales. [Old English *hǣring;* related to Old High German *hāring,* Old Frisian *hēring,* Dutch *haring*]

herringbone ('hɛrɪŋˌbəʊn) *n* **1a** a pattern used in textiles, brickwork, etc., consisting of two or more rows of short parallel strokes slanting in alternate directions to form a series of parallel Vs or zigzags. **1b** (*as modifier*): *a herringbone pattern.* **2** *Skiing.* a method of ascending a slope by walking with the skis pointing outwards and one's weight on the inside edges. ◆ *vb* **3** to decorate (textiles, brickwork, etc.) with herringbone. **4** (*intr*) *Skiing.* to ascend a slope in herringbone fashion.

herringbone bond *n* a type of bricklaying in which the bricks are laid on the slant to form a herringbone pattern.

herringbone gear *n* a gearwheel having two sets of helical teeth, one set inclined at an acute angle to the other so that V-shaped teeth are formed. Also called: **double-helical gear.**

herring gull *n* a common gull, *Larus argentatus,* that has a white plumage with black-tipped wings and pink legs.

Herriot *n* **1** (*French* ɛrjo) **Édouard** (edwar). 1872–1957, French Radical statesman and writer; premier (1924–25; 1932). **2** ('hɛrɪət) **James.** real name *James Alfred Wight.* 1916–95, British veterinary surgeon and writer. His books based on his experiences in Yorkshire have been adapted for television and films.

hers (hɜːz) *pron* **1** something or someone belonging to or associated with her: *hers is the nicest dress; that cat is hers.* **2 of hers.** belonging to or associated with her. [C14 *hires;* see HER]

Herschel ('hɜːʃəl) *n* **1 Caroline Lucretia.** 1750–1848, British astronomer, born in Germany, noted for her catalogue of nebulae and star clusters: sister of Sir William Herschel. **2** Sir **John Frederick William.** 1792–1871, British astronomer. He discovered and catalogued over 525 nebulae and star clusters. **3** his father, Sir **(Frederick) William,** original name *Friedrich Wilhelm Herschel.* 1738–1822, British astronomer, born in Germany. He constructed a reflecting telescope, which led to his discovery of the planet Uranus (1781), two of its satellites, and two of the satellites of Saturn. He also discovered the motions of binary stars.

herself (hə'sɛlf) *pron* **1a** the reflexive form of *she* or *her.* **1b** (intensifier): *the queen herself signed the letter.* **2** (*preceded by a copula*) her normal or usual self: *she looks herself again after the operation.* **3** *Irish and Scot.* the wife or woman of the house: *is herself at home?*

Herstmonceux *or* **Hurstmonceux** ('hɜːstmənˌsuː, -ˌsəʊ) *n* a village in S England, in E Sussex north of Eastbourne: 15th-century castle, site of the Royal Observatory, which was transferred from Greenwich between 1948 and 1958, until 1990.

Hertford ('hɑːtfəd) *n* a town in SE England, administrative centre of Hertfordshire. Pop.: 21 665 (1991).

Hertfordshire ('hɑːtfədˌʃɪə, -ʃə) *n* a county of S England, bordering on Greater London in the south: mainly low-lying, with the Chiltern Hills in the northwest; largely agricultural; expanding light industries, esp. in the new towns. Administrative centre: Hertford. Pop.: 1 005 400 (1994 est.). Area: 1634 sq. km (631 sq. miles).

Hertogenbosch (*Dutch* hɛrtoːxən'bɔs) *n* **'s.** See **'s Hertogenbosch.**

Herts (hɑːts) *abbrev. for* Hertfordshire.

hertz (hɜːts) *n, pl* **hertz.** the derived SI unit of frequency; the frequency of a periodic phenomenon that has a periodic time of 1 second; 1 cycle per second. Symbol: Hz [C20: named after Heinrich Rudolph HERTZ]

Hertz (hɜːts; *German* hɛrts) *n* **1 Gustav** ('gustaf). 1887–1975, German atomic physicist. He provided evidence for the quantum theory by his research with Franck on the effects produced by bombarding atoms with electrons: they shared the Nobel prize for physics (1925). **2 Heinrich Rudolph** ('hainrɪç 'ruːdɔlf). 1857–94, German physicist. He was the first to produce electromagnetic waves artificially. ► **'Hertzian** *adj*

Hertzian wave *n* an electromagnetic wave with a frequency in the range from about 3 × 10^{10} hertz to about 1.5 × 10^5 hertz. [C19: named after H. R. HERTZ]

Hertzog ('hɜːtsɒg) *n* **James Barry Munnik.** 1866–1942, South African statesman; prime minister (1924–39): founded the Nationalist Party (1913), advocating complete South African independence from Britain; opposed South African participation in World Wars I and II.

Hertzsprung (*Danish* hɛrdsbrɔŋ) *n* **Ejnar** ('aɪnar). 1873–1967, Danish astronomer: he discovered the existence of giant and dwarf stars, originating one form of the Hertzsprung-Russell diagram.

Hertzsprung-Russell diagram ('hɜːtssprʌŋ'rʌsᵊl) *n* a graph in which the spectral types of stars are plotted against their absolute magnitudes. Stars fall into different groupings in different parts of the graph. See also **main sequence.** [C20: named after Ejnar HERTZSPRUNG and Henry N. RUSSELL]

Herzegovina (ˌhɜːtsəgəʊ'viːnə) *or* **Hercegovina** *n* a region in Bosnia-Herzegovina: originally under Austro-Hungarian rule; became part of the province of Bosnia-Herzegovina (1878), which was a constituent republic of Yugoslavia (1946–92).

Herzen (*Russian* 'gjɛrtsən) *n* **Aleksandr (Ivanovich)** (alɛk'sandr i'vaːnovitʃ). 1812–70, Russian socialist political philosopher: best known for his autobiography *My Past and Thoughts* (1861–67).

Herzl (*German* 'hɛrtsəl) *n* **Theodor** ('teːodoːr). 1860–1904, Austrian writer, born in Hungary; founder of the Zionist movement. In *The Jewish State* (1896), he advocated resettlement of the Jews in a state of their own.

Herzog (*German* 'hɛrtsoːk) *n* **1 Roman.** born 1934, German politician; president of Germany from 1994. **2 Werner** ('vɛrnər). born 1942, German film director. His films include *Signs of Life* (1967), *Fata Morgana* (1970), *Fitzcarraldo* (1982), and *Scream from Stone* (1991).

he's (hiːz) *contraction of* he is *or* he has.

Heseltine ('hɛzəlˌtaɪn) *n* **1 Michael (Ray Dibden).** born 1933, British Conservative politician; secretary of state for defence (1983–86); secretary of state for the environment (1990–92); secretary of state for industry (1992–95); deputy prime minister and first secretary of state (1995–97). **2 Philip Arnold.** See (Peter) **Warlock.**

Heshvan (xɛʃ'vɑn) *n* a variant spelling of **Cheshvan.**

Hesiod ('hɛsɪˌɒd) *n* 8th century B.C., Greek poet and the earliest author of didactic verse. His two complete extant works are the *Works and Days,* dealing with the agricultural seasons, and the *Theogony,* concerning the origin of the world and the genealogies of the gods. ▸ **ˌHesi'odic** *adj*

Hesione (hɪ'saɪənɪ) *n Greek myth.* daughter of King Laomedon, rescued by Hercules from a sea monster.

hesitant ('hɛzɪtᵊnt) *adj* wavering, hesitating, or irresolute. ▸ **'hesitance** *or* **'hesitancy** *n* ▸ **'hesitantly** *adv*

hesitate ('hɛzɪˌteɪt) *vb* (*intr*) **1** to hold back or be slow in acting; be uncertain. **2** to be unwilling or reluctant (to do something). **3** to stammer or pause in speaking. [C17: from Latin *haesitāre,* from *haerēre* to cling to] ▸ **'hesiˌtater** *or* **'hesiˌtator** *n* ▸ **'hesiˌtatingly** *adv* ▸ **ˌhesi'tation** *n* ▸ **'hesiˌtative** *adj*

Hesperia (hɛ'spɪərɪə) *n* a poetic name used by the ancient Greeks for Italy and by the Romans for Spain or beyond. [Latin, from Greek: land of the west, from *hesperos* western]

Hesperian (hɛ'spɪərɪən) *adj* **1** *Poetic.* western. **2** of or relating to the Hesperides. ◆ *n* **3** a native or inhabitant of a western land.

Hesperides (hɛ'spɛrɪˌdiːz) *pl n Greek myth.* **1** the daughters of Hesperus, nymphs who kept watch with a dragon over the garden of the golden apples in the Islands of the Blessed. **2** (*functioning as sing*) the gardens themselves. **3** another name for the **Islands of the Blessed.** ▸ **Hesperidian** (ˌhɛspə'rɪdɪən) *or* **ˌHesper'idean** *adj*

hesperidin (hɛ'spɛrɪdɪn) *n* a glycoside extracted from orange peel or other citrus fruits and used to treat capillary fragility. [C19: from New Latin HESPERIDIUM + -IN]

hesperidium (ˌhɛspə'rɪdɪəm) *n Botany.* the fruit of citrus plants, in which the flesh consists of fluid-filled hairs and is protected by a tough rind. [C19: New Latin; alluding to the fruit in the garden of the HESPERIDES]

Hesperus ('hɛspərəs) *n* an evening star, esp. Venus. [from Latin, from Greek *Hesperos,* from *hesperos* western]

Hess (hɛs) *n* **1** Dame **Myra.** 1890–1965, English pianist. **2 (Walther Richard) Rudolf** ('ruːdɔlf). 1894–1987, German Nazi leader. He made a secret flight to Scotland (1941) to negotiate peace with Britain but was held as a prisoner of war; later sentenced to life imprisonment at the Nuremberg trials (1946); committed suicide. **3 Victor Francis.** 1883–1964, U.S. physicist, born in Austria: pioneered the investigation of cosmic rays: shared the Nobel prize for physics (1936).

Hesse[1] (hɛs) *n* a state of central Germany, formed in 1945 from the former Prussian province of Hesse-Nassau and part of the former state of Hesse; part of West Germany until 1990. Capital: Wiesbaden. Pop.: 6 009 900 (1996 est.). Area: 21 111 sq. km (8151 sq. miles). German name: **Hessen** ('hɛsᵊn).

Hesse[2] (hɛs; *German* 'hɛsə) *n* **Hermann** ('hɛrman). 1877–1962, German novelist, short-story writer, and poet. His novels include *Der Steppenwolf* (1927) and *Das Glasperlenspiel* (1943): Nobel prize for literature 1946.

Hesse-Nassau *n* a former province of Prussia, now part of the state of Hesse, Germany; part of West Germany until 1990.

hessian ('hɛsɪən) *n* a coarse jute fabric similar to sacking, used for bags, upholstery, etc. [C18: from HESSE[1] + -IAN]

Hessian ('hɛsɪən) *n* **1** a native or inhabitant of Hesse. **2a** a Hessian soldier in any of the mercenary units of the British Army in the War of American Independence or the Napoleonic Wars. **2b** *U.S.* any German mercenary in the British Army during the War of American Independence. **3** *Chiefly U.S.* a mercenary or ruffian. ◆ *adj* **4** of or relating to Hesse or its inhabitants.

Hessian boots *pl n* men's high boots with tassels around the top, fashionable in England in the early 19th century.

Hessian fly *n* a small dipterous fly, *Mayetiola destructor,* whose larvae damage wheat, barley, and rye: family *Cecidomyidae* (gall midges). [C18: so called because it was thought to have been introduced into America by Hessian soldiers]

hessite ('hɛsaɪt) *n* a black or grey metallic mineral consisting of silver telluride in cubic crystalline form. Formula: Ag_2Te. [C19: from German *Hessit;* named after Henry *Hess,* 19th-century chemist of Swiss origin who worked in Russia; see -ITE[1]]

hessonite ('hɛsəˌnaɪt) *n* an orange-brown variety of grossularite garnet. Also called: **essonite, cinnamon stone.** [C19: from French, from Greek *hēssōn* less, inferior + -ITE[1]; so called because it is less hard than genuine hyacinth]

hest (hɛst) *n* an archaic word for **behest.** [Old English *hǣs;* related to *hātan* to promise, command]

Hestia ('hɛstɪə) *n Greek myth.* the goddess of the hearth. Roman counterpart: **Vesta.**

Hesychast ('hɛsɪˌkæst) *n Greek Orthodox Church.* a member of a school of mysticism developed by the monks of Mount Athos in the 14th century. [C18: from Medieval Latin *hesychasta* mystic, from Greek *hēsukhastēs,* from *hēsukhazein* to be tranquil, from *hēsukhos* quiet] ▸ **ˌHesy'chastic** *adj*

het[1] (hɛt) *n Slang.* short for **heterosexual.**

het[2] (hɛt) *vb* **1** *Archaic or dialect.* a past tense and past participle of **heat.** ◆ *adj* **2** a Scot. word for **hot.** ◆ See also **het up.**

hetaera (hɪ'tɪərə) *or* **hetaira** (hɪ'taɪrə) *n, pl* **-taerae** (-'tɪəriː) *or* **-tairai** (-'taɪraɪ). (esp. in ancient Greece) a female prostitute, esp. an educated courtesan. [C19: from Greek *hetaira* concubine] ▸ **he'taeric** *or* **he'tairic** *adj*

hetaerism (hɪ'tɪərɪzəm) *or* **hetairism** (hɪ'taɪrɪzəm) *n* **1** the state of being a concubine. **2** *Sociol., anthropol.* a social system attributed to some primitive societies, in which women are communally shared. ▸ **he'taerist** *or* **he'tairist** *n* ▸ **ˌhetae'ristic** *or* **ˌhetai'ristic** *adj*

heterarchy ('hɛtərɑːkɪ) *n Maths, linguistics.* a formal structure, usually represented by a diagram of connected nodes, without any single permanent uppermost node. Compare **hierarchy** (sense 5), **tree** (sense 6). [from Greek *heteros* other, different + *archē* sovereignty]

hetero ('hɛtərəʊ) *n, pl* **-os.,** *adj Informal.* short for **heterosexual.**

hetero- *combining form.* other, another, or different: *heterodyne; heterophony; heterosexual.* Compare **homo-.** [from Greek *heteros* other]

heteroblastic (ˌhɛtərəʊ'blæstɪk) *adj Botany.* (of a plant or plant part) showing a marked difference in form between the juvenile and the adult structures. Compare **homoblastic.**

heterocercal (ˌhɛtərəʊ'sɜːkᵊl) *adj Ichthyol.* of or possessing a tail in which the vertebral column turns upwards and extends into the upper, usually larger, lobe, as in sharks. Compare **homocercal.** [C19: from HETERO- + Greek *kerkos* tail]

heterochlamydeous (ˌhɛtərəʊklə'mɪdɪəs) *adj* (of a plant) having a perianth consisting of distinct sepals and petals. Compare **homochlamydeous.**

heterochromatic (ˌhɛtərəʊkrəʊ'mætɪk) *adj* **1** of or involving many different colours. **2** *Physics.* consisting of or concerned with different frequencies or wavelengths. ▸ **ˌhetero'chromatism** *n*

heterochromatin (ˌhɛtərəʊ'krəʊmətɪn) *n* the part of a chromosome that stains strongly with basic dyes in the interphase of cell division and has little genetic activity. Compare **euchromatin.**

heterochromosome (ˌhɛtərəʊ'krəʊməˌsəʊm) *n* an atypical chromosome, esp. a sex chromosome.

heterochromous (ˌhɛtərəʊ'krəʊməs) *adj* (esp. of plant parts) of different colours: *the heterochromous florets of a daisy flower.*

heteroclite ('hɛtərəˌklaɪt) *adj also* **heteroclitic** (ˌhɛtərə'klɪtɪk). **1** (esp. of the form of a word) irregular or unusual. ◆ *n* **2** an irregularly formed word. [C16: from Late Latin *heteroclitus* declining irregularly, from Greek *heteroklitos,* from HETERO- + *klinein* to bend, inflect]

heterocyclic (ˌhɛtərəʊ'saɪklɪk, -'sɪk-) *adj* (of an organic compound) containing a closed ring of atoms, at least one of which is not a carbon atom. Compare **homocyclic.**

heterodactyl (ˌhɛtərəʊ'dæktɪl) *adj* **1** (of the feet of certain birds) having the first and second toes directed backwards and the third and fourth forwards. ◆ *n* **2** a bird with heterodactyl feet. ◆ Compare **zygodactyl.**

heterodont ('hɛtərəˌdɒnt) *adj* (of most mammals) having teeth of different types. Compare **homodont.**

heterodox ('hɛtərəʊˌdɒks) *adj* **1** at variance with established, orthodox, or accepted doctrines or beliefs. **2** holding unorthodox doctrines or opinions. [C17: from Greek *heterodoxos* holding another opinion, from HETERO- + *doxa* opinion] ▸ **'heteroˌdoxy** *n*

heterodyne ('hɛtərəʊˌdaɪn) *vb* **1** *Electronics.* to combine by intermodulation (two alternating signals, esp. radio signals) to produce two signals having frequencies corresponding to the sum and the difference of the original frequencies. See also **superheterodyne receiver.** ◆ *adj* **2** produced by, operating by, or involved in heterodyning two signals.

heteroecious (ˌhɛtə'riːʃəs) *adj* (of parasites, esp. rust fungi) undergoing different stages of the life cycle on different host species. Compare **autoecious.** [from HETERO- + *-oecious,* from Greek *oikia* house] ▸ **ˌheter'oecism** *n*

heterogamete (ˌhɛtərəʊgæ'miːt) *n* a gamete that differs in size and form from the one with which it unites in fertilization. Compare **isogamete.**

heterogametic (ˌhɛtərəʊgə'mɛtɪk) *adj Genetics.* denoting the sex that possesses dissimilar sex chromosomes. In humans and many other mammals it is the male sex, possessing one X-chromosome and one Y-chromosome. Compare **homogametic.**

heterogamy (ˌhɛtə'rɒgəmɪ) *n* **1** a type of sexual reproduction in which the gametes differ in both size and form. Compare **isogamy. 2** a condition in which different types of reproduction occur in successive generations of an organism. **3** the presence of both male and female flowers in one inflorescence. Compare **homogamy** (sense 1). ▸ **ˌheterˈogamous** *adj*

heterogeneous (ˌhɛtərəʊˈdʒiːnɪəs) *adj* **1** composed of unrelated or differing parts or elements. **2** not of the same kind or type. **3** *Chem.* of, composed of, or concerned with two or more different phases. Compare **homogeneous.** [C17: from Medieval Latin *heterogeneus,* from Greek *heterogenēs,* from HETERO- + *genos* sort] ▸ **heterogeneity** (ˌhɛtərəʊdʒɪˈniːɪtɪ) *or* **ˌheteroˈgeneousness** *n* ▸ **ˌheteroˈgeneously** *adv*

heterogenesis (ˌhɛtərəʊˈdʒɛnɪsɪs) *n* another name for **alternation of generations** or **abiogenesis.** ▸ **heterogenetic** (ˌhɛtərəʊdʒɪˈnɛtɪk) *or* **ˌheteroˈgenic** *adj* ▸ **ˌheterogeˈnetically** *adv*

heterogenous (ˌhɛtəˈrɒdʒɪnəs) *adj Biology, med.* not originating within the body; of foreign origin: *a heterogenous skin graft.* Compare **autogenous.**

heterogony (ˌhɛtəˈrɒgənɪ) *n* **1** *Biology.* the alternation of parthenogenetic and sexual generations in rotifers and similar animals. **2** the condition in plants, such as the primrose, of having flowers that differ from each other in the length of their stamens and styles. Compare **homogony.** ▸ **ˌheterˈogonous** *adj* ▸ **ˌheterˈogonously** *adv*

heterograft (ˈhɛtərəʊˌgrɑːft) *n* a tissue graft obtained from a donor of a different species from the recipient.

heterography (ˌhɛtəˈrɒgrəfɪ) *n* **1** the phenomenon of different letters or sequences of letters representing the same sound in different words, as for example *-ight* and *-ite* in *blight* and *bite.* **2** any writing system in which this phenomenon occurs. ▸ **heterographic** (ˌhɛtərəʊˈgræfɪk) *or* **ˌheteroˈgraphical** *adj*

heterogynous (ˌhɛtəˈrɒdʒɪnəs) *adj* (of ants, bees, etc.) having two types of female, one fertile and the other infertile.

heterokaryon (ˌhɛtərəʊˈkærɪɒn) *n Biology.* a fungal cell or mycelium containing two or more nuclei of different genetic constitution. [from HETERO- + *karyon,* from Greek *karuon* kernel]

heterolecithal (ˌhɛtərəʊˈlɛsɪθəl) *adj* (of the eggs of birds) having an unequally distributed yolk. Compare **isolecithal.** [C19: HETERO- + Greek *lekithos* egg yolk]

heterologous (ˌhɛtəˈrɒləgəs) *adj* **1** *Pathol.* of, relating to, or designating cells or tissues not normally present in a particular part of the body. **2** (esp. of parts of an organism or of different organisms) differing in structure or origin. ▸ **ˌheterˈology** *n*

heterolysis (ˌhɛtəˈrɒlɪsɪs) *n* **1** the dissolution of the cells of one organism by the lysins of another. Compare **autolysis. 2** Also called: **heterolytic fission.** *Chem.* the dissociation of a molecule into two ions with opposite charges. Compare **homolysis.** ▸ **heterolytic** (ˌhɛtərəʊˈlɪtɪk) *adj*

heteromerous (ˌhɛtəˈrɒmərəs) *adj Biology.* having or consisting of parts that differ, esp. in number.

heteromorphic (ˌhɛtərəʊˈmɔːfɪk) *or* **heteromorphous** *adj Biology.* **1** differing from the normal form in size, shape, and function. **2** (of pairs of homologous chromosomes) differing from each other in size or form. **3** (esp. of insects) having different forms at different stages of the life cycle. ▸ **ˌheteroˈmorphism** *or* **ˌheteroˈmorphy** *n*

heteronomous (ˌhɛtəˈrɒnɪməs) *adj* **1** subject to an external law, rule, or authority. Compare **autonomous. 2** (of the parts of an organism) differing in the manner of growth, development, or specialization. **3** (in the philosophy of Kant) directed to an end other than duty for its own sake. Compare **autonomous** (sense 4b). ▸ **ˌheterˈonomously** *adv* ▸ **ˌheterˈonomy** *n*

heteronym (ˈhɛtərəʊˌnɪm) *n* one of two or more words pronounced differently but spelt alike: *the two English words spelt "bow" are heteronyms.* Compare **homograph.** [C17: from Late Greek *heteronumos,* from Greek HETERO- + *onoma* name] ▸ **heteronymous** (ˌhɛtəˈrɒnɪməs) *adj* ▸ **ˌheterˈonymously** *adv*

Heteroousian (ˌhɛtərəʊˈuːsɪən, -ˈaʊsɪən) *n* **1** a Christian who maintains that God the Father and God the Son are different in substance. ◆ *adj* **2** of or relating to this belief. [C17: from Late Greek *heteroousios,* from Greek HETERO- + *ousia* nature]

heterophony (ˌhɛtəˈrɒfənɪ) *n* the simultaneous performance of different versions of the same melody by different voices or instruments.

heterophyllous (ˌhɛtərəʊˈfɪləs, ˌhɛtəˈrɒfɪləs) *adj* (of plants such as arrowhead) having more than one type of leaf on the same plant. Also: **anisophyllous.** ▸ **ˈheteroˌphylly** *n*

heteroplasty (ˈhɛtərəʊˌplæstɪ) *n, pl* **-ties.** the surgical transplantation of tissue obtained from another person or animal. ▸ **ˌheteroˈplastic** *adj*

heteroploid (ˈhɛtərəʊˌplɔɪd) *adj* **1** of a chromosome number that is neither the haploid nor diploid number characteristic of the species. ◆ *n* **2** such a chromosome number.

heteropolar (ˌhɛtərəʊˈpəʊlə) *adj* a less common word for **polar** (sense 5a). ▸ **heteropolarity** (ˌhɛtərəʊpəʊˈlærɪtɪ) *n*

heteropterous (ˌhɛtəˈrɒptərəs) *or* **heteropteran** *adj* of, relating to, or belonging to the *Heteroptera,* a suborder of hemipterous insects, including bedbugs, water bugs, etc., in which the forewings are membranous but have leathery tips. Compare **homopterous.** [C19: from New Latin *Heteroptera,* from HETERO- + Greek *pteron* wing]

heteroscedastic (ˌhɛtərəʊskɪˈdæstɪk) *adj Statistics.* **1** (of several distributions) having different variances. **2** (of a bivariate or multivariate distribution) not having any variable whose variance is the same for all values of the other or others. **3** (of a random variable) having different variances for different values of the others in a multivariate distribution. ◆ Compare **homoscedastic.** [C20: from HETERO- + *scedastic,* from Greek *skedasis* a scattering, dispersal] ▸ **heteroscedasticity** (ˌhɛtərəʊskɪdæsˈtɪsɪtɪ) *n*

heterosexism (ˌhɛtərəʊˈsɛkˌsɪzəm) *n* discrimination on the basis of sexual orientation, practised by heterosexuals against homosexuals. ▸ **ˌheteroˈsexist** *adj, n*

heterosexual (ˌhɛtərəʊˈsɛksjʊəl) *n* **1** a person who is sexually attracted to the opposite sex. ◆ *adj* **2** of or relating to heterosexuality. ◆ Compare **homosexual.**

heterosexuality (ˌhɛtərəʊˌsɛksjʊˈælɪtɪ) *n* sexual attraction to or sexual relations with a person or persons of the opposite sex. Compare **homosexuality.**

heterosis (ˌhɛtəˈrəʊsɪs) *n Biology.* another name for **hybrid vigour.** [C19: from Late Greek: alteration, from Greek *heteroioun* to alter, from *heteros* other, different]

heterosporous (ˌhɛtəˈrɒspərəs) *adj* (of seed plants and some ferns) producing megaspores and microspores. Compare **homosporous.** ▸ **ˌheterˈospory** *n*

heterostyly (ˈhɛtərəˌstaɪlɪ) *n* the condition in certain plants, such as primroses, of having styles of different lengths, each type of style in flowers on different plants, which ensures cross-pollination. [C20: from Greek, from *heteros* different + *stylos* pillar] ▸ **ˌheteroˈstylous** *adj*

heterotaxis (ˌhɛtərəʊˈtæksɪs), **heterotaxy,** *or* **heterotaxia** *n* an abnormal or asymmetrical arrangement of parts, as of the organs of the body or the constituents of a rock. ▸ **ˌheteroˈtactic, ˌheteroˈtactous,** *or* **ˌheteroˈtaxic** *adj*

heterothallic (ˌhɛtərəʊˈθælɪk) *adj* **1** (of some algae and fungi) having male and female reproductive organs on different thalli. **2** (of some fungi) having sexual reproduction that occurs only between two self-sterile mycelia. ◆ Compare **homothallic.** [C20: from HETERO- + Greek *thallos* green shoot, young twig] ▸ **ˌheteroˈthallism** *n*

heterotopia (ˌhɛtərəʊˈtəʊpɪə) *or* **heterotopy** (ˌhɛtəˈrɒtəpɪ) *n* abnormal displacement of a bodily organ or part. [C19: from New Latin, from HETERO- + Greek *topos* place] ▸ **ˌheteroˈtopic** *or* **ˌheterˈotopous** *adj*

heterotrophic (ˌhɛtərəʊˈtrɒfɪk) *adj* (of animals and some plants) using complex organic compounds to manufacture their own organic constituents. Compare **autotrophic.** [C20: from HETERO- + Greek *trophikos* concerning food, from *trophē* nourishment] ▸ **ˈheteroˌtroph** *n*

heterotypic (ˌhɛtərəʊˈtɪpɪk) *or* **heterotypical** *adj* denoting or relating to the first nuclear division of meiosis, in which the chromosome number is halved. Compare **homeotypic.**

heterozygote (ˌhɛtərəʊˈzaɪgəʊt, -ˈzɪgəʊt) *n* an animal or plant that is heterozygous; a hybrid. Compare **homozygote.** ▸ **ˌheterozyˈgosis** *n*

heterozygous (ˌhɛtərəʊˈzaɪgəs) *adj Genetics.* (of an organism) having dissimilar alleles for any one gene: *heterozygous for eye colour.* Compare **homozygous.**

heth *or* **cheth** (hɛt; *Hebrew* xɛt) *n* the eighth letter of the Hebrew alphabet (ח), transliterated as *h* and pronounced as a pharyngeal fricative. [from Hebrew]

hetman (ˈhɛtmən) *n, pl* **-mans.** another word for **ataman.** [C18: from Polish, from German *Hauptmann* headman]

het up *adj* angry; excited: *don't get het up.*

heuchera (ˈhjuːkərə) *n* any plant of the N. American genus *Heuchera,* with low-growing heart-shaped leaves and mostly red flowers carried in sprays on slender graceful stems: family *Saxifragaceae.* See also **alumroot.** [named after J. H. *Heucher* (1677–1747), German doctor and botanist]

heulandite (ˈhjuːlənˌdaɪt) *n* a white, grey, red, or brown zeolite mineral that consists essentially of hydrated calcium aluminium silicate in the form of elongated tabular crystals. Formula: $Ca_2(Al_4Si_{14})O_{36}.12H_2O$. [C19: named after H. *Heuland,* 19th-century English mineral collector; see -ITE[1]]

heuristic (hjʊəˈrɪstɪk) *adj* **1** helping to learn; guiding in discovery or investigation. **2** (of a method of teaching) allowing pupils to learn things for themselves. **3a** *Maths, science, philosophy.* using or obtained by exploration of possibilities rather than by following set rules. **3b** *Computing.* denoting a rule of thumb for solving a problem without the exhaustive application of an algorithm: *a heuristic solution.* ◆ *n* **4** (*pl*) the science of heuristic procedure. [C19: from New Latin *heuristicus,* from Greek *heuriskein* to discover] ▸ **heuˈristically** *adv*

heuristics (hjʊəˈrɪstɪks) *n* (*functioning as sing*) *Maths, logic.* a method or set of rules for solving problems other than by algorithm. See also **algorithm** (sense 1), **artificial intelligence.**

hevea (ˈhiːvjə) *n* any tree of the South American euphorbiaceous genus *Hevea,* having a milky sap which provides rubber: used esp. in electrical insulation. [C19: New Latin from native name *hevé*]

Hevelius (*German* heˈveːlius) *n* **Johannes** (joˈhanəs). 1611–87, German astronomer, who published one of the first detailed maps of the lunar surface.

Hever Castle (ˈhiːvə) *n* a Tudor mansion near Edenbridge in Kent: home of Anne Boleyn before her marriage; Italian garden added in the 20th century by the Astor family.

Hevesy (*Hungarian* ˈhɛvɛʃi) *n* **Georg von** (ˈgeːɔrg fɔn). 1885–1966, Hungarian chemist. He worked on radioactive tracing and, with D. Coster, discovered the element hafnium (1923): Nobel prize for chemistry 1943.

hew (hjuː) *vb* **hews, hewing, hewed, hewed** *or* **hewn** (hjuːn). **1** to strike (something, esp. wood) with cutting blows, as with an axe. **2** (*tr;* often foll. by *out*) to shape or carve from a substance. **3** (*tr;* often foll. by *away, down, from, off,* etc.) to sever from a larger or another portion. **4** (*intr;* often foll. by *to*) *U.S. and Canadian.* to conform (to a code, principle, etc.). [Old English *hēawan;* related to Old Norse *heggva,* Old Saxon *hāwa,* Old High German *houwan,* Latin *cūdere* to beat] ▸ **ˈhewer** *n*

HEW (in the U.S.) *abbrev. for* Department of Health, Education, and Welfare.

Hewish (ˈhjuːɪʃ) *n* **Antony.** born 1924, British radio astronomer, noted esp. for his role in the discovery of pulsars (1967): shared the Nobel prize for physics 1974.

hex[1] (hɛks) *n* **a** short for **hexadecimal notation** *or* **hexadecimal. b** (*as modifier*): *hex code.*

hex[2] (hɛks) *Informal.* ◆ *vb* **1** (*tr*) to bewitch. ◆ *n* **2** an evil spell or symbol of bad luck. **3** a witch. [C19: via Pennsylvania Dutch from German *Hexe* witch, from

Middle High German *hecse,* perhaps from Old High German *hagzissa;* see HAG[1]] ▸ **'hexer** *n*

hex. *abbrev. for:* **1** hexachord. **2** hexagon. **3** hexagonal.

hexa- *or before a vowel* **hex-** *combining form.* six: *hexachord; hexameter.* [from Greek, from *hex* SIX]

hexachlorocyclohexane (ˌhɛksəˌklɔːrəˌsaɪkləʊ'hɛkseɪn) *n* a white or yellowish powder existing in many isomeric forms. A mixture of isomers, including lindane, is used as an insecticide. Formula: $C_6H_6Cl_6$.

hexachloroethane (ˌhɛksəˌklɔːrəʊ'ɛθeɪn) *or* **hexachlorethane** *n* a colourless crystalline insoluble compound with a camphor-like odour: used in pyrotechnics and explosives. Formula: C_2Cl_6.

hexachlorophene (ˌhɛksə'klɔːrəfiːn) *n* an insoluble almost odourless white bactericidal substance used in antiseptic soaps, deodorants, etc. Formula: $(C_6HCl_3OH)_2CH_2$.

hexachord ('hɛksəˌkɔːd) *n* (in medieval musical theory) any of three diatonic scales based upon C, F, and G, each consisting of six notes, from which solmization was developed.

hexacosanoic acid (ˌhɛksəkəʊsə'nəʊɪk) *n* a white insoluble odourless wax present in beeswax, carnauba, and Chinese wax. Formula: $CH_3(CH_2)_{24}COOH$. Also called: **cerotic acid.**

hexad ('hɛksæd) *n* **1** a group or series of six. **2** the number or sum of six. [C17: from Greek *hexas,* from *hex* six] ▸ **hex'adic** *adj*

hexadecane ('hɛksədɛˌkeɪn, ˌhɛksə'dɛkeɪn) *n* the systematic name for **cetane.** [C19: from HEXA- + DECA- + -ANE]

hexadecanoic acid ('hɛksəˌdɛkənəʊɪk) *n* the systematic name for **palmitic acid.**

hexadecimal notation *or* **hexadecimal** (ˌhɛksə'dɛsɪməl) *n* a number system having a base 16; the symbols for the numbers 0–9 are the same as those used in the decimal system, and the numbers 10–15 are usually represented by the letters A–F. The system is used as a convenient way of representing the internal binary code of a computer.

hexaemeron (ˌhɛksə'ɛmərɒn) *or* **hexahemeron** *n* **a** the period of six days in which God created the world. **b** the account of the Creation in Genesis 1. [C16: via Late Latin from Greek, from *hexaēmeros* (adj) of six days, from HEXA- + *hēmera* day] ▸ ˌ**hexa'emeric** *or* ˌ**hexa'hemeric** *adj*

hexagon ('hɛksəgən) *n* a polygon having six sides.

hexagonal (hɛk'sægənᵊl) *adj* **1** having six sides and six angles. **2** of or relating to a hexagon. **3** *Crystallog.* relating or belonging to the crystal system characterized by three equal coplanar axes inclined at 60° to each other and a fourth longer or shorter axis at right angles to their plane. See also **trigonal.** ▸ **hex'agonally** *adv*

hexagram ('hɛksəˌgræm) *n* **1** a star-shaped figure formed by extending the sides of a regular hexagon to meet at six points. **2** a group of six broken or unbroken lines which may be combined into 64 different patterns, as used in the *I Ching.* ▸ ˌ**hexa'grammoid** *adj, n*

hexahedron (ˌhɛksə'hiːdrən) *n* a solid figure having six plane faces. A **regular hexahedron** (cube) has square faces. See also **polyhedron.** ▸ ˌ**hexa'hedral** *adj*

hexahydrate (ˌhɛksə'haɪdreɪt) *n* a hydrate, such as magnesium chloride, $MgCl_2.6H_2O$, with six molecules of water per molecule of substance. ▸ ˌ**hexa'hydrated** *adj*

hexahydropiridine (ˌhɛksəhaɪdrəʊ'pɪrɪˌdiːn) *n* the systematic name for **piperidine.**

hexahydropyrazine (ˌhɛksəhaɪdrəʊ'paɪrəˌziːn) *n* the systematic name for **piperazine.**

hexamerous (hɛk'sæmərəs) *or* **hexameral** *adj* (esp. of the parts of a plant) arranged in groups of six. ▸ **hex'amerism** *n*

hexameter (hɛk'sæmɪtə) *n Prosody.* **1** a verse line consisting of six metrical feet. **2** (in Greek and Latin epic poetry) a verse line of six metrical feet, of which the first four are usually dactyls or spondees, the fifth almost always a dactyl, and the sixth a spondee or trochee. ▸ **hexametric** (ˌhɛksə'mɛtrɪk), **hex'ametral,** *or* ˌ**hexa'metrical** *adj*

hexamethylenetetramine (ˌhɛksəˌmɛθɪliːn'tɛtrəˌmiːn) *n* a colourless crystalline organic compound used as a urinary antiseptic. Formula: $C_6H_{12}N_4$. Also called: **hexamine, methenamine.**

hexamine ('hɛksəmiːn) *n* **1** another name for **hexamethylenetetramine. 2** a type of fuel produced in small solid blocks or tablets for use in miniature camping stoves.

hexane ('hɛkseɪn) *n* a liquid alkane existing in five isomeric forms that are found in petroleum and used as solvents, esp. the isomer with a straight chain of carbon atoms (*n*-hexane). Formula: C_6H_{14}. [C19: from HEXA- + -ANE]

hexangular (hɛk'sæŋgjʊlə) *adj* having six angles.

hexanoic acid (ˌhɛksə'nəʊɪk) *n* an insoluble oily carboxylic acid found in coconut and palm oils and in milk. Formula: $C_5H_{11}COOH$. [C20: from HEXANE + *-oic*]

hexapla ('hɛksəplə) *n* an edition of the Old Testament compiled by Origen, containing six versions of the text. [C17: from Greek *hexaploos* sixfold] ▸ **'hexaplar, hexaplaric** (ˌhɛksə'plærɪk), *or* **hexaplarian** (ˌhɛksə'plɛərɪən) *adj*

hexapod ('hɛksəˌpɒd) *n* any arthropod of the class *Hexapoda* (or *Insecta);* an insect.

hexapody (hɛk'sæpədɪ) *n, pl* **-dies.** *Prosody.* a verse measure consisting of six metrical feet. ▸ **hexapodic** (ˌhɛksə'pɒdɪk) *adj*

hexastich ('hɛksəˌstɪk) *or* **hexastichon** (hɛk'sæstɪˌkɒn) *n Prosody.* a poem, stanza, or strophe that consists of six lines. ▸ ˌ**hexa'stichic** *adj*

hexastyle ('hɛksəˌstaɪl) *Architect.* ◆ *n* **1** a portico or façade with six columns. ◆ *adj* **2** having six columns.

Hexateuch ('hɛksəˌtjuːk) *n* the first six books of the Old Testament. [C19: from HEXA- + Greek *teukhos* a book] ▸ **'Hexaˌteuchal** *adj*

hexavalent (ˌhɛksə'veɪlənt) *adj Chem.* having a valency of six. Also: **sexivalent.**

hexone ('hɛksəʊn) *n* another name for **methyl isobutyl ketone.**

hexosan ('hɛksəˌsæn) *n* any of a group of polysaccharides that yield hexose on hydrolysis.

hexose ('hɛksəʊs, -əʊz) *n* a monosaccharide, such as glucose, that contains six carbon atoms per molecule.

hexyl ('hɛksɪl) *n* (*modifier*) of, consisting of, or containing the group of atoms C_6H_{13}, esp. the isomeric form of this group, $CH_3(CH_2)_4CH_2$-: *a hexyl group or radical.*

hexylresorcinol (ˌhɛksɪlrɪ'zɔːsɪˌnɒl) *n* a yellowish-white crystalline phenol that has a fatty odour and sharp taste; 2,4- dihydroxy-1-hexylbenzene: used for treating bacterial infections of the urinary tract. Formula: $C_{12}H_{18}O_2$.

hey (heɪ) *interj* **1** an expression indicating surprise, dismay, discovery, etc., or calling for another's attention. **2 hey presto.** an exclamation used by conjurors to herald the climax of a trick. [C13: compare Old French *hay,* German *hei,* Swedish *hej*]

heyday ('heɪˌdeɪ) *n* the time of most power, popularity, vigour, etc.; prime. [C16: probably based on HEY]

Heyduck ('haɪdʊk) *n* a variant spelling of **Haiduk.**

Heyer ('heɪə) *n* **Georgette.** 1902–74, British historical novelist and writer of detective stories, noted esp. for her romances of the Regency period.

Heyerdahl (*Norwegian* 'hɛiərdaːl) *n* **Thor** (tɔː). born 1914, Norwegian anthropologist. In 1947 he demonstrated that the Polynesians could originally have been migrants from South America, by sailing from Peru to the Pacific Islands of Tuamotu in the *Kon-Tiki,* a raft made of balsa wood. DNA testing in the late 1990s indicated that such a migration did not actually take place.

Heysham ('heɪʃəm) *n* a port in NW England, in NW Lancashire. Pop. (with Morecambe): 46 657 (1991).

Heywood[1] ('heɪˌwʊd) *n* a town in NW England, in Rochdale unitary authority, Greater Manchester near Bury. Pop.: 29 286 (1991).

Heywood[2] ('heɪˌwʊd) *n* **1 John.** ?1497–?1580, English dramatist, noted for his comic interludes. **2 Thomas.** ?1574–1641, English dramatist, noted esp. for his domestic drama *A Woman Killed with Kindness* (1607).

Hezbollah (ˌhɛzbə'lɑː) *or* **Hizbollah** *n* an organization of militant Shiite Muslims based in Lebanon. [C20: Arabic, literally: party of God]

Hezekiah (ˌhɛzə'kaɪə) *n* a king of Judah ?715–?687 B.C., noted for his religious reforms (II Kings 18–19). Douay spelling: **Ezechias.** [from Hebrew *hizqīyyāhū* God has strengthened]

hf *abbrev. for* half.

Hf *the chemical symbol for* hafnium.

HF *or* **h.f.** *abbrevs. for* high frequency.

hg *abbrev. for* hectogram.

Hg *the chemical symbol for* mercury. [from New Latin HYDRARGYRUM]

HG *abbrev. for:* **1** High German. **2** His (*or* Her) Grace. **3** (in Britain) Home Guard.

HGH *abbrev. for* human growth hormone.

hgt *abbrev. for* height.

HGV (formerly, in Britain) *abbrev. for* heavy goods vehicle.

HH *abbrev. for* **1** His (*or* Her) Highness. **2** His Holiness (title of the Pope). ◆ **3** (on Brit. pencils) *symbol for* double hard.

hhd *abbrev. for* hogshead.

H-hour *n Military.* the specific hour at which any operation commences. Also called: **zero hour.**

hi[1] (haɪ) *sentence substitute.* an informal word for **hello.** [C20: originally U.S., from HIYA]

hi[2] (haɪ) *interj* an expression used to attract attention. [C15: *hy;* compare HEY]

HI *abbrev. for:* **1** Hawaii (state). **2** Hawaiian Islands.

Hialeah (ˌhaɪə'liːə) *n* a city in SE Florida, near Miami: racetrack. Pop.: 204 684 (1996 est.).

hiatus (haɪ'eɪtəs) *n, pl* **-tuses** *or* **-tus. 1** (esp. in manuscripts) a break or gap where something is missing. **2** a break or interruption in continuity. **3** a break between adjacent vowels in the pronunciation of a word. **4** *Anatomy.* a natural opening or aperture; foramen. **5** *Anatomy.* a less common word for **vulva.** [C16: from Latin: gap, cleft, aperture, from *hiāre* to gape, yawn] ▸ **hi'atal** *adj*

hiatus hernia *or* **hiatal hernia** *n* protrusion of part of the stomach through the diaphragm at the oesophageal opening.

Hiawatha (ˌhaɪə'wɒθə) *n* a 16th-century Onondaga Indian chief: credited with the organization of the Five Nations.

Hib (hɪb) *n acronym for Haemophilus influenzae* type b: a vaccine against a type of bacterial meningitis, administered to children.

hibachi (hɪ'bɑːtʃɪ) *n* a portable brazier for heating and cooking food. [from Japanese, from *hi* fire + *bachi* bowl]

hibakusha (hɪ'bɑːkʊʃə) *n, pl* **-sha** *or* **-shas.** a survivor of either of the atomic-bomb attacks on Hiroshima and Nagasaki in 1945. [C20: from Japanese, from *hibaku* exposed + *-sha* -person]

hibernaculum (ˌhaɪbə'nækjʊləm) *or* **hibernacle** ('haɪbəˌnækᵊl) *n, pl* **-ula** (-jʊlə) *or* **-les.** *Rare.* **1** the winter quarters of a hibernating animal. **2** the protective case or covering of a plant bud or animal. [C17: from Latin: winter residence; see HIBERNATE]

hibernal (haɪ'bɜːnᵊl) *adj* of or occurring in winter. [C17: from Latin *hībernālis,* from *hiems* winter]

hibernate ('haɪbəˌneɪt) *vb* (*intr*) **1** (of some mammals, reptiles, and amphibians) to pass the winter in a dormant condition with metabolism greatly slowed down. Compare **aestivate. 2** to cease from activity. [C19: from Latin *hībernāre* to spend the winter, from *hībernus* of winter, from *hiems* winter] ▸ ˌ**hiber'nation** *n* ▸ **'hiberˌnator** *n*

Hibernia (haɪ'bɜːnɪə) *n* the Roman name for **Ireland**[1]: used poetically in later times. ▸ **Hi'bernian** *adj, n*

Hibernicism (haɪ'bɜːnɪˌsɪzəm) *or* **Hibernianism** (haɪ'bɜːnɪəˌnɪzəm) *n* an Irish expression, idiom, trait, custom, etc.

Hiberno- (haɪ'bɜːnəʊ) *combining form.* denoting Irish or Ireland: *Hiberno-English.*

hibiscus (haɪ'bɪskəs) *n, pl* **-cuses.** any plant of the chiefly tropical and subtropical malvaceous genus *Hibiscus,* esp. *H. rosa-sinensis,* cultivated for its large brightly coloured flowers. [C18: from Latin, from Greek *hibiskos* marsh mallow]

hic (hɪk) *interj* a representation of the sound of a hiccup.

hiccup ('hɪkʌp) *n* **1** a spasm of the diaphragm producing a sudden breathing in followed by a closing of the glottis, resulting in a sharp sound. Technical name: **singultus. 2** the state or condition of having such spasms. **3** *Informal.* a minor difficulty or problem. ◆ *vb* **-cups, -cuping, -cuped** *or* **-cups, -cupping, -cupped. 4** (*intr*) to make a hiccup or hiccups. **5** (*tr*) to utter with a hiccup or hiccups. ◆ Also: **hiccough** ('hɪkʌp). [C16: of imitative origin]

hic jacet *Latin.* (hɪk 'jæket) (on gravestones) here lies.

hick (hɪk) *n Informal.* **a** a country person; bumpkin. **b** (*as modifier*): *hick ideas.* [C16: after *Hick,* familiar form of *Richard*]

hickey ('hɪkɪ) *n* **1** *U.S. and Canadian informal.* an object or gadget: used as a name when the correct name is forgotten, etc.; doodah. **2** *U.S. and Canadian informal.* a mark on the skin, esp. a lovebite. **3** *Printing.* a spot on a printed sheet caused by an imperfection or a speck on the printing plate. [C20: of unknown origin]

Hickok ('hɪkɒk) *n* **James Butler,** known as *Wild Bill Hickok.* 1837–76, U.S. frontiersman and marshal.

hickory ('hɪkərɪ) *n, pl* **-ries. 1** any juglandaceous tree of the chiefly North American genus *Carya,* having nuts with edible kernels and hard smooth shells. See also **pecan, pignut** (sense 1), **bitternut** (sense 1), **shagbark. 2** the hard tough wood of any of these trees. **3** the nut of any of these trees. **4** a switch or cane made of hickory wood. [C17: from earlier *pohickery,* from Algonquian *pawcohiccora* food made from ground hickory nuts]

hid (hɪd) *vb* the past tense and a past participle of **hide**[1].

hidalgo (hɪ'dælgəʊ; *Spanish* i'ðalγo) *n, pl* **-gos** (-gəʊz; *Spanish* -γos). a member of the lower nobility in Spain. [C16: from Spanish, from Old Spanish *fijo dalgo* nobleman, from Latin *filius* son + *dē* of + *aliquid* something]

Hidalgo (hɪ'dælgəʊ; *Spanish* i'ðalγo) *n* a state of central Mexico: consists of a high plateau, with the Sierra Madre Oriental in the north and east; ancient remains of Teltec culture (at Tula); rich mineral resources. Capital: Pachuca. Pop.: 2 111 782 (1995 est.). Area: 20 987 sq. km (8103 sq. miles).

HIDB *abbrev. for* Highlands and Islands Development Board.

hidden ('hɪdᵊn) *vb* **1** a past participle of **hide**[1]. ◆ *adj* **2** concealed or obscured: *a hidden cave; a hidden meaning.* ► **'hiddenly** *adv* ► **'hiddenness** *n*

hidden agenda *n* a hidden motive or intention behind an overt action, policy, etc.

hidden hand *n* an unknown force or influence believed to be the cause of certain, often unfortunate, events.

hiddenite ('hɪdəˌnaɪt) *n* a green transparent variety of the mineral spodumene, used as a gemstone. [C19: named after W. E. *Hidden* (1853–1918), American mineralogist who discovered it]

hide[1] (haɪd) *vb* **hides, hiding, hid** (hɪd), **hidden** ('hɪdᵊn) *or* **hid. 1** to put or keep (oneself or an object) in a secret place; conceal (oneself or an object) from view or discovery: *to hide a pencil; to hide from the police.* **2** (*tr*) to conceal or obscure: *the clouds hid the sun.* **3** (*tr*) to keep secret. **4** (*tr*) to turn (one's head, eyes, etc.) away. ◆ *n* **5** *Brit.* a place of concealment, usually disguised to appear as part of the natural environment, used by hunters, birdwatchers, etc. U.S. and Canadian equivalent: **blind.** ◆ See also **hide-out.** [Old English *hȳdan;* related to Old Frisian *hēda,* Middle Low German *hüden,* Greek *keuthein*] ► **'hidable** *adj* ► **'hider** *n*

hide[2] (haɪd) *n* **1** the skin of an animal, esp. the tough thick skin of a large mammal, either tanned or raw. **2** *Informal.* the human skin. **3** *Austral. and N.Z. informal.* impudence. ◆ *vb* **hides, hiding, hided. 4** (*tr*) *Informal.* to flog. [Old English *hȳd;* related to Old Norse *hūth,* Old Frisian *hēd,* Old High German *hūt,* Latin *cutis* skin, Greek *kutos;* see CUTICLE] ► **'hideless** *adj*

hide[3] (haɪd) *n* an obsolete Brit. unit of land measure, varying in magnitude from about 60 to 120 acres. [Old English *hīgid;* related to *hīw* family, household, Latin *cīvis* citizen]

hide-and-seek *or U.S. and Canadian* **hide-and-go-seek** *n* a game in which one player covers his eyes and waits while the others hide, and then he tries to find them.

hideaway ('haɪdəˌweɪ) *n* a hiding place or secluded spot.

hidebound ('haɪdˌbaʊnd) *adj* **1** restricted by petty rules, a conservative attitude, etc. **2** (of cattle, etc.) having the skin closely attached to the flesh as a result of poor feeding. **3** (of trees) having a very tight bark that impairs growth.

hideous ('hɪdɪəs) *adj* **1** extremely ugly; repulsive: *a hideous person.* **2** terrifying and horrific. [C13: from Old French *hisdos,* from *hisde* fear; of uncertain origin] ► **'hideously** *adv* ► **'hideousness** *or* **hideosity** (ˌhɪdɪ'ɒsɪtɪ) *n*

hide-out *n* **1** a hiding place, esp. a remote place used by outlaws, etc.; hideaway. ◆ *vb* **hide out.** (*intr*) **2** to remain deliberately concealed, esp. for a prolonged period of time.

Hideyoshi Toyotomi (ˌhiːde'jɔːʃɪ ˌtɔːjɔː'tɔːmɪ) *n* 1536–98, Japanese military dictator (1582–98). He unified all Japan (1590).

hiding[1] ('haɪdɪŋ) *n* **1** the state of concealment (esp. in the phrase **in hiding**). **2** **hiding place.** a place of concealment.

hiding[2] ('haɪdɪŋ) *n* **1** *Informal.* a flogging; beating. **2 be on a hiding to nothing.** to be bound to fail; to face impossible odds.

hidrosis (hɪ'drəʊsɪs) *n* **1** a technical word for **perspiration** or **sweat. 2** any skin disease affecting the sweat glands. **3** Also called: **hyperhidrosis** (ˌhaɪpəhɪ'drəʊsɪs, -haɪ'drəʊsɪs). *Pathol.* excessive perspiration. [C18: via New Latin from Greek: sweating, from *hidrōs* sweat] ► **hidrotic** (hɪ'drɒtɪk) *adj*

hidy-hole *or* **hidey-hole** ('haɪdɪˌhəʊl) *n Informal.* a hiding place.

hie (haɪ) *vb* **hies, hieing** *or* **hying, hied.** *Archaic or poetic.* to hurry; hasten; speed. [Old English *hīgian* to strive]

hieland ('hiːlənd) *adj Scot. dialect.* **1** a variant of **Highland. 2** characteristic of Highlanders, esp. alluding to their supposed gullibility or foolishness in towns or cities.

hiemal ('haɪəməl) *adj* a less common word for **hibernal.** [C16: from Latin *hiems* winter; see HIBERNATE]

hieracosphinx (ˌhaɪə'reɪkəʊˌsfɪŋks) *n, pl* **-sphinxes** *or* **-sphinges** (-ˌsfɪndʒiːz). (in ancient Egyptian art) a hawk-headed sphinx. [C18: from Greek *hierax* hawk + SPHINX]

hierarch ('haɪəˌrɑːk) *n* **1a** a person in a position of high priestly authority. **1b** a person holding high rank in a religious hierarchy. **2** a person at a high level in a hierarchy. ► ˌ**hier'archal** *adj*

hierarchy ('haɪəˌrɑːkɪ) *n, pl* **-chies. 1** a system of persons or things arranged in a graded order. **2** a body of persons in holy orders organized into graded ranks. **3** the collective body of those so organized. **4** a series of ordered groupings within a system, such as the arrangement of plants and animals into classes, orders, families, etc. **5** *Linguistics, etc.* a formal structure, usually represented by a diagram of connected nodes, with a single uppermost element. Compare **ordering, heterarchy, tree** (sense 6). **6** government by an organized priesthood. [C14: from Medieval Latin *hierarchia,* from Late Greek *hierarkhia,* from *hierarkhēs* high priest; see HIERO-, -ARCHY] ► ˌ**hier'archical** *or* ˌ**hier'archic** *adj* ► ˌ**hier'archically** *adv* ► **'hierˌarchism** *n*

hieratic (ˌhaɪə'rætɪk) *adj also* **hieratical. 1** of or relating to priests. **2** of or relating to a cursive form of hieroglyphics used by priests in ancient Egypt. **3** of or relating to styles in art that adhere to certain fixed types or methods, as in ancient Egypt. ◆ *n* **4** the hieratic script of ancient Egypt. [C17: from Latin *hierāticus,* from Greek *hieratikos,* from *hiereus* a priest, from *hieros* holy] ► ˌ**hier'atically** *adv*

hiero- *or before a vowel* **hier-** *combining form.* holy or divine: *hierocracy; hierarchy.* [from Greek, from *hieros*]

hierocracy (ˌhaɪə'rɒkrəsɪ) *n, pl* **-cies.** government by priests or ecclesiastics. ► **hierocratic** (ˌhaɪərə'krætɪk) *or* ˌ**hiero'cratical** *adj*

hierodule ('haɪərəˌdjuːl) *n* (in ancient Greece) a temple slave, esp. a sacral prostitute. [C19: from Greek *hierodoulos,* from HIERO- + *doulos* slave] ► ˌ**hiero'dulic** *adj*

hieroglyphic (ˌhaɪərə'glɪfɪk) *adj also* **hieroglyphical. 1** of or relating to a form of writing using picture symbols, esp. as used in ancient Egypt. **2** written with hieroglyphic symbols. **3** difficult to read or decipher. ◆ *n also* **hieroglyph. 4** a picture or symbol representing an object, concept, or sound. **5** a symbol or picture that is difficult to read or decipher. [C16: from Late Latin *hieroglyphicus,* from Greek *hieroglyphikos,* from HIERO- + *gluphē* carving, from *gluphein* to carve] ► ˌ**hiero'glyphically** *adv* ► **hieroglyphist** (ˌhaɪərə'glɪfɪst, ˌhaɪə'rɒg-) *n*

hieroglyphics (ˌhaɪərə'glɪfɪks) *n* (*functioning as sing or pl*) **1** a form of writing, esp. as used in ancient Egypt, in which pictures or symbols are used to represent objects, concepts, or sounds. **2** difficult or undecipherable writing.

hierogram ('haɪərəˌgræm) *n* a sacred symbol.

hierology (ˌhaɪə'rɒlədʒɪ) *n, pl* **-gies. 1** sacred literature. **2** a biography of a saint. ► **hierologic** (ˌhaɪərə'lɒdʒɪk) *or* ˌ**hiero'logical** *adj* ► ˌ**hier'ologist** *n*

Hieronymus (ˌhaɪə'rɒnɪməs) *n* **Eusebius** (juː'siːbɪəs). the Latin name of (Saint) **Jerome.** ► **Hieronymic** (ˌhaɪərə'nɪmɪk) *or* ˌ**Hiero'nymian** *adj*

hierophant ('haɪərəˌfænt) *n* **1** (in ancient Greece) an official high priest of religious mysteries, esp. those of Eleusis. **2** a person who interprets and explains esoteric mysteries. [C17: from Late Latin *hierophanta,* from Greek *hierophantēs,* from HIERO- + *phainein* to reveal] ► ˌ**hiero'phantic** *adj* ► ˌ**hiero'phantically** *adv*

hifalutin (ˌhaɪfə'luːtɪn) *adj* a variant spelling of **highfalutin.**

hi-fi ('haɪ'faɪ) *n Informal.* **1a** short for **high fidelity. 1b** (*as modifier*): *hi-fi equipment.* **2** a set of high-quality sound-reproducing equipment.

Higgins ('hɪgɪnz) *n* **Alex,** known as *Hurricane Higgins.* born 1949, Northern Irish snooker player.

higgle ('hɪgᵊl) *vb* a less common word for **haggle.** ► **'higgler** *n*

higgledy-piggledy ('hɪgᵊldɪ'pɪgᵊldɪ) *Informal.* ◆ *adj, adv* **1** in a jumble. ◆ *n* **2** a muddle.

Higgs particle (hɪgs) *n Physics.* an elementary particle with zero spin and mass greater than zero, predicted to exist by electroweak theory and other gauge theories. [C20: named after Peter *Higgs* (born 1929), British theoretical physicist]

high (haɪ) *adj* **1** being a relatively great distance from top to bottom; tall: *a high building.* **2** situated at or extending to a relatively great distance above the ground or above sea level: *a high plateau.* **3a** (*postpositive*) being a specified distance from top to bottom: *three feet high.* **3b** (*in combination*): *a seven-foot-high wall.* **4** extending from an elevation: *a high dive.* **5** (*in combination*) coming up to a specified level: *knee-high.* **6** being at its peak or point of culmination: *high noon.* **7** of greater than average height: *a high collar.* **8** greater than normal in degree, intensity, or amount: *high prices; a high temperature; a high wind.* **9** of large or relatively large numerical value: *high frequency; high voltage; high mileage.* **10** (of sound) acute in pitch; having a high frequency. **11** (of latitudes) situated relatively far north or south from the equator. **12** (of meat) slightly decomposed or tainted, regarded as enhancing the flavour of game. **13** of great eminence; very important: *the high priestess.* **14** exalted in style or character; elevated: *high drama.* **15** expressing or feeling contempt or arrogance: *high words.* **16** elated; cheerful: *high spirits.* **17** (*predicative*) *Informal.* overexcited: *by the end of term the children are really high.* **18** *Informal.*

being in a state of altered consciousness, characterized esp. by euphoria and often induced by the use of alcohol, narcotics, etc. **19** luxurious or extravagant: *high life.* **20** advanced in complexity or development: *high finance.* **21** (of a gear) providing a relatively great forward speed for a given engine speed. Compare **low**[1] (sense 21). **22** *Phonetics.* of, relating to, or denoting a vowel whose articulation is produced by raising the back of the tongue towards the soft palate or the blade towards the hard palate, such as for the *ee* in English *see* or *oo* in English *moon.* Compare **low**[1] (sense 20). **23** (*cap. when part of name*) formal and elaborate in style: *High Mass.* **24** (*usually cap.*) of or relating to the High Church. **25** remote, esp. in time. **26** *Cards.* **26a** having a relatively great value in a suit. **26b** able to win a trick. **27 high and dry.** stranded; helpless; destitute. **28 high and low.** in all places; everywhere. **29 high and mighty.** *Informal.* arrogant. **30 high as a kite.** *Informal.* **30a** very drunk. **30b** overexcited. **30c** euphoric from drugs. **31 high opinion.** a favourable opinion. ◆ *adv* **32** at or to a height: *he jumped high.* **33** in a high manner. **34** *Nautical.* close to the wind with sails full. ◆ *n* **35** a high place or level. **36** *Informal.* a state of altered consciousness, often induced by alcohol, narcotics, etc. **37** another word for **anticyclone. 38** short for **high school. 39** (*cap*) (esp. in Oxford) the High Street. **40** *Electronics.* the voltage level in a logic circuit corresponding to logical one. Compare **low**[1] (sense 30). **41 on high. 41a** at a height. **41b** in heaven. [Old English *hēah;* related to Old Norse *hār,* Gothic *hauhs,* Old High German *hōh* high, Lithuanian *kaũkas* bump, Russian *kúchča* heap, Sanskrit *kuča* bosom]

high altar *n* the principal altar of a church.

High Arctic *n* the regions of Canada, esp. the northern islands, within the Arctic Circle.

highball ('haɪˌbɔːl) *Chiefly U.S.* ◆ *n* **1** a long iced drink consisting of a spirit base with water, soda water, etc. **2** (originally in railway use) a signal that the way ahead is clear and one may proceed. ◆ *vb* **3** (*intr*) to move at great speed. **4** (*tr*) to drive (a vehicle) at great speed. [C19: (in sense 2) from the early railway signal consisting of a ball hoisted to the top of a pole]

highbinder ('haɪˌbaɪndə) *n U.S. informal.* **1** a gangster. **2** a corrupt politician. **3** (formerly) a member of a Chinese-American secret society that engaged in blackmail, murder, etc. [C19: named after the *High-binders,* a New York city gang]

highborn ('haɪˌbɔːn) *adj* of noble or aristocratic birth.

highboy ('haɪˌbɔɪ) *n U.S. and Canadian.* a tall chest of drawers in two sections, the lower section being a lowboy. Brit. equivalent: **tallboy.**

high brass *n* brass containing 65 per cent copper and 35 per cent zinc, used for most applications.

highbrow ('haɪˌbraʊ) *Often disparaging.* ◆ *n* **1** a person of scholarly and erudite tastes. ◆ *adj also* **highbrowed. 2** appealing to highbrows: *highbrow literature.*

high camp *n* a sophisticated form of **camp**[2] (the style).

high-carbon steel *n* steel containing between 0.5 and 1.5 per cent carbon.

highchair ('haɪˌtʃɛə) *n* a long-legged chair for a child, esp. one with a table-like tray used at meal times.

High Church *n* **1** the party or movement within the Church of England stressing continuity with Catholic Christendom, the authority of bishops, and the importance of sacraments, rituals, and ceremonies. Compare **Broad Church, Low Church.** ◆ *adj* **High-Church. 2** of or relating to this party or movement. ▸ **'High-'Churchman** *n*

high-class *adj* **1** of very good quality; superior: *a high-class grocer.* **2** belonging to, associated with, or exhibiting the characteristics of an upper social class: *a high-class lady; a high-class prostitute.*

high-coloured *adj* (of the complexion) deep red or purplish; florid.

high comedy *n* comedy set largely among cultured and articulate people and featuring witty dialogue. Compare **low comedy.** ▸ **high comedian** *n*

high command *n* the commander-in-chief and senior officers of a nation's armed forces.

high commissioner *n* **1** the senior diplomatic representative sent by one Commonwealth country to another instead of an ambassador. **2** the head of an international commission. **3** the chief officer in a colony or other dependency.

high country *n* (often preceded by *the*) sheep pastures in the foothills of the Southern Alps, New Zealand.

High Court *n* **1** a shortened form of: **1a** (in England and Wales) High Court of Justice. **1b** (in Scotland) High Court of Justiciary. **2** (in New Zealand) a court of law inferior to the Court of Appeal; formerly called: **Supreme Court.**

High Court of Justice *n* (in England) one of the two divisions of the Supreme Court of Judicature. See also **Court of Appeal.**

High Court of Justiciary *n* the senior criminal court in Scotland, to which all cases of murder and rape and all cases involving heavy penalties are referred.

high day *n* a day of celebration; festival (esp. in the phrase **high days and holidays**).

high definition television *n* a television system offering a picture with superior definition, using 1000 or more scanning lines, and possibly a higher field repetition rate to reduce flicker effects. Abbrev.: **HDTV.**

high-density *adj Computing.* (of a floppy disk) having a relatively high storage capacity, usually of 1.2 or 1.44 megabytes.

high-end *adj* (*prenominal*) (esp. of computers, electronic equipment, etc.) of the greatest power or sophistication.

high-energy physics *n* another name for **particle physics.**

higher ('haɪə) *adj* **1** the comparative of **high.** ◆ *n* (*usually cap.*) (in Scotland) **2a** the advanced level of the Scottish Certificate of Education. **2b** (*as modifier*): *Higher Latin.* **3** a pass in a particular subject at Higher level: *she has four Highers.*

higher criticism *n* the use of scientific techniques of literary criticism to establish the sources of the books of the Bible. Compare **lower criticism.**

higher education *n* education and training at colleges, universities, polytechnics, etc.

higher mathematics *n* (*functioning as sing*) mathematics, including number theory and topology, that is more abstract than normal arithmetic, algebra, geometry, and trigonometry.

higher-rate tax *n* (in Britain) a rate of income tax that is higher than the basic rate and becomes payable on taxable income in excess of a specified limit.

higher-up *n Informal.* a person of higher rank or in a superior position.

highest common factor *n* the largest number or quantity that is a factor of each member of a group of numbers or quantities. Abbrev.: **HCF, h.c.f.** Also called: **greatest common divisor.**

high explosive *n* an extremely powerful chemical explosive, such as TNT or gelignite.

highfalutin, hifalutin (ˌhaɪfə'luːtɪn), *or* **highfaluting** *adj Informal.* pompous or pretentious. [C19: from HIGH + *-falutin,* perhaps variant of *fluting,* from FLUTE]

high fashion *n* another name for **haute couture.**

high fidelity *n* **a** the reproduction of sound using electronic equipment that gives faithful reproduction with little or no distortion. **b** (*as modifier*): *a high-fidelity amplifier.* ◆ Often shortened to **hi-fi.**

high-five *Slang.* ◆ *n* **1** a gesture of greeting or congratulation in which two people slap raised right palms together. ◆ *vb* **2** to greet or congratulate (a person) in this way.

high-flown *adj* extravagant or pretentious in conception or intention: *high-flown ideas.*

high-flyer *or* **high-flier** *n* **1** a person who is extreme in aims, ambition, etc. **2** a person of great ability, esp. in a career. ▸ **ˌhigh-'flying** *adj, n*

high frequency *n* a radio-frequency band or radio frequency lying between 30 and 3 megahertz. Abbrev.: **HF.**

High German *n* **1** the standard German language, historically developed from the form of West Germanic spoken in S Germany. Abbrev.: **HG.** See also **German, Low German. 2** any of the German dialects of S Germany, Austria, or Switzerland.

high-handed *adj* tactlessly overbearing and inconsiderate. ▸ **ˌhigh-'handedly** *adv* ▸ **ˌhigh-'handedness** *n*

high hat *n* another name for **top hat.**

high-hat *adj* **1** *Informal.* snobbish and arrogant. ◆ *vb* **-hats, -hatting, -hatted.** (*tr*) **2** *Informal, chiefly U.S. and Canadian.* to treat in a snobbish or offhand way. ◆ *n* **3** *Informal.* a snobbish person. **4** two facing brass cymbals triggered by means of a foot pedal.

High Holidays *pl n Judaism.* the festivals of Rosh Hashanah and Yom Kippur, the period of repentance in the first ten days of the Jewish new year. Also called: **Days of Awe, Yamim Nora'im.**

high hurdles *n* (*functioning as sing*) a race in which competitors leap over hurdles 42 inches (107 cm) high.

highjack ('haɪˌdʒæk) *vb, n* a less common spelling of **hijack.** ▸ **'highˌjacker** *n*

high jinks *or* **hijinks** ('haɪˌdʒɪŋks) *n* lively enjoyment.

high jump *n* **1a** (usually preceded by *the*) an athletic event in which a competitor has to jump over a high bar set between two vertical supports. **1b** (*as modifier*): *high-jump techniques.* **2 be for the high jump.** *Brit. informal.* to be liable to receive a severe reprimand or punishment. ▸ **high jumper** *n* ▸ **high jumping** *n*

high-key *adj* (of a photograph, painting, etc.) having a predominance of light grey tones or light colours. Compare **low-key** (sense 3).

high-keyed *adj* **1** having a high pitch; shrill. **2** *U.S.* highly strung. **3** bright in colour.

highland ('haɪlənd) *n* **1** relatively high ground. **2** (*modifier*) of or relating to a highland. ▸ **'highlander** *n*

Highland ('haɪlənd) *n* **1** a council area in N Scotland, formed in 1975 (as Highland Region) from Caithness, Sutherland, Nairnshire, most of Inverness-shire, and Ross and Cromarty except for the Outer Hebrides. Administrative centre: Inverness. Pop.: 206 900 (1996 est.). Area: 25 149 sq. km (9710 sq. miles). **2** (*modifier*) of, relating to, or denoting the Highlands of Scotland.

Highland cattle *n* a breed of cattle with shaggy hair, usually reddish-brown in colour, and long horns.

Highland Clearances *pl n* in Scotland, the removal, often by force, of the people from some parts of the Highlands to make way for sheep, during the eighteenth and nineteenth centuries. Also called: **the Clearances.**

Highland dress *n* **1** the historical costume, including the plaid, kilt or filibeg, and bonnet, as worn by Highland clansmen and soldiers. **2** a modern version of this worn for formal occasions.

Highlander ('haɪləndə) *n* **1** a native of the Highlands of Scotland. **2** a member of a Scottish Highland regiment.

Highland fling *n* a vigorous Scottish solo dance.

Highland Games *n* (*functioning as sing or pl*) a meeting in which competitions in sport, piping, and dancing are held: originating in the Highlands of Scotland.

Highlands ('haɪləndz) *n* **the. 1a** the part of Scotland that lies to the northwest of the great fault that runs from Dumbarton to Stonehaven. **1b** a smaller area consisting of the mountainous north of Scotland: distinguished by Gaelic culture. **2** (*often not cap.*) the highland region of any country.

high-level *adj* (of conferences, talks, etc.) involving very important people.

high-level language *n* a computer programming language that resembles natural language or mathematical notation and is designed to reflect the requirements of a problem; examples include Ada, BASIC, C, COBOL, FORTRAN, Pascal. See also **machine code.**

high-level waste *n* radioactive waste material, such as spent nuclear fuel, having a high activity and thus needing constant cooling for several decades by its producers before it can be disposed of. Compare **intermediate-level waste, low-level waste.**

highlife ('haɪˌlaɪf) *n* **a** a style of music combining West African elements with U.S. jazz forms, found esp. in the cities of West Africa. **b** (*as modifier*): *a highlife band.*

highlight ('haɪˌlaɪt) *n* **1** an area of the lightest tone in a painting, drawing, photograph, etc. **2** the most exciting or memorable part of an event or period of time. **3** (*often pl*) a bleached blond streak in the hair. ◆ *vb* (*tr*) **4** *Painting, drawing, photog., etc.* to mark (any brightly illuminated or prominent part of a form or figure) with light tone. **5** to bring notice or emphasis to. **6** to be the highlight of. **7** to produce blond streaks in (the hair) by bleaching.

highlighter ('haɪˌlaɪtə) *n* **1** a cosmetic cream or powder applied to the face to highlight the cheekbones, eyes, etc. **2** a fluorescent felt-tip pen used as a marker to emphasize a section of text without obscuring it.

highly ('haɪlɪ) *adv* **1** (intensifier): *highly pleased; highly disappointed.* **2** with great approbation or favour: *we spoke highly of it.* **3** in a high position: *placed highly in class.* **4** at or for a high price or cost.

highly strung *or U.S. and Canadian* **high-strung** *adj* tense and easily upset; excitable; nervous.

High Mass *n* a solemn and elaborate sung Mass. Compare **Low Mass.**

high-minded *adj* **1** having or characterized by high moral principles. **2** *Archaic.* arrogant; haughty. ▸ ˌ**high-'mindedly** *adv* ▸ ˌ**high-'mindedness** *n*

high-muck-a-muck *n* a conceited or haughty person. [C19: from Chinook Jargon *hiu muckamuck,* literally: plenty (of) food]

highness ('haɪnɪs) *n* the condition of being high or lofty.

Highness ('haɪnɪs) *n* (preceded by *Your, His,* or *Her*) a title used to address or refer to a royal person.

high-octane *adj* **1** (of petrol) having a high octane number. **2** *Informal.* dynamic, forceful, or intense: *high-octane drive and efficiency.*

high-pass filter *n Electronics.* a filter that transmits all frequencies above a specified value, substantially attenuating frequencies below this value. Compare **low-pass filter, band-pass filter.**

high-pitched *adj* **1** pitched high in volume or tone. See **high** (sense 10). **2** (of a roof) having steeply sloping sides. **3** (of an argument, style, etc.) lofty or intense.

high place *n Old Testament.* a place of idolatrous worship, esp. a hilltop.

high places *pl n* positions and offices of influence and importance: *a scandal in high places.*

high point *n* a moment or occasion of great intensity, interest, happiness, etc.: *the award marked a high point in his life.*

high-powered *adj* **1** (of an optical instrument or lens) having a high magnification: *a high-powered telescope.* **2** dynamic and energetic; highly capable. **3** possessing great strength, power, etc.: *a high-powered engine.*

high-pressure *adj* **1** having, using, involving, or designed to withstand a pressure above normal pressure: *a high-pressure gas; a high-pressure cylinder.* **2** *Informal.* (of selling) persuasive in an aggressive and persistent manner.

high priest *n* **1** *Judaism.* the priest of highest rank who alone was permitted to enter the holy of holies of the tabernacle and Temple. **2** *Mormon Church.* a priest of the order of Melchizedek priesthood. **3** Also (*fem*) **high priestess.** the head of a group or cult. ▸ **high priesthood** *n*

high profile *n* **a** a position or approach characterized by a deliberate seeking of prominence or publicity. **b** (*as modifier*): *a high-profile campaign.* ◆ Compare **low profile.**

high relief *n* relief in which forms and figures stand out from the background to half or more than half of their natural depth. Also called: **alto-relievo.**

High Renaissance *n* **a the.** the period from about the 1490s to the 1520s in painting, sculpture, and architecture in Europe, esp. in Italy, when the Renaissance ideals were considered to have been attained through the mastery of Leonardo, Michelangelo, and Raphael. **b** (*as modifier*): *High Renaissance art.*

high-rise *adj* **a** (*prenominal*) of or relating to a building that has many storeys, esp. one used for flats or offices: *a high-rise block.* Compare **low-rise. b** (*as n*): *a high-rise in Atlanta.*

high-risk *adj* denoting a group, part, etc., that is particularly subject or exposed to a danger.

highroad ('haɪˌrəʊd) *n* **1** a main road; highway. **2** (usually preceded by *the*) the sure way: *the highroad to fame.*

high roller *n Slang, chiefly U.S. and Canadian.* a person who spends money extravagantly or gambles recklessly. ▸ **high rolling** *n, adj*

high school *n* **1** *Brit.* another term for **grammar school. 2** *U.S. and N.Z.* a secondary school from grade 7 to grade 12. **3** *Canadian.* a secondary school, the grades covered depending on the province.

high seas *pl n* (*sometimes sing*) the open seas of the world, outside the jurisdiction of any one nation.

high season *n* the most popular time of year at a holiday resort, etc.

Highsmith ('haɪˌsmɪθ) *n* **Patricia.** 1921–95, U.S. author of crime fiction. Her novels include *Strangers on a Train* (1950) and *Ripley's Game* (1974).

high society *n* **a** the upper classes, esp. when fashionable. **b** (*as modifier*): *her high-society image.*

high-sounding *adj* another term for **high-flown.**

high-speed *adj Photog.* **1** employing or requiring a very short exposure time: *high-speed film.* **2** recording or making exposures at a rate usually exceeding 50 and up to several million frames per second. **3** working, moving, or operating at a high speed.

high-speed steel *n* any of various steels that retain their hardness at high temperatures and are thus suitable for making tools used on lathes and other high-speed machines.

high-spirited *adj* vivacious, bold, or lively. ▸ ˌ**high-'spiritedly** *adv* ▸ ˌ**high-'spiritedness** *n*

high spot *n Informal.* another word for **highlight** (sense 2).

high-stepper *n* a horse trained to lift its feet high off the ground when walking or trotting.

High Street (*often not caps.*) *n* (usually preceded by *the*) **1** *Brit.* the main street of a town, usually where the principal shops are situated. **2** the market constituted by the general public. **3** (*modifier*) geared to meet the requirements of, and readily available for purchase by, the general public: *High-Street fashion.*

hight (haɪt) *vb* (*tr; used only as a past tense in the passive or as a past participle*) *Archaic and poetic.* to name; call: *a maid hight Mary.* [Old English *heht,* from *hatan* to call; related to Old Norse *heita,* Old Frisian *hēta,* Old High German *heizzan*]

high table *n* (*sometimes caps.*) the table, sometimes elevated, in the dining hall of a school, college, etc., at which the principal teachers, fellows, etc., sit.

hightail ('haɪˌteɪl) *vb* (*intr*) *Informal, chiefly U.S. and Canadian.* to go or move in a great hurry. Also: **hightail it.**

High Tatra *n* another name for the **Tatra Mountains.**

high tea *n Brit.* See **tea** (sense 4c).

high tech (tɛk) *n* a variant spelling of **hi tech.**

high technology *n* highly sophisticated, often electronic, techniques used in manufacturing and other processes.

high-tension *n* (*modifier*) subjected to, carrying, or capable of operating at a relatively high voltage: *a high-tension wire.* Abbrev.: **HT.**

high tide *n* **1a** the tide at its highest level. **1b** the time at which it reaches this. **2** a culminating point.

high time *Informal.* ◆ *adv* **1** the latest possible time; a time that is almost too late: *it's high time you mended this shelf.* ◆ *n* **2** Also called: **high old time.** an enjoyable and exciting time.

high-toned *adj* **1** having a superior social, moral, or intellectual quality. **2** affectedly superior. **3** high in tone.

high tops *pl n* training shoes that reach above the ankles.

high treason *n* an act of treason directly affecting a sovereign or state.

high-up *n Informal.* a person who holds an important or influential position.

highveld ('haɪˌfɛlt, -ˌvɛlt) *n* **the.** the high-altitude grassland region of E South Africa.

high water *n* **1** another name for **high tide** (sense 1). **2** the state of any stretch of water at its highest level, as during a flood. ◆ Abbrev.: **HW.**

high-water mark *n* **1a** the level reached by sea water at high tide or by other stretches of water in flood. **1b** the mark indicating this level. **2** the highest point.

highway ('haɪˌweɪ) *n* **1** a public road that all may use. **2** *Now chiefly U.S. and Canadian except in legal contexts.* a main road, esp. one that connects towns or cities. **3** a main route for any form of transport. **4** a direct path or course.

Highway Code *n* (in Britain) a booklet compiled by the Department of Transport for the guidance of users of public roads.

highwayman ('haɪˌweɪmən) *n, pl* **-men.** (formerly) a robber, usually on horseback, who held up travellers.

highway robbery *n Informal.* blatant overcharging.

high wire *n* a tightrope stretched high in the air for balancing acts.

High Wycombe ('wɪkəm) *n* a town in S central England, in S Buckinghamshire: furniture industry. Pop.: 71 718 (1991).

HIH *abbrev. for* His (*or* Her) Imperial Highness.

hi-hat *n* a variant spelling of **high-hat** (sense 4).

hijab (hɪ'dʒæb, hɛ'dʒɑːb) *or* **hejab** *n* a covering for the head and face, worn by Muslim women. [from Arabic, literally: curtain]

hijack *or* **highjack** ('haɪˌdʒæk) *vb* **1** (*tr*) to seize, divert, or appropriate (a vehicle or the goods it carries) while in transit: *to hijack an aircraft.* **2** to rob (a person or vehicle) by force: *to hijack a traveller.* **3** (esp. in the U.S. during Prohibition) to rob (a bootlegger or smuggler) of his illicit goods or to steal (illicit goods) in transit. ◆ *n* **4** the act or an instance of hijacking. [C20: of unknown origin] ▸ '**hiˌjacker** *or* '**highˌjacker** *n*

Hijaz (hiː'dʒæz) *n* a variant spelling of **Hejaz.**

Hijrah ('hɪdʒrə) *n* a variant of **Hegira.**

hike (haɪk) *vb* **1** (*intr*) to walk a long way, usually for pleasure or exercise, esp. in the country. **2** (usually foll. by *up*) to pull or be pulled; hitch. **3** (*tr*) to increase (a price). ◆ *n* **4** a long walk. **5** a rise in prices, wages, etc. [C18: of uncertain origin] ▸ '**hiker** *n*

hike out *vb* (*intr, adv*) *Naut.* the U.S. and Canadian term for **sit out** (sense 3).

hilarious (hɪ'lɛərɪəs) *adj* very funny or merry. [C19: from Latin *hilaris* glad, from Greek *hilaros*] ▸ **hi'lariously** *adv* ▸ **hi'lariousness** *n*

hilarity (hɪ'lærɪtɪ) *n* mirth and merriment; cheerfulness.

Hilary of Poitiers ('hɪlərɪ) *n* **Saint.** ?315–?367 A.D., French bishop, an opponent of Arianism. Feast day: Jan. 13 or 14.

Hilary term *n* the spring term at Oxford University, the Inns of Court, and some other educational establishments. [C16: named after Saint HILARY OF POITIERS]

Hilbert ('hɪlbət) *n* **David** ('dɑːfɪt). 1862–1943, German mathematician, who made outstanding contributions to the theories of number fields and invariants and to geometry.

Hildebrand ('hɪldəˌbrænd) *n* the monastic name of **Gregory VII.** ▸ ˌ**Hildeˈbrandian** *adj, n* ▸ '**HildeˌbrandIne** *adj*

Hildegard of Bingen ('hɪldəgɑːd; 'bɪŋən) *n* **Saint.** 1098–1179, German abbess, poet, composer, and mystic.

Hildesheim (*German* 'hɪldəshaim) *n* a city in N central Germany, in Lower Saxony: a member of the Hanseatic League. Pop.: 106 101 (1996 est.).

hill (hɪl) *n* **1a** a conspicuous and often rounded natural elevation of the earth's surface, less high or craggy than a mountain. **1b** (*in combination*): *a hillside; a* *hilltop.* **2a** a heap or mound made by a person or animal. **2b** (*in combination*): *a dunghill.* **3** an incline; slope. **4 over the hill. 4a** *Informal.* beyond one's prime. **4b** *Military slang.* absent without leave or deserting. **5 up hill and down dale.** strenuously and persistently. ♦ *vb* (*tr*) **6** to form into a hill or mound. **7** to cover or surround with a mound or heap of earth. ♦ See also **hills.** [Old English *hyll;* related to Old Frisian *holla* head, Latin *collis* hill, Low German *hull* hill] ► **'hiller** *n* ► **'hilly** *adj*

Hill (hɪl) *n* **1 Archibald Vivian.** 1886–1977, British biochemist, noted for his research into heat loss in muscle contraction: shared the Nobel prize for physiology or medicine (1922). **2 Damon Graham Devereux,** son of Graham Hill. born 1960, British motor-racing driver; Formula One world champion (1996). **3 David Octavius.** 1802–70, Scottish painter and portrait photographer, noted esp. for his collaboration with the chemist Robert Adamson (1821–48). **4 Geoffrey (William).** born 1932, British poet: his books include *King Log* (1968), *Mercian Hymns* (1971), *The Mystery of the Charity of Charles Péguy* (1983), and *The Triumph of Love* (1999). **5 Graham.** 1929–75, British motor-racing driver: world champion (1962, 1968). **6 Octavia.** 1838–1912, British housing reformer; a founder of the National Trust. **7** Sir **Rowland.** 1795–1879, British originator of the penny postage. **8 Susan (Elizabeth).** born 1942, British novelist and writer of short stories: her books include *I'm the King of the Castle* (1970) and *The Woman in Black* (1983).

Hilla ('hɪlə) *n* a market town in central Iraq, on a branch of the Euphrates: built partly of bricks from the nearby site of Babylon. Pop.: 268 834 (1987). Also called: **Al Hillah.**

Hillary ('hɪlərɪ) *n* Sir **Edmund.** born 1919, New Zealand explorer and mountaineer. He and his Sherpa guide, Tenzing Norgay, were the first to reach the summit of Mount Everest (1953); New Zealand ambassador to India (1984–89).

hillbilly ('hɪl,bɪlɪ) *n, pl* **-lies. 1** *Usually disparaging.* an unsophisticated person, esp. from the mountainous areas in the southeastern U.S. **2** another name for **country and western.** [C20: from HILL + *Billy* (the nickname)]

hill climb *n* a competition in which motor vehicles attempt singly to ascend a steep slope as fast as possible.

hill country *n N.Z.* (in North Island) elevated pasture land for sheep or cattle.

Hillel ('hɪlɛl, -lәl) *n* ?60 B.C.–?9 A.D., rabbi, born in Babylonia; president of the Sanhedrin. He was the first to formulate principles of biblical interpretation.

Hiller ('hɪlə) *n* Dame **Wendy.** born 1912, British actress. Her many films include *Pygmalion* (1938), *Major Barbara* (1940), and *Separate Tables* (1958).

hillfort ('hɪl,fɔːt) *n Archaeol.* a hilltop fortified with ramparts and ditches, dating from the second millennium B.C.

Hilliard ('hɪlɪəd) *n* **Nicholas.** 1537–1619, English miniaturist, esp. of portraits.

Hillingdon ('hɪlɪŋdən) *n* a residential borough of W Greater London. Pop.: 243 000 (1994 est.). Area: 110 sq. km (43 sq. miles).

hill mynah *n* a starling, *Gracula religiosa,* of S and SE Asia: a popular cage bird because of its ability to talk. Also called: **Indian grackle.**

hillock ('hɪlək) *n* a small hill or mound. [C14 *hilloc,* from HILL + -OCK] ► **'hillocked** *or* **'hillocky** *adj*

hills (hɪlz) *pl n* **1 the.** a hilly and often remote region. **2 as old as the hills.** very old.

hill station *n* (in northern India) a settlement or resort at a high altitude.

hilt (hɪlt) *n* **1** the handle or shaft of a sword, dagger, etc. **2 to the hilt.** to the full. ♦ *vb* **3** (*tr*) to supply with a hilt. [Old English; related to Old Norse *hjalt,* Old Saxon *helta* oar handle, Old High German *helza*]

Hilton ('hɪltən) *n* **Walter.** died 1396, English mystical writer: author of *The Scale of Perfection.*

hilum ('haɪləm) *n, pl* **-la** (-lə). **1** *Botany.* **1a** a scar on the surface of a seed marking its point of attachment to the seed stalk (funicle). **1b** the nucleus of a starch grain. **2** a rare word for **hilus.** [C17: from Latin: trifle; see NIHIL]

hilus ('haɪləs) *n* a deep fissure or depression on the surface of a bodily organ around the point of entrance or exit of vessels, nerves, or ducts. [C19: via New Latin from Latin: a trifle] ► **'hilar** *adj*

Hilversum ('hɪlvəsəm; *Dutch* 'hɪlvərsym) *n* a city in the central Netherlands, in North Holland province: Dutch radio and television centre. Pop.: 84 213 (1994).

him (hɪm; *unstressed* ɪm) *pron* (*objective*) **1** refers to a male person or animal: *they needed him; she baked him a cake; not him again!* **2** *Chiefly U.S.* a dialect word for **himself** when used as an indirect object: *he ought to find him a wife.* [Old English *him,* dative of *hē* HE[1]]

USAGE See at **me**[1].

HIM *abbrev. for* His (*or* Her) Imperial Majesty.

Himachal Pradesh (hɪ'mɑːtʃəl prɑː'deʃ) *n* a state of N India, in the W Himalayas: rises to about 6700 m (22 000 ft.) and is densely forested. Capital: Simla. Pop.: 5 530 000 (1994 est.). Area: 55 658 sq. km (21 707 sq. miles).

Himalayan cat *n* the U.S. name for **colourpoint cat.**

Himalayas (,hɪmə'leɪəz, hɪ'mɑːljəz) *pl n* **the.** a vast mountain system in S Asia, extending 2400 km (1500 miles) from Kashmir (west) to Assam (east), between the valleys of the Rivers Indus and Brahmaputra: covers most of Nepal, Sikkim, Bhutan, and the S edge of Tibet; the highest range in the world, with several peaks over 7500 m (25 000 ft.). Highest peak: Mount Everest, 8848 m (29 028 ft.). ► **,Hima'layan** *adj*

Himalia (hɪ'mɑːlɪə) *n Astronomy.* a satellite of Jupiter in an intermediate orbit.

himation (hɪ'mætɪ,ɒn) *n, pl* **-ia** (-ɪə). (in ancient Greece) a cloak draped around the body. [C19: from Greek: a little garment, from *heima* dress, from *hennunai* to clothe]

Himeji ('hiːmɛ,dʒiː) *n* a city in central Japan, on W Honshu: cotton textile centre. Pop.: 470 986 (1995).

Himmler (*German* 'hɪmlər) *n* **Heinrich** ('hainrɪç). 1900–45, German Nazi leader, head of the SS and the Gestapo (1936–45); committed suicide.

Hims (hɪmz) *n* a former name of **Homs.**

himself (hɪm'sɛlf; *medially often* ɪm'sɛlf) *pron* **1a** the reflexive form of *he* or *him.* **1b** (intensifier): *the king himself waved to me.* **2** (*preceded by a copula*) his normal or usual self: *he seems himself once more.* **3** *Irish and Scot.* the man of the house: *how is himself?* [Old English *him selfum,* dative singular of *hē self;* see HE[1], SELF]

Himyarite ('hɪmjə,raɪt) *n* **1** a member of an ancient people of SW Arabia, sometimes regarded as including the Sabeans. ♦ *adj* **2** of or relating to this people or their culture. [C19: named after *Himyar* legendary king in ancient Yemen]

Himyaritic (,hɪmjə'rɪtɪk) *n* **1** the extinct language of the Himyarites, belonging to the SE Semitic subfamily of the Afro-Asiatic family. ♦ *adj* **2** of, relating to, or using this language.

hin (hɪn) *n* a Hebrew unit of capacity equal to about 12 pints or 3.5 litres. [from Late Latin, from Greek, from Hebrew *hīn,* from Egyptian *hnw*]

Hinayana (,hiːnə'jɑːnə) *n* **a** any of various early forms of Buddhism. **b** (*as modifier*): *Hinayana Buddhism.* [from Sanskrit *hīnayāna,* from *hīna* lesser + *yāna* vehicle] ► **,Hina'yanist** *n* ► **,Hinaya'nistic** *adj*

Hinckley ('hɪŋklɪ) *n* a town in central England, in Leicestershire. Pop.: 40 608 (1991 est.).

hind[1] (haɪnd) *adj* **hinder, hindmost** *or* **hindermost.** (*prenominal*) (esp. of parts of the body) situated at the back or rear: *a hind leg.* [Old English *hindan* at the back, related to German *hinten;* see BEHIND, HINDER[2]]

hind[2] (haɪnd) *n, pl* **hinds** *or* **hind. 1** the female of the deer, esp. the red deer when aged three years or more. **2** any of several marine serranid fishes of the genus *Epinephelus,* closely related and similar to the gropers. [Old English *hind;* related to Old High German *hinta,* Greek *kemas* young deer, Lithuanian *szmúlas* hornless]

hind[3] (haɪnd) *n* (formerly) **1** a simple peasant. **2** (in N Britain) a skilled farm worker. **3** a steward. [Old English *hīne,* from *hīgna,* genitive plural of *hīgan* servants]

Hind. *abbrev. for:* **1** Hindi. **2** Hindu. **3** Hindustan. **4** Hindustani.

hindbrain ('haɪnd,breɪn) *n* the nontechnical name for **rhombencephalon.**

Hindemith (*German* 'hɪndəmɪt) *n* **Paul** (paul). 1895–1963, German composer and musical theorist, who opposed the twelve-tone technique. His works include the song cycle *Das Marienleben* (1923) and the opera *Mathis der Maler* (1938).

Hindenburg[1] ('hɪndənbʊrk) *n* the German name for **Zabrze.**

Hindenburg[2] ('hɪndən,bɜːg; *German* 'hɪndənbʊrk) *n* **Paul von Beneckendorff und von** (paul fɔn 'bɛnəkəndɔrf unt fɔn). 1847–1934, German field marshal and statesman; president (1925–34). During World War I he directed German strategy together with Ludendorff (1916–18).

Hindenburg line *n* a line of strong fortifications built by the German army near the Franco-Belgian border in 1916–17: breached by the Allies in August 1918. [C20: named after P. von HINDENBURG]

hinder[1] ('hɪndə) *vb* **1** to be or get in the way of (someone or something); hamper. **2** (*tr*) to prevent. [Old English *hindrian;* related to Old Norse *hindra,* Old High German *hintarōn*] ► **'hinderer** *n* ► **'hindering** *adj, n*

hinder[2] ('haɪndə) *adj* (*prenominal*) situated at or further towards the back or rear; posterior. [Old English; related to Old Norse *hindri* latter, Gothic *hindar* beyond, Old High German *hintar* behind]

hindgut ('haɪnd,gʌt) *n* **1** the part of the vertebrate digestive tract comprising the colon and rectum. **2** the posterior part of the digestive tract of arthropods. ♦ See also **foregut, midgut.**

Hindi ('hɪndɪ) *n* **1** a language or group of dialects of N central India. It belongs to the Indic branch of the Indo-European family and is closely related to Urdu. See also **Hindustani. 2** a formal literary dialect of this language, the official language of India, usually written in Nagari script. **3** a person whose native language is Hindi. [C18: from Hindi *hindī,* from *Hind* India, from Old Persian *Hindu* the river Indus]

hindmost ('haɪnd,məʊst) *or* **hindermost** ('haɪndə,məʊst) *adj* furthest back; last.

Hindoo ('hɪnduː, hɪn'duː) *n, pl* **-doos,** *adj* an older spelling of **Hindu.** ► **Hindooism** ('hɪndu,ɪzəm) *n*

hindquarter ('haɪnd,kwɔːtə) *n* **1** one of the two back quarters of a carcass of beef, lamb, etc. **2** (*pl*) the rear, esp. of a four-legged animal.

hindrance ('hɪndrəns) *n* **1** an obstruction or snag; impediment. **2** the act of hindering; prevention.

hindsight ('haɪnd,saɪt) *n* **1** the ability to understand, after something has happened, what should have been done or what caused the event. **2** a firearm's rear sight.

Hindu *or* **Hindoo** ('hɪnduː, hɪn'duː) *n, pl* **-dus** *or* **-doos. 1** a person who adheres to Hinduism. **2** an inhabitant or native of Hindustan or India, esp. one adhering to Hinduism. ♦ *adj* **3** relating to Hinduism, Hindus, or India. [C17: from Persian *Hindū,* from *Hind* India; see HINDI]

Hinduism *or* **Hindooism** ('hɪndu,ɪzəm) *n* the complex of beliefs, values, and customs comprising the dominant religion of India, characterized by the worship of many gods, including Brahma as supreme being, a caste system, belief in reincarnation, etc.

Hindu Kush (kʊʃ, kuːʃ) *pl n* a mountain range in central Asia, extending about 800 km (500 miles) east from the Koh-i-Baba Mountains of central Afghanistan to the Pamirs. Highest peak: Tirich Mir, 7690 m (25 230 ft.).

Hindustan (,hɪndʊ'stɑːn) *n.* **1** the land of the Hindus, esp. India north of the Deccan and excluding Bengal. **2** the general area around the Ganges where Hindi is the predominant language. **3** the areas of India where Hinduism predominates, as contrasted with those areas where Islam predominates.

Hindustani, Hindoostani (,hɪndʊ'stɑːnɪ), *or* **Hindostani** (,hɪndəʊ'stɑːnɪ) *n* **1** the dialect of Hindi spoken in Delhi: used as a lingua franca throughout India. **2** a group of languages or dialects consisting of all spoken forms of Hindi and Urdu considered together. ◆ *adj* **3** of or relating to these languages or Hindustan.

Hines (haɪnz) *n* **Earl,** known as *Earl "Fatha" Hines.* 1905–83, U.S. jazz pianist, conductor, and songwriter.

hinge (hɪndʒ) *n* **1** a device for holding together two parts such that one can swing relative to the other, typically having two interlocking metal leaves held by a pin about which they pivot. **2** *Anatomy.* a type of joint, such as the knee joint, that moves only backwards and forwards; a joint that functions in only one plane. Technical name: **ginglymus. 3** a similar structure in invertebrate animals, such as the joint between the two halves of a bivalve shell. **4** something on which events, opinions, etc., turn. **5** Also called: **mount.** *Philately.* a small thin transparent strip of gummed paper for affixing a stamp to a page. ◆ *vb* **6** (*tr*) to attach or fit a hinge to (something). **7** (*intr;* usually foll. by *on* or *upon*) to depend (on). **8** (*intr*) to hang or turn on or as if on a hinge. [C13: probably of Germanic origin; compare Middle Dutch *henge;* see HANG] ► **hinged** *adj* ► **'hingeless** *adj* ► **'hinge,like** *adj*

hinny[1] ('hɪnɪ) *n, pl* **-nies.** the sterile hybrid offspring of a male horse and a female donkey or ass. Compare **mule**[1] (sense 1). [C17: from Latin *hinnus,* from Greek *hinnos*]

hinny[2] ('hɪnɪ) *vb* **-nies, -nying, -nied.** a less common word for **whinny.**

hinny[3] ('hɪnɪ) *n Scot. and northern English dialect.* a term of endearment, esp. for a woman or child. [variant of HONEY]

Hinshelwood ('hɪnʃəl,wʊd) *n* Sir **Cyril Norman.** 1897–1967, English chemist, who shared the Nobel prize for chemistry (1956) for the study of reaction kinetics.

hint (hɪnt) *n* **1** a suggestion or implication given in an indirect or subtle manner: *he dropped a hint.* **2** a helpful piece of advice or practical suggestion. **3** a small amount; trace. ◆ *vb* **4** (when *intr,* often foll. by *at;* when *tr, takes a clause as object*) to suggest or imply indirectly. [C17: of uncertain origin] ► **'hinter** *n* ► **'hinting** *n* ► **'hintingly** *adv*

hinterland ('hɪntə,lænd) *n* **1** land lying behind something, esp. a coast or the shore of a river. **2** remote or undeveloped areas of a country. **3** an area located near and dependent on a large city, esp. a port. [C19: from German, from *hinter* behind + *land* LAND; see HINDER[2]]

hip[1] (hɪp) *n* **1** (*often pl*) either side of the body below the waist and above the thigh, overlying the lateral part of the pelvis and its articulation with the thighbones. **2** another name for **pelvis** (sense 1). **3** short for **hip joint. 4** the angle formed where two sloping sides of a roof meet or where a sloping side meets a sloping end. [Old English *hype;* related to Old High German *huf,* Gothic *hups,* Dutch *heup*] ► **'hipless** *adj* ► **'hip,like** *adj*

hip[2] (hɪp) *n* the berry-like brightly coloured fruit of a rose plant: a swollen receptacle, rich in vitamin C, containing several small hairy achenes. Also called: **rosehip.** [Old English *héopa;* related to Old Saxon *hiopo,* Old High German *hiufo,* Dutch *joop,* Norwegian dialect *hjūpa*]

hip[3] (hɪp) *interj* an exclamation used to introduce cheers (in the phrase **hip, hip, hurrah**). [C18: of unknown origin]

hip[4] (hɪp) *or* **hep** *adj* **hipper, hippest** *or* **hepper, heppest.** *Slang.* **1** aware of or following the latest trends in music, ideas, fashion, etc. **2** (*often postpositive;* foll. by *to*) informed (about). [C20: variant of earlier *hep*]

hip bath *n* a portable bath in which the bather sits.

hipbone ('hɪp,bəʊn) *n* the nontechnical name for **innominate bone.**

hip flask *n* a small metal flask for spirits, etc., often carried in a hip pocket.

hip-hop ('hɪp,hɒp) *n* a U.S. pop culture movement of the 1980s comprising rap music, graffiti, and break dancing.

hip-huggers *pl n Chiefly U.S.* trousers that begin at the hips instead of the waist. Usual Brit. word: **hipsters.**

hip joint *n* the ball-and-socket joint that connects each leg to the trunk of the body, in which the head of the femur articulates with the socket (acetabulum) of the pelvis.

hipparch ('hɪpɑːk) *n* (in ancient Greece) a cavalry commander. [C17: from Greek *hippos* horse + -ARCH]

Hipparchus[1] (hɪ'pɑːkəs) *n* **1** 2nd century B.C., Greek astronomer. He discovered the precession of the equinoxes, calculated the length of the solar year, and developed trigonometry. **2** died 514 B.C., tyrant of Athens (527–514).

Hipparchus[2] (hɪ'pɑːkəs) *n* a large crater in the SW quadrant of the moon, about 130 kilometres in diameter.

hippeastrum (hɪpɪ'æstrəm) *n* any plant of the South American amaryllidaceous genus *Hippeastrum:* cultivated for their large funnel-shaped typically red flowers. [C19: New Latin, from Greek *hippeus* knight + *astron* star]

hipped[1] (hɪpt) *adj* **1a** having a hip or hips. **1b** (*in combination*)*: broad-hipped; low-hipped.* **2** (esp. of cows, sheep, reindeer, elk, etc.) having an injury to the hip, such as a dislocation of the bones. **3** *Architect.* having a hip or hips. See also **hipped roof.**

hipped[2] (hɪpt) *adj* (*often postpositive;* foll. by *on*) *U.S. and Canadian dated slang.* very enthusiastic (about). [C20: from HIP[4]]

hipped roof *n* a roof having sloping ends and sides.

hippie ('hɪpɪ) *n* a variant spelling of **hippy**[1].

hippo ('hɪpəʊ) *n, pl* **-pos.** *Informal.* **1** short for **hippopotamus. 2** *S. Africa.* an armoured police car.

hippocampus (,hɪpəʊ'kæmpəs) *n, pl* **-pi** (-paɪ). **1** a mythological sea creature with the forelegs of a horse and the tail of a fish. **2** any marine teleost fish of the genus *Hippocampus,* having a horselike head. See **sea horse. 3** an area of cerebral cortex that forms a ridge in the floor of the lateral ventricle of the brain, which in cross section has the shape of a sea horse. It functions as part of the limbic system. [C16: from Latin, from Greek *hippos* horse + *kampos* a sea monster] ► **,hippo'campal** *adj*

hip pocket *n* a pocket at the back of a pair of trousers.

hippocras ('hɪpəʊ,kræs) *n* an old English drink of wine flavoured with spices. [C14 *ypocras,* from Old French: HIPPOCRATES, probably referring to a filter called *Hippocrates' sleeve*]

Hippocrates (hɪ'pɒkrə,tiːz) *n* ?460–?377 B.C., Greek physician, commonly regarded as the father of medicine. ► **,Hippo'cratic** *or* **,Hippo'cratical** *adj*

Hippocratic oath *n* an oath taken by a doctor to observe a code of medical ethics derived from that of Hippocrates.

Hippocrene ('hɪpəʊ,kriːn, ,hɪpəʊ'kriːnɪ) *n* a spring on Mount Helicon in Greece, said to engender poetic inspiration. [C17: via Latin from Greek *hippos* horse + *krēnē* spring] ► **,Hippo'crenian** *adj*

hippodrome ('hɪpə,drəʊm) *n* **1** a music hall, variety theatre, or circus. **2** (in ancient Greece or Rome) an open-air course for horse and chariot races. [C16: from Latin *hippodromos,* from Greek *hippos* horse + *dromos* a race]

hippogriff *or* **hippogryph** ('hɪpəʊ,grɪf) *n* a monster of Greek mythology with a griffin's head, wings, and claws and a horse's body. [C17: from Italian *ippogrifo,* from *ippo-* horse (from Greek *hippos*) + *grifo* GRIFFIN[1]]

Hippolyta (hɪ'pɒlɪtə) *or* **Hippolyte** (hɪ'pɒlɪ,tiː) *n Greek myth.* a queen of the Amazons, slain by Hercules in battle for her belt, which he obtained as his ninth labour.

Hippolytus (hɪ'pɒlɪtəs) *n Greek myth.* a son of Theseus, killed after his stepmother Phaedra falsely accused him of raping her. ► **Hip'polytan** *adj*

Hippomenes (hɪ'pɒmɪ,niːz) *n Greek myth.* the husband, in some traditions, of Atalanta.

hippopotamus (,hɪpə'pɒtəməs) *n, pl* **-muses** *or* **-mi** (-,maɪ). **1** a very large massive gregarious artiodactyl mammal, *Hippopotamus amphibius,* living in or around the rivers of tropical Africa: family *Hippopotamidae.* It has short legs and a thick skin sparsely covered with hair. **2 pigmy hippopotamus.** a related but smaller animal, *Choeropsis liberiensis.* [C16: from Latin, from Greek *hippopotamos* river horse, from *hippos* horse + *potamos* river]

Hippo Regius ('hɪpəʊ 'riːdʒɪəs) *n* an ancient Numidian city, adjoining present-day Annaba, Algeria. Often shortened to **Hippo.**

hippuric acid (hɪ'pjʊərɪk) *n* a crystalline solid excreted in the urine of mammals. Formula: $C_9H_9NO_3$.

hippy[1] *or* **hippie** ('hɪpɪ) *n, pl* **-pies. a** (esp. during the 1960s) a person whose behaviour, dress, use of drugs, etc., implied a rejection of conventional values. **b** (*as modifier*)*: hippy language.* [C20: see HIP[4]]

hippy[2] ('hɪpɪ) *adj* **-pier, -piest.** *Informal.* (esp. of a woman) having large hips.

hip roof *n* a roof having sloping ends and sides.

hipster ('hɪpstə) *n* **1** *Slang, now rare.* **1a** an enthusiast of modern jazz. **1b** an outmoded word for **hippy**[1]. **2** (*modifier*) (of trousers) cut so that the top encircles the hips.

hipsters ('hɪpstəz) *pl n Brit.* trousers cut so that the top encircles the hips. Usual U.S. word: **hip-huggers.**

hiragana (,hɪərə'gɑːnə) *n* one of the Japanese systems of syllabic writing based on Chinese cursive ideograms. The more widely used of the two current systems, it is employed in newspapers and general literature. Compare **katakana.** [from Japanese: flat kana]

Hiram ('haɪərəm) *n* 10th century B.C., king of Tyre, who supplied Solomon with materials and craftsmen for the building of the Temple (II Samuel 5:11; I Kings 5:1–18).

hircine ('hɜːsaɪn, -sɪn) *adj* **1** *Archaic.* of or like a goat, esp. in smell. **2** *Literary.* lustful; lascivious. [C17: from Latin *hircīnus,* from *hircus* goat]

hire ('haɪə) *vb* (*tr*) **1** to acquire the temporary use of (a thing) or the services of (a person) in exchange for payment. **2** to employ (a person) for wages. **3** (often foll. by *out*) to provide (something) or the services of (oneself or others) for an agreed payment, usually for an agreed period. **4** (*tr;* foll. by *out*) *Chiefly Brit.* to pay independent contractors for (work to be done). ◆ *n* **5a** the act of hiring or the state of being hired. **5b** (*as modifier*)*: a hire car.* **6a** the price paid or payable for a person's services or the temporary use of something. **6b** (*as modifier*)*: the hire charge.* **7 for** *or* **on hire.** available for service or temporary use in exchange for payment. [Old English *hȳrian;* related to Old Frisian *hēra* to lease, Middle Dutch *hūren*] ► **'hirable** *or* **'hireable** *adj* ► **'hirer** *n*

hireling ('haɪəlɪŋ) *n Derogatory.* a person who works only for money, esp. one paid to do something unpleasant. [Old English *hȳrling;* related to Dutch *huurling;* see HIRE, -LING[1]]

hire-purchase *n Brit.* **a** a system for purchasing merchandise, such as cars or furniture, in which the buyer takes possession of the merchandise on payment of a deposit and completes the purchase by paying a series of regular instalments while the seller retains ownership until the final instalment is paid. **b** (*as modifier*)*: hire-purchase legislation.* Abbrev.: **HP, h.p.** U.S. and Canadian equivalents: **installment plan, instalment plan.**

Hiri Motu ('hɪərɪ 'məʊtuː) *n* another name for **Motu** (the language).

hiring-fair *n* (formerly, in rural areas) a fair or market at which agricultural labourers were hired.

Hirohito (,hɪərəʊ'hiːtəʊ) *n* 1901–89, emperor of Japan 1926–89. In 1946 he became a constitutional monarch.

Hiroshige (,hɪərəʊ'ʃiːgeɪ) *n* **Ando** ('ɑːndəʊ). 1797–1858, Japanese artist, esp. of colour wood-block prints.

Hiroshima (,hɪrɒ'ʃiːmə, hɪ'rɒʃɪmə) *n* a port in SW Japan, on SW Honshu on the delta of the Ota River: largely destroyed on August 6, 1945, by the first atomic bomb to be used in warfare, dropped by the U.S., which killed over 75 000 of its inhabitants. Pop.: 1 108 868 (1995).

hirple ('hɪrpᵊl) *Scot.* ◆ *vb* (*intr*) **1** to limp. ◆ *n* **2** a limping gait. [C15: of unknown origin]

Hirst (hɜːst) *n* **Damien.** born 1965, British artist, noted for his works featuring dead animals preserved in tanks of formaldehyde.

hirsute ('hɜːsjuːt) *adj* **1** covered with hair. **2** (of plants or their parts) covered with long but not stiff hairs. **3** (of a person) having long, thick, or untrimmed hair. [C17: from Latin *hirsūtus* shaggy; related to Latin *horrēre* to bristle, *hirtus* hairy; see HORRID] ▸ **'hirsuteness** *n*

hirudin (hɪ'ruːdɪn) *n Med.* an anticoagulant extracted from the mouth glands of leeches. [C20: from Latin *hirudin-, hirudo* leech + -IN]

hirundine (hɪ'rʌndɪn, -daɪn) *adj* **1** of or resembling a swallow. **2** belonging to the bird family *Hirundinidae,* which includes swallows and martins. [C19: from Late Latin *hirundineus,* from Latin *hirundō* a swallow]

his (hɪz; *unstressed* ɪz) *determiner* **1a** of, belonging to, or associated with him: *his own fault; his knee; I don't like his being out so late.* **1b** (*as pronoun*): *his is on the left; that book is his.* **2 his and hers.** (of paired objects) for a man and woman respectively. ◆ *pron* **3 of his.** belonging to or associated with him. [Old English *his,* genitive of *hē* HE[1] and of *hit* IT]

Hispania (hɪ'spænɪə) *n* the Iberian peninsula in the Roman world.

Hispanic (hɪ'spænɪk) *adj* **1** relating to, characteristic of, or derived from Spain or the Spanish. ◆ *n* **2** *U.S.* a U.S. citizen of Spanish or Latin-American descent.

Hispanicism (hɪ'spænɪˌsɪzəm) *n* a word or expression borrowed from Spanish or modelled on the form of a Spanish word or expression.

Hispanicize *or* **Hispanicise** (hɪ'spænɪˌsaɪz) *vb* (*tr*) to make Spanish, as in custom or culture; bring under Spanish control or influence. ▸ **His'panicist** *n* ▸ **HisˌpaniciˈzatIon** *or* **Hisˌpaniciˈsation** *n*

Hispaniola (ˌhɪspən'jəʊlə; *Spanish* ispa'ɲola) *n* the second largest island in the Caribbean, in the Greater Antilles: divided politically into Haiti and the Dominican Republic; discovered in 1492 by Christopher Columbus, who named it La Isla Española. Area: 18 703 sq. km (29 418 sq. miles). Former name: **Santo Domingo.**

hispid ('hɪspɪd) *adj Biology.* covered with stiff hairs or bristles. [C17: from Latin *hispidus* bristly] ▸ **his'pidity** *n*

hiss (hɪs) *n* **1** a voiceless fricative sound like that of a prolonged *s.* **2** such a sound uttered as an exclamation of derision, contempt, etc., esp. by an audience or crowd. **3** *Electronics.* receiver noise with a continuous spectrum, caused by thermal agitation, shot noise, etc. ◆ *interj* **4** an exclamation of derision or disapproval. ◆ *vb* **5** (*intr*) to produce or utter a hiss. **6** (*tr*) to express with a hiss, usually to indicate derision or anger. **7** (*tr*) to show derision or anger towards (a speaker, performer, etc.) by hissing. [C14: of imitative origin] ▸ **'hisser** *n*

Hiss (hɪs) *n* **Alger.** 1904–96, U.S. politician: imprisoned (1950–54) for perjury in connection with alleged espionage activities.

hist (hɪst) *interj* an exclamation used to attract attention or as a warning to be silent.

hist. *abbrev. for:* **1** histology. **2** historical. **3** history.

histaminase (hɪ'stæmɪˌneɪs) *n* an enzyme, occurring in the digestive system, that inactivates histamine by removal of its amino group. Also called: **diamine oxidase.**

histamine ('hɪstəˌmiːn, -mɪn) *n* an amine formed from histidine and released by the body tissues in allergic reactions, causing irritation. It also stimulates gastric secretions, dilates blood vessels, and contracts smooth muscle. Formula: $C_5H_9N_3$. See also **antihistamine.** [C20: from HIST(IDINE) + -AMINE] ▸ **histaminic** (ˌhɪstə'mɪnɪk) *adj*

histidine ('hɪstɪˌdiːn, -dɪn) *n* a nonessential amino acid that occurs in most proteins: a precursor of histamine.

histiocyte ('hɪstɪəˌsaɪt) *n Physiol.* a macrophage that occurs in connective tissue. [C20: alteration of German *histiozyt,* from Greek *histion* a little web, from *histos* web + -CYTE] ▸ **histiocytic** (ˌhɪstɪə'sɪtɪk) *adj*

histo- *or before a vowel* **hist-** *combining form.* indicating animal or plant tissue: *histology; histamine.* [from Greek, from *histos* web]

histochemistry (ˌhɪstəʊ'kemɪstrɪ) *n* the chemistry of tissues, such as liver and bone, often studied with the aid of a microscope. ▸ **ˌhisto'chemical** *adj*

histocompatibility (ˌhɪstəʊkəmˌpætɪ'bɪlɪtɪ) *n* the degree of similarity between the histocompatibility antigens of two individuals. Histocompatibility determines whether an organ transplant will be tolerated. ▸ **ˌhistocom'patible** *adj*

histocompatibility antigen *n* a molecule occurring on the surface of tissue cells that can take several different forms. The differences between histocompatibility antigens are inherited and determine organ transplant rejection.

histogen ('hɪstəˌdʒen) *n* any of several distinct regions in a plant that differentiate to produce new tissue.

histogenesis (ˌhɪstəʊ'dʒenɪsɪs) *or* **histogeny** (hɪ'stɒdʒənɪ) *n* the formation of tissues and organs from undifferentiated cells. ▸ **histogenetic** (ˌhɪstəʊdʒə'netɪk) *or* **ˌhisto'genic** *adj* ▸ **ˌhistoge'netically** *or* **ˌhisto'genically** *adv*

histogram ('hɪstəˌgræm) *n* a statistical graph that represents the frequency of values of a quantity by vertical rectangles of varying heights and widths. The width of the rectangles is in proportion to the class interval under consideration, and their areas represent the relative frequency of the phenomenon in question. See also **stem-and-leaf diagram.** [C20: perhaps from HISTO(RY) + -GRAM]

histoid ('hɪstɔɪd) *adj* (esp. of a tumour) **1** resembling normal tissue. **2** composed of one kind of tissue.

histology (hɪ'stɒlədʒɪ) *n* **1** the study, esp. the microscopic study, of the tissues of an animal or plant. **2** the structure of a tissue or organ. ▸ **histological** (ˌhɪstə'lɒdʒɪkᵊl) *or* **ˌhisto'logic** *adj* ▸ **ˌhisto'logically** *adv* ▸ **his'tologist** *n*

histolysis (hɪ'stɒlɪsɪs) *n* the disintegration of organic tissues. ▸ **histolytic** (ˌhɪstə'lɪtɪk) *adj* ▸ **ˌhisto'lytically** *adv*

histone ('hɪstəʊn) *n* any of a group of basic proteins present in cell nuclei and implicated in the spatial organization of DNA.

histopathology (ˌhɪstəʊpə'θɒlədʒɪ) *n* the study of the microscopic structure of diseased tissues. ▸ **histopathological** (ˌhɪstəʊˌpæθə'lɒdʒɪkᵊl) *adj*

histoplasmosis (ˌhɪstəʊplæz'məʊsɪs) *n* a severe fungal disease of the lungs caused by *Histoplasma capsulatum.*

historian (hɪ'stɔːrɪən) *n* a person who writes or studies history, esp. one who is an authority on it.

historiated (hɪ'stɔːrɪˌeɪtɪd) *adj* decorated with flowers or animals. Also: **storiated.** [C19: from Medieval Latin *historiāre* to tell a story in pictures, from Latin *historia* story]

historic (hɪ'stɒrɪk) *adj* **1** famous or likely to become famous in history; significant. **2** a less common word for **historical** (senses 1–5). **3** Also: **secondary.** *Linguistics.* (of Latin, Greek, or Sanskrit verb tenses) referring to past time.

USAGE A distinction is usually made between *historic* (important, significant) and *historical* (pertaining to history): *a historic decision; a historical perspective.*

historical (hɪ'stɒrɪkᵊl) *adj* **1** belonging to or typical of the study of history: *historical methods.* **2** concerned with or treating of events of the past: *historical accounts.* **3** based on or constituting factual material as distinct from legend or supposition. **4** based on or inspired by history: *a historical novel.* **5** occurring or prominent in history. **6** a less common word for **historic** (sense 1). ▸ **his'torically** *adv* ▸ **his'toricalness** *n*

USAGE See at **historic.**

historical-cost accounting *n* a method of accounting that values assets at the original cost. In times of high inflation profits can be overstated. Compare **current-cost accounting.**

historical geology *n* the branch of geology concerned with the evolution of the earth from its origins to the present.

historical linguistics *n* (*functioning as sing*) the study of language as it changes in the course of time, with a view either to discovering general principles of linguistic change or to establishing the correct genealogical classification of particular languages. Also called: **diachronic linguistics.** Compare **descriptive linguistics.**

historical materialism *n* the part of Marxist theory maintaining that social structures derive from economic structures and that these are transformed as a result of class struggles, each ruling class producing another, which will overcome and destroy it, the final phase being the emergence of a communist society.

historical method *n* a means of learning about something by considering its origins and development.

historical present *n* the present tense used to narrate past events, usually employed in English for special effect or in informal use, as in *a week ago I'm walking down the street and I see this accident.*

historical school *n* **1** a group of 19th-century German economists who maintained that modern economies evolved from historical institutions. **2** the school of jurists maintaining that laws are based on social and historical circumstances rather than made by a sovereign power.

historic episcopate *n Christian Church.* the derivation of the episcopate of a Church in historic succession from the apostles.

historicism (hɪ'stɒrɪˌsɪzəm) *n* **1** the belief that natural laws govern historical events which in turn determine social and cultural phenomena. **2** the doctrine that each period of history has its own beliefs and values inapplicable to any other, so that nothing can be understood independently of its historical context. **3** the conduct of any enquiry in accordance with these views. **4** excessive emphasis on history, historicism, past styles, etc. ▸ **his'toricist** *n, adj*

historicity (ˌhɪstə'rɪsɪtɪ) *n* historical authenticity.

Historic Places Trust *n* (in New Zealand) the statutory body concerned with the conservation of historic buildings, esp. with ancient Maori sites.

historiographer (hɪˌstɔːrɪ'ɒgrəfə) *n* **1** a historian, esp. one concerned with historical method and the writings of other historians. **2** a historian employed to write the history of a group or public institution.

historiography (ˌhɪstɔːrɪ'ɒgrəfɪ) *n* **1** the writing of history. **2** the study of the development of historical method, historical research, and writing. **3** any body of historical literature. ▸ **historiographic** (hɪˌstɔːrɪə'græfɪk) *or* **hisˌtorio'graphical** *adj*

history ('hɪstərɪ, 'hɪstrɪ) *n, pl* **-ries. 1a** a record or account, often chronological in approach, of past events, developments, etc. **1b** (*as modifier*): *a history book; a history play.* **2** all that is preserved or remembered of the past, esp. in written form. **3** the discipline of recording and interpreting past events involving human beings. **4** past events, esp. when considered as an aggregate. **5** an event in the past, esp. one that has been forgotten or reduced in importance: *their quarrel was just history.* **6** the past, background, previous experiences, etc., of a thing or person: *the house had a strange history.* **7** a play that depicts or is based on historical events. **8** a narrative relating the events of a character's life: *the history of Joseph Andrews.* ◆ Abbrev. (for senses 1,2,3): **hist.** [C15: from Latin *historia,* from Greek: enquiry, from *historein* to narrate, from *histōr* judge]

histrionic (ˌhɪstrɪ'ɒnɪk) *or* **histrionical** *adj* **1** excessively dramatic, insincere, or artificial: *histrionic gestures.* **2** *Now rare.* dramatic. ◆ *n* **3** (*pl*) melodramatic displays of temperament. **4** *Rare.* (*pl, functioning as sing*) dramatics. [C17: from Late Latin *histriōnicus* of a player, from *histriō* actor] ▸ **ˌhistri'onically** *adv*

hit (hɪt) *vb* **hits, hitting, hit.** (*mainly tr*) **1** (*also intr*) to deal (a blow or stroke) to (a person or thing); strike: *the man hit the child.* **2** to come into violent contact with: *the car hit the tree.* **3** to reach or strike with a missile, thrown object, etc.: *to hit a target.* **4** to make or cause to make forceful contact; knock or bump: *I hit my arm on the table.* **5** to propel or cause to move by striking: *to hit a ball.* **6** *Cricket.* to score (runs). **7** to affect (a person, place, or thing) suddenly or adversely: *his illness hit his wife very hard.* **8** to become suddenly apparent to (a person): *the reason for his behaviour hit me and made the whole episode clear.* **9** to achieve or reach: *to hit the jackpot; unemployment hit a new high.* **10** to experience or encounter: *I've hit a slight snag here.* **11** *Slang.* to murder (a rival criminal) in fulfilment of an underworld contract or vendetta. **12** to accord or suit (esp. in the phrase **hit one's fancy**). **13** to guess correctly or find out by accident: *you have hit the answer.* **14** *Informal.* to set out on (a road, path, etc.): *let's hit the road.* **15** *Informal.* to arrive or appear in: *he will hit town tomorrow night.* **16** *Informal, chiefly U.S. and Canadian.* to demand or request from: *he hit me for a pound.* **17** *Slang.* to drink an excessive amount of (alcohol): *to hit the bottle.* **18 hit it.** *Music, slang.* start playing. **19 hit the sack** (*or* **hay**). *Slang.* to go to bed. **20 not know what has hit one.** to be completely taken by surprise. ◆ *n* **21** an impact or collision. **22** a shot, blow, etc., that reaches its object. **23** an apt, witty, or telling remark. **24** *Informal.* **24a** a person or thing that gains wide appeal: *she's a hit with everyone.* **24b** (*as modifier*): *a hit record.* **25** *Informal.* a stroke of luck. **26** *Slang.* **26a** a murder carried out as the result of an underworld vendetta or rivalry. **26b** (*as modifier*): *a hit squad.* **27** *Slang.* a drag on a cigarette, a swig from a bottle, a line of a drug, or an injection of heroin. **28** *Computing slang.* a single visit to a website. **29 make** (*or* **score**) **a hit with.** *Informal.* to make a favourable impression on. ◆ See also **hit off, hit on, hit out.** [Old English *hittan,* from Old Norse *hitta*]

Hitachi (hɪ'tætʃɪ) *n* a city in Japan, in E Honshu: a centre of the electronics industry. Pop.: 199 241 (1995).

hit-and-miss *adj Informal.* random; haphazard: *a hit-and-miss affair; the technique is very hit and miss.* Also: **hit or miss.**

hit-and-run *adj* (*prenominal*) **1a** involved in or denoting a motor-vehicle accident in which the driver leaves the scene without stopping to give assistance, inform the police, etc. **1b** (*as n*): *a hit-and-run.* **2** (of an attack, raid, etc.) relying on surprise allied to a rapid departure from the scene of operations for the desired effect: *hit-and-run tactics.* **3** *Baseball.* denoting a play in which a base runner begins to run as the pitcher throws the ball to the batter.

hitch (hɪtʃ) *vb* **1** to fasten or become fastened with a knot or tie, esp. temporarily. **2** (often foll. by *up*) to connect (a horse, team, etc.); harness. **3** (*tr;* often foll. by *up*) to pull up (the trousers, a skirt, etc.) with a quick jerk. **4** (*intr*) *Chiefly U.S.* to move in a halting manner: *to hitch along.* **5** to entangle or become entangled: *the thread was hitched on the reel.* **6** (*tr; passive*) *Slang.* to marry (esp. in the phrase **get hitched**). **7** *Informal.* to obtain (a ride or rides) by hitchhiking. ◆ *n* **8** an impediment or obstacle, esp. one that is temporary or minor: *a hitch in the proceedings.* **9** a knot for fastening a rope to posts, other ropes, etc., that can be undone by pulling against the direction of the strain that holds it. **10** a sudden jerk; tug; pull: *he gave it a hitch and it came loose.* **11** *Chiefly U.S.* a hobbling gait: *to walk with a hitch.* **12** a device used for fastening. **13** *Informal.* a ride obtained by hitchhiking. **14** *U.S. and Canadian slang.* a period of time spent in prison, in the army, etc. [C15: of uncertain origin] ▸ **'hitcher** *n*

Hitchcock ('hɪtʃ,kɒk) *n* Sir **Alfred** (**Joseph**). 1899–1980, English film director, noted for his mastery in creating suspense. His films include *The Thirty-Nine Steps* (1935), *Rebecca* (1940), *Psycho* (1960), and *The Birds* (1963).

hitchhike ('hɪtʃ,haɪk) *vb* (*intr*) to travel by obtaining free lifts in motor vehicles. ▸ **'hitch,hiker** *n*

hitching post *n* a post or rail to which the reins of a horse, etc., are tied.

hi tech *or* **high tech** (tɛk) *n* **1** short for **high technology. 2** a style of interior design using features of industrial equipment. ◆ *adj* **hi-tech** *or* **high-tech. 3** designed for or using high technology. **4** of or in the interior design style. ◆ Compare **low tech.**

hither ('hɪðə) *adv* **1** Also (archaic): **hitherward, hitherwards.** to or towards this place (esp. in the phrase **come hither**). **2 hither and thither.** this way and that, as in a state of confusion. ◆ *adj* **3** *Archaic or dialect.* (of a side or part, esp. of a hill or valley) nearer; closer. [Old English *hider;* related to Old Norse *hethra* here, Gothic *hidrē,* Latin *citrā* on this side, *citrō*]

hithermost ('hɪðə,məʊst) *adj Now rare.* nearest to this place or in this direction.

hitherto ('hɪðə'tuː) *adv* **1** until this time: *hitherto, there have been no problems.* **2** *Archaic.* to this place or point.

Hitler ('hɪtlə) *n* **1 Adolf** ('aːdɔlf). Grandmother's maiden name and father's original surname *Schicklgrüber.* 1889–1945, German dictator, born in Austria. After becoming president of the National Socialist German Workers' Party (Nazi party), he attempted to overthrow the government of Bavaria (1923). While in prison he wrote *Mein Kampf,* expressing his philosophy of the superiority of the Aryan race and the inferiority of the Jews. He was appointed chancellor of Germany (1933), transforming it from a democratic republic into the totalitarian Third Reich, of which he became Führer in 1934. He established concentration camps to exterminate the Jews, rearmed the Rhineland (1936), annexed Austria (1938) and Czechoslovakia, and invaded Poland (1939), which precipitated World War II. He committed suicide. **2** a person who displays dictatorial characteristics.

Hitlerism ('hɪtlə,rɪzəm) *n* the policies, principles, and methods of the Nazi party as developed by Adolf Hitler.

hit list *n Informal.* **1** a list of people to be murdered: *a terrorist hit list.* **2** a list of targets to be eliminated in some way: *a hit list of pits to be closed.*

hit man *n Slang.* a hired assassin, esp. one employed by gangsters.

hit off *vb* **1** (*tr, adv*) to represent or mimic accurately. **2 hit it off.** *Informal.* to have a good relationship with.

hit on *vb* (*tr, prep*) **1** to strike. **2** Also: **hit upon.** to discover unexpectedly or guess correctly. **3** *U.S. and Canadian. slang.* to make sexual advances to.

hit out *vb* (*intr, adv;* often foll. by *at*) **1** to direct blows forcefully and vigorously. **2** to make a verbal attack (upon someone).

hit parade *n Old-fashioned.* a listing or playing of the current most popular songs.

hitter ('hɪtə) *n* **1** *Informal.* a boxer who has a hard punch rather than skill or finesse. **2** a person who hits something.

Hittite ('hɪtaɪt) *n* **1** a member of an ancient people of Anatolia, who built a great empire in N Syria and Asia Minor in the second millennium B.C. **2** the extinct language of this people, deciphered from cuneiform inscriptions found at Boğazköy and elsewhere. It is clearly related to the Indo-European family of languages, although the precise relationship is disputed. ◆ *adj* **3** of or relating to this people, their civilization, or their language.

hit wicket *n Cricket.* an instance of a batsman breaking the wicket with the bat or a part of the body while playing a stroke and so being out.

HIV *abbrev. for* human immunodeficiency virus; the cause of AIDS. Two strains have been identified: HIV-1 and HIV-2.

hive (haɪv) *n* **1** a structure in which social bees live and rear their young. **2** a colony of social bees. **3** a place showing signs of great industry (esp. in the phrase **a hive of activity**). **4** a teeming crowd; multitude. **5** an object in the form of a hive. ◆ *vb* **6** to cause (bees) to collect or (of bees) to collect inside a hive. **7** to live or cause to live in or as if in a hive. **8** (*tr*) (of bees) to store (honey, pollen, etc.) in the hive. **9** (*tr;* often foll. by *up* or *away*) to store, esp. for future use: *he used to hive away a small sum every week.* [Old English *hӯf;* related to Westphalian *hüwe,* Old Norse *hūfr* ship's hull, Latin *cūpa* barrel, Greek *kupē,* Sanskrit *kūpa* cave] ▸ **'hive,like** *adj*

hive bee *n* another name for **honeybee.**

hive dross *n* another name for **propolis.**

hive off *vb* (*adv*) **1** to transfer or be transferred from a larger group or unit. **2** (*usually tr*) to transfer (profitable activities of a nationalized industry) back to private ownership.

hives (haɪvz) *n* (*functioning as sing or pl*) *Pathol.* a nontechnical name for **urticaria.** [C16: of uncertain origin]

hiya ('haɪjə, ,haɪ'jɑː) *sentence substitute.* an informal term of greeting. [C20: shortened from *how are you?*]

Hizbollah (,hɪzbə'lɑː) *n* a variant spelling of **Hezbollah.**

HJ (on gravestones) *abbrev. for* hic jacet. [Latin: here lies]

HJS (on gravestones) *abbrev. for* hic jacet sepultus. [Latin: here lies buried]

HK **1** *abbrev. for* House of Keys (Manx Parliament). **2** *international car registration for* Hong Kong.

HKJ *international car registration for* (Hashemite Kingdom of) Jordan.

hl *symbol for* hectolitre.

HL (in Britain) *abbrev. for* House of Lords.

HLA system *n* human leucocyte antigen system; a group of the most important antigens responsible for tissue compatibility, together with the genes that encode them. For tissue and organ transplantation to be successful there needs to be a minimum number of HLA differences between the donor's and recipient's tissue.

hm *symbol for* hectometre.

HM *abbrev. for:* **1** His (*or* Her) Majesty. **2** heavy metal (sense 1). **3** headmaster; headmistress.

h'm (*spelling pron* hmmm) *interj* used to indicate hesitation, doubt, assent, pleasure, etc.

HMAS *abbrev. for* His (*or* Her) Majesty's Australian Ship.

HMCS *abbrev. for* His (*or* Her) Majesty's Canadian Ship.

HMG *abbrev. for* His (*or* Her) Majesty's Government.

HMI (in Britain) *abbrev. for* Her Majesty's Inspector; a government official who examines and supervises schools.

H.M.S. *or* **HMS** *abbrev. for:* **1** His (*or* Her) Majesty's Service. **2** His (*or* Her) Majesty's Ship.

HMSO (formerly, in Britain) *abbrev. for* His (*or* Her) Majesty's Stationery Office.

HNC (in Britain) *abbrev. for* Higher National Certificate; a qualification recognized by many national technical and professional institutions.

HND (in Britain) *abbrev. for* Higher National Diploma; a qualification in technical subjects equivalent to an ordinary degree.

ho[1] (həʊ) *interj* **1** Also: **ho-ho.** an imitation or representation of the sound of a deep laugh. **2** an exclamation used to attract attention, announce a destination, etc.: *what ho! land ho! westward ho!* [C13: of imitative origin; compare Old Norse *hó,* Old French *ho!* halt!]

ho[2] (həʊ) *n U.S. Black slang.* a derogatory term for a woman. [C20: from Black or Southern U.S. pronunciation of WHORE]

Ho *the chemical symbol for* holmium.

HO *or* **H.O.** *abbrev. for:* **1** head office. **2** *Brit. government.* Home Office.

ho. *abbrev. for* house.

hoactzin (həʊ'æktsɪn) *n* a variant of **hoatzin.**

hoar (hɔː) *n* **1** short for **hoarfrost.** ◆ *adj* **2** *Rare.* covered with hoarfrost. **3** *Archaic.* a poetic variant of **hoary.** [Old English *hār;* related to Old Norse *hārr,* Old High German *hēr,* Old Slavonic *sěrŭ* grey]

hoard (hɔːd) *n* **1** an accumulated store hidden away for future use. **2** a cache of ancient coins, treasure, etc. ◆ *vb* **3** to gather or accumulate (a hoard). [Old English *hord;* related to Old Norse *hodd,* Gothic *huzd,* German *Hort,* Swedish *hydda* hut] ▸ **'hoarder** *n*

USAGE *Hoard* is sometimes wrongly written where *horde* is meant: *hordes* (not *hoards*) *of tourists.*

hoarding ('hɔːdɪŋ) *n* **1** a large board used for displaying advertising posters, as by a road. Also called (esp. U.S. and Canadian): **billboard. 2** a temporary wooden fence erected round a building or demolition site. [C19: from C15 *hoard* fence, from Old French *hourd* palisade, of Germanic origin, related to Gothic *haurds,* Old Norse *hurth* door]

hoarfrost ('hɔː,frɒst) *n* a deposit of needle-like ice crystals formed on the ground by direct condensation at temperatures below freezing point. Also called: **white frost.**

hoarhound ('hɔː,haʊnd) *n* a variant spelling of **horehound.**

hoarse (hɔːs) *adj* **1** gratingly harsh or raucous in tone. **2** low, harsh, and lacking in intensity: *a hoarse whisper.* **3** having a husky voice, as through illness, shouting, etc. [C14: of Scandinavian origin; related to Old Norse *hās*, Old Saxon *hēs*] ▸ 'hoarsely *adv* ▸ 'hoarseness *n*

hoarsen ('hɔːsᵊn) *vb* to make or become hoarse.

hoary ('hɔːrɪ) *adj* **hoarier, hoariest.** **1** having grey or white hair. **2** white or whitish-grey in colour. **3** ancient or venerable. ▸ **'hoarily** *adv* ▸ **'hoariness** *n*

hoary cress *n* a perennial cruciferous Mediterranean plant, *Cardaria* (or *Lepidium*) *draba*, with small white flowers: a widespread troublesome weed.

hoast (host) *Scot.* ◆ *n* **1** a cough. ◆ *vb* (*intr*) **2** to cough. [from Old Norse]

hoatching ('həutʃɪŋ) *adj Scot.* infested; swarming: *this food's hoatching with flies.* [of unknown origin]

hoatzin (həu'ætsɪn) *or* **hoactzin** *n* a unique South American gallinaceous bird, *Opisthocomus hoazin*, with a brownish plumage, a very small crested head, and clawed wing digits in the young: family *Opisthocomidae.* [C17: from American Spanish, from Nahuatl *uatzin* pheasant]

hoax (həuks) *n* **1** a deception, esp. a practical joke. ◆ *vb* **2** (*tr*) to deceive or play a joke on (someone). [C18: probably from HOCUS] ▸ **'hoaxer** *n*

hob[1] (hɒb) *n* **1** the flat top part of a cooking stove, or a separate flat surface, containing hotplates or burners. **2** a shelf beside an open fire, for keeping kettles, etc., hot. **3** a steel pattern used in forming a mould or die in cold metal. **4** a hard steel rotating cutting tool used in machines for cutting gears. ◆ *vb* **hobs, hobbing, hobbed.** **5** (*tr*) to cut or form with a hob. [C16: variant of obsolete *hubbe*, of unknown origin; perhaps related to HUB]

hob[2] (hɒb) *n* **1** a hobgoblin or elf. **2 raise** *or* **play hob.** *U.S. informal.* to cause mischief or disturbance. **3** a male ferret. [C14: variant of *Rob*, short for *Robin* or *Robert*] ▸ **'hob,like** *adj*

Hobart ('həubɑːt) *n* a port in Australia, capital of the island state of Tasmania on the estuary of the Derwent: excellent natural harbour; University of Tasmania (1890). Pop.: 194 700 (1995 est.).

Hobbema ('hɒbɪmə; *Dutch* 'hɔbəmaː) *n* **Meindert** ('maɪndərt). 1638–1709, Dutch painter of peaceful landscapes, usually including a watermill.

Hobbes (hɒbz) *n* **Thomas.** 1588–1679, English political philosopher. His greatest work is the *Leviathan* (1651), which contains his defence of absolute sovereignty. ▸ **'Hobbesian** *n, adj*

Hobbism ('hɒbɪzəm) *n* the mechanistic political philosophy of Hobbes, which stresses the necessity for a powerful sovereign to control human beings. ▸ **'Hobbist** *n*

hobbit ('hɒbɪt) *n* one of an imaginary race of half-size people living in holes. [C20: coined by J. R. R. Tolkien, with the meaning "hole-builder"] ▸ **'hobbitry** *n*

hobble ('hɒbᵊl) *vb* **1** (*intr*) to walk with a lame awkward movement. **2** (*tr*) to fetter the legs of (a horse) in order to restrict movement. **3** to progress unevenly or with difficulty. **4** (*tr*) to hamper or restrict (the actions or scope of a person, organization, etc.). ◆ *n* **5** a strap, rope, etc., used to hobble a horse. **6** a limping gait. **7** *Brit. dialect.* a difficult or embarrassing situation. ◆ Also (for senses 2, 5): **hopple.** [C14: probably from Low German; compare Flemish *hoppelen*, Middle Dutch *hobbelen* to stammer] ▸ **'hobbler** *n*

hobbledehoy (,hɒbᵊldɪ'hɔɪ) *n Archaic or dialect.* a clumsy or bad-mannered youth. [C16: from earlier *hobbard de hoy*, of uncertain origin]

hobble skirt *n* a long skirt, popular between 1910 and 1914, cut so narrow at the ankles that it hindered walking.

Hobbs (hɒbz) *n* Sir **John Berry,** known as *Jack Hobbs.* 1882–1963, English cricketer: scored 197 centuries.

hobby[1] ('hɒbɪ) *n, pl* **-bies.** **1** an activity pursued in spare time for pleasure or relaxation. **2** *Archaic or dialect.* a small horse or pony. **3** short for **hobbyhorse** (sense 1). **4** an early form of bicycle, without pedals. [C14 *hobyn*, probably variant of proper name *Robin*; compare DOBBIN] ▸ **'hobbyist** *n*

hobby[2] ('hɒbɪ) *n, pl* **-bies.** any of several small Old World falcons, esp. the European *Falco subbuteo*, formerly used in falconry. [C15: from Old French *hobet*, from *hobe* falcon; probably related to Middle Dutch *hobbelen* to roll, turn]

hobbyhorse ('hɒbɪ,hɔːs) *n* **1** a toy consisting of a stick with a figure of a horse's head at one end. **2** another word for **rocking horse.** **3** a figure of a horse attached to a performer's waist in a pantomime, morris dance, etc. **4** a favourite topic or obsessive fixed idea (esp. in the phrase **on one's hobbyhorse**). ◆ *vb* **5** (*intr*) *Nautical.* (of a vessel) to pitch violently. [C16: from HOBBY[1], originally a small horse, hence sense 3; then generalized to apply to any pastime]

hobday ('hɒb,deɪ) *vb* (*tr*) to alleviate (a breathing problem in certain horses) by the surgical operation of pinning back the vocal fold. [C20: named after F. T. *Hobday* (1869–1939), English veterinary surgeon, who devised the operation] ▸ **'hob,dayed** *adj*

hobgoblin (,hɒb'gɒblɪn) *n* **1** an evil or mischievous goblin. **2** a bogey; bugbear. [C16: from HOB[2] + GOBLIN]

hobnail ('hɒb,neɪl) *n* **a** a short nail with a large head for protecting the soles of heavy footwear. **b** (*as modifier*): *hobnail boots.* [C16: from HOB[1] (in the archaic sense: peg) + NAIL] ▸ **'hob,nailed** *adj*

hobnob ('hɒb,nɒb) *vb* **-nobs, -nobbing, -nobbed.** (*intr*; often foll. by *with*) **1** to socialize or talk informally. **2** *Obsolete.* to drink (with). [C18: from *hob or nob* to drink to one another in turns, hence, to be familiar, ultimately from Old English *habban* to HAVE + *nabban* not to have]

hobo ('həubəu) *n, pl* **-bos** *or* **-boes.** *Chiefly U.S. and Canadian.* **1** a tramp; vagrant. **2** a migratory worker, esp. an unskilled labourer. [C19 (U.S.): origin unknown] ▸ **'hoboism** *n*

Hoboken ('həubəukən) *n* a city in N Belgium, in Antwerp province, on the River Scheldt. Pop.: 35 000 (latest est.).

hobson-jobson (,hɒbsᵊn'dʒɒbsᵊn) *n* another word for **folk etymology.** [C19: Anglo-Indian folk-etymological variant of Arabic *yā Hasan! yā Husayn!* O Hasan! O Husain! (ritual lament for the grandsons of Mohammed); influenced by the surnames *Hobson* and *Jobson*]

Hobson's choice ('hɒbsᵊnz) *n* the choice of taking what is offered or nothing at all. [C16: named after Thomas *Hobson* (1544–1631), English liveryman who gave his customers no choice but had them take the nearest horse]

Hochheimer ('hɒk,haɪmə; *German* 'hoːxhaimər) *n* a German white wine from the area around Hochheim near Mainz. Also called: **'Hoch,heim.**

Hochhuth (*German* 'hoːxhuːt) *n* **Rolf** (rɔlf). born 1933, Swiss dramatist. His best-known works are the controversial documentary drama *The Representative* (1963), on the papacy's attitude to the Jews in World War II, *Soldiers* (1967), *German Love Story* (1980), and *Wessis in Weimar* (1992).

Ho Chi Minh ('həu 'tʃiː 'mɪn) *n* original name *Nguyen That Tan.* 1890–1969, Vietnamese statesman; president of North Vietnam (1954–69). He headed the Vietminh (1941), which won independence for Vietnam from the French (1954).

Ho Chi Minh City *n* a port in S Vietnam, 97 km (60 miles) from the South China Sea, on the Saigon River: captured by the French in 1859; merged with adjoining Cholon in 1932; capital of the former Republic of Vietnam (South Vietnam) from 1954 to 1976; university (1917); U.S. headquarters during the Vietnam War. Pop.: 4 322 300 (1993 est.). Former name (until 1976): **Saigon.**

hock[1] (hɒk) *n* **1** the joint at the tarsus of a horse or similar animal, pointing backwards and corresponding to the human ankle. **2** the corresponding joint in domestic fowl. ◆ *vb* **3** another word for **hamstring.** [C16: short for *hockshin*, from Old English *hōhsinu* heel sinew]

hock[2] (hɒk) *n* **1** any of several white wines from the German Rhine. **2** (not in technical usage) any dry white wine. [C17: short for obsolete *hockamore* HOCHHEIMER]

hock[3] (hɒk) *Informal, chiefly U.S. and Canadian.* ◆ *vb* **1** (*tr*) to pawn or pledge. ◆ *n* **2** the state of being in pawn (esp. in the phrase **in hock**). **3 in hock. 3a** in prison. **3b** in debt. [C19: from Dutch *hok* prison, debt] ▸ **'hocker** *n*

hockey[1] ('hɒkɪ) *n* **1** Also called (esp. U.S. and Canadian): **field hockey. 1a** a game played on a field by two opposing teams of 11 players each, who try to hit a ball into their opponents' goal using long sticks curved at the end. **1b** (*as modifier*): *hockey stick; hockey ball.* **2** See **ice hockey.** [C19: from earlier *hawkey*, of unknown origin]

hockey[2] ('hɒkɪ) *n East Anglian dialect.* **a** the feast at harvest home; harvest supper. **b** (*as modifier*): *the hockey cart.* Also: **hawkey, horkey.** [C16: of unknown origin]

Hockney ('hɒknɪ) *n* **David.** born 1937, English painter, best known for his etchings, such as those to Cavafy's poems (1966), naturalistic portraits such as *Mr and Mrs Clark and Percy* (1971), and for paintings of water, swimmers, and swimming pools.

Hocktide ('hɒk,taɪd) *n Brit. history.* a former festival celebrated on the second Monday and Tuesday after Easter. [C15: from *hock-*, *hoke-* (of unknown origin) + TIDE[1]]

hocus ('həukəs) *vb* **-cuses, -cusing, -cused** *or* **-cuses, -cussing, -cussed.** (*tr*) *Now rare.* **1** to take in; trick. **2** to stupefy, esp. with a drug. **3** to add a drug to (a drink).

hocus-pocus ('həukəs'pəukəs) *n* **1** trickery or chicanery. **2** mystifying jargon. **3** an incantation used by conjurors or magicians when performing tricks. **4** conjuring skill or practice. ◆ *vb* **-cuses, -cusing, -cused** *or* **-cuses, -cussing, -cussed.** **5** to deceive or trick (someone). [C17: perhaps a dog-Latin formation invented by jugglers]

hod (hɒd) *n* **1** an open metal or plastic box fitted with a handle, for carrying bricks, mortar, etc. **2** a tall narrow coal scuttle. [C14: perhaps alteration of C13 dialect *hot*, from Old French *hotte* pannier, creel, probably from Germanic]

hod carrier *n* a labourer who carries the materials in a hod for a plasterer, bricklayer, etc. Also called: **hodman.**

hodden ('hɒdᵊn) *or* **hoddin** ('hɒdɪn) *n* a coarse homespun cloth produced in Scotland: **hodden grey** is made by mixing black and white wools. [C18: Scottish, of obscure origin]

Hodeida (hɒ'deɪdə) *n* a port in N Yemen, on the Red Sea; formerly in North Yemen. Pop.: 246 068 (1993 est.).

Hodge (hɒdʒ) *n* a typical name for a farm labourer; rustic. [C14 *hogge*, from familiar form of *Roger*]

hodgepodge ('hɒdʒ,pɒdʒ) *n* a variant (esp. U.S. and Canadian) of **hotchpotch.**

Hodgkin ('hɒdʒkɪn) *n* **1** Sir **Alan Lloyd.** 1914–98, English physiologist. With A. F. Huxley, he explained the conduction of nervous impulses in terms of the physical and chemical changes involved: shared the Nobel prize for physiology or medicine (1963). **2 Dorothy Crowfoot.** 1910–94, English chemist and crystallographer, who determined the three-dimensional structure of insulin: Nobel prize for chemistry (1964).

Hodgkin's disease *n* a malignant disease, a form of lymphoma, characterized by enlargement of the lymph nodes, spleen, and liver. Also called: **lymphoadenoma, lymphogranulomatosis.** [C19: named after Thomas *Hodgkin* (1798–1866), London physician, who first described it]

hodman ('hɒdmən) *n, pl* **-men.** *Brit.* another name for a **hod carrier.**

hodograph ('hɒdə,grɑːf, -græf) *n* a curve of which the radius vector represents the velocity of a moving particle. [C19: from Greek *hodos* way + -GRAPH] ▸ **,hodo'graphic** *adj*

hodometer (hɒ'dɒmɪtə) *n U.S.* another name for **odometer.** ▸ **ho'dometry** *n*

hodoscope ('hɒdə,skəup) *n Physics.* any device for tracing the path of a charged particle, esp. a particle found in cosmic rays. [C20: from Greek *hodos* way, path + -SCOPE]

hoe (həu) *n* **1** any of several kinds of long-handled hand implement equipped with a light blade and used to till the soil, eradicate weeds, etc. ◆ *vb* **hoes, hoeing, hoed. 2** to dig, scrape, weed, or till (surface soil) with or as if with a hoe. [C14: via Old French *houe* from Germanic: compare Old High German *houwā, houwan* to HEW, German *Haue* hoe] ▶ **'hoer** *n* ▶ **'hoe,like** *adj*

hoedown ('həʊ,daʊn) *n U.S. and Canadian.* **1** a boisterous square dance. **2** a party at which hoedowns are danced.

hoe in *vb* (*intr, adv*) *Austral. and N.Z. informal.* to eat food heartily.

hoe into *vb* (*intr, prep*) *Austral. and N.Z. informal.* to eat (food) heartily.

Hoek van Holland ('hu:k fɑn 'hɔlɑnt) *n* the Dutch name for the **Hook of Holland.**

Hofei ('həʊ'feɪ) *n* a variant transliteration of the Chinese name for **Hefei.**

Hoffman ('hɒfmən) *n* **Dustin** (**Lee**) ('dʌstɪn). born 1937, U.S. stage and film actor. His films include *The Graduate* (1967), *Midnight Cowboy* (1969), *All the President's Men* (1976), *Kramer vs Kramer* (1979), *Rain Man* (1989), *Accidental Hero* (1992), and *Wag the Dog* (1998).

Hofmann ('hɒfmən) *n* **Hans.** 1880–1966, U.S. painter, born in Germany: a pioneer of the abstract expressionist style.

Hofmannsthal (*German* 'ho:fmanstaːl) *n* **Hugo von** ('hu:go fɔn). 1874–1929, Austrian lyric poet and dramatist, noted as the librettist for Richard Strauss' operas, esp. *Der Rosenkavalier* (1911), *Elektra* (1909), and *Ariadne auf Naxos* (1912).

Hofuf (hʊ'fu:f) *n* another name for **Al Hufuf.**

hog (hɒg) *n* **1** a domesticated pig, esp. a castrated male weighing more than 102 kg. **2** *U.S. and Canadian.* any artiodactyl mammal of the family *Suidae;* pig. **3** Also: **hogg.** *Brit. dialect., Austral., and N.Z.* another name for **hogget. 4** *Informal.* a selfish, greedy or slovenly person. **5** *Nautical.* a stiff brush, for scraping a vessel's bottom. **6** *Nautical.* the amount or extent to which a vessel is hogged. Compare **sag** (sense 6). **7** another word for **camber** (sense 4). **8** *Slang, chiefly U.S.* a large powerful motorcycle. **9 go the whole hog.** *Informal.* to do something thoroughly or unreservedly: *if you are redecorating one room, why not go the whole hog and paint the entire house?* **10 live high on the hog.** *Informal, chiefly U.S.* to have an extravagant lifestyle. ◆ *vb* **hogs, hogging, hogged.** (*tr*) **11** *Slang.* to take more than one's share of. **12** to arch (the back) like a hog. **13** to cut (the mane) of (a horse) very short. [Old English *hogg,* from Celtic; compare Cornish *hoch*] ▶ **'hogger** *n* ▶ **'hog,like** *adj*

hogan ('həʊgən) *n* a wooden dwelling covered with earth, typical of the Navaho Indians of N America. [from Navaho]

Hogarth ('həʊgɑːθ) *n* **William.** 1697–1764, English engraver and painter. He is noted particularly for his series of engravings satirizing the vices and affectations of his age, such as *A Rake's Progress* (1735) and *Marriage à la Mode* (1745). ▶ **Ho'garthian** *adj*

hogback ('hɒg,bæk) *n* **1** Also called: **hog's back.** a narrow ridge with sides that consist of steeply inclined rock strata. **2** *Archaeol.* a Saxon or Scandinavian tomb with sloping sides.

hog badger *n* a SE Asian badger, *Arctonyx collaris,* with a piglike mobile snout. Also called: **sand badger.**

hog cholera *n* the U.S. term for **swine fever.**

hogfish ('hɒg,fɪʃ) *n, pl* **-fish** *or* **-fishes. 1** a wrasse, *Lachnolaimus maximus,* that occurs in the Atlantic off the SE coast of North America. The head of the male resembles a pig's snout. **2** another name for **pigfish** (sense 1).

Hogg (hɒg) *n* **1 James,** known as *the Ettrick Shepherd.* 1770–1835, Scottish poet and writer. His works include the volume of poems *The Queen's Wake* (1813) and the novel *The Confessions of a Justified Sinner* (1824). **2 Quintin.** See (1st Baron) **Hailsham of St Marylebone.**

hogged (hɒgd) *adj Nautical.* (of a vessel) having a keel that droops at both ends. Compare **sag** (sense 6).

hogget ('hɒgɪt) *n Brit. dialect, Austral., and N.Z.* **1** a sheep up to the age of one year that has yet to be sheared. **2** the meat of this sheep.

hoggin ('hɒgɪn) *or* **hogging** ('hɒgɪŋ) *n* a finely sifted gravel used for making paths or roads. [C19: perhaps the same as *hogging* from HOG in the sense of arching the back, from the shape given to a road to facilitate drainage]

hoggish ('hɒgɪʃ) *adj* selfish, gluttonous, or dirty. ▶ **'hoggishly** *adv* ▶ **'hoggishness** *n*

Hogmanay (,hɒgmə'neɪ) *n* (*sometimes not cap.*) **a** New Year's Eve in Scotland. **b** (*as modifier*): *a Hogmanay party.* See also **first-foot.** [C17: Scottish and Northern English, perhaps from Norman French *hoguinane,* from Old French *aguillanneuf* the last day of the year; also, a New Year's eve gift]

hognosed skunk ('hɒg,nəʊzd) *n* any of several American skunks of the genus *Conepatus,* esp. *C. leuconotus,* having a broad snoutlike nose.

hognose snake ('hɒg,nəʊz) *n* any North American nonvenomous colubrid snake of the genus *Heterodon,* having a trowel-shaped snout and inflating the body when alarmed. Also called: **puff adder.**

hognut ('hɒg,nʌt) *n* another name for **pignut** (sense 1).

hog peanut *n* a North American leguminous climbing plant, *Amphicarpa bracteata,* having fleshy curved one-seeded pods, which ripen in or on the ground.

hog's fennel *n* any of several Eurasian umbelliferous marsh plants of the genus *Peucedanum,* esp. *P. officinale,* having clusters of small whitish flowers.

hogshead ('hɒgz,hɛd) *n* **1** a unit of capacity, used esp. for alcoholic beverages. It has several values, being 54 imperial gallons in the case of beer and 52.5 imperial gallons in the case of wine. **2** a large cask used for shipment of wines and spirits. [C14: of obscure origin]

hogtie ('hɒg,taɪ) *vb* **-ties, -tying, -tied.** (*tr*) *Chiefly U.S.* **1** to tie together the legs or the arms and legs of. **2** to impede, hamper, or thwart.

Hogue (*French* ɔg) *n* See **La Hogue.**

hogwash ('hɒg,wɒʃ) *n* **1** nonsense. **2** pigswill.

hogweed ('hɒg,wi:d) *n* any of several coarse weedy plants, esp. cow parsnip. See also **giant hogweed.**

Hohenlinden (*German* ho:ən'lɪndən) *n* a village in S Germany, in Bavaria east of Munich: scene of the defeat of the Austrians by the French during the Napoleonic Wars (1800).

Hohenlohe ('həʊən,ləʊə; *German* ho:ən'lo:ə) *n* **Chlodwig** ('klo:tvɪç), Prince of Hohenlohe-Schillingsfürst. 1819–1901, Prussian statesman; chancellor of the German empire (1894–1900).

Hohenstaufen ('həʊən,ʃtaʊfən; *German* ho:ən'ʃtaufən) *n* a German princely family that provided rulers of Germany (1138–1208, 1215–54), Sicily (1194–1268), and the Holy Roman Empire (1138–1254).

Hohenzollern ('həʊən,zɒlən; *German* ho:ən'tsɔlərn) *n* a German noble family, the younger (Franconian) branch of which provided rulers of Brandenburg (1417–1701) and Prussia (1701–1918). The last kings of Prussia (1871–1918) were also emperors of Germany.

Hohhot ('hɒ'hɒt), **Huhehot,** *or* **Hu-ho-hao-t'e** *n* a city in N China, capital of Inner Mongolia Autonomous Region (since 1954); previously capital of the former Suiyüan province; Inner Mongolia University (1957). Pop.: 652 534 (1990 est.).

ho-hum ('həʊ,hʌm) *adj Informal.* lacking interest or inspiration; dull; mediocre: *a ho-hum collection of new releases.*

hoick (hɔɪk) *vb Informal.* to rise or raise abruptly and sharply: *to hoick an aircraft.* [C20: of unknown origin]

hoicks (hɔɪks) *interj* a cry used to encourage hounds to hunt. Also: **yoicks.**

hoiden ('hɔɪdᵊn) *n* a variant spelling of **hoyden.** ▶ **'hoidenish** *adj* ▶ **'hoidenishness** *n*

hoi polloi (,hɔɪ pə'lɔɪ) *pl n Often derogatory.* the masses; common people. [Greek, literally: the many]

hoist (hɔɪst) *vb* **1** (*tr*) to raise or lift up, esp. by mechanical means. **2 hoist with one's own petard.** See **petard** (sense 2). ◆ *n* **3** any apparatus or device for hoisting. **4** the act of hoisting. **5** See **rotary clothesline. 6** *Nautical.* **6a** the amidships height of a sail bent to the yard with which it is hoisted. Compare **drop** (sense 15). **6b** the difference between the set and lowered positions of this yard. **7** *Nautical.* the length of the luff of a fore-and-aft sail. **8** *Nautical.* a group of signal flags. **9** the inner edge of a flag next to the staff. Compare **fly**[1] (sense 25). [C16: variant of *hoise,* probably from Low German; compare Dutch *hijschen,* German *hissen*] ▶ **'hoister** *n*

hoity-toity (,hɔɪtɪ'tɔɪtɪ) *adj Informal.* arrogant or haughty: *we have had enough of her hoity-toity manner.* [C17: rhyming compound based on C16 *hoit* to romp, of obscure origin]

hoke (həʊk) *vb* (*tr;* usually foll. by *up*) to overplay (a part, etc.). [C20: perhaps from HOKUM]

hokey ('həʊkɪ) *adj Slang, chiefly U.S. and Canadian.* **1** corny; sentimental. **2** contrived; phoney. [C20: from HOKUM]

hokey cokey ('həʊkɪ 'kəʊkɪ) *n* a Cockney song with a traditional dance routine to match the words.

hokey-pokey (,həʊkɪ'pəʊkɪ) *n* another word for **hocus-pocus** (senses 1, 2).

Hokkaido (hɒ'kaɪdəʊ) *n* the second largest and northernmost of the four main islands of Japan, separated from Honshu by the Tsugaru Strait and from the island of Sakhalin, Russia, by La Pérouse Strait: constitutes an autonomous administrative division. Capital: Sapporo. Pop.: 5 692 000 (1995). Area: 78 508 sq. km (30 312 sq. miles).

hokku ('hɒku:) *n, pl* **-ku.** *Prosody.* another word for **haiku.** [from Japanese, from *hok* beginning + *ku* hemistich]

hokonui (həʊkə'nu:i:) *n N.Z. obsolete.* illicit whisky. [from *Hokonui,* district of Southland region, N.Z.]

hokum ('həʊkəm) *n Slang.* **1** claptrap; bunk. **2** obvious or hackneyed material of a sentimental nature in a play, film, etc. [C20: probably a blend of HOCUS-POCUS and BUNKUM]

Hokusai ('həʊkʊ,saɪ, ,həʊkʊ'saɪ) *n* **Katsushika** (,kætsu:'ʃi:kə). 1760–1849, Japanese artist, noted for the draughtsmanship of his colour wood-block prints, which influenced the impressionists.

hol- *combining form.* a variant of **holo-** before a vowel.

Holarctic (həʊ'lɑ:ktɪk) *adj* of or denoting a zoogeographical region consisting of the Palaearctic and Nearctic regions. [C19: from HOLO- + ARCTIC]

Holbein (*German* 'hɔlbain) *n* **1 Hans** (hans), known as *Holbein the Elder.* 1465–1524, German painter. **2** his son, **Hans,** known as *Holbein the Younger.* 1497–1543, German painter and engraver; court painter to Henry VIII of England (1536–43). He is noted particularly for his portraits, such as those of Erasmus (1524; 1532) and Sir Thomas More (1526).

Holberg ('hɒlbɜ:g) *n* **Ludvig,** Baron. 1684–1754, Danish playwright, poet, and historian, born in Norway: considered the founder of modern Danish literature.

hold[1] (həʊld) *vb* **holds, holding, held** (hɛld). **1** to have or keep (an object) with or within the hands, arms, etc.; clasp. **2** (*tr*) to support or bear: *to hold a drowning man's head above water.* **3** to maintain or be maintained in a specified state or condition: *to hold one's emotions in check; hold firm.* **4** (*tr*) to set aside or reserve: *they will hold our tickets until tomorrow.* **5** (when *intr, usually used in commands*) to restrain or be restrained from motion, action, departure, etc.: *hold that man until the police come.* **6** (*intr*) to remain fast or unbroken: *that cable won't hold much longer.* **7** (*intr*) (of the weather) to remain dry and bright: *how long will the weather hold?* **8** (*tr*) to keep the attention of: *her singing held the audience.* **9** (*tr*) to engage in or carry on: *to hold a meeting.* **10** (*tr*) to have the ownership, possession, etc., of: *he holds a law degree from London; who's holding the ace of spades?* **11** (*tr*) to have the use of or responsibility for: *to hold the office of director.* **12** (*tr*) to have the space or capacity for: *the carton will hold only eight books.* **13** (*tr*) to be able to control the outward effects of drinking beer, spirits, etc.: *he can hold his drink well.* **14** (often foll. by *to* or *by*) to remain or cause to remain committed to: *hold him to his promise; he held by his views in spite of opposition.* **15** (*tr; takes a clause as object*) to claim: *he* *holds that the theory is incorrect.* **16** (*intr*) to remain relevant, valid, or true: *the old philosophies don't hold nowadays.* **17** (*tr*) to keep in the mind: *to hold affection for someone.* **18** (*tr*) to regard or consider in a specified manner: *I hold him very dear.* **19** (*tr*) to guard or defend successfully: *hold the fort against the attack.* **20** (*intr*) to continue to go: *hold on one's way.* **21** (sometimes foll. by *on*) *Music.* to sustain the sound of (a note) throughout its specified duration: *to hold on a semibreve for its full value.* **22** (*tr*) *Computing.* to retain (data) in a storage device after copying onto another storage device or onto another location in the same device. Compare **clear** (sense 49). **23** (*tr*) to be in possession of illegal drugs. **24 hold (good) for.** to apply or be relevant to: *the same rules hold for everyone.* **25 hold it! 25a** stop! wait! **25b** stay in the same position! as when being photographed. **26 hold one's head high.** to conduct oneself in a proud and confident manner. **27 hold one's own.** to maintain one's situation or position esp. in spite of opposition or difficulty. **28 hold one's peace** *or* **tongue.** to keep silent. **29 hold water.** to prove credible, logical, or consistent. **30 there is no holding him.** he is so spirited or resolute that he cannot be restrained. ◆ *n* **31** the act or method of holding fast or grasping, as with the hands. **32** something to hold onto, as for support or control. **33** an object or device that holds fast or grips something else so as to hold it fast. **34** controlling force or influence: *she has a hold on him.* **35** a short delay or pause. **36 on hold.** in a state of temporary postponement or delay. **37** a prison or a cell in a prison. **38** *Wrestling.* a way of seizing one's opponent: *a wrist hold.* **39** *Music.* a pause or fermata. **40a** a tenure or holding, esp. of land. **40b** (*in combination*): *leasehold; freehold; copyhold.* **41** a container. **42** *Archaic.* a fortified place. **43 get hold of. 43a** to obtain. **43b** to come into contact with. **44 no holds barred.** all limitations removed. ◆ See also **hold back, hold down, hold forth, hold in, hold off, hold on, hold out, hold over, hold together, hold-up, hold with.** [Old English *healdan;* related to Old Norse *halla,* Gothic *haldan,* German *halten*] ▸ **'holdable** *adj*

hold[2] (həʊld) *n* the space in a ship or aircraft for storing cargo. [C16: variant of HOLE]

holdall ('həʊldˌɔːl) *n Brit.* a large strong bag with handles. Usual U.S. and Canadian name: **carryall.**

hold back *vb* (*adv*) **1** to restrain or be restrained. **2** (*tr*) to withhold: *he held back part of the payment.* ◆ *n* **holdback. 3** a strap of the harness joining the breeching to the shaft, so that the horse can hold back the vehicle. **4** something that restrains or hinders.

hold down *vb* (*tr, adv*) **1** to restrain or control. **2** *Informal.* to manage to retain or keep possession of: *to hold down two jobs at once.*

holden ('həʊldən) *vb Archaic or dialect.* a past participle of **hold**[1].

holder ('həʊldə) *n* **1** a person or thing that holds. **2a** a person, such as an owner, who has possession or control of something. **2b** (*in combination*): *householder.* **3** *Law.* a person who has possession of a bill of exchange, cheque, or promissory note that he is legally entitled to enforce. ▸ **'holder,ship** *n*

Hölderlin (*German* 'hœldərliːn) *n* **Friedrich** ('friːdrɪç). 1770–1843, German lyric poet, whose works include the poems *Menon's Lament for Diotima* and *Bread and Wine* and the novel *Hyperion* (1797–99).

holdfast ('həʊldˌfɑːst) *n* **1a** the act of gripping strongly. **1b** such a grip. **2** any device used to secure an object, such as a hook, clamp, etc. **3** the organ of attachment of a seaweed or related plant.

hold forth *vb* (*adv*) **1** (*intr*) to speak for a long time or in public. **2** (*tr*) to offer (an attraction or enticement).

hold in *vb* (*tr, adv*) **1** to curb, control, or keep in check. **2** to conceal or restrain (feelings).

holding ('həʊldɪŋ) *n* **1** land held under a lease and used for agriculture or similar purposes. **2** (*often pl*) property to which the holder has legal title, such as land, stocks, shares, and other investments. **3** *Sport.* the obstruction of an opponent with the hands or arms, esp. in boxing. ◆ *adj* **4** *Austral. informal.* in funds; having money.

holding company *n* a company with controlling shareholdings in one or more other companies.

holding operation *n* a plan or procedure devised to prolong the existing situation.

holding paddock *n Austral. and N.Z.* a paddock in which cattle or sheep are kept temporarily, as before shearing, etc.

holding pattern *n* the oval or circular path of an aircraft flying around an airport awaiting permission to land.

hold off *vb* (*adv*) **1** (*tr*) to keep apart or at a distance. **2** (*intr;* often foll. by *from*) to refrain (from doing something): *he held off buying the house until prices fell slightly.*

hold on *vb* (*intr, adv*) **1** to maintain a firm grasp: *she held on with all her strength.* **2** to continue or persist. **3** (foll. by *to*) to keep or retain: *hold on to those stamps as they'll soon be valuable.* **4** to keep a telephone line open. ◆ *interj* **5** *Informal.* stop! wait!

hold out *vb* (*adv*) **1** (*tr*) to offer or present. **2** (*intr*) to last or endure. **3** (*intr*) to continue to resist or stand firm, as a city under siege or a person refusing to succumb to persuasion. **4** *Chiefly U.S.* to withhold (something due or expected). **5 hold out for.** to wait patiently or uncompromisingly for (the fulfilment of one's demands). **6 hold out on.** *Informal.* to delay in or keep from telling (a person) some new or important information. ◆ *n* **holdout.** *U.S.* **7** a person, country, organization, etc., that continues to resist or refuses to change: *Honecker was one of the staunchest holdouts against reform.* **8** a person, country, organization, etc., that declines to cooperate or participate: *they remain the only holdouts to signing the accord.*

hold over *vb* (*tr, mainly adv*) **1** to defer consideration of or action on. **2** to postpone for a further period. **3** to prolong (a note, chord, etc.) from one bar to the next. **4** (*prep*) to intimidate (a person) with (a threat). ◆ *n* **holdover.** *U.S. and Canadian informal.* **5** an elected official who continues in office after his term has expired. **6** a performer or performance continuing beyond the original engagement.

hold together *vb* (*adv*) **1** to cohere or remain or cause to cohere or remain in one piece: *your old coat holds together very well.* **2** to stay or cause to stay united: *the children held the family together.*

hold-up *n* **1** a robbery, esp. an armed one. **2** a delay; stoppage. **3** *U.S.* an excessive charge; extortion. ◆ *vb* **hold up.** (*adv*) **4** (*tr*) to delay; hinder: *we were held up by traffic.* **5** (*tr*) to keep from falling; support. **6** (*tr*) to stop forcibly or waylay in order to rob, esp. using a weapon. **7** (*tr*) to exhibit or present: *he held up his achievements for our admiration.* **8** (*intr*) to survive or last: *how are your shoes holding up?* **9** *Bridge.* to refrain from playing a high card, so delaying the establishment of (a suit).

hold with *vb* (*intr, prep*) to support; approve of.

hole (həʊl) *n* **1** an area hollowed out in a solid. **2** an opening made in or through something. **3** an animal's hiding place or burrow. **4** *Informal.* an unattractive place, such as a town or a dwelling. **5** *Informal.* a cell or dungeon. **6** *U.S. informal.* a small anchorage. **7** a fault (esp. in the phrase **pick holes in**). **8** *Slang.* a difficult and embarrassing situation. **9** the cavity in various games into which the ball must be thrust. **10** (on a golf course) **10a** the cup on each of the greens. **10b** each of the divisions of a course (usually 18) represented by the distance between the tee and a green. **10c** the score made in striking the ball from the tee into the hole. **11** *Physics.* **11a** a vacancy in a nearly full band of quantum states of electrons in a semiconductor or an insulator. Under the action of an electric field holes behave as carriers of positive charge. **11b** (*as modifier*): *hole current.* **11c** a vacancy in the nearly full continuum of quantum states of negative energy of fermions. A hole appears as the antiparticle of the fermion. **12 hole in the wall.** *Informal.* a small dingy place, esp. one difficult to find. **13 in holes.** so worn as to be full of holes: *his socks were in holes.* **14 in the hole.** *Chiefly U.S.* **14a** in debt. **14b** (of a card, the **hole card,** in stud poker) dealt face down in the first round. **15 make a hole in.** to consume or use a great amount of (food, drink, money, etc.): *to make a hole in a bottle of brandy.* ◆ *vb* **16** to make a hole or holes in (something). **17** (when *intr,* often foll. by *out*) *Golf.* to hit (the ball) into the hole. [Old English *hol;* related to Gothic *hulundi,* German *Höhle,* Old Norse *hylr* pool, Latin *caulis* hollow stem; see HOLLOW] ▸ **'holey** *adj*

hole-and-corner *adj* (*usually prenominal*) *Informal.* furtive or secretive.

hole in one *Golf.* ◆ *n* **1** a shot from the tee that finishes in the hole. ◆ *vb* **2** (*intr*) to score a hole in one. ◆ Also (esp. U.S.): **ace.**

hole in the heart *n* **a** a defect of the heart in which there is an abnormal opening in any of the walls dividing the four heart chambers. **b** (*as modifier*): *a hole-in-the-heart operation.*

hole up *vb* (*intr, adv*). **1** (of an animal) to hibernate, esp. in a cave. **2** *Informal.* to hide or remain secluded.

Holguín (*Spanish* ɔl'ɣin) *n* a city in NE Cuba, in Holguín province: trading centre. Pop.: 242 085 (1994 est.).

Holi ('hɒˌliː) *n* a Hindu spring festival, celebrated for two to five days, commemorating Krishna's dalliance with the cowgirls. Bonfires are lit and coloured powder and water thrown over celebrants. [named after *Holika,* legendary female demon]

-holic *suffix forming nouns.* indicating a person having an abnormal desire for or dependence on: *workaholic; chocoholic.* [C20: on the pattern of *alcoholic*]

holiday ('hɒlɪˌdeɪ, -dɪ) *n* **1** (*often pl*) *Chiefly Brit.* **1a** a period in which a break is taken from work or studies for rest, travel, or recreation. U.S. and Canadian word: **vacation. 1b** (*as modifier*): *a holiday mood.* **2** a day on which work is suspended by law or custom, such as a religious festival, bank holiday, etc. Related adj: **ferial.** ◆ *vb* **3** (*intr*) *Chiefly Brit.* to spend a holiday. [Old English *hāligdæg,* literally: holy day]

Holiday ('hɒlɪˌdeɪ) *n* **Billie.** real name *Eleanora Fagan;* known as *Lady Day.* 1915–59, U.S. jazz singer.

holiday camp *n Brit.* a place, esp. one at the seaside, providing accommodation, recreational facilities, etc., for holiday-makers.

holiday-maker *n Brit.* a person who goes on holiday. U.S. and Canadian equivalents: **vacationer, vacationist.**

holily ('həʊlɪlɪ) *adv* in a holy, devout, or sacred manner.

holiness ('həʊlɪnɪs) *n* the state or quality of being holy.

Holiness ('həʊlɪnɪs) *n* (preceded by *his* or *your*) a title once given to all bishops, but now reserved for the pope.

Holinshed ('hɒlɪnʃed) *or* **Holingshed** *n* **Raphael.** died ?1580, English chronicler. His *Chronicles of England, Scotland, and Ireland* (1577) provided material for Shakespeare's historical and legendary plays.

holism ('həʊlɪzəm) *n* **1** any doctrine that a system may have properties over and above those of its parts and their organization. **2** the treatment of any subject as a whole integrated system, esp., in medicine, the consideration of the complete person, physically and psychologically, in the treatment of a disease. See also **alternative medicine. 3** *Philosophy.* one of a number of methodological theses holding that the significance of the parts can only be understood in terms of their contribution to the significance of the whole and that the latter must therefore be epistemologically prior. Compare **reductionism, atomism** (sense 2). [C20: from HOLO- + -ISM] ▸ **ho'listic** *adj* ▸ **ho'listically** *adv*

Holkar State (hɒl'kɑː) *n* a former state of central India, ruled by the Holkar dynasty of Maratha rulers of Indore (18th century until 1947).

Holkham Hall ('həʊlkəm, 'hɒlkəm) *n* a Palladian mansion near Wells in Norfolk: built 1734–59 by William Kent for Thomas Coke.

holland ('hɒlənd) *n* a coarse linen cloth, used esp. for furnishing. [C15: after HOLLAND[1], where it was made]

Holland[1] ('hɒlənd) *n* **1** another name for the **Netherlands. 2** a county of the Holy Roman Empire, corresponding to the present-day North and South Holland provinces of the Netherlands. **3 Parts of.** an area in E England constituting a former administrative division of Lincolnshire.

Holland[2] ('hɒlənd) *n* **1 Henry.** 1745–1806, British neoclassical architect. His work includes Brooks's Club (1776) and Carlton House (1783), both in London. **2 Sir Sidney George.** 1893–1961, New Zealand statesman; prime minister of New Zealand (1949–57).

hollandaise sauce (ˌhɒlən'deɪz, 'hɒlənˌdeɪz) *n* a rich sauce of egg yolks, butter, vinegar, etc., served esp. with fish. [C19: from French *sauce hollandaise* Dutch sauce]

Hollander ('hɒləndə) *n* another name for a **Dutchman.**

Hollandia (hɒ'lændɪə) *n* a former name of **Jayapura.**

Hollands ('hɒləndz) *n* Dutch gin, often sold in stone bottles. [C18: from Dutch *hollandsch genever*]

holler ('hɒlə) *Informal.* ◆ *vb* **1** to shout or yell (something). ◆ *n* **2** a shout; call. [variant of C16 *hollow,* from *holla,* from French *holà* stop! (literally: ho there!)]

Holliger (*German* 'hɔlɪgə) *n* **Heinz** (haints). born 1939, Swiss oboist and composer.

hollo ('hɒləʊ), **holla** ('hɒlə), *or* **holloa** (hə'ləʊ) *n, pl* **-los, -las,** *or* **-loas** (-'ləʊz), *interj* **1** a cry for attention, or of encouragement. ◆ *vb* **2** (*intr*) to shout. [C16: from French *holà* ho there!]

hollow ('hɒləʊ) *adj* **1** having a hole, cavity, or space within; not solid. **2** having a sunken area; concave. **3** recessed or deeply set: *hollow cheeks.* **4** (of sounds) as if resounding in a hollow place. **5** without substance or validity. **6** hungry or empty. **7** insincere; cynical. **8 a hollow leg** *or* **hollow legs.** the capacity to eat or drink a lot without ill effects. ◆ *adv* **9 beat (someone) hollow.** *Brit. informal.* to defeat (someone) thoroughly and convincingly. ◆ *n* **10** a cavity, opening, or space in or within something. **11** a depression or dip in the land. ◆ *vb* (often foll. by *out,* usually when *tr*) **12** to make or become hollow. **13** to form (a hole, cavity, etc.) or (of a hole, etc.) to be formed. [C12: from *holu,* inflected form of Old English *holh* cave; related to Old Norse *holr,* German *hohl;* see HOLE] ▸ **'hollowly** *adv* ▸ **'hollowness** *n*

hollow-back *n Pathol.* the nontechnical name for **lordosis.** Compare **hunchback.**

hollow-eyed *adj* with the eyes appearing to be sunk into the face, as from excessive fatigue.

hollowware ('hɒləʊˌwɛə) *n* hollow articles made of metal, china, etc., such as pots, jugs, and kettles. Compare **flatware** (sense 2).

holly ('hɒlɪ) *n, pl* **-lies. 1** any tree or shrub of the genus *Ilex,* such as the Eurasian *I. aquifolium,* having bright red berries and shiny evergreen leaves with prickly edges. **2** branches of any of these trees, used for Christmas decorations. **3 holly oak.** another name for **holm oak.** ◆ See also **sea holly.** [Old English *holegn;* related to Old Norse *hulfr,* Old High German *hulis,* German *Hulst,* Old Slavonic *kolja* prick]

Holly ('hɒlɪ) *n* **Buddy.** real name *Charles Harden Holley.* 1936–59, U.S. rock-and-roll singer, guitarist, and songwriter. His hits (all 1956–59) include "That'll be the Day", "Maybe Baby", "Peggy Sue", "Oh, Boy", "Think it over", and "It doesn't Matter anymore".

hollyhock ('hɒlɪˌhɒk) *n* a tall widely cultivated malvaceous plant, *Althaea rosea,* with stout hairy stems and spikes of white, yellow, red, or purple flowers. Also called (U.S.): **rose mallow.** [C16: from HOLY + *hock,* from Old English *hoc* mallow]

Hollywood ('hɒlɪˌwʊd) *n* **1** a NW suburb of Los Angeles, California: centre of the American film industry. Pop.: 250 000 (1985 est.). **2a** the American film industry. **2b** (*as modifier*): *a Hollywood star.*

holm[1] (həʊm) *n Dialect, chiefly northwestern English.* **1** an island in a river or lake. **2** low flat land near a river. [Old English *holm* sea, island; related to Old Saxon *holm* hill, Old Norse *holmr* island, Latin *culmen* tip]

holm[2] (həʊm) *n* **1** short for **holm oak. 2** *Chiefly Brit.* a dialect word for **holly.** [C14: variant of obsolete *holin,* from Old English *holegn* HOLLY]

Holmes (həʊmz) *n* **1 Oliver Wendell.** 1809–94, U.S. author, esp. of humorous essays, such as *The Autocrat of the Breakfast Table* (1858) and its sequels. **2** his son, **Oliver Wendell.** 1841–1935, U.S. jurist, noted for his liberal judgments.

holmic ('hɒlmɪk) *adj* of or containing holmium.

holmium ('hɒlmɪəm) *n* a malleable silver-white metallic element of the lanthanide series. Symbol: Ho; atomic no.: 67; atomic wt.: 164.93032; valency: 3; relative density: 8.795; melting pt.: 1474°C; boiling pt.: 2700°C. [C19: from New Latin *Holmia* Stockholm]

holm oak *n* an evergreen Mediterranean oak tree, *Quercus ilex,* with prickly leaves resembling holly. Also called: **holm, holly oak, ilex.**

holo- *or before a vowel* **hol-** *combining form.* whole or wholly: *holograph; holotype; Holarctic.* [from Greek *holos*]

holobenthic (ˌhɒlə'bɛnθɪk) *adj* (of an animal) completing its life cycle in the ocean depths.

holoblastic (ˌhɒlə'blæstɪk) *adj Embryol.* of or showing cleavage of the entire zygote into blastomeres, as in eggs with little yolk. Compare **meroblastic.** ▸ ˌ**holo'blastically** *adv*

Holocaine ('hɒləˌkeɪn) *n* a trademark for **phenacaine.**

holocaust ('hɒləˌkɔːst) *n* **1** great destruction or loss of life or the source of such destruction, esp. fire. **2** (*usually cap.*) **the.** Also called: **Churban, Shoah.** the mass murder by the Nazis of the Jews of continental Europe between 1940 and 1945. **3** a rare word for **burnt offering.** [C13: from Late Latin *holocaustum* whole burnt offering, from Greek *holokauston,* from HOLO- + *kaustos,* from *kaiein* to burn] ▸ ˌ**holo'caustal** *or* ˌ**holo'caustic** *adj*

Holocene ('hɒləˌsiːn) *adj* **1** of, denoting, or formed in the second and most recent epoch of the Quaternary period, which began 10 000 years ago at the end of the Pleistocene. ◆ *n* **2 the.** the Holocene epoch or rock series. ◆ Also: **Recent.**

holocrine ('hɒləkrɪn) *adj* (of the secretion of glands) characterized by disintegration of the entire glandular cell in releasing its product, as in sebaceous glands. Compare **merocrine, apocrine.** [C20: from HOLO- + Greek *krinein* to separate, decide]

holocrystalline (ˌhɒlə'krɪstəˌlaɪn) *adj* (of igneous rocks) having only crystalline components and no glass. Compare **hemicrystalline.**

holoenzyme (ˌhɒləʊ'ɛnzaɪm) *n* an active enzyme consisting of a protein component (apoenzyme) and its coenzyme.

Holofernes (ˌhɒlə'fɜːniːz, hə'lɒfəˌniːz) *n* the Assyrian general, who was killed by the biblical heroine Judith.

hologram ('hɒləˌgræm) *n* a photographic record produced by illuminating the object with coherent light (as from a laser) and, without using lenses, exposing a film to light reflected from this object and to a direct beam of coherent light. When interference patterns on the film are illuminated by the coherent light a three-dimensional image is produced.

holograph ('hɒləˌgræf, -ˌgrɑːf) *n* **a** a book or document handwritten by its author; original manuscript; autograph. **b** (*as modifier*): *a holograph document.*

holography (hɒ'lɒgrəfɪ) *n* the science or practice of producing holograms. ▸ **holographic** (ˌhɒlə'græfɪk) *adj* ▸ ˌ**holo'graphically** *adv*

holohedral (ˌhɒlə'hiːdrəl) *adj* (of a crystal) exhibiting all the planes required for the symmetry of the crystal system. ▸ ˌ**holo'hedrism** *n*

holomorphic (ˌhɒlə'mɔːfɪk) *adj Maths.* another word for **analytic** (sense 5).

holophrastic (ˌhɒlə'fræstɪk) *adj* **1** denoting the stage in a child's acquisition of syntax when most utterances are single words. **2** (of languages) tending to express in one word what would be expressed in several words in other languages; polysynthetic. [C19: from HOLO- + Greek *phrastikos* expressive, from *phrazein* to express]

holophytic (ˌhɒlə'fɪtɪk) *adj* (of plants) capable of synthesizing their food from inorganic molecules, esp. by photosynthesis. ▸ **holophyte** ('hɒləˌfaɪt) *n*

holoplankton (ˌhɒlə'plæŋktən) *n* organisms, such as diatoms and algae, that spend all stages of their life cycle as plankton. Compare **meroplankton.**

holothurian (ˌhɒlə'θjʊərɪən) *n* **1** any echinoderm of the class *Holothuroidea,* including the sea cucumbers, having a leathery elongated body with a ring of tentacles around the mouth. ◆ *adj* **2** of, relating to, or belonging to the *Holothuroidea.* [C19: from New Latin *Holothūria* name of type genus, from Latin: water polyp, from Greek *holothourion,* of obscure origin]

holotype ('hɒləˌtaɪp) *n Biology.* another name for **type specimen.** ▸ **holotypic** (ˌhɒlə'tɪpɪk) *adj*

holozoic (ˌhɒlə'zəʊɪk) *adj* (of animals) obtaining nourishment by feeding on plants or other animals.

holp (həʊlp) *vb Archaic or dialect.* a past tense of **help.**

holpen ('həʊlpən) *vb Archaic.* a past participle of **help.**

hols (hɒlz) *pl n Brit. school slang.* holidays.

Holst (həʊlst) *n* **Gustav (Theodore).** 1874–1934, English composer. His works include operas, choral music, and orchestral music such as the suite *The Planets* (1917).

Holstein[1] ('həʊlstaɪn) *n* the usual U.S. and Canadian name for **Friesian** (the cattle).

Holstein[2] (*German* 'hɔlʃtain) *n* a region of N Germany, in S Schleswig-Holstein: in early times a German duchy of Saxony; became a duchy of Denmark in 1474; finally incorporated into Prussia in 1866.

holster ('həʊlstə) *n* **1** a sheathlike leather case for a pistol, attached to a belt or saddle. **2** *Mountaineering.* a similar case for an ice axe or piton hammer. [C17: via Dutch *holster* from Germanic; compare Old Norse *hulstr* sheath, Old English *heolstor* darkness, Gothic *hulistr* cover] ▸ **'holstered** *adj*

holt[1] (həʊlt) *n Archaic or poetic.* a wood or wooded hill. [Old English *holt;* related to Old Norse *holt,* Old High German *holz,* Old Slavonic *kladŭ* log, Greek *klados* twig]

holt[2] (həʊlt) *n* the burrowed lair of an animal, esp. an otter. [C16: a phonetic variant of HOLD[2]]

Holt (həʊlt) *n* **Harold Edward.** 1908–67, Australian statesman; prime minister (1966–67); believed drowned.

holus-bolus ('həʊləs'bəʊləs) *adv Informal.* all at once. [C19: pseudo-Latin based on *whole bolus;* see BOLUS]

holy ('həʊlɪ) *adj* **holier, holiest. 1** of, relating to, or associated with God or a deity; sacred. **2** endowed or invested with extreme purity or sublimity. **3** devout, godly, or virtuous. **4 holier-than-thou.** offensively sanctimonious or self-righteous: *a holier-than-thou attitude.* **5 holy terror. 5a** a difficult or frightening person. **5b** *Irish informal.* a person who is an active gambler, womanizer, etc. ◆ *n, pl* **-lies. 6a** a sacred place. **6b the holy.** (*functioning as pl*) persons or things invested with holiness. [Old English *hālig, hǣlig;* related to Old Saxon *hēlag,* Gothic *hailags,* German *heilig;* see HALLOW]

Holy Alliance *n* **1** a document advocating government according to Christian principles that was signed in 1815 by the rulers of Russia, Prussia, and Austria. **2** the informal alliance that resulted from this agreement.

Holy Bible *n* another name for the **Bible.**

Holy City *n* **the. 1** Jerusalem, esp. when regarded as the focal point of the religions of Judaism, Christianity, or Islam. **2** *Christianity.* heaven regarded as the perfect counterpart of Jerusalem. **3** any city regarded as especially sacred by a particular religion.

Holy Communion *n* **1** the celebration of the Eucharist. **2** the consecrated elements of the Eucharist. ◆ Often shortened to **Communion.**

holy day *n* a day on which a religious festival is observed.

holy day of obligation *n* a major feastday of the Roman Catholic Church on which Catholics are bound to attend Mass and refrain from servile work.

Holy Family *n* **the.** *Christianity.* the infant Jesus, Mary, and St Joseph.

Holy Father *n R.C. Church.* a title of the pope.

Holy Ghost *n* another name for the **Holy Spirit.**

Holy Grail *n* **1** Also called: **Grail, Sangraal.** (in medieval legend) the bowl used by Jesus at the Last Supper. It was allegedly brought to Britain by Joseph of Arimathea, where it became the quest of many knights. **2** *Informal.* any desired ambition or goal: *the Holy Grail of infrared astronomy.* [C14: *grail* from Old French *graal,* from Medieval Latin *gradālis* bowl, of unknown origin]

Holyhead ('hɒlɪ,hɛd) *n* a town in NW Wales, in Anglesey, the chief town of Holy Island: a port on the N coast. Pop.: 11 796 (1991).

Holy Hour *n* **1** *R.C. Church.* an hour set aside for prayer and reflection. **2** (*not caps.*) *Irish informal.* a period during the afternoon when public houses are obliged to close by law.

Holy Innocents' Day *n* Dec. 28, a day commemorating the massacre of male children at Bethlehem by Herod's order (Matthew 2:16); Childermas.

Holy Island *n* **1** an island off the NE coast of Northumberland, linked to the mainland by road but accessible only at low water: site of a monastery founded by St Aidan in 635. Also called: **Lindisfarne. 2** an island off the NW coast of Anglesey. Area: about 62 sq. km (24 sq. miles).

Holy Joe *n Informal.* **1** a minister or chaplain. **2** any sanctimonious or self-righteous person.

Holy Land *n* **the.** another name for **Palestine** (sense 1).

holy Mary *n Irish.* a pietistic person: *he's a real holy Mary.*

Holyoake ('həʊlɪ,əʊk) *n* Sir **Keith Jacka** ('dʒækə). 1904–83, New Zealand politician; prime minister (1957; 1960–72); governor general (1977–80).

Holy Office *n R.C. Church.* a congregation established in 1542 as the final court of appeal in heresy trials; it now deals with matters of doctrine.

holy of holies *n* **1** any place of special sanctity. **2** (*caps.*) the innermost compartment of the Jewish tabernacle, and later of the Temple, where the Ark was enshrined.

holy orders *pl n* **1** the sacrament or rite whereby a person is admitted to the Christian ministry. **2** the grades of the Christian ministry. **3** the rank or status of an ordained Christian minister. ♦ See also **orders.**

holy place *n* **1** the outer chamber of a Jewish sanctuary. **2** a place of pilgrimage.

Holy Roller *n Derogatory.* a member of a sect that expresses religious fervour in an ecstatic or frenzied way.

Holy Roman Empire *n* the complex of European territories under the rule of the Frankish or German king who bore the title of Roman emperor, beginning with the coronation of Charlemagne in 800 A.D. The last emperor, Francis II, relinquished his crown in 1806.

holy rood *n* **1** a cross or crucifix, esp. one placed upon the rood screen in a church. **2** (*often cap.*) the cross on which Christ was crucified.

Holyroodhouse (,hɒlɪru:d'haʊs) *n* a royal palace in Edinburgh in Scotland: official residence of the Queen when in Scotland; begun in 1501 by James IV of Scotland; scene of the murder of David Rizzio in 1566.

Holy Saturday *n* the Saturday before Easter Sunday.

Holy Scripture *n* another term for **Scripture.**

Holy See *n R.C. Church.* **1** the see of the pope as bishop of Rome and head of the Church. **2** the Roman curia.

Holy Sepulchre *n New Testament.* the tomb in which the body of Christ was laid after the Crucifixion.

Holy Spirit *or* **Ghost** *n Christianity.* the third person of the Trinity.

holystone ('həʊlɪ,stəʊn) *n* **1** a soft sandstone used for scrubbing the decks of a vessel. ♦ *vb* **2** (*tr*) to scrub (a vessel's decks) with a holystone. [C19: perhaps so named from its being used in a kneeling position]

holy synod *n* the governing body of any of the Orthodox Churches.

Holy Thursday *n R.C. Church.* **1** another name for **Maundy Thursday. 2** a rare name for **Ascension Day.**

holy war *n* a war waged in the cause of a religion.

holy water *n* water that has been blessed by a priest for use in symbolic rituals of purification.

Holy Week *n* the week preceding Easter Sunday.

Holy Willie ('wɪlɪ) *n* a person who is hypocritically pious. [C18: from Burns' *Holy Willie's Prayer*]

Holy Writ *n* another term for **Scripture.**

Holy Year *n R.C. Church.* a period of remission from sin, esp. one granted every 25 years.

hom (hɒm) *or* **homa** ('hɒmə) *n* **1** a sacred plant of the Parsees and ancient Persians. **2** a drink made from this plant. [from Persian, from Avestan *haoma*]

homage ('hɒmɪdʒ) *n* **1** a public show of respect or honour towards someone or something (esp. in the phrases **pay** *or* **do homage to**). **2** (in feudal society) **2a** the act of respect and allegiance made by a vassal to his lord. See also **fealty. 2b** something done in acknowledgment of vassalage. ♦ *vb* (*tr*) **3** *Archaic or poetic.* to render homage to. [C13: from Old French, from *home* man, from Latin *homo*]

hombre[1] ('ɒmbreɪ, -brɪ) *n Western U.S.* a slang word for **man.** [C19: from Spanish: man]

hombre[2] ('hɒmbə) *n* a variant of **ombre.**

homburg ('hɒmbɜ:g) *n* a man's hat of soft felt with a dented crown and a stiff upturned brim. [C20: named after *Homburg,* in Germany, town where it was originally made]

home (həʊm) *n* **1** the place or a place where one lives: *have you no home to go to?* **2** a house or other dwelling. **3** a family or other group living in a house or other place. **4** a person's country, city, etc., esp. viewed as a birthplace, a residence during one's early years, or a place dear to one. **5** the environment or habitat of a person or animal. **6** the place where something is invented, founded, or developed: *the U.S. is the home of baseball.* **7a** a building or organization set up to care for orphans, the aged, etc. **7b** an informal name for a **mental home. 8** *Sport.* one's own ground: *the match is at home.* **9a** the objective towards which a player strives in certain sports. **9b** an area where a player is safe from attack. **10** *Lacrosse.* **10a** one of two positions of play nearest the opponents' goal. **10b** a player assigned to such a position: *inside home.* **11** *Baseball.* another name for **home plate. 12** *N.Z. informal, obsolete.* Britain, esp. England. **13 a home from home.** a place other than one's own home where one can be at ease. **14 at home. 14a** in one's own home or country. **14b** at ease, as if at one's own home. **14c** giving an informal party at one's own home. **14d** *Brit.* such a party. **15 at home in, on,** *or* **with.** familiar or conversant with. **16 home and dry.** *Brit. informal.* definitely safe or successful: *we will not be home and dry until the votes have been counted.* Austral. and N.Z. equivalent: **home and hosed. 17 near home.** concerning one deeply. ♦ *adj* (*usually prenominal*) **18** of, relating to, or involving one's home, country, etc.; domestic. **19** (of an activity) done in one's house: *home taping.* **20** effective or deadly: *a home thrust.* **21** *Sport.* relating to one's own ground: *a home game.* **22** *U.S.* central; principal: *the company's home office.* ♦ *adv* **23** to or at home: *I'll be home tomorrow.* **24** to or on the point. **25** to the fullest extent: *hammer the nail home.* **26** (of nautical gear) into or in the best or proper position: *the boom is home.* **27 bring home to. 27a** to make clear to. **27b** to place the blame on. **28 come home.** *Nautical.* (of an anchor) to fail to hold. **29 come home to.** to become absolutely clear to. **30 nothing to write home about.** *Informal.* to be of no particular interest: *the film was nothing to write home about.* ♦ *vb* **31** (*intr*) (of birds and other animals) to return home accurately from a distance. **32** (often foll. by *on* or *onto*) to direct or be directed onto a point or target, esp. by automatic navigational aids. **33** to send or go home. **34** to furnish with or have a home. **35** (*intr;* often foll. by *in* or *in on*) to be directed towards a goal, target, etc. [Old English *hām;* related to Old Norse *heimr,* Gothic *haims,* Old High German *heim,* Dutch *heem,* Greek *kōmi* village] ► **'home,like** *adj*

Home (hju:m) *n* **Baron.** See (Baron) **Home of the Hirsel.**

home aid *n N.Z.* another name for **home help.**

home-alone *adj Informal.* (esp. of a young child) left in a house, flat, etc. unattended.

home banking *n* a system whereby a person at home or in an office can use a computer with a modem to call up information from a bank or to transfer funds electronically.

homebody ('həʊm,bɒdɪ) *n, pl* **-bodies.** *Informal.* a person whose life and interests are centred on the home.

homeboy ('həʊm,bɔɪ) *n Slang, chiefly U.S.* **1** a close friend. **2** a person from one's home town or neighbourhood. [C20: U.S. rap-music usage] ► **'home,girl** *fem n*

homebred ('həʊm,brɛd) *adj* **1** raised or bred at home. **2** lacking sophistication or cultivation; crude.

home-brew *n* a beer or other alcoholic drink brewed at home rather than commercially. ► **'home-'brewed** *adj*

homecoming ('həʊm,kʌmɪŋ) *n* **1** the act of coming home. **2** *U.S.* an annual celebration held by a university, college, or school, for former students.

Home Counties *pl n* the counties surrounding London.

home economics *n* (*functioning as sing or pl*) the study of diet, budgeting, child care, textiles, and other subjects concerned with running a home. ► **home economist** *n*

home farm *n Brit.* (esp. formerly) a farm belonging to and providing food for a large country house.

home ground *n* a familiar area or topic.

home-grown *adj* (esp. of fruit and vegetables) produced in one's own country, district, estate, or garden.

Home Guard *n* **1** a volunteer part-time military force recruited for the defence of the United Kingdom in World War II. **2** (in various countries) a civil defence and reserve militia organization.

home help *n Social welfare.* (in Britain and New Zealand) **1** a person, usually a woman, who is paid to do domestic chores for persons unable to look after themselves adequately. **2** Also called: **home care.** such a service provided by a local authority social services department to those whom it judges most need it. ♦ Also called (N.Z.): **home aid.**

homeland ('həʊm,lænd) *n* **1** the country in which one lives or was born. **2** the official name for a **Bantustan.**

homelands movement *n Austral.* the programme to resettle native Australians on their tribal lands.

homeless ('həʊmlɪs) *adj* **a** having nowhere to live. **b** (*as collective n;* preceded by *the*): *the homeless.* ► **'homelessness** *n*

home loan *n* an informal name for **mortgage** (sense 1).

homely ('həʊmlɪ) *adj* **-lier, -liest. 1** characteristic of or suited to the ordinary home; unpretentious. **2** (of a person) **2a** *Brit.* warm and domesticated in manner or appearance. **2b** *Chiefly U.S. and Canadian.* plain or ugly. ► **'homeliness** *n*

home-made *adj* **1** (esp. of cakes, jam, and other foods) made at home or on the premises, esp. of high-quality ingredients. **2** crudely fashioned.

homemaker ('həʊm,meɪkə) *n* **1** *Chiefly U.S. and Canadian.* a person, esp. a housewife, who manages a home. **2** *U.S. and Canadian.* a social worker who manages a household during the incapacity of the housewife. ► **'home,making** *n, adj*

homeo-, homoeo-, *or* **homoio-** *combining form.* like or similar: *homeomorphism.* [from Latin *homoeo-,* from Greek *homoio-,* from *homos* same]

Home Office *n Brit. government.* the national department responsible for the maintenance of law and order, immigration control, and all other domestic affairs not specifically assigned to another department.

Home of the Hirsel (hju:m; 'hɜ:səl) *n* Baron, title of *Sir Alec Douglas-Home,* formerly 14th Earl of Home. 1903–95, British Conservative statesman: he renounced his earldom to become prime minister of Great Britain and Northern Ireland (1963–64); foreign secretary (1970–74).

homeomorphism *or* **homoeomorphism** (ˌhəʊmɪəˈmɔːfɪzəm) *n* **1** the property, shown by certain chemical compounds, of having the same crystal form but different chemical composition. **2** *Maths.* a one-to-one correspondence, continuous in both directions, between the points of two geometric figures or between two topological spaces. ► **ˌhomeoˈmorphic, ˌhomeoˈmorphous,** *or* **ˌhomoeoˈmorphic, ˌhomoeoˈmorphous** *adj*

homeopathy *or* **homoeopathy** (ˌhəʊmɪˈɒpəθɪ) *n* a method of treating disease by the use of small amounts of a drug that, in healthy persons, produces symptoms similar to those of the disease being treated. Compare **allopathy.** ► **homeopathic** *or* **homoeopathic** (ˌhəʊmɪəˈpæθɪk) *adj* ► **ˌhomeoˈpathically** *or* **ˌhomoeoˈpathically** *adv* ► **homeopathist, homoeopathist** (ˌhəʊmɪˈɒpəθɪst) *or* **homeopath, homoeopath** (ˈhəʊmɪəˌpæθ) *n*

homeostasis *or* **homoeostasis** (ˌhəʊmɪəʊˈsteɪsɪs) *n* **1** the maintenance of metabolic equilibrium within an animal by a tendency to compensate for disrupting changes. **2** the maintenance of equilibrium within a social group, person, etc. ► **homeostatic** *or* **homoeostatic** (ˌhəʊmɪəʊˈstætɪk) *adj*

homeotypic (ˌhəʊmɪəʊˈtɪpɪk), **homeotypical** *or* **homoeotypic, homoeotypical** *adj* denoting or relating to the second nuclear division of meiosis, which resembles mitosis. Compare **heterotypic.**

homeowner (ˈhəʊmˌəʊnə) *n* a person who owns the house in which he or she lives. ► **ˌhomeˈownership** *n*

home page *n Computing.* (on a website) the main document relating to an individual or institution that provides introductory information about a website with links to the actual details of services or information provided.

home plate *n Baseball.* a flat often five-sided piece of hard rubber or other material that serves to define the area over which the pitcher must throw the ball for a strike and that a base runner must safely reach on his way from third base to score a run. Also called: **plate, home, home base.**

homer (ˈhəʊmə) *n* **1** another word for **homing pigeon. 2** *U.S. and Canadian.* an informal word for **home run.**

Homer (ˈhəʊmə) *n* **1** c. 800 B.C., Greek poet to whom are attributed the *Iliad* and the *Odyssey*. Almost nothing is known of him, but it is thought that he was born on the island of Chios and was blind. **2 Winslow.** 1836–1910, U.S. painter, noted for his seascapes and scenes of working life.

home range *n Ecology.* the area in which an animal normally ranges.

Homeric (həʊˈmerɪk) *or* **Homerian** (həʊˈmɪərɪən) *adj* **1** of, relating to, or resembling Homer or his poems. **2** imposing or heroic. **3** of or relating to the archaic form of Greek used by Homer. See **epic.** ► **Hoˈmerically** *adv*

Homeric laughter *n* loud unrestrained laughter, as that of the gods.

home rule *n* **1** self-government, esp. in domestic affairs. **2** *U.S. government.* the partial autonomy of cities and (in some states) counties, under which they manage their own affairs, with their own charters, etc., within the limits set by the state constitution and laws. **3** the partial autonomy sometimes granted to a national minority or a colony.

Home Rule *n* self-government for Ireland: the goal of the Irish Nationalists from about 1870 to 1920.

home run *n Baseball.* a hit that enables the batter to run round all four bases, usually by hitting the ball out of the playing area.

Home Secretary *n Brit. government.* short for **Secretary of State for the Home Department;** the head of the Home Office.

homesick (ˈhəʊmˌsɪk) *adj* depressed or melancholy at being away from home and family. ► **ˈhomeˌsickness** *n*

homespun (ˈhəʊmˌspʌn) *adj* **1** having plain or unsophisticated character. **2** woven or spun at home. ◆ *n* **3** cloth made at home or made of yarn spun at home. **4** a cloth resembling this but made on a power loom.

homestead (ˈhəʊmˌsted, -stɪd) *n* **1** a house or estate and the adjoining land, buildings, etc., esp. a farm. **2** (in the U.S.) a house and adjoining land designated by the owner as his fixed residence and exempt under the homestead laws from seizure and forced sale for debts. **3** (in western Canada) a piece of land, usually 160 acres, granted to a settler by the federal government. **4** *Austral. and N.Z.* the owner's or manager's residence on a sheep or cattle station; in New Zealand the term includes all outbuildings.

Homestead Act *n* **1** an act passed by the U.S. Congress in 1862 making available to settlers 160-acre tracts of public land for cultivation. **2** (in Canada) a similar act passed by the Canadian Parliament in 1872.

homesteader (ˈhəʊmˌstedə) *n* **1** a person owning a homestead. **2** *U.S. and Canadian.* a person who acquires or possesses land under a homestead law. **3** a person taking part in a homesteading scheme.

homesteading (ˈhəʊmˌstedɪŋ) *n* (in Britain) **a** a scheme whereby council tenants are enabled to buy derelict property from the council and renovate it with the aid of Government grants. **b** (*as modifier*): *a homesteading scheme.*

homestead law *n* (in the U.S. and Canada) any of various laws conferring certain privileges on owners of homesteads.

home straight *n* **1** *Horse racing.* the section of a racecourse forming the approach to the finish. **2** the final stage of an undertaking or journey. ◆ Also (chiefly U.S.) **home stretch.**

home teacher *n Brit.* a teacher who educates ill or disabled children in their homes.

home truth *n* (*often pl*) an unpleasant fact told to a person about himself.

home unit *n Austral. and N.Z.* a self-contained residence which is part of a series of similar residences. Often shortened to **unit.**

homeward (ˈhəʊmwəd) *adj* **1** directed or going home. **2** (of a ship, part of a voyage, etc.) returning to the home port. ◆ *adv also* **homewards. 3** towards home.

homework (ˈhəʊmˌwɜːk) *n* **1** school work done out of lessons, esp. at home. **2** any preparatory study. **3** work done at home for pay.

homeworker (ˈhəʊmˌwɜːkə) *n* a person who does paid work at home, rather than in an office.

homey (ˈhəʊmɪ) *adj* **homier, homiest. 1** a variant spelling (esp. U.S.) of **homy.** ◆ *n* **2** *N.Z. informal.* a British person. ► **ˈhomeyness** *n*

homicidal (ˌhɒmɪˈsaɪdᵊl) *adj* **1** of, involving, or characterized by homicide. **2** likely to commit homicide: *a homicidal maniac.* ► **ˌhomiˈcidally** *adv*

homicide (ˈhɒmɪˌsaɪd) *n* **1** the killing of a human being by another person. **2** a person who kills another. [C14: from Old French, from Latin *homo* man + *caedere* to slay]

homie (ˈhəʊmɪ) *n Slang, chiefly U.S.* short for **homeboy** *or* **homegirl.**

homiletic (ˌhɒmɪˈletɪk) *or* **homiletical** *adj* **1** of or relating to a homily or sermon. **2** of, relating to, or characteristic of homiletics. ► **ˌhomiˈletically** *adv*

homiletics (ˌhɒmɪˈletɪks) *n* (*functioning as sing*) the art of preaching or writing sermons. [C17: from Greek *homilētikos* cordial, from *homilein* to converse with; see HOMILY]

homily (ˈhɒmɪlɪ) *n, pl* **-lies. 1** a sermon or discourse on a moral or religious topic. **2** moralizing talk or writing. [C14: from Church Latin *homīlia,* from Greek: discourse, from *homilein* to converse with, from *homilos* crowd, from *homou* together + *ilē* crowd] ► **ˈhomilist** *n*

homing (ˈhəʊmɪŋ) *n* (*modifier*) **1** *Zoology.* relating to the ability to return home after travelling great distances: *homing instinct.* **2** (of an aircraft, a missile, etc.) capable of guiding itself onto a target or to a specified point.

homing guidance *n* a method of missile guidance in which internal equipment enables it to steer itself onto the target, as by sensing the target's heat radiation.

homing pigeon *n* any breed of pigeon developed for its homing instinct, used for carrying messages or for racing. Also called: **homer.**

hominid (ˈhɒmɪnɪd) *n* **1** any primate of the family *Hominidae,* which includes modern man (*Homo sapiens*) and the extinct precursors of man. ◆ *adj* **2** of, relating to, or belonging to the *Hominidae.* [C19: via New Latin from Latin *homo* man + -ID[2]]

hominoid (ˈhɒmɪˌnɔɪd) *adj* **1** of or like man; manlike. **2** of, relating to, or belonging to the primate superfamily *Hominoidea,* which includes the anthropoid apes and man. ◆ *n* **3** a hominoid animal. [C20: from Latin *homin-, homo* man + -OID]

hominy (ˈhɒmɪnɪ) *n Chiefly U.S.* coarsely ground maize prepared as a food by boiling in milk or water. [C17: probably of Algonquian origin]

hominy grits *pl n U.S.* finely ground hominy. Often shortened to **grits.**

homo (ˈhəʊməʊ) *n, pl* **-mos.** *Informal.* short for **homosexual.**

Homo (ˈhəʊməʊ) *n* a genus of hominids including modern man (see ***Homo sapiens***) and several extinct species of primitive man, including *H. habilis* and *H. erectus.* [Latin: man]

homo- *combining form.* being the same or like: *homologous; homosexual.* Compare **hetero-.** [via Latin from Greek, from *homos* same]

homoblastic (ˌhəʊməˈblæstɪk) *adj* (of a plant or plant part) showing no difference in form between the juvenile and the adult structures. Compare **heteroblastic.**

homocentric (ˌhəʊməʊˈsentrɪk, ˌhɒm-) *adj* having the same centre; concentric. ► **ˌhomoˈcentrically** *adv*

homocercal (ˌhəʊməʊˈsɜːkᵊl, ˌhɒm-) *adj Ichthyol.* of or possessing a symmetrical tail that extends beyond the end of the vertebral column, as in most bony fishes. Compare **heterocercal.** [C19: from HOMO- + Greek *kerkos* tail]

homochlamydeous (ˌhəʊməkləˈmɪdɪəs) *adj* (of a plant) having a perianth in which the sepals and petals are fused together and indistinguishable. Compare **heterochlamydeous.**

homochromatic (ˌhəʊməʊkrəʊˈmætɪk, ˌhɒm-) *adj* a less common word for **monochromatic** (sense 1). ► **homochromatism** (ˌhəʊməʊˈkrəʊməˌtɪzəm, ˌhɒm-) *n*

homochromous (ˌhəʊməˈkrəʊməs, ˌhɒm-) *adj* (esp. of plant parts) of only one colour.

homocyclic (ˌhəʊməʊˈsaɪklɪk, -ˈsɪk-, ˌhɒm-) *adj* (of an organic compound) containing a closed ring of atoms of the same kind, esp. carbon atoms. Compare **heterocyclic.**

homodont (ˈhəʊməˌdɒnt) *adj* (of most nonmammalian vertebrates) having teeth that are all of the same type. Compare **heterodont.** [C19: from HOMO- + -ODONT]

homoeo- *combining form.* a variant of **homeo-.**

homoeroticism (ˌhəʊməʊɪˈrɒtɪˌsɪzəm) *or* **homoerotism** (ˌhəʊməʊˈerəˌtɪzəm) *n* eroticism centred on or aroused by persons of one's own sex. ► **ˌhomoeˈrotic** *adj*

homogametic (ˌhəʊməgəˈmetɪk) *adj Genetics.* denoting the sex that possesses two similar sex chromosomes. In humans and many other mammals it is the female sex, possessing two X-chromosomes. Compare **heterogametic.**

homogamy (hɒˈmɒgəmɪ) *n* **1** a condition in which all the flowers of an inflorescence are either of the same sex or hermaphrodite. Compare **heterogamy** (sense 3). **2** the maturation of the anthers and stigmas of a flower at the same time, ensuring self-pollination. Compare **dichogamy.** ► **hoˈmogamous** *adj*

homogenate (hɒˈmɒdʒɪnɪt, -ˌneɪt) *n* a substance produced by homogenizing. [C20: from HOMOGENIZE + -ATE[1]]

homogeneous (ˌhəʊməˈdʒiːnɪəs, ˌhɒm-) *adj* **1** composed of similar or identical parts or elements. **2** of uniform nature. **3** similar in kind or nature. **4** having a constant property, such as density, throughout. **5** *Maths.* **5a** (of a polynomial) containing terms of the same degree with respect to all the variables, as in $x^2 + 2xy + y^2$. **5b** (of a function) containing a set of variables such that when each is multiplied by a constant, this constant can be eliminated without altering the value of the function, as in $\cos x/y + x/y$. **5c** (of an equation) containing a homogeneous function made equal to 0. **6** *Chem.* of, composed of, or concerned with a single phase. Compare **heterogeneous.** ◆ Also (for senses 1–4): **homogenous.** ► **homogeneity** (ˌhəʊməʊdʒɪˈniːɪtɪ, ˌhɒm-) *n* ► **ˌhomoˈgeneously** *adv* ► **ˌhomoˈgeneousness** *n*

homogenize *or* **homogenise** (hɒ'mɒdʒɪ,naɪz) *vb* **1** (*tr*) to break up the fat globules in (milk or cream) so that they are evenly distributed. **2** to make or become homogeneous. ▸ **ho,mogeni'zation** *or* **ho,mogeni'sation** *n* ▸ **ho'moge,nizer** *or* **ho'moge,niser** *n*

homogenous (hə'mɒdʒɪnəs) *adj* **1** another word for **homogeneous** (senses 1–4). **2** of, relating to, or exhibiting homogeny.

homogeny (hɒ'mɒdʒɪnɪ) *n Biology.* similarity in structure of individuals or parts because of common ancestry. [C19: from Greek *homogeneia* community of origin, from *homogenēs* of the same kind]

homogony (hɒ'mɒgənɪ) *n* the condition in a plant of having stamens and styles of the same length in all the flowers. Compare **heterogony** (sense 2). ▸ **ho'mogonous** *adj* ▸ **ho'mogonously** *adv*

homograft ('hɒmə,grɑːft) *n* a tissue graft obtained from an organism of the same species as the recipient.

homograph ('hɒmə,græf, -,grɑːf) *n* one of a group of words spelt in the same way but having different meanings. Compare **heteronym.** ▸ **,homo'graphic** *adj*

homoio- *combining form.* a variant of **homeo-.**

homoiothermic (həʊ,mɔɪə'θɜːmɪk) *or* **homothermal** *adj* (of birds and mammals) having a constant body temperature, usually higher than the temperature of the surroundings; warm-blooded. Compare **poikilothermic.** ▸ **ho'moio,thermy** *or* **'homo,thermy** *n*

Homoiousian (,həʊmɔɪ'uːsɪən, -'aʊ-, ,hɒm-) *n* **1** a Christian who believes that the Son is of like (and not identical) substance with the Father. Compare **Homoousian.** ◆ *adj* **2** of or relating to the Homoiousians. [C18: from Late Greek *homoiousios* of like substance, from Greek *homoio-* like + *ousia* nature] ▸ **,Homoi'ousianism** *n*

homologate (hɒ'mɒlə,geɪt) *vb* (*tr*) **1** *Law, chiefly Scots.* to approve or ratify (a deed or contract, esp. one that is defective). **2** *Law.* to confirm (a proceeding, etc.). **3** to recognize (a particular type of car or car component) as a production model or component rather than a prototype, as in making it eligible for a motor race. [C17: from Medieval Latin *homologāre* to agree, from Greek *homologein* to approve, from *homologos* agreeing, from HOMO- + *legein* to speak] ▸ **ho,molo'gation** *n*

homologize *or* **homologise** (hɒ'mɒlə,dʒaɪz) *vb* to be, show to be, or make homologous. ▸ **ho'molo,gizer** *or* **ho'molo,giser** *n*

homologous (həʊ'mɒləgəs, hɒ-), **homological** (,həʊmə'lɒdʒɪkᵊl, ,hɒm-), *or* **homologic** *adj* **1** having a related or similar position, structure, etc. **2** *Chem.* (of a series of organic compounds) having similar characteristics and structure but differing by a number of CH_2 groups. **3** *Med.* **3a** (of two or more tissues) identical in structure. **3b** (of a vaccine) prepared from the infecting microorganism. **4** *Biology.* (of organs and parts) having the same evolutionary origin but different functions: *the wing of a bat and the paddle of a whale are homologous.* Compare **analogous** (sense 2). **5** *Maths.* (of elements) playing a similar role in distinct figures or functions. ▸ **,homo'logically** *adv*

homologous chromosomes *pl n* two chromosomes, one of paternal origin, the other of maternal origin, that are identical in appearance and pair during meiosis.

homolographic (həʊ,mɒlə'græfɪk) *or* **homalographic** *adj Cartography.* another term for **equal-area.**

homologue *or U.S.* (*sometimes*) **homolog** ('hɒmə,lɒg) *n* **1** *Biology.* a homologous part or organ. **2** *Chem.* any homologous compound.

homology (həʊ'mɒlədʒɪ) *n, pl* **-gies. 1** the condition of being homologous. **2** *Chem.* the similarities in chemical behaviour shown by members of a homologous series. **3** *Zoology.* the measurable likenesses between animals, as used in grouping them according to the theory of cladistics. [C17: from Greek *homologia* agreement, from *homologos* agreeing; see HOMOLOGATE]

homolosine projection (hɒ'mɒlə,saɪn) *n* a map projection of the world on which the oceans are distorted to allow for greater accuracy in representing the continents, combining the sinusoidal and equal-area projections. [C20: from HOMOLOGRAPHIC + SINE[1]]

homolysis (hɒ'mɒlɪsɪs) *n* the dissociation of a molecule into two neutral fragments. Also called: **homolytic fission.** Compare **heterolysis** (sense 2). ▸ **homolytic** (,həʊməʊ'lɪtɪk, ,hɒm-) *adj*

homomorphism (,həʊməʊ'mɔːfɪzəm, ,hɒm-) *or* **homomorphy** *n Biology.* similarity in form, as of the flowers of a plant. ▸ **,homo'morphic** *or* **,homo'morphous** *adj*

homonym ('hɒmənɪm) *n* **1** one of a group of words pronounced or spelt in the same way but having different meanings. Compare **homograph, homophone. 2** a person with the same name as another. **3** *Biology.* a specific or generic name that has been used for two or more different organisms. [C17: from Latin *homōnymum*, from Greek *homōnumon*, from *homōnumos* of the same name; see HOMO-, -ONYM] ▸ **,homo'nymic** *or* **ho'monymous** *adj* ▸ **,homo'nymity** *or* **ho'monymy** *n*

Homoousian (,həʊməʊ'uːsɪən, -'aʊ-, ,hɒm-) *n* **1** a Christian who believes that the Son is of the same substance as the Father. Compare **Homoiousian.** ◆ *adj* **2** of or relating to the Homoousians. [C16: from Late Greek *homoousios* of the same substance, from Greek HOMO- + *ousia* nature] ▸ **,Homo'ousianism** *n*

homophile ('həʊmə,faɪl, 'hɒm-) *n* a rare word for **homosexual.**

homophobia (,həʊməʊ'fəʊbɪə) *n* intense hatred or fear of homosexuals or homosexuality. [C20: from HOMO(SEXUAL) + -PHOBIA] ▸ **'homo,phobe** *n* ▸ **,homo'phobic** *adj*

homophone ('hɒmə,fəʊn) *n* **1** one of a group of words pronounced in the same way but differing in meaning or spelling or both, as for example *bear* and *bare.* **2** a written letter or combination of letters that represents the same speech sound as another: *"ph" is a homophone of "f" in English.*

homophonic (,hɒmə'fɒnɪk) *adj* **1** of or relating to homophony. **2** of or relating to music in which the parts move together rather than independently. ▸ **,homo'phonically** *adv*

homophonous (hɒ'mɒfənəs) *adj* of, relating to, or denoting a homophone.

homophony (hɒ'mɒfənɪ) *n* **1** the linguistic phenomenon whereby words of different origins become identical in pronunciation. **2** part music composed in a homophonic style.

homophyly (hɒ'mɒfəlɪ) *n* resemblance due to common ancestry. [C19: from Greek, from HOMO- + PHYLUM] ▸ **homophyllic** (,həʊmə'fɪlɪk, ,hɒm-) *adj*

homoplastic (,həʊməʊ'plæstɪk, ,hɒm-) *adj* **1** (of a tissue graft) derived from an individual of the same species as the recipient. **2** another word for **analogous** (sense 2). ▸ **,homo'plastically** *adv* ▸ **'homo,plasty** *n* ▸ **homoplasy** ('həʊməʊ,pleɪsɪ,'hɒm-) *n*

homopolar (,həʊməʊ'pəʊlə) *adj Chem.* of uniform charge; not ionic; covalent: *a homopolar bond.* ▸ **homopolarity** (,həʊməʊpəʊ'lærɪtɪ, ,hɒm-) *n*

homopterous (həʊ'mɒptərəs) *or* **homopteran** *adj* of, relating to, or belonging to the *Homoptera,* a suborder of hemipterous insects, including cicadas, aphids, and scale insects, having wings of a uniform texture held over the back at rest. Compare **heteropterous.** [C19: from Greek *homopteros,* from HOMO- + *pteron* wing]

homorganic (,həʊmɔː'gænɪk, ,hɒm-) *adj Phonetics.* (of a consonant) articulated at the same point in the vocal tract as a consonant in a different class. Thus ŋ is the homorganic nasal of *k.*

Homo sapiens ('sæpɪ,ɛnz) *n* the specific name of modern man; the only extant species of the genus *Homo.* This species also includes extinct types of primitive man such as Cro-Magnon man. See also **man** (sense 5). [New Latin, from Latin *homo* man + *sapiens* wise]

homoscedastic (,həʊməʊskɪ'dæstɪk) *adj Statistics.* **1** (of several distributions) having equal variance. **2** (of a bivariate or multivariate distribution) having one variable whose variance is the same for all values of the other or others. **3** (of a random variable) having this property. ◆ Compare **heteroscedastic.** [C20: from HOMO- + *scedastic,* from Greek *skedasis* a scattering, dispersal] ▸ **homoscedasticity** (,həʊməʊskɪdæs'tɪsɪtɪ) *n*

homosexual (,həʊməʊ'sɛksjʊəl, ,hɒm-) *n* **1** a person who is sexually attracted to members of the same sex. ◆ *adj* **2** of or relating to homosexuals or homosexuality. **3** of or relating to the same sex. ◆ Compare **heterosexual.**

homosexuality (,həʊməʊ,sɛksjʊ'ælɪtɪ, ,hɒm-) *n* sexual attraction to or sexual relations with members of the same sex. Compare **heterosexuality.**

homosporous (hɒ'mɒspərəs, ,həʊməʊ'spɔːrəs) *adj* (of some ferns) producing spores of one kind only, which develop into hermaphrodite gametophytes. Compare **heterosporous.** ▸ **homospory** (həʊ'mɒspərɪ) *n*

homotaxis (,həʊməʊ'tæksɪs, ,hɒm-) *n* similarity of composition and arrangement in rock strata of different ages or in different regions. ▸ **,homo'taxic** *or* **,homo'taxial** *adj* ▸ **,homo'taxially** *adv*

homothallic (,həʊməʊ'θælɪk) *adj* (of some algae and fungi) having both male and female reproductive organs on the same thallus, which is self-fertilizing. Compare **heterothallic.** [C20: from HOMO- + Greek *thallos* green shoot] ▸ **,homo'thallism** *n*

homothermal (,həʊməʊ'θɜːməl, ,hɒm-) *adj* another word for **homoiothermic.**

homozygote (,həʊməʊ'zaɪgəʊt, -'zɪg-, ,hɒm-) *n* an animal or plant that is homozygous and breeds true to type. Compare **heterozygote.** ▸ **,homozy'gosis** *n* ▸ **homozygotic** (,həʊməʊzaɪ'gɒtɪk, -zɪ-, ,hɒm-) *adj*

homozygous (,həʊməʊ'zaɪgəs, -'zɪg-, ,hɒm-) *adj Genetics.* (of an organism) having identical alleles for any one gene: *these two fruit flies are homozygous for red eye colour.* Compare **heterozygous.** ▸ **,homo'zygously** *adv*

Homs (hɒms) *or* **Hums** (hʊms) *n* a city in W Syria, near the Orontes River: important in Roman times as the capital of Phoenicia-Lebanesia. Pop.: 644 204 (1994 est.). Ancient name: **Emesa** ('ɛmesə). Former name: **Hims.**

homunculus (hɒ'mʌŋkjʊləs) *n, pl* **-li** (-,laɪ). **1** a miniature man; midget. **2** (in early biological theory) a fully-formed miniature human being existing in a spermatozoon or egg. ◆ Also called: **homuncule** (həʊ'mʌŋkjuːl). [C17: from Latin, diminutive of *homo* man] ▸ **ho'muncular** *adj*

homy *or esp. U.S.* **homey** ('həʊmɪ) *adj* **homier, homiest.** like a home, esp. in comfort or informality; cosy. ▸ **'hominess** *or esp. U.S.* **'homeyness** *n*

hon. *abbrev. for:* **1** honorary. **2** honourable.

Hon. *abbrev. for* Honourable (title).

honan ('həʊ'næn) *n* (*sometimes cap.*) a silk fabric of rough weave. [C20: from *Honan,* former name of HENAN, where it is made]

Honan ('həʊ'næn) *n* a variant transliteration of the Chinese name for **Henan.**

honcho ('hɒntʃəʊ) *Informal, chiefly U.S.* ◆ *n, pl* **-chos. 1** the person in charge; the boss. ◆ *vb* **2** to supervise or be in charge of. [C20: from Japanese *han'chō* group leader]

Hond. *abbrev. for* Honduras.

Hondo ('hɒndəʊ) *n* another name for **Honshu.**

Honduras (hɒn'djʊərəs) *n* **1** a republic in Central America: an early centre of Mayan civilization; colonized by the Spanish from 1524 onwards; gained independence in 1821. Official language: Spanish; English is also widely spoken. Religion: Roman Catholic majority. Currency: lempira. Capital: Tegucigalpa. Pop.: 5 919 000 (1998 est.). Area: 112 088 sq. km (43 277 sq. miles). **2 Gulf of.** an inlet of the Caribbean, on the coasts of Honduras, Guatemala, and Belize. ▸ **Hon'duran** *adj, n*

hone[1] (həʊn) *n* **1** a fine whetstone, esp. for sharpening razors. **2** a tool consisting of a number of fine abrasive slips held in a machine head, rotated and reciprocated to impart a smooth finish to cylinder bores, etc. ◆ *vb* **3** (*tr*) to sharpen or polish with or as if with a hone. [Old English *hān* stone; related to Old Norse *hein*]

USAGE *Hone* is sometimes wrongly used where *home* is meant: *this device makes it easier to home in on* (not *hone in on*) *the target.*

hone[2] (həun) *vb* (*intr*) *Dialect.* **1** (often foll. by *for* or *after*) to yearn or pine. **2** to moan or grieve. [C17: from Old French *hogner* to growl, probably of Germanic origin; compare Old High German *hōnen* to revile]

Honecker (*German* 'hɒnɛkər) *n* **Erich** ('eːrɪç). 1912–94, German statesman; head of state of East Germany (1976–89).

Honegger ('hɒnɪgə; *French* ɔnɛgɛr) *n* **Arthur** (artyr). 1892–1955, French composer, one of Les Six. His works include the oratorios *King David* (1921) and *Joan of Arc at the Stake* (1935), and *Pacific 231* (1924) for orchestra.

honest ('ɒnɪst) *adj* **1** not given to lying, cheating, stealing, etc.; trustworthy. **2** not false or misleading; genuine. **3** just or fair: *honest wages.* **4** characterized by sincerity and candour: *an honest appraisal.* **5** without pretensions or artificial traits: *honest farmers.* **6** *Archaic.* (of a woman) respectable. **7 honest broker.** a mediator in disputes, esp. international ones. **8 make an honest woman of.** to marry (a woman, esp. one who is pregnant) to prevent scandal. **9 honest Injun.** (*interj*) *School slang.* genuinely, really. **10 honest to God** (*or* **goodness**). **10a** (*adj*) completely authentic. **10b** (*interj*) an expression of affirmation or surprise. [C13: from Old French *honeste,* from Latin *honestus* distinguished, from *honōs* HONOUR] ▸ **'honestness** *n*

honestly ('ɒnɪstlɪ) *adv* **1** in an honest manner. **2** (intensifier): *I honestly don't believe it.* ◆ *interj* **3** an expression of disgust, surprise, etc.

honesty ('ɒnɪstɪ) *n, pl* **-ties. 1** the condition of being honest. **2** sincerity or fairness. **3** *Archaic.* virtue or respect. **4** a purple-flowered SE European cruciferous plant, *Lunaria annua,* cultivated for its flattened silvery pods, which are used for indoor decoration. Also called: **moonwort, satinpod.**

honesty box *n* a container into which members of the public are trusted to place payments when there is no attendant to collect them.

honewort ('həun,wɜːt) *n* **1** a European umbelliferous plant, *Trinia glauca,* with clusters of small white flowers. **2** any of several similar and related plants. [C17: apparently from obsolete dialect *hone* a swelling, of obscure origin; the plant was believed to relieve swellings]

honey ('hʌnɪ) *n* **1** a sweet viscid substance made by bees from nectar and stored in their nests or hives as food. It is spread on bread or used as a sweetening agent. **2** any similar sweet substance, esp. the nectar of flowers. **3** anything that is sweet or delightful. **4** (*often cap.*) *Chiefly U.S. and Canadian.* a term of endearment. **5** *Informal, chiefly U.S. and Canadian.* something considered to be very good of its kind: *a honey of a car.* **6** (*modifier*) of, concerned with, or resembling honey. ◆ *vb* **honeys, honeying, honeyed** *or* **honied. 7** (*tr*) to sweeten with or as if with honey. **8** (often foll. by *up*) to talk to (someone) in a fond or flattering way. [Old English *huneg;* related to Old Norse *hunang,* Old Saxon *hanig,* German *Honig,* Greek *knēkos* yellowish, Sanskrit *kánaka-* gold] ▸ **'honey-,like** *adj*

honey badger *n* another name for **ratel.**

honey bear *n* another name for **kinkajou** (sense 1) or **sun bear.**

honeybee ('hʌnɪ,biː) *n* any of various social honey-producing bees of the genus *Apis,* esp. *A. mellifera,* which has been widely domesticated as a source of honey and beeswax. Also called: **hive bee.**

honeybunch ('hʌnɪ,bʌntʃ) *or* **honeybun** ('hʌnɪ,bʌn) *n Informal, chiefly U.S.* honey; darling: a term of endearment.

honey buzzard *n* a common European bird of prey, *Pernis apivorus,* having broad wings and a typically dull brown plumage with white-streaked underparts: family *Accipitridae* (hawks, buzzards, etc.). It feeds on grubs and honey from bees' nests.

honeycomb ('hʌnɪ,kəum) *n* **1** a waxy structure, constructed by bees in a hive, that consists of adjacent hexagonal cells in which honey is stored, eggs are laid, and larvae develop. **2** something resembling this in structure or appearance. **3** *Zoology.* another name for **reticulum** (sense 2). ◆ *vb* (*tr*) **4** to pierce or fill with holes, cavities, etc. **5** to permeate: *honeycombed with spies.*

honeycomb moth *n* another name for the **wax moth.**

honey creeper *n* **1** any small tropical American songbird of the genus *Dacnis* and related genera, closely related to the tanagers and buntings, having a slender downward-curving bill and feeding on nectar. **2** any bird of the family *Drepanididae* of Hawaii.

honeydew ('hʌnɪ,djuː) *n* **1** a sugary substance excreted by aphids and similar insects. **2** a similar substance exuded by certain plants. **3** short for **honeydew melon.** ▸ **'honey,dewed** *adj*

honeydew melon *n* a variety of muskmelon with a smooth greenish-white rind and sweet greenish flesh.

honey-eater ('hʌnɪ,iːtə) *n* any small arboreal songbird of the Australasian family *Meliphagidae,* having a downward-curving bill and a brushlike tongue specialized for extracting nectar from flowers.

honeyed *or* **honied** ('hʌnɪd) *adj Poetic.* **1** flattering or soothing. **2** made sweet or agreeable: *honeyed words.* **3** of, full of, or resembling honey. ▸ **'honeyedly** *or* **'honiedly** *adv*

honey fungus *n* an edible basidiomycetous fungus, *Armillaria mellea,* having a yellow-spotted cap and wrinkled stems, parasitic on the roots of woody plants, which it may kill by root rot. It spreads by thin black underground strands. Also called: **bootlace fungus.**

honey guide *n* any small bird of the family *Indicatoridae,* inhabiting tropical forests of Africa and Asia and feeding on beeswax, honey, and insects: order *Piciformes* (woodpeckers, etc.).

honey locust *n* **1** a thorny mimosaceous tree, *Gleditsia triacanthos* of E North America, that has long pods containing a sweet-tasting pulp. **2** another name for **mesquite.**

honey mesquite *n* another name for **mesquite.**

honeymoon ('hʌnɪ,muːn) *n* **1a** a holiday taken by a newly married couple. **1b** (*as modifier*): *a honeymoon cottage.* **2** a holiday considered to resemble a honeymoon: *a second honeymoon.* **3** the early, usually calm period of a relationship, such as a political or business one. ◆ *vb* **4** (*intr*) to take a honeymoon. [C16: traditionally explained as an allusion to the feelings of married couples as changing with the phases of the moon] ▸ **'honey,mooner** *n*

honey mouse *or* **phalanger** *n* a small agile Australian marsupial, *Tarsipes spenserae,* having dark-striped pale brown fur, a long prehensile tail, and a very long snout and tongue with which it feeds on honey, pollen, and insects: family *Phalangeridae.* Also called: **honeysucker.**

honey plant *n* any of various plants that are particularly useful in providing bees with nectar.

honeysucker ('hʌnɪ,sʌkə) *n* **1** any bird, esp. a honey-eater, that feeds on nectar. **2** another name for **honey mouse.**

honeysuckle ('hʌnɪ,sʌk^{ə}l) *n* **1** any temperate caprifoliaceous shrub or vine of the genus *Lonicera:* cultivated for their fragrant white, yellow, or pink tubular flowers. **2** any of several similar plants. **3** any of various Australian trees or shrubs of the genus *Banksia,* having flowers in dense spikes: family *Proteaceae.* [Old English *hunigsūce,* from HONEY + SUCK; see SUCKLE] ▸ **'honey,suckled** *adj*

honeysuckle ornament *n Arts.* another term for **anthemion.**

honey-sweet *adj* sweet or endearing.

honeytrap ('hʌnɪ,træp) *n Informal.* a scheme in which a victim is lured into a compromising sexual situation to provide an opportunity for blackmail.

hong (hɒŋ) *n* **1** (in China) a factory, warehouse, etc. **2** (formerly, in Canton) a foreign commercial establishment. [C18: from Chinese (Cantonese dialect)]

hongi ('hɒŋiː) *n N.Z.* a form of salutation expressed by touching noses. [Maori]

Hong Kong (,hɒŋ 'kɒŋ) *n* **1** a Special Administrative Region of S China, with some autonomy; formerly a British Crown Colony: consists of Hong Kong Island, leased by China to Britain from 1842 until 1997, Kowloon Peninsula, Stonecutters Island, the New Territories (mainland), leased by China in 1898 for a 99-year period, and over 230 small islands; important entrepôt trade and manufacturing centre, esp. for textiles and other consumer goods; university (1912). Administrative centre: Victoria. Pop.: 6 660 000 (1998 est.). Area: 1046 sq. km (404 sq. miles). **2** an island in Hong Kong region, south of Kowloon Peninsula: contains the capital, Victoria. Pop.: 996 183 (latest est.). Area: 75 sq. km (29 sq. miles).

Hong-wu ('hɒŋ'wuː) *or* **Hung-wu** *n* title of *Chu Yuan-Zhang* (or *Chu Yüan-Chang*), 1328–98, first emperor (1368–98) of the Ming dynasty, uniting China under his rule by 1382.

Hong Xiu Quan ('hɒŋ 'ʃjuː 'tʃwɑːn) *or* **Hung Hsiu-Ch'uan** *n* 1814–64, Chinese religious leader and revolutionary. Claiming (1851) to be Christ's brother, he led the Taiping rebellion; committed suicide when it was defeated.

Honiara (,həunɪ'ɑːrə) *n* the capital of the Solomon Islands, on NW Guadalcanal Island. Pop.: 43 643 (1996 est.).

honied ('hʌnɪd) *adj* a variant spelling of **honeyed.** ▸ **'honiedly** *adv*

honi soit qui mal y pense *French.* (ɔni swa ki mal i pɑ̃s) shamed be he who thinks evil of it: the motto of the Order of the Garter.

Honiton ('hɒnɪt^{ə}n, 'hʌn-) *or* **Honiton lace** *n* a type of lace with a floral sprig pattern. [C19: named after *Honiton,* Devon, where it was first made]

honk (hɒŋk) *n* **1** a representation of the sound made by a goose. **2** any sound resembling this, esp. a motor horn. ◆ *vb* **3** to make or cause (something) to make such a sound. **4** (*intr*) *Brit.* a slang word for **vomit.**

honker ('hɒŋkə) *n* **1** a person or thing that honks. **2** *Canadian.* an informal name for the **Canada goose. 3** *Slang.* a nose, esp. a large nose.

honky ('hɒŋkɪ) *n, pl* **honkies.** *Derogatory slang, chiefly U.S.* a White man or White men collectively. [C20: of unknown origin]

honky-tonk ('hɒŋkɪ,tɒŋk) *n* **1** *U.S. and Canadian slang.* **1a** a cheap disreputable nightclub, bar, etc. **1b** (*as modifier*): *a honky-tonk district.* **2** a style of ragtime piano-playing, esp. on a tinny-sounding piano. **3** a type of country music, usually performed by a small band with electric and steel guitars. **4** (*as modifier*): *honky-tonk music.* [C19: rhyming compound based on HONK]

Honolulu (,hɒnə'luːluː) *n* a port in Hawaii, on S Oahu Island: the state capital. Pop.: 423 475 (1996 est.).

honor ('ɒnə) *n, vb* the U.S. spelling of **honour.**

honorarium (,ɒnə'rɛərɪəm) *n, pl* **-iums** *or* **-ia** (-ɪə). a fee paid for a nominally free service. [C17: from Latin: something presented on being admitted to a post of HONOUR]

honorary ('ɒnərərɪ, 'ɒnrərɪ) *adj* (*usually prenominal*) **1a** (esp. of a position, title, etc.) held or given only as an honour, without the normal privileges or duties: *an honorary degree.* **1b** (of a secretary, treasurer, etc.) unpaid. **2** having such a position or title. **3** depending on honour rather than legal agreement.

honorific (,ɒnə'rɪfɪk) *adj* **1** showing or conferring honour or respect. **2a** (of a pronoun, verb inflection, etc.) indicating the speaker's respect for the addressee or his acknowledgment of inferior status. **2b** (*as n*): *a Japanese honorific.* ▸ **,honor'ifically** *adv*

honoris causa *Latin.* (hɒ'nɔːrɪs 'kauzɑː) for the sake of honour.

honour *or U.S.* **honor** ('ɒnə) *n* **1** personal integrity; allegiance to moral principles. **2a** fame or glory. **2b** a person or thing that wins this for another: *he is an honour to the school.* **3** (*often pl*) great respect, regard, esteem, etc., or an outward sign of this. **4** (*often pl*) high or noble rank. **5** a privilege or pleasure: *it is an honour to serve you.* **6** a woman's virtue or chastity. **7a** *Bridge, poker, etc.* any of the top five cards in a suit or any of the four aces at no trumps. **7b** *Whist.* any of the top four cards. **8** *Golf.* the right to tee off first. **9 do honour to. 9a** to pay homage to. **9b** to be a credit to. **10 do the honours. 10a** to serve as host or hostess. **10b** to perform a social act, such as carving meat, proposing a toast, etc. **11 honour bright.** *Brit. school slang.* an exclamation pledging honour. **12 in honour bound.** under a moral obligation. **13 in honour of.** out of respect for. **14 on** (*or* **upon**) **one's honour.** on the pledge of one's word or good name. ◆ *vb* (*tr*) **15** to hold in respect or esteem. **16** to show courteous behaviour towards. **17** to worship. **18** to confer a distinction upon. **19** to accept and then pay when due (a cheque, draft, etc.). **20** to keep (one's promise);

fulfil (a previous agreement). **21** to bow or curtsy to (one's dancing partner). ◆ See also **honours.** [C12: from Old French *onor,* from Latin *honor* esteem] ▸ **'honourer** *or U.S.* **'honorer** *n* ▸ **'honourless** *or U.S.* **'honorless** *adj*

Honour ('ɒnə) *n* (preceded by *Your, His,* or *Her*) **a** a title used to or of certain judges. **b** (in Ireland) a form of address in general use.

honourable *or U.S.* **honorable** ('ɒnərəbᵊl, 'ɒnrəbᵊl) *adj* **1** possessing or characterized by high principles: *honourable intentions.* **2** worthy of or entitled to honour or esteem. **3** consistent with or bestowing honour. ▸ **'honourableness** *or U.S.* **'honorableness** *n* ▸ **'honourably** *or U.S.* **'honorably** *adv*

Honourable *or U.S.* **Honorable** ('ɒnərəbᵊl, 'ɒnrəbᵊl) *adj* (*prenominal*) **the.** a title of respect placed before a name: employed before the names of various officials in the English-speaking world, as a courtesy title in Britain for the children of viscounts and barons and the younger sons of earls, and in Parliament by one member speaking of another. Abbrev.: **Hon.**

honourable discharge *n* See **discharge** (sense 15).

Honour Moderations *pl n* (at Oxford University) the first public examination, in which candidates are placed into one of three classes of honours. Sometimes shortened to **Moderations** or **Mods.**

honours *or U.S.* **honors** ('ɒnəz) *pl n* **1** observances of respect. **2** (*often cap.*) **2a** (in a university degree or degree course) a rank of the highest academic standard. **2b** (*as modifier*): *an honours degree.* Abbrev.: **Hons.** Compare **general** (sense 9), **pass** (sense 35). **3** a high mark awarded for an examination; distinction. **4 last** (*or* **funeral**) **honours.** observances of respect at a funeral. **5 military honours.** ceremonies performed by troops in honour of royalty, at the burial of an officer, etc.

honour school *n* (at Oxford University) one of the courses of study leading to an honours degree.

honours list *n Brit.* a list of those who have had or are having an honour, esp. a peerage or membership of an order of chivalry, conferred on them.

honours of war *pl n Military.* the honours granted by the victorious to the defeated, esp. as of marching out with all arms and flags flying.

Hon. Sec. *abbrev. for* Honorary Secretary.

Honshu ('hɒnʃuː) *n* the largest of the four main islands of Japan, between the Pacific and the Sea of Japan; regarded as the Japanese mainland; includes a number of offshore islands and contains most of the main cities. Pop.: 100 995 000 (1995). Area: 230 448 sq. km (88 976 sq. miles). Also called: **Hondo.**

hoo (huː) *pron West Yorkshire and south Lancashire dialect.* she. [from Old English *heo*]

hooch *or* **hootch** (huːtʃ) *n Informal, chiefly U.S. and Canadian.* alcoholic drink, esp. illicitly distilled spirits. [C20: shortened from Tlingit *Hootchinoo,* name of a tribe that distilled a type of liquor]

Hooch *or* **Hoogh** (huːtʃ; *Dutch* hoːx) *n* **Pieter de** ('piːtər də). 1629–?1684, Dutch genre painter, noted esp. for his light effects.

hood[1] (hʊd) *n* **1** a loose head covering either attached to a cloak or coat or made as a separate garment. **2** something resembling this in shape or use. **3** the U.S. and Canadian name for **bonnet** (of a car). **4** the folding roof of a convertible car. **5** a hoodlike garment worn over an academic gown, indicating its wearer's degree and university. **6** *Falconry.* a close-fitting cover, placed over the head and eyes of a falcon to keep it quiet when not hunting. **7** *Biology.* a structure or marking, such as the fold of skin on the head of a cobra, that covers or appears to cover the head or some similar part. ◆ *vb* **8** (*tr*) to cover or provide with or as if with a hood. [Old English *hōd;* related to Old High German *huot* hat, Middle Dutch *hoet,* Latin *cassis* helmet; see HAT] ▸ **'hoodless** *adj* ▸ **'hood,like** *adj*

hood[2] (hʊd) *n Slang.* short for **hoodlum** (gangster).

Hood (hʊd) *n* **1 Robin.** See **Robin Hood. 2 Samuel,** 1st Viscount. 1724–1816, British admiral. He fought successfully against the French during the American Revolution and the French Revolutionary Wars. **3 Thomas.** 1799–1845, British poet and humorist: his work includes protest poetry, such as *The Song of the Shirt* (1843) and *The Bridge of Sighs* (1844).

-hood *suffix forming nouns.* **1** indicating state or condition of being: *manhood.* **2** indicating a body of persons: *knighthood; priesthood.* [Old English *-hād*]

'hood (hʊd) *n Slang, chiefly U.S.* short for **neighbourhood.**

hooded ('hʊdɪd) *adj* **1** covered with, having, or shaped like a hood. **2** (of eyes) having heavy eyelids that appear to be half closed.

hooded crow *n* a subspecies of the carrion crow, *Corvus corone cornix,* that has a grey body and black head, wings, and tail. Also called (Scot.): **hoodie** ('hʊdɪ), **hoodie crow.**

hooded seal *n* a large greyish earless seal, *Cystophora cristata,* of the N Atlantic and Arctic Oceans, having an inflatable hoodlike sac over the nasal region. Also called: **bladdernose.**

hoodlum ('huːdləm) *n* **1** a petty gangster or ruffian. **2** a lawless youth. [C19: perhaps from Southern German dialect *Haderlump* ragged good-for-nothing] ▸ **'hoodlumism** *n*

hoodman-blind *n Brit., archaic.* blind man's buff.

hood mould *n* another name for **dripstone** (sense 2).

hoodoo ('huːduː) *n, pl* **-doos. 1** a variant of **voodoo. 2** *Informal.* a person or thing that brings bad luck. **3** *Informal.* bad luck. **4** (in the western U.S. and Canada) a strangely shaped column of rock. ◆ *vb* **-doos, -dooing, -dooed. 5** (*tr*) *Informal.* to bring bad luck to. [C19: variant of VOODOO] ▸ **'hoodooism** *n*

hoodwink ('hʊd,wɪŋk) *vb* (*tr*) **1** to dupe; trick. **2** *Obsolete.* to cover or hide. [C16: originally, to cover the eyes with a hood, blindfold] ▸ **'hood,winker** *n*

hooey ('huːɪ) *n, interj Slang.* nonsense; rubbish. [C20: of unknown origin]

hoof (huːf) *n, pl* **hooves** (huːvz) *or* **hoofs. 1a** the horny covering of the end of the foot in the horse, deer, and all other ungulate mammals. **1b** (*in combination*): *a hoofbeat.* Related adj: **ungular. 2** the foot of an ungulate mammal. **3** a hoofed animal. **4** *Facetious.* a person's foot. **5 on the hoof. 5a** (of livestock) alive. **5b** in an impromptu manner: *he did his thinking on the hoof.* ◆ *vb* **6** (*tr*) to kick or trample with the hoofs. **7 hoof it.** *Slang.* **7a** to walk. **7b** to dance. [Old English *hōf;* related to Old Norse *hōfr,* Old High German *huof* (German *Huf*), Sanskrit *saphás*] ▸ **'hoofless** *adj* ▸ **'hoof,like** *adj*

hoofbound ('huːf,baʊnd) *adj Vet. science.* (of a horse) having dry contracted hooves, with resultant pain and lameness.

hoofed (huːft) *adj* **a** having a hoof or hoofs. **b** (*in combination*): *four-hoofed; cloven-hoofed.*

hoofer ('huːfə) *n Slang.* a professional dancer, esp. a tap-dancer.

Hooft (*Dutch* hoːft) *n* **Pieter Corneliszoon** ('piːtər kɔr'neːlisoːn). 1581–1647, Dutch poet, historian, and writer: noted esp. for his love poetry and his 27-volume *History of the Netherlands* (1626–47).

Hoogh (*Dutch* hoːx) *n* See (Pieter de) **Hooch.**

Hooghly ('huːglɪ) *n* a river in NE India, in West Bengal: the westernmost and commercially most important channel by which the River Ganges enters the Bay of Bengal. Length: 232 km (144 miles).

hoo-ha ('huː,hɑː) *n* a noisy commotion or fuss. [C20: of unknown origin]

hook (hʊk) *n* **1** a piece of material, usually metal, curved or bent and used to suspend, catch, hold, or pull something. **2** short for **fish-hook. 3** a trap or snare. **4** *Chiefly U.S.* something that attracts or is intended to be an attraction. **5** something resembling a hook in design or use. **6a** a sharp bend or angle in a geological formation, esp. a river. **6b** a sharply curved spit of land. **7** *Boxing.* a short swinging blow delivered from the side with the elbow bent. **8** *Cricket.* a shot in which the ball is hit square on the leg side with the bat held horizontally. **9** *Golf.* a shot that causes the ball to swerve sharply from right to left. **10** *Surfing.* the top of a breaking wave. **11** Also called: **hookcheck.** *Ice hockey.* the act of hooking an opposing player. **12** *Music.* a stroke added to the stem of a written or printed note to indicate time values shorter than a crotchet. **13** a catchy musical phrase in a pop song. **14** another name for a **sickle. 15** a nautical word for **anchor. 16 by hook or (by) crook.** by any means. **17 get the hook.** *U.S. and Canadian slang.* to be dismissed from employment. **18 hook, line, and sinker.** *Informal.* completely: *he fell for it hook, line, and sinker.* **19 off the hook. 19a** *Slang.* out of danger; free from obligation or guilt. **19b** (of a telephone receiver) not on the support, so that incoming calls cannot be received. **20 on one's own hook.** *Slang, chiefly U.S.* on one's own initiative. **21 on the hook.** *Slang.* **21a** waiting. **21b** in a dangerous or difficult situation. **22 sling one's hook.** *Brit. slang.* to leave. ◆ *vb* **23** (often foll. by *up*) to fasten or be fastened with or as if with a hook or hooks. **24** (*tr*) to catch (something, such as a fish) on a hook. **25** to curve like or into the shape of a hook. **26** (*tr*) (of bulls, elks, etc.) to catch or gore with the horns. **27** (*tr*) to make (a rug) by hooking yarn through a stiff fabric backing with a special instrument. **28** (*tr;* often foll. by *down*) to cut (grass or herbage) with a sickle: *to hook down weeds.* **29** *Boxing.* to hit (an opponent) with a hook. **30** *Ice hockey.* to impede (an opposing player) by catching hold of him with the stick. **31** *Golf.* to play (a ball) with a hook. **32** *Rugby.* to obtain and pass (the ball) backwards from a scrum to a member of one's team, using the feet. **33** *Cricket.* to play (a ball) with a hook. **34** (*tr*) *Informal.* to trick. **35** (*tr*) a slang word for **steal. 36 hook it.** *Slang.* to run or go quickly away. ◆ See also **hook-up.** [Old English *hōc;* related to Middle Dutch *hōk,* Old Norse *haki*] ▸ **'hookless** *adj* ▸ **'hook,like** *adj*

hookah *or* **hooka** ('hʊkə) *n* an oriental pipe for smoking marijuana, tobacco, etc., consisting of one or more long flexible stems connected to a container of water or other liquid through which smoke is drawn and cooled. Also called: **hubble-bubble, kalian, narghile, water pipe.** [C18: from Arabic *huqqah*]

hook and eye *n* a fastening for clothes consisting of a small hook hooked onto a small metal or thread loop.

Hooke (hʊk) *n* **Robert.** 1635–1703, English physicist, chemist, and inventor. He formulated Hooke's law (1678), built the first Gregorian telescope, and invented a balance spring for watches.

hooked (hʊkt) *adj* **1** bent like a hook. **2** having a hook or hooks. **3** caught or trapped. **4** a slang word for **married. 5.** *Slang.* addicted to a drug. **6** (often foll. by *on*) obsessed (with). ▸ **hookedness** ('hʊkɪdnɪs) *n*

hooker[1] ('hʊkə) *n* **1** a commercial fishing boat using hooks and lines instead of nets. **2** a sailing boat of the west of Ireland formerly used for cargo and now for pleasure sailing and racing. [C17: from Dutch *hoeker*]

hooker[2] ('hʊkə) *n* **1** a person or thing that hooks. **2** *U.S. and Canadian slang.* **2a** a draught of alcoholic drink, esp. of spirits. **2b** a prostitute. **3** *Rugby.* the central forward in the front row of a scrum whose main job is to hook the ball.

Hooker ('hʊkə) *n* **1** Sir **Joseph Dalton.** 1817–1911, British botanist; director of Kew Gardens (1865–85). **2 Richard.** 1554–1600, British theologian, who influenced Anglican theology with *The Laws of Ecclesiastical Polity* (1593–97). **3** Sir **William Jackson.** 1785–1865, British botanist; first director of Kew Gardens: father of Sir Joseph Dalton Hooker.

Hooke's law *n* the principle that the stress imposed on a solid is directly proportional to the strain produced, within the elastic limit. [C18: named after R. HOOKE]

hooknose ('hʊk,nəʊz) *n* a nose with a pronounced outward and downward curve; aquiline nose. ▸ **'hook,nosed** *adj*

Hook of Holland *n* **the. 1** a cape on the SW coast of the Netherlands, in South Holland province. **2** a port on this cape. ◆ Dutch name: **Hoek van Holland.**

hook-tip *n* **1** any of several moths of the genus *Daepana,* characterized by the hooked point on each forewing. **2 beautiful hook-tip.** a similar but unrelated species, *Laspeyria flexula.*

hook-up *n* **1** the contact of an aircraft in flight with the refuelling hose of a tanker aircraft. **2** an alliance or relationship, esp. an unlikely one, between people, countries, etc. **3** the linking of broadcasting equipment or stations to transmit a special programme. ♦ *vb* **hook up** (*adv*). **4** to connect (two or more people or things). **5** (often foll. by *with*) *Slang.* to get married (to).

hookworm ('hʊk,wɜ:m) *n* any parasitic blood-sucking nematode worm of the family *Ancylostomatidae,* esp. *Ancylostoma duodenale* or *Necator americanus,* both of which cause disease. They have hooked mouthparts and enter their hosts by boring through the skin.

hookworm disease *n* the nontechnical name for **ancylostomiasis.**

hooky *or* **hookey** ('hʊkɪ) *n Informal, chiefly U.S., Canadian, and N.Z.* truancy, usually from school (esp. in the phrase **play hooky**). [C20: perhaps from *hook it* to escape]

hooley *or* **hoolie** ('hu:lɪ) *n, pl* **-leys** *or* **-lies.** *Chiefly Irish and N.Z.* a lively party. [C19: of unknown origin]

hooligan ('hu:lɪgən) *n Slang.* a rough lawless young person. [C19: perhaps variant of *Houlihan,* Irish surname] ▸ **'hooliganism** *n*

hoon (hu:n) *n Austral. & N.Z. informal.* a hooligan. [of unknown origin]

hoop[1] (hu:p) *n* **1** a rigid circular band of metal or wood. **2** something resembling this. **3a** a band of iron that holds the staves of a barrel or cask together. **3b** (*as modifier*): *hoop iron.* **4** a child's toy shaped like a hoop and rolled on the ground or whirled around the body. **5** *Croquet.* any of the iron arches through which the ball is driven. **6a** a light curved frame to spread out a skirt. **6b** (*as modifier*): *a hoop skirt; a hoop petticoat.* **7** *Basketball.* the round metal frame to which the net is attached to form the basket. **8** a large ring through which performers or animals jump. **9** *Jewellery.* **9a** an earring consisting of one or more circles of metal, plastic, etc. **9b** the part of a finger ring through which the finger fits. **10** *Austral. informal.* a jockey. **11 go** *or* **be put through the hoop.** to be subjected to an ordeal. ♦ *vb* **12** (*tr*) to surround with or as if with a hoop. [Old English *hōp;* related to Dutch *hoep,* Old Norse *hōp* bay, Lithuanian *kabē* hook] ▸ **hooped** *adj* ▸ **'hoop,like** *adj*

hoop[2] (hu:p) *n, vb* a variant spelling of **whoop.**

hooper ('hu:pə) *n* a rare word for **cooper.**

hoopla ('hu:plɑ:) *n* **1** *Brit.* a fairground game in which a player tries to throw a hoop over an object and so win it. **2** *U.S. and Canadian slang.* noise; bustle. **3** *U.S. slang.* nonsense; ballyhoo. [C20: see WHOOP, LA[2]]

hoopoe ('hu:pu:) *n* an Old World bird, *Upupa epops,* having a pinkish-brown plumage with black-and-white wings and an erectile crest: family *Upupidae,* order *Coraciiformes* (kingfishers, etc.). [C17: from earlier *hoopoop,* of imitative origin; compare Latin *upupa*]

hoop pine *n* a fast-growing timber tree of Australia, *Araucaria cunninghamii,* having rough bark with hoop-like cracks around the trunk and branches: family *Araucariaceae.*

hoop snake *n* any of various North American snakes, such as the mud snake (*Farancia abacura*), that were formerly thought to hold the tail in the mouth and roll along like a hoop.

hooray (hu:'reɪ) *interj, n, vb* **1** a variant of **hurrah.** ♦ *interj* **2** Also: **hooroo** (hu:'ru:). *Austral. and N.Z.* goodbye; cheerio.

Hooray Henry ('hu:,reɪ) *n, pl* **Hooray Henries** *or* **-rys.** a young upper-class man, often with affectedly hearty voice and manners. Sometimes shortened to **Hooray.**

hoosegow *or* **hoosgow** ('hu:sgaʊ) *n U.S.* a slang word for **jail.** [C20: from Mexican Spanish *jusgado* prison, from Spanish: court of justice, from *juzgar* to judge, from Latin *jūdicāre,* from *judex* a JUDGE; compare JUG]

hoot[1] (hu:t) *n* **1** the mournful wavering cry of some owls. **2** a similar sound, such as that of a train whistle. **3** a jeer of derision. **4** *Informal.* an amusing person or thing. **5 not give a hoot.** not to care at all. ♦ *vb* **6** (often foll. by *at*) to jeer or yell (something) contemptuously (at someone). **7** (*tr*) to drive (political speakers, actors on stage, etc.) off or away by hooting. **8** (*intr*) to make a hoot. **9** (*intr*) *Brit.* to blow a horn. [C13 *hoten,* of imitative origin]

hoot[2] (hu:t) *or* **hoots** (hu:ts) *interj* an exclamation of impatience or dissatisfaction: a supposed Scotticism. [C17: of unknown origin]

hoot[3] (hu:t) *n Austral. and N.Z.* a slang word for **money.** [from Maori *utu* price]

hootch (hu:tʃ) *n* a variant spelling of **hooch.**

hootenanny ('hu:t(ə),nænɪ) *or* **hootnanny** ('hu:t,nænɪ) *n, pl* **-nies. 1.** *U.S. and Canadian.* an informal performance by folk singers. **2** *Chiefly U.S.* something the name of which is unspecified or forgotten. [C20: of unknown origin]

hooter ('hu:tə) *n Chiefly Brit.* **1** a person or thing that hoots, esp. a car horn. **2** *Slang.* a nose.

hoot owl *n* any owl that utters a hooting cry, as distinct from a screech owl.

Hoover[1] ('hu:və) *n* **1** *Trademark.* a type of vacuum cleaner. ♦ *vb* (*usually not cap.*) **2** to vacuum-clean (a carpet, furniture, etc.). **3** (*tr;* often foll. by *up*) to consume or dispose of (something) quickly and completely: *he hoovered up his grilled fish.*

Hoover[2] ('hu:və) *n* **1 Herbert (Clark).** 1874–1964, U.S. statesman; 31st president of the U.S. (1929–33). He organized relief for Europe during and after World War I, but as president he lost favour after his failure to alleviate the effects of the Depression. **2 J(ohn) Edgar.** 1895–1972, U.S. lawyer: director of the FBI (1924–72). He used new scientific methods to combat crime, including the first fingerprint file.

Hoover Dam *n* a dam in the western U.S., on the Colorado River on the border between Nevada and Arizona; forms Lake Mead. Height: 222 m (727 ft.). Length: 354 m (1180 ft.). Former name (1933–47): **Boulder Dam.**

hooves (hu:vz) *n* a plural of **hoof.**

hop[1] (hɒp) *vb* **hops, hopping, hopped. 1** (*intr*) to make a jump forwards or upwards, esp. on one foot. **2** (*intr*) (esp. of frogs, birds, rabbits, etc.) to move forwards in short jumps. **3** (*tr*) to jump over: *he hopped the hedge.* **4** (*intr*) *Informal.* to move or proceed quickly (in, on, out of, etc.): *hop on a bus.* **5** (*tr*) *Informal.* to cross (an ocean) in an aircraft: *they hopped the Atlantic in seven hours.* **6** (*tr*) *U.S. and Canadian informal.* to travel by means of (an aircraft, bus, etc.): *he hopped a train to Chicago.* **7** *U.S. and Canadian.* to bounce or cause to bounce: *he hopped the flat stone over the lake's surface.* **8** (*intr*) *U.S. and Canadian informal.* to begin intense activity, esp. work. **9** (*intr*) another word for **limp**[1]. **10 hop it** (*or* **off**). *Brit. slang.* to go away. ♦ *n* **11** the act or an instance of hopping. **12** *Old-fashioned informal.* a dance, esp. one at which popular music is played: *we're all going to the school hop tonight.* **13** *Informal.* a trip, esp. in an aircraft. **14** *U.S.* a bounce, as of a ball. **15 on the hop.** *Informal.* **15a** active or busy. **15b** *Brit.* unawares or unprepared: *the new ruling caught me on the hop.* ♦ See also **hop into.** [Old English *hoppian;* related to Old Norse *hoppa* to hop, Middle Low German *hupfen*]

hop[2] (hɒp) *n* **1** any climbing plant of the N temperate genus *Humulus,* esp. *H. lupulus,* which has green conelike female flowers and clusters of small male flowers: family *Cannabiaceae* (or *Cannabidaceae*). See also **hops. 2 hop garden.** a field of hops. **3** *Obsolete slang.* opium or any other narcotic drug. [C15: from Middle Dutch *hoppe;* related to Old High German *hopfo,* Norwegian *hupp* tassel]

hop clover *n* the U.S. name for **hop trefoil.**

hope (həʊp) *n* **1** (*sometimes pl*) a feeling of desire for something and confidence in the possibility of its fulfilment: *his hope for peace was justified; their hopes were dashed.* **2** a reasonable ground for this feeling: *there is still hope.* **3** a person or thing that gives cause for hope. **4** a thing, situation, or event that is desired: *my hope is that prices will fall.* **5 not a hope** *or* **some hope.** used ironically to express little confidence that expectations will be fulfilled. ♦ *vb* **6** (*tr; takes a clause as object or an infinitive*) to desire (something) with some possibility of fulfilment: *we hope you can come; I hope to tell you.* **7** (*intr;* often foll. by *for*) to have a wish (for a future event, situation, etc.). **8** (*tr; takes a clause as object*) to trust, expect, or believe: *we hope that this is satisfactory.* [Old English *hopa;* related to Old Frisian *hope,* Dutch *hoop,* Middle High German *hoffe*] ▸ **'hoper** *n*

Hope (həʊp) *n* **1 Anthony,** real name *Sir Anthony Hope Hawkins.* 1863–1933, English novelist; author of *The Prisoner of Zenda* (1894). **2 Bob,** real name *Leslie Townes Hope.* born 1903, U.S. comedian and comic actor, born in England. His films include *The Cat and the Canary* (1939), *Road to Morocco* (1942), and *The Paleface* (1947). He was awarded an honorary knighthood in 1998.

hope chest *n* the U.S., Canadian, and N.Z. name for **bottom drawer.**

hopeful ('həʊpfʊl) *adj* **1** having or expressing hope. **2** giving or inspiring hope; promising. ♦ *n* **3** a person considered to be on the brink of success (esp. in the phrase **a young hopeful**). ▸ **'hopefulness** *n*

hopefully ('həʊpfʊlɪ) *adv* **1** in a hopeful manner. **2** *Informal.* it is hoped: *hopefully they will be married soon.*

USAGE The use of *hopefully* to mean *it is hoped* used to be considered incorrect by some people but has now become acceptable in informal contexts.

Hopeh *or* **Hopei** ('həʊ'peɪ) *n* a variant transliteration of the Chinese name for **Hebei.**

hopeless ('həʊplɪs) *adj* **1** having or offering no hope. **2** impossible to analyse or solve. **3** unable to learn, function, etc. **4** *Informal.* without skill or ability. ▸ **'hopelessly** *adv* ▸ **'hopelessness** *n*

hophead ('hɒp,hed) *n Slang, chiefly U.S.* a heroin or opium addict. [C20: from obsolete slang *hop* opium; see HOP[2]]

Hopi ('həʊpɪ) *n* **1** (*pl* **-pis** *or* **-pi**) a member of a North American Indian people of NE Arizona. **2** the language of this people, belonging to the Shoshonean subfamily of the Uto-Aztecan family. [from Hopi *Hópi* peaceful]

hop into *vb* (*intr, prep*) *Austral. and N.Z. slang.* **1** to attack (a person). **2** to start or set about (a task).

Hopkins ('hɒpkɪnz) *n* **1** Sir **Anthony.** born 1937, Welsh actor: his films include *The Silence of the Lambs* (1991), *Shadowlands* (1994), *Surviving Picasso* (1996), and *Meet Joe Black* (1999). **2** Sir **Frederick Gowland** ('gaʊlənd). 1861–1947, British biochemist, who pioneered research into what came to be called vitamins: shared the Nobel prize for physiology or medicine (1929). **3 Gerard Manley.** 1844–89, British poet and Jesuit priest, who experimented with sprung rhythm in his highly original poetry. **4 Harry L(loyd).** 1890–1946, U.S. administrator. During World War II he was a personal aide to President Roosevelt and administered the lend-lease programme.

hoplite ('hɒplaɪt) *n* (in ancient Greece) a heavily armed infantryman. [C18: from Greek *hoplitēs,* from *hoplon* weapon, from *hepein* to prepare] ▸ **hoplitic** (hɒp'lɪtɪk) *adj*

hoplology (hɒp'lɒlədʒɪ) *n* the study of weapons or armour. [C19: from Greek, from *hoplon* weapon + -LOGY] ▸ **hop'lologist** *n*

hopper ('hɒpə) *n* **1** a person or thing that hops. **2** a funnel-shaped chamber or reservoir from which solid materials can be discharged under gravity into a receptacle below, esp. for feeding fuel to a furnace, loading a railway truck with grain, etc. **3** a machine used for picking hops. **4** any of various long-legged hopping insects, esp. the grasshopper, leaf hopper, and immature locust. **5** Also called: **hoppercar.** an open-topped railway truck for bulk transport of loose minerals, etc., unloaded through doors on the underside. **6** *Computing.* a device for holding punched cards and feeding them to a card punch or card reader.

Hopper ('hɒpə) *n* **Edward.** 1882–1967, U.S. painter, noted for his realistic depiction of everyday scenes.

hop-picker *n* a person employed or a machine used to pick hops.

hopping ('hɒpɪŋ) *n* **1** the action of a person or animal that hops. **2** *Tyneside dialect.* a fair, esp. (**the Hoppings**) an annual fair in Newcastle. ♦ *adj* **3 hopping mad.** in a terrible rage.

hopple ('hɒp(ə)l) *vb, n* a less common word for **hobble** (senses 2, 5). ▸ **'hoppler** *n*

Hoppus foot ('hɒpəs) *n* a unit of volume equal to 1.27 cubic feet, applied to timber in the round, the cross-sectional area being taken as the square of one quarter of the circumference. [C20: named after Edward *Hoppus,* 18th-century English surveyor]

hops (hɒps) *pl n* the dried ripe flowers, esp. the female flowers, of the hop plant, used to give a bitter taste to beer.

hopsack ('hɒp,sæk) *n* **1** a roughly woven fabric of wool, cotton, etc., used for clothing. **2** Also called: **hopsacking.** a coarse fabric used for bags, etc., made generally of hemp or jute.

hopscotch ('hɒp,skɒtʃ) *n* a children's game in which a player throws a small stone or other object to land in one of a pattern of squares marked on the ground and then hops over to it to pick it up. [C19: HOP[1] + SCOTCH[1]]

hop, step, and jump *n* **1** an older term for **triple jump. 2** Also called: **hop, skip, and jump.** a short distance: *the shops are only a hop, step, and jump from our house.*

hop trefoil *n* a leguminous plant, *Trifolium campestre,* of N temperate grasslands, with globular yellow flower heads and trifoliate leaves. U.S. and Canadian name: **hop clover.**

hor. *abbrev. for:* **1** horizon. **2** horizontal.

hora ('hɔːrə) *n* a traditional Israeli or Romanian circle dance. [from Modern Hebrew *hōrāh,* from Romanian *horă,* from Turkish]

Horace ('hɒrɪs) *n* Latin name *Quintus Horatius Flaccus.* 65–8 B.C., Roman poet and satirist: his verse includes the lyrics in the *Epodes* and the *Odes,* the *Epistles* and *Satires,* and the *Ars Poetica.*

Horae ('hɔːriː) *pl n Classical myth.* the goddesses of the seasons. Also called: **the Hours.** [Latin: hours]

horal ('hɔːrəl) *adj* a less common word for **hourly.** [C18: from Late Latin *hōrālis* of an HOUR]

horary ('hɔːrərɪ) *adj Archaic.* **1** relating to the hours. **2** hourly. [C17: from Medieval Latin *hōrārius;* see HOUR]

Horatian (hə'reɪʃən) *adj* of, relating to, or characteristic of Horace or his poetry.

Horatian ode *n* an ode of several stanzas, each of the same metrical pattern. Also called: **Sapphic ode.**

Horatius Cocles (hɒ'reɪʃɪəs 'kəukliːz) *n* a legendary Roman hero of the 6th century B.C., who defended a bridge over the Tiber against Lars Porsena.

horde (hɔːd) *n* **1** a vast crowd; throng; mob. **2** a local group of people in a nomadic society. **3** a nomadic group of people, esp. an Asiatic group. **4** a large moving mass of animals, esp. insects. ◆ *vb* **5** (*intr*) to form, move in, or live in a horde. [C16: from Polish *horda,* from Turkish *ordū* camp; compare *Urdu*]

USAGE *Horde* is sometimes wrongly written where *hoard* is meant: *a hoard* (not *horde*) *of gold coins.*

hordein ('hɔːdiːɪn) *n* a simple protein, rich in proline, that occurs in barley. [C19: from French *hordéine,* from Latin *hordeum* barley + French *-ine* -IN]

Hordern ('hɔːdən) *n* Sir **Michael** (**Murray**). 1911–95, British actor.

Horeb ('hɔːrɛb) *n Bible.* a mountain, probably Mount Sinai.

horehound *or* **hoarhound** ('hɔː,haund) *n* **1** Also called: **white horehound.** a downy perennial herbaceous Old World plant, *Marrubium vulgare,* with small white flowers that contain a bitter juice formerly used as a cough medicine and flavouring: family *Labiatae* (labiates). See also **black horehound. 2 water horehound.** another name for **bugleweed** (sense 1). [Old English *hārhūne,* from *hār* grey + *hūne* horehound, of obscure origin]

hori ('hɔːriː) *n, pl* **horis.** *N.Z. informal, derogatory.* a Maori. [Maori]

horizon (hə'raɪzᵊn) *n* **1** Also called: **visible horizon, apparent horizon.** the apparent line that divides the earth and the sky. **2** *Astronomy.* **2a** Also called: **sensible horizon.** the circular intersection with the celestial sphere of the plane tangential to the earth at the position of the observer. **2b** Also called: **celestial horizon.** the great circle on the celestial sphere, the plane of which passes through the centre of the earth and is parallel to the sensible horizon. **3** the range or limit of scope, interest, knowledge, etc. **4** a layer of rock within a stratum that has a particular composition, esp. of fossils, by which the stratum may be dated. **5** a layer in a soil profile having particular characteristics. See **A horizon, B horizon, C horizon. 6 on the horizon.** likely or about to happen or appear. [C14: from Latin, from Greek *horizōn kuklos* limiting circle, from *horizein* to limit, from *horos* limit] ▸ **ho'rizonless** *adj*

horizontal (,hɒrɪ'zɒntᵊl) *adj* **1** parallel to the plane of the horizon; level; flat. Compare **vertical** (sense 1). **2** of or relating to the horizon. **3** measured or contained in a plane parallel to that of the horizon. **4** applied uniformly or equally to all members of a group. **5** *Economics.* relating to identical stages of commercial activity: *horizontal integration.* ◆ *n* **6** a horizontal plane, position, line, etc. ▸ **,hori'zontalness** *or* **,horizon'tality** *n* ▸ **,hori'zontally** *adv*

horizontal bar *n Gymnastics.* a raised bar on which swinging and vaulting exercises are performed. Also called: **high bar.**

horizontal mobility *n Sociol.* the movement of groups or individuals to positions that differ from those previously held but do not involve any change in class, status, or power. Compare **vertical mobility.** See also **upward mobility, downward mobility.**

horizontal stabilizer *n* the U.S. name for **tailplane.**

horizontal union *n* another name (esp. U.S.) for **craft union.**

Horkheimer (*German* 'hɔrkhaɪmər) *n* **Max.** 1895–1973, German social theorist of the Frankfurt school. His books include *Eclipse of Reason* (1947) and *Critical Theory* (1968).

horme ('hɔːmɪ) *n* (in the psychology of C. G. Jung) fundamental vital energy. [C20: from Greek *hormē* impulse] ▸ **'hormic** *adj*

hormone ('hɔːməun) *n* **1** a chemical substance produced in an endocrine gland and transported in the blood to a certain tissue, on which it exerts a specific effect. **2** an organic compound produced by a plant that is essential for growth. **3** any synthetic substance having the same effects. [C20: from Greek *hormōn,* from *horman* to stir up, urge on, from *hormē* impulse, assault] ▸ **hor'monal** *adj*

hormone replacement therapy *n* a form of oestrogen treatment used to control menopausal symptoms and in the prevention of osteoporosis. Abbrev.: **HRT.**

Hormuz (hɔː'muːz, 'hɔːmʌz) *or* **Ormuz** *n* an island off the SE coast of Iran, in the **Strait of Hormuz**: ruins of the ancient city of Hormuz, a major trading centre in the Middle Ages. Area: about 41 sq. km (16 sq. miles).

horn (hɔːn) *n* **1** either of a pair of permanent outgrowths on the heads of cattle, antelopes, sheep, etc., consisting of a central bony core covered with layers of keratin. Related adjs.: **corneous, keratoid. 2** the outgrowth from the nasal bone of a rhinoceros, consisting of a mass of fused hairs. **3** any hornlike projection or process, such as the eyestalk of a snail. **4** the antler of a deer. **5a** the constituent substance, mainly keratin, of horns, hooves, etc. **5b** (*in combination*): *horn-rimmed spectacles.* **6** a container or device made from this substance or an artificial substitute: *a shoe horn; a drinking horn.* **7** an object or part resembling a horn in shape, such as the points at either end of a crescent, the point of an anvil, the pommel of a saddle, or a cornucopia. **8** a primitive musical wind instrument made from the horn of an animal. **9** any musical instrument consisting of a pipe or tube of brass fitted with a mouthpiece, with or without valves. See **hunting horn, French horn, cor anglais. 10** *Jazz slang.* any wind instrument. **11a** a device for producing a warning or signalling noise. **11b** (*in combination*): *a foghorn.* **12** (*usually pl*) the hornlike projection attributed to certain devils, deities, etc. **13** (*usually pl*) the imaginary hornlike parts formerly supposed to appear on the forehead of a cuckold. **14** Also called: **horn balance.** an extension of an aircraft control surface that projects in front of the hinge providing aerodynamic assistance in moving the control. **15a** Also called: **acoustic horn, exponential horn.** a hollow conical device coupled to the diaphragm of a gramophone to control the direction and quality of the sound. **15b** a similar device attached to an electrical loudspeaker, esp. in a public-address system. **15c** Also called: **horn antenna.** a microwave aerial, formed by flaring out the end of a waveguide. **16** *Geology.* another name for **pyramidal peak. 17** a stretch of land or water shaped like a horn. **18** *Brit. taboo slang.* an erection of the penis. **19** *Bible.* a symbol of power, victory, or success: *in my name shall his horn be exalted.* **20 blow one's own horn.** *U.S. and Canadian.* to boast about oneself; brag. Brit. equivalent: **blow one's own trumpet. 21 draw** (*or* **pull**) **in one's horns. 21a** to suppress or control one's feelings, esp. of anger, enthusiasm, or passion. **21b** to withdraw a previous statement. **21c** to economize. **22 on the horns of a dilemma. 22a** in a situation involving a choice between two equally unpalatable alternatives. **22b** in an awkward situation. ◆ *vb* (*tr*) **23** to provide with a horn or horns. **24** to gore or butt with a horn. ◆ See also **horn in.** [Old English; related to Old Norse *horn,* Gothic *haurn,* Latin *cornu* horn] ▸ **'hornless** *adj* ▸ **'horn,like** *adj*

Horn (hɔːn) *n* **Cape.** See **Cape Horn.**

hornbeam ('hɔːn,biːm) *n* **1** any tree of the betulaceous genus *Carpinus,* such as *C. betulus* of Europe and Asia, having smooth grey bark and hard white wood. **2** the wood of any of these trees. ◆ Also called: **ironwood.** [C14: from HORN + BEAM, referring to its tough wood]

hornbill ('hɔːn,bɪl) *n* any bird of the family *Bucerotidae* of tropical Africa and Asia, having a very large bill with a basal bony protuberance: order *Coraciiformes* (kingfishers, etc.).

hornblende ('hɔːn,blɛnd) *n* a black or greenish-black mineral of the amphibole group, found in igneous and metamorphic rocks. Composition: calcium magnesium iron sodium aluminium aluminosilicate. General formula: $Ca_2Na(Mg,Fe)_4(Al,Fe)(Si,Al)_8O_{22}$. Crystal structure: monoclinic. [C18: from German *Horn* horn + BLENDE] ▸ **,horn'blendic** *adj*

hornbook ('hɔːn,buk) *n* **1** a page bearing a religious text or the alphabet, held in a frame with a thin window of flattened cattle horn over it. **2** any elementary primer.

horned (hɔːnd) *adj* having a horn, horns, or hornlike parts. ▸ **hornedness** ('hɔːnɪdnɪs) *n*

horned owl *n* any large owl of the genus *Bubo,* having prominent ear tufts: family *Strigidae.*

horned poppy *n* any of several Eurasian papaveraceous plants of the genera *Glaucium* and *Roemeria,* having large brightly coloured flowers and long curved seed capsules.

horned pout *n* a North American catfish, *Ameiurus* (or *Ictalurus*) *nebulosus,* with a sharp spine on the dorsal and pectoral fins and eight long barbels around the mouth: family *Ameiuridae.* Also called: **brown bullhead.**

horned toad *or* **lizard** *n* any small insectivorous burrowing lizard of the genus *Phrynosoma,* inhabiting desert regions of America, having a flattened toadlike body covered with spines: family *Iguanidae* (iguanas).

horned viper *n* a venomous snake, *Cerastes cornutus,* that occurs in desert regions of N Africa and SW Asia and has a small horny spine above each eye: family *Viperidae* (vipers). Also called: **sand viper.**

hornet ('hɔːnɪt) *n* **1** any of various large social wasps of the family *Vespidae,* esp. *Vespa crabro* of Europe, that can inflict a severe sting. **2 hornet's nest.** a strongly unfavourable reaction (often in the phrase **stir up a hornet's nest**). [Old English *hyrnetu;* related to Old Saxon *hornut,* Old High German *hornuz*]

hornet clearwing *n* See **clearwing.**

hornfels ('hɔːnfɛlz) *n* a hard compact fine-grained metamorphic rock formed by the action of heat on clay rocks. Also called: **hornstone.** [German: literally, horn rock]

horn in *vb* (*intr, adv;* often foll. by *on*) *Slang.* to interrupt or intrude: *don't horn in on our conversation.*

Horn of Africa *n* a region of NE Africa, comprising Somalia and adjacent territories.

horn of plenty *n* **1** another term for **cornucopia. 2** an edible basidiomycetous fungus, *Craterellus cornucopioides,* related to the chanterelle and like it funnel shaped but dark brown inside and dark grey outside: found in broad-leaved woodland.

hornpipe ('hɔːn,paɪp) *n* **1** an obsolete reed instrument with a mouthpiece made of horn. **2** an old British solo dance to a hornpipe accompaniment, traditionally performed by sailors. **3** a piece of music for such a dance.

horns and halo effect *n* a tendency to allow one's judgement of another person, esp. in a job interview, to be unduly influenced by an unfavourable (horns) or favourable (halo) first impression based on appearances.

horn silver *n* another name for **cerargyrite.**

hornstone ('hɔːn,stəun) *n* another name for **chert** or **hornfels.** [C17: translation of German *Hornstein;* so called from its appearance]

hornswoggle ('hɔːn,swɒgᵊl) *vb* (*tr*) *Slang.* to cheat or trick; bamboozle. [C19: of unknown origin]

horntail ('hɔːn,teɪl) *n* any of various large wasplike insects of the hymenopterous family *Siricidae,* the females of which have a strong stout ovipositor and lay their eggs in the wood of felled trees. Also called: **wood wasp.**

hornwort ('hɔːn,wɜːt) *n* any aquatic plant of the genus *Ceratophyllum,* forming submerged branching masses in ponds and slow-flowing streams: family *Ceratophyllaceae.*

hornwrack ('hɔːn,ræk) *n* a yellowish bryozoan or sea mat sometimes found on beaches after a storm.

horny ('hɔːnɪ) *adj* **hornier, horniest. 1** of, like, or hard as horn. **2** having a horn or horns. **3** *Slang.* **3a** sexually aroused. **3b** provoking or intended to provoke sexual arousal. **3c** sexually eager or lustful. ► **'hornily** *adv* ► **'horniness** *n*

horol. *abbrev. for* horology.

horologe ('hɒrə,lɒdʒ) *n* a rare word for **timepiece.** [C14: from Latin *hōrologium,* from Greek *hōrologion,* from *hōra* HOUR + *-logos* from *legein* to tell]

horologist (hɒ'rɒlədʒɪst) *or* **horologer** (hɒ'rɒlədʒə) *n* a person skilled in horology, esp. an expert maker of timepieces.

horologium (,hɒrə'ləudʒɪəm) *n, pl* **-gia** (-dʒɪə). **1** a clocktower. **2** Also called: **horologion.** (in the Eastern Church) a liturgical book of the offices for the canonical hours, corresponding to the Western breviary. [C17: from Latin; see HOROLOGE]

Horologium (,hɒrə'ləudʒɪəm) *n, Latin genitive* **Horologii** (,hɒrə'ləudʒɪaɪ). a faint constellation in the S hemisphere lying near Eridanus and Hydrus.

horology (hɒ'rɒlədʒɪ) *n* the art or science of making timepieces or of measuring time. ► **horologic** (,hɒrə'lɒdʒɪk) *or* **,horo'logical** *adj*

horopter (hɒ'rɒptə) *n Optics.* the locus of all points in space that stimulate points on each eye that yield the same visual direction as each other. [C18: from Greek *horos* boundary + *optēr,* from *ops* eye]

horoscope ('hɒrə,skəup) *n* **1** the prediction of a person's future based on a comparison of the zodiacal data for the time of birth with the data from the period under consideration. **2** the configuration of the planets, the sun, and the moon in the sky at a particular moment. **3** Also called: **chart.** a diagram showing the positions of the planets, sun, moon, etc., at a particular time and place. [Old English *horoscopus,* from Latin, from Greek *hōroskopos* ascendant birth sign, from *hōra* HOUR + -SCOPE] ► **horoscopic** (,hɒrə'skɒpɪk) *adj*

horoscopy (hɒ'rɒskəpɪ) *n, pl* **-pies.** the casting and interpretation of horoscopes.

Horowitz ('hɒrəvɪts) *n* **Vladimir.** 1904–89, Russian virtuoso pianist, in the U.S. from 1928.

horrendous (hɒ'rendəs) *adj* another word for **horrific.** [C17: from Latin *horrendus* fearful, from *horrēre* to bristle, shudder, tremble; see HORROR] ► **hor'rendously** *adv*

horrible ('hɒrəbᵊl) *adj* **1** causing horror; dreadful. **2** disagreeable; unpleasant. **3** *Informal.* cruel or unkind. [C14: via Old French from Latin *horribilis,* from *horrēre* to tremble] ► **'horribleness** *n*

horribly ('hɒrɪblɪ) *adv* **1** in a horrible manner. **2** (intensifier): *I'm horribly bored.*

horrid ('hɒrɪd) *adj* **1** disagreeable; unpleasant: *a horrid meal.* **2** repulsive or frightening. **3** *Informal.* unkind. [C16 (in the sense: bristling, shaggy): from Latin *horridus* prickly, rough, from *horrēre* to bristle] ► **'horridly** *adv* ► **'horridness** *n*

horrific (hɒ'rɪfɪk, hə-) *adj* provoking horror; horrible. ► **hor'rifically** *adv*

horrify ('hɒrɪ,faɪ) *vb* **-fies, -fying, -fied.** (*tr*) **1** to cause feelings of horror in; terrify; frighten. **2** to dismay or shock greatly. ► **,horrifi'cation** *n* ► **'horrified** *adj* ► **'horri,fying** *adj* ► **'horri,fyingly** *adv*

horripilation (hɒ,rɪpɪ'leɪʃən) *n Physiol.* **1** a technical name for **goose flesh. 2** the erection of any short bodily hairs. [C17: from Late Latin *horripilātiō* a bristling, from Latin *horrēre* to stand on end + *pilus* hair]

horror ('hɒrə) *n* **1** extreme fear; terror; dread. **2** intense loathing; hatred. **3** (*often pl*) a thing or person causing fear, loathing, etc. **4** (*modifier*) having a frightening subject, esp. a supernatural one: *a horror film.* [C14: from Latin: a trembling with fear; compare HIRSUTE]

horrors ('hɒrəz) *pl n* **1** *Slang.* a fit of depression or anxiety. **2** *Informal.* See **delirium tremens.** ♦ *interj* **3** an expression of dismay, sometimes facetious.

horror-struck *or* **horror-stricken** *adj* shocked; horrified.

Horsa ('hɔːsə) *n* died ?455 A.D., leader, with his brother Hengist, of the first Jutish settlers in Britain. See also **Hengist.**

hors concours *French.* (ɔr kõkur) *adj* (*postpositive*), *adv* **1** (of an artist, exhibitor, etc.) excluded from competing. **2** without equal; unrivalled. [literally: out of the competition]

hors de combat *French.* (ɔr də kõba) *adj* (*postpositive*), *adv* disabled or injured. [literally: out of (the) fight]

hors d'oeuvre (ɔː 'dɜːvr; *French* ɔr dœvrə) *n, pl* **hors d'oeuvre** *or* **hors d'oeuvres** ('dɜːvr; *French* dœvrə). an additional dish served as an appetizer, usually before the main meal. [C18: from French, literally: outside the work, not part of the main course]

horse (hɔːs) *n* **1** a domesticated perissodactyl mammal, *Equus caballus,* used for draught work and riding: family *Equidae.* Related adj: **equine. 2** the adult male of this species; stallion. **3 wild horse. 3a** a horse (*Equus caballus*) that has become feral. **3b** another name for **Przewalski's horse. 4a** any other member of the family *Equidae,* such as the zebra or ass. **4b** (*as modifier*): *the horse family.* **5** (*functioning as pl*) horsemen, esp. cavalry: *a regiment of horse.* **6** Also called: **buck.** *Gymnastics.* a padded apparatus on legs, used for vaulting, etc. **7** a narrow board supported by a pair of legs at each end, used as a frame for sawing or as a trestle, barrier, etc. **8** a contrivance on which a person may ride and exercise. **9** a slang word for **heroin. 10** *Mining.* a mass of rock within a vein of ore. **11** *Nautical.* a rod, rope, or cable, fixed at the ends, along which something may slide by means of a thimble, shackle, or other fitting; traveller. **12** *Chess.* an informal name for **knight. 13** *Informal.* short for **horsepower. 14** (*modifier*) drawn by a horse or horses: *a horse cart.* **15 be** (*or* **get**) **on one's high horse.** *Informal.* to be disdainfully aloof. **16 flog a dead horse.** See **flog** (sense 6). **17 hold one's horses.** to hold back; restrain oneself. **18 a horse of another** *or* **a different colour.** a completely different topic, argument, etc. **19 horses for courses.** a policy, course of action, etc. modified slightly to take account of specific circumstances without departing in essentials from the original. **20 the horse's mouth.** the most reliable source. **21 to horse!** an order to mount horses. ♦ *vb* **22** (*tr*) to provide with a horse or horses. **23** to put or be put on horseback. **24** (*tr*) to move (something heavy) into position by sheer physical strength. [Old English *hors;* related to Old Frisian *hors,* Old High German *hros,* Old Norse *hross*] ► **'horseless** *adj* ► **'horse,like** *adj*

horse around *or* **about** *vb* (*intr, adv*) *Informal.* to indulge in horseplay.

horseback ('hɔːs,bæk) *n* **a** a horse's back (esp. in the phrase **on horseback**). **b** (*as modifier*): *horseback riding.*

horse bean *n* another name for **broad bean.**

horsebox ('hɔːs,bɒks) *n Brit.* a van or trailer used for carrying horses.

horse brass *n* a decorative brass ornament, usually circular, originally attached to a horse's harness.

horse chestnut *n* **1** any of several trees of the genus *Aesculus,* esp. the Eurasian *A. hippocastanum,* having palmate leaves, erect clusters of white, pink, or red flowers, and brown shiny inedible nuts enclosed in a spiky bur: family *Hippocastanaceae.* **2** Also called: **conker.** the nut of this tree. [C16: so called from its having been used in the treatment of respiratory disease in horses]

horseflesh ('hɔːs,flɛʃ) *n* **1** horses collectively. **2** the flesh of a horse, esp. edible horse meat.

horsefly ('hɔːs,flaɪ) *n, pl* **-flies.** any large stout-bodied dipterous fly of the family *Tabanidae,* the females of which suck the blood of mammals, esp. horses, cattle, and man. Also called: **gadfly, cleg.**

horse gentian *n* any caprifoliaceous plant of the genus *Triosteum,* of Asia and North America, having small purplish-brown flowers. Also called: **feverwort.**

Horse Guards *pl n* **1** the cavalry regiment that, together with the Life Guards, comprises the cavalry part of the British sovereign's Household Brigade. **2** their headquarters in Whitehall, London: also the headquarters of the British Army.

horsehair ('hɔːs,hɛə) *n* **a** a hair taken chiefly from the tail or mane of a horse, used in upholstery and for fabric, etc. **b** (*as modifier*): *a horsehair mattress.*

horsehair toadstool *or* **fungus** *n* a small basidiomycetous fungus, *Marasmius androsaceus,* having a rusty coloured cap and very slender black stems. It is related to the fairy ring mushroom, but is commonly found among conifers and heather.

horsehair worm *n* another name for **hairworm** (sense 2).

Horsehead nebula ('hɔːs,hɛd) *n Astronomy.* a dark nebula lying in the constellation of Orion and resembling the head of a horse.

horsehide ('hɔːs,haɪd) *n* **1** the hide of a horse. **2** leather made from this hide. **3** (*modifier*) made of horsehide.

horse latitudes *pl n Nautical.* the latitudes near 30°N or 30°S at sea, characterized by baffling winds, calms, and high barometric pressure. [C18: referring either to the high mortality of horses on board ship in these latitudes or to *dead horse* (nautical slang: advance pay), which sailors expected to work off by this stage of a voyage]

horse laugh *n* a coarse, mocking, or raucous laugh; guffaw.

horseleech ('hɔːs,liːtʃ) *n* **1** any of several large carnivorous freshwater leeches of the genus *Haemopis,* esp. *H. sanguisuga.* **2** an archaic name for a **veterinary surgeon.**

horse mackerel *n* **1** Also called: **scad.** a mackerel-like carangid fish, *Trachurus trachurus,* of European Atlantic waters, with a row of bony scales along the lateral line. Sometimes called (U.S.): **saurel. 2** any of various large tunnies or related fishes.

horseman ('hɔːsmən) *n, pl* **-men. 1** a person who is skilled in riding or horsemanship. **2** a person who rides a horse. ► **'horse,woman** *fem n*

horsemanship ('hɔːsmən,ʃɪp) *n* **1** the art of riding on horseback. **2** skill in riding horses.

horse marine *n U.S.* **1** (formerly) a mounted marine or cavalryman serving in a ship. **2** someone out of his natural element, as if a member of an imaginary body of marine cavalry.

horsemint ('hɔːs,mɪnt) *n* **1** a hairy European mint plant, *Mentha longifolia,* with small mauve flowers: family *Labiatae* (labiates). **2** any of several similar and related plants, such as *Monarda punctata* of North America.

horse mushroom *n* a large edible agaricaceous field mushroom, *Agaricus arvensis,* with a white cap and greyish gills.

horse nettle *n* a weedy solanaceous North American plant, *Solanum carolinense,* with yellow prickles, white or blue flowers, and yellow berries.

Horsens (*Danish* 'hɔrsəns) *n* a port in Denmark, in E Jutland at the head of **Horsens Fjord**. Pop.: 55 252 (1995).

horse opera *n Informal.* another term for **Western** (sense 4).

horse pistol *n* a large holstered pistol formerly carried by horsemen.

horseplay ('hɔːsˌpleɪ) *n* rough, boisterous, or rowdy play.

horsepower ('hɔːsˌpaʊə) *n* **1** an fps unit of power, equal to 550 foot-pounds per second (equivalent to 745.7 watts). **2** a U.S. standard unit of power, equal to 746 watts. ◆ Abbrevs.: **HP, h.p.**

horsepower-hour *n* an fps unit of work or energy equal to the work done by 1 horsepower in 1 hour. 1 horsepower-hour is equivalent to 2.686×10^6 joules.

horseradish ('hɔːsˌrædɪʃ) *n* **1** a coarse Eurasian cruciferous plant, *Armoracia rusticana,* cultivated for its thick white pungent root. **2** the root of this plant, which is ground and combined with vinegar, etc., to make a sauce.

horse sense *n* another term for **common sense**.

horseshit ('hɔːsˌʃɪt) *n Taboo slang.* rubbish; nonsense.

horseshoe ('hɔːsˌʃuː) *n* **1** a piece of iron shaped like a U with the ends curving inwards that is nailed to the underside of the hoof of a horse to protect the soft part of the foot from hard surfaces: commonly thought to be a token of good luck. **2** an object of similar shape. ◆ *vb* **-shoes, -shoeing, -shoed. 3** (*tr*) to fit with a horseshoe; shoe.

horseshoe arch *n* an arch formed in the shape of a horseshoe, esp. as used in Moorish architecture.

horseshoe bat *n* any of numerous large-eared Old World insectivorous bats, mostly of the genus *Rhinolophus,* with a fleshy growth around the nostrils, used in echolocation: family *Rhinolophidae.*

horseshoe crab *n* any marine chelicerate arthropod of the genus *Limulus,* of North America and Asia, having a rounded heavily armoured body with a long pointed tail: class *Merostomata.* Also called: **king crab**.

horseshoes ('hɔːsˌʃuːz) *n* (*functioning as sing*) a game in which the players try to throw horseshoes so that they encircle a stake in the ground some distance away.

horsetail ('hɔːsˌteɪl) *n* **1** any tracheophyte plant of the genus *Equisetum,* having jointed stems with whorls of small dark toothlike leaves and producing spores within conelike structures at the tips of the stems: phylum *Sphenophyta.* **2** a stylized horse's tail formerly used as the emblem of a pasha, the number of tails increasing with rank.

horse trading *n* hard bargaining to obtain equal concessions by both sides in a dispute.

horseweed ('hɔːsˌwiːd) *n* the U.S. name for **Canadian fleabane** (see **fleabane** (sense 3)).

horsewhip ('hɔːsˌwɪp) *n* **1** a whip, usually with a long thong, used for managing horses. ◆ *vb* **-whips, -whipping, -whipped. 2** (*tr*) to flog with such a whip. ► **'horseˌwhipper** *n*

horsey *or* **horsy** ('hɔːsɪ) *adj* **horsier, horsiest. 1** of or relating to horses: *a horsey smell.* **2** dealing with or devoted to horses. **3** like a horse: *a horsey face.* ► **'horsily** *adv* ► **'horsiness** *n*

horst (hɔːst) *n* a ridge of land that has been forced upwards between two parallel faults. **[C20: from German: thicket]**

hort. *abbrev. for:* **1** horticultural. **2** horticulture.

Horta[1] (*Portuguese* 'ɔrtə) *n* a port in the Azores, on the SE coast of Fayal Island.

Horta[2] ('ɔːtə) *n* **Victor.** 1861–1947, Belgian architect, best known for his early buildings in Art Nouveau style.

hortatory ('hɔːtətərɪ, -trɪ) *or* **hortative** ('hɔːtətɪv) *adj* tending to exhort; encouraging. **[C16: from Late Latin** *hortātōrius,* **from Latin** *hortārī* **to** EXHORT**]** ► **hor'tation** *n* ► **'hortatorily** *or* **'hortatively** *adv*

Hortense (*French* ɔrtɑ̃s) *n* See (Eugénie Hortense de) **Beauharnais**.

Horthy (*Hungarian* 'horti) *n* **Miklós** ('mikloːʃ), full name *Horthy de Nagybánya.* 1868–1957, Hungarian admiral: suppressed Kun's Communist republic (1919); regent of Hungary (1920–44).

horticulture ('hɔːtɪˌkʌltʃə) *n* the art or science of cultivating gardens. **[C17: from Latin** *hortus* **garden +** CULTURE, **on the model of** AGRICULTURE**]** ► **ˌhorti'cultural** *adj* ► **ˌhorti'culturally** *adv* ► **ˌhorti'culturalist** *or* **ˌhorti'culturist** *n*

hortus siccus ('hɔːtəs 'sɪkəs) *n* a less common name for **herbarium**. **[C17: Latin, literally: dry garden]**

Horus ('hɔːrəs) *n* a solar god of Egyptian mythology, usually depicted with a falcon's head. **[via Late Latin from Greek** *Hōros,* **from Egyptian** *Hur* **hawk]**

Hos. *Bible. abbrev. for* Hosea.

hosanna (həʊ'zænə) *interj* **1** an exclamation of praise, esp. one to God. ◆ *n* **2** the act of crying "hosanna". **[Old English** *osanna,* **via Late Latin from Greek, from Hebrew** *hōshi 'āh nnā* **save now, we pray]**

hose[1] (həʊz) *n* **1** a flexible pipe, for conveying a liquid or gas. ◆ *vb* **2** (sometimes foll. by *down*) to wash, water, or sprinkle (a person or thing) with or as if with a hose. **[C15: later use of** HOSE[2]**]**

hose[2] (həʊz) *n, pl* **hose** *or* **hosen. 1** stockings, socks, and tights collectively. **2** *History.* a man's garment covering the legs and reaching up to the waist; worn with a doublet. **3 half-hose.** socks. **[Old English** *hosa;* **related to Old High German** *hosa,* **Dutch** *hoos,* **Old Norse** *hosa***]**

Hosea (həʊ'zɪə) *n Old Testament.* **1** a Hebrew prophet of the 8th century B.C. **2** the book containing his oracles.

hosier ('həʊzɪə) *n* a person who sells stockings, etc.

hosiery ('həʊzɪərɪ) *n* stockings, socks, and knitted underclothing collectively.

hosp. *abbrev. for* hospital.

hospice ('hɒspɪs) *n, pl* **hospices. 1** a nursing home that specializes in caring for the terminally ill. **2** Also called: **hospitium** (hɒ'spɪtɪəm), *pl* **hospitia** (hɒ'spɪtɪə). *Archaic.* a place of shelter for travellers, esp. one kept by a monastic order. **[C19: from French, from Latin** *hospitium* **hospitality, from** *hospes* **guest,** HOST[1]**]**

hospitable ('hɒspɪtəb^{ə}l, hɒ'spɪt-) *adj* **1** welcoming to guests or strangers. **2** fond of entertaining. **3** receptive: *hospitable to new ideas.* **[C16: from Medieval Latin** *hospitāre* **to receive as a guest, from Latin** *hospes* **guest,** HOST[1]**]** ► **'hospitableness** *n* ► **'hospitably** *adv*

hospital ('hɒspɪt^{ə}l) *n* **1** an institution for the medical, surgical, obstetric, or psychiatric care and treatment of patients. **2** (*modifier*) having the function of a hospital: *a hospital ship.* **3** a repair shop for something specified: *a dolls' hospital.* **4** *Archaic.* a charitable home, hospice, or school. **[C13: from Medieval Latin** *hospitāle* **hospice, from Latin** *hospitālis* **relating to a guest, from** *hospes, hospit-* **guest,** HOST[1]**]**

hospital corner *n* a corner of a made-up bed in which the bedclothes have been neatly and securely folded, esp. as in hospitals.

Hospitalet (*Spanish* ɔspita'lɛt) *n* a city in NE Spain, a SW suburb of Barcelona. Pop.: 262 501 (1995 est.).

hospitality (ˌhɒspɪ'tælɪtɪ) *n, pl* **-ties. 1** kindness in welcoming strangers or guests. **2** receptiveness.

hospitality suite *n* a room or suite, as at a conference, where free drinks are offered.

hospitalization *or* **hospitalisation** (ˌhɒspɪtəlaɪ'zeɪʃən) *n* **1** the act or an instance of being hospitalized. **2** the duration of a stay in a hospital.

hospitalize *or* **hospitalise** ('hɒspɪtəˌlaɪz) *vb* (*tr*) to admit or send (a person) into a hospital.

hospitaller *or U.S.* **hospitaler** ('hɒspɪtələ) *n* a person, esp. a member of certain religious orders, dedicated to hospital work, ambulance services, etc. **[C14: from Old French** *hospitalier,* **from Medieval Latin** *hospitālārius,* **from** *hospitāle* **hospice; see** HOSPITAL**]**

Hospitaller *or U.S.* **Hospitaler** ('hɒspɪtələ) *n* a member of the order of the Knights Hospitallers.

hospodar ('hɒspəˌdɑː) *n* (formerly) the governor or prince of Moldavia or Wallachia under Ottoman rule. **[C17: via Romanian from Ukrainian, from** *hospod'* **lord; related to Russian** *gospodin* **courtesy title, Old Slavonic** *gospodĭ* **lord]**

host[1] (həʊst) *n* **1** a person who receives or entertains guests, esp. in his own home. **2a** a country or organization which provides facilities for and receives visitors to an event. **2b** (*as modifier*): *the host nation.* **3** the compere of a show or television programme. **4** *Biology.* **4a** an animal or plant that nourishes and supports a parasite. **4b** an animal, esp. an embryo, into which tissue is experimentally grafted. **5** *Computing.* a computer connected to a network and providing facilities to other computers and their users. **6** the owner or manager of an inn. ◆ *vb* **7** to be the host of (a party, programme, etc.): *to host one's own show.* **8** (*tr*) *U.S. informal.* to leave (a restaurant) without paying the bill. **[C13: from French** *hoste,* **from Latin** *hospes* **guest, foreigner, from** *hostis* **enemy]**

host[2] (həʊst) *n* **1** a great number; multitude. **2** an archaic word for **army**. **[C13: from Old French** *hoste,* **from Latin** *hostis* **stranger, enemy]**

Host (həʊst) *n* the bread consecrated in the Eucharist. **[C14: from Old French** *oiste,* **from Latin** *hostia* **victim]**

hosta ('hɒstə) *n* any plant of the liliaceous genus *Hosta,* of China and Japan: cultivated esp. for their ornamental foliage. **[C19: New Latin, named after N. T.** *Host* **(1761–1834), Austrian physician]**

hostage ('hɒstɪdʒ) *n* **1** a person given to or held by a person, organization, etc., as a security or pledge or for ransom, release, exchange for prisoners, etc. **2** the state of being held as a hostage. **3** any security or pledge. **4 give hostages to fortune.** to place oneself in a position in which misfortune may strike through the loss of what one values most. **[C13: from Old French, from** *hoste* **guest,** HOST[1]**]**

hostel ('hɒst^{ə}l) *n* **1** a building providing overnight accommodation, as for the homeless, etc. **2** See **youth hostel**. **3** *Brit.* a supervised lodging house for nurses, workers, etc. **4** *Archaic.* another word for **hostelry**. **[C13: from Old French, from Medieval Latin** *hospitāle* **hospice; see** HOSPITAL**]**

hosteller *or U.S.* **hosteler** ('hɒstələ) *n* **1** a person who stays at youth hostels. **2** an archaic word for **innkeeper**.

hostelling *or U.S.* **hosteling** ('hɒstəlɪŋ) *n* the practice of staying at youth hostels when travelling.

hostelry ('hɒstəlrɪ) *n, pl* **-ries.** *Archaic or facetious.* an inn.

hostel school *n* (in N Canada) a government boarding school for Indian and Inuit students.

hostess ('həʊstɪs) *n* **1** a woman acting as host. **2** a woman who receives and entertains patrons of a club, restaurant, etc. **3** See **air hostess**.

hostie ('həʊstɪ) *n Austral. informal.* short for **air hostess**.

hostile ('hɒstaɪl) *adj* **1** antagonistic; opposed. **2** of or relating to an enemy. **3** unfriendly. ◆ *n* **4** a hostile person; enemy. **[C16: from Latin** *hostīlis,* **from** *hostis* **enemy]** ► **'hostilely** *adv*

hostile witness *n* a witness who gives evidence against the party calling him.

hostility (hɒ'stɪlɪtɪ) *n, pl* **-ties. 1** enmity or antagonism. **2** an act expressing enmity or opposition. **3** (*pl*) fighting; warfare.

hostler ('ɒslə) *n* another name (esp. Brit.) for **ostler**.

hot (hɒt) *adj* **hotter, hottest. 1** having a relatively high temperature. **2** having a temperature higher than desirable. **3** causing or having a sensation of bodily heat. **4** causing a burning sensation on the tongue: *hot mustard; a hot curry.* **5** expressing or feeling intense emotion, such as embarrassment, anger, or lust. **6** intense or vehement: *a hot argument.* **7** recent; fresh; new: *a hot trial; hot from the press.* **8** *Ball games.* (of a ball) thrown or struck hard, and so difficult to respond to. **9** much favoured or approved: *a hot tip; a hot favourite.* **10** *Informal.* having a dangerously high level of radioactivity: *a hot laboratory.* **11** *Slang.* (of goods or money) stolen, smuggled, or otherwise illegally obtained. **12** *Slang.* (of people) being sought by the police. **13** (of a colour) intense; striking: *hot pink.* **14** close or following closely: *hot on the scent.* **15** *Informal.* at a dangerously high electric potential: *a hot terminal.* **16** *Physics.* having an energy level higher than that of the ground state: *a hot atom.* **17** *Slang.* impressive or good of its kind (esp. in the phrase **not so hot**). **18** *Jazz slang.* arousing great excitement or enthusiasm by inspired improvisation, strong rhythms, etc. **19** *Informal.* dangerous or unpleasant (esp. in the phrase **make it hot for someone**). **20** (in various searching or guessing games) very near the answer or object to be found. **21** *Metallurgy.* (of a process) at a sufficiently high temperature for metal to be in a soft workable state. **22** *Austral. and N.Z. informal.* (of a price, charge, etc.) excessive. **23 give it (to someone) hot.** to punish or thrash (someone). **24 hot on.** *Informal.* **24a** very severe: *the police are hot on drunk drivers.* **24b** particularly skilled at or knowledgeable about: *he's hot on vintage cars.* **25 hot under the collar.** *Informal.* aroused with anger, annoyance, etc. **26 in hot water.** *Informal.* in trouble, esp. with those in authority. ◆ *adv* **27** in a hot manner; hotly. ◆ See also **hots, hot up.** [Old English *hāt;* related to Old High German *heiz,* Old Norse *heitr,* Gothic *heito* fever] ► **'hotly** *adv* ► **'hotness** *n*

hot air *n Informal.* empty and usually boastful talk.

hot-air balloon *n* a lighter-than-air craft in which air heated by a flame is trapped in a large fabric bag.

Hotan ('həʊ'tæn), **Hotien,** *or* **Ho-t'ien** ('həʊ'tjɛn) *n* **1** an oasis in W China, in the Taklimakan Shamo desert of central Xinjiang Uygur Autonomous Region, around the seasonal Hotan River. **2** the chief town of this oasis, situated at the foot of the Kunlun Mountains. Pop.: 71 600 (1986 est.). Also called: **Khotan, Hetian.**

hotbed ('hɒt,bɛd) *n* **1** a glass-covered bed of soil, usually heated by fermenting material, used for propagating plants, forcing early vegetables, etc. **2** a place offering ideal conditions for the growth of an idea, activity, etc., esp. one considered bad: *a hotbed of insurrection.*

hot-blooded *adj* **1** passionate or excitable. **2** (of a horse) being of thoroughbred stock. ► **,hot-'bloodedness** *n*

hotchpot ('hɒtʃ,pɒt) *n Property law.* the collecting of property so that it may be redistributed in equal shares, esp. on the intestacy of a parent who has given property to his children in his lifetime. [C14: from Old French *hochepot,* from *hocher* to shake, of Germanic origin + POT[1]]

hotchpotch ('hɒtʃ,pɒtʃ) *or esp. U.S. and Canadian* **hodgepodge** *n* **1** a jumbled mixture. **2** a thick soup or stew made from meat and vegetables. [C15: variant of HOTCHPOT]

hot cockles *n* (*functioning as sing*) (formerly) a children's game in which one blindfolded player has to guess which other player has hit him.

hot cross bun *n* a yeast bun with spices, currants, and sometimes candied peel, marked with a cross and traditionally eaten on Good Friday.

hot-desking ('dɛskɪŋ) *n* the practice of not assigning permanent desks in a workplace, so that employees may work at any available desk.

hot dog[1] *n* a sausage, esp. a frankfurter, served hot in a long roll split lengthways. [C20: from the supposed resemblance of the sausage to a dachshund]

hot dog[2] *n* **1** *Chiefly U.S.* a person who performs showy acrobatic manoeuvres when skiing or surfing. ◆ *vb* **hot-dog, -dogs, -dogging, -dogged.** **2** (*intr*) to perform a series of manoeuvres in skiing, surfing, etc., esp. in a showy manner. [C20: from U.S. *hot dog!,* exclamation of pleasure, approval, etc.]

hotel (həʊ'tɛl) *n* a commercially run establishment providing lodging and usually meals for guests, and often containing a public bar. [C17: from French *hôtel,* from Old French *hostel;* see HOSTEL]

Hotel (həʊ'tɛl) *n Communications.* a code word for the letter *h.*

hotelier (həʊ'tɛljeɪ) *n* an owner or manager of one or more hotels.

hot fence *n N.Z.* an electric fence surrounding a farm.

hot flush *or U.S.* **hot flash** *n* a sudden unpleasant hot feeling in the skin, caused by endocrine imbalance, esp. experienced by women at menopause.

hotfoot ('hɒt,fʊt) *adv* **1** with all possible speed; quickly. ◆ *vb* **2** to move quickly.

hothead ('hɒt,hɛd) *n* an excitable or fiery person.

hot-headed *adj* impetuous, rash, or hot-tempered. ► **,hot-'headedly** *adv* ► **,hot-'headedness** *n*

hothouse ('hɒt,haʊs) *n* **1a** a greenhouse in which the temperature is maintained at a fixed level above that of the surroundings. **1b** (*as modifier*): *a hothouse plant.* **2** a place offering ideal conditions for the growth of an idea, activity, etc.: *the cultural hothouse of Europe and America.* **3** an environment where there is great pressure: *showjumping is a tough, hothouse world.*

Hotien *or* **Ho-t'ien** ('həʊ'tjɛn) *n* a variant transliteration of the Chinese name for **Hotan.**

hot key *n Computing.* a single key on the keyboard of a computer which carries out a series of commands.

hotline ('hɒt,laɪn) *n* **1** a direct telephone, teletype, or other communications link between heads of government, for emergency use. **2** any such direct line kept for urgent use.

hot link *n* a word or phrase in a hypertext document that when selected by mouse or keyboard causes information that has been associated with that word or phrase to be displayed. See **hypertext.**

hot metal *n* **a** metallic type cast into shape in the molten state. **b** (*as modifier*): *hot-metal printing.*

hot money *n* capital transferred from one financial centre to another seeking the highest interest rates or the best opportunity for short-term gain, esp. from changes in exchange rates.

hot pants *pl n* **1** very brief skin-tight shorts, worn by young women. **2** *Taboo slang.* a feeling of sexual arousal: *he has hot pants for her.*

hot pepper *n* **1** any of several varieties of the pepper *Capsicum frutescens,* esp. chilli pepper. **2** the pungent usually small fruit of any of these plants.

hotplate ('hɒt,pleɪt) *n* **1** an electrically heated plate on a cooker. **2** a portable device, heated electrically or by spirit lamps, etc., on which food can be kept warm.

hotpot ('hɒt,pɒt) *n* **1** *Brit.* a baked stew or casserole made with meat or fish and covered with a layer of potatoes. **2** *Austral. slang.* a heavily backed horse.

hot potato *n Slang.* an awkward or delicate matter.

hot-press *n* **1** a machine for applying a combination of heat and pressure to give a smooth surface to paper, to express oil from it, etc. ◆ *vb* **2** (*tr*) to subject (paper, cloth, etc.) to heat and pressure to give it a smooth surface or extract oil.

hot rod *n* a car with an engine that has been radically modified to produce increased power.

hots (hɒts) *pl n* **the.** *Slang.* intense sexual desire; lust (esp. in the phrase **have the hots for someone**).

hot seat *n* **1** *Informal.* a precarious, difficult, or dangerous position. **2** *U.S.* a slang term for **electric chair.**

hot shoe *n Photog.* an accessory shoe on a camera through which electrical contact is made to an electronic flash device.

hotshot ('hɒt,ʃɒt) *n Informal.* an important person or expert, esp. when showy.

hot spot *n* **1** an area of potential violence or political unrest. **2** a lively nightclub or other place of entertainment. **3a** any local area of high temperature in a part of an engine, etc. **3b** part of the inlet manifold of a paraffin engine that is heated by exhaust gases to vaporize the fuel. **4** *Med.* **4a** a small area on the surface of or within a body with an exceptionally high concentration of radioactivity or of some chemical or mineral considered harmful. **4b** a similar area that generates an abnormal amount of heat, as revealed by thermography. **5** *Genetics.* a part of a chromosome that has a tendency for mutation or recombination.

hot spring *n* a natural spring of mineral water at a temperature of 21°C (70°F) or above, found in areas of volcanic activity. Also called: **thermal spring.**

hotspur ('hɒt,spɜː) *n* an impetuous or fiery person. [C15: from *Hotspur,* nickname of Sir Henry PERCY]

Hotspur ('hɒt,spɜː) *n* **Harry.** nickname of (Sir Henry) **Percy.**

hot stuff *n Informal.* **1** a person, object, etc., considered important, attractive, sexually exciting, etc. **2** a pornographic or erotic book, play, film, etc.

Hottentot ('hɒtᵊn,tɒt) *n Offensive.* **1** (*pl* **-tot** *or* **-tots**) another name for the **Khoikhoi** people. **2** any of the languages of this people, belonging to the Khoisan family. [C17: from Afrikaans, of uncertain origin]

Hottentot fig *n* a perennial plant, *Mesembryanthemum* (or *Carpobrotus*) *edule,* originally South African, having fleshy prostrate leaves, showy yellow or purple flowers, and edible fruits.

hottie ('hɒtɪ) *n Austral. and N.Z. informal.* a hot-water bottle.

hotting ('hɒtɪŋ) *n Informal.* the practice of stealing fast cars and putting on a show of skilful but dangerous driving. ► **'hotter** *n*

hottish ('hɒtɪʃ) *adj* fairly hot.

hot up *vb* (*adv*) *Informal.* **1** to make or become more exciting, active, or intense: *the chase was hotting up.* **2** (*tr*) another term for **soup up.**

hot-water bottle *n* a receptacle, now usually made of rubber, designed to be filled with hot water, used for warming a bed or parts of the body.

hot-wire *vb* (*tr*) *Slang.* to start the engine of (a motor vehicle) by bypassing the ignition switch.

hot-work *vb* (*tr*) to shape (metal) when hot.

hot zone *n Computing.* a variable area towards the end of a line of text that informs the operator that a decision must be taken as to whether to hyphenate or begin a new line.

houdah ('haʊdə) *n* a variant spelling of **howdah.**

Houdan ('huːdæn) *n* a breed of light domestic fowl originally from France, with a distinctive full crest. [C19: named after *Houdan,* village near Paris where the breed originated]

Houdini (huː'diːnɪ) *n* **Harry,** real name *Ehrich Weiss.* 1874–1926, U.S. magician and escapologist.

Houdon (*French* udɔ̃) *n* **Jean Antoine** (ʒɑ̃ ɑ̃twan). 1741–1828, French neoclassical portrait sculptor.

hough (hɒk) *Brit.* ◆ *n* **1** another word for **hock**[1]. **2** (hɒx). in Scotland, a cut of meat corresponding to shin. ◆ *vb* (*tr*) **3** to hamstring (cattle, horses, etc.). [C14: from Old English *hōh* heel]

Houghton-le-Spring ('haʊtᵊnlə'sprɪŋ) *n* a town in N England, in Sunderland unitary authority, Tyne and Wear: coal-mining. Pop.: 35 100 (1991).

hoummos, houmous, *or* **houmus** ('huːməs) *n* variant spellings of **hummus.**

hound[1] (haʊnd) *n* **1a** any of several breeds of dog used for hunting. **1b** (*in combination*): *an otterhound; a deerhound.* **2 the hounds.** a pack of foxhounds, etc. **3** a dog, esp. one regarded as annoying. **4** a despicable person. **5** (in hare and hounds) a runner who pursues a hare. **6** *Slang, chiefly U.S. and Canadian.* an enthusiast: *an autograph hound.* **7** short for **houndfish.** See also **nursehound.** **8 ride to hounds** *or* **follow the hounds.** to take part in a fox hunt with hounds. ◆ *vb* (*tr*) **9** to pursue or chase relentlessly. **10** to urge on. [Old English *hund;* related to Old High German *hunt,* Old Norse *hundr,* Gothic *hunds*] ► **'hounder** *n*

hound[2] (haʊnd) *n* **1** either of a pair of horizontal bars that reinforce the running gear of a horse-drawn vehicle. **2** *Nautical.* either of a pair of fore-and-aft braces that serve as supports for a topmast. [C15: of Scandinavian origin; related to Old Norse *hūnn* knob, cube]

houndfish ('haʊnd,fɪʃ) *n, pl* **-fish** *or* **-fishes.** a name given to various small sharks or dogfish. See also **nursehound.**

hound's-tongue *n* any boraginaceous weedy plant of the genus *Cynoglossum,* esp. the Eurasian *C. officinale,* which has small reddish-purple flowers and spiny fruits. Also called: **dog's-tongue.** [Old English *hundestunge,* translation of Latin *cynoglōssos,* from Greek *kunoglōssos,* from *kuōn* dog + *glōssa* tongue; referring to the shape of its leaves]

hound's-tooth check *n* a pattern of broken or jagged checks, esp. one printed on or woven into cloth. Also called: **dog's-tooth check, dogtooth check.**

Hounslow ('haʊnzləʊ) *n* a borough of Greater London, on the River Thames: site of London's first civil airport (1919). Pop.: 202 700 (1994 est.). Area: 59 sq. km (23 sq. miles).

Houphouet-Boigny (*French* ufwɛbwaɲi) *n* **Félix** (feliks). 1905–93, Côte d'Ivoire statesman; president of the Côte d'Ivoire (1960–93).

hour (aʊə) *n* **1** a period of time equal to 3600 seconds; 1/24th of a calendar day. Related adjs.: **horal, horary. 2** any of the points on the face of a timepiece that indicate intervals of 60 minutes. **3 the hour.** an exact number of complete hours: *the bus leaves on the hour.* **4** the time of day as indicated by a watch, clock, etc. **5** the period of time allowed for or used for something: *the lunch hour; the hour of prayer.* **6** a special moment or period: *our finest hour.* **7 the hour.** the present time: *the man of the hour.* **8** the distance covered in an hour: *we live an hour from the city.* **9** *Astronomy.* an angular measurement of right ascension equal to 15° or a 24th part of the celestial equator. **10 one's hour. 10a** a time of success, fame, etc. **10b** Also: **one's last hour.** the time of one's death: *his hour had come.* **11 take one's hour.** *Irish informal.* to do something in a leisurely manner. ◆ See also **hours.** [C13: from Old French *hore,* from Latin *hōra,* from Greek: season]

hour angle *n* the angular distance along the celestial equator from the meridian of the observer to the hour circle of a particular celestial body.

hour circle *n* a great circle on the celestial sphere passing through the celestial poles and a specified point, such as a star.

hourglass ('aʊə,glɑːs) *n* **1** a device consisting of two transparent chambers linked by a narrow channel, containing a quantity of sand that takes a specified time to trickle to one chamber from the other. **2** (*modifier*) well-proportioned with a small waist: *an hourglass figure.*

hour hand *n* the pointer on a timepiece that indicates the hour. Compare **minute hand, second hand.**

houri ('hʊərɪ) *n, pl* **-ris. 1** (in Muslim belief) any of the nymphs of Paradise. **2** any alluring woman. [C18: from French, from Persian *hūri,* from Arabic *hūr,* plural of *haurā'* woman with dark eyes]

hourlong ('aʊə,lɒŋ) *adj, adv* lasting an hour.

hourly ('aʊəlɪ) *adj* **1** of, occurring, or done every hour. **2** done in or measured by the hour: *we are paid an hourly rate.* **3** continual or frequent. ◆ *adv* **4** every hour. **5** at any moment or time.

hours (aʊəz) *pl n* **1** a period regularly or customarily appointed for work, business, etc. **2** one's times of rising and going to bed (esp. in the phrases **keep regular, irregular,** or **late hours**). **3 the small hours.** the hours just after midnight. **4 till all hours.** until very late. **5** an indefinite period of time. **6** Also called (in the Roman Catholic Church): **canonical hours. 6a** the seven times of the day laid down for the recitation of the prayers of the divine office. **6b** the prayers recited at these times.

Hours (aʊəz) *pl n* another word for the **Horae.**

house *n* (haʊs), *pl* **houses** ('haʊzɪz). **1a** a building used as a home; dwelling. **1b** (*as modifier*): *house dog.* **2** the people present in a house, esp. its usual occupants. **3a** a building used for some specific purpose. **3b** (*in combination*): *a schoolhouse.* **4** (*often cap.*) a family line including ancestors and relatives, esp. a noble one: *the House of York.* **5a** a commercial company; firm: *a publishing house.* **5b** (*as modifier*): *house style; a house journal.* **6** an official deliberative or legislative body, such as one chamber of a bicameral legislature. **7** a quorum in such a body (esp. in the phrase **make a house**). **8** a dwelling for a religious community. **9** *Astrology.* any of the 12 divisions of the zodiac. See also **planet** (sense 3). **10a** any of several divisions, esp. residential, of a large school. **10b** (*as modifier*): *house spirit.* **11a** a hotel, restaurant, bar, inn, club, etc., or the management of such an establishment. **11b** (*as modifier*): *house rules.* **11c** (*in combination*): *steakhouse.* **12** (*modifier*) (of wine) sold unnamed by a restaurant, at a lower price than wines specified on the wine list: *the house red.* **13** the audience in a theatre or cinema. **14** an informal word for **brothel. 15** a hall in which an official deliberative or legislative body meets. **16** See **full house. 17** *Curling.* the 12-foot target circle around the tee. **18** *Nautical.* any structure or shelter on the weather deck of a vessel. **19 bring the house down.** *Theatre.* to win great applause. **20 house and home.** an emphatic form of **home. 21 keep open house.** to be always ready to provide hospitality. **22 like a house on fire.** *Informal.* very well, quickly, or intensely. **23 on the house.** (usually of drinks) paid for by the management of the hotel, bar, etc. **24 put one's house in order.** to settle or organize one's affairs. **25 safe as houses.** *Brit.* very secure. ◆ *vb* (haʊz). **26** (*tr*) to provide with or serve as accommodation. **27** to give or receive shelter or lodging. **28** (*tr*) to contain or cover, esp. in order to protect. **29** (*tr*) to fit (a piece of wood) into a mortise, joint, etc. **30** (*tr*) *Nautical.* **30a** to secure or stow. **30b** to secure (a topmast). **30c** to secure and stow (an anchor). [Old English *hūs;* related to Old High German *hūs,* Gothic *gudhūs* temple, Old Norse *hūs* house] ▸ **'houseless** *adj*

House (haʊs) **the.** *n* **1** See **House of Commons. 2** *Brit. informal.* the Stock Exchange.

house agent *n Brit.* another name for **estate agent.**

house arrest *n* confinement to one's own home.

houseboat ('haʊs,bəʊt) *n* a stationary boat or barge used as a home.

housebound ('haʊs,baʊnd) *adj* unable to leave one's house because of illness, injury, etc.

houseboy ('haʊs,bɔɪ) *n* a male domestic servant.

housebreaking ('haʊs,breɪkɪŋ) *n Criminal law.* the act of entering a building as a trespasser for an unlawful purpose. Assimilated with burglary, 1968. ▸ **'house,breaker** *n*

house-broken *adj* another word for **house-trained.**

housecarl ('haʊs,kɑːl) *n* (in medieval Europe) a household warrior of Danish kings and noblemen. [Old English *hūscarl,* from Old Norse *hūskarl* manservant, from *hūs* HOUSE + *karl* man; see CHURL]

housecoat ('haʊs,kəʊt) *n* a woman's loose robelike informal garment.

house-craft *n* skill in domestic management.

house factor *n* a Scottish term for **estate agent.**

housefather ('haʊs,fɑːðə) *n* a man in charge of the welfare of a particular group of children in an institution such as a children's home or approved school. ▸ **'house,mother** *fem n*

housefly ('haʊs,flaɪ) *n, pl* **-flies.** a common dipterous fly, *Musca domestica,* that frequents human habitations, spreads disease, and lays its eggs in carrion, decaying vegetables, etc.: family *Muscidae.*

house group *or* **church** *n* a group of Christians who regularly meet to worship, study the Bible, etc. in someone's house.

house guest *n* a guest at a house, esp. one who stays for a comparatively long time.

household ('haʊs,həʊld) *n* **1** the people living together in one house collectively. **2** (*modifier*) of, relating to, or used in the running of a household; domestic: *household management.*

householder ('haʊs,həʊldə) *n* a person who owns or rents a house. ▸ **'house,holder,ship** *n*

household gods *pl n* **1** (in ancient Rome) deities of the home; lares and penates. **2** *Brit. informal.* the essentials of domestic life.

household name *or* **word** *n* a person or thing that is very well known.

household troops *pl n* the infantry and cavalry regiments that carry out escort and guard duties for a head of state.

househusband ('haʊs,hʌzbənd) *n* a married man who keeps house, usually without having paid employment.

housekeeper ('haʊs,kiːpə) *n* **1** a person, esp. a woman, employed to run a household. **2 good** (*or* **bad**) **housekeeper.** a person who is (or is not) an efficient and thrifty domestic manager.

housekeeping ('haʊs,kiːpɪŋ) *n* **1** the running of a household. **2** money allocated for the running of a household. **3** organization and tidiness in general, as of an office, shop, etc. **4** the general maintenance of a computer storage system, including removal of obsolete files, documentation, etc.

housel ('haʊzᵊl) *n* **1** a medieval name for **Eucharist.** ◆ *vb* **-sels, -selling, -selled** *or U.S.* **-sels, -seling, -seled. 2** (*tr*) to give the Eucharist to (someone). [Old English *hūsl;* related to Gothic *hunsl* sacrifice, Old Norse *hūsl*]

houseleek ('haʊs,liːk) *n* any Old World crassulaceous plant of the genus *Sempervivum,* esp. *S. tectorum,* which has a rosette of succulent leaves and pinkish flowers: grows on walls. Also called: **hen-and-chickens.**

house lights *pl n* the lights in the auditorium of a theatre, cinema, etc.

houseline ('haʊs,laɪn) *n Nautical.* tarred marline. Also called: **housing.**

housemaid ('haʊs,meɪd) *n* a girl or woman employed to do housework, esp. one who is resident in the household.

housemaid's knee *n* inflammation and swelling of the bursa in front of the kneecap, caused esp. by constant kneeling on a hard surface. Technical name: **prepatellar bursitis.**

houseman ('haʊsmən) *n, pl* **-men.** *Med.* a junior doctor who is a member of the medical staff of a hospital. U.S. and Canadian equivalent: **intern.**

house martin *n* a Eurasian swallow, *Delichon urbica,* with a slightly forked tail and a white and bluish-black plumage.

housemaster ('haʊs,mɑːstə) *n* a teacher, esp. in a boarding school, responsible for the pupils in his house. ▸ **housemistress** ('haʊs,mɪstrɪs) *fem n*

house moth *n* either of two species of micro moth, esp. the **brown house moth** (*Hofmannophila pseudospretella*) which, although it usually inhabits birds' nests, sometimes enters houses where its larvae can be very destructive of stored fabrics and foodstuffs.

house mouse *n* any of various greyish mice of the Old World genus *Mus,* esp. *M. musculus,* a common household pest in most parts of the world: family *Muridae.*

House music *or* **House** *n* a type of disco music of the late 1980s, based on funk, with fragments of other recordings edited in electronically.

House of Assembly *n* a legislative assembly or the lower chamber of such an assembly, esp. in various British colonies and countries of the Commonwealth.

house of cards *n* **1** a tiered structure created by balancing playing cards on their edges. **2** an unstable situation, plan, etc.

House of Commons *n* (in Britain, Canada, etc.) the lower chamber of Parliament.

house of correction *n* (formerly) a place of confinement for persons convicted of minor offences.

house of God *n* a church, temple, or chapel.

house of ill repute *or* **ill fame** *n* a euphemistic name for **brothel.**

House of Keys *n* the lower chamber of the legislature of the Isle of Man.

House of Lords *n* (in Britain) the upper chamber of Parliament, composed of the peers of the realm.

House of Representatives *n* **1** (in the U.S.) the lower chamber of Congress. **2** (in Australia) the lower chamber of Parliament. **3** the sole chamber of New Zealand's Parliament: formerly the lower chamber. **4** (in the U.S.) the lower chamber in many state legislatures.

House of the People *n* another name for **Lok Sabha.**

house organ *n* a periodical published by an organization for its employees or clients.

house party *n* **1** a party, usually in a country house, at which guests are invited to stay for several days. **2** the guests who are invited.

house physician *or* **doctor** *n* a physician who lives in a hospital or other institution where he is employed. Compare **resident** (sense 7).

house plant *n* a plant that can be grown indoors.

house-proud *adj* proud of the appearance, cleanliness, etc., of one's house, sometimes excessively so.

houseroom ('haʊsˌrʊm, -ˌruːm) *n* **1** room for storage or lodging. **2 give (something) houseroom.** (*used with a negative*) to have or keep (something) in one's house: *I wouldn't give that vase houseroom.*

Houses of Parliament *n* (in Britain) **1** the building in which the House of Commons and the House of Lords assemble. **2** these two chambers considered together.

house sparrow *n* a small Eurasian weaverbird, *Passer domesticus,* now established in North America and Australia. It has a brown streaked plumage with grey underparts. Also called (U.S.): **English sparrow.**

house spider *n* any largish dark spider of the genus *Tegenaria* that is common in houses, such as the cardinal spider.

house style *n* a set of rules concerning spellings, typography, etc., observed by editorial and printing staff in a particular publishing or printing company.

house-train *vb* (*tr*) *Brit.* to train (pets) to urinate and defecate outside the house or in a special place. ▸ **'house-ˌtrained** *adj*

House Un-American Activities Committee *n* the former name of the **Internal Security Committee** of the U.S. House of Representatives: notorious for its anti-Communist investigations in the late 1940s and 1950s.

house-warming *n* **a** a party given after moving into a new home. **b** (*as modifier*): *a house-warming party.*

housewife ('haʊsˌwaɪf) *n pl* **-wives. 1** a woman, typically a married woman, who keeps house, usually without having paid employment. **2** ('hʌzɪf) Also called: **hussy, huswife.** *Chiefly Brit.* a small sewing kit issued to soldiers. ▸ **housewifery** ('haʊsˌwɪfərɪ, -ˌwɪfrɪ) *n*

housewifely ('haʊsˌwaɪflɪ) *adj* prudent and neat; domestic: *housewifely virtues.* ▸ **'houseˌwifeliness** *n*

housework ('haʊsˌwɜːk) *n* the work of running a home, such as cleaning, cooking, etc. ▸ **'houseˌworker** *n*

housey-housey ('haʊzɪ'haʊzɪ) *n* another name for **bingo** or **lotto. [C20:** so called from the cry of "house!" shouted by the winner of a game, probably from FULL HOUSE**]**

housing[1] ('haʊzɪŋ) *n* **1a** houses or dwellings collectively. **1b** (*as modifier*): *a housing problem.* **2** the act of providing with accommodation. **3** a hole, recess, groove, or slot made in one wooden member to receive another. **4** a part designed to shelter, cover, contain, or support a component, such as a bearing, or a mechanism, such as a pump or wheel: *a bearing housing; a motor housing; a wheel housing.* **5** another word for **houseline.**

housing[2] ('haʊzɪŋ) *n* (*often pl*) *Archaic.* another word for **trappings** (sense 2). **[C14:** from Old French *houce* covering, of Germanic origin**]**

housing association *n Social welfare.* (in Britain) a non-profit-making body whose purpose is to build, convert, or improve houses for letting at fair rents.

housing benefit *n Social welfare.* (in Britain) a payment made by a local authority in the form of a rent rebate to a council tenant, a rent allowance to a private tenant, or a rate rebate to a tenant or home-owner.

housing estate *n* a planned area of housing, often with its own shops and other amenities.

housing project *n U.S.* a housing development built and maintained by a local authority, usually intended for people with a low or moderate income.

housing scheme *n* **1** a local-authority housing plan. **2** the houses built according to such a plan; housing estate. ◆ Often shortened to **scheme.**

Housman ('haʊsmən) *n* **A(lfred) E(dward).** 1859–1936, English poet and classical scholar, author of *A Shropshire Lad* (1896) and *Last Poems* (1922).

Houston ('hjuːstən) *n* an inland port in SE Texas, linked by the **Houston Ship Canal** to the Gulf of Mexico and the Gulf Intracoastal Waterway: capital of the Republic of Texas (1837–39; 1842–45); site of the Manned Spacecraft Center (1964). Pop.: 1 744 058 (1996 est.).

houstonia (huː'stəʊnɪə) *n* any small North American rubiaceous plant of the genus *Houstonia,* having blue, white or purple flowers. **[C19:** named after Dr. William *Houston* (died 1733), Scottish botanist**]**

houting ('haʊtɪŋ) *n* a European whitefish, *Coregonus oxyrhynchus,* that lives in salt water but spawns in freshwater lakes: a valued food fish. **[C19:** from Dutch, from Middle Dutch *houtic,* of uncertain origin**]**

hove (həʊv) *vb Chiefly nautical.* a past tense and past participle of **heave.**

Hove (həʊv) *n* a town and coastal resort in S England, in Brighton and Hove unitary authority, East Sussex. Pop.: 67 602 (1991).

hovel ('hʌvᵊl, 'hɒv-) *n* **1** a ramshackle dwelling place. **2** an open shed for livestock, carts, etc. **3** the conical building enclosing a kiln. ◆ *vb* **-els, -elling, -elled** *or U.S.* **-els, -eling, -eled. 4** to shelter or be sheltered in a hovel. **[C15:** of unknown origin**]**

hover ('hɒvə) *vb* (*intr*) **1** to remain suspended in one place. **2** (of certain birds, esp. hawks) to remain in one place in the air by rapidly beating the wings. **3** to linger uncertainly in a nervous or solicitous way. **4** to be in a state of indecision: *she was hovering between the two suitors.* ◆ *n* **5** the act of hovering. **[C14:** *hoveren,* variant of *hoven,* of obscure origin**]** ▸ **'hoverer** *n* ▸ **'hoveringly** *adv*

hovercraft ('hɒvəˌkrɑːft) *n* a vehicle that is able to travel across both land and water on a cushion of air. The cushion is produced by a fan continuously forcing air under the vehicle.

hover fly *n* any dipterous fly of the family *Syrphidae,* with a typically hovering flight, esp. *Syrphus ribesii,* which mimics a wasp.

hoverport ('hɒvəˌpɔːt) *n* a port for hovercraft.

hovertrain ('hɒvəˌtreɪn) *n* a train that moves over a concrete track and is supported while in motion by a cushion of air supplied by powerful fans.

how[1] (haʊ) *adv* **1** in what way? in what manner? by what means?: *how did it happen?* Also used in indirect questions: *tell me how he did it.* **2** to what extent?: *how tall is he?* **3** how good? how well? what...like?: *how did she sing? how was the holiday?* **4 how about?** used to suggest something: *how about asking her? how about a cup of tea?* **5 how are you?** what is your state of health? **6 how come?** *Informal.* what is the reason (that)?: *how come you told him?* **7 how's that for...? 7a** is this satisfactory as regards...: *how's that for size?* **7b** an exclamation used to draw attention to a quality, deed, etc.: *how is that for endurance?* **8 how's that? 8a** what is your opinion? **8b** *Cricket.* Also written: **howzat** (haʊ'zæt). (an appeal to the umpire) is the batsman out? **9 how now?** *or* **how so?** *Archaic.* what is the meaning of this? **10** Also: **as how.** *Not standard.* that: *he told me as how the shop was closed.* **11** in whatever way: *do it how you wish.* **12** used in exclamations to emphasize extent: *how happy I was!* **13 and how!** (intensifier) very much so! **14 here's how!** (as a toast) good health! ◆ *n* **15** the way a thing is done: *the how of it.* **[**Old English *hū;* related to Old Frisian *hū,* Old High German *hweo***]**

how[2] (haʊ) *sentence substitute.* a greeting supposed to be or have been used by American Indians and often used humorously. **[C19:** of Siouan origin; related to Dakota *háo***]**

Howard ('haʊəd) *n* **1 Catherine.** ?1521–42, fifth wife of Henry VIII of England; beheaded. **2 Charles,** Lord Howard of Effingham and 1st Earl of Nottingham. 1536–1624, Lord High Admiral of England (1585–1618). He commanded the fleet that defeated the Spanish Armada (1588). **3** Sir **Ebenezer.** 1850–1928, English town planner, who introduced garden cities. **4 Henry.** See (Earl of) **Surrey. 5 John.** 1726–90, English prison reformer. **6 John Winston.** born 1939, Australian politician; prime minister of Australia from 1996. **7 Leslie.** real name *Leslie Howard Stainer.* 1890–1943, British actor of Hungarian descent. His many films included *The Scarlet Pimpernel* (1938), *Pygmalion* (1938), and *Gone With the Wind* (1939). **8 Trevor.** 1916–88, British actor. His many films include *Brief Encounter* (1946), *The Third Man* (1949), *Ryan's Daughter* (1970), and *White Mischief* (1987).

howbeit (haʊ'biːɪt) *Archaic.* ◆ *sentence connector.* **1** however. ◆ *conj* **2** (*subordinating*) though; although.

howdah *or* **houdah** ('haʊdə) *n* a seat for riding on an elephant's back, esp. one with a canopy. **[C18:** from Hindi *haudah,* from Arabic *haudaj* load carried by elephant or camel**]**

how do you do *sentence substitute.* **1** Also: **how do?, how d'ye do?** a formal greeting said by people who are being introduced to each other or are meeting for the first time. ◆ *n* **how-do-you-do. 2** *Informal.* a difficult situation.

howdy ('haʊdɪ) *sentence substitute. Chiefly U.S.* an informal word for **hello. [C16:** from the phrase *how d'ye do***]**

howe (haʊ) *n Scot. and northern English dialect.* a depression in the earth's surface, such as a basin or valley. **[C16:** from HOLE**]**

Howe (haʊ) *n* **1 Elias.** 1819–67, U.S. inventor of the sewing machine (1846). **2 Howe of Aberavon,** Baron, title of (*Richard Edward*) *Geoffrey Howe.* born 1926, British Conservative politician; Chancellor of the Exchequer (1979–83); foreign secretary (1983–89); deputy prime minister (1989–90). **3 Richard,** 4th Viscount Howe. 1726–99, British admiral: served (1776–78) in the War of American Independence and commanded the Channel fleet against France, winning the Battle of the Glorious First of June (1794). **4** his brother, **William,** 5th Viscount Howe. 1729–1814, British general; commander in chief (1776–78) of British forces in the War of American Independence.

howe'er (haʊ'ɛə) *sentence connector, adv* a poetic contraction of **however.**

Howel Dda ('haʊəl 'ðɑː) *n* See **Hywel Dda.**

however (haʊ'ɛvə) *sentence connector.* **1** still; nevertheless. **2** on the other hand; yet. ◆ *adv* **3** by whatever means; in whatever manner. **4** (*used with adjectives expressing or admitting of quantity or degree*) no matter how: *however long it takes, finish it.* **5** an emphatic form of **how**[1] (sense 1).

howf *or* **howff** (haʊf, həʊf) *n Scot.* a haunt, esp. a public house. **[C16:** of uncertain origin**]**

howitzer ('haʊɪtsə) *n* a cannon having a short or medium barrel with a low muzzle velocity and a steep angle of fire. **[C16:** from Dutch *houwitser,* from German *Haubitze,* from Czech *houfnice* stone-sling**]**

howk (haʊk) *vb Scot.* to dig (out or up). **[C17:** from earlier *holk***]**

howl (haʊl) *n* **1** a long plaintive cry or wail characteristic of a wolf or hound. **2** a similar cry of pain or sorrow. **3** *Slang.* **3a** a person or thing that is very funny. **3b** a prolonged outburst of laughter. **4** *Electronics.* an unwanted prolonged high-pitched sound produced by a sound-producing system as a result of feedback. ◆ *vb* **5** to express in a howl or utter such cries. **6** (*intr*) (of the wind, etc.) to make a wailing noise. **7** (*intr*) *Informal.* to shout or laugh. **[C14:** *houlen;* related to Middle High German *hiuweln,* Middle Dutch *hūlen,* Danish *hyle***]**

Howland Island ('haʊlənd) *n* a small island in the central Pacific, near the equator northwest of Phoenix Island: U.S. airfield. Area: 2.6 sq. km (1 sq. mile).

howl down *vb* (*tr, adv*) to prevent (a speaker) from being heard by shouting disapprovingly.

howler ('haʊlə) *n* **1** Also called: **howler monkey.** any large New World monkey of the genus *Alouatta,* inhabiting tropical forests in South America and having a loud howling cry. **2** *Informal.* a glaring mistake. **3** *Brit.* (formerly) a device that produces a loud tone in a telephone receiver to attract attention when the receiver is incorrectly replaced. **4** a person or thing that howls.

howlet ('haʊlɪt) *n Archaic, poetic.* another word for **owl. [C15:** diminutive of *howle* OWL**]**

howling ('haʊlɪŋ) *adj* (*prenominal*) *Informal.* (intensifier): *a howling success; a howling error.* ▸ **'howlingly** *adv*

Howlin' Wolf ('haʊlɪn) *n* real name *Chester Burnett.* 1910–76, U.S. blues singer and songwriter.

howlround ('haʊlˌraʊnd) *n* the condition, resulting in a howling noise, when sound from a loudspeaker is fed back into the microphone of a public-address or recording system. Also called: **'howlˌback.**

Howrah ('haʊrə) *n* an industrial city in E India, in West Bengal on the Hooghly River opposite Calcutta. Pop.: 950 435 (1991).

howsoever (ˌhaʊsəʊˈɛvə) *sentence connector, adv* a less common word for **however**.

how-to *adj* (of a book or guide) giving basic instructions to the lay person on how to do or make something, esp. as a hobby or for practical purposes: *a how-to book on carpentry*.

howtowdie (haʊˈtaʊdɪ) *n* a Scottish dish of boiled chicken with poached eggs and spinach. [C18: from Old French *hétoudeau, estaudeau* a fat young chicken for cooking]

howzit (ˈhaʊzɪt) *sentence substitute. S. African.* an informal word for **hello**. [C20: from the phrase *how is it?*]

Hoxha (*Albanian* ˈhodʒa) *n* **Enver** (ˈɛmvɛr). 1908–85, Albanian statesman: founded the Albanian Communist Party in 1941 and was its first secretary (1954–85).

hoy[1] (hɔɪ) *n Nautical.* **1** a freight barge. **2** a coastal fishing and trading vessel, usually sloop-rigged, used during the 17th and 18th centuries. [C15: from Middle Dutch *hoei*]

hoy[2] (hɔɪ) *interj* a cry used to attract attention or drive animals. [C14: variant of HEY]

hoya (ˈhɔɪə) *n* any plant of the asclepiadaceous genus *Hoya,* of E Asia and Australia, esp. the waxplant. [C19: named after Thomas *Hoy* (died 1821), English gardener]

hoyden *or* **hoiden** (ˈhɔɪdᵊn) *n* a wild boisterous girl; tomboy. [C16: perhaps from Middle Dutch *heidijn* heathen] ▸ **ˈhoydenish** *or* **ˈhoidenish** *adj* ▸ **ˈhoydenishness** *or* **ˈhoidenishness** *n*

Hoylake (ˈhɔɪˌleɪk) *n* a town and resort in NW England, in Wirral unitary authority, Merseyside, on the Irish Sea. Pop.: 25 554 (1991).

Hoyle[1] (hɔɪl) *n* an authoritative book of rules for card games. [after Edmond *Hoyle* (1672–1769), English authority on games, its compiler]

Hoyle[2] (hɔɪl) *n* Sir **Fred**. born 1915, English astronomer and writer: his books include *The Nature of the Universe* (1950) and *Frontiers of Astronomy* (1955), and science-fiction writings.

HP *or* **h.p.** *abbrev. for:* **1** *Brit.* hire purchase. **2** horsepower. **3** high pressure. **4** (in Britain) Houses of Parliament.

HPV *abbrev. for* human papilloma virus.

HQ *or* **h.q.** *abbrev. for* headquarters.

hr *abbrev. for* hour.

HR *abbrev. for:* **1** *Brit.* Home Rule. **2** *U.S.* House of Representatives. **3** *international car registration for* Croatia.

Hradec Králové (*Czech* ˈhradɛts ˈkraːlɔvɛː) *n* a town in the N Czech Republic, on the Elbe River. Pop.: 100 528 (1996 est.). German name: **Königgrätz**.

HRE *abbrev. for* Holy Roman Emperor *or* Empire.

HRH *abbrev. for* His (*or* Her) Royal Highness.

HRT *abbrev. for* hormone replacement therapy.

Hrvatska (ˈhrvaːtskaː) *n* the Serbo-Croat name for **Croatia**.

hryvna (ˈhrʌvnə) *or* **hryvnya** (ˈhrʌvnjə) *n* the standard monetary unit of the Ukraine, divided into 100 kopiykas.

HS *abbrev. for:* **1** High School. **2** (in Britain) Home Secretary.

h.s. *abbrev. for* hoc sensu. [Latin: in this sense]

HSH *abbrev. for* His (*or* Her) Serene Highness.

Hsi (ʃiː) *n* a variant spelling of **Xi**.

Hsia Kuei (ˈʃjɑː ˈkweɪ) *n* See **Xia Gui**.

Hsia-men (ˈʃjɑːˈmɛn) *n* a transliteration of the modern Chinese name for **Amoy**.

Hsian (ʃjɑːn) *n* a variant transliteration of the Chinese name for **Xi An**.

Hsiang (ʃjɑːŋ) *n* a variant transliteration of the Chinese name for **Xiang**.

Hsin-hai-lien (ˈʃɪn ˈhaɪ ˈljɛn) *n* a variant transliteration of the Chinese name for **Lianyungang**.

Hsining (ˈʃiːˈnɪŋ) *n* a variant transliteration of the Chinese name for **Xining**.

Hsinking (ˈʃɪnˈkɪŋ) *n* the former name (1932–45) of **Changchun**.

HSM *abbrev. for* His (*or* Her) Serene Majesty.

HST (in Britain) *abbrev. for* high speed train.

Hsüan-tsang (ˈʃwɑːn ˈtsæŋ) *n* a variant transliteration of the Chinese name for **Xuan Zang**.

Hsüan-tsung (ˈʃwɑːn ˈtsʊŋ) *n* a variant transliteration of the Chinese name for **Xuan Zong**.

Hsüan T'ung (ˈʃwɑːn ˈtʊŋ) *n* a variant transliteration of the Chinese name for **Xuan-tong**.

Hsü-chou (ˈʃuːˈtʃaʊ) *n* a variant transliteration of the Chinese name for **Xuzhou**.

Hsün-tzu (ˈtʃʊn ˈdʒɪ) *n* a variant transliteration of the Chinese name for **Xun Zi**.

ht *abbrev. for* height.

HT *Physics. abbrev. for* high tension.

HTLV *abbrev. for* human T-cell lymphotrophic virus: any one of a small family of viruses that cause certain rare diseases in the T-cells of human beings; for instance, HTLV I causes a form of leukaemia.

HTML *abbrev. for* hypertext markup language: a text description language that is used for electronic publishing, esp. on the World Wide Web.

HTTP *abbrev. for* hypertext transfer protocol, used esp. on the World Wide Web. See also **hypertext**.

Hts (in place names) *abbrev. for* Heights.

Hua Guo Feng (ˈhwɑː gwəʊ ˈfɛʃ) *or* **Hua Kuo-feng** (ˈhwɑː kwəʊ ˈfɛŋ) *n* born *c.* 1920, Chinese Communist statesman; prime minister of China 1976–80.

Huainan (ˈhwaɪˈnæn) *n* a city in E China, in Anhui province north of Hefei. Pop.: 1 200 000 (1991 est.).

Huambo (*Portuguese* ˈwambu) *n* a town in central Angola: designated by the Portuguese as the future capital of the country. Pop.: 400 000 (1995 est.). Former name (1928–73): **Nova Lisboa**.

Huang Hai (ˈhwæŋ ˈhaɪ) *n* the Pinyin transliteration of the Chinese name for the **Yellow Sea**.

Huang Ho (ˈhwæŋ ˈhəʊ) *n* the Pinyin transliteration of the Chinese name for the **Yellow River**.

Huang Hua (hwæŋ hwɑː) *n* born 1913, Chinese Communist statesman; minister for foreign affairs (1976–83).

Huáscar (*Spanish* uaskar) *n* died 1533, Inca ruler (1525–33): murdered by his half brother Atahualpa.

Huascarán (*Spanish* uaskaˈran) *or* **Huascán** (*Spanish* uasˈkan) *n* an extinct volcano in W Peru, in the Peruvian Andes: the highest peak in Peru; avalanche in 1962 killed over 3000 people. Height: 6768 m (22 205 ft.).

hub (hʌb) *n* **1** the central portion of a wheel, propeller, fan, etc., through which the axle passes. **2** the focal point. [C17: probably variant of HOB[1]]

hub-and-spoke *n* (*modifier*) denoting a method of organizing intercontinental air traffic in which one major airport is used as a feeder for local airports. Sometimes shortened to **hub**.

Hubble (ˈhʌbᵊl) *n* **Edwin Powell**. 1889–1953, U.S. astronomer, noted for his investigations of nebulae and the recession of the galaxies.

hubble-bubble (ˈhʌbᵊlˈbʌbᵊl) *n* **1** another name for **hookah**. **2** hubbub; turmoil. **3** a bubbling or gargling sound. [C17: rhyming jingle based on BUBBLE]

Hubble classification *n* a method of classifying galaxies depending on whether they are elliptical, spiral, barred spiral, or irregular. [C20: named after E. P. HUBBLE]

Hubble constant *n* the rate at which the universe expands, a value derived from the ratio of recession velocity to distance for galaxies beyond the Local Group. It is currently estimated to lie in the range 50–100 km s^{-1} $megaparsec^{-1}$.

Hubble's law *n Astronomy.* a law stating that the velocity of recession of a galaxy is proportional to its distance from the observer.

Hubble telescope *n* a telescope launched into orbit around the earth in 1990 to provide information about the universe in the visible, infrared, and ultraviolet ranges. [C20: named after E.P. HUBBLE]

hubbub (ˈhʌbʌb) *n* **1** a confused noise of many voices. **2** uproar. [C16: probably from Irish *hooboobbes;* compare Scottish Gaelic *ubub!* an exclamation of contempt]

hubby (ˈhʌbɪ) *n, pl* **-bies**. an informal word for **husband**. [C17: by shortening and altering]

hubcap (ˈhʌbˌkæp) *n* a metal cap fitting onto the hub of a wheel, esp. a stainless steel or chromium-plated one.

Hubei (ˈhuːˈbeɪ), **Hupeh,** *or* **Hupei** *n* a province of central China: largely low-lying with many lakes. Capital: Wuhan. Pop.: 57 720 000 (1996 est.). Area: 187 500 sq. km (72 394 sq. miles).

Hubli (ˈhuːblɪ) *n* a city in W India, in NW Mysore: incorporated with Dharwar in 1961; educational and trading centre. Pop. (with Dharwar): 648 298 (1991).

hubris (ˈhjuːbrɪs) *or* **hybris** *n* **1** pride or arrogance. **2** (in Greek tragedy) an excess of ambition, pride, etc., ultimately causing the transgressor's ruin. [C19: from Greek] ▸ **huˈbristic** *or* **hyˈbristic** *adj*

huckaback (ˈhʌkəˌbæk) *n* a coarse absorbent linen or cotton fabric used for towels and informal shirts, etc. Also called: **huck** (hʌk). [C17: of unknown origin]

huckery (ˈhʌkərɪ) *adj N.Z. informal.* ugly.

huckle (ˈhʌkᵊl) *n Rare.* **1** the hip or haunch. **2** a projecting or humped part. [C16: diminutive of Middle English *huck* hip, haunch; perhaps related to Old Norse *hūka* to squat]

huckleberry (ˈhʌkᵊlˌbɛrɪ) *n, pl* **-ries**. **1** any American ericaceous shrub of the genus *Gaylussacia,* having edible dark blue berries with large seeds. **2** the fruit of any of these shrubs. **3** another name for **blueberry**. **4** a Brit. name for **whortleberry** (sense 1). [C17: probably a variant of *hurtleberry,* of unknown origin]

hucklebone (ˈhʌkᵊlˌbəʊn) *n Archaic.* **1** the anklebone; talus. **2** the hipbone; innominate bone.

huckster (ˈhʌkstə) *n* **1** a person who uses aggressive or questionable methods of selling. **2** *Now rare.* a person who sells small articles or fruit in the street. **3** *U.S.* a person who writes for radio or television advertisements. ◆ *vb* **4** (*tr*) to peddle. **5** (*tr*) to sell or advertise aggressively or questionably. **6** to haggle (over). [C12: perhaps from Middle Dutch *hoekster,* from *hoeken* to carry on the back] ▸ **ˈhucksterism** *n*

HUD *abbrev. for* head-up display.

Huddersfield (ˈhʌdəzˌfiːld) *n* a town in N England, in Kirklees unitary authority, West Yorkshire, on the River Colne: textile industry. Pop.: 143 726 (1991).

huddle (ˈhʌdᵊl) *n* **1** a heaped or crowded mass of people or things. **2** *Informal.* a private or impromptu conference (esp. in the phrase **go into a huddle**). ◆ *vb* **3** to crowd or cause to crowd or nestle closely together. **4** (often foll. by *up*) to draw or hunch (oneself), as through cold. **5** (*intr*) *Informal.* to meet and confer privately. **6** (*tr*) *Chiefly Brit.* to do (something) in a careless way. **7** (*tr*) *Rare.* to put on (clothes) hurriedly. [C16: of uncertain origin; compare Middle English *hoderen* to wrap up] ▸ **ˈhuddler** *n*

Huddleston (ˈhʌdᵊlstən) *n* **Trevor**. 1913–98, British Anglican prelate; suffragan bishop of Stepney (1968–78) and bishop of Mauritius (1978–83); president of the Anti-Apartheid Movement (1981–94).

hudibrastic (ˌhjuːdɪˈbræstɪk) *adj* mock-heroic in style. [C18: after *Hudibras,* poem (1663–68) by Samuel Butler]

Hudson (ˈhʌdsən) *n* **1 Henry**. died 1611, English navigator: he explored the Hudson River (1609) and Hudson Bay (1610), where his crew mutinied and cast him adrift to die. **2 W(illiam) H(enry)**. 1841–1922, British naturalist and novelist, born in Argentina, noted esp. for his romance *Green Mansions* (1904) and the autobiographical *Far Away and Long Ago* (1918).

Hudson Bay *n* an inland sea in NE Canada: linked with the Atlantic by **Hud-**

son Strait; the S extension forms James Bay; discovered in 1610 by Henry Hudson. Area (excluding James Bay): 647 500 sq. km (250 000 sq. miles).

Hudson River *n* a river in E New York State, flowing generally south into Upper New York Bay: linked to the Great Lakes, the St Lawrence Seaway, and Lake Champlain by the New York State Barge Canal and the canalized Mohawk River. Length: 492 km (306 miles).

Hudson's Bay Company *n* an English company chartered in 1670 to trade in all parts of North America drained by rivers flowing into Hudson Bay.

Hudson seal *n* muskrat fur that has been dressed and dyed to resemble sealskin.

hue (hju:) *n* **1** the attribute of colour that enables an observer to classify it as red, green, blue, purple, etc., and excludes white, black, and shades of grey. See also **colour. 2** a shade of a colour. **3** aspect; complexion: *a different hue on matters.* [Old English *hīw* beauty; related to Old Norse *hȳ* fine hair, Gothic *hiwi* form]

Hué (*French* ɥe) *n* a port in central Vietnam, on the delta of the **Hué River** near the South China Sea: former capital of the kingdom of Annam, of French Indochina (1883–1946), and of Central Vietnam (1946–54). Pop.: 219 149 (1992 est.).

hue and cry *n* **1** (formerly) the pursuit of a suspected criminal with loud cries in order to raise the alarm. **2** any loud public outcry. **[C16:** from Anglo-French *hu et cri,* from Old French *hue* outcry, from *huer* to shout, from *hu!* shout of warning + *cri* CRY**]**

hued (hju:d) *adj Archaic or poetic.* **a** having a hue or colour as specified. **b** (*in combination*): *rosy-hued dawn.*

Huelva (*Spanish* 'uelβa) *n* a port in SW Spain, between the estuaries of the Odiel and Tinto Rivers: exports copper and other ores. Pop.: 145 712 (1995 est.).

Huesca (*Spanish* 'ueska) *n* a city in NE Spain: Roman town, site of Quintus Sertorius' school (76 B.C.); 15th-century cathedral and ancient palace of Aragonese kings. Pop.: 50 020 (1991). Latin name: **Osca** ('ɒskə).

huff (hʌf) *n* **1** a passing mood of anger or pique (esp. in the phrase **in a huff**). ◆ *vb* **2** to make or become angry or resentful. **3** (*intr*) to blow or puff heavily. **4** Also: **blow.** *Draughts.* to remove (an opponent's draught) from the board for failure to make a capture. **5** (*tr*) *Obsolete.* to bully. **6 huffing and puffing.** empty threats or objections; bluster. **[C16:** of imitative origin; compare PUFF**]** ▸ **'huffish** *or* **'huffy** *adj* ▸ **'huffily** *or* **huffishly** *adv* ▸ **'huffiness** *or* **'huffishness** *n*

Hufuf (hu'fu:f) *n* See **Al Hufuf.**

hug (hʌg) *vb* **hugs, hugging, hugged.** (*mainly tr*) **1** (*also intr*) to clasp (another person or thing) tightly or (of two people) to cling close together; embrace. **2** to keep close to a shore, kerb, etc. **3** to cling to (beliefs, etc.); cherish. **4** to congratulate (oneself); be delighted with (oneself). ◆ *n* **5** a tight or fond embrace. **[C16:** probably of Scandinavian origin; related to Old Norse *hugga* to comfort, Old English *hogian* to take care of**]** ▸ **'huggable** *adj* ▸ **'hugger** *n*

huge (hju:dʒ) *adj* extremely large in size, amount, or scope. Archaic form: **hugeous. [C13:** from Old French *ahuge,* of uncertain origin**]** ▸ **'hugeness** *n*

hugely ('hju:dʒlɪ) *adv* very much; enormously.

hugger-mugger ('hʌgə,mʌgə) *n* **1** confusion. **2** *Rare.* secrecy. ◆ *adj, adv Archaic.* **3** with secrecy. **4** in confusion. ◆ *vb Obsolete.* **5** (*tr*) to keep secret. **6** (*intr*) to act secretly. **[C16:** of uncertain origin**]**

Huggins ('hʌgɪnz) *n* Sir **William.** 1824–1910, British astronomer. He pioneered the use of spectroscopy in astronomy and discovered the red shift in the lines of a stellar spectrum.

Hugh Capet ('hju: 'kæpɪt, 'keɪpɪt) *n* See (Hugh) **Capet.**

Hughes (hju:z) *n* **1 Howard.** 1905–76, U.S. industrialist, aviator, and film producer. He became a total recluse during the last years of his life. **2** (**James Mercer**) **Langston.** 1902–67, U.S. Black poet and writer. His collections include *The Weary Blues* (1926) and *The Panther and the Lash* (1967). **3 Richard** (**Arthur Warren**). 1900–76, British novelist. He wrote *A High Wind in Jamaica* (1929), *In Hazard* (1938), and *The Fox in the Attic* (1961). **4 Ted,** full name *Edward James Hughes.* 1930–98, British poet: his works include *The Hawk in the Rain* (1957), *Crow* (1970), and *Birthday Letters* (1998). Poet laureate (1984–98). **5 Thomas.** 1822–96, British novelist; author of *Tom Brown's Schooldays* (1857). **6 William Morris.** 1864–1952, Australian statesman, born in England: prime minister of Australia (1915–23).

hug-me-tight *n* a woman's knitted jacket.

Hugo ('hju:gəʊ; *French* ygo) *n* **Victor** (**Marie**) (viktɔr). 1802–85, French poet, novelist, and dramatist; leader of the romantic movement in France. His works include the volumes of verse *Les Feuilles d'automne* (1831) and *Les Contemplations* (1856), the novels *Notre-Dame de Paris* (1831) and *Les Misérables* (1862), and the plays *Hernani* (1830) and *Ruy Blas* (1838).

Huguenot ('hju:gə,nəʊ, -,nɒt) *n* **1** a French Calvinist, esp. of the 16th or 17th centuries. ◆ *adj* **2** designating the French Protestant Church. **[C16:** from French, from Genevan dialect *eyguenot* one who opposed annexation by Savoy, ultimately from Swiss German *Eidgenoss* confederate; influenced by *Hugues,* surname of 16th-century Genevan burgomaster**]** ▸ **,Hugue'notic** *adj* ▸ **'Hugue,notism** *n*

huh (*spelling pron* hʌ) *interj* an exclamation of derision, bewilderment, inquiry, etc.

Huhehot (,hu:hɪ'hɒt ,hu:ɪ-) *or* **Hu-ho-hao-t'e** (,hu:həʊ-haʊ'teɪ) *n* a variant transliteration of the Chinese name for **Hohhot.**

huhu ('hu:hu:) *n* a New Zealand beetle, *Prionoplus reticularis,* with a hairy body. **[**Maori**]**

hui ('hu:ɪ) *n, pl* **huies.** *N.Z.* **1** a Maori social gathering. **2** *Informal.* any party. **[**Maori**]**

huia ('hu:ɪjə) *n* an extinct bird of New Zealand, *Heteralocha acutirostris,* prized by early Maoris for its distinctive tail feathers. **[**Maori**]**

hula ('hu:lə) *or* **hula-hula** *n* a Hawaiian dance performed by a woman. **[**from Hawaiian**]**

Hula Hoop *n Trademark.* a light hoop that is whirled around the body by movements of the waist and hips.

hula skirt *n* a skirt made of long grass attached to a waistband and worn by hula dancers.

hulk (hʌlk) *n* **1** the body of an abandoned vessel. **2** *Disparaging.* a large or unwieldy vessel. **3** *Disparaging.* a large ungainly person or thing. **4** (*often pl*) the frame or hull of a ship, used as a storehouse, etc., or (esp. in 19th-century Britain) as a prison. ◆ *vb* **5** (*intr*) *Brit. informal.* to move clumsily. **6** (*intr;* often foll. by *up*) to rise massively. **[**Old English *hulc,* from Medieval Latin *hulca,* from Greek *holkas* barge, from *helkein* to tow**]**

hulking ('hʌlkɪŋ) *adj* big and ungainly. Also: **'hulky.**

hull (hʌl) *n* **1** the main body of a vessel, tank, flying boat, etc. **2** the shell or pod of peas or beans; the outer covering of any fruit or seed; husk. **3** the persistent calyx at the base of a strawberry, raspberry, or similar fruit. **4** the outer casing of a missile, rocket, etc. ◆ *vb* **5** to remove the hulls from (fruit or seeds). **6** (*tr*) to pierce the hull of (a vessel, tank, etc.). **[**Old English *hulu;* related to Old High German *helawa,* Old English *helan* to hide**]** ▸ **'huller** *n* ▸ **'hull-less** *adj*

Hull[1] (hʌl) *n* **1** a port in NE England, in Kingston upon Hull unitary authority, East Riding of Yorkshire: the largest fishing port in Britain; university (1929). Pop.: 310 636 (1991). Official name: **Kingston upon Hull. 2** a city in SE Canada, in SW Quebec on the River Ottawa: a centre of the timber trade and associated industries. Pop.: 60 707 (1991).

Hull[2] (hʌl) *n* **Cordell.** 1871–1955, U.S. statesman; secretary of state (1933–44). He helped to found the U.N.: Nobel peace prize 1945.

hullabaloo *or* **hullaballoo** (,hʌləbə'lu:) *n, pl* **-loos.** loud confused noise, esp. of protest; commotion. **[C18:** perhaps from interjection HALLO + Scottish *baloo* lullaby**]**

hull down *adj* **1** (of a ship) having its hull concealed by the horizon. **2** (of a tank) having only its turret visible.

hullo (hʌ'ləʊ) *sentence substitute, n* a variant of **hello.**

Hulme (hju:m) *n* **T**(**homas**) **E**(**rnest**). 1883–1917, English literary critic and poet; a proponent of imagism.

hum (hʌm) *vb* **hums, humming, hummed. 1** (*intr*) to make a low continuous vibrating sound like that of a prolonged *m.* **2** (*intr*) (of a person) to sing with the lips closed. **3** (*intr*) to utter an indistinct sound, as in hesitation; hem. **4** (*intr*) *Informal.* to be in a state of feverish activity. **5** (*intr*) *Brit. and Irish slang.* to smell unpleasant. **6** (*intr*) *Austral. slang.* to scrounge. **7 hum and haw.** See **hem**[2] (sense 3). ◆ *n* **8** a low continuous murmuring sound. **9** *Electronics.* an undesired low-frequency noise in the output of an amplifier or receiver, esp. one caused by the power supply. **10** *Austral. slang.* a scrounger; cadger. **11** *Brit. and Irish slang.* an unpleasant odour. ◆ *interj, n* **12** an indistinct sound of hesitation, embarrassment, etc.; hem. **[C14:** of imitative origin; compare Dutch *hommelen,* Old High German *humbal* bumblebee**]** ▸ **'hummer** *n*

human ('hju:mən) *adj* **1** of, characterizing, or relating to man and mankind: *human nature.* **2** consisting of people: *the human race; a human chain.* **3** having the attributes of man as opposed to animals, divine beings, or machines: *human failings.* **4a** kind or considerate. **4b** natural. ◆ *n* **5** a human being; person. ◆ Related prefix: **anthropo-. [C14:** from Latin *hūmānus;* related to Latin *homō* man**]** ▸ **'human-,like** *adj* ▸ **'humanness** *n*

human being *n* a member of any of the races of *Homo sapiens;* person; man, woman, or child.

human capital *n Economics.* the abilities and skills of any individual, esp. those acquired through investment in education and training, that enhance potential income earning.

humane (hju:'meɪn) *adj* **1** characterized by kindness, mercy, sympathy, etc. **2** inflicting as little pain as possible: *a humane killing.* **3** civilizing or liberal (esp. in the phrases **humane studies, humane education**). **[C16:** variant of HUMAN**]** ▸ **hu'manely** *adv* ▸ **hu'maneness** *n*

humane society *n* an organization for promotion of humane ideals, esp. in dealing with animals.

human interest *n* (in a newspaper story, news broadcasting, etc.) reference to individuals and their emotions.

humanism ('hju:mə,nɪzəm) *n* **1** the denial of any power or moral value superior to that of humanity; the rejection of religion in favour of a belief in the advancement of humanity by its own efforts. **2** a philosophical position that stresses the autonomy of human reason in contradistinction to the authority of the Church. **3** (*often cap.*) a cultural movement of the Renaissance, based on classical studies. **4** interest in the welfare of people. ▸ **'humanist** *n* ▸ **,human'istic** *adj*

humanistic psychology *n* approach to psychology advocated by some that emphasizes feelings and emotions and the better understanding of the self in terms of observation of oneself and one's relations with others.

humanitarian (hju:,mænɪ'teərɪən) *adj* **1** having the interests of mankind at heart. **2** of or relating to ethical or theological humanitarianism. ◆ *n* **3** a philanthropist. **4** an adherent of humanitarianism.

humanitarianism (hju:,mænɪ'teərɪə,nɪzəm) *n* **1** humanitarian principles. **2** *Ethics.* **2a** the doctrine that man's duty is to strive to promote the welfare of mankind. **2b** the doctrine that man can achieve perfection through his own resources. **3** *Theol.* the belief that Jesus Christ was only a mortal man. ▸ **hu,mani'tarianist** *n*

humanity (hju:'mænɪtɪ) *n, pl* **-ties. 1** the human race. **2** the quality of being human. **3** kindness or mercy. **4** (*pl*) (usually preceded by *the*) the study of literature, philosophy, and the arts. **5** the study of Ancient Greek and Roman language, literature, etc.

humanize *or* **humanise** ('hju:mə,naɪz) *vb* **1** to make or become human. **2** to make or become humane. ▸ ˌhumaniˈzation *or* ˌhumaniˈsation *n* ▸ ˈhumanˌizer *or* ˈhumanˌiser *n*

humankind (ˌhju:mənˈkaɪnd) *n* the human race; humanity.

USAGE See at **mankind.**

humanly (ˈhju:mənlɪ) *adv* **1** by human powers or means. **2** in a human or humane manner.

human nature *n* **1** the qualities common to humanity. **2** ordinary human behaviour, esp. considered as less than perfect. **3** *Sociol.* the unique elements that form a basic part of human life and distinguish it from other animal life.

humanoid (ˈhju:məˌnɔɪd) *adj* **1** like a human being in appearance. ◆ *n* **2** a being with human rather than anthropoid characteristics. **3** (in science fiction) a robot or creature resembling a human being.

human papilloma virus *n* any one of a class of viruses that cause tumours, including warts, in humans. Certain strains infect the cervix and have been implicated as a cause of cervical cancer. Abbrev.: **HPV**

human resources *pl n* **1a** the workforce of an organization. **1b** (*as modifier*): *human-resources management; human-resources officer.* **2** the contribution to an employing organization which its workforce could provide in effort, skills, knowledge, etc.

human rights *pl n* the rights of individuals to liberty, justice, etc.

Humber (ˈhʌmbə) *n* an estuary in NE England, into which flow the Rivers Ouse and Trent: flows east into the North Sea; navigable for large ocean-going ships as far as Hull; crossed by the **Humber Bridge** (1981), a single-span suspension bridge with a main span of 1410 m (4626 ft.). Length: 64 km (40 miles).

Humberside (ˈhʌmbəˌsaɪd) *n* a former county of N England around the Humber estuary, formed in 1974 from parts of the East and West Ridings of Yorkshire and N Lincolnshire: replaced in 1996 by the unitary authorities of East Riding of Yorkshire, Kingston upon Hull, North Lincolnshire (Lincolnshire), and North East Lincolnshire (Lincolnshire).

humble (ˈhʌmbᵊl) *adj* **1** conscious of one's failings. **2** unpretentious; lowly: *a humble cottage; my humble opinion.* **3** deferential or servile. ◆ *vb* (*tr*) **4** to cause to become humble; humiliate. **5** to lower in status. [C13: from Old French, from Latin *humilis* low, from *humus* the ground] ▸ ˈ**humbled** *adj* ▸ ˈ**humbleness** *n* ▸ ˈ**humbler** *n* ▸ ˈ**humbling** *adj* ▸ ˈ**humblingly** *adv* ▸ ˈ**humbly** *adv*

humblebee (ˈhʌmbᵊlˌbi:) *n* another name for the **bumblebee.** [C15: related to Middle Dutch *hommel* bumblebee, Old High German *humbal;* see HUM]

humble pie *n* **1** (formerly) a pie made from the heart, entrails, etc., of a deer. **2 eat humble pie.** to behave or be forced to behave humbly; be humiliated. [C17: earlier *an umble pie,* by mistaken word division from *a numble pie,* from *numbles* offal of a deer, from Old French *nombles,* ultimately from Latin *lumbulus* a little loin, from *lumbus* loin]

Humboldt (ˈhʌmbəult; *German* ˈhumbɔlt) *n* **1** Baron (**Friedrich Heinrich**) **Alexander von** (aleˈksandər fɔn). 1769–1859, German scientist, who made important scientific explorations in Central and South America (1799–1804). In *Kosmos* (1845–62), he provided a comprehensive description of the physical universe. **2** his brother, Baron (**Karl**) **Wilhelm von** (ˈvɪlhɛlm fɔn). 1767–1835, German philologist and educational reformer.

Humboldt Current *n* a cold ocean current of the S Pacific, flowing north along the coasts of Chile and Peru. Also called: **Peru Current.**

humbucker (ˈhʌmˌbʌkə) *n* a twin-coil guitar pick-up.

humbug (ˈhʌmˌbʌg) *n* **1** a person or thing that tricks or deceives. **2** nonsense; rubbish. **3** *Brit.* a hard boiled sweet, usually flavoured with peppermint and often having a striped pattern. ◆ *vb* **-bugs, -bugging, -bugged. 4** to cheat or deceive (someone). [C18: of unknown origin] ▸ ˈ**humˌbugger** *n* ▸ ˈ**humˌbuggery** *n*

humdinger (ˈhʌmˌdɪŋə) *n Slang.* **1** something unusually large: *a humdinger of a recession.* **2** an excellent person or thing: *a humdinger of a party.* [C20: of unknown origin]

humdrum (ˈhʌmˌdrʌm) *adj* **1** ordinary; dull. ◆ *n* **2** a monotonous routine, task, or person. [C16: rhyming compound, probably based on HUM] ▸ ˈ**humˌdrumness** *n*

Hume (hju:m) *n* **1** (**George**) **Basil.** 1923–99, English Roman Catholic Benedictine monk and cardinal; archbishop of Westminster (1976–99. **2 David.** 1711–76, Scottish empiricist philosopher, economist, and historian, whose sceptic philosophy restricted human knowledge to that which can be perceived by the senses. His works include *A Treatise of Human Nature* (1740), *An Enquiry concerning the Principles of Morals* (1751), *Political Discourses* (1752), and *History of England* (1754–62). **3 John.** born 1937, Northern Ireland politician; leader of the Social Democratic and Labour Party (SDLP) from 1979. Nobel peace prize jointly with David Trimble in 1998. ▸ ˈ**Humism** *n*

humectant (hju:ˈmɛktənt) *adj* **1** producing moisture. ◆ *n* **2** a substance added to another substance to keep it moist. [C17: from Latin *ūmectāre* to wet, from *ūmēre* to be moist, from *ūmor* moisture; see HUMOUR]

humeral (ˈhju:mərəl) *adj* **1** *Anatomy.* of or relating to the humerus. **2** of or near the shoulder.

humeral veil *n R.C. Church.* a silk shawl worn by a priest at High Mass, etc. Often shortened to **veil.**

humerus (ˈhju:mərəs) *n, pl* **-meri** (-məˌraɪ). **1** the bone that extends from the shoulder to the elbow. **2** the corresponding bone in other vertebrates. [C17: from Latin *umerus;* related to Gothic *ams* shoulder, Greek *ōmos*]

Hume's law *n* the philosophical doctrine that an evaluative statement cannot be derived from purely factual premises, often formulated as: *one can't derive an "ought" from an "is".* See also **naturalistic fallacy.** [named after David HUME]

humic (ˈhju:mɪk) *adj* of, relating to, or derived from humus: *humic acids.* [C19: from Latin *humus* ground + -IC]

humicole (ˈhju:mɪˌkəul) *n* any plant that thrives on humus. ▸ **humicolous** (hju:ˈmɪkələs) *adj*

humid (ˈhju:mɪd) *adj* moist; damp: *a humid day.* [C16: from Latin *ūmidus,* from *ūmēre* to be wet; see HUMECTANT, HUMOUR] ▸ ˈ**humidly** *adv* ▸ ˈ**humidness** *n*

humidifier (hju:ˈmɪdɪˌfaɪə) *n* a device for increasing or controlling the water vapour in a room, building, etc.

humidify (hju:ˈmɪdɪˌfaɪ) *vb* **-fies, -fying, -fied.** (*tr*) to make (air) humid or damp. ▸ **huˌmidifiˈcation** *n*

humidistat (hju:ˈmɪdɪˌstæt) *n* a device for maintaining constant humidity. Also called: **hygrostat.**

humidity (hju:ˈmɪdɪtɪ) *n* **1** the state of being humid; dampness. **2** a measure of the amount of moisture in the air. See **relative humidity, absolute humidity.**

humidor (ˈhju:mɪˌdɔ:) *n* a humid place or container for storing cigars, tobacco, etc.

humify (ˈhju:mɪˌfaɪ) *vb* **-fies, -fying, -fied.** to convert or be converted into humus. ▸ ˌ**humifiˈcation** *n*

humiliate (hju:ˈmɪlɪˌeɪt) *vb* (*tr*) to lower or hurt the dignity or pride of. [C16: from Late Latin *humiliāre,* from Latin *humilis* HUMBLE] ▸ **huˈmiliˌated** *adj* ▸ **huˈmiliˌating** *adj* ▸ **huˈmiliˌatingly** *adv* ▸ **huˌmiliˈation** *n* ▸ **humiliative** (hju:ˈmɪljətɪv) *adj* ▸ **huˈmiliˌator** *n* ▸ **huˈmiliatory** *adj*

humility (hju:ˈmɪlɪtɪ) *n, pl* **-ties.** the state or quality of being humble.

hummel (ˈhʌmᵊl) *adj Scot.* **1** (of cattle) hornless. **2** (of grain) awnless. [C15: of Germanic origin; compare Low German *hummel* hornless animal]

Hummel (ˈhuməl) *n* **Johann Nepomuk** (joˈhan ˈne:pomuk). 1778–1837, German composer and pianist.

hummingbird (ˈhʌmɪŋˌbɜ:d) *n* any very small American bird of the family *Trochilidae,* having a brilliant iridescent plumage, long slender bill, and wings specialized for very powerful vibrating flight: order *Apodiformes.*

hummingbird moth *n U.S.* another name for the **hawk moth.**

humming top *n* a top that hums as it spins.

hummock (ˈhʌmək) *n* **1** a hillock; knoll. **2** a ridge or mound of ice in an ice field. **3** Also called: **hammock.** *Chiefly southern U.S.* a wooded area lying above the level of an adjacent marsh. [C16: of uncertain origin; compare HUMP, HAMMOCK] ▸ ˈ**hummocky** *adj*

hummus, hoummos, *or* **houmous** (ˈhuməs) *n* a creamy dip originating in the Middle East, made from puréed chickpeas, tahina, etc. [from Turkish *humus*]

USAGE Avoid confusion with **humus.**

humungous *or esp. U.S.* **humongous** (hju:ˈmɒŋgəs, -ˈmʌŋgəs) *adj U.S. slang.* exceptionally large; huge or enormous. [C20: of uncertain origin]

humoral (ˈhju:mərəl) *adj* **1** *Immunol.* denoting or relating to a type of immunity caused by free antibodies circulating in the blood. **2** *Obsolete.* of or relating to the four bodily fluids (humours).

humoresque (ˌhju:məˈrɛsk) *n* a short lively piece of music. [C19: from German *Humoreske,* ultimately from English HUMOUR]

humorist (ˈhju:mərɪst) *n* a person who acts, speaks, or writes in a humorous way. ▸ ˌ**humorˈistic** *adj*

humorous (ˈhju:mərəs) *adj* **1** funny; comical; amusing. **2** displaying or creating humour. **3** *Archaic.* another word for **capricious.** ▸ ˈ**humorously** *adv* ▸ ˈ**humorousness** *n*

humour *or U.S.* **humor** (ˈhju:mə) *n* **1** the quality of being funny. **2** Also called: **sense of humour.** the ability to appreciate or express that which is humorous. **3** situations, speech, or writings that are thought to be humorous. **4a** a state of mind; temper; mood. **4b** (*in combination*): *ill humour; good humour.* **5** temperament or disposition. **6** a caprice or whim. **7** any of various fluids in the body, esp. the aqueous humour and vitreous humour. **8** Also called: **cardinal humour.** *Archaic.* any of the four bodily fluids (blood, phlegm, choler or yellow bile, melancholy or black bile) formerly thought to determine emotional and physical disposition. **9 out of humour.** in a bad mood. ◆ *vb* (*tr*) **10** to attempt to gratify; indulge: *he humoured the boy's whims.* **11** to adapt oneself to: *to humour someone's fantasies.* [C14: from Latin *humor* liquid; related to Latin *ūmēre* to be wet, Old Norse *vökr* moist, Greek *hugros* wet] ▸ ˈ**humourful** *or U.S.* ˈ**humorful** *adj* ▸ ˈ**humourless** *or U.S.* ˈ**humorless** *adj* ▸ ˈ**humourlessness** *or U.S.* ˈ**humorlessness** *n*

humoursome *or U.S.* **humorsome** (ˈhju:məsəm) *adj* **1** capricious; fanciful. **2** inclined to humour (someone).

hump (hʌmp) *n* **1** a rounded protuberance or projection, as of earth, sand, etc. **2** *Pathol.* a rounded deformity of the back in persons with kyphosis, consisting of a convex spinal curvature. **3** a rounded protuberance on the back of a camel or related animal. **4 the hump.** *Brit. informal.* a fit of depression or sulking (esp. in the phrase **it gives me the hump**). **5 over the hump.** past the largest or most difficult portion of work, time, etc. ◆ *vb* **6** to form or become a hump; hunch; arch. **7** (*tr*) *Brit. slang.* to carry or heave. **8** *Taboo slang.* to have sexual intercourse with (someone). **9 hump one's swag.** *Austral. and N.Z. informal.* (of a tramp) to carry one's belongings from place to place on one's back. [C18: probably from earlier HUMPBACKED] ▸ ˈ**humpˌlike** *adj*

humpback (ˈhʌmpˌbæk) *n* **1** another word for **hunchback. 2** Also called: **humpback whale.** a large whalebone whale, *Megaptera novaeangliae,* closely related and similar to the rorquals but with a humped back and long flippers: family *Balaenopteridae.* **3** a Pacific salmon, *Oncorhynchus gorbuscha,* the male of which has a humped back and hooked jaws. **4** Also called: **humpback bridge.** *Brit.* a road bridge having a sharp incline and decline and usually a narrow roadway. [C17: alteration of earlier *crumpbacked,* perhaps influenced by HUNCHBACK; perhaps related to Dutch *homp* lump] ▸ ˈ**humpˌbacked** *adj*

Humperdinck (*German* ˈhumpərdɪŋk) *n* **Engelbert** (ˈɛŋəlbɛrt). 1854–1921, German composer, esp. of operas, including *Hansel and Gretel* (1893).

humph (*spelling pron* hʌmf) *interj* an exclamation of annoyance, dissatisfaction, scepticism, etc.

Humphrey ('hʌmfrɪ) *n* **1 Duke.** See (Humphrey, Duke of) **Gloucester. 2 Hubert Horatio.** 1911–78, U.S. statesman; vice-president of the U.S. under President Johnson (1965–69).

Humphreys Peak ('hʌmfrɪz) *n* a mountain in N central Arizona, in the San Francisco Peaks: the highest peak in the state. Height: 3862 m (12 670 ft.).

Humphries ('hʌmfrɪz) *n* **(John) Barry.** born 1934, Australian comic actor and writer, best known for creating the character Dame Edna Everage.

humpty ('hʌmptɪ) *n Brit.* a low padded seat; pouffe. **[C20:** from *humpty* hunchbacked, perhaps influenced by *Humpty Dumpty* (nursery rhyme)**]**

humpty dumpty ('hʌmptɪ 'dʌmptɪ) *n Chiefly Brit.* **1** a short fat person. **2** a person or thing that once overthrown or broken cannot be restored or mended. **[C18:** after the nursery rhyme *Humpty Dumpty***]**

humpy[1] ('hʌmpɪ) *adj* **humpier, humpiest. 1** full of humps. **2** *Brit. informal.* angry or gloomy. ► **'humpiness** *n*

humpy[2] ('hʌmpɪ) *n, pl* **humpies.** *Austral.* a primitive hut. **[C19:** from a native Australian language**]**

Hums (hʊms) *n* a variant of **Homs.**

hum tone *n* a note produced by a bell when struck, lying an octave or (in many English bells) a sixth or seventh below the strike tone. Also called (esp. Brit.): **hum note.**

humus ('hju:məs) *n* a dark brown or black colloidal mass of partially decomposed organic matter in the soil. It improves the fertility and water retention of the soil and is therefore important for plant growth. **[C18:** from Latin: soil, earth**]**

USAGE Avoid confusion with **hummus.**

Hun (hʌn) *n* **1** a member of any of several Asiatic nomadic peoples speaking Mongoloid or Turkic languages who dominated much of Asia and E Europe from before 300 B.C., invading the Roman Empire in the 4th and 5th centuries A.D. **2** *Informal.* (esp. in World War I) a derogatory name for a **German. 3** *Informal.* a vandal. **[**Old English *Hūnas,* from Late Latin *Hūnī,* from Turkish *Hun-yū***]** ► **'Hun,like** *adj*

Hunan ('hu:'næn) *n* a province of S China, between the Yangtze River and the Nan Ling Mountains: drained chiefly by the Xiang and Yüan Rivers; valuable mineral resources. Capital: Changsha. Pop.: 63 920 000 (1996 est.). Area: 210 500 sq. km (82 095 sq. miles).

hunch (hʌntʃ) *n* **1** an intuitive guess or feeling. **2** another word for **hump. 3** a lump or large piece. ◆ *vb* **4** to bend or draw (oneself or a part of the body) up or together. **5** (*intr;* usually foll. by *up*) to sit in a hunched position. **[C16:** of unknown origin**]**

hunchback ('hʌntʃ,bæk) *n* **1** a person having an abnormal convex curvature of the thoracic spine. **2** such a curvature. ◆ Also called: **humpback.** See **kyphosis.** Compare **hollow-back. [C18:** from earlier *hunchbacked, huckbacked* humpbacked, influenced by *bunchbacked,* from *bunch* (in obsolete sense of *hump*) + BACKED**]** ► **'hunch,backed** *adj*

hundred ('hʌndrəd) *n, pl* **-dreds** *or* **-dred. 1** the cardinal number that is the product of ten and ten; five score. See also **number** (sense 1). **2** a numeral, 100, C, etc., representing this number. **3** (*often pl*) a large but unspecified number, amount, or quantity: *there will be hundreds of people there.* **4 the hundreds. 4a** the numbers 100 to 109: *the temperature was in the hundreds.* **4b** the numbers 100 to 199: *his score went into the hundreds.* **4c** the numbers 100 to 999: *the price was in the hundreds.* **5** (*pl*) the 100 years of a specified century: *in the sixteen hundreds.* **6** something representing, represented by, or consisting of 100 units. **7** *Maths.* the position containing a digit representing that number followed by two zeros: *in 4376, 3 is in the hundred's place.* **8** an ancient division of a county in England, Ireland, and parts of the U.S. ◆ *determiner* **9a** amounting to or approximately a hundred: *a hundred reasons for that.* **9b** (*as pronoun*): *the hundred I chose.* **10** amounting to 100 times a particular scientific quantity: *a hundred volts.* Related prefix: **hecto-. [**Old English; related to Old Frisian *hunderd,* Old Norse *hundrath,* German *hundert,* Gothic *hund,* Latin *centum,* Greek *hekaton***]**

hundred days *pl n French history.* the period between Napoleon Bonaparte's arrival in Paris from Elba on March 20, 1815, and his abdication on June 29, 1815.

hundred-percenter *n U.S.* an extreme or unjustified nationalist. ► **'hundred-per'centism** *n*

hundreds and thousands *pl n* tiny beads of brightly coloured sugar, used in decorating cakes, sweets, etc.

hundredth ('hʌndrədθ) *adj* **1** (*usually prenominal*) **1a** being the ordinal number of 100 in numbering or counting order, position, time, etc. **1b** (*as n*): *the hundredth in line.* ◆ *n* **2a** one of 100 approximately equal parts of something. **2b** (*as modifier*): *a hundredth part.* **3** one of 100 equal divisions of a particular scientific quantity. Related prefix: **centi-**: *centimetre.* **4** the fraction equal to one divided by 100 (1/100).

hundredweight ('hʌndrəd,weɪt) *n, pl* **-weights** *or* **-weight. 1** Also called: **long hundredweight.** *Brit.* a unit of weight equal to 112 pounds or 50.802 35 kilograms. **2** Also called: **short hundredweight.** *U.S. and Canadian.* a unit of weight equal to 100 pounds or 45.359 24 kilograms. **3** Also called: **metric hundredweight.** a metric unit of weight equal to 50 kilograms. ◆ Abbrev. (for senses 1, 2): **cwt.**

Hundred Years' War *n* the series of wars fought intermittently between England and France from 1337–1453: after early victories the English were expelled from all of France except Calais.

hung (hʌŋ) *vb* **1** the past tense and past participle of **hang** (except in the sense of *to execute* or in the idiom *I'll be hanged*). ◆ *adj* **2a** (of a legislative assembly) not having a party with a working majority: *a hung parliament.* **2b** unable to reach a decision: *a hung jury.* **2c** (of a situation) unable to be resolved. **3 hung over.** *Informal.* suffering from the effects of a hangover. **4 hung up.** *Slang.* **4a** impeded by some difficulty or delay. **4b** in a state of confusion; emotionally disturbed. **5 hung up on.** *Slang.* obsessively or exclusively interested in: *he's hung up on modern art these days.*

Hung. *abbrev. for:* **1** Hungarian. **2** Hungary.

Hungarian (hʌŋ'gɛərɪən) *n* **1** the official language of Hungary, also spoken in Romania and elsewhere, belonging to the Finno-Ugric family and most closely related to the Ostyak and Vogul languages of NW Siberia. **2** a native, inhabitant, or citizen of Hungary. **3** a Hungarian-speaking person who is not a citizen of Hungary. ◆ *adj* **4** of or relating to Hungary, its people, or their language. ◆ Compare **Magyar.**

Hungarian goulash *n* the full name of **goulash.**

Hungary ('hʌŋgərɪ) *n* a republic in central Europe: Magyars first unified under Saint Stephen, the first Hungarian king (1001–38); taken by the Hapsburgs from the Turks at the end of the 17th century; gained autonomy with the establishment of the dual monarchy of Austria-Hungary (1867) and became a republic in 1918; passed under Communist control in 1949; a popular rising in 1956 was suppressed by Soviet troops; a multi-party democracy replaced Communism in 1989 after mass protests. It consists chiefly of the Middle Danube basin and plains. Official language: Hungarian. Religion: Christian majority. Currency: forint. Capital: Budapest. Pop.: 10 117 000 (1998 est.). Area: 93 030 sq. km (35 919 sq. miles). Hungarian name: **Magyarország.**

hunger ('hʌŋgə) *n* **1** a feeling of pain, emptiness, or weakness induced by lack of food. **2** an appetite, desire, need, or craving: *hunger for a woman.* ◆ *vb* **3** to have or cause to have a need or craving for food. **4** (*intr;* usually foll. by *for* or *after*) to have a great appetite or desire (for). **[**Old English *hungor;* related to Old High German *hungar,* Old Norse *hungr,* Gothic *hūhrus***]**

hunger march *n* a procession of protest or demonstration by the unemployed.

hunger strike *n* a voluntary fast undertaken, usually by a prisoner, as a means of protest. ► **hunger striker** *n*

Hung Hsiu-ch'uan ('hʌŋ 'ʃju: 'tʃwɑ:n) *n* See **Hong Xiu Quan.**

Hungnam (,huŋ'næm) *n* a port in E North Korea, on the Sea of Japan southeast of Hamhung. Pop.: 260 000 (latest est.).

hungry ('hʌŋgrɪ) *adj* **-grier, -griest. 1** desiring food. **2** experiencing pain, weakness, or nausea through lack of food. **3** (*postpositive;* foll. by *for*) having a craving, desire, or need (for). **4** expressing or appearing to express greed, craving, or desire. **5** lacking fertility; poor. **6** *N.Z.* (of timber) dry and bare. ► **'hungrily** *or* **'hungeringly** *adv* ► **'hungriness** *n*

Hung-wu ('hʌŋ 'wu:) *n* See **Hong-wu.**

hunk (hʌŋk) *n* **1** a large piece. **2** Also called: **hunk of a man.** *Slang.* a well-built, sexually attractive man. **[C19:** probably related to Flemish *hunke;* compare Dutch *homp* lump**]**

hunker ('hʌŋkə) *vb* (*intr*) (often foll. by *down*) to squat; crouch.

hunkers ('hʌŋkəz) *pl n* haunches. **[C18:** of uncertain origin**]**

hunks (hʌŋks) *n* (*functioning as sing*) *Rare.* **1** a crotchety old person. **2** a miserly person. **[C17:** of unknown origin**]**

hunky-dory (,hʌŋkɪ'dɔ:rɪ) *adj Informal.* very satisfactory; fine. **[C20:** of uncertain origin**]**

Hunnish ('hʌnɪʃ) *adj* **1** of, relating to, or characteristic of the Huns. **2** barbarously destructive; vandalistic. ► **'Hunnishly** *adv* ► **'Hunnishness** *n*

hunt (hʌnt) *vb* **1** to seek out and kill or capture (game or wild animals) for food or sport. **2** (*intr;* often foll. by *for*) to look (for); search (for): *to hunt for a book; to hunt up a friend.* **3** (*tr*) to use (hounds, horses, etc.) in the pursuit of wild animals, game, etc.: *to hunt a pack of hounds.* **4** (*tr*) to search or draw (country) to hunt wild animals, game, etc.: *to hunt the parkland.* **5** (*tr;* often foll. by *down*) to track or chase diligently, esp. so as to capture: *to hunt down a criminal.* **6** (*tr; usually passive*) to persecute; hound. **7** (*intr*) (of a gauge indicator, engine speed, etc.) to oscillate about a mean value or position. **8** (*intr*) (of an aircraft, rocket, etc.) to oscillate about a flight path. ◆ *n* **9** the act or an instance of hunting. **10** chase or search, esp. of animals or game. **11** the area of a hunt. **12** a party or institution organized for the pursuit of wild animals or game, esp. for sport. **13** the participants in or members of such a party or institution. ◆ See also **hunt down, hunt up. [**Old English *huntian;* related to Old English *hentan,* Old Norse *henda* to grasp**]** ► **'huntedly** *adv*

Hunt (hʌnt) *n* **1 Henry,** known as *Orator Hunt.* 1773–1835, British radical, who led the mass meeting that ended in the Peterloo Massacre (1819). **2 (William) Holman.** 1827–1910, British painter; a founder of the Pre-Raphaelite Brotherhood (1848). **3 James.** 1947–93, British motor-racing driver: world champion 1976. **4 (Henry Cecil) John,** Baron. 1910–98, British army officer and mountaineer. He planned and led the expedition that first climbed Mount Everest (1953). **5 (James Henry) Leigh** (li:). 1784–1859, British poet and essayist: a founder of *The Examiner* (1808) in which he promoted the work of Keats and Shelley.

huntaway ('hʌntə,weɪ) *n N.Z.* a dog trained to drive sheep at a long distance from the shepherd.

hunt down *vb* (*adv*) **1** (*tr*) to pursue successfully by diligent searching and chasing: *they finally hunted down the killer in Mexico.* **2** (*intr*) (of a bell) to be rung progressively later during a set of changes.

hunted ('hʌntɪd) *adj* harassed and worn: *he has a hunted look.*

hunter ('hʌntə) *n* **1** a person or animal that seeks out and kills or captures game. Fem. equivalent: **huntress** ('hʌntrɪs). **2a** a person who looks diligently for something. **2b** (*in combination*): *a fortune-hunter.* **3** a specially bred horse used in hunting, usually characterized by strength and stamina. **4** a specially bred dog used to hunt game. **5** a watch with a hinged metal lid or case (**hunting case**) to protect the crystal. Also called: **hunting watch.** See also **half-hunter.**

Hunter ('hʌntə) *n* **1 John.** 1728–93, British physician, noted for his investigation of venereal and other diseases. **2** his brother, **William.** 1718–83, British anatomist and obstetrician.

hunter-gatherer *Anthropol.* ◆ *adj* **1** (of a society, lifestyle, etc.) surviving by hunting animals and gathering plants for subsistence. ◆ *n* **2** a member of such a society.

hunter-killer *adj* denoting a type of naval vessel, esp. a submarine, designed and equipped to pursue and destroy enemy craft.

hunter's moon *n* the full moon following the harvest moon.

hunting ('hʌntɪŋ) *n* **a** the pursuit and killing or capture of game and wild animals, regarded as a sport. **b** (*as modifier*): *hunting boots; hunting lodge.* Related adj: **venatic.**

hunting cat *or* **leopard** *n* another name for **cheetah.**

Huntingdon[1] ('hʌntɪŋdən) *n* a town in E central England, in Cambridgeshire: birthplace of Oliver Cromwell. Pop. (with Godmanchester): 15 575 (1991).

Huntingdon[2] ('hʌntɪŋdən) *n* **Selina,** Countess of Huntingdon. 1707–91, English religious leader, who founded a Calvinistic Methodist sect.

Huntingdonshire ('hʌntɪŋdən,ʃɪə, -ʃə) *n* (until 1974) a former county of E England, now part of Cambridgeshire.

hunting ground *n* **1** the area of a hunt. **2** Also called: **happy hunting ground.** any place containing a supply of what is wanted or in which a search is conducted: *some resorts are a happy hunting ground for souvenirs.*

hunting horn *n* **1** a long straight metal tube with a flared end and a cylindrical bore, used in giving signals in hunting. See **horn** (sense 9). **2** an obsolete brass instrument from which the modern French horn was developed.

hunting knife *n* a knife used for flaying and cutting up game and sometimes for killing it.

hunting spider *n* another name for **wolf spider.**

Huntington's disease *n* a rare hereditary type of chorea, marked by involuntary jerky movements, impaired speech, and increasing dementia. Former name: **Huntington's chorea.** [C19: named after George *Huntington* (1850–1916), U.S. neurologist]

huntsman ('hʌntsmən) *n, pl* **-men. 1** a person who hunts. **2** a person who looks after and trains hounds, beagles, etc., and manages them during a hunt.

huntsman's-cup *n U.S.* any of various pitcher plants of the genus *Sarracenia,* whose leaves are modified to form tubular pitchers.

Huntsville ('hʌntsvɪl) *n* a city in NE Alabama: space-flight and guided-missile research centre. Pop.: 170 424 (1996 est.).

hunt the slipper *n* a children's game in which the players look for a hidden slipper or other object, such as a thimble (**hunt the thimble**).

hunt up *vb* (*adv*) **1** (*tr*) to search for, esp. successfully: *I couldn't hunt up a copy of it anywhere.* **2** (*intr*) (of a bell) to be rung progressively earlier during a set of changes.

Hunyadi (*Hungarian* 'hunjɔdi) *n* **János** ('ja:noʃ). ?1387–1456, Hungarian general, who led Hungarian resistance to the Turks, defeating them notably at Belgrade (1456).

Huon pine ('hju:ɒn) *n* a taxaceous tree, *Dacrydium franklinii,* of Australasia, SE Asia, and Chile, with scalelike leaves and cup-shaped berry-like fruits. [named after the *Huon* River, Tasmania]

Hupeh *or* **Hupei** ('xu:'peɪ) *n* a variant transliteration of the Chinese name for **Hubei.**

huppah ('hʊpə) *n* a variant spelling of **chuppah.**

Hurban *Hebrew.* (*Hebrew* xu:r'bɑn; *Yiddish* 'xu:rbᵊn) *n* a variant spelling of **Churban.**

Hurd (hɜ:d) *n* **Douglas** (**Richard**), Baron Hurd of Westwell. born 1930, British Conservative politician; home secretary (1985–89); foreign secretary (1989–95).

hurdies ('hʌrdɪz) *pl n Scot.* the buttocks or haunches. [C16: of unknown origin]

hurdle ('hɜ:dᵊl) *n* **1a** *Athletics.* one of a number of light barriers over which runners leap in certain events. **1b** a low barrier used in certain horse races. **2** an obstacle to be overcome: *the next hurdle in his career.* **3** a light framework of interlaced osiers, wattle, etc., used as a temporary fence. **4** *Brit.* a sledge on which criminals were dragged to their executions. ◆ *vb* **5** to jump (a hurdle, etc.), as in racing. **6** (*tr*) to surround with hurdles. **7** (*tr*) to overcome. [Old English *hyrdel;* related to Gothic *haurds* door, Old Norse *hurth* door, Old High German *hurd,* Latin *crātis,* Greek *kurtos* basket] ▸ **'hurdler** *n*

hurdle rate *n Finance.* the rate of return that a proposed project must provide if it is to be worth considering: usually calculated as the cost of the capital involved adjusted by a risk factor.

hurds (hɜ:dz) *pl n* another word for **hards.**

hurdy-gurdy ('hɜ:dɪ'gɜ:dɪ) *n, pl* **-dies. 1** any mechanical musical instrument, such as a barrel organ. **2** a medieval instrument shaped like a viol in which a rosined wheel rotated by a handle sounds the strings. [C18: rhyming compound, probably of imitative origin]

hurl (hɜ:l) *vb* **1** (*tr*) to throw or propel with great force. **2** (*tr*) to utter with force; yell: *to hurl insults.* **3** (hʌrl). *Scot.* to transport or be transported in a driven vehicle. ◆ *n* **4** the act or an instance of hurling. **5** (hʌrl). *Scot.* a ride in a driven vehicle. [C13: probably of imitative origin] ▸ **'hurler** *n*

hurley ('hɜ:lɪ) *n* **1** *Chiefly Brit.* another word for **hurling** (the game). **2** Also called: **hurley stick.** the stick used in playing hurling.

hurling ('hɜ:lɪŋ) *n* a traditional Irish game resembling hockey and lacrosse, played with sticks and a ball between two teams of 15 players each.

hurly-burly ('hɜ:lɪ'bɜ:lɪ) *n, pl* **hurly-burlies. 1** confusion or commotion. ◆ *adj* **2** turbulent. [C16: from earlier *hurling and burling,* rhyming phrase based on *hurling* in obsolete sense of uproar]

Huron ('hjʊərən) *n* **1 Lake.** a lake in North America, between the U.S. and Canada: the second largest of the Great Lakes. Area: 59 570 sq. km (23 000 sq. miles). **2** (*pl* **-rons** *or* **-ron**) a member of a North American Indian people formerly living in the region east of Lake Huron. **3** the Iroquoian language of this people.

hurrah (hʊ'rɑ:), **hooray** (hu:'reɪ), *or* **hurray** (hʊ'reɪ) *interj, n* **1** a cheer of joy, victory, etc. ◆ *vb* **2** to shout "hurrah". [C17: probably from German *hurra;* compare HUZZAH]

hurricane ('hʌrɪkᵊn, -keɪn) *n* **1** a severe, often destructive storm, esp. a tropical cyclone. **2a** a wind of force 12 or above on the Beaufort scale. **2b** (*as modifier*): *a wind of hurricane force.* **3** anything acting like such a wind. [C16: from Spanish *huracán,* from Taino *hurakán,* from *hura* wind]

hurricane deck *n* a ship's deck that is covered by a light deck as a sunshade.

hurricane lamp *n* a paraffin lamp, with a glass covering to prevent the flame from being blown out. Also called: **storm lantern.**

hurried ('hʌrɪd) *adj* performed with great or excessive haste: *a hurried visit.* ▸ **'hurriedly** *adv* ▸ **'hurriedness** *n*

hurry ('hʌrɪ) *vb* **-ries, -rying, -ried. 1** (*intr;* often foll. by *up*) to hasten (to do something); rush. **2** (*tr;* often foll. by *along*) to speed up the completion, progress, etc., of. ◆ *n* **3** haste. **4** urgency or eagerness. **5 in a hurry.** *Informal.* **5a** easily: *you won't beat him in a hurry.* **5b** willingly: *we won't go there again in a hurry.* [C16 *horyen,* probably of imitative origin; compare Middle High German *hurren;* see SCURRY] ▸ **'hurrying** *n, adj* ▸ **'hurryingly** *adv*

hurry-scurry *adv* **1** in frantic haste. ◆ *adj* **2** hasty and disorderly. ◆ *n* **3** disordered haste. ◆ *vb* (*intr*) **4** to rush about in confusion. [C18: reduplication of HURRY; compare HELTER-SKELTER]

hurst (hɜ:st) *n Archaic.* **1** a wood. **2** a sandbank. [Old English *hyrst;* related to Old High German *hurst*]

Hurstmonceux ('hɜ:stmən,su:, -,səʊ) *n* a variant spelling of **Herstmonceux.**

hurt[1] (hɜ:t) *vb* **hurts, hurting, hurt. 1** to cause physical pain to (someone or something). **2** to cause emotional pain or distress to (someone). **3** to produce a painful sensation in (someone): *the bruise hurts.* **4** (*intr*) *Informal.* to feel pain. ◆ *n* **5** physical, moral, or mental pain or suffering. **6** a wound, cut, or sore. **7** damage or injury; harm. ◆ *adj* **8** injured or pained physically or emotionally: *a hurt knee; a hurt look.* [C12 *hurten* to hit, from Old French *hurter* to knock against, probably of Germanic origin; compare Old Norse *hrūtr* ram, Middle High German *hurt* a collision] ▸ **'hurter** *n*

hurt[2] (hɜ:t) *or* **whort** (hwɜ:t) *n Southern English dialect.* another name for **whortleberry.**

hurter ('hɜ:tə) *n* an object or part that gives protection, such as a concrete block that protects a building from traffic or the shoulder of an axle against which the hub strikes. [C14 *hurtour,* from Old French *hurtoir* something that knocks or strikes, from *hurter* to HURT[1]]

hurtful ('hɜ:tfʊl) *adj* causing distress or injury: *to say hurtful things.* ▸ **'hurtfully** *adv* ▸ **'hurtfulness** *n*

hurtle ('hɜ:tᵊl) *vb* **1** to project or be projected very quickly, noisily, or violently. **2** (*intr*) *Rare.* to collide or crash. [C13 *hurtlen,* from *hurten* to strike; see HURT[1]]

Hus (*Czech* hʊs) *n* **Jan** (jan). the Czech name of (John) **Huss.**

Husain (hʊ'seɪn, -'saɪn) *n* **1** ?629–680 A.D., Islamic caliph, the son of Ali and Fatima and the grandson of Mohammed. **2** a variant of **Hussein.**

husband ('hʌzbənd) *n* **1** a woman's partner in marriage. **2** *Archaic.* **2a** a manager of an estate. **2b** a frugal person. ◆ *vb* **3** to manage or use (resources, finances, etc.) thriftily. **4** *Archaic.* **4a** (*tr*) to find a husband for. **4b** (of a woman) to marry (a man). **5** (*tr*) *Obsolete.* to till (the soil). [Old English *hūsbonda,* from Old Norse *hūsbōndi,* from *hūs* house + *bōndi* one who has a household, from *bōa* to dwell] ▸ **'husbander** *n* ▸ **'husbandless** *adj*

husbandman ('hʌzbəndmən) *n, pl* **-men.** *Archaic.* a farmer.

husbandry ('hʌzbəndrɪ) *n* **1** farming, esp. when regarded as a science, skill, or art. **2** management of affairs and resources.

Husein ibn-Ali (hʊ'seɪn 'ɪbᵊn'ɑ:lɪ, 'ælɪ, hʊ'saɪn) *n* 1856–1931, first king of Hejaz (1916–24): initiated the Arab revolt against the Turks (1916–18); forced to abdicate by ibn-Saud.

hush[1] (hʌʃ) *vb* **1** to make or become silent; quieten. **2** to soothe or be soothed. ◆ *n* **3** stillness; silence. **4** an act of hushing. ◆ *interj* **5** a plea or demand for silence. [C16: probably from earlier *husht* quiet!, the *-t* being thought to indicate a past participle] ▸ **hushed** *adj*

hush[2] (hʌʃ) *Mining, northern English.* ◆ *vb* (*tr*) **1** to run water over the ground to erode (surface soil), revealing the underlying strata and any valuable minerals present. **2** to wash (an ore) by removing particles of earth with rushing water. ◆ *n* **3** a gush of water, esp. when artificially produced. [C18: of imitative origin]

hushaby ('hʌʃə,baɪ) *interj* **1** used in quietening a baby or child to sleep. ◆ *n* **2** a lullaby. [C18: from HUSH[1] + *by,* as in BYE-BYE]

hush-hush *adj Informal.* (esp. of official work, documents, etc.) secret; confidential.

hush money *n Slang.* money given to a person, such as an accomplice, to ensure that something is kept secret.

hush up *vb* (*tr, adv*) to suppress information or rumours about.

husk (hʌsk) *n* **1** the external green or membranous covering of certain fruits and seeds. **2** any worthless outer covering. ◆ *vb* **3** (*tr*) to remove the husk from. [C14: probably based on Middle Dutch *huusken* little house, from *hūs* house; related to Old English *hosu* husk, *hūs* HOUSE] ▸ **'husker** *n* ▸ **'husk,like** *adj*

husky[1] ('hʌskɪ) *adj* **huskier, huskiest. 1** (of a voice, an utterance, etc.) slightly hoarse or rasping. **2** of, like, or containing husks. **3** *Informal.* big, strong, and well-built. [C19: probably from HUSK, from the toughness of a corn husk] ▸ **'huskily** *adv* ▸ **'huskiness** *n*

husky[2] ('hʌskɪ) *n, pl* **huskies.** a breed of Arctic sled dog with a thick dense coat, pricked ears, and a curled tail. [C19: probably based on ESKIMO]

huss (hʌs) *n* the flesh of the European dogfish, when used as food. [C15 *husk, huske,* C16 *huss*: of obscure origin]

Huss (hʌs) *n* **John,** Czech name *Jan Hus.* ?1372–1415, Bohemian religious reformer. Influenced by Wycliffe, he anticipated the Reformation in denouncing doctrines and abuses of the Church. His death at the stake precipitated the Hussite wars in Bohemia and Moravia.

hussar (hʊ'zɑː) *n* **1a** a member of any of various light cavalry regiments in European armies, renowned for their elegant dress. **1b** (*pl; cap. when part of a name*): *the Queen's own Hussars.* **2** a Hungarian horseman of the 15th century. **[C15:** from Hungarian *huszár* hussar, formerly freebooter, from Old Serbian *husar,* from Old Italian *corsaro* CORSAIR**]**

Hussein (hʊ'seɪn) *n* **1** Also: **Husain.** 1935–99, king of Jordan (1952–99). **2 Saddam** (sæ'dæm). born 1937, Iraqi politician: president (from 1979) and prime minister (from 1994) of Iraq. He led Iraq into the Iran-Iraq War (1980–88) and the Gulf War (1991).

Husserl (*German* 'hʊsərl) *n* **Edmund** ('ɛtmʊnt). 1859–1938, German philosopher; founder of phenomenology.

Hussite ('hʌsaɪt) *n* **1** an adherent of the religious ideas of John Huss in the 14th century or a member of the movement initiated by him. ◆ *adj* **2** of or relating to John Huss, his teachings, followers, etc. ► **'Hussism** *or* **'Hussitism** *n*

hussy ('hʌsɪ, -zɪ) *n, pl* **-sies. 1** *Contemptuous.* a shameless or promiscuous woman. **2** *Dialect.* a folder for needles, thread, etc. **[C16** (in the sense: housewife): from *hussif* HOUSEWIFE**]**

hustings ('hʌstɪŋz) *n* (*functioning as pl or sing*) **1** *Brit.* (before 1872) the platform on which candidates were nominated for Parliament and from which they addressed the electors. **2** the proceedings at a parliamentary election. **3** political campaigning. **[C11:** from Old Norse *hūsthing,* from *hūs* HOUSE + *thing* assembly**]**

hustle ('hʌsᵊl) *vb* **1** to shove or crowd (someone) roughly. **2** to move or cause to move hurriedly or furtively: *he hustled her out of sight.* **3** (*tr*) to deal with or cause to proceed hurriedly: *to hustle legislation through.* **4** *Slang.* to earn or obtain (something) forcefully. **5** *U.S. and Canadian slang.* (of procurers and prostitutes) to solicit. ◆ *n* **6** an instance of hustling. **7** undue activity. **8** a disco dance of the 1970s. **[C17:** from Dutch *husselen* to shake, from Middle Dutch *hutsen***]** ► **'hustler** *n*

hustle up *vb* (*tr*) *Informal, chiefly U.S. and Canadian.* to prepare quickly.

Huston ('hjuːstən) *n* **John.** 1906–87, U.S. film director. His films include *The Treasure of the Sierra Madre* (1947), for which he won an Oscar, *The African Queen* (1951), *The Man Who Would Be King* (1975), *Prizzi's Honour* (1985), and *The Dead* (1987).

hut (hʌt) *n* **1** a small house or shelter, usually made of wood or metal. **2 the.** *Austral.* (on a sheep or cattle station) accommodation for the shearers, stockmen, etc. **3** *N.Z.* a shelter for mountaineers, skiers, etc. ◆ *vb* **4** to furnish with or live in a hut. **[C17:** from French *hutte,* of Germanic origin; related to Old High German *hutta* a crude dwelling**]** ► **'hut,like** *adj*

hutch (hʌtʃ) *n* **1** a cage, usually of wood and wire mesh, for small animals. **2** *Informal, derogatory.* a small house. **3** a cart for carrying ore. **4** a trough, esp. one used for kneading dough or (in mining) for washing ore. ◆ *vb* **5** (*tr*) to store or keep in or as if in a hutch. **[C14** *hucche,* from Old French *huche,* from Medieval Latin *hutica,* of obscure origin**]**

Hutcheson ('hʌtʃɪsən) *n* **Francis.** 1694–1746, Scottish philosopher: he published books on ethics and aesthetics, including *System of Moral Philosophy* (1755).

hutchie ('hʌtʃɪ) *n Austral.* a groundsheet draped over an upright stick, used as a temporary shelter. **[C20:** from HUTCH**]**

hut circle *n Archaeol.* a circle of earth or stones representing the site of a prehistoric hut.

hutment ('hʌtmənt) *n Chiefly military.* a number or group of huts.

Hutton ('hʌtᵊn) *n* **1 James.** 1726–97, Scottish geologist, regarded as the founder of modern geology. **2** Sir **Leonard,** known as *Len Hutton.* 1916–90, English cricketer; the first professional captain of England (1953).

Hutu ('huː,tuː) *n, pl* **-tu** *or* **-tus.** a member of a Negroid people of Rwanda and Burundi.

hutzpah ('xʊtspə) *n* a variant spelling of **chutzpah.**

Huxley ('hʌkslɪ) *n* **1 Aldous** (**Leonard**) ('ɔːldəs). 1894–1963, British novelist and essayist, noted particularly for his novel *Brave New World* (1932), depicting a scientifically controlled civilization of human robots. **2** his half-brother, Sir **Andrew Fielding,** born 1917, English biologist: noted for his research into nerve cells and the mechanism by which nerve impulses are transmitted; Nobel prize for physiology or medicine shared with Alan Hodgkin and John Eccles 1963; president of the Royal Society (1980–85). **3** brother of Aldous, Sir **Julian** (**Sorrel**). 1887–1975, English biologist; first director-general of UNESCO (1946–48). His works include *Essays of a Biologist* (1923) and *Evolution: the Modern Synthesis* (1942). **4** their grandfather, **Thomas Henry.** 1825–95, English biologist, the leading British exponent of Darwin's theory of evolution; his works include *Man's Place in Nature* (1863) and *Evolution and Ethics* (1893).

Hu Yaobang (xuː jau'bɑːŋ) *n* 1915–89, Chinese statesman; leader of the Chinese Communist Party (1981–87).

Huygens ('haɪgənz; *Dutch* 'hœixəns) *n* **Christiaan** ('kristiː,aːn). 1629–95, Dutch physicist: first formulated the wave theory of light.

Huygens' eyepiece *n Physics.* a telescope eyepiece consisting of two planoconvex lenses separated by a distance equal to half the sum of their focal lengths, which are in the ratio of three to one, and oriented so that their curved surfaces face the incident light. **[C19:** named after C. HUYGENS**]**

Huysmans (*French* ʁismɑ̃s) *n* **Joris Karl** (ʒɔris karl). 1848–1907, French novelist of the Decadent school, whose works include *À rebours* (1884).

huzzah (hə'zɑː) *interj, n, vb* an archaic word for **hurrah. [C16:** of unknown origin**]**

HV *or* **h.v.** *abbrev. for* high voltage.

HW *or* **h.w.** *abbrev. for:* **1** high water. **2** *Cricket.* hit wicket.

hwan (hwɑːn, wɑːn) *n* another name for **won**[2] (senses 1, 2). **[**Korean**]**

Hwange ('hwæŋgeɪ) *n* a town in W Zimbabwe: coal mines. Pop.: 40 000 (1989 est.). Former name (until 1982): **Wankie.**

Hwang Hai ('wæŋ 'haɪ) *n* a variant transliteration of the Chinese name for the **Yellow Sea.**

Hwang Ho ('wæŋ 'həʊ) *n* a variant transliteration of the Chinese name for the **Yellow River.**

HWM *abbrev. for* high-water mark.

hwyl ('huːɪl) *n* emotional fervour, as in the recitation of poetry. **[C19:** Welsh**]**

hyacinth ('haɪəsɪnθ) *n* **1** any liliaceous plant of the Mediterranean genus *Hyacinthus,* esp. any cultivated variety of *H. orientalis,* having a thick flower stalk bearing white, blue, or pink fragrant flowers. **2** the flower or bulb of such a plant. **3** any similar or related plant, such as the grape hyacinth. **4** Also called: **jacinth.** a red or reddish-brown transparent variety of the mineral zircon, used as a gemstone. **5** *Greek myth.* a flower which sprang from the blood of the dead Hyacinthus. **6** any of the varying colours of the hyacinth flower or stone. **[C16:** from Latin *hyacinthus,* from Greek *huakinthos***]** ► **hyacinthine** (,haɪə'sɪnθaɪn) *adj*

Hyacinthus (,haɪə'sɪnθəs) *n Greek myth.* a youth beloved of Apollo and inadvertently killed by him. At the spot where the youth died, Apollo caused a flower to grow.

Hyades[1] ('haɪə,diːz) *or* **Hyads** ('haɪædz) *pl n* an open cluster of stars in the constellation Taurus. Compare **Pleiades**[2]. **[C16:** via Latin from Greek *huades,* perhaps from *huein* to rain**]**

Hyades[2] ('haɪə,diːz) *pl n Greek myth.* seven nymphs, daughters of Atlas, whom Zeus placed among the stars after death.

hyaena (haɪ'iːnə) *n* a variant spelling of **hyena.** ► **hy'aenic** *adj*

hyalin ('haɪəlɪn) *n* glassy translucent substance, such as occurs in certain degenerative skin conditions or in hyaline cartilage.

hyaline ('haɪəlɪn) *adj* **1** *Biology.* clear and translucent, with no fibres or granules. **2** *Archaic.* transparent. ◆ *n* **3** *Archaic.* a glassy transparent surface. **[C17:** from Late Latin *hyalinus,* from Greek *hualinos* of glass, from *hualos* glass**]**

hyaline cartilage *n* a common type of cartilage with a translucent matrix containing little fibrous tissue.

hyalite ('haɪə,laɪt) *n* a clear and colourless variety of opal in globular form.

hyalo- *or before a vowel* **hyal-** *combining form.* of, relating to, or resembling glass: *hyaloplasm.* **[**from Greek *hualos* glass**]**

hyaloid ('haɪə,lɔɪd) *adj Anatomy, zoology.* clear and transparent; glassy; hyaline. **[C19:** from Greek *hualoeidēs***]**

hyaloid membrane *n* the delicate transparent membrane enclosing the vitreous humour of the eye.

hyaloplasm ('haɪələʊ,plæzəm) *n* the clear nongranular constituent of cell cytoplasm. ► **,hyalo'plasmic** *adj*

hyaluronic acid (,haɪəlʊ'rɒnɪk) *n* a viscous polysaccharide with important lubricating properties, present, for example, in the synovial fluid in joints. **[C20:** HYALO- + Greek *ouron* urine + -IC**]** ► **,hyalu'ronic** *adj*

hyaluronidase (,haɪəlʊ'rɒnɪ,deɪs, -,deɪz) *n* an enzyme that breaks down hyaluronic acid, thus decreasing the viscosity of the medium containing the acid. **[C20:** HYALO- + Greek *ouron* urine + -ID[3] + -ASE**]**

hybrid ('haɪbrɪd) *n* **1** an animal or plant resulting from a cross between genetically unlike individuals. Hybrids between different species are usually sterile. **2** anything of mixed ancestry. **3** a word, part of which is derived from one language and part from another, such as *monolingual,* which has a prefix of Greek origin and a root of Latin origin. ◆ *adj* **4** denoting or being a hybrid; of mixed origin. **5** *Physics.* (of an electromagnetic wave) having components of both electric and magnetic field vectors in the direction of propagation. **6** *Electronics.* **6a** (of a circuit) consisting of transistors and valves. **6b** (of an integrated circuit) consisting of one or more fully integrated circuits and other components, attached to a ceramic substrate. Compare **monolithic** (sense 3). **[C17:** from Latin *hibrida* offspring of a mixed union (human or animal)**]** ► **'hybridism** *n* ► **hy'bridity** *n*

hybrid antibody *n* a synthetic antibody that is able to combine with two different antigens.

hybrid bill *n* (in Parliament) a public bill to which the standing orders for private business apply; a bill having a general application as well as affecting certain private interests.

hybrid computer *n* a computer that uses both analogue and digital techniques.

hybridize *or* **hybridise** ('haɪbrɪ,daɪz) *vb* to produce or cause to produce hybrids; crossbreed. ► **'hybrid,izable** *or* **'hybrid,isable** *adj* ► **,hybridi'zation** *or* **,hybridi'sation** *n* ► **'hybrid,izer** *or* **'hybrid,iser** *n*

hybridoma (,haɪbrə'dəʊmə) *n* a hybrid cell formed by the fusion of two different types of cell, esp. one capable of producing antibodies, but of limited lifespan, fused with an immortal tumour cell. **[C20:** from HYBRID + -OMA**]**

hybrid rock *n* an igneous rock formed by molten magma incorporating preexisting rock through which it passes.

hybrid vigour *n Biology.* the increased size, strength, etc., of a hybrid as compared to either of its parents. Also called: **heterosis.**

hybris ('haɪbrɪs) *n* a variant of **hubris.** ► **hy'bristic** *adj*

hydantoin (haɪ'dæntəʊɪn) *n* a colourless odourless crystalline compound present in beet molasses: used in the manufacture of pharmaceuticals and synthetic resins. Formula: $C_3H_4N_2O_2$. **[C20:** from HYD(ROGEN + *all*)*antoin* product occurring in allantoic fluid**]**

hydathode ('haɪdə,θəʊd) *n* a pore in plants, esp. on the leaves, specialized for excreting water. **[C19:** from Greek, from *hudor* water + *hodos* way**]**

hydatid ('haɪdətɪd) *n* **1** a large bladder containing encysted larvae of the tapeworm *Echinococcus:* causes serious disease in man. **2** a sterile fluid-filled cyst produced in man and animals during infestation by *Echinococcus* larval forms. Also called: **hydatid cyst.** [C17: from Greek *hudatis* watery vesicle, from *hudōr, hudat-* water]

Hyde[1] (haɪd) *n* a town in NW England, in Tameside unitary authority, Greater Manchester; textiles, footwear, engineering. Pop.: 30 666 (1991).

Hyde[2] (haɪd) *n* **1 Douglas.** 1860–1949, Irish scholar and author; first president of Eire (1938–45). **2 Edward.** See (1st Earl of) **Clarendon.**

Hyde Park *n* a park in W central London: popular for open-air meetings.

Hyderabad (ˈhaɪdərəˌbɑːd, -ˌbæd, ˈhaɪdrə-) *n* **1** a city in S central India, capital of Andhra Pradesh state and capital of former Hyderabad state; university (1918). Pop.: 3 145 939 (1991). **2** a former state of S India: divided in 1956 between the states of Andhra Pradesh, Mysore, and Maharashtra. **3** a city in SW Pakistan, on the River Indus: seat of the University of Sind (1947). Pop.: 795 000 (latest est.).

Hyder Ali *or* **Haidar Ali** (ˈhaɪdər ˈɑːlɪ) *n* 1722–82, Indian ruler of Mysore (1766–82), who waged two wars against the British in India (1767–69; 1780–82).

hydnocarpate (ˌhɪdnəʊˈkɑːpeɪt) *n* any salt or ester of hydnocarpic acid.

hydnocarpic acid (ˌhɪdnəʊˈkɑːpɪk) *n* a cyclic fatty acid occurring in the form of its glycerides in chaulmoogra oil. Formula: $C_{16}H_{28}O_2$. [C20: from Greek *hudnon* truffle + *karpos* fruit + -IC]

hydr- *combining form.* a variant of **hydro-** before a vowel.

hydra (ˈhaɪdrə) *n, pl* **-dras** *or* **-drae** (-driː). **1** any solitary freshwater hydroid coelenterate of the genus *Hydra,* in which the body is a slender polyp with tentacles around the mouth. **2** a persistent trouble or evil: *the hydra of the Irish problem.* [C16: from Latin, from Greek *hudra* water serpent; compare OTTER]

Hydra[1] (ˈhaɪdrə) *n Greek myth.* a monster with nine heads, each of which, when struck off, was replaced by two new ones.

Hydra[2] (ˈhaɪdrə) *n, Latin genitive* **Hydrae** (ˈhaɪdriː). a very long faint constellation lying mainly in the S hemisphere and extending from near Virgo to Cancer.

hydracid (haɪˈdræsɪd) *n* an acid, such as hydrochloric acid, that does not contain oxygen.

hydragogue (ˈhaɪdrəˌgɒg) *n Med.* any purgative that causes evacuation of water from the bowels.

hydrangea (haɪˈdreɪndʒə) *n* any shrub or tree of the Asian and American genus *Hydrangea,* cultivated for their large clusters of white, pink, or blue flowers: family *Hydrangeaceae.* [C18: from New Latin, from Greek *hudōr* water + *angeion* vessel: probably from the cup-shaped fruit]

hydrant (ˈhaɪdrənt) *n* an outlet from a water main, usually consisting of an upright pipe with a valve attached, from which water can be tapped for fighting fires. See also **fire hydrant.** [C19: from HYDRO- + -ANT]

hydranth (ˈhaɪdrænθ) *n* a polyp in a colony of hydrozoan coelenterates that is specialized for feeding rather than reproduction. [C19: from HYDRA + Greek *anthos* flower]

hydrargyria (ˌhaɪdrɑːˈdʒɜːrɪə) *or* **hydrargyrism** (haɪˈdrɑːdʒɪrɪzəm) *n Med.* mercury poisoning. [C17: see HYDRARGYRUM]

hydrargyrum (haɪˈdrɑːdʒɪrəm) *n* an obsolete name for **mercury** (sense 1). [C16: from New Latin, from Latin *hydrargyrus* from Greek *hydrarguros,* from HYDRO- + *arguros* silver] ▸ **hydrargyric** (ˌhaɪdrɑːˈdʒɪrɪk) *adj*

hydrastine (haɪˈdræstiːn, -tɪn) *n* a white poisonous alkaloid extracted from the roots of the goldenseal: has been used in medicine (in the form of one of its water-soluble salts) to contract the uterus and arrest haemorrhage. Formula: $C_{21}H_{21}NO_6$. [C19: from HYDRAST(IS) + -INE[2]]

hydrastinine (haɪˈdræstɪˌniːn) *n* a colourless crystalline water-soluble compound whose pharmacological action resembles that of hydrastine. Formula: $C_{11}H_{13}NO_3$.

hydrastis (haɪˈdræstɪs) *n* any ranunculaceous plant of the genus *Hydrastis,* of Japan and E North America, such as goldenseal, having showy foliage and ornamental red fruits. [C18: New Latin, from Greek HYDRO- + *-astis,* of unknown origin]

hydrate (ˈhaɪdreɪt) *n* **1** a chemical compound containing water that is chemically combined with a substance and can usually be expelled without changing the constitution of the substance. **2** a chemical compound that can dissociate reversibly into water and another compound. For example sulphuric acid (H_2SO_4) dissociates into sulphur trioxide (SO_3) and water (H_2O). **3** (*not in technical usage*) a chemical compound, such as a carbohydrate, that contains hydrogen and oxygen atoms in the ratio two to one. ◆ *vb* **4** to undergo or cause to undergo treatment or impregnation with water. [C19: from HYDRO- + -ATE[1]] ▸ **hyˈdration** *n* ▸ **ˈhydrator** *n*

hydrated (ˈhaɪdreɪtɪd) *adj* (of a compound) chemically bonded to water molecules.

hydraulic (haɪˈdrɒlɪk) *adj* **1** operated by pressure transmitted through a pipe by a liquid, such as water or oil. **2** of, concerned with, or employing liquids in motion. **3** of or concerned with hydraulics. **4** hardening under water: *hydraulic cement.* [C17: from Latin *hydraulicus* of a water organ, from Greek *hudraulikos,* from *hudraulos* water organ, from HYDRO- + *aulos* pipe, reed instrument] ▸ **hyˈdraulically** *adv*

hydraulic brake *n* a type of brake, used in motor vehicles, in which the braking force is transmitted from the brake pedal to the brakes by a liquid under pressure.

hydraulic coupling *n* another name for **torque converter.**

hydraulic press *n* a press that utilizes liquid pressure to enable a small force applied to a small piston to produce a large force on a larger piston. The small piston moves through a proportionately greater distance than the larger.

hydraulic ram *n* **1** the larger or working piston of a hydraulic press. **2** a form of water pump utilizing the kinetic energy of running water to provide static pressure to raise water to a reservoir higher than the source.

hydraulics (haɪˈdrɒlɪks) *n* (*functioning as sing*) another name for **fluid mechanics.**

hydraulic suspension *n* a system of motor-vehicle suspension using hydraulic members, often with hydraulic compensation between front and rear systems (**hydroelastic suspension**).

hydrazide (ˈhaɪdrəˌzaɪd) *n* any of a class of chemical compounds that result when hydrogen in hydrazine or any of its derivatives is replaced by an acid radical.

hydrazine (ˈhaɪdrəˌziːn, -zɪn) *n* a colourless basic liquid made from sodium hypochlorite and ammonia: a strong reducing agent, used chiefly as a rocket fuel. Formula: N_2H_4. [C19: from HYDRO- + AZO- + -INE[2]]

hydrazoic acid (ˌhaɪdrəˈzəʊɪk) *n* a colourless highly explosive liquid. Formula: HN_3. See also **azide.**

hydria (ˈhaɪdrɪə) *n* (in ancient Greece and Rome) a large water jar. [C19: from Latin, from Greek *hudria,* from *hudōr* water]

hydric (ˈhaɪdrɪk) *adj* **1** of or containing hydrogen. **2** containing or using moisture.

hydride (ˈhaɪdraɪd) *n* any compound of hydrogen with another element, including ionic compounds such as sodium hydride (NaH), covalent compounds such as borane (B_2H_6), and the transition metal hydrides formed when certain metals, such as palladium, absorb hydrogen.

hydrilla (haɪˈdrɪlə) *n* any aquatic plant of the Eurasian genus *Hydrilla,* growing underwater and forming large masses: used as an oxygenator in aquaria and pools. It was introduced in the S U.S. where it has become a serious problem, choking fish and hindering navigation. [C20: New Latin, probably from HYDRA]

hydriodic acid (ˌhaɪdrɪˈɒdɪk) *n* the colourless or pale yellow aqueous solution of hydrogen iodide: a strong acid. [C19: from HYDRO- + IODIC]

hydro[1] (ˈhaɪdrəʊ) *n, pl* **-dros.** *Brit.* (esp. formerly) a hotel or resort, often near a spa, offering facilities for hydropathic treatment.

hydro[2] (ˈhaɪdrəʊ) *adj* **1** short for **hydroelectric.** ◆ *n* **2** a Canadian name for **electricity** as supplied to a residence, business, institution, etc.

hydro- *or sometimes before a vowel* **hydr-** *combining form.* **1** indicating or denoting water, liquid, or fluid: *hydrolysis; hydrodynamics.* **2** indicating the presence of hydrogen in a chemical compound: *hydrochloric acid.* **3** indicating a hydroid: *hydrozoan.* [from Greek *hudōr* water]

hydroacoustics (ˌhaɪdrəʊəˈkuːstɪks) *n* (*functioning as sing*) *Physics.* the study of sound travelling through water.

hydrobromic acid (ˌhaɪdrəʊˈbrəʊmɪk) *n* the colourless or faintly yellow aqueous solution of hydrogen bromide: a strong acid.

hydrocarbon (ˌhaɪdrəʊˈkɑːbᵊn) *n* any organic compound containing only carbon and hydrogen, such as the alkanes, alkenes, alkynes, terpenes, and arenes.

hydrocele (ˈhaɪdrəʊˌsiːl) *n* an abnormal collection of fluid in any saclike space, esp. around the testicles. [C16: from HYDRO- + -CELE]

hydrocellulose (ˌhaɪdrəʊˈsɛljʊˌləʊs, -ˌləʊz) *n* a gelatinous material consisting of hydrated cellulose, made by treating cellulose with water, acids, or alkalis: used in making paper, viscose rayon, and mercerized cotton.

hydrocephalus (ˌhaɪdrəʊˈsɛfələs) *or* **hydrocephaly** (ˌhaɪdrəʊˈsɛfəlɪ) *n* accumulation of cerebrospinal fluid within the ventricles of the brain because its normal outlet has been blocked by congenital malformation or disease. In infancy it usually results in great enlargement of the head. Nontechnical name: **water on the brain.** ▸ **hydrocephalic** (ˌhaɪdrəʊsɪˈfælɪk), **ˌhydroˈcephaloid,** *or* **ˌhydroˈcephalous** *adj*

hydrochloric acid (ˌhaɪdrəˈklɒrɪk) *n* the colourless or slightly yellow aqueous solution of hydrogen chloride: a strong acid used in many industrial and laboratory processes. Formerly called: **muriatic acid.**

hydrochloride (ˌhaɪdrəˈklɔːraɪd) *n* a quaternary salt formed by the addition of hydrochloric acid to an organic base, such as aniline hydrochloride, $[C_6H_5NH_3]^+ Cl^-$.

hydrocoral (ˌhaɪdrəˈkɒrəl) *or* **hydrocoralline** *n* any hydrozoan coelenterate of the order *Milleporina* (or *Hydrocorallinae*), which includes the millepores. [C20: from HYDRO- + CORAL]

hydrocortisone (ˌhaɪdrəʊˈkɔːtɪˌzəʊn) *n* the principal glucocorticoid secreted by the adrenal cortex; 17-hydroxycorticosterone. The synthesized form is used mainly in treating rheumatic, allergic, and inflammatory disorders. Formula: $C_{21}H_{30}O_5$. Also called: **cortisol.**

hydrocyanic acid (ˌhaɪdrəʊsaɪˈænɪk) *n* another name for **hydrogen cyanide,** esp. when in aqueous solution.

hydrodynamic (ˌhaɪdrəʊdaɪˈnæmɪk, -dɪ-) *or* **hydrodynamical** *adj* **1** of or concerned with the mechanical properties of fluids. **2** of or concerned with hydrodynamics. ▸ **ˌhydrodyˈnamically** *adv*

hydrodynamics (ˌhaɪdrəʊdaɪˈnæmɪks, -dɪ-) *n* **1** (*functioning as sing*) the branch of science concerned with the mechanical properties of fluids, esp. liquids. Also called: **hydromechanics.** See also **hydrokinetics, hydrostatics. 2** another name for **hydrokinetics.**

hydroelastic suspension (ˌhaɪdrəʊɪˈlæstɪk) *n* See **hydraulic suspension.**

hydroelectric (ˌhaɪdrəʊɪˈlɛktrɪk) *adj* **1** generated by the pressure of falling water: *hydroelectric power.* **2** of or concerned with the generation of electricity by water pressure: *a hydroelectric scheme.* ▸ **hydroelectricity** (ˌhaɪdrəʊɪlɛkˈtrɪsɪtɪ, -ˌiːlɛk-) *n*

hydrofluoric acid (ˌhaɪdrəʊfluːˈɒrɪk) *n* the colourless aqueous solution of hydrogen fluoride: a strong acid that attacks glass.

hydrofoil (ˈhaɪdrəˌfɔɪl) *n* **1** a fast light vessel the hull of which is raised out of the water on one or more pairs of fixed vanes. **2** any of these vanes.

hydroforming (ˈhaɪdrəʊˌfɔːmɪŋ) *n Chem.* **1** the catalytic reforming of petroleum to increase the proportion of aromatic and branched-chain hydrocarbons. **2** *Engineering.* a forming process in which a metal component is shaped by a metal punch forced against a die, consisting of a flexible bag containing a fluid.

hydrogel ('haɪdrəˌdʒɛl) *n* a gel in which the liquid constituent is water.

hydrogen ('haɪdrɪdʒən) *n* **a** a flammable colourless gas that is the lightest and most abundant element in the universe. It occurs mainly in water and in most organic compounds and is used in the production of ammonia and other chemicals, in the hydrogenation of fats and oils, and in welding. Symbol: H; atomic no.: 1; atomic wt.: 1.00794; valency: 1; density: 0.08988 kg/m^3; melting pt.: –259.34°C; boiling pt.: –252.87°C. See also **deuterium, tritium. b** (*as modifier*): *hydrogen bomb.* [C18: from French *hydrogène,* from HYDRO- + -GEN; so called because its combustion produces water]

hydrogenate ('haɪdrədʒɪˌneɪt, haɪ'drɒdʒɪˌneɪt), **hydrogenize,** *or* **hydrogenise** ('haɪdrədʒɪˌnaɪz, haɪ'drɒdʒɪˌnaɪz) *vb* to undergo or cause to undergo a reaction with hydrogen: *to hydrogenate ethylene.* ▸ **ˌhydrogen'ation, ˌhydrogeni'zation,** *or* **ˌhydrogeni'sation** *n* ▸ **'hydrogenˌator** *n*

hydrogen bomb *n* a type of bomb in which energy is released by fusion of hydrogen nuclei to give helium nuclei. The energy required to initiate the fusion is provided by the detonation of an atomic bomb, which is surrounded by a hydrogen-containing substance such as lithium deuteride. Also called: **H-bomb.** See also **fusion bomb.**

hydrogen bond *n* a weak chemical bond between an electronegative atom, such as fluorine, oxygen, or nitrogen, and a hydrogen atom bound to another electronegative atom. Hydrogen bonds are responsible for the properties of water and many biological molecules.

hydrogen bromide *n* **1** a colourless pungent gas used in organic synthesis. Formula: HBr. **2** an aqueous solution of hydrogen bromide; hydrobromic acid.

hydrogen carbonate *n* another name for **bicarbonate.**

hydrogen chloride *n* **1** a colourless pungent corrosive gas obtained by the action of sulphuric acid on sodium chloride: used in making vinyl chloride and other organic chemicals. Formula: HCl. **2** an aqueous solution of hydrogen chloride; hydrochloric acid.

hydrogen cyanide *n* a colourless poisonous liquid with a faint odour of bitter almonds, usually made by a catalysed reaction between ammonia, oxygen, and methane. It forms prussic acid in aqueous solution and is used for making plastics and dyes and as a war gas. Formula: HCN. Also called: **hydrocyanic acid.**

hydrogen embrittlement (ɪm'brɪtᵊlmənt) *n Engineering.* the weakening of metal by the sorption of hydrogen during a pickling process, such as that used in plating.

hydrogen fluoride *n* **1** a colourless poisonous corrosive gas or liquid made by reaction between calcium fluoride and sulphuric acid: used as a fluorinating agent and catalyst. Formula: HF. **2** an aqueous solution of hydrogen fluoride; hydrofluoric acid.

hydrogen iodide *n* **1** a colourless poisonous corrosive gas obtained by a catalysed reaction between hydrogen and iodine vapour: used in making iodides. Formula: HI. **2** an aqueous solution of this gas; hydriodic acid.

hydrogen ion *n* **1** an ionized hydrogen atom, occurring in plasmas and in aqueous solutions of acids, in which it is solvated by one or more water molecules; proton. Formula: H^+ **2** an ionized hydrogen molecule; hydrogen molecular ion. Formula: H_2^+

hydrogenize *or* **hydrogenise** ('haɪdrədʒɪˌnaɪz, haɪ'drɒdʒɪˌnaɪz) *vb* variants of **hydrogenate.** ▸ **ˌhydrogeni'zation** *or* **ˌhydrogeni'sation** *n*

hydrogenolysis (ˌhaɪdrəʊdʒɪ'nɒlɪsɪs) *n* a chemical reaction in which a compound is decomposed by hydrogen.

hydrogenous (haɪ'drɒdʒɪnəs) *adj* of or containing hydrogen.

hydrogen peroxide *n* a colourless oily unstable liquid, usually used in aqueous solution. It is a strong oxidizing agent used as a bleach for textiles, wood pulp, hair, etc., and as an oxidizer in rocket fuels. Formula: H_2O_2.

hydrogen sulphate *n* another name for **bisulphate.**

hydrogen sulphide *n* a colourless poisonous soluble flammable gas with an odour of rotten eggs: used as a reagent in chemical analysis. Formula: H_2S. Also called: **sulphuretted hydrogen.**

hydrogen sulphite *n* another name for **bisulphite.**

hydrogen tartrate *n* another name for **bitartrate.**

hydrogeology (ˌhaɪdrədʒɪ'ɒlədʒɪ) *n* the branch of geology dealing with the waters below the earth's surface and with the geological aspects of surface waters. ▸ **ˌhydrogeo'logical** *adj* ▸ **ˌhydroge'ologist** *n*

hydrograph ('haɪdrəˌgrɑːf, -ˌgræf) *n* a graph showing the seasonal variation in the level, velocity, or discharge of a body of water.

hydrography (haɪ'drɒgrəfɪ) *n* **1** the study, surveying, and mapping of the oceans, seas, and rivers. Compare **hydrology. 2** the oceans, seas, and rivers as represented on a chart. ▸ **hy'drographer** *n* ▸ **hydrographic** (ˌhaɪdrə'græfɪk) *or* **ˌhydro'graphical** *adj* ▸ **ˌhydro'graphically** *adv*

hydroid ('haɪdrɔɪd) *adj* **1** of or relating to the *Hydroida,* an order of colonial hydrozoan coelenterates that have the polyp phase dominant. **2** (of coelenterate colonies or individuals) having or consisting of hydra-like polyps. ♦ *n* **3** a hydroid colony or individual. [C19: from HYDRA + -OID]

hydrokinetic (ˌhaɪdrəʊkɪ'nɛtɪk, -kaɪ-) *or* **hydrokinetical** *adj* **1** of or concerned with fluids that are in motion. **2** of or concerned with hydrokinetics.

hydrokinetics (ˌhaɪdrəʊkɪ'nɛtɪks, -kaɪ-) *n* (*functioning as sing*) the branch of science concerned with the mechanical behaviour and properties of fluids in motion, esp. of liquids. Also called: **hydrodynamics.**

hydrolase ('haɪdrəˌleɪz) *n* an enzyme, such as an esterase, that controls hydrolysis.

hydrologic cycle *n* another name for **water cycle.**

hydrology (haɪ'drɒlədʒɪ) *n* the study of the distribution, conservation, use, etc., of the water of the earth and its atmosphere. ▸ **hydrologic** (ˌhaɪdrə'lɒdʒɪk) *or* **ˌhydro'logical** *adj* ▸ **ˌhydro'logically** *adv* ▸ **hy'drologist** *n*

hydrolysate (haɪ'drɒlɪˌseɪt) *n* a substance or mixture produced by hydrolysis. [C20: from HYDROLYSIS + -ATE[1]]

hydrolyse *or U.S.* **hydrolyze** ('haɪdrəˌlaɪz) *vb* to subject to or undergo hydrolysis. ▸ **'hydroˌlysable** *or U.S.* **'hydroˌlyzable** *adj* ▸ **ˌhydroly'sation** *or U.S.* **ˌhydroly'zation** *n* ▸ **'hydroˌlyser** *or U.S.* **'hydroˌlyzer** *n*

hydrolysis (haɪ'drɒlɪsɪs) *n* a chemical reaction in which a compound reacts with water to produce other compounds.

hydrolyte ('haɪdrəˌlaɪt) *n* a substance subjected to hydrolysis.

hydrolytic (ˌhaɪdrə'lɪtɪk) *adj* of, concerned with, producing, or produced by hydrolysis.

hydromagnetics (ˌhaɪdrəʊmæg'nɛtɪks) *n* another name for **magnetohydrodynamics.** ▸ **ˌhydromag'netic** *adj*

hydromancy ('haɪdrəʊˌmænsɪ) *n* divination by water. ▸ **'hydroˌmancer** *n* ▸ **ˌhydro'mantic** *adj*

hydromechanics (ˌhaɪdrəʊmɪ'kænɪks) *n* another name for **hydrodynamics.** ▸ **ˌhydrome'chanical** *adj*

hydromedusa (ˌhaɪdrəʊmɪ'djuːsə) *n, pl* **-sas** *or* **-sae** (-siː). the medusa form of hydrozoan coelenterates. ▸ **ˌhydrome'dusan** *adj*

hydromel ('haɪdrəʊˌmɛl) *n Archaic.* another word for **mead** (the drink). [C15: from Latin, from Greek *hudromeli,* from HYDRO- + *meli* honey]

hydrometallurgy (ˌhaɪdrəʊ'mɛtᵊˌlɜːdʒɪ, -mɛ'tælədʒɪ) *n* a technique for the recovery of a metal from an aqueous medium in which the metal or the gangue is preferentially dissolved. ▸ **ˌhydroˌmetal'lurgical** *adj*

hydrometeor (ˌhaɪdrəʊ'miːtɪə) *n* any weather condition produced by water in the atmosphere, such as rain or snow. ▸ **ˌhydroˌmeteoro'logical** *adj* ▸ **ˌhydroˌmeteor'ology** *n*

hydrometer (haɪ'drɒmɪtə) *n* an instrument for measuring the relative density of a liquid, usually consisting of a sealed graduated tube with a weighted bulb on one end, the relative density being indicated by the length of the unsubmerged stem. ▸ **hydrometric** (ˌhaɪdrəʊ'mɛtrɪk) *or* **ˌhydro'metrical** *adj* ▸ **ˌhydro'metrically** *adv* ▸ **hy'drometry** *n*

hydronaut ('haɪdrəʊˌnɔːt) *n U.S. Navy.* a person trained to operate deep submergence vessels. [C20: from Greek, from HYDRO- + *-naut,* as in *aeronaut, astronaut*]

hydronium ion (haɪ'drəʊnɪəm) *n Chem.* another name for **hydroxonium ion.** [C20: from HYDRO- + (AMM)ONIUM]

hydropathy (haɪ'drɒpəθɪ) *n* a pseudoscientific method of treating disease by the use of large quantities of water both internally and externally. Also called: **water cure.** Compare **hydrotherapy.** ▸ **hydropathic** (ˌhaɪdrəʊ'pæθɪk) *or* **ˌhydro'pathical** *adj* ▸ **hy'dropathist** *or* **'hydroˌpath** *n*

hydrophane ('haɪdrəʊˌfeɪn) *n* a white partially opaque variety of opal that becomes translucent in water. ▸ **hydrophanous** (haɪ'drɒfənəs) *adj*

hydrophilic (ˌhaɪdrəʊ'fɪlɪk) *adj Chem.* tending to dissolve in, mix with, or be wetted by water: *a hydrophilic colloid.* Compare **hydrophobic.** ▸ **'hydroˌphile** *n*

hydrophilous (haɪ'drɒfɪləs) *adj Botany.* growing in or pollinated by water. ▸ **hy'drophily** *n*

hydrophobia (ˌhaɪdrə'fəʊbɪə) *n* **1** another name for **rabies. 2** a fear of drinking fluids, esp. that of a person with rabies, because of painful spasms when trying to swallow. Compare **aquaphobia.**

hydrophobic (ˌhaɪdrə'fəʊbɪk) *adj* **1** of or relating to hydrophobia. **2** *Chem.* tending not to dissolve in, mix with, or be wetted by water: *a hydrophobic colloid.* Compare **hydrophilic.**

hydrophone ('haɪdrəˌfəʊn) *n* an electroacoustic transducer that converts sound or ultrasonic waves travelling through water into electrical oscillations.

hydrophyte ('haɪdrəʊˌfaɪt) *n* a plant that grows only in water or very moist soil. ▸ **hydrophytic** (ˌhaɪdrəʊ'fɪtɪk) *adj*

hydroplane ('haɪdrəʊˌpleɪn) *n* **1** a motorboat equipped with hydrofoils or with a shaped bottom that raises its hull out of the water at high speeds. **2** an attachment to an aircraft to enable it to glide along the surface of water. **3** another name (esp. U.S.) for a **seaplane. 4** a horizontal vane on the hull of a submarine for controlling its vertical motion. ♦ *vb* **5** (*intr*) (of a boat) to rise out of the water in the manner of a hydroplane.

hydroponics (ˌhaɪdrəʊ'pɒnɪks) *n* (*functioning as sing*) a method of cultivating plants by growing them in gravel, etc., through which water containing dissolved inorganic nutrient salts is pumped. Also called: **aquiculture.** [C20: from HYDRO- + (GEO)PONICS] ▸ **ˌhydro'ponic** *adj* ▸ **ˌhydro'ponically** *adv*

hydropower ('haɪdrəʊˌpaʊə) *n* hydroelectric power.

hydroquinone (ˌhaɪdrəʊkwɪ'nəʊn) *or* **hydroquinol** (ˌhaɪdrəʊ'kwɪnɒl) *n* a white crystalline soluble phenol used as a photographic developer; 1,4-dihydroxybenzene. Formula: $C_6H_4(OH)_2$. Also called: **quinol.**

hydroscope ('haɪdrəˌskəʊp) *n* any instrument for making observations of underwater objects. ▸ **hydroscopic** (ˌhaɪdrə'skɒpɪk) *or* **ˌhydro'scopical** *adj*

hydrosere ('haɪdrəʊsɪə) *n* a sere that begins in an aquatic environment.

hydroski ('haɪdrəʊˌskiː) *n* a hydrofoil used on some seaplanes to provide extra lift when taking off.

hydrosol ('haɪdrəˌsɒl) *n Chem.* a sol that has water as its liquid phase.

hydrosome ('haɪdrəˌsəʊm) *or* **hydrosoma** (ˌhaɪdrə'səʊmə) *n Zoology.* the body of a colonial hydrozoan. [C19: from *hydro-,* from HYDRA + -SOME[3]]

hydrosphere ('haɪdrəˌsfɪə) *n* the watery part of the earth's surface, including oceans, lakes, water vapour in the atmosphere, etc. ▸ **ˌhydro'spheric** *adj*

hydrostat ('haɪdrəʊˌstæt) *n* a device that detects the presence of water as a prevention against drying out, overflow, etc., esp. one used as a warning in a steam boiler.

hydrostatic (ˌhaɪdrəʊ'stætɪk) *or* **hydrostatical** *adj* **1** of or concerned with fluids that are not in motion: *hydrostatic pressure.* **2** of or concerned with hydrostatics. ▸ **ˌhydro'statically** *adv*

hydrostatic balance *n* a balance for finding the weight of an object submerged in water in order to determine the upthrust on it and thus determine its relative density.

hydrostatics (ˌhaɪdrəʊˈstætɪks) *n* (*functioning as sing*) the branch of science concerned with the mechanical properties and behaviour of fluids that are not in motion. See also **hydrodynamics.**

hydrosulphate (ˌhaɪdrəʊˈsʌlfeɪt) *n* any quaternary acid salt formed by addition of an organic base to sulphuric acid, such as aniline hydrosulphate, $C_6H_5NH_3HSO_4$.

hydrosulphide (ˌhaɪdrəʊˈsʌlfaɪd) *n* any salt derived from hydrogen sulphide by replacing one of its hydrogen atoms with a metal atom. Technical name: **hydrogen sulphide.**

hydrosulphite (ˌhaɪdrəʊˈsʌlfaɪt) *n* another name (not in technical usage) for **dithionite.** [C20: from HYDROSULPH(UROUS) + -ITE[2]]

hydrosulphurous acid (ˌhaɪdrəʊˈsʌlfərəs) *n* another name (not in technical usage) for **dithionous acid.**

hydrotaxis (ˌhaɪdrəʊˈtæksɪs) *n* the directional movement of an organism or cell in response to the stimulus of water. ▸ ˌ**hydroˈtactic** *adj*

hydrotherapeutics (ˌhaɪdrəʊˌθerəˈpjuːtɪks) *n* (*functioning as sing*) the branch of medical science concerned with hydrotherapy. ▸ ˌ**hydroˌtheraˈpeutic** *adj*

hydrotherapy (ˌhaɪdrəʊˈθerəpɪ) *n Med.* the treatment of certain diseases by the external use of water, esp. by exercising in water in order to mobilize stiff joints or strengthen weakened muscles. Also called: **water cure.** Compare **hydropathy.** ▸ **hydrotherapic** (ˌhaɪdrəʊθɪˈræpɪk) *adj* ▸ ˌ**hydroˈtherapist** *n*

hydrothermal (ˌhaɪdrəʊˈθɜːməl) *adj* of or relating to the action of water under conditions of high temperature, esp. in forming rocks and minerals. ▸ ˌ**hydroˈthermally** *adv*

hydrothorax (ˌhaɪdrəʊˈθɔːræks) *n Pathol.* an accumulation of fluid in one or both pleural cavities, often resulting from disease of the heart or kidneys. ▸ **hydrothoracic** (ˌhaɪdrəʊθɔːˈræsɪk) *adj*

hydrotropism (haɪˈdrɒtrəˌpɪzəm) *n* the directional growth of plants in response to the stimulus of water. ▸ **hydrotropic** (ˌhaɪdrəʊˈtrɒpɪk) *adj* ▸ ˌ**hydroˈtropically** *adv*

hydrous (ˈhaɪdrəs) *adj* **1** containing water. **2** (of a chemical compound) combined with water molecules: *hydrous copper sulphate,* $CuSO_4.5H_2O$.

hydrovane (ˈhaɪdrəʊˌveɪn) *n* a vane on a seaplane conferring stability on water (a sponson) or facilitating take off (a hydrofoil).

hydroxide (haɪˈdrɒksaɪd) *n* **1** a base or alkali containing the ion OH^-. **2** any compound containing an -OH group.

hydroxonium ion (ˌhaɪdrɒkˈsəʊnɪəm) *n* a positive ion, H_3O^+, formed by the attachment of a proton to a water molecule: occurs in solutions of acids and behaves like a hydrogen ion. Also called: **hydronium ion.**

hydroxy (haɪˈdrɒksɪ) *adj* (of a chemical compound) containing one or more hydroxyl groups. [C19: HYDRO- + OXY(GEN)]

hydroxy- *combining form.* (in chemical compounds) indicating the presence of one or more hydroxyl groups or ions. [from HYDRO- + OXY(GEN)]

hydroxy acid *n* **1** any acid, such as sulphuric acid, containing hydroxyl groups in its molecules. **2** any of a class of carboxylic acids that contain both a hydroxyl group and a carboxyl group in their molecules.

hydroxyl (haɪˈdrɒksɪl) *n* (*modifier*) of, consisting of, or containing the monovalent group -OH or the ion OH^-: *a hydroxyl group or radical.* ▸ ˌ**hydroxˈylic** *adj*

hydroxylamine (haɪˌdrɒksɪləˈmiːn, -ˈæmɪn, -ˈsaɪləˌmiːn) *n* a colourless crystalline compound that explodes when heated: a reducing agent. Formula: NH_2OH.

hydroxyproline (haɪˌdrɒksɪˈprəʊliːn, -lɪn) *n* an amino acid occurring in some proteins, esp. collagen. Formula: $(OH)C_4H_7N(COOH)$.

hydroxytryptamine (haɪˌdrɒksɪˈtrɪptəmiːn) *n* 5-hydroxytryptamine: another name for **serotonin.** Abbrev.: **5HT.**

hydrozoan (ˌhaɪdrəʊˈzəʊən) *n* **1** any colonial or solitary coelenterate of the class *Hydrozoa,* which includes the hydra, Portuguese man-of-war, and the sertularians. ◆ *adj* **2** of, relating to, or belonging to the *Hydrozoa.*

Hydrus (ˈhaɪdrəs) *n, Latin genitive* **Hydri** (ˈhaɪdraɪ). a constellation near the S celestial pole lying close to Eridanus and Tucana and containing part of the Small Magellanic cloud. [C17: from Latin, from Greek *hudros* water serpent, from *hudōr* water]

hyena *or* **hyaena** (haɪˈiːnə) *n* any of several long-legged carnivorous doglike mammals of the genera *Hyaena* and *Crocuta,* such as *C. crocuta* (**spotted** or **laughing hyena**), of Africa and S Asia: family *Hyaenidae,* order *Carnivora* (carnivores). See also **strandwolf.** [C16: from Medieval Latin, from Latin *hyaena,* from Greek *huaina,* from *hus* hog] ▸ **hyˈenic** *or* **hyˈaenic** *adj*

hyetal (ˈhaɪɪtᵊl) *adj* of or relating to rain, rainfall, or rainy regions. [C19: from Greek *huetos* rain + -AL[1]]

hyeto- *or before a vowel* **hyet-** *combining form.* indicating rain. [from Greek *huetos*]

hyetograph (ˈhaɪɪtəˌgrɑːf, -ˌgræf) *n* **1** a chart showing the distribution of rainfall of a particular area, usually throughout a year. **2** a self-recording rain gauge.

hyetography (ˌhaɪɪˈtɒgrəfɪ) *n* the study of the distribution and recording of rainfall. ▸ **hyetographic** (ˌhaɪɪtəˈgræfɪk) *or* ˌ**hyetoˈgraphical** *adj* ▸ ˌ**hyetoˈgraphically** *adv*

Hygeia (haɪˈdʒiːə) *n* the Greek goddess of health. ▸ **Hyˈgeian** *adj*

hygiene (ˈhaɪdʒiːn) *n* **1** Also called: **hygienics.** the science concerned with the maintenance of health. **2** clean or healthy practices or thinking: *personal hygiene.* [C18: from New Latin *hygiēna,* from Greek *hugieinē,* from *hugieinos* healthful, from *hugiēs* healthy]

hygienic (haɪˈdʒiːnɪk) *adj* promoting health or cleanliness; sanitary. ▸ **hyˈgienically** *adv*

hygienics (haɪˈdʒiːnɪks) *n* (*functioning as sing*) another word for **hygiene** (sense 1).

hygienist (ˈhaɪdʒiːnɪst), **hygeist,** *or* **hygieist** (ˈhaɪdʒiːɪst) *n* a person skilled in the practice of hygiene. See also **dental hygienist.**

hygristor (haɪˈgrɪstə) *n* an electronic component the resistance of which varies with humidity. [C20: from HYGRO- + (RES)ISTOR]

hygro- *or before a vowel* **hygr-** *combining form.* indicating moisture: *hygrometer.* [from Greek *hugros* wet]

hygrograph (ˈhaɪgrəˌgrɑːf, -ˌgræf) *n* an automatic hygrometer that produces a graphic record of the humidity of the air.

hygrometer (haɪˈgrɒmɪtə) *n* any of various instruments for measuring humidity. ▸ **hygrometric** (ˌhaɪgrəˈmɛtrɪk) *adj* ▸ ˌ**hygroˈmetrically** *adv* ▸ **hyˈgrometry** *n*

hygrophilous (haɪˈgrɒfɪləs) *adj* (of a plant) growing in moist places. ▸ **hygrophile** (ˈhaɪgrəʊˌfaɪl) *n*

hygrophyte (ˈhaɪgrəˌfaɪt) *n* any plant that grows in wet or waterlogged soil. ▸ **hygrophytic** (ˌhaɪgrəˈfɪtɪk) *adj*

hygroscope (ˈhaɪgrəˌskəʊp) *n* any device that indicates the humidity of the air without necessarily measuring it.

hygroscopic (ˌhaɪgrəˈskɒpɪk) *adj* (of a substance) tending to absorb water from the air. ▸ ˌ**hygroˈscopically** *adv* ▸ **hygroscopicity** (ˌhaɪgrəskəʊˈpɪsɪtɪ) *n*

hygrostat (ˈhaɪgrəˌstæt) *n* another name for **humidistat.**

hying (ˈhaɪɪŋ) *vb* a present participle of **hie.**

Hyksos (ˈhɪksɒs) *n, pl* **-sos.** a member of a nomadic Asian people, probably Semites, who controlled Egypt from 1720 B.C. until 1560 B.C. [from Greek *Huksōs* name of ruling dynasty in Egypt, from Egyptian *hq'sʼsw* ruler of the lands of the nomads]

hyla (ˈhaɪlə) *n* any tree frog of the genus *Hyla,* such as *H. leucophyllata* (**white-spotted hyla**) of tropical America. [C19: from New Latin, from Greek *hulē* forest, wood]

hylo- *or before a vowel* **hyl-** *combining form.* **1** indicating matter (as distinguished from spirit): *hylozoism.* **2** indicating wood: *hylophagous.* [from Greek *hulē* wood]

hylomorphism (ˌhaɪləˈmɔːfɪzəm) *n* the philosophical doctrine that identifies matter with the first cause of the universe.

hylophagous (haɪˈlɒfəgəs) *adj* (esp. of insects) feeding on wood. [C19: from Greek *hulophagos,* from *hulē* wood + *phagein* to devour]

hylotheism (ˌhaɪləˈθiːɪzəm) *n* the doctrine that God is identical to matter.

hylozoism (ˌhaɪləˈzəʊɪzəm) *n* the philosophical doctrine that life is one of the properties of matter. [C17: HYLO- + Greek *zōē* life] ▸ ˌ**hyloˈzoic** *adj* ▸ ˌ**hyloˈzoist** *n* ▸ ˌ**hylozoˈistic** *adj* ▸ ˌ**hylozoˈistically** *adv*

hymen (ˈhaɪmɛn) *n Anatomy.* a fold of mucous membrane that partly covers the entrance to the vagina and is usually ruptured when sexual intercourse takes place for the first time. [C17: from Greek: membrane] ▸ **ˈhymenal** *adj*

Hymen (ˈhaɪmɛn) *n* the Greek and Roman god of marriage.

hymeneal (ˌhaɪmɛˈniːəl) *adj* **1** *Chiefly poetic.* of or relating to marriage. ◆ *n* **2** a wedding song or poem.

hymenium (haɪˈmiːnɪəm) *n, pl* **-nia** (-nɪə) *or* **-niums.** (in basidiomycetous and ascomycetous fungi) a layer of cells some of which produce the spores.

hymenophore (haɪˈmiːnəʊˌfɔː) *n Botany.* the fruiting body of some basidiomycetous fungi. [from HYMENIUM + -PHORE]

hymenopteran (ˌhaɪmɪˈnɒptərən) *or* **hymenopteron** *n, pl* **-terans, -tera** (-tərə), *or* **-terons.** any hymenopterous insect.

hymenopterous (ˌhaɪmɪˈnɒptərəs) *or* **hymenopteran** *adj* of, relating to, or belonging to the *Hymenoptera,* an order of insects, including bees, wasps, ants, and sawflies, having two pairs of membranous wings and an ovipositor specialized for stinging, sawing, or piercing. [C19: from Greek *humenopteros* membrane wing; see HYMEN, -PTEROUS]

Hymettus (haɪˈmɛtəs) *n* a mountain in SE Greece, in Attica east of Athens: famous for its marble and for honey. Height: 1032 m (3386 ft.). Modern Greek name: **Imittós.** ▸ **Hyˈmettian** *or* **Hyˈmettic** *adj*

hymn (hɪm) *n* **1** a Christian song of praise sung to God or a saint. **2** a similar song praising other gods, a nation, etc. ◆ *vb* **3** to express (praises, thanks, etc.) by singing hymns. [C13: from Latin *hymnus,* from Greek *humnos*] ▸ **hymnic** (ˈhɪmnɪk) *adj* ▸ **ˈhymnˌlike** *adj*

hymnal (ˈhɪmnᵊl) *n* **1** a book of hymns. ◆ *adj* **2** of, relating to, or characteristic of hymns.

hymn book *n* a book containing the words and music of hymns.

hymnist (ˈhɪmnɪst), **hymnodist** (ˈhɪmnədɪst), *or* **hymnographer** (hɪmˈnɒgrəfə) *n* a person who composes hymns.

hymnody (ˈhɪmnədɪ) *n* **1** the composition or singing of hymns. **2** hymns collectively. ◆ Also called: **hymnology.** [C18: from Medieval Latin *hymnōdia,* from Greek *humnōidia,* from *humnōidein* to chant a hymn, from HYMN + *aeidein* to sing] ▸ **hymnodical** (hɪmˈnɒdɪkᵊl) *adj*

hymnology (hɪmˈnɒlədʒɪ) *n* **1** the study of hymn composition. **2** another word for **hymnody.** ▸ **hymnologic** (ˌhɪmnəˈlɒdʒɪk) *or* ˌ**hymnoˈlogical** *adj* ▸ **hymˈnologist** *n*

hyoid (ˈhaɪɔɪd) *adj also* **hyoidal** *or* **hyoidean. 1** of or relating to the hyoid bone. ◆ *n also* **hyoid bone. 2** the horseshoe-shaped bone that lies at the base of the tongue and above the thyroid cartilage. **3** a corresponding bone or group of bones in other vertebrates. [C19: from New Latin *hyoīdes,* from Greek *huoeidēs* having the shape of the letter UPSILON, from *hu* upsilon + -OID]

hyoscine (ˈhaɪəˌsiːn) *n* another name for **scopolamine.** [C19: from HYOSC(YAMUS) + -INE[2]]

hyoscyamine (ˌhaɪəˈsaɪəˌmiːn, -mɪn) *n* a poisonous alkaloid occurring in henbane and related plants: an optically active isomer of atropine, used in medicine in a similar way. Formula: $C_{17}H_{23}NO_3$.

hyoscyamus (ˌhaɪəˈsaɪəməs) *n* any plant of the solanaceous genus *Hyoscyamus,* of Europe, Asia, and N Africa, including henbane. **[C18:** from New Latin, from Greek *huoskuamos,* from *hus* pig + *kuamos* bean; the plant was thought to be poisonous to pigs**]**

hyp. *abbrev. for:* **1** hypotenuse. **2** hypothesis. **3** hypothetical.

hyp- *prefix* a variant of **hypo-** before a vowel: *hypabyssal.*

hypabyssal (ˌhɪpəˈbɪsᵊl) *adj* (of igneous rocks) derived from magma that has solidified close to the surface of the earth in the form of dykes, sills, etc.

hypaesthesia *or U.S.* **hypesthesia** (ˌhɪpiːsˈθiːzɪə, ˌhaɪ-) *n Pathol.* a reduced sensibility to touch. ► **hypaesthesic** *or U.S.* **hypesthesic** (ˌhɪpiːsˈθiːsɪk, ˌhaɪ-) *adj*

hypaethral *or U.S.* **hypethral** (hɪˈpiːθrəl, haɪ-) *adj* (esp. of a classical temple) having no roof. **[C18:** from Latin *hypaethrus* uncovered, from Greek *hupaithros,* from HYPO- + *aithros* clear sky**]**

hypalgesia (ˌhaɪpælˈdʒiːzɪə, -sɪə) *n Pathol.* diminished sensitivity to pain. ► **ˌhypalˈgesic** *adj*

hypallage (haɪˈpæləˌdʒiː) *n Rhetoric.* a figure of speech in which the natural relations of two words in a statement are interchanged, as in *the fire spread the wind.* **[C16:** via Late Latin from Greek *hupallagē* interchange, from HYPO- + *allassein* to exchange**]**

hypanthium (haɪˈpænθɪəm) *n, pl* **-thia** (-θɪə). *Botany.* the cup-shaped or flat receptacle of perigynous flowers. **[C19:** from New Latin, from HYPO- + Greek *anthion* a little flower, from *anthos* flower**]** ► **hyˈpanthial** *adj*

Hypatia (haɪˈpeɪʃɪə) *n* died 415 A.D., **Neo-Platonist** philosopher and politician, who lectured at Alexandria. She was murdered by a Christian mob.

hype[1] (haɪp) *Slang.* ◆ *n* **1** a hypodermic needle or injection. ◆ *vb* **2** (*intr;* usually foll. by *up*) to inject oneself with a drug. **3** (*tr*) to stimulate artificially or excite. **[C20:** shortened from HYPODERMIC**]**

hype[2] (haɪp) *n* **1** a deception or racket. **2** intensive or exaggerated publicity or sales promotion: *media hype.* **3** the person or thing so publicized. ◆ *vb* (*tr*) **4** to market or promote (a product) using exaggerated or intensive publicity. **5** to falsify or rig (something). **6** (in the pop-music business) to buy (copies of a particular record) in such quantity as to increase its ratings in the charts. **[C20:** of unknown origin**]** ► **ˈhyper** *n* ► **ˈhyping** *n*

hyped up *adj Slang.* stimulated or excited by or as if by the effect of a stimulating drug.

hyper (ˈhaɪpə) *adj Informal.* overactive; overexcited. **[C20:** probably independent use of HYPER-**]**

hyper- *prefix* **1** above, over, or in excess: *hypercritical.* **2** (in medicine) denoting an abnormal excess: *hyperacidity.* **3** indicating that a chemical compound contains a greater than usual amount of an element: *hyperoxide.* **[**from Greek *huper* over**]**

hyperacidity (ˌhaɪpərəˈsɪdɪtɪ) *n* excess acidity of the gastrointestinal tract, esp. the stomach, producing a burning sensation. ► **ˌhyperˈacid** *adj*

hyperactive (ˌhaɪpərˈæktɪv) *adj* abnormally active. ► **ˌhyperˈaction** *n* ► **ˌhyperacˈtivity** *n*

hyperaemia *or U.S.* **hyperemia** (ˌhaɪpərˈiːmɪə) *n Pathol.* an excessive amount of blood in an organ or part. ► **ˌhyperˈaemic** *or U.S.* **ˌhyperˈemic** *adj*

hyperaesthesia *or U.S.* **hyperesthesia** (ˌhaɪpəriːsˈθiːzɪə) *n Pathol.* increased sensitivity of any of the sense organs, esp. of the skin to cold, heat, pain, etc. ► **hyperaesthetic** *or U.S.* **hyperesthetic** (ˌhaɪpəriːsˈθɛtɪk) *adj*

hyperbaric (ˌhaɪpəˈbærɪk) *adj* of, concerned with, or operating at pressures higher than normal.

hyperbaton (haɪˈpɜːbəˌtɒn) *n Rhetoric.* a figure of speech in which the normal order of words is reversed, as in *cheese I love.* **[C16:** via Latin from Greek, literally: an overstepping, from HYPER- +*bainein* to step**]**

hyperbola (haɪˈpɜːbələ) *n, pl* **-las** *or* **-le** (-ˌliː). a conic section formed by a plane that cuts both bases of a cone; it consists of two branches asymptotic to two intersecting fixed lines and has two foci. Standard equation: $x^2/a^2 - y^2/b^2 = 1$ where $2a$ is the distance between the two intersections with the *x*-axis and $b = a\sqrt{(e^2 - 1)}$, where *e* is the eccentricity. **[C17:** from Greek *huperbolē,* literally: excess, extravagance, from HYPER- + *ballein* to throw**]**

hyperbole (haɪˈpɜːbəlɪ) *n* a deliberate exaggeration used for effect: *he embraced her a thousand times.* **[C16:** from Greek: from HYPER- + *bolē* a throw, from *ballein* to throw**]** ► **hyˈperbolism** *n*

hyperbolic (ˌhaɪpəˈbɒlɪk) *or* **hyperbolical** *adj* **1** of or relating to a hyperbola. **2** *Rhetoric.* of or relating to a hyperbole. ► **ˌhyperˈbolically** *adv*

hyperbolic function *n* any of a group of functions of an angle expressed as a relationship between the distances of a point on a hyperbola to the origin and to the coordinate axes. The group includes sinh (**hyperbolic sine**), cosh (**hyperbolic cosine**), tanh (**hyperbolic tangent**), sech (**hyperbolic secant**), cosech (**hyperbolic cosecant**), and coth (**hyperbolic cotangent**).

hyperbolize *or* **hyperbolise** (haɪˈpɜːbəˌlaɪz) *vb* to express (something) by means of hyperbole.

hyperboloid (haɪˈpɜːbəˌlɔɪd) *n* a geometric surface consisting of one sheet, or of two sheets separated by a finite distance, whose sections parallel to the three coordinate planes are hyperbolas or ellipses. Equations: $x^2/a^2 + y^2/b^2 - z^2/c^2 = 1$ (one sheet) or $x^2/a^2 - y^2/b^2 - z^2/c^2 = 1$ (two sheets) where *a, b,* and *c* are constants.

Hyperborean (ˌhaɪpəˈbɔːrɪən) *n* **1** *Greek myth.* one of a people believed to have lived beyond the North Wind in a sunny land. **2** an inhabitant of the extreme north. ◆ *adj* **3** (*sometimes not cap.*) of or relating to the extreme north. **4** of or relating to the Hyperboreans. **[C16:** from Latin *hyperboreus,* from Greek *huperboreos,* from HYPER- + *Boreas* the north wind**]**

hypercapnia (ˌhaɪpəˈkæpnɪə) *n* an excess of carbon dioxide in the blood. Also: **hypercarbia. [**from HYPER- + Greek *kapnos* smoke**]** ► **ˌhyperˈcapnic** *adj*

hypercatalectic (ˌhaɪpəˌkætəˈlɛktɪk) *adj Prosody.* (of a line of verse) having extra syllables after the last foot.

hypercharge (ˈhaɪpəˌtʃɑːdʒ) *n* a property of baryons that is used to account for the absence of certain strong interaction decays.

hypercholesterolaemia *or U.S.* **hypercholesterolemia** (ˌhaɪpəkəˌlɛstərɒlˈiːmɪə) *n* the condition of having high levels of cholesterol in the blood. See **hyperlipidaemia.**

hypercorrect (ˌhaɪpəkəˈrɛkt) *adj* **1** excessively correct or fastidious. **2** resulting from or characterized by hypercorrection. ► **ˌhypercorˈrectness** *n*

hypercorrection (ˌhaɪpəkəˈrɛkʃən) *n* a mistaken correction to text or speech made through a desire to avoid nonstandard pronunciation or grammar: *"between you and I" is a hypercorrection of "between you and me".*

hypercritical (ˌhaɪpəˈkrɪtɪkᵊl) *adj* excessively or severely critical; carping; captious. ► **ˌhyperˈcritic** *n* ► **ˌhyperˈcritically** *adv* ► **ˌhyperˈcritiˌcism** *n*

hypercube (ˈhaɪpəˌkjuːb) *n Maths.* a figure in a space of four or more dimensions having all its sides equal and all its angles right angles.

hyperdulia (ˌhaɪpədjuˈlɪə) *n R.C. Church.* special veneration accorded to the Virgin Mary. Compare **dulia, latria. [C16:** from Latin HYPER- + Medieval Latin *dulia* service**]** ► **ˌhyperˈdulic** *or* **ˌhyperˈdulical** *adj*

hyperemia (ˌhaɪpərˈiːmɪə) *n Pathol.* the usual U.S. spelling of **hyperaemia.** ► **ˌhyperˈemic** *adj*

hyperesthesia (ˌhaɪpərisˈθiːzɪə) *n Pathol.* the usual U.S. spelling of **hyperaesthesia.** ► **ˌhyperesˈthetic** *adj*

hypereutectic (ˌhaɪpəjuːˈtɛktɪk) *or* **hypereutectoid** *adj* (of a mixture or alloy with two components) containing more of the minor component than a eutectic mixture. Compare **hypoeutectic.**

hyperextension (ˌhaɪpərɪkˈstɛnʃən) *n* extension of an arm or leg beyond its normal limits.

hyperfine structure (ˈhaɪpəˌfaɪn) *n* the splitting of a spectral line of an atom or molecule into two or more closely spaced components as a result of interaction of the electrons with the magnetic moments of the nuclei or with external fields. Compare **fine structure.** See also **Stark, Zeeman effect.**

hyperfocal distance (ˌhaɪpəˈfəʊkᵊl) *n* the distance from a camera lens to the point beyond which all objects appear sharp and clearly defined.

hypergamy (haɪˈpɜːgəmɪ) *n* **1** *Anthropol.* a custom that forbids a woman to marry a man of lower social status. **2** any marriage with a partner of higher social status. **[C19:** from HYPER- + -GAMY**]** ► **ˌhyperˈgamous** *adj*

hypergeometric (ˌhaɪpədʒɪəˈmɛtrɪk) *adj* of or relating to operations or series that transcend ordinary geometrical operations or series.

hyperglycaemia *or U.S.* **hyperglycemia** (ˌhaɪpəglaɪˈsiːmɪə) *n Pathol.* an abnormally large amount of sugar in the blood. **[C20:** from HYPER- + GLYCO- + -AEMIA**]** ► **ˌhyperglyˈcaemic** *or U.S.* **ˌhyperglyˈcemic** *adj*

hypergolic (ˌhaɪpəˈgɒlɪk) *adj* (of a rocket fuel) able to ignite spontaneously on contact with an oxidizer. **[C20:** from German *Hypergol* (perhaps from HYP(ER-) + ERG[1] + -OL[2]) + -IC**]**

hypericum (haɪˈpɛrɪkəm) *n* any herbaceous plant or shrub of the temperate genus *Hypericum*: family *Hypericaceae.* See **rose of Sharon** (sense 1), **Saint John's wort. [C16:** via Latin from Greek *hupereikon,* from HYPER- + *ereikē* heath**]**

hyperinflation (ˌhaɪpərɪnˈfleɪʃən) *n* extremely high inflation, usually over 50 per cent per month, often involving social disorder. Also called: **galloping inflation.**

hyperinsulinism (ˌhaɪpərˈɪnsjʊlɪˌnɪzəm) *n Pathol.* an excessive amount of insulin in the blood, producing hypoglycaemia, caused by oversecretion of insulin by the pancreas or overdosage of insulin in treating diabetes. See **insulin reaction.**

Hyperion[1] (haɪˈpɪərɪən) *n Greek myth.* a Titan, son of Uranus and Gaea, father of Helios (sun), Selene (moon), and Eos (dawn).

Hyperion[2] (haɪˈpɪərɪən) *n* an outer satellite of the planet Saturn.

hyperkeratosis (ˌhaɪpəˌkɛrəˈtəʊsɪs) *n Pathol.* overgrowth and thickening of the outer layer of the skin. ► **hyperkeratotic** (ˌhaɪpəˌkɛrəˈtɒtɪk) *adj*

hyperkinesia (ˌhaɪpəkɪˈniːzɪə, -kaɪ-) *or* **hyperkinesis** (ˌhaɪpəkɪˈniːsɪs, -kaɪ-) *n Pathol.* **1** excessive movement, as in a muscle spasm. **2** extreme overactivity in children. **[C20:** from HYPER- + *-kinesia* from Greek *kinēsis* movement, from *kinein* to move**]** ► **hyperkinetic** (ˌhaɪpəkɪˈnɛtɪk, -kaɪ-) *adj*

hyperlipidaemia *or U.S.* **hyperlipidemia** (ˌhaɪpəˌlɪpɪˈdiːmɪə) *n* an abnormally high level of lipids, esp. cholesterol, in the blood, predisposing to atherosclerosis and other arterial diseases.

hypermania (ˌhaɪpəˈmeɪnɪə) *n Psychol.* a condition of extreme mania.

hypermarket (ˈhaɪpəˌmɑːkɪt) *n Brit.* a huge self-service store, usually built on the outskirts of a town. **[C20:** translation of French *hypermarché***]**

hypermedia (ˈhaɪpəˌmiːdɪə) *n* computer software and hardware that allows users to interact with text, graphics, sound, and video, each of which can be accessed from within any of the others. Compare **hypertext.**

hypermeter (haɪˈpɜːmɪtə) *n Prosody.* a verse line containing one or more additional syllables. ► **hypermetric** (ˌhaɪpəˈmɛtrɪk) *or* **ˌhyperˈmetrical** *adj*

hypermetropia (ˌhaɪpəmɪˈtrəʊpɪə) *or* **hypermetropy** (ˌhaɪpəˈmɛtrəpɪ) *n Pathol.* variants of **hyperopia. [C19:** from Greek *hupermetros* beyond measure (from HYPER- + *metron* measure) + -OPIA**]** ► **hypermetropic** (ˌhaɪpəmɪˈtrɒpɪk) *or* **ˌhypermeˈtropical** *adj*

hypermnesia (ˌhaɪpəmˈniːzɪə) *n Psychol.* an unusually good ability to remember, found in some mental disorders and possibly in hypnosis. **[C20:** New Latin, from HYPER- + *-mnesia,* formed on the model of AMNESIA**]**

hypermodern school (ˌhaɪpəˈmɒdən) *n* a name given by S. G. Tartakower to a style of chess typified by Richard Reti and A. I. Nimzowitsch and characterized by control of the centre from the flanks.

hyperon (ˈhaɪpəˌrɒn) *n Physics.* any baryon that is not a nucleon. **[C20:** from HYPER- + -ON**]**

hyperopia (ˌhaɪpəˈrəʊpɪə) *n* inability to see near objects clearly because the images received by the eye are focused behind the retina; long-sightedness. Also called: **hypermetropia, hypermetropy.** Compare **myopia, presbyopia.** ► **hyperopic** (ˌhaɪpəˈrɒpɪk).

hyperorexia (ˌhaɪpərɒˈrɛksɪə) *n* compulsive overeating. [C20: from HYPER- + Greek *orexis* appetite]

hyperosmia (ˌhaɪpəˈrɒzmɪə) *n* an abnormally acute sense of smell. [C20: from HYPER- + Greek *osmē* odour]

hyperostosis (ˌhaɪpərɒˈstəʊsɪs) *n, pl* **-ses** (-siːz). *Pathol.* **1** an abnormal proliferation of bony tissue. **2** a bony growth arising from the root of a tooth or from the surface of a bone. ► **hyperostotic** (ˌhaɪpərɒˈstɒtɪk) *adj*

hyperparasite (ˌhaɪpəˈpærəˌsaɪt) *n* an organism that is parasitic on another parasite.

hyperphagia (ˌhaɪpəˈfeɪdʒɪə) *n Psychol.* compulsive overeating over a prolonged period.

hyperphysical (ˌhaɪpəˈfɪzɪkᵊl) *adj* beyond the physical; supernatural or immaterial. ► **ˌhyperˈphysically** *adv*

hyperpituitarism (ˌhaɪpəpɪˈtjuːɪtəˌrɪzəm) *n Pathol.* overactivity of the pituitary gland, sometimes resulting in acromegaly or gigantism. ► **ˌhyperpiˈtuitary** *adj*

hyperplane (ˈhaɪpəˌpleɪn) *n Maths.* a higher dimensional analogue of a plane in three dimensions.

hyperplasia (ˌhaɪpəˈpleɪzɪə) *n* enlargement of a bodily organ or part resulting from an increase in the total number of cells. Compare **hypertrophy.** ► **hyperplastic** (ˌhaɪpəˈplæstɪk) *adj*

hyperploid (ˈhaɪpəˌplɔɪd) *adj Biology.* having or relating to a chromosome number that slightly exceeds an exact multiple of the haploid number. ► **ˈhyperˌploidy** *n*

hyperpnoea *or U.S.* **hyperpnea** (ˌhaɪpəpˈniːə, ˌhaɪpəˈniːə) *n* an increase in the breathing rate or in the depth of breathing, as after strenuous exercise. [C20: from New Latin, from HYPER- + Greek *pnoia* breath, from *pnein* to breathe]

hyperprosexia (ˌhaɪpəprɒˈsɛksɪə) *n Psychol.* a condition in which the whole attention is occupied by one object or idea to the exclusion of others. [C20: from HYPER- + Greek *prosexein* to heed]

hyperpyrexia (ˌhaɪpəpaɪˈrɛksɪə) *n Pathol.* an extremely high fever, with a temperature of 41°C (106°F) or above. Also called: **hyperthermia, hyperthermy.** ► **hyperpyretic** (ˌhaɪpəpaɪˈrɛtɪk) *or* **ˌhyperpyˈrexial** *adj*

hypersensitive (ˌhaɪpəˈsɛnsɪtɪv) *adj* **1** having unduly vulnerable feelings. **2** abnormally sensitive to an allergen, a drug, or other agent. ► **ˌhyperˈsensitiveness** *or* **ˌhyperˌsensiˈtivity** *n*

hypersensitize *or* **hypersensitise** (ˌhaɪpəˈsɛnsɪˌtaɪz) *vb* (*tr*) to treat (a photographic emulsion), usually after manufacture and shortly before exposure, to increase its speed. ► **ˌhyperˌsensitiˈzation** *or* **ˌhyperˌsensitiˈsation** *n*

hypersonic (ˌhaɪpəˈsɒnɪk) *adj* concerned with or having a velocity of at least five times that of sound in the same medium under the same conditions. ► **ˌhyperˈsonics** *n*

hyperspace (ˌhaɪpəˈspeɪs) *n* **1** *Maths.* space having more than three dimensions: often used to describe a multi-dimensional environment. **2** (in science fiction) a theoretical dimension within which conventional space-time relationship does not apply. ► **hyperspatial** (ˌhaɪpəˈspeɪʃəl) *adj*

hypersthene (ˈhaɪpəˌsθiːn) *n* a green, brown, or black pyroxene mineral consisting of magnesium iron silicate in orthorhombic crystalline form. Formula: $(Mg,Fe)_2Si_2O_6$. [C19: from HYPER- + Greek *sthenos* strength] ► **hypersthenic** (ˌhaɪpəˈsθɛnɪk) *adj*

hypertension (ˌhaɪpəˈtɛnʃən) *n Pathol.* abnormally high blood pressure. ► **hypertensive** (ˌhaɪpəˈtɛnsɪv) *adj, n*

hypertext (ˈhaɪpəˌtɛkst) *n* computer software and hardware that allows users to create, store, and view text and move between related items easily and in a non-sequential way; a word or phrase can be selected to link users to another part of the same document or to a different document.

hyperthermia (ˌhaɪpəˈθɜːmɪə) *or* **hyperthermy** (ˌhaɪpəˈθɜːmɪ) *n Pathol.* variants of **hyperpyrexia.** ► **ˌhyperˈthermal** *adj*

hyperthymia (ˌhaɪpəˈθaɪmɪə) *n* excessive emotionalism. [C20: from HYPER- + Greek *thymos* spirit]

hyperthyroidism (ˌhaɪpəˈθaɪrɔɪˌdɪzəm) *n* overproduction of thyroid hormone by the thyroid gland, causing nervousness, insomnia, sweating, palpitation, and sensitivity to heat. Also called: **thyrotoxicosis.** See **exophthalmic goitre.** ► **ˌhyperˈthyroid** *adj, n*

hypertonic (ˌhaɪpəˈtɒnɪk) *adj* **1** (esp. of muscles) being in a state of abnormally high tension. **2** (of a solution) having a higher osmotic pressure than that of a specified, generally physiological, solution. Compare **hypotonic, isotonic.** ► **hypertonicity** (ˌhaɪpətəʊˈnɪsɪtɪ) *n*

hypertrophy (haɪˈpɜːtrəfɪ) *n, pl* **-phies. 1** enlargement of an organ or part resulting from an increase in the size of the cells. Compare **atrophy, hyperplasia.** ♦ *vb* **-phies, -phying, -phied. 2** to undergo or cause to undergo this condition. ► **hypertrophic** (ˌhaɪpəˈtrɒfɪk) *adj*

hyperventilation (ˌhaɪpəˌvɛntɪˈleɪʃən) *n* an increase in the depth, duration, and rate of breathing, sometimes resulting in cramp and dizziness. ► **ˌhyperˈventilate** *vb*

hypervitaminosis (ˌhaɪpəˌvɪtəmɪˈnəʊsɪs, -ˌvaɪ-) *n Pathol.* the condition resulting from the chronic excessive intake of vitamins. [C20: from HYPER- + VITAMIN + -OSIS]

hypesthesia (ˌhɪpiːsˈθiːzɪə, ˌhaɪ-) *n* the usual U.S. spelling of **hypaesthesia.** ► **hypesthesic** (ˌhɪpiːsˈθiːsɪk, ˌhaɪ-) *adj*

hypethral (hɪˈpiːθrəl, haɪ-) *adj* the usual U.S. spelling of **hypaethral.**

hypha (ˈhaɪfə) *n, pl* **-phae** (-fiː). any of the filaments that constitute the body (mycelium) of a fungus. [C19: from New Latin, from Greek *huphē* web] ► **ˈhyphal** *adj*

hyphen (ˈhaɪfᵊn) *n* **1** the punctuation mark (-), used to separate the parts of some compound words, to link the words of a phrase, and between syllables of a word split between two consecutive lines of writing or printing. ♦ *vb* **2** (*tr*) another word for **hyphenate.** [C17: from Late Latin (meaning: the combining of two words), from Greek *huphen* (adv) together, from HYPO- + *heis* one]

hyphenate (ˈhaɪfᵊˌneɪt) *or* **hyphen** *vb* (*tr*) to separate (syllables, words, etc.) with a hyphen. ► **ˌhyphenˈation** *n*

hyphenated (ˈhaɪfᵊˌneɪtɪd) *adj* **1** containing or linked with a hyphen. **2** *Chiefly U.S.* having a nationality denoted by a hyphenated word: *American-Irish.*

hyphen help *n* a word processing function that assists the operator to identify automatically those words that can be hyphenated at the end of a line of text.

hypnagogic *or* **hypnogogic** (ˌhɪpnəˈɡɒdʒɪk) *adj Psychol.* of or relating to the state just before one is fully asleep. See also **hypnagogic image, hypnopompic.** [C19: from French *hypnagogique*; see HYPNO-, -AGOGIC]

hypnagogic image *n Psychol.* an image experienced by a person just before falling asleep, which often resembles a hallucination.

hypno- *or before a vowel* **hypn-** *combining form.* **1** indicating sleep: *hypnophobia.* **2** relating to hypnosis: *hypnotherapy.* [from Greek *hupnos* sleep]

hypnoanalysis (ˌhɪpnəʊəˈnælɪsɪs) *n Psychol.* psychoanalysis conducted on a hypnotized person. ► **hypnoanalytic** (ˌhɪpnəʊˌænəˈlɪtɪk) *adj*

hypnogenesis (ˌhɪpnəʊˈdʒɛnɪsɪs) *n Psychol.* the induction of sleep or hypnosis. ► **hypnogenetic** (ˌhɪpnəʊdʒɪˈnɛtɪk) *adj* ► **ˌhypnogeˈnetically** *adv*

hypnoid (ˈhɪpˌnɔɪd) *or* **hypnoidal** (hɪpˈnɔɪdᵊl) *adj Psychol.* of or relating to a state resembling sleep or hypnosis.

hypnology (hɪpˈnɒlədʒɪ) *n Psychol.* the study of sleep and hypnosis. ► **hypnologic** (ˌhɪpnəˈlɒdʒɪk) *or* **ˌhypnoˈlogical** *adj* ► **hypˈnologist** *n*

hypnopaedia (ˌhɪpnəʊˈpiːdɪə) *n* the learning of lessons heard during sleep. [C20: from HYPNO- + Greek *paideia* education]

hypnopompic (ˌhɪpnəʊˈpɒmpɪk) *adj Psychol.* relating to the state existing between sleep and full waking, characterized by the persistence of dreamlike imagery. See also **hypnagogic.** [C20: from HYPNO- + Greek *pompē* a sending forth, escort + -IC; see POMP]

Hypnos (ˈhɪpnɒs) *n Greek myth.* the god of sleep. Roman counterpart: **Somnus.** Compare **Morpheus.** [Greek: sleep]

hypnosis (hɪpˈnəʊsɪs) *n, pl* **-ses** (-siːz). an artificially induced state of relaxation and concentration in which deeper parts of the mind become more accessible: used clinically to reduce reaction to pain, to encourage free association, etc. See also **autohypnosis.**

hypnotherapy (ˌhɪpnəʊˈθɛrəpɪ) *n* the use of hypnosis in the treatment of emotional and psychogenic problems. ► **ˌhypnoˈtherapist** *n*

hypnotic (hɪpˈnɒtɪk) *adj* **1** of, relating to, or producing hypnosis or sleep. **2** (of a person) susceptible to hypnotism. ♦ *n* **3** a drug or agent that induces sleep. **4** a person susceptible to hypnosis. [C17: from Late Latin *hypnōticus*, from Greek *hupnōtikos*, from *hupnoun* to put to sleep, from *hupnos* sleep] ► **hypˈnotically** *adv*

hypnotism (ˈhɪpnəˌtɪzəm) *n* **1** the scientific study and practice of hypnosis. **2** the process of inducing hypnosis.

hypnotist (ˈhɪpnətɪst) *n* a person skilled in the theory and practice of hypnosis.

hypnotize *or* **hypnotise** (ˈhɪpnəˌtaɪz) *vb* (*tr*) **1** to induce hypnosis in (a person). **2** to charm or beguile; fascinate. ► **ˈhypnoˌtizable** *or* **ˈhypnoˌtisable** *adj* ► **ˌhypnoˌtizaˈbility** *or* **ˌhypnoˌtisaˈbility** *n* ► **ˌhypnotiˈzation** *or* **ˌhypnotiˈsation** *n* ► **ˈhypnoˌtizer** *or* **ˈhypnoˌtiser** *n*

hypo[1] (ˈhaɪpəʊ) *n* another name for **sodium thiosulphate,** esp. when used as a fixer in photographic developing. [C19: shortened from HYPOSULPHITE]

hypo[2] (ˈhaɪpəʊ) *n, pl* **-pos.** *Informal.* short for **hypodermic syringe.**

hypo- *or before a vowel* **hyp-** *prefix* **1** under, beneath, or below: *hypodermic.* **2** lower; at a lower point: *hypogastrium.* **3** less than: *hypoploid.* **4** (in medicine) denoting a deficiency or an abnormally low level: *hypothyroid.* **5** incomplete or partial: *hypoplasia.* **6** indicating that a chemical compound contains an element in a lower oxidation state than usual: *hypochlorous acid.* [from Greek, from *hupo* under]

Hypo- *prefix* indicating a plagal mode in music: *Hypodorian.* [from Greek: beneath (it lies a fourth below the corresponding authentic mode)]

hypoacidity (ˌhaɪpəʊəˈsɪdɪtɪ) *n Med.* abnormally low acidity, as of the contents of the stomach.

hypoallergenic (ˈhaɪpəʊˌæləˈdʒɛnɪk) *adj* (of cosmetics, earrings, etc.) not likely to cause an allergic reaction.

hypoblast (ˈhaɪpəˌblæst) *n* **1** Also called: **endoblast.** *Embryol.* the inner layer of an embryo at an early stage of development that becomes the endoderm at gastrulation. **2** a less common name for **endoderm.** ► **ˌhypoˈblastic** *adj*

hypocaust (ˈhaɪpəˌkɔːst) *n* an ancient Roman heating system in which hot air circulated under the floor and between double walls. [C17: from Latin *hypocaustum*, from Greek *hupokauston* room heated from below, from *hupokaiein* to light a fire beneath, from HYPO- + *kaiein* to burn]

hypocentre (ˈhaɪpəʊˌsɛntə) *n* **1** Also called: **ground zero.** the point on the ground immediately below the centre of explosion of a nuclear bomb in the atmosphere. **2** another term for **focus** (sense 6).

hypochlorite (ˌhaɪpəˈklɔːraɪt) *n* any salt or ester of hypochlorous acid.

hypochlorous acid (ˌhaɪpəˈklɔːrəs) *n* an unstable acid known only in solution and in the form of its salts, formed when chlorine dissolves in water: a strong oxidizing and bleaching agent. Formula: HOCl.

hypochondria (ˌhaɪpəˈkɒndrɪə) *n* chronic abnormal anxiety concerning the state of one's health, even in the absence of any evidence of disease on medical examination. Also called: **hypochondriasis** (ˌhaɪpəʊkɒnˈdraɪəsɪs). [C18: from Late Latin: the abdomen, supposedly the seat of melancholy, from Greek *hupokhondria,* from *hupokhondrios* of the upper abdomen, from HYPO- + *khondros* cartilage]

hypochondriac (ˌhaɪpəˈkɒndrɪˌæk) *n* **1** a person suffering from hypochondria. ◆ *adj also* **hypochondriacal** (ˌhaɪpəkɒnˈdraɪək°l). **2** relating to or suffering from hypochondria. **3** *Anatomy.* of or relating to the hypochondrium. ▸ **ˌhypochonˈdriacally** *adv*

hypochondrium (ˌhaɪpəˈkɒndrɪəm) *n, pl* **-dria** (-drɪə). *Anatomy.* the upper region of the abdomen on each side of the epigastrium, just below the lowest ribs. [C17: from New Latin, from Greek *hupokhondrion;* see HYPOCHONDRIA]

hypocorism (haɪˈpɒkəˌrɪzəm) *n* **1** a pet name, esp. one using a diminutive affix: *"Sally" is a hypocorism for "Sarah".* **2** another word for **euphemism** (sense 1). [C19: from Greek *hupokorisma,* from *hupokorizesthai* to use pet names, from *hypo-* beneath + *korizesthai,* from *korē* girl, *koros* boy] ▸ **hypocoristic** (ˌhaɪpəkɔːˈrɪstɪk) *adj* ▸ **ˌhypocoˈristically** *adv*

hypocotyl (ˌhaɪpəˈkɒtɪl) *n* the part of an embryo plant between the cotyledons and the radicle. [C19: from HYPO- + COTYL(EDON)] ▸ **ˌhypoˈcotylous** *adj*

hypocrisy (hɪˈpɒkrəsɪ) *n, pl* **-sies. 1** the practice of professing standards, beliefs, etc., contrary to one's real character or actual behaviour, esp. the pretence of virtue and piety. **2** an act or instance of this.

hypocrite (ˈhɪpəkrɪt) *n* a person who pretends to be what he is not. [C13: from Old French *ipocrite,* via Late Latin, from Greek *hupokritēs* one who plays a part, from *hupokrinein* to feign, from *krinein* to judge] ▸ **ˌhypoˈcritical** *adj* ▸ **ˌhypoˈcritically** *adv*

hypocrystalline (ˌhaɪpəʊˈkrɪstəˌlaɪn) *adj* another word for **hemicrystalline.**

hypocycloid (ˌhaɪpəˈsaɪklɔɪd) *n* a curve described by a point on the circumference of a circle as the circle rolls around the inside of a fixed coplanar circle. Compare **epicycloid, cycloid** (sense 4). ▸ **ˌhypocyˈcloidal** *adj*

hypoderm (ˈhaɪpəˌdɜːm) *n* a variant of **hypodermis.** ▸ **ˌhypoˈdermal** *adj*

hypodermic (ˌhaɪpəˈdɜːmɪk) *adj* **1** of or relating to the region of the skin beneath the epidermis. **2** injected beneath the skin. ◆ *n* **3** a hypodermic syringe or needle. **4** a hypodermic injection. ▸ **ˌhypoˈdermically** *adv*

hypodermic syringe *n Med.* a type of syringe consisting of a hollow cylinder, usually of glass or plastic, a tightly fitting piston, and a hollow needle (**hypodermic needle**), used for withdrawing blood samples, injecting medicine, etc.

hypodermis (ˌhaɪpəˈdɜːmɪs) *or* **hypoderm** *n* **1** *Botany.* a layer of thick-walled supportive or water-storing cells beneath the epidermis in some plants. **2** *Zoology.* the epidermis of arthropods, annelids, etc., which secretes and is covered by a cuticle. [C19: from HYPO- + EPIDERMIS]

Hypodorian (ˌhaɪpəˈdɔːrɪən) *adj Music.* denoting a plagal mode represented by the ascending diatonic scale from A to A. Compare **Dorian** (sense 3). See **Hypo-.**

hypoeutectic (ˌhaɪpəʊjuːˈtɛktɪk) *or* **hypoeutectoid** *adj* (of a mixture or alloy with two components) containing less of the minor component than a eutectic mixture. Compare **hypereutectic.**

hypogastrium (ˌhaɪpəˈgæstrɪəm) *n, pl* **-tria** (-trɪə). *Anatomy.* the lower front central region of the abdomen, below the navel. [C17: from New Latin, from Greek *hupogastrion,* from HYPO- + *gastrion,* diminutive of *gastēr* stomach] ▸ **ˌhypoˈgastric** *adj*

hypogeal (ˌhaɪpəˈdʒiːəl) *or* **hypogeous** *adj* **1** occurring or living below the surface of the ground. **2** *Botany.* of or relating to seed germination in which the cotyledons remain below the ground, because of the growth of the epicotyl. [C19: from Latin *hypogēus,* from Greek *hupogeios,* from HYPO- + *gē* earth]

hypogene (ˈhaɪpəˌdʒiːn) *adj* formed, taking place, or originating beneath the surface of the earth. Compare **epigene.** ▸ **hypogenic** (ˌhaɪpəˈdʒɛnɪk) *adj*

hypogenous (haɪˈpɒdʒɪnəs) *adj Botany.* produced or growing on the undersurface, esp. (of fern spores) growing on the undersurface of the leaves.

hypogeous (ˌhaɪpəˈdʒiːəs) *adj* another word for **hypogeal.**

hypogeum (ˌhaɪpəˈdʒiːəm) *n, pl* **-gea** (-ˈdʒiːə). an underground vault, esp. one used for burials. [C18: from Latin, from Greek *hupogeion;* see HYPOGEAL]

hypoglossal (ˌhaɪpəˈglɒs°l) *adj* **1** situated beneath the tongue. ◆ *n* **2** short for **hypoglossal nerve.**

hypoglossal nerve *n* the twelfth cranial nerve, which supplies the muscles of the tongue.

hypoglycaemia *or U.S.* **hypoglycemia** (ˌhaɪpəʊglaɪˈsiːmɪə) *n Pathol.* an abnormally small amount of sugar in the blood. [C20: from HYPO- + GLYCO- + -AEMIA] ▸ **ˌhypoglyˈcaemic** *or U.S.* **ˌhypoglyˈcemic** *adj*

hypognathous (haɪˈpɒgnəθəs) *adj* **1** having a lower jaw that protrudes beyond the upper jaw. **2** (of insects) having downturned mouthparts. ▸ **hyˈpognathism** *n*

hypogynous (haɪˈpɒdʒɪnəs) *adj* **1** (of a flower) having the gynoecium situated above the other floral parts, as in the buttercup. **2** of or relating to the parts of a flower arranged in this way. ▸ **hyˈpogyny** *n*

hypoid gear (ˈhaɪpɔɪd) *n* a gear having a tooth form generated by a hypocycloidal curve; used extensively in motor vehicle transmissions to withstand a high surface loading. [C20: *hypoid,* shortened from HYPOCYCLOID]

hypolimnion (ˌhaɪpəʊˈlɪmnɪən) *n* the lower and colder layer of water in a lake. [C20: from HYPO- + Greek *limnion,* diminutive of *limnē* lake]

Hypolydian (ˌhaɪpəˈlɪdɪən) *adj Music.* denoting a plagal mode represented by the diatonic scale from D to D. Compare **Lydian** (sense 2). See **Hypo-.**

hypomania (ˌhaɪpəʊˈmeɪnɪə) *n Psychiatry.* an abnormal condition of extreme excitement, milder than mania but characterized by great optimism and overactivity and often by reckless spending of money. ▸ **hypomanic** (ˌhaɪpəʊˈmænɪk) *adj*

hyponasty (ˈhaɪpəˌnæstɪ) *n* increased growth of the lower surface of a plant part, resulting in an upward bending of the part. Compare **epinasty.** ▸ **ˌhypoˈnastic** *adj* ▸ **ˌhypoˈnastically** *adv*

hyponitrite (ˌhaɪpəˈnaɪtraɪt) *n* any salt or ester of hyponitrous acid.

hyponitrous acid (ˌhaɪpəˈnaɪtrəs) *n* a white soluble unstable crystalline acid: an oxidizing and reducing agent. Formula: $H_2N_2O_2$.

hyponym (ˈhaɪpəʊnɪm) *n* a word whose meaning is included in that of another word: *'scarlet', 'vermilion', and 'crimson' are hyponyms of 'red'.* Compare **superordinate** (sense 3), **synonym, antonym.** [C20: from HYPO- + Greek *onoma* name] ▸ **hyponymy** (haɪˈpɒnəmɪ) *n*

hypophosphate (ˌhaɪpəˈfɒsfeɪt) *n* any salt or ester of hypophosphoric acid.

hypophosphite (ˌhaɪpəˈfɒsfaɪt) *n* any salt of hypophosphorous acid.

hypophosphoric acid (ˌhaɪpəfɒsˈfɒrɪk) *n* a crystalline odourless deliquescent solid: a tetrabasic acid produced by the slow oxidation of phosphorus in moist air. Formula: $H_4P_2O_6$.

hypophosphorous acid (ˌhaɪpəˈfɒsfərəs) *n* a colourless or yellowish oily liquid or white deliquescent solid: a monobasic acid and a reducing agent. Formula: H_3PO_2.

hypophyge (haɪˈpɒfɪdʒɪ) *n Architect.* another name for **apophyge.**

hypophysis (haɪˈpɒfɪsɪs) *n, pl* **-ses** (-ˌsiːz). the technical name for **pituitary gland.** [C18: from Greek: outgrowth, from HYPO- + *phuein* to grow] ▸ **hypophyseal** *or* **hypophysial** (ˌhaɪpəˈfɪzɪəl, haɪˌpɒfɪˈsɪəl) *adj*

hypopituitarism (ˌhaɪpəpɪˈtjuːɪtəˌrɪzəm) *n Pathol.* underactivity of the pituitary gland. ▸ **ˌhypopiˈtuitary** *adj*

hypoplasia (ˌhaɪpəʊˈpleɪzɪə) *or* **hypoplasty** (ˈhaɪpəʊˌplæstɪ) *n Pathol.* incomplete development of an organ or part. ▸ **hypoplastic** (ˌhaɪpəʊˈplæstɪk) *adj*

hypoploid (ˈhaɪpəˌplɔɪd) *adj* having or designating a chromosome number that is slightly less than a multiple of the haploid number. ▸ **ˈhypoˌploidy** *n*

hypopnoea *or U.S.* **hypopnea** (haɪˈpɒpnɪə, ˌhaɪpəˈniːə) *n Pathol.* abnormally shallow breathing, usually accompanied by a decrease in the breathing rate. [C20: New Latin, from HYPO- + Greek *pnoia* breath, from *pnein* to breathe]

hyposensitize *or* **hyposensitise** (ˌhaɪpəʊˈsɛnsɪˌtaɪz) *vb (tr)* to desensitize; render less sensitive. ▸ **ˌhypoˌsensitiˈzation** *or* **ˌhypoˌsensitiˈsation** *n*

hypostasis (haɪˈpɒstəsɪs) *n, pl* **-ses** (-ˌsiːz). **1** *Metaphysics.* the essential nature of a substance as opposed to its attributes. **2** *Christianity.* **2a** any of the three persons of the Godhead, together constituting the Trinity. **2b** the one person of Christ in which the divine and human natures are united. **3** the accumulation of blood in an organ or part as the result of poor circulation. **4** another name for **epistasis** (sense 3). [C16: from Late Latin: substance, from Greek *hupostasis* foundation, from *huphistasthai* to stand under, from HYPO- + *histanai* to cause to stand] ▸ **hypostatic** (ˌhaɪpəˈstætɪk) *or* **ˌhypoˈstatical** *adj* ▸ **ˌhypoˈstatically** *adv*

hypostasize *or* **hypostasise** (haɪˈpɒstəˌsaɪz) *vb* another word for **hypostatize.** ▸ **hyˌpostasiˈzation** *or* **hyˌpostasiˈsation** *n*

hypostatize *or* **hypostatise** (haɪˈpɒstəˌtaɪz) *vb (tr)* **1** to regard or treat as real. **2** to embody or personify. ▸ **hyˌpostatiˈzation** *or* **hyˌpostatiˈsation** *n*

hyposthenia (ˌhaɪpɒsˈθiːnɪə) *n Pathol.* a weakened condition; lack of strength. [C19: from HYPO- + Greek *sthenos* strength] ▸ **hyposthenic** (ˌhaɪpɒsˈθɛnɪk) *adj*

hypostyle (ˈhaɪpəʊˌstaɪl) *adj* **1** having a roof supported by columns. ◆ *n* **2** a building constructed in this way.

hyposulphite (ˌhaɪpəˈsʌlfaɪt) *n* **1** another name for **sodium thiosulphate,** esp. when used as a photographic fixer. Often shortened to **hypo. 2** another name for **dithionite.**

hyposulphurous acid (ˌhaɪpəˈsʌlfərəs) *n* another name for **dithionous acid.**

hypotaxis (ˌhaɪpəʊˈtæksɪs) *n Grammar.* the subordination of one clause to another by a conjunction. Compare **parataxis.** ▸ **hypotactic** (ˌhaɪpəʊˈtæktɪk) *adj*

hypotension (ˌhaɪpəʊˈtɛnʃən) *n Pathol.* abnormally low blood pressure. ▸ **hypotensive** (ˌhaɪpəʊˈtɛnsɪv) *adj*

hypotenuse (haɪˈpɒtɪˌnjuːz) *n* the side in a right-angled triangle that is opposite the right angle. Abbrev.: **hyp.** [C16: from Latin *hypotēnūsa,* from Greek *hupoteinousa grammē* subtending line, from *hupoteinein* to subtend, from HYPO- + *teinein* to stretch]

hypoth. *abbrev. for:* **1** hypothesis. **2** hypothetical.

hypothalamus (ˌhaɪpəˈθæləməs) *n, pl* **-mi** (-ˌmaɪ). a neural control centre at the base of the brain, concerned with hunger, thirst, satiety, and other autonomic functions. ▸ **hypothalamic** (ˌhaɪpəθəˈlæmɪk) *adj*

hypothec (haɪˈpɒθɪk) *n Roman and Scots law.* a charge on property in favour of a creditor. [C16: from Late Latin *hypotheca* a security, from Greek *hupothēkē* deposit, pledge, from *hupotithenai* to deposit as a security, place under, from HYPO- + *tithenai* to place]

hypotheca (ˌhaɪpəʊˈθiːkə) *n, pl* **-cae** (-siː). the inner and younger layer of the cell wall of a diatom. Compare **epitheca.** [from HYPO- + THECA]

hypothecate (haɪˈpɒθɪˌkeɪt) *vb (tr) Law.* to pledge (personal property or a ship) as security for a debt without transferring possession or title. See also **bottomry.** ▸ **hyˌpotheˈcation** *n* ▸ **hyˈpotheˌcator** *n*

hypothermal (ˌhaɪpəʊˈθɜːməl) *adj* **1** of, relating to, or characterized by hypothermia. **2** (of rocks and minerals) formed at great depth under conditions of high temperature.

hypothermia (ˌhaɪpəʊˈθɜːmɪə) *n* **1** *Pathol.* an abnormally low body temperature, as induced in the elderly by exposure to cold weather. **2** *Med.* the intentional reduction of normal body temperature, as by ice packs, to reduce the patient's metabolic rate: performed esp. in heart and brain surgery.

hypothesis (haɪˈpɒθɪsɪs) *n, pl* **-ses** (-ˌsiːz). **1** a suggested explanation for a group of facts or phenomena, either accepted as a basis for further verification (**working hypothesis**) or accepted as likely to be true. Compare **theory** (sense 5). **2** an assumption used in an argument without it being endorsed; a supposition. **3** an unproved theory; a conjecture. [C16: from Greek, from *hupotithenai* to propose, suppose, literally: put under; see HYPO-, THESIS] ▸ **hyˈpothesist** *n*

hypothesis testing *n Statistics.* the theory, methods, and practice of testing a hypothesis concerning the parameters of a population distribution (the **null hypothesis**) against another (the **alternative hypothesis**) which will be accepted only if its probability exceeds a predetermined significance level, generally on the basis of statistics derived from random sampling from the given population. Compare **statistical inference.**

hypothesize *or* **hypothesise** (haɪˈpɒθɪˌsaɪz) *vb* to form or assume as a hypothesis. ▸ **hyˈpotheˌsizer** *or* **hyˈpotheˌsiser** *n*

hypothetical (ˌhaɪpəˈθɛtɪkᵊl) *or* **hypothetic** *adj* **1** having the nature of a hypothesis. **2** assumed or thought to exist. **3** *Logic.* another word for **conditional** (sense 4). **4** existing only as an idea or concept: *a time machine is a hypothetical device.* ▸ ˌ**hypoˈthetically** *adv*

hypothetical imperative *n* (esp. in the moral philosophy of Kant) any conditional rule of action, concerned with means and ends rather than with duty for its own sake. Compare **categorical imperative.**

hypothetico-deductive (ˌhaɪpəˈθɛtɪkəʊdɪˈdʌktɪv) *adj* pertaining to or governed by the supposed method of scientific progress whereby a general hypothesis is tested by deducing predictions that may be experimentally tested. When such a prediction is falsified the theory is rejected and a new hypothesis is required.

hypothymia (haɪpəˈθaɪmɪə) **1** a state of depression. **2** a diminished emotional response. **[**C20: from HYPO- + Greek *thymos* spirit**]**

hypothyroidism (ˌhaɪpəʊˈθaɪrɔɪˌdɪzəm) *n Pathol.* **1** insufficient production of thyroid hormones by the thyroid gland. **2** any disorder, such as cretinism or myxoedema, resulting from this. ▸ ˌ**hypoˈthyroid** *n, adj*

hypotonic (ˌhaɪpəˈtɒnɪk) *adj* **1** *Pathol.* (of muscles) lacking normal tone or tension. **2** (of a solution) having a lower osmotic pressure than that of a specified, generally physiological, solution. Compare **hypertonic, isotonic.** ▸ **hypotonicity** (ˌhaɪpətəˈnɪsɪtɪ) *n*

hypoxanthine (ˌhaɪpəˈzænθiːn, -θɪn) *n* a white or colourless crystalline compound that is a breakdown product of nucleoproteins. Formula: $C_5H_4N_4O$.

hypoxia (haɪˈpɒksɪə) *n* deficiency in the amount of oxygen delivered to the body tissues. **[**C20: from HYPO- + OXY-[2] + -IA**]** ▸ **hypoxic** (haɪˈpɒksɪk) *adj*

Hypsilantis *or* **Hypsilantes** (*Greek* ˌipsiˈlandis) *n* variants of **Ypsilanti.**

hypso- *or before a vowel* **hyps-** *combining form.* indicating height: *hypsometry.* **[**from Greek *hupsos***]**

hypsochromic (ˌhɪpsəˈkrəʊmɪk) *adj Chem.* denoting or relating to a shift to a shorter wavelength in the absorption spectrum of a compound. ▸ ˈ**hypsoˌchrome** *n*

hypsography (hɪpˈsɒgrəfɪ) *n* **1** the scientific study and mapping of the earth's topography above sea level. **2** topography or relief, or a map showing this. **3** another name for **hypsometry.** ▸ **hypsographic** (ˌhɪpsəˈgræfɪk) *or* ˌ**hypsoˈgraphical** *adj*

hypsometer (hɪpˈsɒmɪtə) *n* **1** an instrument for measuring altitudes by determining the boiling point of water at a given altitude. **2** any instrument used to calculate the heights of trees by triangulation.

hypsometry (hɪpˈsɒmɪtrɪ) *n* (in mapping) the establishment of height above sea level. Also called: **hypsography.** ▸ **hypsometric** (ˌhɪpsəˈmɛtrɪk) *or* ˌ**hypsoˈmetrical** *adj* ▸ ˌ**hypsoˈmetrically** *adv* ▸ **hypˈsometrist** *n*

hyracoid (ˈhaɪrəˌkɔɪd) *adj* **1** of, relating to, or belonging to the mammalian order *Hyracoidea,* which contains the hyraxes. ◆ *n* **2** a hyrax. ▸ ˌ**hyraˈcoidean** *adj, n*

hyrax (ˈhaɪræks) *n, pl* **hyraxes** *or* **hyraces** (ˈhaɪrəˌsiːz). any agile herbivorous mammal of the family *Procaviidae* and order *Hyracoidea,* of Africa and SW Asia, such as *Procavia capensis* (**rock hyrax**). They resemble rodents but have feet with hooflike toes. Also called: **dassie.** **[**C19: from New Latin, from Greek *hurax* shrewmouse; probably related to Latin *sōrex***]**

Hyrcania (hɜːˈkeɪnɪə) *n* an ancient district of Asia, southeast of the Caspian Sea. ▸ **Hyrˈcanian** *adj*

hyson (ˈhaɪsᵊn) *n* a Chinese green tea, the early crop of which is known as **young hyson** and the inferior leaves as **hyson skin.** **[**C18: from Chinese (Cantonese) *hei-ch'un* bright spring**]**

hyssop (ˈhɪsəp) *n* **1** a widely cultivated Asian plant, *Hyssopus officinalis,* with spikes of small blue flowers and aromatic leaves, used as a condiment and in perfumery and folk medicine: family *Labiatae* (labiates). **2** any of several similar or related plants such as the hedge hyssop. **3** a Biblical plant, used for sprinkling in the ritual practices of the Hebrews. **[**Old English *ysope,* from Latin *hyssōpus,* from Greek *hussōpos,* of Semitic origin; compare Hebrew *ēzōv***]**

hysterectomize *or* **hysterectomise** (ˌhɪstəˈrɛktəˌmaɪz) *vb* (*tr*) to perform a hysterectomy on (someone).

hysterectomy (ˌhɪstəˈrɛktəmɪ) *n, pl* **-mies.** surgical removal of the uterus.

hysteresis (ˌhɪstəˈriːsɪs) *n Physics.* the lag in a variable property of a system with respect to the effect producing it as this effect varies, esp. the phenomenon in which the magnetic induction of a ferromagnetic material lags behind the changing external field. **[**C19: from Greek *husterēsis* coming late, from *husteros* coming after**]** ▸ **hysteretic** (ˌhɪstəˈrɛtɪk) *adj* ▸ ˌ**hysterˈetically** *adv*

hysteresis loop *n* a closed curve showing the variation of the magnetic induction of a ferromagnetic material with the external magnetic field producing it, when this field is changed through a complete cycle.

hysteria (hɪˈstɪərɪə) *n* **1** a mental disorder characterized by emotional outbursts, susceptibility to autosuggestion, and, often, symptoms such as paralysis that mimic the effects of physical disorders. ◆ See also **conversion disorder. 2** any frenzied emotional state, esp. of laughter or crying. **[**C19: from New Latin, from Latin *hystericus* HYSTERIC**]**

hysteric (hɪˈstɛrɪk) *n* **1** a hysterical person. ◆ *adj* **2** hysterical. ◆ See also **hysterics.** **[**C17: from Latin *hystericus* literally: of the womb, from Greek *husterikos,* from *hustera* the womb; from the belief that hysteria in women originated in disorders of the womb**]**

hysterical (hɪˈstɛrɪkᵊl) *or* **hysteric** *adj* **1** of or suggesting hysteria: *hysterical cries.* **2** suffering from hysteria. **3** *Informal.* wildly funny. ▸ **hysˈterically** *adv*

hysterics (hɪˈstɛrɪks) *n* (*functioning as pl or sing*) **1** an attack of hysteria. **2** *Informal.* wild uncontrollable bursts of laughter.

hystero- *or before a vowel* **hyster-** *combining form.* **1** indicating the uterus: *hysterotomy.* **2** hysteria: *hysterogenic.* **[**from Greek *hustera* womb**]**

hysterogenic (ˌhɪstərəˈdʒɛnɪk) *adj* inducing hysteria. **[**C20: from HYSTERIA + -GENIC**]** ▸ **hysterogeny** (ˌhɪstəˈrɒdʒənɪ) *n*

hysteroid (ˈhɪstəˌrɔɪd) *or* **hysteroidal** *adj* resembling hysteria.

hysteron proteron (ˈhɪstəˌrɒn ˈprɒtəˌrɒn) *n* **1** *Logic.* a fallacious argument in which the proposition to be proved is assumed as a premise. **2** *Rhetoric.* a figure of speech in which the normal order of two sentences, clauses, etc., is reversed: *bred and born* (*for born and bred*). **[**C16: from Late Latin, from Greek *husteron proteron* the latter (placed as) former**]**

hysterotomy (ˌhɪstəˈrɒtəmɪ) *n, pl* **-mies.** surgical incision into the uterus.

hystricomorph (hɪˈstraɪkəʊˌmɔːf) *n* **1** any rodent of the suborder *Hystricomorpha,* which includes porcupines, cavies, agoutis, and chinchillas. ◆ *adj also* **hystricomorphic** (hɪˌstraɪkəʊˈmɔːfɪk). **2** of, relating to, or belonging to the *Hystricomorpha.* **[**C19: from Latin *hystrix* porcupine, from Greek *hustrix***]**

Hywel Dda *or* **Howel Dda** (ˈhaʊəl ˈðɑː) *n* known as *Hywel the Good.* died 950 A.D., Welsh prince. He united S and N Wales and codified Welsh law.

Hz *Symbol for* hertz.

Ii

i *or* **I** (aɪ) *n, pl* **i's, I's,** *or* **Is. 1** the ninth letter and third vowel of the modern English alphabet. **2** any of several speech sounds represented by this letter, in English as in *bite* or *hit.* **3a** something shaped like an I. **3b** (*in combination*): *an I-beam.* **4 dot the i's and cross the t's.** to pay meticulous attention to detail.

i *symbol for* the imaginary number $\sqrt{-1}$.

I[1] (aɪ) *pron* (*subjective*) refers to the speaker or writer. [C12: reduced form of Old English *ic;* compare Old Saxon *ik,* Old High German *ih,* Sanskrit *ahám*]

I[2] *symbol for:* **1** *Chem.* iodine. **2** *Physics.* current. **3** *Physics.* isospin. **4** *Logic.* a particular affirmative categorial statement, such as *some men are married,* often symbolized as **SiP**. Compare **A, E, O**[1]. [from Latin (*aff*)*i*(*rmo*) I affirm] **5** *the Roman numeral for* one. See **Roman numerals. 6** *international car registration for* Italy.

i. *abbrev. for:* **1** *Grammar.* intransitive. **2** *Dentistry.* incisor. **3** *Banking.* interest.

I. *abbrev. for:* **1** Independence. **2** Independent. **3** Institute. **4** International. **5** Island *or* Isle.

-i *suffix forming adjectives.* of or relating to a region or people, esp. of the Middle East: *Iraqi; Bangladeshi.* [from an adjectival suffix in Semitic and in Indo-Iranian languages]

-i- *connective vowel.* used between elements in a compound word: *cuneiform, coniferous.* Compare **-o-**. [from Latin, stem vowel of nouns and adjectives in combination]

Ia. *or* **IA** *abbrev. for* Iowa.

-ia *suffix forming nouns.* **1** occurring in place names: *Albania; Columbia.* **2** occurring in names of diseases and pathological disorders: *pneumonia; aphasia.* **3** occurring in words denoting condition or quality: *utopia.* **4** occurring in names of botanical genera: *acacia; poinsettia.* **5** occurring in names of zoological classes: *Reptilia.* **6** occurring in collective nouns borrowed from Latin: *marginalia; memorabilia; regalia.* [(for senses 1–4) New Latin, from Latin and Greek, suffix of feminine nouns; (for senses 5–6) from Latin, neuter plural suffix]

IAA *abbrev. for* indoleacetic acid.

IAAF *abbrev. for* International Amateur Athletic Federation

IAEA *abbrev. for* International Atomic Energy Agency.

IAF *abbrev. for* Indian Air Force.

-ial *suffix forming adjectives.* of; relating to; connected with: *managerial.* [from Latin *-iālis,* adj. suffix; compare -AL[1]]

iamb (ˈaɪæm, ˈaɪæmb) *or* **iambus** (aɪˈæmbəs) *n, pl* **iambs, iambi** (aɪˈæmbaɪ), *or* **iambuses.** *Prosody.* **1** a metrical foot consisting of two syllables, a short one followed by a long one (⏑–). **2** a line of verse of such feet. [C19 *iamb,* from C16 *iambus,* from Latin, from Greek *iambos*]

iambic (aɪˈæmbɪk) *Prosody.* ◆ *adj* **1** of, relating to, consisting of, or using an iamb or iambs. **2** (in Greek literature) denoting a type of satirical verse written in iambs. ◆ *n* **3** a metrical foot, line, or stanza of verse consisting of iambs. **4** a type of ancient Greek satirical verse written in iambs. ▸ **iˈambically** *adv*

-ian *suffix.* a variant of **-an**: *Etonian; Johnsonian.* [from Latin *-iānus*]

-iana *suffix forming nouns.* a variant of **-ana**.

IAP *abbrev. for* Internet access provider: a company that provides organizations or individuals with access to the Internet.

Iapetus (aɪˈæpɪtəs) *n* a large outer satellite of the planet Saturn.

IARU *abbrev. for* International Amateur Radio Union.

IAS *Aeronautics. abbrev. for* indicated air speed.

Iaşi (*Romanian* ˈjaʃj) *n* a city in NE Romania: capital of Moldavia (1565–1859); university (1860). Pop.: 339 889 (1994 est.). German name: **Jassy**.

-iasis *or* **-asis** *n combining form.* (in medicine) indicating a diseased condition: *psoriasis.* Compare **-osis** (sense 2). [from New Latin, from Greek, suffix of action]

IATA (aɪˈɑːtə, iːˈɑːtə) *n acronym for* International Air Transport Association.

iatric (aɪˈætrɪk) *or* **iatrical** *adj* relating to medicine or physicians; medical. [C19: from Greek *iatrikos* of healing, from *iasthai* to heal]

-iatrics *n combining form.* indicating medical care or treatment: *paediatrics.* Compare **-iatry.** [from IATRIC]

iatrogenic (aɪˌætrəʊˈdʒɛnɪk) *adj* **1** *Med.* (of an illness or symptoms) induced in a patient as the result of a physician's words or action. **2** *Social welfare.* (of a problem) induced by the means of treating a problem but ascribed to the continuing natural development of the problem being treated. ▸ **iatrogenicity** (aɪˌætrəʊdʒɪˈnɪsɪtɪ) *n*

-iatry *n combining form.* indicating healing or medical treatment: *psychiatry.* Compare **-iatrics.** [from New Latin *-iatria,* from Greek *iatreia* the healing art, from *iatros* healer, physician] ▸ **-iatric** *adj combining form.*

ib. See **ibid.**

IBA (in Britain) *abbrev. for* Independent Broadcasting Authority.

Ibadan (ɪˈbædᵊn) *n* a city in SW Nigeria, capital of Oyo state: university (1948). Pop.: 1 432 000 (1996 est.).

Ibagué (*Spanish* iβaˈɣe) *n* a city in W central Colombia. Pop.: 419 883 (1997 est.).

Ibáñez (*Spanish* iˈβaɲeθ) *n* See (Vicente) **Blasco Ibáñez**.

Ibarruri (*Spanish* iˈβarruri) *n* **Dolores** (doˈlores). real name of (La) **Pasionaria**.

I-beam *n* a rolled steel joist or a girder with a cross section in the form of a capital letter *I.* Compare **H-beam.**

Iberia (aɪˈbɪərɪə) *n* **1** the Iberian Peninsula. **2** an ancient region in central Asia, south of the Caucasus corresponding approximately to present-day Georgia.

Iberian (aɪˈbɪərɪən) *n* **1** a member of a group of ancient Caucasoid peoples who inhabited the Iberian Peninsula in preclassical and classical times. See also **Celtiberian. 2** a native or inhabitant of the Iberian Peninsula; a Spaniard or Portuguese. **3** a native or inhabitant of ancient Iberia in the Caucasus. ◆ *adj* **4** denoting, or relating to the pre-Roman peoples of the Iberian Peninsula or of Caucasian Iberia. **5** of or relating to the Iberian Peninsula, its inhabitants, or any of their languages.

Iberian Peninsula *n* a peninsula of SW Europe, occupied by Spain and Portugal.

iberis (aɪˈbɪərɪs) *n* any plant of the annual or perennial Eurasian genus *Iberis,* 12 to 25 cm (6-12 in.) in height, with white or purple flowers. *I. amara* and *I. umbellata* are the garden candytuft. Family *Cruciferae.* [New Latin, from *Iberia* Spain, where many species are common]

Ibero- (ˈaɪbərəʊ) *combining form.* indicating Iberia or Iberian: *Ibero-Caucasian.*

Ibert (*French* ibɛr) *n* **Jacques** (**François Antoine**) (ʒak). 1890–1962, French composer; his works include the humorous orchestral *Divertissement* (1930).

Iberville (*French* ibɛrvil) *n* **Pierre le Moyne** (pjɛr lə mwan), Sieur d'. 1661–1706, French-Canadian explorer, who founded (1700) the first French colony in Louisiana.

ibex (ˈaɪbɛks) *n, pl* **ibexes, ibices** (ˈɪbɪˌsiːz, ˈaɪ-), *or* **ibex.** any of three wild goats, *Capra ibex, C. caucasica,* or *C. pyrenaica,* of mountainous regions of Europe, Asia, and North Africa, having large backward-curving horns. [C17: from Latin: chamois]

Ibibio (ɪˈbɪbɪəʊ) *n* **1** (*pl* **-os** *or* **-o**) a member of a Negroid people of SE Nigeria, living esp. in and around Calabar. **2** Also called: **Efik.** the language of this people.

ibid. *or* **ib.** (in annotations, bibliographies, etc., when referring to a book, article, chapter, or page previously cited) *abbrev. for* ibidem. [Latin: in the same place]

ibis (ˈaɪbɪs) *n, pl* **ibises** *or* **ibis.** any of various wading birds of the family *Threskiornithidae,* such as *Threskiornis aethiopica* (**sacred ibis**), that occur in warm regions and have a long thin down-curved bill: order *Ciconiiformes* (herons, storks, etc.). Compare **wood ibis.** [C14: via Latin from Greek, from Egyptian *hby*]

Ibiza *or* **Iviza** (*Spanish* iˈβiθa) *n* **1** a Spanish island in the W Mediterranean, one of the Balearic Islands: hilly, with a rugged coast; tourism. Pop.: 45 000 (1986). Area: 541 sq. km (209 sq. miles). **2** the capital of Ibiza, a port on the south of the island. Pop.: 16 000 (latest est.).

-ible *suffix forming adjectives.* a variant of **-able.** ▸ **-ibly** *suffix forming adverbs.* ▸ **-ibility** *suffix forming nouns.*

ibn-al-Arabi (ˌɪbᵊnælɑːˈrɑːbɪ) *n* **Muhyi-l-din.** 1165–1240, Muslim mystic and poet, born in Spain, noted for his influence on Sufism.

ibn-Batuta (ˌɪbᵊnbæˈtuːtɑː) *n* 1304–?68, Arab traveller, who wrote the *Rihlah,* an account of his travels (1325–54) in Africa and Asia.

ibn-Ezra (ˌɪbᵊnˈɛzrə) *n* **Abraham Ben Meir.** 1093–1167, Jewish poet, scholar, and traveller, born in Spain.

ibn-Gabirol (ˌɪbᵊnˌgɑːˈbiːrɔːl) *n* **Solomon.** ?1021–?58, Jewish philosopher and poet, born in Spain. His work *The Fountain of Life* influenced Western medieval philosophers.

ibn-Khaldun (ˌɪbᵊnˌkɑːlˈduːn) *n* 1332–1406, Arab historian and philosopher. His *Kitab al-'ibar* (*Book of Examples*) is a history of Islam.

ibn-Rushd (ˌɪbᵊnˈrʊʃt) *n* the Arabic name of **Averroës.**

ibn-Saud (ˌɪbᵊnˈsaʊd) *n* **Abdul-Aziz** (æbˈdʊlæˈziːz). 1880–1953, first king of Saudi Arabia (1932–53).

ibn-Sina (ˌɪbᵊnˈsiːnə) *n* the Arabic name of **Avicenna.**

Ibo *or* **Igbo** (ˈiːbəʊ) *n* **1** (*pl* **-bos** *or* **-bo**) a member of a Negroid people of W Africa, living chiefly in S Nigeria. **2** the language of this people, belonging to the Kwa branch of the Niger-Congo family: one of the chief literary and cultural languages of S Nigeria.

Ibrahim Pasha (ˌɪbrəˈhiːm ˈpɑːʃə) *n* 1789–1848, Albanian general; son of Mehemet Ali, whom he succeeded as viceroy of Egypt (1848).

IBRD *abbrev. for* International Bank for Reconstruction and Development (the World Bank).

Ibsen (ˈɪbsən) *n* **Henrik** (ˈhɛnrɪk). 1828–1906, Norwegian dramatist and poet. After his early verse plays *Brand* (1866) and *Peer Gynt* (1867), he began the series of social dramas in prose, including *A Doll's House* (1879), *Ghosts* (1881), and *The Wild Duck* (1886), which have had a profound influence on modern drama. His later plays, such as *Hedda Gabler* (1890) and *The Master Builder* (1892), are more symbolic.

ibuprofen (aɪˈbjuːprəʊfən) *n* a drug, isobutylphenylpropionic acid, that relieves pain and reduces inflammation: used to treat arthritis and muscular strains. Formula: $C_{13}H_{18}O_2$.

IC *abbrev. for:* **1** internal-combustion. **2** *Electronics.* integrated circuit. **3** (in transformational grammar) immediate constituent. **4** *Astrology.* Imum Coeli: the point on the ecliptic lying directly opposite the Midheaven.

i/c *abbrev. for* in charge (of).

-ic *suffix forming adjectives.* **1** of, relating to, or resembling: *allergic; Germanic; periodic.* See also **-ical**. **2** (in chemistry) indicating that an element is chemically combined in the higher of two possible valence states: *ferric; stannic.* Compare **-ous** (sense 2). [from Latin *-icus* or Greek *-ikos; -ic* also occurs in nouns that represent a substantive use of adjectives (*magic*) and in nouns borrowed directly from Latin or Greek (*critic, music*)]

Içá ('iːsɑː; *Portuguese* i'sa) *n* the Brazilian part of the **Putumayo River**.

ICA *abbrev. for:* **1** (in Britain) Institute of Contemporary Arts. **2** International Cooperation Administration.

-ical *suffix forming adjectives.* a variant of **-ic**, but in some words having a less literal application than corresponding adjectives ending in *-ic: economical; fanatical.* [from Latin *-icālis*] ▸ **-ically** *suffix forming adverbs.*

ICAO *abbrev. for* International Civil Aviation Organization.

Icaria (aɪ'kɛərɪə, ɪ-) *n* a Greek island in the Aegean Sea, in the Southern Sporades group. Area: 256 sq. km (99 sq. miles). Modern Greek name: **Ikaría**. Also called: **Nikaria**.

Icarian[1] (aɪ'kɛərɪən, ɪ-) *adj* of or relating to Icarus.

Icarian[2] (aɪ'kɛərɪən, ɪ-) *adj* **1** of or relating to Icaria or its inhabitants. ◆ *n* **2** an inhabitant of Icaria.

Icarian Sea *n* the part of the Aegean Sea between the islands of Patmos and Leros and the coast of Asia Minor, where, according to legend, Icarus fell into the sea.

Icarus ('ɪkərəs, 'aɪ-) *n Greek myth.* the son of Daedalus, with whom he escaped from Crete, flying with wings made of wax and feathers. Heedless of his father's warning he flew too near the sun, causing the wax to melt, and fell into the Aegean and drowned.

ICBM *abbrev. for* intercontinental ballistic missile: a missile with a range greater than 5500 km.

ice (aɪs) *n* **1** water in the solid state, formed by freezing liquid water. Related adj: **glacial**. **2** a portion of ice cream. **3** *Slang.* a diamond or diamonds. **4** the field of play in ice hockey. **5** *Slang.* a concentrated and highly potent form of methamphetamine with dangerous side effects. **6** **break the ice. 6a** to relieve shyness, etc., esp. between strangers. **6b** to be the first of a group to do something. **7** **cut no ice.** *Informal.* to fail to make an impression. **8** **on ice.** in abeyance; pending. **9** **on thin ice.** unsafe or unsafely; vulnerable or vulnerably. ◆ *vb* **10** (often foll. by *up, over,* etc.) to form or cause to form ice; freeze. **11** (*tr*) to mix with ice or chill (a drink, etc.). **12** (*tr*) to cover (a cake, etc.) with icing. **13** (*tr*) *U.S. slang.* to kill. [Old English *īs;* compare Old High German *īs,* Old Norse *īss*] ▸ **'iceless** *adj* ▸ **'ice,like** *adj*

ICE (in Britain) *abbrev. for* Institution of Civil Engineers.

Ice. *abbrev. for* Iceland(ic).

ice age *n* another name for **glacial period**.

ice axe *n* a light axe used by mountaineers for cutting footholds in snow or ice, to provide an anchor point, or to control a slide on snow; it has a spiked tip and a head consisting of a pick and an adze.

ice bag *n* **1** a waterproof bag used as an ice pack. **2** a strong bag, usually made of canvas and equipped with two handles, used for carrying blocks of ice.

ice beer *n* a beer that is chilled after brewing so that any water is turned to ice and then removed.

iceberg ('aɪsbɜːg) *n* **1** a large mass of ice floating in the sea, esp. a mass that has broken off a polar glacier. **2** **tip of the iceberg.** the small visible part of something, esp. a problem or difficulty, that is much larger. **3** *Slang, chiefly U.S.* a person considered to have a cold or reserved manner. [C18: probably part translation of Middle Dutch *ijsberg* ice mountain; compare Norwegian *isberg*]

iceberg lettuce *n* a type of lettuce with very crisp pale leaves tightly enfolded.

iceblink ('aɪs,blɪŋk) *n* **1** Also called: **blink**. a yellowish-white reflected glare in the sky over an ice field. **2** a coastal ice cliff.

ice block *n Scot., Austral., and N.Z.* a flavoured frozen water ice: in Australia and New Zealand, sometimes on a stick.

iceboat ('aɪs,bəʊt) *n* another name for **icebreaker** (sense 1) or **ice yacht**.

icebound ('aɪs,baʊnd) *adj* covered or made immobile by ice; frozen in: *an icebound ship.*

icebox ('aɪs,bɒks) *n* **1** a compartment in a refrigerator for storing or making ice. **2** an insulated cabinet packed with ice for storing food.

icebreaker ('aɪs,breɪkə) *n* **1** Also called: **iceboat**. a vessel with a reinforced bow for breaking up the ice in bodies of water to keep channels open for navigation. **2** any tool or device for breaking ice into smaller pieces. **3** something intended to relieve mutual shyness at a gathering of strangers.

icecap ('aɪs,kæp) *n* a thick mass of glacial ice and snow that permanently covers an area of land, such as either of the polar regions or the peak of a mountain.

ice cream *n* a kind of sweetened frozen liquid, properly made from cream and egg yolks but often made from milk or a custard base, flavoured in various ways.

ice-cream cone *or* **cornet** *n* **1** a conical edible wafer for holding ice cream. **2** such a cone containing ice cream.

ice-cream soda *n Chiefly U.S.* ice cream served in a tall glass of carbonated water and a little milk, usually flavoured in various ways.

iced (aɪst) *adj* **1** covered, coated, or chilled with ice. **2** covered with icing: *iced cakes.*

ice dance *n* any of a number of dances, mostly based on ballroom dancing, performed by a couple skating on ice. ▸ **ice dancer** *n* ▸ **ice dancing** *n*

icefall ('aɪs,fɔːl) *n* a very steep part of a glacier that has deep crevasses and resembles a frozen waterfall.

ice field *n* **1** a very large flat expanse of ice floating in the sea; large ice floe. **2** a large mass of ice permanently covering an extensive area of land.

ice fish *n* any percoid fish of the family *Chaenichthyidae,* of Antarctic seas, having a semitransparent scaleless body.

ice floe *n* a sheet of ice, of variable size, floating in the sea. See also **ice field** (sense 1).

ice foot *n* a narrow belt of ice permanently attached to the coast in polar regions.

ice hockey *n* a game played on ice by two opposing teams of six players each, who wear skates and try to propel a flat puck into their opponents' goal with long sticks having an offset flat blade at the end.

ice house *n* a building for storing ice.

Içel (iː'tʃel) *n* another name for **Mersin**.

Icel. *abbrev. for* Iceland(ic).

Iceland ('aɪslənd) *n* an island republic in the N Atlantic, regarded as part of Europe: settled by Norsemen, who established a legislative assembly in 930; under Danish rule (1380–1918); gained independence in 1918 and became a republic in 1944; contains large areas of glaciers, snowfields, and lava beds with many volcanoes and hot springs (the chief source of domestic heat); inhabited chiefly along the SW coast. The economy is based largely on fishing. Official language: Icelandic. Official religion: Evangelical Lutheran. Currency: krona. Capital: Reykjavik. Pop.: 276 000 (1998 est.). Area: 102 828 sq. km (39 702 sq. miles).

Iceland agate *n* another name for **obsidian**.

Icelander ('aɪs,lændə, 'aɪsləndə) *n* a native, citizen, or inhabitant of Iceland.

Icelandic (aɪs'lændɪk) *adj* **1** of, relating to, or characteristic of Iceland, its people, or their language. ◆ *n* **2** the official language of Iceland, belonging to the North Germanic branch of the Indo-European family. See also **Old Icelandic**.

Iceland moss *n* a lichen, *Cetraria islandica,* of arctic regions and N Europe, with brownish edible fronds.

Iceland poppy *n* any of various widely cultivated arctic poppies, esp. *Papaver nudicaule,* with white or yellow nodding flowers.

Iceland spar *n* a pure transparent variety of calcite with double-refracting crystals used in making polarizing microscopes.

ice lolly *n Brit. informal.* an ice cream or water ice on a stick. Also called: **lolly**. U.S. and Canadian equivalent (trademark): **Popsicle**.

ice machine *n* a machine that automatically produces ice for use in drinks, etc.

ice maiden *n* a beautiful but aloof woman.

ice man *n Chiefly U.S.* a man who sells or delivers ice.

ice needle *n Meteorol.* one of many needle-like ice crystals that form cirrus clouds in clear cold weather.

Iceni (aɪ'siːnaɪ) *pl n* an ancient British tribe that rebelled against the Romans in 61 A.D. under Queen Boudicca.

ice pack *n* **1** a bag or folded cloth containing ice, applied to a part of the body, esp. the head, to cool, reduce swelling, etc. **2** another name for **pack ice**. **3** a sachet containing a gel that can be frozen or heated and that retains its temperature for an extended period of time, used esp. in cool bags.

ice pick *n* a pointed tool used for breaking ice.

ice plant *n* a low-growing plant, *Mesembryanthemum* (or *Cryophytum*) *crystallinum,* of southern Africa, with fleshy leaves covered with icelike hairs and pink or white rayed flowers: family *Aizoaceae.*

ice point *n* the temperature at which a mixture of ice and water are in equilibrium at a pressure of one atmosphere. It is 0° on the Celsius scale and 32° on the Fahrenheit scale. Compare **steam point**.

ice screw *n Mountaineering.* a screwed tubular or solid steel rod with a ring at one end for inserting into ice as an anchor point.

ice sheet *n* a thick layer of ice covering a large area of land for a long time, esp. the layer that covered much of the N hemisphere during the last glacial period.

ice shelf *n* a thick mass of ice that is permanently attached to the land but projects into and floats on the sea.

ice show *n* any entertainment performed by ice-skaters.

ice skate *n* **1** a boot having a steel blade fitted to the sole to enable the wearer to glide swiftly over ice. **2** the steel blade on such a boot or shoe. ◆ *vb* **ice-skate. 3** (*intr*) to glide swiftly over ice on ice skates. ▸ **'ice-,skater** *n*

ice station *n* a scientific research station in polar regions, where ice movement, weather, and environmental conditions are monitored.

ice water *n* **1** water formed from ice. **2** Also called: **iced water**. drinking water cooled by refrigeration or the addition of ice.

ice yacht *n* a sailing craft having a cross-shaped frame with a cockpit and runners for travelling over ice. Also called: **iceboat**.

ICFTU *abbrev. for* International Confederation of Free Trade Unions.

Ichang *or* **I-ch'ang** ('iː'tʃæŋ) *n* a variant transliteration of the Chinese name of **Yichang**.

I.Chem.E. *abbrev. for* Institution of Chemical Engineers.

I Ching ('iː 'tʃɪŋ) *n* an ancient Chinese book of divination and a source of Confucian and Taoist philosophy. Answers to questions and advice may be obtained by referring to the text accompanying one of 64 hexagrams, selected at random. Also called: **Book of Changes**.

ich-laut ('ɪç,laut, 'ɪk-) *n* (*sometimes cap.*) *Phonetics.* the voiceless palatal fricative sound that is written as *ch* in German *ich,* often allophonic with the ach-laut. See also **ach-laut**. [from German, from *ich* I + *laut* sound]

ichneumon (ɪk'njuːmən) *n* a mongoose, *Herpestes ichneumon,* of Africa and S Europe, having greyish-brown speckled fur. [C16: via Latin from Greek, literally: tracker, hunter, from *ikhneuein* to track, from *ikhnos* a footprint; so named from the animal's alleged ability to locate the eggs of crocodiles]

ichneumon fly *or* **wasp** *n* any hymenopterous insect of the family *Ichneumonidae,* whose larvae are parasitic in caterpillars and other insect larvae.

ichnite ('ɪknaɪt) *or* **ichnolite** ('ɪknə,laɪt) *n* a fossilized footprint. [C19: from Greek *ikhnos* footprint, track + -ITE[1]]

ichnography (ɪk'nɒgrəfɪ) *n* **1** the art of drawing ground plans. **2** the ground plan of a building, factory, etc. [C16: from Latin *ichnographia,* from Greek *ikhnographia,* from *ikhnos* trace, track] ▸ **ichnographic** (ˌɪknəˈɡræfɪk) *or* **ˌichno-ˈgraphical** *adj* ▸ **ˌichnoˈgraphically** *adv*

ichnology (ɪkˈnɒlədʒɪ) *n* the study of fossil footprints. [C19: from Greek *ikhnos* footprint, track] ▸ **ichnological** (ˌɪknəˈlɒdʒɪkᵊl) *adj*

ichor (ˈaɪkɔː) *n* **1** *Greek myth.* the fluid said to flow in the veins of the gods. **2** *Pathol.* a foul-smelling watery discharge from a wound or ulcer. [C17: from Greek *ikhōr,* of obscure origin] ▸ **ˈichorous** *adj*

ichth. *abbrev. for* ichthyology.

ichthyic (ˈɪkθɪɪk) *adj* of, relating to, or characteristic of fishes. [C19: from Greek, from *ikhthus* fish]

ichthyo- *or before a vowel* **ichthy-** *combining form.* indicating or relating to fishes: *ichthyology.* [from Latin, from Greek *ikhthus* fish]

ichthyoid (ˈɪkθɪˌɔɪd) *adj also* **ichthyoidal. 1** resembling a fish. ♦ *n* **2** a fishlike vertebrate.

ichthyol. *or* **ichth.** *abbrev. for* ichthyology.

ichthyolite (ˈɪkθɪəˌlaɪt) *n Rare.* any fossil fish. ▸ **ichthyolitic** (ˌɪkθɪəˈlɪtɪk) *adj*

ichthyology (ˌɪkθɪˈɒlədʒɪ) *n* the study of the physiology, history, economic importance, etc., of fishes. ▸ **ichthyologic** (ˌɪkθɪəˈlɒdʒɪk) *or* **ˌichthyoˈlogical** *adj* ▸ **ˌichthyoˈlogically** *adv* ▸ **ˌichthyˈologist** *n*

ichthyophagous (ˌɪkθɪˈɒfəɡəs) *adj* feeding on fish. ▸ **ichthyophagy** (ˌɪkθɪˈɒfədʒɪ) *n*

ichthyornis (ˌɪkθɪˈɔːnɪs) *n* an extinct Cretaceous sea bird of the genus *Ichthyornis,* thought to have resembled a tern. [C19: New Latin, from ICHTHY- + Greek *ornis* bird]

ichthyosaur (ˈɪkθɪəˌsɔː) *or* **ichthyosaurus** (ˌɪkθɪəˈsɔːrəs) *n, pl* **-saurs, -sauruses,** *or* **-sauri** (-ˈsɔːraɪ). any extinct marine Mesozoic reptile of the order *Ichthyosauria,* which had a porpoise-like body with dorsal and tail fins and paddle-like limbs. See also **plesiosaur.**

ichthyosis (ˌɪkθɪˈəʊsɪs) *n* a congenital disease in which the skin is coarse, dry, and scaly. Also called: **xeroderma.** Nontechnical name: **fishskin disease.** ▸ **ichthyotic** (ˌɪkθɪˈɒtɪk) *adj*

ICI *abbrev. for* Imperial Chemical Industries.

-ician *suffix forming nouns.* indicating a person skilled or involved in a subject or activity: *physician; beautician.* [from French *-icien;* see -IC, -IAN]

icicle (ˈaɪsɪkᵊl) *n* a hanging spike of ice formed by the freezing of dripping water. [C14: from ICE + *ickel,* from Old English *gicel* icicle, related to Old Norse *jökull* large piece of ice, glacier] ▸ **ˈicicled** *adj*

icily (ˈaɪsɪlɪ) *adv* in an icy or reserved manner.

iciness (ˈaɪsɪnɪs) *n* **1** the condition of being icy or very cold. **2** a manner that is cold or reserved; aloofness.

icing (ˈaɪsɪŋ) *n* **1** Also called (esp. U.S. and Canadian): **frosting.** a sugar preparation, variously flavoured and coloured, for coating and decorating cakes, biscuits, etc. **2** the formation of ice, as on a ship or aircraft, due to the freezing of moisture in the atmosphere. **3** any unexpected extra or bonus (esp. in **icing on the cake**).

icing sugar *n Brit.* a very finely ground sugar used for icings, confections, etc. U.S. term: **confectioners' sugar.**

ICJ *abbrev. for* International Court of Justice.

icon *or* **ikon** (ˈaɪkɒn) *n* **1** a representation of Christ, the Virgin Mary, or a saint, esp. one painted in oil on a wooden panel, depicted in a traditional Byzantine style and venerated in the Eastern Church. **2** an image, picture, representation, etc. **3** a symbol resembling or analogous to the thing it represents. **4** a person regarded as a sex symbol or as a symbol of a belief or cultural movement. **5** a pictorial representation of a facility available on a computer system, that enables the facility to be activated by means of a screen cursor rather than by a textual instruction. [C16: from Latin, from Greek *eikōn* image, from *eikenai* to be like]

iconic (aɪˈkɒnɪk) *or* **iconical** *adj* **1** relating to, resembling, or having the character of an icon. **2** (of memorial sculptures, esp. those depicting athletes of ancient Greece) having a fixed conventional style.

iconic memory *n Psychol.* the temporary persistence of visual impressions after the stimulus has been removed. Compare **echoic memory.**

Iconium (aɪˈkəʊnɪəm) *n* the ancient name for **Konya.**

icono- *or before a vowel* **icon-** *combining form.* indicating an image or likeness: *iconology.* [from Greek: ICON]

iconoclasm (aɪˈkɒnəˌklæzəm) *n* the acts or beliefs of an iconoclast.

iconoclast (aɪˈkɒnəˌklæst) *n* **1** a person who attacks established or traditional concepts, principles, laws, etc. **2a** a destroyer of religious images or sacred objects. **2b** an adherent of the heretical movement within the Greek Orthodox Church from 725 to 842 A.D., which aimed at the destruction of icons and religious images. [C16: from Late Latin *iconoclastes,* from Late Greek *eikonoklastēs,* from *eikōn* icon + *klastēs* breaker] ▸ **iˌconoˈclastic** *adj* ▸ **iˌconoˈclastically** *adv*

iconography (ˌaɪkɒˈnɒɡrəfɪ) *n, pl* **-phies. 1a** the symbols used in a work of art or art movement. **1b** the conventional significance attached to such symbols. **2** a collection of pictures of a particular subject, such as Christ. **3** the representation of the subjects of icons or portraits, esp. on coins. ▸ **ˌicoˈnographer** *n* ▸ **iconographic** (aɪˌkɒnəˈɡræfɪk) *or* **iˌconoˈgraphical** *adj*

iconolatry (ˌaɪkɒˈnɒlətrɪ) *n* the worship or adoration of icons as idols. ▸ **ˌicoˈnolater** *n* ▸ **ˌicoˈnolatrous** *adj*

iconology (ˌaɪkɒˈnɒlədʒɪ) *n* **1** the study or field of art history concerning icons. **2** icons collectively. **3** the symbolic representation or symbolism of icons. ▸ **iconological** (aɪˌkɒnəˈlɒdʒɪkᵊl) *adj* ▸ **ˌicoˈnologist** *n*

iconomatic (aɪˌkɒnəˈmætɪk) *adj* employing pictures to represent not objects themselves but the sound of their names. [C19: from Greek, from *eikon* image + *onoma* name] ▸ **iconomaticism** (aɪˌkɒnəˈmætɪˌsɪzəm) *n*

iconoscope (aɪˈkɒnəˌskəʊp) *n* a television camera tube in which an electron beam scans a photoemissive surface, converting an optical image into electrical pulses.

iconostasis (ˌaɪkəʊˈnɒstəsɪs) *or* **iconostas** (aɪˈkɒnəˌstæs) *n, pl* **iconostases** (ˌaɪkəʊˈnɒstəˌsiːz *or* aɪˈkɒnəˌstæsɪz) *Eastern Church.* a screen with doors and icons set in tiers, which separates the bema (sanctuary) from the nave. [C19: Church Latin, from Late Greek *eikonostasion* shrine, literally: area where images are placed, from ICONO- + *histanai* to stand]

icosahedron (ˌaɪkəsəˈhiːdrən) *n, pl* **-drons** *or* **-dra** (-drə). a solid figure having 20 faces. The faces of a **regular icosahedron** are equilateral triangles. [C16: from Greek *eikosaedron,* from *eikosi* twenty + *-edron* -HEDRON] ▸ **ˌicosaˈhedral** *adj*

icositetrahedron (ˌaɪkəsɪˌtetrəˈhiːdrən) *n, pl* **-drons** *or* **-dra** (-drə). a solid figure having 24 trapezoid faces, as occurring in some crystals.

ICS *abbrev. for* Indian Civil Service.

-ics *suffix forming nouns; functioning as sing* **1** indicating a science, art, or matters relating to a particular subject: *aeronautics; politics.* **2** indicating certain activities or practices: *acrobatics.* [plural of *-ic,* representing Latin *-ica,* from Greek *-ika,* as in *mathēmatika* mathematics]

ICSH *abbrev. for* interstitial-cell-stimulating hormone.

icterus (ˈɪktərəs) *n* **1** *Pathol.* another name for **jaundice. 2** a yellowing of plant leaves, caused by excessive cold or moisture. [C18: from Latin: yellow bird, the sight of which reputedly cured jaundice, from Greek *ikteros*] ▸ **icteric** (ɪkˈterɪk) *adj*

Ictinus (ɪkˈtaɪnəs) *n* 5th century B.C., Greek architect, who designed the Parthenon with Callicrates.

ictus (ˈɪktəs) *n, pl* **-tuses** *or* **-tus. 1** *Prosody.* metrical or rhythmic stress in verse feet, as contrasted with the stress accent on words. **2** *Med.* a sudden attack or stroke. [C18: from Latin *icere* to strike] ▸ **ˈictal** *adj*

ICU *abbrev. for* intensive care unit.

icy (ˈaɪsɪ) *adj* **icier, iciest. 1** made of, covered with, or containing ice. **2** resembling ice. **3** freezing or very cold. **4** cold or reserved in manner; aloof.

icy pole *n* the Australian name for an **ice lolly.**

id (ɪd) *n Psychoanal.* the mass of primitive instincts and energies in the unconscious mind that, modified by the ego and the superego, underlies all psychic activity. [C20: New Latin, from Latin: it; used to render German *Es*]

ID *abbrev. for:* **1** Idaho. **2** identification. **3** Also: **i.d.** inside diameter. **4** Intelligence Department. **5** Also **i.d.** intradermal.

id. *abbrev. for* idem.

Id. *abbrev. for* Idaho.

I'd (aɪd) *contraction of* I had *or* I would.

-id[1] *suffix forming nouns.* **1** indicating the names of meteor showers that appear to radiate from a specified constellation: *Orionids* (from Orion). **2** indicating a particle, body, or structure of a specified kind: *energid.* [from Latin *-id-, -is,* from Greek, feminine suffix of origin]

-id[2] *suffix forming nouns and adjectives.* **1** indicating members of a zoological family: *cyprinid.* **2** indicating members of a dynasty: *Seleucid; Fatimid.* [from New Latin *-idae* or *-ida,* from Greek *-idēs* suffix indicating offspring]

-id[3] *suffix forming nouns.* a variant of **-ide.**

Ida (ˈaɪdə) *n* **Mount. 1** a mountain in central Crete: the highest on the island; in ancient times associated with the worship of Zeus. Height: 2456 m (8057 ft). Modern Greek name: **Idhi. 2** a mountain in NW Turkey, southeast of the site of ancient Troy. Height: 1767 m (5797 ft.). Turkish name: **Kaz Daği.**

IDA *abbrev. for* International Development Association.

Ida. *abbrev.for* Idaho.

-idae *suffix forming nouns.* indicating names of zoological families: *Felidae; Hominidae.* [New Latin, from Latin, from Greek *-idai,* suffix indicating offspring]

Idaho (ˈaɪdəˌhəʊ) *n* a state of the northwestern U.S.: consists chiefly of ranges of the Rocky Mountains, with the Snake River basin in the south; important for agriculture (**Idaho potatoes**), livestock, and silver-mining. Capital: Boise. Pop.: 1 210 232 (1997 est.). Area: 216 413 sq. km (83 557 sq. miles). Abbrevs.: **Id., Ida.,** or (with zip code) **ID** ▸ **ˈIdaˌhoan** *adj, n*

IDB *Chiefly S. African. abbrev. for* illicit diamond buying.

IDC *abbrev. for* industrial development certificate.

ID card *n* a card or document that serves to identify a person, or to prove his age, membership, etc.

IDD *abbrev. for* international direct dialling.

ide (aɪd) *n* another name for the **silver orfe.** See **orfe.** [C19: from New Latin *idus,* from Swedish *id*]

-ide *or* **-id** *suffix forming nouns.* **1** (*added to the combining form of the nonmetallic or electronegative elements*) indicating a binary compound: *sodium chloride.* **2** indicating an organic compound derived from another: *acetanilide.* **3** indicating one of a class of compounds or elements: *peptide; lanthanide.* [from German *-id,* from French *oxide* OXIDE, based on the suffix of *acide* ACID]

idea (aɪˈdɪə) *n* **1** any content of the mind, esp. the conscious mind. **2** the thought of something: *the very idea appals me.* **3** a mental representation of something: *she's got a good idea of the layout of the factory.* **4** the characterization of something in general terms; concept: *the idea of a square circle is self-contradictory.* **5** an individual's conception of something: *his idea of honesty is not the same as yours and mine.* **6** the belief that something is the case: *he has the idea that what he's doing is right.* **7** a scheme, intention, plan, etc.: *here's my idea for the sales campaign.* **8** a vague notion or indication; inkling: *he had no idea of what life would be like in Africa.* **9** significance or purpose: *the idea of the game is to discover the murderer.* **10** *Philosophy.* **10a** a private mental object, regarded as the immediate object of thought or perception. **10b** a Platonic Idea or Form. **11** *Music.* a thematic phrase or figure; motif. **12** *Obsolete.* a mental image. **13 get ideas.** to become ambitious, restless, etc. **14 not one's idea of.** not what one regards as (hard work, a holiday, etc.). **15 that's an**

idea. that is worth considering. **16 the very idea!** that is preposterous, unreasonable, etc. [C16: via Late Latin from Greek: model, pattern, notion, from *idein* to see] ▸ **i'dealess** *adj*

USAGE It is usually considered correct to say that someone has *the idea of doing* something, rather than *the idea to do* it: *he had the idea of taking* (not *the idea to take*) *a short holiday.*

Idea (aɪ'dɪə) *n* another name for **Form.**

ideal (aɪ'dɪəl) *n* **1** a conception of something that is perfect, esp. that which one seeks to attain. **2** a person or thing considered to represent perfection: *he's her ideal.* **3** something existing only as an idea. **4** a pattern or model, esp. of ethical behaviour. ◆ *adj* **5** conforming to an ideal. **6** of, involving, or existing in the form of an idea. **7** *Philosophy.* **7a** of or relating to a highly desirable and possible state of affairs. **7b** of or relating to idealism. ▸ **ideality** (ˌaɪdɪ'ælɪtɪ) *n* ▸ **i'deally** *adv* ▸ **i'dealness** *n*

ideal crystal *n Chem.* a crystal in which there are no defects or impurities.

ideal element *n* any element added to a mathematical theory in order to eliminate special cases. The ideal element i = √–1 allows all algebraic equations to be solved and the point at infinity (**ideal point**) ensures that any two lines in projective geometry intersect.

ideal gas *n* a hypothetical gas which obeys Boyle's law exactly at all temperatures and pressures, and which has internal energy that depends only upon the temperature. Measurements upon real gases are extrapolated to zero pressure to obtain results in agreement with theories relating to an ideal gas, especially in thermometry. Also called: **perfect gas.**

idealism (aɪ'dɪəˌlɪzəm) *n* **1** belief in or pursuance of ideals. **2** the tendency to represent things in their ideal forms, rather than as they are. **3** any of a group of philosophical doctrines that share the monistic view that material objects and the external world do not exist in reality independently of the human mind but are variously creations of the mind or constructs of ideas. Compare **materialism** (sense 2), **dualism** (sense 2). ▸ **i'dealist** *n* ▸ **iˌdeal'istic** *adj* ▸ **iˌdeal'istically** *adv*

idealization *or* **idealisation** (aɪˌdɪəlaɪ'zeɪʃən) *n* **1** the representation of something as ideal. **2** a conception of something that dwells on its advantages and ignores its deficiencies. **3** a general theoretical account of natural phenomena that ignores features that are difficult to accommodate within a theory.

idealize *or* **idealise** (aɪ'dɪəˌlaɪz) *vb* **1** to consider or represent (something) as ideal. **2** (*tr*) to portray as ideal; glorify. **3** (*intr*) to form an ideal or ideals. ▸ **i'dealˌizer** *or* **i'dealˌiser** *n*

ideas of reference *pl n* a schizophrenic symptom in which the patient thinks that things completely disconnected from him are influencing him or conveying messages to him.

ideatum (ˌaɪdɪ'eɪtəm) *n, pl* **-ata** (-'eɪtə). *Philosophy.* the objective reality with which human ideas are supposed to correspond. [C18: New Latin, from Latin: IDEA]

idée fixe *French.* (ide fiks) *n, pl* ***idées fixes*** (ide fiks). a fixed idea; obsession.

idée reçue *French.* (ide rəsy) *n, pl* ***idées reçues*** (ide rəsy). a generally held opinion or concept. [literally: received idea]

idem *Latin.* ('aɪdem, 'ɪdɛm) *pron, adj* the same: used to refer to an article, chapter, etc., previously cited.

idempotent ('aɪdəmˌpəʊtənt, 'ɪd-) *adj Maths.* (of a matrix, transformation, etc.) not changed in value following multiplication by itself. [C20: from Latin *idem* same + POTENT[1]]

identic (aɪ'dɛntɪk) *adj* **1** *Diplomacy.* (esp. of opinions expressed by two or more governments) having the same wording or intention regarding another power: *identic notes.* **2** an obsolete word for **identical.**

identical (aɪ'dɛntɪkᵊl) *adj* **1** Also called: **numerically identical.** being one and the same individual: *Cicero and Tully are identical.* **2** Also called: **quantitatively identical.** exactly alike, equal, or agreeing. **3** designating either or both of a pair of twins of the same sex who developed from a single fertilized ovum that split into two. Compare **fraternal** (sense 3). ▸ **i'dentically** *adv* ▸ **i'denticalness** *n*

identical proposition *n Logic.* a necessary truth, esp. a categorial identity, such as *whatever is triangular has three sides.*

identification (aɪˌdɛntɪfɪ'keɪʃən) *n* **1** the act of identifying or the state of being identified. **2a** something that identifies a person or thing. **2b** (*as modifier*): *an identification card.* **3** *Psychol.* **3a** the process of recognizing specific objects as the result of remembering. **3b** the process by which one incorporates aspects of another person's personality. **3c** the transferring of a response from one situation to another because the two bear similar features. See also **generalization** (sense 3).

identification parade *n* a group of persons including one suspected of having committed a crime assembled for the purpose of discovering whether a witness can identify the suspect.

identify (aɪ'dɛntɪˌfaɪ) *vb* **-fies, -fying, -fied.** (*mainly tr*) **1** to prove or recognize as being a certain person or thing; determine the identity of. **2** to consider as the same or equivalent. **3** (*also intr;* often foll. by *with*) to consider (oneself) as similar to another. **4** to determine the taxonomic classification of (a plant or animal). **5** (*intr;* usually foll. by *with*) *Psychol.* to engage in identification. ▸ **i'dentiˌfiable** *adj* ▸ **i'dentiˌfiably** *adv* ▸ **i'dentiˌfier** *n*

Identikit (aɪ'dɛntɪˌkɪt) *n Trademark.* **1a** a set of transparencies of various typical facial characteristics that can be superimposed on one another to build up, on the basis of a description, a picture of a person sought by the police. **1b** (*as modifier*): *an Identikit picture.* **2** (*modifier*) artificially created by copying different elements in an attempt to form a whole: *an identikit pop group.*

identity (aɪ'dɛntɪtɪ) *n, pl* **-ties. 1** the state of having unique identifying characteristics held by no other person or thing. **2** the individual characteristics by which a person or thing is recognized. **3** Also called: **numerical identity.** the property of being one and the same individual: *his loss of memory did not affect his identity.* **4** Also called: **qualitative identity.** the state of being the same in nature, quality, etc.: *they were linked by the identity of their tastes.* **5** the state of being the same as a person or thing described or claimed: *the identity of the stolen goods has not yet been established.* **6** identification of oneself as: *moving to London destroyed his Welsh identity.* **7** *Logic.* **7a** that relation that holds only between any entity and itself. **7b** an assertion that that relation holds, as *Cicero is Tully.* **8** *Maths.* **8a** an equation that is valid for all values of its variables, as in $(x - y)(x + y) = x^2 - y^2$. Often denoted by the symbol ≡ **8b** Also called: **identity element.** a member of a set that when operating on another member, *x*, produces that member *x:* *the identity for multiplication of numbers is 1 since x.1 = 1.x = x.* See also **inverse** (sense 2b). **9** *Austral. and N.Z. informal.* a well-known person, esp. in a specified locality; figure (esp. in the phrase **an old identity**). [C16: from Late Latin *identitās,* from Latin *idem* the same]

identity card *n* a card that establishes a person's identity, esp. one issued to all members of the population in wartime, to the staff of an organization, etc.

identity theory *n Philosophy.* a form of materialism which holds mental states to be identical with certain states of the brain and so to have no separate existence, but regards this identity as contingent so that mentalistic and physicalistic language are not held to be synonymous. See also **anomalous monism, materialism** (sense 2).

ideo- *combining form.* of or indicating idea or ideas: *ideology.* [from French *idéo-,* from Greek *idea* IDEA]

ideogram ('ɪdɪəʊˌgræm) *or* **ideograph** ('ɪdɪəʊˌgrɑːf, -ˌgræf) *n* **1** a sign or symbol, used in such writing systems as those of China or Japan, that directly represents a concept, idea, or thing rather than a word or set of words for it. **2** any graphic sign or symbol, such as %, @, &, etc.

ideography (ˌɪdɪ'ɒgrəfɪ) *n* the use of ideograms to communicate ideas.

ideologist (ˌaɪdɪ'ɒlədʒɪst) *n* **1** a person who supports a particular ideology, esp. a political theorist. **2** a person who studies an ideology or ideologies. **3** a theorist or visionary. ◆ Also called: **ideologue** ('aɪdɪəˌlɒg).

ideology (ˌaɪdɪ'ɒlədʒɪ) *n, pl* **-gies. 1** a body of ideas that reflects the beliefs and interests of a nation, political system, etc. and underlies political action. **2** *Philosophy, sociology.* the set of beliefs by which a group or society orders reality so as to render it intelligible. **3** speculation that is imaginary or visionary. **4** the study of the nature and origin of ideas. ▸ **ideological** (ˌaɪdɪə'lɒdʒɪkᵊl) *or* **ˌideo'logic** *adj* ▸ **ˌideo'logically** *adv*

ideomotor (ˌaɪdɪə'məʊtə) *adj Physiol.* designating automatic muscular movements stimulated by ideas, as in absent-minded acts.

ides (aɪdz) *n* (*functioning as sing*) (in the Roman calendar) the 15th day in March, May, July, and October and the 13th day of each other month. See also **calends, nones.** [C15: from Old French, from Latin *īdūs* (plural), of uncertain origin]

id est *Latin.* ('ɪd 'est) the full form of **i.e.**

Idhi ('iði) *n* a transliteration of the Modern Greek name for (Mount) **Ida** (sense 1).

idio- *combining form.* indicating peculiarity, isolation, or that which pertains to an individual person or thing: *idiolect.* [from Greek *idios* private, separate]

idioblast ('ɪdɪəʊˌblæst) *n* a plant cell that differs from those around it in the same tissue. ▸ **ˌidio'blastic** *adj*

idiocy ('ɪdɪəsɪ) *n, pl* **-cies. 1** (*not in technical usage*) severe mental retardation. **2** foolishness or senselessness; stupidity. **3** a foolish act or remark.

idioglossia (ˌɪdɪəʊ'glɒsɪə) *n* **1** a private language, as invented by a child or between two children, esp. twins. **2** a pathological condition in which a person's speech is so severely distorted that it is unintelligible. [C19: from Greek *idios* private, separate + *glossa* tongue]

idiogram ('ɪdɪəʊˌgræm) *n* another name for **karyogram.**

idiographic (ˌɪdɪəʊ'græfɪk) *adj Psychol.* of or relating to the study of individuals. Compare **nomothetic.**

idiolect ('ɪdɪəˌlɛkt) *n* the variety or form of a language used by an individual. ▸ **ˌidio'lectal** *or* **ˌidio'lectic** *adj*

idiom ('ɪdɪəm) *n* **1** a group of words whose meaning cannot be predicted from the meanings of the constituent words, as for example (*It was raining*) *cats and dogs.* **2** linguistic usage that is grammatical and natural to native speakers of a language. **3** the characteristic vocabulary or usage of a specific human group or subject. **4** the characteristic artistic style of an individual, school, period, etc. [C16: from Latin *idiōma* peculiarity of language, from Greek; see IDIO-] ▸ **idiomatic** (ˌɪdɪə'mætɪk) *or* **ˌidio'matical** *adj* ▸ **ˌidio'matically** *adv* ▸ **ˌidio'maticalness** *n*

idiomorphic (ˌɪdɪəʊ'mɔːfɪk) *adj* (of minerals) occurring naturally in the form of well-developed crystals. ▸ **ˌidio'morphically** *adv* ▸ **ˌidio'morphism** *n*

idiopathy (ˌɪdɪ'ɒpəθɪ) *n, pl* **-thies.** any disease of unknown cause. ▸ **idiopathic** (ˌɪdɪəʊ'pæθɪk) *adj*

idiophone ('ɪdɪəˌfəʊn) *n Music.* a percussion instrument, such as a cymbal or xylophone, made of naturally sonorous material. ▸ **idiophonic** (ˌɪdɪə'fɒnɪk) *adj*

idioplasm ('ɪdɪəʊˌplæzəm) *n* another name for **germ plasm.** ▸ **ˌidio'plasmic** *or* **idioplasmatic** (ˌɪdɪəʊplæz'mætɪk) *adj*

idiosyncrasy (ˌɪdɪəʊ'sɪŋkrəsɪ) *n, pl* **-sies. 1** a tendency, type of behaviour, mannerism, etc., of a specific person; quirk. **2** the composite physical or psychological make-up of a specific person. **3** an abnormal reaction of an individual to specific foods, drugs, or other agents. [C17: from Greek *idiosunkrasia,* from IDIO- + *sunkrasis* mixture, temperament, from *sun-* SYN- + *kerannunai* to mingle] ▸ **idiosyncratic** (ˌɪdɪəʊsɪŋ'krætɪk) *adj* ▸ **ˌidiosyn'cratically** *adv*

idiot ('ɪdɪət) *n* **1** a person with severe mental retardation. **2** a foolish or senseless person. [C13: from Latin *idiōta* ignorant person, from Greek *idiōtēs* private person, one who lacks professional knowledge, ignoramus; see IDIO-]

idiot board *n* a slang name for **Autocue.**

idiot box *n Slang.* a television set.
idiotic (ˌɪdɪˈɒtɪk) *adj* of or resembling an idiot; foolish; senseless. ▸ **ˌidiˈotically** *adv* ▸ **ˌidiˈoticalness** *n*
idiotism (ˈɪdɪəˌtɪzəm) *n* **1** an archaic word for **idiocy. 2** an obsolete word for **idiom.**
idiot savant (ˈiːdjəʊ sæˈvɑ̃, ˈɪdɪət ˈsævənt) *n, pl* **idiots savants** (ˈiːdjəʊ sæˈvɑ̃) *or* **idiot savants.** a person of subnormal intelligence who performs brilliantly at some specialized intellectual task, such as giving the day of the week for any calendar date past or present. [C19: from French: knowledgeable idiot]
idiot tape *n Printing.* an input tape for a typesetting machine that contains text only, the typographical instructions being supplied by the typesetting machine itself.
idle (ˈaɪdᵊl) *adj* **1** unemployed or unoccupied; inactive. **2** not operating or being used. **3** (of money) not being used to earn interest or dividends. **4** not wanting to work; lazy. **5** (*usually prenominal*) frivolous or trivial: *idle pleasures.* **6** ineffective or powerless; fruitless; vain. **7** without basis; unfounded. ◆ *vb* **8** (when *tr*, often foll. by *away*) to waste or pass (time) fruitlessly or inactively: *he idled the hours away.* **9** (*intr*) to loiter or move aimlessly. **10** (*intr*) (of a shaft, etc.) to turn without doing useful work. **11** (*intr*) Also (Brit.): **tick over.** (of an engine) to run at low speed with the transmission disengaged. **12** (*tr*) *U.S. and Canadian.* to cause to be inactive or unemployed. [Old English *īdel;* compare Old High German *ītal* empty, vain] ▸ **ˈidleness** *n* ▸ **ˈidly** *adv*
idle pulley *or* **idler pulley** *n* a freely rotating trolley used to control the tension or direction of a belt. Also called: **idler.**
idler (ˈaɪdlə) *n* **1** a person who idles. **2** another name for **idle pulley** *or* **idle wheel. 3** *Nautical.* a ship's crew member, such as a carpenter, sailmaker, etc., whose duties do not include standing regular watches.
idler shaft *n* a shaft carrying one or more gearwheels that idles between a driver shaft and a driven shaft, usually to reverse the direction of rotation or provide different spacing of gearwheels, esp. in a gearbox.
idle time *n Commerce.* time during which a machine or a worker could be working but is not, as when one job has been completed and tooling or materials for the next are not complete or available. Compare **downtime.**
idle wheel *n* a gearwheel interposed between two others to transmit torque without changing the direction of rotation to the velocity ratio. Also called: **idler.**
IDN *abbrev. for* in Dei nomine. Also: **IND.** [Latin: in the name of God]
Ido (ˈiːdəʊ) *n* an artificial language; a modification of Esperanto. [C20: offspring, from Greek *-id* daughter of]
idocrase (ˈaɪdəˌkreɪs, ˈɪd-) *n* another name for **vesuvianite.** [C19: from French, from Greek *eidos* form + *krasis* a mingling]
idol (ˈaɪdᵊl) *n* **1** a material object, esp. a carved image, that is worshipped as a god. **2** *Christianity, Judaism.* any being (other than the one God) to which divine honour is paid. **3** a person who is revered, admired, or highly loved. [C13: from Late Latin *īdōlum,* from Latin: image, from Greek *eidōlon,* from *eidos* shape, form]
idolatrize *or* **idolatrise** (aɪˈdɒləˌtraɪz) *vb* **1** (*tr*) a less common word for **idolize. 2** (*intr*) to indulge in the worship of idols. ▸ **iˈdolaˌtrizer** *or* **iˈdolaˌtriser** *n*
idolatry (aɪˈdɒlətrɪ) *n* **1** the worship of idols. **2** great devotion or reverence. ▸ **iˈdolater** *n or* **iˈdolatress** *fem n* ▸ **iˈdolatrous** *adj* ▸ **iˈdolatrously** *adv* ▸ **iˈdolatrousness** *n*
idolize *or* **idolise** (ˈaɪdəˌlaɪz) *vb* **1** (*tr*) to admire or revere greatly. **2** (*tr*) to worship as an idol. **3** (*intr*) to worship idols. ▸ **iˈdolism, ˌidoliˈzation** *or* **ˌidoliˈsation** *n* ▸ **ˈidolist, ˈidolˌizer** *or* **ˈidolˌiser** *n*
idolum (ɪˈdəʊləm) *n* **1** a mental picture; idea. **2** a false idea, fallacy. [C17: from Latin: IDOL]
Idomeneus (aɪˈdɒmɪˌnjuːs) *n Greek myth.* a king of Crete who fought on the Greek side in the Trojan War.
IDP *abbrev. for* integrated data processing.
Id-ul-Adha (ˈiːdʊlˌɑːdə) *n* an annual Muslim festival marking the end of the pilgrimage to Mecca. Animals are sacrificed and their meat shared among the poor. [from Arabic *id ul adha* festival of sacrifice]
Id-ul-Fitr (ˌɪdˌʊlˈfɪtᵊr) *n* an annual Muslim festival marking the end of Ramadan, involving the exchange of gifts and a festive meal. [from Arabic *id ul fitr* festival of fast-breaking]
Idun (ˈiːdʊn) *or* **Ithunn** *n Norse myth.* the goddess of spring who guarded the apples that kept the gods eternally young; wife of Bragi.
idyll *or U.S.* (*sometimes*) **idyl** (ˈɪdɪl) *n* **1** a poem or prose work describing an idealized rural life, pastoral scenes, etc. **2** any simple narrative or descriptive piece in poetry or prose. **3** a charming or picturesque scene or event. **4** a piece of music with a calm or pastoral character. [C17: from Latin *Tdyllium,* from Greek *eidullion,* from *eidos* shape, (literary) form]
idyllic (ɪˈdɪlɪk, aɪ-) *adj* **1** of or relating to an idyll. **2** charming; picturesque. ▸ **iˈdyllically** *adv*
idyllist *or U.S.* **idylist** (ˈɪdɪlɪst) *n* a writer of idylls.
IE *abbrev. for* Indo-European (languages).
i.e. *abbrev. for* id est. [Latin: that is (to say); in other words]
-ie *suffix forming nouns.* a variant of **-y**[2].
iechyd da (ˈjækiːˌdɑː; *Welsh* ˈjexəd dɑː) *interj Welsh.* a drinking toast; good health; cheers. [Welsh: good health]
IEE *abbrev. for* Institution of Electrical Engineers.
Ieper (ˈiːpər) *n* the Flemish name for **Ypres.**
-ier *suffix forming nouns.* a variant of **-eer:** *brigadier.* [from Old English *-ere* -ER[1] or (in some words) from Old French *-ier,* from Latin *-ārius* -ARY]
Ieyasu (ˌiːjeˈjɑːsuː) *n* a variant spelling of (Tokugawa) **Iyeyasu.**
if (ɪf) *conj* (*subordinating*) **1** in case that, or on condition that: *if you try hard it might work; if he were poor, would you marry him?* **2** used to introduce an indirect question. In this sense, *if* approaches the meaning of *whether.* **3** even though: *an attractive if awkward girl.* **4a** used to introduce expressions of desire, with *only: if I had only known.* **4b** used to introduce exclamations of surprise, dismay, etc.: *if this doesn't top everything!* **5 as if.** as it would be if; as though: *he treats me as if I were junior to him.* ◆ *n* **6** an uncertainty or doubt: *the big if is whether our plan will work at all.* **7** a condition or stipulation: *I won't have any ifs or buts.* [Old English *gif;* related to Old Saxon *ef* if, Old High German *iba* whether, if]
IF *or* **i.f.** *Electronics. abbrev. for* intermediate frequency.
IFA *abbrev. for* independent financial adviser.
IFC *abbrev. for* International Finance Corporation.
Ife (ˈiːfɪ) *n* a town in W central Nigeria: one of the largest and oldest Yoruba towns; university (1961); centre of the cocoa trade. Pop.: 296 800 (1996 est.).
-iferous *suffix forming adjectives.* containing or yielding: *carboniferous.*
iff (ɪf) *conj Logic.* a shortened form of *if and only if:* it indicates that the two sentences so connected are necessary and sufficient conditions for one another. Usually *iff* is used for equivalence in the metalanguage, rather than as the biconditional in the object language.
IFF *Military abbrev. for* Identification, Friend or Foe: a system using radar transmissions to which equipment carried by friendly forces automatically responds with a precoded signal.
iffy (ˈɪfɪ) *adj Informal.* uncertain or subject to contingency: *this scheme sounds a bit iffy.* [C20: from IF + -Y[1]]
Ifni (*Spanish* ˈifni) *n* a former Spanish province in S Morocco, on the Atlantic: returned to Morocco in 1969.
IFR *Aeronautics. abbrev. for* instrument flying regulations.
IFS *abbrev. for* Irish Free State (now called Republic of Ireland).
-ify *suffix forming verbs.* a variant of **-fy:** *intensify.* ▸ **-ification** *suffix forming nouns.*
IG *abbrev. for:* **1** Indo-Germanic (languages). **2** Inspector General.
Igbo (ˈiːbəʊ) *n, pl* **-bo** *or* **-bos.** a variant spelling of **Ibo.**
Igdrasil (ˈɪgdrəsɪl) *n* a variant spelling of **Yggdrasil.**
IGFET (ˈɪgfet) *n* insulated-gate field-effect transistor; a type of field-effect transistor having one or more semiconductor gate electrodes. Compare **JFET.**
igloo *or* **iglu** (ˈɪgluː) *n, pl* **-loos** *or* **-lus. 1** a dome-shaped Eskimo house, usually built of blocks of solid snow. **2** a hollow made by a seal in the snow over its breathing hole in the ice. [C19: from Eskimo *igdlu* house]
IGM *Chess. abbrev. for* International Grandmaster.
ign. *abbrev. for:* **1** ignites. **2** ignition. **3** ignotus. [Latin: unknown]
Ignatiev (ɪgˈnɑːtjef) *n* Count **Nikolai Pavlovich.** 1832–1908, Russian diplomat and politician. As ambassador to Turkey (1864–77), he negotiated the Treaty of San Stefano (1878) ending the Russo-Turkish War.
Ignatius (ɪgˈneɪʃɪəs) *n* **Saint,** surnamed *Theophorus.* died ?110 A.D., bishop of Antioch. His seven letters, written on his way to his martyrdom in Rome, give valuable insight into the early Christian Church. Feast day: Oct. 17 or Dec. 17 or 20.
Ignatius Loyola (lɔɪˈəʊlə) *n* **Saint.** 1491–1556, Spanish ecclesiastic. He founded the Society of Jesus (1534) and was its first general (1541–56). His *Spiritual Exercises* (1548) remains the basic manual for the training of Jesuits. Feast day: July 31.
igneous (ˈɪgnɪəs) *adj* **1** (of rocks) derived from magma or lava that has solidified on or below the earth's surface. Compare **sedimentary, metamorphic** (sense 2). **2** of or relating to fire. [C17: from Latin *igneus* fiery, from *ignis* fire]
ignescent (ɪgˈnesᵊnt) *adj* **1** giving off sparks when struck, as a flint. **2** capable of bursting into flame. ◆ *n* **3** an ignescent substance. [C19: from Latin *ignescere* to become inflamed]
ignimbrite (ˈɪgnɪmˌbraɪt) *n* a rock formed by the deposition at high temperature and the consolidation of a nuée ardente, being a complicated mixture of volcanic materials welded together by heat, hot gases, and pressure. Also called: **welded tuft.** See **tuft.** [C20: from Latin *ign(is)* fire + *imbr(is), imber* shower of rain + -ITE[1]]
ignis fatuus (ˈɪgnɪs ˈfætjʊəs) *n, pl* **ignes fatui** (ˈɪgniːz ˈfætjʊˌaɪ). another name for **will-o'-the-wisp.** [C16: from Medieval Latin, literally: foolish fire]
ignite (ɪgˈnaɪt) *vb* **1** to catch fire or set fire to; burn or cause to burn. **2** (*tr*) *Chem.* to heat strongly. [C17: from Latin *ignīre* to set alight, from *ignis* fire] ▸ **igˈnitable** *or* **igˈnitible** *adj* ▸ **igˌnitaˈbility** *or* **igˌnitiˈbility** *n*
igniter (ɪgˈnaɪtə) *n* **1** a person or thing that ignites. **2** a fuse to fire explosive charges. **3** an electrical device for lighting a gas turbine. **4** a subsidiary electrode in an ignitron.
ignition (ɪgˈnɪʃən) *n* **1** the act or process of initiating combustion. **2** the process of igniting the fuel in an internal-combustion engine. **3** (usually preceded by *the*) the devices used to ignite the fuel in an internal-combustion engine.
ignition coil *n* an induction coil that supplies the high voltage to the sparking plugs of an internal-combustion engine.
ignition key *n* the key used in a motor vehicle to turn the switch that connects the battery to the ignition system and other electrical devices.
ignitron (ɪgˈnaɪtrɒn, ˈɪgnɪˌtrɒn) *n* a mercury-arc rectifier controlled by a subsidiary electrode, the igniter, partially immersed in a mercury cathode. A current passed between igniter and cathode forms a hot spot sufficient to strike an arc between cathode and anode. [C20: from IGNITER + ELECTRON]
ignoble (ɪgˈnəʊbᵊl) *adj* **1** dishonourable; base; despicable. **2** of low birth or origins; humble; common. **3** of low quality; inferior. **4** *Falconry.* **4a** designating short-winged hawks that capture their quarry by swiftness and adroitness of flight. Compare **noble** (sense 7). **4b** designating quarry which is inferior or unworthy of pursuit by a particular species of hawk or falcon. [C16: from Latin *ignōbilis,* from IN-[1] + Old Latin *gnōbilis* NOBLE] ▸ **ˌignoˈbility** *or* **igˈnobleness** *n* ▸ **igˈnobly** *adv*
ignominy (ˈɪgnəˌmɪnɪ) *n, pl* **-minies. 1** disgrace or public shame; dishonour. **2**

a cause of disgrace; a shameful act. [C16: from Latin *ignōminia* disgrace, from *ig-* (see IN-[2]) + *nōmen* name, reputation] ▸ ˌ**igno'minious** *adj* ▸ ˌ**igno'miniously** *adv* ▸ ˌ**igno'miniousness** *n*

ignoramus (ˌɪgnəˈreɪməs) *n, pl* **-muses.** an ignorant person; fool. [C16: from legal Latin, literally: we have no knowledge of, from Latin *ignōrāre* to be ignorant of; see IGNORE; modern usage originated from the use of *Ignoramus* as the name of an unlettered lawyer in a play by G. Ruggle, 17th-century English dramatist]

ignorance (ˈɪgnərəns) *n* lack of knowledge, information, or education; the state of being ignorant.

ignorant (ˈɪgnərənt) *adj* **1** lacking in knowledge or education; unenlightened. **2** (*postpositive*; often foll. by *of*) lacking in awareness or knowledge (of): *ignorant of the law.* **3** resulting from or showing lack of knowledge or awareness: *an ignorant remark.* ▸ ˈ**ignorantly** *adv*

ignoratio elenchi (ˌɪgnəˈreɪʃɪəʊ ɪˈlɛŋkaɪ) *n Logic.* **1** a purported refutation of a proposition that does not in fact prove it false but merely establishes a related but strictly irrelevant proposition. **2** the fallacy of arguing in this way. [Latin: an ignorance of proof, translating Greek *elenchou agnoia*]

ignore (ɪgˈnɔː) *vb* (*tr*) **1** to fail or refuse to notice; disregard. ◆ *n* **2** *Austral. informal.* disregard: *to treat someone with ignore.* [C17: from Latin *ignōrāre* not to know, from *ignārus* ignorant of, from *i-* IN-[1] + *gnārus* knowing; related to Latin *noscere* to know] ▸ **ig'norable** *adj* ▸ **ig'norer** *n*

ignotum per ignotius *Latin.* (ɪgˈnəʊtʊm pər ɪgˈnəʊtɪʊs) *n* an explanation that is obscurer than the thing to be explained. [literally: the unknown by means of the more unknown]

Igorot (ˌɪgəˈrəʊt, ˌiːgə-) *or* **Igorrote** (ˌɪgəˈrəʊtɪ, ˌiːgə-) *n, pl* **-rot, -rots** *or* **-rote, -rotes.** a member of a Negrito people of the mountains of N Luzon in the Philippines: noted as early exponents of mining.

Igraine (ɪˈgreɪn) *or* **Ygerne** *n* the mother of King Arthur.

Iguaçú *or* **Iguassú** (*Portuguese* iguaˈsu) *n* a river in SE South America, rising in S Brazil and flowing west to join the Paraná River, forming part of the border between Brazil and Argentina. Length: 1200 km (745 miles).

Iguaçú Falls *n* a waterfall on the border between Brazil and Argentina, on the Iguaçú River: divided into hundreds of separate falls by forested rocky islands. Width: about 4 km (2.5 miles). Height: 82 m (269 ft.).

iguana (ɪˈgwɑːnə) *n* **1** either of two large tropical American arboreal herbivorous lizards of the genus *Iguana,* esp. *I. iguana* (**common iguana**), having a greyish-green body with a row of spines along the back: family *Iguanidae.* **2** Also called: **iguanid** (ɪˈgwɑːnɪd). any other lizard of the tropical American family *Iguanidae.* **3** another name for **leguaan.** [C16: from Spanish, from Arawak *iwana*] ▸ **i'guanian** *n, adj*

iguanodon (ɪˈgwɑːnəˌdɒn) *n* a massive herbivorous long-tailed bipedal dinosaur of the genus *Iguanodon,* common in Europe and N Africa in Jurassic and Cretaceous times: suborder *Ornithopoda* (ornithopods). [C19: New Latin, from IGUANA + Greek *odōn* tooth]

IGY *abbrev. for* International Geophysical Year.

IHC (in New Zealand) *abbrev. for* intellectually handicapped child.

ihram (ɪˈrɑːm) *n* the customary white robes worn by Muslim pilgrims to Mecca, symbolizing a sacred or consecrated state. [C18: from Arabic *ihrām,* from *harama* he forbade]

IHS the first three letters of the name Jesus in Greek (ΙΗΣΟΥΣ), often used as a Christian emblem.

iid *Statistics. abbrev. for* independent identically distributed (of random variables).

IJssel *or* **Yssel** (ˈaɪsəl; *Dutch* ˈɛisəl) *n* a river in the central Netherlands: a distributary of the Rhine, flowing north to the IJsselmeer. Length: 116 km (72 miles).

IJsselmeer *or* **Ysselmeer** (*Dutch* ɛisəlˈmeːr) *n* a shallow lake in the NW Netherlands; formed from the S part of the Zuider Zee by the construction of the **IJsselmeer Dam** in 1932; salt water gradually replaced by fresh water from the IJssel River; fisheries (formerly marine fish, now esp. eels). Area: (before reclamation) 3690 sq. km (1425 sq. miles). Estimated final area: 1243 sq. km (480 sq. miles). English name: **Ijssel Lake.**

ikan (ˈiːkan) *n* (in Malaysia) fish used esp. in names of cooked dishes: *assam ikan.* [from Malay]

Ikaría (ikaˈria) *n* a transliteration of the Modern Greek name for **Icaria.**

ikat (ˈaɪkæt) *n* a method of creating patterns in fabric by tie-dyeing the yarn before weaving. [C20: from Malay, literally: to tie, bind]

ikebana (ˌiːkəˈbɑːnə) *n* the Japanese decorative art of flower arrangement.

Ikeja (ɪˈkeɪjə) *n* a town in SW Nigeria, capital of Lagos state: residential and industrial suburb of Lagos. Pop.: 63 870 (latest est.).

Ikhnaton (ɪkˈnɑːtən) *n* a variant of **Akhenaten.**

ikon (ˈaɪkɒn) *n* a variant spelling of **icon.**

IL *abbrev. for:* **1** Illinois. **2** *international car registration for* Israel.

il- *prefix* variant of **in-**[1] and **in-**[2] before *l.*

ilang-ilang (ˈiːlæŋˈiːlæŋ) *n* a variant spelling of **ylang-ylang.**

-ile *suffix forming adjectives and nouns.* indicating capability, liability, or a relationship with something: *agile; fragile; juvenile.* [via French from Latin or directly from Latin *-ilis*]

ILEA (ˈɪlɪə) *n* (formerly) *abbrev. or acronym for* Inner London Education Authority.

ileac (ˈɪlɪˌæk) *or* **ileal** (ˈɪlɪəl) *adj* **1** *Anatomy.* of or relating to the ileum. **2** *Pathol.* of or relating to ileus.

Île-de-France (*French* ildəfrɑ̃s) *n* **1** a region of N France, in the Paris Basin: part of the duchy of France in the 10th century. **2** a former name (1715–1810) for **Mauritius.**

Île du Diable (il dy djɑblə) *n* the French name for **Devil's Island.**

ileitis (ˌɪlɪˈaɪtɪs) *n* inflammation of the ileum.

ileo- *or before a vowel* **ile-** *combining form.* indicating the ileum: *ileostomy.*

ileostomy (ˌɪlɪˈɒstəmɪ) *n, pl* **-mies.** the surgical formation of a permanent opening through the abdominal wall into the ileum.

Îles Comores (il kɔmɔr) *n* the French name for the **Comoros.**

Îles du Salut (il dy saly) *n* the French name for the **Safety Islands.**

Ilesha (ɪˈleɪʃə) *n* a town in W Nigeria. Pop.: 378 400 (1996 est.).

Îles Mascareignes (il maskarɛɲ) *n* the French name for the **Mascarene Islands.**

Îles sous le Vent (il su lə vɑ̃) *n* the French name for the **Leeward Islands** (sense 3).

ileum (ˈɪlɪəm) *n* **1** the part of the small intestine between the jejunum and the caecum. **2** the corresponding part in insects. [C17: New Latin, from Latin *īlium, īleum* flank, groin, of obscure origin]

ileus (ˈɪlɪəs) *n* obstruction of the intestine, esp. the ileum, by mechanical occlusion or as the result of distension of the bowel following loss of muscular action. [C18: from Latin *īleos* severe colic, from Greek *eileos* a rolling, twisting, from *eilein* to roll]

ilex (ˈaɪlɛks) *n* **1** any of various trees or shrubs of the widely distributed genus *Ilex,* such as the holly and inkberry: family *Aquifoliaceae.* **2** another name for the **holm oak.** [C16: from Latin]

ilia (ˈɪlɪə) *n* the plural of **ilium.**

Ilia (ˈɪlɪə) *n* (in Roman legend) the daughter of Aeneas and Lavinia, who, according to some traditions, was the mother of Romulus and Remus. See also **Rhea Silvia.**

Ilía (iˈlia) *n* a transliteration of the Modern Greek name for **Elia**[1].

iliac (ˈɪlɪˌæk) *adj Anatomy.* of or relating to the ilium.

Iliad (ˈɪlɪəd) *n* a Greek epic poem describing the siege of Troy, attributed to Homer and probably composed before 700 B.C. ▸ **Iliadic** (ˌɪlɪˈædɪk) *adj*

Iliamna (ˌɪlɪˈæmnə) *n* **1** a lake in SW Alaska: the largest lake in Alaska. Length: about 130 km (80 miles). Width: 40 km (25 miles). **2** a volcano in SW Alaska, northwest of Iliamna Lake. Height: 3076 m (10 092 ft.).

Iligan (ɪˈliːgən) *n* a city in the Philippines, a port on the N coast of Mindanao. Pop.: 209 639 (1994 est.).

Ilion (ˈɪlɪən) *n* a transliteration of the Greek name for ancient **Troy.**

ilium (ˈɪlɪəm) *n, pl* **-ia** (-ɪə). the uppermost and widest of the three sections of the hipbone.

Ilium (ˈɪlɪəm) *n* the Latin name for ancient **Troy.**

ilk[1] (ɪlk) *n* **1** a type; class; sort (esp. in the phrase **of that, his, her,** etc., **ilk**): *people of that ilk should not be allowed here.* **2 of that ilk.** *Scot.* of the place of the same name: used to indicate that the person named is proprietor or laird of the place named: *Moncrieff of that ilk.* [Old English *ilca* the same family, same kind; related to Gothic *is* he, Latin *is,* Old English *gelīc* like]

USAGE Although the use of *ilk* in the sense of sense 1 is sometimes condemned as being the result of a misunderstanding of the original Scottish expression *of that ilk,* it is nevertheless well established and generally acceptable.

ilk[2] (ɪlk) *or* **ilka** (ˈɪlkə) *determiner Scot.* each; every. [Old English *ǣlc* each (+A[1])]

Ilkeston (ˈɪlkɪstən) *n* a town in N central England, in SE Derbyshire. Pop.: 35 134 (1991).

Ilkley (ˈɪlklɪ) *n* a town in N England, in West Yorkshire: nearby is **Ilkley Moor** (to the south). Pop.: 13 530 (1991).

ill (ɪl) *adj* **worse, worst. 1** (*usually postpositive*) not in good health; sick. **2** characterized by or intending evil, harm, etc.; hostile: *ill deeds.* **3** causing or resulting in pain, harm, adversity, etc.: *ill effects.* **4** ascribing or imputing evil to something referred to: *ill repute.* **5** promising an unfavourable outcome; unpropitious: *an ill omen.* **6** harsh; lacking kindness: *ill will.* **7** not up to an acceptable standard; faulty: *ill manners.* **8 ill at ease.** unable to relax; uncomfortable. ◆ *n* **9** evil or harm: *to wish a person ill.* **10** a mild disease. **11** misfortune; trouble. ◆ *adv* **12** badly: *the title ill befits him.* **13** with difficulty; hardly: *he can ill afford the money.* **14** not rightly: *she ill deserves such good fortune.* [C11 (in the sense: evil): from Old Norse *illr* bad]

ill. *abbrev. for:* **1** illustrated. **2** illustration.

Ill. *abbrev. for* Illinois.

I'll (aɪl) *contraction of* I will *or* I shall.

ill-advised *adj* **1** acting without reasonable care or thought: *you would be ill-advised to sell your house now.* **2** badly thought out; not or insufficiently considered: *an ill-advised plan of action.* ▸ ˌ**ill-ad'visedly** *adv*

ill-affected *adj* (often foll. by *towards*) not well disposed; disaffected.

Illampu (*Spanish* iʎamˈpu) *n* one of the two peaks of Mount **Sorata.**

ill-assorted *adj* badly matched; incompatible.

illation (ɪˈleɪʃən) *n* a rare word for **inference.** [C16: from Late Latin *illātiō* a bringing in, from Latin *illātus* brought in, from *inferre* to bring in, from IN-[2] + *ferre* to bear, carry]

illative (ɪˈleɪtɪv) *adj* **1** of or relating to illation; inferential. **2** *Grammar.* denoting a word or morpheme used to signal inference, for example *so* or *therefore.* **3** (in the grammar of Finnish and other languages) denoting a case of nouns expressing a relation of motion or direction, usually translated by the English prepositions *into* or *towards.* Compare **elative** (sense 1). ◆ *n* **4** *Grammar.* **4a** the illative case. **4b** an illative word or speech element. [C16: from Late Latin *illātīvus* inferring, concluding] ▸ **il'latively** *adv*

Illawarra (ˌɪləˈwɒrə) *n* **1** a coastal district of E Australia, in S New South Wales. Pop.: 342 700 (1991). **2** an Australian breed of shorthorn dairy cattle noted for its high milk yield and ability to survive on poor pastures.

ill-behaved *adj* poorly behaved; lacking good manners.

ill-bred *adj* badly brought up; lacking good manners. ▸ ˌ**ill-'breeding** *n*

ill-considered *adj* done without due consideration; not thought out: *an ill-considered decision.*

ill-defined *adj* imperfectly defined; having no clear outline.

ill-disposed *adj* (often foll. by *towards*) not kindly disposed.

Ille-et-Vilaine (*French* ilevilen) *n* a department of NW France, in E Brittany. Capital: Rennes. Pop.: 836 700 (1995). Area: 6992 sq. km (2727 sq. miles).

illegal (ɪ'liːgᵊl) *adj* **1** forbidden by law; unlawful; illicit. **2** unauthorized or prohibited by a code of official or accepted rules. ◆ *n* **3** a person who has entered or attempted to enter a country illegally. ▸ **il'legally** *adv* ▸ **,ille'gality** *n*

illegalize *or* **illegalise** (ɪ'liːgə,laɪz) *vb (tr)* to make illegal. ▸ **il,legali'zation** *or* **il,legali'sation** *n*

illegible (ɪ'lɛdʒɪbᵊl) *adj* unable to be read or deciphered. ▸ **il,legi'bility** *or* **il'legibleness** *n* ▸ **il'legibly** *adv*

illegitimate (,ɪlɪ'dʒɪtɪmɪt) *adj* **1** born of parents who were not married to each other at the time of birth; bastard. **2** forbidden by law; illegal; unlawful. **3** contrary to logic; incorrectly reasoned. ◆ *n* **4** an illegitimate person; bastard. ▸ **,ille'gitimacy** *or* **,ille'gitimateness** *n* ▸ **,ille'gitimately** *adv*

ill-fated *adj* doomed or unlucky: *an ill-fated marriage.*

ill-favoured *or U.S.* **ill-favored** *adj* **1** unattractive or repulsive in appearance; ugly. **2** offensive, disagreeable, or objectionable. ▸ **,ill-'favouredly** *or U.S.* **,ill-'favoredly** *adv* ▸ **,ill-'favouredness** *or U.S.* **,ill-'favoredness** *n*

ill feeling *n* hostile feeling; animosity.

ill-founded *adj* not founded on true or reliable premises; unsubstantiated: *an ill-founded rumour.*

ill-gotten *adj* obtained dishonestly or illegally (esp. in the phrase **ill-gotten gains**).

ill humour *n* a disagreeable or sullen mood; bad temper. ▸ **,ill-'humoured** *adj* ▸ **,ill-'humouredly** *adv*

illiberal (ɪ'lɪbərəl) *adj* **1** narrow-minded; prejudiced; bigoted; intolerant. **2** not generous; mean. **3** lacking in culture or refinement. ▸ **il,liber'ality, il'liberalness,** *or* **il'liberalism** *n* ▸ **il'liberally** *adv*

Illich ('ɪlɪtʃ) *n* **Ivan.** born 1926. U.S. teacher and writer, born in Austria. His books include *Deschooling Society* (1971), *Medical Nemesis* (1975), and *In the Mirror of the Past* (1991).

illicit (ɪ'lɪsɪt) *adj* **1** another word for **illegal. 2** not allowed or approved by common custom, rule, or standard: *illicit sexual relations.* ▸ **il'licitly** *adv* ▸ **il'licitness** *n*

Illimani (*Spanish* iʎi'mani) *n* a mountain in W Bolivia, in the Andes near La Paz. Height: 6882 m (22 580 ft.).

illimitable (ɪ'lɪmɪtəbᵊl) *adj* limitless; boundless. ▸ **il,limita'bility** *or* **il'limitableness** *n* ▸ **il'limitably** *adv*

illinium (ɪ'lɪnɪəm) *n Chem.* the former name for **promethium.** [C20: New Latin, from ILLINOIS + -IUM]

Illinois (,ɪlɪ'nɔɪ) *n* **1** a state of the N central U.S., in the Midwest: consists of level prairie crossed by the Illinois and Kaskaskia Rivers; mainly agricultural. Capital: Springfield. Pop.: 11 895 849 (1997 est.). Area: 144 858 sq. km (55 930 sq. miles). Abbrevs.: **Ill.** or (with zip code) **IL 2** a river in Illinois, flowing SW to the Mississippi. Length: 439 km (273 miles). ▸ **Illinoisan** (,ɪlɪ'nɔɪən), **Illinoian** (,ɪlɪ'nɔɪən), *or* **Illinoisian** (,ɪlɪ'nɔɪzɪən) *n, adj*

illiquid (ɪ'lɪkwɪd) *adj* **1** (of an asset) not easily convertible into cash. **2** (of an enterprise, organization, etc.) deficient in liquid assets.

illite ('ɪlaɪt) *n* a clay mineral of the mica group, found in shales and mudstones. Crystal structure: monoclinic. [C20: named after ILLINOIS, where it was first found]

illiterate (ɪ'lɪtərɪt) *adj* **1** unable to read and write. **2** violating accepted standards in reading and writing: *an illiterate scrawl.* **3** uneducated, ignorant, or uncultured: *scientifically illiterate.* ◆ *n* **4** an illiterate person. ▸ **il'literacy** *or* **il'literateness** *n* ▸ **il'literately** *adv*

ill-judged *adj* rash; ill-advised.

ill-mannered *adj* having bad manners; rude; impolite. ▸ **,ill-'manneredly** *adv*

ill-natured *adj* naturally unpleasant and mean. ▸ **,ill-'naturedly** *adv* ▸ **,ill-'naturedness** *n*

illness ('ɪlnɪs) *n* **1** a disease or indisposition; sickness. **2** a state of ill health. **3** *Obsolete.* wickedness.

illocution (,ɪlə'kjuːʃən) *n Philosophy.* an act performed by a speaker by virtue of uttering certain words, as for example the acts of promising or of threatening. Also called: **illocutionary act.** See also **performative.** Compare **perlocution.** [C20: from IL- + LOCUTION] ▸ **,illo'cutionary** *adj*

illogic (ɪ'lɒdʒɪk) *n* reasoning characterized by lack of logic; illogicality.

illogical (ɪ'lɒdʒɪkᵊl) *adj* **1** characterized by lack of logic; senseless or unreasonable. **2** disregarding logical principles. ▸ **illogicality** (ɪ,lɒdʒɪ'kælɪtɪ) *or* **il'logicalness** *n* ▸ **il'logically** *adv*

ill-omened *adj* doomed to be unlucky; ill-fated.

ill-sorted *adj* badly arranged or matched; ill-assorted.

ill-starred *adj* unlucky; unfortunate; ill-fated.

ill temper *n* bad temper; irritability. ▸ **,ill-'tempered** *adj* ▸ **,ill-'temperedly** *adv*

ill-timed *adj* occurring at or planned for an unsuitable time.

ill-treat *vb (tr)* to behave cruelly or harshly towards; misuse; maltreat. ▸ **,ill-'treatment** *n*

illude (ɪ'luːd) *vb Literary.* to trick or deceive. [C15: from Latin *illūdere* to sport with, from *lūdus* game]

illume (ɪ'luːm) *vb (tr)* a poetic word for **illuminate.** [C17: shortened from ILLUMINE]

illuminance (ɪ'luːmɪnəns) *n* the luminous flux incident on unit area of a surface. It is measured in lux. Symbol: E_v Sometimes called: **illumination.** Compare **irradiance.**

illuminant (ɪ'luːmɪnənt) *n* **1** something that provides or gives off light. ◆ *adj* **2** giving off light; illuminating.

illuminate *vb* (ɪ'luːmɪ,neɪt). **1** *(tr)* to throw light in or into; light up: *to illuminate a room.* **2** *(tr)* to make easily understood; clarify. **3** to adorn, decorate, or be decorated with lights. **4** *(tr)* to decorate (a letter, page, etc.) by the application of colours, gold, or silver. **5** *(intr)* to become lighted up. ◆ *adj* (ɪ'luːmɪnɪt, -,neɪt). **6** *Archaic.* made clear or bright with light; illuminated. ◆ *n* (ɪ'luːmɪnɪt, -,neɪt). **7** a person who has or claims to have special enlightenment. [C16: from Latin *illūmināre* to light up, from *lūmen* light] ▸ **il'luminative** *adj* ▸ **il'lumi,nator** *n*

illuminati (ɪ,luːmɪ'nɑːtiː) *pl n, sing* **-to** (-təʊ). a group of persons claiming exceptional enlightenment on some subject, esp. religion. [C16: from Latin, literally: the enlightened ones, from *illūmināre* to ILLUMINATE]

Illuminati (ɪ,luːmɪ'nɑːtiː) *pl n, sing* **-to** (-təʊ). **1** any of several groups of illuminati, esp. in 18th-century France. **2** a group of religious enthusiasts of 16th-century Spain who were persecuted by the Inquisition. **3** a masonic sect founded in Bavaria in 1778 claiming that the illuminating grace of Christ resided in it alone. **4** a rare name for the Rosicrucians.

illuminating (ɪ'luːmɪ,neɪtɪŋ) *adj* serving to inform or clarify; instructive. ▸ **il'lumi,natingly** *adv*

illumination (ɪ,luːmɪ'neɪʃən) *n* **1** the act of illuminating or the state of being illuminated. **2** a source of light. **3** *(often pl) Chiefly Brit.* a light or lights, esp. coloured lights, used as decoration in streets, parks, etc. **4** spiritual or intellectual enlightenment; insight or understanding. **5** the act of making understood; clarification. **6** decoration in colours, gold, or silver used on some manuscripts or printed works. **7** *Physics.* another name (not in technical usage) for **illuminance.** ▸ **il,lumi'national** *adj*

illumine (ɪ'luːmɪn) *vb* a literary word for **illuminate.** [C14: from Latin *illūmināre* to make light; see ILLUMINATE] ▸ **il'luminable** *adj*

illuminism (ɪ'luːmɪ,nɪzəm) *n* **1** belief in and advocation of special enlightenment. **2** the tenets and principles of the Illuminati or of any of several religious or political movements initiated by them. ▸ **il'luminist** *n*

ill-use *vb* ('ɪl'juːz). **1** to use badly or cruelly; abuse; maltreat. ◆ *n* ('ɪl'juːs), *also* **ill-usage. 2** harsh or cruel treatment; abuse.

illusion (ɪ'luːʒən) *n* **1** a false appearance or deceptive impression of reality: *the mirror gives an illusion of depth.* **2** a false or misleading perception or belief; delusion: *he has the illusion that he is really clever.* **3** *Psychol.* a perception that is not true to reality, having been altered subjectively in some way in the mind of the perceiver. See also **hallucination. 4** a very fine gauze or tulle used for trimmings, veils, etc. [C14: from Latin *illūsiō* deceit, from *illūdere;* see ILLUDE] ▸ **il'lusionary** *or* **il'lusional** *adj* ▸ **il'lusioned** *adj*

illusionism (ɪ'luːʒə,nɪzəm) *n* **1** *Philosophy.* the doctrine that the external world exists only in illusory sense perceptions. **2** the use of highly illusory effects in art or decoration, esp. the use of perspective in painting to create an impression of three-dimensional reality.

illusionist (ɪ'luːʒənɪst) *n* **1** a person given to illusions; visionary; dreamer. **2** *Philosophy.* a person who believes in illusionism. **3** an artist who practises illusionism. **4** a conjuror; magician. ▸ **il,lusion'istic** *adj*

illusory (ɪ'luːsərɪ) *or* **illusive** (ɪ'luːsɪv) *adj* producing, produced by, or based on illusion; deceptive or unreal. ▸ **il'lusorily** *or* **il'lusively** *adv* ▸ **il'lusoriness** *or* **il'lusiveness** *n*

USAGE *Illusive* is sometimes wrongly used where *elusive* is meant: *they fought hard, but victory remained elusive* (not *illusive*).

illust. *or* **illus.** *abbrev. for:* **1** illustrated. **2** illustration.

illustrate ('ɪlə,streɪt) *vb* **1** to clarify or explain by use of examples, analogy, etc. **2** *(tr)* to be an example or demonstration of. **3** *(tr)* to explain or decorate (a book, text, etc.) with pictures. **4** *(tr)* an archaic word for **enlighten.** [C16: from Latin *illustrāre* to make light, explain, from *lustrāre* to purify, brighten; see LUSTRUM] ▸ **'illus,tratable** *adj* ▸ **'illus,trative** *adj* ▸ **'illus,tratively** *adv* ▸ **'illus,trator** *n*

illustration (,ɪlə'streɪʃən) *n* **1** pictorial matter used to explain or decorate a text. **2** an example or demonstration: *an illustration of his ability.* **3** the act of illustrating or the state of being illustrated. ▸ **,illus'trational** *adj*

illustrious (ɪ'lʌstrɪəs) *adj* **1** of great renown; famous and distinguished. **2** glorious or great: *illustrious deeds.* **3** *Obsolete.* shining. [C16: from Latin *illustris* bright, distinguished, famous, from *illustrāre* to make light; see ILLUSTRATE] ▸ **il'lustriously** *adv* ▸ **il'lustriousness** *n*

illuviation (ɪ,luːvɪ'eɪʃən) *n* the process by which a material (**illuvium**), which includes colloids and mineral salts, is washed down from one layer of soil to a lower layer. [C20: from Latin *illuviēs* dirt, mud, from IL- + *-luviēs*, from *lavere* to wash] ▸ **il'luvial** *adj*

ill will *n* hostile feeling; enmity; antagonism.

Illyria (ɪ'lɪrɪə) *n* an ancient region of uncertain boundaries on the E shore of the Adriatic Sea, including parts of present-day Croatia, Montenegro, and Albania.

Illyrian (ɪ'lɪrɪən) *n* **1** a member of the group of related Indo-European peoples who occupied Illyria from the late third millennium to the early first millennium B.C. **2** the extinct and almost unrecorded language of these peoples: of uncertain relationship within the Indo-European family, but thought by some to be the ancestor of modern Albanian. ◆ *adj* **3** of, characteristic of, or relating to Illyria, its people, or their language.

Illyricum (ɪ'lɪrɪkəm) *n* a Roman province founded after 168 B.C., based on the coastal area of Illyria.

Ilmen ('ɪlmən) *n* **Lake.** a lake in NW Russia, in the Novgorod Region: drains through the Volkhov River into Lake Ladoga. Area: between 780 sq. km (300 sq. miles) and 2200 sq. km (850 sq. miles), according to the season.

ilmenite ('ɪlmɪ,naɪt) *n* a black mineral found in igneous rocks as sedimentary deposits and in veins. It is the chief source of titanium. Composition: iron titanium oxide. Formula: $FeTiO_3$. Crystal structure: hexagonal (rhombohedral). [C19: from *Ilmen,* mountain range in the southern Urals, Russia, + -ITE[1]]

ILO *abbrev. for* International Labour Organisation.

Iloilo (,iːləʊ'iːləʊ) *n* a port in the W central Philippines, on SE Panay Island. Pop.: 302 200 (1994 est.).

Ilorin (ɪ'lɒrɪn) *n* a city in W Nigeria, capital of Kwara state: agricultural trade centre. Pop.: 475 800 (1996 est.).

ILR (in Britain) *abbrev. for* Independent Local Radio.

ILS *Aeronautics. abbrev. for* instrument landing system.

Ilyushin (*Russian* il'juːʃɪn) *n* **Sergei Vladimirovich** (sɪr'gei vladi'miːrovɪtʃ). 1894–1977, Soviet aircraft designer. He designed the dive bomber Il-2 Stormovik and the jet airliner Il-62.

IM *abbrev. for:* **1** Also: **i.m.** intramuscular. **2** *Chess.* International Master.

I'm (aɪm) *contraction of* I am.

im- *prefix* a variant of **in-**[1] and **in-**[2] before *b, m,* and *p.*

image ('ɪmɪdʒ) *n* **1** a representation or likeness of a person or thing, esp. in sculpture. **2** an optically formed reproduction of an object, such as one formed by a lens or mirror. **3** a person or thing that resembles another closely; double or copy. **4** a mental representation or picture; idea produced by the imagination. **5** the personality presented to the public by a person, organization, etc.: *a criminal charge is not good for a politician's image.* See also **corporate image. 6** the pattern of light that is focused onto the retina of the eye. **7** *Psychol.* the mental experience of something that is not immediately present to the senses, often involving memory. See also **imagery, body image, hypnagogic image. 8** a personification of a specified quality; epitome: *the image of good breeding.* **9** a mental picture or association of ideas evoked in a literary work, esp. in poetry. **10** a figure of speech, such as a simile or metaphor. **11** *Maths.* (of a point) the value of a function, f(*x*), corresponding to the point *x*. **12** an obsolete word for **apparition.** ◆ *vb (tr)* **13** to picture in the mind; imagine. **14** to make or reflect an image of. **15** *Computing.* to project or display on a screen or visual display unit. **16** to portray or describe. **17** to be an example or epitome of; typify. [C13: from Old French *imagene,* from Latin *imāgō* copy, representation; related to Latin *imitārī* to IMITATE] ▸ **'imageable** *adj* ▸ **'imageless** *adj*

image converter *or* **tube** *n* a device for producing a visual image formed by other electromagnetic radiation such as infrared or ultraviolet radiation or X-rays.

image enhancement *n* a method of improving the definition of a video picture by a computer program, which reduces the lowest grey values to black and the highest to white: used for pictures from microscopes, surveillance cameras, and scanners.

image intensifier *or* **tube** *n* any of various devices for amplifying the intensity of an optical image, sometimes used in conjunction with an image converter.

image orthicon *n* a television camera tube in which electrons, emitted from a photoemissive surface in proportion to the intensity of the incident light, are focused onto the target causing secondary emission of electrons.

image printer *n Computing.* a printer which uses optical technology to produce an image of a complete page from digital input.

imagery ('ɪmɪdʒrɪ, -dʒərɪ) *n, pl* **-ries. 1** figurative or descriptive language in a literary work. **2** images collectively. **3** *Psychol.* **3a** the materials or general processes of the imagination. **3b** the characteristic kind of mental images formed by a particular individual. See also **image** (sense 7), **imagination** (sense 1). **4** *Military.* the presentation of objects reproduced photographically (by infrared or electronic means) as prints or electronic displays.

image tube *n* another name for **image converter** or **image intensifier.**

imaginal (ɪ'mædʒɪnᵊl) *adj* **1** of, relating to, or resembling an imago. **2** of or relating to an image.

imaginary (ɪ'mædʒɪnərɪ, -dʒɪnrɪ) *adj* **1** existing in the imagination; unreal; illusory. **2** *Maths.* involving or containing imaginary numbers. The imaginary part of a complex number, *z*, is usually written Imz. ▸ **im'aginarily** *adv* ▸ **im'aginariness** *n*

imaginary number *n* any complex number of the form *a* + i*b, where b* is not zero and i = √−1.

imaginary part *n* the coefficient *b* in a complex number *a* + i*b*, where i = √−1.

imagination (ɪˌmædʒɪ'neɪʃən) *n* **1** the faculty or action of producing ideas, esp. mental images of what is not present or has not been experienced. **2** mental creative ability. **3** the ability to deal resourcefully with unexpected or unusual problems, circumstances, etc. **4** (in romantic literary criticism, esp. that of S. T. Coleridge) a creative act of perception that joins passive and active elements in thinking and imposes unity on the poetic material. Compare **fancy** (sense 9). ▸ **imˌagi'national** *adj*

imaginative (ɪ'mædʒɪnətɪv) *adj* **1** produced by or indicative of a vivid or creative imagination: *an imaginative story.* **2** having a vivid imagination. ▸ **im'aginatively** *adv* ▸ **im'aginativeness** *n*

imagine (ɪ'mædʒɪn) *vb* **1** (when *tr, may take a clause as object*) to form a mental image of. **2** (when *tr, may take a clause as object*) to think, believe, or guess. **3** (*tr; takes a clause as object*) to suppose; assume: *I imagine he'll come.* **4** (*tr; takes a clause as object*) to believe or assume without foundation: *he imagines he knows the whole story.* **5** an archaic word for **plot**[1]. ◆ *sentence substitute.* **6** Also: **imagine that!** an exclamation of surprise. [C14: from Latin *imāginārī* to fancy, picture mentally, from *imāgō* likeness; see IMAGE] ▸ **im'aginable** *adj* ▸ **im'aginably** *adv* ▸ **im'aginer** *n*

imagism ('ɪmɪˌdʒɪzəm) *n* a poetic movement in England and America between 1912 and 1917, initiated chiefly by Ezra Pound, advocating the use of ordinary speech and the precise presentation of images. ▸ **'imagist** *n, adj* ▸ **ˌimag'istic** *adj* ▸ **ˌimag'istically** *adv*

imago (ɪ'meɪgəʊ) *n, pl* **imagoes** *or* **imagines** (ɪ'mædʒəˌniːz). **1** an adult sexually mature insect produced after metamorphosis. **2** *Psychoanal.* an idealized image of another person, usually a parent, acquired in childhood and carried in the unconscious in later life. [C18: New Latin, from Latin: likeness; see IMAGE]

imam (ɪ'mɑːm) *or* **imaum** (ɪ'mɑːm, ɪ'mɔːm) *n Islam.* **1** a leader of congregational prayer in a mosque. **2** a caliph, as leader of a Muslim community. **3** an honorific title applied to eminent doctors of Islam, such as the founders of the orthodox schools. **4** any of a succession of either seven or twelve religious leaders of the Shiites, regarded by their followers as divinely inspired. [C17: from Arabic: leader, from *amma* he guided]

imamate (ɪ'mɑːmeɪt) *n Islam.* **1** the region or territory governed by an imam. **2** the office, rank, or period of office of an imam.

IMarE *abbrev. for* Institute of Marine Engineers.

imaret (ɪ'mɑːrɛt) *n* (in Turkey) a hospice for pilgrims or travellers. [C17: from Turkish, from Arabic *'imārah* hospice, building, from *amara* he built]

imbalance (ɪm'bæləns) *n* a lack of balance, as in emphasis, proportion, etc.: *the political imbalance of the programme.*

imbecile ('ɪmbɪˌsiːl, -ˌsaɪl) *n* **1** *Psychol.* a person of very low intelligence (IQ of 25 to 50), usually capable only of guarding himself against danger and of performing simple mechanical tasks under supervision. **2** *Informal.* an extremely stupid person; dolt. ◆ *adj also* **imbecilic** (ˌɪmbɪ'sɪlɪk). **3** of or like an imbecile; mentally deficient; feeble-minded. **4** stupid or senseless: *an imbecile thing to do.* [C16: from Latin *imbēcillus* feeble (physically or mentally)] ▸ **'imbeˌcilely** *or* **ˌimbe'cilically** *adv* ▸ **ˌimbe'cility** *n*

imbed (ɪm'bɛd) *vb* **-beds, -bedding, -bedded.** a less common spelling of **embed.**

imbibe (ɪm'baɪb) *vb* **1** to drink (esp. alcoholic drinks). **2** *Literary.* to take in or assimilate (ideas, facts, etc.): *to imbibe the spirit of the Renaissance.* **3** (*tr*) to take in as if by drinking: *to imbibe fresh air.* **4** to absorb or cause to absorb liquid or moisture; assimilate or saturate. [C14: from Latin *imbibere,* from *bibere* to drink] ▸ **im'biber** *n*

imbibition (ˌɪmbɪ'bɪʃən) *n* **1** *Chem.* the absorption or adsorption of a liquid by a gel or solid. **2** *Photog.* the absorption of dyes by gelatine, used in some colour printing processes. **3** *Obsolete.* the act of imbibing.

imbricate *adj* ('ɪmbrɪkɪt, -ˌkeɪt), *also* **imbricated. 1** *Architect.* relating to or having tiles, shingles, or slates that overlap. **2** *Botany.* (of leaves, scales, etc.) overlapping each other. ◆ *vb* ('ɪmbrɪˌkeɪt). **3** (*tr*) to decorate with a repeating pattern resembling scales or overlapping tiles. [C17: from Latin *imbricāre* to cover with overlapping tiles, from *imbrex* pantile] ▸ **'imbricately** *adv* ▸ **ˌimbri'cation** *n*

imbroglio (ɪm'brəʊlɪˌəʊ) *n, pl* **-glios. 1** a confused or perplexing political or interpersonal situation. **2** *Obsolete.* a confused heap; jumble. [C18: from Italian, from *imbrogliare* to confuse, EMBROIL]

Imbros ('ɪmbrəs) *n* a Turkish island in the NE Aegean Sea, west of the Gallipoli Peninsula: occupied by Greece (1912–14) and Britain (1914–23). Area: 280 sq. km (108 sq. miles). Turkish name: **Imroz.**

imbrue *or* **embrue** (ɪm'bruː) *vb* **-brues, -bruing, -brued.** (*tr*) *Rare.* **1** to stain, esp. with blood. **2** to permeate or impregnate. [C15: from Old French *embreuver,* from Latin *imbibere* IMBIBE] ▸ **im'bruement** *or* **em'bruement** *n*

imbue (ɪm'bjuː) *vb* **-bues, -buing, -bued.** (*tr;* usually foll. by *with*) **1** to instil or inspire (with ideals, principles, etc.): *his sermons were imbued with the spirit of the Reformation.* **2** *Rare.* to soak, esp. with moisture, dye, etc. [C16: from Latin *imbuere* to stain, accustom] ▸ **im'buement** *n*

IMCO *abbrev. for* Intergovernmental Maritime Consultative Organization: the department of the United Nations concerned with international maritime safety, antipollution regulations, etc.

IMechE *abbrev. for* Institution of Mechanical Engineers.

IMF *abbrev. for* International Monetary Fund.

Imhotep (ɪm'həʊtɛp) *n* c. 2600 B.C., Egyptian physician and architect. After his death he was worshipped as a god; the Greeks identified him with Asclepius.

imidazole (ˌɪmɪd'æzəʊl, -ɪdə'zəʊl) *n* **1** Also called: **glyoxaline, iminazole.** a white crystalline basic heterocyclic compound; 1,3-diazole. Formula: $C_3H_4N_2$. **2** any substituted derivative of this compound. [C19: from IMIDE + AZOLE]

imide ('ɪmaɪd) *n* any of a class of organic compounds whose molecules contain the divalent group -CONHCO-. [C19: alteration of AMIDE] ▸ **imidic** (ɪ'mɪdɪk) *adj*

imine (ɪ'miːn, 'ɪmiːn) *n* any of a class of organic compounds in which a nitrogen atom is bound to one hydrogen atom and to two alkyl or aryl groups. They contain the divalent group NH. [C19: alteration of AMINE]

IMinE *abbrev. for* Institution of Mining Engineers.

iminourea (ɪˌmiːnəʊjʊə'rɪə) *n* another name for **guanidine.**

imipramine (ɪ'mɪprəˌmiːn) *n* a tricyclic antidepressant drug. Formula: $C_{19}H_{24}N_2$. [C20: from IMI(DE) + PR(OPYL) + AMINE]

imit. *abbrev. for:* **1** imitation. **2** imitative.

imitate ('ɪmɪˌteɪt) *vb (tr)* **1** to try to follow the manner, style, character, etc., of or take as a model: *many writers imitated the language of Shakespeare.* **2** to pretend to be or to impersonate, esp. for humour; mimic. **3** to make a copy or reproduction of; duplicate; counterfeit. **4** to make or be like; resemble or simulate: *her achievements in politics imitated her earlier successes in business.* [C16: from Latin *imitārī;* see IMAGE] ▸ **imitable** ('ɪmɪtəbᵊl) *adj* ▸ **ˌimita'bility** *or* **'imitableness** *n* ▸ **'imiˌtator** *n*

imitation (ˌɪmɪ'teɪʃən) *n* **1** the act, practice, or art of imitating; mimicry. **2** an instance or product of imitating, such as a copy of the manner of a person; impression. **3a** a copy or reproduction of a genuine article; counterfeit. **3b** (*as modifier*): *imitation jewellery.* **4** (in contrapuntal or polyphonic music) the repetition of a phrase or figure in one part after its appearance in another, as in a fugue. **5** a literary composition that adapts the style of an older work to the writer's own purposes. ▸ **ˌimi'tational** *adj*

imitative ('ɪmɪtətɪv) *adj* **1** imitating or tending to imitate or copy. **2** characterized by imitation. **3** copying or reproducing the features of an original, esp. in an inferior manner: *imitative painting.* **4** another word for **onomatopoeic.** ▸ **'imitatively** *adv* ▸ **'imitativeness** *n*

Imittós (ˌimi'tɔs) *n* a transliteration of the Modern Greek name for **Hymettus.**

immaculate (ɪ'mækjʊlɪt) *adj* **1** completely clean; extremely tidy: *his clothes* *were immaculate.* **2** completely flawless, etc.: *an immaculate rendering of the symphony.* **3** morally pure; free from sin or corruption. **4** *Biology.* of only one colour, with no spots or markings. [C15: from Latin *immaculātus,* from IM- (not) + *macula* blemish] ▸ **imˈmaculacy** *or* **imˈmaculateness** *n* ▸ **imˈmaculately** *adv*

Immaculate Conception *n Christian theol., R.C. Church.* the doctrine that the Virgin Mary was conceived without any stain of original sin.

immanent (ˈɪmənənt) *adj* **1** existing, operating, or remaining within; inherent. **2** of or relating to the pantheistic conception of God, as being present throughout the universe. Compare **transcendent** (sense 3). [C16: from Latin *immanēre* to remain in, from IM- (in) + *manēre* to stay] ▸ **ˈimmanence** *or* **ˈimmanency** *n* ▸ **ˈimmanently** *adv*

immanentism (ˈɪmənənˌtɪzəm) *n* belief in the immanence of God. ▸ **ˈimmanentist** *n*

Immanuel *or* **Emmanuel** (ɪˈmænjuəl) *n Bible.* the child whose birth was foretold by Isaiah (Isaiah 7:14) and who in Christian tradition is identified with Jesus. [from Hebrew *ʿimmānū'el,* literally: God with us]

immaterial (ˌɪməˈtɪərɪəl) *adj* **1** of no real importance; inconsequential. **2** not formed of matter; incorporeal; spiritual. ▸ **ˌimmaˌteriˈality** *or* **ˌimmaˈterialness** *n* ▸ **ˌimmaˈterially** *adv*

immaterialism (ˌɪməˈtɪərɪəˌlɪzəm) *n Philosophy.* **1** the doctrine that the material world exists only in the mind. **2** the doctrine that only immaterial substances or spiritual beings exist. See also **idealism** (sense 3). ▸ **ˌimmaˈterialist** *n*

immaterialize *or* **immaterialise** (ˌɪməˈtɪərɪəˌlaɪz) *vb* (*tr*) to make immaterial.

immature (ˌɪməˈtjʊə, -ˈtʃʊə) *adj* **1** not fully grown or developed. **2** deficient in maturity; lacking wisdom, insight, emotional stability, etc. **3** *Geography.* a less common term for **youthful** (sense 4). ▸ **ˌimmaˈturity** *or* **ˌimmaˈtureness** *n* ▸ **ˌimmaˈturely** *adv*

immeasurable (ɪˈmɛʒərəbᵊl) *adj* incapable of being measured, esp. by virtue of great size; limitless. ▸ **imˌmeasuraˈbility** *or* **imˈmeasurableness** *n* ▸ **imˈmeasurably** *adv*

immediate (ɪˈmiːdɪət) *adj* (*usually prenominal*) **1** taking place or accomplished without delay: *an immediate reaction.* **2** closest or most direct in effect or relationship: *the immediate cause of his downfall.* **3** having no intervening medium; direct in effect: *an immediate influence.* **4** contiguous in space, time, or relationship: *our immediate neighbour.* **5** present; current: *the immediate problem is food.* **6** *Philosophy.* of or relating to an object or concept that is directly known or intuited. **7** *Logic.* (of an inference) deriving its conclusion from a single premise, esp. by conversion or obversion of a categorial statement. [C16: from Medieval Latin *immediātus,* from Latin IM- (not) + *mediāre* to be in the middle; see MEDIATE] ▸ **imˈmediacy** *or* **imˈmediateness** *n*

immediate annuity *n* an annuity that starts less than a year after its purchase. Compare **deferred annuity.**

immediate constituent *n* a constituent of a linguistic construction at the first step in an analysis; for example, the immediate constituents of a sentence are the subject and the predicate.

immediately (ɪˈmiːdɪətlɪ) *adv* **1** without delay or intervention; at once; instantly: *it happened immediately.* **2** very closely or directly: *this immediately concerns you.* **3** near or close by: *he's somewhere immediately in this area.* ♦ *conj* **4** (*subordinating*) *Chiefly Brit.* at the same time as; as soon as: *immediately he opened the door, there was a gust of wind.*

immedicable (ɪˈmɛdɪkəbᵊl) *adj* (of wounds) unresponsive to treatment. ▸ **imˈmedicableness** *n* ▸ **imˈmedicably** *adv*

Immelmann turn *or* **Immelmann** (ˈɪməlˌmɑːn, -mən) *n* an aircraft manoeuvre used to gain height while reversing the direction of flight. It consists of a half loop followed by a half roll. [C20: named after Max *Immelmann* (1890–1916), German aviator]

immemorial (ˌɪmɪˈmɔːrɪəl) *adj* originating in the distant past; ancient (postpositive in the phrase **time immemorial**). [C17: from Medieval Latin *immemoriālis,* from Latin IM- (not) + *memoria* MEMORY] ▸ **ˌimmeˈmorially** *adv*

immense (ɪˈmɛns) *adj* **1** unusually large; huge; vast. **2** without limits; immeasurable. **3** *Informal.* very good; excellent. [C15: from Latin *immensus,* literally: unmeasured, from IM- (not) + *mensus* measured, from *mētīrī* to measure] ▸ **imˈmensely** *adv* ▸ **imˈmenseness** *n*

immensity (ɪˈmɛnsɪtɪ) *n, pl* **-ties. 1** the state or quality of being immense; vastness; enormity. **2** enormous expanse, distance, or volume: *the immensity of space.* **3** *Informal.* a huge amount: *an immensity of wealth.*

immensurable (ɪˈmɛnʃərəbᵊl) *adj* a less common word for **immeasurable.**

immerge (ɪˈmɜːdʒ) *vb* an archaic word for **immerse.** [C17: from Latin *immergere* to IMMERSE] ▸ **imˈmergence** *n*

immerse (ɪˈmɜːs) *vb* (*tr*) **1** (often foll. by *in*) to plunge or dip into liquid. **2** (*often passive;* often foll. by *in*) to involve deeply; engross: *to immerse oneself in a problem.* **3** to baptize by immersion. [C17: from Latin *immergere,* from IM- (in) + *mergere* to dip] ▸ **imˈmersible** *adj*

immersed (ɪˈmɜːst) *adj* **1** sunk or submerged. **2** (of plants) growing completely submerged in water. **3** (of a plant or animal organ) embedded in another organ or part. **4** involved deeply; engrossed.

immerser (ɪˈmɜːsə) *n* an informal term for **immersion heater.**

immersion (ɪˈmɜːʃən) *n* **1** a form of baptism in which part or the whole of a person's body is submerged in the water. **2** Also called: **ingress.** *Astronomy.* the disappearance of a celestial body prior to an eclipse or occultation. **3** the act of immersing or state of being immersed.

immersion heater *n* an electrical device, usually thermostatically controlled, for heating the liquid in which it is immersed, esp. as a fixture in a domestic hot-water tank.

immersionism (ɪˈmɜːʃəˌnɪzəm) *n* the doctrine that immersion is the only true and valid form of Christian baptism. ▸ **imˈmersionist** *n*

immesh (ɪˈmɛʃ) *vb* a variant of **enmesh.**

immethodical (ˌɪmɪˈθɒdɪkᵊl) *adj* lacking in method or planning; disorganized. ▸ **ˌimmeˈthodically** *adv* ▸ **ˌimmeˈthodicalness** *n*

immigrant (ˈɪmɪɡrənt) *n* **1a** a person who immigrates. Compare **emigrant. 1b** (*as modifier*): *an immigrant community.* **2** *Brit.* a person who has been settled in a country of which he is not a native for less than ten years. **3** an animal or plant that lives or grows in a region to which it has recently migrated.

immigrate (ˈɪmɪˌɡreɪt) *vb* **1** (*intr*) to come to a place or country of which one is not a native in order to settle there. Compare **emigrate. 2** (*intr*) (of an animal or plant) to migrate to a new geographical area. **3** (*tr*) to introduce or bring in as an immigrant. [C17: from Latin *immigrāre* to go into, from IM- + *migrāre* to move] ▸ **ˌimmiˈgration** *n* ▸ **ˌimmiˈgrational** *or* **ˈimmiˌgratory** *adj* ▸ **ˈimmiˌgrator** *n*

imminent (ˈɪmɪnənt) *adj* **1** liable to happen soon; impending. **2** *Obsolete.* jutting out or overhanging. [C16: from Latin *imminēre* to project over, from IM- (in) + *-minēre* to project; related to *mons* mountain] ▸ **ˈimminence** *or* **ˈimminentness** *n* ▸ **ˈimminently** *adv*

Immingham (ˈɪmɪŋəm) *n* a port in NE England, in North East Lincolnshire unitary authority, Lincolnshire: docks opened in 1912, principally for the exporting of coal; now handles chiefly bulk materials, esp. imported iron ore. Pop.: 12 278 (1991).

immingle (ɪˈmɪŋɡᵊl) *vb Archaic.* to blend or mix together; intermingle.

immiscible (ɪˈmɪsɪbᵊl) *adj* (of two or more liquids) incapable of being mixed to form a homogeneous substance: *oil and water are immiscible.* ▸ **imˌmisciˈbility** *n* ▸ **imˈmiscibly** *adv*

immitigable (ɪˈmɪtɪɡəbᵊl) *adj Rare.* unable to be mitigated; relentless; unappeasable. ▸ **imˈmitigably** *adv* ▸ **imˌmitigaˈbility** *n*

immix (ɪˈmɪks) *vb* (*tr*) *Archaic.* to mix in; commix. ▸ **imˈmixture** *n*

immobile (ɪˈməʊbaɪl) *adj* **1** not moving; motionless. **2** not able to move or be moved; fixed. ▸ **immobility** (ˌɪməʊˈbɪlɪtɪ) *n*

immobilism (ɪˈməʊbɪˌlɪzəm) *n* a political policy characterized by inertia and antipathy to change.

immobilize *or* **immobilise** (ɪˈməʊbɪˌlaɪz) *vb* (*tr*) **1** to make or become immobile: *to immobilize a car.* **2** *Finance.* **2a** to remove (specie) from circulation and hold it as a reserve. **2b** to convert (circulating capital) into fixed capital. ▸ **imˌmobiliˈzation** *or* **imˌmobiliˈsation** *n* ▸ **imˈmobiˌlizer** *or* **imˈmobiˌliser** *n*

immoderate (ɪˈmɒdərɪt, ɪˈmɒdrɪt) *adj* **1** lacking in moderation; excessive: *immoderate demands.* **2** *Obsolete.* venial; intemperate: *immoderate habits.* ▸ **imˈmoderately** *adv* ▸ **imˌmoderˈation** *or* **imˈmoderateness** *n*

immodest (ɪˈmɒdɪst) *adj* **1** indecent, esp. with regard to sexual propriety; improper. **2** bold, impudent, or shameless. ▸ **imˈmodestly** *adv* ▸ **imˈmodesty** *n*

immolate (ˈɪməʊˌleɪt) *vb* (*tr*) **1** to kill or offer as a sacrifice, esp. by fire. **2** *Literary.* to sacrifice (something highly valued). [C16: from Latin *immolāre* to sprinkle an offering with sacrificial meal, sacrifice, from IM- (in) + *mola* spelt grain; see MILL[1]] ▸ **ˌimmoˈlation** *n* ▸ **ˈimmoˌlator** *n*

immoral (ɪˈmɒrəl) *adj* **1** transgressing accepted moral rules; corrupt. **2** sexually dissolute; profligate or promiscuous. **3** unscrupulous or unethical: *immoral trading.* **4** tending to corrupt or resulting from corruption: *an immoral film; immoral earnings.* ▸ **imˈmorally** *adv*

immoralist (ɪˈmɒrəlɪst) *n* a person who advocates or practises immorality.

immorality (ˌɪməˈrælɪtɪ) *n, pl* **-ties. 1** the quality, character, or state of being immoral. **2** immoral behaviour, esp. in sexual matters; licentiousness; profligacy or promiscuity. **3** an immoral act.

immortal (ɪˈmɔːtᵊl) *adj* **1** not subject to death or decay; having perpetual life. **2** having everlasting fame; remembered throughout time. **3** everlasting; perpetual; constant. **4** of or relating to immortal beings or concepts. ♦ *n* **5** an immortal being. **6** (*often pl*) a person who is remembered enduringly, esp. an author: *Dante is one of the immortals.* ▸ **ˌimmorˈtality** *n* ▸ **imˈmortally** *adv*

immortalize *or* **immortalise** (ɪˈmɔːtəˌlaɪz) *vb* (*tr*) **1** to give everlasting fame to, as by treating in a literary work: *Macbeth was immortalized by Shakespeare.* **2** to give immortality to. ▸ **imˌmortaliˈzation** *or* **imˌmortaliˈsation** *n* ▸ **imˈmortalˌizer** *or* **imˈmortalˌiser** *n*

Immortals (ɪˈmɔːtᵊlz) *pl n* **1** (*sometimes not cap.*) the gods of ancient Greece and Rome. **2** (in ancient Persia) the royal bodyguard or a larger elite unit of 10 000 men. **3** the members of the French Academy.

immortelle (ˌɪmɔːˈtɛl) *n* any of various plants, mostly of the family *Compositae* (composites), that retain their colour when dried, esp. *Xeranthemum annuum.* Also called: **everlasting, everlasting flower.** [C19: from French (*fleur*) *immortelle* everlasting (flower)]

immotile (ɪˈməʊtaɪl) *adj* (esp. of living organisms or their parts) not capable of moving spontaneously and independently. ▸ **immotility** (ˌɪməʊˈtɪlɪtɪ) *n*

immovable *or* **immoveable** (ɪˈmuːvəbᵊl) *adj* **1** unable to move or be moved; fixed; immobile. **2** unable to be diverted from one's intentions; steadfast. **3** unaffected by feeling; impassive. **4** unchanging; unalterable. **5** (of feasts, holidays, etc.) occurring on the same date every year. **6** *Law.* **6a** (of property) not liable to be removed; fixed. **6b** of or relating to immoveables. Compare **movable.** ▸ **imˌmovaˈbility, imˌmoveaˈbility** *or* **imˈmovableness, imˈmoveableness** *n* ▸ **imˈmovably** *or* **imˈmoveably** *adv*

immoveables (ɪˈmuːvəbᵊlz) *pl n* (in most foreign legal systems) real property.

immune (ɪˈmjuːn) *adj* **1** protected against a specific disease by inoculation or as the result of innate or acquired resistance. **2** relating to or conferring immunity: *an immune body* (see **antibody**). **3** (*usually postpositive;* foll. by *to*) unsusceptible (to) or secure (against): *immune to inflation.* **4** exempt from obligation, penalty, etc. ◆ *n* 5 an immune person or animal. [C15: from Latin *immūnis* exempt from a public service, from IM- (not) + *mūnus* duty]

immune complex *or* **immunocomplex** (ˈɪmjʊnəʊˌkɒmplɛks) *n* a complex formed between an antibody and an antigen.

immune response *n* the reaction of an organism's body to foreign materials (antigens), including the production of antibodies.

immunity (ɪˈmjuːnɪtɪ) *n, pl* **-ties.** 1 the ability of an organism to resist disease, either through the activities of specialized blood cells or antibodies produced by them in response to natural exposure or inoculation (**active immunity**) or by the injection of antiserum or the transfer of antibodies from a mother to her baby via the placenta or breast milk (**passive immunity**). See also **acquired immunity, natural immunity. 2** freedom from obligation or duty, esp. exemption from tax, duty, legal liability, etc. **3** any special privilege granting immunity. **4** the exemption of ecclesiastical persons or property from various civil obligations or liabilities.

immunize *or* **immunise** (ˈɪmjʊˌnaɪz) *vb* to make immune, esp. by inoculation. ▸ **ˌimmuniˈzation** *or* **ˌimmuniˈsation** *n* ▸ **ˈimmuˌnizer** *or* **ˈimmuˌniser** *n*

immuno- *or before a vowel* **immun-** *combining form.* indicating immunity or immune: *immunology.*

immunoassay (ˌɪmjʊnəʊˈæseɪ) *n Immunol.* a technique of identifying a substance, esp. a protein, through its action as an antigen. ▸ **ˈimmunoˌassayist** *n*

immunochemistry (ˌɪmjʊnəʊˈkɛmɪstrɪ) *n* the study of the chemical reactions of immunity.

immunocompetence (ˌɪmjʊnəʊˈkɒmpɪtəns) *n* the capacity of the immune system to carry out its function of distinguishing alien from endogenous material; ability of the body to resist disease.

immunocompromised (ˌɪmjʊnəʊˈkɒmprəmaɪzd) *adj* having an impaired immune system and therefore incapable of an effective immune response, usually as a result of disease, such as AIDS, that damages the immune system.

immunodeficiency (ˌimjʊnəʊdɪˈfɪʃənsɪ) *n* a deficiency in or breakdown of a person's immune system.

immunoelectrophoresis (ˌɪmjʊnəʊɪˌlɛktrəʊfəˈriːsɪs) *n* a technique for identifying the antigens in a blood serum, which are separated into fractions by electrophoresis.

immunofluorescence (ˌɪmjʊnəʊflʊəˈrɛsəns) *n* a method used to determine the location of antibodies or antigens in which the antibodies or antigens are labelled with a fluorescent dye.

immunogen (ɪˈmjuːnəʊdʒən) *n* 1 any substance that evokes an immune response. **2** any substance that stimulates immunity.

immunogenetics (ˌɪmjʊnəʊdʒɪˈnɛtɪks) *n* (*functioning as sing*) the study of the relationship between immunity and genetics. ▸ **ˌimmunogeˈnetic** *or* **ˌimmunogeˈnetical** *adj*

immunogenic (ˌɪmjʊnəʊˈdʒɛnɪk) *adj* causing or producing immunity or an immune response. ▸ **ˌimmunoˈgenically** *adv*

immunoglobulin (ˌɪmjʊnəʊˈglɒbjʊlɪn) *n* any of five classes of proteins, all of which show antibody activity. The most abundant ones are **immunoglobulin G** (**IgG**) and **immunoglobulin A** (**IgA**).

immunological tolerance *n* the absence of antibody production in response to the presence of antigens, usually as a result of previous exposure to the antigens.

immunology (ˌɪmjʊˈnɒlədʒɪ) *n* the branch of biological science concerned with the study of immunity. ▸ **immunologic** (ˌɪmjʊnəˈlɒdʒɪk) *or* **ˌimmunoˈlogical** *adj* ▸ **ˌimmunoˈlogically** *adv* ▸ **ˌimmuˈnologist** *n*

immunoreaction (ɪˌmjuːnəʊrɪˈækʃən) *n* the reaction between an antigen and its antibody.

immunosuppression (ˌɪmjʊnəʊsəˈprɛʃən) *n* medical suppression of the body's immune system, esp. in order to reduce the likelihood of rejection of a transplanted organ.

immunosuppressive (ˌɪmjʊnəʊsəˈprɛsɪv) *n* 1 any drug used for immunosuppression. ◆ *adj* **2** of or relating to such a drug. ▸ **ˌimmunosupˈpressant** *n, adj*

immunotherapy (ˌɪmjʊnəʊˈθɛrəpɪ) *n Med.* the treatment of disease by stimulating the body's production of antibodies. ▸ **immunotherapeutic** (ˌɪmjʊnəʊˈθɛrəpjuːtɪk) *adj*

immure (ɪˈmjʊə) *vb* (*tr*) **1** *Archaic or literary.* to enclose within or as if within walls; imprison. **2** to shut (oneself) away from society. **3** *Obsolete.* to build into or enclose within a wall. [C16: from Medieval Latin *immūrāre,* from Latin IM- (in) + *mūrus* a wall] ▸ **imˈmurement** *n*

immutable (ɪˈmjuːtəbəl) *adj* unchanging through time; unalterable; ageless: *immutable laws.* ▸ **imˌmutaˈbility** *or* **imˈmutableness** *n* ▸ **imˈmutably** *adv*

Imo (ˈiːməʊ) *n* a state of SE Nigeria, formed in 1976 from part of East-Central State. Capital: Owerri. Pop.: 2 779 028 (1995 est.). Area: 5530 sq. km (2135 sq. miles).

imp (ɪmp) *n* **1** a small demon or devil; mischievous sprite. **2** a mischievous child. ◆ *vb* **3** (*tr*) *Falconry.* to insert (new feathers) into the stumps of broken feathers in order to repair the wing of a hawk or falcon. [Old English *impa* bud, graft, hence offspring, child, from *impian* to graft, ultimately from Greek *emphutos* implanted, from *emphuein* to implant, from *phuein* to plant]

imp. *abbrev. for:* **1** imperative. **2** imperfect. **3** imperial. **4** impersonal. **5** import. **6** important. **7** importer. **8** imprimatur.

Imp. *abbrev. for:* **1** Imperator. [Latin: Emperor] **2** Imperatrix. [Latin: Empress] **3** Imperial.

impact *n* (ˈɪmpækt). **1** the act of one body, object, etc., striking another; collision. **2** the force with which one thing hits another or with which two objects collide. **3** the impression made by an idea, cultural movement, social group, etc.: *the impact of the Renaissance on Medieval Europe.* ◆ *vb* (ɪmˈpækt). **4** to drive or press (an object) firmly into (another object, thing, etc.) or (of two objects) to be driven or pressed firmly together. **5** to have an impact or strong effect (on). [C18: from Latin *impactus* pushed against, fastened on, from *impingere* to thrust at, from *pangere* to drive in] ▸ **imˈpaction** *n*

impact adhesive *n* a glue designed to give adhesion when two coated surfaces are pressed together.

impacted (ɪmˈpæktɪd) *adj* **1** (of a tooth) unable to erupt, esp. because of being wedged against another tooth below the gum. **2** (of a fracture) having the jagged broken ends wedged into each other.

impactive (ɪmˈpæktɪv) *adj* **1** of or relating to a physical impact. **2** making a strong impression.

impact printer *n* any printing device in which the printing surface strikes the paper, such as a traditional typewriter or a line printer. See also **non-impact printer.**

impair (ɪmˈpɛə) *vb* (*tr*) to reduce or weaken in strength, quality, etc.: *his hearing was impaired by an accident.* [C14: from Old French *empeirer* to make worse, from Late Latin *pējorāre,* from Latin *pejor* worse; see PEJORATIVE] ▸ **imˈpairable** *adj* ▸ **imˈpairer** *n* ▸ **imˈpairment** *n*

impala (ɪmˈpɑːlə) *n, pl* **-las** *or* **-la.** an antelope, *Aepyceros melampus,* of southern and eastern Africa, having lyre-shaped horns and able to move with enormous leaps when disturbed. [from Zulu]

impale *or* **empale** (ɪmˈpeɪl) *vb* (*tr*) **1** (often foll. by *on, upon,* or *with*) to pierce with a sharp instrument: *they impaled his severed head on a spear.* **2** *Archaic.* to enclose with pales or fencing; fence in. **3** *Heraldry.* to charge (a shield) with two coats of arms placed side by side. [C16: from Medieval Latin *impālāre,* from Latin IM- (in) + *pālus* PALE[2]] ▸ **imˈpalement** *or* **emˈpalement** *n* ▸ **imˈpaler** *or* **emˈpaler** *n*

impalpable (ɪmˈpælpəbᵊl) *adj* **1** imperceptible, esp. to the touch: *impalpable shadows.* **2** difficult to understand; abstruse. ▸ **imˌpalpaˈbility** *n* ▸ **imˈpalpably** *adv*

impanation (ˌɪmpæˈneɪʃən) *n Christianity.* the embodiment of Christ in the consecrated bread and wine of the Eucharist. [C16: from Medieval Latin *impanātiō,* from *impanātus* embodied in bread, from Latin IM- (in) + *panis* bread]

impanel (ɪmˈpænᵊl) *vb* **-els, -elling, -elled** *or U.S.* **-els, -eling, -eled.** a variant spelling (esp. U.S.) of **empanel.** ▸ **imˈpanelment** *n*

imparadise (ɪmˈpærədaɪs) *vb* (*tr*) **1** to make blissfully happy; enrapture. **2** to make into or like paradise.

imparipinnate (ˌɪmpærɪˈpɪneɪt, -ˈpɪnɪt) *adj* (of pinnate leaves) having a terminal unpaired leaflet. Compare **paripinnate.**

imparisyllabic (ɪmˌpærsɪˈlæbɪk) *adj* (of a noun or verb in inflected languages) having inflected forms with different numbers of syllables. Compare **parisyllabic.**

imparity (ɪmˈpærɪtɪ) *n, pl* **-ties.** a less common word for **disparity** (sense 1). [C16: from Late Latin *imparitās,* from Latin *impar* unequal]

impart (ɪmˈpɑːt) *vb* (*tr*) **1** to communicate (information); relate. **2** to give or bestow (something, esp. an abstract quality): *to impart wisdom.* [C15: from Old French *impartir,* from Latin *impertīre,* from IM- (in) + *partīre* to share, from *pars* part] ▸ **imˈpartable** *adj* ▸ **ˌimparˈtation** *or* **imˈpartment** *n* ▸ **imˈparter** *n*

impartial (ɪmˈpɑːʃəl) *adj* not prejudiced towards or against any particular side or party; fair; unbiased. ▸ **imˌpartiˈality** *or* **imˈpartialness** *n* ▸ **imˈpartially** *adv*

impartible (ɪmˈpɑːtəbᵊl) *adj* **1** *Law.* (of land, an estate, etc.) incapable of partition; indivisible. **2** capable of being imparted. ▸ **imˌpartiˈbility** *n* ▸ **imˈpartibly** *adv*

impassable (ɪmˈpɑːsəbᵊl) *adj* (of terrain, roads, etc.) not able to be travelled through or over. ▸ **imˌpassaˈbility** *or* **imˈpassableness** *n* ▸ **imˈpassably** *adv*

impasse (æmˈpɑːs, ˈæmpɑːs, ɪmˈpɑːs, ˈɪmpɑːs) *n* a situation in which progress is blocked; an insurmountable difficulty; stalemate; deadlock. [C19: from French; see IM-, PASS]

impassible (ɪmˈpæsəbᵊl) *adj Rare.* **1** not susceptible to pain or injury. **2** impassive or unmoved. ▸ **imˌpassiˈbility** *or* **imˈpassibleness** *n* ▸ **imˈpassibly** *adv*

impassion (ɪmˈpæʃən) *vb* (*tr*) to arouse the passions of; inflame.

impassioned (ɪmˈpæʃənd) *adj* filled with passion; fiery; inflamed: *an impassioned appeal.* ▸ **imˈpassionedly** *adv* ▸ **imˈpassionedness** *n*

impassive (ɪmˈpæsɪv) *adj* **1** not revealing or affected by emotion; reserved. **2** calm; serene; imperturbable. **3** *Rare.* unconscious or insensible. ▸ **imˈpassively** *adv* ▸ **imˈpassiveness** *or* **impassivity** (ˌɪmpæˈsɪvɪtɪ) *n*

impaste (ɪmˈpeɪst) *vb* (*tr*) to apply paint thickly to. [C16: from Italian *impastare,* from *pasta* PASTE[1]] ▸ **impastation** (ˌɪmpæsˈteɪʃən) *n*

impasto (ɪmˈpæstəʊ) *n* **1** paint applied thickly, so that brush and palette knife marks are evident. **2** the technique of applying paint in this way. [C18: from Italian, from *impastare;* see IMPASTE]

impatience (ɪmˈpeɪʃəns) *n* **1** lack of patience; intolerance of or irritability with anything that impedes or delays. **2** restless desire for change and excitement.

impatiens (ɪmˈpeɪʃɪˌɛnz) *n, pl* **-ens.** any balsaminaceous plant of the genus *Impatiens,* such as balsam, touch-me-not, busy Lizzie, and policeman's helmet. [C18: New Latin from Latin: impatient; from the fact that the ripe pods burst open when touched]

impatient (ɪmˈpeɪʃənt) *adj* **1** lacking patience; easily irritated at delay, opposition, etc. **2** exhibiting lack of patience: *an impatient retort.* **3** (*postpositive;* foll. by *of*) intolerant (of) or indignant (at): *impatient of indecision.* **4** (*postpositive;* often foll. by *for*) restlessly eager (for something or to do something). ▸ **imˈpatiently** *adv*

impeach (ɪmˈpiːtʃ) *vb* (*tr*) **1** *Criminal law.* to bring a charge or accusation against. **2** *Brit. criminal law.* to accuse of a crime, esp. of treason or some other offence against the state. **3** *Chiefly U.S.* to charge (a public official) with an offence committed in office. **4** to challenge or question (a person's honesty, integrity, etc.). [C14: from Old French *empeechier,* from Late Latin *impedicāre* to entangle, catch, from Latin IM- (in) + *pedica* a fetter, from *pēs* foot] ▸ **imˈpeacher** *n*

impeachable (ɪmˈpiːtʃəbᵊl) *adj* **1** capable of being impeached or accused. **2** (of an offence) making a person liable to impeachment. ▸ **imˌpeachaˈbility** *n*

impeachment (ɪmˈpiːtʃmənt) *n* **1** *Rare.* (in England) committal by the House of Commons, esp. of a minister of the Crown, for trial by the House of Lords. The last instance occurred in 1805. **2** (in the U.S.) a proceeding brought against a federal government official. **3** an accusation or charge. **4** *Obsolete.* discredit; reproach.

impearl (ɪmˈpɜːl) *vb* (*tr*) *Archaic or poetic.* **1** to adorn with pearls. **2** to form into pearl-like shapes or drops.

impeccable (ɪmˈpɛkəbᵊl) *adj* **1** without flaw or error; faultless: *an impeccable record.* **2** *Rare.* incapable of sinning. [C16: from Late Latin *impeccābilis* sinless, from Latin IM- (not) + *peccāre* to sin] ▸ **imˌpeccaˈbility** *n* ▸ **imˈpeccably** *adv*

impeccant (ɪmˈpɛkənt) *adj* not sinning; free from sin. [C18: from IM- (not) + Latin *peccant-,* from *peccāre* to sin] ▸ **imˈpeccancy** *n*

impecunious (ˌɪmpɪˈkjuːnɪəs) *adj* without money; penniless. [C16: from IM- (not) + *-pecunious,* from Latin *pecūniōsus* wealthy, from *pecūnia* money] ▸ **ˌimpeˈcuniously** *adv* ▸ **ˌimpeˈcuniousness** *or* **impecuniosity** (ˌɪmpɪkjuːnɪˈɒsɪtɪ) *n*

impedance (ɪmˈpiːdᵊns) *n* **1** a measure of the opposition to the flow of an alternating current equal to the square root of the sum of the squares of the resistance and the reactance, expressed in ohms. Symbol: *Z* **2** a component that offers impedance. **3** Also called: **acoustic impedance.** the ratio of the sound pressure in a medium to the rate of alternating flow of the medium through a specified surface due to the sound wave. Symbol: Z_a **4** Also called: **mechanical impedance.** the ratio of the mechanical force, acting in the direction of motion, to the velocity of the resulting vibration. Symbol: Z_m

impede (ɪmˈpiːd) *vb* (*tr*) to restrict or retard in action, progress, etc.; hinder; obstruct. [C17: from Latin *impedīre* to hinder, literally: shackle the feet, from *pēs* foot] ▸ **imˈpeder** *n* ▸ **imˈpedingly** *adv*

impediment (ɪmˈpɛdɪmənt) *n* **1** a hindrance or obstruction. **2** a physical defect, esp. one of speech, such as a stammer. **3** (*pl* **-ments** *or* **-menta** (-ˈmɛntə)) *Law.* an obstruction to the making of a contract, esp. a contract of marriage by reason of closeness of blood or affinity. ▸ **imˌpediˈmental** *or* **imˌpediˈmentary** *adj*

impedimenta (ɪmˌpɛdɪˈmɛntə) *pl n* **1** the baggage and equipment carried by an army. **2** any objects or circumstances that impede progress. **3** a plural of **impediment** (sense 3). [C16: from Latin, plural of *impedīmentum* hindrance; see IMPEDE]

impedor (ɪmˈpiːdə) *n Physics.* a component, such as an inductor or resistor, that offers impedance.

impel (ɪmˈpɛl) *vb* **-pels, -pelling, -pelled.** (*tr*) **1** to urge or force (a person) to an action; constrain or motivate. **2** to push, drive, or force into motion. [C15: from Latin *impellere* to push against, drive forward, from IM- (in) + *pellere* to drive, push, strike] ▸ **imˈpellent** *n, adj*

impeller (ɪmˈpɛlə) *n* **1** the vaned rotating disc of a centrifugal pump, compressor, etc. **2** a compressor or centrifugal pump having such an impeller.

impend (ɪmˈpɛnd) *vb* (*intr*) **1** (esp. of something threatening) to be about to happen; be imminent. **2** (foll. by *over*) *Rare.* to be suspended; hang. [C16: from Latin *impendēre* to overhang, from *pendēre* to hang] ▸ **imˈpendence** *or* **imˈpendency** *n* ▸ **imˈpending** *adj*

impenetrable (ɪmˈpɛnɪtrəbᵊl) *adj* **1** incapable of being pierced through or penetrated: *an impenetrable forest.* **2** incapable of being understood; incomprehensible: *impenetrable jargon.* **3** incapable of being seen through: *impenetrable gloom.* **4** not susceptible to ideas, influence, etc.: *impenetrable ignorance.* **5** *Physics.* (of a body) incapable of occupying the same space as another body. ▸ **imˌpenetraˈbility** *n* ▸ **imˈpenetrableness** *n* ▸ **imˈpenetrably** *adv*

impenitent (ɪmˈpɛnɪtənt) *adj* not sorry or penitent; unrepentant. ▸ **imˈpenitence, imˈpenitency,** *or* **imˈpenitentness** *n* ▸ **imˈpenitently** *adv*

impennate (ɪmˈpɛneɪt) *adj Rare.* (of birds) lacking true functional wings or feathers.

imper. *abbrev. for* imperative.

imperative (ɪmˈpɛrətɪv) *adj* **1** extremely urgent or important; essential. **2** peremptory or authoritative: *an imperative tone of voice.* **3** Also: **imperatival** (ɪmˌpɛrəˈtaɪvᵊl). *Grammar.* denoting a mood of verbs used in giving orders, making requests, etc. In English the verb root without any inflections is the usual form, as for example *leave* in *Leave me alone.* ◆ *n* **4** something that is urgent or essential. **5** an order or command. **6** *Grammar.* **6a** the imperative mood. **6b** a verb in this mood. [C16: from Late Latin *imperātīvus,* from Latin *imperāre* to command] ▸ **imˈperatively** *adv* ▸ **imˈperativeness** *n*

imperator (ˌɪmpəˈrɑːtɔː) *n* **1a** (in imperial Rome) a title of the emperor. **1b** (in republican Rome) a temporary title of honour bestowed upon a victorious general. **2** a less common word for **emperor.** [C16: from Latin: commander, from *imperāre* to command] ▸ **imperatorial** (ɪmˌpɛrəˈtɔːrɪəl) *adj* ▸ **imˌperaˈtorially** *adv* ▸ **ˌimpeˈratorˌship** *n*

imperceptible (ˌɪmpəˈsɛptɪbᵊl) *adj* too slight, subtle, gradual, etc., to be perceived. ▸ **ˌimperˌceptiˈbility** *or* **ˌimperˈceptibleness** *n* ▸ **ˌimperˈceptibly** *adv*

imperceptive (ˌɪmpəˈsɛptɪv) *adj, also* **impercipient** (ˌɪmpə-ˈsɪpɪənt). lacking in perception; obtuse. ▸ **ˌimperˈception** *n* ▸ **ˌimperˈceptively** *adv* ▸ **ˌimpercepˈtivity, ˌimperˈceptiveness,** *or* **ˌimperˈcipience** *n*

imperf. *abbrev. for:* **1** Also: **impf.** imperfect. **2** (of stamps) imperforate.

imperfect (ɪmˈpɜːfɪkt) *adj* **1** exhibiting or characterized by faults, mistakes, etc.; defective. **2** not complete or finished; deficient. **3** *Botany.* **3a** (of flowers) lacking functional stamens or pistils. **3b** (of fungi) not undergoing sexual reproduction. **4** *Grammar.* denoting a tense of verbs used most commonly in describing continuous or repeated past actions or events, as for example *was walking* as opposed to *walked.* **5** *Law.* (of a trust, an obligation, etc.) lacking some necessary formality to make effective or binding; incomplete; legally unenforceable. See also **executory** (sense 1). **6** *Music.* **6a** (of a cadence) proceeding to the dominant from the tonic, subdominant, or any chord other than the dominant. **6b** of or relating to all intervals other than the fourth, fifth, and octave. Compare **perfect** (sense 9). ◆ *n* **7** *Grammar.* **7a** the imperfect tense. **7b** a verb in this tense. ▸ **imˈperfectly** *adv* ▸ **imˈperfectness** *n*

imperfect competition *n Economics.* the market situation that exists when one or more of the necessary conditions for perfect competition do not hold.

imperfection (ˌɪmpəˈfɛkʃən) *n* **1** the condition or quality of being imperfect. **2** a fault or defect.

imperfective (ˌɪmpəˈfɛktɪv) *Grammar.* ◆ *adj* **1** denoting an aspect of the verb in some languages, including English, used to indicate that the action is in progress without regard to its completion. Compare **perfective.** ◆ *n* **2a** the imperfective aspect of a verb. **2b** a verb in this aspect. ▸ **ˌimperˈfectively** *adv*

imperforate (ɪmˈpɜːfərɪt, -ˌreɪt) *adj* **1** not perforated. **2** (of a postage stamp) not provided with perforation or any other means of separation. Abbrev.: **imperf.** Compare **perforate. 3** *Anatomy.* (of a bodily part, such as the anus) without the normal opening. ▸ **imˌperfoˈration** *n*

imperia (ɪmˈpɪərɪə) *n* the plural of **imperium.**

imperial (ɪmˈpɪərɪəl) *adj* **1** of or relating to an empire, emperor, or empress. **2** characteristic of or befitting an emperor; majestic; commanding. **3** characteristic of or exercising supreme authority; imperious. **4** (esp. of products and commodities) of a superior size or quality. **5** (*usually prenominal*) (of weights, measures, etc.) conforming to standards or definitions legally established in Britain: *an imperial gallon.* ◆ *n* **6** any of various book sizes, esp. 7½ by 11 inches (**imperial octavo**) or (chiefly Brit.) 11 by 15 inches (**imperial quarto**). **7** a size of writing or printing paper, 23 by 31 inches (U.S. and Canadian) or 22 by 30 inches (Brit.). **8** (formerly) a Russian gold coin originally worth ten roubles. **9** *U.S.* **9a** the top of a carriage, such as a diligence. **9b** a luggage case carried there. **10** *Architect.* a dome that has a point at the top. **11** a small tufted beard popularized by the emperor Napoleon III. **12** a member of an imperial family, esp. an emperor or empress. **13** a red deer having antlers with fourteen points. [C14: from Late Latin *imperiālis,* from Latin *imperium* command, authority, empire] ▸ **imˈperially** *adv* ▸ **imˈperialness** *n*

Imperial (ɪmˈpɪərɪəl) *adj* **1** (*sometimes not cap.*) of or relating to a specified empire, such as the British Empire. ◆ *n* **2** a supporter or soldier of the Holy Roman Empire.

imperial gallon *n* a formal name for **gallon** (sense 1).

imperialism (ɪmˈpɪərɪəˌlɪzəm) *n* **1** the policy or practice of extending a state's rule over other territories. **2** an instance or policy of aggressive behaviour by one state against another. **3** the extension or attempted extension of authority, influence, power, etc., by any person, country, institution, etc.: *cultural imperialism.* **4** a system of imperial government or rule by an emperor. **5** the spirit, character, authority, etc., of an empire. **6** advocacy of or support for any form of imperialism. ▸ **imˈperialist** *adj, n* ▸ **imˌperialˈistic** *adj* ▸ **imˌperialˈistically** *adv*

Imperial War Museum *n* a museum in London, founded in 1920, containing material related to military operations involving British and Commonwealth forces since 1914.

imperil (ɪmˈpɛrɪl) *vb* (*tr*) to place in danger or jeopardy; endanger. ▸ **imˈperilment** *n*

imperious (ɪmˈpɪərɪəs) *adj* **1** domineering; arrogant; overbearing. **2** *Rare.* urgent; imperative. [C16: from Latin *imperiōsus* from *imperium* command, power] ▸ **imˈperiously** *adv* ▸ **imˈperiousness** *n*

imperishable (ɪmˈpɛrɪʃəbᵊl) *adj* **1** not subject to decay or deterioration: *imperishable goods.* **2** not likely to be forgotten: *imperishable truths.* ▸ **imˌperishaˈbility** *or* **imˈperishableness** *n* ▸ **imˈperishably** *adv*

imperium (ɪmˈpɪərɪəm) *n, pl* **-ria** (-rɪə). **1** (in ancient Rome) the supreme power, held esp. by consuls and emperors, to command and administer in military, judicial, and civil affairs. **2** the right to command; supreme power. **3** a less common word for **empire.** [C17: from Latin: command, empire, from *imperāre* to command; see EMPEROR]

impermanent (ɪmˈpɜːmənənt) *adj* not permanent; fleeting; transitory. ▸ **imˈpermanence** *or* **imˈpermanency** *n* ▸ **imˈpermanently** *adv*

impermeable (ɪmˈpɜːmɪəbᵊl) *adj* (of a substance) not allowing the passage of a fluid through interstices; not permeable. ▸ **imˌpermeaˈbility** *or* **imˈpermeableness** *n* ▸ **imˈpermeably** *adv*

impermissible (ˌɪmpəˈmɪsɪbᵊl) *adj* not permissible; not allowed. ▸ **ˌimperˌmissiˈbility** *n* ▸ **ˌimperˈmissibly** *adv*

impers. *abbrev. for* impersonal.

imperscriptible (ˌɪmpəˈskrɪptɪbᵊl) *adj* not supported by written authority. [C19: from IM- (not) + Latin *perscribere* to write down]

impersonal (ɪmˈpɜːsənᵊl) *adj* **1** without reference to any individual person; objective: *an impersonal assessment.* **2** devoid of human warmth or sympathy; cold: *an impersonal manner.* **3** not having human characteristics: *an impersonal God.* **4** *Grammar.* (of a verb) having no logical subject. Usually in English the pronoun *it* is used in such cases as a grammatical subject, as for example in *It is raining.* **5** *Grammar.* (of a pronoun) not denoting a person. ▸ **imˌpersonˈality** *n* ▸ **imˈpersonally** *adv*

impersonalize *or* **impersonalise** (ɪm'pɜːsənəˌlaɪz) *vb.* (*tr*) to make impersonal, esp. to rid of such human characteristics as sympathy, warmth, etc.; dehumanize. ▸ **imˌpersonali'zation** *or* **imˌpersonali'sation** *n*

impersonate (ɪm'pɜːsəˌneɪt) *vb* (*tr*) **1** to pretend to be (another person). **2** to imitate the character, mannerisms, etc., of (another person). **3** *Rare.* to play the part or character of. **4** an archaic word for **personify.** ▸ **imˌperson'ation** *n* ▸ **im'personˌator** *n*

impertinence (ɪm'pɜːtɪnəns) *or* **impertinency** *n* **1** disrespectful behaviour or language; rudeness; insolence. **2** an impertinent act, gesture, etc. **3** *Rare.* lack of pertinence; irrelevance; inappropriateness.

impertinent (ɪm'pɜːtɪnənt) *adj* **1** rude; insolent; impudent. **2** irrelevant or inappropriate. [C14: from Latin *impertinēns* not belonging, from Latin IM- (not) + *pertinēre* to be relevant; see PERTAIN] ▸ **im'pertinently** *adv*

imperturbable (ˌɪmpɜː'tɜːbəbᵊl) *adj* not easily perturbed; calm; unruffled. ▸ **ˌimperˌturba'bility** *or* **ˌimper'turbableness** *n* ▸ **ˌimper'turbably** *adv* ▸ **imperturbation** (ˌɪmpɜːtɜː'beɪʃən) *n*

impervious (ɪm'pɜːvɪəs) *or* **imperviable** *adj* **1** not able to be penetrated, as by water, light, etc.; impermeable. **2** (*often postpositive;* foll. by *to*) not able to be influenced (by) or not receptive (to): *impervious to argument.* ▸ **im'perviously** *adv* ▸ **im'perviousness** *n*

impetigo (ˌɪmpɪ'taɪgəʊ) *n* a contagious bacterial skin disease characterized by the formation of pustules that develop into yellowish crusty sores. [C16: from Latin: scabby eruption, from *impetere* to assail; see IMPETUS; for form, compare VERTIGO] ▸ **impetiginous** (ˌɪmpɪ'tɪdʒɪnəs) *adj*

impetrate ('ɪmpɪˌtreɪt) *vb* (*tr*) **1** to supplicate or entreat for, esp. by prayer. **2** to obtain by prayer. [C16: from Latin *impetrāre* to procure by entreaty, from *-petrāre,* from *patrāre* to bring to pass, of uncertain origin; perhaps related to Latin *pater* a father] ▸ **ˌimpe'tration** *n* ▸ **'impetrative** *adj* ▸ **'impeˌtrator** *n*

impetuous (ɪm'petjʊəs) *adj* **1** liable to act without consideration; rash; impulsive. **2** resulting from or characterized by rashness or haste. **3** *Poetic.* moving with great force or violence; rushing: *the impetuous stream hurtled down the valley.* [C14: from Late Latin *impetuōsus* violent; see IMPETUS] ▸ **im'petuously** *adv* ▸ **im'petuousness** *or* **impetuosity** (ɪmˌpetjʊ'ɒsɪtɪ) *n*

impetus ('ɪmpɪtəs) *n, pl* **-tuses. 1** an impelling movement or force; incentive or impulse; stimulus. **2** *Physics.* the force that sets a body in motion or that tends to resist changes in a body's motion. [C17: from Latin: attack, from *impetere* to assail, from IM- (in) + *petere* to make for, seek out]

impf. *or* **imperf.** *abbrev. for* imperfect.

imp. gal. *or* **imp. gall.** *abbrev. for* imperial gallon.

Imphal (ɪm'fɑːl, 'ɪmfəl) *n* a city in NE India, capital of Manipur Territory, on the Manipur River: formerly the seat of the Manipur kings: site of a major Anglo-Indian victory over the Japanese (1944), which was a turning point in the British recovery of Burma (now called Myanmar). Pop.: 198 535 (1991).

impi ('ɪmpɪ) *n, pl* **-pi** *or* **-pies.** a group of Bantu warriors. [C19: Nguni: regiment, army]

impiety (ɪm'paɪɪtɪ) *n, pl* **-ties. 1** lack of reverence or proper respect for a god. **2** any lack of proper respect. **3** an impious act.

impinge (ɪm'pɪndʒ) *vb* **1** (*intr;* usually foll. by *on* or *upon*) to encroach or infringe; trespass: *to impinge on someone's time.* **2** (*intr;* usually foll. by *on, against,* or *upon*) to collide (with); strike. [C16: from Latin *impingere* to drive at, dash against, from *pangere* to fasten, drive in] ▸ **im'pingement** *n* ▸ **im'pinger** *n*

impingement attack *n Metallurgy.* a form of corrosion of metals caused by erosion of the oxide layer by a moving fluid in which there are suspended particles or air bubbles.

impious ('ɪmpɪəs) *adj* **1** lacking piety or reverence for a god; ungodly. **2** lacking respect; undutiful. ▸ **'impiously** *adv* ▸ **'impiousness** *n*

impish ('ɪmpɪʃ) *adj* of or resembling an imp; mischievous. ▸ **'impishly** *adv* ▸ **'impishness** *n*

implacable (ɪm'plækəbᵊl) *adj* **1** incapable of being placated or pacified; unappeasable. **2** inflexible; intractable. ▸ **imˌplaca'bility** *or* **im'placableness** *n* ▸ **im'placably** *adv*

implacental (ˌɪmplə'sentᵊl) *adj* another word for **aplacental.**

implant *vb* (ɪm'plɑːnt). (*tr*) **1** to establish firmly; inculcate; instil: *to implant sound moral principles.* **2** to plant or embed; infix; entrench. **3** *Surgery.* **3a** to graft (a tissue) into the body. **3b** to insert (a radioactive substance, hormone, etc.) into the tissues. ◆ *n* ('ɪmˌplɑːnt). **4** anything implanted, esp. surgically, such as a tissue graft or hormone. ▸ **im'planter** *n*

implantation (ˌɪmplɑːn'teɪʃən) *n* **1** the act of implanting or the state of being implanted. **2** Also called: **nidation.** the attachment of the blastocyst of a mammalian embryo to the wall of the uterus of the mother.

implausible (ɪm'plɔːzəbᵊl) *adj* not plausible; provoking disbelief; unlikely. ▸ **imˌplausi'bility** *or* **im'plausibleness** *n* ▸ **im'plausibly** *adv*

implead (ɪm'pliːd) *vb* (*tr*) *Law, rare.* **1a** to sue or prosecute. **1b** to bring an action against. **2** to accuse. [C13: from Anglo-French *empleder;* see IM-, PLEAD] ▸ **im'pleadable** *adj* ▸ **im'pleader** *n*

implement *n* ('ɪmplɪmənt). **1** a piece of equipment; tool or utensil: *gardening implements.* **2** something used to achieve a purpose; agent. ◆ *vb* ('ɪmplɪˌment). (*tr*) **3** to carry out; put into action; perform: *to implement a plan.* **4** *Archaic.* to complete, satisfy, or fulfil. [C17: from Late Latin *implēmentum,* literally: a filling up, from Latin *implēre* to fill up, satisfy, fulfil] ▸ **ˌimple'mental** *adj* ▸ **ˌimplemen'tation** *n* ▸ **'impleˌmenter** *or* **'impleˌmentor** *n*

implicate ('ɪmplɪˌkeɪt) *vb* (*tr*) **1** to show to be involved, esp. in a crime. **2** to involve as a necessary inference; imply: *his protest implicated censure by the authorities.* **3** to affect intimately: *this news implicates my decision.* **4** *Rare.* to intertwine or entangle. [C16: from Latin *implicāre* to involve, from IM- + *plicāre* to fold] ▸ **implicative** (ɪm'plɪkətɪv) *adj* ▸ **im'plicatively** *adv*

implication (ˌɪmplɪ'keɪʃən) *n* **1** the act of implicating or the state of being implicated. **2** something that is implied; suggestion: *the implication of your silence is that you're bored.* **3** *Logic.* **3a** the operator that forms a sentence from two given sentences and corresponds to the English *if... then....* **3b** a sentence so formed. Usually written p→q or p⊃q, where p,q are the component sentences, it is true except when p (the antecedent) is true and q (the consequent) is false. **3c** the relation between such sentences. ▸ **ˌimpli'cational** *adj*

implicature (ɪm'plɪkətʃə) *n Logic, philosophy.* **1** a proposition inferred from the circumstances of utterances of another proposition rather than from its literal meaning, as when an academic referee writes *the candidate's handwriting is excellent* to convey that he has nothing relevant to commend. **2** the relation between the uttered and the inferred statement.

implicit (ɪm'plɪsɪt) *adj* **1** not explicit; implied; indirect: *there was implicit criticism in his voice.* **2** absolute and unreserved; unquestioning: *you have implicit trust in him.* **3** (*when postpositive,* foll. by *in*) contained or inherent: *to bring out the anger implicit in the argument.* **4** *Maths.* (of a function) having an equation of the form $f(x,y) = 0$, in which y cannot be directly expressed in terms of x, as in $xy + x^2 + y^3x^2 = 0$. Compare **explicit**[1] (sense 4). **5** *Obsolete.* intertwined. [C16: from Latin *implicitus,* variant of *implicātus* interwoven; see IMPLICATE] ▸ **im'plicitly** *adv* ▸ **im'plicitness** *or* **im'plicity** *n*

implied (ɪm'plaɪd) *adj* hinted at or suggested; not directly expressed: *an implied criticism.* ▸ **impliedly** (ɪm'plaɪɪdlɪ) *adv*

implode (ɪm'pləʊd) *vb* **1** to collapse or cause to collapse inwards in a violent manner as a result of external pressure: *the vacuum flask imploded.* **2** (*tr*) to pronounce (a consonant) with or by implosion. ◆ Compare **explode.** [C19: from IM- + (EX)PLODE]

implore (ɪm'plɔː) *vb* (*tr*) **1** to beg or ask (someone) earnestly (to do something); plead with; beseech. **2** to ask earnestly or piteously for; supplicate; beg: *to implore someone's mercy.* [C16: from Latin *implōrāre,* from IM- + *plōrāre* to bewail] ▸ **ˌimplo'ration** *n* ▸ **im'ploratory** *adj* ▸ **im'plorer** *n* ▸ **im'ploringly** *adv*

implosion (ɪm'pləʊʒən) *n* **1** the act or process of imploding: *the implosion of a light bulb.* **2** *Phonetics.* the suction or inhalation of breath employed in the pronunciation of an ingressive consonant.

implosive (ɪm'pləʊsɪv) *adj* **1** pronounced by or with implosion. ◆ *n* **2** an implosive consonant. ▸ **im'plosively** *adv*

imply (ɪm'plaɪ) *vb* **-plies, -plying, -plied.** (*tr; may take a clause as object*) **1** to express or indicate by a hint; suggest: *what are you implying by that remark?* **2** to suggest or involve as a necessary consequence. **3** *Logic.* to enable (a conclusion) to be inferred. **4** *Obsolete.* to entangle or enfold. [C14: from Old French *emplier,* from Latin *implicāre* to involve; see IMPLICATE]

USAGE See at **infer.**

impolder (ɪm'pəʊldə) *or* **empolder** *vb* to make into a polder; reclaim (land) from the sea. [C19: from Dutch *inpolderen,* see IN-[2], POLDER]

impolicy (ɪm'pɒlɪsɪ) *n, pl* **-cies.** the act or an instance of being unjudicious or impolitic.

impolite (ˌɪmpə'laɪt) *adj* discourteous; rude; uncivil. ▸ **ˌimpo'litely** *adv* ▸ **ˌimpo'liteness** *n*

impolitic (ɪm'pɒlɪtɪk) *adj* not politic or expedient; unwise. ▸ **im'politicly** *adv* ▸ **im'politicness** *n*

imponderabilia (ɪmˌpɒndərə'bɪlɪə) *pl n* imponderables. [C20: New Latin]

imponderable (ɪm'pɒndərəbᵊl, -drəbᵊl) *adj* **1** unable to be weighed or assessed. ◆ *n* **2** something difficult or impossible to assess. ▸ **imˌpondera'bility** *or* **im'ponderableness** *n* ▸ **im'ponderably** *adv*

imponent (ɪm'pəʊnənt) *n* a person who imposes a duty, etc.

import *vb* (ɪm'pɔːt, 'ɪmpɔːt). **1** to buy or bring in (goods or services) from a foreign country. Compare **export. 2** (*tr*) to bring in from an outside source: *to import foreign words into the language.* **3** *Rare.* to signify or be significant; mean; convey: *to import doom.* ◆ *n* ('ɪmpɔːt). **4** (*often pl*) **4a** goods (**visible imports**) or services (**invisible imports**) that are bought from foreign countries. **4b** (*as modifier*): *an import licence.* **5** significance or importance: *a man of great import.* **6** meaning or signification. **7** *Informal.* a sportsman who is not native to the country in which he or she plays. [C15: from Latin *importāre* to carry in, from IM- + *portāre* to carry] ▸ **im'portable** *adj* ▸ **imˌporta'bility** *n* ▸ **im'porter** *n*

importance (ɪm'pɔːtᵊns) *n* **1** the state of being important; significance. **2** social status; standing; esteem: *a man of importance.* **3** *Obsolete.* **3a** meaning or signification. **3b** an important matter. **3c** importunity.

important (ɪm'pɔːtᵊnt) *adj* **1** of great significance or value; outstanding: *Voltaire is an important writer.* **2** of social significance; notable; eminent; esteemed: *an important man in the town.* **3** (*when postpositive,* usually foll. by *to*) specially relevant or of great concern (to); valued highly (by): *your wishes are important to me.* **4** an obsolete word for **importunate.** [C16: from Old Italian *importante,* from Medieval Latin *importāre* to signify, be of consequence, from Latin: to carry in; see IMPORT] ▸ **im'portantly** *adv*

USAGE The use of *more importantly* as in *more importantly, the local council is opposed to this proposal* has become very common, but many people still prefer to use *more important.*

importation (ˌɪmpɔː'teɪʃən) *n* **1** the act, business, or process of importing goods or services. **2** an imported product or service.

importunate (ɪm'pɔːtjʊnɪt) *adj* **1** persistent or demanding; insistent. **2** *Rare.* troublesome; annoying. ▸ **im'portunately** *adv* ▸ **im'portunateness** *n*

importune (ɪm'pɔːtjuːn) *vb* (*tr*) **1** to harass with persistent requests; demand of (someone) insistently. **2** to beg for persistently; request with insistence. **3** *Obsolete.* **3a** to anger or annoy. **3b** to force; impel. [C16: from Latin *importūnus* tiresome, from *im-* IN-[1] + *-portūnus* as in *opportūnus* OPPORTUNE] ▸ **im'portunely** *adv* ▸ **im'portuner** *n* ▸ **,impor'tunity** *or* **im'portunacy** *n*

impose (ɪm'pəʊz) *vb* (usually foll. by *on* or *upon*) **1** (*tr*) to establish as something to be obeyed or complied with; enforce: *to impose a tax on the people.* **2** to force (oneself, one's presence, etc.) on another or others; obtrude. **3** (*intr*) to take advantage, as of a person or quality: *to impose on someone's kindness.* **4** (*tr*) *Printing.* to arrange pages so that after printing and folding the pages will be in the correct order. **5** (*tr*) to pass off deceptively; foist: *to impose a hoax on someone.* **6** (*tr*) (of a bishop or priest) to lay (the hands) on the head of a candidate for certain sacraments. [C15: from Old French *imposer,* from Latin *impōnere* to place upon, from *pōnere* to place, set] ▸ **im'posable** *adj* ▸ **im'poser** *n*

imposing (ɪm'pəʊzɪŋ) *adj* grand or impressive: *an imposing building.* ▸ **im'posingly** *adv* ▸ **im'posingness** *n*

imposing stone *or* **table** *n Printing.* a flat hard surface upon which pages printed from hot metal are imposed.

imposition (,ɪmpə'zɪʃən) *n* **1** the act of imposing. **2** something that is imposed unfairly on someone. **3** (in Britain) a task set as a school punishment. **4** the arrangement of pages for printing so that the finished work will have its pages in the correct order.

impossibility (ɪm,pɒsə'bɪlɪtɪ, ,ɪmpɒs-) *n, pl* **-ties. 1** the state or quality of being impossible. **2** something that is impossible.

impossible (ɪm'pɒsəb**ə**l) *adj* **1** incapable of being done, undertaken, or experienced. **2** incapable of occurring or happening. **3** absurd or inconceivable; unreasonable: *it's impossible to think of him as a bishop.* **4** *Informal.* intolerable; outrageous: *those children are impossible.* ▸ **im'possibleness** *n* ▸ **im'possibly** *adv*

impossible figure *n* a picture of an object that at first sight looks three-dimensional but cannot be a two-dimensional projection of a real three-dimensional object, for example a picture of a staircase that re-enters itself while appearing to ascend continuously. Also called: **Escher figure.**

impost[1] ('ɪmpəʊst) *n* **1** a tax, esp. a customs duty. **2** *Horse racing.* the specific weight that a particular horse must carry in a handicap race. ◆ *vb* **3** (*tr*) *U.S.* to classify (imported goods) according to the duty payable on them. [C16: from Medieval Latin *impostus* tax, from Latin *impositus* imposed; see IMPOSE] ▸ **'imposter** *n*

impost[2] ('ɪmpəʊst) *n Architect.* a member at the top of a wall, pier, or column that supports an arch, esp. one that has a projecting moulding. [C17: from French *imposte,* from Latin *impositus* placed upon; see IMPOSE]

impostor *or* **imposter** (ɪm'pɒstə) *n* a person who deceives others, esp. by assuming a false identity; charlatan. [C16: from Late Latin: deceiver; see IMPOSE]

impostume (ɪm'pɒstjuːm) *or* **imposthume** (ɪm'pɒsθuːm) *n* an archaic word for **abscess.** [C15: from Old French *empostume,* from Late Latin *apostēma,* from Greek, literally: separation (of pus), from *aphistanai* to remove, from *histanai* to stand]

imposture (ɪm'pɒstʃə) *n* the act or an instance of deceiving others, esp. by assuming a false identity. [C16: from French, from Late Latin *impostūra,* from Latin *impōnere;* see IMPOSE] ▸ **impostrous** (ɪm'pɒstrəs), **impostorous** (ɪm'pɒstərəs), *or* **im'posturous** *adj*

impotent ('ɪmpətənt) *adj* **1** (*when postpositive, often takes an infinitive*) lacking sufficient strength; powerless. **2** (esp. of males) unable to perform sexual intercourse. **3** *Obsolete.* lacking self-control; unrestrained. ▸ **'impotence, 'impotency,** *or* **'impotentness** *n* ▸ **'impotently** *adv*

impound (ɪm'paʊnd) *vb* (*tr*) **1** to confine (stray animals, illegally parked cars, etc.) in a pound. **2a** to seize (chattels, etc.) by legal right. **2b** to take possession of (a document, evidence, etc.) and hold in legal custody. **3** to collect (water) in a reservoir or dam, as for irrigation. **4** to seize or appropriate. ▸ **im'poundable** *adj* ▸ **im'poundage** *or* **im'poundment** *n* ▸ **im'pounder** *n*

impoverish (ɪm'pɒvərɪʃ) *vb* (*tr*) **1** to make poor or diminish the quality of: *to impoverish society by cutting the grant to the arts.* **2** to deprive (soil, etc.) of fertility. [C15: from Old French *empovrir, from povre* POOR] ▸ **im'poverisher** *n* ▸ **im'poverishment** *n*

impower (ɪm'paʊə) *vb* a less common spelling of **empower.**

impracticable (ɪm'præktɪkəb**ə**l) *adj* **1** incapable of being put into practice or accomplished; not feasible. **2** unsuitable for a desired use; unfit. **3** an archaic word for **intractable.** ▸ **im,practica'bility** *or* **im'practicableness** *n* ▸ **im'practicably** *adv*

impractical (ɪm'præktɪk**ə**l) *adj* **1** not practical or workable: *an impractical solution.* **2** not given to practical matters or gifted with practical skills: *he is intelligent but too impractical for commercial work.* ▸ **im,practi'cality** *or* **im'practicalness** *n* ▸ **im'practically** *adv*

imprecate ('ɪmprɪ,keɪt) *vb* **1** (*intr*) to swear, curse, or blaspheme. **2** (*tr*) to invoke or bring down (evil, a curse, etc.): *to imprecate disaster on the ship.* **3** (*tr*) to put a curse on. [C17: from Latin *imprecārī* to invoke, from *im-* IN-[2] + *precārī* to PRAY] ▸ **'impre,catory** *adj*

imprecation (,ɪmprɪ'keɪʃən) *n* **1** the act of imprecating. **2** a malediction; curse.

imprecise (,ɪmprɪ'saɪs) *adj* not precise; inexact or inaccurate. ▸ **,impre'cisely** *adv* ▸ **imprecision** (,ɪmprɪ'sɪʒən) *or* **,impre'ciseness** *n*

impredicative (,ɪmprə'dɪkətɪv) *adj Logic.* (of a definition) given in terms that require quantification over a range that includes that which is to be defined, as *having all the properties of a great general* where one of the properties as ascribed must be that property itself. Compare **predicative** (sense 2).

impregnable[1] (ɪm'prɛgnəb**ə**l) *adj* **1** unable to be broken into or taken by force: *an impregnable castle.* **2** unable to be shaken or overcome: *impregnable self-confidence.* **3** incapable of being refuted: *an impregnable argument.* [C15 *imprenable,* from Old French, from IM- (not) + *prenable* able to be taken, from *prendre* to take] ▸ **im,pregna'bility** *or* **im'pregnableness** *n* ▸ **im'pregnably** *adv*

impregnable[2] (ɪm'prɛgnəb**ə**l) *or* **impregnatable** (,ɪmprɛg'neɪtəb**ə**l) *adj* able to be impregnated; fertile.

impregnate *vb* ('ɪmprɛg,neɪt). (*tr*) **1** to saturate, soak, or infuse: *to impregnate a cloth with detergent.* **2** to imbue or permeate; pervade. **3** to cause to conceive; make pregnant. **4** to fertilize (an ovum). **5** to make (land, soil, etc.) fruitful. ◆ *adj* (ɪm'prɛgnɪt, -,neɪt). **6** pregnant or fertilized. [C17: from Late Latin *impraegnāre* to make pregnant, from Latin *im-* IN-[2] + *praegnans* PREGNANT] ▸ **,impreg'nation** *n* ▸ **im'pregnator** *n*

impresa (ɪm'preɪzə) *or* **imprese** (ɪm'priːz) *n* an emblem or device, usually a motto, as on a coat of arms. [C16: from Italian, literally: undertaking, hence deed of chivalry, motto, from *imprendere* to undertake; see EMPRISE]

impresario (,ɪmprə'sɑːrɪ,əʊ) *n, pl* **-sarios. 1** a producer or sponsor of public entertainments, esp. musical or theatrical ones. **2** the director or manager of an opera, ballet, or other performing company. [C18: from Italian, literally: one who undertakes; see IMPRESA]

imprescriptible (,ɪmprɪ'skrɪptəb**ə**l) *adj Law.* immune or exempt from prescription. ▸ **,impre,scripti'bility** *n* ▸ **,impre'scriptibly** *adv*

impress[1] *vb* (ɪm'prɛs). (*tr*) **1** to make an impression on; have a strong, lasting, or favourable effect on: *I am impressed by your work.* **2** to produce (an imprint, etc.) by pressure in or on (something): *to impress a seal in wax; to impress wax with a seal.* **3** (often foll. by *on*) to stress (something to a person); urge; emphasize: *to impress the danger of a situation on someone.* **4** to exert pressure on; press. **5** *Electronics.* to apply (a voltage) to a circuit or device. ◆ *n* ('ɪmprɛs). **6** the act or an instance of impressing. **7** a mark, imprint, or effect produced by impressing. [C14: from Latin *imprimere* to press into, imprint, from *premere* to PRESS[1]] ▸ **im'presser** *n* ▸ **im'pressible** *adj*

impress[2] *vb* (ɪm'prɛs). **1** to commandeer or coerce (men or things) into government service; press-gang. ◆ *n* ('ɪmprɛs). **2** the act of commandeering or coercing into government service; impressment. [C16: see *im-* IN-[2], PRESS[2]]

impression (ɪm'prɛʃən) *n* **1** an effect produced in the mind by a stimulus; sensation: *he gave the impression of wanting to help.* **2** an imprint or mark produced by pressing: *he left the impression of his finger in the mud.* **3** a vague idea, consciousness, or belief: *I had the impression we had met before.* **4** a strong, favourable, or remarkable effect: *he made an impression on the managers.* **5** the act of impressing or the state of being impressed. **6** *Printing.* **6a** the act, process, or result of printing from type, plates, etc. **6b** one of a number of printings of a publication printed from the same setting of type with no or few alterations. Compare **edition** (sense 2). **6c** the total number of copies of a publication printed at one time. **7** *Dentistry.* an imprint of the teeth and gums, esp. in wax or plaster, for use in preparing crowns, inlays, or dentures. **8** an imitation or impersonation: *he did a funny impression of the politician.* ▸ **im'pressional** *adj* ▸ **im'pressionally** *adv*

impressionable (ɪm'prɛʃənəb**ə**l, -'prɛʃnə-) *adj* easily influenced or characterized by susceptibility to influence: *an impressionable child; an impressionable age.* ▸ **im,pressiona'bility** *or* **im'pressionableness** *n*

impressionism (ɪm'prɛʃə,nɪzəm) *n* **1** (*often cap.*) a movement in French painting, developed in the 1870s chiefly by Monet, Renoir, Pissarro, and Sisley, having the aim of objectively recording experience by a system of fleeting impressions, esp. of natural light effects. **2** the technique in art, literature, or music of conveying experience by capturing fleeting impressions of reality or of mood.

impressionist (ɪm'prɛʃənɪst) *n* **1** (*usually cap.*) any of the French painters of the late 19th century who were exponents of impressionism. **2** (*sometimes cap.*) any artist, composer, or writer who uses impressionism. **3** an entertainer who impersonates famous people. ◆ *adj* **4** (*often cap.*) denoting, of, or relating to impressionism or the exponents of this style. ▸ **im,pression'istic** *adj*

impressive (ɪm'prɛsɪv) *adj* capable of impressing, esp. by size, magnificence, etc.; awe-inspiring; commanding. ▸ **im'pressively** *adv* ▸ **im'pressiveness** *n*

impressment (ɪm'prɛsmənt) *n* the commandeering or conscription of things or men into government service.

impressure (ɪm'prɛʃə) *n* an archaic word for **impression.** [C17: see IMPRESS[1], -URE; formed on the model of PRESSURE]

imprest (ɪm'prɛst) *n* **1** a fund of cash from which a department or other unit pays incidental expenses, topped up periodically from central funds. **2** *Chiefly Brit.* an advance from government funds for the performance of some public business or service. **3** *Brit.* (formerly) an advance payment of wages to a sailor or soldier. [C16: probably from Italian *imprestare* to lend, from Latin *in-* towards + *praestāre* to pay, from *praestō* at hand; see PRESTO]

imprimatur (,ɪmprɪ'meɪtə, -'mɑː-) *n* **1** *R.C. Church.* a licence granted by a bishop certifying the Church's approval of a book to be published. **2** sanction, authority, or approval, esp. for something to be printed. [C17: New Latin, literally: let it be printed]

imprimis (ɪm'praɪmɪs) *adv Archaic.* in the first place. [C15: from Latin phrase *in prīmīs,* literally: among the first things]

imprint *n* ('ɪmprɪnt). **1** a mark or impression produced by pressure, printing, or stamping. **2** a characteristic mark or indication; stamp: *the imprint of great sadness on his face.* **3** the publisher's name and address, usually with the date of publication, in a book, pamphlet, etc. **4** the printer's name and address on any printed matter. ◆ *vb* (ɪm'prɪnt). **5** to produce (a mark, impression, etc.) on (a surface) by pressure, printing, or stamping: *to imprint a seal on wax; to imprint wax with a seal.* **6** to establish firmly; impress; stamp: *to imprint the details on one's mind.* **7** (of young animals) to undergo the process of imprinting. ▸ **im'printer** *n*

imprinting (ɪm'prɪntɪŋ) *n* the development through exceptionally fast learning in young animals of recognition of and attraction to members of their own species or to surrogates.

imprison (ɪmˈprɪzən) *vb* (*tr*) to confine in or as if in prison. ▸ **imˈprisoner** *n* ▸ **imˈprisonment** *n*

improbable (ɪmˈprɒbəbᵊl) *adj* not likely or probable; doubtful; unlikely. ▸ **imˌprobaˈbility** *or* **imˈprobableness** *n* ▸ **imˈprobably** *adv*

improbity (ɪmˈprəʊbɪtɪ) *n, pl* **-ties.** dishonesty, wickedness, or unscrupulousness.

impromptu (ɪmˈprɒmptjuː) *adj* **1** unrehearsed; spontaneous; extempore. **2** produced or done without care or planning; improvised. ◆ *adv* **3** in a spontaneous or improvised way: *he spoke impromptu.* ◆ *n* **4** something that is impromptu. **5** a short piece of instrumental music, sometimes improvisatory in character. [C17: from French, from Latin *in promptū* in readiness, from *promptus* (adj) ready, PROMPT]

improper (ɪmˈprɒpə) *adj* **1** lacking propriety; not seemly or fitting. **2** unsuitable for a certain use or occasion; inappropriate: *an improper use for a tool.* **3** irregular or abnormal. ▸ **imˈproperly** *adv* ▸ **imˈproperness** *n*

improper fraction *n* a fraction in which the numerator has a greater absolute value or degree than the denominator, as 7/6 or $(x^2 + 3)/(x + 1)$.

improper integral *n* a definite integral having one or both limits infinite or having an integrand that becomes infinite within the limits of integration.

impropriate *vb* (ɪmˈprəʊprɪˌeɪt). **1** (*tr*) to transfer (property, rights, etc.) from the Church into lay hands. ◆ *adj* (ɪmˈprəʊprɪɪt, -ˌeɪt). **2** transferred in this way. [C16: from Medieval Latin *impropriāre* to make one's own, from Latin *im-* IN-[2] + *propriāre* to APPROPRIATE] ▸ **imˌpropriˈation** *n* ▸ **imˈpropriˌator** *n*

impropriety (ˌɪmprəˈpraɪɪtɪ) *n, pl* **-ties. 1** lack of propriety; indecency; indecorum. **2** an improper act or use. **3** the state of being improper.

improv (ˈɪmprɒv) *n* improvisational comedy.

improve (ɪmˈpruːv) *vb* **1** to make or become better in quality; ameliorate. **2** (*tr*) to make (buildings, land, etc.) more valuable by additions or betterment. **3** (*intr;* usually foll. by *on* or *upon*) to achieve a better standard or quality in comparison (with): *to improve on last year's crop.* ◆ *n* **4 on the improve.** *Austral. informal.* improving. [C16: from Anglo-French *emprouer* to turn to profit, from *en prou* into profit, from *prou* profit, from Late Latin *prōde* beneficial, from Latin *prōdesse* to be advantageous, from PRO-[1] + *esse* to be] ▸ **imˈprovable** *adj* ▸ **imˌprovaˈbility** *or* **imˈprovableness** *n* ▸ **imˈprovably** *adv* ▸ **imˈprover** *n* ▸ **imˈprovingly** *adv*

improvement (ɪmˈpruːvmənt) *n* **1** the act of improving or the state of being improved. **2** something that improves, esp. an addition or alteration. **3** alteration of the structure, fixtures, fittings, or decor of a building without changing its function. Compare **conversion** (sense 9). **4** (*usually pl*) *Austral. and N.Z.* a building or other works on a piece of land, adding to its value.

improvident (ɪmˈprɒvɪdənt) *adj* **1** not provident; thriftless, imprudent, or prodigal. **2** heedless or incautious; rash. ▸ **imˈprovidence** *n* ▸ **imˈprovidently** *adv*

improvisation (ˌɪmprəvaɪˈzeɪʃən) *n* **1** the act or an instance of improvising. **2** a product of improvising; something improvised. ▸ **ˌimproviˈsational** *or* **improvisatory** (ˌɪmprəˈvaɪzətərɪ, -ˈvɪz-, ˌɪmprəvaɪˈzeɪtərɪ, -trɪ) *adj*

improvise (ˈɪmprəˌvaɪz) *vb* **1** to perform or make quickly from materials and sources available, without previous planning. **2** to perform (a poem, play, piece of music, etc.), composing as one goes along. [C19: from French, from Italian *improvvisare*, from Latin *imprōvīsus* unforeseen, from IM- (not) + *prōvīsus*, from *prōvidēre* to foresee; see PROVIDE] ▸ **ˈimproˌviser** *n*

imprudent (ɪmˈpruːdᵊnt) *adj* not prudent; rash, heedless, or indiscreet. ▸ **imˈprudence** *n* ▸ **imˈprudently** *adv*

impudence (ˈɪmpjʊdəns) *or* **impudency** *n* **1** the quality of being impudent. **2** an impudent act or statement. [C14: from Latin *impudēns* shameless, from IM- (not) + *pudēns* modest; see PUDENCY]

impudent (ˈɪmpjʊdənt) *adj* **1** mischievous, impertinent, or disrespectful. **2** an obsolete word for **immodest.** ▸ **ˈimpudently** *adv* ▸ **ˈimpudentness** *n*

impudicity (ˌɪmpjʊˈdɪsɪtɪ) *n Rare.* immodesty. [C16: from Old French *impudicite*, from Latin *impudīcus* shameless, from IN-[1] + *pudīcus* modest, virtuous]

impugn (ɪmˈpjuːn) *vb* (*tr*) to challenge or attack as false; assail; criticize. [C14: from Old French *impugner*, from Latin *impugnāre* to fight against, attack, from IM- + *pugnāre* to fight] ▸ **imˈpugnable** *adj* ▸ **impugnation** (ˌɪmpʌgˈneɪʃən) *or* **imˈpugnment** *n* ▸ **imˈpugner** *n*

impuissant (ɪmˈpjuːɪsᵊnt, ɪmˈpwiː-) *adj* powerless, ineffectual, feeble, or impotent. [C17: from French: powerless] ▸ **imˈpuissance** *n*

impulse (ˈɪmpʌls) *n* **1** an impelling force or motion; thrust; impetus. **2** a sudden desire, whim, or inclination: *I bought it on an impulse.* **3** an instinctive drive; urge. **4** tendency; current; trend. **5** *Physics.* **5a** the product of the average magnitude of a force acting on a body and the time for which it acts. **5b** the change in the momentum of a body as a result of a force acting upon it. **6** *Physiol.* See **nerve impulse. 7** *Electronics.* a less common word for **pulse**[1] (sense 2). **8 on impulse.** spontaneously or impulsively. [C17: from Latin *impulsus* a pushing against, incitement, from *impellere* to strike against; see IMPEL]

impulse buying *n* the buying of retail merchandise prompted by a whim on seeing the product displayed. ▸ **impulse buyer** *n*

impulse turbine *n* a turbine in which the expansion of the fluid is completed in a static nozzle, the torque being produced by the change in momentum of the fluid impinging on curved rotor blades. Compare **reaction turbine.**

impulsion (ɪmˈpʌlʃən) *n* **1** the act of impelling or the state of being impelled. **2** motion produced by an impulse; propulsion. **3** a driving force; compulsion.

impulsive (ɪmˈpʌlsɪv) *adj* **1** characterized by actions based on sudden desires, whims, or inclinations rather than careful thought: *an impulsive man.* **2** based on emotional impulses or whims; spontaneous: *an impulsive kiss.* **3** forceful, inciting, or impelling. **4** (of physical forces) acting for a short time; not continuous. **5** (of a sound) brief, loud, and having a wide frequency range. ▸ **imˈpulsively** *adv* ▸ **imˈpulsiveness** *n*

impundulu (ɪmˈpunˌdulu) *n S. African.* a mythical bird associated with witchcraft, frequently manifested as the secretary bird. [from Nguni *mpundulu*]

impunity (ɪmˈpjuːnɪtɪ) *n, pl* **-ties. 1** exemption or immunity from punishment or recrimination. **2** exemption or immunity from unpleasant consequences: *a successful career marked by impunity from early mistakes.* **3 with impunity. 3a** with no unpleasant consequences. **3b** with no care or heed for such consequences. [C16: from Latin *impūnitās* freedom from punishment, from *impūnis* unpunished, from IM- (not) + *poena* punishment]

impure (ɪmˈpjʊə) *adj* **1** not pure; combined with something else; tainted or sullied. **2** (in certain religions) **2a** (of persons) ritually unclean and as such debarred from certain religious ceremonies. **2b** (of foodstuffs, vessels, etc.) debarred from certain religious uses. **3** (of a colour) mixed with another colour or with black or white. **4** of more than one origin or style, as of architecture or other design. ▸ **imˈpurely** *adv* ▸ **imˈpureness** *n*

impurity (ɪmˈpjʊərɪtɪ) *n, pl* **-ties. 1** the quality of being impure. **2** an impure thing, constituent, or element: *impurities in the water.* **3** *Electronics.* a small quantity of an element added to a pure semiconductor crystal to control its electrical conductivity. See also **acceptor** (sense 2), **donor** (sense 5).

imputable (ɪmˈpjuːtəbᵊl) *adj* capable of being imputed; attributable; ascribable. ▸ **imˌputaˈbility** *or* **imˈputableness** *n* ▸ **imˈputably** *adv*

imputation system *n* a taxation system in which some, or all, of the corporation tax on a company is treated as a tax credit on account of the income tax paid by its shareholders on their dividends. See also **advance corporation tax.**

impute (ɪmˈpjuːt) *vb* (*tr*) **1** to attribute or ascribe (something dishonest or dishonourable, esp. a criminal offence) to a person. **2** to attribute to a source or cause: *I impute your success to nepotism.* **3** *Commerce.* to give (a notional value) to goods or services when the real value is unknown. [C14: from Latin *imputāre*, from IM- + *putāre* to think, calculate] ▸ **ˌimpuˈtation** *n* ▸ **imˈputative** *adj* ▸ **imˈputer** *n*

impv. *abbrev. for* imperative.

Imran Khan (ˈɪmrɑːn ˈkɑːn) *n* full name *Imran Ahmad Khan Niazi.* born 1952, Pakistani cricketer: played for Worcestershire (1971–76) and Sussex (1977–88); captained Pakistan (1982–84; 1985–87; 1988–92). He stood unsuccessfully in Pakistan's 1997 elections.

Imroz (ˈimrɔz) *n* the Turkish name for **Imbros.**

IMS *abbrev. for* Indian Medical Service.

IMunE *abbrev. for* Institution of Municipal Engineers.

in (ɪn) *prep* **1** inside; within: *no smoking in the auditorium.* **2** at a place where there is: *lying in the shade; walking in the rain.* **3** indicating a state, situation, or condition: *in a deep sleep; standing in silence.* **4** before or when (a period of time) has elapsed: *come back in one year.* **5** using (a language, etc.) as a means of communication: *written in code.* **6** concerned or involved with, esp. as an occupation: *in journalism.* **7** while or by performing the action of; as a consequence of or by means of: *in crossing the street he was run over.* **8** used to indicate goal or purpose: *in honour of the president.* **9** (used of certain animals) about to give birth to; pregnant with (specified offspring): *in foal; in calf.* **10** a variant of **into:** *she fell in the water; he tore the paper in two.* **11 have it in one.** (often foll. by an infinitive) to have the ability (to do something). **12 in it.** *Austral. informal.* joining in; taking part. **13 in that** *or* **in so far as.** (*conj*) because or to the extent that; inasmuch as: *I regret my remark in that it upset you.* **14 nothing, very little, quite a bit,** *etc.,* **in it.** no, a great, etc., difference or interval between two things. ◆ *adv* (*particle*) **15** in or into a particular place; inward or indoors: *come in; bring him in.* **16** so as to achieve office, power, or authority: *the Conservatives got in at the last election.* **17** so as to enclose: *block in; cover in a hole.* **18** (in certain games) so as to take one's turn or one's team's turn at a certain aspect of the play; taking one's innings: *you have to get the other side out before you go in.* **19** *Brit.* (of a fire) alight: *do you keep the fire in all night?* **20** (*in combination*) indicating an activity or gathering, esp. one organized to protest against something: *teach-in; work-in.* **21 in at.** present at (the beginning, end, etc.). **22 in between.** between. **23 in for.** about to be affected by (something, esp. something unpleasant): *you're in for a shock.* **24 in on.** acquainted with or sharing in: *I was in on all his plans.* **25 in with.** associated with; friendly with; regarded highly by. **26 have (got) it in for.** *Informal.* to wish or intend harm towards. ◆ *adj* **27** (*stressed*) fashionable; modish: *the in thing to do.* **28** *N.Z.* competing: *you've got to be in to win.* ◆ *n* **29 ins and outs.** intricacies or complications; details: *the ins and outs of a computer system.* [Old English; compare Old High German *in,* Welsh *yn,* Old Norse *ī,* Latin *in,* Greek *en*]

In *the chemical symbol for* indium.

IN *abbrev. for* Indiana.

in. *abbrev. for* inch(es).

in-[1], **il-, im-,** *or* **ir-** *prefix* not; non-: *incredible; insincere; illegal; imperfect; irregular.* Compare **un-**[1]. [from Latin *in-;* related to *ne-, nōn* not]

in-[2], **il-, im-,** *or* **ir-** *prefix* **1** in; into; towards; within; on: *infiltrate; immigrate.* **2** having an intensive or causative function: *inflame; imperil.* [from IN (prep, adv)]

-in *suffix forming nouns.* **1** indicating a neutral organic compound, including proteins, glucosides, and glycerides: *insulin; digitoxin; tripalmitin.* **2** indicating an enzyme in certain nonsystematic names: *pepsin.* **3** indicating a pharmaceutical substance: *penicillin; riboflavin; aspirin.* **4** indicating a chemical substance in certain nonsystematic names: *coumarin.* [from New Latin *-ina;* compare -INE[2]]

inability (ˌɪnəˈbɪlɪtɪ) *n* lack of ability or means; incapacity.

in absentia *Latin.* (ɪn æbˈsɛntɪə) *adv* in the absence of (someone indicated): *he was condemned in absentia.*

inaccessible (ˌɪnækˈsɛsəbᵊl) *adj* not accessible; unapproachable. ▸ **ˌinacˌcesˈsiˈbility** *or* **ˌinacˈcessibleness** *n* ▸ **ˌinacˈcessibly** *adv*

inaccuracy (ɪn'ækjʊrəsɪ) *n, pl* **-cies.** 1 lack of accuracy; imprecision. 2 an error, a mistake, or a slip.
inaccurate (ɪn'ækjʊrɪt) *adj* not accurate; imprecise, inexact, or erroneous. ▶ **in'accurately** *adv* ▶ **in'accurateness** *n*
inaction (ɪn'ækʃən) *n* lack of action; idleness; inertia.
inactivate (ɪn'æktɪ,veɪt) *vb (tr)* to render inactive. ▶ **in,acti'vation** *n*
inactive (ɪn'æktɪv) *adj* 1 idle or inert; not active. 2 sluggish, passive, or indolent. 3 *Military.* of or relating to persons or equipment not in active service. 4 *Chem.* (of a substance) having little or no reactivity. 5 (of an element, isotope, etc.) having little or no radioactivity. ▶ **in'actively** *adv* ▶ **,inac'tivity** *or* **in'activeness** *n*
inadequate (ɪn'ædɪkwɪt) *adj* 1 not adequate; insufficient. 2 not capable or competent; lacking. ▶ **in'adequacy** *n* ▶ **in'adequately** *adv*
inadmissible (,ɪnəd'mɪsəbᵊl) *adj* not admissible or allowable. ▶ **,inad,missi'bility** *n* ▶ **,inad'missibly** *adv*
inadvertence (,ɪnəd'vɜːtᵊns) *or* **inadvertency** *n* 1 lack of attention; heedlessness. 2 an instance or an effect of being inadvertent; oversight; slip.
inadvertent (,ɪnəd'vɜːtᵊnt) *adj* 1 failing to act carefully or considerately; inattentive. 2 resulting from heedless action; unintentional. ▶ **,inad'vertently** *adv*
inadvisable (,ɪnəd'vaɪzəbᵊl) *adj* 1 not advisable; not recommended. 2 unwise; imprudent. ▶ **,inad,visa'bility** *or* **,inad'visableness** *n* ▶ **,inad'visably** *adv*
-inae *suffix forming plural proper nouns.* occurring in names of zoological subfamilies: *Felinae.* [New Latin, from Latin, feminine plural of *-īnus* -INE[1]]
in aeternum *Latin.* (ɪn iː'tɜːnəm) *n* forever; eternally.
inalienable (ɪn'eɪljənəbᵊl) *adj* not able to be transferred to another; not alienable: *the inalienable rights of the citizen.* ▶ **in,aliena'bility** *or* **in'alienableness** *n* ▶ **in'alienably** *adv*
inalterable (ɪn'ɔːltərəbᵊl) *adj* not alterable; unalterable. ▶ **in,altera'bility** *or* **in'alterableness** *n* ▶ **in'alterably** *adv*
inamorata (ɪn,æmə'rɑːtə, ,ɪnæmə-) *or (masc)* **inamorato** (ɪn,æmə'rɑːtəʊ, ,ɪnæmə-) *n, pl* **-tas** *or (masc)* **-tos.** a person with whom one is in love; lover. [C17: from Italian *innamorata, innamorato,* from *innamorare* to cause to fall in love, from *amore* love, from Latin *amor*]
in-and-in *adj* (of breeding) carried out repeatedly among closely related individuals of the same species to eliminate or intensify certain characteristics.
inane (ɪ'neɪn) *adj* senseless, unimaginative, or empty; unintelligent: *inane remarks.* [C17: from Latin *inānis* empty] ▶ **in'anely** *adv*
inanga ('iːnʌŋə) *n* another name for the New Zealand **whitebait** (sense 2). [Maori]
inanimate (ɪn'ænɪmɪt) *adj* 1 lacking the qualities or features of living beings; not animate: *inanimate objects.* 2 lacking any sign of life or consciousness; appearing dead. 3 lacking vitality; spiritless; dull. ▶ **in'animately** *adv* ▶ **in'animateness** *or* **inanimation** (ɪn,ænɪ'meɪʃən) *n*
inanition (,ɪnə'nɪʃən) *n* 1 exhaustion resulting from lack of food. 2 mental, social, or spiritual weakness or lassitude. [C14: from Late Latin *inānītio* emptiness, from Latin *inānis* empty; see INANE]
inanity (ɪ'nænɪtɪ) *n, pl* **-ties.** 1 lack of intelligence or imagination; senselessness; silliness. 2 a senseless action, remark, etc. 3 an archaic word for **emptiness.**
inappellable (,ɪnə'peləbᵊl) *adj* incapable of being appealed against, as a court decision; unchallengeable. [C19: from IN-[1] + Latin *appellāre* to APPEAL]
inappetence (ɪn'æpɪtəns) *or* **inappetency** *n Rare.* lack of appetite or desire. ▶ **in'appetent** *adj*
inapplicable (ɪn'æplɪkəbᵊl, ,ɪnə'plɪk-) *adj* not applicable or suitable; irrelevant. ▶ **in,applica'bility** *or* **in'applicableness** *n* ▶ **in'applicably** *adv*
inapposite (ɪn'æpəzɪt) *adj* not appropriate or pertinent; unsuitable. ▶ **in'appositely** *adv* ▶ **in'appositeness** *n*
inappreciable (,ɪnə'priːʃəbᵊl) *adj* 1 incapable of being appreciated. 2 imperceptible; negligible. ▶ **,inap'preciably** *adv*
inappreciative (,ɪnə'priːʃətɪv) *adj* lacking appreciation; unappreciative. ▶ **,inap'preciatively** *adv* ▶ **,inap,preci'ation** *or* **,inap'preciativeness** *n*
inapprehensive (,ɪnæprɪ'hensɪv) *adj* 1 not perceiving or feeling fear or anxiety; untroubled. 2 *Rare.* unable to understand; imperceptive. ▶ **,inappre'hensively** *adv* ▶ **,inappre'hensiveness** *n*
inapproachable (,ɪnə'prəʊtʃəbᵊl) *adj* not accessible; unapproachable; unfriendly. ▶ **,inap,proacha'bility** *adv* ▶ **,inap'proachably** *adv*
inappropriate (,ɪnə'prəʊprɪɪt) *adj* not fitting or appropriate; unsuitable or untimely. ▶ **,inap'propriately** *adv* ▶ **,inap'propriateness** *n*
inapt (ɪn'æpt) *adj* 1 not apt or fitting; inappropriate. 2 lacking skill; inept. ▶ **in'apti,tude** *or* **in'aptness** *n* ▶ **in'aptly** *adv*
inarch (ɪn'ɑːtʃ) *vb (tr)* to graft (a plant) by uniting stock and scion while both are still growing independently.
inarticulate (,ɪnɑː'tɪkjʊlɪt) *adj* 1 unable to express oneself fluently or clearly; incoherent. 2 (of speech, language, etc.) unclear or incomprehensible; unintelligible: *inarticulate grunts.* 3 unable to speak; dumb. 4 unable to be expressed; unvoiced: *inarticulate suffering.* 5 *Biology.* having no joints, segments, or articulation. ▶ **,inar'ticulately** *adv* ▶ **,inar'ticulateness** *or* **,inar'ticulacy** *n*
inartificial (,ɪnɑːtɪ'fɪʃəl) *adj Archaic.* 1 not artificial; real; natural. 2 inartistic. ▶ **,inarti'ficially** *adv*
inartistic (,ɪnɑː'tɪstɪk) *adj* lacking in artistic skill, appreciation, etc.; Philistine. ▶ **,inar'tistically** *adv*
inasmuch as (,ɪnəz'mʌtʃ) *conj (subordinating)* 1 in view of the fact that; seeing that; since. 2 to the extent or degree that; in so far as.
inattentive (,ɪnə'tentɪv) *adj* not paying attention; heedless; negligent. ▶ **,inat'tention** *or* **,inat'tentiveness** *n* ▶ **,inat'tentively** *adv*
inaudible (ɪn'ɔːdəbᵊl) *adj* not loud enough to be heard; not audible. ▶ **in,audi'bility** *or* **in'audibleness** *n* ▶ **in'audibly** *adv*
inaugural (ɪn'ɔːgjʊrəl) *adj* 1 characterizing or relating to an inauguration. ◆ *n* 2 a speech made at an inauguration, esp. by a president of the U.S.
inaugurate (ɪn'ɔːgjʊ,reɪt) *vb (tr)* 1 to commence officially or formally; initiate. 2 to place in office formally and ceremonially; induct. 3 to open ceremonially; dedicate formally: *to inaugurate a factory.* [C17: from Latin *inaugurāre,* literally: to take omens, practise augury, hence to install in office after taking auguries; see IN-[2], AUGUR] ▶ **in,augu'ration** *n* ▶ **in'augu,rator** *n* ▶ **inauguratory** (ɪn'ɔːgjʊrətərɪ, -trɪ) *adj*
Inauguration Day *n* the day on which the inauguration of a president of the U.S. takes place, Jan. 20.
inauspicious (,ɪnɔː'spɪʃəs) *adj* not auspicious; unlucky. ▶ **,inaus'piciously** *adv* ▶ **,inaus'piciousness** *n*
inbd *abbrev. for* inboard (on an aircraft, a boat, etc.).
inbeing ('ɪn,biːɪŋ) *n* 1 existence in something else; inherence. 2 basic and inward nature; essence.
in-between *adj* 1 intermediate: *he's at the in-between stage, neither a child nor an adult.* ◆ *n* 2 an intermediate person or thing.
inboard ('ɪn,bɔːd) *adj* 1 (esp. of a boat's motor or engine) situated within the hull. Compare **outboard** (sense 1). 2 situated between the wing tip of an aircraft and its fuselage: *an inboard engine.* ◆ *adv* 3 towards the centre line of or within a vessel, aircraft, etc.
in-bond shop *n Caribbean.* a duty-free shop.
inborn ('ɪn'bɔːn) *adj* existing from birth; congenital; innate.
inbound ('ɪn,baʊnd) *adj* coming in; inward bound: *an inbound ship.*
inbreathe (ɪn'briːð) *vb (tr) Rare.* to infuse or imbue.
inbred ('ɪn'bred) *adj* 1 produced as a result of inbreeding. 2 deeply ingrained; innate: *inbred good manners.*
inbreed ('ɪn'briːd) *vb* **-breeds, -breeding, -bred.** 1 to breed from unions between closely related individuals, esp. over several generations. 2 *(tr)* to develop within; engender. ▶ **'in'breeding** *n, adj*
in-built *adj* built-in, integral.
inby (ɪn'baɪ) *adv* 1 *Scot.* into the house or an inner room; inside; within. 2 *Scot. and northern English dialect.* towards or near the house. ◆ *adj* 3 *Scot. and northern English dialect.* located near or nearest to the house: *the inby field.* [C18: from IN (adv) + BY (adv)]
inc. *abbrev. for:* 1 included. 2 including. 3 inclusive. 4 income. 5 incomplete. 6 increase.
Inc. *or* **inc.** (esp. after the names of U.S. business organizations) *abbrev. for* incorporated. Brit. equivalent: **Ltd.**
Inca ('ɪŋkə) *n, pl* **-ca** *or* **-cas.** 1 a member of a South American Indian people whose great empire centred on Peru lasted from about 1100 A.D. to the Spanish conquest in the early 1530s and is famed for its complex culture. 2 the ruler or king of this empire or any member of his family. 3 the language of the Incas. See also **Quechua.** [C16: from Spanish, from Quechua *inka* king] ▶ **'Incan** *adj*
incalculable (ɪn'kælkjʊləbᵊl) *adj* beyond calculation; unable to be predicted or determined. ▶ **in,calcula'bility** *or* **in'calculableness** *n* ▶ **in'calculably** *adv*
incalescent (,ɪnkə'lesᵊnt) *adj Chem.* increasing in temperature. [C17: from Latin *incalescere,* from IN-[2] + *calescere* to grow warm, from *calēre* to be warm] ▶ **,inca'lescence** *n*
in camera (ɪn 'kæmərə) *adv, adj* 1 in a private or secret session; not in public. 2 *Law.* 2a in the privacy of a judge's chambers. 2b in a court not open to the public. [Latin: in the chamber]
incandesce (,ɪnkæn'des) *vb (intr)* to exhibit incandescence.
incandescence (,ɪnkæn'desəns) *or* **incandescency** *n* 1 the emission of light by a body as a consequence of raising its temperature. Compare **luminescence.** 2 the light produced by raising the temperature of a body.
incandescent (,ɪnkæn'desᵊnt) *adj* 1 emitting light as a result of being heated to a high temperature; red-hot or white-hot. 2 *Informal.* extremely angry; raging. [C18: from Latin *incandescere* to become hot, glow, from IN-[2] + *candescere* to grow bright, from *candēre* to be white; see CANDID] ▶ **,in-can'descently** *adv*
incandescent lamp *n* a source of light that contains a heated solid, such as an electrically heated filament.
incantation (,ɪnkæn'teɪʃən) *n* 1 ritual recitation of magic words or sounds. 2 the formulaic words or sounds used; a magic spell. [C14: from Late Latin *incantātiō* an enchanting, from *incantāre* to repeat magic formulas, from Latin, from IN-[2] + *cantāre* to sing; see ENCHANT] ▶ **,incan'tational** *or* **in'cantatory** *adj*
incapable (ɪn'keɪpəbᵊl) *adj* 1 (when *postpositive,* often foll. by *of*) not capable (of); lacking the ability (to). 2 powerless or helpless, as through injury or intoxication. 3 (*postpositive;* foll. by *of*) not susceptible (to); not admitting (of): *a problem incapable of solution.* ▶ **in,capa'bility** *or* **in'capableness** *n* ▶ **in'capably** *adv*
incapacitant (,ɪnkə'pæsɪtənt) *n* a substance that can temporarily incapacitate a person, used esp. as a weapon in biological warfare.
incapacitate (,ɪnkə'pæsɪ,teɪt) *vb (tr)* 1 to deprive of power, strength, or capacity; disable. 2 to deprive of legal capacity or eligibility. ▶ **,inca,paci'tation** *n*
incapacity (,ɪnkə'pæsɪtɪ) *n, pl* **-ties.** 1 lack of power, strength, or capacity; inability. 2 *Law.* 2a legal disqualification or ineligibility. 2b a circumstance causing this.
Incaparina (ɪn,kæpə'riːnə) *n* a cheap high-protein food made of cottonseed, sorghum flours, maize, yeast, etc., used, esp. in Latin America, to prevent protein-deficiency diseases. [C20: from *Institute of Nutrition in Central America and Panama* + (F)ARINA]
incapsulate (ɪn'kæpsjʊ,leɪt) *vb* a less common spelling of **encapsulate.** ▶ **in,capsu'lation** *n*

in-car *adj* installed or provided within a car: *an in-car hi-fi system.*

incarcerate (ɪnˈkɑːsəˌreɪt). *vb (tr)* to confine or imprison. [C16: from Medieval Latin *incarcerāre,* from Latin IN-[2] + *carcer* prison] ▸ **inˌcarcerˈation** *n* ▸ **inˈcarcerˌator** *n*

incardinate (ɪnˈkɑːdɪˌneɪt) *vb (tr) R.C. Church.* to transfer (a cleric) to the jurisdiction of a new bishop. [C17: from Late Latin *incardināre,* from IN-[2] + *cardinālis* CARDINAL]

incardination (ɪnˌkɑːdɪˈneɪʃən) *n* **1** the official acceptance by one diocese of a clergyman from another diocese. **2** the promotion of a clergyman to the status of a cardinal.

incarnadine (ɪnˈkɑːnəˌdaɪn) *Archaic or literary.* ◆ *vb* **1** *(tr)* to tinge or stain with red. ◆ *adj* **2** of a pinkish or reddish colour similar to that of flesh or blood. [C16: from French *incarnadin* flesh-coloured, from Italian, from Late Latin *incarnātus* made flesh, INCARNATE]

incarnate *adj* (ɪnˈkɑːnɪt, -neɪt). *(usually immediately postpositive)* **1** possessing bodily form, esp. the human form: *a devil incarnate.* **2** personified or typified: *stupidity incarnate.* **3** (esp. of plant parts) flesh-coloured or pink. ◆ *vb* (ɪnˈkɑːneɪt). *(tr)* **4** to give a bodily or concrete form to. **5** to be representative or typical of. [C14: from Late Latin *incarnāre* to make flesh, from Latin IN-[2] + *carō* flesh]

incarnation (ˌɪnkɑːˈneɪʃən) *n* **1** the act of manifesting or state of being manifested in bodily form, esp. human form. **2** a bodily form assumed by a god, etc. **3** a person or thing that typifies or represents some quality, idea, etc.: *the weasel is the incarnation of ferocity.*

Incarnation (ˌɪnkɑːˈneɪʃən) *n* **1** *Christian theol.* the assuming of a human body by the Son of God. **2** *Christianity.* the presence of God on Earth in the person of Jesus.

incarvillea (ˌɪnkɑːˈvɪlɪə) *n* any plant of the genus *Incarvillea,* native to China, of which some species are grown as garden or greenhouse plants for their large usually carmine-coloured trumpet-shaped flowers, esp. *I. delavayi:* family *Bignoniaceae.* [named after Pierre *d'Incarville* (1706–57), French missionary]

incase (ɪnˈkeɪs) *vb* a variant spelling of **encase.** ▸ **inˈcasement** *n*

incautious (ɪnˈkɔːʃəs) *adj* not careful or cautious. ▸ **inˈcautiously** *adv* ▸ **inˈcautiousness** *or* **inˈcaution** *n*

incendiarism (ɪnˈsɛndɪəˌrɪzəm) *n* **1** the act or practice of illegal burning; arson. **2** (esp. formerly) the creation of civil strife or violence for political reasons.

incendiary (ɪnˈsɛndɪərɪ) *adj* **1** of or relating to the illegal burning of property, goods, etc. **2** tending to create strife, violence, etc.; inflammatory. **3** (of a substance) capable of catching fire, causing fires, or burning readily. ◆ *n, pl* **-aries. 4** a person who illegally sets fire to property, goods, etc.; arsonist. **5** (esp. formerly) a person who stirs up civil strife, violence, etc., for political reasons; agitator. **6** Also called: **incendiary bomb.** a bomb that is designed to start fires. **7** an incendiary substance, such as phosphorus. [C17: from Latin *incendiārius* setting alight, from *incendium* fire, from *incendere* to kindle]

incense[1] (ˈɪnsɛns) *n* **1** any of various aromatic substances burnt for their fragrant odour, esp. in religious ceremonies. **2** the odour or smoke so produced. **3** any pleasant fragrant odour; aroma. **4** *Rare.* homage or adulation. ◆ *vb* **5** to burn incense in honour of (a deity). **6** *(tr)* to perfume or fumigate with incense. [C13: from Old French *encens,* from Church Latin *incensum,* from Latin *incendere* to kindle] ▸ **ˌincenˈsation** *n*

incense[2] (ɪnˈsɛns) *vb (tr)* to enrage greatly. [C15: from Latin *incensus* set on fire, from *incendere* to kindle] ▸ **inˈcensement** *n*

incensory (ˈɪnsɛnsərɪ) *n, pl* **-ries.** a less common name for a **censer.** [C17: from Medieval Latin *incensorium*]

incentive (ɪnˈsɛntɪv) *n* **1** a motivating influence; stimulus. **2a** an additional payment made to employees as a means of increasing production. **2b** *(as modifier): an incentive scheme.* ◆ *adj* **3** serving to incite to action. [C15: from Late Latin *incentīvus* (adj), from Latin: striking up, setting the tune, from *incinere* to sing, from IN-[2] + *canere* to sing] ▸ **inˈcentively** *adv*

incept (ɪnˈsɛpt) *vb (tr)* **1** (of organisms) to ingest (food). **2** *Brit.* (formerly) to take a master's or doctor's degree at a university. ◆ *n* **3** *Botany.* a rudimentary organ. [C19: from Latin *inceptus* begun, attempted, from *incipere* to begin, take in hand, from IN-[2] + *capere* to take] ▸ **inˈceptor** *n*

inception (ɪnˈsɛpʃən) *n* the beginning, as of a project or undertaking.

inceptive (ɪnˈsɛptɪv) *adj* **1** beginning; incipient; initial. **2** Also called: **inchoative.** *Grammar.* denoting an aspect of verbs in some languages used to indicate the beginning of an action. ◆ *n* **3** *Grammar.* **3a** the inceptive aspect of verbs. **3b** a verb in this aspect. ▸ **inˈceptively** *adv*

incertitude (ɪnˈsɜːtɪˌtjuːd) *n* **1** uncertainty; doubt. **2** a state of mental or emotional insecurity.

incessant (ɪnˈsɛsᵊnt) *adj* not ceasing; continual. [C16: from Late Latin *incessāns,* from Latin IN-[1] + *cessāre* to CEASE] ▸ **inˈcessancy** *or* **inˈcessantness** *n* ▸ **inˈcessantly** *adv*

incest (ˈɪnsɛst) *n* sexual intercourse between two persons commonly regarded as too closely related to marry. [C13: from Latin *incestus* incest (from adj: impure, defiled), from IN-[1] + *castus* CHASTE]

incestuous (ɪnˈsɛstjʊəs) *adj* **1** relating to or involving incest: *an incestuous union.* **2** guilty of incest. **3** *Obsolete.* resulting from incest: *an incestuous bastard.* **4** resembling incest in excessive or claustrophobic intimacy. ▸ **inˈcestuously** *adv* ▸ **inˈcestuousness** *n*

inch[1] (ɪntʃ) *n* **1** a unit of length equal to one twelfth of a foot or 0.0254 metre. **2** *Meteorol.* **2a** an amount of precipitation that would cover a surface with water one inch deep: *five inches of rain fell in January.* **2b** a unit of pressure equal to a mercury column one inch high in a barometer. **3** a very small distance, degree, or amount. **4 every inch.** in every way; completely: *he was every inch an aristocrat.* **5 inch by inch.** gradually; little by little. **6 within an inch of.** very close to. ◆ *vb* **7** to move or be moved very slowly or in very small steps: *the car inched forward.* **8** *(tr;* foll. by *out)* to defeat (someone) by a very small margin. [Old English *ynce,* from Latin *uncia* twelfth part; see OUNCE[1]]

inch[2] (ɪntʃ) *n Scot. and Irish.* a small island. [C15: from Gaelic *innis* island; compare Welsh *ynys*]

inchmeal (ˈɪntʃˌmiːl) *adv* gradually; inch by inch or little by little. [C16: from INCH[1] + *-mele,* from Old English *mælum* quantity taken at one time; compare PIECEMEAL]

inchoate *adj* (ɪnˈkəʊeɪt, -ˈkəʊɪt). **1** just beginning; incipient. **2** undeveloped; immature; rudimentary. **3** (of a legal document, promissory note, etc.) in an uncompleted state; not yet made specific or valid. ◆ *vb* (ɪnˈkəʊeɪt). *(tr)* **4** to begin. [C16: from Latin *incohāre* to make a beginning, literally: to hitch up, from IN-[2] + *cohum* yokestrap] ▸ **inˈchoately** *adv* ▸ **inˈchoateness** *n* ▸ **ˌinchoˈation** *n* ▸ **inchoative** (ɪnˈkəʊətɪv) *adj*

Inchon *or* **Incheon** (ˈɪnˈtʃɒn) *n* a port in W South Korea, on the Yellow Sea: the chief port for Seoul: site of a major strategic amphibious assault by UN troops, liberating Seoul (Sept. 15, 1950). Pop.: 2 307 618 (1995). Former name: **Chemulpo.**

inchworm (ˈɪntʃˌwɜːm) *n* another name for a **measuring worm.**

incidence (ˈɪnsɪdəns) *n* **1** degree, extent, or frequency of occurrence; amount: *a high incidence of death from pneumonia.* **2** the act or manner of impinging on or affecting by proximity or influence. **3** *Physics.* the arrival of a beam of light or particles at a surface. See also **angle of incidence. 4** *Geometry.* the partial coincidence of two configurations, such as a point that lies on a circle.

incident (ˈɪnsɪdənt) *n* **1** a distinct or definite occurrence; event. **2** a minor, subsidiary, or related event or action. **3** a relatively insignificant event that might have serious consequences, esp. in international politics. **4** a public disturbance: *the police had reports of an incident outside a pub.* ◆ *adj* **5** *(postpositive;* foll. by *to)* related (to) or dependent (on). **6** (when *postpositive,* often foll. by *to)* having a subsidiary or minor relationship (with). **7** (esp. of a beam of light or particles) arriving at or striking a surface: *incident electrons.* [C15: from Medieval Latin *incidens* an event, from Latin *incidere,* literally: to fall into, hence befall, happen, from IN-[2] + *cadere* to fall]

incidental (ˌɪnsɪˈdɛntᵊl) *adj* **1** happening in connection with or resulting from something more important; casual or fortuitous. **2** *(postpositive;* foll. by *to)* found in connection (with); related (to). **3** *(postpositive;* foll. by *upon)* caused (by). **4** occasional or minor: *incidental expenses.* ◆ *n* **5** *(often pl)* an incidental or minor expense, event, or action. ▸ **ˌinciˈdentalness** *n*

incidentally (ˌɪnsɪˈdɛntəlɪ) *adv* **1** as a subordinate or chance occurrence. **2** *(sentence modifier)* by the way.

incidental music *n* background music for a film, television programme, etc.

incinerate (ɪnˈsɪnəˌreɪt) *vb* to burn up completely; reduce to ashes. [C16: from Medieval Latin *incinerāre,* from Latin IN-[2] + *cinis* ashes] ▸ **inˌcinerˈation** *n*

incinerator (ɪnˈsɪnəˌreɪtə) *n* a furnace or apparatus for incinerating something, esp. refuse.

incipient (ɪnˈsɪpɪənt) *adj* just starting to be or happen; beginning. [C17: from Latin *incipiēns,* from *incipere* to begin, take in hand, from IN-[2] + *capere* to take] ▸ **inˈcipience** *or* **inˈcipiency** *n* ▸ **inˈcipiently** *adv*

incipit (ˈɪnkɪpɪt) *Latin.* here begins: used as an introductory word at the beginning of some medieval manuscripts.

incise (ɪnˈsaɪz) *vb (tr)* to produce (lines, a design, etc.) by cutting into the surface of (something) with a sharp tool. [C16: from Latin *incīdere* to cut into, from IN-[2] + *caedere* to cut]

incised (ɪnˈsaɪzd) *adj* **1** cut into or engraved: *an incised surface.* **2** made by cutting or engraving: *an incised design.* **3** (of a wound) cleanly cut, as with a surgical knife. **4** having margins that are sharply and deeply indented: *an incised leaf.*

incisiform (ɪnˈsaɪzɪˌfɔːm) *adj Zoology.* having the shape of an incisor tooth.

incision (ɪnˈsɪʒən) *n* **1** the act of incising. **2** a cut, gash, or notch. **3** a cut made with a knife during a surgical operation. **4** any indentation in an incised leaf. **5** *Rare.* incisiveness.

incisive (ɪnˈsaɪsɪv) *adj* **1** keen, penetrating, or acute. **2** biting or sarcastic; mordant: *an incisive remark.* **3** having a sharp cutting edge: *incisive teeth.* ▸ **inˈcisively** *adv* ▸ **inˈcisiveness** *n*

incisor (ɪnˈsaɪzə) *n* a chisel-edged tooth at the front of the mouth. In man there are four in each jaw.

incisure (ɪnˈsaɪʒə) *n Anatomy.* an incision or notch in an organ or part. ▸ **inˈcisural** *adj*

incite (ɪnˈsaɪt) *vb (tr)* to stir up or provoke to action. [C15: from Latin *incitāre,* from IN-[2] + *citāre* to excite] ▸ **ˌinciˈtation** *n* ▸ **inˈcitement** *n* ▸ **inˈciter** *n* ▸ **inˈcitingly** *adv*

incivility (ɪnsɪˈvɪlɪtɪ) *n, pl* **-ties. 1** lack of civility or courtesy; rudeness. **2** an impolite or uncivil act or remark.

incl. *abbrev. for:* **1** including. **2** inclusive.

inclement (ɪnˈklɛmənt) *adj* **1** (of weather) stormy, severe, or tempestuous. **2** harsh, severe, or merciless. ▸ **inˈclemency** *or* **inˈclementness** *n* ▸ **inˈclemently** *adv*

inclinable (ɪnˈklaɪnəbᵊl) *adj* **1** *(postpositive;* usually foll. by *to)* having an inclination or tendency (to); disposed (to). **2** capable of being inclined.

inclination (ˌɪnklɪˈneɪʃən) *n* **1** (often foll. by *for, to, towards,* or an infinitive) a particular disposition, esp. a liking or preference; tendency: *I've no inclination for such dull work.* **2** the degree of deviation from a particular plane, esp. a horizontal or vertical plane. **3** a sloping or slanting surface; incline. **4** the act of inclining or the state of being inclined. **5** the act of bowing or nodding the head. **6** *Maths.* **6a** the angle between a line on a graph and the positive limb of the *x*-axis. **6b** the smaller dihedral angle between one plane and another. **7** *Astronomy.* the angle between the plane of the orbit of a planet or comet and another plane, usually that of the ecliptic. 8 *Physics*. another name for **dip** (sense 27). ► ,**incli'national** *adj*

incline *vb* (ɪn'klaɪn). 1 to deviate or cause to deviate from a particular plane, esp. a vertical or horizontal plane; slope or slant. 2 (when *tr*, may take an infinitive) to be disposed or cause to be disposed (towards some attitude or to do something): *he inclines towards levity; that does not incline me to think that you are right*. 3 to bend or lower (part of the body, esp. the head), as in a bow or in order to listen. 4 **incline one's ear**. to listen favourably (to). ◆ *n* ('ɪnklaɪn, ɪn'klaɪn). 5 an inclined surface or slope; gradient. 6 short for **inclined railway**. [C13: from Latin *inclīnāre* to cause to lean, from *clīnāre* to bend; see LEAN[1]] ► **in'cliner** *n*

inclined (ɪn'klaɪnd) *adj* 1 (*postpositive*; often foll. by *to*) having a disposition; tending. 2 sloping or slanting.

inclined plane *n* a plane whose angle to the horizontal is less than a right angle.

inclined railway *n Chiefly U.S.* a cable railway used on particularly steep inclines unsuitable for normal adhesion locomotives.

inclinometer (,ɪnklɪ'nɒmɪtə) *n* 1 an aircraft instrument for indicating the angle that an aircraft makes with the horizontal. 2 another name for **dip circle**.

inclose (ɪn'kləʊz) *vb* a less common spelling of **enclose**. ► **in'closable** *adj* ► **in'closer** *n* ► **in'closure** *n*

include (ɪn'klu:d) *vb* (*tr*) 1 to have as contents or part of the contents; be made up of or contain. 2 to add as part of something else; put in as part of a set, group, or category. 3 to contain as a secondary or minor ingredient or element. [C15 (in the sense: to enclose): from Latin *inclūdere* to enclose, from IN-[2] + *claudere* to close] ► **in'cludable** *or* **in'cludible** *adj*

included (ɪn'klu:dɪd) *adj* (of the stamens or pistils of a flower) not protruding beyond the corolla. ► **in'cludedness** *n*

include out *vb* (*tr, adv*) *Informal*. to exclude: *you can include me out of that deal*.

inclusion (ɪn'klu:ʒən) *n* 1 the act of including or the state of being included. 2 something included. 3 *Geology*. a solid fragment, liquid globule, or pocket of gas enclosed in a mineral or rock. 4 *Maths*. 4a the relation between two sets that obtains when all the members of the first are members of the second. Symbol: $x \subseteq y$. 4b **strict** *or* **proper inclusion**. the relation that obtains between two sets when the first includes the second but not vice versa. Symbol: $x \subset y$. 5 *Engineering*. a foreign particle in a metal, such as a particle of metal oxide.

inclusion body *n Pathol*. any of the small particles found in cells infected with certain viruses.

inclusive (ɪn'klu:sɪv) *adj* 1 (*postpositive*; foll. by *of*) considered together (with): *capital inclusive of profit*. 2 (*postpositive*) including the limits specified: *Monday to Friday inclusive is five days*. 3 comprehensive. 4 *Logic*. (of a disjunction) true if at least one of its component propositions is true. Compare **exclusive** (sense 10). ► **in'clusively** *adv* ► **in'clusiveness** *n*

inclusive language *n* language that avoids the use of certain expressions or words that might be considered to exclude particular groups of people, esp. gender-specific words, such as "man", "mankind", and masculine pronouns, the use of which might be considered to exclude women.

inclusive or *n Logic*. the connective that gives the value *true* to a disjunction if either or both of the disjuncts are true. Also called: **inclusive disjunction**. Compare **exclusive or**.

incoercible (,ɪnkəʊ'ɜ:səbᵊl) *adj* 1 unable to be coerced or compelled. 2 (of a gas) not capable of being liquefied by pressure alone.

incog. *abbrev. for* incognito.

incogitable (ɪn'kɒdʒɪtəbᵊl) *adj Rare*. not to be contemplated; unthinkable. ► **in,cogita'bility** *n*

incogitant (ɪn'kɒdʒɪtənt) *adj Rare*. thoughtless. [C17: from Latin *incōgitāns*, from IN-[1] + *cōgitāre* to think]

incognito (,ɪnkɒg'ni:təʊ, ɪn'kɒgnɪtəʊ) *or* (*fem*) **incognita** *adv, adj* (*postpositive*) 1 under an assumed name or appearance; in disguise. ◆ *n, pl* **-tos** *or* (*fem*) **-tas**. 2 a person who is incognito. 3 the assumed name or disguise of such a person. [C17: from Italian, from Latin *incognitus* unknown, from IN-[1] + *cognitus* known]

incognizant (ɪn'kɒgnɪzənt) *adj* (*when postpositive*, often foll. by *of*) unaware (of). ► **in'cognizance** *n*

incoherent (,ɪnkəʊ'hɪərənt) *adj* 1 lacking in clarity or organization; disordered. 2 unable to express oneself clearly; inarticulate. 3 *Physics*. (of two or more waves) having the same frequency but not the same phase: *incoherent light*. ► ,**inco'herence**, ,**inco'herency**, *or* ,**inco'herentness** *n* ► ,**inco'herently** *adv*

incombustible (,ɪnkəm'bʌstəbᵊl) *adj* 1 not capable of being burnt; fireproof. ◆ *n* 2 an incombustible object or material. ► ,**incom,busti'bility** *or* ,**incom'bustibleness** *n* ► ,**incom'bustibly** *adv*

income ('ɪnkʌm, 'ɪnkəm) *n* 1 the amount of monetary or other returns, either earned or unearned, accruing over a given period of time. 2 receipts; revenue. 3 *Rare*. an inflow or influx. [C13 (in the sense: arrival, entrance): from Old English *incumen* a coming in]

income bond *n* a bond that pays interest at a rate in direct proportion to the issuer's earnings.

income group *n* a group in a given population having incomes within a certain range.

incomer ('ɪnkʌmə) *n* a person who comes to live in a place in which he was not born.

incomes policy *n* See **prices and incomes policy**.

income support *n* (in Britain, formerly) a social security payment for people on very low incomes.

income tax *n* a personal tax, usually progressive, levied on annual income subject to certain deductions.

incoming ('ɪn,kʌmɪŋ) *adj* 1 coming in; entering. 2 about to come into office; succeeding. 3 (of interest, dividends, etc.) being received; accruing. ◆ *n* 4 the act of coming in; entrance. 5 (*usually pl*) income or revenue.

incommensurable (,ɪnkə'mɛnʃərəbᵊl) *adj* 1 incapable of being judged, measured, or considered comparatively. 2 (*postpositive*; foll. by *with*) not in accordance; incommensurate. 3 *Maths*. 3a not having a common factor other than 1, such as 2 and $\sqrt{-5}$. 3b not having units of the same dimension. 3c unrelated to another measurement by integral multiples. ◆ *n* 4 something incommensurable. ► ,**incom,mensura'bility** *or* ,**incom'mensurableness** *n* ► ,**incom'mensurably** *adv*

incommensurate (,ɪnkə'mɛnʃərɪt) *adj* 1 (when *postpositive*, often foll. by *with*) not commensurate; disproportionate. 2 incommensurable. ► ,**incom'mensurately** *adv* ► ,**incom'mensurateness** *n*

incommode (,ɪnkə'məʊd) *vb* (*tr*) to bother, disturb, or inconvenience. [C16: from Latin *incommodāre* to be troublesome, from *incommodus* inconvenient, from IN-[1] + *commodus* convenient; see COMMODE]

incommodious (,ɪnkə'məʊdɪəs) *adj* 1 insufficiently spacious; cramped. 2 troublesome or inconvenient. ► ,**incom'modiously** *adv* ► ,**incom'modiousness** *n*

incommodity (,ɪnkə'mɒdɪtɪ) *n, pl* **-ties**. a less common word for **inconvenience**.

incommunicable (,ɪnkə'mju:nɪkəbᵊl) *adj* 1 incapable of being communicated. 2 an obsolete word for **incommunicative**. ► ,**incom,munica'bility** *or* ,**incom'municableness** *n* ► ,**incom'municably** *adv*

incommunicado (,ɪnkə,mju:nɪ'kɑ:dəʊ) *adv, adj* (*postpositive*) deprived of communication with other people, as while in solitary confinement. [C19: from Spanish *incomunicado*, from *incomunicar* to deprive of communication; see IN-[1], COMMUNICATE]

incommunicative (,ɪnkə'mju:nɪkətɪv) *adj* tending not to communicate with others; taciturn. ► ,**incom'municatively** *adv* ► ,**incom'municativeness** *n*

incommutable (,ɪnkə'mju:təbᵊl) *adj* incapable of being commuted; unalterable. ► ,**incom,muta'bility** *or* ,**incom'mutableness** *n* ► ,**incom'mutably** *adv*

incomparable (ɪn'kɒmpərəbᵊl, -prəbᵊl) *adj* 1 beyond or above comparison; matchless; unequalled. 2 lacking a basis for comparison; not having qualities or features that can be compared. ► **in,compara'bility** *or* **in'comparableness** *n* ► **in'comparably** *adv*

incompatible (,ɪnkəm'pætəbᵊl) *adj* 1 incapable of living or existing together in peace or harmony; conflicting or antagonistic. 2 opposed in nature or quality; inconsistent. 3 (of an office, position, etc.) only able to be held by one person at a time. 4 *Med*. (esp. of two drugs or two types of blood) incapable of being combined or used together; antagonistic. 5 *Logic*. (of two propositions) unable to be both true at the same time. 6 (of plants) 6a not capable of forming successful grafts. 6b incapable of self-fertilization. 7 *Maths*. another word for **inconsistent** (sense 4). ◆ *n* 8 (*often pl*) a person or thing that is incompatible with another. ► ,**incom,pati'bility** *or* ,**incom'patibleness** *n* ► ,**incom'patibly** *adv*

incompetent (ɪn'kɒmpɪtənt) *adj* 1 not possessing the necessary ability, skill, etc. to do or carry out a task; incapable. 2 marked by lack of ability, skill, etc. 3 *Law*. not legally qualified: *an incompetent witness*. 4 (of rock strata, folds, etc.) yielding readily to pressure so as to undergo structural deformation. ◆ *n* 5 an incompetent person. ► **in'competence** *or* **in'competency** *n* ► **in'competently** *adv*

incomplete (,ɪnkəm'pli:t) *adj* 1 not complete or finished. 2 not completely developed; imperfect. 3 *Logic*. 3a (of a formal theory) not so constructed that the addition of a non-theorem to the axioms renders it inconsistent. 3b (of an expression) not having a reference of its own but requiring completion by another expression. ► ,**incom'pletely** *adv* ► ,**incom'pleteness** *or* ,**incom'pletion** *n*

incompliant (,ɪnkəm'plaɪənt) *adj* not compliant; unyielding or inflexible. ► ,**incom'pliance** *or* ,**incom'pliancy** *n* ► ,**incom'pliantly** *adv*

incomprehensible (,ɪnkɒmprɪ'hɛnsəbᵊl, ɪn,kɒm-) *adj* 1 incapable of being understood; unintelligible. 2 *Archaic*. limitless; boundless. ► ,**incom-pre,hensi'bility** *or* ,**incompre'hensibleness** *n* ► ,**incompre'hensibly** *adv*

incomprehension (,ɪnkɒmprɪ'hɛnʃən, ɪn,kɒm-) *n* inability or failure to comprehend; lack of understanding.

incomprehensive (,ɪnkɒmprɪ'hɛnsɪv, ɪn,kɒm-) *adj* not comprehensive; limited in range or scope. ► ,**incompre'hensively** *adv* ► ,**incompre'hensiveness** *n*

incompressible (,ɪnkəm'prɛsəbᵊl) *adj* incapable of being compressed or condensed. ► ,**incom,pressi'bility** *or* ,**incom'pressibleness** *n* ► ,**incom'pressibly** *adv*

incomputable (,ɪnkəm'pju:təbᵊl) *adj* incapable of being computed; incalculable. ► ,**incom,puta'bility** *n* ► ,**incom'putably** *adv*

inconceivable (,ɪnkən'si:vəbᵊl) *adj* incapable of being conceived, imagined, or considered. ► ,**incon,ceiva'bility** *or* ,**incon'ceivableness** *n* ► ,**incon'ceivably** *adv*

inconclusive (,ɪnkən'klu:sɪv) *adj* not conclusive or decisive; not finally settled; indeterminate. ► ,**incon'clusively** *adv* ► ,**incon'clusiveness** *n*

incondensable *or* **incondensible** (,ɪnkən'dɛnsəbᵊl) *adj* incapable of being condensed. ► ,**incon,densa'bility** *or* ,**incon,densi'bility** *n*

incondite (ɪn'kɒndɪt, -daɪt) *adj Rare*. 1 poorly constructed or composed. 2 rough or crude. [C17: from Latin *inconditus*, from IN-[1] + *conditus*, from *condere* to put together] ► **in'conditely** *adv*

inconformity (,ɪnkən'fɔ:mɪtɪ) *n* lack of conformity; irregularity.

incongruity (,ɪnkɒŋ'gru:ɪtɪ) *n, pl* **-ties**. 1 something incongruous. 2 the state or quality of being incongruous.

incongruous (ɪn'kɒŋgrʊəs) *or* **incongruent** *adj* 1 (when *postpositive*, foll.

by *with* or *to*) incompatible with (what is suitable); inappropriate. **2** containing disparate or discordant elements or parts. ► **in'congruously** *or* **in'congruently** *adv* ► **in'congruousness** *or* **in'congruence** *n*

inconsecutive (ˌɪnkən'sɛkjʊtɪv) *adj* not consecutive; not in sequence. ► **ˌincon'secutively** *adv* ► **ˌincon'secutiveness** *n*

inconsequential (ˌɪnkɒnsɪ'kwɛnʃəl, ɪnˌkɒn-) *or* **inconsequent** (ɪn'kɒnsɪkwənt) *adj* **1** not following logically as a consequence. **2** trivial or insignificant. **3** not in a logical sequence; haphazard. ► **ˌinconseˌquenti'ality, ˌinconse'quentialness, in'consequence,** *or* **in'consequentness** *n* ► **ˌinconse'quentially** *or* **in'consequently** *adv*

inconsiderable (ˌɪnkən'sɪdərəbᵊl) *adj* **1** relatively small. **2** not worthy of consideration; insignificant. ► **ˌincon'siderableness** *n* ► **ˌincon'siderably** *adv*

inconsiderate (ˌɪnkən'sɪdərɪt) *adj* **1** lacking in care or thought for others; heedless; thoughtless. **2** *Rare.* insufficiently considered. ► **ˌincon'siderately** *adv* ► **ˌincon'siderateness** *or* **ˌinconˌsider'ation** *n*

inconsistency (ˌɪnkən'sɪstənsɪ) *n, pl* **-cies. 1** lack of consistency or agreement; incompatibility. **2** an inconsistent feature or quality. **3** *Logic.* **3a** the property of being inconsistent. **3b** a self-contradictory proposition.

inconsistent (ˌɪnkən'sɪstənt) *adj* **1** lacking in consistency, agreement, or compatibility; at variance. **2** containing contradictory elements. **3** irregular or fickle in behaviour or mood. **4** Also: **incompatible.** *Maths.* (of two or more equations) not having one common set of values of the variables: $x + 2y = 5$ and $x + 2y = 6$ are inconsistent. **5** *Logic.* (of a set of propositions) enabling an explicit contradiction to be validly derived. ► **ˌincon'sistently** *adv*

inconsolable (ˌɪnkən'səʊləbᵊl) *adj* incapable of being consoled or comforted; disconsolate. ► **ˌinconˌsola'bility** *or* **ˌincon'solableness** *n* ► **ˌincon'solably** *adv*

inconsonant (ɪn'kɒnsənənt) *adj* lacking in harmony or compatibility; discordant. ► **in'consonance** *n* ► **in'consonantly** *adv*

inconspicuous (ˌɪnkən'spɪkjʊəs) *adj* not easily noticed or seen; not prominent or striking. ► **ˌincon'spicuously** *adv* ► **ˌincon'spicuousness** *n*

inconstant (ɪn'kɒnstənt) *adj* **1** not constant; variable. **2** fickle. ► **in'constancy** *n* ► **in'constantly** *adv*

inconsumable (ˌɪnkən'sjuːməbᵊl) *adj* **1** incapable of being consumed or used up. **2** *Economics.* providing an economic service without being consumed, as currency. ► **ˌincon'sumably** *adv*

incontestable (ˌɪnkən'tɛstəbᵊl) *adj* incapable of being contested or disputed. ► **ˌinconˌtesta'bility** *or* **ˌincon'testableness** *n* ► **ˌincon'testably** *adv*

incontinent[1] (ɪn'kɒntɪnənt) *adj* **1** lacking in restraint or control, esp. sexually. **2** relating to or exhibiting involuntary urination or defecation. **3** (foll. by *of*) having little or no control (over). **4** unrestrained; uncontrolled. [C14: from Old French, from Latin *incontinens,* from IN-[1] + *continere* to hold, restrain] ► **in'continence** *or* **in'continency** *n* ► **in'continently** *adv*

incontinent[2] (ɪn'kɒntɪnənt) *or* **incontinently** *adv* obsolete words for **immediately.** [C15: from Late Latin *in continentī tempore,* literally: in continuous time, that is, with no interval]

incontrollable (ˌɪnkən'trəʊləbᵊl) *adj* a less common word for **uncontrollable.** ► **ˌincon'trollably** *adv*

incontrovertible (ˌɪnkɒntrə'vɜːtəbᵊl, ɪnˌkɒn-) *adj* incapable of being contradicted or disputed; undeniable. ► **ˌincontroˌverti'bility** *or* **ˌincontro'vertibleness** *n* ► **ˌincontro'vertibly** *adv*

inconvenience (ˌɪnkən'viːnjəns, -'viːnɪəns) *n* **1** the state or quality of being inconvenient. **2** something inconvenient; a hindrance, trouble, or difficulty. ◆ *vb* **3** (*tr*) to cause inconvenience to; trouble or harass.

inconvenient (ˌɪnkən'viːnjənt, -'viːnɪənt) *adj* not convenient; troublesome, awkward, or difficult. ► **ˌincon'veniently** *adv*

inconvertible (ˌɪnkən'vɜːtəbᵊl) *adj* **1** incapable of being converted or changed. **2** (of paper currency) **2a** not redeemable for gold or silver specie. **2b** not exchangeable for another currency. ► **ˌinconˌverti'bility** *or* **ˌincon'vertibleness** *n* ► **ˌincon'vertibly** *adv*

inconvincible (ˌɪnkən'vɪnsəbᵊl) *adj* refusing or not able to be convinced. ► **ˌinconˌvinci'bility** *or* **ˌincon'vincibleness** *n* ► **ˌincon'vincibly** *adv*

incoordinate (ˌɪnkəʊ'ɔːdɪnɪt) *adj* **1** not coordinate; unequal in rank, order, or importance. **2** uncoordinated.

incoordination (ˌɪnkəʊˌɔːdɪ'neɪʃən) *n* **1** lack of coordination or organization. **2** *Pathol.* a lack of muscular control when making a voluntary movement.

incorp. *or* **incor.** *abbrev. for* incorporated.

incorporable (ɪn'kɔːpərəbᵊl) *adj* capable of being incorporated or included.

incorporate[1] *vb* (ɪn'kɔːpəˌreɪt). **1** to include or be included as a part or member of a united whole. **2** to form or cause to form a united whole or mass; merge or blend. **3** to form (individuals, an unincorporated enterprise, etc.) into a corporation or other organization with a separate legal identity from that of its owners or members. ◆ *adj* (ɪn'kɔːpərɪt, -prɪt). **4** combined into a whole; incorporated. **5** formed into or constituted as a corporation. [C14 (in the sense: put into the body of something else): from Late Latin *incorporāre* to embody, from Latin IN-[2] + *corpus* body] ► **in'corporative** *adj* ► **inˌcorpo'ration** *n*

incorporate[2] (ɪn'kɔːpərɪt, -prɪt) *adj* an archaic word for **incorporeal.** [C16: from Late Latin *incorporātus,* from Latin IN-[1] + *corporātus* furnished with a body]

incorporated (ɪn'kɔːpəˌreɪtɪd) *adj* **1** united or combined into a whole. **2** organized as a legal corporation, esp. in commerce. Abbrev.: **Inc.** *or* **inc.** ► **in'corpoˌratedness** *n*

incorporating (ɪn'kɔːpəˌreɪtɪŋ) *adj Linguistics.* another word for **polysynthetic.**

incorporator (ɪn'kɔːpəˌreɪtə) *n* **1** a person who incorporates. **2** *U.S. commerce.* **2a** any of the signatories of a certificate of incorporation. **2b** any of the original members of a corporation.

incorporeal (ˌɪnkɔː'pɔːrɪəl) *adj* **1** without material form, body, or substance. **2** spiritual or metaphysical. **3** *Law.* having no material existence but existing by reason of its annexation of something material, such as an easement, touchline, copyright, etc.: *an incorporeal hereditament.* ► **ˌincor'poreally** *adv* ► **incorporeity** (ɪnˌkɔːpə'riːɪtɪ) *or* **ˌincorpore'ality** *n*

incorrect (ˌɪnkə'rɛkt) *adj* **1** false; wrong: *an incorrect calculation.* **2** not fitting or proper: *incorrect behaviour.* ► **ˌincor'rectly** *adv* ► **ˌincor'rectness** *n*

incorrigible (ɪn'kɒrɪdʒəbᵊl) *adj* **1** beyond correction, reform, or alteration. **2** firmly rooted; ineradicable. **3** *Philosophy.* (of a belief) having the property that whoever honestly believes it cannot be mistaken. Compare **defeasible** (sense 2). ◆ *n* **4** a person or animal that is incorrigible. ► **inˌcorrigi'bility** *or* **in'corrigibleness** *n* ► **in'corrigibly** *adv*

incorrupt (ˌɪnkə'rʌpt) *adj* **1** free from corruption; pure. **2** free from decay; fresh or untainted. **3** (of a manuscript, text, etc.) relatively free from error or alteration. ► **ˌincor'ruptly** *adv* ► **ˌincor'ruption** *or* **ˌincor'ruptness** *n*

incorruptible (ˌɪnkə'rʌptəbᵊl) *adj* **1** incapable of being corrupted; honest; just. **2** not subject to decay or decomposition. ► **ˌincorˌrupti'bility** *or* **ˌincor'ruptibleness** *n* ► **ˌincor'ruptibly** *adv*

Incoterms ('ɪnkəˌtɜːmz) *n* a glossary of terms used in international commerce and trade, published by the International Chamber of Commerce.

incr. *abbrev. for:* **1** increase. **2** increased. **3** increasing.

incrassate *adj* (ɪn'kræsɪt, -eɪt), *also* **incrassated. 1** *Biology.* thickened or swollen: *incrassate cell walls.* **2** *Obsolete.* fattened or swollen. ◆ *vb* (ɪn'kræseɪt). **3** *Obsolete.* to make or become thicker. [C17: from Late Latin *incrassāre,* from Latin *crassus* thick, dense] ► **ˌincras'sation** *n*

increase *vb* (ɪn'kriːs). **1** to make or become greater in size, degree, frequency, etc.; grow or expand. ◆ *n* ('ɪnkriːs). **2** the act of increasing; augmentation. **3** the amount by which something increases. **4 on the increase.** increasing, esp. becoming more frequent. [C14: from Old French *encreistre,* from Latin *incrēscere,* from IN-[2] + *crēscere* to grow] ► **in'creasable** *adj* ► **increasedly** (ɪn'kriːsɪdlɪ) *or* **in'creasingly** *adv* ► **in'creaser** *n*

increate (ˌɪnkrɪ'eɪt, 'ɪnkrɪˌeɪt) *adj Archaic, poetic.* (esp. of gods) never having been created. ► **ˌincre'ately** *adv*

incredible (ɪn'krɛdəbᵊl) *adj* **1** beyond belief or understanding; unbelievable. **2** *Informal.* marvellous; amazing. ► **inˌcredi'bility** *or* **in'credibleness** *n* ► **in'credibly** *adv*

incredulity (ˌɪnkrɪ'djuːlɪtɪ) *n* lack of belief; scepticism.

incredulous (ɪn'krɛdjʊləs) *adj* (often foll. by *of*) not prepared or willing to believe (something); unbelieving. ► **in'credulously** *adv* ► **in'credulousness** *n*

increment ('ɪnkrɪmənt) *n* **1** an increase or addition, esp. one of a series. **2** the act of increasing; augmentation. **3** *Maths.* a small positive or negative change in a variable or function. Symbol: Δ, as in Δx or Δf. [C15: from Latin *incrēmentum* growth, INCREASE] ► **incremental** (ˌɪnkrɪ'mɛntᵊl) *adj*

incremental plotter *n* a device that plots graphs on paper from computer-generated instructions. See also **microfilm plotter.**

incremental recorder *n Computing.* a device for recording data as it is generated, usually on paper tape or magnetic tape, and feeding it into a computer.

increscent (ɪn'krɛsᵊnt) *adj* (esp. of the moon) increasing in size; waxing. [C16: from Latin *incrēscēns*]

incretion (ɪn'kriːʃən) *n Physiol.* **1** direct secretion into the bloodstream, esp. of a hormone from an endocrine gland. **2** the substance so secreted. [C20: from IN-[2] + (SE)CRETION] ► **in'cretionary** *or* **incretory** ('ɪnkrɪtərɪ, -trɪ) *adj*

incriminate (ɪn'krɪmɪˌneɪt) *vb* (*tr*) **1** to imply or suggest the guilt or error of (someone). **2** to charge with a crime or fault. [C18: from Late Latin *incrīmināre* to accuse, from Latin *crīmen* accusation; see CRIME] ► **inˌcrimi'nation** *n* ► **in'crimiˌnator** *n* ► **in'criminatory** *adj*

incross ('ɪnkrɒs) *n* **1** a plant or animal produced by continued inbreeding. ◆ *vb* **2** to inbreed or produce by inbreeding.

incrust (ɪn'krʌst) *vb* a variant spelling of **encrust.** ► **in'crustant** *n, adj* ► **ˌincrus'tation** *n*

incubate ('ɪnkjʊˌbeɪt) *vb* **1** (of birds) to supply (eggs) with heat for their development, esp. by sitting on them. **2** to cause (eggs, embryos, bacteria, etc.) to develop, esp. in an incubator or culture medium. **3** (*intr*) (of eggs, embryos, bacteria, etc.) to develop in favourable conditions, esp. in an incubator. **4** (*intr*) (of disease germs) to remain inactive in an animal or human before causing disease. **5** to develop or cause to develop gradually; foment or be fomented. [C18: from Latin *incubāre* to lie upon, hatch, from IN-[2] + *cubāre* to lie down] ► **ˌincu'bation** *n* ► **ˌincu'bational** *adj* ► **'incuˌbative** *or* **'incuˌbatory** *adj*

incubation period *n Med.* the time between exposure to an infectious disease and the appearance of the first signs or symptoms. Sometimes shortened to **incubation.**

incubator ('ɪnkjʊˌbeɪtə) *n* **1** *Med.* an enclosed transparent boxlike apparatus for housing prematurely born babies under optimum conditions until they are strong enough to survive in the normal environment. **2** a container kept at a constant temperature in which birds' eggs can be artificially hatched or bacterial cultures grown. **3** a person, animal, or thing that incubates.

incubus ('ɪnkjʊbəs) *n, pl* **-bi** (-ˌbaɪ) *or* **-buses. 1** a demon believed in folklore to lie upon sleeping persons, esp. to have sexual intercourse with sleeping women. Compare **succubus. 2** something that oppresses, worries, or disturbs greatly, esp. a nightmare or obsession. [C14: from Late Latin, from *incubāre* to lie upon; see INCUBATE]

incudes (ɪn'kjuːdiːz) *n* the plural of **incus.**

inculcate ('ɪnkʌlˌkeɪt, ɪn'kʌlkeɪt) *vb* (*tr*) to instil by forceful or insistent repetition. [C16: from Latin *inculcāre* to tread upon, ram down, from IN-[2] + *calcāre* to trample, from *calx* heel] ► **ˌincul'cation** *n* ► **'inculˌcator** *n*

inculpable (ɪn'kʌlpəbᵊl) *adj* incapable of being blamed or accused; guiltless. ► **inˌculpa'bility** *or* **in'culpableness** *n* ► **in'culpably** *adv*

inculpate ('ɪnkʌl,peɪt, ɪn'kʌlpeɪt) *vb (tr)* to incriminate; cause blame to be imputed to. [C18: from Late Latin *inculpāre,* from Latin *culpāre* to blame, from *culpa* fault, blame] ▸ **,incul'pation** *n* ▸ **inculpative** (ɪn'kʌlpətɪv) *or* **inculpatory** (ɪn'kʌlpətərɪ, -trɪ) *adj*

incult (ɪn'kʌlt) *adj Rare.* **1** (of land) uncultivated; untilled; naturally wild. **2** lacking refinement and culture. [C16: from Latin *incultus,* from IN-[1] + *colere* to till]

incumbency (ɪn'kʌmbənsɪ) *n, pl* **-cies. 1** the state or quality of being incumbent. **2** the office, duty, or tenure of an incumbent.

incumbent (ɪn'kʌmbənt) *adj* **1** *Formal.* (often *postpositive* and foll. by *on* or *upon* and an infinitive) morally binding or necessary; obligatory: *it is incumbent on me to attend.* **2** (usually *postpositive* and foll. by *on*) resting or lying (on). ◆ *n* **3** a person who holds an office, esp. a clergyman holding a benefice. [C16: from Latin *incumbere* to lie upon, devote one's attention to, from IN-[2] + *-cumbere,* related to Latin *cubāre* to lie down] ▸ **in'cumbently** *adv*

incumber (ɪn'kʌmbə) *vb* a less common spelling of **encumber.** ▸ **in'cumberingly** *adv* ▸ **in'cumbrance** *n*

incunabula (,ɪnkju'næbjʊlə) *pl n, sing* **-lum** (-ləm). **1** any book printed before 1500. **2** the infancy or earliest stages of something; beginnings. [C19: from Latin, originally: swaddling clothes, hence beginnings, from IN-[2] + *cūnābula* cradle] ▸ **,incu'nabular** *adj*

incur (ɪn'kɜː) *vb* **-curs, -curring, -curred.** *(tr)* **1** to make oneself subject to (something undesirable); bring upon oneself. **2** to run into or encounter. [C16: from Latin *incurrere* to run into, from *currere* to run] ▸ **in'currable** *adj*

incurable (ɪn'kjʊərəbᵊl) *adj* **1** (esp. of a disease) not curable; unresponsive to treatment. ◆ *n* **2** a person having an incurable disease. ▸ **in,cura'bility** *or* **in'curableness** *n* ▸ **in'curably** *adv*

incurious (ɪn'kjʊərɪəs) *adj* not curious; indifferent or uninterested. ▸ **incuriosity** (ɪn,kjʊərɪ'ɒsɪtɪ) *or* **in'curiousness** *n* ▸ **in'curiously** *adv*

incurrence (ɪn'kʌrəns) *n* the act or state of incurring.

incurrent (ɪn'kʌrənt) *adj* **1** (of anatomical ducts, tubes, channels, etc.) having an inward flow. **2** flowing or running in an inward direction. [C16: from Latin *incurrēns* running into; see INCUR]

incursion (ɪn'kɜːʃən) *n* **1** a sudden invasion, attack, or raid. **2** the act of running or leaking into; penetration. [C15: from Latin *incursiō* onset, attack, from *incurrere* to run into; see INCUR] ▸ **incursive** (ɪn'kɜːsɪv) *adj*

incurvate *vb* ('ɪnkɜː,veɪt), *also* **incurve** (ɪn'kɜːv). **1** to curve or cause to curve inwards. ◆ *adj* (ɪn'kɜːvɪt, -veɪt). **2** curved inwards. [C16: from Latin *incurvāre (vb)*] ▸ **,incur'vation** *n* ▸ **incurvature** (ɪn'kɜːvətʃə) *n*

incus ('ɪŋkəs) *n, pl* **incudes** (ɪn'kjuːdiːz). the central of the three small bones in the middle ear of mammals. Nontechnical name: **anvil.** Compare **malleus, stapes.** [C17: from Latin: anvil, from *incūdere* to forge] ▸ **incudate** ('ɪŋkjʊ,deɪt) *or* **incudal** ('ɪŋkjʊdᵊl) *adj*

incuse (ɪn'kjuːz) *n* **1** a design stamped or hammered onto a coin. ◆ *vb* **2** to impress (a design) in a coin or to impress (a coin) with a design by hammering or stamping. ◆ *adj* **3** stamped or hammered onto a coin. [C19: from Latin *incūsus* hammered; see INCUS]

Ind (ɪnd) *n* **1** a poetic name for **India. 2** an obsolete name for the **Indies.**

IND 1 Also: **IDN** *abbrev. for* in nomine Dei. [Latin: in the name of God] ◆ **2** *international car registration for* India.

ind. *abbrev. for:* **1** independence. **2** independent. **3** index. **4** indicative. **5** indirect. **6** industrial. **7** industry.

Ind. *abbrev. for:* **1** Independent. **2** India. **3** Indian. **4** Indiana. **5** Indies.

indaba (ɪn'dɑːbə) *n* **1** *Anthropol., history.* (among Bantu peoples of southern Africa) a meeting to discuss a serious topic. **2** *S. African informal.* a matter of concern or for discussion. [C19: from Zulu: topic]

indamine ('ɪndə,miːn, -mɪn) *n* **1** an organic base used in the production of the dye safranine. Formula: $NH_2C_6H_4N{:}C_6H_4{:}NH$ **2** any of a class of organic bases with a similar structure to this compound. Their salts are unstable blue and green dyes. [C20: from INDIGO + AMINE]

indebted (ɪn'dɛtɪd) *adj* (*postpositive*) **1** owing gratitude for help, favours, etc; obligated. **2** owing money.

indebtedness (ɪn'dɛtɪdnɪs) *n* **1** the state of being indebted. **2** the total of a person's debts.

indecency (ɪn'diːsənsɪ) *n, pl* **-cies. 1** the state or quality of being indecent. **2** an indecent act, etc.

indecent (ɪn'diːsᵊnt) *adj* **1** offensive to standards of decency, esp. in sexual matters. **2** unseemly or improper (esp. in the phrase **indecent haste**). ▸ **in'decently** *adv*

indecent assault *n* the act of taking indecent liberties with a person without his or her consent.

indecent exposure *n* the offence of indecently exposing parts of one's body in public, esp. the genitals.

indeciduous (,ɪndɪ'sɪdjʊəs) *adj* **1** (of leaves) not deciduous. **2** another word for **evergreen** (sense 1).

indecipherable (,ɪndɪ'saɪfərəbᵊl, -frəbᵊl) *adj* not decipherable; illegible. ▸ **,inde,ciphera'bility** *or* **,inde'cipherableness** *n* ▸ **,inde'cipherably** *adv*

indecisive (,ɪndɪ'saɪsɪv) *adj* **1** (of a person) vacillating; irresolute. **2** not decisive or conclusive. ▸ **,inde'cision** *or* **,inde'cisiveness** *n* ▸ **,inde'cisively** *adv*

indeclinable (,ɪndɪ'klaɪnəbᵊl) *adj* (of a noun or pronoun) having only one form; not declined for case or number. ▸ **,inde'clinableness** *n* ▸ **,inde'clinably** *adv*

indecorous (ɪn'dɛkərəs) *adj* improper or ungraceful; unseemly. ▸ **in'decorously** *adv* ▸ **in'decorousness** *n*

indecorum (,ɪndɪ'kɔːrəm) *n* indecorous behaviour or speech; unseemliness.

indeed (ɪn'diːd) *sentence connector.* **1** certainly; actually: *indeed, it may never happen.* ◆ *adv* **2** (intensifier): *that is indeed amazing.* **3** or rather; what is more: *a comfortable, indeed wealthy family.* ◆ *interj* **4** an expression of doubt, surprise, etc.

indef. *abbrev. for* indefinite.

indefatigable (,ɪndɪ'fætɪgəbᵊl) *adj* unable to be tired out; unflagging. [C16: from Latin *indēfatīgābilis,* from IN-[1] + *dēfatīgāre,* from *fatīgāre* to tire] ▸ **,inde,fatiga'bility** *or* **,inde'fatigableness** *n* ▸ **,inde'fatigably** *adv*

indefeasible (,ɪndɪ'fiːzəbᵊl) *adj Law.* not liable to be annulled or forfeited. ▸ **,inde,feasi'bility** *or* **,inde'feasibleness** *n* ▸ **,inde'feasibly** *adv*

indefectible (,ɪndɪ'fɛktɪbᵊl) *adj* **1** not subject to decay or failure. **2** flawless. ▸ **,inde,fecti'bility** *n* ▸ **,inde'fectibly** *adv*

indefensible (,ɪndɪ'fɛnsəbᵊl) *adj* **1** not justifiable or excusable. **2** capable of being disagreed with; untenable. **3** incapable of defence against attack. ▸ **,inde,fensi'bility** *or* **,inde'fensibleness** *n* ▸ **,inde'fensibly** *adv*

indefinable (,ɪndɪ'faɪnəbᵊl) *adj* incapable of being defined or analysed: *there was an indefinable sense of terror.* ▸ **,inde'finableness** *n* ▸ **,inde'finably** *adv*

indefinite (ɪn'dɛfɪnɪt) *adj* **1** not certain or determined; unsettled. **2** without exact limits; indeterminate: *an indefinite number.* **3** vague, evasive, or unclear. **4** Also: **indeterminate.** *Botany.* **4a** too numerous to count: *indefinite stamens.* **4b** capable of continued growth at the tip of the stem, which does not terminate in a flower: *an indefinite inflorescence.* ▸ **in'definitely** *adv* ▸ **in'definiteness** *n*

indefinite article *n Grammar.* a determiner that expresses nonspecificity of reference, such as *a, an,* or *some.* Compare **definite article.**

indefinite integral *n Maths.* **a** any function whose derivative is the given function, as x^2, $x^2 + 3$, $x^2 - 5$, etc. of $2x$. **b** the schema representing all such functions, here $x^2 + k$. **c** the symbolic representation of this as a function of the given function, written $\int f(x)dx$ where $f(x)$ is the given function. **d** the symbol $\int$.

indefinite pronoun *n Grammar.* a pronoun having no specific referent, such as *someone, anybody,* or *nothing.*

indehiscent (,ɪndɪ'hɪsᵊnt) *adj* (of fruits) not dehiscent; not opening to release seeds. ▸ **,inde'hiscence** *n*

indelible (ɪn'dɛlɪbᵊl) *adj* **1** incapable of being erased or obliterated. **2** making indelible marks: *indelible ink.* [C16: from Latin *indēlēbilis* indestructible, from IN-[1] + *delēre* to destroy] ▸ **in,deli'bility** *or* **in'delibleness** *n* ▸ **in'delibly** *adv*

indelicate (ɪn'dɛlɪkɪt) *adj* **1** coarse, crude, or rough. **2** offensive, embarrassing, or tasteless. ▸ **in'delicacy** *or* **in'delicateness** *n* ▸ **in'delicately** *adv*

indemnify (ɪn'dɛmnɪ,faɪ) *vb* **-fies, -fying, -fied.** *(tr)* **1** to secure against future loss, damage, or liability; give security for; insure. **2** to compensate for loss, injury, expense, etc.; reimburse. ▸ **in,demnifi'cation** *n* ▸ **in'demni,fier** *n*

indemnity (ɪn'dɛmnɪtɪ) *n, pl* **-ties. 1** compensation for loss or damage; reimbursement. **2** protection or insurance against future loss or damage. **3** legal exemption from penalties or liabilities incurred through one's acts or defaults. **4** (in Canada) the salary paid to a member of Parliament or of a legislature. **5 act of indemnity.** an act of Parliament granting exemption to public officers from technical penalties that they may have been compelled to incur. [C15: from Late Latin *indemnitās,* from *indemnis* uninjured, from Latin IN-[1] + *damnum* damage]

indemonstrable (,ɪndɪ'mɒnstrəbᵊl) *adj* incapable of being demonstrated or proved. ▸ **,inde,monstra'bility** *n* ▸ **,inde'monstrably** *adv*

indene ('ɪndiːn) *n* a colourless liquid hydrocarbon extracted from petroleum and coal tar and used in making synthetic resins. Formula: C_9H_8. [C20: from INDOLE + -ENE]

indent[1] *vb* (ɪn'dɛnt). (*mainly tr*) **1** to place (written or printed matter, etc.) in from the margin, as at the beginning of a paragraph. **2** to cut or tear (a document, esp. a contract or deed in duplicate) so that the irregular lines may be matched to confirm its authenticity. **3** *Chiefly Brit.* (in foreign trade) to place an order for (foreign goods), usually through an agent. **4** (when *intr,* foll. by *for, on,* or *upon*) *Chiefly Brit.* to make an order on (a source or supply) or for (something). **5** to notch (an edge, border, etc.); make jagged. **6** to bind (an apprentice, etc.) by indenture. ◆ *n* ('ɪn,dɛnt). **7** *Chiefly Brit.* (in foreign trade) an order for foreign merchandise, esp. one placed with an agent. **8** *Chiefly Brit.* an official order for goods. **9** (in the late 18th-century U.S.) a certificate issued by federal and state governments for the principal or interest due on the public debt. **10** another word for **indenture. 11** another word for **indentation** (sense 4). [C14: from Old French *endenter,* from EN-[1] + *dent* tooth, from Latin *dēns*] ▸ **in'denter** *or* **in'dentor** *n*

indent[2] *vb* (ɪn'dɛnt). **1** *(tr)* to make a dent or depression in. ◆ *n* ('ɪn,dɛnt). **2** a dent or depression. [C15: from IN-[2] + DENT[1]]

indentation (,ɪndɛn'teɪʃən) *n* **1** a hollowed, notched, or cut place, as on an edge or on a coastline. **2** a series of hollows, notches, or cuts. **3** the act of indenting or the condition of being indented. **4** Also called: **indention, indent.** the leaving of space or the amount of space left between a margin and the start of an indented line.

indention (ɪn'dɛnʃən) *n* another word for **indentation** (sense 4).

indenture (ɪn'dɛntʃə) *n* **1** any deed, contract, or sealed agreement between two or more parties. **2** (formerly) a deed drawn up in duplicate, each part having correspondingly indented edges for identification and security. **3** (*often pl*) a contract between an apprentice and his master. **4** a formal or official list or certificate authenticated for use as a voucher, etc. **5** a less common word for **indentation.** ◆ *vb* **6** *(intr)* to enter into an agreement by indenture. **7** *(tr)* to bind (an apprentice, servant, etc.) by indenture. **8** *(tr) Obsolete.* to indent or wrinkle. ▸ **in'denture,ship** *n*

independence (,ɪndɪ'pɛndəns) *n* the state or quality of being independent. Also called: **independency.**

Independence (,ɪndɪ'pɛndəns) *n* a city in W Missouri, near Kansas City: starting point for the Santa Fe, Oregon, and California Trails (1831–44). Pop.: 110 303 (1996 est.).

Independence Day *n* the official name for the **Fourth of July**.

independency (ˌɪndɪˈpɛndənsɪ) *n, pl* **-cies. 1** a territory or state free from the control of any other power. **2** another word for **independence**.

Independency (ˌɪndɪˈpɛndənsɪ) *n* (esp. in the Congregational Church) the principle upholding the independence of each local church or congregation.

independent (ˌɪndɪˈpɛndənt) *adj* **1** free from control in action, judgment, etc.; autonomous. **2** not dependent on anything else for function, validity, etc.; separate: *two independent units make up this sofa*. **3** not reliant on the support, esp. financial support, of others. **4** capable of acting for oneself or on one's own: *a very independent little girl*. **5** providing a large unearned sum towards one's support (esp. in the phrases **independent income, independent means**). **6** living on an unearned income. **7** *Maths.* (of a system of equations) not linearly dependent. See also **independent variable. 8** *Statistics.* **8a** (of two or more variables) distributed so that the value taken by one variable will have no effect on that taken by another or others. **8b** (of two or more events) such that the probability of all occurring equals the product of their individual probabilities. Compare **statistical dependence. 9** *Logic.* (of a set of propositions) **9a** not validly derivable from one another, so that if the propositions are the axioms of some theory none can be dispensed with. **9b** not logically related, so that in no case can the truth value of one be inferred from those of the others. ◆ *n* **10** an independent person or thing. **11** a person who is not affiliated to or who acts independently of a political party. ► **ˌindeˈpendently** *adv*

Independent (ˌɪndɪˈpɛndənt) *n* **1** (in England) a member of the Congregational Church. ◆ *adj* **2** of or relating to Independency.

independent clause *n Grammar.* a main or coordinate clause. Compare **dependent clause.**

independent school *n* **1** (in Britain) a school that is neither financed nor controlled by the government or local authorities. **2** (in Australia) a school that is not part of the state system.

independent variable *n* **1** Also called: **argument.** a variable in a mathematical equation or statement whose value determines that of the dependent variable: in $y = f(x)$, x is the independent variable. **2** *Statistics.* Also called: **predictor.** the variable which an experimenter deliberately manipulates in order to observe its relationship with some other quantity, or which defines the distinct conditions in an experiment. See also **experimental condition.**

in-depth *adj* carefully worked out, detailed and thorough: *an in-depth study*.

indescribable (ˌɪndɪˈskraɪbəbᵊl) *adj* beyond description; too intense, extreme, etc., for words. ► **ˌindeˌscribaˈbility** *or* **ˌindeˈscribableness** *n* ► **ˌindeˈscribably** *adv*

indestructible (ˌɪndɪˈstrʌktəbᵊl) *adj* incapable of being destroyed; very durable. ► **ˌindeˌstructiˈbility** *or* **ˌindeˈstructibleness** *n* ► **ˌindeˈstructibly** *adv*

indeterminable (ˌɪndɪˈtɜːmɪnəbᵊl) *adj* **1** incapable of being ascertained. **2** incapable of being settled. ► **ˌindeˈterminableness** *n* ► **ˌindeˈterminably** *adv*

indeterminacy principle *n* another name for **uncertainty principle.**

indeterminate (ˌɪndɪˈtɜːmɪnɪt) *adj* **1** uncertain in extent, amount, or nature. **2** not definite; inconclusive: *an indeterminate reply*. **3** unable to be predicted, calculated, or deduced. **4** *Physics, etc.* (of an effect) not obeying the law of causality; noncausal. **5** *Maths.* **5a** having no numerical meaning, as 0.00 and 0/0. **5b** (of an equation) having more than one variable and an unlimited number of solutions. **6** *Botany.* another word for **indefinite** (sense 4). **7** (of a structure, framework, etc.) comprising forces that cannot be fully analysed, esp. by vector analysis. ► **ˌindeˈterminacy, ˌindeˌtermiˈnation,** *or* **ˌindeˈterminateness** *n* ► **ˌindeˈterminately** *adv*

indeterminate sentence *n Law.* a prison sentence the length of which depends on the prisoner's conduct.

indeterminism (ˌɪndɪˈtɜːmɪˌnɪzəm) *n* the philosophical doctrine that behaviour is not entirely determined by motives. ► **ˌindeˈterminist** *n, adj* ► **ˌindeˌterminˈistic** *adj*

index (ˈɪndɛks) *n, pl* **-dexes** *or* **-dices** (-dɪˌsiːz). **1** an alphabetical list of persons, places, subjects, etc., mentioned in the text of a printed work, usually at the back, and indicating where in the work they are referred to. **2** See **thumb index. 3** *Library science.* a systematic list of book titles or author's names, giving cross-references and the location of each book; catalogue. **4** an indication, sign, or token. **5** a pointer, needle, or other indicator, as on an instrument. **6** *Maths.* **6a** another name for **exponent** (sense 4). **6b** a number or variable placed as a superscript to the left of a radical sign indicating by its value the root to be extracted, as in $\sqrt[3]{8} = 2$. **6c** a subscript or superscript to the right of a variable to show that the variable should be considered over a range of specified values: x_i *for the index* $i = 3$ *includes* x_1, x_2, and x_3. **7** a numerical scale by means of which variables, such as levels of the cost of living, can be compared with each other or with some base number. **8** a number or ratio indicating a specific characteristic, property, etc.: *refractive index*. **9** Also called: **fist.** a printer's mark (☛) used to indicate notes, paragraphs, etc. **10** *Obsolete.* a table of contents or preface. ◆ *vb (tr)* **11** to put an index in (a book). **12** to enter (a word, item, etc.) in an index. **13** to point out; indicate. **14** to index-link. **15** to move (a machine or a workpiece held in a machine tool) so that one particular operation will be repeated at certain defined intervals. [C16: from Latin: pointer, hence forefinger, title, index, from *indicāre* to disclose, show; see INDICATE] ► **ˈindexer** *n* ► **ˈindexless** *adj*

indexation (ˌɪndɛkˈseɪʃən) or **index-linking** *n* the act of making wages, interest rates, etc., index-linked.

index case *n Med.* the first case of a disease.

index finger *n* the finger next to the thumb. Also called: **forefinger.**

index fossil *n* a fossil species that characterizes and is used to delimit a geological zone. Also called: **zone fossil.**

index futures *pl n* a form of financial futures based on projected movement of a share price index, such as the Financial Times Stock Exchange 100 Share Index.

indexical (ɪnˈdɛksɪkᵊl) *adj* **1** arranged as or relating to an index or indexes. ◆ *n* **2** *Logic, linguistics.* a term whose reference depends on the context of utterance, such as *I, you, here, now,* or *tomorrow*. Also: **deictic.**

indexing head *n* a circular plate mounted to rotate on its centre, inscribed with concentric circles, each accurately divided, the dimensions being marked by drilled holes. The plate can be moved round with a workpiece to facilitate the accurate location of holes or other machining operations on the workpiece.

Index Librorum Prohibitorum *Latin.* (ˈɪndɛks laɪˈbrɔːrʊm prəʊˌhɪbɪˈtɔːrʊm) *n R.C. Church.* (formerly) an official list of proscribed books. Often called: **the Index.** [C17, literally: list of forbidden books]

index-linked *adj* (of wages, interest rates, etc.) directly related to the cost-of-living index and rising or falling accordingly.

index number *n Statistics.* a statistic indicating the relative change occurring in each successive period of time in the price, volume, or value of a commodity or in a general economic variable, such as the price level, national income, or gross output, with reference to a previous base period conventionally given the number 100.

Index of Industrial Production *n* (in Britain) an index produced by the Central Statistical Office showing changes in the production of the primary British industries.

index of refraction *n* another name for **refractive index.**

India (ˈɪndɪə) *n* **1** a republic in S Asia: history dates from the Indus Valley civilization (3rd millennium B.C.); came under British supremacy in 1763 and passed to the British Crown in 1858; nationalist movement arose under Gandhi (1869–1948); Indian subcontinent divided into Pakistan (Muslim) and India (Hindu) in 1947; became a republic within the Commonwealth in 1950. It consists chiefly of the Himalayas, rising over 7500 m (25 000 ft.) in the extreme north, the Ganges plain in the north, the Thar Desert in the northwest, the Chota Nagpur plateau in the northeast, and the Deccan Plateau in the south. Official and administrative languages: Hindi and English; each state has its own language. Religion: Hindu majority, Muslim minority. Currency: rupee. Capital: New Delhi. Pop.: 984 004 000 (1998 est.). Area: 3 268 100 sq. km (1 261 813 sq. miles). Hindi name: **Bharat. 2** *Communications.* a code word for the letter *i*.

Indiaman (ˈɪndɪəmən) *n, pl* **-men.** (formerly) a large merchant ship engaged in trade with India.

Indian (ˈɪndɪən) *n* **1** a native, citizen, or inhabitant of the Republic of India. **2** an American Indian. **3** (*not in scholarly usage*) any of the languages of the American Indians. ◆ *adj* **4** of, relating to, or characteristic of India, its inhabitants, or any of their languages. **5** of, relating to, or characteristic of the American Indians or any of their languages.

Indiana (ˌɪndɪˈænə) *n* a state of the N central U.S., in the Midwest: consists of an undulating plain, with sand dunes and lakes in the north and limestone caves in the south. Capital: Indianapolis. Pop.: 5 864 108 (1997 est.). Area: 93 491 sq. km (36 097 sq. miles). Abbrevs.: **Ind.** or (with zip code) **IN** ► **ˌIndiˈanian** *adj, n*

Indian agent *n* an official who represents the U.S. or Canadian government to a group of North American Indians.

Indianapolis (ˌɪndɪəˈnæpəlɪs) *n* a city in central Indiana: the state capital. Pop.: 746 737 (1996 est.).

Indian bread *n* another name for **corn bread.**

Indian cholera *n* another name for **cholera.**

Indian club *n* a bottle-shaped club, usually used in pairs by gymnasts, jugglers, etc.

Indian corn *n* another name for **maize** (sense 1).

Indian Desert *n* another name for the **Thar Desert.**

Indian Empire *n* British India and the Indian states under indirect British control, which gained independence as India and Pakistan in 1947.

Indian file *n* another term for **single file.**

Indian giver *n U.S. and Canadian offensive.* a person who asks for the return of a present he has given. ► **Indian giving** *n*

Indian hemp *n* **1** another name for **hemp,** esp. the variety *Cannabis indica,* from which several narcotic drugs are obtained. **2** Also called: **dogbane.** a perennial American apocynaceous plant, *Apocynum cannabinum,* whose fibre was formerly used by the Indians to make rope.

Indian ink *or esp. U.S. and Canadian* **India ink** *n* **1** a black pigment made from a mixture of lampblack and a binding agent such as gelatine or glue: usually formed into solid cakes and sticks. **2** a black liquid ink made from this pigment. ◆ Also called: **China ink, Chinese ink.**

Indian liquorice *n* a woody leguminous tropical Asian climbing plant, *Abrus precatorius,* with scarlet black-spotted poisonous seeds, used as beads, and roots used as a substitute for liquorice. Also called: **jequirity.**

Indian list *n Informal.* (in Canada) a list of persons to whom spirits may not be sold. Also called: **interdict list.**

Indian mallow *n* a tall malvaceous weedy North American plant, *Abutilon theophrasti,* with small yellow flowers and large velvety leaves.

Indian meal *n* another name for **corn meal.**

Indian millet *n* another name for **durra.**

Indian mulberry *n* a small rubiaceous tree, *Morinda citrifolia,* of SE Asia and Australasia, with rounded yellow fruits: yields red and yellow dyes.

Indian Mutiny *n* a revolt of Indian troops (1857–59) that led to the transfer of the administration of India from the East India Company to the British Crown.

Indian National Congress *n* the official name for **Congress** (the political party).

Indian Ocean *n* an ocean bordered by Africa in the west, Asia in the north, and Australia in the east and merging with the Antarctic Ocean in the south. Average depth: 3900 m (13 000 ft.). Greatest depth (off the Sunda Islands): 7450 m (24 442 ft.). Area: about 73 556 000 sq. km (28 400 000 sq. miles).

Indian pipe *n* a white or pinkish saprophytic woodland plant, *Monotropa uniflora,* of the N hemisphere, with a solitary nodding flower resembling a pipe: family *Monotropaceae.*

Indian red *n* **1** a red pigment containing ferric oxide, used in paints and cosmetics and produced by oxidizing iron salts. **2** a type of red soil containing ferric oxide, found in S Asia and used as a pigment and metal polish.

Indian reserve *or* **reservation** *n* See **reservation** (sense 4).

Indian rice *n* **1** an annual erect aquatic North American grass, *Zizania aquatica,* with edible purplish-black grain. **2** the grain of this plant. ◆ Also called: **wild rice.**

Indian rope-trick *n* the supposed Indian feat of climbing an unsupported rope.

Indian sign *n U.S.* a magic spell designed to place the victim in one's power or bring him bad luck.

Indian States and Agencies *pl n* another name for the **Native States.**

Indian summer *n* **1** a period of unusually settled warm weather after the end of summer proper. **2** a period of ease and tranquillity or of renewed productivity towards the end of a person's life or of an epoch. ◆ See also **Saint Martin's summer.** [originally U.S.: probably so named because it was first noted in regions occupied by American Indians]

Indian sweater *n* another name for **Cowichan sweater.**

Indian Territory *n* the territory established in the early 19th century in present-day Oklahoma, where Indians were forced to settle by the U.S. government. The last remnant was integrated into the new state of Oklahoma in 1907.

Indian tobacco *n* a poisonous North American campanulaceous plant, *Lobelia inflata,* with small pale blue flowers and rounded inflated seed capsules.

India paper *n* **1** a thin soft opaque printing paper made in the Orient. **2** another name (not in technical usage) for **Bible paper.**

India print *n* a colourful cotton fabric, with a block-printed pattern, made in India.

India rubber *n* another name for **rubber**[1] (sense 1).

Indic ('ɪndɪk) *adj* **1** denoting, belonging to, or relating to a branch of Indo-European consisting of the Indo-European languages of India, including Sanskrit, Hindi and Urdu, Punjabi, Gujerati, Bengali, and Sinhalese. ◆ *n* **2** this group of languages. ◆ Also: **Indo-Aryan.**

indic. *abbrev. for:* **1** indicating. **2** indicative. **3** indicator.

indican ('ɪndɪkən) *n* a compound secreted in the urine, usually in the form of its potassium salt; indoxylsulphuric acid. Formula: $C_8H_6NOSO_2OH$. [C19: from Latin *indicum* INDIGO + -AN]

indicant ('ɪndɪkənt) *n* something that indicates.

indicate ('ɪndɪˌkeɪt) *vb* (*tr*) **1** (*may take a clause as object*) to be or give a sign or symptom of; imply: *cold hands indicate a warm heart.* **2** to point out or show. **3** (*may take a clause as object*) to state briefly; suggest: *he indicated what his feelings were.* **4** (of instruments) to show a reading of: *the speedometer indicated 50 miles per hour.* **5** (*usually passive*) to recommend or require: *surgery seems to be indicated for this patient.* [C17: from Latin *indicāre* to point out, from IN-[2] + *dicāre* to proclaim; compare INDEX] ▸ **'indiˌcatable** *adj* ▸ **indicatory** (ɪn'dɪkətərɪ, -trɪ) *adj*

indicated horsepower *n* the power output of a piston engine calculated from the mean effective pressure in the cylinder as derived from an indicator diagram and the speed of the engine in revolutions per minute.

indication (ˌɪndɪ'keɪʃən) *n* **1** something that serves to indicate or suggest; sign: *an indication of foul play.* **2** the degree or quantity represented on a measuring instrument or device. **3** the action of indicating. **4** something that is indicated as advisable, necessary, or expedient.

indicative (ɪn'dɪkətɪv) *adj* **1** (*usually postpositive;* foll. by *of*) serving as a sign; suggestive: *indicative of trouble ahead.* **2** *Grammar.* denoting a mood of verbs used chiefly to make statements. Compare **subjunctive** (sense 1). ◆ *n* **3** *Grammar.* **3a** the indicative mood. **3b** a verb in the indicative mood. ◆ Abbrev.: **indic.** ▸ **in'dicatively** *adv*

indicator ('ɪndɪˌkeɪtə) *n* **1** something that provides an indication, esp. of trends. See **economic indicator. 2** a device to attract attention, such as the pointer of a gauge or a warning lamp. **3** an instrument that displays certain operating conditions in a machine, such as a gauge showing temperature, speed, pressure, etc. **4a** a device that records or registers something, such as the movements of a lift, or that shows information, such as arrival and departure times of trains. **4b** (*as modifier*): *indicator light.* **5** Also called: **blinker.** a device for indicating that a motor vehicle is about to turn left or right, esp. two pairs of lights that flash when operated or a pair of trafficators. **6** Also called: **dial gauge.** a delicate measuring instrument used to determine small differences in the height of mechanical components. It consists of a spring-loaded plunger that operates a pointer moving over a circular scale. **7** *Chem.* **7a** a substance used in titrations to indicate the completion of a chemical reaction, usually by a change of colour. **7b** a substance, such as litmus, that indicates the presence of an acid or alkali. **8** Also called: **indicator species.** *Ecology.* **8a** a plant or animal species that thrives only under particular environmental conditions and therefore indicates these conditions where it is found. **8b** a species of plant or animal whose well-being confirms the well-being of other species in the area.

indicator diagram *n* a graphical or other representation of the cyclic variations of pressure and volume within the cylinder of a reciprocating engine obtained by using an indicator.

indices ('ɪndɪˌsiːz) *n* a plural of **index.**

indicia (ɪn'dɪʃɪə) *pl n, sing* **-cium** (-ʃɪəm). distinguishing markings or signs; indications. [C17: from Latin, plural of *indicium* a notice, from INDEX] ▸ **in'dicial** *adj*

indicolite ('ɪndɪkəˌlaɪt) *or* **indigolite** *n* a form of tourmaline ranging in colour from pale blue to blue-black. [C19: from Spanish *indico* INDIGO + -LITE]

indict (ɪn'daɪt) *vb* (*tr*) to charge (a person) with crime, esp. formally in writing; accuse. [C14: alteration of *enditen* to INDITE] ▸ **ˌindict'ee** *n* ▸ **in'dicter** *or* **in'dictor** *n*

USAGE See at **indite.**

indictable (ɪn'daɪtəb°l) *adj Criminal law.* **1** (of a person) liable to be indicted. **2** (of a crime) that makes a person liable to be indicted. ▸ **in'dictably** *adv*

indiction (ɪn'dɪkʃən) *n* (in the Roman Empire and later in various medieval kingdoms) **1** a recurring fiscal period of 15 years, often used as a unit for dating events. **2** a particular year in this period or the number assigned it. **3** (from the reign of Constantine the Great) **3a** a valuation of property made every 15 years as a basis for taxation. **3b** the tax based on this valuation. [C14: from Latin *indictiō* declaration, announcement of a tax; see INDITE] ▸ **in'dictional** *adj*

indictment (ɪn'daɪtmənt) *n Criminal law.* **1** a formal written charge of crime formerly referred to and presented on oath by a grand jury. **2** any formal accusation of crime. **3** *Scot.* a charge of crime brought at the instance of the Lord Advocate. **4** the act of indicting or the state of being indicted.

indie ('ɪndɪ) *n Informal.* **a** an independent record company. **b** (*as modifier*): *the indie charts.*

Indies ('ɪndɪz) *n* **the. 1** the territories of S and SE Asia included in the East Indies, India, and Indochina. **2** See **East Indies. 3** See **West Indies.**

indifference (ɪn'dɪfrəns, -fərəns) *n* **1** the fact or state of being indifferent; lack of care or concern. **2** lack of quality; mediocrity. **3** lack of importance; insignificance. **4** See **principle of indifference.**

indifferent (ɪn'dɪfrənt, -fərənt) *adj* **1** (often foll. by *to*) showing no care or concern; uninterested: *he was indifferent to my pleas.* **2** unimportant; immaterial. **3a** of only average or moderate size, extent, quality, etc. **3b** not at all good; poor. **4** showing or having no preferences; impartial. **5** *Biology.* **5a** (of cells or tissues) not differentiated or specialized. **5b** (of a species) occurring in two or more different communities. [C14: from Latin *indifferēns* making no distinction] ▸ **in'differently** *adv*

indifferentism (ɪn'dɪfrənˌtɪzəm, -fərən-) *n* systematic indifference, esp. in matters of religion. ▸ **in'differentist** *n*

indigene ('ɪndɪˌdʒiːn) *or* **indigen** ('ɪndɪdʒən) *n* an indigenous person, animal, or thing; native.

indigenous (ɪn'dɪdʒɪnəs) *adj* (when *postpositive,* foll. by *to*) **1** originating or occurring naturally (in a country, region, etc.); native. **2** innate (to); inherent (in). [C17: from Latin *indigenus,* from *indigena* indigene, from *indi-* in + *gignere* to beget] ▸ **in'digenously** *adv* ▸ **in'digenousness** *or* **indigenity** (ˌɪndɪ'dʒenɪtɪ) *n*

indigent ('ɪndɪdʒənt) *adj* **1** so poor as to lack even necessities; very needy. **2** (usually foll. by *of*) *Archaic.* lacking (in) or destitute (of). ◆ *n* **3** an impoverished person. [C14: from Latin *indigēre* to need, from *egēre* to lack] ▸ **'indigence** *n* ▸ **'indigently** *adv*

indigested (ˌɪndɪ'dʒestɪd) *adj Archaic.* undigested.

indigestible (ˌɪndɪ'dʒestəb°l) *adj* **1** incapable of being digested or difficult to digest. **2** difficult to understand or absorb mentally: *an indigestible book.* ▸ **ˌindiˌgesti'bility** *or* **ˌindi'gestibleness** *n* ▸ **ˌindi'gestibly** *adv*

indigestion (ˌɪndɪ'dʒestʃən) *n* difficulty in digesting food, accompanied by abdominal pain, heartburn, and belching. Technical name: **dyspepsia.**

indigestive (ˌɪndɪ'dʒestɪv) *adj* relating to or suffering from indigestion; dyspeptic.

indign (ɪn'daɪn) *adj Obsolete or poetic.* **1** undeserving; unworthy. **2** unseemly; disgraceful. **3** not deserved. [C15: from Old French *indigne,* from Latin *indignus* unworthy, from IN-[1] + *dignus* worthy; see DIGNITY]

indignant (ɪn'dɪgnənt) *adj* feeling or showing indignation. [C16: from Latin *indignārī* to be displeased with] ▸ **in'dignantly** *adv*

indignation (ˌɪndɪg'neɪʃən) *n* anger or scorn aroused by something felt to be unfair, unworthy, or wrong.

indignity (ɪn'dɪgnɪtɪ) *n, pl* **-ties. 1** injury to one's self-esteem or dignity; humiliation. **2** *Obsolete.* disgrace or disgraceful character or conduct.

indigo ('ɪndɪˌgəʊ) *n, pl* **-gos** *or* **-goes. 1** Also called: **indigotin.** a blue vat dye originally obtained from plants but now made synthetically. **2** any of various tropical plants of the leguminous genus *Indigofera,* such as the anil, that yield this dye. Compare **wild indigo. 3a** any of a group of colours that have the same blue-violet hue; a spectral colour. **3b** (*as adj*): *an indigo carpet.* [C16: from Spanish *indico,* via Latin from Greek *Indikos* of India] ▸ **indigotic** (ˌɪndɪ'gɒtɪk) *adj*

indigo blue *n, adj* (**indigo-blue** *when prenominal*). the full name for **indigo** (the colour and the dye).

indigo bunting, bird, *or* **finch** *n* a North American bunting, *Passerina cyanea,* the male of which is bright blue and the female brown.

indigoid ('ɪndɪˌgɔɪd) *adj* **1** of, concerned with, or resembling indigo or its blue colour. ◆ *n* **2** any of a number of synthetic dyes or pigments related in chemical structure to indigo.

indigolite ('ɪndɪgəˌlaɪt) *n* a variant spelling of **indicolite.**

indigo snake *n* a dark-blue nonvenomous North American colubrid snake, *Drymarchon corais couperi.*

indigotin (ɪn'dɪgətɪn, ˌɪndɪ'gəʊ-) *n* another name for **indigo** (the dye). [C19: from INDIGO + -IN]

indirect (ˌɪndɪ'rekt) *adj* **1** deviating from a direct course or line; roundabout; circuitous. **2** not coming as a direct effect or consequence; secondary: *indirect benefits.* **3** not straightforward, open, or fair; devious or evasive: *an indirect in-*

sult. **4** (of a title or an inheritance) not inherited in an unbroken line of succession from father to son. ▸ ˌ**indiˈrectly** *adv* ▸ ˌ**indiˈrectness** *n*

indirect costs *pl n* another name for **overheads**.

indirection (ˌɪndɪˈrɛkʃən) *n* **1** indirect procedure, courses, or methods. **2** lack of direction or purpose; aimlessness. **3** indirect dealing; deceit.

indirect labour *n Commerce.* work done in administration and sales rather than in the manufacturing of a product. Compare **direct labour** (sense 1).

indirect lighting *n* reflected or diffused light from a concealed source.

indirect object *n Grammar.* a noun, pronoun, or noun phrase indicating the recipient or beneficiary of the action of a verb and its direct object, as *John* in the sentence *I bought John a newspaper.* Compare **direct object**.

indirect proof *n Logic, maths.* proof of a conclusion by showing its negation to be self-contradictory; reductio ad absurdum. Compare **direct** (sense 17).

indirect question *n* a question reported in indirect speech, as in *She asked why you came.* Compare **direct question**.

indirect speech *or esp. U.S.* **indirect discourse** *n* the reporting of something said or written by conveying what was meant rather than repeating the exact words, as in the sentence *He asked me whether I would go* as opposed to *He asked me, "Will you go?"* Also called: **reported speech**.

indirect tax *n* a tax levied on goods or services rather than on individuals or companies. Compare **direct tax**. ▸ **indirect taxˈation** *n*

indiscernible (ˌɪndɪˈsɜːnəbᵊl) *adj* **1** incapable of being discerned. **2** scarcely discernible or perceptible. ▸ ˌ**indisˈcernibleness** *or* ˌ**indiscerniˈbility** *n* ▸ ˌ**indisˈcernibly** *adv*

indiscipline (ɪnˈdɪsɪplɪn) *n* lack of discipline.

indiscreet (ˌɪndɪˈskriːt) *adj* not discreet; imprudent or tactless. ▸ ˌ**indisˈcreetly** *adv* ▸ ˌ**indisˈcreetness** *n*

indiscrete (ˌɪndɪˈskriːt) *adj* not divisible or divided into parts. ▸ ˌ**indisˈcretely** *adv* ▸ ˌ**indisˈcreteness** *n*

indiscretion (ˌɪndɪˈskrɛʃən) *n* **1** the characteristic or state of being indiscreet. **2** an indiscreet act, remark, etc. ▸ ˌ**indisˈcretionary** *adj*

indiscriminate (ˌɪndɪˈskrɪmɪnɪt) *adj* **1** lacking discrimination or careful choice; random or promiscuous. **2** jumbled; confused. ▸ ˌ**indisˈcriminately** *adv* ▸ ˌ**indisˈcriminateness** *n* ▸ ˌ**indisˌcrimiˈnation** *n*

indispensable (ˌɪndɪˈspɛnsəbᵊl) *adj* **1** absolutely necessary; essential. **2** not to be disregarded or escaped: *an indispensable role.* ◆ *n* **3** an indispensable person or thing. ▸ ˌ**indisˌpensaˈbility** *or* ˌ**indisˈpensableness** *n* ▸ ˌ**indisˈpensably** *adv*

indispose (ˌɪndɪˈspəuz) *vb (tr)* **1** to make unwilling or opposed; disincline. **2** to cause to feel ill. **3** to make unfit (for something or to do something).

indisposed (ˌɪndɪˈspəuzd) *adj* **1** sick or ill. **2** unwilling. [C15: from Latin *indispositus* disordered] ▸ **indisposition** (ˌɪndɪspəˈzɪʃən) *n*

indisputable (ˌɪndɪˈspjuːtəbᵊl) *adj* beyond doubt; not open to question. ▸ ˌ**indisˌputaˈbility** *or* ˌ**indisˈputableness** *n* ▸ ˌ**indisˈputably** *adv*

indissoluble (ˌɪndɪˈsɒljubᵊl) *adj* incapable of being dissolved or broken; permanent. ▸ ˌ**indisˌsoluˈbility** *or* ˌ**indisˈsolubleness** *n* ▸ ˌ**indisˈsolubly** *adv*

indistinct (ˌɪndɪˈstɪŋkt) *adj* incapable of being clearly distinguished, as by the eyes, ears, or mind; not distinct. ▸ ˌ**indisˈtinctly** *adv* ▸ ˌ**indisˈtinctness** *n*

indistinctive (ˌɪndɪˈstɪŋktɪv) *adj* **1** without distinctive qualities. **2** unable to make distinctions; undiscriminating. ▸ ˌ**indisˈtinctively** *adv* ▸ ˌ**indisˈtinctiveness** *n*

indistinguishable (ˌɪndɪˈstɪŋgwɪʃəbᵊl) *adj* **1** (*often postpositive;* foll. by *from*) identical or very similar (to): *twins indistinguishable from one another.* **2** not easily perceptible; indiscernible. ▸ ˌ**indisˌtinguishaˈbility** *or* ˌ**indisˈtinguishableness** *n* ▸ ˌ**indisˈtinguishably** *adv*

indite (ɪnˈdaɪt) *vb (tr)* **1** *Archaic.* to write. **2** *Obsolete.* to dictate. [C14: from Old French *enditer,* from Latin *indīcere* to declare, from IN-[2] + *dīcere* to say] ▸ **inˈditement** *n* ▸ **inˈditer** *n*

USAGE *Indite* and *inditement* are sometimes wrongly used where *indict* and *indictment* are meant: *he was indicted* (not *indited*) *for fraud.*

indium (ˈɪndɪəm) *n* a rare soft silvery metallic element associated with zinc ores: used in alloys, electronics, and electroplating. Symbol: In; atomic no.: 49; atomic wt.: 114.82; valency: 1, 2, or 3; relative density: 7.31; melting pt.: 156.63°C; boiling pt.: 2073°C. [C19: New Latin, from INDIGO + -IUM]

indiv. *or* **individ.** *abbrev. for* individual.

indivertible (ˌɪndɪˈvɜːtɪbᵊl) *adj* incapable of being diverted or turned aside. ▸ ˌ**indiˈvertibly** *adv*

individual (ˌɪndɪˈvɪdjuəl) *adj* **1** of, relating to, characteristic of, or meant for a single person or thing. **2** separate or distinct, esp. from others of its kind; particular: *please mark the individual pages.* **3** characterized by unusual and striking qualities; distinctive. **4** *Obsolete.* indivisible; inseparable. ◆ *n* **5** a single person, esp. when regarded as distinct from others. **6** *Biology.* **6a** a single animal or plant, esp. as distinct from a species. **6b** a single member of a compound organism or colony. **7** *Logic.* **7a** Also called: **particular**. an object as opposed to a property or class. **7b** an element of the domain of discourse of a theory. [C15: from Medieval Latin *indīviduālis,* from Latin *indīviduus* indivisible, from IN-[1] + *dīviduus* divisible, from *dīvidere* to DIVIDE] ▸ ˌ**indiˈvidually** *adv*

individualism (ˌɪndɪˈvɪdjuəˌlɪzəm) *n* **1** the action or principle of asserting one's independence and individuality; egoism. **2** an individual quirk or peculiarity. **3** another word for **laissez faire** (sense 1). **4** *Philosophy.* the doctrine that only individual things exist and that therefore classes or properties have no reality. Compare **Platonism, realism** (sense 5).

individualist (ˌɪndɪˈvɪdjuəlɪst) *n* **1** a person who shows independence and individuality in his behaviour, opinions, or actions. **2** an advocate of individualism. ▸ ˌ**indiˌvidualˈistic** *adj* ▸ ˌ**indiˌvidualˈistically** *adv*

individuality (ˌɪndɪˌvɪdjuˈælɪtɪ) *n, pl* **-ties**. **1** distinctive or unique character or personality: *a work of great individuality.* **2** the qualities that distinguish one person or thing from another; identity. **3** the state or quality of being a separate entity; discreteness.

individualize *or* **individualise** (ˌɪndɪˈvɪdjuəˌlaɪz) *vb (tr)* **1** to make or mark as individual or distinctive in character. **2** to consider or treat individually; particularize. **3** to make or modify so as to meet the special requirements of a person. ▸ ˌ**indiˌvidualiˈzation** *or* ˌ**indiˌvidualiˈsation** *n* ▸ ˌ**indiˈvidualˌizer** *or* ˌ**indiˈvidualˌiser** *n*

individuate (ˌɪndɪˈvɪdjuˌeɪt) *vb (tr)* **1** to give individuality or an individual form to. **2** to distinguish from others of the same species or group; individualize. ▸ ˌ**indiˈviduˌator** *n*

individuation (ˌɪndɪˌvɪdjuˈeɪʃən) *n* **1** the act or process of individuating. **2** (in the psychology of Jung) the process by which the wholeness of the individual is established through the integration of consciousness and the collective unconscious. **3** *Zoology.* the development of separate but mutually interdependent units, as in the development of zooids forming a colony.

indivisible (ˌɪndɪˈvɪzəbᵊl) *adj* **1** unable to be divided. **2** *Maths.* leaving a remainder when divided by a given number: *8 is indivisible by 3.* ▸ ˌ**indiˌvisiˈbility** *or* ˌ**indiˈvisibleness** *n* ▸ ˌ**indiˈvisibly** *adv*

Indo- (ˈɪndəu-) *combining form.* denoting India or Indian: *Indo-European.*

Indo-Aryan *adj* **1** another word for **Indic** (sense 1). ◆ *n* **2** another name for **Indic** (sense 2). **3** a native speaker of an Indo-Aryan language.

Indochina *or* **Indo-China** *n* (ˈɪndəuˈtʃaɪnə) **1** Also called: **Farther India**. a peninsula in SE Asia, between India and China: consists of Myanmar, Thailand, Laos, Cambodia, Vietnam, and Malaysia. **2** the former French colonial possessions of Cochin China, Annam, Tonkin, Laos, and Cambodia. ▸ ˈ**Indo-chiˈnese** *or* ˈ**Indo-Chiˈnese** *adj, n*

indocile (ɪnˈdəusaɪl) *adj* difficult to discipline or instruct. ▸ **indocility** (ˌɪndəuˈsɪlɪtɪ) *n*

indoctrinate (ɪnˈdɒktrɪˌneɪt) *vb (tr)* **1** to teach (a person or group of people) systematically to accept doctrines, esp. uncritically. **2** *Rare.* to impart learning to; instruct. ▸ **inˌdoctriˈnation** *n* ▸ **inˈdoctriˌnator** *n*

Indo-European *adj* **1** denoting, belonging to, or relating to a family of languages that includes English and many other culturally and politically important languages of the world: a characteristic feature, esp. of the older languages such as Latin, Greek, and Sanskrit, is inflection showing gender, number, and case. **2** denoting or relating to the hypothetical parent language of this family, primitive Indo-European. **3** denoting, belonging to, or relating to any of the peoples speaking these languages. ◆ *n* **4** the Indo-European family of languages. **5** Also called: **primitive Indo-European, Proto-Indo-European**. the reconstructed hypothetical parent language of this family. **6** a member of the prehistoric people who spoke this language. **7** a descendant of this people or a native speaker of an Indo-European language.

Indo-Germanic *adj, n Obsolete.* another term for **Indo-European**.

Indo-Hittite *n* the Indo-European family of languages: used by scholars who regard Hittite not as a branch of Indo-European but as a related language.

Indo-Iranian *adj* **1** of or relating to the Indic and Iranian branches of the Indo-European family of languages. ◆ *n* **2** this group of languages, sometimes considered as forming a single branch of Indo-European.

indole (ˈɪndəul) *or* **indol** (ˈɪndəul, -dɒl) *n* a white or yellowish crystalline heterocyclic compound extracted from coal tar and used in perfumery, medicine, and as a flavouring agent; 1-benzopyrrole. Formula: C_8H_7N. [C19: from IND(IGO) + -OLE[1]]

indoleacetic acid (ˌɪndəuləˈsiːtɪk, -ˈsetɪk) *n* an auxin that causes elongation of the cells of plant stems. Formula: $C_{10}H_9NO_2$. Abbrev.: **IAA**.

indolebutyric acid (ˌɪndəulbjuːˈtɪrɪk) *n* a synthetic auxin used for stimulating plant growth and root formation. Formula: $C_8H_6N(CH_2)_3COOH$.

indolent (ˈɪndələnt) *adj* **1** disliking work or effort; lazy; idle. **2** *Pathol.* causing little pain: *an indolent tumour.* **3** (esp. of a painless ulcer) slow to heal. [C17: from Latin *indolēns* not feeling pain, from IN-[1] + *dolēns,* from *dolēre* to grieve, cause distress] ▸ ˈ**indolence** *n* ▸ ˈ**indolently** *adv*

Indologist (ɪnˈdɒlədʒɪst) *n* a student of Indian literature, history, philosophy, etc. ▸ **Inˈdology** *n*

indomethacin (ˌɪndəuˈmɛθəsɪn) *n* a drug administered orally to relieve pain, fever, and inflammation, esp. in rheumatoid arthritis. Formula: $C_{19}H_{16}ClNO_4$. [C20: from INDOLE + METH- + ACETIC ACID + -IN]

indomitable (ɪnˈdɒmɪtəbᵊl) *adj* (of courage, pride, etc.) difficult or impossible to defeat or subdue. [C17: from Late Latin *indomitābilis,* from Latin *indomitus* untamable, from IN-[1] + *domitus* subdued, from *domāre* to tame] ▸ **inˌdomitaˈbility** *or* **inˈdomitableness** *n* ▸ **inˈdomitably** *adv*

Indonesia (ˌɪndəuˈniːzɪə) *n* a republic in SE Asia, in the Malay Archipelago, consisting of the main islands of Sumatra, Java and Madura, Bali, Sulawesi (Celebes), Lombok, Sumbawa, Flores, the Moluccas, Timor, part of Borneo (Kalimantan), Irian Jaya, and over 3000 small islands in the Indian and Pacific Oceans: became the Dutch East Indies in 1798; declared independence in 1945; became a republic in 1950; illegally annexed East Timor in 1975. Official language: Bahasa Indonesia. Religion: Muslim majority. Currency: rupiah. Capital: Jakarta. Pop.: 202 957 000 (1998 est.). Area: 1 919 317 sq. km (741 052 sq. miles). Former names (1798–1945): **Dutch East Indies, Netherlands East Indies**.

Indonesian (ˌɪndəuˈniːzɪən) *adj* **1** of or relating to Indonesia, its people, or their language. ◆ *n* **2** a native or inhabitant of Indonesia. **3** another name for **Bahasa Indonesia**.

indoor (ˈɪnˌdɔː) *adj (prenominal)* of, situated in, or appropriate to the inside of a house or other building: *an indoor tennis court; indoor amusements.*

indoors (ˌɪnˈdɔːz) *adv, adj (postpositive)* inside or into a house or other building.

Indo-Pacific *adj* **1** of or relating to the region of the Indian and W Pacific Oceans off the coast of SE Asia. ◆ *n* **2** a hypothetical family of languages relating the languages of New Guinea other than Malayo-Polynesian. Tentative affiliations with Malayo-Polynesian or Australian languages have been suggested.

indophenol (ˌɪndəʊˈfiːnɒl) *n* **1** a derivative of quinonimine. Formula: $HOC_6H_4NC_6H_4O$. **2** any of a class of derivatives of this compound, esp. one of the blue or green dyes that are used for wool and cotton. **[C19:** from INDIGO + PHENOL**]**

Indore (ɪnˈdɔː) *n* **1** a city in central India, in W Madhya Pradesh. Pop.: 1 091 674 (1991). **2** a former state of central India: became part of Madhya Bharat in 1948, which in turn became part of Madhya Pradesh in 1956.

indorse (ɪnˈdɔːs) *vb* a variant spelling of **endorse.** ▸ **inˈdorsable** *adj* ▸ **inˈdorsement** *n* ▸ **inˈdorser** *or* **inˈdorsor** *n*

indorsee (ˌɪndɔːˈsiː, ɪnˈdɔːsiː) *n* a variant of **endorsee.**

indoxyl (ɪnˈdɒksɪl) *n* a yellow water-soluble crystalline compound occurring in woad as its glucoside and in urine as its ester. Formula: C_8H_7NO. See also **indican.** **[C19:** from INDIGO + HYDROXYL**]**

Indra (ˈɪndrə) *n Hinduism.* the most celebrated god of the Rig-Veda, governing the weather and dispensing rain.

indraught *or U.S.* **indraft** (ˈɪnˌdrɑːft) *n* **1** the act of drawing or pulling in. **2** an inward flow, esp. of air.

indrawn (ˌɪnˈdrɔːn) *adj* **1** drawn or pulled in. **2** inward looking or introspective.

Indre (*French* ɛ̃drə) *n* a department of central France in the Centre region. Capital: Châteauroux. Pop.: 234 400 (1995). Area: 6906 sq. km (2693 sq. miles).

Indre-et-Loire (*French* ɛ̃drəelwar) *n* a department of W central France in the Centre region: contains many famous châteaux along the Loire. Capital: Tours. Pop.: 545 800 (1995). Area: 6158 sq. km (2402 sq. miles).

indris (ˈɪndrɪs) *or* **indri** (ˈɪndrɪ) *n, pl* **-dris. 1** a large Madagascan arboreal lemuroid primate, *Indri indri,* with thick silky fur patterned in black, white, and fawn: family *Indriidae.* **2 woolly indris.** a related nocturnal Madagascan animal, *Avahi laniger,* with thick grey-brown fur and a long tail. **[C19:** from French: lemur, from Malagasy *indry!* look! mistaken for the animal's name**]**

indubitable (ɪnˈdjuːbɪtəbᵊl) *adj* incapable of being doubted; unquestionable. **[C18:** from Latin *indubitābilis,* from IN-[1] + *dubitāre* to doubt**]** ▸ **inˌdubitaˈbility** *or* **inˈdubitableness** *n* ▸ **inˈdubitably** *adv*

induc. *abbrev. for* induction.

induce (ɪnˈdjuːs) *vb (tr)* **1** (often foll. by an infinitive) to persuade or use influence on. **2** to cause or bring about. **3** *Med.* to initiate or hasten (labour), as by administering a drug to stimulate uterine contractions. **4** *Logic, obsolete.* to assert or establish (a general proposition, hypothesis, etc.) by induction. **5** to produce (an electromotive force or electrical current) by induction. **6** to transmit (magnetism) by induction. **[C14:** from Latin *indūcere* to lead in, from *dūcere* to lead**]** ▸ **inˈducer** *n* ▸ **inˈducible** *adj*

induced drag *n* the former name for **trailing vortex drag.**

inducement (ɪnˈdjuːsmənt) *n* **1** the act of inducing. **2** a means of inducing; persuasion; incentive. **3** *Law.* (in pleading) the introductory part that leads up to and explains the matter in dispute.

induct (ɪnˈdʌkt) *vb (tr)* **1** to bring in formally or install in an office, place, etc.; invest. **2** (foll. by *to* or *into*) to initiate in knowledge (of). **3** *U.S.* to enlist for military service; conscript. **4** *Physics.* another word for **induce** (senses 5, 6). **[C14:** from Latin *inductus* led in, past participle of *indūcere* to introduce; see INDUCE**]**

inductance (ɪnˈdʌktəns) *n* **1** Also called: **induction.** the property of an electric circuit as a result of which an electromotive force is created by a change of current in the same circuit (see **self-inductance**) or in a neighbouring circuit (see **mutual inductance**). It is usually measured in henries. Symbol: *L* **2** Also called: **inductor.** a component, such as a coil, in an electrical circuit, the main function of which is to produce inductance.

inductee (ˌɪndʌkˈtiː) *n U.S.* a military conscript.

inductile (ɪnˈdʌktaɪl) *adj* not ductile, pliant, or yielding. ▸ **ˌinducˈtility** *n*

induction (ɪnˈdʌkʃən) *n* **1** the act of inducting or state of being inducted. **2** the act of inducing. **3** (in an internal-combustion engine) the part of the action of a piston by which mixed air and fuel are drawn from the carburettor to the cylinder. **4** *Logic.* **4a** a process of reasoning, used esp. in science, by which a general conclusion is drawn from a set of premises, based mainly on experience or experimental evidence. The conclusion goes beyond the information contained in the premises, and does not follow necessarily from them. Thus an inductive argument may be highly probable, yet lead from true premises to a false conclusion. **4b** a conclusion reached by this process of reasoning. Compare **deduction** (sense 4). **5** the process by which electrical or magnetic properties are transferred, without physical contact, from one circuit or body to another. See also **inductance. 6** *Biology.* the effect of one tissue, esp. an embryonic tissue, on the development of an adjacent tissue. **7** *Biochem.* the process by which synthesis of an enzyme is stimulated by the presence of its substrate. **8** *Maths, logic.* **8a** a method of proving a proposition that all integers have a property, by first proving that 1 has the property and then that if the integer *n* has it so has *n* + 1. **8b** the application of recursive rules. **9a** a formal introduction or entry into an office or position. **9b** (*as modifier*): *induction course; induction period.* **10** *U.S.* the formal enlistment of a civilian into military service. **11** an archaic word for **preface.** ▸ inˈ**ductional** *adj*

induction coil *n* a transformer for producing a high voltage from a low voltage. It consists of a cylindrical primary winding of few turns, a concentric secondary winding of many turns, and often a common soft-iron core. Sometimes shortened to **coil.**

induction hardening *n* a process in which the outer surface of a metal component is rapidly heated by means of induced eddy currents. After rapid cooling the resulting phase transformations produce a hard wear-resistant skin.

induction heating *n* the heating of a conducting material as a result of the electric currents induced in it by an externally applied alternating magnetic field.

induction loop system *n* a system enabling partially deaf people to hear dialogue and sound in theatres, cinemas, etc., consisting of a loop of wire placed round the perimeter of a designated area. This emits an electromagnetic signal which is picked up by a hearing aid. Often shortened to **induction loop.**

induction motor *n* a type of brushless electric motor in which an alternating supply fed to the windings of the stator creates a magnetic field that induces a current in the windings of the rotor. Rotation of the rotor results from the interaction of the magnetic field created by the rotor current with the field of the stator.

inductive (ɪnˈdʌktɪv) *adj* **1** relating to, involving, or operated by electrical or magnetic induction: *an inductive reactance.* **2** *Logic, maths.* of, relating to, or using induction: *inductive reasoning.* **3** serving to induce or cause. **4** a rare word for **introductory. 5** *Biology.* producing a reaction within an organism, esp. induction in embryonic tissue. ▸ **inˈductively** *adv* ▸ **inˈductiveness** *n*

inductor (ɪnˈdʌktə) *n* **1** a person or thing that inducts. **2** another name for an **inductance** (sense 2).

indue (ɪnˈdjuː) *vb* **-dues, -duing, -dued.** a variant spelling of **endue.**

indulge (ɪnˈdʌldʒ) *vb* **1** (when *intr,* often foll. by *in*) to yield to or gratify (a whim or desire for): *to indulge a desire for new clothes; to indulge in new clothes.* **2** (*tr*) to yield to the wishes of; pamper: *to indulge a child.* **3** (*tr*) to allow oneself the pleasure of something: *at Christmas he liked to indulge himself.* **4** (*tr*) *Commerce.* to allow (a debtor) an extension of time for payment of (a bill, etc.). **5** (*intr*) *Informal.* to take alcoholic drink, esp. to excess. **[C17:** from Latin *indulgēre* to concede, from *-dulgēre,* probably related to Greek *dolikhos* long, Gothic *tulgus* firm**]** ▸ **inˈdulger** *n* ▸ **inˈdulgingly** *adv*

indulgence (ɪnˈdʌldʒəns) *n* **1** the act of indulging or state of being indulgent. **2** a pleasure, habit, etc., indulged in; extravagance: *fur coats are an indulgence.* **3** liberal or tolerant treatment. **4** something granted as a favour or privilege. **5** *R.C. Church.* a remission of the temporal punishment for sin after its guilt has been forgiven. **6** *Commerce.* an extension of time granted as a favour for payment of a debt or as fulfilment of some other obligation. **7** Also called: **Declaration of Indulgence.** a royal grant during the reigns of Charles II and James II of England giving Nonconformists and Roman Catholics a measure of religious freedom. ◆ *vb (tr)* **8** *R.C. Church.* to designate as providing indulgence: *indulgenced prayers.*

indulgent (ɪnˈdʌldʒənt) *adj* showing or characterized by indulgence. ▸ **inˈdulgently** *adv*

induline (ˈɪndjʊˌlaɪn) *or* **indulin** (ˈɪndjʊlɪn) *n* any of a class of blue dyes obtained from aniline and aminoazobenzene. **[C19:** from INDIGO + -ULE + -INE[2]**]**

indult (ɪnˈdʌlt) *n R.C. Church.* a faculty granted by the Holy See allowing a specific deviation from the Church's common law. **[C16:** from Church Latin *indultum* a privilege, from Latin *indulgēre* to INDULGE**]**

indumentum (ɪndjuˈmɛntəm) *n, pl* **-ta** *or* **-tums.** *Biology.* an outer covering, such as hairs or down on a plant or leaf, feathers, fur, etc. **[C19:** Latin, literally: garment**]**

induna (ɪnˈduːnə) *n* (in South Africa) a Black African overseer in a factory, mine, etc. **[C20:** from Zulu *nduna* an official**]**

induplicate (ɪnˈdjuːplɪkɪt, -ˌkeɪt) *or* **induplicated** *adj* (of the parts of a bud) bent or folded inwards with the edges touching but not overlapping. ▸ **inˌdupliˈcation** *n*

indurate *Rare.* ◆ *vb* (ˈɪndjʊˌreɪt). **1** to make or become hard or callous. **2** to make or become hardy. ◆ *adj* (ˈɪndjʊrɪt). **3** hardened, callous, or unfeeling. **[C16:** from Latin *indūrāre* to make hard; see ENDURE**]** ▸ **ˌinduˈration** *n* ▸ **ˈinduˌrative** *adj*

Indus[1] (ˈɪndəs) *n* a faint constellation in the S hemisphere lying between Telescopium and Tucano.

Indus[2] (ˈɪndəs) *n* a river in S Asia, rising in SW Tibet in the Kailas Range of the Himalayas and flowing northwest through Kashmir, then southwest across Pakistan to the Arabian Sea: important throughout history, esp. for the Indus Civilization (about 3000 to 1500 B.C.), and for irrigation. Length: about 2900 km (1800 miles).

indusium (ɪnˈdjuːzɪəm) *n, pl* **-sia** (-zɪə). **1** a membranous outgrowth on the undersurface of fern leaves that covers and protects the developing spores. **2** an enveloping membrane, such as the amnion. **[C18:** New Latin, from Latin: tunic, from *induere* to put on**]** ▸ **inˈdusial** *adj*

industrial (ɪnˈdʌstrɪəl) *adj* **1** of, relating to, derived from, or characteristic of industry. **2** employed in industry: *the industrial workforce.* **3** relating to or concerned with workers in industry: *industrial conditions.* **4** used in industry: *industrial chemicals.* ▸ **inˈdustrially** *adv*

industrial action *n Brit.* any action, such as a strike or go-slow, taken by employees in industry to protest against working conditions, redundancies, etc.

industrial archaeology *n* the study of past industrial machines, works, etc. ▸ **industrial archaeologist** *n*

industrial democracy *n* control of an organization by the people who work for it, esp. by workers holding positions on its board of directors.

industrial design *n* the art or practice of designing any object for manufacture. ▸ **industrial designer** *n*

industrial development certificate *n* (in Britain) a certificate issued by the Department of the Environment to an industrial organization wishing to build or extend a factory, which has to accompany an application for planning permission. Abbrev.: **IDC.**

industrial diamond *n* a small often synthetic diamond, valueless as a gemstone, used in cutting tools, abrasives, etc.

industrial disease *n* any disease to which workers in a particular industry are prone.

industrial espionage *n* attempting to obtain trade secrets by dishonest means, as by telephone- or computer-tapping, infiltration of a competitor's workforce, etc.

industrial estate *n Brit.* another name for **trading estate.** U.S. equivalent: **industrial park.**
industrialism (ɪn'dʌstrɪə,lɪzəm) *n* an organization of society characterized by large-scale mechanized manufacturing industry rather than trade, farming, etc.
industrialist (ɪn'dʌstrɪəlɪst) *n* a person who has a substantial interest in the ownership or control of industrial enterprise.
industrialize *or* **industrialise** (ɪn'dʌstrɪə,laɪz) *vb* **1** (*tr*) to develop industry on an extensive scale in (a country, region, etc.). **2** (*intr*) (of a country, region, etc.) to undergo the development of industry on an extensive scale. ► **in,dustriali'zation** *or* **in,dustriali'sation** *n*
industrial medicine *n* the study and practice of the health care of employees of large organizations, including measures to prevent accidents, industrial diseases, and stress in the workforce and to monitor the health of executives.
industrial melanism *n* See **melanism** (sense 1).
industrial misconduct *n* behaviour by an employee which is considered to be negligent or irregular to such an extent that disciplinary action may be taken, usually by agreement between management and the employee's representatives.
industrial psychology *n* the scientific study of human behaviour and cognitive processes in relation to the working environment.
industrial relations *n* **1** (*functioning as pl*) those aspects of collective relations between management and workers' representatives which are normally covered by collective bargaining. **2** (*functioning as sing*) the management of relations between the employers or managers of an enterprise and their employees.
Industrial Revolution *n* **the.** the transformation in the 18th and 19th centuries of first Britain and then other W European countries and the U.S. into industrial nations.
industrials (ɪn'dʌstrɪəlz) *pl n* stocks, shares, and bonds of industrial enterprises.
industrial-strength *adj Chiefly humorous.* extremely strong or powerful: *industrial-strength tea.*
industrial tribunal *n* (in Northern Ireland and formerly elsewhere in the UK) a tribunal that rules on disputes between employers and employees regarding unfair dismissal, redundancy, etc.
industrial union *n* a labour organization in which all workers in a given industry are eligible for membership. Compare **craft union.**
Industrial Workers of the World *n* **the.** an international revolutionary federation of industrial unions founded in Chicago in 1905: banned in the U.S. in 1949. Abbrev.: **IWW.** See also **Wobbly.**
industrious (ɪn'dʌstrɪəs) *adj* **1** hard-working, diligent, or assiduous. **2** an obsolete word for **skilful.** ► **in'dustriously** *adv* ► **in'dustriousness** *n*
industry ('ɪndəstrɪ) *n, pl* **-tries. 1** organized economic activity concerned with manufacture, extraction and processing of raw materials, or construction. **2** a branch of commercial enterprise concerned with the output of a specified product or service: *the steel industry.* **3a** industrial ownership and management interests collectively, as contrasted with labour interests. **3b** manufacturing enterprise collectively, as opposed to agriculture. **4** diligence; assiduity. [C15: from Latin *industria* diligence, from *industrius* active, of uncertain origin]
indwell (ɪn'dwel) *vb* **-dwells, -dwelling, -dwelt. 1** (*tr*) (of a spirit, principle, etc.) to inhabit; suffuse. **2** (*intr*) to dwell; exist. ► **in'dweller** *n*
Indy, d' (*French* dɛ̃di) *n* **Vincent** (vɛ̃sɔ̃). See (Vincent) **d'Indy.**
Indy Car racing ('ɪndɪ) *n* a U.S. form of professional motor racing around banked oval tracks. [C20: named after the *Indianapolis 500* motor race]
Ine ('ɪnə, 'ɪnɪ) *n* died after 726, king of Wessex (688–726).
-ine[1] *suffix forming adjectives.* **1** of, relating to, or belonging to: *saturnine.* **2** consisting of or resembling: *crystalline.* [from Latin *-īnus,* from Greek *-inos*]
-ine[2] *suffix forming nouns.* **1** indicating a halogen: *chlorine.* **2** indicating a nitrogenous organic compound, including amino acids, alkaloids, and certain other bases: *alanine; nicotine; purine.* **3** Also: **-in.** indicating a chemical substance in certain nonsystematic names: *glycerine.* **4** indicating a mixture of hydrocarbons: *benzine.* **5** an obsolete equivalent of **-yne.** [via French from Latin *-ina* (from *-inus*) and Greek *-inē*]
inearth (ɪn'ɜːθ) *vb* (*tr*) a poetic word for **bury.**
inebriant (ɪn'iːbrɪənt) *adj* **1** causing intoxication, esp. drunkenness. ◆ *n* **2** something that inebriates.
inebriate *vb* (ɪn'iːbrɪ,eɪt). (*tr*) **1** to make drunk; intoxicate. **2** to arouse emotionally; make excited. ◆ *n* (ɪn'iːbrɪɪt). **3** a person who is drunk, esp. habitually. ◆ *adj* (ɪn'iːbrɪɪt). *also* **inebriated. 4** drunk, esp. habitually. [C15: from Latin *inēbriāre,* from IN-[2] + *ēbriāre* to intoxicate, from *ēbrius* drunk] ► **in,ebri'ation** *n* ► **inebriety** (,ɪnɪ'braɪɪtɪ) *n*
inedible (ɪn'ɛdɪbᵊl) *adj* not fit to be eaten; uneatable. ► **in,edi'bility** *n*
inedited (ɪn'ɛdɪtɪd) *adj* **1** not edited. **2** not published.
ineducable (ɪn'ɛdjukəbᵊl) *adj* incapable of being educated, esp. on account of mental retardation. ► **in,educa'bility** *n*
ineffable (ɪn'ɛfəbᵊl) *adj* **1** too great or intense to be expressed in words; unutterable. **2** too sacred to be uttered. **3** indescribable; indefinable. [C15: from Latin *ineffābilis* unutterable, from IN-[1] + *effābilis,* from *effārī* to utter, from *fārī* to speak] ► **in,effa'bility** *or* **in'effableness** *n* ► **in'effably** *adv*
ineffaceable (,ɪnɪ'feɪsəbᵊl) *adj* incapable of being effaced; indelible. ► **,inef,facea'bility** *n* ► **,inef'faceably** *adv*
ineffective (,ɪnɪ'fɛktɪv) *adj* **1** having no effect. **2** incompetent or inefficient. ► **,inef'fectively** *adv* ► **,inef'fectiveness** *n*
ineffectual (,ɪnɪ'fɛktʃuəl) *adj* **1** having no effect or an inadequate effect. **2** lacking in power or forcefulness; impotent: *an ineffectual ruler.* ► **,inef,fectu'ality** *or* **,inef'fectualness** *n* ► **,inef'fectually** *adv*
inefficacious (,ɪnɛfɪ'keɪʃəs) *adj* failing to produce the desired effect. ► **,ineffi'caciously** *adv* ► **inefficacy** (ɪn'ɛfɪkəsɪ), **,ineffi'caciousness,** *or* **inefficacity** (,ɪnɛfɪ'kæsɪtɪ) *n*
inefficient (,ɪnɪ'fɪʃənt) *adj* **1** unable to perform a task or function to the best advantage; wasteful or incompetent. **2** unable to produce the desired result. ► **,inef'ficiency** *n* ► **,inef'ficiently** *adv*
inelastic (,ɪnɪ'læstɪk) *adj* **1** not elastic; not resilient. **2** *Physics.* (of collisions) involving an overall decrease in translational kinetic energy. ► **ine'lastically** *adv* ► **inelasticity** (,ɪnɪlæs'tɪsɪtɪ) *n*
inelegant (ɪn'ɛlɪgənt) *adj* **1** lacking in elegance or refinement; unpolished or graceless. **2** coarse or crude. ► **in'elegance** *or* **in'elegancy** *n* ► **in'elegantly** *adv*
ineligible (ɪn'ɛlɪdʒəbᵊl) *adj* **1** (often foll. by *for* or an infinitive) not fit or qualified: *ineligible for a grant; ineligible to vote.* ◆ *n* **2** an ineligible person. ► **in,eligi'bility** *or* **in'eligibleness** *n* ► **in'eligibly** *adv*
ineloquent (ɪn'ɛləkwənt) *adj* lacking eloquence or fluency of expression. ► **in'eloquence** *n* ► **in'eloquently** *adv*
ineluctable (,ɪnɪ'lʌktəbᵊl) *adj* (esp. of fate) incapable of being avoided; inescapable. [C17: from Latin *inēluctābilis,* from IN-[1] + *ēluctārī* to escape, from *luctārī* to struggle] ► **,ine,lucta'bility** *n* ► **,ine'luctably** *adv*
ineludible (,ɪnɪ'luːdəbᵊl) *adj* a rare word for **inescapable.** ► **,ine,ludi'bility** *n* ► **,ine'ludibly** *adv*
inept (ɪn'ɛpt) *adj* **1** awkward, clumsy, or incompetent. **2** not suitable, appropriate, or fitting; out of place. [C17: from Latin *ineptus,* from IN-[1] + *aptus* fitting, suitable] ► **in'epti,tude** *n* ► **in'eptly** *adv* ► **in'eptness** *n*
inequable (ɪn'ɛkwəbᵊl) *adj* uneven; not uniform.
inequality (,ɪnɪ'kwɒlɪtɪ) *n, pl* **-ties. 1** the state or quality of being unequal; disparity. **2** an instance of disparity. **3** lack of smoothness or regularity. **4** social or economic disparity. **5** *Maths.* **5a** a statement indicating that the value of one quantity or expression is not equal to another, as in $x \neq y$: x may be greater than y, denoted by $x > y$, or less than y, denoted by $x < y$. **5b** the relation of being unequal. **6** *Astronomy.* a departure from uniform orbital motion.
inequitable (ɪn'ɛkwɪtəbᵊl) *adj* not equitable; unjust or unfair. ► **in'equitableness** *n* ► **in'equitably** *adv*
inequity (ɪn'ɛkwɪtɪ) *n, pl* **-ties. 1** lack of equity; injustice; unfairness. **2** an unjust or unfair act, sentence, etc.
ineradicable (,ɪnɪ'rædɪkəbᵊl) *adj* not able to be removed or rooted out; inextirpable: *an ineradicable disease.* ► **,ine'radicableness** *n* ► **,ine'radicably** *adv*
inerrable (ɪn'ɛrəbᵊl) *or* **inerrant** (ɪn'ɛrənt) *adj* less common words for **infallible.** ► **in,erra'bility, in'errableness,** *or* **in'errancy** *n* ► **in'errably** *adv*
inert (ɪn'ɜːt) *adj* **1** having no inherent ability to move or to resist motion. **2** inactive, lazy, or sluggish. **3** having only a limited ability to react chemically; unreactive. [C17: from Latin *iners* unskilled, from IN-[1] + *ars* skill; see ART[1]] ► **in'ertly** *adv* ► **in'ertness** *n*
inert gas *n* **1** Also called: **noble gas, rare gas, argonon.** any of the unreactive gaseous elements helium, neon, argon, krypton, xenon, and radon. **2** (loosely) any gas, such as carbon dioxide, that is nonoxidizing.
inertia (ɪn'ɜːʃə, -ʃɪə) *n* **1** the state of being inert; disinclination to move or act. **2** *Physics.* **2a** the tendency of a body to preserve its state of rest or uniform motion unless acted upon by an external force. **2b** an analogous property of other physical quantities that resist change: *thermal inertia.* ► **in'ertial** *adj*
inertia force *n* an imaginary force supposed to act upon an accelerated body, equal in magnitude and opposite in direction to the resultant of the real forces. It is used in the theory of dynamics originated by d'Alembert.
inertial force *n* an imaginary force which an accelerated observer postulates so that he can use the equations appropriate to an inertial observer. See also **Coriolis force.**
inertial fusion *n Physics.* a type of nuclear fusion induced by impact, as by pulses of laser radiation or high-energy charged particles, rather than by high temperature.
inertial guidance *or* **navigation** *n* a method of controlling the flight path of a missile by instruments contained within it. Velocities or distances covered, computed from the acceleration measured by these instruments, are compared with stored data and used to control the speed and direction of the missile. Compare **celestial guidance, terrestrial guidance.**
inertial mass *n* the mass of a body as determined by its momentum, as opposed to gravitational mass. The acceleration of a falling body is inversely proportional to its inertial mass but directly proportional to its gravitational mass: as all falling bodies have the same constant acceleration the two types of mass must be equal.
inertial observer *n* a hypothetical observer who is not accelerated with respect to an inertial system. Newton's laws of motion and the special theory of relativity apply to the measurements which would be made by such observers.
inertial system *n* a frame of reference within which bodies are not accelerated unless acted upon by external forces. Also called: **inertial reference frame.**
inertia-reel seat belt *n* a type of car seat belt in which the belt is free to unwind from a metal drum except when the drum locks as a result of rapid deceleration.
inertia selling *n* (in Britain) the illegal practice of sending unrequested goods to householders followed by a bill for the price of the goods if they do not return them.
inescapable (,ɪnɪ'skeɪpəbᵊl) *adj* incapable of being escaped or avoided. ► **,ines'capably** *adv*
inescutcheon (,ɪnɪ'skʌtʃən) *n Heraldry.* a small shield-shaped charge in the centre of a shield.
in esse (ɪn 'ɛsɪ) *adj* actually existing. Compare **in posse.** [Latin, literally: in being]

inessential (ˌɪnɪ'sɛnʃəl) *adj* 1 not necessary. ◆ *n* 2 anything that is not essential. ▸ **ˌinesˌsenti'ality** *n*

inessive (ɪn'ɛsɪv) *adj* 1 (in the grammar of Finnish and related languages) denoting a case of nouns, etc., used when indicating the location of the referent. ◆ *n* 2 the inessive case. [C20: from Latin *inesse* to be in]

inestimable (ɪn'ɛstɪməbᵊl) *adj* 1 not able to be estimated; immeasurable. 2 of immeasurable value. ▸ **inˌestima'bility** *or* **in'estimableness** *n* ▸ **in'estimably** *adv*

inevitable (ɪn'ɛvɪtəbᵊl) *adj* 1 unavoidable. 2 sure to happen; certain. ◆ *n* 3 (often preceded by *the*) something that is unavoidable. [C15: from Latin *inēvītābilis,* from IN-[1] + *ēvītābilis,* from *ēvītāre* to shun, from *vītāre* to avoid] ▸ **inˌevita'bility** *or* **in'evitableness** *n* ▸ **in'evitably** *adv*

inexact (ˌɪnɪg'zækt) *adj* not exact or accurate. ▸ **ˌinex'actiˌtude** *or* **ˌinex'actness** *n* ▸ **ˌinex'actly** *adv*

inexcusable (ˌɪnɪk'skjuːzəbᵊl) *adj* not able to be excused or justified. ▸ **ˌinexˌcusa'bility** *or* **ˌinex'cusableness** *n* ▸ **ˌinex'cusably** *adv*

inexhaustible (ˌɪnɪg'zɔːstəbᵊl) *adj* 1 incapable of being used up; endless: *inexhaustible patience.* 2 incapable or apparently incapable of becoming tired; tireless. ▸ **ˌinexˌhausti'bility** *or* **ˌinex'haustibleness** *n* ▸ **ˌinex'haustibly** *adv*

inexistent (ˌɪnɪg'zɪstənt) *adj* a rare word for **nonexistent.** ▸ **ˌinex'istence** *or* **ˌinex'istency** *n*

inexorable (ɪn'ɛksərəbᵊl) *adj* 1 not able to be moved by entreaty or persuasion. 2 relentless. [C16: from Latin *inexōrābilis,* from IN-[1] + *exōrābilis,* from *exōrāre* to prevail upon, from *ōrāre* to pray] ▸ **inˌexora'bility** *or* **in'exorableness** *n* ▸ **in'exorably** *adv*

inexpedient (ˌɪnɪk'spiːdɪənt) *adj* not suitable, advisable, or judicious. ▸ **ˌinex'pedience** *or* **ˌinex'pediency** *n* ▸ **ˌinex'pediently** *adv*

inexpensive (ˌɪnɪk'spɛnsɪv) *adj* not expensive; cheap. ▸ **ˌinex'pensively** *adv* ▸ **ˌinex'pensiveness** *n*

inexperience (ˌɪnɪk'spɪərɪəns) *n* lack of experience or of the knowledge and understanding derived from experience. ▸ **ˌinex'perienced** *adj*

inexpert (ɪn'ɛkspɜːt) *adj* not expert; unskilled or unskilful; inept. ▸ **in'expertly** *adv* ▸ **in'expertness** *n*

inexpiable (ɪn'ɛkspɪəbᵊl) *adj* 1 incapable of being expiated; unpardonable. 2 *Archaic.* implacable. ▸ **in'expiableness** *n* ▸ **in'expiably** *adv*

inexplicable (ˌɪnɪk'splɪkəbᵊl, ɪn'ɛksplɪkəbᵊl) *or* **inexplainable** *adj* not capable of explanation; unexplainable. ▸ **ˌinexplica'bility, ˌinex'plicableness** *or* **ˌinexˌplaina'bility, ˌinex'plainableness** *n* ▸ **ˌinex'plicably** *or* **ˌinex'plainably** *adv*

inexplicit (ˌɪnɪk'splɪsɪt) *adj* not explicit, clear, or precise; vague. ▸ **ˌinex'plicitly** *adv* ▸ **ˌinex'plicitness** *n*

inexpressible (ˌɪnɪk'sprɛsəbᵊl) *adj* too great, etc., to be expressed or uttered; indescribable. ▸ **ˌinexˌpressi'bility** *or* **ˌinex'pressibleness** *n* ▸ **ˌinex'pressibly** *adv*

inexpressive (ˌɪnɪk'sprɛsɪv) *adj* 1 lacking in expression: *an inexpressive face.* 2 an archaic word for **inexpressible.** ▸ **ˌinex'pressively** *adv* ▸ **ˌinex'pressiveness** *n*

inexpugnable (ˌɪnɪk'spʌgnəbᵊl) *adj* a rare word for **impregnable**[1]. ▸ **ˌinexˌpugna'bility** *or* **ˌinex'pugnableness** *n* ▸ **ˌinex'pugnably** *adv*

inexpungible (ˌɪnɪks'pʌndʒɪbᵊl) *adj* incapable of being expunged.

inextensible (ˌɪnɪk'stɛnsəbᵊl) *adj* not capable of extension. ▸ **ˌinexˌtensi'bility** *n*

in extenso *Latin.* (ɪn ɪk'stɛnsəʊ) *adv* at full length.

inextinguishable (ˌɪnɪk'stɪŋgwɪʃəbᵊl) *adj* not able to be extinguished, quenched, or put to an end. ▸ **ˌinex'tinguishableness** *n* ▸ **ˌinex'tinguishably** *adv*

inextirpable (ˌɪnɪk'stɜːpəbᵊl) *adj* not able to be extirpated; ineradicable. ▸ **ˌinex'tirpableness** *n*

in extremis *Latin.* (ɪn ɪk'striːmɪs) *adv* 1 in extremity; in dire straits. 2 at the point of death. [literally: in the furthest reaches]

inextricable (ˌɪnɛks'trɪkəbᵊl) *adj* 1 not able to be escaped from: *an inextricable dilemma.* 2 not able to be disentangled, etc.: *an inextricable knot.* 3 extremely involved or intricate. ▸ **ˌinextrica'bility** *or* **ˌinex'tricableness** *n* ▸ **ˌinex'tricably** *adv*

INF *abbrev. for* intermediate-range nuclear forces: land-based missiles and aircraft with a range between 500 and 5000 km.

inf. *abbrev. for:* 1 inferior. 2 infinitive. 3 influence. 4 information. 5 infra. [Latin: below; after; later]

Inf. *or* **inf.** *abbrev. for* infantry.

infallibilism (ɪn'fælɪbᵊˌlɪzəm) *n R.C. Church.* the principle of papal infallibility. ▸ **in'fallibilist** *n*

infallible (ɪn'fæləbᵊl) *adj* 1 not fallible; not liable to error. 2 not liable to failure; certain; sure: *an infallible cure.* 3 completely dependable or trustworthy. ◆ *n* 4 a person or thing that is incapable of error or failure. ▸ **inˌfalli'bility** *or* **in'fallibleness** *n* ▸ **in'fallibly** *adv*

infamize *or* **infamise** ('ɪnfəˌmaɪz) *vb* (*tr*) to make infamous.

infamous ('ɪnfəməs) *adj* 1 having a bad reputation; notorious. 2 causing or deserving a bad reputation; shocking: *infamous conduct.* 3 *Criminal law.* (formerly) 3a (of a person) deprived of certain rights of citizenship on conviction of certain offences. 3b (of a crime or punishment) entailing such deprivation. ▸ **'infamously** *adv* ▸ **'infamousness** *n*

infamy ('ɪnfəmɪ) *n, pl* **-mies.** 1 the state or condition of being infamous. 2 an infamous act or event. [C15: from Latin *infāmis* of evil repute, from IN-[1] + *fāma* FAME]

infancy ('ɪnfənsɪ) *n, pl* **-cies.** 1 the state or period of being an infant; childhood. 2 an early stage of growth or development. 3 infants collectively. 4 the period of life prior to attaining legal majority (reached at 21 under common law, at 18 by statute); minority nonage.

infant ('ɪnfənt) *n* 1 a child at the earliest stage of its life; baby. 2 *Law.* another word for **minor** (sense 10). 3 *Brit.* a young schoolchild, usually under the age of seven. 4 a person who is beginning or inexperienced in an activity. 5 (*modifier*) 5a of or relating to young children or infancy. 5b designed or intended for young children. ◆ *adj* 6 in an early stage of development; nascent: *an infant science or industry.* 7 *Law.* of or relating to the legal status of infancy. [C14: from Latin *infāns,* literally: speechless, from IN-[1] + *fārī* to speak] ▸ **'infantˌhood** *n*

infanta (ɪn'fæntə) *n* (formerly) 1 a daughter of a king of Spain or Portugal. 2 the wife of an infante. [C17: from Spanish or Portuguese, feminine of INFANTE]

infante (ɪn'fæntɪ) *n* (formerly) a son of a king of Spain or Portugal, esp. one not heir to the throne. [C16: from Spanish or Portuguese, literally: INFANT]

infanticide (ɪn'fæntɪˌsaɪd) *n* 1 the killing of an infant. 2 the practice of killing newborn infants, still prevalent in some primitive tribes. 3 a person who kills an infant. ▸ **inˌfanti'cidal** *adj*

infantile ('ɪnfənˌtaɪl) *adj* 1 like a child in action or behaviour; childishly immature; puerile. 2 of, relating to, or characteristic of infants or infancy. 3 in an early stage of development. ▸ **infantility** (ˌɪnfən'tɪlɪtɪ) *n*

infantile paralysis *n* a former name for **poliomyelitis.**

infantilism (ɪn'fæntɪˌlɪzəm) *n* 1 *Psychol.* 1a a condition in which an older child or adult is mentally or physically undeveloped. 1b isolated instances of infantile behaviour in mature persons. 2 childish speech; baby talk.

infant prodigy *n* an exceptionally talented child.

infantry ('ɪnfəntrɪ) *n, pl* **-tries. a.** soldiers or units of soldiers who fight on foot with small arms. **b** (*as modifier*): *an infantry unit.* Abbrevs.: **Inf., inf.** [C16: from Italian *infanteria,* from *infante* boy, foot soldier; see INFANT]

infantryman ('ɪnfəntrɪmən) *n, pl* **-men.** a soldier belonging to the infantry.

infant school *n* (in England and Wales) a school for children aged between 5 and 7. Compare **junior school.**

infarct (ɪn'fɑːkt) *n* a localized area of dead tissue (necrosis) resulting from obstruction of the blood supply to that part, esp. by an embolus. Also called: **infarction.** [C19: via New Latin from Latin *infarctus* stuffed into, from *farcīre* to stuff] ▸ **in'farcted** *adj*

infarction (ɪn'fɑːkʃən) *n* 1 the formation or development of an infarct. 2 another word for **infarct.**

infatuate *vb* (ɪn'fætjʊˌeɪt). (*tr*) 1 to inspire or fill with foolish, shallow, or extravagant passion. 2 to cause to act foolishly. ◆ *adj* (ɪn'fætjʊɪt, -ˌeɪt). 3 an archaic word for **infatuated.** ◆ *n* (ɪn'fætjʊɪt, -ˌeɪt). 4 *Literary.* a person who is infatuated. [C16: from Latin *infatuāre,* from IN-[2] + *fatuus* FATUOUS]

infatuated (ɪn'fætjʊˌeɪtɪd) *adj* (often foll. by *with*) possessed by a foolish or extravagant passion, esp. for another person. ▸ **in'fatuˌatedly** *adv*

infatuation (ɪnˌfætjʊ'eɪʃən) *n* 1 the act of infatuating or state of being infatuated. 2 foolish or extravagant passion. 3 an object of foolish or extravagant passion.

infeasible (ɪn'fiːzəbᵊl) *adj* a less common word for **impracticable.** ▸ **inˌfeasi'bility** *or* **in'feasibleness** *n*

infect (ɪn'fɛkt) *vb* (*mainly tr*) 1 to cause infection in; contaminate (an organism, wound, etc.) with pathogenic microorganisms. 2 (*also intr*) to affect or become affected with a communicable disease. 3 to taint, pollute, or contaminate. 4 to affect, esp. adversely, as if by contagion. 5 *Computing.* to affect or become affected with a computer virus. 6 *Chiefly international law.* to taint with crime or illegality; expose to penalty or subject to forfeiture. ◆ *adj* 7 *Archaic.* contaminated or polluted with or as if with a disease; infected. [C14: from Latin *inficere* to dip into, stain, from *facere* to make] ▸ **in'fector** *or* **in'fecter** *n*

infection (ɪn'fɛkʃən) *n* 1 invasion of the body by pathogenic microorganisms. 2 the resulting condition in the tissues. 3 an infectious disease. 4 the act of infecting or state of being infected. 5 an agent or influence that infects. 6 persuasion or corruption, as by ideas, perverse influences, etc.

infectious (ɪn'fɛkʃəs) *adj* 1 (of a disease) capable of being transmitted. Compare **contagious.** 2 (of a disease) caused by microorganisms, such as bacteria, viruses, or protozoa. 3 causing or transmitting infection. 4 tending or apt to spread, as from one person to another: *infectious mirth.* 5 *International law.* 5a tainting or capable of tainting with illegality. 5b rendering liable to seizure or forfeiture. ▸ **in'fectiously** *adv* ▸ **in'fectiousness** *n*

infectious hepatitis *n* any form of hepatitis caused by viruses. See **hepatitis A, hepatitis B.**

infectious mononucleosis *n* an acute infectious disease, caused by Epstein-Barr virus, characterized by fever, sore throat, swollen and painful lymph nodes, and abnormal lymphocytes in the blood. Also called: **glandular fever.**

infective (ɪn'fɛktɪv) *adj* 1 capable of causing infection. 2 a less common word for **infectious.** ▸ **in'fectively** *adv* ▸ **in'fectiveness** *or* **ˌinfec'tivity** *n*

infecund (ɪn'fiːkənd) *adj* a less common word for **infertile.** ▸ **infecundity** (ˌɪnfɪ'kʌndɪtɪ) *n*

infelicitous (ˌɪnfɪ'lɪsɪtəs) *adj* 1 not felicitous; unfortunate. 2 inappropriate or unsuitable. ▸ **ˌinfe'licitously** *adv*

infelicity (ˌɪnfɪ'lɪsɪtɪ) *n, pl* **-ties.** 1 the state or quality of being unhappy or unfortunate. 2 an instance of bad luck or mischance; misfortune. 3 something, esp. a remark or expression, that is inapt or inappropriate.

infer (ɪn'fɜː) *vb* **-fers, -ferring, -ferred.** (when *tr, may take a clause as object*) 1 to conclude (a state of affairs, supposition, etc.) by reasoning from evidence; deduce. 2 (*tr*) to have or lead to as a necessary or logical consequence; indicate. 3 (*tr*) to hint or imply. [C16: from Latin *inferre* to bring into, from *ferre* to bear, carry] ▸ **in'ferable, in'ferible, in'ferrable,** *or* **in'ferrible** *adj* ▸ **in'ferably** *adv* ▸ **in'ferrer** *n*

USAGE The use of *infer* to mean *imply* is common in both speech and writing, but is regarded by many people as incorrect.

inference ('ɪnfərəns, -frəns) *n* 1 the act or process of inferring. 2 an inferred conclusion, deduction, etc. 3 any process of reasoning from premises to a conclusion. **4** *Logic.* the specific mode of reasoning used. See also **deduction** (sense 4), **induction** (sense 4).

inferencing (ˈɪnfərənsɪŋ) *n Psycholinguistics.* the practice of inferring the meaning of an unfamiliar word or expression from the meaning of familiar words occurring with it in a context together with one's knowledge of or beliefs about the world.

inferential (ˌɪnfəˈrɛnʃəl) *adj* of, relating to, or derived from inference. ▸ **ˌinferˈentially** *adv*

inferential statistics *n (functioning as sing)* another name for **statistical inference.**

inferior (ɪnˈfɪərɪə) *adj* **1** lower in value or quality. **2** lower in rank, position, or status; subordinate. **3** not of the best; mediocre; commonplace. **4** lower in position; situated beneath. **5** (of a plant ovary) enclosed by and fused with the receptacle so that it is situated below the other floral parts. **6** *Astronomy.* **6a** orbiting or occurring between the sun and the earth: *an inferior planet; inferior conjunction.* **6b** lying below the horizon. **7** *Printing.* (of a character) printed at the foot of an ordinary character, as the 2 in H_2O. ◆ *n* **8** an inferior person. **9** *Printing.* an inferior character. [C15: from Latin: lower, from *inferus* low] ▸ **inferiority** (ɪnˌfɪərɪˈɒrɪtɪ) *n* ▸ **inˈferiorly** *adv*

inferior court *n* **1** a court of limited jurisdiction. **2** any court other than the Supreme Court of Judicature.

inferiority complex *n Psychiatry.* a disorder arising from the conflict between the desire to be noticed and the fear of being humiliated, characterized by aggressiveness or withdrawal into oneself.

inferior planet *n* either of the planets Mercury and Venus, whose orbits lie inside that of the earth.

infernal (ɪnˈfɜːnᵊl) *adj* **1** of or relating to an underworld of the dead. **2** deserving hell or befitting its occupants; diabolic; fiendish. **3** *Informal.* irritating; confounded. [C14: from Late Latin *infernālis,* from *infernus* hell, from Latin (adj): lower, hellish; related to Latin *inferus* low] ▸ **ˌinferˈnality** *n* ▸ **inˈfernally** *adv*

infernal machine *n Archaic.* a usually disguised explosive device or booby trap.

inferno (ɪnˈfɜːnəʊ) *n, pl* **-nos. 1** *(sometimes cap.;* usually preceded by *the)* hell; the infernal region. **2** any place or state resembling hell, esp. a conflagration. [C19: from Italian, from Late Latin *infernus* hell]

infertile (ɪnˈfɜːtaɪl) *adj* **1** not capable of producing offspring; sterile. **2** (of land) not productive; barren. ▸ **inˈfertilely** *adv* ▸ **infertility** (ˌɪnfəˈtɪlɪtɪ) *n*

infest (ɪnˈfɛst) *vb (tr)* **1** to inhabit or overrun in dangerously or unpleasantly large numbers. **2** (of parasites such as lice) to invade and live on or in (a host). [C15: from Latin *infestāre* to molest, from *infestus* hostile] ▸ **ˌinfesˈtation** *n* ▸ **inˈfester** *n*

infeudation (ˌɪnfjuˈdeɪʃən) *n* **1** (in feudal society) **1a** the act of putting a vassal in possession of a fief. **1b** the deed conferring such possession. **1c** the consequent relationship of lord and vassal. **2** the granting of tithes to laymen.

infibulate (ɪnˈfɪbjuˌleɪt) *vb (tr) Rare.* to enclose (esp. the genitals, to prevent sexual intercourse) with a clasp. [C17: from Latin *infībulāre,* from IN-[2] + *fibula* clasp, FIBULA] ▸ **inˌfibuˈlation** *n*

infidel (ˈɪnfɪdᵊl) *n* **1** a person who has no religious belief; unbeliever. ◆ *adj* **2** rejecting a specific religion, esp. Christianity or Islam. **3** of, characteristic of, or relating to unbelievers or unbelief. [C15: from Medieval Latin *infidēlis,* from Latin (adj): unfaithful, from IN-[1] + *fidēlis* faithful; see FEAL]

infidelity (ˌɪnfɪˈdɛlɪtɪ) *n, pl* **-ties. 1** lack of faith or constancy, esp. sexual faithfulness. **2** lack of religious faith; disbelief. **3** an act or instance of disloyalty.

infield (ˈɪnˌfiːld) *n* **1** *Cricket.* the area of the field near the pitch. Compare **outfield. 2** *Baseball.* **2a** the area of the playing field enclosed by the base lines and extending beyond them towards the outfield. **2b** the positions of the first baseman, second baseman, shortstop, third baseman, and sometimes the pitcher, collectively. Compare **outfield. 3** *Agriculture.* **3a** the part of a farm nearest to the farm buildings. **3b** land from which crops are regularly taken.

infielder (ˈɪnˌfiːldə) *or* **infieldsman** (ˈɪnfiːldzmən) *n* a player positioned in the infield.

infighting (ˈɪnˌfaɪtɪŋ) *n* **1** *Boxing.* combat at close quarters in which proper blows are inhibited and the fighters try to wear down each other's strength. **2** intense competition, as between members of the same organization, esp. when kept secret from outsiders. ▸ **ˈinˌfighter** *n*

infill (ˈɪnfɪl) *or* **infilling** (ˈɪnfɪlɪŋ) *n* **1** the act of filling or closing gaps, etc., in something, such as a row of buildings. **2** material used to fill a cavity, gap, hole, etc.

infiltrate (ˈɪnfɪlˌtreɪt) *vb* **1** to undergo or cause to undergo the process in which a fluid passes into the pores or interstices of a solid; permeate. **2** *Military.* to pass undetected through (an enemy-held line or position). **3** to gain or cause to gain entrance or access surreptitiously: *they infiltrated the party structure.* ◆ *n* **4** something that infiltrates. **5** *Pathol.* any substance that passes into and accumulates within cells, tissues, or organs. [C18: from IN-[2] + FILTRATE] ▸ **ˌinfilˈtration** *n* ▸ **ˈinfilˌtrative** *adj* ▸ **ˈinfilˌtrator** *n*

infimum (ˈɪnfɪməm) *n, pl* **-ma.** *Maths.* the greatest lower bound.

infin. *abbrev. for* infinitive.

infinite (ˈɪnfɪnɪt) *adj* **1a** having no limits or boundaries in time, space, extent, or magnitude. **1b** *(as n;* preceded by *the): the infinite.* **2** extremely or immeasurably great or numerous: *infinite wealth.* **3** all-embracing, absolute, or total: *God's infinite wisdom.* **4** *Maths.* **4a** having an unlimited or uncountable number of digits, factors, terms, members, etc.: *an infinite series.* **4b** (of a set) able to be put in a one-to-one correspondence with part of itself. **4c** (of an integral) having infinity as one or both limits of integration. Compare **finite** (sense 2). ▸ **ˈinfinitely** *adv* ▸ **ˈinfiniteness** *n*

infinitesimal (ˌɪnfɪnɪˈtɛsɪməl) *adj* **1** infinitely or immeasurably small. **2** *Maths.* of, relating to, or involving a small change in the value of a variable that approaches zero as a limit. ◆ *n* **3** *Maths.* an infinitesimal quantity. ▸ **ˌinfiniˈtesimally** *adv*

infinitesimal calculus *n* another name for **calculus** (sense 1).

infinitive (ɪnˈfɪnɪtɪv) *n Grammar.* a form of the verb not inflected for grammatical categories such as tense and person and used without an overt subject. In English, the infinitive usually consists of the word *to* followed by the verb. ▸ **infinitival** (ˌɪnfɪnɪˈtaɪvᵊl) *adj* ▸ **inˈfinitively** *or* **ˌinfiniˈtivally** *adv*

infinitive marker *n Grammar.* a word or affix occurring with the verb stem in the infinitive, such as *to* in *to make.*

infinitude (ɪnˈfɪnɪˌtjuːd) *n* **1** the state or quality of being infinite. **2** an infinite extent, quantity, degree, etc.

infinity (ɪnˈfɪnɪtɪ) *n, pl* **-ties. 1** the state or quality of being infinite. **2** endless time, space, or quantity. **3** an infinitely or indefinitely great number or amount. **4** *Optics, photog.* a point that is far enough away from a lens, mirror, etc., for the light emitted by it to fall in parallel rays on the surface of the lens, etc. **5** *Physics.* a dimension or quantity of sufficient size to be unaffected by finite variations. **6** *Maths.* **6a** the concept of a value greater than any finite numerical value. **6b** the reciprocal of zero. **7** a distant hypothetical point at which two parallel lines are assumed to meet. ◆ Symbol (for senses 4-7): ∞

infirm (ɪnˈfɜːm) *adj* **1a** weak in health or body, esp. from old age. **1b** *(as collective n;* preceded by *the): the infirm.* **2** lacking moral certainty; indecisive or irresolute. **3** not stable, sound, or secure: *an infirm structure; an infirm claim.* **4** *Law.* (of a law, custom, etc.) lacking legal force; invalid. ▸ **inˈfirmly** *adv* ▸ **inˈfirmness** *n*

infirmary (ɪnˈfɜːmərɪ) *n, pl* **-ries.** a place for the treatment of the sick or injured; dispensary; hospital.

infirmity (ɪnˈfɜːmɪtɪ) *n, pl* **-ties. 1** the state or quality of being infirm. **2** physical weakness or debility; frailty. **3** a moral flaw or failing.

infix *vb* (ɪnˈfɪks, ˈɪnˌfɪks). **1** *(tr)* to fix firmly in. **2** *(tr)* to instil or inculcate. **3** *Grammar.* to insert (an affix) or (of an affix) to be inserted into the middle of a word. ◆ *n* (ˈɪnˌfɪks). **4** *Grammar.* an affix inserted into the middle of a word. ▸ **ˌinfixˈation** *or* **infixion** (ɪnˈfɪkʃən) *n*

infl. *abbrev. for:* **1** influence. **2** influenced.

in flagrante delicto (ɪn fləˈgræntɪ dɪˈlɪktəʊ) *adv Chiefly Law.* while committing the offence; red-handed. Also: **flagrante delicto.** [Latin, literally: with the crime still blazing]

inflame (ɪnˈfleɪm) *vb* **1** to arouse or become aroused to violent emotion. **2** *(tr)* to increase or intensify; aggravate. **3** to produce inflammation in (a tissue, organ, or part) or (of a tissue, etc.) to become inflamed. **4** to set or be set on fire; kindle. **5** *(tr)* to cause to redden. ▸ **inˈflamer** *n* ▸ **inˈflamingly** *adv*

inflammable (ɪnˈflæməbᵊl) *adj* **1** liable to catch fire; flammable. **2** readily aroused to anger or passion. ◆ *n* **3** something that is liable to catch fire. ▸ **inˌflammaˈbility** *or* **inˈflammableness** *n* ▸ **inˈflammably** *adv*

USAGE See at **flammable.**

inflammation (ˌɪnfləˈmeɪʃən) *n* **1** the reaction of living tissue to injury or infection, characterized by heat, redness, swelling, and pain. **2** the act of inflaming or the state of being inflamed.

inflammatory (ɪnˈflæmətərɪ, -trɪ) *adj* **1** characterized by or caused by inflammation. **2** tending to arouse violence, strong emotion, etc. ▸ **inˈflammatorily** *adv*

inflatable (ɪnˈfleɪtəbᵊl) *n* **1** any of various large air-filled objects made of strong plastic or rubber, used for children to play on at fairs, carnivals, etc. ◆ *adj* **2** capable of being inflated.

inflate (ɪnˈfleɪt) *vb* **1** to expand or cause to expand by filling with gas or air. **2** *(tr)* to cause to increase excessively; puff up; swell: *to inflate one's opinion of oneself.* **3** *(tr)* to cause inflation of (prices, money, etc.). **4** *(tr)* to raise in spirits; elate. **5** *(intr)* to undergo economic inflation. [C16: from Latin *inflāre* to blow into, from *flāre* to blow] ▸ **inˈflatedly** *adv* ▸ **inˈflatedness** *n* ▸ **inˈflater** *or* **inˈflator** *n*

inflation (ɪnˈfleɪʃən) *n* **1** the act of inflating or state of being inflated. **2** *Economics.* a progressive increase in the general level of prices brought about by an expansion in demand or the money supply (**demand-pull inflation**) or by autonomous increases in costs (**cost-push inflation**). Compare **deflation. 3** *Informal.* the rate of increase of prices.

inflationary (ɪnˈfleɪʃənərɪ) *adj* of, relating to, causing, or characterized by inflation: *inflationary wage claims.*

inflationary gap *n* the excess of total spending in an economy over the value, at current prices, of the output it can produce.

inflationary spiral *n* the situation in which price and income increases may each induce further rises in the other.

inflationism (ɪnˈfleɪʃəˌnɪzəm) *n* the advocacy or policy of inflation through expansion of the supply of money and credit. ▸ **inˈflationist** *n, adj*

inflect (ɪnˈflɛkt) *vb* **1** *Grammar.* to change (the form of a word) or (of a word) to change in form by inflection. **2** *(tr)* to change (the voice) in tone or pitch; modulate. **3** *(tr)* to cause to deviate from a straight or normal line or course; bend. [C15: from Latin *inflectere* to curve round, alter, from *flectere* to bend] ▸ **inˈflectedness** *n* ▸ **inˈflective** *adj* ▸ **inˈflector** *n*

inflection *or* **inflexion** (ɪnˈflɛkʃən) *n* **1** modulation of the voice. **2** *Grammar.* a change in the form of a word, usually modification or affixation, signalling change in such grammatical functions as tense, voice, mood, person, gender, number, or case. **3** an angle or bend. **4** the act of inflecting or the state of being inflected. **5** *Maths.* a change in curvature from concave to convex or vice versa. See also **point of inflection.** ▸ **inˈflectional** *or* **inˈflexional** *adj* ▸ **inˈflectionally** *or* **inˈflexionally** *adv* ▸ **inˈflectionless** *or* **inˈflexionless** *adj*

inflexed (ɪnˈflɛkst) *adj Biology.* curved or bent inwards and downwards towards the axis: *inflexed leaves.*

inflexible (ɪnˈflɛksəbᵊl) *adj* **1** not flexible; rigid; stiff. **2** obstinate; unyielding. **3**

without variation; unalterable; fixed. [C14: from Latin *inflexībilis;* see INFLECT] ▸ **in,flexi'bility** *or* **in'flexibleness** *n* ▸ **in'flexibly** *adv*

inflict (ɪn'flɪkt) *vb* (*tr*) **1** (often foll. by *on* or *upon*) to impose (something unwelcome, such as pain, oneself, etc.). **2** *Rare.* to cause to suffer; afflict (with). **3** to deal out (blows, lashes, etc.). [C16: from Latin *inflīgere* to strike (something) against, dash against, from *flīgere* to strike] ▸ **in'flictable** *adj* ▸ **in'flicter** *or* **in'flictor** *n* ▸ **in'fliction** *n* ▸ **in'flictive** *adj*

in-flight *adj* provided during flight in an aircraft: *in-flight meals.*

inflorescence (,ɪnflɔː'rɛsəns) *n* **1** the part of a plant that consists of the flower-bearing stalks. **2** the arrangement of the flowers on the stalks. **3** the process of flowering; blossoming. [C16: from New Latin *inflōrēscentia,* from Late Latin *inflōrescere* to blossom, from *flōrescere* to bloom] ▸ **,inflo'rescent** *adj*

inflow ('ɪn,fləʊ) *n* **1** something, such as a liquid or gas, that flows in. **2** the amount or rate of flowing in. **3** Also called: **inflowing.** the act of flowing in; influx.

influence ('ɪnflʊəns) *n* **1** an effect of one person or thing on another. **2** the power of a person or thing to have such an effect. **3** power or sway resulting from ability, wealth, position, etc. **4** a person or thing having influence. **5** *Astrology.* an ethereal fluid or occult power regarded as emanating from the stars and affecting a person's actions, future, etc. **6 under the influence.** *Informal.* drunk. ◆ *vb* (*tr*) **7** to persuade or induce. **8** to have an effect upon (actions, events, etc.); affect. [C14: from Medieval Latin *influentia* emanation of power from the stars, from Latin *influere* to flow into, from *fluere* to flow] ▸ **'influenceable** *adj* ▸ **'influencer** *n*

influent ('ɪnflʊənt) *adj also* **inflowing. 1** flowing in. ◆ *n* **2** something flowing in, esp. a tributary. **3** *Ecology.* an organism that has a major effect on the nature of its community.

influential (,ɪnflʊ'ɛnʃəl) *adj* having or exerting influence. ▸ **,influ'entially** *adv*

influenza (,ɪnflʊ'ɛnzə) *n* a highly contagious and often epidemic viral disease characterized by fever, prostration, muscular aches and pains, and inflammation of the respiratory passages. Also called: **grippe.** Informal name: **flu.** [C18: from Italian, literally: INFLUENCE, hence, incursion, epidemic (first applied to influenza in 1743)] ▸ **,influ'enzal** *adj*

influx ('ɪn,flʌks) *n* **1** the arrival or entry of many people or things. **2** the act of flowing in; inflow. **3** the mouth of a stream or river. [C17: from Late Latin *influxus,* from *influere;* see INFLUENCE]

info ('ɪnfəʊ) *n Informal.* short for **information.**

infold (ɪn'fəʊld) *vb* a variant spelling of **enfold.** ▸ **in'folder** *n* ▸ **in'foldment** *n*

infomercial (,ɪnfə'mɜːʃəl) *n* a short film, usually for television, which advertises a product or service in an informative way. [C20: from INFO + (COM)MERCIAL]

infopreneurial (,ɪnfəʊprə'nɜːrɪəl) *adj* of or relating to the manufacture or sales of electronic office or factory equipment designed to distribute information: *an infopreneurial industry.* [C20: INFO(RMATION) + (ENTRE)PRENEUR + -IAL]

inform[1] (ɪn'fɔːm) *vb* **1** (*tr;* often foll. by *of* or *about*) to give information to; tell. **2** (*tr;* often foll. by *of* or *about*) to make conversant (with). **3** (*intr;* often foll. by *against* or *on*) to give information regarding criminals, as to the police, etc. **4** to give form to. **5** to impart some essential or formative characteristic to. **6** (*tr*) to animate or inspire. **7** (*tr*) *Obsolete.* **7a** to train or educate. **7b** to report. [C14: from Latin *informāre* to give form to, describe, from *formāre* to FORM] ▸ **in'formable** *adj* ▸ **informedly** (ɪn'fɔːmɪdlɪ) *adv* ▸ **in'formingly** *adv*

inform[2] (ɪn'fɔːm) *adj Archaic.* without shape; unformed. [C16: from Latin *informis* from IN-[1] + *forma* shape]

informal (ɪn'fɔːməl) *adj* **1** not of a formal, official, or stiffly conventional nature: *an informal luncheon.* **2** appropriate to everyday life or use: *informal clothes.* **3** denoting or characterized by idiom, vocabulary, etc., appropriate to everyday conversational language rather than to formal written language. **4** denoting a second-person pronoun in some languages used when the addressee is regarded as a friend or social inferior: *In French the pronoun "tu" is informal, while "vous" is formal.* ▸ **in'formally** *adv*

informality (,ɪnfɔː'mælɪtɪ) *n, pl* **-ties. 1** the condition or quality of being informal. **2** an informal act.

informal settlement *n S. African euphemistic.* a squatter camp.

informal vote *n Austral. and N.Z.* an invalid vote or ballot.

informant (ɪn'fɔːmənt) *n* a person who gives information about a thing, a subject being studied, etc.

informatics (,ɪnfə'mætɪks) *n* (*functioning as sing*) another term for **information science.**

information (,ɪnfə'meɪʃən) *n* **1** knowledge acquired through experience or study. **2** knowledge of specific and timely events or situations; news. **3** the act of informing or the condition of being informed. **4a** an office, agency, etc., providing information. **4b** (*as modifier*)*: information service.* **5a** a charge or complaint made before justices of the peace, usually on oath, to institute summary criminal proceedings. **5b** a complaint filed on behalf of the Crown, usually by the attorney general. **6** *Computing.* **6a** the meaning given to data by the way in which it is interpreted. **6b** another word for **data** (sense 2). ▸ **,infor'mational** *adj*

information processing *n Computing.* the combined processing of numerical data, graphics, text, etc.

information question *n* another term for **WH question.**

information retrieval *n Computing.* the process of recovering specific information from stored data.

information science *n* the science of the collection, evaluation, organization, and dissemination of information, often employing computers.

information superhighway *n* **1** the concept of a worldwide network of computers capable of transferring all types of digital information at high speed. **2** another name for the **Internet.** ◆ *Also called:* **information highway.**

information technology *n* the technology of the production, storage, and communication of information using computers and microelectronics. Abbrev.: **IT.**

information theory *n* a collection of mathematical theories, based on statistics, concerned with methods of coding, transmitting, storing, retrieving, and decoding information.

informative (ɪn'fɔːmətɪv) *or* **informatory** *adj* providing information; instructive. ▸ **in'formatively** *adv* ▸ **in'formativeness** *n*

informed (ɪn'fɔːmd) *adj* **1** having much knowledge or education; learned or cultured. **2** based on information: *an informed judgment.*

informer (ɪn'fɔːmə) *n* **1** a person who informs against someone, esp. a criminal. **2** a person who provides information: *he was the President's financial informer.*

infotainment (,ɪnfəʊ'teɪnmənt) *n* (in television) the practice of presenting serious or instructive subjects in a style designed primarily to be entertaining. [C20: from INFO + (ENTER)TAINMENT]

infra *Latin.* ('ɪnfrə) *adv* (esp. in textual annotation) below; further on.

infra- *prefix* below; beneath; after: *infrasonic; infralapsarian.* [from Latin *infrā*]

infracostal (,ɪnfrə'kɒstᵊl) *adj Anatomy.* situated beneath the ribs.

infract (ɪn'frækt) *vb* (*tr*) to violate or break (a law, an agreement, etc.). [C18: from Latin *infractus* broken off, from *infringere;* see INFRINGE] ▸ **in'fraction** *n* ▸ **in'fractor** *n*

infra dig ('ɪnfrə 'dɪg) *adj* (*postpositive*) *Informal.* beneath one's dignity. [C19: from Latin phrase *infrā dignitātem*]

infralapsarian (,ɪnfrəlæp'sɛərɪən) *n Christian theol., chiefly Calvinist.* a person who believes that foreknowledge of the Fall preceded God's decree of who was predestined to salvation and who was not. Compare **supralapsarian.** [C18: from INFRA- + *lapsarian* (see SUPRALAPSARIAN)] ▸ **,infralap'sarianism** *n*

infrangible (ɪn'frændʒɪbᵊl) *adj* **1** incapable of being broken. **2** not capable of being violated or infringed. [C16: from Late Latin *infrangibilis,* from Latin IN-[1] + *frangere* to break] ▸ **in,frangi'bility** *or* **in'frangibleness** *n* ▸ **in'frangibly** *adv*

infrared (,ɪnfrə'rɛd) *n* **1** the part of the electromagnetic spectrum with a longer wavelength than light but a shorter wavelength than radio waves; radiation with wavelength between 0.8 micrometres and 1 millimetre. ◆ *adj* **2** of, relating to, using, or consisting of radiation lying within the infrared: *infrared radiation.*

infrared astronomy *n* the study of radiations from space in the infrared region of the electromagnetic spectrum.

infrared photography *n* photography using film with an emulsion that is sensitive to infrared light, enabling it to be used in misty weather, in darkened interiors, or at night. It has applications in aerial surveys, the detection of forgeries, etc.

infrasound ('ɪnfrə,saʊnd) *n* soundlike waves having a frequency below the audible range, that is, below about 16Hz. ▸ **infrasonic** (,ɪnfrə'sɒnɪk) *adj*

infraspecific (,ɪnfrəspə'sɪfɪk) *adj Biology.* occurring within or affecting all members of a species: *infraspecific variation.*

infrastructure ('ɪnfrə,strʌktʃə) *n* **1** the basic structure of an organization, system, etc. **2** the stock of fixed capital equipment in a country, including factories, roads, schools, etc., considered as a determinant of economic growth.

infrequent (ɪn'friːkwənt) *adj* rarely happening or present; only occasional. ▸ **in'frequency** *or* **in'frequence** *n* ▸ **in'frequently** *adv*

infringe (ɪn'frɪndʒ) *vb* **1** (*tr*) to violate or break (a law, an agreement, etc.). **2** (*intr;* foll. by *on* or *upon*) to encroach or trespass. [C16: from Latin *infringere* to break off, from *frangere* to break] ▸ **in'fringement** *n* ▸ **in'fringer** *n*

infulae ('ɪnfjʊliː) *pl n, sing* **-la** (-lə). the two ribbons hanging from the back of a bishop's mitre. [C17: from Latin, plural of *infula,* woollen fillet worn on forehead by ancient Romans during religious rites]

infundibular (,ɪnfʌn'dɪbjʊlə) *adj* funnel-shaped. [C18: from INFUNDIBULUM]

infundibuliform (,ɪnfʌn'dɪbjʊlɪ,fɔːm) *adj* (of plant parts) shaped like a funnel.

infundibulum (,ɪnfʌn'dɪbjʊləm) *n, pl* **-la** (-lə). *Anatomy.* any funnel-shaped part, esp. the stalk connecting the pituitary gland to the base of the brain. [C18: from Latin: funnel, from *infundere* to INFUSE] ▸ **,infun'dibulate** *adj*

infuriate *vb* (ɪn'fjʊərɪ,eɪt). **1** (*tr*) to anger; annoy. ◆ *adj* (ɪn'fjʊərɪɪt). **2** *Archaic.* furious; infuriated. [C17: from Medieval Latin *infuriāre* (vb); see IN-[2], FURY] ▸ **in'furiately** *adv* ▸ **in'furi,ating** *adj* ▸ **in'furiatingly** *adv* ▸ **in,furi'ation** *n*

infuscate (ɪn'fʌskeɪt) *or* **infuscated** *adj* (esp. of the wings of an insect) tinged with brown. [C17: from Latin *infuscāre* to darken, from *fuscus* dark]

infuse (ɪn'fjuːz) *vb* **1** (*tr;* often foll. by *into*) to instil or inculcate. **2** (*tr;* foll. by *with*) to inspire; emotionally charge. **3** to soak or be soaked in order to extract flavour or other properties. **4** *Rare.* (foll. by *into*) to pour. [C15: from Latin *infundere* to pour into] ▸ **in'fuser** *n*

infuser (ɪn'fjuːzə) *n* any device used to make an infusion, esp. a tea maker.

infusible[1] (ɪn'fjuːzəbᵊl) *adj* not fusible; not easily melted; having a high melting point. [C16: from IN-[1] + FUSIBLE] ▸ **in,fusi'bility** *or* **in'fusibleness** *n*

infusible[2] (ɪn'fjuːzəbᵊl) *adj* capable of being infused. [C17: from INFUSE + -IBLE] ▸ **in,fusi'bility** *or* **in'fusibleness** *n*

infusion (ɪn'fjuːʒən) *n* **1** the act of infusing. **2** something infused. **3** an extract obtained by soaking. **4** *Med.* introduction of a liquid, such as a saline solution, into a vein. ▸ **infusive** (ɪn'fjuːsɪv) *adj*

infusionism (ɪn'fjuːʒə,nɪzəm) *n Christian theol.* the doctrine that at the birth of each individual a pre-existing soul is implanted in his body, to remain there for the duration of his earthly life. ▸ **in'fusionist** *n, adj*

infusorial earth (ˌɪnfjuˈzɔːrɪəl) *n* another name for **diatomaceous earth**. See **diatomite**.

infusorian (ˌɪnfjuˈzɔːrɪən) *n Obsolete*. **1** any of the microscopic organisms, such as protozoans and rotifers, found in infusions of organic material. **2** any member of the subclass *Ciliata* (see **ciliate** (sense 3)). ◆ *adj* **3** of or relating to infusorians. **[C18:** from New Latin *Infusoria* former class name; see INFUSE] ▸ ˌ**infuˈsorial** *adj*

-ing[1] *suffix forming nouns*. **1** (*from verbs*) the action of, process of, result of, or something connected with the verb: *coming; meeting; a wedding; winnings*. **2** (*from other nouns*) something used in, consisting of, involving, etc.: *tubing; soldiering*. **3** (*from other parts of speech*): *an outing*. [Old English *-ing, -ung*]

-ing[2] *suffix*. **1** forming the present participle of verbs: *walking; believing*. **2** forming participial adjectives: *a growing boy; a sinking ship*. **3** forming adjectives not derived from verbs: *swashbuckling*. [Middle English *-ing, -inde*, from Old English *-ende*]

-ing[3] *suffix forming nouns*. a person or thing having a certain quality or being of a certain kind: *sweeting; whiting*. [Old English *-ing*; related to Old Norse *-ingr*]

ingather (ɪnˈgæðə) *vb* (*tr*) to gather together or in (a harvest). ▸ **inˈgatherer** *n*

Inge (ɪŋ) *n* **William Ralph**, known as *the Gloomy Dean*. 1860–1954, English theologian, noted for his pessimism; dean of St Paul's Cathedral (1911–34).

ingeminate (ɪnˈdʒɛmɪˌneɪt) *vb* (*tr*) *Rare*. to repeat; reiterate. **[C16:** from Latin *ingemināre* to redouble, from IN-[2] + *gemināre* to GEMINATE] ▸ **inˌgemiˈnation** *n*

ingenerate[1] (ɪnˈdʒɛnərɪt) *adj Rare*. inherent, intrinsic, or innate. **[C17:** from Late Latin *ingenerātus* not generated; see IN-[1], GENERATE]

ingenerate[2] (ɪnˈdʒɛnəˌreɪt) *vb* (*tr*) *Archaic*. to produce within; engender. **[C16:** from Latin *ingenerāre*; see IN-[2], GENERATE] ▸ **inˌgenerˈation** *n*

Ingenhousz (ˈɪŋgənˌhaʊs) *n* **Jan** (jɑn). 1730–99, Dutch plant physiologist and physician, who discovered photosynthesis.

ingenious (ɪnˈdʒiːnjəs, -nɪəs) *adj* **1** possessing or done with ingenuity; skilful or clever. **2** *Obsolete*. having great intelligence; displaying genius. **[C15:** from Latin *ingeniōsus*, from *ingenium* natural ability; see ENGINE] ▸ **inˈgeniously** *adv* ▸ **inˈgeniousness** *n*

ingénue (ˌænʒeɪˈnjuː; *French* ɛ̃ʒeny) *n* an artless, innocent, or inexperienced girl or young woman. **[C19:** from French, feminine of *ingénu* INGENUOUS]

ingenuity (ˌɪndʒɪˈnjuːɪtɪ) *n, pl* **-ties**. **1** inventive talent; cleverness. **2** an ingenious device, act, etc. **3** *Archaic*. frankness; candour. **[C16:** from Latin *ingenuitās* a freeborn condition, outlook consistent with such a condition, from *ingenuus* native, freeborn (see INGENUOUS); meaning influenced by INGENIOUS]

ingenuous (ɪnˈdʒɛnjʊəs) *adj* **1** naive, artless, or innocent. **2** candid; frank; straightforward. **[C16:** from Latin *ingenuus* freeborn, worthy of a freeman, virtuous, from IN-[2] + *-genuus*, from *gignere* to beget] ▸ **inˈgenuously** *adv* ▸ **inˈgenuousness** *n*

ingest (ɪnˈdʒɛst) *vb* (*tr*) **1** to take (food or liquid) into the body. **2** (of a jet engine) to suck in (an object, a bird, etc.). **[C17:** from Latin *ingerere* to put into, from IN-[2] + *gerere* to carry; see GEST] ▸ **inˈgestible** *adj* ▸ **inˈgestion** *n* ▸ **inˈgestive** *adj*

ingesta (ɪnˈdʒɛstə) *pl n* nourishment taken into the body through the mouth.

ingle (ˈɪŋgᵊl) *n Archaic or dialect*. a fire in a room or a fireplace. **[C16:** probably from Scots Gaelic *aingeal* fire]

Ingleborough (ˈɪŋgᵊlbərə, -brə) *n* a mountain in N England, in North Yorkshire: potholes. Height: 723 m (2373 ft.).

inglenook (ˈɪŋgᵊlˌnʊk) *n Brit*. a corner by a fireplace; chimney corner.

inglorious (ɪnˈglɔːrɪəs) *adj* **1** without courage or glory; dishonourable, shameful, or disgraceful. **2** unknown or obscure. ▸ **inˈgloriously** *adv* ▸ **inˈgloriousness** *n*

ingo (ˈɪŋgəʊ) *n Scot*. a reveal. Also **ingoing**.

ingoing (ˈɪnˌgəʊɪŋ) *adj* **1** coming or going in; entering. ◆ *n* **2** (*often pl*) *English law*. the sum paid by a new tenant for fixtures left behind by the outgoing tenant. **3** *Scot*. another word for **ingo**.

Ingolstadt (*German* ˈɪŋɡɔlʃtat) *n* a city in S central Germany, in Bavaria on the River Danube: oil-refining. Pop.: 111 979 (1996 est.).

ingot (ˈɪŋgət) *n* **1** a piece of cast metal obtained from a mould in a form suitable for storage, transporting, and further use. ◆ *vb* **2** (*tr*) to shape (metal) into ingots. **[C14:** perhaps from IN-[2] + Old English *goten*, past participle of *geotan* to pour]

ingot iron *n* a type of steel containing a small amount of carbon and very small quantities of other elements.

ingraft (ɪnˈgrɑːft) *vb* a variant spelling of **engraft**. ▸ **inˈgraftment** *or* ˌ**ingrafˈtation** *n*

ingrain *or* **engrain** *vb* (ɪnˈgreɪn). (*tr*) **1** to impress deeply on the mind or nature; instil. **2** *Archaic*. to dye into the fibre of (a fabric). ◆ *adj* (ˈɪnˌgreɪn). **3** variants of **ingrained**. **4** (of woven or knitted articles, esp. rugs and carpets) made of dyed yarn or of fibre that is dyed before being spun into yarn. ◆ *n* (ˈɪnˌgreɪn). **5a** a carpet made from ingrained yarn. **5b** such yarn. **[C18:** from the phrase *dyed in grain* dyed with kermes through the fibre]

ingrained *or* **engrained** (ɪnˈgreɪnd) *adj* **1** deeply impressed or instilled: *his fears are deeply ingrained*. **2** (*prenominal*) complete or inveterate; utter: *an ingrained fool*. **3** (esp. of dirt) worked into or through the fibre, grain, pores, etc. ▸ **ingrainedly** *or* **engrainedly** (ɪnˈgreɪnɪdlɪ) *adv* ▸ **inˈgrainedness** *or* **enˈgrainedness** *n*

ingrate (ˈɪngreɪt, ɪnˈgreɪt) *Archaic*. ◆ *n* **1** an ungrateful person. ◆ *adj* **2** ungrateful. **[C14:** from Latin *ingrātus* (*adj*), from IN-[1] + *grātus* GRATEFUL] ▸ **ˈingrately** *adv*

ingratiate (ɪnˈgreɪʃɪˌeɪt) *vb* (*tr*; often foll. by *with*) to place (oneself) purposely in the favour (of another). **[C17:** from Latin, from IN-[2] + *grātia* grace, favour] ▸ **inˈgratiˌating** *or* **inˈgratiatory** *adj* ▸ **inˈgratiˌatingly** *adv* ▸ **inˌgratiˈation** *n*

ingratitude (ɪnˈgrætɪˌtjuːd) *n* lack of gratitude; ungratefulness; thanklessness.

ingravescent (ˌɪngrəˈvɛsᵊnt) *adj Rare*. (esp. of a disease) becoming more severe. **[C19:** from Latin *ingravescere* to become heavier, from *gravescere* to grow heavy, from *gravis* heavy] ▸ ˌ**ingraˈvescence** *n*

ingredient (ɪnˈgriːdɪənt) *n* a component of a mixture, compound, etc., esp. in cooking. **[C15:** from Latin *ingrediēns* going into, from *ingredī* to enter; see INGRESS]

Ingres (*French* ɛ̃grə) *n* **Jean Auguste Dominique** (ʒɑ̃ ogyst dɔminik). 1780–1867, French classical painter, noted for his draughtsmanship.

ingress (ˈɪngrɛs) *n* **1** the act of going or coming in; an entering. **2** a way in; entrance. **3** the right or permission to enter. **4** *Astronomy*. another name for **immersion** (sense 2). **[C15:** from Latin *ingressus*, from *ingredī* to go in, from *gradī* to step, go] ▸ **ingression** (ɪnˈgrɛʃən) *n*

ingressive (ɪnˈgrɛsɪv) *adj* **1** of or concerning ingress. **2** (of a speech sound) pronounced with an inhalation rather than exhalation of breath. ◆ *n* **3** an ingressive speech sound, such as a Zulu click. ▸ **inˈgressiveness** *n*

in-group *n Sociol*. a highly cohesive and relatively closed social group characterized by the preferential treatment reserved for its members and the strength of loyalty between them. Compare **out-group**.

ingrowing (ˈɪnˌgrəʊɪŋ) *adj* **1** (esp. of a toenail) growing abnormally into the flesh. **2** growing within or into.

ingrown (ˈɪnˌgrəʊn, ɪnˈgrəʊn) *adj* **1** (esp. of a toenail) grown abnormally into the flesh; covered by adjacent tissues. **2** grown within; native; innate. **3** excessively concerned with oneself, one's own particular group, etc. **4** ingrained.

ingrowth (ˈɪnˌgrəʊθ) *n* **1** the act of growing inwards: *the ingrowth of a toenail*. **2** something that grows inwards.

inguinal (ˈɪŋgwɪnᵊl) *adj Anatomy*. of or relating to the groin. **[C17:** from Latin *inguinālis*, from *inguen* groin]

ingulf (ɪnˈgʌlf) *vb* a variant spelling of **engulf**. ▸ **inˈgulfment** *n*

ingurgitate (ɪnˈgɜːdʒɪˌteɪt) *vb* to swallow (food) with greed or in excess; gorge. **[C16:** from Latin *ingurgitāre* to flood, from IN-[2] + *gurges* abyss] ▸ **inˌgurgiˈtation** *n*

Ingush (ɪŋˈguːʃ) *n, pl* **-gushes** *or* **-gush**. a member of a people of S central Russia, speaking a Circassian language and chiefly inhabiting the Ingush Republic.

Ingush Republic *n* a constituent republic of S Russia: part of the Checheno-Ingush Autonomous Republic from 1936 until 1992. Capital: Nazran. Also called: **Ingushetia** (ɪŋguːˈʃɛtɪə).

inhabit (ɪnˈhæbɪt) *vb* **-its, -iting, -ited**. **1** (*tr*) to live or dwell in; occupy. **2** (*intr*) *Archaic*. to abide or dwell. **[C14:** from Latin *inhabitāre*, from *habitāre* to dwell] ▸ **inˈhabitable** *adj* ▸ **inˌhabitaˈbility** *n* ▸ **inˌhabiˈtation** *n*

inhabitant (ɪnˈhæbɪtənt) *n* a person or animal that is a permanent resident of a particular place or region. ▸ **inˈhabitancy** *or* **inˈhabitance** *n*

inhalant (ɪnˈheɪlənt) *adj* **1** (esp. of a volatile medicinal preparation) inhaled for its soothing or therapeutic effect. **2** inhaling. ◆ *n* **3** an inhalant medicinal preparation.

inhalation (ˌɪnhəˈleɪʃən) *n* **1** the act of inhaling; breathing in of air or other vapours. **2** an inhalant preparation.

inhalator (ˈɪnhəˌleɪtə) *n* a device for issuing a vapour which is breathed in to ease discomfort of or provide medication for the respiratory system.

inhale (ɪnˈheɪl) *vb* to draw (breath) into the lungs; breathe in. **[C18:** from IN-[2] + Latin *halāre* to breathe]

inhaler (ɪnˈheɪlə) *n* **1** a device for breathing in therapeutic vapours, esp. one for relieving nasal congestion. **2** a person who inhales.

Inhambane (ˌɪnjəmˈbɑːnə) *n* a port in SE Mozambique on an inlet of the Mozambique Channel (**Inhambane Bay**). Pop.: 64 274 (1986).

inharmonious (ˌɪnhɑːˈməʊnɪəs) *adj* **1** Also: **inharmonic** (ˌɪnhɑːˈmɒnɪk). lacking harmony; discordant. **2** lacking accord or agreement. ▸ ˌ**inharˈmoniously** *adv* ▸ ˌ**inharˈmoniousness** *n*

inhaul (ˈɪnˌhɔːl) *or* **inhauler** *n Nautical*. a line for hauling in a sail.

inhere (ɪnˈhɪə) *vb* (*intr*; foll. by *in*) to be an inseparable part (of). **[C16:** from Latin *inhaerēre* to stick in, from *haerēre* to stick]

inherence (ɪnˈhɪərəns, -ˈhɛr-) *or* **inherency** *n* **1** the state or condition of being inherent. **2** *Metaphysics*. the relation of attributes, elements, etc., to the subject of which they are predicated, esp. if they are its essential constituents.

inherent (ɪnˈhɪərənt, -ˈhɛr-) *adj* existing as an inseparable part; intrinsic. ▸ **inˈherently** *adv*

inherit (ɪnˈhɛrɪt) *vb* **-its, -iting, -ited**. **1** to receive (property, a right, title, etc.) by succession or under a will. **2** (*intr*) to succeed as heir. **3** (*tr*) to possess (a characteristic) through genetic transmission. **4** (*tr*) to receive (a position, attitude, property, etc.) from a predecessor. **[C14:** from Old French *enheriter*, from Late Latin *inhērēditāre* to appoint an heir, from Latin *hērēs* HEIR] ▸ **inˈherited** *adj* ▸ **inˈheritor** *n* ▸ **inˈheritress** *or* **inˈheritrix** *fem n*

inheritable (ɪnˈhɛrɪtəbᵊl) *adj* **1** capable of being transmitted by heredity from one generation to a later one. **2** capable of being inherited. **3** *Rare*. capable of inheriting; having the right to inherit. ▸ **inˌheritaˈbility** *or* **inˈheritableness** *n* ▸ **inˈheritably** *adv*

inheritance (ɪnˈhɛrɪtəns) *n* **1** *Law*. **1a** hereditary succession to an estate, title, etc. **1b** the right of an heir to succeed to property on the death of an ancestor. **1c** something that may legally be transmitted to an heir. **2** the act of inheriting. **3** something inherited; heritage. **4** the derivation of characteristics of one generation from an earlier one by heredity. **5** *Obsolete*. hereditary rights.

inheritance tax *n* **1** (in Britain) a tax introduced in 1986 to replace capital transfer tax, consisting of a percentage levied on that part of an inheritance exceeding a specified allowance, and scaled charges on gifts made within seven years of death. **2** (in the U.S.) a state tax imposed on an inheritance according to its size and the relationship of the beneficiary to the deceased.

inhesion (ɪn'hiːʒən) *n* a less common word for **inherence** (sense 1). [C17: from Late Latin *inhaesiō*, from *inhaerēre* to INHERE]

inhibit (ɪn'hɪbɪt) *vb* (*tr*) **-its, -iting, -ited. 1** to restrain or hinder (an impulse, a desire, etc.). **2** to prohibit; forbid. **3** to stop, prevent, or decrease the rate of (a chemical reaction). **4** *Electronics.* **4a** to prevent the occurrence of (a particular signal) in a circuit. **4b** to prevent the performance of (a particular operation). [C15: from Latin *inhibēre* to restrain, from IN-[2] + *habēre* to have] ▸ **in'hibitable** *adj* ▸ **in'hibitive** *or* **in'hibitory** *adj*

inhibition (ˌɪnɪ'bɪʃən, ˌɪnhɪ-) *n* **1** the act of inhibiting or the condition of being inhibited. **2** *Psychol.* **2a** a mental state or condition in which the varieties of expression and behaviour of an individual become restricted. **2b** the weakening of a learned response usually as a result of extinction or because of the presence of a distracting stimulus. **2c** (in psychoanalytical theory) the unconscious restraining of an impulse. See also **repression. 3** the process of stopping or retarding a chemical reaction. **4** *Physiol.* the suppression of the function or action of an organ or part, as by stimulation of its nerve supply. **5** *Church of England.* an episcopal order suspending an incumbent.

inhibitor (ɪn'hɪbɪtə) *n* **1** Also called: **inhibiter.** a person or thing that inhibits. **2** Also called: **anticatalyst.** a substance that retards or stops a chemical reaction. Compare **catalyst. 3** *Biochem.* **3a** a substance that inhibits the action of an enzyme. **3b** a substance that inhibits a metabolic or physiological process: *a plant growth inhibitor.* **4** any impurity in a solid that prevents luminescence. **5** an inert substance added to some rocket fuels to inhibit ignition on certain surfaces.

inhomogeneous (ɪnˌhəʊmə'dʒiːnɪəs, -ˌhɒm-) *adj* not homogeneous or uniform. ▸ **inhomogeneity** (ɪnˌhəʊmədʒɪ'niːɪtɪ, -ˌhɒm-) *n*

inhospitable (ɪn'hɒspɪtəb^əl, ˌɪnhɒ'spɪt-) *adj* **1** not hospitable; unfriendly. **2** (of a region, an environment, etc.) lacking a favourable climate, terrain, etc. ▸ **in'hospitableness** *n* ▸ **in'hospitably** *adv*

inhospitality (ˌɪnhɒspɪ'tælɪtɪ, ɪnˌhɒs-) *n* the state or attitude of being inhospitable or unwelcoming.

in-house *adj, adv* within an organization or group: *an in-house job; the job was done in-house.*

inhuman (ɪn'hjuːmən) *adj* **1** Also: **inhumane** (ˌɪnhjuː'meɪn). lacking humane feelings, such as sympathy, understanding, etc.; cruel; brutal. **2** not human. ▸ **ˌinhu'manely** *adv* ▸ **in'humanly** *adv* ▸ **in'humanness** *n*

inhumanity (ˌɪnhjuː'mænɪtɪ) *n, pl* **-ties. 1** lack of humane qualities. **2** an inhumane act, decision, etc.

inhume (ɪn'hjuːm) *vb* (*tr*) to inter; bury. [C17: from Latin *inhumāre*, from IN-[2] + *humus* ground] ▸ **ˌinhu'mation** *n* ▸ **in'humer** *n*

inimical (ɪ'nɪmɪk^əl) *adj* **1** adverse or unfavourable. **2** not friendly; hostile. [C17: from Late Latin *inimīcālis*, from *inimīcus*, from IN-[1] + *amīcus* friendly; see ENEMY] ▸ **in'imically** *adv* ▸ **in'imicalness** *or* **inˌimi'cality** *n*

inimitable (ɪ'nɪmɪtəb^əl) *adj* incapable of being duplicated or imitated; unique. ▸ **inˌimita'bility** *or* **in'imitableness** *n* ▸ **in'imitably** *adv*

inion ('ɪnɪən) *n Anatomy.* the most prominent point at the back of the head, used as a point of measurement in craniometry. [C19: from Greek: back of the head]

iniquity (ɪ'nɪkwɪtɪ) *n, pl* **-ties. 1** lack of justice or righteousness; wickedness; injustice. **2** a wicked act; sin. [C14: from Latin *inīquitās*, from *inīquus* unfair, from IN-[1] + *aequus* even, level; see EQUAL] ▸ **in'iquitous** *adj* ▸ **in'iquitously** *adv* ▸ **in'iquitousness** *n*

init. *abbrev. for:* **1** initial. **2** initio. [Latin: in the beginning]

initial (ɪ'nɪʃəl) *adj* **1** of, at, or concerning the beginning. ◆ *n* **2** the first letter of a word, esp. a person's name. **3** *Printing.* a large sometimes highly decorated letter set at the beginning of a chapter or work. **4** *Botany.* a cell from which tissues and organs develop by division and differentiation; a meristematic cell. ◆ *vb* **-tials, -tialling, -tialled** *or U.S.* **-tials, -tialing, -tialed. 5** (*tr*) to sign with one's initials, esp. to indicate approval; endorse. [C16: from Latin *initiālis* of the beginning, from *initium* beginning, literally: an entering upon, from *inīre* to go in, from IN-[2] + *īre* to go] ▸ **in'itialer** *or* **in'itialler** *n* ▸ **in'itially** *adv*

initialize *or* **initialise** (ɪ'nɪʃəˌlaɪz) *vb* (*tr*) to assign an initial value to (a variable or storage location) in a computer program. ▸ **inˌitiali'zation** *or* **inˌitiali'sation** *n*

initiate *vb* (ɪ'nɪʃɪˌeɪt). (*tr*) **1** to begin or originate. **2** to accept (new members) into an organization such as a club, through often secret ceremonies. **3** to teach fundamentals to: *she initiated him into the ballet.* ◆ *adj* (ɪ'nɪʃɪɪt, -ˌeɪt). **4** initiated; begun. ◆ *n* (ɪ'nɪʃɪɪt, -ˌeɪt). **5** a person who has been initiated, esp. recently. **6** a beginner; novice. [C17: from Latin *initiāre* (vb), from *initium*; see INITIAL] ▸ **in'itiatory** *adj*

initiation (ɪˌnɪʃɪ'eɪʃən) *n* **1** the act of initiating or the condition of being initiated. **2** the often secret ceremony initiating new members into an organization.

initiative (ɪ'nɪʃɪətɪv, -'nɪʃətɪv) *n* **1** the first step or action of a matter; commencing move: *he took the initiative; a peace initiative.* **2** the right or power to begin or initiate something: *he has the initiative.* **3** the ability or attitude required to begin or initiate something. **4** *Government.* **4a** the right or power to introduce legislation, etc., in a legislative body. **4b** the procedure by which citizens originate legislation, as in many American states and Switzerland. **5 on one's own initiative.** without being prompted. ◆ *adj* **6** of or concerning initiation or serving to initiate; initiatory. ▸ **in'itiatively** *adv*

initiator (ɪ'nɪʃɪeɪtə) *n* **1** a person or thing that initiates. **2** *Chem.* a substance that starts a chain reaction. **3** *Chem.* an explosive used in detonators. ▸ **in'itiˌatress** *or* **in'itiˌatrix** *fem n*

inject (ɪn'dʒɛkt) *vb* (*tr*) **1** *Med.* to introduce (a fluid) into (the body of a person or animal) by means of a syringe or similar instrument. **2** (foll. by *into*) to introduce (a new aspect or element): *to inject humour into a scene.* **3** to interject (a comment, idea, etc.). **4** to place (a rocket, satellite, etc.) in orbit. [C17: from Latin *injicere* to throw in, from *jacere* to throw] ▸ **in'jectable** *adj*

injection (ɪn'dʒɛkʃən) *n* **1** fluid injected into the body, esp. for medicinal purposes. **2** something injected. **3** the act of injecting. **4a** the act or process of introducing fluid under pressure, such as fuel into the combustion chamber of an engine. **4b** (*as modifier*): *injection moulding.* **5** *Maths.* a function or mapping for which $f(x) = f(y)$ only if $x = y$ and for which the image of every element of the domain is contained in the image space. See also **surjection, bijection.** ▸ **in'jective** *adj*

injector (ɪn'dʒɛktə) *n* **1** a person or thing that injects. **2** a device for spraying fuel into the combustion chamber of an internal-combustion engine. **3** a device for forcing water into a steam boiler. Also called: **inspirator.**

injudicious (ˌɪndʒʊ'dɪʃəs) *adj* not discreet; imprudent. ▸ **ˌinju'diciously** *adv* ▸ **ˌinju'diciousness** *n*

Injun ('ɪndʒən) *n* **1** *U.S.* an informal or dialect word for (American) **Indian. 2 honest Injun.** (*interj*) *Slang.* genuinely; really.

injunction (ɪn'dʒʌŋkʃən) *n* **1** *Law.* an instruction or order issued by a court to a party to an action, esp. to refrain from some act, such as causing a nuisance. **2** a command, admonition, etc. **3** the act of enjoining. [C16: from Late Latin *injunctiō*, from Latin *injungere* to ENJOIN] ▸ **in'junctive** *adj* ▸ **in'junctively** *adv*

injure ('ɪndʒə) *vb* (*tr*) **1** to cause physical or mental harm or suffering to; hurt or wound. **2** to offend, esp. by an injustice. [C16: back formation from INJURY] ▸ **'injurable** *adj* ▸ **'injured** *adj* ▸ **'injurer** *n*

injurious (ɪn'dʒʊərɪəs) *adj* **1** causing damage or harm; deleterious; hurtful. **2** abusive, slanderous, or libellous. ▸ **in'juriously** *adv* ▸ **in'juriousness** *n*

injury ('ɪndʒərɪ) *n, pl* **-ries. 1** physical damage or hurt. **2** a specific instance of this: *a leg injury.* **3** harm done to a reputation. **4** *Law.* a violation or infringement of another person's rights that causes him harm and is actionable at law. **5** an obsolete word for **insult.** [C14: from Latin *injūria* injustice, wrong, from *injūriōsus* acting unfairly, wrongful, from IN-[1] + *jūs* right]

injury benefit *n* (in the British National Insurance scheme) a weekly payment to a person injured while at work, varying according to the degree of injury.

injury time *n Soccer, rugby, etc.* extra playing time added on to compensate for time spent attending to injured players during the match. Also called: **stoppage time.**

injustice (ɪn'dʒʌstɪs) *n* **1** the condition or practice of being unjust or unfair. **2** an unjust act.

ink (ɪŋk) *n* **1** a fluid or paste used for printing, writing, and drawing. **2** a dark brown fluid ejected into the water for self-concealment by an octopus or related mollusc from a gland (**ink sac**) near the anus. ◆ *vb* (*tr*) **3** to mark with ink. **4** to coat (a printing surface) with ink. ◆ See also **ink in, ink up.** [C13: from Old French *enque*, from Late Latin *encaustum* a purplish-red ink, from Greek *enkauston* purple ink, from *enkaustos* burnt in, from *enkaiein* to burn in; see EN-[2], CAUSTIC] ▸ **'inker** *n*

Inkatha (ɪn'kɑːtə) *n* a South African Zulu organization founded by Chief Mangosouthu Buthelezi in 1975 as a paramilitary group seeking nonracial democracy; won four seats in South Africa's first nonracial elections in 1994. [C20: Zulu name for the grass coil used by Zulu women carrying loads on their heads, the many strands of which provide its strength and cohesion]

inkberry ('ɪŋkˌbɛrɪ) *n, pl* **-ries. 1** a North American holly tree, *Ilex glabra*, with black berry-like fruits. **2** another name for the **pokeweed. 3** the fruit of either of these plants.

inkblot ('ɪŋkˌblɒt) *n Psychol.* an abstract patch of ink, one of ten commonly used in the Rorschach test.

ink-cap *n* any of several saprotrophic agaricaceous fungi of the genus *Coprinus*, whose caps disintegrate into a black inky fluid after the spores mature. It includes the **shaggy ink-cap** (*Coprinus comatus*), also called **lawyer's wig,** a distinctive fungus having a white cylindrical cap covered with shaggy white or brownish scales.

Inkerman ('ɪŋkəmən; *Russian* inkɪr'man) *n* a village in the Ukraine, in the S Crimea east of Sevastopol: scene of a battle during the Crimean War in which British and French forces defeated the Russians (1854).

inkhorn ('ɪŋkˌhɔːn) *n* (formerly) a small portable container for ink, usually made from horn.

inkhorn term *n* an affectedly learned and obscure borrowing from another language, esp. Greek or Latin.

ink in *vb* (*adv*) **1** (*tr*) to use ink to go over pencil lines in (a drawing). **2** to apply ink to (a printing surface) in preparing to print from it. **3** to arrange or confirm definitely.

ink jet *n* a method of printing using electrostatic fields to control the direction of streams of electrically charged ink.

inkle ('ɪŋk^əl) *n* **1** a kind of linen tape used for trimmings. **2** the thread or yarn from which this tape is woven. [C16: of unknown origin]

inkling ('ɪŋklɪŋ) *n* a slight intimation or suggestion; suspicion. [C14: probably from *inclen* to hint at; related to Old English *inca*]

inkstand ('ɪŋkˌstænd) *n* a stand or tray on which are kept writing implements and containers for ink.

ink up *vb* (*adv*) to apply ink to (a printing machine) in preparing it for operation.

inkwell ('ɪŋkˌwɛl) *n* a small container for pen ink, often let into the surface of a desk.

inky ('ɪŋkɪ) *adj* **inkier, inkiest. 1** resembling ink, esp. in colour; dark or black. **2** of, containing, or stained with ink: *inky fingers.* ▸ **'inkiness** *n*

INLA *abbrev. for* Irish National Liberation Army; a Republican paramilitary organization in Ireland.

inlace (ɪn'leɪs) *vb* a variant spelling of **enlace.**

inlaid ('ɪnˌleɪd, ɪn'leɪd) *adj* **1** set in the surface, as a design in wood. **2** having such a design or inlay: *an inlaid table.*

inland *adj* ('ɪnlənd). **1** of, concerning, or located in the interior of a country or region away from a sea or border. **2** *Chiefly Brit.* operating within a country or region; domestic; not foreign. ◆ *n* ('ɪnˌlænd, -lənd). **3** the interior of a country or region. ◆ *adv* ('ɪnˌlænd, -lənd). **4** towards or into the interior of a country or region. ▸ **'inlander** *n*

inland bill *n* a bill of exchange that is both drawn and made payable in the same country. Compare **foreign bill.**

Inland Revenue *n* (in Britain and New Zealand) a government board that administers and collects major direct taxes, such as income tax, corporation tax, and capital gains tax. Abbrev.: **IR.**

Inland Sea *n* a sea in SW Japan, between the islands of Honshu, Shikoku, and Kyushu. Japanese name: **Seto Naikai.**

in-law *n* **1** a relative by marriage. ◆ *adj* **2** (*postpositive; in combination*) related by marriage: *a father-in-law.* [C19: back formation from *father-in-law,* etc.]

inlay *vb* (ɪn'leɪ), **-lays, -laying, -laid.** (*tr*) **1** to decorate (an article, esp. of furniture, or a surface) by inserting pieces of wood, ivory, etc., into prepared slots in the surface. ◆ *n* ('ɪnˌleɪ). **2** *Dentistry.* a filling, made of gold, porcelain, etc., inserted into a cavity and held in position by cement. **3** decoration made by inlaying. **4** an inlaid article, surface, etc. ▸ **'inˌlaid** *adj* ▸ **'inˌlayer** *n*

inlet *n* ('ɪnˌlet). **1** a narrow inland opening of the coastline. **2** an entrance or opening. **3** the act of letting someone or something in. **4** something let in or inserted. **5a** a passage, valve, or part through which a substance, esp. a fluid, enters a device or machine. **5b** (*as modifier*): *an inlet valve.* ◆ *vb* (ɪn'let), **-lets, -letting, -let.** **6** (*tr*) to insert or inlay.

inlier ('ɪnˌlaɪə) *n* an outcrop of rocks that is entirely surrounded by younger rocks.

in-line *adj* **1** denoting a linked sequence of manufacturing processes. **2** denoting an internal-combustion engine having its cylinders arranged in a line.

in-line skate *n* another name for **Rollerblade.**

in loc. cit. (in textual annotation) *abbrev. for* in loco citato. [Latin: in the place cited]

in loco parentis *Latin.* (ɪn 'ləʊkəʊ pə'rɛntɪs) in place of a parent: said of a person acting in a parental capacity.

inly ('ɪnlɪ) *adv Poetic.* inwardly; intimately.

inlying ('ɪnˌlaɪɪŋ) *adj* situated within or inside.

inmate ('ɪnˌmeɪt) *n* **1** a person who is confined to an institution such as a prison or hospital. See also **resident** (sense 2). **2** *Obsolete.* a person who lives with others in a house.

in medias res *Latin.* (ɪn 'miːdɪˌæs 'reɪs) in or into the middle of events or a narrative. [literally: into the midst of things, taken from a passage in Horace's *Ars Poetica*]

in mem. *abbrev. for* in memoriam.

in memoriam (ɪn mɪ'mɔːrɪəm) in memory of; as a memorial to: used in obituaries, epitaphs, etc. [Latin]

inmesh (ɪn'mɛʃ) *vb* a variant spelling of **enmesh.**

inmigrant ('ɪnˌmaɪgrənt) *adj* **1** coming in from another area of the same country: *an inmigrant worker.* ◆ *n* **2** an inmigrant person or animal.

inmost ('ɪnˌməʊst) *adj* another word for **innermost.**

inn (ɪn) *n* **1** a pub or small hotel providing food and accommodation. **2** (formerly, in England) a college or hall of residence for students, esp. of law, now only in the names of such institutions as the **Inns of Court.** [Old English; compare Old Norse *inni* inn, house, place of refuge]

Inn (ɪn) *n* a river in central Europe, rising in Switzerland in Graubünden and flowing northeast through Austria and Bavaria to join the River Danube at Passau: forms part of the border between Austria and Germany. Length: 514 km (319 miles).

innards ('ɪnədz) *pl n Informal.* **1** the internal organs of the body, esp. the viscera. **2** the interior parts or components of anything, esp. the working parts. [C19: colloquial variant of *inwards*]

innate (ɪ'neɪt, 'ɪneɪt) *adj* **1** existing in a person or animal from birth; congenital; inborn. **2** being an essential part of the character of a person or thing. **3** instinctive; not learned: *innate capacities.* **4** *Botany.* (of anthers) joined to the filament by the base only. **5** (in rationalist philosophy) (of ideas) present in the mind before any experience and knowable by pure reason. [C15: from Latin, from *innascī* to be born in, from *nascī* to be born] ▸ **in'nately** *adv* ▸ **in'nateness** *n*

innate releasing mechanism *n Psychol.* the process by which a stimulus evokes a response when the connection between the two is inborn. Abbrev.: **IRM.**

inner ('ɪnə) *adj* (*prenominal*) **1** being or located further inside: *an inner room.* **2** happening or occurring inside: *inner movement.* **3** relating to the soul, mind, spirit, etc.: *inner feelings.* **4** more profound or obscure; less apparent: *the inner meaning.* **5** exclusive or private: *inner regions of the party.* **6** *Chem.* (of a compound) having a cyclic structure formed or apparently formed by reaction of one functional group in a molecule with another group in the same molecule: *an inner ester.* ◆ *n* **7** Also called: **red.** *Archery.* **7a** the red innermost ring on a target. **7b** a shot which hits this ring. ▸ **'innerly** *adv* ▸ **'innerness** *n*

inner bar *n Brit.* all Queen's or King's Counsel collectively.

inner child *n Psychol.* the part of the psyche believed to retain feelings as they were experienced in childhood.

inner city *n* **a** the parts of a city in or near its centre, esp. when they are associated with poverty, unemployment, substandard housing, etc. **b** (*as modifier*): *inner-city schools.*

inner-directed *adj* guided by one's own conscience and values rather than external pressures to conform. Compare **other-directed.** ▸ **'inner-di'rection** *n*

inner ear *n* another name for **internal ear.**

Inner Hebrides *pl n* See **Hebrides.**

Inner Light *or* **Word** *n Quakerism.* the presence and inner working of God in the soul acting as a guiding spirit that is superior even to Scripture and unites man to Christ.

inner man *or* (*fem*) **inner woman** *n* **1** the mind or soul. **2** *Jocular.* the stomach or appetite.

Inner Mongolia *n* an autonomous region of NE China: consists chiefly of the Mongolian plateau, with the Gobi Desert in the north and the Great Wall of China in the south. Capital: Hohhot. Pop.: 22 840 000 (1996 est.). Area: 1 177 500 sq. km (459 225 sq. miles).

innermost ('ɪnəˌməʊst) *adj* **1** being or located furthest within; central. **2** intimate; private: *innermost beliefs.*

inner planet *n* any of the planets Mercury, Venus, earth, and Mars, whose orbits lie inside the asteroid belt.

inner space *n* **1** the environment beneath the surface of the sea. **2** the human mind regarded as being as unknown or as unfathomable as space.

Inner Temple *n* (in England) one of the four legal societies in London that together form the Inns of Court.

inner tube *n* an inflatable rubber tube that fits inside a pneumatic tyre casing.

innervate ('ɪnɜːˌveɪt) *vb* (*tr*) **1** to supply nerves to (a bodily organ or part). **2** to stimulate (a bodily organ or part) with nerve impulses. ▸ **ˌinner'vation** *n*

innerve (ɪ'nɜːv) *vb* (*tr*) to supply with nervous energy; stimulate.

inning ('ɪnɪŋ) *n* **1** *Baseball.* a division of the game consisting of a turn at bat and a turn in the field for each side. **2** *Archaic.* the reclamation of land from the sea. [Old English *innung* a going in, from *innian* to go in]

innings ('ɪnɪŋz) *n* **1** (*functioning as sing*) *Cricket.* **1a** the batting turn of a player or team. **1b** the runs scored during such a turn. **2** (*sometimes sing*) a period of opportunity or action. **3** (*functioning as pl*) land reclaimed from the sea.

Inniskilling (ˌɪnɪs'kɪlɪŋ) *n* the former name of **Enniskillen.**

innkeeper ('ɪnˌkiːpə) *n* an owner or manager of an inn.

innocence ('ɪnəsəns) *n* the quality or state of being innocent. Archaic word: **innocency** ('ɪnəsənsɪ). [C14: from Latin *innocentia* harmlessness, from *innocēns* doing no harm, blameless, from IN-[1] + *nocēns* harming, from *nocēre* to hurt, harm; see NOXIOUS]

innocent ('ɪnəsənt) *adj* **1** not corrupted or tainted with evil or unpleasant emotion; sinless; pure. **2** not guilty of a particular crime; blameless. **3** (*postpositive; foll. by of*) free (of); lacking: *innocent of all knowledge of history.* **4a** harmless or innocuous: *an innocent game.* **4b** not cancerous: *an innocent tumour.* **5** credulous, naive, or artless. **6** simple-minded; slow-witted. ◆ *n* **7** an innocent person, esp. a young child or an ingenuous adult. **8** a simple-minded person; simpleton. ▸ **'innocently** *adv*

Innocent II *n* original name *Gregorio Papareschi.* died 1143, pope (1130–43). He condemned Abelard's teachings.

Innocent III *n* original name *Giovanni Lotario de' Conti.* ?1161–1216, pope (1198–1216), under whom the temporal power of the papacy reached its height. He instituted the Fourth Crusade (1202) and a crusade against the Albigenses (1208), and called the fourth Lateran Council (1215).

Innocent IV *n* original name *Sinibaldo de' Fieschi.* died 1254, pope (1243–54); an unrelenting enemy of Emperor Frederick II and his heirs.

innocuous (ɪ'nɒkjʊəs) *adj* having little or no adverse or harmful effect; harmless. [C16: from Latin *innocuus* harmless, from IN-[1] + *nocēre* to harm] ▸ **in'nocuously** *adv* ▸ **in'nocuousness** *or* **innocuity** (ˌɪnə'kjuːɪtɪ) *n*

innominate (ɪ'nɒmɪnɪt) *adj* **1** having no name; nameless. **2** a less common word for **anonymous.**

innominate bone *n* either of the two bones that form the sides of the pelvis, consisting of three fused components, the ilium, ischium, and pubis. Nontechnical name: **hipbone.**

in nomine (ɪn 'nɒmɪˌneɪ, -ˌniː) *n Music.* any of several pieces of music of the 16th or 17th centuries for keyboard or for a consort of viols, based on a cantus firmus derived from the Vespers antiphon *Gloria tibi Trinitas.* [from Latin *in nomine Jesu* in the name of Jesus, the first words of an introit for which this type of music was originally composed]

innovate ('ɪnəˌveɪt) *vb* to invent or begin to apply (methods, ideas, etc.). [C16: from Latin *innovāre* to renew, from IN-[2] + *novāre* to make new, from *novus* new] ▸ **'innoˌvative** *or* **'innoˌvatory** *adj* ▸ **'innoˌvator** *n*

innovation (ˌɪnə'veɪʃən) *n* **1** something newly introduced, such as a new method or device. **2** the act of innovating. ▸ **ˌinno'vational** *adj* ▸ **ˌinno'vationist** *n*

innoxious (ɪ'nɒkʃəs) *adj* not noxious; harmless. ▸ **in'noxiously** *adv* ▸ **in'noxiousness** *n*

Innsbruck ('ɪnzbrʊk) *n* a city in W Austria, on the River Inn at the foot of the Brenner Pass: tourist centre. Pop.: 118 112 (1991).

Inns of Court *pl n* (in England) the four private unincorporated societies in London that function as a law school and have the exclusive privilege of calling candidates to the English bar. See **Lincoln's Inn, Inner Temple, Middle Temple, Gray's Inn.**

innuendo (ˌɪnjʊ'ɛndəʊ) *n, pl* **-dos** *or* **-does.** **1** an indirect or subtle reference, esp. one made maliciously or indicating criticism or disapproval; insinuation. **2** *Law.* (in pleading) a word introducing an explanatory phrase, usually in parenthesis. **3** *Law.* (in an action for defamation) **3a** an explanation of the construction put upon words alleged to be defamatory where the defamatory meaning is not apparent. **3b** the words thus explained. [C17: from Latin, literally: by hinting, from *innuendum,* gerund of *innuere* to convey by a nod, from IN-[2] + *nuere* to nod]

Innuit ('ɪnjuːɪt) *n* a variant spelling of **Inuit.**

innumerable (ɪ'njuːmərəbᵊl, ɪ'njuːmrəbᵊl) *or* **innumerous** *adj* so many as to be uncountable; extremely numerous. ▸ **inˌnumera'bility** *or* **in'numerableness** *n* ▸ **in'numerably** *adv*

innumerate (ɪ'njuːmərɪt) *adj* **1** having neither knowledge nor understanding of mathematics or science. ◆ *n* **2** an innumerate person. ▸ **in'numeracy** *n*

innutrition (ˌɪnjuːˈtrɪʃən) *n* lack or absence of nutrition. Compare **malnutrition**. ▸ ˌ**innuˈtritious** *adj*

inobservance (ˌɪnəbˈzɜːvəns) *n* **1** heedlessness. **2** lack of compliance with or adherence to a law, religious duty, etc. ▸ ˌ**inobˈservant** *adj* ▸ ˌ**inobˈservantly** *adv*

inoculable (ɪˈnɒkjʊləbᵊl) *adj* capable of being inoculated. ▸ **inˌoculaˈbility** *n*

inoculate (ɪˈnɒkjʊˌleɪt) *vb* **1** to introduce (the causative agent of a disease) into the body of (a person or animal), in order to induce immunity. **2** (*tr*) to introduce (microorganisms, esp. bacteria) into (a culture medium). **3** (*tr*) to cause to be influenced or imbued, as with ideas or opinions. **[C15:** from Latin *inoculāre* to implant, from IN-[2] + *oculus* eye, bud**]** ▸ **inˌocuˈlation** *n* ▸ **inˈoculative** *adj* ▸ **inˈocuˌlator** *n*

inoculum (ɪˈnɒkjʊləm) *or* **inoculant** *n, pl* **-la** (-lə) *or* **-lants**. *Med.* the substance used in giving an inoculation. **[C20:** New Latin; see INOCULATE**]**

inodorous (ɪnˈəʊdərəs) *adj* odourless; having no odour.

in-off *n Billiards.* a shot that goes into a pocket after striking another ball.

inoffensive (ˌɪnəˈfɛnsɪv) *adj* **1** not giving offence; unobjectionable. **2** not unpleasant, poisonous, or harmful. ▸ ˌ**inofˈfensively** *adv* ▸ ˌ**inofˈfensiveness** *n*

inofficious (ˌɪnəˈfɪʃəs) *adj* contrary to moral obligation, as the disinheritance of a child by his parents: *an inofficious will.* ▸ ˌ**inofˈficiously** *adv* ▸ ˌ**inofˈficiousness** *n*

Inönü (ˈiːnɜːˌnuː, ˌɪnɜːˈnuː) *n* **Ismet** (ɪsˈmɛt, ˈɪsmɛt). 1884–1973, Turkish statesman; president of Turkey (1938–50) and prime minister (1923–37; 1961–65).

inoperable (ɪnˈɒpərəbᵊl, -ˈɒprə-) *adj* **1** incapable of being implemented or operated; unworkable. **2** *Surgery.* not suitable for operation without risk, esp. (of a malignant tumour) because metastasis has rendered surgery useless. ▸ **inˌoperaˈbility** *or* **inˈoperableness** *n* ▸ **inˈoperably** *adv*

inoperative (ɪnˈɒpərətɪv, -ˈɒprə-) *adj* **1** not operating. **2** useless or ineffective. ▸ **inˈoperativeness** *n*

inopportune (ɪnˈɒpəˌtjuːn) *adj* not opportune; inappropriate or badly timed. ▸ **inˈopporˌtunely** *adv* ▸ **inˈopporˌtuneness** *or* **inˌopporˈtunity** *n*

inordinate (ɪnˈɔːdɪnɪt) *adj* **1** exceeding normal limits; immoderate. **2** unrestrained, as in behaviour or emotion; intemperate. **3** irregular or disordered. **[C14:** from Latin *inordinātus* disordered, from IN-[1] + *ordināre* to put in order**]** ▸ **inˈordinacy** *or* **inˈordinateness** *n* ▸ **inˈordinately** *adv*

inorg. *abbrev. for* inorganic.

inorganic (ˌɪnɔːˈgænɪk) *adj* **1** not having the structure or characteristics of living organisms; not organic. **2** relating to or denoting chemical compounds that do not contain carbon. Compare **organic** (sense 4). **3** not having a system, structure, or ordered relation of parts; amorphous. **4** not resulting from or produced by growth; artificial. **5** *Linguistics.* denoting or relating to a sound or letter introduced into the pronunciation or spelling of a word at some point in its history. ▸ ˌ**inorˈganically** *adv*

inorganic chemistry *n* the branch of chemistry concerned with the elements and all their compounds except those containing carbon. Some simple carbon compounds, such as oxides, carbonates, etc., are treated as inorganic. Compare **organic chemistry**.

inosculate (ɪnˈɒskjʊˌleɪt) *vb* **1** *Physiol.* (of small blood vessels) to communicate by anastomosis. **2** to unite or be united so as to be continuous; blend. **3** to intertwine or cause to intertwine. **[C17:** from IN-[2] + Latin *ōsculāre* to equip with an opening, from *ōsculum,* diminutive of *ōs* mouth**]** ▸ **inˌoscuˈlation** *n*

inositol (ɪˈnəʊsɪˌtɒl) *n* a cyclic alcohol, one isomer of which (*i*-inositol) is present in yeast and is a growth factor for some organisms; cyclohexanehexol. Formula: $C_6H_{12}O_6$. **[C19:** from Greek *in-, is* sinew + -OSE[2] + -ITE[1] + -OL[1]**]**

inotropic (ˌɪnəˈtrɒpɪk, ˌaɪnə-) *adj* affecting or controlling the contraction of muscles, esp. those of the heart: *inotropic drugs.* **[C20:** from Greek, from *is* (stem *in-*) tendon + -TROPIC**]**

inpatient (ˈɪnˌpeɪʃənt) *n* a patient living in the hospital where he is being treated. Compare **outpatient**.

in perpetuum *Latin.* (ɪn pɜːˈpɛtjʊəm) for ever.

in personam (ɪn pɜːˈsəʊnæm) *adj Law.* (of a judicial act) directed against a specific person or persons. Compare **in rem**. **[**Latin**]**

in petto (ɪn ˈpɛtəʊ) *adj R.C. Church.* not disclosed: used of the names of cardinals designate. **[**Italian, literally: in the breast**]**

in posse (ɪn ˈpɒsɪ) *adj* possible; potential. Compare **in esse**. **[**Latin, literally: in possibility**]**

in propria persona *Latin.* (ɪn ˈprəʊprɪə pɜːˈsəʊnə) *adv Chiefly law.* in person; personally.

input (ˈɪnˌpʊt) *n* **1** the act of putting in. **2** that which is put in. **3** (*often pl*) a resource required for industrial production, such as capital goods, labour services, raw materials, etc. **4** *Electronics.* **4a** the signal or current fed into a component or circuit. **4b** the terminals, or some other point, to which the signal is applied. **5** *Computing.* the data fed into a computer from a peripheral device. **6** (*modifier*) of or relating to electronic, computer, or other input: *input program.* ♦ *vb* **7** (*tr*) to insert (data) into a computer.

input device *n Computing.* a peripheral device that accepts data and feeds it into a computer.

input/output *n Computing.* **1** the data or information that is passed into or out of a computer. Abbrev.: **I/O.** **2** (*modifier*) concerned with or relating to such passage of data or information.

input-output analysis *n Economics.* an analysis of production relationships between the industries of an economy involving a study of each industry's inputs and outputs, esp. as used in social accounting.

inqilab (ˈɪnkɪˌlɑːb) *n* (in India, Pakistan, etc.) revolution (esp. in the phrase **inqilab zindabad** long live the revolution). **[**Urdu**]**

inquest (ˈɪnˌkwɛst) *n* **1** an inquiry into the cause of an unexplained, sudden, or violent death, or as to whether or not property constitutes treasure trove, held by a coroner, in certain cases with a jury. **2** *Informal.* any inquiry or investigation. **[C13:** from Medieval Latin *inquēsta,* from Latin IN-[2] + *quaesītus* investigation, from *quaerere* to examine**]**

inquietude (ɪnˈkwaɪɪˌtjuːd) *n* restlessness, uneasiness, or anxiety. ▸ **inquiet** (ɪnˈkwaɪət) *adj* ▸ **inˈquietly** *adv*

inquiline (ˈɪnkwɪˌlaɪn) *n* **1** an animal that lives in close association with another animal without harming it. See also **commensal** (sense 1). ♦ *adj* **2** of or living as an inquiline. **[C17:** from Latin *inquilīnus* lodger, from IN-[2] + *colere* to dwell**]** ▸ **inquilinism** (ˈɪnkwɪlɪˌnɪzəm) *or* **inquilinity** (ˌɪnkwɪˈlɪnɪtɪ) *n* ▸ **inquilinous** (ˌɪnkwɪˈlaɪnəs) *adj*

inquire *or* **enquire** (ɪnˈkwaɪə) *vb* **1a** to seek information; ask: *she inquired his age; she inquired about rates of pay.* **1b** (foll. by *of*) to ask (a person) for information: *I'll inquire of my aunt when she is coming.* **2** (*intr*; often foll. by *into*) to make a search or investigation. **[C13:** from Latin *inquīrere* from IN-[2] + *quaerere* to seek**]** ▸ **inˈquirer** *or* **enˈquirer** *n*

inquiring (ɪnˈkwaɪərɪŋ) *adj* seeking or tending to seek answers, information, etc.: *an inquiring mind.* ▸ **inˈquiringly** *adv*

inquiry *or* **enquiry** (ɪnˈkwaɪərɪ) *n* **1** a request for information; a question. **2** an investigation, esp. a formal one conducted into a matter of public concern by a body constituted for that purpose by a government, local authority, or other organization.

inquisition (ˌɪnkwɪˈzɪʃən) *n* **1** the act of inquiring deeply or searchingly; investigation. **2** a deep or searching inquiry, esp. a ruthless official investigation of individuals in order to suppress revolt or root out the unorthodox. **3** an official inquiry, esp. one held by a jury before an officer of the Crown. **4** another word for **inquest** (sense 2). **[C14:** from legal Latin *inquīsītiō,* from *inquīrere* to seek for; see INQUIRE**]** ▸ ˌ**inquiˈsitional** *adj* ▸ ˌ**inquiˈsitionist** *n*

Inquisition (ˌɪnkwɪˈzɪʃən) *n History.* a judicial institution of the Roman Catholic Church (1232–1820) founded to discover and suppress heresy. See also **Spanish Inquisition**.

inquisitive (ɪnˈkwɪzɪtɪv) *adj* **1** excessively curious, esp. about the affairs of others; prying. **2** eager to learn; inquiring. ▸ **inˈquisitively** *adv* ▸ **inˈquisitiveness** *n*

inquisitor (ɪnˈkwɪzɪtə) *n* **1** a person who inquires, esp. deeply, searchingly, or ruthlessly. **2** (*often cap.*) an official of the ecclesiastical court of the Inquisition.

Inquisitor-General *n, pl* **Inquisitors-General**. *History.* the head of the Spanish court of Inquisition.

inquisitorial (ɪnˌkwɪzɪˈtɔːrɪəl) *adj* **1** of, relating to, or resembling inquisition or an inquisitor. **2** offensively curious; prying. **3** *Law.* denoting criminal procedure in which one party is both prosecutor and judge, or in which the trial is held in secret. Compare **accusatorial** (sense 2). ▸ **inˌquisiˈtorially** *adv* ▸ **inˌquisiˈtorialness** *n*

inquorate (ɪnˈkwɔːreɪt) *adj Brit.* not consisting of or being a quorum: *this meeting is inquorate.*

in re (ɪn ˈreɪ) *prep* in the matter of: used esp. in bankruptcy proceedings. **[C17:** from Latin**]**

in rem (ɪn ˈrɛm) *adj Law.* (of a judicial act) directed against property rather than against a specific person. Compare **in personam**. **[**Latin, literally: against the matter**]**

in rerum natura *Latin.* (ɪn ˈrɛərʊm næˈtʊərə) in the nature of things.

INRI *abbrev. for* Iesus Nazarenus Rex Iudaeorum (the inscription placed over Christ's head during the Crucifixion). **[**Latin: Jesus of Nazareth, King of the Jews**]**

inroad (ˈɪnˌrəʊd) *n* **1** an invasion or hostile attack; raid or incursion. **2** an encroachment or intrusion.

inrush (ˈɪnˌrʌʃ) *n* a sudden usually overwhelming inward flow or rush; influx. ▸ ˈ**inˌrushing** *n, adj*

INS *abbrev. for* International News Service.

ins. *abbrev. for:* **1** inches. **2** inspector. **3** insulated. **4** insulation. **5** insurance.

insalivate (ɪnˈsælɪˌveɪt) *vb* (*tr*) to saturate (food) with saliva during mastication. ▸ **inˌsaliˈvation** *n*

insalubrious (ˌɪnsəˈluːbrɪəs) *adj* not salubrious; unpleasant, unhealthy, or sordid. ▸ ˌ**insaˈlubriously** *adv* ▸ **insalubrity** (ˌɪnsəˈluːbrɪtɪ) *n*

insane (ɪnˈseɪn) *adj* **1a** mentally deranged; crazy; of unsound mind. **1b** (*as collective n; preceded by the*): *the insane.* **2** characteristic of a person of unsound mind: *an insane stare.* **3** irresponsible; very foolish; stupid. ▸ **inˈsanely** *adv* ▸ **inˈsaneness** *n*

insanitary (ɪnˈsænɪtərɪ, -trɪ) *adj* not sanitary; dirty or infected. ▸ **inˈsanitariness** *or* **inˌsaniˈtation** *n*

insanity (ɪnˈsænɪtɪ) *n, pl* **-ties**. **1** relatively permanent disorder of the mind; state or condition of being insane. **2** *Law.* (not in strict legal usage) a state of mind characterized by the inability to distinguish right from wrong. **3** utter folly; stupidity.

insatiable (ɪnˈseɪʃəbᵊl, -ʃɪə-) *or* **insatiate** (ɪnˈseɪʃɪɪt) *adj* not able to be satisfied or satiated; greedy or unappeasable. ▸ **inˌsatiaˈbility, inˈsatiableness,** *or* **inˈsatiateness** *n* ▸ **inˈsatiably** *or* **inˈsatiately** *adv*

inscape (ˈɪnskeɪp) *n* the essential inner nature of a person, an object, etc. **[C19:** from IN-[2] + *-scape,* as in LANDSCAPE; coined by Gerard Manley HOPKINS**]**

inscribe (ɪnˈskraɪb) *vb* (*tr*) **1** to make, carve, or engrave (writing, letters, a design, etc.) on (a surface such as wood, stone, or paper). **2** to enter (a name) on a list or in a register. **3** to sign one's name on (a book, photograph, etc.) before presentation to another person. **4** to draw (a geometric construction such as a circle, polygon, etc.) inside another construction so that the two are in contact but do not intersect. Compare **circumscribe** (sense 3). **[C16:** from Latin *inscrībere;* see INSCRIPTION**]** ▸ **inˈscribable** *adj* ▸ **inˈscribableness** *n* ▸ **inˈscriber** *n*

inscription (ɪnˈskrɪpʃən) *n* **1** something inscribed, esp. words carved or engraved on a coin, tomb, etc. **2** a signature or brief dedication in a book or on a work of art. **3** the act of inscribing. **4** *Philosophy, linguistics.* an element of written language, esp. a sentence. Compare **utterance**[1] (sense 3). [C14: from Latin *inscriptiō* a writing upon, from *inscrībere* to write upon, from IN-[2] + *scrībere* to write] ▸ **in'scriptional** *or* **in'scriptive** *adj* ▸ **in'scriptively** *adv*

inscrutable (ɪn'skru:təbᵊl) *adj* incomprehensible; mysterious or enigmatic. [C15: from Late Latin *inscrūtābilis,* from Latin IN-[1] + *scrūtārī* to examine] ▸ **in,scruta'bility** *or* **in'scrutableness** *n* ▸ **in'scrutably** *adv*

insect ('ɪnsɛkt) *n* **1** any small air-breathing arthropod of the class *Insecta,* having a body divided into head, thorax, and abdomen, three pairs of legs, and (in most species) two pairs of wings. Insects comprise about five sixths of all known animal species, with a total of over one million named species. Related adj: **entomic.** **2** (loosely) any similar invertebrate, such as a spider, tick, or centipede. **3** a contemptible, loathsome, or insignificant person. [C17: from Latin *insectum* (animal that has been) cut into, insect, from *insecāre,* from IN-[2] + *secāre* to cut; translation of Greek *entomon* insect] ▸ **in'sectean, in'sectan,** *or* **in'sectile** *adj* ▸ **'insect-,like** *adj*

insectarium (,ɪnsɛk'tɛərɪəm) *or* **insectary** (ɪn'sɛktərɪ) *n, pl* **-tariums, -taria** (-'tɛərɪə), *or* **-taries.** a place where living insects are kept, bred, and studied.

insecticide (ɪn'sɛktɪ,saɪd) *n* a substance used to destroy insect pests. ▸ **in,secti'cidal** *adj*

insectivore (ɪn'sɛktɪ,vɔ:) *n* **1** any placental mammal of the order *Insectivora,* being typically small, with simple teeth, and feeding on invertebrates. The group includes shrews, moles, and hedgehogs. **2** any animal or plant that derives nourishment from insects.

insectivorous (,ɪnsɛk'tɪvərəs) *adj* **1** feeding on or adapted for feeding on insects: *insectivorous plants.* **2** of or relating to the order *Insectivora.*

insectivorous bat *n* any bat of the suborder *Microchiroptera,* typically having large ears and feeding on insects. The group includes common bats (*Myotis* species), vampire bats, etc. Compare **fruit bat.**

insecure (,ɪnsɪ'kjʊə) *adj* **1** anxious or afraid; not confident or certain. **2** not adequately protected: *an insecure fortress.* **3** unstable or shaky. ▸ **,inse'curely** *adv* ▸ **,inse'cureness** *n* ▸ **,inse'curity** *n*

inselberg ('ɪnzᵊl,bɜ:g) *n* an isolated rocky hill rising abruptly from a flat plain. [from German, from *Insel* island + *Berg* mountain]

inseminate (ɪn'sɛmɪ,neɪt) *vb (tr)* **1** to impregnate (a female) with semen. **2** to introduce (ideas or attitudes) into the mind of (a person or group). [C17: from Latin *insēmināre,* from IN-[2] + *sēmināre* to sow, from *sēmen* seed] ▸ **in,semi'nation** *n* ▸ **in'semi,nator** *n*

insensate (ɪn'sɛnseɪt, -sɪt) *adj* **1** lacking sensation or consciousness. **2** insensitive; unfeeling. **3** foolish; senseless. ▸ **in'sensately** *adv* ▸ **in'sensateness** *n*

insensible (ɪn'sɛnsəbᵊl) *adj* **1** lacking sensation or consciousness. **2** (foll. by *of* or *to*) unaware (of) or indifferent (to): *insensible to suffering.* **3** thoughtless or callous. **4** a less common word for **imperceptible.** ▸ **in,sensi'bility** *or* **in'sensibleness** *n* ▸ **in'sensibly** *adv*

insensitive (ɪn'sɛnsɪtɪv) *adj* **1** lacking sensitivity; unfeeling. **2** lacking physical sensation. **3** (*postpositive;* foll. by *to*) not sensitive (to) or affected (by): *insensitive to radiation.* ▸ **in'sensitively** *adv* ▸ **in'sensitiveness** *or* **in,sensi'tivity** *n*

insentient (ɪn'sɛnʃɪənt) *adj Rare.* lacking consciousness or senses; inanimate. ▸ **in'sentience** *or* **in'sentiency** *n*

inseparable (ɪn'sɛpərəbᵊl, -'sɛprə-) *adj* incapable of being separated or divided. ▸ **in,separa'bility** *or* **in'separableness** *n* ▸ **in'separably** *adv*

insert *vb* (ɪn'sɜ:t). *(tr)* **1** to put in or between; introduce. **2** to introduce, as into text, such as a newspaper; interpolate. ◆ *n* ('ɪnsɜ:t). **3** something inserted. **4a** a folded section placed in another for binding in with a book. **4b** a printed sheet, esp. one bearing advertising, placed loose between the leaves of a book, periodical, etc. **5** another word for **cut-in** (sense 6). [C16: from Latin *inserere* to plant in, ingraft, from IN-[2] + *serere* to join] ▸ **in'sertable** *adj* ▸ **in'serter** *n*

inserted (ɪn'sɜ:tɪd) *adj* **1** *Anatomy.* (of a muscle) attached to the bone that it moves. **2** *Botany.* (of parts of a plant) growing from another part, as stamens from the corolla.

insertion (ɪn'sɜ:ʃən) *n* **1** the act of inserting or something that is inserted. **2** a word, sentence, correction, etc., inserted into text, such as a newspaper. **3** a strip of lace, embroidery, etc., between two pieces of material. **4** *Anatomy.* the point or manner of attachment of a muscle to the bone that it moves. **5** *Botany.* the manner or point of attachment of one part to another. ▸ **in'sertional** *adj*

insertion element *or* **sequence** *n Genetics.* a section of DNA that has been inserted into another chromosome. See **transposon.**

in-service *adj* denoting training that is given to employees during the course of employment: *an in-service course.*

insessorial (,ɪnsɛ'sɔ:rɪəl) *adj* **1** (of feet or claws) adapted for perching. **2** (of birds) having insessorial feet. [C19: from New Latin *Insessōrēs* birds that perch, from Latin: perchers, from *insidēre* to sit upon, from *sedēre* to sit]

inset *vb* (ɪn'sɛt), **-sets, -setting, -set.** **1** *(tr)* to set or place in or within; insert. ◆ *n* ('ɪn,sɛt). **2** something inserted. **3** *Printing.* **3a** a small map or diagram set within the borders of a larger one. **3b** another name for **insert** (sense 4). **4** a piece of fabric inserted into a garment, as to shape it or for decoration. **5** a flowing in, as of the tide. ▸ **'in,setter** *n*

inshallah (ɪn'ʃælə) *sentence substitute. Islam.* if Allah wills it. [C19: from Arabic]

inshore ('ɪn'ʃɔ:) *adj* **1** in or on the water, but close to the shore: *inshore weather.* ◆ *adv, adj* **2** towards the shore from the water: *an inshore wind; we swam inshore.*

inshrine (ɪn'ʃraɪn) *vb* a variant spelling of **enshrine.**

inside *n* ('ɪn'saɪd). **1** the interior; inner or enclosed part or surface. **2** the side of a path away from the road or adjacent to a wall. **3** (*also pl*) *Informal.* the internal organs of the body, esp. the stomach and bowels. **4** **inside of.** in a period of time less than; within. **5** **inside out.** with the inside facing outwards. **6** **know (something) inside out.** to know thoroughly or perfectly. ◆ *prep* (,ɪn'saɪd). **7** in or to the interior of; within or to within; on the inside of. ◆ *adj* ('ɪn,saɪd). **8** on or of an interior; on the inside: *an inside door.* **9** (*prenominal*) arranged or provided by someone within an organization or building, esp. illicitly: *the raid was an inside job; inside information.* ◆ *adv* (,ɪn'saɪd). **10** within or to within a thing or place; indoors. **11** by nature; fundamentally: *inside, he's a good chap.* **12** *Slang.* in or into prison.

USAGE See at **outside.**

inside forward *n Soccer.* (esp. formerly) one of two players (the **inside right** and the **inside left**) having mainly midfield and attacking roles.

inside job *n Informal.* a crime committed with the assistance of someone associated with the victim, such as a person employed on the premises burgled.

inside lane *n Athletics.* the inside, and therefore the shortest, route around a circular or oval multi-lane running track.

insider (,ɪn'saɪdə) *n* **1** a member of a specified group. **2** a person with access to exclusive information.

insider dealing *or* **trading** *n* dealing in company securities on a recognized stock exchange, with a view to making a profit or avoiding a loss, by a person who has confidential information about the securities that, if generally known, would affect their price. Its practice by those connected with a company is illegal. ▸ **insider dealer** *or* **trader** *n*

inside track *n* **1** the inner and therefore shorter side of a racecourse. **2** *Informal.* a position of advantage: *the local man has the inside track in this contest.*

insidious (ɪn'sɪdɪəs) *adj* **1** stealthy, subtle, cunning, or treacherous. **2** working in a subtle or apparently innocuous way, but nevertheless deadly: *an insidious illness.* [C16: from Latin *insidiōsus* cunning, from *insidiae* an ambush, from *insidēre* to sit in; see INSESSORIAL] ▸ **in'sidiously** *adv* ▸ **in'sidiousness** *n*

insight ('ɪn,saɪt) *n* **1** the ability to perceive clearly or deeply; penetration. **2** a penetrating and often sudden understanding, as of a complex situation or problem. **3** *Psychol.* **3a** the capacity for understanding one's own or another's mental processes. **3b** the immediate understanding of the significance of an event or action. **4** *Psychiatry.* the ability to understand one's own problems, sometimes used to distinguish between psychotic and neurotic disorders. ▸ **'in,sightful** *adj*

insignia (ɪn'sɪgnɪə) *n, pl* **-nias** *or* **-nia.** **1** a badge or emblem of membership, office, or dignity. **2** a distinguishing sign or mark. ◆ Also called (rare): **insigne** (ɪn'sɪgni:). [C17: from Latin: marks, badges, from *insignis* distinguished by a mark, prominent, from IN-[2] + *signum* mark]

insignificant (,ɪnsɪg'nɪfɪkənt) *adj* **1** having little or no importance; trifling. **2** almost or relatively meaningless. **3** small or inadequate: *an insignificant wage.* **4** not distinctive in character, etc. ▸ **,insig'nificance** *or* **,insig'nificancy** *n* ▸ **,insig'nificantly** *adv*

insincere (,ɪnsɪn'sɪə) *adj* lacking sincerity; hypocritical. ▸ **,insin'cerely** *adv* ▸ **insincerity** (,ɪnsɪn'sɛrɪtɪ) *n*

insinuate (ɪn'sɪnjʊ,eɪt) *vb* **1** (*may take a clause as object*) to suggest by indirect allusion, hints, innuendo, etc. **2** *(tr)* to introduce subtly or deviously. **3** *(tr)* to cause (someone, esp. oneself) to be accepted by gradual approaches or manoeuvres. [C16: from Latin *insinuāre* to wind one's way into, from IN-[2] + *sinus* curve] ▸ **in'sinuative** *or* **in'sinuatory** *adj* ▸ **in'sinu,ator** *n*

insinuation (ɪn,sɪnjʊ'eɪʃən) *n* **1** an indirect or devious hint or suggestion. **2** the act or practice of insinuating.

insipid (ɪn'sɪpɪd) *adj* **1** lacking spirit; boring. **2** lacking taste; unpalatable. [C17: from Latin *insipidus,* from IN-[1] + *sapidus* full of flavour, SAPID] ▸ **,insi'pidity** *or* **in'sipidness** *n* ▸ **in'sipidly** *adv*

insipience (ɪn'sɪpɪəns) *n Archaic.* lack of wisdom. [C15: from Latin *insipientia,* from IN-[1] + *sapientia* wisdom; see SAPIENT] ▸ **in'sipient** *adj* ▸ **in'sipiently** *adv*

insist (ɪn'sɪst) *vb* (when *tr, takes a clause as object;* when *intr,* usually foll. by *on* or *upon*) **1** to make a determined demand (for): *he insisted that his rights be respected; he insisted on his rights.* **2** to express a convinced belief (in) or assertion (of): *he insisted that she was mad; he insisted on her madness.* [C16: from Latin *insistere* to stand upon, urge, from IN-[2] + *sistere* to stand] ▸ **in'sister** *n* ▸ **in'sistingly** *adv*

insistent (ɪn'sɪstənt) *adj* **1** making continual and persistent demands. **2** demanding notice or attention; compelling: *the insistent cry of a bird.* ▸ **in'sistence** *or* **in'sistency** *n* ▸ **in'sistently** *adv*

in situ *Latin.* (ɪn 'sɪtju:) *adv, adj* (*postpositive*) **1** in the natural, original, or appropriate position. **2** *Pathol.* (esp. of a cancerous growth or tumour) not seen to be spreading from a localized position.

insnare (ɪn'snɛə) *vb* a less common spelling of **ensnare.** ▸ **in'snarement** *n* ▸ **in'snarer** *n*

insobriety (,ɪnsəʊ'braɪɪtɪ) *n* lack of sobriety; intemperance.

in so far as *or* **insofar as** (,ɪnsəʊ'fɑ:) *adv* to the degree or extent that.

insolate ('ɪnsəʊ,leɪt) *vb (tr)* to expose to sunlight, as for bleaching. [C17: from Latin *insōlāre* to place in the sun, from IN-[2] + *sōl* sun]

insolation (,ɪnsəʊ'leɪʃən) *n* **1** the quantity of solar radiation falling upon a body or planet, esp. per unit area. **2** exposure to the sun's rays. **3** another name for **sunstroke.**

insole ('ɪn,səʊl) *n* **1** the inner sole of a shoe or boot. **2** a loose additional inner sole used to give extra warmth, comfort, etc.

insolent ('ɪnsələnt) *adj* offensive, impudent, or disrespectful. [C14: from Latin *insolens,* from IN-[1] + *solēre* to be accustomed] ▸ **'insolence** *n* ▸ **'insolently** *adv*

insoluble (ɪn'sɒljʊbᵊl) *adj* **1** incapable of being dissolved; incapable of forming a solution, esp. in water. **2** incapable of being solved. ▸ **in,solu'bility** *or* **in'solubleness** *n* ▸ **in'solubly** *adv*

insolvable (ɪnˈsɒlvəbᵊl) *adj* another word for **insoluble** (sense 2). ▸ **inˌsolvaˈbility** *n* ▸ **inˈsolvably** *adv*

insolvency provision *n Brit.* the right of employees of a firm that goes bankrupt or into receivership to receive money owed to them as wages, etc.

insolvent (ɪnˈsɒlvənt) *adj* **1** (of a person, company, etc.) having insufficient assets to meet debts and liabilities; bankrupt. **2** of or relating to bankrupts or bankruptcy. ◆ *n* **3** a person who is insolvent; bankrupt. ▸ **inˈsolvency** *n*

insomnia (ɪnˈsɒmnɪə) *n* chronic inability to fall asleep or to enjoy uninterrupted sleep. Related adj: **agrypnotic.** [C18: from Latin, from *insomnis* sleepless, from *somnus* sleep] ▸ **inˈsomnious** *adj*

insomniac (ɪnˈsɒmnɪˌæk) *adj* **1** exhibiting or causing insomnia. ◆ *n* **2** a person experiencing insomnia.

insomuch (ˌɪnsəʊˈmʌtʃ) *adv* **1** (foll. by *as* or *that*) to such an extent or degree. **2** (foll. by *as*) because of the fact (that); inasmuch (as).

insouciant (ɪnˈsuːsɪənt) *adj* carefree or unconcerned; light-hearted. [C19: from French, from IN-[1] + *souciant* worrying, from *soucier* to trouble, from Latin *sollicitāre;* compare SOLICITOUS] ▸ **inˈsouciance** *n* ▸ **inˈsouciantly** *adv*

insoul (ɪnˈsəʊl) *vb* (*tr*) a variant of **ensoul.**

insp. *abbrev. for:* **1** inspected. **2** inspector.

inspan (ɪnˈspæn) *vb* **-spans, -spanning, -spanned.** (*tr*) *Chiefly S. African.* to harness (animals) to (a vehicle); yoke. [C19: from Afrikaans, from Middle Dutch *inspannen,* from *spannen* to stretch, yoke; see SPAN[1]]

inspect (ɪnˈspɛkt) *vb* (*tr*) **1** to examine closely, esp. for faults or errors. **2** to scrutinize officially (a document, military personnel on ceremonial parade, etc.). [C17: from Latin *inspicere,* from *specere* to look] ▸ **inˈspectable** *adj* ▸ **inˈspectingly** *adv* ▸ **inˈspection** *n* ▸ **inˈspectional** *adj* ▸ **inˈspective** *adj*

inspection chamber *n* a more formal name for **manhole** (sense 1).

inspection pit *n* a hole in the floor of a garage etc. from which the underside of a vehicle can be examined and serviced.

inspector (ɪnˈspɛktə) *n* **1** a person who inspects, esp. an official who examines for compliance with regulations, standards, etc. **2** a police officer ranking below a superintendent or chief inspector and above a sergeant. ▸ **inˈspectoral** *or* **inspectorial** (ˌɪnspɛkˈtɔːrɪəl) *adj* ▸ **inˈspectorˌship** *n*

inspectorate (ɪnˈspɛktərɪt) *n* **1** the office, rank, or duties of an inspector. **2** a body of inspectors. **3** a district under an inspector.

inspector general *n, pl* **inspectors general. 1** the head of an inspectorate or inspection system; an officer with wide investigative powers. **2** a staff officer of the military, air, or naval service with the responsibility of conducting inspections and investigations.

inspector of taxes *n* an official of the Inland Revenue whose work is to assess individuals' income tax liability.

insphere (ɪnˈsfɪə) *vb* a variant spelling of **ensphere.**

inspiration (ˌɪnspɪˈreɪʃən) *n* **1** stimulation or arousal of the mind, feelings, etc., to special or unusual activity or creativity. **2** the state or quality of being so stimulated or aroused. **3** someone or something that causes this state. **4** an idea or action resulting from such a state. **5** the act or process of inhaling; breathing in.

inspirational (ˌɪnspɪˈreɪʃənᵊl) *adj* **1** of, relating to, or tending to arouse inspiration; inspiring. **2** resulting from inspiration; inspired. ▸ **ˌinspiˈrationally** *adv*

inspirator (ˈɪnspɪˌreɪtə) *n* a device for drawing in or injecting a vapour, liquid, etc. Also called: **injector.**

inspiratory (ɪnˈspaɪərətərɪ, -trɪ) *adj* of or relating to inhalation or the drawing in of air.

inspire (ɪnˈspaɪə) *vb* **1** to exert a stimulating or beneficial effect upon (a person); animate or invigorate. **2** (*tr;* foll. by *with* or *to; may take an infinitive*) to arouse (with a particular emotion or to a particular action); stir. **3** (*tr*) to prompt or instigate; give rise to: *her beauty inspired his love.* **4** (*tr; often passive*) to guide or arouse by divine influence or inspiration. **5** to take or draw (air, gas, etc.) into the lungs; inhale. **6** (*tr*) *Archaic.* **6a** to breathe into or upon. **6b** to breathe life into. [C14 (in the sense: to breathe upon, blow into): from Latin *inspīrāre,* from *spīrāre* to breathe] ▸ **inˈspirable** *adj* ▸ **inˈspirative** *adj* ▸ **inˈspirer** *n* ▸ **inˈspiringly** *adv*

inspired (ɪnˈspaɪəd) *adj* **1** aroused or guided by or as if aroused or guided by divine inspiration: *an inspired performance; she was like one inspired.* **2** extremely accurate or apt but based on intuition rather than knowledge or logical deduction: *an inspired guess.*

inspirit (ɪnˈspɪrɪt) *vb* (*tr*) to fill with vigour; inspire. ▸ **inˈspiriter** *n* ▸ **inˈspiritingly** *adv* ▸ **inˈspiritment** *n*

inspissate (ɪnˈspɪseɪt) *vb Archaic.* to thicken, as by evaporation. [C17: from Late Latin *inspissātus* thickened, from Latin *spissāre* to thicken, from *spissus* thick] ▸ **ˌinspisˈsation** *n* ▸ **ˈinspisˌsator** *n*

inst. *abbrev. for:* **1** instant (this month). **2** instantaneous. **3** instrumental.

Inst. *abbrev. for:* **1** Institute. **2** Institution.

instability (ˌɪnstəˈbɪlɪtɪ) *n, pl* **-ties. 1** lack of stability or steadiness. **2** tendency to variable or unpredictable behaviour. **3** *Physics.* a sudden deformation of a plasma due to a weakening of the confining field.

instable (ɪnˈsteɪbᵊl) *adj* a less common word for **unstable.**

install *or* **instal** (ɪnˈstɔːl) *vb* **-stalls, -stalling, -stalled** *or* **-stals, -stalling, -stalled.** (*tr*) **1** to place (machinery, equipment, etc.) in position and connect and adjust for use. **2** to transfer (computer software) from a distribution file to a permanent location on disk, and prepare it for its particular environment and application. **3** to put in a position, rank, etc. **4** to settle (a person, esp. oneself) in a position or state: *she installed herself in an armchair.* [C16: from Medieval Latin *installāre,* from IN-[2] + *stallum* STALL[1]] ▸ **inˈstaller** *n*

installant (ɪnˈstɔːlənt) *n* **a** a person who installs another in an office, etc. **b** (*as modifier*): *an installant bishop.*

installation (ˌɪnstəˈleɪʃən) *n* **1** the act of installing or the state of being installed. **2** a large device, system, or piece of equipment that has been installed. **3** a military establishment usually serving in a support role. **4** an art exhibit often involving video or moving parts where the relation of the parts to the whole is important to the interpretation of the piece.

installment plan *or esp. Canadian* **instalment plan** *n* the U.S. and Canadian name for **hire-purchase.**

instalment[1] *or U.S.* **installment** (ɪnˈstɔːlmənt) *n* **1** one of the portions, usually equal, into which a debt is divided for payment at specified intervals over a fixed period. **2** a portion of something that is issued, broadcast, or published in parts, such as a serial in a magazine. [C18: from obsolete *estallment,* probably from Old French *estaler* to fix, hence to agree rate of payment, from *estal* something fixed, place, from Old High German *stal* STALL[1]]

instalment[2] *or U.S.* **installment** (ɪnˈstɔːlmənt) *n* another word for **installation** (sense 1).

instance (ˈɪnstəns) *n* **1** a case or particular example. **2 for instance.** for or as an example. **3** a specified stage in proceedings; step (in the phrases **in the first, second,** etc., **instance**). **4** urgent request or demand (esp. in the phrase **at the instance of**). **5** *Logic.* **5a** an expression derived from another by instantiation. **5b** See **substitution** (sense 4b). **6** *Archaic.* motive or reason. ◆ *vb* (*tr*) **7** to cite as an example. [C14 (in the sense: case, example): from Medieval Latin *instantia* example, (in the sense: urgency) from Latin: a being close upon, presence, from *instāns* pressing upon, urgent; see INSTANT]

instancy (ˈɪnstənsɪ) *n Rare.* **1** the quality of being urgent or imminent. **2** instantaneousness; immediateness.

instant (ˈɪnstənt) *n* **1** a very brief time; moment. **2** a particular moment or point in time: *at the same instant.* **3 on the instant.** immediately; without delay. ◆ *adj* **4** immediate; instantaneous. **5** (esp. of foods) prepared or designed for preparation with very little time and effort: *instant coffee.* **6** urgent or imperative. **7** (*postpositive*) *Rare except when abbreviated in formal correspondence.* **7a** of the present month: *a letter of the 7th instant.* Abbrev.: **inst.** Compare **proximo, ultimo. 7b** currently under consideration. ◆ *adv* **8** a poetic word for **instantly.** [C15: from Latin *instāns,* from *instāre* to be present, press closely, from IN-[2] + *stāre* to stand]

instantaneous (ˌɪnstənˈteɪnɪəs) *adj* **1** occurring with almost no delay; immediate. **2** happening or completed within a moment: *instantaneous death.* **3** *Maths.* **3a** occurring at or associated with a particular instant. **3b** equal to the limit of the average value of a given variable as the time interval over which the variable is considered approaches zero: *instantaneous velocity.* ▸ **ˌinstanˈtaneously** *adv* ▸ **ˌinstanˈtaneousness** *or* **instantaneity** (ɪnˌstæntəˈniːɪtɪ) *n*

instanter (ɪnˈstæntə) *adv Law.* without delay; (in connection with pleading) the same day or within 24 hours. [C17: from Latin: urgently, from *instans* INSTANT]

instantiate (ɪnˈstænʃɪˌeɪt) *vb* (*tr*) to represent by an instance. [C20: from Latin *instantia* (see INSTANCE) + -ATE[1]]

instantiation (ɪnˌstænʃɪˈeɪʃən) *n* **1** the act or an instance of instantiating. **2** the representation of (an abstraction) by a concrete example. **3** *Logic.* **3a** the process of deriving an individual statement from a general one by replacing the variable with a name or other referring expression. **3b** the valid inference of an instance from a universally quantified statement, as *David is rational* from *all men are rational.* **3c** a statement so derived.

instantly (ˈɪnstəntlɪ) *adv* **1** immediately; at once. **2** *Archaic.* urgently or insistently.

instant replay *n* another name for **action replay.**

instar (ˈɪnstɑː) *n* the stage in the development of an insect between any two moults. [C19: New Latin from Latin: image]

instate (ɪnˈsteɪt) *vb* (*tr*) to place in a position or office; install. ▸ **inˈstatement** *n*

instauration (ˌɪnstɔːˈreɪʃən) *n Rare.* restoration or renewal. [C17: from Latin *instaurātiō,* from *instaurāre* to renew] ▸ **ˈinstauˌrator** *n*

instead (ɪnˈstɛd) *adv* **1** as a replacement, substitute, or alternative. **2 instead of.** (*prep*) in place of or as an alternative to. [C13: from phrase *in stead* in place]

instep (ˈɪnˌstɛp) *n* **1** the middle section of the human foot, forming the arch between the ankle and toes. **2** the part of a shoe, stocking, etc., covering this. [C16: probably from IN-[2] + STEP]

instigate (ˈɪnstɪˌgeɪt) *vb* (*tr*) **1** to bring about, as by incitement or urging: *to instigate rebellion.* **2** to urge on to some drastic or inadvisable action. [C16: from Latin *instīgāre* to stimulate, incite; compare Greek *stizein* to prick] ▸ **ˈinstiˌgatingly** *adv* ▸ **ˌinstiˈgation** *n* ▸ **ˈinstiˌgative** *adj* ▸ **ˈinstiˌgator** *n*

instil *or U.S.* **instill** (ɪnˈstɪl) *vb* **-stils** *or* **-stills, -stilling, -stilled.** (*tr*) **1** to introduce gradually; implant or infuse. **2** *Rare.* to pour in or inject in drops. [C16: from Latin *instillāre* to pour in a drop at a time, from *stillāre* to drip] ▸ **inˈstiller** *n* ▸ **inˈstilment,** *U.S.* **inˈstillment,** *or* **ˌinstilˈlation** *n*

instinct (ˈɪnstɪŋkt) *n* **1** the innate capacity of an animal to respond to a given stimulus in a relatively fixed way. **2** inborn intuitive power. **3** a natural and apparently innate aptitude. ◆ *adj* (ɪnˈstɪŋkt) **4** *Rare.* (*postpositive;* often foll. by *with*) **4a** animated or impelled (by). **4b** imbued or infused (with). [C15: from Latin *instinctus* roused, from *instinguere* to incite; compare INSTIGATE]

instinctive (ɪnˈstɪŋktɪv) *or* **instinctual** *adj* **1** of, relating to, or resulting from instinct. **2** conditioned so as to appear innate: *an instinctive movement in driving.* ▸ **inˈstinctively** *or* **inˈstinctually** *adv*

institute (ˈɪnstɪˌtjuːt) *vb* (*tr*) **1** to organize; establish. **2** to initiate: *to institute a practice.* **3** to establish in a position or office; induct. **4** (foll. by *in* or *into*) to install (a clergyman) in a church. ◆ *n* **5** an organization founded for particular work, such as education, promotion of the arts, or scientific research. **6** the building where such an organization is situated. **7** something instituted, esp. a rule, custom, or precedent. [C16: from Latin *instituere,* from *statuere* to place, stand] ▸ **'insti,tutor** *or* **'insti,tuter** *n*

institutes ('ɪnstɪ,tju:ts) *pl n* a digest or summary, esp. of laws.

Institutes ('ɪnstɪ,tju:ts) *pl n* **1** an introduction to legal study in ancient Rome, compiled by order of Justinian and divided into four books forming part of the Corpus Juris Civilis. **2** short for **Institutes of the Christian Religion,** the book by Calvin, completed in 1536 and constituting the basic statement of the Reformed faith, that repudiates papal authority and postulates the doctrines of justification by faith alone and predestination.

institution (,ɪnstɪ'tju:ʃən) *n* **1** the act of instituting. **2** an organization or establishment founded for a specific purpose, such as a hospital, church, company, or college. **3** the building where such an organization is situated. **4** an established custom, law, or relationship in a society or community. **5** Also called: **institutional investor.** a large organization, such as an insurance company, bank, or pension fund, that has substantial sums to invest on a stock exchange. **6** *Informal.* a constant feature or practice: *Jones' drink at the bar was an institution.* **7** the appointment or admission of an incumbent to an ecclesiastical office or pastoral charge. **8** *Christian theol.* the creation of a sacrament by Christ, esp. the Eucharist. ▸ **,insti'tutionary** *adj*

institutional (,ɪnstɪ'tju:ʃənᵊl) *adj* **1** of, relating to, or characteristic of institutions. **2** dull, routine, and uniform: *institutional meals.* **3** relating to principles or institutes, esp. of law. ▸ **,insti'tutionally** *adv*

institutionalism (,ɪnstɪ'tju:ʃənə,lɪzəm) *n* the system of or belief in institutions. ▸ **,insti'tutionalist** *n*

institutionalize *or* **institutionalise** (,ɪnstɪ'tju:ʃənə,laɪz) *vb* **1** (*tr; often passive*) to subject to the deleterious effects of confinement in an institution: *a mental patient who was institutionalized into boredom and apathy.* **2** (*tr*) to place in an institution. **3** to make or become an institution. ▸ **,insti,tutionali'zation** *or* **,insti,tutionali'sation** *n*

institutive ('ɪnstɪ,tju:tɪv) *adj* **1** concerned with instituting and establishing. **2** established by custom or law. ▸ **'insti,tutively** *adv*

in-store *adj* available or taking place within a department store: *in-store banking facilities.*

instr. *abbrev. for:* **1** instructor. **2** instrument. **3** instrumental.

instruct (ɪn'strʌkt) *vb* (*tr*) **1** to direct to do something; order. **2** to teach (someone) how to do (something). **3** to furnish with information; apprise. **4** *Law, chiefly Brit.* **4a** (esp. of a client to his solicitor or a solicitor to a barrister) to give relevant facts or information to. **4b** to authorize (a barrister or solicitor) to conduct a case on a person's behalf: *to instruct counsel.* [C15: from Latin *instruere* to construct, set in order, equip, teach, from *struere* to build] ▸ **in'structible** *adj*

instruction (ɪn'strʌkʃən) *n* **1** a direction; order. **2** the process or act of imparting knowledge; teaching; education. **3** *Computing.* a part of a program consisting of a coded command to the computer to perform a specified function. ▸ **in'structional** *adj*

instructions (ɪn'strʌkʃənz) *pl n* **1** directions, orders, or recommended rules for guidance, use, etc. **2** *Law.* the facts and details relating to a case given by a client to his solicitor or by a solicitor to a barrister with directions to conduct the case: *to take instructions.*

instructive (ɪn'strʌktɪv) *adj* serving to instruct or enlighten; conveying information. ▸ **in'structively** *adv* ▸ **in'structiveness** *n*

instructor (ɪn'strʌktə) *n* **1** someone who instructs; teacher. **2** *U.S. and Canadian.* a university teacher ranking below assistant professor. ▸ **in'structor,ship** *n* ▸ **instructress** (ɪn'strʌktrɪs) *fem n*

instrument *n* ('ɪnstrəmənt). **1** a mechanical implement or tool, esp. one used for precision work: *surgical instrument.* **2** *Music.* any of various contrivances or mechanisms that can be played to produce musical tones or sounds. **3** an important factor or agency in something: *her evidence was an instrument in his arrest.* **4** *Informal.* a person used by another to gain an end; dupe; tool. **5** a measuring device, such as a pressure gauge or ammeter. **6a** a device or system for use in navigation or control, esp. of aircraft. **6b** (*as modifier*): *instrument landing.* **7** a formal legal document. ◆ *vb* ('ɪnstrə,mɛnt). (*tr*) **8** another word for **orchestrate** (sense 1). **9** to equip with instruments. [C13: from Latin *instrūmentum* tool, equipment, from *instruere* to erect, furnish; see INSTRUCT]

instrumental (,ɪnstrə'mɛntᵊl) *adj* **1** serving as a means or influence; helpful. **2** of, relating to, or characterized by an instrument or instruments. **3** played by or composed for musical instruments. **4** *Grammar.* denoting a case of nouns, etc., in certain inflected languages, indicating the instrument used in performing an action, usually translated into English using the prepositions *with* or *by means of.* ◆ *n* **5** a piece of music composed for instruments rather than for voices. **6** *Grammar.* **6a** the instrumental case. **6b** a word or speech element in the instrumental case. ▸ **,instrumen'tality** *n* ▸ **,instru'mentally** *adv*

instrumentalism (,ɪnstrə'mɛntə,lɪzəm) *n* **1** a system of pragmatic philosophy holding that ideas are instruments, that they should guide our actions and can change the world, and that their value consists not in their truth but in their success. **2** an antirealist philosophy of science that holds that theories are not true or false but are merely tools for deriving predictions from observational data.

instrumentalist (,ɪnstrə'mɛntəlɪst) *n* **1** a person who plays a musical instrument. **2** *Philosophy.* a person who believes in the doctrines of instrumentalism. ◆ *adj* **3** of or relating to instrumentalism.

instrumental learning *n Psychol.* a method of training in which the reinforcement is made contingent on the occurrence of the response. Compare **classical conditioning.**

instrumentation (,ɪnstrəmɛn'teɪʃən) *n* **1** the instruments specified in a musical score or arrangement. **2** another word for **orchestration. 3** the study of the characteristics of musical instruments. **4** the use of instruments or tools. **5** means; agency.

instrument flying *n* the navigation of an aircraft by the use of instruments only.

instrument landing *n* an aircraft landing relying only upon instruments and ground radio devices, usually made when visibility is very poor.

instrument panel *or* **board** *n* **1** a panel on which instruments are mounted, as on a car. See also **dashboard. 2** an array of instruments, gauges, etc., mounted to display the condition or performance of a machine.

insubordinate (,ɪnsə'bɔ:dɪnɪt) *adj* **1** not submissive to authority; disobedient or rebellious. **2** not in a subordinate position or rank. ◆ *n* **3** an insubordinate person. ▸ **,insub'ordinately** *adv* ▸ **,insub,ordi'nation** *n*

insubstantial (,ɪnsəb'stænʃəl) *adj* **1** not substantial; flimsy, tenuous, or slight. **2** imaginary; unreal. ▸ **,insub,stanti'ality** *n* ▸ **,insub'stantially** *adv*

insufferable (ɪn'sʌfərəbᵊl) *adj* intolerable; unendurable. ▸ **in'sufferableness** *n* ▸ **in'sufferably** *adv*

insufficiency (,ɪnsə'fɪʃənsɪ) *n* **1** Also called: **,insuf'ficience.** the state of being insufficient. **2** *Pathol.* failure in the functioning of an organ, tissue, etc.: *cardiac insufficiency.*

insufficient (,ɪnsə'fɪʃənt) *adj* not sufficient; inadequate or deficient. ▸ **,insuf'ficiently** *adv*

insufflate ('ɪnsʌ,fleɪt) *vb* **1** (*tr*) to breathe or blow (something) into (a room, area, etc.). **2** *Med.* to blow (air, medicated powder, etc.) into the lungs or into a body cavity. **3** (*tr*) to breathe or blow upon (someone or something) as a ritual or sacramental act, esp. so as to symbolize the influence of the Holy Spirit. ▸ **,insuf'flation** *n* ▸ **'insuf,flator** *n*

insula ('ɪnsjʊlə) *n, pl* **-lae** (-,li:). a pyramid-shaped area of the brain within each cerebral hemisphere beneath parts of the frontal and temporal lobes. Also called: **island of Reil.** [Latin, literally: island]

insular ('ɪnsjʊlə) *adj* **1** of, relating to, or resembling an island. **2** remote, detached, or aloof. **3** illiberal or narrow-minded. **4** isolated or separated. [C17: from Late Latin *insulāris,* from Latin *insula* island, ISLE] ▸ **'insularism** *or* **insularity** (,ɪnsjʊ'lærɪtɪ) *n* ▸ **'insularly** *adv*

insulate ('ɪnsjʊ,leɪt) *vb* (*tr*) **1** to prevent or reduce the transmission of electricity, heat, or sound to or from (a body, device, or region) by surrounding with a nonconducting material. **2** to isolate or detach. [C16: from Late Latin *insulātus:* made into an island]

insulating tape *n Brit.* adhesive tape, impregnated with a moisture-repelling substance, used to insulate exposed electrical conductors. U.S. and Canadian name: **friction tape.**

insulation (,ɪnsjʊ'leɪʃən) *n* **1** Also called: **insulant** ('ɪnsjʊlənt). material used to insulate a body, device, or region. **2** the act or process of insulating.

insulator ('ɪnsjʊ,leɪtə) *n* any material or device that insulates, esp. a material with a very low electrical conductivity or thermal conductivity or something made of such a material.

insulin ('ɪnsjʊlɪn) *n* a protein hormone, secreted in the pancreas by the islets of Langerhans, that controls the concentration of glucose in the blood. Insulin deficiency results in diabetes mellitus. [C20: from New Latin *insula* islet (of the pancreas) + -IN]

insulin reaction *or* **shock** *n* the condition in a diabetic resulting from an overdose of insulin, causing a sharp drop in the blood sugar level with tremor, profuse sweating, and convulsions. See also **hyperinsulinism.**

insult *vb* (ɪn'sʌlt). **1** (*tr*) to treat, mention, or speak to rudely; offend; affront. **2** (*tr*) *Obsolete.* to assault; attack. ◆ *n* ('ɪnsʌlt). **3** an offensive or contemptuous remark or action; affront; slight. **4** a person or thing producing the effect of an affront: *some television is an insult to intelligence.* **5** *Med.* an injury or trauma. **6 add insult to injury.** to make an unfair or unacceptable situation even worse. [C16: from Latin *insultāre* to jump upon, from IN-[2] + *saltāre* to jump] ▸ **in'sulter** *n*

insuperable (ɪn'su:pərəbᵊl, -prəbᵊl, -'sju:-) *adj* incapable of being overcome; insurmountable. ▸ **in,supera'bility** *or* **in'superableness** *n* ▸ **in'superably** *adv*

insupportable (,ɪnsə'pɔ:təbᵊl) *adj* **1** incapable of being endured; intolerable; insufferable. **2** incapable of being supported or justified; indefensible. ▸ **,insup'portableness** *n* ▸ **,insup'portably** *adv*

insuppressible (,ɪnsə'prɛsəbᵊl) *adj* incapable of being suppressed, overcome, or muffled: *an insuppressible giggle.* ▸ **,insup'pressibly** *adv*

insurable interest *n Law.* a financial or other interest in the life or property covered by an insurance contract, without which the contract cannot be enforced.

insurance (ɪn'ʃʊərəns, -'ʃɔ:-) *n* **1a** the act, system, or business of providing financial protection for property, life, health, etc., against specified contingencies, such as death, loss, or damage, and involving payment of regular premiums in return for a policy guaranteeing such protection. **1b** the state of having such protection. **1c** Also called: **insurance policy.** the policy providing such protection. **1d** the pecuniary amount of such protection. **1e** the premium payable in return for such protection. **1f** (*as modifier*): *insurance agent; insurance broker; insurance company.* **2** a means of protecting or safeguarding against risk or injury.

insure (ɪn'ʃʊə, -'ʃɔ:) *vb* **1** (often foll. by *against*) to guarantee or protect (against risk, loss, etc.): *we insured against disappointment by making an early reservation.* **2** (often foll. by *against*) to issue (a person) with an insurance policy or take out an insurance policy (on): *his house was heavily insured against fire; after all his car accidents the company refuses to insure him again.* **3** another word (esp. U.S.) for **ensure** (senses 1, 2). ◆ Also (rare) (for senses 1, 2): **ensure.** ▸ **in'surable** *adj* ▸ **in,sura'bility** *n*

insured (ɪn'ʃʊəd, -'ʃɔ:d) *adj* **1** covered by insurance: *an insured risk.* ◆ *n* **2** the person, persons, or organization covered by an insurance policy.

insurer (ɪn'ʃʊərə, -'ʃɔ:-) *n* **1** a person or company offering insurance policies in return for premiums. **2** a person or thing that insures.

insurgence (ɪn'sɜːdʒəns) *n* rebellion, uprising, or riot.
insurgent (ɪn'sɜːdʒənt) *adj* **1** rebellious or in revolt, as against a government in power or the civil authorities. ◆ *n* **2** a person who takes part in an uprising or rebellion; insurrectionist. **3** *International law.* a person or group that rises in revolt against an established government or authority but whose conduct does not amount to belligerency. [C18: from Latin *insurgēns* rising upon or against, from *insurgere* to rise up, from *surgere* to rise] ▸ **in'surgency** *n*
insurmountable (ˌɪnsə'maʊntəbəl) *adj* incapable of being overcome; insuperable. ▸ **ˌinsurˌmounta'bility** *or* **ˌinsur'mountableness** *n* ▸ **ˌinsur'mountably** *adv*
insurrection (ˌɪnsə'rɛkʃən) *n* the act or an instance of rebelling against a government in power or the civil authorities; insurgency. [C15: from Late Latin *insurrectiō*, from *insurgere* to rise up] ▸ **ˌinsur'rectional** *adj* ▸ **ˌinsur'rectionary** *n, adj* ▸ **ˌinsur'rectionism** *n* ▸ **ˌinsur'rectionist** *n, adj*
insusceptible (ˌɪnsə'sɛptəbəl) *adj* (when *postpositive,* usually foll. by *to*) not capable of being affected (by); not susceptible (to). ▸ **ˌinsusˌcepti'bility** *n* ▸ **ˌinsus'ceptibly** *adv*
inswing ('ɪnˌswɪŋ) *n Cricket.* the movement of a bowled ball from off to leg through the air. Compare **outswing.**
inswinger ('ɪnˌswɪŋə) *n* **1** *Cricket.* a ball bowled so as to move from off to leg through the air. **2** *Soccer.* a ball kicked, esp. from a corner, so as to move through the air in a curve towards the goal or the centre.
int. *abbrev. for:* **1** interest. **2** interim. **3** interior. **4** internal. **5** Also: **Int.** international. **6** interpreter. **7** intelligence (military).
intact (ɪn'tækt) *adj* untouched or unimpaired; left complete or perfect. [C15: from Latin *intactus* not touched, from *tangere* to touch] ▸ **in'tactness** *n*
intaglio (ɪn'tɑːlɪˌəʊ) *n, pl* **-lios** *or* **-li** (-ljiː). **1** a seal, gem, etc., ornamented with a sunken or incised design, as opposed to a design in relief. Compare **cameo. 2** the art or process of incised carving. **3** a design, figure, or ornamentation carved, engraved, or etched into the surface of the material used. **4** any of various printing techniques using an etched or engraved plate. The whole plate is smeared with ink, the surface wiped clean, and the ink in the recesses then transferred to the paper or other material. **5** an incised die used to make a design in relief. [C17: from Italian, from *intagliare* to engrave, from *tagliare* to cut, from Late Latin *tāliāre;* see TAILOR] ▸ **intagliated** (ɪn'tɑːlɪˌeɪtɪd) *adj*
intake ('ɪnˌteɪk) *n* **1** a thing or a quantity taken in: *an intake of students.* **2** the act of taking in. **3** the opening through which fluid enters a duct or channel, esp. the air inlet of a jet engine. **4** a ventilation shaft in a mine. **5** a contraction or narrowing: *an intake in a garment.*
intangible (ɪn'tændʒɪbəl) *adj* **1** incapable of being perceived by touch; impalpable. **2** imprecise or unclear to the mind: *intangible ideas.* **3** (of property or a business asset) saleable though not possessing intrinsic productive value. ◆ *n* **4** something that is intangible. ▸ **inˌtangi'bility** *or* **in'tangibleness** *n* ▸ **in'tangibly** *adv*
intarsia (ɪn'tɑːsɪə) *or* **tarsia** *n* **1** a decorative or pictorial mosaic of inlaid wood or sometimes ivory of a style developed in the Italian Renaissance and used esp. on wooden wall panels. **2** the art or practice of making such mosaics. **3** (in knitting) an individually worked motif. [C19: changed from Italian *intarsio*]
integer ('ɪntɪdʒə) *n* **1** any rational number that can be expressed as the sum or difference of a finite number of units, being a member of the set ...–3, –2, –1, 0, 1, 2, 3... **2** an individual entity or whole unit. [C16: from Latin: untouched, entire, from *tangere* to touch]
integral *adj* ('ɪntɪgrəl, ɪn'tɛgrəl). **1** (often foll. by *to*) being an essential part (of); intrinsic (to). **2** intact; entire. **3** formed of constituent parts; united. **4** *Maths.* **4a** of or involving an integral. **4b** involving or being an integer. ◆ *n* ('ɪntɪgrəl). **5** *Maths.* the sum of a large number of infinitesimally small quantities, summed either between stated limits (**definite integral**) or in the absence of limits (**indefinite integral**). Symbol: ∫ **6** a complete thing; whole. ▸ **integrality** (ˌɪntɪ'grælɪtɪ) *n* ▸ **'integrally** *adv*
integral calculus *n* the branch of calculus concerned with the determination of integrals and their application to the solution of differential equations, the determination of areas and volumes, etc. Compare **differential calculus.**
integrand ('ɪntɪˌgrænd) *n* a mathematical function to be integrated. [C19: from Latin: to be integrated]
integrant ('ɪntəgrənt) *adj* **1** part of a whole; integral; constituent. ◆ *n* **2** an integrant thing or part.
integrate *vb* ('ɪntɪˌgreɪt). **1** to make or be made into a whole; incorporate or be incorporated. **2** (*tr*) to designate (a school, park, etc.) for use by all races or groups; desegregate. **3** to amalgamate or mix (a racial or religious group) with an existing community. **4** *Maths.* to perform an integration on (a quantity, expression, etc.). ◆ *adj* ('ɪntɪgrɪt). **5** made up of parts; integrated. [C17: from Latin *integrāre;* see INTEGER] ▸ **integrable** ('ɪntəgrəbəl) *adj* ▸ **ˌintegra'bility** *n* ▸ **'inteˌgrative** *adj*
integrated ('ɪntɪˌgreɪtɪd) *adj* **1** characterized by integration. **2** denoting a works which combines various processes normally carried out at different locations: *an integrated steelworks.* **3** *Biology.* denoting a virus the DNA of which is incorporated into the chromosomes of the host cell.
integrated circuit *n* a very small electronic circuit consisting of an assembly of elements made from a chip of semiconducting material, such as crystalline silicon. Abbrev.: **IC.**
integrated school *n* (in New Zealand) a private or church school that has joined the state school system.
integration (ˌɪntɪ'greɪʃən) *n* **1** the act of combining or adding parts to make a unified whole. **2** the act of amalgamating a racial or religious group with an existing community. **3** the combination of previously racially segregated social facilities into a nonsegregated system. **4** *Psychol.* organization into a unified pattern, esp. of different aspects of the personality into a hierarchical system of functions. **5** the assimilation of nutritive material by the body during the process of anabolism. **6** *Maths.* an operation used in calculus in which the integral of a function or variable is determined; the inverse of differentiation. ▸ **ˌinte'grationist** *n*
integrative bargaining ('ɪntɪˌgreɪtɪv) *n Industrial relations.* a type of bargaining in which all parties involved recognize that there are common problems requiring mutual resolution.
integrator ('ɪntɪˌgreɪtə) *n* **1** a person or thing that integrates, esp. a mechanical instrument that determines the value of a definite integral, as the area under a curve. See also **planimeter. 2** *Computing.* **2a** an arithmetic component with two input variables, *x* and *y*, whose output variable *z* is proportional to the integral of *y* with respect to *x*. **2b** an arithmetic component whose output variable is proportional to the integral of the input variable with respect to elapsed time.
integrity (ɪn'tɛgrɪtɪ) *n* **1** adherence to moral principles; honesty. **2** the quality of being unimpaired; soundness. **3** unity; wholeness. [C15: from Latin *integritās;* see INTEGER]
integument (ɪn'tɛgjʊmənt) *n* any outer protective layer or covering, such as a cuticle, seed coat, rind, or shell. [C17: from Latin *integumentum,* from *tegere* to cover] ▸ **inˌtegu'mental** *or* **inˌtegu'mentary** *adj*
intellect ('ɪntɪˌlɛkt) *n* **1** the capacity for understanding, thinking, and reasoning, as distinct from feeling or wishing. **2** a mind or intelligence, esp. a brilliant one: *his intellect is wasted on that job.* **3** *Informal.* a person possessing a brilliant mind; brain. **4** those possessing the greatest mental power: *the intellect of a nation.* [C14: from Latin *intellectus* comprehension, intellect, from *intellegere* to understand; see INTELLIGENCE] ▸ **ˌintel'lective** *adj* ▸ **ˌintel'lectively** *adv*
intellection (ˌɪntɪ'lɛkʃən) *n* **1** mental activity; thought. **2** an idea or thought.
intellectual (ˌɪntɪ'lɛktʃʊəl) *adj* **1** of or relating to the intellect, as opposed to the emotions. **2** appealing to or characteristic of people with a developed intellect: *intellectual literature.* **3** expressing or enjoying mental activity. ◆ *n* **4** a person who enjoys mental activity and has highly developed tastes in art, literature, etc. **5** a person who uses or works with his intellect. **6** a highly intelligent person. ▸ **ˌintelˌlectu'ality** *or* **ˌintel'lectualness** *n* ▸ **ˌintel'lectually** *adv*
intellectualism (ˌɪntɪ'lɛktʃʊəˌlɪzəm) *n* **1** development and exercise of the intellect. **2** the placing of excessive value on the intellect, esp. with disregard for the emotions. **3** *Philosophy.* **3a** the doctrine that reason is the ultimate criterion of knowledge. **3b** the doctrine that deliberate action is consequent on a process of conscious or subconscious reasoning. ▸ **ˌintel'lectualist** *n, adj* ▸ **ˌintelˌlectual'istic** *adj* ▸ **ˌintelˌlectual'istically** *adv*
intellectualize *or* **intellectualise** (ˌɪntɪ'lɛktʃʊəˌlaɪz) *vb* **1** to make or become intellectual. **2** (*tr*) to treat or consider in an intellectual way; rationalize. ▸ **ˌintelˌlectuali'zation** *or* **ˌintelˌlectuali'sation** *n* ▸ **ˌintel'lectualˌizer** *or* **ˌintel'lectualˌiser** *n*
intellectual property *n* an intangible asset, such as a copyright or patent.
intelligence (ɪn'tɛlɪdʒəns) *n* **1** the capacity for understanding; ability to perceive and comprehend meaning. **2** good mental capacity: *a person of intelligence.* **3** *Old-fashioned.* news; information. **4** military information about enemies, spies, etc. **5** a group or department that gathers or deals with such information. **6** (*often cap.*) an intelligent being, esp. one that is not embodied. **7** (*modifier*) of or relating to intelligence: *an intelligence network.* [C14: from Latin *intellegentia,* from *intellegere* to discern, comprehend, literally: choose between, from INTER- + *legere* to choose] ▸ **inˌtelli'gential** *adj*
intelligence quotient *n* a measure of the intelligence of an individual derived from results obtained from specially designed tests. The quotient is traditionally derived by dividing an individual's mental age by his chronological age and multiplying the result by 100. Abbrev.: **IQ.**
intelligencer (ɪn'tɛlɪdʒənsə) *n Archaic.* an informant or spy.
intelligence test *n* any of a number of tests designed to measure a person's mental skills. See also **Binet-Simon scale.**
intelligent (ɪn'tɛlɪdʒənt) *adj* **1** having or indicating intelligence. **2** having high intelligence; clever. **3** indicating high intelligence; perceptive: *an intelligent guess.* **4** guided by reason; rational. **5** (of computerized functions) able to modify action in the light of ongoing events. **6** (*postpositive;* foll. by *of*) *Archaic.* having knowledge or information: *they were intelligent of his whereabouts.* ▸ **in'telligently** *adv*
intelligent card *n* another name for **smart card.**
intelligent knowledge-based system *n* a computer system in which the properties of a database and an expert system are combined to enable the system to store and process data and make deductions from stored data. Abbrev.: **IKBS.**
intelligentsia (ɪnˌtɛlɪ'dʒɛntsɪə) *n* (usually preceded by *the*) the educated or intellectual people in a society or community. [C20: from Russian *intelligentsiya,* from Latin *intellegentia* INTELLIGENCE]
intelligent terminal *n* a computer operating terminal that can carry out some data processing, as well as sending data to and receiving it from a central processor.
intelligible (ɪn'tɛlɪdʒəbəl) *adj* **1** able to be understood; comprehensible. **2** *Philosophy.* **2a** capable of being apprehended by the mind or intellect alone. **2b** (in metaphysical systems such as those of Plato or Kant) denoting that metaphysical realm which is accessible to the intellect as opposed to the world of mere phenomena accessible to the senses. [C14: from Latin *intellegibilis;* see INTELLECT] ▸ **inˌtelligi'bility** *or* **in'telligibleness** *n* ▸ **in'telligibly** *adv*
Intelsat ('ɪntɛlˌsæt) *n* any of the series of communications satellites operated by the International Telecommunications Satellite Consortium.
intemerate (ɪn'tɛmərɪt) *adj Rare.* not defiled; pure; unsullied. [C15: from Latin *intemerātus* undefiled, pure, from IN-[1] + *temerāre* to darken, violate, from *temere* rashly] ▸ **in'temerately** *adv* ▸ **in'temerateness** *n*
intemperate (ɪn'tɛmpərɪt, -prɪt) *adj* **1** consuming alcoholic drink habitually

or to excess. **2** indulging bodily appetites to excess; immoderate. **3** unrestrained: *intemperate rage.* **4** extreme or severe: *an intemperate climate.* ▸ **in'temperance** *or* **in'temperateness** *n* ▸ **in'temperately** *adv*

intend (ɪn'tɛnd) *vb* **1** (*may take a clause as object*) to propose or plan (something or to do something); have in mind; mean. **2** (*tr;* often foll. by *for*) to design or destine (for a certain purpose, person, etc.): *that shot was intended for the President.* **3** (*tr*) to mean to express or indicate: *what do his words intend?* **4** (*intr*) to have a purpose as specified; mean: *he intends well.* **5** (*tr*) *Archaic.* to direct or turn (the attention, eyes, etc.). [C14: from Latin *intendere* to stretch forth, give one's attention to, from *tendere* to stretch] ▸ **in'tender** *n*

intendance (ɪn'tɛndəns) *n* **1** any of various public departments, esp. in France. **2** a less common word for **superintendence.**

intendancy (ɪn'tɛndənsɪ) *n* **1** the position or work of an intendant. **2** intendants collectively. **3** *History.* the district or area administered by an intendant.

intendant (ɪn'tɛndənt) *n* **1** *History.* a provincial or colonial official of France, Spain, or Portugal. **2** a senior administrator in some countries, esp. in Latin America. **3** a superintendent or manager.

intended (ɪn'tɛndɪd) *adj* **1** planned or future. ♦ *n* **2** *Informal.* a person whom one is to marry; fiancé or fiancée.

intendment (ɪn'tɛndmənt) *n* **1** the meaning of something as fixed or understood by the law. **2** *Obsolete.* intention, design, or purpose.

intenerate (ɪn'tɛnəˌreɪt) *vb* (*tr*) *Rare.* to soften or make tender. [C16: from IN-[2] + Latin *tener* delicate, TENDER[1]] ▸ **inˌtener'ation** *n*

intens. *abbrev. for:* **1** intensifier. **2** intensive.

intense (ɪn'tɛns) *adj* **1** of extreme force, strength, degree, or amount: *intense heat.* **2** characterized by deep or forceful feelings: *an intense person.* [C14: from Latin *intensus* stretched, from *intendere* to stretch out; see INTEND] ▸ **in'tensely** *adv* ▸ **in'tenseness** *n*

USAGE *Intense* is sometimes wrongly used where *intensive* is meant: *the land is under intensive* (not *intense*) *cultivation. Intensely* is sometimes wrongly used where *intently* is meant: *he listened intently* (not *intensely*).

intensifier (ɪn'tɛnsɪˌfaɪə) *n* **1** a person or thing that intensifies. **2** a word, esp. an adjective or adverb, that has little semantic content of its own but that serves to intensify the meaning of the word or phrase that it modifies: *awfully* and *up* are intensifiers in the phrases *awfully sorry* and *cluttered up.* **3** a substance, esp. one containing silver or uranium, used to increase the density of a photographic film or plate. Compare **reducer** (sense 1).

intensify (ɪn'tɛnsɪˌfaɪ) *vb* **-fies, -fying, -fied. 1** to make or become intense or more intense. **2** (*tr*) to increase the density of (a photographic film or plate). ▸ **inˌtensifi'cation** *n*

intension (ɪn'tɛnʃən) *n* **1** *Logic.* **1a** the set of characteristics or properties by which the referent or referents of a given word are determined: thus, the intension of *marsupial* is the set containing the characteristics *suckling its young* and *having a pouch.* Compare **extension** (sense 11a). **1b** See **subjective intension. 2** a rare word for **intensity, determination,** or **intensification.**

intensional (ɪn'tɛnʃənᵊl) *adj Logic.* (of a predicate) incapable of explanation solely in terms of the set of objects to which it is applicable; requiring explanation in terms of meaning or understanding. Compare **extensional.** See also **opaque context, Electra paradox.** ▸ **in'tensionally** *adv*

intensional object *n Logic, philosophy.* the object of a propositional attitude that may or may not exist, as in *Robert is dreaming of the pot of gold at the end of the rainbow.* This must be an intensional (or opaque) context, for otherwise, since there is no pot of gold, Robert would be dreaming of nothing.

intensity (ɪn'tɛnsɪtɪ) *n, pl* **-ties. 1** the state or quality of being intense. **2** extreme force, degree, or amount. **3** *Physics.* **3a** a measure of field strength or of the energy transmitted by radiation. See **radiant intensity, luminous intensity. 3b** (of sound in a specified direction) the average rate of flow of sound energy, usually in watts, for one period through unit area at right angles to the specified direction. Symbol: *I* **4** Also called: **earthquake intensity.** *Geology.* a measure of the size of an earthquake based on observation of the effects of the shock at the earth's surface. Specified on the Mercalli scale. See **Mercalli scale, Richter scale.**

intensive (ɪn'tɛnsɪv) *adj* **1** involving the maximum use of land, time, or some other resource: *intensive agriculture; an intensive course.* **2** (*usually in combination*) using one factor of production proportionately more than others, as specified: *capital-intensive; labour-intensive.* **3** *Agriculture.* involving or farmed using large amounts of capital or labour to increase production from a particular area. Compare **extensive** (sense 3). **4** denoting or relating to a grammatical intensifier. **5** denoting or belonging to a class of pronouns used to emphasize a noun or personal pronoun, such as *himself* in the sentence *John himself did it.* In English, intensive pronouns are identical in form with reflexive pronouns. **6** of or relating to intension. **7** *Physics.* of or relating to a property, measurement, etc., that is independent of mass. Compare **extensive** (sense 4). ♦ *n* **8** an intensifier or intensive pronoun or grammatical construction. ▸ **in'tensively** *adv* ▸ **in'tensiveness** *n*

intensive care *n* extensive and continuous care and treatment provided for an acutely ill patient, usually in a specially designated section (**intensive care unit**) of a hospital.

intent (ɪn'tɛnt) *n* **1** something that is intended; aim; purpose; design. **2** the act of intending. **3** *Law.* the will or purpose with which one does an act. **4** implicit meaning; connotation. **5 to all intents and purposes.** for all practical purposes; virtually. ♦ *adj* **6** firmly fixed; determined; concentrated: *an intent look.* **7** (*postpositive;* usually foll. by *on* or *upon*) having the fixed intention (of); directing one's mind or energy (to): *intent on committing a crime.* [C13 (in the sense: intention): from Late Latin *intentus* aim, intent, from Latin: a stretching out; see INTEND] ▸ **in'tently** *adv* ▸ **in'tentness** *n*

intention (ɪn'tɛnʃən) *n* **1** a purpose or goal; aim: *it is his intention to reform.* **2** *Law.* the resolve or design with which a person does or refrains from doing an act, a necessary ingredient of certain offences. **3** *Med.* a natural healing process, as by **first intention,** in which the edges of a wound cling together with no tissue between, or by **second intention,** in which the wound edges adhere with granulation tissue. **4** (*usually pl*) design or purpose with respect to a proposal of marriage (esp. in the phrase **honourable intentions**). **5** an archaic word for **meaning** or **intentness.**

intentional (ɪn'tɛnʃənᵊl) *adj* **1** performed by or expressing intention; deliberate. **2** of or relating to intention or purpose. **3** *Philosophy.* **3a** of or relating to the capacity of the mind to refer to different kinds of objects. **3b** (of an object) existing only as the object of some mental attitude rather than in reality, as *a unicorn* in *she hopes to meet a unicorn.* See also **intensional.** ▸ **inˌtention'ality** *n* ▸ **in'tentionally** *adv*

inter (ɪn'tɜː) *vb* **-ters, -terring, -terred.** (*tr*) to place (a body) in the earth; bury, esp. with funeral rites. [C14: from Old French *enterrer,* from Latin IN-[2] + *terra* earth]

inter. *abbrev. for* intermediate.

inter- *prefix* **1** between or among: *international.* **2** together, mutually, or reciprocally: *interdependent; interchange.* [from Latin]

interact (ˌɪntər'ækt) *vb* (*intr*) to act on or in close relation with each other.

interaction (ˌɪntər'ækʃən) *n* **1** a mutual or reciprocal action or influence. **2** *Physics.* the transfer of energy between elementary particles, between a particle and a field, or between fields. See **strong interaction, electromagnetic interaction, fundamental interaction, gravitational interaction, weak interaction,** and **electroweak interaction.** ▸ **ˌinter'actional** *adj*

interactionism (ˌɪntər'ækʃəˌnɪzəm) *n Philosophy.* the dualistic doctrine that holds that mind and body have a causal effect upon one another, as when pricking one's finger (physical) causes pain (mental), or an embarrassing memory (mental) causes one to blush (physical). Compare **parallelism** (sense 3).

interactive (ˌɪntər'æktɪv) *adj* **1** allowing or relating to continuous two-way transfer of information between a user and the central point of a communication system, such as a computer or television. **2** (of two or more persons, forces, etc.) acting upon or in close relation with each other; interacting. ▸ **ˌinterac'tivity** *n*

interactive engineering *n* another name for **concurrent engineering.**

interactive video *n* a computer-optical disk system that displays still or moving video images as determined by computer program and user needs.

inter alia *Latin.* ('ɪntər 'eɪlɪə) *adv* among other things.

inter alios *Latin.* ('ɪntər 'eɪlɪəʊs) *adv* among other people.

interatomic (ˌɪntərə'tɒmɪk) *adj* existing or occurring between or among atoms. Compare **intra-atomic.**

interbedded (ˌɪntə'bɛdɪd) *adj Geology.* occurring between beds, esp. (of laval rock) occurring between strata of a different origin.

interbrain ('ɪntəˌbreɪn) *n Anatomy.* a nontechnical word for **diencephalon.**

interbreed (ˌɪntə'briːd) *vb* **-breeds, -breeding, -bred. 1** (*intr*) to breed within a single family or strain so as to produce particular characteristics in the offspring. **2** another term for **crossbreed** (sense 1).

interbroker dealer (ˌɪntə'brəʊkə) *n Stock Exchange.* a specialist who matches the needs of different market makers and facilitates dealings between them.

intercalary (ɪn'tɜːkələrɪ) *adj* **1** (of a day, month, etc.) inserted in the calendar. **2** (of a particular year) having one or more days inserted. **3** inserted, introduced, or interpolated. **4** *Botany.* growing between the upper branches and the lower branches or bracts on a stem. [C17: from Latin *intercalārius;* see INTERCALATE] ▸ **in'tercalarily** *adv*

intercalate (ɪn'tɜːkəˌleɪt) *vb* (*tr*) **1** to insert (one or more days) into the calendar. **2** to interpolate or insert. [C17: from Latin *intercalāre* to insert, proclaim that a day has been inserted, from INTER- + *calāre* to proclaim] ▸ **inˌterca'lation** *n* ▸ **in'tercalative** *adj*

intercede (ˌɪntə'siːd) *vb* (*intr*) **1** (often foll. by *in*) to come between parties or act as mediator or advocate: *to intercede in the strike.* **2** *Roman history.* (of a tribune or other magistrate) to interpose a veto. [C16: from Latin *intercēdere* to intervene, from INTER- + *cēdere* to move] ▸ **ˌinter'ceder** *n*

intercellular (ˌɪntə'sɛljʊlə) *adj Biology.* between or among cells: *intercellular fluid.*

intercensal (ˌɪntə'sɛnsəl) *adj* (of population figures, etc.) estimated at a time between official censuses. [C19: from INTER- + *censal,* irregularly formed from CENSUS]

intercept *vb* (ˌɪntə'sɛpt). (*tr*) **1** to stop, deflect, or seize on the way from one place to another; prevent from arriving or proceeding. **2** *Sport.* to seize or cut off (a pass) on its way from one opponent to another. **3** *Maths.* to cut off, mark off, or bound (some part of a line, curve, plane, or surface). ♦ *n* ('ɪntəˌsɛpt). **4** *Maths.* **4a** a point at which two figures intersect. **4b** the distance from the origin to the point at which a line, curve, or surface cuts a coordinate axis. **4c** an intercepted segment. **5** *Sport, U.S. and Canadian.* the act of intercepting an opponent's pass. [C16: from Latin *intercipere* to seize before arrival, from INTER- + *capere* to take] ▸ **ˌinter'ception** *n* ▸ **ˌinter'ceptive** *adj*

interceptor *or* **intercepter** (ˌɪntə'sɛptə) *n* **1** a person or thing that intercepts. **2** a fast highly manoeuvrable fighter aircraft used to intercept enemy aircraft.

intercession (ˌɪntə'sɛʃən) *n* **1** the act or an instance of interceding. **2** the act of interceding or offering petitionary prayer to God on behalf of others. **3** such petitionary prayer. **4** *Roman history.* the interposing of a veto by a tribune or

ˌinteral'lied *adj* **ˌinter'bank** *adj* **ˌinter'branch** *adj*

other magistrate. [C16: from Latin *intercessio;* see INTERCEDE] ▸ **ˌinterˈcessional** *or* **ˌinterˈcessory** *adj* ▸ **ˌinterˈcessor** *n* ▸ **ˌintercesˈsorial** *adj*

interchange *vb* (ˌɪntəˈtʃeɪndʒ). **1** to change places or cause to change places; alternate; exchange; switch. ◆ *n* (ˈɪntəˌtʃeɪndʒ). **2** the act of interchanging; exchange or alternation. **3** a motorway junction of interconnecting roads and bridges designed to prevent streams of traffic crossing one another. ▸ **ˌinterˈchangeable** *adj* ▸ **ˌinterˌchangeaˈbility** *or* **ˌinterˈchangeableness** *n* ▸ **ˌinterˈchangeably** *adv*

Intercity (ˌɪntəˈsɪtɪ) *adj* (in Britain) *Trademark.* denoting a fast train or passenger rail service, esp. between main towns.

interclavicle (ˌɪntəˈklævɪkᵊl) *n* a membrane bone between and beneath the clavicles, present in some fossil amphibians, all reptiles except snakes, and monotremes. ▸ **interclavicular** (ˌɪntəkləˈvɪkjʊlə) *adj*

intercolumniation (ˌɪntəkəˌlʌmnɪˈeɪʃən) *n Architect.* **1** the horizontal distance between two adjacent columns. **2** the system of spacing for a set of columns. [C17: from Latin *intercolumnium* space between two columns] ▸ **ˌintercoˈlumnar** *adj*

intercom (ˈɪntəˌkɒm) *n Informal.* an internal telephone system for communicating within a building, an aircraft, etc. [C20: short for *intercommunication*]

intercommunicate (ˌɪntəkəˈmjuːnɪˌkeɪt) *vb* (*intr*) **1** to communicate mutually. **2** to interconnect, as two rooms. ▸ **ˌintercomˈmunicable** *adj* ▸ **ˌintercomˌmunicaˈbility** *n* ▸ **ˌintercomˌmuniˈcation** *n* ▸ **ˌintercomˈmunicative** *adj* ▸ **ˌintercomˈmuniˌcator** *n*

intercommunion (ˌɪntəkəˈmjuːnjən) *n* association between Churches, involving esp. mutual reception of Holy Communion.

intercontinental ballistic missile (ˌɪntəˌkɒntɪˈnɛntᵊl) *n* a missile that follows a ballistic trajectory and has the range to carry a nuclear bomb over 5500 km. Abbrev.: **ICBM.**

interconversion (ˌɪntəkənˈvɜːʃən) *n* a process in which two things are each converted into the other, often as the result of chemical or physical activity.

intercooler (ˌɪntəˈkuːlə) *n* a heat exchanger used in a supercharger or turbocharger.

intercostal (ˌɪntəˈkɒstᵊl) *adj Anatomy.* between the ribs: *intercostal muscles.* [C16: via New Latin from Latin INTER- + *costa* rib]

intercourse (ˈɪntəˌkɔːs) *n* **1** communication or exchange between individuals; mutual dealings. **2** See **sexual intercourse.** [C15: from Medieval Latin *intercursus* business, from Latin *intercurrere* to run between, from *currere* to run]

intercrop (ˌɪntəˈkrɒp) *n* **1** a crop grown between the rows of another crop. ◆ *vb* **-crops, -cropping, -cropped. 2** to grow (one crop) between the rows of (another).

intercross (ˌɪntəˈkrɒs) *vb, n* another word for **crossbreed.**

intercurrent (ˌɪntəˈkʌrənt) *adj* **1** occurring during or in between; intervening. **2** *Pathol.* (of a disease) occurring during the course of another disease. ▸ **ˌinterˈcurrence** *n* ▸ **ˌinterˈcurrently** *adv*

intercut (ˌɪntəˈkʌt) *vb* **-cuts, -cutting, -cut.** *Films.* another word for **crosscut.**

interdental (ˌɪntəˈdɛntᵊl) *adj* **1** situated between teeth. **2** *Phonetics.* (of a consonant) pronounced with the tip of the tongue lying between the upper and lower front teeth, as for the *th* sounds in English *thin* and *then.* ▸ **ˌinterˈdentally** *adv*

interdict *n* (ˈɪntəˌdɪkt, -ˌdaɪt). **1** *R.C. Church.* the exclusion of a person or all persons in a particular place from certain sacraments and other benefits, although not from communion. **2** *Civil law.* any order made by a court or official prohibiting an act. **3** *Scots Law.* an order having the effect of an injunction. **4** *Roman history.* **4a** an order of a praetor commanding or forbidding an act. **4b** the procedure by which this order was sought. ◆ *vb* (ˌɪntəˈdɪkt, -ˈdaɪt). (*tr*) **5** to place under legal or ecclesiastical sanction; prohibit; forbid. **6** *Military.* to destroy (an enemy's lines of communication) by firepower. [C13: from Latin *interdictum* prohibition, from *interdīcere* to forbid, from INTER- + *dīcere* to say] ▸ **ˌinterˈdictive** *or* **ˌinterˈdictory** *adj* ▸ **ˌinterˈdictively** *adv* ▸ **ˌinterˈdictor** *n*

interdiction (ˌɪntəˈdɪkʃən) *n* **1** the act of interdicting or state of being interdicted. **2** an interdict.

interdict list *n* another name for **Indian list.**

interdigitate (ˌɪntəˈdɪdʒɪˌteɪt) *vb* (*intr*) to interlock like the fingers of clasped hands. [C19: from INTER- + Latin *digitus* (see DIGIT) + -ATE[1]]

interdisciplinary (ˌɪntəˈdɪsɪˌplɪnərɪ) *adj* involving two or more academic disciplines.

interest (ˈɪntrɪst, -tərɪst) *n* **1** the sense of curiosity about or concern with something or someone: *an interest in butterflies.* **2** the power of stimulating such a sense: *to have great interest.* **3** the quality of such stimulation. **4** something in which one is interested; a hobby or pursuit. **5** (*often pl*) benefit; advantage: *she always acted in her own interest.* **6** (*often pl*) **6a** a right, share, or claim, esp. in a business or property. **6b** the business, property, etc., in which a person has such concern. **7a** a charge for the use of credit or borrowed money. **7b** such a charge expressed as a percentage per time unit of the sum borrowed or used. **8** (*often pl*) a section of a community, etc., whose members have common aims: *we must not offend the landed interest.* **9 declare an interest.** to make known one's connection, esp. a prejudicial connection, with an affair. ◆ *vb* (*tr*) **10** to arouse or excite the curiosity or concern of. **11** to cause to become involved in something; concern. [C15: from Latin: it concerns, from *interesse;* from INTER- + *esse* to be]

interested (ˈɪntrɪstɪd, -tərɪs-) *adj* **1** showing or having interest. **2** (*usually prenominal*) personally involved or implicated: *the interested parties met to discuss the business.* ▸ **ˈinterestedly** *adv* ▸ **ˈinterestedness** *n*

interesting (ˈɪntrɪstɪŋ, -tərɪs-) *adj* inspiring interest; absorbing. ▸ **ˈinterestingly** *adv* ▸ **ˈinterestingness** *n*

interest-rate futures *pl n* financial futures based on projected movements of interest rates.

interface *n* (ˈɪntəˌfeɪs). **1** *Physical chem.* a surface that forms the boundary between two bodies, liquids, or chemical phases. **2** a common point or boundary between two things, subjects, etc. **3** an electrical circuit linking one device, esp. a computer, with another. ◆ *vb* (ˌɪntəˈfeɪs). **4** (*tr*) to design or adapt the input and output configurations of (two electronic devices) so that they may work together compatibly. **5** to be or become an interface (with). **6** to be or become interactive (with). ▸ **interfacial** (ˌɪntəˈfeɪʃəl) *adj* ▸ **ˌinterˈfacially** *adv*

interfacing (ˈɪntəˌfeɪsɪŋ) *n* **1** a piece of fabric sewn beneath the facing of a garment, usually at the inside of the neck, armholes, etc., to give shape and firmness. **2** another name for **interlining.**

interfascicular (ˌɪntəfəˈsɪkjʊlə) *adj Botany.* between the vascular bundles of the stem: *interfascicular cambium.*

interfere (ˌɪntəˈfɪə) *vb* (*intr*) **1** (often foll. by *in*) to interpose, esp. meddlesomely or unwarrantedly; intervene. **2** (often foll. by *with*) to come between or in opposition; hinder; obstruct. **3** (foll. by *with*) *Euphemistic.* to assault sexually. **4** to strike one against the other, as a horse's legs. **5** *Physics.* to cause or produce interference. [C16: from Old French *s'entreferir* to collide, from *entre-* INTER- + *ferir* to strike, from Latin *ferīre*] ▸ **ˌinterˈferer** *n* ▸ **ˌinterˈfering** *adj* ▸ **ˌinterˈferingly** *adv*

interference (ˌɪntəˈfɪərəns) *n* **1** the act or an instance of interfering. **2** *Physics.* the process in which two or more coherent waves combine to form a resultant wave in which the displacement at any point is the vector sum of the displacements of the individual waves. If the individual waves converge the resultant is a system of fringes. Two waves of equal or nearly equal intensity moving in opposite directions combine to form a standing wave. **3** Also called: **radio interference.** any undesired signal that tends to interfere with the reception of radio waves. **4** *Aeronautics.* the effect on the flow pattern around a body of objects in the vicinity. ▸ **interferential** (ˌɪntəfəˈrɛnʃəl) *adj*

interference fit *n Engineering.* a match between the size and shape of two parts, such that force is required for assembly as one part is slightly larger than the other.

interferometer (ˌɪntəfəˈrɒmɪtə) *n* **1** *Physics.* any acoustic, optical, or microwave instrument that uses interference patterns or fringes to make accurate measurements of wavelength, wave velocity, distance, etc. **2** *Astronomy.* a radio telescope consisting of two or more radio antennas separated by a known distance and connected to the same receiver so that radio waves from a source in space undergo interference, enabling the position of the source to be accurately determined. ▸ **interferometric** (ˌɪntəˌfɛrəˈmɛtrɪk) *adj* ▸ **ˌinterˌferoˈmetrically** *adv* ▸ **ˌinterferˈometry** *n*

interferon (ˌɪntəˈfɪərɒn) *n Biochem.* any of a family of proteins made by cells in response to virus infection that prevent the growth of the virus. Some interferons can prevent cell growth and have been tested for use in cancer therapy. [C20: from INTERFERE + -ON]

interfertile (ˌɪntəˈfɜːtaɪl) *adj* (of plants and animals) able to interbreed. ▸ **ˌinterferˈtility** *n*

interfile (ˌɪntəˈfaɪl) *vb* (*tr*) **1** to place (one or more items) among other items in a file or arrangement. **2** to combine (two or more sets of items) in one file or arrangement.

interflow (ˌɪntəˈfləʊ) *vb* (*intr*) to flow together; merge.

interfluent (ɪnˈtɜːflʊənt) *adj* flowing together; merging. [C17: from Latin *interfluere,* from INTER- + *fluere* to flow]

interfluve (ˈɪntəˌfluːv) *n* a ridge or area of land dividing two river valleys. [C20: back formation from *interfluvial,* from INTER- + Latin *fluvius* river] ▸ **ˌinterˈfluvial** *adj*

interfuse (ˌɪntəˈfjuːz) *vb* **1** to diffuse or mix throughout or become so diffused or mixed; intermingle. **2** to blend or fuse or become blended or fused. ▸ **ˌinterˈfusion** *n*

intergenerational mobility (ˌɪntəˌdʒɛnəˈreɪʃənᵊl) *n Sociol.* movement within or between social classes and occupations, the change occurring from one generation to the next. Compare **intragenerational mobility.**

interglacial (ˌɪntəˈgleɪsɪəl, -ʃəl) *adj* **1** occurring or formed between periods of glacial action. ◆ *n* **2** a period of comparatively warm climate between two glaciations, esp. of the Pleistocene epoch.

intergrade *vb* (ˌɪntəˈgreɪd). **1** (*intr*) (esp. of biological species, etc.) to merge one into another. ◆ *n* (ˈɪntəˌgreɪd). **2** an intermediate stage or form. ▸ **ˌintergraˈdation** *n* ▸ **ˌintergraˈdational** *adj* ▸ **ˌinterˈgradient** *adj*

interim (ˈɪntərɪm) *adj* **1** (*prenominal*) temporary, provisional, or intervening: *interim measures to deal with the emergency.* ◆ *n* **2** (usually preceded by *the*) the intervening time; the meantime (esp. in the phrase **in the interim**). ◆ *adv* **3** *Rare.* meantime. [C16: from Latin: meanwhile]

Interim (ˈɪntərɪm) *n* any of three provisional arrangements made during the

ˌinterˈclass *adj*
ˌinterˈclub *adj*
ˌintercolˈlegiate *adj*
ˌintercomˈmunity *adj*
ˌinterˈcompany *adj*
ˌinterconˈnect *vb*
ˌinterconˈnection *n*
ˌinterˌcontiˈnental *adj*
ˌinterconˈvertible *adj*
ˌinterˈcounty *adj*
ˌinterdeˌnomiˈnational *adj*
ˌinterˌdepartˈmental *adj*
ˌinterdeˈpend *vb*
ˌinterdeˈpendence *n*
ˌinterdeˈpendency *n*
ˌinterdeˈpendent *adj*
ˌintergaˈlactic *adj*
ˌinterˌgovernˈmental *adj*
ˌinterˈgroup *adj*

Reformation by the German emperor and Diet to regulate religious differences between Roman Catholics and Protestants.

Interim Standard Atmosphere *n* an agreed theoretical description of the atmosphere for altitudes between 50 and 80 km, pending refinement by further measurements. See **International Standard Atmosphere.**

interior (ɪn'tɪərɪə) *n* **1** a part, surface, or region that is inside or on the inside: *the interior of Africa.* **2** inner character or nature. **3** a film or scene shot inside a building, studio, etc. **4** a picture of the inside of a room or building, as in a painting or stage design. **5** the inside of a building or room, with respect to design and decoration. ◆ *adj* **6** of, situated on, or suitable for the inside; inner. **7** coming or acting from within; internal. **8** of or involving a nation's domestic affairs; internal. **9** (esp. of one's spiritual or mental life) secret or private; not observable. [C15: from Latin (adj), comparative of *inter* within] ▸ **in'teriorly** *adv*

Interior (ɪn'tɪərɪə) *n* (*in titles;* usually preceded by *the*) the domestic or internal affairs of any of certain countries: *Department of the Interior.*

interior angle *n* **1** an angle of a polygon contained between two adjacent sides. **2** any of the four angles made by a transversal that lie inside the region between the two intersected lines.

interior decoration *n* **1** the colours, furniture, etc., of the interior of a house, etc. **2** Also called: **interior design.** the art or business of an interior decorator.

interior decorator *n* **1** Also called: **interior designer.** a person whose profession is the planning of the decoration and furnishings of the interior of houses, shops, etc. **2** a person whose profession is the painting and wallpapering of houses.

interiorize *or* **interiorise** (ɪn'tɪərɪəˌraɪz) *vb* (*tr*) another word for **internalize.**

interior monologue *n* a literary attempt to present the mental processes of a character before they are formed into regular patterns of speech or logical sequence. See also **stream of consciousness.**

interior-sprung *adj* (esp. of a mattress) containing springs.

interj. *abbrev. for* interjection.

interjacent (ˌɪntə'dʒeɪsᵊnt) *adj* located in between; intervening. [C16: from Latin *interjacēnt-*, from *interjacēre,* from INTER- + *jacēre* to lie]

interject (ˌɪntə'dʒɛkt) *vb* (*tr*) **1** to interpose abruptly or sharply; interrupt with; throw in: *she interjected clever remarks.* **2** *Archaic.* to come between; interpose. [C16: from Latin *interjicere* to place between, from *jacere* to throw] ▸ ˌ**inter'jector** *n*

interjection (ˌɪntə'dʒɛkʃən) *n* **1** a word or remark expressing emotion; exclamation. **2** the act of interjecting. **3** a word or phrase that is characteristically used in syntactic isolation and that usually expresses sudden emotion; expletive. Abbrev.: **interj.** ▸ ˌ**inter'jectional,** ˌ**inter'jectory,** *or* ˌ**inter'jectural** *adj* ▸ ˌ**inter'jectionally** *adv*

interlace (ˌɪntə'leɪs) *vb* **1** to join together (patterns, fingers, etc.) by crossing, as if woven; intertwine. **2** (*tr*) to mingle or blend in an intricate way. **3** (*tr;* usually foll. by *with*) to change the pattern of; diversify; intersperse: *to interlace a speech with humour.* ▸ **interlacedly** (ˌɪntə'leɪsɪdlɪ) *adv* ▸ ˌ**inter'lacement** *n*

interlaced scanning *n* a system of scanning a television picture, first along the even-numbered lines, then along the odd-numbered lines, in one complete scan.

Interlaken ('ɪntəˌlɑːkən) *n* a town and resort in central Switzerland, situated between Lakes Brienz and Thun on the River Aar. Pop.: 4 900 (1987 est.).

interlaminate (ˌɪntə'læmɪˌneɪt) *vb* (*tr*) to place, stick, or insert (a sheet, layer, etc.) between (other layers). ▸ ˌ**inter'laminar** *adj* ▸ ˌ**interˌlami'nation** *n*

interlap (ˌɪntə'læp) *vb* **-laps, -lapping, -lapped.** a less common word for **overlap.**

interlard (ˌɪntə'lɑːd) *vb* (*tr*) **1** to scatter thickly in or between; intersperse: *to interlard one's writing with foreign phrases.* **2** to occur frequently in; be scattered in or through: *foreign phrases interlard his writings.*

interlay *vb* (ˌɪntə'leɪ). **-lays, -laying, -laid** (-'leɪd). **1** (*tr*) to insert (layers) between; interpose: *to interlay gold among the silver; to interlay the silver with gold.* ◆ *n* ('ɪntəˌleɪ). **2** material, such as paper, placed between a printing plate and its base, either all over in order to bring it up to type height, or in places in order to achieve the correct printing pressure all over the plate.

interleaf ('ɪntəˌliːf) *n, pl* **-leaves.** a blank leaf inserted between the leaves of a book.

interleave (ˌɪntə'liːv) *vb* (*tr*) **1** (often foll. by *with*) to intersperse (with), esp. alternately, as the illustrations in a book (with protective leaves). **2** to provide (a book) with blank leaves for notes, etc., or to protect illustrations.

interleukin (ˌɪntə'luːkɪn) *n* a substance extracted from white blood cells that stimulates their activity against infection and may be used to combat some forms of cancer.

interlibrary loan (ˌɪntə'laɪbrərɪ) *n* **1** a system by which libraries borrow publications from other libraries. **2a** an instance of such borrowing. **2b** a publication so borrowed.

interline[1] (ˌɪntə'laɪn) *or* **interlineate** (ˌɪntə'lɪnɪˌeɪt) *vb* (*tr*) to write or print (matter) between the lines of (a text, book, etc.). ▸ '**interˌlining** *or* ˌ**interˌline'ation** *n*

interline[2] (ˌɪntə'laɪn) *vb* (*tr*) to provide (a part of a garment, such as a collar or cuff) with a second lining, esp. of stiffened material. ▸ '**interˌliner** *n*

interlinear (ˌɪntə'lɪnɪə) *or* **interlineal** *adj* **1** written or printed between lines of text. **2** written or printed with the text in different languages or versions on alternate lines. ▸ ˌ**inter'linearly** *or* ˌ**inter'lineally** *adv*

interlinear spacing *n* See **leading** [2].

interlingua (ˌɪntə'lɪŋgwə) *n* **1** (*usually cap.*) an artificial language based on words common to English and the Romance languages. **2** any artificial language used to represent the meaning of natural languages, as for purposes of machine translation. [C20: from Italian, from INTER- + *lingua* language]

interlining ('ɪntəˌlaɪnɪŋ) *n* the material used to interline parts of garments, now often made of reinforced paper.

interlock *vb* (ˌɪntə'lɒk). **1** to join or be joined firmly, as by a mutual interconnection of parts. ◆ *n* ('ɪntəˌlɒk). **2** the act of interlocking or the state of being interlocked. **3** a device, esp. one operated electromechanically, used in a logic circuit to prevent an activity being initiated unless preceded by certain events. **4** a closely knitted fabric. ◆ *adj* ('ɪntəˌlɒk). **5** (of fabric) closely knitted. ▸ '**interˌlocker** *n*

interlocking directorates *pl n* boards of directors of different companies having sufficient members in common to ensure that the companies involved are under the same control.

interlocution (ˌɪntəlɒ'kjuːʃən) *n* conversation, discussion, or dialogue.

interlocutor (ˌɪntə'lɒkjʊtə) *n* **1** a person who takes part in a conversation. **2** Also called: **middleman.** the man in the centre of a troupe of minstrels who engages the others in talk or acts as announcer. **3** *Scots Law.* a decree by a judge. ▸ ˌ**inter'locutress,** ˌ**inter'locutrice,** *or* ˌ**inter'locutrix** *fem n*

interlocutory (ˌɪntə'lɒkjʊtərɪ, -trɪ) *adj* **1** *Law.* pronounced during the course of proceedings; provisional: *an interlocutory injunction.* **2** interposed, as into a conversation, narrative, etc. **3** of, relating to, or characteristic of dialogue. ▸ ˌ**inter'locutorily** *adv*

interloper ('ɪntəˌləʊpə) *n* **1** an intruder. **2** a person who introduces himself into professional or social circles where he does not belong. **3** a person who interferes in matters that are not his concern. **4** a person who trades unlawfully. [C17: from INTER- + *loper,* from Middle Dutch *loopen* to leap]

interlude ('ɪntəˌluːd) *n* **1** a period of time or different activity between longer periods, processes, or events; episode or interval. **2** *Theatre.* a short dramatic piece played separately or as part of a longer entertainment, common in 16th-century England. **3** a brief piece of music, dance, etc., given between the sections of another performance. [C14: from Medieval Latin *interlūdium,* from Latin INTER- + *lūdus* play]

interlunation (ˌɪntəluː'neɪʃən) *n* the period between the old and new moons during which the moon is invisible. See **new moon.** ▸ ˌ**inter'lunar** *adj*

intermarry (ˌɪntə'mærɪ) *vb* **-ries, -rying, -ried.** (*intr*) **1** (of different groups, races, religions, creeds, etc.) to become connected by marriage. **2** to marry within one's own family, clan, group, etc. ▸ ˌ**inter'marriage** *n*

intermeddle (ˌɪntə'mɛdᵊl) *vb* (*intr*) *Rare.* another word for **meddle.** [C14 *entremedle,* from Anglo-Norman *entremedler,* from Old French; see INTER- + MEDDLE]

intermediary (ˌɪntə'miːdɪərɪ) *n, pl* **-aries. 1** a person who acts as a mediator or agent between parties. **2** something that acts as a medium or means. **3** an intermediate state or period. ◆ *adj* **4** acting as an intermediary. **5** situated, acting, or coming between; intermediate.

intermediate *adj* (ˌɪntə'miːdɪɪt). **1** occurring or situated between two points, extremes, places, etc.; in between. **2** (of a class, course, etc.) suitable for learners with some degree of skill or competence. **3** *Physics.* (of a neutron) having an energy between 100 and 100 000 electronvolts. **4** *Geology.* (of such igneous rocks as syenite) containing between 55 and 66 per cent silica. ◆ *n* (ˌɪntə'miːdɪɪt). **5** something intermediate. **6** a substance formed during one of the stages of a chemical process before the desired product is obtained. ◆ *vb* (ˌɪntə'miːdɪˌeɪt). **7** (*intr*) to act as an intermediary or mediator. [C17: from Medieval Latin *intermediāre* to intervene, from Latin INTER- + *medius* middle] ▸ ˌ**inter'mediacy** *or* ˌ**inter'mediateness** *n* ▸ ˌ**inter'mediately** *adv* ▸ ˌ**interˌmedi'ation** *n* ▸ ˌ**inter'mediˌator** *n*

intermediate-acting *adj* (of a drug) intermediate in its effects between long- and short-acting drugs. Compare **long-acting, short-acting.**

intermediate frequency *n Electronics.* the frequency to which the signal carrier frequency is changed in a superheterodyne receiver and at which most of the amplification takes place.

intermediate host *n* an animal that acts as host to a parasite that has not yet become sexually mature.

intermediate-level waste *n* radioactive waste material, such as reactor and processing-plant components, that is solidified before being mixed with concrete and stored in steel drums in deep mines or beneath the seabed in concrete chambers. Compare **high-level waste, low-level waste.**

intermediate range ballistic missile *n* a missile that follows a ballistic trajectory with a medium range, normally of the order of 750–1500 miles. Abbrev.: **IRBM.**

intermediate school *n N.Z.* a school for children aged between 11 and 13.

intermediate treatment *n Social welfare.* a form of child care for young people in trouble that involves neither custody nor punishment and provides opportunities to learn constructive patterns of behaviour to replace potentially criminal ones.

intermediate vector boson *n Physics.* a hypothetical particle believed to mediate the weak interaction between elementary particles.

interment (ɪn'tɜːmənt) *n* burial, esp. with ceremonial rites.

intermezzo (ˌɪntə'mɛtsəʊ) *n, pl* **-zos** *or* **-zi** (-tsiː). **1** a short piece of instrumental music composed for performance between the acts or scenes of an opera, drama, etc. **2** an instrumental piece either inserted between two longer move-

ˌ**inter'link** *vb*

ments in an extended composition or intended for independent performance. **3** another name for **interlude** (sense 3). **[C19:** from Italian, from Late Latin *intermedium* interval; see INTERMEDIATE**]**

intermigration (ˌɪntəmaɪˈgreɪʃən) *n* migration between two groups of people, animals, etc., resulting in an exchange of habitat.

interminable (ɪnˈtɜːmɪnəbᵊl) *adj* endless or seemingly endless because of monotony or tiresome length. ► **inˌterminaˈbility** *or* **inˈterminableness** *n* ► **inˈterminably** *adv*

intermission (ˌɪntəˈmɪʃən) *n* **1** an interval, as between parts of a film. **2** a period between events or activities; pause. **3** the act of intermitting or the state of being intermitted. **[C16:** from Latin *intermissiō*, from *intermittere* to leave off, INTERMIT**]** ► **ˌinterˈmissive** *adj*

intermit (ˌɪntəˈmɪt) *vb* **-mits, -mitting, -mitted.** to suspend (activity) or (of activity) to be suspended temporarily or at intervals. **[C16:** from Latin *intermittere* to leave off, from INTER- + *mittere* to send**]** ► **ˌinterˈmittingly** *adv* ► **ˌinterˈmittor** *n*

intermittent (ˌɪntəˈmɪtᵊnt) *adj* occurring occasionally or at regular or irregular intervals; periodic. ► **ˌinterˈmittence** *or* **ˌinterˈmittency** *n* ► **ˌinterˈmittently** *adv*

intermittent claudication *n Pathol.* pain and cramp in the calf muscles, aggravated by walking and caused by an insufficient supply of blood.

intermittent fever *n* any fever, such as malaria, characterized by intervals of periodic remission.

intermixture (ˌɪntəˈmɪkstʃə) *n* **1** the act of intermixing or state of being intermixed. **2** another word for **mixture. 3** an additional constituent or ingredient.

intermodal (ˌɪntəˈməʊdᵊl) *adj* **1** (of a transport system) using different modes of conveyance in conjunction, such as ships, aircraft, road vehicles, etc. **2** (of a container) able to be carried by different modes of conveyance without being unpacked. **3** *Psychol.* denoting an interaction between different senses.

intermodulation (ˈɪntəˌmɒdjʊˈleɪʃən) *n Electronics.* **a** interaction between two signals in electronic apparatus such that each affects the amplitude of the other. **b** (*as modifier*): *intermodulation distortion.*

intermolecular (ˌɪntəməˈlɛkjʊlə) *adj* occurring among or between molecules.

intermontane (ˌɪntəmɒnˈteɪn) *adj* occurring or situated between mountain ranges: *an intermontane basin.*

intern *vb* **1** (ɪnˈtɜːn). (*tr*) to detain or confine (foreign or enemy citizens, ships, etc.), esp. during wartime. **2** (ˈɪntɜːn). (*intr*) *Chiefly U.S.* to serve or train as an intern. ◆ *n* (ˈɪntɜːn). **3** another word for **internee. 4** Also: **interne.** the approximate U.S. and Canadian equivalent of a British **houseman. 5** *Chiefly U.S.* a student teacher. **6** *Chiefly U.S.* a student or recent graduate receiving practical training in a working environment. ◆ *adj* (ɪnˈtɜːn). **7** an archaic word for **internal. [C19:** from Latin *internus* internal**]**

internal (ɪnˈtɜːnᵊl) *adj* **1** of, situated on, or suitable for the inside; inner. **2** coming or acting from within; interior. **3** involving the spiritual or mental life; subjective. **4** of or involving a nation's domestic as opposed to foreign affairs. **5** *Education.* denoting assessment by examiners who are employed at the candidate's place of study. **6** situated within, affecting, or relating to the inside of the body. ◆ *n* **7** *Euphemistic.* a medical examination of the vagina or uterus. **[C16:** from Medieval Latin *internālis*, from Late Latin *internus* inward**]** ► **ˌinterˈnality** *or* **inˈternalness** *n* ► **inˈternally** *adv*

internal-combustion engine *n* a heat engine in which heat is supplied by burning the fuel in the working fluid (usually air).

internal ear *n* the part of the ear that consists of the cochlea, vestibule, and semicircular canals. Also called: **inner ear, labyrinth.**

internal energy *n* the thermodynamic property of a system that changes by an amount equal to the work done on the system when it suffers an adiabatic change. It is the sum of the kinetic and potential energies of its constituent atoms, molecules, etc. Symbol: *U* or *E*

internalize *or* **internalise** (ɪnˈtɜːnəˌlaɪz) *vb* (*tr*) *Psychol., sociol.* to make internal, esp. to incorporate within oneself (values, attitudes, etc.) through learning or socialization. Compare **introject.** Also: **interiorize.** ► **inˌternaliˈzation** *or* **inˌternaliˈsation** *n*

internal market *n* a system in which goods and services are sold by the provider to a range of purchasers within the same organization, who compete to establish the price of the product.

internal medicine *n* the branch of medical science concerned with the diagnosis and nonsurgical treatment of disorders of the internal structures of the body.

internal rate of return *n* an interest rate giving a net present value of zero when applied to the expected cash flow of a project. Its value, compared to the cost of the capital involved, is used to determine the project's viability.

internal resistance *n Physics.* the resistance of a cell, accumulator, etc., usually given as $(E\text{-}V)/I$, where E is the emf of the cell, and V the potential difference between terminals when it is delivering a current I.

internal revenue *n U.S.* government income derived from taxes, etc., within the country.

internal rhyme *n Prosody.* rhyme that occurs between words within a verse line.

internal secretion *n Physiol.* a secretion, esp. a hormone, that is absorbed directly into the blood.

internat. *abbrev. for* international.

international (ˌɪntəˈnæʃənᵊl) *adj* **1** of, concerning, or involving two or more nations or nationalities. **2** established by, controlling, or legislating for several nations: *an international court; international fishing rights.* **3** available for use by all nations: *international waters.* ◆ *n* **4** *Sport.* **4a** a contest between two national teams. **4b** a member of these teams. ► **ˌinterˌnationˈality** *n* ► **ˌinterˈnationally** *adv*

International (ˌɪntəˈnæʃənᵊl) *n* **1** any of several international socialist organizations. See **Comintern, First International, Labour and Socialist International, Second International, Socialist International, Trotskyist International, Vienna Union. 2** a member of any of these organizations.

International Atomic Time *n* the scientific standard of time based on the SI unit, the second, used by means of atomic clocks and satellites to synchronize the time standards of the major nations. Abbrev.: **TAI.**

International Bank for Reconstruction and Development *n* the official name for the **World Bank.** Abbrev.: **IBRD.**

International Brigade *n* a military force that fought on the Republican side in the Spanish Civil War, consisting of volunteers (predominantly socialists and communists) from many countries.

international candle *n* a former international unit of luminous intensity, originally defined in terms of a standard candle and later in terms of a pentane-burning lamp. It has now been replaced by the candela.

International Court of Justice *n* a court established in the Hague to settle disputes brought by nations that are parties to the Statute of the Court. Also called: **World Court.**

International Criminal Police Organization *n* See **Interpol.**

International Date Line *n* the line approximately following the 180° meridian from Greenwich on the east side of which the date is one day earlier than on the west. Also called: **date line.**

International Development Association *n* an organization set up in 1960 to provide low-interest loans to developing countries. It is part of the World Bank Group. Abbrev: **IDA.**

Internationale (ˌɪntənæʃəˈnɑːl) *n* **the.** a revolutionary socialist hymn, first sung in 1871 in France. **[C19:** shortened from French *chanson internationale* international song**]**

International Finance Corporation *n* an organization that invests directly in private companies and makes or guarantees loans to private investors. It is affiliated to the World Bank and is part of the World Bank Group. Abbrev.: **IFC.**

International Geophysical Year *n* the 18-month period from July 1, 1957, to Dec. 31, 1958, during which a number of nations agreed to cooperate in a geophysical research programme. Abbrev.: **IGY.**

International Gothic *n* a style in art during the late 14th and early 15th centuries characterized by elegant stylization of illuminated manuscripts, mosaics, stained glass, etc., and by increased interest in secular themes. Major contributors were Simone Martini, Giotto, and Pisanello.

International Grandmaster *n Chess.* See **grandmaster** (sense 2).

internationalism (ˌɪntəˈnæʃənəˌlɪzəm) *n* **1** the ideal or practice of cooperation and understanding between nations. **2** the state or quality of being international.

internationalist (ˌɪntəˈnæʃənəlɪst) *n* **1** an advocate of internationalism. **2** a person versed in international law. **3** (*cap.*) a member of an International.

internationalize *or* **internationalise** (ˌɪntəˈnæʃənəˌlaɪz) *vb* (*tr*) **1** to make international. **2** to put under international control. ► **ˌinterˌnationaliˈzation** *or* **ˌinterˌnationaliˈsation** *n*

International Labour Organisation *n* a special agency of the United Nations responsible for research and recommendations in the field of labour conditions and practices: founded in 1919 in affiliation to the League of Nations. Abbrev.: **ILO.**

international law *n* the body of rules generally recognized by civilized nations as governing their conduct towards each other and towards each other's subjects.

International Master *n Chess.* the second highest title awarded by the FIDE to a player: won by obtaining a certain number of points during specific international chess tournaments. Often shortened to **master.** Compare **grandmaster** (sense 2).

International Modernism *n* See **International Style.**

International Monetary Fund *n* an international financial institution organized in 1945 to promote international trade by increasing the exchange stability of the major currencies. A fund is maintained out of which member nations with temporary balance-of-payments deficits may make withdrawals. Abbrev.: **IMF.**

international Morse code *n* the full name for **Morse code.**

international nautical mile *n* the full name for **nautical mile** (sense 1).

International Phonetic Alphabet *n* a series of signs and letters propagated by the Association Phonétique Internationale for the representation of human speech sounds. It is based on the Roman alphabet but supplemented by modified signs or symbols from other writing systems, and is usually employed in its revised form of 1951. Abbrev.: **IPA.**

international pitch *n Music.* the frequency of 435 hertz assigned to the A above middle C, widely used until 1939. See **pitch**[1] (sense 28b).

International Practical Temperature Scale *n* a temperature scale adopted by international agreement in 1968 based on thermodynamic temperature and using experimental values to define 11 fixed points. The lowest is the triple point of an equilibrium mixture of orthohydrogen and parahydrogen (−259.34°C) and the highest the freezing point of gold (1064.43°C).

ˌinterˈmingle *vb*	**ˌinterˈmix** *vb*	**ˌinterˈplanetary** *adj*

international screw thread *n Engineering.* a metric system for screw threads relating the pitch to the diameter.

international sea and swell scale *n* another name for the **Douglas scale.**

International Standard Atmosphere *n* a theoretical vertical distribution of the physical properties of the atmosphere up to an altitude of 50 km established by international agreement. It permits the standardization of aircraft instruments and performance of all types of flying vehicles.

International Standards Organization *n* an international organization for the standardization of units of measurement, technical terminology, etc. Founded in its present form in 1947, it has a secretariat in Geneva. Abbrev.: **ISO.**

International Style *or* **Modernism** *n* a twentieth-century architectural style characterized by undecorated rectilinear forms and the use of glass, steel, and reinforced concrete.

International Telecommunications Union *n* a special agency of the United Nations, founded in 1947, that is responsible for the international allocation and registration of frequencies for communications and the regulation of telegraph, telephone, and radio services: originally established in 1865 as the International Telegraph Union.

international telegram *n* a telemessage sent from the UK to a foreign country.

interne ('ɪntɜːn) *n* a variant spelling of **intern** (sense 4).

internecine (ˌɪntəˈniːsaɪn) *adj* **1** mutually destructive or ruinous; maiming both or all sides: *internecine war.* **2** of or relating to slaughter or carnage; bloody. **3** of or involving conflict within a group or organization. **[**C17: from Latin *internecīnus,* from *internecāre* to destroy, from *necāre* to kill**]**

internee (ˌɪntɜːˈniː) *n* a person who is interned, esp. an enemy citizen in wartime or a terrorism suspect.

Internet ('ɪntəˌnɛt) *n* **the.** the single worldwide computer network that interconnects other computer networks, on which end-user services, such as World Wide Web sites or data archives, are located, enabling data and other information to be exchanged. Also called: the **Net.**

interneuron (ˌɪntəˈnjʊərɒn) *n Physiol.* any neuron that connects afferent and efferent neurons in a reflex arc. Also called: **internuncial neuron.**

internist ('ɪntɜːnɪst, ɪnˈtɜːnɪst) *n* a physician who specializes in internal medicine.

internment (ɪnˈtɜːnmənt) *n* **a** the act of interning or state of being interned, esp. of enemy citizens in wartime or of terrorism suspects. **b** *(as modifier): an internment camp.*

internode ('ɪntəˌnəʊd) *n* **1** the part of a plant stem between two nodes. **2** the part of a nerve fibre between two nodes of Ranvier. ▸ **ˌinterˈnodal** *adj*

internship ('ɪntɜːnʃɪp) *n Chiefly U.S. and Canadian.* the position of being an intern or the period during which a person is an intern.

internuncial (ˌɪntəˈnʌnʃəl) *adj* **1** *Physiol.* (esp. of neurons) interconnecting. See **internode. 2** of, relating to, or emanating from a papal internuncio.

internuncio (ˌɪntəˈnʌnʃɪˌəʊ) *n, pl* **-cios. 1** an ambassador of the pope ranking immediately below a nuncio. **2** a messenger, agent, or go-between. **[**C17: from Italian *internunzio,* from Latin *internuntius,* from INTER- + *nuntius* messenger**]**

interoceptor (ˌɪntərəʊˈsɛptə) *n Physiol.* a sensory receptor of an internal organ (excluding the muscles). Compare **exteroceptor, proprioceptor. [**C20: from INTER(IOR) + (RE)CEPTOR**]** ▸ **ˌinteroˈceptive** *adj*

interosculate (ˌɪntərˈɒskjʊˌleɪt) *vb (intr) Biology.* (of two different species or groups of organisms) to share certain characteristics. ▸ **ˌinterˌoscuˈlation** *n*

interpage (ˌɪntəˈpeɪdʒ) *vb (tr)* **1** to print (matter) on intervening pages. **2** to insert (intervening pages) into a book.

interpellant (ˌɪntəˈpɛlənt) *adj* **1** causing an interpellation. ◆ *n* **2** a deputy who interpellates.

interpellate (ɪnˈtɜːpeˌleɪt) *vb (tr) Parliamentary procedure.* (in European legislatures) to question (a member of the government) on a point of government policy, often interrupting the business of the day. **[**C16: from Latin *interpellāre* to disturb, from INTER- + *pellere* to push**]** ▸ **inˌterpelˈlation** *n* ▸ **inˈterpelˌlator** *n*

interpenetrate (ˌɪntəˈpɛnɪˌtreɪt) *vb* **1** to penetrate (something) thoroughly; pervade. **2** to penetrate each other or one another mutually. ▸ **ˌinterˈpenetrable** *adj* ▸ **ˌinterˈpenetrant** *adj* ▸ **ˌinterˌpeneˈtration** *n* ▸ **ˌinterˈpenetrative** *adj* ▸ **ˌinterˈpenetratively** *adv*

interpersonal (ˌɪntəˈpɜːsənᵊl) *adj* between persons; involving personal relationships.

interphase ('ɪntəˌfeɪz) *n Biology.* the period between two divisions of a cell.

interphone ('ɪntəˌfəʊn) *n* a telephone system for linking different rooms within a building, ship, etc.

interplay ('ɪntəˌpleɪ) *n* reciprocal and mutual action and reaction, as in circumstances, events, or personal relations.

interplead (ˌɪntəˈpliːd) *vb* **-pleads, -pleading; -pleaded, -plead** (-ˈplɛd), *or* **-pled.** *(intr) Law.* to institute interpleader proceedings.

interpleader (ˌɪntəˈpliːdə) *n Law.* **1** a process by which a person holding money or property claimed by two or more parties and having no interest in it himself can require the claimants to litigate with each other to determine the issue. **2** a person who interpleads.

Interpol ('ɪntəˌpɒl) *n acronym for* International Criminal Police Organization, an association of over 100 national police forces, devoted chiefly to fighting international crime.

interpolate (ɪnˈtɜːpəˌleɪt) *vb* **1** to insert or introduce (a comment, passage, etc.) into (a conversation, text, etc.). **2** to falsify or alter (a text, manuscript, etc.) by the later addition of (material, esp. spurious or valueless passages). **3** *(intr)* to make additions, interruptions, or insertions. **4** *Maths.* to estimate (a value of a function) between the values already known or determined. Compare **extrapolate** (sense 1). **[**C17: from Latin *interpolāre* to give a new appearance to, from INTER- + *polīre* to POLISH**]** ▸ **inˈterpoˌlater** *or* **inˈterpoˌlator** *n* ▸ **inˈterpolative** *adj*

interpolation (ɪnˌtɜːpəˈleɪʃən) *n* **1** the act of interpolating or the state of being interpolated. **2** something interpolated.

interpose (ˌɪntəˈpəʊz) *vb* **1** to put or place between or among other things. **2** to introduce (comments, questions, etc.) into a speech or conversation; interject. **3** to exert or use power, influence, or action in order to alter or intervene in (a situation). **[**C16: from Old French *interposer,* from Latin *interpōnere,* from INTER- + *pōnere* to put**]** ▸ **ˌinterˈposable** *adj* ▸ **ˌinterˈposal** *n* ▸ **ˌinterˈposer** *n*

interposition (ˌɪntəpəˈzɪʃən) *n* **1** something interposed. **2** the act of interposing or the state of being interposed.

interpret (ɪnˈtɜːprɪt) *vb* **1** *(tr)* to clarify or explain the meaning of; elucidate. **2** *(tr)* to construe the significance or intention of: *to interpret a smile as an invitation.* **3** *(tr)* to convey or represent the spirit or meaning of (a poem, song, etc.) in performance. **4** *(intr)* to act as an interpreter; translate orally. **[**C14: from Latin *interpretārī,* from *interpres* negotiator, one who explains, from INTER- + *-pres,* probably related to *pretium* PRICE**]** ▸ **inˈterpretable** *adj* ▸ **inˌterpretaˈbility** *or* **inˈterpretableness** *n* ▸ **inˈterpretably** *adv*

interpretation (ɪnˌtɜːprɪˈteɪʃən) *n* **1** the act or process of interpreting or explaining; elucidation. **2** the result of interpreting; an explanation. **3** a particular view of an artistic work, esp. as expressed by stylistic individuality in its performance. **4** explanation, as of the environment, a historical site, etc., provided by the use of original objects, personal experience, visual display material, etc. **5** *Logic.* an allocation of significance to the terms of a purely formal system, by specifying ranges for the variables, denotations for the individual constants, etc.; a function from the formal language to such elements of a possible world. ▸ **inˌterpreˈtational** *adj*

interpretative (ɪnˈtɜːprɪtətɪv) *or* **interpretive** (ɪnˈtɜːprɪtɪv) *adj* of, involving, or providing interpretation; expository. ▸ **inˈterpretatively** *or* **inˈterpretively** *adv*

interpreter (ɪnˈtɜːprɪtə) *n* **1** a person who translates orally from one language into another. **2** a person who interprets the work of others. **3** *Computing.* **3a** a program that translates a second program to machine code one statement at a time and causes the execution of the resulting code as soon as the translation is completed. **3b** a machine that interprets the holes in a punched card and prints the corresponding characters on that card. ▸ **inˈterpreterˌship** *n* ▸ **inˈterpretress** *fem n*

interpretive centre *n* (at a place of interest, such as a country park, historical site, etc.) a building or group of buildings that provides interpretation of the place of interest through a variety of media, such as video displays and exhibitions of material, and, often, includes facilities such as refreshment rooms and gift shops. Also called: **visitor centre.**

interpretive semantics *n (functioning as sing)* a school of semantic theory based on the doctrine that the rules that relate sentences to their meanings form an autonomous system, separate from the rules that determine what is grammatical in a language. Compare **generative semantics.**

interquartile range (ˌɪntəˈkwɔːtaɪl) *n Statistics.* the difference between the value of a variable below which lie 25 per cent of the population, and that below which lie 75 per cent: a measure of the spread of the distribution.

interradial (ˌɪntəˈreɪdɪəl) *adj* situated between two radii or rays, esp. between the radii of a sea urchin or similar animal. ▸ **ˌinterˈradially** *adv*

interregnum (ˌɪntəˈrɛgnəm) *n, pl* **-nums** *or* **-na** (-nə). **1** an interval between two reigns, governments, incumbencies, etc. **2** any period in which a state lacks a ruler, government, etc. **3** a period of absence of some control, authority, etc. **4** a gap in a continuity. **[**C16: from Latin, from INTER- + *regnum* REIGN**]** ▸ **ˌinterˈregnal** *adj*

interrelate (ˌɪntərɪˈleɪt) *vb* to place in or come into a mutual or reciprocal relationship. ▸ **ˌinterreˈlation** *n* ▸ **ˌinterreˈlationˌship** *n*

interrex (ˌɪntəˈrɛks) *n, pl* **interreges** (ˌɪntəˈriːdʒiːz). a person who governs during an interregnum; provisional ruler. **[**C16: from Latin, from INTER- + *rēx* king**]**

interrog. *abbrev. for:* **1** interrogate. **2** interrogation. **3** interrogative.

interrogate (ɪnˈtɛrəˌgeɪt) *vb* to ask questions (of), esp. to question (a witness in court, spy, etc.) closely. **[**C15: from Latin *interrogāre* to question, examine, from *rogāre* to ask**]** ▸ **inˈterroˌgatingly** *adv*

interrogation (ɪnˌtɛrəˈgeɪʃən) *n* **1** the technique, practice, or an instance of interrogating. **2** a question or query. **3** *Telecomm.* the transmission of one or more triggering pulses to a transponder. ▸ **inˌterroˈgational** *adj*

interrogation mark *n* a less common term for **question mark.**

interrogative (ˌɪntəˈrɒgətɪv) *adj* **1** asking or having the nature of a question. **2** denoting a form or construction used in asking a question. **3** denoting or belonging to a class of words, such as *which* and *whom,* that are determiners, adjectives, or pronouns and serve to question which individual referent or referents are intended. Compare **demonstrative, relative.** ◆ *n* **4** an interrogative word, phrase, sentence, or construction. **5** a question mark. ▸ **ˌinterˈrogatively** *adv*

ˌinterproˈfessional *adj*
ˌinterproˈvincial *adj*
ˌinterˈracial *adj*
ˌinterˈregional *adj*
ˌinterreˈligious *adj*

interrogator (ɪnˈtɛrəˌgeɪtə) *n* **1** a person who interrogates. **2** a radio or radar transmitter used to send interrogating signals.

interrogatories (ˌɪntəˈrɒgətərɪz, -trɪz) *pl n Law.* written questions asked by one party to a suit, to which the other party has to give written answers under oath.

interrogatory (ˌɪntəˈrɒgətərɪ, -trɪ) *adj* **1** expressing or involving a question. ◆ *n, pl* **-tories. 2** a question or interrogation. ► ˌ**interˈrogatorily** *adv*

interrupt (ˌɪntəˈrʌpt) *vb* **1** to break the continuity of (an action, event, etc.) or hinder (a person) by intrusion. **2** (*tr*) to cease to perform (some action). **3** (*tr*) to obstruct (a view). **4** to prevent or disturb (a conversation, discussion, etc.) by questions, interjections, or comment. ◆ *n* **5** the signal to initiate the stopping of the running of one computer program in order to run another, after which the running of the original program is usually continued. **[C15:** from Latin *interrumpere,* from INTER- + *rumpere* to break] ► ˌ**interˈruptible** *adj* ► ˌ**interˈruptive** *adj* ► ˌ**interˈruptively** *adv*

interrupted (ˌɪntəˈrʌptɪd) *adj* **1** broken, discontinued, or hindered. **2** (of plant organs, esp. leaves) not evenly spaced along an axis. **3** Also: **deceptive.** *Music.* (of a cadence) progressing from the dominant chord to any other, such as the subdominant or submediant. ► ˌ**interˈruptedly** *adv*

interrupted screw *n* a screw with a slot or slots cut into the thread, esp. one used in the breech of some guns permitting both engagement and release of the block by a partial turn of the screw.

interrupter *or* **interruptor** (ˌɪntəˈrʌptə) *n* **1** a person or thing that interrupts. **2** an electromechanical device for opening and closing an electric circuit.

interruption (ˌɪntəˈrʌpʃən) *n* **1** something that interrupts, such as a comment, question, or action. **2** an interval or intermission. **3** the act of interrupting or the state of being interrupted.

interscholastic (ˌɪntəskəˈlæstɪk) *adj* **1** (of sports events, competitions, etc.) occurring between two or more schools. **2** representative of various schools.

inter se *Latin.* (ˈɪntə ˈseɪ) *adv* among or between themselves.

intersect (ˌɪntəˈsɛkt) *vb* **1** to divide, cut, or mark off by passing through or across. **2** (esp. of roads) to cross (each other). **3** *Maths.* (often foll. by *with*) to have one or more points in common (with another configuration). **[C17:** from Latin *intersecāre* to divide, from INTER- + *secāre* to cut]

intersection (ˌɪntəˈsɛkʃən, ˈɪntəˌsɛk-) *n* **1** a point at which things intersect, esp. a road junction. **2** the act of intersecting or the state of being intersected. **3** *Maths.* **3a** a point or set of points common to two or more geometric configurations. **3b** Also called: **product.** the set of elements that are common to two sets. **3c** the operation that yields that set from a pair of given sets. Symbol: ∩, as in $A \cap B$. ► ˌ**interˈsectional** *adj*

intersex (ˈɪntəˌsɛks) *n Zoology.* an individual with characteristics intermediate between those of a male and a female. Compare **gynandromorph, hermaphrodite** (sense 1).

intersexual (ˌɪntəˈsɛksjʊəl) *adj* **1** occurring or existing between the sexes. **2** relating to or being an intersex. ► ˌ**interˌsexuˈality** *or* ˌ**interˈsexualism** *n* ► ˌ**interˈsexually** *adv*

interspace *vb* (ˌɪntəˈspeɪs). **1** (*tr*) to make or occupy a space between. ◆ *n* (ˈɪntəˌspeɪs). **2** space between or among things. ► **interspatial** (ˌɪntəˈspeɪʃəl) *adj* ► ˌ**interˈspatially** *adv*

interspecific (ˌɪntəspəˈsɪfɪk) *adj* hybridized from, relating to, or occurring between different species: *interspecific competition.*

intersperse (ˌɪntəˈspɜːs) *vb* (*tr*) **1** to scatter or distribute among, between, or on. **2** to diversify (something) with other things scattered here and there. **[C16:** from Latin *interspargere,* from INTER- + *spargere* to sprinkle] ► **interspersedly** (ˌɪntəˈspɜːsɪdlɪ) *adv* ► **interspersion** (ˌɪntəˈspɜːʃən) *or* ˌ**interˈspersal** *n*

interstadial (ˌɪntəˈsteɪdɪəl) *adj, n* another word for **interglacial. [C20:** from New Latin, from INTER- + *stadium* stage]

interstate (ˈɪntəˌsteɪt) *adj* **1** between or involving two or more of the states of the U.S., Australia, etc. ◆ *adv* **2** *Austral.* to or into another state.

interstellar medium (ˌɪntəˈstɛlə) *n* the matter occurring between the stars of our Galaxy, largely in the spiral arms, and consisting mainly of huge clouds of ionized, neutral, or molecular hydrogen. Abbrev.: **ISM.**

interstice (ɪnˈtɜːstɪs) *n* (*usually pl*) **1** a minute opening or crevice between things. **2** *Physics.* the space between adjacent atoms in a crystal lattice. **[C17:** from Latin *interstitium* interval, from *intersistere,* from INTER- + *sistere* to stand]

interstitial (ˌɪntəˈstɪʃəl) *adj* **1** of or relating to an interstice or interstices. **2** *Physics.* forming or occurring in an interstice: *an interstitial atom.* **3** *Chem.* containing interstitial atoms or ions: *an interstitial compound.* **4** *Anatomy, zoology.* occurring in the spaces between organs, tissues, etc.: *interstitial cells.* ◆ *n* **5** *Chem.* an atom or ion situated in the interstices of a crystal lattice. ► ˌ**interˈstitially** *adv*

interstitial-cell-stimulating hormone *n* another name for **luteinizing hormone.**

interstratify (ˌɪntəˈstrætɪˌfaɪ) *vb* **-fies, -fying, -fied.** (*tr; usually passive*) to arrange (a series of rock strata) in alternating beds. ► ˌ**interˌstratifiˈcation** *n*

intertexture (ˌɪntəˈtɛkstʃə) *n* **1** the act or process of interweaving or the condition of having been interwoven. **2** something that has been interwoven.

intertidal (ˌɪntəˈtaɪdᵊl) *adj* of or relating to the zone of the shore between the high-water mark and low-water mark.

intertrigo (ˌɪntəˈtraɪgəʊ) *n* chafing between two moist closely opposed skin surfaces, as at the armpit. **[C18:** from INTER- + *-trigo,* from Latin *terere* to rub]

Intertropical Convergence Zone (ˌɪntəˈtrɒpɪkᵊl) *n Meteorol.* the zone of converging trade winds along the equator causing rising air currents and low atmospheric pressure. Abbrev.: **ITCZ.**

intertwine (ˌɪntəˈtwaɪn) *vb* to unite or be united by twisting or twining together. Also: **intertwist.** ► ˌ**interˈtwinement** *n* ► ˌ**interˈtwiningly** *adv*

interval (ˈɪntəvəl) *n* **1** the period of time marked off by or between two events, instants, etc. **2** the distance between two points, objects, etc. **3** a pause or interlude, as between periods of intense activity. **4** *Brit.* a short period between parts of a play, concert, film, etc.; intermission. **5** *Music.* the difference of pitch between two notes, either sounded simultaneously (**harmonic interval**) or in succession as in a musical part (**melodic interval**). An interval is calculated by counting the (inclusive) number of notes of the diatonic scale between the two notes: *the interval between C and G is a fifth.* **6** the ratio of the frequencies of two sounds. **7** *Maths.* **7a** the set containing all real numbers or points between two given numbers or points, called the endpoints. A **closed interval** includes the endpoints, but an **open interval** does not. **7b** the set of points in *n*-dimensional space where coordinates satisfy the inequalities $a_i \leqslant x_i \leqslant b_i$ (**closed interval**) or $a_i < x_i < b_i$ (**open interval**) where $a_i < b_i$. **8 at intervals. 8a** occasionally or intermittently. **8b** with spaces between. **[C13:** from Latin *intervallum,* literally: space between two palisades, from INTER- + *vallum* palisade, rampart] ► **intervallic** (ˌɪntəˈvælɪk) *adj*

interval estimate *n Statistics.* an interval within which the true value of a parameter of a population is stated to lie with a predetermined probability on the basis of sampling statistics. Compare: **point estimate.**

intervalometer (ˌɪntəvəˈlɒmɪtə) *n* an automatic device used to trigger an operation at regular intervals, esp. such a device operating the shutter of a camera.

interval scale *n Statistics.* a scale of measurement of data according to which the differences between values can be quantified in absolute but not relative terms and for which any zero is merely arbitrary: for instance, dates are measured on an interval scale since differences can be measured in years, but no sense can be given to a ratio of times. Compare **ordinal scale, ratio scale, nominal scale.**

interval signal *n* a characteristic snatch of music, chimes, etc., transmitted as an identifying signal by a radio station between programme items.

interval training *n* a method of athletic training using alternate sprinting and jogging. Also called: **fartlek.**

intervene (ˌɪntəˈviːn) *vb* (*intr*) **1** (often foll. by *in*) to take a decisive or intrusive role (in) in order to modify or determine events or their outcome. **2** (foll. by *in* or *between*) to come or be (among or between). **3** (of a period of time) to occur between events or points in time. **4** (of an event) to disturb or hinder a course of action. **5** *Economics.* to take action to affect the market forces of an economy, esp. to maintain the stability of a currency. **6** *Law.* to interpose and become a party to a legal action between others, esp. in order to protect one's interests. **[C16:** from Latin *intervenīre* to come between, from INTER- + *venīre* to come] ► ˌ**interˈvener** *or* ˌ**interˈvenor** *n*

intervening variable (ˌɪntəˈviːnɪŋ) *n Maths, psychol., etc.* a hypothetical variable postulated to account for the way in which a set of independent variables control a set of dependent variables.

intervention (ˌɪntəˈvɛnʃən) *n* **1** the act of intervening. **2** any interference in the affairs of others, esp. by one state in the affairs of another. **3** *Economics.* the action of a central bank in supporting the international value of a currency by buying large quantities of the currency to keep the price up. **4** *Commerce.* the action of the EU in buying up surplus produce when the market price drops to a certain value. ► ˌ**interˈventional** *adj*

interventional radiology (ˌɪntəˈvɛnʃənᵊl) *n* an application of radiology that enables minimally invasive surgery to be performed with the aid of simultaneous radiological imaging of the field of operation within the body.

interventionist (ˌɪntəˈvɛnʃənɪst) *adj* **1** of, relating to, or advocating intervention, esp. in the affairs of a foreign country. ◆ *n* **2** an interventionist person or state. ► ˌ**interˈventionism** *n*

intervention price *n Commerce.* the price at which the EU intervenes to buy surplus produce.

intervertebral disc (ˌɪntəˈvɜːtəbrəl) *n* any of the cartilaginous discs between individual vertebrae, acting as shock absorbers.

interview (ˈɪntəˌvjuː) *n* **1** a conversation with or questioning of a person, usually conducted for television, radio, or a newspaper. **2** a formal discussion, esp. one in which an employer assesses an applicant for a job. ◆ *vb* **3** to conduct an interview with (someone). **[C16:** from Old French *entrevue;* see INTER-, VIEW] ► ˌ**interviewˈee** *n* ► ˈ**interˌviewer** *n*

inter vivos *Latin.* (ˈɪntə ˈviːvɒs) *adj Law.* between living people: *an inter vivos gift.*

intervocalic (ˌɪntəvəʊˈkælɪk) *adj* pronounced or situated between vowels. ► ˌ**intervoˈcalically** *adv*

interwar (ˌɪntəˈwɔː) *adj* of or happening in the period between World War I and World War II.

interweave (ˌɪntəˈwiːv) *vb* **-weaves, -weaving, -wove** *or* **-weaved; -woven, -wove,** *or* **-weaved.** to weave, blend, or twine together; intertwine. Also: **interwork.** ► ˌ**interˈweavement** *n* ► ˈ**interˌweaver** *n*

intestate (ɪnˈtɛsteɪt, -tɪt) *adj* **1a** (of a person) not having made a will. **1b** (of property) not disposed of by will. ◆ *n* **2** a person who dies without having made a will. ◆ Compare **testate. [C14:** from Latin *intestātus,* from IN-[1] + *testātus,* from *testārī* to bear witness, make a will, from *testis* a witness] ► **inˈtestacy** *n*

ˌ**interˈstellar** *adj*
ˌ**interˈtribal** *adj*
ˌ**interˈurban** *adj*
ˌ**interˈvarsity** *adj*
ˌ**interˈvertebral** *adj*

intestinal flora *n* harmless microorganisms that inhabit the lumen of the intestinal tract.

intestine (ɪnˈtɛstɪn) *n* (*usually pl*) the part of the alimentary canal between the stomach and the anus. See **large intestine, small intestine.** Related adj: **alvine.** [C16: from Latin *intestīnum* gut, from *intestīnus* internal, from *intus* within] ▸ **intestinal** (ɪnˈtɛstɪnᵊl, ˌɪntɛsˈtaɪnᵊl) *adj* ▸ **inˈtestinally** *adv*

inti (ˈɪntɪ) *n* a former monetary unit of Peru. [C20: from Quechua]

intifada (ˌɪntɪˈfɑːdə) *n* the Palestinian uprising against Israel in the West Bank and Gaza Strip that started at the end of 1987. [C20: Arabic, literally: uprising]

intima (ˈɪntɪmə) *n, pl* **-mae** (-ˌmiː). *Anatomy, zoology.* the innermost layer of an organ or part, esp. of a blood vessel. [C19: from Latin, feminine of *intimus* innermost; see INTIMATE[1]] ▸ **ˈintimal** *adj*

intimacy (ˈɪntɪməsɪ) *n, pl* **-cies. 1** close or warm friendship or understanding; personal relationship. **2** (*often pl*) *Euphemistic.* sexual relations.

intimate[1] (ˈɪntɪmɪt) *adj* **1** characterized by a close or warm personal relationship: *an intimate friend.* **2** deeply personal, private, or secret. **3** (*often postpositive;* foll. by *with*) *Euphemistic.* having sexual relations (with). **4a** (*postpositive;* foll. by *with*) having a deep or unusual knowledge (of) **4b** (of knowledge) deep; extensive. **5** having a friendly, warm, or informal atmosphere: *an intimate nightclub.* **6** of or relating to the essential part or nature of something; intrinsic. **7** denoting the informal second person of verbs and pronouns in French and other languages. ◆ *n* **8** a close friend. [C17: from Latin *intimus* very close friend, from (adj): innermost, deepest, from *intus* within] ▸ **ˈintimately** *adv* ▸ **ˈintimateness** *n*

intimate[2] (ˈɪntɪˌmeɪt) *vb* (*tr; may take a clause as object*) **1** to hint; suggest. **2** to proclaim; make known. [C16: from Late Latin *intimāre* to proclaim, from Latin *intimus* innermost] ▸ **ˈintiˌmater** *n*

intimation (ˌɪntɪˈmeɪʃən) *n* **1** a hint or suggestion. **2** *Rare.* an announcement or notice.

intimidate (ɪnˈtɪmɪˌdeɪt) *vb* (*tr*) **1** to make timid or frightened; scare. **2** to discourage, restrain, or silence illegally or unscrupulously, as by threats or blackmail. [C17: from Medieval Latin *intimidāre,* from Latin IN-[2] + *timidus* fearful, from *timor* fear] ▸ **inˈtimiˌdating** *adj* ▸ **inˌtimiˈdation** *n* ▸ **inˈtimiˌdator** *n*

intinction (ɪnˈtɪŋkʃən) *n Christianity.* the practice of dipping the Eucharistic bread into the wine at Holy Communion. [C16: from Late Latin *intinctiō* a dipping in, from Latin *intingere* to dip in, from *tingere* to dip]

intine (ˈɪntɪn, -tiːn, -taɪn) *n* the inner membrane of a pollen grain or a spore. Compare **extine.** [C19: from Latin *intimus* innermost + -INE[1]]

intitule (ɪnˈtɪtjuːl) *vb* (*tr*) *Parliamentary procedure.* (in Britain) to entitle (an Act). [C15: from Old French *intituler,* from Latin *titulus* TITLE]

intl *abbrev. for* international.

into (ˈɪntuː; *unstressed* ˈɪntə) *prep* **1** to the interior or inner parts of: *to look into a case.* **2** to the middle or midst of so as to be surrounded by: *into the water; into the bushes.* **3** against; up against: *he drove into a wall.* **4** used to indicate the result of a transformation or change: *he changed into a monster.* **5** *Maths.* used to indicate a dividend: *three into six is two.* **6** *Informal.* interested or enthusiastically involved in: *I'm really into Freud these days.*

intolerable (ɪnˈtɒlərəbᵊl) *adj* **1** more than can be tolerated or endured; insufferable. **2** *Informal.* extremely irritating or annoying. ▸ **inˌtoleraˈbility** *or* **inˈtolerableness** *n* ▸ **inˈtolerably** *adv*

intolerant (ɪnˈtɒlərənt) *adj* **1** lacking respect for practices and beliefs other than one's own. **2** (*postpositive;* foll. by *of*) not able or willing to tolerate or endure: *intolerant of noise.* ▸ **inˈtolerance** *n* ▸ **inˈtolerantly** *adv*

intonate (ˈɪntəʊˌneɪt) *vb* (*tr*) **1** to pronounce or articulate (continuous connected speech) with a characteristic rise and fall of the voice. **2** a less common word for **intone.**

intonation (ˌɪntəʊˈneɪʃən) *n* **1** the sound pattern of phrases and sentences produced by pitch variation in the voice. **2** the act or manner of intoning. **3** an intoned, chanted, or monotonous utterance; incantation. **4** *Music.* the opening of a piece of plainsong, sung by a soloist. **5** *Music.* **5a** the correct or accurate pitching of intervals. **5b** the capacity to play or sing in tune. See also **just intonation.** ▸ **ˌintoˈnational** *adj*

intonation pattern *or* **contour** *n Linguistics.* a characteristic series of musical pitch levels that serves to distinguish between questions, statements, and other types of utterance in a language.

intone (ɪnˈtəʊn) *vb* **1** to utter, recite, or sing (a chant, prayer, etc.) in a monotonous or incantatory tone. **2** (*intr*) to speak with a particular or characteristic intonation or tone. **3** to sing (the opening phrase of a psalm, etc.) in plainsong. [C15: from Medieval Latin *intonare,* from IN-[2] + TONE] ▸ **inˈtoner** *n*

intorsion (ɪnˈtɔːʃən) *n Botany.* a spiral twisting in plant stems or other parts.

in toto *Latin.* (ɪn ˈtəʊtəʊ) *adv* totally; entirely; completely.

intoxicant (ɪnˈtɒksɪkənt) *n* **1** anything that causes intoxication. ◆ *adj* **2** causing intoxication.

intoxicate (ɪnˈtɒksɪˌkeɪt) *vb* (*tr*) **1** (of an alcoholic drink) to produce in (a person) a state ranging from euphoria to stupor, usually accompanied by loss of inhibitions and control; make drunk; inebriate. **2** to stimulate, excite, or elate so as to overwhelm. **3** (of a drug) to poison. [C16: from Medieval Latin, from *intoxicāre* to poison, from Latin *toxicum* poison; see TOXIC] ▸ **inˈtoxicable** *adj* ▸ **inˈtoxiˌcating** *adj* ▸ **inˈtoxiˌcatingly** *adv* ▸ **inˈtoxiˌcative** *adj* ▸ **inˈtoxiˌcator** *n*

intoxication (ɪnˌtɒksɪˈkeɪʃən) *n* **1** drunkenness; inebriation. **2** great elation. **3** the act of intoxicating. **4** poisoning.

intr. *abbrev. for* intransitive.

intra- *prefix* within; inside: *intravenous.* [from Latin *intrā* on the inside, within; see INTERIOR]

intra-atomic (ˌɪntrəəˈtɒmɪk) *adj* existing or occurring within an atom or atoms. Compare **interatomic.**

intracapsular (ˌɪntrəˈkæpsjʊlə) *adj Anatomy.* within a capsule, esp. within the capsule of a joint.

intracardiac (ˌɪntrəˈkɑːdɪˌæk) *adj* within the heart.

intracellular (ˌɪntrəˈsɛljʊlə) *adj Biology.* situated or occurring inside a cell or cells. ▸ **ˌintraˈcellularly** *adv*

Intracoastal Waterway (ˌɪntrəˈkəʊstᵊl) *n* short for **Atlantic Intracoastal Waterway.**

intracranial (ˌɪntrəˈkreɪnɪəl) *adj* within the skull.

intractable (ɪnˈtræktəbᵊl) *adj* **1** difficult to influence or direct: *an intractable disposition.* **2** (of a problem, illness, etc.) difficult to solve, alleviate, or cure. **3** difficult to shape or mould, esp. with the hands. ▸ **inˌtractaˈbility** *or* **inˈtractableness** *n* ▸ **inˈtractably** *adv*

intracutaneous (ˌɪntrəkjuːˈteɪnɪəs) *adj Anatomy.* within the skin. Also: **intradermal.** ▸ **ˌintracuˈtaneously** *adv*

intradermal (ˌɪntrəˈdɜːməl) *or* **intradermic** *adj Anatomy.* other words for **intracutaneous.** Abbrev. (esp. of an injection) **ID, i.d.** ▸ **ˌintraˈdermally** *or* **ˌintraˈdermically** *adv*

intrados (ɪnˈtreɪdɒs) *n, pl* **-dos** *or* **-doses.** *Architect.* the inner curve or surface of an arch or vault. Compare **extrados.** [C18: from French, from INTRA- + *dos* back, from Latin *dorsum*]

intrafascicular (ˌɪntrəfəˈsɪkjʊlə) *adj Botany.* between the xylem and phloem elements of a vascular bundle: *intrafascicular cambium.*

intragenerational mobility (ˌɪntrəˌdʒɛnəˈreɪʃənᵊl) *n Sociol.* movement within or between social classes and occupations, the change occurring within an individual's lifetime. Compare **intergenerational mobility.**

intramolecular (ˌɪntrəməˈlɛkjʊlə) *adj* occurring within a molecule or molecules.

intramural (ˌɪntrəˈmjʊərəl) *adj* **1** *Education, chiefly U.S. and Canadian.* operating within or involving those in a single establishment. **2** *Anatomy.* within the walls of a cavity or hollow organ. ▸ **ˌintraˈmurally** *adv*

intramuscular (ˌɪntrəˈmʌskjʊlə) *adj Anatomy.* within a muscle: *an intramuscular injection.* Abbrev. (esp. of an injection): **IM, i.m.** ▸ **ˌintraˈmuscularly** *adv*

intranational (ˌɪntrəˈnæʃənᵊl) *adj* within one nation.

intranet (ˈɪntrəˌnɛt) *n Computing.* an internal network that makes use of Internet technology. [C20: from INTRA- + NET[1] (sense 8), modelled on INTERNET]

intrans. *abbrev. for* intransitive.

intransigent (ɪnˈtrænsɪdʒənt) *adj* **1** not willing to compromise; obstinately maintaining an attitude. ◆ *n, also* **intransigentist. 2** an intransigent person, esp. in politics. [C19: from Spanish *los intransigentes* the uncompromising (ones), a name adopted by certain political extremists, from IN-[1] + *transigir* to compromise, from Latin *transigere* to settle; see TRANSACT] ▸ **inˈtransigence** *or* **inˈtransigency** *n* ▸ **inˈtransigently** *adv*

intransitive (ɪnˈtrænsɪtɪv) *adj* **1a** denoting a verb when it does not require a direct object. **1b** denoting a verb that customarily does not require a direct object: *"to faint" is an intransitive verb.* **1c** (*as n*) a verb in either of these categories. **2** denoting an adjective or noun that does not require any particular noun phrase as a referent. **3** *Logic, maths.* (of a relation) having the property that if it holds between one argument and a second, and between the second and a third, it must fail to hold between the first and the third: *"being the mother of" is an intransitive relation.* ◆ Compare **transitive, pseudo-intransitive.** ▸ **inˈtransitively** *adv* ▸ **inˌtransiˈtivity** *or* **inˈtransitiveness** *n*

intranuclear (ˌɪntrəˈnjuːklɪə) *adj* situated or occurring within a nucleus.

intraocular (ˌɪntrəˈɒkjʊlə) *adj Anatomy.* within an eyeball.

intrapartum (ˌɪntrəˈpɑːtəm) *adj Med.* of or relating to childbirth or delivery: *intrapartum care.* [C20: New Latin, from INTRA- + *partum,* from *partus* birth]

intrapreneur (ˌɪntrəprəˈnɜː) *n* a person who while remaining within a larger organization uses entrepreneurial skills to develop a new product or line of business as a subsidiary of the organization. [C20: from INTRA- + (ENTRE)PRENEUR]

intraspecific (ˌɪntrəspəˈsɪfɪk) *adj* relating to or occurring between members of the same species: *intraspecific competition.*

intrastate (ˌɪntrəˈsteɪt) *adj Chiefly U.S.* of, relating to, or confined within a single state, esp. a state of the U.S.

intratelluric (ˌɪntrətəˈljʊərɪk) *adj* (of rocks and their constituents, processes, etc.) formed or occurring below the surface of the earth.

intrauterine (ˌɪntrəˈjuːtəraɪn) *adj* within the womb.

intrauterine device *n* a metal or plastic device, in the shape of a loop, coil, or ring, inserted into the uterus to prevent conception. Abbrev.: **IUD.**

intravasation (ɪnˌtrævəˈseɪʃən) *n* the passage of extraneous material, such as pus, into a blood or lymph vessel. Compare **extravasation.**

intravenous (ˌɪntrəˈviːnəs) *adj Anatomy.* within a vein: *an intravenous injection.* Abbrevs. (esp. of an injection): **IV, i.v.** ▸ **ˌintraˈvenously** *adv*

in-tray *n* a tray for incoming papers requiring attention.

intrazonal soil (ˌɪntrəˈzəʊnᵊl) *n* a soil that has a well-developed profile determined by relief, parent material, age, etc.

intreat (ɪnˈtriːt) *vb* an archaic spelling of **entreat.** ▸ **inˈtreatingly** *adv* ▸ **inˈtreatment** *n*

intrench (ɪnˈtrɛntʃ) *vb* a less common spelling of **entrench.** ▸ **inˈtrencher** *n* ▸ **inˈtrenchment** *n*

intrepid (ɪnˈtrɛpɪd) *adj* fearless; daring; bold. [C17: from Latin *intrepidus,* from IN-[1] + *trepidus* fearful, timid] ▸ **ˌintreˈpidity** *or* **inˈtrepidness** *n* ▸ **inˈtrepidly** *adv*

intricate (ˈɪntrɪkɪt) *adj* **1** difficult to understand; obscure; complex; puzzling. **2** entangled or involved: *intricate patterns.* [C15: from Latin *intrīcāre* to entangle, perplex, from IN-[2] + *trīcae* trifles, perplexities] ▸ **ˈintricacy** *or* **ˈintricateness** *n* ▸ **ˈintricately** *adv*

intrigant *or* **intriguant** (ˈɪntrɪgənt; *French* ɛ̃trigɑ̃) *or* (*fem*) **intrigante** *or*

intriguante (ˌɪntrɪˈgɒnt; *French* ɛ̃trigɑ̃t) *n Archaic.* a person who intrigues; intriguer.

intrigue *vb* (ɪnˈtriːg), **-trigues, -triguing, -trigued. 1** (*tr*) to make interested or curious: *I'm intrigued by this case, Watson.* **2** (*intr*) to make secret plots or employ underhand methods; conspire. **3** (*intr; often foll. by* with) to carry on a clandestine love affair. ◆ *n* (ɪnˈtriːg, ˈɪntriːg). **4** the act or an instance of secret plotting, etc. **5** a clandestine love affair. **6** the quality of arousing interest or curiosity; beguilement. [C17: from French *intriguer,* from Italian *intrigare,* from Latin *intrīcāre;* see INTRICATE] ▸ **inˈtriguer** *n*

intriguing (ɪnˈtriːgɪŋ) *adj* arousing great interest or curiosity: *an intriguing mystery.* ▸ **inˈtriguingly** *adv*

intrinsic (ɪnˈtrɪnsɪk) *or* **intrinsical** *adj* **1** of or relating to the essential nature of a thing; inherent. **2** *Anatomy.* situated within or peculiar to a part: *intrinsic muscles.* [C15: from Late Latin *intrinsecus* from Latin, inwardly, from *intrā* within + *secus* alongside; related to *sequī* to follow] ▸ **inˈtrinsically** *adv*

intrinsic factor *n Biochem.* a glycoprotein, secreted by the stomach, the presence of which is necessary for the absorption of cyanocobalamin (vitamin B_{12}) in the intestine.

intrinsic semiconductor *n* an almost pure semiconductor to which no impurities have been added and in which the electron and hole densities are equal at thermal equilibrium. Also called: **i-type semiconductor.**

intro (ˈɪntrəʊ) *n, pl* **-tros.** *Informal.* short for **introduction.**

intro. *or* **introd.** *abbrev. for:* **1** introduction. **2** introductory.

intro- *prefix* in, into, or inward: *introvert.* [from Latin *intrō* towards the inside, inwardly, within]

introduce (ˌɪntrəˈdjuːs) *vb* (*tr*) **1** (often foll. by *to*) to present (someone) by name (to another person) or (two or more people to each other). **2** (foll. by *to*) to cause to experience for the first time: *to introduce a visitor to beer.* **3** to present for consideration or approval, esp. before a legislative body: *to introduce a draft bill.* **4** to bring in; establish: *to introduce decimal currency.* **5** to present (a radio or television programme, etc.) verbally. **6** (foll. by *with*) to start: *he introduced his talk with some music.* **7** (often foll. by *into*) to insert or inject: *he introduced the needle into his arm.* **8** to place (members of a species of plant or animal) in a new environment with the intention of producing a resident breeding population. [C16: from Latin *intrōdūcere* to bring inside, from INTRO- + *dūcere* to lead] ▸ **ˌintroˈducer** *n* ▸ **ˌintroˈducible** *adj*

introduction (ˌɪntrəˈdʌkʃən) *n* **1** the act of introducing or fact of being introduced. **2** a presentation of one person to another or others. **3** a means of presenting a person to another person, group, etc., such as a **letter of introduction** or reference. **4** a preliminary part, as of a book, speech, etc. **5** *Music.* **5a** an instrumental passage preceding the entry of a soloist, choir, etc. **5b** an opening passage in a movement or composition that precedes the main material. **6** something that has been or is introduced, esp. something that is not native to an area, country, etc. **7** a basic or elementary work of instruction, reference, etc. **8** *Logic.* (qualified by the name of an operation) a syntactic rule specifying the conditions under which a formula or statement containing the specified operator may be derived from others: *conjunction-introduction; negation-introduction.*

introductory (ˌɪntrəˈdʌktərɪ, -trɪ) *adj* serving as an introduction; preliminary; prefatory. ▸ **ˌintroˈductorily** *adv* ▸ **ˌintroˈductoriness** *n*

introgression (ˌɪntrəˈgrɛʃən) *n* the introduction of genes from the gene pool of one species into that of another during hybridization.

introit (ˈɪntrɔɪt) *n R.C. Church, Church of England.* a short prayer said or sung as the celebrant is entering the sanctuary to celebrate Mass or Holy Communion. [C15: from Church Latin *introitus* introit, from Latin: entrance, from *introīre* to go in, from INTRO- + *īre* to go] ▸ **inˈtroital** *adj*

introject (ˌɪntrəˈdʒɛkt) *vb Psychol.* **1** (*intr*) (esp. of a child) to incorporate ideas of others, or (in fantasy) of objects. **2** to turn (feelings for another) towards oneself. ◆ Compare **project.** See also **internalize.**

introjection (ˌɪntrəˈdʒɛkʃən) *n Psychol.* the act or process of introjecting. [C20: from INTRO- + (PRO)JECTION] ▸ **ˌintroˈjective** *adj*

intromission (ˌɪntrəˈmɪʃən) *n* a less common word for **insertion** or **introduction.** ▸ **ˌintroˈmissive** *adj*

intromit (ˌɪntrəˈmɪt) *vb* **-mits, -mitting, -mitted.** (*tr*) *Rare.* to enter or insert or allow to enter or be inserted. [C15: from Latin *intrōmittere* to send in, from INTRO- + *mittere* to send] ▸ **ˌintroˈmissible** *adj* ▸ **ˌintroˌmissiˈbility** *n* ▸ **ˌintroˈmittent** *adj* ▸ **ˌintroˈmitter** *n*

intron (ˈɪntrɒn) *n Biochem.* a stretch of DNA that interrupts a gene and does not contribute to the specification of a protein. Compare **exon**[2]. [C20: from *intr(agenic) (regi)on*]

introrse (ɪnˈtrɔːs) *adj Botany.* turned inwards or towards the axis, as anthers that shed their pollen towards the centre of the flower. [C19: from Latin *introrsus,* contraction of *intrōversus,* from INTRO- + *versus* turned, from *vertere* to turn] ▸ **inˈtrorsely** *adv*

introspect (ˌɪntrəˈspɛkt) *vb* (*intr*) to examine and analyse one's own thoughts and feelings.

introspection (ˌɪntrəˈspɛkʃən) *n* the examination of one's own thoughts, impressions, and feelings, esp. for long periods. [C17: from Latin *intrōspicere* to look within, from INTRO- + *specere* to look] ▸ **ˌintroˈspectional** *or* **ˌintroˈspective** *adj* ▸ **ˌintroˈspectionist** *n* ▸ **ˌintroˈspectively** *adv* ▸ **ˌintroˈspectiveness** *n*

introversion (ˌɪntrəˈvɜːʃən) *n* **1** *Psychol.* the directing of interest inwards towards one's own thoughts and feelings rather than towards the external world or making social contacts. **2** *Pathol.* the turning inside out of a hollow organ or part. ◆ Compare **extroversion.** ▸ **ˌintroˈversive** *or* **ˌintroˈvertive** *adj*

introvert *n* (ˈɪntrəˌvɜːt). **1** *Psychol.* a person prone to introversion. ◆ *adj* (ˈɪntrəˌvɜːt). **2** Also: **introverted.** characterized by introversion. ◆ *vb* (ˌɪntrəˈvɜːt). **3** (*tr*) *Pathol.* to turn (a hollow organ or part) inside out. ◆ Compare **extrovert.** [C17: see INTRO-, INVERT]

intrude (ɪnˈtruːd) *vb* **1** (often foll. by *into, on,* or *upon*) to put forward or interpose (oneself, one's views, something) abruptly or without invitation. **2** *Geology.* to force or thrust (rock material, esp. molten magma) or (of rock material) to be thrust between solid rocks. [C16: from Latin *intrūdere* to thrust in, from IN-[2] + *trūdere* to thrust] ▸ **inˈtrudingly** *adv*

intruder (ɪnˈtruːdə) *n* a person who enters a building, grounds, etc., without permission.

intrusion (ɪnˈtruːʒən) *n* **1** the act or an instance of intruding; an unwelcome visit, interjection, etc.: *an intrusion on one's privacy.* **2a** the movement of magma from within the earth's crust into spaces in the overlying strata to form igneous rock. **2b** any igneous rock formed in this way. **3** *Property law.* an unlawful entry onto land by a stranger after determination of a particular estate of freehold and before the remainderman or reversioner has made entry. ▸ **inˈtrusional** *adj*

intrusive (ɪnˈtruːsɪv) *adj* **1** characterized by intrusion or tending to intrude. **2** (of igneous rocks) formed by intrusion. Compare **extrusive** (sense 2). **3** *Phonetics.* relating to or denoting a speech sound that is introduced into a word or piece of connected speech for a phonetic rather than a historical or grammatical reason, such as the (r) often pronounced between *idea* and *of* in *the idea of it.* ▸ **inˈtrusively** *adv* ▸ **inˈtrusiveness** *n*

intrust (ɪnˈtrʌst) *vb* a less common spelling of **entrust.** ▸ **inˈtrustment** *n*

intubate (ˈɪntjʊˌbeɪt) *vb* (*tr*) *Med.* to insert a tube or cannula into (a hollow organ); cannulate. ▸ **ˌintuˈbation** *n*

INTUC (ˈɪntʌk) *n acronym for* Indian National Trade Union Congress.

intuit (ɪnˈtjuːɪt) *vb* to know or discover by intuition. ▸ **inˈtuitable** *adj*

intuition (ˌɪntjʊˈɪʃən) *n* **1** knowledge or belief obtained neither by reason nor by perception. **2** instinctive knowledge or belief. **3** a hunch or unjustified belief. **4** *Philosophy.* immediate knowledge of a proposition or object such as Kant's account of our knowledge of sensible objects. **5** the supposed faculty or process by which we obtain any of these. [C15: from Late Latin *intuitiō* a contemplation, from Latin *intuērī* to gaze upon, from *tuērī* to look at] ▸ **ˌintuˈitional** *adj* ▸ **ˌintuˈitionally** *adv*

intuitionism (ˌɪntjuˈɪʃəˌnɪzəm) *or* **intuitionalism** *n* **1** (in ethics) **1a** the doctrine that there are moral truths discoverable by intuition. **1b** the doctrine that there is no single principle by which to resolve conflicts between intuited moral rules. ◆ See also **deontological. 2** *Philosophy.* the theory that general terms are used of a variety of objects in accordance with perceived similarities. Compare **nominalism, Platonism. 3** *Logic.* the doctrine that logical axioms rest on prior intuitions concerning time, negation, and provability. **4a** the theory that mathematics cannot intelligibly comprehend the properties of infinite sets, and that only what can be shown to be provable can be justifiably asserted. **4b** the reconstruction of mathematics or logic in accordance with this view. ◆ Compare **formalism, logicism, finitism. 5** the doctrine that knowledge, esp. of the external world, is acquired by intuition. ▸ **ˌintuˈitionist** *or* **ˌintuˈitionalist** *n*

intuitive (ɪnˈtjuːɪtɪv) *adj* **1** resulting from intuition: *an intuitive awareness.* **2** of, characterized by, or involving intuition. ▸ **inˈtuitively** *adv* ▸ **inˈtuitiveness** *n*

intumesce (ˌɪntjuˈmɛs) *vb* (*intr*) to swell or become swollen; undergo intumescence. [C18: from Latin *intumescere,* from *tumescere* to begin to swell, from *tumēre* to swell]

intumescence (ˌɪntjuˈmɛsəns) *or* **intumescency** *n* **1** *Pathol.* a swelling up, as with blood or other fluid. **2** *Pathol.* a swollen organ or part. **3** *Chem.* the swelling of certain substances on heating, often accompanied by the escape of water vapour. ▸ **ˌintuˈmescent** *adj*

intussuscept (ˌɪntəssəˈsɛpt) *vb* (*tr; usually passive*) *Pathol.* to turn or fold (an organ or a part) inwards; invaginate. ▸ **ˌintussusˈceptive** *adj*

intussusception (ˌɪntəssəˈsɛpʃən) *n* **1** *Pathol.* invagination of a tubular organ or part, esp. the telescoping of one section of the intestinal tract into a lower section, causing obstruction. **2** *Biology.* growth in the surface area of a cell by the deposition of new particles between the existing particles of the cell wall. Compare **apposition** (sense 3). [C18: from Latin *intus* within + *susceptiō* a taking up]

intwine (ɪnˈtwaɪn) *vb* a less common spelling of **entwine.** ▸ **inˈtwinement** *n*

Inuit *or* **Innuit** (ˈɪnjuːɪt) *n, pl* **-it** *or* **-its.** an Eskimo of N America or Greenland, as distinguished from one from Asia or the Aleutian Islands: the general name for an Eskimo in Canada. Compare **Yupik.** [from Eskimo *inuit* the people, pl of *inuk* a man]

Inuktitut (ɪˈnʊktəˌtʊt) *n Canadian.* the language of the Inuit; Eskimo. [from Eskimo *inuk* man + *titut* speech]

inulin (ˈɪnjʊlɪn) *n* a fructose polysaccharide present in the tubers and rhizomes of some plants. Formula: $(C_6H_{10}O_5)_n$. [C19: from Latin *inula* elecampane + -IN]

inunction (ɪnˈʌŋkʃən) *n* **1** the application of an ointment to the skin, esp. by rubbing. **2** the ointment so used. **3** the act of anointing; anointment. [C15: from Latin *inunguere* to anoint, from *unguere;* see UNCTION]

inundate (ˈɪnʌnˌdeɪt) *vb* (*tr*) **1** to cover completely with water; overflow; flood; swamp. **2** to overwhelm, as if with a flood: *to be inundated with requests.* [C17: from Latin *inundāre* to flood, from *unda* wave] ▸ **ˈinundant** *or* **inˈundatory** *adj* ▸ **ˌinunˈdation** *n* ▸ **ˈinunˌdator** *n*

inurbane (ˌɪnɜːˈbeɪn) *adj Rare.* not urbane; lacking in courtesy or polish. ▸ **inurbanity** (ˌɪnɜːˈbænɪtɪ) *n* ▸ **ˌinurˈbanely** *adv*

inure *or* **enure** (ɪˈnjʊə) *vb* **1** (*tr; often passive;* often foll. by *to*) to cause to accept or become hardened to; habituate. **2** (*intr*) (esp. of a law, etc.) to come into operation; take effect. [C15 *enuren* to accustom, from *ure* use, from Old

French *euvre* custom, work, from Latin *opera* works, plural of *opus*] ▸ **inur-edness** *or* **enuredness** (ɪ'njuərɪdnɪs) *n* ▸ **in'urement** *or* **en'urement** *n*

inurn (ɪn'ɜ:n) *vb (tr)* **1** to place (esp. cremated ashes) in an urn. **2** a less common word for **inter.** ▸ **in'urnment** *n*

in utero *Latin.* (ɪn 'ju:tə,rəʊ) *adv* within the womb.

inutile (ɪn'ju:taɪl) *adj Rare.* useless; unprofitable. ▸ **in'utilely** *adv* ▸ **,inu'til-ity** *n*

inv. *abbrev. for:* **1** invented. **2** invention. **3** inventor. **4** invoice.

in vacuo *Latin.* (ɪn 'vækjʊ,əʊ) *adv* **1** in a vacuum. **2** in isolation; without reference to facts or evidence.

invade (ɪn'veɪd) *vb* **1** to enter (a country, territory, etc.) by military force. **2** *(tr)* to occupy in large numbers; overrun; infest. **3** *(tr)* to trespass or encroach upon (privacy, etc.). **4** *(tr)* to enter and spread throughout, esp. harmfully; pervade. **5** (of plants, esp. weeds) to become established in (a place to which they are not native). [C15: from Latin *invādere,* from *vādere* to go] ▸ **in'vadable** *adj* ▸ **in'vader** *n*

invaginate *vb* (ɪn'vædʒɪ,neɪt). **1** *Pathol.* to push one section of (a tubular organ or part) back into itself so that it becomes ensheathed; intussuscept. **2** *(intr)* (of the outer layer of an organism or part) to undergo invagination. ◆ *adj* (ɪn'vædʒɪnɪt, -,neɪt). **3** (of an organ or part) folded back upon itself. [C19: from Medieval Latin *invāgīnāre,* from Latin IN-[2] + *vāgīna* sheath] ▸ **in'vagi-nable** *adj*

invagination (ɪn,vædʒɪ'neɪʃən) *n* **1** *Pathol.* the process of invaginating or the condition of being invaginated; intussusception. **2** *Pathol.* an invaginated organ or part. **3** an infolding of the outer layer of cells of an organism or part of an organism so as to form a pocket in the surface, as in the embryonic development of a gastrula from a blastula.

invalid[1] ('ɪnvə,li:d, -lɪd) *n* **1a** a person suffering from disablement or chronic ill health. **1b** *(as modifier): an invalid chair.* ◆ *adj* **2** suffering from or disabled by injury, sickness, etc. ◆ *vb (tr)* **3** to cause to become an invalid; disable. **4** (usually foll. by *out; often passive*) *Chiefly Brit.* to require (a member of the armed forces) to retire from active service through wounds or illness. [C17: from Latin *invalidus* infirm, from IN-[1] + *validus* strong] ▸ **,inva'lidity** *n*

invalid[2] (ɪn'vælɪd) *adj* **1** not valid; having no cogency or legal force. **2** *Logic.* (of an argument) having a conclusion that does not follow from the premises: it may be false when the premises are all true; not valid. [C16: from Medieval Latin *invalidus* without legal force; see INVALID[1]] ▸ **invalidity** (,ɪnvə'lɪdɪtɪ) *or* **in'validness** *n* ▸ **in'validly** *adv*

invalidate (ɪn'vælɪ,deɪt) *vb (tr)* **1** to render weak or ineffective, as an argument. **2** to take away the legal force or effectiveness of; annul, as a contract. ▸ **in,vali'dation** *n* ▸ **in'vali,dator** *n*

invalidism ('ɪnvəlɪ,dɪzəm) *n* **1** the state of being an invalid, esp. by reason of ill health. **2** a state of being abnormally preoccupied with one's physical health.

invalidity benefit *n* (in the British National Insurance scheme) a weekly payment to a person who has been off work through illness for more than six months. Abbrev.: **IVB.**

invaluable (ɪn'væljʊəbᵊl) *adj* having great value that is impossible to calculate; priceless. ▸ **in'valuableness** *n* ▸ **in'valuably** *adv*

Invar (ɪn'vɑ:) *n Trademark.* an alloy containing iron (63.8 per cent), nickel (36 per cent), and carbon (0.2 per cent). It has a very low coefficient of expansion and is used for the balance springs of watches, etc. [C20: shortened from INVARIABLE]

invariable (ɪn'vɛərɪəbᵊl) *adj* **1** not subject to alteration; unchanging. ◆ *n* **2** a mathematical quantity having an unchanging value; a constant. ▸ **in,vari-a'bility** *or* **in'variableness** *n* ▸ **in'variably** *adv*

invariant (ɪn'vɛərɪənt) *n* **1** *Maths.* an entity, quantity, etc., that is unaltered by a particular transformation of coordinates: *a point in space, rather than its coordinates, is an invariant.* ◆ *adj* **2** *Maths.* (of a relationship or a property of a function, configuration, or equation) unaltered by a particular transformation of coordinates. **3** a rare word for **invariable.** ▸ **in'variance** *or* **in'variancy** *n*

invasion (ɪn'veɪʒən) *n* **1** the act of invading with armed forces. **2** any encroachment or intrusion: *an invasion of rats.* **3** the onset or advent of something harmful, esp. of a disease. **4** *Pathol.* the spread of cancer from its point of origin into surrounding tissues. **5** the movement of plants to an area to which they are not native.

invasive (ɪn'veɪsɪv) *adj* **1** of or relating to an invasion, intrusion, etc. **2** relating to or denoting cancer at the stage at which it has spread from its site of origin to other tissues. **3** (of surgery) involving making a relatively large incision in the body to gain access to the target of the surgery, as opposed to making a small incision or gaining access endoscopically through a natural orifice.

invective (ɪn'vektɪv) *n* **1** vehement accusation or denunciation, esp. of a bitterly abusive or sarcastic kind. ◆ *adj* **2** characterized by or using abusive language, bitter sarcasm, etc. [C15: from Late Latin *invectīvus* reproachful, scolding, from Latin *invectus* carried in; see INVEIGH] ▸ **in'vectively** *adv* ▸ **in'vectiveness** *n*

inveigh (ɪn'veɪ) *vb (intr;* foll. by *against)* to speak with violent or invective language; rail. [C15: from Latin *invehī,* literally: to be carried in, hence, assail physically or verbally, from IN-[2] + *vehī* to be carried, ride] ▸ **in'veigher** *n*

inveigle (ɪn'vi:gᵊl, -'veɪ-) *vb (tr;* often foll. by *into* or an infinitive) to lead (someone into a situation) or persuade (to do something) by cleverness or trickery; cajole: *to inveigle customers into spending more.* [C15: from Old French *avogler* to blind, deceive, from *avogle* blind, from Medieval Latin *ab oculis* without eyes] ▸ **in'veiglement** *n* ▸ **in'veigler** *n*

invent (ɪn'vent) *vb* **1** to create or devise (new ideas, machines, etc.). **2** to make up (falsehoods); fabricate. [C15: from Latin *invenīre* to find, come upon, from IN-[2] + *venīre* to come] ▸ **in'ventible** *or* **in'ventable** *adj*

invention (ɪn'venʃən) *n* **1** the act or process of inventing. **2** something that is invented. **3** *Patent law.* the discovery or production of some new or improved process or machine that is both useful and is not obvious to persons skilled in the particular field. **4** creative power or ability; inventive skill. **5** *Euphemistic.* a fabrication; lie. **6** (in traditional rhetoric) one of the five steps in preparing a speech or discourse: the process of finding suitable topics on which to talk or write. **7** *Music.* a short piece consisting of two or three parts usually in imitative counterpoint. **8** *Sociol.* the creation of a new cultural pattern or trait. ▸ **in'ventional** *adj* ▸ **in'ventionless** *adj*

inventive (ɪn'ventɪv) *adj* **1** skilled or quick at contriving; ingenious; resourceful. **2** characterized by inventive skill: *an inventive programme of work.* **3** of or relating to invention. ▸ **in'ventively** *adv* ▸ **in'ventiveness** *n*

inventor (ɪn'ventə) *n* a person who invents, esp. as a profession. ▸ **in'ven-tress** *fem n*

inventory ('ɪnvəntərɪ, -trɪ) *n* **1** a detailed list of articles, goods, property, etc. **2** *(often pl) Accounting, chiefly U.S.* **2a** the amount or value of a firm's current assets that consist of raw materials, work in progress, and finished goods; stock. **2b** such assets individually. ◆ *vb* **-tories, -torying, -toried. 3** *(tr)* to enter (items) in an inventory; make a list of. [C16: from Medieval Latin *inventōrium;* see INVENT] ▸ **'inventoriable** *adj* ▸ **,inven'torial** *adj* ▸ **,in-ven'torially** *adv*

inveracity (,ɪnvə'ræsɪtɪ) *n, pl* **-ties.** *Formal or euphemistic.* **1** lying; untruthfulness. **2** an untruth; lie.

Inveraray (,ɪnvə'rɛərɪ) *n* a town in W Scotland, in Argyll and Bute: Inveraray Castle is the seat of the Dukes of Argyll. Pop.: 512 (1991).

Invercargill (,ɪnvə'kɑ:gɪl) *n* a city in New Zealand, on South Island: regional trading centre for sheep and agricultural products. Pop.: 51 600 (1995 est.).

Inverclyde (,ɪnvə'klaɪd) *n* a council area of W central Scotland: created in 1996 from part of Strathclyde region. Administrative centre: Greenock. Pop.: 89 990 (1996 est.). Area: 162 sq. km (63 sq. miles).

Inverness (,ɪnvə'nɛs) *n* **1** a town in N Scotland, administrative centre of Highland: tourism and specialized engineering. Pop.: 41 234 (1991). **2** *(sometimes not cap.)* an overcoat with a removable cape.

Inverness-shire (,ɪnvə'nɛs,ʃɪə, -ʃə) *n* (until 1975) a county of NW Scotland, now part of Highland.

inverse (ɪn'vɜ:s, 'ɪnvɜ:s) *adj* **1** opposite or contrary in effect, sequence, direction, etc. **2** *Maths.* **2a** (of a relationship) containing two variables such that an increase in one results in a decrease in the other: *the volume of a gas is in inverse ratio to its pressure.* **2b** (of an element) operating on a specified member of a set to produce the identity of the set: *the additive inverse element of x is −x, the multiplicative inverse element of x is 1/x.* **3** *(usually prenominal)* upside-down; inverted: *in an inverse position.* ◆ *n* **4** *Maths.* **4a** another name for **reciprocal** (sense 7). **4b** an inverse element. **5** *Logic.* a categorial proposition derived from another by changing both the proposition and its subject from affirmative to negative, or vice versa, as *all immortals are angels* from *no mortals are angels.* [C17: from Latin *inversus,* from *invertere* to INVERT] ▸ **in'versely** *adv*

inverse function *n* a function whose independent variable is the dependent variable of a given trigonometric or hyperbolic function: *the inverse function of* sin *x* is arcsin *y (also written* $\sin^{-1} y$).

inverse square law *n* any natural law in which the magnitude of a physical quantity varies inversely with the square of the distance from its source.

inversion (ɪn'vɜ:ʃən) *n* **1** the act of inverting or state of being inverted. **2** something inverted, esp. a reversal of order, mutual functions, etc.: *an inversion of their previous relationship.* **3** Also called: **anastrophe.** *Rhetoric.* the reversal of a normal order of words. **4** *Chem.* **4a** the conversion of a dextrorotatory solution of sucrose into a laevorotatory solution of glucose and fructose by hydrolysis. **4b** any similar reaction in which the optical properties of the reactants are opposite to those of the products. **5** *Music.* **5a** the process or result of transposing the notes of a chord (esp. a triad) such that the root, originally in the bass, is placed in an upper part. When the bass note is the third of the triad, the resulting chord is the **first inversion;** when it is the fifth, the resulting chord is the **second inversion.** See also **root position. 5b** (in counterpoint) the modification of a melody or part in which all ascending intervals are replaced by corresponding descending intervals and vice versa. **5c** the modification of an interval in which the higher note becomes the lower or the lower one the higher. See **complement** (sense 8). **6** *Pathol.* abnormal positioning of an organ or part, as in being upside down or turned inside out. **7** *Psychiatry.* **7a** the adoption of the role or characteristics of the opposite sex. **7b** another word for **homosexuality. 8** *Meteorol.* an abnormal condition in which the layer of air next to the earth's surface is cooler than an overlying layer. **9** *Anatomy, phonetics.* another word for **retroflexion** (sense 2). **10** *Computing.* an operation by which each digit of a binary number is changed to the alternative digit, as *10110* to *01001.* **11** *Genetics.* a type of chromosomal mutation in which a section of a chromosome, and hence the order of its genes, is reversed. **12** *Logic.* the process of deriving the inverse of a categorial proposition. **13** *Maths.* a transformation of the set of points *P* to the new set of points *P′* about a fixed point *O* such that $OP.OP' = a^2$, where *a* is a constant and *P* and *P′* lie on a straight line through *O* and on the same side of it. ▸ **in'versive** *adj*

invert *vb* (ɪn'vɜ:t). **1** to turn or cause to turn upside down or inside out. **2** *(tr)* to reverse in effect, sequence, direction, etc. **3** *(tr) Phonetics.* **3a** to turn (the tip of the tongue) up and back. **3b** to pronounce (a speech sound) by retroflexion. **4** *Logic.* to form the inverse of a categorial proposition. ◆ *n* ('ɪnvɜ:t). **5** *Psychiatry.* **5a** a person who adopts the role of the opposite sex. **5b** another word for **homosexual. 6** *Architect.* **6a** the lower inner surface of a drain, sewer, etc. Compare **soffit** (sense 2). **6b** an arch that is concave upwards, esp. one used in foundations. [C16: from Latin *invertere,* from IN-[2] + *vertere* to turn] ▸ **in'vertible** *adj* ▸ **in,verti'bility** *n*

invertase (ɪn'vɜ:teɪz) *n* an enzyme, occurring in the intestinal juice of animals and in yeasts, that hydrolyses sucrose to glucose and fructose. Also called: **sac-charase.**

invertebrate (ɪn'vɜːtɪbrɪt, -ˌbreɪt) *n* **1** any animal lacking a backbone, including all species not classified as vertebrates. ◆ *adj also* **in'vertebral. 2** of, relating to, or designating invertebrates.

inverted comma *n* another term for **quotation mark.**

inverted mordent *n Music.* a melodic ornament consisting of the rapid single or double alternation of a principal note with a note one degree higher. Also called: **upper mordent.** See also **pralltriller.**

inverted pleat *n Dressmaking.* a box pleat reversed so that the fullness of the material is turned inwards.

inverted snob *n* a person who scorns the conventions or attitudes of his own class or social group by attempting to identify with people of a supposedly lower class.

inverter *or* **invertor** (ɪn'vɜːtə) *n* **1** any device for converting a direct current into an alternating current. **2** *Computing.* another name for **NOT circuit.**

invert sugar ('ɪnvɜːt) *n* a mixture of fructose and glucose obtained by the inversion of sucrose.

invest (ɪn'vɛst) *vb* **1** (often foll. by *in*) to lay out (money or capital in an enterprise, esp. by purchasing shares) with the expectation of profit. **2** (*tr;* often foll. by *in*) to devote (effort, resources, etc., to a project). **3** (*tr;* often foll. by *in* or *with*) *Archaic or ceremonial.* to clothe or adorn (in some garment, esp. the robes of an office): *to invest a king in the insignia of an emperor.* **4** (*tr;* often foll. by *in*) to install formally or ceremoniously (in an official position, rank, etc.). **5** (*tr;* foll. by *in* or *with*) to place (power, authority, etc., in) or provide (with power or authority): *to invest new rights in the monarchy.* **6** (*tr; usually passive;* foll. by *in* or *with*) to provide or endow (a person with qualities, characteristics, etc.): *he was invested with great common sense.* **7** (*tr;* foll. by *with*) *Usually poetic.* to cover or adorn, as if with a coat or garment: *when spring invests the trees with leaves.* **8** (*tr*) *Rare.* to surround with military forces; besiege. **9** (*intr;* foll. by *in*) *Informal.* to purchase; buy. [C16: from Medieval Latin *investīre* to clothe, from Latin, from *vestīre,* from *vestis* a garment] ▶ **in'vestable** *or* **in'vestible** *adj* ▶ **in'vestor** *n*

investigate (ɪn'vɛstɪˌgeɪt) *vb* to inquire into (a situation or problem, esp. a crime or death) thoroughly; examine systematically, esp. in order to discover the truth. [C16: from Latin *investīgāre* to search after, from IN-[2] + *vestīgium* track; see VESTIGE] ▶ **in'vestigable** *adj* ▶ **in'vestigative** *or* **in'vestigatory** *adj*

investigation (ɪnˌvɛstɪ'geɪʃən) *n* the act or process of investigating; a careful search or examination in order to discover facts, etc. ▶ **inˌvesti'gational** *adj*

investigator (ɪn'vɛstɪˌgeɪtə) *n* a person who investigates, such as a private detective.

investiture (ɪn'vɛstɪtʃə) *n* **1** the act of presenting with a title or with the robes and insignia of an office or rank. **2** (in feudal society) the formal bestowal of the possessory right to a fief or other benefice. **3** a less common word for **investment** (sense 7). ▶ **in'vestitive** *adj*

investment (ɪn'vɛstmənt) *n* **1a** the act of investing money. **1b** the amount invested. **1c** an enterprise, asset, etc., in which money is or can be invested. **2a** the act of investing effort, resources, etc. **2b** the amount invested. **3** *Economics.* the amount by which the stock of capital (plant, machinery, materials, etc.) in an enterprise or economy changes. **4** *Biology.* the outer layer or covering of an organ, part, or organism. **5** a less common word for **investiture** (sense 1). **6** the act of investing or state of being invested, as with an official robe, a specific quality, etc. **7** *Rare.* the act of besieging with military forces, works, etc.

investment analyst *n* a specialist in forecasting the prices of stocks and shares.

investment bond *n* a single-premium life-assurance policy in which a fixed sum is invested in an asset-backed fund.

investment trust *n* a financial enterprise that invests its subscribed capital in securities for its investors' benefit.

inveterate (ɪn'vɛtərɪt) *adj* **1** long established, esp. so as to be deep-rooted or ingrained: *an inveterate feeling of hostility.* **2** (*prenominal*) settled or confirmed in a habit or practice, esp. a bad one; hardened: *an inveterate smoker.* **3** *Obsolete.* full of hatred; hostile. [C16: from Latin *inveterātus* of long standing, from *inveterāre* to make old, from IN-[2] + *vetus* old] ▶ **in'veteracy** *or* **in'veterateness** *n* ▶ **in'veterately** *adv*

inviable (ɪn'vaɪəbᵊl) *adj* not viable, esp. financially; not able to survive: *an inviable company.* ▶ **inˌvia'bility** *or* **in'viableness** *n* ▶ **in'viably** *adv*

invidious (ɪn'vɪdɪəs) *adj* **1** incurring or tending to arouse resentment, unpopularity, etc.: *an invidious task.* **2** (of comparisons or distinctions) unfairly or offensively discriminating. **3** *Obsolete.* grudging; envious. [C17: from Latin *invidiōsus* full of envy, from *invidia* ENVY] ▶ **in'vidiously** *adv* ▶ **in'vidiousness** *n*

invigilate (ɪn'vɪdʒɪˌleɪt) *vb* (*intr*) **1** *Brit.* to watch examination candidates, esp. to prevent cheating. U.S. word: **proctor. 2** *Archaic.* to keep watch. [C16: from Latin *invigilāre* to watch over, from IN-[2] + *vigilāre* to keep watch; see VIGIL] ▶ **inˌvigi'lation** *n* ▶ **in'vigiˌlator** *n*

invigorate (ɪn'vɪgəˌreɪt) *vb* (*tr*) to give vitality and vigour to; animate; brace; refresh: *to be invigorated by fresh air.* [C17: from IN-[2] + Latin *vigor* VIGOUR] ▶ **in'vigorˌatingly** *adv* ▶ **inˌvigor'ation** *n* ▶ **in'vigorative** *adj* ▶ **in'vigoratively** *adv* ▶ **in'vigorˌator** *n*

invincible (ɪn'vɪnsəbᵊl) *adj* **1** incapable of being defeated; unconquerable. **2** unable to be overcome; insuperable: *invincible prejudices.* [C15: from Late Latin *invincibilis,* from Latin IN-[1] + *vincere* to conquer] ▶ **inˌvinci'bility** *or* **in'vincibleness** *n* ▶ **in'vincibly** *adv*

in vino veritas *Latin.* (ɪn 'viːnəʊ 'vɛrɪˌtæs) in wine there is truth; people speak the truth when they are drunk.

inviolable (ɪn'vaɪələbᵊl) *adj* that must not or cannot be transgressed, dishonoured, or broken; to be kept sacred: *an inviolable oath.* ▶ **inˌviola'bility** *or* **in'violableness** *n* ▶ **in'violably** *adv*

inviolate (ɪn'vaɪəlɪt, -ˌleɪt) *adj* **1** free from violation, injury, disturbance, etc. **2** a less common word for **inviolable.** ▶ **in'violacy** *or* **in'violateness** *n* ▶ **in'violately** *adv*

invisible (ɪn'vɪzəbᵊl) *adj* **1** not visible; not able to be perceived by the eye: *invisible rays.* **2** concealed from sight; hidden. **3** not easily seen or noticed: *invisible mending.* **4** kept hidden from public view; secret; clandestine. **5** *Economics.* of or relating to services rather than goods in relation to the invisible balance: *invisible earnings.* ◆ *n* **6** *Economics.* an invisible item of trade; service. ▶ **inˌvisi'bility** *or* **in'visibleness** *n* ▶ **in'visibly** *adv*

invisible balance *n Economics.* the difference in value between total exports of services plus payment of property incomes from abroad and total imports of services plus payment abroad of property incomes. Compare **balance of trade.**

invisible ink *n* a liquid used for writing that does not become visible until it has been treated with chemicals, heat, ultraviolet light, etc.

invitation (ˌɪnvɪ'teɪʃən) *n* **1a** the act of inviting, such as an offer of entertainment or hospitality. **1b** (*as modifier*): *an invitation dance; an invitation race.* **2** the act of enticing or attracting; allurement.

invitatory (ɪn'vaɪtətərɪ, -trɪ) *adj* **1** serving as or conveying an invitation. ◆ *n, pl* **-tories. 2** any of various invitations to prayer, such as Psalm 95 in a religious service.

invite *vb* (ɪn'vaɪt). (*tr*) **1** to ask (a person or persons) in a friendly or polite way (to do something, attend an event, etc.): *he invited them to dinner.* **2** to make a request for, esp. publicly or formally: *to invite applications.* **3** to bring on or provoke; give occasion for: *you invite disaster by your actions.* **4** to welcome or tempt. ◆ *n* ('ɪnvaɪt). **5** an informal word for **invitation.** [C16: from Latin *invītāre* to invite, entertain, from IN-[2] + *-vītāre,* probably related to Greek *hiesthai* to be desirous of] ▶ **in'viter** *n*

inviting (ɪn'vaɪtɪŋ) *adj* tempting; alluring; attractive. ▶ **in'vitingly** *adv* ▶ **in'vitingness** *n*

in vitro (ɪn 'viːtrəʊ) *adv, adj* (of biological processes or reactions) made to occur outside the body of the organism in an artificial environment. [New Latin, literally: in glass]

in vitro fertilization *n* a technique enabling some women who are unable to conceive to bear children. Egg cells removed from a woman's ovary are fertilized by sperm in vitro; some of the resulting fertilized egg cells are incubated until the blastocyst stage and then implanted into her uterus. Abbrev.: **IVF.**

in vivo (ɪn 'viːvəʊ) *adv, adj* (of biological processes or experiments) occurring or carried out in the living organism. [New Latin, literally: in a living (thing)]

invocate ('ɪnvəˌkeɪt) *vb* an archaic word for **invoke.** ▶ **invocative** (ɪn'vɒkətɪv) *adj* ▶ **'invoˌcator** *n*

invocation (ˌɪnvə'keɪʃən) *n* **1** the act of invoking or calling upon some agent for assistance. **2** a prayer asking God for help, forgiveness, etc., esp. as part of a religious service. **3** an appeal for inspiration and guidance from a Muse or deity at the beginning of a poem. **4a** the act of summoning a spirit or demon from another world by ritual incantation or magic. **4b** the incantation used in this act. ▶ **ˌinvo'cational** *adj* ▶ **invocatory** (ɪn'vɒkətərɪ, -trɪ) *adj*

invoice ('ɪnvɔɪs) *n* **1** a document issued by a seller to a buyer listing the goods or services supplied and stating the sum of money due. ◆ *vb* **2** (*tr*) **2a** to present (a customer) with an invoice. **2b** to list (merchandise sold) on an invoice. [C16: from earlier *invoyes,* from Old French *envois,* plural of *envoi* message; see ENVOY[1]]

invoke (ɪn'vəʊk) *vb* (*tr*) **1** to call upon (an agent, esp. God or another deity) for help, inspiration, etc. **2** to put (a law, penalty, etc.) into use: *the union invoked the dispute procedure.* **3** to appeal to (an outside agent or authority) for confirmation, corroboration, etc. **4** to implore or beg (help, etc.). **5** to summon (a spirit, demon, etc.); conjure up. [C15: from Latin *invocāre* to call upon, appeal to, from *vocāre* to call] ▶ **in'vocable** *adj* ▶ **in'voker** *n*

USAGE *Invoke* is sometimes wrongly used where *evoke* is meant: *this proposal evoked* (not *invoked*) *a strong reaction.*

involucel (ɪn'vɒljʊˌsɛl) *or* **involucellum** (ɪnˌvɒljʊ'sɛləm) *n, pl* **-cels** *or* **-cella** (-'sɛlə). a ring of bracts at the base of the florets of a compound umbel. [C19: from New Latin *involūcellum* a little cover; see INVOLUCRE] ▶ **inˌvolu'cellate** *or* **inˌvolu'cellated** *adj*

involucre ('ɪnvəˌluːkə) *or* **involucrum** (ˌɪnvə'luːkrəm) *n, pl* **-cres** *or* **-cra** (-krə). a ring of bracts at the base of an inflorescence in such plants as the *Compositae.* [C16 (in the sense: envelope): from New Latin *involucrum,* from Latin: wrapper, from *involvere* to wrap; see INVOLVE] ▶ **ˌinvo'lucral** *adj* ▶ **ˌinvo'lucrate** *adj*

involuntary (ɪn'vɒləntərɪ, -trɪ) *adj* **1** carried out without one's conscious wishes; not voluntary; unintentional. **2** *Physiol.* (esp. of a movement or muscle) performed or acting without conscious control. ▶ **in'voluntarily** *adv* ▶ **in'voluntariness** *n*

involute *adj* ('ɪnvəˌluːt), *also* **involuted. 1** complex, intricate, or involved. **2** *Botany.* (esp. of petals, leaves, etc., in bud) having margins that are rolled inwards. **3** (of certain shells) closely coiled so that the axis is obscured. ◆ *n* ('ɪnvəˌluːt). **4** *Geom.* the curve described by the free end of a thread as it is wound around another curve, the **evolute,** such that its normals are tangential to the evolute. ◆ *vb* (ˌɪnvə'luːt). **5** (*intr*) to become involute. [C17: from Latin *involūtus,* from *involvere;* see INVOLVE] ▶ **'invoˌlutely** *adv* ▶ **ˌinvo'lutedly** *adv*

involute gear *n* a gear tooth form that is generated by involute geometry.

involution (ˌɪnvə'luːʃən) *n* **1** the act of involving or complicating or the state of being involved or complicated. **2** something involved or complicated. **3** *Zoology.* degeneration or structural deformation. **4** *Biology.* an involute formation or structure. **5** *Physiol.* reduction in size of an organ or part, as of the uterus following childbirth or as a result of ageing. **6** an algebraic operation in which a number, variable, expression etc., is raised to a specified power. Compare **evo-**

lution (sense 5). 7 *Grammar.* an involved construction, such as one in which the subject is separated from the predicate by an additional clause. ▸ **ˌinvoˈlutional** *adj*

involve (ɪnˈvɒlv) *vb (tr)* **1** to include or contain as a necessary part: *the task involves hard work.* **2** to have an effect on; spread to: *the investigation involved many innocent people.* **3** (*often passive;* usually foll. by *in* or *with*) to concern or associate significantly: *many people were involved in the crime.* **4** (*often passive*) to make complicated; tangle: *the situation was further involved by her disappearance.* **5** *Rare, often poetic.* to wrap or surround. **6** *Maths, obsolete.* to raise to a specified power. [C14: from Latin *involvere* to roll in, surround, from IN-[2] + *volvere* to roll] ▸ **inˈvolvement** *n* ▸ **inˈvolver** *n*

involved (ɪnˈvɒlvd) *adj* **1** complicated; difficult to comprehend: *an involved literary style.* **2** (*usually postpositive*) concerned or implicated: *one of the men involved.* **3** (*postpositive;* foll. by *with*) *Euphemistic.* having sexual relations: *she was involved with a number of men.*

invt. *or* **invty** *abbrev. for* inventory.

invulnerable (ɪnˈvʌlnərəbᵊl, -ˈvʌlnrəbᵊl) *adj* **1** incapable of being wounded, hurt, damaged, etc., either physically or emotionally. **2** incapable of being damaged or captured: *an invulnerable fortress.* ▸ **inˌvulneraˈbility** *or* **inˈvulnerableness** *n* ▸ **inˈvulnerably** *adv*

invultuation (ɪnˌvʌltʃuˈeɪʃən) *n* the use of or the act of making images of people, animals, etc., for witchcraft. [C19: from Medieval Latin *invultuāre* to make a likeness, from IN-[2] + *vultus* likeness]

inward (ˈɪnwəd) *adj* **1** going or directed towards the middle of or into something. **2** situated within; inside. **3** of, relating to, or existing in the mind or spirit: *inward meditation.* **4** of one's own country or a specific country: *inward investment.* ◆ *adv* **5** a variant of **inwards** (sense 1). ◆ *n* **6** the inward part; inside. ▸ **ˈinwardness** *n*

inwardly (ˈɪnwədlɪ) *adv* **1** within the private thoughts or feelings; secretly: *inwardly troubled, he kept smiling.* **2** not aloud: *to laugh inwardly.* **3** with reference to the inside or inner part; internally. **4** *Archaic.* intimately; essentially: *the most inwardly concerned of the plotters.*

inwards *adv* (ˈɪnwədz) *also* **inward.** **1** towards the interior or middle of something. **2** in, into, or towards the mind or spirit. ◆ *pl n* (ˈɪnədz). **3** a variant spelling of **innards.**

inweave (ɪnˈwiːv) *vb* **-weaves, -weaving, -wove** *or* **-weaved; -woven** *or* **-weaved.** *(tr)* to weave together into or as if into a design, fabric, etc.; interweave.

inwrap (ɪnˈræp) *vb* **-wraps, -wrapping, -wrapped.** a less common spelling of **enwrap.**

inwrought (ˌɪnˈrɔːt) *adj* **1** worked or woven into material, esp. decoratively. **2** *Rare.* blended with other things.

in-your-face *adj Slang.* aggressive and confrontational: *provocative in-your-face activism.*

Io[1] (ˈaɪəʊ) *n Greek myth.* a maiden loved by Zeus and turned into a white heifer by either Zeus or Hera.

Io[2] (ˈaɪəʊ) *n* the innermost of the four Galilean satellites of Jupiter, displaying intense volcanic activity. Diameter: 3630 km; orbital radius: 422 000 km.

Io[3] *the chemical symbol for* ionium.

I/O *abbrev. for* input/output.

Ioánnina (*Greek* jɔˈanina) *or* **Yanina** *n* a city in NW Greece: belonged to the Serbs (1349–1430) and then the Turks (until 1913); seat of Ali Pasha, the "Lion of Janina", from 1788 to 1822. Pop.: 56 496 (1991 est.). Serbian name: **Janina.**

IOC *abbrev. for* International Olympic Committee.

iodate (ˈaɪəˌdeɪt) *n* **1** a salt of iodic acid. ◆ *vb* **2** *(tr)* another word for **iodize.** ▸ **ˌioˈdation** *n*

iodic (aɪˈɒdɪk) *adj* of or containing iodine, esp. in the pentavalent state.

iodic acid *n* a colourless or pale yellow soluble crystalline substance that forms acidic aqueous solutions. Used as a reagent and disinfectant. Formula: HIO_3.

iodide (ˈaɪəˌdaɪd) *n* **1** a salt of hydriodic acid, containing the iodide ion, I^-. **2** a compound containing an iodine atom, such as methyl iodide, CH_3I.

iodine (ˈaɪəˌdiːn) *n* a bluish-black element of the halogen group that sublimates into a violet irritating gas. Its compounds are used in medicine and photography and in dyes. The radioisotope **iodine-131** (**radioiodine**), with a half-life of 8 days, is used in the diagnosis and treatment of thyroid disease. Symbol: I; atomic no.: 53; atomic wt.: 126.90447; valency: 1, 3, 5, or 7; relative density: 4.93; melting pt.: 113.5°C; boiling pt.: 184.35°C. [C19: from French *iode,* from Greek *iōdēs* rust-coloured, but taken to mean violet-coloured, through a mistaken derivation from *ion* violet]

iodism (ˈaɪəˌdɪzəm) *n* poisoning induced by ingestion of iodine or its compounds.

iodize *or* **iodise** (ˈaɪəˌdaɪz) *vb (tr)* to treat or react with iodine or an iodine compound. Also: **iodate.** ▸ **ˌiodiˈzation** *or* **ˌiodiˈsation** *n* ▸ **ˈioˌdizer** *or* **ˈioˌdiser** *n*

iodo- *or before a vowel* **iod-** *combining form.* indicating iodine: *iodoform; iodism.*

iodoform (aɪˈɒdəˌfɔːm) *n* a yellow crystalline insoluble volatile solid with a penetrating sweet odour made by heating alcohol with iodine and an alkali: used as an antiseptic. Formula: CHI_3. Systematic name: **triiodomethane.**

iodometry (ˌaɪəˈdɒmɪtrɪ) *n Chem.* a procedure used in volumetric analysis for determining the quantity of substance present that contains, liberates, or reacts with iodine. ▸ **iodometric** (ˌaɪədəʊˈmetrɪk) *or* **ˌiodoˈmetrical** *adj* ▸ **ˌiodoˈmetrically** *adv*

iodopsin (ˌaɪəˈdɒpsɪn) *n* a violet light-sensitive pigment in the cones of the retina of the eye. Also called: **visual violet.** See also **rhodopsin.**

iodous (aɪˈɒdəs) *adj* **1** of or containing iodine, esp. in the trivalent state. **2** concerned with or resembling iodine.

iolite (ˈaɪəˌlaɪt) *n* another name for **cordierite.** [C19: from Greek *ion* a violet + -LITE]

IOM *abbrev. for* Isle of Man.

Io moth *n* an American saturniid moth, *Automeris io,* bright yellow with a blue-and-pink eyelike spot on each of the hind wings. [C19: after Io (who was tormented by a gadfly), referring to the sting of the larva]

ion (ˈaɪən, -ɒn) *n* an electrically charged atom or group of atoms formed by the loss or gain of one or more electrons. See also **cation, anion.** [C19: from Greek, literally: going, from *ienai* to go]

-ion *suffix forming nouns.* indicating an action, process, or state: *creation; objection.* Compare **-ation, -tion.** [from Latin *-iōn-, -io*]

Iona (aɪˈəʊnə) *n* an island off the W coast of Scotland, in the Inner Hebrides: site of St Columba's monastery (founded in 563) and an important early centre of Christianity. Area: 854 ha (2112 acres).

IONARC *abbrev. for* Indian Ocean National Association for Regional Cooperation.

ion engine *n* a type of rocket engine in which thrust is obtained by the electrostatic acceleration of charged positive ions. Compare **plasma engine.**

Ionesco (ˌiːəˈnɛskəʊ; *French* jɔnɛsko) *n* **Eugène** (øʒɛn). 1912–94, French dramatist, born in Romania; a leading exponent of the theatre of the absurd. His plays include *The Bald Prima Donna* (1950) and *Rhinoceros* (1960).

ion exchange *n* the process in which ions are exchanged between a solution and an insoluble solid, usually a resin. It is used to soften water, to separate radioactive isotopes, and to purify certain industrial chemicals.

Ionia (aɪˈəʊnɪə) *n* an ancient region of W central Asia Minor, including adjacent Aegean islands: colonized by Greeks in about 1100 B.C.

Ionian (aɪˈəʊnɪən) *n* **1** a member of a Hellenic people who settled in Attica in about 1100 B.C. and later colonized the islands and E coast of the Aegean Sea. ◆ *adj* **2** of or relating to this people or their dialect of Ancient Greek; Ionic. **3** of or relating to Ionia. **4** *Music.* relating to or denoting an authentic mode represented by the ascending natural diatonic scale from C to C and forming the basis of the modern major key. See also **Hypo-.**

Ionian Islands *pl n* a group of Greek islands in the Ionian Sea, consisting of Corfu, Cephalonia, Zante, Levkas, Ithaca, Cythera, and Paxos: ceded to Greece in 1864. Pop.: 193 734 (1991). Area: 2307 sq. km (891 sq. miles).

Ionian Sea *n* the part of the Mediterranean Sea between SE Italy, E Sicily, and Greece.

ionic (aɪˈɒnɪk) *adj* of, relating to, or occurring in the form of ions.

Ionic (aɪˈɒnɪk) *adj* **1** of, denoting, or relating to one of the five classical orders of architecture, characterized by fluted columns and capitals with scroll-like ornaments. See also **Doric, Composite, Tuscan, Corinthian.** **2** of or relating to Ionia, its inhabitants, or their dialect of Ancient Greek. **3** *Prosody.* of, relating to, designating, or employing Ionics in verse. ◆ *n* **4** one of four chief dialects of Ancient Greek; the dialect spoken in Ionia. Compare **Aeolic, Arcadic, Doric.** See also **Attic** (sense 3). **5** (in classical prosody) a type of metrical foot having either two long followed by two short syllables (**greater Ionic**), or two short followed by two long syllables (**lesser Ionic**).

ionic bond *n* another name for **electrovalent bond.**

ion implantation *n* a technique used in the manufacture of semiconductor devices in which impurities are implanted by means of beams of electrically accelerated ions.

ionium (aɪˈəʊnɪəm) *n Obsolete.* a naturally occurring radioisotope of thorium with a mass number of 230. Symbol: Io [C20: from New Latin, from ION + -IUM]

ionization *or* **ionisation** (ˌaɪənaɪˈzeɪʃən) *n* **a** the formation of ions as a result of a chemical reaction, high temperature, electrical discharge, or radiation. **b** (*as modifier*): *ionization temperature; ionization current.*

ionization chamber *n* a device for detecting and measuring ionizing radiation, consisting of a tube containing a low pressure gas and two electrodes between which a high voltage is maintained. The current between the electrodes is a function of the intensity of the radiation.

ionization potential *n* the energy required to remove an electron from an atom, molecule, or radical, measured in electronvolts. Symbol: *I* Compare **electron affinity.**

ionize *or* **ionise** (ˈaɪəˌnaɪz) *vb* to change or become changed into ions. ▸ **ˈionˌizable** *or* **ˈionˌisable** *adj* ▸ **ˈionˌizer** *or* **ˈionˌiser** *n*

ionizing radiation *n* electromagnetic or corpuscular radiation that is able to cause ionization.

ionone (ˈaɪəˌnəʊn) *n* **1** a yellowish liquid mixture of two isomers with an odour of violets, extracted from certain plants and used in perfumery. **2** either of these two isomers. Formula: $C_{13}H_{20}O$.

ionopause (aɪˈɒnəˌpɔːz) *n* the transitional zone in the atmosphere between the ionosphere and the exosphere, about 644 km (400 miles) from the earth's surface.

ionophore (aɪˈɒnəˌfɔː) *n* a chemical compound capable of forming a complex with an ion and transporting it through a biological membrane. [C20: from ION + -O- + -PHORE]

ionosphere (aɪˈɒnəˌsfɪə) *n* a region of the earth's atmosphere, extending from about 60 kilometres to 1000 km above the earth's surface, in which there is a high concentration of free electrons formed as a result of ionizing radiation entering the atmosphere from space. See also **D region, E region, F region.** ▸ **ionospheric** (aɪˌɒnəˈsfɛrɪk) *adj*

ionospheric wave *n* another name for **sky wave.**

ionotropy (ˌaɪəˈnɒtrəpɪ) *n Chem.* the reversible interconversion of a pair of organic isomers as a result of the migration of an ionic part of the molecule.

ion rocket *n* a rocket propelled by an ion engine.

iontophoresis (aɪˌɒntəʊfəˈriːsɪs) *n Biochem.* a technique for studying neurotransmitters in the brain by the application of experimental solutions to the tissues through fine glass electrodes. [C20: from Greek *iont-, ion,* from *ienai* to go + -PHORESIS]

IOOF *abbrev. for* Independent Order of Oddfellows.

iota (aɪˈəʊtə) *n* **1** the ninth letter in the Greek alphabet (Ι, ι), a vowel or semivowel, transliterated as *i* or *j*. **2** (*usually used with a negative*) a very small amount; jot (esp. in the phrase **not one** *or* **an iota**). [C16: via Latin from Greek, of Semitic origin; see JOT]

iotacism (aɪˈəʊtəˌsɪzəm) *n* a tendency of vowels and diphthongs, esp. in Modern Greek, to acquire the pronunciation of the vowel iota (iː).

IOU *n* a written promise or reminder to pay a debt. [C17: representing *I owe you*]

-ious *suffix forming adjectives from nouns.* characterized by or full of: *ambitious; religious; suspicious.* Compare **-eous.** [from Latin *-ius* and *-iōsus* full of]

IOW *abbrev. for* Isle of Wight.

Iowa (ˈaɪəʊə) *n* a state of the N central U.S., in the Midwest: consists of rolling plains crossed by many rivers, with the Missouri forming the western border and the Mississippi the eastern. Capital: Des Moines. Pop.: 2 852 423 (1997 est.). Area: 144 887 sq. km (55 941 sq. miles). Abbrevs.: **Ia.** or (with zip code) **IA** ▸ **Iowan** (ˈaɪəʊən) *adj, n*

IPA *abbrev. for* International Phonetic Alphabet.

Ipatieff (ɪˈpætjɛf) *n* **Vladimir Nikolaievich** (ˈvlædɪmɪə ˌnɪkəˈlaɪəvɪtʃ). 1867–1952, U.S. physicist, born in Russia. He discovered the structure of isoprene (1897) and later developed high-octane fuels.

ipecacuanha (ˌɪpɪˌkækjuˈænə) *or* **ipecac** (ˈɪpɪˌkæk) *n* **1** a low-growing South American rubiaceous shrub, *Cephaelis ipecacuanha.* **2** a drug prepared from the dried roots of this plant, used as a purgative and emetic. [C18: from Portuguese, from Tupi *ipekaaguéne,* from *ipeh* low + *kaa* leaves + *guéne* vomit]

Iphigenia (ˌɪfɪdʒɪˈnaɪə) *n Greek myth.* the daughter of Agamemnon, taken by him to be sacrificed to Artemis, who saved her life and made her a priestess.

I-pin (ɪˈpɪn) *n* a variant transliteration of the Chinese name for **Yibin.**

Ipoh (ˈiːpəʊ) *n* a city in Malaysia, capital of Perak state: tin-mining centre. Pop.: 382 633 (1991).

ipomoea (ˌɪpəˈmɪə, ˌaɪ-) *n* **1** any tropical or subtropical convolvulaceous plant of the genus *Ipomoea,* such as the morning-glory, sweet potato, and jalap, having trumpet-shaped flowers. **2** the dried root of a Mexican species, *I. orizabensis,* which yields a cathartic resin. [C18: New Latin, from Greek *ips* worm + *homoios* like]

ippon (ˈɪpɒn) *n Judo, karate.* a winning point awarded in a sparring competition for a perfectly executed technique. [C20: Japanese, literally: one point]

Ipsambul (ˌɪpsæmˈbuːl) *n* another name for **Abu Simbel.**

ipse dixit *Latin.* (ˈɪpseɪ ˈdɪksɪt) *n* an arbitrary and unsupported assertion. [C16, literally: he himself said it]

ipsilateral (ˌɪpsɪˈlætərəl) *adj* on or affecting the same side of the body. [C20: irregularly formed from Latin *ipse* self + LATERAL]

ipsissima verba *Latin.* (ɪpˈsɪsɪmə ˈvɜːbə) *pl n* the very words; verbatim.

ipso facto (ˈɪpsəʊ ˈfæktəʊ) *adv* by that very fact or act: *ipso facto his guilt was apparent.* [from Latin]

ipso jure (ˈɪpsəʊ ˈjʊərɪ) *adv* by the law itself; by operation of law. [from Latin]

Ipsus (ˈɪpsəs) *n* an ancient town in Asia Minor, in S Phrygia: site of a decisive battle (301 B.C.) in the Wars of the Diadochi in which Lysimachus and Seleucus defeated Antigonus and Demetrius.

Ipswich (ˈɪpswɪtʃ) *n* a town in E England, administrative centre of Suffolk, at the head of the Orwell estuary: manufactures agricultural and industrial machinery. Pop.: 130 157 (1991).

IQ *abbrev. for* intelligence quotient.

i.q. *abbrev. for* idem quod. [Latin: the same as]

Iqaluit (ɪˈkælʊɪt) *n* a town in N Canada, capital of Nunavut. Pop.: 3700 (1999 est.). Former name: **Frobisher Bay.**

Iqbal (ˈɪkbal) *n* Sir **Muhammad** (mʊˈhæməd). 1875–1938, Indian Muslim poet, philosopher, and political leader, who advocated the establishment of separate nations for Indian Hindus and Muslims and is generally regarded as the originator of Pakistan.

Iquique (*Spanish* iˈkike) *n* a port in N Chile: oil refineries. Pop.: 152 592 (1995 est.).

Iquitos (*Spanish* iˈkitɔs) *n* an inland port in NE Peru, on the Amazon 3703 km (2300 miles) from the Atlantic: head of navigation for large steamers. Pop.: 274 759 (1993).

Ir *the chemical symbol for* iridium.

IR *abbrev. for:* **1** infrared. **2** (in Britain) Inland Revenue. ◆ **3** *international car registration for* Iran.

Ir. *abbrev. for:* **1** Ireland. **2** Irish.

ir- *prefix* a variant of **in-**[1] and **in-**[2] before *r.*

IRA *abbrev. for* Irish Republican Army.

iracund (ˈaɪərəˌkʌnd) *adj Rare.* easily angered. [C19: from Latin *īrācundus,* from *īra* anger] ▸ **ˌiraˈcundity** *n*

irade (ɪˈrɑːdɛ) *n* a written edict of a Muslim ruler. [C19: from Turkish: will, desire, from Arabic *irādah*]

Iráklion (*Greek* iˈrakliɔn) *n* a port in Greece, in N Crete: former capital of Crete (until 1841); ruled by Venetians (13th–17th centuries). Pop.: 117 167 (1991). Italian name: **Candia.** Also called: **Heraklion, Herakleion.**

Iran (ɪˈrɑːn) *n* a republic in SW Asia, between the Caspian Sea and the Persian Gulf: consists chiefly of a high central desert plateau almost completely surrounded by mountains, a semitropical fertile region along the Caspian coast, and a hot and dry area beside the Persian Gulf. Oil is the most important export. Official language: Farsi (Persian). Official religion: Muslim majority. Currency: rial. Capital: Tehran. Pop.: 61 531 000 (1998 est.). Area: 1 647 050 sq. km (635 932 sq. miles). Former name (until 1935): **Persia.** Official name: **Islamic Republic of Iran.** See also **Persian Empire.**

Iran. *abbrev. for* Iranian.

Iranian (ɪˈreɪnɪən) *n* **1** a native, citizen, or inhabitant of Iran. **2** a branch of the Indo-European family of languages, divided into **West Iranian** (including Old Persian, Pahlavi, modern Persian, Kurdish, Baluchi, and Tajik) and **East Iranian** (including Avestan, Sogdian, Pashto, and Ossetic). **3** the modern Persian language. ◆ *adj* **4** relating to, denoting, or characteristic of Iran, its inhabitants, or their language; Persian. **5** belonging to or relating to the Iranian branch of Indo-European.

Iran-Iraq War *n* the war (1980–88) fought by Iran and Iraq, following the Iraqi invasion of disputed border territory in Iran. It ended indecisively with no important gains on either side: Iraq subsequently (1990) conceded the disputed territory. Also called: **Gulf War.**

Iraq (ɪˈrɑːk) *n* a republic in SW Asia, on the Persian Gulf: coextensive with ancient Mesopotamia; became a British mandate in 1920, independent in 1932, and a republic in 1958. The Iraqi invasion of Kuwait (1990) was condemned by the United Nations and led to the Gulf War (1991), in which Iraq was defeated by U.S.-led UN forces. Iraq consists chiefly of the mountains of Kurdistan in the northeast, part of the Syrian Desert, and the lower basin of the Rivers Tigris and Euphrates. Oil is the major export. Official language: Arabic; Kurdish is official in the Kurdish Autonomous Region only. Official religion: Muslim. Currency: dinar. Capital: Baghdad. Pop.: 21 722 000 (1998 est.). Area: 438 446 sq. km (169 284 sq. miles). ▸ **Iraqi** (ɪˈrɑːkɪ) *adj, n*

IRAS *abbrev. for* Infrared Astronomical Satellite, a pioneering international earth-orbiting satellite that during 1983 made an all-sky survey at infrared wavelengths.

irascible (ɪˈræsɪbᵊl) *adj* **1** easily angered; irritable. **2** showing irritability: *an irascible action.* [C16: from Late Latin *īrascibilis,* from Latin *īra* anger] ▸ **iˌrasciˈbility** *or* **iˈrascibleness** *n* ▸ **iˈrascibly** *adv*

irate (aɪˈreɪt) *adj* **1** incensed with anger; furious. **2** marked by extreme anger: *an irate letter.* [C19: from Latin *īrātus* enraged, from *īrascī* to be angry] ▸ **iˈrately** *adv*

Irbid (ˈɪrbɪd) *n* a town in NW Jordan. Pop.: 208 201 (1994).

Irbil (ˈɪəbɪl) *n* a variant of **Erbil.**

IRBM *abbrev. for* intermediate range ballistic missile.

ire (aɪə) *n Literary.* anger; wrath. [C13: from Old French, from Latin *īra*] ▸ **ˈireful** *adj* ▸ **ˈirefully** *adv* ▸ **ˈirefulness** *n* ▸ **ˈireless** *adj*

Ire. *abbrev. for* Ireland.

Ireland[1] (ˈaɪələnd) *n* **1** an island off NW Europe: part of the British Isles, separated from Britain by the North Channel, the Irish Sea, and St George's Channel; contains large areas of peat bog, with mountains that rise over 900 m (3000 ft.) in the southwest and several large lakes. It was conquered by England in the 16th and early 17th centuries and ruled as a dependency until 1801, when it was united with Great Britain until its division in 1921 into the Irish Free State and Northern Ireland. Latin name: **Hibernia. 2 Republic of.** Also called: **Irish Republic, Southern Ireland.** a republic in NW Europe occupying most of Ireland: established as the Irish Free State (a British dominion) in 1921 and declared a republic in 1949; joined the Common Market (now the European Union) in 1973. Official languages: Irish (Gaelic) and English. Currency: euro and punt. Capital: Dublin. Pop.: 3 647 000 (1998 est.). Area: 70 285 sq. km (27 137 sq. miles). Gaelic name: **Eire.** ◆ See also **Northern Ireland.**

Ireland[2] (ˈaɪələnd) *n* **John** (**Nicholson**). 1879–1962, English composer, esp. of songs.

Irene (aɪˈriːnɪ) *n* **1** ?752–803 A.D., Byzantine ruler (780–90, 792–97, joint ruler with her son Constantine VI; 797–802). She is venerated as a saint in the Greek Orthodox Church. **2** *Greek myth.* the goddess of peace.

irenic, eirenic (aɪˈriːnɪk, -ˈrɛn-) *or* **irenical, eirenical** *adj* tending to conciliate or promote peace. [C19: from Greek *eirēnikos,* from *eirēnē* peace] ▸ **iˈrenically** *or* **eiˈrenically** *adv*

irenicon (aɪˈriːnɪˌkɒn) *n* a variant spelling of **eirenicon.**

irenics (aɪˈriːnɪks, -ˈrɛn-) *n* (*functioning as sing*) that branch of theology that is concerned with unity between Christian sects and denominations.

Ireton (ˈaɪətᵊn) *n* **Henry.** 1611–51, English Parliamentarian general in the Civil War; son-in-law of Oliver Cromwell. His plan for a constitutional monarchy was rejected by Charles I (1647), whose death warrant he signed; lord deputy of Ireland (1650–51).

Irian Barat (ˈɪərɪən ˈbærɑːt) *n* the former Indonesian name for **Irian Jaya.**

Irian Jaya *n* the W part of the island of New Guinea: formerly under Dutch rule, becoming a province of Indonesia in 1963. Capital: Jayapura. Pop.: 1 956 300 (1995 est.). Area: 416 990 sq. km (161 000 sq. miles). Former names (until 1963): **Dutch New Guinea, Netherlands New Guinea.** English name: **West Irian.**

iridaceous (ˌɪrɪˈdeɪʃəs, ˌaɪ-) *adj* of, relating to, or belonging to the *Iridaceae,* a family of monocotyledonous plants, including iris, crocus, and gladiolus, having swordlike leaves and showy flowers.

iridectomy (ˌɪrɪˈdɛktəmɪ, ˌaɪ-) *n, pl* **-mies.** surgical removal of part of the iris.

iridescent (ˌɪrɪˈdɛsᵊnt) *adj* displaying a spectrum of colours that shimmer and change due to interference and scattering as the observer's position changes. [C18: from IRIDO- + -ESCENT] ▸ **ˌiriˈdescence** *n* ▸ **ˌiriˈdescently** *adv*

iridic (aɪˈrɪdɪk, ɪˈrɪd-) *adj* **1** of or containing iridium, esp. in the tetravalent state. **2** of or relating to the iris of the eye.

iridium (aɪˈrɪdɪəm, ɪˈrɪd-) *n* a very hard inert yellowish-white transition element that is the most corrosion-resistant metal known. It occurs in platinum ores and is used as an alloy with platinum. Symbol: Ir; atomic no.: 77; atomic wt.: 192.22; valency: 3 or 4; relative density: 22.42; melting pt.: 2447°C; boiling pt.: 4428°C. [C19: New Latin, from IRIDO- + -IUM; from its colourful appearance when dissolving in certain acids]

irido- *or before a vowel* **irid-** *combining form.* **1** denoting the iris of the eye or the genus of plants: *iridectomy; iridaceous.* **2** denoting a rainbow: *iridescent.* [from Latin *irid-*, IRIS]

iridocyte ('ɪrɪdəʊˌsaɪt) *n Zoology.* a guanine-containing cell in the skin of fish and some cephalopods, giving these animals their iridescence.

iridology (ˌɪrɪ'dɒlədʒɪ) *n* the practice of examining the iris of the eye as a method of medical diagnosis. ▸ ˌ**iri'dologist** *n*

iridosmine (ˌɪrɪ'dɒsmaɪn, ˌaɪrɪ-) *or* **iridosmium** *n* other names for **osmiridium.** [C19: from IRIDO- + OSM(IUM) + -INE[2]]

iridotomy (ˌɪrɪ'dɒtəmɪ, ˌaɪrɪ-) *n, pl* **-mies.** surgical incision into the iris, esp. to create an artificial pupil.

iris ('aɪrɪs) *n, pl* **irises** *or* **irides** ('aɪrɪˌdiːz, 'ɪrɪ-). **1** the coloured muscular diaphragm that surrounds and controls the size of the pupil. **2** Also called: **fleur-de-lys.** any plant of the iridaceous genus *Iris,* having brightly coloured flowers composed of three petals and three drooping sepals. See also **flag**[2], **orris**[1], **stinking iris. 3** Also called: **rainbow quartz.** a form of quartz that reflects light polychromatically from internal fractures. **4** a rare or poetic word for **rainbow. 5** something resembling a rainbow; iridescence. **6** short for **iris diaphragm.** [C14: from Latin: rainbow, iris (flower), crystal, from Greek]

Iris ('aɪrɪs) *n* the goddess of the rainbow along which she travelled to earth as a messenger of the gods.

iris diaphragm *n* an adjustable diaphragm that regulates the amount of light entering an optical instrument, esp. a camera. It usually consists of a number of thin metal leaves arranged so that they open out into an approximately circular aperture. Sometimes shortened to **iris.**

Irish ('aɪrɪʃ) *adj* **1** of, relating to, or characteristic of Ireland, its people, their Celtic language, or their dialect of English. **2** *Informal, offensive.* ludicrous or illogical. ◆ *n* **3 the Irish.** (*functioning as pl*) the natives or inhabitants of Ireland. **4** another name for **Irish Gaelic.**

Irish bull *n* a ludicrously illogical statement. See also **bull**[2].

Irish coffee *n* hot coffee mixed with Irish whiskey and topped with double cream.

Irish elk *n* an extinct Eurasian giant deer of the Pleistocene genus *Megaloceros,* which had antlers up to 4 metres across.

Irish Free State *n* a former name for the (Republic of) **Ireland** (1921–37).

Irish Gaelic *n* the Goidelic language of the Celts of Ireland, now spoken mainly along the west coast; an official language of the Republic of Ireland since 1921.

Irishism ('aɪrɪˌʃɪzəm) *n* an Irish custom or idiom.

Irishman ('aɪrɪʃmən) *or* (*fem*) **Irishwoman** *n, pl* **-men** *or* **-women.** a native, citizen, or inhabitant of Ireland or a descendant of one.

Irish moss *n* another name for **carrageen.**

Irish potato *n Chiefly U.S.* another name for the **potato.**

Irish Republic *n* See **Ireland**[1] (sense 2).

Irish Republican Army *n* a militant organization of Irish nationalists founded with the aim of striving for a united independent Ireland by means of guerrilla warfare. Abbrev.: **IRA.**

Irish Sea *n* an arm of the North Atlantic Ocean between Great Britain and Ireland.

Irish setter *n* a breed of setter developed in Ireland, having a flat soft brownish-red coat. Also called: **red setter.**

Irish stew *n* a white stew made of mutton, lamb, or beef, with potatoes, onions, etc.

Irish terrier *n* a breed of terrier with a wiry wheaten or reddish coat.

Irish water spaniel *n* a breed of dog used to hunt duck and having a dense coat of a purplish-liver colour that falls in tight ringlets covering the whole body except for the face and tail.

Irish whiskey *n* any of the whiskeys made in Ireland, usually from malt and subject to three distillations.

Irish wolfhound *n* a large breed of hound with a rough thick coat.

iritis (aɪ'raɪtɪs) *n* inflammation of the iris of the eye. ▸ **iritic** (aɪ'rɪtɪk) *adj*

irk (ɜːk) *vb* (*tr*) to irritate, vex, or annoy. [C13 *irken* to grow weary; probably related to Old Norse *yrkja* to work]

irksome ('ɜːksəm) *adj* causing vexation, annoyance, or boredom; troublesome or tedious. ▸ **'irksomely** *adv* ▸ **'irksomeness** *n*

Irkutsk (*Russian* ir'kutsk) *n* a city in S Russia; situated on the Trans-Siberian railway; university (1918); one of the largest industrial centres in Siberia, esp. for heavy engineering. Pop.: 585 000 (1995 est.).

IRL *international car registration for* Republic of Ireland.

IRM *abbrev. for* innate releasing mechanism.

IRO *abbrev. for:* **1** (in Britain) Inland Revenue Office. **2** International Refugee Organization.

iroko (ɪ'rəʊkəʊ) *n, pl* **-kos. 1** a tropical African hardwood tree of the genus *Chlorophora.* **2** the hard reddish-brown wood of this tree. [C19: from Yoruba]

iron ('aɪən) *n* **1a** a malleable ductile silvery-white ferromagnetic metallic element occurring principally in haematite and magnetite. It is widely used for structural and engineering purposes. See also **steel, cast iron, wrought iron, pig iron.** Symbol: Fe; atomic no.: 26; atomic wt.: 55.847; valency: 2,3,4, or 6; relative density: 7.874; melting pt.: 1538°C; boiling pt.: 2862°C. Related adjs.: **ferric, ferrous.** Related prefix: **ferro-. 1b** (*as modifier*): *iron railings.* **2** any of certain tools or implements made of iron or steel, esp. for use when hot: *a grappling iron; a soldering iron.* **3** an appliance for pressing fabrics using dry heat or steam, esp. a small electrically heated device with a handle and a weighted flat bottom. **4** any of various golf clubs with narrow metal heads, numbered from 1 to 9 according to the slant of the face, used esp. for approach shots: *a No. 6 iron.* **5** an informal word for **harpoon** (sense 1). **6** *U.S. slang.* a splintlike support for a malformed leg. **7** great hardness, strength, or resolve: *a will of iron.* **8** *Astronomy. short for* iron meteorite. **9** See **shooting iron. 10 strike while the iron is hot.** to act at an opportune moment. ◆ *adj* **11** very hard, immovable, or implacable: *iron determination.* **12** very strong; extremely robust: *an iron constitution.* **13** cruel or unyielding: *he ruled with an iron hand.* **14 an iron fist.** a cruel and unyielding attitude or approach. See also **velvet** (sense 6). ◆ *vb* **15** to smooth (clothes or fabric) by removing (creases or wrinkles) using a heated iron; press. **16** (*tr*) to furnish or clothe with iron. **17** (*tr*) *Rare.* to place (a prisoner) in irons. ◆ See also **iron out, irons.** [Old English *irēn;* related to Old High German *īsan,* Old Norse *jārn;* compare Old Irish *īarn*] ▸ **'ironer** *n* ▸ **'ironless** *adj* ▸ **'ironˌlike** *adj*

iron age *n Classical myth.* the last and worst age in the history of the world.

Iron Age *n* **a** the period following the Bronze Age characterized by the extremely rapid spread of iron tools and weapons, which began in the Middle East about 1100 B.C. **b** (*as modifier*): *an Iron-Age weapon.*

ironbark ('aɪənˌbɑːk) *n* any of several Australian eucalyptus trees that have hard rough bark.

ironbound ('aɪənˌbaʊnd) *adj* **1** bound with iron. **2** unyielding; inflexible. **3** (of a coast) rocky; rugged.

Iron Chancellor *n* **the.** nickname of (Prince Otto Eduard Leopold von) **Bismarck.**

ironclad *adj* (ˌaɪən'klæd). **1** covered or protected with iron: *an ironclad warship.* **2** inflexible; rigid: *an ironclad rule.* **3** not able to be assailed or contradicted: *an ironclad argument.* ◆ *n* ('aɪənˌklæd). **4** a large wooden 19th-century warship with armoured plating.

Iron Cross *n* the highest decoration for bravery awarded to the German armed forces in wartime: instituted in 1813.

Iron Curtain *n* **a** (formerly) the guarded border between the countries of the Soviet bloc and the rest of Europe. **b** (*as modifier*): *Iron Curtain countries.*

Iron Duke *n* **the.** nickname of (1st Duke of) **Wellington.**

Iron Gate *or* **Iron Gates** *n* a gorge of the River Danube on the border between Romania and Yugoslavia. Length: 3 km (2 miles). Romanian name: **Porţile de Fier.**

iron glance *n* another name for **haematite.**

iron grey *n* **a** a neutral or dark grey colour. **b** (*as adj*): *iron-grey hair.*

Iron Guard *n* a Romanian fascist party that ceased to exist after World War II.

iron hand *n* harsh or rigorous control; overbearing or autocratic force: *he ruled with an iron hand.*

iron horse *n Archaic.* a steam-driven railway locomotive.

ironic (aɪ'rɒnɪk) *or* **ironical** *adj* of, characterized by, or using irony. ▸ **i'ronically** *adv* ▸ **i'ronicalness** *n*

ironing ('aɪənɪŋ) *n* **1** the act of ironing washed clothes. **2** clothes that are to be or that have been ironed.

ironing board *n* a board, usually on legs, with a suitable covering on which to iron clothes.

ironize *or* **ironise** ('aɪrəˌnaɪz) *vb* **1** (*intr*) to use or indulge in irony. **2** (*tr*) to make ironic or use ironically. ▸ **'ironist** *n*

iron lung *n* **1** an airtight metal cylinder enclosing the entire body up to the neck and providing artificial respiration when the respiratory muscles are paralysed, as by poliomyelitis. **2** *Irish informal.* a gas container used in dispensing beer.

iron maiden *n* a medieval instrument of torture, consisting of a hinged case (often shaped in the form of a woman) lined with iron spikes, which was forcibly closed on the victim.

iron man *n Austral.* an event at a surf carnival in which contestants compete at swimming, surfing, running, etc.

ironmaster ('aɪənˌmɑːstə) *n Brit.* a manufacturer of iron, esp. (formerly) the owner of an ironworks.

iron meteorite *n* a meteorite that is composed mainly of iron and nickel.

ironmonger ('aɪənˌmʌŋgə) *n Brit.* a dealer in metal utensils, hardware, locks, etc. U.S. and Canadian equivalent: **hardware dealer.** ▸ **'ironˌmongery** *n*

iron out *vb* (*tr, adv*) **1** to smooth, using a heated iron. **2** to put right or settle (a problem or difficulty) as a result of negotiations or discussions. **3** *Austral. informal.* to knock unconscious.

iron pan *n Geology.* a hard layer of precipitated iron salts often found below the surface of sands and gravels.

iron pyrites ('paɪraɪts) *n* another name for **pyrite.**

iron rations *pl n* emergency food supplies, esp. for military personnel in action. See also **K ration.**

irons ('aɪənz) *pl n* **1** fetters or chains (often in the phrase **in** or **into irons**). **2 in irons.** *Nautical.* (of a sailing vessel) headed directly into the wind without steerageway. **3 have several irons in the fire.** to be involved in many projects, activities, etc.

Irons ('aɪənz) *n* **Jeremy.** born 1948, British film and stage actor. His films include *The French Lieutenant's Woman* (1981), *The Mission* (1986), *Reversal of Fortune* (1990), and *House of the Spirits* (1993).

Ironside ('aɪənˌsaɪd) *n* nickname of **Edmund II** of England.

ironsides ('aɪənˌsaɪdz) *n* **1** a person with great stamina or resistance. **2** an ironclad ship. **3** (*often cap.*) (in the English Civil War) **3a** the cavalry regiment trained and commanded by Oliver Cromwell. **3b** Cromwell's entire army.

ironstone ('aɪənˌstəʊn) *n* **1** any rock consisting mainly of an iron-bearing ore. **2** Also called: **ironstone china.** a tough durable earthenware.

ironware ('aɪənˌwɛə) *n* domestic articles made of iron.

ironwood ('aɪənˌwʊd) *n* **1** any of various betulaceous trees, such as hornbeam, that have very hard wood. **2** a Californian rosaceous tree, *Lyonothamnus floribundus,* with very hard wood. **3** any of various other trees with hard wood, such as the mopani. **4** the wood of any of these trees.

ironwork ('aɪənˌwɜːk) *n* **1** work done in iron, esp. decorative work. **2** the craft or practice of working in iron. ◆ See also **ironworks.**

ironworker ('aɪənˌwɜːkə) *n* **1** a person who works in an ironworks. **2** a person who makes articles of iron.

ironworks (ˈaɪən,wɜːks) *n* (*sometimes functioning as sing*) a building in which iron is smelted, cast, or wrought.

irony[1] (ˈaɪrənɪ) *n, pl* **-nies.** **1** the humorous or mildly sarcastic use of words to imply the opposite of what they normally mean. **2** an instance of this, used to draw attention to some incongruity or irrationality. **3** incongruity between what is expected to be and what actually is, or a situation or result showing such incongruity. **4** See **dramatic irony. 5** *Philosophy.* See **Socratic irony.** [C16: from Latin *ironia,* from Greek *eirōneia,* from *eirōn* dissembler, from *eirein* to speak]

irony[2] (ˈaɪənɪ) *adj* of, resembling, or containing iron.

Iroquoian (,ɪrəˈkwɔɪən) *n* **1** a family of North American Indian languages including Cherokee, Mohawk, Seneca, Oneida, and Onondaga: probably related to Siouan. ♦ *adj* **2** of or relating to the Iroquois, their culture, or their languages.

Iroquois (ˈɪrə,kwɔɪ, -,kwɔɪz) *n, pl* **-quois. 1** a member of any of a group of North American Indian peoples formerly living between the Hudson River and the St Lawrence and Lake Erie. See also **Five Nations, Six Nations. 2** any of the Iroquoian languages. ♦ *adj* **3** of or relating to the Iroquois, their language, or their culture.

IRQ *international car registration for* Iraq.

irradiance (ɪˈreɪdɪəns) *n* the radiant flux incident on unit area of a surface. It is measured in watts per square metre. Symbol: E_e Also called: **irradiation.** Compare **illuminance.**

irradiant (ɪˈreɪdɪənt) *adj* radiating light; shining brightly.

irradiate (ɪˈreɪdɪ,eɪt) *vb* **1** (*tr*) *Physics.* to subject to or treat with light or other electromagnetic radiation or with beams of particles. **2** (*tr*) to expose (food) to electromagnetic radiation to kill bacteria and retard deterioration. **3** (*tr*) to make clear or bright intellectually or spiritually; illumine. **4** a less common word for **radiate** (sense 1). **5** (*intr*) *Obsolete.* to become radiant. ▸ **irˈradiative** *adj* ▸ **irˈradi,ator** *n*

irradiation (ɪ,reɪdɪˈeɪʃən) *n* **1** the act or process of irradiating or the state of being irradiated. **2** the apparent enlargement of a brightly lit object when it is viewed against a dark background. **3** a shaft of light; beam or ray. **4** *Med.* **4a** the therapeutic or diagnostic use of radiation, esp. X-rays. **4b** exposure of a patient to such radiation. **5** another name for **radiation** or **irradiance.**

irrational (ɪˈræʃənᵊl) *adj* **1** inconsistent with reason or logic; illogical; absurd. **2** incapable of reasoning. **3a** *Maths.* (of an equation, etc.) containing one or more variables in irreducible radical form or raised to a fractional power: $\sqrt{(x^2 + 1)} = x^{5/3}$. **3b** (*as n*): *an irrational.* **4** *Prosody.* (in Greek or Latin verse) **4a** of or relating to a metrical irregularity, usually the occurrence of a long syllable instead of a short one. **4b** denoting a metrical foot where such an irregularity occurs. ▸ **irˈrationally** *adv* ▸ **irˈrationalness** *n*

irrationality (ɪ,ræʃəˈnælɪtɪ) *or* **irrationalism** *n* **1** the state or quality of being irrational. **2** irrational thought, action, or behaviour.

irrational number *n* any real number that cannot be expressed as the ratio of two integers, such as π.

Irrawaddy (,ɪrəˈwɒdɪ) *n* the main river in Myanmar, rising in the north in two headstreams and flowing south through the whole length of Myanmar, to enter the Andaman Sea by nine main mouths. Length: 2100 km (1300 miles).

irreclaimable (,ɪrɪˈkleɪməbᵊl) *adj* not able to be reclaimed. ▸ **,irre,claimaˈbility** *or* **,irreˈclaimableness** *n* ▸ **,irreˈclaimably** *adv*

irreconcilable (ɪˈrɛkᵊn,saɪləbᵊl, ɪ,rɛkᵊnˈsaɪ-) *adj* **1** not able to be reconciled; uncompromisingly conflicting; incompatible. ♦ *n* **2** a person or thing that is implacably hostile or uncompromisingly opposed. **3** (*usually pl*) one of various principles, ideas, etc., that are incapable of being brought into agreement. ▸ **ir,recon,cilaˈbility** *or* **irˈrecon,cilableness** *n* ▸ **irˈrecon,cilably** *adv*

irrecoverable (,ɪrɪˈkʌvərəbᵊl, -ˈkʌvrə-) *adj* **1** not able to be recovered or regained. **2** not able to be remedied or rectified. ▸ **,irreˈcoverableness** *n* ▸ **,irreˈcoverably** *adv*

irrecusable (,ɪrɪˈkjuːzəbᵊl) *adj* not able to be rejected or challenged, as evidence, etc. ▸ **,irreˈcusably** *adv*

irredeemable (,ɪrɪˈdiːməbᵊl) *adj* **1** (of bonds, debentures, shares, etc.) without a date of redemption of capital; incapable of being bought back directly or paid off. **2** (of paper money) not convertible into specie. **3** (of a sinner) not able to be saved or reformed. **4** (of a loss) not able to be recovered; irretrievable. **5** not able to be improved or rectified; irreparable. ▸ **,irre,deemaˈbility** *or* **,irreˈdeemableness** *n* ▸ **,irreˈdeemably** *adv*

irredentist (,ɪrɪˈdɛntɪst) *n* **1** a person who favours the acquisition of territory that once was part of his country or is considered to have been. ♦ *adj* **2** of, relating to, or advocating this belief. [C19: from Italian *irredentista,* from the phrase *Italia irredenta,* literally: Italy unredeemed, from *ir-* IN-[1] + *redento* redeemed, from Latin *redemptus* bought back; see REDEEM] ▸ **,irreˈdentism** *n*

Irredentist (,ɪrɪˈdɛntɪst) *n* (*sometimes not cap.*) a member of an Italian association prominent in 1878 that sought to recover for Italy certain neighbouring regions (***Italia irredenta***) with a predominantly Italian population that were under foreign control.

irreducible (,ɪrɪˈdjuːsɪbᵊl) *adj* **1** not able to be reduced or lessened. **2** not able to be brought to a simpler or reduced form. **3** *Maths.* **3a** (of a polynomial) unable to be factorized into polynomials of lower degree, as $(x^2 + 1)$. **3b** (of a radical) incapable of being reduced to a rational expression, as $\sqrt{(x + 1)}$. ▸ **,irre,duciˈbility** *or* **,irreˈducibleness** *n* ▸ **,irreˈducibly** *adv*

irreflexive (,ɪrɪˈflɛksɪv) *adj Logic.* (of a relation) failing to hold between each member of its domain and itself: *'... is distinct from ...' is irreflexive.* Compare **reflexive** (sense 4), **nonreflexive.**

irrefragable (ɪˈrɛfrəgəbᵊl) *adj* not able to be denied or refuted; indisputable. [C16: from Late Latin *irrefrāgābilis,* from Latin IR- + *refrāgārī* to resist, thwart] ▸ **ir,refragaˈbility** *or* **irˈrefragableness** *n* ▸ **irˈrefragably** *adv*

irrefrangible (,ɪrɪˈfrændʒəbᵊl) *adj* **1** not to be broken or transgressed; inviolable. **2** *Physics.* incapable of being refracted. ▸ **,irre,frangiˈbility** *or* **,irreˈfrangibleness** *n* ▸ **,irreˈfrangibly** *adv*

irrefutable (ɪˈrɛfjutəbᵊl, ,ɪrɪˈfjuːtəbᵊl) *adj* impossible to deny or disprove; incontrovertible. ▸ **ir,refutaˈbility** *or* **irˈrefutableness** *n* ▸ **irˈrefutably** *adv*

irreg. *abbrev. for* irregular(ly).

irregular (ɪˈrɛgjulə) *adj* **1** lacking uniformity or symmetry; uneven in shape, position, arrangement, etc. **2** not occurring at expected or equal intervals: *an irregular pulse.* **3** differing from the normal or accepted practice or routine. **4** not according to established standards of behaviour; unconventional. **5** (of the formation, inflections, or derivations of a word) not following the usual pattern of formation in a language, as English plurals ending other than in *-s* or *-es.* **6** of or relating to guerrillas or volunteers not belonging to regular forces: *irregular troops.* **7** (of flowers) having any of their parts, esp. petals, differing in size, shape, etc.; asymmetric. **8** *U.S.* (of merchandise) not up to the manufacturer's standards or specifications; flawed; imperfect. ♦ *n* **9** a soldier not in a regular army. **10** (*often pl*) *U.S.* imperfect or flawed merchandise. Compare **second**[1] (sense 15). ▸ **irˈregularly** *adv*

irregularity (ɪ,rɛgjuˈlærɪtɪ) *n, pl* **-ties. 1** the state or quality of being irregular. **2** something irregular, such as a bump in a smooth surface. **3** a breach of a convention or normal procedure.

irrelative (ɪˈrɛlətɪv) *adj* **1** unrelated. **2** a rare word for **irrelevant.** ▸ **irˈrelatively** *adv* ▸ **irˈrelativeness** *n*

irrelevant (ɪˈrɛləvənt) *adj* not relating or pertinent to the matter at hand; not important. ▸ **irˈrelevance** *or* **irˈrelevancy** *n* ▸ **irˈrelevantly** *adv*

irrelievable (,ɪrɪˈliːvəbᵊl) *adj* not able to be relieved.

irreligion (,ɪrɪˈlɪdʒən) *n* **1** lack of religious faith. **2** indifference or opposition to religion. ▸ **,irreˈligionist** *n* ▸ **,irreˈligious** *adj* ▸ **,irreˈligiously** *adv* ▸ **,irreˈligiousness** *n*

irremeable (ɪˈrɛmɪəbᵊl, ɪˈriː-) *adj Archaic or poetic.* affording no possibility of return. [C16: from Latin *irremeābilis,* from IR- + *remeāre* to return, from RE- + *meāre* to go] ▸ **irˈremeably** *adv*

irremediable (,ɪrɪˈmiːdɪəbᵊl) *adj* not able to be remedied; incurable or irreparable. ▸ **,irreˈmediableness** *n* ▸ **,irreˈmediably** *adv*

irremissible (,ɪrɪˈmɪsəbᵊl) *adj* **1** unpardonable; inexcusable. **2** that must be done, as through duty or obligation. ▸ **,irre,missiˈbility** *or* **,irreˈmissibleness** *n* ▸ **,irreˈmissibly** *adv*

irremovable (,ɪrɪˈmuːvəbᵊl) *adj* not able to be removed. ▸ **,irre,movaˈbility** *or* **,irreˈmovableness** *n* ▸ **,irreˈmovably** *adv*

irreparable (ɪˈrɛpərəbᵊl, ɪˈrɛprəbᵊl) *adj* not able to be repaired or remedied; beyond repair. ▸ **ir,reparaˈbility** *or* **irˈreparableness** *n* ▸ **irˈreparably** *adv*

irrepealable (,ɪrɪˈpiːləbᵊl) *adj* not able to be repealed. ▸ **,irre,pealaˈbility** *or* **,irreˈpealableness** *n* ▸ **,irreˈpealably** *adv*

irreplaceable (,ɪrɪˈpleɪsəbᵊl) *adj* not able to be replaced: *an irreplaceable antique.* ▸ **,irreˈplaceably** *adv*

irrepleviable (,ɪrɪˈplɛvɪəbᵊl) *or* **irreplevisable** (,ɪrɪˈplɛvɪsəbᵊl) *adj Law.* not able to be replevied. [C16: see *ir-* IN-[1], REPLEVIN]

irrepressible (,ɪrɪˈprɛsəbᵊl) *adj* not capable of being repressed, controlled, or restrained. ▸ **,irre,pressiˈbility** *or* **,irreˈpressibleness** *n* ▸ **,irreˈpressibly** *adv*

irreproachable (,ɪrɪˈprəʊtʃəbᵊl) *adj* not deserving reproach; blameless. ▸ **,irre,proachaˈbility** *or* **,irreˈproachableness** *n* ▸ **,irreˈproachably** *adv*

irresistible (,ɪrɪˈzɪstəbᵊl) *adj* **1** not able to be resisted or refused; overpowering: *an irresistible impulse.* **2** very fascinating or alluring: *an irresistible woman.* ▸ **,irre,sistiˈbility** *or* **,irreˈsistibleness** *n* ▸ **,irreˈsistibly** *adv*

irresoluble (ɪˈrɛzəljubᵊl) *adj* **1** a less common word for **insoluble. 2** *Archaic.* not capable of being relieved. ▸ **ir,resoluˈbility** *n* ▸ **irˈresolubly** *adv*

irresolute (ɪˈrɛzə,luːt) *adj* lacking resolution; wavering; hesitating. ▸ **irˈreso,lutely** *adv* ▸ **irˈreso,luteness** *or* **ir,resoˈlution** *n*

irresolvable (,ɪrɪˈzɒlvəbᵊl) *adj* **1** not able to be resolved into parts or elements. **2** not able to be solved; insoluble. ▸ **,irre,solvaˈbility** *or* **,irreˈsolvableness** *n* ▸ **,irreˈsolvably** *adv*

irrespective (,ɪrɪˈspɛktɪv) *adj* **1 irrespective of.** (*prep*) without taking account of; regardless of. ♦ *adv* **2** *Informal.* regardless; without due consideration: *he carried on with his plan irrespective.* ▸ **,irreˈspectively** *adv*

irrespirable (ɪˈrɛspɪrəbᵊl, ,ɪrɪˈspaɪərəbᵊl) *adj* not fit for breathing or incapable of being breathed.

irresponsible (,ɪrɪˈspɒnsəbᵊl) *adj* **1** not showing or done with due care for the consequences of one's actions or attitudes; reckless. **2** not capable of bearing responsibility. **3** *Archaic.* not answerable to a higher authority for one's actions. ▸ **,irre,sponsiˈbility** *or* **,irreˈsponsibleness** *n* ▸ **,irreˈsponsibly** *adv*

irresponsive (,ɪrɪˈspɒnsɪv) *adj* not responsive. ▸ **,irreˈsponsively** *adv* ▸ **,irreˈsponsiveness** *n*

irretentive (,ɪrɪˈtɛntɪv) *adj* not retentive. ▸ **,irreˈtentiveness** *n*

irretrievable (,ɪrɪˈtriːvəbᵊl) *adj* not able to be retrieved, recovered, or repaired. ▸ **,irre,trievaˈbility** *or* **,irreˈtrievableness** *n* ▸ **,irreˈtrievably** *adv*

irreverence (ɪˈrɛvərəns, ɪˈrɛvrəns) *n* **1** lack of due respect or veneration; disrespect. **2** a disrespectful remark or act. ▸ **irˈreverent** *or* **ir,reveˈrential** *adj* ▸ **irˈreverently** *adv*

irreversible (,ɪrɪˈvɜːsəbᵊl) *adj* **1** not able to be reversed: *the irreversible flow of time.* **2** not able to be revoked or repealed; irrevocable. **3** *Chem., physics.* capable of changing or producing a change in one direction only: *an irreversible reaction.* **4** *Thermodynamics.* (of a change, process, etc.) occurring through a number of intermediate states that are not all in thermodynamic equilibrium. ▸ **,irre,versiˈbility** *or* **,irreˈversibleness** *n* ▸ **,irreˈversibly** *adv*

irrevocable (ɪˈrɛvəkəbᵊl) *adj* not able to be revoked, changed, or undone; unalterable. ▸ **ir,revocaˈbility** *or* **irˈrevocableness** *n* ▸ **irˈrevocably** *adv*

irrigate (ˈɪrɪ,geɪt) *vb* **1** to supply (land) with water by means of artificial canals, ditches, etc., esp. to promote the growth of food crops. **2** *Med.* to bathe or wash out a bodily part, cavity, or wound. **3** (*tr*) to make fertile, fresh, or vital by or as if by watering. [C17: from Latin *irrigāre,* from *rigāre* to moisten, conduct water] ▸ **'irrigable** *adj* ▸ **,irri'gation** *n* ▸ **,irri'gational** *or* **'irri,gative** *adj* ▸ **'irri,gator** *n*

irriguous (ɪ'rɪgjʊəs) *adj Archaic or poetic.* well-watered; watery. [C17: from Latin *irriguus* supplied with water, from *riguus* watered; see IRRIGATE]

irritable ('ɪrɪtəbᵊl) *adj* **1** quickly irritated; easily annoyed; peevish. **2** (of all living organisms) capable of responding to such stimuli as heat, light, and touch. **3** *Pathol.* abnormally sensitive. ▸ **,irrita'bility** *n* ▸ **'irritableness** *n* ▸ **'irritably** *adv*

irritable bowel syndrome *n Med.* a chronic condition of recurring abdominal pain with constipation or diarrhoea or both.

irritant ('ɪrɪtənt) *adj* **1** causing irritation; irritating. ◆ *n* **2** something irritant. ▸ **'irritancy** *n*

irritate ('ɪrɪ,teɪt) *vb* **1** to annoy or anger (someone). **2** (*tr*) *Biology.* to stimulate (an organism or part) to respond in a characteristic manner. **3** (*tr*) *Pathol.* to cause (a bodily organ or part) to become excessively stimulated, resulting in inflammation, tenderness, etc. [C16: from Latin *irrītāre* to provoke, exasperate] ▸ **'irri,tator** *n*

irritation (,ɪrɪ'teɪʃən) *n* **1** something that irritates. **2** the act of irritating or the condition of being irritated. ▸ **'irri,tative** *adj*

irrupt (ɪ'rʌpt) *vb* (*intr*) **1** to enter forcibly or suddenly. **2** (of a plant or animal population) to enter a region suddenly and in very large numbers. **3** (of a population) to increase suddenly and greatly. [C19: from Latin *irrumpere* to rush into, invade, from *rumpere* to break, burst] ▸ **ir'ruption** *n*

irruptive (ɪ'rʌptɪv) *adj* **1** irrupting or tending to irrupt. **2** of, involving, or causing irruption. **3** (of igneous rocks) intrusive. ▸ **ir'ruptively** *adv*

IRS (in the U.S.) *abbrev. for* Internal Revenue Service

Irtysh *or* **Irtish** (ɪə'tɪʃ) *n* a river in central Asia, rising in China in the Altai Mountains and flowing west through Kazakhstan, then northwest into Russia to join the Ob River as its chief tributary. Length: 4444 km (2760 miles).

Irvine ('ɜːvɪn) *n* a town on the W coast of Scotland, the administrative centre of North Ayrshire: designated a new town in 1966. Pop.: 32 988 (1991).

Irving ('ɜːvɪŋ) *n* **1** Sir **Henry.** real name *John Henry Brodribb.* 1838–1905, English actor and manager of the Lyceum Theatre in London (1878–1902). **2** **Washington.** 1783–1859, U.S. essayist and short-story writer, noted for *The Sketch Book of Geoffrey Crayon* (1820), which contains the stories *Rip Van Winkle* and *The Legend of Sleepy Hollow.*

is (ɪz) *vb* (used with *he, she, it,* and with singular nouns) a form of the present tense (indicative mood) of **be.** [Old English; compare Old Norse *es,* German *ist,* Latin *est,* Greek *esti*]

IS *international car registration for* Iceland. [Icelandic *Ísland*]

Is. *abbrev. for:* **1** Also: **Isa.** *Bible.* Isaiah. **2** Island(s) *or* Isle(s).

is- *combining form.* variant of **iso-** before a vowel: *isentropic.*

ISA[1] *Aeronautics. abbrev. for:* **1** International Standard Atmosphere. **2** Interim Standard Atmosphere.

ISA[2] ('aɪsə) *n acronym for* individual savings account: a tax-free savings scheme introduced in Britain in 1999.

Isaac ('aɪzək) *n* an Old Testament patriarch, the son of Abraham and Sarah and father of Jacob and Esau (Genesis 17; 21–27).

Isabella[1] (,ɪzə'bɛlə) *or* **Isabel** ('ɪzə,bɛl) *n* **a** a greyish-yellow colour. **b** Also: **Isabelline** (,ɪzə'bɛliːn). (*as adj*): *an Isabella mohair coat.* [C17: from the name *Isabella;* original reference uncertain]

Isabella[2] (,ɪzə'bɛlə) *n* original name *Elizabeth Farnese.* 1692–1766, second wife (1714–46) of Philip V of Spain and mother of Charles III of Spain.

Isabella I *n* known as *Isabella the Catholic.* 1451–1504, queen of Castile (1474–1504) and, with her husband, Ferdinand V, joint ruler of Castile and Aragon (1479–1504).

Isabella II *n* 1830–1904, queen of Spain (1833–68), whose accession precipitated the first Carlist war (1833–39). She was deposed in a revolution.

Isabella of France *n* 1292–1358, wife (1308–27) of Edward II of England, whom, aided by her lover, Roger de Mortimer, she deposed; mother of Edward III.

isagoge ('aɪsə,gəʊdʒɪ, ,aɪsə'gəʊ-) *n* an academic introduction to a specialized subject field or area of research. [C17: from Latin, from Greek *eisagōgē,* from *eisagein* to introduce, from *eis-* into + *agein* to lead]

isagogics (,aɪsə'gɒdʒɪks) *n* (*usually functioning as sing*) introductory studies, esp. in the history of the Bible. ▸ **,isa'gogic** *adj*

Isaiah (aɪ'zaɪə) *n Old Testament.* **1** the first of the major Hebrew prophets, who lived in the 8th century B.C. **2** the book of his and others' prophecies.

isallobar (aɪ'sælə,bɑː) *n Meteorol.* a line on a map running through places experiencing equal pressure changes.

Isar ('iːzɑː) *n* a river in central Europe, rising in W Austria and flowing generally northeast through S Germany into the Danube. Length: over 260 km (160 miles).

isatin ('aɪsətɪn) *or* **isatine** ('aɪsə,tiːn) *n* a yellowish-red crystalline compound soluble in hot water, used for the preparation of vat dyes. Formula: $C_8H_5NO_2$. [C19: from Latin *isatis* woad + -IN] ▸ **,isa'tinic** *adj*

Isauria (aɪ'sɔːrɪə) *n* an ancient district of S central Asia Minor, chiefly on the N slopes of the W Taurus Mountains. ▸ **I'saurian** *adj, n*

ISBN *abbrev. for* International Standard Book Number.

Iscariot (ɪ'skærɪət) *n* See **Judas** (Iscariot).

ischaemia *or* **ischemia** (ɪ'skiːmɪə) *n Pathol.* an inadequate supply of blood to an organ or part, as from an obstructed blood flow. [C19: from Greek *iskhein* to restrict, + -EMIA] ▸ **ischaemic** *or* **ischemic** (ɪ'skɛmɪk) *adj*

Ischia ('iːskjɑː, 'ɪskɪə) *n* a volcanic island in the Tyrrhenian Sea, at the N end of the Bay of Naples. Area: 47 sq. km (18 sq. miles).

ischium ('ɪskɪəm) *n, pl* **-chia** (-kɪə). one of the three sections of the hipbone, situated below the ilium. [C17: from Latin: hip joint, from Greek *iskhion*] ▸ **'ischial** *adj*

ISD *abbrev. for* international subscriber dialling.

ISDN *abbrev. for* integrated services digital network: a rapid telecommunications network, combining data transfer and telephony.

-ise *suffix forming verbs.* a variant of **-ize.**

USAGE See at **-ize.**

isentropic (,aɪsɛn'trɒpɪk) *adj* having or taking place at constant entropy.

Isère (*French* izɛr) *n* **1** a department of SE France, in Rhône-Alpes region. Capital: Grenoble. Pop.: 1 064 600 (1995). Area: 7904 sq. km (3083 sq. miles). **2** a river in SE France, rising in the Graian Alps and flowing west and southwest to join the River Rhône near Valence. Length: 290 km (180 miles).

Iseult, Yseult (ɪ'suːlt), *or* **Isolde** (ɪ'zəʊldə) *n* (in Arthurian legend) **1** an Irish princess wed to Mark, king of Cornwall, but in love with his knight Tristan. **2** (in another account) the daughter of the king of Brittany, married to Tristan.

Isfahan (,ɪsfə'hɑːn) *or* **Eşfahān** *n* a city in central Iran: the second largest city in the country; capital of Persia in the 11th century and from 1598 to 1722. Pop.: 1 220 595 (1994 est.). Ancient name: **Aspadana** (,æspə'dɑːnə).

-ish *suffix forming adjectives.* **1** of or belonging to a nationality or group: *Scottish.* **2** *Often derogatory.* having the manner or qualities of; resembling: *slavish; prudish; boyish.* **3** somewhat; approximately: *yellowish; sevenish.* **4** concerned or preoccupied with: *bookish.* [Old English *-isc;* related to German *-isch,* Greek *-iskos*]

Isherwood ('ɪʃə,wʊd) *n* **Christopher,** full name *Christopher William Bradshaw-Isherwood.* 1904–86, U.S. novelist and dramatist, born in England. His works include the novel *Goodbye to Berlin* (1939) and three verse plays written in collaboration with W.H. Auden.

Ishiguro (,ɪʃɪ'gʊrəʊ) *n* **Kazuo** (kæt'zuːəʊ). born 1954, British novelist, born in Japan. His novels include *An Artist of the Floating World* (1986) and the Booker-prizewinning *The Remains of the Day* (1989).

Ishmael ('ɪʃmeɪəl) *n* **1** the son of Abraham and Hagar, Sarah's handmaid: the ancestor of 12 Arabian tribes (Genesis 21:8–21; 25:12–18). **2** a bandit chieftain, who defied the Babylonian conquerors of Judah and assassinated the governor appointed by Nebuchadnezzar (II Kings 25:25; Jeremiah 40:13–41:18). **3** *Rare.* an outcast.

Ishmaelite ('ɪʃmeɪə,laɪt) *n* **1** a supposed descendant of Ishmael; a member of a desert people of Old Testament times. **2** *Rare.* an outcast. ▸ **'Ishmael,itism** *n*

Ishtar ('ɪʃtɑː) *n* the principal goddess of the Babylonians and Assyrians; divinity of love, fertility, and war.

Isidore of Seville ('ɪzɪdɔː) *n* **Saint,** Latin name *Isidorus Hispalensis.* ?560–636 A.D., Spanish archbishop and scholar, noted for his *Etymologies,* an encyclopedia. Feast day: April 4.

isinglass ('aɪzɪŋ,glɑːs) *n* **1** a gelatine made from the air bladders of freshwater fish, used as a clarifying agent and adhesive. **2** another name for **mica.** [C16: from Middle Dutch *huysenblase,* literally: sturgeon bladder; influenced by English GLASS]

Isis[1] ('aɪsɪs) *n* the local name for the River Thames at Oxford.

Isis[2] ('aɪsɪs) *n* an ancient Egyptian fertility goddess, depicted as a woman with a cow's horns, between which was the disc of the sun; wife and sister of Osiris.

Iskander Bey (ɪs'kændə beɪ) *n* the Turkish name for **Scanderbeg.**

Iskenderun (ɪs'kɛndə,ruːn) *n* a port in S Turkey, on the **Gulf of Iskenderun.** Pop.: 153 871 (1995 est.). Former name: **Alexandretta.**

Isl. *abbrev. for:* **1** Island. **2** Isle.

Islam ('ɪzlɑːm) *n* **1** Also called: **Islamism** (ɪz'lɑːmɪzəm, 'ɪzləmɪzəm). the religion of Muslims, having the Koran as its sacred scripture and teaching that there is only one God and that Mohammed is his prophet; Mohammedanism. **2a** Muslims collectively and their civilization. **2b** the countries where the Muslim religion is predominant. [C19: from Arabic: surrender (to God), from *aslama* to surrender] ▸ **Is'lamic** *adj*

Islamabad (ɪz'lɑːmə,bɑːd) *n* the capital of Pakistan, in the north on the Potwar Plateau: site chosen in 1959; surrounded by the Capital Territory of Islamabad for 909 sq. km (351 sq. miles). Pop.: 204 364 (1995 est.).

Islamist ('ɪz,ləmɪst) *adj* **1** supporting or advocating Islamic fundamentalism. ◆ *n* **2** a supporter or advocate of Islamic fundamentalism.

Islamize *or* **Islamise** ('ɪzlə,maɪz) *vb* (*tr*) to convert or subject to the influence of Islam. ▸ **,Islami'zation** *or* **,Islami'sation** *n*

island ('aɪlənd) *n* **1** a mass of land that is surrounded by water and is smaller than a continent. **2** See **traffic island.** **3** *Anatomy.* a part, structure, or group of cells distinct in constitution from its immediate surroundings. ◆ Related adj: **insular.** ◆ *vb* (*tr*) *Rare.* **4** to cause to become an island. **5** to intersperse with islands. **6** to place on an island; insulate; isolate. [Old English *īgland,* from *īg* island + LAND; *s* inserted through influence of ISLE] ▸ **'island-,like** *adj*

island arc *n* an arc-shaped chain of islands, such as the Aleutian Islands or the Japanese Islands, usually lying at the edge of a Benioff zone, indicating volcanic activity where the oceanic lithosphere is descending into the earth's interior.

islander ('aɪləndə) *n* **1** a native or inhabitant of an island. **2** (*cap.*) *N.Z.* a native or inhabitant of the Pacific Islands.

island of Reil (raɪl) *n* another name for **insula.** [after Johann *Reil* (died 1813), German physician]

Islands ('aɪləndz) *pl n N.Z.* **the.** the islands of the South Pacific.

islands council *n* (in Scotland since 1975) any of the three divisions (Orkney, Shetland, and the Western Isles) into which the Scottish islands are divided for purposes of local government. See also **region** (sense 6).

Islands of the Blessed *pl n Greek myth.* lands where the souls of heroes and good men were taken after death. Also called: **Hesperides.**

island universe *n* a former name for **galaxy.**

Islay ('aɪlə, 'aɪleɪ) *n* an island off the W coast of Scotland: the southernmost of the Inner Hebrides; separated from the island of Jura by the **Sound of Islay.** Pop.: 3500 (latest est.). Area: 606 sq. km (234 sq. miles).

isle (aɪl) *n Poetic except when cap. and part of place name.* an island, esp. a small one. [C13: from Old French *isle,* from Latin *insula* island]

Isle of Dogs *n* See (Isle of) **Dogs.**

Isle of Man *n* See (Isle of) **Man.**

Isle of Pines *n* the former name of the (Isle of) **Youth.**

Isle of Sheppey *n* See (Isle of) **Sheppey.**

Isle of Wight *n* See (Isle of) **Wight.**

Isle of Youth *n* See (Isle of) **Youth.**

Isle Royale (ˈrɔɪəl) *n* an island in the northeast U.S., in NW Lake Superior: forms, with over 100 surrounding islands, **Isle Royale National Park.** Area: 541 sq. km (209 sq. miles).

islet (ˈaɪlɪt) *n* a small island. [C16: from Old French *islette;* see ISLE]

islets of Langerhans *or* **islands of Langerhans** (ˈlæŋəˌhæns) *pl n* small groups of endocrine cells in the pancreas that secrete the hormones insulin and glucagon. [C19: named after Paul *Langerhans* (1847–88), German physician]

Islington (ˈɪzlɪŋtən) *n* a borough of N Greater London. Pop.: 175 200 (1994 est.). Area: 16 sq. km (6 sq. miles).

ism (ˈɪzəm) *n Informal, often derogatory.* an unspecified doctrine, system, or practice.

ISM *abbrev. for* interstellar medium.

-ism *suffix forming nouns.* **1** indicating an action, process, or result: *criticism; terrorism.* **2** indicating a state or condition: *paganism.* **3** indicating a doctrine, system, or body of principles and practices: *Leninism; spiritualism.* **4** indicating behaviour or a characteristic quality: *heroism.* **5** indicating a characteristic usage, esp. of a language: *colloquialism; Scotticism.* **6** indicating prejudice on the basis specified: *sexism; ageism.* [from Old French *-isme,* from Latin *-ismus,* from Greek *-ismos*]

Ismaili *or* **Isma'ili** (ˌɪzmɑːˈiːlɪ) *n Islam.* **1** a Shiah sect whose adherents believe that Ismail, son of the sixth imam, was the rightful seventh imam. **2** (*pl* **-lis**) Also called: **Ismailian** (ˌɪzmɑːɪˈliːən). a member of this sect.

Ismailia (ˌɪzmaɪˈlɪə) *n* a city in NE Egypt, on the Suez Canal: founded in 1863 by the former Suez Canal Company; devastated by Israeli troops in the October War (1973). Pop.: 255 000 (1992 est.).

Ismail Pasha (ˌɪzmɑːˈiːl ˈpɑːʃə) *n* 1830–95, viceroy (1863–66) and khedive (1867–79) of Egypt, who brought his country close to bankruptcy. He was forced to submit to Anglo-French financial control (1876) and to abdicate (1879).

isna *or* **isnae** (ˈɪznɪ) *vb Scot.* is not.

isn't (ˈɪzᵊnt) *vb contraction of* is not.

ISO *abbrev. for* **1** International Standards Organization. **2** Imperial Service Order (a Brit. decoration).

iso- *or before a vowel* **is-** *combining form.* **1** equal or identical: *isomagnetic.* **2** indicating that a chemical compound is an isomer of a specified compound: *isobutane; isocyanic acid.* [from Greek *isos* equal]

isoagglutination (ˌaɪsəʊəˌgluːtɪˈneɪʃən) *n* the agglutination of red blood cells of an organism by the blood serum of another organism of the same species. ▶ **ˌisoagˈglutinative** *adj*

isoagglutinin (ˌaɪsəʊəˈgluːtɪnɪn) *n* an antibody that causes agglutination of red blood cells in animals of the same species from which it was derived.

isoamyl acetate (ˌaɪsəʊˈæmɪl) *n* a colourless volatile compound used as a solvent for cellulose lacquers and as a flavouring. Formula: $(CH_3)_2CHCH_2CH_2OOCCH_3$.

isoantigen (ˌaɪsəʊˈæntɪdʒən) *n Immunol.* an antigen that stimulates antibody production in different members of the same species.

isobar (ˈaɪsəʊˌbɑː) *n* **1** a line on a map connecting places of equal atmospheric pressure, usually reduced to sea level for purposes of comparison, at a given time or period. **2** *Physics.* any of two or more atoms that have the same mass number but different atomic numbers: *tin-115 and indium-115 are isobars.* Compare **isotope.** [C19: from Greek *isobarēs* of equal weight, from ISO- + *baros* weight] ▶ **ˈisobarˌism** *n*

isobaric (ˌaɪsəʊˈbærɪk) *adj* **1** Also: **isopiestic.** having equal atmospheric pressure. **2** of or relating to isobars.

isobaric spin *n* See **isospin.**

isobath (ˈaɪsəʊˌbæθ) *n* a line on a map connecting points of equal underwater depth. [C19: from Greek *isobathēs* of equal depth, from ISO- + *bathos* depth] ▶ **ˌisoˈbathic** *adj*

isobilateral (ˌaɪsəʊbaɪˈlætərəl) *adj Botany.* (esp. of a leaf) capable of being divided into symmetrical halves along two different planes.

isocheim *or* **isochime** (ˈaɪsəʊˌkaɪm) *n* a line on a map connecting places with the same mean winter temperature. [C19: from ISO- + Greek *kheima* winter weather] ▶ **ˌisoˈcheimal, ˌisoˈcheimenal,** *or* **ˌisoˈchimal** *adj*

isochor *or* **isochore** (ˈaɪsəʊˌkɔː) *n* a line on a graph showing the variation of the temperature of a fluid with its pressure, when the volume is kept constant. [C19: from ISO- + Greek *khōros* place, space] ▶ **ˌisoˈchoric** *adj*

isochromatic (ˌaɪsəʊkrəʊˈmætɪk) *adj* **1a** having the same colour. **1b** of uniform colour. **2** *Photog.* (of an early type of emulsion) sensitive to green light in addition to blue light but not to red light.

isochronal (aɪˈsɒkrənᵊl) *or* **isochronous** *adj* **1** having the same duration; equal in time. **2** occurring at equal time intervals; having a uniform period of vibration or oscillation. [C17: from New Latin *isochronus,* from Greek *isokhronos,* from ISO- + *khronos* time] ▶ **iˈsochronally** *or* **iˈsochronously** *adv* ▶ **iˈsochroˌnism** *n*

isochrone (ˈaɪsəʊˌkrəʊn) *n* a line on a map or diagram connecting places from which it takes the same time to travel to a certain point.

isochronize *or* **isochronise** (aɪˈsɒkrəˌnaɪz) *vb* (*tr*) to make isochronal.

isochroous (aɪˈsɒkrəʊəs) *adj* of uniform colour.

isoclinal (ˌaɪsəʊˈklaɪnᵊl) *or* **isoclinic** (ˌaɪsəʊˈklɪnɪk) *adj* **1** sloping in the same direction and at the same angle. **2** *Geology.* (of folds) having limbs that are parallel to each other. ◆ *n* **3** Also called: **isocline, isoclinal line.** an imaginary line connecting points on the earth's surface having equal angles of dip.

isocline (ˈaɪsəʊˌklaɪn) *n* **1** a series of rock strata with isoclinal folds. **2** another name for **isoclinal** (sense 3).

isocracy (aɪˈsɒkrəsɪ) *n, pl* **-cies. 1** a form of government in which all people have equal powers. **2** equality of political power. ▶ **isocratic** (ˌaɪsəʊˈkrætɪk) *adj*

Isocrates (aɪˈsɒkrəˌtiːz) *n* 436–338 B.C., Athenian rhetorician and teacher.

isocyanic acid (ˌaɪsəʊsaɪˈænɪk) *n* a hypothetical acid known only in the form of its compounds. Formula: HNCO.

isocyanide (ˌaɪsəʊˈsaɪəˌnaɪd) *n* any salt or ester of isocyanic acid. Also called: **carbylamine, isonitrile.**

isodiametric (ˌaɪsəʊˌdaɪəˈmɛtrɪk) *adj* **1** having diameters of the same length. **2** (of a crystal) having three equal axes. **3** (of a cell or similar body) having a similar diameter in all planes.

isodiaphere (ˌaɪsəʊˈdaɪəˌfɪə) *n* one of two or more nuclides in which the difference between the number of neutrons and the number of protons is the same: *a nuclide that has emitted an alpha particle, and its decay product, are isodiapheres.*

isodimorphism (ˌaɪsəʊdaɪˈmɔːfɪzəm) *n* a property of a dimorphous substance such that it is isomorphous with another dimorphous substance in both its forms. ▶ **ˌisodiˈmorphous** *or* **ˌisodiˈmorphic** *adj*

isodose (ˈaɪsəʊˌdəʊs) *n Med.* a dose of radiation applied to a part of the body in radiotherapy that is equal to the dose applied to a different part.

isodynamic (ˌaɪsəʊdaɪˈnæmɪk) *adj Physics.* **1** having equal force or strength. **2** of or relating to an imaginary line on the earth's surface connecting points of equal horizontal magnetic intensity.

isoelectric (ˌaɪsəʊɪˈlɛktrɪk) *adj* having the same electric potential.

isoelectric point *n Biochem.* the pH value at which the net electric charge of a molecule, such as a protein or amino acid, is zero.

isoelectronic (ˌaɪsəʊɪlɛkˈtrɒnɪk) *adj* (of atoms, radicals, or ions) having an equal number of electrons or a similar configuration of electrons.

isoenzyme (ˌaɪsəʊˈɛnzaɪm) *n* another name for **isozyme.** ▶ **isoenzymic** (ˌaɪsəʊɛnˈzaɪmɪk, -ˈzɪm-) *adj*

isogamete (ˌaɪsəʊgæˈmiːt) *n* a gamete that is similar in size and form to the one with which it unites in fertilization. Compare **heterogamete.** ▶ **isogametic** (ˌaɪsəʊgæˈmɛtɪk) *adj*

isogamy (aɪˈsɒgəmɪ) *n* (in some algae and fungi) sexual fusion of gametes of similar size and form. Compare **heterogamy** (sense 1). ▶ **iˈsogamous** *adj*

isogenous (aɪˈsɒdʒɪnəs) *adj Biology.* **1** of similar origin, as parts derived from the same embryonic tissue. **2** Also: **isogenic** (ˌaɪsəʊˈdʒɛnɪk). genetically uniform. ▶ **iˈsogeny** *n*

isogeotherm (ˌaɪsəʊˈdʒiːəʊˌθɜːm) *n* an imaginary line below the surface of the earth connecting points of equal temperature. ▶ **ˌisoˌgeoˈthermal** *or* **ˌisoˌgeoˈthermic** *adj*

isogloss (ˈaɪsəʊˌglɒs) *n* a line drawn on a map around the area in which a linguistic feature is to be found, such as a particular pronunciation of a given word. ▶ **ˌisoˈglossal** *or* **ˌisoˈglottic** *adj*

isogon (ˈaɪsəʊˌgɒn) *n* an equiangular polygon.

isogonic (ˌaɪsəʊˈgɒnɪk) *or* **isogonal** (aɪˈsɒgənᵊl) *adj* **1** *Maths.* having, making, or involving equal angles. ◆ *n* **2** Also called: **isogonic line, isogonal line, isogone.** *Physics.* an imaginary line connecting points on the earth's surface having equal magnetic declination.

isogram (ˈaɪsəʊˌgræm) *n* another name for **isopleth.**

isohel (ˈaɪsəʊˌhɛl) *n* a line on a map connecting places with an equal period of sunshine. [C20: from ISO- + Greek *hēlios* sun]

isohydric (ˌaɪsəʊˈhaɪdrɪk) *adj Chem.* having the same acidity or hydrogen-ion concentration.

isohyet (ˌaɪsəʊˈhaɪɪt) *n* a line on a map connecting places having equal rainfall. [C19: from ISO- + *-hyet,* from Greek *huetos* rain]

isolate *vb* (ˈaɪsəˌleɪt). (*tr*) **1** to place apart; cause to be alone. **2** *Med.* to quarantine (a person or animal) having or suspected of having a contagious disease. **3** to obtain (a compound) in an uncombined form. **4** to obtain pure cultures of (bacteria, esp. those causing a particular disease). **5** *Electronics.* to prevent interaction between (circuits, components, etc.); insulate. ◆ *n* (ˈaɪsəlɪt). **6** an isolated person or group. [C19: back formation from *isolated,* via Italian from Latin *insulātus,* literally: made into an island; see INSULATE] ▶ **ˈisolable** *adj* ▶ **ˌisolaˈbility** *n* ▶ **ˈisoˌlator** *n*

isolated pawn *n Chess.* a pawn without pawns of the same colour on neighbouring files.

isolating (ˈaɪsəˌleɪtɪŋ) *adj Linguistics.* another word for **analytic.**

isolation (ˌaɪsəˈleɪʃən) *n* **1** the act of isolating or the condition of being isolated. **2** (of a country, party, etc.) nonparticipation in or withdrawal from international politics. **3** *Med.* **3a** social separation of a person who has or is suspected of having a contagious disease. Compare **quarantine. 3b** (*as modifier*): *an isolation hospital.* **4** *Sociol.* a lack of contact between persons, groups, or whole societies. **5** *Social psychol.* the failure of an individual to maintain contact with others or genuine communication where interaction with others persists. **6 in isolation.** without regard to context, similar matters, etc.

isolationism (ˌaɪsəˈleɪʃəˌnɪzəm) *n* **1** a policy of nonparticipation in or withdrawal from international affairs. **2** an attitude favouring such a policy. ▶ **ˌisoˈlationist** *n, adj*

isolative (ˈaɪsəˌleɪtɪv, ˈaɪsələtɪv) *adj* **1** (of a sound change) occurring in all linguistic environments, as the change of Middle English /iː/ to Modern English /aɪ/, as in *time.* Compare **combinative** (sense 2). **2** of, relating to, or concerned with isolation.

Isolde (iˈzɔldə) *n* the German name of **Iseult.**

isolecithal (ˌaɪsəʊˈlɛsɪθəl) *adj* (of the ova of mammals and certain other vertebrates) having an evenly distributed yolk. Compare **heterolecithal.**

isoleucine (ˌaɪsəʊˈluːsiːn, -sɪn) *n* an essential amino acid that occurs in proteins and is formed by protein hydrolysis.

isolex (ˈaɪsəˌlɛks) *n Linguistics.* an isogloss marking off the area in which a particular item of vocabulary is found. **[C20:** from ISO(GLOSS) + Greek *lex(is)* word**]**

isoline (ˈaɪsəʊˌlaɪn) *n* another term for **isopleth.**

isologous (aɪˈsɒləgəs) *adj* (of two or more organic compounds) having a similar structure but containing different atoms of the same valency. **[C19:** from ISO- + (HOMO)LOGOUS**]** ▸ **isologue** (ˈaɪsəʊˌlɒg) *n*

isomagnetic (ˌaɪsəʊmægˈnɛtɪk) *adj* **1** having equal magnetic induction or force. ◆ *n* **2** Also called: **isomagnetic line.** an imaginary line connecting points on the earth's surface having equal magnetic intensity.

isomer (ˈaɪsəmə) *n* **1** *Chem.* a compound that exhibits isomerism with one or more other compounds. **2** *Physics.* a nuclide that exhibits isomerism with one or more other nuclides. ▸ **isomeric** (ˌaɪsəˈmɛrɪk) *adj*

isomerase (aɪˈsɒməreɪs) *n* any enzyme that catalyses the conversion of one isomeric form of a compound to another.

isomerism (aɪˈsɒməˌrɪzəm) *n* **1** the existence of two or more compounds having the same molecular formula but a different arrangement of atoms within the molecule. See also **stereoisomerism, optical isomerism. 2** the existence of two or more nuclides having the same atomic numbers and mass numbers but different energy states.

isomerize *or* **isomerise** (aɪˈsɒməˌraɪz) *vb Chem.* to change or cause to change from one isomer to another. ▸ **iˌsomeriˈzation** *or* **iˌsomeriˈsation** *n*

isomerous (aɪˈsɒmərəs) *adj* **1** having an equal number of parts or markings. **2** (of flowers) having floral whorls with the same number of parts. Compare **anisomerous.**

isometric (ˌaɪsəʊˈmɛtrɪk) *adj also* **isometrical. 1** having equal dimensions or measurements. **2** *Physiol.* of or relating to muscular contraction that does not produce shortening of the muscle. **3** (of a crystal or system of crystallization) having three mutually perpendicular equal axes. **4** *Crystallog.* another word for **cubic** (sense 4). **5** *Prosody.* having or made up of regular feet. **6** (of a method of projecting a drawing in three dimensions) having the three axes equally inclined and all lines drawn to scale. ◆ *n* **7** Also called: **isometric drawing.** a drawing made in this way. **8** Also called: **isometric line.** a line on a graph showing variations of pressure with temperature at constant volume. **[C19:** from Greek *isometria* (see ISO- + -METRY) + -IC**]** ▸ **ˌisoˈmetrically** *adv*

isometrics (ˌaɪsəʊˈmɛtrɪks) *n* (*functioning as sing*) physical exercise involving isometric contraction of muscles.

isometropia (ˌaɪsəʊmɪˈtrəʊpɪə) *n Ophthalmol.* equal refraction of the two eyes. **[**from Greek *isometros* of equal measure + -OPIA**]**

isometry (aɪˈsɒmɪtrɪ) *n* **1** *Maths.* rigid motion of a plane or space such that the distance between any two points before and after this motion is unaltered. **2** equality of height above sea level.

isomorph (ˈaɪsəʊˌmɔːf) *n* a substance or organism that exhibits isomorphism.

isomorphism (ˌaɪsəʊˈmɔːfɪzəm) *n* **1** *Biology.* similarity of form, as in different generations of the same life cycle. **2** *Chem.* the existence of two or more substances of different composition in a similar crystalline form. **3** *Maths.* a one-to-one correspondence between the elements of two or more sets, such as those of Arabic and Roman numerals, and between the sums or products of the elements of one of these sets and those of the equivalent elements of the other set or sets. ▸ **ˌisoˈmorphic** *or* **ˌisoˈmorphous** *adj*

isoniazid (ˌaɪsəʊˈnaɪəzɪd) *n* a soluble colourless crystalline compound used to treat tuberculosis. Formula: $C_6H_7N_3O$. **[C20** *isoni(cotinic acid hydr)azid(e)***]**

isonome (ˈaɪsəʊˌnəʊm) *n Botany.* a line on a chart connecting points of equal abundance values of a plant species sampled in different sections of an area. Isonomes of different species from the same area are compared in studies of plant distribution. **[C20:** from ISO- + Greek *nomos* rule, law**]**

isonomy (aɪˈsɒnəmɪ) *n* **1** the equality before the law of the citizens of a state. **2** the equality of civil or political rights. ▸ **isonomic** (ˌaɪsəʊˈnɒmɪk) *or* **iˈsonomous** *adj*

isooctane (ˌaɪsəʊˈɒkteɪn) *n* a colourless liquid alkane hydrocarbon produced from petroleum and used in standardizing petrol. Formula: $(CH_3)_3CCH_2CH(CH_3)_2$. See also **octane number.**

isopach (ˈaɪsəʊˌpæk) *or* **isopachyte** (ˌaɪsəʊˈpækaɪt) *n Geology.* a line on a map connecting points below which a particular rock stratum has the same thickness. **[C20:** from ISO- + Greek *pakhus* thick, *pakhutēs* thickness**]**

isophone (ˈaɪsəˌfəʊn) *n Linguistics.* an isogloss marking off an area in which a particular feature of pronunciation is found. **[C20:** from *iso-* (as in ISOGLOSS) + *-phone* (as in PHONEME)**]**

isopiestic (ˌaɪsəʊpaɪˈɛstɪk) *adj* another word for **isobaric** (sense 1). **[C19:** from ISO- + Greek *piestos* compressible, from *piezein* to press**]** ▸ **ˌisopiˈestically** *adv*

isopleth (ˈaɪsəʊˌplɛθ) *n* a line on a map connecting places registering the same amount or ratio of some geographical or meteorological phenomenon or phenomena. Also called: **isogram, isoline. [C20:** from Greek *isoplēthēs* equal in number, from ISO- + *plēthos* multitude, great number**]**

isopod (ˈaɪsəʊˌpɒd) *n* **1** any crustacean of the order *Isopoda,* including woodlice and pill bugs, in which the body is flattened dorsoventrally. ◆ *adj* **2** of, relating to, or belonging to the *Isopoda.* ▸ **isopodan** (aɪˈsɒpədən) *or* **iˈsopodous** *adj*

isoprene (ˈaɪsəʊˌpriːn) *n* a colourless volatile liquid with a penetrating odour: used in making synthetic rubbers. Formula: $CH_2{:}CHC(CH_3){:}CH_2$. Systematic name: **methylbuta-1,3-diene. [C20:** from ISO- + PR(OPYL) + -ENE**]**

isopropyl (ˌaɪsəʊˈprəʊpɪl) *n* (*modifier*) of, consisting of, or containing the group of atoms $(CH_3)_2CH$-, derived from propane: *an isopropyl group or radical.*

isopycnic (ˌaɪsəʊˈpɪknɪk) *n* a line on a map connecting points of equal atmospheric density. **[C19:** from ISO- + Greek *puknos* thick**]**

ISO rating *n Photog.* a classification of film speed in which a doubling of the ISO number represents a doubling in sensitivity; for example, ISO 400 film requires half the exposure of ISO 200 under the same conditions. The system uses identical numbers to the obsolete ASA rating. **[C20:** from *I*nternational *S*tandards *O*rganization**]**

isorhythmic (ˌaɪsəˈrɪðmɪk) *adj Music.* (of medieval motets) having a cantus firmus that is repeated according to a strict system of internal reiterated note values.

isosceles (aɪˈsɒsɪˌliːz) *adj* **1** (of a triangle) having two sides of equal length. **2** (of a trapezium) having the two nonparallel sides of equal length. **[C16:** from Late Latin, from Greek *isoskelēs,* from ISO- + *skelos* leg**]**

isoseismal (ˌaɪsəʊˈsaɪzməl) *adj* **1** of or relating to equal intensity of earthquake shock. ◆ *n* **2** a line on a map connecting points at which earthquake shocks are of equal intensity. ◆ Also: **isoseismic.**

isosmotic (ˌaɪsɒzˈmɒtɪk) *adj* another word for **isotonic** (sense 3).

isospin (ˈaɪsəʊˌspɪn) *n* a quantity used in the classification of elementary particles. Particles which have very similar properties except for those associated with their charge are regarded as forms of the same fundamental particle with different components of the isospin in a certain direction in an imaginary space. Also called: **isobaric spin, isotopic spin.**

isospondylous (ˌaɪsəˈspɒndᵊləs) *adj* of, relating to, or belonging to the *Isospondyli* (or *Clupeiformes*), an order of soft-finned teleost fishes that includes the herring, salmon, trout, and pike. **[C20:** from ISO- + Greek *spondulos* vertebra**]**

isostasy (aɪˈsɒstəsɪ) *n* the state of balance, or equilibrium, which sections of the earth's lithosphere (whether continental or oceanic) are thought ultimately to achieve when the vertical forces upon them remain unchanged. The lithosphere floats upon the semifluid asthenosphere below. If a section of lithosphere is loaded, as by ice, it will slowly subside to a new equilibrium position; if a section of lithosphere is reduced in mass, as by erosion, it will slowly rise to a new equilibrium position. **[C19:** ISO- + *-stasy,* from Greek *stasis* a standing**]** ▸ **isostatic** (ˌaɪsəʊˈstætɪk) *adj*

isostemonous (ˌaɪsəʊˈstiːmənəs, -ˈstɛm-) *adj Botany.* (of a flower) having the stamens arranged in a single whorl and equal to the number of petals. **[C19:** from ISO- + Greek *-stemonus* relating to a STAMEN**]**

isosteric (ˌaɪsəʊˈstɛrɪk) *adj* (of two different molecules) having the same number of atoms and the same number and configuration of valency electrons, as carbon dioxide and nitrous oxide.

isotach (ˈaɪsəʊˌtæk) *n* a line on a map connecting points of equal wind speed. **[**from ISO- + Greek *takhos* speed**]**

isotactic (ˌaɪsəʊˈtæktɪk) *adj Chem.* (of a stereospecific polymer) having identical steric configurations of the groups on each asymmetric carbon atom on the chain. Compare **syndiotactic.**

isoteniscope (ˌaɪsəʊˈtɛnɪˌskəʊp) *n Chem.* an instrument used to measure vapour pressure. **[C20:** from ISO- + TEN(SION) + -I- + -SCOPE**]**

isothere (ˈaɪsəʊˌθɪə) *n* a line on a map linking places with the same mean summer temperature. Compare **isocheim. [C19:** from ISO- + Greek *theros* summer**]** ▸ **isotheral** (aɪˈsɒθərəl) *adj*

isotherm (ˈaɪsəʊˌθɜːm) *n* **1** a line on a map linking places of equal temperature. **2** *Physics.* a curve on a graph that connects points of equal temperature. ◆ Also called: **isothermal, isothermal line.**

isothermal (ˌaɪsəʊˈθɜːməl) *adj* **1** (of a process or change) taking place at constant temperature. **2** of or relating to an isotherm. ◆ *n* **3** another word for **isotherm.** ▸ **ˌisoˈthermally** *adv*

isotone (ˈaɪsəˌtəʊn) *n* one of two or more atoms of different atomic number that contain the same number of neutrons.

isotonic (ˌaɪsəʊˈtɒnɪk) *adj* **1** *Physiol.* (of two or more muscles) having equal tension. **2** (of a drink) designed to replace the fluid and salts lost from the body during strenuous exercise. **3** Also: **isosmotic.** (of two solutions) having the same osmotic pressure, commonly having physiological osmotic pressure. Compare **hypertonic, hypotonic. 4** *Music.* of, relating to, or characterized by the equal intervals of the well-tempered scale: *isotonic tuning.* ▸ **isotonicity** (ˌaɪsəʊtəʊˈnɪsɪtɪ) *n*

isotope (ˈaɪsəˌtəʊp) *n* one of two or more atoms with the same atomic number that contain different numbers of neutrons. **[C20:** from ISO- + Greek *topos* place**]** ▸ **isotopic** (ˌaɪsəˈtɒpɪk) *adj* ▸ **ˌisoˈtopically** *adv* ▸ **isotopy** (aɪˈsɒtəpɪ) *n*

isotopic spin *n* See **isospin.**

isotron (ˈaɪsəˌtrɒn) *n Physics.* a device for separating small quantities of isotopes by ionizing them and separating the ions by a mass spectrometer. **[C20:** from ISOTOPE + -TRON**]**

isotropic (ˌaɪsəʊˈtrɒpɪk) *or* **isotropous** (aɪˈsɒtrəpəs) *adj* **1** having uniform physical properties in all directions. **2** *Biology.* not having predetermined axes: *isotropic eggs.* ▸ **ˌisoˈtropically** *adv* ▸ **iˈsotropy** *n*

isozyme (ˈaɪsəʊˌzaɪm) *n* any of a set of structural variants of an enzyme occurring in different tissues in a single species. Also called: **isoenzyme. [**from ISO- + (EN)ZYME**]** ▸ **isozymic** (ˌaɪsəʊˈzaɪmɪk, -ˈzɪm-) *adj*

ISP *abbrev. for* Internet service provider, a business providing its customers with connection to the Internet and other related services.

I-spy *n* a game in which one player specifies the initial letter of the name of an object that he can see, which the other players then try to guess.

Israel (ˈɪzreɪəl, -rɪəl) *n* **1** a republic in SW Asia, on the Mediterranean Sea: established in 1948, in the former British mandate of Palestine, as a primarily Jewish state; 8 disputes with Arab neighbours (who did not recognize the state of Israel), erupted into full-scale wars in 1948, 1956, 1967 (the Six Day War), and 1973 (the Yom Kippur War). In 1993 Israel agreed to grant autonomous status to the Gaza Strip and the West Bank, according to the terms of a peace agreement with the P.L.O. Official languages: Hebrew and Arabic. Religion: Jewish majority, Muslim and Christian minorities. Currency: shekel. Capital (international recognition withheld as East Jerusalem was annexed (1967) by Israel: UN recognized capital: Tel Aviv): Jerusalem. Pop.: 5 740 000 (1998 est.). Area (including Golan Heights and East Jerusalem): 21 946 sq. km (8473 sq. miles). **2a** the ancient kingdom of the 12 Hebrew tribes at the SE end of the Mediterranean. **2b** the kingdom in the N part of this region formed by the ten northern tribes of Israel in the 10th century B.C. and destroyed by the Assyrians in 721 B.C. **3** *Informal.* the Jewish community throughout the world.

Israeli (ɪzˈreɪlɪ) *n, pl* **-lis** *or* **-li. 1** a citizen or inhabitant of the state of Israel. ◆ *adj* **2** of, relating to, or characteristic of the state of Israel or its inhabitants.

Israelite (ˈɪzrɪəˌlaɪt, -rə-) *n* **1** *Bible.* a member of the ethnic group claiming descent from Jacob; a Hebrew. **2** *Bible.* a citizen of the kingdom of Israel (922 to 721 B.C.) as opposed to Judah. **3** a member of any of various Christian sects who regard themselves as God's chosen people. **4** an archaic word for a **Jew**.

Israfil (ˈɪzrəˌfiːl), **Israfel** (ˈɪzrəˌfɛl), *or* **Israfeel** (ˈɪzrəˌfiːl) *n Koran.* the archangel who will sound the trumpet on the Day of Judgment, heralding the end of the world.

Issachar (ˈɪsəˌkɑː) *n Old Testament.* **1** the fifth son of Jacob by his wife Leah (Genesis 30:17–18). **2** the tribe descended from this patriarch. **3** the territory of this tribe.

Issigonis (ˌɪsɪˈɡəʊnɪs) *n* Sir **Alec** (**Arnold Constantine**). 1906–88, British car designer born in Smyrna. He is noted for his designs for the Morris Minor (1948) and the Mini (1959).

issuable (ˈɪʃjuəbᵊl) *adj* **1** capable of issuing or being issued. **2** *Chiefly law.* open to debate or litigation. **3** authorized to be issued. ▸ **ˈissuably** *adv*

issuance (ˈɪʃjuəns) *n* the act of issuing.

issuant (ˈɪʃjuənt) *adj Archaic or heraldry.* emerging or issuing.

issue (ˈɪʃjuː) *n* **1** the act of sending or giving out something; supply; delivery. **2** something issued; an edition of stamps, a magazine, etc. **3** the number of identical items, such as banknotes or shares in a company, that become available at a particular time. **4** the act of emerging; outflow; discharge. **5** something flowing out, such as a river. **6** a place of outflow; outlet. **7** the descendants of a person; offspring; progeny. **8** a topic of interest or discussion. **9** an important subject requiring a decision. **10** an outcome or consequence; result. **11** *Pathol.* **11a** a suppurating sore. **11b** discharge from a wound. **12** *Law.* the matter remaining in dispute between the parties to an action after the pleadings. **13** the yield from or profits arising out of land or other property. **14** *Military.* the allocation of items of government stores, such as food, clothing, and ammunition. **15** *Library science.* **15a** the system for recording current loans. **15b** the number of books loaned in a specified period. **16** *Obsolete.* an act, deed, or proceeding. **17 at issue. 17a** under discussion. **17b** in disagreement. **18 force the issue.** to compel decision on some matter. **19 join issue. 19a** to join in controversy. **19b** to submit an issue for adjudication. **20 take issue.** to disagree. ◆ *vb* **-sues, -suing, -sued. 21** to come forth or emerge or cause to come forth or emerge. **22** to publish or deliver (a newspaper, magazine, etc.). **23** (*tr*) to make known or announce. **24** (*intr*) to originate or proceed. **25** (*intr*) to be a consequence; result. **26** (*intr; foll. by in*) to end or terminate. **27** (*tr*) **27a** to give out or allocate (equipment, a certificate, etc.) officially to someone. **27b** (foll. by *with*) to supply officially (with). **[C13:** from Old French *eissue* way out, from *eissir* to go out, from Latin *exīre*, from EX-[1] + *īre* to go**]** ▸ **ˈissueless** *adj* ▸ **ˈissuer** *n*

issue price *n Stock Exchange.* the price at which a new issue of shares is offered to the public.

issuing house *n Brit.* a financial institution that engages in finding capital for established companies or for private firms wishing to convert to public companies, by issuing shares on their behalf.

Issus (ˈɪsəs) *n* an ancient town in S Asia Minor, in Cilicia north of present-day Iskenderun: scene of a battle (333 B.C.) in which Alexander the Great defeated the Persians.

Issyk-Kul (*Russian* isˈsikˈkulj) *n* a lake in NE Kyrgyzstan in the Tian Shan mountains, at an altitude of 1609 m (5280 ft.): one of the largest mountain lakes in the world. Area: 6200 sq. km (2390 sq. miles).

-ist *suffix.* **1** (*forming nouns*) a person who performs a certain action or is concerned with something specified: *motorist; soloist.* **2** (*forming nouns*) a person who practises in a specific field: *physicist; typist.* **3** (*forming nouns and adjectives*) a person who advocates a particular doctrine, system, etc., or relating to such a person or the doctrine advocated: *socialist.* **4** (*forming nouns and adjectives*) a person characterized by a specified trait, tendency, etc., or relating to such a person or trait: *purist.* **5** (*forming nouns and adjectives*) a person who is prejudiced on the basis specified: *sexist; ageist.* **[**via Old French from Latin *-ista, -istēs,* from Greek *-istēs***]**

istana (iːˈstana) *n* (in Malaysia) a royal palace. **[**from Malay**]**

Istanbul (ˌɪstænˈbuːl) *n* a port in NW Turkey, on the western (European) shore of the Bosporus: the largest city in Turkey; founded in about 660 B.C. by Greeks; refounded by Constantine the Great in 330 A.D. as the capital of the Eastern Roman Empire; taken by the Turks in 1453 and remained capital of the Ottoman Empire until 1922; industrial centre for shipbuilding, textiles, etc. Pop.: 7 774 169 (1995 est.). Ancient name: **Byzantium.** Former name (330–1926): **Constantinople.**

Isth. *or* **isth.** *abbrev. for* isthmus.

isthmian (ˈɪsθmɪən) *adj* relating to or situated in an isthmus.

Isthmian (ˈɪsθmɪən) *adj* relating to or situated in the Isthmus of Corinth or the Isthmus of Panama.

Isthmian Games *n* a Panhellenic festival celebrated every other year in ancient Corinth.

isthmus (ˈɪsməs) *n, pl* **-muses** *or* **-mi** (-maɪ). **1** a narrow strip of land connecting two relatively large land areas. **2** *Anatomy.* **2a** a narrow band of tissue connecting two larger parts of a structure. **2b** a narrow passage connecting two cavities. **[C16:** from Latin, from Greek *isthmos***]** ▸ **ˈisthmoid** *adj*

-istic *suffix forming adjectives.* equivalent to a combination of **-ist** and **-ic** but in some words having a less specific or literal application and sometimes a mildly pejorative force, as compared with corresponding adjectives ending in **-ist**: *communistic; impressionistic.* **[**from Latin *-isticus,* from Greek *istikos***]**

istle (ˈɪstlɪ) *or* **ixtle** *n* a fibre obtained from various tropical American agave and yucca trees used in making carpets, cord, etc. **[C19:** from Mexican Spanish *ixtle,* from Nahuatl *ichtli***]**

Istria (ˈɪstrɪə) *n* a peninsula in the N Adriatic Sea: passed from Italy to Yugoslavia (except for Trieste) in 1947 and to Croatia in 1991. ▸ **ˈIstrian** *n, adj*

it (ɪt) *pron* (*subjective or objective*) **1** refers to a nonhuman, animal, plant, or inanimate thing, or sometimes to a small baby: *it looks dangerous; give it a bone.* **2** refers to an unspecified or implied antecedent or to a previous or understood clause, phrase, etc.: *it is impossible; I knew it.* **3** used to represent human life or experience either in totality or in respect of the present situation: *how's it going?; I've had it; to brazen it out.* **4** used as a formal subject (or object), referring to a following clause, phrase, or word: *it helps to know the truth; I consider it dangerous to go on.* **5** used in the nominative as the formal grammatical subject of impersonal verbs. When *it* functions absolutely in such sentences, not referring to any previous or following clause or phrase, the context is nearly always a description of the environment or of some physical sensation: *it is raining; it hurts.* **6** (used as complement with *be*) *Informal.* the crucial or ultimate point: *the steering failed and I thought that was it.* ◆ *n* **7** (in children's games) the player whose turn it is to try to touch another. Compare **he**[1] (sense 5b). **8** *Informal.* **8a** sexual intercourse. **8b** sex appeal. **9** *Informal.* a desirable quality or ability: *he's really got it.* **[**Old English *hit***]**

IT *abbrev. for* information technology.

It. *abbrev. for:* **1** Italian. **2** Italy.

ITA (in Britain) *abbrev. for* Independent Television Authority: now superseded by the IBA.

i.t.a. *or* **ITA** *abbrev. for* initial teaching alphabet, a partly phonetic alphabet used to teach reading.

itacolumite (ˌɪtəˈkɒljʊˌmaɪt) *n* a fine-grained micaceous sandstone that occurs in thin flexible slabs. **[C19:** named after *Itacolumi* mountain in Brazil where it is found**]**

itaconic acid (ˌɪtəˈkɒnɪk) *n* a white colourless crystalline carboxylic acid obtained by the fermentation of carbohydrates and used in the manufacture of synthetic resins. Formula: CH_2:C(COOH)CH_2COOH.

ital. *abbrev. for* italic.

Ital. *abbrev. for:* **1** Italian. **2** Italy.

Italia (iˈtaːlja) *n* the Italian name for **Italy.**

Italia irredenta *Italian.* (irreˈdɛnta) *n* See **Irredentist.**

Italian (ɪˈtæljən) *n* **1** the official language of Italy and one of the official languages of Switzerland: the native language of approximately 60 million people. It belongs to the Romance group of the Indo-European family, and there is a considerable diversity of dialects. **2** a native, citizen, or inhabitant of Italy, or a descendant of one. **3** See **Italian vermouth.** ◆ *adj* **4** relating to, denoting, or characteristic of Italy, its inhabitants, or their language.

Italianate (ɪˈtæljənɪt, -ˌneɪt) *or* **Italianesque** (ɪˌtæljəˈnɛsk) *adj* Italian in style or character.

Italian East Africa *n* a former Italian territory in E Africa, formed in 1936 from the possessions of Eritrea, Italian Somaliland, and Ethiopia: taken by British forces in 1941.

Italian greyhound *n* a breed of dog like a miniature greyhound.

Italianism (ɪˈtæljəˌnɪzəm) *or* **Italicism** (ɪˈtælɪˌsɪzəm) *n* **1** an Italian custom or style. **2** Italian quality or life, or the cult of either.

Italianize *or* **Italianise** (ɪˈtæljəˌnaɪz) *vb* to make or become Italian or like an Italian person or thing. ▸ **Iˌtalianiˈzation** *or* **Iˌtalianiˈsation** *n*

Italian sixth *n* (in musical harmony) an augmented sixth chord characterized by having a major third and an augmented sixth above the root.

Italian Somaliland *n* a former Italian colony in E Africa, united with British Somaliland in 1960 to form the independent republic of Somalia.

Italian sonnet *n* another term for **Petrarchan sonnet.**

Italian vermouth *n* sweet vermouth.

italic (ɪˈtælɪk) *adj* **1** Also: **Italian.** of, relating to, or denoting a style of handwriting with the letters slanting to the right. ◆ *n* **2** a style of printing type modelled on this, chiefly used to indicate emphasis, a foreign word, etc. Compare **roman**[1]. **3** (*often pl*) italic type or print. **[C16** (after an edition of Virgil (1501) printed in Venice and dedicated to Italy): from Latin *Italicus* of Italy, from Greek *Italikos***]**

Italic (ɪˈtælɪk) *n* **1** a branch of the Indo-European family of languages that includes many of the ancient languages of Italy, such as Venetic and the Osco-Umbrian group, Latin, which displaced them, and the Romance languages. ◆ *adj* **2** denoting, relating to, or belonging to this group of languages, esp. the extinct ones.

italicize *or* **italicise** (ɪˈtælɪˌsaɪz) *vb* **1** to print (textual matter) in italic type. **2** (*tr*) to underline (letters, words, etc.) with a single line to indicate italics. ▸ **iˌtaliciˈzation** *or* **iˌtaliciˈsation** *n*

Italo- (ɪˈtæləʊ-) *combining form.* indicating Italy or Italian: *Italophobia; Italo-German.*

Italy (ˈɪtəlɪ) *n* a republic in S Europe, occupying a peninsula in the Mediterranean between the Tyrrhenian and the Adriatic Seas, with the islands of Sardinia and Sicily to the west: first united under the Romans but became fragmented into numerous political units in the Middle Ages; united kingdom proclaimed in 1861; under the dictatorship of Mussolini (1922–43); became a republic in 1946; a member of the European Union. It is generally mountainous, with the Alps in the north and the Apennines running the length of the peninsula. Official language: Italian. Religion: Roman Catholic majority. Currency: euro and lira. Capital: Rome. Pop.: 57 650 000 (1998 est.). Area: 301 247 sq. km (116 312 sq. miles). Italian name: **Italia.**

Itar Tass (ɪ'tɑː tæs) *n* a news agency serving Russia, eastern Europe, and central Asia, created in 1992 to replace the former Soviet news agency Tass. [Information Telegraph Agency of Russia, Telegraph Agency of Sovereign States]

ITC (in Britain) *abbrev. for* Independent Television Commission.

itch (ɪtʃ) *n* **1** an irritation or tickling sensation of the skin causing a desire to scratch. **2** a restless desire. **3** any skin disorder, such as scabies, characterized by intense itching. ◆ *vb* **4** (*intr*) to feel or produce an irritating or tickling sensation. **5** (*intr*) to have a restless desire (to do something). **6** *Not standard.* to scratch (the skin). **7** **itching palm.** a grasping nature; avarice. **8** **have itchy feet.** to be restless; have a desire to travel. [Old English *gīccean* to itch, of Germanic origin] ▸ **'itchy** *adj* ▸ **'itchiness** *n*

itch mite *n* any mite of the family *Sarcoptidae,* all of which are skin parasites, esp. *Sarcoptes scabei,* which causes scabies.

-ite[1] *suffix forming nouns.* **1** a native or inhabitant of: *Israelite.* **2** a follower or advocate of; a member or supporter of a group: *Luddite; labourite.* **3** (in biology) indicating a division of a body or organ: *somite.* **4** indicating a mineral or rock: *nephrite; peridotite.* **5** indicating a commercial product: *vulcanite.* [via Latin *-ita* from Greek *-itēs* or directly from Greek]

-ite[2] *suffix forming nouns.* indicating a salt or ester of an acid having a name ending in *-ous: a nitrite is a salt of nitrous acid.* [from French, arbitrary alteration of -ATE[1]]

item *n* ('aɪtəm). **1** a thing or unit, esp. included in a list or collection. **2** *Bookkeeping.* an entry in an account. **3** a piece of information, detail, or note: *a news item.* **4** *Informal.* two people having a romantic or sexual relationship. ◆ *vb* ('aɪtəm). **5** (*tr*) an archaic word for **itemize.** ◆ *adv* ('aɪtɛm). **6** likewise; also. [C14 (adv) from Latin: in like manner]

itemize *or* **itemise** ('aɪtəˌmaɪz) *vb* (*tr*) to put on a list or make a list of. ▸ **ˌitemi'zation** *or* **ˌitemi'sation** *n*

item veto *n* (in the U.S.) the power of a state governor to veto items in bills without vetoing the entire measure.

Iténez (i'teneθ) *n* the Spanish name for the **Guaporé.**

iterate ('ɪtəˌreɪt) *vb* (*tr*) to say or do again; repeat. [C16: from Latin *iterāre,* from *iterum* again] ▸ **'iterant** *adj* ▸ **ˌiter'ation** *or* **'iterance** *n*

iterative ('ɪtərətɪv) *adj* **1** repetitious or frequent. **2** *Maths, logic.* another word for **recursive.** **3** *Grammar.* another word for **frequentative.** ▸ **'iteratively** *adv* ▸ **'iterativeness** *n*

Ithaca ('ɪθəkə) *n* a Greek island in the Ionian Sea, the smallest of the Ionian Islands: regarded as the home of Homer's Odysseus. Area: 93 sq. km (36 sq. miles). Modern Greek name: **Itháki** (i'θaki). ▸ **'Ithacan** *n, adj*

ither ('ɪðər) *determiner* a Scot. word for **other.**

Ithunn ('iːðʊn) *n* a variant of **Idun.**

ithyphallic (ˌɪθɪ'fælɪk) *adj* **1** *Prosody.* (in classical verse) of or relating to the usual metre in hymns to Bacchus. **2** of or relating to the phallus carried in the ancient festivals of Bacchus. **3** (of sculpture and graphic art) having or showing an erect penis. ◆ *n* **4** *Prosody.* a poem in ithyphallic metre. [C17: from Late Latin, from Greek *ithuphallikos,* from *ithuphallos* erect phallus, from *ithus* straight + *phallos* PHALLUS]

itinerancy (ɪ'tɪnərənsɪ, aɪ-) *or* **itineracy** *n* **1** the act of itinerating. **2** *Chiefly Methodist Church.* the system of appointing a minister to a circuit of churches or chapels. **3** itinerants collectively.

itinerant (ɪ'tɪnərənt, aɪ-) *adj* **1** itinerating. **2** working for a short time in various places, esp. as a casual labourer. ◆ *n* **3** an itinerant worker or other person. [C16: from Late Latin *itinerārī* to travel, from *iter* a journey] ▸ **i'tinerantly** *adv*

itinerary (aɪ'tɪnərərɪ, ɪ-) *n, pl* **-aries.** **1** a plan or line of travel; route. **2** a record of a journey. **3** a guidebook for travellers. ◆ *adj* **4** of or relating to travel or routes of travel. **5** a less common word for **itinerant.**

itinerate (aɪ'tɪnəˌreɪt, ɪ-) *vb* (*intr*) to travel from place to place. ▸ **iˌtiner'ation** *n*

-itious *suffix forming adjectives.* having the nature of; characterized by: *nutritious; suppositious.* [from Latin *-icius, -itious*]

-itis *suffix forming nouns.* **1** indicating inflammation of a specified part: *tonsillitis.* **2** *Informal.* indicating a preoccupation with or imaginary condition of illness caused by: *computeritis; telephonitis.* [New Latin, from Greek, feminine of *-itēs* belonging to; see -ITE[1]]

it'll ('ɪtᵊl) *contraction of* it will *or* it shall.

Ito ('iːtəʊ) *n* Prince **Hirobumi** (ˌhɪərə'buːmɪ). 1841–1909, Japanese statesman; premier (1884–88; 1892–96; 1898; 1900–01). He led the movement to modernize Japan and helped to draft the Meiji constitution (1889); assassinated.

ITO *abbrev. for* International Trade Organization.

-itol *suffix forming nouns.* indicating that certain chemical compounds are polyhydric alcohols: *inisitol; sorbitol.* [from -ITE[2] + -OL[1]]

its (ɪts) *determiner* **a** of, belonging to, or associated in some way with it: *its left rear wheel.* **b** (*as pronoun*): *each town claims its is the best.*

it's (ɪts) *contraction of* it is *or* it has.

itself (ɪt'sɛlf) *pron* **1a** the reflexive form of **it.** **1b** (intensifier)*: even the money itself won't convince me.* **2** (*preceded by a copula*) its normal or usual self: *my cat isn't itself today.*

itsy-bitsy ('ɪtsɪ'bɪtsɪ) *or* **itty-bitty** ('ɪtɪ'bɪtɪ) *adj Informal.* very small; tiny. [C20: baby talk alteration of *little bit*]

ITU *abbrev. for:* **1** Intensive Therapy Unit. **2** International Telecommunications Union.

Itúrbide (*Spanish* 'iβtureðe) *n* **Agustín de** (aɣus'tin de). 1783–1824, Mexican nationalist and emperor (1822–23). He was forced to abdicate and later executed.

ITV (in Britain) *abbrev. for* Independent Television.

-ity *suffix forming nouns.* indicating state or condition: *technicality.* [from Old French *-ite,* from Latin *-itās*]

i-type semiconductor *n* another name for **intrinsic semiconductor.**

IU *abbrev. for:* **1** immunizing unit. **2** international unit.

IU(C)D *abbrev. for* intrauterine (contraceptive) device.

Iulus (aɪ'juːləs) *n* **1** another name for **Ascanius.** **2** the son of Ascanius, founder of the Julian gens or clan.

-ium *or sometimes* **-um** *suffix forming nouns.* **1** indicating a metallic element: *platinum; barium.* **2** (in chemistry) indicating groups forming positive ions: *ammonium chloride; hydroxonium ion.* **3** indicating a biological structure: *syncytium.* [New Latin, from Latin, from Greek *-ion,* diminutive suffix]

i.v. *abbrev. for:* **1** initial velocity. **2** Also: **IV.** intravenous(ly).

Ivan III ('aɪvən) *n* known as *Ivan the Great.* 1440–1505, grand duke of Muscovy (1462–1505). He expanded Muscovy, defeated the Tatars (1480), and assumed the title of Ruler of all Russia (1472).

Ivan IV *n* known as *Ivan the Terrible.* 1530–84, grand duke of Muscovy (1533–47) and first tsar of Russia (1547–84). He conquered Kazan (1552), Astrakhan (1556), and Siberia (1581), but was defeated by Poland in the Livonian War (1558–82) after which his rule became increasingly oppressive.

Ivanovo (*Russian* ɪ'vanəvə) *n* a city in W central Russia, on the Uvod River: textile centre. Pop.: 474 000 (1995 est.). Former name (1871–1932): **Ivanovo-Voznesensk** (-vəznɪ'sjensk).

IVB *abbrev. for* invalidity benefit.

I've (aɪv) *contraction of* I have.

-ive *suffix.* **1** (*forming adjectives*) indicating a tendency, inclination, character, or quality: *divisive; prohibitive; festive; massive.* **2** (*forming nouns of adjectival origin*): *detective; expletive.* [from Latin *-īvus*]

ivermectin (ˌaɪvə'mɛktɪn) *n* a drug that kills parasitic nematode worms, mites, and insects. It is used to treat a variety of parasitic infections in domestic animals and has shown encouraging results in preliminary trials for treating onchocerciasis in humans.

Ives (aɪvz) *n* **1** **Charles Edward.** 1874–1954, U.S. composer, noted for his innovative use of polytonality, polyrhythms, and quarter tones. His works include *Second Piano Sonata: Concord* (1915), five symphonies, chamber music, and songs. **2** **Frederick Eugene.** 1856–1937, U.S. inventor of halftone photography.

IVF *abbrev. for* in vitro fertilization.

ivied ('aɪvɪd) *adj* covered with ivy.

Iviza (*Spanish* i'βiθa) *n* a variant spelling of **Ibiza.**

Ivorian (aɪ'vɔːrɪən) *n* **1** a native or inhabitant of the Côte d'Ivoire. ◆ *adj* **2** of or relating to the Côte d'Ivoire or its inhabitants.

ivories ('aɪvərɪz, -vrɪz) *pl n Slang.* **1** the keys of a piano. **2** another word for **teeth.** **3** another word for **dice.**

ivory ('aɪvərɪ, -vrɪ) *n, pl* **-ries.** **1a** a hard smooth creamy white variety of dentine that makes up a major part of the tusks of elephants, walruses, and similar animals. **1b** (*as modifier*): *ivory ornaments.* **2** a tusk made of ivory. **3a** a yellowish-white colour; cream. **3b** (*as adj*): *ivory shoes.* **4** a substance resembling elephant tusk. **5** an ornament, etc., made of ivory. **6** **black ivory.** *Obsolete.* Black slaves collectively. ◆ See also **ivories.** [C13: from Old French *ivurie,* from Latin *evoreus* made of ivory, from *ebur* ivory; related to Greek *elephas* ivory, ELEPHANT] ▸ **'ivory-ˌlike** *adj*

Ivory ('aɪvərɪ) *n* **James.** born 1928, U.S. film director. With the producer Ismael Merchant, his films include *Shakespeare Wallah* (1964), *Heat and Dust* (1983), *A Room With a View* (1986), and *A Soldier's Daughter Never Cries* (1998).

ivory black *n* a black pigment obtained by grinding charred scraps of ivory in oil.

Ivory Coast *n* **the.** the former name (until 1986) of **Côte d'Ivoire.**

ivory gull *n* a white gull, *Pagophila* (or *Larus*) *eburneus,* mostly confined to arctic regions.

ivory nut *n* **1** the seed of the ivory palm, which contains an ivory-like substance used to make buttons, etc. **2** any similar seed from other palms. ◆ Also called: **vegetable ivory.**

ivory palm *n* a low-growing South American palm tree, *Phytelephas macrocarpa,* that yields the ivory nut.

ivory tower ('taʊə) *n* **a** seclusion or remoteness of attitude regarding real problems, everyday life, etc. **b** (*as modifier*): *ivory-tower aestheticism.* ▸ **ˌivory-'towered** *adj*

ivorywood ('aɪvərɪˌwʊd) *n* **1** the yellowish-white wood of an Australian tree, *Siphonodon australe,* used for engraving, inlaying, and turnery. **2** the tree itself: family *Siphonodontaceae.*

IVR *abbrev. for* International Vehicle Registration.

ivy ('aɪvɪ) *n, pl* **ivies.** **1** any woody climbing or trailing araliaceous plant of the Old World genus *Hedera,* esp. *H. helix,* having lobed evergreen leaves and black berry-like fruits. **2** any of various other climbing or creeping plants, such as Boston ivy, poison ivy, and ground ivy. [Old English *īfig;* related to Old High German *ebah,* perhaps to Greek *iphuon* a plant] ▸ **'ivy-ˌlike** *adj*

Ivy League *n U.S.* **a the.** a group of eight universities (Brown, Columbia, Cornell, Dartmouth College, Harvard, Princeton, the University of Pennsylvania, and Yale) that have similar academic and social prestige in the U.S. to Oxford and Cambridge in Britain. **b** (*as modifier*): *an Ivy-League education.*

iwi ('iːwɪ) *n N.Z.* a Maori tribe. [Maori]

iwis *or* **ywis** (ɪ'wɪs) *adv* an archaic word for **certainly.** [C12: from Old English *gewiss* certain]

Iwo ('iːwəʊ) *n* a city in SW Nigeria. Pop.: 362 000 (1996 est.).

Iwo Jima ('dʒiːmə) *n* an island in the W Pacific, about 1100 km (700 miles) south of Japan: one of the Volcano Islands; scene of prolonged fighting between U.S. and Japanese forces until taken by the U.S. in 1945; returned to Japan in 1968. Area: 20 sq. km (8 sq. miles).

IWW *abbrev. for* Industrial Workers of the World.

ixia ('ɪksɪə) *n* any plant of the iridaceous genus *Ixia,* of southern Africa, having showy ornamental funnel-shaped flowers. [C18: New Latin from Greek *ixos* mistletoe, birdlime prepared from mistletoe berries]

Ixion (ɪk'saɪən) *n Greek myth.* a Thessalian king punished by Zeus for his love of Hera by being bound to a perpetually revolving wheel. ► **Ixionian** (ˌɪksɪ'əʊnɪən) *adj*

Ixtaccihuatl *or* **Iztaccihuatl** (ˌiːstək'siːwətᵊl) *n* a dormant volcano in central Mexico, southeast of Mexico City. Height: (central peak) 5286 m (17 342 ft.).

ixtle ('ɪkstlɪ, 'ɪst-) *n* a variant of **istle.**

Iyar *or* **Iyyar** (i'jar) *n* (in the Jewish calendar) the second month of the year according to biblical reckoning and the eighth month of the civil year, usually falling within April and May. [from Hebrew]

Iyeyasu *or* **Ieyasu** (ˌiːjeɪ'jɑːsuː) *n* **Tokugawa** (ˌtɒkuː'gɑːwə). 1542–1616, Japanese general and statesman; founder of the Tokugawa shogunate (1603–1867).

izard ('ɪzəd) *n* (esp. in the Pyrenees) another name for **chamois.**

-ize *or* **-ise** *suffix forming verbs.* **1** to cause to become, resemble, or agree with: *legalize.* **2** to become; change into: *crystallize.* **3** to affect in a specified way; subject to: *hypnotize.* **4** to act according to some practice, principle, policy, etc.: *economize.* [from Old French *-iser,* from Late Latin *-izāre,* from Greek *-izein*]

USAGE In Britain and the U.S. *-ize* is the preferred ending for many verbs, but *-ise* is equally acceptable in British English. Certain words (chiefly those not formed by adding the suffix to an existing word) are, however, always spelt with *-ise* in both Britain and the U.S.: *advertise, revise.*

Izetbegović (ˌɪzət'bɛgəvɪtʃ) *n* **Alija** ('æljə). born 1925, Bosnia and Herzegovinian politician: he led the country to independence in 1992, when he became president.

Izhevsk (*Russian* i'ʒɛfsk) *n* an industrial city in central Russia, capital of the Udmurt Republic. Pop.: 654 000 (1995 est.).

Izmir ('ɪzmɪə) *n* a port in W Turkey, on the **Gulf of Izmir:** the third largest city in the country; university (1955). Pop.: 2 017 699 (1995 est.). Former name: **Smyrna.**

Izmit ('ɪzmɪt) *n* a town in NW Turkey, on the **Gulf of Izmit.** Pop.: 275 800 (1994 est.).

Iznik (ɪz'nɪk) *n* the modern Turkish name of **Nicaea.**

Iztaccihuatl (ˌiːstək'siːwətᵊl) *n* a variant spelling of **Ixtaccihuatl.**

izzard ('ɪzəd) *n Archaic.* the letter *Z.* [C18: from earlier *ezed,* probably from Old French *et zède,* literally: and zed]

Jj

j *or* **J** (dʒeɪ) *n, pl* **j's, J's,** *or* **Js. 1** the tenth letter and seventh consonant of the modern English alphabet. **2** a speech sound represented by this letter, in English usually a voiced palato-alveolar affricate, as in *jam.*

j *symbol for:* **1** *Maths.* the unit vector along the *y*-axis. **2** the imaginary number $\sqrt{-1}$.

J *symbol for:* **1** *Cards.* jack. **2** joule(s). **3** current density. ◆ **4** *international car registration for* Japan.

J. *abbrev. for:* **1** Journal. **2** (*pl* **JJ.**) Judge. **3** (*pl* **JJ.**) Justice.

JA *abbrev. for:* **1** Also: **J/A.** *Banking.* joint account. **2** Judge Advocate. ◆ **3** *international car registration for* Jamaica.

Ja. *abbrev. for* January.

jaap (jɑːp) *n S. African offensive.* a simpleton or country bumpkin. [from Afrikaans]

jab (dʒæb) *vb* **jabs, jabbing, jabbed. 1** to poke or thrust sharply. **2** to strike with a quick short blow or blows. ◆ *n* **3** a sharp poke or stab. **4** a quick short blow, esp. (in boxing) a straight punch with the leading hand. **5** *Informal.* an injection: *polio jabs.* [C19: originally Scottish variant of JOB] ▸ **ˈjabbingly** *adv*

Jabalpur *or* **Jubbulpore** (ˌdʒʌbəlˈpʊə) *n* a city in central India, in central Madhya Pradesh. Pop.: 741 927 (1991).

jabber (ˈdʒæbə) *vb* **1** to speak or say rapidly, incoherently, and without making sense; chatter. ◆ *n* **2** such talk. [C15: of imitative origin; compare GIBBER[1]] ▸ **ˈjabberer** *n*

jabberwocky (ˈdʒæbəˌwɒkɪ) *n, pl* **-wockies.** nonsense verse. [C19: coined by Lewis Carroll as the title of a poem in *Through the Looking Glass* (1871)]

Jabir ibn Hayyan (ˈdʒɑːbɪə ˌiːbᵊn hɑːˈjɑːn) *n* ?721–?815. Arab alchemist, whose many works enjoyed enormous esteem among later alchemists, such as Geber.

jabiru (ˈdʒæbɪˌruː) *n* **1** a large white tropical American stork, *Jabiru mycteria,* with a dark naked head and a dark bill. **2** Also called: **black-necked stork, policeman bird.** a large Australian stork, *Xenorhyncus asiaticus,* having a white plumage, dark green back and tail, and red legs. **3** another name for **saddlebill. 4** (*not in ornithological usage*) another name for **wood ibis.** [C18: via Portuguese from Tupi-Guarani]

jaborandi (ˌdʒæbəˈrændɪ) *n* **1** any of several tropical American rutaceous shrubs of the genus *Pilocarpus,* esp. *P. jaborandi.* **2** the dried leaves of any of these plants, used to induce sweating. [C19: from Portuguese, from Tupi-Guarani *yaborandí*]

jabot (ˈʒæbəʊ) *n* a frill or ruffle on the breast or throat of a garment, originally to hide the closure of a shirt. [C19: from French: bird's crop, jabot; compare Old French *gave* throat]

jacamar (ˈdʒækəˌmɑː) *n* any bird of the tropical American family *Galbulidae,* having an iridescent plumage and feeding on insects: order *Piciformes* (woodpeckers, etc.). [C19: from French, from Tupi *jacamá-ciri*]

jaçana (ˌʒɑːsəˈnɑː, ˌdʒæ-) *n* any bird of the family *Jacanidae,* of tropical and subtropical marshy regions, having long legs and very long toes that enable walking on floating plants: order *Charadriiformes.* Also called: **lily-trotter.** [C18: from Portuguese *jaçanã,* from Tupi-Guarani *jasaná*]

jacaranda (ˌdʒækəˈrændə) *n* **1** any bignoniaceous tree of the tropical American genus *Jacaranda,* having fernlike leaves and pale purple flowers and widely cultivated in temperate areas of Australia. **2** the fragrant ornamental wood of any of these trees. **3** any of several related or similar trees or their wood. [C18: from Portuguese, from Tupi-Guarani *yacarandá*]

jacaré (ˈdʒækəreɪ) *n* another name for **cayman.** [C18: from Portuguese, from Tupi *jacaré*]

jacinth (ˈdʒæsɪnθ) *n* another name for **hyacinth** (sense 4). [C13: from Medieval Latin *jacinthus,* from Latin *hyacinthus* plant, precious stone; see HYACINTH]

jack[1] (dʒæk) *n* **1** a man or fellow. **2** a sailor. **3** the male of certain animals, esp. of the ass or donkey. **4** a mechanical or hydraulic device for exerting a large force, esp. to raise a heavy weight such as a motor vehicle. **5** any of several mechanical devices that replace manpower, such as a contrivance for rotating meat on a spit. **6** one of four playing cards in a pack, one for each suit, bearing the picture of a young prince; knave. **7** *Bowls.* a small usually white bowl at which the players aim with their own bowls. **8** *Electrical engineering.* a female socket with two or more terminals designed to receive a male plug (**jack plug**) that either makes or breaks the circuit or circuits. **9** a flag, esp. a small flag flown at the bow of a ship indicating the ship's nationality. Compare **Union Jack. 10** *Nautical.* either of a pair of crosstrees at the head of a topgallant mast used as standoffs for the royal shrouds. **11** a part of the action of a harpsichord, consisting of a fork-shaped device on the end of a pivoted lever on which a plectrum is mounted. **12** any of various tropical and subtropical carangid fishes, esp. those of the genus *Caranx,* such as *C. hippos* (**crevalle jack**). **13** Also called: **jackstone.** one of the pieces used in the game of jacks. **14** short for **applejack, bootjack, jackass, jackfish, jack rabbit,** and **lumberjack. 15** *U.S.* a slang word for **money. 16 every man jack.** everyone without exception. ◆ *adj* **17 jack of.** *Austral. slang.* tired or fed up with (something). ◆ *vb* (*tr*) **18** to lift or push (an object) with a jack. **19** Also: **jacklight.** *U.S. and Canadian.* to hunt (fish or game) by seeking them out or dazzling them with a flashlight. ◆ See also **jack in, jacks, jack up.** [C16 *jakke,* variant of *Jankin,* diminutive of *John*]

jack[2] *or* **jak** (dʒæk) *n* short for **jackfruit** *or* **jakfruit.** [C17: from Portuguese *jaca;* see JACKFRUIT]

jack[3] (dʒæk) *n* **1** a short sleeveless coat of armour of the Middle Ages, consisting usually of a canvas base with metal plates. **2** *Archaic.* a drinking vessel, often of leather. [C14: from Old French *jaque,* of uncertain origin]

Jack (dʒæk) *n* **I'm all right, Jack.** *Brit. informal.* **a** a remark indicating smug and complacent selfishness. **b** (*as modifier*)*: an "I'm all right, Jack" attitude.*

jackal (ˈdʒækɔːl) *n* **1** any of several African or S Asian canine mammals of the genus *Canis,* closely related to the dog, having long legs and pointed ears and muzzle: predators and carrion-eaters. **2** a person who does menial tasks for another. **3** a villain, esp. a swindler. [C17: from Turkish *chakāl,* from Persian *shagāl,* from Sanskrit *srgāla*]

jackanapes (ˈdʒækəˌneɪps) *n* **1** a conceited impertinent person. **2** a mischievous child. **3** *Archaic.* a monkey. [C16: variant of *Jakken-apes,* literally: Jack of the ape, nickname of William de la Pole (1396–1450), first Duke of Suffolk, whose badge showed an ape's ball and chain]

jackass (ˈdʒækˌæs) *n* **1** a male donkey. **2** a stupid person; fool. **3 laughing jackass.** another name for **kookaburra.** [C18: from JACK[1] (male) + ASS[1]]

jack bean *n* a tropical American leguminous plant, *Canavalia ensiformis,* that has clusters of purple flowers and long pods and is grown in the southern U.S. for forage.

jackboot (ˈdʒækˌbuːt) *n* **1** an all-leather military boot, extending up to or above the knee. **2a** arbitrary, cruel, and authoritarian rule or behaviour. **2b** (*as modifier*)*: jackboot tactics.* ▸ **ˈjackˌbooted** *adj*

jack-by-the-hedge *n* another name for **garlic mustard.**

jackdaw (ˈdʒækˌdɔː) *n* a large common Eurasian passerine bird, *Corvus monedula,* in which the plumage is black and dark grey: noted for its thieving habits: family *Corvidae* (crows). [C16: from JACK[1] + DAW]

Jackeen (dʒæˈkiːn) *n Irish.* a slick self-assertive lower-class Dubliner. [C19: from proper name *Jack* + *-een,* Irish diminutive suffix, from Irish Gaelic *-ín*]

jackeroo *or* **jackaroo** (ˌdʒækəˈruː) *n, pl* **-roos.** *Austral. informal.* a young male management trainee on a sheep or cattle station. [C19: from JACK[1] + (KANG)AROO]

jacket (ˈdʒækɪt) *n* **1** a short coat, esp. one that is hip-length and has a front opening and sleeves. **2** something that resembles this or is designed to be worn around the upper part of the body: *a life jacket.* **3** any exterior covering or casing, such as the insulating cover of a boiler. **4** the part of the cylinder block of an internal-combustion engine that encloses the coolant. **5** See **dust jacket. 6a** the skin of a baked potato. **6b** (*as modifier*)*: jacket potatoes.* **7** a metal casing used in certain types of ammunition. **8** *U.S.* a cover to protect a gramophone record. Brit. name: **sleeve. 9** *Chiefly U.S.* a folder or envelope to hold documents. ◆ *vb* **10** (*tr*) to put a jacket on (someone or something). [C15: from Old French *jaquet* short jacket, from *jacque* peasant, from proper name *Jacques* James] ▸ **ˈjacketed** *adj* ▸ **ˈjacket-ˌlike** *adj*

jackfish (ˈdʒækˌfɪʃ) *n, pl* **-fish** *or* **-fishes.** a popular name for **pike** (the fish), esp. when small.

Jack Frost *n* a personification of frost or winter.

jackfruit *or* **jakfruit** (ˈdʒækˌfruːt) *n* **1** a tropical Asian moraceous tree, *Artocarpus heterophyllus.* **2** the edible fruit of this tree, which resembles breadfruit and can weigh up to 27 kilograms (60 pounds). ◆ Sometimes shortened to **jack** *or* **jak.** [C19: from Portuguese *jaca,* from Malayalam *cakka*]

Jack-go-to-bed-at-noon *n* another name for **goatsbeard** (sense 1).

jackhammer (ˈdʒækˌhæmə) *n* a hand-held hammer drill, driven by compressed air, for drilling rocks, etc.

Jackie *or* **Jacky** (ˈdʒækɪ) *n, pl* **Jackies.** *Austral. offensive slang.* **1** a native Australian. **2** native Australians collectively. **3 sit up like Jackie.** to sit bolt upright, esp. cheekily.

jack in *vb* (*tr, adv*) *Slang.* to abandon or leave (an attempt or enterprise).

jack-in-office *n* a self-important petty official.

jack-in-the-box *n, pl* **jack-in-the-boxes** *or* **jacks-in-the-box.** a toy consisting of a figure on a compressed spring in a box, which springs out when the lid is opened.

jack-in-the-green *n* (in England, formerly) a man who wore or supported a leaf-covered wooden framework while dancing in May-Day celebrations.

jack-in-the-pulpit *n* **1** an E North American aroid plant, *Arisaema triphyllum,* having a leaflike spathe partly arched over a clublike spadix. **2** *Brit.* another name for **cuckoopint.**

Jack Ketch (kɛtʃ) *n Brit. archaic.* a hangman. [C18: after *John Ketch* (died 1686), public executioner in England]

jackknife (ˈdʒækˌnaɪf) *n, pl* **-knives. 1** a knife with the blade pivoted to fold into a recess in the handle. **2** a former name for a type of dive in which the diver bends at the waist in midair, with his legs straight and his hands touching his feet, finally straightening out and entering the water headfirst: forward pike dive. ◆ *vb* (*intr*) **3** (of an articulated lorry) to go out of control in such a way that the trailer swings round at an angle to the cab. **4** to make a jackknife dive.

jack ladder *n* another name for **Jacob's ladder** (sense 2).

Jacklin ('dʒæklɪn) *n* **Tony,** full name *Anthony Jacklin.* Born 1944. English golfer: won the British Open Championship (1969) and the U.S. Open Championship (1970).

jack of all trades *n, pl* **jacks of all trades.** a person who undertakes many different kinds of work.

jack-o'-lantern *n* **1** a lantern made from a hollowed pumpkin, which has holes cut in it to represent a human face. **2** a will-o'-the-wisp or similar phenomenon.

jack pine *n* a coniferous tree, *Pinus banksiana,* of North America, having paired needle-like leaves and small cones that remain on the branches for many years: family *Pinaceae.*

jack plane *n* a carpenter's plane, usually with a wooden body, used for rough planing of timber.

jackpot ('dʒæk,pɒt) *n* **1** any large prize, kitty, or accumulated stake that may be won in gambling, such as a pool in poker that accumulates until the betting is opened with a pair of jacks or higher. **2 hit the jackpot. 2a** to win a jackpot. **2b** *Informal.* to achieve great success, esp. through luck. **[C20:** probably from JACK[1] (playing card) + POT[1]**]**

jack rabbit *n* any of various W North American hares, such as *Lepus townsendi* (**white-tailed jack rabbit**), having long hind legs and large ears. **[C19:** shortened from *jackass-rabbit,* referring to its long ears**]**

jack rafter *n* a short rafter used in a hip roof.

Jack Robinson *n* **before you could** (*or* **can**) **say Jack Robinson.** extremely quickly or suddenly.

Jack Russell *n* a small short-legged terrier having a white coat with tan, black, or lemon markings: there are rough- and smooth-haired varieties. Also called: **Jack Russell terrier. [**named after John *Russell* (1795–1883), English clergyman who developed the breed**]**

jacks (dʒæks) *n* (*functioning as sing*) a game in which bone, metal, or plastic pieces (**jackstones**) are thrown and then picked up in various groups between bounces or throws of a small ball. Sometimes called: **knucklebones. [C19:** shortened from *jackstones,* variant of *checkstones* pebbles**]**

jackscrew ('dʒæk,skruː) *n* another name for **screw jack.**

jackshaft ('dʒæk,ʃɑːft) *n* a short length of shafting that transmits power from an engine or motor to a machine.

jacksie *or* **jacksy** ('dʒæksɪ) *n Brit. slang.* the buttocks or anus. Also called **jaxie, jaxy. [C19:** probably from JACK[1]**]**

jacksmelt ('dʒæk,smɛlt) *n, pl* **-smelts** *or* **-smelt.** a marine teleost food fish, *Atherinopsis californiensis,* of American coastal waters of the North Pacific: family *Atherinidae* (silversides).

jacksnipe ('dʒæk,snaɪp) *n, pl* **-snipe** *or* **-snipes. 1** a small Eurasian short-billed snipe, *Lymnocryptes minima.* **2** any of various similar birds, such as the pectoral sandpiper.

Jackson[1] ('dʒæksən) *n* a city in and state capital of Mississippi, on the Pearl River. Pop.: 192 923 (1996 est.).

Jackson[2] ('dʒæksən) *n* **1 Andrew.** 1767–1845, U.S. statesman, general, and lawyer; seventh president of the U.S. (1829–37). He became a national hero after successfully defending New Orleans from the British (1815). During his administration the spoils system was introduced and the national debt was fully paid off. **2 Colin (Ray).** born 1967, British athlete, broke world record for 110 m hurdles in 1993 (12.91 seconds) and for the 60 m hurdles in 1994 (7.3 seconds). **3 Glenda.** born 1936, British stage, film, and television actress, and Labour politician. Her films include *Women in Love* (1969) for which she won an Oscar, *The Music Lovers* (1970), *Sunday Bloody Sunday* (1971), and *Turtle Diary* (1985); became a member of parliament in 1992. **4 Jesse (Louis).** born 1941, U.S. Democrat politician and clergyman; Black campaigner for minority rights. **5 Michael (Joe).** born 1958, U.S. pop singer, lead vocalist with the Jacksons (originally the Jackson 5) (1969–86). His solo albums include *Thriller* (1982) and *Bad* (1989). **6 Thomas Jonathan,** known as *Stonewall Jackson.* 1824–63, Confederate general in the American Civil War, noted particularly for his command at the first Battle of Bull Run (1861). ► **Jacksonian** (dʒæk'səʊnɪən) *adj, n*

Jacksonville ('dʒæksən,vɪl) *n* a port in NE Florida: the leading commercial centre of the southeast. Pop.: 679 792 (1996 est.).

jackstay ('dʒæk,steɪ) *n Nautical.* **1** a metal rod, wire rope, or wooden batten to which an edge of a sail is fastened along a yard. **2** a support for the parrel of a yard.

jackstraws ('dʒæk,strɔːz) *n* (*functioning as sing*) another name for **spillikins.**

Jack Tar *n Now chiefly literary.* a sailor.

Jack-the-lad *n Slang.* a young man who is regarded as a brash, loud show-off.

Jack-the-rags *n South Wales dialect.* a rag-and-bone man.

Jack the Ripper *n* an unidentified murderer who killed at least seven prostitutes in London's East End between August and November 1888.

jack towel *n* another name for **roller towel.**

jack up *vb* (*adv*) **1** (*tr*) to increase (prices, salaries, etc.). **2** (*tr*) to raise an object, such as a car, with or as with a jack. **3** (*intr*) *Slang.* to inject oneself with a drug, usually heroin. **4** (*intr*) *Austral. informal.* to refuse to comply; rebel, esp. collectively. **5** *N.Z. informal.* to initiate, organize, or procure.

Jacky ('dʒækɪ) *n* See **Jackie.**

Jacky Howe *n Austral. informal.* (formerly) a sleeveless flannel shirt worn by shearers. **[C19:** named after *Jacky Howe* (1855–1922) who was the world champion shearer in 1892**]**

Jacob ('dʒeɪkəb) *n* **1** *Old Testament.* the son of Isaac, twin brother of Esau, and father of the twelve patriarchs of Israel. **2** Also called: **Jacob sheep.** any of an ancient breed of sheep having a fleece with dark brown patches and two or four horns. **[**sense 2 in allusion to Genesis 30:40**]**

Jacobean (,dʒækə'bɪən) *adj* **1** *History.* characteristic of or relating to James I of England or to the period of his rule (1603–25). **2** of or relating to the style of furniture current at this time, characterized by the use of dark brown carved oak. **3** denoting, relating to, or having the style of architecture used in England during this period, characterized by a combination of late Gothic and Palladian motifs. ◆ *n* **4** any writer or other person who lived in the reign of James I. **[C18:** from New Latin *jacōbaeus,* from *Jacōbus* James**]**

Jacobi *n* **1** (dʒæ'kəʊbɪ). **Derek (George).** born 1938, British actor. **2** (*German* ja'koːbi). **Karl Gustav Jacob** (karl 'gʊstaf 'jaːkɔp). 1804–51, German mathematician. Independently of N. H. Abel, he discovered elliptic functions (1829). He also made important contributions to the study of determinants and differential equations.

Jacobian (dʒə'kəʊbɪən) *or* **Jacobian determinant** *n Maths.* a function from *n* equations in *n* variables whose value at any point is the *n x n* determinant of the partial derivatives of those equations evaluated at that point. **[**named after K. G. J. JACOBI**]**

Jacobin ('dʒækəbɪn) *n* **1** a member of the most radical club founded during the French Revolution, which overthrew the Girondists in 1793 and, led by Robespierre, instituted the Reign of Terror. **2** a leftist or extreme political radical. **3** a French Dominican friar. **4** (*sometimes not cap.*) a variety of fancy pigeon with a hood of feathers swept up over and around the head. ◆ *adj* **5** of, characteristic of, or relating to the Jacobins or their policies. **[C14:** from Old French, from Medieval Latin *Jacōbīnus,* from Late Latin *Jacōbus* James; applied to the Dominicans, from the proximity of the church of *St Jacques* (St James) to their first convent in Paris; the political club originally met in the convent in 1789**]** ► **,Jaco'binic** *or* **,Jaco'binical** *adj* ► **,Jaco'binically** *adv* ► **'Jacobinism** *n*

Jacobite ('dʒækə,baɪt) *n* **1** *British history.* an adherent of James II after his overthrow in 1688, or of his descendants in their attempts to regain the throne. **2** a member of the Monophysite Church of Syria, which became a schismatic church in 451 A.D. **[C17:** from Late Latin *Jacōbus* James + -ITE[1]**]** ► **Jacobitic** (,dʒækə'bɪtɪk) *adj* ► **'Jaco,bitism** *n*

Jacobite Rebellion *n* **the.** *British history.* **1** the unsuccessful Jacobite rising of 1715 led by James Francis Edward Stuart. **2** the last Jacobite rising (1745-46) led by Charles Edward Stuart, the Young Pretender, which after initial successes was crushed at Culloden.

Jacobsen (*Danish* 'jakɔbsən) *n* **Arne** ('arnə). 1902–71, Danish architect and designer. His buildings include the Town Hall at Rodovre (1955).

Jacob sheep *n* See **Jacob** (sense 2).

Jacob's ladder *n* **1** *Old Testament.* the ladder reaching up to heaven that Jacob saw in a dream (Genesis 28:12–17). **2** Also called: **jack ladder.** a ladder made of wooden or metal steps supported by ropes or chains. **3** a North American polemoniaceous plant, *Polemonium caeruleum,* with blue flowers and a ladder-like arrangement of leaves. **4** any of several similar or related plants.

Jacob's staff *n* a medieval instrument for measuring heights and distances.

jacobus (dʒə'kəʊbəs) *n, pl* **-buses.** an English gold coin minted in the reign of James I. **[C17:** from Late Latin: James**]**

jaconet ('dʒækənɪt) *n* a light cotton fabric used for clothing, bandages, etc. **[C18:** from Urdu *jagannāthī,* from *Jagannāthpūrī,* India, where it was originally made**]**

Jacopo della Quercia (*Italian* 'jaːkopo ,dela 'kwɛrtʃa) *n* ?1374–1438, Italian Renaissance sculptor: best known for his marble reliefs of scenes from Genesis around the portal of S. Petronio, Bologna (1425–35).

Jacquard ('dʒækɑːd, dʒə'kɑːd; *French* ʒakar) *n* **1** Also called: **Jacquard weave.** a fabric in which the design is incorporated into the weave instead of being printed or dyed on. **2** Also called: **Jacquard loom.** the loom that produces this fabric. **[C19:** named after Joseph M. *Jacquard* (1752–1834), French inventor**]**

Jacquerie *French.* (ʒakri) *n* the revolt of the N French peasants against the nobility in 1358. **[C16:** from Old French: the peasantry, from *jacque* a peasant, from *Jacques* James, from Late Latin *Jacōbus***]**

jactation (dʒæk'teɪʃən) *n* **1** *Rare.* the act of boasting. **2** *Pathol.* another word for **jactitation** (sense 3). **[C16:** from Latin *jactātiō* bragging, from *jactāre* to flourish, from *jacere* to throw**]**

jactitation (,dʒæktɪ'teɪʃən) *n* **1** the act of boasting. **2** a false boast or claim that tends to harm another person, esp. a false assertion that one is married to another, formerly actionable at law. **3** Also called: **jactation.** *Pathol.* restless tossing in bed, characteristic of severe fevers and certain mental disorders. **[C17:** from Medieval Latin *jactitātiō,* from Latin *jacitāre* to utter publicly, from *jactitāre* to toss about; see JACTATION**]**

Jacuzzi (dʒə'kuːzɪ) *n, pl* **-zis. 1** *Trademark.* a system of underwater jets that keep the water in a bath or pool constantly agitated. **2** (*sometimes not cap.*) a bath or pool equipped with this. **[C20:** named after Candido and Roy Jacuzzi, who developed and marketed it**]**

jade[1] (dʒeɪd) *n* **1a** a semiprecious stone consisting of either jadeite or nephrite. It varies in colour from white to green and is used for making ornaments and jewellery. **1b** (*as modifier*): *jade ornaments.* **2** the green colour of jade. **[C18:** from French, from Italian *giada,* from obsolete Spanish *piedra de ijada* colic stone (literally: stone of the flank, because it was believed to cure renal colic); *ijada,* from Vulgar Latin *īliata* (unattested) flanks, from Latin *īlia,* plural of *īlium;* see ILEUM**]** ► **'jade,like** *adj*

jade[2] (dʒeɪd) *n* **1** an old overworked horse; nag; hack. **2** *Derogatory or facetious.* a woman considered to be ill-tempered or disreputable. ◆ *vb* **3** to exhaust or make exhausted from work or use. **[C14:** of unknown origin**]** ► **'jadish** *adj* ► **'jadishly** *adv* ► **'jadishness** *n*

jaded ('dʒeɪdɪd) *adj* **1** exhausted or dissipated. **2** satiated. ► **'jadedly** *adv* ► **'jadedness** *n*

jade green *n, adj* **a** a colour varying from yellowish-green to bluish-green. **b** (*as adj*): *a jade-green carpet.*

jadeite ('dʒeɪdaɪt) *n* a usually green or white mineral of the clinopyroxene group, found in igneous and metamorphic rocks. It is used as a gemstone (jade).

Composition: sodium aluminium silicate. Formula: $NaAlSi_2O_6$. Crystal structure: monoclinic.

Jadotville (*French* ʒadovil) *n* the former name of **Likasi.**

j'adoube *French.* (ʒadub) *interj Chess.* an expression of an intention to touch a piece in order to adjust its placement rather than to make a move. [literally: I adjust]

jaeger ('jeɪgə) *n* **1** *Military.* a marksman in certain units of the German or Austrian armies. **2** a member of a light or mountain infantry unit in some European armies. **3** *U.S. and Canadian.* any of several skuas of the genus *Stercorarius.* **4** *Rare.* a hunter or hunter's attendant. ◆ Also (for senses 1, 2, 4): **jager** or **jäger.** [C18: from German *Jäger* hunter, from *jagen* to hunt; see YACHT]

Jael ('dʒeɪəl) *n Old Testament.* the woman who killed Sisera when he took refuge in her tent (Judges 4:17–21).

Jaén (xa'en) *n* a city in S Spain. Pop.: 113 141 (1995 est.).

Jaffa ('dʒæfə, 'dʒɑː-) *n* **1** a port in W Israel, on the Mediterranean: incorporated into Tel Aviv in 1950; an old Canaanite city. Biblical name: **Joppa.** Hebrew name: **Yafo. 2** a large variety of orange, having a thick skin.

Jaffna ('dʒæfnə) *n* a port in N Sri Lanka: for many centuries the capital of a Tamil kingdom. Pop.: 129 000 (1990 est.).

jag[1] *or* **jagg** (dʒæg) *vb* **jags, jagging, jagged. 1** (*tr*) to cut unevenly; make jagged. **2** *Austral.* to catch (fish) by impaling them on an unbaited hook. ◆ *n, vb* **3** *Scot.* an informal word for **jab** (senses 3, 5). ◆ *n* **4** a jagged notch or projection. [C14: of unknown origin]

jag[2] (dʒæg) *n Slang.* **1a** intoxication from drugs or alcohol. **1b** a bout of drinking or drug taking. **2** a period of uncontrolled activity: *a crying jag.* [of unknown origin]

Jag (dʒæg) *n Informal.* a Jaguar car: often understood as a symbol of affluence.

JAG *abbrev. for* Judge Advocate General.

jaga ('dʒaga) (in Malaysia) ◆ *n* **1** a guard; sentry. ◆ *vb* **2** (*tr*) to guard or watch: *jaga the door.* [from Malay]

Jagannath, Jagganath ('dʒʌgəˌnɑːt, -ˌnɔːt), *or* **Jagannatha** (ˌdʒʌgə'nɑːθə) *n Hinduism.* other names for **Juggernaut.**

jäger ('jeɪgə) *n* See **jaeger.**

jagged ('dʒægɪd) *adj* having sharp projecting notches; ragged; serrate. ▸ **'jaggedly** *adv* ▸ **'jaggedness** *n*

Jagger ('dʒægə) *n* **Mick,** full name *Michael Philip Jagger.* born 1943, English rock singer and songwriter: lead vocalist with the Rolling Stones.

jaggery, jaggary, *or* **jagghery** ('dʒægərɪ) *n* a coarse brown sugar made in the East Indies from the sap of the date palm. [C16: from Hindi *jāgrī*; compare Sanskrit *śárkarā* gritty substance, sugar]

jaggy ('dʒægɪ) *adj* **-gier, -giest. 1** a less common word for **jagged. 2** *Scot.* prickly.

jaguar ('dʒægjʊə) *n* a large feline mammal, *Panthera onca,* of S North America, Central America, and N South America, similar to the leopard but with a shorter tail and larger spots on its coat. [C17: from Portuguese, from Tupi *jaguara,* Guarani *yaguara*]

jaguarondi (ˌdʒægwə'rɒndɪ) *or* **jaguarundi** (ˌdʒægwə'rʌndɪ) *n, pl* **-dis.** a feline mammal, *Felis yagouaroundi,* of Central and South America, with a reddish or grey coat, short legs, and a long tail. See also **eyra.** [C19: via Portuguese from Tupi]

Jahveh ('jɑːveɪ) *or* **Jahweh** ('jɑːweɪ) *n* variant of **Yahweh.**

Jahvist ('jɑːvɪst) *or* **Jahwist** ('jɑːwɪst) *n* variant of **Yahwist.**

Jahwism ('jɑːwɪzᵊm) *or* **Jahvism** ('jɑːvɪzəm) *n* variants of **Yahwism** *or* **Yahvism.** ▸ **Jah'wistic** *or* **Jah'vistic** *adj*

jai (dʒæ) *n Indian.* victory (to). [Hindi *jaya* victory]

jai alai ('haɪ 'laɪ, 'haɪ əˌlaɪ, ˌhaɪ ə'laɪ) *n* a version of pelota played by two or four players. [via Spanish from Basque, from *jai* game, festival + *alai* merry]

Jai Hind ('dʒæ 'hɪnd) victory to India: a political slogan and a form of greeting in India. [Hindi, from *jaya* victory + *Hind* India]

jail *or* **gaol** (dʒeɪl) *n* **1** a place for the confinement of persons convicted and sentenced to imprisonment or of persons awaiting trial to whom bail is not granted. ◆ *vb* **2** (*tr*) to confine in prison. [C13: from Old French *jaiole* cage, from Vulgar Latin *caveola* (unattested), from Latin *cavea* enclosure; see CAGE: the two spellings derive from the forms of the word that developed in two different areas of France, and the spelling *gaol* represents a pronunciation in use until the 17th century] ▸ **'jailless** *or* **'gaolless** *adj* ▸ **'jail-like** *or* **'gaol-like** *adj*

jailbird *or* **gaolbird** ('dʒeɪlˌbɜːd) *n* a person who is or has been confined to jail, esp. repeatedly; convict.

jailbreak *or* **gaolbreak** ('dʒeɪlˌbreɪk) *n* an escape from jail.

jail delivery *n* **1** forcible and illegal liberation of prisoners from jail. **2** *English law.* (formerly) a commission issued to assize judges when they come to a circuit town authorizing them to try all prisoners and release those acquitted.

jailer, jailor, *or* **gaoler** ('dʒeɪlə) *n* a person in charge of prisoners in a jail.

jail fever *n* a former name for **typhus,** once a common disease in jails.

jailhouse ('dʒeɪlˌhaʊs) *n Southern U.S.* a jail; prison.

Jain (dʒaɪn) *or* **Jaina** ('dʒaɪnə) *n* **1** an adherent of Jainism. **2** one of the saints believed to be the founders of Jainism. ◆ *adj* **3** of or relating to Jainism or the Jains. [C19: from Hindi *jaina* saint, literally: overcomer, from Sanskrit]

Jainism ('dʒaɪˌnɪzəm) *n* an ancient Hindu religion, which has its own scriptures and believes that the material world is eternal, progressing endlessly in a series of vast cycles. ▸ **'Jainist** *n, adj*

Jaipur (dʒaɪ'pʊə) *n* a city of great beauty in N India, capital of Rajasthan state: University of Rajasthan (1947). Pop.: 1 458 183 (1991).

Jakarta *or* **Djakarta** (dʒə'kɑːtə) *n* the capital of Indonesia, in N West Java: founded in 1619 and ruled by the Dutch until 1945; the chief trading centre of the East in the 17th century; University of Indonesia (1947). Pop.: 9 160 500 (1995 est.). Former name (until 1949): **Batavia.**

jake (dʒeɪk) *adj Austral. and N.Z. slang.* **1** satisfactory; all right. **2 she's jake.** everything is under control. [probably from the name *Jake*]

jakes (dʒeɪks) *n* **1** an archaic slang word for **lavatory. 2** *Southwestern English dialect.* human excrement. [C16: probably from French *Jacques* James]

Jakobson ('jɑːkəbsən) *n* **Roman** (**Osipovič**). 1896–1982, U.S. linguist, born in Russia. His publications include *Children's Speech* (1941) and *Fundamentals of Language* (1956).

Jalandhar ('dʒælænˌdɑː) *n* a city in NW India, in central Punjab. Pop.: 509 510 (1991).

jalap *or* **jalop** ('dʒæləp) *n* **1** a Mexican convolvulaceous plant, *Exogonium* (or *Ipomoea*) *purga.* **2** any of several similar or related plants. **3** the dried and powdered root of any of these plants, used as a purgative. **4** the resin obtained from any of these plants. [C17: from French, from Mexican Spanish *jalapa,* short for *purga de Jalapa* purgative of Jalapa] ▸ **jalapic** (dʒə'læpɪk) *adj*

Jalapa (*Spanish* xa'lapa) *n* a city in E central Mexico, capital of Veracruz State, at an altitude of 1427 m (4681 ft.): resort. Pop.: 288 331 (1990).

jalapeño (dʒælə'piːnəʊ; *Spanish* xala'penjo) *n* a very hot type of green chilli pepper, used esp. in Mexican cookery. Also: **jalapeño pepper.** [Mexican Spanish]

Jalisco (*Spanish* xa'lisko) *n* a state of W Mexico, on the Pacific: crossed by the Sierra Madre; valuable mineral resources. Capital: Guadalajara. Pop.: 5 990 054 (1995 est.). Area: 80 137 sq. km (30 934 sq. miles).

jalopy *or* **jaloppy** (dʒə'lɒpɪ) *n, pl* **-lopies** *or* **-loppies.** *Informal.* a dilapidated old car. [C20: of unknown origin]

jalouse (dʒə'luːz) *vb Scot.* to suspect; infer. [C19: from French *jalouser* to be jealous of]

jalousie ('ʒælʊˌziː) *n* **1** a window blind or shutter constructed from angled slats of wood, plastic, etc. **2** a window made of similarly angled slats of glass. [C19: from Old French *gelosie* latticework screen, literally: JEALOUSY, perhaps because one can look through the screen without being seen]

jam[1] (dʒæm) *vb* **jams, jamming, jammed. 1** (*tr*) to cram or wedge into or against something: *to jam paper into an incinerator.* **2** (*tr*) to crowd or pack: *cars jammed the roads.* **3** to make or become stuck or locked: *the switch has jammed.* **4** (*tr*; often foll. by *on*) to activate suddenly (esp. in the phrase **jam on the brakes**). **5** (*tr*) to block; congest: *to jam the drain with rubbish.* **6** (*tr*) to crush, bruise, or squeeze; smash. **7** *Radio.* to prevent the clear reception of (radio communications or radar signals) by transmitting other signals on the same frequency. **8** (*intr*) *Musicians' slang.* to play in a jam session. ◆ *n* **9** a crowd or congestion in a confined space: *a traffic jam.* **10** the act of jamming or the state of being jammed. **11** *Informal.* a difficult situation; predicament: *to help a friend out of a jam.* **12** See **jam session.** [C18: probably of imitative origin; compare CHAMP[1]] ▸ **'jammer** *n*

jam[2] (dʒæm) *n* **1** a preserve containing fruit, which has been boiled with sugar until the mixture sets. **2** *Slang.* something desirable: *you want jam on it.* [C18: perhaps from JAM[1] (the act of squeezing)]

Jam. *abbrev. for* **1** Jamaica. **2** *Bible.* James.

Jamaica (dʒə'meɪkə) *n* an island and state in the Caribbean: colonized by the Spanish from 1494 onwards, large numbers of Black slaves being imported; captured by the British in 1655 and established as a colony in 1866; gained full independence in 1962; a member of the Commonwealth. Exports: chiefly bauxite and alumina, sugar, and bananas. Official language: English. Religion: Protestant majority. Currency: Jamaican dollar. Capital: Kingston. Pop.: 2 254 000 (1998 est.). Area: 10 992 sq. km (4244 sq. miles). ▸ **Ja'maican** *n, adj*

Jamaican ebony *n* another name for **cocuswood.**

Jamaica pepper *n* another name for **allspice.**

Jamaica rum *n* a highly flavoured rum produced in Jamaica.

jamb *or* **jambe** (dʒæm) *n* **1** a vertical side member of a doorframe, window frame, or lining. **2** a vertical inside face of an opening in a wall. [C14: from Old French *jambe* leg, jamb, from Late Latin *gamba* hoof, hock, from Greek *kampē* joint]

jambalaya (ˌdʒʌmbə'laɪə) *n* a Creole dish made of shrimps, ham, rice, onions, etc. [C19: from Louisiana French, from Provençal *jambalaia* chicken and rice stew]

jambeau ('dʒæmbəʊ), **jambart** ('dʒæmbɑːt), *or* **jamber** ('dʒæmbə) *n, pl* **-beaux** (-bəʊz), **-barts,** *or* **-bers.** (*often pl*) other words for **greave.** [C14: from Anglo-French, from *jambe* leg; see JAMB]

Jambi *or* **Djambi** ('dʒæmbɪ) *n* a port in W Indonesia, in SE Sumatra on the Hari River. Pop.: 410 400 (1995 est.). Also called: **Telanaipura.**

jambo ('dʒambɔ) *sentence substitute.* an E African salutation. [C20: from Swahili]

jamboree (ˌdʒæmbə'riː) *n* **1** a large and often international gathering of Scouts. **2** a party or spree. [C19: of uncertain origin]

James (dʒeɪmz) *n* **1 Henry.** 1843–1916, British novelist, short-story writer, and critic, born in the U.S. Among his novels are *Washington Square* (1880), *The Portrait of a Lady* (1881), *The Bostonians* (1886), *The Wings of the Dove* (1902), *The Ambassadors* (1903), and *The Golden Bowl* (1904). **2 Jesse** (**Woodson**). 1847–82, U.S. outlaw. **3 P**(**hyllis**) **D**(**orothy**), Baroness James of Holland Park. born 1920, British detective novelist. Her books include *Death of an Expert Witness* (1977), *Original Sin* (1994), and *A Certain Justice* (1997). **4 William,** brother of Henry James. 1842–1910, U.S. philosopher and psychologist, whose theory of pragmatism is expounded in *Essays in Radical Empiricism* (1912). His other works include *The Will to Believe* (1897), *The Principles of Psychology* (1890), and *The Varieties of Religious Experience* (1902). **5** *New Testament.* **5a** known as *James the Great.* one of the twelve apostles, a son of Zebedee and brother to John the apostle (Matthew 4:21). Feast day: July 25 or April 30. **5b** known as *James the Less.* one of the twelve apostles, son of Alphaeus (Matthew 10:3). Feast day: May 3 or Oct. 9. **5c** known as *James the brother of the Lord.* a brother or close relative of Jesus (Mark 6:3; Galatians

1:19). Feast day: Oct. 23. **5d** the book ascribed to his authorship (in full **The Epistle of James**).

James I *n* **1** called *the Conqueror.* 1208–76, king of Aragon (1216–76). He captured the Balearic Islands and Valencia from the Muslims, thus beginning Aragonese expansion in the Mediterranean. **2** 1394–1437, king of Scotland (1406–37), second son of Robert III. **3** 1566–1625, king of England and Ireland (1603–25) and, as James VI, king of Scotland (1567–1625), in succession to Elizabeth I of England and his mother, Mary Queen of Scots, respectively. He alienated Parliament by his assertion of the divine right of kings, his favourites, esp. the Duke of Buckingham, and his subservience to Spain.

James II *n* **1** 1430–60, king of Scotland (1437–60), son of James I. **2** 1633–1701, king of England, Ireland, and, as James VII, of Scotland (1685–88); son of Charles I. His pro-Catholic sympathies and arbitrary rule caused the Whigs and Tories to unite in inviting his eldest surviving daughter, Mary, and her husband, William of Orange, to take the throne as joint monarchs. James was defeated at the Boyne (1690) when he attempted to regain the throne.

James III *n* 1451–88, king of Scotland (1460–88), son of James II.

James IV *n* 1473–1513, king of Scotland (1488–1513), son of James III; he invaded England (1496) in support of Perkin Warbeck; he was killed at Flodden.

James V *n* 1512–42, king of Scotland (1513–42), son of James IV.

James VI *n* title as king of Scotland of **James I** of England and Ireland.

James VII *n* title as king of Scotland of **James II** of England and Ireland.

James Bay *n* the S arm of Hudson Bay, in central Canada. Area: 108 780 sq. km (42 000 sq. miles).

Jamesian *or* **Jamesean** ('dʒeɪmzɪən) *adj* relating to or characteristic of Henry James or his brother, William.

James-Lange theory ('dʒeɪmz'lɑːŋgə) *n Psychol.* a theory that emotions are caused by bodily sensations; for example, we are sad because we weep. [named after William JAMES + Carl *Lange* (1834–1900), Danish psychologist]

Jameson ('dʒeɪms°n) *n* Sir **Leander Starr.** 1853–1917, British administrator in South Africa, who led an expedition into the Transvaal in 1895 in an unsuccessful attempt to topple its Boer regime (the **Jameson Raid**); prime minister of Cape Colony (1904–08).

Jamestown ('dʒeɪmz,taʊn) *n* a ruined village in E Virginia, on **Jamestown Island** (a peninsula in the James River): the first permanent settlement by the English in America (1607); capital of Virginia (1607–98); abandoned in 1699.

jamming ('dʒæmɪŋ) *n Mountaineering.* a rock-climbing technique in which holds are got by wedging the hands and feet in suitable cracks.

Jammu ('dʒʌmuː) *n* a city in N India, winter capital of the state of Jammu and Kashmir. Pop.: 206 135 (1991).

Jammu and Kashmir *n* the official name for the part of **Kashmir** under Indian control.

jammy ('dʒæmɪ) *adj* **-mier, -miest. 1** covered with or tasting like jam. **2** *Brit. slang.* lucky: *jammy so-and-sos!*

Jamnagar (,dʒæmnə'gɑː) *n* a city in India, in Gujarat: noted for its palaces and temples: cement, pottery, textiles. Pop.: 294 344 (1989).

jam-packed *adj* crowded, packed, or filled to capacity.

jampan ('dʒæm,pæn) *n* a type of sedan chair used in India. [C19: from Bengali *jhāmpān*]

jam session *n Slang.* an unrehearsed or improvised jazz or rock performance. [C20: probably from JAM[1]]

Jamshedpur (,dʒʌmʃed'pʊə) *n* a city in NE India, in SE Bihar: large iron and steel works (1907–11); a major industrial centre. Pop.: 457 061 (1989).

Jamshid *or* **Jamshyd** (dʒæm'ʃiːd) *n Persian myth.* a ruler of the peris who was punished for bragging that he was immortal by being changed into human form. He then became a great king of Persia. See also **peri.**

Jan. *abbrev. for* January.

Janáček (*Czech* 'janaːtʃɛk) *n* **Leoš** ('lɛɔʃ). 1854–1928, Czech composer. His music is influenced by Czech folksong and speech rhythms and is remarkable for its integration of melody and language. His works include the operas *Jenufa* (1904) and *The Cunning Little Vixen* (1924), the *Glagolitic Mass* (1927), as well as orchestral and chamber music and songs.

Jana Sangh ('dʒʌnə 'sʌŋg) *n* a political party in India. [Hindi, literally: people's party]

Janata ('dʒʌnətɑː) *n* **1** (in India) the general public; the people. **2** a political party in India: founded in 1976 and came to power in 1977. [Hindi]

Jandal ('dʒænd°l) *n N.Z. trademark.* a type of sandal with a strip of material between the big toe and the other toes and over the foot.

jane (dʒeɪn) *n Slang, chiefly U.S.* a girl or woman.

Janeite ('dʒeɪ,naɪt) *n* a devotee of the works of Jane Austen.

Jane's (dʒeɪnz) *n* any of several periodical publications such as *Fighting Ships* and *All the World's Aircraft.* [C20: named after Frederick Thomas *Jane* (1865–1916), British naval writer and artist]

Janet (*French* ʒanɛ) *n* **Pierre Marie Félix** (pjɛr mari feliks). 1859–1947, French psychologist and neurologist, noted particularly for his work on the origins of hysteria.

jangle ('dʒæŋg°l) *vb* **1** to sound or cause to sound discordantly, harshly, or unpleasantly: *the telephone jangled.* **2** (*tr*) to produce a jarring effect on: *the accident jangled his nerves.* **3** an archaic word for **wrangle.** ◆ *n* **4** a harsh, unpleasant ringing noise. **5** an argument or quarrel. [C13: from Old French *jangler,* of Germanic origin; compare Middle Dutch *jangelen* to whine, complain] ▸ **'jangler** *n*

Janiculum (dʒə'nɪkjʊləm) *n* a hill in Rome across the River Tiber from the Seven Hills.

Janina ('janiːna) *n* the Serbian name for **Ioánnina.**

janissary ('dʒænɪsərɪ) *or* **janizary** ('dʒænɪzərɪ) *n, pl* **-saries** *or* **-zaries.** an infantryman in the Turkish army, originally a member of the sovereign's personal guard, from the 14th to the early 19th century. [C16: from French *janissaire,* from Italian *giannizzero,* from Turkish *yeniçeri,* from *yeni* new + *çeri* soldiery]

janitor ('dʒænɪtə) *n* **1** *Scot., U.S., and Canadian.* the caretaker of a building, esp. a school. **2** *Chiefly U.S. and Canadian.* a person employed to clean and maintain a building, esp. the public areas in a block of flats or office building; porter. [C17: from Latin: doorkeeper, from *jānua* door, entrance, from *jānus* covered way (compare JANUS[1]); related to Latin *īre* to go] ▸ **janitorial** (,dʒænɪ'tɔːrɪəl) *adj* ▸ **'janitress** *fem n*

Jan Mayen ('jæn 'maɪən) *n* an island in the Arctic Ocean, between Greenland and N Norway: volcanic, with large glaciers; former site of Dutch whaling stations; annexed to Norway in 1929. Area: 373 sq. km (144 sq. miles).

Jansen ('dʒæns°n) *n* **Cornelis** (kɔː'niːlɪs). Latin name *Cornelius Jansenius.* 1585–1638, Dutch Roman Catholic theologian. In *Augustinus* (1640) he defended the teachings of St. Augustine, esp. on free will, grace, and predestination.

Jansenism ('dʒænsə,nɪzəm) *n* **1** *R.C. Church.* the doctrine of Cornelis Jansen and his disciples, who maintained that salvation was limited to those subject to a supernatural determinism, the rest being destined to perdition. **2** the religious movement arising from these doctrines. ▸ **'Jansenist** *n, adj* ▸ **,Jansen'istic** *or* **,Jansen'istical** *adj*

jansky ('dʒænskɪ) *n, pl* **-skys.** a unit of flux density equal to 10^{-26} W m^{-2} Hz^{-1}, used in radio astronomy. Symbol: Jy [C20: named after K. G. JANSKY]

Jansky ('dʒænskɪ) *n* **Karl Guthe.** 1905–50, U.S. electrical engineer. He discovered a source of radio waves outside the solar system (1932) and pioneered radio astronomy.

January ('dʒænjʊərɪ) *n, pl* **-aries.** the first month of the year, consisting of 31 days. [C14: from Latin *Jānuārius,* from adj: (month) of JANUS[1]]

Janus[1] ('dʒeɪnəs) *n* the Roman god of doorways, passages, and bridges. In art he is depicted with two heads facing opposite ways. [C16: from Latin, from *jānus* archway]

Janus[2] ('dʒeɪnəs) *n* a small inner satellite of Saturn.

Janus-faced *adj* two-faced; hypocritical; deceitful.

Jap (dʒæp) *n, adj Informal, often derogatory.* short for **Japanese.**

Jap. *abbrev. for* Japan(ese).

japan (dʒə'pæn) *n* **1** a glossy durable black lacquer originally from the Orient, used on wood, metal, etc. **2** work decorated and varnished in the Japanese manner. **3** a liquid used as a paint drier. ◆ *adj* **4** relating to or varnished with japan. ◆ *vb* **-pans, -panning, -panned. 5** (*tr*) to lacquer with japan or any similar varnish.

Japan (dʒə'pæn) *n* an archipelago and empire in E Asia, extending for 3200 km (2000 miles) between the Sea of Japan and the Pacific and consisting of the main islands of Hokkaido, Honshu, Shikoku, and Kyushu and over 3000 smaller islands: feudalism abolished in 1871, followed by industrialization and expansion of territories, esp. during World Wars I and II, when most of SE Asia came under Japanese control; dogma of the emperor's divinity abolished in 1946 under a new democratic constitution; rapid economic growth has made Japan the most industrialized nation in the Far East. Official language: Japanese. Religion: Shintoist majority, large Buddhist minority. Currency: yen. Capital: Tokyo. Pop.: 126 398 000 (1998 est.). Area: 369 660 sq. km (142 726 sq. miles). Japanese names: **Nippon, Nihon.**

Japan Current *n* a warm ocean current flowing northeastwards off the E coast of Japan towards the North Pacific. Also called: **Kuroshio.**

Japanese (,dʒæpə'niːz) *adj* **1** of, relating to, or characteristic of Japan, its people, or their language. ◆ *n* **2** (*pl* **-nese.**) a native or inhabitant of Japan or a descendant of one. **3** the official language of Japan: the native language of approximately 100 million people: considered by some scholars to be part of the Altaic family of languages.

Japanese andromeda *n* an ericaceous Japanese shrub, *Pieris japonica,* with drooping clusters of small bell-shaped white flowers.

Japanese beetle *n* a scarabaeid beetle, *Popillia japonica,* that eats the leaves and fruits of various plants: accidentally introduced into the U.S. from Japan.

Japanese cedar *n* another name for **cryptomeria.**

Japanese ivy *n* another name for **Virginia creeper** (sense 2).

Japanese lantern *n* another name for **Chinese lantern** (sense 1).

Japanese persimmon *n* an Asian persimmon tree, *Diospyros kaki,* with red or orange edible fruit. Also called: **kaki.**

Japanese river fever *n* another name for **scrub typhus.**

Japanese slippers *pl n* (in Malaysia) casual sandals; flip-flops.

Japanese stranglehold *n* a wrestling hold in which an opponent's wrists are pulled to cross his arms in front of his own neck and exert pressure on his windpipe.

Japanese umbrella pine *n* a single aberrant species of pine, *Sciadopitys verticillata,* in which the leaves are fused in pairs and the crown is spire-shaped.

Japan wax *or* **tallow** *n* a yellow wax obtained from the berries of plants of the genus *Rhus.* It is used in making matches, soaps, candles, and polishes.

jape (dʒeɪp) *n* **1** a jest or joke. ◆ *vb* **2** to joke or jest (about). [C14: perhaps from Old French *japper* to bark, yap, of imitative origin] ▸ **'japer** *n* ▸ **'japery** *n* ▸ **'japingly** *adv*

Japheth ('dʒeɪfɛθ) *n Old Testament.* the second son of Noah, traditionally regarded as the ancestor of a number of non-Semitic nations (Genesis 10:1–5).

Japhetic (dʒeɪ'fɛtɪk) *adj* denoting a discredited grouping of languages that postulated a relationship between Basque, Etruscan, and Georgian among others. [C19: from New Latin *Japheti* descendants of JAPHETH + -IC]

japonica (dʒə'pɒnɪkə) *n* **1** Also called: **Japanese quince.** a Japanese rosaceous shrub, *Chaenomeles japonica,* cultivated for its red flowers and yellowish fruit. **2** another name for the **camellia.** [C19: from New Latin, feminine of *japonicus* Japanese, from *Japonia* JAPAN]

Japurá (*Portuguese* ʒapu'ra) *n* a river in NW South America, rising in SW Colombia and flowing southeast across Colombia and Brazil to join the Amazon near Tefé: known as the Caquetá in Colombia. Length: about 2800 km (1750 miles). Spanish name: **Yapurá.**

Jaques-Dalcroze (*French* ʒakdalkroz) *n* **Émile** (emil). 1865–1950, Swiss composer and teacher: invented eurythmics.

jar[1] (dʒɑː) *n* **1** a wide-mouthed container that is usually cylindrical, made of glass or earthenware, and without handles. **2** Also: **'jarful.** the contents or quantity contained in a jar. **3** *Brit. informal.* a glass of alcoholic drink, esp. beer: *to have a jar with someone.* **4** *Obsolete.* a measure of electrical capacitance. **[C16:** from Old French *jarre,* from Old Provençal *jarra,* from Arabic *jarrah* large earthen vessel**]**

jar[2] (dʒɑː) *vb* **jars, jarring, jarred. 1** to vibrate or cause to vibrate. **2** to make or cause to make a harsh discordant sound. **3** (often foll. by *on*) to have a disturbing or painful effect (on the nerves, mind, etc.). **4** (*intr*) to disagree; clash. ◆ *n* **5** a jolt or shock. **6** a harsh discordant sound. **[C16:** probably of imitative origin; compare Old English *cearran* to creak**]** ▸ **'jarring** *adj* ▸ **'jarringly** *adv*

jar[3] (dʒɑː) *n* **on a** (*or* **the**) **jar.** (of a door) slightly open; ajar. **[C17** (in the sense: turn): from earlier *char,* from Old English *cierran* to turn; see AJAR[1]**]**

jardinière (ˌʒɑːdɪ'njɛə) *n* **1** an ornamental pot or trough for plants. **2** a garnish of fresh vegetables, cooked, diced, and served around a dish of meat. **[C19:** from French, feminine of *jardinier* gardener, from *jardin* GARDEN**]**

jargon[1] ('dʒɑːgən) *n* **1** specialized language concerned with a particular subject, culture, or profession. **2** language characterized by pretentious syntax, vocabulary, or meaning. **3** gibberish. **4** another word for **pidgin.** ◆ *vb* **5** (*intr*) to use or speak in jargon. **[C14:** from Old French, perhaps of imitative origin; see GARGLE**]**

jargon[2] ('dʒɑːgɒn) *or* **jargoon** (dʒɑː'guːn) *n Mineralogy.* a golden yellow, smoky, or colourless variety of zircon. **[C18:** from French, from Italian *giargone,* ultimately from Persian *zargūn* of the golden colour; see ZIRCON**]**

jargonize *or* **jargonise** ('dʒɑːgəˌnaɪz) *vb* **1** (*tr*) to translate into jargon. **2** (*intr*) to talk in jargon. ▸ **ˌjargoni'zation** *or* **ˌjargoni'sation** *n*

jarl (jɑːl) *n Medieval history.* a Scandinavian chieftain or noble. **[C19:** from Old Norse; see EARL**]** ▸ **'jarldom** *n*

Jarlsberg ('jɑːlzbɜːg) *n Trademark.* a hard mild-tasting yellow-coloured cheese with holes in it. **[C20:** after *Jarlsberg,* Norway, where it originated**]**

jarosite ('dʒærəˌsaɪt) *n* a yellow to brown secondary mineral consisting of basic hydrated sulphate of iron and potassium in masses or hexagonal crystals. Formula: $KFe_3(SO_4)_2(OH)_6$. **[C19:** from *Barranco Jaroso,* in Almeria, Spain + -ITE[1]**]**

jarp (dʒɑːp) *or* **jaup** (dʒɔːp) *vb* (*tr*) *Northeast English dialect.* to strike or smash, esp. to break the shell of (an egg) at Easter. **[**from Scottish *jaup, jawp* to dash or splash like water: perhaps of imitative origin**]**

jarrah ('dʒærə) *n* a widely planted Australian eucalyptus tree, *Eucalyptus marginata,* that yields a valuable timber. **[**from a native Australian language**]**

Jarrett ('dʒærɪt) *n* **Keith.** born 1945, U.S. jazz pianist and composer.

Jarrow ('dʒærəʊ) *n* a port in NE England, in South Tyneside unitary authority, Tyne and Wear: ruined monastery where the Venerable Bede lived and died; its unemployed marched on London in the 1930s; shipyards, oil installations, iron and steel works. Pop.: 29 325 (1991 est.).

Jarry (*French* ʒari) *n* **Alfred** (alfred). 1873–1907, French dramatist and poet, who initiated the theatre of the absurd with his play *Ubu Roi* (1896).

Jaruzelski (*Polish* jaruː'ʒɛlski) *n* **Wojciech** ('vɔɪtʃɛk). born 1923, Polish statesman and soldier; prime minister (1981–85); head of state 1985–90 (as president from 1989).

jarvey *or* **jarvie** ('dʒɑːvɪ) *n Brit. informal, obsolete.* a hackney coachman. **[C19:** from *Jarvey,* familiar form of personal name *Jarvis***]**

Jas. *abbrev. for* James.

jasmine ('dʒæsmɪn, 'dʒæz-) *n* **1** Also called: **jessamine.** any oleaceous shrub or climbing plant of the tropical and subtropical genus *Jasminum,* esp. *J. officinalis:* widely cultivated for their white, yellow, or red fragrant flowers, which are used in making perfume and in flavouring tea. See also **winter jasmine. 2** any of several other shrubs with fragrant flowers, such as the Cape jasmine, yellow jasmine, and frangipani (**red jasmine**). **3** a light to moderate yellow colour. **[C16:** from Old French *jasmin,* from Arabic *yāsamīn,* from Persian *yāsmīn***]**

Jason ('dʒeɪsᵊn) *n Greek myth.* the hero who led the Argonauts in quest of the Golden Fleece. He became the husband of Medea, whom he later abandoned for Glauce.

jaspé ('dʒæspeɪ) *adj* resembling jasper; variegated. **[C19:** from French, from *jasper* to marble**]**

jasper ('dʒæspə) *n* **1** an opaque impure microcrystalline form of quartz, red, yellow, brown, or dark green in colour, used as a gemstone and for ornamental decoration. **2** Also called: **jasper ware.** a dense hard stoneware, invented in 1775 by Wedgwood, capable of being stained throughout its substance with metallic oxides and used as background for applied classical decoration. **[C14:** from Old French *jaspe,* from Latin *jaspis,* from Greek *iaspis,* of Semitic origin; related to Assyrian *ashpū,* Arabic *yashb,* Hebrew *yāshpheh***]**

Jasper National Park ('dʒæspə) *n* a national park in SW Canada, in W Alberta in the Rockies: wildlife sanctuary. Area: 10 900 sq. km (4200 sq. miles).

Jaspers (*German* 'jaspərs) *n* **Karl** (karl). 1883–1969, German existentialist philosopher.

Jassy ('jasi) *n* the German name for **Iaşi.**

Jat (dʒɑːt) *n, pl* **Jat** *or* **Jats.** a member of an Indo-European people widely dispersed throughout the Punjab, Rajputana, and Uttar Pradesh.

Jataka Tales ('dʒɑːtəkə) *pl n* a body of literature comprising accounts of previous lives of the Buddha.

jato ('dʒeɪtəʊ) *n, pl* **-tos.** *Aeronautics.* jet-assisted takeoff. **[C20** *j(et-)a(ssisted) t(ake)o(ff)***]**

jaundice ('dʒɔːndɪs) *n* **1** Also called: **icterus.** yellowing of the skin and whites of the eyes due to the abnormal presence of bile pigments in the blood, as in hepatitis. **2** a mental state of bitterness, jealousy, and ill humour resulting in distorted judgment. ◆ *vb* **3** to distort (the judgment, etc.) adversely: *jealousy had jaundiced his mind.* **4** to affect with or as if with jaundice. **[C14:** from Old French *jaunisse,* from *jaune* yellow, from Latin *galbinus* yellowish, from *galbus***]** ▸ **'jaundiced** *adj*

jaunt (dʒɔːnt) *n* **1** a short pleasurable excursion; outing. ◆ *vb* **2** (*intr*) to go on such an excursion. **[C16:** of unknown origin**]** ▸ **'jauntingly** *adv*

jaunting car *or* **jaunty car** *n* a light two-wheeled one-horse car, formerly widely used in Ireland.

jaunty ('dʒɔːntɪ) *adj* **-tier, -tiest. 1** sprightly, self-confident, and cheerful; brisk: *a jaunty step.* **2** smart; trim: *a jaunty hat.* **[C17:** from French *gentil* noble; see GENTEEL**]** ▸ **'jauntily** *adv* ▸ **'jauntiness** *n*

Jaurès (*French* ʒorɛs) *n* **Jean Léon** (ʒɑ̃ leɔ̃). 1859–1914, French politician and writer, who founded the socialist paper *l'Humanité* (1904), and united the French socialist movement into a single party (1905); assassinated.

Jav. *abbrev. for* Javanese.

Java[1] ('dʒɑːvə) *n* an island of Indonesia, south of Borneo, from which it is separated by the **Java Sea:** politically the most important island of Indonesia; it consists chiefly of active volcanic mountains and is densely forested. It came under Dutch control in 1596 and became part of Indonesia in 1949. It is one of the most densely populated areas in the world. Capital: Jakarta. Pop. (with Madura): 102 910 500 (1995 est.). Area: 132 174 sq. km (51 032 sq. miles). ▸ **'Javan** *n, adj*

Java[2] ('dʒɑːvə) *n Trademark.* a programming language especially applicable to the World Wide Web. **[C20:** named after *Java* coffee, said to be consumed in large quantities by the language's creators**]**

Java man *n* a type of primitive man, *Homo erectus* (formerly called *Pithecanthropus erectus*), that lived in the middle Palaeolithic Age in Java. Also called: **Trinil man.**

Javanese (ˌdʒɑːvə'niːz) *adj* **1** of, relating to, or characteristic of Java, its people, or the Javanese language. ◆ *n* **2** (*pl* **-nese.**) a native or inhabitant of Java. **3** a Malayo-Polynesian language of Central and Eastern Java.

Javari *or* **Javary** (*Portuguese* ʒava'ri) *n* a river in South America, flowing northeast as part of the border between Peru and Brazil to join the Amazon. Length: about 1050 km (650 miles). Spanish name: **Yavarí.**

Java sparrow *n* a small grey-and-pink finchlike Indonesian weaverbird, *Padda oryzivora:* a popular cage bird.

javelin ('dʒævlɪn) *n* **1** a long pointed spear thrown as a weapon or in competitive field events. **2 the javelin.** the event or sport of throwing the javelin. **[C16:** from Old French *javeline,* variant of *javelot,* of Celtic origin**]**

Javel water *or* **Javelle water** ('dʒævᵊl, dʒə'vɛl) *n* **1** an aqueous solution containing sodium hypochlorite and some sodium chloride, used as a bleach and disinfectant. **2** Also called: **eau de Javelle.** a similar solution made from potassium carbonate and chlorine. **[C19:** partial translation of French *eau de Javel,* from *Javel,* formerly a town, now part of Paris**]**

jaw (dʒɔː) *n* **1** the part of the skull of a vertebrate that frames the mouth and holds the teeth. In higher vertebrates it consists of the **upper jaw** (maxilla) fused to the cranium and the **lower jaw** (mandible). Related adjs: **gnathal, gnathic. 2** the corresponding part of an invertebrate, esp. an insect. **3** a pair or either of a pair of hinged or sliding components of a machine or tool designed to grip an object. **4** *Slang.* **4a** impudent talk; cheek. **4b** idle conversation; chat. **4c** moralizing talk; a lecture. ◆ *vb* **5** (*intr*) *Slang.* **5a** to talk idly; chat; gossip. **5b** to lecture. ◆ See also **jaws. [C14:** probably from Old French *joue* cheek; related to Italian *gota* cheek**]** ▸ **'jawˌlike** *adj*

jawan (dʒə'wɑːn) *n* (in India) **1** a soldier. **2** a young man. **[**Urdu: young man**]**

Jawara ('dʒɑːwərə) *n* Sir **Dawda** ('dɔːdə). born 1924, Gambian statesman; president of The Gambia (1970–94); overthrown in a military coup.

jawbone ('dʒɔːˌbəʊn) *n* **1** a nontechnical name for **mandible** or (less commonly) **maxilla.** ◆ *vb* **2** *U.S.* to try to persuade or bring pressure to bear (on) by virtue of one's high office or position, esp. in urging compliance with official policy.

jawbreaker ('dʒɔːˌbreɪkə) *n* **1** Also called: **jawcrusher.** a device having hinged jaws for crushing rocks and ores. **2** *Informal.* a word that is hard to pronounce. ▸ **'jawˌbreaking** *adj* ▸ **'jawˌbreakingly** *adv*

jaws (dʒɔːz) *pl n* **1** the narrow opening of some confined place such as a gorge. **2 the jaws.** a dangerously close position: *the jaws of death.*

jaws of life *pl n* (*functioning as sing*) powerful shears used for cutting a vehicle open after a collision.

Jaxartes (dʒæk'sɑːtiːz) *n* the ancient name for **Syr Darya.**

jay (dʒeɪ) *n* **1** any of various passerine birds of the family *Corvidae* (crows), esp. the Eurasian *Garrulus glandarius,* with a pinkish-brown body, blue-and-black wings, and a black-and-white crest. See also **blue jay. 2** a foolish or gullible person. **[C13:** from Old French *jai,* from Late Latin *gāius,* perhaps from proper name *Gāius***]**

Jay (dʒeɪ) *n* **John.** 1745–1829, American statesman, jurist, and diplomat; first chief justice of the Supreme Court (1789–95). He negotiated the treaty with Great Britain (**Jay's treaty,** 1794), that settled outstanding disputes.

Jaya ('dʒɑːjə) *or* **Djaja** *n* **Mount.** a mountain in E Indonesia, in Irian Jaya in the Sudirman Range: the highest mountain in New Guinea. Height: 5039 m (16 532 ft.). Former names: (Mount) **Carstensz, Sukarno Peak.**

Jayapura (ˌdʒɑːjɑː'pʊərə) *or* **Djajapura** *n* a port in NE Indonesia, capital of Irian Jaya, on the N coast. Pop.: 180 400 (1995 est.). Former names: **Sukarnapura, Kotabaru, Hollandia.**

Jayawardene (ˌdʒeɪə'wɑːdɪnə) *n* **Junius Richard.** 1906–96, Sri Lankan statesman; prime minister (1977–78) and first president of Sri Lanka (1978–89).

Jaycee ('dʒeɪ'siː) *n Austral, N.Z., U.S., and Canadian.* a young person who belongs to a junior chamber of commerce. [C20: from the initials of *J*(unior) *C*(hamber), short for *United States Junior Chamber of Commerce*]

jaywalk ('dʒeɪˌwɔːk) *vb* (*intr*) to cross or walk in a street recklessly or illegally. [C20: from JAY (sense 2)] ► **'jayˌwalker** *n* ► **'jayˌwalking** *n*

jazz (dʒæz) *n* **1a** a kind of music of African-American origin, characterized by syncopated rhythms, solo and group improvisation, and a variety of harmonic idioms and instrumental techniques. It exists in a number of styles. Compare **blues.** See also: **bebop, bop, Dixieland, free** (sense 7), **hard bop, harmolodics, mainstream** (sense 2), **modern jazz, New Orleans jazz, swing** (sense 28), **trad. 1b** (*as modifier*): *a jazz band.* **1c** (*in combination*): *a jazzman.* **2** *Informal.* enthusiasm or liveliness. **3** *Slang.* rigmarole; paraphernalia: *legal papers and all that jazz.* **4** *African-American slang, obsolete.* sexual intercourse. ◆ *vb* **5** (*intr*) to play or dance to jazz music. **6** *African-American slang, obsolete.* to have sexual intercourse with (a person). [C20: of unknown origin] ► **'jazzer** *n*

jazz age *n* (*often caps.*) **the.** (esp. in the U.S.) the period between the end of World War I and the beginning of the Depression during which jazz became popular. [C20: popularized by F. Scott FITZGERALD, who called a collection of his short stories *Tales of the Jazz Age* (1922)]

jazz up *vb* (*tr, adv*) *Informal.* **1** to imbue (a piece of music) with jazz qualities, esp. by improvisation or a quicker tempo. **2** to make more lively, gaudy, or appealing.

jazzy ('dʒæzɪ) *adj* **jazzier, jazziest.** *Informal.* **1** of, characteristic of, or resembling jazz music. **2** gaudy or flashy: *a jazzy car.* ► **'jazzily** *adv* ► **'jazziness** *n*

JC *abbrev. for* jurisconsult.

J.C. *abbrev. for:* **1** Jesus Christ. **2** Julius Caesar.

JCB *n Trademark.* a type of construction machine with a hydraulically operated shovel on the front and an excavator arm on the back. [named from the initials of *J*(oseph) *C*(yril) *B*(amford) (born 1916), its English manufacturer]

JCD *abbrev. for:* **1** Doctor of Canon Law. [Latin: *Juris Canonici Doctor*] **2** Doctor of Civil Law. [Latin: *Juris Civilis Doctor*]

JCL *Computing. abbrev. for* Job Control Language.

JCR *abbrev. for* junior common room.

JCS *abbrev. for* Joint Chiefs of Staff.

jct. *or* **jctn** *abbrev. for* junction.

JD *abbrev. for:* **1** Doctor of Laws. [Latin: *Jurum Doctor*] **2** juvenile delinquent.

jealous ('dʒɛləs) *adj* **1** suspicious or fearful of being displaced by a rival: *a jealous lover.* **2** (often *postpositive* and foll. by *of*) resentful (of) or vindictive (towards), esp. through envy: *a child jealous of his brother.* **3** (often *postpositive* and foll. by *of*) possessive and watchful in the maintenance or protection (of): *jealous of one's reputation.* **4** characterized by or resulting from jealousy. **5** *Obsolete except in biblical use.* demanding exclusive loyalty: *a jealous God.* **6** an obsolete word for **zealous.** [C13: from Old French *gelos,* from Medieval Latin *zēlōsus,* from Late Latin *zēlus* emulation, jealousy, from Greek *zēlos* ZEAL] ► **'jealously** *adv* ► **'jealousness** *n*

jealousy ('dʒɛləsɪ) *n, pl* **-ousies.** the state or quality of being jealous.

jean (dʒiːn) *n* a tough twill-weave cotton fabric used for hard-wearing trousers, overalls, etc. See also **jeans.** [C16: short for *jean fustian,* from *Gene* GENOA]

Jean (*French* ʒɑ̃) *n* born 1921, grand duke of Luxembourg from 1964.

Jean de Meung (*French* ʒɑ̃ də mœ̃) *n* real name *Jean Clopinel.* ?1250–?1305, French poet, who continued Guillaume de Lorris' *Roman de la Rose.* His portion of the poem consists of some 18 000 lines and contains satirical attacks on women and the Church.

Jeanne d'Arc (ʒan dark) *n* the French name of **Joan of Arc.**

Jean Paul (*French* ʒɑ̃ pɔl) *n* real name *Johann Paul Friedrich Richter.* 1763–1825, German novelist.

jeans (dʒiːnz) *pl n* informal trousers for casual wear, made esp. of denim or corduroy. [plural of JEAN]

Jeans (dʒiːnz) *n* Sir **James Hopwood.** 1877–1946, English astronomer, physicist, and mathematician, best known for his popular books on astronomy. He made important contributions to the kinetic theory of gases and the theory of stellar evolution.

jebel *or* **djebel** ('dʒɛbᵊl) *n* a hill or mountain in an Arab country.

Jebel Musa ('dʒɛbᵊl 'muːsə) *n* a mountain in NW Morocco, near the Strait of Gibraltar: one of the Pillars of Hercules. Height: 850 m (2790 ft.).

Jedda ('dʒɛdə) *n* another name for **Jidda.**

jeelie *or* **jeely** ('dʒiːlɪ) *n Scot.* jelly or jam.

Jeep (dʒiːp) *n Trademark.* a small military road vehicle with four-wheel drive. [C20: probably from the initials *GP,* for *general purpose* (*vehicle*)]

jeepers *or* **jeepers creepers** ('dʒiːpəz 'kriːpəz) *interj U.S. and Canadian slang.* a mild exclamation of surprise. [C20: euphemism for *Jesus*]

Jeeps (dʒiːps) *n* **Dickie.** born 1931, English Rugby Union footballer: halfback for England (1956–62) and the British Lions (1959–62).

jeer (dʒɪə) *vb* **1** (often foll. by *at*) to laugh or scoff (at a person or thing); mock. ◆ *n* **2** a remark or cry of derision; gibe; taunt. [C16: of unknown origin] ► **'jeerer** *n* ► **'jeering** *adj, n* ► **'jeeringly** *adv*

jefe (*Spanish* 'xefe) *n* (in Spanish-speaking countries) a military or political leader. [Spanish, from French *chef* CHIEF]

Jefferies ('dʒɛfrɪz) *n* **Richard.** 1848–87, British writer and naturalist, noted for his observation of English country life: his books include *Bevis* (1882) and collections of essays such as *The Open Air* (1885).

Jefferson ('dʒɛfəsᵊn) *n* **Thomas.** 1743–1826, U.S. statesman: secretary of state (1790–93); third president (1801–09). He was the chief drafter of the Declaration of Independence (1776), the chief opponent of the centralizing policies of the Federalists under Hamilton, and effected the Louisiana Purchase (1803). ► **Jeffersonian** (ˌdʒɛfə'səʊnɪən) *adj, n*

Jefferson City *n* a city in central Missouri, the state capital, on the Missouri River. Pop.: 35 481 (1990).

Jeffrey ('dʒɛfrɪ) *n* **Francis,** Lord. 1773–1850, Scottish judge and literary critic. As editor of the *Edinburgh Review* (1803–29), he was noted for the severity of his criticism of the romantic poets, esp. Wordsworth.

Jeffreys ('dʒɛfrɪz) *n* **George,** 1st Baron Jeffreys of Wem. ?1645–89, English judge, notorious for his brutality at the "Bloody Assizes" (1685), where those involved in Monmouth's rebellion were tried.

jehad (dʒɪ'hæd) *n* a variant spelling of **jihad.**

Jehol (dʒə'hɒl) *n* **1** a former province of NE China, north of the Great Wall: divided among Hebei, Liaoning, and Inner Mongolia in 1956. Area: 192 380 sq. km (74 278 sq. miles). **2** a region of NE China, in Hebei and Liaoning provinces: mountainous.

Jehoshaphat (dʒɪ'hɒʃəˌfæt, -'hɒs-) *n Old Testament.* **1** the king of Judah (?873–?849 B.C.) (I Kings 22:41–50). **2 Valley of Jehoshaphat.** the site of Jehovah's apocalyptic judgment upon the nations (Joel 4:14).

Jehovah (dʒɪ'həʊvə) *n Old Testament.* the personal name of God, revealed to Moses on Mount Horeb (Exodus 3). [C16: from Medieval Latin, from Hebrew YHVH: the original vocalization was considered too sacred to be pronounced and the vowels of Eloah (God) were therefore substituted in the Masoretic text, whence Yetto Vah]

Jehovah's Witness *n* a member of a Christian Church of American origin, the followers of which believe that the end of the present world system of government is near, that all other Churches and religions are false or evil, that all war is unlawful, and that the civil law must be resisted whenever it conflicts with their Church's own religious principles.

Jehovist (dʒɪ'həʊvɪst) *n* **1** another name for the **Yahwist. 2** a person who maintains that the name YHVH in the Hebrew text of the Old Testament was originally pronounced *Jehovah.* ◆ *adj* **3** of or relating to the Yahwist source of the Pentateuch. ► **Je'hovism** *n* ► **Jehovistic** (ˌdʒiːhəʊ'vɪstɪk) *adj*

Jehu ('dʒiːhjuː) *n* **1** *Old Testament.* the king of Israel (?842–?815 B.C.); the slayer of Jezebel (II Kings 9:11–30). **2** a fast driver, esp. one who is reckless (from the phrase **to drive like Jehu.** II Kings 9:20).

jejune (dʒɪ'dʒuːn) *adj* **1** simple; naive; unsophisticated. **2** insipid; dull; dry. **3** lacking nourishment; insubstantial or barren. [C17: from Latin *jējūnus* hungry, empty] ► **je'junely** *adv* ► **je'juneness** *or* **je'junity** *n*

jejunostomy (dʒɪdʒuː'nɒstəmɪ) *n* the surgical formation of an opening from the jejunum to the surface of the body, through which food may be introduced.

jejunum (dʒɪ'dʒuːnəm) *n* the part of the small intestine between the duodenum and the ileum. [C16: from Latin, from *jējūnus* empty; from the belief that the jejunum is empty after death] ► **je'junal** *adj*

Jekyll ('dʒɛkᵊl) *n* **Gertrude.** 1843–1932, British landscape gardener: noted for her simplicity of design and use of indigenous plants.

Jekyll and Hyde ('dʒɛkᵊl; haɪd) *n* **a** a person with two distinct personalities, one good, the other evil. **b** (*as modifier*): *a Jekyll-and-Hyde personality.* [C19: after the principal character of Robert Louis Stevenson's novel *The Strange Case of Dr Jekyll and Mr Hyde* (1886)]

jell *or* **gel** (dʒɛl) *vb* **jells, jelling, jelled** *or* **gels, gelling, gelled. 1** to make or become gelatinous; congeal. **2** (*intr*) to assume definite form: *his ideas have jelled.* ◆ *n* **3** *U.S.* an informal word for **jelly.** [C19: back formation from JELLY[1]]

jellaba *or* **jellabah** ('dʒɛləbə) *n* a kind of loose cloak with a hood, worn esp. in North Africa and the Middle East. [from Arabic *jallabah*]

Jellicoe ('dʒɛlɪˌkəʊ) *n* **John Rushworth,** 1st Earl Jellicoe. 1859–1935, British admiral, who commanded the Grand Fleet at the Battle of Jutland (1916), which incapacitated the German fleet for the rest of World War I.

jellied ('dʒɛlɪd) *adj* **1** congealed into jelly, esp. by cooling. **2** containing, set in, or coated with jelly.

jellies ('dʒɛlɪz) *pl n Brit. slang.* gelatine capsules of temazepam, dissolved and injected as a recreational drug. [C20: shortened from GELATINE]

jellify ('dʒɛlɪˌfaɪ) *vb* **-fies, -fying, -fied.** to make into or become jelly. ► **ˌjellifi'cation** *n*

Jell-o ('dʒɛləʊ) *n Trademark.* (in U.S. and Canada) jelly.

jelly[1] ('dʒɛlɪ) *n, pl* **-lies. 1** a fruit-flavoured clear dessert set with gelatine. U.S. and Canadian trademark: **Jell-o. 2** a preserve made from the juice of fruit boiled with sugar and used as jam. **3** a savoury food preparation set with gelatine or with a strong gelatinous stock and having a soft elastic consistency: *calf's-foot jelly.* **4** anything having the consistency of jelly. **5** *Informal.* a coloured gelatine filter that can be fitted in front of a stage or studio light. ◆ *vb* **-lies, -lying, -lied. 6** to jellify. [C14: from Old French *gelee* frost, jelly, from *geler* to set hard, from Latin *gelāre,* from *gelu* frost] ► **'jelly-ˌlike** *adj*

jelly[2] ('dʒɛlɪ) *n Brit.* a slang name for **gelignite.**

jelly baby *n Brit.* a small sweet made from a gelatinous substance formed to resemble a baby in shape.

jelly bag *n* a muslin bag used to strain off the juice from the fruit in making jelly (the preserve).

jellybean ('dʒɛlɪˌbiːn) *n* a bean-shaped sweet with a brightly coloured coating around a gelatinous filling.

jellyfish ('dʒɛlɪˌfɪʃ) *n, pl* **-fish** *or* **-fishes. 1** any marine medusoid coelenterate of the class *Scyphozoa,* having a gelatinous umbrella-shaped body with trailing tentacles. **2** any other medusoid coelenterate. **3** *Informal.* a weak indecisive person.

jelly fungus *n* a member of any of three orders (*Auriculariales, Tremellales,* and *Dacrymycetales*) of basidiomycetous fungi that grow on trees and have a jelly-like consistency when wet. They include the conspicuous **yellow brain fungus** (*Tremella mesenterica*), the black **witch's butter** (*Exidia plana*), and the pinky-red **jew's-ear** (*Auricularia auricula-judae*).

jelly mould *n* **1** a mould made of glass, copper, etc., used to make a jelly in a decorative shape. **2** the N.Z. term for **jelly fungus.**

jelutong ('dʒɛlə,tɒŋ) *n* **1** a Malaysian apocynaceous tree of the genus *Dyera*, esp. *D. costulata.* **2** the latex obtained from this tree, used in the manufacture of chewing gum. **3** the wood of this tree. [C19: from Malay]

jemadar ('dʒɛmə,dɑː) *n* **1** a native junior officer belonging to a locally raised regiment serving as mercenaries in India, esp. with the British Army (until 1947). **2** an officer in the Indian police. [C18: from Urdu *jama 'dār*, from Persian *jama 'at* body of men + *dār* having]

Jemappes (*French* ʒəmap) *n* a town in SW Belgium, in Hainaut province west of Mons: scene of a battle (1792) during the French Revolutionary Wars, in which the French defeated the Austrians. Pop.: 18 100 (latest est.).

jembe ('dʒɛmbɛ) *n E African.* a hoe. [C19: from Swahili]

jemmy ('dʒɛmɪ) *or U.S.* **jimmy** *n, pl* **-mies. 1** a short steel crowbar used, esp. by burglars, for forcing doors and windows. ◆ *vb* **-mies, -mying, -mied. 2** (*tr*) to prise (something) open with a jemmy. [C19: from the pet name for *James*]

Jena (*German* 'jeːna) *n* a city in E central Germany, in Thuringia: university (1558), at which Hegel and Schiller taught; site of the battle (1806) in which Napoleon Bonaparte defeated the Prussians; optical and precision instrument industry. Pop.: 101 061 (1996 est.).

je ne sais quoi *French.* (ʒənsekwa) *n* an indefinable quality, esp. of personality. [literally: I don't know what]

Jenghis Khan ('dʒɛŋgɪs 'kɑːn) *n* See **Genghis Khan.**

Jenkins ('dʒɛŋkɪnz) *n* **Roy (Harris),** Baron Jenkins of Hillhead. born 1920, British Social Democrat politician; president of the Common Market Commission (1977–80); originally a Labour politician; cofounder of the Social Democratic Party (1981); leader of party (1982–83); Chancellor of Oxford University from 1987.

Jenner ('dʒɛnə) *n* **1 Edward.** 1749–1823, English physician, who discovered vaccination by showing that injections of cowpox virus produce immunity against smallpox (1796). **2** Sir **William.** 1815–98, English physician and pathologist, who differentiated between typhus and typhoid fevers (1849).

jennet, genet, *or* **gennet** ('dʒɛnɪt) *n* **1** Also called: **jenny.** a female donkey or ass. **2** a small Spanish riding horse. [C15: from Old French *genet*, from Catalan *ginet,* horse of the type used by the *Zenete*, from Arabic *Zanātah* the Zenete, a Moorish people renowned for their horsemanship]

jenny ('dʒɛnɪ) *n, pl* **-nies. 1** a hand-operated machine for turning up the edge of a piece of sheet metal in preparation for making a joint. **2** the female of certain animals or birds, esp. a donkey, ass, or wren. **3** short for **spinning jenny. 4** *Billiards, etc.* an in-off. See **long jenny, short jenny.** [C17: from the name *Jenny*, diminutive of *Jane*]

Jensen (*Danish* 'jɛnsən) *n* **Johannes Vilhelm** (jo'hanəs 'vɪlhelm). 1873–1950, Danish novelist, poet, and essayist: best known for his novel sequence about the origins of mankind *The Long Journey* (1908–22). Nobel prize for literature 1944.

jeopardize *or* **jeopardise** ('dʒɛpə,daɪz) *vb* (*tr*) **1** to risk; hazard: *he jeopardized his job by being persistently unpunctual.* **2** to put in danger; imperil.

jeopardy ('dʒɛpədɪ) *n* (usually preceded by *in*) **1** danger of injury, loss, death, etc.; risk; peril; hazard: *his health was in jeopardy.* **2** *Law.* danger of being convicted and punished for a criminal offence. See also **double jeopardy.** [C14: from Old French *jeu parti,* literally: divided game, hence uncertain issue, from *jeu* game, from Latin *jocus* joke, game + *partir* to divide, from Latin *partīrī*]

Jephthah ('dʒɛfθə) *n Old Testament.* a judge of Israel, who sacrificed his daughter in fulfilment of a vow (Judges 11:12–40). Douay spelling: **Jephte** ('dʒɛftə).

jequirity *or* **jequerity** (dʒɪ'kwɪrɪtɪ) *n, pl* **-ties. 1** other names for **Indian liquorice. 2 jequirity bean.** the seed of the Indian liquorice. [C19: from Portuguese *jequiriti,* from Tupi-Guarani *jekiriti*]

Jer. *Bible. abbrev. for* Jeremiah.

Jerba ('dʒɜːbə) *n* a variant spelling of **Djerba.**

jerbil ('dʒɜːbɪl) *n* a variant spelling of **gerbil.**

jerboa (dʒɜː'bəʊə) *n* any small nocturnal burrowing rodent of the family *Dipodidae,* inhabiting dry regions of Asia and N Africa, having pale sandy fur, large ears, and long hind legs specialized for jumping. [C17: from New Latin, from Arabic *yarbū'*]

jeremiad (,dʒɛrɪ'maɪəd) *n* a long mournful lamentation or complaint.

Jeremiah (,dʒɛrɪ'maɪə) *n* **1** *Old Testament.* **1a** a major prophet of Judah from about 626 to 587 B.C. **1b** the book containing his oracles. **2** a person who habitually prophesies doom or denounces contemporary society.

jerepigo (,dʒɛrə'piːgəʊ) *n S. African.* a usually red heavy dessert wine. [from Portuguese *geropiga*]

Jerez (*Spanish* xe'reθ) *n* a town in SW Spain: famous for the making of sherry. Pop.: 191 394 (1995 est.). Official name: **Jerez de la Frontera** (xe'reð ðe la frɔn'tera). Former name: **Xeres.**

Jericho ('dʒɛrɪ,kəʊ) *n* a village in the West Bank near the N end of the Dead Sea, 251 m (825 ft.) below sea level: on the site of an ancient city, the first place to be taken by the Israelites under Joshua after entering the Promised Land in the 14th century B.C. (Joshua 6).

jerid (dʒə'riːd) *n* a wooden javelin used in Muslim countries in military displays on horseback. Also: **jereed, jerreed.**

jerk[1] (dʒɜːk) *vb* **1** to move or cause to move with an irregular or spasmodic motion. **2** to throw, twist, pull, or push (something) abruptly or spasmodically. **3** (*tr;* often foll. by *out*) to utter (words, sounds, etc.) in a spasmodic, abrupt, or breathless manner. ◆ *n* **4** an abrupt or spasmodic movement. **5** an irregular jolting motion: *the car moved with a jerk.* **6** (*pl*) Also called: **physical jerks.** *Brit. informal.* physical exercises. **7** (*pl*) *U.S.* a slang word for **chorea. 8** *Slang, chiefly U.S. and Canadian.* a person regarded with contempt, esp. a stupid or ignorant person. [C16: probably variant of *yerk* to pull stitches tight in making a shoe; compare Old English *gearcian* to make ready] ▸ **'jerker** *n* ▸ **'jerking** *adj, n*

jerk[2] (dʒɜːk) *vb* (*tr*) **1** to preserve (venison, beef, etc.) by cutting into thin strips and curing by drying in the sun. ◆ *n* **2** Also called: **jerky.** jerked meat, esp. beef. [C18: back formation from *jerky,* from CHARQUI]

jerkin ('dʒɜːkɪn) *n* **1** a sleeveless and collarless short jacket worn by men or women. **2** a man's sleeveless and collarless fitted jacket, often made of leather, worn in the 16th and 17th centuries. [C16: of unknown origin]

jerk off *or U.S.* **jack off** *vb* (*adv often reflexive*) *Taboo slang.* (of a male) to masturbate.

jerkwater ('dʒɜːk,wɔːtə) *adj U.S. and Canadian slang.* inferior and insignificant: *a jerkwater town.* [C19: originally referring to railway locomotives for which water was taken on in buckets from streams along the route]

jerky[1] ('dʒɜːkɪ) *adj* **jerkier, jerkiest.** characterized by jerks; spasmodic. ▸ **'jerkily** *adv* ▸ **'jerkiness** *n*

jerky[2] ('dʒɜːkɪ) *n* another word for **jerk**[2] (sense 2).

jeroboam (,dʒɛrə'bəʊəm) *n* a wine bottle holding the equivalent of four normal bottles (approximately 104 ounces). Also called: **double-magnum.** [C19: humorous allusion to JEROBOAM (sense 1), described as a "mighty man of valour" (I Kings 11:28) who "made Israel to sin" (I Kings 14:16)]

Jeroboam (,dʒɛrə'bəʊəm) *n Old Testament.* **1** the first king of the northern kingdom of Israel (?922–?901 B.C.). **2** king of the northern kingdom of Israel (?786–?746 B.C.).

Jerome (dʒə'rəʊm) *n* **1 Saint.** Latin name *Eusebius Hieronymus.* ?347–?420 A.D., Christian monk and scholar, whose outstanding work was the production of the Vulgate. Feast day: Sept. 30. **2 Jerome K(lapka).** 1859–1927, English humorous writer; author of *Three Men in a Boat* (1889).

jerreed (dʒə'riːd) *n* a variant spelling of **jerid.**

jerry ('dʒɛrɪ) *n, pl* **-ries. 1** *Brit.* an informal word for **chamber pot. 2** short for **jeroboam.**

Jerry ('dʒɛrɪ) *n, pl* **-ries.** *Brit. slang.* **1** a German, esp. a German soldier. **2** the Germans collectively: *Jerry didn't send his bombers out last night.*

jerry-build *vb* **-builds, -building, -built.** (*tr*) to build (houses, flats, etc.) badly using cheap materials. ▸ **'jerry-,builder** *n*

jerry can *n* a flat-sided can with a capacity of between 4.5 and 5 gallons used for storing or transporting liquids, esp. motor fuel: originally a German design adopted by the British Army during World War II. [C20: from JERRY]

jersey ('dʒɜːzɪ) *n* **1** a knitted garment covering the upper part of the body. **2a** a machine-knitted slightly elastic cloth of wool, silk, nylon, etc., used for clothing. **2b** (*as modifier*): *a jersey suit.* **3** a football shirt. [C16: from JERSEY, from the woollen sweaters traditionally worn by the fishermen]

Jersey ('dʒɜːzɪ) *n* **1** an island in the English Channel, the largest of the Channel Islands: forms, with two other islands, the bailiwick of Jersey; colonized from Normandy in the 11th century and still officially French-speaking; noted for finance, market gardening, dairy farming, and tourism. Capital: St Helier. Pop.: 85 600 (1998 est.). Area: 116 sq. km (45 sq. miles). **2** a breed of dairy cattle producing milk with a high butterfat content, originating from the island of Jersey.

Jersey City *n* an industrial city in NE New Jersey, opposite Manhattan on a peninsula between the Hudson and Hackensack Rivers: part of the Port of New York; site of one of the greatest railway terminals in the world. Pop.: 229 039 (1996 est.).

Jerusalem (dʒə'ruːsələm) *n* **1** the capital of Israel (recognition of this has been withheld by a number of countries pending completion of negotiations on Palestinian autonomy), situated in the Judaean hills: became capital of the Hebrew kingdom after its capture by David around 1000 B.C.; destroyed by Nebuchadnezzar of Babylon in 586 B.C.; taken by the Romans in 63 B.C.; devastated in 70 A.D. and 135 A.D. during the Jewish rebellions against Rome; fell to the Arabs in 637 and to the Seljuk Turks in 1071; ruled by Crusaders from 1099 to 1187 and by the Egyptians and Turks until conquered by the British (1917); centre of the British mandate of Palestine from 1920 to 1948, when the Arabs took the old city and the Jews held the new city; unified after the Six Day War (1967) under the Israelis; the holy city of Jews, Christians, and Muslims. Pop.: 591 400 (1997 est.). **2a the New Jerusalem.** *Christianity.* Heaven. **2b** any ideal city.

Jerusalem artichoke *n* **1** a North American sunflower, *Helianthus tuberosus,* widely cultivated for its underground edible tubers. **2** the tuber of this plant, which is cooked and eaten as a vegetable. ◆ See also **artichoke** (senses 1, 2). [C17: by folk etymology from Italian *girasole articiocco;* see GIRASOL]

Jerusalem cherry *n* a small South American solanaceous shrub, *Solanum pseudo-capsicum,* cultivated as a house plant for its white flowers and inedible reddish cherry-like fruit.

Jerusalem cross *n* a cross the equal arms of which end in a bar. Also called: **cross potent.**

Jerusalem oak *n* a weedy North American chenopodiaceous plant, *Chenopodium botrys,* that has lobed leaves and smells of turpentine.

Jerusalem syndrome *n* a delusive condition affecting some visitors to Jerusalem in which the sufferer identifies with a major figure from his or her religious background.

Jervis Bay ('dʒɑːvɪs) *n* an inlet of the Pacific in SE Australia, on the coast of S New South Wales: part of the Australian Capital Territory: site of the Royal Australian Naval College.

Jespersen ('jɛspəsᵊn, 'dʒɛs-) *n* **(Jens) Otto (Harry).** 1860–1943, Danish philologist: author of *Modern English Grammar* (1909–31).

jess (dʒɛs) *Falconry.* ◆ *n* **1** a short leather strap, one end of which is permanently attached to the leg of a hawk or falcon while the other can be attached to a leash. ◆ *vb* **2** (*tr*) to put jesses on (a hawk or falcon). [C14: from Old French *ges,* from Latin *jactus* a throw, from *jacere* to throw] ▸ **jessed** *adj*

jessamine ('dʒɛsəmɪn) *n* another name for **jasmine** (sense 1).

Jesse ('dʒɛsɪ) *n Old Testament.* the father of David (I Samuel 16).

Jesselton ('dʒɛsəltən) *n* the former name of **Kota Kinabalu.**

Jesse window *n* a window in a church with a representation of Christ's descent from Jesse, usually in the form of a genealogical tree.

jessie ('dʒɛsɪ) *n Slang.* an effeminate, weak, or cowardly boy or man.

jest (dʒɛst) *n* **1** something done or said for amusement; joke. **2** a frivolous mood or attitude; playfulness; fun: *to act in jest.* **3** a jeer or taunt. **4** an object of derision; laughing stock; butt. ◆ *vb* **5** to act or speak in an amusing, teasing, or frivolous way; joke. **6** to make fun of (a person or thing); scoff or mock. [C13: variant of GEST] ▸ **'jestful** *adj* ▸ **'jesting** *adj, n* ▸ **'jestingly** *adv*

jester ('dʒɛstə) *n* a professional clown employed by a king or nobleman, esp. at courts during the Middle Ages.

Jesu ('dʒiːzjuː) *n* a poetic name for or vocative form of **Jesus.** [C17: from Late Latin, vocative of JESUS]

Jesuit ('dʒɛzjʊɪt) *n* **1** a member of a Roman Catholic religious order (the **Society of Jesus**) founded by Ignatius Loyola in 1534 with the aims of defending the papacy and Catholicism against the Reformation and to undertake missionary work among the heathen. **2** (*sometimes not cap.*) *Informal, offensive.* a person given to subtle and equivocating arguments; casuist. [C16: from New Latin *Jēsuita,* from Late Latin *Jēsus* + *-ita* -ITE[1]] ▸ **,Jesu'itic** *or* **,Jesu'itical** *adj* ▸ **Jesu'itically** *adv*

Jesuitism ('dʒɛzjʊɪ,tɪzəm) *or* **Jesuitry** *n* **1** theology or practices of the Jesuits. **2** *Informal, offensive.* subtle and equivocating arguments; casuistry.

Jesus ('dʒiːzəs) *n* **1** Also called: **Jesus Christ, Jesus of Nazareth.** ?4 B.C.–?29 A.D., founder of Christianity, born in Bethlehem and brought up in Nazareth as a Jew. He is believed by Christians to be the Son of God and to have been miraculously conceived by the Virgin Mary, wife of Joseph. With 12 disciples, he undertook two missionary journeys through Galilee, performing miracles, teaching, and proclaiming the coming of the Kingdom of God. His revolutionary Sermon on the Mount (Matthew 5–8), which preaches love, humility, and charity, the essence of his teaching, aroused the hostility of the Pharisees. After the Last Supper with his disciples, he was betrayed by Judas and crucified. He is believed by Christians to have risen from his tomb after three days, appeared to his disciples several times, and ascended to Heaven after 40 days. **2** *Son of Sirach.* 3rd century B.C., author of the Apocryphal book of Ecclesiasticus. ◆ *interj also* **Jesus wept. 3** *Taboo slang.* used to express intense surprise, dismay, etc. [via Latin from Greek *Iēsous,* from Hebrew *Yeshūa',* shortened from *Yehōshūa'* God is help, JOSHUA]

Jesus freak *n Informal.* a member of any of various Christian groups that combine a hippy communal way of life with zealous evangelicalism.

jet[1] (dʒɛt) *n* **1** a thin stream of liquid or gas forced out of a small aperture or nozzle. **2** an outlet or nozzle for emitting such a stream. **3** a jet-propelled aircraft. **4** *Astronomy.* a long thin feature extending from an active galaxy and usually observed at radio wavelengths. ◆ *vb* **jets, jetting, jetted. 5** to issue or cause to issue in a jet: *water jetted from the hose; he jetted them with water.* **6** to transport or be transported by jet aircraft. [C16: from Old French *jeter* to throw, from Latin *jactāre* to toss about, frequentative of *jacere* to throw]

jet[2] (dʒɛt) *n* **a** a hard black variety of lignite that takes a brilliant polish and is used for jewellery, ornaments, etc. **b** (*as modifier*): *jet earrings.* [C14: from Old French *jaiet,* from Latin *gagātēs,* from Greek *lithos gagatēs* stone of *Gagai,* a town in Lycia, Asia Minor]

JET (dʒɛt) *n acronym for* Joint European Torus; an apparatus at Culham, Oxfordshire, for research into energy production by nuclear fusion.

jet black *n* **a** a deep black colour. **b** (*as adj*): *jet-black hair.*

jet-boat *n N.Z.* a power boat that is powered and steered by a jet of water under pressure.

jet condenser *n* a steam condenser in which steam is condensed by jets of water.

jeté (ʒə'teɪ) *n Ballet.* a step in which the dancer springs from one leg and lands on the other. [French, literally: thrown, from *jeter;* see JET[1]]

jet engine *n* a gas turbine, esp. one fitted to an aircraft.

Jethro ('dʒɛθrəʊ) *n Old Testament.* a Midianite priest, the father-in-law of Moses (Exodus 3:1; 4:18).

jet lag *n* a general feeling of fatigue and disorientation often experienced by travellers by jet aircraft who cross several time zones in relatively few hours.

jetliner ('dʒɛt,laɪnə) *n* a commercial airliner powered by jet engines.

jet pipe *n* the duct attached to the rear of a gas turbine through which the exhaust gases are discharged, esp. one fitted to an aircraft engine.

jet plane *n* an aircraft powered by one or more jet engines.

jetport ('dʒɛt,pɔːt) *n* an airport for jet planes.

jet-propelled *adj* **1** driven by jet propulsion. **2** *Informal.* very fast.

jet propulsion *n* **1** propulsion by means of a jet of fluid. **2** propulsion by means of a gas turbine, esp. when the exhaust gases provide the propulsive thrust.

jetsam *or* **jetsom** ('dʒɛtsəm) *n* **1** that portion of the equipment or cargo of a vessel thrown overboard to lighten her, as during a storm. Compare **flotsam** (sense 1), **lagan. 2** another word for **flotsam** (sense 2). [C16: shortened from JETTISON]

jet set *n* **a** a rich and fashionable social set the members of which travel widely for pleasure. **b** (*as modifier*): *jet-set travellers.* ▸ **'jet-,setter** *n* ▸ **'jet-,setting** *adj*

jet ski *n* **1** *Trademark.* a small self-propelled vehicle for one person resembling a scooter, which skims across water on a flat keel, and is steered by means of handlebars. ◆ *vb* **jet-ski, -skis, -skiing, -skied** *or* **-ski'd.** (*intr*) **2** to ride a jet ski. ▸ **jet skier** *n* ▸ **jet skiing** *n*

jet stream *n* **1** *Meteorol.* a narrow belt of high-altitude winds (about 12 000 metres high) moving east at high speeds and having an important effect on frontogenesis. **2** the jet of exhaust gases produced by a gas turbine, rocket motor, etc.

jettison ('dʒɛtɪsᵊn, -zᵊn) *vb* (*tr*) **-sons, -soning, -soned. 1** to throw away; abandon: *to jettison old clothes.* **2** to throw overboard. ◆ *n* **3** another word for **jetsam** (sense 1). [C15: from Old French *getaison,* ultimately from Latin *jactātiō* a tossing about; see JACTATION]

jetton ('dʒɛtᵊn) *n* a counter or token, esp. a chip used in such gambling games as roulette. [C18: from French *jeton,* from *jeter* to cast up (accounts); see JET[1]]

jetty[1] ('dʒɛtɪ) *n, pl* **-ties. 1** a structure built from a shore out into the water to direct currents or protect a harbour. **2** a landing pier; dock. [C15: from Old French *jetee* projecting part, literally: something thrown out, from *jeter* to throw; see JET[1]]

jetty[2] ('dʒɛtɪ) *adj* of or resembling jet, esp. in colour or polish. ▸ **'jettiness** *n*

jeu d'esprit (*French* ʒø dɛspri) *n, pl* ***jeux d'esprit*** (ʒø dɛspri). a light-hearted display of wit or cleverness, esp. in literature. [literally: play of spirit]

jeunesse dorée *French.* (ʒœnɛs dɔre) *n* rich and fashionable young people. [literally: gilded youth]

Jevons ('dʒɛvᵊnz) *n* **William Stanley.** 1835–82, English economist and logician: introduced the concept of final or marginal utility in *The Theory of Political Economy* (1871).

Jew (dʒuː) *n* **1** a member of the Semitic people who are notionally descended from the ancient Israelites, are spread throughout the world, and are linked by loose cultural or religious ties. **2** a person whose religion is Judaism. ◆ See also **Hebrew, Israeli, Israelite.** [C12: from Old French *juiu,* from Latin *jūdaeus,* from Greek *ioudaios,* from Hebrew *yehūdī,* from *yehūdāh* JUDAH]

Jew-baiting *n* active persecution or harassment of Jews. ▸ **'Jew-,baiter** *n*

jewel ('dʒuːəl) *n* **1** a precious or semiprecious stone; gem. **2** a person or thing resembling a jewel in preciousness, brilliance, etc. **3** a gemstone, often synthetically produced, used as a bearing in a watch. **4** a piece of jewellery. **5** an ornamental glass boss, sometimes faceted, used in stained glasswork. **6 jewel in the crown.** the most valuable, esteemed, or successful person or thing of a number: *who will be the jewel in the crown of English soccer?* ◆ *vb* **-els, -elling, -elled** *or U.S.* **-els, -eling, -eled. 7** (*tr*) to fit or decorate with a jewel or jewels. [C13: from Old French *jouel,* perhaps from *jeu* game, from Latin *jocus*] ▸ **'jewelled** *or U.S.* **'jeweled** *adj* ▸ **'jewel-,like** *adj*

jewelfish ('dʒuːəl,fɪʃ) *n, pl* **-fish** *or* **-fishes.** an African cichlid, *Hemichromis bimaculatus*: a beautifully coloured and popular aquarium fish.

jeweller *or U.S.* **jeweler** ('dʒuːələ) *n* a person whose business is the cutting, polishing, or setting of gemstones or the making, repairing, or selling of jewellery.

jeweller's rouge *n* a finely powdered form of ferric oxide used as a metal polish. Also called: **crocus.** See also **colcothar.**

jewellery *or U.S.* **jewelry** ('dʒuːəlrɪ) *n* **1** objects that are worn for personal adornment, such as bracelets, rings, necklaces, etc., considered collectively. **2** the art or business of a jeweller.

Jewess ('dʒuːɪs) *n* a Jewish girl or woman.

jewfish ('dʒuː,fɪʃ) *n, pl* **-fish** *or* **-fishes. 1** any of various large dark serranid fishes, such as *Mycteroperca bonaci,* of warm or tropical seas. **2** *Austral.* a freshwater catfish. [C17: of uncertain origin]

Jewish ('dʒuːɪʃ) *adj* **1** of, relating to, or characteristic of Jews. ◆ *n* **2** a less common word for **Yiddish.** ▸ **'Jewishly** *adv* ▸ **'Jewishness** *n*

Jewish Autonomous Region *n* an administrative division of SE Russia, in E Siberia: colonized by Jews in 1928; largely agricultural. Capital: Birobidzhan. Pop.: 216 000 (1995 est.). Area: 36 000 sq. km (13 895 sq. miles). Also called: **Birobidzhan, Birobijan.**

Jewish calendar *n* the lunisolar calendar used by the Jews, in which time is reckoned from 3761 BC, regarded as the year of the Creation. The months, Nisan, Iyar, Sivan, Tammuz, Av, Elul, Tishri, Cheshvan, Kislev, Tevet, Shevat, and Adar, have either 29 or 30 days. Originally a new month was declared when the new moon was sighted in Jerusalem, but when this became impossible, a complex formula was devised to keep Rosh Chodesh near to the new moon. In addition, to keep the harvest festivals in the right seasons, there is a Metonic cycle of 14 years, in five of which an additional month is added after Shevat (see **Adar**). The year according to biblical reckoning begins with Nisan, and the civil year begins with Tishri; the years are numbered from Tishri. Also called: **Hebrew calendar.**

jew lizard *n* a large Australian lizard, *Amphibolus barbatus,* having a pouch beneath the jaw that is distended when the animal is threatened. Also called: **bearded lizard** *or* **dragon.**

Jewry ('dʒʊərɪ) *n, pl* **-ries. 1a** Jews collectively. **1b** the Jewish religion or culture. **2** *Archaic.* (sometimes found in street names in England) a quarter of a town inhabited by Jews. **3 the.** (in some anti-semitic literature) the Jews conceived of as an organized force seeking world domination. **4** *Archaic.* the land of Judaea.

jew's-ear *n* See **jelly fungus.**

jew's-harp *n* a musical instrument consisting of a small lyre-shaped metal frame held between the teeth, with a steel tongue plucked with the finger. Changes in pitch are produced by varying the size of the mouth cavities.

Jezebel ('dʒɛzə,bɛl, -bᵊl) *n* **1** *Old Testament.* the wife of Ahab, king of Israel: she fostered the worship of Baal and tried to destroy the prophets of Israel (I Kings 18:4–13); she was killed by Jehu (II Kings 9:29–37). **2** (*sometimes not cap.*) a shameless or scheming woman.

Jezreel ('dʒɛzrɪəl) *n* **Plain of.** another name for **Esdraelon.** ▸ **'Jezreel,ite** *n*

JFET ('dʒeɪfɛt) *n acronym for* junction field-effect transistor; a type of field-effect transistor in which the semiconductor gate region or regions form one or more p-n junctions with the conduction channel. Compare **IGFET.**

JFK *abbrev. for* John Fitzgerald Kennedy.

Jhabvala (dʒæb'vɑːlə) *n* **Ruth Prawer,** original name *Ruth Prawer.* born 1927, British writer living in India and the U.S., born in Germany to Polish parents:

author of the Booker-prizewinning novel *Heat and Dust* (1975) and scripts for films by James Ivory.

Jhansi ('dʒɑːnsɪ) *n* a city in central India, in SW Uttar Pradesh: scene of a mutiny against the British in 1857. Pop.: 300 850 (1991).

jhatka ('dʒætkə) *n* the slaughter of animals for food according to Sikh law. [Punjabi]

Jhelum ('dʒiːləm) *n* a river in Pakistan and Kashmir, rising in W central Kashmir and flowing northwest through the Vale of Kashmir, then southwest into N West Punjab to join the Chenab River: important for irrigation, having the Mangla Dam (Pakistan), completed in 1967. Length: about 720 km (450 miles).

JHVH *or* **JHWH** *Old Testament.* variants of **YHVH**.

-ji (-dziː) *Indian.* a suffix placed after a person's name or title as a mark of respect. [Hindi]

Jiang Jie Shi ('dʒjæŋ 'dʒjː 'ʃː) *n* See **Chiang Kai-shek**.

Jiang Jing Guo ('dʒjæŋ 'dʒɪŋ 'gwəʊ) *n* See **Chiang Ching-kuo**.

Jiang Qing ('dʒjæŋ 'tʃɪŋ) *or* **Chiang Ch'ing** *n* 1913–91, Chinese Communist actress and politician; widow of Mao Tse-tung. She was a leading member of the Gang of Four.

Jiangsu ('dʒjæŋ'suː) *or* **Kiangsu** *n* a province of E China, on the Yellow Sea: consists mostly of the marshy delta of the Yangtze River, with some of China's largest cities and most densely populated areas. Capital: Nanjing. Pop.: 70 660 000 (1996 est.). Area: 102 200 sq. km (39 860 sq. miles).

Jiangxi ('dʒjæŋ'ʃiː) *or* **Kiangsi** *n* a province of SE central China, in the basins of the Kan River and the Poyang Lake: mineral resources include coal and tungsten. Capital: Nanchang. Pop.: 40 630 000 (1996 est.). Area: 164 800 sq. km (64 300 sq. miles).

Jiang Zemin ('dʒjæŋ ʒeɪ'mɪn) *n* born 1926, Chinese Communist politician: president from 1993.

Jiazhou ('dʒjæ'dʒəʊ) *or* **Kiaochow** *n* a territory of NE China, in SE Shandong province, surrounding **Jiazhou Bay** (an inlet of the Yellow Sea): leased to Germany from 1898 to 1914. Area: about 520 sq. km (200 sq. miles).

jib[1] (dʒɪb) *n* **1** *Nautical.* any triangular sail set forward of the foremast of a vessel. **2 cut of someone's jib.** someone's manner, behaviour, style, etc. **3** *Obsolete.* **3a** the lower lip, usually when it protrudes forwards in a grimace. **3b** the face or nose. [C17: of unknown origin]

jib[2] (dʒɪb) *vb* **jibs, jibbing, jibbed.** (*intr*) *Chiefly Brit.* **1** (often foll. by *at*) to be reluctant (to); hold back (from); balk (at). **2** (of an animal) to stop short and refuse to go forwards: *the horse jibbed at the jump.* **3** *Nautical.* variant of **gybe**. [C19: of unknown origin] ▸ **'jibber** *n*

jib[3] (dʒɪb) *n* the projecting arm of a crane or the boom of a derrick, esp. one that is pivoted to enable it to be raised or lowered. [C18: probably based on GIBBET]

jib[4] (dʒɪb) *n* (*often pl*) *South Wales dialect.* a contortion of the face; a face: *stop making jibs.* [special use of JIB[1] (in the sense: lower lip, face)]

jibbons ('dʒɪbᵊnz) *pl n Southwest Brit. dialect.* spring onions. [from Norman French *chiboule,* variant of French *ciboule* onion, ultimately from Latin *capulla* an onion patch, from *caepa* an onion]

jib boom *n Nautical.* a spar forming an extension of the bowsprit.

jibe[1] (dʒaɪb), **jib,** *or* **jibb** (dʒɪb) *vb, n Nautical.* variants of **gybe**.

jibe[2] (dʒaɪb) *vb* a variant spelling of **gibe**[1]. ▸ **'jiber** *n* ▸ **'jibingly** *adv*

jibe[3] (dʒaɪb) *vb* (*intr*) *Informal.* to agree; accord; harmonize. [C19: of unknown origin]

jib-headed *adj Nautical.* **1** (of a sail) pointed at the top or head. **2** (of a sailing vessel or rig) having sails that are triangular.

Jibouti *or* **Jibuti** (dʒɪ'buːtɪ) *n* variant spellings of **Djibouti**.

JICTAR ('dʒɪktɑː) *n acronym for* Joint Industry Committee for Television Advertising Research.

Jidda ('dʒɪdə) *or* **Jedda** *n* a port in W Saudi Arabia, on the Red Sea: the diplomatic capital of the country; the port of entry for Mecca, 80 km (50 miles) east. Pop.: 1 500 000 (1991 est.).

jiffy ('dʒɪfɪ) *or* **jiff** (dʒɪf) *n, pl* **jiffies** *or* **jiffs.** *Informal.* a very short time: *wait a jiffy.* [C18: of unknown origin]

Jiffy bag *n Trademark.* a thickly padded but light envelope in which articles such as books are placed for protection in the post.

jig (dʒɪg) *n* **1** any of several old rustic kicking and leaping dances. **2** a piece of music composed for or in the rhythm of this dance, usually in six-eight time. **3** a mechanical device designed to hold and locate a component during machining and to guide the cutting tool. **4** *Angling.* any of various spinning lures that wobble when drawn through the water. **5** Also called: **jigger**. *Mining.* a device for separating ore or coal from waste material by agitation in water. **6** *Obsolete.* a joke or prank. ◆ *vb* **jigs, jigging, jigged. 7** to dance (a jig). **8** to jerk or cause to jerk up and down rapidly. **9** (often foll. by *up*) to fit or be fitted in a jig. **10** (*tr*) to drill or cut (a workpiece) in a jig. **11** *Mining.* to separate ore or coal from waste material using a jig. **12** (*intr*) to produce or manufacture a jig. **13** *Austral. slang.* to play truant from school. [C16 (originally: a dance or the music for it; applied to various modern devices because of the verbal sense: to jerk up and down rapidly): of unknown origin]

Jigawa (ˌdʒɪ'gɑːwə) *n* a state of N Nigeria. Capital: Dutse. Pop.: 3 164 134 (1995 est.). Area (including Kano state): 43 285 sq. km (16 712 sq. miles).

jigger[1] ('dʒɪgə) *n* **1** a person or thing that jigs. **2** *Golf.* an iron, now obsolete, with a thin blade, used for hitting long shots from a bare lie. **3** any of a number of mechanical devices having a vibratory or jerking motion. **4** a light lifting tackle used on ships. **5** a small glass, esp. for whisky, with a capacity of about one and a half ounces. **6** *N.Z.* a light hand- or power-propelled vehicle used on railway lines. **7** *Engineering.* a type of hydraulic lift in which a hydraulic ram operates the lift through a block and tackle which increases the length of the stroke. **8** *Canadian.* a device used when setting a gill net beneath ice. **9** *Mining.* another word for **jig** (sense 5). **10** *Nautical.* short for **jiggermast**. **11** *Billiards.* another word for **bridge**[1] (sense 10). **12** *U.S. and Canadian informal.* a device or thing the name of which is unknown or temporarily forgotten. **13** *Liverpool dialect.* an alleyway.

jigger[2] *or* **jigger flea** ('dʒɪgə) *n* other names for the **chigoe** (sense 1).

jiggered ('dʒɪgəd) *adj* (*postpositive*) **1** *Informal.* damned; blowed: *I'm jiggered if he'll get away with it.* **2** (sometimes foll. by *up*) *Scot. and Northern English dialect.* tired out. [C19: probably euphemism for *buggered;* see BUGGER]

jiggermast ('dʒɪgəˌmɑːst) *n Nautical.* any small mast on a sailing vessel, esp. the mizzenmast of a yawl. Sometimes shortened to **jigger**.

jiggery-pokery ('dʒɪgərɪ'pəʊkərɪ) *n Informal, chiefly Brit.* dishonest or deceitful behaviour or business; trickery. [C19: from Scottish dialect *joukery-pawkery*]

jiggle ('dʒɪgᵊl) *vb* **1** to move or cause to move up and down or to and fro with a short jerky motion: *to jiggle the door handle.* ◆ *n* **2** a short jerky motion. [C19: frequentative of JIG; compare JOGGLE] ▸ **'jiggly** *adj*

jigsaw ('dʒɪgˌsɔː) *n* **1** a mechanical saw with a fine steel blade for cutting intricate curves in sheets of material. **2** See **jigsaw puzzle**. [C19: from JIG (to jerk up and down rapidly) + SAW[1]]

jigsaw puzzle *n* a puzzle in which the player has to reassemble a picture that has been mounted on a wooden or cardboard base and cut into a large number of irregularly shaped interlocking pieces.

jihad *or* **jehad** (dʒɪ'hæd) *n* **1** *Islam.* a holy war against infidels undertaken by Muslims in defence of the Islamic faith. **2** *Islam.* the personal struggle of the individual believer against evil and persecution. **3** *Rare.* a crusade in support of a cause. [C19: from Arabic *jihād* a conflict]

Jilin ('dʒiː'lɪn) *or* **Kirin** *n* **1** a province of NE China, in central Manchuria. Capital: Changchun. Pop.: 25 920 000 (1996 est.). Area: 187 000 sq. km (72 930 sq. miles). **2** Also called: **Chi-lin** ('tʃiː'lɪn). a river port in NE China, in N central Jilin province on the Songhua River. Pop.: 1 270 000 (1991 est.).

jill (dʒɪl) *n Dialect.* a variant spelling of **gill**[4] (sense 2).

jillaroo (ˌdʒɪlə'ruː) *n, pl* **-roos.** *Austral. informal.* a female jackeroo.

jillion ('dʒɪljən) *n Informal.* an extremely large number or amount: *jillions of pounds.* [C20: fanciful coinage based on MILLION, BILLION, etc.] ▸ **'jillionth** *adj*

Jilolo (dʒaɪ'ləʊləʊ) *n* a variant spelling of **Djailolo**. See **Halmahera**.

Jilong ('dʒiː'lʊŋ) *n* the Pinyin transliteration of the Chinese name for **Chilung**.

jilt (dʒɪlt) *vb* **1** (*tr*) to leave or reject (a lover), esp. without previous warning: *she was jilted at the altar.* ◆ *n* **2** a woman who jilts a lover. [C17: from dialect *jillet* flighty girl, diminutive of proper name *Gill*] ▸ **'jilter** *n*

jim crow ('dʒɪm 'krəʊ) *n* (*often caps.*) *U.S.* **1a** the policy or practice of segregating Blacks. **1b** (*as modifier*): *jim-crow laws.* **2a** a derogatory term for Black. **2b** (*as modifier*): *a jim-crow saloon.* **3** an implement for bending iron bars or rails. **4** a crowbar fitted with a claw. [C19: from *Jim Crow,* name of song used as the basis of an act by Thomas Rice (1808–60), American entertainer] ▸ **'jim-'crowism** *n*

Jiménez (*Spanish* xi'meneθ) *n* **Juan Ramón** (xwan ra'mɔn). 1881–1958, Spanish lyric poet. His most famous work is *Platero y yo* (1917), a prose poem: Nobel prize for literature 1956.

Jiménez de Cisneros (*Spanish* xi'meneð ðe θiz'nerɔs) *n* **Francisco** (fran'θisko). 1436–1517, Spanish cardinal and statesman; regent of Castile (1506–07) and Spain (1516–17) and grand inquisitor for Castile and León (1507–17). Also called: **Ximenes de Cisneros, Ximenez de Cisneros.**

jimjams ('dʒɪmˌdʒæmz) *pl n* **1** a slang word for **delirium tremens**. **2** a state of nervous tension, excitement, or anxiety. **3** *Informal.* pyjamas. [C19: whimsical formation based on JAM[1]]

jimmy ('dʒɪmɪ) *n, pl* **-mies,** *vb* **-mies, -mying, -mied.** the U.S. word for **jemmy**.

Jimmy ('dʒɪmɪ) *n Central Scot. urban dialect.* an informal term of address to a male stranger.

Jimmy Woodser (ˌdʒɪmɪ 'wʊdzə) *n Austral. informal.* **1** a man who drinks by himself. **2** a drink taken alone.

jimson weed ('dʒɪmsᵊn) *n* the U.S. and Canadian name for **thorn apple** (sense 1). [C17: from earlier *Jamestown weed,* from *Jamestown,* Virginia]

Jinan ('dʒiː'næn), **Chinan,** *or* **Tsinan** *n* an industrial city in NE China, capital of Shandong province; probably over 3000 years old. Pop.: 2 320 000 (1991 est.).

Jingdezhen ('dʒɪŋ'dɛdʒɛn), **Fowliang,** *or* **Fou-liang** *n* a city in SE China, in NE Jiangxi province east of Lake Poyang: famous for its porcelain industry, established in the sixth century. Pop.: 281 183 (1990 est.).

Jinghis Khan ('dʒɪŋgɪs 'kɑːn) *n* See **Genghis Khan**.

jingle ('dʒɪŋgᵊl) *vb* **1** to ring or cause to ring lightly and repeatedly. **2** (*intr*) to sound in a manner suggestive of jingling: *a jingling verse.* ◆ *n* **3** a sound of metal jingling: *the jingle of the keys.* **4** a catchy and rhythmic verse, song, etc., esp. one used in advertising. [C16: probably of imitative origin; compare Dutch *jengelen*] ▸ **'jingler** *n* ▸ **'jingly** *adj*

jingo ('dʒɪŋgəʊ) *n, pl* **-goes. 1** a loud and bellicose patriot; chauvinist. **2** jingoism. **3 by jingo.** an exclamation of surprise. [C17: originally perhaps a euphemism for *Jesus;* applied to bellicose patriots after the use of *by Jingo!* in the refrain of a 19th-century music-hall song] ▸ **'jingoish** *adj*

jingoism ('dʒɪŋgəʊˌɪzəm) *n* the belligerent spirit or foreign policy of jingoes; chauvinism. ▸ **'jingoist** *n, adj* ▸ **ˌjingo'istic** *adj* ▸ **ˌjingo'istically** *adv*

Jinja ('dʒɪndʒə) *n* a town in Uganda, on the N shore of Lake Victoria. Pop.: 60 979 (1991).

Jinjiang ('dʒɪn'dʒjæŋ), **Chinkiang,** *or* **Cheng-chiang** *n* a port in E China, in S Jiangsu at the confluence of the Yangtze River and the Grand Canal. Pop.: 368 316 (1990 est.).

jink (dʒɪŋk) *vb* **1** to move swiftly or jerkily or make a quick turn in order to dodge or elude. ◆ *n* **2** a jinking movement. [C18: of Scottish origin, imitative of swift movement]

jinker ('dʒɪŋkə) *n Austral.* a vehicle for transporting timber, consisting of a tractor and two sets of wheels for supporting the logs. [of unknown origin]

jinks (dʒɪŋks) *pl n* boisterous or mischievous play (esp. in the phrase **high jinks**). [C18: of unknown origin]

jinn (dʒɪn) *n (often functioning as sing)* the plural of **jinni**.

Jinnah ('dʒɪnə) *n* **Mohammed Ali**. 1876–1948, Indian Muslim statesman. He campaigned for the partition of India into separate Hindu and Muslim states, becoming first governor general of Pakistan (1947–48).

jinni, jinnee, djinni, *or* **djinny** (dʒɪ'ni:, 'dʒɪnɪ) *n, pl* **jinn** *or* **djinn** (dʒɪn). a being or spirit in Muslim belief who could assume human or animal form and influence man by supernatural powers. [C17: from Arabic]

jinrikisha, jinricksha, jinrickshaw, *or* **jinriksha** (dʒɪn'rɪkʃɔ:, -ʃə) *n* other names for **rickshaw**. [C19: from Japanese, from *jin* man + *riki* power + *sha* carriage]

jinx (dʒɪŋks) *n* **1** an unlucky or malevolent force, person, or thing. ◆ *vb* **2** (*tr*) to be or put a jinx on. [C20: perhaps from New Latin *Jynx* genus name of the wryneck, from Greek *iunx* wryneck, the name of a bird used in magic]

Jinzhou ('dʒɪn'dʒəʊ), **Chin-Chou,** *or* **Chin-chow** *n* a city in NE China, in SW Liaoning province. Pop.: 569 518 (1990 est.). Former name (1913–47): **Chin-hsien.**

jipijapa (ˌhi:pi:'hɑ:pɑ:) *n* a palmlike plant, *Carludovica palmata,* of central and South America, whose fanlike leaves are bleached for making panama hats: family *Cyclanthaceae*. [American Spanish, after *Jipijapa,* Ecuador]

jism ('dʒɪzəm) *or* **jissom** ('dʒɪsəm) *n Taboo.* informal words for **semen**. [of unknown origin]

JIT *abbrev. for* **just-in-time.**

jitney ('dʒɪtnɪ) *n U.S., now rare.* **1** a small bus that carries passengers for a low price, originally five cents. **2** *Slang.* a nickel; five cents. [C20: of unknown origin]

jitter ('dʒɪtə) *Informal.* ◆ *vb* **1** (*intr*) to be anxious or nervous. ◆ *n* **2 the jitters.** nervousness and anxiety. **3** *Electronics.* small rapid variations in the amplitude or timing of a waveform arising from fluctuations in the voltage supply, mechanical vibrations, etc. [C20: of unknown origin] ▸ **'jittery** *adj* ▸ **'jitteriness** *n*

jitterbug ('dʒɪtəˌbʌg) *n* **1** a fast jerky American dance, usually to a jazz accompaniment, that was popular in the 1940s. **2** a person who dances the jitterbug. **3** a highly nervous or excitable person. ◆ *vb* **-bugs, -bugging, -bugged. 4** (*intr*) to perform such a dance.

jiujitsu *or* **jiujutsu** (dʒu:'dʒɪtsu:) *n* variant spellings of **jujitsu**.

jive (dʒaɪv) *n* **1** a style of lively and jerky dance performed to jazz and, later, to rock and roll, popular esp. in the 1940s and 1950s. **2** Also called: **jive talk.** a variety of American slang spoken chiefly by Blacks, esp. jazz musicians. **3a** *Slang, chiefly U.S.* deliberately misleading or deceptive talk. **3b** (*as modifier*): jive talk. ◆ *vb* **4** (*intr*) to dance the jive. **5** *Slang, chiefly U.S.* to mislead; tell lies (to). [C20: of unknown origin] ▸ **'jiver** *n*

jizz (dʒɪz) *n* a term for the total combination of characteristics that serve to identify a particular species of bird or plant. [origin obscure]

JJ. *abbrev. for:* **1** Judges. **2** Justices.

jnd *abbrev. for* just noticeable difference.

Jnr *abbrev. for* junior.

jo *or* **joe** (dʒəʊ) *n, pl* **joes.** a Scot. word for **sweetheart**. [C16: alteration of JOY]

Joab ('dʒəʊæb) *n Old Testament.* the successful commander of King David's forces and the slayer of Abner and Absalom (II Samuel 2:18–23; 3:24–27; 18:14–15).

Joachim *n* **1** ('jo:axɪm). **Joseph** ('jo:zɛf). 1831–1907, Hungarian violinist and composer. **2** ('dʒəʊəkɪm). **Saint.** 1st century B.C., traditionally the father of the Virgin Mary; feast day: July 25 or Sept. 9.

Joachim of Fiore ('fjɔ:reɪ) *n* ?1132–1202 A.D., Italian mystic and philosopher, best known for teaching that history can be divided into three ages, those of the Father, Son, and Holy Ghost.

Joan (dʒəʊn) *n* **1** known as *the Fair Maid of Kent.* 1328–85, wife of Edward the Black Prince; mother of Richard II. **2 Pope.** legendary female pope, first mentioned in the 13th century: said to have been elected while disguised as a man and to have died in childbirth.

joannes (dʒəʊ'æni:z) *n, pl* **-nes.** a variant of **johannes**.

Joan of Arc *n* **Saint**, known as *the Maid of Orléans;* French name *Jeanne d'Arc.* ?1412–31, French national heroine, who led the army that relieved Orléans in the Hundred Years' War, enabling Charles VII to be crowned at Reims (1429). After being captured (1430), she was burnt at the stake as a heretic. She was canonized in 1920. Feast day: May 30.

João Pessoa (*Portuguese* 'ʒuãum pe'soa) *n* a port in NE Brazil, capital of Paraíba state. Pop.: 497 306 (1991).

job (dʒɒb) *n* **1** an individual piece of work or task. **2** an occupation; post of employment. **3** an object worked on or a result produced from working. **4** a duty or responsibility: *her job was to cook the dinner.* **5** *Informal.* a difficult task or problem: *I had a job to contact him.* **6** a state of affairs: *make the best of a bad job; it's a good job I saw you.* **7** *Informal.* a damaging piece of work: *he really did a job on that.* **8** *Informal.* a crime, esp. a robbery or burglary. **9** *Informal.* an article or specimen: *the new car was a nice little job.* **10** an instance of jobbery. **11** *Computing.* a unit of work for a computer consisting of a single complete task submitted by a user. **12 jobs for the boys.** appointments given to or created for allies or favourites. **13 on the job. 13a** actively engaged in one's employment. **13b** *Brit. taboo.* engaged in sexual intercourse. **14 just the job.** exactly what was required. ◆ *vb* **jobs, jobbing, jobbed. 15** (*intr*) to work by the piece or at casual jobs. **16** to make a private profit out of (a public office, etc.). **17** (*intr; usually foll. by in*) **17a** to buy and sell (goods or services) as a middleman: *he jobs in government surplus.* **17b** *Brit.* to buy and sell stocks and shares as a stockjobber: *he jobs in blue chips.* **18** (*tr;* often foll. by *out*) to apportion (a contract, work, etc.) among several contractors, workers, etc. [C16: of uncertain origin]

Job (dʒəʊb) *n* **1** *Old Testament.* **1a** a Jewish patriarch, who maintained his faith in God in spite of the afflictions sent by God to test him. **1b** the book containing Job's pleas to God under these afflictions, attempted explanations of them by his friends, and God's reply to him. **2** any person who withstands great suffering without despairing.

job analysis *n* the analysis of the contents of a job in order to provide a job description for such purposes as fitting the job into a grading structure or matching individual capabilities to job requirements.

jobber ('dʒɒbə) *n* **1** *Brit.* short for **stockjobber** (sense 1). **2** a person who jobs.

jobbery ('dʒɒbərɪ) *n* the practice of making private profit out of a public office; corruption or graft.

jobbing ('dʒɒbɪŋ) *adj* working on occasional jobs or by the piece rather than in a regular job: *a jobbing gardener.*

jobbing printer *n* one who prints mainly commercial and display work rather than books or newspapers.

Jobcentre ('dʒɒbˌsɛntə) *n Brit.* any of a number of government offices having premises usually situated in or near the main shopping area of a town in which people seeking jobs can consult displayed advertisements in informal surroundings.

Jobclub ('dʒɒbˌklʌb) *n* a group of unemployed people organized through a Jobcentre, which meets every day and is given advice on job seeking to increase its members' chances of finding employment.

Job Corps (dʒɒb) *n U.S.* a Federal organization established in 1964 to train unemployed youths in order to make it easier for them to find work.

job description *n* a detailed written account, agreed between management and worker, of all the duties and responsibilities which together make up a particular job.

job enlargement *n* a widening of the range of tasks performed by an employee in order to provide variety in the activities undertaken.

job evaluation *n* the analysis of the relationship between jobs in an organization: often used as a basis for a wages structure.

jobless ('dʒɒblɪs) *adj* **a** unemployed. **b** (*as collective n;* preceded by *the*): *the jobless.* ▸ **'joblessness** *n*

job lot *n* **1** a miscellaneous collection of articles sold as a lot. **2** a collection of cheap or trivial items.

job rotation *n* the practice of transferring an employee from one work station or activity to another during the working day in order to add variety to a job: often used in assembly line work.

job satisfaction *n* the extent to which a person's hopes, desires, and expectations about the employment he is engaged in are fulfilled.

Job's comforter *n* a person who, while purporting to give sympathy, succeeds only in adding to distress.

jobseeker's allowance ('dʒɒbˌsi:kəz) *n* (in Britain) a National Insurance or social security payment for unemployed people; replaced unemployment benefit in 1996. Abbrev.: **JSA.**

job sharing *n* the division of a job between two or more people such that each covers the same job for complementary parts of the day or week. ▸ **job sharer** *n*

Job's-tears *n* **1** (*functioning as sing*) a tropical Asian grass, *Coix lacryma-jobi,* cultivated for its white beadlike modified leaves, which contain edible seeds. **2** (*functioning as pl*) the beadlike structures of this plant, used as rosary or ornamental beads.

jobsworth ('dʒɒbzˌwɜ:θ) *n Informal.* a person in a position of minor authority who invokes the letter of the law in order to avoid any action requiring initiative, cooperation, etc. [C20: from *it's more than my job's worth to ...*]

Jocasta (dʒəʊ'kæstə) *n Greek myth.* a queen of Thebes, the wife of Laius, who married Oedipus without either of them knowing he was her son.

Jochum (*German* 'jɔxʊm) *n* **Eugen** ('ɔyge:n). 1902–87, German orchestral conductor.

jock (dʒɒk) *n* **1** *Informal.* short for **disc jockey**. **2** *Informal.* short for **jockstrap**. **3** *U.S. informal.* an athlete. **4** *N.Z. mining.* a pointed bar of steel inserted into the wheel of a mine vehicle and used for emergency braking.

Jock (dʒɒk) *n* a slang word or term of address for a Scot.

jockey ('dʒɒkɪ) *n* **1** a person who rides horses in races, esp. as a profession or for hire. ◆ *vb* **2a** (*tr*) to ride (a horse) in a race. **2b** (*intr*) to ride as a jockey. **3** (*intr*) (often foll. by *for*) to try to obtain an advantage by manoeuvring, esp. literally in a race or metaphorically, as in a struggle for power (esp. in the phrase **jockey for position**). **4** to trick or cheat (a person). [C16 (in the sense: lad): from name *Jock* + -EY]

jockey cap *n* a cap with a long peak projecting from the forehead.

Jockey Club *n Brit.* the governing body that regulates and controls horse-racing both on the flat and over jumps.

jocko ('dʒɒkəʊ) *n, pl* **-os.** a W African name for **chimpanzee**. [C19: from French, based on Bantu *ngeko*]

jockstrap ('dʒɒkˌstræp) *n* an elasticated belt with a pouch worn by men, esp. athletes, to support the genitals. Also called: **athletic support.** [C20: from slang *jock* penis + STRAP]

jocose (dʒə'kəʊs) *adj* characterized by humour; merry. [C17: from Latin *jocōsus* given to jesting, from *jocus* JOKE] ▸ **jo'cosely** *adv* ▸ **jo'coseness** *or* **jocosity** (dʒə'kɒsɪtɪ) *n*

jocular ('dʒɒkjʊlə) *adj* **1** characterized by joking and good humour. **2** meant lightly or humorously; facetious. [C17: from Latin *joculāris,* from *joculus* little JOKE] ▸ **jocularity** (ˌdʒɒkjʊ'lærɪtɪ) *n* ▸ **'jocularly** *adv*

jocund ('dʒɒkənd) *adj* of a humorous temperament; merry. [C14: from Late

Latin *jocundus,* from Latin *jūcundus* pleasant, from *juvāre* to please] ▸ **jocundity** (dʒəʊ'kʌndɪtɪ) *or* '**jocundness** *n* ▸ '**jocundly** *adv*

Jodhpur (ˌdʒɒd'pʊə) *n* **1** a former state of NW India, one of the W Rajputana states: now part of Rajasthan. **2** a walled city in NW India, in W Rajasthan: university (1962). Pop.: 666 279 (1991). ▸ **Jodhpuri** ('dʒɒdpʊrɪ) *adj*

Jodhpuri coat *n* a coat worn by men in India, similar to but shorter than a sherwani. [named after JODHPUR]

jodhpurs ('dʒɒdpəz) *pl n* **1** riding breeches, loose-fitting around the hips and tight-fitting from the thighs to the ankles. **2** Also called: **jodhpur boots.** ankle-length leather riding boots. [C19: from the town JODHPUR]

Jodl (*German* 'joːdəl) *n* **Alfred** ('alfreːt). 1890–1946, German general, largely responsible for German strategy during World War II: executed as a war criminal.

Jodo ('dʒəʊˌdəʊ) *n* a Japanese Buddhist sect teaching salvation through faith in Buddha. [from Japanese]

Jodrell Bank ('dʒɒdrəl) *n* an astronomical observatory in NW England, in Cheshire: radio telescope with a steerable parabolic dish, 75 m (250 ft.) in diameter.

Joe (dʒəʊ) *n* (*sometimes not cap.*) *Slang.* **1** *U.S. and Canadian.* a man or fellow. **2** *U.S.* a GI; soldier.

Joe Blake *n Austral.* **1** *Rhyming slang.* a snake. **2 the Joe Blakes.** the DT's.

Joe Bloggs (blɒgz) *n Brit. slang.* an average or typical man. U.S., Canadian, and Austral. equivalent: **Joe Blow.** See also **Joe Six-Pack.**

Joel ('dʒəʊəl) *n Old Testament.* **1** a Hebrew prophet. **2** the book containing his oracles.

Joe Public *n Slang.* the general public.

joe-pye weed ('dʒəʊ'paɪ) *n U.S. and Canadian.* any of several North American plants of the genus *Eupatorium,* esp. *E. purpureum,* having pale purplish clusters of flower heads lacking rays: family *Compositae* (composites). [C19: of unknown origin]

joes (dʒəʊz) *pl n Austral. informal.* **the.** a fit of depression. [short for *the Joe Blakes*]

Joe Six-Pack ('sɪksˌpæk) *n U.S. slang.* an average or typical man.

Joe Soap *n* **1** *Brit. slang.* a person who is regarded as unintelligent and imposed upon as a stooge or scapegoat. **2** the N.Z. term for **Joe Bloggs.**

joey ('dʒəʊɪ) *n Austral. informal.* **1** a young kangaroo. **2** a young animal or child. [C19: from a native Australian language]

Joey Hooker ('dʒəʊɪ 'hʊkə) *n* another name for **gallant soldier** (a plant).

Joffre (*French* ʒɔfrə) *n* **Joseph Jacques Césaire** (ʒozɛf ʒak sezɛr). 1852–1931, French marshal. He commanded the French army (1914–16) and was largely responsible for the Allies' victory at the Marne (1914), which halted the German advance on Paris.

jog[1] (dʒɒg) *vb* **jogs, jogging, jogged. 1** (*intr*) to run or move slowly or at a jog trot, esp. for physical exercise. **2** (*intr;* foll. by *on* or *along*) to continue in a plodding way. **3** (*tr*) to jar or nudge slightly; shake lightly. **4** (*tr*) to remind; stimulate: *please jog my memory.* **5** (*tr*) *Printing.* to even up the edges of (a stack of paper); square up. ◆ *n* **6** the act of jogging. **7** a slight jar or nudge. **8** a jogging motion; trot. [C14: probably variant of *shog* to shake, influenced by dialect *jot* to jolt]

jog[2] (dʒɒg) *n U.S. and Canadian.* **1** a sharp protruding point in a surface; jag. **2** a sudden change in course or direction. [C18: probably variant of JAG[1]]

jogger ('dʒɒgə) *n* **1** a person who runs at a jog trot over some distance for exercise, usually regularly. **2** *N.Z.* a cart with rubber-tyred wheels used on a farm.

jogger's nipple *n Informal.* painful inflammation of the nipple, caused by friction with a garment when running for long distances.

jogging ('dʒɒgɪŋ) *n* running at a slow regular pace usually over a long distance as part of an exercise routine.

joggle ('dʒɒgᵊl) *vb* **1** to shake or move (someone or something) with a slightly jolting motion. **2** (*tr*) to join or fasten (two pieces of building material) by means of a joggle. ◆ *n* **3** the act of joggling. **4** a slight irregular shake; jolt. **5** a joint between two pieces of building material by means of a projection on one piece that fits into a notch in the other; dowel. **6** a shoulder designed to take the thrust of a strut or brace. [C16: frequentative of JOG[1]] ▸ '**joggler** *n*

joggle post *n* a post or beam consisting of two timbers joined to each other by joggles.

Jogjakarta (ˌdʒəʊgjɑː'kɑːtɑː, ˌdʒɒg-) *n* a variant spelling of **Yogyakarta.**

jog trot *n* **1** an easy bouncy gait, esp. of a horse, midway between a walk and a trot. **2** a monotonous or regular way of living or doing something. ◆ *vb* **jog-trot, -trots, -trotting, -trotted. 3** (*intr*) to move at a jog trot.

johannes (dʒəʊ'hæniːz) *or* **joannes** *n, pl* **-nes.** a Portuguese gold coin minted in the early 18th century. [C18: after *Joannes* (King John V) of Portugal, whose name was inscribed on the coin]

Johannesburg (dʒəʊ'hænɪsˌbɜːg) *n* a city in N South Africa, in Gauteng province: South Africa's largest city and chief industrial centre; grew with the establishment in 1886 of the gold-mining industry; University of Witwatersrand (1922). Pop.: 1 712 507 (1991).

john (dʒɒn) *n* **1** *Chiefly U.S. and Canadian.* a slang word for **lavatory** (sense 1). **2** *Austral. slang.* short for **John Hop.** [C20: special use of the proper name]

John (dʒɒn) *n* **1** *New Testament.* **1a** the apostle John, the son of Zebedee, identified with the author of the fourth Gospel, three epistles, and the book of Revelation. Feast day: Dec. 27 or Sept. 26. **1b** the fourth Gospel. **1c** any of three epistles (in full **The First, Second,** and **Third Epistles of John**). **2** See **John the Baptist. 3** known as *John Lackland.* 1167–1216, king of England (1199–1216); son of Henry II. He succeeded to the throne on the death of his brother Richard I, having previously tried to usurp the throne. War with France led to the loss of most of his French possessions. After his refusal to recognize Stephen Langton as archbishop of Canterbury an interdict was imposed on England (1208–14). In 1215 he was compelled by the barons to grant the Magna Carta. **4** called *the Fearless.* 1371–1419, duke of Burgundy (1404–19). His attempt to control the mad king Charles VI and his murder of the king's brother led to civil war: assassinated. **5 Augustus (Edwin).** 1878–1961, British painter, esp. of portraits. **6 Barry.** born 1945, Welsh Rugby Union footballer: halfback for Wales (1966–72) and the British Lions (1968–71). **7** Sir **Elton (Hercules).** original name *Reginald Dwight.* born 1947, British rock pianist, composer, and singer; his hits include "Goodbye Yellow Brick Road" (1973) and "Candle in the Wind 1997" (1997), a tribute to Diana, Princess of Wales. **8 Gwen,** sister of Augustus John. 1876–1939, British painter, working in France: noted esp. for her portraits of women.

John I *n* **1** surnamed *Tzimisces.* 925–976 A.D., Byzantine emperor (969–976): extended Byzantine power into Bulgaria and Syria. **2** called *the Great.* 1357–1433, king of Portugal (1385–1433). He secured independence for Portugal by his victory over Castile (1385) and initiated Portuguese overseas expansion.

John II *n* **1** called *the Good.* 1319–64, king of France (1350–64): captured by the English at Poitiers (1356) and forced to sign treaties (1360) surrendering SW France to England. **2** called *the Perfect.* 1455–95, king of Portugal (1481–95): sponsored Portuguese expansion in the New World and reduced the power of the aristocracy. **3** surnamed *Casimir Vasa.* 1609–72, king of Poland (1648–68), who lost much territory to neighbouring countries: abdicated.

John III *n* **1** 1507–57, king of Portugal (1521–57): his reign saw the expansion of the Portuguese empire overseas but the start of economic decline at home. **2** surnamed *Sobieski.* 1624–96, king of Poland (1674–96). He raised the Turkish siege of Vienna (1683).

John IV *n* called *the Fortunate.* 1604–56, king of Portugal (1640–56). As duke of Braganza he led a revolt against Spanish rule and became king: lost most of Portugal's Asian possessions to the Dutch.

John VI *n* ?1769–1826, king of Portugal (1816–26): recognized the independence of Brazil (1825).

John XXII *n* original name *Jacques Duèse.* ?1244–1334, pope (1316–34), residing at Avignon; involved in a long conflict with the Holy Roman Emperor Louis IV and opposed the Franciscan Spirituals.

John XXIII *n* original name *Angelo Giuseppe Roncalli.* 1881–1963, pope (1958–63). He promoted ecumenism and world peace and summoned the second Vatican Council (1962–65).

John Barleycorn *n Usually humorous.* the personification of alcoholic drink, esp. of malt spirits.

John Birch Society *n U.S. politics.* a fanatical right-wing association organized along semisecret lines to fight Communism. [C20: named after *John Birch* (killed by Chinese communists 1945), American USAF captain whom its members regarded as the first cold-war casualty]

John Bull *n* **1** a personification of England or the English people. **2** a typical Englishman. [C18: name of a character intended to be representative of the English nation in *The History of John Bull* (1712) by John Arbuthnot] ▸ **John Bullish** *adj* ▸ **John Bullishness** *n* ▸ **John Bullism** *n*

John Chrysostom ('krɪsəstəm) *n* **Saint.** ?345–407 A.D., Greek bishop and theologian; one of the Fathers of the Greek Church, noted for his eloquence. Feast day: Sept. 13.

John Doe *n* See **Doe.**

John Dory ('dɔːrɪ) *n* a European dory (the fish), *Zeus faber,* having a deep compressed body, spiny dorsal fins, and massive mobile jaws. [C18: from proper name *John* + DORY[1]; on the model of DOE]

Johne's disease ('jəʊnəz) *n* an infectious disease of ruminants characterized by chronic inflammation of the bowel and caused by *Mycobacterium paratuberculosis,* a bacterium that can be transmitted in milk and is a possible cause of Crohn's disease in humans. [C20: named after H. A. *Johne* (1839–1910), German veterinary surgeon]

John Hancock *n U.S. and Canadian informal.* a person's signature: *put your John Hancock on this form.* Also called **John Henry.** [after *John* HANCOCK, from his clear and legible signature on the American Declaration of Independence]

John Hop *n Austral. slang.* a policeman. [rhyming slang for COP[1]]

johnny ('dʒɒnɪ) *n, pl* **-nies.** *Brit.* **1** (*often cap.*) *Informal.* a man or boy; chap. **2** a slang word for **condom.**

johnny cake *or* **johnny-cake** *n* **1** *U.S.* a type of thin flat corn bread baked on a griddle. **2** *Austral.* a thin cake of flour and water paste cooked in the ashes of a fire or in a pan.

Johnny Canuck ('dʒɒnɪ kə'nʌk) *n Canadian.* **1** an informal name for a **Canadian. 2** a personification of Canada.

Johnny-come-lately *n, pl* **Johnny-come-latelies** *or* **Johnnies-come-lately.** *Slang.* a brash newcomer, novice, or recruit.

Johnny-jump-up *n U.S. and Canadian.* any of several violaceous plants, esp. the wild pansy. [C19: so called from its quick growth]

Johnny raw *n Slang.* a novice; new recruit.

Johnny Reb *n U.S. informal.* (in the American Civil War) a Confederate soldier. [C19: from REBEL (n)]

John of Austria *n* called *Don John.* 1547–78, Spanish general: defeated the Turks at Lepanto (1571).

John of Damascus *n* **Saint.** ?675–749 A.D., Syrian theologian, who defended the veneration of icons and images against the iconoclasts. Feast day: Dec. 4.

John of Gaunt (gɔːnt) *n* Duke of Lancaster. 1340–99, son of Edward III: virtual ruler of England during the last years of his father's reign and during Richard II's minority. [*Gaunt,* variant of GHENT, where he was born]

John of Leyden ('laɪdᵊn) *n* original name *Jan Bockelson.* ?1509–36, Dutch Anabaptist leader. He established a theocracy in Münster (1534) but was tortured to death after the city was recaptured (1535) by its prince bishop.

John of Salisbury *n* died 1180, English ecclesiastic and scholar; bishop of Chartres (1176–80). He supported Thomas à Becket against Henry II.

John of the Cross *n* **Saint.** original name *Juan de Yepis y Alvarez.* 1542–91, Spanish Carmelite monk, poet, and mystic. He founded the Discalced Carmelites with Saint Teresa (1568). Feast day: Dec. 14.

John o'Groats (ə'grəʊts) *n* a village at the northeasternmost tip of the Scottish mainland: considered to be the northernmost point of the mainland of Great Britain although Dunnet Head, slightly to the west, lies further north. See also **Land's End.**

John Paul I *n* original name *Albino Luciani.* 1912–78, pope (1978) whose brief 33-day reign was characterized by a simpler papal style and anticipated an emphasis on pastoral rather than administrative priorities.

John Paul II *n* original name *Karol Wojtyla.* born 1920, pope from 1978, born in Poland: the first non-Italian to be elected since 1522.

Johns (dʒɒnz) *n* **Jasper.** born 1930, U.S. artist, noted for his collages and constructions.

Johnson ('dʒɒnsᵊn) *n* **1 Amy.** 1903–41, British aviator, who made several record flights, including those to Australia (1930) and to Cape Town and back (1936). **2 Andrew.** 1808–75, U.S. Democrat statesman who was elected vice president under the Republican Abraham Lincoln; 17th president of the U.S. (1865–69), became president after Lincoln's assassination. His lenience towards the South after the American Civil War led to strong opposition from radical Republicans, who tried to impeach him. **3 Jack.** 1878–1946, U.S. boxer; world heavyweight champion (1908–15). **4 Lionel (Pigot).** 1867–1902, British poet and critic, best known for his poems "Dark Angel" and "By the Statue of King Charles at Charing Cross". **5 Lyndon Baines,** known as *LBJ.* 1908–73, U.S. Democrat statesman; 36th president of the U.S. (1963–69). His administration carried the Civil Rights Acts of 1964 and 1965, but he lost popularity by increasing U.S. involvement in the Vietnam war. **6 Michael (Duane).** born 1967, U.S. athlete: world (1995) and Olympic (1996) 200- and 400-metre gold medallist. **7 Robert.** ?1898–1937, U.S. blues singer and guitarist. **8 Samuel,** known as *Dr. Johnson.* 1709–84, British lexicographer, critic, and conversationalist, whose greatest works are his *Dictionary* (1755), his edition of Shakespeare (1765), and his *Lives of the Most Eminent English Poets* (1779–81). His fame, however, rests as much on Boswell's biography of him as on his literary output.

Johnson grass *n* a persistent perennial Mediterranean grass, *Sorghum halepense,* cultivated for hay and pasture in the U.S. where it also grows as a weed. See also **sorghum.** [C19: named after William *Johnson* (died 1859), American agriculturalist who introduced it]

Johnsonian (dʒɒn'səʊnɪən) *adj* of, relating to, or characteristic of Samuel Johnson, his works, or his style of writing.

John the Baptist *n* **Saint.** *New Testament.* the son of Zacharias and Elizabeth and the cousin and forerunner of Jesus, whom he baptized. He was beheaded by Herod (Matthew 14:1–2). Feast day: June 24.

John Thomas *n Slang.* a taboo name for **penis.**

Johore (dʒəʊ'hɔː) *n* a state of Malaysia, on the S Malay Peninsula: mostly forested, with large swamps; bauxite- and iron-mining. Capital: Johore Bahru. Pop.: 2 106 700 (1993 est.). Area: 18 984 sq. km (7330 sq. miles).

Johore Bahru ('bɑːruː) *n* a city in S Malaysia, capital of Johore state: important trading centre, situated at the sole crossing point of **Johore Strait** (between Malaya and Singapore Island). Pop.: 328 646 (1991).

joie de vivre *French.* (ʒwa də vivrə) *n* joy of living; enjoyment of life; ebullience.

join (dʒɔɪn) *vb* **1** to come or bring together; connect. **2** to become a member of (a club, organization, etc.). **3** (*intr; often foll. by with*) to become associated or allied. **4** (*intr; usually foll. by in*) to take part. **5** (*tr*) to meet (someone) as a companion. **6** (*tr*) to become part of; take a place in or with. **7** (*tr*) to unite (two people) in marriage. **8** (*tr*) *Geom.* to connect with a straight line or a curve. **9** (*tr*) an informal word for **adjoin. 10 join battle.** to start fighting. **11 join duty.** *Indian.* to report for work after a period of leave or a strike. **12 join hands. 12a** to hold one's own hands together. **12b** (of two people) to hold each other's hands. **12c** (usually foll. by *with*) to work together in an enterprise or task. ◆ *n* **13** a joint; seam. **14** the act of joining. **15** *Maths.* another name for **union** (sense 9). ◆ See also **join up.** [C13: from Old French *joindre* from Latin *jungere* to yoke] ▸ **'joinable** *adj*

joinder ('dʒɔɪndə) *n* **1** the act of joining, esp. in legal contexts. **2** *Law.* **2a** (in pleading) the stage at which the parties join issue (**joinder of issue**). **2b** the joining of two or more persons as coplaintiffs or codefendants (**joinder of parties**). **2c** the joining of two or more causes in one suit. [C17: from French *joindre* to JOIN]

joiner ('dʒɔɪnə) *n* **1** *Chiefly Brit.* a person trained and skilled in making finished woodwork, such as windows, doors, and stairs. **2** a person or thing that joins. **3** *Informal.* a person who joins many clubs, causes, etc.

joinery ('dʒɔɪnərɪ) *n* **1** the skill or craft of a joiner. **2** work made by a joiner.

joint (dʒɔɪnt) *n* **1** a junction of two or more parts or objects. **2** the part or space between two such junctions. **3** *Anatomy.* the junction between two or more bones, usually formed of connective tissue and cartilage. **4** the point of connection between movable parts in invertebrates, esp. insects and other arthropods. Related adj: **articular. 5** the part of a plant stem from which a branch or leaf grows. **6** one of the parts into which a carcass of meat is cut by the butcher, esp. for roasting. **7** *Geology.* a crack in a rock along which no displacement has occurred. **8** *Slang.* **8a** a disreputable establishment, such as a bar or nightclub. **8b** *Often facetious.* a dwelling or meeting place. **9** *Slang.* a cannabis cigarette. **10 out of joint. 10a** dislocated. **10b** out of order or disorganized. **11 put someone's nose out of joint.** See **nose** (sense 18). ◆ *adj* **12** shared by or belonging to two or more: *joint property.* **13** created by combined effort. **14** sharing with others or with one another: *joint rulers.* **15** *Law.* (of persons) combined in ownership or obligation; regarded as a single entity in law. ◆ *vb* (*tr*) **16** to provide with or fasten by a joint or joints. **17** to plane the edge of (a board, etc.) into the correct shape for a joint. **18** to cut or divide (meat, fowl, etc.) into joints or at a joint. ▸ **'jointly** *adv*

joint account *n* a bank account registered in the name of two or more persons, any of whom may make deposits and withdrawals.

joint consultation *n* a formal system of communication between the management of an organization and the employees' representatives used prior to taking decisions affecting the workforce, usually effected through a joint consultative committee.

joint density function *n Statistics.* a function of two or more random variables from which can be obtained a single probability that all the variables in the function will take specified values or fall within specified intervals.

jointed ('dʒɔɪntɪd) *adj* **1a** having a joint or joints. **1b** (*in combination*): *large-jointed.* **2** (of a plant stem or similar part) marked with constrictions, at which the stem breaks into separate portions. ▸ **'jointedly** *adv* ▸ **'jointedness** *n*

jointer ('dʒɔɪntə) *n* **1** a tool for pointing mortar joints, as in brickwork. **2** Also called: **jointing plane.** a long plane for shaping the edges of planks so that they can be fitted together. **3** a person or thing that makes joints.

joint resolution *n U.S.* a resolution passed by both houses of a bicameral legislature, signed by the chief executive and legally binding.

jointress ('dʒɔɪntrɪs) *n Law.* a woman entitled to a jointure.

joint stock *n* capital funds held in common and usually divided into shares between the owners.

joint-stock company *n* **1** *Brit.* a business enterprise characterized by its separate legal existence and the sharing of ownership between shareholders, whose liability is limited. **2** *U.S.* a business enterprise whose owners are issued shares of transferable stock but do not enjoy limited liability.

jointure ('dʒɔɪntʃə) *n* **1** *Law.* **1a** provision made by a husband for his wife by settling property upon her at marriage for her use after his death. **1b** the property so settled. **2** *Obsolete.* the act of joining or the condition of being joined. [C14: from Old French, from Latin *junctūra* a joining]

jointworm ('dʒɔɪnt,wɜːm) *n U.S.* the larva of chalcid flies of the genus *Harmolita,* esp. *H. tritici,* which form galls on the stems of cereal plants.

join up *vb* (*adv*) **1** (*intr*) to become a member of a military or other organization; enlist. **2** (often foll. by *with*) to unite or connect.

Joinville (*French* ʒwɛ̃vil) *n* **Jean de** (ʒɑ̃ də). ?1224–1317, French chronicler, noted for his *Histoire de Saint Louis* (1309).

joist (dʒɔɪst) *n* **1** a beam made of timber, steel, or reinforced concrete, used in the construction of floors, roofs, etc. See also **rolled-steel joist.** ◆ *vb* **2** (*tr*) to construct (a floor, roof, etc.) with joists. [C14: from Old French *giste* beam supporting a bridge, from Vulgar Latin *jacitum* (unattested) support, from *jacēre* to lie]

jojoba (həʊ'həʊbə) *n* a shrub or small tree of SW North America, *Simmondsia californica,* that has edible seeds containing a valuable oil used in cosmetics. [Mexican Spanish]

joke (dʒəʊk) *n* **1** a humorous anecdote. **2** something that is said or done for fun; prank. **3** a ridiculous or humorous circumstance. **4** a person or thing inspiring ridicule or amusement; butt. **5** a matter to be joked about or ignored. **6 joking apart.** seriously: said to recall a discussion to seriousness after there has been joking. **7 no joke.** something very serious. ◆ *vb* **8** (*intr*) to tell jokes. **9** (*intr*) to speak or act facetiously or in fun. **10** to make fun of (someone); tease. [C17: from Latin *jocus* a jest] ▸ **'jokey** *or* **'joky** *adj* ▸ **'jokingly** *adv*

joker ('dʒəʊkə) *n* **1** a person who jokes, esp. in an obnoxious manner. **2** *Slang, often derogatory.* a person: *who does that joker think he is?* **3** an extra playing card in a pack, which in many card games can substitute for or rank above any other card. **4** *Chiefly U.S.* a clause or phrase inserted in a legislative bill in order to make the bill inoperative or to alter its apparent effect.

Jokjakarta (,dʒəʊkjɑː'kɑːtɑː, ,dʒɒk-) *n* a variant spelling of **Yogyakarta.**

jol (dʒɒl) *S. African slang.* ◆ *n* **1** a party. ◆ *vb* **jolling, jolled. 2** (*intr*) to have a good time.

jolie laide *French.* (ʒɔli lɛd) *n, pl* **jolies laides** (ʒɔli lɛd). a woman whose ugliness forms her chief fascination. [literally: pretty (attractive) ugly woman]

Joliot-Curie (*French* ʒɔljokyri) *n* **Jean-Frédéric** (ʒɑ̃frederik), 1900–58, and his wife, **Irène** (irɛn), 1897–1956, French physicists: shared the Nobel prize for chemistry in 1935 for discovering artificial radioactivity.

Jolliet (*French* ʒɔljɛ) *n* **Louis.** 1645–1700, French-Canadian explorer, with Jaques Marquette, of the Mississippi river.

jollification (,dʒɒlɪfɪ'keɪʃən) *n* a merry festivity.

jollify ('dʒɒlɪ,faɪ) *vb* **-fies, -fying, -fied.** to be or cause to be jolly.

jollities ('dʒɒlɪtɪz) *pl n Brit.* a party or celebration.

jollity ('dʒɒlɪtɪ) *n, pl* **-ties.** the condition of being jolly.

jolly ('dʒɒlɪ) *adj* **-lier, -liest. 1** full of good humour; jovial. **2** having or provoking gaiety and merrymaking; festive. **3** greatly enjoyable; pleasing. ◆ *adv* **4** *Brit.* (intensifier): *you're jolly nice.* ◆ *vb* **-lies, -lying, -lied.** (*tr*) *Informal.* **5** (often foll. by *up* or *along*) to try to make or keep (someone) cheerful. **6** to make goodnatured fun of. ◆ *n* **7** *Informal, chiefly Brit.* a festivity or celebration. **8** *Informal, chiefly Brit.* a trip, esp. one made for pleasure by a public official or committee at public expense. **9** *Brit. slang.* a Royal Marine. [C14: from Old French *jolif,* probably from Old Norse *jōl* YULE] ▸ **'jolliness** *n*

jolly boat *n* **1** a small boat used as a utility tender for a vessel. **2** a small sailing boat used for pleasure. [C18: *jolly* probably from Danish *jolle* YAWL[1]]

Jolly Roger *n* the traditional pirate flag, consisting of a white skull and crossbones on a black field.

Jolo (həʊ'ləʊ) *n* an island in the SW Philippines: the main island of the Sulu Archipelago. Pop.: 360 588 (1980). Area: 893 sq. km (345 sq. miles).

Jolson ('dʒəʊlsən) *n* **Al,** real name *Asa Yoelson.* 1886–1950, U.S. singer and film actor, born in Russia; star of the first talking picture *The Jazz Singer* (1927).

jolt (dʒəʊlt) *vb* (*tr*) **1** to bump against with a jarring blow; jostle. **2** to move in a jolting manner. 3 to surprise or shock. ◆ *n* 4 a sudden jar or blow. 5 an emotional shock. [C16: probably blend of dialect *jot* to jerk and dialect *joll* to bump] ▸ **'jolter** *n* ▸ **'joltingly** *adv* ▸ **'jolty** *adj*

Jon. *Bible. abbrev. for* Jonah.

Jonah ('dʒəʊnə) *or* **Jonas** ('dʒəʊnəs) *n* 1 *Old Testament.* 1a a Hebrew prophet who, having been thrown overboard from a ship in which he was fleeing from God, was swallowed by a great fish and vomited onto dry land. 1b the book in which his adventures are recounted. 2 a person believed to bring bad luck to those around him; a jinx. ▸ **,Jonah'esque** *adj*

Jonathan[1] ('dʒɒnəθən) *n* a variety of red apple that ripens in early autumn. [C19: named after *Jonathan* Hasbrouk (died 1846), American jurist]

Jonathan[2] *n Old Testament.* the son of Saul and David's close friend, who was killed in battle (I Samuel 31; II Samuel 1:19–26).

Jones (dʒəʊnz) *n* 1 **Daniel.** 1881–1967, British phonetician. 2 **Daniel.** 1912–93, Welsh composer. He wrote nine symphonies and much chamber music. 3 **David.** 1895–1974, British artist and writer: his literary works, which combine poetry and prose, include *In Parenthesis* (1937), an account of World War I, and *The Anathemata* (1952). 4 **Inigo** ('ɪnɪgəʊ). 1573–1652, English architect and theatrical designer, who introduced Palladianism to England. His buildings include the Banqueting Hall of Whitehall. He also designed the settings for court masques, being the first to use the proscenium arch and movable scenery in England. 5 **John Paul,** original name *John Paul.* 1747–92, U.S. naval commander, born in Scotland: noted for his part in the War of American Independence. 6 **(Everett) Le Roi** ('liːrɔɪ), Muslim name *Imanu Amiri Baraka.* born 1934, U.S. Black poet, dramatist, and political figure. 7 **Robert Tyre,** known as *Bobby Jones.* 1902–71, U.S. golfer.

Jongkind (*Dutch* 'jɔŋkɪnt) *n* **Johann Barthold** (joː'hɑn 'bartɔlt). 1819–91, Dutch landscape painter and etcher, working in Paris: best known for his atmospheric seascapes.

jongleur (*French* ʒɔ̃glœr) *n* (in medieval France) an itinerant minstrel. [C18: from Old French *jogleour,* from Latin *joculātor* joker, jester; see JUGGLE]

Jönköping (*Swedish* 'jœntçøːpiŋ) *n* a city in S Sweden, on the S shore of Lake Vättern: scene of the conclusion of peace between Sweden and Denmark in 1809. Pop.: 115 636 (1997 est.).

jonnock ('dʒɒnək) *or* **jannock** ('dʒænək) *Dialect.* ◆ *adj* 1 (*usually postpositive*) genuine; real. ◆ *adv* 2 honestly; truly; genuinely. [of uncertain origin]

jonquil ('dʒɒŋkwɪl) *n* a Eurasian amaryllidaceous plant, *Narcissus jonquilla* with long fragrant yellow or white short-tubed flowers. [C17: from French *jonquille,* from Spanish *junquillo,* diminutive of *junco* reed; see JUNCO]

Jonson ('dʒɒns°n) *n* **Ben.** 1572–1637, English dramatist and poet, who developed the "comedy of humours", in which each character is used to satirize one particular humour or temperament. His plays include *Volpone* (1606), *The Alchemist* (1610), and *Bartholomew Fair* (1614), and he also wrote court masques.

jook (dʒʊk) *or* **chook** *Caribbean informal.* ◆ *vb* 1 (*tr*) to poke or puncture (the skin). ◆ *n* 2 a jab or the resulting wound. [C20: of uncertain origin]

Joplin ('dʒɒplɪn) *n* 1 **Janis.** 1943–70, U.S. rock singer, noted for her hoarse and passionate style. Her albums include *Cheap Thrills* (1968) and *Pearl* (1971). 2 **Scott.** 1868–1917, U.S. pianist and composer: creator of ragtime.

Joppa ('dʒɒpə) *n* the biblical name of **Jaffa,** the port from which Jonah embarked (Jonah 1:3).

Jordaens (*Flemish* jɔr'daːns) *n* **Jacob** ('jaːkɔp). 1593–1678, Flemish painter, noted for his naturalistic depiction of peasant scenes.

Jordan[1] ('dʒɔːd°n) *n* 1 a kingdom in SW Asia: coextensive with the biblical Moab, Gilead, and Edom; made a League of Nations mandate and emirate under British control in 1922 and became an independent kingdom in 1946; territories west of the River Jordan and the Jordanian part of Jerusalem (intended to be part of an autonomous Palestine) were occupied by Israel after the war of 1967. It contains part of the Great Rift Valley and consists mostly of desert. Official language: Arabic. Official religion: (Sunni) Muslim. Currency: dinar. Capital: Amman. Pop.: 4 682 000 (1998 est.). Area: 89 185 sq. km (34 434 sq. miles). Official name: **Hashemite Kingdom of Jordan.** Former name (1922–49): **Trans-Jordan.** 2 the chief and only perennial river of Israel and Jordan, rising in several headstreams in Syria and Lebanon, and flowing south through the Sea of Galilee to the Dead Sea: occupies the N end of the Great Rift Valley system and lies mostly below sea level. Length: over 320 km (200 miles). ▸ **Jordanian** (dʒɔː'deɪnɪən) *adj, n*

Jordan[2] ('dʒɔːd°n) *n* **Michael (Jeffrey).** born 1963, U.S. basketball player.

Jordan almond *n* 1 a large variety of Spanish almond used in confectionery. 2 a sugar-coated almond. [C15: by folk etymology from earlier *jardyne almaund,* literally: garden almond, from Old French *jardin* GARDEN]

jorum ('dʒɔːrəm) *n* a large drinking bowl or vessel or its contents: *a jorum of punch.* [C18: probably named after *Jorum,* who brought vessels of silver, gold, and brass to King David (II Samuel 8:10)]

Jos (dʒɒs) *n* a city in central Nigeria, capital of Plateau state on the **Jos Plateau:** major centre of the tin-mining industry. Pop.: 206 300 (1996 est.).

joseph ('dʒəʊzɪf) *n* a woman's floor-length riding coat with a small cape, worn esp. in the 18th century. [perhaps from the story of Joseph and his long coat (Genesis 37:3)]

Joseph ('dʒəʊzɪf) *n* 1 *Old Testament.* 1a the eleventh son of Jacob and one of the 12 patriarchs of Israel (Genesis 30:2–24). 1b either or both of two tribes descended from his sons Ephraim and Manasseh. 2 **Saint.** *New Testament.* the husband of Mary the mother of Jesus (Matthew 1:16–25). Feast day: Mar. 19.

Joseph II *n* 1741–90, Holy Roman emperor (1765–90); son of Francis I. He ruled Austria jointly with his mother, Maria Theresa, until her death (1780). He reorganized taxation, abolished serfdom, curtailed the feudal power of the nobles, and asserted his independence from the pope.

Joseph Bonaparte Gulf *n* an inlet of the Timor Sea in N Australia. Width: 360 km (225 miles).

Josephine ('dʒəʊzəˌfiːn) *n* **Empress,** previous name *Joséphine de Beauharnais;* real name *Marie Joséphine Tascher de la Pagerie.* 1763–1814, empress of France as wife of Napoleon Bonaparte (1796–1809).

Joseph of Arimathea (ˌærɪmə'θɪːə) *n* **Saint.** *New Testament.* a wealthy member of the Sanhedrin, who obtained the body of Jesus after the Crucifixion and laid it in his own tomb (Matthew 27:57–60). Feast day: Mar. 17 or July 31.

Josephson effect ('dʒəʊzɪfsən) *n Physics.* any one of the phenomena which occur when an electric current passes through a very thin insulating layer between two superconducting substances. The applications include the very precise standardization of the volt. [C20: named after Brian David *Josephson* (born 1940), English physicist; shared the Nobel prize for physics in 1973]

Josephus (dʒəʊ'siːfəs) *n* **Flavius** ('fleɪvɪəs). real name *Joseph ben Matthias.* ?37–?100 A.D., Jewish historian and general; author of *History of the Jewish War* and *Antiquities of the Jews.*

josh (dʒɒʃ) *Slang.* ◆ *vb* 1 to tease (someone) in a bantering way. ◆ *n* 2 a teasing or bantering joke. [C19: perhaps from JOKE, influenced by BOSH[1]] ▸ **'josher** *n*

Josh. *Bible. abbrev. for* Joshua.

Joshua ('dʒɒʃʊə) *n Old Testament.* 1 Moses' successor, who led the Israelites in the conquest of Canaan. 2 the book recounting his deeds. Douay spelling: **Josue** ('dʒɒsjuiː).

Joshua tree *n* a treelike desert yucca plant, *Yucca brevifolia,* of the southwestern U.S., with sword-shaped leaves and greenish-white flowers. [named after the prophet *Joshua,* alluding to the extended branches of the tree]

Josiah (dʒəʊ'saɪə) *n* died ?609 B.C., king of Judah (?640–?609). After the discovery of a book of law (probably Deuteronomy) in the Temple he began a programme of religious reform. Douay spelling: **Josias** (dʒəʊ'saɪəs).

Jospin (*French* ʒospɛ̃) *n* **Lionel (Robert).** born 1937, French politician; prime minister from 1997.

Josquin des Prés (*French* ʒɔskɛ̃ de pre) *n* See **des Prés.**

joss (dʒɒs) *n* a Chinese deity worshipped in the form of an idol. [C18: from pidgin English, from Portuguese *deos* god, from Latin *deus*]

josser ('dʒɒsə) *n Slang.* 1 *Brit.* a simpleton; fool. 2 *Brit.* a fellow; chap. 3 *Austral.* a clergyman. [C19: from JOSS + -ER[1]]

joss house *n* a Chinese temple or shrine where an idol or idols are worshipped.

joss stick *n* a stick of dried perfumed paste, giving off a fragrant odour when burnt as incense.

jostle ('dʒɒs°l) *vb* 1 to bump or push (someone) roughly. 2 to come or bring into contact. 3 to force (one's way) by pushing. ◆ *n* 4 the act of jostling. 5 a rough bump or push. [C14: see JOUST] ▸ **'jostlement** *n* ▸ **'jostler** *n*

jot (dʒɒt) *vb* **jots, jotting, jotted.** 1 (*tr;* usually foll. by *down*) to write a brief note of. ◆ *n* 2 (*used with a negative*) a little bit (in phrases such as **not to care (or give) a jot**). [C16: from Latin *jota,* from Greek *iōta,* of Semitic origin; see IOTA]

jota (*Spanish* 'xɔta) *n* a Spanish dance with castanets in fast triple time, usually to a guitar and voice accompaniment. [Spanish, probably modification of Old Spanish *sota,* from *sotar* to dance, from Latin *saltāre*]

jotter ('dʒɒtə) *n* a small notebook.

jotting ('dʒɒtɪŋ) *n* something jotted down.

Jotun *or* **Jotunn** ('jɔːtʊn) *n Norse myth.* any of a race of giants. [from Old Norse *jötunn* giant; related to EAT]

Jotunheim *or* **Jotunnheim** ('jɔːtʊnˌheɪm) *n Norse myth.* the home of the giants in the northeast of Asgard. [from Old Norse, from *jötunn* giant + *heimr* world, HOME]

joual (ʒwɑːl) *n* nonstandard Canadian French dialect, esp. as associated with ill-educated speakers. [from the pronunciation in this dialect of French *cheval* horse]

jougs (dʒʊgz) *pl n Scot. history.* an iron ring, fastened by a chain to a wall, post, or tree, in which an offender was held by the neck: common in Scotland from the 16th to 18th century. [C16: probably from French *joug* yoke]

jouk (dʒʊk) *Scot.* ◆ *vb* 1 to duck or dodge. ◆ *n* 2 a sudden evasive movement. [C16: of uncertain origin]

joule (dʒuːl) *n* the derived SI unit of work or energy; the work done when the point of application of a force of 1 newton is displaced through a distance of 1 metre in the direction of the force. 1 joule is equivalent to 1 watt-second, 10^7 ergs, 0.2390 calories, or 0.738 foot-pound. Symbol: J [C19: named after J. P. JOULE]

Joule (dʒuːl) *n* **James Prescott.** 1818–89, English physicist, who evaluated the mechanical equivalent of heat and contributed to the study of heat and electricity.

Joule effect *n Physics.* 1 the production of heat as the result of a current flowing through a conductor. See **Joule's law** (sense 1). 2 an increase in length of certain ferromagnetic materials when longitudinally magnetized.

Joule's law *n* 1 *Physics.* the principle that the heat produced by an electric current is equal to the product of the resistance of the conductor, the square of the current, and the time for which it flows. 2 *Thermodynamics.* the principle that at constant temperature the internal energy of an ideal gas is independent of volume. Real gases change their internal energy with volume as a result of intermolecular forces. [C19: named after J. P. JOULE]

Joule-Thomson effect *n* a change in temperature of a thermally insulated gas when it is forced through a small hole or a porous material. For each gas there is a temperature of inversion above which the change is positive and below which it is negative. Also called: **Joule-Kelvin effect.** [C20: named after J. P. JOULE and Sir William Thomson, 1st Baron KELVIN]

jounce (dʒaʊns) *vb* 1 to shake or jolt or cause to shake or jolt; bounce. ◆ *n* 2 a jolting movement; shake; bump. [C15: probably a blend of dialect *joll* to bump + BOUNCE]

jour. *abbrev. for:* **1** journal. **2** journalist. **3** journeyman.

journal ('dʒɜːnᵊl) *n* **1** a newspaper or periodical. **2** a book in which a daily record of happenings, etc., is kept. **3** an official record of the proceedings of a legislative body. **4** *Book-keeping.* **4a** one of several books in which transactions are initially recorded to facilitate subsequent entry in the ledger. **4b** another name for **daybook. 5** the part of a shaft or axle in contact with or enclosed by a bearing. **6** a plain cylindrical bearing to support a shaft or axle. **[C14:** from Old French: daily, from Latin *diurnālis;* see DIURNAL**]**

journal box *n Machinery.* a case enclosing or supporting a journal, often used as a means of retaining the lubricant.

journalese (ˌdʒɜːnᵊ'liːz) *n Derogatory.* a superficial cliché-ridden style of writing regarded as typical of newspapers.

journalism ('dʒɜːnᵊˌlɪzəm) *n* **1** the profession or practice of reporting about, photographing, or editing news stories for one of the mass media. **2** newspapers and magazines collectively; the press. **3** the material published in a newspaper, magazine, etc.: *this is badly written journalism.* **4** news reports presented factually without analysis.

journalist ('dʒɜːnᵊlɪst) *n* **1** a person whose occupation is journalism. **2** a person who keeps a journal.

journalistic (ˌdʒɜːnᵊ'lɪstɪk) *adj* of, relating to, or characteristic of journalism or journalists. ▸ ˌ**journal'istically** *adv*

journalize *or* **journalise** ('dʒɜːnᵊˌlaɪz) *vb* to record (daily events) in a journal. ▸ ˌ**journali'zation** *or* ˌ**journali'sation** *n* ▸ '**journalˌizer** *or* '**journalˌiser** *n*

journey ('dʒɜːnɪ) *n* **1** a travelling from one place to another; trip or voyage. **2a** the distance travelled in a journey. **2b** the time taken to make a journey. ◆ *vb* **3** *(intr)* to make a journey. **[C13:** from Old French *journee* a day, a day's travelling, from Latin *diurnum* day's portion; see DIURNAL**]** ▸ '**journeyer** *n*

journeyman ('dʒɜːnɪmən) *n, pl* **-men. 1** a craftsman, artisan, etc., who is qualified to work at his trade in the employment of another. **2** a competent workman. **3** (formerly) a worker hired on a daily wage. **[C15:** from JOURNEY (in obsolete sense: a day's work) + MAN**]**

journeywork ('dʒɜːnɪˌwɜːk) *n Rare.* **1** necessary, routine, and menial work. **2** the work of a journeyman.

journo ('dʒɜːnəʊ) *n, pl* **journos.** *Slang.* a journalist.

joust (dʒaʊst) *History.* ◆ *n* **1** a combat between two mounted knights tilting against each other with lances. A tournament consisted of a series of such engagements. ◆ *vb* **2** *(intr;* often foll. by *against* or *with)* to encounter or engage in such a tournament: *he jousted with five opponents.* **[C13:** from Old French *jouste,* from *jouster* to fight on horseback, from Vulgar Latin *juxtāre* (unattested) to come together, from Latin *juxtā* close**]** ▸ '**jouster** *n*

j'ouvert ('ʒuːvɛət) *n Chiefly Caribbean.* the eve of Mardi gras; the Monday morning on which the festivities begin. **[**from French *jour ouvert* the day having been opened**]**

Jove (dʒəʊv) *n* **1** another name for **Jupiter**[1]. **2 by Jove.** an exclamation of surprise or excitement. **[C14:** from Old Latin *Jovis* Jupiter**]**

jovial ('dʒəʊvɪəl) *adj* having or expressing convivial humour; jolly. **[C16:** from Latin *joviālis* of (the planet) Jupiter, considered by astrologers to foster good humour**]** ▸ ˌ**jovi'ality** *or* '**jovialness** *n* ▸ '**jovially** *adv*

Jovian[1] ('dʒəʊvɪən) *adj* **1** of or relating to the god Jove (Jupiter). **2** of, occurring on, or relating to the planet Jupiter. **3** of or relating to the giant planets Jupiter, Saturn, Uranus, and Neptune: *the Jovian planets.* **[C16:** from Old Latin *Jovis* Jupiter**]**

Jovian[2] ('dʒəʊvɪən) *n* full name *Flavius Claudius Jovianus.* ?331–364 A.D., Roman emperor (363–64): he made peace with Persia, relinquishing Roman provinces beyond the Tigris, and restored privileges to the Christians.

Jowett ('dʒaʊɪt) *n* **Benjamin.** 1817–93, British classical scholar and educator: translated the works of Plato.

jowl[1] (dʒaʊl) *n* **1** the jaw, esp. the lower one. **2** *(often pl)* a cheek, esp. a prominent one. **3 cheek by jowl.** See **cheek** (sense 7). **[**Old English *ceafl* jaw; related to Middle High German *kivel,* Old Norse *kjaptr***]** ▸ **jowled** *adj*

jowl[2] (dʒaʊl) *n* **1** fatty flesh hanging from the lower jaw. **2** a similar fleshy part in animals, such as the wattle of a fowl or the dewlap of a bull. **[**Old English *ceole* throat; compare Old High German *kela***]**

joy (dʒɔɪ) *n* **1** a deep feeling or condition of happiness or contentment. **2** something causing such a feeling; a source of happiness. **3** an outward show of pleasure or delight; rejoicing. **4** *Brit. informal.* success; satisfaction: *I went to the bank for a loan, but got no joy.* ◆ *vb* **5** *(intr)* to feel joy. **6** *(tr) Obsolete.* to make joyful; gladden. **[C13:** from Old French *joie,* from Latin *gaudium* joy, from *gaudēre* to be glad**]**

joyance ('dʒɔɪəns) *n Archaic.* a joyous feeling or festivity.

Joyce (dʒɔɪs) *n* **1 James (Augustine Aloysius).** 1882–1941, Irish novelist and short-story writer. He profoundly influenced the development of the modern novel by his use of complex narrative techniques, esp. stream of consciousness and parody, and of compound and coined words. His works include the novels *Ulysses* (1922) and *Finnegans Wake* (1939) and the short stories *Dubliners* (1914). **2 William,** known as *Lord Haw-Haw.* 1906–46, British broadcaster of Nazi propaganda to Britain, who was executed for treason.

Joycean ('dʒɔɪsɪən) *adj* **1** of, relating to, or like, James Joyce or his works. ◆ *n* **2** a student or admirer of Joyce or his works.

joyful ('dʒɔɪfʊl) *adj* **1** full of joy; elated. **2** expressing or producing joy: *a joyful look; a joyful occasion.* ▸ '**joyfully** *adv* ▸ '**joyfulness** *n*

joyless ('dʒɔɪlɪs) *adj* having or producing no joy or pleasure. ▸ '**joylessly** *adv* ▸ '**joylessness** *n*

joyous ('dʒɔɪəs) *adj* **1** having a happy nature or mood. **2** joyful. ▸ '**joyously** *adv* ▸ '**joyousness** *n*

joypop ('dʒɔɪˌpɒp) *vb* **-pops, -popping, -popped.** *(intr) Slang.* to take addictive drugs occasionally without becoming addicted.

joyride *n* **1** a ride taken for pleasure in a car, esp. in a stolen car driven recklessly. ◆ *vb* **joy-ride, -rides, -riding, -rode, -ridden. 2** *(intr)* to take such a ride. ▸ '**joyˌrider** *n* ▸ '**joyˌriding** *n*

joystick ('dʒɔɪˌstɪk) *n* **1** *Informal.* the control stick of an aircraft or of any of various machines. **2** *Computing.* a lever by means of which the movement of a cursor on a screen may be controlled.

JP *abbrev. for* Justice of the Peace.

J/psi particle *n* a type of elementary particle thought to be formed from charmed quarks. See **charm**[1] (sense 7).

Jr *or* **jr** *abbrev. for* junior.

JSA (in Britain) *abbrev. for* jobseeker's allowance.

JSD *abbrev. for* Doctor of Juristic Science.

jt *abbrev. for* joint.

Juan Carlos (*Spanish* xwan 'karlɔs) *n* born 1938, king of Spain from 1975: nominated by Franco as the first king of the restored Spanish monarchy that was to follow his death.

Juan de Fuca ('dʒuːən dɪ 'fjuːkə; *Spanish* xwan de 'fuka) *n* **Strait of.** a strait between Vancouver Island (Canada) and NW Washington (U.S.). Length: about 129 km (80 miles). Width: about 24 km (15 miles).

Juan Fernández Islands ('dʒuːən fə'nændez; *Spanish* xwan fɛr'nandɛθ) *pl n* a group of three islands in the S Pacific Ocean, administered by Chile: volcanic and wooded. Area: about 180 sq. km (70 sq. miles).

Juantorena (*Spanish* xwanto'rena) *n* **Alberto** (al'βɛrto). born 1951, Cuban runner: won the 400 metres and the 800 metres in the 1976 Olympic Games.

Juárez[1] (*Spanish* 'xwarɛθ) *n* short for **Ciudad Juárez.**

Juárez[2] (Spanish 'xwarɛθ) *n* **Benito Pablo** (be'nito 'paβlo). 1806–72, Mexican statesman. As president (1861–65; 1867–72) he thwarted Napoleon III's attempt to impose an empire under Maximilian and introduced many reforms.

juba ('dʒuːbə) *n* a lively African-American dance developed in the southern U.S. **[C19:** of Zulu origin**]**

Juba ('dʒuːbə) *n* a river in NE Africa, rising in S central Ethiopia and flowing south across Somalia to the Indian Ocean: the chief river of Somalia. Length: about 1660 km (1030 miles).

Jubal ('dʒuːbᵊl) *n Old Testament.* the alleged inventor of musical instruments (Genesis 4:21).

jubbah ('dʒʊbə) *n* a long loose outer garment with wide sleeves, worn by Muslim men and women, esp. in India. **[C16:** from Arabic**]**

Jubbulpore (ˌdʒʌbᵊl'pʊə) *n* a variant spelling of **Jabalpur.**

jube[1] ('dʒuːbɪ) *n* **1** a gallery or loft over the rood screen in a church or cathedral. **2** another name for **rood screen. [C18:** from French *jubé,* from opening words of Medieval Latin prayer *Jube, Domine, benedicere* Bid, Lord, a blessing; probably from the deacon's standing by the rood screen or in the rood loft to pronounce this prayer**]**

jube[2] (dʒuːb) *n Austral. and N.Z. informal.* any jelly-like sweet. **[C20:** shortened from JUJUBE**]**

jubilant ('dʒuːbɪlənt) *adj* feeling or expressing great joy. **[C17:** from Latin *jūbilāns* shouting for joy, from *jūbilāre* to give a joyful cry, from *jūbilum* a shout, wild cry**]** ▸ '**jubilance** *or* '**jubilancy** *n* ▸ '**jubilantly** *adv*

jubilate ('dʒuːbɪˌleɪt) *vb (intr)* **1** to have or express great joy; rejoice. **2** to celebrate a jubilee. **[C17:** from Latin *jūbilāre* to raise a shout of joy; see JUBILANT**]**

Jubilate (ˌdʒuːbɪ'lɑːtɪ) *n* **1** *R.C. Church, Church of England.* the 100th psalm used as a canticle in the liturgy. **2** a musical setting of this psalm. **[**from the opening word (*Jubilate* make a joyful noise) of the Vulgate version**]**

jubilation (ˌdʒuːbɪ'leɪʃən) *n* a feeling of great joy and celebration.

jubilee ('dʒuːbɪˌliː, ˌdʒuːbɪ'liː) *n* **1** a time or season for rejoicing. **2** a special anniversary, esp. a 25th or 50th one. **3** *R.C. Church.* a specially appointed period, now ordinarily every 25th year, in which special indulgences are granted. **4** *Old Testament.* a year that was to be observed every 50th year, during which Hebrew slaves were to be liberated, alienated property was to be restored, etc. **5** a less common word for **jubilation. [C14:** from Old French *jubile,* from Late Latin *jubilaeus,* from Late Greek *iōbēlaios,* from Hebrew *yōbhēl* ram's horn, used for the proclamation of the year of jubilee; influenced by Latin *jūbilāre* to shout for joy**]**

JUD *abbrev. for* Doctor of Canon and Civil Law. **[**Latin *Juris Utriusque Doctor***]**

Jud. *Bible. abbrev. for:* **1** Also: **Judg.** Judges. **2** Judith.

Judaea *or* **Judea** (dʒuː'dɪə) *n* the S division of ancient Palestine, succeeding the kingdom of Judah: a Roman province during the time of Christ. ▸ **Ju'daean** *or* **Ju'dean** *adj, n*

Judaeo- *or U.S.* **Judeo-** (dʒuː'deɪəʊ-, dʒuː'diːəʊ-) *combining form.* relating to Judaism: *Judaeo-Christian.*

Judaeo-German *n* another name for **Yiddish.**

Judaeo-Spanish *n* another name for **Ladino.**

Judah ('dʒuːdə) *n Old Testament.* **1** the fourth son of Jacob, one of whose descendants was to be the Messiah (Genesis 29:35; 49:8–12). **2** the tribe descended from him. **3** the tribal territory of his descendants which became the nucleus of David's kingdom and, after the kingdom had been divided into Israel and Judah, the southern kingdom of Judah, with Jerusalem as its centre. Douay spelling: **Juda.**

Judah ha-Levi (hɑː'liːvaɪ) *n* ?1075–1141, Jewish poet and philosopher, born in Spain; his major works include the collection in *Diwan* and the prose work *Sefer ha-Kuzari,* which presented his philosophy of Judaism in dialogue form.

Judah ha-Nasi (hɑːnɑː'siː) *n* ?135–?220 A.D., rabbi and patriarch of the Sanhedrin, who compiled the Mishnah.

Judaic (dʒuː'deɪɪk) *or* **Judaical** *adj* **1** of or relating to the Jews or Judaism. **2** a less common word for **Jewish.** ▸ **Ju'daically** *adv*

Judaica (dʒuː'deɪɪkə) *pl n* **1** the literature, customs, culture, etc., of the Jews. **2** books or artefacts of Jewish interest, esp. as a collection. **[**Latin, literally: Jewish matters**]**

Judaism ('dʒuːdeɪˌɪzəm) *n* **1** the religion of the Jews, based on the Old Testament and the Talmud and having as its central point a belief in the one God as transcendent creator of all things and the source of all righteousness. **2** the religious and cultural traditions, customs, attitudes, and way of life of the Jews. ▸ **ˌJudaˈistic** *adj*

Judaize *or* **Judaise** (ˈdʒuːdeɪˌaɪz) *vb* **1** to conform or bring into conformity with Judaism. **2** (*tr*) to convert to Judaism. **3** (*tr*) to imbue with Jewish principles. ▸ **ˌJudaiˈzation** *or* **ˌJudaiˈsation** *n* ▸ **ˈJudaˌizer** *or* **ˈJudaˌiser** *n*

judas (ˈdʒuːdəs) *n* (*sometimes cap.*) a peephole or a very small window in a door. Also called: **judas window, judas hole.** [C19: after *Judas Iscariot*]

Judas (ˈdʒuːdəs) *n* **1** *New Testament.* the apostle who betrayed Jesus to his enemies for 30 pieces of silver (Luke 22:3–6, 47–48). Full name: **Judas Iscariot. 2** a person who betrays a friend; traitor. **3** a brother or relative of James and also of Jesus (Matthew 13:55). This figure, Thaddaeus, and Jude were probably identical. ◆ *adj* **4** denoting an animal or bird used to lure others of its kind or lead them to slaughter.

Judas Maccabaeus (ˌmækəˈbiːəs) *n* Jewish leader, whose revolt (166–161 B.C.) against the Seleucid kingdom of Antiochus IV (Epiphanes) enabled him to recapture Jerusalem and rededicate the Temple.

Judas tree *n* small Eurasian leguminous tree, *Cercis siliquastrum,* with pinkish-purple flowers that bloom before the leaves appear: popularly thought to be the tree on which Judas hanged himself. See also **redbud.**

judder (ˈdʒʌdə) *Informal, chiefly Brit.* ◆ *vb* **1** (*intr*) to shake or vibrate. ◆ *n* **2** abnormal vibration in a mechanical system, esp. due to grabbing between friction surfaces, as in the clutch of a motor vehicle. **3** a juddering motion. [probably blend of JAR[2] + SHUDDER]

judder bar *n* a N.Z. name for **sleeping policeman.**

Jude (dʒuːd) *n* **1** a book of the New Testament (in full **The Epistle of Jude**). **2** **Saint.** Also called: **Judas.** the author of this, stated to be the brother of James (Jude 1) and almost certainly identical with Thaddaeus (Matthew 10:2–4). Feast day: Oct. 28 or June 19.

Judea (dʒuːˈdɪə) *n* a variant spelling of **Judaea.**

Judezmo (dʒʊˈdezməʊ) *n* another name for **Ladino.** [from Ladino: Jewish]

judge (dʒʌdʒ) *n* **1** a public official with authority to hear cases in a court of law and pronounce judgment upon them. Compare **magistrate, justice** (senses 5, 6). Related adj: **judicial. 2** a person who is appointed to determine the result of contests or competitions. **3** a person qualified to comment critically: *a good judge of antiques.* **4** a leader of the peoples of Israel from Joshua's death to the accession of Saul. ◆ *vb* **5** to hear and decide upon (a case at law). **6** (*tr*) to pass judgment on; sentence. **7** (when *tr, may take a clause as object or an infinitive*) to decide or deem (something) after inquiry or deliberation. **8** to determine the result of (a contest or competition). **9** to appraise (something) critically. **10** (*tr; takes a clause as object*) to believe (something) to be the case; suspect. [C14: from Old French *jugier,* from Latin *jūdicāre* to pass judgment, from *jūdex* a judge] ▸ **ˈjudgeable** *adj* ▸ **ˈjudgeless** *adj* ▸ **ˈjudgeˌlike** *adj* ▸ **ˈjudger** *n* ▸ **ˈjudgingly** *adv*

judge advocate *n, pl* **judge advocates.** an officer who superintends proceedings at a military court martial.

judge advocate general *n, pl* **judge advocates general** *or* **judge advocate generals.** the civil adviser to the Crown on matters relating to courts martial and on military law generally.

judge-made *adj* based on a judge's interpretation or decision (esp. in the phrase **judge-made law**).

Judges (ˈdʒʌdʒɪz) *n* (*functioning as sing*) the book of the Old Testament recounting the history of Israel under the warrior champions and national leaders known as judges from the death of Joshua to the birth of Samuel.

judgeship (ˈdʒʌdʒˌʃɪp) *n* the position, office, or function of a judge.

judges' rules *pl n* (in English law) a set of rules, not legally binding, governing the behaviour of police towards suspects, as in administering a caution to a person under arrest.

judgment *or* **judgement** (ˈdʒʌdʒmənt) *n* **1** the faculty of being able to make critical distinctions and achieve a balanced viewpoint; discernment. **2a** the verdict pronounced by a court of law. **2b** an obligation arising as a result of such a verdict, such as a debt. **2c** the document recording such a verdict. **2d** (*as modifier*): *a judgment debtor.* **3** the formal decision of one or more judges at a contest or competition. **4** a particular decision or opinion formed in a case in dispute or doubt. **5** an estimation: *a good judgment of distance.* **6** criticism or censure. **7** *Logic.* **7a** the act of establishing a relation between two or more terms, esp. as an affirmation or denial. **7b** the expression of such a relation. **8** **against one's better judgment.** contrary to a more appropriate or preferred course of action. **9 sit in judgment. 9a** to preside as judge. **9b** to assume the position of critic. **10 in someone's judgment.** in someone's opinion.

Judgment (ˈdʒʌdʒmənt) *n* **1** the estimate by God of the ultimate worthiness or unworthiness of the individual (the **Particular Judgment**) or of all mankind (the **General Judgment** or **Last Judgment**). **2** God's subsequent decision determining the final destinies of all individuals.

judgmental *or* **judgemental** (dʒʌdʒˈmentᵊl) *adj* of or denoting an attitude in which judgments about other people's conduct are made.

Judgment Day *n* the occasion of the Last (or General) Judgment by God at the end of the world. Also called: **Day of Judgment.** See **Last Judgment.**

judicable (ˈdʒuːdɪkəbᵊl) *adj* capable of being judged, esp. in a court of law.

judicative (ˈdʒuːdɪkətɪv) *adj* **1** having the function of trying causes. **2** competent to judge and pass sentence.

judicator (ˈdʒuːdɪˌkeɪtə) *n* a person who acts as a judge.

judicatory (ˈdʒuːdɪkətərɪ) *adj* **1** of or relating to the administration of justice. ◆ *n* **2** a court of law. **3** the administration of justice. ▸ **ˌjudicaˈtorial** *adj*

judicature (ˈdʒuːdɪkətʃə) *n* **1** the administration of justice. **2** the office, function, or power of a judge. **3** the extent of authority of a court or judge. **4** a body of judges or persons exercising judicial authority; judiciary. **5** a court of justice or such courts collectively.

judicial (dʒuːˈdɪʃəl) *adj* **1** of or relating to the administration of justice. **2** of or relating to judgment in a court of law or to a judge exercising this function. **3** inclined to pass judgment; discriminating. **4** allowed or enforced by a court of law: *a decree of judicial separation.* **5** having qualities appropriate to a judge. **6** giving or seeking judgment, esp. determining or seeking determination of a contested issue. [C14: from Latin *jūdiciālis* belonging to the law courts, from *jūdicium* judgment, from *jūdex* a judge] ▸ **juˈdicially** *adv*

Judicial Committee of the Privy Council *n* the highest appellate court for Britain's dependencies and for some dominions of the Commonwealth.

judicial separation *n Family law.* a decree prohibiting a man and wife from cohabiting but not dissolving the marriage. See also **a mensa et thoro.** Compare **divorce.**

judiciary (dʒuːˈdɪʃɪərɪ, -ˈdɪʃərɪ) *adj* **1** of or relating to courts of law, judgment, or judges. ◆ *n, pl* **-aries. 2** the branch of the central authority in a state concerned with the administration of justice. Compare **executive** (sense 2), **legislature. 3** the system of courts in a country. **4** the judges collectively; bench.

judicious (dʒuːˈdɪʃəs) *adj* having or proceeding from good judgment. ▸ **juˈdiciously** *adv* ▸ **juˈdiciousness** *n*

Judith (ˈdʒuːdɪθ) *n* **1** the heroine of one of the books of the Apocrypha, who saved her native town by decapitating Holofernes. **2** the book recounting this episode.

judo (ˈdʒuːdəʊ) *n* **a** the modern sport derived from jujitsu, in which the object is to throw, hold to the ground, or otherwise force an opponent to submit, using the minimum of physical effort. **b** (*as modifier*): *a judo throw.* [Japanese, from *jū* gentleness + *dō* way] ▸ **ˈjudoist** *n*

judogi (dʒʊˈdəʊgɪ) *n* a white two-piece cotton costume worn during judo contests. [from Japanese]

judoka (ˈdʒuːdəʊˌkæ) *n* a competitor or expert in judo. [Japanese; see JUDO]

Judy (ˈdʒuːdɪ) *n, pl* **-dies. 1** the wife of Punch in the children's puppet show *Punch and Judy.* See **Punch. 2** (*often not cap.*) *Brit. slang.* a girl or woman.

jug (dʒʌg) *n* **1** a vessel for holding or pouring liquids, usually having a handle and a spout or lip. U.S. equivalent: **pitcher. 2** *Austral. and N.Z.* such a vessel used as a kettle: *an electric jug.* **3** *U.S.* a large vessel with a narrow mouth. **4** Also called: **jugful.** the amount of liquid held by a jug. **5** *Brit. informal.* a glass of alcoholic drink, esp. beer. **6** a slang word for **jail.** ◆ *vb* **jugs, jugging, jugged. 7** to stew or boil (meat, esp. hare) in an earthenware container. **8** (*tr*) *Slang.* to put in jail. [C16: probably from *Jug,* nickname from girl's name *Joan*]

jugal (ˈdʒuːgᵊl) *adj* **1** of or relating to the zygomatic bone. ◆ *n* **2** Also called: **jugal bone.** other names for **zygomatic bone.** [C16: from Latin *jugālis* of a yoke, from *jugum* a yoke]

jugate (ˈdʒuːgeɪt, -gɪt) *adj* (esp. of compound leaves) having parts arranged in pairs. [C19: from New Latin *jugātus* (unattested), from Latin *jugum* a yoke]

jug band *n* a small group playing folk or jazz music, using empty jugs that are played by blowing across their openings to produce bass notes.

Jugendstil *German.* (ˈjuːgəntʃtiːl) *n* another name for **Art Nouveau.** [from *Jugend* literally: youth, name of illustrated periodical that first appeared in 1896, + *Stil* STYLE]

jugged hare *n* a stew of hare cooked in an earthenware pot or casserole.

juggernaut (ˈdʒʌgəˌnɔːt) *n* **1** any terrible force, esp. one that destroys or that demands complete self-sacrifice. **2** *Brit.* a very large lorry for transporting goods by road, esp. one that travels throughout Europe.

Juggernaut (ˈdʒʌgəˌnɔːt) *n Hinduism.* **1** a crude idol of Krishna worshipped at Puri and throughout Orissa and Bengal. At an annual festival the idol is wheeled through the town on a gigantic chariot and devotees are supposed to have formerly thrown themselves under the wheels. **2** a form of Krishna miraculously raised by Brahma from the state of a crude idol to that of a living god. [C17: from Hindi *Jagannath,* from Sanskrit *Jagannātha* lord of the world (that is, Vishnu, chief of the Hindu gods), from *jagat* world + *nātha* lord]

juggins (ˈdʒʌgɪnz) *n Brit. informal.* a silly person; simpleton. [C19: special use of the surname *Juggins*]

juggle (ˈdʒʌgᵊl) *vb* **1** to throw and catch (several objects) continuously so that most are in the air all the time, as an entertainment. **2** to arrange or manipulate (facts, figures, etc.) so as to give a false or misleading picture. **3** (*tr*) to keep (several activities) in progress, esp. with difficulty. ◆ *n* **4** an act of juggling. [C14: from Old French *jogler* to perform as a jester, from Latin *joculārī* to jest, from *jocus* a jest] ▸ **ˈjugglery** *n*

juggler (ˈdʒʌglə) *n* **1** a person who juggles, esp. a professional entertainer. **2** a person who fraudulently manipulates facts or figures.

juglandaceous (ˌdʒuːglænˈdeɪʃəs) *adj* of, relating to, or belonging to the *Juglandaceae,* a family of trees that includes walnut and hickory. [C19: via New Latin from Latin *juglans* walnut, from *ju-,* shortened from *Jovi-* of Jupiter + *glans* acorn]

Jugoslavia (ˌjuːgəʊˈslɑːvɪə) *n* a variant spelling of **Yugoslavia.** ▸ **ˈJugoˌslav** *or* **ˌJugoˈslavian** *adj, n*

jugular (ˈdʒʌgjʊlə) *adj* **1** of, relating to, or situated near the throat or neck. **2** of, having, or denoting pelvic fins situated in front of the pectoral fins: *a jugular fish.* ◆ *n* **3** short for **jugular vein. 4 go for the jugular.** to make a savage and destructive attack on an enemy's weakest point. [C16: from Late Latin *jugulāris,* from Latin *jugulum* throat]

jugular vein *n* any of three large veins of the neck that return blood to the heart from the head and face.

jugulate (ˈdʒʌgjʊˌleɪt) *vb* (*tr*) *Rare.* to check (a disease) by extreme measures or remedies. [C17 (in the obsolete sense: kill by cutting the throat of): from Latin *jugulāre,*from *jugulum* throat, from *jugum* yoke] ▸ **ˌjuguˈlation** *n*

jugum (ˈdʒuːgəm) *n* **1** a small process at the base of each forewing in certain insects by which the forewings are united to the hindwings during flight. **2** *Botany.* a pair of opposite leaflets. [C19: from Latin, literally: YOKE]

Jugurtha (dʒuː'gɜːθə) *n* died 104 B.C., king of Numidia (?112–104), who waged war against the Romans (the **Jugurthine War,** 112–105) and was defeated and executed.

juice (dʒuːs) *n* **1** any liquid that occurs naturally in or is secreted by plant or animal tissue: *the juice of an orange; digestive juices.* **2** *Informal.* **2a** fuel for an engine, esp. petrol. **2b** electricity. **2c** alcoholic drink. **3a** vigour or vitality. **3b** essence or fundamental nature. **4 stew in one's own juice.** See **stew**[1] (sense 10). [C13: from Old French *jus,* from Latin] ▸ **'juiceless** *adj*

juicer *n* a kitchen appliance, usually operated by electricity, for extracting juice from fruits and vegetables. Also called: **juice extractor.**

juice up *vb* (*tr, adv*) **1** *U.S. slang.* to make lively: *to juice up a party.* **2** (*often passive*) to cause to be drunk: *he got juiced up on Scotch last night.*

juicy ('dʒuːsɪ) *adj* **juicier, juiciest. 1** full of juice. **2** provocatively interesting; spicy: *juicy gossip.* **3** *Slang.* voluptuous or seductive: *she's a juicy bit.* **4** *Chiefly U.S. and Canadian.* profitable: *a juicy contract.* ▸ **'juicily** *adv* ▸ **'juiciness** *n*

Juiz de Fora (*Portuguese* ʒu'iʃ di 'fɔra) *n* a city in SE Brazil, in Minas Gerais state on the Rio de Janeiro–Belo Horizonte railway: textiles. Pop.: 377 538 (1991).

jujitsu, jujutsu, *or* **jiujutsu** (dʒuː'dʒɪtsuː) *n* the traditional Japanese system of unarmed self-defence perfected by the samurai. See also **judo.** [C19: from Japanese, from *jū* gentleness + *jutsu* art]

juju ('dʒuːdʒuː) *n* **1** an object superstitiously revered by certain W African peoples and used as a charm or fetish. **2** the power associated with a juju. **3** a taboo effected by a juju. **4** any process in which a mystery is exploited to confuse people. [C19: probably from Hausa *djudju* evil spirit, fetish] ▸ **'jujuism** *n* ▸ **'jujuist** *n*

jujube ('dʒuːdʒuːb) *n* **1** any of several Old World spiny rhamnaceous trees of the genus *Ziziphus,* esp. *Z. jujuba,* that have small yellowish flowers and dark red edible fruits. See also **Christ's-thorn. 2** the fruit of any of these trees. **3** a chewy sweet made of flavoured gelatine and sometimes medicated to soothe sore throats. ◆ Also called (for senses 1, 2): **Chinese date.** [C14: from Medieval Latin *jujuba,* modification of Latin *zīzyphum,* from Greek *zizuphon*]

jukebox ('dʒuːk,bɒks) *n* a coin-operated machine, usually found in pubs, clubs, etc., that contains records, CDs, or videos, which are played when selected by a customer. [C20: from Gullah *juke* bawdy (as in *juke house* brothel) + BOX[1]]

jukskei ('jʊk,skeɪ) *n S. African.* a game in which a peg is thrown over a fixed distance at a stake driven into the ground. [from Afrikaans *juk* yoke + *skei* pin]

Jul. *abbrev. for* July.

julep ('dʒuːlɪp) *n* **1** a sweet drink, variously prepared and sometimes medicated. **2** *Chiefly U.S.* short for **mint julep.** [C14: from Old French, from Arabic *julāb,* from Persian *gulāb* rose water, from *gul* rose + *āb* water]

Julian[1] ('dʒuːljən, -lɪən) *n* known as *Julian the Apostate;* Latin name *Flavius Claudius Julianus.* 331–363 A.D., Roman emperor (361–363), who attempted to revive paganism in the Roman empire while remaining tolerant to Christians and Jews.

Julian[2] ('dʒuːljən, -lɪən) *adj* **1** of or relating to Julius Caesar. **2** denoting or relating to the Julian calendar.

Juliana (,dʒʊlɪ'ɑːnə; *Dutch* jyːliː'aːnaː) *n* full name *Juliana Louise Emma Marie Wilhelmina.* born 1909, queen of the Netherlands (1948–80). She abdicated in favour of her eldest daughter Beatrix.

Julian Alps *pl n* a mountain range in Slovenia: an E range of the Alps.

Julian calendar *n* the calendar introduced by Julius Caesar in 46 B.C., identical to the present calendar in all but two aspects: the beginning of the year was not fixed on Jan. 1 and leap years occurred every fourth year and in every centenary year. Compare **Gregorian calendar.**

Julian of Norwich *n* ?1342–?1413, English mystic and anchoress: best known for the *Revelations of Divine Love* describing her visions.

julienne (,dʒuːlɪ'en) *adj* **1** (of vegetables) cut into thin shreds. ◆ *n* **2** a clear consommé to which a mixture of such vegetables has been added. [French, from name *Jules, Julien,* or *Julienne*]

Juliet (dʒʊlɪ'et) *n Communications.* a code word for the letter *j.*

Juliet cap ('dʒuːlɪɪt) *n* a close-fitting decorative cap, worn esp. by brides. [C20: after the heroine of Shakespeare's *Romeo and Juliet* (1594)]

Julius II ('dʒuːljəs, -lɪəs) *n* original name *Guiliano della Rovere.* 1443–1513, pope (1503–13). He completed the restoration of the Papal States to the Church, began the building of St Peter's, Rome (1506), and patronized Michelangelo, Raphael, and Bramante.

Julius Caesar *n* See **Caesar.**

Jullundur ('dʒʌləndə) *n* the former name of **Jalandhar.**

July (dʒuː'laɪ, dʒə-, dʒʊ-) *n, pl* **-lies.** the seventh month of the year, consisting of 31 days. [C13: from Anglo-French *julie,* from Latin *Jūlius,* after Gaius *Julius* CAESAR, in whose honour it was named]

Jumada (dʒʊ'mɑːdə) *n* either the fifth or the sixth month of the Muslim year, known respectively as **Jumada I** and **Jumada II.** [Arabic]

jumar ('dʒuːmə) *n Mountaineering.* **1** Also called: **jumar clamp.** a clamp with a handle that can move freely up a rope on which it is clipped but locks when downward pressure is applied. ◆ *vb* (*intr*) **2** to climb (up a fixed rope) using jumars. [C20: Swiss name]

jumble ('dʒʌmbᵊl) *vb* **1** to mingle (objects, papers, etc.) in a state of disorder. **2** (*tr; usually passive*) to remember in a confused form; muddle. ◆ *n* **3** a disordered mass, state, etc. **4** *Brit.* articles donated for a jumble sale. **5** Also called: **jumbal.** a small thin cake, usually ring-shaped. [C16: of uncertain origin] ▸ **'jumbler** *n* ▸ **'jumbly** *adj*

jumble sale *n* a sale of miscellaneous articles, usually cheap and predominantly secondhand, in aid of charity. U.S. and Canadian equivalent: **rummage sale.**

jumbo ('dʒʌmbəʊ) *n, pl* **-bos. 1** *Informal.* **1a** a very large person or thing. **1b** (*as modifier*): *a jumbo box of detergent.* **2** See **jumbo jet.** [C19: after the name of a famous elephant exhibited by P. T. Barnum, from Swahili *jumbe* chief]

jumboize *or* **jumboise** ('dʒʌmbəʊ,aɪz) *vb* (*tr*) to extend (a ship, esp. a tanker) by cutting out the middle part and inserting a new larger part between the original bow and stern. [C20: from JUMBO + -IZE]

jumbo jet *n Informal.* a type of large jet-propelled airliner that carries several hundred passengers.

jumbuck ('dʒʌm,bʌk) *n Austral. archaic.* an informal word for **sheep.** [C19: from a native Australian language]

Jumna ('dʒʌmnə) *n* a river in N India, rising in Uttar Pradesh in the Himalayas and flowing south and southeast to join the Ganges just below Allahabad (a confluence held sacred by Hindus). Length: 1385 km (860 miles).

jump (dʒʌmp) *vb* **1** (*intr*) to leap or spring clear of the ground or other surface by using the muscles in the legs and feet. **2** (*tr*) to leap over or clear (an obstacle): *to jump a gap.* **3** (*tr*) to cause to leap over an obstacle: *to jump a horse over a hedge.* **4** (*intr*) to move or proceed hastily (into, onto, out of, etc.): *she jumped into a taxi and was off.* **5** (*tr*) *Informal.* to board so as to travel illegally on: *he jumped the train as it was leaving.* **6** (*intr*) to parachute from an aircraft. **7** (*intr*) to jerk or start, as with astonishment, surprise, etc.: *she jumped when she heard the explosion.* **8** to rise or cause to rise suddenly or abruptly. **9** to pass or skip over (intervening objects or matter): *she jumped a few lines and then continued reading.* **10** (*intr*) to change from one thing to another, esp. from one subject to another. **11** (*tr*) to drill by means of a jumper. **12** (*intr*) (of a film) **12a** to have sections of a continuous sequence omitted, as through faulty cutting. **12b** to flicker, as through faulty alignment of the film. **13** (*tr*) *U.S.* to promote in rank, esp. unexpectedly or to a higher rank than expected. **14** (*tr*) to start (a car) using jump leads. **15** *Draughts.* to capture (an opponent's piece) by moving one of one's own pieces over it to an unoccupied square. **16** (*intr*) *Bridge.* to bid in response to one's partner at a higher level than is necessary, to indicate a strong hand. **17** (*tr*) to come off (a track, rail, etc.): *the locomotive jumped the rails.* **18** (*intr*) (of the stylus of a record player) to be jerked out of the groove. **19** (*intr*) *Slang.* to be lively: *the party was jumping when I arrived.* **20** (*tr*) *Informal.* to attack without warning: *thieves jumped the old man as he walked through the park.* **21** (*tr*) *Informal.* (of a driver or a motor vehicle) to pass through (a red traffic light) or move away from (traffic lights) before they change to green. **22** (*tr*) *Brit. slang.* (of a man) to have sexual intercourse with. **23 jump bail.** to forfeit one's bail by failing to appear in court, esp. by absconding. **24 jump down someone's throat.** *Informal.* to address or reply to someone with unexpected sharpness. **25 jump ship.** to desert, esp. to leave a ship in which one is legally bound to serve. **26 jump the queue.** See **queue-jump. 27 jump to it.** *Informal.* to begin something quickly and efficiently. ◆ *n* **28** an act or instance of jumping. **29** a space, distance, or obstacle to be jumped or that has been jumped. **30** a descent by parachute from an aircraft. **31** *Sport.* any of several contests involving a jump: *the high jump.* **32** a sudden rise: *the jump in prices last month.* **33** a sudden or abrupt transition. **34** a sudden jerk or involuntary muscular spasm, esp. as a reaction of surprise. **35** a step or degree: *one jump ahead.* **36** *Draughts.* a move that captures an opponent's piece by jumping over it. **37** *Films.* **37a** a break in continuity in the normal sequence of shots. **37b** (*as modifier*): *a jump cut.* **38** *Computing.* another name for **branch** (sense 7). **39** *Brit. slang.* an act of sexual intercourse. **40 on the jump.** *Informal, chiefly U.S. and Canadian.* **40a** in a hurry. **40b** busy and energetic. **41 take a running jump.** *Brit. informal.* a contemptuous expression of dismissal. ◆ See also **jump at, jump-off, jump on, jump-up.** [C16: probably of imitative origin; compare Swedish *gumpa* to jump] ▸ **'jumpable** *adj* ▸ **'jumpingly** *adv*

jump at *vb* (*intr, prep*) to be glad to accept: *I would jump at the chance of going.*

jump ball *n Basketball.* a ball thrown high by the referee between two opposing players to put it in play, as after a stoppage in which no foul or violation was committed.

jump bid *n Bridge.* a bid by the responder at a higher level than is necessary.

jumped-up *adj Informal.* suddenly risen in significance, esp. when appearing arrogant.

jumper[1] ('dʒʌmpə) *n* **1** *Chiefly Brit.* a knitted or crocheted garment covering the upper part of the body. **2** the U.S. and Canadian term for **pinafore dress.** [C19: from obsolete *jump* man's loose jacket, variant of *jupe,* from Old French, from Arabic *jubbah* long cloth coat]

jumper[2] ('dʒʌmpə) *n* **1** a boring tool that works by repeated impact, such as a steel bit in a hammer drill used in boring rock. **2** Also called: **jumper cable, jumper lead.** a short length of wire used to make a connection, usually temporarily, between terminals or to bypass a component. **3** a type of sled with a high crosspiece. **4** a person or animal that jumps. **5** *Irish derogatory slang.* a person who changes religion; a convert.

jumping bean *n* a seed of any of several Mexican euphorbiaceous plants, esp. species of *Sebastiania,* that contains a moth caterpillar whose movements cause it to jerk about.

jumping gene *n* a fragment of nucleic acid, such as a plasmid or a transposon, that can become incorporated into the DNA of a cell.

jumping jack *n* **1** a firework having a long narrow tube filled with gunpowder, folded like an accordion so that when lit it burns with small explosions causing it to jump along the ground. **2** a toy figure of a man with jointed limbs that can be moved by pulling attached strings.

jumping mouse *n* any long-tailed small mouselike rodent of the family *Zapodidae,* of North America, E Asia, and N and E Europe, having long hind legs specialized for leaping.

jumping-off place *or* **point** *n* **1** a starting point, as in an enterprise. **2** a final or extreme condition. 3 *Canadian.* a place where one leaves civilization to go into the wilderness. 4 *U.S.* a very remote spot.

jumping spider *n* any spider of the family *Salticidae,* esp. *Attulus saltator,* that catch their prey by hunting and can jump considerable distances.

jump jet *n* a fixed-wing jet aircraft that is capable of landing and taking off vertically.

jump jockey *n Brit.* a jockey who rides in steeplechases, as opposed to one who rides in flat races.

jump leads (li:dz) *pl n* two heavy cables fitted with crocodile clips used to start a motor vehicle with a discharged battery by connecting the battery to an external battery. U.S. and Canadian name: **jumper cables.**

jump-off *n* **1** an extra round in a showjumping contest when two or more horses are equal first, the fastest round deciding the winner. ◆ *vb* **jump off. 2** (*intr, adv*) to begin or engage in a jump-off.

jump on *vb* (*intr, prep*) *Informal.* to reprimand or attack suddenly and forcefully.

jump seat *n* **1** a folding seat for temporary use, as on the flight deck of some aircraft for an additional crew member. **2** *Brit.* a folding seat in a motor vehicle such as in a London taxi.

jump shot *n Basketball.* a shot at the basket made by a player releasing the ball at the highest point of a leap.

jump-start *vb* **1** to start the engine of (a car) by pushing or rolling it and then engaging the gears or (of a car) to start in this way. ◆ *n* **2** the act of starting a car in this way. ◆ Also (Brit.): **bump-start.**

jump suit *n* a one-piece garment of combined trousers and jacket or shirt.

jump-up *n* **1** (in the Caribbean) an occasion of mass dancing and merrymaking, as in a carnival. ◆ *vb* **jump up.** (*intr, adv*) **2** to stand up quickly and suddenly. **3** (in the Caribbean) to take part in a jump-up.

jumpy ('dʒʌmpɪ) *adj* **jumpier, jumpiest. 1** nervous or apprehensive. **2** moving jerkily or fitfully. ▸ **'jumpily** *adv* ▸ **'jumpiness** *n*

Jun. *abbrev. for:* **1** June. **2** Also: **jun.** junior.

Junagadh (ˌdʒu:nəˈgæd) *n* a town in India, in Gujarat: noted for its Buddhist caves and temples. Pop.: 130 484 (1991).

junc. *abbrev. for* junction.

juncaceous (dʒʌŋˈkeɪʃəs) *adj* of, relating to, or belonging to the *Juncaceae,* a family of grasslike plants with small brown flowers: includes the rushes and woodrushes. Compare **cyperaceous.** [**C19:** via New Latin from Latin *juncus* a rush]

junco ('dʒʌŋkəʊ) *n, pl* **-cos** *or* **-coes.** any North American bunting of the genus *Junco,* having a greyish plumage with white outer tail feathers. [**C18:** from Spanish: a rush, a marsh bird, from Latin *juncus* rush]

junction ('dʒʌŋkʃən) *n* **1** a place where several routes, lines, or roads meet, link, or cross each other: *a railway junction.* **2** a point on a motorway where traffic may leave or join it. **3** *Electronics.* **3a** a contact between two different metals or other materials: *a thermocouple junction.* **3b** a transition region between regions of differing electrical properties in a semiconductor: *a p-n junction.* **4** a connection between two or more conductors or sections of transmission lines. **5** the act of joining or the state of being joined. [**C18:** from Latin *junctiō* a joining, from *junctus* joined, from *jungere* to join] ▸ **'junctional** *adj*

junction box *n* an earthed enclosure within which wires or cables can be safely connected.

junction transistor *n* a bipolar transistor consisting of two p-n junctions combined to form either an n-p-n or a p-n-p transistor, having the three electrodes, the emitter, base, and collector.

juncture ('dʒʌŋktʃə) *n* **1** a point in time, esp. a critical one (often in the phrase **at this juncture**). **2** *Linguistics.* **2a** a pause in speech or a feature of pronunciation that introduces, accompanies, or replaces a pause. **2b** the set of phonological features signalling a division between words, such as those that distinguish *a name* from *an aim.* **3** a less common word for **junction.**

Jundiaí (*Portuguese* ʒundiaˈi) *n* an industrial city in SE Brazil, in São Paulo state. Pop.: 253 177 (1991).

June (dʒu:n) *n* the sixth month of the year, consisting of 30 days. [**Old English** *iunius,* from Latin *junius,* probably from *Junius* name of Roman gens]

Juneau ('dʒu:nəʊ) *n* a port in SE Alaska: state capital. Pop.: 26 751 (1990).

Juneberry ('dʒu:nˌbɛrɪ) *n, pl* **-ries.** another name for **serviceberry** (senses 1, 2).

June bug *or* **beetle** *n* any of various large brown North American scarabaeid beetles that are common in late spring and early summer, esp. any of the genus *Polyphylla.* Also called: **May beetle, May bug.**

Jung (jʊŋ) *n* **Carl Gustav** (karl ˈgʊstaf). 1875–1961, Swiss psychologist. His criticism of Freud's emphasis on the sexual instinct ended their early collaboration. He went on to found analytical psychology, developing the concepts of the collective unconscious and its archetypes and of the extrovert and introvert as the two main psychological types.

Jungfrau (*German* ˈjʊŋfrau) *n* a mountain in S Switzerland, in the Bernese Alps south of Interlaken. Height: 4158 m (13 642 ft.).

Junggar Pendi ('dʒʊŋˈgɛər ˈpɛnˈdi:), **Dzungaria,** *or* **Zungaria** *n* an arid region of W China, in N Xinjiang Uygur between the Altai Mountains and the Tian Shan.

Jungian ('jʊŋɪən) *adj* of, following, or relating to C. G. Jung, his system of psychoanalysis, or to analytical psychology.

jungle ('dʒʌŋgᵊl) *n* **1** an equatorial forest area with luxuriant vegetation, often almost impenetrable. **2** any dense or tangled thicket or growth. **3** a place of intense competition or ruthless struggle for survival: *the concrete jungle.* **4** a type of fast electronic dance music, originating in the early 1990s, which combines elements of techno and ragga. **5** *U.S. slang.* (esp. in the Depression) a gathering place for the unemployed, etc. [**C18:** from Hindi *jangal,* from Sanskrit *jāngala* wilderness] ▸ **'jungly** *adj*

jungle fever *n* a serious malarial fever occurring in the East Indies.

jungle fowl *n* **1** any small gallinaceous bird of the genus *Gallus,* of S and SE Asia, the males of which have an arched tail and a combed and wattled head: family *Phasianidae* (pheasants). *G. gallus* (**red jungle fowl**) is thought to be the ancestor of the domestic fowl. **2** *Austral.* any of several megapodes, esp. *Megapodius freycinet.*

jungle gym *n* a climbing frame for young children. [**from a trademark**]

jungle juice *n* a slang name for alcoholic liquor, esp. home-made liquor.

junior ('dʒu:njə) *adj* **1** lower in rank or length of service; subordinate. **2** younger in years: *junior citizens.* **3** of or relating to youth or childhood: *junior pastimes.* **4** *Brit.* of or relating to schoolchildren between the ages of 7 and 11 approximately. **5** *U.S.* of, relating to, or designating the third year of a four-year course at college or high school. ◆ *n* **6** *Law.* (in England) any barrister below the rank of Queen's Counsel. **7** a junior person. **8** *Brit.* a junior schoolchild. **9** *U.S.* a junior student. [**C17:** from Latin: younger, from *juvenis* young]

Junior ('dʒu:njə) *adj* being the younger: usually used after a name to distinguish the son from the father with the same first name or names: *Charles Parker, Junior.* Abbrevs.: **Jnr, Jr, Jun., Junr.**

junior college *n U.S. and Canadian.* **1** an educational establishment providing a two-year course that either terminates with an associate degree or is the equivalent of the freshman and sophomore years of a four-year undergraduate course. **2** the junior section of a college or university.

junior common room *n* (in certain universities and colleges) a common room for the use of students. Compare **senior common room, middle common room.**

junior lightweight *n* **a** a professional boxer weighing 126–130 pounds (57–59 kg). **b** (*as modifier*): *a junior-lightweight bout.*

junior middleweight *n* **a** a professional boxer weighing 147–154 pounds (66.5–70 kg). **b** (*as modifier*): *the junior-middleweight championship.* Compare **light middleweight.**

junior school *n* (in England and Wales) a school for children aged between 7 and 11. Compare **infant school.**

junior technician *n* a rank in the RAF senior to aircraftman: comparable to that of private in the army.

junior welterweight *n* **a** a professional boxer weighing 135–140 pounds (61–63.5 kg). **b** (*as modifier*): *a junior-welterweight fight.* Compare **light welterweight.**

juniper ('dʒu:nɪpə) *n* **1** any coniferous shrub or small tree of the genus *Juniperus,* of the N hemisphere, having purple berry-like cones. The cones of *J. communis* (**common** or **dwarf juniper**) are used as a flavouring in making gin. See also **red cedar** (sense 1). **2** any of various similar trees, grown mainly as ornamentals. **3** *Old Testament.* one of the trees used in the building of Solomon's temple (I Kings 6:15, 34) and for shipbuilding (Ezekiel 27:5). [**C14:** from Latin *jūniperus,* of obscure origin]

Junius ('dʒu:njəs) *n* pen name of the anonymous author of a series of letters (1769–72) attacking the ministries of George III of England: now generally believed to have been written by Sir Philip Francis.

junk[1] (dʒʌŋk) *n* **1** discarded or secondhand objects, etc., collectively. **2** *Informal.* **2a** rubbish generally. **2b** nonsense: *the play was absolute junk.* **3** *Slang.* any narcotic drug, esp. heroin. ◆ *vb* **4** (*tr*) *Informal.* to discard as junk; scrap. [**C15** *jonke* old useless rope]

junk[2] (dʒʌŋk) *n* a sailing vessel used in Chinese waters and characterized by a very high poop, flat bottom, and square sails supported by battens. [**C17:** from Portuguese *junco,* from Javanese *jon;* related to Dutch *jonk*]

junk bond *n Finance.* a security that offers a high yield but often involves a high risk of default.

Junker ('jʊŋkə) *n* **1** *History.* any of the aristocratic landowners of Prussia who were devoted to maintaining their identity and extensive social and political privileges. **2** an arrogant, narrow-minded, and tyrannical German army officer or official. **3** (formerly) a young German nobleman. [**C16:** from German, from Old High German *junchērro* young lord, from *junc* young + *hērro* master, lord] ▸ **'Junkerdom** *n* ▸ **'Junkerism** *n*

Junkers ('jʊŋkəz) *n* **Hugo.** 1859–1935, German aircraft designer. His military aircraft were used in both World Wars.

junket ('dʒʌŋkɪt) *n* **1** an excursion, esp. one made for pleasure at public expense by a public official or committee. **2** a sweet dessert made of flavoured milk set to a curd with rennet. **3** a feast or festive occasion. ◆ *vb* **4** (*intr*) (of a public official, committee, etc.) to go on a junket. **5** to have or entertain with a feast or festive gathering. [**C14** (in the sense: rush basket, hence custard served on rushes): from Old French (dialect) *jonquette,* from *jonc* rush, from Latin *juncus* reed] ▸ **'junketer, 'junketter,** *or* **ˌjunke'teer** *n*

junk food *n* food that is low in nutritional value, often highly processed or ready-prepared, and eaten instead of or in addition to well-balanced meals.

junkie *or* **junky** ('dʒʌŋkɪ) *n, pl* **junkies.** an informal word for **drug addict,** esp. one who injects heroin into himself.

junk mail *n* untargeted mail advertising goods or services.

junkman ('dʒʌŋkˌmæn) *n, pl* **-men.** the U.S. and Canadian term for **rag-and-bone man.**

junk shop *n* **1** a shop selling miscellaneous secondhand goods. **2** *Derogatory.* a shop selling antiques.

junkyard ('dʒʌŋkˌjɑ:d) *n* a place where junk is stored or collected for sale.

Juno[1] ('dʒu:nəʊ) *n* **1** (in Roman tradition) the queen of the Olympian gods. Greek counterpart: **Hera. 2** a woman of stately bearing and regal beauty.

Juno[2] ('dʒu:nəʊ) *n Astronomy.* the fourth largest known asteroid (approximate diameter 240 kilometres) and one of the four brightest.

Junoesque (ˌdʒu:nəʊˈɛsk) *adj* having stately bearing and regal beauty like the goddess Juno.

Junr *or* **junr** *abbrev. for* junior.

junta ('dʒʊntə, 'dʒʌn-; *chiefly U.S.* 'hʊntə) *n* **1** a group of military officers holding the power in a country, esp. after a coup d'état. **2** Also called: **junto.** a small group of men; cabal, faction, or clique. **3** a legislative or executive council in some parts of Latin America. [C17: from Spanish: council, from Latin *junctus* joined, from *jungere* to JOIN]

junto ('dʒʊntəʊ, 'dʒʌn-) *n, pl* **-tos.** a variant of **junta** (sense 2). [C17: variant of JUNTA]

Jupiter[1] ('dʒu:pɪtə) *n* (in Roman tradition) the king and ruler of the Olympian gods. Greek counterpart: **Zeus.**

Jupiter[2] ('dʒu:pɪtə) *n* the largest of the planets and the fifth from the sun. It has 16 satellites and is surrounded by a transient planar ring system consisting of dust particles. Mean distance from sun: 778 million km; period of revolution around sun: 11.86 years; period of axial rotation: 9.83 hours; diameter and mass: 11.2 and 317.9 times that of earth respectively.

jupon ('ʒu:pɒn) *n* a short close-fitting sleeveless padded garment, used in the late 14th and early 15th centuries with armour. Also called: **gipon.** [C15: from Old French, from Old French *jupe;* see JUMPER[1]]

jura ('dʒʊərə) *n* the plural of **jus.**

Jura ('dʒʊərə) *n* **1** a department of E France, in Franche-Comté region. Capital: Lons-le-Saunier. Pop.: 252 100 (1995). Area: 5055 sq. km (1971 sq. miles). **2** a canton of Switzerland, bordering the French frontier: formed in 1979 from part of Bern. Capital: Delémont. Pop.: 69 188 (1996 est.). Area: 838 sq. km (323 sq. miles). **3** an island off the W coast of Scotland, in the Inner Hebrides, separated from the mainland by the **Sound of Jura.** Pop. (with Colonsay): 250 (latest est.). Area: 381 sq. km (147 sq. miles). **4** a mountain range in W central Europe, between the Rivers Rhine and Rhône: mostly in E France, extending into W Switzerland. **5** a range of mountains in the NE quadrant of the moon lying on the N border of the Mare Imbrium.

jural ('dʒʊərəl) *adj* **1** of or relating to law or to the administration of justice. **2** of or relating to rights and obligations. [C17: from Latin *iūs* law + -AL[1]] ► **'jurally** *adv*

Jurassic (dʒʊ'ræsɪk) *adj* **1** of, denoting, or formed in the second period of the Mesozoic era, between the Triassic and Cretaceous periods, lasting for 45 million years during which dinosaurs and ammonites flourished. ◆ *n* **2 the.** the Jurassic period or rock system. [C19: from French *jurassique,* after the JURA (Mountains)]

jurat ('dʒʊəræt) *n* **1** *Law.* a statement at the foot of an affidavit, naming the parties, stating when, where, and before whom it was sworn, etc. **2** (in England) a municipal officer of the Cinque Ports, having a similar position to that of an alderman. **3** (in France and the Channel Islands) a magistrate. [C16: from Medieval Latin *jūrātus* one who has been sworn, from Latin *jūrāre* to swear]

juratory ('dʒʊərətərɪ, -trɪ) *adj Law.* of, relating to, or expressed in an oath.

JurD *abbrev. for* Doctor of Law. [Latin: *Juris Doctor*]

jurel (hu:'rɛl) *n* any of several carangid food fishes of the genus *Caranx,* of warm American Atlantic waters. [C18: from Spanish, from Catalan *sorell,* from Late Latin *saurus* horse mackerel, from Greek *sauros* lizard]

juridical (dʒʊ'rɪdɪk°l) *or* **juridic** *adj* of or relating to law, to the administration of justice, or to the office or function of a judge; legal. [C16: from Latin *jūridicus,* from *iūs* law + *dicere* to say] ► **ju'ridically** *adv*

juridical days *pl n Law.* days on which the courts are in session. Compare **dies non.**

jurisconsult (ˌdʒʊərɪs'kɒnsʌlt) *n* **1** a person qualified to advise on legal matters. **2** a master of jurisprudence. [C17: from Latin *jūris consultus;* see JUS, CONSULT]

jurisdiction (ˌdʒʊərɪs'dɪkʃən) *n* **1** the right or power to administer justice and to apply laws. **2** the exercise or extent of such right or power. **3** power or authority in general. [C13: from Latin *jūrisdictiō* administration of justice; see JUS, DICTION] ► **ˌjuris'dictional** *adj* ► **ˌjuris'dictionally** *adv* ► **ˌjuris'dictive** *adj*

jurisp. *abbrev. for* jurisprudence.

jurisprudence (ˌdʒʊərɪs'pru:d°ns) *n* **1** the science or philosophy of law. **2** a system or body of law. **3** a branch of law: *medical jurisprudence.* [C17: from Latin *jūris prūdentia;* see JUS, PRUDENCE] ► **jurisprudential** (ˌdʒʊərɪspru:'dɛnʃəl) *adj* ► **ˌjurispru'dentially** *adv*

jurisprudent (ˌdʒʊərɪs'pru:d°nt) *adj* **1** skilled in jurisprudence or versed in the principles of law. ◆ *n* **2** a jurisprudent person.

jurist ('dʒʊərɪst) *n* **1** a person versed in the science of law, esp. Roman or civil law. **2** a writer on legal subjects. **3** a student or graduate of law. **4** (in the U.S.) a lawyer. [C15: from French *juriste,* from Medieval Latin *jūrista;* see JUS]

juristic (dʒʊ'rɪstɪk) *or* **juristical** *adj* **1** of or relating to jurists. **2** of, relating to, or characteristic of the study of law or the legal profession. ► **ju'ristically** *adv*

juristic act *n* **1** a proceeding designed to have a legal effect. **2** an act by an individual aimed at altering, terminating, or otherwise affecting a legal right.

juror ('dʒʊərə) *n* **1** a member of a jury. **2** a person whose name is included on a panel from which a jury is selected. **3** a person who takes an oath. [C14: from Anglo-French *jurour,* from Old French *jurer* to take an oath, from Latin *jūrāre*]

Juruá (*Portuguese* ʒu'rua) *n* a river in South America, rising in E central Peru and flowing northeast across NW Brazil to join the Amazon. Length: 1900 km (1200 miles).

jury[1] ('dʒʊərɪ) *n, pl* **-ries. 1** a group of, usually twelve, people sworn to deliver a true verdict according to the evidence upon a case presented in a court of law. See also **grand jury, petit jury. 2** a body of persons appointed to judge a competition and award prizes. **3 the jury is still out.** *Informal.* it has not yet been decided or agreed on. [C14: from Old French *juree,* from *jurer* to swear; see JUROR]

jury[2] ('dʒʊərɪ) *adj Chiefly nautical.* (in combination) makeshift: *jury-rigged.* [C17: of unknown origin]

jury box *n* an enclosure where the jury sit in court.

juryman ('dʒʊərɪmən) *or* (*fem*) **jurywoman** *n, pl* **-men** *or* **-women.** a member of a jury.

jury process *n* the writ used to summon jurors.

jury-rigged *adj Chiefly nautical.* set up in a makeshift manner, usually as a result of the loss of regular gear.

jus (dʒʌs) *n, pl* **jura** ('dʒʊərə). *Law.* **1** a right, power, or authority. **2** law in the abstract or as a system, as distinguished from specific enactments. [Latin: law]

jus. *or* **just.** *abbrev. for* justice.

jus canonicum (kə'nɒnɪkəm) *n* canon law. [from Latin]

jus civile (sɪ'vi:lɪ) *n* **1** the civil law of the Roman state. **2** the body of law derived from the principles of this law. Compare **jus gentium, jus naturale.** [from Latin]

jus divinum (dɪ'vi:nəm) *n* divine law. [from Latin]

jus gentium ('dʒɛntɪəm) *n Roman law.* those rules of law common to all nations. [from Latin]

jus naturale (ˌnætju'reɪlɪ) *n Roman law.* **1** (originally) a system of law based on fundamental ideas of right and wrong; natural law. **2** (in later usage) another term for **jus gentium.** [from Latin]

jus sanguinis ('sæŋgwɪnɪs) *n Law.* the principle that a person's nationality at birth is the same as that of his natural parents. Compare **jus soli.** [Latin, literally: law of blood]

jussive ('dʒʌsɪv) *adj Grammar.* another word for **imperative** (sense 3). [C19: from Latin *jūssus* ordered, from *jubēre* to command]

jus soli ('səʊlaɪ) *n Law.* the principle that a person's nationality at birth is determined by the territory within which he was born. Compare **jus sanguinis.** [from Latin, literally: law of soil]

just *adj* (dʒʌst). **1a** fair or impartial in action or judgment. **1b** (*as collective n; preceded by the): the just.* **2** conforming to high moral standards; honest. **3** consistent with justice: *a just action.* **4** rightly applied or given; deserved: *a just reward.* **5** legally valid; lawful: *a just inheritance.* **6** well-founded; reasonable: *just criticism.* **7** correct, accurate, or true: *a just account.* ◆ *adv* (dʒʌst; *unstressed* dʒəst). **8** used with forms of *have* to indicate an action performed in the very recent past: *I have just closed the door.* **9** at this very instant: *he's just coming in to land.* **10** no more than; merely; only: *just an ordinary car.* **11** exactly; precisely: *that's just what I mean.* **12** by a small margin; barely: *he just got there in time.* **13** (intensifier): *it's just wonderful to see you.* **14** *Informal.* indeed; with a vengeance: *isn't it just.* **15 just about. 15a** at the point of starting (to do something). **15b** very nearly; almost: *I've just about had enough.* **16 just a moment, second,** *or* **minute.** an expression requesting the hearer to wait or pause for a brief period of time. **17 just now. 17a** a very short time ago. **17b** at this moment. **17c** *S. African informal.* in a little while. **18 just on.** having reached exactly: *it's just on five o'clock.* **19 just so. 19a** an expression of complete agreement or of unwillingness to dissent. **19b** arranged with precision. [C14: from Latin *jūstus* righteous, from *jūs* justice] ► **'justly** *adv* ► **'justness** *n*

USAGE The use of *just* with *exactly* (*it's just exactly what they want*) is redundant and should be avoided: *it's exactly what they want.*

justice ('dʒʌstɪs) *n* **1** the quality or fact of being just. **2** *Ethics.* **2a** the principle of fairness that like cases should be treated alike. **2b** a particular distribution of benefits and burdens fairly in accordance with a particular conception of what are to count as like cases. **2c** the principle that punishment should be proportionate to the offence. **3** the administration of law according to prescribed and accepted principles. **4** conformity to the law; legal validity. **5** a judge of the Supreme Court of Judicature. **6** short for **justice of the peace. 7** good reason (esp. in the phrase **with justice**): *he was disgusted by their behaviour, and with justice.* **8 do justice to. 8a** to show to full advantage: *the picture did justice to her beauty.* **8b** to show full appreciation of by action: *he did justice to the meal.* **8c** to treat or judge fairly. **9 do oneself justice.** to make full use of one's abilities. **10 bring to justice.** to capture, try, and usually punish (a criminal, an outlaw, etc.). [C12: from Old French, from Latin *jūstitia,* from *justus* JUST]

justice court *n* an inferior court presided over by a justice of the peace.

justice of the peace *n* a lay magistrate, appointed by the crown or acting *ex officio,* whose function is to preserve the peace in his area, try summarily such cases as are within his jurisdiction, and perform miscellaneous administrative duties.

justice of the peace court *n* (in Scotland, formerly) a court with limited criminal jurisdiction held by justices of the peace in counties: replaced in 1975 by the **district court.**

justiceship ('dʒʌstɪsˌʃɪp) *n* the rank or office of a justice.

justiciable (dʒʌ'stɪʃɪəb°l) *adj* **1** capable of being determined by a court of law. **2** liable to be brought before a court for trial; subject to jurisdiction. ► **jusˌticia'bility** *n*

justiciar (dʒʌ'stɪʃɪˌɑ:) *n English legal history.* the chief political and legal officer from the time of William I to that of Henry III, who deputized for the king in his absence and presided over the kings' courts. Also called: **justiciary.** ► **jus'ticiarˌship** *n*

justiciary (dʒʌ'stɪʃɪərɪ) *adj* **1** of or relating to the administration of justice. ◆ *n, pl* **-aries. 2** an officer or administrator of justice; judge. **3** another word for **justiciar.**

justifiable ('dʒʌstɪˌfaɪəb°l) *adj* capable of being justified; understandable. ► **ˌjustiˌfia'bility** *or* **'justiˌfiableness** *n* ► **'justiˌfiably** *adv*

justifiable homicide *n* lawful killing, as in the execution of a death sentence.

justification (ˌdʒʌstɪfɪ'keɪʃən) *n* **1** reasonable grounds for complaint, defence, etc. **2** the act of justifying; proof, vindication, or exculpation. **3** *Theol.* **3a** the act of justifying. **3b** the process of being justified or the condition of having been justified. **4** Also called: **justification by faith.** *Protestant theol.* the doctrine that God vindicates only those who repent and believe in Jesus. **5** *Print-*

ing, computing. the process of adjusting interword spacing in text or data so that both right and left margins are straight. **6** *Computing.* the process of moving data right or left so that the first or last character occurs in a predefined position.

justificatory ('dʒʌstɪfɪˌkeɪtərɪ, -trɪ) *or* **justificative** ('dʒʌstɪfɪˌkeɪtɪv) *adj* serving as justification or capable of justifying; vindicatory.

justify ('dʒʌstɪˌfaɪ) *vb* **-fies, -fying, -fied.** (*mainly tr*) **1** (*often passive*) to prove or see to be just or valid; vindicate: *he was certainly justified in taking the money.* **2** to show to be reasonable; warrant or substantiate: *his behaviour justifies our suspicion.* **3** to declare or show to be free from blame or guilt; absolve. **4** *Law.* **4a** to show good reason in court for (some action taken). **4b** to show adequate grounds for doing (that with which a person is charged): *to justify a libel.* **5** (*also intr*) *Printing, computing.* to adjust the spaces between words in (a line of type or data) so that it is of the required length or (of a line of type or data) to fit exactly. **6a** *Protestant theol.* to account or declare righteous by the imputation of Christ's merits to the sinner. **6b** *R.C. theol.* to change from sinfulness to righteousness by the transforming effects of grace. **7** (*also intr*) *Law.* to prove (a person) to have sufficient means to act as surety, etc., or (of a person) to qualify to provide bail or surety. **[C14:** from Old French *justifier,* from Latin *justificāre,* from *jūstus* JUST + *facere* to make**]** ► **'justiˌfier** *n*

Justinian I (dʒʌ'stɪnɪən) *n* called *the Great;* Latin name *Flavius Anicius Justinianus.* 483–565 A.D., Byzantine emperor (527–565). He recovered North Africa, SE Spain, and Italy, largely owing to the brilliance of generals such as Belisarius. He sponsored the Justinian Code.

Justinian II *n* 669–711 A.D., Byzantine emperor (685–95, 705–11). Banished (695) after a revolt against his oppressive rule, he regained the throne with the help of the Bulgars. He was killed in a second revolt.

Justinian Code *n* a compilation of Roman imperial law made by order of Justinian I, forming part of the **Corpus Juris Civilis.**

Justin Martyr ('dʒʌstɪn) *n* **Saint.** ?100–?165 A.D., Christian apologist and philosopher. Feast day: June 1.

just-in-time *adj* denoting or relating to an industrial method in which waste of resources is eliminated or reduced by producing production-line components, etc., as they are required, rather than holding large stocks. Abbrev.: **JIT.**

just intonation *n* a form of tuning employing the pitch intervals of the untempered natural scale, sometimes employed in the playing of the violin, cello, etc.

justle ('dʒʌsᵊl) *vb* a less common word for **jostle.**

just noticeable difference *n Psychol.* another name for **difference threshold.** Abbrev.: **jnd.**

jut (dʒʌt) *vb* **juts, jutting, jutted. 1** (*intr;* often foll. by *out*) to stick out or overhang beyond the surface or main part; protrude or project. ◆ *n* **2** something that juts out. **[C16:** variant of JET[1]**]** ► **'jutting** *adj*

jute (dʒuːt) *n* **1** either of two Old World tropical yellow-flowered herbaceous plants, *Corchorus capsularis* or *C. olitorius,* cultivated for their strong fibre: family *Tiliaceae.* **2** this fibre, used in making sacks, rope, etc. **[C18:** from Bengali *jhuto,* from Sanskrit *jūta* braid of hair, matted hair**]**

Jute (dʒuːt) *n* a member of one of various Germanic tribes, some of whom invaded England in the 6th century A.D., settling in Kent.

Jutish ('dʒuːtɪʃ) *adj* **1** of or relating to the Jutes. ◆ *n* **2** another name for **Kentish.**

Jutland ('dʒʌtlənd) *n* a peninsula of N Europe: forms the continental portion of Denmark and geographically includes the N part of the German province of Schleswig-Holstein, while politically it includes only the mainland of Denmark and the islands north of Limfjorden; a major but inconclusive naval battle was fought off its NW coast in 1916 between the British and German fleets. Danish name: **Jylland.** ► **'Jutlander** *n*

juvenal ('dʒuːvɪnᵊl) *adj Ornithol.* a variant spelling (esp. U.S.) of **juvenile** (sense 4).

Juvenal ('dʒuːvɪnᵊl) *n* Latin name *Decimus Junius Juvenalis.* ?60–?140 A.D., Roman satirist. In his 16 verse satires, he denounced the vices of imperial Rome.

juvenescence (ˌdʒuːvɪ'nɛsəns) *n* **1** youth or immaturity. **2** the act or process of growing from childhood to youth. **3** restoration of youth; rejuvenation.

juvenescent (ˌdʒuːvɪ'nɛsᵊnt) *adj* becoming or being young or youthful. **[C19:** from Latin *juvenēscere* to grow up, regain strength, from *juvenis* youthful**]**

juvenile ('dʒuːvɪˌnaɪl) *adj* **1** young, youthful, or immature. **2** suitable or designed for young people: *juvenile pastimes.* **3** (of animals or plants) not yet fully mature. **4** of or denoting young birds that have developed their first plumage of adult feathers. **5** *Geology.* occurring at the earth's surface for the first time; new: *juvenile water; juvenile gases.* ◆ *n* **6** a juvenile person, animal, or plant. **7** an actor who performs youthful roles. **8** a book intended for young readers. **[C17:** from Latin *juvenīlis* youthful, from *juvenis* young**]** ► **'juveˌnilely** *adv* ► **'juveˌnileness** *n*

juvenile court *n* the former name for **youth court.**

juvenile delinquency *n* antisocial or criminal conduct by juvenile delinquents.

juvenile delinquent *n* a child or young person guilty of some offence, act of vandalism, or antisocial behaviour or whose conduct is beyond parental control and who may be brought before a juvenile court.

juvenile hormone *n* a hormone, secreted by insects from a pair of glands behind the brain, that promotes the growth of larval characteristics and inhibits metamorphosis.

juvenilia (ˌdʒuːvɪ'nɪlɪə) *pl n* works of art, literature, or music produced in youth or adolescence, before the artist, author, or composer has formed a mature style. **[C17:** from Latin, literally: youthful things; see JUVENILE**]**

juvenility (ˌdʒuːvɪ'nɪlɪtɪ) *n, pl* **-ties. 1** the quality or condition of being juvenile, esp. of being immature. **2** (*often pl*) a juvenile act or manner. **3** juveniles collectively.

juxtapose (ˌdʒʌkstə'pəʊz) *vb* (*tr*) to place close together or side by side. **[C19:** back formation from *juxtaposition,* from Latin *juxta* next to + POSITION**]** ► **ˌjuxtapo'sition** *n* ► **ˌjuxtapo'sitional** *adj*

JWV *abbrev. for* Jewish War Veterans.

Jylland ('jylan) *n* the Danish name for **Jutland.**

k *or* **K** (keɪ) *n, pl* **k's, K's,** *or* **Ks. 1** the 11th letter and 8th consonant of the modern English alphabet. **2** a speech sound represented by this letter, usually a voiceless velar stop, as in *kitten.* **3** See **five Ks.**

k *symbol for:* **1** kilo(s). **2** *Maths.* the unit vector along the *z*-axis.

K *symbol for:* **1** kelvin(s). **2** *Chess.* king. **3** *Chem.* potassium. [from New Latin *kalium*] **4** *Physics.* kaon. **5** *Currency.* **5a** kina. **5b** kip. **5c** kopeck. **5d** kwacha. **5e** kyat. **6** one thousand. [from KILO-] **7** *Computing.* **7a** a unit of 1024 words, bits, or bytes. **7b** (not in technical usage) 1000. **8** *international car registration for* Cambodia.

K *or* **K.** *abbrev. for* Köchel: indicating the serial number in the catalogue (1862) of the works of Mozart made by Ludwig von Köchel, (1800–1877).

k. *abbrev. for:* **1** karat. **2** Also: **K.** king.

K2 *n* a mountain in the Karakoram Range on the Kashmir-Xinjiang Uygur AR border: the second highest mountain in the world. Height: 8611 m (28 250 ft.). Also called: **Godwin Austen, Dapsang.**

ka (kɑ:) *n* (in ancient Egypt) an attendant spirit supposedly dwelling as a vital force in a man or statue. [from Egyptian]

Kaaba *or* **Caaba** ('kɑ:bə) *n* a cube-shaped building in Mecca, the most sacred Muslim pilgrim shrine, into which is built the black stone believed to have been given by Gabriel to Abraham. Muslims turn in its direction when praying. [from Arabic *ka'bah,* from *ka'b* cube]

kab (kæb) *n* a variant spelling of **cab**[2].

kabaka (ka'baka) *n* any of the former rulers of the Baganda people of S Uganda. [C19: from Luganda]

Kabalega Falls (ˌkɑ:bə'leɪgə) *pl n* rapids on the lower Victoria Nile, about 35 km (22 miles) east of Lake Albert, where the Nile drops 120 m (400 ft.).

kabaragoya (kəˌbɑ:rə'gəʊjə) *n* a very large monitor lizard, *Varanus salvator,* of SE Asia: it grows to a length of three metres. Also called: **Malayan monitor.** [perhaps Tagalog]

Kabardian (kə'bɑ:dɪən) *n* **1** a member of a Circassian people of the North West Caucasus. **2** the Eastern dialect of the Circassian language. Compare **Adygei.**

Kabardino-Balkar Republic (ˌkæbə'di:nəʊˌbælkə) *n* a constituent republic of S Russia, on the N side of the Caucasus Mountains. Capital: Nalchik. Pop.: 787 000 (1995 est.). Area: 12 500 sq. km (4825 sq. miles). Also called: **Kabardino-Balkaria** (kæbəˌdi:nəʊbæl'kɑ:rɪə).

kabaddi (kə'bɑ:dɪ) *n* a game played between two teams of seven players, in which individuals take turns to chase and try to touch members of the opposing team without being captured by them. [Tamil]

kabbala *or* **kabala** (kə'bɑ:lə) *n* variant spellings of **cabbala.** ► **kabbalism** *or* **kabalism** ('kæbəˌlɪzəm) *n* ► **'kabbalist** *or* **'kabalist** *n* ► **ˌkabba'listic** *or* **ˌkaba'listic** *adj*

Kabila (kæ'bi:lə) *n* **Laurent** (*French* lorã). born 1940, Zaïrese (now Congolese) politician and guerrilla leader: he overthrew former president Mobutu and renamed Zaïre, becoming president of the Democratic Republic of Congo in 1997.

Kabinett (ˌkæbɪ'nɛt) *n* a dry, usually white, wine produced in Germany, made from mature grapes with no added sugar. [C20: from German, literally: cabinet]

Kabir (kə'bɪə) *n* 1440–1518, Indian religious leader who pioneered a religious movement that combined elements of Islam and Hinduism and is considered the precursor of Sikhism.

kabob (kə'bɒb) *n* another name for **kebab.**

kabuki (kæ'bu:kɪ) *n* a form of Japanese drama based on popular legends and characterized by elaborate costumes, stylized acting, and the use of male actors for all roles. See also **No**[1]. [Japanese, from *ka* singing + *bu* dancing + *ki* art]

Kabul (kə'bʊl, 'kɔ:b^{ə}l) *n* **1** the capital of Afghanistan, in the northeast of the country at an altitude of 1800 m (5900 ft.) on the **Kabul River**: over 3000 years old, with a strategic position commanding passes through the Hindu Kush and main routes to the Khyber Pass; destroyed and rebuilt many times; capital of the Mogul Empire from 1504 until 1738 and of Afghanistan from 1773; university (1932). Pop.: 700 000 (1993 est.). **2** a river in Afghanistan and Pakistan, rising in the Hindu Kush and flowing east into the Indus at Attock, Pakistan. Length: 700 km (435 miles).

Kabyle (kə'baɪl) *n* **1** (*pl* **-byles** *or* **-byle**) a member of a Berber people inhabiting the E Atlas Mountains in Tunisia and Algeria. **2** the dialect of Berber spoken by this people. [C19: from Arabic *qabā'il,* plural of *qabīlah* tribe]

kachang puteh ('katʃaŋ pu:'teɪ) *n* (in Malaysia) roasted or fried nuts or beans. [from Malay, literally: white beans]

Kachera (kʌ'tʃerrə) *or* **Kacha** ('kʌtʃə) *n* short trousers traditionally worn by Sikhs as a symbol of their religious and cultural loyalty: originally worn for ease of horse riding. See also **five Ks.** [Punjabi]

kachina (kə'tʃi:nə) *n* any of the supernatural beings believed by the Hopi Indians to be the ancestors of living humans. [from Hopi *qačina* supernatural]

kadaitcha (kə'daɪtʃə) *n* a variant spelling of **kurdaitcha.**

Kádár ('kɑ:dɑ:r) *n* **János** ('jɑ:nɒʃ). 1912–89, Hungarian statesman; Communist prime minister of Hungary (1956–58; 1961–65) and first secretary of the Communist Party (1956–88).

Kaddish ('kædɪʃ) *n, pl* **Kaddishim** (kæ'dɪʃɪm). *Judaism.* **1** an ancient Jewish liturgical prayer largely written in Aramaic and used in various forms to separate sections of the liturgy. Mourners have the right to recite some of these in public prayer during the year after, and on the anniversary of, a death. **2 say Kaddish.** to be a mourner. [C17: from Aramaic *qaddīsh* holy]

kadi ('kɑ:dɪ, 'keɪdɪ) *n, pl* **-dis.** a variant spelling of **cadi.**

Kaduna (kə'du:nə) *n* **1** a state of N Nigeria. Capital: Kaduna. Pop.: 4 438 007 (1995 est.). Area: 46 053 sq. km (17 781 sq. miles). Former name (until 1976): **North-Central State. 2** a city in N central Nigeria, capital of Kaduna state on the **Kaduna River** (a principal tributary of the Niger). Pop.: 342 200 (1996 est.).

Kaesŏng (ˌkeɪ'sɒŋ) *n* a city in SW North Korea: former capital of Korea (938–1392). Pop.: 120 000 (1987 est.).

Kaffir *or* **Kafir** ('kæfə) *n, pl* **-firs** *or* **-fir. 1** *Offensive.* **1a** (in southern Africa) any Black African. **1b** (*as modifier*): *Kaffir farming.* **2** a former name for the **Xhosa** language. **3** *Offensive.* (among Muslims) a non-Muslim or infidel. [C19: from Arabic *kāfir* infidel, from *kafara* to deny, refuse to believe]

kaffir beer *n S. African.* beer made from sorghum (kaffir corn) or millet.

kaffirboom ('kæfəˌbʊəm) *n S. African.* a deciduous flowering tree, *Erythrina caffra,* having large clusters of brilliant orange or scarlet flowers. [from KAFFIR + Afrikaans *boom* tree]

kaffir corn *or U.S.* (*sometimes*) **kafir corn** *n* a Southern African variety of sorghum, cultivated in dry regions for its grain and as fodder. Sometimes shortened to **kaffir** or (U.S.) **kafir.**

kaffiyeh (kæ'fi:jə) *n* a variant of **keffiyeh.**

Kaffraria (kæ'frɛərɪə) *n* a former region of S central South Africa: inhabited chiefly by the Kaffirs; British Kaffraria was a crown colony established in 1853 in the southwest of the region and annexed to Cape Colony in 1865. ► **Kaf'frarian** *adj, n*

Kafir ('kæfə) *n, pl* **-irs** *or* **-ir. 1** another name for the **Nuri. 2** a variant spelling of **Kaffir.** [C19: from Arabic; see KAFFIR]

Kafiristan (ˌkæfɪrɪ'stɑ:n) *n* the former name of **Nuristan.**

Kafka ('kæfkə; *Czech* 'kafka) *n* **Franz** (frants). 1883–1924, Czech novelist writing in German. In his two main novels *The Trial* (1925) and *The Castle* (1926), published posthumously against his wishes, he portrays man's fear, isolation, and bewilderment in a nightmarish dehumanized world. ► **Kafkaesque** (ˌkæfkə'ɛsk) *adj*

kaftan *or* **caftan** ('kæftæn, -ˌtɑ:n) *n* **1** a long coatlike garment, usually worn with a belt and made of rich fabric, worn in the East. **2** an imitation of this, worn, esp. by women, in the West, consisting of a loose dress with long wide sleeves. [C16: from Turkish *qaftān*]

Kagera (kæ'gɛrə) *n* a river in E Africa, rising in headstreams on the border between Tanzania and Rwanda and flowing east to Lake Victoria: the most remote headstream of the Nile and largest tributary of Lake Victoria. Length: about 480 km (300 miles).

Kagoshima (ˌkægɒ'ʃi:mə) *n* a port in SW Japan, on S Kyushu. Pop.: 546 294 (1995).

kagoul *or* **kagoule** (kə'gu:l) *n* variant spellings of **cagoule.**

kagu ('kɑ:gu:) *n* a crested nocturnal bird, *Rhynochetos jubatus,* with a red bill and greyish plumage: occurs only in New Caledonia and is nearly extinct: family *Rhynochetidae,* order *Gruiformes* (cranes, rails, etc.). [native name in New Caledonia]

kahawai ('kɑ:həˌwaɪ) *n* a large food and game fish of Australian and New Zealand coastal waters, *Arripis trutta,* that is greenish grey to silvery underneath and spotted with brown: resembles a salmon but is in fact a marine perch. Also called: **Australian salmon.** [Maori]

kahikatea (ˌkaɪkə'tɪə) *n* a tall New Zealand coniferous tree, *Podocarpus dacrydioides,* valued for its timber and resin. Also called: **white pine.** [Maori]

Kahn (kɑ:n) *n* **1 Herman.** 1922–83, U.S. mathematician and futurologist; director of the Hudson Institute (1961–83). **2 Louis I(sadore).** 1901–74, U.S. architect, noted for his art museums at Yale (1951–53), Fort Worth (1966–72), and New Haven (1969–74).

kai (kaɪ) *n N.Z.* food. [Maori, from Melanesian pidgin *kaikai*]

kaiak ('kaɪæk) *n* a variant of **kayak.**

Kaieteur Falls (ˌkaɪə'tʊə) *pl n* a waterfall in Guyana, on the Potaro River. Height: 226 m (741 ft.). Width: about 107 m (350 ft.).

kaif (kaɪf) *n* a variant of **kif.**

Kaifeng ('kaɪ'fɛŋ) *n* a city in E China, in N Henan on the Yellow River: one of the oldest cities in China and its capital (as Pien-liang) from 907 to 1126. Pop.: 507 763 (1990 est.).

kaik (kaɪk) *n N.Z.* the South Island dialect word for **kainga.**

kail (keɪl) *n* a variant spelling of **kale.**

kailyard ('keɪlˌjɑ:d) *n* a variant spelling of **kaleyard.**

kai moana (maʊ'ænə) *n N.Z.* seafood. [Maori]

kain (keɪn) *n History.* a variant spelling of **cain.**

kainga ('kaɪŋə) *n* (in New Zealand) a Maori village or small settlement. Also called (on South Island): **kaik.** [Maori]

kainite ('kaɪnaɪt) *n* a white mineral consisting of potassium chloride and magnesium sulphate: a fertilizer and source of potassium salts. Formula: $KCl.MgSO_4.3H_2O$. [C19: from German *Kainit,* from Greek *kainos* new + -ITE[1]]

kainogenesis (ˌkaɪnəʊˈdʒɛnɪsɪs) *n* another name for **caenogenesis**. ▸ **kainogenetic** (ˌkaɪnəʊdʒəˈnɛtɪk) *adj* ▸ ˌ**kainogeˈnetically** *adv*

Kairouan (*French* kɛrwɑ̃), **Kairwan,** *or* **Qairwan** (kaɪəˈwɑːn) *n* a city in NE Tunisia: one of the holy cities of Islam; pilgrimage and trading centre. Pop.: 102 600 (1994).

Kaiser[1] (ˈkaɪzə) *n* (*sometimes not cap.*) *History.* **1** any German emperor, esp. Wilhelm II (1888–1918). **2** *Obsolete.* any Austro-Hungarian emperor. **[C16:** from German, ultimately from Latin *Caesar* emperor, from the cognomen of Gaius Julius CAESAR**]** ▸ ˈ**kaiserdom** *or* ˈ**kaiserism** *n*

Kaiser[2] (*German* ˈkaizər) *n* **Georg** (ˈgeːɔrk). 1878–1945, German expressionist dramatist.

Kaiserslautern (*German* kaizərsˈlautərn) *n* a city in W Germany, in S Rhineland-Palatinate. Pop.: 102 002 (1996 est.).

kaizen *Japanese.* (kaɪˈzɛn) *n* a philosophy of continuous improvement of working practices that underlies total quality management and just-in-time business techniques. **[**literally: improvement**]**

kak (kʌk) *n S. African taboo.* **1** faeces. **2** rubbish. **[**Afrikaans**]**

kaka (ˈkɑːkə) *n* a New Zealand parrot, *Nestor meridionalis,* with a long compressed bill. **[C18:** from Maori, perhaps imitative of its call**]**

kaka beak *n* an evergreen climbing shrub, *Clianthus puniceus,* having pinnate leaves and clusters of bright red flowers in the shape of a parrot's beak. It is native to New Zealand but now rare except in cultivation. Also called: **red kowhai.**

kakapo (ˈkɑːkəˌpəʊ) *n, pl* **-pos.** a ground-living nocturnal parrot, *Strigops habroptilus,* of New Zealand, resembling an owl. **[C19:** from Maori, literally: night kaka**]**

kakemono (ˌkækɪˈməʊnəʊ) *n, pl* **-nos.** a Japanese paper or silk wall hanging, usually long and narrow, with a picture or inscription on it and a roller at the bottom. **[C19:** from Japanese, from *kake* hanging + *mono* thing**]**

kaki (ˈkɑːkɪ) *n, pl* **kakis.** another name for **Japanese persimmon.** **[**Japanese**]**

kala-azar (ˌkɑːləəˈzɑː) *n* a tropical infectious disease caused by the protozoan *Leishmania donovani* in the liver, spleen, etc., characterized by fever and weight loss; visceral leishmaniasis. **[**from Assamese *kālā* black + *āzār* disease**]**

Kalahari (ˌkæləˈhɑːrɪ) *n* **the.** an extensive arid plateau of South Africa, Namibia, and Botswana: inhabited by Bushmen. Area: 260 000 sq. km (100 000 sq. miles). Also called: **Kalahari Desert.**

Kalamazoo (ˌkæləməˈzuː) *n* a city in SW Michigan, midway between Detroit and Chicago: aircraft, missile parts. Pop.: 77 460 (1996 est.).

kalanchoe (ˌkælənˈkəʊɪ) *n* any plant of the tropical succulent genus *Kalanchoe,* grown as pot plants for their small brightly coloured flowers, sometimes scented, and their dark shiny leaves: family *Crassulaceae.* **[**New Latin, from the Chinese name of one of the species**]**

Kalashnikov (kəˈlæʃnɪˌkɒf) *n* a Russian-made automatic rifle. See also **AK-47.** **[C20:** named after Mikhail *Kalashnikov* (born 1919), its designer**]**

Kalat *or* **Khelat** (kəˈlɑːt) *n* a region of SW Pakistan, in S Baluchistan: formerly a princely state ruled by the Khan of Kalat, which joined Pakistan in 1948.

kale *or* **kail** (keɪl) *n* **1** a cultivated variety of cabbage, *Brassica oleracea acephala,* with crinkled leaves: used as a potherb. See also **collard. 2** *Scot.* a cabbage. **3** *U.S. slang.* money. ◆ Compare (for senses 1, 2) **sea kale.** **[**Old English *cāl;* see COLE**]**

kaleidoscope (kəˈlaɪdəˌskəʊp) *n* **1** an optical toy for producing symmetrical patterns by multiple reflections in inclined mirrors enclosed in a tube. Loose pieces of coloured glass, paper, etc., are placed between transparent plates at the far end of the tube, which is rotated to change the pattern. **2** any complex pattern of frequently changing shapes and colours. **3** a complicated set of circumstances. **[C19:** from Greek *kalos* beautiful + *eidos* form + -SCOPE**]** ▸ **kaleidoscopic** (kəˌlaɪdəˈskɒpɪk) *adj* ▸ **kaˌleidoˈscopically** *adv*

kalends (ˈkælɪndz) *pl n* a variant spelling of **calends.**

Kalevala (ˌkɑːləˈvɑːlə; *Finnish* ˈkɑlɛvɑlɑ) *n Finnish legend.* **1** the land of the hero Kaleva, who performed legendary exploits. **2** the Finnish national epic in which these exploits are recounted, compiled by Elias Lönnrot from folk poetry in 1835 to 1849. **[**Finnish, from *kaleva* of a hero + *-la* dwelling place, home**]**

kaleyard *or* **kailyard** (ˈkeɪlˌjɑːd; *Scot.* -ˌjard) *n Scot.* a vegetable garden. **[C19:** literally: cabbage garden**]**

kaleyard school *or* **kailyard school** *n* a group of writers who depicted the sentimental and homely aspects of life in the Scottish Lowlands from about 1880 to 1914. The best known contributor to the school was J. M. Barrie.

Kalgan (ˈkɑːlˈgɑːn) *n* a former name of **Zhangjiakou.**

Kalgoorlie (kælˈgʊəlɪ) *n* a city in Western Australia, adjoining the town of Boulder: a centre of the Coolgardie gold rushes of the early 1890s; declining gold resources superseded by the discovery of nickel ore in 1966. Pop.: 26 079 (including Boulder) (1991).

kali (ˈkælɪ, ˈkeɪ-) *n* another name for **saltwort** (sense 1).

Kali (ˈkɑːlɪ) *n* the Hindu goddess of destruction, consort of Siva. Her cult was characterized by savagery and cannibalism.

kalian (kælˈjɑːn) *n* another name for **hookah.** **[C19:** from Persian, from Arabic *qalyān***]**

Kalidasa (ˌkælɪˈdɑːsə) *n* ?5th century A.D., Indian dramatist and poet, noted for his romantic verse drama *Sakuntala.*

kalif (ˈkeɪlɪf, ˈkæl-) *n* a variant spelling of **caliph.**

Kalimantan (ˌkælɪˈmæntən) *n* the Indonesian name for Borneo: applied to the Indonesian part of the island only, excluding the Malaysian states of Sabah and Sarawak and the sultanate of Brunei. Pop.: 6 723 086 (1980).

Kalinin[1] (*Russian* kaˈlinin) *n* the former name (until 1991) of **Tver.**

Kalinin[2] (*Russian* kaˈlinin) *n* **Mikhail Ivanovich** (mixaˈil iˈvanəvitʃ). 1875–1946, Soviet statesman: titular head of state (1919–46); a founder of *Pravda* (1912).

Kaliningrad (*Russian* kəlininˈgrat) *n* a port in W Russia, on the Pregolya River: severely damaged in World War II as the chief German naval base on the Baltic; ceded to the Soviet Union in 1945 and is now Russia's chief Baltic naval base. Pop.: 419 000 (1995 est.). Former name (until 1946): **Königsberg.**

Kalisz (*Polish* ˈkaliʃ) *n* a town in central Poland, on an island in the Prosna River: textile industry. Pop.: 106 800 (1996 est.). Ancient name: **Calissia** (kəˈlɪsɪə).

Kaliyuga (ˌkɑːlɪˈjuːgə) *n* (in Hindu mythology) the fourth (present) age of the world, characterized by total decadence.

Kalmar (*Swedish* ˈkalmar) *n* a port in SE Sweden, partly on the mainland and partly on a small island in the **Sound of Kalmar,** opposite Öland: scene of the signing of the Union of Kalmar, which united Sweden, Denmark, and Norway into a single monarchy (1397–1523). Pop.: 58 070 (1994).

kalmia (ˈkælmɪə) *n* any evergreen ericaceous shrub of the North American genus *Kalmia,* having showy clusters of white or pink flowers. See also: **mountain laurel.** **[C18:** named after Peter *Kalm* (1715–79), Swedish botanist and pupil of Linnaeus**]**

Kalmuck (ˈkælmʌk) *or* **Kalmyk** (ˈkælmɪk) *n* **1** (*pl* **-mucks, -muck** *or* **-myks, -myk**) a member of a Mongoloid people of Buddhist tradition, who migrated from W China in the 17th century. **2** the language of this people, belonging to the Mongolic branch of the Altaic family.

Kalmuck Republic *or* **Kalmyk Republic** *n* a constituent republic of S Russia, on the Caspian Sea: became subject to Russia in 1646. Capital: Elista. Pop.: 320 000 (1995 est.). Area: 76 100 sq. km (29 382 sq. miles). Also called: **Kalmykia.**

kalong (ˈkɑːlɒŋ) *n* any fruit bat of the genus *Pteropus;* a flying fox. **[**Javanese**]**

kalpa (ˈkælpə) *n* (in Hindu cosmology) a period in which the universe experiences a cycle of creation and destruction. **[C18:** Sanskrit**]**

kalpak (ˈkælpæk) *n* a variant spelling of **calpac.**

kalsomine (ˈkælsəˌmaɪn, -mɪn) *n, v.* a variant of **calcimine.**

Kaluga (*Russian* kaˈlugə) *n* a city in central Russia, on the Oka River. Pop.: 347 000 (1995 est.).

Kama[1] (*Russian* ˈkamə) *n* a river in central Russia, rising in the Ural Mountains and flowing to the River Volga, of which it is the largest tributary. Length: 2030 km (1260 miles).

Kama[2] (ˈkɑːmə) *n* the Hindu god of love. **[**from Sanskrit**]**

kamacite (ˈkæməˌsaɪt) *n* an alloy of iron and nickel, occurring in meteorites. **[C19:** from (obsolete) German *Kamacit,* from Greek *kamax* shaft, pole + -ITE[1]**]**

Kamakura (ˌkæməˈkʊərə) *n* a city in central Japan, on S Honshu: famous for its Great Buddha (Daibutsu), a 13th-century bronze, 15 m (49 ft.) high. Pop.: 170 319 (1995 est.).

kamala (kəˈmɑːlə, ˈkæmələ) *n* **1** an East Indian euphorbiaceous tree, *Mallotus philippinensis.* **2** a powder obtained from the seed capsules of this tree, used as a dye and formerly as a worm powder. **[C19:** from Sanskrit, probably of Dravidian origin; compare Kanarese *kōmale***]**

Kamasutra (ˌkɑːməˈsuːtrə) *n* **the.** an ancient Hindu text on erotic pleasure and other topics. **[**Sanskrit: book on love, from *kāma* love + *sūtra* thread**]**

Kamchatka (*Russian* kamˈtʃatkə) *n* a peninsula in E Russia, between the Sea of Okhotsk and the Bering Sea. Length: about 1200 km (750 miles). ▸ **Kamˈchatkan** *adj, n*

kame (keɪm) *n* an irregular mound or ridge of gravel, sand, etc., deposited by water derived from melting glaciers. **[C19:** Scottish and northern English variant of COMB**]**

Kamensk-Uralski (*Russian* ˈkamɪnskuˈraljskij) *n* an industrial city in S Russia. Pop.: 197 000 (1995 est.).

Kamerad *German.* (kaməˈraːt; *English* ˈkæməˌrɑːd) *n* a shout of surrender, used by German soldiers. **[**German: COMRADE**]**

Kamerlingh-Onnes (*Dutch* ˈkamərlɪŋ ˈɔnəs) *n* **Heike** (ˈhaɪkə). 1853–1926, Dutch physicist: a pioneer of the physics of low-temperature materials and discoverer (1911) of superconductivity. Nobel prize for physics 1913.

Kamerun (ˈkaməruːn) *n* the German name for **Cameroon.**

Kamet (ˈkɑːmɛt, ˈkʌmeɪt) *n* a mountain in N India, in Uttar Pradesh in the Himalayas. Height: 7756 m (25 447 ft.).

kami (ˈkɑːmɪ) *n, pl* **-mi.** a divine being or spiritual force in Shinto. **[C18:** from Japanese: god, lord**]**

kamikaze (ˌkæmɪˈkɑːzɪ) *n* (*often cap.*) **1** (in World War II) one of a group of Japanese pilots who performed suicidal missions by crashing their aircraft, loaded with explosives, into an enemy target, esp. a ship. **2** an aircraft used for such a mission. **3** (*modifier*) (of an action) undertaken or (of a person) undertaking an action in the knowledge that it will result in the death of the person performing it in order that maximum damage may be inflicted on an enemy: *a kamikaze attack; a kamikaze bomber.* **4** (*modifier*) extremely foolhardy and possibly self-defeating: *kamikaze pricing.* **[C20:** from Japanese, from *kami* divine + *kaze* wind**]**

kamilaroi (ˈkæmələrɔɪ) *n* an Australian Aboriginal language formerly used in NW New South Wales.

Kammerer (*German* ˈkamərər) *n* **Paul.** 1880–1926, Austrian zoologist: noted for his controversial experiments, esp. with the midwife toad, apparently demonstrating the inheritance of acquired characteristics. Accused of fraud, he committed suicide.

Kampala (kæmˈpɑːlə) *n* the capital and largest city of Uganda, in Central region on Lake Victoria: Makerere University (1961). Pop.: 954 000 (1995 est.).

kampong (ˈkæmpɒŋ, kæmˈpɒŋ) *n* (in Malaysia) a village. **[C19:** from Malay**]**

Kampuchea (ˌkæmpuˈtʃɪə) *n* the name of Cambodia from 1976 until 1989. During the Vietnamese occupation of Cambodia (1979–89) exiled Cambodian factions, including the Khmer Rouge, formed the Coalition Government of Democratic Kampuchea (CGDK). The pro-Vietnamese government reverted to the name Cambodia in 1989. In 1993 all factions of the CGDK participated in democratic elections, except for the Khmer Rouge who continued guerrilla activities. See also **Cambodia.** ▸ ˌ**Kampuˈchean** *adj, n*

kamseen (kæm'si:n) *or* **kamsin** ('kæmsɪn) *n* variants of **khamsin.**

Kan. *abbrev. for* Kansas.

kana ('kɑ:nə) *n* the Japanese syllabary, which consists of two written varieties. See **hiragana, katakana.** [C18: from Japanese, literally: borrowed or provisional letters; compare KANJI, which are regarded as real letters]

Kanak (kə'næk) *n* a native or inhabitant of New Caledonia who seeks independence from France. [C20: from Hawaiian: man]

Kanaka (kə'nækə, 'kænəkə) *n* **1** (esp. in Hawaii) a native Hawaiian. **2** (*often not cap.*) *Austral.* any native of the South Pacific islands, esp. (formerly) one abducted to work in Australia. [C19: from Hawaiian: man, human being]

kanamycin (,kænə'maɪsɪn) *n* an antibiotic obtained from the soil bacterium *Streptomyces kanamyceticus,* used in the treatment of various infections, esp. those caused by Gram-negative bacteria. Formula: $C_{18}H_{36}N_4O_{11}$. [C20: from New Latin *kanamyceticus*]

Kananga (kə'næŋgə) *n* a city in the SW Democratic Republic of the Congo (formerly Zaïre): a commercial centre on the railway from Lubumbashi to Port Francqui. Pop.: 393 030 (1994 est.). Former name (until 1966): **Luluabourg.**

Kanara *or* **Canara** (kə'nɑ:rə) *n* a region of SW India, in Karnataka on the Deccan Plateau and the W Coast. Area: about 155 000 sq. km (60 000 sq. miles).

Kanarese *or* **Canarese** (,kænə'ri:z) *n* **1** (*pl* **-rese**) a member of a people of S India living chiefly in Kanara. **2** the language of this people; Kannada.

Kanazawa (,kænə'zɑ:wə) *n* a port in central Japan, on W Honshu: textile and porcelain industries. Pop.: 453 977 (1995).

kanban *Japanese.* ('kænbæn) *n* **1** a just-in-time manufacturing process in which the movements of materials through a process are recorded on specially designed cards. **2** any of the cards used for ordering materials in such a system. [literally: advertisement hoarding]

Kanchenjunga (,kæntʃən'dʒʌŋgə) *n* a variant spelling of **Kangchenjunga.**

Kanchipuram (kɑ:n'tʃi:pərəm) *n* a city in SE India, in Tamil Nadu: a sacred Hindu town known as "the Benares of the South"; textile industries. Pop.: 144 955 (1991).

Kandahar (,kændə'hɑ:) *n* a city in S Afghanistan: an important trading centre, built by Ahmad Shah Durrani (1724–73) as his capital on the site of several former cities. Pop.: 237 500 (1990 est.).

Kandinsky (*Russian* kan'dinskij) *n* **Vasili** (va'silij). 1866–1944, Russian expressionist painter and theorist, regarded as the first to develop an entirely abstract style: a founder of *der Blaue Reiter.*

Kandy ('kændɪ) *n* a city in central Sri Lanka: capital of the kingdom of Kandy from 1480 until 1815, when occupied by the British; sacred Buddhist temple; University of Sri Lanka. Pop.: 104 000 (1990 est.).

kanga *or* **khanga** ('kɑ:ŋgɑ:) *n* a piece of gaily decorated thin cotton cloth used as a garment by women in E Africa. [from Swahili]

kangaroo (,kæŋgə'ru:) *n, pl* **-roos. 1** any large herbivorous marsupial of the genus *Macropus* and related genera, of Australia and New Guinea, having large powerful hind legs, used for leaping, and a long thick tail: family *Macropodidae.* See also **rat kangaroo, tree kangaroo. 2** (*usually pl*) *Stock Exchange.* an Australian share, esp. in mining, land, or a tobacco company. ◆ *vb* **-roos, -rooing, -rooed. 3** *Informal.* (of a car) to move forward or to cause (a car) to move forward with short sudden jerks, as a result of improper use of the clutch. [C18: probably from a native Australian language] ► **,kanga'roo-,like** *adj*

kangaroo closure *n Parliamentary procedure.* a form of closure in which the chairman or speaker selects certain amendments for discussion and excludes others. Compare **guillotine** (sense 4).

kangaroo court *n* an irregular court, esp. one set up by prisoners in a jail or by strikers to judge strikebreakers.

kangaroo dog *n* an Australian breed of large rough-haired dog that resembles a greyhound and is bred to hunt kangaroos.

kangaroo grass *n* a tall widespread Australian grass, *Themeda australis,* which is highly palatable to cattle and is used for fodder.

Kangaroo Island *n* an island in the Indian Ocean, off South Australia. Area: 4350 sq. km (1680 sq. miles).

kangaroo paw *n* any plant of the Australian genus *Anigozanthos,* having green-and-red hairy flowers: family *Haemodoraceae.*

kangaroo rat *n* **1** any small leaping rodent of the genus *Dipodomys,* related to the squirrels and inhabiting desert regions of North America, having a stocky body and very long hind legs and tails: family *Heteromyidae.* **2** Also called: **kangaroo mouse.** any of several leaping murine rodents of the Australian genus *Notomys.*

kangaroo vine *n* See **cissus.**

Kangchenjunga, Kanchenjunga (,kæntʃən'dʒʌŋgə), *or* **Kinchinjunga** *n* a mountain on the border between Nepal and Sikkim, in the Himalayas: the third highest mountain in the world. Height: 8598 m (28 208 ft.).

Kang-de ('kæŋ'deɪ) *or* **Kang-te** ('kæŋ'teɪ) *n* title as emperor of Manchukuo of (Henry) **Pu-yi.**

Kangha ('kʌŋhə) *n* the comb traditionally worn by Sikhs as a symbol of their religious and cultural loyalty: originally worn to keep the hair clean. See also **five Ks.** [Punjabi *kanghā*]

KaNgwane (,kɑ:ᵊŋ'gwɑ:neɪ) *n* (formerly) a Bantu homeland in South Africa; replaced in 1994. Capital: Schoemansdal. Former name: **Swazi Territory.**

kanji ('kændʒɪ, 'kɑ:n-) *n, pl* **-ji** *or* **-jis. 1** a Japanese writing system using characters mainly derived from Chinese ideograms. **2** a character in this system. [Japanese, from Chinese *han* Chinese + *zi* character]

Kannada ('kɑ:nədə, 'kæn-) *n* a language of S India belonging to the Dravidian family of languages: the state language of Karnataka, also spoken in Madras and Maharashtra. Also called: **Kanarese.**

Kannon (kɑnon) *n* the Japanese name for **Kuan Yin.**

Kano ('kɑ:nəʊ, 'keɪnəʊ) *n* **1** a state of N Nigeria: consists of wooded savanna in the south and scrub vegetation in the north. Capital: Kano. Pop.: 6 297 165 (1995 est.). Area: 20 131 sq. km (7773 sq. miles). **2** a city in N Nigeria, capital of Kano state: transport and market centre. Pop.: 674 100 (1996 est.).

Kanpur (kɑ:n'pʊə) *n* an industrial city in NE India, in S Uttar Pradesh on the River Ganges: scene of the massacre by Nana Sahib of British soldiers and European families and his later defeat by British forces in 1857. Pop.: 1 874 409 (1991). Former name: **Cawnpore.**

Kans. *abbrev. for* Kansas.

Kansas ('kænzəs) *n* a state of the central U.S.: consists of undulating prairie, drained chiefly by the Arkansas, Kansas, and Missouri Rivers; mainly agricultural. Capital: Topeka. Pop.: 2 594 840 (1997 est.). Area: 213 096 sq. km (82 277 sq. miles). Abbrevs.: **Kan., Kans.,** or (with zip code) **KS** ► **'Kansan** *adj, n*

Kansas City *n* **1** a city in W Missouri, at the confluence of the Missouri and Kansas Rivers: important centre of livestock and meat-packing industry. Pop.: 441 259 (1996 est.). **2** a city in NE Kansas, adjacent to Kansas City, Missouri. Pop.: 142 654 (1996 est.).

Kansu ('kæn'su:) *n* a variant transliteration of the Chinese name for **Gansu.**

Kant (kænt; *German* kant) *n* **Immanuel** (ɪ'ma:nue:l). 1724–1804, German idealist philosopher. He sought to determine the limits of man's knowledge in *Critique of Pure Reason* (1781) and propounded his system of ethics as guided by the categorical imperative in *Critique of Practical Reason* (1788).

kantar (kæn'tɑ:) *n* a unit of weight used in E Mediterranean countries, equivalent to 100 pounds or 45 kilograms but varying from place to place. [C16: from Arabic *qinṭār,* from Late Greek *kentēnarion* weight of a hundred pounds, from Late Latin *centēnārium,* from *centum* hundred]

Kantian ('kæntɪən) *adj* (of a philosophical theory) derived from or analogous to a position of Kant, esp. his doctrines that there are synthetic a priori propositions which order our experience but are not derived from it, that metaphysical conclusions can be inferred from the nature of possible experience, that duty is to be done for its own sake and not as a means to any other end, and that there is a world of things-in-themselves to be distinguished from mere phenomena. See also **transcendental argument, transcendental idealism, categorical imperative, noumenon.** ► **'Kantian,ism** *or* **'Kantism** *n*

KANU ('kɑ:nu:) *n acronym for* Kenya African National Union.

kanzu ('kænzu) *n* a long garment, usually white, with long sleeves, worn by E African men. [C20: from Swahili]

Kaohsiung, Kao-hsiung ('kaʊ'ʃjuŋ) *or* **Gaoxiong** *n* a port in SW Taiwan, on the South China Sea: the chief port of the island. Pop.: 1 426 518 (1996 est.). Japanese name: **Takao.**

Kaolack ('kɑ:əʊ,læk, 'kaʊlæk) *n* a port in SW Senegal, on the Saloum River. Pop.: 181 000 (1995 est.).

kaoliang (,keɪəʊlɪ'æŋ) *n* any of various E Asian varieties of the sorghum *Sorghum vulgare.* [from Chinese *kao* tall + *liang* grain]

kaolin *or* **kaoline** ('keɪəlɪn) *n* a fine white clay used for the manufacture of hard-paste porcelain and bone china and in medicine as a poultice and gastrointestinal absorbent. Also called: **china clay, china stone.** [C18: from French, from Chinese *Kaoling* Chinese mountain where supplies for Europe were first obtained, from *kao* high + *ling* hill] ► **,kao'linic** *adj* ► **,kaolin'ize** *vb*

kaolinite ('keɪəlɪ,naɪt) *n* a white or grey clay mineral consisting of hydrated aluminium silicate in triclinic crystalline form, the main constituent of kaolin. Formula: $Al_2Si_2O_5(OH)_4$.

kaon ('keɪɒn) *n* a meson that has a positive or negative charge and a rest mass of about 996 electron masses, or no charge and a rest mass of 964 electron masses. Also called: **K-meson.** [C20: *ka* representing the letter *k* + (MES)ON]

kapellmeister (kæ'pel,maɪstə) *n, pl* **-ter.** a variant spelling of **capellmeister.**

Kapfenberg (*German* 'kapfənbɛrk) *n* an industrial town in E Austria, in Styria. Pop.: 23 490 (1991).

kaph (kɔ:f, kɑ:f; *Hebrew* kaf) *n* the 11th letter of the Hebrew alphabet (כ or, at the end of a word, ך) transliterated as *k* or, when final, *kh.* [Hebrew, literally: palm of the hand]

Kapil Dev ('kæpɪl 'dev) *n* (**Ramlal**) **Nikhanj** (nɪ'kændʒ). born 1959, Indian cricketer: captain of India (1983–84).

Kapitza (kə'pitsa) *n* **Piotr Leonidovich** ('pjɔtᵊr liə'nidovitʃ). 1894–1984, Russian physicist. He worked in England and the USSR, doing research in several areas, particularly cryogenics; Nobel prize for physics in 1978.

kapok ('keɪpɒk) *n* a silky fibre obtained from the hairs covering the seeds of a tropical bombacaceous tree, *Ceiba pentandra* (**kapok tree** or **silk-cotton tree**): used for stuffing pillows, etc., and for sound insulation. Also called: **silk cotton.** [C18: from Malay]

Kaposi's sarcoma (kæ'pəʊsɪz) *n* a form of skin cancer found in Africans and more recently in victims of AIDS. [C20: named after Moritz Kohn *Kaposi* (1837–1902), Austrian dermatologist who first described the sores that characterize the disease]

kappa ('kæpə) *n* the tenth letter in the Greek alphabet (Κ, κ), a consonant, transliterated as *c* or *k.* [Greek, of Semitic origin]

kaput (kæ'pʊt) *adj* (*postpositive*) *Informal.* ruined, broken, or not functioning. [C20: from German *kaputt* done for, from French *être capot* to have made no tricks (literally: to be hoodwinked), from *capot* hooded cloak]

Kara ('kʌrə) *n* the steel bangle traditionally worn by Sikhs as a symbol of their religious and cultural loyalty, symbolizing unity with God: originally worn as a wristguard by swordsmen. See also **five Ks.** [Punjabi *karā*]

karabiner (,kærə'bi:nə) *n Mountaineering.* a metal clip with a spring for attaching to a piton, belay, etc. Also called: **snaplink, krab.** [shortened from German *Karabinerhaken,* literally: carbine hook, that is, one used to attach carbines to a belt]

Karachai-Cherkess Republic (kərʌ'tʃaɪtʃeə'kɛs) *or* **Karachayevo-Cherkess Republic** (kərʌ'tʃaɪevəʊtʃeə'kɛs) *n* a constituent republic of W Russia, on the N side of the Caucasus Mountains. Capital: Cherkessk. Pop.: 435 000

(1995 est.). Area: 14 100 sq. km (5440 sq. miles). Also called: **Karachai-Cherkessia** (kærəˌtʃaɪtʃɛə'kɛsɪə).

Karachi (kə'rɑːtʃɪ) *n* a port in S Pakistan, on the Arabian Sea: capital of Pakistan (1947–60); university (1950); chief port: commercial and industrial centre. Pop.: 9 863 000 (1995 est.).

Karafuto (ˌkɑːrɑː'fuːtɔ) *n* transliteration of the Japanese name for **Sakhalin**.

Karaganda (*Russian* kərəgan'da) *n* a city in E central Kazakhstan, founded in 1857: a major coal-mining and industrial centre. Pop.: 573 700 (1995 est.). Also called: **Qaraghandy**.

Karaite ('kɛərəˌaɪt) *n* **1** a member of a Jewish sect originating in the 8th century A.D., which rejected the Talmud, favoured strict adherence to and a literal interpretation of the Bible, and attempted to deduce a code of life from it. ♦ *adj* **2** of, relating to, or designating the Karaite sect. [C18: from Hebrew *qārāīm* members of the sect, scripturalists, from *qārā* to read]

Karajan (*German* 'ka:rajan) *n* **Herbert von** ('hɛrbɛrt fɔn). 1908–89, Austrian conductor.

Kara-Kalpak (kə'rɑːkəl'pɑːk) *n* **1** (*pl* **-paks** *or* **-pak**) a member of a Mongoloid people of central Asia. **2** the language of this people, belonging to the Turkic branch of the Altaic family.

Kara-Kalpak Autonomous Republic (kə'rɑːkəl'pɑːk) *n* an administrative division in NW Uzbekistan, on the Aral Sea: came under Russian rule by stages from 1873 until Uzbekistan became independent in 1991. Capital: Nukus. Pop.: 1 343 000 (1993 est.). Area: 165 600 sq. km (63 900 sq. miles). Also called: **Kara-Kalpakia** (kə'rɑːkəl'pɑːkɪə), **Kara-Kalpakstan** (kə'rɑːkəlˌpɑːkˌstæn, -'stɑːn).

Karakoram *or* **Karakorum** (ˌkærə'kɔːrəm) *n* a mountain system in N Kashmir, extending for about 480 km (300 miles) from northwest to southeast: contains the second highest peak in the world (K2); crossed by several high passes, notably the **Karakoram Pass,** 5575 m (18 290 ft.).

Karakorum (ˌkærə'kɔːrəm) *n* a ruined city in Mongolia: founded in 1220 by Ghenghis Khan; destroyed by Kublai Khan when his brother rebelled against him, after Kublai Khan had moved his capital to Peking (now Beijing).

karakul *or* **caracul** ('kærəkᵊl) *n* **1** a breed of sheep of central Asia having coarse black, grey, or brown hair: the lambs have soft curled usually black hair. **2** the fur prepared from these lambs. ♦ See also **Persian lamb.** [C19: from Russian, from the name of a region in Bukhara where the sheep originated]

Kara Kum (*Russian* kəra 'kum) *n* a desert in Turkmenistan, covering most of the country: extensive areas now irrigated. Area: about 300 000 sq. km (120 000 sq. miles).

Karamanlis (*Greek* karaman'lis) *n* **Konstantinos** (kɔnstan'tinɔs). 1907–98, Greek statesman; prime minister of Greece (1955–58; 1958–61; 1961–63; 1974–80): president of Greece (1980–85; 1990–95).

karaoke (ˌkɑːrə'əʊkɪ) *n* **a** an entertainment of Japanese origin in which people take it in turns to sing well-known songs over a prerecorded backing tape. **b** (*as modifier*): *a karaoke bar.* [from Japanese, from *kara* empty + *ōkesutora* orchestra]

Kara Sea ('kɑːrə) *n* a shallow arm of the Arctic Ocean off the N coast of Russia: ice-free for about three months of the year.

karat ('kærət) *n* the usual U.S. and Canadian spelling of **carat** (sense 2).

karate (kə'rɑːtɪ) *n* **a** a traditional Japanese system of unarmed combat, employing smashes, chops, kicks, etc., made with the hands, feet, elbows, or legs. **b** (*as modifier*): *karate chop.* [Japanese, literally: empty hand, from *kara* empty + *te* hand]

karateka (kə'rɑːtɪˌkæ) *n* a competitor or expert in karate. [Japanese; see KARATE]

Karbala ('kɑːbələ) *or* **Kerbela** *n* a town in central Iraq: the chief holy city of Iraq and centre of Shiah Muslim pilgrimage; burial place of Mohammed's grandson Husain. Pop.: 296 705 (1987).

Karelia (kə'riːlɪə; *Russian* ka'reljə) *n* **1** a region of NE Europe, formerly in Finland but annexed in several stages by the former Soviet Union: corresponds roughly to the Karelian Republic in Russia. **2** another name for the **Karelian Republic.**

Karelian (kə'riːlɪən) *adj* **1** of or relating to Karelia, its people, or their language. ♦ *n* **2** a native or inhabitant of Karelia. **3** the dialect of Finnish spoken in Karelia.

Karelian Republic *n* a constituent republic of NW Russia between the White Sea and Lakes Onega and Ladoga. Capital: Petrozavodsk. Pop.: 789 000 (1995 est.). Area: 172 400 sq. km (66 560 sq. miles). Also called: **Karelia.**

Karelian Isthmus *n* a strip of land, now in Russia, between the Gulf of Finland and Lake Ladoga: annexed by the former Soviet Union after the Russo-Finnish War (1939–40).

Karen (kə'rɛn) *n* **1** (*pl* **-rens** *or* **-ren**) a member of a Thai people of Myanmar. **2** the language of this people, probably related to Thai and belonging to the Sino-Tibetan family.

Kariba (kə'riːbə) *n* **Lake.** a lake on the Zambia-Zimbabwe border, created by the building of the **Kariba Dam** across the Zambezi for hydroelectric power. Length: 282 km (175 miles).

Karitane (ˌkærɪ'tɑːnɪ) *n* short for **Karitane nurse.**

Karitane hospital *n N.Z.* a hospital for young babies and their mothers. [from *Karitane,* a town on South Island, New Zealand, headquarters of the PLUNKET SOCIETY]

Karitane nurse *n N.Z.* a nurse trained in the care of young babies and their mothers according to the principles of the Plunket Society. Often shortened to **Karitane.**

Karl-Marx-Stadt (*German* karl'marksʃtat) *n* the former name (1953–90) of **Chemnitz.**

Karloff ('kɑːlɒf) *n* **Boris,** real name *William Pratt.* 1887–1969, English film actor, famous for his roles in horror films, esp. *Frankenstein* (1931).

Karlovy Vary (*Czech* 'karlɔvi 'vari) *n* a city in the W Czech Republic, at the confluence of the Tepla and Ohře Rivers: warm mineral springs. Pop.: 56 290 (1991). German name: **Karlsbad** *or* **Carlsbad** ('karlsbaːt).

Karlskrona ('kɑːlsˌkrəʊnə) *n* a port in S Sweden: Sweden's main naval base since 1680. Pop.: 60 642 (1994).

Karlsruhe (*German* 'karlsruːə) *n* a city in SW Germany, in Baden-Württemberg: capital of the former Baden state. Pop.: 275 690 (1996 est.).

karma ('kɑːmə) *n* **1** *Hinduism, Buddhism.* the principle of retributive justice determining a person's state of life and the state of his reincarnations as the effect of his past deeds. **2** *Theosophy.* the doctrine of inevitable consequence. **3** destiny or fate. [C19: from Sanskrit: action, effect, from *karoti* he does] ▸ **'karmic** *adj*

Kármán vortex street ('kɑːmən) *n* a regular stream of vortices shed from a body placed in a fluid stream: investigated by Kármán who advanced a formula for the frequency of the shed vortices in terms of the stream velocity and the dimensions of the body. See also **vortex street.** [named after Theodore Von *Kármán* (1881–1963), Hungarian-born engineer]

Karnak ('kɑːnæk) *n* a village in E Egypt, on the Nile: site of the N part of the ruins of ancient Thebes.

Karnataka (kə'nɑːtəkə) *n* a state of S India, on the Arabian Sea: consists of a narrow coastal plain rising to the South Deccan plateau; mainly agricultural. Capital: Bangalore. Pop.: 44 977 201 (1991). Area: 191 791 sq. km (74 051 sq. miles). Former name (1956–73): **Mysore.**

Karnatak music (kə'nɑːtək) *n* the classical music of South India.

Kärnten ('kɛrntən) *n* the German name for **Carinthia.**

Karoo *or* **Karroo** (kə'ruː) *n, pl* **-roos.** (*often not cap.*) **1** any of several high arid plateaus in South Africa, esp. the **Central Karoo** and the **Little Karoo** . The highveld, north of the Central Karoo, is sometimes called the **Northern Karoo. 2** a period or rock system in Southern Africa equivalent to the period or system extending from the Upper Carboniferous to the Lower Jurassic: divided into **Lower** and **Upper Karoo.**♦ *adj* **3** of, denoting, or formed in the Karoo period. [C18: from Afrikaans *karo,* probably from Khoikhoi *garo* desert]

kaross (kə'rɒs) *n* a garment of skins worn by indigenous peoples in southern Africa. [C18: from Afrikaans *karos,* perhaps from Dutch *kuras,* from French *cuirasse* CUIRASS]

Karpov (*Russian* 'karpəf) *n* **Anatoly** (ana'tɔlij). born 1951, Russian chess player: world champion (1975–85; 1993).

karri ('kɑːrɪ) *n, pl* **-ris. 1** an Australian eucalyptus tree, *Eucalyptus diversifolia.* **2** the durable wood of this tree, used esp. for construction. [from a native Australian language]

karst (kɑːst) *n* (*modifier*) denoting the characteristic scenery of a limestone region, including underground streams, gorges, etc. [C19: German, from *Karst,* limestone plateau near Trieste] ▸ **'karstic** *adj*

kart (kɑːt) *n* a light low-framed vehicle with small wheels and engine used for recreational racing. Also called: **go-cart, go-kart.**

karyo- *or* **caryo-** *combining form.* indicating the nucleus of a cell: *karyogamy.* [from New Latin, from Greek *karuon* kernel, nut]

karyogamy (ˌkærɪ'ɒgəmɪ) *n Biology.* the fusion of two gametic nuclei during fertilization. ▸ **karyogamic** (ˌkærɪə'gæmɪk) *adj*

karyogram ('kærɪəˌgræm) *n* a diagram or photograph of the chromosomes of a cell, arranged in homologous pairs and in a numbered sequence. Also called: **idiogram.**

karyokinesis (ˌkærɪəʊkɪ'niːsɪs, -kaɪ-) *n* another name for **mitosis.** [C19: from KARYO- + Greek *kinēsis* movement] ▸ **karyokinetic** (ˌkærɪəʊkɪ'nɛtɪk, -kaɪ-) *adj*

karyology (ˌkærɪ'ɒlədʒɪ) *n* the study of cell nuclei, esp. with reference to the structure of the chromosomes. ▸ **ˌkary'ologist** *n*

karyolymph ('kærɪəʊˌlɪmf) *n* the liquid portion of the nucleus of a cell.

karyolysis (ˌkærɪ'ɒlɪsɪs) *n Cytology.* the disintegration of a cell nucleus, which occurs on death of the cell. [C20: from Greek, from *karyon* a nut + -LYSIS] ▸ **karyolytic** (ˌkærɪə'lɪtɪk) *adj*

karyoplasm ('kærɪəʊˌplæzəm) *n* another name for **nucleoplasm.** ▸ **ˌkaryo'plasmic** *adj*

karyosome ('kærɪəʊˌsəʊm) *n* **1** any of the dense aggregates of chromatin in the nucleus of a cell: thought to be thickened segments of chromosomes. **2** the nucleus of a cell.

karyotin (ˌkærɪ'əʊtɪn) *n* a less common word for **chromatin.** [from KARYO- + (CHROMA)TIN]

karyotype ('kærɪəˌtaɪp) *n* **1** the appearance of the chromosomes in a somatic cell of an individual or species, with reference to their number, size, shape, etc. ♦ *vb* (*tr*) **2** to determine the karyotype of (a cell). ▸ **karyotypic** (ˌkærɪə'tɪpɪk) *or* **ˌkaryo'typical** *adj*

Kasai (kɑː'saɪ) *n* a river in southwestern Africa, rising in central Angola and flowing east then north as part of the border between Angola and the Democratic Republic of the Congo (formerly Zaïre), continuing northwest through the Democratic Republic of the Congo to the River Congo. Length: 2154 km (1338 miles).

kasbah *or* **casbah** ('kæzbɑː) *n* (*sometimes cap.*) **1** the citadel of any of various North African cities. **2** the quarter in which a kasbah is located. Compare **medina.** [from Arabic *kaṣbạ* citadel]

kasha ('kɑːʃə) *n* a dish originating in Eastern Europe, consisting of boiled or baked buckwheat. [from Russian]

kasher *Hebrew.* ('kɑːʃə) *vb* (*tr*) *Judaism.* to make fit for use; render kosher: for instance, to remove excess blood from (meat) by the prescribed process of washing and salting, or to remove all trace of previous nonkosher substances from (a utensil) by heating, immersion, etc. See also **kosher.** [see KOSHER]

Kashi ('kɑː'ʃiː) *or* **Kashgar** ('kɑːʃ'gɑː) *n* an oasis city in W China, in W Xinjiang Uygur AR. Pop.: 174 570 (1990 est.).

kashmir (ˈkæʃmɪə) *n* a variant spelling of **cashmere.**

Kashmir (kæʃˈmɪə) *n* a region of SW central Asia: from the 16th century ruled by the Moguls, Afghanis, Sikhs, and British successively; since 1947 disputed between India, Pakistan, and China; 84 000 sq. km (33 000 sq. miles) in the northwest are held by Pakistan and known as Azad Kashmir (Free Kashmir); 42 735 sq. km (16 496 sq. miles) in the east are held by China; the remainder was in 1956 officially incorporated into India as the state of Jammu and Kashmir; traversed by the Himalaya and Karakoram mountain ranges and the Rivers Jhelum and Indus; a fruit-growing and cattle-grazing region, with a woollen industry. Capitals: (Azad Kashmir) Muzaffarabad; (Jammu and Kashmir) Srinagar (summer), Jammu (winter).

Kashmir goat *n* a Himalayan breed of goat having an undercoat of silky wool from which cashmere wool is obtained.

Kashmiri (kæʃˈmɪərɪ) *adj* **1** of or relating to Kashmir, its people, or their language. ◆ *n* **2** (*pl* **-miris** *or* **-miri**) a member of the people of Kashmir. **3** the state language of Kashmir, belonging to the Dardic group of the Indo-European family of languages. ► **Kashˈmirian** *adj, n*

kashruth *or* ***kashrut*** *Hebrew.* (kaʃˈruːt) *n* **1** the condition of being fit for ritual use in general. **2** the system of dietary laws which require ritual slaughter, the removal of excess blood from meat, and the complete separation of milk and meat, and prohibit such foods as pork and shellfish. ◆ See also **kosher** (sense 1). [literally: appropriateness, fitness]

Kasparov (ˈkæspərɒf) *n* **Garry** (ˈgærɪ), real name *Gary Weinstein.* born 1963, Armenian-Jewish chess player, born in Azerbaijan: world champion (1985–93).

Kassa (ˈkɔʃʃɔ) *n* the Hungarian name for **Košice.**

Kassala (kəˈsɑːlə) *n* a city in the E Sudan: founded as a fort by the Egyptians in 1834. Pop.: 234 270 (1993).

Kassel *or* **Cassel** (*German* ˈkasəl) *n* a city in central Germany, in Hesse; capital of Westphalia (1807–13) and of the Prussian province of Hesse-Nassau (1866–1945). Pop.: 201 573 (1996 est.).

Kastrop-Rauxel (*German* ˈkastrɔpˈrauksəl) *n* a variant spelling of **Castrop-Rauxel.**

kat (kæt, kɑːt) *n* a variant spelling of **khat.**

kata (ˈkætə) *n* an exercise consisting of a sequence of the specific movements of a martial art, used in training and designed to show skill in technique. [C20: Japanese, literally: shape, pattern]

kata- *prefix* a variant of **cata-.**

katabasis (kəˈtæbəsɪs) *n, pl* **-ses** (-ˌsiːz). **1** the retreat of the Greek mercenaries of Cyrus the Younger, after his death at Cunaxa, from the Euphrates to the Black Sea in 401–400 B.C. under the leadership of Xenophon: recounted in his *Anabasis.* Compare **anabasis. 2** *Literary.* a retreat. [C19: from Greek: a going down, from *katabainein* to go down]

katabatic (ˌkætəˈbætɪk) *adj* (of winds) blowing downhill through having become denser with cooling, esp. at night when heat is lost from the earth's surface. Compare **anabatic.**

katabolism (kəˈtæbəˌlɪzəm) *n* a variant spelling of **catabolism.** ► **katabolic** (ˌkætəˈbɒlɪk) *adj* ► ˌ**kataˈbolically** *adv*

katakana (ˌkɑːtəˈkɑːnə) *n* one of the two systems of syllabic writing employed for the representation of Japanese, based on Chinese ideograms. It is used mainly for foreign or foreign-derived words. [Japanese, from *kata* side + KANA]

Katanga (kəˈtæŋgə) *n* the former name (until 1972) of **Shaba.**

Katar (kæˈtɑː) *n* a variant spelling of **Qatar.**

Kathak (ˈkʌtək) *n* a form of N Indian classical dancing that tells a story. [Bengali: narrator, from Sanskrit *kathayati* he tells]

Kathakali (ˌkɑːθəˈkɑːlɪ) *n pl* **-lis.** a form of dance drama of S India using mime and based on Hindu literature. [from Malayalam, from *katha* story + *kali* play]

Katharevusa *or* **Katharevousa** (ˌkɑːθəˈrɛvəˌsɑː) *n* a literary style of Modern Greek, derived from the Attic dialect of Ancient Greek and including many archaic features. Compare **Demotic.**

katharometer (ˌkæθəˈrɒmɪtə) *n Chem.* an instrument used for the analysis of gases by measurement of thermal conductivity.

Kathiawar (ˌkætɪəˈwɑː) *n* a large peninsula of W India, in Gujarat between the Gulf of Kutch and the Gulf of Cambay. Area: about 60 690 sq. km (23 430 sq. miles).

katipo (ˈkætɪˌpəʊ, ˈkɑːd-) *n, pl* **-pos.** a small venomous spider, *Latrodectus katipo,* of New Zealand, commonly black with a red or orange stripe on the abdomen. [Maori]

Katmai (ˈkætmaɪ) *n* **Mount.** a volcano in SW Alaska, in the Aleutian Range: erupted in 1912 forming the Valley of Ten Thousand Smokes, a region with numerous fumaroles; established as **Katmai National Monument,** 10 917 sq. km (4215 sq. miles), in 1918. Height: 2100 m (7000 ft.). Depth of crater: 1130 m (3700 ft.). Width of crater: about 4 km (2.5 miles).

Katmandu *or* **Kathmandu** (ˌkætmænˈduː) *n* the capital of Nepal, in the east at the confluence of the Baghmati and Vishnumati Rivers. Pop.: 535 000 (1993 est.).

Katowice (*Polish* katɔˈvitsɛ) *n* an industrial city in S Poland. Pop.: 354 200 (1996 est.). Former name (1953–56): **Stalinogrod.**

Katrine (ˈkætrɪn) *n* **Loch.** a lake in central Scotland, east of Loch Lomond: noted for its associations with Sir Walter Scott's *Lady of the Lake.* Length: about 13 km (8 miles).

Katsina (kætˈsiːnə) *n* a city in N Nigeria, in Kaduna state: a major intellectual and cultural centre of the Hausa people (16th–18th centuries). Pop.: 206 500 (1996 est.).

Kattegat *or* **Cattegat** (ˈkætɪˌgæt) *n* a strait between Denmark and Sweden: linked by the Sound, the Great Belt, and the Little Belt with the Baltic Sea and by the Skagerrak with the North Sea.

katydid (ˈkeɪtɪˌdɪd) *n* any typically green long-horned grasshopper of the genus *Microcentrum* and related genera, living among the foliage of trees in North America. [C18: of imitative origin]

Katz (ˈkæts) *n* Sir **Bernard.** born 1911, British neurophysiologist, born in Germany. Shared the Nobel prize for physiology or medicine (1970) with Julius Axelrod and Ulf von Euler.

katzenjammer (ˈkætsənˌdʒæmə) *n Chiefly U.S.* **1** a confused uproar. **2** a hangover. [German, literally: hangover, from *Katzen* cats + *jammer* misery, wailing]

Kauai (kɑːˈwɑːiː) *n* a volcanic island in NW Hawaii, northwest of Oahu. Chief town: Lihue. Pop.: 50 947 (1990). Area: 1433 sq. km (553 sq. miles).

Kauffmann (ˈkaufmən) *n* **Angelica** (andʒeˈlikə). 1741–1807, Swiss painter, who worked chiefly in England.

Kaufman (ˈkaufmən) *n* **George S(imon).** 1889–1961, U.S. dramatist who, with Moss Hart, collaborated on many Broadway comedy hits.

kaumatua (kaʊˈmɑːtuːə) *n N.Z.* a senior member of a tribe; elder. [Maori]

Kaunas (ˈkaʊnəs) *n* a city in central Lithuania at the confluence of the Neman and Viliya Rivers: ceded by Poland to Russia in 1795; became the provisional capital of Lithuania (1920–40); incorporated into the Soviet Union 1944–91; university (1922). Pop.: 410 800 (1996 est.). Russian name: **Kovno.**

Kaunda (kɑːˈʊndə) *n* **Kenneth (David).** born 1924, Zambian statesman. He became Zambia's first president (1964–91); in 1997 he was accused of treason and arrested.

Kaur (ˈkaʊr) *n* a title assumed by a Sikh woman when she becomes a full member of the community. [from Punjabi, literally: princess]

kauri (ˈkaʊrɪ) *n, pl* **-ris. 1** a New Zealand coniferous tree, *Agathis australis,* with oval leaves and round cones: family *Araucariaceae.* **2** the wood or resin of this tree. [C19: Maori]

kauri gum *n* a hard resin from the kauri tree, found usually as a fossil in the soil where an extinct tree once grew: used chiefly in making varnishes.

kava (ˈkɑːvə) *n* **1** a Polynesian shrub, *Piper methysticum:* family *Piperaceae.* **2** a drink prepared from the aromatic roots of this shrub. [C18: from Polynesian (Tongan): bitter]

Kavália (kəˈvæljə; *Greek* kaˈvala) *n* a port in E Greece, in Macedonia East and Thrace region on the **Bay of Kavália:** an important Macedonian fortress of the Byzantine empire; ceded to Greece by Turkey after the Balkan War (1912–13). Pop.: 58 576 (1991). Ancient name: **Neapolis.**

Kaveri (ˈkɔːvərɪ) *n* a variant spelling of **Cauvery.**

Kavir Desert (kæˈvɪə) *n* another name for the **Dasht-i-Kavir.**

kawakawa (ˈkɑːwəˌkɑːwə) *n* an aromatic shrub or small tree of New Zealand, *Macropiper excelsum:* held to be sacred by the Maoris. Also called: **peppertree.** [Maori]

Kawasaki (ˌkɑːwəˈsɑːkɪ) *n* an industrial port in central Japan, on SE Honshu, between Tokyo and Yokohama. Pop.: 1 202 811 (1995).

Kawasaki's disease (ˌkæwəˈsækɪ) *n* a disease of children that causes a rash, fever, and swelling of the lymph nodes and often damages the heart muscle. [C20: named after T. *Kawasaki,* Japanese physician who first described it]

Kay (keɪ) *n* **Sir.** (in Arthurian legend) the braggart foster brother and steward of King Arthur.

kayak *or* **kaiak** (ˈkaɪæk) *n* **1** a small light canoe-like boat used by Eskimos, consisting of a light frame covered with watertight animal skins. **2** a fibreglass or canvas-covered canoe of similar design. [C18: from Eskimo (Greenland dialect)]

kayo *or* **KO** (ˈkeɪˈəʊ) *n, pl* **kayos,** *vb,* **kayoes** *or* **kayos, kayoing, kayoed.** *Boxing, slang.* another term for **knockout** or **knock out.** [C20: from the initial letters of *knock out*]

Kayseri (ˌkaɪseˈriː; *Turkish* ˈkaiseri) *n* a city in central Turkey: trading centre since ancient times as the chief city of Cappadocia. Pop.: 463 759 (1995 est.). Ancient name: **Caesarea Mazaca.**

kazachok (ˌkɑːzəˈtʃɒk) *n* a Russian folk dance in which the performer executes high kicks from a squatting position. [Russian]

Kazakh *or* **Kazak** (kəˈzɑːk, kɑː-) *n* **1** (*pl* **-zakhs** *or* **-zaks**) a member of a traditionally Muslim Mongoloid people of Kazakhstan. **2** the language of this people, belonging to the Turkic branch of the Altaic family.

Kazakhstan, *or* **Kazakstan** (ˌkɑːzɑːkˈstæn, -ˈstɑːn). *n* a republic in central Asia: conquered by Mongols in the 13th century; came under Russian control in the 18th and 19th centuries; was a Soviet republic from 1936 until it gained independence in 1991. It has rich mineral deposits and agriculture is important. Official language: Kazakh. Religion: nonreligious, Muslim, and Christian. Official currency: tenge. Capital: Akmola. Pop.: 15 797 000 (1998 est.). Area: 2 715 100 sq. km (1 048 030 sq. miles).

Kazan[1] (kəˈzæn, -ˈzɑːn; *Russian* kaˈzanj) *n* a city in W Russia, capital of the Tatar Autonomous Republic on the River Volga: capital of an independent khanate in the 15th century; university (1804); a major industrial centre. Pop.: 1 085 000 (1995 est.).

Kazan[2] (kəˈzɑːn) *n* **Elia** (ˈiːljə), real name *Elia Kazanjoglous.* born 1909, U.S. stage and film director and writer, born in Turkey. His films include *Gentleman's Agreement* (1947) and *On the Waterfront* (1954) for both of which he won Oscars, and *East of Eden* (1955).

Kazan Retto (kɑːˈzɑːn ˈrɛtəʊ) *n* transliteration of the Japanese name for the **Volcano Islands.**

Kazantzakis (*Greek* kazanˈdzakis) *n* **Nikos** (ˈnikɔs). 1885–1957, Greek novelist, poet, and dramatist, noted esp. for his novels *Zorba the Greek* (1946) and *Christ Recrucified* (1954) and his epic poem *The Odyssey* (1938).

Kazbek (kɑːzˈbɛk) *n* **Mount.** an extinct volcano in N Georgia in the central Caucasus Mountains. Height: 5047 m (16 558 ft.).

Kaz Daği (ˈkaz ˈdɑj) *n* the Turkish name for (Mount) **Ida** (sense 2).

kazoo (kəˈzuː) *n, pl* **-zoos.** a cigar-shaped musical instrument of metal or plastic with a membranous diaphragm of thin paper that vibrates with a nasal sound when the player hums into it. [C20: probably imitative of the sound produced]

kb *abbrev. for* kilobar.

KB (in Britain) *abbrev. for:* **1** King's Bench. **2** Knight Bachelor. **3** *Computing.* kilobyte. **4** *Chess. symbol for* king's bishop.

KBE *abbrev. for* Knight (Commander of the Order) of the British Empire.

KBP *Chess. symbol for* king's bishop's pawn.

kbyte *Computing. abbrev. for* kilobyte.

kc *abbrev. for* kilocycle.

KC (in Britain) *abbrev. for* **1** King's Counsel. **2** Kennel Club.

kcal *abbrev. for* kilocalorie.

KCB *abbrev. for* Knight Commander of the Bath (a Brit. title).

KCMG *abbrev. for* Knight Commander (of the Order) of St Michael and St George (a Brit. title).

Kčs. *abbrev. for* koruna. [Czech *koruna československá*]

KCVO *abbrev. for* Knight Commander of the Royal Victorian Order (a Brit. title).

KD *or* **k.d.** *Commerce. abbrev. for* knocked down: indicating furniture, machinery, etc., in separate parts.

KE *abbrev. for* kinetic energy.

kea ('keɪə) *n* a large New Zealand parrot, *Nestor notabilis,* with brownish-green plumage. [C19: from Maori, imitative of its call]

Kéa ('kɛa) *n* transliteration of the Modern Greek name for **Keos.**

Kean (kiːn) *n* **Edmund.** ?1789–1833, English actor, noted for his Shakespearean roles.

Keating ('kiːtɪŋ) *n* **Paul.** born 1944, Australian Labor politician; prime minister of Australia (1991–96).

Keaton ('kiːtᵊn) *n* **Buster,** real name *Joseph Francis Keaton.* 1895–1966, U.S. film comedian who starred in silent films such as *The Navigator* (1924), *The General* (1926), and *Steamboat Bill Junior* (1927).

Keats (kiːts) *n* **John.** 1795–1821, English poet. His finest poetry is contained in *Lamia and other Poems* (1820), which includes *The Eve of St Agnes, Hyperion,* and the odes *On a Grecian Urn, To a Nightingale, To Autumn,* and *To Psyche.*

kebab (kə'bæb) *n* a dish consisting of small pieces of meat, tomatoes, onions, etc., threaded onto skewers and grilled, generally over charcoal. Also called: **shish kebab, kabob, cabob.** [C17: via Urdu from Arabic *kabāb* roast meat]

Keble ('kiːbᵊl) *n* **John.** 1792–1866, English clergyman. His sermon on national apostasy (1833) is considered to have inspired the Oxford Movement.

Kechua ('kɛtʃwə) *n* a variant of **Quechua.**

keck[1] (kɛk) *vb (intr) Chiefly U.S.* **1** to retch or feel nausea. **2** to feel or express disgust. [C17: of imitative origin]

keck[2] (kɛk) *n* another name for **cow parsnip** and **cow parsley.** [C17: from KEX, which was mistaken as a plural (as if *kecks*)]

kecks *or* keks (kɛks) *pl n N English dialect.* trousers. [C19: from obsolete *kicks* breeches]

Kecskemét (*Hungarian* 'kɛtʃkemeːt) *n* a city in central Hungary: vineyards and fruit farms. Pop.: 105 000 (1997 est.).

ked (kɛd) *n* See **sheep ked.** [C16: of unknown origin]

Kedah ('kɛdə) *n* a state of NW Malaysia: under Thai control until it came under the British in 1909; the chief exports are rice, tin, and rubber. Capital: Alor Star. Pop.: 1 412 000 (1993 est.). Area: 9425 sq. km (3639 sq. miles).

keddah ('kɛdə) *n* a variant spelling of **kheda.**

kedge (kɛdʒ) *Nautical.* ♦ *vb* **1** to draw (a vessel) along by hauling in on the cable of a light anchor that has been dropped at some distance from it, or (of a vessel) to be drawn in this fashion. ♦ *n* **2** a light anchor, used esp. for kedging. [C15: from *caggen* to fasten]

kedgeree (ˌkɛdʒə'riː) *n Chiefly Brit.* a dish consisting of rice, cooked flaked fish, and hard-boiled eggs. [C17: from Hindi *khicarī,* from Sanskrit *khiccā,* of obscure origin]

Kediri (kɪ'dɪərɪ) *n* a city in Indonesia, in E Java: commercial centre. Pop.: 261 300 (1995 est.).

Kedleston Hall ('kɛdᵊlstən) *n* a mansion near Derby in Derbyshire: rebuilt (1759–65) for the Curzon family by Matthew Brettingham, James Paine, and Robert Adam.

Kedron ('kɛdrɒn) *or* **Kidron** *n Bible.* a ravine under the eastern wall of Jerusalem.

keef (kiːf) *n* a variant spelling of **kif.**

Keegan ('kiːgən) *n* **Kevin.** born 1951, English footballer; manager of Newcastle United (1992–97); England coach from 1999.

keek (kiːk) *n, vb* a Scot. word for **peep**[1]. [C18: probably from Middle Dutch *kīken* to look]

keel[1] (kiːl) *n* **1** one of the main longitudinal structural members of a vessel to which the frames are fastened and that may extend into the water to provide lateral stability. **2 on an even keel.** well-balanced; steady. **3** any structure corresponding to or resembling the keel of a ship, such as the central member along the bottom of an aircraft fuselage. **4** *Biology.* a ridgelike part; carina. **5** a poetic word for **ship.** ♦ *vb* **6** to capsize. ♦ See also **keel over.** [C14: from Old Norse *kjölr;* related to Middle Dutch *kiel,* KEEL[2]] ► '**keel-less** *adj*

keel[2] (kiːl) *n Eastern English dialect.* **1** a flat-bottomed vessel, esp. one used for carrying coal. **2** a measure of coal equal to about 21 tons. [C14 *kele,* from Middle Dutch *kiel;* compare Old English *cēol* ship]

keel[3] (kiːl) *n* **1** red ochre stain used for marking sheep, timber, etc. ♦ *vb (tr)* **2** to mark with this stain. [Old English *cēlan,* from *cōl* COOL]

keel[4] (kiːl) *vb* an archaic word for **cool** (esp. in the phrase **keel the pot**). [C15: probably from Scottish Gaelic *cīl*]

keel[5] (kiːl) *n* a fatal disease of young ducks, characterized by intestinal bleeding. [C19: from KEEL[1]; see KEEL OVER]

keelage ('kiːlɪdʒ) *n* a fee charged by certain ports to allow a ship to dock.

keel arch *n* another name for **ogee arch.**

keelboat ('kiːlˌbəʊt) *n* a river boat with a shallow draught and a keel, used for freight and moved by towing, punting, or rowing.

keelhaul ('kiːlˌhɔːl) *vb (tr)* **1** to drag (a person) by a rope from one side of a vessel to the other through the water under the keel. **2** to rebuke harshly. [C17: from Dutch *kielhalen;* see KEEL[1], HAUL]

keelie ('kiːlɪ) *n Scot.* **1** a kestrel. **2** an urban ruffian; lower-class town or city dweller, esp. Glaswegian. [C19: of uncertain origin]

Keeling Islands ('kiːlɪŋ) *pl n* another name for the **Cocos Islands.**

keel over *vb (adv)* **1** to turn upside down; capsize. **2** *(intr) Informal.* to collapse suddenly.

keelson ('kɛlsən, 'kiːl-) *or* **kelson** *n* a longitudinal beam fastened to the keel of a vessel for strength and stiffness. [C17: probably from Low German *kielswin,* keel swine, ultimately of Scandinavian origin]

Keelung ('kiː'lʊŋ) *n* another name for **Chilung.**

keen[1] (kiːn) *adj* **1** eager or enthusiastic. **2** *(postpositive;* foll. by *on)* fond (of); devoted (to): *keen on a girl; keen on golf.* **3** intellectually acute: *a keen wit.* **4** (of sight, smell, hearing, etc.) capable of recognizing fine distinctions. **5** having a sharp cutting edge or point. **6** extremely cold and penetrating: *a keen wind.* **7** intense or strong: *a keen desire.* **8** *Chiefly Brit.* extremely low so as to be competitive: *keen prices.* **9** *Slang, chiefly U.S. and Canadian.* very good. [Old English *cēne;* related to Old High German *kuoni* brave, Old Norse *koenn* wise; see CAN[1], KNOW] ► '**keenly** *adv* ► '**keenness** *n*

keen[2] (kiːn) *vb (intr)* **1** to lament the dead. ♦ *n* **2** a dirge or lament for the dead. [C19: from Irish Gaelic *caoine,* from Old Irish *coīnim* I wail] ► '**keener** *n*

keep (kiːp) *vb* **keeps, keeping, kept** (kɛpt). **1** *(tr)* to have or retain possession of. **2** *(tr)* to have temporary possession or charge of: *keep my watch for me during the game.* **3** *(tr)* to store in a customary place: *I keep my books in the desk.* **4** to remain or cause to remain in a specified state or condition: *keep the dog quiet; keep ready.* **5** to continue or cause to continue: *keep the beat; keep in step.* **6** *(tr)* to have or take charge or care of: *keep the shop for me till I return.* **7** *(tr)* to look after or maintain for use, pleasure, etc.: *to keep chickens; keep two cars.* **8** *(tr)* to provide for the upkeep or livelihood of. **9** *(tr)* to support financially, esp. in return for sexual favours: *he keeps a mistress in the country.* **10** to confine or detain or be confined or detained. **11** to withhold or reserve or admit of withholding or reserving: *your news will keep till later.* **12** *(tr)* to refrain from divulging or violating: *to keep a secret; keep one's word.* **13** to preserve or admit of preservation. **14** *(tr;* sometimes foll. by *up)* to observe with due rites or ceremonies: *to keep Christmas.* **15** *(tr)* to maintain by writing regular records in: *to keep a diary.* **16** (when *intr,* foll. by *in, on, to,* etc.) to stay in, on, or at (a place or position): *please keep your seats; keep to the path.* **17** *(tr)* to associate with (esp. in the phrase **keep bad company**). **18** *(tr)* to maintain in existence: *to keep court in the palace.* **19** *(tr) Chiefly Brit.* to have habitually in stock: *this shop keeps all kinds of wool.* **20 how are you keeping?** how are you? **21 keep tabs on.** *Informal.* to keep a watchful eye on. **22 keep track of.** See **track** (sense 14). **23 keep time.** See **time** (sense 42). **24 keep wicket.** to play as wicketkeeper in the game of cricket. **25 you can keep it.** *Informal.* I have no interest in what you are offering. ♦ *n* **26** living or support: *he must work for his keep.* **27** *Archaic.* charge or care. **28** Also called: **dungeon, donjon.** the main tower within the walls of a medieval castle or fortress. **29 for keeps.** *Informal.* **29a** completely; permanently. **29b** for the winner or possessor to keep permanently. ♦ See also **keep at, keep away, keep back, keep down, keep from, keep in, keep off, keep on, keep out, keep to, keep under, keep up.** [Old English *cēpan* to observe; compare Old Saxon *kapōn* to look, Old Norse *kōpa* to stare]

keep at *vb (prep)* **1** *(intr)* to persevere with or persist in. **2** *(tr)* to constrain (a person) to continue doing (a task).

keep away *vb (adv;* often foll. by *from)* **1** to refrain or prevent from coming (near). **2** to stop using, touching, etc.

keep back *vb (adv;* often foll. by *from)* **1** *(tr)* to refuse to reveal or disclose. **2** to prevent, be prevented, or refrain from advancing, entering, etc.

keep down *vb (adv, mainly tr)* **1** to repress; hold in submission. **2** to restrain or control: *he had difficulty keeping his anger down.* **3** to cause not to increase or rise: *prices were kept down for six months.* **4** *(intr)* not to show oneself to one's opponents; lie low. **5** to cause (food) to stay in the stomach; not vomit.

keeper ('kiːpə) *n* **1** a person in charge of animals, esp. in a zoo. **2** a person in charge of a museum, collection, or section of a museum. **3** a person in charge of other people, such as a warder in a jail. **4** See **goalkeeper, wicketkeeper, gamekeeper. 5** a person who keeps something. **6** a device, such as a clip, for keeping something in place. **7** a soft iron or steel bar placed across the poles of a permanent magnet to close the magnetic circuit when it is not in use. ► '**keeperless** *adj* ► '**keeperˌship** *n*

keeper ring *n* another name for **guard ring.**

keep fit *n* **a** exercises designed to promote physical fitness if performed regularly. **b** *(as modifier): keep-fit classes.*

keep from *vb (prep)* **1** (foll. by a gerund) to prevent or restrain (oneself or another); refrain or cause to refrain. **2** *(tr)* to protect or preserve from.

keep in *vb (mainly adv)* **1** *(intr; also prep)* to stay indoors. **2** *(tr)* to restrain (an emotion); repress. **3** *(tr)* to detain (a schoolchild) after hours as a punishment. **4** (of a fire) to stay alight or to cause (a fire) to stay alight. **5** *(tr, prep)* to allow a constant supply of: *her prize money kept her in new clothes for a year.* **6 keep in with.** to maintain good relations with.

keeping ('kiːpɪŋ) *n* **1** conformity or harmony (esp. in the phrases **in** *or* **out of keeping**). **2** charge or care: *valuables in the keeping of a bank.*

keepnet ('kiːpˌnɛt) *n* a cylindrical net strung on wire hoops and sealed at one end, suspended in water by anglers to keep alive the fish they have caught.

keep off *vb* **1** to stay or cause to stay at a distance (from). **2** *(prep)* not to eat or drink or prevent from eating or drinking. **3** *(prep)* to avoid or cause to avoid (a topic). **4** *(intr, adv)* not to start: *the rain kept off all day.*

keep on *vb (adv)* **1** to continue or persist in (doing something): *keep on running.* **2** *(tr)* to continue to wear. **3** *(tr)* to continue to employ: *the firm kept on only ten men.* **4** *(intr; foll. by about)* to persist in talking (about). **5** *(intr; foll. by at)* to nag (a person).

keep out *vb (adv)* **1** to remain or cause to remain outside. **2 keep out of. 2a** to remain or cause to remain unexposed to: *keep out of the sun.* **2b** to avoid or cause to avoid: *the boss is in an angry mood, so keep out of his way.*

keepsake ('kiːpˌseɪk) *n* a gift that evokes memories of a person or event with which it is associated.

keep to *vb (prep)* **1** to adhere to or stand by or cause to adhere to or stand by: *to keep to a promise.* **2** to confine or be confined to. **3 keep to oneself. 3a** *(intr)* to avoid the society of others. **3b** *(tr)* to refrain from sharing or disclosing. **4 keep oneself to oneself.** to avoid the society of others.

keep under *vb* **1** to remain or cause to remain below (a surface). **2** *(tr, adv)* to cause to remain unconscious. **3** *(tr, adv)* to hold in submission.

keep up *vb (adv)* **1** *(tr)* to maintain (prices, one's morale) at the present level. **2** *(intr)* to maintain a pace or rate set by another. **3** *(intr; often foll. by with)* to remain informed: *to keep up with technological developments.* **4** *(tr)* to maintain in good condition. **5** *(tr)* to hinder (a person) from going to bed at night: *the excitement kept the children up well past their bedtime.* **6 keep it up.** to continue a good performance. **7 keep one's chin up.** to keep cheerful under difficult circumstances. **8 keep one's end up.** to maintain one's stance or position against opposition or misfortune. **9 keep up with.** to remain in contact with, esp. by letter. **10 keep up with (the Joneses).** *Informal.* to compete with (one's neighbours) in material possessions, etc.

keeshond ('keɪsˌhɒnd, 'kiːs-) *n, pl* **-honds** *or* **-honden** (-ˌhɒndᵊn). a breed of dog of the spitz type with a shaggy greyish coat and tightly curled tail, originating in Holland. [C20: from Dutch, probably from *Kees* nickname for *Cornelis* Cornelius, from Latin + *hond* HOUND[1]]

Keewatin (kiː'weɪtɪn) *n* a former administrative district of the Northwest Territories of Canada stretching from the district of Mackenzie to Hudson Bay; became part of Nunavut in 1999: mostly tundra. Area: 590 930 sq. km (228 160 sq. miles).

kef (kɛf) *n* a variant of **kif.**

keffiyeh (kɛ'fiːjə), **kaffiyeh,** *or* **kufiyah** *n* a cotton headdress worn by Arabs. [C19: from Arabic, perhaps from Late Latin *cofea* COIF]

Keflavík ('kɛfləˌvɪk) *n* a port in SW Iceland: Nato airbase, fishing. Pop.: 7627 (1994).

keftedes (kɛf'tɛðɛs) *n* a Greek dish of meatballs cooked with herbs and onions. [C20: from Modern Greek]

keg (kɛg) *n* **1** a small barrel with a capacity of between five and ten gallons. **2** *Brit.* **2a** an aluminium container in which beer is transported and stored. **2b** Also called: **keg beer.** beer kept in a keg: it is infused with gas and served under pressure. [C17: variant of Middle English *kag,* of Scandinavian origin; related to Old Norse *kaggi* cask]

kegler ('kɛglə) *or* **kegeler** ('kɛgələ) *n Informal, chiefly U.S.* a participant in a game of tenpin bowling. [from German, from *Kegel* pin, from Old High German *kegil* peg]

Keighley ('kiːθlɪ) *n* a town in N England, in Bradford unitary authority, West Yorkshire, on the River Aire: textile industry. Pop.: 49 567 (1991).

Keijo (ˌkeɪ'dʒəʊ) *n* transliteration of the Japanese name for **Seoul.**

keister *or* **keester** ('kiːstə) *n Slang, chiefly U.S.* **1** the rump; buttocks. **2** a suitcase, trunk, or box. [C20: of uncertain origin]

Keitel ('kaɪtᵊl) *n* **Wilhelm** ('vɪlhɛlm). 1882–1946, German field marshal; chief of the supreme command of the armed forces (1938–45). He was convicted at the Nuremberg trials and executed.

keitloa ('kaɪtləʊə, 'keɪt-) *n* a southern African variety of the black two-horned rhinoceros, *Diceros bicornis.* [C19: from Tswana *khetlwa*]

Kekkonen (*Finnish* 'kɛkkɔnɛn) *n* **Urho** ('urhɔ). (1900–86), Finnish statesman; president (1956–81).

keks (kɛks) *pl n* a variant spelling of **kecks.**

Kekulé formula ('kɛkjəˌleɪ) *n* a representation of the benzene molecule as six carbon atoms at the corners of a regular hexagon with alternate double and single bonds joining them and with one hydrogen atom bound to each carbon atom. See **benzene ring.** [C19: named after F. A. KEKULÉ VON STRADONITZ]

Kekulé von Stradonitz (*German* 'kekule fɔn 'ʃtradonɪts) *n* **(Friedrich) August** ('ogyst). 1829–96, German chemist. His elucidation of the concepts of valence and single, double, and triple bonds enabled him to suggest the structure of many molecules, notably benzene (**Kekulé structure**).

Kelantan (kɛ'læntən, kɪˌlæn'tæn) *n* a state of NE Malaysia: under Thai control until it came under the British in 1909; produces rice and rubber. Capital: Kota Bharu. Pop.: 1 221 700 (1993 est.). Area: 14 930 sq. km (5765 sq. miles).

Keller ('kɛlə) *n* **1 Gottfried.** 1819–90, Swiss novelist and short-story writer, who wrote in German: noted esp. for the novel *Der Grüne Heinrich* (1855, rewritten 1880). **2 Helen (Adams).** 1880–1968, U.S. author and lecturer. Blind and deaf from infancy, she was taught to read, write, and speak and became noted for her work for the handicapped.

Kells (kɛlz) *n* a town in the Republic of Ireland, in Co. Meath: *The Book of Kells,* an illuminated manuscript of the Gospels, was produced at the monastery here in the 8th century. Pop.: 2187 (1991).

Kelly ('kɛlɪ) *n* **1 Gene,** full name *Eugene Curran Kelly.* 1912–96, U.S. dancer, choreographer, film actor, and director. His many films include *An American in Paris* (1951) and *Singin' in the Rain* (1952). **2 Grace.** 1929–82, U.S. film actress. Her films included *High Noon* (1952) and *High Society* (1956). She married Prince Rainier III of Monaco in 1956 and died following a car crash. **3 Ned.** 1855–80, Australian horse and cattle thief and bushranger, active in Victoria: captured by the police and hanged. **4 (as) game as Ned Kelly.** See **game**[1] (sense 25).

Kelmscott Manor ('kɛlmzˌkɒt) *n* a Tudor house near Lechlade in Oxfordshire: home (1871–96) of William Morris.

keloid *or* **cheloid** ('kiːlɔɪd) *n Pathol.* a hard smooth pinkish raised growth of scar tissue at the site of an injury, tending to occur more frequently in dark-skinned races. [C19: from Greek *khēlē* claw] ▸ **ke'loidal** *or* **che'loidal** *adj*

kelp (kɛlp) *n* **1** any large brown seaweed, esp. any species of *Laminaria.* **2** the ash of such seaweed, used as a source of iodine and potash. [C14: of unknown origin]

kelpie[1] *or* **kelpy** ('kɛlpɪ) *n, pl* **-pies.** an Australian breed of sheepdog, originally developed from Scottish collies, having a smooth coat of various colours and erect ears. [named after a particular specimen of the breed, c. 1870]

kelpie[2] ('kɛlpɪ) *n* (in Scottish folklore) a water spirit in the form of a horse that drowned its riders. [C18: probably related to Scottish Gaelic *cailpeach* heifer, of obscure origin]

kelson ('kɛlsən) *n* a variant of **keelson.**

kelt (kɛlt) *n* a salmon that has recently spawned and is usually in poor condition. [C14: of unknown origin]

Kelt (kɛlt) *n* a variant of **Celt.** ▸ **'Keltic** *adj* ▸ **'Keltically** *adv* ▸ **'KeltiˌcismA** *n* ▸ **'Kelticist** *or* **'Keltist** *n*

kelter ('kɛltə) *n* a variant of **kilter.**

kelvin ('kɛlvɪn) *n* the basic SI unit of thermodynamic temperature; the fraction 1/273.16 of the thermodynamic temperature of the triple point of water. Symbol: K

Kelvin ('kɛlvɪn) *n* **William Thomson,** 1st Baron Kelvin. 1824–1907, British physicist, noted for his work in thermodynamics, inventing the Kelvin scale, and in electricity, pioneering undersea telegraphy.

Kelvin scale *n* a thermodynamic temperature scale based upon the efficiencies of ideal heat engines. The zero of the scale is absolute zero. Originally the degree was equal to that on the Celsius scale but it is now defined so that the triple point of water is exactly 273.16 kelvins. The International Practical Temperature Scale (1968) realizes the Kelvin scale over a wide range of temperatures. Compare **Rankine scale.**

kelyphitic rim *n Geology.* a mineral shell enclosing another mineral in an igneous rock, formed by reaction of the interned mineral with the surrounding rock. [C19: from Greek *keluphos* pod + *-itic;* see -ITE[1]]

Kemal Atatürk (kɛ'mɑːl 'ætəˌtɜːk) *n* See **Atatürk.** ▸ **Ke'malism** *n* ▸ **Ke'malist** *n, adj*

Kemble ('kɛmbᵊl) *n* **1 Frances Anne,** known as *Fanny.* 1809–93, English actress, in the U.S. from 1832. **2** her uncle, **John Philip.** 1757–1823, English actor and theatrical manager.

Kemerovo (*Russian* 'kjemɪrəvə) *n* a city in S Russia: a major coal-mining centre of the Kuznetsk Basin, with important chemical plants. Pop.: 503 000 (1995 est.). Former name (until 1932): **Shcheglovsk.**

kemp (kɛmp) *n* a coarse hair or strand of hair, esp. one in a fleece that resists dyeing. [C14: from Old Norse *kampr* beard, moustache] ▸ **'kempy** *adj*

Kempe (kɛmp) *n* **1 Margery.** ?1373–?1440, English mystic. Her autobiography, *The Book of Margery Kempe,* describes her mystical experiences and pilgrimages in Europe and Palestine. **2** (*German* 'kɛmpə) **Rudolf** ('ruːdɔlf). 1910–76, German orchestral conductor, noted esp. for his interpretations of Wagner.

Kempis ('kɛmpɪs) *n* **Thomas à.** ?1380–1471, German Augustinian monk, generally regarded as the author of the devotional work *The Imitation of Christ.*

kempt (kɛmpt) *adj* (of hair) tidy; combed. See also **unkempt.** [C20: back formation from *unkempt;* originally past participle of dialect *kemb* to COMB]

ken (kɛn) *n* **1** range of knowledge or perception (esp. in the phrases **beyond** *or* **in one's ken**). ◆ *vb* **kens, kenning, kenned** *or* **kent** (kɛnt). **2** *Scot. and northern English dialect.* to know. **3** *Scot. and northern English dialect.* to understand; perceive. **4** *(tr) Archaic.* to see. [Old English *cennan;* related to Old Norse *kenna* to perceive, Old High German *kennen* to make known; see CAN[1]]

Ken. *abbrev. for* Kentucky.

kenaf (kə'næf) *n* another name for **ambary.** [from Persian]

Kendal ('kɛndᵊl) *n* a town in NW England, in Cumbria: a gateway town to the Lake District, with an ancient woollen industry. Pop.: 25 461 (1991).

Kendal green *n* **1** a green woollen cloth, formerly worn by foresters. **2** the colour of this cloth, produced by a dye obtained from the woad plant. See also **dyer's-greenweed.** [C14: from *Kendal,* where it originated]

Kendall ('kɛndəl) *n* **Edward Calvin.** 1886–1972, U.S. biochemist, who isolated the hormone thyroxine (1916). He shared the Nobel prize for physiology or medicine (1950) with Phillip Hench and Tadeus Reichstein for their work on hormones.

kendo ('kɛndəʊ) *n* the Japanese art of fencing with pliable bamboo staves or, sometimes, real swords: strict conventions are observed. [from Japanese]

Kendrew ('kɛndruː) *n* Sir **John Cowdery.** 1917–97, British biochemist. Using X-ray diffraction he discovered the structure of myoglobin, for which he shared a Nobel Prize (1962) with Max Perutz.

Keneally (kə'nælɪ) *n* **Thomas (Michael).** born 1935, Australian writer. His novels include the Booker prizewinner *Schindler's Ark* (1982); other works are *The Playmaker* (1987) and *The Great Shame* (1998).

Kenilworth ('kɛnɪlˌwɜːθ) *n* a town in central England, in Warwickshire: ruined 12th-century castle, subject of Sir Walter Scott's novel *Kenilworth.* Pop.: 21 623 (1991).

Kénitra (*French* kenitra) *n* another name for **Mina Hassan Tani.**

Kennedy[1] ('kɛnɪdɪ) *n* **Cape.** a former name (1963–73) of (Cape) **Canaveral.**

Kennedy[2] ('kɛnɪdɪ) *n* **1 Charles Peter.** born 1959, British politician, leader of the Liberal Democrats from 1999. **2 Edward (Moore),** known as *Ted.* born 1932, U.S. Democrat politician; senator since 1962. **3** his brother, **John (Fitzgerald),** known as *JFK.* 1917–63, U.S. Democrat statesman; 35th president of the U.S. (1961–63), the first Roman Catholic and the youngest man ever to be president. He demanded the withdrawal of Soviet missiles from Cuba (1962) and prepared civil rights reforms; assassinated. **4 Nigel (Paul).** born 1956, British violinist, noted for his flamboyant style. **5 Robert (Francis),** known as *Bobby,* brother of John Kennedy. 1925–68, U.S. Democrat statesman; attorney general (1961–64) and senator for New York (1965–68); assassinated.

kennel[1] ('kɛnᵊl) *n* **1** a hutlike shelter for a dog. U.S. name: **doghouse. 2** (*usually pl*) an establishment where dogs are bred, trained, boarded, etc. **3** the lair of a fox or other animal. **4** a ramshackle house; hovel. **5** a pack of hounds. ◆ *vb* **-nels, -nelling, -nelled** *or U.S.* **-nels, -neling, -neled. 6** to put or go into a kennel; keep or stay in a kennel. **[C14:** from Old French *chenil,* from Vulgar Latin *canīle* (unattested), from Latin *canis* dog**]**

kennel[2] ('kɛnᵊl) *n Archaic.* an open sewer or street gutter. **[C16:** variant of *cannel* CHANNEL[1]**]**

Kennelly ('kɛnəlɪ) *n* **Arthur Edwin.** 1861–1939, U.S. electrical engineer: independently of Heaviside, he predicted the existence of an ionized layer in the upper atmosphere, known as the Kennelly-Heaviside layer or E region.

Kennelly-Heaviside layer *n* See **E region.**

Kenneth I ('kɛnɪθ) *n* surnamed *MacAlpine.* died 858, king of the Scots of Dalriada and of the Picts (?844–858): considered the first Scottish king.

kenning ('kɛnɪŋ) *n* a conventional metaphoric name for something, esp. in Old Norse and Old English poetry, such as Old English *bānhūs* (bone house) for "body". **[C14:** from Old Norse, from *kenna;* see KEN**]**

Kenny ('kɛnɪ) *n* **1 Brett.** born 1961, Australian rugby league player. **2 Yvonne.** born 1950, Australian opera singer.

Kenny method *or* **treatment** ('kɛnɪ) *n* a method of treating poliomyelitis by applying hot moist packs to the affected muscles alternated by passive and later active movement of the muscles. **[C20:** named after Sister Elizabeth *Kenny,* 1886–1952, Australian nurse who developed it**]**

keno, keeno, kino, *or* **quino** ('ki:no) *n U.S. and Canadian.* a game of chance similar to bingo. **[C19:** of unknown origin**]**

kenogenesis (ˌki:nəʊ'dʒɛnɪsɪs) *n* a secondary U.S. spelling of **caenogenesis.** ▸ **kenogenetic** (ˌki:nəʊdʒə'nɛtɪk) *adj* ▸ **ˌkenogeˈnetically** *adv*

kenosis (kɪ'nəʊsɪs) *n Christianity.* Christ's voluntary renunciation of certain divine attributes, in order to identify himself with mankind (Philippians 2:6–7). **[C19:** from Greek: an emptying, from *kenoun* to empty from *kenos* empty**]** ▸ **kenotic** (kɪ'nɒtɪk) *adj, n*

Kensington and Chelsea ('kɛnzɪŋtən) *n* a borough of Greater London, on the River Thames: **Kensington Palace** (17th century) and gardens. Pop.: 151 500 (1994 est.). Area: 12 sq. km (5 sq. miles).

kenspeckle ('kɛnˌspɛkᵊl) *adj Scot.* easily seen or recognized. **[C18:** from dialect *kenspeck,* of Scandinavian origin; compare Old Norse *kennispecki* power of recognition; related to KEN**]**

kent (kɛnt) *vb* a past tense and past participle of **ken.**

Kent[1] (kɛnt) *n* a county of SE England, on the English Channel: the first part of Great Britain to be colonized by the Romans; one of the seven kingdoms of Anglo-Saxon England until absorbed by Wessex in the 9th century A.D. Apart from the Downs it is mostly low-lying and agricultural, specializing in fruit and hops. Administrative centre: Maidstone. Pop.: 1 546 300 (1994 est.). Area: 3731 sq. km (1440 sq. miles).

Kent[2] (kɛnt) *n* **William.** ?1685–1748, English architect, landscape gardener, and interior designer.

kente ('kɛntɪ) *n* **1** Also called: **kente cloth.** a brightly coloured handwoven cloth of Ghana, usually with some gold thread. **2** the toga made of this cloth. **[**from a Ghanaian language, possibly Akan**]**

kentia ('kɛntɪə) *n* a plant name formerly used to include palms now allotted to several different genera and still used commercially to denote the feather palm genus *Howea,* native to Lord Howe Island, popular as greenhouse or house plants for their decorative arching foliage: family *Palmaceae.* **[**named after W. *Kent* (fl. c. 1800), Dutch traveller and botanist**]**

Kentish ('kɛntɪʃ) *adj* **1** of or relating to Kent. ◆ *n* **2** Also called: **Jutish.** the dialect of Old and Middle English spoken in Kent. See also **Anglian, West Saxon.**

Kentish glory *n* a moth, *Endromis versicolora,* common in north and central Europe, having brown variegated front wings and, in the male, orange hindwings.

kentledge ('kɛntlɪdʒ) *n Nautical.* scrap metal used as ballast in a vessel. **[C17:** perhaps from Old French *quintelage* ballast, from *quintal* hundredweight, ultimately from Arabic *qintār;* see KANTAR**]**

Kentucky (kɛn'tʌkɪ) *n* **1** a state of the S central U.S.: consists of an undulating plain in the west, the Bluegrass region in the centre, the Tennessee and Ohio River basins in the southwest, and the Appalachians in the east. Capital: Frankfort. Pop.: 3 908 124 (1997 est.). Area: 102 693 sq. km (39 650 sq. miles). Abbrevs.: **Ken., Ky.** or (with zip code) **KY 2** a river in central Kentucky, rising in the Cumberland Mountains and flowing northwest to the Ohio River. Length: 417 km (259 miles). ▸ **Kenˈtuckian** *adj, n*

Kentucky bluegrass *n* a Eurasian grass, *Poa pratensis,* grown for forage and naturalized throughout North America.

Kentucky coffee tree *n* a North American leguminous tree, *Gymnocladus dioica,* whose seeds, in brown curved pulpy pods, were formerly used as a coffee substitute.

Kentucky Derby *n* a race for three-year-old horses run annually since 1875 at Louisville, Kentucky.

Kenwood House ('kɛnwʊd) *n* a 17th century mansion on Hampstead Heath in London: remodelled and decorated by Robert Adam: contains the Iveagh bequest, a noted art collection.

Kenya ('kɛnjə, 'ki:njə) *n* **1** a republic in E Africa, on the Indian Ocean: became a British protectorate in 1895 and a colony in 1920; gained independence in 1963 and is a member of the Commonwealth. Coffee constitutes about a third of the total exports. Official languages: Swahili and English. Religions: Christian majority, animist minority. Currency: shilling. Capital: Nairobi. Pop.: 28 337 000 (1998 est.). Area: 582 647 sq. km (224 960 sq. miles). **2 Mount.** an extinct volcano in central Kenya: the second highest mountain in Africa; girth at 2400 m (8000 ft.) is about 150 km (95 miles). The regions above 3200 m (10 500 ft.) constitute **Mount Kenya National Park.** Height: 5200 m (17 058 ft.). ▸ **ˈKenyan** *adj, n*

Kenyatta (kɛn'jætə) *n* **Jomo** ('dʒəʊməʊ). ?1891–1978, Kenyan statesman: imprisoned as a suspected leader of the Mau Mau revolt (1953–59); elected president of the Kenya African National Union (1961); prime minister of independent Kenya (1963) and president (1964–78).

Keos ('keɪɒs) *n* an island in the Aegean Sea, in the NW Cyclades. Pop.: 1700 (latest est.). Area: 174 sq. km (67 sq. miles). Italian name: **Zea.** Modern Greek name: **Kéa.**

kep (kɛp) *vb* **keps, kepping, keppit** ('kɛpɪt). (*tr*) *Scot. and northern English dialect.* to catch. **[**from KEEP (in obsolete sense: to put oneself in the way of)**]**

Kephallinía (ˌkɛfali'nia; *English* ˌkɛfə'li:nɪə) *n* transliteration of the Modern Greek name for **Cephalonia.**

kepi ('keɪpi:) *n, pl* **kepis.** a military cap with a circular top and a horizontal peak. **[C19:** from French *képi,* from German (Swiss dialect) *käppi* a little cap, from *kappe* CAP**]**

Kepler[1] ('kɛplə) *n* **Johannes** (jo'hanəs). 1571–1630, German astronomer. As discoverer of Kepler's laws of planetary motion he is regarded as one of the founders of modern astronomy.

Kepler[2] ('kɛplə) *n* a small crater in the NW quadrant of the moon, centre of a large bright ray system.

Kepler's laws *pl n* three laws of planetary motion published by Kepler between 1609 and 1619. The first states that the orbit of a planet describes an ellipse with the sun at one focus. The second states that, during one orbit, the straight line joining the sun and a planet sweeps out equal areas in equal times. The third states that the squares of the periods of any two planets are proportional to the cubes of their orbital major axes.

kept (kɛpt) *vb* **1** the past tense and past participle of **keep. 2 kept woman.** *Censorious.* a woman maintained by a man as his mistress.

Kerala ('kɛrələ, kə'rɑ:lə) *n* a state of SW India, on the Arabian Sea: formed in 1956, it includes the former state of Travancore-Cochin; has the highest population density of any Indian state. Capital: Trivandrum. Pop.: 30 555 000 (1994 est.). Area: 38 863 sq. km (15 005 sq. miles).

keramic (kɪ'ræmɪk) *adj* a rare variant of **ceramic.**

keramics (kɪ'ræmɪks) *n* a rare variant of **ceramics.**

keratin ('kɛrətɪn) *or* **ceratin** *n* a fibrous protein that occurs in the outer layer of the skin and in hair, nails, feathers, hooves, etc.

keratinize *or* **keratinise** (kɪ'rætɪˌnaɪz, 'kɛrətɪ-) *vb* to become or cause to become impregnated with keratin. ▸ **keˌratiniˈzation** *or* **keˌratiniˈsation** *n*

keratitis (ˌkɛrə'taɪtɪs) *n* inflammation of the cornea.

kerato- *or before a vowel* **kerat-** *combining form.* **1** indicating horn or a horny substance: *keratin; keratogenous.* **2** indicating the cornea: *keratoplasty.* **[**from Greek *kerat-, keras* horn**]**

keratogenous (ˌkɛrə'tɒdʒɪnəs) *adj* developing or causing the growth of horny tissue.

keratoid ('kɛrəˌtɔɪd) *adj* resembling horn; horny.

keratoplasty ('kɛrətəʊˌplæstɪ) *n, pl* **-ties.** plastic surgery of the cornea, esp. involving corneal grafting. ▸ **ˌkeratoˈplastic** *adj*

keratose ('kɛrəˌtəʊs, -ˌtəʊz) *adj* (esp. of certain sponges) having a horny skeleton.

keratosis (ˌkɛrə'təʊsɪs) *n Pathol.* **1** any skin condition marked by a horny growth, such as a wart. **2** a horny growth.

keratotomy (ˌkɛrə'tɒtəmɪ) *n* surgical incision of the cornea.

kerb *or U.S. and Canadian* **curb** (kɜ:b) *n* **1** a line of stone or concrete forming an edge between a pavement and a roadway. ◆ *vb* **2** (*tr*) to provide with or enclose with a kerb. **[C17:** from Old French *courbe* bent, from Latin *curvus;* see CURVE**]**

kerbaya ('kɛrbaja) *n* a blouse worn by Malay women. **[**from Malay**]**

kerb crawling *n* the act of driving slowly along the edge of the pavement seeking to entice someone into the car for sexual purposes. ▸ **kerb crawler** *n*

kerb drill *n* a pedestrian's procedure for crossing a road safely, esp. as taught to children.

Kerbela ('kɜ:bələ) *n* a variant of **Karbala.**

kerbing *or U.S. and Canadian* **curbing** ('kɜ:bɪŋ) *n* **1** material used for a kerb. **2** a less common word for **kerb** (sense 1).

kerb market *n Stock Exchange.* **1** an after-hours street market. **2** a street market dealing in unquoted securities.

kerbstone *or U.S. and Canadian* **curbstone** ('kɜ:bˌstəʊn) *n* one of a series of stones that form a kerb.

kerb weight *n* the weight of a motor car without occupants, luggage, etc.

Kerch (*Russian* kjertʃ) *n* a port in the S Ukraine on the **Kerch Peninsula** and the **Strait of Kerch** (linking the Black Sea with the Sea of Azov): founded as a Greek colony in the 6th century B.C.; ceded to Russia in 1774; iron-mining, steel production, and fishing. Pop.: 175 000 (1996 est.).

kerchief ('kɜ:tʃɪf) *n* a piece of cloth worn tied over the head or around the neck. **[C13:** from Old French *cuevrechef,* from *covrir* to COVER + *chef* head; see CHIEF**]** ▸ **ˈkerchiefed** *adj*

kerel ('kerəl) *n S. African.* a chap or fellow. **[C19:** Afrikaans**]**

Kerenski *or* **Kerensky** (kə'rɛnskɪ; *Russian* 'kjerɪnskij) *n* **Aleksandr Fyodorovich** (alɪk'sandr 'fjɔdərəvitʃ). 1881–1970, Russian liberal revolutionary leader; prime minister (July–October 1917): overthrown by the Bolsheviks.

kerf (kɜ:f) *n* the cut made by a saw, an axe, etc. **[**Old English *cyrf* a cutting; related to Old English *ceorfan* to CARVE**]**

kerfuffle, carfuffle, *or* **kurfuffle** (kəˈfʌfᵊl) *n* **1** *Informal, chiefly Brit.* commotion; disorder; agitation. ◆ *vb* **2** (*tr*) *Scot.* to put into disorder or disarray; ruffle or disarrange. [from Scottish *curfuffle, carfuffle,* from Scottish Gaelic *car* twist, turn + *fuffle* to disarrange]

Kerguelen (ˈkɜːgɪlɪn) *n* an archipelago in the S Indian Ocean: consists of one large volcanic island (Kerguelen or Desolation Island) and 300 small islands; part of the French Southern and Antarctic Territories.

Kerkrade (*Dutch* ˈkɛrkraːdə) *n* a town in the SE Netherlands, in Limburg: one of the oldest coal-mining centres in Europe. Pop.: 52 848 (1994).

Kérkyra (ˈkɛrkira) *n* transliteration of the Modern Greek name for **Corfu.**

kerma (ˈkɜːmə) *n Physics.* the quotient of the sum of the initial kinetic energies of all the charged particles liberated by indirectly ionizing radiation in a volume element of a material divided by the mass of the volume element. The SI unit is the gray. [C20: *k*(inetic) *e*(nergy) *r*(eleased per unit) *ma*(ss)]

Kerman (kəˈmɑːn) *n* a city in SE Iran: carpet-making centre. Pop.: 349 626 (1994 est.).

Kermanshah (ˌkɜːmænˈʃɑː) *n* the former name (until 1987) of **Bakhtaran.**

kermes (ˈkɜːmɪz) *n* **1** the dried bodies of female scale insects of the genus *Kermes,* esp. *K. ilices* of Europe and W Asia, used as a red dyestuff. **2** a small evergreen Eurasian oak tree, *Quercus coccifera:* the host plant of kermes scale insects. [C16: from French *kermès,* from Arabic *qirmiz,* from Sanskrit *krmija-* red dye, literally: produced by a worm, from *krmi* worm + *ja-* produced]

kermis *or* **kirmess** (ˈkɜːmɪs) *n* **1** (formerly, esp. in Holland and Northern Germany) an annual country festival or carnival. **2** *U.S. and Canadian.* a similar event, esp. one held to collect money for charity. [C16: from Middle Dutch *kercmisse,* from *kerc* church + *misse* MASS; originally a festival held to celebrate the dedication of a church]

kern[1] *or* **kerne** (kɜːn) *n* **1** the part of the character on a piece of printer's type that projects beyond the body. ◆ *vb* **2** (*tr*) to furnish (a typeface) with a kern. [C17: from French *carne* corner of type, projecting angle, ultimately from Latin *cardō* hinge]

kern[2] (kɜːn) *n* **1** a lightly armed foot soldier in medieval Ireland or Scotland. **2** a troop of such soldiers. **3** *Archaic.* a loutish peasant. [C14: from Middle Irish *cethern* band of foot soldiers, from *cath* battle]

kern[3] (kɜːn) *n Engineering.* the central area of a wall, column, etc., through which all compressive forces pass. [from German *Kern* core, heart]

Kern (kɜːn) *n* **Jerome (David).** 1885–1945, U.S. composer of musical comedies, esp. *Show Boat* (1927).

kernel (ˈkɜːnᵊl) *n* **1** the edible seed of a nut or fruit within the shell or stone. **2** the grain of a cereal, esp. wheat, consisting of the seed in a hard husk. **3** the central or essential part of something. ◆ *vb* **-nels, -nelling, -nelled** *or U.S.* **-nels, -neling, -neled. 4** (*intr*) *Rare.* to form kernels. [Old English *cyrnel* a little seed, from *corn* seed; see CORN[1]] ► **ˈkernel-less** *adj*

kerning (ˈkɜːnɪŋ) *n Printing.* the adjustment of space between the letters of words to improve the appearance of text matter.

kernite (ˈkɜːnaɪt) *n* a light soft colourless or white mineral consisting of a hydrated sodium borate in monoclinic crystalline form: an important source of borax and other boron compounds. Formula: $Na_2B_4O_7.4H_2O$. [C20: from *Kern* County, California, where it was found + -ITE[1]]

kernmantel rope (ˈkɜːnˌmæntᵊl) *n Mountaineering.* a rope made of many straight nylon fibres within a plaited sheath; used for its tensile strength, freedom from twisting, and elasticity. [C20: from German *Kernmantel,* from *Kern* core + *Mantel* coat, casing]

kero (ˈkɛrəʊ) *n Austral. and N.Z.* short for **kerosene.**

kerogen (ˈkɛrədʒən) *n* the solid organic material found in some rocks, such as oil shales, that produces hydrocarbons similar to petroleum when heated. [C20: from Greek *kērо(s)* wax + -GEN]

kerosene *or* **kerosine** (ˈkɛrəˌsiːn) *n* **1** another name (esp. U.S. and Canadian) for **paraffin** (sense 1). **2** the general name for paraffin as a fuel for jet aircraft. [C19: from Greek *kēros* wax + -ENE]

USAGE The spelling *kerosine* is now the preferred form in technical and industrial usage.

Kerouac (ˈkɛrʊˌæk) *n* **Jack,** real name *Jean-Louis Lebris de Kérouac.* 1922–69, U.S. novelist and poet of the Beat Generation. His works include *On the Road* (1957) and *Big Sur* (1962).

Kerr (kɜː) *n* Sir **John Robert.** 1914–91, Australian public servant. As governor general of Australia (1974–77), he dismissed the Labor prime minister Gough Whitlam (1975) amid great controversy.

Kerr effect *n* **1** Also called: **electro-optical effect.** the production of double refraction in certain transparent substances by the application of a strong electric field. **2** Also called: **magneto-optical effect.** a slight elliptical polarization of plane polarized light when reflected from one of the poles of a strong magnet. [C19: named after John *Kerr* (1824–1907), Scottish physicist]

Kerry (ˈkɛrɪ) *n* **1** a county of SW Republic of Ireland, in W Munster province: mostly mountainous (including the highest peaks in Ireland), with a deeply indented coast and many offshore islands. County town: Tralee. Pop.: 126 000 (1996). Area: 4701 sq. km (1815 sq. miles). **2** a small black breed of dairy cattle, originally from Kerry.

Kerry blue terrier *n* an Irish breed of terrier with a soft silky wavy coat of a silvery-grey or smoky blue colour.

kersey (ˈkɜːzɪ) *n* **1** a smooth woollen cloth used for overcoats, etc. **2** a twilled woollen cloth with a cotton warp. [C14: probably from *Kersey,* village in Suffolk]

kerseymere (ˈkɜːzɪˌmɪə) *n* a fine soft woollen cloth of twill weave. [C18: from KERSEY + (CASSI)MERE]

kerygma (ˌkɛˈrɪgmə) *n Christianity.* the essential news of Jesus, as preached by the early Christians to elicit faith rather than to educate or instruct. [from Greek: preaching, proclamation]

Kesey (ˈkiːsɪ) *n* **Ken.** born 1935, U.S. novelist, best-known for *One Flew Over the Cuckoo's Nest* (1962).

Kesh (keɪʃ) *n* the beard and uncut hair, covered by the turban, traditionally worn by Sikhs as a symbol of their religious and cultural loyalty, symbolizing the natural life. See also **five Ks.** [Punjabi *keś*]

Kesselring (ˈkɛsᵊlrɪŋ) *n* **Albert** (ˈalbɛrt). 1885–1960, German field marshal. He commanded the Luftwaffe attacks on Poland, France, and Britain (1939–40), and was supreme commander in Italy (1943–45) and on the western front (1945).

Kesteven (ˈkɛstɪvᵊn, kɛˈstiːvᵊn) *n* **Parts of.** an area in E England constituting a former administrative division of Lincolnshire.

kestrel (ˈkɛstrəl) *n* any of several small falcons, esp. the European *Falco tinnunculus,* that tend to hover against the wind and feed on small mammals on the ground. [C15: changed from Old French *cresserele,* from *cressele* rattle, from Vulgar Latin *crepicella* (unattested), from Latin *crepitāre* to crackle, from *crepāre* to rustle]

Keswick (ˈkɛzɪk) *n* a market town in NW England, in Cumbria in the Lake District: tourist centre. Pop.: 4836 (1991).

ketamine (ˈkɛtəmiːn) *n* a drug, chemically related to PCP, that is used in medicine as a general anaesthetic, being administered by injection; cyclohexylamine.

ketch (kɛtʃ) *n* a two-masted sailing vessel, fore-and-aft rigged, with a tall mainmast and a mizzen stepped forward of the rudderpost. Compare **yawl**[1] (sense 1). [C15 *cache,* probably from *cacchen* to hunt; see CATCH]

ketchup (ˈkɛtʃəp), **catchup,** *or* **catsup** *n* any of various piquant sauces containing vinegar: *tomato ketchup.* [C18: from Chinese (Amoy) *kōetsiap* brine of pickled fish, from *kōe* seafood + *tsiap* sauce]

ketene (ˈkiːtiːn, ˈkɛt-) *n* a colourless irritating toxic gas used as an acetylating agent in organic synthesis. Formula: CH_2:CO. Also called: **ethonone.**

keto- *or before a vowel* **ket-** *combining form.* indicating that a chemical compound is a ketone or is derived from a ketone: *ketose; ketoxime.*

keto-enol tautomerism (ˈkiːtəʊˈiːnɒl) *n Chem.* tautomerism in which the tautomers are an enol and a keto form. The change occurs by transfer of a hydrogen atom within the molecule.

keto form (ˈkiːtəʊ) *n* the form of tautomeric compounds when they are ketones rather than enols. See **keto-enol tautomerism.**

ketogenic (ˌkiːtəʊˈdʒɛnɪk) *adj Med.* forming or able to stimulate the production of ketone bodies: *a ketogenic diet.*

ketonaemia *or U.S.* **ketonemia** (ˌkiːtəʊˈniːmɪə) *n Pathol.* an excess of ketone bodies in the blood.

ketone (ˈkiːtəʊn) *n* any of a class of compounds with the general formula R′COR, where R and R′ are alkyl or aryl groups. See also **acetone.** [C19: from German *Keton,* from *Aketon* ACETONE] ► **ketonic** (kɪˈtɒnɪk) *adj*

ketone body *n Biochem.* any of three compounds (acetoacetic acid, 3-hydroxybutanoic acid, and acetone) produced when fatty acids are broken down in the liver to provide a source of energy. Excess ketone bodies are present in the blood and urine of people unable to use glucose as an energy source, as in diabetes and starvation. Also called: **acetone body.**

ketone group *n Chem.* the functional group of ketones: a carbonyl group attached to the carbon atoms of two other organic groups.

ketonuria (ˌkiːtəʊˈnjʊərɪə) *n Pathol.* the presence of ketone bodies in the urine.

ketose (ˈkiːtəʊz) *n* any monosaccharide that contains a ketone group.

ketosis (kɪˈtəʊsɪs) *n Pathol.* the condition resulting from excess production of ketone bodies.

ketoxime (kiːˈtɒksiːm) *n* an oxime formed by reaction between hydroxylamine and a ketone.

Kettering (ˈkɛtərɪŋ) *n* a town in central England, in Northamptonshire: footwear industry. Pop.: 47 186 (1991).

kettle (ˈkɛtᵊl) *n* **1** a metal container with a handle and spout for boiling water. **2** any of various metal containers for heating liquids, cooking fish, etc. **3** a large metal vessel designed to withstand high temperatures, used in various industrial processes such as refining and brewing. **4** short for **kettle hole.** [C13: from Old Norse *ketill;* related to Old English *cietel* kettle, Old High German *kezzil;* all ultimately from Latin *catillus* a little pot, from *catīnus* pot]

kettledrum (ˈkɛtᵊlˌdrʌm) *n* a percussion instrument of definite pitch, consisting of a hollow bowl-like hemisphere covered with a skin or membrane, supported on a tripod or stand. The pitch may be adjusted by means of screws or pedals, which alter the tension of the skin. ► **ˈkettleˌdrummer** *n*

kettle hole *n* a round hollow formed by the melting of a mass of buried ice. Often shortened to **kettle.**

kettle of fish *n* **1** a situation; state of affairs (often used ironically in the phrase **a pretty** or **fine kettle of fish**). **2** case; matter for consideration: *that's quite a different kettle of fish.*

ketubah (kɘtuˈbaː) *n Judaism.* the contract that states the obligations within Jewish marriage. [from Hebrew, literally: document]

keV *abbrev. for* kilo-electronvolt.

kevel (ˈkɛvᵊl) *n* **1** *Nautical.* a strong bitt or bollard for securing heavy hawsers. **2** *Building trades.* a hammer having an edged end and a pointed end, used for breaking and rough-shaping stone. [C14: from Old Northern French *keville,* from Latin *clāvicula* a little key, from *clāvis* key]

Kevlar (ˈkɛvˌlɑː) *n Trademark.* a synthetic fibre, consisting of long-chain polyamides, having high tensile strength and temperate resistance.

Kew (kjuː) *n* part of the Greater London borough of Richmond-upon-Thames, on the River Thames: famous for **Kew Gardens** (the Royal Botanic Gardens), established in 1759 and given to the nation in 1841.

kewpie doll (ˈkjuːpɪ) *n U.S. and Canadian.* **1** any brightly coloured doll, commonly given as a prize at carnivals. **2** (*caps.*) *Trademark.* a doll having rosy cheeks and a curl of hair on its head. [C20: *kewpie,* perhaps from *Cupid*]

kex (kɛks) *n* **1** any of several large hollow-stemmed umbelliferous plants, such as cow parsnip and chervil. **2** the dried stalks of any of these plants. [C14: of obscure origin]

key[1] (kiː) *n* **1** a metal instrument, usually of a specifically contoured shape, that is made to fit a lock and, when rotated, operates the lock's mechanism. **2** any instrument that is rotated to operate a valve, clock winding mechanism, etc. **3** a small metal peg or wedge inserted into keyways. **4** any of a set of levers operating a typewriter, computer, etc. **5** any of the visible parts of the lever mechanism of a musical keyboard instrument that when depressed set in motion the action that causes the instrument to sound. **6a** Also called: **tonality.** any of the 24 major and minor diatonic scales considered as a corpus of notes upon which a piece of music draws for its tonal framework. **6b** the main tonal centre in an extended composition: *a symphony in the key of F major.* **6c** the tonic of a major or minor scale. **6d** See **tuning key. 7** something that is crucial in providing an explanation or interpretation: *the key to adult behaviour lies in childhood.* **8** a means of achieving a desired end: *the key to happiness.* **9** a means of access or control: *Gibraltar is the key to the Mediterranean.* **10** a list of explanations of symbols, codes, etc. **11** a text that explains or gives information about a work of literature, art, or music. **12** Also called: **key move.** the correct initial move in the solution of a set problem. **13** *Biology.* a systematic list of taxonomic characteristics, used to identify animals or plants. **14** *Photog., painting.* the dominant tonal value and colour intensity of a picture. See also **low-key** (sense 3), **high-key. 15** *Electrical engineering.* **15a** a hand-operated device for opening or closing a circuit or for switching circuits. **15b** a hand-operated switch that is pressed to transmit coded signals, esp. Morse code. **16** the grooving or scratching of a surface or the application of a rough coat of plaster, etc., to provide a bond for a subsequent finish. **17** pitch: *he spoke in a low key.* **18** a characteristic mood or style: *a poem in a melancholic key.* **19** level of intensity: *she worked herself up to a high key.* **20** *Railways.* a wooden wedge placed between a rail and a chair to keep the rail firmly in place. **21** a wedge for tightening a joint or for splitting stone or timber. **22** short for **keystone** (sense 1). **23** *Botany.* any dry winged fruit, esp. that of the ash. **24** (*modifier*) of great importance: *a key issue.* **25** (*modifier*) *Photog.* determining the tonal value of a photograph: *flesh colour is an important key tone.* ◆ *vb* (*mainly tr*) **26** (foll. by *to*) to harmonize (with): *to key one's actions to the prevailing mood.* **27** to adjust or fasten with a key or some similar device. **28** to provide with a key or keys. **29** (often foll. by *up*) to locate the position of (a piece of copy, artwork, etc.) on a layout by the use of symbols. **30** (*also intr*) another word for **keyboard** (sense 3). **31** to include a distinguishing device in (an advertisement, etc.), so that responses to it can be identified. **32** to provide a keystone for (an arch). ◆ See also **key in, key up.** [Old English *cǣg*; related to Old Frisian *kēi*, Middle Low German *keie* spear] ▸ **'keyless** *adj*

key[2] (kiː) *n* a variant spelling of **cay.**

keyboard ('kiːˌbɔːd) *n* **1a** a complete set of keys, usually hand-operated, as on a piano, organ, typewriter, or typesetting machine. **1b** (*as modifier*): *a keyboard instrument.* **2** (*often pl*) a musical instrument, esp. an electronic one, played by means of a keyboard. ◆ *vb* **3** to set (a text) in type, onto magnetic tape, or into some other medium, by using a keyboard machine. ▸ **'keyˌboarder** *n*

keyboardist ('kiːˌbɔːdɪst) *n* a person who plays a keyboard instrument, esp. an electronic musical instrument.

key fruit *n* another name for **samara.**

key grip *n Chiefly U.S.* the person in charge of moving and setting up camera tracks and scenery in a film or television studio. See also **grip**[1] (sense 11).

keyhole ('kiːˌhəʊl) *n* **1** an aperture in a door or a lock case through which a key may be passed to engage the lock mechanism. **2** any small aperture resembling a keyhole in shape or function.

keyhole surgery *n* surgery carried out through a very small incision.

key in *vb* (*tr, adv*) to enter (information or instructions) in a computer or other device by means of a keyboard or keypad.

key light *n Television, photog., etc.* the main stage or studio light that gives the required overall intensity of illumination.

key-man assurance *n* an assurance policy taken out, esp. by a small company, on the life of a senior executive whose death would create a serious loss.

key money *n* a fee payment required from a new tenant of a house or flat before he moves in.

Keynes (keɪnz) *n* **John Maynard,** 1st Baron Keynes. 1883–1946, English economist. In *The General Theory of Employment, Interest and Money* (1936) he argued that unemployment was characteristic of an unregulated market economy and therefore to achieve a high level of employment it was necessary for governments to manipulate the overall level of demand through monetary and fiscal policies (including, when appropriate, deficit financing). He helped to found the International Monetary Fund and the World Bank. ▸ **'Keynesian** *adj, n* ▸ **'KeynesianˌIsm** *n*

keynote ('kiːˌnəʊt) *n* **1a** a central or determining principle in a speech, literary work, etc. **1b** (*as modifier*): *a keynote speech.* **2** the note upon which a scale or key is based; tonic. ◆ *vb* (*tr*) **3** to deliver a keynote address to (a political convention, etc.). **4** to outline (political issues, policy, etc.) in or as in a keynote address.

keypad ('kiːˌpæd) *n* **1** a small keyboard with push buttons, as on a pocket calculator, remote control unit for a television, etc. **2** *Computing.* a data input device consisting of a limited number of keys, each with nominated functions.

key punch *n* **1** Also called: **card punch.** a device having a keyboard that is operated manually to transfer data onto punched cards, paper tape, etc. ◆ *vb* **key-punch. 2** to transfer (data) onto punched cards, paper tape, etc., by using a key punch.

keys (kiːz) *interj Scot. dialect.* a children's cry for truce or respite from the rules of a game. [origin uncertain]

key signature *n Music.* a group of sharps or flats appearing at the beginning of each stave line to indicate the key in which a piece, section, etc., is to be performed.

key stage *n Brit. Education.* any one of four broad age-group divisions (5–7; 7–11; 11–14; 14–16) to which each level of the National Curriculum applies.

keystone ('kiːˌstəʊn) *n* **1** Also called: **headstone, quoin.** the central stone at the top of an arch or the top stone of a dome or vault. **2** something that is necessary to connect or support a number of other related things.

keystroke ('kiːˌstrəʊk) *n* a single operation of the mechanism of a typewriter or keyboard-operated typesetting machine by the action of a key.

key up *vb* (*tr, adv*) to raise the intensity, excitement, tension, etc., of.

keyway ('kiːˌweɪ) *n* a longitudinal slot cut into a component to accept a key that engages with a similar slot on a mating component to prevent relative motion of the two components.

keyword ('kiːˌwɜːd) *n* **1** a word used as a key to a code. **2** any significant word or phrase, esp. a word used to describe the contents of a document.

kg 1 *abbrev. for* keg. ◆ **2** *symbol for* kilogram.

KG *abbrev. for* Knight of the Order of the Garter (a Brit. title).

KGB *abbrev.* the former Soviet secret police, founded in 1954. Compare **GRU.** [from Russian *Komitet Gosudarstvennoi Bezopasnosti* State Security Committee]

Khabarovsk (*Russian* xa'barəfsk) *n* a port in E Russia, on the Amur River: it was the administrative centre of the whole Soviet Far Eastern territory until 1938; a major industrial centre. Pop.: 618 000 (1995 est.).

Khachaturian (ˌkɑːtʃə'tʊərɪən; *Russian* xətʃətu'rjan) *n* **Aram Ilich** ('arəm ilj'jitʃ). 1903–78, Russian composer. His works, which often incorporate Armenian folk tunes, include a piano concerto and the ballets *Gayaneh* (1942) and *Spartacus* (1954).

khaddar ('kɑːdə) *or* **khadi** ('kɑːdɪ) *n* a cotton cloth of plain weave, produced in India. [from Hindi *khādar*]

Khadijah (ˌkɑ'diːdʒə) *n* 554–619 A.D., the first wife of the Prophet Mohammed, regarded as the first convert to Islam.

Khafre ('kæfreɪ, 'kɑːfreɪ) *n* Greek name *Chephren.* king of Egypt (*c.* 2550 B.C.) of the 4th dynasty. He built the second pyramid and is thought to have built the Sphinx at Giza.

Khakass Republic (kə'kæs) *n* a constituent republic of S central Russia, in the Krasnoyarsk Territory: formed in 1930. Capital: Abakan. Pop.: 583 000 (1995 est.). Area: 61 900 sq. km (23 855 sq. miles). Also called **Khakassia** (kə'kæsɪə; *Russian* xə'kasɪjə).

khaki ('kɑːkɪ) *n, pl* **-kis. 1a** a dull yellowish-brown colour. **1b** (*as adj*): *a khaki background.* **2a** a hard-wearing fabric of this colour, used esp. for military uniforms. **2b** (*as modifier*): *a khaki jacket.* [C19: from Urdu, from Persian: dusty, from *khāk* dust]

khaki election *n Brit.* a general election held during or immediately after a war, esp. one in which the war has an effect on how people vote. [C20: first used of the 1900 general election, during which the conduct of the Boer war was an election issue]

Khalid ibn Abdul Aziz ('kɑːlɪd 'ɪb[ə]n 'æbdʊlə'ziːz) *n* 1913–82, king and President of the Council of Ministers of Saudi Arabia (1975–82).

khalif ('keɪlɪf, 'kæl-) *n* a variant spelling of **caliph.**

Khalkha ('kælkə) *n* the dialect of Mongolian that is the official language of Mongolia.

Khalkidíki (xalkiðí'ki) *n* transliteration of the Modern Greek name for **Chalcidice.**

Khalkís (xal'kis) *n* transliteration of the Modern Greek name for **Chalcis.**

Khalsa ('kælsə) *n* an order of the Sikh religion, founded (1699) by Guru Gobind Singh. Members vow to wear the five Ks, to eat only ritually killed meat, and to refrain from committing adultery or cutting their hair.

Khama ('kɑːmə) *n* Sir **Seretse** (sə'rɛtsɪ). 1921–80, Botswana statesman; the first president of Botswana (1966–80).

khamsin ('kæmsɪn, kæm'siːn), **kamseen,** *or* **kamsin** *n* a hot southerly wind blowing from about March to May, esp. in Egypt. [C17: from Arabic, literally: fifty]

khan[1] (kɑːn) *n* **1a** (formerly) a title borne by medieval Chinese emperors and Mongol and Turkic rulers: usually added to a name: *Kublai Khan.* **1b** such a ruler. **2** a title of respect borne by important personages in Afghanistan and central Asia. [C14: from Old French *caan,* from Medieval Latin *caanus,* from Turkish *khān,* contraction of *khāqān* ruler]

khan[2] (kɑːn) *n* an inn in Turkey, certain Arab countries, etc.; caravanserai. [C14: via Arabic from Persian]

Khan (kɑːn) *n* **Imran.** See **Imran Khan.**

khanate ('kɑːneɪt, 'kæn-) *n* **1** the territory ruled by a khan. **2** the position or rank of a khan.

khanda ('kʌndə) *n* a double-edged sword that appears as the emblem on the Sikh flag and is used in the Amrit ceremony to stir the amrit.

khanga ('kæŋgə) *n* a variant spelling of **kanga.**

Khaniá (xa'nja) *n* transliteration of the Modern Greek name for **Canea.**

kharif (kə'riːf) *n* (in Pakistan, India, etc.) a crop that is harvested at the beginning of winter. Compare **rabi.** [Urdu, ultimately from Arabic *kharafa* to gather]

Kharkov (*Russian* 'xarjkəf) *n* a city in the E Ukraine: capital of the Ukrainian Soviet Socialist Republic (1917–34); university (1805). Pop.: 1 555 000 (1996 est.).

Khartoum *or* **Khartum** (kɑː'tuːm) *n* the capital of the Sudan, at the junction of the Blue and the White Nile: with adjoining Khartoum North and Omdurman, the largest conurbation in the country; destroyed by the Mahdists in 1885 when General Gordon was killed; seat of the Anglo-Egyptian government of the Sudan until 1954, then capital of the new republic. Pop.: 924 505 (1993).

khat *or* **kat** (kæt, kɑːt) *n* **1** a white-flowered evergreen shrub, *Catha edulis,* of

Africa and Arabia, whose leaves have narcotic properties. **2** the leaves of this shrub, chewed or prepared as a drink. [C19: from Arabic *qāt*]

khayal (kəˈjɑːl) *n* a kind of Indian classical vocal music. [Urdu: literally: thought, imagination]

Khayyám (kaɪˈɑːm) *n* **Omar.** See **Omar Khayyám.**

khazi (ˈkɑːzɪ) *n Slang.* a lavatory; toilet. [C19: from *casa, case* a brothel, from Italian *casa* a house; modern spelling probably influenced by KHAKI]

kheda, khedah, *or* **keddah** (ˈkɛdə) *n* (in India, Myanmar, etc.) an enclosure into which wild elephants are driven to be captured. [from Hindi]

khedive (kɪˈdiːv) *n* the viceroy of Egypt under Ottoman suzerainty (1867–1914). [C19: from French *khédive,* from Turkish *hidiv,* from Persian *khidīw* prince] ▸ **kheˈdival** *or* **kheˈdivial** *adj* ▸ **kheˈdivate** *or* **kheˈdiviate** *n*

Khelat (kəˈlɑːt) *n* a variant spelling of **Kalat.**

Kherson (*Russian* xɪrˈsɔn) *n* a port in the S Ukraine on the Dnieper River near the Black Sea: shipyards. Pop.: 363 000 (1996 est.).

Khingan Mountains (ˈʃɪŋˈɑːn) *pl n* a mountain system of NE China, in W Manchuria. Highest peak: 2034 m (6673 ft.).

Khíos (ˈçɪɔs) *n* transliteration of the Modern Greek name for **Chios.**

Khirbet Qumran (ˈkɪəbɛt ˈkʊmrɑːn) *n* an archaeological site in NW Jordan, near the NW shore of the Dead Sea: includes the caves where the Dead Sea Scrolls were found.

Khiva (*Russian* xiˈva) *n* a former khanate of W Asia, on the Amu Darya River: divided between the former Uzbek and Turkmen Soviet Socialist Republics in 1924.

Khmer (kmɛə, kmɜː) *n* **1** a member of a people of Cambodia, noted for a civilization that flourished from about 800 A.D. to about 1370, remarkable for its architecture. **2** the language of this people, belonging to the Mon-Khmer family: the official language of Kampuchea. ◆ *adj* **3** of or relating to this people or their language. ▸ **ˈKhmerian** *adj*

Khmer Republic *n* the former official name (1970–76) of **Kampuchea.**

Khmer Rouge (ruːʒ) *n* the Kampuchean communist party, which seized power (1975) in a civil war: in exile since 1979, dispersed in 1999.

Khoikhoi (kɔɪˈkɔɪ *or* xɔɪˈxɔɪ) *n* **1** a member of a race of people of Southern Africa, of short stature and a dark yellowish-brown complexion, who formerly occupied the region near the Cape of Good Hope and are now almost extinct. **2** any of the languages of this people, belonging to the Khoisan family.

Khoisan (ˈkɔɪsɑːn, kɔɪˈsɑːn) *n* **1** a family of languages spoken in southern Africa by the Khoikhoi and Bushmen and by two small groups in Tanzania. A characteristic phonological feature of these languages is the use of suction stops (clicks). ◆ *adj* **2** denoting, relating to, or belonging to this family of languages.

Khojent, Khodzhent (*Russian* xadˈʒɛnt) *or* **Khujand** (*Russian* xuˈjænd) *n* a town in Tajikistan on the Syr Darya River: one of the oldest towns in central Asia; textile industries. Pop.: 164 500 (1991 est.). Former name (1936–91): **Leninabad.**

Khomeini (ˈxɔmeɪniː) *n* **Ruholla** (ˈruhɒˈlɑː), known as *Ayatollah Khomeini.* 1900–89, Iranian Shiite Muslim religious and political leader. Following the overthrow of the shah of Iran (1979) he returned from exile and instituted an Islamic republic. His rule saw deteriorating relations with the West and war (1980–88) with Iraq.

Khotan (ˈkəʊˈtɑːn) *n* another name for **Hotan.**

Khrushchev (kruːsˈtʃɒf, ˈkrʊstʃɒf; *Russian* xruˈʃtʃɔf) *n* **Nikita Sergeyevich** (niˈkitə sɪrˈgjejɪvitʃ). 1894–1971, Soviet statesman; premier of the Soviet Union (1958–64). After Stalin's death he became first secretary of the Soviet Communist Party (1953–64) and initiated a policy to remove the influence of Stalin (1956). As premier, he pursued a policy of peaceful coexistence with the West, but alienated Communist China.

Khufu (ˈkuːfuː) *n* the original name of **Cheops.**

Khujand (*Russian* xuˈjænd) *n* a variant spelling of **Khojent.**

Khulna (ˈkʊlnɑː) *n* a city in S Bangladesh. Pop.: 731 000 (1991).

khurta (ˈkʊətə) *n* a variant spelling of **kurta.**

khuskhus (ˈkʊskʊs) *n* an aromatic perennial Indian grass, *Vetiveria zizanioides* (or *Andropogon squarrosus*), whose roots are woven into mats, fans, and baskets. [Hindi]

Khyber Pass (ˈkaɪbə) *n* a narrow pass over the Safed Koh Range between Afghanistan and Pakistan, over which came the Persian, Greek, Tatar, Mogul, and Afghan invasions of India; scene of bitter fighting between the British and Afghans (1838–42, 1878–80). Length: about 53 km (33 miles). Highest point: 1072 m (3518 ft.).

kHz *symbol for* kilohertz.

kiaat (ˈkiːɑːt) *n* **1** a tropical African leguminous tree, *Pterocarpus angolensis.* **2** the wood of this tree, used for furniture, floors, etc. [C19: Afrikaans, from Dutch, probably from Malay *kaju* wood]

kiang (kɪˈæŋ) *n* a variety of the wild ass, *Equus hemionus,* that occurs in Tibet and surrounding regions. Compare **onager.** [C19: from Tibetan *rkyan*]

Kiangsi (ˈkjæŋˈsiː) *n* a variant transliteration of the Chinese name for **Jiangxi.**

Kiangsu (ˈkjæŋˈsuː) *n* a variant transliteration of the Chinese name for **Jiangsu.**

Kiaochow (ˈkjaʊˈtʃaʊ) *n* a variant transliteration of the Chinese name for **Jiazhou.**

kia ora (ˌkɪə ˈɔːrə) *sentence substitute. N.Z.* greetings! good luck! [Maori, literally: be well!]

kibble[1] (ˈkɪbᵊl) *n Brit.* a bucket used in wells or in mining for hoisting. [C17: from German *kübel;* related to Old English *cyfel,* ultimately from Medieval Latin *cuppa* CUP]

kibble[2] (ˈkɪbᵊl) *vb (tr)* to grind into small pieces. [C18: of unknown origin]

kibbutz (kɪˈbʊts) *n, pl* **kibbutzim** (ˌkɪbʊtˈsiːm). a collective agricultural settlement in modern Israel, owned and administered communally by its members and on which children are reared collectively. [C20: from Modern Hebrew *qibbūs:* gathering, from Hebrew *qibbūtz*]

kibe (kaɪb) *n* a chilblain, esp. an ulcerated one on the heel. [C14: probably from Welsh *cibi,* of obscure origin]

kibitka (kɪˈbɪtkə) *n* **1** (in Russia) a covered sledge or wagon. **2** a felt tent used among the Tatars of central Asia. **3** a Tatar family. [C18: Russian, from Tatar *kibits*]

kibitz (ˈkɪbɪts) *vb (intr) U.S. and Canadian informal.* to interfere or offer unwanted advice, esp. as a spectator at a card game. [C20: from Yiddish *kibitzen,* from German *kiebitzen* to be an onlooker, from *Kiebitz* busybody, literally: plover] ▸ **ˈkibitzer** *n*

kiblah *or* **kibla** (ˈkɪblɑː) *n Islam.* the direction of Mecca, to which Muslims turn in prayer, indicated in mosques by a niche (mihrab) in the wall. [C18: from Arabic *qiblah* that which is placed opposite; related to *qabala* to be opposite]

kibosh (ˈkaɪˌbɒʃ) *Slang.* ◆ *n* **1 put the kibosh on.** to put a stop to; prevent from continuing; halt. ◆ *vb* **2** *(tr) Rare.* to put a stop to. [C19: of unknown origin]

kick (kɪk) *vb* **1** *(tr)* to drive or impel with the foot. **2** *(tr)* to hit with the foot or feet. **3** *(intr)* to strike out or thrash about with the feet, as in fighting or swimming. **4** *(intr)* to raise a leg high, as in dancing. **5** (of a gun, etc.) to recoil or strike in recoiling when fired. **6** *(tr) Rugby.* **6a** to make (a conversion or a drop goal) by means of a kick. **6b** to score (a goal) by means of a kicked conversion. **7** *(tr) Soccer.* to score (a goal) by a kick. **8** *(intr) Cricket.* (of a ball) to rear up sharply. **9** *(intr; sometimes foll. by against) Informal.* to object or resist. **10** *(intr) Informal.* to be active and in good health (esp. in the phrase **alive and kicking**). **11** *Informal.* to change gear in (a car, esp. a racing car): *he kicked into third and passed the bigger car.* **12** *(tr) Informal.* to free oneself of (an addiction, etc.): *to kick heroin; to kick the habit.* **13 kick against the pricks.** See **prick** (sense 20). **14 kick into touch. 14a** *Rugby, soccer.* to kick the ball out of the playing area and into touch. See **touch** (sense 15). **14b** *Informal.* to take some temporizing action so that a problem is shelved or a decision postponed. **15 kick one's heels.** to wait or be kept waiting. **16 kick over the traces.** See **trace**[2] (sense 3). **17 kick the bucket.** *Slang.* to die. **18 kick up one's heels.** *Informal.* to enjoy oneself without inhibition. ◆ *n* **19** a thrust or blow with the foot. **20** any of certain rhythmic leg movements used in swimming. **21** the recoil of a gun or other firearm. **22** *Informal.* a stimulating or exciting quality or effect (esp. in the phrases **get a kick out of** or **for kicks**). **23** *Informal.* the sudden stimulating or intoxicating effect of strong alcoholic drink or certain drugs. **24** *Informal.* power or force. **25** *Slang.* a temporary enthusiasm: *he's on a new kick every week.* **26 kick in the pants.** *Slang.* **26a** a reprimand or scolding designed to produce greater effort, enthusiasm, etc., in the person receiving it. **26b** a setback or disappointment. **27 kick in the teeth.** *Slang.* a humiliating rebuff. ◆ See also **kick about, kickback, kick in, kick off, kick out, kick up, kick upstairs.** [C14 *kiken,* perhaps of Scandinavian origin] ▸ **ˈkickable** *adj*

kick about *or* **around** *vb (mainly adv) Informal.* **1** *(tr)* to treat harshly. **2** *(tr)* to discuss (ideas, etc.) informally. **3** *(intr)* to wander aimlessly. **4** *(intr)* to lie neglected or forgotten. **5** *(intr; also prep)* to be present in (some place).

kickback (ˈkɪkˌbæk) *n* **1** a strong reaction. **2** part of an income paid to a person having influence over the size or payment of the income, esp. by some illegal arrangement. ◆ *vb* **kick back.** *(adv)* **3** *(intr)* to have a strong reaction. **4** *(intr)* (esp. of a gun) to recoil. **5** to pay a kickback to (someone).

kick boxing *n* a martial art that resembles boxing but permits blows with the feet as well as punches.

kickdown (ˈkɪkˌdaʊn) *n* a method of changing gear in a car with automatic transmission, by fully depressing the accelerator.

kicker (ˈkɪkə) *n* **1** a person or thing that kicks. **2** *Sport.* a player in a rugby or occasionally a soccer team whose task is to attempt to kick conversions, penalty goals, etc. **3** *U.S. and Canadian slang.* a hidden and disadvantageous factor, such as a clause in a contract. **4** *Informal.* any light outboard motor for propelling a boat.

kick in *vb (adv)* **1** *(intr)* to start or become activated. **2** *(tr) Chiefly Austral. and N.Z. informal.* to contribute.

kick off *vb (intr, adv)* **1** to start play in a game of football by kicking the ball from the centre of the field. **2** *Informal.* to commence a discussion, job, etc. ◆ *n* **kickoff. 3a** a place kick from the centre of the field in a game of football. **3b** the time at which the first such kick is due to take place: *kickoff is at 2.30 p.m.* **4** *Informal.* **4a** the beginning of something. **4b for a kickoff.** to begin with.

kick on *vb (adv) Informal.* to continue.

kick out *vb (tr, adv) Informal.* to eject or dismiss.

kick pleat *n* a back pleat at the hem of a straight skirt to allow the wearer greater ease in walking.

kickshaw (ˈkɪkˌʃɔː) *or* **kickshaws** *n* **1** a valueless trinket. **2** *Archaic.* a small elaborate or exotic delicacy. [C16: back formation from *kickshaws,* by folk etymology from French *quelque chose* something]

kicksorter (ˈkɪkˌsɔːtə) *n Physics.* a multichannel pulse-height analyser used esp. to distinguish between isotopes by sorting their characteristic pulses (kicks).

kickstand (ˈkɪkˌstænd) *n* a short metal bar attached to and pivoting on the bottom of the frame of a motorcycle or bicycle, which when kicked into a vertical position holds the stationary vehicle upright.

kick-start (ˈkɪkˌstɑːt) *vb (tr)* **1** to start (a motorcycle engine) by means of a pedal that is kicked downwards. **2** *Informal.* to make (something) active, functional, or productive again. ◆ *n* **3** an action or event resulting in the reactivation of something. ▸ **ˈkick-ˌstarter** *n*

kick turn *n Skiing.* a standing turn performed by swivelling each ski separately through 180°.

kick up *vb (adv)* **1** *Informal.* to cause (trouble, a fuss, etc.). **2 kick up bobsy-die.** See **bobsy-die.**

kick upstairs *vb (tr, adv) Informal.* to promote to a nominally higher but effectively powerless position.

kid[1] (kɪd) *n* **1** the young of a goat or of a related animal, such as an antelope. **2** soft smooth leather made from the hide of a kid. **3** *Informal.* **3a** a young person; child. **3b** *(modifier)* younger or being still a child: *kid brother; kid sister.* **4** **our kid.** *Liverpool dialect.* my younger brother or sister. ◆ *vb* **kids, kidding, kidded. 5** (of a goat) to give birth to (young). [C12: of Scandinavian origin; compare Old Norse *kith,* Shetland Islands *kidi* lamb] ▸ **'kiddishness** *n* ▸ **'kid,like** *adj*

kid[2] (kɪd) *vb* **kids, kidding, kidded.** (sometimes foll. by *on* or *along*) *Informal.* **1** *(tr)* to tease or deceive for fun. **2** *(intr)* to behave or speak deceptively for fun. **3** *(tr)* to delude or fool (oneself) into believing (something): *don't kid yourself that no-one else knows.* [C19: probably from KID[1]] ▸ **'kidder** *n* ▸ **'kiddingly** *adv*

kid[3] (kɪd) *n* a small wooden tub. [C18: probably variant of KIT[1] (in the sense: barrel)]

Kid (kɪd) *n* **Thomas.** a variant spelling of (Thomas) **Kyd.**

Kidd (kɪd) *n* **William,** known as *Captain Kidd.* 1645–1701, Scottish privateer, pirate, and murderer; hanged.

Kidderminster ('kɪdə,mɪnstə) *n* **1** a town in W central England, in N Worcestershire on the River Stour: carpet industry. Pop.: 54 644 (1991 est.). **2** a type of ingrain reversible carpet originally made at Kidderminster.

kiddle ('kɪdᵊl) *n Brit., archaic.* a device, esp. a barrier constructed of nets and stakes, for catching fish in a river or in the sea. [C13: from Anglo-French, from Old French *quidel,* of obscure origin]

Kiddush ('kɪdəʃ; *Hebrew* kɪ'duʃ) *n Judaism.* **1** a special blessing said before a meal on sabbaths and festivals, usually including the blessing for wine or bread. **2** a reception usually for the congregants after a service at which drinks and snacks are served and this grace is said. [from Hebrew *qiddūsh* sanctification]

kiddy *or* **kiddie** ('kɪdɪ) *n, pl* **-dies.** *Informal.* an affectionate word for **child.**

kid glove *n* **1** a glove made of kidskin. **2 handle with kid gloves.** to treat with great tact or caution. ◆ *adj* **kidglove. 3** overdelicate or overrefined. **4** diplomatic; tactful: *a kidglove approach.*

kidnap ('kɪdnæp) *vb* **-naps, -napping, -napped** *or U.S.* **-naps, -naping, -naped.** *(tr)* to carry off and hold (a person), usually for ransom. [C17: KID[1] + obsolete *nap* to steal; see NAB] ▸ **'kidnapper** *n* ▸ **'kidnapping** *or U.S.* **'kidnaping** *n*

kidney ('kɪdnɪ) *n* **1** either of two bean-shaped organs at the back of the abdominal cavity in man, one on each side of the spinal column. They maintain water and electrolyte balance and filter waste products from the blood, which are excreted as urine. Related adjs.: **nephritic, renal. 2** the corresponding organ in other animals. **3** the kidneys of certain animals used as food. **4** class, type, or disposition (esp. in the phrases **of the same** or **a different kidney**). [C14: of uncertain origin] ▸ **'kidney,like** *adj*

kidney bean *n* **1** any of certain bean plants having kidney-shaped seeds, esp. the French bean and scarlet runner. **2** the seed of any of these beans.

kidney machine *n* another name for **artificial kidney.** See **haemodialysis.**

kidney ore *n Geology.* a form of hematite that occurs in kidney-shaped masses.

kidney-shaped *adj* shaped like an oval with an inward curve at one side.

kidney stone *n* **1** *Pathol.* a hard mass formed in the kidney, usually composed of oxalates, phosphates, and carbonates. Also called: **renal calculus. 2** *Mineralogy.* another name for **nephrite.**

kidney vetch *n* a silky papilionaceous perennial plant, *Anthyllis vulneraria,* of Europe and N Africa, with yellow or orange flowers. Also called: **ladies' fingers.**

kidology (kɪ'dɒlədʒɪ) *n Brit. informal.* the art or practice of bluffing or deception. [C20: from KID[2] + -OLOGY]

Kidron ('kiːdrən) *n* a variant of **Kedron.**

kidskin ('kɪd,skɪn) *n* a soft smooth leather made from the hide of a young goat. Often shortened to **kid.**

kids' stuff *n Slang.* **1** something considered fit only for children. **2** something considered simple or easy.

kidstakes ('kɪd,steɪks) *pl n Austral. informal.* pretence; nonsense: *cut the kidstakes!*

kief (kiːf) *n* a variant spelling of **kif.**

kiekie ('kɪə,kɪə, 'kiː,kiː) *n* a climbing bush plant, *Freycinetia banksii,* of New Zealand, having elongated leaves and edible berries. [Maori]

Kiel (kiːl) *n* a port in N Germany, capital of Schleswig-Holstein state, on the **Kiel Canal** (connecting the North Sea with the Baltic): joined the Hanseatic League in 1284; became part of Denmark in 1773 and passed to Prussia in 1866; an important naval base in World Wars I and II; shipbuilding and engineering industries. Pop.: 246 033 (1996 est.).

Kielce (*Polish* 'kjɛltsɛ) *n* an industrial city in S Poland. Pop.: 213 700 (1996 est.).

kier (kɪə) *n* a vat in which cloth is bleached. [C16: from Old Norse *ker* tub; related to Old High German *kar*]

Kierkegaard ('kɪəkə,gɑːd; *Danish* 'kirgəgɔːr) *n* **Søren Aabye** ('søːrən 'ɔːby). 1813–55, Danish philosopher and theologian. He rejected organized Christianity and anticipated the existentialists in emphasizing man's moral responsibility and freedom of choice. His works include *Either/Or* (1843), *The Concept of Dread* (1844), and *The Sickness unto Death* (1849). ▸ **,Kierke'gaardian** *adj*

kieselguhr ('kiːzᵊl,guə) *n* an unconsolidated form of **diatomite.** [C19: from German *Kieselgur,* from *Kiesel* flint, pebble + *Gur* loose earthy deposit]

kieserite ('kiːzə,raɪt) *n* a white mineral consisting of hydrated magnesium sulphate. Formula: $MgSO_4.H_2O$. [C19: named after Dietrich G. *Kieser* (died 1862), German physician; see -ITE[1]]

Kiev ('kiːæf; *Russian* 'kijɪf) *n* the capital of the Ukraine, on the Dnieper River: formed the first Russian state by the late 9th century; university (1834). Pop.: 2 630 000 (1996 est.).

kif (kɪf, kiːf), **kaif, keef, kef,** *or* **kief** *n* **1** another name for **marijuana. 2** any drug or agent that when smoked is capable of producing a euphoric condition. **3** the euphoric condition produced by smoking marijuana. [C20: from Arabic *kayf* pleasure]

Kigali (kɪ'gɑːlɪ) *n* the capital of Rwanda, in the central part. Pop.: 232 733 (1991).

Kigoma-Ujiji (kɪ'gəʊmə uː'dʒiːdʒɪ) *n* a city in W Tanzania, on the shore of Lake Tanganyika; formed by the merger of the towns of Kigoma and Ujiji in the 1960s.

kike (kaɪk) *n U.S. and Canadian slang.* an offensive word for **Jew.** [C20: probably variant of *kiki,* reduplication of *-ki,* common name-ending among Jews from Slavic countries]

Kikládhes (ki'klaðɛs) *n* transliteration of the Modern Greek name for **Cyclades.**

kikoi ('kiːkɔɪ) *n* (in E Africa) **a** a piece of cotton cloth with coloured bands, worn wrapped around the body. **b** *(as modifier): kikoi material.* [C20: from Swahili]

kikumon ('kɪkuː,mɒn) *n* the chrysanthemum emblem of the imperial family of Japan. [Japanese]

Kikuyu (kɪ'kuːjuː) *n* **1** *(pl* **-yus** *or* **-yu)** a member of a Negroid people of E Africa, living chiefly in Kenya on the high foothills around Mount Kenya. **2** the language of this people, belonging to the Bantu group of the Niger-Congo family.

Kilauea (,kiːlɑːuː'eɪə) *n* a crater on the E side of Mauna Loa volcano, on SE Hawaii Island: the world's largest active crater. Height: 1247 m (4090 ft.). Width: 3 km (2 miles).

Kildare (kɪl'dɛə) *n* a county of E Republic of Ireland, in Leinster province: mostly low-lying and fertile. County town: Naas. Pop.: 135 000 (1996). Area: 1694 sq. km (654 sq. miles).

kilderkin ('kɪldəkɪn) *n* **1** an obsolete unit of liquid capacity equal to 16 or 18 Imperial gallons or of dry capacity equal to 16 or 18 wine gallons. **2** a cask capable of holding a kilderkin. [C14: from Middle Dutch *kindekijn,* from *kintal* hundredweight, from Medieval Latin *quintale;* see KENTLEDGE]

kiley ('kaɪlɪ) *n* a variant spelling of **kylie.**

kilim (kɪ'lim, 'kiːlɪm) *n* a pileless woven rug of intricate design made in the Middle East. [C19: from Turkish, from Persian *kilīm*]

Kilimanjaro (,kɪlɪmən'dʒɑːrəʊ) *n* a volcanic massif in N Tanzania: the highest peak in Africa; extends from east to west for 80 km (50 miles). Height: 5895 m (19 340 ft.).

Kilkenny (kɪl'kɛnɪ) *n* **1** a county of SE Republic of Ireland, in Leinster province: mostly agricultural. County town: Kilkenny. Pop.: 75 000 (1996). Area: 2062 sq. km (796 sq. miles). **2** a market town in SE Republic of Ireland, county town of Co. Kilkenny: capital of the ancient kingdom of Ossory. Pop.: 9500 (latest est.).

kill[1] (kɪl) *vb (mainly tr)* **1** *(also intr;* when *tr,* sometimes foll. by *off)* to cause the death of (a person or animal). **2** to put an end to; destroy: *to kill someone's interest.* **3** to make (time) pass quickly, esp. while waiting for something. **4** to deaden (sound). **5** *Informal.* to tire out; exhaust: *the effort killed him.* **6** *Informal.* to cause to suffer pain or discomfort: *my shoes are killing me.* **7** *Informal.* to cancel, cut, or delete: *to kill three lines of text.* **8** *Informal.* to quash, defeat, or veto: *the bill was killed in the House of Lords.* **9** *Informal.* to switch off; stop: *to kill a motor.* **10** *(also intr) Informal.* to overcome with attraction, laughter, surprise, etc.: *she was dressed to kill; his gags kill me.* **11** *Slang.* to consume (alcoholic drink) entirely: *he killed three bottles of rum.* **12** *Tennis, squash, etc.* to hit (a ball) so hard or so accurately that the opponent cannot return it. **13** *Soccer.* to bring (a moving ball) under control; trap. **14 kill oneself.** *Informal.* to overexert oneself: *don't kill yourself.* **15 kill two birds with one stone.** to achieve two results with one action. ◆ *n* **16** the act of causing death, esp. at the end of a hunt, bullfight, etc. **17** the animal or animals killed during a hunt. **18** *N.Z.* the seasonal tally of stock slaughtered at a freezing works. **19** the destruction of a battleship, tank, etc. **20 in at the kill.** present at the end or climax of some undertaking. [C13 *cullen;* perhaps related to Old English *cwellan* to kill; compare German (Westphalian dialect) *küllen;* see QUELL]

kill[2] (kɪl) *n U.S.* a channel, stream, or river (chiefly as part of place names). [C17: from Middle Dutch *kille;* compare Old Norse *kīll* small bay, creek]

Killarney (kɪ'lɑːnɪ) *n* a town in SW Republic of Ireland, in Co. Kerry: a tourist centre near the **Lakes of Killarney.** Pop.: 7250 (1991).

killdeer ('kɪl,dɪə) *n, pl* **-deer** *or* **-deers.** a large brown-and-white North American plover, *Charadrius vociferus,* with two black breast bands and a noisy cry. [C18: of imitative origin]

killer ('kɪlə) *n* **1a** a person or animal that kills, esp. habitually. **1b** *(as modifier): a killer shark.* **2** something, esp. a task or activity, that is particularly taxing or exhausting. **3** *Austral. and N.Z.* an animal selected to be slaughtered for food.

killer bee *n* an African honeybee, or one of its hybrids originating in Brazil, that is extremely aggressive when disturbed.

killer cell *n* a type of white blood cell that is able to kill cells, such as cancer cells and cells infected with viruses.

killer whale *n* a predatory black-and-white toothed whale, *Orcinus orca,* with a large erect dorsal fin, most common in cold seas: family *Delphinidae.* Also called: **killer, grampus, orc.**

killick ('kɪlɪk) *or* **killock** ('kɪlək) *n Nautical.* a small anchor, esp. one made of a heavy stone. [C17: of unknown origin]

Killiecrankie (,kɪlɪ'kræŋkɪ) *n* a pass in central Scotland, in the Grampians: scene of a battle (1689) in which the Jacobites defeated William III's forces but lost their leader, Viscount Dundee.

killifish ('kɪlɪ,fɪʃ) *n, pl* **-fish** *or* **-fishes.** any of various chiefly American minnow-like cyprinodont fishes of the genus *Fundulus* and related genera, of fresh and brackish waters: used as aquarium fishes, to control mosquitoes, and as anglers' bait. [C19: see KILL[2], FISH]

killikinick (,kɪlɪkɪ'nɪk) *n* a variant of **kinnikinnick.**

killing ('kɪlɪŋ) *Informal.* ◆ *adj* **1** very tiring; exhausting: *a killing pace.* **2** extremely funny; hilarious. **3** causing death; fatal. ◆ *n* **4** the act of causing death; slaying. **5** a sudden stroke of success, usually financial, as in speculations on the stock market (esp. in the phrase **make a killing**). ► **'killingly** *adv*

killjoy ('kɪlˌdʒɔɪ) *n* a person who spoils other people's pleasure.

kill-time *n* **a** an occupation that passes the time. **b** (*as modifier*): *kill-time pursuits.*

Kilmarnock (kɪl'mɑːnək) *n* a town in SW Scotland, the administrative centre of East Ayrshire: associations with Robert Burns; engineering and textile industries; whisky blending. Pop.: 44 307 (1991).

kiln (kɪln) *n* **1** a large oven for burning, drying, or processing something, such as porcelain or bricks. ◆ *vb* **2** (*tr*) to fire or process in a kiln. [Old English *cylen,* from Late Latin *culīna* kitchen, from Latin *coquere* to COOK]

Kilner jar ('kɪlnə) *n Trademark.* a glass preserving jar with an airtight lid, used for bottling fruit or vegetables.

kilo[1] ('kiːləʊ) *n, pl* **kilos.** short for **kilogram** *or* **kilometre.**

kilo[2] ('kiːləʊ) *n Communications.* a code word for the letter *k.*

kilo- *prefix* **1** denoting 10^3 (1000): *kilometre.* Symbol: k **2** (in computer technology) denoting 2^{10} (1024): *kilobyte:* in computer usage, *kilo-* is restricted to sizes of storage (e.g. *kilobit*) when it means 1024; in other computer contexts it retains its usual meaning of 1000. [from French, from Greek *khilioi* thousand]

kilobyte ('kɪləˌbaɪt) *n Computing.* 1024 bytes. Abbrevs.: **KB, kbyte.** See also kilo- (sense 2).

kilocalorie ('kɪləʊˌkælərɪ) *n* another name for **Calorie.**

kilocycle ('kɪləʊˌsaɪkəl) *n* short for kilocycle per second: a former unit of frequency equal to 1 kilohertz.

kilogram ('kɪləʊˌgræm) *n* **1** one thousand grams. **2** the basic SI unit of mass, equal to the mass of the international prototype held by the *Bureau International des Poids et Mesures.* One kilogram is equivalent to 2.204 62 pounds. Symbol: kg

kilogram calorie *n* another name for **Calorie.**

kilohertz ('kɪləʊˌhɜːts) *n* one thousand hertz; one thousand cycles per second. Symbol: kHz

kilometre *or U.S.* **kilometer** ('kɪləˌmiːtə, kɪ'lɒmɪtə) *n* one thousand metres, equal to 0.621 371 miles. Symbol: km ► **kilometric** (ˌkɪləʊ'metrɪk) *or* **ˌkilo'metrical** *adj*

kiloton ('kɪləʊˌtʌn) *n* **1** one thousand tons. **2** an explosive power, esp. of a nuclear weapon, equal to the power of 1000 tons of TNT. Abbrev.: **kt.**

kilovolt ('kɪləʊˌvəʊlt) *n* one thousand volts. Symbol: kV

kilowatt ('kɪləʊˌwɒt) *n* one thousand watts. Symbol: kW

kilowatt-hour *n* a unit of energy equal to the work done by a power of 1000 watts in one hour. Symbol: kWh

kilt (kɪlt) *n* **1** a knee-length pleated skirt, esp. one in tartan, as worn by men in Highland dress. ◆ *vb* (*tr*) **2** to tuck (the skirt) up around one's body. **3** to put pleats in (cloth, a skirt, etc.). [C18: of Scandinavian origin; compare Danish *kilte* to tuck up, Old Swedish *kilta* lap] ► **'kilted** *adj* ► **'kiltˌlike** *adj*

kilter ('kɪltə) *or* **kelter** *n* working order or alignment (esp. in the phrases **off kilter, out of kilter**). [C17: origin unknown]

Kilung ('kiː'lʊŋ) *n* another name for **Chilung.**

Kilvert ('kɪlvət) *n* **Francis.** 1840–79, British clergyman and diarist. His diary (published 1938–40) gives a vivid account of life in the Welsh Marches in the 1870s.

Kimberley ('kɪmbəlɪ) *n* **1** a city in central South Africa, in Northern Cape province: besieged (1899–1900) for 126 days during the Boer War; diamond-mining and -marketing centre, with heavy engineering works. Pop.: 183 000 (1995 est.). **2** Also called: **the Kimberleys.** a plateau region of NW Australia, in N Western Australia: consists of rugged mountains surrounded by grassland. Area: about 360 000 sq. km (140 000 sq. miles).

kimberlite ('kɪmbəˌlaɪt) *n* an intrusive igneous rock consisting largely of peridotite and often containing diamonds. [C19: from KIMBERLEY + -ITE[1]]

Kim Il Sung (kim il sʌŋ) *n* 1912–94, North Korean statesman and marshal; prime minister (1948–72) and president (1972–94) of North Korea.

kimono (kɪ'məʊnəʊ) *n, pl* **-nos.** **1** a loose sashed ankle-length garment with wide sleeves, worn in Japan. **2** any garment copied from this. [C19: from Japanese: clothing, from *kiru* to wear + *mono* thing] ► **ki'monoed** *adj*

kin (kɪn) *n* **1** a person's relatives collectively; kindred. **2** a class or group with similar characteristics. **3** See **next of kin.** ◆ *adj* **4** (*postpositive*) related by blood. **5** a less common word for **akin.** [Old English *cyn;* related to Old Norse *kyn* family, Old High German *kind* child, Latin *genus* kind]

-kin *suffix forming nouns.* small: *lambkin.* [from Middle Dutch, of West Germanic origin; compare German *-chen*]

kina ('kiːnə) *n* the standard monetary unit of Papua New Guinea, divided into 100 toeas. [from a Papuan language]

Kinabalu (ˌkɪnəbə'luː) *n* a mountain in Malaysia, on N Borneo in central Sabah: the highest peak in Borneo. Height: 4125 m (13 533 ft.).

kinaesthesia (ˌkɪnɪs'θiːzɪə, ˌkaɪn-), **kinaesthesis** *or U.S.* **kinesthesia, kinesthesis** *n* the sensation by which bodily position, weight, muscle tension, and movement are perceived. Also called: **muscle sense.** [C19: from New Latin, from Greek *kinein* to move + AESTHESIA] ► **kinaesthetic** *or U.S.* **kinesthetic** (ˌkɪnɪs'θetɪk, ˌkaɪn-) *adj*

kinase ('kaɪneɪz, 'kɪn-) *n* **1** any enzyme that can convert an inactive zymogen to the corresponding enzyme. **2** any enzyme that brings about the phosphorylation of a molecule. [C20: from KIN(ETIC) + -ASE]

Kincardineshire (kɪn'kɑːdɪnˌʃɪə, -ʃə) *n* a former county of E Scotland: became part of Grampian region in 1975 and part of Aberdeenshire in 1996. Also called: **the Mearns.**

Kinchinjunga (ˌkɪntʃɪn'dʒʌŋgə) *n* a variant of **Kangchenjunga.**

kincob ('kɪŋkɒb) *n* a fine silk fabric embroidered with threads of gold or silver, of a kind made in India. [C18: from Urdu *kimkhāb*]

kind[1] (kaɪnd) *adj* **1** having a friendly or generous nature or attitude. **2** helpful to others or to another: *a kind deed.* **3** considerate or humane. **4** cordial; courteous (esp. in the phrase **kind regards**). **5** pleasant; agreeable; mild: *a kind climate.* **6** *Informal.* beneficial or not harmful: *a detergent that is kind to the hands.* **7** *Archaic.* loving. [Old English *gecynde* natural, native; see KIND[2]]

kind[2] (kaɪnd) *n* **1** a class or group having characteristics in common; sort; type: *two of a kind; what kind of creature?* **2** an instance or example of a class or group, esp. a rudimentary one: *heating of a kind.* **3** essential nature or character: *the difference is one of kind rather than degree.* **4** *Archaic.* gender or sex. **5** *Archaic.* nature; the natural order. **6 in kind. 6a** (of payment) in goods or produce rather than in money. **6b** with something of the same sort: *to return an insult in kind.* **7 kind of.** (*adv*) *Informal.* somewhat; rather: *kind of tired.* [Old English *gecynd* nature; compare Old English *cyn* KIN, Gothic *kuni* race, Old High German *kikunt,* Latin *gens*]

USAGE The mixture of plural and singular constructions, although often used informally with *kind* and *sort*, should be avoided in serious writing: *children enjoy those kinds* (not *those kind*) *of stories; these sorts* (not *these sort*) *of distinctions are becoming blurred.*

kindergarten ('kɪndəˌgɑːtən) *n* a class or small school for young children, usually between the ages of four and six to prepare them for primary education. Often shortened (in Australia) to **kinder** or (in Australia and New Zealand) to **kindy** or **kindie.** [C19: from German, literally: children's garden] ► **'kinderˌgartener** *n*

kind-hearted *adj* characterized by kindness; sympathetic. ► **ˌkind-'heartedly** *adv* ► **ˌkind-'heartedness** *n*

kindle ('kɪndəl) *vb* **1** to set alight or start to burn. **2** to arouse or be aroused: *the project kindled his interest.* **3** to make or become bright. [C12: from Old Norse *kynda,* influenced by Old Norse *kyndill* candle] ► **'kindler** *n*

kindless ('kaɪndlɪs) *adj Archaic.* **1** heartless. **2** against nature; unnatural. ► **'kindlessly** *adv*

kindling ('kɪndlɪŋ) *n* material for starting a fire, such as dry wood, straw, etc.

kindly ('kaɪndlɪ) *adj* **-lier, -liest.** **1** having a sympathetic or warm-hearted nature. **2** motivated by warm and sympathetic feelings: *a kindly act.* **3** pleasant, mild, or agreeable: *a kindly climate.* **4** *Archaic.* natural; normal. ◆ *adv* **5** in a considerate or humane way. **6** with tolerance or forbearance: *he kindly forgave my rudeness.* **7** cordially; pleasantly: *he greeted us kindly.* **8** please (often used to express impatience or formality): *will you kindly behave yourself!* **9** *Archaic.* in accordance with nature; appropriately. **10 take kindly.** to react favourably. ► **'kindliness** *n*

kindness ('kaɪndnɪs) *n* **1** the practice or quality of being kind. **2** a kind, considerate, or helpful act.

kindred ('kɪndrɪd) *adj* **1** having similar or common qualities, origin, etc. **2** related by blood or marriage. **3 kindred spirit.** a person with whom one has something in common. ◆ *n* **4** relationship by blood. **5** similarity in character. **6** a person's relatives collectively. [C12 *kinred,* from KIN + *-red,* from Old English *rǣden* rule, from *rǣdan* to rule] ► **'kindredness** *or* **'kindredˌship** *n*

kindy *or* **kindie** ('kɪndɪ) *n Austral. and N.Z. informal.* short for **kindergarten.**

kine (kaɪn) *n* (*functioning as pl*) an archaic word for **cows** or **cattle.** [Old English *cȳna* of cows, from *cū* COW[1]]

kinematics (ˌkɪnɪ'mætɪks, ˌkaɪ-) *n* (*functioning as sing*) the study of the motion of bodies without reference to mass or force. Compare **dynamics** (sense 1). [C19: from Greek *kinēma* movement; see CINEMA, -ICS] ► **ˌkine'matic** *adj* ► **ˌkine'matically** *adv*

kinematic viscosity *n* a measure of the resistance to flow of a fluid, equal to its absolute viscosity divided by its density. Symbol: ν

kinematograph (ˌkɪnɪ'mætəˌgrɑːf, ˌkaɪnɪ-, -ˌgræf) *n* a variant of **cinematograph.** ► **kinematographer** (ˌkɪnəmə'tɒgrəfə) *n* ► **kinematographic** (ˌkɪnɪˌmætə'græfɪk, ˌkaɪnɪ-) *adj* ► **ˌkinema'tography** *n*

kinescope ('kɪnəskəʊp) *n* the U.S. name for **television tube.**

kinesics (kɪ'niːsɪks) *n* (*functioning as sing*) the study of the role of body movements, such as winking, shrugging, etc., in communication.

kinesiology (kɪˌniːsɪ'ɒlədʒɪ) *n* the study of the mechanics and anatomy of human muscles.

kinesis (kɪ'niːsɪs, kaɪ-) *n Biology.* the nondirectional movement of an organism or cell in response to a stimulus, the rate of movement being dependent on the strength of the stimulus.

kinesthesia (ˌkɪnɪs'θiːzɪə, ˌkaɪn-) *or* **kinesthesis** *n* the usual U.S. spelling of **kinaesthesia.**

kinetheodolite (ˌkɪnəθɪ'ɒdəˌlaɪt) *n* a type of theodolite containing a cine camera instead of a telescope and giving continuous film of a moving target together with a record of its altitude and azimuth: used in tracking a missile, satellite, etc.

kinetic (kɪ'netɪk, kaɪ-) *adj* relating to, characterized by, or caused by motion. [C19: from Greek *kinētikos,* from *kinein* to move] ► **ki'netically** *adv*

kinetic art *n* art, esp. sculpture, that moves or has moving parts.

kinetic energy *n* the energy of motion of a body, equal to the work it would do if it were brought to rest. The **translational kinetic energy** depends on motion through space, and for a rigid body of constant mass is equal to the product of half the mass times the square of the speed. The **rotational kinetic energy** depends on rotation about an axis, and for a body of constant moment of inertia is equal to the product of half the moment of inertia times the square of the angular velocity. In relativistic physics kinetic energy is equal to the product of the increase of mass caused by motion times the square of the speed of light. The SI unit is the joule but the electronvolt is often used in atomic physics. Symbol: E_k, K, or T Abbrev.: **KE.**

kinetics (kɪˈnɛtɪks, kaɪ-) *n* (*functioning as sing*) **1** another name for **dynamics** (sense 2). **2** the branch of mechanics, including both dynamics and kinematics, concerned with the study of bodies in motion. **3** the branch of dynamics that excludes the study of bodies at rest. **4** the branch of chemistry concerned with the rates of chemical reactions.

kinetic theory *n* **the.** a theory of gases postulating that they consist of particles of negligible size moving at random and undergoing elastic collisions. In full: **Kinetic theory of gases.**

kinetoplast (kɪˈnɛtəˌplæst, -ˈniː-, -ˌplɑːst) *n* a small granular cell body close to the nucleus in some flagellate protozoans. Also called: **kinetonucleus** (kɪˌnɛtəʊˈnjuːklɪəs). [C20: from Greek; see KINETIC, -PLAST]

kinfolk (ˈkɪnˌfəʊk) *pl n Chiefly U.S. and Canadian.* another word for **kinsfolk.**

king (kɪŋ) *n* **1** a male sovereign prince who is the official ruler of an independent state; monarch. Related adjs.: **royal, regal, monarchical. 2a** a ruler or chief: *king of the fairies.* **2b** (*in combination*): *the pirate king.* **3a** a person, animal, or thing considered as the best or most important of its kind. **3b** (*as modifier*): *a king bull.* **4** any of four playing cards in a pack, one for each suit, bearing the picture of a king. **5** the most important chess piece, although theoretically the weakest, being able to move only one square at a time in any direction. See also **check** (sense 30), **checkmate. 6** *Draughts.* a piece that has moved entirely across the board and has been crowned, after which it may move backwards as well as forwards. **7 king of kings. 7a** God. **7b** a title of any of various oriental monarchs. ◆ *vb* (*tr*) **8** to make (someone) a king. **9 king it.** to act in a superior fashion. [Old English *cyning;* related to Old High German *kunig* king, Danish *konge*] ► **ˈkingˌhood** *n* ► **ˈkingless** *adj* ► **ˈkingˌlike** *adj*

King (kɪŋ) *n* **1 B.B.,** real name *Riley B. King.* born 1925, U.S. blues singer and guitarist. **2 Billie Jean** (née *Moffitt*). born 1943, U.S. tennis player: Wimbledon champion 1966–68, 1972–73, and 1975; U.S. champion 1967, 1971–72, and 1974. **3 Martin Luther.** 1929–68, U.S. Baptist minister and civil-rights leader. He advocated nonviolence in his campaigns against the segregation of Blacks in the South: assassinated: Nobel Peace Prize 1964. **4 William Lyon Mackenzie.** 1874–1950, Canadian Liberal statesman; prime minister (1921–26; 1926–30; 1935–48).

kingbird (ˈkɪŋˌbɜːd) *n* any of several large American flycatchers of the genus *Tyrannus,* esp. *T. tyrannus* (**eastern kingbird** *or* **bee martin**).

kingbolt (ˈkɪŋˌbəʊlt) *or* **king rod** *n* **a** the pivot bolt that connects the body of a horse-drawn carriage to the front axle and provides the steering joint. **b** a similar bolt placed between a railway carriage and the bogies.

King Charles spaniel *n* **1** a toy breed of spaniel with a short turned-up nose and a domed skull. **2 cavalier King Charles spaniel.** a similar breed that is slightly larger and has a longer nose. [C17: named after Charles II of England, who popularized the breed]

king cobra *n* a very large venomous tropical Asian elapid snake, *Ophiophagus hannah,* that feeds on snakes and other reptiles and extends its neck into a hood when alarmed. Also called: **hamadryad.**

King Country *n* **the.** an area in the centre of North Island, New Zealand: home of the King Movement, a nineteenth-century Maori separatist movement.

king crab *n* another name for the **horseshoe crab.**

kingcraft (ˈkɪŋˌkrɑːft) *n Archaic.* the art of ruling as a king, esp. by diplomacy and cunning.

kingcup (ˈkɪŋˌkʌp) *n Brit.* any of several yellow-flowered ranunculaceous plants, esp. the marsh marigold.

kingdom (ˈkɪŋdəm) *n* **1** a territory, state, people, or community ruled or reigned over by a king or queen. **2** any of the three groups into which natural objects may be divided: the animal, plant, and mineral kingdoms. **3** *Biology.* any of the major categories into which living organisms are classified. Modern systems recognize five kingdoms: *Prokaryotae* (bacteria), *Protoctista* (algae, protozoans, etc.), *Fungi, Plantae,* and *Animalia.* **4** *Theol.* the eternal sovereignty of God. **5** an area of activity, esp. mental activity, considered as being the province of something specified: *the kingdom of the mind.* ► **ˈkingdomless** *adj*

kingdom come *n* **1** the next world; life after death. **2** *Informal.* the end of the world (esp. in the phrase **until kingdom come**). **3** *Informal.* unconsciousness or death.

kingfish (ˈkɪŋˌfɪʃ) *n, pl* **-fish** *or* **-fishes. 1** any marine sciaenid food and game fish of the genus *Menticirrhus,* occurring in warm American Atlantic coastal waters. **2** another name for **opah** (the fish). **3** any of various other large food fishes, esp. the Spanish mackerel.

kingfisher (ˈkɪŋˌfɪʃə) *n* any coraciiform bird of the family *Alcedinidae,* esp. the Eurasian *Alcedo atthis,* which has a greenish-blue and orange plumage. Kingfishers have a large head, short tail, and long sharp bill and tend to live near open water and feed on fish. [C15: originally *king's fisher*]

king-hit *Austral. informal.* ◆ *n* **1** a knockout blow, esp. an unfair one. ◆ *vb* **-hits, -hitting, -hit.** (*tr*) **2** to deliver a knockout blow to.

King James Version *or* **Bible** *n* **the.** another name for the **Authorized Version.**

kingklip (ˈkɪŋˌklɪp) *n S. African.* an edible eel-like marine fish.

kinglet (ˈkɪŋlɪt) *n* **1** *Often derogatory.* the king of a small or insignificant territory. **2** *U.S. and Canadian.* any of various small warblers of the genus *Regulus,* having a black-edged yellow crown: family *Muscicapidae.*

kingly (ˈkɪŋlɪ) *adj* **-lier, -liest. 1** appropriate to a king; majestic. **2** royal. ◆ *adv* **3** *Poetic or archaic.* in a manner appropriate to a king. ► **ˈkingliness** *n*

kingmaker (ˈkɪŋˌmeɪkə) *n* a person who has control over appointments to positions of authority.

king-of-arms *n, pl* **kings-of-arms. 1** the highest rank of heraldic officer, itself divided into the ranks of Garter, Clarenceaux, and Norroy and Ulster. In Scotland the first is Lyon. **2** a person holding this rank.

king of the castle *n Chiefly Brit.* **1** a children's game in which each child attempts to stand alone on a mound, sandcastle, etc., by pushing other children off it. **2** *Informal.* a person who is in a commanding or superior position.

king of the herrings *n* another name for **oarfish** or **rabbitfish** (sense 1).

king penguin *n* a large penguin, *Aptenodytes patagonica,* found on islands bordering the Antarctic Circle.

kingpin (ˈkɪŋˌpɪn) *n* **1** the most important person in an organization. **2** the crucial or most important feature of a theory, argument, etc. **3** Also called (Brit.): **swivel pin.** a pivot pin that provides a steering joint in a motor vehicle by securing the stub axle to the axle beam. **4** *Tenpin bowling.* the front pin in the triangular arrangement of the ten pins. **5** (in ninepins) the central pin in the diamond pattern of the nine pins.

king post *n* a vertical post connecting the apex of a triangular roof truss to the tie beam. Also called: **joggle post.** Compare **queen post.**

king prawn *n* any of several large prawns of the genus *Penaeus,* which are fished commercially in Australian waters.

Kings (kɪŋz) *n* (*functioning as sing*) *Old Testament.* (in versions based on the Hebrew, including the Authorized Version) either of the two books called **I** and **II Kings,** recounting the histories of the kings of Judah and Israel.

king salmon *n* another name for **Chinook salmon.**

King's Bench *n* (when the sovereign is male) another name for **Queen's Bench Division.**

King's Counsel *n* (when the sovereign is male) another name for **Queen's Counsel.**

King's English *n* (esp. when the British sovereign is male) standard Southern British English.

king's evidence *n* (when the sovereign is male) another name for **queen's evidence** (esp. in the phrase **turn king's evidence**).

king's evil *n* **the.** *Pathol.* a former name for **scrofula.** [C14: from the belief that the king's touch would heal scrofula]

Kingsford-Smith (ˈkɪŋzfədˈsmɪθ) *n* Sir **Charles** (**Edward**). 1897–1935, Australian aviator and pioneer (with Charles Ulm) of trans-Pacific and trans-Tasman flights.

king's highway *n* (in Britain, esp. when the sovereign is male) any public road or right of way.

kingship (ˈkɪŋʃɪp) *n* **1** the position or authority of a king. **2** the skill or practice of ruling as a king.

king-size *or* **king-sized** *adj* larger or longer than a standard size.

Kingsley (ˈkɪŋzlɪ) *n* **1 Ben.** born 1943, British actor. He won an Oscar for his performance in the title role of the film *Gandhi* (1982). **2 Charles.** 1819–75, British clergyman and author. His works include the historical romances *Westward Ho!* (1855) and *Hereward the Wake* (1866) and the children's story *The Water Babies* (1863). **3** his brother, **Henry.** 1830–76, British novelist, editor, and journalist, who spent some time in Australia. His works include *Ravenshoe* (1861) and the Anglo-Australian novels *The Recollections of Geoffrey Hamlyn* (1859) and *The Hillyars and the Burtons* (1865).

King's Lynn (ˈkɪŋz ˈlɪn) *n* a market town in E England, in Norfolk on the estuary of the Great Ouse near the Wash: a leading port in the Middle Ages. Pop.: 41 281 (1991). Also called: **Lynn, Lynn Regis.**

king snake *n* any nonvenomous North American colubrid snake of the genus *Lampropeltis,* feeding on other snakes, small mammals, etc.

king's peace *n* **1** (in early medieval England) the protection secured by the king for particular people or places. **2** (in medieval England) the general peace secured to the entire realm by the law administered in the king's name.

King's proctor *n* (in England when the sovereign is male) an official empowered to intervene in divorce and certain other cases when it is alleged that facts are being suppressed.

King's Regulations *pl n* (in Britain and the Commonwealth when the sovereign is male) the code of conduct for members of the armed forces that deals with discipline, aspects of military law, etc.

King's Scout *n* (in Britain and the Commonwealth when the sovereign is male) another name for **Queen's Scout.** U.S. equivalent: **Eagle Scout.**

king's shilling *or, when the sovereign was female,* **queen's shilling** *n* **1** (until 1879) a shilling paid to new recruits to the British army. **2 take the king's** (*or* **queen's**) **shilling.** *Brit. archaic.* to enlist in the army.

King's speech *n* (in Britain and the dominions of the Commonwealth when the sovereign is male) another name for the **speech from the throne.**

Kingston (ˈkɪŋstən) *n* **1** the capital and chief port of Jamaica, on the SE coast: University of the West Indies. Pop.: 103 771 (1991). **2** a port in SE Canada, in SE Ontario: the chief naval base of Lake Ontario and a large industrial centre; university (1841). Pop.: 56 597 (1991). **3** short for **Kingston upon Thames.**

Kingston upon Hull *n* **1** the official name of **Hull**[1]. **2** a unitary authority in NE England, in the East Riding of Yorkshire: formerly (1974–96) part of the county of Humberside. Pop.: 265 000 (1994 est.). Area: 71 sq. km (27 sq. miles).

Kingston upon Thames *n* a borough of SW Greater London, on the River Thames: formed in 1965 by the amalgamation of several former boroughs of Surrey. Pop.: 138 500 (1994 est.). Area: 38 sq. km (15 sq. miles).

Kingstown (ˈkɪŋzˌtaʊn) *n* the capital of St Vincent and the Grenadines: a port and resort. Pop.: 15 466 (1991).

Kingwana (kɪŋˈwɑːnə) *n* a language of the Democratic Republic of the Congo (formerly Zaïre) in W Africa, closely related to Swahili and used as a lingua franca.

kingwood (ˈkɪŋˌwʊd) *n* **1** the hard fine-grained violet-tinted wood of a Brazilian leguminous tree, *Dalbergia cearensis,* used in cabinetwork. **2** the tree yielding this wood.

kinin (ˈkaɪnɪn) *n* **1** any of a group of polypeptides in the blood that cause dilation of the blood vessels and make smooth muscles contract. **2** another name for **cytokinin.** [C20: from Greek *kin(ēma)* motion + -IN]

kink (kɪŋk) *n* **1** a sharp twist or bend in a wire, rope, hair, etc., esp. one caused when it is pulled tight. **2** a crick in the neck or similar muscular spasm. **3** a flaw or minor difficulty in some undertaking or project. **4** a flaw or idiosyncrasy of personality; quirk. **5** *Brit. informal.* a sexual deviation. **6** *U.S.* a clever or unusual idea. ◆ *vb* **7** to form or cause to form a kink. [C17: from Dutch: a curl in a rope; compare Middle Low German *kinke* kink, Old Norse *kinka* to nod]

kinkajou ('kɪŋkəˌdʒuː) *n* **1** Also called: **honey bear, potto.** an arboreal fruit-eating mammal, *Potos flavus,* of Central and South America, with a long prehensile tail: family *Procyonidae* (raccoons) order *Carnivora* (carnivores). **2** another name for **potto** (sense 1). [C18: from French *quincajou,* from Algonquian; related to Ojibwa *gwīngwâage* wolverine]

kinky ('kɪŋkɪ) *adj* **kinkier, kinkiest. 1** *Slang.* given to unusual, abnormal, or deviant sexual practices. **2** *Informal.* exhibiting unusual idiosyncrasies of personality; quirky; eccentric. **3** *Informal.* attractive or provocative in a bizarre way: *kinky clothes.* **4** tangled or tightly looped, as a wire or rope. **5** tightly curled, as hair. ▸ **'kinkily** *adv* ▸ **'kinkiness** *n*

kinnikinnick, kinnikinic (ˌkɪnɪkɪ'nɪk), *or* **killikinick** *n* **1** the dried leaves and bark of certain plants, sometimes with tobacco added, formerly smoked by some North American Indians. **2** any of the plants used for such a preparation, such as the sumach *Rhus glabra.* [C18: from Algonquian, literally: that which is mixed; related to Natick *kinukkinuk* mixture]

Kinnock ('kɪnək) *n* **Neil** (**Gordon**). born 1942, British Labour politician, born in Wales; leader of the Labour Party (1983–92); European Commissioner from 1994 and vice-president of the European Commission from 1999.

kino ('kiːnəʊ) *n* a dark red resin obtained from various tropical plants, esp. an Indian leguminous tree, *Pterocarpus marsupium,* used as an astringent and in tanning. Also called: **kino gum.** [C18: of West African origin; related to Mandingo *keno*]

Kinross-shire (kɪn'rɒsˌʃɪə, -ʃə) *n* a former county of E central Scotland: became part of Tayside region in 1975 and part of Perth and Kinross in 1996.

kin selection *n Biology.* natural selection resulting from altruistic behaviour by animals towards members of the same species, esp. their offspring or other relatives.

Kinsey ('kɪnzɪ) *n* **Alfred Charles.** 1894–1956, U.S. zoologist, who directed a survey of human sexual behaviour.

kinsfolk ('kɪnzˌfəʊk) *pl n* one's family or relatives.

Kinshasa (kɪn'ʃɑːzə, -'ʃɑːsə) *n* the capital of the Democratic Republic of the Congo (formerly Zaïre), on the River Congo opposite Brazzaville: became capital of the Belgian Congo in 1929 and of Zaïre in 1960; university (1954). Pop.: 4 655 313 (1994 est.). Former name (until 1966): **Léopoldville.**

kinship ('kɪnʃɪp) *n* **1** blood relationship. **2** the state of having common characteristics or a common origin.

kinsman ('kɪnzmən) *n, pl* **-men. 1** a blood relation or a relation by marriage. **2** a member of the same race, tribe, or ethnic stock. ▸ **'kinsˌwoman** *fem n*

kiosk ('kiːɒsk) *n* **1** a small sometimes movable booth from which cigarettes, newspapers, light refreshments, etc., are sold. **2** *Chiefly Brit.* a telephone box. **3** *Chiefly U.S.* a thick post on which advertisements are posted. **4** (in Turkey, Iran, etc., esp. formerly) a light open-sided pavilion. [C17: from French *kiosque* bandstand, from Turkish *kösk,* from Persian *kūshk* pavilion]

Kioto (kɪ'əʊtəʊ, 'kjəʊ-) *n* a variant spelling of **Kyoto.**

kip[1] (kɪp) *Slang.* ◆ *n* **1** *Brit.* sleep or slumber: *to get some kip.* **2** *Brit.* a bed or lodging. **3** *Obsolete* (*except Irish*). a brothel. ◆ *vb* **kips, kipping, kipped.** (*intr*) **4** *Brit.* to sleep or take a nap. **5** *Brit.* (foll. by *down*) to prepare for sleep. [C18: of uncertain origin; apparently related to Danish *kippe* common alehouse]

kip[2] (kɪp) *or* **kipskin** ('kɪpˌskɪn) *n* the hide of a young animal, esp. a calf or lamb. [C16: from Middle Dutch *kipp;* related to Middle Low German *kip,* Old Norse *kippa* bundle]

kip[3] (kɪp) *n* a unit of weight equal to one thousand pounds. [C20: from KI(LO)[1] + P(OUND)[2]]

kip[4] (kɪp) *n* the standard monetary unit of Laos, divided into 100 at. [from Thai]

kip[5] (kɪp) *n Austral.* a small board used to spin the coins in two-up. [C19: from KEP]

Kipling ('kɪplɪŋ) *n* (**Joseph**) **Rudyard** ('rʌdjəd). 1865–1936, English poet, short-story writer, and novelist, born in India. His works include *Barrack-Room Ballads* (1892), the two *Jungle Books* (1894, 1895), *Stalky and Co.* (1899), *Kim* (1901), and the *Just So Stories* (1902): Nobel prize for literature 1907.

kippa (ki'pa) *n Judaism.* a skullcap worn by orthodox male Jews at all times and by others for prayer, esp. a crocheted one worn by those with a specifically religious Zionist affiliation.

kipper[1] ('kɪpə) *n* **1** a fish, esp. a herring, that has been cleaned, salted, and smoked. **2** a male salmon during the spawning season. **3** *Austral. archaic derogatory slang.* an Englishman. ◆ *vb* **4** (*tr*) to cure (a fish, esp. a herring) by salting and smoking. [Old English *cypera,* perhaps from *coper* COPPER[1]; referring to its colour]

kipper[2] ('kɪpə) *n* native Australian youth who has completed an initiation rite. [from a native Australian language]

Kipp's apparatus (kɪps) *n* a laboratory apparatus for producing a gas, usually hydrogen sulphide, by the action of a liquid on a solid without heating. [C19: named after Petrus Jacobus *Kipp* (1808–84), Dutch chemist]

kir (kɜː, kir) *n* a drink made from dry white wine and cassis. [named after Canon F. *Kir* (1876–1968), mayor of Dijon, who is said to have invented it]

kirby grip ('kɜːbɪ) *n Brit.* a hairgrip consisting of a piece of metal bent over to form a tight clip and having the upper part ridged to prevent it slipping on the hair. [from *Kerbigrip,* trademark for the original such hairgrip]

Kirchhoff (*German* 'kɪrçhɔf) *n* **Gustav Robert** ('gʊstaf 'roːbɛrt). 1824–87, German physicist. With Bunsen he developed the method of spectrum analysis that led to their discovery of caesium (1860) and rubidium (1861): also worked on electrical networks.

Kirchhoff's laws *pl n* two laws describing the flow of currents in electric circuits. The first states that the algebraic sum of all the electric currents meeting at any point in a circuit is zero. The second states that in a closed loop of a circuit the algebraic sum of the products of the resistances and the currents flowing through them is equal to the algebraic sum of all the electromotive forces acting in the loop.

Kirchner (*German* kɪrçnər) *n* **Ernst Ludwig.** 1880–1938, German expressionist painter and printmaker; a founder of the group *die Brücke* (1905).

Kirghiz *or* **Kirgiz** ('kɜːgɪz) *n* a variant spelling of **Kyrgyz.**

Kirghizia *or* **Kirgizia** (kɜː'gɪzɪə) *n* the former Russian name for **Kyrgyzstan.**

Kirghiz Steppe *n* a variant spelling of **Kyrgyz Steppe.**

Kiribati (ˌkɪrɪ'bætɪ) *n* an independent republic in the W Pacific: comprises 33 islands including Banaba (Ocean Island), the Gilbert and Phoenix Islands, and eight of the Line Islands; part of the British colony of the Gilbert and Ellice Islands until 1975; became self-governing in 1977 and gained full independence in 1979 as the Republic of Kiribati; a member of the Commonwealth. Official languages: English, I-Kiribati (Gilbertese) is widely spoken. Religion: Christian majority. Currency: Australian dollar. Capital: Bairiki islet, in Tarawa atoll. Pop.: 84 000 (1998 est.). Area: 684 sq. km (264 sq. miles).

kirigami (ˌkɪrɪ'gɑːmɪ) *n* the art, originally Japanese, of folding and cutting paper into decorative shapes. Compare **origami.** [C20: from Japanese]

Kirin ('kiː'rɪn) *n* a variant transliteration of the Chinese name for **Jilin.**

Kiritimati ('kɪrɪtɪ'mɑːtɪ) *n* an island in the central Pacific, in Kiribati: one of the Line Islands; the largest atoll in the world. Pop.: 2537 (1990). Former name: **Christmas Island.**

kirk (kɜːk; *Scot.* kɪrk) *n* **1** a Scot. word for **church. 2** a Scottish church. [C12: from Old Norse *kirkja,* from Old English *cirice* CHURCH]

Kirk[1] (kɜːk; *Scot.* kɪrk) *n* **the.** *Informal.* the Presbyterian Church of Scotland.

Kirk[2] (kɜːk) *n* **Norman.** 1923–74, prime minister of New Zealand (1972–74).

Kirkby[1] ('kɜːbɪ) *n* a town in NW England, in Knowsley unitary authority, Merseyside. Pop.: 43 017 (1991).

Kirkby[2] (kɜːbɪ) *n* **Emma.** born 1949, British soprano, specializing in performances of early music with period instruments.

Kirkcaldy (kɜː'kɔːdɪ) *n* a port in E Scotland, in SE Fife on the Firth of Forth. Pop.: 47 155 (1991).

Kirkcudbrightshire (kɜː'kuːbrɪˌʃɪə, -ʃə) *n* a former county of SW Scotland, part of Dumfries and Galloway since 1975.

Kirklees (ˌkɜːk'liːz) *n* a unitary authority in N England, in West Yorkshire. Pop.: 386 900 (1994 est.). Area: 410 sq. km (158 sq. miles).

kirkman ('kɜːkmən; 'kɪrk-) *n, pl* **-men.** *Scot.* **1** a member or strong upholder of the Kirk. **2** a churchman; clergyman.

Kirkpatrick (kɜːk'pætrɪk) *n* **Mount.** a mountain in Antarctica, in S Victoria Land in the Queen Alexandra Range. Height: 4528 m (14 856 ft.).

kirk session *n* the lowest court of the Presbyterian Church.

Kirkuk (kɜː'kʊk, 'kɜːkʊk) *n* a city in NE Iraq: centre of a rich oilfield with pipelines to the Mediterranean. Pop.: 418 624 (1987).

Kirkwood gap ('kɜːkwʊd) *n* any of the regions of the asteroid belt between Mars and Jupiter in which few asteroids orbit as a result of Jupiter's perturbing influence. [C19: named after Daniel Kirkwood, who first explained them]

Kirkwall ('kɜːkˌwɔːl) *n* a town on the N coast of Mainland in the Orkney Islands: administrative centre of the island authority of Orkney: cathedral built by Norsemen (begun in 1137). Pop.: 6469 (1991).

Kirlian photography ('kɜːlɪən) *n* a process that is said to record directly on photographic film the field radiation of electricity emitted by an object to which an electric charge has been applied. [C20: named after Semyan D. and Valentina K. *Kirlian,* Russian researchers who described the process]

Kirman (kɪə'mɑːn) *n, pl* **-mans.** a Persian carpet or rug. [named after KERMAN, Iran]

kirmess ('kɜːmɪs) *n* a variant spelling of **kermis.**

Kirov[1] (*Russian* 'kirəf) *n* a city in NW Russia, on the Vyatka River: an early trading centre; engineering industries. Pop.: 464 000 (1995 est.). Former name (1780–1934): **Vyatka.**

Kirov[2] (*Russian* 'kirəf) *n* **Sergei Mironovich** (sɪr'gjej mi'rɔnəvitʃ). 1888–1934, Soviet politician; one of Stalin's chief aides. His assassination was the starting point for Stalin's purge of the Communist Party (1934–38).

Kirovabad (*Russian* kirəva'bat) *n* See **Gandzha.**

Kirovograd (*Russian* kirəva'grat) *n* a city in the S central Ukraine on the Ingul River: manufacturing centre of a rich agricultural area. Pop.: 276 000 (1996 est.). Former names: **Yelisavetgrad** (until 1924), **Zinovievsk** (1924–36).

Kirpan (kɪr'pɑːn) the short sword traditionally carried by Sikhs as a symbol of their religious and cultural loyalty, symbolizing protection for the weak. See also **five Ks.** [Punjabi *kirpān*]

Kirsch (kɪəʃ) *or* **Kirschwasser** ('kɪəʃˌvɑːsə) *n* a brandy distilled from cherries, made chiefly in the Black Forest in Germany and in the Jura and Vosges districts of France. [German *Kirschwasser* cherry water]

kirtan ('kɪrtɑn) *n Hinduism.* devotional singing, usually accompanied by musical instruments. [from Sanskrit *kīrtanam* praise, eulogy]

kirtle ('kɜːtᵊl) *n Archaic.* **1** a woman's skirt or dress. **2** a man's coat. [Old English *cyrtel,* probably from *cyrtan* to shorten, ultimately from Latin *curtus* cut short]

Kiruna (*Swedish* 'kiːruna) *n* a town in N Sweden: iron-mining centre. Pop.: 26 150 (1990).

Kirundi (kɪ'rʊndɪ) *n* the official language of Burundi, belonging to the Bantu group of the Niger-Congo family and closely related to Rwanda.

Kisangani (ˌkɪsæŋ'gɑːnɪ) *n* a city in the N Democratic Republic of the Congo (formerly Zaïre), at the head of navigation of the River Congo below Stanley Falls: Université Libre du Congo (1963). Pop.: 417 517 (1994 est.). Former name (until 1966): **Stanleyville.**

kish (kɪʃ) *n Metallurgy.* graphite formed on the surface of molten iron that contains a large amount of carbon. [C19: perhaps changed from German *Kies* gravel; related to Old High German *kisil* pebble]

Kishinev (*Russian* kiʃiˈnjɔf) *n* the capital of Moldova on the Byk River: manufacturing centre of a rich agricultural region; university (1945). Pop.: 662 000 (1994 est.). Romanian name: **Chişinău.**

kishke (ˈkɪʃkə) *n* a beef or fowl intestine or skin stuffed with flour, onion, etc., and boiled and roasted. [Yiddish: gut, probably from Russian *kishka*]

Kislev (kiˈslev) *n* (in the Jewish calendar) the ninth month of the year according to biblical reckoning and the third month of the civil year, usually falling within November and December. [from Hebrew]

Kismayu (kɪsˈmɑːjuː) *n* another name for **Chisimaio.**

kismet (ˈkɪzmɛt, ˈkɪs-) *n* **1** *Islam.* the will of Allah. **2** fate or destiny. [C19: from Turkish, from Persian *qismat,* from Arabic, *qasama* he divided]

kiss (kɪs) *vb* **1** (*tr*) to touch with the lips or press the lips against as an expression of love, greeting, respect, etc. **2** (*intr*) to join lips with another person in an act of love or desire. **3** to touch (each other) lightly: *their hands kissed.* **4** *Billiards.* (of balls) to touch (each other) lightly while moving. ◆ *n* **5** the act of kissing; a caress with the lips. Related adj: **oscular. 6** a light touch. **7** a small light sweet or cake, such as one made chiefly of egg white and sugar: *coffee kisses.* ◆ See also **kiss off.** [Old English *cyssan,* from *coss;* compare Old High German *kussen,* Old Norse *kyssa*] ► **ˈkissable** *adj*

kissagram (ˈkɪsəˌgræm) *n* a greetings service in which a person is employed to present greetings by kissing the person celebrating. [C20: blend of *kiss* and *telegram*]

kiss-and-tell *modifier.* denoting the practice of publicizing one's former sexual relationship with a celebrity, esp. in the tabloid press: *a kiss-and-tell interview.*

kiss curl *n Brit.* a circular curl of hair pressed flat against the cheek or forehead. U.S. and Canadian term: **spit curl.**

kissel (ˈkɪsəl) *n* a Russian dessert of sweetened fruit purée thickened with arrowroot. [from Russian *kisel'*]

kisser (ˈkɪsə) *n* **1** a person who kisses, esp. in a way specified: *a good kisser.* **2** a slang word for **mouth** or **face.**

kissing bug *n* a North American assassin bug, *Melanolestes picipes,* with a painful bite, usually attacking the lips or cheeks of man.

Kissinger (ˈkɪsɪndʒə) *n* **Henry (Alfred).** born 1923, U.S. academic and diplomat, born in Germany; assistant to President Nixon for national security affairs (1969–75); Secretary of State (1973–77): shared the Nobel peace prize 1973.

kissing gate *n* a gate set in a U- or V-shaped enclosure, allowing only one person to pass through at a time.

kiss of death *n* an act or relationship that has fatal or disastrous consequences. [from Judas' kiss that betrayed Jesus in the garden of Gethsemane (Mark 14:44–45)]

kiss off *Slang, chiefly U.S. and Canadian.* ◆ *vb* **1** (*tr, adv*) to ignore or dismiss rudely and abruptly. ◆ *n* **kiss-off. 2** a rude and abrupt dismissal.

kiss of life *n* **the. 1** mouth-to-mouth resuscitation in which a person blows gently into the mouth of an unconscious person, allowing the lungs to deflate after each blow. **2** something that revitalizes or reinvigorates.

kist[1] (kɪst) *n Scot. and northern English dialect.* a large chest or coffer. [C14: from Old Norse *kista;* see CHEST]

kist[2] (kɪst) *n Archaeol.* a variant spelling of **cist**[2].

kist[3] (kɪst) *n S. African.* a large wooden chest in which linen is stored, esp. one used to store a bride's trousseau. [from Afrikaans, from Dutch: CHEST]

Kistna (ˈkɪstnə) *n* another name for the (River) **Krishna.**

Kisumu (kɪˈsuːmuː) *n* a port in W Kenya, in Nyanza province on the NE shore of Lake Victoria: fishing and trading centre. Pop.: 201 100 (1991 est.).

kit[1] (kɪt) *n* **1** a set of tools, supplies, construction materials, etc., for use together or for a purpose: *a first-aid kit; a model aircraft kit.* **2** the case or container for such a set. **3a** a set of pieces of equipment ready to be assembled. **3b** (*as modifier*): *kit furniture.* **4a** clothing and other personal effects, esp. those of a traveller or soldier: *safari kit; battle kit.* **4b** *Informal.* clothing in general (esp. in the phrase **get one's kit off**). **5 the whole kit** *or* **kit and caboodle.** *Informal.* everything or everybody. ◆ See also **kit out.** [C14: from Middle Dutch *kitte* tankard]

kit[2] (kɪt) *n* a kind of small violin, now obsolete, used esp. by dancing masters in the 17th–18th centuries. [C16: of unknown origin]

kit[3] (kɪt) *n* **1** an informal or diminutive name for **kitten. 2** a cub of various small mammals, such as the ferret or fox. [C16: by shortening]

kit[4] (kɪt) *n N.Z.* a plaited flax basket. [from Maori *kete*]

Kitagawa Utamaro *n* See (Kitagawa) **Utamaro.**

Kitaj (ˈkaɪtæʒ) *n* **R. B.** born 1932, U.S. painter working in Britain, noted for such large figurative works as *If Not, Not* (1976).

Kitakyushu (ˌkiːtəˈkjuːʃuː) *n* a port in Japan, on N Kyushu: formed in 1963 by the amalgamation of the cities of Wakamatsu, Yahata, Tobata, Kokura, and Moji; one of Japan's largest industrial centres. Pop.: 1 019 562 (1995).

kitbag (ˈkɪtˌbæg) *n* a canvas or other bag for a serviceman's kit.

kitchen (ˈkɪtʃɪn) *n* **a** a room or part of a building equipped for preparing and cooking food. **b** (*as modifier*): *a kitchen table.* [Old English *cycene,* ultimately from Late Latin *coquīna,* from Latin *coquere* to COOK; see KILN]

kitchen cabinet *n* a group of unofficial advisers to a political leader, esp. when considered to be more influential than the official cabinet.

Kitchener[1] (ˈkɪtʃɪnə) *n* an industrial town in SE Canada, in S Ontario: founded in 1806 as Dutch Sand Hills, it was renamed Berlin in 1830 and Kitchener in 1916. Pop.: 168 282 (1991).

Kitchener[2] (ˈkɪtʃɪnə) *n* **Horatio Herbert,** 1st Earl Kitchener of Khartoum. 1850–1916, British field marshal. As head of the Egyptian army (1892–98), he expelled the Mahdi from the Sudan (1898), occupying Khartoum; he also commanded British forces (1900–02) in the Boer War and (1902–09) in India. He conducted the mobilization of the British army for World War I as war minister (1914–16); he was drowned on his way to Russia.

kitchenette *or* **kitchenet** (ˌkɪtʃɪˈnɛt) *n* a small kitchen or part of another room equipped for use as a kitchen.

kitchen garden *n* a garden where vegetables and sometimes also fruit are grown. ► **kitchen gardener** *n*

kitchen kaffir *n* a derogatory term for **Fanagalo.**

kitchen midden *n Archaeology.* the site of a large mound of domestic refuse marking a prehistoric settlement: usually including bones, potsherds, seashells, etc.

kitchen police *pl n U.S.* soldiers who have been detailed to work in the kitchen, esp. as a punishment. Abbrev.: **KP.**

kitchen sink *n* **1** a sink in a kitchen for washing dishes, vegetables, etc. **2 everything but the kitchen sink.** everything that can be conceived of. **3** (*modifier*) denoting a type of drama or painting of the 1950s depicting the sordid aspects of domestic reality.

kitchen tea *n Austral. and N.Z.* a party held before a wedding to which female guests bring items of kitchen equipment as wedding presents.

kitchenware (ˈkɪtʃɪnˌwɛə) *n* pots and pans, knives, forks, spoons, and other utensils used in the kitchen.

kite[1] (kaɪt) *n* **1** a light frame covered with a thin material flown in the wind at the end of a length of string. **2** *Brit. slang.* an aeroplane. **3** (*pl*) *Nautical.* any of various light sails set in addition to the working sails of a vessel. **4** any diurnal bird of prey of the genera *Milvus, Elanus,* etc., typically having a long forked tail and long broad wings and usually preying on small mammals and insects: family *Accipitridae* (hawks, etc.). **5** *Archaic.* a person who preys on others. **6** *Commerce.* a negotiable paper drawn without any actual transaction or assets and designed to obtain money on credit, give an impression of affluence, etc. **7 fly a kite.** See **fly**[1] (sense 14). **8 high as a kite.** See **high** (sense 30). ◆ *vb* **9** to issue (fictitious papers) to obtain credit or money. **10** (*tr*) *U.S. and Canadian.* to write (a cheque) in anticipation of sufficient funds to cover it. **11** (*intr*) to soar and glide. [Old English *cӯta;* related to Middle High German *küze* owl, Old Norse *kӯta* to quarrel] ► **ˈkiter** *n*

kite[2] (kəɪt) *n* a variant spelling of **kyte.**

kite fighting *n* (in Malaysia) a game in which one player attempts to cut the string of his opponent's kite with the string of his own. See also **glass string.**

kite flying *n Commerce.* the practice of drawing cheques on deposits which are already committed, assuming that the delay in clearing the cheque will allow time to replenish the account. Also called: **kiting.**

Kitemark *n Brit.* the official mark of quality and reliability, in the form of a kite, on articles approved by the British Standards Institution.

kitenge (kiːˈtɛŋgɛ) *n E African.* **a** a thick cotton cloth measuring 114 × 213 cm (45 × 84 inches), used in making garments. **b** (*as modifier*): *a kitenge dress.* [C20: from Swahili]

kit fox *n* another name for **swift fox.**

kith (kɪθ) *n* one's friends and acquaintances (esp. in the phrase **kith and kin**). [Old English *cӯthth,* from *cūth;* see UNCOUTH]

kithara (ˈkɪθərə) *n* a variant of **cithara.**

Kíthira (ˈkiθira) *n* transliteration of the Modern Greek name for **Cythera.**

kit out *or* **up** *vb* **kits, kitting, kitted.** (*tr, adv*) *Chiefly Brit.* to provide with (a kit of personal effects and necessities).

kitsch (kɪtʃ) *n* **a** tawdry, vulgarized, or pretentious art, literature, etc., usually with popular or sentimental appeal. **b** (*as modifier*): *a kitsch plaster bust of Beethoven.* [C20: from German] ► **ˈkitschy** *adj*

kittel (ˈkiːtəl) *n* a white garment used as a shroud or worn by traditional Jews on Yom Kippur. [from German *Kittel,* smock]

kitten (ˈkɪtən) *n* **1** a young cat. **2 have kittens.** Also: **have a canary.** *Brit. informal.* to react with disapproval, anxiety, etc.: *she had kittens when she got the bill.* U.S. equivalent: **have a cow.** ◆ *vb* **3** (of cats) to give birth to (young). [C14: from Old Northern French *caton,* from CAT[1]; probably influenced by Middle English *kiteling*] ► **ˈkitten-ˌlike** *adj*

kittenish (ˈkɪtənɪʃ) *adj* **1** like a kitten; lively. **2** (of a woman) flirtatious, esp. coyly flirtatious. ► **ˈkittenishly** *adv* ► **ˈkittenishness** *n*

kitten moth *n* any of three prominent moths, notably the **poplar kitten** (*furcula bifida*), that have larvae like those of the related puss moth.

kittiwake (ˈkɪtɪˌweɪk) *n* either of two oceanic gulls of the genus *Rissa,* esp. *R. tridactyla,* having a white plumage with pale grey black-tipped wings and a square-cut tail. [C17: of imitative origin]

kittle (ˈkɪtəl) *Scot.* ◆ *adj* **1** capricious and unpredictable. ◆ *vb* **2** to be troublesome or puzzling to (someone). **3** to tickle. [C16: probably from Old Norse *kitla* to TICKLE]

kitty[1] (ˈkɪtɪ) *n, pl* **-ties.** a diminutive or affectionate name for a **kitten** or **cat**[1]. [C18: see KIT[3]]

kitty[2] (ˈkɪtɪ) *n, pl* **-ties. 1** the pool of bets in certain gambling games. **2** any shared fund of money, etc. **3** (in bowls) the jack. [C19: see KIT[1]]

kitty-cornered *adj* a variant of **cater-cornered.**

Kitty Hawk (ˈkɪtɪ hɔːk) *n* a village in NE North Carolina, near Kill Devil Hill, where the Wright brothers made the first aeroplane flight in the U.S. (1903).

Kitwe (ˈkɪtweɪ) *n* a city in N Zambia: commercial centre of the Copper Belt. Pop.: 338 207 (1990).

Kitzbühel (ˈkɪtsbuəl) *n* a town in W Austria, in the Tirol: centre for winter sports. Pop.: 8223 (1991).

Kiushu (ˈkjuːʃuː) *n* a variant spelling of **Kyushu.**

kiva (ˈkiːvə) *n* a large underground or partly underground room in a Pueblo Indian village, used chiefly for religious ceremonies. [from Hopi]

Kivu (ˈkiːvuː) *n* **Lake.** a lake in central Africa, between the Democratic Republic of the Congo (formerly Zaïre) and Rwanda at an altitude of 1460 m (4790 ft.). Area: 2698 sq. km (1042 sq. miles). Depth: (maximum) 475 m (1558 ft.).

Kiwanis (kɪ'wɑːnɪs) *n* a North American organization of men's clubs founded in 1915 to promote community service. [C20: alleged to be from an American Indian language: to make oneself known] ▸ **Ki'wanian** *n*

kiwi ('kiːwiː) *n, pl* **kiwis.** 1 any nocturnal flightless New Zealand bird of the genus *Apteryx*, having a long beak, stout legs, and weakly barbed feathers: order *Apterygiformes* (see **ratite**). 2 short for **kiwi fruit.** 3 *Informal except in New Zealand.* a New Zealander. [C19: from Maori, of imitative origin]

kiwi fruit *n* the edible oval fruit of the kiwi plant, *Actinidia chinensis*, a climbing plant native to Asia but grown extensively in New Zealand; it has a brown fuzzy skin and pale green flesh. Also called: **Chinese gooseberry.**

Kizil Irmak (kɪ'zɪl ɪə'mɑːk) *n* a river in Turkey, rising in the Kizil Dag and flowing southwest, northwest, and northeast to the Black Sea: the longest river in Asia Minor. Length: about 1150 km (715 miles). Ancient name: **Halys** ('heɪlɪs).

KKK *abbrev. for* Ku Klux Klan.

KKt *Chess. symbol for* king's knight.

KKtP *Chess. symbol for* king's knight's pawn.

kl *symbol for* kilolitre.

Klagenfurt (*German* 'klaːgənfʊrt) *n* a city in S Austria, capital of Carinthia province: tourist centre. Pop.: 89 415 (1991).

Klaipeda (*Russian* 'klajpɪdə) *n* a port in Lithuania on the Baltic: shipbuilding and fish canning. Pop.: 206 400 (1993 est.). German name: **Memel.**

Klan (klæn) *n* (usually preceded by *the*) short for **Ku Klux Klan.** ▸ **'Klanism** *n*

klangfarbe ('klɑːŋˌfɑːbə) *n* (*often cap.*) instrumental timbre or tone colour. [German: tone colour]

Klansman ('klænzmən) *n, pl* **-men.** a member of the Ku Klux Klan.

Klausenburg ('klauzənbʊrk) *n* the German name for **Cluj.**

klaxon *or* **claxon** ('klæksᵊn) *n* a type of loud horn formerly used on motor vehicles. [C20: former trademark, from the name of the manufacturing company]

Kléber (*French* klebɛr) *n* **Jean Baptiste** (ʒɑ̃ batist). 1753–1800, French general, who succeeded Napoleon as commander in Egypt (1799); assassinated.

Klebs-Löffler bacillus ('klɛbz'lʌflə; *German* 'kleːps'lœflər) *n* a rodlike Gram-positive bacterium, *Corynebacterium diphtheriae*, that causes diphtheria: family *Corynebacteriaceae.* [C19: named after Edwin *Klebs* (1834–1913) and Friedrich A. J. *Löffler* (1852–1915), German bacteriologists]

Klee (*German* kleː) *n* **Paul** (paul). 1879–1940, Swiss painter and etcher. A founder member of *der Blaue Reiter*, he subsequently evolved an intensely personal style of unusual fantasy and wit.

Kleenex ('kliːnɛks) *n, pl* **-ex** *or* **-exes.** *Trademark.* a kind of soft paper tissue, used esp. as a handkerchief.

Klein (klaɪn) *n* 1 **Calvin** (**Richard**). born 1942, U.S. fashion designer. 2 **Melanie.** 1882–1960, Austrian psychoanalyst resident in England (from 1926), noted for her work on child behaviour.

Klein bottle (klaɪn) *n Maths.* a three-dimensional surface having no interior, formed by inserting the smaller end of an open tapered tube through the surface of the tube and making this end contiguous with the other end. [named after Felix *Klein* (1849–1925) German mathematician]

kleinhuisie ('kleɪnˈheɪsɪ) *n S. African.* an outside lavatory. [C20: Afrikaans: literally, little house]

Kleist (klaɪst) *n* (**Bernd**) **Heinrich** (**Wilhelm**) **von** ('hainrɪç fɔn). 1777–1811, German dramatist, poet, and short-story writer. His plays include *The Broken Pitcher* (1808), *Penthesilea* (1808), and *The Prince of Homburg* (published 1821).

Klemperer ('klɛmpərə) *n* **Otto.** 1885–1973, orchestral conductor, born in Germany. He was best known for his interpretations of Beethoven.

klepht (klɛft) *n* any of the Greeks who fled to the mountains after the 15th-century Turkish conquest of Greece and whose descendants survived as brigands into the 19th century. [C19: from Modern Greek *klephtēs*, from Greek *kleptēs* thief] ▸ **'klephtic** *adj*

kleptomania (ˌklɛptəʊ'meɪnɪə) *n Psychol.* a strong impulse to steal, esp. when there is no obvious motivation. [C19: *klepto-* from Greek *kleptēs* thief, from *kleptein* to steal + -MANIA] ▸ **ˌklepto'maniˌac** *n*

kletterschuh ('klɛtəʃuː) *n, pl* **kletterschuhe** ('klɛtəˌʃuːə) a lightweight climbing boot with a canvas or suede upper and Vibram (originally felt or cord) sole. Also called: **klett.** [C20: from German: climbing shoe]

klieg light (kliːg) *n* an intense carbon-arc light used for illumination in producing films. [C20: named after John H. *Kliegl* (1869–1959) and his brother Anton (1872–1927), German-born American inventors in the field of lighting]

Klimt (klɪmt) *n* **Gustav** ('gʊstaf). 1862–1918, Austrian painter. He founded the Vienna Sezession (1897), a group of painters influenced by Art Nouveau.

Kline (klaɪn) *n* **Franz** (frænts). 1910–62, U.S. abstract expressionist painter. His works are characterized by heavy black strokes on a white or grey background.

Klint (klɪnt) *n* **Kaara** (kɑːrə). 1888–1954, Danish furniture designer; founder of the contemporary Scandinavian style.

klipspringer ('klɪpˌsprɪŋə) *n* a small agile antelope, *Oreotragus oreotragus*, inhabiting rocky regions of Africa south of the Sahara. [C18: from Afrikaans, from Dutch *klip* rock (see CLIFF) + *springer*, from *springen* to SPRING]

Klondike ('klɒndaɪk) *n* 1 a region of NW Canada, in the Yukon in the basin of the Klondike River: site of rich gold deposits, discovered in 1896 but largely exhausted by 1910. Area: about 2100 sq. km (800 sq. miles). 2 a river in NW Canada, rising in the Yukon and flowing west to the Yukon River. Length: about 145 km (90 miles).

klondyker *or* **klondiker** ('klɒnˌdaɪkə) *n Brit.* an East European factory ship. [C20: from the gold miners who took part in the 19th century gold rush to the KLONDIKE]

klong (klɒŋ) *n* a type of canal in Thailand. [from Thai]

kloof (kluːf) *n* a mountain pass or gorge in southern Africa. [C18: from Afrikaans, from Middle Dutch *clove* a cleft; see CLEAVE[1]]

klootchman ('kluːtʃmən) *n, pl* **-mans** *or* **-men.** *Northwestern Canadian.* an Indian woman; squaw. Also called: **klootch, klooch.** [C19: from Chinook Jargon, from Nootka *hlotssma* woman, wife]

Klopstock (*German* 'klɔpʃtɔk) *n* **Friedrich Gottlieb** ('friːdrɪç 'gɔtliːp). 1724–1803, German poet, noted for his religious epic *Der Messias* (1748–73) and for his odes.

klutz (klʌts) *n U.S. and Canadian slang.* a clumsy or stupid person. [from German *Klotz* dolt; compare CLOT] ▸ **'klutzy** *adj*

klystron ('klɪstrɒn, 'klaɪ-) *n* an electron tube for the amplification or generation of microwaves by means of velocity modulation. [C20: *klys-*, from Greek *klus-*, *kluzein* to wash over, break over + -TRON]

km *symbol for* kilometre.

K-meson *n* another name for **kaon.**

kn *abbrev. for:* 1 *Nautical.* knot. 2 krona. 3 krone.

KN *Chess. symbol for* king's knight.

knack (næk) *n* 1 a skilful, ingenious, or resourceful way of doing something. 2 a particular talent or aptitude, esp. an intuitive one. [C14: probably variant of *knak* sharp knock, rap, of imitative origin]

knacker ('nækə) *Brit.* ◆ *n* 1 a person who buys up old horses for slaughter. 2 a person who buys up old buildings and breaks them up for scrap. 3 (*usually pl*) *Slang.* another word for **testicle.** 4 *Irish slang.* a despicable person. ◆ *vb* 5 (*tr; usually passive*) *Slang.* to exhaust; tire. [C16: probably from *nacker* saddler, probably of Scandinavian origin; compare Old Norse *hnakkur* saddle] ▸ **'knackered** *adj*

knacker's yard *n Brit.* 1 a slaughterhouse for horses. 2 *Informal.* destruction because of being beyond all usefulness (esp. in the phrase **ready for the knacker's yard**).

knackwurst *or* **knockwurst** ('nɒkˌwɜːst) *n* a short fat highly seasoned sausage. [German, from *knacken* to make a cracking sound + *Wurst* sausage]

knag (næg) *n* 1 a knot in wood. 2 a wooden peg. [C15: perhaps from Low German *knagge*]

knap[1] (næp) *n Dialect.* the crest of a hill. [Old English *cnæpp* top; compare Old Norse *knappr* knob]

knap[2] (næp) *vb* **knaps, knapping, knapped.** (*tr*) *Dialect.* to hit, hammer, or chip. [C15 (in the sense: to strike with a sharp sound): of imitative origin; compare Dutch *knappen* to crack] ▸ **'knapper** *n*

knapping hammer *n* a hammer used for breaking and shaping stones.

knapsack ('næpˌsæk) *n* a canvas or leather bag carried strapped on the back or shoulder. [C17: from Low German *knappsack*, probably from *knappen* to bite, snap + *sack* bag; related to Dutch *knapzak*; see SACK[1]]

knapweed ('næpˌwiːd) *n* any of several plants of the genus *Centaurea*, having purplish thistle-like flowers: family *Compositae* (composites). See also **centaury** (sense 2), **hardheads.** [C15 *knopwed*; see KNOP, WEED[1]]

knar (nɑː) *n* a variant of **knur.** [C14 *knarre* rough stone, knot on a tree; related to Low German *knarre*] ▸ **knarred** *or* **'knarry** *adj*

knave (neɪv) *n* 1 *Archaic.* a dishonest man; rogue. 2 another word for **jack** (the playing card). 3 *Obsolete.* a male servant. [Old English *cnafa*; related to Old High German *knabo* boy] ▸ **'knavish** *adj* ▸ **'knavishly** *adv* ▸ **'knavishness** *n*

knavery ('neɪvərɪ) *n, pl* **-eries.** 1 a deceitful or dishonest act. 2 dishonest conduct; trickery.

knawel ('nɔːəl) *n* any of several Old World caryophyllaceous plants of the genus *Scleranthus*, having heads of minute petal-less flowers. [C16: from German *Knauel*, literally: ball of yarn, from Old High German *kliuwa* ball]

knead (niːd) *vb* (*tr*) 1 to work and press (a soft substance, such as bread dough) into a uniform mixture with the hands. 2 to squeeze, massage, or press with the hands. 3 to make by kneading. [Old English *cnedan*; related to Old Saxon *knedan*, Old Norse *knotha*] ▸ **'kneader** *n*

Knebworth House ('nɛbwɜːθ) *n* a Tudor mansion in Knebworth in Hertfordshire: home of Sir Edward Bulwer-Lytton; decorated (1843) in the Gothic style.

knee (niː) *n* 1 the joint of the human leg connecting the tibia and fibula with the femur and protected in front by the patella. Technical name: **genu.** Related adj: **genicular.** 2a the area surrounding and above this joint. 2b (*modifier*) reaching or covering the knee: *knee breeches; knee socks.* 3 a corresponding or similar part in other vertebrates. 4 the part of a garment that covers the knee. 5 the upper surface of a seated person's thigh: *the child sat on her mother's knee.* 6 anything resembling a knee in action, such as a device pivoted to allow one member angular movement in relation to another. 7 anything resembling a knee in shape, such as an angular bend in a pipe. 8 any of the hollow rounded protuberances that project upwards from the roots of the swamp cypress: thought to aid respiration in waterlogged soil. 9 **bend** *or* **bow the knee.** to kneel or submit. 10 **bring someone to his knees.** to force someone into submission. 11 **bring something to its knees.** to cause something to be in a weakened or impoverished state. ◆ *vb* **knees, kneeing, kneed.** 12 (*tr*) to strike, nudge, or push with the knee. [Old English *cnēow*; compare Old High German *kneo*, Old Norse *knē*, Latin *genu*]

kneecap ('niːˌkæp) *n* 1 *Anatomy.* a nontechnical name for **patella.** 2 another word for **poleyn.** ◆ *vb* **-caps, -capping, -capped.** (*tr*) 3 (esp. of certain terrorist groups) to shoot (a person) in the kneecap, esp. as an act of retaliation.

knee-deep *adj* 1 so deep as to reach or cover the knees: *knee-deep mud.* 2 (*postpositive;* often foll. by *in*) 2a sunk or covered to the knees: *knee-deep in sand.* 2b immersed; deeply involved: *knee-deep in work.*

knee drop *n* a wrestling attack in which a wrestler lifts his opponent and drops him onto his bent knee.

knee-high *adj* 1 another word for **knee-deep** (sense 1). 2 as high as the knee: *a knee-high child.*

kneehole ('niːˌhəʊl) *n* **a** a space for the knees, esp. under a desk. **b** (*as modifier*): *a kneehole desk.*

knee jerk *n* 1 *Physiol.* Also called: **patellar reflex.** an outward reflex kick of the lower leg caused by a sharp tap on the tendon just below the patella. ◆ *modifier.* **kneejerk.** 2 made or occurring as a predictable and automatic response, without thought: *kneejerk support.*

kneel (ni:l) *vb* **kneels, kneeling, knelt** *or* **kneeled.** 1 (*intr*) to rest, fall, or support oneself on one's knees. ◆ *n* 2 the act or position of kneeling. [Old English *cnēowlian;* see KNEE] ▸ **'kneeler** *n*

knee-length *adj* reaching to the knee: *a knee-length skirt; knee-length boots.*

kneepad ('ni:,pæd) *n* any of several types of protective covering for the knees. Also called: **kneecap.**

kneepan ('ni:,pæn) *n Anatomy.* another word for **patella.**

knees-up *n, pl* **knees-ups.** *Brit. informal.* 1 a boisterous dance involving the raising of alternate knees. 2 a lively noisy party or celebration, esp. one with dancing. [C20: from the song "Knees up Mother Brown" to which the dance is performed]

kneidel ('kneɪdᵊl, 'knaɪ-) *n* (in Jewish cookery) a small dumpling, usually served in chicken soup. [from Yiddish]

knell (nel) *n* 1 the sound of a bell rung to announce a death or a funeral. 2 something that precipitates or indicates death or destruction. ◆ *vb* 3 (*intr*) to ring a knell. 4 (*tr*) to proclaim or announce by or as if by a tolling bell. [Old English *cnyll;* related to Middle High German *knüllen* to strike, Dutch *knallen* to bang]

Kneller ('nɛlə) *n* Sir **Godfrey.** ?1646–1723, portrait painter at the English court, born in Germany.

knelt (nɛlt) *vb* a past tense and past participle of **kneel.**

Knesset *or* **Knesseth** ('knɛsɪt) *n* the unicameral parliament of Israel. [Hebrew, literally: gathering]

knew (nju:) *vb* the past tense of **know.**

Knickerbocker ('nɪkə,bɒkə) *n U.S.* 1 a descendant of the original Dutch settlers of New York. 2 an inhabitant of New York. [C19: named after Diedrich *Knickerbocker,* fictitious Dutchman alleged to be the author of Washington Irving's *History of New York* (1809)]

knickerbocker glory *n* a rich confection consisting of layers of ice cream, jelly, cream, and fruit served in a tall glass.

knickerbockers ('nɪkə,bɒkəz) *pl n* baggy breeches fastened with a band at the knee or above the ankle. Also called (U.S.): **knickers.** [C19: regarded as the traditional dress of the Dutch settlers in America; see KNICKERBOCKER]

knickers ('nɪkəz) *pl n* 1 an undergarment for women covering the lower trunk and sometimes the thighs and having separate legs or leg-holes. 2 a U.S. variant of **knickerbockers.** 3 **get one's knickers in a twist.** *Slang.* to become agitated, flustered, or upset. [C19: contraction of KNICKERBOCKERS]

knick-knack *or* **nick-nack** ('nɪk,næk) *n* 1 a cheap ornament; trinket. 2 an ornamental article of furniture, dress, etc. [C17: by reduplication from *knack,* in obsolete sense: toy] ▸ **'knick-,knackery** *or* **'nick-,nackery** *n*

knickpoint *or esp. U.S.* **nickpoint** ('nɪk,pɔɪnt) *n* a break in the slope of a river profile caused by renewed erosion by a rejuvenated river. [C20: partial translation of German *Knickpunkt,* from *knicken* to bend + *Punkt* POINT]

knife (naɪf) *n, pl* **knives** (naɪvz). 1 a cutting instrument consisting of a sharp-edged often pointed blade of metal fitted into a handle or onto a machine. 2 a similar instrument used as a weapon. 3 **have one's knife in someone.** to have a grudge against or victimize someone. 4 **twist the knife.** to make a bad situation worse in a deliberately malicious way. 5 **the knives are out for (someone).** *Brit.* people are determined to harm or put a stop to (someone): *the knives are out for Stevens.* 6 **under the knife.** undergoing a surgical operation. ◆ *vb* (*tr*) 7 to cut, stab, or kill with a knife. 8 to betray, injure, or depose in an underhand way. [Old English *cnīf;* related to Old Norse *knīfr,* Middle Low German *knīf*] ▸ **'knife,like** *adj* ▸ **'knifer** *n*

knife edge *n* 1 the sharp cutting edge of a knife. 2 any sharp edge. 3 a sharp-edged wedge of hard material on which the beam of a balance pivots or about which a pendulum is suspended. 4 a critical point in the development of a situation, process of making a decision, etc.

knife grinder *n* a person who makes and sharpens knives, esp. an itinerant one.

knife pleat *n* a single pleat turned in one direction.

knife-point *n* 1 the tip of a knife blade. 2 **at knife-point.** under threat of being stabbed.

kniferest ('naɪf,rest) *n* a support on which a carving knife or carving fork is placed at the table.

knife switch *n* an electric switch in which a flat metal blade, hinged at one end, is pushed between fixed contacts.

knight (naɪt) *n* 1 (in medieval Europe) 1a (originally) a person who served his lord as a mounted and heavily armed soldier. 1b (later) a gentleman invested by a king or other lord with the military and social standing of this rank. 2 (in modern times) a person invested by a sovereign with a nonhereditary rank and dignity usually in recognition of personal services, achievements, etc. A British knight bears the title *Sir* placed before his name: *Sir Winston Churchill.* 3 a chess piece, usually shaped like a horse's head, that moves either two squares horizontally and one square vertically or one square horizontally and two squares vertically. 4 a heroic champion of a lady or of a cause or principle. 5 a member of the Roman class of the equites. ◆ *vb* 6 (*tr*) to make (a person) a knight; dub. [Old English *cniht* servant; related to Old High German *kneht* boy]

Knight (naɪt) *n* Dame **Laura.** 1887–1970, British painter, noted for her paintings of Gypsies, the ballet, and the circus.

knight bachelor *n, pl* **knights bachelors** *or* **knights bachelor.** 1 a person who has been knighted but who does not belong to any of the orders of knights. 2 another name for a **bachelor** (sense 3).

knight banneret *n, pl* **knights bannerets.** another name for a **banneret.**

knight errant *n, pl* **knights errant.** (esp. in medieval romance) a knight who wanders in search of deeds of courage, chivalry, etc.

knight errantry *n* 1 the practices of a knight errant. 2 quixotic behaviour or practices.

knighthead ('naɪt,hɛd) *n Nautical.* either of a pair of vertical supports for each side of the bowsprit. [C18: originally decorated with carvings of knights' heads]

knighthood ('naɪthʊd) *n* 1 the order, dignity, or rank of a knight. 2 the qualities of a knight; knightliness. 3 knights collectively.

knightly ('naɪtlɪ) *adj* of, relating to, resembling, or befitting a knight. ▸ **'knightliness** *n*

knight marshal *n* another name for **marshal** (sense 5).

knight of the road *n Informal or facetious.* 1 a tramp. 2 a commercial traveller. 3 a lorry driver. 4 *Obsolete.* a highwayman.

Knights Hospitallers *n* 1 Also called: **Knights of St John of Jerusalem.** a military religious order founded about the time of the first crusade (1096–99) among European crusaders. It took its name from a hospital and hostel in Jerusalem. Full name: **Knights of the Hospital of St John of Jerusalem.** 2 See **Hospitaller.**

Knights of St. Columba *n* an international, semi-secret fraternal and charitable order for Catholic laymen, which originated in New Haven, Connecticut in 1882 (the **Knights of Columbus**).

Knights of the Round Table *n* (in Arthurian legend) an order of knights created by King Arthur.

Knight Templar *n, pl* **Knights Templars** *or* **Knights Templar.** another term for **Templar.**

kniphofia (nɪ'fəʊfɪə) *n* any plant of the perennial southern African genus *Kniphofia,* some species of which are cultivated for their conical spikes of bright red or yellow drooping tubular flowers: family *Liliaceae.* Also called: **red-hot poker.** [named after J. H. *Kniphof* (1704–1763), German doctor and botanist]

knish (knɪʃ) *n* a piece of dough stuffed with potato, meat, or some other filling and baked or fried. [Yiddish, from Russian *knysh* cake; compare Polish *knysz*]

knit (nɪt) *vb* **knits, knitting, knitted** *or* **knit.** 1 to make (a garment, etc.) by looping and entwining (yarn, esp. wool) by hand by means of long eyeless needles (**knitting needles**) or by machine (**knitting machine**). 2 to join or be joined together closely. 3 to draw (the brows) together or (of the brows) to come together, as in frowning or concentrating. 4 (of a broken bone) to join together; heal. ◆ *n* 5a a fabric or garment made by knitting. 5b (*in combination*): *a heavy knit.* [Old English *cnyttan* to tie in; related to Middle Low German *knütten* to knot together; see KNOT[1]] ▸ **'knittable** *adj* ▸ **'knitter** *n*

knitting ('nɪtɪŋ) *n* **a** knitted work or the process of producing it. **b** (*as modifier*): *a knitting machine.*

knitwear ('nɪt,wɛə) *n* knitted clothes, esp. sweaters.

knives (naɪvz) *n* the plural of **knife.**

knob (nɒb) *n* 1 a rounded projection from a surface, such as a lump on a tree trunk. 2 a handle of a door, drawer, etc., esp. one that is rounded. 3 a round hill or knoll or morainic ridge. 4 *Brit. taboo.* a slang word for **penis.** 5 **and the same to you with (brass) knobs on.** *Brit. informal.* the same to you but even more so. ◆ *vb* **knobs, knobbing, knobbed.** 6 (*tr*) to supply or ornament with knobs. 7 (*intr*) to form into a knob; bulge. [C14: from Middle Low German *knobbe* knot in wood; see KNOP] ▸ **'knobby** *adj* ▸ **'knob,like** *adj*

knobbly ('nɒblɪ) *adj* **-blier, -bliest.** having or covered with small knobs; bumpy.

knobkerrie ('nɒb,kɛrɪ) *or* **knobstick** ('nɒb,stɪk) *n* a stick with a round knob at the end, used as a club or missile by South African tribesmen. [C19: from Afrikaans *knopkierie,* from *knop* knob, from Middle Dutch *cnoppe* + *kierie* stick, from Khoikhoi *kīrri*]

knock (nɒk) *vb* 1 (*tr*) to give a blow or push to; strike. 2 (*intr*) to rap sharply with the knuckles, a hard object, etc., esp. to capture attention: *to knock at the door.* 3 (*tr*) to make or force by striking: *to knock a hole in the wall.* 4 (*intr;* usually foll. by *against*) to collide (with). 5 (*tr*) to bring into a certain condition by hitting or pushing: *to knock someone unconscious.* 6 (*tr*) *Informal.* to criticize adversely; belittle: *to knock someone's work.* 7 (*intr*) Also: **pink.** (of an internal-combustion engine) to emit a characteristic metallic noise as a result of faulty combustion. 8 (*intr*) (of a bearing, esp. one in an engine) to emit a regular characteristic sound as a result of wear. 9 *Brit. slang.* to have sexual intercourse with (a person). 10 **knock (a person) into the middle of next week.** *Informal.* to hit (a person) with a very heavy blow. 11 **knock one's head against.** to have a violent or unpleasant encounter with (adverse facts or circumstances). 12 **knock on the head.** 12a to daze or kill (a person) by striking on the head. 12b effectively to prevent the further development of (a plan). ◆ *n* 13a a blow, push, or rap: *he gave the table a knock.* 13b the sound so caused. 14 the sound of knocking in an engine or bearing. 15 *Informal.* a misfortune, rebuff, or setback. 16 *Informal.* unfavourable criticism. 17 *Informal.* (in cricket) an innings or a spell of batting. ◆ See also **knock about, knock back, knock down, knock off, knock-on, knockout, knock up.** [Old English *cnocian,* of imitative origin; related to Old Norse *knoka* to hit]

knock about *or* **around** *vb* 1 (*intr, adv*) to wander about aimlessly. 2 (*intr, prep*) to travel about, esp. as resulting in varied or exotic experience: *he's knocked about the world a bit.* 3 (*intr, adv;* foll. by *with*) to associate: *to knock about with a gang.* 4 (*tr, adv*) to treat brutally: *he knocks his wife about.* 5 (*tr, adv*) to consider or discuss informally: *to knock an idea about.* ◆ *n* **knockabout.** 6 a sailing vessel, usually sloop-rigged, without a bowsprit and with a single jib. ◆ *adj* **knockabout.** 7 rough; boisterous: *knockabout farce.*

knock back *vb* (*tr, adv*) 1 *Informal.* to drink, esp. quickly. 2 *Informal.* to cost. 3 *Slang.* to reject or refuse: *you cannot possibly knock back such an offer.* 4

Slang. to come as an unpleasant surprise to; disconcert. ◆ *n* **knock-back. 5** *Slang.* a refusal or rejection. **6** *Prison slang.* failure to obtain parole.

knock down *vb (tr, adv)* **1** to strike to the ground with a blow, as in boxing. **2** (in auctions) to declare (an article) sold, as by striking a blow with a gavel. **3** to demolish. **4** to dismantle, for ease of transport. **5** *Informal.* to reduce (a price, etc.). **6** *Austral. slang.* to spend (a cheque). **7** *Austral. slang.* to drink. ◆ *adj* **knockdown.** *(prenominal)* **8** overwhelming; powerful: *a knockdown blow.* **9** *Chiefly Brit.* cheap: *I got the table at a knockdown price.* **10** easily dismantled: *knockdown furniture.* ◆ *n* **knockdown. 11** *U.S. and Austral. slang.* an introduction: *will you give me a knockdown to her?*

knocker ('nɒkə) *n* **1** an object, usually ornamental and made of metal, attached to a door by a hinge and used for knocking. **2** *Informal.* a person who finds fault or disparages. **3** *(usually pl) Slang.* a female breast. **4** a person or thing that knocks. **5 on the knocker.** *Austral. and N.Z. informal.* promptly; at once: *you pay on the knocker here.*

knock-for-knock *adj* designating an agreement between vehicle insurers that in the event of an accident each will pay for the damage to the vehicle insured with him without attempting to establish blame for the accident.

knocking copy *n* advertising or publicity material designed to denigrate a competing product.

knocking-shop *n Brit.* a slang word for **brothel.**

knock-knee *n* a condition in which the legs are bent inwards causing the knees to touch when standing. Technical name: **genu valgum.** ▸ **ˌknock-'kneed** *adj*

knock off *vb (mainly adv)* **1** *(intr, also prep) Informal.* to finish work: *we knocked off an hour early.* **2** *(tr) Informal.* to make or do hastily or easily: *to knock off a novel in a week.* **3** *(tr; also prep) Informal.* to reduce the price of (an article) by (a stated amount). **4** *(tr) Slang.* to kill. **5** *(tr) Slang.* to rob or steal: *to knock off a bank; to knock off a watch.* **6** *(tr) Slang.* to stop doing something, used as a command: *knock it off!* **7** *(tr) Slang.* to have sexual intercourse with; to seduce.

knock-on *adj* **1** resulting inevitably but indirectly from another event or circumstance: *the works closed with the direct loss of 3000 jobs and many more from the knock-on effect on the area.* ◆ *n* **2** *Rugby.* the infringement of playing the ball forward with the hand or arm. ◆ *vb* **knock on** *(adv)* **3** *Rugby.* to play (the ball) forward with the hand or arm.

knockout ('nɒkˌaʊt) *n* **1** the act of rendering unconscious. **2** a blow that renders an opponent unconscious. **3a** a competition in which competitors are eliminated progressively. **3b** *(as modifier): a knockout contest.* **4** a series of absurd invented games, esp. obstacle races, involving physical effort or skill. **5** *Informal.* a person or thing that is overwhelmingly impressive or attractive: *she's a knockout.* ◆ *vb* **knock out.** *(tr, adv)* **6** to render unconscious, esp. by a blow. **7** *Boxing.* to defeat (an opponent) by a knockout. **8** to destroy, damage, or injure badly. **9** to eliminate, esp. in a knockout competition. **10** *Informal.* to overwhelm or amaze, esp. with admiration or favourable reaction: *I was knocked out by that new song.* **11** to remove the ashes from (one's pipe) by tapping.

knockout drops *pl n Slang.* a drug secretly put into someone's drink to cause stupefaction. See also **Mickey Finn.**

knock up *vb (adv, mainly tr)* **1** Also: **knock together.** *Informal.* to assemble quickly; improvise: *to knock up a set of shelves.* **2** *Brit. informal.* to waken; rouse: *to knock someone up early.* **3** *Slang.* to make pregnant. **4** *Brit. informal.* to exhaust: *the heavy work knocked him up.* **5** *Cricket.* to score (runs). **6** *(intr) Tennis, squash, etc.* to practise or hit the ball about informally, esp. before a match. ◆ *n* **knock-up. 7** a practice session at tennis, squash, or a similar game.

knockwurst ('nɒkˌwɜːst) *n* a variant spelling of **knackwurst.**

Knole (nəʊl) *n* a mansion in Sevenoaks in Kent: built (1454) for Thomas Bourchier, Archbishop of Canterbury; later granted to the Sackville family, who made major alterations (1603–08).

knoll[1] (nəʊl) *n* a small rounded hill. [Old English *cnoll;* compare Old Norse *knollr* hilltop] ▸ **'knolly** *adj*

knoll[2] (nəʊl) *n, vb* an archaic or dialect word for **knell.** ▸ **'knoller** *n*

knop (nɒp) *n Archaic.* a knob, esp. an ornamental one. [C14: from Germanic; compare Middle Dutch *cnoppe* bud, Old High German *knopf*]

Knossos *or* **Cnossus** ('nɒsəs, 'knɒs-) *n* a ruined city in N central Crete: remains of the Minoan Bronze Age civilization.

knot[1] (nɒt) *n* **1** any of various fastenings formed by looping and tying a piece of rope, cord, etc., in upon itself, to another piece of rope, or to another object. **2** a prescribed method of tying a particular knot. **3** a tangle, as in hair or string. **4** a decorative bow or fastening, as of ribbon or braid. **5** a small cluster or huddled group. **6** a tie or bond: *the marriage knot.* **7** a difficult problem. **8** a protuberance or lump of plant tissues, such as that occurring on the trunks of certain trees. **9a** a hard mass of wood at the point where a branch joins the trunk of a tree. **9b** a cross section of this, usually roundish and cross-grained, visible in a piece of timber. **10** a sensation of constriction, caused by tension or nervousness: *his stomach was tying itself in knots.* **11a** *Pathol.* a lump of vessels or fibres formed in a part, as in a muscle. **11b** *Anatomy.* a protuberance on an organ or part. **12** a unit of speed used by nautical vessels and aircraft, being one nautical mile (about 1.15 statute miles or 1.85 km) per hour. **13** one of a number of equally spaced knots on a log line used to indicate the speed of a ship in nautical miles per hour. **14 at a rate of knots.** very fast. **15 tie (someone) in knots.** to completely perplex or confuse (someone). **16 tie the knot.** *Informal.* to get married. ◆ *vb* **knots, knotting, knotted. 17** *(tr)* to tie or fasten in a knot. **18** to form or cause to form into a knot. **19** *(tr)* to ravel or entangle or become ravelled or entangled. **20** *(tr)* to make (an article or a design) by tying thread in an interlaced pattern of ornamental knots, as in macramé. [Old English *cnotta;* related to Old High German *knoto,* Old Norse *knūtr*] ▸ **'knotter** *n* ▸ **'knotless** *adj* ▸ **'knotˌlike** *adj*

knot[2] (nɒt) *n* a small northern sandpiper, *Calidris canutus,* with a short bill and grey plumage. [C15: of unknown origin]

knot garden *n* (esp. formerly) a formal garden of intricate design.

knotgrass ('nɒtˌgrɑːs) *n* **1** Also called: **allseed.** a polygonaceous weedy plant, *Polygonum aviculare,* whose small green flowers produce numerous seeds. **2** any of several related plants.

knothole ('nɒtˌhəʊl) *n* a hole in a piece of wood where a knot has been.

knotted ('nɒtɪd) *adj* **1** (of wood, rope, etc.) having knots. **2 get knotted!** *Brit. slang.* used as a response to express disapproval or rejection.

knotting ('nɒtɪŋ) *n* **1** a sealer applied over knots in new wood before priming to prevent resin from exuding. **2** (esp. formerly) a kind of decorative knotted fancywork.

knotty ('nɒtɪ) *adj* **-tier, -tiest. 1** (of wood, rope, etc.) full of or characterized by knots. **2** extremely difficult or intricate. ▸ **'knottily** *adv* ▸ **'knottiness** *n*

knotweed ('nɒtˌwiːd) *n* any of several polygonaceous plants of the genus *Polygonum,* having small flowers and jointed stems.

knotwork ('nɒtˌwɜːk) *n* ornamentation consisting of a mass of intertwined and knotted cords.

knout (naʊt) *n* a stout whip used formerly in Russia as an instrument of punishment. [C17: from Russian *knut,* of Scandinavian origin; compare Old Norse *knūtr* knot]

know (nəʊ) *vb* **knows, knowing, knew** (njuː), **known** (nəʊn). *(mainly tr)* **1** *(also intr; may take a clause as object)* to be or feel certain of the truth or accuracy of (a fact, etc.). **2** to be acquainted or familiar with: *she's known him five years.* **3** to have a familiarity or grasp of, as through study or experience: *he knows French.* **4** *(also intr; may take a clause as object)* to understand, be aware of, or perceive (facts, etc.): *he knows the answer now.* **5** (foll. by *how*) to be sure or aware of (how to be or do something). **6** to experience, esp. deeply: *to know poverty.* **7** to be intelligent, informed, or sensible enough (to do something): *she knew not to go home yet.* **8** *(may take a clause as object)* to be able to distinguish or discriminate. **9** *Archaic.* to have sexual intercourse with. **10 I know what.** I have an idea. **11 know what's what.** to know how one thing or things in general work. **12 you know.** *Informal.* a parenthetical filler phrase used to make a pause in speaking or add slight emphasis to a statement. **13 you never know.** things are uncertain. ◆ *n* **14 in the know.** *Informal.* aware or informed. [Old English *gecnāwan;* related to Old Norse *knā* I can, Latin *noscere* to come to know] ▸ **'knowable** *adj* ▸ **'knower** *n*

know-all *n Informal, disparaging.* a person who pretends or appears to know a great deal.

know-how *n Informal.* **1** ingenuity, aptitude, or skill; knack. **2** commercial and saleable knowledge of how to do a particular thing; experience.

knowing ('nəʊɪŋ) *adj* **1** suggesting secret information or knowledge. **2** wise, shrewd, or clever. **3** deliberate; intentional. ◆ *n* **4 there is no knowing.** one cannot tell. ▸ **'knowingly** *adv* ▸ **'knowingness** *n*

knowledge ('nɒlɪdʒ) *n* **1** the facts, feelings or experiences known by a person or group of people. **2** the state of knowing. **3** awareness, consciousness, or familiarity gained by experience or learning. **4** erudition or informed learning. **5** specific information about a subject. **6** sexual intercourse (obsolete except in the legal phrase **carnal knowledge**). **7 come to one's knowledge.** to become known to one. **8 to my knowledge. 8a** as I understand it. **8b** as I know. **9 grow out of one's knowledge.** *Irish.* to behave in a presumptuous or conceited manner.

knowledgeable *or* **knowledgable** ('nɒlɪdʒəbᵊl) *adj* possessing or indicating much knowledge. ▸ **'knowledgeableness** *or* **'knowledgableness** *n* ▸ **'knowledgeably** *or* **'knowledgably** *adv*

known (nəʊn) *vb* **1** the past participle of **know.** ◆ *adj* **2** specified and identified: *a known criminal.* ◆ *n* **3** a fact or entity known.

Knowsley ('nəʊzlɪ) *n* a unitary authority of NW England, in Merseyside. Pop.: 154 000 (1994 est.). Area: 97 sq. km (38 sq. miles).

Knox (nɒks) *n* **1 John.** ?1514–72, Scottish theologian and historian. After exile in England and on the Continent (1547–59), he returned to Scotland in 1559 and established the Presbyterian Church of Scotland (1560). His chief historical work was the *History of the Reformation in Scotland* (1586). **2 Ronald (Arbuthnott).** 1888–1957, British priest and author. A convert to Roman Catholicism, he is noted for his translation of the Vulgate (1945–49).

Knox-Johnston (ˌnɒks'dʒɒnstən) *n* Sir **Robin (William Robert Patrick).** born 1939, British yachtsman. He was the first to sail round the world alone nonstop (1968–69).

Knoxville ('nɒksvɪl) *n* an industrial city in E Tennessee, on the Tennessee River: state capital (1796–1812; 1817–19). Pop.: 167 535 (1996 est.).

KNP *Chess. symbol for* king's knight's pawn.

Knt *abbrev. for* Knight.

knuckle ('nʌkᵊl) *n* **1** a joint of a finger, esp. that connecting a finger to the hand. **2** a joint of veal, pork, etc., consisting of the part of the leg below the knee joint, often used in making stews or stock. **3** the cylindrical portion of a hinge through which the pin passes. **4** an angle joint between two members of a structure. **5 near the knuckle.** *Informal.* approaching indecency. ◆ *vb* **6** *(tr)* to rub or press with the knuckles. **7** *(intr)* to keep the knuckles on the ground while shooting a marble. ◆ See also **knuckle down, knuckle under.** [C14: related to Middle High German *knöchel,* Middle Low German *knoke* bone, Dutch *knok*] ▸ **'knuckly** *adj*

knucklebone ('nʌkᵊlˌbəʊn) *n* any bone forming part of a knuckle or knuckle joint.

knucklebones ('nʌkᵊlˌbəʊnz) *n (functioning as sing)* a less common name for **jacks** (the game).

knuckle down *vb (intr, adv) Informal.* to apply oneself diligently: *to knuckle down to some work.*

knuckle-duster *n* (*often pl*) a metal bar fitted over the knuckles, often with holes for the fingers, for inflicting injury by a blow with the fist.

knucklehead ('nʌkᵊl,hɛd) *n Informal.* fool; idiot. ▸ **'knuckle,headed** *adj*

knuckle joint *n* **1** any of the joints of the fingers. **2** *Mechanical engineering.* a hinged joint between two rods, often a ball and socket joint.

knuckle under *vb* (*intr, adv*) to give way under pressure or authority; yield.

knur, knurr (nɜː), *or* **knar** *n* a knot or protuberance in a tree trunk or in wood. [C16 *knor;* related to Middle High German *knorre* knot; compare KNAR]

knurl *or* **nurl** (nɜːl) *vb* (*tr*) **1** to impress with a series of fine ridges or serrations. ♦ *n* **2** a small ridge, esp. one of a series providing a rough surface that can be gripped. [C17: probably from KNUR]

knurly ('nɜːlɪ) *adj* **knurlier, knurliest.** a rare word for **gnarled.**

Knussen ('nʌsən) *n* (**Stuart**) **Oliver.** born 1952, British composer and conductor. His works include the opera *Where the Wild Things Are* (1981) and three symphonies.

Knut (kə'njuːt) *n* a variant spelling of **Canute.**

KO *or* **k.o.** ('keɪ'əʊ) *vb* **KO's, KO'ing, KO'd; k.o.'s, k.o.'ing, k.o.'d,** *n, pl* **KO's** *or* **k.o.'s.** a slang term for **knock out** or **knockout.**

koa ('kəʊə) *n* **1** a Hawaiian mimosaceous tree, *Acacia koa,* yielding a hard wood. **2** the reddish wood of this tree, used esp. for furniture. [C19: from Hawaiian]

koala *or* **koala bear** (kəʊ'ɑːlə) *n* a slow-moving Australian arboreal marsupial, *Phascolarctus cinereus,* having dense greyish fur and feeding on eucalyptus leaves and bark. Also called (Austral.): **native bear.** [from a native Australian language]

koan ('kəʊæn) *n* (in Zen Buddhism) a problem or riddle that admits no logical solution. [from Japanese]

kob (kɒb) *n* any of several species of African antelope, esp. *Kobus kob:* similar to waterbucks. [C20: from a Niger-Congo language; compare Wolof *koba,* Fulani *kōba*]

Kobarid ('kəʊbə,riːd; *Serbo-Croat* 'kɔba,rid) *n* a village in Slovenia on the Isonzo River: part of Italy until 1947; scene of the defeat of the Italians by Austro-German forces (1917). Italian name: **Caporetto.**

Kobe ('kəʊbɪ) *n* a port in S Japan, on S Honshu on Osaka Bay: formed in 1889 by the amalgamation of Hyogo and Kobe; a major industrial complex, producing ships, steel, and rubber goods. Pop.: 1 423 830 (1995).

København (købən'haun) *n* the Danish name for **Copenhagen.**

Koblenz *or* **Coblenz** (*German* 'koːblɛnts) *n* a city in W central Germany, in the Rhineland-Palatinate at the confluence of the Rivers Moselle and Rhine: ruled by the archbishop-electors of Trier from 1018 until occupied by the French in 1794; passed to Prussia in 1815, becoming capital of the Rhine Province (1824–1945) and of the Rhineland-Palatinate (1946–50); wine trade centre. Pop.: 109 219 (1996 est.). Latin name: **Confluentes** (,kɒnflʊ'ɛntiːz).

kobold ('kɒbəʊld) *n German myth.* **1** a mischievous household sprite. **2** a spirit that haunts subterranean places, such as mines. [C19: from German; see COBALT]

Koch (*German* kɔx) *n* **Robert** ('roːbɛrt). 1843–1910, German bacteriologist, who isolated the anthrax bacillus (1876), the tubercle bacillus (1882), and the cholera bacillus (1883): Nobel prize for physiology or medicine 1905.

Köchel (*German* 'kœçəl) *n* See **K.**

Kochi (kəʊ'tʃiː) *n* a port in SW Japan, on central Shikoku on Urado Bay. Pop.: 322 077 (1995 est.).

kochia ('kəʊkɪə) *n* any plant of the widely distributed annual genus *Kochia,* esp. *K. Scoparia trichophila,* grown for its foliage, which turns dark red in the late summer: family *Chenopodiaceae.* Also called: **burning bush, summer cypress.** [named after W. D. J. *Koch* (1771–1849), German botanist]

Kodály (*Hungarian* 'kodaːj) *n* **Zoltán** ('zoltaːn). 1882–1967, Hungarian composer. His works were often inspired by native folk songs and include the comic opera *Háry János* (1926) and *Psalmus Hungaricus* (1923) for chorus and orchestra.

Kodiak ('kəʊdɪ,æk) *n* an island in S Alaska, in the Gulf of Alaska: site of the first European settlement in Alaska, made by Russians in 1784. Pop.: 13 309 (1990). Area: 8974 sq. km (3465 sq. miles).

Kodiak bear *or* **Kodiak** *n* a large variety of the brown bear, *Ursus arctos,* inhabiting the west coast of Alaska and neighbouring islands, esp. Kodiak.

Kodok ('kəʊdɒk) *n* the modern name for **Fashoda.**

koeksister ('kʊk,sɪstə) *n S. African.* a plaited doughnut deep-fried and soaked in syrup. [Afrikaans, but possibly of Malay origin]

koel ('kəʊəl) *n* any of several parasitic cuckoos of the genus *Eudynamys,* esp. *E. scolopacea,* of S and SE Asia and Australia. [C19: from Hindi, from Sanskrit *kokila*]

Koestler ('kɜːstlə) *n* **Arthur.** 1905–83, British writer, born in Hungary. Of his early antitotalitarian novels *Darkness at Noon* (1940) is outstanding. His later works, *The Sleepwalkers* (1959), *The Act of Creation* (1964), and *The Ghost in the Machine* (1967) reflect his interest in science, philosophy, and psychology. He committed suicide.

kofta ('kɒftə) *n* an Indian dish of seasoned minced meat shaped into small balls and cooked. [Urdu]

koftgar ('kɒftgɑː) *n* (in India) a person skilled in the art of inlaying steel with gold (**koftgari**). [C19: Urdu]

Kofu ('kəʊfuː) *n* a city in central Japan, on S Honshu: textiles. Pop.: 201 123 (1995 est.).

Kogi ('kəʊgɪ) *n* a state of W Nigeria. Capital: Lokoja. Pop.: 2 346 946 (1995 est.).

koha ('kəʊhə) *n N.Z.* a gift or donation, esp. of cash. [Maori]

kohanga reo (kə'hɑŋgə 'rɛɔ) *n N.Z.* an infant class in which the lessons are conducted in Maori. [Maori, literally: language nest]

Koheleth (kəʊ'hɛlɪθ) *n Old Testament.* Ecclesiastes or its author, traditionally believed to be Solomon. [from Hebrew *qōheleth*]

Kohen *or* **Cohen** (kɒ'hɛn, kɔɪn) *n Judaism.* a member of the priestly family of the Tribe of Levi, descended from Aaron, who has certain ritual privileges in the synagogue service. [from Hebrew, literally: priest]

Kohima ('kəʊhɪ,mɑː) *n* a city in NE India, capital of Nagaland, near the Burmese border: centre of fierce fighting in World War II, when it was surrounded by the Japanese but not captured (1944). Pop.: 21 545 (latest est.).

Koh-i-noor, Kohinor, *or* **Kohinur** (,kəʊɪ'nʊə) *n* a very large oval Indian diamond, part of the British crown jewels since 1849, weighing 108.8 carats. [C19: from Persian *Kōh-i-nūr,* literally: mountain of light, from *kōh* mountain + Arabic *nūr* light]

kohl (kəʊl) *n* a cosmetic powder used, originally esp. in Muslim and Asian countries, to darken the area around the eyes. It is usually powdered antimony sulphide. [C18: from Arabic *kohl;* see ALCOHOL]

Kohl (kəʊl) *n* **Helmut** ('hɛlmuːt). born 1930, German statesman: chancellor of West Germany (1982–90) and of Germany (1990–98).

Köhler (*German* 'køːlər) *n* **Wolfgang** ('vɔlfgaŋ). 1887–1967, German psychologist, a leading exponent of Gestalt psychology.

kohlrabi (kəʊl'rɑːbɪ) *n, pl* **-bies.** a cultivated variety of cabbage, *Brassica oleracea caulorapa* (or *gongylodes*), whose thickened stem is eaten as a vegetable. Also called: **turnip cabbage.** [C19: from German, from Italian *cavoli rape* (pl), from *cavolo* cabbage (from Latin *caulis*) + *rapa* turnip (from Latin); influenced by German *Kohl* cabbage]

Kohoutek (kə'huːtɛk) *n* a comet of almost parabolic orbit that reached its closest approach to the sun in Dec. 1973. [C20: named after Luboš *Kohoutek,* Czech astronomer working in Germany who discovered it in March, 1973]

koi (kɔɪ) *n* any of various ornamental forms of the common carp. [Japanese]

koine ('kɔɪniː) *n* a common language among speakers of different languages; lingua franca. [from Greek *koinē dialektos* common language]

Koine ('kɔɪniː) *n* (*sometimes not cap.*) **the.** the Ancient Greek dialect that was the lingua franca of the empire of Alexander the Great and was widely used throughout the E Mediterranean area in Roman times.

kokako ('kəʊ,kɑːkəʊ) *n, pl* **-kos.** a dark grey long-tailed wattled crow of New Zealand, *Callaeas cinerea.* [Maori]

Kokand (*Russian* ka'kant) *n* a city in NE Uzbekistan, in the Fergana valley. Pop.: 184 000 (1996).

kokanee (kəʊ'kænɪ) *n* a landlocked salmon, *Oncorhynchus nerka kennerlyi,* of lakes in W North America: a variety of sockeye. [probably from *Kokanee* Creek, in SE British Columbia]

kokobeh ('kʌkʌbɛ) *adj* (of certain fruit) having a rough skin: *kokobeh breadfruit.* [from Twi: leprosy]

Koko Nor ('kəʊ'kəʊ 'nɔː) *or* **Kuku Nor** *n* a lake in W China, in Qinghai province in the NE Tibetan Highlands at an altitude of about 3000 m (10 000 ft.): the largest lake in China. Area: about 4100 sq. km (1600 sq. miles). Chinese name: **Qinghai.**

Kokoschka (*German* ko'kɔʃka, 'kɔkɔʃka) *n* **Oskar** ('ɔskar). 1886–1980, Austrian expressionist painter and dramatist, noted for his landscapes and portraits.

Kokura (,kəʊkə'rɑː) *n* a former city in SW Japan, on N Kyushu: merged with adjacent townships in 1963 to form the new city of **Kitakyushu.**

kola ('kəʊlə) *n* a variant spelling of **cola**[1].

kola nut *n* a variant spelling of **cola nut.**

Kola Peninsula ('kəʊlə) *n* a peninsula in NW Russia, between the Barents and White Seas: forms most of the Murmansk region. Area: about 130 000 sq. km (50 000 sq. miles).

Kolar Gold Fields (kəʊ'lɑː) *n* a city in S India, in SE Karnataka: a major gold-mining centre since 1881. Pop.: 83 219 (1991 est.).

Kolding (*Danish* 'kɔleŋ) *n* a port in Denmark, in E Jutland at the head of **Kolding Fjord** (an inlet of the Little Belt). Pop.: 59 558 (1995).

Kolhapur (,kəʊlhɑː'pʊə) *n* a city in W India, in S Maharashtra: university (1963). Pop.: 406 370 (1991).

kolinsky (kə'lɪnskɪ) *n, pl* **-skies. 1** any of various Asian minks, esp. *Mustela sibirica* of Siberia. **2** the rich tawny fur of this animal. [C19: from Russian *kolinski* of *Kola:* see KOLA PENINSULA]

Kolkata ('kolkɑːtə) *n* the official name of **Calcutta.**

kolkhoz, kolkhos (kɒl'hɔːz; *Russian* kal'xɔs), *or* **kolkoz** (kɒl'kɔːz) *n* a Russian collective farm. [C20: from Russian, short for *kollektivnoe khozyaistvo* collective farm]

Kollwitz (*German* 'kɔlvɪts) *n* **Käthe** ('kɛːtə). 1867–1945, German lithographer and sculptress.

Kolmar ('kɔlmar) *n* the German name for **Colmar.**

Kolmogorov (,kɒlmɒ'gɔːrɒf) *n* **Andrei Nikolaevich** (an'drjej nika'lajəvitʃ). (1903–87), Soviet mathematician, who made important contributions to the theoretical foundations of probability.

Köln (kœln) *n* the German name for **Cologne.**

Kol Nidre (kɔːl 'nɪdreɪ; *Hebrew* kɔl niː'dre) *n Judaism.* **1** the evening service with which Yom Kippur begins. **2** the opening prayer of that service, declaring null in advance any purely religious vows one may come to make in the coming year. [Aramaic *kōl nidhrē* all the vows; the prayer's opening words]

kolo ('kəʊləʊ) *n, pl* **-los. 1** a Serbian folk dance in which a circle of people dance slowly around one or more dancers in the centre. **2** a piece of music composed for or in the rhythm of this dance. [Serbo-Croat, from Old Slavonic: wheel; related to Old English *hwēol* WHEEL]

Kolomna (*Russian* ka'lɔmnə) *n* a city in the W central Russia, at the confluence of the Moskva and Oka Rivers: railway engineering centre. Pop.: 154 000 (1995 est.).

Kolozsvár ('koloʒvaːr) *n* the Hungarian name for **Cluj.**

Kolyma (*Russian* kəli'ma) *n* a river in NE Russia, rising in the Kolyma Mountains north of the Sea of Okhotsk and flowing generally north to the East Siberian Sea. Length: 2600 km (1615 miles).

Kolyma Range *n* a mountain range in NE Russia, in NE Siberia, extending about 1100 km (700 miles) between the Kolyma River and the Sea of Okhotsk. Highest peak: 1862 m (6109 ft.).

Komati (kəˈmɑːtɪ, ˈkəʊmətɪ) *n* a river in southern Africa, rising in E South Africa and flowing east through Swaziland and Mozambique to the Indian Ocean at Delagoa Bay. Length: about 800 km (500 miles).

komatik (ˈkəʊmætɪk) *n* a sledge having wooden runners and crossbars bound with rawhide, used by Eskimos. [C20: from Eskimo (Labrador)]

Komi (ˈkəʊmɪ) *n* **1** (*pl* **Komi** *or* **Komis**) a member of a Finno-Ugric people living chiefly in the Komi Republic, in the NW Urals. **2** the Finno-Ugric language of this people; Zyrian.

Komi Republic (ˈkəʊmɪ) *n* a constituent republic of NW Russia: annexed by the princes of Moscow in the 14th century. Capital: Syktyvkar. Pop.: 1 203 000 (1995 est.). Area: 415 900 sq. km (160 540 sq. miles).

Kommunarsk (*Russian* kəmuˈnarsk) *n* the former name (until 1992) of **Alchevsk.**

Kommunizma Peak (*Russian* kəmuˈnjizmə) *n* a mountain in SE Tajikistan in the Pamirs: the highest mountain in the former Soviet Union. Height: 7495 m (24 590 ft.). Former name: **Stalin Peak.**

Komodo dragon *or* **lizard** (kəˈməʊdəʊ) *n* the largest monitor lizard, *Varanus komodoensis,* of Komodo and other East Indian islands: grows to a length of 3 m (about 10 ft.) and a weight of 135 kilograms (about 300 lbs.).

komondor (ˈkɒmənˌdɔː) *n* a large powerful dog of an ancient Hungarian breed, originally used for sheep herding. It has a very long white coat that hangs in woolly or matted locks.

Komsomol (ˌkɒmsəˈmɒl, ˈkɒmsəˌmɒl; *Russian* kəmsaˈmɔl) *n* (formerly) the youth association of the Soviet Union for 14- to 26-year-olds. [C20: from Russian, from *Kom(munisticheski) So(yuz) Mol(odezhi)* Communist Union of Youth]

Komsomolsk (*Russian* kəmsaˈmɔljsk) *n* an industrial city in W Russia, on the Amur River: built by members of the Komsomol (Communist youth league) in 1932. Pop.: 309 000 (1995 est.).

Konakry *or* **Konakri** (*French* kɔnakri) *n* variant spellings of **Conakry.**

kondo (ˈkɒndəʊ) *n, pl* **-dos.** (in Uganda) a thief or armed robber. [C20: from Luganda]

koneke (ˈkɒnˌɛkɪ) *n N.Z.* a farm vehicle with runners in front and wheels at the rear. [Maori]

Kongo (ˈkɒŋgəʊ) *n* **1** (*pl* **-gos** *or* **-go**) a member of a Negroid people of Africa living in the tropical forests of the Democratic Republic of the Congo (formerly Zaïre), the Congo Republic, and Angola. **2** the language of this people, belonging to the Bantu group of the Niger-Congo family.

kongoni (kəŋˈgəʊnɪ) *n, pl* **-ni.** an E African hartebeest, *Alcelaphus buselaphus.* See **hartebeest** (sense 1). [Swahili]

Kongur Shan (ˈkʊŋguə ˈʃæn), **Kungur,** *or* **Qungur** *n* a mountain in China, in W Xinjiang Uygur: the highest peak in the Pamirs. Height: 7719 m (25 325 ft.).

Kong Zi (ˈkʊŋ ziː) *n* the Pinyin transliteration of the Chinese name for **Confucius.**

Königgrätz (køːnɪçˈgrɛːts) *n* the German name for **Hradec Králové.**

Königsberg (ˈkɜːnɪgzˌbɜːg; *German* ˈkøːnɪçsbɛrk) *n* the former name (until 1946) of **Kaliningrad.**

Königshütte (ˈkøːnɪçshytə) *n* the German name for **Chorzów.**

konimeter (kəʊˈnɪmɪtə) *n* a device for collecting samples of dust, etc., in the air by sucking the air through a hole and allowing it to pass over a glass plate coated with grease on which the particles collect. [C20: from Greek *konia* dust + -METER]

koniology *or* **coniology** (ˌkəʊnɪˈɒlədʒɪ) *n* the study of atmospheric dust and its effects. [C20: from Greek *konia* dust + -LOGY]

Konstanz (ˈkɔnstants) *n* the German name for **Constance.**

Konya *or* **Konia** (ˈkɔːnjɑː) *n* a city in SW central Turkey: in ancient times a Phrygian city and capital of Lycaonia. Pop.: 584 785 (1995 est.). Ancient name: **Iconium.**

koodoo (ˈkuːduː) *n* a variant spelling of **kudu.**

kook (kuːk) *n U.S. and Canadian informal.* an eccentric, crazy, or foolish person. [C20: probably from CUCKOO]

kookaburra (ˈkʊkəˌbʌrə) *n* a large arboreal Australian kingfisher, *Dacelo novaeguineae* (or *gigas*), with a cackling cry. Also called: **laughing jackass.** [C19: from a native Australian language]

kooky *or* **kookie** (ˈkuːkɪ) *adj* **kookier, kookiest.** *Informal.* crazy, eccentric, or foolish.

Kooning (ˈkuːnɪŋ) *n* **Willem de** (ˈwɪləm də). 1904–97, U.S. abstract expressionist painter, born in Holland.

koori (ˈkʊərɪ) *n, pl* **-ries.** a native Australian. [C19: from a native Australian language]

Kootenay *or* **Kootenai** (ˈkuːtᵊniː, ˈkuːtneɪ) *n* a river in W North America, rising in SE British Columbia and flowing south into NW Montana, then north into Idaho before re-entering British Columbia, broadening into **Kootenay Lake,** then flowing to the Columbia River. Length: 655 km (407 miles).

kop (kɒp) *n* a prominent isolated hill or mountain in southern Africa. See **inselberg.** [from Afrikaans: head, hence high part; compare German *Kopf* head; see COP[2]]

kopeck, kopek, *or* **copeck** (ˈkəʊpɛk) *n* a monetary unit of Russia and Belarus worth one hundredth of a rouble: coins are still used as tokens for coin-operated machinery although the kopeck itself is virtually valueless. [Russian *kopeika,* from *kopye* lance; so called because of the representation of Tsar Ivan IV on the coin with a lance in his hand]

Kopeisk *or* **Kopeysk** (*Russian* kaˈpjejsk) *n* a city in SW central Russia, in Chelyabinsk province: lignite mining. Pop.: 78 300 (1991 est.). Former name: **Kopi** (ˈkɔpi).

koph *or* **qoph** (kɒf) *n* the 19th letter in the Hebrew alphabet (ק) transliterated as *q,* and pronounced as a velar or uvular stop. [from Hebrew *qoph;* see QOPH]

kopje *or* **koppie** (ˈkɒpɪ) *n* a small isolated hill. [C19: from Afrikaans *koppie,* from Dutch *kopje,* literally: a little head, from *kop* head; see KOP]

koppa (ˈkɒpə) *n* a consonantal letter in the Greek alphabet pronounced like kappa (K) with the point of articulation further back in the throat. It became obsolete in classical (Attic) Greek orthography, but was passed on to the Romans who incorporated it into their alphabet as Q. [Greek, of Semitic origin]

kora (ˈkɔːrə) *n* a West African instrument with twenty-one strings, combining features of the harp and the lute.

Koran (kɔːˈrɑːn) *n* the sacred book of Islam, believed by Muslims to be the infallible word of God dictated to Mohammed through the medium of the angel Gabriel. Also: **Qur'an.** [C17: from Arabic *qur'ān* reading, book; related to *qara'a* to read, recite] ► **Koˈranic** *adj*

Korat cat (ˈkɔːræt) *n* a rare type of cat originating in Thailand that has a blue-grey coat and, in the adult, brilliant green eyes. [named after the *Korat* Plateau in Thailand]

Korbut (*Russian* ˈkɔrbut) *n* **Olga** (ˈɔljgə). born 1955, Soviet gymnast: noted for her highly individualistic style, which greatly increased the popularity of the sport, esp. following her performance in the 1972 Olympic Games.

Korçë (*Albanian* ˈkortʃə) *n* a market town in SE Albania. Pop.: 67 100 (1991 est.).

Korchnoi (ˈkɔːtʃˌnɔɪ) *n* **Victor.** born 1931, Soviet-born chess player: Soviet champion 1960, 1962, and 1964: defected to the West in 1976.

Korda (ˈkɔːdə) *n* Sir **Alexander,** real name *Sandor Kellner.* 1893–1956, British film producer and director, born in Hungary: his films include *The Scarlet Pimpernel* (1934), *Anna Karenina* (1948), and *The Third Man* (1949).

Kordofan (ˌkɔːdəʊˈfæn) *n* a region of the central Sudan: consists of a plateau with rugged uplands (the Nuba Mountains). Area: 380 548 sq. km (146 930 sq. miles).

Kordofanian (ˌkɔːdəʊˈfeɪnɪən) *n* **1** a group of languages spoken in the Kordofan and Nuba Hills of the S Sudan: classed as an independent family, probably distantly related to Niger-Congo. ◆ *adj* **2** denoting, relating to, or belonging to this group of languages. **3** of or relating to Kordofan.

Korea (kəˈriːə) *n* a former country in E Asia, now divided into two separate countries, North Korea and South Korea. Korea occupied the peninsula between the Sea of Japan and the Yellow Sea: an isolated vassal of Manchu China for three centuries until the opening of ports to Japanese trade in 1876; gained independence in 1895; annexed to Japan in 1910 and divided in 1945 into two occupation zones (Russian in the north, American in the south), which became North Korea and South Korea in 1948. Japanese name (1910–45): **Chosen.** See **North Korea, South Korea.**

Korean (kəˈriːən) *adj* **1** of or relating to Korea, its people, or their language. ◆ *n* **2** a native or inhabitant of Korea. **3** the official language of North and South Korea, considered by some scholars to be part of the Altaic family of languages.

Korean War *n* the war (1950–53) fought between North Korea, aided by Communist China, and South Korea, supported by the U.S. and other members of the UN.

Korea Strait *n* a strait between South Korea and SW Japan, linking the Sea of Japan with the East China Sea.

korero (ˈkɒrərɔː) *n, pl* **-ros.** *N.Z.* a talk or discussion; meeting. [Maori]

korfball (ˈkɔːfˌbɔːl) *n* a game similar to basketball, in which each team consists of six men and six women. [C20: from Dutch *korfbal* basketball]

Kórinthos (ˈkɔrinθɔs) *n* transliteration of the Modern Greek name for **Corinth.**

korma *or* **qorma** (ˈkɔːmə) *n* any of a variety of Indian dishes consisting of meat or vegetables braised with water, stock, yogurt, or cream. [from Urdu]

Korsakoffian (ˌkɔːsəˈkɒfɪən) *adj* **1** relating to or suffering from Korsakoff's psychosis. ◆ *n* **2** a person suffering from Korsakoff's psychosis.

Korsakoff's psychosis *or* **syndrome** (ˈkɔːsəkɒfs) *n* a mental illness involving severe confusion and inability to retain recent memories, usually caused by alcoholism. [C19: named after Sergei *Korsakoff* (1854–1900), Russian neuropsychiatrist, who described it]

Kortrijk (ˈkɔrtrɛik) *n* the Flemish name for **Courtrai.**

koru (ˈkɒruː) *n N.Z.* a stylized curved pattern used esp. in carving. [Maori]

koruna (kɒˈruːnə) *n* **1** the standard monetary unit of the Czech Republic, divided into 100 halers. **2** the standard monetary unit of Slovakia, divided into 100 haliers. [Czech, from Latin *corōna* crown, wreath; see CROWN]

Korzybski (kɔːˈzɪbskɪ) *n* **Alfred** (**Habdank Skarbek**). 1879–1950, U.S. originator of the theory and study of general semantics, born in Poland.

kos (kəʊs) *n, pl* **kos.** an Indian unit of distance having different values in different localities. It is usually between 1 and 3 miles or 1 and 5 kilometres. Also called: **coss.** [from Hindi *kōs*]

Kos *or* **Cos** (kɒs) *n* an island in the SE Aegean Sea, in the Greek Dodecanese Islands: separated from SW Turkey by the **Kos Channel;** settled in ancient times by Dorians and became famous for literature and medicine. Pop.: 21 000 (latest est.). Area: 282 sq. km (109 sq. miles).

Kosciusko[1] (ˌkɒsɪˈʌskəʊ) *n* **Mount.** a mountain in Australia, in SE New South Wales in the Australian Alps: the highest peak in Australia. Height: 2230 m (7316 ft.).

Kosciusko[2] (ˌkɒsɪˈʌskəʊ) *n* **Thaddeus,** Polish name *Tadeusz Kościusko.* 1746–1817, Polish general: fought for the colonists in the American War of Independence and led an unsuccessful revolt against the partitioning of Poland (1794).

kosher (ˈkəʊʃə) *adj* **1** *Judaism.* conforming to religious law; fit for use: esp., (of food) prepared in accordance with the dietary laws. See also **kasher, kashruth.** **2** *Informal.* **2a** genuine or authentic. **2b** legitimate or proper. [C19: from Yiddish, from Hebrew *kāshēr* right, proper]

Košice (*Czech* ˈkɔʃitse) *n* a city in E Slovakia: passed from Hungary to Czechoslovakia in 1920 and to Slovakia in 1993. Pop.: 240 915 (1996 est.). Hungarian name: **Kassa.**

Kosovo (*Serbo-Croat* 'kɔsɔvɔ) *n* a region in S central Yugoslavia, in SW Serbia: became an autonomous region in 1946; chiefly Albanian in population since the 13th century, it was deprived of its autonomous status by Serbia after declaring independence in 1990; Serb suppression of violent separatists escalated to a policy of ethnic cleansing in 1998, provoking NATO airstrikes against Serbia in 1999: mainly a plateau. Capital: Priština. Pop.: 1 989 000 (1995 est.). Area: 10 887 sq. km (4203 sq. miles). Full name: **Kosovo-Metohija** (*Serbo-Croat* 'kɔsɔvɔmɛˌtɔhija).

Kossoff ('kɒsɒf) *n* **Leon.** born 1926, British painter, esp. of London scenes.

Kossuth (*Hungarian* 'koʃu:t) *n* **Lajos** ('lɔjoʃ). 1802–94, Hungarian statesman. He led the revolution against Austria (1848) and was provisional governor (1849), but he fled when the revolt was suppressed (1849).

Kostroma (*Russian* kəstra'ma) *n* a city in W central Russia, on the River Volga: fought over bitterly by Novgorod, Tver, and Moscow, until annexed by Moscow in 1329; textile centre. Pop.: 285 000 (1995 est.).

Kosygin (*Russian* ka'sigin) *n* **Aleksei Nikolayevich** (alɪk'sjej nika'lajɪvitʃ). 1904–80, Soviet statesman; premier of the Soviet Union (1964–80).

Kota *or* **Kotah** ('kəʊtə) *n* a city in NW India, in Rajasthan on the Chambal River: textile industry. Pop.: 537 371 (1991).

Kotabaru ('kəʊtə'bɑ:ru:) *n* a former name of **Jayapura.**

Kota Bharu *or* **Bahru** ('kəʊtə 'bɑ:ru:) *n* a port in NE Peninsular Malaysia: capital of Kelantan state on the delta of the Kelantan River. Pop.: 219 713 (1991).

Kota Kinabalu ('kəʊtə ˌkɪnəbə'lu:) *n* a port in Malaysia, capital of Sabah state on the South China Sea: exports timber and rubber. Pop.: 208 484 (1991). Former name: **Jesselton.**

koto ('kəʊtəʊ) *n, pl* **kotos.** a Japanese stringed instrument, consisting of a rectangular wooden body over which are stretched silk strings, which are plucked with plectrums or a nail-like device. [Japanese]

kotuku ('kəʊtʊku:) *n, pl* **-ku.** *N.Z.* the white heron, *Egretta alba,* having brilliant white plumage, black legs and yellow eyes and bill. [Maori]

koulibiaca *or* **coulibiaca** (ˌkəʊlɪ'bjɑ:kə) *n* a Russian baked dish consisting of flaked fish mixed with semolina encased in pastry. [from Russian]

koumis ('ku:mɪs) *n* a variant spelling of **kumiss.**

kouprey ('ku:preɪ) *n* a large wild member of the cattle tribe, *Box sauveli,* of SE Asia, having a blackish-brown body and white legs: an endangered species. [C20: from French, from a Cambodian native name, from Pali *gō* cow + Khmer *brai* forest]

Kovno ('kɔvnə) *n* transliteration of the Russian name for **Kaunas.**

Kovrov (*Russian* kav'rɔf) *n* a city in W central Russia, on the Klyazma River: textiles and heavy engineering. Pop.: 162 000 (1995 est.).

Koweit (kəʊ'weɪt) *n* a variant of **Kuwait.**

kowhai ('kəʊwaɪ; 'kəʊfaɪ) *n N.Z.* a small leguminous tree, *Sophora tetraptera,* of New Zealand and Chile, with clusters of yellow flowers. [C19: from Maori]

Kowloon ('kaʊ'lu:n) *n* **1** a peninsula of SE China, opposite Hong Kong Island: part of the former British colony of Hong Kong. Area: 10 sq. km (3.75 sq. miles). **2** a port in Hong Kong, on Kowloon Peninsula. Pop.: 1 990 000 (1994 est.).

kowtow (ˌkaʊ'taʊ) *vb* (*intr*) **1** to touch the forehead to the ground as a sign of deference: a former Chinese custom. **2** (often foll. by *to*) to be servile or obsequious (towards). ◆ *n* **3** the act of kowtowing. [C19: from Chinese *k'o t'ou,* from *k'o* to strike, knock + *t'ou* head] ▸ ˌ**kow'tower** *n*

Kozhikode (ˌkəʊʒɪ'kəʊd) *n* a port in SW India, in W Kerala on the Malabar coast: important European trading post (1511–1765): formerly calico-manufacturing. Pop.: 420 000 (1991). Former name: **Calicut.**

KP *abbrev. for:* **1** Knight (of the Order) of St Patrick. **2** *U.S. military.* kitchen police. ◆ **3** *Chess. symbol for* king's pawn.

kph *abbrev. for* kilometres per hour.

Kr 1 *Currency. symbol for:* **1a** krona. **1b** krone. **2** *the chemical symbol for* krypton.

KR *Chess. symbol for* king's rook.

kr. *abbrev. for:* **1** krona. **2** krone.

Kra (krɑ:) *n* **Isthmus of.** an isthmus of SW Thailand, between the Bay of Bengal and the Gulf of Siam: the narrowest part of the Malay Peninsula. Width: about 56 km (35 miles).

kraal (krɑ:l) *S. African.* ◆ *n* **1** a hut village in southern Africa, esp. one surrounded by a stockade. **2** an enclosure for livestock. ◆ *adj* **3** denoting or relating to the tribal aspects of the Black African way of life. ◆ *vb* **4** (*tr*) to enclose (livestock) in a kraal. [C18: from Afrikaans, from Portuguese *curral* pen; see CORRAL]

Krafft-Ebing (*German* 'kraft'e:bɪŋ) *n* **Richard** ('rɪçart), Baron von Krafft-Ebing. 1840–1902, German neurologist and psychiatrist who pioneered the systematic study of sexual behaviour in *Psychopathia Sexualis* (1886).

kraft (krɑ:ft) *n* strong wrapping paper, made from pulp processed with a sulphate solution. [from German: force]

Kragujevac (*Serbo-Croat* 'kragujevats) *n* a town in E central Yugoslavia, in Serbia; capital of Serbia (1818–39); automobile industry. Pop.: 147 305 (1991).

krait (kraɪt) *n* any nonaggressive brightly coloured venomous elapid snake of the genus *Bungarus,* of S and SE Asia. [C19: from Hindi *karait,* of obscure origin]

Krakatoa (ˌkrɑ:kə'təʊə, ˌkrækə'təʊə) *or* **Krakatau** (ˌkrɑ:kə'taʊ, ˌkrækə'taʊ) *n* a volcanic island in Indonesia, in the Sunda Strait between Java and Sumatra: partially destroyed by its eruption in 1883, the greatest in recorded history. Further eruptions 44 years later formed a new island, **Anak Krakatau** ("Child of Krakatau"). Also called: **Rakata.**

Krakau ('krɑ:kaʊ) *n* the German name for **Cracow.**

kraken ('krɑ:kən) *n* a legendary sea monster of gigantic size believed to dwell off the coast of Norway. [C18: from Norwegian, of obscure origin]

Kraków ('krakuf) *n* the Polish name for **Cracow.**

Kramatorsk (*Russian* krəma'tɔrsk) *n* a city in the E Ukraine: a major industrial centre of the Donets Basin. Pop.: 197 000 (1996 est.).

krameria (krə'mɪərɪə) *n* another name for **rhatany** (plant or drug). [C18: New Latin, named (by Linnaeus) after J. G. H. *Kramer,* an Austrian botanist]

Kranj (krɑ:nj) *n* the Slovene name for **Carniola.**

krans (krɑ:ns) *n S. African.* a sheer rock face; precipice. [C18: from Afrikaans]

Krasnodar (*Russian* krəsna'dar) *n* an industrial city in SW Russia, on the Kuban River. Pop.: 646 000 (1995 est.). Former name (until 1920): **Yekaterinodar.**

Krasnoyarsk (*Russian* krəsna'jarsk) *n* a city in E central Russia, on the Yenisei River: the country's largest hydroelectric power station is nearby. Pop.: 869 000 (1995 est.).

K ration *n* a small package containing emergency rations used by U.S. and Allied forces in the field in World War II. [C20: *K,* from the initial of the surname of Ancel *Keys* (born 1904), U.S. physiologist who instigated it]

Kraut (kraʊt) *n, adj Slang.* a derogatory word for **German.** [from German (*Sauer*)*kraut,* literally: (pickled) cabbage]

Krebs (krebz) *n* Sir **Hans Adolf.** 1900–81, British biochemist, born in Germany, who shared a Nobel prize for physiology or medicine (1953) for the discovery of the **Krebs cycle.**

Krebs cycle *n* a stage of tissue respiration: a series of biochemical reactions occurring in mitochondria in the presence of oxygen by which acetate, derived from the break down of foodstuffs, is converted to carbon dioxide and water, with the release of energy. Also called: **citric acid cycle, tricarboxylic acid cycle.** [C20: named after H. A. KREBS]

Krefeld ('kreɪfɛld; *German* 'kre:fɛlt) *n* a city in Germany, in W North Rhine-Westphalia: textile industries. Pop.: 249 606 (1996 est.).

Kreisler (*German* 'kraislər) *n* **Fritz** (frɪts). 1875–1962, U.S. violinist, born in Austria.

Kremenchug (*Russian* krɪmɪn'tʃuk) *n* an industrial city in the E central Ukraine on the Dnieper River. Pop.: 246 000 (1996 est.).

kremlin ('krɛmlɪn) *n* the citadel of any Russian city. [C17: from obsolete German *Kremelin,* from Russian *kreml*]

Kremlin ('krɛmlɪn) *n* **1** the 12th-century citadel in Moscow, containing the former Imperial Palace, three Cathedrals, and the offices of the Russian government. **2** (formerly) the central government of the Soviet Union.

Kremlinology (ˌkrɛmlɪn'ɒlədʒɪ) *n* (formerly) the study and analysis of the policies and practices of the Soviet government. ▸ ˌ**Kremlin'ologist** *n*

Krems (*German* krɛms) *n* a town in NE Austria, in Lower Austria on the River Danube. Pop.: 22 830 (1991).

kreplach ('krɛplɑ:k, -lɑ:x) *pl n* small filled dough casings usually served in soup. [C20: from Yiddish]

kreutzer *or* **kreuzer** ('krɔɪtsə) *n* any of various former copper and silver coins of Germany or Austria. [C16: from German *Kreuzer,* from *Kreuz* cross, from Latin *crux;* referring to the cross originally stamped upon such coins]

kriegspiel ('kri:gˌspi:l) *n* **1** (*sometimes cap.*) another word for **war game. 2** a variation of chess in which each player has his own board and men and does not see his opponent's board and men. The moves are regulated by an umpire on a third board out of sight of both players. [C19: from German *Kriegsspiel* war game]

Kriemhild ('kri:mhɪlt) *or* **Kriemhilde** ('kri:mˌhɪldə) *n* (in the *Nibelungenlied*) the wife of Siegfried. She corresponds to Gudrun in Norse mythology.

krill (krɪl) *n, pl* **krill.** any small shrimplike marine crustacean of the order *Euphausiacea:* the principal food of whalebone whales. [C20: from Norwegian *kril* young fish]

krimmer *or* **crimmer** ('krɪmə) *n* a tightly curled light grey fur obtained from the skins of lambs from the Crimean region. [C20: from German, from *Krim* CRIMEA]

Krio ('kri:əʊ) *n* **1** the English-based creole widely used as a lingua franca in Sierra Leone. Its principal language of admixture is Yoruba. **2** (*pl* **-os**) a native speaker of Krio. **3** (*modifier*) of or relating to the Krio language or Krios: *Krio poetry.* [alteration of CREOLE]

Kriol ('krɪɒl) *n* a creole language used by Aboriginal communities in the northern regions of Australia, developed from Northern Territory pidgin.

kris (krɪs) *n* a Malayan and Indonesian stabbing or slashing knife with a scalloped edge. Also called: **crease, creese.** [C16: from Malay *kris*]

Krishna[1] ('krɪʃnə) *n* a river in S India, rising in the Western Ghats and flowing generally southeast to the Bay of Bengal. Length: 1300 km (800 miles). Also called: **Kistna.**

Krishna[2] ('krɪʃnə) *n Hinduism.* the most celebrated of the Hindu deities, whose life story is told in the *Mahabharata.* [via Hindi from Sanskrit, literally: dark, black] ▸ '**Krishnaism** *n*

Krishna Menon ('kri:ʃnə 'mɛnən) *n* **Vengalil Krishnan** ('vɛŋgəlɪl 'kri:ʃnən). See (Vengalil Krishnan Krishna) **Menon.**

Kriss Kringle (ˌkrɪs 'krɪŋgᵊl) *n Chiefly U.S.* another name for **Santa Claus.** [changed from German *Christkindl* little Christ child, from CHRIST + *Kindl,* from *Kind* child]

Kristeva (krɪs'teɪvə) *n* **Julia.** born 1941, French semiotician, born in Bulgaria. Her works include *La Révolution du langage poétique* (1974) and *Polylogue* (1977).

Kristiania (ˌkrɪstɪ'ɑ:nɪə) *n* a former name (1877–1924) of **Oslo.**

Kristiansand *or* **Christiansand** ('krɪstʃənˌsænd; *Norwegian* kristian'san) *n* a port in S Norway, on the Skagerrak: shipbuilding. Pop.: 65 543 (1990).

Kristiansen ('krɪstʃənsən) *n* **Ingrid.** born 1956, Norwegian long-distance runner: former London marathon winner: world 10 000 metres record holder (1986–93).

Kristianstad ('krɪstʃənˌstɑ:d; *Swedish* kri'ʃansta:d) *n* a town in S Sweden:

founded in 1614 as a Danish fortress, it was finally acquired by Sweden in 1678. Pop.: 73 543 (1994).

Kríti ('kriti) *n* transliteration of the Modern Greek name for **Crete.**

Krivoy Rog (*Russian* kri'vɔj 'rɔk) *n* a city in the SE Ukraine: founded in the 17th century by Cossacks; iron-mining centre; iron- and steelworks. Pop.: 720 000 (1996 est.).

KRL *abbrev. for* knowledge representation language (in artificial intelligence).

kromesky (krə'mɛskɪ) *n, pl* **-kies.** a croquette consisting of a piece of bacon wrapped round minced meat or fish. [C19: from Russian *kromochka,* diminutive of *kroma* slice of bread]

krona ('krəʊnə) *n, pl* **kronor** ('krəʊnə). the standard monetary unit of Sweden, divided into 100 öre.

króna ('krəʊnə) *n, pl* **-nur** (-nə). the standard monetary unit of Iceland, divided into 100 aurar.

krone[1] ('krəʊnə) *n, pl* **-ner** (-nə). **1** the standard monetary unit of Denmark and its dependencies, divided into 100 øre. **2** the standard monetary unit of Norway, divided into 100 øre. [C19: from Danish or Norwegian, from Middle Low German *krōne,* ultimately from Latin *corōna* CROWN]

krone[2] ('krəʊnə) *n, pl* **-nen** (-nən). **1** a former German gold coin worth ten marks. **2** a former Austrian monetary unit. [C19: from German, literally: crown; see KRONE[1]]

Kronecker delta ('krɒnɪkə) *n Maths.* a function of two variables, i and j, that has a value of zero unless $i = j$, when it has a value of unity. Symbol: δ_{ij} [named after Leopold *Kronecker* (1823–91), German mathematician]

Kronos ('krəʊnɒs) *n* a variant of **Cronus.**

Kronstadt *n* **1** (*Russian* kran'ʃtat). a port in NW Russia, on Kotlin island in the Gulf of Finland: naval base. Pop.: 44 400 (1994 est.). **2** ('kro:nʃtat). the German name for **Braşov.**

kroon (kru:n) *n, pl* **kroons** *or* **krooni** ('kru:nɪ). the standard monetary unit of Estonia, divided into 100 cents. [Estonian *kron,* from German *krone* KRONE[2]]

Kropotkin (*Russian* kra'pɒtkin) *n* Prince **Peter,** Russian name *Pyotr Alexeyevich.* 1842–1921, Russian anarchist: his books include *Mutual Aid* (1902) and *Modern Science and Anarchism* (1903).

KRP *Chess. symbol for* king's rook's pawn.

Kruger ('kru:gə) *n* **Stephanus Johannes Paulus** ('stɛfənʊs jəʊ'hænɪs 'pɔ:lʊs), known as *Oom Paul.* 1825–1904, Boer statesman; president of the Transvaal (1883–1900). His opposition to Cecil Rhodes and his denial of civil rights to the Uitlanders led to the Boer War (1899–1902).

Kruger National Park *n* a wildlife sanctuary in NE South Africa: the world's largest game reserve. Area: over 21 700 sq. km (8400 sq. miles).

Krugerrand ('kru:gə,rænd) *n* a South African coin used for investment only and containing 1 troy ounce of gold. [C20: from S.J.P. KRUGER + RAND[1]]

Krugersdorp ('kru:gəz,dɔ:p) *n* a city in NE South Africa, on the Witwatersrand, at an altitude of 1722 m (5650 ft.): a gold-, manganese-, and uranium-mining centre. Pop.: 74 000 (latest est.).

kruller ('krʌlə) *n* a variant spelling of **cruller.**

krummholz ('krʊm,həʊlts) *n Botany.* the zone of stunted wind-blown trees growing at high altitudes just above the timber line. [C20: from German *krumm* bent + *Holz* wood]

krummhorn ('krʌm,hɔ:n) *n* a variant spelling of **crumhorn.**

Krupp (krʊp, krʌp) *n* a German family of steel and armaments manufacturers, including **Alfred,** 1812–87, his son **Friedrich Alfred,** 1854–1902, and the latter's son-in-law, **Gustav Krupp von Bohlen und Halbach,** 1870–1950.

Krušné Hory ('krʊʃnɛ 'hɔrɪ) *n* the Czech name for the **Erzgebirge.**

Krym *or* **Krim** (krɪm) *n* transliteration of the Russian name for **Crimea.**

krypton ('krɪptɒn) *n* an inert gaseous element occurring in trace amounts in air and used in fluorescent lights and lasers. Symbol: Kr; atomic no.: 36; atomic wt.: 83.80; valency: 0; density: 3.733 kg/m^3; melting pt.: –157.37°C; boiling pt.: –153.23±0.10°C. [C19: from Greek, from *kruptos* hidden; see CRYPT]

krytron ('kraɪtrɒn) *n Electronics.* a type of fast electronic gas-discharge switch, used as a trigger in nuclear weapons.

KS *abbrev. for* Kansas.

Kshatriya ('kʃætrɪə) *n* a member of the second of the four main Hindu castes, the warrior caste. [C18: from Sanskrit, from *kshatra* rule]

KStJ *abbrev. for* Knight of the Order of St John.

kt *abbrev. for:* **1** karat. **2** *Nautical.* knot.

Kt 1 Also: **Knt.** *abbrev. for* knight. ◆ **2** Also: **N.** *Chess. symbol for* knight.

KT *abbrev. for:* **1** Knight of the Order of the Thistle (a Brit. title). **2** Knight Templar.

kt. *abbrev. for* kiloton.

K/T boundary *n Geology.* **a** Cretaceous/Tertiary boundary: the time zone comprising the end of the Cretaceous and the beginning of the Tertiary periods. **b** (*as modifier*): *K/T boundary sediments.* [C20: *K* and *T,* symbols for Cretaceous and Tertiary, respectively]

Kuala Lumpur ('kwɑ:lə 'lʊmpʊə, -pə) *n* a city in Malaysia, in the SW Malay Peninsula: formerly (until 2000) the capital of Malaysia; became capital of the Federated Malay States in 1895, and of Malaysia in 1963; capital of Selangor state from 1880 to 1973, when it was made a federal territory. Pop.: 1 145 075 (1991).

Kuan Yin *or* **Kwan Yin** (kwan jɪn) *n* a female Chinese Bodhisattva of compassion, regarded as the protector of women and children and patron of sailors. Japanese name: **Kannon.** [from Chinese: one who hears the sounds of the world]

Kuban (*Russian* ku'banj) *n* a river in SW Russia, rising in the Caucasus Mountains and flowing north and northwest to the Sea of Azov. Length: 906 km (563 miles).

Kubelik (*Czech* 'kubɛli:k) *n* **Raphael** ('ra:faɛl). 1914–96, Czech conductor and composer.

Kublai Khan ('ku:blaɪ 'kɑ:n) *n* ?1216–94, Mongol emperor of China: grandson of Genghis Khan. He completed his grandfather's conquest of China by overthrowing the Sung dynasty (1279) and founded the Yuan dynasty (1279–1368).

Kubrick ('kju:brɪk) *n* **Stanley.** 1928–99, U.S. film writer, director, and producer. He directed *Lolita* (1962), *Dr Strangelove* (1963), *2001: A Space Odyssey* (1968), *A Clockwork Orange* (1971), *The Shining* (1980), *Full Metal Jacket* (1987), and *Eyes Wide Shut* (1999).

Kuch Bihar ('ku:tʃ bɪ'hɑ:) *n* a variant spelling of **Cooch Behar.**

kuchen ('ku:xən) *n* a breadlike cake containing apple, nuts, and sugar, originating from Germany. [German: CAKE]

Kuching ('ku:tʃɪŋ) *n* a port in E Malaysia, capital of Sarawak state, on the Sarawak River 24 km (15 miles) from its mouth. Pop.: 147 729 (1991).

kudos ('kju:dɒs) *n* (*functioning as sing*) acclaim, glory, or prestige. [C18: from Greek]

kudu *or* **koodoo** ('ku:du:) *n* either of two spiral-horned antelopes, *Tragelaphus strepsiceros* (**greater kudu**) or *T. imberbis* (**lesser kudu**), which inhabit the bush of Africa. [C18: from Afrikaans *koedoe,* probably from Khoi]

kudzu ('kʊdzu:) *n* a hairy leguminous climbing plant, *Pueraria thunbergiana,* of China and Japan, with trifoliate leaves and purple fragrant flowers. [from Japanese *kuzu*]

kueh ('kɒeɪ) *n* (*functioning as sing or pl*) (in Malaysia) any cake of Malay, Chinese, or Indian origin. [from Malay]

Kuenlun ('kʊn'lʊn) *n* a variant spelling of **Kunlun.**

Kufic *or* **Cufic** ('ku:fɪk, 'kju:-) *adj* **1** of, relating to, or denoting an early form of the Arabic alphabet employed in making copies of the Koran. ◆ *n* **2** the script formed by the letters of this alphabet.

kufiyah (kʊ'fi:jə) *n* a variant of **keffiyeh.**

Kuibyshev *or* **Kuybyshev** (*Russian* 'kujbɪʃəf) *n* the former name (until 1991) of **Samara.**

Ku Klux Klan ('ku: 'klʌks 'klæn) *n* **1** a secret organization of White Southerners formed after the U.S. Civil War to fight Black emancipation and Northern domination. **2** a secret organization of White Protestant Americans, mainly in the South, who use violence against Blacks, Jews, and other minority groups. [C19 *Ku Klux,* probably based on Greek *kuklos* CIRCLE + *Klan* CLAN] ▶ **Ku Kluxer** *or* **Ku Klux Klanner** *n* ▶ **Ku Kluxism** *n*

kukri ('kʊkrɪ) *n, pl* **-ris.** a knife with a curved blade that broadens towards the point, esp. as used by Gurkhas. [from Hindi]

Kuku Nor ('ku:'ku: 'nɔ:) *n* a variant of **Koko Nor.**

kula ('ku:lə) *n* a ceremonial gift exchange practised among a group of islanders in the W Pacific, used to establish relations between islands. [of Melanesian origin]

kulak ('ku:læk) *n* (in Russia after 1906) a member of the class of peasants who became proprietors of their own farms. After the October Revolution the kulaks opposed collectivization of land, but in 1929 Stalin initiated their liquidation. [C19: from Russian: fist, hence, tightfisted person; related to Turkish *kol* arm]

kulan ('ku:,lɑ:n) *n* the Asiatic wild ass of the Russian steppes, probably a variety of kiang or onager. [C18: from Kirghiz]

kulfi ('kʊlfɪ) *n* an Indian dessert made by freezing milk which has been concentrated by boiling away some of the water in it, and flavoured with nuts and cardamom seeds.

Kultur (kʊl'tʊə) *n* (often used ironically) German civilization, esp. as characterized by authoritarianism and earnestness. [German, from Latin *cultūra* CULTURE]

Kulturkampf (kʊl'tʊə,kæmpf, 'kʊltə-) *n* the struggle of the Prussian state against the Roman Catholic Church (1872–87), which took the form of laws designed to bring education, marriage, etc., under the control of the state. [German: culture struggle]

Kulun ('ku:'lu:n) *n* the Chinese name for **Ulan Bator.**

Kum (kʊm) *n* a variant spelling of **Qom.**

Kumamoto (,kʊmə'məʊtəʊ) *n* a city in SW Japan, on W central Kyushu: Kumamoto Medical University (1949). Pop.: 650 322 (1995).

Kumaratunge (,kʊmə'rɑtʊŋgə) *n* **Chandrika** ('tʃʊn,drɪkə) **Bandaranaike.** born 1945, Sri Lankan politician: prime minister (1994); president from 1994.

Kumasi (ku:'mæsɪ) *n* a city in S Ghana: seat of Ashanti kings since 1663; university (1961); market town for a cocoa-producing region. Pop.: 385 192 (1988 est.).

Kumayri (*Russian* ,kumaɪ'rɪ) *n* a city in NW Armenia: textile centre. Pop.: 120 000 (1989). Former names (1840–1924): **Aleksandropol,** (1924–91): **Leninakan.**

kumbaloi (,kʊmbə'lɔɪ) *pl n* another name for **worry beads.** [C20: Modern Greek]

kumera *or* **kumara** ('ku:mərə) *n* the N.Z. name for **sweet potato.** [Maori]

kumiss, koumiss, koumis, *or* **koumyss** ('ku:mɪs) *n* a drink made from fermented mare's or other milk, drunk by certain Asian tribes, esp. in Russia or used for dietetic and medicinal purposes. [C17: from Russian *kumys,* from Kazan Tatar *kumyz*]

kumite ('kuimɪ,teɪ) *n Karate, etc.* freestyle sparring or fighting. [C20: Japanese, literally: sparring]

kümmel ('kʊməl; *German* 'kyməl) *n* a German liqueur flavoured with aniseed and cumin. [C19: from German *Kümmel,* from Old High German *kumil,* probably variant of *kumin* CUMIN]

kummerbund ('kʌmə,bʌnd) *n* a variant spelling of **cummerbund.**

kumquat *or* **cumquat** ('kʌmkwɒt) *n* **1** any of several small Chinese trees of the rutaceous genus *Fortunella.* **2** the small round orange fruit of such a tree, with a sweet rind, used in preserves and confections. [C17: from Chinese (Cantonese) *kam kwat,* representing Mandarin Chinese *chin chü* golden orange]

Kun (kuːn) *n* **Béla** ('beːlɔ). 1886–?1937, Hungarian Communist leader, president of the short-lived Communist republic in Hungary (1919). He was forced into exile and died in a Stalinist purge.

kuna ('kuːnə) *n* the standard monetary unit of Croatia, divided into 100 lipas.

Kundera ('kʌndərə) *n* **Milan.** born 1929, Czech novelist living in France. His novels include *The Book of Laughter and Forgetting* (1979), *The Unbearable Lightness of Being* (1984), and *Slowness* (1996).

Küng (kʊŋ) *n* **Hans.** born 1928, Swiss Roman Catholic theologian, who questioned the doctrine of infallibility: his licence to teach was withdrawn in 1979. His books include *Global Responsibility* (1991).

kung fu ('kʌŋ 'fuː) *n* a Chinese martial art combining principles of karate and judo. **[**from Chinese: martial art**]**

K'ung Fu-tse ('kʊŋ 'fuː'tseɪ) *n* the Chinese name of **Confucius.**

Kungur ('kʊŋgʊə) *n* a variant transliteration of the Chinese name for **Kongur Shan.**

Kunlun, Kuenlun, *or* **Kwenlun** ('kʊn'lʊn) *n* a mountain range in China, between the Tibetan plateau and the Tarim Basin, extending over 1600 km (1000 miles) east from the Pamirs: the largest mountain system of Asia. Highest peak: Ulugh Muztagh, 7723 m (25 338 ft.).

Kunming *or* **K'un-ming** ('kʊn'mɪŋ) *n* a city in SW China, capital of Yunnan province, near Lake Tien: important during World War II as a Chinese military centre, American air base, and transport terminus for the Burma Road; Yunnan University (1934). Pop.: 1 520 000 (1991 est.).

kunzite ('kʊntsaɪt) *n* a lilac-coloured transparent variety of the mineral spodumene: a gemstone. **[**C20: named after George F. *Kunz* (1856–1932), U.S. gem expert**]**

Kuomintang ('kwəʊ'mɪn'tæŋ) *n* the political party founded by Sun Yat-sen in 1911 and dominant in China from 1928 until 1949 under the leadership of Chiang Kai-shek. Since then it has been the official ruling party of Taiwan. **[**C20: from Chinese (Mandarin): National People's Party, from *kuo* nation + *min* people + *tang* party**]**

Kuopio (*Finnish* 'kwɔpjɔ) *n* a city in S central Finland. Pop.: 83 955 (1994).

Kura (kʊ'rɑː) *n* a river in W Asia, rising in NE Turkey and flowing across Georgia and Azerbaijan to the Caspian Sea. Length: 1515 km (941 miles).

kurchatovium (ˌkɜːtʃə'təʊvɪəm) *n* another name for **rutherfordium,** esp. as used in the former Soviet Union. **[**C20: from Russian, named after I. V. *Kurchatov* (1903–60), Soviet physicist**]**

Kurd (kɜːd) *n* a member of a nomadic people living chiefly in E Turkey, N Iraq, and W Iran.

kurdaitcha (kə'daɪtʃə) *n* (in certain Central Australian Aboriginal tribes) the man with the mission of avenging the death of a tribesman. Also: **kadaitcha.**

kurdaitcha shoes *pl n* (in certain Central Australian Aboriginal tribes) the emu-feather shoes worn by the kurdaitcha on his mission so that his footsteps may not be traced. Also: **kadaitcha shoes.**

Kurdish ('kɜːdɪʃ) *n* **1** the language of the Kurds, belonging to the West Iranian branch of the Indo-European family. ◆ *adj* **2** of or relating to the Kurds or their language.

Kurdistan, Kurdestan, *or* **Kordestan** (ˌkɜːdɪ'stɑːn) *n* a large plateau and mountainous region, between the Caspian Sea and the Black Sea, south of the Caucasus. Area: over 29 000 sq. km (74 000 sq. miles).

Kure (kuː'reɪ) *n* a port in SW Japan, on SW Honshu: a naval base; shipyards. Pop.: 209 477 (1995 est.).

Kurgan (*Russian* kur'gan) *n* a city in W Russia, on the Tobol River: industrial centre for an agricultural region. Pop.: 363 000 (1995 est.).

kuri ('kuːrɪ) *n, pl* **-ris.** *N.Z.* a mongrel dog. Also called **goorie.** **[**Maori**]**

Kuril Islands *or* **Kurile Islands** (kʊ'riːl) *pl n* a chain of 56 volcanic islands off the NE coast of Asia, extending for 1200 km (750 miles) from the S tip of the Kamchatka Peninsula to NE Hokkaido. Area: 14 990 sq. km (6020 sq. miles). Japanese name: **Chishima.**

Kurland ('kʊələnd) *n* a variant spelling of **Courland.**

Kurosawa (ˌkʊərə'sɑːwə) *n* **Akira** (ə'kɪərə). 1910–98, Japanese film director. His works include *Rashomon* (1950), *The Seven Samurai* (1954), *The Throne of Blood* (1957), *Kagemusha* (1980), *Ran* (1985), and *Madadayo* (1993).

Kuroshio (kə'rəʊʃɪˌəʊ) *n* another name for **Japan Current.**

kurrajong *or* **currajong** ('kʌrəˌdʒɒŋ) *n* any of various Australian trees or shrubs, esp. *Brachychiton populneum,* a sterculiaceous tree that yields a tough durable fibre. **[**C19: from a native Australian language**]**

kursaal ('kɜːzᵊl) *n* **1** a public room at a health resort. **2** an amusement park at a seaside or other resort. **[**from German, literally: cure room**]**

Kursk (*Russian* kursk) *n* a city in W Russia: industrial centre of an agricultural region: scene of a major Soviet victory (1943). Pop.: 442 000 (1995 est.).

kurta *or* **khurta** ('kʊətə) *n* a long loose garment like a shirt without a collar worn in India. **[**Hindi**]**

kurtosis (kə'təʊsɪs) *n Statistics.* a measure of the concentration of a distribution around its mean, esp. the statistic $B_2 = m_4/m^2_2$ where m_2 and m_4 are respectively the second and fourth moment of the distribution around the mean. In a normal distribution $B_2 = 3$. See also **platykurtic, mesokurtic, leptokurtic.** Compare **skewness.** **[**from Greek: curvature, from *kurtos* arched**]**

kuru ('kʊruː) *n* a degenerative disease of the nervous system, restricted to certain tribes in New Guinea, marked by loss of muscular control and thought to be caused by a slow virus. **[**C20: from a native name**]**

kuruş (kʊ'ruːʃ) *n, pl* **-ruş.** a Turkish monetary unit worth one hundredth of a lira. Also called: **piastre.** **[**from Turkish**]**

Kurzeme ('kʊrzɛmɛ) *n* the Latvian name for **Courland.**

Kush (kʌʃ, kʊʃ) *n* a variant spelling of **Cush.**

Kuskokwim ('kʌskəˌkwɪm) *n* a river in SW Alaska, rising in the Alaska Range and flowing generally southwest to **Kuskokwim Bay,** an inlet of the Bering Sea. Length: about 970 km (600 miles).

Kutaisi (*Russian* kuta'isi) *n* an industrial city in W Georgia on the Rioni River: one of the oldest towns of the Caucasus. Pop.: 240 600 (1994 est.).

Kutch *or* **Cutch** (kʌtʃ) *n* **1** a former state of W India, on the **Gulf of Kutch** (an inlet of the Arabian Sea): part of Gujarat state since 1960. **2 Rann of.** an extensive salt waste in W central India, and S Pakistan: consists of the Great Rann in the north and the Little Rann in the southeast; seasonal alternation between marsh and desert; some saltworks. In 1968 an international tribunal awarded about 10 per cent of the border area to Pakistan. Area: 23 000 sq. km (9000 sq. miles).

kutu ('kuːtuː) *n N.Z.* a slang word for **body louse** (see **louse** (sense 1)). Also called: **cootie.** **[**Maori**]**

Kutuzov (*Russian* ku'tuzəf) *n* Prince **Mikhail Ilarionovich** (mixa'il ilərі'ɔnəvitʃ). 1745–1813, Russian field marshal, who harried the French army under Napoleon throughout their retreat from Moscow (1812–13).

Kuwait (kʊ'weɪt) *or* **Koweit** *n* **1** a state on the NW coast of the Persian Gulf: came under British protection in 1899 and gained independence in 1961; invaded by Iraq in 1990; liberated by U.S.-led UN forces 1991 in the Gulf War: mainly desert. The economy is dependent on oil. Official language: Arabic. Official religion: Muslim. Currency: dinar. Capital: Kuwait. Pop.: 1 866 000 (1998 est.). Area: 28 859 sq. km (9375 sq. miles). **2** the capital of Kuwait: a port on the Persian Gulf. Pop.: 28 859 (1995). ▸ **Ku'waiti** *or* **Ko'waiti** *adj, n*

Kuznets ('kuznɪtz) *n* **Simon.** 1901–85, U.S. economist born in Russia. His books include *National Income and its Composition (1919–1938)* (1941) and *Economic Growth of Nations* (1971). He was awarded the Nobel Prize for economics in 1971.

Kuznetsk Basin (*Russian* kuz'njetsk) *or* **Kuzbass** (*Russian* kuz'bas) *n* a region of S Russia, in the Kemerovo Region of W Siberia: the richest coalfield in the country, with reserves of iron ore. Chief industrial centre: Novokuznetsk. Area: about 69 900 sq. km (27 000 sq. miles).

kV *abbrev. for* kilovolt.

KV *abbrev. for* Köchel Verzeichnis. See **K** **[**German, literally: Köchel catalogue**]**

Kvaløy (*Norwegian* 'kvaːlœj) *n* two islands in the Arctic Ocean, off the N coast of Norway: **North Kvaløy,** 329 sq. km (127 sq. miles), and **South Kvaløy,** 735 sq. km (284 sq. miles).

kvass, kvas, *or* **quass** (kvɑːs) *n* an alcoholic drink of low strength made in Russia and E Europe from cereals and stale bread. **[**C16: from Russian *kvas;* related to Old Slavic *kvasŭ* yeast, Latin *cāseus* cheese**]**

kvetch (kvetʃ) *vb (intr) Slang, chiefly U.S.* to complain or grumble, esp. incessantly. **[**C20: from Yiddish *kvetshn,* literally: to squeeze, press**]**

kW *abbrev. for* kilowatt.

Kwa (kwɑː) *n* **1** a group of languages, now generally regarded as a branch of the Niger-Congo family, spoken in an area of W Africa extending from the Ivory Coast to E Nigeria and including Akan, Ewe, Yoruba, and Ibo. ◆ *adj* **2** relating to or belonging to this group of languages.

kwacha ('kwɑːtʃɑː) *n* **1** the standard monetary unit of Zambia, divided into 100 ngwee. **2** the standard monetary unit of Malawi, divided into 100 tambala. **[**from a native word in Zambia**]**

Kwajalein ('kwɑːdʒəˌleɪn) *n* an atoll in the W Pacific, in the W Marshall Islands, in the central part of the Ralik Chain. Length: about 125 km (78 miles).

Kwakiutl (ˌkwɑːkɪ'uːtᵊl) *n* **1** (*pl* **-utl** *or* **-utls**) a member of a North American Indian people of N Vancouver Island and the adjacent mainland. **2** the language of this people, belonging to the Wakashan family.

Kwangchow ('kwæŋ'tʃaʊ) *n* a variant transliteration of the Chinese name for **Canton.**

Kwangchowan ('kwæŋ'tʃaʊ'wɑːn) *n* a territory of SE China, in SW Kwantung province: leased to France as part of French Indochina from 1898 to 1945. Area: 842 sq. km (325 sq. miles).

Kwangju ('kwæŋ'dʒuː) *n* a city in SW South Korea: an important military base during the Korean War; cotton textile industry. Pop.: 1 257 504 (1995).

Kwangsi-Chuang Autonomous Region ('kwæŋ'siː'tʃwæŋ) *n* a variant transliteration of the Chinese name for **Guangxi Zhuang Autonomous Region.**

Kwangtung ('kwæŋ'tʊŋ) *n* a variant transliteration of the Chinese name for **Guangdong.**

Kwantung Leased Territory (ˌkwæn'tʊŋ) *n* a strategic territory of NE China, at the S tip of the Liaotung Peninsula of Manchuria: leased forcibly by Russia in 1898; taken over by Japan in 1905; occupied by the Soviet Union in 1945 and subsequently returned to China on the condition of shared administration; made part of Liaoning province by China in 1954. Area: about 3400 sq. km (1300 sq. miles). Also called: **Kuan-tung.**

kwanza ('kwænzə) *n* the standard monetary unit of Angola, divided into 100 lwei. **[**from a Bantu language**]**

Kwara ('kwɑːrə) *n* a state of W Nigeria: mainly wooded savanna. Capital: Ilorin. Pop.: 1 751 464 (1995 est.). Area: 36 825 sq. km (14 218 sq. miles).

kwashiorkor (ˌkwæʃɪ'ɔːkə) *n* severe malnutrition of infants and young children, esp. soon after weaning, resulting from dietary deficiency of protein. **[**C20: from a native word in Ghana**]**

KwaZulu (kwɑː'zuːluː) *n* (formerly) a Bantu homeland in South Africa, in Natal: abolished in 1993 and replaced by KwaZulu/Natal in 1994. Capital: Ulundi.

KwaZulu/Natal (kwɑːˌzuːluːnə'tæl, -'tɑːl) *n* a province of NE South Africa; replaced the former province of Natal in 1994: service industries. Capital: Ulundi. Pop.: 8 713 100 (1995 est.). Area: 92 180 sq. km (35 591 sq. miles).

Kwedien (kwɪ'diːn) *n* a young African boy, esp. one who has not yet undergone the rites of initiation. **[**from Xhosa *inKwenkwe* boy**]**

Kweichow *or* **Kueichou** ('kweɪ'tʃaʊ) *n* a variant transliteration of the Chinese name for **Guizhou.**

Kweilin *or* **Kuei-lin** ('kweɪ'lɪn) *n* a variant transliteration of the Chinese name for **Guilin.**

Kweisui (ˈkweɪˈsweɪ) *n* the former name of **Hohhot.**

Kweiyang *or* **Kuei-yang** (ˈkweɪˈjæŋ) *n* a variant transliteration of the Chinese name for **Guiyang.**

kwela (ˈkweɪlə, ˈkwɛlə) *n* a type of pop music popular among the Black communities of South Africa. [C20: said to be from Zulu or Xhosa: jump up]

kWh *abbrev. for* kilowatt-hour.

KWIC (kwɪk) *n acronym for* key word in context (esp. in the phrase **KWIC index**).

KWOC (kwɒk) *n acronym for* key word out of context.

KWT *international car registration for* Kuwait.

Ky (kiː) *n* **Nguyen Kao** (ˈŋˈguːjɛn ˈkaʊ). born 1930, Vietnamese military and political leader: premier of South Vietnam (1965–67); vice president (1967–71).

Ky. *or* **KY** *abbrev. for* Kentucky.

kyanite (ˈkaɪəˌnaɪt) *n* a variant spelling of **cyanite.** ▸ **kyanitic** (ˌkaɪəˈnɪtɪk) *adj*

kyanize *or* **kyanise** (ˈkaɪəˌnaɪz) *vb* (*tr*) to treat (timber) with corrosive sublimate to make it resistant to decay. [C19: after J. H. *Kyan* (died 1850), English inventor of the process] ▸ **ˌkyaniˈzation** *or* **ˌkyaniˈsation** *n*

kyat (kɪˈɑːt) *n* the standard monetary unit of Myanmar, divided into 100 pyas. [from Burmese]

Kyd *or* **Kid** (kɪd) *n* **Thomas.** 1558–94, English dramatist, noted for his revenge play *The Spanish Tragedy* (1586).

kyle (kaɪl) *n Scot.* (esp. in place names) a narrow strait or channel: *Kyle of Lochalsh.* [C16: from Gaelic *caol,* from *caol* narrow]

kylie *or* **kiley** (ˈkaɪlɪ) *n Austral.* a boomerang that is flat on one side and convex on the other. [C19: from a native Australian language]

kylin (ˈkiːˈlɪn) *n* (in Chinese art) a mythical animal of composite form. [C19: from Chinese *ch'i-lin,* literally: male-female]

kylix *or* **cylix** (ˈkaɪlɪks, ˈkɪl-) *n, pl* **-likes** (-lɪˌkiːz). a shallow two-handled drinking vessel used in ancient Greece. [C19: from Greek *kulix* cup; compare CHALICE]

kyloe (ˈkaɪləʊ) *n* a breed of small long-horned long-haired beef cattle from NW Scotland. [C19: of uncertain origin]

kymograph (ˈkaɪməˌgrɑːf, -ˌgræf) *or* **cymograph** *n* **1** *Med.* a rotatable drum for holding paper on which a tracking stylus continuously records variations in blood pressure, respiratory movements, etc. **2** *Phonetics.* this device as applied to the measurement of variations in the muscular action of the articulatory organs. **3** an instrument for recording the angular oscillations of an aircraft in flight. [C20: from Greek *kuma* wave + -GRAPH] ▸ **ˌkymoˈgraphic** *or* **ˌcymoˈgraphic** *adj*

Kymric (ˈkɪmrɪk) *n, adj* a variant spelling of **Cymric.**

Kymry (ˈkɪmrɪ) *pl n* a variant spelling of **Cymry.**

Kynewulf (ˈkɪnəˌwʊlf) *n* a variant spelling of **Cynewulf.**

Kyongsong (ˈkjɔːŋˈsɔːŋ) *n* another name for **Seoul.**

Kyoto *or* **Kioto** (kɪˈəʊtəʊ, ˈkjəʊ-) *n* a city in central Japan, on S Honshu: the capital of Japan from 794 to 1868; cultural centre, with two universities (1875, 1897). Pop.: 1 463 601 (1995).

kype (kaɪp) *n* the hook on the lower jaw of a mature male salmon. [from Scot. *kip, kipp* anything beaked or hooked; perhaps related to Low German *kippe* point, tip]

kyphosis (kaɪˈfəʊsɪs) *n Pathol.* backward curvature of the thoracic spine, of congenital origin or resulting from injury or disease; hunchback. See also **Pott's disease.** Compare **lordosis, scoliosis.** [C19: from New Latin, from Greek *kuphōsis,* from *kuphos* humpbacked] ▸ **kyphotic** (kaɪˈfɒtɪk) *adj*

Kyrgyz (ˈkɪəgɪz) *n* **1** (*pl* **-ghiz** or **-giz**) a member of a Mongoloid people of central Asia, inhabiting Kyrgyzstan and a vast area of central Siberia. **2** the language of this people, belonging to the Turkic branch of the Altaic family.

Kyrgyzstan (ˈkɪəgɪzˌstɑːn, -ˌstæn), **Kirghizstan,** *or* **Kirgizstan** *n* a republic in central Asia: came under Russian rule in the 19th century, became a Soviet republic in 1936 and gained independence in 1991; it has deposits of minerals, oil, and gas. Official languages: Kirghiz and Russian. Religion: nonreligious, Muslim. Currency: som. Capital: Bishkek. Pop.: 4 691 000 (1998 est.). Area: 198 500 sq. km (76 460 sq. miles).

Kyrgyz Steppe *n* a vast steppe region in central Kazakhstan. Also called: (the) **Steppes.**

Kyrie eleison (ˈkɪrɪɪ əˈleɪsᵊn) *n* **1** a formal invocation used in the liturgies of the Roman Catholic, Greek Orthodox, and Anglican Churches. **2** a musical setting of this. Often shortened to **Kyrie.** [C14: via Late Latin from Late Greek *kurie, eleēson* Lord, have mercy]

kyte *or* **kite** (kəɪt) *n Scot.* the belly. [C16: of uncertain origin]

Kythera (ˈkɪθɪrə) *n* a variant spelling of **Cythera.**

kyu (kjuː) *n Judo.* **1** one of the five student grades for inexperienced competitors. **2** a student in the kyu grades. ◆ Compare **dan**[2]. [from Japanese]

Kyushu *or* **Kiushu** (ˈkjuːʃuː) *n* an island of SW Japan: the southernmost of Japan's four main islands, with over 300 surrounding small islands; coalfield and chemical industries. Chief cities: Fukuoka, Kitakyushu, and Nagasaki. Pop.: 13 424 000 (1995). Area: 35 659 sq. km (13 768 sq. miles).

Kyzyl Kum (*Russian* kiˈzil ˈkum) *n* a desert in Kazakhstan and Uzbekistan.

Ll

l *or* **L** (ɛl) *n, pl* **l's, L's,** *or* **Ls. 1** the 12th letter and ninth consonant of the modern English alphabet. **2** a speech sound represented by this letter, usually a lateral, as in *label.* **3a** something shaped like an L. **3b** (*in combination*): *an L-shaped room.*

l *symbol for:* **1** litre. **2** *Physics.* lepton number.

L *symbol for:* **1** ell (unit). **2** lambert(s). **3** large. **4** Latin. **5** (on British motor vehicles) learner driver. **6** *Physics.* length. **7** live. **8** *Currency.* **8a** Usually written £. pound. [Latin: *libra*] **8b** lempira. **8c** lek. **8d** leu. **8e** lire. **9** *Aeronautics.* lift. **10** *Electronics.* inductor (in circuit diagrams). **11** *Physics.* latent heat. **12** *Physics.* self-inductance. **13** *Chem.* the Avogadro constant. **14** *the Roman numeral for* 50. See **Roman numerals.** ♦ **15** *international car registration for* Luxembourg.

L. *or* **l.** *abbrev. for:* **1** lake. **2** law. **3** leaf. **4** league. **5** left. **6** length. **7** liber. [Latin: book] **8** (*pl* **LL.** *or* **ll.**) line. **9** link. **10** low.

L. *abbrev. for:* **1** *Politics.* Liberal. **2** (in titles) Licentiate. **3** Linnaeus. **4** (fraternal) Lodge.

la[1] (lɑː) *n Music.* a variant spelling of **lah.**

la[2] (lɔː) *interj* an exclamation of surprise or emphasis. [Old English *lā* LO]

La *the chemical symbol for* lanthanum.

LA *abbrev. for:* **1** Legislative Assembly. **2** Library Association. **3** local agent. **4** Los Angeles. **5** Louisiana.

La. *abbrev. for* Louisiana.

laager *or* **lager** (ˈlɑːgə) *n* **1** (in Africa) a camp, esp. one defended by a circular formation of wagons. **2** *Military.* a place where armoured vehicles are parked. ♦ *vb* **3** to form (wagons) into a laager. **4** (*tr*) to park (armoured vehicles) in a laager. [C19: from Afrikaans *lager,* via German from Old High German *legar* bed, lair]

Laaland (*Danish* ˈlɔlan) *n* a variant spelling of **Lolland.**

lab (læb) *n Informal.* short for: **1** laboratory. **2** Labrador retriever.

lab. *abbrev. for:* **1** laboratory. **2** labour.

Lab. *abbrev. for:* **1** *Politics.* Labour. **2** Labrador.

Laban (ˈleɪbᵊn) *n Old Testament.* the father-in-law of Jacob, father of Leah and Rachel (Genesis 29:16).

labarum (ˈlæbərəm) *n, pl* **-ra** (-rə). **1** a standard or banner carried in Christian religious processions. **2** the military standard bearing a Christian monogram used by Constantine the Great. [C17: from Late Latin, of obscure origin]

labdanum (ˈlæbdənəm) *or* **ladanum** *n* a dark resinous juice obtained from various rockroses of the genus *Cistus,* used in perfumery and in the manufacture of fumigants and medicinal plasters. [C16: Latin, from Greek *ladanon,* from *lēdon* rockrose, from Semitic]

Labe (ˈlabɛ) *n* the Czech name for the (River) **Elbe.**

labefaction (ˌlæbɪˈfækʃən) *or* **labefactation** (ˌlæbɪfækˈteɪʃən) *n Rare.* deterioration; weakening. [C17: from Late Latin *labefactiō,* from Latin *labefacere* shake, from *lābī* to fall + *facere* to make]

label (ˈleɪbᵊl) *n* **1** a piece of paper, card, or other material attached to an object to identify it or give instructions or details concerning its ownership, use, nature, destination, etc.; tag. **2** a brief descriptive phrase or term given to a person, group, school of thought, etc.: *the label "Romantic" is applied to many different kinds of poetry.* **3** a word or phrase heading a piece of text to indicate or summarize its contents. **4** a trademark or company or brand name on certain goods, esp. on gramophone records. **5** another name for **dripstone** (sense 2). **6** *Heraldry.* a charge consisting of a horizontal line across the chief of a shield with three or more pendants: the charge of an eldest son. **7** *Computing.* a group of characters, such as a number or a word, appended to a particular statement in a program to allow its unique identification. **8** *Chem.* a radioactive element used in a compound to trace the mechanism of a chemical reaction. ♦ *vb* **-bels, -belling, -belled** *or U.S.* **-bels, -beling, -beled.** (*tr*) **9** to fasten a label to. **10** to mark with a label. **11** to describe or classify in a word or phrase: *to label someone a liar.* **12** to make (one or more atoms in a compound) radioactive, for use in determining the mechanism of a reaction. [C14: from Old French, from Germanic; compare Old High German *lappa* rag] ▸ **ˈlabeller** *n*

labellum (ləˈbɛləm) *n, pl* **-la** (-lə). **1** the part of the corolla of certain plants, esp. orchids, that forms a distinct, often lobed, lip. **2** a lobe at the tip of the proboscis of a fly. [C19: New Latin, diminutive of Latin *labrum* lip] ▸ **laˈbelloid** *adj*

labia (ˈleɪbɪə) *n* the plural of **labium.**

labial (ˈleɪbɪəl) *adj* **1** of, relating to, or near lips or labia. **2** *Music.* producing sounds by the action of an air stream over a narrow liplike fissure, as in a flue pipe of an organ. **3** *Phonetics.* relating to a speech sound whose articulation involves movement or use of the lips: *a labial click.* ♦ *n* **4** Also called: **labial pipe.** *Music.* an organ pipe with a liplike fissure. **5** *Phonetics.* a speech sound such as English *p* or *m,* whose articulation involves movement or use of the lips. [C16: from Medieval Latin *labiālis,* from Latin *labium* lip] ▸ **ˌlabiˈality** *n* ▸ **ˈlabially** *adv*

labialize *or* **labialise** (ˈleɪbɪəˌlaɪz) *vb* (*tr*) *Phonetics.* to pronounce with articulation involving rounded lips, such as for (k) before a close back vowel (uː) as in English *cool.* ▸ **ˈlabialˌism, ˌlabialiˈzation,** *or* **ˌlabialiˈsation** *n*

labia majora (məˈdʒɔːrə) *pl n* the two elongated outer folds of skin in human females surrounding the vaginal orifice. [C18: New Latin: greater lips]

labia minora (mɪˈnɔːrə) *pl n* the two small inner folds of skin in human females forming the margins of the vaginal orifice. [C18: New Latin: smaller lips]

labiate (ˈleɪbɪˌeɪt, -ɪt) *n* **1** any plant of the family *Labiatae,* having square stems, aromatic leaves, and a two-lipped corolla: includes mint, thyme, sage, rosemary, etc. ♦ *adj* **2** of, relating to, or belonging to the family *Labiatae.* [C18: from New Latin *labiātus,* from Latin *labium* lip]

Labiche (*French* labiʃ) *n* **Eugène Marin** (øʒɛn marɛ̃). 1815–88, French dramatist, noted for his farces of middle-class life, which include *Le Chapeau de paille d'Italie* (1851) and *Le Voyage de Monsieur Perrichon* (1860).

labile (ˈleɪbɪl) *adj* **1** *Chem.* (of a compound) prone to chemical change. **2** liable to change or move. [C15: via Late Latin *lābilis,* from Latin *lābī* to slide, slip] ▸ **lability** (ləˈbɪlɪtɪ) *n*

labio- *or before a vowel* **labi-** *combining form.* relating to or formed by the lips and (another organ or part): *labiodental.* [from Latin *labium* lip]

labiodental (ˌleɪbɪəʊˈdɛntᵊl) *Phonetics.* ♦ *adj* **1** pronounced by bringing the bottom lip into contact or near contact with the upper teeth, as for the fricative (f) in English *fat, puff.* ♦ *n* **2** a labiodental consonant.

labionasal (ˌleɪbɪəʊˈneɪzᵊl) *Phonetics.* ♦ *adj* **1** pronounced by making a complete closure of the air passage at the lips and lowering the soft palate allowing air to escape through the nasal cavity. ♦ *n* **2** a labionasal consonant, such as *m.*

labiovelar (ˌleɪbɪəʊˈviːlə) *Phonetics.* ♦ *adj* **1** relating to or denoting a speech sound pronounced with simultaneous articulation at the soft palate and the lips. ♦ *n* **2** a labiovelar speech sound, such as some pronunciations of the consonant spelt *q* in English.

labium (ˈleɪbɪəm) *n, pl* **-bia** (-bɪə). **1** a lip or liplike structure. **2** any one of the four lip-shaped folds of the female vulva. See **labia majora, labia minora. 3** the fused pair of appendages forming the lower lip of insects. **4** the lower lip of the corolla of labiate flowers. [C16: New Latin, from Latin: lip]

lablab (ˈlæbˌlæb) *n* **1** a twining leguminous plant, *Dolichos lablab* (or *Lablab niger*), of tropical Africa. **2** the edible pod or bean of this plant. [from Arabic]

labor (ˈleɪbə) *vb, n* the U.S. spelling of **labour.**

laboratory (ləˈbɒrətərɪ, -trɪ; *U.S.* ˈlæbrəˌtɔːrɪ) *n, pl* **-ries. 1a** a building or room equipped for conducting scientific research or for teaching practical science. **1b** (*as modifier*): *laboratory equipment.* **2** a place where chemicals or medicines are manufactured. ♦ Often shortened to **lab.** See also **language laboratory.** [C17: from Medieval Latin *labōrātōrium* workshop, from Latin *labōrāre* to LABOUR]

Labor Day *n* **1** (in the U.S. and Canada) a public holiday in honour of labour, held on the first Monday in September. **2** (in Australia) a public holiday observed on different days in different states.

laborious (ləˈbɔːrɪəs) *adj* **1** involving great exertion or long effort. **2** given to working hard. **3** (of literary style, etc.) not fluent. ▸ **laˈboriously** *adv* ▸ **laˈboriousness** *n*

Labor Party *n* one of the chief political parties of Australia, generally supporting the interests of organized labour.

labour *or U.S.* **labor** (ˈleɪbə) *n* **1** productive work, esp. physical toil done for wages. **2a** the people, class, or workers involved in this, esp. in contrast to management, capital, etc. **2b** (*as modifier*): *a labour dispute; labour relations.* **3a** difficult or arduous work or effort. **3b** (*in combination*): *labour-saving.* **4** a particular job or task, esp. of a difficult nature. **5a** the process or effort of childbirth or the time during which this takes place. **5b** (*as modifier*): *labour pains.* **6 labour of love.** something done for pleasure rather than gain. ♦ *vb* **7** (*intr*) to perform labour; work. **8** (*intr;* foll. by *for,* etc.) to strive or work hard (for something). **9** (*intr;* usually foll. by *under*) to be burdened (by) or be at a disadvantage (because of): *to labour under a misapprehension.* **10** (*intr*) to make one's way with difficulty. **11** (*tr*) to deal with or treat too persistently: *to labour a point.* **12** (*intr*) (of a woman) to be in labour. **13** (*intr*) (of a ship) to pitch and toss. [C13: via Old French from Latin *labor;* perhaps related to *lābī* to fall] ▸ **ˈlabouringly** *or U.S.* **ˈlaboringly** *adv*

Labour and Socialist International *n* **the.** an international association of socialist parties formed in Hamburg in 1923: destroyed by World War II. Also called: **Second International.**

labour camp *n* **1** a penal colony involving forced labour. **2** a camp for migratory labourers.

Labour Day *n* a public holiday in many countries in honour of labour, usually held on May 1. See also **Labor Day.**

laboured *or U.S.* **labored** (ˈleɪbəd) *adj* **1** (of breathing) performed with difficulty. **2** showing effort; contrived; lacking grace or fluency. ▸ **ˈlabouredly** *or U.S.* **ˈlaboredly** *adv* ▸ **ˈlabouredness** *or U.S.* **ˈlaboredness** *n*

labourer *or U.S.* **laborer** (ˈleɪbərə) *n* a person engaged in physical work, esp. of an unskilled kind.

labour exchange *n Brit.* a former name for **employment office.**

labour-intensive *adj* of or denoting a task, organization, industry, etc., in which a high proportion of the costs are due to wages, salaries, etc.

labourism *or U.S.* **laborism** (ˈleɪbəˌrɪzəm) *n* **1** the dominance of the working classes. **2** a political, social, or economic system that favours such dominance. **3** support for workers' rights.

labourist *or U.S.* **laborist** ('leɪbərɪst) *n* **1** a person who supports workers' rights. **2** a supporter of labourism.
Labourite ('leɪbəˌraɪt) *n* an adherent of the Labour Party.
labour law *n* those areas of law which appertain to the relationship between employers and employees and between employers and trade unions.
Labour Party *n* **1** a British political party, formed in 1900 as an amalgam of various trade unions and socialist groups, generally supporting the interests of organized labour and advocating democratic socialism and social equality. **2** any similar party in any of various other countries.
labour relations *pl n* **a** collective relations between the management of an organization and its employees or employees' representatives. **b** a set of such relations in a wider context, such as in an industry, or in a national economy.
labra ('leɪbrə, 'læb-) *n* the plural of **labrum.**
Labrador ('læbrəˌdɔː) *n* **1** Also called: **Labrador-Ungava.** a large peninsula of NE Canada, on the Atlantic, the Gulf of St. Lawrence, Hudson Strait, and Hudson Bay: contains most of the province of Quebec and the mainland part of Newfoundland; geologically part of the Canadian Shield. Area: 1 619 000 sq. km (625 000 sq. miles). **2** Also called: **Coast of Labrador.** a region of NE Canada, on the Atlantic and consisting of the mainland part of Newfoundland province. **3** (*often not cap.*) short for **Labrador retriever.**
Labrador Current *n* a cold ocean current flowing southwards off the coast of Labrador and meeting the warm Gulf Stream, causing dense fogs off Newfoundland.
labradorescent (ˌlæbrədɔː'rɛsənt) *adj* (of minerals) displaying a brilliant play of colours, as that shown by some forms of labradorite.
labradorite (ˌlæbrə'dɔːraɪt) *n* a blue, green, or reddish-brown feldspar mineral of the plagioclase series: used as a decorative stone. Formula: $CaAl_2Si_2O_8$. $NaAlSi_3O_8$. [C18: named after LABRADOR, where it was found; see -ITE[1]]
Labrador retriever *n* a powerfully-built variety of retriever with a short dense usually black or golden-brown coat. Often shortened to **Labrador** or (informal) **lab.**
Labrador tea *n* **1** either of two arctic evergreen ericaceous shrubs, *Ledum groenlandicum* or *L. palustre* var. *decumbens.* **2** (in Canada) an infusion brewed from the leaves of either of these plants.
labret ('leɪbrɛt) *n* a piece of bone, shell, etc.; inserted into the lip as an ornament by certain peoples. [C19: from Latin *labrum* lip]
labroid ('læbrɔɪd, 'leɪ-) *or* **labrid** ('læbrɪd) *n* **1** any percoid fish of the family *Labridae* (wrasses). ◆ *adj* **2** of or relating to the *Labridae.* [C19: from New Latin *Labroidea,* from Latin *lābrus* a fish, from *labrum* lip]
labrum ('leɪbrəm, 'læb-) *n, pl* **-bra** (-brə). a lip or liplike part, such as the cuticular plate forming the upper lip of insects. [C19: New Latin, from Latin]
La Bruyère (*French* la bryjɛr) *n* **Jean de** (ʒɑ̃ də). 1645–96, French moralist, noted for his *Caractères* (1688), satirical character studies, including portraits of contemporary public figures.
Labuan (lə'buːən) *n* an island in Malaysia, off the NW coast of Borneo: part of the Straits Settlements until 1946, when transferred to North Borneo. Chief town: Victoria. Area: 98 sq. km (38 sq. miles).
laburnum (lə'bɜːnəm) *n* any papilionaceous tree or shrub of the Eurasian genus *Laburnum,* having clusters of yellow drooping flowers: all parts of the plant are poisonous. [C16: New Latin, from Latin]
labyrinth ('læbərɪnθ) *n* **1** a mazelike network of tunnels, chambers, or paths, either natural or man-made. Compare **maze** (sense 1). **2** any complex or confusing system of streets, passages, etc. **3** a complex or intricate situation. **4a** any system of interconnecting cavities, esp. those comprising the internal ear. **4b** another name for **internal ear. 5** *Electronics.* an enclosure behind a high-performance loudspeaker, consisting of a series of air chambers designed to absorb unwanted sound waves. [C16: via Latin from Greek *laburinthos,* of obscure origin]
Labyrinth ('læbərɪnθ) *n Greek myth.* a huge maze constructed for King Minos in Crete by Daedalus to contain the Minotaur.
labyrinth fish *n* any tropical freshwater spiny-finned fish of the family *Anabantidae* of SE Asia and Africa, having a lunglike respiratory organ. See also **anabantid.**
labyrinthine (ˌlæbə'rɪnθaɪn), **labyrinthian** (ˌlæbə'rɪnθɪən), *or* **labyrinthic** (ˌlæbə'rɪnθɪk) *adj* **1** of or relating to a labyrinth. **2** resembling a labyrinth in complexity. ▸ ˌ**laby'rinthically** *adv*
labyrinthitis (ˌlæbərɪn'θaɪtɪs) *n* inflammation of the inner ear, causing loss of balance, vertigo, and vomiting. Also called: **otitis interna.**
labyrinthodont (ˌlæbə'rɪnθəˌdɒnt) *n* any primitive amphibian of the order *Labyrinthodontia,* of late Devonian to Triassic times, having teeth with much-folded dentine. [C19: from Greek *laburinthos* LABYRINTH + -ODONT]
lac[1] (læk) *n* a resinous substance secreted by certain lac insects, used in the manufacture of shellac. [C16: from Dutch *lak* or French *laque,* from Hindi *lākh* resin, ultimately from Sanskrit *lākshā*]
lac[2] (lɑːk) *n* a variant spelling of **lakh.**
LAC *Brit. abbrev. for* leading aircraftman.
Lacan (*French* lakɑ̃) *n* **Jacques** (ʒak). 1901–81, French psychoanalyst, who reinterpreted Freud in terms of structural linguistics: an important influence on structuralist thought.
Laccadive, Minicoy, and Amindivi Islands ('lækədɪv, 'mɪnɪˌkɔɪ, ˌʌmən'diːviː) *pl n* the former name (until 1973) of the **Lakshadweep Islands.**
laccolith ('lækəlɪθ) *or* **laccolite** ('lækəˌlaɪt) *n* a dome of igneous rock between two layers of older sedimentary rock: formed by the intrusion of magma, forcing the overlying strata into a dome. [C19: from Greek *lakkos* cistern + -LITH] ▸ ˌ**lacco'lithic** *or* **laccolitic** (ˌlækə'lɪtɪk) *adj*
lace (leɪs) *n* **1** a delicate decorative fabric made from cotton, silk, etc., woven in an open web of different symmetrical patterns and figures. **2** a cord or string drawn through holes or eyelets or around hooks to fasten a shoe or garment. **3** ornamental braid often used on military uniforms, etc. **4** a dash of spirits added to a beverage. ◆ *vb* **5** to fasten (shoes, etc.) with a lace. **6** (*tr*) to draw (a cord or thread) through holes, eyes, etc., as when tying shoes. **7** (*tr*) to compress the waist of (someone), as with a corset. **8** (*tr*) to add a small amount of alcohol or drugs to (food or drink). **9** (*tr; usually passive* and foll. by *with*) to streak or mark with lines or colours: *the sky was laced with red.* **10** (*tr*) to intertwine; interlace. **11** (*tr*) *Informal.* to give a sound beating to. [C13 *las,* from Old French *laz,* from Latin *laqueus* noose] ◆ See also **lace into, lace up.** ▸ **'lace,like** *adj* ▸ **'lacer** *n*
lacebark ('leɪsbɑːk) *n* another name for **ribbonwood.**
lace bug *n* a small bug of the family *Tingidae,* having a delicate pattern in the wing venation. They are plant feeders and include the **thistle lace bugs** (*Tingis cardui* and *T. ampliata*) and the **rhododendron bug** (*Stephanitis rhododendri*).
Lacedaemon (ˌlæsɪ'diːmən) *n* another name for **Sparta** or **Laconia.**
Lacedaemonian (ˌlæsɪdɪ'məʊnɪən) *adj, n* another word for **Spartan.**
lace into *vb* (*intr, prep*) to attack violently, either verbally or physically.
lacerant ('læsərənt) *adj* painfully distressing; harrowing.
lacerate *vb* ('læsəˌreɪt). (*tr*) **1** to tear (the flesh, etc.) jaggedly. **2** to hurt or harrow (the feelings, etc.). ◆ *adj* ('læsəˌreɪt, -rɪt). **3** having edges that are jagged or torn; lacerated: *lacerate leaves.* [C16: from Latin *lacerāre* to tear, from *lacer* mangled] ▸ **'lacerable** *adj* ▸ ˌ**lacera'bility** *n* ▸ ˌ**lacer'ation** *n* ▸ **'lacerative** *adj*
Lacerta (lə'sɜːtə) *n, Latin genitive* **Lacertae** (lə'sɜːtiː). a small faint constellation in the N hemisphere, part of which is crossed by the Milky Way, lying between Cygnus and Andromeda. [Latin: lizard]
lacertilian (ˌlæsə'tɪlɪən) *n also* **lacertian** (lə'sɜːʃən). **1** any reptile of the suborder *Lacertilia* (lizards). ◆ *adj* **2** of, relating to, or belonging to the *Lacertilia.* [C19: New Latin, from Latin *lacerta* lizard]
lace up *vb* **1** (*tr, adv*) to tighten or fasten (clothes or footwear) with laces. ◆ *adj* **lace-up. 2** (of footwear) to be fastened with laces. ◆ *n* **lace-up. 3** a lace-up shoe or boot.
lacewing ('leɪsˌwɪŋ) *n* any of various neuropterous insects, esp. any of the families *Chrysopidae* (**green lacewings**) and *Hemerobiidae* (**brown lacewings**), having lacy wings and preying on aphids and similar pests.
laches ('lætʃɪz) *n Law.* negligence or unreasonable delay in pursuing a legal remedy. [C14 *lachesse,* via Old French *lasche* slack, from Latin *laxus* LAX]
Lachesis ('lækɪsɪs) *n Greek myth.* one of the three Fates. [via Latin from Greek, from *lakhesis* destiny, from *lakhein* to befall by lot]
Lachlan ('lɒklən) *n* a river in SE Australia, rising in central New South Wales and flowing northwest then southwest to the Murrumbidgee River. Length: about 1450 km (900 miles). [named after *Lachlan* Macquarie, governor of New South Wales (1809–21)]
lachryma Christi ('lækrəmə 'krɪstɪ) *n* a red or white wine from the bay of Naples in S Italy. [C17: from Latin: Christ's tear]
lachrymal ('lækrɪməl) *adj* a variant spelling of **lacrimal.**
lachrymator ('lækrɪˌmeɪtə) *n* a variant spelling of **lacrimator.**
lachrymatory ('lækrɪmətərɪ, -trɪ) *n, pl* **-ries. 1** a small vessel found in ancient tombs, formerly thought to hold the tears of mourners. ◆ *adj* **2** a variant spelling of **lacrimatory.**
lachrymose ('lækrɪˌməʊs, -ˌməʊz) *adj* **1** given to weeping; tearful. **2** mournful; sad. [C17: from Latin *lacrimōsus,* from *lacrima* a tear] ▸ **'lachry,mosely** *adv* ▸ **lachrymosity** (ˌlækrɪ'mɒsɪtɪ) *n*
lacing ('leɪsɪŋ) *n* **1** *Chiefly Brit.* a course of bricks, stone, etc., for strengthening a rubble or flint wall. **2** another word for **lace** (senses 2, 3). **3** *Informal.* a severe beating (esp. in the phrase **give someone a lacing**).
laciniate (lə'sɪnɪˌeɪt, -ɪt) *or* **laciniated** *adj* **1** *Biology.* jagged: *a laciniate leaf.* **2** having a fringe. [C17: from Latin *lacinia* flap] ▸ **la,cini'ation** *n*
lac insect (læk) *n* any of various homopterous insects of the family *Lacciferidae,* esp. *Laccifer lacca* of India, the females of which secrete lac.
lack (læk) *n* **1** an insufficiency, shortage, or absence of something required or desired. **2** something that is required but is absent or in short supply. ◆ *vb* **3** (when *intr;* often foll. by *in* or *for*) to be deficient (in) or have need (of): *to lack purpose.* [C12: related to Middle Dutch *laken* to be wanting]
lackadaisical (ˌlækə'deɪzɪk[ə]l) *adj* **1** lacking vitality and purpose. **2** lazy or idle, esp. in a dreamy way. [C18: from earlier *lackadaisy,* extended form of LACKADAY] ▸ ˌ**lacka'daisically** *adv* ▸ ˌ**lacka'daisicalness** *n*
lackaday ('lækəˌdeɪ) *interj Archaic.* another word for **alas.** [C17: from *alack the day*]
lacker ('lækə) *n* a variant spelling of **lacquer.**
lackey ('lækɪ) *n* **1** a servile follower; hanger-on. **2** a liveried male servant or valet. **3** a person who is treated like a servant. ◆ *vb* **4** (when *intr,* often foll. by *for*) to act as a lackey (to). ◆ Also (rare): **'lacquey.** [C16: via French *laquais,* from Old French, perhaps from Catalan *lacayo, alacayo;* perhaps related to ALCALDE]
lackey moth *n* a bombycid moth, *Malacosoma neustria,* whose brightly striped larvae live at first in a communal web often on fruit trees, of which they may become a pest.
lacklustre *or U.S.* **lackluster** ('lækˌlʌstə) *adj* lacking force, brilliance, or vitality.
Laclos (*French* laklo) *n* **Pierre Choderlos de** (pjɛr ʃɔdɛrlo də). 1741–1803, French soldier and writer, noted for his novel in epistolary form *Les Liaisons dangereuses* (1782).
Laconia (lə'kəʊnɪə) *n* an ancient country of S Greece, in the SE Peloponnese, of which Sparta was the capital: corresponds to the present-day department of Lakonia. ▸ **La'conian** *n, adj*
laconic (lə'kɒnɪk) *or* **laconical** *adj* (of a person's speech) using few words;

terse. [C16: via Latin from Greek *Lakōnikos,* from *Lakōn* Laconian, Spartan; referring to the Spartans' terseness of speech] ▸ **la'conically** *adv*

laconism ('lækəˌnɪzəm) *or* **laconicism** (lə'kɒnɪˌsɪzəm) *n Rare.* **1** economy of expression. **2** a terse saying.

La Coruña (*Spanish* la ko'ruɲa) *n* a port in NW Spain, on the Atlantic: point of departure for the Spanish Armada (1588); site of the defeat of the French by the English under Sir John Moore in the Peninsular War (1809). Pop.: 254 822 (1995 est.). English name: **Corunna.**

lacquer ('lækə) *n* **1** a hard glossy coating made by dissolving cellulose derivatives or natural resins in a volatile solvent. **2** a black resinous substance, obtained from certain trees, used to give a hard glossy finish to wooden furniture. **3 lacquer tree.** Also called: **varnish tree.** an E Asian anacardiaceous tree, *Rhus verniciflua,* whose stem yields a toxic exudation from which black lacquer is obtained. **4** Also called: **hair lacquer.** a mixture of shellac and alcohol for spraying onto the hair to hold a style in place. **5** *Art.* decorative objects coated with such lacquer, often inlaid. ◆ *vb* (*tr*) **6** to apply lacquer to. [C16: from obsolete French *lacre* sealing wax, from Portuguese *laca* LAC[1]] ▸ **'lacquerer** *n*

lacrimal, lachrymal, *or* **lacrymal** ('lækrɪməl) *adj* of or relating to tears or to the glands that secrete tears. [C16: from Medieval Latin *lachrymālis,* from Latin *lacrima* a tear]

lacrimal duct *n* a short tube in the inner corner of the eyelid through which tears drain into the nose. Nontechnical name: **tear duct.**

lacrimal gland *n* the compound gland that secretes tears and lubricates the surface of the eye and the conjunctiva of the eyelid.

lacrimation (ˌlækrɪ'meɪʃən) *n* the secretion of tears.

lacrimator, lachrymator, *or* **lacrymator** ('lækrɪˌmeɪtə) *n* a substance causing an increase in the flow of tears. See **tear gas.**

lacrimatory, lachrymatory, *or* **lacrymatory** ('lækrɪmətərɪ, -trɪ) *adj* of, causing, or producing tears.

lacrosse (lə'krɒs) *n* a ball game invented by American Indians, now played by two teams who try to propel a ball into each other's goal by means of long-handled hooked sticks that are loosely strung with a kind of netted pouch. [C19: Canadian French: the hooked stick, crosier]

lactalbumin (læk'tælbjʊmɪn) *n* a protein occurring in milk that contains all the amino acids essential to man. See also **caseinogen.** [C19: from LACTO- + ALBUMIN]

lactam ('læktæm) *n Chem.* any of a group of inner amides, derived from amino acids, having the characteristic group -CONH-. [C20: from LACT(ONE) + AM(IDE)]

lactase ('lækteɪs, -teɪz) *n* any of a group of enzymes that hydrolyse lactose to glucose and galactose. [C20: from LACTO- + -ASE]

lactate[1] ('lækteɪt) *n* an ester or salt of lactic acid. [C18: from LACTO- + -ATE[1]]

lactate[2] ('lækteɪt) *vb* (*intr*) (of mammals) to produce or secrete milk.

lactation (læk'teɪʃən) *n* **1** the secretion of milk from the mammary glands after parturition. **2** the period during which milk is secreted. ▸ **lac'tational** *adj* ▸ **lac'tationally** *adv*

lacteal ('læktɪəl) *adj* **1** of, relating to, or resembling milk. **2** (of lymphatic vessels) conveying or containing chyle. ◆ *n* **3** any of the lymphatic vessels conveying chyle from the small intestine to the thoracic duct. [C17: from Latin *lacteus* of milk, from *lac* milk] ▸ **'lacteally** *adv*

lactescent (læk'tesᵊnt) *adj* **1** (of plants and certain insects) secreting a milky fluid. **2** milky or becoming milky. [C18: from Latin *lactescēns,* from *lactescĕre* to become milky, from *lact-, lac* milk] ▸ **lac'tescence** *n*

lactic ('læktɪk) *adj* relating to or derived from milk. [C18: from Latin *lact-, lac* milk]

lactic acid *n* a colourless syrupy carboxylic acid found in sour milk and many fruits and used as a preservative (**E270**) for foodstuffs, such as soft margarine, and for making pharmaceuticals and adhesives. Formula: $CH_3CH(OH)COOH$. Systematic name: **2-hydroxypropanoic acid.**

lactiferous (læk'tɪfərəs) *adj* **1** producing, conveying, or secreting milk or a milky fluid: *lactiferous ducts.* **2** *Botany.* containing latex; laticiferous. [C17: from Latin *lactifer,* from *lact-, lac* milk] ▸ **lac'tiferousness** *n*

lacto- *or before a vowel* **lact-** *combining form.* indicating milk: *lactobacillus.* [from Latin *lact-, lac* milk]

lactobacillus (ˌlæktəʊbə'sɪləs) *n, pl* **-li** (-laɪ). any Gram-positive rod-shaped bacterium of the genus *Lactobacillus,* which ferments carbohydrates: family *Lactobacillaceae.*

lactoflavin (ˌlæktəʊ'fleɪvɪn) *n* a less common name for **riboflavin.**

lactogenic (ˌlæktə'dʒenɪk) *adj* inducing lactation: *lactogenic hormone.* See also **prolactin.**

lactoglobulin (ˌlæktəʊ'glɒbjʊlɪn) *n Biochem.* any of a number of globular proteins found in milk.

lactometer (læk'tɒmɪtə) *n* a hydrometer used to measure the relative density of milk and thus determine its quality. Also called: **galactometer.**

lactone ('læktəʊn) *n* any of a class of organic compounds formed from hydroxy acids and containing the group -C(CO)OC-, where the carbon atoms are part of a ring. ▸ **lactonic** (læk'tɒnɪk) *adj*

lactoprotein (ˌlæktəʊ'prəʊtiːn) *n* any protein, such as lactalbumin or caseinogen, that is present in milk.

lactoscope ('læktəˌskəʊp) *n* an instrument for measuring the amount of cream in milk.

lactose ('læktəʊs, -təʊz) *n* a white crystalline disaccharide occurring in milk and used in the manufacture of pharmaceuticals and baby foods. Formula: $C_{12}H_{22}O_{11}$. Also called: **milk sugar.**

lactosuria (ˌlæktəʊ'sjʊərɪə) *n Med.* the presence of lactose in the urine.

lacto-vegetarian *n* a vegetarian whose diet includes dairy produce and eggs.

La Cumbre (lə 'kuːmbreɪ) *n* another name for the **Uspallata Pass.**

lacuna (lə'kjuːnə) *n, pl* **-nae** (-niː) *or* **-nas. 1** a gap or space, esp. in a book or manuscript. **2** *Biology.* a cavity or depression, such as any of the spaces in the matrix of bone. **3** another name for **coffer** (sense 3). [C17: from Latin *lacūna* pool, cavity, from *lacus* lake] ▸ **la'cunose, la'cunal,** *or* **la'cunary** *adj* ▸ **lacunosity** (ˌlækjʊ'nɒsɪtɪ) *n*

lacunar (lə'kjuːnə) *n, pl* **lacunars** *or* **lacunaria** (ˌlækjʊ'neərɪə). **1** Also called: **lequear.** a ceiling, soffit, or vault having coffers. **2** another name for **coffer** (sense 3). ◆ *adj* **3** of, relating to, or containing a lacuna or lacunas. [C17: from Latin *lacūnar* panelled ceiling, from *lacūna* cavity; see LACUNA]

lacustrine (lə'kʌstraɪn) *adj* **1** of or relating to lakes. **2** living or growing in or on the shores of a lake. [C19: from Italian *lacustre,* from Latin *lacus* lake]

LACW *Brit. abbrev. for* leading aircraftwoman.

lacy ('leɪsɪ) *adj* **lacier, laciest.** made of or resembling lace. ▸ **'lacily** *adv* ▸ **'laciness** *n*

lad (læd) *n* **1** a boy or young man. **2** *Informal.* a familiar form of address for any male. **3** a lively or dashing man or youth (esp. in the phrase **a bit of a lad**). **4** *Brit.* a boy or man who looks after horses. [C13 *ladde;* perhaps of Scandinavian origin]

ladanum ('lædənəm) *n* another name for **labdanum.**

ladder ('lædə) *n* **1** a portable framework of wood, metal, rope, etc., in the form of two long parallel members connected by several parallel rungs or steps fixed to them at right angles, for climbing up or down. **2** any hierarchy conceived of as having a series of ascending stages, levels, etc: *the social ladder.* **3a** anything resembling a ladder. **3b** (*as modifier*): *ladder stitch.* **4** Also called: **run.** *Chiefly Brit.* a line of connected stitches that have come undone in knitted material, esp. stockings. **5** See **ladder tournament.** ◆ *vb* **6** *Chiefly Brit.* to cause a line of interconnected stitches in (stockings, etc.) to undo, as by snagging, or (of a stocking) to come undone in this way. [Old English *hlǣdder;* related to Old High German *leitara*]

ladder back *n* a type of chair in which the back is constructed of horizontal slats between two uprights.

ladder tournament *n* a tournament in a sport or game in which each contestant in a list attempts to defeat and displace the contestant above him. Also called: **ladder.**

laddie ('lædɪ) *n Chiefly Scot.* a familiar term for a male, esp. a young man; lad.

laddish ('lædɪʃ) *adj Informal, usu. derogatory.* characteristic of male adolescents or young men, esp. by being rowdy, macho, or immature: *laddish behaviour.*

lade[1] (leɪd) *vb* **lades, lading, laded, laden** ('leɪdᵊn) *or* **laded. 1** to put cargo or freight on board (a ship, etc.) or (of a ship, etc.) to take on cargo or freight. **2** (*tr; usually passive* and foll. by *with*) to burden or oppress. **3** (*tr; usually passive* and foll. by *with*) to fill or load. **4** to remove (liquid) with or as if with a ladle. [Old English *hladen* to load; related to Dutch *laden*] ▸ **'lader** *n*

lade[2] (led, leɪd) *n Scot.* a watercourse, esp. a millstream. [of uncertain origin]

laden ('leɪdᵊn) *vb* **1** a past participle of **lade**[1]. ◆ *adj* **2** weighed down with a load; loaded. **3** encumbered; burdened.

la-di-da, lah-di-dah, *or* **la-de-da** (ˌlɑːdiː'dɑː) *adj* **1** *Informal.* affecting exaggeratedly genteel manners or speech. ◆ *n* **2** a la-di-da person. [C19: mockingly imitative of affected speech]

ladies *or* **ladies' room** *n* (*functioning as sing*) *Informal.* a women's public lavatory.

ladies' fingers *n* (*functioning as sing or pl*) another name for **kidney vetch** or **okra.**

ladies' gallery *n* (in Britain, formerly) **1** a gallery in the old House of Commons set aside for women spectators. **2** a portion of the strangers' gallery of the new House of Commons similarly reserved.

ladies' man *or* **lady's man** *n* a man who is fond of, attentive to, and successful with women.

ladies'-tresses *n* (*functioning as sing or pl*) a variant spelling of **lady's-tresses.**

Ladin (læ'diːn) *n* a Rhaetian dialect spoken in parts of South Tyrol. Compare **Friulian, Romansch.** [C19: from Italian *ladino,* from Latin *latīnus* Latin]

lading ('leɪdɪŋ) *n* a load; cargo; freight.

ladino (lə'diːnəʊ) *n, pl* **-nos.** an Italian variety of white clover grown as a forage crop in North America. [C20: perhaps from Italian *ladino* (see LADIN), referring to a person or thing from the Italian-speaking area of Switzerland, where the clover is grown]

Ladino (lə'diːnəʊ) *n* a language of Sephardic Jews, based on Spanish with some Hebrew elements and usually written in Hebrew characters. Also called: **Judaeo-Spanish, Judezmo.** [from Spanish: Latin]

Ladislaus I ('lædɪsˌlɔːs) *or* **Ladislas** ('lædɪsˌlæs) *n* **Saint.** 1040–95, king of Hungary (1077–95). He extended his country's boundaries and suppressed paganism. Feast day: June 27.

ladle ('leɪdᵊl) *n* **1** a long-handled spoon having a deep bowl for serving or transferring liquids: *a soup ladle.* **2** a large bucket-shaped container for transferring molten metal. ◆ *vb* **3** (*tr*) to lift or serve out with or as if with a ladle. [Old English *hlædel,* from *hladan* to draw out] ▸ **'ladleˌful** *n*

ladle out *vb* (*tr, adv*) *Informal.* to distribute (money, gifts, etc.) generously.

Ladoga (*Russian* 'ladəgə) *n* **Lake.** a lake in NW Russia, in the SW Karelian Republic: the largest lake in Europe; drains through the River Neva into the Gulf of Finland. Area: about 18 000 sq. km (7000 sq. miles). Russian name: **Ladozhskoye Ozero** ('ladəʃskəjə 'ɔzɪrə).

Ladrone Islands (lə'drəʊn) *pl n* the former name (1521–1668) of the **Mariana Islands.**

lad's love *n* another name for **southernwood.**

lady ('leɪdɪ) *n, pl* **-dies. 1** a woman regarded as having the characteristics of a good family and high social position; female counterpart of **gentleman** (sense 1). **2a** a polite name for a woman. **2b** (*as modifier*): *a lady doctor.* **3** an informal name for **wife. 4 lady of the house.** the female head of the household. **5**

History. a woman with proprietary rights and authority, as over a manor. Compare **lord** (sense 3). [Old English *hlǣfdīge,* from *hlāf* bread + *dīge* kneader, related to *dāh* dough]

Lady ('leɪdɪ) *n, pl* **-dies. 1** (in Britain) a title of honour borne by various classes of women of the peerage. **2 my lady.** a term of address to holders of the title Lady, used esp. by servants. **3 Our Lady.** a title of the Virgin Mary. **4** *Archaic.* an allegorical prefix for the personifications of certain qualities: *Lady Luck.* **5** *Chiefly Brit.* the term of address by which certain positions of respect are prefaced when held by women: *Lady Chairman.*

ladybird ('leɪdɪˌbɜːd) *n* any of various small brightly coloured beetles of the family *Coccinellidae,* such as *Adalia bipunctata* (**two-spotted ladybird**), which has red elytra marked with black spots. Usual U.S. and Canadian name: **ladybug.** [C18: named after Our *Lady,* the Virgin Mary]

lady bountiful *n* an ostentatiously charitable woman. [after a character in George Farquhar's play *The Beaux' Stratagem* (1707)]

Lady Chapel *n* a chapel within a church or cathedral, dedicated to the Virgin Mary.

Lady Day *n* March 25, the feast of the Annunciation of the Virgin Mary; one of the four quarter days in England, Wales and Ireland. Also called: **Annunciation Day.**

lady fern *n* a large, graceful, but variable fern, *Athyrium filix-femina,* with bipinnate fronds, commonly found on damp acid soils in woods and on hillsides.

ladyfinger ('leɪdɪˌfɪŋgə) *or* **lady's finger** *n* a small finger-shaped sponge cake.

ladyfy *or* **ladify** ('leɪdɪˌfaɪ) *vb* **-fies, -fying, -fied.** (*tr*) to make a lady of (someone).

lady-in-waiting *n, pl* **ladies-in-waiting.** a lady of a royal household who attends a queen or princess.

lady-killer *n Informal.* a man who is, or thinks he is, irresistibly fascinating to women. ▸ **'lady-ˌkilling** *n, adj*

ladylike ('leɪdɪˌlaɪk) *adj* **1** like or befitting a lady in manners and bearing; refined and fastidious. **2** *Derogatory.* (of a man) effeminate. ▸ **'ladyˌlikeness** *n*

ladylove ('leɪdɪˌlʌv) *n Now rare.* a beloved woman.

Lady Macbeth strategy *n Informal.* a strategy in a takeover battle in which a third party makes a bid acceptable to the target company, appearing to act as a white knight but subsequently joining forces with the original (unwelcome) bidder. [C20: after *Lady Macbeth* in Shakespeare's *Macbeth* (1605)]

lady mayoress *n Brit.* the wife of a lord mayor.

Lady Muck *n Informal, usu. derogatory.* an ordinary woman behaving or being treated as if she were aristocratic. See also **Lord Muck.**

Lady of the Lake *n* (in Arthurian legend) a mysterious supernatural being sometimes identified with **Vivian.**

lady orchid *n* a tall graceful orchid, *Orchis purpurea,* with faintly scented purple-brown and green flowers with a pinkish or white lip. [C19: named from a fancied resemblance to a lady in regency dress and bonnet]

lady's bedstraw *n* a Eurasian rubiaceous plant, *Galium verum,* with clusters of small yellow flowers.

lady's finger *n* another name for **bhindi.**

Ladyship ('leɪdɪʃɪp) *n* (preceded by *your* or *her*) a title used to address or refer to any peeress except a duchess.

lady's maid *n* a personal servant to a woman, esp. in matters of dress and toilet.

lady's man *n* a variant spelling of **ladies' man.**

lady's mantle *n* any of various rosaceous plants of the N temperate genus *Alchemilla,* having small green flowers.

Ladysmith ('leɪdɪˌsmɪθ) *n* a city in E South Africa: besieged by Boers for four months (1899–1900) during the Boer War. Pop.: 56 599 (1989).

lady's-slipper *n* any of various orchids of the Eurasian genus *Cypripedium,* esp. *C. calceolus,* having reddish or purple flowers. See also **moccasin flower, cypripedium.**

lady's-smock *n* a N temperate cruciferous plant, *Cardamine pratensis,* with white or rose-pink flowers. Also called: **cuckooflower.**

lady's-thumb *n* the usual U.S. name for **red shank** (the plant).

lady's-tresses *or* **ladies'-tresses** *n* (*functioning as sing or pl*) any of various orchids of the genus *Spiranthes,* having spikes of small white fragrant flowers.

Laënnec (*French* laɛnɛk) *n* **René Théophile Hyacinthe** (rəne teɔfil jasɛ̃t). 1781–1826, French physician, who invented the stethoscope.

Laertes (leɪ'ɜːtiːz) *n Greek myth.* the father of Odysseus.

laetrile ('leɪəˌtraɪl) *n* an extract of peach stones sold as a cure for cancer but judged useless and possibly dangerous by medical scientists.

laevo- *or U.S.* **levo-** *combining form.* **1** on or towards the left: *laevorotatory.* **2** (in chemistry) denoting a laevorotatory compound: *laevulose.* [from Latin *laevus* left]

laevogyrate (ˌliːvəʊ'dʒaɪreɪt) *adj* another word for **laevorotatory.**

laevorotation (ˌliːvəʊrəʊ'teɪʃən) *n* **1** a rotation to the left. **2** an anticlockwise rotation of the plane of polarization of plane-polarized light as a result of its passage through a crystal, liquid, or solution. ◆ Compare **dextrorotation.**

laevorotatory (ˌliːvəʊ'rəʊtətərɪ, -trɪ) *or* **laevorotary** *adj* of, having, or causing laevorotation. Also: **laevogyrate.**

laevulin ('lɛvjʊlɪn) *n* a polysaccharide occurring in the tubers of certain helianthus plants. [C19: from LAEVULOSE + -IN]

laevulose ('lɛvjʊˌləʊs, -ˌləʊz) *n* another name for **fructose.** [C19: from LAEVO- + -ULE + -OSE[2]]

Lafayette *or* **La Fayette** (*French* lafajɛt) *n* **1 Marie Joseph Paul Yves Roch Gilbert du Motier** (mari ʒozɛf pɔl iv rɔk ʒilbɛr dy mɔtje), Marquis de Lafayette. 1757–1834, French general and statesman. He fought on the side of the colonists in the War of American Independence and, as commander of the National Guard (1789–91; 1830), he played a leading part in the French Revolution and the revolution of 1830. **2 Marie-Madeleine** (marimadlɛn), Comtesse de Lafayette. 1634–93, French novelist, noted for her historical romance *La Princesse de Clèves* (1678).

Laffer curve ('læfə) *n Economics.* a curve on a graph showing government tax revenue plotted against percentage tax rates. It has been used to show that a cut in a high tax rate can increase government revenue. [C20: named after Arthur *Laffer* (born 1940), U.S. economist]

La Fontaine (*French* la fɔ̃tɛn) *n* **Jean de** (ʒɑ̃ də). 1621–95, French poet, famous for his *Fables* (1668–94).

Laforgue (*French* lafɔrg) *n* **Jules** (ʒyl). 1860–87, French symbolist poet. An originator of free verse, he had a considerable influence on modern poetry.

LAFTA ('læftə) *n acronym for* Latin American Free Trade Area, the name before 1981 of the Latin American Integration Association. See **LAIA.**

lag[1] (læg) *vb* **lags, lagging, lagged.** (*intr*) **1** (often foll. by *behind*) to hang (back) or fall (behind) in movement, progress, development, etc. **2** to fall away in strength or intensity. **3** to determine an order of play in certain games, as by rolling marbles towards a line or, in billiards, hitting cue balls up the table against the top cushion in an attempt to bring them back close to the headrail. ◆ *n* **4** the act or state of slowing down or falling behind. **5** the interval of time between two events, esp. between an action and its effect. **6** an act of lagging in a game, such as billiards. [C16: of obscure origin]

lag[2] (læg) *Slang.* ◆ *n* **1** a convict or ex-convict (esp. in the phrase **old lag**). **2** a term of imprisonment. ◆ *vb* **lags, lagging, lagged. 3** (*tr*) to arrest or put in prison. [C19: of unknown origin]

lag[3] (læg) *vb* **lags, lagging, lagged. 1** (*tr*) to cover (a pipe, cylinder, etc.) with lagging to prevent loss of heat. ◆ *n* **2** the insulating casing of a steam cylinder, boiler, etc.; lagging. **3** a stave or lath. [C17: of Scandinavian origin; related to Swedish *lagg* stave]

lagan ('lægən) *or* **ligan** ('laɪgən) *n* goods or wreckage on the sea bed, sometimes attached to a buoy to permit recovery. Compare **flotsam, jetsam.** [C16: from Old French *lagan,* probably of Germanic origin; compare Old Norse *lögn* dragnet]

Lag b'Omer *Hebrew.* (lag bə'ɔmɛr; *English* læg 'bəʊmə) *n* a Jewish holiday celebrated on the 18th day of Iyar. [Hebrew, literally: 33rd (day) of the Omer]

lagena (lə'dʒiːnə) *n* **1** a bottle with a narrow neck. **2** an outgrowth of the sacculus in the ear of fishes and amphibians, thought to be homologous to the cochlea of mammals. [C19: Latin, a flask, from Greek *lagēnos*]

lager[1] ('lɑːgə) *n* a light-bodied effervescent beer, fermented in a closed vessel using yeasts that sink to the bottom of the brew. Compare **ale.** [C19: from German *Lagerbier* beer for storing, from *Lager* storehouse]

lager[2] ('lɑːgə) *n* a variant spelling of **laager.**

Lagerkvist (*Swedish* 'lɑːgərkvist) *n* **Pär** (**Fabian**) (pæːr). 1891–1974, Swedish novelist and dramatist. His works include the novels *The Dwarf* (1944) and *Barabbas* (1950): Nobel prize for literature 1951.

Lagerlöf (*Swedish* 'lɑːgərløːv) *n* **Selma** ('sɛlma). 1858–1940, Swedish novelist, noted esp. for her children's classic *The Wonderful Adventures of Nils* (1906–07): Nobel prize for literature 1909.

lager lout *n* a rowdy or aggressive young drunk male.

laggard ('lægəd) *n* **1** a person who lags behind. **2** a dawdler or straggler. ◆ *adj* **3** *Rare.* sluggish, slow, or dawdling. ▸ **'laggardly** *adv* ▸ **'laggardness** *n*

lagging ('lægɪŋ) *n* **1** insulating material wrapped around pipes, boilers, etc., or laid in a roof loft, to prevent loss of heat. **2** the act or process of applying lagging. **3** a wooden frame used to support an arch during construction.

lagniappe *or* **lagnappe** (læn'jæp, 'lænjæp) *n U.S.* **1** a small gift, esp. one given to a customer who makes a purchase. **2** something given or obtained as a gratuity or bonus. [C19: Louisiana French, from American Spanish *la ñapa,* from Quechua *yápa* addition]

lagomorph ('lægəʊˌmɔːf) *n* any placental mammal of the order *Lagomorpha,* having two pairs of upper incisors specialized for gnawing: includes pikas, rabbits, and hares. [C19: via New Latin from Greek *lagōs* hare; see -MORPH] ▸ **ˌlago'morphic** *or* **ˌlago'morphous** *adj*

lagoon (lə'guːn) *n* **1** a body of water cut off from the open sea by coral reefs or sand bars. **2** any small body of water, esp. one adjoining a larger one. ◆ Also (rare): **la'gune.** [C17: from Italian *laguna,* from Latin *lacūna* pool; see LACUNA]

Lagoon Islands *pl n* a former name of **Tuvalu.**

Lagos ('leɪgɒs) *n* **1** the former capital and chief port of Nigeria, on the Bight of Benin: first settled in the sixteenth century; a slave market until the nineteenth century; ceded to Britain (1861); university (1962). Pop.: 1 484 000 (1995 est.). **2** a state of SW Nigeria. Capital: Ikeja. Pop.: 6 357 253 (1995 est.). Area: 3345 sq. km (1292 sq. miles).

Lagrange (*French* lagrɑ̃ʒ) *n* Comte **Joseph Louis** (ʒozɛf lwi). 1736–1813, French mathematician and astronomer, noted particularly for his work on harmonics, mechanics, and the calculus of variations. ▸ **Lagrangian** (lə'greɪndʒɪən) *adj*

Lagrangian point *n Astronomy.* one of five points in the plane of revolution of two bodies in orbit around their common centre of gravity, at which a third body of negligible mass can remain in equilibrium with respect to the other two bodies. [named after J. L. LAGRANGE]

La Granja (*Spanish* la 'graŋxa) *n* another name for **San Ildefonso.**

lag screw *n* a woodscrew with a square head. [from LAG[3]; the screw was originally used to fasten barrel staves]

Lagting *or* **Lagthing** ('lɑːgtɪŋ) *n* the upper chamber of the Norwegian parliament. See also **Storting, Odelsting.** [Norwegian, from *lag* law + *ting* parliament]

La Guaira *or* **La Guayra** (*Spanish* la 'gwaira) *n* the chief seaport of Venezuela, on the Caribbean. Pop.: 26 669 (1990 est.).

La Guardia (lə'gwɑːdɪə) *n* **Fiorello H**(**enry**) (ˌfɪə'rɛləʊ). 1882–1947, U.S. politician. As mayor of New York (1933–45), he organized slum-clearance and labour safeguard schemes and suppressed racketeering.

lah (lɑː) *n Music.* (in tonic sol-fa) the sixth note of any major scale; submediant. [C14: see GAMUT]

lahar ('lɑːhɑː) *n* a landslide of volcanic debris mixed with water down the sides of a volcano, usually precipitated by heavy rainfall. [C20: from Javanese: lava]

lah-di-dah (ˌlɑːdiː'dɑː) *adj, n Informal.* a variant spelling of **la-di-da.**

Lahnda ('lɑːndə) *n* a language or group of dialects of Pakistan, belonging to the Indic branch of the Indo-European family and closely related to Punjabi.

La Hogue (*French* la ɔg) *n* a roadstead off the NW coast of France: scene of the defeat of the French by the Dutch and English fleet (1692).

Lahore (lə'hɔː) *n* **1** a city in NE Pakistan: capital of the former province of West Pakistan (1955–70); University of the Punjab (1882). Pop.: 5 085 000 (1995 est.). **2** a variety of large domestic fancy pigeon having a black-and-white plumage.

Lahti (*Finnish* 'lɑhti) *n* a town in S Finland: site of the main Finnish radio and television stations; furniture industry. Pop.: 94 706 (1994).

LAIA *abbrev. for* Latin American Integration Association (before 1981, known as the Latin American Free Trade Area). An economic group, its members are Argentina, Bolivia, Brazil, Chile, Colombia, Ecuador, Mexico, Paraguay, Peru, Uruguay, and Venezuela.

Laibach ('laibax) *n* the German name for **Ljubljana.**

laic ('leɪɪk) *adj also* **laical. 1** of or involving the laity; secular. ◆ *n* **2** a rare word for **layman.** [C15: from Late Latin *lāicus* LAY[3]] ▸ **'laically** *adv* ▸ **'laicism** *n*

laicize *or* **laicise** ('leɪɪˌsaɪz) *vb (tr)* to withdraw clerical or ecclesiastical character or status from (an institution, building, etc.). ▸ **ˌlaici'zation** *or* **ˌlaici'sation** *n*

laid (leɪd) *vb* the past tense and past participle of **lay**[1].

laid-back *adj Informal.* relaxed in style, character, or behaviour; easy-going and unhurried.

laid paper *n* paper with a regular mesh impressed upon it by the dandy roller on a paper-making machine. Compare **wove paper.**

laik (leɪk) *vb Northern English dialect.* **1** (when *intr,* often foll. by *about*) to play (a game, etc.). **2** (*intr*) to be on holiday, esp. to take a day off work. **3** (*intr*) to be unemployed. [C14: *leiken,* from Old Norse *leika;* related to Old English *lacan* to manoeuvre; compare LARK[2]]

Lailat-ul-Qadr (ˌleɪlætʊl'kɑːdə) *n* a night of study and prayer observed annually by Muslims to mark the communication of the Koran: it usually follows the 27th day of Ramadan. [from Arabic: night of determination]

lain (leɪn) *vb* the past participle of **lie**[2].

Laine (leɪn) *n* **Cleo** ('kliːəʊ), full name *Clementina Dinah Laine.* born 1927, British jazz singer, noted esp. for her recordings with her husband John Dankworth.

Laing (læŋ) *n* **R**(**onald**) **D**(**avid**). 1927–89, Scottish psychiatrist; his best known books include *The Divided Self* (1960), *The Politics of Experience and the Bird of Paradise* (1967), and *Knots* (1970).

Laingian ('læŋɪən) *adj* **1** of or based on R. D. Laing's theory that mental illnesses are understandable as natural responses to stress in family and social situations. ◆ *n* **2** a follower or adherent of Laing's teaching.

lair[1] (lɛə) *n* **1** the resting place of a wild animal. **2** *Informal.* a place of seclusion or hiding. **3** an enclosure or shed for farm animals. **4** *Scot.* the ground for a grave in a cemetery. ◆ *vb* **5** (*intr*) (esp. of a wild animal) to retreat to or rest in a lair. **6** (*tr*) to drive or place (an animal) in a lair. [Old English *leger;* related to LIE[2] and Old High German *leger* bed]

lair[2] (ler) *n, vb* a Scot. word for **mire.** [from Old Norse *leir* mud]

lair[3] (lɛə) *Austral. slang.* ◆ *n* **1** a flashy man who shows off. ◆ *vb* **2** (*intr;* foll. by *up* or *around*) to behave or dress like a lair. [perhaps from LEER]

lairage ('lɛərɪdʒ) *n* accommodation for farm animals, esp. at docks or markets.

laird (lɛəd; *Scot.* lerd) *n Scot.* a landowner, esp. of a large estate. [C15: Scottish variant of LORD]

lairy ('lɛərɪ) *adj* **lairier, lairiest.** gaudy or flashy. [C20: from LEERY]

laissez aller *or* ***laisser aller*** *French.* (lese ale) *n* lack of constraint; freedom. [literally: let go]

laissez faire *or* **laisser faire** *French.* (lese fɛr; *English* ˌlɛseɪ 'fɛə) *n* **1a** Also called: **individualism.** the doctrine of unrestricted freedom in commerce, esp. for private interests. **1b** (*as modifier*): *a laissez-faire economy.* **2** indifference or noninterference, esp. in the affairs of others. [French, literally: let (them) act] ▸ **ˌlaissez-'faireism** *or* **ˌlaisser-'faireism** *n*

laissez passer *or* ***laisser passer*** *French.* (lese pase) *n* a document granting unrestricted access or movement to its holder. [literally: let pass]

laity ('leɪɪtɪ) *n* **1** laymen, as distinguished from clergymen. **2** all people not of a specific occupation. [C16: from LAY[3]]

Laius ('laɪəs) *n Greek myth.* a king of Thebes, killed by his son Oedipus, who did not know of their relationship.

lake[1] (leɪk) *n* **1** an expanse of water entirely surrounded by land and unconnected to the sea except by rivers or streams. Related adj: **lacustrine. 2** anything resembling this. **3** a surplus of a liquid commodity: *a wine lake.* [C13: *lac,* via Old French from Latin *lacus* basin]

lake[2] (leɪk) *n* **1** a bright pigment used in textile dyeing and printing inks, produced by the combination of an organic colouring matter with an inorganic compound, usually a metallic salt, oxide, or hydroxide. See also **mordant. 2** a red dye obtained by combining a metallic compound with cochineal. [C17: variant of LAC[1]]

Lake District *n* a region of lakes and mountains in NW England, in Cumbria: includes England's largest lake (Windermere) and highest mountain (Scafell Pike); national park; literary associations (the Lake Poets); tourist region. Also called: **Lakeland.**

lake dwelling *n* a dwelling, esp. in prehistoric villages, constructed on platforms supported by wooden piles driven into the bottom of a lake. ▸ **lake dweller** *n*

lake herring *n* **1** another name for **cisco. 2** another name for **powan.**

Lakeland ('leɪkˌlænd) *n* **1** another name for the **Lake District.** ◆ *adj* **2** of or relating to the Lake District.

Lakeland terrier *n* a wire-haired breed of terrier, originally from the Lake District and used for hunting.

Lake of the Woods *n* a lake in N central North America, mostly in W Northern Ontario, Canada: fed chiefly by the Rainy River; drains into Lake Winnipeg by the Winnipeg River; many islands; tourist region. Area: 3846 sq. km (1485 sq. miles).

Lake Poets *pl n* the English poets Wordsworth, Coleridge, and Southey, who lived in and drew inspiration from the Lake District at the beginning of the 19th century.

laker ('leɪkə) *n* a cargo vessel used on lakes.

Lake Success *n* a village in SE New York State, on W Long Island: headquarters of the United Nations Security Council from 1946 to 1951. Pop.: 2450 (1990 est.).

lakh *or* **lac** (lɑːk) *n* (in India) the number 100 000, esp. when referring to this sum of rupees. [C17: from Hindi *lākh,* ultimately from Sanskrit *lakshā* a sign]

laksa ('læksa) *n* (in Malaysia) a dish of Chinese origin consisting of rice noodles served in curry or hot soup. [from Malay: ten thousand]

Lakshadweep Islands (læk'ʃædwiːp) *pl n* a group of 26 coral islands and reefs in the Arabian Sea, off the SW coast of India: a union territory of India since 1956. Administrative centre: Kavaratti Island. Pop.: 56 000 (1994 est.). Area: 28 sq. km (11 sq. miles). Former name (until 1973): **Laccadive, Minicoy, and Amindivi Islands.**

Lakshmi ('lɑːkʃmɪ) *n Hinduism.* the goddess of wealth and prosperity, and the consort of the god Vishnu. [from Sanskrit *Lākṣmi,* literally: wealth, splendour]

laky ('leɪkɪ) *adj* **lakier, lakiest.** of the reddish colour of the pigment lake.

Lala ('lɑːlɑː) *n* a title or form of address, equivalent to *Mr,* used in India. [Hindi]

lalang ('lɑːlɑːŋ) *n* a coarse weedy Malaysian grass, *Imperata arundinacea.* [Malay]

lalapalooza (ˌlɒləpə'luːzə) *n* a variant spelling of **lollapalooza.**

-lalia *combining form.* indicating a speech defect or abnormality: *coprolalia; echolalia.* [New Latin, from Greek *lalia* chatter, from *lalein* to babble]

La Línea (*Spanish* la 'linea) *n* a town in SW Spain, on the Bay of Gibraltar. Pop.: 57 000 (latest est.). Official name: **La Línea de la Concepción** (ðe la ˌkonθep'θjon).

Lalique (*French* lalik) *n* **René** (**Jules**) (rəne). 1860–1945, French Art-Nouveau jeweller, glass-maker, and designer: noted esp. for his frosted glassware.

Lallans ('lælənz) *or* **Lallan** ('lælən) *n* **1** a literary version of the variety of English spoken and written in the Lowlands of Scotland. **2** (*modifier*) of or relating to the Lowlands of Scotland or their dialects. [Scottish variant of LOWLANDS]

lallation (læ'leɪʃən) *n Phonetics.* a defect of speech consisting of the pronunciation of (r) as (l). [C17: from Latin *lallāre* to sing lullaby, of imitative origin]

lallygag ('lælɪˌgæg) *or* **lollygag** *vb* **-gags, -gagging, -gagged.** (*intr*) *U.S.* to loiter aimlessly. [C20: of unknown origin]

Lalo ('lɑːləʊ) *n* (**Victor-Antoine-**)**Édouard** (edwar). 1823–92, French composer of Spanish descent. His works include the *Symphonie espagnole* (1873) and the ballet *Namouna* (1882).

lam[1] (læm) *vb* **lams, lamming, lammed.** *Slang.* **1** (*tr*) to thrash or beat. **2** (*intr;* usually foll. by *into* or *out*) to make a sweeping stroke or blow. [C16: from Scandinavian; related to Old Norse *lemja*]

lam[2] (læm) *U.S. and Canadian slang.* ◆ *n* **1** a sudden flight or escape, esp. to avoid arrest. **2 on the lam. 2a** making an escape. **2b** in hiding. ◆ *vb* **lams, lamming, lammed. 3** (*intr*) to escape or flee. [C19: perhaps from LAM[1] (hence, to be off)]

lam. *abbrev. for* laminated.

Lam. *Bible. abbrev. for* Lamentations.

lama ('lɑːmə) *n* a priest or monk of Lamaism. [C17: from Tibetan *blama*]

Lamaism ('lɑːməˌɪzəm) *n* the Mahayana form of Buddhism of Tibet and Mongolia. See also **Dalai Lama.** ▸ **'Lamaist** *n, adj* ▸ **ˌLama'istic** *adj*

La Mancha (*Spanish* la 'mantʃa) *n* a plateau of central Spain, between the mountains of Toledo and the hills of Cuenca: traditionally associated with episodes in *Don Quixote.* Average height: 600 m (2000 ft.).

La Manche (*French* la mɑ̃ʃ) *n* See **Manche** (sense 2).

Lamarck (*French* lamark) *n* **Jean Baptiste Pierre Antoine de Monet** (ʒɑ̃ batist pjɛr ɑ̃twan də mɔnɛ), Chevalier de Lamarck. 1744–1829, French naturalist. He outlined his theory of organic evolution (Lamarckism) in *Philosophie zoologique* (1809).

Lamarckian (lɑː'mɑːkɪən) *adj* **1** of or relating to Lamarck. ◆ *n* **2** a supporter of Lamarckism.

Lamarckism (lɑː'mɑːkɪzəm) *n* the theory of organic evolution proposed by Lamarck, based on the principle that characteristics of an organism modified during its lifetime are inheritable. See also **acquired characteristic, Neo-Lamarckism.**

Lamartine (*French* lamartin) *n* **Alphonse Marie Louis de Prat de** (alfɔ̃s mari lwi də pra də). 1790–1869, French romantic poet, historian, and statesman: his works include *Méditations poétiques* (1820) and *Histoire des Girondins* (1847).

lamasery ('lɑːməsərɪ) *n, pl* **-series.** a monastery of lamas. [C19: from French *lamaserie,* from LAMA + French *-serie,* from Persian *serāī* palace]

lamb (læm) *n* **1** the young of a sheep. **2** the meat of a young sheep. **3** a person, esp. a child, who is innocent, meek, good, etc. **4** a person easily deceived. **5 like**

a lamb to the slaughter. 5a without resistance. 5b innocently. ◆ vb 6 (intr) Also lamb down. (of a ewe) to give birth. 7 (tr; used in the passive) (of a lamb) to be born. 8 (intr) (of a shepherd) to tend the ewes and newborn lambs at lambing time. ◆ See also lamb down. [Old English lamb, from Germanic; compare German Lamm, Old High German and Old Norse lamb] ▸ 'lamb,like adj

Lamb[1] (læm) n the. a title given to Christ in the New Testament.

Lamb[2] (læm) n 1 Charles, pen name Elia. 1775–1834, English essayist and critic. He collaborated with his sister Mary on Tales from Shakespeare (1807). His other works include Specimens of English Dramatic Poets (1808) and the largely autobiographical essays collected in Essays of Elia (1823; 1833). 2 William. See (2nd Viscount) Melbourne. 3 Willis Eugene. born 1913, U.S. physicist. He detected the small difference in energy between two states of the hydrogen atom (Lamb shift). Nobel prize for physics 1955.

lambada (læm'bɑːdə) n 1 an erotic dance, originating in Brazil, performed by two people who hold each other closely and gyrate their hips in synchronized movements. 2 the music that accompanies the lambada, combining salsa, calypso, and reggae. [C20: from Portuguese, literally: the snapping of a whip]

Lambaréné (French lɑ̃barene) n a town in W Gabon on the Ogooué River: site of the hospital built by Albert Schweitzer, who died and was buried there (1965). Pop.: 50 000 (1985 est.).

lambast (læm'bæst) or **lambaste** (læm'beɪst) vb (tr) 1 to beat or whip severely. 2 to reprimand or scold. [C17: perhaps from LAM[1] + BASTE[3]]

lambda ('læmdə) n the 11th letter of the Greek alphabet (Λ, λ), a consonant transliterated as l. [C14: from Greek, from Semitic; related to LAMED]

lambda calculus n Logic, computing. a formalized description of functions and the way in which they combine, developed by Alonzo Church and used in the theory of certain high-level programming languages. [C20: from the use of the symbol lambda (λ) to represent the mathematical functions]

lambdacism ('læmdə,sɪzəm) n Phonetics. 1 excessive use or idiosyncratic pronunciation of l. 2 another word for lallation. [C17: from Late Latin labdacismus, from Greek]

lambdoid ('læmdɔɪd) or **lambdoidal** adj 1 having the shape of the Greek letter lambda. 2 of or denoting the suture near the back of the skull between the occipital and parietal bones. [C16: via French from Greek lambdoeidēs]

lamb down vb (tr, adv) 1 another term for lamb (sense 6). 2 Austral. informal. to persuade (someone) to spend all his money.

lambent ('læmbənt) adj 1 (esp. of a flame) flickering softly over a surface. 2 glowing with soft radiance. 3 (of wit or humour) light or brilliant. [C17: from the present participle of Latin lambere to lick] ▸ 'lambency n ▸ 'lambently adv

lambert ('læmbət) n the cgs unit of illumination, equal to 1 lumen per square centimetre. Symbol: L [named after J. H. Lambert (1728–77), German mathematician and physicist]

Lambert ('læmbət) n Constant. 1905–51, English composer and conductor. His works include much ballet music and The Rio Grande (1929), a work for chorus, orchestra, and piano, using jazz idioms.

Lambeth ('læmbəθ) n 1 a borough of S Greater London, on the Thames: contains Lambeth Palace (the London residence of the Archbishop of Canterbury). Pop.: 260 700 (1994 est.). Area: 27 sq. km (11 sq. miles). 2 the Archbishop of Canterbury in his official capacity.

Lambeth Conference n the decennial conference of Anglican bishops, begun in 1867. See also Lambeth Quadrilateral.

Lambeth Quadrilateral n the four essentials agreed upon at the Lambeth Conference of 1888 for a United Christian Church, namely, the Holy Scriptures, the Apostles' Creed, the sacraments of baptism and Holy Communion, and the historic episcopate.

Lambeth walk n Chiefly Brit. a line dance popular in the 1930s.

lambing ('læmɪŋ) n 1a the birth of lambs. 1b (as modifier): lambing time. 2 the shepherd's work of tending the ewes and newborn lambs at this time.

lambkin ('læmkɪn) or **lambie** n 1 a small or young lamb. 2 a term of affection for a small endearing child.

Lamb of God n a title given to Christ in the New Testament, probably with reference to his sacrificial death.

lambrequin ('læmbrɪkɪn, 'læmbə-) n 1 an ornamental hanging covering the edge of a shelf or the upper part of a window or door. 2a a border pattern giving a draped effect, used on ceramics, etc. 2b (as modifier): a lambrequin pattern. 3 (often pl) a scarf worn over a helmet. 4 Heraldry. another name for mantling. [C18: from French, from Dutch lamperkin (unattested), diminutive of lamper veil]

lamb's ears n (functioning as sing) a perennial herb, Stachys lanata, planted for its foliage, which is covered with white woolly down; the purplish or striped flowers are small. Also called: lamb's tongue, (Scot.) lamb's lugs.

lamb's fry n 1 Brit. lamb's offal, esp. lamb's testicles, as food. 2 Austral. and N.Z. lamb's liver as food.

lambskin ('læm,skɪn) n 1 the skin of a lamb, esp. with the wool still on. 2a a material or garment prepared from this skin. 2b (as modifier): a lambskin coat. 3 a cotton or woollen fabric resembling this skin.

lamb's lettuce n another name for corn salad.

lamb's-quarters n, pl lamb's-quarters. a U.S. name for fat hen.

lamb's tails pl n the pendulous catkins of the hazel tree.

lamb's wool n a fine soft wool obtained from a lamb at its first shearing. b (as modifier): lamb's-wool jumpers.

LAMDA ('læmdə) n acronym for London Academy of Music and Dramatic Art.

lame[1] (leɪm) adj 1 disabled or crippled in the legs or feet. 2 painful or weak: a lame back. 3 weak; unconvincing: a lame excuse. 4 not effective or enthusiastic: a lame try. 5 U.S. slang. conventional or uninspiring. ◆ vb 6 (tr) to make lame. [Old English lama; related to Old Norse lami, German lahm] ▸ 'lamely adv ▸ 'lameness n

lame[2] (leɪm) n one of the overlapping metal plates used in armour after about 1330; splint. [C16: via Old French from Latin lāmina a thin plate, LAMINA]

lamé ('lɑːmeɪ) n a a fabric of silk, cotton, or wool interwoven with threads of metal. b (as modifier): a gold lamé gown. [from French, from Old French lame gold or silver thread, thin plate, from Latin lāmina thin plate]

lamebrain ('leɪm,breɪn) n Informal. a stupid or slow-witted person.

lamed ('lɑːmɪd; Hebrew 'lamɛd) n the 12th letter in the Hebrew alphabet (ל), transliterated as l. Also: lamedh ('lamɛd). [from Hebrew, literally: ox goad (from its shape)]

lame duck n 1 a person or thing that is disabled or ineffectual. 2 Stock Exchange. a speculator who cannot discharge his liabilities. 3 a company with a large workforce and high prestige that is unable to meet foreign competition without government support. 4 U.S. 4a an elected official or body of officials remaining in office in the interval between the election and inauguration of a successor. 4b (as modifier): a lame-duck president. 5 (modifier) U.S. designating a term of office after which the officeholder will not run for re-election.

lamella (lə'mɛlə) n, pl -lae (-liː) or -las. 1 a thin layer, plate, or membrane, esp. any of the calcified layers of which bone is formed. 2 Botany. 2a any of the spore-bearing gills of a mushroom. 2b any of the membranes in a chloroplast. 2c Also called: middle lamella. a layer of pectin cementing together adjacent cells. 3 one of a number of timber, metal, or concrete members connected along a pattern of intersecting diagonal lines to form a framed vaulted roof structure. 4 any thin sheet of material or thin layer in a fluid. [C17: New Latin, from Latin, diminutive of lāmina thin plate] ▸ la'mellar, lamellate ('læmɪ,leɪt, -lɪt; lə'mɛleɪt, -lɪt), or lamellose (lə'mɛləʊs, 'læmɪ,ləʊs) adj ▸ la'mellarly or 'lamellately adv ▸ 'lamel,lated adj ▸ ,lamel'lation n ▸ lamellosity (,læmə'lɒsɪtɪ) n

lamelli- combining form. indicating lamella or lamellae: lamellibranch.

lamellibranch (lə'mɛlɪ,bræŋk) n, adj another word for bivalve (senses 1, 2). [C19: from New Latin lamellibranchia plate-gilled (animals); see LAMELLA, BRANCHIA] ▸ la,melli'branchiate adj, n

lamellicorn (lə'mɛlɪ,kɔːn) n 1 any beetle of the superfamily Lamellicornia, having flattened terminal plates to the antennae: includes the scarabs and stag beetles. ◆ adj 2 of, relating to, or belonging to the Lamellicornia. 3 designating antennae with platelike terminal segments. [C19: from New Latin Lamellicornia plate-horned (animals)]

lamelliform (lə'mɛlɪ,fɔːm) adj shaped like a lamella; platelike: lamelliform antennae.

lamellirostral (lə,mɛlɪ'rɒstrəl) or **lamellirostrate** (lə,mɛlɪ'rɒstreɪt) adj (of ducks, geese, etc.) having a bill fringed with thin plates on the inner edge for straining water from food. [C19: from New Latin lāmellirostris, from LAMELLA + rostrum beak]

lament (lə'mɛnt) vb 1 to feel or express sorrow, remorse, or regret (for or over). ◆ n 2 an expression of sorrow. 3 a poem or song in which a death is lamented. [C16: from Latin lāmentum] ▸ la'menter n ▸ la'mentingly adv

lamentable ('læməntəbᵊl) adj 1 wretched, deplorable, or distressing. 2 an archaic word for mournful. ▸ 'lamentableness n ▸ 'lamentably adv

lamentation (,læmɛn'teɪʃən) n 1 a lament; expression of sorrow. 2 the act of lamenting.

Lamentations (,læmɛn'teɪʃənz) n (functioning as sing) 1 a book of the Old Testament, traditionally ascribed to the prophet Jeremiah, lamenting the destruction of Jerusalem. 2 a musical setting of these poems.

lamented (lə'mɛntɪd) adj grieved for or regretted (often in the phrase late lamented): our late lamented employer. ▸ la'mentedly adv

Lamerie ('læmərɪ) n Paul de. 1688–1751, English silversmith of French Huguenot descent, noted for his lavish rococo designs.

lamia ('leɪmɪə) n, pl -mias or -miae (-mɪ,iː). 1 Classical myth. one of a class of female monsters depicted with a snake's body and a woman's head and breasts. 2 a vampire or sorceress. [C14: via Latin from Greek Lamia]

lamina ('læmɪnə) n, pl -nae (-,niː) or -nas. 1 a thin plate, esp. of bone or mineral. 2 Botany. the flat blade of a leaf, petal, or thallus. [C17: New Latin, from Latin: thin plate] ▸ 'laminar or laminose ('læmɪ,nəʊs, -,nəʊz) adj

laminar flow n nonturbulent motion of a fluid in which parallel layers have different velocities relative to each other. Compare turbulent flow. See also streamline flow.

laminaria (,læmɪ'nɛərɪə) n any brown seaweed of the genus Laminaria, having large fluted leathery fronds. [C19: genus name formed from Latin lamina plate]

laminarin (,læmɪ'nɑːrɪn) n a carbohydrate, consisting of repeated glucose units, that is the main storage product of brown algae. [C20: from LAMINAR(IA) + -IN]

laminate vb ('læmɪ,neɪt). 1 (tr) to make (material in sheet form) by bonding together two or more thin sheets. 2 to split or be split into thin sheets. 3 (tr) to beat, form, or press (material, esp. metal) into thin sheets. 4 (tr) to cover or overlay with a thin sheet of material. ◆ n ('læmɪ,neɪt, -nɪt). 5 a material made by bonding together two or more sheets. ◆ adj ('læmɪ,neɪt, -nɪt). 6 having or composed of lamina; laminated. [C17: from New Latin lāminātus plated] ▸ laminable ('læmɪnəbᵊl) adj ▸ 'lami,nator n

laminated ('læmɪ,neɪtɪd) adj 1 composed of thin sheets (of plastic, wood, etc.) superimposed and bonded together by synthetic resins, usually under heat and pressure. 2 covered with a thin protective layer of plastic or synthetic resin. 3 another word for laminate (sense 6).

lamination (,læmɪ'neɪʃən) n 1 the act of laminating or the state of being laminated. 2 a layered structure. 3 a layer; lamina. 4 one of a set of iron plates forming the core of an electrical transformer. 5 Geology. laminar stratification, typically shown by shales.

laminectomy (ˌlæmɪˈnɛktəmɪ) *n, pl* **-mies.** surgical incision into the backbone to gain access to the spinal cord. Also called: **rachiotomy.**

lamington (ˈlæmɪŋtən) *n Austral. and N.Z.* a cube of sponge cake coated in chocolate and dried coconut. **[C20** (in the earlier sense: a homburg hat): named after Baron *Lamington,* governor of Queensland (1896–1901)**]**

laminitis (ˌlæmɪˈnaɪtɪs) *n* inflammation of the laminated tissue structure to which the hoof of a horse is attached. Also called: **founder. [C19:** from New Latin, from LAMINA + -ITIS**]**

Lammas (ˈlæməs) *n* **1** *R.C. Church.* Aug. 1, held as a feast, commemorating St. Peter's miraculous deliverance from prison. **2** Also called: **Lammas Day.** the same day formerly observed in England as a harvest festival. In Scotland Lammas is a quarter day. **[**Old English *hlāfmæsse* loaf mass**]**

Lammastide (ˈlæməsˌtaɪd) *n Archaic.* the season of Lammas.

lammergeier *or* **lammergeyer** (ˈlæməˌgaɪə) *n* a rare vulture, *Gypaetus barbatus,* of S Europe, Africa, and Asia, with dark wings, a pale breast, and black feathers around the bill: family *Accipitridae* (hawks). Also called: **bearded vulture. [C19:** from German *Lämmergeier,* from *Lämmer* lambs + *Geier* vulture**]**

lamp (læmp) *n* **1a** any of a number of devices that produce illumination: *an electric lamp; a gas lamp; an oil lamp.* **1b** (*in combination*)*: lampshade.* **2** a device for holding one or more electric light bulbs: *a table lamp.* **3** a vessel in which a liquid fuel is burned to supply illumination. **4** any of a variety of devices that produce radiation, esp. for therapeutic purposes: *an ultraviolet lamp.* **[C13** *lampe,* via Old French from Latin *lampas,* from Greek, from *lampein* to shine**]**

lampas[1] (ˈlæmpəs) *or* **lampers** (ˈlæmpəz) *n* a swelling of the mucous membrane of the hard palate of horses. **[C16:** from Old French; origin obscure**]**

lampas[2] (ˈlæmpəs) *n* an ornate damask-like cloth of cotton or silk and cotton, used in upholstery. **[C14** (a kind of crepe): probably from Middle Dutch *lampers***]**

lampblack (ˈlæmpˌblæk) *n* a finely divided form of almost pure carbon produced by the incomplete combustion of organic compounds, such as natural gas, used in making carbon electrodes and dynamo brushes and as a pigment.

lamp chimney *n* a glass tube that surrounds the wick in an oil lamp.

Lampedusa[1] (ˌlæmpɪˈdjuːzə) *n* an island in the Mediterranean, between Malta and Tunisia. Area: about 21 sq. km (8 sq. miles).

Lampedusa[2] (ˌlæmpɪˈdjuːzə) *n* **Giuseppe Tomasi di.** 1896–1957, Italian novelist: author of the historical novel *The Leopard* (1958).

lamper eel (ˈlæmpə) *n* another name for **lamprey. [C19** *lamper,* variant of LAMPREY**]**

lampern (ˈlæmpən) *n* a migratory European lamprey, *Lampetra fluviatilis,* that spawns in rivers. Also called: **river lamprey. [C14** *laumprun,* from Old French, from *lampreie* LAMPREY**]**

lampion (ˈlæmpɪən) *n* an oil-burning lamp. **[C19:** from French via Italian *lampione,* from Old French *lampe* LAMP**]**

lamplighter (ˈlæmpˌlaɪtə) *n* **1** (formerly) a person who lit and extinguished street lamps, esp. gas ones. **2** *Chiefly U.S. and Canadian.* any of various devices used to light lamps.

lampoon (læmˈpuːn) *n* **1** a satire in prose or verse ridiculing a person, literary work, etc. ◆ *vb* **2** (*tr*) to attack or satirize in a lampoon. **[C17:** from French *lampon,* perhaps from *lampons* let us drink (frequently used as a refrain in poems)**]** ▸ **lamˈpooner** *or* **lamˈpoonist** *n* ▸ **lamˈpoonery** *n*

lamppost (ˈlæmpˌpəʊst) *n* a post supporting a lamp, esp. in a street.

lamprey (ˈlæmprɪ) *n* any eel-like cyclostome vertebrate of the family *Petromyzonidae,* having a round sucking mouth for clinging to and feeding on the blood of other animals. Also called: **lamper eel.** See also **sea lamprey. [C13:** from Old French *lamproie,* from Late Latin *lamprēda;* origin obscure**]**

lamprophyre (ˈlæmprəˌfaɪə) *n* any of a group of basic igneous rocks consisting of feldspar and ferromagnesian minerals, esp. biotite: occurring as dykes and minor intrusions. **[**from Greek *lampros* bright + *-phyre,* from PORPHYRY**]**

lamp shell *n* another name for a **brachiopod. [C19:** from its likeness in shape to an ancient Roman oil lamp**]**

lamp standard *n* a tall metal or concrete post supporting a street lamp.

LAN *abbrev. for* local area network.

lanai (lɑːˈnɑːɪ, ləˈnaɪ) *n* a Hawaiian word for **veranda.**

Lanai (lɑːˈnɑːɪ, ləˈnaɪ) *n* an island in central Hawaii, west of Maui Island. Pop.: 2426 (1990). Area: 363 sq. km. (140 sq. miles).

Lanarkshire (ˈlænəkˌʃɪə, -ʃə) *n* a historical county of S Scotland: became part of Strathclyde region in 1975; since 1996 administered by the council areas of North Lanarkshire, South Lanarkshire, and Glasgow.

lanate (ˈleɪneɪt) *or* **lanose** (ˈleɪnəʊs, -nəʊz) *adj Biology.* having or consisting of a woolly covering of hairs. **[C18:** from Latin *lānātus,* from *lāna* wool**]**

Lancashire (ˈlæŋkəˌʃɪə, -ʃə) *n* **1** a county of NW England, on the Irish Sea: became a county palatine in 1351 and a duchy attached to the Crown; much reduced in size after the 1974 boundary changes, losing the Furness district to Cumbria and much of the south to Greater Manchester, Merseyside, and Cheshire. It was traditionally a cotton textiles manufacturing region. Administrative centre: Preston. Pop.: 1 424 000 (1994 est.). Area: 3063 sq. km (1182 sq. miles). Abbrev.: **Lancs. 2** a mild whitish-coloured cheese with a crumbly texture.

Lancaster[1] (ˈlæŋkəstə, ˈlæŋˌkæstə) *n* the English royal house that reigned from 1399 to 1461.

Lancaster[2] (ˈlæŋkəstə) *n* a city in NW England, former county town of Lancashire, on the River Lune: castle (built on the site of a Roman camp); university (1964). Pop.: 44 497 (1991).

Lancastrian (læŋˈkæstrɪən) *n* **1** a native or resident of Lancashire or Lancaster. **2** an adherent of the house of Lancaster in the Wars of the Roses. Compare **Yorkist.** ◆ *adj* **3** of or relating to Lancashire or Lancaster. **4** of or relating to the house of Lancaster.

lance (lɑːns) *n* **1** a long weapon with a pointed head used by horsemen to unhorse or injure an opponent. **2** a similar weapon used for hunting, whaling, etc. **3** *Surgery.* another name for **lancet. 4** short for **sand lance** (another name for **sand eel**). ◆ *vb* (*tr*) **5** to pierce (an abscess or boil) with a lancet to drain off pus. **6** to pierce with or as if with a lance. **[C13** *launce,* from Old French *lance,* from Latin *lancea***]**

lance corporal *n* a noncommissioned officer of the lowest rank in the British Army.

lancejack (ˈlɑːnsˌdʒæk) *n Brit. military slang.* a lance corporal.

lancelet (ˈlɑːnslɪt) *n* any of several marine animals of the genus *Branchiostoma* (formerly *Amphioxus*), esp. *B. lanceolatus,* that are closely related to the vertebrates: subphylum *Cephalochordata* (cephalochordates). Also called: **amphioxus. [C19:** referring to the slender shape**]**

Lancelot (ˈlɑːnslət) *n* (in Arthurian legend) one of the Knights of the Round Table; the lover of Queen Guinevere.

lanceolate (ˈlɑːnsɪəˌleɪt, -lɪt) *adj* narrow and tapering to a point at each end: *lanceolate leaves.* **[C18:** from Late Latin *lanceolātus,* from *lanceola* small LANCE**]**

lancer (ˈlɑːnsə) *n* **1** (formerly) a cavalryman armed with a lance. **2a** a member of a regiment retaining such a title. **2b** (*pl; cap. when part of a name*)*: the 21st Lancers.* ◆ See also **lancers.**

lance rest *n* **1** a hinged bracket on the breastplate of a medieval horseman on which the lance was rested in a charge. **2** a similar structure on a knight's saddle.

lancers (ˈlɑːnsəz) *n* (*functioning as sing*) **1** a quadrille for eight or sixteen couples. **2** a piece of music composed for this dance.

lance sergeant *n* a corporal acting as a sergeant, usually on a temporary basis and without additional pay.

lancet (ˈlɑːnsɪt) *n* **1** Also called: **lance.** a pointed surgical knife with two sharp edges. **2** short for **lancet arch** or **lancet window. [C15** *lancette,* from Old French: small LANCE**]**

lancet arch *n* a narrow acutely pointed arch having two centres of equal radii. Sometimes shortened to **lancet.** Also called: **acute arch, Gothic arch, pointed arch, ogive.**

lanceted (ˈlɑːnsɪtɪd) *adj Architect.* having one or more lancet arches or windows.

lancet fish *n* either of two deep-sea teleost fishes, *Alepisaurus ferox* or *A. borealis,* having a long body with a long sail-like dorsal fin: family *Alepisauridae.*

lancet window *n* a narrow window having a lancet arch. Sometimes shortened to **lancet.**

lancewood (ˈlɑːnsˌwʊd) *n* **1** any of various tropical trees, esp. *Oxandra lanceolata,* yielding a tough elastic wood: family *Annonaceae.* **2** the wood of any of these trees.

Lanchow *or* **Lan-chou** (ˈlænˈtʃaʊ) *n* a variant transliteration of the Chinese name for **Lanzhou.**

lancinate (ˈlɑːnsɪˌneɪt) *adj* (esp. of pain) sharp or cutting. **[C17:** from Latin *lancinātus* pierced, rent; related to *lacer* mangled**]** ▸ **ˌlanciˈnation** *n*

Lancs (læŋks) *abbrev. for* Lancashire.

land (lænd) *n* **1** the solid part of the surface of the earth as distinct from seas, lakes, etc. Related adj: **terrestrial. 2a** ground, esp. with reference to its use, quality, etc. **2b** (*in combination*)*: land-grabber.* **3** rural or agricultural areas as contrasted with urban ones. **4** farming as an occupation or way of life. **5** *Law.* **5a** any tract of ground capable of being owned as property, together with any buildings on it, extending above and below the surface. **5b** any hereditament, tenement, or other interest; realty. **6a** a country, region, or area. **6b** the people of a country, etc. **7** a realm, sphere, or domain. **8** *Economics.* the factor of production consisting of all natural resources. **9** the unindented part of a grooved surface, esp. one of the ridges inside a rifle bore. **10 how the land lies.** the prevailing conditions or state of affairs. ◆ *vb* **11** to transfer (something) or go from a ship or boat to the shore: *land the cargo.* **12** (*intr*) to come to or touch shore. **13** to come down or bring (something) down to earth after a flight or jump. **14** to come or bring to some point, condition, or state. **15** (*tr*) *Angling.* to retrieve (a hooked fish) from the water. **16** (*tr*) *Informal.* to win or obtain: *to land a job.* **17** (*tr*) *Informal.* to deliver (a blow). ◆ See also **lands, land up, land with. [**Old English; compare Old Norse, Gothic *land,* Old High German *lant***]** ▸ **ˈlandless** *adj* ▸ **ˈlandlessness** *n*

Land (lænd) *n* **Edwin Herbert.** 1909–91, U.S. inventor of the Polaroid Land camera.

Land (*German* lant) *n, pl* ***Länder*** (ˈlɛndər) **a** any of the federal states of Germany. **b** any of the provinces of Austria. **[**German**]**

land agent *n* **1** a person who administers a landed estate and its tenancies. **2** a person who acts as an agent for the sale of land. ▸ **land agency** *n*

landammann (ˈlændəmən) *n* (*sometimes cap.*) the chairman of the governing council in any of several Swiss cantons. **[C18:** Swiss German, from *Land* country + *Ammann,* from *Amt* office + *Mann* MAN**]**

landau (ˈlændɔː) *n* a four-wheeled carriage, usually horse-drawn, with two folding hoods that meet over the middle of the passenger compartment. **[C18:** named after *Landau,* (a town in Bavaria) where it was first made**]**

Landau (*Russian* lanˈdau) *n* **Lev Davidovich** (ljef daˈvidəvitʃ). 1908–68, Soviet physicist, noted for his researches on quantum theory and his work on the theories of solids and liquids: Nobel prize for physics 1962.

landaulet *or* **landaulette** (ˌlændɔːˈlɛt) *n* **1** a small landau. **2** *U.S.* an early type of car with a folding hood over the passenger seats and an open driver's seat.

land bank *n* a bank that issues banknotes on the security of property.

land bridge *n* (in zoogeography) a connecting tract of land between two continents, enabling animals to pass from one continent to the other.

land crab *n* any of various crabs, esp. of the tropical family *Gecarcinidae,* that are adapted to a partly terrestrial life.

Landdrost ('lændrɒst) *n S. African history.* the chief magistrate of a district. [C18: Afrikaans, from Dutch *land* country + *drost* sheriff, bailiff]

landed ('lændɪd) *adj* **1** owning land: *landed gentry.* **2** consisting of or including land: *a landed estate.*

Landes (*French* lɑ̃d) *n* **1** a department of SW France, in Aquitaine region. Capital: Mont-de-Marsan. Pop.: 318 300 (1995). Area: 9364 sq. km (3652 sq. miles). **2** a region of SW France, on the Bay of Biscay: occupies most of the Landes department and parts of Gironde and Lot-et-Garonne; consists chiefly of the most extensive forest in France. Area: 14 000 sq. km (5400 sq. miles).

Landeshauptmann ('lɑːndɪsˌhauptmən) *n* the head of government in an Austrian state. [C20: from German, from *Land* country + *Hauptmann* leader]

landfall ('lændˌfɔːl) *n* **1** the act of sighting or nearing land, esp. from the sea. **2** the land sighted or neared.

landfill ('lændˌfɪl) *n* **a** disposal of waste material by burying it under layers of earth. **b** (*as modifier*): *landfill sites.*

land forces *pl n* armed forces serving on land.

landform ('lændˌfɔːm) *n Geology.* any natural feature of the earth's surface, such as valleys and mountains.

land girl *n* a girl or woman who does farm work, esp. in wartime.

land grant *n* **1** *U.S. and Canadian.* a grant of public land to a college, railway, etc. **2** (*modifier*) *U.S.* designating a state university established with such a grant.

landgrave ('lændˌgreɪv) *n German history.* **1** (from the 13th century to 1806) a count who ruled over a specified territory. **2** (after 1806) the title of any of various sovereign princes in central Germany. [C16: via German, from Middle High German *lantgrāve,* from *lant* land + *grāve* count]

landgraviate (lænd'greɪvɪɪt, -ˌeɪt) *or* **landgravate** ('lændgrəˌveɪt) *n* the domain or position of a landgrave or landgravine.

landgravine ('lændgrəˌviːn) *n* **1** the wife or widow of a landgrave. **2** a woman who held the rank of landgrave.

land-holder *n* a person who owns or occupies land. ▸ **'land-ˌholding** *adj, n*

landing ('lændɪŋ) *n* **1a** the act of coming to land, esp. after a flight or sea voyage. **1b** (*as modifier*): *landing place.* **2** a place of disembarkation. **3** the floor area at the top of a flight of stairs or between two flights of stairs.

landing beacon *n* a radio transmitter that emits a landing beam.

landing beam *n* a radio beam transmitted from a landing field to enable aircraft to make an instrument landing.

landing craft *n Military.* any small vessel designed for the landing of troops and equipment on beaches.

landing field *n* an area of land on which aircraft land and from which they take off.

landing gear *n* another name for **undercarriage** (sense 1).

landing net *n Angling.* a loose long-handled net on a triangular frame for lifting hooked fish from the water.

landing speed *n* the minimum air speed at which an aircraft lands safely.

landing stage *n* a platform used for landing goods and passengers from a vessel.

landing strip *n* another name for **airstrip.**

landlady ('lændˌleɪdɪ) *n, pl* **-dies. 1** a woman who owns and leases property. **2** a landlord's wife. **3** a woman who owns or runs a lodging house, pub, etc.

ländler (*German* 'lɛntlər) *n* **1** an Austrian country dance in which couples spin and clap. **2** a piece of music composed for or in the rhythm of this dance, in three-four time. [German, from dialect *Landl* Upper Austria]

land line *n* a telecommunications wire or cable laid over land.

landlocked ('lændˌlɒkt) *adj* **1** (of a country) completely surrounded by land. **2** (esp. of lakes) completely or almost completely surrounded by land. **3** (esp. of certain salmon) living in fresh water that is permanently isolated from the sea.

landloper ('lændˌləupə) *n Scot.* a vagabond or vagrant. [C16: from Dutch, from LAND + *loopen* to run, LEAP]

landlord ('lændˌlɔːd) *n* **1** a man who owns and leases property. **2** a man who owns or runs a lodging house, pub, etc. **3** *Brit. archaic.* the lord of an estate.

landlordism ('lændlɔːˌdɪzəm) *n* the system by which land under private ownership is rented for a fixed sum to tenants.

landlubber ('lændˌlʌbə) *n Nautical.* any person having no experience at sea. [C18: LAND + LUBBER]

landmark ('lændˌmɑːk) *n* **1** a prominent or well-known object in or feature of a particular landscape. **2** an important or unique decision, event, fact, discovery, etc. **3** a boundary marker or signpost.

landmass ('lændˌmæs) *n* a large continuous area of land, as opposed to seas or islands.

land mine *n Military.* an explosive charge placed in the ground, usually detonated by stepping or driving on it.

land office *n U.S. and Canadian.* an office that administers the sale of public land.

land-office business *n U.S. and Canadian informal.* a booming or thriving business.

land of milk and honey *n* **1** *Old Testament.* the land of natural fertility promised to the Israelites by God (Ezekiel 20:6). **2** any fertile land, state, etc.

land of Nod *n* **1** *Old Testament.* a region to the east of Eden to which Cain went after he had killed Abel (Genesis 4:14). **2** an imaginary land of sleep.

Land of the Midnight Sun *n* **1** any land north of the Arctic Circle, which has continuous daylight throughout the short summer, esp. N parts of Norway, Sweden, and Finland. **2** an informal name for **Lapland.**

Landor ('lændɔː) *n* **Walter Savage.** 1775–1864, English poet, noted also for his prose works, including *Imaginary Conversations* (1824–29).

landowner ('lændˌəunə) *n* a person who owns land. ▸ **'landˌownerˌship** *n* ▸ **'landˌowning** *n, adj*

Landowska (*Polish* lan'dɔfska) *n* **Wanda** ('vanda). 1877–1959, U.S. harpsichordist, born in Poland.

land-poor *adj* owning much unprofitable land and lacking the money to maintain its fertility or improve it.

landrace ('lændˌreɪs) *n* **1** *Chiefly Brit.* a white very long-bodied lop-eared breed of pork pig. **2** *Botany.* an ancient or primitive cultivated variety of a crop plant. [from Danish, literally: land race]

land rail *n* another name for **corncrake.**

land reform *n* the redistributing of large agricultural holdings among the landless.

Landrost ('lændrɒst) *n* a variant spelling of **Landdrost.**

lands (lændz) *pl n* **1** holdings in land. **2** *S. African.* the part of a farm on which crops are grown.

landscape ('lændˌskeɪp) *n* **1** an extensive area of land regarded as being visually distinct: *ugly slagheaps dominated the landscape.* **2** a painting, drawing, photograph, etc., depicting natural scenery. **3a** the genre including such pictures. **3b** (*as modifier*): *landscape painter.* **4** the distinctive features of a given area of intellectual activity, regarded as an integrated whole: *the landscape of the European imagination.* ◆ *adj* **5** *Printing.* **5a** (of a publication or an illustration in a publication) of greater width than height. Compare **portrait** (sense 3). **5b** (of a page) carrying an illustration or table printed at right angles to the normal text. ◆ *vb* **6** (*tr*) to improve the natural features of (a garden, park, etc.), as by creating contoured features and planting trees. **7** (*intr*) to work as a landscape gardener. [C16 *landskip* (originally a term in painting), from Middle Dutch *lantscap* region; related to Old English *landscipe* tract of land, Old High German *lantscaf* region]

landscape gardening *n* the art of laying out grounds in imitation of natural scenery. Also called: **landscape architecture.** ▸ **landscape gardener** *n*

landscapist ('lændˌskeɪpɪst) *n* a painter of landscapes.

Landseer ('lænsɪə) *n* Sir **Edwin Henry.** 1802–73, English painter, noted for his studies of animals.

Land's End *n* a granite headland in SW England, on the SW coast of Cornwall: the westernmost point of England.

landshark ('lændˌʃɑːk) *n Informal.* a person who makes inordinate profits by buying and selling land.

Landshut (*German* 'lantshuːt) *n* a city in SE Germany, in Bavaria: Trausnitz castle (13th century); manufacturing centre for machinery and chemicals. Pop.: 59 670 (1991).

landside ('lændˌsaɪd) *n* **1** the part of an airport farthest from the aircraft, the boundary of which is the security check, customs, passport control, etc. Compare **airside. 2** the part of a plough that slides along the face of the furrow wall on the opposite side to the mouldboard.

landsknecht ('læntskəˌnɛkt) *n* a mercenary foot soldier in late 15th-, 16th-, and 17th-century Europe, esp. a German pikeman. [German, literally: land-knight]

landslide ('lændˌslaɪd) *n* **1** Also called: **landslip. 1a** the sliding of a large mass of rock material, soil, etc., down the side of a mountain or cliff. **1b** the material dislodged in this way. **2a** an overwhelming electoral victory. **2b** (*as modifier*): *a landslide win.*

Landsmål ('lɑːntsmoːl) *n* another name for **Nynorsk.**

landsman[1] ('lændzmən) *n, pl* **-men. 1** a person who works or lives on land, as distinguished from a seaman. **2** a person with no experience at sea.

landsman[2] ('lændzmən) *n, pl* **-men.** a Jewish compatriot from the same area of origin as another. [from Yiddish]

Landsteiner (*German* 'lantˌʃtaɪnər) *n* **Karl** (karl). 1868–1943, Austrian immunologist, who discovered (1900) human blood groups and introduced the ABO classification system. He also discovered (1940) the Rhesus (Rh) factor in blood and researched into poliomyelitis. Nobel prize for physiology or medicine (1930).

Landsturm *German.* ('lantʃturm) *n* (in German-speaking countries) **1** a reserve force; militia. **2** a general levy in wartime. [C19: literally: landstorm; originally a summons to arms by means of storm-warning bells]

Landtag ('lɑːntˌtɑːk) *n* **1** the legislative assembly of each state in present-day Germany and Austria. **2** the estates of principalities in medieval and modern Germany. **3** the assembly of numerous states in 19th-century Germany. [C16: German: land assembly]

land tax *n* (formerly) a tax payable annually by virtue of ownership of land, abolished in Britain in 1963.

land up *vb* (*adv, usually intr*) to arrive or cause to arrive at a final point: *after a summer in Europe, he suddenly landed up at home.*

landwaiter ('lændˌweɪtə) *n* an officer of the Custom House.

landward ('lændwəd) *adj* **1** lying, facing, or moving towards land. **2** in the direction of the land. ◆ *adv* **3** a variant of **landwards.**

landwards ('lændwədz) *or* **landward** *adv* towards land.

land with *vb* (*tr, prep*) to give to, so as to put in difficulties; cause to be burdened with: *why did you land me with this extra work?*

lane[1] (leɪn) *n* **1a** a narrow road or way between buildings, hedges, fences, etc. **1b** (*cap. as part of a street name*): *Drury Lane.* **2a** any of the parallel strips into which the carriageway of a major road or motorway is divided. **2b** any narrow well-defined route or course for ships or aircraft. **3** one of the parallel strips into which a running track or swimming bath is divided for races. **4** the long strip of wooden flooring down which balls are bowled in a bowling alley. [Old English *lane, lanu,* of Germanic origin; related to Middle Dutch *lāne* lane]

lane[2] (leɪn) *adj Scot. dialect.* **1** lone or alone. **2** (**on**) **one's lane.** on one's own.

Lanfranc ('lænfræŋk) *n* ?1005–89, Italian ecclesiastic and scholar; archbishop of Canterbury (1070–89) and adviser to William the Conqueror. He instituted many reforms in the English Church.

lang (læŋ) *adj* a Scot. word for **long.**

Lang (læŋ) *n* **1 Cosmo Gordon,** 1st Baron Lang of Lambeth. 1864–1945, British churchman; archbishop of Canterbury (1928–42). **2 Fritz.** 1890–1976, Austrian film director, later in the U.S., most notable for his silent films, such as *Metropolis* (1926), *M* (1931), and *The Testament of Dr. Mabuse* (1932). **3 Jack (John Thomas).** 1876–1975, controversial Labor premier of New South Wales from 1925–27 and from 1930–32, who introduced much social welfare legislation and was dismissed by the governor, Sir Philip Game, in 1932 for acting unconstitutionally.

lang. *abbrev. for* language.

langar ('lʌnga:) *n Sikhism.* **a** the dining hall in a gurdwara. **b** the food served, given to all regardless of caste or religion as a gesture of equality. [Punjabi]

Lange ('lɒŋɪ) *n* **David (Russell).** born 1942, New Zealand statesman: leader of the Labour Party from 1983: prime minister (1984–89).

Langer ('læŋə) *n* **Bernhard** ('bɛrnhart). born 1957, German professional golfer: won the U.S. Masters Championship (1985, 1993).

Langerhans islets ('læŋə,hæns) *or* **islands** *n Anatomy.* see **islets of Langerhans.**

Langland ('læŋlənd) *n* **William.** ?1332–?1400, English poet. The allegorical religious poem in alliterative verse, *The Vision of William concerning Piers the Plowman,* is attributed to him.

langlauf ('la:ŋ,laʊf) *n* cross-country skiing. [German, literally: long run] ► **langläufer** ('la:ŋ,lɔɪfə) *n*

Langley ('læŋlɪ) *n* **Samuel Pierpont,** 1834–1906, U.S. astronomer and physicist: invented the bolometer (1878) and pioneered the construction of heavier-than-air flying machines.

Langmuir ('læŋmjʊə) *n* **Irving.** 1881–1957, U.S. chemist. He developed the gas-filled tungsten lamp and the atomic hydrogen welding process: Nobel prize for chemistry 1932.

Langobard ('læŋgə,ba:d) *n* a less common name for a **Lombard.** [C18: from Late Latin *Langobardicus* Lombard]

Langobardic (,læŋgə'ba:dɪk) *n* **1** the language of the ancient Lombards: a dialect of Old High German. ◆ *adj* **2** of or relating to the Lombards or their language.

langouste ('lɒŋgu:st, lɒŋ'gu:st) *n* another name for the **spiny lobster.** [French, from Old Provençal *langosta,* perhaps from Latin *lōcusta* lobster, locust]

langoustine (,lɒŋgu:'sti:n) *n* a large prawn or small lobster. [from French, diminutive of LANGOUSTE]

langrage ('læŋgrɪdʒ), **langrel** ('læŋgrəl), *or* **langridge** *n* shot consisting of scrap iron packed into a case, formerly used in naval warfare. [C18: of unknown origin]

Langres Plateau (*French* lɑ̃grə) *n* a calcareous plateau of E France north of Dijon between the Seine and the Saône, reaching over 580 m (1900 ft.): forms a watershed between rivers flowing to the Mediterranean and to the English Channel.

langsyne (,læŋ'saɪn, -'saɪn) *Scot.* ◆ *adv* **1** long ago; long since. ◆ *n* **2** times long past, esp. those fondly remembered. See also **auld lang syne.** [C16: Scottish: long since]

Langton ('læŋtən) *n* **Stephen.** ?1150–1228, English cardinal; archbishop of Canterbury (1213–28). He was consecrated archbishop by Pope Innocent III in 1207 but was kept out of his see by King John until 1213. He was partly responsible for the Magna Carta (1215).

Langtry ('læŋtrɪ) *n* **Lillie,** known as *the Jersey Lily,* real name *Émilie Charlotte le Breton.* 1852–1929, English actress, noted for her beauty and for her friendship with Edward VII.

language ('læŋgwɪdʒ) *n* **1** a system for the expression of thoughts, feelings, etc., by the use of spoken sounds or conventional symbols. **2** the faculty for the use of such systems, which is a distinguishing characteristic of man as compared with other animals. **3** the language of a particular nation or people: *the French language.* **4** any other systematic or nonsystematic means of communicating, such as gesture or animal sounds: *the language of love.* **5** the specialized vocabulary used by a particular group: *medical language.* **6** a particular manner or style of verbal expression: *your language is disgusting.* **7** *Computing.* See **programming language. 8 speak the same language.** to communicate with understanding because of common background, values, etc. [C13: from Old French *langage,* ultimately from Latin *lingua* tongue]

language laboratory *n* a room equipped with tape recorders, etc., for learning foreign languages.

langue (la:ŋg) *n Linguistics.* language considered as an abstract system or a social institution, being the common possession of a speech community. Compare **parole** (sense 5). [C19: from French: language]

langue de chat ('la:ŋ də 'ʃa:) *n* **1** a flat sweet finger-shaped biscuit. **2** a piece of chocolate having the same shape. [French: cat's tongue]

Languedoc (*French* lɑ̃gdɔk) *n* **1** a former province of S France, lying between the foothills of the Pyrenees and the River Rhône: formed around the countship of Toulouse in the 13th century; important production of bulk wines. **2** a wine from this region.

langue d'oc *French.* (lɑ̃g dɔk) *n* the group of medieval French dialects spoken in S France: often regarded as including Provençal. Compare ***langue d'oïl.*** [literally: language of *oc* (form for the Provençal *yes*), ultimately from Latin *hoc* this]

Languedoc-Roussillon (*French* lɑ̃gdɔkrusijɔ̃) *n* a region of S France, on the Gulf of Lions: consists of the departments of Lozère, Gard, Hérault, Aude, and Pyrénées-Orientales; mainly mountainous with a coastal plain.

langue d'oïl *French.* (lɑ̃g dɔj) *n* the group of medieval French dialects spoken in France north of the Loire; the medieval basis of modern French. [literally: language of *oïl* (the northern form for *yes*), ultimately from Latin *hoc ille* (*fecit*) this he (did)]

languet ('læŋgwɛt) *n Rare.* anything resembling a tongue in shape or function. [C15: from Old French *languette,* diminutive of *langue* tongue]

languid ('læŋgwɪd) *adj* **1** without energy or spirit. **2** without interest or enthusiasm. **3** sluggish; inactive. [C16: from Latin *languidus,* from *languēre* to languish] ► **'languidly** *adv* ► **'languidness** *n*

languish ('læŋgwɪʃ) *vb* (*intr*) **1** to lose or diminish in strength or energy. **2** (often foll. by *for*) to be listless with desire; pine. **3** to suffer deprivation, hardship, or neglect: *to languish in prison.* **4** to put on a tender, nostalgic, or melancholic expression. [C14 *languishen,* from Old French *languiss-,* stem of *languir,* ultimately from Latin *languēre*] ► **'languishing** *adj* ► **'languishingly** *adv* ► **'languishment** *n*

languor ('læŋgə) *n* **1** physical or mental laziness or weariness. **2** a feeling of dreaminess and relaxation. **3** oppressive silence or stillness. [C14 *langour,* via Old French from Latin *languor,* from *languēre* to languish; the modern spelling is directly from Latin]

languorous ('læŋgərəs) *adj* **1** characterized by or producing languor. **2** another word for **languid.** ► **'languorously** *adv* ► **'languorousness** *n*

langur (lʌŋ'gʊə) *n* any of various agile arboreal Old World monkeys of the genus *Presbytis* and related genera, of S and SE Asia having a slender body, long tail and hands, and long hair surrounding the face. [Hindi, perhaps related to Sanskrit *lāngūla* tailed]

laniard ('lænjəd) *n* a variant spelling of **lanyard.**

laniary ('lænɪərɪ) *adj* **1** (esp. of canine teeth) adapted for tearing. ◆ *n, pl* **-aries. 2** a tooth adapted for tearing. [C19: from Latin *lanius* butcher, from *laniāre* to tear]

laniferous (lə'nɪfərəs) *or* **lanigerous** (lə'nɪdʒərəs) *adj Biology.* bearing wool or fleecy hairs resembling wool. [C17: from Latin *lānifer,* from *lāna* wool]

lank (læŋk) *adj* **1** long and limp. **2** thin or gaunt. [Old English *hlanc* loose] ► **'lankly** *adv* ► **'lankness** *n*

Lankester ('læŋkɪstə) *n* Sir **Edwin Ray.** 1847–1929, English zoologist, noted particularly for his work in embryology and study of protozoans.

lanky ('læŋkɪ) *adj* **lankier, lankiest.** tall, thin, and loose-jointed. ► **'lankily** *adv* ► **'lankiness** *n*

lanner ('lænə) *n* **1** a large falcon, *Falco biarmicus,* of Mediterranean regions, N Africa, and S Asia. **2** *Falconry.* the female of this falcon. Compare **lanneret.** [C15: from Old French (*faucon*) *lanier* cowardly (falcon), from Latin *lanārius* wool worker, coward; referring to its sluggish flight and timid nature]

lanneret ('lænə,rɛt) *n* the male or tercel of the lanner falcon. [C15: diminutive of LANNER]

lanolin ('lænəlɪn) *or* **lanoline** ('lænəlɪn, -,li:n) *n* a yellowish viscous substance extracted from wool, consisting of a mixture of esters of fatty acids: used in some ointments. Also called: **wool fat.** [C19: via German from Latin *lāna* wool + *oleum* oil; see -IN] ► **lanolated** ('lænə,leɪtɪd) *adj*

lanose ('leɪnəʊs, -nəʊz) *adj* another word for **lanate.** [C19: from Latin *lānosus*] ► **lanosity** (leɪ'nɒsɪtɪ) *n*

Lansbury ('lænzbərɪ) *n* **George.** 1859–1940, British Labour politician, who led the Labour Party in opposition (1931–35). A committed pacifist, he resigned over the party's reaction to Mussolini's seizure of Ethiopia.

Lansdowne ('lænzdaʊn) *n* **1st Marquess of.** See (William Petty Fitzmaurice) **Shelburne.**

Lansing ('lænsɪŋ) *n* a city in S Michigan, on the Grand River: the state capital. Pop.: 125 736 (1996 est.).

Lansker line ('lænskə) *n* (in Pembrokeshire) the linguistic and ethnic division between the Welsh-speaking north and the English-speaking south. [C19: from Pembrokeshire dialect *lansker* boundary]

lansquenet ('lænskə,nɛt) *n* **1** a gambling game of chance. **2** an archaic spelling of **landsknecht.** [from French]

lantana (læn'teɪnə, -'ta:-) *n* any verbenaceous shrub or herbaceous plant of the tropical American genus *Lantana,* having spikes of yellow or orange flowers. It was introduced into Australia, where it is now regarded as a troublesome weed. [C18: New Latin, from Italian dialect *lantana* wayfaring tree]

lantern ('læntən) *n* **1** a light with a transparent or translucent protective case. **2** a structure on top of a dome or roof having openings or windows to admit light or air. **3** the upper part of a lighthouse that houses the light. **4** *Photog.* short for **magic lantern.** [C13: from Latin *lanterna,* from Greek *lamptēr* lamp, from *lampein* to shine]

lantern fish *n* any small deep-sea teleost fish of the family *Myctophidae,* having a series of luminescent spots along the body.

lantern fly *n* any of various tropical insects of the homopterous family *Fulgoridae,* many species of which have a snoutlike process formerly thought to emit light.

lantern jaw *n* (when *pl,* refers to upper and lower jaw; when *sing* usually to lower jaw) a long hollow jaw that gives the face a drawn appearance. ► **'lantern-,jawed** *adj*

lantern pinion *or* **wheel** *n* a type of gearwheel, now used only in clocks, consisting of two parallel circular discs connected by a number of pins running parallel to the axis.

lantern slide *n* (formerly) a photographic slide for projection, used in a magic lantern.

lanthanide ('lænθə,naɪd) *or* **lanthanon** ('lænθə,nɒn) *n* any element of the lanthanide series. Also called: **rare earth, rare-earth element.** [C19: from LANTHANUM + -IDE]

lanthanide series *n* a class of 15 chemically related elements with atomic numbers from 57 (lanthanum) to 71 (lutetium).

lanthanum ('lænθənəm) *n* a silvery-white ductile metallic element of the lanthanide series, occurring principally in bastnaesite and monazite: used in pyrophoric alloys, electronic devices, and in glass manufacture. Symbol: La; atomic no.: 57; atomic wt.: 138.9055; valency: 3; relative density: 6.145; melting pt.: 918°C; boiling pt.: 3464°C. [C19: New Latin, from Greek *lanthanein* to lie unseen]

lanthorn ('lænt,hɔːn, 'læntən) *n* an archaic word for **lantern.**

lanugo (lə'njuːgəʊ) *n, pl* **-gos.** a layer of fine hairs, esp. the covering of the human fetus before birth. [C17: from Latin: down, from *lāna* wool] ▸ **lanuginous** (lə'njuːdʒɪnəs) *or* **la'nugi,nose** *adj* ▸ **la'nuginousness** *n*

Lanús (*Spanish* la'nus) *n* a city in E Argentina: a S suburb of Buenos Aires. Pop.: 466 755 (1991).

lanyard *or* **laniard** ('lænjəd) *n* **1** a cord, esp. one worn around the neck, to hold a whistle, knife, etc. **2** a cord with an attached hook used in firing certain types of cannon. **3** *Nautical.* a line rove through deadeyes for extending or tightening standing rigging. [C15 *lanyer,* from French *lanière,* from *lasne* strap, probably of Germanic origin]

Lanzhou, Lanchow, *or* **Lan-chou** ('læn'dʒəʊ) *n* a city in N China, capital of Gansu province, on the Yellow River: situated on the main route between China and the West. Pop.: 1 510 000 (1991 est.).

Lao (laʊ) *or* **Laotian** ('laʊʃɪən) *n* **1** (*pl* **Lao, Laos,** *or* **Laotians**) a member of a Buddhist people of Laos and NE Thailand, related to the Thais. **2** the language of this people, closely related to Thai. ◆ *adj* **3** of or relating to this people or their language or to Laos.

LAO *international car registration for* Laos.

Laoag (lɑː'wɑːg) *n* a city in the N Philippines, on NW Luzon: trade centre for an agricultural region. Pop.: 84 000 (1990 est.).

Laocoon (leɪ'ɒkəʊ,ɒn) *n Greek myth.* a priest of Apollo at Troy who warned the Trojans against the wooden horse left by the Greeks; killed with his twin sons by two sea serpents.

Laodicea (,leɪəʊdɪ'sɪə) *n* the ancient name of several Greek cities in W Asia, notably of **Latakia.**

laodicean (,leɪəʊdɪ'sɪən) *adj* **1** lukewarm and indifferent, esp. in religious matters. ◆ *n* **2** a person having a lukewarm attitude towards religious matters. [C17: referring to the early Christians of Laodicea (Revelation 3:14–16)]

Laoighis ('leɪʃ) *n* a variant spelling of **Laois.**

Laois ('leɪʃ) *n* a county of central Republic of Ireland, in Leinster province: formerly boggy but largely reclaimed for agriculture. County town: Portlaoise. Pop.: 53 000 (1996). Area: 1719 sq. km (664 sq. miles). Also called: **Laoighis, Leix.** Former name: **Queen's County.**

Laomedon (leɪ'ɒmɪ,dɒn) *n Greek myth.* the founder and ruler of Troy, who cheated Apollo and Poseidon of their wage for constructing the city's walls; the father of Priam.

Laos (laʊz, laʊs) *n* a republic in SE Asia: first united as the kingdom of Lan Xang ("million elephants") in 1353, after being a province of the Khmer Empire for about four centuries; made part of French Indochina in 1893 and gained independence in 1949; became a republic in 1975. It is generally forested and mountainous, with the Mekong River running almost the whole length of the W border. Official language: Lao. Religion: Buddhist majority, tribal religions. Currency: kip. Capital: Vientiane. Pop.: 5 261 000 (1998 est.). Area: 236 800 sq. km (91 429 sq. miles). Official name: **People's Democratic Republic of Laos.** ▸ **Laotian** ('laʊʃɪən) *adj, n*

Lao Zi ('laʊ'zɪə) *or* **Lao-tzu** ('laʊ'tsuː) *n* ?604–?531 B.C., Chinese philosopher, traditionally regarded as the founder of Taoism and the author of the *Tao-te Ching.*

lap^1 (læp) *n* **1** the area formed by the upper surface of the thighs of a seated person. **2** Also called: **lapful.** the amount held in one's lap. **3** a protected place or environment: *in the lap of luxury.* **4** any of various hollow or depressed areas, such as a hollow in the land. **5** the part of one's clothing that covers the lap. **6 drop in someone's lap.** give someone the responsibility of. **7 in the lap of the gods.** beyond human control and power. [Old English *læppa* flap; see LOBE, LAPPET, LOP^2]

lap^2 (læp) *n* **1** one circuit of a racecourse or track. **2** a stage or part of a journey, race, etc. **3a** an overlapping part or projection. **3b** the extent of overlap. **4** the length of material needed to go around an object. **5** a rotating disc coated with fine abrasive for polishing gemstones. **6** any device for bedding mechanical components together using a fine abrasive to polish the mating surfaces. **7** *Metallurgy.* a defect in rolled metals caused by the folding of a fin onto the surface. **8** a sheet or band of fibres, such as cotton, prepared for further processing. ◆ *vb* **laps, lapping, lapped. 9** (*tr*) to wrap or fold (around or over): *he lapped a bandage around his wrist.* **10** (*tr*) to enclose or envelop in: *he lapped his wrist in a bandage.* **11** to place or lie partly or completely over or project beyond. **12** (*tr; usually passive*) to envelop or surround with comfort, love, etc.: *lapped in luxury.* **13** (*intr*) to be folded. **14** (*tr*) to overtake (an opponent) in a race so as to be one or more circuits ahead. **15** (*tr*) to polish or cut (a workpiece, gemstone, etc.) with a fine abrasive, esp. to hone (mating metal parts) against each other with an abrasive. **16** to form (fibres) into a sheet or band. [C13 (in the sense: to wrap): probably from LAP^1] ▸ **'lapper** *n*

lap^3 (læp) *vb* **laps, lapping, lapped. 1** (of small waves) to wash against (a shore, boat, etc.), usually with light splashing sounds. **2** (often foll. by *up*) (esp. of animals) to scoop (a liquid) into the mouth with the tongue. ◆ *n* **3** the act or sound of lapping. **4** a thin food for dogs or other animals. ◆ See also **lap up.** [Old English *lapian;* related to Old High German *laffan,* Latin *lambere,* Greek *laptein*] ▸ **'lapper** *n*

La Palma (*Spanish* la 'palma) *n* an island in the N Atlantic, in the NW Canary Islands: administratively part of Spain. Chief town: Santa Cruz de la Palma. Pop.: 77 000 (latest est.). Area: 725 sq. km (280 sq. miles).

laparoscope ('læpərə,skəʊp) *n* a medical instrument consisting of a tube that is inserted through the abdominal wall and illuminated to enable a doctor to view the internal organs. [C19 (applied to various instruments used to examine the abdomen) and C20 (in the specific modern sense): from Greek *lapara* (see LAPAROTOMY) + -SCOPE] ▸ **,lapa'roscopy** *n*

laparotomy (,læpə'rɒtəmɪ) *n, pl* **-mies. 1** surgical incision through the abdominal wall, esp. to investigate the cause of an abdominal disorder. **2** surgical incision into the loin. [C19: from Greek *lapara* flank, from *laparos* soft + -TOMY]

La Paz (læ 'pæz; *Spanish* la 'paθ) *n* a city in W Bolivia, at an altitude of 3600 m (12 000 ft.): seat of government since 1898 (though Sucre is still the official capital); the country's largest city; founded in 1548 by the Spaniards; university (1830). Pop.: 784 976 (1993 est.).

lapboard ('læp,bɔːd) *n* a flat board that can be used on the lap as a makeshift table or desk.

lap-chart *n Motor racing.* a log of every lap covered by each car in a race, showing the exact position throughout.

lap dancing *n* a form of entertainment in which scantily dressed women dance erotically for individual members of the audience.

lap dissolve *n Films.* the technique of allowing the end of one scene to overlap the beginning of the next scene by fading out the former while fading in the latter.

lapdog ('læp,dɒg) *n* **1** a pet dog small and docile enough to be cuddled in the lap. **2** *Informal.* a person who attaches himself to someone in admiration or infatuation.

lapel (lə'pel) *n* the continuation of the turned or folded back collar on a suit coat, jacket, etc. [C18: from LAP^1] ▸ **la'pelled** *adj*

lapheld ('læp,held) *adj* (esp. of a personal computer) small enough to be used on one's lap; portable.

lapidary ('læpɪdərɪ) *n, pl* **-daries. 1** a person whose business is to cut, polish, set, or deal in gemstones. ◆ *adj* **2** of or relating to gemstones or the work of a lapidary. **3** Also: **lapidarian** (,læpɪ'deərɪən). engraved, cut, or inscribed in a stone or gemstone. **4** of sufficiently high quality to be engraved on a stone: *a lapidary inscription.* [C14: from Latin *lapidārius,* from *lapid-, lapis* stone] ▸ **,lapi'darian** *adj*

lapidate ('læpɪ,deɪt) *vb* (*tr*) *Literary.* **1** to pelt with stones. **2** to kill by stoning. [C17: from Latin *lapidāre,* from *lapis* stone] ▸ **,lapi'dation** *n*

lapidicolous (,læpɪ'dɪkələs) *adj Zoology.* living under stones.

lapidify (lə'pɪdɪ,faɪ) *vb* **-fies, -fying, -fied.** to change into stone. [C17: from French *lapidifier,* from Medieval Latin *lapidificāre,* ultimately from Latin *lapis* stone] ▸ **la,pidifi'cation** *n*

lapillus (lə'pɪləs) *n, pl* **-li** (-laɪ). a small piece of lava thrown from a volcano. [C18: Latin: little stone]

lapis lazuli *or* **lazuli** ('læpɪs) *n* **1** a brilliant blue variety of the mineral lazurite, used as a gemstone. **2** the deep blue colour of lapis lazuli. ◆ Also called: **lapis.** [C14: from Latin *lapis* stone + Medieval Latin *lazulī,* from *lazulum,* from Arabic *lāzaward,* from Persian *lāzhuward,* of obscure origin]

Lapith ('læpɪθ) *n, pl* **Lapithae** ('læpɪ,θiː) *or* **Lapiths.** *Greek myth.* a member of a people in Thessaly who at the wedding of their king, Pirithoüs, fought the drunken centaurs.

lap joint *n* a joint made by placing one member over another and fastening them together. Also called: **lapped joint.** ▸ **'lap-,jointed** *adj*

Laplace (*French* laplas) *n* **Pierre Simon** (pjɛr simɔ̃), Marquis de Laplace. 1749–1827, French mathematician, physicist, and astronomer. He formulated the nebular hypothesis (1796). He also developed the theory of probability.

Laplace operator *n Maths.* the operator $\partial^2/\partial x^2 + \partial^2/\partial y^2 + \partial^2/\partial z^2$, used in differential analysis. Symbol: ∇^2 Also called: **Laplacian** (lə'pleɪʃɪən).

Lapland ('læp,lænd) *n* an extensive region of N Europe, mainly within the Arctic Circle: consists of the N parts of Norway, Sweden, Finland, and the Kola Peninsula of the extreme NW of Russia. Also called (informal): **Land of the Midnight Sun.** ▸ **'Lap,lander** *n*

La Plata (*Spanish* la 'plata) *n* **1** a port in E Argentina, near the Río de la Plata estuary: founded in 1882 and modelled on Washington DC; university (1897). Pop.: 642 979 (1991). **2** See (Río de la) **Plata.**

lap of honour *n* a ceremonial circuit of a racing track, etc., by the winner of a race.

Lapp (læp) *n* **1** a member of a nomadic people living chiefly in N Scandinavia and the Kola Peninsula of Russia. **2** the language of this people, belonging to the Finno-Ugric family. ◆ *adj* **3** of or relating to this people or their language. ▸ **'Lappish** *adj, n*

lappet ('læpɪt) *n* **1** a small hanging flap or piece of lace, etc., such as one dangling from a headdress. **2** *Zoology.* a lobelike hanging structure, such as the wattle on a bird's head. [C16: from LAP^1 + -ET] ▸ **'lappeted** *adj*

lappet moth *n* a large purple-brown hairy eggar moth, *Gastropacha quercifolia,* whose grey furry caterpillars have lappets on each flank.

Lapsang Souchong ('læpsæŋ suː'ʃɒŋ) *n* a large-leafed variety of China tea with a slightly smoky flavour.

lapse (læps) *n* **1** a drop in standard of an isolated or temporary nature: *a lapse of justice.* **2** a break in occurrence, usage, etc.: *a lapse of five weeks between letters.* **3** a gradual decline or a drop to a lower degree, condition, or state: *a lapse from high office.* **4** a moral fall. **5** *Law.* the termination of some right, interest, or privilege, as by neglecting to exercise it or through failure of some contingency. **6** *Insurance.* the termination of coverage following a failure to pay the premiums. ◆ *vb* (*intr*) **7** to drop in standard or fail to maintain a norm. **8** to decline gradually or fall in status, condition, etc. **9** to be discontinued, esp. through negligence or other failure. **10** (usually foll. by *into*) to drift or slide (into a condition): *to lapse into sleep.* **11** (often foll. by *from*) to turn away (from beliefs or norms). **12** *Law.* (of a devise or bequest) to become void, as on the beneficiary's predeceasing the testator. **13** (of time) to slip away. [C15: from Latin *lāpsus* error, from *lābī* to glide] ▸ **'lapsable** *or* **'lapsible** *adj* ▸ **lapsed** *adj* ▸ **'lapser** *n*

lapse rate *n* the rate of change of any meteorological factor with altitude, esp. atmospheric temperature, which usually decreases at a rate of 0.6°C per 100 metres (**environmental lapse rate**). Unsaturated air loses about 1°C per 100 m (**dry adiabatic lapse rate**), whereas saturated air loses an average 0.5°C per 100 m (**saturated adiabatic lapse rate**).

lapstrake ('læp,streɪk) *or* **lapstreak** ('læp,striːk) *Nautical.* ◆ *adj* **1** another term for **clinker-built.** ◆ *n* **2** a clinker-built boat. [C18: from LAP[2] + STRAKE]

lapsus ('læpsəs) *n, pl* **-sus.** *Formal.* a lapse or error. [from Latin: LAPSE]

lapsus linguae ('lɪŋgwiː) *n* a slip of the tongue. [Latin]

Laptev Sea ('læptɪf) *n* a shallow arm of the Arctic Ocean, along the N coast of Russia between the Taimyr Peninsula and the New Siberian Islands. Former name: **Nordenskjöld Sea.**

laptop ('læp,tɒp) *or* **laptop computer** *n* a personal computer that is small and light enough to be operated on the user's lap. Compare **palmtop computer.**

lap up *vb (tr, adv)* **1** to eat or drink. **2** to relish or delight in: *he laps up old horror films.* **3** to believe or accept eagerly and uncritically: *he laps up tall stories.*

lapwing ('læp,wɪŋ) *n* any of several plovers of the genus *Vanellus,* esp. *V. vanellus,* typically having a crested head, wattles, and spurs. Also called: **green plover, pewit, peewit.** [C17: altered form of Old English *hlēapewince* plover, from *hlēapan* to LEAP + *wincian* to jerk, WINK[1]]

lar (lɑː) *n* the singular of **lares.** See **lares and penates.** [Latin]

LAR *international car registration for* Libya.

Lara ('lɑːrə) *n* **Brian Charles.** born 1970, Trinidadian cricketer: captain of Trinidad from 1990, he plays for Warwickshire (since 1994); world record score of 501 runs in one innings.

larboard ('lɑːbəd) *n, adj Nautical.* a former word for **port**[2]. [C14 *laddeborde* (changed to *larboard* by association with *starboard*), from *laden* to load + *borde* BOARD]

larceny ('lɑːsɪnɪ) *n, pl* **-nies.** *Law.* (formerly) a technical word for **theft.** [C15: from Old French *larcin,* from Latin *lātrōcinium* robbery, from *latrō* robber] ▸ **'larcenist** *or* **'larcener** *n* ▸ **'larcenous** *adj* ▸ **'larcenously** *adv*

larch (lɑːtʃ) *n* **1** any coniferous tree of the genus *Larix,* having deciduous needle-like leaves and egg-shaped cones: family *Pinaceae.* **2** the wood of any of these trees. [C16: from German *Lärche,* ultimately from Latin *larix*]

lard (lɑːd) *n* **1** the rendered fat from a pig, esp. from the abdomen, used in cooking. **2** *Informal.* excess fat on a person's body. ◆ *vb (tr)* **3** to prepare (lean meat, poultry, etc.) by inserting small strips of bacon or fat before cooking. **4** to cover or smear (foods) with lard. **5** to add extra material to (speech or writing); embellish. [C15: via Old French from Latin *lāridum* bacon fat] ▸ **'lard,like** *adj* ▸ **'lardy** *adj*

larder ('lɑːdə) *n* a room or cupboard, used as a store for food. [C14: from Old French *lardier,* from LARD]

larder beetle *n* See **dermestid.**

Lardner ('lɑːdnə) *n* **Ring(old Wilmer).** 1885–1933, U.S. short-story writer and journalist, whose best-known works are collected in *How to Write Short Stories* (1924) and *The Love Nest* (1926).

lardon ('lɑːdᵊn) *or* **lardoon** (lɑː'duːn) *n* a strip of fat used in larding meat. [C15: from Old French, from LARD]

lard pig *n* a large type of pig used principally for lard.

lardy cake ('lɑːdɪ) *n Brit.* a rich sweet cake made of bread dough, lard, sugar, and dried fruit.

Laredo (lə'reɪdəʊ) *n* a city in the U.S., in Texas, on the Mexican border: founded by the Spanish in 1755 on the Rio Grande. Pop.: 164 899 (1996 est.).

lares and penates ('lɛəriːz, 'lɑː-) *pl n* **1** *Roman myth.* **1a** household gods. **1b** statues of these gods kept in the home. **2** the valued possessions of a household.

large (lɑːdʒ) *adj* **1** having a relatively great size, quantity, extent, etc.; big. **2** of wide or broad scope, capacity, or range; comprehensive: *a large effect.* **3** having or showing great breadth of understanding: *a large heart.* **4** *Nautical.* (of the wind) blowing from a favourable direction. **5** *Rare.* overblown; pretentious. **6** generous. **7** *Obsolete.* (of manners and speech) gross; rude. ◆ *n* **8 at large. 8a** (esp. of a dangerous criminal or wild animal) free; not confined. **8b** roaming freely, as in a foreign country. **8c** as a whole; in general. **8d** in full detail; exhaustively. **8e ambassador-at-large.** See **ambassador** (sense 4). **9 in (the) large.** as a totality or on a broad scale. ◆ *adv* **10** *Nautical.* with the wind blowing from a favourable direction. **11 by and large. 11a** *(sentence modifier)* generally; as a rule: *by and large, the man is the breadwinner.* **11b** *Nautical.* towards and away from the wind. **12 loom large.** to be very prominent or important. [C12 (originally: generous): via Old French from Latin *largus* ample, abundant] ▸ **'largeness** *n*

Large Black *n* a heavy black breed of pig with long lop ears: used for crossbreeding.

large calorie *n* another name for **Calorie.**

large-format *adj* of or relating to a camera with an image area of 5 inches by 4 inches or more.

large-handed *adj* generous; profuse.

large-hearted *adj* kind; sympathetic. Also: **large-souled.**

large intestine *n* the part of the alimentary canal consisting of the caecum, colon, and rectum. It extracts moisture from food residues, which are later excreted as faeces. Compare **small intestine.**

largely ('lɑːdʒlɪ) *adv* **1** principally; to a great extent. **2** on a large scale or in a large manner.

large-minded *adj* generous or liberal in attitudes. ▸ **,large-'mindedly** *adv* ▸ **,large-'mindedness** *n*

largemouth bass ('lɑːdʒ,maʊθ 'bæs) *n* a common North American freshwater black bass, *Micropterus salmoides:* a popular game fish.

largen ('lɑːdʒən) *vb (tr)* another word for **enlarge.**

large-scale *adj* **1** wide-ranging or extensive. **2** (of maps and models) constructed or drawn to a big scale.

large-scale integration *n Electronics.* the process of integrating several thousand circuits on a single silicon chip. Abbrev.: **LSI.**

largesse *or* **largess** (lɑː'dʒɛs) *n* **1** the generous bestowal of gifts, favours, or money. **2** the things so bestowed. **3** generosity of spirit or attitude. [C13: from Old French, from LARGE]

large white *n* **1** Also called: **cabbage white.** a large white butterfly, *Pieris brassicae,* with scanty black markings, the larvae of which feed on brassica leaves. **2** *(often caps.)* a white large-bodied breed of pig commonly kept for pork, bacon, and for fattening.

larghetto (lɑː'gɛtəʊ) *Music.* ◆ *adj, adv* **1** to be performed moderately slowly. ◆ *n, pl* **-tos. 2** a piece or passage to be performed in this way. [Italian: diminutive of LARGO]

largish ('lɑːdʒɪʃ) *adj* fairly large.

largo ('lɑːgəʊ) *Music.* ◆ *adj, adv* **1** to be performed slowly and broadly. ◆ *n, pl* **-gos. 2** a piece or passage to be performed in this way. [C17: from Italian, from Latin *largus* LARGE]

lari *or* **laari** (lɑːrɪ) *n* the standard monetary unit of Georgia, divided into 100 tetri.

Lariam ('lærɪæm) *n Trademark.* a preparation of the drug mefloquine, used in the treatment and prevention of malaria.

lariat ('lærɪət) *n U.S. and Canadian.* **1** another word for **lasso. 2** a rope for tethering animals. [C19: from Spanish *la reata* the LASSO]

larine ('læraɪn, -rɪn) *adj* **1** of, relating to, or resembling a gull. **2** of, relating to, or belonging to the suborder *Lari,* which contains the gulls, terns, skuas, and skimmers. [C20: via New Latin from *Larus* genus name, from Greek *laros* a kind of gull]

Larisa *or* **Larissa** (lə'rɪsə; *Greek* 'larisa) *n* a city in E Greece, in E Thessaly: fortified by Justinian; annexed to Greece in 1881. Pop.: 113 426 (1991).

lark[1] (lɑːk) *n* **1** any brown songbird of the predominantly Old World family *Alaudidae,* esp. the skylark: noted for their singing. **2** short for **titlark** or **meadowlark. 3** *(often cap.)* any of various slender but powerful fancy pigeons, such as the **Coburg Lark. 4 up with the lark.** up early in the morning. [Old English *lāwerce, lǣwerce,* of Germanic origin; related to German *Lerche,* Icelandic *lǣvirki*]

lark[2] (lɑːk) *Informal.* ◆ *n* **1** a carefree adventure or frolic. **2** a harmless piece of mischief. **3 what a lark!** how amusing! ◆ *vb (intr)* **4** (often foll. by *about*) to have a good time by frolicking. **5** to play a prank. [C19: originally slang, perhaps related to LAIK] ▸ **'larker** *n* ▸ **'larkish** *adj* ▸ **'larkishness** *n* ▸ **'larky** *adj*

Larkin ('lɑːkɪn) *n* **Philip.** 1922–85, English poet: his verse collections include *The Less Deceived* (1955) and *The Whitsun Weddings* (1964).

larkspur ('lɑːk,spɜː) *n* any of various ranunculaceous plants of the genus *Delphinium,* with spikes of blue, pink, or white irregular spurred flowers. [C16: LARK[1] + SPUR]

Larmor precession ('lɑːmɔː) *n* precession of the orbit of an electron in an atom that is subjected to a magnetic field. [C20: named after Sir Joseph *Larmor* (1857–1942), British physicist]

larn (lɑːn) *vb Not standard.* **1** *Facetious.* to learn. **2** *(tr)* to teach (someone) a lesson: *that'll larn you!* [C18: from a dialect form of LEARN]

larnax ('lɑːnæks) *n Archaeol.* a coffin made of terracotta. [from Greek; perhaps related to Late Greek *narnax* chest]

Larne (lɒːn) *n* a district of NE Northern Ireland, in Co. Antrim. Pop.: 29 419 (1991). Area: 336 sq. km (130 sq. miles).

larney ('lɑːnɪ) *S. African.* ◆ *n* **1** a white person. **2** a rich person. ◆ *adj* **3** (of clothes) smart. [C20: probably from an Indian language]

La Rochefoucauld (*French* la rɔʃfuko) *n* **François** (frɑ̃swa), Duc de La Rochefoucauld. 1613–80, French writer. His best-known work is *Réflexions ou sentences et maximes morales* (1665), a collection of epigrammatic and cynical observations on human nature.

La Rochelle (*French* la rɔʃɛl) *n* a port in W France, on the Bay of Biscay: a Huguenot stronghold until its submission through famine to Richelieu's forces after a long siege (1627–28). Pop.: 71 094 (1990).

Larousse (*French* larus) *n* **Pierre Athanase** (pjer atanɑz). 1817–75, French grammarian, lexicographer, and encyclopedist. He edited and helped to compile the *Grand Dictionnaire universel du XIX siècle* (1866–76).

larrigan ('lærɪgən) *n* a knee-high oiled leather moccasin boot worn by trappers, etc. [C19: of unknown origin]

larrikin ('lærɪkɪn) *n Austral. and N.Z. slang.* **a** a mischievous person. **b** *(as modifier): a larrikin bloke.* [C19: from English dialect: a mischievous youth]

larrup ('lærəp) *vb (tr) Dialect.* to beat or flog. [C19: of unknown origin] ▸ **'larruper** *n*

Larry ('lærɪ) *n Brit., Austral., and N.Z. informal.* **(as) happy as Larry.** extremely happy. [of uncertain origin]

larum ('lærəm) *n* an archaic word for **alarm.**

larva ('lɑːvə) *n, pl* **-vae** (-viː). an immature free-living form of many animals that develops into a different adult form by metamorphosis. [C18: (C17 in the original Latin sense: ghost): New Latin] ▸ **'larval** *adj*

larvicide ('lɑːvɪ,saɪd) *n* a chemical used for killing larvae. ▸ **,larvi'cidal** *adj*

Larwood ('lɑːwʊd) *n* **Harold.** 1904–95, English cricketer. An outstanding fast bowler, he played 21 times for England between 1926 and 1932.

laryngeal (,lærɪn'dʒiːəl, lə'rɪndʒɪəl) *or* **laryngal** (lə'rɪŋgᵊl) *adj* **1** of or relating to the larynx. **2** *Phonetics.* articulated at the larynx; glottal. [C18: from New Latin *laryngeus* of the LARYNX] ▸ **laryn'geally** *adv*

laryngitis (,lærɪn'dʒaɪtɪs) *n* inflammation of the larynx. ▸ **laryngitic** (,lærɪn'dʒɪtɪk) *adj*

laryngo- *or before a vowel* **laryng-** *combining form.* indicating the larynx: *laryngoscope.*

laryngology (ˌlærɪŋˈgɒlədʒɪ) *n* the branch of medicine concerned with the larynx and its diseases. ▸ **laryngological** (ləˌrɪŋgəˈlɒdʒɪkəl) *or* **laˌryngoˈlogic** *adj* ▸ **laˌryngoˈlogically** *adv* ▸ **ˌlarynˈgologist** *n*

laryngoscope (ləˈrɪŋgəˌskəʊp) *n* a medical instrument for examining the larynx. ▸ **laryngoscopic** (ləˌrɪŋgəˈskɒpɪk) *adj* ▸ **laˌryngoˈscopically** *adv* ▸ **laryngoscopist** (ˌlærɪŋˈgɒskəpɪst) *n* ▸ **ˌlarynˈgoscopy** *n*

laryngotomy (ˌlærɪŋˈgɒtəmɪ) *n, pl* **-mies.** surgical incision into the larynx.

larynx (ˈlærɪŋks) *n, pl* **larynges** (ləˈrɪndʒiːz) *or* **larynxes.** a cartilaginous and muscular hollow organ forming part of the air passage to the lungs: in higher vertebrates it contains the vocal cords. [C16: from New Latin *larynx,* from Greek *larunx*]

lasagne *or* **lasagna** (ləˈzænjə, -ˈsæn-) *n* **1** a form of pasta consisting of wide flat sheets. **2** any of several dishes made from layers of lasagne and meat, cheese, etc. [from Italian *lasagna,* from Latin *lasanum* cooking pot]

La Salle[1] (lə ˈsæl) *n* a city in SE Canada, in Quebec: a S suburb of Montreal. Pop.: 73 804 (1991).

La Salle[2] (*French* la sal) *n* Sieur **Robert Cavelier de** (rɔbɛr kavəlje də). 1643–87, French explorer and fur trader in North America; founder of Louisiana (1682).

La Scala (la ˈskaːla) *n* the chief opera house in Italy, in Milan (opened 1776).

lascar (ˈlæskə) *n* a sailor from the East Indies. [C17: from Urdu *lashkar* soldier, from Persian: the army]

Lascaux (*French* lasko) *n* site of a cave in SW France, in the Dordogne: contains Palaeolithic wall drawings and paintings.

lascivious (ləˈsɪvɪəs) *adj* **1** lustful; lecherous. **2** exciting sexual desire. [C15: from Late Latin *lascīviōsus,* from Latin *lascīvia* wantonness, from *lascīvus*] ▸ **lasˈciviously** *adv* ▸ **lasˈciviousness** *n*

Lasdun (ˈlæzdən) *n* Sir **Denys.** born 1914, British architect. He is best known for the University of East Anglia (1968) and the National Theatre in London (1976).

lase (leɪz) *vb* (*intr*) (of a substance, such as carbon dioxide or ruby) to be capable of acting as a laser.

laser (ˈleɪzə) *n* **1** a source of high-intensity optical, infrared, or ultraviolet radiation produced as a result of stimulated emission maintained within a solid, liquid, or gaseous medium. The photons involved in the emission process all have the same energy and phase so that the laser beam is monochromatic and coherent, allowing it to be brought to a fine focus. **2** any similar source producing a beam of any electromagnetic radiation, such as infrared or microwave radiation. See also **maser.** [C20: from *l*ight *a*mplification by *s*timulated *e*mission of *r*adiation]

laser card *n Computing.* another name for **smart card.**

laser printer *n* a quiet high-quality computer printer that uses a laser beam shining on a photoconductive drum to produce characters, which are then transferred to paper.

laser ring gyro *n Aeronautics.* a system of aerial navigation in which rotation is sensed by the measuring of the frequency shift of laser light in a closed circuit in a horizontal plane.

laser treatment *n* any of various medical and surgical techniques using lasers, such as the removal of small growths.

lash[1] (læʃ) *n* **1** a sharp cutting blow from a whip or other flexible object: *twenty lashes was his punishment.* **2** the flexible end or ends of a whip. **3** a cutting or hurtful blow to the feelings, as one caused by ridicule or scolding. **4** a forceful beating or impact, as of wind, rain, or waves against something. **5 have a lash (at).** *Austral. and N.Z. informal.* to make an attempt at or take part in (something). **6** See **eyelash.** ◆ *vb* (*tr*) **7** to hit (a person or thing) sharply with a whip, rope, etc., esp. as a punishment. **8** (of rain, waves, etc.) to beat forcefully against. **9** to attack with words, ridicule, etc. **10** to flick or wave sharply to and fro: *the restless panther lashed his tail.* **11** to urge or drive with or as if with a whip: *to lash the audience into a violent mood.* ◆ See also **lash out.** [C14: perhaps imitative] ▸ **ˈlasher** *n* ▸ **ˈlashingly** *adv*

lash[2] (læʃ) *vb* (*tr*) to bind or secure with rope, string, etc. [C15: from Old French *lachier,* ultimately from Latin *laqueāre* to ensnare, from *laqueus* noose] ▸ **ˈlasher** *n*

-lashed *adj* having eyelashes as specified: *long-lashed.*

lashing[1] (ˈlæʃɪŋ) *n* **1** a whipping; flogging. **2** a scolding. **3** (*pl;* usually foll. by *of*) *Brit. informal.* large amounts; lots.

lashing[2] (ˈlæʃɪŋ) *n* rope, cord, etc., used for binding or securing.

Lashio (ˈlæʃɪˌəʊ) *n* a town in NE central Myanmar: starting point of the Burma Road to Chongqing, China.

Lashkar (ˈlʌʃkə) *n* a former city in N India, in Madhya Pradesh: capital of the former states of Gwalior and Madhya Bharat; now part of the city of Gwalior.

lash out *vb* (*intr, adv*) **1** to burst into or resort to verbal or physical attack. **2** *Brit. informal.* to be extravagant, as in spending.

lash-up (ˈlæʃˌʌp) *n* **a** Also called: **hook-up.** a temporary connection of equipment for experimental or emergency use. **b** (*as modifier*): *lash-up equipment.*

Lasker (ˈlæskə) *n* **Emanuel.** 1868–1941, German chess player: world champion (1894–1921).

lasket (ˈlæskɪt) *n* a loop at the foot of a sail onto which an extra sail may be fastened. [C18: perhaps an alteration of French *lacet* LATCHET, through the influence of GASKET]

Laski (ˈlæskɪ) *n* **Harold (Joseph).** 1893–1950, English political scientist and socialist leader.

Las Palmas (*Spanish* las ˈpalmas) *n* a port in the central Canary Islands, on NE Grand Canary: a major fuelling port on the main shipping route between Europe and South America. Pop.: 372 270 (1986).

La Spezia (*Italian* la ˈspettsia) *n* a port in NW Italy, in Liguria, on the **Gulf of Spezia:** the chief naval base in Italy. Pop.: 100 458 (1992).

lass (læs) *n* a girl or young woman. [C13: origin uncertain]

Lassa (ˈlɑːsə) *n* a variant spelling of **Lhasa.**

Lassa fever *n* a serious viral disease of Central West Africa, characterized by high fever and muscular pains. [named after *Lassa,* the village in Nigeria where it was first identified]

Lassalle (*German* laˈsal) *n* **Ferdinand** (ˈferdinant). 1825–64, German socialist and writer: a founder of the first German workers' political party (1863), which later became the Social Democratic Party.

Lassen Peak (ˈlæsən) *n* a volcano in S California, in the S Cascade Range. An area of 416 sq. km (161 sq. miles) was established as **Lassen Volcanic National Park** in 1916. Height: 3187 m (10 457 ft.).

lassi (ˈlæsɪ) *n* a cold drink made with yoghurt or buttermilk and flavoured with sugar, salt, or a mild spice.

lassie (ˈlæsɪ) *n Informal.* a little lass; girl.

lassitude (ˈlæsɪˌtjuːd) *n* physical or mental weariness. [C16: from Latin *lassitūdō,* from *lassus* tired]

lasso (læˈsuː, ˈlæsəʊ) *n, pl* **-sos** *or* **-soes. 1** a long rope or thong with a running noose at one end, used (esp. in America) for roping horses, cattle, etc.; lariat. ◆ *vb* **-sos** *or* **-soes; -soing, -soed. 2** (*tr*) to catch with or as if with a lasso. [C19: from Spanish *lazo,* ultimately from Latin *laqueus* noose] ▸ **lasˈsoer** *n*

Lassus (ˈlæsəs) *n* **Roland de.** Italian name *Orlando di Lasso.* ?1532–94, Flemish composer, noted for his mastery in both sacred and secular music.

last[1] (lɑːst) *adj* (*often prenominal*) **1** being, happening, or coming at the end or after all others: *the last horse in the race.* **2** being or occurring just before the present; most recent: *last Thursday.* **3 last but not least.** coming last in order but nevertheless important. **4 last but one.** next to last. **5** only remaining: *one's last cigarette.* **6** most extreme; utmost. **7** least suitable, appropriate, or likely: *he was the last person I would have chosen.* **8** (esp. relating to the end of a person's life or of the world) **8a** final or ultimate: *last rites.* **8b** (*cap.*): *the Last Judgment.* **9** (*postpositive*) *Liverpool dialect.* inferior, unpleasant, or contemptible: *this ale is last.* ◆ *adv* **10** after all others; at or in the end: *he came last.* **11a** most recently: *he was last seen in the mountains.* **11b** (*in combination*): *last-mentioned.* **12** (*sentence modifier*) as the last or latest item. ◆ *n* **13 the last. 13a** a person or thing that is last. **13b** the final moment; end. **14** one's last moments before death. **15** the last thing a person can do (esp. in the phrase **breathe one's last**). **16** the final appearance, mention, or occurrence: *we've seen the last of him.* **17 at last.** in the end; finally. **18 at long last.** finally, after difficulty, delay, or irritation. ◆ See also **last out.** [variant of Old English *latest, lætest,* superlative of LATE]

USAGE Since *last* can mean either *after all others* or *most recent,* it is better to avoid using this word where ambiguity might arise as in *her last novel. Final* or *latest* should be used in such contexts to avoid ambiguity.

last[2] (lɑːst) *vb* **1** (when *intr,* often foll. by *for*) to remain in being (for a length of time); continue: *his hatred lasted for several years.* **2** to be sufficient for the needs of (a person) for (a length of time): *it will last us until Friday.* **3** (when *intr,* often foll. by *for*) to remain fresh, uninjured, or unaltered (for a certain time or duration): *he lasted for three hours underground.* [Old English *lǣstan;* related to Gothic *laistjan* to follow] ▸ **ˈlaster** *n*

last[3] (lɑːst) *n* **1** the wooden or metal form on which a shoe or boot is fashioned or repaired. ◆ *vb* **2** (*tr*) to fit (a shoe or boot) on a last. [Old English *lǣste,* from *lāst* footprint; related to Old Norse *leistr* foot, Gothic *laists*] ▸ **ˈlaster** *n*

last[4] (lɑːst) *n* a unit of weight or capacity having various values in different places and for different commodities. Commonly used values are 2 tons, 2000 pounds, 80 bushels, or 640 gallons. [Old English *hlæst* load; related to *hladan* to LADE[1]]

last-cyclic *adj Transformational grammar.* denoting rules that apply only to main clauses. Compare **cyclic** (sense 6), **post-cyclic.**

last-ditch *n* (*modifier*) made or done as a last desperate attempt or effort in the face of opposition.

last-gasp *n* (*modifier*) done in desperation at the last minute: *a last-gasp attempt to save the talks.*

lasting (ˈlɑːstɪŋ) *adj* **1** permanent or enduring. ◆ *n* **2** a strong durable closely woven fabric used for shoe uppers, etc. ▸ **ˈlastingly** *adv* ▸ **ˈlastingness** *n*

Last Judgment *n* **the.** the occasion, after the resurrection of the dead at the end of the world, when, according to biblical tradition, God will decree the final destinies of all men according to the good and evil in their earthly lives. Also called: **the Last Day, Doomsday, Judgment Day.**

lastly (ˈlɑːstlɪ) *adv* **1** at the end or at the last point. ◆ *sentence connector.* **2** in the end; finally: *lastly, he put on his jacket.*

last-minute *n* (*modifier*) given or done at the latest possible time: *last-minute preparations.*

last name *n* another term for **surname** (sense 1).

last out *vb* (*intr, adv*) **1** to be sufficient for one's needs: *how long will our supplies last out?* **2** to endure or survive: *some old people don't last out the winter.*

last post *n* (in the British military services) **1** a bugle call that orders men to retire for sleep. **2** a similar call sounded at military funerals.

last quarter *n* one of the four principal phases of the moon, occurring between full moon and new moon, when half the lighted surface is visible. Compare **first quarter.**

last rites *pl n Christianity.* religious rites prescribed for those close to death.

last straw *n* **the.** the final irritation or problem that stretches one's endurance or patience beyond the limit. [from the proverb, "It is the last straw that breaks the camel's back"]

Last Supper *n* **the.** the meal eaten by Christ with his disciples on the night before his Crucifixion, during which he is believed to have instituted the Eucharist.

last thing *adv* as the final action, esp. before retiring to bed at night.

Las Vegas (læs 'veɪgəs) *n* a city in SE Nevada: famous for luxury hotels and casinos. Pop.: 376 906 (1996 est.).

lat. *abbrev. for* latitude.

Lat. *abbrev. for* Latin.

latah ('lɑːtə) *n* a psychological condition, observed esp. in Malaysian cultures, in which an individual, after experiencing a shock, becomes anxious and suggestible, often imitating the actions of another person. [C19: from Malay]

Latakia *or* **Lattakia** (ˌlætə'kiːə) *n* the chief port of Syria, in the northwest: tobacco industry. Pop.: 306 535 (1994 est.). Latin name: **Laodicea ad Mare.**

latch (lætʃ) *n* **1** a fastening for a gate or door that consists of a bar that may be slid or lowered into a groove, hole, etc. **2** a spring-loaded door lock that can be opened by a key from outside. **3** Also called: **latch circuit.** *Electronics.* a logic circuit that transfers the input states to the output states when signalled, the output thereafter remaining insensitive to changes in input status until signalled again. ◆ *vb* **4** to fasten, fit, or be fitted with or as if with a latch. [Old English *læccan* to seize, of Germanic origin; related to Greek *lazesthai*]

latchet ('lætʃɪt) *n Archaic.* a shoe fastening, such as a thong or lace. [C14: from Old French *lachet,* from *las* LACE]

latchkey ('lætʃˌkiː) *n* **1** a key for an outside door or gate, esp. one that lifts a latch. **2a** a supposed freedom from restrictions. **2b** (*as modifier*): *a latchkey existence.*

latchkey child *n* a child who has to let himself in at home on returning from school, as his parents are out at work.

latch on *vb* (*intr, adv;* often foll. by *to*) *Informal.* **1** to attach oneself (to): *to latch on to a new acquaintance.* **2** to understand: *he suddenly latched on to what they were up to.* **3** *U.S. and Canadian.* to obtain; get.

latchstring ('lætʃˌstrɪŋ) *n* a length of string fastened to a latch and passed through a hole in the door so that it can be opened from the other side.

late (leɪt) *adj* **1** occurring or arriving after the correct or expected time: *the train was late.* **2** (*prenominal*) occurring, scheduled for, or being at a relatively advanced time: *a late marriage.* **3** (*prenominal*) towards or near the end: *the late evening.* **4** at an advanced time in the evening or at night: *it was late.* **5** (*prenominal*) occurring or being just previous to the present time: *his late remarks on industry.* **6** (*prenominal*) having died, esp. recently: *my late grandfather.* **7** (*prenominal*) just preceding the present or existing person or thing; former: *the late manager of this firm.* **8 of late.** recently; lately. ◆ *adv* **9** after the correct or expected time: *he arrived late.* **10** at a relatively advanced age: *she married late.* **11** recently; lately: *as late as yesterday he was selling books.* **12 late hours.** rising and going to bed later than is usual. **13 late in the day. 13a** at a late or advanced stage. **13b** too late. [Old English *læt;* related to Old Norse *latr,* Gothic *lats*] ► **'lateness** *n*

USAGE Since *late* can mean *deceased,* many people think it is better to avoid using this word to refer to the person who held a post or position before its present holder: *the previous* (not *the late*) *editor of* The Times.

latecomer ('leɪtˌkʌmə) *n* a person or thing that comes late.

lated ('leɪtɪd) *adj* an archaic word for **belated.**

lateen (lə'tiːn) *adj Nautical.* denoting a rig with a triangular sail (**lateen sail**) bent to a yard hoisted to the head of a low mast, used esp. in the Mediterranean. [C18: from French *voile latine* Latin sail]

lateenrigged (lə'tiːnˌrɪgd) *adj Nautical.* rigged with a lateen sail.

Late Greek *n* the Greek language from about the 3rd to the 8th centuries A.D. Compare **Medieval Greek, Koine.**

Late Latin *n* the form of written Latin used from the 3rd to the 7th centuries A.D. See also **Biblical Latin, Medieval Latin.**

lately ('leɪtlɪ) *adv* in recent times; of late.

latency period *n Psychoanal.* a period according to Freud, from the age of about five to puberty, when sexual interest is diminished.

La Tène (læ 'tɛn) *adj* of or relating to a Celtic culture in Europe from about the 5th to the 1st centuries B.C., characterized by a distinctive type of curvilinear decoration. See also **Hallstatt.** [C20: from *La Tène,* a part of Lake Neuchâtel, Switzerland, where remains of this culture were first discovered]

latent ('leɪtᵊnt) *adj* **1** potential but not obvious or explicit. **2** (of buds, spores, etc.) dormant. **3** *Pathol.* (esp. of an infectious disease) not yet revealed or manifest. **4** (of a virus) inactive in the host cell, its nucleic acid being integrated into, and replicated with, the host cell's DNA. **5** *Psychoanal.* relating to that part of a dream expressive of repressed desires: *latent content.* Compare **manifest** (sense 2). [C17: from Latin *latēnt-,* from *latens* present participle of *latēre* to lie hidden] ► **'latency** *n* ► **'latently** *adv*

latent heat *n* (*no longer in technical usage*) the heat evolved or absorbed by unit mass (**specific latent heat**) or unit amount of substance (**molar latent heat**) when it changes phase without change of temperature.

latent image *n Photog.* the invisible image produced by the action of light, etc., on silver halide crystals suspended in the emulsion of a photographic material. It becomes visible after development.

latent learning *n Psychol.* learning mediated neither by reward nor by the expectation of reward.

latent period *n* **1** the incubation period of an infectious disease, before symptoms appear. **2** another name for **latent time.**

latent time *n Psychol.* the time from the onset of a stimulus to that of the response. Also called: **latency, reaction time.**

later ('leɪtə) *adj, adv* **1** the comparative of **late.** ◆ *adv* **2** afterwards; subsequently. **3 see you later.** an expression of farewell. **4 sooner or later.** eventually; inevitably.

lateral ('lætərəl) *adj* **1** of or relating to the side or sides: *a lateral blow.* **2** *Phonetics.* (of a speech sound like *l*) pronounced with the tip of the tongue touching the centre of the alveolar ridge, leaving space on one or both sides for the passage of the airstream. ◆ *n* **3** a lateral object, part, passage, or movement. **4** *Phonetics.* a lateral speech sound. [C17: from Latin *laterālis,* from *latus* side] ► **'laterally** *adv*

laterality (ˌlætə'rælɪtɪ) *n Psychol.* the difference in the mental functions controlled by the left and right cerebral hemispheres of the brain.

lateral line system *n* a system of sensory organs in fishes and aquatic amphibians consisting of a series of cells on the head and along the sides of the body that detect pressure changes and vibrations.

lateral thinking *n* a way of solving problems by rejecting traditional methods and employing unorthodox and apparently illogical means.

Lateran ('lætərən) *n* **the. 1** Also called: **Lateran palace.** a palace in Rome, formerly the official residence of the popes. **2** any of five ecumenical councils held in this palace between 1123 and 1512. **3** the basilica of Saint John Lateran, the cathedral church of Rome. [from Latin: the district is named after the ancient Roman family *Plautii Laterani*]

laterigrade ('lætərɪˌgreɪd) *adj Zoology.* (of some crabs) having a gait characterized by sideways movement.

laterite ('lætəˌraɪt) *n* any of a group of deposits consisting of residual insoluble deposits of ferric and aluminium oxides: formed by weathering of rocks in tropical regions. [C19: from Latin *later* brick, tile] ► **lateritic** (ˌlætə'rɪtɪk) *adj*

lateroversion (ˌlætərəʊ'vɜːʃən) *n* abnormal lateral displacement of a bodily organ or part, esp. of the uterus. [C20: from LATERAL + *-version,* from Latin *versiō* a turning]

latest ('leɪtɪst) *adj, adv* **1** the superlative of **late.** ◆ *adj* **2** most recent, modern, or new: *the latest fashions.* ◆ *n* **3 at the latest.** no later than the time specified. **4 the latest.** *Informal.* the most recent fashion or development.

latex ('leɪtɛks) *n, pl* **latexes** *or* **latices** ('lætɪˌsiːz). **1** a whitish milky fluid containing protein, starch, alkaloids, etc., that is produced by many plants. Latex from the rubber tree is used in the manufacture of rubber. **2** a suspension of synthetic rubber or plastic in water, used in the manufacture of synthetic rubber products, etc. [C19: New Latin, from Latin: liquid, fluid]

lath (lɑːθ) *n, pl* **laths** (lɑːðz, lɑːθs). **1** one of several thin narrow strips of wood used to provide a supporting framework for plaster, tiles, etc. **2** expanded sheet metal, wire mesh, etc., used to provide backing for plaster or rendering. **3** any thin strip of wood. ◆ *vb* **4** (*tr*) to attach laths to (a ceiling, roof, floor, etc.). [Old English *lætt;* related to Dutch *lat,* Old High German *latta*] ► **'lathˌlike** *adj*

lathe[1] (leɪð) *n* **1** a machine for shaping, boring, facing, or cutting a screw thread in metal, wood, etc., in which the workpiece is turned about a horizontal axis against a fixed tool. ◆ *vb* **2** (*tr*) to shape, bore, or cut a screw thread in or on (a workpiece) on a lathe. [perhaps C15 *lath* a support, of Scandinavian origin; compare Old Danish *lad* lathe, Old English *hlæd* heap]

lathe[2] (leɪð) *n Brit. history.* any of the former administrative divisions of Kent. [Old English *læth* district]

lather ('lɑːðə, 'læ-) *n* **1** foam or froth formed by the action of soap or a detergent in water. **2** foam formed by other liquid, such as the sweat of a horse. **3** *Informal.* a state of agitation or excitement. ◆ *vb* **4** to coat or become coated with lather. **5** (*intr*) to form a lather. [Old English *lēathor* soap; related to Old Norse *lauthr* foam] ► **'lathery** *adj*

lathi ('lɑːtɪ) *n* a long heavy wooden stick used as a weapon in India, esp. by the police. [Hindi]

lathy ('lɑːθɪ) *adj* **lathier, lathiest.** resembling a lath, esp. in being tall and thin.

lathyrism ('læθəˌrɪzəm) *n* a neurological disease often resulting in weakness and paralysis of the legs: caused by eating the pealike seeds of the leguminous plant *Lathyrus sativus.*

latices ('lætɪˌsiːz) *n* a plural of **latex.**

laticifer (lə'tɪsɪfə) *n Botany.* a cell or group of cells in a plant that contains latex. [C19: from New Latin *latic-* LATEX + -FER] ► **laticiferous** (ˌlætɪ'sɪfərəs) *adj*

latifundium (ˌlætɪ'fʌndɪəm) *n, pl* **-dia** (-dɪə). a large agricultural estate, esp. one worked by slaves in ancient Rome. [C17: from Latin *lātus* broad + *fundus* farm, estate]

Latimer ('lætəmə) *n* **Hugh.** ?1485–1555, English Protestant bishop: burnt at the stake for refusing to disavow his Protestant beliefs when Mary I assumed the throne.

latimeria (ˌlætɪ'mɪərɪə) *n* any coelacanth fish of the genus *Latimeria.* [C20: named after Marjorie Courtenay-*Latimer* (born 1902), South African museum curator]

Latin ('lætɪn) *n* **1** the language of ancient Rome and the Roman Empire and of the educated in medieval Europe, which achieved its classical form during the 1st century B.C. Having originally been the language of Latium, belonging to the Italic branch of the Indo-European family, it later formed the basis of the Romance group. See **Late Latin, Low Latin, Medieval Latin, New Latin, Old Latin.** See also **Romance. 2** a member of any of those peoples whose languages are derived from Latin. **3** an inhabitant of ancient Latium. ◆ *adj* **4** of or relating to the Latin language, the ancient Latins, or Latium. **5** characteristic of or relating to those peoples in Europe and Latin America whose languages are derived from Latin. **6** of or relating to the Roman Catholic Church. **7** denoting or relating to the Roman alphabet. [Old English *latin* and *læden* Latin, language, from Latin *Latīnus* of Latium]

Latina (*Italian* la'tiːna) *n* a city in W central Italy, in Lazio: built as a planned town in 1932 on reclaimed land of the Pontine Marshes. Pop.: 110 233 (1996 est.). Former name (until 1947): **Littoria.**

Latin alphabet *n* another term for **Roman alphabet.**

Latin America *n* those areas of America whose official languages are Spanish and Portuguese, derived from Latin: South America, Central America, Mexico, and certain islands in the Caribbean. ► **Latin American** *n, adj*

Latinate ('lætɪˌneɪt) *adj* (of writing, vocabulary, etc.) imitative of or derived from Latin.

Latin Church *n* the Roman Catholic Church.

Latin cross *n* a cross the lowest arm of which is longer than the other three.

Latinism ('lætɪˌnɪzəm) *n* a word, idiom, or phrase borrowed from Latin.

Latinist ('lætɪnɪst) *n* a person who studies or is proficient in Latin.

Latinity (lə'tɪnɪtɪ) *n* **1** facility in the use of Latin. **2** Latin style, esp. in literature.

Latinize *or* **Latinise** ('lætɪˌnaɪz) *vb (tr)* **1** to translate into Latin or Latinisms. **2** to transliterate into the Latin alphabet. **3** to cause to acquire Latin style or customs. **4** to bring Roman Catholic influence to bear upon (the form of religious ceremonies, etc.). ▸ **ˌLatiniˈzation** *or* **ˌLatiniˈsation** *n* ▸ **ˈLatinˌizer** *or* **ˈLatinˌiser** *n*

Latino (læ'tiːnəʊ) *n, pl,* **-nos.** *U.S.* an inhabitant of the U.S. who is of Latin American origin. ▸ **La'tinna** *fem n*

Latin Quarter *n* an area of Paris, on the S bank of the River Seine: contains the city's main educational establishments; centre for students and artists.

Latin square *n* (in statistical analysis) one of a set of square arrays of *n* rows and columns, esp. as used in statistics and studied in combinatorial analysis, built up from *n* different symbols so that no symbol occurs more than once in any row or column.

latish ('leɪtɪʃ) *adj* rather late.

latitude ('lætɪˌtjuːd) *n* **1a** an angular distance in degrees north or south of the equator (latitude 0°), equal to the angle subtended at the centre of the globe by the meridian between the equator and the point in question. **1b** *(often pl)* a region considered with regard to its distance from the equator. See **longitude** (sense 1). **2** scope for freedom of action, thought, etc.; freedom from restriction: *his parents gave him a great deal of latitude.* **3** *Photog.* the range of exposure over which a photographic emulsion gives an acceptable negative. **4** *Astronomy.* See **celestial latitude.** [C14: from Latin *lātitūdō,* from *lātus* broad] ▸ **ˌlatiˈtudinal** *adj* ▸ **ˌlatiˈtudinally** *adv*

latitudinarian (ˌlætɪˌtjuːdɪ'nɛərɪən) *adj* **1** permitting or marked by freedom of attitude or behaviour, esp. in religious matters. **2** *(sometimes cap.)* of or relating to a school of thought within the Church of England in the 17th century that minimized the importance of divine authority in matters of doctrine and stressed the importance of reason and personal judgment. ◆ *n* **3** a person with latitudinarian views. [C17: from Latin *lātitūdō* breadth, LATITUDE, influenced in form by TRINITARIAN] ▸ **ˌlatiˌtudiˈnarianism** *n*

Latium ('leɪʃɪəm) *n* an ancient territory in W central Italy, in modern Lazio, on the Tyrrhenian Sea: inhabited by the Latin people from the 10th century B.C. until dominated by Rome (4th century B.C.). Italian name: **Lazio.**

Latona (lə'təʊnə) *n* the Roman name of **Leto.**

Latour *(French* latur) *n* **Maurice Quentin de** (mɔris kɑ̃tɛ̃ də) 1704–88, French pastelist noted for the vivacity of his portraits.

La Tour *(French* la tur) *n* **Georges de** (ʒɔrʒ də). ?1593–1652, French painter, esp. of candlelit religious scenes.

La Trappe *(French* la trap) *n* a monastery in NW France, in the village of Soligny-la-Trappe northeast of Alençon: founded in about 1140, site of the Trappist reform of Cistercian order in 1664.

latria (lə'traɪə) *n R.C. Church, theol.* the adoration that may be offered to God alone. [C16: via Latin from Greek *latreia* worship]

latrine (lə'triːn) *n* a lavatory, as in a barracks, camp, etc. [C17: from French, from Latin *lātrīna,* shortened form of *lavātrīna* bath, from *lavāre* to wash]

-latry *n combining form.* indicating worship of or excessive veneration of: *idolatry; Mariolatry.* [from Greek *-latria,* from *latreia* worship] ▸ **-latrous** *adj combining form.*

lats (læts) *n, pl* **lati** ('læti:). the standard monetary unit of Latvia, divided into 100 santimi.

latte ('læteɪ, 'lɑːteɪ) *n* coffee made with hot milk. [C20: from Italian *(caffè e) latte* (coffee and) milk]

latten ('lætᵊn) *n* metal or alloy, esp. brass, made in thin sheets. [C14: from Old French *laton,* of unknown origin]

latter ('lætə) *adj (prenominal)* **1a** denoting the second or second mentioned of two: distinguished from *former.* **1b** *(as n; functioning as sing or pl): the latter is not important.* **2** near or nearer the end: *the latter part of a film.* **3** more advanced in time or sequence; later.

USAGE *The latter* should only be used to refer to the second of two items: *many people choose to go by hovercraft rather than use the ferry, but I prefer the latter.* The last of three or more items can be referred to as *the last-named.*

latter-day *adj* present-day; modern.

Latter-day Saint *n* a more formal name for a **Mormon.**

latterly ('lætəlɪ) *adv* recently; lately.

lattermost ('lætəˌməʊst) *adj* a less common word for **last**[1].

lattice ('lætɪs) *n* **1** Also called: **ˈlatticeˌwork.** an open framework of strips of wood, metal, etc., arranged to form an ornamental pattern. **2a** a gate, screen, etc., formed of such a framework. **2b** *(as modifier): a lattice window.* **3** something, such as a decorative or heraldic device, resembling such a framework. **4** an array of objects or points in a periodic pattern in two or three dimensions, esp. an array of atoms, ions, etc., in a crystal or an array of points indicating their positions in space. See also **Bravais lattice.** ◆ *vb* **5** to make, adorn, or supply with a lattice or lattices. [C14: from Old French *lattis,* from *latte* LATH] ▸ **ˈlatticed** *adj*

lattice energy *n Chem.* the energy required to separate the ions of a crystal to an infinite distance, usually expressed in joules per mole.

latus rectum ('lɑːtəs 'rɛktəm) *n, pl* **latera recta** ('lætərə 'rɛktə). *Geometry.* a chord that passes through the focus of a conic and is perpendicular to the major axis. [C18: New Latin: straight side]

Latvia ('lætvɪə) *n* a republic in NE Europe, on the Gulf of Riga and the Baltic Sea: ruled by Poland, Sweden, and Russia since the 13th century, Latvia was independent from 1919 until 1940 and was a Soviet republic (1940–91), gaining its independence after conflict with Soviet forces; it is mostly forested. Official language: Latvian. Religion: nonreligious, Christian. Currency: lats. Capital: Riga. Pop.: 2 445 000 (1998 est.). Area: 63 700 sq. km (25 590 sq. miles).

Latvian ('lætvɪən) *adj* **1** of or relating to Latvia, its people, or their language. ◆ *n* **2** Also called: **Lettish.** the official language of Latvia: closely related to Lithuanian and belonging to the Baltic branch of the Indo-European family. **3** a native or inhabitant of Latvia.

laud (lɔːd) *Literary.* ◆ *vb* **1** *(tr)* to praise or glorify. ◆ *n* **2** praise or glorification. [C14: vb from Latin *laudāre;* n. from *laudēs,* pl. of Latin *laus* praise] ▸ **ˈlauder** *n*

Laud (lɔːd) *n* **William.** 1573–1645, English prelate; archbishop of Canterbury (1633–45). His persecution of Puritans and his High Church policies in England and Scotland were a cause of the Civil War; he was impeached by the Long Parliament (1640) and executed.

Lauda *(German* 'lauda) *n* **Niki** ('nɪki). born 1949, Austrian motor-racing driver: world champion 1975, 1977, 1984.

laudable ('lɔːdəbᵊl) *adj* deserving or worthy of praise; admirable; commendable. ▸ **ˈlaudableness** *or* **ˌlaudaˈbility** *n* ▸ **ˈlaudably** *adv*

laudanum ('lɔːdᵊnəm) *n* **1** a tincture of opium. **2** (formerly) any medicine of which opium was the main ingredient. [C16: New Latin, name chosen by Paracelsus for a preparation probably containing opium, perhaps based on LABDANUM]

laudation (lɔː'deɪʃən) *n* a formal word for **praise.**

laudatory ('lɔːdətərɪ, -trɪ) *or* **laudative** *adj* expressing or containing praise; eulogistic.

Lauder ('lɔːdə) *n* Sir **Harry.** real name *Hugh MacLennan.* 1870–1950, Scottish ballad singer and music-hall comedian.

Laudian ('lɔːdɪən) *adj Church of England.* of or relating to the High-Church standards set up for the Church of England by Archbishop Laud.

lauds (lɔːdz) *n (functioning as sing or pl) Chiefly R.C. Church.* the traditional morning prayer of the Western Church, constituting with matins the first of the seven canonical hours. [C14: see LAUD]

Laue *(German* 'lauə) *n* **Max Theodor Felix von** (maks 'teːodoːr 'feːlɪks fɔn). 1879–1960, German physicist. He pioneered the technique of measuring the wavelengths of X-rays by their diffraction by crystals and contributed to the theory of relativity: Nobel prize for physics 1914.

laugh (lɑːf) *vb* **1** *(intr)* to express or manifest emotion, esp. mirth or amusement, typically by expelling air from the lungs in short bursts to produce an inarticulate voiced noise, with the mouth open. **2** *(intr)* (esp. of certain mammals or birds) to make a noise resembling a laugh. **3** *(tr)* to utter or express with laughter: *he laughed his derision at the play.* **4** *(tr)* to bring or force (someone, esp. oneself) into a certain condition by laughter: *he laughed himself sick.* **5** *(intr;* foll. by *at)* to make fun (of); jeer (at). **6** (intr; foll. by *over)* to read or discuss something with laughter. **7 don't make me laugh.** *Informal.* I don't believe you for a moment. **8 laugh all the way to the bank.** *Informal.* to be unashamedly pleased at making a lot of money. **9 laugh in a person's face.** to show open contempt or defiance towards a person. **10 laugh like a drain.** *Informal.* to laugh loudly and coarsely. **11 laugh up one's sleeve.** to laugh or have grounds for amusement, self-satisfaction, etc., secretly. **12 laugh on the other side of one's face.** to show sudden disappointment or shame after appearing cheerful or confident: **13 be laughing.** *Informal.* to be in a favourable situation. ◆ *n* **14** the act or an instance of laughing. **15** a manner of laughter. **16** *Informal.* a person or thing that causes laughter: *that holiday was a laugh.* **17 the last laugh.** the final success in an argument, situation, etc., after previous defeat. ◆ See also **laugh away, laugh down, laugh off.** [Old English *læhan, hliehhen;* related to Gothic *hlahjan,* Dutch *lachen*] ▸ **ˈlaugher** *n* ▸ **ˈlaughing** *n, adj* ▸ **ˈlaughingly** *adv*

laughable ('lɑːfəbᵊl) *adj* **1** producing scorn; ludicrous: *he offered me a laughable sum for the picture.* **2** arousing laughter. ▸ **ˈlaughableness** *n* ▸ **ˈlaughably** *adv*

laugh away *vb (tr, adv)* **1** to dismiss or dispel (something unpleasant) by laughter. **2** to make (time) pass pleasantly by jesting.

laugh down *vb (tr, adv)* to silence by laughing contemptuously.

laughing gas *n* another name for **nitrous oxide.**

laughing hyena *n* another name for the **spotted hyena** (see **hyena**).

laughing jackass *n* another name for the **kookaburra.**

laughing stock *n* an object of humiliating ridicule: *his mistakes have made him a laughing stock.*

laugh off *vb (tr, adv)* to treat or dismiss lightly, esp. with stoicism: *he laughed off his injuries.*

laughter ('lɑːftə) *n* **1** the action of or noise produced by laughing. **2** the experience or manifestation of mirth, amusement, scorn, or joy. [Old English *hleahtor;* related to Old Norse *hlātr*]

Laughton ('lɔːtᵊn) *n* **Charles.** 1899–1962, U.S. actor, born in England: noted esp. for his films of the 1930s, such as *The Private Life of Henry VIII* (1933), for which he won an Oscar, and *Mutiny on the Bounty* (1935).

launce (lɑːns) *n* another name for the **sand eel.**

Launceston ('lɔːnsəstən) *n* a city in Australia, the chief port of the island state of Tasmania on the Tamar River, 64 km (40 miles) from Bass Strait. Pop.: 93 347 (1991).

launch[1] (lɔːntʃ) *vb* **1** to move (a vessel) into the water. **2** to move (a newly built vessel) into the water for the first time. **3** *(tr)* **3a** to start off or set in motion: *to launch a scheme.* **3b** to put (a new product) on the market. **4** *(tr)* to propel with force. **5** to involve (oneself) totally and enthusiastically: *to launch oneself into work.* **6** *(tr)* to set (a missile, spacecraft, etc.) into motion. **7** *(tr)* to catapult (an aircraft), as from the deck of an aircraft carrier. **8** *(intr;* foll. by *into)* to start talking or writing (about): *he launched into a story.* **9** *(intr;* usually foll. by *out)* to start (out) on a fresh course. **10** *(intr;* usually foll. by *out) Informal.* to spend a lot of money. ◆ *n* **11** an act or instance of launching. [C14: from Anglo-

French *lancher,* from Late Latin *lanceāre* to use a lance, hence, to set in motion. See LANCE]

launch[2] (lɔːntʃ) *n* **1** a motor driven boat used chiefly as a transport boat. **2** the largest of the boats of a man-of-war. [**C17**: via Spanish *lancha* and Portuguese from Malay *lancharan* boat, from *lanchar* speed]

launcher ('lɔːntʃə) *n* any installation, vehicle, or other device for launching rockets, missiles, or other projectiles.

launch pad *or* **launching pad** *n* **1** a platform from which a spacecraft, rocket, etc., is launched. **2** an effective starting point for a career, enterprise, or campaign.

launch shoe *or* **launching shoe** *n* an attachment to an aircraft from which a missile is launched.

launch vehicle *or* **launching vehicle** *n* **1** a rocket, without its payload, used to launch a spacecraft. **2** another name for **booster** (sense 2).

launch window *n* the limited period during which a spacecraft can be launched on a particular mission.

launder ('lɔːndə) *vb* **1** to wash, sometimes starch, and often also iron (clothes, linen, etc.). **2** (*intr*) to be capable of being laundered without shrinking, fading, etc. **3** (*tr*) to process (something acquired illegally) to make it appear respectable, esp. to process illegally acquired funds through a legitimate business or to send them to a foreign bank for subsequent transfer to a home bank. ◆ *n* **4** a water trough, esp. one used for washing ore in mining. [**C14** (n, meaning: a person who washes linen): changed from *lavender* washerwoman, from Old French *lavandiere,* ultimately from Latin *lavāre* to wash] ▸ **'launderer** *n*

Launderette (ˌlɔːndə'rɛt, lɔːn'drɛt) *n Brit. and N.Z. trademark.* a commercial establishment where clothes can be washed and dried, using coin-operated machines. Also called (U.S., Canadian, and N.Z.): **Laundromat.**

laundress ('lɔːndrɪs) *n* a woman who launders clothes, sheets, etc., for a living.

laundrette (lɔːn'drɛt) *n* a variant of **Launderette.**

Laundromat ('lɔːndrəˌmæt) *n Trademark.* a U.S., Canadian, and N.Z. name for **Launderette.**

laundry ('lɔːndrɪ) *n, pl* **-dries. 1** a place where clothes and linen are washed and ironed. **2** the clothes or linen washed and ironed. **3** the act of laundering. [**C16**: changed from **C14** *lavendry;* see LAUNDER]

laundryman ('lɔːndrɪmən) *or* (*fem*) **laundrywoman** *n, pl* **-men** *or* **-women. 1** a person who collects or delivers laundry. **2** a person who works in a laundry.

lauraceous (lɔː'reɪʃəs) *adj* of, relating to, or belonging to the *Lauraceae,* a family of aromatic trees and shrubs having leathery leaves: includes the laurels and avocado.

Laurasia (lɔː'reɪʃə) *n* one of the two ancient supercontinents produced by the first split of the even larger supercontinent Pangaea about 200 million years ago, comprising what are now North America, Greenland, Europe, and Asia (excluding India). See also **Gondwanaland, Pangaea.** [**C20**: from New Latin *Laur(entia)* (referring to the ancient N American landmass, from *Laurentian* strata of the Canadian Shield) + *(Eur)asia*]

laureate ('lɔːrɪɪt) *adj* (*usually immediately postpositive*) **1** *Literary.* crowned with laurel leaves as a sign of honour. **2** *Archaic.* made of laurel. ◆ *n* **3** short for **poet laureate. 4** a person honoured with an award for art or science: *a Nobel laureate.* **5** *Rare.* a person honoured with the laurel crown or wreath. [**C14**: from Latin *laureātus,* from *laurea* LAUREL] ▸ **'laureateˌship** *n* ▸ **laureation** (ˌlɔːrɪ'eɪʃən) *n*

laurel ('lɒrəl) *n* **1** Also called: **bay, bay laurel, sweet bay, true laurel.** a small Mediterranean lauraceous evergreen tree, *Laurus nobilis,* with glossy aromatic leaves, used for flavouring in cooking, and small blackish berries. **2** a similar and related tree, *Laurus canariensis,* of the Canary Islands and Azores. **3** short for **cherry laurel** or **mountain laurel. 4 spurge laurel.** a European thymelaeaceous evergreen shrub, *Daphne laureola,* with glossy leaves and small green flowers. **5 spotted** or **Japan laurel.** an evergreen cornaceous shrub, *Aucuba japonica,* of S and SE Asia, the female of which has yellow-spotted leaves. **6** (*pl*) a wreath of true laurel, worn on the head as an emblem of victory or honour in classical times. **7** (*pl*) honour, distinction, or fame. **8 look to one's laurels.** to be on guard against one's rivals. **9 rest on one's laurels.** to be satisfied with distinction won by past achievements and cease to strive for further achievements. ◆ *vb* **-rels, -relling, -relled** *or U.S.* **-rels, -reling, -reled. 10** (*tr*) to crown with laurels. [**C13** *lorer,* from old French *lorier* laurel tree, ultimately from Latin *laurus*]

Laurel and Hardy ('lɒrəl; 'hɑːdɪ) *n* a team of U.S. film comedians, **Stan Laurel,** 1890–1965, born in Britain, the thin one, and his partner, **Oliver Hardy,** 1892–1957, the fat one.

Laurentian (lɔː'rɛnʃən) *adj* **1** Also: **Lawrentian.** of or resembling the style of D. H. or T. E. Lawrence. **2** of, relating to, or situated near the St. Lawrence River.

Laurentian Mountains *pl n* a range of low mountains in E Canada, in Quebec between the St Lawrence River and Hudson Bay. Highest point: 1191 m (3905 ft.). Also called: **Laurentides** ('lɔːrənˌtaɪdz).

Laurentian Shield *n* another name for the **Canadian Shield.** Also called: **Laurentian Plateau.**

lauric acid ('lɔːrɪk, 'lɒ-) *n* another name for **dodecanoic acid.** [**C19**: from Latin *laurus* laurel; from its occurrence in the berries of the laurel (*Laurus nobilis*)]

Laurier ('lɒrɪə) *n* Sir **Wilfrid.** 1841–1919, Canadian Liberal statesman; the first French-Canadian prime minister (1896–1911).

laurustinus (ˌlɔːrə'staɪnəs) *n* a Mediterranean caprifoliaceous shrub, *Viburnum tinus,* with glossy evergreen leaves and white or pink fragrant flowers. [**C17**: from New Latin, from Latin *laurus* laurel]

lauryl alcohol ('lɔːrɪl, 'lɒ-) *n* a water-insoluble crystalline solid used in the manufacture of detergents; 1-dodecanol. Formula: $CH_3(CH_2)_{10}CH_2OH$. [**C20**: from LAUR(IC ACID) + -YL]

Lausanne (ləʊ'zæn; *French* lozan) *n* a city in W Switzerland, capital of Vaud canton, on Lake Geneva; cultural and commercial centre; university (1537). Pop.: 116 795 (1995 est.).

Lautrec (*French* lo'trɛk) *n* See (Henri de) **Toulouse-Lautrec.**

lav (læv) *n Brit. informal.* short for **lavatory.**

lava ('lɑːvə) *n* **1** magma emanating from volcanoes and other vents. **2** any extrusive igneous rock formed by the cooling and solidification of lava. [**C18**: from Italian (Neapolitan dialect), from Latin *lavāre* to wash]

lavabo (lə'veɪbəʊ) *n, pl* **-boes** *or* **-bos.** *Chiefly R.C. Church.* **1a** the ritual washing of the celebrant's hands after the offertory at Mass. **1b** (*as modifier*): *lavabo basin; lavabo towel.* **2** another name for **washbasin. 3** a trough for washing in a convent or monastery. [**C19**: from Latin: I shall wash, the opening of Psalm 26:6]

lavage ('lævɪdʒ, læ'vɑːʒ) *n Med.* the washing out of a hollow organ by flushing with water. [**C19**: via French, from Latin *lavāre* to wash]

Laval[1] (lə'væl) *n* a city in SE Canada, in Quebec: a NW suburb of Montreal. Pop.: 314 398 (1991).

Laval[2] (*French* laval) *n* **Pierre** (pjɛr). 1883–1945, French statesman. He was premier of France (1931–32; 1935–36) and premier of the Vichy government (1942–44). He was executed for collaboration with Germany.

lava lamp *n* a decorative type of lamp in which a luminous viscous material moves in constantly changing shapes. [**C20**: from the resemblance of the shapes to molten lava in water]

lava-lava *n* a draped skirtlike garment of printed cotton or calico worn by Polynesians. [Samoan]

lavatera (ˌlævə'tɪərə) *n* any plant of the genus *Lavatera,* closely resembling mallow and grown for their purple, white, or rose-coloured flowers: family *Malvaceae.* [named after the two brothers *Lavater,* 18th-century Swiss doctors and naturalists]

lavation (læ'veɪʃən) *n Formal or literary.* the act or process of washing. [**C17**: from Latin *lavātio,* from *lavāre* to wash] ▸ **la'vational** *adj*

lavatorial (ˌlævə'tɔːrɪəl) *adj* **1** of or in the style of decoration supposed to typify public lavatories: *white lavatorial tiling.* **2** characterized by excessive mention of lavatories and the excretory functions; vulgar or scatological: *lavatorial humour.*

lavatory ('lævətərɪ, -trɪ) *n, pl* **-ries. 1** Also called: **toilet, water closet, WC. 1a** a sanitary installation for receiving and disposing of urine and faeces, consisting of a bowl fitted with a water-flushing device and connected to a drain. **1b** a room containing such an installation. **2** the washing place in a convent or monastic establishment. [**C14**: from Late Latin *lavātōrium,* from Latin *lavāre* to wash]

lavatory paper *n Brit.* another name for **toilet paper.**

lave (leɪv) *vb* an archaic word for **wash.** [Old English *lafian,* perhaps from Latin *lavāre* to wash]

lavender ('lævəndə) *n* **1** any of various perennial shrubs or herbaceous plants of the genus *Lavandula,* esp. *L. vera,* cultivated for its mauve or blue flowers and as the source of a fragrant oil (**oil of lavender**): family *Labiatae* (labiates). See also **spike lavender.** Compare **sea lavender. 2** the dried parts of *L. vera,* used to perfume clothes. **3a** a pale or light bluish-purple to a very pale violet colour. **3b** (*as adj*): *lavender socks.* **4** perfume scented with lavender. [**C13**: *lavendre,* via French from Medieval Latin *lavendula,* of obscure origin]

lavender bag *n* a small fabric bag filled with dried lavender flowers and placed amongst clothes or linen to scent them.

lavender water *n* a perfume made of essential oils of lavender and alcohol.

laver[1] ('leɪvə) *n* **1** *Old Testament.* a large basin of water used by the priests for ritual ablutions. **2** the font or the water of baptism. [**C14**: from Old French *laveoir,* from Late Latin *lavātōrium* washing place]

laver[2] ('lɑːvə) *n* any of several seaweeds of the genus *Porphyra* and related genera, with edible fronds: phylum *Rhodophyta* (red algae). [**C16**: from Latin]

Laver ('leɪvə) *n* **Rod**(**ney**). born 1938, Australian tennis player: Wimbledon champion 1961, 1962, 1968, 1969; U.S. champion 1962, 1969.

laver bread ('lɑːvə) *n* laver seaweed fried as a breakfast food; popular in Wales.

laverock ('lævərək; *Scot. also* 'levərək, 'levrək) *n* a Scot. and northern English dialect word for **skylark** (bird). [Old English *lǣwerce* LARK[1]]

lavish ('lævɪʃ) *adj* **1** prolific, abundant, or profuse. **2** generous; unstinting; liberal. **3** extravagant; prodigal; wasteful: *lavish expenditure.* ◆ *vb* **4** (*tr*) to give, expend, or apply abundantly, generously, or in profusion. [**C15**: adj use of *lavas* profusion, from Old French *lavasse* torrent, from Latin *lavāre* to wash] ▸ **'lavisher** *n* ▸ **'lavishly** *adv* ▸ **'lavishment** *n* ▸ **'lavishness** *n*

Lavoisier (*French* lavwazje) *n* **Antoine Laurent** (ɑ̃twan lɔrɑ̃). 1743–94, French chemist; one of the founders of modern chemistry. He disproved the phlogiston theory, named oxygen, and discovered its importance in respiration and combustion.

lavolta (lə'vɒltə) *n* another word for **volta.** [**C16**: from Italian *la volta* the turn; see VOLTA]

law[1] (lɔː) *n* **1** a rule or set of rules, enforceable by the courts, regulating the government of a state, the relationship between the organs of government and the subjects of the state, and the relationship or conduct of subjects towards each other. **2a** a rule or body of rules made by the legislature. See **statute law. 2b** a rule or body of rules made by a municipal or other authority. See **bylaw. 3a** the condition and control enforced by such rules. **3b** (*in combination*): *lawcourt.* **4** a rule of conduct: *a law of etiquette.* **5** one of a set of rules governing a particular field of activity: *the laws of tennis.* **6 the law. 6a** the legal or judicial system. **6b** the profession or practice of law. **6c** *Informal.* the police or a policeman. **7** a binding force or statement: *his word is law.* **8** Also called: **law of nature.** a generalization based on a recurring fact or event. **9** the science or knowledge of law; jurisprudence. **10** the principles originating and formerly applied only in courts of common law. Compare **equity** (sense 3). **11** a general principle, formula, or rule describing a phenomenon in mathematics, science, philosophy, etc.: *the laws of thermodynamics.* **12** *Judaism.* (*cap.*; preceded by *the*) **12a** short for **Law of Moses. 12b** the English term for **Torah.** ♦ See also **Oral Law, Written Law. 13 a law unto itself (oneself, etc.)** a person or thing that is outside established laws. **14 go to law.** to resort to legal proceedings on some matter. **15 lay down the law.** to speak in an authoritative or dogmatic manner. **16 reading (of) the Law.** *Judaism.* that part of the morning service on Sabbaths, festivals, and Mondays and Thursdays during which a passage is read from the Torah scrolls. **17 take the law into one's own hands.** to ignore or bypass the law when redressing a grievance. Related adjs: **judicial, jural, juridical, legal.** [Old English *lagu,* from Scandinavian; compare Icelandic *lög* (pl) things laid down, law]

law[2] (lɔː) *n Scot.* a hill, esp. one rounded in shape. [Old English *hlǣw*]

law[3] (lɔː) *adj* a Scot. word. for **low**[1].

Law (lɔː) *n* **1 Andrew Bonar** (ˈbɒnə). 1858–1923, British Conservative statesman, born in Canada; prime minister (1922–23). **2 Denis.** born 1940, Scottish footballer and television and radio commentator on the sport. **3 John.** 1671–1729, Scottish financier. He founded the first bank in France (1716) and the Mississippi Scheme for the development of Louisiana (1717), which collapsed due to excessive speculation. **4 William.** 1686–1761, British Anglican divine, best known for *A Serious Call to a Holy and Devout Life* (1728).

law-abiding *adj* adhering more or less strictly to the laws: *a law-abiding citizen.* ▸ **ˈlaw-aˌbidingness** *n*

law agent *n* (in Scotland) a solicitor holding a certificate from the Law Society of Scotland and thereby entitled to appear for a client in any Sheriff Court.

law-and-order *n* (*modifier*) favouring or advocating strong measures to suppress crime and violence: *a law-and-order candidate.*

lawbreaker (ˈlɔːˌbreɪkə) *n* **1** a person who breaks the law. **2** *Informal.* something that does not conform with legal standards or requirements. ▸ **ˈlawˌbreaking** *n, adj*

law centre *n Brit.* an independent service financed by a local authority, which provides free legal advice and information to the general public.

Lawes (lɔːz) *n* **1 Henry.** 1596–1662, English composer, noted for his music for Milton's masque *Comus* (1634) and for his settings of some of Robert Herrick's poems. **2** his brother, **William.** 1602–45, English composer, noted for his harmonically experimental instrumental music.

Law French *n* a set of Anglo-Norman terms used in English laws and law books.

lawful (ˈlɔːfʊl) *adj* allowed, recognized, or sanctioned by law; legal. ▸ **ˈlawfully** *adv* ▸ **ˈlawfulness** *n*

lawgiver (ˈlɔːˌgɪvə) *n* **1** the giver of a code of laws. **2** Also called: **lawmaker.** a maker of laws. ▸ **ˈlawˌgiving** *n, adj*

lawin *or* **lawing** (ˈlɔːɪn) *n Scot.* a bill or reckoning. [C16: from Old Norse *lag* market price]

lawks (lɔːks) *interj Brit.* an expression of surprise or dismay. [C18: variant of *Lord!,* probably influenced in form by ALACK]

lawless (ˈlɔːlɪs) *adj* **1** without law. **2** disobedient to the law. **3** contrary to or heedless of the law. **4** uncontrolled; unbridled: *lawless rage.* ▸ **ˈlawlessly** *adv* ▸ **ˈlawlessness** *n*

Law Lords *pl n* (in Britain) members of the House of Lords who sit as the highest court of appeal, although in theory the full House of Lords has this role.

lawman (ˈlɔːmən) *n, pl* **-men.** *Chiefly U.S.* an officer of the law, such as a policeman or sheriff.

law merchant *n Mercantile law.* the body of rules and principles determining the rights and obligations of the parties to commercial transactions; commercial law.

lawn[1] (lɔːn) *n* **1** a flat and usually level area of mown and cultivated grass. **2** an archaic or dialect word for **glade.** [C16: changed form of C14 *launde,* from Old French *lande,* of Celtic origin; compare Breton *lann* heath; related to LAND] ▸ **ˈlawny** *adj*

lawn[2] (lɔːn) *n* a fine linen or cotton fabric, used for clothing. [C15: probably from *Laon,* a town in France where linen was made] ▸ **ˈlawny** *adj*

lawn mower *n* a hand-operated or power-operated machine with rotary blades for cutting grass on lawns.

lawn tennis *n* **1** tennis played on a grass court. **2** the formal name for **tennis.**

law of averages *n* (popularly) the expectation that a possible event is bound to occur regularly with a frequency approximating to its probability, as in the (actually false) example: *after five heads in a row the law of averages makes tails the better bet.* Compare **law of large numbers.**

law of effect *n Psychol.* another name for **Thorndike's Law** (see **Thorndike,** sense 1).

law of large numbers *n* the fundamental statistical result that the average of a sequence of *n* identically distributed independent random variables tends to their common mean as *n* tends to infinity, whence the frequency of the occurrence of an event in *n* independent repetitions of an experiment tends to its probability.

Law of Moses *n* **1** the first five books of the Old Testament; Pentateuch. **2** *Judaism.* a law or body of laws derived from the Torah in accordance with interpretations (the Oral Law) traditionally believed to have been given to Moses on Mount Sinai together with the Written Law.

law of nations *n* another term for **international law.**

law of nature *n* **1** an empirical truth of great generality, conceived of as a physical (but not a logical) necessity, and consequently licensing counterfactual conditionals. **2** a system of morality conceived of as grounded in reason. See **natural law** (sense 2), **nomological** (sense 2). **3** See **law** (sense 8).

law of supply and demand *n* the theory that prices are determined by the interaction of supply and demand: an increase in supply will lower prices if not accompanied by increased demand, and an increase in demand will raise prices unless accompanied by increased supply.

law of the jungle *n* a state of ruthless competition or self-interest.

law of thermodynamics *n* **1** any of three principles governing the relationships between different forms of energy. The **first law of thermodynamics** (law of conservation of energy) states that the change in the internal energy of a system is equal to the sum of the heat added to the system and the work done on it. The **second law of thermodynamics** states that heat cannot be transferred from a colder to a hotter body within a system without net changes occurring in other bodies within that system; in any irreversible process, entropy always increases. The **third law of thermodynamics** (Nernst heat theorem) states that it is impossible to reduce the temperature of a system to absolute zero in a finite number of steps. **2** Also called: **zeroth law of thermodynamics.** the principle that if two bodies are each in thermal equilibrium with a third body then the first two bodies are in thermal equilibrium with each other.

Lawrence (ˈlɒrəns) *n* **1 Saint.** died 258 A.D., Roman martyr: according to tradition he was roasted to death on a gridiron. Feast day: Aug. 10. **2 D(avid) H(erbert).** 1885–1930, British novelist, poet, and short-story writer. Many of his works deal with the destructiveness of modern industrial society, contrasted with the beauty of nature and instinct, esp. the sexual impulse. His novels include *Sons and Lovers* (1913), *The Rainbow* (1915), *Women in Love* (1920), and *Lady Chatterley's Lover* (1928). **3 Ernest Orlando.** 1901–58, U.S. physicist, who invented the cyclotron (1931): Nobel prize for physics 1939. **4 Gertrude.** 1898–1952, British actress, noted esp. for her roles in comedies such as Noël Coward's *Private Lives* (1930). **5** Sir **Thomas.** 1769–1830, British portrait painter. **6 T(homas) E(dward),** known as *Lawrence of Arabia.* 1888–1935, British soldier and writer. He took a major part in the Arab revolt against the Turks (1916–18), proving himself an outstanding guerrilla leader. He described his experiences in *The Seven Pillars of Wisdom* (1926).

lawrencium (lɒˈrɛnsɪəm, lɔː-) *n* a transuranic element artificially produced from californium. Symbol: Lr; atomic no.: 103; half-life of most stable isotope, ^{256}Lr: 35 seconds; valency: 3. [C20: named after Ernest O. LAWRENCE]

Lawrentian (lɔːˈrɛnʃən) *adj* relating to or characteristic of D.H. Lawrence.

Law Society *n* (in England or Scotland) the professional body of solicitors, established in 1825 and entrusted with the registration of solicitors (requiring the passing of certain examinations) and the regulation of professional conduct.

Lawson (ˈlɔːsən) *n* **Henry Archibald.** 1867–1922, Australian poet and short-story writer, whose work is taken as being most representative of the Australian outback, esp. in *While the Billy Boils* (1896) and *Joe Wilson and his Mates* (1901).

law stationer *n* **1** a stationer selling articles used by lawyers. **2** *Brit.* a person who makes handwritten copies of legal documents.

lawsuit (ˈlɔːˌsuːt, -ˌsjuːt) *n* a proceeding in a court of law brought by one party against another, esp. a civil action.

law term *n* **1** an expression or word used in law. **2** any of various periods of time appointed for the sitting of law courts.

lawyer (ˈlɔːjə, ˈlɔɪə) *n* **1** a member of the legal profession, esp. a solicitor. See also **advocate, barrister, solicitor. 2** a popular name for **burbot** (a fish). [C14: from LAW[1]]

lawyer's wig *n* another name for the **shaggy ink-cap:** see **ink-cap.**

lawyer vine *n Austral.* any of various kinds of entangling and thorny vegetation, esp. in tropical areas. Also called: **lawyer cane, lawyer palm.**

lax (læks) *adj* **1** lacking firmness; not strict. **2** lacking precision or definition. **3** not taut. **4** *Phonetics.* (of a speech sound) pronounced with little muscular effort and consequently having relatively imprecise accuracy of articulation and little temporal duration. In English the vowel *i* in *bit* is lax. **5** (of flower clusters) having loosely arranged parts. [C14 (originally used with reference to the bowels): from Latin *laxus* loose] ▸ **ˈlaxly** *adv* ▸ **ˈlaxity** *or* **ˈlaxness** *n*

laxation (lækˈseɪʃən) *n* **1** the act of making lax or the state of being lax. **2** *Physiol.* another word for **defecation.** [C14: from Latin *laxātio,* from *laxāre* to slacken]

laxative (ˈlæksətɪv) *n* **1** an agent stimulating evacuation of faeces. ♦ *adj* **2** stimulating evacuation of faeces. [C14 (originally: relaxing): from Medieval Latin *laxātīvus,* from Latin *laxāre* to loosen]

Laxness (ˈlaxsnes) *n* **Halldór (Kiljan)** (ˈhaldoʊr). 1902–98, Icelandic novelist, noted for his treatment of rural working life in Iceland. His works include *Salka Valka* (1932) and *Independent People* (1935). Nobel prize for literature 1955.

lay[1] (leɪ) *vb* **lays, laying, laid** (leɪd). (*mainly tr*) **1** to put in a low or horizontal position; cause to lie: *to lay a cover on a bed.* **2** to place, put, or be in a particular state or position: *he laid his finger on his lips.* **3** (*intr*) *Dialect or not standard.* to be in a horizontal position; lie: *he often lays in bed all the morning.* **4** (sometimes foll. by *down*) to establish as a basis: *to lay a foundation for discussion.* **5** to place or dispose in the proper position: *to lay a carpet.* **6** to arrange (a table) for eating a meal. **7** to prepare (a fire) for lighting by arranging fuel in the grate. **8** (*also intr*) (of birds, esp. the domestic hen) to produce (eggs). **9** to present or put forward: *he laid his case before the magistrate.* **10** to impute or attribute: *all the blame was laid on him.* **11** to arrange, devise, or prepare: *to lay a trap.* **12** to place, set, or locate: *the scene is laid in London.* **13** to apply on or as if on a surface: *to lay a coat of paint.* **14** to impose as a penalty or burden: *to lay a fine.* **15** to make (a bet) with (someone): *I lay you five to one on Prince.* **16** to cause to settle: *to lay the dust.* **17** to allay; suppress: *to lay a rumour.* **18** to bring down forcefully: *to lay a whip on someone's back.* **19** *Taboo slang.* to have sexual intercourse with. **20** to press down or make smooth: *to lay the nap of cloth.* **21** to cut (small trunks or branches of shrubs or trees) halfway through and bend them diagonally to form a hedge: *to lay a hedge.* **22** to arrange and twist together (strands) in order to form (a rope, cable, etc.). **23** *Military.* to apply settings of elevation and training to (a weapon) prior to firing. **24** (foll. by *on*) *Hunting.* to put (hounds or other dogs) onto a scent. **25** another word for **inlay. 26** (*intr;* often foll. by *to* or *out*) *Dialect or informal.* to plan, scheme, or devise. **27** (*intr*) *Nautical.* to move or go, esp. into a specified position or direction: *to lay close to the wind.* **28 lay aboard.** *Nautical.* (formerly) to move alongside a warship to board it. **29 lay a course. 29a** *Nautical.* to sail on a planned course without tacking. **29b** to plan an action. **30 lay bare.** to reveal or explain: *he laid bare his plans.* **31 lay hands on.** See **hands** (sense 12). **32 lay hold of.** to seize or grasp. **33 lay oneself open.** to make oneself vulnerable (to criticism, attack, etc.): *by making such a statement he laid himself open to accusations of favouritism.* **34 lay open.** to reveal or disclose. **35 lay siege to.** to besiege (a city, etc.). ◆ *n* **36** the manner or position in which something lies or is placed. **37** *Taboo slang.* **37a** an act of sexual intercourse. **37b** a sexual partner. **38** a portion of the catch or the profits from a whaling or fishing expedition. **39** the amount or direction of hoist in the strands of a rope. ◆ See also **layabout, lay aside, lay away, lay-by, lay down, lay in, lay into, lay off, lay on, lay out, lay over, lay to, lay up.** [Old English *lecgan;* related to Gothic *lagjan,* Old Norse *leggja*]

USAGE In careful English, the verb *lay* is used with an object and *lie* without one: *the soldier laid down his arms; the Queen laid a wreath; the book was lying on the table; he was lying on the floor.* In informal English, *lay* is frequently used for *lie: the book was laying on the table.* All careful writers and speakers observe the distinction even in informal contexts.

lay[2] (leɪ) *vb* the past tense of **lie**[2].

lay[3] (leɪ) *adj* **1** of, involving, or belonging to people who are not clergy. **2** nonprofessional or nonspecialist; amateur. [C14: from Old French *lai,* from Late Latin *lāicus,* ultimately from Greek *laos* people]

lay[4] (leɪ) *n* **1** a ballad or short narrative poem, esp. one intended to be sung. **2** a song or melody. [C13: from Old French *lai,* perhaps of Germanic origin]

layabout (ˈleɪəˌbaʊt) *n* **1** a lazy person; loafer. ◆ *vb* **lay about. 2** (*prep,* usually *intr* or *reflexive*) *Old-fashioned.* to hit out with violent and repeated blows in all directions.

Layamon (ˈlaɪəmən) *or* **Lawman** (ˈlɔːmən) *n* 12th-century English poet and priest; author of the *Brut,* a chronicle providing the earliest version of the Arthurian story in English.

lay analyst *n* a person without medical qualifications who practises psychoanalysis.

Layard (lɛəd) *n* Sir **Austen Henry.** 1817–94, English archaeologist, noted for his excavations at Nimrud and Nineveh.

lay aside *vb* (*tr, adv*) **1** to abandon or reject. **2** to store or reserve for future use.

lay away *vb* (*tr, adv*) **1** to store or reserve for future use. **2** to reserve (merchandise) for future delivery, while payments are being made.

layback (ˈleɪˌbæk) *n Mountaineering.* a technique for climbing cracks by pulling on one side of the crack with the hands and pressing on the other with the feet.

lay brother *or (fem)* **lay sister** *n* a person who has taken the vows of a religious order but is not ordained and not bound to divine office.

lay-by *n* **1** *Brit.* a place for drivers to stop at the side of a main road. **2** *Nautical.* an anchorage in a narrow waterway, away from the channel. **3** a small railway siding where rolling stock may be stored or parked. **4** *Austral. and N.Z.* a system of payment whereby a buyer pays a deposit on an article, which is reserved for him until he has paid the full price. ◆ *vb* **lay by** (*adv*) **5** (*tr*) to set aside or save for future needs. **6** Also: **lay to.** to cause (a sailing vessel) to stop in open water or (of a sailing vessel) to stop.

lay days *pl n* **1** *Commerce.* the number of days permitted for the loading or unloading of a ship without payment of demurrage. **2** *Nautical.* the time during which a ship is kept from sailing because of loading, bad weather, etc.

lay down *vb* (*tr, adv*) **1** to place on the ground, etc. **2** to relinquish or discard: *to lay down one's life.* **3** to formulate (a rule, principle, etc.). **4** to build or begin to build: *the railway was laid down as far as Manchester.* **5** to record (plans) on paper. **6** to convert (land) into pasture. **7** to store or stock: *to lay down wine.* **8** *Informal.* to wager or bet. **9** (*tr, adv*) *Informal.* to record (tracks) in a studio.

layer (ˈleɪə) *n* **1** a thickness of some homogeneous substance, such as a stratum or a coating on a surface. **2** one of four levels of vegetation defined in ecological studies: the ground or moss layer, the field or herb layer, the shrub layer, and the tree layer. **3** a laying hen. **4** *Horticulture.* **4a** a shoot or branch rooted during layering. **4b** a plant produced as a result of layering. ◆ *vb* **5** to form or make a layer of (something). **6** to take root or cause to take root by layering. [C14 *leyer, legger,* from LAY[1] + -ER[1]]

layer cake *n* a cake made in layers with a filling.

layering (ˈleɪərɪŋ) *n* **1** *Horticulture.* a method of propagation that induces a shoot or branch to take root while it is still attached to the parent plant. **2** *Geology.* the banded appearance of certain igneous rocks, each band being of a different mineral composition.

layette (leɪˈɛt) *n* a complete set of articles, including clothing, bedclothes, and other accessories, for a newborn baby. [C19: from French, from Old French, from *laie,* from Middle Dutch *laege* box]

lay figure *n* **1** an artist's jointed dummy, used in place of a live model, esp. for studying effects of drapery. **2** a person considered to be subservient or unimportant. [C18: from obsolete *layman,* from Dutch *leeman,* literally: jointman]

lay in *vb* (*tr, adv*) to accumulate and store: *we must lay in food for the party.*

laying on of hands *n* (in Christian ordination, confirmation, faith healing, etc.) the act of laying hands on a person's head to confer spiritual blessing.

lay into *vb* (*intr, prep*) *Informal.* **1** to attack forcefully. **2** to berate severely.

layman (ˈleɪmən) *or (fem)* **laywoman** *n, pl* **-men** *or* **-women. 1** a person who is not a clergyman. **2** a person who does not have specialized or professional knowledge of a subject: *science for the layman.*

lay off *vb* **1** (*tr, adv*) to suspend (workers) from employment with the intention of re-employing them at a later date: *the firm had to lay off 100 men.* **2** (*intr*) *Informal.* to leave (a person, thing, or activity) alone: *lay off me, will you!* **3** (*tr, adv*) to mark off the boundaries of. **4** (*tr, adv*) *Soccer.* to pass or deflect (the ball) to a team-mate, esp. one in a more advantageous position. **5** *Gambling.* another term for **hedge** (sense 10). ◆ *n* **lay-off. 6** the act of suspending employees. **7** a period of imposed unemployment.

lay on *vb* (*tr, adv*) **1** to provide or supply: *to lay on entertainment.* **2** *Brit.* to install: *to lay on electricity.* **3 lay it on.** *Informal.* **3a** to exaggerate, esp. when flattering. **3b** to charge an exorbitant price. **3c** to punish or strike harshly.

lay out *vb* (*tr, adv*) **1** to arrange or spread out. **2** to prepare (a corpse) for burial or cremation. **3** to plan or contrive. **4** *Informal.* to spend (money), esp. lavishly. **5** *Informal.* to knock unconscious. **6** *Informal.* to exert (oneself) or put (oneself) to an effort: *he laid himself out to please us.* ◆ *n* **layout. 7** the arrangement or plan of something, such as a building. **8** the arrangement of written material, photographs, or other artwork on an advertisement or page in a book, newspaper, etc. **9** a preliminary plan indicating this. **10** a drawing showing the relative disposition of parts in a machine, etc. **11** the act of laying out. **12** something laid out. **13** the formation of cards on the table in various games, esp. in patience. **14** *Informal, chiefly U.S.* a residence or establishment, esp. a large one.

lay over *U.S. and Canadian.* ◆ *vb* (*adv*) **1** (*tr*) to postpone for future action. **2** (*intr*) to make a temporary stop in a journey. ◆ *n* **layover. 3** a break in a journey, esp. in waiting for a connection.

lay reader *n* **1** *Church of England.* a person licensed by a bishop to conduct religious services other than the Eucharist. **2** *R.C. Church.* a layman chosen from among the congregation to read the epistle at Mass and sometimes other prayers.

layshaft (ˈleɪˌʃɑːft) *n* an auxiliary shaft in a gearbox, running parallel to the main shaft, to and from which drive is transferred to enable varying ratios to be obtained.

lay to *vb* (*intr adv*) *Nautical.* **1** to bring a vessel into a haven. **2** another term for **heave to.**

lay up *vb* (*tr, adv*) **1** to store or reserve for future use. **2** (*usually passive*) *Informal.* to incapacitate or confine through illness.

lazar (ˈlæzə) *n* an archaic word for **leper.** [C14: via Old French and Medieval Latin, after LAZARUS] ▸ **ˈlazar-ˌlike** *adj*

lazaretto (ˌlæzəˈrɛtəʊ), **lazaret,** *or* **lazarette** (ˌlæzəˈrɛt) *n, pl* **-rettos, -rets,** *or* **-rettes. 1** Also called: **glory hole.** *Nautical.* a small locker at the stern of a boat or a storeroom between decks of a ship. **2** Also called: **lazar house, pesthouse.** (formerly) a hospital for persons with infectious diseases, esp. leprosy. [C16: Italian, from *lazzaro* LAZAR]

Lazarus (ˈlæzərəs) *n New Testament.* **1** the brother of Mary and Martha, whom Jesus restored to life (John 11–12). **2** the beggar who lay at the gate of the rich man Dives in Jesus' parable (Luke 16:19–31).

laze (leɪz) *vb* **1** (*intr*) to be indolent or lazy. **2** (*tr;* often foll. by *away*) to spend (time) in indolence. ◆ *n* **3** the act or an instance of idling. [C16: back formation from LAZY]

Lazio (ˈlattsjo) *n* **1** a region of W central Italy, on the Tyrrhenian Sea: includes the plain of the lower Tiber, the reclaimed Pontine Marshes, and Campagna. Capital: Rome. Pop.: 5 202 098 (1996 est.). **2** the Italian name for **Latium.**

lazuli (ˈlæzjʊˌlaɪ) *n* short for **lapis lazuli.**

lazulite (ˈlæzjʊˌlaɪt) *n* a blue mineral, consisting of hydrated magnesium iron phosphate, occurring in metamorphic rocks. Formula: $(Mg,Fe)Al_2(PO_4)_2(OH)_2$. [C19: from Medieval Latin *lāzulum* azure, LAPIS LAZULI]

lazurite (ˈlæzjʊˌraɪt) *n* a rare blue mineral consisting of a sodium aluminium silicate and sulphide: used as the gemstone lapis lazuli. Formula: $Na_{4-5}Al_3Si_3O_{12}S$. [C19: from Medieval Latin *lāzur* LAPIS LAZULI]

lazy (ˈleɪzɪ) *adj* **lazier, laziest. 1** not inclined to work or exertion. **2** conducive to or causing indolence. **3** moving in a languid or sluggish manner: *a lazy river.* **4** (of a brand letter or mark on livestock) shown as lying on its side. [C16: origin uncertain] ▸ **ˈlazily** *adv* ▸ **ˈlaziness** *n*

lazy bed *n* (in parts of Scotland and Ireland, formerly) a patch in which potatoes were cultivated by laying them on the surface and covering them with kelp and with soil from a trench on either side of the bed.

lazybones (ˈleɪzɪˌbəʊnz) *n Informal.* a lazy person.

lazy daisy stitch *n* an embroidery stitch consisting of a long chain stitch, usually used in making flower patterns.

lazy Susan *n* a revolving tray, often divided into sections, for holding condiments, etc.

lazy tongs *pl n* a set of tongs with extensible arms to allow objects to be grasped or handled at a distance.

lb *abbrev. for:* **1** *Cricket.* leg bye. **2** Also: **lb.** pound (weight). [Latin: *libra*]

LB *international car registration for* Liberia.

lbf *abbrev. for* pound force. See **pound**[2] (sense 4).

LBJ *abbrev. for* Lyndon Baines Johnson.

LBO *abbrev. for* leveraged buyout.

LBV *abbrev. for* Late Bottled Vintage: applied to port wine that has been matured in casks for six years and is then ready for drinking.

lbw *Cricket. abbrev. for* leg before wicket.

lc *abbrev. for:* **1** left centre (of a stage, etc.). **2** loco citato. [Latin: in the place cited] **3** *Printing.* lower case.

LC (in the U.S.) *abbrev. for* Library of Congress.

L/C, l/c, *or* **lc** *abbrev. for* letter of credit.

lcd *or* **LCD** *abbrevs. for* lowest common denominator.

LCD *abbrev. for* liquid-crystal display.

l'chaim (ləˈxɑjim) *interj, n* a variant spelling of **lechaim.**

LCJ *Brit. abbrev. for* Lord Chief Justice.

LCL *or* **lcl** *Commerce. abbrev. for* less than carload lot.

lcm *or* **LCM** *abbrev. for* lowest common multiple.

L/Cpl *abbrev. for* lance corporal.

ld *abbrev. for* load.

Ld *abbrev. for* Lord (title).

LD *abbrev. for:* **1** lethal dosage: usually used with a subscript numeral showing what percentage of a test group of animals dies as a result of either being fed a substance being tested on them or being exposed to ionizing radiation, esp. in the median lethal dose: LD_{50}. **2** Low Dutch.

L-D converter *n Metallurgy.* a vessel in which steel is made from pig iron by blowing oxygen into the molten metal through a water-cooled tube. [C20: L(inz)-D(onawitz), from the Austrian towns of *Linz* and *Donawitz,* where the process was first used successfully]

Ldg *abbrev. for* leading: *Ldg seaman.*

LDL *abbrev. for* low-density lipoprotein.

L-dopa (ɛl'dəupə) *n* a substance occurring naturally in the body and used to treat Parkinson's disease. Formula: $C_9H_{11}NO_4$. Also called: **levodopa.** [C20: from *L-d(ihydr)o(xy)p(henyl)a(lanine)*]

L-driver *n Brit.* a learner-driver: a person who is learning to drive, has not yet passed the official driving test, and must be accompanied by a qualified driver and display L-plates on the car.

LDS *abbrev. for:* **1** Latter-day Saints. **2** laus Deo semper. [Latin: praise be to God for ever] **3** (in Britain) Licentiate in Dental Surgery.

LE *abbrev. for* lupus erythematosus.

-le *suffix forming verbs.* denoting repeated or continuous action, often of a diminutive nature: *twiddle; wriggle; wrestle.* [from Middle English *-len,* Old English *-lian,* with similar significance]

lea[1] (li:) *n* **1** *Poetic.* a meadow or field. **2** land that has been sown with grass seed. [Old English *lēah;* related to German dialect *loh* thicket]

lea[2] (li:) *n* **1** a unit for measuring lengths of yarn, usually taken as 80 yards for wool, 120 yards for cotton and silk, and 300 yards for linen. **2** a measure of yarn expressed as the length per unit weight, usually the number of leas per pound. [C14: of uncertain origin]

LEA (in Britain) *abbrev. for* Local Education Authority.

lea. *abbrev. for:* **1** league. **2** leather.

leach[1] (li:tʃ) *vb* **1** to remove or be removed from a substance by a percolating liquid. **2** to lose or cause to lose soluble substances by the action of a percolating liquid. **3** another word for **percolate** (senses 1, 2). ♦ *n* **4** the act or process of leaching. **5** a substance that is leached or the constituents removed by leaching. **6** a porous vessel for leaching. [C17: variant of obsolete *letch* to wet, perhaps from Old English *leccan* to water; related to LEAK] ▸ **'leacher** *n*

leach[2] (li:tʃ) *n* a variant spelling of **leech**[2].

Leach (li:tʃ) *n* **Bernard** (**Howell**). 1887–1979, British potter, born in Hong Kong.

leachate ('li:tʃeɪt) *n* water that carries salts dissolved out of materials through which it has percolated, esp. polluted water from a refuse tip.

Leacock ('li:kɒk) *n* **Stephen Butler.** 1869–1944, Canadian humorist and economist: his comic works include *Literary Lapses* (1910) and *Frenzied Fiction* (1917).

lead[1] (li:d) *vb* **leads, leading, led** (lɛd). **1** to show the way to (an individual or a group) by going with or ahead: *lead the party into the garden.* **2** to guide or be guided by holding, pulling, etc.: *he led the horse by its reins.* **3** (*tr*) to cause to act, feel, think, or behave in a certain way; induce; influence: *he led me to believe that he would go.* **4** (*tr*) to phrase a question to (a witness) that tends to suggest the desired answer. **5** (when *intr,* foll. by *to*) (of a road, route, etc.) to serve as the means of reaching a place. **6** (*tr*) to go ahead so as to indicate (esp. in the phrase **lead the way**). **7** to guide, control, or direct: *to lead an army.* **8** (*tr*) to direct the course of or conduct (water, a rope or wire, etc.) along or as if along a channel. **9** to initiate the action of (something); have the principal part in (something): *to lead a discussion.* **10** to go at the head of or have the top position in (something): *he leads his class in geography.* **11** (*intr;* foll. by *with*) to have as the first or principal item: *the newspaper led with the royal birth.* **12** *Music.* **12a** *Brit.* to play first violin in (an orchestra). **12b** (*intr*) (of an instrument or voice) to be assigned an important entry in a piece of music. **13** to direct and guide (one's partner) in a dance. **14** (*tr*) **14a** to pass or spend: *I lead a miserable life.* **14b** to cause to pass a life of a particular kind: *to lead a person a dog's life.* **15** (*intr;* foll. by *to*) to tend (to) or result (in): *this will only lead to misery.* **16** to initiate a round of cards by putting down (the first card) or to have the right to do this: *she led a diamond.* **17** (*tr*) to aim at a point in front of (a moving target) in shooting, etc., in order to allow for the time of flight. **18** (*intr*) *Boxing.* to make an offensive blow, esp. as one's habitual attacking punch: *southpaws lead with their right.* **19 lead astray.** to mislead so as to cause error or wrongdoing. **20 lead by the nose.** See **nose** (sense 12). ♦ *n* **21a** the first, foremost, or most prominent place. **21b** (*as modifier*): *lead singer.* **22** example, precedence, or leadership: *the class followed the teacher's lead.* **23** an advance or advantage held over others: *the runner had a lead of twenty yards.* **24** anything that guides or directs; indication; clue. **25** another name for **leash. 26** the act or prerogative of playing the first card in a round of cards or the card so played. **27** the principal role in a play, film, etc., or the person playing such a role. **28a** the principal news story in a newspaper: *the scandal was the lead in the papers.* **28b** the opening paragraph of a news story. **28c** (*as modifier*): *lead story.* **29** *Music.* an important entry assigned to one part usually at the beginning of a movement or section. **30** a wire, cable, or other conductor for making an electrical connection. **31** *Boxing.* **31a** one's habitual attacking punch. **31b** a blow made with this. **32** *Nautical.* the direction in which a rope runs. **33** a deposit of metal or ore; lode. **34** the firing of a gun, missile, etc., ahead of a moving target to correct for the time of flight of the projectile. ♦ See also **lead off, lead on, lead up to.** [Old English *lǣdan;* related to *līthan* to travel, Old High German *līdan* to go]

lead[2] (lɛd) *n* **1** a heavy toxic bluish-white metallic element that is highly malleable: occurs principally as galena and used in alloys, accumulators, cable sheaths, paints, and as a radiation shield. Symbol: Pb; atomic no.: 82; atomic wt.: 207.2; valency: 2 or 4; relative density: 11.35; melting pt.: 327.502°C; boiling pt.: 1750°C. Related adjs.: **plumbic, plumbeous, plumbous. 2** a lead weight suspended on a line used to take soundings of the depth of water. **3 swing the lead.** to malinger or make up excuses. **4** lead weights or shot, as used in cartridges, fishing lines, etc. **5** a thin grooved strip of lead for holding small panes of glass or pieces of stained glass. **6** (*pl*) **6a** thin sheets or strips of lead used as a roof covering. **6b** a flat or low-pitched roof covered with such sheets. **7** *Printing.* a thin strip of type metal used for spacing between lines of hot-metal type. Compare **reglet** (sense 2). **8a** graphite or a mixture containing graphite, clay, etc., used for drawing. **8b** a thin stick of this material, esp. the core of a pencil. **9** (*modifier*) of, consisting of, relating to, or containing lead. **10 go down like a lead balloon.** See **balloon** (sense 9). ♦ *vb* (*tr*) **11** to fill or treat with lead. **12** to surround, cover, or secure with lead or leads. **13** *Printing.* to space (type) by use of leads. [Old English; related to Dutch *lood,* German *Lot*] ▸ **'leadless** *adj* ▸ **'leady** *adj*

lead acetate (lɛd) *n* a white crystalline toxic solid used in dyeing cotton and in making varnishes and enamels. Formula: $Pb(CH_3CO)_2$. Systematic name: **lead(II) acetate.** Also called: **sugar of lead.**

lead arsenate (lɛd) *n* a white insoluble toxic crystalline powder used as an insecticide and fungicide. Formula: $Pb_3(AsO_4)_2$.

Leadbelly ('lɛd,bɛlɪ) *n* real name *Huddie Ledbetter.* 1888–1949, U.S. blues singer and guitarist.

lead chromate (lɛd) *n Chem.* a yellow solid used as a pigment, as in chrome yellow. Formula: $PbCrO_4$.

lead colic (lɛd) *n* a symptom of lead poisoning characterized by intense abdominal pain. Also called: **painter's colic.**

leaded ('lɛdɪd) *adj* **1** (of windows) composed of small panes of glass held in place by thin grooved strips of lead: *leaded lights.* **2** (of petrol) containing tetraethyl lead in order to improve combustion.

leaden ('lɛdᵊn) *adj* **1** heavy and inert. **2** laboured or sluggish: *leaden steps.* **3** gloomy, spiritless, or lifeless. **4** made partly or wholly of lead. **5** of a dull greyish colour: *a leaden sky.* ▸ **'leadenly** *adv* ▸ **'leadenness** *n*

leader ('li:də) *n* **1** a person who rules, guides, or inspires others; head. **2** *Music.* **2a** Also called (esp. U.S. and Canadian): **concertmaster.** the principal first violinist of an orchestra, who plays solo parts, and acts as the conductor's deputy and spokesman for the orchestra. **2b** *U.S.* a conductor or director of an orchestra or chorus. **3a** the first man on a climbing rope. **3b** the leading horse or dog in a team. **4** *Chiefly U.S. and Canadian.* an article offered at a sufficiently low price to attract customers. See also **loss leader. 5** a statistic or index that gives an advance indication of the state of the economy. **6** *Chiefly Brit.* Also called: **leading article.** the leading editorial in a newspaper. **7** *Angling.* another word for **trace**[2] (sense 2) or **cast** (sense 32a). **8** *Nautical.* another term for **fairlead. 9** a strip of blank film or tape used to facilitate threading a projector, developing machine, etc., and to aid identification. **10** (*pl*) *Printing.* rows of dots or hyphens used to guide the reader's eye across a page, as in a table of contents. **11** *Botany.* any of the long slender shoots that grow from the stem or branch of a tree: usually removed during pruning. **12** *Brit.* a member of the Government having primary authority in initiating legislative business (esp. in the phrases **Leader of the House of Commons** and **Leader of the House of Lords**). **13** the senior barrister, usually a Queen's Counsel, in charge of the conduct of a case. Compare **junior** (sense 6). ▸ **'leaderless** *adj*

leadership ('li:dəʃɪp) *n* **1** the position or function of a leader. **2** the period during which a person occupies the position of leader: *during her leadership very little was achieved.* **3a** the ability to lead. **3b** (*as modifier*): *leadership qualities.* **4** the leaders as a group of a party, union, etc.: *the union leadership is now very reactionary.*

lead glass (lɛd) *n* glass that contains lead oxide as a flux.

lead-in ('li:d,ɪn) *n* **1a** an introduction to a subject. **1b** (*as modifier*): *a lead-in announcement.* **2** the connection between a radio transmitter, receiver, etc., and the aerial or transmission line.

leading[1] ('li:dɪŋ) *adj* **1** guiding, directing, or influencing. **2** (*prenominal*) principal or primary. **3** in the first position: *the leading car in the procession.* **4** *Maths.* (of a coefficient) associated with the term of highest degree in a polynomial containing one variable: *in* $5x^2 + 2x + 3$, *5 is the leading coefficient.* ▸ **'leadingly** *adv*

leading[2] ('lɛdɪŋ) *n Printing.* the spacing between lines of photocomposed or digitized type. Also called **interlinear spacing.**

leading aircraftman ('li:dɪŋ) *n Brit. airforce.* the rank above aircraftman. ▸ **leading aircraftwoman** *fem n*

leading article ('li:dɪŋ) *n Journalism.* **1** another term for **leader** (sense 6). **2** *Chiefly U.S.* the article given most prominence in a magazine or newspaper.

leading dog *n N.Z.* a dog trained to lead a flock of sheep to prevent them breaking or stampeding.

leading edge ('li:dɪŋ) *n* **1** the forward edge of a propeller blade, aerofoil, or wing. Compare **trailing edge. 2** *Electrical engineering.* the part of a pulse signal that has an increasing amplitude. ♦ *modifier.* **leading-edge. 3** advanced; foremost: *leading-edge technology.*

leading light ('li:dɪŋ) *n* **1** an important or outstanding person, esp. in an organization or cause. **2** *Nautical.* a less common term for **range light.**

leading man ('li:dɪŋ) *n* a man who plays the main part in a film, play, etc. ▸ **leading lady** *fem n*

leading note ('li:dɪŋ) *n Music.* **1** another word for **subtonic. 2** (esp. in cadences) a note, usually the subtonic of a scale, that tends most naturally to resolve to the note lying one semitone above it.

leading question ('li:dɪŋ) *n* a question phrased in a manner that tends to suggest the desired answer, such as *What do you think of the horrible effects of pollution?*

leading rating *n* a rank in the Royal Navy comparable but junior to that of a corporal in the army.

leading reins *or U.S. and Canadian* **leading strings** ('li:dɪŋ) *pl n* **1** straps or a harness and strap used to assist and control a child who is learning to walk. **2** excessive guidance or restraint.

lead line (lɛd) *n Nautical.* a length of line for swinging a lead, marked at various points to indicate multiples of fathoms.

lead monoxide (lɛd) *n* a poisonous insoluble oxide of lead existing in red and yellow forms: used in making glass, glazes, and cements, and as a pigment. Formula: PbO. Systematic name: **lead(II) oxide.** Also called: **litharge, plumbous oxide.**

lead off (li:d) *vb (adv)* **1** to initiate the action of (something); begin. ◆ *n* **lead-off. 2** an initial move or action. **3** a person or thing that begins something.

lead on (li:d) *vb (tr, adv)* to lure or entice, esp. into trouble or wrongdoing.

lead pencil (lɛd) *n* a pencil in which the writing material is a thin stick of a graphite compound.

lead poisoning (lɛd) *n* **1** Also called: **plumbism, saturnism.** acute or chronic poisoning by lead or its salts, characterized by abdominal pain, vomiting, convulsions, and coma. **2** *U.S. slang.* death or injury resulting from being shot with bullets.

lead screw (li:d) *n* a threaded rod that drives the tool carriage in a lathe when screw cutting, etc.

leadsman ('lɛdzmən) *n, pl* **-men.** *Nautical.* a sailor who takes soundings with a lead line.

lead tetraethyl (lɛd) *n* another name for **tetraethyl lead.**

lead time (li:d) *n* **1** *Manufacturing.* the time between the design of a product and its production. **2** *Commerce.* the time from the placing of an order to the delivery of the goods.

lead up to (li:d) *vb (intr, adv + prep)* **1** to act as a preliminary or introduction to. **2** to approach (a topic) gradually or cautiously.

leadwort ('lɛd,wɜ:t) *n* any shrub of the plumbaginaceous genus *Plumbago,* of tropical and subtropical regions, with red, blue, or white flowers.

leaf (li:f) *n, pl* **leaves** (li:vz). **1** the main organ of photosynthesis and transpiration in higher plants, usually consisting of a flat green blade attached to the stem directly or by a stalk. Related adjs.: **foliar, foliate. 2** foliage collectively. **3 in leaf.** (of shrubs, trees, etc.) having a full complement of foliage leaves. **4** one of the sheets of paper in a book. **5** a hinged, sliding, or detachable part, such as an extension to a table. **6** metal in the form of a very thin flexible sheet: *gold leaf.* **7** a foil or thin strip of metal in a composite material; lamina. **8** short for **leaf spring. 9** the inner or outer wall of a cavity wall. **10** a crop that is harvested in the form of leaves. **11** a metal strip forming one of the laminations in a leaf spring. **12** a slang word for **marijuana. 13 take a leaf out of** (*or* **from**) **someone's book.** to imitate someone, esp. in one particular course of action. **14 turn over a new leaf.** to begin a new and improved course of behaviour. ◆ *vb* **15** (when *intr,* usually foll. by *through*) to turn (through pages, sheets, etc.) cursorily. **16** (*intr*) (of plants) to produce leaves. [Old English; related to Gothic *laufs,* Icelandic *lauf*] ▸ **'leafless** *adj* ▸ **'leaflessness** *n* ▸ **'leaf,like** *adj*

leafage ('li:fɪdʒ) *n* a less common word for **foliage.**

leaf beet *n* another name for **chard.**

leaf beetle *n* any of a large family of beetles (*Chrysomelidae*) that includes more than 25,000 species, mostly leaf feeders and mostly brightly coloured, with a metallic sheen. It includes the notorious **Colorado beetle,** the **bloody-nosed beetle,** and the **flea beetles** (*Phyllotreta* species) which attack young cabbage plants.

leaf-climber *n* a plant that climbs by using leaves specialized as tendrils.

leafcutter ant ('li:f,kʌtə) *n* any of various South American ants of the genus *Atta* that cut pieces of leaves and use them as fertilizer for the fungus on which they feed.

leafcutter bee *n* any of various solitary bees of the genus *Megachile* that nest in soil or rotten wood, constructing the cells in which they lay their eggs from pieces of leaf.

leaf fat *n* the dense fat that accumulates in layers around the kidneys of certain animals, esp. pigs.

leaf gap *n Botany.* a region of parenchyma cells in the vascular tissue of flowering plants and some ferns, situated above a leaf trace.

leaf-hopper *n* any homopterous insect of the family *Cicadellidae,* including various pests of crops.

leaf insect *n* any of various mostly tropical Asian insects of the genus *Phyllium* and related genera, having a flattened leaflike body: order *Phasmida.* See also **stick insect.**

leaf-lard *n* lard prepared from the leaf fat of a pig.

leaflet ('li:flɪt) *n* **1** a printed and usually folded sheet of paper for distribution, usually free and containing advertising material or information about a political party, charity, etc. **2** any of the subdivisions of a compound leaf such as a fern leaf. **3** any small leaf or leaflike part. ◆ *vb* **4** to distribute printed leaflets (to): *they leafleted every flat in the area.* ▸ **'leafleter** *n*

leaf miner *n* **1** any of various insect larvae that bore into and feed on leaf tissue, esp. the larva of dipterous flies of the genus *Philophylla* (family *Trypetidae*) and the caterpillar of moths of the family *Gracillariidae.* **2** the adult insect of any of these larvae.

leaf monkey *n* another name for **langur.**

leaf mould *n* **1** a nitrogen-rich material consisting of decayed leaves, etc., used as a fertilizer. **2** any of various fungus diseases affecting the leaves of certain plants.

leaf sheath *n Botany.* a sheath covering the base of a grass stem.

leaf sight *n* a folding rear sight on certain rifles.

leaf spot *n* any of various plant diseases, usually caused by fungi: characterized by dark lesions on the leaves.

leaf spring *n* **1** one of a number of metal strips bracketed together in length to form a compound spring. **2** the compound spring so formed.

leafstalk ('li:f,stɔ:k) *n* the stalk attaching a leaf to a stem or branch. Technical name: **petiole.**

leaf trace *n Botany.* a vascular bundle connecting the vascular tissue of the stem with that of a leaf.

leafy ('li:fɪ) *adj* **leafier, leafiest. 1** covered with or having leaves. **2** resembling a leaf or leaves. ▸ **'leafiness** *n*

league[1] (li:g) *n* **1** an association or union of persons, nations, etc., formed to promote the interests of its members. **2** an association of sporting clubs that organizes matches between member teams of a similar standard. **3** a class, category, or level: *he is not in the same league.* **4 in league (with).** working or planning together with. **5** (*modifier*) of, involving, or belonging to a league: *a league game; a league table.* ◆ *vb* **leagues, leaguing, leagued. 6** to form or be formed into a league. [C15: from Old French *ligue,* from Italian *liga,* ultimately from Latin *ligāre* to bind]

league[2] (li:g) *n* an obsolete unit of distance of varying length. It is commonly equal to 3 miles. [C14 *leuge,* from Late Latin *leuga, leuca,* of Celtic origin]

league football *n* **1** Also called: **league.** *Chiefly Austral.* rugby league football. **2** *Austral.* an Australian Rules competition conducted within a league rather than a football association.

League of Nations *n* an international association of states founded in 1920 with the aim of preserving world peace: dissolved in 1946.

leaguer[1] ('li:gə) *n Archaic.* **1** an encampment, esp. of besiegers. **2** the siege itself. [C16: from Dutch *leger* siege; related to LAIR[1]]

leaguer[2] ('li:gə) *n Chiefly U.S. and Canadian.* a member of a league.

league table *n Brit.* **1** a tabulated comparison of clubs or teams competing in a sporting league. **2** a set of statistics used to compare the performance of a number of individuals, groups, or institutions: *a league table of examination results.*

Leah ('lɪə) *n Old Testament.* the first wife of Jacob and elder sister of Rachel, his second wife (Genesis 29).

leak (li:k) *n* **1a** a crack, hole, etc., that allows the accidental escape or entrance of fluid, light, etc. **1b** such escaping or entering fluid, light, etc. **2 spring a leak.** to develop a leak. **3** something resembling this in effect: *a leak in the defence system.* **4** the loss of current from an electrical conductor because of faulty insulation, etc. **5** a disclosure, often intentional, of secret information. **6** the act or an instance of leaking. **7** a slang word for **urination.** ◆ *vb* **8** to enter or escape or allow to enter or escape through a crack, hole, etc. **9** (when *intr,* often foll. by *out*) to disclose (secret information), often intentionally, or (of secret information) to be disclosed. **10** (*intr*) a slang word for **urinate.** [C15: from Scandinavian; compare Old Norse *leka* to drip] ▸ **'leaker** *n*

leakage ('li:kɪdʒ) *n* **1** the act or an instance of leaking. **2** something that escapes or enters by a leak. **3** *Commerce.* an allowance made for partial loss (of stock, etc.) due to leaking. **4** *Physics.* **4a** an undesired flow of electric current, neutrons, etc., **4b** (*as modifier*): *leakage current.*

Leakey ('li:kɪ) *n* **1 Louis Seymour Bazett** ('bæzɪt). 1903–72, British anthropologist and archaeologist, settled in Kenya. He discovered fossil remains of manlike apes in E Africa. **2** his son **Richard.** born 1944, Kenyan anthropologist, who discovered the remains of primitive man over 2 million years old in E Africa.

leaky ('li:kɪ) *adj* **leakier, leakiest.** leaking or tending to leak. ▸ **'leakiness** *n*

leal (li:l) *adj Archaic or Scot.* loyal; faithful. [C13: from Old French *leial,* from Latin *lēgālis* LEGAL; related to LOYAL] ▸ **'leally** *adv* ▸ **lealty** ('li:əltɪ) *n*

Leamington Spa ('lɛmɪŋtən) *n* a town in central England, in central Warwickshire: saline springs. Pop.: 55 396 (1991). Official name: **Royal Leamington Spa.**

lean[1] (li:n) *vb* **leans, leaning; leaned** *or* **leant. 1** (foll. by *against, on,* or *upon*) to rest or cause to rest against a support. **2** to incline or cause to incline from a vertical position. **3** (*intr;* foll. by *to* or *towards*) to have or express a tendency or leaning. **4 lean over backwards.** *Informal.* to make a special effort, esp. in order to please. ◆ *n* **5** the condition of inclining from a vertical position. ◆ See also **lean on.** [Old English *hleonian, hlinian;* related to Old High German *hlinēn,* Latin *clīnāre* to INCLINE]

lean[2] (li:n) *adj* **1** (esp. of a person or an animal) having no surplus flesh or bulk; not fat or plump. **2** not bulky or full. **3** (of meat) having little or no fat. **4** not rich, abundant, or satisfying. **5** (of a mixture of fuel and air) containing insufficient fuel and too much air: *a lean mixture.* **6** (of printer's type) having a thin appearance. **7** (of a paint) containing relatively little oil. **8** (of an ore) not having a high mineral content. **9** (of concrete) made with a small amount of cement. ◆ *n* **10** the part of meat that contains little or no fat. [Old English *hlǣne,* of Germanic origin] ▸ **'leanly** *adv* ▸ **'leanness** *n*

Lean (li:n) *n* Sir **David.** 1908–91, English film director. His films include *In Which We Serve* (1942), *Blithe Spirit* (1945), *Brief Encounter* (1946), *Great Expectations* (1946), *Oliver Twist* (1948), *The Bridge on the River Kwai* (1957), *Lawrence of Arabia* (1962), *Dr Zhivago* (1965), and *A Passage to India* (1984).

lean-burn *adj* (esp. of an internal-combustion engine) designed to use a lean mixture of fuel and air in order to reduce petrol consumption and exhaust emissions.

Leander (lɪ'ændə) *n* (in Greek legend) a youth of Abydos, who drowned in the Hellespont in a storm on one of his nightly visits to Hero, his beloved. See also **Hero**[1].

leaning ('li:nɪŋ) *n* a tendency or inclination.

lean on *vb (intr, prep)* **1** Also: **lean upon.** to depend on for advice, support, etc. **2** *Informal.* to exert pressure on (someone), as by threats or intimidation.

leant (lɛnt) *vb* a past tense and past participle of **lean**[1].

lean-to *n, pl* **-tos. 1** a roof that has a single slope with its upper edge adjoining a wall or building. **2** a shed or outbuilding with such a roof.

leap (liːp) *vb* **leaps, leaping; leapt** *or* **leaped. 1** (*intr*) to jump suddenly from one place to another. **2** (*intr; often foll. by at*) to move or react quickly. **3** (*tr*) to jump over. **4** to come into prominence rapidly: *the thought leapt into his mind.* **5** (*tr*) to cause (an animal, esp. a horse) to jump a barrier. ◆ *n* **6** the act of jumping. **7** a spot from which a leap was or may be made. **8** the distance of a leap. **9** an abrupt change or increase. **10** Also called (U.S. and Canadian): **skip.** *Music.* a relatively large melodic interval, esp. in a solo part. **11 a leap in the dark.** an action performed without knowledge of the consequences. **12 by leaps and bounds.** with unexpectedly rapid progress. [Old English *hlēapan;* related to Gothic *hlaupan,* German *laufen*] ▸ **'leaper** *n*

leapfrog ('liːp,frɒg) *n* **1** a children's game in which each player in turn leaps over the others' bent backs, leaning on them with the hands and spreading the legs wide. ◆ *vb* **-frogs, -frogging, -frogged. 2a** (*intr*) to play leapfrog. **2b** (*tr*) to leap in this way over (something). **3** to advance or cause to advance by jumps or stages.

leap second *n* a second added to or removed from a scale for reckoning time on one particular occasion, to synchronize it with another scale.

leapt (lɛpt, liːpt) *vb* a past tense and past participle of **leap.**

leap year *n* a calendar year of 366 days, February 29 (**leap day**) being the additional day, that occurs every four years (those whose number is divisible by four) except for century years whose number is not divisible by 400. It offsets the difference between the length of the solar year (365.2422 days) and the calendar year of 365 days.

Lear (lɪə) *n* **Edward.** 1812–88, English humorist and painter, noted for his illustrated nonsense poems and limericks.

lea-rig ('liː,rɪg) *n Scot.* a ridge of unploughed land. [Old English *lǣghrycg*]

learn (lɜːn) *vb* **learns, learning; learned** (lɜːnd) *or* **learnt. 1** (when *tr, may take a clause as object*) to gain knowledge of (something) or acquire skill in (some art or practice). **2** (*tr*) to commit to memory. **3** (*tr*) to gain by experience, example, etc. **4** (*intr;* often foll. by *of* or *about*) to become informed; know. **5** *Not standard.* to teach. [Old English *leornian;* related to Old High German *lirnen*] ▸ **'learnable** *adj* ▸ **'learner** *n*

learned ('lɜːnɪd) *adj* **1** having great knowledge or erudition. **2** involving or characterized by scholarship. **3** (*prenominal*) a title applied in referring to a member of the legal profession, esp. to a barrister: *my learned friend.* ▸ **'learnedly** *adv* ▸ **'learnedness** *n*

learned helplessness *n* the act of giving up trying as a result of consistent failure to be rewarded in life, thought to be a cause of depression.

learner's chain *n N.Z.* an inexperienced team of slaughtermen working in a freezing works.

learning ('lɜːnɪŋ) *n* **1** knowledge gained by study; instruction or scholarship. **2** the act of gaining knowledge. **3** *Psychol.* any relatively permanent change in behaviour that occurs as a direct result of experience.

learning curve *n* a graphical representation of progress in learning: *I'm still only half way up the learning curve.*

learnt (lɜːnt) *vb* a past tense and past participle of **learn.**

lease[1] (liːs) *n* **1** a contract by which property is conveyed to a person for a specified period, usually for rent. **2** the instrument by which such property is conveyed. **3** the period of time for which it is conveyed. **4** a prospect of renewed health, happiness, etc.: *a new lease of life.* ◆ *vb* (*tr*) **5** to grant possession of (land, buildings, etc.) by lease. **6** to take a lease of (property); hold under a lease. [C15: via Anglo-French from Old French *lais* (n), from *laissier* to let go, from Latin *laxāre* to loosen] ▸ **'leasable** *adj* ▸ **'leaser** *n*

lease[2] (liːz) *n Dialect.* open pasture or common. [Old English *lǣs;* perhaps related to Old Norse *lāth* property]

leaseback ('liːs,bæk) *n* a property transaction in which the buyer leases the property to the seller.

leasehold ('liːs,həʊld) *n* **1** land or property held under a lease. **2** the tenure by which such property is held. **3** (*modifier*) held under a lease.

leaseholder ('liːs,həʊldə) *n* **1** a person in possession of leasehold property. **2** a tenant under a lease.

leash (liːʃ) *n* **1** a line or rope used to walk or control a dog or other animal; lead. **2** something resembling this in function: *he kept a tight leash on his emotions.* **3** *Hunting.* three of the same kind of animal, usually hounds, foxes, or hares. **4 straining at the leash.** eagerly impatient to begin something. ◆ *vb* **5** (*tr*) to control or secure by or as if by a leash. [C13: from Old French *laisse,* from *laissier* to loose (hence, to let a dog run on a leash), ultimately from Latin *laxus* LAX]

least (liːst) *determiner* **1a the.** the superlative of **little:** *you have the least talent of anyone.* **1b** (*as pronoun; functioning as sing*): *least isn't necessarily worst.* **2 at least. 2a** if nothing else: *you should at least try.* **2b** at the least. **3 at the least.** Also: **at least.** at the minimum: *at the least you should earn a hundred pounds.* **4 in the least.** (*usually used with a negative*) in the slightest degree; at all: *I don't mind in the least.* ◆ *adv* **5 the least.** superlative of **little:** *they travel the least of all.* ◆ *adj* **6** of very little importance or rank. [Old English *lǣst,* superlative of *lǣssa* LESS]

least common denominator *n* another name for **lowest common denominator.**

least common multiple *n* another name for **lowest common multiple.**

least squares *n* a method for determining the best value of an unknown quantity relating one or more sets of observations or measurements, esp. to find a curve that best fits a set of data. It states that the sum of the squares of the deviations of the experimentally determined value from its optimum value should be a minimum.

leastways ('liːst,weɪz) *or U.S. and Canadian* **leastwise** *adv Informal.* at least; anyway; at any rate.

leat (liːt) *n Brit.* a trench or ditch that conveys water to a mill wheel. [Old English *-gelǣt* (as in *wætergelǣt* water channel), from LET[1]]

leather ('lɛðə) *n* **1a** a material consisting of the skin of an animal made smooth and flexible by tanning, removing the hair, etc. **1b** (*as modifier*): *leather goods.* Related adjs.: **coriaceous, leathern. 2** (*pl*) leather clothes, esp. as worn by motorcyclists. **3** the flap of a dog's ear. ◆ *vb* (*tr*) **4** to cover with leather. **5** to whip with or as if with a leather strap. [Old English *lether-* (in compound words); related to Old High German *leder,* Old Norse *lethr-*]

leatherback ('lɛðə,bæk) *n* a large turtle, *Dermochelys coriacea,* of warm and tropical seas, having a ridged leathery carapace: family *Dermochelidae.* Also called (in Britain): **leathery turtle.**

leather beetle *n* see **dermestid.**

leatherette (,lɛðə'rɛt) *n* an imitation leather made from paper, cloth, etc.

leatherhead ('lɛðə,hɛd) *n* another name for **friarbird.**

Leatherhead ('lɛðə,hɛd) *n* a town in S England, in Surrey. Pop.: 42 903 (1991).

leatherjacket ('lɛðə,dʒækɪt) *n* **1** any of various tropical carangid fishes of the genera *Oligoplites* and *Scomberoides,* having a leathery skin. **2** any of various brightly coloured tropical triggerfishes of the genus *Monacanthus* and related genera. **3** the greyish-brown tough-skinned larva of certain craneflies, esp. of the genus *Tipula,* which destroy the roots of grasses, etc.

leathern ('lɛðən) *adj Archaic.* made of or resembling leather.

leatherneck ('lɛðə,nɛk) *n Slang.* a member of the U.S. Marine Corps. [from the custom of facing the neckband of their uniform with leather]

leatherwood ('lɛðə,wʊd) *n* **1** Also called: **wicopy.** a North American thymelaeaceous shrub, *Dirca palustris,* with pale yellow flowers and tough flexible branches. **2** any of various Australian shrubs of the family *Cunoniaceae.*

leathery ('lɛðərɪ) *adj* having the appearance or texture of leather, esp. in toughness. ▸ **'leatheriness** *n*

leave[1] (liːv) *vb* **leaves, leaving, left.** (*mainly tr*) **1** (*also intr*) to go or depart (from a person or place). **2** to cause to remain behind, often by mistake, in a place: *he often leaves his keys in his coat.* **3** to cause to be or remain in a specified state: *paying the bill left him penniless.* **4** to renounce or abandon: *to leave a political movement.* **5** to refrain from consuming or doing something: *the things we have left undone.* **6** to result in; cause: *childhood problems often leave emotional scars.* **7** to allow to be or remain subject to another person or thing: *leave the past to look after itself.* **8** to entrust or commit: *leave the shopping to her.* **9** to submit in place of one's personal appearance: *will you leave your name and address?* **10** to pass in a specified direction: *flying out of the country, we left the cliffs on our left.* **11** to be survived by (members of one's family): *he leaves a wife and two children.* **12** to bequeath or devise: *he left his investments to his children.* **13** (*tr*) to have as a remainder: *37 – 14 leaves 23.* **14** *Not standard.* to permit; let. **15 leave be.** *Informal.* to leave undisturbed. **16 leave go** *or* **hold of.** *Not standard.* to stop holding. **17 leave it at that.** *Informal.* to take a matter no further. **18 leave much to be desired.** to be very unsatisfactory. **19 leave (someone) alone. 19a** Also: **let alone.** See **let**[1] (sense 7). **19b** to permit to stay or be alone. **20 leave someone to himself.** not to control or direct someone. ◆ See also **leave behind, leave off, leave out.** [Old English *lǣfan;* related to *belīfan* to be left as a remainder] ▸ **'leaver** *n*

leave[2] (liːv) *n* **1** permission to do something: *he was granted leave to speak.* **2 by** *or* **with your leave.** with your permission. **3** permission to be absent, as from a place of work or duty: *leave of absence.* **4** the duration of such absence: *ten days' leave.* **5** a farewell or departure (esp. in the phrase **take (one's) leave**). **6 on leave.** officially excused from work or duty. **7 take leave (of).** to say farewell (to). **8 take leave of one's senses.** to go mad or become irrational. [Old English *lēaf;* related to *alӯfan* to permit, Middle High German *loube* permission]

leave[3] (liːv) *vb* **leaves, leaving, leaved.** (*intr*) to produce or grow leaves.

leave behind *vb* (*tr*) **1** (*adv*) to forget or neglect to bring or take. **2** to cause to remain as a result or sign of something: *the storm left a trail of damage behind.* **3** to pass: *once the wind came up, we soon left the land behind us.*

leaved (liːvd) *adj* **a** having a leaf or leaves; leafed. **b** (*in combination*): *a five-leaved stem.*

leaven ('lɛvᵊn) *n also* **leavening. 1** any substance that produces fermentation in dough or batter, such as yeast, and causes it to rise. **2** a piece of such a substance kept to ferment a new batch of dough. **3** an agency or influence that produces a gradual change. ◆ *vb* (*tr*) **4** to cause fermentation in (dough or batter). **5** to pervade, causing a gradual change, esp. with some moderating or enlivening influence. [C14: via Old French ultimately from Latin *levāmen* relief, (hence, raising agent, leaven), from *levāre* to raise]

Leavenworth ('lɛvᵊn,wɜːθ, -wəθ) *n* a city in NE Kansas, on the Missouri River: the state's oldest city, founded in 1854 by proslavery settlers from Missouri. Pop.: 38 495 (1990).

leave of absence *n* **1** permission to be absent from work or duty. **2** the period of absence.

leave off *vb* **1** (*intr*) to stop; cease. **2** (*tr, adv*) to stop wearing or using.

leave out *vb* (*tr, adv*) **1** to cause to remain in the open: *you can leave your car out tonight.* **2** to omit or exclude.

leaves (liːvz) *n* the plural of **leaf.**

leave-taking *n* the act of departing; a farewell.

leavings ('liːvɪŋz) *pl n* something remaining, such as food on a plate, residue, refuse, etc.

Leavis ('liːvɪs) *n* **F(rank) R(aymond).** 1895–1978, English literary critic. He edited *Scrutiny* (1932–53) and his books include *The Great Tradition* (1948) and *The Common Pursuit* (1952). ▸ **'Leavis,ite** *adj, n*

Lebanon ('lɛbənən) *n* (sometimes preceded by *the*) a republic in W Asia, on the Mediterranean: an important centre of the Phoenician civilization in the third millennium B.C.; part of the Ottoman Empire from 1516 until 1919; gained independence in 1941 (effective by 1945). Official language: Arabic; French and

English are also widely spoken. Religion: Muslim and Christian. Currency: Lebanese pound. Capital: Beirut. Pop.: 3 506 000 (1998 est.). Area: 10 400 sq. km (4015 sq. miles). ▸ **Lebanese** (ˌlɛbəˈniːz) *adj, n*

Lebanon Mountains *pl n* a mountain range in central Lebanon, extending across the whole country parallel with the Mediterranean coast. Highest peak: 3104 m (10 184 ft.). Arabic name: **Jebel Liban** (ˈdʒɛbəl ˈliːbɑːn).

leben (ˈlɛbən) *n* a semiliquid food made from curdled milk in N Africa and the Levant. [C17: from Arabic *laban*]

Lebensraum (ˈleɪbənzˌraʊm) *n* territory claimed by a nation or state on the grounds that it is necessary for survival or growth. [German, literally: living space]

lebkuchen (ˈleɪbˌkuːkən) *n pl* **-chen.** a biscuit, originating from Germany, usually containing honey, spices, etc. [German: literally, loaf cake]

Leblanc (*French* ləblɑ̃) *n* **Nicolas** (nikɔla). ?1742–1806, French chemist, who invented a process for the manufacture of soda from common salt.

Lebowa (ləˈbəʊə) *n* a former Bantu homeland in NE South Africa, consisting of three separate territories with several smaller exclaves: abolished in 1993.

Lebrun (*French* ləbrœ̃) *n* **1 Albert** (albɛr). 1871–1950, French statesman; president (1932–40). **2** Also: **Le Brun. Charles** (ʃarl). 1619–90, French historical painter. He was court painter to Louis XIV and executed much of the decoration of the palace of Versailles.

LEC (lɛk) *n acronym for* Local Enterprise Company. See **Training Agency.**

Le Carré (lə ˈkæreɪ) *n* **John,** real name *David John Cornwell.* born 1931, English novelist, esp. of spy thrillers such as *The Spy who came in from the Cold* (1963), *Tinker, Tailor, Soldier, Spy* (1974), *Smiley's People* (1980), *A Perfect Spy* (1986), and *The Tailor of Panama* (1996).

Le Cateau (*French* lə kato) *n* a town in NE France: site (August 26, 1914) of the largest British battle since Waterloo, which led to the disruption of the German attack on the Allies. Pop.: 9205 (latest est.).

Lecce (*Italian* ˈlettʃe) *n* a walled city in SE Italy, in Puglia: Greek and Roman remains. Pop.: 100 046 (1996 est.).

lech *or* **letch** (lɛtʃ) *Informal.* ◆ *vb* **1** (*intr;* usually foll. by *after*) to behave lecherously (towards); lust (after). ◆ *n* **2** a lecherous act or indulgence. [C19: back formation from LECHER]

Lech (lɛk; *German* lɛç) *n* a river in central Europe, rising in SW Austria and flowing generally north through S Germany to the River Danube. Length: 285 km (177 miles).

lechaim, lehaim, *or* **l'chaim** (ləˈxɑjim) *Judaism.* ◆ *interj* **1** a drinking toast. ◆ *n* **2** a small drink with which to toast something or someone. [from Hebrew, literally: to life]

Le Chatelier's principle (lə ʃæˈtɛljeɪz) *n Chem.* the principle that if a system in chemical equilibrium is subjected to a disturbance it tends to change in a way that opposes this disturbance. [C19: named after H. L. *Le Chatelier* (1850–1936), French chemist]

lecher (ˈlɛtʃə) *n* a promiscuous or lewd man. [C12: from Old French *lecheor* lecher, from *lechier* to lick, of Germanic origin; compare Old High German *leccōn* to lick]

lecherous (ˈlɛtʃərəs) *adj* characterized by or inciting lechery. ▸ **ˈlecherously** *adv*

lechery (ˈlɛtʃərɪ) *n, pl* **-eries.** unrestrained and promiscuous sexuality.

lecithin (ˈlɛsɪθɪn) *n Biochem.* any of a group of phospholipids that are found in many plant and animal tissues, esp. egg yolk: used in making candles, cosmetics, and inks, and as an emulsifier and stabilizer in foods (**E322**). Systematic name: **phosphatidylcholine.** [C19: from Greek *lekithos* egg yolk]

lecithinase (ləˈsɪθɪˌneɪs) *n* any of a group of enzymes that remove the fatty-acid residue from lecithins: present in the venom of many snakes.

Lecky (ˈlɛkɪ) *n* **William Edward Hartpole** (ˈhɑːtˌpəʊl). 1838–1903, Irish historian; author of *The History of England in the 18th Century* (1878–90).

Leclanché cell (ləˈklɑːnʃeɪ) *n Electrical engineering.* a primary cell with a carbon anode, surrounded by crushed carbon and manganese dioxide in a porous container, immersed in an electrolyte of aqueous ammonium chloride into which the zinc cathode dips. The common dry battery is a form of Leclanché cell. [C19: named after Georges *Leclanché* (1839–82), French engineer]

Leconte de Lisle (*French* ləkɔ̃t də lil) *n* **Charles Marie René** (ʃarl mari rəne). 1818–94, French Parnassian poet.

Le Corbusier (*French* lə kɔrbyzje) *n* real name *Charles Édouard Jeanneret.* 1887–1965, French architect and town planner, born in Switzerland. He is noted for his use of reinforced concrete and for his modular system, which used units of a standard size. His works include Unité d'Habitation at Marseilles (1946–52) and the city of Chandigarh, India (1954).

Le Creusot (*French* lə krøzo) *n* a town in E central France: metal, machinery, and armaments industries. Pop.: 33 274 (1983 est.).

lect. *abbrev. for:* **1** lecture. **2** lecturer.

lectern (ˈlɛktən) *n* **1** a reading desk or support in a church. **2** any similar desk or support. [C14: from Old French *lettrun,* from Late Latin *lectrum,* ultimately from *legere* to read]

lectin (ˈlɛktɪn) *n* a type of protein possessing high affinity for a specific sugar; lectins are often highly toxic. [C20: from Latin *lectus,* past participle of *legere* to select + -IN]

lection (ˈlɛkʃən) *n* a variant reading of a passage in a particular copy or edition of a text. [C16: from Latin *lectio* a reading, from *legere* to read, select]

lectionary (ˈlɛkʃənərɪ) *n, pl* **-aries.** a book containing readings appointed to be read at divine services. [C15: from Church Latin *lectiōnārium,* from *lectio* LECTION]

lector (ˈlɛktɔː) *n* **1** a lecturer or reader in certain universities. **2** *R.C. Church.* **2a** a person appointed to read lessons at certain services. **2b** (in convents or monastic establishments) a member of the community appointed to read aloud during meals. [C15: from Latin, from *legere* to read] ▸ **lectorate** (ˈlɛktərɪt) *or* **ˈlectorˌship** *n*

lecture (ˈlɛktʃə) *n* **1** a discourse on a particular subject given or read to an audience. **2** the text of such a discourse. **3** a method of teaching by formal discourse. **4** a lengthy reprimand or scolding. ◆ *vb* **5** to give or read a lecture (to an audience or class). **6** (*tr*) to reprimand at length. [C14: from Medieval Latin *lectūra* reading, from *legere* to read]

lecturer (ˈlɛktʃərə) *n* **1** a person who lectures. **2** a teacher in higher education without professorial status.

lectureship (ˈlɛktʃəˌʃɪp) *n* **1** the office or position of lecturer. **2** an endowment financing a series of lectures.

lecythus (ˈlɛsɪθəs) *n, pl* **-thi** (-θaɪ). (in ancient Greece) a vase with a narrow neck. [from Greek *lēkuthos*]

led (lɛd) *vb* the past tense and past participle of **lead**[1].

LED *Electronics. abbrev. for* light-emitting diode.

Leda[1] (ˈliːdə) *n Greek myth.* a queen of Sparta who was the mother of Helen and Pollux by Zeus, who visited her in the form of a swan.

Leda[2] (ˈliːdə) *n Astronomy.* a small satellite of Jupiter in an intermediate orbit.

LED display *n* a flat-screen device in which an array of light-emitting diodes can be selectively activated to display numerical and alphabetical information, used esp. in pocket calculators, digital timepieces, measuring instruments, and in some microcomputers.

Lederberg (ˈlɛdəˌbɜːg) *n* **Joshua.** born 1925, U.S. geneticist, who discovered the phenomenon of transduction in bacteria. Nobel prize for physiology or medicine 1958 with George Beadle and Edward Tatum.

lederhosen (ˈleɪdəˌhəʊzən) *pl n* leather shorts with H-shaped braces, worn by men in Austria, Bavaria, etc. [German: leather trousers]

ledge (lɛdʒ) *n* **1** a narrow horizontal surface resembling a shelf and projecting from a wall, window, etc. **2** a layer of rock that contains an ore; vein. **3** a ridge of rock that lies beneath the surface of the sea. **4** a narrow shelflike rock projection on a cliff or mountain. [C14 *legge,* perhaps from *leggen* to LAY[1]] ▸ **ˈledgy** *or* **ledged** *adj*

ledger (ˈlɛdʒə) *n* **1** *Book-keeping.* the principal book in which the commercial transactions of a company are recorded. **2** a flat horizontal slab of stone. **3** a horizontal scaffold pole fixed to two upright poles for supporting the outer ends of putlogs. **4** *Angling.* **4a** a wire trace that allows the weight to rest on the bottom and the bait to float freely. **4b** (*as modifier*): *ledger tackle.* ◆ *vb* **5** (*intr*) *Angling.* to fish using a ledger. [C15 *legger* book retained in a specific place, probably from *leggen* to LAY[1]]

ledger board *n* **1** a timber board forming the top rail of a fence or balustrade. **2** Also called: **ribbon strip.** a timber board fixed horizontally to studding to support floor joists.

ledger line *n* **1** *Music.* a short line placed above or below the staff to accommodate notes representing pitches above or below the staff. **2** *Angling.* a line using ledger tackle.

lee (liː) *n* **1** a sheltered part or side; the side away from the direction from which the wind is blowing. **2 by the lee.** *Nautical.* so that the wind is blowing on the wrong side of the sail. **3 under the lee.** *Nautical.* towards the lee. ◆ *adj* **4** (*prenominal*) *Nautical.* on, at, or towards the side or part away from the wind: *on a lee shore.* Compare **weather** (sense 5). [Old English *hlēow* shelter; related to Old Norse *hlé*]

Lee[1] (liː) *n* a river in SW Republic of Ireland, flowing east into Cork Harbour. Length: about 80 km (50 miles).

Lee[2] (liː) *n* **1 Bruce,** original name *Lee Yuen Kam.* 1940–73, U.S. film actor and kung fu expert who starred in such films as *Enter the Dragon* (1973). **2 Gypsy Rose,** original name *Rose Louise Hovick.* 1914–70, U.S. striptease and burlesque artiste, who appeared in the Ziegfeld Follies (1936) and in films. **3 Laurie** (ˈlɒrɪ). 1914–97, British poet and writer, best known for the autobiographical *Cider with Rosie* (1959). **4 Richard Henry.** 1732–94, American Revolutionary statesman, who moved the resolution in favour of American independence (1776). **5 Robert E(dward).** 1807–70, American general; commander-in-chief of the Confederate armies in the Civil War. **6 Spike,** real name *Shelton Jackson Lee.* born 1957, U.S. film director: his films include *She's Gotta Have It* (1985), *Malcolm X* (1992), and *He Got Game* (1998). **7 T(sung)-D(ao)** (tsuːŋ daʊ). born 1926, U.S. physicist, born in China. With Yang he disproved the principle that parity is always conserved and shared the Nobel prize for physics in 1957.

leeboard (ˈliːˌbɔːd) *n Nautical.* one of a pair of large adjustable paddle-like boards that may be lowered along the lee side to reduce sideways drift or leeway.

leech[1] (liːtʃ) *n* **1** any annelid worm of the class *Hirudinea,* which have a sucker at each end of the body and feed on the blood or tissues of other animals. See also **horseleech, medicinal leech. 2** a person who clings to or preys on another person. **3a** an archaic word for **physician. 3b** (*in combination*): *leechcraft.* **4 cling like a leech.** to cling or adhere persistently to something. ◆ *vb* **5** (*tr*) to use leeches to suck the blood of (a person), as a method of medical treatment. [Old English *lǣce, lœce;* related to Middle Dutch *lieke*] ▸ **ˈleechˌlike** *adj*

leech[2] *or* **leach** (liːtʃ) *n Nautical.* the after edge of a fore-and-aft sail or either of the vertical edges of a squaresail. [C15: of Germanic origin; compare Dutch *lijk*]

Leeds[1] (liːdz) *n* **1** a city in N England, in Leeds unitary authority, West Yorkshire on the River Aire: linked with Liverpool and Goole by canals; a former centre of the clothing industry; university (1904). Pop.: 424 194 (1991). **2** a unitary authority in N England, in West Yorkshire. Pop.: 724 400 (1994 est.). Area 562 sq. km (217 sq. miles).

Leeds[2] (liːdz) *n* **1st Duke of.** See (1st Earl of) **Danby.**

Leeds Castle *n* a castle near Maidstone in Kent: the home of several medieval queens of England.

leek (liːk) *n* **1** Also called: **scallion.** an alliaceous plant, *Allium porrum,* with a slender white bulb, cylindrical stem, and broad flat overlapping leaves: used in cooking. **2** any of several related species, such as *A. ampeloprasum* (wild leek). **3** a leek, or a representation of one, as a national emblem of Wales. [Old English *lēac;* related to Old Norse *laukr,* Old High German *louh*]

leer (lɪə) *vb* **1** (*intr*) to give an oblique, sneering, or suggestive look or grin. ◆ *n* **2** such a look. [C16: perhaps verbal use of obsolete *leer* cheek, from Old English *hlēor*] ► **'leering** *adj, n* ► **'leeringly** *adv*

leery *or* **leary** ('lɪərɪ) *adj* **leerier, leeriest** *or* **learier, leariest. 1** *Now chiefly dialect.* knowing or sly. **2** *Slang.* (foll. by *of*) suspicious or wary. [C18: perhaps from obsolete sense (to look askance) of LEER] ► **'leeriness** *or* **'leariness** *n*

lees (liːz) *pl n* the sediment from an alcoholic drink. [C14: plural of obsolete *lee,* from Old French, probably from Celtic; compare Irish *lige* bed]

leet[1] (liːt) *n English history.* **1** Also called: **court-leet.** a special kind of manorial court that some lords were entitled to hold. **2** the jurisdiction of this court. [C15: from Anglo-French, of unknown origin]

leet[2] (liːt) *n Scot.* a list of candidates for an office. [C15: perhaps from Anglo-French *litte,* variant of LIST[1]]

Leeuwarden (*Dutch* 'leːwɑrdə) *n* a city in the N Netherlands, capital of Friesland province. Pop.: 87 464 (1994).

Leeuwenhoek ('leɪvᵊn,huːk, *Dutch* 'leːwənhuːk) *n* **Anton van** ('ɑntɔn vɑn). 1632–1723, Dutch microscopist, whose microscopes enabled him to give the first accurate description of blood corpuscles, spermatozoa, and microbes.

leeward ('liːwəd; *nautical* 'luːəd) *Chiefly nautical.* ◆ *adj* **1** of, in, or moving to the quarter towards which the wind blows. ◆ *n* **2** the point or quarter towards which the wind blows. **3** the side towards the lee. ◆ *adv* **4** towards the lee. ◆ Compare **windward.**

Leeward Islands ('liːwəd) *pl n* **1** a group of islands in the Caribbean, in the N Lesser Antilles between Puerto Rico and Martinique. **2** a former British colony in the E Caribbean (1871–1956), consisting of Antigua, Barbuda, Redonda, Saint Kitts, Nevis, Anguilla, Montserrat, and the British Virgin Islands. **3** a group of islands in the S Pacific, in French Polynesia in the W Society Archipelago: Huahiné, Raiatéa, Tahaa, Bora-Bora, and Maupiti. Pop.: 22 232 (1988). French name: **Îles sous le Vent.**

lee wave *n Meteorol.* a stationary wave sometimes formed in an air stream on the leeward side of a hill or mountain range.

leeway ('liː,weɪ) *n* **1** room for free movement within limits, as in action or expenditure. **2** sideways drift of a boat or aircraft.

Le Fanu ('lɛfənjuː) *n* **(Joseph) Sheridan.** 1814–73, Irish writer, best known for his stories of mystery and the supernatural, esp. *Uncle Silas* (1864) and the collection *In a Glass Darkly* (1872).

Lefkoşa (lef'koʃə) *n* the Turkish name for **Nicosia.**

left[1] (lɛft) *adj* **1** (*usually prenominal*) of or designating the side of something or someone that faces west when the front is turned towards the north. **2** (*usually prenominal*) worn on a left hand, foot, etc. **3** (*sometimes cap.*) of or relating to the political or intellectual left. **4** (*sometimes cap.*) radical or progressive, esp. as compared to less radical or progressive groups, persons, etc. ◆ *adv* **5** on or in the direction of the left. ◆ *n* **6** a left side, direction, position, area, or part. Related adjs.: **sinister, sinistral. 7** (*often cap.*) the supporters or advocates of varying degrees of social, political, or economic change, reform, or revolution designed to promote the greater freedom, power, welfare, or comfort of the common people. **8 to the left.** radical in the methods, principles, etc., employed in striving to achieve such change. **9** *Boxing.* **9a** a blow with the left hand. **9b** the left hand. [Old English *left* idle, weak, variant of *lyft-* (in *lyftādl* palsy, literally: left-disease); related to Middle Dutch *lucht* left]

left[2] (lɛft) *vb* the past tense and past participle of **leave**[1].

Left Bank *n* a district of Paris, on the S bank of the River Seine; frequented by artists, students, etc.

left-field *adj Informal.* regarded as being outside the mainstream; unconventional. [C20: from baseball term *left field,* the area of the outfield to the batter's left, regarded as the scene of little action]

left-footer *n Informal.* (esp. in Ireland and Scotland) a Roman Catholic. [C20: from the Northern Irish saying that farm workers in Eire use the left foot to push a spade when digging]

left-hand *adj* (*prenominal*) **1** of, relating to, located on, or moving towards the left: *this car is left-hand drive; a left-hand bend.* **2** for use by the left hand; left-handed.

left-handed *adj* **1** using the left hand with greater ease than the right. **2** performed with the left hand. **3** designed or adapted for use by the left hand. **4** worn on the left hand. **5** awkward or clumsy. **6** ironically ambiguous: *a left-handed compliment.* **7** turning from right to left; anticlockwise. **8** *Law.* another term for **morganatic.** ◆ *adv* **9** with the left hand. ► **,left-'handedly** *adv* ► **,left-'handedness** *n*

left-hander *n* **1** a blow with the left hand. **2** a left-handed person.

leftist ('lɛftɪst) *adj* **1** of, tending towards, or relating to the political left or its principles. ◆ *n* **2** a person who supports or belongs to the political left. ► **'leftism** *n*

left-luggage office *n Brit.* a place at a railway station, airport, etc., where luggage may be left for a small charge with an attendant for safekeeping. U.S. and Canadian name: **checkroom.**

leftover ('lɛft,əʊvə) *n* **1** (*often pl*) an unused portion or remnant, as of material or of cooked food. ◆ *adj* **2** left as an unused portion or remnant.

leftward ('lɛftwəd) *adj* **1** on or towards the left. ◆ *adv* **2** a variant of **leftwards.**

leftwards ('lɛftwədz) *or* **leftward** *adv* towards or on the left.

left wing *n* **1** (*often cap.*) the leftist faction of an assembly, party, group, etc.; the radical or progressive wing. **2** the units of an army situated on the left of a battle position. **3** *Sport.* **3a** the left-hand side of the field of play from the point of view of either team facing its opponents' goal. **3b** a player positioned in this area in certain games. ◆ *adj* **left-wing. 4** of, belonging to, or relating to the political left wing. ► **,left-'winger** *n*

lefty ('lɛftɪ) *n, pl* **lefties.** *Informal.* **1** a left-winger. **2** *Chiefly U.S. and Canadian.* a left-handed person.

leg (lɛg) *n* **1a** either of the two lower limbs, including the bones and fleshy covering of the femur, tibia, fibula, and patella. **1b** (*as modifier*): *leg guard; leg rest.* Related adj: **crural. 2** any similar or analogous structure in animals that is used for locomotion or support. **3** this part of an animal, esp. the thigh, used for food: *leg of lamb.* **4** something similar to a leg in appearance or function, such as one of the four supporting members of a chair. **5** a branch, limb, or part of a forked or jointed object. **6** the part of a garment that covers the leg. **7** a section or part of a journey or course. **8** a single stage, lap, length, etc., in a relay race. **9** *Austral. and N.Z.* either one of two races on which a cumulative bet has been placed. **10** either the opposite or adjacent side of a right-angled triangle. **11** *Nautical.* **11a** the distance travelled without tacking. **11b** (in yacht racing) the course between any two marks. **12** one of a series of games, matches, or parts of games. **13** *Cricket.* **13a** the side of the field to the left of a right-handed batsman as he faces the bowler. **13b** (*as modifier*): *a leg slip; leg stump.* **14 give (someone) a leg up. 14a** to help (someone) to climb an obstacle by pushing upwards. **14b** to help (someone) to advance. **15 not have a leg to stand on.** to have no reasonable or logical basis for an opinion or argument. **16 on his, its, etc., last legs.** (of a person or thing) worn out; exhausted. **17 pull (someone's) leg.** *Informal.* to tease, fool, or make fun of (someone). **18 shake a leg.** *Informal.* **18a** to hurry up: usually used in the imperative. **18b** to dance. **19 show a leg.** *Informal.* to get up in the morning. **20 stretch one's legs.** See **stretch** (sense 17). ◆ *vb* **legs, legging, legged. 21** (*tr*) *Obsolete.* to propel (a canal boat) through a tunnel by lying on one's back and walking one's feet along the tunnel roof. **22 leg it.** *Informal.* to walk, run, or hurry. [C13: from Old Norse *leggr,* of obscure origin] ► **'leg,like** *adj*

leg. *abbrev. for:* **1** legal. **2** legate. **3** legato. **4** legislation. **5** legislative. **6** legislature.

legacy ('lɛgəsɪ) *n, pl* **-cies. 1** a gift by will, esp. of money or personal property. **2** something handed down or received from an ancestor or predecessor. **3** (*modifier*) surviving computer systems, hardware, or software: *legacy network: legacy application.* [C14 (meaning: office of a legate), C15 (meaning: bequest): from Medieval Latin *lēgātia* commission; see LEGATE]

legal ('liːgᵊl) *adj* **1** established by or founded upon law; lawful. **2** of or relating to law. **3** recognized, enforceable, or having a remedy at law rather than in equity. **4** relating to or characteristic of the profession of law. [C16: from Latin *lēgālis,* from *lēx* law] ► **'legally** *adv*

legal aid *n* financial assistance available to persons unable to meet the full cost of legal proceedings.

legal cap *n U.S.* ruled writing paper, about 8 by 13½ inches with the fold at the top, for use by lawyers.

legalese (,liːgə'liːz) *n* the conventional language in which legal documents, etc., are written.

legal holiday *n U.S.* any of several weekdays which are observed as national holidays. Also called (Canadian): **statutory holiday.** Brit. equivalent: **bank holiday.**

legalism ('liːgə,lɪzəm) *n* strict adherence to the law, esp. the stressing of the letter of the law rather than its spirit. ► **'legalist** *n, adj* ► **,legal'istic** *adj* ► **,legal'istically** *adv*

legality (lɪ'gælɪtɪ) *n, pl* **-ties. 1** the state or quality of being legal or lawful. **2** adherence to legal principles.

legalize *or* **legalise** ('liːgə,laɪz) *vb* (*tr*) **1** to make lawful or legal. **2** to confirm or validate (something previously unlawful). ► **,legali'zation** *or* **,legali'sation** *n*

legal medicine *n* another name for **forensic medicine.**

legal positivism *n* another name for **positivism** (sense 2).

legal separation *n* another term (esp. U.S.) for **judicial separation.**

legal tender *n* currency in specified denominations that a creditor must by law accept in redemption of a debt.

Legaspi (le'gæspɪ) *n* a port in the Philippines, on SE Luzon on the Gulf of Albay. Pop.: 125 128 (1994 est.).

legate ('lɛgɪt) *n* **1** a messenger, envoy, or delegate. **2** *R.C. Church.* an emissary to a foreign state representing the Pope. [Old English, via Old French from Latin *lēgātus* deputy, from *lēgāre* to delegate; related to *lēx* law] ► **'legate,ship** *n* ► **legatine** ('lɛgə,taɪn) *adj*

legatee (,lɛgə'tiː) *n* a person to whom a legacy is bequeathed. Compare **devisee.**

legation (lɪ'geɪʃən) *n* **1** a diplomatic mission headed by a minister. **2** the official residence and office of a diplomatic minister. **3** the act of sending forth a diplomatic envoy. **4** the mission or business of a diplomatic envoy. **5** the rank or office of a legate. [C15: from Latin *lēgātiō,* from *lēgātus* LEGATE] ► **le'gationary** *adj*

legato (lɪ'gɑːtəʊ) *Music.* ◆ *adj, adv* **1** to be performed smoothly and connectedly. ◆ *n, pl* **tos. 2a** a style of playing in which no perceptible gaps are left between notes. **2b** (*as modifier*): *a legato passage.* [C19: from Italian, literally: bound]

legator (,lɛgə'tɔː) *n* a person who gives a legacy or makes a bequest. [C17: from Latin, from *lēgāre* to bequeath; see LEGATE] ► **,lega'torial** *adj*

leg before wicket *n Cricket.* a manner of dismissal on the grounds that a batsman has been struck on the leg by a bowled ball that otherwise would have hit the wicket. Abbrev.: **lbw.**

leg break *n Cricket.* a bowled ball that spins from leg to off on pitching.

leg bye *n Cricket.* a run scored after the ball has hit the batsman's leg or some other part of his body, except his hand, without touching the bat. Abbrev.: **lb.**

legend ('lɛdʒənd) *n* **1** a popular story handed down from earlier times whose truth has not been ascertained. **2** a group of such stories: *the Arthurian legend.* **3** a modern story that has taken on the characteristics of a traditional legendary tale. **4** a person whose fame or notoriety makes him a source of exaggerated or romanticized tales or exploits. **5** an inscription or title, as on a coin or beneath a coat of arms. **6** explanatory matter accompanying a table, map, chart, etc. **7a** a story of the life of a saint. **7b** a collection of such stories. **[C14** (in the sense: a saint's life or a collection of saints' lives): from Medieval Latin *legenda* passages to be read, from Latin *legere* to read**]** ▸ **'legendry** *n*

legendary ('lɛdʒəndərɪ, -drɪ) *adj* **1** of or relating to legend. **2** celebrated or described in a legend or legends. **3** very famous or notorious.

Legendre (*French* ləʒɑ̃drə) *n* **Adrien Marie** (adriɛ̃ mari). 1752–1833, French mathematician, noted for his work on the theory of numbers, the theory of elliptical functions, and the method of least squares.

Léger (*French* leʒe) *n* **Fernand** (fɛrnɑ̃). 1881–1955, French cubist painter, influenced by industrial technology.

legerdemain (ˌlɛdʒədə'meɪn) *n* **1** another name for **sleight of hand. 2** cunning deception or trickery. **[C15:** from Old French: light of hand**]** ▸ **ˌleger-de'mainist** *n*

leger line ('lɛdʒə) *n* a variant spelling of **ledger line.**

leges ('liːdʒiːz) *n* the plural of **lex.**

legged ('lɛgɪd, lɛgd) *adj* **a** having a leg or legs. **b** (*in combination*): *three-legged; long-legged.*

leggings ('lɛgɪŋz) *pl n* **1** an extra outer covering for the lower legs. **2** close-fitting trousers worn by women and children. ▸ **'legginged** *adj*

leggy ('lɛgɪ) *adj* **-gier, -giest. 1** having unusually long legs. **2** (of a woman) having long and shapely legs. **3** (of a plant) having an unusually long and weak stem. ▸ **'legginess** *n*

leghorn ('lɛgˌhɔːn) *n* **1** a type of Italian wheat straw that is woven into hats. **2** any hat made from this straw when plaited. **[C19:** named after LEGHORN (Livorno)**]**

Leghorn *n* **1** ('lɛgˌhɔːn). the English name for **Livorno. 2** (lɛ'gɔːn). a breed of domestic fowl laying white eggs.

legible ('lɛdʒəbᵊl) *adj* **1** (of handwriting, print, etc.) able to be read or deciphered. **2** able to be discovered; discernible. **[C14:** from Late Latin *legibilis,* from Latin *legere* to read**]** ▸ **ˌlegi'bility** *or* **'legibleness** *n* ▸ **'legibly** *adv*

legion ('liːdʒən) *n* **1** a military unit of the ancient Roman army made up of infantry with supporting cavalry, numbering some three to six thousand men. **2** any large military force: *the French Foreign Legion.* **3** (*usually cap.*) an association of ex-servicemen: *the British Legion.* **4** (*often pl*) any very large number, esp. of people. ◆ *adj* **5** (*usually postpositive*) very large or numerous. **[C13:** from Old French, from Latin *legio,* from *legere* to choose**]**

legionary ('liːdʒənərɪ) *adj* **1** of or relating to a legion. ◆ *n, pl* **-aries. 2** a soldier belonging to a legion.

legionary ant *n* another name for the **army ant.**

legionnaire (ˌliːdʒə'nɛə) *n* (*often cap.*) a member of certain military forces or associations, such as the French Foreign Legion or the British Legion.

legionnaire's *or* **legionnaires' disease** *n* a serious, sometimes fatal, infection, caused by the bacterium *Legionella pneumophila,* which has symptoms similar to those of pneumonia: believed to be spread by inhalation of contaminated water vapour from showers and air-conditioning plants. **[C20:** after the outbreak at a meeting of the American Legion at Philadelphia in 1976**]**

Legion of Honour *n* an order for civil or military merit instituted by Napoleon in France in 1802. French name: **Légion d'honneur** (leʒjɔ̃ dɔnœr).

legis. *abbrev. for:* **1** legislation. **2** legislative. **3** legislature.

legislate ('lɛdʒɪsˌleɪt) *vb* **1** (*intr*) to make or pass laws. **2** (*tr*) to bring into effect by legislation. **[C18:** back formation from LEGISLATOR**]**

legislation (ˌlɛdʒɪs'leɪʃən) *n* **1** the act or process of making laws; enactment. **2** the laws so made.

legislative ('lɛdʒɪslətɪv) *adj* **1** of or relating to legislation. **2** having the power or function of legislating: *a legislative assembly.* **3** of or relating to a legislature. ◆ *n* **4** *Rare.* another word for **legislature.** ▸ **'legislatively** *adv*

legislative assembly *n* (*often caps.*) **1** the bicameral legislature in 28 states of the U.S. **2** the lower chamber of the bicameral state legislatures in several Commonwealth countries, such as Australia. **3** the unicameral legislature in most Canadian provinces. **4** any assembly with legislative powers.

legislative council *n* (*often caps.*) **1** the upper chamber of certain bicameral legislatures, such as those of the Indian and Australian states. **2** the unicameral legislature of certain colonies or dependent territories. **3** (in the U.S.) a committee composed of members of both chambers of a state legislature, that meets to discuss problems, construct a legislative programme, etc.

legislator ('lɛdʒɪsˌleɪtə) *n* **1** a person concerned with the making or enactment of laws. **2** a member of a legislature. **[C17:** from Latin *lēgis lātor,* from *lēx* law + *lātor* from *lātus,* past participle of *ferre* to bring**]** ▸ **'legisˌlatorˌship** *n* ▸ **'legisˌlatress** *fem n*

legislatorial (ˌlɛdʒɪslə'tɔːrɪəl) *adj* of or relating to a legislator or legislature.

legislature ('lɛdʒɪsˌleɪtʃə) *n* a body of persons vested with power to make, amend, and repeal laws. Compare **executive, judiciary.**

legist ('liːdʒɪst) *n* a person versed in the law. **[C15:** from Medieval Latin *lēgista,* from *lēx* law**]**

legit (lɪ'dʒɪt) *Slang.* ◆ *adj* **1** short for **legitimate.** ◆ *n* **2** legitimate or professionally respectable drama.

legitimate *adj* (lɪ'dʒɪtɪmɪt). **1** born in lawful wedlock; enjoying full filial rights. **2** conforming to established standards of usage, behaviour, etc. **3** based on correct or acceptable principles of reasoning. **4** reasonable, sensible, or valid: *a legitimate question.* **5** authorized, sanctioned by, or in accordance with law. **6** of, relating to, or ruling by hereditary right: *a legitimate monarch.* **7** of or relating to a body of famous long-established plays as distinct from films, television, vaudeville, etc.: *the legitimate theatre.* ◆ *vb* (lɪ'dʒɪtɪˌmeɪt). **8** (*tr*) to make, pronounce, or show to be legitimate. **[C15:** from Medieval Latin *lēgitimātus* made legal, from *lēx* law**]** ▸ **le'gitimacy** *or* **le'gitimateness** *n* ▸ **le'gitimately** *adv* ▸ **leˌgiti'mation** *n*

legitimist (lɪ'dʒɪtɪmɪst) *n* **1** a monarchist who supports the rule of a legitimate dynasty or of its senior branch. **2** (formerly) a supporter of the elder line of the Bourbon family in France. **3** a supporter of legitimate authority. ◆ *adj also* **legitimistic. 4** of or relating to legitimists. ▸ **le'gitimism** *n*

legitimize, legitimise (lɪ'dʒɪtɪˌmaɪz) *or* **legitimatize, legitimatise** (lɪ'dʒɪtɪməˌtaɪz) *vb* (*tr*) to make legitimate; legalize. ▸ **leˌgitimi'zation, leˌgitimi'sation** *or* **leˌgitimati'zation, leˌgitimati'sation** *n*

legless ('lɛglɪs) *adj* **1** without legs. **2** *Informal.* very drunk.

legman ('lɛgmən) *n, pl* **-men.** *Chiefly U.S. and Canadian.* **1** a newsman who reports on news stories from the scene of action or original source. **2** a person employed to run errands, collect information, etc., outside an office.

Legnica (*Polish* lɛg'nitsa) *n* an industrial town in SW Poland. Pop.: 108 000 (1996 est.). German name: **Liegnitz.**

Lego ('lɛgəʊ) *n Trademark.* a construction toy consisting of plastic bricks and other standardized components that fit together with studs. **[C20:** from Danish *leg godt* play well**]**

leg-of-mutton *or* **leg-o'-mutton** *n* (*modifier*) (of a sail, sleeve, etc.) tapering sharply or having a triangular profile.

leg-pull *n Brit. informal.* a practical joke or mild deception.

legroom ('lɛgˌruːm) *n* room to move one's legs comfortably, as in a car.

leg rope *Austral. and N.Z.* ◆ *n* **1** a rope used to secure an animal by its hind leg. ◆ *vb* **leg-rope.** (*tr*) **2** to restrain (an animal) by a leg rope.

leguaan ('lɛgjʊən, 'lɛguˌɑːn) *n S. African.* a large amphibious monitor lizard of the genus *Varanus,* esp. *V. niloticus* (the **water leguaan**), which can grow up to 2 or 3 m. Also called: **iguana. [C19:** Dutch, from French *l'iguane* the iguana**]**

legume ('lɛgjuːm, lɪ'gjuːm) *n* **1** the long dry dehiscent fruit produced by leguminous plants; a pod. **2** any table vegetable of the superfamily *Leguminosae,* esp. beans or peas. **3** any leguminous plant. **[C17:** from French *légume,* from Latin *legūmen* bean, from *legere* to pick (a crop)**]**

legumin (lɪ'gjuːmɪn) *n* a protein obtained mainly from the seeds of leguminous plants. **[C19:** from LEGUME**]**

leguminous (lɪ'gjuːmɪnəs) *adj* of, relating to, or belonging to the *Leguminosae* (or *Fabaceae*), a superfamily of flowering plants having pods (or legumes) as fruits and root nodules enabling storage of nitrogen-rich material: includes mimosaceous, caesalpiniaceous, and papilionaceous plants. **[C17:** from Latin *legūmen;* see LEGUME**]**

legwarmer ('lɛgˌwɔːmə) *n* one of a pair of garments resembling stockings without feet, usually knitted and brightly coloured, often worn over jeans, tights, etc. or during exercise.

legwork ('lɛgˌwɜːk) *n Informal.* work that involves travelling on foot or as if on foot.

lehaim (lə'xɑjim) *interj, n* a variant spelling of **lechaim.**

Lehár ('leɪhɑː, lɪ'hɑː) *n* **Franz** (frants). 1870–1948, Hungarian composer of operettas, esp. *The Merry Widow* (1905).

Le Havre (lə 'hɑːvrə; *French* lə ɑvrə) *n* a port in N France, on the English Channel at the mouth of the River Seine: transatlantic trade; oil refining. Pop.: 197 219 (1990).

Lehmann ('leɪmən) *n* **1 Lilli** ('lɪlɪ). 1848–1929, German soprano. **2 Lotte** ('lɒtə). 1888–1976, U.S. soprano, born in Germany. **3 Rosamond (Nina).** 1903–90, British novelist. Her books include *Dusty Answer* (1927), *Invitation to the Waltz* (1932), and *The Echoing Grove* (1953).

Lehmbruck (*German* 'leːmbrʊk) *n* **Wilhelm** ('vɪlhɛlm). 1881–1919, German sculptor and graphic artist.

lehr (lɪə) *n* a long tunnel-shaped oven used for annealing glass. **[**from German: pattern, model**]**

lei[1] (leɪ) *n* (in Hawaii) a garland of flowers, worn around the neck. **[**from Hawaiian**]**

lei[2] (leɪ) *n* the plural of **leu.**

Leibnitz *or* **Leibniz** ('laɪbnɪts) *n* Baron **Gottfried Wilhelm von** ('gɔtfriːt 'vɪlhɛlm fɔn). 1646–1716, German rationalist philosopher and mathematician. He conceived of the universe as a hierarchy of independent units or monads, synchronized by pre-established harmony. His works include *Théodicée* (1710) and *Monadologia* (1714). He also devised a system of calculus, independently of Newton. ▸ **Leib'nitzian** *adj*

Leibnitz Mountains *pl n* a mountain range on the SW limb of the moon, containing the highest peaks (10 000 metres) on the moon.

Leibnitz's law *n Logic, philosophy.* **1** the principle that two expressions satisfy exactly the same predicates if and only if they both refer to the same subject. **2** the weaker principle that if *a=b* whatever is true of *a* is true of *b.*

Leicester[1] ('lɛstə) *n* **1** a city in central England, in Leicester unitary authority, on the River Soar: administrative centre of Leicestershire: Roman remains and a ruined Norman castle; university (1918); light engineering, hosiery, and footwear industries. Pop.: 293 400 (1994 est.). **2** a unitary authority in Central England, mainly comprising Leicester city, in Leicestershire. Pop.: 295 700 (1995 est.). Area: 73 sq. km (28 sq. miles). short for **Leicestershire. 3** a breed of sheep with long wool, originally from Leicestershire. **4** a fairly mild dark orange whole-milk cheese, similar to Cheddar.

Leicester[2] ('lɛstə) *n* **Earl of.** title of *Robert Dudley.* ?1532–88, English courtier; favourite of Elizabeth I. He led an unsuccessful expedition to the Netherlands (1585–87).

Leicestershire ('lɛstəˌʃɪə, -ʃə) *n* a county of central England: absorbed the small historical county of Rutland in 1974; Rutland and Leicester city became independent unitary authorities in 1997: largely agricultural. Administrative centre:

Leicester. Pop.: 592 700 (1995 est.). Area: 2553 sq. km (834 sq. miles). Shortened form: **Leicester.** Abbrev.: **Leics.**

Leichhardt ('laɪk,hɑːt; *German* 'laiçhart) *n* **Friedrich Wilhelm Ludwig** ('friːdrɪç 'vɪlhɛlm 'luːtvɪç). 1813–48, Australian explorer, born in Prussia. He disappeared during an attempt to cross Australia from East to West.

Leics *abbrev. for* Leicestershire.

Leiden *or* **Leyden** ('laɪdᵊn; *Dutch* 'lɛidə) *n* a city in the W Netherlands, in South Holland province: residence of the Pilgrim Fathers for 11 years before they sailed for America in 1620; university (1575). Pop.: 115 473 (1995 est.).

Leif Ericson ('liːf 'ɛrɪksən) *n* See **Ericson.**

Leigh[1] (liː) *n* a town in NW England, in Wigan unitary authority, Greater Manchester: engineering industries. Pop.: 43 150 (1991).

Leigh[2] (liː) *n* **1 Mike.** born 1943, British dramatist and theatre, film, and television director, noted for his use of improvisation. His plays include *Abigail's Party* (1977), and his films include *High Hopes* (1988) and *Secrets and Lies* (1996). **2 Vivien,** real name *Vivian Hartley.* 1913–67, English stage and film actress. Her films include *Gone with the Wind* (1939) and *A Streetcar Named Desire* (1951), for both of which she won Oscars.

Leigh Fermor ('fɛːmɔː) *n* See (Patrick Leigh) **Fermor.**

Leighton ('leɪtən) *n* **Frederic,** 1st Baron Leighton of Stretton. 1830–96, British painter and sculptor of classical subjects: president of the Royal Academy (1878).

Leinster ('lɛnstə) *n* a province of E and SE Republic of Ireland: it consists of the counties of Carlow, Dublin, Kildare, Kilkenny, Laois, Longford, Louth, Meath, Offaly, Westmeath, Wexford, and Wicklow. Pop.: 1 922 000 (1996). Area: 19 632 sq. km (7580 sq. miles).

Leipzig ('laɪpsɪg; *German* 'laiptsɪç) *n* a city in E central Germany, in Saxony: famous fairs, begun about 1170; publishing and music centre; university (1409); scene of a decisive defeat for Napoleon Bonaparte in 1813. Pop.: 470 778 (1996 est.).

Leiria (*Portuguese* lei'riə) *n* a city in central Portugal: site of the first printing press in Portugal (1466). Pop.: 96 583 (1981).

leishmania (liːʃ'meɪnɪə) *n* any parasitic flagellate protozoan of the genus *Leishmania:* occurs in man and animals and causes certain skin diseases. **[C20:** New Latin, named after Sir W.B. *Leishman* (1865–1926), Scottish bacteriologist**]**

leishmaniasis (,liːʃmə'naɪəsɪs) *or* **leishmaniosis** (liːʃ,meɪnɪ'əʊsɪs, -,mæn-) *n* any disease, such as kala-azar, caused by protozoa of the genus *Leishmania.*

leister ('liːstə) *n* **1** a spear with three or more prongs for spearing fish, esp. salmon. ◆ *vb* **2** (*tr*) to spear (a fish) with a leister. **[C16:** from Scandinavian; related to Old Norse *ljōstr,* from *ljōsta* to stab**]**

leisure ('lɛʒə; *U.S. also* 'liːʒər) *n* **1a** time or opportunity for ease, relaxation, etc. **1b** (*as modifier*): *leisure activities.* **2** ease or leisureliness. **3 at leisure. 3a** having free time for ease, relaxation, etc. **3b** not occupied or engaged. **3c** without hurrying. **4 at one's leisure.** when one has free time. **[C14:** from Old French *leisir;* ultimately from Latin *licēre* to be allowed**]**

leisure centre *n* a building designed to provide facilities for a range of leisure pursuits, such as a sports hall, café, and meeting rooms.

leisured ('lɛʒəd) *adj* **1** (*usually prenominal*) having much leisure, as through unearned wealth: *the leisured classes.* **2** unhurried or relaxed: *in a leisured manner.*

leisurely ('lɛʒəlɪ) *adj* **1** unhurried; relaxed. ◆ *adv* **2** without haste; in a relaxed way. ▸ **'leisureliness** *n*

Leith (liːθ) *n* a port in SE Scotland, on the Firth of Forth: part of Edinburgh since 1920.

leitmotif *or* **leitmotiv** ('laɪtməʊ,tiːf) *n* **1** *Music.* a recurring short melodic phrase or theme used, esp. in Wagnerian music dramas, to suggest a character, thing, etc. **2** an often repeated word, phrase, image, or theme in a literary work. **[C19:** from German *leitmotiv* leading motif**]**

Leitrim ('liːtrɪm) *n* a county of N Republic of Ireland in Connacht province, on Donegal Bay: agricultural. County town: Carrick-on-Shannon. Pop.: 25 000 (1996). Area: 1525 sq. km (589 sq. miles).

Leix (liːʃ) *n* another name for **Laois.**

Leizhou ('leɪ'dʒəʊ) *or* **Luichow Peninsula** *n* a peninsula of SE China, in SW Guangdong province, separated from Hainan Island by Hainan Strait.

lek[1] (lɛk) *n* **1** a small area in which birds of certain species, notably the black grouse, gather for sexual display and courtship. **2** the act or practice of so gathering. **[C19:** perhaps from dialect *lake* (vb) from Old English *lácan* to frolic, fight, or perhaps from Swedish *leka* to play**]**

lek[2] (lɛk) *n* the standard monetary unit of Albania, divided into 100 qintars. **[**from Albanian**]**

lekker ('lɛkə) *adj S. African slang.* **1** pleasing or enjoyable. **2** tasty. **[C20:** Afrikaans, from Dutch**]**

Lely ('liːlɪ) *n* Sir **Peter.** Dutch name *Pieter van der Faes.* 1618–80, Dutch portrait painter in England.

LEM (lɛm) *n acronym for* lunar excursion module.

Lemaître (*French* ləmɛtr) *n Abbé* **Georges (Édouard)** (ʒɔrʒ). 1894–1966, Belgian astronomer and priest, who first proposed the big-bang theory of the universe (1927).

leman ('lɛmən, 'liː-) *n Archaic.* **1** a beloved; sweetheart. **2** a lover or mistress. **[**C13 *lemman, leofman,* from *leof* dear, LIEF + MAN**]**

Léman (lemɑ̃) *n* **Lac.** the French name for (Lake) **Geneva.**

Le Mans (*French* lə mɑ̃) *n* a city in NW France: scene of the first experiments in motoring and flying; annual motor race. Pop.: 148 465 (1990).

Lemberg ('lɛmbɛrk) *n* the German name for **Lviv.**

lemma[1] ('lɛmə) *n, pl* **-mas** *or* **-mata** (-mətə). **1** a subsidiary proposition, assumed to be valid, that is used in the proof of another proposition. **2** *Linguistics.* a word considered as its citation form together with all the inflected forms. For example, the lemma *go* consists of *go* together with *goes, going, went,* and *gone.* **3** an argument or theme, esp. when used as the subject or title of a composition. **[C16** (meaning: proposition), **C17** (meaning: title, theme): via Latin from Greek: premise, from *lambanein* to take (for granted)**]**

lemma[2] ('lɛmə) *n, pl* **-mas** *or* **-mata** (-mətə). the outer of two bracts surrounding each floret of a grass inflorescence. **[C19:** from Greek: rind, from *lepein* to peel**]**

lemmatize *or* **lemmatise** ('lɛmə,taɪz) *vb* (*tr*) *Linguistics.* to group together the inflected forms of (a word) for analysis as a single item. ▸ **,lemmati'zation** *or* **,lemmati'sation** *n*

lemming ('lɛmɪŋ) *n* **1** any of various volelike rodents of the genus *Lemmus* and related genera, of northern and arctic regions of Europe, Asia, and North America: family *Cricetidae.* The Scandinavian variety, *Lemmus lemmus,* migrates periodically when its population reaches a peak. **2** a member of any large group following an unthinking course towards mass destruction. **[C17:** from Norwegian; related to Latin *latrāre* to bark**]** ▸ **'lemming-,like** *adj*

lemniscate ('lɛmnɪskɪt) *n* a closed plane curve consisting of two symmetrical loops meeting at a node. Equation: $(x^2 + y^2)^2 = a^2(x^2 - y^2)$, where *a* is the greatest distance from the curve to the origin. The symbol for infinity (∞) is an example.

lemniscus (lɛm'nɪskəs) *n, pl* **-nisci** (-'nɪsaɪ, -'nɪskiː). *Anatomy.* a technical name for **fillet** (sense 9). **[C19:** New Latin, from Latin, from Greek *lēmniskos* ribbon**]**

Lemnos ('lɛmnɒs) *n* a Greek island in the N Aegean Sea: famous for its medicinal earth (**Lemnian seal**). Chief town: Kastron. Pop.: 16 000 (latest est.). Area: 477 sq. km (184 sq. miles). Modern Greek name: **Límnos.** ▸ **Lemnian** ('lɛmnɪən) *adj, n*

lemon ('lɛmən) *n* **1** a small Asian evergreen tree, *Citrus limon,* widely cultivated in warm and tropical regions, having pale green glossy leaves and edible fruits. Related adjs.: **citric, citrine, citrous. 2a** the yellow oval fruit of this tree, having juicy acidic flesh rich in vitamin C. **2b** (*as modifier*): *a lemon jelly.* **3** Also called: **lemon yellow. 3a** a greenish-yellow or strong yellow colour. **3b** (*as adj*): *lemon wallpaper.* **4** a distinctive tart flavour made from or in imitation of the lemon. **5** *Slang.* a person or thing considered to be useless or defective. **[C14:** from Medieval Latin *lemōn-,* from Arabic *laymūn***]** ▸ **'lemonish** *adj* ▸ **'lemon-,like** *adj*

lemonade (,lɛmə'neɪd) *n* a drink made from lemon juice, sugar, and water or from carbonated water, citric acid, etc.

lemon balm *n* the full name of **balm** (sense 5).

lemon cheese *or* **curd** *n* a soft paste made from lemons, sugar, eggs, and butter, used as a spread or filling.

lemon drop *n* a lemon-flavoured boiled sweet.

lemon fish *n* another name for **cobia.**

lemon geranium *n* a cultivated geraniaceous plant, *Pelargonium limoneum,* with lemon-scented leaves.

lemon grass *n* a perennial grass, *Cymbopogon citratus,* with a large flower spike: used in cooking and grown in tropical regions as the source of an aromatic oil (**lemon grass oil**).

lemon sole *n* a European flatfish, *Microstomus kitt,* with a variegated brown body: highly valued as a food fish: family *Pleuronectidae.*

lemon squash *n Brit.* a drink made from a sweetened lemon concentrate and water.

lemon squeezer *n* **1** any of various devices for extracting the juice from citrus fruit. **2** *N.Z. informal.* a peaked hat with four indentations worn by the army on ceremonial occasions.

lemon verbena *n* a tropical American verbenaceous shrub, *Lippia citriodora,* with slender lemon-scented leaves yielding an oil used in perfumery.

lemonwood ('lɛmən,wʊd) *n* a small tree, *Pittosporum eugenioides,* of New Zealand having a white bark and lemon-scented flowers.

lemony ('lɛmənɪ) *adj* **1** having or resembling the taste or colour of a lemon. **2** *Austral. slang.* angry or irritable.

lempira (lɛm'pɪərə) *n* the standard monetary unit of Honduras, divided into 100 centavos. **[**American Spanish, after *Lempira,* Indian chief who opposed the Spanish**]**

lemur ('liːmə) *n* **1** any Madagascan prosimian primate of the family *Lemuridae,* such as *Lemur catta* (the **ring-tailed lemur**). They are typically arboreal, having foxy faces and long tails. **2** any similar or closely related animal, such as a loris or indris. **[C18:** New Latin, adapted from Latin *lemurēs* ghosts; so named by Linnaeus for its ghost-like face and nocturnal habits**]** ▸ **'lemur-,like** *adj*

lemures ('lɛmjʊ,riːz) *pl n Roman myth.* the spirits of the dead. **[**Latin: see LEMUR**]**

lemuroid ('lɛmjʊ,rɔɪd) *or* **lemurine** ('lɛmjʊ,raɪn, -rɪn) *adj* **1** of, relating to, or belonging to the superfamily *Lemuroidea,* which includes the lemurs and indrises. **2** resembling or closely related to a lemur. ◆ *n* **3** an animal that resembles or is closely related to a lemur.

Lena ('liːnə; *Russian* 'ljɛnə) *n* a river in Russia, rising in S Siberia and flowing generally north through the Sakha Republic to the Laptev Sea by an extensive delta: the longest river in Russia. Length: 4271 km (2653 miles).

lend (lɛnd) *vb* **lends, lending, lent** (lɛnt). **1** (*tr*) to permit the use of (something) with the expectation of return of the same or an equivalent. **2** to provide (money) temporarily, often at interest. **3** (*intr*) to provide loans, esp. as a profession. **4** (*tr*) to impart or contribute (something, esp. some abstract quality): *her presence lent beauty.* **5** (*tr*) to provide, esp. in order to assist or support: *he lent his skill to the company.* **6 lend an ear.** to listen. **7 lend itself.** to possess the right characteristics or qualities for: *the novel lends itself to serialization.* **8 lend oneself.** to give support, cooperation, etc. **[C15** *lende* (originally the past tense), from Old English *lǣnan,* from *lǣn* LOAN[1]; related to Icelandic *lāna,* Old High German *lēhanōn***]** ▸ **'lender** *n*

lender of last resort *n* the central bank of a country with authority for controlling its banking system.

lending library *n* **1** Also called (esp. U.S.): **circulating library.** the department of a public library providing books for use outside the building. **2** a small commercial library.

Lendl ('lɛndᵊl) *n* **Ivan** (iː'væn, -'vɑːn). born 1960, Czech tennis player; U.S. Open champion (1985–87).

lend-lease *n* (during World War II) the system organized by the U.S. in 1941 by which equipment and services were provided for countries fighting Germany.

Lenglen (*French* lɑ̃glɑ̃) *n* **Suzanne** (syzan). 1899–1938, French tennis player: Wimbledon champion (1919-25).

length (lɛŋkθ, lɛŋθ) *n* **1** the linear extent or measurement of something from end to end, usually being the longest dimension or, for something fixed, the longest horizontal dimension. **2** the extent of something from beginning to end, measured in some more or less regular units or intervals: *the book was 600 pages in length.* **3** a specified distance, esp. between two positions or locations: *the length of a race.* **4** a period of time, as between specified limits or moments. **5** something of a specified, average, or known size or extent measured in one dimension, often used as a unit of measurement: *a length of cloth.* **6** a piece or section of something narrow and long: *a length of tubing.* **7** the quality, state, or fact of being long rather than short. **8** (*usually pl*) the amount of trouble taken in pursuing or achieving something (esp. in the phrase **to great lengths**). **9** (*often pl*) the extreme or limit of action (in phrases such as **to any length(s), to what length(s) would someone go,** etc.). **10** *Prosody, phonetics.* the metrical quantity or temporal duration of a vowel or syllable. **11** the distance from one end of a rectangular swimming bath to the other. Compare **width** (sense 4). **12** *Prosody.* the quality of a vowel, whether stressed or unstressed, that distinguishes it from another vowel of similar articulatory characteristics. Thus (iː) in English *beat* is of greater length than (ɪ) in English *bit.* **13** *Cricket.* the distance from the batsman at which the ball pitches. **14** *Bridge.* a holding of four or more cards in a suit. **15** *N.Z. informal.* the general idea; the main purpose. **16 at length. 16a** in depth; fully. **16b** eventually. **16c** for a long time; interminably. [Old English *lengthu;* related to Middle Dutch *lengede,* Old Norse *lengd*]

lengthen ('lɛŋkθən, 'lɛŋθən) *vb* to make or become longer. ▸ **'lengthener** *n*

lengthman ('lɛŋkθmən, 'lɛŋθ-) *n, pl* **-men.** *Brit.* a person whose job it is to maintain a particular length of road or railway line.

lengthways ('lɛŋkθ,weɪz, 'lɛŋθ-) *or* **lengthwise** *adv, adj* in, according to, or along the direction of length.

lengthy ('lɛŋkθɪ, 'lɛŋθɪ) *adj* **lengthier, lengthiest.** of relatively great or tiresome extent or duration. ▸ **'lengthily** *adv* ▸ **'lengthiness** *n*

lenient ('liːnɪənt) *adj* **1** showing or characterized by mercy or tolerance. **2** *Archaic.* caressing or soothing. [C17: from Latin *lēnīre* to soothe, from *lēnis* soft] ▸ **'leniency** *or* **'lenience** *n* ▸ **'leniently** *adv*

Lenin ('lɛnɪn) *n* **Vladimir Ilyich** (vla'dimir ilj'jitʃ), original surname *Ulyanov.* 1870–1924, Russian statesman and Marxist theoretician; first premier of the Soviet Union. He formed the Bolsheviks (1903) and led them in the October Revolution (1917), which established the Soviet Government. He adopted the New Economic Policy (1921) after the Civil War had led to the virtual collapse of the Russian economy, formed the Comintern (1919), and was the originator of the guiding doctrine of the Soviet Union, Marxism-Leninism. After the Soviet Union broke up in 1991, many statues of Lenin were demolished.

Leninabad (*Russian* lɪnina'bat) *n* the former name (1937–91) of **Khojent.**

Leninakan (*Russian* lɪnina'kan) *n* the former name (1925–91) of **Kumayri.**

Leningrad ('lɛnɪn,græd; *Russian* lɪnin'grat) *n* the former name (1937–91) of **Saint Petersburg.**

Leninism ('lɛnɪ,nɪzəm) *n* **1** the political and economic theories of Lenin. **2** another name for **Marxism-Leninism.** ▸ **'Leninist** *or* **'Leninite** *n, adj*

Lenin Peak *n* a mountain in Tajikistan; the highest peak in the Trans Alai Range. Height: 7134 m (23 406 ft.).

lenis ('liːnɪs) *Phonetics.* ◆ *adj* **1** (of a consonant) articulated with weak muscular tension. ◆ *n, pl* **lenes** ('liːniːz). **2** a consonant, such as English *b* or *v,* pronounced with weak muscular force. ◆ Compare **fortis.** [C19: from Latin: gentle]

lenitive ('lɛnɪtɪv) *adj* **1** soothing or alleviating pain or distress. ◆ *n* **2** a lenitive drug. [C16: from Medieval Latin *lēnītīvus,* from Latin *lēnīre* to soothe]

lenity ('lɛnɪtɪ) *n, pl* **-ties.** the state or quality of being lenient. [C16: from Latin *lēnitās* gentleness, from *lēnis* soft]

Lennon ('lɛnən) *n* **John** (**Ono**), original name *John Winston Lennon.* 1940–80, English rock guitarist, singer, and songwriter: member of the Beatles (1962–70). His subsequent recordings, many in collaboration with his wife Yoko Ono, include "Instant Karma" (1970), *Imagine* (1971), and *Double Fantasy* (1980). He was assassinated by a demented fan.

leno ('liːnəʊ) *n, pl* **-nos. 1** (in textiles) a weave in which the warp yarns are twisted together in pairs between the weft or filling yarns. **2** a fabric of this weave. [C19: probably from French *linon* lawn, from *lin* flax, from Latin *līnum.* See LINEN]

Leno ('liːnəʊ) *n* **Dan,** original name *George Galvin.* 1860–1904, British music-hall entertainer, noted esp. for his pantomime performances: he died insane.

Le Nôtre (*French* lə notrə) *n* **André** (ɑ̃dre). 1613–1700, French landscape gardener, who created the gardens at Versailles for Louis XIV.

lens (lɛnz) *n* **1** a piece of glass or other transparent material, used to converge or diverge transmitted light and form optical images. **2** Also called: **compound lens.** a combination of such lenses for forming images or concentrating a beam of light. **3** a device that diverges or converges a beam of electromagnetic radiation, sound, or particles. See **electron lens. 4** *Anatomy.* See **crystalline lens.** Related adj: **lenticular.** [C17: from Latin *lēns* lentil, referring to the similarity of a lens to the shape of a lentil]

Lens (lenz; *French* lɑ̃) *n* an industrial town in N France, in the Pas de Calais department; badly damaged in both World Wars. Pop (town).: 35 278 (1990), with a conurbation of 323 174 (1990).

lens hood *n Photog.* an extension piece fixed to a camera lens to shield it from a direct light source.

lent (lɛnt) *vb* the past tense and past participle of **lend.**

Lent (lɛnt) *n* **1** *Christianity.* the period of forty weekdays lasting from Ash Wednesday to Holy Saturday, observed as a time of penance and fasting commemorating Jesus' fasting in the wilderness. **2** (*modifier*) falling within or associated with the season before Easter: *Lent observance.* **3** (*pl*) (at Cambridge University) Lent term boat races. [Old English *lencten, lengten* spring, literally: lengthening (of hours of daylight)]

lentamente (,lɛntə'mɛntɪ) *adv Music.* to be played slowly. [C18: Italian, from LENTO]

lenten ('lɛntən) *adj* **1** (*often cap.*) of or relating to Lent. **2** *Archaic or literary.* spare, plain, or meagre: *lenten fare.* **3** *Archaic.* cold, austere, or sombre: *a lenten lover.*

lentic ('lɛntɪk) *adj Ecology.* of, relating to, or inhabiting still water: *a lentic fauna.* Compare **lotic.** [C20: from Latin *lentus* slow]

lenticel ('lɛntɪ,sɛl) *n* any of numerous pores in the stem of a woody plant allowing exchange of gases between the plant and the exterior. [C19: from New Latin *lenticella,* from Latin *lenticula* diminutive of *lēns* LENTIL] ▸ **lenticellate** (,lɛntɪ'sɛlɪt) *adj*

lenticle ('lɛntɪkᵊl) *n Geology.* a lens-shaped layer of mineral or rock embedded in a matrix of different constitution.

lenticular (lɛn'tɪkjʊlə) *or* **lentiform** ('lɛntɪ,fɔːm) *adj* **1** Also: **lentoid** ('lɛntɔɪd). shaped like a biconvex lens. **2** of or concerned with a lens or lenses. **3** shaped like a lentil seed. **4** of or relating to a galaxy with a large central bulge, small disc, but no spiral arms, intermediate in shape between spiral and elliptical galaxies. [C17: from Latin *lenticulāris* like a LENTIL]

lentigo (lɛn'taɪgəʊ) *n, pl* **lentigines** (lɛn'tɪdʒɪ,niːz). a technical name for a **freckle.** [C14: from Latin, from *lēns* LENTIL] ▸ **len'tiginous** *or* **len'tiginose** *adj*

lentil ('lɛntɪl) *n* **1** a small annual leguminous plant, *Lens culinaris,* of the Mediterranean region and W Asia, having edible brownish convex seeds. **2** any of the seeds of this plant, which are cooked and eaten as a vegetable, in soups, etc. [C13: from Old French *lentille,* from Latin *lenticula,* diminutive of *lēns* lentil]

lentissimo (lɛn'tɪsɪ,məʊ) *adj, adv Music.* to be played very slowly. [Italian, superlative of *lento* slow]

lentivirus ('lɛntɪ,vaɪrəs) *n* any of a group of slowly acting viruses, often affecting the nervous system. [C20: from Latin *lentus* slow + VIRUS]

lent lily *n* another name for the **daffodil.**

lento ('lɛntəʊ) *Music.* ◆ *adj, adv* **1** to be performed slowly. ◆ *n, pl* **-tos. 2** a movement or passage performed in this way. [C18: Italian, from Latin *lentus* slow]

Lent term *n* the spring term at Cambridge University and some other educational establishments.

Lenya ('lɛnjə) *n* **Lotte** ('lɒtɪ), original name *Caroline Blamauer.* 1900–81, Austrian singer and actress, associated esp. with the songs of her husband Kurt Weill.

Lenz's law ('lɛntsɪz) *n Physics.* the principle that the direction of the current induced in a circuit by a changing magnetic field is such that the magnetic field produced by this current will oppose the original field. [C19: named after H. F. E. *Lenz* (1804–65), German physicist]

Leo[1] ('liːəʊ) *n* a name for a lion, used in children's tales, fables, etc. [from Latin: lion]

Leo[2] ('liːəʊ) *n, Latin genitive* **Leonis** (liː'əʊnɪs). **1** *Astronomy.* a zodiacal constellation in the N hemisphere, lying between Cancer and Virgo on the ecliptic, that contains the star Regulus and the radiant of the Leonid meteor shower. **2** *Astrology.* **2a** Also called: the **Lion.** the fifth sign of the zodiac, symbol ♌, having a fixed fire classification and ruled by the sun. The sun is in this sign between about July 23 and Aug. 22. **2b** a person born during a period when the sun is in this sign. ◆ *adj* **3** *Astrology.* born under or characteristic of Leo. ◆ Also (for senses 2b, 3): **Leonian** (liː'əʊnɪən).

Leo I ('liːəʊ) *n* **Saint,** known as *Leo the Great.* ?390–461 A.D., pope (440–461). He extended the authority of the papacy in the West and persuaded Attila not to attack Rome (452). Feast day: Nov. 10 or Feb. 18.

Leo III *n* **1** called *the Isaurian.* ?675–741 A.D., Byzantine emperor (717–41): he checked Arab expansionism and began the policy of iconoclasm, which divided the empire for the next century. **2 Saint.** ?750–816 A.D., pope (795–816). He crowned Charlemagne emperor of the Romans (800). Feast day: June 12.

Leo IX *n* **Saint,** original name *Bruno of Egisheim.* 1002–54, pope (1049–54): first of the great medieval reforming popes. Conflict with the Eastern Church led to the schism between Rome and Constantinople (1054). Feast day: April 19.

Leo X *n* original name *Giovanni de' Medici.* 1475–1521, pope (1513–21): noted for his patronage of Renaissance art and learning; excommunicated Luther (1521).

Leo XIII *n* original name *Gioacchino Pecci.* 1810–1903, pope (1878–1903). His many important encyclicals include *Rerum novarum* (1891) on the need for Roman Catholics to take action on various social problems.

Leoben (*German* le'oːbən) *n* a city in E central Austria, in Styria on the Mur River: lignite mining. Pop.: 28 504 (1991).

Leo Minor *n* a small faint constellation in the N hemisphere lying near Leo and Ursa Major.

León (*Spanish* le'ɔn) *n* **1** a region and former kingdom of NW Spain, which united with Castile in 1230. **2** a city of NW Spain: capital of the kingdom of León (10th century). Pop.: 147 780 (1995 est.). **3** a city in central Mexico, in W

Guanajuato state: commercial centre of a rich agricultural region. Pop.: 867 920 (1990). Official name **León de los Aldamas** (de los 'aldamas). **4** a city in W Nicaragua: one of the oldest towns of Central America, founded in 1524; capital of Nicaragua until 1855; university (1812). Pop.: 171 375 (1994 est.).

Leonard ('lɛnəd) *n* **Sugar Ray**, real name *Ray Charles Leonard.* born 1956, U.S. boxer: the first man to have won world titles at five officially recognized weights.

Leonardo da Vinci (ˌliːəˈnɑːdəu də 'vɪntʃɪ) *n* 1452–1519, Italian painter, sculptor, architect, and engineer: the most versatile talent of the Italian Renaissance. His most famous paintings include *The Virgin of the Rocks* (1483–85), the *Mona Lisa* (or *La Gioconda,* 1503), and the *Last Supper* (?1495–97). His numerous drawings, combining scientific precision in observation with intense imaginative power, reflect the breadth of his interests, which ranged over biology, physiology, hydraulics, and aeronautics. He invented the first armoured tank and foresaw the invention of aircraft and submarines. ▸ **Leonardesque** (ˌliːənɑːˈdɛsk) *adj*

Leonardo of Pisa *n* See (Leonardo) **Fibonacci.**

Leoncavallo (*Italian* leoŋka'vallo) *n* **Ruggiero** (rud'dʒɛːro). 1858–1919, Italian composer of operas, notably *I Pagliacci* (1892).

leone (liːˈəunɪ) *n* the standard monetary unit of Sierra Leone, divided into 100 cents. [C20: from SIERRA LEONE]

Leonid ('liːənɪd) *n, pl* **Leonids** *or* **Leonides** (lɪ'ɒnɪˌdiːz). any member of a meteor shower that is usually insignificant, but more spectacular every 33 years, and occurs annually in mid-November, appearing to radiate from a point in the constellation Leo. [C19: from New Latin *Leōnidēs,* from *leō* lion]

Leonidas (lɪ'ɒnɪˌdæs) *n* died 480 B.C., king of Sparta (?490–480), hero of the Battle of Thermopylae, in which he was killed by the Persians under Xerxes.

leonine ('liːəˌnaɪn) *adj* of, characteristic of, or resembling a lion. [C14: from Latin *leōnīnus,* from *leō* lion]

Leonine ('liːəˌnaɪn) *adj* **1** connected with one of the popes called Leo: an epithet applied to: **a** a district of Rome on the right bank of the Tiber fortified by Pope Leo IV (**Leonine City**); **b** certain prayers in the Mass prescribed by Leo XIII. ◆ *n* **2** Also called: **Leonine verse. 2a** a type of medieval hexameter or elegiac verse having internal rhyme. **2b** a type of English verse with internal rhyme.

Leonov (*Russian* lɪ'ɔnəf) *n* **Aleksei Arkhipovich** (alɪk'sjej ar'xipɪvitʃ). born 1934, Soviet cosmonaut; the first man to walk in space (1965).

leontopodium (lɪˌɒntə'pəudɪəm) *n* any plant of the Eurasian alpine genus *Leontopodium,* esp. *L. alpinum.* See **edelweiss.** [New Latin, from Greek *leōn* lion + *podion,* diminutive of *pous* foot (from the shape of the flowers)]

leopard ('lɛpəd) *n* **1** Also called: **panther.** a large feline mammal, *Panthera pardus,* of forests of Africa and Asia, usually having a tawny yellow coat with black rosette-like spots. **2** any of several similar felines, such as the snow leopard and cheetah. **3 clouded leopard.** a feline, *Neofelis nebulosa,* of SE Asia and Indonesia with a yellowish-brown coat marked with darker spots and blotches. **4** *Heraldry.* a stylized leopard, painted as a lion with the face turned towards the front. **5** the pelt of a leopard. [C13: from Old French *lepart,* from Late Latin *leōpardus,* from Late Greek *leópardos,* from *leōn* lion + *pardos* PARD[2] (the leopard was thought to be the result of cross-breeding)] ▸ '**leopardess** *fem n*

Leopardi (*Italian* leo'pardi) *n* Count **Giacomo** ('dʒaːkomo). 1798–1837, Italian poet and philosopher, noted esp. for his lyrics, collected in *I Canti* (1831).

leopard lily *n* a North American lily plant, *Lilium pardalinum,* cultivated for its large orange-red flowers, with brown-spotted petals and long stamens.

leopard moth *n* a nocturnal European moth, *Zeuzera pyrina,* having white wings and body, both marked with black spots: family *Cossidae.*

leopard's-bane *n* any of several Eurasian perennial plants of the genus *Doronicum,* esp. *D. plantagineum,* having clusters of yellow flowers: family *Compositae* (composites).

Leopold I ('lɪəˌpəuld) *n* **1** 1640–1705, Holy Roman Emperor (1658–1705). His reign was marked by wars with Louis XIV of France and with the Turks. **2** 1790–1865, first king of the Belgians (1831–65).

Leopold II *n* **1** 1747–92, Holy Roman Emperor (1790–92). He formed an alliance with Prussia against France (1792) after the downfall of his brother-in-law Louis XVI. **2** 1835–1909, king of the Belgians (1865–1909); son of Leopold I. He financed Stanley's explorations in Africa, becoming first sovereign of the Congo Free State (1885).

Leopold III *n* 1901–83, king of the Belgians (1934–51); son of Albert I. His surrender to the Nazis (1940) forced his eventual abdication in favour of his son, Baudouin.

Léopoldville ('lɪəpəuldˌvɪl; *French* leɔpɔlvil) *n* the former name (until 1966) of **Kinshasa.**

leotard ('lɪəˌtɑːd) *n* **1** a tight-fitting garment covering the body from the shoulders down to the thighs and worn by acrobats, ballet dancers, etc. **2** (*pl*) *U.S. and Canadian.* another name for **tights** (sense 1b). [C19: named after Jules *Léotard,* French acrobat]

Lepanto *n* **1** (*Italian* 'lɛːpanto) a port in W Greece, between the Gulfs of Corinth and Patras: scene of a naval battle (1571) in which the Turkish fleet was defeated by the fleets of the Holy League. Pop.: 8170 (latest est.). Greek name: **Návpaktos. 2** (lɪ'pæntəu). **Gulf of.** another name for the (Gulf of) **Corinth.**

Lepaya (lɪ'pɑːjə) *n* a variant spelling of **Liepāja.**

Lepcha ('lɛptʃə) *n* **1** (*pl* **-cha** *or* **-chas**) a member of a Mongoloid people of Sikkim. **2** the language of this people, belonging to the Tibeto-Burman branch of the Sino-Tibetan family. ◆ *adj* **3** of or relating to this people or their language.

leper ('lɛpə) *n* **1** a person who has leprosy. **2** a person who is ignored or despised. [C14: via Late Latin from Greek *lepra,* noun use of *lepros* scaly, from *lepein* to peel]

lepido- *or before a vowel* **lepid-** *combining form.* scale or scaly: *lepidopterous.* [from Greek *lepis* scale; see LEPER]

lepidolite (lɪ'pɪdəˌlaɪt, 'lɛpɪdəˌlaɪt) *n* a lilac, pink, or greyish mica consisting of a hydrous silicate of lithium, potassium, aluminium, and fluorine, containing rubidium as an impurity: a source of lithium and rubidium. Formula: $K_2Li_3Al_4Si_7O_{21}(OH,F)_3$.

lepidopteran (ˌlɛpɪ'dɒptərən) *n, pl* **-terans** *or* **-tera** (-tərə), *also* **lepidopteron. 1** any of numerous insects of the order *Lepidoptera,* typically having two pairs of wings covered with fragile scales, mouthparts specialized as a suctorial proboscis, and caterpillars as larvae: comprises the butterflies and moths. ◆ *adj also* **lepidopterous. 2** of, relating to, or belonging to the order *Lepidoptera.* [C19: from New Latin *lepidoptera,* from LEPIDO- + Greek *pteron* wing]

lepidopterist (ˌlɛpɪ'dɒptərɪst) *n* a person who studies or collects moths and butterflies.

lepidosiren (ˌlɛpɪdəu'saɪərən) *n* a South American lungfish, *Lepidosiren paradoxa,* having an eel-shaped body and whiplike paired fins.

lepidote ('lɛpɪˌdəut) *adj Biology.* covered with scaly leaves or spots. [C19: via New Latin *lepidōtus,* from Greek, from *lepis* scale]

Lepidus ('lɛpɪdəs) *n* **Marcus Aemilius** ('mɑːkəs iːˈmɪlɪəs). died ?13 B.C., Roman statesman: formed the Second Triumvirate with Octavian (later Augustus) and Mark Antony.

Lepontine Alps (lɪ'pɒntaɪn) *pl n* a range of the S central Alps, in S Switzerland and N Italy. Highest peak: Monte Leone, 3553 m (11 657 ft.).

leporid ('lɛpərɪd) *adj* **1** of, relating to, or belonging to the *Leporidae,* a family of lagomorph mammals having long ears and limbs and a short tail: includes rabbits and hares. ◆ *n* **2** any animal belonging to the family *Leporidae.* [C19: from Latin *lepus* hare]

leporine ('lɛpəˌraɪn) *adj* of, relating to, or resembling a hare. [C17: from Latin *leporīnus,* from *lepus* hare]

Leppard ('lɛpəd) *n* **Raymond.** born 1927, British conductor and musicologist, in the U.S. from 1977: noted esp. for his revivals of early opera.

LEPRA ('lɛprə) *n acronym for* Leprosy Relief Association.

leprechaun ('lɛprəˌkɔːn) *n* (in Irish folklore) a mischievous elf, often believed to have a treasure hoard. [C17: from Irish Gaelic *leipreachān,* from Middle Irish *lūchorpān,* from *lū* small + *corp* body, from Latin *corpus* body]

leprosarium (ˌlɛprə'sɛərɪəm) *n, pl* **-ia** (-ɪə). a hospital or other centre for the treatment or care of lepers. [C20: from Medieval Latin: see LEPER]

leprose ('lɛprəus, -rəuz) *adj Biology.* having or denoting a whitish scurfy surface.

leprosy ('lɛprəsɪ) *n Pathol.* a chronic infectious disease occurring mainly in tropical and subtropical regions, characterized by the formation of painful inflamed nodules beneath the skin and disfigurement and wasting of affected parts, caused by the bacillus *Mycobacterium leprae.* Also called: **Hansen's disease.** [C16: from LEPROUS + -Y[3]]

leprous ('lɛprəs) *adj* **1** having leprosy. **2** relating to or resembling leprosy. **3** *Biology.* a less common word for **leprose.** [C13: from Old French, from Late Latin *leprosus,* from *lepra* LEPER] ▸ '**leprously** *adv* ▸ '**leprousness** *n*

-lepsy *or sometimes* **-lepsia** *n combining form.* indicating a seizure or attack: *catalepsy.* [from New Latin *-lepsia,* from Greek, from *lēpsis* a seizure, from *lambanein* to seize] ▸ **-leptic** *adj combining form.*

leptin ('lɛptɪn) *n* a protein, produced by fat cells in the body, that acts on the brain to regulate the amount of additional fat laid down in the body. [C20: from LEPTO- + -IN]

lepto- *or before a vowel* **lept-** *combining form.* fine, slender, or slight: *leptosome.* [from Greek *leptos* thin, literally: peeled, from *lepein* to peel]

leptocephalic (ˌlɛptəusɪ'fælɪk) *or* **leptocephalous** (ˌlɛptəu'sɛfələs) *adj* having a narrow skull.

leptocephalus (ˌlɛptəu'sɛfələs) *n, pl* **-li** (-ˌlaɪ). the slender transparent oceanic larva of eels of the genus *Anguilla* that migrates from its hatching ground in the Caribbean to European freshwater habitats.

leptocercal (ˌlɛptəu'sɜːkᵊl) *adj Zoology.* having a long thin tail. [from LEPTO- + Greek *kerkos* tail]

leptodactylous (ˌlɛptəu'dæktɪləs) *adj Zoology.* having slender digits.

leptokurtic (ˌlɛptəu'kɜːtɪk) *adj Statistics.* (of a distribution) having kurtosis B_2 greater than 3, more heavily concentrated about the mean than a normal distribution. Compare **platykurtic, mesokurtic.** [C20: from LEPTO- + Greek *kurtos* arched, bulging + -IC]

lepton[1] ('lɛptɒn) *n, pl* **-ta** (-tə). **1** a Greek monetary unit worth one hundredth of a drachma. **2** a small coin of ancient Greece. [from Greek *lepton* (*nomisma*) small (coin)]

lepton[2] ('lɛptɒn) *n Physics.* any of a group of elementary particles and their antiparticles, such as an electron, muon, or neutrino, that participate in electromagnetic and weak interactions and have a half-integral spin. [C20: from LEPTO- + -ON] ▸ **lep'tonic** *adj*

lepton number *n Physics.* a quantum number describing the behaviour of elementary particles, equal to the number of leptons present minus the number of antileptons. It is thought to be conserved in all processes. Symbol: **l**

leptophyllous (ˌlɛptəu'fɪləs) *adj* (of plants) having long slender leaves.

leptorrhine ('lɛptərɪn) *adj* another word for **catarrhine** (sense 2).

leptosome ('lɛptəˌsəum) *n* a person with a small bodily frame and a slender physique. ▸ ˌ**lepto'somic** *or* **leptosomatic** (ˌlɛptəusə'mætɪk) *adj*

leptospirosis (ˌlɛptəuspaɪ'rəusɪs) *n* any of several infectious diseases caused by spirochaete bacteria of the genus *Leptospira,* transmitted to man by animals and characterized by jaundice, meningitis, and kidney failure. Also called: **Weil's disease.** [C20: from New Latin *Leptospira* (LEPTO- + Greek *speira* coil + -OSIS)]

leptotene ('lɛptəuˌtiːn) *n* the first stage of the prophase of meiosis during which the nuclear material becomes resolved into slender single-stranded chromosomes. [C20: from LEPTO- + *-tene,* from Greek *tainia* band, filament]

Lepus ('lɛpəs, 'li:-) *n, Latin genitive* **Leporis** ('lɛpərɪs). a small constellation in the S hemisphere lying between Orion and Columba. [New Latin, from Latin: hare]

lequear (lə'kwɪə) *n* another name for **lacunar** (sense 1).

Lérida (*Spanish* 'leriða) *n* a city in NE Spain, in Catalonia: commercial centre of an agricultural region. Pop.: 114 367 (1995 est.).

Lermontov (*Russian* 'ljɛrməntəf) *n* **Mikhail Yurievich** (mixa'il 'jurjɪvitʃ). 1814–41, Russian novelist and poet: noted esp. for the novel *A Hero of Our Time* (1840).

Lerner ('lɜ:nə) *n* **Alan Jay.** 1914–86, U.S. songwriter and librettist. With Frederick Loewe he wrote *My Fair Lady* (1956) and *Camelot* (1960) as well as a number of film scripts, including *Gigi* (1958).

Lerwick ('lɜ:wɪk) *n* a town in Scotland, administrative centre of the island authority of Shetland, on the island of Mainland: the most northerly town in the British Isles; knitwear, oil refining. Pop.: 7500 (1987 est.).

Le Sage *or* **Lesage** (*French* lə saʒ) *n* **Alain-René** (alɛ̃rəne). 1668–1747, French novelist and dramatist, author of the picaresque novel *Gil Blas* (1715–35).

lesbian ('lɛzbɪən) *n* **1** a female homosexual. ♦ *adj* **2** of or characteristic of lesbians. [C19: from the homosexuality attributed to Sappho] ▸ **'lesbianism** *n*

Lesbian ('lɛzbɪən) *n* **1** a native or inhabitant of Lesbos. **2** the Aeolic dialect of Ancient Greek spoken in Lesbos. ♦ *adj* **3** of or relating to Lesbos. **4** of or relating to the poetry of Lesbos, esp. that of Sappho.

Lesbos ('lɛzbɒs) *n* an island in the E Aegean, off the NW coast of Turkey: a centre of lyric poetry, led by Alcaeus and Sappho (6th century B.C.); annexed to Greece in 1913. Chief town: Mytilene. Pop.: 105 082 (1991). Area: 1630 sq. km (630 sq. miles). Modern Greek name: **Lésvos.** Former name: **Mytilene.**

Les Cayes (leɪ 'keɪ; *French* le kaj) *n* a port in SW Haiti, on the S Tiburon Peninsula. Pop.: 45 904 (1992). Also called: **Cayes.** Former name: **Aux Cayes.**

lese-majesty ('li:z'mædʒɪstɪ) *n* **1** any of various offences committed against the sovereign power in a state; treason. **2** an attack on authority or position. [C16: from French *lèse majesté,* from Latin *laesa mājestās* wounded majesty]

lesion ('li:ʒən) *n* **1** any structural change in a bodily part resulting from injury or disease. **2** an injury or wound. [C15: via Old French from Late Latin *laesiō* injury, from Latin *laedere* to hurt]

Lesotho (lɪ'su:tu, lə'səutəu) *n* a kingdom in southern Africa, forming an enclave in the Republic of South Africa: annexed to British Cape Colony in 1871; made a protectorate in 1884; gained independence in 1966; a member of the Commonwealth. It is generally mountainous, with temperate grasslands throughout. Languages: Sesotho and English. Religion: Christian majority. Currency: loti. Capital: Maseru. Pop.: 2 090 000 (1998 est.). Area: 30 344 sq. km (11 716 sq. miles). Former name (1884–1966): **Basutoland.**

less (lɛs) *determiner* **1a** the comparative of **little** (sense 1): *less sugar; less spirit than before.* **1b** (*as pronoun; functioning as sing or pl*): *she has less than she needs; the less you eat, the less you want.* **2** (usually preceded by *no*) lower in rank or importance: *no less a man than the president; St. James the Less.* **3 no less.** *Informal.* used to indicate surprise or admiration, often sarcastic, at the preceding statement: *she says she's been to Italy, no less.* **4 less of.** to a smaller extent or degree: *we see less of John these days; less of a success than I'd hoped.* ♦ *adv* **5** the comparative of *a little: she walks less than she should; less quickly; less beautiful.* **6 much** *or* **still less.** used to reinforce a negative: *we don't like it, still less enjoy it.* **7 think less of.** to have a lower opinion of. ♦ *prep* **8** subtracting; minus: *three weeks less a day.* [Old English *lǣssa* (adj), *lǣs* (adv, n)]

USAGE *Less* should not be confused with *fewer. Less* refers strictly only to quantity and not to number: *there is less water than before. Fewer* means smaller in number: *there are fewer people than before.*

-less *suffix forming adjectives.* **1** without; lacking: *speechless.* **2** not able to (do something) or not able to be (done, performed, etc.): *countless.* [Old English *-lās,* from *lēas* lacking]

lessee (lɛ'si:) *n* a person to whom a lease is granted; a tenant under a lease. [C15: via Anglo-French from Old French *lessé,* from *lesser* to LEASE[1]] ▸ **les'seeship** *n*

lessen ('lɛsᵊn) *vb* **1** to make or become less. **2** (*tr*) to make little of.

Lesseps ('lɛsəps; *French* lesɛps) *n* Vicomte **Ferdinand Marie de** (fɛrdinɑ̃ mari də). 1805–94, French diplomat: directed the construction of the Suez Canal (1859–69) and the unsuccessful first attempt to build the Panama Canal (1881–89).

lesser ('lɛsə) *adj* not as great in quantity, size, or worth.

Lesser Antilles *pl n* **the.** a group of islands in the Caribbean, including the Leeward Islands, the Windward Islands, Barbados, and the Netherlands Antilles. Also called: **Caribbees.**

lesser celandine *n* a Eurasian ranunculaceous plant, *Ranunculus ficaria,* having yellow flowers and heart-shaped leaves. Also called: **pilewort.** Compare **greater celandine.**

lesser panda *n* See **panda** (sense 2).

Lesser Sunda Islands *pl n* the former name of **Nusa Tenggara.**

Lessing ('lɛsɪŋ) *n* **1 Doris (May).** born 1919, English novelist and short-story writer, brought up in Rhodesia: her novels include the five-novel sequence *Children of Violence* (1952–69), *The Golden Notebook* (1962), *Memoirs of a Survivor* (1974), a series of science-fiction works (1979–83), *The Good Terrorist* (1985), and *Love Again* (1996). **2 Gotthold Ephraim** ('gɔthɔlt 'e:fraɪm). 1729–81, German dramatist and critic. His plays include *Miss Sara Sampson* (1755), the first German domestic tragedy, and *Nathan der Weise* (1779). He is noted for his criticism of French classical dramatists, and for his treatise on aesthetics *Laokoon* (1766).

lesson ('lɛsᵊn) *n* **1a** a unit, or single period of instruction in a subject; class: *an hour-long music lesson.* **1b** the content of such a unit. **2** material assigned for individual study. **3** something from which useful knowledge or principles can be learned; example. **4** the principles, knowledge, etc., gained. **5** a reprimand or punishment intended to correct. **6** a portion of Scripture appointed to be read at divine service. ♦ *vb* **7** (*tr*) *Rare.* to censure or punish. [C13: from Old French *leçon,* from Latin *lēctiō,* from *legere* to read]

lessor ('lɛsɔ:, lɛ'sɔ:) *n* a person who grants a lease of property.

lest (lɛst) *conj* (*subordinating; takes* should *or a subjunctive vb*) **1** so as to prevent any possibility that: *he fled the country lest he be captured and imprisoned.* **2** (*after verbs or phrases expressing fear, worry, anxiety, etc.*) for fear that; in case: *he was alarmed lest she should find out.* [Old English *thē lǣste,* earlier *thӯ lǣs the,* literally: whereby less that]

Lésvos ('lɛzvɔs) *n* transliteration of the Modern Greek name for **Lesbos.**

let[1] (lɛt) *vb* **lets, letting, let.** (*tr;* usually takes an infinitive without *to* or an implied infinitive) **1** to permit; allow: *she lets him roam around.* **2** (*imperative or dependent imperative*) **2a** used as an auxiliary to express a request, proposal, or command, or to convey a warning or threat: *let's get on; just let me catch you here again!* **2b** (in mathematical or philosophical discourse) used as an auxiliary to express an assumption or hypothesis: *let "a" equal "b".* **2c** used as an auxiliary to express resigned acceptance of the inevitable: *let the worst happen.* **3a** to allow the occupation of (accommodation) in return for rent. **3b** to assign (a contract for work). **4** to allow or cause the movement of (something) in a specified direction: *to let air out of a tyre.* **5** *Irish informal.* to utter: *to let a cry.* **6 let alone.** (*conj*) much less; not to mention: *I can't afford wine, let alone champagne.* **7 let** *or* **leave alone** *or* **be.** to refrain from annoying or interfering with: *let the poor cat alone.* **8 let go.** See **go**[1] (sense 59). **9 let loose. 9a** to set free. **9b** *Informal.* to make (a sound or remark) suddenly: *he let loose a hollow laugh.* **9c** *Informal.* to discharge (rounds) from a gun or guns: *they let loose a couple of rounds of ammunition.* ♦ *n* **10** *Brit.* the act of letting property or accommodation: *the majority of new lets are covered by the rent regulations.* ♦ See also **let down, let in, let into, let off, let on, let out, let through, let up.** [Old English *lǣtan* to permit; related to Gothic *lētan,* German *lassen*]

let[2] (lɛt) *n* **1** an impediment or obstruction (esp. in the phrase **without let or hindrance**). **2** *Tennis, squash, etc.* **2a** a minor infringement or obstruction of the ball, requiring a point to be replayed. **2b** the point so replayed. ♦ *vb* **lets, letting, letted** *or* **let. 3** (*tr*) *Archaic.* to hinder; impede. [Old English *lettan* to hinder, from *læt* LATE; related to Old Norse *letja*]

-let *suffix forming nouns.* **1** small or lesser: *booklet; starlet.* **2** an article of attire or ornament worn on a specified part of the body: *anklet.* [from Old French *-elet,* from Latin *-āle,* neuter of adj suffix *-ālis* or from Latin *-ellus,* diminutive suffix]

letch (lɛtʃ) *vb, n* a variant spelling of **lech.** [C18: perhaps back formation from LECHER]

Letchworth ('lɛtʃwəθ, -,wɜ:θ) *n* a town in SE England, in N Hertfordshire: the first garden city in Great Britain (founded in 1903). Pop.: 31 418 (1991).

let down *vb* (*tr, mainly adv*) **1** (*also prep*) to lower. **2** to fail to fulfil the expectations of (a person); disappoint. **3** to undo, shorten, and resew (the hem) so as to lengthen (a dress, skirt, etc.). **4** to untie (long hair that is bound up) and allow to fall loose. **5** to deflate: *to let down a tyre.* ♦ *n* **letdown. 6** a disappointment. **7** the gliding descent of an aircraft in preparation for landing.

lethal ('li:θəl) *adj* **1** able to cause or causing death. **2** of or suggestive of death. [C16: from Latin *lēthālis,* from *lētum* death] ▸ **lethality** (li:'θælɪtɪ) *n* ▸ **'lethally** *adv*

lethal dose *n* the amount of a drug or other agent that if administered to an animal or human will prove fatal. Abbrev.: **LD.** See also **median lethal dose.**

lethargy ('lɛθədʒɪ) *n, pl* **-gies. 1** sluggishness, slowness, or dullness. **2** an abnormal lack of energy, esp. as the result of a disease. [C14: from Late Latin *lēthargīa,* from Greek *lēthargos* drowsy, from *lēthē* forgetfulness] ▸ **lethargic** (lɪ'θɑ:dʒɪk) *or* **le'thargical** *adj* ▸ **le'thargically** *adv*

Lethbridge ('lɛθbrɪdʒ) *n* a city in Canada, in S Alberta: coal-mining. Pop.: 60 974 (1991).

Lethe ('li:θɪ) *n* **1** *Greek myth.* a river in Hades that caused forgetfulness in those who drank its waters. **2** forgetfulness. [C16: via Latin from Greek, from *lēthē* oblivion] ▸ **Lethean** (lɪ'θi:ən) *adj*

let in *vb* (*tr, adv*) **1** to allow to enter. **2 let in for.** to involve (oneself or another) in (something more than is expected): *he let himself in for a lot of extra work.* **3 let in on.** to allow (someone) to know about or participate in.

let into *vb* (*tr, prep*) **1** to allow to enter. **2** to put into the surface of: *to let a pipe into the wall.* **3** to allow (someone) to share (a secret).

Leto ('li:təu) *n* the mother by Zeus of Apollo and Artemis. Roman name: **Latona.**

let off *vb* (*tr, mainly adv*) **1** (*also prep*) to allow to disembark or leave. **2** to explode or fire (a bomb, gun, etc.). **3** (*also prep*) to excuse from (work or other responsibilities): *I'll let you off for a week.* **4** to allow to get away without the expected punishment, work, etc. **5** to let (accommodation) in portions. **6** to release (liquid, air, etc.). **7 let off steam.** See **steam** (sense 6). **8 let (someone) off with.** to give (a light punishment) to (someone).

let on *vb* (*adv;* when *tr, takes a clause as object*) *Informal.* **1** to allow (something, such as a secret) to be known; reveal: *he never let on that he was married.* **2** (*tr*) to cause or encourage to be believed; pretend.

let out *vb* (*adv, mainly tr*) **1** to give vent to; emit: *to let out a howl.* **2** to allow to go or run free; release. **3** (*may take a clause as object*) to reveal (a secret). **4** to make available to tenants, hirers, or contractors. **5** to permit to flow out: *to let air out of the tyres.* **6** to make (a garment) larger, as by unpicking (the seams) and sewing nearer the outer edge. ♦ *n* **let-out. 7** a chance to escape.

LETS (lɛts) *n acronym for* Local Exchange and Trading System: an economic system in which members of a community exchange goods and services using a cashless local currency.

let's (lɛts) *contraction of* let us: used to express a suggestion, command, etc., by the speaker to himself and his hearers.

Lett (lɛt) *n* another name for a **Latvian**.

letter ('lɛtə) *n* **1** any of a set of conventional symbols used in writing or printing a language, each symbol being associated with a group of phonetic values in the language; character of the alphabet. **2** a written or printed communication addressed to a person, company, etc., usually sent by post in an envelope. Related adj: **epistolary. 3** (often preceded by *the*) the strict legalistic or pedantic interpretation of the meaning of an agreement, document, etc.; exact wording as distinct from actual intention (esp. in the phrase **the letter of the law**). Compare **spirit**[1] (sense 10). **4** *Printing, archaic.* a style of typeface: *a fancy letter.* **5 to the letter. 5a** following the literal interpretation or wording exactly. **5b** attending to every detail. ♦ *vb* **6** to write or mark letters on (a sign, etc.), esp. by hand. **7** (*tr*) to set down or print using letters. ♦ See also **letters**. [C13: from Old French *lettre,* from Latin *littera* letter of the alphabet] ▸ **'letterer** *n*

letter bomb *n* a thin explosive device inside an envelope, detonated when the envelope is opened.

letter box *n Chiefly Brit.* **1a** a slot, usually covered with a hinged flap, through which letters, etc. are delivered to a building. **1b** a private box into which letters, etc., are delivered. **2** Also called: **postbox.** a public box into which letters, etc., are put for collection and delivery.

letterboxing ('lɛtə,bɒksɪŋ) *n* a method of formatting film that enables all of a wide-screen film to be transmitted on a television screen, resulting in a blank strip of screen above and below the picture.

letter card *n* **1** a card, usually one on which the postage is prepaid, that is sealed by being folded in half so that its gummed edges come into contact with each other. **2** a long card consisting of a number of postcard views, with space for writing a letter on the backs, that is folded like a concertina for posting.

lettered ('lɛtəd) *adj* **1** well educated in literature, the arts, etc. **2** literate. **3** of or characterized by learning or culture. **4** printed or marked with letters.

letterhead ('lɛtə,hɛd) *n* a sheet of paper printed with one's address, name, etc., for writing a letter on.

letter-high *adj* another term for **type-high.**

lettering ('lɛtərɪŋ) *n* **1** the act, art, or technique of inscribing letters on to something. **2** the letters so inscribed.

letter of advice *n* a commercial letter giving a specific notification, such as the consignment of goods.

letter of attorney *n* a less common term for **power of attorney.**

letter of credit *n* **1** a letter issued by a bank entitling the bearer to draw funds up to a specified maximum from that bank or its agencies. **2** a letter addressed by a bank instructing the addressee to allow the person named to draw a specified sum on the credit of the addressor bank.

letter of intent *n* a letter indicating that the writer has the serious intention of doing something, such as signing a contract in the circumstances specified. It does not constitute either a promise or a contract.

letter of introduction *n* a letter given by one person to another, as an introduction to a third party.

letter of marque *or* **letters of marque** *n* **1** a licence granted by a state to a private citizen to arm a ship and seize merchant vessels of another nation. **2** a similar licence issued by a nation allowing a private citizen to seize goods or citizens of another nation. ♦ Also called: **letter of marque and reprisal.**

letter-perfect *adj* another term (esp. in the U.S.) for **word-perfect.**

letterpress ('lɛtə,prɛs) *n* **1a** a method of printing in which ink is transferred from raised surfaces to paper by pressure; relief printing. **1b** matter so printed. **2** text matter as distinct from illustrations.

letter-quality printing *n Computing.* high-quality output in printed form from a printer linked to a word processor. Compare **draft-quality printing.**

letters ('lɛtəz) *n* (*functioning as pl or sing*) **1** literary knowledge, ability, or learning: *a man of letters.* **2** literary culture in general. **3** an official title, degree, etc., indicated by an abbreviation: *letters after one's name.*

letterset ('lɛtə,sɛt) *n* a method of rotary printing in which ink is transferred from raised surfaces to paper via a rubber-covered cylinder. [C20: from LETTER(PRESS) + (OFF)SET)

letters of administration *pl n Law.* a formal document nominating a specified person to take over, administer, and dispose of an estate when there is no executor to carry out the testator's will.

letters of credence *or* **letters credential** *pl n* a formal document accrediting a diplomatic officer to a foreign court or government.

letters patent *pl n* See **patent** (sense 1).

let through *vb* (*tr*) to allow to pass (through): *the invalid was let through to the front of the queue.*

Lettish ('lɛtɪʃ) *n, adj* another word for **Latvian.**

lettre de cachet *French.* (lɛtrə də kaʃɛ) *n, pl* ***lettres de cachet*** (lɛtrə də kaʃɛ). *French history.* a letter under the sovereign's seal, often authorizing imprisonment without trial. [literally: letter with a seal]

lettuce ('lɛtɪs) *n* **1** any of various plants of the genus *Lactuca,* esp. *L. sativa,* which is cultivated in many varieties for its large edible leaves: family *Compositae* (composites). **2** the leaves of any of these varieties, which are eaten in salads. **3** any of various plants that resemble true lettuce, such as lamb's lettuce and sea lettuce. [C13: probably from Old French *laitues,* pl. of *laitue,* from Latin *lactūca,* from *lac-* milk, because of its milky juice]

let up *vb* (*intr, adv*) **1** to diminish, slacken, or stop. **2** (foll. by *on*) *Informal.* to be less harsh (towards someone). ♦ *n* **let-up. 3** *Informal.* a lessening or abatement.

leu ('leɪu:) *n, pl* **lei** (leɪ). the standard monetary unit of Romania and Moldova, divided into 100 bani. [from Romanian: lion]

Leucas ('lu:kəs) *n* a variant spelling of **Leukas.**

leucine ('lu:si:n) *or* **leucin** ('lu:sɪn) *n* an essential amino acid found in many proteins.

Leucippus (lu:'sɪpəs) *n* 5th century B.C. Greek philosopher, who originated the atomist theory of matter, developed by his disciple, Democritus.

leucite ('lu:saɪt) *n* a grey or white mineral consisting of potassium aluminium silicate: a source of potash for fertilizers and of aluminium. Formula: $KAlSi_2O_6$. ▸ **leucitic** (lu:'sɪtɪk) *adj*

leuco-, leuko- *or before a vowel* **leuc-, leuk-** *combining form.* white or lacking colour: *leucocyte; leucorrhoea; leukaemia.* [from Greek *leukos* white]

leuco base ('lu:kəʊ) *n* a colourless compound formed by reducing a dye so that the original dye can be regenerated by oxidation.

leucoblast *or esp. U.S.* **leukoblast** ('lu:kəʊ,blɑ:st) *n* an immature leucocyte.

leucocratic (,lu:kə'krætɪk) *adj* (of igneous rocks) light-coloured because of a low content of ferromagnesian minerals. [C20: from German *leukokrat,* from LEUCO- + Greek *kratein* to rule]

leucocyte *or esp. U.S.* **leukocyte** ('lu:kə,saɪt) *n* any of the various large unpigmented cells in the blood of vertebrates. Also called: **white blood cell, white (blood) corpuscle.** See also **lymphocyte, granulocyte, monocyte.** ▸ **leucocytic** *or esp. U.S.* **leukocytic** (,lu:kə'sɪtɪk) *adj*

leucocytosis *or esp. U.S.* **leukocytosis** (,lu:kəʊsaɪ'təʊsɪs) *n* a gross increase in the number of white blood cells in the blood, usually as a response to an infection. ▸ **leucocytotic** *or esp. U.S.* **leukocytotic** (,lu:kəʊsaɪ'tɒtɪk) *adj*

leucoderma *or esp. U.S.* **leukoderma** (,lu:kəʊ'dɜ:mə) *n* any area of skin that is white from congenital (**albinism**; see **albino**) or acquired absence or loss of melanin pigmentation. Also called: **vitiligo.** ▸ **,leuco'dermal, ,leuco'dermic** *or esp. U.S.* **,leuko'dermal, ,leuko'dermic** *adj*

leucoma (lu:'kəʊmə) *n Pathol.* a white opaque scar of the cornea.

leucomaine ('lu:kə,meɪn) *n Biochem.* any of a group of toxic amines produced during animal metabolism. [C20: from LEUCO- + *-maine,* as in *ptomaine*]

leucopenia *or esp. U.S.* **leukopenia** (,lu:kəʊ'pi:nɪə) *n Pathol.* an abnormal reduction in the number of white blood cells in the blood, characteristic of certain diseases. [C19: from LEUCO- + Greek *penia* poverty] ▸ **,leuco'penic** *or esp. U.S.* **,leuko'penic** *adj*

leucoplast ('lu:kə,plæst) *or* **leucoplastid** *n* any of the small colourless bodies occurring in the cytoplasm of plant cells and used for storing food material, esp. starch.

leucopoiesis *or esp. U.S.* **leukopoiesis** (,lu:kəʊpɔɪ'i:sɪs) *n Physiol.* formation of leucocytes in the body. Also called: **leucocytopoiesis.** ▸ **leucopoietic** *or esp. U.S.* **leukopoietic** (,lu:kəʊpɔɪ'ɛtɪk) *adj*

leucorrhoea *or esp. U.S.* **leukorrhea** (,lu:kə'ri:ə) *n Pathol.* a white or yellowish discharge of mucous material from the vagina, often an indication of infection. ▸ **,leucor'rhoeal** *or esp. U.S.* **,leukor'rheal** *adj*

leucotomy (lu:'kɒtəmɪ) *n* the surgical operation of cutting some of the nerve fibres in the frontal lobes of the brain for treating intractable mental disorders. See also **lobotomy.** [C20: from LEUCO- (with reference to the white brain tissue) + -TOMY]

Leuctra ('lu:ktrə) *n* an ancient town in Greece southwest of Thebes in Boeotia: site of a victory of Thebes over Sparta (371 B.C.), which marked the end of Spartan military supremacy in Greece.

leukaemia *or esp. U.S.* **leukemia** (lu:'ki:mɪə) *n* an acute or chronic disease characterized by a gross proliferation of leucocytes, which crowd into the bone marrow, spleen, lymph nodes, etc., and suppress the blood-forming apparatus. [C19: from LEUCO- + Greek *haima* blood]

Leukas *or* **Leucas** ('lu:kəs) *n* another name for **Levkás.**

leuko- *combining form.* a variant of **leuco-.**

leukotriene (,lu:kəʊ'traɪi:n) *n* one of a class of products of metabolic conversion of arachidonic acid; the active constituents of slow-reacting substance, responsible for bronchial constriction, contraction of smooth muscle, and inflammatory processes. [C20: from *leukocyte,* in which they were discovered + *triene* from the conjugated triene unit that they contain]

Leuven ('lø:və) *n* the Flemish name for **Louvain.**

lev (lɛf) *n, pl* **leva** ('lɛvə). the standard monetary unit of Bulgaria, divided into 100 stotinki. [from Bulgarian: lion]

Lev. *Bible. abbrev. for* Leviticus.

Levalloisian (,lɛvə'lɔɪzɪən) *or* **Levallois** (lə'vælwɑ:) *adj* of or relating to a Lower Palaeolithic culture in W Europe, characterized by a method of flaking flint tools so that one side of the core is flat and the other domed.

levant[1] (lɪ'vænt) *n* a type of leather made from the skins of goats, sheep, or seals, having a pattern of irregular creases. [C19: shortened from *Levant morocco* (type of leather)]

levant[2] (lɪ'vænt) *vb* (*intr*) *Brit.* to bolt or abscond, esp. to avoid paying debts. [C18: perhaps from Spanish *levantar (el campo)* to break (camp)]

Levant (lɪ'vænt) *n* **the.** a former name for the area of the E Mediterranean now occupied by Lebanon, Syria, and Israel. [C15: from Old French, from the present participle of *lever* to raise (referring to the rising of the sun in the east), from Latin *levāre*]

levanter[1] (lɪ'væntə) *n* (*sometimes cap.*) **1** an easterly wind in the W Mediterranean area, esp. in the late summer. **2** an inhabitant of the Levant.

levanter[2] (lɪ'væntə) *n Brit.* a person who bolts or absconds.

levantine ('lɛvən,taɪn) *n* a cloth of twilled silk.

Levantine ('lɛvən,taɪn) *adj* **1** of or relating to the Levant. ♦ *n* **2** (esp. formerly) an inhabitant of the Levant.

levator (lɪ'veɪtə, -tɔ:) *n* **1** *Anatomy.* any of various muscles that raise a part of the body. **2** *Surgery.* an instrument for elevating a part or structure. [C17: New Latin, from Latin *levāre* to raise]

levee[1] ('lɛvɪ) *n U.S.* **1** an embankment alongside a river, produced naturally by sedimentation or constructed by man to prevent flooding. **2** an embankment that surrounds a field that is to be irrigated. **3** a landing place on a river; quay. **[C18:** from French, from Medieval Latin *levāta,* from Latin *levāre* to raise**]**

levee[2] ('lɛvɪ, 'lɛveɪ) *n* **1** a formal reception held by a sovereign just after rising from bed. **2** (in Britain) a public court reception for men, held in the early afternoon. **[C17:** from French, variant of *lever* a rising, from Latin *levāre* to raise**]**

level ('lɛvᵊl) *adj* **1** on a horizontal plane. **2** having a surface of completely equal height. **3** being of the same height as something else. **4** (of quantities to be measured, as in recipes) even with the top of the cup, spoon, etc. **5** equal to or even with (something or someone else). **6** not having or showing inconsistency or irregularities. **7** Also: **level-headed.** even-tempered; steady. ♦ *vb* **-els, -elling, -elled** *or U.S.* **-els, -eling, -eled. 8** (*tr;* sometimes foll. by *off*) to make (a surface) horizontal, level, or even. **9** to make (two or more people or things) equal, as in position or status. **10** (*tr*) to raze to the ground. **11** (*tr*) to knock (a person) down by or as if by a blow. **12** (*tr*) to direct (a gaze, criticism, etc.) emphatically at someone. **13** (*intr;* often foll. by *with*) *Informal.* to be straightforward and frank. **14** (*intr;* foll. by *off* or *out*) to manoeuvre an aircraft into a horizontal flight path after a dive, climb, or glide. **15** (often foll. by *at*) to aim (a weapon) horizontally. **16** *Surveying.* to determine the elevation of a section of (land), sighting through a levelling instrument to a staff at successive pairs or points. ♦ *n* **17** a horizontal datum line or plane. **18** a device, such as a spirit level, for determining whether a surface is horizontal. **19** a surveying instrument consisting basically of a telescope with a spirit level attached, used for measuring relative heights of land. See **Abney level, dumpy level. 20** a reading of the difference in elevation of two points taken with such an instrument. **21** position or status in a scale of values. **22** amount or degree of progress; stage. **23** a specified vertical position; altitude. **24** a horizontal line or plane with respect to which measurement of elevation is based: *sea level.* **25** a flat even surface or area of land. **26** a horizontal passage or drift in a mine. **27** any of the successive layers of material that have been deposited with the passage of time to build up and raise the height of the land surface. **28** *Physics.* the ratio of the magnitude of a physical quantity to an arbitrary magnitude: *sound-pressure level.* **29 do one's level best.** to make every possible effort; try one's utmost. **30 find one's level.** to find one's most suitable place socially, professionally, etc. **31 on a level.** on the same horizontal plane as another. **32 on the level.** *Informal.* sincere, honest, or genuine. **[C14:** from Old French *livel,* from Vulgar Latin *lībellum* (unattested), from Latin *lībella,* diminutive of *lībra* scales**]** ► **'levelly** *adv* ► **'levelness** *n*

level crossing *n Brit.* a point at which a railway and a road cross, esp. one with barriers that close the road when a train is scheduled to pass. U.S. and Canadian name: **grade crossing.**

level descriptor (dɪ'skrɪptə) *n Brit. Education.* one of a set of criteria used to assess the performance of a pupil in a particular subject.

level-headed *adj* even-tempered, balanced, and reliable; steady. ► **,level-'headedly** *adv* ► **,level-'headedness** *n*

leveller *or U.S.* **leveler** ('lɛvələ) *n* **1** a person or thing that levels. **2** a person who works for the abolition of inequalities.

Levellers ('lɛvələz) *n* **the.** *English history.* a radical group on the Parliamentarian side during the Civil War that advocated republicanism, freedom of worship, etc.

levelling screw *n* a screw, often one of three, for adjusting the level of an apparatus.

level of attainment *n Brit. Education.* one of ten groupings, each with its own attainment criteria based on pupil age and ability, within which a pupil is assessed.

level pegging *Brit. informal.* ♦ *n* **1** equality between two contestants. ♦ *adj* **2** (of two contestants) equal.

level playing field *n* a situation in which none of the competing parties has an advantage at the outset of a competitive activity.

Leven ('liːvᵊn) *n* **Loch. 1** a lake in E central Scotland: one of the shallowest of Scottish lochs, with seven islands, on one of which Mary Queen of Scots was imprisoned (1567–8). Length: 6 km (3.7 miles). Width: 4 km (2.5 miles). **2** a sea loch in W Scotland, extending for about 14 km (9 miles) east from Loch Linnhe.

lever ('liːvə) *n* **1** a rigid bar pivoted about a fulcrum, used to transfer a force to a load and usually to provide a mechanical advantage. **2** any of a number of mechanical devices employing this principle. **3** a means of exerting pressure in order to accomplish something; strategic aid. ♦ *vb* **4** to prise or move (an object) with a lever. **[C13:** from Old French *leveour,* from *lever* to raise, from Latin *levāre,* from *levis* light**]** ► **'lever-,like** *adj*

leverage ('liːvərɪdʒ, -vrɪdʒ) *n* **1** the action of a lever. **2** the mechanical advantage gained by employing a lever. **3** power to accomplish something; strategic advantage. **4** the enhanced power available to a large company: *the supermarket chains have greater leverage than single-outlet enterprises.* **5** U.S. word for **gearing** (sense 3). **6** the use made by a company of its limited assets to guarantee the substantial loans required to finance its business.

leveraged buyout ('liːvərɪdʒd) *n* a takeover bid in which a small company makes use of its limited assets, and those of the usually larger target company, to raise the loans required to finance the takeover. Abbrev.: **LBO.**

leveret ('lɛvərɪt, -vrɪt) *n* a young hare, esp. one less than one year old. **[C15:** from Norman French *levrete,* diminutive of *levre,* from Latin *lepus* hare**]**

Leverhulme ('liːvə,hjuːm) *n* **William Hesketh,** 1st Viscount. 1851-1925, English soap manufacturer and philanthropist, who founded (1881) the model industrial town Port Sunlight.

Leverkusen (*German* 'leːvər,kuːzən) *n* a town in NW Germany, in North Rhine-Westphalia on the Rhine: chemical industries. Pop.: 162 252 (1996 est.).

Leverrier (*French* ləverje) *n* **Urbain Jean Joseph** (yrbɛ̃ ʒɑ̃ ʒozɛf). 1811–77, French astronomer: calculated the existence and position of the planet Neptune.

Levi[1] ('liːvaɪ) *n* **1** *Old Testament.* **1a** the third son of Jacob and Leah and the ancestor of the tribe of Levi (Genesis 29:34). **1b** the priestly tribe descended from this patriarch (Numbers 18:21–24). **2** *New Testament.* another name for **Matthew** (the apostle).

Levi[2] (*Italian* 'lɛːvi) *n* **1 Carlo.** 1902–75, Italian physician, painter, and writer. Best known for his novel *Christ Stopped at Eboli* (1947), his other works include *The Watch* (1952) and *Words are Stones* (1958). **2 Primo** ('priːməʊ). 1919–87, Italian novelist. His book *If This is a Man* (1947) relates his experiences in Auschwitz. Other books include *The Periodic Table* (1956) and *The Drowned and the Saved* (1988), published after his suicide.

Levi[3] ('liːvaɪ; *Hebrew* 'levi) *or* **Levite** ('liːvaɪt) *n Judaism.* a descendant of the tribe of Levi who has certain privileges in the synagogue service.

leviable ('lɛvɪəbᵊl) *adj* **1** (of taxes, tariffs, etc.) liable to be levied. **2** (of goods, etc.) liable to bear a levy; taxable.

leviathan (lɪ'vaɪəθən) *n* **1** *Bible.* a monstrous beast, esp. a sea monster. **2** any huge or powerful thing. **[C14:** from Late Latin, ultimately from Hebrew *liwyāthān,* of obscure origin**]**

levigate ('lɛvɪ,geɪt) *vb Chem.* **1** (*tr*) to grind into a fine powder or a smooth paste. **2** to form or cause to form a homogeneous mixture, as in the production of gels. **3** (*tr*) to suspend (fine particles) by grinding in a liquid, esp. as a method of separating fine from coarse particles. ♦ *adj* **4** *Botany.* having a smooth polished surface; glabrous. **[C17:** from Latin *lēvigāre,* from *lēvis* smooth**]** ► **,levi'gation** *n* ► **'levi,gator** *n*

levin ('lɛvɪn) *n* an archaic word for **lightning. [C13:** probably from Scandinavian; compare Danish *lygnild***]**

levirate ('lɛvɪrɪt) *n* the practice, required by Old Testament law, of marrying the widow of one's brother. **[C18:** from Latin *lēvir* a husband's brother**]** ► **leviratic** (,lɛvɪ'rætɪk) *or* **,levi'ratical** *adj*

Levi's ('liːvaɪz) *pl n Trademark.* jeans, usually blue and made of denim.

Lévi-Strauss ('lɛvɪ'straʊs; *French* levistros) *n* **Claude** (klod). born 1908, French anthropologist, leading exponent of structuralism. His books include *The Elementary Structures of Kinship* (1969), *Totemism* (1962), *The Savage Mind* (1966), *Mythologies* (1964–71), and *Saudades do Brazil* (Memories of Brazil; 1994).

Levit. *Bible. abbrev. for* Leviticus.

levitate ('lɛvɪ,teɪt) *vb* **1** to rise or cause to rise and float in the air, without visible agency, attributed, esp. formerly, to supernatural causes. **2** (*tr*) *Med.* to support (a patient) on a cushion of air in the treatment of severe burns. **[C17:** from Latin *levis* light + *-tate,* as in *gravitate***]** ► **,levi'tation** *n* ► **'levi,tator** *n*

Levite ('liːvaɪt) *n* **1** *Old Testament.* a member of the priestly tribe of Levi. **2** *Judaism.* another word for **Levi**[3].

Levitical (lɪ'vɪtɪkᵊl) *or* **Levitic** *adj* **1** of or relating to the Levites. **2** of or relating to the book of Leviticus containing moral precepts and many of the laws concerning the Temple ritual and construction. ► **Le'vitically** *adv*

Leviticus (lɪ'vɪtɪkəs) *n Old Testament.* the third book of the Old Testament, containing Levitical law and ritual precepts.

levity ('lɛvɪtɪ) *n, pl* **-ties. 1** inappropriate lack of seriousness. **2** fickleness or instability. **3** *Archaic.* lightness in weight. **[C16:** from Latin *levitās* lightness, from *levis* light**]**

Levkás (lɛf'kæs), **Leukas** *or* **Leucas** *n* a Greek island in the Ionian Sea, in the Ionian Islands. Pop.: 22 000 (latest est.). Area: 295 sq. km (114 sq. miles). Italian name: **Santa Maura.**

Levkosia (lɛf'kəʊsɪə) *or* **Leukosia** *n* the Greek name for **Nicosia.**

levo- *combining form.* a U.S. variant of **laevo-. [**from Latin *laevus* left, on the left**]**

levodopa (,liːvəʊ'dəʊpə) *n* another name for **L-dopa.**

levy ('lɛvɪ) *vb* **levies, levying, levied.** (*tr*) **1** to impose and collect (a tax, tariff, fine, etc.). **2** to conscript troops for service. **3** to seize or attach (property) in accordance with the judgment of a court. ♦ *n, pl* **levies. 4a** the act of imposing and collecting a tax, tariff, etc. **4b** the money so raised. **5a** the conscription of troops for service. **5b** a person conscripted in this way. **[C15:** from Old French *levée* a raising, from *lever,* from Latin *levāre* to raise**]** ► **'levier** *n*

Lévy-Bruhl (levibrul) *n* **Lucien** (lysjɛ̃). 1857–1939, French anthropologist and philosopher, noted for his study of the psychology of primitive peoples.

levy en masse ('lɛvɪ ɒn 'mæs) *n* the conscription of the civilian population in large numbers in the face of impending invasion. Also called: **levée en masse** (*French* ləveɑ̃ mas).

lewd (luːd) *adj* **1** characterized by or intended to excite crude sexual desire; obscene. **2** *Obsolete.* **2a** wicked. **2b** ignorant. **[C14:** from Old English *lǣwde* lay, ignorant; see LAY[3]**]** ► **'lewdly** *adv* ► **'lewdness** *n*

Lewes ('luːɪs) *n* a market town in S England, administrative centre of East Sussex, on the River Ouse: site of a battle (1264) in which Henry III was defeated by Simon de Montfort. Pop.: 15 376 (1991).

lewis ('luːɪs) *or* **lewisson** *n* a lifting device for heavy stone blocks consisting of a number of curved pieces of metal fitting into a dovetailed recess cut into the stone. **[C18:** perhaps from the name of the inventor**]**

Lewis[1] ('luːɪs) *n* the N part of the island of Lewis with Harris, in the Outer Hebrides. Area: 1634 sq. km (631 sq. miles).

Lewis[2] ('luːɪs) *n* **1 Carl.** full name *Frederick Carleton Lewis.* born 1961, U.S. athlete; winner of the long jump, 100 metres, 200 metres, and 4 × 100 metres relay at the 1984 Olympic Games; winner of the 100 metres in the 1988 Olympic Games; winner of the long jump in the 1992 and 1996 Olympic Games. **2** See (Cecil) **Day-Lewis. 3 C(live) S(taples).** 1898–1963, English novelist, critic, and Christian apologist, noted for his critical work, *Allegory of Love* (1936), his theological study, *The Screwtape Letters* (1942), and for his children's books chronicling the land of Narnia. **4 Matthew Gregory,** known as *Monk Lewis.* 1775–1818, English novelist and dramatist, noted for his Gothic horror story

The Monk (1796). **5 Meriwether.** 1774–1807, American explorer who, with William Clark, led an overland expedition from St. Louis to the Pacific Ocean (1804–06). **6 (John) Saunders** ('sɔːndəz). 1893–1985, Welsh poet, dramatist, critic, and politician: founder (1926) and president (1926–39) of the Welsh Nationalist Party. **7 (Harry) Sinclair.** 1885–1951, U.S. novelist. He satirized the complacency and philistinism of American small-town life, esp. in *Main Street* (1920) and *Babbitt* (1922): Nobel prize for literature 1930. **8 Wally.** born 1959, Australian rugby league player. **9 (Percy) Wyndham.** 1884–1957, British painter, novelist, and critic, born in the U.S.: a founder of vorticism. His writings include *Time and Western Man* (1927), *The Apes of God* (1930), and the trilogy *The Human Age* (1928–55).

Lewis acid *n* a substance capable of accepting a pair of electrons from a base to form a covalent bond. Compare **Lewis base.** [C20: named after G. N. *Lewis* (1875–1946), U.S. chemist]

Lewis base *n* a substance capable of donating a pair of electrons to an acid to form a covalent bond. Compare **Lewis acid.** [C20: named after G. N. *Lewis*; see LEWIS ACID]

Lewis gun *n* a light air-cooled drum-fed gas-operated machine gun used chiefly in World War I. [C20: named after I. N. *Lewis* (1858–1931), U.S. soldier]

Lewisham ('luːɪʃəm) *n* a borough of S Greater London, on the River Thames. Pop.: 242 400 (1994 est.). Area: 35 sq. km (13 sq. miles).

lewisite ('luːɪˌsaɪt) *n* a colourless oily poisonous liquid with an odour resembling that of geraniums, having a powerful vesicant action and used as a war gas; 1-chloro-2-dichloroarsinoethene. Formula: $ClCH{:}CHAsCl_2$. [C20: named after W. L. *Lewis* (1878–1943), U.S. chemist]

Lewis with Harris *or* **Lewis and Harris** *n* an island in the Outer Hebrides, separated from the NW coast of Scotland by the Minch: consists of Lewis in the north and Harris in the south; many lakes and peat moors; economy based chiefly on the Harris tweed industry, with some fishing. Chief town: Stornoway. Pop.: 23 500 (latest est.). Area: 2134 sq. km (824 sq. miles).

lex (lɛks) *n, pl* **leges** ('liːdʒiːz). **1** a system or body of laws. **2** a particular specified law. [Latin]

lex. *abbrev. for* lexicon.

lexeme ('lɛksiːm) *n Linguistics.* a minimal meaningful unit of language, the meaning of which cannot be understood from that of its component morphemes. *Take off* (in the senses to mimic, to become airborne, etc.) is a lexeme, as well as the independent morphemes *take* and *off.* [C20: from LEX(ICON) + -EME]

lexical ('lɛksɪkᵊl) *adj* **1** of or relating to items of vocabulary in a language. **2** of or relating to a lexicon. ► **lexicality** (ˌlɛksɪ'kælɪtɪ) *n* ► **'lexically** *adv*

lexical decision task *n Psychol.* an experimental task in which subjects have to decide as fast as possible whether a given letter string is a word.

lexical insertion *n Generative grammar.* the process in which actual morphemes of a language are substituted either for semantic material or for place-fillers in the course of a derivation of a sentence.

lexicalize *or* **lexicalise** ('lɛksɪkəˌlaɪz) *vb Linguistics.* to form (a word or lexeme) or (of a word or lexeme) to be formed from constituent morphemes, words, or lexemes, as to form *cannot* from *can* and *not.* ► **ˌlexicali'zation** *or* **ˌlexicali'sation** *n*

lexical meaning *n* the meaning of a word in relation to the physical world or to abstract concepts, without reference to any sentence in which the word may occur. Compare **grammatical meaning, content word.**

lexical order *n* the arrangement of a set of items in accordance with a recursive algorithm, such as the entries in a dictionary whose order depends on their first letter unless these are the same in which case it is the second which decides, and so on.

lexicog. *abbrev. for:* **1** lexicographical. **2** lexicography.

lexicography (ˌlɛksɪ'kɒɡrəfɪ) *n* the process or profession of writing or compiling dictionaries. ► **ˌlexi'cographer** *n* ► **lexicographic** (ˌlɛksɪkə'ɡræfɪk) *or* **ˌlexico'graphical** *adj* ► **ˌlexico'graphically** *adv*

lexicology (ˌlɛksɪ'kɒlədʒɪ) *n* the study of the overall structure and history of the vocabulary of a language. ► **lexicological** (ˌlɛksɪkə'lɒdʒɪkᵊl) *adj* ► **ˌlexico'logically** *adv* ► **ˌlexi'cologist** *n*

lexicon ('lɛksɪkən) *n* **1** a dictionary, esp. one of an ancient language such as Greek or Hebrew. **2** a list of terms relating to a particular subject. **3** the vocabulary of a language or of an individual. **4** *Linguistics.* the set of all the morphemes of a language. [C17: New Latin, from Greek *lexikon,* n use of *lexikos* relating to words, from Greek *lexis* word, from *legein* to speak]

lexicostatistics (ˌlɛksɪkəʊstə'tɪstɪks) *n* (*functioning as sing*) the statistical study of the vocabulary of a language, with special attention to the historical links with other languages. See also **glottochronology.**

lexigram ('lɛksɪˌɡræm) *n* a figure or symbol that represents a word. [C20: from Greek *lexis* word + -GRAM]

lexigraphy (lɛk'sɪɡrəfɪ) *n* a system of writing in which each word is represented by a sign. [C19: from Greek *lexis* word + -GRAPHY]

Lexington ('lɛksɪŋtən) *n* **1** a city in NE central Kentucky, in the bluegrass region: major centre for horse-breeding. Pop.: 239 942 (1996 est.). **2** a city in Massachusetts, northwest of Boston: site of the first action (1775) of the War of American Independence. Pop.: 28 974 (1990).

lexis ('lɛksɪs) *n* the totality of vocabulary items in a language, including all forms having lexical meaning or grammatical function. [C20: from Greek *lexis* word]

lex loci ('ləʊsaɪ, -kiː) *n* the law of the place. [from Latin]

lex non scripta (nɒn 'skrɪptə) *n* the unwritten law; common law. [from Latin]

lex scripta *n* the written law; statute law. [from Latin]

lex talionis (ˌtælɪ'əʊnɪs) *n* the law of revenge or retaliation. [C16: New Latin]

ley (leɪ, liː) *n* **1** arable land put down to grass; grassland or pastureland. **2** Also called: **ley line.** a line joining two prominent points in the landscape, thought to be the line of a prehistoric track. [C14: variant of LEA[1]]

Leyden[1] ('laɪdᵊn; *Dutch* 'lɛidə) *n* a variant spelling of **Leiden.**

Leyden[2] ('laɪdᵊn) *n* See **Lucas van Leyden.**

Leyden jar *n Physics.* an early type of capacitor consisting of a glass jar with the lower part of the inside and outside coated with tin foil. [C18: first made in Leiden]

ley farming *n* the alternation at intervals of several years of crop growing and grassland pasture.

Leyte ('leɪteɪ) *n* an island in the central Philippines, in the Visayan Islands. Chief town: Tacloban. Pop.: 1 362 050 (1990). Area: 7215 sq. km (2786 sq. miles).

Leyte Gulf *n* an inlet of the Pacific in the E Philippines, east of Leyte and south of Samar: scene of a battle (Oct. 23–26, 1944) during World War II, in which the Americans defeated almost the entire Japanese navy, thereby ensuring ultimate Allied victory.

LF *Radio. abbrev. for* low frequency.

LG *abbrev. for* Low German.

lg. *or* **lge** *abbrev. for* large.

lgth *abbrev. for* length.

LGU *abbrev. for* Ladies' Golf Union.

LGV (in Britain) *abbrev. for* large goods vehicle.

lh *or* **LH** *abbrev. for* left hand.

LH *abbrev. for* luteinizing hormone.

Lhasa *or* **Lassa** ('lɑːsə) *n* a city in SW China, capital of Tibet AR, at an altitude of 3606 m (11 830 ft.): for centuries the sacred city of Lamaism and residence of the Dalai Lamas from the 17th century until 1950; known as the Forbidden City because it was closed to Westerners until the beginning of the 20th century; annexed by China in 1951. The Dalai Lama fled after an unsuccessful revolt against Chinese rule in 1959. Pop.: 106 885 (1990 est.).

lhasa apso ('lɑːsə 'æpsəʊ) *n, pl* **lhasa apsos.** a small dog of a Tibetan breed having a long straight dense coat, often gold or greyish, and a well-feathered tail carried curled over its back. [Tibetan]

lhd *abbrev. for* left-hand drive.

LH-RH *abbrev. for* luteinizing hormone-releasing hormone.

li (liː) *n* a Chinese unit of length, approximately equal to 590 yards. [from Chinese]

Li *the chemical symbol for* lithium.

LI *abbrev. for:* **1** Long Island. **2** Light Infantry.

liabilities (ˌlaɪə'bɪlɪtɪz) *pl n Accounting.* business obligations incurred but not discharged and entered as claims on the assets shown on the balance sheet. Compare **assets** (sense 1).

liability (ˌlaɪə'bɪlɪtɪ) *n, pl* **-ties. 1** the state of being liable. **2** a financial obligation. **3** a hindrance or disadvantage. **4** likelihood or probability.

liable ('laɪəbᵊl) *adj* (*postpositive*) **1** legally obliged or responsible; answerable. **2** susceptible or exposed; subject. **3** probable, likely, or capable: *it's liable to happen soon.* [C15: perhaps via Anglo-French, from Old French *lier* to bind, from Latin *ligāre*] ► **'liableness** *n*

USAGE The use of *liable to* to mean *likely to* was formerly considered incorrect, but is now acceptable.

liaise (lɪ'eɪz) *vb* (*intr;* usually foll. by *with*) to communicate and maintain contact (with). [C20: back formation from LIAISON]

liaison (lɪ'eɪzɒn) *n* **1** communication and contact between groups or units. **2** (*modifier*) of or relating to liaison between groups or units: *a liaison officer.* **3** a secretive or adulterous sexual relationship. **4** the relationship between military units necessary to ensure unity of purpose. **5** (in the phonology of several languages, esp. French) the pronunciation of a normally silent consonant at the end of a word immediately before another word commencing with a vowel, in such a way that the consonant is taken over as the initial sound of the following word. Liaison is seen between French *ils* (il) and *ont* (ɔ̃), to give *ils ont* (il zɔ̃). **6** any thickening for soups, sauces, etc., such as egg yolks or cream. [C17: via French from Old French, from *lier* to bind, from Latin *ligāre*]

liaison officer *n* **1** a person who liaises between groups or units. **2** *N.Z.* a university official who oversees the operation of the accrediting system in schools.

Liákoura ('ljakura) *n* transliteration of the Modern Greek name for (Mount) **Parnassus.**

liana (lɪ'ɑːnə) *or* **liane** (lɪ'ɑːn) *n* any of various woody climbing plants of tropical forests. [C19: changed from earlier *liane* (through influence of French *lier* to bind), from French, of obscure origin] ► **li'anoid** *adj*

Lianyungang ('ljæn'jʊŋ'ɡæŋ), **Sinhailien,** *or* **Hsin-hai-lien** *n* a city in E China, near the coast of Jiangsu. Pop.: 354 139 (1990 est.).

Liao (ljaʊ) *n* a river in NE China, rising in SE Inner Mongolia and flowing northeast then southwest to the Gulf of Liaodong. Length: about 1100 km (700 miles).

Liaodong ('ljaʊ'dʊŋ) *or* **Liaotung** ('ljaʊ'tʊŋ) *n* **1** a peninsula of NE China, in S Manchuria extending south into the Yellow Sea: forms the S part of Liaoning province. **2 Gulf of.** the N part of the Gulf of Chihli, west of the peninsula of Liaodong.

Liaoning ('ljaʊ'nɪŋ) *n* a province of NE China, in S Manchuria. Capital: Shenyang. Pop.: 40 920 000 (1996 est.). Area: 150 000 sq. km (58 500 sq. miles).

Liaoyang ('ljaʊ'jæŋ) *n* a city in NE China, in S Manchuria, in Liaoning province: a regional capital in the early dynasties. Pop.: 492 559 (1990 est.).

liar ('laɪə) *n* a person who has lied or lies repeatedly.

liard (lɪ'ɑːd) *n* a former small coin of various European countries. [C16: after G. *Liard,* French minter]

Liard ('liːɑːd, liː'ɑːd, -'ɑː) *n* a river in W Canada, rising in the SE Yukon and flowing east and then northwest to the Mackenzie River. Length: 885 km (550 miles).

liar paradox *n Logic.* the paradox that *this statement is false* is true only if it is false and false only if it is true: attributed to Epimenides the Cretan in the form *all Cretans are liars.*

Lias ('laɪəs) *n* the lowest series of rocks of the Jurassic system. **[C15** (referring to a kind of limestone), **C19** (geological sense) from Old French *liois,* perhaps from *lie* lees, dregs, so called from its appearance**]** ▸ **Liassic** (laɪ'æsɪk) *adj*

liatris (laɪ'ætrɪs) *n* see **blazing star** (sense 2). **[C18:** New Latin, of uncertain origin**]**

lib (lɪb) *n Informal, sometimes derogatory.* short for **liberation** (sense 2).

lib. *abbrev. for:* **1** liber. **[**Latin: book**] 2** librarian. **3** library.

Lib. *abbrev. for* Liberal.

libation (laɪ'beɪʃən) *n* **1a** the pouring out of wine, etc., in honour of a deity. **1b** the liquid so poured out. **2** *Usually facetious.* an alcoholic drink. **[C14:** from Latin *lībātiō,* from *lībāre* to pour an offering of drink**]** ▸ **li'bational** *or* **li'bationary** *adj*

Libau ('li:bau) *n* the German name for **Liepāja.**

Libava (lɪ'bavə) *n* transliteration of the Russian name for **Liepāja.**

Libby ('lɪbɪ) *n* **Willard Frank.** 1908–80, U.S. chemist, who devised the technique of radiocarbon dating: Nobel prize for chemistry 1960.

libeccio (lɪ'betʃɪəu) *or* **libecchio** (lɪ'bekɪəu) *n* a strong westerly or southwesterly wind blowing onto the W coast of Corsica. **[**Italian, via Latin, from Greek *libs***]**

libel ('laɪbᵊl) *n* **1** *Law.* **1a** the publication of defamatory matter in permanent form, as by a written or printed statement, picture, etc. **1b** the act of publishing such matter. **2** any defamatory or unflattering representation or statement. **3** *Ecclesiastical law.* a plaintiff's written statement of claim. **4** *Scots Law.* the formal statement of a charge. ◆ *vb* **-bels, -belling, -belled** *or U.S.* **-bels, -beling, -beled.** *(tr)* **5** *Law.* to make or publish a defamatory statement or representation about (a person). **6** to misrepresent injuriously. **7** *Ecclesiastical law.* to bring an action against (a person) in the ecclesiastical courts. **[C13** (in the sense: written statement), hence **C14** legal sense: a plaintiff's statement, via Old French from Latin *libellus* a little book, from *liber* a book**]** ▸ **'libeller** *or* **'libelist** *n* ▸ **'libellous** *or* **'libelous** *adj*

libellant *or U.S.* **libelant** ('laɪbᵊlənt) *n* **1** a party who brings an action in the ecclesiastical courts by presenting a libel. **2** a person who publishes a libel.

libellee *or U.S.* **libelee** (ˌlaɪbᵊ'li:) *n* a person against whom a libel has been filed in an ecclesiastical court.

liber ('laɪbə) *n* a rare name for **phloem. [C18:** from Latin, in original sense: tree bark**]**

liberal ('lɪbərəl, 'lɪbrəl) *adj* **1** relating to or having social and political views that favour progress and reform. **2** relating to or having policies or views advocating individual freedom. **3** giving and generous in temperament or behaviour. **4** tolerant of other people. **5** abundant; lavish: *a liberal helping of cream.* **6** not strict; free: *a liberal translation.* **7** of or relating to an education that aims to develop general cultural interests and intellectual ability. ◆ *n* **8** a person who has liberal ideas or opinions. **[C14:** from Latin *līberālis* of freedom, from *līber* free**]** ▸ **'liberally** *adv* ▸ **'liberalness** *n*

Liberal ('lɪbərəl, 'lɪbrəl) *n* **1** a member or supporter of a Liberal Party or Liberal Democrat party. ◆ *adj* **2** of or relating to a Liberal Party.

liberal arts *pl n* the fine arts, humanities, sociology, languages, and literature. Often shortened to **arts.**

Liberal Democrat *n* a member or supporter of the Liberal Democrats.

Liberal Democrats *pl n* (in Britain) a political party with centrist policies; established in 1988 as the Social and Liberal Democrats when the Liberal Party merged with the Social Democratic Party; renamed Liberal Democrats in 1989.

liberalism ('lɪbərəˌlɪzəm, 'lɪbrə-) *n* **1** liberal opinions, practices, or politics. **2** a movement in modern Protestantism that rejects biblical authority. ▸ **'liberalist** *n, adj* ▸ **ˌliberal'istic** *adj*

liberality (ˌlɪbə'rælɪtɪ) *n, pl* **-ties. 1** generosity; bounty. **2** the quality or condition of being liberal.

liberalize *or* **liberalise** ('lɪbərəˌlaɪz, 'lɪbrə-) *vb* to make or become liberal. ▸ **ˌliberali'zation** *or* **ˌliberali'sation** *n* ▸ **'liberalˌizer** *or* **'liberalˌiser** *n*

Liberal Party *n* **1** one of the former major political parties in Britain; in 1988 merged with the Social Democratic Party to form the Social and Liberal Democrats; renamed the Liberal Democrats in 1989. **2** one of the major political parties in Australia, a conservative party, generally opposed to the Labor Party. **3** one of the major political parties in Canada, generally representing viewpoints between those of the Progressive Conservative Party and the New Democratic Party. **4** any other party supporting liberal policies.

liberal studies *n (functioning as sing) Brit.* a supplementary arts course for those specializing in scientific, technical, or professional studies.

Liberal Unionist *n* a Liberal who opposed Gladstone's policy of Irish Home Rule in 1886 and after. ▸ **Liberal Unionism** *n*

liberate ('lɪbəˌreɪt) *vb (tr)* **1** to give liberty to; make free. **2** to release (something, esp. a gas) from chemical combination during a chemical reaction. **3** to release from occupation or subjugation by a foreign power. **4** to free from social prejudices or injustices. **5** *Euphemistic or facetious.* to steal. ▸ **'liberˌator** *n*

liberated ('lɪbəˌreɪtɪd) *adj* **1** given liberty; freed; released. **2** released from occupation or subjugation by a foreign power. **3** (esp. in feminist theory) not bound by traditional sexual and social roles.

liberation (ˌlɪbə'reɪʃən) *n* **1** a liberating or being liberated. **2** the seeking of equal status or just treatment for or on behalf of any group believed to be discriminated against: *women's liberation; animal liberation.* ▸ **ˌliber'ationist** *n, adj*

liberation theology *n* the belief that Christianity involves not only faith in the teachings of the Church but also a commitment to change social and political conditions from within in societies in which it is considered exploitation and oppression exist.

Liberec (*Czech* 'liberɛts) *n* a city in the N Czech Republic, on the Neisse River: a centre of the German Sudeten movement in 1938. Pop.: 100 604 (1996 est.). German name: **Reichenberg.**

Liber Extra ('laɪbər 'ɛkstrə) *n* See **Decretals. [**Latin: book of additional (decretals)**]**

Liberia (laɪ'bɪərɪə) *n* a republic in W Africa, on the Atlantic: originated in 1822 as a home for freed Afro-American slaves, with land purchased by the American Colonization Society; republic declared in 1847; exports are predominantly rubber and iron ore. Official language: English. Religion: Christian majority, also animist. Currency: dollar. Capital: Monrovia. Pop.: 2 772 000 (1998 est.). Area: 111 400 sq. km (43 000 sq. miles). ▸ **Li'berian** *adj, n*

libero (*Italian* 'li:bero) *n* another name for **sweeper** (sense 3).

libertarian (ˌlɪbə'tɛərɪən) *n* **1** a believer in freedom of thought, expression, etc. **2** *Philosophy.* a believer in the doctrine of free will. Compare **determinism.** ◆ *adj* **3** of, relating to, or characteristic of a libertarian. **[C18:** from LIBERTY**]** ▸ **ˌliber'tarianism** *n*

liberticide (lɪ'bɜ:tɪˌsaɪd) *n* **1** a destroyer of freedom. **2** the destruction of freedom. ▸ **liˌberti'cidal** *adj*

libertine ('lɪbəˌti:n, -ˌtaɪn) *n* **1** a morally dissolute person. ◆ *adj* **2** morally dissolute. **[C14** (in the sense: freedman, dissolute person): from Latin *lībertīnus* freedman, from *lībertus* freed, from *līber* free**]** ▸ **'liberˌtinage** *or* **'libertinˌism** *n*

liberty ('lɪbətɪ) *n, pl* **-ties. 1** the power of choosing, thinking, and acting for oneself; freedom from control or restriction. **2** the right or privilege of access to a particular place; freedom. **3** *(often pl)* a social action regarded as being familiar, forward, or improper. **4** *(often pl)* an action that is unauthorized or unwarranted in the circumstances: *he took liberties with the translation.* **5a** authorized leave granted to a sailor. **5b** *(as modifier): liberty man; liberty boat.* **6 at liberty.** free, unoccupied, or unrestricted. **7 take liberties (with).** to be overfamiliar or overpresumptuous. **8 take the liberty (of** *or* **to).** to venture or presume (to do something). **[C14:** from Old French *liberté,* from Latin *lībertās,* from *līber* free**]**

liberty bodice *n* a sleeveless vest-like undergarment made from thick cotton and covering the upper part of the body, formerly worn esp. by young children.

liberty cap *n* **1** a cap of soft felt worn as a symbol of liberty, esp. during the French Revolution, from the practice in ancient Rome of giving a freed slave such a cap. **2** a poisonous hallucinogenic basidiomycetous fungus, *Psilocybe semilanceata,* yellowish-brown with a distinctive pointed cap, found in groups in grassland.

liberty hall *n (sometimes caps.) Informal.* a place or condition of complete liberty.

liberty horse *n* (in a circus) a riderless horse that performs movements to verbal commands.

Liberty Island *n* a small island in upper New York Bay: site of the Statue of Liberty. Area: 5 hectares (12 acres). Former name (until 1956): **Bedloe's Island.**

liberty ship *n* a supply ship of World War II.

Libia ('li:bja) *n* the Italian name for **Libya.**

libidinous (lɪ'bɪdɪnəs) *adj* **1** characterized by excessive sexual desire. **2** of or relating to the libido. ▸ **li'bidinously** *adv* ▸ **li'bidinousness** *n*

libido (lɪ'bi:dəu) *n, pl* **-dos. 1** *Psychoanal.* psychic energy emanating from the id. **2** sexual urge or desire. **[C20** (in psychoanalysis): from Latin: desire**]** ▸ **libidinal** (lɪ'bɪdɪnᵊl) *adj* ▸ **li'bidinally** *adv*

libra ('laɪbrə) *n, pl* **-brae** (-bri:). an ancient Roman unit of weight corresponding to 1 pound, but equal to about 12 ounces. **[C14:** from Latin, literally: scales**]**

Libra ('li:brə) *n, Latin genitive* **Librae** ('li:bri:). **1** *Astronomy.* a small faint zodiacal constellation in the S hemisphere, lying between Virgo and Scorpius on the ecliptic. **2** *Astrology.* **2a** Also called: the **Scales,** the **Balance.** the seventh sign of the zodiac, symbol ♎, having a cardinal air classification and ruled by the planet Venus. The sun is in this sign between about Sept. 23 and Oct. 22. **2b** a person born under this sign. ◆ *adj* **3** *Astrology.* born under or characteristic of Libra. ◆ Also (for senses 2b, 3): **Libran** ('li:brən).

librarian (laɪ'brɛərɪən) *n* a person in charge of or assisting in a library.

librarianship (laɪ'brɛərɪənʃɪp, laɪ-) *n* the professional administration of library resources and services. Also called: **library science.**

library ('laɪbrərɪ) *n, pl* **-braries. 1** a room or set of rooms where books and other literary materials are kept. **2** a collection of literary materials, films, CDs, children's toys, etc., kept for borrowing or reference. **3** the building or institution that houses such a collection: *a public library.* **4** a set of books published as a series, often in a similar format. **5** *Computing.* a collection of standard programs and subroutines for immediate use, usually stored on disk or some other storage device. **6** a collection of specific items for reference or checking against: *a library of genetic material.* **[C14:** from Old French *librairie,* from Medieval Latin *librāris,* n. use of Latin *librārius* relating to books, from *liber* book**]**

library edition *n* an edition of a book having a superior quality of paper, binding, etc.

librate ('laɪbreɪt) *vb (intr)* **1** to oscillate or waver. **2** to hover or be balanced. **[C17:** from Latin *librātus,* from *librāre* to balance**]** ▸ **libratory** ('laɪbrətərɪ, -trɪ) *adj*

libration (laɪ'breɪʃən) *n* **1** the act or an instance of oscillating. **2** a real or apparent oscillation of the moon enabling approximately nine per cent of the surface facing away from earth to be seen. ▸ **li'brational** *adj*

librettist (lɪ'brɛtɪst) *n* the author of a libretto.

libretto (lɪ'brɛtəu) *n, pl* **-tos** *or* **-ti** (-ti:). a text written for and set to music in an opera, etc. **[C18:** from Italian, diminutive of *libro* book**]**

Libreville (*French* librəvil) *n* the capital of Gabon, in the west on the estuary of the Gabon River: founded as a French trading post in 1843 and expanded with the settlement of freed slaves in 1848. Pop.: 362 386 (1993).

libriform ('laɪbrɪˌfɔːm) *adj* (of a fibre of woody tissue) elongated and having a pitted thickened cell wall.

Librium ('lɪbrɪəm) *n Trademark.* a preparation of the drug chlordiazepoxide used as a tranquillizer. See also **benzodiazepine.**

Libya ('lɪbɪə) *n* a republic in N Africa, on the Mediterranean: became an Italian colony in 1912; divided after World War II into Tripolitania and Cyrenaica (under British administration) and Fezzan (under French); gained independence in 1951; monarchy overthrown by a military junta in 1969. It consists almost wholly of desert and is a major exporter of oil. Official language: Arabic. Official religion: (Sunni) Muslim. Currency: Libyan dinar. Capital: Tripoli. Pop.: 5 691 000 (1998 est.). Area: 1 760 000 sq. km (680 000 sq. miles). Official name: **Al-Jumhuria al-Arabia allibya** (-ˌdʒæmə'hɪriːjθ).

Libyan ('lɪbɪən) *adj* **1** of or relating to Libya, its people, or its language. ♦ *n* **2** a native or inhabitant of Libya. **3** the extinct Hamitic language of ancient Libya.

Libyan Desert *n* a desert in N Africa, in E Libya, W Egypt, and the NW Sudan: the NE part of the Sahara.

lice (laɪs) *n* the plural of **louse.**

licence *or U.S.* **license** ('laɪsəns) *n* **1** a certificate, tag, document, etc., giving official permission to do something. **2** formal permission or exemption. **3** liberty of action or thought; freedom. **4** intentional disregard of or deviation from conventional rules to achieve a certain effect: *poetic licence.* **5** excessive freedom. **6** licentiousness. **[C14:** via Old French and Medieval Latin *licentia* permission, from Latin: freedom, from *licet* it is allowed**]**

license ('laɪsəns) *vb* (*tr*) **1** to grant or give a licence for (something, such as the sale of alcohol). **2** to give permission to or for. ▸ **'licensable** *adj* ▸ **'licenser** *or* **'licensor** *n*

licensed aircraft engineer *n* the official name for **ground engineer.**

licensee (ˌlaɪsən'siː) *n* a person who holds a licence, esp. one to sell alcoholic drink.

license plate *or Canadian* **licence plate** *n* the U.S. and Canadian term for **numberplate.**

licentiate (laɪ'senʃɪɪt) *n* **1** a person who has received a formal attestation of professional competence to practise a certain profession or teach a certain skill or subject. **2** a degree between that of bachelor and doctor awarded now only by certain chiefly European universities. **3** a person who holds this degree. **4** *Chiefly Presbyterian Church.* a person holding a licence to preach. **[C15:** from Medieval Latin *licentiātus,* from *licentiāre* to permit**]** ▸ **li'centiateˌship** *n* ▸ **liˌcenti'ation** *n*

licentious (laɪ'senʃəs) *adj* **1** sexually unrestrained or promiscuous. **2** *Now rare.* showing disregard for convention. **[C16:** from Latin *licentiōsus* capricious, from *licentia* LICENCE**]** ▸ **li'centiously** *adv* ▸ **li'centiousness** *n*

lichee (ˌlaɪ'tʃiː) *n* a variant spelling of **litchi.**

lichen ('laɪkən, 'lɪtʃən) *n* **1** an organism that is formed by the symbiotic association of a fungus and an alga or cyanobacterium and occurs as crusty patches or bushy growths on tree trunks, bare ground, etc. Lichens are now classified as a phylum of fungi (*Mycophycophyta*). **2** *Pathol.* any of various eruptive disorders of the skin. **[C17:** via Latin from Greek *leikhēn,* from *leikhein* to lick**]** ▸ **'lichened** *adj* ▸ **'lichen-ˌlike** *adj* ▸ **'lichenˌoid** *adj* ▸ **'lichenous** *or* **'lichenˌose** *adj*

lichenin ('laɪkənɪn) *n* a complex polysaccharide occurring in certain species of mosses.

lichenology (ˌlaɪkə'nɒlədʒɪ, ˌlɪ-) *n* the study of the structure, physiology, and ecology of lichens.

Lichfield ('lɪtʃˌfiːld) *n* a city in central England, in SE Staffordshire: cathedral with three spires (13th-14th century); birthplace of Samuel Johnson, during whose lifetime the **Lichfield Group** (a literary circle) flourished. Pop.: 28 666 (1991).

lich gate (lɪtʃ) *n* a variant spelling of **lych gate.**

lichi (ˌlaɪ'tʃiː) *n* a variant spelling of **litchi.**

licht (lɪxt) *n, adj, vb* a Scot. word for **light**[1] and **light**[2].

Lichtenstein ('lɪktənˌstaɪn) *n* **Roy.** 1923–97, U.S. pop artist.

licit ('lɪsɪt) *adj* a less common word for **lawful.** **[C15:** from Latin *licitus* permitted, from *licēre* to be permitted**]** ▸ **'licitly** *adv* ▸ **'licitness** *n*

lick (lɪk) *vb* **1** (*tr*) to pass the tongue over, esp. in order to taste or consume. **2** to flicker or move lightly over or round (something): *the flames licked around the door.* **3** (*tr*) *Informal.* **3a** to defeat or vanquish. **3b** to flog or thrash. **3c** to be or do much better than. **4 lick into shape.** to put into a satisfactory condition: from the former belief that bear cubs were born formless and had to be licked into shape by their mother. **5 lick one's lips.** to anticipate or recall something with glee or relish. **6 lick one's wounds.** to retire after a defeat or setback in order to husband one's resources. **7 lick the boots of.** See **boot**[1] (sense 14). ♦ *n* **8** an instance of passing the tongue over something. **9** a small amount: *a lick of paint.* **10** Also called: **salt lick.** a block of compressed salt or chemical matter provided for domestic animals to lick for medicinal purposes. **11** a place to which animals go to lick exposed natural deposits of salt. **12** *Informal.* a hit; blow. **13** *Slang.* a short musical phrase, usually on one instrument. **14** *Informal.* speed; rate of movement: *he was going at quite a lick when he hit it.* **15 a lick and a promise.** something hastily done, esp. a hurried wash. **[**Old English *liccian;* related to Old High German *leckon,* Latin *lingere,* Greek *leikhein***]** ▸ **'licker** *n*

lick-alike *adj Irish informal.* very similar: *he and his father are lick-alike.*

lickerish *or* **liquorish** ('lɪkərɪʃ) *adj Archaic.* **1** lecherous or lustful. **2** greedy; gluttonous. **3** appetizing or tempting. **[C16:** changed from C13 *lickerous,* via Norman French from Old French *lechereus* lecherous; see LECHER**]** ▸ **'lickerishly** *or* **'liquorishly** *adv* ▸ **'lickerishness** *or* **'liquorishness** *n*

lickety-split ('lɪkɪtɪ'splɪt) *adv U.S. and Canadian informal.* very quickly; speedily. **[C19:** from LICK + SPLIT**]**

licking ('lɪkɪŋ) *n Informal.* **1** a beating. **2** a defeat.

lickspittle ('lɪkˌspɪtᵊl) *n* a flattering or servile person.

licorice ('lɪkərɪs) *n* the usual U.S. and Canadian spelling of **liquorice.**

lictor ('lɪktə) *n* one of a group of ancient Roman officials, usually bearing fasces, who attended magistrates, etc. **[C16** *lictor,* **C14** *littour,* from Latin *ligāre* to bind**]**

lid (lɪd) *n* **1** a cover, usually removable or hinged, for a receptacle: *a saucepan lid; a desk lid.* **2** short for **eyelid. 3** *Botany.* another name for **operculum** (sense 2). **4** *U.S. dated slang.* a quantity of marijuana, usually an ounce. **5 dip one's lid.** *Austral. informal.* to raise one's hat as a greeting, etc. **6 flip one's lid.** *Slang.* to become crazy or angry. **7 put the lid on.** *Informal.* **7a** *Brit.* to be the final blow to. **7b** to curb, prevent, or discourage. **8 take the lid off.** *Informal.* to make startling or spectacular revelations about. **[**Old English *hlid;* related to Old Friesian *hlid,* Old High German *hlit* cover**]** ▸ **'lidded** *adj*

Liddell Hart ('lɪdᵊl 'hɑːt) *n* Sir **Basil Henry.** 1895–1970, British military strategist and historian: he advocated the development of mechanized warfare before World War II.

Lidice (*Czech* 'lidjtse) *n* a mining village in the Czech Republic: destroyed by the Germans in 1942 in reprisal for the assassination of Reinhard Heydrich; rebuilt as a national memorial.

lidless ('lɪdlɪs) *adj* **1** having no lid or top. **2** (of animals) having no eyelids. **3** *Archaic.* vigilant and watchful.

lido ('liːdəʊ) *n, pl* **-dos.** *Brit.* a public place of recreation, including a pool for swimming or water sports. **[C20:** after the *Lido,* island bathing beach near Venice, from Latin *litus* shore**]**

lidocaine ('laɪdəˌkeɪn) *n* the U.S. name for **lignocaine. [C20:** from *acetanilid* + *-caine* as in *cocaine***]**

lie[1] (laɪ) *vb* **lies, lying, lied. 1** (*intr*) to speak untruthfully with intent to mislead or deceive. **2** (*intr*) to convey a false impression or practise deception: *the camera does not lie.* ♦ *n* **3** an untrue or deceptive statement deliberately used to mislead. **4** something that is deliberately intended to deceive. **5 give the lie to. 5a** to disprove. **5b** to accuse of lying. ♦ Related adj: **mendacious. [**Old English *lyge* (n), *lēogan* (vb); related to Old High German *liogan,* Gothic *liugan***]**

lie[2] (laɪ) *vb* **lies, lying, lay** (leɪ), **lain** (leɪn). (*intr*) **1** (often foll. by *down*) to place oneself or be in a prostrate position, horizontal to the ground. **2** to be situated, esp. on a horizontal surface: *the pencil is lying on the desk; India lies to the south of Russia.* **3** to be buried: *here lies Jane Brown.* **4** (*copula*) to be and remain (in a particular state or condition): *to lie dormant.* **5** to stretch or extend: *the city lies before us.* **6** (usually foll. by *on* or *upon*) to rest or weigh: *my sins lie heavily on my mind.* **7** (usually foll. by *in*) to exist or consist inherently: *strength lies in unity.* **8** (foll. by *with*) **8a** to be or rest (with): *the ultimate decision lies with you.* **8b** *Archaic.* to have sexual intercourse (with). **9** (of an action, claim, appeal, etc.) to subsist; be maintainable or admissible. **10** *Archaic.* to stay temporarily. **11 lie in state.** See **state** (sense 13). **12 lie low. 12a** to keep or be concealed or quiet. **12b** to wait for a favourable opportunity. ♦ *n* **13** the manner, place, or style in which something is situated. **14** the hiding place or lair of an animal. **15** *Golf.* **15a** the position of the ball after a shot: *a bad lie.* **15b** the angle made by the shaft of the club before the upswing. **16 lie of the land. 16a** the topography of the land. **16b** the way in which a situation is developing or people are behaving. ♦ See also **lie down, lie in, lie to, lie up. [**Old English *licgan* akin to Old High German *ligen* to lie, Latin *lectus* bed**]**

USAGE See at **lay**[1].

Lie (liː) *n* **Trygve Halvdan** ('trygvə 'halðan). 1896–1968, Norwegian statesman; first secretary-general of the United Nations (1946–52).

Liebfraumilch ('liːbfrauˌmɪlk; *German* 'liːpfraumɪlç) *or* **Liebfrauenmilch** (*German* liːp'frauənmɪlç) *n* a white table wine from the Rhine vineyards. **[**German: from *Liebfrau* the Virgin Mary + *Milch* milk; after *Liebfrauenstift* convent in Worms where the wine was originally made**]**

Liebig (*German* 'liːbɪç) *n* **Justus** ('justus), Baron von Liebig. 1803–73, German chemist, who founded agricultural chemistry. He also contributed to organic chemistry, esp. to the concept of radicals, and discovered chloroform.

Liebig condenser *n Chem.* a laboratory condenser consisting of a glass tube surrounded by a glass envelope through which cooling water flows.

Liebknecht (*German* 'liːpkneçt) *n* **1 Karl** (karl). 1871–1919, German socialist leader: with Rosa Luxemburg he led an unsuccessful Communist revolt (1919) and was assassinated. **2** his father, **Wilhelm** ('vɪlhelm). 1826–1900, German socialist leader and journalist, a founder (1869) of what was to become (1891) the German Social Democratic Party.

Liechtenstein ('lɪktənˌstaɪn; *German* 'lɪçtənʃtain) *n* a small mountainous principality in central Europe on the Rhine: formed in 1719 by the uniting of the lordships of Schellenburg and Vaduz, which had been purchased by the Austrian family of Liechtenstein; customs union formed with Switzerland in 1924. Official language: German. Religion: Roman Catholic majority. Currency: Swiss franc. Capital: Vaduz. Pop.: 31 400 (1998 est.). Area: 160 sq. km (62 sq. miles). ▸ **'Liechtenˌsteiner** *adj, n*

lied (liːd; *German* liːt) *n, pl* **lieder** ('liːdə; *German* 'liːdər). *Music.* any of various musical settings for solo voice and piano of a romantic or lyrical poem, for which composers such as Schubert, Schumann, and Wolf are famous. **[**from German: song**]**

lie detector *n* a polygraph used esp. by a police interrogator to detect false or devious answers to questions, a sudden change in one or more involuntary physiological responses being considered a manifestation of guilt, fear, etc. See **polygraph** (sense 1), **galvanic skin response.**

lie down *vb* (*intr, adv*) **1** to place oneself or be in a prostrate position in order to rest or sleep. **2** to accept without protest or opposition (esp. in the phrases **lie down under, take something lying down**). ♦ *n* **lie-down. 3** a rest.

lief (liːf) *adv* **1** *Now rare.* gladly; willingly: *I'd as lief go today as tomorrow.* ♦ *adj* **2** *Archaic.* **2a** ready; glad. **2b** dear; beloved. **[**Old English *leof;* related to *lufu* love**]**

liege (liːdʒ) *adj* **1** (of a lord) owed feudal allegiance (esp. in the phrase **liege lord**). **2** (of a vassal or servant) owing feudal allegiance: *a liege subject.* **3** of or relating to the relationship or bond between liege lord and liegeman: *liege homage.* **4** faithful; loyal. ◆ *n* **5** a liege lord. **6** a liegeman or true subject. [C13: from Old French *lige,* from Medieval Latin *līticus,* from *lītus, laetus* serf, of Germanic origin]

Liège (lɪˈeɪʒ; *French* ljɛʒ) *n* **1** a province of E Belgium: formerly a principality of the Holy Roman Empire, much larger than the present-day province. Pop.: 1 013 729 (1996 est.). Area: 3877 sq. km (1497 sq. miles). **2** a city in E Belgium, capital of Liège province: the largest French-speaking city in Belgium; river port and industrial centre. Pop.: 190 525 (1996 est.). ◆ Flemish name: **Luik.**

liegeman (ˈliːdʒˌmæn) *n, pl* **-men. 1** (formerly) the subject of a sovereign or feudal lord; vassal. **2** a loyal follower.

Liegnitz (ˈliːgnɪts) *n* the German name for **Legnica.**

lie in *vb* (*intr, adv*) **1** to remain in bed late in the morning. **2** to be confined in childbirth. ◆ *n* **lie-in. 3** a long stay in bed in the morning.

lien (ˈliːən, liːn) *n Law.* a right to retain possession of another's property pending discharge of a debt. [C16: via Old French from Latin *ligāmen* bond, from *ligāre* to bind]

lienal (ˈlaɪənᵊl) *adj* of or relating to the spleen. [C19: from Latin *lien* SPLEEN]

lientery (ˈlaɪəntərɪ, -trɪ) *n Pathol.* the passage of undigested food in the faeces. [C16: from French, from Medieval Latin, from Greek *leienteria,* from *leios* smooth + *enteron* intestine] ▸ ˌ**lienˈteric** *adj*

Liepāja *or* **Lepaya** (lɪˈpɑːjə) *n* a port in W Latvia on the Baltic Sea; founded by the Teutonic Knights in 1263: a naval and industrial centre, with a fishing fleet. Pop.: 100 271 (1995 est.). Russian name: **Libava.** German name: **Libau.**

lierne (lɪˈɜːn) *n Architect.* a short secondary rib that connects the intersections of the primary ribs, esp. as used in Gothic vaulting. [C19: from French, perhaps related to *lier* to bind]

Liestal (*German* ˈliːstaːl) *n* a city in NW Switzerland, capital of Basel-Land demicanton. Pop.: 12 161 (1987 est.).

lie to *vb* (*intr, adv*) *Nautical.* (of a vessel) to be hove to with little or no swinging.

Lietuva (lɪəˈtuːvə) *n* the Lithuanian name for **Lithuania.**

lieu (ljuː, luː) *n* stead; place (esp. in the phrases **in lieu, in lieu of**). [C13: from Old French, ultimately from Latin *locus* place]

lie up *vb* (*intr, adv*) **1** to go into or stay in one's room or bed, as through illness. **2** to be out of commission or use: *my car has been lying up for months.*

Lieut *abbrev. for* lieutenant. Also: **Lt.**

lieutenant (lɛfˈtɛnənt; *U.S.* luːˈtɛnənt) *n* **1** a military officer holding commissioned rank immediately junior to a captain. **2** a naval officer holding commissioned rank immediately junior to a lieutenant commander. **3** *U.S.* an officer in a police or fire department ranking immediately junior to a captain. **4** a person who holds an office in subordination to or in place of a superior. [C14: from Old French, literally: place-holding] ▸ **lieuˈtenancy** *n*

lieutenant colonel *n* an officer holding commissioned rank immediately junior to a colonel in certain armies, air forces, and marine corps.

lieutenant commander *n* an officer holding commissioned rank in certain navies immediately junior to a commander.

lieutenant general *n* an officer holding commissioned rank in certain armies, air forces, and marine corps immediately junior to a general.

lieutenant governor *n* **1** a deputy governor. **2** (in the U.S.) an elected official who acts as deputy to a state governor and succeeds him if he dies. **3** **lieutenant-governor.** (in Canada) the representative of the Crown in a province: appointed by the federal government acting for the Crown.

Lifar (*Russian* ljiˈfar) *n* **Serge** (sɛrʒ). 1905–86, Russian ballet dancer and choreographer: ballet master at the Paris Opera Ballet (1932–58). His ballets include *Prométhée* (1929), *Icare* (1935), and *Phèdre* (1950).

life (laɪf) *n, pl* **lives** (laɪvz). **1** the state or quality that distinguishes living beings or organisms from dead ones and from inorganic matter, characterized chiefly by metabolism, growth, and the ability to reproduce and respond to stimuli. Related adjs.: **animate, vital. 2** the period between birth and death. **3** a living person or being: *to save a life.* **4** the time between birth and the present time. **5a** the remainder or extent of one's life. **5b** (*as modifier*): *a life sentence; life membership; life subscription; life work.* **6** short for **life imprisonment. 7** the amount of time that something is active or functioning: *the life of a battery.* **8** a present condition, state, or mode of existence: *my life is very dull here.* **9a** a biography. **9b** (*as modifier*): *a life story.* **10a** a characteristic state or mode of existence: *town life.* **10b** (*as modifier*): *life style.* **11** the sum or course of human events and activities. **12** liveliness or high spirits: *full of life.* **13** a source of strength, animation, or vitality: *he was the life of the show.* **14** all living things, taken as a whole: *there is no life on Mars; plant life.* **15** sparkle, as of wines. **16** strong or high flavour, as of fresh food. **17** (*modifier*) *Arts.* drawn or taken from a living model: *life drawing; a life mask.* **18** *Physics.* another name for **lifetime. 19** (in certain games) one of a number of opportunities of participation. **20 as large as life.** *Informal.* real and living. **21 larger than life.** in an exaggerated form. **22 come to life. 22a** to become animate or conscious. **22b** to be realistically portrayed or represented. **23 for dear life.** urgently or with extreme vigour or desperation. **24 for the life of me (him, her,** etc.) though trying desperately. **25 go for your life.** *Austral. and N.Z. informal.* an expression of encouragement. **26 a matter of life and death.** a matter of extreme urgency. **27 not on your life.** *Informal.* certainly not. **28 the life and soul.** *Informal.* a person regarded as the main source of merriment and liveliness: *the life and soul of the party.* **29 the life of Riley.** *Informal.* an easy life. **30 to the life.** (of a copy or image) resembling the original exactly. **31 to save (one's) life.** *Informal.* in spite of all considerations or attempts: *he couldn't play football to save his life.* **32 the time of one's life.** a memorably enjoyable time. **33 true to life.** faithful to reality. [Old English *līf;* related to Old High German *lib,* Old Norse *līf* life, body]

life assurance *n* a form of insurance providing for the payment of a specified sum to a named beneficiary on the death of the policyholder. Also called: **life insurance.**

life belt *n* a ring filled with buoyant material or air, used to keep a person afloat when in danger of drowning.

lifeblood (ˈlaɪfˌblʌd) *n* **1** the blood, considered as vital to sustain life. **2** the essential or animating force.

lifeboat (ˈlaɪfˌbəʊt) *n* **1** a boat, propelled by oars or a motor, used for rescuing people at sea, escaping from a sinking ship, etc. **2** *Informal.* a fund set up by the dealers in a market to rescue any member who may become insolvent as a result of a collapse in market prices.

life buoy *n* any of various kinds of buoyant device for keeping people afloat in an emergency.

life cycle *n* the series of changes occurring in an animal or plant between one development stage and the identical stage in the next generation.

life estate *n* property that may be held only for the extent of the holder's lifetime.

life expectancy *n* the statistically determined average number of years of life remaining after a specified age for a given group of individuals. Also called: **expectation of life.**

life form *n* **1** *Biology.* the characteristic overall form and structure of a mature organism on the basis of which it can be classified. **2** any living creature. **3** (in science fiction) an alien.

lifeguard (ˈlaɪfˌgɑːd) *n* a person present at a beach or pool to guard people against the risk of drowning. Also called: **life-saver.**

Life Guards *pl n* (in Britain) a cavalry regiment forming part of the Household Brigade, who wear scarlet jackets and white plumes in their helmets.

life history *n* **1** the series of changes undergone by an organism between fertilization of the egg and death. **2** the series of events that make up a person's life.

life imprisonment *n* (in Britain) an indeterminate sentence always given for murder and as a maximum sentence in several other crimes. There is no remission, although the Home Secretary may order the prisoner's release on licence.

life instinct *n Psychoanal.* the instinct for reproduction and self-preservation.

life insurance *n* another name for **life assurance.**

life interest *n* interest (esp. from property) that is payable to a person during his life but ceases with his death.

life jacket *n* an inflatable sleeveless jacket worn to keep a person afloat when in danger of drowning.

lifeless (ˈlaɪflɪs) *adj* **1** without life; inanimate; dead. **2** not sustaining living organisms. **3** having no vitality or animation. **4** unconscious. ▸ ˈ**lifelessly** *adv* ▸ ˈ**lifelessness** *n*

lifelike (ˈlaɪfˌlaɪk) *adj* closely resembling or representing life. ▸ ˈ**lifeˌlikeness** *n*

lifeline (ˈlaɪfˌlaɪn) *n* **1** a line thrown or fired aboard a vessel for hauling in a hawser for a breeches buoy. **2** any rope or line attached to a vessel or trailed from it for the safety of passengers, crew, swimmers, etc. **3** a line by which a deep-sea diver is raised or lowered. **4** a vital line of access or communication.

lifelong (ˈlaɪfˌlɒŋ) *adj* lasting for or as if for a lifetime.

life mask *n* a cast taken from the face of a living person, usually using plaster of Paris.

life peer *n Brit.* a peer whose title lapses at his death.

life preserver *n* **1** *Brit.* a club or bludgeon, esp. one kept for self-defence. **2** *U.S. and Canadian.* a life belt or life jacket.

lifer (ˈlaɪfə) *n Informal.* a prisoner sentenced to life imprisonment.

life raft *n* a raft for emergency use at sea.

life-saver *n* **1** the saver of a person's life. **2** another name for **lifeguard. 3** *Informal.* a person or thing that gives help in time of need. ▸ ˈ**life-ˌsaving** *adj, n*

life science *n* any one of the branches of science concerned with the structure and behaviour of living organisms, such as biology, botany, zoology, physiology, or biochemistry. Compare **physical science.** See also **social science.**

life-size *or* **life-sized** *adj* representing actual size.

life space *n Psychol.* a spatial representation of all the forces that control a person's behaviour.

life span *n* the period of time during which a human being, animal, machine, etc., may be expected to live or function under normal conditions.

lifestyle (ˈlaɪfˌstaɪl) *n* **1** a set of attitudes, habits, or possessions associated with a particular person or group. **2** such attitudes, etc., regarded as fashionable or desirable. **3** *N.Z.* **3a** a luxurious semirural manner of living. **3b** (*as modifier*): *a lifestyle property.*

lifestyle business *n* a small business in which the owners are more anxious to pursue interests that reflect their lifestyle than to make more than a comfortable living.

life-support *adj* of or providing the equipment required to sustain human life in an unnatural environment, such as in space, or in severe illness or disability.

life table *n* another name for **mortality table.**

lifetime (ˈlaɪfˌtaɪm) *n* **1a** the length of time a person or animal is alive. **1b** (*as modifier*): *a lifetime supply.* **2** the length of time that something functions, is useful, etc.. **3** *Physics.* the average time of existence of an unstable or reactive entity, such as a nucleus or elementary particle, etc.; mean life.

Liffey (ˈlɪfɪ) *n* a river in E Republic of Ireland, rising in the Wicklow Mountains and flowing west, then northeast through Dublin into Dublin Bay. Length: 80 km (50 miles).

Lifford (ˈlɪfərd) *n* the county town of Donegal, Republic of Ireland; market town. Pop.: 1461 (1986).

LIFO (ˈlaɪfəʊ) *acronym for* last in, first out (as an accounting principle in sorting stock). Compare **FIFO.**

lift[1] (lɪft) *vb* **1** to rise or cause to rise upwards from the ground or another support to a higher place: *to lift a sack.* **2** to move or cause to move upwards: *to lift one's eyes.* **3** (*tr*) to take hold of in order to carry or remove: *to lift something down from a shelf.* **4** (*tr*) to raise in status, spirituality, estimation, etc.: *his position lifted him from the common crowd.* **5** (*tr*) to revoke or rescind: *to lift tax restrictions.* **6** to make or become audible or louder: *to lift one's voice in song.* **7** (*tr*) to take (plants or underground crops) out of the ground for transplanting or harvesting. **8** (*intr*) to disappear by lifting or as if by lifting: *the fog lifted.* **9** to transport in a vehicle. **10** (*tr*) *Informal.* to take unlawfully or dishonourably; steal. **11** (*tr*) *Informal.* to make dishonest use of (another person's idea, writing, etc.); plagiarize. **12** (*tr*) *Slang.* to arrest. **13** (*tr*) to perform a face-lift on. **14** (*tr*) *U.S. and Canadian.* to pay off (a mortgage, etc.). ◆ *n* **15** the act or an instance of lifting. **16** the power or force available or used for lifting. **17a** *Brit.* a platform, compartment, or cage raised or lowered in a vertical shaft to transport persons or goods in a building. U.S. and Canadian word: **elevator. 17b** See **chairlift, ski lift. 18** the distance or degree to which something is lifted. **19** a usually free ride as a passenger in a car or other vehicle. **20** a rise in the height of the ground. **21** a rise in morale or feeling of cheerfulness usually caused by some specific thing or event. **22** the force required to lift an object. **23** a layer of the heel of a shoe, etc., or a detachable pad inside the shoe to give the wearer added height. **24** aid; help. **25** *Mining.* **25a** the thickness of ore extracted in one operation. **25b** a set of pumps used in a mine. **26a** the component of the aerodynamic forces acting on a wing, etc., at right angles to the airflow. **26b** the upward force exerted by the gas in a balloon, airship, etc. **27** See **airlift** (sense 1). [C13: from Scandinavian; related to Old Norse *lypta,* Old English *lyft* sky; compare LOFT] ▸ **'liftable** *adj* ▸ **'lifter** *n*

lift[2] (lɪft) *n Scot.* the sky. [Old English *lyft*]

liftboy ('lɪftˌbɔɪ) *or* **liftman** *n, pl* **-boys** *or* **-men.** a person who operates a lift, esp. in large public or commercial buildings and hotels.

lifting body *n* a wingless aircraft or spacecraft that derives its aerodynamic lift from the shape of its body.

liftoff ('lɪftˌɒf) *n* **1** the initial movement or ascent of a rocket from its launch pad. **2** the instant at which this occurs. ◆ *vb* **lift off. 3** (*intr, adv*) (of a rocket) to leave its launch pad.

lift pump *n* a pump that raises a fluid to a higher level. It usually consists of a piston and vertical cylinder with flap or ball valves in both piston and cylinder base. Compare **force pump.**

lig (lɪg) *Brit. slang.* ◆ *n* **1** (esp. in the entertainment industry and the media) a function at which free entertainment and refreshments are available. ◆ *vb* **ligs, ligging, ligged. 2** (*intr*) to attend such a function in order to take advantage of free entertainment and refreshments; freeload. [C20: origin uncertain] ▸ **'ligger** *n* ▸ **'ligging** *n*

ligament ('lɪgəmənt) *n* **1** *Anatomy.* any one of the bands or sheets of tough fibrous connective tissue that restrict movement in joints, connect various bones or cartilages, support muscles, etc. **2** any physical or abstract connection or bond. [C14: from Medieval Latin *ligāmentum,* from Latin (in the sense: bandage), from *ligāre* to bind]

ligamentous (ˌlɪgə'mɛntəs), **ligamental,** *or* **ligamentary** *adj* relating to or shaped like a ligament.

ligan ('laɪgən) *n* a variant of **lagan.**

ligand ('lɪgənd, 'laɪ-) *n Chem.* an atom, molecule, radical, or ion forming a complex with a central atom. [C20: from Latin *ligandum,* gerund of *ligāre* to bind]

ligase ('laɪˌgeɪz) *n* any of a class of enzymes that catalyse the formation of covalent bonds and are important in the synthesis and repair of biological molecules, such as DNA.

ligate ('laɪgeɪt) *vb* (*tr*) to tie up or constrict (something) with a ligature. [C16: from Latin *ligātus,* from *ligāre* to bind] ▸ **li'gation** *n* ▸ **ligative** ('lɪgətɪv) *adj*

ligature ('lɪgətʃə, -ˌtʃʊə) *n* **1** the act of binding or tying up. **2** something used to bind. **3** a link, bond, or tie. **4** *Surgery.* a thread or wire for tying around a vessel, duct, etc., as for constricting the flow of blood to a part. **5** *Printing.* a character of two or more joined letters, such as, ﬁ, ﬂ, ﬃ, ﬄ. **6** *Music.* **6a** a slur or the group of notes connected by it. **6b** (in plainsong notation) a symbol indicating two or more notes grouped together. ◆ *vb* **7** (*tr*) to bind with a ligature; ligate. [C14: from Late Latin *ligātūra,* ultimately from Latin *ligāre* to bind]

liger ('laɪgə) *n* the hybrid offspring of a female tiger and a male lion.

Ligeti (*Hungarian* 'ligeti) *n* **György** (djørdj). born 1923, Hungarian composer, resident in Vienna. His works, noted for their experimentalism, include *Atmosphères* (1961) for orchestra, *Volumina* (1962) for organ, and a requiem mass (1965).

light[1] (laɪt) *n* **1** the medium of illumination that makes sight possible. **2** Also called: **visible radiation.** electromagnetic radiation that is capable of causing a visual sensation and has wavelengths from about 380 to about 780 nanometres. **3** (*not in technical usage*) electromagnetic radiation that has a wavelength outside this range, esp. ultraviolet radiation: *ultraviolet light.* **4** the sensation experienced when electromagnetic radiation within the visible spectrum falls on the retina of the eye. Related prefix: **photo-. 5** anything that illuminates, such as a lamp or candle. **6** See **traffic light. 7** a particular quality or type of light: *a good light for reading.* **8a** illumination from the sun during the day; daylight. **8b** the time this appears; daybreak; dawn. **9** anything that allows the entrance of light, such as a window or compartment of a window. **10** the condition of being visible or known (esp. in the phrases **bring** *or* **come to light**). **11** an aspect or view: *he saw it in a different light.* **12** mental understanding or spiritual insight. **13** a person considered to be an authority or leader. **14** brightness of countenance, esp. a sparkle in the eyes. **15a** the act of igniting or kindling something, such as a cigarette. **15b** something that ignites or kindles, esp. in a specified manner, such as a spark or flame. **15c** something used for igniting or kindling, such as a match. **16** See **lighthouse. 17a** the effect of illumination on objects or scenes, as created in a picture. **17b** an area of brightness in a picture, as opposed to shade. **18** a poetic or archaic word for **eyesight. 19** the answer to a clue in a crossword. **20 in (the) light of.** in view of; taking into account; considering. **21 light at the end of the tunnel.** hope for the ending of a difficult or unpleasant situation. **22 out like a light.** quickly asleep or unconscious. **23 see the light. 23a** to gain sudden insight into or understanding of something. **23b** to experience a religious conversion. **24 see the light (of day). 24a** to come into being. **24b** to come to public notice. **25 shed** (*or* **throw**) **light on.** to clarify or supply additional information on. **26 stand in a person's light.** to stand so as to obscure a person's vision. **27 strike a light. 27a** (*vb*) to ignite something, esp. a match, by friction. **27b** (*interj*) *Brit.* an exclamation of surprise. ◆ *adj* **28** full of light; well-lighted. **29** (of a colour) reflecting or transmitting a large amount of light: *light yellow.* Compare **medium** (sense 2), **dark** (sense 2). **30** *Phonetics.* relating to or denoting an (l) pronounced with front vowel resonance; clear: *the French "l" is much lighter than that of English.* Compare **dark** (sense 9). ◆ *vb* **lights, lighting, lighted** *or* **lit** (lɪt). **31** to ignite or cause to ignite. **32** (often foll. by *up*) to illuminate or cause to illuminate. **33** to make or become cheerful or animated. **34** (*tr*) to guide or lead by light. ◆ See also **lights**[1], **light up.** [Old English *lēoht;* related to Old High German *lioht,* Gothic *liuhath,* Latin *lux*] ▸ **'lightish** *adj* ▸ **'lightless** *adj*

light[2] (laɪt) *adj* **1** not heavy; weighing relatively little. **2** having relatively low density: *magnesium is a light metal.* **3** lacking sufficient weight; not agreeing with standard or official weights. **4** not great in degree, intensity, or number: *light rain; a light eater.* **5** without burdens, difficulties, or problems; easily borne or done: *a light heart; light work.* **6** graceful, agile, or deft: *light fingers.* **7** not bulky or clumsy. **8** not serious or profound; entertaining: *light verse.* **9** without importance or consequence; insignificant: *no light matter.* **10** frivolous or capricious. **11** loose in morals. **12** dizzy or unclear: *a light head.* **13** (of bread, cake, etc.) spongy or well leavened. **14** easily digested: *a light meal.* **15** relatively low in alcoholic content: *a light wine.* **16** (of a soil) having a crumbly texture. **17** (of a vessel, lorry, etc.) **17a** designed to carry light loads. **17b** not loaded. **18** carrying light arms or equipment: *light infantry.* **19** (of an industry) engaged in the production of small consumer goods using light machinery. Compare **heavy** (sense 10). **20** *Aeronautics.* (of an aircraft) having a maximum take-off weight less than 5670 kilograms (12 500 pounds). **21** *Chem.* (of an oil fraction obtained from coal tar) having a boiling range between about 100° and 210°C. **22** (of a railway) having a narrow gauge, or in some cases a standard gauge with speed or load restrictions not applied to a main line. **23** *Bridge.* **23a** (of a bid) made on insufficient values. **23b** (of a player) having failed to take sufficient tricks to make his contract. **24** *Phonetics, prosody.* (of a syllable, vowel, etc.) unaccented or weakly stressed; short. Compare **heavy** (sense 13). See also **light**[1] (sense 30). **25** *Phonetics.* the least of three levels of stress in an utterance, in such languages as English. **26 light on.** *Informal.* lacking a sufficient quantity of (something). **27 make light of.** to treat as insignificant or trifling. ◆ *adv* **28** a less common word for **lightly. 29** with little equipment, baggage, etc.: *to travel light.* ◆ *vb* **lights, lighting, lighted** *or* **lit** (lɪt). (*intr*) **30** (esp. of birds) to settle or land after flight. **31** to get down from a horse, vehicle, etc. **32** (foll. by *on* or *upon*) to come upon unexpectedly. **33** to strike or fall on: *the choice lighted on me.* ◆ See also **light into, light out, lights**[2]. [Old English *lēoht;* related to Dutch *licht,* Gothic *leihts*] ▸ **'lightish** *adj* ▸ **'lightly** *adv* ▸ **'lightness** *n*

Light (laɪt) *n* **1** God regarded as a source of illuminating grace and strength. **2** *Quakerism.* short for **Inner Light.**

light air *n* very light air movement of force one on the Beaufort scale.

light box *n* a light source contained in a box and covered with a diffuser, used for viewing photographic transparencies, negatives, etc.

light breeze *n* a very light wind of force two on the Beaufort scale.

light bulb *n* a glass bulb containing a gas, such as argon or nitrogen, at low pressure and enclosing a thin metal filament that emits light when an electric current is passed through it. Sometimes shortened to **bulb.**

light-emitting diode *n* a diode of semiconductor material, such as gallium arsenide, that emits light when a forward bias is applied, the colour depending on the semiconductor material: used as off/on indicators. Abbrev.: **LED.**

lighten[1] ('laɪtᵊn) *vb* **1** to become or make light. **2** (*intr*) to shine; glow. **3** (*intr*) (of lightning) to flash. **4** (*tr*) an archaic word for **enlighten.**

lighten[2] ('laɪtᵊn) *vb* **1** to make or become less heavy. **2** to make or become less burdensome or oppressive; mitigate. **3** to make or become more cheerful or lively.

light engine *n* a railway locomotive in motion without drawing any carriages or wagons. U.S. equivalent: **wildcat.**

lightening ('laɪtᵊnɪŋ) *n Obstetrics.* the sensation, experienced by many women late in pregnancy when the head of the fetus enters the pelvis, of a reduction in pressure on the diaphragm.

lighter[1] ('laɪtə) *n* **1** a small portable device for providing a naked flame or red-hot filament to light cigarettes, etc. **2** a person or thing that ignites something.

lighter[2] ('laɪtə) *n* a flat-bottomed barge used for transporting cargo, esp. in loading or unloading a ship. [C15: probably from Middle Dutch; compare C16 Dutch *lichter*]

lighterage ('laɪtərɪdʒ) *n* **1** the conveyance or loading and unloading of cargo by means of a lighter. **2** the charge for this service.

lighter than air *adj* (**lighter-than-air** *when prenominal*). **1** having a lower density than that of air. **2** of or relating to an aircraft, such as a balloon or airship, that depends on buoyancy for support in the air.

light face *n* **1** *Printing.* a weight of type characterized by light thin lines. Compare **bold face.** ◆ *adj also* **light-faced. 2** (of type) having this weight.

light-fast *adj* (of a dye or dyed article) unaffected by light.

light-fingered *adj* having nimble or agile fingers, esp. for thieving or picking pockets. ▸ **ˌlight-'fingeredness** *n*

light flyweight *n* **a** an amateur boxer weighing not more than 48 kg (106 pounds). **b** (*as modifier*): *a light-flyweight fight.*

light-footed *adj* having a light or nimble tread. ► **ˌlight-ˈfootedly** *adv* ► **ˌlight-ˈfootedness** *n*

light-headed *adj* **1** frivolous in disposition or behaviour. **2** giddy; feeling faint or slightly delirious. ► **ˌlight-ˈheadedly** *adv* ► **ˌlight-ˈheadedness** *n*

light-hearted *adj* cheerful or carefree in mood or disposition. ► **ˌlight-ˈheartedly** *adv* ► **ˌlight-ˈheartedness** *n*

light heavyweight *n* **1** Also called (in Brit.): **cruiserweight. 1a** a professional boxer weighing 160–175 pounds (72.5–79.5 kg). **1b** an amateur boxer weighing 75–81 kg (165–179 pounds). **1c** (*as modifier*): *a light-heavyweight bout.* **2** a wrestler in a similar weight category (usually 192–214 pounds (87–97 kg)).

light horse *n* lightly armed and highly mobile cavalry. ► **ˌlight-ˈhorseman** *n*

lighthouse (ˈlaɪtˌhaʊs) *n* a fixed structure in the form of a tower equipped with a light visible to mariners for warning them of obstructions, for marking harbour entrances, etc.

lighting (ˈlaɪtɪŋ) *n* **1** the act or quality of illumination or ignition. **2** the apparatus for supplying artificial light effects to a stage, film, or television set. **3** the distribution of light on an object or figure, as in painting, photography, etc.

lighting cameraman *n Films.* the person who designs and supervises the lighting of scenes to be filmed.

lighting-up time *n* the time when vehicles are required by law to have their lights switched on.

light into *vb* (*intr, prep*) *Informal.* to assail physically or verbally.

light meter *n* another name for **exposure meter.**

light middleweight *n* **a** an amateur boxer weighing 67–71 kg (148–157 pounds). **b** (*as modifier*): *a light-middleweight bout.* Compare **junior middleweight.**

light music *n* music for popular entertainment.

lightness (ˈlaɪtnɪs) *n* the attribute of an object or colour that enables an observer to judge the extent to which the object or colour reflects or transmits incident light. See also **colour.**

lightning (ˈlaɪtnɪŋ) *n* **1** a flash of light in the sky, occurring during a thunderstorm and caused by a discharge of electricity, either between clouds or between a cloud and the earth. Related adjs.: **fulgurous, fulminous. 2** (*modifier*) fast and sudden: *a lightning raid.* [C14: variant of *lightening*]

lightning arrester *n* a device that protects electrical equipment, such as an aerial, from an excessive voltage resulting from a lightning discharge or other accidental electric surge, by discharging it to earth.

lightning bug *n U.S. and Canadian.* another name for the **firefly.**

lightning chess *n* rapid chess in which either each move has a fixed time allowed (usually 10 seconds) or each player is allotted a fixed time (often 5 minutes) for all his moves. U.S. name: **rapid transit chess.**

lightning conductor *or* **rod** *n* a metal strip terminating in a series of sharp points, attached to the highest part of a building, etc., to discharge the electric field before it can reach a dangerous level and cause a lightning strike.

light opera *n* another term for **operetta.**

light out *vb* (*intr, adv*) *Informal.* to depart quickly, as if being chased.

light pen *n Computing.* **a** a rodlike device which, when applied to the screen of a cathode-ray tube, can detect the time of passage of the illuminated spot across that point thus enabling a computer to determine the position on the screen being pointed at. **b** a penlike device, used to read bar codes, that emits light and determines the intensity of that light as reflected from a small area of an adjacent surface.

light pollution *n* the glow from street and domestic lighting that obscures the night sky and hinders the observation of faint stars.

light rail *n* a transport system using small trains or trams, often serving parts of a large metropolitan area.

light reaction *n Botany.* the stage of photosynthesis during which light energy is absorbed by chlorophyll and transformed into chemical energy stored in ATP. Compare **dark reaction.**

lights[1] (laɪts) *pl n* a person's ideas, knowledge, or understanding: *he did it according to his lights.*

lights[2] (laɪts) *pl n* the lungs, esp. of sheep, bullocks, and pigs, used for feeding pets and occasionally in human food. [C13: plural noun use of LIGHT[2], referring to the light weight of the lungs]

light-sensitive *adj Physics.* (of a surface) having a photoelectric property, such as the ability to generate a current, change its electrical resistance, etc., when exposed to light.

lightship (ˈlaɪtˌʃɪp) *n* a ship equipped as a lighthouse and moored where a fixed structure would prove impracticable.

light show *n* a kaleidoscopic display of moving lights, etc., projected onto a screen, esp. during pop concerts.

lightsome[1] (ˈlaɪtsəm) *adj Archaic or poetic.* **1** lighthearted. **2** airy or buoyant. **3** not serious; frivolous. ► **ˈlightsomely** *adv* ► **ˈlightsomeness** *n*

lightsome[2] (ˈlaɪtsəm) *adj Archaic or poetic.* **1** producing or reflecting light. **2** full of or flooded with light.

lights out *n* **1** the time when those resident at an institution, such as soldiers in barracks or children at a boarding school, are expected to retire to bed. **2** a fanfare or other signal indicating or signifying this.

light table *n Printing.* a translucent surface of ground glass or a similar substance, illuminated from below and used for the examination of positive or negative film, and for the make-up of photocomposed pages.

light trap *n* any mechanical arrangement that allows some form of movement to take place while excluding light, such as a light-proof door or the lips of a film cassette.

light up *vb* (*adv*) **1** to light a cigarette, pipe, etc. **2** to illuminate or cause to illuminate. **3** to make or become cheerful or animated.

light water *n* a name for water (H_2O), as distinct from heavy water.

lightweight (ˈlaɪtˌweɪt) *adj* **1** of a relatively light weight. **2** not serious; trivial. ◆ *n* **3** a person or animal of a relatively light weight. **4a** a professional boxer weighing 130–135 pounds (59–61 kg). **4b** an amateur boxer weighing 57–60 kg (126–132 pounds). **4c** (*as modifier*): *the lightweight contender.* **5** a wrestler in a similar weight category (usually 115–126 pounds (52–57 kg)). **6** *Informal.* a person of little importance or influence.

light welterweight *n* **a** an amateur boxer weighing 60–63.5 kg (132–140 pounds). **b** (*as modifier*): *the light welterweight champion.* Compare **junior welterweight.**

light year *n* a unit of distance used in astronomy, equal to the distance travelled by light in one year, i.e. 9.4607×10^{12} kilometres or 0.3066 parsecs.

lignaloes (laɪˈnæləʊz, lɪg-) *n* (*functioning as sing*) another name for **eaglewood** (sense 2). [C14 *ligne aloes,* from Medieval Latin *lignum aloēs* wood of the aloe]

ligneous (ˈlɪgnɪəs) *adj* of or resembling wood. [C17: from Latin *ligneus,* from *lignum* wood]

ligni-, ligno-, *or before a vowel* **lign-** *combining form.* indicating wood: *lignocellulose.* [from Latin *lignum* wood]

lignicolous (lɪgˈnɪkələs) *or* **lignicole** (ˈlɪgnɪˌkəʊl) *adj* growing or living on or in wood. [C19: LIGNI- + -COLOUS]

ligniform (ˈlɪgnɪˌfɔːm) *adj* having the appearance of wood.

lignify (ˈlɪgnɪˌfaɪ) *vb* **-fies, -fying, -fied.** *Botany.* to make or become woody as a result of the deposition of lignin in the cell walls. ► **ˌlignifiˈcation** *n*

lignin (ˈlɪgnɪn) *n* a complex polymer occurring in certain plant cell walls making the plant rigid.

lignite (ˈlɪgnaɪt) *n* a brown carbonaceous sedimentary rock with woody texture that consists of accumulated layers of partially decomposed vegetation deposited in the late Cretaceous period: used as a fuel. Fixed carbon content: 46–60 per cent; calorific value: 1.28×10^7 to 1.93×10^7 J/kg (5500 to 8300 Btu/lb). Also called: **brown coal.** ► **lignitic** (lɪgˈnɪtɪk) *adj*

lignivorous (lɪgˈnɪvərəs) *adj* (of animals) feeding on wood.

lignocaine (ˈlɪgnəˌkeɪn) *n* a powerful local anaesthetic administered by injection, or topically to mucous membranes. Formula: $C_{14}H_{22}N_2O.HCl.H_2O$. U.S. name: **lidocaine.** [C20: from LIGNO- + *caine,* on the model of *cocaine*]

lignocellulose (ˌlɪgnəʊˈsɛljʊˌləʊs, -ˌləʊz) *n* a compound of lignin and cellulose that occurs in the walls of xylem cells in woody tissue.

lignum (ˈlɪgnəm) *n Austral.* another name for **polygonum.**

lignum vitae (ˈvaɪtɪ) *n* **1** either of two zygophyllaceous tropical American trees, *Guaiacum officinale* or *G. sanctum,* having blue or purple flowers. **2** the heavy resinous wood of either of these trees, which is used in machine bearings, casters, etc.: formerly thought to have medicinal properties. ◆ See also **guaiacum.** [New Latin, from Late Latin, literally: wood of life]

ligroin (ˈlɪgrəʊɪn) *n* a volatile fraction of petroleum containing aliphatic hydrocarbons of the paraffin series. It has an approximate boiling point range of 70°–130°C and is used as a solvent. [origin unknown]

ligula (ˈlɪgjʊlə) *n, pl* **-lae** (-ˌliː) *or* **-las. 1** *Entomol.* the terminal part of the labium of an insect consisting of paired lobes. **2** a variant spelling of **ligule.** [C18: New Latin; see LIGULE] ► **ˈligular** *adj* ► **ˈliguˌloid** *adj*

ligulate (ˈlɪgjʊlɪt, -ˌleɪt) *adj* **1** having the shape of a strap. **2** *Biology.* of, relating to, or having a ligule or ligula.

ligule (ˈlɪgjuːl) *or* **ligula** *n* **1** a strap-shaped membranous outgrowth at the junction between the leaf blade and sheath in many grasses. **2** a strap-shaped corolla, such as that of the ray flower in the daisy. [C19: via French, from Latin *ligula* strap, variant of *lingula,* from *lingua* tongue]

ligure (ˈlɪgjʊə) *n Old Testament.* any of the 12 precious stones used in the breastplates of high priests. [C14: from Late Latin *ligūrius,* from Late Greek *ligurion*]

Liguria (lɪˈgjʊərɪə) *n* a region of NW Italy, on the **Ligurian Sea** (an arm of the Mediterranean): the third smallest of the regions of Italy. Pop.: 1 658 513 (1996 est.). Area: 5410 sq. km (2089 sq. miles). ► **Liˈgurian** *adj, n*

likable *or* **likeable** (ˈlaɪkəbᵊl) *adj* easy to like; pleasing. ► **ˈlikableness** *or* **ˈlikeableness** *n*

Likasi (lɪˈkɑːsɪ) *n* a city in the S Democratic Republic of the Congo (formerly Zaïre): a centre of copper and cobalt production. Pop.: 299 118 (1994 est.). Former name: **Jadotville.**

like[1] (laɪk) *adj* **1** (*prenominal*) similar; resembling. ◆ *prep* **2** similar to; similarly to; in the manner of: *acting like a maniac; he's so like his father.* **3** used correlatively to express similarity in certain proverbs: *like mother, like daughter.* **4** such as: *there are lots of ways you might amuse yourself—like taking a long walk, for instance.* ◆ *adv* **5** a dialect word for **likely. 6** *Not standard.* as it were: often used as a parenthetic filler: *there was this policeman just staring at us, like.* ◆ *conj* **7** *Not standard.* as though; as if: *you look like you've just seen a ghost.* **8** in the same way as; in the same way that: *she doesn't dance like you do.* ◆ *n* **9** the equal or counterpart of a person or thing, esp. one respected or prized: *compare like with like; her like will never be seen again.* **10 the like.** similar things: *dogs, foxes, and the like.* **11 the likes** (*or* **like**) **of.** people or things similar to (someone or something specified): *we don't want the likes of you around here.* [shortened from Old English *gelīc;* compare Old Norse *glīkr* and *līkr* like]

USAGE The use of *like* to mean *such as* was formerly thought to be undesirable in formal writing, but has now become acceptable. It was also thought that *as* rather than *like* should be used to mean *in the same way that*, but now both *as* and *like* are acceptable: *they hunt and catch fish as/like their ancestors used to.* The use of *look like* and *seem like* before a clause, although very common, is thought by many people to be incorrect or non-standard: *it looks as though he won't come* (not *it looks like he won't come*).

like[2] (laɪk) *vb* **1** (*tr*) to find (something) enjoyable or agreeable or find it enjoyable or agreeable (to do something): *he likes boxing; he likes to hear music.* **2** (*tr*) to be fond of. **3** (*tr*) to prefer or wish (to do something): *we would like you to go.* **4** (*tr*) to feel towards; consider; regard: *how did she like it?* **5** (*intr*) to feel disposed or inclined; choose; wish. **6** (*tr*) *Archaic.* to please; agree with: *it likes me not to go.* ♦ *n* **7** (*usually pl*) a favourable feeling, desire, preference, etc. (esp. in the phrase **likes and dislikes**). [Old English *līcian;* related to Old Norse *līka,* Dutch *lijken*]

-like *suffix forming adjectives.* **1** resembling or similar to: *lifelike; springlike.* **2** having the characteristics of: *childlike; ladylike.* [from LIKE[1] (prep)]

likelihood (ˈlaɪklɪˌhʊd) *or* **likeliness** *n* **1** the condition of being likely or probable; probability. **2** something that is probable. **3** *Statistics.* the probability of a given sample being randomly drawn regarded as a function of the parameters of the population. The likelihood ratio is the ratio of this to the maximized likelihood. See also **maximum likelihood.**

likely (ˈlaɪklɪ) *adj* **1** (usually foll. by an infinitive) tending or inclined; apt: *likely to rain.* **2** probable: *a likely result.* **3** believable or feasible; plausible. **4** appropriate for a purpose or activity. **5** having good possibilities of success: *a likely candidate.* **6** *Dialect, chiefly U.S.* attractive, agreeable, or enjoyable: *her likely ways won her many friends.* ♦ *adv* **7** probably or presumably. **8 as likely as not.** very probably. [C14: from Old Norse *līkligr*]

USAGE *Likely* as an adverb is preceded by another, intensifying adverb, as in *it will very likely rain* or *it will most likely rain.* Its use without an intensifier, as in *it will likely rain* is regarded as unacceptable by most users of British English, though it is common in colloquial U.S. English.

like-minded *adj* agreeing in opinions, goals, etc. ▸ **ˌlike-ˈmindedly** *adv* ▸ **ˌlike-ˈmindedness** *n*

liken (ˈlaɪkən) *vb* (*tr*) to see or represent as the same or similar; compare. [C14: from LIKE[1] (adj)]

likeness (ˈlaɪknɪs) *n* **1** the condition of being alike; similarity. **2** a painted, carved, moulded, or graphic image of a person or thing. **3** an imitative appearance; semblance.

likewise (ˈlaɪkˌwaɪz) *adv* **1** in addition; moreover; also. **2** in like manner; similarly.

liking (ˈlaɪkɪŋ) *n* **1** the feeling of a person who likes; fondness. **2** a preference, inclination, or pleasure.

likuta (liːˈkuːtɑː) *n, pl* **makuta** (mɑːˈkuːtɑː). (formerly) a coin used in Zaïre. [C20: from Congolese]

lilac (ˈlaɪlək) *n* **1** Also called: **syringa.** any of various Eurasian oleaceous shrubs or small trees of the genus *Syringa,* esp. *S. vulgaris* (**common lilac**) which has large sprays of purple or white fragrant flowers. **2 French lilac.** another name for **goat's-rue** (sense 1). **3a** a light or moderate purple colour, sometimes with a bluish or reddish tinge. **3b** (*as adj*): *a lilac carpet.* [C17: via French from Spanish, from Arabic *līlak,* changed from Persian *nīlak* bluish, from *nīl* blue]

lilangeni (ˈlɪlɑːŋˌgeɪnɪ) *n, pl* **emalangeni** (ˈɛmɑːlɑːŋˌgeɪnɪ) the standard monetary unit of Swaziland, divided into 100 cents.

Lilburne (ˈlɪlˌbɜːn) *n* **John.** ?1614–57, English Puritan pamphleteer and leader of the Levellers, a radical group prominent during the Civil War.

liliaceous (ˌlɪlɪˈeɪʃəs) *adj* of, relating to, or belonging to the *Liliaceae,* a family of plants having showy flowers and a bulb or bulblike organ: includes the lily, tulip, bluebell, and onion. [C18: from Late Latin *līliāceus,* from *līlium* lily]

Lilienthal (*German* ˈliːliəntaːl) *n* **Otto** (ˈɔto). 1848–96, German aeronautical engineer, a pioneer of glider design.

Lilith (ˈlɪlɪθ) *n* **1** (in the Old Testament and in Jewish folklore) a female demon, who attacks children. **2** (in Talmudic literature) Adam's first wife. **3** a witch notorious in medieval demonology.

Liliuokalani (liːˌliːʊəʊkɑːˈlɑːniː) *n* **Lydia Kamekeha** (ˌkɑːmeɪˈkeɪhɑː). 1838–1917, queen and last sovereign of the Hawaiian Islands (1891–95).

Lille (*French* lil) *n* an industrial city in N France: the medieval capital of Flanders; forms with Roubaix and Tourcoing one of the largest conurbations in France. Pop.: 178 301 (1990).

Lille Bælt (ˈlilə ˈbɛld) *n* the Danish name for the **Little Belt.**

Lillee (ˈlɪlɪ) *n* **Dennis** (**Keith**). born 1949, Australian cricketer who, by the end of the 1982–83 season, had taken what was then a world record total of 355 wickets in 65 tests.

Lilliputian (ˌlɪlɪˈpjuːʃɪən) *n* **1** a tiny person or being. ♦ *adj* **2** tiny; very small. **3** petty or trivial. [C18: from *Lilliput,* an imaginary country of tiny inhabitants in Swift's *Gulliver's Travels* (1726)]

lilly-pilly (ˈlɪlɪˌpɪlɪ) *n Austral.* a tall myrtaceous tree, *Eugenia smithii,* having dark green leaves, spikes of feathery flowers, and white to purplish edible berries.

Lilo (ˈlaɪləʊ) *n, pl* **-los.** *Trademark.* a type of inflatable plastic or rubber mattress.

Lilongwe (lɪˈlɒŋwɪ) *n* the capital of Malawi, in the central part west of Lake Malawi. Pop.: 395 500 (1994 est.).

lilt (lɪlt) *n* **1** (in music) a jaunty rhythm. **2** a buoyant motion. ♦ *vb* (*intr*) **3** (of a melody) to have a lilt. **4** to move in a buoyant manner. [C14 *lulten,* origin obscure] ▸ **ˈlilting** *adj*

lily (ˈlɪlɪ) *n, pl* **lilies. 1** any liliaceous perennial plant of the N temperate genus *Lilium,* such as the Turk's-cap lily and tiger lily, having scaly bulbs and showy typically pendulous flowers. **2** the bulb or flower of any of these plants. **3** any of various similar or related plants, such as the water lily, plantain lily, and day lily. [Old English, from Latin *līlium;* related to Greek *leirion* lily] ▸ **ˈlilyˌlike** *adj*

lily iron *n* a harpoon, the head of which is detachable. [C19: from the shape of its shaft, which resembles lily leaves]

lily-livered *adj* cowardly; timid.

lily of the valley *n, pl* **lilies of the valley.** a small liliaceous plant, *Convallaria majalis,* of Eurasia and North America cultivated as a garden plant, having two long oval leaves and spikes of white bell-shaped flowers.

lily pad *n* any of the floating leaves of a water lily.

lily-trotter *n* another name for **jaçana.**

lily-white *adj* **1** of a pure white: *lily-white skin.* **2** *Informal.* pure; irreproachable. **3** *U.S. informal.* **3a** discriminating against Blacks: *a lily-white club.* **3b** racially segregated.

Lima (ˈliːmə) *n* **1** the capital of Peru, near the Pacific coast on the Rímac River: the centre of Spanish colonization in South America; university founded in 1551 (the oldest in South America); an industrial centre with a port at nearby Callao. Pop. (city): 421 570 (1995 est.), with a conurbation of 6 022 213 (1995). **2** *Communications.* a code word for the letter *L.*

lima bean (ˈlaɪmə, ˈliː-) *n* **1** any of several varieties of the bean plant, *Phaseolus lunatus* (or *P. limensis*), native to tropical America but cultivated in the U.S. for its flat pods containing pale green edible seeds. **2** the seed of such a plant. ♦ See also **butter bean.** [C19: named after LIMA]

limacine (ˈlɪməˌsaɪn, -sɪn, ˈlaɪ-) *adj* **1** of, or relating to slugs, esp. those of the genus *Limax.* **2** Also: **limaciform** (lɪˈmæsɪˌfɔːm). resembling a slug. [C19: from New Latin, from Latin *līmax,* from *līmus* mud]

limaçon (ˈlɪməˌsɒn) *n* a heart-shaped curve generated by a point lying on a line at a fixed distance from the intersection of the line with a fixed circle, the line rotating about a point on the circumference of the circle. [French, literally: snail (so named by Pascal)]

Limassol (ˈlɪməˌsɒl) *n* a port in S Cyprus: trading centre. Pop.: 143 400 (1994 est.). Ancient name: **Lemessus** (ləˈmɛsəs).

Limavady (ˌlɪməˈvædɪ) *n* a district of N Northern Ireland, in Co. Londonderry. Pop.: 29 567 (1991). Area: 586 sq. km (226 sq. miles).

limb[1] (lɪm) *n* **1** an arm or leg, or the analogous part on an animal, such as a wing. **2** any of the main branches of a tree. **3** a branching or projecting section or member; extension. **4** a person or thing considered to be a member, part, or agent of a larger group or thing. **5** *Chiefly Brit.* a mischievous child (esp. in **limb of Satan** *or* **limb of the devil**). **6 out on a limb. 6a** in a precarious or questionable position. **6b** *Brit.* isolated, esp. because of unpopular opinions. ♦ *vb* **7** (*tr*) a rare word for **dismember.** [Old English *lim;* related to Old Norse *limr*] ▸ **limbed** *adj* ▸ **ˈlimbless** *adj*

limb[2] (lɪm) *n* **1** the edge of the apparent disc of the sun, a moon, or a planet. **2** a graduated arc attached to instruments, such as the sextant, used for measuring angles. **3** *Botany.* **3a** the expanded upper part of a bell-shaped corolla. **3b** the expanded part of a leaf, petal, or sepal. **4** either of the two halves of a bow. **5** Also called: **fold limb.** either of the sides of a geological fold. [C15: from Latin *limbus* edge]

limbate (ˈlɪmbeɪt) *adj Biology.* having an edge or border of a different colour from the rest: *limbate flowers.* [C19: from Late Latin *limbātus* bordered, from LIMBUS]

limbed (lɪmd) *adj* **a** having limbs. **b** (*in combination*): *short-limbed; strong-limbed.*

limber[1] (ˈlɪmbə) *adj* **1** capable of being easily bent or flexed; pliant. **2** able to move or bend freely; agile. [C16: origin uncertain] ▸ **ˈlimberly** *adv* ▸ **ˈlimberness** *n*

limber[2] (ˈlɪmbə) *n* **1** part of a gun carriage, consisting of an axle, pole, and two wheels, that is attached to the rear of an item of equipment, esp. field artillery. ♦ *vb* **2** (usually foll. by *up*) to attach the limber (to a gun, etc.). [C15 *lymour* shaft of a gun carriage, origin uncertain]

limber[3] (ˈlɪmbə) *n* (*often pl*) *Nautical.* (in the bilge of a vessel) a fore-and-aft channel through a series of holes in the frames (**limber holes**) where water collects and can be pumped out. [C17: probably changed from French *lumière* hole (literally: light)]

limber up *vb* (*adv*) **1** (*intr*) (esp. in sports) to exercise in order to be limber and agile. **2** (*tr*) to make flexible.

limbic system (ˈlɪmbɪk) *n* the part of the brain bordering on the corpus callosum: concerned with basic emotion, hunger, and sex. [C19 *limbic,* from French *limbique,* from *limbe* limbus, from New Latin *limbus,* from Latin: border]

limbo[1] (ˈlɪmbəʊ) *n, pl* **-bos. 1** (*often cap.*) *Christianity.* the supposed abode of infants dying without baptism and the just who died before Christ. **2** an imaginary place for lost, forgotten, or unwanted persons or things. **3** an unknown intermediate place or condition between two extremes: *in limbo.* **4** a prison or confinement. [C14: from Medieval Latin *in limbo* on the border (of hell)]

limbo[2] (ˈlɪmbəʊ) *n, pl* **-bos.** a Caribbean dance in which dancers pass, while leaning backwards, under a bar. [C20: origin uncertain]

Limbourg (lɛ̃bur) *n* the French name for **Limburg**[1] (sense 3).

Limburg[1] (ˈlɪmbɜːg; *Dutch* ˈlɪmbyrx) *n* **1** a medieval duchy of W Europe: divided between the Netherlands and Belgium in 1839. **2** a province of the SE Netherlands: contains a coalfield and industrial centres. Capital: Maastricht. Pop.: 1 133 700 (1996 est.). Area: 2253 sq. km (809 sq. miles). **3** a province of NE Belgium: contains the industrial regions of the Kempen coalfield. Capital: Hassett. Pop.: 775 302 (1996 est.). Area: 2422 sq. km (935 sq. miles). French name: **Limbourg.**

Limburg[2] (*Dutch* ˈlɪmbyrx) *or* **Limbourg** *n* **de.** active ?1400–?1416, a Dutch family of manuscript illuminators. The three brothers Pol, Herman, and Jehanequin are best known for illustrating the *Très Riches Heures du Duc de Berry,* one of the finest examples of the International Gothic style.

Limburger (ˈlɪmbɜːgə) *n* a semihard white cheese of very strong smell and flavour. Also called: **Limburg cheese.**

limbus (ˈlɪmbəs) *n, pl* **-bi** (-baɪ). *Anatomy.* the edge or border of any of various structures or parts. [C15: from Latin: edge] ▸ **ˈlimbic** *adj*

lime[1] (laɪm) *n* **1** short for **quicklime, birdlime, slaked lime. 2** *Agriculture.* any of certain calcium compounds, esp. calcium hydroxide, spread as a dressing on lime-deficient land. ◆ *vb (tr)* **3** to spread (twigs, etc.) with birdlime. **4** to spread a calcium compound upon (land) to improve plant growth. **5** to catch (animals, esp. birds) with or as if with birdlime. **6** to whitewash or cover (a wall, ceiling, etc.) with a mixture of lime and water (**limewash**). [Old English *līm;* related to Icelandic *līm* glue, Latin *līmus* slime]

lime[2] (laɪm) *n* **1** a small Asian citrus tree, *Citrus aurantifolia,* with stiff sharp spines and small round or oval greenish fruits. **2a** the fruit of this tree, having acid fleshy pulp rich in vitamin C. **2b** (*as modifier*): *lime juice.* ◆ *adj* **3** having the flavour of lime fruit. [C17: from French, from Provençal, from Arabic *līmah*]

lime[3] (laɪm) *n* a European linden tree, *Tilia europaea,* planted in many varieties for ornament. [C17: changed from obsolete *line,* from Old English *lind* LINDEN]

lime[4] (laɪm) *vb (intr) Caribbean slang.* (of young people) to sit or stand around on the pavement. [of unknown origin]

limeade (ˌlaɪmˈeɪd) *n* a drink made from sweetened lime juice and plain or carbonated water.

lime burner *n* a person whose job it is to burn limestone to make lime.

lime green *n* **a** a moderate greenish-yellow colour. **b** (*as adj*): *a lime-green dress.*

limekiln (ˈlaɪmˌkɪln) *n* a kiln in which calcium carbonate is calcined to produce quicklime.

limelight (ˈlaɪmˌlaɪt) *n* **1 the.** a position of public attention or notice (esp. in the phrase **in the limelight**). **2a** a type of lamp, formerly used in stage lighting, in which light is produced by heating lime to white heat. **2b** Also called: **calcium light.** brilliant white light produced in this way. ▸ **ˈlimeˌlighter** *n*

limen (ˈlaɪmɛn) *n, pl* **limens** *or* **limina** (ˈlɪmɪnə). *Psychol.* another term for **threshold** (sense 4). See also **liminal.** [C19: from Latin]

lime pit *n* (in tanning) a pit containing lime in which hides are placed to remove the hair.

limerick (ˈlɪmərɪk) *n* a form of comic verse consisting of five anapaestic lines of which the first, second, and fifth have three metrical feet and rhyme together and the third and fourth have two metrical feet and rhyme together. [C19: allegedly from *will you come up to Limerick?,* a refrain sung between nonsense verses at a party]

Limerick (ˈlɪmərɪk) *n* **1** a county of SW Republic of Ireland, in N Munster province: consists chiefly of an undulating plain with rich pasture and mountains in the south. County town: Limerick. Pop.: 165 000 (1996). Area: 2686 sq. km (1037 sq. miles). **2** a port in SW Republic of Ireland, county town of Limerick, at the head of the Shannon estuary. Pop.: 74 900 (1995 est.).

limes (ˈlaɪmiːz) *n, pl* **limites** (ˈlɪmɪˌtiːz). the fortified boundary of the Roman Empire. [from Latin]

limestone (ˈlaɪmˌstəʊn) *n* a sedimentary rock consisting mainly of calcium carbonate, deposited as the calcareous remains of marine animals or chemically precipitated from the sea: used as a building stone and in the manufacture of cement, lime, etc.

limestone pavement *n Geology.* a horizontal surface of exposed limestone in which the joints have been enlarged, cutting the surface into roughly rectangular blocks. See also **clint, grike.**

limewater (ˈlaɪmˌwɔːtə) *n* **1** a clear colourless solution of calcium hydroxide in water, sometimes used in medicine as an antacid. **2** water that contains dissolved lime or calcium salts, esp. calcium carbonate or calcium sulphate.

limey (ˈlaɪmɪ) *U.S. and Canadian slang.* ◆ *n* **1** a British person. **2** a British sailor or ship. ◆ *adj* **3** British. [abbreviated from C19 *lime-juicer,* because British sailors were required to drink lime juice as a protection against scurvy]

limicoline (laɪˈmɪkəˌlaɪn, -lɪn) *adj* of, relating to, or belonging to the *Charadrii,* a suborder of birds containing the plovers, sandpipers, snipes, oystercatchers, avocets, etc. [C19: from New Latin *Limicolae* former name of order, from Latin *līmus* mud + *colere* to inhabit]

limicolous (laɪˈmɪkələs) *adj* (of certain animals) living in mud or muddy regions.

liminal (ˈlɪmɪnᵊl) *adj Psychol.* relating to the point (or threshold) beyond which a sensation becomes too faint to be experienced. [C19: from Latin *līmen* threshold]

limit (ˈlɪmɪt) *n* **1** (*sometimes pl*) the ultimate extent, degree, or amount of something: *the limit of endurance.* **2** (*often pl*) the boundary or edge of a specific area: *the city limits.* **3** (*often pl*) the area of premises within specific boundaries. **4** the largest quantity or amount allowed. **5** *Maths.* **5a** a value to which a function $f(x)$ approaches as closely as desired as the independent variable approaches a specified value ($x = a$) or approaches infinity. **5b** a value to which a sequence a_n approaches arbitrarily close as n approaches infinity. **5c** the limit of a sequence of partial sums of a convergent infinite series: *the limit of* $1 + ½ + ¼ + ⅛ + \ldots$ *is 2.* **6** *Maths.* one of the two specified values between which a definite integral is evaluated. **7 the limit.** *Informal.* a person or thing that is intolerably exasperating. **8 off limits. 8a** out of bounds. **8b** forbidden to do or use: *smoking was off limits everywhere.* **9 within limits.** to a certain or limited extent: *I approve of it within limits.* ◆ *vb (tr)* **-its, -iting, -ited. 10** to restrict or confine, as to area, extent, time, etc. **11** *Law.* to agree, fix, or assign specifically. [C14: from Latin *līmes* boundary] ▸ **ˈlimitable** *adj* ▸ **ˈlimitableness** *n* ▸ **ˈlimitless** *adj* ▸ **ˈlimitlessly** *adv* ▸ **ˈlimitlessness** *n*

limitarian (ˌlɪmɪˈtɛərɪən) *n Christianity.* a person who regards salvation as limited to only a part of mankind.

limitary (ˈlɪmɪtərɪ, -trɪ) *adj* **1** of, involving, or serving as a limit. **2** restricted or limited.

limitation (ˌlɪmɪˈteɪʃən) *n* **1** something that limits a quality or achievement. **2** the act of limiting or the condition of being limited. **3** *Law.* a certain period of time, legally defined, within which an action, claim, etc., must be commenced. **4** *Property law.* a restriction upon the duration or extent of an estate.

limited (ˈlɪmɪtɪd) *adj* **1** having a limit; restricted; confined. **2** without fullness or scope; narrow. **3** (of governing powers, sovereignty, etc.) restricted or checked, by or as if by a constitution, laws, or an assembly: *limited government.* **4** *U.S. and Canadian.* (of a train) stopping only at certain stations and having only a set number of cars for passengers. **5** *Chiefly Brit.* (of a business enterprise) owned by shareholders whose liability for the enterprise's debts is restricted. ◆ *n* **6** *U.S. and Canadian.* a limited train, bus, etc. ▸ **ˈlimitedly** *adv* ▸ **ˈlimitedness** *n*

limited company *n Brit.* a company whose owners enjoy limited liability for the company's debts and losses.

limited edition *n* an edition of something such as a book, plate, etc., that is limited to a specified number.

limited liability *n Brit.* liability restricted to the unpaid portion (if any) of the par value of the shares of a limited company. It is a feature of share ownership.

limited monarchy *n* another term for **constitutional monarchy.**

limited war *n* a war in which the belligerents do not seek the total destruction of the enemy, esp. one in which nuclear weapons are deliberately not used.

limiter (ˈlɪmɪtə) *n* an electronic circuit that produces an output signal whose positive or negative amplitude, or both, is limited to some predetermined value above which the peaks become flattened. Also called: **clipper.**

limit man *n* (in a handicap sport or game) the competitor with the maximum handicap.

limit point *n Maths.* a point in a topological space such that there is at least one other point of the space in every neighbourhood of the given point: *0 is the limit point of the sequence* 1, ½, ¼, ⅛,.... Also called: **accumulation point.**

limitrophe (ˈlɪmɪˌtrəʊf) *adj* (of a country or region) on or near a frontier. [C19: via French from Late Latin *limitrophus,* from *limit-* LIMIT + Greek *-trophus* supporting; originally referring to borderland that supported frontier troops]

limivorous (lɪˈmɪvərəs) *adj* (of certain invertebrate animals) feeding on mud. [C19: from Latin *līmus* mud + -VOROUS]

limn (lɪm) *vb (tr)* **1** to represent in drawing or painting. **2** *Archaic.* to describe in words. **3** an obsolete word for **illuminate.** [C15: from Old French *enluminer* to illumine (a manuscript) from Latin *inlūmināre* to brighten, from *lūmen* light] ▸ **limner** (ˈlɪmnə) *n*

limnetic (lɪmˈnɛtɪk) *adj* of, relating to, or inhabiting the open water of lakes down to the depth of light penetration: *the limnetic zone.* [C20: from Greek *limnē* pool]

limnology (lɪmˈnɒlədʒɪ) *n* the study of bodies of fresh water with reference to their plant and animal life, physical properties, geographical features, etc. [C20: from Greek *limnē* lake] ▸ **limnological** (ˌlɪmnəˈlɒdʒɪkᵊl) *or* **ˌlimnoˈlogic** *adj* ▸ **ˌlimnoˈlogically** *adv* ▸ **limˈnologist** *n*

limnophilous (lɪmˈnɒfɪləs) *adj* (of animals) living in lakes or freshwater marshes.

Límnos (ˈlimnɔs) *n* transliteration of the Modern Greek name for **Lemnos.**

limo (ˈlɪməʊ) *n, pl* **-mos.** *Informal.* short for **limousine.**

Limoges (lɪˈməʊʒ; *French* limɔʒ) *n* a city in S central France, on the Vienne River: a centre of the porcelain industry since the 18th century. Pop.: 175 646 (1990).

limonene (ˈlɪməˌniːn) *n* a liquid optically active terpene with a lemon-like odour, found in lemon, orange, peppermint, and other essential oils and used as a wetting agent and in the manufacture of resins. Formula: $C_{10}H_{16}$. [C19: from New Latin *limonum* lemon]

limonite (ˈlaɪməˌnaɪt) *n* a common brown, black, or yellow amorphous secondary mineral that consists of hydrated ferric oxides and is a source of iron. Formula: $FeO(OH).nH_2O$. [C19: probably from Greek *leimōn,* translation of earlier German name, *Wiesenerz* meadow ore] ▸ **limonitic** (ˌlaɪməˈnɪtɪk) *adj*

Limousin (*French* limuzɛ̃) *n* a region and former province of W central France, in the W part of the Massif Central.

limousine (ˈlɪməˌziːn, ˌlɪməˈziːn) *n* **1** any large and luxurious car, esp. one that has a glass division between the driver and passengers. **2** a former type of car in which the roof covering the rear seats projects over the driver's compartment. [C20: from French, literally: cloak (originally one worn by shepherds in *Limousin*), hence later applied to the car]

limp[1] (lɪmp) *vb (intr)* **1** to walk with an uneven step, esp. with a weak or injured leg. **2** to advance in a labouring or faltering manner. ◆ *n* **3** an uneven walk or progress. [C16: probably a back formation from obsolete *limphalt* lame, from Old English *lemphealt;* related to Middle High German *limpfen* to limp] ▸ **ˈlimper** *n* ▸ **ˈlimping** *adj, n* ▸ **ˈlimpingly** *adv*

limp[2] (lɪmp) *adj* **1** not firm or stiff. **2** not energetic or vital. **3** (of the binding of a book) not stiffened with boards. [C18: probably of Scandinavian origin; related to Icelandic *limpa* looseness] ▸ **ˈlimply** *adv* ▸ **ˈlimpness** *n*

limpet (ˈlɪmpɪt) *n* **1** any of numerous marine gastropods, such as *Patella vulgata* (**common limpet**) and *Fissurella* (or *Diodora*) *apertura* (**keyhole limpet**), that have a conical shell and are found clinging to rocks. **2** any of various similar freshwater gastropods, such as *Ancylus fluviatilis* (**river limpet**). **3** (*modifier*) relating to or denoting certain weapons that are attached to their targets by magnetic or adhesive properties and resist removal: *limpet mines.* [Old English *lempedu,* from Latin *lepas,* from Greek]

limpid (ˈlɪmpɪd) *adj* **1** clear or transparent. **2** (esp. of writings, style, etc.) free from obscurity. **3** calm; peaceful. [C17: from French *limpide,* from Latin *limpidus* clear] ▸ **limˈpidity** *or* **ˈlimpidness** *n* ▸ **ˈlimpidly** *adv*

limpkin (ˈlɪmpkɪn) *n* a rail-like wading bird, *Aramus guarauna,* of tropical American marshes, having dark brown plumage with white markings and a wailing cry: order *Gruiformes* (cranes, rails, etc.). Also called: **courlan.** [C19: named from its awkward gait]

Limpopo (lɪmˈpəʊpəʊ) *n* a river in SE Africa, rising in E South Africa and flowing northeast, then southeast as the border between South Africa and Zimbabwe and through Mozambique to the Indian Ocean. Length: 1770 km (1100 miles).

limp-wristed *adj* ineffectual; effete.

limulus ('lɪmjʊləs) *n, pl* **-li** (-ˌlaɪ). any horseshoe crab of the genus *Limulus*, esp. *L. polyphemus*. [C19: from New Latin (name of genus), from Latin *līmus* sidelong]

limy[1] ('laɪmɪ) *adj* **limier, limiest.** **1** of, like, or smeared with birdlime. **2** containing or characterized by the presence of lime. ▸ **'liminess** *n*

limy[2] ('laɪmɪ) *adj* **limier, limiest.** of or tasting of lime (the fruit).

lin. *abbrev. for:* **1** lineal. **2** linear.

linac ('lɪnæk) *n* short for **linear accelerator.**

Linacre ('lɪnəkə) *n* **Thomas.** ?1460–1524, English humanist and physician: founded the Royal College of Physicians (1518).

linage *or* **lineage** ('laɪnɪdʒ) *n* **1** the number of lines in a piece of written or printed matter. **2** payment for written material calculated according to the number of lines. **3** a less common word for **alignment.**

linalool (lɪ'næləʊˌɒl, 'lɪnəˌluːl) *or* **linalol** ('lɪnəˌlɒl) *n* an optically active colourless fragrant liquid found in many essential oils and used in perfumery. Formula: $C_{10}H_{18}O$. [from LIGNALOES + -OL[1]]

Linares (*Spanish* li'nares) *n* a city in S Spain: site of Scipio Africanus' defeat of the Carthaginians (208 B.C.); lead mines. Pop.: 57 210 (1991).

Lin Biao ('lɪn 'bjaʊ) See **Lin Piao.**

linchpin *or* **lynchpin** ('lɪntʃˌpɪn) *n* **1** a pin placed transversely through an axle to keep a wheel in position. **2** a person or thing regarded as an essential or coordinating element: *the linchpin of the company.* [C14 *lynspin*, from Old English *lynis*]

Lincoln[1] ('lɪŋkən) *n* **1** a city in E central England, administrative centre of Lincolnshire: an important ecclesiastical and commercial centre in the Middle Ages; Roman ruins, a castle (founded by William the Conqueror) and a famous cathedral (begun in 1086). Pop.: 80 281 (1991). Latin name: **Lindum** ('lɪndəm). **2** a city in SE Nebraska: state capital; University of Nebraska (1869). Pop.: 209 192 (1996 est.). **3** short for **Lincolnshire. 4** a breed of long-woolled sheep, originally from Lincolnshire.

Lincoln[2] ('lɪŋkən) *n* **Abraham.** 1809–65, U.S. Republican statesman; 16th president of the U.S. His fame rests on his success in saving the Union in the Civil War (1861–65) and on his emancipation of slaves (1863); assassinated by Booth.

Lincoln Center *n* a centre for the performing arts in New York City, including theatres, a library, and a school. Official name: **Lincoln Center for the Performing Arts.**

Lincoln green *n, adj* **1a** a yellowish-green or brownish-green colour. **1b** (*as adj*): *a Lincoln-green suit.* **2** a cloth of this colour. [C16: so named after a green fabric formerly made at LINCOLN]

Lincolnshire ('lɪŋkənˌʃɪə, -ʃə) *n* a county of E England, on the North Sea and the Wash: mostly low-lying and fertile, with fenland around the Wash and hills (the **Lincoln Wolds**) in the east; one of the main agricultural counties of Great Britain: the geographical and ceremonial county includes the unitary authorities of North Lincolnshire and North East Lincolnshire (both part of Humberside county from 1974 to 1996). Administrative centre: Lincoln. Pop. (including unitary authorities): 922 600 (1996 est.). Area (including unitary authorities): 7604 sq. km (2936 sq. miles). Abbrev.: **Lincs.**

Lincoln's Inn *n* one of the four legal societies in London which together form the Inns of Court.

lincrusta (lɪn'krʌstə) *n* a type of wallpaper having a hard embossed surface. [C19: from Latin *linum* flax + *crusta* rind]

Lincs (lɪŋks) *abbrev. for* Lincolnshire.

linctus ('lɪŋktəs) *n, pl* **-tuses.** a syrupy medicinal preparation, taken to relieve coughs and sore throats. [C17 (in the sense: medicine to be licked with the tongue): from Latin, past participle of *lingere* to lick]

Lind (lɪnd) *n* **1 James.** 1716–94, British physician. He demonstrated (1754) that citrus fruits can cure and prevent scurvy, a remedy adopted by the British navy in 1796. **2 Jenny,** original name *Johanna Maria Lind Goldschmidt.* 1820–87, Swedish coloratura soprano.

lindane ('lɪndeɪn) *n* a white poisonous crystalline powder with a slight musty odour: used as an insecticide, weedkiller, and, in low concentrations, in treating scabies; 1,2,3,4,5,6-hexachlorocyclohexane. Formula: $C_6H_6Cl_6$. [C20: named after T. van der *Linden*, Dutch chemist]

Lindbergh ('lɪndbɜːg, 'lɪnbɜːg) *n* **Charles Augustus.** 1902–74, U.S. aviator, who made the first solo nonstop flight across the Atlantic (1927).

Lindemann ('lɪndəmən) *n* **Frederick Alexander,** 1st Viscount Cherwell. 1886–1957, British physicist, born in Germany; Churchill's scientific adviser during World War II.

linden ('lɪndən) *n* any of various tiliaceous deciduous trees of the N temperate genus *Tilia*, having heart-shaped leaves and small fragrant yellowish flowers: cultivated for timber and as shade trees. See also **lime**[3], **basswood.** [C16: n use of obsolete adj *linden*, from Old English *linde* lime tree]

Lindesnes ('lɪndɪsˌnɛs) *n* a cape at the S tip of Norway, projecting into the North Sea. Also called: (the) **Naze.**

Lindisfarne ('lɪndɪsˌfɑːn) *n* another name for **Holy Island.**

Lindsay ('lɪndzɪ) *n* **1** See (Sir David) **Lyndsay. 2** (**Nicholas**) **Vachel** ('veɪtʃəl). 1879–1931, U.S. poet; best known for *General William Booth* (1913) and *The Congo* (1914). **3 Norman Alfred William.** 1879–1969, Australian artist and writer.

Lindsey ('lɪndzɪ) *n* **Parts of.** an area in E England constituting a former administrative division of Lincolnshire.

Lindwall ('lɪndˌwɔːl) *n* **Ray**(**mond Russell**). 1921–96, Australian cricketer. A fast bowler, he played for Australia 61 times between 1946 and 1958.

line[1] (laɪn) *n* **1** a narrow continuous mark, as one made by a pencil, pen, or brush across a surface. **2** such a mark cut into or raised from a surface. **3** a thin indented mark or wrinkle. **4** a straight or curved continuous trace having no breadth that is produced by a moving point. **5** *Maths.* **5a** any straight one-dimensional geometrical element whose identity is determined by two points. A **line segment** lies between any two points on a line. **5b** a set of points (x, y) that satisfies the equation $y = mx + c$, where m is the gradient and c is the intercept with the y-axis. **6** a border or boundary: *the county line.* **7** *Sport.* **7a** a white or coloured band indicating a boundary or division on a field, track, etc. **7b** a mark or imaginary mark at which a race begins or ends. **8** *American football.* **8a** See **line of scrimmage. 8b** the players arranged in a row on either side of the line of scrimmage at the start of each play. **9** a specified point of change or limit: *the dividing line between sanity and madness.* **10a** the edge or contour of a shape, as in sculpture or architecture, or a mark on a painting, drawing, etc., defining or suggesting this. **10b** the sum or type of such contours or marks, characteristic of a style or design: *the line of a draughtsman; the line of a building.* **11** anything long, flexible, and thin, such as a wire or string: *a washing line; a fishing line.* **12** a telephone connection: *a direct line to New York.* **13a** a conducting wire, cable, or circuit for making connections between pieces of electrical apparatus, such as a cable for electric-power transmission, telecommunications, etc. **13b** (*as modifier*): *the line voltage.* **14** a system of travel or transportation, esp. over agreed routes: *a shipping line.* **15** a company operating such a system. **16** a route between two points on a railway. **17** *Chiefly Brit.* **17a** a railway track, including the roadbed, sleepers, etc. **17b** one of the rails of such a track. **18** *N.Z.* a roadway usually in a rural area. **19** a course or direction of movement or advance: *the line of flight of a bullet.* **20** a course or method of action, behaviour, etc.: *take a new line with him.* **21** a policy or prescribed course of action or way of thinking (often in the phrases **bring** *or* **come into line**). **22** a field of study, interest, occupation, trade, or profession: *this book is in your line.* **23** alignment; true (esp. in the phrases **in line, out of line**). **24** one kind of product or article: *a nice line in hats.* **25** *N.Z.* a collection of bales of wool all of the one type. **26** a row of persons or things: *a line of cakes on the conveyor belt.* **27** a chronological or ancestral series, esp. of people: *a line of prime ministers.* **28** a row of words printed or written across a page or column. **29** a unit of verse consisting of the number of feet appropriate to the metre being used and written or printed with the words in a single row. **30** a short letter; note: *just a line to say thank you.* **31** a piece of useful information or hint about something: *give me a line on his work.* **32** one of a number of narrow horizontal bands forming a television picture. **33** *Physics.* a narrow band in an electromagnetic spectrum, resulting from a transition in an atom of a gas. **34** *Music.* **34a** any of the five horizontal marks that make up the stave. Compare **space** (sense 9). **34b** the musical part or melody notated on one such set. **34c** a discernible shape formed by sequences of notes or musical sounds: *a meandering melodic line.* **34d** (in polyphonic music) a set of staves that are held together with a bracket or brace. **35** a unit of magnetic flux equal to 1 maxwell. **36** a defensive or fortified position, esp. one that marks the most forward position in war or a national boundary: *the front line.* **37 line ahead** *or* **line abreast.** a formation adopted by a naval unit for manoeuvring. **38** a formation adopted by a body or a number of military units when drawn up abreast. **39** the combatant forces of certain armies and navies, excluding supporting arms. **40** *Fencing.* one of four divisions of the target on a fencer's body, considered as areas to which specific attacks are made. **41** the scent left by a fox. **42a** the equator (esp. in the phrase **crossing the line**). **42b** any circle or arc on the terrestrial or celestial sphere. **43** the amount of insurance written by an underwriter for a particular risk. **44** a U.S. and Canadian word for **queue. 45** *Slang.* a portion of a powdered drug for snorting. **46** *Slang.* something said for effect, esp. to solicit for money, sex, etc.: *he gave me his usual line.* **47 above the line. 47a** *Account.* denoting entries above a horizontal line on a profit and loss account, separating those that establish the profit or loss from those that show how the profit is distributed. **47b** denoting revenue transactions rather than capital transactions in a nation's accounts. **47c** *Marketing.* expenditure on media advertising through an agency, rather than internally arranged advertising, such as direct mail, free samples, etc. **47d** *Bridge.* denoting bonus points, marked above the horizontal line on the score card. **48 below the line. 48a** *Account.* denoting entries below a horizontal line on a profit and loss account, separating those that establish the profit or loss from those that show how the profit is distributed. **48b** denoting capital transactions rather than revenue transactions in a nation's accounts. **48c** *Marketing.* denoting expenditure on advertising by other means than the traditional media, such as the provision of free gifts, special displays, direct-mail shots, etc. **48d** *Bridge.* denoting points scored towards game and rubber, marked below the horizontal line on the score card. **49 all along the line. 49a** at every stage in a series. **49b** in every detail. **50 do a line** (**with**). *Irish and Austral. informal.* to associate (with a person of the opposite sex) regularly; go out (with): *he is doing a line with her.* **51 draw the line** (**at**). to reasonably object (to) or set a limit (on): *her father draws the line at her coming in after midnight.* **52 get a line on.** *Informal.* to obtain information about. **53 hold the line. 53a** to keep a telephone line open. **53b** *Football.* to prevent the opponents from taking the ball forward. **53c** (of soldiers) to keep formation, as when under fire. **54 in line for.** in the running for; a candidate for: *he's in line for a directorship.* **55 in line with.** conforming to. **56 in the line of duty.** as a necessary and usually undesired part of the performance of one's responsibilities. **57 lay** *or* **put on the line. 57a** to pay money. **57b** to speak frankly and directly. **57c** to risk (one's career, reputation, etc.) on something. **58 shoot a line.** *Informal.* to try to create a false image, as by boasting or exaggerating. **59 step out of line.** to fail to conform to expected standards, attitudes, etc. **60 toe the line.** to conform to expected standards, attitudes, etc. ◆ *vb* **61** (*tr*) to mark with a line or lines. **62** (*tr*) to draw or represent with a line or lines. **63** (*tr*) to be or put as a border to: *tulips lined the lawns.* **64** to place in or form a row, series, or alignment. ◆ See also **lines, line-up.** [C13: partly from Old French *ligne*, ultimately from Latin *līnea,* n. use of *līneus* flaxen, from *līnum* flax; partly from Old English *līn,* ultimately also from Latin *līnum* flax] ▸ **'linable** *or* **'lineable** *adj* ▸ **lined** *adj* ▸ **'line,like** *adj* ▸ **'liny** *or* **'liney** *adj*

line[2] (laɪn) *vb (tr)* **1** to attach an inside covering to (a garment, curtain, etc.), as for protection, to hide the seaming, or so that it should hang well. **2** to cover or fit the inside of: *to line the walls with books.* **3** to fill plentifully: *a purse lined with money.* **4** to reinforce the back of (a book) with fabric, paper, etc. [**C14**: ultimately from Latin *līnum* flax, since linings were often made of linen]

lineage[1] ('lɪnɪɪdʒ) *n* **1** direct descent from an ancestor, esp. a line of descendants from one ancestor. **2** a less common word for **derivation.** [**C14**: from Old French *lignage,* from Latin *līnea* LINE[1]]

lineage[2] ('laɪnɪdʒ) *n* a variant spelling of **linage.**

lineal ('lɪnɪəl) *adj* **1** being in a direct line of descent from an ancestor. **2** of, involving, or derived from direct descent. **3** a less common word for **linear.** [**C14**: via Old French from Late Latin *līneālis,* from Latin *līnea* LINE[1]] ▸ **'lineally** *adv*

lineament ('lɪnɪəmənt) *n (often pl)* **1** a facial outline or feature. **2** a distinctive characteristic or feature. **3** *Geology.* any long natural feature on the surface of the earth, such as a fault, esp. as revealed by aerial photography. [**C15**: from Latin: line, from *līneāre* to draw a line] ▸ **lineamental** (,lɪnɪə'mentᵊl) *adj*

linear ('lɪnɪə) *adj* **1** of, in, along, or relating to a line. **2** of or relating to length. **3** resembling, represented by, or consisting of a line or lines. **4** having one dimension. **5** designating a style in the arts, esp. painting, that obtains its effects through line rather than colour or light and in which the edges of forms and planes are sharply defined. Compare **painterly. 6** *Maths.* of or relating to the first degree: *a linear equation.* **7** narrow and having parallel edges: *a linear leaf.* **8** *Electronics.* **8a** (of a circuit, etc.) having an output that is directly proportional to input: *linear amplifier.* **8b** having components arranged in a line. [**C17**: from Latin *līneāris* of or by means of lines] ▸ **linearity** (,lɪnɪ'ærɪtɪ) *n* ▸ **'linearly** *adv*

Linear A *n* a hitherto undeciphered script, partly syllabic and partly ideographic, found on tablets and pottery in Crete and dating mainly from the 15th century B.C.

linear accelerator *n* an accelerator in which charged particles are accelerated along a linear path by potential differences applied to a number of electrodes along their path. Sometimes shortened to **linac.**

Linear B *n* an ancient system of writing, apparently a modified form of Linear A, found on clay tablets and jars of the second millennium B.C. The earliest excavated examples, dating from about 1400, came from Knossos, in Crete, but all the later finds are at Pylos and Mycenae on the Greek mainland, dating from the 14th–12th centuries. The script is generally accepted as being an early representation of Mycenaean Greek.

linear equation *n* a polynomial equation of the first degree, such as $x + y = 7$.

linear measure *n* a unit or system of units for the measurement of length. Also called: **long measure.**

linear motor *n* a form of electric motor in which the stator and the rotor are linear and parallel. It can be used to drive a train, one part of the motor being in the locomotive, the other in the track.

linear perspective *n* the branch of perspective in which the apparent size and shape of objects and their position with respect to foreground and background are established by actual or suggested lines converging on the horizon.

linear programming *n Maths.* a technique used in economics, etc., for determining the maximum or minimum of a linear function of non-negative variables subject to constraints expressed as linear equalities or inequalities.

lineate ('lɪnɪɪt, -,eɪt) *or* **lineated** *adj* marked with lines; streaked. [**C17**: from Latin *līneātus* drawn with lines]

lineation (,lɪnɪ'eɪʃən) *n* **1** the act of marking with lines. **2** an arrangement of or division into lines. **3** an outline or contour. **4** any linear arrangement involving rocks or minerals, such as a series of parallel rock strata.

linebacker ('laɪn,bækə) *n* a defensive player in American or Canadian football who is positioned just behind the line of scrimmage.

line block *n* a letterpress printing block made by a photoengraving process without the use of a screen.

line breeding *n* selective inbreeding that produces individuals possessing one or more of the favourable characteristics of their common ancestor.

line call *n Tennis.* the judgment of the umpire or linesman as to whether the ball has landed in or out of court.

linecaster ('laɪn,kɑːstə) *n* a typesetting machine that casts metal type in lines.

line composition *n Printing.* type produced on a linecaster.

line dancing *n* a form of dancing performed by rows of people to country and western music.

line drawing *n* a drawing made with lines only, gradations in tone being provided by the spacing and thickness of the lines.

line-engraving *n* **1** the art or process of hand-engraving in intaglio and copper plate. **2** a plate so engraved. **3** a print taken from such a plate. ▸ **'line-en,graver** *n*

Line Islands *pl n* a group of coral islands in the central Pacific, including Tabuaeran, Teraina, and Kiritimati: part of Kiribati, with Palmyra and Jarvis administered by the U.S.

Lineker ('lɪnɪkə) *n* **Gary Winston.** born 1960, English footballer: played for England (1986–92; captain 1991–92); his clubs included Barcelona (1986–89) and Tottenham Hotspur (1989–92).

lineman ('laɪnmən) *n, pl* **-men. 1** another name for **platelayer. 2** a person who does the chaining, taping, or marking of points for a surveyor. **3** *Austral. and N.Z.* (formerly) the member of a beach life-saving team who controlled the line used to help drowning swimmers and surfers. **4** *American football.* a member of the row of players who start each down, positioned on either side of the line of scrimmage. **5** *U.S. and Canadian.* another word for **linesman** (sense 2).

line management *n Commerce.* those managers in an organization who are responsible for the main activity or product of the organization, as distinct from those, such as transport, accounting, or personnel, who provide services to the line management. ▸ **line manager** *n*

linen ('lɪnɪn) *n* **1a** a hard-wearing fabric woven from the spun fibres of flax. **1b** *(as modifier): a linen tablecloth.* **2** yarn or thread spun from flax fibre. **3** clothes, sheets, tablecloths, etc., made from linen cloth or from a substitute such as cotton. **4** See **linen paper.** [Old English *linnen,* ultimately from Latin *līnum* flax, LINE[2]]

linen paper *n* paper made from flax fibres or having a similar texture.

line of battle *n* a formation adopted by a military or naval force when preparing for action.

line of credit *n U.S. and Canadian.* another name for **credit line.**

line of fire *n* the flight path of a missile discharged or to be discharged from a firearm.

line of force *n* a line in a field of force, such as an electric or magnetic field, for which the tangent at any point is the direction of the force at that point.

line of scrimmage *n American football.* an imaginary line, parallel to the goal lines, on which the ball is placed at the start of a down and on either side of which the offense and defense line up.

line of sight *n* **1** the straight line along which an observer looks or a beam of radiation travels. **2** *Ophthalmol.* another term for **line of vision.**

line of vision *n Ophthalmol.* a straight line extending from the fovea centralis of the eye to an object on which the eye is focused. Also called: **line of sight.**

lineolate ('lɪnɪə,leɪt) *or* **lineolated** *adj Biology.* marked with very fine parallel lines. [**C19**: from Latin *līneola,* diminutive of *līnea* LINE[1]]

line-out *n Rugby Union.* the method of restarting play when the ball goes into touch, the forwards forming two parallel lines at right angles to the touchline and jumping for the ball when it is thrown in.

line printer *n* an electromechanical device that prints a line of characters at a time rather than a character at a time, at speeds from about 200 to 3000 lines per minute: used in printing and in computer systems.

liner[1] ('laɪnə) *n* **1** a passenger ship or aircraft, esp. one that is part of a commercial fleet. **2** See **freightliner. 3** Also called: **eye liner.** a cosmetic used to outline the eyes, consisting of a liquid or cake mixed with water and applied by brush or a grease pencil. **4** a person or thing that uses lines, esp. in drawing or copying.

liner[2] ('laɪnə) *n* **1** a material used as a lining. **2** a person who supplies or fits linings. **3** *Engineering.* a sleeve, usually of a metal that will withstand wear or corrosion, fixed inside or outside a structural component: *cylinder liner.*

liner notes *pl n* the U.S. name for **sleeve notes.**

lines (laɪnz) *pl n* **1** general appearance or outline: *a car with fine lines.* **2** a plan of procedure or construction: *built on traditional lines.* **3a** the spoken words of a theatrical presentation. **3b** the words of a particular role: *he forgot his lines.* **4** *Informal, chiefly Brit.* a marriage certificate: *marriage lines.* **5** luck, fate, or fortune (esp. in the phrase **hard lines**). **6a** rows of buildings, temporary stabling, etc., in a military camp: *transport lines.* **6b** a defensive position, row of trenches, or other fortification: *we broke through the enemy lines.* **7a** a school punishment of writing the same sentence or phrase out a specified number of times. **7b** the phrases or sentences so written out: *a hundred lines.* **8 read between the lines.** to understand or find an implicit meaning in addition to the obvious one.

linesman ('laɪnzmən) *n, pl* **-men. 1** an official who helps the referee or umpire in various sports, esp. by indicating when the ball has gone out of play. **2** *Chiefly Brit.* a person who installs, maintains, or repairs telephone or electric-power lines. U.S. and Canadian name: **lineman.**

line squall *n* a squall or series of squalls along a cold front.

line-up *n* **1** a row or arrangement of people or things assembled for a particular purpose: *the line-up for the football match.* **2** the members of such a row or arrangement. **3** an identity parade. ◆ *vb* **line up.** *(adv)* **4** to form, put into, or organize a line-up. **5** *(tr)* to produce, organize, and assemble: *they lined up some questions.* **6** *(tr)* to align.

ling[1] (lɪŋ) *n, pl* **ling** *or* **lings. 1** any of several gadoid food fishes of the northern coastal genus *Molva,* esp. *M. molva,* having an elongated body with long fins. **2** another name for **burbot** (a fish). [**C13**: probably from Low German; related to LONG[1]]

ling[2] (lɪŋ) *n* another name for **heather** (sense 1). [**C14**: from Old Norse *lyng*] ▸ **'lingy** *adj*

ling. *abbrev. for* linguistics.

-ling[1] *suffix forming nouns.* **1** *Often disparaging.* a person or thing belonging to or associated with the group, activity, or quality specified: *nestling; underling.* **2** used as a diminutive: *duckling.* [Old English *-ling,* of Germanic origin; related to Icelandic *-lingr,* Gothic *-lings*]

-ling[2] *suffix forming adverbs.* in a specified condition, manner, or direction: *darkling; sideling.* [Old English *-ling,* adverbial suffix]

lingam ('lɪŋgəm) *or* **linga** ('lɪŋgə) *n* **1** (in Sanskrit grammar) the masculine gender. **2a** the Hindu phallic image of the god Siva. **2b** the penis. [**C18**: from Sanskrit]

Lingayen Gulf ('lɪŋgɑː'jɛn) *n* a large inlet of the South China Sea in the Philippines, on the NW coast of Luzon: site of Japanese landing in 1941 invasion.

lingcod ('lɪŋ,kɒd) *n, pl* **-cod** *or* **-cods.** any scorpaenoid food fish of the family *Ophiodontidae,* esp. *Ophiodon elongatus,* of the North Pacific Ocean.

linger ('lɪŋgə) *vb (mainly intr)* **1** to delay or prolong departure. **2** to go in a slow or leisurely manner; saunter. **3** to remain just alive for some time prior to death. **4** to persist or continue, esp. in the mind. **5** to be slow to act; dither; procrastinate. [**C13** (northern dialect) *lengeren* to dwell, from *lengen* to prolong, from Old English *lengan;* related to Old Norse *lengja;* see LONG[1]] ▸ **'lingerer** *n* ▸ **'lingering** *adj* ▸ **'lingeringly** *adv*

lingerie ('lænʒərɪ) *n* **1** women's underwear and nightwear. **2** *Archaic.* linen goods collectively. [C19: from French, from *linge,* from Latin *līneus* linen, from *līnum* flax]

lingo ('lɪŋgəʊ) *n, pl* **-goes.** *Informal.* any foreign or unfamiliar language, jargon, etc. [C17: perhaps from LINGUA FRANCA; compare Portuguese *lingoa* tongue]

lingua ('lɪŋgwə) *n, pl* **-guae** (-gwiː). *Anatomy.* **1** the technical name for **tongue. 2** any tongue-like structure. [C17: Latin]

lingua franca ('fræŋkə) *n, pl* **lingua francas** *or* **linguae francae** ('frænsiː). **1** a language used for communication among people of different mother tongues. **2** a hybrid language containing elements from several different languages used in this way. **3** any system of communication providing mutual understanding. [C17: Italian, literally: Frankish tongue]

Lingua Franca *n* a particular lingua franca spoken from the time of the Crusades to the 18th century in the ports of the Mediterranean, based on Italian, Spanish, French, Arabic, Greek, and Turkish.

lingual ('lɪŋgwəl) *adj* **1** *Anatomy.* of or relating to the tongue or a part or structure resembling a tongue. **2a** *Rare.* of or relating to language or languages. **2b** (*in combination*): *polylingual.* **3** articulated with the tongue. ♦ *n* **4** a lingual consonant, such as Scots (r). ► **'lingually** *adv*

linguiform ('lɪŋgwɪˌfɔːm) *adj* shaped like a tongue.

linguine *or* **linguini** (lɪŋ'gwiːnɪ) *n* a kind of pasta in the shape of thin flat strands. [from Italian: small tongues]

linguist ('lɪŋgwɪst) *n* **1** a person who has the capacity to learn and speak foreign languages. **2** a person who studies linguistics. **3** *West African, esp. Ghanaian.* the spokesman for a chief. [C16: from Latin *lingua* tongue]

linguistic (lɪŋ'gwɪstɪk) *adj* **1** of or relating to language. **2** of or relating to linguistics. ► **lin'guistically** *adv*

linguistic atlas *n* an atlas showing the distribution of distinctive linguistic features of languages or dialects.

linguistic borrowing *n* another name for **loan word.**

linguistic geography *n* the study of the distribution of dialectal speech elements. ► **linguistic geographer** *n*

linguistic philosophy *n* the approach to philosophy common in the mid 20th century that tends to see philosophical problems as arising from inappropriate theoretical use of language and therefore as being resolved by detailed attention to the common use of expressions.

linguistics (lɪŋ'gwɪstɪks) *n* (*functioning as sing*) the scientific study of language. See also **historical linguistics, descriptive linguistics.**

lingulate ('lɪŋgjʊˌleɪt) *or* **lingulated** *adj* shaped like a tongue: *a lingulate leaf.* [C19: from Latin *lingulātus*]

linhay ('lɪnɪ) *n Dialect.* a farm building with an open front. [C17: of unknown origin]

liniment ('lɪnɪmənt) *n* a medicated liquid, usually containing alcohol, camphor, and an oil, applied to the skin to relieve pain, stiffness, etc. [C15: from Late Latin *linīmentum,* from *linere* to smear, anoint]

linin ('laɪnɪn) *n* the network of viscous material in the nucleus of a cell that connects the chromatin granules. [C19: from Latin *līnum* flax + -IN]

lining ('laɪnɪŋ) *n* **1a** material used to line a garment, curtain, etc. **1b** (*as modifier*): *lining satin.* **2** a material, such as mull or brown paper, used to strengthen the back of a book. **3** *Civil engineering.* a layer of concrete, brick, or timber, etc., used in canals to prevent them leaking or in tunnels to prevent them falling in. **4** any material used as an interior covering.

link[1] (lɪŋk) *n* **1** any of the separate rings, loops, or pieces that connect or make up a chain. **2** something that resembles such a ring, loop, or piece. **3** a road, rail, air, or sea connection, as between two main routes. **4** a connecting part or episode. **5** a connecting piece in a mechanism, often having pivoted ends. **6** Also called: **radio link.** a system of transmitters and receivers that connect two locations by means of radio and television signals. **7** a unit of length equal to one hundredth of a chain. 1 link of a Gunter's chain is equal to 7.92 inches, and of an engineer's chain to 1 foot. **8 weak link.** an unreliable person or thing within an organization or system. ♦ *vb* **9** (often foll. by *up*) to connect or be connected with or as if with links. **10** (*tr*) to connect by association, etc. [C14: from Scandinavian; compare Old Norse *hlekkr* link] ► **'linkable** *adj*

link[2] (lɪŋk) *n* (formerly) a torch used to light dark streets. [C16: perhaps from Latin *lychnus,* from Greek *lukhnos* lamp]

linkage ('lɪŋkɪdʒ) *n* **1** the act of linking or the state of being linked. **2** a system of interconnected levers or rods for transmitting or regulating the motion of a mechanism. **3** *Electronics.* the product of the total number of lines of magnetic flux and the number of turns in a coil or circuit through which they pass. **4** *Genetics.* the occurrence of two genes close together on the same chromosome so that they are unlikely to be separated during crossing over and tend to be inherited as a single unit.

linkboy ('lɪŋkˌbɔɪ) *or* **linkman** *n, pl* **-boys** *or* **-men.** (formerly) a boy who carried a torch for pedestrians in dark streets.

linked list *n Computing.* a list in which each item contains both data and a pointer to one or both neighbouring items, thus eliminating the need for the data items to be ordered in memory.

linker ('lɪŋkə) *n* **1** *Computing.* a program that adjusts two or more machine-language program segments so that they may be simultaneously loaded and executed as a unit. **2** (in systemic grammar) a word that links one word, phrase, sentence, or clause to another; a co-ordinating conjunction or a sentence connector. Compare **binder** (sense 11).

linkman ('lɪŋkmən) *n, pl* **-men. 1** a presenter of a television or radio programme, esp. a sports transmission, consisting of a number of outside broadcasts from different locations. **2** another word for **linkboy.**

link motion *n* a mechanism controlling the valves of a steam engine, consisting of a slotted link terminating in a pair of eccentrics.

Linköping (*Swedish* 'lintçøːpiŋ) *n* a city in S Sweden: a political and ecclesiastical centre in the Middle Ages; engineering industry. Pop.: 131 898 (1997 est.).

links (lɪŋks) *pl n* **1a** short for **golf links. 1b** (*as modifier*): *a links course.* **2** *Chiefly Scot.* undulating sandy ground near the shore. [Old English *hlincas* plural of *hlinc* ridge]

Link trainer *n Trademark.* a ground-training device for training pilots and air-crew in the use of flight instruments. Compare **flight simulator.** [named after E. A. *Link* (1904–81), its U.S. inventor]

linkup ('lɪŋkˌʌp) *n* **1** the establishing of a connection or union between objects, groups, organizations, etc. **2** the connection or union established.

linkwork ('lɪŋkˌwɜːk) *n* **1** something made up of links. **2** a mechanism consisting of a series of links to impart or control motion; linkage.

Linlithgow (lɪn'lɪθgəʊ) *n* **1** a town in SE Scotland, in West Lothian: ruined palace, residence of Scottish kings and birthplace of Mary, Queen of Scots. Pop.: 11 866 (1991). **2** the former name of **West Lothian.**

linn (lɪn) *n Chiefly Scot.* **1** a waterfall or a pool at the foot of it. **2** a ravine or precipice. [C16: probably from a confusion of two words, Scottish Gaelic *linne* pool and Old English *hlynn* torrent]

Linnaeus (lɪ'niːəs, -'neɪ-) *n* **Carolus** ('kærələs), original name *Carl von Linné.* 1707–78, Swedish botanist, who established the binomial system of biological nomenclature that forms the basis of modern classification.

Linnean *or* **Linnaean** (lɪ'niːən, -'neɪ-) *adj* **1** of or relating to Linnaeus. **2** relating to the system of classification of plants and animals using binomial nomenclature.

linnet ('lɪnɪt) *n* **1** a brownish Old World finch, *Acanthis cannabina*: the male has a red breast and forehead. **2** Also called: **house finch.** a similar and related North American bird, *Carpodacus mexicanus.* [C16: from Old French *linotte,* ultimately from Latin *līnum* flax (because the bird feeds on flaxseeds)]

Linnhe ('lɪnɪ) *n* **Loch.** a sea loch of W Scotland, at the SW end of the Great Glen. Length: about 32 km (20 miles).

lino ('laɪnəʊ) *n* short for **linoleum.**

linocut ('laɪnəʊˌkʌt) *n* **1** a design cut in relief on linoleum mounted on a wooden block. **2** a print made from such a design.

linoleate (lɪ'nəʊlɪˌeɪt) *n* an ester or salt of linoleic acid.

linoleic acid (ˌlɪnəʊ'liːɪk) *n* a colourless oily essential fatty acid found in many natural oils, such as linseed: used in the manufacture of soaps, emulsifiers, and driers. Formula: $C_{18}H_{32}O_2$. [C19: from Latin *linum* flax + OLEIC ACID; so named because it is found in linseed oil]

linolenic acid (ˌlɪnəʊ'lenɪk, -'liː-) *n* a colourless unsaturated essential fatty acid found in drying oils, such as linseed oil, and used in making paints and synthetic resins; 9,12,15-octadecatrienoic acid. Formula: $C_{18}H_{30}O_2$.

linoleum (lɪ'nəʊlɪəm) *n* a sheet material made of hessian, jute, etc., coated under pressure and heat with a mixture of powdered cork, linseed oil, rosin, and pigment, used as a floor covering. Often shortened to **lino.** [C19: from Latin *līnum* flax + *oleum* oil]

lino tile *n* a tile made of linoleum or a similar substance, used as a floor covering.

Linotype ('laɪnəʊˌtaɪp) *n* **1** *Trademark.* a typesetting machine, operated by a keyboard, that casts an entire line on one solid slug of metal. **2** type produced by such a machine.

Lin Piao ('lɪn 'pjaʊ) *or* **Lin Biao** *n* 1908–71, Chinese Communist general and statesman. He became minister of defence (1959) and second in rank to Mao Tse-tung (1966). He fell from grace and is reported to have died in an air crash while attempting to flee to the Soviet Union.

linsang ('lɪnsæŋ) *n* any of several forest-dwelling viverrine mammals, *Poiana richardsoni* of W Africa or either of the two species of *Prionodon* of S Asia: closely related to the genets, having a very long tail and a spotted or banded coat of thick fur. [C19: Malay]

linseed ('lɪnˌsiːd) *n* another name for **flaxseed.** [Old English *līnsǣd,* from *līn* flax + *sǣd* seed]

linseed oil *n* a yellow oil extracted from seeds of the flax plant. It has great drying qualities and is used in making oil paints, printer's ink, linoleum, etc.

linsey-woolsey ('lɪnzɪ'wʊlzɪ) *n* **1** a thin rough fabric of linen warp and coarse wool or cotton filling. **2** a strange nonsensical mixture or confusion. [C15: probably from *Lindsey,* Suffolk village where the fabric was first made + WOOL (with rhyming suffix *-sey*)]

linstock ('lɪnˌstɒk) *n* a long staff holding a lighted match, formerly used to fire a cannon. [C16: from Dutch *lontstok,* from *lont* match + *stok* stick]

lint (lɪnt) *n* **1** an absorbent cotton or linen fabric with the nap raised on one side, used to dress wounds, etc. **2** shreds of fibre, yarn, etc. **3** *Chiefly U.S.* staple fibre for making cotton yarn. [C14: probably from Latin *linteus* made of linen, from *līnum* flax] ► **'linty** *adj*

lintel ('lɪntᵊl) *n* a horizontal beam, as over a door or window. [C14: via Old French probably from Late Latin *līmitāris* (unattested) of the boundary, influenced in meaning by *līminaris* of the threshold]

linter ('lɪntə) *n* **1** a machine for stripping the short fibres of ginned cotton seeds. **2** (*pl*) the fibres so removed.

lintie ('lɪntɪ) *n* a Scot. word for **linnet** (sense 1).

lintwhite ('lɪntˌwaɪt) *n Archaic or poetic, chiefly Scot.* the linnet. [Old English *līnetwige,* probably from *līn* flax + *-twige,* perhaps related to Old High German *zwigon* to pluck]

linum ('laɪnəm) *n* any plant of the annual or perennial genus *Linum,* of temperate regions, esp. *L. grandiflorum,* from N Africa, cultivated for its showy red or blue flowers: family *Linaceae.* See also **flax.** [Latin, from Greek *linon* flax]

Linz (lɪnts) *n* a port in N Austria, capital of Upper Austria, on the River Danube: cultural centre; steelworks. Pop.: 203 044 (1991). Latin name: **Lentia** ('lɛntɪə, 'lɛnsɪə).

lion ('laɪən) *n* **1** a large gregarious predatory feline mammal, *Panthera leo,* of

open country in parts of Africa and India, having a tawny yellow coat and, in the male, a shaggy mane. Related adj: **leonine. 2** a conventionalized lion, the principal beast used as an emblem in heraldry. It has become the national emblem of Great Britain. **3** a courageous, strong, or bellicose person. **4** a celebrity or idol who attracts much publicity and a large following. **5 beard the lion in his den.** to approach a feared or influential person, esp. in order to ask a favour. **6 the lion's share.** the largest portion. [Old English *līo, lēo* (Middle English *lioun,* from Anglo-French *liun*), both from Latin *leo,* Greek *leōn*]
Lion ('laɪən) *n* **the.** the constellation Leo, the fifth sign of the zodiac.
lioness ('laɪənɪs) *n* a female lion.
lionfish ('laɪən,fɪʃ) *n, pl* **-fish** *or* **-fishes.** any of various scorpion fishes of the tropical Pacific genus *Pterois,* having a striped body and elongated spiny fins.
lion-hearted *adj* very brave; courageous. ▸ **'lion-,heartedly** *adv* ▸ **'lion,heartedness** *n*
lionize *or* **lionise** ('laɪə,naɪz) *vb* (*tr*) to treat as or make into a celebrity. ▸ **,lioni'zation** *or* **,lioni'sation** *n* ▸ **'lion,izer** *or* **'lion,iser** *n*
Lions ('laɪənz) *n* **Gulf of.** a wide bay of the Mediterranean off the S coast of France, between the Spanish border and Toulon. French name: **Golfe du Lion** (gɔlf dy ljɔ̃).
Lions Club *n* any of the local clubs that form the International Association of Lions Clubs, formed in the U.S. in 1917 to foster local and international good relations and service to the community.
lip (lɪp) *n* **1** *Anatomy.* **1a** either of the two fleshy folds surrounding the mouth, playing an important role in the production of speech sounds, retaining food in the mouth, etc. Related adj: **labial. 1b** (*as modifier*): *lip salve.* **2** the corresponding part in animals, esp. mammals. **3** any structure resembling a lip, such as the rim of a crater, the margin of a gastropod shell, etc. **4** a nontechnical word for **labium** and **labellum** (sense 1). **5** *Slang.* impudent talk or backchat. **6** the embouchure and control in the lips needed to blow wind and brass instruments. **7 bite one's lip. 7a** to stifle one's feelings. **7b** to be annoyed or irritated. **8 button (up) one's lip.** *Slang.* to stop talking: often imperative. **9 keep a stiff upper lip.** to maintain one's courage or composure during a time of trouble without giving way to or revealing one's emotions. **10 lick** *or* **smack one's lips.** to anticipate or recall something with glee or relish. ◆ *vb* **lips, lipping, lipped. 11** (*tr*) to touch with the lip or lips. **12** (*tr*) to form or be a lip or lips for. **13** (*tr*) *Rare.* to murmur or whisper. **14** (*intr*) to use the lips in playing a wind instrument. [Old English *lippa;* related to Old High German *leffur,* Norwegian *lepe,* Latin *labium*] ▸ **'lipless** *adj* ▸ **'lip,like** *adj*
lip- *combining form.* a variant of **lipo-** before a vowel.
lipaemia *or U.S.* **lipemia** (lɪ'piːmɪə) *n Pathol.* an abnormally large amount of fat in the blood. [from Greek *lipos* fat + -AEMIA]
Lipari Islands ('lɪpərɪ) *pl n* a group of volcanic islands under Italian administration off the N coast of Sicily: remains that form a continuous record from Neolithic times. Chief town: Lipari. Pop.: 10 300 (1987 est.). Area: 114 sq. km (44 sq. miles). Also called: **Aeolian Islands.** Italian name: **Isole Eolie** ('iːzole e'ɔːlje).
lipase ('laɪpeɪs, 'lɪpeɪs) *n* any of a group of fat-digesting enzymes produced in the stomach, pancreas, and liver and also occurring widely in the seeds of plants. [C19: from Greek *lipos* fat + -ASE]
Lipchitz ('lɪpʃɪts) *n* **Jacques** (ʒɑːk). 1891–1973, U.S. sculptor, born in Lithuania: he pioneered cubist sculpture.
Li Peng ('liː 'pɛŋ) *n* born 1928, Chinese Communist politician: premier (prime minister) from 1988.
Lipetsk (*Russian* 'lipitsk) *n* a city in central Russia, on the Voronezh River: steelworks. Pop.: 474 000 (1995 est.).
lip gloss *n* a cosmetic preparation applied to the lips to give a sheen.
lipid *or* **lipide** ('laɪpɪd, 'lɪpɪd) *n Biochem.* any of a large group of organic compounds that are esters of fatty acids (**simple lipids,** such as fats and waxes) or closely related substances (**compound lipids,** such as phospholipids): usually insoluble in water but soluble in alcohol and other organic solvents. They are important structural materials in living organisms. Former name: **lipoid.** [C20: from French *lipide,* from Greek *lipos* fat]
Lipizzaner (,lɪpɪt'sɑːnə) *n* a breed of riding and carriage horse used by the Spanish Riding School in Vienna and nearly always grey in colour. [German, after *Lipizza,* near Trieste, where these horses were bred]
lip microphone *n* a microphone designed and shaped to be held close to the mouth, for use in noisy environments.
Li Po *or* **Li T'ai-po** ('liː 'taɪ 'pəʊ) *n* ?700–762 A.D., Chinese poet. His lyrics deal mostly with wine, nature, and women and are remarkable for their imagery.
lipo- *or before a vowel* **lip-** *combining form.* fat or fatty: *lipoprotein.* [from Greek *lipos* fat]
lipogenesis (,lɪpəʊ'dʒɛnɪsɪs) *adj Biochem.* the synthesis of fatty acids in the body from glucose and other substrates.
lipogram ('lɪpəʊ,græm) *n* a piece of writing from which all words containing a particular letter have been deliberately omitted.
lipography (lɪ'pɒgrəfɪ) *n* the accidental omission of words or letters in writing. [C19: from Greek *lip-,* stem of *leipein* to omit + -GRAPHY]
lipoic acid *n Biochem.* a sulphur-containing fatty acid, regarded as an element of the vitamin B complex, minute amounts of which are required for carbohydrate metabolism.
lipoid ('lɪpɔɪd, 'laɪ-) *adj also* **lipoidal. 1** resembling fat; fatty. ◆ *n* **2** a fatlike substance, such as wax. **3** *Biochem.* a former name for **lipid.**
lipolysis (lɪ'pɒlɪsɪs) *n Chem.* the hydrolysis of fats resulting in the production of carboxylic acids and glycerol. ▸ **lipolytic** (,lɪpəʊ'lɪtɪk) *adj*
lipoma (lɪ'pəʊmə) *n, pl* **-mas** *or* **-mata** (-mətə). *Pathol.* a tumour composed of fatty tissue. [C19: New Latin] ▸ **lipomatous** (lɪ'pɒmətəs) *adj*
lipophilic (,lɪpəʊ'fɪlɪk) *or* **lipotropic** (,lɪpəʊ'trɒpɪk, ,laɪ-) *adj Chem.* having an affinity for lipids.
lipoplast ('lɪpəʊ,plɑːst) *or* **lipidoplast** ('lɪpɪdəʊ,plɑːst) *n Botany.* a small particle in plant cytoplasm, esp. that of seeds, in which fat is stored.
lipopolysaccaride (,lɪpəʊ,pɒlɪ'sækə,raɪd) *n* a molecule, consisting of lipid and polysaccharide components, that is the main constituent of the cell walls of Gram-negative bacteria.
lipoprotein (,lɪpəʊ'prəʊtiːn, ,laɪ-) *n* any of a group of proteins to which a lipid molecule is attached, important in the transport of lipids in the bloodstream. They exist in two main forms: high-density lipoproteins and low-density lipoproteins. See also **low-density lipoprotein.**
liposome ('lɪpəʊ,səʊm) *n* a particle formed by lipids, consisting of a double layer similar to a natural biological membrane, enclosing an aqueous compartment.
liposuction ('lɪpəʊ,sʌkʃən) *n* a cosmetic surgical operation in which subcutaneous fat is removed from the body by suction.
lipotropic (,lɪpəʊ'trɒpɪk) *adj Biochem.* (of a substance) increasing the utilization of fat by the tissues.
Lippe ('lɪpə) *n* **1** a former state of NW Germany, now part of the German state of North Rhine-Westphalia: part of West Germany until 1990. **2** a river in NW Germany, flowing west to the Rhine. Length: about 240 km (150 miles).
-lipped *adj* having a lip or lips as specified: *tight-lipped.*
Lippershey ('lɪpəs,haɪ) *or* **Lippersheim** ('lɪpəs,haɪm) *n* **Hans.** died ?1619, Dutch lens grinder, who built the first telescope.
Lippi (*Italian* 'lippi) *n* **1 Filippino** (filip'piːno). ?1457–1504, Italian painter of the Florentine school. **2** his father, **Fra Filippo** (fra fi'lippo). ?1406–69, Italian painter of the Florentine school, noted particularly for his frescoes at Prato Cathedral (1452–64).
Lippizaner (,lɪpɪt'zɑːnə) *n* a variant spelling of **Lipizzaner.**
Lippmann ('lɪpmən; *French* lipman) *n* **Gabriel** (gabriɛl). 1845–1921, French physicist. He devised the earliest process of colour photography: Nobel prize for physics 1908.
lippy[1] ('lɪpɪ) *adj* **-pier, -piest.** insolent or cheeky.
lippy[2] ('lɪpɪ) *n Informal.* lipstick.
lip-read ('lɪp,riːd) *vb* **-reads, -reading, -read** (-'rɛd). to interpret (words) by lip-reading.
lip-reading *n* a method used by the deaf to comprehend spoken words by interpreting movements of the speaker's lips. Also called: **speech-reading.** ▸ **'lip-,reader** *n*
lip service *n* insincere support or respect expressed but not put into practice.
lipstick ('lɪp,stɪk) *n* a cosmetic for colouring the lips, usually in the form of a stick.
lip-synch *or* **lip-sync** ('lɪp,sɪŋk) *vb* to mouth (prerecorded words) on television or film.
lipuria (lɪ'pjʊərɪə) *n Pathol.* the presence of fat in the urine.
liq. *abbrev. for:* **1** liquid. **2** liquor.
liquate ('laɪkweɪt) *vb* (*tr;* often foll. by *out*) to separate one component of (an alloy, impure metal, or ore) by heating so that the more fusible part melts. [C17: from Latin *liquāre* to dissolve] ▸ **li'quation** *n*
liquefacient (,lɪkwɪ'feɪʃənt) *n* **1** a substance that liquefies or causes liquefaction. ◆ *adj* **2** becoming or causing to become liquid. [C19: from Latin *liquefacere* to make LIQUID]
liquefied natural gas *n* a mixture of various gases, esp. methane, liquefied under pressure for transportation and used as an engine fuel. Abbrev.: **LNG.**
liquefied petroleum gas *n* a mixture of various petroleum gases, esp. propane and butane, stored as a liquid under pressure and used as an engine fuel. See also **bottled gas.** Abbrev.: **LPG** *or* **LP gas.**
liquefy ('lɪkwɪ,faɪ) *vb* **-fies, -fying, -fied.** (esp. of a gas) to become or cause to become liquid. [C15: via Old French from Latin *liquefacere* to make liquid] ▸ **liquefaction** (,lɪkwɪ'fækʃən) *n* ▸ **,lique'factive** *adj* ▸ **'lique,fiable** *adj* ▸ **'lique,fier** *n*
liquesce (lɪ'kwɛs) *vb* (*intr*) to become liquid.
liquescent (lɪ'kwɛsᵊnt) *adj* (of a solid or gas) becoming or tending to become liquid. [C18: from Latin *liquescere*] ▸ **li'quescence** *or* **li'quescency** *n*
liqueur (lɪ'kjʊə; *French* likœr) *n* **1a** any of several highly flavoured sweetened spirits such as kirsch or cointreau, intended to be drunk after a meal. **1b** (*as modifier*): *liqueur glass.* **2** a small hollow chocolate sweet containing liqueur. [C18: from French; see LIQUOR]
liquid ('lɪkwɪd) *n* **1** a substance in a physical state in which it does not resist change of shape but does resist change of size. Compare **gas** (sense 1), **solid** (sense 1). **2** a substance that is a liquid at room temperature and atmospheric pressure. **3** *Phonetics.* a frictionless continuant, esp. (l) or (r). ◆ *adj* **4** of, concerned with, or being a liquid or having the characteristic state of liquids: *liquid wax.* **5** shining, transparent, or brilliant. **6** flowing, fluent, or smooth. **7** (of assets) in the form of money or easily convertible into money. [C14: via Old French from Latin *liquidus,* from *liquēre* to be fluid] ▸ **'liquidly** *adv* ▸ **'liquidness** *n*
liquid air *n* air that has been liquefied by cooling. It is a pale blue and consists mainly of liquid oxygen (boiling pt.: -182.9°C) and liquid nitrogen (boiling pt.: -195.7°C): used in the production of pure oxygen, nitrogen, and the inert gases, and as a refrigerant.
liquidambar (,lɪkwɪd'æmbə) *n* **1** any deciduous tree of the hamamelidaceous genus *Liquidambar,* of Asia and North and Central America, with star-shaped leaves, and exuding a yellow aromatic balsam. See also **sweet gum. 2** the balsam of this tree, used in medicine. See also **storax** (sense 3). [C16: New Latin, from Latin *liquidus* liquid + Medieval Latin *ambar* AMBER]
liquidate ('lɪkwɪ,deɪt) *vb* **1a** to settle or pay off (a debt, claim, etc.). **1b** to determine by litigation or agreement the amount of (damages, indebtedness, etc.). **2a** to terminate the operations of (a commercial firm, bankrupt estate, etc.) by assessment of liabilities and appropriation of assets for their settlement. **2b** (of a

commercial firm, etc.) to terminate operations in this manner. **3** (*tr*) to convert (assets) into cash. **4** (*tr*) to eliminate or kill.

liquidation (ˌlɪkwɪˈdeɪʃən) *n* **1a** the process of terminating the affairs of a business firm, etc., by realizing its assets to discharge its liabilities. **1b** the state of a business firm, etc., having its affairs so terminated (esp. in the phrase **to go into liquidation**). **2** destruction; elimination.

liquidator (ˈlɪkwɪˌdeɪtə) *n* a person assigned to supervise the liquidation of a business concern and whose legal authorization, rights, and duties differ according to whether the liquidation is compulsory or voluntary.

liquid crystal *n* a liquid that has some crystalline characteristics, such as the presence of different optical properties in different directions; a substance in a mesomorphic state. See also **smectic, nematic.**

liquid-crystal display *n* a flat-screen display in which an array of liquid-crystal elements can be selectively activated to generate an image, an electric field applied to each element altering its optical properties; it is used, for example, in portable computers, digital watches, and calculators. Abbrev.: **LCD.**

liquid fire *n* inflammable petroleum or other liquid used as a weapon of war in flamethrowers, etc.

liquid glass *n* another name for **water glass.**

liquidity (lɪˈkwɪdɪtɪ) *n* **1** the possession of sufficient liquid assets to discharge current liabilities. **2** the state or quality of being liquid.

liquidity preference *n Economics.* the desire to hold money rather than other assets, in Keynsian theory based on motives of transactions, precaution, and speculation.

liquidity ratio *n* the ratio of those assets that can easily be exchanged for money to the total assets of a bank or other financial institution. Also called: **liquid assets ratio.**

liquidize *or* **liquidise** (ˈlɪkwɪˌdaɪz) *vb* **1** to make or become liquid; liquefy. **2** (*tr*) to pulverize (food) in a liquidizer so as to produce a fluid.

liquidizer *or* **liquidiser** (ˈlɪkwɪˌdaɪzə) *n* a kitchen appliance with blades for cutting and puréeing vegetables, blending liquids, etc. Also called: **blender.**

liquid measure *n* a unit or system of units for measuring volumes of liquids or their containers.

liquid oxygen *n* the clear pale blue liquid state of oxygen produced by liquefying air and allowing the nitrogen to evaporate: used in rocket fuels. Also called: **lox.**

liquid paraffin *n* a colourless almost tasteless oily liquid obtained by petroleum distillation and used as a laxative. Also called (esp. U.S. and Canadian): **mineral oil.**

liquor (ˈlɪkə) *n* **1** any alcoholic drink, esp. spirits, or such drinks collectively. **2** any liquid substance, esp. that in which food has been cooked. **3** *Pharmacol.* a solution of a pure substance in water. **4** *Brewing.* warm water added to malt to form wort. **5 in liquor.** drunk; intoxicated. ◆ *vb* **6** *Brewing.* to steep (malt) in warm water to form wort; mash. **[**C13: via Old French from Latin, from *liquēre* to be liquid**]**

liquorice *or U.S. and Canadian* **licorice** (ˈlɪkərɪs, -ərɪʃ) *n* **1** a perennial Mediterranean leguminous shrub, *Glycyrrhiza glabra,* having spikes of pale blue flowers and flat red-brown pods. **2** the dried root of this plant, used as a laxative and in confectionery. **3** a sweet having a liquorice flavour. **[**C13: via Anglo-Norman and Old French from Late Latin *liquirītia,* from Latin *glycyrrhīza,* from Greek *glukurrhiza,* from *glukus* sweet + *rhiza* root**]**

liquorish (ˈlɪkərɪʃ) *adj* **1** a variant spelling of **lickerish. 2** *Brit.* a variant of **liquorice.** ▸ **ˈliquorishly** *adv* ▸ **ˈliquorishness** *n*

liquor store *n U.S. and Canadian.* See **package store.**

liquor up *vb* (*adv*) *U.S. and Canadian slang.* to become or cause to become drunk.

lira (ˈlɪərə; *Italian* ˈliːra) *n, pl* **lire** (ˈlɪərɪ; *Italian* ˈliːre) *or* **liras. 1** the standard monetary unit of Italy and San Marino. **2** Also called: **pound.** the standard monetary unit of Turkey, divided into 100 kuruş. **3** the standard monetary unit of Malta, divided into 100 cents or 1000 mils. **[**Italian, from Latin *lībra* pound**]**

liriodendron (ˌlɪrɪəʊˈdɛndrən) *n, pl* **-drons** *or* **-dra** (-drə). either of the two deciduous trees of the magnoliaceous genus *Liriodendron,* the tulip tree of North America or *L. chinense* of China. **[**C18: New Latin, from Greek *leiron* lily + *dendron* tree**]**

liripipe (ˈlɪrɪˌpaɪp) *or* **liripoop** (ˈlɪrɪˌpuːp) *n* the tip of a graduate's hood. **[**C14: Medieval Latin *liripipium,* origin obscure**]**

Lisbon (ˈlɪzbən) *n* the capital and chief port of Portugal, in the southwest on the Tagus estuary: became capital in 1256; subject to earthquakes and severely damaged in 1755; university (1911). Pop.: 677 790 (1991). Portuguese name: **Lisboa** (liʒˈboə).

Lisburn (ˈlɪzbɜːn) *n* **1** a town in Northern Ireland in Lisburn district, Co. Antrim, noted for its linen industry: headquarters of the British Army in Northern Ireland. Pop.: 42 110 (1991). **2** a district of S Northern Ireland, in Co. Antrim and Co. Down. Pop.: 99 458 (1991). Area: 446 sq. km (172 sq. miles).

Lisieux (*French* lizjø) *n* a town in NW France: Roman Catholic pilgrimage centre, for its shrine of St Thérèse, who lived there. Pop.: 24 506 (1990).

lisle (laɪl) *n* **a** a strong fine cotton thread or fabric. **b** (*as modifier*): *lisle stockings.* **[**C19: named after *Lisle* (now Lille), town in France where this type of thread was originally manufactured**]**

lisp (lɪsp) *n* **1** the articulation of *s* and *z* like or nearly like the *th* sounds in English *thin* and *then* respectively. **2** the habit or speech defect of pronouncing *s* and *z* in this manner. **3** the sound of a lisp in pronunciation. ◆ *vb* **4** to use a lisp in the pronunciation of (speech). **5** to speak or pronounce imperfectly or haltingly. **[**Old English *āwlispian,* from *wlisp* lisping (adj), of imitative origin; related to Old High German *lispen***]** ▸ **ˈlisper** *n* ▸ **ˈlisping** *adj, n* ▸ **ˈlispingly** *adv*

LISP (lɪsp) *n* a high-level computer-programming language suitable for work in artificial intelligence. **[**C20: from *lis(t) p(rocessing)***]**

lis pendens (lɪs ˈpɛndɛnz) *n* **1** a suit pending in a court that concerns the title to land. **2** a notice filed to warn interested persons of such a suit. **[**Latin: pending lawsuit**]**

Lissajous figure (ˈliːsəˌʒuː, ˌliːsəˈʒuː) *n* a curve traced out by a point that undergoes two simple harmonic motions in mutually perpendicular directions. The shape of these curves is characteristic of the relative phases and frequencies of the motion; they are used to determine the frequencies and phases of alternating voltages. **[**C19: named after Jules A. *Lissajous* (1822–80), French physicist**]**

lissom *or* **lissome** (ˈlɪsəm) *adj* **1** supple in the limbs or body; lithe; flexible. **2** agile; nimble. **[**C19: variant of LITHESOME**]** ▸ **ˈlissomly** *or* **ˈlissomely** *adv* ▸ **ˈlissomness** *or* **ˈlissomeness** *n*

list[1] (lɪst) *n* **1** an item-by-item record of names or things, usually written or printed one under the other. **2** *Computing.* a linearly ordered data structure. **3 be on the danger list.** to be in a critical medical or physical condition. ◆ *vb* **4** (*tr*) to make a list of. **5** (*tr*) to include in a list. **6** (*tr*) *Brit.* to declare to be a listed building. **7** (*tr*) *Stock Exchange.* to obtain an official quotation for (a security) so that it may be traded on the recognized market. **8** an archaic word for **enlist. [**C17: from French, ultimately related to LIST[2]; compare Italian *lista* list of names (earlier: border, strip, as of paper), Old High German *līsta* border**]** ▸ **ˈlistable** *adj*

list[2] (lɪst) *n* **1** a border or edging strip, esp. of cloth. **2** a less common word for **selvage. 3** a strip of bark, sapwood, etc., trimmed from a board or plank. **4** another word for **fillet** (sense 8). **5** a strip, band, ridge or furrow. **6** *Agriculture.* a ridge in ploughed land formed by throwing two furrows together. ◆ *vb* (*tr*) **7** to border with or as if with a list or lists. **8** *Agriculture.* to plough (land) so as to form lists. **9** to cut a list from (a board, plank, etc.). ◆ See also **lists. [**Old English *līst;* related to Old High German *līsta***]**

list[3] (lɪst) *vb* **1** (esp. of ships) to lean over or cause to lean over to one side. ◆ *n* **2** the act or an instance of leaning to one side. **[**C17: origin unknown**]**

list[4] (lɪst) *Archaic.* ◆ *vb* **1** to be pleasing to (a person). **2** (*tr*) to desire or choose. ◆ *n* **3** a liking or desire. **[**Old English *lystan;* related to Old High German *lusten* and Gothic *lūston* to desire**]**

list[5] (lɪst) *vb* an archaic or poetic word for **listen. [**Old English *hlystan;* related to Old Norse *hlusta***]**

listed building *n* (in Britain) a building officially recognized as having special historical or architectural interest and therefore protected from demolition or alteration.

listed company *n Stock Exchange.* a company whose shares are quoted on the main market of the London Stock Exchange.

listed security *n Stock Exchange.* a security that is quoted on the main market of the London Stock Exchange and appears in its *Official List of Securities.* Compare **Third Market, unlisted securities market.**

listel (ˈlɪstᵊl) *n* another name for **fillet** (sense 8). **[**C16: via French from Italian *listello,* diminutive of *lista* band, LIST[2]**]**

listen (ˈlɪsᵊn) *vb* (*intr*) **1** to concentrate on hearing something. **2** to take heed; pay attention: *I told you many times but you wouldn't listen.* **[**Old English *hlysnan;* related to Old High German *lūstrēn***]** ▸ **ˈlistener** *n*

listenable (ˈlɪsᵊnəbᵊl) *adj* easy or pleasant to listen to. ▸ **ˌlistenaˈbility** *n*

listen in *vb* (*intr, adv;* often foll. by *to*) **1** to listen to the radio. **2** to intercept radio communications. **3** to listen but not contribute (to a discussion), esp. surreptitiously.

listening post *n* **1** *Military.* a forward position set up to obtain early warning of enemy movement. **2** any strategic position or place for obtaining information about another country or area.

lister (ˈlɪstə) *n U.S. and Canadian agriculture.* a plough with a double mouldboard designed to throw soil to either side of a central furrow. Also called: **lister plough, middlebreaker, middle buster. [**C19: from LIST[2]**]**

Lister (ˈlɪstə) *n* **Joseph,** 1st Baron Lister. 1827–1912, British surgeon, who introduced the use of antiseptics.

listeria (lɪsˈtɪərɪə) *n* any rodlike Gram-positive bacterium of the genus *Listeria,* esp. *L. monocytogenes,* the cause of listeriosis. **[**C20: named after Joseph LISTER**]** ▸ **lisˈterial** *adj*

listeriosis (lɪˌstɪərɪˈəʊsɪs) *n* a serious form of food poisoning, caused by bacteria of the genus *Listeria.* Its symptoms can include meningitis and in pregnant women it may cause damage to the fetus.

Listerism (ˈlɪstəˌrɪzəm) *n Surgery.* the use of or theory of using antiseptic techniques.

listing (ˈlɪstɪŋ) *n* **1** a list or an entry in a list. **2** *Computing.* a printed copy of a program or file in a form that can be read by humans. **3** a place on the Official List of Securities of the London Stock Exchange obtained by a company that has fulfilled the listing requirements and whose shares are quoted on the main market. **4** (*pl*) lists of concerts, films, and other events printed in newspapers or magazines, showing details, such as times and venues.

listless (ˈlɪstlɪs) *adj* disinclined for any effort or exertion; lacking vigour, enthusiasm, or energy. **[**C15: from *list* desire + -LESS**]** ▸ **ˈlistlessly** *adv* ▸ **ˈlistlessness** *n*

Liston (ˈlɪstən) *n* **Sonny,** real name *Charles.* 1922–70, U.S. boxer: former world heavyweight champion.

list price *n* the selling price of merchandise as quoted in a catalogue or advertisement.

list renting *n* the practice of renting a list of potential customers to a direct-mail seller of goods or to the fund raisers of a charity.

lists (lɪsts) *pl n* **1** *History.* **1a** the enclosed field of combat at a tournament. **1b** the barriers enclosing the field at a tournament. **2** any arena or scene of conflict, controversy, etc. **3 enter the lists.** to engage in a conflict, controversy, etc. [C14: plural of LIST[2] (border, boundary)]

Liszt (lɪst) *n* **Franz** (frants). 1811–86, Hungarian composer and pianist. The greatest piano virtuoso of the 19th century, he originated the symphonic poem, pioneered the one-movement sonata form, and developed new harmonic combinations. His works include the symphonies *Faust* (1861) and *Dante* (1867), piano compositions and transcriptions, songs, and church music.

lit (lɪt) *vb* **1** a past tense and past participle of **light**[1]. **2** an alternative past tense and past participle of **light**[2].

lit. *abbrev. for:* **1** literal(ly). **2** literary. **3** literature.

Li T'ai-po ('li: 'taɪ'pəʊ) *n* See **Li Po.**

litany ('lɪtənɪ) *n, pl* **-nies. 1** *Christianity.* **1a** a form of prayer consisting of a series of invocations, each followed by an unvarying response. **1b the Litany.** the general supplication in this form included in the Book of Common Prayer. **2** any long or tedious speech or recital. [C13: via Old French from Medieval Latin *litanīa* from Late Greek *litaneia* prayer, ultimately from Greek *litē* entreaty]

litas ('li:tɑ:s) *n, pl* **litai** ('li:teɪ). the standard monetary unit of Lithuania, divided into 100 centai.

litchi, lichee, lichi, *or* **lychee** (ˌlaɪ'tʃi:) *n* **1** a Chinese sapindaceous tree, *Litchi chinensis,* cultivated for its round edible fruits. **2** the fruit of this tree, which has whitish juicy pulp. [C16: from Cantonese *lai chi*]

lite (laɪt) *adj* **1** (of food and drink) containing few calories or little alcohol or fat. **2** denoting a more restrained or less extreme version of a person or thing: *reggae lite.* [C20: variant spelling of LIGHT[2]]

-lite *n combining form.* (in names of minerals) stone: *chrysolite.* Compare **-lith.** [from French *-lite* or *-lithe,* from Greek *lithos* stone]

liter ('li:tə) *n* the U.S. spelling of **litre.**

literacy ('lɪtərəsɪ) *n* **1** the ability to read and write. **2** the ability to use language proficiently.

literae humaniores ('lɪtəˌri: hju:ˌmænɪ'ɔ:ri:z) *n* (at Oxford University) the faculty concerned with Greek and Latin literature, ancient history, and philosophy; classics. [Latin, literally: the more humane letters]

literal ('lɪtərəl) *adj* **1** in exact accordance with or limited to the primary or explicit meaning of a word or text. **2** word for word. **3** dull, factual, or prosaic. **4** consisting of, concerning, or indicated by letters. **5** true; actual. **6** *Maths.* containing or using coefficients and constants represented by letters: $ax^2 + b$ is a literal expression. Compare **numerical** (sense 3a). ◆ *n* **7** Also called: **literal error.** a misprint or misspelling in a text. [C14: from Late Latin *litterālis* concerning letters, from Latin *littera* LETTER] ▸ **'literalness** *or* **literality** (ˌlɪtə'rælɪtɪ) *n*

literalism ('lɪtərəˌlɪzəm) *n* **1** the disposition to take words and statements in their literal sense. **2** literal or realistic portrayal in art or literature. ▸ **'literalist** *n* ▸ **ˌliteral'istic** *adj* ▸ **ˌliteral'istically** *adv*

literally ('lɪtərəlɪ) *adv* **1** in a literal manner. **2** (intensifier): *there were literally thousands of people.*

USAGE The use of *literally* as an intensifier is common, esp. in informal contexts. In some cases, it provides emphasis without adding to the meaning: *the house was literally only five minutes walk away.* Often, however, its use results in absurdity: *the news was literally an eye-opener to me.* It is therefore best avoided in formal contexts.

literary ('lɪtərərɪ, 'lɪtrərɪ) *adj* **1** of, relating to, concerned with, or characteristic of literature or scholarly writing: *a literary discussion; a literary style.* **2** versed in or knowledgeable about literature: *a literary man.* **3** (of a word) formal; not colloquial. [C17: from Latin *litterārius* concerning reading and writing. See LETTER] ▸ **'literarily** *adv* ▸ **'literariness** *n*

literary agent *n* a person who manages the business affairs of an author. ▸ **literary agency** *n*

literate ('lɪtərɪt) *adj* **1** able to read and write. **2** educated; learned. **3** used to words rather than numbers as a means of expression. Compare **numerate.** ◆ *n* **4** a literate person. [C15: from Latin *litterātus* learned. See LETTER] ▸ **'literately** *adv*

literati (ˌlɪtə'rɑ:ti:) *pl n* literary or scholarly people. [C17: from Latin]

literatim (ˌlɪtə'rɑ:tɪm) *adv* letter for letter. [C17: from Medieval Latin, from Latin *littera* LETTER]

literation (ˌlɪtə'reɪʃən) *n* the use of letters to represent sounds or words.

literator ('lɪtəˌreɪtə) *n* another word for **littérateur.** [C18: from Latin, from *littera* letter]

literature ('lɪtərɪtʃə, 'lɪtrɪ-) *n* **1** written material such as poetry, novels, essays, etc., esp. works of imagination characterized by excellence of style and expression and by themes of general or enduring interest. **2** the body of written work of a particular culture or people: *Scandinavian literature.* **3** written or printed matter of a particular type or on a particular subject: *scientific literature; the literature of the violin.* **4** printed material giving a particular type of information: *sales literature.* **5** the art or profession of a writer. **6** *Obsolete.* learning. [C14: from Latin *litterātūra* writing; see LETTER]

lith. *abbrev. for:* **1** lithograph. **2** lithography.

Lith. *abbrev. for* Lithuania(n).

-lith *n combining form.* indicating stone or rock: *megalith.* Compare **-lite.** [from Greek *lithos* stone]

litharge ('lɪθɑ:dʒ) *n* another name for **lead monoxide.** [C14: via Old French from Latin *lithargyrus,* from Greek, from *lithos* stone + *arguros* silver]

lithe (laɪð) *adj* flexible or supple. [Old English (in the sense: gentle; C15: supple); related to Old High German *lindi* soft, Latin *lentus* slow] ▸ **'lithely** *adv* ▸ **'litheness** *n*

lithesome ('laɪðsəm) *adj* a less common word for **lissom.** [C18: from LITHE + -SOME[1]]

lithia ('lɪθɪə) *n* **1** another name for **lithium oxide. 2** lithium present in mineral waters as lithium salts. [C19: New Latin, ultimately from Greek *lithos* stone]

lithiasis (lɪ'θaɪəsɪs) *n Pathol.* the formation of a calculus. [C17: New Latin; see LITHO-, -IASIS]

lithia water *n* a natural or artificial mineral water that contains lithium salts.

lithic ('lɪθɪk) *adj* **1** of, relating to, or composed of stone: *a lithic sandstone.* **2** *Pathol.* of or relating to a calculus or calculi, esp. one in the urinary bladder. **3** of or containing lithium. [C18: from Greek *lithikos* stony]

-lithic *adj combining form.* (in anthropology) relating to the use of stone implements in a specified cultural period: *Neolithic.* [from Greek *lithikos,* from *lithos* stone]

lithification (ˌlɪθɪfɪ'keɪʃən) *n* the consolidation of a loosely deposited sediment into a hard sedimentary rock.

lithium ('lɪθɪəm) *n* a soft silvery element of the alkali metal series: the lightest known metal, used as an alloy hardener, as a reducing agent, and in batteries. Symbol: Li; atomic no.: 3; atomic wt.: 6.941; valency: 1; relative density: 0.534; melting pt.: 180.6°C; boiling pt.: 1342°C. [C19: New Latin, from LITHO- + -IUM]

lithium carbonate *n* a white crystalline solid used in the treatment of manic-depressive illness and mania. Formula: Li_2CO_3.

lithium oxide *n* a white crystalline compound. It absorbs carbon dioxide and water vapour.

litho ('laɪθəʊ) *n, pl* **-thos,** *adj, adv* short for **lithography, lithograph, lithographic,** or **lithographically.**

litho. *or* **lithog.** *abbrev. for:* **1** lithograph. **2** lithography.

litho- *or before a vowel* **lith-** *combining form.* stone: *lithograph.* [from Latin, from Greek, from *lithos* stone]

lithogenous (lɪ'θɒdʒɪnəs) *adj* (of animals, esp. certain corals) rock-building.

lithograph ('lɪθəˌgrɑ:f, -ˌgræf) *n* **1** a print made by lithography. ◆ *vb* **2** (*tr*) to reproduce (pictures, text, etc.) by lithography. ▸ **lithographic** (ˌlɪθə'græfɪk) *or* **ˌlitho'graphical** *adj* ▸ **ˌlitho'graphically** *adv*

lithography (lɪ'θɒgrəfɪ) *n* a method of printing from a metal or stone surface on which the printing areas are not raised but made ink-receptive while the non-image areas are made ink-repellent. [C18: from New Latin *lithographia, from* LITHO- + -GRAPHY] ▸ **li'thographer** *n*

lithoid ('lɪθɔɪd) *or* **lithoidal** (lɪ'θɔɪd[ə]l) *adj* resembling stone or rock. [C19: from Greek *lithoeidēs,* from *lithos* stone]

lithol. *abbrev. for* lithology.

lithology (lɪ'θɒlədʒɪ) *n* **1** the physical characteristics of a rock, including colour, composition, and texture. **2** the study of rocks. ▸ **lithologic** (ˌlɪθə'lɒdʒɪk) *or* **ˌlitho'logical** *adj* ▸ **ˌlitho'logically** *adv* ▸ **li'thologist** *n*

lithomarge ('lɪθəˌmɑ:dʒ) *n* a smooth compact type of kaolin: white or reddish and often mottled. [C18: from New Latin *lithomarga* from LITHO- + Latin *marga* marl]

lithometeor (ˌlɪθə'mi:tɪə) *n* a mass of solid particles, such as dust, sand, etc., suspended in the atmosphere.

lithophyte ('lɪθəˌfaɪt) *n* **1** a plant that grows on rocky or stony ground. **2** an organism, such as a coral, that is partly composed of stony material. ▸ **lithophytic** (ˌlɪθə'fɪtɪk) *adj*

lithopone ('lɪθəˌpəʊn) *n* a white pigment consisting of a mixture of zinc sulphide, zinc oxide, and barium sulphate. [C20: from LITHO- + Greek *ponos* work]

lithosol ('lɪθəˌsɒl) *n Chiefly U.S.* a type of azonal soil consisting chiefly of unweathered or partly weathered rock fragments, usually found on steep slopes. [C20: from LITHO- + Latin *solum* soil]

lithosphere ('lɪθəˌsfɪə) *n* the rigid outer layer of the earth, having an average thickness of about 75 km and comprising the earth's crust and the solid part of the mantle above the asthenosphere.

lithotomy (lɪ'θɒtəmɪ) *n, pl* **-mies.** the surgical removal of a calculus, esp. one in the urinary bladder. [C18: via Late Latin from Greek, from LITHO- + -TOMY] ▸ **lithotomic** (ˌlɪθə'tɒmɪk) *or* **ˌlitho'tomical** *adj* ▸ **li'thotomist** *n*

lithotripsy ('lɪθəʊˌtrɪpsɪ) *n* the use of ultrasound, often generated by a lithotripter, to pulverize kidney stones and gallstones *in situ.* [C20: from LITHO- + Greek *thruptein* to crush]

lithotripter ('lɪθəˌtrɪptə) *n* a machine that pulverizes kidney stones by ultrasound as an alternative to their surgical removal.

lithotrity (lɪ'θɒtrɪtɪ) *n, pl* **-ties.** *Surgery.* the crushing of a calculus in the bladder by means of an instrument (**lithotrite**) so that it can be expelled by urinating. [C19: from LITHO- + Latin *trītus,* from *terere* to crush]

Lithuania (ˌlɪθju'eɪnɪə) *n* a republic in NE Europe, on the Baltic Sea: a grand duchy in medieval times; united with Poland in 1569; occupied by Russia in 1795 and by Germany during World War I; independent Lithuania formed in 1918, but occupied by Soviet troops in 1919 and then by Poland; became a Soviet republic in 1940; unilaterally declared independence from the Soviet Union in 1990; recognized as independent in 1991. Official language: Lithuanian. Religion: Roman Catholic majority. Currency: litas. Capital: Vilnius. Pop.: 3 704 000 (1998 est.). Area: 65 200 sq. km (25 174 sq. miles). Also called: **Lithuanian Republic.** Lithuanian name: **Lietuva.**

Lithuanian (ˌlɪθju'eɪnɪən) *adj* **1** of, relating to, or characteristic of Lithuania, its people, or their language. ◆ *n* **2** the official language of Lithuania: belonging to the Baltic branch of the Indo-European family. **3** a native or inhabitant of Lithuania.

litigable ('lɪtɪgəb[ə]l) *adj Law.* that may be the subject of litigation.

litigant ('lɪtɪgənt) *n* **1** a party to a lawsuit. ◆ *adj* **2** engaged in litigation.

litigate ('lɪtɪˌgeɪt) *vb* **1** to bring or contest (a claim, action, etc.) in a lawsuit. **2** (*intr*) to engage in legal proceedings. [C17: from Latin *lītigāre,* from *līt-,* stem of *līs* lawsuit + *agere* to carry on] ▸ **'litiˌgator** *n*

litigation (ˌlɪtɪˈɡeɪʃən) *n* **1** the act or process of bringing or contesting a lawsuit. **2** a judicial proceeding or contest.

litigious (lɪˈtɪdʒəs) *adj* **1** excessively ready to go to law. **2** of or relating to litigation. **3** inclined to dispute or disagree. [C14: from Latin *lītigiōsus* quarrelsome, from *lītigium* strife] ▸ **liˈtigiously** *adv* ▸ **liˈtigiousness** *n*

litmus (ˈlɪtməs) *n* a soluble powder obtained from certain lichens. It turns red under acid conditions and blue under basic conditions and is used as an indicator. [C16: perhaps from Scandinavian; compare Old Norse *litmosi*, from *litr* dye + *mosi* moss]

litmus test *n* **1** a test to establish the acidity or alkalinity of a mixture. **2** a critical indication of future success or failure.

litotes (ˈlaɪtəʊˌtiːz) *n, pl* **-tes.** understatement for rhetorical effect, esp. when achieved by using negation with a term in place of using an antonym of that term, as in "She was not a little upset" for "She was extremely upset." [C17: from Greek, from *litos* small]

litre *or U.S.* **liter** (ˈliːtə) *n* **1** one cubic decimetre. **2** (formerly) the volume occupied by 1 kilogram of pure water at 4°C and 760 millimetres of mercury. This is equivalent to 1.000 028 cubic decimetres or about 1.76 pints. [C19: from French, from Medieval Latin *litra*, from Greek: a unit of weight]

LittB *or* **LitB** *abbrev. for* Bachelor of Letters *or* Bachelor of Literature. [Latin: *Litterarum Baccalaureus*]

LittD *or* **LitD** *abbrev. for* Doctor of Letters *or* Doctor of Literature. [Latin: *Litterarum Doctor*]

litter (ˈlɪtə) *n* **1a** small refuse or waste materials carelessly dropped, esp. in public places. **1b** (*as modifier*): *litter bin.* **2** a disordered or untidy condition or a collection of objects in this condition. **3** a group of offspring produced at one birth by a mammal such as a sow. **4** a layer of partly decomposed leaves, twigs, etc., on the ground in a wood or forest. **5** straw, hay, or similar material used as bedding, protection, etc., by animals or plants. **6** See **cat litter. 7** a means of conveying people, esp. sick or wounded people, consisting of a light bed or seat held between parallel sticks. ◆ *vb* **8** to make (a place) untidy by strewing (refuse). **9** to scatter (objects, etc.) about or (of objects) to lie around or upon (anything) in an untidy fashion. **10** (of pigs, cats, etc.) to give birth to (offspring). **11** (*tr*) to provide (an animal or plant) with straw or hay for bedding, protection, etc. [C13 (in the sense: bed): via Anglo-French, ultimately from Latin *lectus* bed]

littérateur (ˌlɪtərəˈtɜː; *French* literatœr) *n* an author, esp. a professional writer. [C19: from French from Latin *litterātor* a grammarian]

litter lout *or U.S. and Canadian* **litterbug** (ˈlɪtəˌbʌɡ) *n Slang.* a person who tends to drop refuse in public places.

little (ˈlɪtᵊl) *determiner* **1** (often preceded by *a*) **1a** a small quantity, extent, or duration of: *the little hope there is left; very little milk.* **1b** (*as pronoun*): *save a little for me.* **2** not much: *little damage was done.* **3 make little of.** See **make** of (sense 3). **4 not a little. 4a** very. **4b** a lot. **5 quite a little.** a considerable amount. **6 think little of.** to have a low opinion of. ◆ *adj* **7** of small or less than average size. **8** young: *a little boy; our little ones.* **9** endearingly familiar; dear: *my husband's little ways.* **10** contemptible, mean, or disagreeable: *your filthy little mind.* **11** (of a region or district) resembling another country or town in miniature: *little Venice.* **12 little game.** a person's secret intention or business: *so that's his little game!* **13 no little.** considerable. ◆ *adv* **14** (usually preceded by *a*) in a small amount; to a small extent or degree; not a lot: *to laugh a little.* **15** (*used preceding a verb*) not at all, or hardly: *he little realized his fate.* **16** not much or often: *we go there very little now.* **17 little by little.** by small degrees. ◆ See also **less, lesser, least, littler, littlest.** [Old English *lȳtel;* related to *lȳr* few, Old High German *luzzil*]

Little America *n* the chief U.S. base in the Antarctic, on the Ross Ice Shelf: first established by Richard Byrd (1928); used for polar exploration.

Little Bear *n* **the.** the English name for **Ursa Minor.**

Little Belt *n* a strait in Denmark, between Jutland and Funen Island, linking the Kattegat with the Baltic. Length: about 48 km (30 miles). Width: up to 29 km (18 miles). Danish name: **Lille Bælt.**

Little Bighorn *n* a river in the W central U.S., rising in N Wyoming and flowing north to the Bighorn River. Its banks were the scene of the defeat (1876) and killing of General Custer and his command by Indians.

Little Corporal *n* **the.** a nickname of Napoleon Bonaparte.

Little Diomede *n* the smaller of the two Diomede Islands in the Bering Strait: administered by the U.S. Area: about 10 sq. km (4 sq. miles).

Little Dipper *n* **the.** a U.S. and Canadian name for **Ursa Minor.**

Little Dog *n* **the.** the English name for **Canis Minor.**

little end *n Brit.* **1** Also called (in vertical engines): **top end.** the smaller end of a connecting rod in an internal-combustion engine or reciprocating pump. Compare: **big end. 2** the bearing surface between the smaller end of a connecting rod and the gudgeon pin.

Little Englander (ˈɪŋɡləndə) *n* **1** (esp. in the 19th century) a person opposed to the extension of the British Empire. **2** *Brit., informal.* a person who perceives most foreign influences on Britain's culture and institutions as damaging or insidious.

little grebe *n* a small brownish European diving bird, *Podiceps ruficollis,* frequenting lakes, family *Podicipitidae* (grebes).

little hours *pl n R.C. Church.* the canonical hours of prime, terce, sext, and nones in the divine office.

Little John *n* one of Robin Hood's companions, noted for his great size and strength.

little magazine *n* a literary magazine that features experimental or other writing of interest to a limited number of readers.

little man *n* **1** a man of no importance or significance. **2** *Brit.* a tradesman or artisan operating on a small scale.

little office *n R.C. Church.* a series of psalms and prayers similar to the divine office but shorter.

little owl *n* a small Old World owl, *Athene noctua,* having a speckled brown plumage and flattish head.

little people *or* **folk** *pl n Folklore.* small supernatural beings, such as elves, pixies, or leprechauns.

littler (ˈlɪtlə) *determiner Not standard.* the comparative of **little.**

Little Rock *n* a city in central Arkansas, on the Arkansas River: state capital. Pop.: 175 752 (1996 est.).

Little Russia *n* a region of the former SW Soviet Union, consisting chiefly of the Ukraine.

Little Russian *n, adj* a former word for **Ukrainian.**

little slam *n Bridge, etc.* the winning of all tricks except one by one side, or the contract to do so. Also called: **small slam.**

littlest (ˈlɪtlɪst) *determiner Not standard.* the superlative of **little.**

Little St Bernard Pass *n* a pass over the Savoy Alps, between Bourg-Saint-Maurice, France, and La Thuile, Italy: 11th-century hospice. Height: 2187 m (7177 ft.).

little theatre *n Theatre, chiefly U.S. and Canadian.* experimental or avant-garde drama, usually amateur, originating from a theatrical movement of the 1920s.

little woman *n* **the.** *Brit., old fashioned.* a facetious term for **wife.**

Littlewood (ˈlɪtᵊlwʊd) *n* (**Maud**) **Joan.** born 1914, British theatre director, who founded the Theatre Workshop Company (1945) with the aim of bringing theatre to the working classes: noted esp. for her production of *Oh, What a Lovely War!* (1963).

littoral (ˈlɪtərəl) *adj* **1** of or relating to the shore of a sea, lake, or ocean. **2** *Biology.* inhabiting the shore of a sea or lake or the shallow waters near the shore: *littoral fauna.* ◆ *n* **3** a coastal or shore region. [C17: from Late Latin *littorālis,* from *lītorālis,* from *lītus* shore]

Littoria (*Italian* litˈtɔːrja) *n* the former name (until 1947) of **Latina.**

lit up *adj Slang.* **1** drunk. **2** drugged, esp. on heroin.

liturgical (lɪˈtɜːdʒɪkᵊl) *or* **liturgic** *adj* **1** of or relating to public worship. **2** of or relating to the liturgy. ▸ **liˈturgically** *adv*

liturgics (lɪˈtɜːdʒɪks) *n* (*functioning as sing*) the study of liturgies. Also called: **liturgiology** (lɪˌtɜːdʒɪˈɒlədʒɪ).

liturgist (ˈlɪtədʒɪst) *n* a student or composer of liturgical forms. ▸ **ˈliturgism** *n* ▸ **ˌliturˈgistic** *adj*

liturgy (ˈlɪtədʒɪ) *n, pl* **-gies. 1** the forms of public services officially prescribed by a Church. **2** (*often cap.*) Also called: **Divine Liturgy.** *Chiefly Eastern Churches.* the Eucharistic celebration. **3** a particular order or form of public service laid down by a Church. [C16: via Medieval Latin, from Greek *leitourgia,* from *leitourgos* minister, from *leit-* people + *ergon* work]

Liu Shao Qi *or* **Liu Shao-ch'i** (ˈljuː ˈʃaʊˈtʃiː) *n* 1898–1974, Chinese Communist statesman; chairman of the People's Republic of China (1959–68); deposed during the Cultural Revolution.

livable *or* **liveable** (ˈlɪvəbᵊl) *adj* **1** (of a room, house, etc.) suitable for living in. **2** worth living; tolerable. **3** (foll. by *with*) pleasant to live (with). ▸ **ˈlivableness, ˈliveableness** *or* **ˌlivaˈbility, ˌliveaˈbility** *n*

live[1] (lɪv) *vb* (*mainly intr*). **1** to show the characteristics of life; be alive. **2** to remain alive or in existence. **3** to exist in a specified way: *to live poorly.* **4** (usually foll. by *in* or *at*) to reside or dwell: *to live in London.* **5** (often foll. by *on*) to continue or last: *the pain still lives in her memory.* **6** (usually foll. by *by*) to order one's life (according to a certain philosophy, religion, etc.). **7** (foll. by *on, upon,* or *by*) to support one's style of life; subsist: *to live by writing.* **8** (foll. by *with*) to endure the effects of (a crime, mistake, etc.). **9** (foll. by *through*) to experience and survive: *he lived through the war.* **10** (*tr*) to pass or spend (one's life, etc.). **11** to enjoy life to the full: *he knows how to live.* **12** (*tr*) to put into practice in one's daily life; express: *he lives religion every day.* **13 live and let live.** to refrain from interfering in others' lives; to be tolerant. **14 where one lives.** *U.S. informal.* in one's sensitive or defenceless position. ◆ See also **live down, live in, live out, live together, live up, live with.** [Old English *libban, lifian;* related to Old High German *libēn,* Old Norse *lifa*]

live[2] (laɪv) *adj* **1** (*prenominal*) showing the characteristics of life. **2** (*usually prenominal*) of, relating to, or abounding in life: *the live weight of an animal.* **3** (*usually prenominal*) of current interest; controversial: *a live issue.* **4** actual: *a real live cowboy.* **5** *Informal.* full of life and energy. **6** (of a coal, ember, etc.) glowing or burning. **7** (esp. of a volcano) not extinct. **8** loaded or capable of exploding: *a live bomb.* **9** *Radio, television, etc.* transmitted or present at the time of performance, rather than being a recording: *a live show.* **10** (of a record) **10a** recorded in concert. **10b** recorded in one studio take, without overdubs or splicing. **11** connected to a source of electric power: *a live circuit.* **12** (esp. of a colour or tone) brilliant or splendid. **13** acoustically reverberant: *a live studio.* **14** *Sport.* (of a ball) in play. **15** (of rocks, ores, etc.) not quarried or mined; native. **16** being in a state of motion or transmitting power; positively connected to a driving member. **17** *Printing.* **17a** (of copy) not yet having been set into type. **17b** (of type that has been set) still in use. ◆ *adv* **18** during, at, or in the form of a live performance: *the show went out live.* [C16: from *on live* ALIVE]

live axle *n* an axle which rotates with the wheel.

live-bearer *n* a fish, esp. a cyprinodont, that gives birth to living young.

live birth *n* the birth of a living child. Compare **stillbirth.**

live centre (laɪv) *n* a conically pointed rod mounted in the headstock of a lathe that locates and turns with the workpiece. Compare **dead centre** (sense 2).

-lived (-lɪvd) *adj* having or having had a life as specified: *short-lived.*

lived-in *adj* having a comfortable, natural, or homely appearance, as if subject to regular use or habitation.

livedo (lɪˈviːdəʊ) *n, pl* **livedos.** *Med.* a reddish discoloured patch on the skin. [from Latin]

live down (lɪv) *vb (tr, adv)* to withstand the effects of (a crime, mistake, etc.) by waiting until others forget or forgive it.

live in (lɪv) *vb (intr, adv)* **1** (of an employee, as in a hospital or hotel) to dwell at one's place of employment. ◆ *adj* **live-in**. **2** living in the place at which one works: *a live-in maid.* **3** living with someone else in that person's home: *a live-in lover.*

livelihood ('laɪvlɪˌhʊd) *n* occupation or employment.

live load (laɪv) *n* a variable weight on a structure, such as moving traffic on a bridge. Also called: **superload**. Compare **dead load**.

livelong ('lɪvˌlɒŋ) *adj Chiefly poetic.* **1** (of time) long or seemingly long, esp. in a tedious way (esp. in the phrase **all the livelong day**). **2** whole; entire. ◆ *n* **3** *Brit.* another name for **orpine**.

lively ('laɪvlɪ) *adj* **-lier, -liest. 1** full of life or vigour. **2** vivacious or animated, esp. when in company. **3** busy; eventful. **4** characterized by mental or emotional intensity; vivid. **5** having a striking effect on the mind or senses. **6** refreshing: *a lively breeze.* **7** springy or bouncy or encouraging springiness: *a lively ball.* **8** (of a boat or ship) readily responsive to the helm. ◆ *adv also* **'livelily. 9** in a brisk manner: *step lively.* **10 look lively.** *(interj)* make haste. ▸ **'liveliness** *n*

liven ('laɪvᵊn) *vb* (usually foll. by *up*) to make or become lively; enliven. ▸ **'livener** *n*

live oak (laɪv) *n* a hard-wooded evergreen oak, *Quercus virginianus,* of S North America: used for shipbuilding.

live out (lɪv) *vb (intr, adv)* (of an employee, as in a hospital or hotel) to dwell away from one's place of employment.

liver[1] ('lɪvə) *n* **1** a multilobed highly vascular reddish-brown glandular organ occupying most of the upper right part of the human abdominal cavity immediately below the diaphragm. It secretes bile, stores glycogen, detoxifies certain poisons, and plays an important part in the metabolism of carbohydrates, proteins, and fat, helping to maintain a correct balance of nutrients. Related adj: **hepatic. 2** the corresponding organ in animals. **3** the liver of certain animals used as food. **4** a reddish-brown colour, sometimes with a greyish tinge. [Old English *lifer;* related to Old High German *lebrav,* Old Norse *lefr,* Greek *liparos* fat] ▸ **'liverless** *adj*

liver[2] ('lɪvə) *n* a person who lives in a specified way: *a fast liver.*

liver extract *n* an extract of raw mammalian liver containing vitamin B_{12}: sometimes used to treat pernicious anaemia.

liver fluke *n* any of various parasitic flatworms, esp. *Fasciola hepatica,* that inhabit the bile ducts of sheep, cattle, etc., and have a complex life cycle: class *Digenea.* See also **trematode**.

liveried ('lɪvərɪd) *adj* (esp. of servants or footmen) wearing livery.

liverish ('lɪvərɪʃ) *adj* **1** *Informal.* having a disorder of the liver. **2** disagreeable; peevish. ▸ **'liverishness** *n*

liver of sulphur *n* a mixture of potassium sulphides used as a fungicide and insecticide and in the treatment of skin diseases.

liver opal *n* a form of opal having a reddish-brown coloration. Also called: **menilite**.

Liverpool[1] ('lɪvəˌpu:l) *n* **1** a city in NW England, in Liverpool unitary authority, Merseyside, on the Mersey estuary: second largest seaport in Great Britain; developed chiefly in the 17th century with the industrialization of S Lancashire; Liverpool University (1881) and John Moore's University. Pop.: 474 000 (1994 est.). **2** a unitary authority in NW England, in Merseyside. Pop.: 474 000 (1994 est.). Area: 113 sq. km (44 sq miles).

Liverpool[2] ('lɪvəˌpu:l) *n* **Robert Banks Jenkinson,** 2nd Earl of Liverpool. 1770–1828, British Tory statesman; prime minister (1812–27). His government was noted for its repressive policies until about 1822, when more liberal measures were introduced by such men as Peel and Canning.

Liverpudlian (ˌlɪvə'pʌdlɪən) *n* **1** a native or inhabitant of Liverpool. ◆ *adj* **2** of or relating to Liverpool. [C19: from LIVERPOOL, with humorous alteration of *pool* to *puddle*]

liver salts *pl n* a preparation of mineral salts used to treat indigestion.

liver sausage *or esp. U.S.* **liverwurst** ('lɪvəˌwɜ:st) *n* a sausage made of or containing liver.

liverwort ('lɪvəˌwɜ:t) *n* any bryophyte plant of the class *Hepaticae,* growing in wet places and resembling green seaweeds or leafy mosses. See also **scale moss**. [late Old English *liferwyrt*]

livery[1] ('lɪvərɪ) *n, pl* **-eries. 1** the identifying uniform, badge, etc., of a member of a guild or one of the servants of a feudal lord. **2** a uniform worn by some menservants and chauffeurs. **3** an individual or group that wears such a uniform. **4** distinctive dress or outward appearance. **5a** the stabling, keeping, or hiring out of horses for money. **5b** *(as modifier): a livery horse.* **6 at livery.** being kept in a livery stable. **7** *Legal history.* an ancient method of conveying freehold land. [C14: via Anglo-French from Old French *livrée* allocation, from *livrer* to hand over, from Latin *līberāre* to set free]

livery[2] ('lɪvərɪ) *adj* **1** of or resembling liver. **2** another word for **liverish**.

livery company *n Brit.* one of the chartered companies of the City of London originating from the craft guilds.

liveryman ('lɪvərɪmən) *n, pl* **-men. 1** *Brit.* a member of a livery company. **2** a worker in a livery stable.

livery stable *n* a stable where horses are accommodated and from which they may be hired out.

lives (laɪvz) *n* the plural of **life**.

live steam (laɪv) *n* steam supplied directly from a boiler at full pressure, before it has performed any work.

livestock ('laɪvˌstɒk) *n (functioning as sing or pl)* cattle, horses, poultry, and similar animals kept for domestic use but not as pets, esp. on a farm or ranch.

live together (lɪv) *vb (intr, adv)* (esp. of an unmarried couple) to dwell in the same house or flat; cohabit.

live trap (laɪv) *n* **1** a box constructed to trap an animal without injuring it. ◆ *vb* **livetrap, -traps, -trapping, -trapped. 2** *(tr)* to catch (an animal) in such a box.

live up (lɪv) *vb* **1** *(intr, adv;* foll. by *to)* to fulfil (an expectation, obligation, principle, etc.). **2 live it up.** *Informal.* to enjoy oneself, esp. flamboyantly.

liveware ('laɪvˌwɛə) *n* the programmers, systems analysts, operating staff, and other personnel working in a computer system. Compare **hardware** (sense 2), **software**.

live wire (laɪv) *n* **1** *Informal.* an energetic or enterprising person. **2** a wire carrying an electric current.

live with (lɪv) *vb (tr, prep)* to dwell with (a person to whom one is not married).

Livia Drusilla ('lɪvɪə dru:'sɪlə) *n* 58 B.C.–29 A.D., Roman noblewoman: wife (from 39 B.C.) of Emperor Augustus and mother of Emperor Tiberius.

livid ('lɪvɪd) *adj* **1** (of the skin) discoloured, as from a bruise or contusion. **2** of a greyish tinge or colour: *livid pink.* **3** *Informal.* angry or furious. [C17: via French from Latin *līvidus,* from *līvēre* to be black and blue] ▸ **'lividly** *adv* ▸ **'lividness** *or* **li'vidity** *n*

living ('lɪvɪŋ) *adj* **1a** possessing life; not dead. **1b** *(as collective n* preceded by *the): the living.* **2** having the characteristics of life (used esp. to distinguish organisms from nonliving matter). **3** currently in use or valid: *living language.* **4** seeming to be real: *a living image.* **5** (of animals or plants) existing in the present age; extant. Compare **extinct** (sense 1). **6** *Geology.* another word for **live**[2] (sense 15). **7** presented by actors before a live audience: *living theatre.* **8** *(prenominal)* (intensifier): *the living daylights.* ◆ *n* **9** the condition of being alive. **10** the manner in which one conducts one's life: *fast living.* **11** the means, esp. the financial means, whereby one lives. **12** *Church of England.* another term for **benefice. 13** *(modifier)* of, involving, or characteristic of everyday life: *living area.* **14** *(modifier)* of or involving those now alive (esp. in the phrase **living memory**).

living death *n* a life or lengthy experience of constant misery.

living fossil *n* an animal or plant, such as the coelacanth and ginkgo, belonging to a group most of whose members are extinct.

living picture *n* another term for **tableau vivant**.

living room *n* a room in a private house or flat used for relaxation and entertainment of guests.

Livingston ('lɪvɪŋstən) *n* a town in SE Scotland, the administrative centre of West Lothian: founded as a new town in 1962. Pop.: 41 647 (1991).

Livingstone ('lɪvɪŋstən) *n* **David.** 1813–73, Scottish missionary and explorer in Africa. After working as a missionary in Botswana, he led a series of expeditions and was the first European to discover Lake Ngami (1849), the Zambezi River (1851), the Victoria Falls (1855), and Lake Malawi (1859). In 1866 he set out to search for the source of the Nile and was found in dire straits and rescued (1871) by the journalist H. M. Stanley.

Livingstone daisy *n* a gardener's name for various species of *Mesembryanthemum,* especially *M. criniflorum,* grown as garden annuals (though several are perennial) for their brightly coloured showy flowers. [C20: of unknown origin]

living wage *n* a wage adequate to permit a wage earner to live and support a family in reasonable comfort.

living will *n* a document stating that if its author becomes terminally ill, his or her life should not be prolonged by artificial means, such as a life-support machine.

Livonia (lɪ'vəʊnɪə) *n* **1** a former Russian province on the Baltic, north of Lithuania: became Russian in 1721; divided between Estonia and Latvia in 1918. **2** a city in SE Michigan, west of Detroit. Pop.: 105 099 (1996 est.). ▸ **Li'vonian** *adj, n*

Livorno *(Italian* li'vorno) *n* a port in W central Italy, in Tuscany on the Ligurian Sea: shipyards; oil-refining. Pop.: 164 569 (1996 est.). English name: **Leghorn**.

livraison *(French* livrɛzɔ̃) *n Rare.* one of the numbers of a book published in parts. [literally: delivery (of goods)]

livre ('li:vrə; *French* livrə) *n* a former French unit of money of account, equal to 1 pound of silver. [C16: via Old French from Latin *lībra* the Roman pound]

Livy ('lɪvɪ) *n* Latin name *Titus Livius.* 59 B.C.–17 A.D., Roman historian; of his history of Rome in 142 books, only 35 survive.

lixiviate (lɪk'sɪvɪˌeɪt) *vb (tr) Chem.* a less common word for **leach**[1] (senses 1, 2). [C17: from LIXIVIUM] ▸ **lix'ivial** *adj* ▸ **lixˌivi'ation** *n*

lixivium (lɪk'sɪvɪəm) *n, pl* **-iums** *or* **-ia** (-ɪə). **1** the alkaline solution obtained by leaching wood ash with water; lye. **2** any solution obtained by leaching. [C17: from Late Latin, from *lix* lye]

lizard ('lɪzəd) *n* **1** any reptile of the suborder *Lacertilia* (or *Sauria),* esp. those of the family *Lacertidae* (Old World lizards), typically having an elongated body, four limbs, and a long tail: includes the geckos, iguanas, chameleons, monitors, and slow worms. Related adjs: **lacertilian, saurian. 2a** leather made from the skin of such an animal. **2b** *(as modifier): a lizard handbag.* [C14: via Old French from Latin *lacerta*]

Lizard ('lɪzəd) *n* **the.** a promontory in SW England, in SW Cornwall: the southernmost point in Great Britain. Also called: **Lizard Head, Lizard Peninsula**.

lizard fish *n* any small teleost fish of the family *Synodontidae,* having a slender body and a lizard-like head and living at the bottom of warm seas.

lizard orchid *n* a European orchid, *Orchis hircina,* rare in Britain, having a tangled spike of purplish and grey-green flowers.

LJ *Brit. abbrev. for* Lord Justice.

Ljubljana (lu:'bljɑ:nə) *n* the capital of Slovenia: capital of Illyria (1816–49); part of Yugoslavia (1918–91); university (1595). Pop.: 269 621 (1996 est.). German name: **Laibach**.

LL *abbrev. for:* **1** Late Latin. **2** Low Latin. **3** Lord Lieutenant.

ll. *abbrev. for* lines (of written matter).

llama ('lɑ:mə) *n* **1** a domesticated South American cud-chewing mammal, *Lama* *glama* (or *L. peruana*), that is used as a beast of burden and is valued for its hair, flesh, and hide: family *Camelidae* (camels). **2** the cloth made from the wool of this animal. **3** any other animal of the genus *Lama*. See **alpaca**[1], **guanaco.** [C17: via Spanish from Quechua]

Llandaff ('lændəf, -dæf) *or* **Llandaf** (*Welsh* hlan'dav) *n* a town in SE Wales, now a suburb of Cardiff; the oldest bishopric in Wales (6th century).

Llandudno (læn'dɪdnəʊ; *Welsh* hlan'dɪdnɔ) *n* a town and resort in NW Wales, in Conwy county borough on the Irish Sea. Pop.: 14 576 (1991).

Llanelli *or* **Llanelly** (θlæ'neθlɪ; *Welsh* hla'nɛhli:) *n* an industrial town in S Wales, in SE Carmarthenshire on an inlet of Carmarthen Bay. Pop.: 44 953 (1991).

Llanfairpwllgwyngyll (*Welsh* hlan,vaɪrpuhl'gwɪngɪhl), **Llanfairpwll,** *or* **Llanfair P. G.** *n* a village in NW Wales, in SE Anglesey: reputed to be the longest place name in Great Britain when unabbreviated; means: St. Mary's Church in the hollow of the white hazel near the rapid whirlpool of Llandysilio of the red cave. Full name: **Llanfairpwllgwyngyllgogerychwyrndrobwllllantysiliogogogoch** (*Welsh* hlan'vaɪrpuhl'gwɪngɪhlgɔ'gerəxwɪrn'drɔbuhl-'hlantə'sɪljɔ'gɔgɔ'gɔx).

Llangollen (*Welsh* hlan'gɒhlɛn) *n* a town in NE Wales, in Denbighshire on the River Dee: International Musical Eisteddfod held annually since 1946. Pop.: 3267 (1991).

llano ('lɑ:nəʊ; *Spanish* 'ʎano) *n, pl* **-nos** (-nəʊz; *Spanish* -nɔs). an extensive grassy treeless plain, esp. in South America. [C17: Spanish, from Latin *plānum* level ground]

Llano Estacado ('lɑ:nəʊ ,estə'kɑ:dəʊ) *n* the S part of the Great Plains of the U.S., extending over W Texas and E New Mexico: oil and natural gas resources. Chief towns: Lubbock and Amarillo. Area: 83 700 sq. km (30 000 sq. miles). Also called: **Staked Plain.**

LLB *abbrev. for* Bachelor of Laws. [Latin: *Legum Baccalaureus*]

LLD *abbrev. for* Doctor of Laws. [Latin: *Legum Doctor*]

Llewellyn (lu:'ɛlɪn) *n* Colonel **Harry.** born 1911, Welsh show-jumping rider: on Foxhunter, he was a member of the British team that won the gold medal at the 1952 Olympic Games.

Llewelyn I *n* See **Llywelyn ap Iorwerth.**

Llewelyn II *n* See **Llywelyn ap Gruffudd.**

Lleyn Peninsula (*Welsh* hli:n) *n* a peninsula in NW Wales between Cardigan Bay and Caernarvon Bay.

LLM *abbrev. for* Master of Laws. [Latin: *Legum Magister*]

Lloyd (lɔɪd) *n* **1 Clive (Hubert).** born 1944, West Indian (Guyanese) cricketer; captained the West Indies (1974–88). **2 Harold (Clayton).** 1893–1971, U.S. comic film actor. **3 Marie,** real name *Matilda Alice Victoria Wood.* 1870–1922, English music-hall entertainer.

Lloyd George *n* **David,** 1st Earl Lloyd George of Dwyfor. 1863–1945, British Liberal statesman: prime minister (1916–22). As chancellor of the exchequer (1908–15) he introduced old age pensions (1908), a radical budget (1909), and an insurance scheme (1911).

Lloyd's (lɔɪdz) *n* an association of London underwriters, set up in the late 17th century. Originally concerned exclusively with marine insurance and a shipping information service, it now subscribes a variety of insurance policies and publishes a daily list (**Lloyd's List**) of shipping data and news. [C17: named after Edward *Lloyd* (died ?1726) at whose coffee house in London the underwriters originally carried on their business]

Lloyd's Register *n* **1** a society formed in 1760 by a group of merchants operating at Lloyd's coffee house to draw up rules concerning the construction of merchant ships. **2** an annual publication giving details of all ships that have been built according to the various classifications established by this society. ◆ In full: **Lloyd's Register of Shipping.**

Lloyd Webber ('wɛbə) *n* Baron **Andrew.** born 1948, English composer. His musicals include *Joseph and the Amazing Technicolour Dreamcoat* (1968), *Jesus Christ Superstar* (1970), and *Evita* (1978), all with lyrics by Tim Rice, and *Cats* (1981), *Starlight Express* (1984), *Phantom of the Opera* (1986), *Aspects of Love* (1989), and *By Jeeves* (1996).

Llywelyn ap Gruffudd ('hləwelɪn æp 'grɪfɪθ) *n* died 1282, prince of Wales (1258–82): the only Welsh ruler to be recognized as such by the English.

Llywelyn ap Iorwerth ('hləwelɪn æp 'jɔ:rweərθ) *n* called *Llywelyn the Great.* died 1240, prince of Gwynedd, N Wales (1194–1238), who extended his rule over most of Wales.

lm *symbol for* lumen.

LMS (in Britain) *abbrev. for* local management of schools: the system of making each school responsible for controlling its total budget, after the budget has been calculated by the Local Education Authority.

LMVD (in New Zealand) *abbrev. for* Licensed Motor Vehicle Dealer.

ln *abbrev. for* (natural) logarithm.

LNG *abbrev. for* liquefied natural gas.

lo (ləʊ) *interj* look! see! (now often in the phrase **lo and behold**). [Old English *lā*]

loach (ləʊtʃ) *n* any carplike freshwater cyprinoid fish of the family *Cobitidae,* of Eurasia and Africa, having a long narrow body with barbels around the mouth. [C14: from Old French *loche,* of obscure origin]

Loach (ləʊtʃ) *n* **Ken(neth).** born 1936, British television and film director; his works for television include *Cathy Come Home* (1966) and his films include *Kes* (1970), *Riff-Raff* (1991), and *My Name is Joe* (1998).

load (ləʊd) *n* **1** something to be borne or conveyed; weight. **2a** the usual amount borne or conveyed. **2b** (*in combination*): *a carload.* **3** something that weighs down, oppresses, or burdens: *that's a load off my mind.* **4** a single charge of a firearm. **5** the weight that is carried by a structure. See also **dead load, live load. 6** *Electrical engineering, electronics.* **6a** a device that receives or dissipates the power from an amplifier, oscillator, generator, or some other source of signals. **6b** the power delivered by a machine, generator, circuit, etc. **7** the force acting on a component in a mechanism or structure. **8** the resistance overcome by an engine or motor when it is driving a machine, etc. **9** an external force applied to a component or mechanism. **10 a load of.** *Informal.* a quantity of: *a load of nonsense.* **11 get a load of.** *Informal.* pay attention to. **12 have a load on.** *U.S. and Canadian slang.* to be intoxicated. **13 shoot one's load.** *Taboo slang.* (of a man) to ejaculate at orgasm. ◆ *vb* (*mainly tr*) **14** (*also intr*) to place or receive (cargo, goods, etc.) upon (a ship, lorry, etc.). **15** to burden or oppress. **16** to supply or beset (someone) with in abundance or overwhelmingly: *they loaded her with gifts.* **17** to cause to be biased: *to load a question.* **18** (*also intr*) to put an ammunition charge into (a firearm). **19** *Photog.* to position (a film, cartridge, or plate) in (a camera). **20** to weight or bias (a roulette wheel, dice, etc.). **21** *Insurance.* to increase (a premium) to cover expenses, etc. **22** to draw power from (an electrical device, such as a generator). **23** to add material of high atomic number to (concrete) to increase its effectiveness as a radiation shield. **24** to increase the power output of (an electric circuit). **25** to increase the work required from (an engine or motor). **26** to apply force to (a mechanism or component). **27** *Computing.* to transfer (a program) to a memory. **28 load the dice. 28a** to add weights to dice in order to bias them. **28b** to arrange to have a favourable or unfavourable position. ◆ See also **loads.** [Old English *lād* course; in meaning, influenced by LADE[1]; related to LEAD[1]]

load displacement *n Nautical.* the total weight of a cargo vessel loaded so that its waterline reaches the summer load line.

loaded ('ləʊdɪd) *adj* **1** carrying a load. **2** (of dice, a roulette wheel, etc.) weighted or otherwise biased. **3** (of a question or statement) containing a hidden trap or implication. **4** charged with ammunition. **5** (of concrete) containing heavy metals, esp. iron or lead, for use in making radiation shields. **6** *Slang.* wealthy. **7** (*postpositive*) *Slang, chiefly U.S. and Canadian.* **7a** drunk. **7b** drugged; influenced by drugs.

loader ('ləʊdə) *n* **1** a person who loads a gun or other firearm. **2** (*in combination*) designating a firearm or machine loaded in a particular way: *breech-loader; top-loader.* **3** *Computing.* a system program that takes a program in a form close to machine code and places it into a memory for execution.

load factor *n* **1** the ratio of the average electric load to the peak load over a period of time. **2** *Aeronautics.* **2a** the ratio of a given external load to the weight of an aircraft. **2b** the actual payload carried by an aircraft as a percentage of its maximum payload.

loading ('ləʊdɪŋ) *n* **1** a load or burden; weight. **2** the addition of an inductance to electrical equipment, such as a transmission line or aerial, to improve its performance. See **loading coil. 3** an addition to an insurance premium to cover expenses, provide a safer profit margin, etc. **4** the ratio of the gross weight of an aircraft to its engine power (**power loading**), wing area (**wing loading**), or some other parameter, or of the gross weight of a helicopter to its rotor disc area (**disc loading**). **5** *Psychol.* the correlation of a factor, such as a personality trait, with a performance score derived from a psychological test. **6** material, such as china clay or size, added to paper, textiles, or similar materials to produce a smooth surface, increase weight, etc. **7** *Austral. and N.Z.* a payment made in addition to a basic wage or salary to reward special skills, compensate for unfavourable conditions, etc.

loading coil *n* an inductance coil inserted at regular intervals and in series with the conductors of a transmission line in order to improve its characteristics.

load line *n Nautical.* a pattern of lines painted on the hull of a ship, approximately midway between the bow and the stern, indicating the various levels that the waterline should reach if the ship is properly loaded under given circumstances.

loads (ləʊdz) *Informal.* ◆ *pl n* **1** (often foll. by *of*) a lot: *loads to eat.* ◆ *adv* **2** (intensifier): *loads better; thanks loads.*

load shedding *n* the act or practice of temporarily reducing the supply of electricity to an area to avoid overloading the generators.

loadstar ('ləʊd,stɑ:) *n* a variant spelling of **lodestar.**

loadstone ('ləʊd,stəʊn) *n* a variant spelling of **lodestone.**

loaf[1] (ləʊf) *n, pl* **loaves** (ləʊvz). **1** a shaped mass of baked bread. **2** any shaped or moulded mass of food, such as cooked meat. **3** *Slang.* the head; sense: *use your loaf!* [Old English *hlāf;* related to Old High German *hleib* bread, Old Norse *hleifr,* Latin *libum* cake]

loaf[2] (ləʊf) *vb* **1** (*intr*) to loiter or lounge around in an idle way. **2** (*tr;* foll. by *away*) to spend (time) idly: *he loafed away his life.* [C19: perhaps back formation from LOAFER]

loafer ('ləʊfə) *n* **1** a person who avoids work; idler. **2** a moccasin-like shoe for casual wear. [C19: perhaps from German *Landläufer* vagabond]

loaf sugar *n* (esp. formerly) **1** a large conical mass of hard refined sugar; sugar loaf. **2** small cube-shaped lumps of this, the form in which it was often sold.

loam (ləʊm) *n* **1** rich soil consisting of a mixture of sand, clay, and decaying organic material. **2** a paste of clay and sand used for making moulds in a foundry, plastering walls, etc. ◆ *vb* **3** (*tr*) to cover, treat, or fill with loam. [Old English *lām;* related to Old Swedish *lēmo* clay, Old High German *leimo*] ► **'loamy** *adj* ► **'loaminess** *n*

loan[1] (ləʊn) *n* **1** the act of lending: *the loan of a car.* **2a** property lent, esp. money lent at interest for a period of time. **2b** (*as modifier*): *loan holder.* **3** the adoption by speakers of one language of a form current in another language. **4** short for **loan word. 5 on loan. 5a** lent out; borrowed. **5b** (esp. of personnel) transferred from a regular post to a temporary one elsewhere. ◆ *vb* **6** to lend (something, esp. money). [C13 *loon, lan,* from Old Norse *lān;* related to Old English *lǣn* loan; compare German *Lehen* fief, *Lohn* wages] ► **'loanable** *adj* ► **'loaner** *n*

loan[2] (ləʊn) *or* **loaning** ('ləʊnɪŋ) *n Scot. and northern English dialect.* **1** a lane. **2** a place where cows are milked. [Old English *lone,* variant of LANE[1]]

loanback ('ləʊnˌbæk) *n* **1** a facility offered by some life-assurance companies in which an individual can borrow from his pension fund. ◆ *vb* **loan back. 2** to make use of this facility.

loan collection *n* a number of works of art lent by their owners for a temporary public exhibition.

Loan Council *n* (in Australia) a statutory body that controls borrowing by the states.

Loanda (ləʊ'ændə) *n* a variant spelling of **Luanda.**

loan shark *n Informal.* a person who lends funds at illegal or exorbitant rates of interest.

loan translation *n* the adoption by one language of a phrase or compound word whose components are literal translations of the components of a corresponding phrase or compound in a foreign language: *English "superman" from German "Übermensch."* Also called: **calque.**

loan word *n* a word adopted, often with some modification of its form, from one language into another.

loath *or* **loth** (ləʊθ) *adj* **1** (usually foll. by *to*) reluctant or unwilling. **2 nothing loath.** willing. [Old English *lāth* (in the sense: hostile); related to Old Norse *leithr*] ▸ **'loathness** *or* **'lothness** *n*

loathe (ləʊð) *vb* (*tr*) to feel strong hatred or disgust for. [Old English *lāthiān,* from LOATH] ▸ **'loather** *n*

loathing ('ləʊðɪŋ) *n* abhorrence; disgust. ▸ **'loathingly** *adv*

loathly[1] ('ləʊθlɪ) *adv* with reluctance; unwillingly.

loathly[2] ('ləʊðlɪ) *adj* an archaic word for **loathsome.**

loathsome ('ləʊðsəm) *adj* causing loathing; abhorrent. ▸ **'loathsomely** *adv* ▸ **'loathsomeness** *n*

loaves (ləʊvz) *n* the plural of **loaf**[1].

lob[1] (lɒb) *Sport.* ◆ *n* **1** a ball struck in a high arc. **2** *Cricket.* a ball bowled in a slow high arc. ◆ *vb* **lobs, lobbing, lobbed. 3** to hit or kick (a ball) in a high arc. **4** *Informal.* to throw, esp. in a high arc. [C14: probably of Low German origin, originally in the sense: something dangling; compare Middle Low German *lobbe* hanging lower lip, Old English *loppe* spider]

lob[2] (lɒb) *n* short for **lobworm.** [C17 (in the sense: pendulous object): related to LOB[1]]

Lobachevsky (*Russian* ləba'tʃefskij) *n* **Nikolai Ivanovich** (nika'laj i'vanəvitʃ). 1793–1856, Russian mathematician; a founder of non-Euclidean geometry.

lobar ('ləʊbə) *adj* of, relating to, or affecting a lobe.

lobate ('ləʊbeɪt) *or* **lobated** *adj* **1** having or resembling lobes. **2** (of birds) having separate toes that are each fringed with a weblike lobe. ▸ **'lobately** *adv*

lobby ('lɒbɪ) *n, pl* **-bies. 1** a room or corridor used as an entrance hall, vestibule, etc. **2** *Chiefly Brit.* a hall in a legislative building used for meetings between the legislators and members of the public. **3** Also called: **division lobby.** *Chiefly Brit.* one of two corridors in a legislative building in which members vote. **4** a group of persons who attempt to influence legislators on behalf of a particular interest. ◆ *vb* **-bies, -bying, -bied. 5** to attempt to influence (legislators, etc.) in the formulation of policy. **6** (*intr*) to act in the manner of a lobbyist. **7** (*tr*) to apply pressure or influence for the passage of (a bill, etc.). [C16: from Medieval Latin *lobia* portico, from Old High German *lauba* arbor, from *laub* leaf] ▸ **'lobbyer** *n*

lobbyist ('lɒbɪɪst) *n* a person employed by a particular interest to lobby. ▸ **'lobbyˌism** *n*

lobe (ləʊb) *n* **1** any rounded projection forming part of a larger structure. **2** any of the subdivisions of a bodily organ or part, delineated by shape or connective tissue. **3** short for **ear lobe. 4** any of the loops that form part of the graphic representation of the radiation pattern of a transmitting aerial. Compare **radiation pattern. 5** any of the parts, not entirely separate from each other, into which a flattened plant part, such as a leaf, is divided. [C16: from Late Latin *lobus,* from Greek *lobos* lobe of the ear or of the liver]

lobectomy (ləʊ'bɛktəmɪ) *n, pl* **-mies.** surgical removal of a lobe from any organ or gland in the body, esp. removal of tissue from the frontal lobe of the brain in an attempt to alleviate mental disorder.

lobelia (ləʊ'biːlɪə) *n* any plant of the genus *Lobelia,* having red, blue, white, or yellow five-lobed flowers with the three lower lobes forming a lip: family *Lobeliaceae.* [C18: from New Latin, named after Matthias de *Lobel* (1538–1616), Flemish botanist]

lobeline ('ləʊbəˌliːn) *n* a crystalline alkaloid extracted from the seeds of the Indian tobacco plant, used as a smoking deterrent and respiratory stimulant. [C19: from LOBELIA]

Lobengula (ˌləʊbən'gjuːlə) *n* ?1836–94, last Matabele king (1870–93); his kingdom was destroyed by the British.

Lobito (*Portuguese* lu'βitu) *n* the chief port in Angola, in the west on **Lobito Bay:** terminus of the railway through Benguela to Mozambique. Pop.: 70 000 (latest est.).

loblolly ('lɒbˌlɒlɪ) *n, pl* **-lies. 1** a southern U.S. pine tree, *Pinus taeda,* with bright red-brown bark, green needle-like leaves, and reddish-brown cones. **2** *Nautical or dialect.* a thick gruel. **3** *U.S. dialect.* a mire; mudhole. [C16: perhaps from dialect *lob* to boil + obsolete dialect *lolly* thick soup]

loblolly boy *or* **man** *n Brit., naval.* (formerly) a boy or man acting as a medical orderly on board ship. [C18: from LOBLOLLY sense 2, applied to a ship's doctor's medicines]

lobo ('ləʊbəʊ) *n, pl* **-bos.** *Western U.S.* another name for **timber wolf.** [Spanish, from Latin *lupus* wolf]

lobola *or* **lobolo** (lɔː'bɔːlə, lə'bəʊ-) *n* (in southern Africa) an African custom by which a bridegroom's family makes a payment in cattle or cash to the bride's family shortly before the marriage. [from Nguni *ukulobola* to give the bride price]

lobotomized *or* **lobotomised** (ləʊ'bɒtəmaɪzd) *adj Informal.* apathetic, sluggish, and zombie-like. [C20: from *lobotomize* (chiefly U.S.) to perform a lobotomy on]

lobotomy (ləʊ'bɒtəmɪ) *n, pl* **-mies. 1** surgical incision into a lobe of any organ. **2** Also called: **prefrontal leucotomy.** surgical interruption of one or more nerve tracts in the frontal lobe of the brain: used in the treatment of intractable mental disorders. [C20: from LOBE + -TOMY]

lobscouse ('lɒbˌskaʊs) *n* a sailor's stew of meat, vegetables, and hardtack. [C18: perhaps from dialect *lob* to boil + *scouse,* broth; compare LOBLOLLY]

lobster ('lɒbstə) *n, pl* **-sters** *or* **-ster. 1** any of several large marine decapod crustaceans of the genus *Homarus,* esp. *H. vulgaris,* occurring on rocky shores and having the first pair of limbs modified as large pincers. **2** any of several similar crustaceans, esp. the spiny lobster. **3** the flesh of any of these crustaceans, eaten as a delicacy. [Old English *loppestre,* from *loppe* spider]

lobster moth *n* a large sombre-hued prominent moth, *Stauropus fagi,* that when at rest resembles dead leaves. The modified thoracic legs of the larva, carried curled over its body, look like a lobster's claw.

lobster Newburg ('njuːbɜːg) *n* lobster cooked in a rich cream sauce flavoured with sherry.

lobster pot *or* **trap** *n* a round basket or trap made of open slats used to catch lobsters.

lobster thermidor ('θɜːmɪˌdɔː) *n* a dish of cooked lobster, replaced in its shell with a creamy cheese sauce.

lobule ('lɒbjuːl) *n* a small lobe or a subdivision of a lobe. [C17: from New Latin *lobulus,* from Late Latin *lobus* LOBE] ▸ **lobular** ('lɒbjʊlə), **lobulate** ('lɒbjʊlɪt), **'lobuˌlated,** *or* **'lobulose** *adj* ▸ **ˌlobu'lation** *n*

lobworm ('lɒbˌwɜːm) *n* **1** another name for **lugworm.** Sometimes shortened to **lob. 2** a large earthworm used as bait in fishing. [C17: from obsolete *lob* lump + WORM]

local ('ləʊkəl) *adj* **1** characteristic of or associated with a particular locality or area. **2** of, concerned with, or relating to a particular place or point in space. **3** *Med.* of, affecting, or confined to a limited area or part. Compare **general** (sense 10), **systemic** (sense 2). **4** (of a train, bus, etc.) stopping at all stations or stops. ◆ *n* **5** a train, bus, etc., that stops at all stations or stops. **6** an inhabitant of a specified locality. **7** *Brit. informal.* a pub close to one's home or place of work. **8** *Med.* short for **local anaesthetic. 9** *U.S. and Canadian.* an item of local interest in a newspaper. **10** *U.S. and Canadian.* a local or regional branch of an association. **11** *Canadian.* a telephone extension. [C15: via Old French from Late Latin *locālis,* from Latin *locus* place, LOCUS] ▸ **'localness** *n*

local anaesthetic *n Med.* a drug that produces local anaesthesia. Often shortened to **local.** See **anaesthesia** (sense 2).

local area network *n Computing.* the linking of a number of different devices by cable within a system. Abbrev.: **LAN.**

local authority *n Brit. and N.Z.* the governing body of a county, district, etc. U.S. equivalent: **local government.**

local colour *n* the characteristic features or atmosphere of a place or time.

locale (ləʊ'kɑːl) *n* a place or area, esp. with reference to events connected with it. [C18: from French *local* (n use of adj); see LOCAL]

local examinations *pl n* any of various examinations, such as the GCE, set by university boards and conducted in local centres, schools, etc.

local government *n* **1** government of the affairs of counties, towns, etc., by locally elected political bodies. **2** the U.S. equivalent of **local authority.**

Local Group *n Astronomy.* the cluster of galaxies to which the Galaxy and the Andromeda Galaxy belong.

localism ('ləʊkəˌlɪzəm) *n* **1** a pronunciation, phrase, etc., peculiar to a particular locality. **2** another word for **provincialism.** ▸ **'localist** *n* ▸ **ˌlocal'istic** *adj*

locality (ləʊ'kælɪtɪ) *n, pl* **-ties. 1** a neighbourhood or area. **2** the site or scene of an event. **3** the fact or condition of having a location or position in space.

localize *or* **localise** ('ləʊkəˌlaɪz) *vb* **1** to make or become local in attitude, behaviour, etc. **2** (*tr*) to restrict or confine (something) to a particular area or part. **3** (*tr*) to assign or ascribe to a particular region. ▸ **'localˌizable** *or* **'localˌisable** *adj* ▸ **ˌlocali'zation** *or* **ˌlocali'sation** *n* ▸ **'localˌizer** *or* **'localˌiser** *n*

local loan *n* (in Britain) a loan issued by a local government authority.

locally ('ləʊkəlɪ) *adv* within a particular area or place.

local option *n* (esp. in Scotland, New Zealand, and the U.S.) the privilege of a municipality, county, etc., to determine by referendum whether a particular activity, esp. the sale of liquor, shall be permitted there.

local oscillator *n Electronics.* the oscillator in a superheterodyne receiver whose output frequency is mixed with the incoming modulated radio-frequency carrier signal to produce the required intermediate frequency.

local sign *n Physiol.* the information from a receptor in the eye or the skin signifying respectively a direction in space or a given point on the body.

local time *n* the time in a particular region or area expressed with reference to the meridian passing through it.

Locarno (*Italian* lo'karno) *n* a town in S Switzerland, in Ticino canton at the N end of Lake Maggiore: tourist resort. Pop.: 14 150 (1990 est.).

Locarno Pact (ləʊ'kɑːnəʊ) *n* a series of treaties, concluded in Locarno, Switzerland in 1925, between Germany, France, Belgium, the United Kingdom, Italy, Poland, and Czechoslovakia. The principal treaty, between Germany, France, and Belgium, concerned the maintenance of their existing frontiers, settlement of disputes by arbitration without resort to force, and the demilitarization of the Rhineland. This treaty was guaranteed by the United Kingdom and Italy but was violated when Germany occupied the Rhineland in 1936. Also called: **Treaties of Locarno.**

locate (ləʊ'keɪt) *vb* **1** (*tr*) to discover the position, situation, or whereabouts of; find. **2** (*tr; often passive*) to situate or place: *located on the edge of the city.* **3** (*intr*) to become established or settled. ▸ **lo'catable** *adj* ▸ **lo'cater** *n*

location (ləʊ'keɪʃən) *n* **1** a site or position; situation. **2** the act or process of locating or the state of being located. **3** a place outside a studio where filming is done: *shot on location.* 4 (in South Africa) **4a** a Black African or Coloured township, usually located near a small town. See also **township** (sense 4). **4b** (formerly) an African tribal reserve. **5** *Computing.* a position in a memory capable of holding a unit of information, such as a word, and identified by its address. **6** *Roman and Scots Law.* the letting out on hire of a chattel or of personal services. [C16: from Latin *locatio,* from *locare* to place]

locative ('lɒkətɪv) *Grammar.* ♦ *adj* **1** (of a word or phrase) indicating place or direction. **2** denoting a case of nouns, etc., that refers to the place at which the action described by the verb occurs. ♦ *n* **3a** the locative case. **3b** a word or speech element in this case. [C19: LOCATE + -IVE, on the model of *vocative*]

loc. cit. (in textual annotation) *abbrev. for* loco citato. [Latin: in the place cited]

loch (lɒx, lɒk) *n* **1** a Scot. word for **lake**[1]. **2** Also called: **sea loch.** a long narrow bay or arm of the sea in Scotland. [C14: from Gaelic]

lochan ('lɒxən, 'lɒkᵊn) *n Scot.* a small inland loch. [C18: Gaelic, diminutive of LOCH]

lochia ('lɒkɪə) *n* a vaginal discharge of cellular debris, mucus, and blood following childbirth. [C17: New Latin from Greek *lokhia,* from *lokhios,* from *lokhos* childbirth] ▸ **'lochial** *adj*

loci ('ləʊsaɪ) *n* the plural of **locus.**

lock[1] (lɒk) *n* **1** a device fitted to a gate, door, drawer, lid, etc., to keep it firmly closed and often to prevent access by unauthorized persons. **2** a similar device attached to a machine, vehicle, etc., to prevent use by unauthorized persons: *a steering lock.* **3a** a section of a canal or river that may be closed off by gates to control the water level and the raising and lowering of vessels that pass through it. **3b** (*as modifier*): *a lock gate.* **4** the jamming, fastening, or locking together of parts. **5** *Brit.* the extent to which a vehicle's front wheels will turn to the right or left: *this car has a good lock.* **6** a mechanism that detonates the charge of a gun. **7 lock, stock, and barrel.** completely; entirely. **8** any wrestling hold in which a wrestler seizes a part of his opponent's body and twists it or otherwise exerts pressure upon it. **9** Also called: **lock forward.** *Rugby.* either of two players who make up the second line of the scrum and apply weight to the forwards in the front line. **10** a gas bubble in a hydraulic system or a liquid bubble in a pneumatic system that stops or interferes with the fluid flow in a pipe, capillary, etc.: *an air lock.* ♦ *vb* **11** to fasten (a door, gate, etc.) or (of a door, etc.) to become fastened with a lock, bolt, etc., so as to prevent entry or exit. **12** (*tr*) to secure (a building) by locking all doors, windows, etc. **13** to fix or become fixed together securely or inextricably. **14** to become or cause to become rigid or immovable: *the front wheels of the car locked.* **15** (when *tr, often passive*) to clasp or entangle (someone or each other) in a struggle or embrace. **16** (*tr*) to furnish (a canal) with locks. **17** (*tr*) to move (a vessel) through a system of locks. **18 lock horns.** (esp. of two equally matched opponents) to become engaged in argument or battle. **19 lock the stable door after the horse has bolted** *or* **been stolen.** to take precautions after harm has been done. ♦ See also **lock on to, lock out, lock up.** [Old English *loc;* related to Old Norse *lok*] ▸ **'lockable** *adj*

lock[2] (lɒk) *n* **1** a strand, curl, or cluster of hair. **2** a tuft or wisp of wool, cotton, etc. **3** (*pl*) *Chiefly literary.* hair, esp. when curly or fine. [Old English *loc;* related to Old Frisian *lok,* Old Norse *lokkr* lock of wool]

lockage ('lɒkɪdʒ) *n* **1** a system of locks in a canal. **2** passage through a lock or the fee charged for such passage.

Locke (lɒk) *n* **1 John.** 1632–1704, English philosopher, who discussed the concept of empiricism in his *Essay Concerning Human Understanding* (1690). He influenced political thought, esp. in France and America, with his *Two Treatises on Government* (1690), in which he sanctioned the right to revolt. **2 Matthew.** ?1630–77, English composer, esp. of works for the stage.

locked-in syndrome *n* a condition in which a person is conscious but unable to move any part of the body except the eyes: results from damage to the brainstem.

locker ('lɒkə) *n* **1a** a small compartment or drawer that may be locked, as one of several in a gymnasium, etc., for clothes and valuables. **1b** (*as modifier*): *a locker room.* **2** a person or thing that locks. **3** *U.S. and Canadian.* a refrigerated compartment for keeping frozen foods, esp. one rented in an establishment.

Lockerbie ('lɒkəbɪ) *n* a town in SW Scotland, in Dumfries and Galloway: scene (1988) of the UK's worst air disaster when a jumbo jet was brought down by a terrorist bomb, killing 270 people, including eleven residents of the town.

locket ('lɒkɪt) *n* a small ornamental case, usually on a necklace or chain, that holds a picture, keepsake, etc. [C17: from French *loquet* latch, diminutive of *loc* LOCK[1]]

lockfast ('lɒk,fɑːst) *adj Scot.* securely fastened with a lock.

lockjaw ('lɒk,dʒɔː) *n Pathol.* a nontechnical name for **trismus** and (often) **tetanus.**

locknut ('lɒk,nʌt) *n* **1** a supplementary nut screwed down upon a primary nut to prevent it from shaking loose. **2** a threaded nut having a feature, such as a nylon insert, to prevent it from shaking loose.

lock on to *vb* (*intr, adv + prep*) (of a radar beam) to automatically follow (a target).

lock out *vb* (*tr, adv*) **1** to prevent from entering by locking a door. **2** to prevent (employees) from working during an industrial dispute, as by closing a factory. ♦ *n* **lockout. 3** the closing of a place of employment by an employer, in order to bring pressure on employees to agree to terms.

locksmith ('lɒk,smɪθ) *n* a person who makes or repairs locks. ▸ **'lock,smithery** *or* **'lock,smithing** *n*

lock step *n* a method of marching in step such that the men follow one another as closely as possible.

lock stitch *n* a sewing-machine stitch in which the top thread interlocks with the bobbin thread.

lock up *vb* (*adv*) **1** (*tr*) Also: **lock in, lock away.** to imprison or confine. **2** to lock or secure the doors, windows, etc., of (a building). **3** (*tr*) to keep or store securely: *secrets locked up in history.* **4** (*tr*) to invest (funds) so that conversion into cash is difficult. **5** *Printing.* to secure (type, etc.) in a chase or in the bed of the printing machine by tightening the quoins. ♦ *n* **lockup. 6** the action or time of locking up. **7** a jail or block of cells. **8** *Brit.* a small shop with no attached quarters for the owner or shopkeeper. **9** *Brit.* a garage or storage place separate from the main premises. **10** *Stock Exchange.* an investment that is intended to be held for a relatively long period. **11** *Printing.* the pages of type held in a chase by the positioning of quoins. ♦ *adj* **12 lock-up.** *Brit. and N.Z.* (of premises) without living accommodation: *a lock-up shop.*

Lockyer ('lɒkjə) *n* Sir **Joseph Norman.** 1836–1920, English astronomer: a pioneer in solar spectroscopy, he was the first to observe helium in the sun's atmosphere (1868).

loco[1] ('ləʊkəʊ) *n Informal.* short for **locomotive.**

loco[2] ('ləʊkəʊ) *adj* **1** *Slang, chiefly U.S.* insane. **2** (of an animal) affected with loco disease. ♦ *n, pl* **-cos. 3** *U.S.* short for **locoweed.** ♦ *vb* (*tr*) **4** to poison with locoweed. **5** *U.S. slang.* to make insane. [C19: via Mexican Spanish from Spanish: crazy]

loco[3] ('ləʊkəʊ) *adj* denoting a price for goods, esp. goods to be exported, that are in a place specified or known, the buyer being responsible for all transport charges from that place: *loco Bristol; a loco price.* [C20: from Latin *locō* from a place]

loco citato *Latin.* ('lɒkəʊ sɪ'tɑːtəʊ) in the place or passage quoted. Abbrevs.: **loc. cit., lc.**

loco disease *or* **poisoning** *n* a disease of cattle, sheep, and horses characterized by paralysis and faulty vision, caused by ingestion of locoweed.

locoism ('ləʊkəʊ,ɪzəm) *n* another word for **loco disease.**

locoman ('ləʊkəʊmən) *n, pl* **-men.** *Brit. informal.* a railwayman, esp. an engine-driver.

locomotion (,ləʊkə'məʊʃən) *n* the act, fact, ability, or power of moving. [C17: from Latin *locō* from a place, ablative of *locus* place + MOTION]

locomotive (,ləʊkə'məʊtɪv) *n* **1a** Also called: **locomotive engine.** a self-propelled engine driven by steam, electricity, or diesel power and used for drawing trains along railway tracks. **1b** (*as modifier*): *a locomotive shed; a locomotive works.* ♦ *adj* **2** of or relating to locomotion. **3** moving or able to move, as by self-propulsion. ▸ **,loco'motively** *adv* ▸ **,loco'motiveness** *n*

locomotor (,ləʊkə'məʊtə) *adj* of or relating to locomotion. [C19: from Latin *locō* from a place, ablative of *locus* place + MOTOR (mover)]

locomotor ataxia *n Pathol.* another name for **tabes dorsalis.**

locoweed ('ləʊkəʊ,wiːd) *n* any of several perennial leguminous plants of the genera *Oxytropis* and *Astragalus* of W North America that cause loco disease in horses, cattle, and sheep.

Locris *or* **Lokris** ('ləʊkrɪs, 'lɒk-) *n* an ancient region of central Greece. ▸ **'Locrian** *or* **'Lokrian** *adj, n*

locular ('lɒkjʊlə) *or* **loculate** ('lɒkjʊ,leɪt, -lɪt) *adj Biology.* divided into compartments by septa: *the locular ovary of a plant.* [C19: from New Latin *loculāris* kept in boxes] ▸ **,locu'lation** *n*

locule ('lɒkjuːl) *or* **loculus** ('lɒkjʊləs) *n, pl* **locules** *or* **loculi** ('lɒkjʊ,laɪ). **1** *Botany.* any of the chambers of an ovary or anther. **2** *Biology.* any small cavity or chamber. [C19: New Latin, from Latin: compartment, from *locus* place]

locum tenens ('ləʊkəm 'tiːnɛnz) *n, pl* **locum tenentes** (tə'nɛntiːz). *Chiefly Brit.* a person who stands in temporarily for another member of the same profession, esp. for a physician, chemist, or clergyman. Often shortened to **locum.** [C17: Medieval Latin: (someone) holding the place (of another)]

locus ('ləʊkəs) *n, pl* **loci** ('ləʊsaɪ). **1** (in many legal phrases) a place or area, esp. the place where something occurred. **2** *Maths.* a set of points or lines whose location satisfies or is determined by one or more specified conditions: *the locus of points equidistant from a given point is a circle.* **3** *Genetics.* the position of a particular gene on a chromosome. [C18: Latin]

locus classicus ('klæsɪkəs) *n, pl* **loci classici** ('klæsɪ,saɪ). an authoritative and often quoted passage from a standard work. [Latin: classical place]

locus sigilli (sɪ'dʒɪlaɪ) *n, pl* **loci sigilli.** the place to which the seal is affixed on legal documents, etc. [Latin]

locus standi ('stændaɪ) *n Law.* the right of a party to appear and be heard before a court. [from Latin: a place for standing]

locust ('ləʊkəst) *n* **1** any of numerous orthopterous insects of the genera *Locusta, Melanoplus,* etc., such as *L. migratoria,* of warm and tropical regions of the Old World, which travels in vast swarms, stripping large areas of vegetation. See also **grasshopper** (sense 1). Compare **seventeen-year locust. 2** Also called: **locust tree, false acacia.** a North American leguminous tree, *Robinia pseudoacacia,* having prickly branches, hanging clusters of white fragrant flowers, and reddish-brown seed pods. **3** the yellowish durable wood of this tree. **4** any of several similar trees, such as the honey locust and carob. [C13 (the insect): from Latin *locusta* locust; applied to the tree (C17) because the pods resemble locusts] ▸ **'locust-,like** *adj*

locust bird *n* any of various pratincoles, esp. *Glareola nordmanni* (**black-winged pratincole**), that feed on locusts.

locution (ləʊ'kjuːʃən) *n* **1** a word, phrase, or expression. **2** manner or style of speech or expression. [C15: from Latin *locūtiō* an utterance, from *loquī* to speak] ▸ **lo'cutionary** *adj*

locutionary act *n Philosophy.* the act of uttering a sentence considered only as such. Compare **illocution, perlocution.**

Lod (lɒd) *n* a town in central Israel, southeast of Tel Aviv: Israel's chief airport. Pop.: 42 000 (1989 est.). Also called: **Lydda.**

lode (ləʊd) *n* **1** a deposit of valuable ore occurring between definite limits in the surrounding rock; vein. **2** a deposit of metallic ore filling a fissure in the surrounding rock. [Old English *lād* course. Compare LOAD]

loden ('ləʊdᵊn) *n* **1** a thick heavy waterproof woollen cloth with a short pile, used to make garments, esp. coats. **2** a dark bluish-green colour, in which the cloth is often made. [German, from Old High German *lodo* thick cloth, perhaps related to Old English *lotha* cloak]

lodestar *or* **loadstar** ('ləʊd,stɑː) *n* **1** a star, esp. the North Star, used in navigation or astronomy as a point of reference. **2** something that serves as a guide or model. [C14: literally, guiding star. See LODE]

lodestone *or* **loadstone** ('ləʊd,stəʊn) *n* **1a** a rock that consists of pure or nearly pure magnetite and thus is naturally magnetic. **1b** a piece of such rock, which can be used as a magnet and which was formerly used as a primitive compass. **2** a person or thing regarded as a focus of attraction. [C16: literally: guiding stone]

lodge (lɒdʒ) *n* **1** *Chiefly Brit.* a small house at the entrance to the grounds of a country mansion, usually occupied by a gatekeeper or gardener. **2** a house or cabin used occasionally, as for some seasonal activity. **3** *U.S. and Canadian.* a central building in a resort, camp, or park. **4** (*cap. when part of a name*) a large house or hotel. **5** a room for the use of porters in a university, college, etc. **6** a local branch or chapter of certain societies. **7** the building used as the meeting place of such a society. **8** the dwelling place of certain animals, esp. the dome-shaped den constructed by beavers. **9** a hut or tent of certain North American Indian peoples. **10** (at Cambridge University) the residence of the head of a college. ◆ *vb* **11** to provide or be provided with accommodation or shelter, esp. rented accommodation. **12** to live temporarily, esp. in rented accommodation. **13** to implant, embed, or fix or be implanted, embedded, or fixed. **14** (*tr*) to deposit or leave for safety, storage, etc. **15** (*tr*) to bring (a charge or accusation) against someone. **16** (*tr;* often foll. by *in* or *with*) to place (authority, power, etc.) in the control (of someone). **17** (*intr;* often foll. by *in*) *Archaic.* to exist or be present (in). **18** (*tr*) (of wind, rain, etc.) to beat down (crops). [C15: from Old French *loge,* perhaps from Old High German *louba* porch] ▸ **'lodgeable** *adj*

Lodge[1] (lɒdʒ) *n* **1 David (John).** born 1935, British novelist and critic. His books include *Changing Places* (1975), *Small World* (1984), *Nice Work* (1988), and *Therapy* (1995). **2** Sir **Oliver (Joseph).** 1851–1940, British physicist, who made important contributions to electromagnetism, radio reception, and attempted to detect the ether. He also studied allegedly psychic phenomena. **3 Thomas.** ?1558–1625, English writer. His romance *Rosalynde* (1590) supplied the plot for Shakespeare's *As You Like It.*

Lodge[2] (lɒdʒ) *n* **the.** the official Canberra residence of the Australian Prime Minister.

lodger ('lɒdʒə) *n* a person who pays rent in return for accommodation in someone else's house.

lodging ('lɒdʒɪŋ) *n* **1** a temporary residence. **2** (*sometimes pl*) sleeping accommodation. **3** (*sometimes pl*) (at Oxford University) the residence of the head of a college. ◆ See also **lodgings.**

lodging house *n* a private home providing accommodation and meals for lodgers.

lodgings ('lɒdʒɪŋz) *pl n* a rented room or rooms in which to live, esp. in another person's house.

lodging turn *n* a period of work or duty, esp. among railway workers, which involves sleeping away from home.

lodgment *or* **lodgement** ('lɒdʒmənt) *n* **1** the act of lodging or the state of being lodged. **2** a blockage or accumulation. **3** a small area gained and held in enemy territory.

Lodi (*Italian* 'lɔːdi) *n* a town in N Italy, in Lombardy: scene of Napoleon's defeat of the Austrians in 1796. Pop.: 42 277 (1993 est.).

lodicule ('lɒdɪ,kjuːl) *n* any of two or three minute scales at the base of the ovary in grass flowers that represent the corolla. [C19: from Latin *lōdīcula,* diminutive of *lōdix* blanket]

Łódź (*Polish* wudʒ) *n* a city in central Poland: the country's second largest city; major centre of the textile industry; university (1945). Pop.: 825 600 (1996 est.).

Loeb (lɜːb; *German* løːp) *n* **Jacques** (ʒɑːk). 1859–1924, U.S. physiologist, born in Germany, noted esp. for his pioneering work on artificial parthenogenesis.

loerie ('laʊrɪ) *n* a variant of **lourie.**

loess ('ləʊɪs; *German* lœs) *n* a light-coloured fine-grained accumulation of clay and silt particles that have been deposited by the wind. [C19: from German *Löss,* from Swiss German dialect *lösch* loose] ▸ **loessial** (ləʊ'ɛsɪəl) *or* **lo'essal** *adj*

Loewe (ləʊ) *n* **Frederick.** 1904–88, U.S. composer of such musical comedies as *Brigadoon* (1947), *My Fair Lady* (1956), and *Camelot* (1960), all with librettos by Alan Jay Lerner.

Loewe *or* **Löwe** (*German* 'løːvə) *n* **(Johann) Karl (Gottfried).** 1796–1869, German composer, esp. of songs, such as *Der Erlkönig* (1818).

Loewi ('ləʊɪ) *n* **Otto.** 1873–1961, U.S. pharmacologist, born in Germany. He shared a Nobel prize for physiology or medicine (1936) with Dale for their work on the chemical transmission of nerve impulses.

lo-fi ('ləʊ'faɪ) *adj Informal.* (of sound reproduction) of or giving an impression of poor quality. [C20: modelled on HI-FI]

Lofoten and Vesterålen (*Norwegian* 'luːfuːtən; 'vɛstəroːlən) *pl n* a group of islands off the NW coast of Norway, within the Arctic Circle. Largest island: Hinny. Pop.: 66 600 (1985 est.). Area: about 5130 sq. km (1980 sq. miles).

loft (lɒft) *n* **1** the space inside a roof. **2** a gallery, esp. one for the choir in a church. **3** a room over a stable used to store hay. **4** *U.S.* an upper storey of a warehouse or factory. **5** a raised house or coop in which pigeons are kept. **6** *Sport.* **6a** (in golf) the angle from the vertical made by the club face to give elevation to a ball. **6b** elevation imparted to a ball. **6c** a lofting stroke or shot. ◆ *vb* (*tr*) **7** *Sport.* to strike or kick (a ball) high in the air. **8** to store or place in a loft. **9** to lay out a full-scale working drawing of (the lines of a vessel's hull). [Late Old English, from Old Norse *lopt* air, ceiling; compare Old Danish and Old High German *loft* (German *Luft* air)]

loftsman ('lɒftsmən) *n, pl* **-men.** a person who reproduces in actual size a draughtsman's design for a ship or an aircraft, working on the floor of a building (**mould loft**) with a large floor area.

lofty ('lɒftɪ) *adj* **loftier, loftiest. 1** of majestic or imposing height. **2** exalted or noble in character or nature. **3** haughty or supercilious. **4** elevated, eminent, or superior. ▸ **'loftily** *adv* ▸ **'loftiness** *n*

log[1] (lɒg) *n* **1a** a section of the trunk or a main branch of a tree, when stripped of branches. **1b** (*modifier*) constructed out of logs: *a log cabin.* **2a** a detailed record of a voyage of a ship or aircraft. **2b** a record of the hours flown by pilots and aircrews. **2c** a book in which these records are made; logbook. **3** a written record of information about transmissions kept by radio stations, amateur radio operators, etc. **4a** a device consisting of a float with an attached line, formerly used to measure the speed of a ship. See also **chip log. 4b heave the log.** to determine a ship's speed with such a device. **5** *Austral.* a claim for better pay and conditions presented by a trade union to an employer. **6 like a log.** without stirring or being disturbed (in the phrase **sleep like a log**). ◆ *vb* **logs, logging, logged. 7** (*tr*) to fell the trees of (a forest, area, etc.) for timber. **8** (*tr*) to saw logs from (trees). **9** (*intr*) to work at the felling of timber. **10** (*tr*) to enter (a distance, event, etc.) in a logbook or log. **11** (*tr*) to record the punishment received by (a sailor) in a logbook. **12** (*tr*) to travel (a specified distance or time) or move at (a specified speed). [C14: origin obscure]

log[2] (lɒg) *n* short for **logarithm.**

-log *combining form.* a U.S. variant of **-logue.**

logagraphia (,lɒgə'græfɪə) *n Med.* inability to express ideas in writing.

logan[1] ('ləʊgən) *or* **logan-stone** *n* other names for **rocking stone.** [C18: from *logging-stone,* from dialect *log* to rock]

logan[2] ('ləʊgən) *n Canadian.* another name for **bogan** (a backwater).

Logan ('ləʊgən) *n* **Mount.** a mountain in NW Canada, in SW Yukon in the St. Elias Range: the highest peak in Canada and the second highest in North America. Height: 6050 m (19 850 ft.).

loganberry ('ləʊgənbərɪ, -brɪ) *n, pl* **-ries. 1** a trailing prickly hybrid rosaceous plant, *Rubus loganobaccus,* cultivated for its edible fruit. **2a** the purplish-red acid fruit of this plant. **2b** (*as modifier*): *loganberry pie.* [C19: named after James H. *Logan* (1841–1928), American judge and horticulturist who first grew it (1881)]

loganiaceous (ləʊ,geɪnɪ'eɪʃəs) *adj* of, relating to, or belonging to the *Loganiaceae,* a tropical and subtropical family of plants that includes nux vomica, pinkroot, and gelsemium. [C19: from New Latin *Logania,* named after James *Logan* (1674–1751) Irish-American botanist]

logaoedic (,lɒgə'iːdɪk) (in classical prosody) ◆ *adj* **1** of or relating to verse in which mixed metres are combined within a single line to give the effect of prose. ◆ *n* **2** a line or verse of this kind. [C19: via Late Latin from Greek *logaoidikos,* from *logos* speech + *aoidē* poetry]

logarithm ('lɒgə,rɪðəm) *n* the exponent indicating the power to which a fixed number, the base, must be raised to obtain a given number or variable. It is used esp. to simplify multiplication and division: if $a^x = M$, then the logarithm of M to the base a (written $\log_a M$) is x. Often shortened to **log.** See also **common logarithm, natural logarithm.** [C17: from New Latin *logarithmus,* coined 1614 by John NAPIER, from Greek, *logos* ratio, reckoning + *arithmos* number]

logarithmic (,lɒgə'rɪðmɪk) *or* **logarithmical** *adj* **1** of, relating to, using, or containing logarithms of a number or variable. **2** consisting of, relating to, or using points or lines whose distances from a fixed point or line are proportional to the logarithms of numbers. ◆ Abbrev.: **log.** ▸ **,loga'rithmically** *adv*

logarithmic function *n* **a** the mathematical function $y = \log x$. **b** a function that can be expressed in terms of this function.

logbook ('lɒg,bʊk) *n* **1** a book containing the official record of trips made by a ship or aircraft; log. **2** *Brit.* (formerly) a document listing the registration, manufacture, ownership and previous owners, etc., of a motor vehicle. Compare **registration document.**

log chip *n Nautical.* the chip of a chip log.

loge (ləʊʒ) *n* **1** a small enclosure or box in a theatre or opera house. **2** the upper section in a theatre or cinema. [C18: French; see LODGE]

logger ('lɒgə) *n* **1** another word for **lumberjack. 2** a tractor or crane for handling logs.

loggerhead ('lɒgə,hɛd) *n* **1** Also called: **loggerhead turtle.** a large-headed turtle, *Caretta caretta,* occurring in most seas: family *Chelonidae.* **2 loggerhead shrike.** a North American shrike, *Lanius ludovicianus,* having a grey head and body, black-and-white wings and tail, and black facial stripe. **3** a tool consisting of a large metal sphere attached to a long handle, used for warming liquids, melting tar, etc. **4** a strong round upright post in a whaleboat for belaying the line of a harpoon. **5** *Archaic or dialect.* a blockhead; dunce. **6 at loggerheads.** engaged in dispute or confrontation. [C16: probably from dialect *logger* wooden block + HEAD] ▸ **'logger,headed** *adj*

loggia ('lɒdʒə, 'lɒdʒɪə) *n, pl* **-gias** *or* **-gie** (-dʒɛ). **1** a covered area on the side of a building, esp. one that serves as a porch. **2** an open balcony in a theatre. [C17: Italian, from French *loge.* See LODGE]

logging ('lɒgɪŋ) *n* the work of felling, trimming, and transporting timber.

logia ('lɒgɪə) *n* **1** a supposed collection of the sayings of Christ held to have been drawn upon by the writers of the gospels. **2** the plural of **logion.**

logic ('lɒdʒɪk) *n* **1** the branch of philosophy concerned with analysing the patterns of reasoning by which a conclusion is properly drawn from a set of premises, without reference to meaning or context. See also **formal logic, deduction** (sense 4), **induction** (sense 4). **2** any particular formal system in which are defined axioms and rules of inference. Compare **formal system, formal language. 3** the system and principles of reasoning used in a specific field of study. **4** a particular method of argument or reasoning. **5** force or effectiveness in argument or dispute. **6** reasoned thought or argument, as distinguished from irrationality. **7** the relationship and interdependence of a series of events, facts, etc. **8 chop logic.** to use excessively subtle or involved logic or argument. **9** *Electronics, computing.* **9a** the principles underlying the units in a computer system that perform arithmetical and logical operations. See also **logic circuit. 9b** (*as modifier*): *a logic element.* [C14: from Old French *logique* from Medieval Latin *logica* (neuter plural, treated in Medieval Latin as feminine singular), from Greek *logikos* concerning speech or reasoning]

logical (ˈlɒdʒɪkᵊl) *adj* **1** relating to, used in, or characteristic of logic. **2** using, according to, or deduced from the principles of logic: *a logical conclusion.* **3** capable of or characterized by clear or valid reasoning. **4** reasonable or necessary because of facts, events, etc.: *the logical candidate.* **5** *Computing.* of, performed by, used in, or relating to the logic circuits in a computer. ► **ˌlogiˈcality** *or* **ˈlogicalness** *n* ► **ˈlogically** *adv*

logical atomism *n* the philosophical theory of Russell and the early Wittgenstein which held that all meaningful expressions must be analysable into atomic elements which refer directly to atomic elements of the real world.

logical consequence *n* the relation that obtains between the conclusion and the premises of a formally valid argument.

logical constant *n* one of the connectives of a given system of formal logic, esp. those of the sentential calculus, *not, and, or,* and *if ... then ....*

logical form *n* the syntactic structure that may be shared by different expressions as abstracted from their content and articulated by the logical constants of a particular logical system, esp. the structure of an argument by virtue of which it can be shown to be formally valid. Thus *John is tall and thin, so John is tall* has the same logical form as *London is large and dirty, so London is large,* namely *P & Q, so P.*

logically possible *adj* capable of being described without self-contradiction.

logical operation *n Computing.* an operation involving the use of logical functions, such as *and* or *or,* that are applied to the input signals of a particular logic circuit.

logical positivism *n* a philosophical theory that holds to be meaningful only those propositions that can be analysed by the tools of logic into elementary propositions that are either tautological or are empirically verifiable. It therefore rejects metaphysics, theology, and sometimes ethics as meaningless.

logical sum *n* another name for **disjunction** (sense 3).

logical truth *n* **1** another term for **tautology** (sense 2). **2** the property of being logically tautologous.

logic array *n Computing.* an integrated circuit consisting of interconnected logic gates.

logic bomb *n Computing.* an unauthorized program that is inserted into a computer system; when activated it interferes with the operation of the computer.

logic circuit *n* an electronic circuit used in computers to perform a logical operation on its two or more input signals. There are six basic circuits, the AND, NOT, NAND, OR, NOR, and exclusive OR circuits, which can be combined into more complex circuits.

logician (lɒˈdʒɪʃən) *n* a person who specializes in or is skilled at logic.

logicism (ˈlɒdʒɪˌsɪzəm) *n* the philosophical theory that all of mathematics can be deduced from logic. Compare **intuitionism, formalism.**

logic level *n* the voltage level representing one or zero in an electronic logic circuit.

logic programming *n* the study or implementation of computer programs capable of discovering or checking proofs of formal expressions or segments.

log in (ˈlɒgɪn) *Computing.* ◆ *vb* **1** Also: **log on.** to enter (an identification number, password, etc.) from a remote terminal to gain access to a multiaccess system. ◆ *n* **2** Also: **login.** the process by which a computer user logs in.

logion (ˈlɒgɪˌɒn) *n, pl* **logia** (ˈlɒgɪə). a saying of Christ regarded as authentic. See also **logia.** [C16: from Greek: a saying, oracle, from *logos* word]

logistic[1] (lɒˈdʒɪstɪk) *n* **1** an uninterpreted calculus or system of symbolic logic. Compare **formal language.** ◆ *adj* **2** *Maths.* (of a curve) having an equation of the form $y = k/(1 + e^{a+bx})$, where *b* is less than zero, and used to describe a continuously increasing function. **3** *Rare.* of, relating to, or skilled in arithmetical calculations. [C17: via French, from Late Latin *logisticus* of calculation, from Greek *logistikos* rational, from *logos* word, reason]

logistic[2] (lɒˈdʒɪstɪk) *or* **logistical** *adj* of or relating to logistics. ► **loˈgistically** *adv*

logistics (lɒˈdʒɪstɪks) *n* (*functioning as sing or pl*) **1** the science of the movement, supplying, and maintenance of military forces in the field. **2** the management of materials flow through an organization, from raw materials through to finished goods. **3** the detailed planning and organization of any large complex operation. [C19: from French *logistique,* from *loger* to LODGE] ► **loˈgistically** *adv* ► **logistician** (ˌlɒdʒɪˈstɪʃən) *n*

log jam *n Chiefly U.S. and Canadian.* **1** blockage caused by the crowding together of a number of logs floating in a river. **2** a deadlock; standstill.

loglog (ˈlɒglɒg) *n* the logarithm of a logarithm (in equations, etc.).

logo (ˈləʊgəʊ, ˈlɒg-) *n, pl* **-os.** short for **logotype** (sense 2).

logo- *combining form.* indicating word or speech: *logogram.* [from Greek; see LOGOS]

log of wood *n N.Z.* **the.** an informal name for **Ranfurly Shield.**

logogram (ˈlɒgəˌgræm) *or* **logograph** (ˈlɒgəˌgrɑːf, -ˌgræf) *n* a single symbol representing an entire morpheme, word, or phrase, as for example the symbol (%) meaning *per cent.* ► **logogrammatic** (ˌlɒgəgrəˈmætɪk), **logographic** (ˌlɒgəˈgræfɪk), *or* **ˌlogoˈgraphical** *adj* ► **ˌlogogramˈmatically** *or* **ˌlogoˈgraphically** *adv*

logography (lɒˈgɒgrəfɪ) *n* (formerly) a method of longhand reporting. ► **loˈgographer** *n*

logogriph (ˈlɒgəʊˌgrɪf) *n* a word puzzle, esp. one based on recombination of the letters of a word. [C16: via French from LOGO- + Greek *griphos* puzzle] ► **ˌlogoˈgriphic** *adj*

logomachy (lɒˈgɒməkɪ) *n, pl* **-chies.** argument about words or the meaning of words. [C16: from Greek *logomakhia,* from *logos* word + *makhē* battle] ► **loˈgomachist** *n*

logopaedics *or U.S.* **logopedics** (ˌlɒgəˈpiːdɪks) *n* (*functioning as sing*) another name for **speech therapy.** ► **ˌlogoˈpaedic** *or U.S.* **ˌlogoˈpedic** *adj*

logorrhoea *or esp. U.S.* **logorrhea** (ˌlɒgəˈrɪə) *n* excessive, uncontrollable, or incoherent talkativeness.

logos (ˈlɒgɒs) *n Philosophy.* reason or the rational principle expressed in words and things, argument, or justification; esp. personified as the source of order in the universe. [C16: from Greek: word, reason, discourse, from *legein* to speak]

Logos (ˈlɒgɒs) *n Christian theol.* the divine Word; the second person of the Trinity incarnate in the person of Jesus.

logotype (ˈlɒgəʊˌtaɪp) *n* **1** *Printing.* a piece of type with several uncombined characters cast on it. **2** Also called: **logo.** a trademark, company emblem, or similar device. ► **ˈlogoˌtypy** *n*

log out (ˈlɒgaʊt) *Computing.* ◆ *vb* **1** Also: **log off.** to disconnect a remote terminal from a multiaccess system by entering (an identification number, password, etc.). ◆ *n* **2** Also: **logout.** the process by which a computer user logs out.

logroll (ˈlɒgˌrəʊl) *vb Chiefly U.S.* to use logrolling in order to procure the passage of (legislation). ► **ˈlogˌroller** *n*

logrolling (ˈlɒgˌrəʊlɪŋ) *n* **1** *U.S.* the practice of undemocratic agreements between politicians involving mutual favours, the trading of votes, etc. **2** another name for **birling.** See **birl**[1].

Logroño (*Spanish* loˈɣroɲo) *n* a walled city in N Spain, on the Ebro River: trading centre of an agricultural region noted for its wine. Pop.: 125 456 (1995 est.).

-logue *or U.S.* **-log** *n combining form.* indicating speech or discourse of a particular kind: *travelogue; monologue.* [from French, from Greek *-logos*]

logway (ˈlɒgˌweɪ) *n* another name for **gangway** (sense 4).

logwood (ˈlɒgˌwʊd) *n* **1** a leguminous tree, *Haematoxylon campechianum,* of the Caribbean and Central America. **2** the heavy reddish-brown wood of this tree, yielding the dye haematoxylin. See also **haematoxylon.**

logy (ˈləʊgɪ) *adj* **logier, logiest.** *Chiefly U.S.* dull or listless. [C19: perhaps from Dutch *log* heavy] ► **ˈloginess** *n*

-logy *n combining form.* **1** indicating the science or study of: *musicology.* **2** indicating writing, discourse, or body of writings: *trilogy; phraseology; martyrology.* [from Latin *-logia,* from Greek, from *logos* word; see LOGOS] ► **-logical** *or* **-logic** *adj combining form.* ► **-logist** *n combining form.*

lohan (ˈləʊˈhɑːn) *n* (*sometimes cap.*) another word for **arhat.**

Lohengrin (ˈləʊɪŋgrɪn) *n* (in German legend) a son of Parzival and knight of the Holy Grail.

loin (lɔɪn) *n* **1** Also called: **lumbus.** *Anatomy.* the part of the lower back and sides between the pelvis and the ribs. Related adj: **lumbar. 2** a cut of meat from this part of an animal. ◆ See also **loins.** [C14: from Old French *loigne,* perhaps from Vulgar Latin *lumbra* (unattested), from Latin *lumbus* loin]

loincloth (ˈlɔɪnˌklɒθ) *n* a piece of cloth worn round the loins. Also called: **breechcloth.**

loins (lɔɪnz) *pl n* **1** the hips and the inner surface of the legs where they join the trunk of the body; crotch. **2a** *Euphemistic.* the reproductive organs. **2b** *Chiefly literary.* the womb.

Loire (*French* lwar) *n* **1** a department of E central France, in Rhône-Alpes region. Capital: St. Étienne. Pop.: 748 500 (1995). Area: 4799 sq. km (1872 sq. miles). **2** a river in France, rising in the Massif Central and flowing north and west in a wide curve to the Bay of Biscay: the longest river in France. Its valley is famous for its wines and châteaux. Length: 1020 km (634 miles). Ancient name: **Liger.**

Loire-Atlantique (*French* lwaratlɑ̃tik) *n* a department of W France, in Pays de la Loire region. Capital: Nantes. Pop.: 1 089 400 (1995). Area: 6980 sq. km (2722 sq. miles).

Loiret (*French* lwarɛ) *n* a department of central France, in Centre region. Capital: Orléans. Pop.: 609 300 (1995). Area: 6812 sq. km (2657 sq. miles).

Loir-et-Cher (*French* lwareʃɛr) *n* a department of N central France, in Centre region. Capital: Blois. Pop.: 312 500 (1995). Area: 6422 sq. km (2505 sq. miles).

loiter (ˈlɔɪtə) *vb* (*intr*) to stand or act aimlessly or idly. [C14: perhaps from Middle Dutch *löteren* to wobble: perhaps related to Old English *lūtian* to lurk] ► **ˈloiterer** *n* ► **ˈloitering** *n, adj*

Loki (ˈləʊkɪ) *n Norse myth.* the god of mischief and destruction.

Lok Sabha (ˈləʊk ˈsʌbə) *n* the lower chamber of India's Parliament. Compare **Rajya Sabha.** [Hindi, from *lok* people + *sabha* assembly]

Lolita (ˌlɒˈliːtə) *n* a sexually precocious young girl. [C20: after the character in Nabokov's novel *Lolita* (1955)]

loll (lɒl) *vb* **1** (*intr*) to lie, lean, or lounge in a lazy or relaxed manner. **2** to hang or allow to hang loosely. ◆ *n* **3** an act or instance of lolling. [C14: perhaps imitative; perhaps related to Middle Dutch *lollen* to doze] ► **ˈloller** *n* ► **ˈlolling** *adj*

Lolland *or* **Laaland** (*Danish* ˈlɔlan) *n* an island of Denmark in the Baltic Sea, south of Sjælland. Pop.: 80 500 (1988 est.). Area: 1240 sq. km (480 sq. miles).

lollapalooza (ˌlɒləpəˈluːzə) *or* **lalapalooza** *n U.S. slang.* something excellent. [origin unknown]

Lollard (ˈlɒləd) *n English history.* a follower of John Wycliffe during the 14th, 15th, and 16th centuries. [C14: from Middle Dutch; mutterer, from *lollen* to mumble (prayers)] ► **ˈLollardy, ˈLollardry,** *or* **ˈLollardism** *n*

lollipop (ˈlɒlɪˌpɒp) *n* **1** a boiled sweet or toffee stuck on a small wooden stick. **2** *Brit.* another word for **ice lolly.** [C18: perhaps from Northern English dialect *lolly* the tongue (compare LOLL) + POP[1]]

lollipop man *or* **lady** *n* (in Britain) a person wearing a white coat and carrying a pole bearing a circular warning sign who stops traffic to allow children travelling to or from school to cross a road safely. Official name: **school crossing patrol.**

lollop ('lɒləp) *vb* (*intr*) *Chiefly Brit.* **1** to walk or run with a clumsy or relaxed bouncing movement. **2** a less common word for **lounge.** [C18: probably from LOLL + *-op* as in GALLOP, to emphasize the contrast in meaning]

lollo rosso ('lɒləu 'rɒsəu) *n* a variety of lettuce originating in Italy, having curly red-tipped leaves and a slightly bitter taste.

lolly ('lɒlɪ) *n, pl* **-lies. 1** an informal word for **lollipop. 2** *Brit.* short for **ice lolly. 3** *Brit., Austral., and N.Z.* a slang word for **money. 4** *Austral. and N.Z. informal.* a sweet, esp. a boiled one. **5 do the** (*or* **one's**) **lolly.** *Austral. informal.* to lose one's temper. [shortened from LOLLIPOP]

lollygag ('lɒlɪˌgæg) *vb* **-gags, -gagging, -gagged.** (*intr*) a variant of **lallygag.**

lolly water *n Austral. and N.Z. informal.* any of various coloured soft drinks.

Lomax ('ləumæks) *n* **Alan.** born 1915, and his father **John Avery** ('eɪvərɪ) (1867–1948), U.S. folklorists.

Lombard[1] ('lɒmbəd, -bɑːd, 'lʌm-) *n* **1** a native or inhabitant of Lombardy. **2** Also called: **Langobard.** a member of an ancient Germanic people who settled in N Italy after 568 A.D. ◆ *adj also* **Lombardic 3** of or relating to Lombardy or the Lombards.

Lombard[2] ('lɒmbəd, -bɑːd, 'lʌm-) *n* **Peter.** ?1100–?60, Italian theologian, noted for his *Sententiarum libri quatuor.*

Lombardi (lɒm'bɑːdɪ) *n* **Vincent Thomas.** 1913–70, American football coach, whose team won the first two Superbowls, and after whom the Superbowl trophy is named.

Lombard Street *n* the British financial and banking world. [C16: from a street in London once occupied by Lombard bankers]

Lombardy ('lɒmbədɪ, 'lʌm-) *n* a region of N central Italy, bordering on the Alps: dominated by prosperous lordships and city-states during the Middle Ages; later ruled by Spain and then by Austria before becoming part of Italy in 1859; intensively cultivated and in parts highly industrialized. Pop.: 8 924 870 (1996 est.). Area: 23 804 sq. km (9284 sq. miles). Italian name: **Lombardia** (ˌlombar'diːa).

Lombardy poplar *n* an Italian poplar tree, *Populus nigra italica,* with upwardly pointing branches giving it a columnar shape.

Lombok ('lɒmbɒk) *n* an island of Indonesia, in the Nusa Tenggara Islands east of Java: came under Dutch rule in 1894; important biologically as being transitional between Asian and Australian in flora and fauna, the line of demarcation beginning at **Lombok Strait** (a channel between Lombok and Bali, connecting the Flores Sea with the Indian Ocean). Chief town: Mataram. Pop.: 2 500 000 (1991). Area: 4730 sq. km (1826 sq. miles).

Lombrosian (lɒm'brəuzɪən) *adj* of or relating to the doctrine propounded by Lombroso that criminals are a product of hereditary and atavistic factors and can be classified as a definite abnormal type.

Lombroso (*Italian* lom'broːso) *n* **Cesare** ('tʃeːzare). 1836–1909, Italian criminologist: he postulated the existence of a criminal type.

Lomé (*French* lɔme) *n* the capital and chief port of Togo, on the Bight of Benin. Pop.: 513 000 (1990 est.).

loment ('ləumɛnt) *or* **lomentum** (ləu'mɛntəm) *n, pl* **-ments** *or* **-menta** (-'mɛntə). the pod of certain leguminous plants, constricted between each seed and breaking into one-seeded portions when ripe. [C19: from Latin *lomentum* bean meal] ▸ **lomentaceous** (ˌləumən'teɪʃəs) *adj*

Lomond ('ləumənd) *n* **1 Loch.** a lake in W Scotland, north of Glasgow: the largest Scottish lake. Length: about 38 km (24 miles). Width: up to 8 km (5 miles). **2** See **Ben Lomond.**

London[1] ('lʌndən) *n* **1** the capital of the United Kingdom, a port in S England on the River Thames near its estuary on the North Sea: consists of the **City** (the financial quarter), the **West End** (the entertainment and major shopping centre), the **East End** (the industrial and dock area), and extensive suburbs. Latin name: **Londinium.** See also **City. 2 Greater.** the administrative area of London, consisting of the City of London and 32 boroughs (13 Inner London boroughs and 19 Outer London boroughs): formed in 1965 from the City, parts of Surrey, Kent, Essex, and Hertfordshire, and almost all of Middlesex: a Mayor of London and a London Assembly will take office in 2000. Pop.: 6 964 400 (1994 est.). Area: 1579 sq. km (610 sq. miles). **3** a city in SE Canada, in SE Ontario on the Thames River: University of Western Ontario (1878). Pop.: 303 165 (1991). ▸ **'Londoner** *n*

London[2] ('lʌndən) *n* **Jack,** full name *John Griffith London.* 1876–1916, U.S. novelist, short-story writer, and adventurer. His works include *Call of the Wild* (1903), *The Sea Wolf* (1904), *The Iron Heel* (1907), and the semiautobiographical *John Barleycorn* (1913).

Londonderry ('lʌndənˌdɛrɪ) *or* **Derry** *n* **1** a historical county of NW Northern Ireland, on the Atlantic: in 1973 replaced for administrative purposes by the districts of Coleraine, Derry, Limavady, and Magherafelt. Area: 2108 sq. km (814 sq. miles). **2** a port in N Northern Ireland, second city of Northern Ireland: given to the City of London in 1613 to be colonized by Londoners; besieged by James II's forces (1688–89). Pop.: 72 334 (1991). ◆ See also **Derry.**

London pride *n* a saxifragaceous plant, a hybrid between *Saxifraga spathularis* and *S. umbrosa,* having a basal rosette of leaves and pinkish-white flowers.

Londrina (*Portuguese* lon'drina) *n* a city in S Brazil, in Paraná: centre of a coffee-growing area. Pop.: 355 062 (1991).

lone (ləun) *adj* (*prenominal*) **1** unaccompanied; solitary. **2** single or isolated: *a lone house.* **3** a literary word for **lonely. 4** unmarried or widowed. [C14: from the mistaken division of ALONE into *a lone*] ▸ **'loneness** *n*

lone hand *n* **1** (in card games such as euchre) an independent player or hand played without a partner. **2 play a lone hand.** to operate without assistance.

lonely ('ləunlɪ) *adj* **-lier, -liest. 1** unhappy as a result of being without the companionship of others: *a lonely man.* **2** causing or resulting from the state of being alone: *a lonely existence.* **3** isolated, unfrequented, or desolate. **4** without companions; solitary. ▸ **'loneliness** *n*

lonely hearts *adj* (*often caps.*) of or for people who wish to meet a congenial companion or marriage partner: *a lonely hearts advertisement.*

lone pair *n Chem.* a pair of valency electrons of opposite spin that are not shared between the atoms in a molecule and are responsible for the formation of coordinate bonds.

loner ('ləunə) *n Informal.* a person or animal who avoids the company of others or prefers to be alone.

lonesome ('ləunsəm) *adj* **1** *Chiefly U.S. and Canadian.* another word for **lonely.** ◆ *n* **2 on** *or* (*U.S.*) **by one's lonesome.** *Informal.* on one's own. ▸ **'lonesomely** *adv* ▸ **'lonesomeness** *n*

lone wolf *n* a person who prefers to be alone.

long[1] (lɒŋ) *adj* **1** having relatively great extent in space on a horizontal plane. **2** having relatively great duration in time. **3a** (*postpositive*) of a specified number of units in extent or duration: *three hours long.* **3b** (*in combination*): *a two-foot-long line.* **4** having or consisting of a relatively large number of items or parts: *a long list.* **5** having greater than the average or expected range: *a long memory.* **6** being the longer or longest of alternatives: *the long way to the bank.* **7** having more than the average or usual quantity, extent, or duration: *a long match.* **8** seeming to occupy a greater time than is really so: *she spent a long afternoon waiting in the departure lounge.* **9** intense or thorough (esp. in the phrase **a long look**). **10** (of drinks) containing a large quantity of nonalcoholic beverage. **11** (of a garment) reaching to the wearer's ankles. **12** *Informal.* (foll. by *on*) plentifully supplied or endowed (with): *long on good ideas.* **13** *Phonetics.* (of a speech sound, esp. a vowel) **13a** of relatively considerable duration. **13b** classified as long, as distinguished from the quality of other vowels. **13c** (in popular usage) denoting the qualities of the five English vowels in such words as *mate, mete, mite, moat, moot,* and *mute.* **14** from end to end; lengthwise. **15** unlikely to win, happen, succeed, etc.: *a long chance.* **16** *Prosody.* **16a** denoting a vowel of relatively great duration or (esp. in classical verse) followed by more than one consonant. **16b** denoting a syllable containing such a vowel. **16c** (in verse that is not quantitative) carrying the emphasis or ictus. **17** *Finance.* having or characterized by large holdings of securities or commodities in anticipation of rising prices: *a long position.* **18** *Cricket.* (of a fielding position) near the boundary: *long leg.* **19** *Informal.* (of people) tall and slender. **20 in the long run.** See **run** (sense 82). **21 long in the tooth.** *Informal.* old or ageing. ◆ *adv* **22** for a certain time or period: *how long will it last?* **23** for or during an extensive period of time: *long into the next year.* **24** at a distant time; quite a bit of time: *long before I met you; long ago.* **25** *Finance.* into a position with more security or commodity holdings than are required by sale contracts and therefore dependent on rising prices for profit: *to go long.* **26 as** (*or* **so**) **long as. 26a** for or during just the length of time that. **26b** inasmuch as; since. **26c** provided that; if. **27 no longer.** not any more; formerly but not now. ◆ *n* **28** a long time (esp. in the phrase **for long**). **29** a relatively long thing, such as a signal in Morse code. **30** a clothing size for tall people, esp. in trousers. **31** *Phonetics.* a long vowel or syllable. **32** *Finance.* a person with large holdings of a security or commodity in expectation of a rise in its price; bull. **33** *Music.* a note common in medieval music but now obsolete, having the time value of two breves. **34 before long.** soon. **35 the long and the short of it.** the essential points or facts. ◆ See also **longs.** [Old English *lang;* related to Old High German *lang,* Old Norse *langr,* Latin *longus*]

long[2] (lɒŋ) *vb* (*intr;* foll. by *for* or an infinitive) to have a strong desire. [Old English *langian;* related to LONG[1]]

long[3] (lɒŋ) *vb* (*intr*) *Archaic.* to belong, appertain, or be appropriate. [Old English *langian* to belong, from *gelang* at hand, belonging to; compare ALONG]

Long (lɒŋ) *n* **Crawford Williamson.** 1815–78, U.S. surgeon. He was the first to use ether as an anaesthetic.

long. *abbrev. for* longitude.

long- *adv* (*in combination*) for or lasting a long time: *long-awaited; long-established; long-lasting.*

long-acting *adj* (of a drug) slowly effective after initial dosage, but maintaining its effects over a long period of time, being slowly absorbed and persisting in the tissues before being excreted. Compare **intermediate-acting, short-acting.**

longan ('lɒŋgən) *or* **lungan** *n* **1** a sapindaceous tree, *Euphoria longan,* of tropical and subtropical Asia, with small yellowish-white flowers and small edible fruits. **2** the fruit of this tree, which is similar to but smaller than the litchi, having white juicy pulp and a single seed. [C18: from Chinese *lung yen* dragon's eye]

long-and-short work *n Architect.* the alternation in masonry of vertical and horizontal blocks of stone.

longanimity (ˌlɒŋgə'nɪmɪtɪ) *n Now rare.* patience or forbearance. [C15: from Late Latin *longanimitās,* from *longanimis* forbearing, from *longus* long + *animus* mind, soul] ▸ **longanimous** (lɒŋ'gænɪməs) *adj*

long arm *n Informal.* **1** power, esp. far-reaching power: *the long arm of the law.* **2 make a long arm.** to reach out for something, as from a sitting position.

Long Beach *n* a city in SW California, on San Pedro Bay: resort and naval base; oil-refining. Pop.: 421 904 (1996 est.).

Longbenton (ˌlɒŋ'bɛntən) *n* a town in N England, in North Tyneside unitary authority, Tyne and Wear. Pop.: 34 630 (1991).

longboat ('lɒŋˌbəut) *n* **1** the largest boat carried aboard a commercial sailing vessel. **2** another term for **longship.**

longbow ('lɒŋˌbəu) *n* a large powerful hand-drawn bow, esp. as used in medieval England.

longcase clock ('lɒŋˌkeɪs) *n* another name for **grandfather clock.**

long-chain *adj Chemistry.* having a relatively long chain of atoms in the molecule.

longcloth ('lɒŋˌklɒθ) *n* **1** a fine plain-weave cotton cloth made in long strips. **2** *U.S.* a light soft muslin.

long-coats *pl n* dress-like garments formerly worn by a baby. Archaic name: **long clothes.**

long-dated *adj* (of a gilt-edged security) having more than 15 years to run before redemption. Compare **medium-dated, short-dated.**

long-day *adj* (of certain plants) able to mature and flower only if exposed to long periods of daylight (more than 12 hours), each followed by a shorter period of darkness. Compare **short-day.**

long-distance *n* **1** (*modifier*) covering relatively long distances: *a long-distance driver.* **2** (*modifier*) (of telephone calls, lines, etc.) connecting points a relatively long way apart. **3** *Chiefly U.S. and Canadian.* a long-distance telephone call. **4** a long-distance telephone system or its operator. ◆ *adv* **5** by a long-distance telephone line: *he phoned long-distance.*

long-drawn-out *adj* over-prolonged or extended.

longe (lʌndʒ, lɒndʒ) *n* an older variant of **lunge**[2]. [C17: via Old French from Latin *longus* LONG[1]]

long-eared owl *n* a slender European owl, *Asio otus,* with long ear tufts: most common in coniferous forests.

Long Eaton ('iːtᵊn) *n* a town in N central England, in SE Derbyshire. Pop.: 44 826 (1991).

longeron ('lɒndʒərən) *n* a main longitudinal structural member of an aircraft. [C20: from French: side support, ultimately from Latin *longus* LONG[1]]

longevity (lɒn'dʒɛvɪtɪ) *n* **1** long life. **2** relatively long duration of employment, service, etc. [C17: from Late Latin *longaevitās,* from Latin *longaevus* long-lived, from *longus* LONG[1] + *aevum* age] ▸ **longevous** (lɒn'dʒiːvəs) *adj*

long face *n* a disappointed, solemn, or miserable facial expression. ▸ ˌ**long-'faced** *adj*

Longfellow ('lɒŋˌfɛləʊ) *n* **Henry Wadsworth.** 1807–82, U.S. poet, noted particularly for his long narrative poems *Evangeline* (1847) and *The Song of Hiawatha* (1855).

long finger *n* **put (something) on the long finger.** *Irish.* to postpone (something) for a long time.

Longford ('lɒŋfəd) *n* **1** a county of N Republic of Ireland, in Leinster province. County town: Longford. Pop.: 30 000 (1996). Area: 1043 sq. km (403 sq. miles). **2** a town in N Republic of Ireland, county town of Co. Longford. Pop.: 6800 (1995 est.).

longhand ('lɒŋˌhænd) *n* ordinary handwriting, in which letters, words, etc., are set down in full, as opposed to shorthand or to typing.

long haul *n* **1** a journey over a long distance, esp. one involving the transport of goods. **2** a lengthy job.

long-headed *adj* astute; shrewd; sagacious. ▸ ˌ**long-'headedly** *adv* ▸ ˌ**long-'headedness** *n*

long hop *n Cricket.* a short-pitched ball, which can easily be hit.

longhorn ('lɒŋˌhɔːn) *n* **1** Also called: **Texas longhorn.** a long-horned breed of beef cattle, usually red or variegated, formerly common in the southwestern U.S. **2** a British breed of beef cattle with long curved horns.

long-horned beetle *n* another name for **longicorn beetle** (see **longicorn** (sense 1)).

long house *n* **1** a long communal dwelling of the Iroquois and other North American Indian peoples. It often served as a council house as well. **2** a long dwelling found in other parts of the world, such as Borneo.

long hundredweight *n* the full name for **hundredweight** (sense 1).

longicorn ('lɒndʒɪˌkɔːn) *n* **1** Also called: **longicorn beetle, long-horned beetle.** any beetle of the family *Cerambycidae,* having a long narrow body, long legs, and long antennae. ◆ *adj* **2** *Zoology.* having or designating long antennae. [C19: from New Latin *longicornis* long-horned]

longing ('lɒŋɪŋ) *n* **1** a prolonged unfulfilled desire or need. ◆ *adj* **2** having or showing desire or need: *a longing look.* ▸ **'longingly** *adv*

Longinus (lɒn'dʒaɪnəs) *n* **Dionysius** (ˌdaɪə'nɪsɪəs). ?2nd century A.D., supposed author of the famous Greek treatise on literary criticism, *On the Sublime.* ▸ **Longinean** (lɒn'dʒɪnɪən) *adj*

longipennate (ˌlɒndʒɪ'pɛneɪt) *adj* (of birds) having long slender wings or feathers.

longirostral (ˌlɒndʒɪ'rɒstrəl) *adj* (of birds) having a long beak.

longish ('lɒŋɪʃ) *adj* rather long.

Long Island *n* an island in SE New York State, separated from the S shore of Connecticut by **Long Island Sound** (an arm of the Atlantic): contains the New York City boroughs of Brooklyn and Queens in the west, many resorts (notably Coney Island), and two large airports (La Guardia and John F. Kennedy). Area: 4462 sq. km (1723 sq. miles).

longitude ('lɒndʒɪˌtjuːd, 'lɒŋg-) *n* **1** distance in degrees east or west of the prime meridian at 0° measured by the angle between the plane of the prime meridian and that of the meridian through the point in question, or by the corresponding time difference. See **latitude** (sense 1). **2** *Astronomy.* short for **celestial longitude.** [C14: from Latin *longitūdō* length, from *longus* LONG[1]]

longitudinal (ˌlɒndʒɪ'tjuːdɪnᵊl, ˌlɒŋg-) *adj* **1** of or relating to longitude or length. **2** placed or extended lengthways. Compare **transverse** (sense 1). **3** *Psychol.* (of a study of behaviour) carried on over a protracted period of time. ▸ ˌ**longi'tudinally** *adv*

longitudinal wave *n* a wave that is propagated in the same direction as the displacement of the transmitting medium. Compare **transverse wave.**

long jenny *n Billiards.* an in-off up the cushion into a far pocket. Compare **short jenny.** [from *Jenny,* pet form of *Janet*]

long johns *pl n Informal.* underpants with long legs.

long jump *n* an athletic contest in which competitors try to cover the farthest distance possible with a running jump from a fixed board or mark. U.S. and Canadian equivalent: **broad jump.** ▸ **long jumping** *n*

longleaf pine ('lɒŋˌliːf) *n* a North American pine tree, *Pinus palustris,* with long needle-like leaves and orange-brown bark: the most important timber tree of the southeastern U.S.

long lease *n* (in England and Wales) a lease, originally for a period of over 21 years, on a whole house of low rent and ratable value, which is the occupants' only or main residence. Under the Leasehold Reform Act (1969) the leaseholder is entitled to buy the freehold, claim an extension of 50 years, or become a statutory tenant.

Longleat House ('lɒŋliːt) *n* an Elizabethan mansion near Warminster in Wiltshire, built (from 1568) by Robert Smythson for Sir John Thynne; the grounds, landscaped by Capability Brown, now contain a famous safari park.

long leg *n Cricket.* **a** a fielding position on the leg side near the boundary almost directly behind the batsman's wicket. **b** a fielder in this position.

long-legged ('lɒŋˌlɛgd, -ˌlɛgɪd) *adj* **1** having long legs. **2** *Informal.* (of a person or animal) able to run fast.

long-lived *adj* having long life, existence, or currency. ▸ ˌ**long-'livedness** *n*

Long March *n* **the.** a journey of about 10 000 km (6000 miles) undertaken (1934–35) by some 100 000 Chinese Communists when they were forced out of their base in Kiangsi in SE China. They made their way to Shensi in NW China; only about 8000 survived the rigours of the journey.

long mark *n* another name for **macron.**

long measure *n* another name for **linear measure.**

long metre *n* a stanzaic form consisting of four octosyllabic lines, used esp. for hymns.

long moss *n* another name for **Spanish moss.**

Longobard ('lɒŋgəˌbɑːd) *n, pl* **-bards** *or* **-bardi** (-ˌbɑːdɪ). a rare name for an ancient **Lombard.** ▸ ˌ**Longo'bardian** *or* ˌ**Longo'bardic** *adj*

long-off *n Cricket.* **a** a fielding position on the off side near the boundary almost directly behind the bowler. **b** a fielder in this position.

long-on *n Cricket.* **a** a fielding position on the leg side near the boundary almost directly behind the bowler. **b** a fielder in this position.

Long Parliament *n English history.* **1** the Parliament summoned by Charles I that assembled on Nov. 3, 1640, was expelled by Cromwell in 1653, and was finally dissolved in 1660. See also **Rump Parliament. 2** the Cavalier Parliament of 1661–79. **3** the Parliament called in Henry IV's reign that met from March 1 to Dec. 22, 1406.

long pig *n Obsolete.* human flesh eaten by cannibals. [translation of a Maori and Polynesian term]

long-playing *adj* of or relating to an LP (long-player).

long primer *n* (formerly) a size of printer's type, approximately equal to 10 point.

long purse *n Informal.* wealth; riches.

long-range *adj* **1** of or extending into the future: *a long-range weather forecast.* **2** (of vehicles, aircraft, etc.) capable of covering great distances without refuelling. **3** (of weapons) made to be fired at a distant target.

longs (lɒŋz) *pl n* **1** full-length trousers. **2** long-dated gilt-edged securities. **3** *Finance.* unsold securities or commodities held in anticipation of rising prices.

long s *n* a lower-case *s,* printed ſ, formerly used in handwriting and printing. Also called: **long ess.**

longship ('lɒŋˌʃɪp) *n* a narrow open vessel with oars and a square sail, used esp. by the Vikings during medieval times.

longshore ('lɒŋˌʃɔː) *adj* situated on, relating to, or along the shore. [C19: shortened form of *alongshore*]

longshore drift *n* the process whereby beach material is gradually shifted laterally as a result of waves meeting the shore at an oblique angle.

longshoreman ('lɒŋˌʃɔːmən) *n, pl* **-men.** a U.S. and Canadian word for **docker**[1].

long shot *n* **1** a competitor, as in a race, considered to be unlikely to win. **2** a bet against heavy odds. **3** an undertaking, guess, or possibility with little chance of success. **4** *Films, television.* a shot where the camera is or appears to be distant from the object to be photographed. **5 by a long shot.** by any means: *he still hasn't finished by a long shot.*

long-sighted *adj* **1** related to or suffering from hyperopia. **2** able to see distant objects in focus. **3** having foresight. ▸ ˌ**long-'sightedly** *adv* ▸ ˌ**long-'sightedness** *n*

Longs Peak *n* a mountain in N Colorado, in the Front Range of the Rockies: the highest peak in the Rocky Mountain National Park. Height: 4345 m (14 255 ft.).

longspur ('lɒŋˌspɜː) *n* any of various Arctic and North American buntings of the genera *Calcarius* and *Rhyncophanes,* all of which have a long claw on the hind toe.

long-standing *adj* existing or in effect for a long time.

long-suffering *adj* **1** enduring pain, unhappiness, etc., without complaint. ◆ *n also* **long-sufferance. 2** long and patient endurance. ▸ ˌ**long-'sufferingly** *adv*

long suit *n* **1a** the longest suit in a hand of cards. **1b** a holding of four or more cards of a suit. **2** *Informal.* an outstanding advantage, personal quality, or talent.

long-tailed tit *n* a small European songbird, *Aegithalos caudatus,* with a black, white, and pink plumage and a very long tail: family *Paridae* (tits).

long-term *adj* **1** lasting, staying, or extending over a long time: *long-term prospects.* **2** *Finance.* maturing after a long period of time: *a long-term bond.*

long-term memory *n Psychol.* that section of the memory storage system in which experiences are stored on a semipermanent basis. Compare **short-term memory.**

longtime ('lɒŋˌtaɪm) *adj* of long standing.

long tin *n Brit.* a tall long loaf of bread.

long tom *n* **1** a long swivel cannon formerly used in naval warfare. **2** a long-range land gun. **3** an army slang name for **cannon** (sense 1).

long ton *n* the full name for **ton**[1] (sense 1).

Longueuil (lɒŋ'geɪl; *French* lɔ̃gœj) *n* a city in SE Canada, in S Quebec: a suburb of Montreal. Pop.: 129 874 (1991).

longueur (*French* lɔ̃gœr) *n* a period of boredom or dullness. [literally: length]

Longus ('lɒŋgəs) *n* ?3rd century A.D., Greek author of the prose romance *Daphnis and Chloe.*

long vacation *n* the long period of holiday in the summer during which universities, law courts, etc., are closed.

long view *n* the consideration of events or circumstances likely to occur in the future.

long wave *n* **a** a radio wave with a wavelength greater than 1000 metres. **b** (*as modifier*): *a long-wave broadcast.*

longways ('lɒŋ,weɪz) *or U.S. and Canadian* **longwise** ('lɒŋ,waɪz) *adv* another word for **lengthways.**

long weekend *n* a weekend holiday extended by a day or days on either side.

long-winded *adj* **1** tiresomely long. **2** capable of energetic activity without becoming short of breath. ► **,long-'windedly** *adv* ► **,long-'windedness** *n*

long-wire aerial *n* a travelling-wave aerial consisting of one or more conductors, the length of which usually exceeds several wavelengths.

Longyearbyen ('lɒŋjɪə,bjɛn) *n* a village on Spitsbergen island, administrative centre of the Svalbard archipelago: coal-mining.

lonicera (lɒ'nɪsərə) *n* See **honeysuckle.**

Lonsdale Belt ('lɒnz,deɪl) *n* (in Britain) a belt conferred as a trophy on professional boxing champions, in various weight categories: if a champion wins it three times it becomes his personal property. [named after Hugh Cecil Lowther, 5th Earl of *Lonsdale* (1857–1944), who presented the first one]

Lons-le-Saunier (*French* lɔ̃ləsonje) *n* a town in E France: saline springs; manufactures sparkling wines. Pop. (conurbation): 210 140 (1990).

loo[1] (lu:) *n, pl* **loos.** *Brit.* an informal word for **lavatory** (sense 1). [C20: perhaps from French *lieux d'aisance* water closet]

loo[2] (lu:) *n, pl* **loos. 1** a gambling card game. **2** a stake used in this game. [C17: shortened form of *lanterloo,* via Dutch from French *lanterelu,* originally a meaningless word from the refrain of a popular song]

loo[3] (lu:) *vb* a variant spelling of **lou.**

looby ('lu:bɪ) *n, pl* **-bies.** a foolish or stupid person. [C14: of unknown origin]

loofah ('lu:fə) *n* **1** the fibrous interior of the fruit of the dishcloth gourd, which is dried, bleached, and used as a bath sponge or for scrubbing. **2** another name for **dishcloth gourd.** ◆ Also called (esp. U.S.): **loofa, luffa.** [C19: from New Latin *luffa,* from Arabic *lūf*]

look (lʊk) *vb* (*mainly intr*) **1** (often foll. by *at*) to direct the eyes (towards): *to look at the sea.* **2** (often foll. by *at*) to direct one's attention (towards): *let's look at the circumstances.* **3** (often foll. by *to*) to turn one's interests or expectations (towards): *to look to the future.* **4** (*copula*) to give the impression of being by appearance to the eye or mind; seem: *that looks interesting.* **5** to face in a particular direction: *the house looks north.* **6** to expect, hope, or plan (to do something): *I look to hear from you soon; he's looking to get rich.* **7** (foll. by *for*) **7a** to search or seek: *I looked for you everywhere.* **7b** to cherish the expectation (of); hope (for): *I look for success.* **8** (foll. by *to*) **8a** to be mindful (of): *to look to the promise one has made.* **8b** to have recourse (to): *look to your swords, men!* **9** to be a pointer or sign: *these early inventions looked towards the development of industry.* **10** (foll. by *into*) to carry out an investigation: *to look into a mystery.* **11** (*tr*) to direct a look at (someone) in a specified way: *she looked her rival up and down.* **12** (*tr*) to accord in appearance with (something): *to look one's age.* **13 look alive** *or* **lively.** hurry up; get busy. **14 look daggers.** See **dagger** (sense 4). **15 look here.** an expression used to attract someone's attention, add emphasis to a statement, etc. **16 look sharp** *or* **smart.** (*imperative*) to hurry up; make haste. **17 not look at.** to refuse to consider: *they won't even look at my offer of £5000.* **18 not much to look at.** unattractive; plain. ◆ *n* **19** the act or an instance of looking: *a look of despair.* **20** a view or sight (of something): *let's have a look.* **21** (*often pl*) appearance to the eye or mind; aspect: *the look of innocence; I don't like the looks of this place.* **22** style; fashion: *the new look for summer.* ◆ *sentence connector.* **23** an expression demanding attention or showing annoyance, determination, etc.: *look, I've had enough of this.* ◆ See also **look after, look back, look down, look forward to, look-in, look on, lookout, look over, look through, look up.** [Old English *lōcian;* related to Middle Dutch *læken,* Old High German *luogen* to look out]

USAGE See at **like.**

look after *vb* (*intr, prep*) **1** to take care of; be responsible for: *she looked after the child while I was out.* **2** to follow with the eyes: *he looked after the girl thoughtfully.*

lookalike ('lʊkə,laɪk) *n* **a** a person, esp. a celebrity, or thing that is the double of another. **b** (*as modifier*): *a lookalike Minister; a lookalike newspaper.*

look back *vb* (*intr, adv*) **1** to cast one's mind to the past. **2 to never look back.** to become increasingly successful: *after his book was published, he never looked back.* **3** *Chiefly Brit.* to pay another visit later.

look down *vb* **1** (*intr, adv;* foll. by *on* or *upon*) to express or show contempt or disdain (for). **2 look down one's nose at.** *Informal.* to be contemptuous or disdainful of.

looker ('lʊkə) *n Informal.* **1** a person who looks. **2** a very attractive person, esp. a woman or girl.

look forward to *vb* (*intr, adv + prep*) to wait or hope for, esp. with pleasure.

look-in *Informal.* ◆ *n* **1** a chance to be chosen, participate, etc. **2** a short visit. ◆ *vb* **look in. 3** (*intr, adv* often foll. by *on*) to pay a short visit.

looking glass *n* **1** a mirror, esp. a ladies' dressing mirror. ◆ *modifier.* **looking-glass. 2** with normal or familiar circumstances reversed; topsy-turvy: *a looking-glass world.* [sense 2 in allusion to Lewis Carroll's *Through the Looking-Glass*]

look on *vb* (*intr*) **1** (*adv*) to be a spectator at an event or incident. **2** (*prep*) Also: **look upon.** to consider or regard: *she looked on the whole affair as a joke; he looks on his mother-in-law with disapproval.* ► **,looker-'on** *n*

lookout ('lʊk,aʊt) *n* **1** the act of keeping watch against danger, etc. **2** a person or persons instructed or employed to keep such a watch, esp. on a ship. **3** a strategic point from which a watch is kept. **4** *Informal.* worry or concern: *that's his lookout.* **5** *Chiefly Brit.* outlook, chances, or view. ◆ *vb* **look out.** (*adv, mainly intr*) **6** to heed one's behaviour; be careful: *look out for the children's health.* **7** to be on the watch: *look out for my mother at the station.* **8** (*tr*) to search for and find: *I'll look out some curtains for your new house.* **9** (foll. by *on* or *over*) to face in a particular direction: *the house looks out over the moor.*

look over *vb* **1** (*intr, prep*) to inspect by making a tour of (a factory, house, etc.): *we looked over the country house.* **2** (*tr, adv*) to examine (a document, letter, etc.): *please look the papers over quickly.* ◆ *n* **lookover. 3** an inspection: often, specifically, a brief or cursory one.

look-see *n Informal.* a brief inspection or look.

look through *vb* **1** (*intr, prep* or *tr, adv*) to examine, esp. cursorily: *he looked through his notes before the lecture.* **2** (*intr, prep*) to ignore (a person) deliberately: *whenever he meets his ex-girlfriend, she looks straight through him.*

look up *vb* (*adv*) **1** (*tr*) to discover (something required to be known) by resorting to a work of reference, such as a dictionary. **2** (*intr*) to increase, as in quality or value: *things are looking up.* **3** (*intr;* foll. by *to*) to have respect (for): *I've always wanted a girlfriend I could look up to.* **4** (*tr*) to visit or make contact with (a person): *I'll look you up when I'm in town.*

loom[1] (lu:m) *n* **1** an apparatus, worked by hand or mechanically (**power loom**), for weaving yarn into a textile. **2** the middle portion of an oar, which acts as a fulcrum swivelling in the rowlock. [C13 (meaning any kind of tool): variant of Old English *gelōma* tool; compare HEIRLOOM]

loom[2] (lu:m) *vb* (*intr*) **1** to come into view indistinctly with an enlarged and often threatening aspect. **2** (of an event) to seem ominously close. **3** (often foll. by *over*) (of large objects) to dominate or overhang. ◆ *n* **4** a rising appearance, as of something far away. [C16: perhaps from East Frisian *lomen* to move slowly]

loom[3] (lu:m) *n Archaic or dialect.* **1** another name for **diver** (the bird). **2** any of various other birds, esp. the guillemot. [C17: from Old Norse *lomr*]

loo mask *n* a half-mask worn during the 18th century for masquerades, etc. Also called: **loup.** [C17 *loo,* from French *loup,* literally: wolf, from Latin *lupus*]

loom-state *adj* (of a woven cotton fabric) not yet dyed.

loon[1] (lu:n) *n* the U.S. and Canadian name for **diver** (the bird). [C17: of Scandinavian origin; related to Old Norse *lōmr*]

loon[2] (lu:n) *n* **1** *Informal.* a simple-minded or stupid person. **2** *Northeast Scot. dialect.* a lad. **3** *Archaic.* a person of low rank or occupation (esp. in the phrase **lord and loon**). [C15: origin obscure]

loony, looney, *or* **luny** ('lu:nɪ) *Slang.* ◆ *adj* **loonier, looniest** *or* **lunier, luniest. 1** lunatic; insane. **2** foolish or ridiculous. ◆ *n, pl* **loonies, looneys,** *or* **lunies. 3** a foolish or insane person. **4** *Canadian.* a Canadian dollar coin with a loon bird on one of its faces. ► **'looniness** *or* **'luniness** *n*

loony bin *n Slang.* a mental hospital or asylum.

loop[1] (lu:p) *n* **1** the round or oval shape formed by a line, string, etc., that curves around to cross itself. **2** any round or oval-shaped thing that is closed or nearly closed. **3** a piece of material, such as string, curved round and fastened to form a ring or handle for carrying by. **4** an intrauterine contraceptive device in the shape of a loop. **5** *Electronics.* **5a** a closed electric or magnetic circuit through which a signal can circulate, as in a feedback control system. **5b** short for **loop aerial. 6** a flight manoeuvre in which an aircraft flies one complete circle in the vertical plane. **7** Also called: **loop line.** *Chiefly Brit.* a railway branch line which leaves the main line and rejoins it after a short distance. **8** *Maths, physics.* a closed curve on a graph: *hysteresis loop.* **9** another name for **antinode. 10** *Anatomy.* **10a** the most common basic pattern of the human fingerprint, formed by several sharply rising U-shaped ridges. Compare **arch**[1] (sense 4b). **10b** a bend in a tubular structure, such as the U-shaped curve in a kidney tubule (**Henle's loop** or **loop of Henle**). **11** *Computing.* a series of instructions in a program, performed repeatedly until some specified condition is satisfied. **12** *Skating.* a jump in which the skater takes off from a back outside edge, makes one, two, or three turns in the air, and lands on the same back outside edge. **13** a group of people to whom information is circulated (esp. in the phrases **in** *or* **out of the loop**). ◆ *vb* **14** (*tr*) to make a loop in or of (a line, string, etc.). **15** (*tr*) to fasten or encircle with a loop or something like a loop. **16** Also: **loop the loop.** to cause (an aircraft) to perform a loop or (of an aircraft) to perform a loop. **17** (*intr*) to move in loops or in a path like a loop. [C14: *loupe,* origin unknown]

loop[2] (lu:p) *n* an archaic word for **loophole.** [C14: perhaps related to Middle Dutch *lupen* to watch, peer]

loop aerial *n* an aerial that consists of one or more coils of wire wound on a frame. Maximum radiation or reception is in the plane of the loop, the minimum occurring at right angles to it. Sometimes shortened to **loop.** Also called: **frame aerial.**

loop diuretic *n Med.* any of a group of diuretics, including frusemide, that act by inhibiting resorption of salts from Henle's loop of the kidney tubule.

looper ('lu:pə) *n* **1** a person or thing that loops or makes loops. **2** another name for a **measuring worm.**

loophole ('lu:p,həʊl) *n* **1** an ambiguity, omission, etc., as in a law, by which one can avoid a penalty or responsibility. **2** a small gap or hole in a wall, esp. one in a fortified wall. ◆ *vb* **3** (*tr*) to provide with loopholes. [C16: from LOOP[2] + HOLE]

loop knot *n* a knot that leaves a loop extending from it.

loopy ('lu:pɪ) *adj* **loopier, loopiest. 1** full of loops; curly or twisted. **2** *Informal.* slightly mad, crazy, or stupid.

Loos (*German* luːs) *n* **Adolf** ('adɔlf). 1870–1933, Austrian architect: a pioneer of modern architecture, noted for his plain austere style in such buildings as Steiner House, Vienna (1910).

loose (luːs) *adj* **1** free or released from confinement or restraint. **2** not close, compact, or tight in structure or arrangement. **3** not fitted or fitting closely: *loose clothing is cooler.* **4** not bundled, packaged, fastened, or put in a container: *loose nails.* **5** inexact; imprecise: *a loose translation.* **6** (of funds, cash, etc.) not allocated or locked away; readily available. **7a** (esp. of women) promiscuous or easy. **7b** (of attitudes, ways of life, etc.) immoral or dissolute. **8** lacking a sense of responsibility or propriety: *loose talk.* **9a** (of the bowels) emptying easily, esp. excessively; lax. **9b** (of a cough) accompanied by phlegm, mucus, etc. **10** (of a dye or dyed article) fading as a result of washing; not fast. **11** *Informal, chiefly U.S. and Canadian.* very relaxed; easy. ◆ *n* **12 the loose.** *Rugby.* the part of play when the forwards close round the ball in a ruck or loose scrum. See **scrum. 13 on the loose. 13a** free from confinement or restraint. **13b** *Informal.* on a spree. ◆ *adv* **14a** in a loose manner; loosely. **14b** (*in combination*): *loose-fitting.* **15 hang loose.** *Informal, chiefly U.S.* to behave in a relaxed, easy fashion. ◆ *vb* **16** (*tr*) to set free or release, as from confinement, restraint, or obligation. **17** (*tr*) to unfasten or untie. **18** to make or become less strict, tight, firmly attached, compact, etc. **19** (when *intr*, often foll. by *off*) to let fly (a bullet, arrow, or other missile). [C13 (in the sense: not bound): from Old Norse *lauss* free; related to Old English *lēas* free from, -LESS] ▸ **'loosely** *adv* ▸ **'looseness** *n*

loosebox ('luːsˌbɒks) *n* an enclosed and covered stall with a door in which an animal can be confined.

loose cannon *n* a person or thing that appears to be beyond control and is potentially a source of unintentional damage.

loose change *n* money in the form of coins suitable for small expenditures.

loose cover *n* a fitted but easily removable cloth cover for a chair, sofa, etc. U.S. and Canadian name: **slipcover.**

loose end *n* **1** a detail that is left unsettled, unexplained, or incomplete. **2 at a loose end.** without purpose or occupation.

loose head *n Rugby.* the prop on the hooker's left in the front row of a scrum. Compare **tight head.**

loose-jointed *adj* **1** supple and easy in movement. **2** loosely built; with ill-fitting joints. ▸ **ˌloose-'jointedness** *n*

loose-leaf *adj* **1** (of a binder, album, etc.) capable of being opened to allow removal and addition of pages. ◆ *n* **2** a serial publication published in loose leaves and kept in such a binder.

loose-limbed *adj* (of a person) having supple limbs.

loosen ('luːsᵊn) *vb* **1** to make or become less tight, fixed, etc. **2** (often foll. by *up*) to make or become less firm, compact, or rigid. **3** (*tr*) to untie. **4** (*tr*) to let loose; set free. **5** (often foll. by *up*) to make or become less strict, severe, etc. **6** (*tr*) to rid or relieve (the bowels) of constipation. [C14: from LOOSE] ▸ **'loosener** *n*

loose order *n Military.* a formation in which soldiers, units, etc., are widely separated from each other.

loose smut *n* a disease of cereal grasses caused by smut fungi of the genus *Ustilago,* in which powdery spore masses replace the host tissue.

loosestrife ('luːsˌstraɪf) *n* **1** any of various primulaceous plants of the genus *Lysimachia,* esp. the yellow-flowered *L. vulgaris* (**yellow loosestrife**). See also **moneywort. 2 purple loosestrife.** Also called: **willowherb.** a purple-flowered lythraceous marsh plant, *Lythrum salicaria.* **3** any of several similar or related plants, such as the primulaceous plant *Naumburgia thyrsiflora* (**tufted loosestrife**). [C16: LOOSE + STRIFE, an erroneous translation of Latin *lysimachia,* as if from Greek *lusimakhos* ending strife, instead of from the name of the supposed discoverer, *Lusimakhos*]

loose-tongued *adj* careless or irresponsible in talking.

loosing *or* **lowsening** ('luːsɪŋ, -zɪŋ, 'lɔɪ-) *n Yorkshire dialect.* a celebration of one's 21st birthday.

loot (luːt) *n* **1** goods stolen during pillaging, as in wartime, during riots, etc. **2** goods, money, etc., obtained illegally. **3** *Informal.* money or wealth. **4** the act of looting or plundering. ◆ *vb* **5** to pillage (a city, settlement, etc.) during war or riots. **6** to steal (money or goods), esp. during pillaging. [C19: from Hindi *lūt*] ▸ **'looter** *n*

lop[1] (lɒp) *vb* **lops, lopping, lopped.** (*tr;* usually foll. by *off*) **1** to sever (parts) from a tree, body, etc., esp. with swift strokes. **2** to cut out or eliminate from as excessive. ◆ *n* **3** a part or parts lopped off, as from a tree. [C15 *loppe* branches cut off; compare LOB[1]] ▸ **'lopper** *n*

lop[2] (lɒp) *vb* **lops, lopping, lopped. 1** to hang or allow to hang loosely. **2** (*intr*) to slouch about or move awkwardly. **3** (*intr*) a less common word for **lope.** [C16: perhaps related to LOP[1]; compare LOB[1]]

lop[3] (lɒp) *n Northern English dialect.* a flea. [probably from Old Norse *hloppa* (unattested) flea, from *hlaupa* to LEAP]

lope (ləʊp) *vb* **1** (*intr*) (of a person) to move or run with a long swinging stride. **2** (*intr*) (of four-legged animals) to run with a regular bounding movement. **3** to cause (a horse) to canter with a long easy stride or (of a horse) to canter in this manner. ◆ *n* **4** a long steady gait or stride. [C15: from Old Norse *hlaupa* to LEAP; compare Middle Dutch *lopen* to run] ▸ **'loper** *n*

lop-eared *adj* (of animals) having ears that droop.

Lope de Vega (*Spanish* 'lope ðe 'βeɣa) *n* full name *Lope Felix de Vega Carpio.* 1562–1635, Spanish dramatist, novelist, and poet. He established the classic form of Spanish drama and was a major influence on European, esp. French, literature. Some 500 of his 1800 plays are extant.

lopho- *combining form.* indicating a crested or tufted part: *lophophore.* [from Greek *lophos* crest]

lophobranch ('ləʊfəˌbræŋk) *n* **1** any teleost fish of the suborder *Lophobranchii,* having the gills arranged in rounded tufts: includes the pipefishes and sea horses. ◆ *adj* **2** of, relating to, or belonging to the *Lophobranchii.* ▸ **lophobranchiate** (ˌləʊfə'bræŋkɪt, -ˌeɪt) *adj*

lophophore ('ləʊfəˌfɔː) *n* a circle or horseshoe of ciliated tentacles surrounding the mouth and used for the capture of food in minute sessile animals of the phyla *Brachiopoda, Phoronida,* and *Ectoprocta.* ▸ **'lopho'phorate** *adj*

lopolith ('lɒpəlɪθ) *n* a saucer-shaped body of intrusive igneous rock, formed by the penetration of magma between the beds or layers of existing rock. Compare **laccolith.** [C20: from Greek *lopas* dish + -LITH]

lopsided (ˌlɒp'saɪdɪd) *adj* **1** leaning or inclined to one side. **2** greater in weight, height, or size on one side. ▸ **ˌlop'sidedly** *adv* ▸ **ˌlop'sidedness** *n*

loq. *abbrev. for* loquitur.

loquacious (lɒ'kweɪʃəs) *adj* characterized by or showing a tendency to talk a great deal. [C17: from Latin *loquāx* from *loquī* to speak] ▸ **lo'quaciously** *adv* ▸ **loquacity** (lɒ'kwæsɪtɪ) *or* **lo'quaciousness** *n*

loquat ('ləʊkwɒt, -kwət) *n* **1** an ornamental evergreen rosaceous tree, *Eriobotrya japonica,* of China and Japan, having reddish woolly branches, white flowers, and small yellow edible plumlike fruits. **2** the fruit of this tree. ◆ Also called: **Japan plum.** [C19: from Chinese (Cantonese) *lō kwat,* literally: rush orange]

loquitur *Latin.* ('lɒkwɪtə) he (or she) speaks: used, esp. formerly, as a stage direction. Usually abbreviated to **loq.**

lor (lɔː) *interj Not standard.* an exclamation of surprise or dismay. [from LORD (interj)]

loran ('lɔːrən) *n* a radio navigation system operating over long distances. Synchronized pulses are transmitted from widely spaced radio stations to aircraft or shipping, the time of arrival of the pulses being used to determine position. [C20: *lo(ng-)ra(nge) n(avigation)*]

Lorca[1] (*Spanish* 'lɔrka) *n* a town in SE Spain, on the Guadalentín River. Pop.: 66 940 (1991).

Lorca[2] (*Spanish* 'lɔrka) *n* **Federico García** (feðe'riko gar'θia). 1898–1936, Spanish poet and dramatist. His poetry, such as *Romancero gitano* (1928), shows his debt to Andalusian folk poetry. His plays include the trilogy *Bodas de sangre* (1933), *Yerma* (1934), and *La Casa de Bernarda Alba* (1936).

lord (lɔːd) *n* **1** a person who has power or authority over others, such as a monarch or master. **2** a male member of the nobility, esp. in Britain. **3** (in medieval Europe) a feudal superior, esp. the master of a manor. Compare **lady** (sense 5). **4** a husband considered as head of the household (archaic except in the facetious phrase **lord and master**). **5** *Astrology.* a planet having a dominating influence. **6 my lord.** a respectful form of address used to a judge, bishop, or nobleman. ◆ *vb* **7** (*tr*) *Now rare.* to make a lord of (a person). **8** to act in a superior manner towards (esp. in the phrase **lord it over**). [Old English *hlāford* bread keeper; see LOAF[1], WARD] ▸ **'lordless** *adj* ▸ **'lordˌlike** *adj*

Lord (lɔːd) *n* **1** a title given to God or Jesus Christ. **2** *Brit.* **2a** a title given to men of high birth, specifically to an earl, marquess, baron, or viscount. **2b** a courtesy title given to the younger sons of a duke or marquess. **2c** the ceremonial title of certain high officials or of a bishop or archbishop: *Lord Mayor; Lord of Appeal; Law Lord; Lord Bishop of Durham.* ◆ *interj* **3** (*sometimes not cap.*) an exclamation of dismay, surprise, etc.: *Good Lord!; Lord only knows!*

Lord Advocate *n* (in Scotland) the chief law officer of the Crown: he acts as public prosecutor and is in charge of the administration of criminal justice.

Lord Chamberlain *n* (in Britain) the chief official of the royal household.

Lord Chancellor *n Brit. government.* the cabinet minister who is head of the judiciary in England and Wales and Speaker of the House of Lords.

Lord Chief Justice *n* the judge who is second only to the Lord Chancellor in the English legal hierarchy; president of one division of the High Court of Justice.

Lord High Chancellor *n* another name for the **Lord Chancellor.**

Lord Howe Island *n* an island in the Tasman Sea, southeast of Australia: part of New South Wales. Area: 17 sq. km (6 sq. miles). Pop.: 300 (1981 est.).

lording ('lɔːdɪŋ) *n* **1** *Archaic.* a gentleman; lord: used in the plural as a form of address. **2** an obsolete word for **lordling.** [Old English *hlāfording,* from *hlāford* LORD + -ING[3], suffix indicating descent]

Lord Justice of Appeal *n* an ordinary judge of the Court of Appeal.

Lord Lieutenant *n* **1** (in Britain) the representative of the Crown in a county. **2** (formerly) the British viceroy in Ireland.

lordling ('lɔːdlɪŋ) *n Now rare.* a young lord.

lordly ('lɔːdlɪ) *adj* **-lier, -liest. 1** haughty; arrogant; proud. **2** of or befitting a lord. ◆ *adv* **3** *Archaic.* in the manner of a lord. ▸ **'lordliness** *n*

Lord Mayor *n* the mayor in the City of London and in certain other important boroughs and large cities.

Lord Muck *n Informal.* an ordinary man behaving or being treated as if he were aristocratic. See also **Lady Muck.**

Lord of Appeal *n Brit.* one of several judges appointed to assist the House of Lords in hearing appeals.

Lord of Hosts *n* Jehovah or God when regarded as having the angelic forces at his command.

Lord of Misrule *n* (formerly, in England) a person appointed master of revels at a Christmas celebration.

Lord of the Flies *n* a name for **Beelzebub.** [translation of Hebrew: see BEELZEBUB]

lordosis (lɔː'dəʊsɪs) *n* **1** *Pathol.* forward curvature of the lumbar spine: congenital or caused by trauma or disease. Nontechnical name: **hollow-back.** Compare **kyphosis, scoliosis. 2** *Zoology.* concave arching of the back occurring in many female animals during sexual stimulation. [C18: New Latin from Greek *lordōsis,* from *lordos* bent backwards] ▸ **lordotic** (lɔː'dɒtɪk) *adj*

Lord President of the Council *n* (in Britain) the Cabinet minister who presides at meetings of the Privy Council.

Lord Privy Seal *n* (in Britain) the senior cabinet minister without official duties.

Lord Protector *n* See **Protector.**

Lord Provost *n* the provost of one of the five major Scottish cities (Edinburgh, Glasgow, Aberdeen, Dundee, and Perth).

Lords (lɔːdz) *n* **the.** short for **House of Lords.**

Lord's (lɔːdz) *n* a cricket ground in N London; headquarters of the MCC.

lords-and-ladies *n* (*functioning as sing*) another name for **cuckoopint.**

Lord's Day *n* **the.** the Christian Sabbath; Sunday.

lordship (ˈlɔːdʃɪp) *n* the position or authority of a lord.

Lordship (ˈlɔːdʃɪp) *n* (preceded by *Your* or *His*) *Brit.* a title used to address or refer to a bishop, a judge of the high court, or any peer except a duke.

Lordship of the Isles *n* an overlordship of the Western Isles of Scotland and adjacent lands instituted in 1266 when Magnus of Norway ceded the Hebrides, the Isle of Man, and Kintyre to the King of Scotland, and claimed by the chiefs of Clan Dougall and later by those of Clan Donald. The title was forfeited to James IV in 1493 and is now held by the eldest son of the sovereign. ▶ **Lord of the Isles** *n*

Lord's Prayer *n* **the.** the prayer taught by Jesus Christ to his disciples, as in Matthew 6:9–13, Luke 11:2–4. Also called: **Our Father, Paternoster** (esp. Latin version).

Lords Spiritual *pl n* the two Anglican archbishops and 24 most senior bishops of England and Wales who sit as members of the House of Lords.

Lord's Supper *n* **the.** another term for **Holy Communion** (I Corinthians 11:20).

Lord's table *n* **the.** *Chiefly Protestantism.* **1** Holy Communion. **2** another name for **altar.**

Lords Temporal *pl n* **the.** (in Britain) peers other than bishops in their capacity as members of the House of Lords.

lordy (ˈlɔːdɪ) *interj Chiefly U.S. and Canadian.* an exclamation of surprise or dismay.

lore[1] (lɔː) *n* **1** collective knowledge or wisdom on a particular subject, esp. of a traditional nature. **2** knowledge or learning. **3** *Archaic.* teaching, or something that is taught. **[**Old English *lār;* related to *leornian* to LEARN**]**

lore[2] (lɔː) *n* **1** the surface of the head of a bird between the eyes and the base of the bill. **2** the corresponding area in a snake or fish. **[C19:** from New Latin *lōrum,* from Latin: strap**]**

Lorelei (ˈlɒrəˌlaɪ) *n* (in German legend) a siren, said to dwell on a rock at the edge of the Rhine south of Koblenz, who lures boatmen to destruction. **[C19:** from German *Lurlei* name of the rock; from a poem by Clemens Brentano (1778–1842)**]**

Loren (*Italian* ˈlɔːren) *n* **Sophia** (soˈfia), real name *Sophia Scicolone.* born 1934, Italian film actress. Her films include *Two Women* (1961) for which she won an Oscar, *The Millionairess* (1961), *Man of La Mancha* (1972), *The Cassandra Crossing* (1977), and *Prêt à Porter* (1994).

Lorentz (*Dutch* ˈloːrənts) *n* **Hendrik Antoon** (ˈhendrɪk ˈantoːn). 1853–1928, Dutch physicist: shared the Nobel prize for physics (1902) with Zeeman for their work on electromagnetic theory.

Lorentz-Fitzgerald contraction *n* the supposed contraction of a body in the direction of its motion through the ether, postulated to explain the result of the Michelson-Morley experiment. The special theory of relativity denies that any such real change can occur in a body as a result of uniform motion but shows that an observer moving with respect to the body will determine an apparent change given by a formula similar to that of Lorentz and Fitzgerald. **[C20:** named after H. A. LORENTZ and G. F. *Fitzgerald* (1851–1901), Irish physicist**]**

Lorentz transformation *n* a set of equations relating the coordinates of space and time used by two hypothetical observers in uniform relative motion. According to the special theory of relativity the laws of physics are invariant under this transformation. **[C20:** named after H. A. LORENTZ**]**

Lorenz (*German* ˈloːrɛnts) *n* **Konrad Zacharias** (ˈkɔnraːt tsaxaˈriːas) 1903–89, Austrian zoologist, who founded ethology. His works include *On Aggression* (1966): shared the Nobel prize for physiology or medicine 1973.

lorgnette (lɔːˈnjɛt) *n* a pair of spectacles or opera glasses mounted on a handle. **[C19:** from French, from *lorgner* to squint, from Old French *lorgne* squinting**]**

lorgnon (*French* lɔrɲɔ̃) *n* **1** a monocle or pair of spectacles. **2** another word for **lorgnette. [C19:** from French, from *lorgner;* see LORGNETTE**]**

lorica (lɒˈraɪkə) *n, pl* **-cae** (-siː, -kiː). **1** the hard outer covering of rotifers, ciliate protozoans, and similar organisms. **2** an ancient Roman cuirass of leather or metal. **[C18:** from New Latin, from Latin: leather cuirass; related to *lōrum* thong**]** ▶ **loricate** (ˈlɒrɪˌkeɪt) *or* **ˈloriˌcated** *adj*

Lorient (*French* lɔrjɑ̃) *n* a port in W France, on the Bay of Biscay. Pop.: 59 437 (1990).

lorikeet (ˈlɒrɪˌkiːt, ˌlɒrɪˈkiːt) *n* any of various small lories, such as *Glossopsitta versicolor* (**varied lorikeet**) or *Trichoglossus moluccanus* (**rainbow lorikeet**). **[C18:** from LORY + *-keet,* as in PARAKEET**]**

lorimer (ˈlɒrɪmə) *or* **loriner** (ˈlɒrɪnə) *n Brit.* (formerly) a person who made bits, spurs, and other small metal objects. **[C15:** from Old French, from *lorain* harness strap, ultimately from Latin *lōrum* strap**]**

loris (ˈlɔːrɪs) *n, pl* **-ris.** any of several omnivorous nocturnal slow-moving prosimian primates of the family *Lorisidae,* of S and SE Asia, esp. *Loris tardigradus* (**slow loris**) and *Nycticebus coucang* (**slender loris**), having vestigial digits and no tails. **[C18:** from French; of uncertain origin**]**

lorn (lɔːn) *adj Poetic.* forsaken or wretched. **[**Old English *loren,* past participle of *-lēosan* to lose**]** ▶ **ˈlornness** *n*

Lorrain (*French* lɔrɛ̃) *n* See **Claude Lorrain.**

Lorraine (lɒˈreɪn; *French* lɔrɛn) *n* **1** a region and former province of E France; ceded to Germany in 1871 after the Franco-Prussian war and regained by France in 1919; rich iron-ore deposits. German name: **Lothringen. 2 Kingdom of.** an early medieval kingdom on the Meuse, Moselle, and Rhine rivers: later a duchy. **3** a former duchy in E France, once the S half of this kingdom.

Lorraine cross *n* See **cross of Lorraine.**

Lorris (*French* lɔris) *n* See **Guillaume de Lorris.**

lorry (ˈlɒrɪ) *n, pl* **-ries. 1** a large motor vehicle designed to carry heavy loads, esp. one with a flat platform. U.S. and Canadian name: **truck.** See also **articulated lorry. 2 off the back of a lorry.** *Brit. informal.* a phrase used humorously to imply that something has been dishonestly acquired: *it fell off the back of a lorry.* **3** any of various vehicles with a flat load-carrying surface, esp. one designed to run on rails. **[C19:** perhaps related to northern English dialect *lurry* to pull, tug**]**

lory (ˈlɔːrɪ) *n, pl* **-ries.** any of various small brightly coloured parrots of Australia and Indonesia, having a brush-tipped tongue with which to feed on nectar and pollen. **[C17:** via Dutch from Malay *lūrī,* variant of *nūrī***]**

Los Alamos (lɒs ˈæləmɒs) *n* a town in the U.S., in New Mexico: the first atomic bomb was developed here. Pop.: 11 455 (1990).

los Angeles (*Spanish* los ˈaŋxeles) *n* See (Victoria) **de los Angeles.**

Los Angeles (lɒs ˈændʒɪˌliːz) *n* a city in SW California, on the Pacific: the second largest city in the U.S., having absorbed many adjacent townships; industrial centre and port, with several universities. Pop.: 3 553 638 (1996 est.). Abbrev.: **LA.**

lose (luːz) *vb* **loses, losing, lost.** (*mainly tr*) **1** to part with or come to be without, as through theft, accident, negligence, etc. **2** to fail to keep or maintain: *to lose one's balance.* **3** to suffer the loss or deprivation of: *to lose a parent.* **4** to cease to have or possess. **5** to fail to get or make use of: *to lose a chance.* **6** (*also intr*) to fail to gain or win (a contest, game, etc.): *to lose the match.* **7** to fail to see, hear, perceive, or understand: *I lost the gist of his speech.* **8** to waste: *to lose money gambling.* **9** to wander from so as to be unable to find: *to lose one's way.* **10** to cause the loss of: *his delay lost him the battle.* **11** to allow to go astray or out of sight: *we lost him in the crowd.* **12** (*usually passive*) to absorb or engross: *he was lost in contemplation.* **13** (*usually passive*) to cause the death or destruction of: *two men were lost in the attack.* **14** to outdistance or elude: *he soon lost his pursuers.* **15** (*intr*) to decrease or depreciate in value or effectiveness: *poetry always loses in translation.* **16** (*also intr*) (of a timepiece) to run slow (by a specified amount): *the clock loses ten minutes every day.* **17** (of a physician) to fail to sustain the life of (a patient). **18** (of a woman) to fail to give birth to (a viable baby), esp. as the result of a miscarriage. **19** *Motor racing slang.* to lose control of (the car), as on a bend: *he lost it going into Woodcote.* **[**Old English *losian* to perish; related to Old English *-lēosan* as in *forlēosan* to forfeit. Compare LOOSE**]** ▶ **ˈlosable** *adj* ▶ **ˈlosableness** *n*

losel (ˈləʊzᵊl) *Archaic or dialect.* ◆ *n* **1** a worthless person. ◆ *adj* **2** (of a person) worthless, useless, or wasteful. **[C14:** from *losen,* from the past participle of LOSE**]**

lose out *vb Informal.* **1** (*intr, adv*) to be defeated or unsuccessful. **2 lose out on.** to fail to secure or make use of: *we lost out on the sale.*

loser (ˈluːzə) *n* **1** a person or thing that loses. **2** a person or thing that seems destined to be taken advantage of, fail, etc.: *a born loser.* **3** *Bridge.* a card that will not take a trick.

Losey (ˈləʊsɪ) *n* **Joseph.** 1909–84, U.S. film director, in Britain from 1952. His films include *The Servant* (1963), *Accident* (1967), *Secret Ceremony* (1968), and *The Go-Between* (1971).

losing (ˈluːzɪŋ) *adj* unprofitable; failing: *the business was a losing concern.*

losings (ˈluːzɪŋz) *pl n* losses, esp. money lost in gambling.

loss (lɒs) *n* **1** the act or an instance of losing. **2** the disadvantage or deprivation resulting from losing: *a loss of reputation.* **3** the person, thing, or amount lost: *a large loss.* **4** (*pl*) military personnel lost by death or capture. **5** (*sometimes pl*) the amount by which the costs of a business transaction or operation exceed its revenue. **6** a measure of the power lost in an electrical system expressed as the ratio of or difference between the input power and the output power. **7** *Insurance.* **7a** an occurrence of something that has been insured against, thus giving rise to a claim by a policyholder. **7b** the amount of the resulting claim. **8 at a loss. 8a** uncertain what to do; bewildered. **8b** rendered helpless (for lack of something): *at a loss for words.* **8c** at less than the cost of buying, producing, or maintaining (something): *the business ran at a loss for several years.* **[C14:** noun probably formed from *lost,* past participle of *losen* to perish, from Old English *lōsian* to be destroyed, from *los* destruction**]**

loss adjuster *n Insurance.* a person qualified to adjust losses incurred through fire, explosion, accident, theft, natural disaster, etc., to agree the loss and the compensation to be paid.

loss leader *n* an article offered below cost in the hope that customers attracted by it will buy other goods.

lossmaker (ˈlɒsˌmeɪkə) *n Brit.* an organization, industry, or enterprise that consistently fails to make a profit. ▶ **ˈlossˌmaking** *adj*

loss ratio *n* the ratio of the annual losses sustained to the premiums received by an insurance company.

lossy (ˈlɒsɪ) *adj* (of a dielectric material, transmission line, etc.) designed to have a high attenuation; dissipating energy: *lossy line.* **[C20:** from LOSS**]**

lost (lɒst) *adj* **1** unable to be found or recovered. **2** unable to find one's way or ascertain one's whereabouts. **3** confused, bewildered, or helpless: *he is lost in discussions of theory.* **4** (sometimes foll. by *on*) not utilized, noticed, or taken advantage of (by): *rational arguments are lost on her.* **5** no longer possessed or existing because of defeat, misfortune, or the passage of time: *a lost art.* **6** destroyed physically: *the lost platoon.* **7** (foll. by *to*) no longer available or open (to). **8** (foll. by *to*) insensible or impervious (to a sense of shame, justice, etc.). **9** (foll. by *in*) engrossed (in): *he was lost in his book.* **10** morally fallen: *a lost woman.* **11** damned: *a lost soul.* **12 get lost.** (*usually imperative*) *Informal.* go away and stay away.

lost cause *n* a cause with no chance of success.

Lost Generation *n* (*sometimes not caps.*) **1** the large number of talented young men killed in World War I. **2** the generation of writers, esp. American authors such as Scott Fitzgerald and Hemingway, active after World War I.

lost tribes *pl n* **the.** *Old Testament.* the ten tribes deported from the N kingdom of Israel in 721 B.C. and believed never to have returned to Palestine.

lot (lɒt) *pron* **1** (*functioning as sing or pl;* preceded by *a*) a great number or quantity: *a lot to do; a lot of people; a lot of trouble.* ◆ *n* **2** a collection of objects, items, or people: *a nice lot of youngsters.* **3** portion in life; destiny; fortune: *it falls to my lot to be poor.* **4** any object, such as a straw or slip of paper, drawn from others at random to make a selection or choice (esp. in the phrase **draw** *or* **cast lots**). **5** the use of lots in making a selection or choice (esp. in the phrase **by lot**). **6** an assigned or apportioned share. **7** an item or set of items for sale in an auction. **8** *Chiefly U.S. and Canadian.* an area of land: *a parking lot.* **9** *U.S. and Canadian.* a piece of land with fixed boundaries. **10** *Chiefly U.S. and Canadian.* a film studio and the site on which it is located. **11 a bad lot.** an unpleasant or disreputable person. **12 cast** *or* **throw in one's lot with.** to join with voluntarily and share the fortunes of. **13 the lot.** the entire amount or number. ◆ *adv* (preceded by *a*) *Informal.* **14** to a considerable extent, degree, or amount; very much: *to delay a lot.* **15** a great deal of the time or often: *to sing madrigals a lot.* ◆ *vb* **lots, lotting, lotted. 16** to draw lots for (something). **17** (*tr*) to divide (land, etc.) into lots. **18** (*tr*) another word for **allot.** ◆ See also **lots.** [Old English *hlot;* related to Old High German *lug* portion of land, Old Norse *hlutr* lot, share]

Lot[1] (lɒt) *n* **1** a department of S central France, in Midi-Pyrénées region. Capital: Cahors. Pop.: 157 000 (1995). Area: 5226 sq. km (2038 sq. miles). **2** a river in S France, rising in the Cevennes and flowing west into the Garonne River. Length: about 483 km (300 miles).

Lot[2] (lɒt) *n Old Testament.* Abraham's nephew: he escaped the destruction of Sodom, but his wife was changed into a pillar of salt for looking back as they fled (Genesis 19).

lota *or* **lotah** ('ləutə) *n* a globular water container, usually of brass, used in India, Myanmar, etc. [C19: from Hindi *lotā*]

Lot-et-Garonne (*French* lɔtegarɔn) *n* a department of SW France, in Aquitaine. Capital: Agen. Pop.: 303 600 (1995). Area: 5385 sq. km (2100 sq. miles).

loth (ləuθ) *adj* a variant spelling of **loath.** ▸ **'lothness** *n*

Lothair I (ləu'θɛə) *n* ?795–855 A.D., Frankish ruler and Holy Roman Emperor (823–30, 833–34, 840–55); son of Louis I, whom he twice deposed from the throne.

Lothair II *n* called *the Saxon.* ?1070–1137, German king (1125–37) and Holy Roman Emperor (1133–37). He was elected German king over the hereditary Hohenstaufen claimant.

Lothario (ləu'θɑːrɪ,əu) *n, pl* **-os.** (*sometimes not cap.*) a rake, libertine, or seducer. [C18: after a seducer in Nicholas Rowe's tragedy *The Fair Penitent* (1703)]

Lothian Region ('ləuðɪən) *n* a former local government region in SE central Scotland, formed in 1975 from East Lothian, most of Midlothian, and West Lothian; replaced in 1996 by the council areas of East Lothian, Midlothian, West Lothian, and Edinburgh.

Lothians ('ləuðɪənz) *pl n* **the.** three historic counties of SE central Scotland (now council areas): East Lothian, West Lothian, and Midlothian (including Edinburgh).

Lothringen ('loːtrɪŋən) *n* the German name for **Lorraine.**

loti ('ləutɪ, 'luːtɪ) *n, pl* **maloti** (mə'ləutɪ, -'luːtɪ). the standard monetary unit of Lesotho, divided into 100 lisente.

lotic ('ləutɪk) *adj Ecology.* of, relating to, or designating natural communities living in rapidly flowing water. Compare **lentic** [C20: from Latin *lotus,* a past participle of *lavāre* to wash]

lotion ('ləuʃən) *n* a liquid preparation having a soothing, cleansing, or antiseptic action, applied to the skin, eyes, etc. [C14: via Old French from Latin *lōtiō* a washing, from *lōtus* past participle of *lavāre* to wash]

lots (lɒts) *Informal.* ◆ *pl n* **1** (often foll. by *of*) great numbers or quantities: *lots of people; to eat lots.* ◆ *adv* **2** a great deal. **3** (intensifier): *the journey is lots quicker by train.*

lottery ('lɒtərɪ) *n, pl* **-teries. 1** a game of chance in which tickets are sold, one or more of which may later qualify the holder for a prize. **2** an activity or endeavour the success of which is regarded as a matter of fate or luck. [C16: from Old French *loterie,* from Middle Dutch *loterije.* See LOT]

lotto ('lɒtəu) *n* **1** Also called: **housey-housey.** a children's game in which numbered discs, counters, etc., are drawn at random and called out, while the players cover the corresponding numbers on cards, the winner being the first to cover all the numbers, a particular row, etc. Compare **bingo. 2** *Austral.* a lottery with cash prizes based on this principle. [C18: from Italian, from Old French *lot,* from Germanic. See LOT]

lotus ('ləutəs) *n* **1** (in Greek mythology) a fruit that induces forgetfulness and a dreamy languor in those who eat it. **2** the plant bearing this fruit, thought to be the date, the jujube, or any of various other plants. **3** any of several water lilies of tropical Africa and Asia, esp. the **white lotus** (*Nymphaea lotus*), which was regarded as sacred in ancient Egypt. **4** a related plant, *Nelumbo nucifera,* which is the sacred lotus of India, China, and Tibet: family *Nelumbonaceae.* **5** a representation of such a plant, common in Hindu, Buddhist, and ancient Egyptian carving and decorative art. **6** any leguminous plant of the genus *Lotus,* of the Old World and North America, having yellow, pink, or white pealike flowers. ◆ Also called (rare): **lotos.** [C16: via Latin from Greek *lōtos,* from Semitic; related to Hebrew *lōt* myrrh]

lotus-eater *n Greek myth.* one of a people encountered by Odysseus in North Africa who lived in indolent forgetfulness, drugged by the fruit of the legendary lotus.

lotus position *n* a seated cross-legged position used in yoga, meditation, etc.

Lotus Sutra *n* a central scripture of Mahayana Buddhism, emphasizing that anyone can attain enlightenment.

lou *or* **loo** (luː) *vb* a Scot. word for **love.**

louche (luːʃ) *adj* shifty or disreputable. [C19: from French, literally: squinting]

loud (laud) *adj* **1** (of sound) relatively great in volume: *a loud shout.* **2** making or able to make sounds of relatively great volume: *a loud voice.* **3** clamorous, insistent, and emphatic: *loud protests.* **4** (of colours, designs, etc.) offensive or obtrusive to look at. **5** characterized by noisy, vulgar, and offensive behaviour. ◆ *adv* **6** in a loud manner. **7 out loud.** audibly, as distinct from silently. [Old English *hlud;* related to Old Swedish *hlūd,* German *laut*] ▸ **'loudly** *adv* ▸ **'loudness** *n*

louden ('laudən) *vb* to make or become louder.

loud-hailer *n* a portable loudspeaker having a built-in amplifier and microphone. Also called (U.S. and Canadian): **bullhorn.**

loudish ('laudɪʃ) *adj* fairly loud; somewhat loud.

loudmouth ('laud,mauθ) *n Informal.* **1** a person who brags or talks too loudly. **2** a person who is gossipy or tactless. ▸ **loudmouthed** ('laud,mauðd, -,mauθt) *adj*

loudspeaker (,laud'spiːkə) *n* a device for converting audio-frequency signals into the equivalent sound waves by means of a vibrating conical diaphragm. Sometimes shortened to **speaker.** Also called: **reproducer.**

loudspeaker van *n* a motor vehicle carrying a public address system. U.S. and Canadian name: **sound truck.**

Lou Gehrig's disease (luː 'gɛrɪg) *n* another name for **amyotrophic lateral sclerosis.** [C20: named after *Lou Gehrig* (1903–41), U.S. baseball player who suffered from it]

lough (lɒx, lɒk) *n* **1** an Irish word for **lake**[1]. **2** a long narrow bay or arm of the sea in Ireland. ◆ Compare **loch.** [C14: from Irish *loch* lake]

Loughborough ('lʌfbərə, -brə) *n* a town in central England, in N Leicestershire: university (1966). Pop.: 46 867 (1991).

louis ('luːɪ; *French* lwi) *n, pl* **louis** ('luːɪz; *French* lwi). short for **louis d'or.**

Louis ('luːɪs) *n* **Joe,** real name *Joseph Louis Barrow,* nicknamed *the Brown Bomber.* 1914–81, U.S. boxer; world heavyweight champion (1937–49).

Louis I ('luːɪ; *French* lwi) *n* known as *Louis the Pious* or *Louis the Debonair.* 778–840 A.D., king of France and Holy Roman Emperor (814–23, 830–33, 834–40): he was twice deposed by his sons.

Louis II *n* **1** known as *Louis the German.* ?804–876 A.D., king of Germany (843–76); son of Louis I. **2** 1845–86, king of Bavaria (1864–86): noted for his extravagant castles and his patronage of Wagner. Declared insane (1886), he drowned himself. **3 de Bourbon.** See (Prince de) **Condé.**

Louis IV *n* known as *Louis the Bavarian.* ?1287–1347, king of Germany (1314–47) and Holy Roman Emperor (1328–47).

Louis V *n* known as *Louis le Fainéant.* ?967–987 A.D., last Carolingian king of France (986–87).

Louis VII *n* known as *Louis le Jeune. c.* 1120–80, king of France (1137–80). He engaged in frequent hostilities (1152–74) with Henry II of England.

Louis VIII *n* known as *Coeur-de-Lion.* 1187–1226, king of France (1223–26). He was offered the English throne by opponents of King John but his invasion failed (1216).

Louis IX *n* known as *Saint Louis.* 1214–70, king of France (1226–70): led the Sixth Crusade (1248–54) and was held to ransom (1250); died at Tunis while on another crusade.

Louis XI *n* 1423–83, king of France (1461–83); involved in a struggle with his vassals, esp. the duke of Burgundy, in his attempt to unite France under an absolute monarchy.

Louis XII *n* 1462–1515, king of France (1498–1515), who fought a series of unsuccessful wars in Italy.

Louis XIII *n* 1601–43, king of France (1610–43). His mother (Marie de Médicis) was regent until 1617; after 1624 he was influenced by his chief minister Richelieu.

Louis XIV *n* known as *le roi soleil* (the Sun King). 1638–1715, king of France (1643–1715); son of Louis XIII and Anne of Austria. Effective ruler from 1661, he established an absolute monarchy. His attempt to establish French supremacy in Europe, waging almost continual wars from 1667 to 1714, ultimately failed. But his reign is regarded as a golden age of French literature and art.

Louis XV *n* 1710–74, king of France (1715–74); great-grandson of Louis XIV. He engaged France in a series of wars, esp. the disastrous Seven Years' War (1756–63), which undermined the solvency and authority of the crown.

Louis XVI *n* 1754–93, king of France (1774–92); grandson of Louis XV. He married Marie Antoinette in 1770 and they were guillotined during the French Revolution.

Louis XVII *n* 1785–95, titular king of France (1793–95) during the Revolution, after the execution of his father Louis XVI; he died in prison.

Louis XVIII *n* 1755–1824, king of France (1814–24); younger brother of Louis XVI. He became titular king after the death of Louis XVII (1795) and ascended the throne at the Bourbon restoration in 1814. He was forced to flee during the Hundred Days.

Louisbourg ('luːɪs,bɜːg) *n* a fortress in Canada, in Nova Scotia on SE Cape Breton Island: founded in 1713 by the French and strongly fortified (1720–40); captured by the British (1758) and demolished; reconstructed as a historic site.

louis d'or (,luːɪ 'dɔː; *French* lwi dɔr) *n, pl* **louis d'or** (,luːɪz 'dɔː; *French* lwi dɔr). **1** a former French gold coin worth 20 francs. **2** an old French coin minted in the reign of Louis XIII. ◆ Often shortened to **louis.** [C17: from French: golden louis, named after Louis XIII]

Louisiana (luː,iːzɪ'ænə) *n* a state of the southern U.S., on the Gulf of Mexico:

originally a French colony; bought by the U.S. in 1803 as part of the Louisiana Purchase; chiefly low-lying. Capital: Baton Rouge. Pop.: 4 351 769 (1997 est.). Area: 116 368 sq. km (44 930 sq. miles). Abbrevs.: **La.** or (with zip code) **LA**

Louisiana Purchase *n* the large region of North America sold by Napoleon I to the U.S. in 1803 for 15 million dollars: consists of the W part of the Mississippi basin. Area: about 2 292 150 sq. km (885 000 sq. miles).

Louis Napoleon *n* the original name of **Napoleon III.**

Louis of Nassau *n* 1538–74, a leader (1568–74) of the revolt of the Netherlands against Spain: died in battle.

Louis Philippe (*French* filip) *n* known as the *Citizen King.* 1773–1850, king of the French (1830–48). His régime became excessively identified with the bourgeoisie and he was forced to abdicate by the revolution of 1848.

Louis Quatorze (kəˈtɔːz) *adj* of or relating to the baroque style of furniture, decoration, and architecture of the time of Louis XIV of France and characterized by massive forms and heavy ornamentation.

Louis Quinze (kænz) *adj* of or relating to the rococo style of the furniture, decoration, and architecture of the time of Louis XV of France.

Louis Seize (sɛz) *adj* of or relating to the style of furniture, decoration, and architecture of the time of Louis XVI of France, belonging to the late French rococo and early neoclassicism.

Louis Treize (trɛz) *adj* of or relating to the style of furniture, decoration, and architecture of the time of Louis XIII of France, with rich decorative features based on classical models.

Louisville (ˈluːɪˌvɪl) *n* a port in N Kentucky, on the Ohio River: site of the annual Kentucky Derby; university (1837). Pop.: 260 689 (1996 est.).

lounge (laʊndʒ) *vb* **1** (*intr;* often foll. by *about* or *around*) to sit, lie, walk, or stand in a relaxed manner. **2** to pass (time) lazily or idly. ◆ *n* **3a** a communal room in a hotel, ship, theatre, etc., used for waiting or relaxing in. **3b** (*as modifier*): *lounge chair.* **4** *Chiefly Brit.* a living room in a private house. **5** Also called: **lounge bar, saloon bar.** *Brit.* a more expensive bar in a pub or hotel. **6** *Chiefly U.S. and Canadian.* **6a** an expensive bar, esp. in a hotel. **6b** short for **cocktail lounge. 7** a sofa or couch, esp. one with a headrest and no back. **8** the act or an instance of lounging. [C16: origin unknown]

lounge lizard *n Informal.* an idle frequenter of places where rich or prominent people gather.

lounger (ˈlaʊndʒə) *n* **1** a comfortable sometimes adjustable couch or extending chair designed for someone to relax on. **2** a loose comfortable leisure garment. **3** a person who lounges.

lounge suit *n* the customary suit of matching jacket and trousers worn by men for the normal business day.

loup[1] (luː) *n* another name for **loo mask.** [C19: from French, from Latin *lupus* wolf]

loup[2] *or* **lowp** (laʊp) *vb, n* a Scot. word for **leap.**

loupe (luːp) *n* a magnifying glass used by jewellers, horologists, etc. [C20: from French (formerly an imperfect precious stone), from Old French, of obscure origin]

louping ill (ˈlaʊpɪŋ, ˈləʊ-) *n* a viral disease of sheep causing muscular twitching and partial paralysis: caused by the bite of an infected tick (*Ixodes ricinus*). [C18 *louping,* from LOUP[2]]

lour *or* **lower** (laʊə) *vb* (*intr*) **1** (esp. of the sky, weather, etc.) to be overcast, dark, and menacing. **2** to scowl or frown. ◆ *n* **3** a menacing scowl or appearance. [C13 *louren* to scowl; compare German *lauern* to lurk] ▸ **ˈlouring** *or* **ˈlowering** *adj* ▸ **ˈlouringly** *or* **ˈloweringly** *adv*

Lourdes (*French* lurd) *n* a town in SW France: a leading place of pilgrimage for Roman Catholics after a peasant girl, Bernadette Soubirous, had visions of the Virgin Mary in 1858. Pop.: 17 100 (1995 est.).

Lourenço Marques (ləˈrɛnsəʊ ˈmɑːk, ˈmɑːks; *Portuguese* loˈrẽsu ˈmarkɪʃ) *n* the former name (until 1975) of **Maputo.**

lourie *or* **loerie** (ˈlaʊrɪ) *n S. African.* any of several species of touraco: louries are divided into two groups, the arboreal species having a mainly green plumage and crimson wings and the species which inhabits the more open savanna areas having a plain grey plumage. [from Malay *luri*]

louse (laʊs) *n, pl* **lice** (laɪs). **1** any wingless bloodsucking insect of the order *Anoplura:* includes *Pediculus capitis* (**head louse**), *Pediculus corporis* (**body louse**), and the crab louse, all of which infest man. Related adj: **pedicular. 2 biting** *or* **bird louse.** any wingless insect of the order *Mallophaga,* such as the chicken louse: external parasites of birds and mammals with biting mouthparts. **3** any of various similar but unrelated insects, such as the plant louse and book louse. **4** *pl* **louses.** *Slang.* an unpleasant or mean person. ◆ *vb* (*tr*) **5** to remove lice from. **6** (foll. by *up*) *Slang.* to ruin or spoil. [Old English *lūs;* related to Old High German, Old Norse *lūs*]

louser (ˈlauzər) *n Irish slang.* a mean nasty person. [C20: from *louse* (*up*) + -ER[1]]

lousewort (ˈlaʊsˌwɜːt) *n* any of various N temperate scrophulariaceous plants of the genus *Pedicularis,* having spikes of white, yellow, or mauve flowers. See also **betony** (sense 3).

lousy (ˈlaʊzɪ) *adj* **lousier, lousiest. 1** *Slang.* very mean or unpleasant: *a lousy thing to do.* **2** *Slang.* inferior or bad: *this is a lousy film.* **3** infested with lice. **4** (foll. by *with*) *Slang.* **4a** provided with an excessive amount (of): *he's lousy with money.* **4b** full of or teeming with. ▸ **ˈlousily** *adv* ▸ **ˈlousiness** *n*

lout[1] (laʊt) *n* a crude or oafish person; boor. [C16: perhaps from LOUT[2]]

lout[2] (laʊt) *vb* (*intr*) *Archaic.* to bow or stoop. [Old English *lūtan;* related to Old Norse *lūta*]

Louth (laʊθ) *n* a county of NE Republic of Ireland, in Leinster province on the Irish Sea: the smallest of the counties. County town: Dundalk. Pop.: 92 000 (1996). Area: 821 sq. km (317 sq. miles).

loutish (ˈlaʊtɪʃ) *adj* characteristic of a lout; unpleasant and uncouth. ▸ **ˈloutishly** *adv* ▸ **ˈloutishness** *n*

Louvain (*French* luvɛ̃) *n* a town in central Belgium, in Flemish Brabant province: capital of the duchy of Brabant (11th–15th centuries) and centre of the cloth trade; university (1426). Pop.: 87 165 (1995 est.). Flemish name: **Leuven.**

louvar (ˈluːvɑː) *n* a large silvery whalelike scombroid fish, *Luvarus imperialis,* that occurs in most tropical and temperate seas and feeds on plankton: family *Luvaridae.* [from Italian (Calabrian and Sicilian dialect) *lùvaru,* perhaps from Latin *ruber* red]

louvre *or U.S.* **louver** (ˈluːvə) *n* **1a** any of a set of horizontal parallel slats in a door or window, sloping outwards to throw off rain and admit air. **1b** Also called: **louvre boards.** the slats together with the frame supporting them. **2** *Architect.* a lantern or turret that allows smoke to escape. [C14: from Old French *lovier,* of obscure origin]

Louvre (*French* luvrə) *n* the national museum and art gallery of France, in Paris: formerly a royal palace, begun in 1546; used for its present purpose since 1793.

louvred *or U.S.* **louvered** (ˈluːvəd) *adj* (of a window, door, etc.) having louvres.

lovable *or* **loveable** (ˈlʌvəbᵊl) *adj* attracting or deserving affection. ▸ **ˌlovaˈbility, ˌloveaˈbility** *or* **ˈlovableness, ˈloveableness** *n* ▸ **ˈlovably** *or* **ˈloveably** *adv*

lovage (ˈlʌvɪdʒ) *n* **1** a European umbelliferous plant, *Levisticum officinale,* with greenish-white flowers and aromatic fruits, which are used for flavouring food. **2** a similar and related plant, *Ligusticum scoticum,* of N Europe. [C14 *loveache,* from Old French *luvesche,* from Late Latin *levisticum,* from Latin *ligusticum,* literally: Ligurian (plant)]

lovat (ˈlʌvət) *n* a yellowish-green or bluish-green mixture, esp. in tweeds or woollens. [named after *Lovat,* Inverness-shire]

love (lʌv) *vb* **1** (*tr*) to have a great attachment to and affection for. **2** (*tr*) to have passionate desire, longing, and feelings for. **3** (*tr*) to like or desire (to do something) very much. **4** (*tr*) to make love to. **5** (*intr*) to be in love. ◆ *n* **6a** an intense emotion of affection, warmth, fondness, and regard towards a person or thing. **6b** (*as modifier*): *love song; love story.* **7** a deep feeling of sexual attraction and desire. **8** wholehearted liking for or pleasure in something. **9** *Christianity.* **9a** God's benevolent attitude towards man. **9b** man's attitude of reverent devotion towards God. **10** Also: **my love.** a beloved person: used esp. as an endearment. **11** *Brit. informal.* a term of address, esp. but not necessarily for a person regarded as likable. **12** (in tennis, squash, etc.) a score of zero. **13 fall in love.** to become in love. **14 for love.** without payment. **15 for love or money.** (*used with a negative*) in any circumstances: *I wouldn't eat a snail for love or money.* **16 for the love of.** for the sake of. **17 in love.** in a state of strong emotional attachment and usually sexual attraction. **18 make love** (**to**). **18a** to have sexual intercourse (with). **18b** *Now archaic.* to engage in courtship (with). ◆ Related adj: **amatory.** [Old English *lufu;* related to Old High German *luba;* compare also Latin *libēre* (originally *lubēre*) to please]

love affair *n* **1** a romantic or sexual relationship, esp. a temporary one, between two people. **2** a great enthusiasm or liking for something: *a love affair with ballet.*

love apple *n* an archaic name for **tomato.**

lovebird (ˈlʌvˌbɜːd) *n* **1** any of several small African parrots of the genus *Agapornis,* often kept as cage birds. **2** another name for **budgerigar. 3** *Informal.* a lover: *the lovebirds are in the garden.*

lovebite (ˈlʌvˌbaɪt) *n* a temporary red mark left on a person's skin by a partner's biting or sucking it during lovemaking.

love child *n Euphemistic.* an illegitimate child; bastard.

love feast *n* **1** Also called: **agape.** (among the early Christians) a religious meal eaten with others as a sign of mutual love and fellowship. **2** a ritual meal modelled upon this.

love game *n Tennis.* a game in which the loser has a score of zero.

love handles *pl n Informal.* folds of excess fat on either side of the waist.

love-in-a-mist *n* an erect S European ranunculaceous plant, *Nigella damascena,* cultivated as a garden plant, having finely cut leaves and white or pale blue flowers. See also **fennelflower.**

love-in-idleness *n* another name for the **wild pansy.**

love knot *n* a stylized bow, usually of ribbon, symbolizing the bond between two lovers. Also called: **lover's knot.**

Lovelace (ˈlʌvˌleɪs) *n* **1 Countess of,** title of *Ada Augusta King.* 1815–52, English mathematician and personal assistant to Charles Babbage: daughter of Lord Byron. She wrote the first computer program. **2 Richard.** 1618–58, English Cavalier poet, noted for *To Althea from Prison* (1642) and *Lucasta* (1649).

loveless (ˈlʌvlɪs) *adj* **1** without love: *a loveless marriage.* **2** receiving or giving no love. ▸ **ˈlovelessly** *adv* ▸ **ˈlovelessness** *n*

love letter *n* **1** a letter or note written by someone to his or her sweetheart or lover. **2** (in Malaysia) a type of biscuit, made from eggs and rice flour and rolled into a cylinder.

love-lies-bleeding *n* any of several amaranthaceous plants of the genus *Amaranthus,* esp. *A. caudatus,* having drooping spikes of small red flowers.

love life *n* the part of a person's life consisting of his or her sexual relationships.

Lovell (ˈlʌvəl) *n* Sir **Bernard.** born 1913, English radio astronomer; founder (1951) and director of Jodrell Bank.

lovelock (ˈlʌvˌlɒk) *n* a long lock of hair worn on the forehead.

lovelorn (ˈlʌvˌlɔːn) *adj* miserable because of unrequited love or unhappiness in love. ▸ **ˈloveˌlornness** *n*

lovely (ˈlʌvlɪ) *adj* **-lier, -liest. 1** very attractive or beautiful. **2** highly pleasing or enjoyable: *a lovely time.* **3** loving and attentive. **4** inspiring love; lovable. ◆ *n, pl* **-lies. 5** *Slang.* a lovely woman. ▸ **ˈloveliness** *n*

lovemaking (ˈlʌvˌmeɪkɪŋ) *n* **1** sexual play and activity between lovers, esp. including sexual intercourse. **2** an archaic word for **courtship.**

love match *n* a betrothal or marriage based on mutual love rather than any other considerations.

love nest *n* a place suitable for or used for making love.

love potion *n* any drink supposed to arouse sexual love in the one who drinks it.

lover ('lʌvə) *n* **1** a person, now esp. a man, who has an extramarital or premarital sexual relationship with another person. **2** (*often pl*) either of the two people involved in a love affair. **3a** someone who loves a specified person or thing: *a lover of music.* **3b** (*in combination*): *a music-lover; a cat-lover.*

love seat *n* a small upholstered sofa for two people.

love set *n Tennis.* a set in which the loser has a score of zero.

lovesick ('lʌvˌsɪk) *adj* pining or languishing because of love. ▸ **'loveˌsickness** *n*

lovey ('lʌvɪ) *n Brit. informal.* another word for **love** (sense 11).

lovey-dovey *adj* making an excessive or ostentatious display of affection.

loving ('lʌvɪŋ) *adj* feeling, showing, or indicating love and affection. ▸ **'lovingly** *adv* ▸ **'lovingness** *n*

loving cup *n* **1** a large vessel, usually two-handled, out of which people drink in turn at a banquet. **2** a similar cup awarded to the winner of a competition.

low[1] (ləʊ) *adj* **1** having a relatively small distance from base to top; not tall or high: *a low hill; a low building.* **2a** situated at a relatively short distance above the ground, sea level, the horizon, or other reference position: *low cloud.* **2b** (*in combination*): *low-lying.* **3a** involving or containing a relatively small amount of something: *a low supply.* **3b** (*in combination*): *low-pressure.* **4a** having little value or quality. **4b** (*in combination*): *low-grade.* **5** of less than the usual or expected height, depth, or degree: *low temperature.* **6a** (of numbers) small. **6b** (of measurements) expressed in small numbers. **7** unfavourable: *a low opinion.* **8** not advanced in evolution: *a low form of plant life.* **9** deep: *a low obeisance.* **10** coarse or vulgar: *a low conversation.* **11a** inferior in culture or status. **11b** (*in combination*): *low-class.* **12** in a physically or mentally depressed or weakened state. **13** designed so as to reveal the wearer's neck and part of the bosom: *a low neckline.* **14** with a hushed tone; quiet or soft: *a low whisper.* **15** of relatively small price or monetary value: *low cost.* **16** *Music.* relating to or characterized by a relatively low pitch. **17** (of latitudes) situated not far north or south of the equator. **18** having little or no money. **19** abject or servile. **20** *Phonetics.* of, relating to, or denoting a vowel whose articulation is produced by moving the back of the tongue away from the soft palate or the blade away from the hard palate, such as for the *a* in English *father.* Compare **high** (sense 22). **21** (of a gear) providing a relatively low forward speed for a given engine speed. **22** (*usually cap.*) of or relating to the Low Church. ◆ *adv* **23** in a low position, level, degree, intensity, etc.: *to bring someone low.* **24** at a low pitch; deep: *to sing low.* **25** at a low price; cheaply: *to buy low.* **26 lay low. 26a** to cause to fall by a blow. **26b** to overcome, defeat or destroy. **27 lie low. 27a** to keep or be concealed or quiet. **27b** to wait for a favourable opportunity. ◆ *n* **28** a low position, level, or degree: *an all-time low.* **29** an area of relatively low atmospheric pressure, esp. a depression. **30** *Electronics.* the voltage level in a logic circuit corresponding to logical zero. Compare **high** (sense 40). [C12 *lāh,* from Old Norse *lāgr;* related to Old Frisian *lēch* low, Dutch *laag*] ▸ **'lowness** *n*

low[2] (ləʊ) *n also* **lowing. 1** the sound uttered by cattle; moo. ◆ *vb* **2** to make or express by a low or moo. [Old English *hlōwan;* related to Dutch *loeien,* Old Saxon *hlōian*]

Low (ləʊ) *n* Sir **David.** 1891–1963, British political cartoonist, born in New Zealand: created Colonel Blimp. See **blimp**[2].

low-alcohol *adj* (of beer or wine) containing only a small amount of alcohol. Compare **alcohol-free.**

lowan ('ləʊən) *n Austral.* another name for **mallee fowl.**

Low Archipelago *n* another name for the **Tuamotu Archipelago.**

lowborn (ˌləʊ'bɔːn) *or* **lowbred** (ˌləʊ'brɛd) *adj Now rare.* of ignoble or common parentage; not royal or noble.

lowboy ('ləʊˌbɔɪ) *n U.S. and Canadian.* a table fitted with drawers.

lowbrow ('ləʊˌbraʊ) *Disparaging.* ◆ *n* **1** a person who has uncultivated or nonintellectual tastes. ◆ *adj also* **lowbrowed. 2** of or characteristic of such a person. ▸ **'lowˌbrowism** *n*

low camp *n* an unsophisticated form of **camp** (the style).

low-carbon steel *n Engineering.* steel containing between 0.04 and 0.25 per cent carbon.

Low Church *n* **1** the school of thought in the Church of England stressing evangelical beliefs and practices. Compare **Broad Church, High Church.** ◆ *adj* **Low-Church. 2** of or relating to this school. ▸ **ˌLow-'Churchman** *n*

low comedy *n* comedy characterized by slapstick and physical action. ▸ **low comedian** *n*

Low Countries *pl n* the lowland region of W Europe, on the North Sea: consists of Belgium, Luxembourg, and the Netherlands.

low-density lipoprotein *n* a lipoprotein that is the form in which cholesterol is transported in the bloodstream to the cells and tissues of the body. High levels of low-density lipoprotein in the blood are associated with atheroma. Abbrev.: **LDL.**

low-down *Informal.* ◆ *adj* **1** mean, underhand, or despicable. ◆ *n* **lowdown. 2** information, esp. secret or true information.

Löwe (*German* 'løːvə) *n* See (Karl) **Loewe.**

Lowell ('ləʊəl) *n* **1 Amy (Lawrence).** 1874–1925, U.S. imagist poet and critic. **2 James Russell.** 1819–91, U.S. poet, essayist, and diplomat, noted for his series of poems in Yankee dialect, *Biglow Papers* (1848; 1867). **3 Robert (Traill Spence).** 1917–77, U.S. poet. His volumes of verse include *Lord Weary's Castle* (1946), *Life Studies* (1959), *For the Union Dead* (1964), and a book of free translations of European poems, *Imitations* (1961).

lower[1] ('ləʊə) *adj* **1** being below one or more other things: *the lower shelf; the lower animals.* **2** reduced in amount or value: *a lower price.* **3** *Maths.* (of a limit or bound) less than or equal to one or more numbers or variables. **4** (*sometimes cap.*) *Geology.* denoting the early part or division of a period, system, formation, etc.: *Lower Silurian.* ◆ *vb* **5** (*tr*) to cause to become low or on a lower level; bring, put, or cause to move down. **6** (*tr*) to reduce or bring down in estimation, dignity, value, etc.: *to lower oneself.* **7** to reduce or be reduced: *to lower one's confidence.* **8** (*tr*) to make quieter: *to lower the radio.* **9** (*tr*) to reduce the pitch of. **10** (*tr*) *Phonetics.* to modify the articulation of (a vowel) by bringing the tongue further away from the roof of the mouth. **11** (*intr*) to diminish or become less. [C12 (comparative of LOW[1]); C17 (vb)] ▸ **'lowerable** *adj*

lower[2] ('laʊə) *vb* a variant spelling of **lour.**

Lower Austria *n* a state of NE Austria: the largest Austrian province, containing most of the Vienna basin. Capital: Sankt Pölten. Pop.: 1 518 000 (1995 est.). Area: 19 170 sq. km (7476 sq. miles). German name: **Niederösterreich.**

Lower California *n* a mountainous peninsula of NW Mexico, between the Pacific and the Gulf of California: administratively divided into the states of Baja California and Baja California Sur. Spanish name: **Baja California.**

Lower Canada *n* (from 1791 to 1841) the official name of the S region of the present-day province of Quebec. Compare **Upper Canada.**

lower case *n* **1** a compositor's type case, in which the small letters are kept. ◆ *adj* **lower-case. 2** of or relating to small letters. ◆ *vb* **lower-case. 3** (*tr*) to print with lower-case letters.

lower chamber *n* another name for a **lower house.**

lower class *n* **1** the social stratum having the lowest position in the social hierarchy. Compare **middle class, upper class, working class.** ◆ *adj* **lower-class. 2** of or relating to the lower class. **3** inferior or vulgar.

lowerclassman (ˌləʊə'klɑːsmən) *n, pl* **-men.** *U.S.* a freshman or sophomore. Also called: **underclassman.**

lower criticism *n* textual criticism, esp. the study of the extant manuscripts of the Scriptures in order to establish the original text. Compare **higher criticism.**

lower deck *n* **1** the deck of a ship situated immediately above the hold. **2** *Informal.* the petty officers and seamen of a ship collectively.

Lower Egypt *n* one of the two main administrative districts of Egypt: consists of the Nile Delta.

lower house *n* one of the two houses of a bicameral legislature: usually the larger and more representative house. Also called: **lower chamber.** Compare **upper house.**

Lower Hutt (hʌt) *n* an industrial town in New Zealand on the S coast of North Island. Pop.: 62 900 (1983).

Lower Lakes *pl n Chiefly Canadian.* Lakes Erie and Ontario.

lower mordent *n* another term for **mordent.**

lowermost ('ləʊəˌməʊst) *adj* lowest.

Lower Palaeolithic *n* **1** the earliest of the three sections of the Palaeolithic, beginning about 3 million years ago and ending about 70 000 B.C. with the emergence of Neanderthal man. ◆ *adj* **2** of or relating to this period.

lower regions *pl n* (usually preceded by *the*) hell.

Lower Saxony *n* a state of N Germany, on the North Sea and including the E Frisian Islands; formerly in West Germany: a leading European producer of petroleum. Capital: Hanover. Pop.: 7 715 400 (1995 est.). Area: 47 408 sq. km (18 489 sq. miles). German name: **Niedersachsen.**

lower school *n* the younger pupils in a secondary school, usually those in the first three or four year groups.

lower world *n* **1** the earth as opposed to heaven or the spiritual world. **2** another name for **hell.**

lowest common denominator *n* the smallest integer or polynomial that is exactly divisible by each denominator of a set of fractions. Abbrevs.: **LCD, lcd.** Also called: **least common denominator.**

lowest common multiple *n* the smallest number or quantity that is exactly divisible by each member of a set of numbers or quantities. Abbrevs.: **LCM, lcm.** Also called: **least common multiple.**

Lowestoft ('ləʊstɒft) *n* a fishing port and resort in E England, in NE Suffolk on the North Sea. Pop.: 62 907 (1991).

low explosive *n* an explosive of relatively low power, as used in firearms.

low frequency *n* a radio-frequency band or a frequency lying between 300 and 30 kilohertz. Abbrev.: **LF.**

Low German *n* a language of N Germany, spoken esp. in rural areas: more closely related to Dutch than to standard High German. Also called: **Plattdeutsch.** Abbrev.: **LG.** See also **German, High German.**

low-key *or* **low-keyed** *adj* **1** having a low intensity or tone. **2** restrained, subdued, or understated. **3** (of a photograph, painting, etc.) having a predominance of dark grey tones or dark colours with few highlights. Compare **high-key.**

lowland ('ləʊlənd) *n* **1** relatively low ground. **2** (*often pl*) a low generally flat region. ◆ *adj* **3** of or relating to a lowland or lowlands. ▸ **'lowlander** *n*

Lowland ('ləʊlənd) *adj* of or relating to the Lowlands of Scotland or the dialect of English spoken there.

Lowlands ('ləʊləndz) *pl n* **the.** a low generally flat region of central Scotland, around the Forth and Clyde valleys, separating the Southern Uplands from the Highlands. ▸ **'Lowlander** *n*

Low Latin *n* any form or dialect of Latin other than the classical, such as Vulgar or Medieval Latin.

low-level language *n* a computer programming language that is closer to machine language than to human language. Compare **high-level language.**

low-level waste *n* waste material contaminated by traces of radioactivity that can be disposed of in steel drums in concrete-lined trenches but not (since 1983) in the sea. Compare **high-level waste, intermediate-level waste.**

lowlife ('ləʊˌlaɪf) *n, pl* **-lifes.** *Slang.* **a** a member or members of the underworld. **b** (*as modifier*): *his lowlife friends.*

lowlight (ˈləʊˌlaɪt) *n* **1** an unenjoyable or unpleasant part of an event. **2** (*usually pl*) a streak of darker colour artificially applied to the hair.

low-loader *n* a road or rail vehicle for heavy loads with a low platform for ease of access.

lowly (ˈləʊlɪ) *Now rare.* ♦ *adj* **-lier, -liest. 1** humble or low in position, rank, status, etc. **2** full of humility; meek. **3** simple, unpretentious, or plain. ♦ *adv* **4** in a low or lowly manner. ▸ **ˈlowliness** *n*

Low Mass *n* a Mass that has a simplified ceremonial form and is spoken rather than sung. Compare **High Mass.**

low-minded *adj* having a vulgar or crude mind and character. ▸ **ˌlow-ˈmindedly** *adv* ▸ **ˌlow-ˈmindedness** *n*

low-necked *adj* (of a woman's garment) having a low neckline.

lowp (laʊp) *vb, n Scot.* a variant spelling of **loup**[2].

low-pass filter *n Electronics.* a filter that transmits all frequencies below a specified value, substantially attenuating frequencies above this value. Compare **high-pass filter, band-pass filter.**

low-pitched *adj* **1** pitched low in tone. **2** (of a roof) having sides with a shallow slope.

low-pressure *adj* **1** having, using, or involving a pressure below normal: *a low-pressure gas.* **2** relaxed or calm.

low profile *n* **1a** a position or attitude characterized by a deliberate avoidance of prominence or publicity. **1b** (*as modifier*): *a low-profile approach.* ♦ *adj* **low-profile. 2** (of a tyre) wide in relation to its height. ♦ Compare **high profile.**

low relief *n* another term for **bas-relief.**

low-rent *adj Informal.* cheap and inferior: *low-rent films.*

low-rise *adj* **1** of or relating to a building having only a few storeys. Compare **high-rise.** ♦ *n* **2** such a building.

lowry *or* **lowrie** (ˈlaʊrɪ) *n* another name for **lory.**

Lowry (ˈlaʊrɪ) *n* **1 L(awrence) S(tephen).** 1887–1976, English painter, noted for his bleak northern industrial scenes, often containing primitive or stylized figures. **2 (Clarence) Malcolm.** 1909–57, British novelist and writer, best known for his semiautobiographical novel *Under the Volcano* (1947).

lowse (lauz, laus) *Scot.* ♦ *adj* **1** loose. ♦ *vb* **2** (*tr*) to release; loose. **3** (*intr*) to finish work. **4 lowsing time.** the time at which work or school finishes; knocking-off time. [a Scot. variant of LOOSE]

low-spirited *adj* depressed, dejected, or miserable. ▸ **ˌlow-ˈspiritedly** *adv* ▸ **ˌlow-ˈspiritedness** *n*

Low Sunday *n* the Sunday after Easter. [probably so named because of its relative unimportance in contrast with Easter Sunday]

low tech *n* **1** short for **low technology. 2** a style of interior design using items associated with low technology. ♦ *adj* **low-tech. 3** of or using low technology. **4** of or in the interior design style. ♦ Compare **hi tech.**

low technology *n* simple unsophisticated technology, often that used for centuries, that is limited to the production of basic necessities.

low-tension *adj* subjected to, carrying, or capable of operating at a low voltage. Abbrev.: **LT.**

low tide *n* **1** the tide when it is at its lowest level or the time at which it reaches this. **2** a lowest point.

lowveld (ˈləʊˌfɛlt, -ˌvɛlt) *n* **the.** another name for **bushveld.**

low-velocity zone *n* a layer or zone in the earth in which the velocity of seismic waves is slightly lower than in the layers above and below. The asthenosphere is thought to be such a zone. See **asthenosphere.**

low water *n* **1** another name for **low tide** (sense 1). **2** the state of any stretch of water at its lowest level. **3** a situation of difficulty or point of least success, excellence, etc.

low-water mark *n* **1** the level reached by seawater at low tide or by other stretches of water at their lowest level. **2** the lowest point or level; nadir.

lox[1] (lɒks) *n* a kind of smoked salmon. [C19: from Yiddish *laks,* from Middle High German *lahs* salmon]

lox[2] (lɒks) *n* short for **liquid oxygen,** esp. when used as an oxidizer for rocket fuels.

loxodromic (ˌlɒksəˈdrɒmɪk) *or* **loxodromical** *adj* of or relating to rhumb lines or to map projections on which rhumb lines appear straight, as on a Mercator projection. [C17: from Greek *loxos* oblique + *dromikos* relating to a course] ▸ **ˌloxoˈdromically** *adv*

loxodromics (ˌlɒksəˈdrɒmɪks) *or* **loxodromy** (lɒkˈsɒdrəmɪ) *n* (*functioning as sing*) the technique of navigating using rhumb lines.

loy (lɔɪ) *n Irish.* a narrow spade with a single footrest. [C18: from Irish Gaelic *láí*]

loyal (ˈlɔɪəl) *adj* **1** having or showing continuing allegiance. **2** faithful to one's country, government, etc. **3** of or expressing loyalty. [C16: from Old French *loial, leial,* from Latin *lēgālis* LEGAL] ▸ **ˈloyally** *adv* ▸ **ˈloyalness** *n*

loyalist (ˈlɔɪəlɪst) *n* a patriotic supporter of his sovereign or government. ▸ **ˈloyalism** *n*

Loyalist (ˈlɔɪəlɪst) *n* **1** (in Northern Ireland) any of the Protestants wishing to retain Ulster's link with Britain. **2** (in North America) an American colonist who supported Britain during the War of American Independence. **3** (during the Spanish Civil War) a supporter of the republican government.

loyalty (ˈlɔɪəltɪ) *n, pl* **-ties. 1** the state or quality of being loyal. **2** (*often pl*) a feeling of allegiance.

loyalty card *n* a swipe card issued by a supermarket or chain store to a customer, used to record credit points awarded for money spent in the store.

Loyang (ˈləʊˈjæŋ) *n* a variant transliteration of the Chinese name for **Luoyang.**

Loyola (lɔɪˈəʊlə) *n* See (Saint) **Ignatius Loyola.**

lozenge (ˈlɒzɪndʒ) *n* **1** Also called: **pastille, troche.** *Med.* a medicated tablet held in the mouth until it has dissolved. **2** *Geometry.* another name for **rhombus. 3** *Heraldry.* a diamond-shaped charge. [C14: from Old French *losange* of Gaulish origin; compare Vulgar Latin *lausa* flat stone]

lozenged (ˈlɒzɪndʒd) *adj* decorated with lozenges.

lozengy (ˈlɒzɪndʒɪ) *adj* (*usually postpositive*) *Heraldry.* divided by diagonal lines to form a lattice.

Lozère (*French* lɔzɛr) *n* a department of S central France, in Languedoc-Roussillon region. Capital: Mende. Pop.: 72 800 (1995). Area: 5180 sq. km (2020 sq. miles).

Lozi (ˈləʊzɪ) *n* the language of the Barotse people of Zambia, belonging to the Bantu group of the Niger-Congo family.

LP[1] *n* **1a** a long-playing gramophone record: usually one 12 inches (30 cm) or 10 inches (25 cm) in diameter, designed to rotate at 33⅓ revolutions per minute. Compare **EP. 1b** (*as modifier*): *an LP sleeve.* **2** long play: a slow-recording facility on a VCR which allows twice the length of material to be recorded on a tape from that of standard play.

LP[2] *abbrev. for* **1** (in Britain) Lord Provost. **2** Also: **lp.** low pressure.

L/P *Printing. abbrev. for* letterpress.

LPG *abbrev. for* liquefied petroleum gas.

L-plate *n Brit.* a white rectangle with an "L" sign fixed to the back and front of a motor vehicle; a red "L" sign is used to show that a driver using it is a learner who has not passed the driving test; a green "L" sign may be displayed by new drivers for up to a year after passing the driving test.

LPO *abbrev. for* London Philharmonic Orchestra.

L'pool *abbrev. for* Liverpool.

LPS (in Britain) *abbrev. for* Lord Privy Seal.

Lr *the chemical symbol for* lawrencium.

LRSC *abbrev. for* Licentiate of the Royal Society of Chemistry.

ls (on a document) the place of the seal. [from Latin *locus sigilli*]

LS *international car registration for* Lesotho.

LSD *n* lysergic acid diethylamide; a crystalline compound prepared from lysergic acid, used in experimental medicine and taken illegally as a hallucinogenic drug. Informal name (as an illegal hallucinogen): **acid.**

L.S.D., £.s.d., *or* **l.s.d.** (in Britain, esp. formerly) *abbrev. for* librae, solidi, denarii. [Latin: pounds, shillings, pence]

LSE *abbrev. for* London School of Economics.

LSI *Electronics. abbrev. for* large scale integration.

LSO *abbrev. for* London Symphony Orchestra.

LSZ (in New Zealand) *abbrev. for* limited speed zone.

lt *abbrev. for:* **1** long ton. **2** (esp. in the U.S.) local time.

Lt *abbrev. for* Lieutenant.

LT 1 *abbrev. for* low-tension. **2** *international car registration for* Lithuania.

LTA *abbrev. for* Lawn Tennis Association.

Lt Cdr *abbrev. for* lieutenant commander.

Lt Col *abbrev. for* lieutenant colonel.

Ltd *or* **ltd** (esp. after the names of British business organizations) *abbrev. for* limited (liability). U.S. equivalent: **Inc.**

Lt Gen *abbrev. for* lieutenant general.

Lt Gov *abbrev. for* lieutenant governor.

Lu *the chemical symbol for* lutetium.

LU *Physics. abbrev. for* loudness unit.

luach (ˈlʊɑx) *n Judaism.* a calendar that shows the dates of festivals and, usually, the times of start and finish of the Sabbath.

Lualaba (ˌluːəˈlɑːbə) *n* a river in the SE Democratic Republic of the Congo (formerly Zaïre), rising in Shaba province and flowing north as the W headstream of the River Congo. Length: about 1800 km (1100 miles).

Luanda *or* **Loanda** (luˈændə) *n* the capital of Angola, a port in the west, on the Atlantic: founded in 1576, it became a centre of the slave trade to Brazil in the 17th and 18th centuries; oil refining. Pop.: 2 250 000 (1995 est.). Official name: **São Paulo de Loanda.**

Luang Prabang (luːˈæŋ prɑːˈbæŋ) *n* a market town in N Laos, on the Mekong River: residence of the monarch of Laos (1946–75). Pop.: 59 800 (1995 est.).

luau (luːˈaʊ, ˈluːaʊ) *n* **1** a feast of Hawaiian food. **2** a dish of taro leaves usually prepared with coconut cream and octopus or chicken. [from Hawaiian *lu'au*]

Luba (ˈluːbə) *n* **1** (*pl* **Luba**) a member of a Negroid people of Africa living chiefly in the S Democratic Republic of the Congo (formerly Zaïre). **2** Also called: **Tshiluba.** the language of this people, belonging to the Bantu group of the Niger-Congo family.

lubber (ˈlʌbə) *n* **1** a big, awkward, or stupid person. **2** short for **landlubber.** [C14 *lobre,* probably from Scandinavian. See LOB[1]] ▸ **ˈlubberly** *adj, adv* ▸ **ˈlubberliness** *n*

lubber line *n* a mark on a ship's compass that designates the fore-and-aft axis of the vessel. Also called: **lubber's line.**

lubber's hole *n Nautical.* a hole in a top or platform on a mast through which a sailor can climb.

Lubbock (ˈlʌbək) *n* a city in NW Texas: cotton market. Pop.: 193 565 (1996 est.).

Lübeck (*German* ˈlyːbɛk) *n* a port in N Germany, in Schleswig-Holstein on the Baltic: the leading member of the Hanseatic League, and a major European commercial centre until the 15th century. Pop.: 216 986 (1996 est.).

Lubitsch (ˈluːbɪtʃ) *n* **Ernst.** 1890–1947, U.S. film director, born in Germany; best known for such sophisticated comedies as *Forbidden Paradise* (1924) and *Ninotchka* (1939).

Lublin (*Polish* ˈlublin) *n* an industrial city in E Poland: provisional seat of the government in 1918 and 1944. Pop.: 353 300 (1996 est.). Russian name: **Lyublin.**

lubra (ˈluːbrə) *n Austral.* an Aboriginal woman. [C19: from a native Australian language]

lubricant (ˈluːbrɪkənt) *n* **1** a lubricating substance, such as oil. ♦ *adj* **2** serving to lubricate. [C19: from Latin *lūbricāns*, present participle of *lūbricāre*. See LUBRICATE]

lubricate ('luːbrɪˌkeɪt) *vb* **1** (*tr*) to cover or treat with an oily or greasy substance so as to lessen friction. **2** (*tr*) to make greasy, slippery, or smooth. **3** (*intr*) to act as a lubricant. [C17: from Latin *lūbricāre*, from *lūbricus* slippery] ▸ ˌ**lubri'cation** *n* ▸ ˌ**lubri'cational** *adj* ▸ '**lubriˌcative** *adj*

lubricator ('luːbrɪˌkeɪtə) *n* **1** a person or thing that lubricates. **2** a device for applying lubricant.

lubricious (luː'brɪʃəs) *or* **lubricous** ('luːbrɪkəs) *adj* **1** *Formal or literary*. lewd, lascivious. **2** *Rare*. oily or slippery. [C16: from Latin *lūbricus*] ▸ **lu'briciously** *or* '**lubricously** *adv*

lubricity (luː'brɪsɪtɪ) *n* **1** *Formal or literary*. lewdness or salaciousness. **2** *Rare*. smoothness or slipperiness. **3** capacity to lubricate. [C15 (lewdness), C17 (slipperiness): from Old French *lubricité*, from Medieval Latin *lubricitās*, from Latin, from *lūbricus* slippery]

lubritorium (ˌluːbrɪ'tɔːrɪəm) *n, pl* **-ria** (-rɪə). *Chiefly U.S.* a place, as in a service station, for the lubrication of motor vehicles. [C20: from LUBRICATE + *-orium*, as in *sanatorium*]

Lubumbashi (ˌluːbʊm'bæʃɪ) *n* a city in the S Democratic Republic of the Congo (formerly Zaïre): founded in 1910 as a copper-mining centre; university (1955). Pop.: 851 381 (1994 est.). Former name (until 1966): **Elisabethville.**

Lucan[1] ('luːkən) *n* Latin name *Marcus Annaeus Lucanus*. 39–65 A.D., Roman poet. His epic poem *Pharsalia* describes the civil war between Caesar and Pompey.

Lucan[2] ('luːkən) *adj* of or relating to St. Luke or St. Luke's gospel.

Lucania (luː'keɪnɪə) *n* the Latin name for **Basilicata.**

lucarne (luː'kɑːn) *n* a type of dormer window. [C16: from French, from Provençal *lucana*, of obscure origin]

Lucas ('luːkəs) *n* **George.** born 1944, U.S. film director, producer, and writer of screenplays. Films include *American Graffiti* (1973) and *Star Wars* (1977) and its prequel *The Phantom Menace* (1999).

Lucas van Leyden ('luːkəs væn 'laɪdᵊn) *n* ?1494–1533, Dutch painter and engraver.

Lucca (*Italian* 'lukka) *n* a city in NW Italy, in Tuscany: centre of a rich agricultural region, noted for the production of olive oil. Pop.: 86 676 (1990 est.). Ancient name: **Luca** ('luːkə).

luce (luːs) *n* another name for the **pike** (the fish). [C14: from Old French *lus*, from Late Latin *lūcius* pike]

lucent ('luːsᵊnt) *adj* brilliant, shining, or translucent. [C16: from Latin *lūcēns*, present participle of *lūcēre* to shine] ▸ '**lucently** *adv*

lucerne (luː'sɜːn) *n Brit.* another name for **alfalfa.**

Lucerne (luː'sɜːn; *French* lysɛrn) *n* **1** a canton in central Switzerland, northwest of Lake Lucerne: joined the Swiss Confederacy in 1332. Pop.: 340 536 (1996 est.). Area: 1494 sq. km (577 sq. miles). **2** a city in central Switzerland, capital of Lucerne canton, on Lake Lucerne: tourist centre. Pop.: 60 600 (1987). **3 Lake.** a lake in central Switzerland: fed and drained chiefly by the River Reuss. Area: 115 sq. km (44 sq. miles). German name: **Vierwaldstättersee.** ◆ German name (for senses 1 and 2): **Luzern.**

Lucian ('luːsɪən) *n* 2nd century A.D., Greek writer, noted esp. for his satirical *Dialogues of the Gods* and *Dialogues of the Dead*.

lucid ('luːsɪd) *adj* **1** readily understood; clear. **2** shining or glowing. **3** *Psychiatry*. of or relating to a period of normality between periods of insane or irresponsible behaviour. [C16: from Latin *lūcidus* full of light, from *lūx* light] ▸ **lu'cidity** *or* '**lucidness** *n* ▸ '**lucidly** *adv*

lucifer ('luːsɪfə) *n* a friction match: originally a trade name for a match manufactured in England in the 19th century.

Lucifer ('luːsɪfə) *n* **1** the leader of the rebellion of the angels: usually identified with Satan. **2** the planet Venus when it rises as the morning star. [Old English, from Latin *Lūcifer*, light-bearer, from *lūx* light + *ferre* to bear]

luciferin (luː'sɪfərɪn) *n Biochem.* a substance occurring in bioluminescent organisms, such as glow-worms and fireflies. It undergoes an enzyme-catalysed oxidation and emits light on decaying to its ground state. [C20: from Latin *lucifer* (literally: light-bearer) + -IN]

luciferous (luː'sɪfərəs) *adj Rare.* bringing or giving light.

lucifugous (luː'sɪfjʊgəs) *adj* avoiding light. [C17: from Latin *lucifugus*, from *lux* (genitive *lūcis*) light + *fugere* to flee + -OUS]

Lucilius (luː'sɪlɪəs) *n* **Gaius** ('gaɪəs). ?180–102 B.C., Roman satirist, regarded as the originator of poetical satire.

Lucina (luː'saɪnə) *n Roman myth.* a title or name given to Juno as goddess of childbirth. [C14: from Latin *lūcīnus* bringing to the light, from *lūx* light]

luck (lʌk) *n* **1** events that are beyond control and seem subject to chance; fortune. **2** success or good fortune. **3** something considered to bring good luck. **4 down on one's luck.** having little or no good luck to the point of suffering hardships. **5 no such luck.** *Informal.* unfortunately not. **6 try one's luck.** to attempt something that is uncertain. ◆ *vb* **7** (*intr*; foll. by *out*) *U.S. and Canadian informal.* to succeed with (something). [C15: from Middle Dutch *luc*; related to Middle High German *gelücke*, late Old Norse *lukka, lykka*]

luckless ('lʌklɪs) *adj* having no luck; unlucky. ▸ '**lucklessly** *adv* ▸ '**lucklessness** *n*

Lucknow ('lʌknaʊ) *n* a city in N India, capital of Uttar Pradesh: capital of Oudh (1775–1856); the British residency was besieged (1857) during the Indian Mutiny. Pop.: 1 619 115 (1991).

luckpenny ('lʌkˌpɛnɪ) *n, pl* **-nies.** *Brit.* **1** a coin kept for luck. **2** a small amount of money returned for luck by a seller to a customer.

lucky ('lʌkɪ) *adj* **luckier, luckiest. 1** having or bringing good fortune. **2** happening by chance, esp. as desired. ▸ '**luckily** *adv* ▸ '**luckiness** *n*

lucky dip *n Brit.* **1** a barrel or box filled with sawdust and small prizes for which children search. **2** *Informal.* an undertaking of uncertain outcome.

lucrative ('luːkrətɪv) *adj* producing a profit; profitable; remunerative. [C15: from Old French *lucratif*; see LUCRE] ▸ '**lucratively** *adv* ▸ '**lucrativeness** *n*

lucre ('luːkə) *n Usually facetious.* money or wealth (esp. in the phrase **filthy lucre**). [C14: from Latin *lūcrum* gain; related to Old English *lēan* reward, German *Lohn* wages]

Lucretia (luː'kriːʃɪə) *n* (in Roman legend) a Roman woman who killed herself after being raped by a son of Tarquin the Proud.

Lucretius (luː'kriːʃɪəs) *n* full name *Titus Lucretius Carus*. ?96–55 B.C., Roman poet and philosopher. In his didactic poem *De rerum natura*, he expounds Epicurus' atomist theory of the universe. ▸ **Lu'cretian** *adj*

lucubrate ('luːkjʊˌbreɪt) *vb* (*intr*) to write or study, esp. at night. [C17: from Latin *lūcubrāre* to work by lamplight] ▸ '**lucuˌbrator** *n*

lucubration (ˌluːkjʊ'breɪʃən) *n* **1** laborious study, esp. at night. **2** (*often pl*) a solemn literary work.

luculent ('luːkjʊlənt) *adj Rare.* **1** easily understood; lucid. **2** bright or shining; glowing. [C15: from Latin *lūculentus* full of light, from *lūx* light] ▸ '**luculently** *adv*

Lucullus (luː'kʌləs) *n* **Lucius Licinius** ('luːsɪəs lɪ'sɪnɪəs). ?110–56 B.C., Roman general and consul, famous for his luxurious banquets. He fought Mithradates VI (74–66). ▸ **Lu'cullan, Lucullean** (ˌluːkʌ'lɪən), *or* ˌ**Lucul'lian** *adj*

Lucy ('luːsɪ) *n* **Saint.** died ?303 A.D., a virgin martyred by Diocletian in Syracuse. Feast day: Dec 13.

lud (lʌd) *Brit.* ◆ *n* **1** lord (in the phrase **my lud, m'lud**): used when addressing a judge in court. ◆ *interj* **2** *Archaic.* an exclamation of dismay or surprise.

Lüda ('luː'dɑː) *or* **Lü-ta** *n* a port in NE China, in S Liaoning province, comprising the two cities of Lü-shun and Dalian at the S end of the Liaodong peninsula: the chief northern port. Pop.: 2 400 000 (1991 est.).

Luddite ('lʌdaɪt) *n English history.* **1** any of the textile workers opposed to mechanization who rioted and organized machine-breaking between 1811 and 1816. **2** any opponent of industrial change or innovation. ◆ *adj* **3** of or relating to the Luddites. [C19: alleged to be named after Ned *Ludd*, an 18th-century Leicestershire workman, who destroyed industrial machinery] ▸ '**Luddism** *n*

Ludendorff (*German* 'luːdəndɔrf) *n* **Erich Friedrich Wilhelm von** ('eːrɪç 'friːdrɪç 'vɪlhɛlm fɔn). 1865–1937, German general, Hindenburg's aide in World War I.

Lüdenscheid (*German* 'lyːdənʃaɪt) *n* a city in W Germany, in North Rhine-Westphalia: manufacturing centre for aluminium and plastics. Pop.: 76 110 (1989 est.).

luderick ('luːdərɪk) *n* an estuarine and rock fish, *Girella tricuspidata*, of Australia, usually black or dark brown in colour: a kind of blackfish. [C19: from a native Australian language]

Lüderitz (*German* 'lyːdərɪts) *n* a port in Namibia: diamond-mining centre. Pop.: 6000 (1990).

Ludhiana (ˌlʊdɪ'ɑːnə) *n* a city in N India, in the central Punjab: Punjab Agricultural University (1962). Pop.: 1 042 740 (1991).

ludic ('luːdɪk) *adj Literary.* playful. [C20: from French *ludique*, from Latin *lūdus* game]

ludicrous ('luːdɪkrəs) *adj* absurd or incongruous to the point of provoking ridicule or laughter. [C17: from Latin *lūdicrus* done in sport, from *lūdus* game; related to *lūdere* to play] ▸ '**ludicrously** *adv* ▸ '**ludicrousness** *n*

Ludlow[1] ('lʌdləʊ) *n Trademark.* a machine for casting type from matrices set by hand, used esp. for headlines.

Ludlow[2] ('lʌdləʊ) *n* a market town in W central England, in Shropshire: castle (11th–16th century). Pop.: 9040 (1991).

ludo ('luːdəʊ) *n Brit.* a simple board game in which players advance counters by throwing dice. [C19: from Latin: I play]

Ludwigsburg (*German* 'luːtvɪçsbʊrk) *n* a city in SW Germany, in Baden-Württemberg north of Stuttgart: expanded in the 18th century around the palace of the dukes of Württemberg. Pop.: 79 340 (1989 est.).

Ludwigshafen (*German* 'luːtvɪçshaːfən) *n* a city in SW Germany, in the Rhineland-Palatinate, on the Rhine: chemical industry. Pop.: 167 369 (1996 est.).

lues ('luːiːz) *n, pl* **lues.** *Rare.* **1** any venereal disease. **2** a pestilence. [C17: from New Latin, from Latin: calamity] ▸ **luetic** (luː'ɛtɪk) *adj* ▸ **lu'etically** *adv*

luff (lʌf) *n* **1** *Nautical.* the leading edge of a fore-and-aft sail. ◆ *vb* **2** *Nautical.* to head (a sailing vessel) into the wind so that her sails flap. **3** (*intr*) *Nautical.* (of a sail) to flap when the wind is blowing equally on both sides. **4** to move the jib of (a crane) or raise or lower the boom of (a derrick) in order to shift a load. [C13 (in the sense: steering gear): from Old French *lof*, perhaps from Middle Dutch *loef* peg of a tiller; compare Old High German *laffa* palm of hand, oar blade, Russian *lapa* paw]

luffa ('lʌfə) *n* **1** any tropical climbing plant of the cucurbitaceous genus *Luffa*, esp. the dishcloth gourd. **2** *U.S.* another name for **loofah.**

Luftwaffe (*German* 'lʊftvafə) *n* the German Air Force. [C20: German, literally: air weapon]

lug[1] (lʌg) *vb* **lugs, lugging, lugged. 1** to carry or drag (something heavy) with great effort. **2** (*tr*) to introduce (an irrelevant topic) into a conversation or discussion. **3** (*tr*) (of a sailing vessel) to carry too much (sail) for the amount of wind blowing. ◆ *n* **4** the act or an instance of lugging. [C14: probably from Scandinavian; apparently related to Norwegian *lugge* to pull by the hair]

lug[2] (lʌg) *n* **1** a projecting piece by which something is connected, supported, or lifted. **2** Also called: **tug.** a leather loop used in harness for various purposes. **3** a box or basket for vegetables or fruit with a capacity of 28 to 40 pounds. **4** *Informal or Scot.* another word for **ear**[1]. **5** *Slang.* a man, esp. a stupid or awkward one. [C15 (Scots dialect) *lugge* ear, perhaps related to LUG[1] (in the sense: to pull by the ear)]

lug[3] (lʌg) *n Nautical.* short for **lugsail.**

lug[4] (lʌg) *n* short for **lugworm.** [C16: origin uncertain]

Luganda (luːˈgændə, -ˈgɑːndə) *n* the language of the Buganda, spoken chiefly in Uganda, belonging to the Bantu group of the Niger-Congo family.

Lugano (luˈgɑːnəʊ) *n* a town in S Switzerland, on Lake Lugano: a financial centre and tourist resort. Pop.: 26 800 (1995 est.).

Lugansk (*Russian* luˈgansk) *n* an industrial city in the E Ukraine, in the Donbass mining region: established in 1795 as an iron-founding centre. Pop.: 487 000 (1996 est.). Former name (1935–91): **Voroshilovgrad.**

luge (luːʒ) *n* **1** a racing toboggan on which riders lie on their backs, descending feet first. ◆ *vb* (*intr*) **2** to ride on a luge. **[C20:** from French**]**

Luger (ˈluːgə) *n Trademark.* a German 9 mm calibre automatic pistol.

luggage (ˈlʌgɪdʒ) *n* suitcases, trunks, etc., containing personal belongings for a journey; baggage. **[C16:** perhaps from LUG[1], influenced in form by BAGGAGE**]**

luggage van *n Brit.* a railway carriage used to transport passengers' luggage, bicycles, etc. U.S. and Canadian name: **baggage car.**

lugger (ˈlʌgə) *n Nautical.* a small working boat rigged with a lugsail. **[C18:** from LUGSAIL**]**

lughole (ˈlʌg,həʊl) *n Brit.* an informal word for **ear**[1]. See also **lug**[2] (sense 4).

Lugo (*Spanish* ˈluɣo) *n* a city in NW Spain: Roman walls; Romanesque cathedral. Pop.: 86 658 (1991). Latin name: **Lucus Augusti** (ˈluːkəs auˈguːstiː, ɔːˈgʌstiː).

lugsail (ˈlʌgsəl) *or* **lug** (lʌg) *n Nautical.* a four-sided sail bent and hoisted on a yard. **[C17:** perhaps from Middle English (now dialect) *lugge* pole, or from *lugge* ear**]**

lug screw *n* a small screw without a head.

lugubrious (luˈguːbrɪəs) *adj* excessively mournful; doleful. **[C17:** from Latin *lūgubris* mournful, from *lūgēre* to grieve**]** ▸ **luˈgubriously** *adv* ▸ **luˈgubriousness** *n*

lugworm (ˈlʌg,wɜːm) *n* any polychaete worm of the genus *Arenicola,* living in burrows on sandy shores and having tufted gills: much used as bait by fishermen. Sometimes shortened to **lug.** Also called: **lobworm. [C17:** of uncertain origin**]**

lug wrench *n* a spanner with a lug or lugs projecting from its jaws to engage the component to be rotated.

Luichow Peninsula (ˈluːˈtʃau) *n* a variant transliteration of the Chinese name for **Leizhou Peninsula.**

Luik (lœik) *n* the Flemish name for **Liège.**

Lukács (ˈluːkætʃ) *n* **Georg** (ˈgeɪɔːk), original name *György.* 1885–1971, Hungarian Marxist philosopher and literary critic, whose works include *History and Class Consciousness* (1923), *Studies in European Realism* (1946), and *The Historical Novel* (1955).

Luke (luːk) *n New Testament.* **1 Saint.** a fellow worker of Paul and a physician (Colossians 4:14). Feast day: Oct 18. **2** the third Gospel, traditionally ascribed to Luke. Related adj: **Lucan.**

lukewarm (ˌluːkˈwɔːm) *adj* **1** (esp. of water) moderately warm; tepid. **2** having or expressing little enthusiasm or conviction. **[C14** *luke* probably from Old English *hlēow* warm; compare German *lauwarm***]** ▸ **ˌlukeˈwarmly** *adv* ▸ **ˌlukeˈwarmness** *n*

Luleå (*Swedish* ˈluːləoː) *n* a port in N Sweden, on the Gulf of Bothnia: industrial and shipbuilding centre; icebound in winter. Pop.: 70 694 (1994).

lull (lʌl) *vb* **1** to soothe (a person or animal) by soft sounds or motions (esp. in the phrase **lull to sleep**). **2** to calm (someone or someone's fears, suspicions, etc.), esp. by deception. ◆ *n* **3** a short period of calm or diminished activity. **[C14:** possibly imitative of crooning sounds; related to Middle Low German *lollen* to soothe, Middle Dutch *lollen* to talk drowsily, mumble**]** ▸ **ˈlulling** *adj*

lullaby (ˈlʌlə,baɪ) *n, pl* **-bies. 1** a quiet song to lull a child to sleep. **2** the music for such a song. ◆ *vb* **-bies, -bying, -bied. 3** (*tr*) to quiet or soothe with or as if with a lullaby. **[C16:** perhaps a blend of LULL + GOODBYE**]**

Lully *n* **1** (*French* lyli). **Jean Baptiste** (ʒɑ̃ batist), Italian name *Giovanni Battista Lulli.* 1632–87, French composer, born in Italy; founder of French opera. With Philippe Quinault as librettist, he wrote operas such as *Alceste* (1674) and *Armide* (1686); as superintendent of music at the court of Louis XIV, he wrote incidental music to comedies by Molière. **2** (ˈlʌlɪ). Also: **Lull** (*Spanish* lul). **Raymond** *or* **Ramón** (raˈmɔn). ?1235–1315, Spanish philosopher, mystic, and missionary. His chief works are *Ars generalis sive magna* and the Utopian novel *Blaquerna.*

lulu (ˈluːluː) *n Slang.* a person or thing considered to be outstanding in size, appearance, etc. **[C19:** probably from the nickname for *Louise***]**

Luluabourg (luːˈluːə,bʊə) *n* the former name (until 1966) of **Kananga.**

lum (lʌm) *n Scot.* a chimney. **[C17:** of obscure origin**]**

lumbago (lʌmˈbeɪgəʊ) *n* pain in the lower back; backache affecting the lumbar region. **[C17:** from Late Latin *lumbāgo,* from Latin *lumbus* loin**]**

lumbar (ˈlʌmbə) *adj* of, near, or relating to the part of the body between the lowest ribs and the hipbones. **[C17:** from New Latin *lumbāris,* from Latin *lumbus* loin**]**

lumbar puncture *n Med.* insertion of a hollow needle into the lower region of the spinal cord to withdraw cerebrospinal fluid, introduce drugs, etc.

lumber[1] (ˈlʌmbə) *n* **1** *Chiefly U.S. and Canadian.* **1a** logs; sawn timber. **1b** cut timber, esp. when sawn and dressed ready for use in joinery, carpentry, etc. **1c** (*as modifier*)*: the lumber trade.* **2** *Brit.* **2a** useless household articles that are stored away. **2b** (*as modifier*)*: lumber room.* ◆ *vb* **3** (*tr*) to pile together in a disorderly manner. **4** (*tr*) to fill up or encumber with useless household articles. **5** *Chiefly U.S. and Canadian.* to convert (the trees) of (a forest) into marketable timber. **6** (*tr*) *Brit. informal.* to burden with something unpleasant, tedious, etc. **7** (*tr*) *Austral.* to arrest; imprison. **[C17:** perhaps from a noun use of LUMBER[2]**]** ▸ **ˈlumberer** *n*

lumber[2] (ˈlʌmbə) *vb* (*intr*) **1** to move awkwardly. **2** an obsolete word for **rumble. [C14** *lomeren;* perhaps related to *lome* LAME[1], Swedish dialect *loma* to move ponderously**]**

lumbering[1] (ˈlʌmbərɪŋ) *n Chiefly U.S. and Canadian.* the business or trade of cutting, transporting, preparing, or selling timber.

lumbering[2] (ˈlʌmbərɪŋ) *adj* **1** awkward in movement. **2** moving with a rumbling sound. ▸ **ˈlumberingly** *adv* ▸ **ˈlumberingness** *n*

lumberjack (ˈlʌmbə,dʒæk) *n* (esp. in North America) a person whose work involves felling trees, transporting the timber, etc. **[C19:** from LUMBER[1] + JACK[1] (man)**]**

lumberjacket (ˈlʌmbə,dʒækɪt) *n* a boldly coloured, usually checked jacket in warm cloth, as worn by lumberjacks. U.S. name: **lumberjack.**

lumberyard (ˈlʌmbə,jɑːd) *n* the U.S. and Canadian word for **timberyard.**

lumbricalis (ˌlʌmbrɪˈkeɪlɪs) *n Anatomy.* any of the four wormlike muscles in the hand or foot. **[C18:** New Latin, from Latin *lumbrīcus* worm**]** ▸ **lumbrical** (ˈlʌmbrɪkᵊl) *adj*

lumbricoid (ˈlʌmbrɪ,kɔɪd) *adj* **1** *Anatomy.* designating any part or structure resembling a worm. **2** of, relating to, or resembling an earthworm. **[C19:** from New Latin *lumbricoides,* from Latin *lumbrīcus* worm**]**

lumen (ˈluːmɪn) *n, pl* **-mens** *or* **-mina** (-mɪnə). **1** the derived SI unit of luminous flux; the flux emitted in a solid angle of 1 steradian by a point source having a uniform intensity of 1 candela. Symbol: lm **2** *Anatomy.* a passage, duct, or cavity in a tubular organ. **3** a cavity within a plant cell enclosed by the cell walls. **[C19:** New Latin, from Latin: light, aperture**]** ▸ **ˈlumenal** *or* **ˈluminal** *adj*

lum-hat (ˌlʌmˈhæt) *n Scot.* a top hat. **[C19:** from LUM**]**

Lumière (*French* lymjɛr) *n* **Auguste Marie Louis Nicolas** (ogyst mari lwi nikɔla). 1862–1954, and his brother, **Louis Jean** (lwi ʒɑ̃), 1864–1948, French chemists and cinema pioneers, who invented a cinematograph and a process of colour photography.

luminance (ˈluːmɪnəns) *n* **1** a state or quality of radiating or reflecting light. **2** a measure (in candelas per square metre) of the brightness of a point on a surface that is radiating or reflecting light. It is the luminous intensity in a given direction of a small element of surface area divided by the orthogonal projection of this area onto a plane at right angles to the direction. Symbol: *L* **[C19:** from Latin *lūmen* light**]**

luminary (ˈluːmɪnərɪ) *n, pl* **-naries. 1** a person who enlightens or influences others. **2** a famous person. **3** *Literary.* something, such as the sun or moon, that gives off light. ◆ *adj* **4** of, involving, or characterized by light or enlightenment. **[C15:** via Old French, from Latin *lūmināre* lamp, from *lūmen* light**]**

luminesce (ˌluːmɪˈnɛs) *vb* (*intr*) to exhibit luminescence. **[**back formation from LUMINESCENT**]**

luminescence (ˌluːmɪˈnɛsəns) *n Physics.* **a** the emission of light at low temperatures by any process other than incandescence, such as phosphorescence or chemiluminescence. **b** the light emitted by such a process. **[C19:** from Latin *lūmen* light**]** ▸ **ˌlumiˈnescent** *adj*

luminosity (ˌluːmɪˈnɒsɪtɪ) *n, pl* **-ties. 1** the condition of being luminous. **2** something that is luminous. **3** *Astronomy.* a measure of the amount of light emitted by a star. **4** *Physics.* the attribute of an object or colour enabling the extent to which an object emits light to be observed. Former name: **brightness.** See also **colour.**

luminous (ˈluːmɪnəs) *adj* **1** radiating or reflecting light; shining; glowing: *luminous colours.* **2** (*not in technical use*) exhibiting luminescence: *luminous paint.* **3** full of light; well-lit. **4** (of a physical quantity in photometry) evaluated according to the visual sensation produced in an observer rather than by absolute energy measurements: *luminous flux; luminous intensity.* Compare **radiant. 5** easily understood; lucid; clear. **6** enlightening or wise. **[C15:** from Latin *lūminōsus* full of light, from *lūmen* light**]** ▸ **ˈluminously** *adv* ▸ **ˈluminousness** *n*

luminous efficacy *n* **1** the quotient of the luminous flux of a radiation and its corresponding radiant flux. Symbol: *K* **2** the quotient of the luminous flux emitted by a source of radiation and the power it consumes. It is measured in lumens per watt. Symbol: η_v, Φ_v

luminous efficiency *n* the efficiency of polychromatic radiation in producing a visual sensation. It is the radiant flux weighed according to the spectral luminous efficiencies of its constituent wavelengths divided by the corresponding radiant flux. Symbol: *V*

luminous energy *n* energy emitted or propagated in the form of light; the product of a luminous flux and its duration, measured in lumen seconds. Symbol: Q_v

luminous exitance *n* the ability of a surface to emit light expressed as the luminous flux per unit area at a specified point on the surface. Symbol: M_v

luminous flux *n* a measure of the rate of flow of luminous energy, evaluated according to its ability to produce a visual sensation. For a monochromatic light it is the radiant flux multiplied by the spectral luminous efficiency of the light. It is measured in lumens. Symbol: Φ_v

luminous intensity *n* a measure of the amount of light that a point source radiates in a given direction. It is expressed by the luminous flux leaving the source in that direction per unit of solid angle. Symbol: I_v

lumisterol (luːˈmɪstə,rɒl) *n Biochem.* a steroid compound produced when ergosterol is exposed to ultraviolet radiation. Formula: $C_{28}H_{44}O$. **[C20:** from Latin *lumin-, lūmen* light + STEROL**]**

lumme *or* **lummy** (ˈlʌmɪ) *interj Brit.* an exclamation of surprise or dismay. **[C19:** alteration of *Lord love me***]**

lummox (ˈlʌməks) *n Informal.* a clumsy or stupid person. **[C19:** origin unknown**]**

lump[1] (lʌmp) *n* **1** a small solid mass without definite shape. **2** *Pathol.* any small swelling or tumour. **3** a collection of things; aggregate. **4** *Informal.* an awkward, heavy, or stupid person. **5** (*pl*) *U.S. informal.* punishment, defeat, or reverses: *he took his lumps.* **6 the lump.** *Brit.* **6a** self-employed workers in the building trade considered collectively, esp. with reference to tax and national insurance evasion. **6b** (*as modifier*)*: lump labour.* **7** (*modifier*) in the form of a lump or lumps: *lump sugar.* **8 a lump in one's throat.** a tight dry feeling in one's throat, usually caused by great emotion. ◆ *vb* **9** (*tr;* often foll. by *together*) to collect into a mass or group. **10** (*intr*) to grow into lumps or become lumpy. **11** (*tr*) to consider as a single group, often without justification. **12** (*tr*) to make or cause lumps in or on. **13** (*intr;* often foll. by *along*) to move or proceed in a heavy manner. **[**C13: probably related to early Dutch *lompe* piece, Scandinavian dialect *lump* block, Middle High German *lumpe* rag**]**

lump[2] (lʌmp) *vb* (*tr*) *Informal.* to tolerate or put up with; endure (in the phrase **lump it**). **[**C16: origin uncertain**]**

lumpectomy (lʌmˈpɛktəmɪ) *n, pl* **-mies.** the surgical removal of a tumour in a breast. **[**C20: from LUMP[1] + -ECTOMY**]**

lumpen (ˈlʌmpᵊn) *adj Informal.* stupid or unthinking. **[**from German *Lump* vagabond, influenced in meaning by *Lumpen* rag, as in LUMPENPROLETARIAT**]**

lumpenproletariat (ˌlʌmpənˌprəʊlɪˈtɛərɪət) *n* (esp. in Marxist theory) the amorphous urban social group below the proletariat, consisting of criminals, tramps, etc. **[**German, literally: ragged proletariat**]**

lumper (ˈlʌmpə) *n U.S.* a stevedore; docker.

lumpfish (ˈlʌmpˌfɪʃ) *n, pl* **-fish** *or* **-fishes. 1** a North Atlantic scorpaenoid fish, *Cyclopterus lumpus,* having a globular body covered with tubercles, pelvic fins fused into a sucker, and an edible roe: family *Cyclopteridae.* **2** any other fish of the family *Cyclopteridae.* ◆ Also called: **lumpsucker. [**C16: *lump* (now obsolete) lumpfish, from Middle Dutch *lumpe,* perhaps related to LUMP[1]**]**

lumpish (ˈlʌmpɪʃ) *adj* **1** resembling a lump. **2** stupid, clumsy, or heavy. ▸ **ˈlumpishly** *adv* ▸ **ˈlumpishness** *n*

lumpsucker (ˈlʌmpˌsʌkə) *n* See **lumpfish.**

lump sum *n* a relatively large sum of money, paid at one time, esp. in cash.

lumpy (ˈlʌmpɪ) *adj* **lumpier, lumpiest. 1** full of or having lumps. **2** (esp. of the sea) rough. **3** (of a person) heavy or bulky. ▸ **ˈlumpily** *adv* ▸ **ˈlumpiness** *n*

lumpy jaw *n Vet. science.* a nontechnical name for **actinomycosis.**

Lumumba (luˈmʊmbə) *n* **Patrice** (pəˈtriːs). 1925–61, Congolese statesman; first prime minister of the Democratic Republic of the Congo (1960); assassinated.

Luna[1] (ˈluːnə) *n* **1** the alchemical name for **silver. 2** the Roman goddess of the moon. Greek counterpart: **Selene. [**from Latin: moon**]**

Luna[2] (ˈluːnə) *or* **Lunik** (ˈluːnɪk) *n* any of a series of Soviet lunar space-probes, one of which, **Luna 9,** made the first soft landing on the moon (1966).

lunacy (ˈluːnəsɪ) *n, pl* **-cies. 1** (formerly) any severe mental illness. **2** foolishness or a foolish act.

luna moth *n* a large American saturniid moth, *Tropaea* (or *Actias*) *luna,* having light green wings with a yellow crescent-shaped marking on each forewing. **[**C19: so named from the markings on its wings**]**

lunar (ˈluːnə) *adj* **1** of or relating to the moon. **2** occurring on, used on, or designed to land on the surface of the moon: *lunar module.* **3** relating to, caused by, or measured by the position or orbital motion of the moon. **4** of or containing silver. **[**C17: from Latin *lūnāris,* from *lūna* the moon**]**

lunar caustic *n* silver nitrate fused into sticks, which were formerly used in cauterizing.

lunar eclipse *n* See under **eclipse** (sense 1).

lunarian (luːˈnɛərɪən) *n* **1** an archaic word for **selenographer. 2** *Myth.* an inhabitant of the moon.

lunar module *n* the module used to carry two of the three astronauts on an Apollo spacecraft to the surface of the moon and back to the spacecraft.

lunar month *n* another name for **synodic month.** See **month** (sense 6).

lunar year *n* See under **year** (sense 6).

lunate (ˈluːneɪt) *or* **lunated** *adj* **1** *Anatomy, botany.* shaped like a crescent. ◆ *n* **2** a crescent-shaped bone forming part of the wrist. **[**C18: from Latin *lūnātus* crescent-shaped, from *lūnāre,* from *lūna* moon**]**

lunatic (ˈluːnətɪk) *adj also* (*rare*) **lunatical** (luːˈnætɪkᵊl). **1** an archaic word for **insane. 2** foolish; eccentric; crazy. ◆ *n* **3** a person who is insane. **[**C13 (adj) via Old French from Late Latin *lūnāticus* crazy, moonstruck, from Latin *lūna* moon**]** ▸ **luˈnatically** *adv*

lunatic asylum *n* another name, usually regarded as offensive, for **mental home.**

lunatic fringe *n* the members of a society or group who adopt or support views regarded as extreme or fanatical.

lunation (luːˈneɪʃən) *n* another name for **synodic month.** See **month** (sense 6).

lunch (lʌntʃ) *n* **1** a meal eaten during the middle of the day. **2** *Caribbean.* (among older people) mid-afternoon tea. ◆ *vb* **3** (*intr*) to eat lunch. **4** (*tr*) to provide or buy lunch for. **[**C16: probably short form of LUNCHEON**]** ▸ **ˈluncher** *n*

luncheon (ˈlʌntʃən) *n* a lunch, esp. a formal one. **[**C16: probably variant of *nuncheon,* from Middle English *noneschench,* from *none* NOON + *schench* drink**]**

luncheon club *n* **1** *Social welfare.* (in Britain) an arrangement or organization for serving hot midday meals for a small charge to old people in clubs or day-centres. **2** a society or group of people who meet regularly for an organized lunch: *a ladies' luncheon club.*

luncheonette (ˌlʌntʃəˈnɛt) *n U.S. and Canadian.* a café or small informal restaurant where light meals and snacks are served.

luncheon meat *n* a ground mixture of meat (often pork) and cereal, usually tinned.

luncheon voucher *n* a voucher worth a specified amount issued to employees and redeemable at a restaurant for food. Abbrev.: **LV.** U.S. equivalent: **meal ticket.**

lunch hour *n* **1** Also called: **lunch break.** a break in the middle of the working day, usually of one hour, during which lunch may be eaten. **2** Also called: **lunch time.** the time at which lunch is usually eaten.

lunchroom (ˈlʌntʃˌruːm, -ˌrʊm) *n U.S. and Canadian.* a room where lunch is served or where students, employees, etc., may eat lunches they bring.

Lund (lʊnd) *n* a city in SE Sweden, northeast of Malmö: founded in about 1020 by the Danish King Canute; the archbishopric for all Scandinavia in the Middle Ages; university (1668). Pop.: 95 895 (1994).

Lundy (ˈlʌndɪ) *n* an island in SW England, in Devon, in the Bristol Channel: now a bird sanctuary. Pop.: 52 (1981).

Lundy's Lane (ˈlʌndɪz) *n* the site, near Niagara Falls, of a major battle (1814) in the War of 1812, in which British and Canadian forces defeated the Americans.

lune[1] (luːn) *n* **1a** a section of the surface of a sphere enclosed between two semicircles that intersect at opposite points on the sphere. **1b** a crescent-shaped figure formed on a plane surface by the intersection of the arcs of two circles. **2** something shaped like a crescent. **3** *R.C. Church.* another word for **lunette** (sense 6). **[**C18: from Latin *lūna* moon**]**

lune[2] (luːn) *n Falconry.* a leash for hawks or falcons. **[**C14 *loigne,* from Old French, from Medieval Latin *longia, longea,* from Latin *longus* LONG[1]**]**

Lüneburg (*German* ˈlyːnəbʊrk) *n* a city in N Germany, in Lower Saxony: capital of the duchy of Brunswick-Lüneburg from 1235 to 1369; prominent Hanse town; saline springs. Pop.: 61 000 (1990 est.).

lunette (luːˈnɛt) *n* **1** anything that is shaped like a crescent. **2** an oval or circular opening to admit light in a dome. **3** a semicircular panel containing a window, mural, or sculpture. **4** a ring attached to a vehicle, into which a hook is inserted so that it can be towed. **5** a type of fortification like a detached bastion. **6** Also called: **lune.** *R.C. Church.* a case fitted with a bracket to hold the consecrated host. **[**C16: from French: crescent, from *lune* moon, from Latin *lūna***]**

Lunéville (*French* lynevil) *n* a city in NE France: scene of the signing of the **Peace of Lunéville** between France and Austria (1801). Pop.: 22 393 (1990).

lung (lʌŋ) *n* **1** either one of a pair of spongy saclike respiratory organs within the thorax of higher vertebrates, which oxygenate the blood and remove its carbon dioxide. **2** any similar or analogous organ in other vertebrates or in invertebrates. **3 at the top of one's lungs.** in one's loudest voice; yelling. ◆ *Related adjs.:* **pneumonic, pulmonary, pulmonic. [**Old English *lungen;* related to Old High German *lungun* lung. Compare LIGHTS[2]**]**

lungan (ˈlʌŋgən) *n* another name for **longan.**

lunge[1] (lʌndʒ) *n* **1** a sudden forward motion. **2** *Fencing.* a thrust made by advancing the front foot and straightening the back leg, extending the sword arm forwards. ◆ *vb* **3** to move or cause to move with a lunge. **4** (*intr*) *Fencing.* to make a lunge. **[**C18: shortened form of obsolete C17 *allonge,* from French *allonger* to stretch out (one's arm), from Late Latin *ēlongāre* to lengthen. Compare ELONGATE**]** ▸ **ˈlunger** *n*

lunge[2] (lʌndʒ) *n* **1** a rope used in training or exercising a horse. ◆ *vb* **2** to exercise or train (a horse) on a lunge. **[**C17: from Old French *longe,* shortened from *allonge,* ultimately from Latin *longus* LONG[1]; related to LUNGE[1]**]**

lungfish (ˈlʌŋˌfɪʃ) *n, pl* **-fish** *or* **-fishes.** any freshwater bony fish of the subclass *Dipnoi,* having an air-breathing lung, fleshy paired fins, and an elongated body. The only living species are those of the genera *Lepidosiren* of South America, *Protopterus* of Africa, and *Neoceratodus* of Australia.

lungi *or* **lungee** (ˈlʊŋgiː) *n* a long piece of cotton cloth worn as a loincloth, sash, or turban by Indian men or as a skirt. **[**C17: Hindi, from Persian**]**

Lungki *or* **Lung-chi** (ˈlʊŋˈkiː) *n* the former name of **Zhangzhou.**

lungworm (ˈlʌŋˌwɜːm) *n* **1** any parasitic nematode worm of the family *Metastrongylidae,* occurring in the lungs of mammals, esp. *Metastrongylus apri* which infects pigs. **2** any of certain other nematodes that are parasitic in the lungs.

lungwort (ˈlʌŋˌwɜːt) *n* **1** any of several Eurasian plants of the boraginaceous genus *Pulmonaria,* esp. *P. officinalis,* which has spotted leaves and clusters of blue or purple flowers: formerly used to treat lung diseases. **2** any of various boraginaceous plants of the N temperate genus *Mertensia,* such as *Mertensia maritima* (sea lungwort), having drooping clusters of tubular usually blue flowers.

Lunik (ˈluːnɪk) *n* another name for **Luna**[2].

lunisolar (ˌluːnɪˈsəʊlə) *adj* resulting from, relating to, or based on the combined gravitational attraction of the sun and moon. **[**C17: from Latin *lūna* moon + SOLAR**]**

lunitidal (ˌluːnɪˈtaɪdᵊl) *adj* of or relating to tidal phenomena as produced by the moon. **[**C19: from Latin *lūna* moon + TIDAL**]**

lunitidal interval *n* the difference in time between the moon crossing a meridian and the following high tide at that meridian.

lunula (ˈluːnjʊlə) *or* **lunule** (ˈluːnjuːl) *n, pl* **-nulae** (-njʊˌliː) *or* **-nules.** the white crescent-shaped area at the base of the human fingernail. Nontechnical name: **half-moon. [**C16: from Latin: small moon, from *lūna***]**

lunulate (ˈluːnjʊˌleɪt) *or* **lunulated** *adj* **1** having markings shaped like crescents: *lunulate patterns on an insect.* **2** Also: **lunular.** shaped like a crescent.

Luo (ləˈwəʊ, ˈluːəʊ) *n* **1** (*pl* **Luo** *or* **Luos**) a member of a cattle-herding Nilotic people living chiefly east of Lake Victoria in Kenya. **2** the language of this people, belonging to the Nilotic group of the Nilo-Saharan family.

Luoyang *or* **Loyang** (ˈləʊˈjæŋ) *n* a city in E China, in N Henan province on the Luo River near its confluence with the Yellow River; an important Buddhist centre in the 5th and 6th centuries; a commercial and industrial centre. Pop.: 1 190 000 (1990 est.).

Lupercalia (ˌluːpɜːˈkeɪlɪə) *n, pl* **-lia** *or* **-lias.** an ancient Roman festival of fertility, celebrated annually on Feb. 15. See also **Saint Valentine's Day. [**Latin, from *Lupercālis* belonging to *Lupercus,* a Roman god of the flocks**]** ▸ **ˌLuperˈcalian** *adj*

lupin *or U.S.* **lupine** (ˈluːpɪn) *n* any papilionaceous plant of the genus *Lupinus,* of North America, Europe, and Africa, with large spikes of brightly coloured flowers and flattened pods. **[**C14: from Latin *lupīnus* wolfish (see LUPINE); from the belief that the plant ravenously exhausted the soil**]**

lupine ('lu:paɪn) *adj* of, relating to, or resembling a wolf. [C17: from Latin *lupīnus*, from *lupus* wolf]

lupulin ('lu:pjʊlɪn) *n* a resinous powder extracted from the female flowers of the hop plant and used as a sedative. [C19: from New Latin *lupulus*, diminutive of *lupus* the hop plant]

lupus ('lu:pəs) *n* any of various ulcerative skin diseases. [C16: via Medieval Latin from Latin: wolf; said to be so called because it rapidly eats away the affected part]

USAGE In current usage the word *lupus* alone is generally understood to signify lupus vulgaris, lupus erythematosus being normally referred to in full or by the abbreviation LE.

Lupus ('lu:pəs) *n, Latin genitive* **Lupi** ('lu:paɪ). a constellation in the S hemisphere lying between Centaurus and Ara.

lupus erythematosus (ˌɛrɪˌθi:mə'təʊsəs) *n* either of two inflammatory diseases of the connective tissue. **Discoid lupus erythematosus** is characterized by a scaly rash over the cheeks and bridge of the nose; **disseminated** or **systemic lupus erythematosus** affects the joints, lungs, kidneys, or skin. Abbrev.: **LE.**

lupus vulgaris (vʌl'gɛərɪs) *n* tuberculosis of the skin, esp. of the face, with the formation of raised translucent nodules. Sometimes shortened to **lupus.**

lur *or* **lure** (lʊə) *n, pl* **lures** ('lʊərɪz). a large bronze musical horn found in Danish peat bogs and probably dating to the Bronze Age. [from Danish (and Swedish and Norwegian) *lur*, from Old Norse *lūthr* trumpet]

lurch[1] (lɜ:tʃ) *vb (intr)* **1** to lean or pitch suddenly to one side. **2** to stagger or sway. ◆ *n* **3** the act or an instance of lurching. [C19: origin unknown] ▸ **'lurching** *adj*

lurch[2] (lɜ:tʃ) *n* **1 leave (someone) in the lurch.** to desert (someone) in trouble. **2** *Cribbage.* the state of a losing player with less than 30 points at the end of a game (esp. in the phrase **in the lurch**). [C16: from French *lourche* a game similar to backgammon, apparently from *lourche* (adj) deceived, probably of Germanic origin]

lurch[3] (lɜ:tʃ) *vb (intr) Archaic or dialect.* to prowl or steal about suspiciously. [C15: perhaps a variant of LURK]

lurcher ('lɜ:tʃə) *n* **1** a crossbred hunting dog, usually a greyhound cross with a collie, esp. one trained to hunt silently. **2** *Archaic.* a person who prowls or lurks. [C16: from LURCH[3]]

lurdan ('lɜ:dᵊn) *Archaic.* ◆ *n* **1** a stupid or dull person. ◆ *adj* **2** dull or stupid. [C14: from Old French *lourdin*, Old French *lourd* heavy, from Latin *lūridus* LURID]

lure (lʊə) *vb (tr)* **1** (sometimes foll. by *away* or *into*) to tempt or attract by the promise of some type of reward. **2** *Falconry.* to entice (a hawk or falcon) from the air to the falconer by a lure. ◆ *n* **3** a person or thing that lures. **4** *Angling.* any of various types of brightly-coloured artificial spinning baits, usually consisting of a plastic or metal body mounted with hooks and trimmed with feathers, etc. See **jig, plug, spoon. 5** *Falconry.* a feathered decoy to which small pieces of meat can be attached and which is equipped with a long thong. [C14: from Old French *loirre* falconer's lure, from Germanic; related to Old English *lathian* to invite] ▸ **'lurer** *n*

Lurex ('lʊərɛks) *n* **1** *Trademark.* a thin metallic thread coated with plastic. **2** fabric containing such thread, which gives it a glittering appearance.

lurgy ('lɜ:gɪ) *n, pl* **-gies.** *Facetious.* any undetermined illness.

Luria ('lʊərɪə) *n* **1 Alexander Romanovich.** 1902–77, Russian psychologist, a pioneer of modern neuropsychology. His most important work concerns the psychological effects of brain tumours. **2 Isaac (ben Solomon).** 1534–72, Jewish mystic living in Egypt and Palestine: noted for his interpretation of the Cabbala.

lurid ('lʊərɪd) *adj* **1** vivid in shocking detail; sensational. **2** horrible in savagery or violence. **3** pallid in colour; wan. **4** glowing with an unnatural glare. [C17: from Latin *lūridus* pale yellow; probably related to *lūtum* a yellow vegetable dye] ▸ **'luridly** *adv* ▸ **'luridness** *n*

Lurie ('lʊərɪ) *n* **Alison.** born 1926, U.S. novelist. Her novels include *Imaginary Friends* (1967), *The War Between the Tates* (1974), and *Foreign Affairs* (1985).

lurk (lɜ:k) *vb (intr)* **1** to move stealthily or be concealed, esp. for evil purposes. **2** to be present in an unobtrusive way; go unnoticed. ◆ *n* **3** *Austral. and N.Z. slang.* a scheme or stratagem for success. [C13: probably frequentative of LOUR; compare Middle Dutch *loeren* to lie in wait] ▸ **'lurker** *n*

lurking ('lɜ:kɪŋ) *adj* **1** lingering and persistent, though unsuspected or unacknowledged: *a lurking suspicion.* **2** dimly perceived: *a lurking shape half concealed in the shadows.*

Lusaka (lu:'zɑ:kə, -'sɑ:kə) *n* the capital of Zambia, in the southeast at an altitude of 1280 m (4200 ft.): became capital of Northern Rhodesia in 1932 and of Zambia in 1964; University of Zambia (1966). Pop.: 982 362 (1990).

Lusatia (lu:'seɪʃɪə) *n* a region of central Europe, lying between the upper reaches of the Elbe and Oder Rivers: now mostly in E Germany, extending into SW Poland; inhabited chiefly by Sorbs.

Lusatian (lu:'seɪʃɪən) *adj* **1** of or relating to Lusatia, its people, or their language. ◆ *n* **2** a native or inhabitant of Lusatia; a Sorb. **3** the Sorbian language.

luscious ('lʌʃəs) *adj* **1** extremely pleasurable, esp. to the taste or smell. **2** very attractive. **3** *Archaic.* cloying. [C15 *lucius, licius*, perhaps a shortened form of DELICIOUS] ▸ **'lusciously** *adv* ▸ **'lusciousness** *n*

lush[1] (lʌʃ) *adj* **1** (of vegetation) abounding in lavish growth. **2** (esp. of fruits) succulent and fleshy. **3** luxurious, elaborate, or opulent. [C15: probably from Old French *lasche* lax, lazy, from Latin *laxus* loose; perhaps related to Old English *lǣc*, Old Norse *lakr* weak, German *lasch* loose] ▸ **'lushly** *adv* ▸ **'lushness** *n*

lush[2] (lʌʃ) *Slang.* ◆ *n* **1** a heavy drinker, esp. an alcoholic. **2** alcoholic drink. ◆ *vb* **3** *U.S. and Canadian.* to drink (alcohol) to excess. [C19: origin unknown]

Lüshun ('lu:'ʃʊn) *n* a port in NE China, in S Liaoning province, at the S end of the Liaodong peninsula; together with the city of Dalian it comprises the port complex of Lüda: jointly held by China and the Soviet Union (1945–55). Former name: **Port Arthur.**

Lusitania (ˌlu:sɪ'teɪnɪə) *n* an ancient region of the W Iberian Peninsula: a Roman province from 27 B.C. to the late 4th century A.D.; corresponds to most of present-day Portugal and the Spanish provinces of Salamanca and Cáceres.

Lusitanian (ˌlu:sɪ'teɪnɪən) *adj* **1** *Chiefly poetic.* of or relating to Lusitania or Portugal. **2** *Biology.* denoting flora or fauna characteristically found only in the warm, moist, west-facing coastal regions of Portugal, Spain, France, and the west and southwest coasts of Great Britain and Ireland.

Luso- *combining form.* indicating Portugal or Portuguese. [from Portuguese *lusitano*, from Latin, from LUSITANIA]

lust (lʌst) *n* **1** a strong desire for sexual gratification. **2** a strong desire or drive. ◆ *vb* **3** (*intr;* often foll. by *after* or *for*) to have a lust (for). [Old English; related to Old High German *lust* desire, Old Norse *losti* sexual desire, Latin *lascīvus* playful, wanton, lustful. Compare LISTLESS]

lustful ('lʌstfʊl) *adj* **1** driven by lust. **2** *Archaic.* vigorous or lusty. ▸ **'lustfully** *adv* ▸ **'lustfulness** *n*

lustral ('lʌstrəl) *adj* **1** of or relating to a ceremony of purification. **2** taking place at intervals of five years; quinquennial. [C16: from Latin *lūstrālis* adj. from LUSTRUM]

lustrate ('lʌstreɪt) *vb (tr)* to purify by means of religious rituals or ceremonies. [C17: from Latin *lūstrāre* to brighten] ▸ **lus'tration** *n* ▸ **lustrative** ('lʌstrətɪv) *adj*

lustre *or U.S.* **luster** ('lʌstə) *n* **1** reflected light; sheen; gloss. **2** radiance or brilliance of light. **3** great splendour of accomplishment, beauty, etc. **4** a substance used to polish or put a gloss on a surface. **5** a vase or chandelier from which hang cut-glass drops. **6** a drop-shaped piece of cut glass or crystal used as a decoration on a chandelier, vase, etc. **7a** a shiny metallic surface on some pottery and porcelain. **7b** (*as modifier*): *lustre decoration.* **8** *Mineralogy.* the way in which light is reflected from the surface of a mineral. It is one of the properties by which minerals are defined. ◆ *vb* **9** to make, be, or become lustrous. [C16: from Old French, from Old Italian *lustro*, from Latin *lustrāre* to make bright; related to LUSTRUM] ▸ **'lustreless** *or U.S.* **'lusterless** *adj* ▸ **'lustrous** *adj*

lustreware *or U.S.* **lusterware** ('lʌstəˌwɛə) *n* pottery or porcelain ware with lustre decoration.

lustring ('lʌstrɪŋ) *or* **lutestring** ('lu:tˌstrɪŋ) *n* a glossy silk cloth, formerly used for clothing, upholstery, etc. [C17: from Italian *lustrino*, from *lustro* LUSTRE]

lustrum ('lʌstrəm) *or* **lustre** *n, pl* **-trums** *or* **-tra** (-trə). a period of five years. [C16: from Latin: ceremony of purification, from *lustrāre* to brighten, purify]

lusty ('lʌstɪ) *adj* **lustier, lustiest. 1** having or characterized by robust health. **2** strong or invigorating: *a lusty brew.* **3** lustful. ▸ **'lustily** *adv* ▸ **'lustiness** *n*

lusus naturae ('lu:sʊs næ'tʊəri:) *n* a freak, mutant, or monster. [C17: Latin: whim of nature]

Lü-ta ('lu:'tɑ:) *n* a variant transliteration of the Chinese name for **Lüda.**

lutanist ('lu:tənɪst) *n* a variant spelling of **lutenist.**

lute[1] (lu:t) *n* an ancient plucked stringed instrument, consisting of a long fingerboard with frets and gut strings, and a body shaped like a sliced pear. [C14: from Old French *lut*, via Old Provençal from Arabic *al 'ūd*, literally: the wood]

lute[2] (lu:t) *n* **1** Also called: **luting.** a mixture of cement and clay used to seal the joints between pipes, etc. **2** *Dentistry.* a thin layer of cement used to fix a crown or inlay in place on a tooth. ◆ *vb* **3** *(tr)* to seal (a joint or surface) with lute. [C14: via Old French ultimately from Latin *lutum* clay]

luteal ('lu:tɪəl) *adj* relating to or characterized by the development of the corpus luteum: *the luteal phase of the oestrous cycle.* [C20: from Latin *lūteus* yellow, relating to *lūtum* a yellow weed]

lutein ('lu:tɪɪn) *n* a xanthophyll pigment, occurring in plants, that has a light-absorbing function in photosynthesis. [C20: from Latin *lūteus* yellow + -IN]

luteinizing hormone ('lu:tɪɪˌnaɪzɪŋ) *n* a gonadotrophic hormone secreted by the anterior lobe of the pituitary gland. In female vertebrates it stimulates ovulation, and in mammals it also induces the conversion of the ruptured follicle into the corpus luteum. In male vertebrates it promotes maturation of the interstitial cells of the testes and stimulates androgen secretion. Abbrev.: **LH.** Also called: **interstitial cell-stimulating hormone.** See also **follicle-stimulating hormone, prolactin.** [C19: from Latin *lūteum* egg yolk, from *lūteus* yellow]

luteinizing hormone-releasing hormone *n* a hypothalamic peptide that stimulates the pituitary gland to release luteinizing hormone. Abbrev.: **LH-RH.**

lutenist ('lu:tənɪst) *or U.S. and Canadian (sometimes)* **lutist** ('lu:tɪst) *n* a person who plays the lute. [C17: from Medieval Latin *lūtānista*, from *lūtāna*, apparently from Old French *lut* LUTE[1]]

luteolin ('lu:tɪəlɪn) *n* a yellow crystalline compound found, in the form of its glycoside, in many plants. Formula: $C_{15}H_{10}O_6$. [C19: via French from New Latin *reseda lūteola*, dyer's rocket, from which this substance is obtained; *lūteola* from Latin *lūteus* yellow]

luteotrophin (ˌlu:tɪəʊ'trəʊfɪn), **luteotrophic hormone,** *or esp. U.S.* **luteotropin, luteotropic hormone** *n* other names for **prolactin.**

luteous ('lu:tɪəs) *adj* of a light to moderate greenish-yellow colour. [C17: from Latin *lūteus* yellow]

lutestring ('lu:tˌstrɪŋ) *n Textiles.* a variant of **lustring.**

Lutetia *or* **Lutetia Parisiorum** (lu:'ti:ʃə pəˌrɪzɪ'ɔ:rəm) *n* an ancient name for **Paris** (the French city).

lutetium *or* **lutecium** (lʊ'ti:ʃɪəm) *n* a silvery-white metallic element of the lanthanide series, occurring in monazite and used as a catalyst in cracking, alkylation, and polymerization. Symbol: Lu; atomic no.: 71; atomic wt.: 174.967; valency: 3; relative density: 9.841; melting pt.: 1663°C; boiling pt.: 3402°C.

[C19: New Latin, from Latin *Lūtētia* ancient name of Paris, home of G. Urbain (1872–1938), French chemist, who discovered it]

Luth. *abbrev. for* Lutheran.

Luther ('lu:θə) *n* **Martin.** 1483–1546, German leader of the Protestant Reformation. As professor of biblical theology at Wittenberg University from 1511, he began preaching the crucial doctrine of justification by faith rather than by works, and in 1517 he nailed 95 theses to the church door at Wittenberg, attacking Tetzel's sale of indulgences. He was excommunicated and outlawed by the Diet of Worms (1521) as a result of his refusal to recant, but he was protected in Wartburg Castle by Frederick III of Saxony (1521–22). He translated the Bible into German (1521–34) and approved Melanchthon's Augsburg Confession (1530), defining the basic tenets of Lutheranism. ▸ **'Lutherism** *n*

Lutheran ('lu:θərən) *n* **1** a follower of Luther or a member of a Lutheran Church. ♦ *adj* **2** of or relating to Luther or his doctrines, the most important being justification by faith alone, consubstantiation, and the authority of the Bible. **3** of or denoting any Protestant Church that follows Luther's doctrines. ▸ **'Lutheranism** *n*

luthern ('lu:θən) *n* another name for **dormer.** [C17: probably from LUCARNE, perhaps influenced by LUTHERAN]

Luthuli *or* **Lutuli** (lu:'tu:lɪ) *n* Chief **Albert John.** 1899–1967, South African political leader. As president of the African National Congress (1952–60), he campaigned for nonviolent resistance to apartheid: Nobel peace prize 1961.

Lutine bell ('lu:ti:n, lu:'ti:n) *n* a bell, taken from the ship *Lutine,* kept at Lloyd's in London and rung before important announcements, esp. the loss of a vessel.

luting ('lu:tɪŋ) *n* **1** another name for **lute**[2] (sense 1). **2** Also called: **luting paste.** a strip of pastry placed around the dish to seal the lid of a pie.

lutist ('lu:tɪst) *n* **1** *U.S. and Canadian.* another word for **lutenist. 2** a person who makes lutes.

lutite ('lu:taɪt) *n* another name for **pelite.** [C20: from Latin *lutum* mud + -ITE[1]]

Luton ('lu:tᵊn) *n* **1** a town in SE central England, in Luton unitary authority, S Bedfordshire: airport; motor-vehicle industries. Pop.: 171 671 (1991). **2** a unitary authority in SE central England, in Bedfordshire. Pop.: 180 800 (1994 est.). Area: 43 sq. km (17 sq. miles).

Luton Hoo (hu:) *n* a mansion near Luton in Bedfordshire: built (1766–67) for the 3rd Earl of Bute by Robert Adam; rebuilt in the 19th century: houses the Wernher Collection of tapestries, porcelain, and paintings.

Lutosławski (*Polish* luto'slavski) *n* **Witold** ('vitɔlt). 1913–94, Polish composer, whose works frequently juxtapose aleatoric and notated writing.

Lutyens ('lʌtʃənz) *n* **1** Sir **Edwin.** 1869–1944, British architect, noted for his neoclassical country houses and his planning of New Delhi, India. **2** his daughter, **Elisabeth.** 1906–83, British composer.

lutz (lu:ts) *n Skating.* a jump in which the skater takes off from the back outside edge of one skate, makes one, two, or three turns in the air, and lands on the back outside edge of the other skate. [C20: of uncertain origin]

Lützen (*German* 'lytsən) *n* a town near Leipzig in E Germany, in Saxony; site of a battle (1632) in the Thirty Years' War in which the army of the Holy Roman Empire under Wallenstein was defeated by the Swedes under Gustavus Adolphus, who died in the battle.

Lützow-Holm Bay ('lutsəʊ'həʊm) *n* an inlet of the Indian Ocean on the coast of Antarctica, between Enderby Land and Queen Maud Land.

luvvie *or* **luvvy** ('lʌvɪ) *n, pl* **-vies.** *Facetious.* a person who is involved in the acting profession or the theatre, esp. one with a tendency to affectation. [C20: from LOVEY]

lux (lʌks) *n, pl* **lux.** the derived SI unit of illumination equal to a luminous flux of 1 lumen per square metre. 1 lux is equivalent to 0.0929 foot-candle. Symbol: lx [C19: from Latin: light]

Lux. *abbrev. for* Luxembourg.

luxate ('lʌkseɪt) *vb (tr) Pathol.* to put (a shoulder, knee, etc.) out of joint; dislocate. [C17: from Latin *luxāre* to displace, from *luxus* dislocated; related to Greek *loxos* oblique] ▸ **lux'ation** *n*

luxe (lʌks, lʊks; *French* lyks) *n* See **de luxe.** [C16: from French from Latin *luxus* extravagance, LUXURY]

Luxembourg ('lʌksəm,bɜ:g; *French* lyksābur) *n* **1** a grand duchy in W Europe: formed the Benelux customs union with Belgium and the Netherlands in 1948 and is now a member of the European Union. Languages: French, German, and Luxemburgish. Religion: Roman Catholic majority. Currency: euro and Luxembourg franc; Belgian franc is also used. Capital: Luxembourg. Pop.: 425 000 (1998 est.). Area: 2586 sq. km (999 sq. miles). **2** the capital of Luxembourg, on the Alzette River: an industrial centre. Pop.: 76 446 (1995 est.). **3** a province in SE Belgium, in the Ardennes. Capital: Arlon. Pop.: 241 339 (1996 est.). Area: 4416 sq. km (1705 sq. miles). ▸ **'Luxembourger** *n*

Luxemburg (*German* 'lʊksəmbʊrk) *n* **Rosa** ('ro:za). 1871–1919, German socialist leader, led an unsuccessful Communist revolt (1919) with Karl Liebknecht and was assassinated.

Luxor ('lʌksɔ:) *n* a town in S Egypt, on the River Nile: the southern part of the site of ancient Thebes; many ruins and tombs, notably the temple built by Amenhotep III (about 1411–1375 B.C.). Pop.: 155 000 (1994 est.).

luxulianite *or* **luxullianite** (lʌk'su:ljə,naɪt) *n* a rare variety of granite containing tourmaline embedded in quartz and feldspar. [C19: named after *Luxulyan,* a village in Cornwall near which it was first found]

luxuriant (lʌg'zjʊərɪənt) *adj* **1** rich and abundant; lush. **2** very elaborate or ornate. **3** extremely productive or fertile. [C16: from Latin *luxuriāns,* present participle of *luxuriāre* to abound to excess] ▸ **lux'uriance** *n* ▸ **lux'uriantly** *adv*

USAGE See at **luxurious.**

luxuriate (lʌg'zjʊərɪ,eɪt) *vb (intr)* **1** (foll. by *in*) to take voluptuous pleasure; revel. **2** to flourish extensively or profusely. **3** to live in a sumptuous way. [C17: from Latin *luxuriāre*] ▸ **lux,uri'ation** *n*

luxurious (lʌg'zjʊərɪəs) *adj* **1** characterized by luxury. **2** enjoying or devoted to luxury. **3** an archaic word for **lecherous.** [C14: via Old French from Latin *luxuriōsus* excessive] ▸ **lux'uriously** *adv* ▸ **lux'uriousness** *n*

USAGE *Luxurious* is sometimes wrongly used where *luxuriant* is meant: *he had a luxuriant* (not *luxurious*) *moustache; the walls were covered with a luxuriant growth of wisteria.*

luxury ('lʌkʃərɪ) *n, pl* **-ries. 1** indulgence in and enjoyment of rich, comfortable, and sumptuous living. **2** (*sometimes pl*) something that is considered an indulgence rather than a necessity. **3** something pleasant and satisfying: *the luxury of independence.* **4** (*modifier*) relating to, indicating, or supplying luxury: *a luxury liner.* [C14 (in the sense: lechery): via Old French from Latin *luxuria* excess, from *luxus* extravagance]

Luzern (lu'tsɛrn) *n* the German name for **Lucerne.**

Luzon (lu:'zɒn) *n* the main and largest island of the Philippines, in the N part of the archipelago, separated from the other islands by the Sibuyan Sea: important agriculturally, producing most of the country's rice, with large forests and rich mineral resources; industrial centres at Manila and Batangas. Capital: Quezon City. Pop.: 32 558 000 (1995 est.). Area: 108 378 sq. km (41 845 sq. miles).

Lv *Currency. abbrev. for* lev(a).

LV 1 (in Britain) *abbrev. for* luncheon voucher. **2** *international car registration for* Latvia.

lv. *abbrev. for* leave (of absence, as from military duty).

Lviv (lvif) *n* an industrial city in the W Ukraine: it has belonged to Poland (1340–1772; 1919–39), Austria (1772–1918), Germany (1939–45), and the Soviet Union (1945–91); Ukrainian cultural centre, with a university (1661). Pop.: 802 000 (1996 est.). Russian name: **Lviv.** Polish name: **Lwów.** German name: **Lemberg.**

Lvov (*Russian* ljvɔf) *n* the Russian name for **Lviv.**

Lw *the former chemical symbol for* lawrencium (now superseded by **Lr**).

LW *abbrev. for:* **1** *Radio.* long wave. **2** low water.

lwl *or* **LWL** *abbrev. for* length waterline; the length of a vessel at the waterline, taken at the centre axis.

LWM *or* **lwm** *abbrev. for* low water mark.

Lwów (lvuf) *n* the Polish name for **Lviv.**

lx *Physics. symbol for* lux.

LXX *symbol for* Septuagint.

-ly[1] *suffix forming adjectives.* **1** having the nature or qualities of: *brotherly; godly.* **2** occurring at certain intervals; every: *daily; yearly.* [Old English *-lic*]

-ly[2] *suffix forming adverbs.* in a certain manner; to a certain degree: *quickly; recently; chiefly.* [Old English *-lice,* from *-lic* -LY[1]]

Lyallpur (,laɪəl'pʊə) *n* the former name (until 1979) of **Faisalabad.**

lyase ('laɪeɪz) *n* any enzyme that catalyses the separation of two parts of a molecule by the formation of a double bond between them. [C20: from Greek *lusis* a loosening + -ASE]

Lyautey (*French* ljote) *n* **Louis Hubert Gonzalve** (lwi ybɛr gõzalv). 1854–1934, French marshal and colonial administrator; resident general in Morocco (1912–25).

lycanthrope ('laɪkən,θrəʊp, laɪ'kænθrəʊp) *n* **1** a werewolf. **2** *Psychiatry.* a person who believes that he is a wolf. [C17: via New Latin, from Greek *lukanthrōpos,* from *lukos* wolf + *anthrōpos* man]

lycanthropy (laɪ'kænθrəpɪ) *n* **1** the supposed magical transformation of a person into a wolf. **2** *Psychiatry.* a delusion in which a person believes that he is a wolf. [C16: from Greek *lukānthropía,* from *lukos* wolf + *anthrōpos* man] ▸ **lycanthropic** (,laɪkən'θrɒpɪk) *adj*

Lycaon (laɪ'keɪɒn) *n Greek myth.* a king of Arcadia said to have offered Zeus a plate of human flesh to learn whether the god was omniscient.

Lycaonia (,lɪkə'əʊnɪə) *n* an ancient region of S Asia Minor, north of the Taurus Mountains; corresponds to present-day S central Turkey.

lycée ('li:seɪ) *n, pl* **-cées** (-seɪz). *Chiefly French.* a secondary school. [C19: French, from Latin: LYCEUM]

lyceum (laɪ'sɪəm) *n* (now chiefly in the names of buildings) **1** a public building for concerts, lectures, etc. **2** *U.S.* a cultural organization responsible for presenting concerts, lectures, etc. **3** another word for **lycée.**

Lyceum (laɪ'sɪəm) *n* **the. 1** a school and sports ground of ancient Athens: site of Aristotle's discussions with his pupils. **2** the Aristotelian school of philosophy. [from Greek *Lukeion,* named after a temple nearby dedicated to *Apollo Lukeios,* an epithet of unknown origin]

lychee (,laɪ'tʃi:) *n* a variant spelling of **litchi.**

lych gate *or* **lich gate** (lɪtʃ) *n* a roofed gate to a churchyard, formerly used during funerals as a temporary shelter for the bier. [C15: *lich,* from Old English *līc* corpse]

lychnis ('lɪknɪs) *n* any caryophyllaceous plant of the genus *Lychnis,* having red, pink, or white five-petalled flowers. See also **ragged robin.** [C17: New Latin, via Latin, from Greek *lukhnis* a red flower; related to *lukhnos* lamp]

Lycia ('lɪsɪə) *n* an ancient region on the coast of SW Asia Minor: a Persian, Rhodian, and Roman province.

Lycian ('lɪsɪən) *adj* **1** of or relating to ancient Lycia, its inhabitants, or their language. ♦ *n* **2** an inhabitant of Lycia. **3** the extinct language of the Lycians, belonging to the Anatolian group or family.

lycopod ('laɪkə,pɒd) *n* another name for a **club moss,** esp. one of the genus *Lycopodium.*

lycopodium (,laɪkə'pəʊdɪəm) *n* any club moss of the genus *Lycopodium,* resembling moss but having woody tissue and spore-bearing cones: family *Lycopodiaceae.* See also **ground pine** (sense 2). [C18: New Latin, from Greek, from *lukos* wolf + *pous* foot]

Lycra ('laɪkrə) *n Trademark.* a type of synthetic elastic fabric and fibre used for tight-fitting garments, such as swimming costumes.

Lycurgus (laɪ'kɜ:gəs) *n* 9th century B.C., Spartan lawgiver. He is traditionally regarded as the founder of the Spartan constitution, military institutions, and educational system.

Lydda ('lɪdə) *n* another name for **Lod**.

lyddite ('lɪdaɪt) *n* **1** an explosive consisting chiefly of fused picric acid. **2** a dense black variety of chert, formerly used as a touchstone. [C19: (sense 1) named after *Lydd,* a town in Kent near which the first tests were made]

Lydgate ('lɪdˌgeɪt) *n* **John.** ?1370–?1450, English poet and monk. His vast output includes devotional works and translations, such as that of a French version of Boccaccio's *The Fall of Princes* (1430–38).

Lydia ('lɪdɪə) *n* an ancient region on the coast of W Asia Minor: a powerful kingdom in the century and a half before the Persian conquest (546 B.C.). Chief town: Sardis.

Lydian ('lɪdɪən) *adj* **1** of or relating to ancient Lydia, its inhabitants, or their language. **2** *Music.* of or relating to an authentic mode represented by the ascending natural diatonic scale from F to F. See also **Hypo-**. Compare **Hypolydian.** ◆ *n* **3** an inhabitant of Lydia. **4** the extinct language of the Lydians, thought to belong to the Anatolian group or family.

lye (laɪ) *n* **1** any solution obtained by leaching, such as the caustic solution obtained by leaching wood ash. **2** a concentrated solution of sodium hydroxide or potassium hydroxide. [Old English *lēag;* related to Middle Dutch *lōghe,* Old Norse *laug* bath, Latin *lavāre* to wash]

Lyell ('laɪəl) *n* Sir **Charles.** 1797–1875, Scottish geologist. In *Principles of Geology* (1830–33) he advanced the theory of uniformitarianism, refuting the doctrine of catastrophism.

lying[1] ('laɪɪŋ) *vb* the present participle and gerund of **lie**[1].

lying[2] ('laɪɪŋ) *vb* the present participle and gerund of **lie**[2].

lying-in *n, pl* **lyings-in. a** confinement in childbirth. **b** *(as modifier): a lying-in hospital.*

lyke-wake ('laɪkˌweɪk) *n Brit.* a watch held over a dead person, often with festivities. [C16: perhaps from Old Norse; see LYCH GATE, WAKE[1]]

Lyle (laɪl) *n* **Sandy,** full name *Alexander Walter Barr Lyle.* born 1958, Scottish professional golfer: won the British Open Championship (1985) and the U.S. Masters (1988).

Lyly ('lɪlɪ) *n* **John.** ?1554–1606, English dramatist and novelist, noted for his two romances, *Euphues, or the Anatomy of Wit* (1578) and *Euphues and his England* (1580), written in an elaborate style. See also **euphuism.**

Lyme disease (laɪm) *n* a disease of domestic animals and humans, caused by the spirochaete *Borrelia burghdorferi* and transmitted by ticks, and variously affecting the joints, heart, and brain. [C20: named after *Lyme,* Connecticut, the town where it was first identified in humans]

lyme grass (laɪm) *n* a N temperate perennial dune grass, *Elymus arenarius,* with a creeping stem and rough bluish leaves. [C18: probably a respelling (influenced by its genus name, *Elymus*) of LIME[1], referring to its stabilizing effect (like lime in mortar)]

Lyme Regis (laɪm 'riːdʒɪs) *n* a resort in S England, in Dorset, on the English Channel: noted for finds of prehistoric fossils. Pop.: 3851 (1991).

Lymington ('lɪmɪŋtən) *n* a market town in S England, in SW Hampshire, on the Solent: yachting centre and holiday resort. Pop.: 13 508 (1991).

lymph (lɪmf) *n* the almost colourless fluid, containing chiefly white blood cells, that is collected from the tissues of the body and transported in the lymphatic system. [C17: from Latin *lympha* water, from earlier *limpa* influenced in form by Greek *numphē* nymph]

lymphadenitis (lɪmˌfædɪ'naɪtɪs, ˌlɪmfæd-) *n* inflammation of a lymph node. [C19: New Latin. See LYMPH, ADENITIS]

lymphadenopathy (lɪmˌfædɪ'nɒpəθɪ, ˌlɪmfæd-) *n* a swelling of the lymph nodes, usually caused by inflammation associated with a viral infection such as rubella.

lymphangial (lɪm'fændʒɪəl) *adj* of or relating to a lymphatic vessel.

lymphangitis (ˌlɪmfæn'dʒaɪtɪs) *n, pl* **-gitides** (-'dʒɪtɪˌdiːz). inflammation of one or more of the lymphatic vessels. [C19: see LYMPH, ANGIO-, -ITIS] ▸ **lymphangitic** (ˌlɪmfæn'dʒɪtɪk) *adj*

lymphatic (lɪm'fætɪk) *adj* **1** of, relating to, or containing lymph: *the lymphatic vessels.* **2** of or relating to the lymphatic system. **3** sluggish or lacking vigour. ◆ *n* **4** a lymphatic vessel. [C17 (meaning: mad): from Latin *lymphāticus.* Original meaning perhaps arose from a confusion between *nymph* and LYMPH; compare Greek *numphaleptos* frenzied] ▸ **lym'phatically** *adv*

lymphatic system *n* an extensive network of capillary vessels that transports the interstitial fluid of the body as lymph to the venous blood circulation.

lymphatic tissue *n* tissue, such as the lymph nodes, tonsils, spleen, and thymus, that produces lymphocytes. Also called: **lymphoid tissue.**

lymph cell *n* another name for **lymphocyte.**

lymph gland *n* a former name for **lymph node.**

lymph node *n* any of numerous bean-shaped masses of tissue, situated along the course of lymphatic vessels, that help to protect against infection by killing bacteria and neutralizing toxins and are the source of lymphocytes.

lympho- *or before a vowel* **lymph-** *combining form.* indicating lymph or the lymphatic system: *lymphogranuloma.*

lymphoblast ('lɪmfəʊˌblɑːst) *n* an abnormal cell consisting of a large nucleus and small cytoplasm that was once thought to be an immature lymphocyte and is now associated with a type of leukaemia (**lymphoblastic leukaemia**). ▸ **lymphoblastic** (ˌlɪmfəʊ'blæstɪk) *adj*

lymphocyte ('lɪmfəʊˌsaɪt) *n* a type of white blood cell formed in lymphoid tissue. See also **B-lymphocyte, T-lymphocyte.** ▸ **lymphocytic** (ˌlɪmfəʊ'sɪtɪk) *adj*

lymphocytopenia (ˌlɪmfəʊˌsaɪtəʊ'piːnɪə) *n Pathol.* an abnormally low level of lymphocytes in the blood. Also called: **lymphopenia.**

lymphocytosis (ˌlɪmfəʊsaɪ'təʊsɪs) *n* an abnormally large number of lymphocytes in the blood: often found in diseases such as glandular fever and smallpox. ▸ **lymphocytotic** (ˌlɪmfəʊsaɪ'tɒtɪk) *adj*

lymphoid ('lɪmfɔɪd) *adj* of or resembling lymph, or relating to the lymphatic system.

lymphoid tissue *n* another name for **lymphatic tissue.**

lymphokine ('lɪmfəʊˌkaɪn) *n Immunol.* a protein, released by lymphocytes, that affects other cells involved in the immune response.

lymphoma (lɪm'fəʊmə) *n, pl* **-mata** (-mətə) *or* **-mas.** any form of cancer of the lymph nodes. Also called: **lymphosarcoma** (ˌlɪmfəʊsɑː'kəʊmə). ▸ **lym'phomatous** *or* **lym'phomaˌtoid** *adj*

lymphopoiesis (ˌlɪmfəʊpɔɪ'iːsɪs) *n, pl* **-ses** (-siːz). the formation of lymphatic tissue or lymphocytes. ▸ **lymphopoietic** (ˌlɪmfəʊpɔɪ'ɛtɪk) *adj*

lyncean (lɪn'siːən) *adj* **1** of or resembling a lynx. **2** *Rare.* having keen sight. [C17: probably via Latin, from Greek *Lunkeios* concerning *Lunkeos,* an Argonaut renowned for his sharpsightedness, from *lunx* lynx]

lynch (lɪntʃ) *vb (tr)* (of a mob) to punish (a person) for some supposed offence by hanging without a trial. [probably after Charles *Lynch* (1736–96), Virginia justice of the peace, who presided over extralegal trials of Tories during the American War of Independence] ▸ **'lyncher** *n* ▸ **'lynching** *n*

Lynch (lɪntʃ) *n* **John,** known as *Jack Lynch.* born 1917, Irish statesman; prime minister of the Republic of Ireland (1966–73; 1977–79).

lynchet ('lɪntʃɪt) *n* a terrace or ridge formed in prehistoric or medieval times by ploughing a hillside. [Old English *hlinc* ridge]

lynch law *n* the practice of condemning and punishing a person by mob action without a proper trial.

Lyndsay *or* **Lindsay** ('lɪndzɪ) *n* Sir **David.** 1486–1554, Scottish poet and courtier, author of *Ane Pleasant Satyre of the Three Estates* (1552).

Lynn[1] (lɪn) *n* another name for **King's Lynn.** Also called: **Lynn Regis** ('riːdʒɪs).

Lynn[2] (lɪn) *n* Dame **Vera,** original name *Vera Margaret Lewis.* born 1917, British singer popular during World War II and known as "the forces' sweetheart". Her best-known songs are "We'll Meet Again" and "White Cliffs of Dover".

lynx (lɪŋks) *n, pl* **lynxes** *or* **lynx. 1** a feline mammal, *Felis lynx* (or *canadensis*), of Europe and North America, with grey-brown mottled fur, tufted ears, and a short tail. Related adj: **lyncean. 2** the fur of this animal. **3 bay lynx.** another name for **bobcat. 4 desert lynx.** another name for **caracal. 5** Also called: **Polish lynx.** a large fancy pigeon from Poland, with spangled or laced markings. [C14: via Latin from Greek *lunx;* related to Old English *lox,* German *Luchs*] ▸ **'lynxˌlike** *adj*

Lynx (lɪŋks) *n, Latin genitive* **Lyncis** ('lɪnsɪs). a faint constellation in the N hemisphere lying between Ursa Major and Cancer.

lynx-eyed *adj* having keen sight.

lyo- *combining form.* indicating dispersion or dissolution: *lyophilic; lyophilize; lyophobic.* [from Greek *luein* to loose]

lyolysis (laɪ'ɒlɪsɪs) *n Chem.* the formation of an acid and a base from the interaction of a salt with a solvent.

Lyon (*French* ljɔ̃) *n* a city in SE central France, capital of Rhône department, at the confluence of the Rivers Rhône and Saône: the third largest city in France; a major industrial centre and river port. Pop.: 422 444 (1990). English name: **Lyons** ('laɪənz). Ancient name: **Lugdunum** (lʊg'duːnəm).

Lyon King of Arms ('laɪən) *n* the chief herald of Scotland. Also called: **Lord Lyon.** [C14: archaic spelling of LION, referring to the figure on the royal shield]

Lyonnais (*French* ljɔnɛ) *n* a former province of E central France, on the Rivers Rhône and Saône: occupied by the present-day departments of Rhône and Loire. Chief town: Lyon.

lyonnaise (ˌlaɪə'neɪz; *French* ljɔnɛz) *adj* (of food) cooked or garnished with onions, usually fried.

Lyonnesse (ˌlaɪə'nɛs) *n* (in Arthurian legend) the mythical birthplace of Sir Tristram, situated in SW England and believed to have been submerged by the sea.

Lyons ('laɪənz) *n* **Joseph Aloysius.** 1879–1939, Australian statesman; prime minister of Australia (1931–39).

lyophilic (ˌlaɪəʊ'fɪlɪk) *adj Chem.* (of a colloid) having a dispersed phase with a high affinity for the continuous phase: *a lyophilic sol.* Compare **lyophobic.**

lyophilize *or* **lyophilise** (laɪ'ɒfɪˌlaɪz) *vb (tr)* to dry (blood, serum, tissue, etc.) by freezing in a high vacuum.

lyophobic (ˌlaɪəʊ'fəʊbɪk) *adj Chem.* (of a colloid) having a dispersed phase with little or no affinity for the continuous phase: *a lyophobic sol.* Compare **lyophilic.**

lyosorption (ˌlaɪəʊ'sɔːpʃən) *n Chem.* the adsorption of a liquid on a solid surface, esp. of a solvent on suspended particles.

Lyra ('laɪərə) *n, Latin genitive* **Lyrae** ('laɪəriː). a small constellation in the N hemisphere lying near Cygnus and Draco and containing the star Vega, an eclipsing binary (**Beta Lyrae**), a planetary nebula (the **Ring Nebula**), and a variable star, **RR Lyrae.**

lyrate ('laɪərɪt) *or* **lyrated** *adj* **1** shaped like a lyre. **2** (of leaves) having a large terminal lobe and smaller lateral lobes. [C18: from New Latin *lyrātus,* Latin from *lyra* LYRE] ▸ **'lyrately** *adv*

lyra viol ('laɪərə) *n* a lutelike musical instrument popular in the 16th and 17th centuries: the forerunner of the mandolin.

lyre (laɪə) *n* **1** an ancient Greek stringed instrument consisting of a resonating tortoise shell to which a crossbar was attached by two projecting arms. It was plucked with a plectrum and used for accompanying songs. **2** any ancient instrument of similar design. **3** a medieval bowed instrument of the violin family. [C13: via Old French from Latin *lyra,* from Greek *lura*]

lyrebird ('laɪəˌbɜːd) *n* either of two pheasant-like Australian birds, *Menura superba* and *M. alberti,* constituting the family *Menuridae:* during courtship displays, the male spreads its tail into the shape of a lyre.

lyric ('lɪrɪk) *adj* **1** (of poetry) **1a** expressing the writer's personal feelings and thoughts. **1b** having the form and manner of a song. **2** of or relating to such poetry. **3** (of a singing voice) having a light quality and tone. **4** intended for singing, esp. (in classical Greece) to the accompaniment of the lyre. ◆ *n* **5** a short poem of songlike quality. **6** (*pl*) the words of a popular song. ◆ Also (for senses 1–3): **lyrical.** [C16: from Latin *lyricus*, from Greek *lurikos*, from *lura* LYRE] ► **'lyrically** *adv* ► **'lyricalness** *n*

lyrical ('lɪrɪk°l) *adj* **1** another word for **lyric** (senses 1–3). **2** enthusiastic; effusive (esp. in the phrase **to wax lyrical**).

lyricism ('lɪrɪˌsɪzəm) *n* **1** the quality or style of lyric poetry. **2** emotional or enthusiastic outpouring.

lyricist ('lɪrɪsɪst) *n* **1** a person who writes the words for a song, opera, or musical play. **2** Also called: **lyrist.** a lyric poet.

lyrism ('lɪrɪzəm) *n* **1** the art or technique of playing the lyre. **2** a less common word for **lyricism.**

lyrist *n* **1** ('laɪərɪst). a person who plays the lyre. **2** ('lɪrɪst). another word for **lyricist** (sense 2).

lys- *combining form.* a variant of **lyso-** before a vowel.

Lysander (laɪ'sændə) *n* died 395 B.C., Spartan naval commander of the Peloponnesian War.

lyse (laɪs, laɪz) *vb* to undergo or cause to undergo lysis.

Lysenko (lɪ'seŋkəʊ; *Russian* li'sjenkə) *n* **Trofim Denisovich** (tra'fim dɪ'nisəvitʃ). 1898–1976, Russian biologist and geneticist.

Lysenkoism (lɪ'seŋkəʊˌɪzəm) *n* a form of Neo-Lamarckism advocated by Lysenko, emphasizing the importance of the inheritance of acquired characteristics.

lysergic acid (lɪ'sɜːdʒɪk, laɪ-) *n* a crystalline compound with a polycyclic molecular structure: used in medical research. Formula $C_{16}H_{16}N_2O_2$. [C20: from (HYDRO)LYS(IS) + ERG(OT) + -IC]

lysergic acid diethylamide (daɪˌeθɪl'eɪmaɪd, -ˌiːθaɪl-) *n* See **LSD.**

Lysias ('lɪsɪˌæs) *n* ?450–?380 B.C., Athenian orator.

Lysimachus (laɪ'sɪməkəs) *n* ?360–281 B.C., Macedonian general under Alexander the Great; king of Thrace (323–281); killed in battle by Seleucus I.

lysimeter (laɪ'sɪmɪtə) *n* an instrument for determining solubility, esp. the amount of water-soluble matter in soil. [C20: from *lysi-* (variant of LYSO-) + -METER]

lysin ('laɪsɪn) *n* any of a group of antibodies or other agents that cause dissolution of cells against which they are directed.

lysine ('laɪsiːn, -sɪn) *n* an essential amino acid that occurs in proteins.

Lysippus (laɪ'sɪpəs) *n* 4th century B.C., Greek sculptor. He introduced a new naturalism into Greek sculpture.

lysis ('laɪsɪs) *n, pl* **-ses** (-siːz). **1** the destruction or dissolution of cells by the action of a particular lysin. **2** *Med.* the gradual reduction in severity of the symptoms of a disease. [C19: New Latin, from Greek, from *luein* to release]

-lysis *n combining form.* indicating a loosening, decomposition, or breaking down: *electrolysis; paralysis.* [from Greek, from *lusis* a loosening; see LYSIS]

Lysithea (laɪ'sɪθɪə) *n Astronomy.* a small satellite of Jupiter in an intermediate orbit.

lyso- *or before a vowel* **lys-** *combining form.* indicating a dissolving or loosening: *lysozyme.* [from Greek *lusis* a loosening]

lysogeny (laɪ'sɒdʒənɪ) *n* the relationship between a bacteriophage and a bacterium in which the virus does not destroy the bacterial cell, its nucleic acid becoming incorporated with that of its host. ► **lysogenic** (ˌlaɪsəʊ'dʒenɪk) *adj*

Lysol ('laɪsɒl) *n Trademark.* a solution containing a mixture of cresols in water, used as an antiseptic and disinfectant.

lysosome ('laɪsəˌsəʊm) *n* any of numerous small particles, containing digestive enzymes, that are present in the cytoplasm of most cells. ► **ˌlyso'somal** *adj*

lysozyme ('laɪsəˌzaɪm) *n* an enzyme occurring in tears, certain body tissues, and egg white: destroys bacteria by hydrolysing polysaccharides in their cell walls. [C20: from LYSO- + (EN)ZYME]

lyssa ('lɪsə) *n Pathol.* a less common word for **rabies.**

-lyte *n combining form.* indicating a substance that can be decomposed or broken down: *electrolyte.* [from Greek *lutos* soluble, from *luein* to loose]

Lytham Saint Anne's ('lɪðəm sənt 'ænz) *n, usually abbreviated to* **Lytham St Anne's.** a resort in NW England, in Lancashire on the Irish Sea. Pop.: 40 866 (1991).

lythraceous (lɪ'θreɪʃəs, laɪ'θreɪ-) *adj* of, relating to, or belonging to the *Lythraceae*, a mostly tropical American family of herbaceous plants, shrubs, and trees that includes purple loosestrife and crape myrtle. [C19: from New Latin *Lythrum* type genus, from Greek *luthron* blood, from the red flowers]

lytic ('lɪtɪk) *adj* **1** relating to, causing, or resulting from lysis. **2** of or relating to a lysin. [C19: Greek *lutikos* capable of loosing]

-lytic *adj combining form.* indicating a loosening or dissolving: *paralytic.* [from Greek, from *lusis;* see -LYSIS]

lytta ('lɪtə) *n, pl* **-tas** *or* **-tae** (-tiː). a rodlike mass of cartilage beneath the tongue in the dog and other carnivores. [C17: New Latin, from Greek *lussa* madness; in dogs, it was believed to be a cause of rabies]

Lyttelton ('lɪt°ltən) *n* **Humphrey.** born 1921, British jazz trumpeter and band leader who influenced the British revival of New Orleans jazz.

Lytton ('lɪt°n) *n* **1st Baron,** title of *Edward George Earle Lytton Bulwer-Lytton.* 1803–73, British novelist, dramatist, and statesman, noted particularly for his historical romances.

Lyublin ('ljublɪn) *n* transliteration of the Russian name for **Lublin.**

Mm

m *or* **M** (ɛm) *n, pl* **m's, M's,** *or* **Ms. 1** the 13th letter and tenth consonant of the modern English alphabet. **2** a speech sound represented by this letter, usually a bilabial nasal, as in *mat.*

m *symbol for:* **1** metre(s). **2** mile(s). **3** milli-. **4** minute(s).

M *symbol for:* **1** mach. **2** medium (size). **3** mega-. **4** *Currency.* mark(s). **5** million. **6** *Astronomy.* Messier catalogue; a catalogue published in 1784, in which 103 nebulae and clusters are listed using a numerical system: *M13 is the globular cluster in Hercules.* **7** Middle. **8** *Physics.* modulus. **9** (in Britain) motorway: *the M1 runs from London to Leeds.* **10** (in Australia) **10a** mature audience (used to describe a category of film certified as suitable for viewing by anyone over the age of 15). **10b** (*as modifier*): *an M film.* **11** *Logic.* the middle term of a syllogism. **12** *Physics.* mutual inductance. **13** *Chem.* molar. ◆ **14** *the Roman numeral for* 1000. See **Roman numerals.** ◆ **15** *international car registration for* Malta.

m. *abbrev. for:* **1** *Cricket.* maiden (over). **2** male. **3** mare. **4** married. **5** masculine. **6** medicine. **7** meridian. **8** month.

M. *abbrev. for:* **1** Majesty. **2** Manitoba. **3** marquis. **4** Master. **5** Medieval. **6** (in titles) Member. **7** Middle. **8** million. **9** Monday. **10** (*pl* **MM.** *or* **MM**) Also: **M** *French.* Monsieur. [French equivalent of *Mr*] **11** mountain.

m- *prefix* short for **meta-** (sense 4).

M'- *prefix* a variant of **Mac-.**

'm *contraction of:* **1** (*vb*) am. **2** (*n*) madam: *yes'm.*

M0 *symbol for* the amount of money in circulation in notes and coin, plus the banks' till money and the banks' balances at the Bank of England. Informal name: **narrow money.**

M1 *symbol for* the amount of money in circulation in notes, coin, current accounts, and deposit accounts transferable by cheque.

M-1 rifle *n* a semiautomatic .30 calibre rifle: the basic infantry weapon of the U.S. Army in World War II and the Korean War. Also called: **Garand rifle.**

M2 *symbol for* the amount of money in circulation in notes and coin plus non-interest-bearing bank deposits, building-society deposits, and National Savings accounts.

M3 *symbol for* the amount of money in circulation given by M1 plus all private-sector bank deposits and certificates of deposit. Former symbol: **£M3** (sterling M3).

M3c *symbol for* the amount of money in circulation given by M3 plus foreign currency bank deposits. Former symbol: **M3** Informal name: **broad money.**

M4 *symbol for* the amount of money in circulation given by M1 plus most private-sector bank deposits and holdings of money-market instruments. Also called: **PSL1.**

M5 *symbol for* the amount of money in circulation given by M4 plus building-society deposits. Also called: **PSL2.**

ma (mɑː) *n* an informal word for **mother**[1].

Ma (mɑː) *n* **Yo-Yo** (ˈjəʊjəʊ). born 1955, U.S. cellist, born in France to Chinese parents.

MA *abbrev. for:* **1** Massachusetts. **2** Master of Arts. **3** *Psychol.* mental age. **4** Military Academy. ◆ **5** *international car registration for* Morocco. [from French *Maroc*]

ma'am (mæm, mɑːm; *unstressed* məm) *n* short for **madam:** used as a title of respect, esp. for female royalty.

maar (mɑː) *n, pl* **maars** *or* **maare** (ˈmɑːrə). (*sometimes cap.*) a coneless volcanic crater that has been formed by a single explosion. [C19: from German]

Maarianhamina (ˈmɑːriɑnhɑminɑ) *n* the Finnish name for **Mariehamn.**

Ma'ariv *Hebrew.* (*Hebrew* mɑɑˈriv; *Yiddish* ˈmɑriv) *n Judaism.* the evening service.

maas (mɑːs) *n S. African.* thick soured milk. [from Nguni *amasi* milk]

Maas (mɑːs) *n* the Dutch name for the **Meuse.**

Maastricht *or* **Maestricht** (ˈmɑːstrɪxt; *Dutch* maːˈstrɪxt) *n* a city in the SE Netherlands near the Belgian and German borders: capital of Limburg province, on the River Maas (Meuse); a European Community treaty (**Maastricht Treaty**) was signed here in 1992, setting out the terms for the creation of the European Union. Pop.: 118 518 (1996 est.).

Mab (mæb) *n* (in English and Irish folklore) a fairy queen said to create and control men's dreams.

mabela (mɑːˈbɛlə) *n S. African.* ground kaffir corn used for making porridge. [from Zulu *amabele* kaffir corn]

Mabinogion (ˌmæbɪˈnɒgɪən) *n* **the.** a collection of Welsh tales based on old Celtic legends and mythology in which magic and the supernatural play a large part. [from Welsh *mabinogi* instruction for young bards]

Mabuse (məˈbjuːz; *French* mabyz) *n* **Jan** (jɑn). original name *Jan Gossaert.* ?1478–?1533, Flemish painter.

mac *or* **mack** (mæk) *n Brit. informal.* short for **mackintosh** (senses 1, 3).

Mac (mæk) *n Chiefly U.S. and Canadian.* an informal term of address to a man. [C20: abstracted from MAC-, prefix of Scottish surnames]

MAC *abbrev. for* multiplexed analogue component: a transmission coding system for colour television using satellite broadcasting.

Mac. *abbrev. for* Maccabees (books of the Apocrypha).

Mac-, Mc-, *or* **M'-** *prefix* (in surnames of Scottish or Irish Gaelic origin) son of: *MacDonald; MacNeice.* [from Goidelic *mac* son of; compare Welsh *mab,* Cornish *mab*]

macabre (məˈkɑːbə, -brə) *adj* **1** gruesome; ghastly; grim. **2** resembling or associated with the danse macabre. [C15: from Old French *danse macabre* dance of death, probably from *macabé* relating to the Maccabees, who were associated with death because of the doctrines and prayers for the dead in II Macc. (12:43–46)] ▸ **maˈcabrely** *adv*

macaco (məˈkɑːkəʊ, -ˈkeɪ-) *n, pl* **-cos.** any of various lemurs, esp. *Lemur macaco,* the males of which are usually black and the females brown. [C18: from French *mococo,* of unknown origin]

macadam (məˈkædəm) *n* a road surface made of compressed layers of small broken stones, esp. one that is bound together with tar or asphalt. [C19: named after John *McAdam* (1756–1836), Scottish engineer, the inventor]

macadamia (ˌmækəˈdeɪmɪə) *n* **1** any tree of the Australian proteaceous genus *Macadamia,* esp. *M. ternifolia,* having clusters of small white flowers and edible nutlike seeds. **2 macadamia nut.** the seed of this tree. [C19: New Latin, named after John *Macadam* (died 1865), Australian chemist]

macadamize *or* **macadamise** (məˈkædəˌmaɪz) *vb* (*tr*) to construct or surface (a road) with macadam. ▸ **macˌadamiˈzation** *or* **macˌadamiˈsation** *n* ▸ **macˈadamˌizer** *or* **macˈadamˌiser** *n*

Macao (məˈkaʊ) *n* a city on the coast of S China, across the estuary of the Zhu Jiang from Hong Kong: chief centre of European trade with China in the 18th century; attained partial autonomy in 1976; formerly (until 1999) a Portuguese overseas province; transit trade with China; tourism. Pop.: 426 000 (1998 est.). Area: 16 sq. km (6 sq. miles). Portuguese name: **Macáu.**

Macapá (*Portuguese* makaˈpa) *n* a town in NE Brazil, capital of the federal territory of Amapá, on the Canal do Norte of the Amazon delta. Pop.: 146 523 (1991).

macaque (məˈkɑːk) *n* any of various Old World monkeys of the genus *Macaca,* inhabiting wooded or rocky regions of Asia and Africa. Typically the tail is short or absent and cheek pouches are present. [C17: from French, from Portuguese *macaco,* from Fiot (a W African language) *makaku,* from *kaku* monkey]

macaroni *or* **maccaroni** (ˌmækəˈrəʊnɪ) *n, pl* **-nis** *or* **-nies. 1** pasta tubes made from wheat flour. **2** (in 18th-century Britain) a dandy who affected foreign manners and style. [C16: from Italian (Neapolitan dialect) *maccarone,* probably from Greek *makaria* food made from barley]

macaronic (ˌmækəˈrɒnɪk) *adj* **1** (of verse) characterized by a mixture of vernacular words jumbled together with Latin words or Latinized words or with words from one or more other foreign languages. ◆ *n* **2** (*often pl*) macaronic verse. [C17: from New Latin *macarōnicus,* literally: resembling macaroni (in lack of sophistication); see MACARONI] ▸ **ˌmacaˈronically** *adv*

macaroni cheese *n* a dish of macaroni with a cheese sauce.

macaroon (ˌmækəˈruːn) *n* a kind of sweet biscuit made of ground almonds, sugar, and egg whites. [C17: via French *macaron* from Italian *maccarone* MACARONI]

Macarthur (məˈkɑːθə) *n* **John.** 1767–1834, Australian military officer, pastoralist, and entrepreneur, born in England. He established the breeding of merino sheep in Australia and was influential in founding the Australian wool industry.

MacArthur (məˈkɑːθə) *n* **Douglas.** 1880–1964, U.S. general. During World War II he became commanding general of U.S. armed forces in the Pacific (1944) and accepted the surrender of Japan, the Allied occupation of which he commanded (1945–51). He was commander in chief of United Nations forces in Korea (1950–51) until dismissed by President Truman.

Macassar (məˈkæsə) *n* a variant spelling of **Makasar.**

Macassar oil *n* an oily preparation formerly put on the hair to make it smooth and shiny. [C19: so called because its ingredients were originally claimed to have come from MAKASAR]

Macáu (məˈkaʊ) *n* the Portuguese name for **Macao.**

Macaulay (məˈkɔːlɪ) *n* **1** Dame **Rose.** 1881–1958, British novelist. Her books include *Dangerous Ages* (1921) and *The Towers of Trebizond* (1956). **2 Thomas Babington,** 1st Baron. 1800–59, English historian, essayist, and statesman. His *History of England from the Accession of James the Second* (1848–61) is regarded as a classic of the Whig interpretation of history.

macaw (məˈkɔː) *n* any large tropical American parrot of the genera *Ara* and *Anodorhynchus,* having a long tail and brilliant plumage. [C17: from Portuguese *macau,* of unknown origin]

Macbeth (məkˈbɛθ, mæk-) *n* died 1057, king of Scotland (1040–57): succeeded Duncan, whom he killed in battle; defeated and killed by Duncan's son Malcolm III.

MacBride (məkˈbraɪd) *n* **Sean** (ʃɔːn). 1904–88, Irish statesman; minister for external affairs (1948–51); chairman of Amnesty International (1961–75); Nobel Peace Prize 1974; UN commissioner for Namibia (1974–76).

McBride (məkˈbraɪd) *n* **Willie John.** born 1940, Irish Rugby Union footballer. A forward, he played for Ireland (1962–75) and the British Lions (1962–74).

Macc. *abbrev. for* Maccabees (books of the Apocrypha).

Maccabean (ˌmækəˈbiːən) *adj* of or relating to the Maccabees or to Judas Maccabaeus.

Maccabees (ˈmækəˌbiːz) *n* **1** a Jewish family of patriots who freed Judaea from

Seleucid oppression (168–142 B.C.). **2** any of four books of Jewish history, including the last two of the Apocrypha.

maccaboy, maccoboy ('mækə,bɔɪ), *or* **maccabaw** ('mækə,bɔː) *n* a dark rose-scented snuff. **[C18:** from French *macouba,* from the name of the district of Martinique where it is made**]**

maccaroni (,mækə'rəʊnɪ) *n, pl* **-nis** *or* **-nies.** a variant spelling of **macaroni.**

McCarthy (mə'kɑːθɪ) *n* **1 Joseph R(aymond).** 1908–57, U.S. Republican senator, who led (1950–54) the notorious investigations of alleged Communist infiltration into the U.S. government. **2 Mary (Therese).** 1912–89, U.S. novelist and critic; her works include *The Group* (1963).

McCarthyism (mə'kɑːθɪ,ɪzəm) *n Chiefly U.S.* **1** the practice of making unsubstantiated accusations of disloyalty or Communist leanings. **2** the use of unsupported accusations for any purpose. **[C20:** after Senator Joseph MCCARTHY**]** ▸ **Mc'Carthyite** *n, adj*

McCartney (mə'kɑːtnɪ) *n* Sir **Paul.** born 1942, English rock musician and songwriter; member of the Beatles (1961–70); leader of Wings (1971–81). His recordings include *Band on the Run* (1973), "Mull of Kintyre" (1977), and *Tug of War* (1982). See also **Beatles.**

Macclesfield ('mækəlz,fiːld) *n* a market town in NW England, in Cheshire: silk industry. Pop.: 50 270 (1991).

McCormack (mə'kɔːmæk) *n* **John.** 1884–1945, Irish tenor: became U.S. citizen 1919.

McCormick (mə'kɔːmɪk) *n* **Cyrus Hall.** 1809–84, U.S. inventor of the reaping machine (1831).

McCoy (mə'kɔɪ) *n Slang.* the genuine person or thing (esp. in the phrase **the real McCoy**). **[C20:** perhaps after Kid *McCoy,* professional name of Norman Selby (1873–1940), American boxer, who was called "the real McCoy" to distinguish him from another boxer of that name**]**

McCullers (mə'kʌləz) *n* **Carson.** 1917–67, U.S. writer, whose novels include *The Heart is a Lonely Hunter* (1940).

MacDiarmid (mək'dɜːmɪd) *n* **Hugh,** pen name of *Christopher Murray Grieve.* 1892–1978, Scottish poet; a founder of the Scottish National Party. His poems include *A Drunk Man Looks at the Thistle* (1926).

Macdonald (mək'dɒnəld) *n* **1 Flora.** 1722–90, Scottish heroine, who helped the Young Pretender to escape to Skye after his defeat at the battle of Culloden (1746). **2** Sir **John Alexander.** 1815–91, Canadian statesman, born in Scotland, who was the first prime minister of the Dominion of Canada (1867–73; 1878–91).

MacDonald (mək'dɒnəld) *n* **(James) Ramsay.** 1866–1937, British statesman, who led the first and second Labour Governments (1924 and 1929–31). He also led a coalition (1931–35), which the majority of the Labour Party refused to support.

Macdonnell Ranges (mək'dɒnəl) *pl n* a mountain system of central Australia, in S central Northern Territory, extending about 160 km (100 miles) east and west of Alice Springs. Highest peak: Mount Ziel, 1510 m (4955 ft.).

mace[1] (meɪs) *n* **1** a club, usually having a spiked metal head, used esp. in the Middle Ages. **2** a ceremonial staff of office carried by certain officials. **3** See **macebearer. 4** an early form of billiard cue. **[C13:** from Old French, probably from Vulgar Latin *mattea* (unattested); apparently related to Latin *mateola* mallet**]**

mace[2] (meɪs) *n* a spice made from the dried aril round the nutmeg seed. **[C14:** formed as a singular from Old French *macis* (wrongly assumed to be plural), from Latin *macir* an oriental spice**]**

Mace (meɪs) *U.S.* ♦ *n* **1** *Trademark.* a liquid causing tears and nausea, used as a spray for riot control, etc. ♦ *vb* **2** *(tr) (sometimes not cap.)* to use Mace on.

macebearer ('meɪs,bεərə) *n* a person who carries a mace in processions or ceremonies.

Maced. *abbrev. for* Macedonia(n).

macedoine (,mæsɪ'dwɑːn) *n* **1** a hot or cold mixture of diced vegetables. **2** a mixture of fruit served in a syrup or in jelly. **3** any mixture; medley. **[C19:** from French, literally: Macedonian, alluding to the mixture of nationalities in Macedonia**]**

Macedon ('mæsɪ,dɒn) *or* **Macedonia** *n* a region of the S Balkans, now divided among Greece, Bulgaria, and Macedonia (Former Yugoslav Republic of Macedonia). As a kingdom in the ancient world it achieved prominence under Philip II (359–336 B.C.) and his son Alexander the Great.

Macedonia (,mæsɪ'dəʊnɪə) *n* **1** a country in SE Europe, comprising the NW half of ancient Macedon: it became part of the kingdom of Serbs, Croats, and Slovenes (subsequently Yugoslavia) in 1913; it declared independence in 1992, but Greece objected to the use of the historical name Macedonia; in 1993 it was recognized by the UN under its current official name (negotiations with Greece over a permanent name have continued). Official language: Macedonian. Religion: Christian majority, Muslim, nonreligious, and Jewish minorities. Currency: denar. Capital: Skopje. Pop.: 2 023 000 (1998 est.). Area: 25 713 sq. km (10 028 sq. miles). Serbian name: **,Makedo'nija.** Official name: **Former Yugoslav Republic of Macedonia** (FYROM). **2** an area of N Greece, comprising the regions of Macedonia Central, Macedonia West, and part of Macedonia East and Thrace. Modern Greek name: **Makedhonia. 3** a district of SW Bulgaria, now occupied by Blagoevgrad province. Area: 6465 sq. km (2496 sq. miles).

Macedonian (,mæsɪ'dəʊnɪən) *adj* **1** of or relating to Macedonia, its inhabitants, or any of their languages or dialects. ♦ *n* **2** a native or inhabitant of Macedonia. **3** the language of the Former Yugoslav Republic of Macedonia, belonging to the south Slavonic branch of the Indo-European family. **4** an extinct language spoken in ancient Macedonia.

Maceió (mase'jɔ) *n* a port in NE Brazil, capital of Alagôas state, on the Atlantic. Pop.: 554 727 (1991).

McEnroe ('mækən,rəʊ) *n* **John (Patrick Jr).** born 1959, U.S. tennis player: U.S. singles champion (1979–81; 1984) and doubles champion (1979; 1981; 1989): Wimbledon singles champion (1981; 1983; 1984) and doubles champion (1979; 1981; 1983; 1984; 1992).

macer ('meɪsə) *n* a macebearer, esp. (in Scotland) an official who acts as usher in a court of law. **[C14:** from Old French *massier,* from *masse* MACE[1]**]**

maceral ('mæsərəl) *n Geology.* any of the organic units that constitute coal: equivalent to any of the mineral constituents of a rock. **[C20:** from Latin *mācerāre* to MACERATE**]**

macerate ('mæsə,reɪt) *vb* **1** to soften or separate or be softened or separated as a result of soaking. **2** to break up or cause to break up by soaking: *macerated peaches.* **3** to become or cause to become thin. **[C16:** from Latin *mācerāre* to soften**]** ▸ **'macer,ater** *or* **'macer,ator** *n* ▸ **'macerative** *adj* ▸ **,macer'ation** *n*

McEwan (mə'kjuːən) *n* **Ian (Russell).** born 1948, British novelist and short-story writer. His books include *First Love, Last Rites* (1975), *The Comfort of Strangers* (1981), *The Child in Time* (1987), *The Innocent* (1990), *Black Dogs* (1992), and *Amsterdam* (1998).

Macgillicuddy's Reeks (mə,gɪlɪ,kʌdɪz 'riːks) *pl n* a range of mountains in SW Republic of Ireland in Kerry: includes Ireland's highest mountain (Carrantuohill).

McGonagall (mə'gɒnəgəl) *n* **William.** 1830–?1902, Scottish writer of doggerel, noted for its bathos, repetitive rhymes, poor scansion, and ludicrous effect.

McGregor (mək'grεgər) *n* **Ewan.** born 1971, Scottish actor; his films include *Shallow Grave* (1994), *Blue Juice* (1995), *Trainspotting* (1996), and *Brassed Off* (1997).

MacGuffin (mə'gʌfɪn) *n* an object or event in a book or a film that serves as the impetus for the plot. **[C20:** coined (c. 1935) by Sir Alfred HITCHCOCK**]**

Mach[1] (mæk) *n* short for **Mach number.**

Mach[2] (*German* max) *n* **Ernst** (εrnst). 1838–1916, Austrian physicist and philosopher. He devised the system of speed measurement using the Mach number. He also founded logical positivism, asserting that the validity of a scientific law is proved only after empirical testing.

mach. *abbrev. for:* **1** machine. **2** machinery. **3** machinist.

Machado (*Portuguese* ma'ʃadu) *n* **Joaquim Maria** (ʒua'kɪ ma'ria). 1839–1908, Brazilian author of novels and short stories, whose novels include *Epitaph of a Small Winner* (1881) and *Dom Casmurro* (1899).

machair ('mæxər) *n Scot.* (in the western Highlands of Scotland) a strip of sandy, grassy, often lime-rich land just above the high-water mark at a sandy shore: used as grazing or arable land. **[C17:** from Scottish Gaelic**]**

machan (mə'tʃɑːn) *n* (in India) a raised platform used in tiger hunting. **[C19:** from Hindi**]**

Machaut (*French* maʃo) *n* **Guillaume de.** (gijom də) c. 1300–77, French composer and poet; a leading exponent of ars nova.

Machel (mə'ʃεl) *n* **Samora (Moises)** (sə'mɔːrə). 1933–86, Mozambique statesman; president of Mozambique from 1975–86.

macher ('mɑxər) *n Yiddish.* an important or influential person: often used ironically. **[**Yiddish, from German, literally: doer**]**

machete (mə'ʃεtɪ, -'tʃεɪ-) *or* **matchet** *n* a broad heavy knife used for cutting or as a weapon, esp. in parts of Central and South America. **[C16** *macheto,* from Spanish *machete,* from *macho* club, perhaps from Vulgar Latin *mattea* (unattested) club**]**

Machiavelli (,mækɪə'vεlɪ) *n* **Niccolò** (nikko'lɔ). 1469–1527, Florentine statesman and political philosopher; secretary to the war council of the Florentine republic (1498–1512). His most famous work is *Il Principe* (*The Prince,* 1532).

Machiavellian *or* **Machiavelian** (,mækɪə'vεlɪən) *adj (sometimes not cap.)* **1** of or relating to the alleged political principles of Machiavelli; cunning, amoral, and opportunist. ♦ *n* **2** a cunning, amoral, and opportunist person, esp. a politician. ▸ **,Machia'vellianism** *or* **,Machia'vellism** *n* ▸ **,Machia'vellist** *adj, n*

machicolate (mə'tʃɪkəʊ,leɪt) *vb (tr)* to construct machicolations at the top of (a wall). **[C18:** from Old French *machicoller,* ultimately from Provençal *machacol,* from *macar* to crush + *col* neck**]**

machicolation (mə,tʃɪkəʊ'leɪʃən) *n* **1** (esp. in medieval castles) a projecting gallery or parapet supported on corbels having openings through which missiles could be dropped. **2** any such opening.

machinate ('mækɪ,neɪt, 'mæʃ-) *vb (usually tr)* to contrive, plan, or devise (schemes, plots, etc.). **[C17:** from Latin *māchinārī* to plan, from *māchina* MACHINE**]** ▸ **'machi,nator** *n*

machination (,mækɪ'neɪʃən, ,mæʃ-) *n* **1** an intrigue, plot, or scheme. **2** the act of devising plots or schemes.

machine (mə'ʃiːn) *n* **1** an assembly of interconnected components arranged to transmit or modify force in order to perform useful work. **2** Also called: **simple machine.** a device for altering the magnitude or direction of a force, esp. a lever, screw, wedge, or pulley. **3** a mechanically operated device or means of transport, such as a car, aircraft, etc. **4** any mechanical or electrical device that automatically performs tasks or assists in performing tasks. **5a** *(modifier)* denoting a firearm that is fully automatic as distinguished from semiautomatic. **5b** *(in combination): machine pistol; machine gun.* **6** any intricate structure or agency: *the war machine.* **7** a mechanically efficient, rigid, or obedient person. **8** an organized body of people that controls activities, policies, etc. **9** (esp. in the classical theatre) a device such as a pulley to provide spectacular entrances and exits for supernatural characters. **10** an event, etc., introduced into a literary work for special effect. ♦ *vb* **11** *(tr)* to shape, cut, or remove (excess material) from (a workpiece) using a machine tool. **12** to use a machine to carry out a process on (something). **[C16:** via French from Latin *māchina* machine, engine, from Doric Greek *makhana* pulley; related to *makhos* device, contrivance] ▸ **ma'chinable** *or* **ma'chineable** *adj* ▸ **ma,china'bility** *n* ▸ **ma'chineless** *adj* ▸ **ma'chine-,like** *adj*

machine bolt *n* a fastening bolt with a machine-cut thread.

machine code *or* **language** *n* instructions for the processing of data in a binary, octal, or hexadecimal code that can be understood and executed by a computer.

machine gun *n* **1a** a rapid-firing automatic gun, usually mounted, from which small-arms ammunition is discharged. **1b** (*as modifier*): *machine-gun fire.* ◆ *vb* **machine-gun, -guns, -gunning, -gunned. 2** (*tr*) to shoot or fire at with a machine gun. ▸ **machine gunner** *n*

machine head *n* a metal peg-and-gear mechanism for tuning a string on an instrument such as a guitar.

machine intelligence *n Brit., now rare.* another term for **artificial intelligence.**

machine learning *n* a branch of artificial intelligence in which a computer generates rules underlying or based on raw data that has been fed into it.

machine moulding *n Engineering.* the process of making moulds and cores for castings by mechanical means, usually by compacting the moulding sand by vibration instead of by ramming down.

machine readable *adj* (of data) in a form in which it can be fed into a computer.

machinery (mə'ʃiːnərɪ) *n, pl* **-eries. 1** machines, machine parts, or machine systems collectively. **2** a particular machine system or set of machines. **3** a system similar to a machine: *the machinery of government.* **4** literary devices used for effect in epic poetry.

machine screw *n* a fastening screw with a machine-cut thread throughout the length of its shank.

machine shop *n* a workshop in which machine tools are operated.

machine tool *n* a power-driven machine, such as a lathe, miller, or grinder, that is used for cutting, shaping, and finishing metals or other materials. ▸ **ma'chine-,tooled** *adj*

machine translation *n* the production of text in one natural language from that in another by means of computer procedures.

machinist (mə'ʃiːnɪst) *n* **1** a person who operates machines to cut or process materials. **2** a maker or repairer of machines.

machismo (mæ'kɪzməʊ, -'tʃɪz-) *n* exaggerated masculine pride. [Mexican Spanish, from Spanish *macho* male, from Latin *masculus* MASCULINE]

Machmeter ('mæk,miːtə) *n* an instrument for measuring the Mach number of an aircraft in flight.

Mach number *n* (*often not cap.*) the ratio of the speed of a body in a particular medium to the speed of sound in that medium. Mach number 1 corresponds to the speed of sound. Often shortened to **Mach.** [C19: named after Ernst MACH]

macho ('mætʃəʊ) *adj* **1** denoting or exhibiting pride in characteristics believed to be typically masculine, such as physical strength, sexual appetite, etc. ◆ *n, pl* **machos. 2** a man who displays such characteristics. [C20: from Spanish: male; see MACHISMO]

machree (mə'kriː) *adj* (*postpositive*) *Irish.* my dear: *mother machree.* [from Irish *mo croidhe*]

machtpolitik ('mɑːxt,pɒlɪtiːk) *n* power politics. [from German]

Machu Picchu ('mɑːtʃuː 'piːktʃuː) *n* a ruined Incan city in S Peru.

machzor *or* ***mahzor*** *Hebrew.* (max'zɔr; *English* mɑːk'zɔː) *n, pl* ***-zorim*** (-zɔ'riːm; *English* -zə'riːm). a Jewish prayer book containing prescribed holiday rituals. [literally: cycle]

Macías Nguema (mə'siːəs ᵊŋ'gweɪmə) *n* the former name (until 1979) of **Bioko.**

McIndoe ('mækɪn,dəʊ) *n* Sir **Archibald Hector.** 1900–60, New Zealand plastic surgeon; noted for his pioneering work with wounded World War II airmen.

macintosh ('mækɪn,tɒʃ) *n* a variant spelling of **mackintosh.**

mack[1] (mæk) *n Brit. informal.* a variant spelling of **mac,** short for **mackintosh** (senses 1, 3).

mack[2] (mæk) *n Slang.* a pimp. [C19: shortened from obsolete *mackerel,* from Old French, of uncertain origin]

Mackay (mə'kaɪ) *n* a port in E Australia, in Queensland: artificial harbour. Pop.: 55 772 (1993).

McKean (mə'kiːn) *n* **Tom.** born 1963, Scottish athlete: European 800 metres gold medallist (1990).

Mackellar (mə'kɛlə) *n* **Dorothea.** 1885–1968, Australian poet, who wrote "My Country", Australia's best known poem.

McKellen (mə'kɛlən) *n* Sir **Ian (Murray).** born 1939, British actor, noted esp. for his Shakespearean roles.

McKenna (mə'kɛnə) *n* **Siobhán** (ʃə'vɔːn). 1923–86, Irish actress, whose notable roles included Pegeen Mike in Synge's *The Playboy of the Western World* and Shaw's Saint Joan.

Mackenzie[1] (mə'kenzɪ) *n* a river in NW Canada, in the Northwest Territories and Nunavut, flowing northwest from Great Slave Lake to the Beaufort Sea: the longest river in Canada; navigable in summer. Length: 1770 km (1100 miles).

Mackenzie[2] (mə'kenzɪ) *n* **1** Sir **Alexander.** ?1755–1820, Scottish explorer and fur trader in Canada. He explored the Mackenzie River (1789) and was the first European to cross America north of Mexico (1793). **2 Alexander.** 1822–92, Canadian statesman; first Liberal prime minister (1873–78). **3** Sir **Compton.** 1883–1972, English author. His works include *Sinister Street* (1913–14) and the comic novel *Whisky Galore* (1947). **4** Sir **Thomas.** 1854–1930, New Zealand statesman born in Scotland: prime minister of New Zealand (1912). **5 William Lyon.** 1795–1861, Canadian journalist and politician, born in Scotland. He led an unsuccessful rebellion against the oligarchic Family Compact (1837).

mackerel ('mækrəl) *n, pl* **-rel** *or* **-rels. 1** a spiny-finned food fish, *Scomber scombrus,* occurring in northern coastal regions of the Atlantic and in the Mediterranean: family *Scombridae.* It has a deeply forked tail and a greenish-blue body marked with wavy dark bands on the back. Compare **Spanish mackerel** (sense 1). **2** any of various other fishes of the family *Scombridae,* such as *Scomber colias* (**Spanish mackerel**) and *S. japonicus* (**Pacific mackerel**). ◆ Compare **horse mackerel.** [C13: from Anglo-French, from Old French *maquerel,* of unknown origin]

mackerel breeze *n* a strong breeze. [C18: so named because the ruffling of the water by the wind aids mackerel fishing]

mackerel shark *n* another name for **porbeagle.**

mackerel sky *n* a sky patterned with cirrocumulus or small altocumulus clouds. [from the similarity to the pattern on a mackerel's back]

Mackerras (mə'kɛrəs) *n* **Charles.** born 1925, Australian conductor, esp. of opera; resident in England.

Mackinac ('mækɪ,nɔː, -,næk) *n* a wooded island in N Michigan, in the **Straits of Mackinac** (a channel between the lower and upper peninsulas of Michigan): an ancient Indian burial ground; state park. Length: 5 km (3 miles).

Mackinaw coat ('mækɪ,nɔː) *n Chiefly U.S. and Canadian.* a thick short double-breasted plaid coat. Also called: **mackinaw.** [C19: named after *Mackinaw,* variant of MACKINAC]

Mackinder (mə'kɪndə) *n* Sir **Halford John.** 1861–1947, British geographer noted esp. for his work in political geography. His writings include *Democratic Ideas and Reality* (1919).

McKinley[1] (mə'kɪnlɪ) *n* **Mount.** a mountain in S central Alaska, in the Alaska Range: the highest peak in North America. Height: 6194 m (20 320 ft.).

McKinley[2] (mə'kɪnlɪ) *n* **William.** 1843–1901, 25th president of the U.S. (1897–1901). His administration was marked by high tariffs and by expansionist policies. He was assassinated.

mackintosh *or* **macintosh** ('mækɪn,tɒʃ) *n* **1** a waterproof raincoat made of rubberized cloth. **2** such cloth. **3** any raincoat. [C19: named after Charles *Macintosh* (1760–1843), who invented it]

Mackintosh ('mækɪn,tɒʃ) *n* **Charles Rennie.** 1868–1928, Scottish architect and artist, exponent of the Art Nouveau style; designer of the Glasgow School of Art (1896).

mackle ('mækᵊl) *or* **macule** ('mækjuːl) *n Printing.* a double or blurred impression caused by shifting paper or type. [C16: via French from Latin *macula* spot, stain]

Maclaurin's series (mə'klɔːrɪnz) *n Maths.* an infinite sum giving the value of a function f(*x*) in terms of the derivatives of the function evaluated at zero: $f(x) = f(0) + (f'(0)x)/1! + (f''(0)x^2)/2! + \ldots$. Also called: **Maclaurin series.** [C18: named after Colin *Maclaurin* (1698–1746), British mathematician who formulated it]

macle ('mækᵊl) *n* another name for **chiastolite** and **twin** (sense 3). [C19: via French from Latin *macula* spot, stain]

Maclean (mə'kleɪn) *n* **1 Donald.** 1913–83, British civil servant, who spied for the Russians: fled to the former Soviet Union (with Guy Burgess) in 1951. **2 Sorley** ('sɔːlɪ). 1911–96, Scottish Gaelic poet. His works include *Dàin do Eimhir agus Dàin Eile* (1943) and *Spring Tide and Neap Tide* (1977).

Macleish (mə'kliːʃ) *n* **Archibald.** 1892–1982, U.S. poet and public official; his works include *Collected Poems* (1952) and *J.B.* (1958).

Macleod (mə'klaʊd) *n* **John James Rickard.** 1876–1935, Scottish physiologist: shared the Nobel prize for physiology or medicine (1923) with Banting for their part in discovering insulin.

McLuhan (mə'kluːən) *n* (**Herbert**) **Marshall.** 1911–80, Canadian author of works analysing the mass media, including *Understanding Media* (1964) and *The Medium is the Message* (1967).

Macmahon (*French* makmaɔ̃) *n* **Marie Edme Patrice Maurice** (mari ɛdmə patris mɔris), Comte de Macmahon. 1808–93, French military commander. He commanded the troops that suppressed the Paris Commune (1871) and was elected president of the Third Republic (1873–79).

McMahon (mək'mɑːən) *n* Sir **William.** 1908–88, Australian statesman; prime minister of Australia (1971–72).

Macmillan (mək'mɪlən) *n* (**Maurice**) **Harold,** 1st Earl of Stockton. 1894–1986, British statesman; Conservative prime minister (1957–63).

MacMillan (mæk'mɪlən) *n* Sir **Kenneth.** 1929–92, British ballet dancer and choreographer; director (1970–77) and principal choreographer (1977–92) of the Royal Ballet.

McMillan (mək'mɪlən) *n* **Edwin M(attison).** 1907–91, U.S. physicist; Nobel prize for chemistry 1951 (with Glenn Seaborg) for the discovery of transuranic elements.

Mcmurdo Sound (mək'mɜːdəʊ) *n* an inlet of the Ross Sea in Antarctica, north of Victoria Land.

McNaughten Rules *or* **McNaghten Rules** (mək'nɔːtᵊn) *pl n* (in English law) a set of rules established by the case of Regina v. McNaughten (1843) by which legal proof of insanity in the commission of a crime depends upon whether or not the accused can show either that he did not know what he was doing or that he is incapable of realizing that what he was doing was wrong.

MacNeice (mək'niːs) *n* **Louis.** 1907–63, British poet, born in Northern Ireland. His works include *Autumn Journal* (1939) and *Solstices* (1961) and a translation of *Agamemnon* (1936).

Macon ('meɪkən) *n* a city in the U.S., in central Georgia, on the Ocmulgee River. Pop.: 113 352 (1996 est.).

Mâcon (*French* makɔ̃) *n* **1** a city in E central France, in the Saône valley: a centre of the wine-producing region of lower Burgundy. Pop.: 39 700 (1995 est.). **2** a red or white wine from the Mâcon area, heavier than the other burgundies.

Maconchy (mə'kɒŋkɪ) *n* Dame **Elizabeth,** married name *Elizabeth LeFanu.* 1907–94, British composer of Irish parentage; noted esp. for her chamber music, which includes 13 string quartets and *Romanza* (1980) for viola and ensemble.

Macpherson (mək'fɜːsᵊn) *n* **James.** 1736–96, Scottish poet and translator. He published supposed translations of the legendary Gaelic poet Ossian, in reality largely his own work.

Macquarie[1] (mə'kwɒrɪ) *n* **Lachlan.** 1762–1824, Australian colonial administrator; Governor of New South Wales (1809–21), noted for his reformist policies towards ex-convicts and for his record in public works such as road-building in the colony.

Macquarie[2] (mə'kwɒrɪ) *n* **1** an Australian island in the Pacific, SE of Tasmania: noted for its species of albatross and penguin. Area: about 168 sq. km (65 sq. miles). **2** a river in SE Australia, in E central New South Wales, rising in the Blue Mountains and flowing NW to the Darling. Length: about 1200 km (750 miles).

McQueen (mə'kwiːn) *n* **Steve.** 1930–80, U.S. film actor, noted for his portrayal of tough characters.

macramé (mə'krɑːmɪ) *n* a type of ornamental work made by knotting and weaving coarse thread into a pattern. **[C19:** via French and Italian from Turkish *makrama* towel, from Arabic *migramah* striped cloth**]**

Macready (mə'kriːdɪ) *n* **William Charles.** 1793–1873, English actor and theatre manager.

macrencephaly (ˌmækrən'sɛfəlɪ) *or (less commonly)* **macrencephalia** (ˌmækrənsɪ'feɪlɪə) *n* the condition of having an abnormally large brain.

macro ('mækrəʊ) *n, pl* **macros. 1** a macro lens. **2** Also: **macro instruction.** a single computer instruction that initiates a set of instructions to perform a specific task.

macro- *or before a vowel* **macr-** *combining form.* **1** large, long, or great in size or duration: *macroscopic.* **2** (in pathology) indicating abnormal enlargement or overdevelopment: *macrocyte.* Compare **micro-** (sense 5). **3** producing larger than life images: *macrophotography.* **[**from Greek *makros* large; compare Latin *macer* MEAGRE**]**

macrobiotics (ˌmækrəʊbaɪ'ɒtɪks) *n (functioning as sing)* a dietary system in which foods are classified according to the principles of Yin and Yang. It advocates diets of whole grains and vegetables grown without chemical additives. **[C20:** from MACRO- + Greek *biotos* life + -ICS**]** ▸ **ˌmacrobi'otic** *adj, n*

macrocarpa (ˌmækrəʊ'kɑːpə) *n* a large coniferous tree of New Zealand, *Cupressus macrocarpa,* used for shelter belts on farms and for rough timber. Also called: **Monterey cypress. [C19:** from New Latin, from Greek MACRO- + *karpos* fruit**]**

macrocephaly (ˌmækrəʊ'sɛfəlɪ) *or (less commonly)* **macrocephalia** (ˌmækrəʊsɪ'feɪlɪə) *n* the condition of having an abnormally large head or skull. ▸ **macrocephalic** (ˌmækrəʊsɪ'fælɪk) *or* **ˌmacro'cephalous** *adj*

macroclimate ('mækrəʊˌklaɪmɪt) *n* the prevailing climate of a large area. ▸ **macroclimatic** (ˌmækrəʊklaɪ'mætɪk) *adj* ▸ **ˌmacrocli'matically** *adv*

macrocosm ('mækrəˌkɒzəm) *n* **1** a complex structure, such as the universe or society, regarded as an entirety, as opposed to microcosms, which have a similar structure and are contained within it. **2** any complex entity regarded as a complete system in itself. ◆ Compare **microcosm. [C16:** via French and Latin from Greek *makros kosmos* great world**]** ▸ **ˌmacro'cosmic** *adj* ▸ **ˌmacro'cosmically** *adv*

macrocyst ('mækrəʊˌsɪst) *n* **1** an unusually large cyst. **2** (in slime moulds) an encysted resting protoplasmic mass. See **plasmodium** (sense 1).

macrocyte ('mækrəʊˌsaɪt) *n Pathol.* an abnormally large red blood cell, over 10 μm in diameter. ▸ **macrocytic** (ˌmækrəʊ'sɪtɪk) *adj*

macrocytosis (ˌmækrəʊsaɪ'təʊsɪs) *n Pathol.* the presence in the blood of macrocytes.

macroeconomics (ˌmækrəʊˌiːkə'nɒmɪks, -ˌɛk-) *n (functioning as sing)* the branch of economics concerned with aggregates, such as national income, consumption, and investment. Compare **microeconomics.** ▸ **ˌmacroˌeco'nomic** *adj*

macroevolution (ˌmækrəʊˌiːvə'luːʃən) *n Biology.* the evolution of large taxonomic groups such as genera and families. ▸ **ˌmacroˌevo'lutionary** *adj*

macrogamete (ˌmækrəʊ'gæmiːt) *or* **megagamete** (ˌmɛgə'gæmiːt) *n* the larger and apparently female of two gametes in conjugating protozoans. Compare **microgamete.**

macroglia (ˌmækrəʊ'glɪə) *n* one of the two types of non-nervous tissue (glia) found in the central nervous system: includes astrocytes. Compare **microglia.**

macroglobulin (ˌmækrəʊ'glɒbjʊlɪn) *n Immunol.* **1** an immunoglobulin of unusually high relative molecular mass, observed in the blood in some diseases. **2** Also called: **immunoglobulin M.** the normal form of this immunoglobulin.

macrograph ('mækrəʊˌgrɑːf, -ˌgræf) *n* a photograph, drawing, etc., in which an object appears as large as or several times larger than the original. ▸ **macrographic** (ˌmækrəʊ'græfɪk) *adj*

macro lens *n* a camera lens used for close-up photography (2–10 cm).

macrolepidoptera (ˌmækrəʊˌlɛpɪ'dɒptərə) *pl n* a collector's name for that part of the lepidoptera that comprises the butterflies and the larger moths (noctuids, geometrids, bombycids, springtails, etc.): a term without taxonomic significance. Compare **microlepidoptera.**

macromere ('mækrəʊˌmɪə) *n Embryol.* any of the large yolk-filled cells formed by unequal cleavage of a fertilized ovum.

macromolecule (ˌmækrəʊ'mɒlɪˌkjuːl) *n* any very large molecule, such as a protein or synthetic polymer. ▸ **macromolecular** (ˌmækrəʊmə'lɛkjʊlə) *adj*

macron ('mækrɒn) *n* a diacritical mark (¯) placed over a letter, used in prosody, in the orthography of some languages, and in several types of phonetic respelling systems, to represent a long vowel. **[C19:** from Greek *makron* something long, from *makros* long**]**

macronucleus (ˌmækrəʊ'njuːklɪəs) *n, pl* **-clei** (-klɪˌaɪ). the larger of the two nuclei in ciliated protozoans, involved in feeding and similar processes. Compare **micronucleus.**

macronutrient (ˌmækrəʊ'njuːtrɪənt) *n* any substance, such as carbon, hydrogen, or oxygen, that is required in large amounts for healthy growth and development.

macrophage ('mækrəʊˌfeɪdʒ) *n* any large phagocytic cell occurring in the blood, lymph, and connective tissue of vertebrates. See also **histiocyte.** ▸ **macrophagic** (ˌmækrəʊ'fædʒɪk) *adj*

macrophagous (mə'krɒfəgəs) *adj Zoology.* (of an animal) feeding on relatively large particles of food.

macrophotography (ˌmækrəʊfə'tɒgrəfɪ) *n* extremely close-up photography in which the image on the film is as large as, or larger than, the object.

macrophysics (ˌmækrəʊ'fɪzɪks) *n (functioning as sing)* the branch of physics concerned with macroscopic systems and objects.

macropsia (mə'krɒpsɪə) *n* the condition of seeing everything in the field of view as larger than it really is, which can occur in diseases of the retina or in some brain disorders.

macropterous (mə'krɒptərəs) *adj* (of certain animals, esp. some types of ant) having large wings.

macroscopic (ˌmækrəʊ'skɒpɪk) *adj* **1** large enough to be visible to the naked eye. Compare **microscopic. 2** comprehensive; concerned with large units. **3** having astronomical dimensions. **4** *Physics.* capable of being described by the statistical properties of a large number of parts. ◆ Also: **megascopic. [C19:** see MACRO-, -SCOPIC**]** ▸ **ˌmacro'scopically** *adv*

macrosociology (ˌmækrəʊˌsəʊsɪ'ɒlədʒɪ) *n* the branch of sociology concerned with the study of human societies on a wide scale. ▸ **ˌmacroˌsocio'logical** *adj*

macrosporangium (ˌmækrəʊspɔː'rændʒɪəm) *n, pl* **-gia** (-dʒɪə). another name for **megasporangium.**

macrospore ('mækrəʊˌspɔː) *n* another name for **megaspore** (sense 1).

macrotous (mə'krəʊtəs) *adj Zoology.* having large ears. **[**from MACRO- + Greek *ous* ear**]**

macruran (mə'kruərən) *n* **1** any decapod crustacean of the group (formerly suborder) *Macrura,* which includes the lobsters, prawns, and crayfish. ◆ *adj also* **macrurous, macrural,** *or* **macruroid. 2** of, relating to, or belonging to the *Macrura.* **[C19:** via New Latin, from Greek *makros* long + *oura* tail**]**

macula ('mækjʊlə) *or* **macule** ('mækjuːl) *n, pl* **-ulae** (-jʊˌliː) *or* **-ules.** *Anatomy.* **1** a small spot or area of distinct colour, esp. the macula lutea. **2** any small discoloured spot or blemish on the skin, such as a freckle. **[C14:** from Latin**]** ▸ **'macular** *adj*

macular degeneration *n* pathological changes in the macula lutea, resulting in loss of central vision: a common cause of blindness in the elderly.

macula lutea ('luːtɪə) *n, pl* **maculae luteae** ('luːtɪˌiː). a small yellowish oval-shaped spot, rich in cones, near the centre of the retina of the eye, where vision is especially sharp. See also **fovea centralis. [**New Latin, literally: yellow spot**]**

maculate *Archaic or literary.* ◆ *vb* ('mækjʊˌleɪt). **1** *(tr)* to spot, stain, or pollute. ◆ *adj* ('mækjʊlɪt). **2** spotted or polluted. **[C15:** from Latin *maculāre* to stain**]**

maculation (ˌmækjʊ'leɪʃən) *n* **1** a pattern of spots, as on certain animals and plants. **2** *Archaic.* the act of maculating or the state of being maculated.

macule ('mækjuːl) *n* **1** *Anatomy.* another name for **macula. 2** *Printing.* another name for **mackle. [C15:** from Latin *macula* spot**]**

Macumba *Portuguese.* (ma'kumba) *n* a religious cult in Brazil that combines Christian and voodoo elements.

mad (mæd) *adj* **madder, maddest. 1** mentally deranged; insane. **2** senseless; foolish: *a mad idea.* **3** (often foll. by *at*) *Informal.* angry; resentful. **4** (foll. by *about, on,* or *over;* often postpositive) wildly enthusiastic (about) or fond (of): *mad about football; football-mad.* **5** extremely excited or confused; frantic: *a mad rush.* **6** temporarily overpowered by violent reactions, emotions, etc.: *mad with grief.* **7** (of animals) **7a** unusually ferocious: *a mad buffalo.* **7b** afflicted with rabies. **8 like mad.** *Informal.* with great energy, enthusiasm, or haste; wildly. **9 mad as a hatter.** crazily eccentric. ◆ *vb* **mads, madding, madded. 10** *U.S. or archaic.* to make or become mad; act or cause to act as if mad. **[**Old English *gemǣded,* past participle of *gemǣdan* to render insane; related to *gemād* insane, and to Old High German *gimeit* silly, crazy, Old Norse *meitha* to hurt, damage**]** ▸ **'maddish** *adj*

MAD (mæd) *n U.S. acronym for* mutual assured destruction: a theory of nuclear deterrence whereby each side in a conflict has the capacity to destroy the other in retaliation for a nuclear attack.

madafu (ma'dafuː) *n E African.* coconut milk. **[C19:** from Swahili**]**

Madag. *abbrev. for* Madagascar.

Madagascar (ˌmædə'gæskə) *n* an island republic in the Indian Ocean, off the E coast of Africa: made a French protectorate in 1895; became autonomous in 1958 and fully independent in 1960; contains unique flora and fauna. Languages: Malagasy and French. Religions: animist and Christian. Currency: franc. Capital: Antananarivo. Pop.: 14 463 000 (1998 est.). Area: 587 041 sq. km (266 657 sq. miles). Official name (since 1975): **Democratic Republic of Madagascar.** Former name (1958–75): **Malagasy Republic.** ▸ **ˌMada'gascan** *n, adj*

Madagascar aquamarine *n* a form of blue beryl from Madagascar, used as a gemstone.

madam ('mædəm) *n, pl* **madams,** *or* (for sense 1) **mesdames** ('meɪˌdæm). **1** a polite term of address for a woman, esp. one considered to be of relatively high social status. **2** a woman who runs a brothel. **3** *Brit. informal.* a precocious or pompous little girl. **[C13:** from Old French *ma dame* my lady**]**

madame ('mædəm; *French* madam) *n, pl* **mesdames** ('meɪˌdæm; *French* medam). a married Frenchwoman: usually used as a title equivalent to *Mrs,* and sometimes extended to older unmarried women to show respect and to women of other nationalities. **[C17:** from French. See MADAM**]**

madcap ('mædˌkæp) *adj* **1** impulsive, reckless, or lively. ◆ *n* **2** an impulsive, reckless, or lively person. **[C16:** from MAD + *cap* (in the figurative sense: head)**]**

mad cow disease *n* an informal name for **BSE**.

madden ('mæd°n) *vb* to make or become mad or angry.

maddening ('mæd°nɪŋ) *adj* **1** serving to send mad. **2** extremely annoying; exasperating. ▸ **'maddeningly** *adv* ▸ **'maddeningness** *n*

madder[1] ('mædə) *n* **1** any of several rubiaceous plants of the genus *Rubia*, esp. the Eurasian *R. tinctoria*, which has small yellow flowers and a red fleshy root. **2** the root of this plant. **3** a dark reddish-purple dye formerly obtained by fermentation of this root; identical to the synthetic dye, alizarin. **4** a red lake obtained from alizarin and an inorganic base; used as a pigment in inks and paints. [Old English *mædere;* related to Middle Dutch *mēde,* Old Norse *mathra*]

madder[2] ('mædə) *adj* the comparative of **mad**.

madding ('mædɪŋ) *adj Archaic.* **1** acting or behaving as if mad: *the madding crowd.* **2** making mad; maddening. ▸ **'maddingly** *adv*

made (meɪd) *vb* **1** the past tense and past participle of **make**[1]. ◆ *adj* **2** artificially produced. **3** (*in combination*) produced or shaped as specified: *handmade.* **4 get** *or* **have it made.** *Informal.* to be assured of success. **5 made of money.** very rich.

made dish *n Cooking.* a dish consisting of a number of different ingredients cooked together.

Madeira (mə'dɪərə; *Portuguese* mə'ðəirə) *n* **1** a group of volcanic islands in the N Atlantic, west of Morocco: constitutes the Portuguese administrative district of Funchal; consists of the chief island, Madeira, Pôrto Santo, and the uninhabited Deserta and Selvagen Islands; gained partial autonomy in 1976. Capital: Funchal. Pop.: 253 800 (1993 est.). Area: 797 sq. km (311 sq. miles). **2** a river in W Brazil, flowing northeast to the Amazon below Manaus. Length: 3241 km (2013 miles). **3** a rich strong fortified white wine made on Madeira.

Madeira cake *n* a kind of rich sponge cake.

madeleine ('mædəlɪn, -ˌleɪn) *n* a small fancy sponge cake. [C19: perhaps after *Madeleine* Paulmier, French pastry cook]

mademoiselle (ˌmædmwə'zɛl; *French* madmwazɛl) *n, pl* **mesdemoiselles** (ˌmeɪdmwə'zɛl; *French* medmwazɛl). **1** a young unmarried French girl or woman: usually used as a title equivalent to *Miss.* **2** a French teacher or governess. [C15: French, from *ma* my + *demoiselle* DAMSEL]

made-up *adj* **1** invented; fictional: *a made-up story.* **2** wearing make-up: *a well made-up woman.* **3** put together; assembled. **4** (of a road) surfaced with tarmac, concrete, etc.

madhouse ('mæd,haus) *n Informal.* **1** a mental hospital or asylum. **2** a state of uproar or confusion.

Madhya Bharat ('mʌdjə 'bɑːrət) *n* a former state of central India: part of Madhya Pradesh since 1956.

Madhya Pradesh ('mʌdjə prɑː'dɛʃ) *n* a state of central India, situated on the Deccan Plateau: the largest Indian state; rich in mineral resources, with several industrial cities. Capital: Bhopal. Pop.: 71 950 000 (1994 est.). Area: 443 446 sq. km (171 215 sq. miles).

Madison[1] ('mædɪs°n) *n* a city in the U.S., in S central Wisconsin, on an isthmus between Lakes Mendota and Monona: the state capital. Pop.: 197 630 (1996 est.).

Madison[2] ('mædɪs°n) *n* **James.** 1751–1836, U.S. statesman; 4th president of the U.S. (1809–17). He helped to draft the U.S. Constitution and Bill of Rights. His presidency was dominated by the War of 1812.

Madison Avenue *n* a street in New York City: a centre of American advertising and public-relations firms and a symbol of their attitudes and methods.

madly ('mædlɪ) *adv* **1** in an insane or foolish manner. **2** with great speed and energy. **3** *Informal.* extremely or excessively: *I love you madly.*

madman ('mædmən) *or (fem)* **madwoman** *n, pl* **-men** *or* **-women.** a person who is insane, esp. one who behaves violently; lunatic.

madness ('mædnɪs) *n* **1** insanity; lunacy. **2** extreme anger, excitement, or foolishness. **3** a nontechnical word for **rabies.**

Madonna[1] (mə'dɒnə) *n* **1** *Chiefly R.C. Church.* a designation of the Virgin Mary. **2** (*sometimes not cap.*) a picture or statue of the Virgin Mary. [C16: Italian, from *ma* my + *donna* lady]

Madonna[2] (mə'dɒnə) *n* full name *Madonna Louise Veronica Ciccone.* born 1958, U.S. rock singer and film actress. Her hits include "Like a Virgin" (1985), "Into the Groove" (1985), and "Ray of Light" (1998). Her films include *Desperately Seeking Susan* (1985), and *Evita* (1996).

Madonna lily *n* a perennial widely cultivated Mediterranean lily plant, *Lilium candidum,* with white trumpet-shaped flowers. Also called: **Annunciation lily.**

madras ('mædrəs, mə'dræs, -'drɑːs) *n* **1a** a strong fine cotton or silk fabric, usually with a woven stripe. **1b** (*as modifier*): *madras cotton.* **2** something made of this, esp. a scarf. **3** a medium-hot curry: *chicken madras.* [C19: so named because the material originated in the MADRAS area]

Madras (mə'drɑːs, -'dræs) *n* **1** a port in SE India, capital of Tamil Nadu, on the Bay of Bengal: founded in 1639 by the English East India Company as **Fort St George;** traditional burial place of St Thomas; university (1857). Pop. (city): 3 841 396 (1991), with a conurbation of 5 421 985 (1991). Official name: **Chennai. 2** the former name (until 1968) for the state of **Tamil Nadu.**

madrasah ('mɑːdrasə) *n Islam.* an educational institution, particularly for Islamic religious instruction. [from Arabic, literally: place of learning]

Madre de Dios (*Spanish* 'maðre ðe 'ðios) *n* a river in NE South America, rising in SE Peru and flowing northeast to the Beni River in N Bolivia. Length: about 965 km (600 miles).

madrepore (ˌmædrɪ'pɔː) *n* any coral of the genus *Madrepora,* many of which occur in tropical seas and form large coral reefs: order *Zoantharia.* [C18: via French from Italian *madrepora* mother-stone, from *madre* mother + *-pora,* from Latin *porus* or Greek *poros* calcareous stone, stalactite] ▸ **ˌmadre'poral, madreporic** (ˌmædrɪ'pɒrɪk), **madreporitic** (ˌmædrɪpə'rɪtɪk), *or* **ˌmadre'porian** *adj*

Madrid (mə'drɪd) *n* the capital of Spain, situated centrally in New Castile: the highest European capital, at an altitude of about 700 m (2300 ft.); a Moorish fortress in the 10th century, captured by Castile in 1083 and made capital of Spain in 1561; university (1836). Pop.: 3 029 734 (1995 est.).

madrigal ('mædrɪg°l) *n* **1** *Music.* a type of 16th- or 17th-century part song for unaccompanied voices with an amatory or pastoral text. Compare **glee** (sense 2). **2** a 14th-century Italian song, related to a pastoral stanzaic verse form. [C16: from Italian, from Medieval Latin *mātricāle* primitive, apparently from Latin *mātrīcālis* of the womb, from *matrīx* womb] ▸ **'madrigalˌesque** *adj* ▸ **madrigalian** (ˌmædrɪ'gælɪən, -'geɪ-) *adj* ▸ **'madrigalist** *n*

madrilène ('mædrɪˌlɛn, -ˌleɪn; *French* madrilɛn) *n* a cold consommé flavoured with tomato juice. [shortened from French *(consommé) madrilène* from Spanish *madrileño* of Madrid]

madroña (mə'drəunjə), **madroño** (mə'drəunjəu), *or* **madrone** (mə'drəunə) *n, pl* **-ñas, -ños,** *or* **-nes.** an ericaceous North American evergreen tree or shrub, *Arbutus menziesii,* with white flowers and red berry-like fruits. See also **strawberry tree.** [C19: from Spanish]

Madura (mə'duərə) *n* an island in Indonesia, off the NE coast of Java: extensive forests and saline springs. Capital: Pamekasan. Area: 5472 sq. km (2113 sq. miles). ▸ **Madurese** (ˌmædjuə'riːz) *adj, n*

Madurai ('mædjuˌraɪ) *n* a city in S India, in S Tamil Nadu: centre of Dravidian culture for over 2000 years; cotton industry. Pop.: 940 989 (1991). Former name: **Madura.**

maduro (mə'duərəu) *adj* **1** (of cigars) dark and strong. ◆ *n, pl* **-ros. 2** a cigar of this type. [Spanish, literally: ripe, from Latin *mātūrus* ripe, MATURE]

madwort ('mædˌwɜːt) *n* **1** a low-growing Eurasian boraginaceous plant, *Asperugo procumbens,* with small blue flowers. **2** any of certain other plants, such as alyssum. [C16: once alleged to be a cure for madness]

madzoon (mɑːd'zuːn) *n* a variant of **matzoon.**

Maeander (miː'ændə) *n* ancient name of the river **Menderes** (sense 1). Also spelled: **Meander.**

Maebashi ('mɑːɛ'bɑːʃiː) *n* a city in central Japan, on central Honshu: centre of sericulture and silk-spinning; university (1949). Pop.: 284 780 (1995).

Maecenas (miː'siːnæs) *n* **1 Gaius** ('gaɪəs). ?70–8 B.C., Roman statesman; adviser to Augustus and patron of Horace and Virgil. **2** a wealthy patron of the arts.

maelstrom ('meɪlstrəum) *n* **1** a large powerful whirlpool. **2** any turbulent confusion. [C17: from obsolete Dutch *maelstroom,* from *malen* to grind, whirl round + *stroom* STREAM]

Maelstrom ('meɪlstrəum) *n* a strong tidal current in a restricted channel in the Lofoten Islands off the NW coast of Norway.

maenad *or* **menad** ('miːnæd) *n* **1** *Classical myth.* a woman participant in the orgiastic rites of Dionysus; bacchante. **2** a frenzied woman. [C16: from Latin *Maenas,* from Greek *mainas* madwoman] ▸ **mae'nadic** *adj* ▸ **mae'nadically** *adv* ▸ **'maenadism** *n*

maestoso (maɪ'stəusəu) *Music.* ◆ *adj, adv* **1** to be performed majestically. ◆ *n* **2** a piece or passage directed to be played in this way. [C18: Italian: majestic, from Latin *māiestās* MAJESTY]

Maestricht ('mɑːstrɪxt; *Dutch* maː'strɪxt) *n* an obsolete spelling of **Maastricht.**

maestro ('maɪstrəu) *n, pl* **-tri** (-trɪ) *or* **-tros. 1** a distinguished music teacher, conductor, or musician. **2** any man regarded as the master of an art: often used as a term of address. **3** See **maestro di cappella.** [C18: Italian: master]

maestro di cappella (dɪ kə'pɛlə) *n* a person in charge of an orchestra, esp. a private one attached to the palace of a prince in Italy during the baroque period. See **kapellmeister.** [Italian: master of the chapel]

Maeterlinck ('meɪtəˌlɪŋk; *French* metɛrlɛ̃k) *n* Comte **Maurice** (mɔris). 1862–1949, Belgian poet and dramatist, noted particularly for his symbolist plays, such as *Pelléas et Mélisande* (1892), which served as the basis for an opera by Debussy, and *L'Oiseau bleu* (1909). Nobel prize for literature 1911.

mae west (meɪ) *n Slang.* an inflatable life jacket, esp. as issued to the U.S. armed forces for emergency use. [C20: after *Mae West,* 1892–1980, American actress, renowned for her generous bust]

Maewo (mɑː'ɛɪwəu) *n* an almost uninhabited island in Vanuatu. Also called: **Aurora.**

Mafeking ('mæfɪˌkɪŋ) *n* the former name (until 1980) of **Mafikeng.**

MAFF (in Britain) *abbrev. for* Ministry of Agriculture, Fisheries, and Food.

maffick ('mæfɪk) *vb* (*intr*) *Brit., archaic.* to celebrate extravagantly and publicly. [C20: back formation from *Mafeking* (now Mafikeng), from the rejoicings at the relief of the siege there in 1900] ▸ **'mafficker** *n*

Mafia *or* **Maffia** ('mæfɪə) *n* **1 the.** an international secret organization founded in Sicily, probably in opposition to tyranny. It developed into a criminal organization and in the late 19th century was carried to the U.S. by Italian immigrants. **2** any group considered to resemble the Mafia. See also **Black Hand, Camorra, Cosa Nostra.** [C19: from Sicilian dialect of Italian, literally hostility to the law, boldness, perhaps from Arabic *mahyah* bragging]

Mafikeng ('mæfɪˌkɛŋ) *n* a town in N South Africa: besieged by the Boers for 217 days (1899–1900) during the second Boer War: administrative headquarters of the British protectorate of Bechuanaland until 1965, although outside its borders. Pop.: 7000 (latest est.). Former name (until 1980): **Mafeking.**

mafioso (ˌmæfɪ'əusəu; *Italian* mafi'oso) *n, pl* **-sos** *or* **-si** (*Italian* -si). a person belonging to the Mafia.

maftir ('mɑftir) *n Judaism.* **1** the final section of the weekly Torah reading. **2** the person to whom it is read, who also reads the Haftarah.

mag[1] (mæg) *n Informal.* See **magazine.**

mag[2] (mæg) *Informal, now chiefly Austral.* ◆ *vb* **mags, magging, magged.** (*intr*) **1** to talk; chatter. ◆ *n* **2** talk; chatter. [C18: from *Mag,* see MAGPIE]

mag. *abbrev. for:* **1** magazine. **2** magnesium. **3** magnetic. **4** magnetism. **5** magnets. **6** magnitude.

magainin (mə'geɪnɪn) *n* any of a series of related substances with antibiotic properties, derived from the skins of frogs. [C20: from Hebrew *magain* a shield]

Magallanes (*Spanish* maɣa'ʎanes) *n* the former name of **Punta Arenas.**

magazine (,mægə'ziːn) *n* **1** a periodical paperback publication containing articles, fiction, photographs, etc. **2** a metal case holding several cartridges used in some kinds of automatic firearms; it is removed and replaced when empty. **3** a building or compartment for storing weapons, explosives, military provisions, etc. **4** a stock of ammunition. **5** a device for continuously recharging a stove or boiler with solid fuel. **6** *Photog.* another name for **cartridge** (sense 5). **7** a rack for automatically feeding a number of slides through a projector. **8** a TV or radio programme made up of a series of short nonfiction items. [C16: via French *magasin* from Italian *magazzino,* from Arabic *makhāzin,* plural of *makhzan* storehouse, from *khazana* to store away]

magdalen ('mægdəlɪn) *or* **magdalene** ('mægdə,liːn, ,mægdə'liːnɪ) *n* **1** *Literary.* a reformed prostitute. **2** *Rare.* a reformatory for prostitutes. [from MARY MAGDALENE]

Magdalena (,mægdə'leɪnə, -'liː-; *Spanish* maɣða'lena) *n* a river in SW Colombia, rising on the E slopes of the Andes and flowing north to the Caribbean near Barranquilla. Length: 1540 km (956 miles).

Magdalena Bay *n* an inlet of the Pacific on the coast of NW Mexico, in Lower California.

Magdalene ('mægdə,liːn, ,mægdə'liːnɪ) *n* See **Mary Magdalene.**

Magdalenian (,mægdə'liːnɪən) *adj* **1** of or relating to the latest Palaeolithic culture in Europe, which ended about 10 000 years ago. ◆ *n* **2** the Magdalenian culture. [C19: from French *magdalénien,* after *La Madeleine,* village in Dordogne, France, near which artefacts of the culture were found]

Magdeburg ('mægdə,bɜːg; *German* 'makdəburk) *n* an industrial city and port in central Germany, on the River Elbe, capital of Saxony-Anhalt: a leading member of the Hanseatic League, whose local laws, the **Magdeburg Laws,** were adopted by many European cities. Pop.: 257 656 (1996 est.).

mage (meɪdʒ) *n* an archaic word for **magician.** [C14: from MAGUS]

Magellan[1] (mə'gelən) *n* **Strait of.** a strait between the mainland of S South America and Tierra del Fuego, linking the S Pacific with the S Atlantic. Length: 600 km (370 miles). Width: up to 32 km (20 miles).

Magellan[2] (mə'gelən) *n* **Ferdinand.** Portuguese name *Fernão de Magalhães.* ?1480–1521, Portuguese navigator in the service of Spain. He commanded an expedition of five ships that set out to sail to the East Indies via the West. He discovered the Strait of Magellan (1520), crossed the Pacific, and reached the Philippines (1521), where he was killed by natives. One of his ships reached Spain (1522) and was therefore the first to circumnavigate the world.

Magellanic Cloud (,mægɪ'lænɪk) *n* either of two small irregular galaxies, the **Large Magellanic Cloud** (Nubecula Major) and the **Small Magellanic Cloud** (Nubecula Minor), lying near the S celestial pole; they are probably satellites of the Galaxy. Distances: 163 000 light years (Large), 196 000 light years (Small).

Magen David *or* **Mogen David** ('mɔːgən 'deɪvɪd) *n Judaism.* another name for the **Star of David.** [C20: from Hebrew *māghēn Dāwīdh* shield of David; see DAVID (sense 1)]

magenta (mə'dʒɛntə) *n* **1a** a deep purplish red that is the complementary colour of green and, with yellow and cyan, forms a set of primary colours. **1b** (*as adj*): *a magenta filter.* **2** another name for **fuchsin.** [C19: named after *Magenta,* Italy, alluding to the blood shed in a battle there (1859)]

maggie ('mægɪ) *n Slang.* a magpie.

Maggiore (,mædʒɪ'ɔːrɪ; *Italian* mad'dʒore) *n* **Lake.** a lake in N Italy and S Switzerland, in the S Lepontine Alps.

maggot ('mægət) *n* **1** the soft limbless larva of dipterous insects, esp. the housefly and blowfly, occurring in decaying organic matter. **2** *Rare.* a fancy or whim. [C14: from earlier *mathek;* related to Old Norse *mathkr* worm, Old English *matha,* Old High German *mado* grub]

maggoty ('mægətɪ) *adj* **1** relating to, resembling, or ridden with maggots. **2** *Slang.* very drunk. **3** *Austral. slang.* annoyed, angry.

Magherafelt ('mæhərə,felt) *n* a district of N Northern Ireland, in Co. Londonderry. Pop.: 36 293 (1991). Area: 572 sq. km (221 sq. miles).

Maghreb *or* **Maghrib** ('mʌgrəb) *n* NW Africa, including Morocco, Algeria, Tunisia, and sometimes Libya. [from Arabic, literally: the West] ▸ **'Maghrebi** *or* **'Maghribi** *adj, n*

magi ('meɪdʒaɪ) *pl n, sing* **magus** ('meɪgəs). **1** the Zoroastrian priests of the ancient Medes and Persians. **2 the three Magi.** the wise men from the East who came to do homage to the infant Jesus (Matthew 2:1–12) and traditionally called Caspar, Melchior, and Balthazar. ▸ **magian** ('meɪdʒɪən) *adj*

magic ('mædʒɪk) *n* **1** the art that, by use of spells, supposedly invokes supernatural powers to influence events; sorcery. **2** the practice of this art. **3** the practice of illusory tricks to entertain other people; conjuring. **4** any mysterious or extraordinary quality or power: *the magic of springtime.* **5 like magic.** very quickly. ◆ *adj also* **magical. 6** of or relating to magic: *a magic spell.* **7** possessing or considered to possess mysterious powers: *a magic wand.* **8** unaccountably enchanting: *magic beauty.* **9** *Informal.* wonderful; marvellous; exciting. ◆ *vb* **-ics, -icking, -icked.** (*tr*) **10** to transform or produce by or as if by magic. **11** (foll. by *away*) to cause to disappear by or as if by magic. [C14: via Old French *magique,* from Greek *magikē* witchcraft, from *magos* MAGUS] ▸ **'magical** *adj* ▸ **'magically** *adv*

magic bullet *n Informal.* any therapeutic agent, esp. one in the early stages of development, reputed to be very effective in treating a condition, such as a malignant tumour, by specifically targeting the diseased tissue.

magic carpet *n* (in fairy stories) a carpet capable of transporting people through the air.

Magic Circle *n* **1** the British association of magicians, traditionally forbidden to reveal any of the secrets of their art. **2** (*not caps.*) a group of influential people involved in a conspiracy.

magic eye *n* a miniature cathode-ray tube in some radio receivers, on the screen of which a pattern is displayed in order to assist tuning.

magician (mə'dʒɪʃən) *n* **1** another term for **conjuror. 2** a person who practises magic. **3** a person who has extraordinary skill, influence, or qualities.

magic lantern *n* an early type of slide projector. Sometimes shortened to **lantern.**

magic mushroom *n Informal.* any of various types of fungi that contain a hallucinogenic substance, esp. *Psilocybe mexicana,* which contains psilocybin.

magic number *n* **1** *Physics.* any of the numbers 2, 8, 20, 28, 50, 82, and 126. Nuclides with these numbers of nucleons appear to have greater stability than other nuclides. **2** *Chem.* a number of atoms that is particularly stable in certain types of compound that have clusters of the same type of atom.

magic realism *or* **magical realism** *n* a style of painting or writing that depicts images or scenes of surreal fantasy in a representational or realistic way. ▸ **magic realist** *or* **magical realist** *n*

magic square *n* a square array of rows of integers arranged so that the sum of the integers is the same when taken vertically, horizontally, or diagonally.

magilp (mə'gɪlp) *n Arts.* a variant spelling of **megilp.**

Maginot line ('mæʒɪ,nəʊ; *French* maʒino) *n* **1** a line of fortifications built by France to defend its border with Germany prior to World War II; it proved ineffective against the German invasion. **2** any line of defence in which blind confidence is placed. [named after André *Maginot* (1877–1932), French minister of war when the fortifications were begun in 1929]

magisterial (,mædʒɪ'stɪərɪəl) *adj* **1** commanding; authoritative. **2** domineering; dictatorial. **3** of or relating to a teacher or person of similar status. **4** of or relating to a magistrate. [C17: from Late Latin *magisteriālis,* from *magister* master] ▸ **,magis'terially** *adv* ▸ **,magis'terialness** *n*

magisterium (,mædʒɪ'stɪərɪəm) *n* the teaching authority or function of the Roman Catholic Church. [C19: see MAGISTERY]

magistery ('mædʒɪstərɪ, -trɪ) *n, pl* **-teries.** *Alchemy.* **1** an agency or substance, such as the philosopher's stone, believed to transmute other substances. **2** any substance capable of healing. [C16: from Medieval Latin *magisterium,* from Latin: mastery, from *magister* master]

magistracy ('mædʒɪstrəsɪ) *or* **magistrature** ('mædʒɪstrə,tjʊə) *n, pl* **-cies** *or* **-tures. 1** the office or function of a magistrate. **2** magistrates collectively. **3** the district under the jurisdiction of a magistrate.

magistral (mə'dʒɪstrəl) *adj* **1** of, relating to, or characteristic of a master. **2** *Pharmacol.* made up according to a special prescription. Compare **officinal. 3** *Fortifications.* determining the location of other fortifications: *the magistral line.* ◆ *n* **4** a fortification in a determining position. [C16: from Latin *magistrālis* concerning a master, from *magister* master] ▸ **magistrality** (,mædʒɪ'strælɪtɪ) *n* ▸ **magistratically** (,mædʒɪ'strætɪkəlɪ) *adv*

magistrate ('mædʒɪ,streɪt, -strɪt) *n* **1** a public officer concerned with the administration of law. Related adj: **magisterial. 2** another name for **justice of the peace. 3** *N.Z.* the former name for **district court judge.** [C17: from Latin *magistrātus,* from *magister* master] ▸ **'magis,trateship** *n*

magistrates' court *n* (in England) a court of summary jurisdiction held before two or more justices of the peace or a stipendiary magistrate to deal with minor crimes, certain civil actions, and preliminary hearings.

Maglemosian *or* **Maglemosean** (,mæglə'məʊzɪən) *n* **1** the first Mesolithic culture of N Europe, dating from 8000 B.C. to about 5000 B.C.: important for the rare wooden objects that have been preserved, such as dugout canoes. ◆ *adj* **2** designating or relating to this culture. [C20: named after the site at *Maglemose,* Denmark, where the culture was first classified]

maglev ('mæg,lɛv) *n* a type of high-speed train that runs on magnets supported by a magnetic field generated around the track. [C20: from *mag(netic) lev(itation)*]

magma ('mægmə) *n, pl* **-mas** *or* **-mata** (-mətə). **1** a paste or suspension consisting of a finely divided solid dispersed in a liquid. **2** hot molten rock, usually formed in the earth's upper mantle, some of which finds its way into the crust and onto the earth's surface, where it solidifies to form igneous rock. [C15, from Latin: dregs (of an ointment), from Greek: salve made by kneading, from *massein* to knead] ▸ **magmatic** (mæg'mætɪk) *adj* ▸ **'magmatism** *n*

magma chamber *n* a reservoir of magma in the earth's upper crust where the magma may reside temporarily on its way from the upper mantle to the earth's surface.

Magna Carta *or* **Magna Charta** ('mægnə 'kɑːtə) *n English history.* the charter granted by King John at Runnymede in 1215, recognizing the rights and privileges of the barons, church, and freemen. [Medieval Latin: great charter]

magna cum laude ('mægnə kʊm 'laʊdeɪ) *Chiefly U.S.* with great praise: the second of three designations for above-average achievement in examinations. Compare **cum laude, summa cum laude.** [Latin]

Magna Graecia ('mægnə 'griːʃɪə) *n* (in the ancient world) S Italy, where numerous colonies were founded by Greek cities. [Latin: Great Greece]

magnanimity (,mægnə'nɪmɪtɪ) *n, pl* **-ties.** generosity. [C14: via Old French from Latin *magnanimitās,* from *magnus* great + *animus* soul]

magnanimous (mæg'nænɪməs) *adj* generous and noble. [C16: from Latin *magnanimus* great-souled] ▸ **mag'nanimously** *adv* ▸ **mag'nanimousness** *n*

magnate ('mægneɪt, -nɪt) *n* **1** a person of power and rank in any sphere, esp. in industry. **2** *History.* a great nobleman. **3** (formerly) a member of the upper chamber in certain European parliaments, as in Hungary. [C15: back formation from earlier *magnates* from Late Latin: great men, plural of *magnās,* from Latin *magnus* great] ▸ **'magnate,ship** *n*

magnesia (mæg'niːʃə) *n* another name for **magnesium oxide.** [C14: via Medieval Latin from Greek *Magnēsia,* of *Magnēs* ancient mineral-rich region] ▸ **mag'nesian, magnesic** (mæg'niːsɪk), *or* **mag'nesial** *adj*

magnesite ('mægnɪ,saɪt) *n* a white, colourless, or lightly tinted mineral consisting of naturally occurring magnesium carbonate in hexagonal crystalline form: a source of magnesium and also used in the manufacture of refractory bricks. Formula: $MgCO_3$. [C19: from MAGNESIUM + -ITE[1]]

magnesium (mæg'niːzɪəm) *n* a light silvery-white metallic element of the alkaline earth series that burns with an intense white flame, occurring principally in magnesite, dolomite, and carnallite: used in light structural alloys, flashbulbs, flares, and fireworks. Symbol: Mg; atomic no.: 12; atomic wt.: 24.3050; valency: 2; relative density: 1.738; melting pt.: 650°C; boiling pt.: 1090°C. [C19: New Latin, from MAGNESIA]

magnesium oxide *n* a white tasteless substance occurring naturally as periclase: used as an antacid and laxative and in refractory materials, such as crucibles and fire bricks. Formula: MgO. Also called: **magnesia.**

magnet ('mægnɪt) *n* **1** a body that can attract certain substances, such as iron or steel, as a result of a magnetic field; a piece of ferromagnetic substance. See also **electromagnet. 2** a person or thing that exerts a great attraction. [C15: via Latin from Greek *magnēs,* shortened from *ho Magnēs lithos* the Magnesian stone. See MAGNESIA]

magnetic (mæg'nɛtɪk) *adj* **1** of, producing, or operated by means of magnetism. **2** of or concerned with a magnet. **3** of or concerned with the magnetism of the earth: *the magnetic equator.* **4** capable of being magnetized. **5** exerting a powerful attraction: *a magnetic personality.* ► **mag'netically** *adv*

magnetic bottle *n* a configuration of magnetic fields for containing the plasma in controlled thermonuclear reactions.

magnetic bubble *n Physics.* a small round magnetic domain induced by a magnetic field in a thin film of magnetic material, used in certain types of computer memories.

magnetic character reader *n* a device that automatically scans and interprets characters printed with magnetic ink. It operates by the process of **magnetic character recognition.**

magnetic compass *n* a compass containing a magnetic needle pivoted in a horizontal plane, that indicates the direction of magnetic north at points on the earth's surface.

magnetic confinement *n* another name for **containment** (sense 3).

magnetic constant *n* the permeability of free space, which has the value $4\pi \times 10^{-7}$ henry per metre. Symbol: M_0 Also called: **absolute permeability.**

magnetic course *n* an aircraft's course in relation to the magnetic north. Also called: **magnetic heading.**

magnetic declination *n* the angle that a compass needle makes with the direction of the geographical north pole at any given point on the earth's surface. Also called: **declination, magnetic variation.**

magnetic dip *or* **inclination** *n* another name for **dip** (sense 27).

magnetic dipole moment *n* a measure of the magnetic strength of a magnet or current-carrying coil, expressed as the torque produced when the magnet or coil is set with its axis perpendicular to unit magnetic field. Symbol: *m, j* Also called: **magnetic moment.** Compare **electromagnetic moment.**

magnetic disk *n Computing.* another name for **disk** (sense 2).

magnetic epoch *n Geology.* a geologically long period of time during which the magnetic field of the earth retains the same polarity. The magnetic field may reverse during such a period for a geologically short period of time (a **magnetic event**).

magnetic equator *n* an imaginary line on the earth's surface, near the equator, at all points on which there is no magnetic dip. Also called: **aclinic line.**

magnetic field *n* a field of force surrounding a permanent magnet or a moving charged particle, in which another permanent magnet or moving charge experiences a force. Compare **electric field.**

magnetic flux *n* **1** a measure of the strength of a magnetic field over a given area, equal to the product of the area and the magnetic flux density through it. Symbol: ϕ **2** a magnetic field.

magnetic flux density *n* a measure of the strength of a magnetic field at a given point, expressed by the force per unit length on a conductor carrying unit current at that point. Symbol: *B* Also called: **magnetic induction.**

magnetic induction *n* another name for **magnetic flux density.**

magnetic ink *n* ink containing particles of a magnetic material used for printing characters for magnetic character recognition.

magnetic ink character recognition *n* the process of reading characters printed in magnetic ink. Abbrev.: **MICR.**

magnetic lens *n* a set of magnets, esp. electromagnets, used to focus or defocus a beam of charged particles in an electron microscope, particle accelerator, or similar device.

magnetic meridian *n* a continuous imaginary line around the surface of the earth passing through both magnetic poles.

magnetic mine *n* a mine designed to activate when a magnetic field such as that generated by the metal of a ship's hull is detected.

magnetic mirror *n Physics.* a configuration of magnetic fields used to confine charged particles, as in a magnetic bottle.

magnetic moment *n* short for **magnetic dipole moment** or **electromagnetic moment.**

magnetic monopole *n* another name for **monopole** (sense 2).

magnetic needle *n* a slender magnetized rod used in certain instruments, such as the magnetic compass, for indicating the direction of a magnetic field.

magnetic north *n* the direction in which a compass needle points, at an angle (the declination) from the direction of true (geographic) north.

magnetic particle inspection *n Engineering.* a method of testing for cracks and other defects in a magnetic material, such as steel, by covering it with a magnetic powder and magnetizing it: any variation in the concentration of the powder indicates a flaw in the material.

magnetic pick-up *n* a type of record player pick-up in which the stylus moves an iron core in a coil, causing a changing magnetic field that produces the current.

magnetic pole *n* **1** either of two regions in a magnet where the magnetic induction is concentrated. **2** either of two variable points on the earth's surface towards which a magnetic needle points, where the lines of force of the earth's magnetic field are vertical.

magnetic resonance *n* the response by atoms, molecules, or nuclei subjected to a magnetic field to radio waves or other forms of energy: used in medicine for scanning (**magnetic resonance imaging**).

magnetics (mæg'nɛtɪks) *n* (*functioning as sing*) the branch of physics concerned with magnetism.

magnetic storm *n* a sudden severe disturbance of the earth's magnetic field, caused by emission of charged particles from the sun.

magnetic stripe *n* (across the back of various types of cheque card, credit card, etc.) a dark stripe of magnetic material consisting of several tracks onto which information may be coded and which may be read or written to electronically.

magnetic tape *n* a long narrow plastic or metal strip coated or impregnated with a ferromagnetic material such as iron oxide, used to record sound or video signals or to store information in computers. Sometimes (informally) shortened to **mag tape.**

magnetic tape unit *or* **drive** *n* a computer device that moves reels of magnetic tape past read-write heads so that data can be transferred to or from the computer.

magnetic variation *n* another name for **magnetic declination.**

magnetism ('mægnɪˌtɪzəm) *n* **1** the property of attraction displayed by magnets. **2** any of a class of phenomena in which a field of force is caused by a moving electric charge. See also **electromagnetism, ferromagnetism, diamagnetism, paramagnetism. 3** the branch of physics concerned with magnetic phenomena. **4** powerful attraction. ► **'magnetist** *n*

magnetite ('mægnɪˌtaɪt) *n* a black magnetic mineral, found in igneous and metamorphic rocks and as a separate deposit. It is a source of iron. Composition: iron oxide. Formula: Fe_3O_4. Crystal structure: cubic. ► **magnetitic** (ˌmægnɪ'tɪtɪk) *adj*

magnetize *or* **magnetise** ('mægnɪˌtaɪz) *vb* (*tr*) **1** to make (a substance or object) magnetic. **2** to attract strongly. **3** an obsolete word for **mesmerize.** ► **ˌmagnet'izable** *or* **ˌmagnet'isable** *adj* ► **ˌmagneti'zation** *or* **ˌmagneti'sation** *n* ► **'magnetˌizer** *or* **'magnetˌiser** *n*

magneto (mæg'niːtəʊ) *n, pl* **-tos.** a small electric generator in which the magnetic field is produced by a permanent magnet, esp. one for providing the spark in an internal-combustion engine. [C19: short for *magnetoelectric generator*]

magneto- *combining form.* indicating magnetism or magnetic properties: *magnetosphere.*

magnetochemistry (mægˌniːtəʊ'kɛmɪstrɪ) *n* the branch of chemistry concerned with the relationship between magnetic and chemical properties. ► **magˌneto'chemical** *adj*

magnetoelectricity (mægˌniːtəʊɪlɛk'trɪsɪtɪ) *n* electricity produced by the action of magnetic fields. ► **magˌnetoe'lectric** *or* **magˌnetoe'lectrical** *adj*

magnetograph (mæg'niːtəʊˌgrɑːf, -ˌgræf) *n* a recording magnetometer, usually used for studying variations in the earth's magnetic field.

magnetohydrodynamics (mægˌniːtəʊˌhaɪdrəʊdaɪ'næmɪks) *n* (*functioning as sing*) **1** the study of the behaviour of conducting fluids, such as liquid metals or plasmas, in magnetic fields. **2** the generation of electricity by subjecting a plasma to a magnetic field and collecting the deflected free electrons. ◆ Abbrev.: **MHD.** ► **magˌnetoˌhydrodynamic** *adj*

magnetometer (ˌmægnɪ'tɒmɪtə) *n* any instrument for measuring the intensity or direction of a magnetic field, esp. the earth's field. ► **magnetometric** (ˌmægnɪtəʊ'mɛtrɪk) *adj* ► **ˌmagne'tometry** *n*

magnetomotive (mægˌniːtəʊ'məʊtɪv) *adj* causing a magnetic flux.

magnetomotive force *n* the agency producing a magnetic flux, considered analogous to the electromotive force in an electric circuit; equal to the circular integral of the magnetic field strength. Symbol: *F*

magneton ('mægnɪˌtɒn, mæg'niːtɒn) *n* **1** Also called: **Bohr magneton.** a unit of magnetic moment equal to $eh/4\pi m$ where *e* and *m* are the charge and mass of an electron and *h* is the Planck constant. It has the value $9.274\ 096 \times 10^{-24}$ joule per tesla. Symbol: β or m_B **2** Also called: **nuclear magneton.** a similar unit equal to $\beta m/M$ where *M* is the mass of the proton. [C20: from MAGNET + (ELECTR)ON]

magnetosphere (mæg'niːtəʊˌsfɪə) *n* the region surrounding a planet, such as the earth, in which the behaviour of charged particles is controlled by the planet's magnetic field. ► **magnetospheric** (mægˌniːtəʊ'sfɛrɪk) *adj*

magnetostatics (mægˌniːtəʊ'stætɪks) *n* (*functioning as sing*) *Physics.* the study of steady-state magnetic fields.

magnetostriction (mægˌniːtəʊ'strɪkʃən) *n* a change in dimensions of a ferromagnetic material that is subjected to a magnetic field. [C19: from MAGNETO- + CONSTRICTION] ► **magˌneto'strictive** *adj*

magnetron ('mægnɪˌtrɒn) *n* a two-electrode electronic valve used with an applied magnetic field to generate high-power microwave oscillations, esp. for use in radar. [C20: from MAGNET + ELECTRON]

magnet school *n* a school that provides a focus on one subject area throughout its curriculum in order to attract, often from an early age, pupils who wish to specialize in this subject.

magnet steel *n Engineering.* steel used for the manufacture of permanent magnets, often having a high cobalt content and smaller amounts of nickel, aluminium, or copper.

magnific (mæg'nɪfɪk) *or* **magnifical** *adj Archaic.* magnificent, grandiose, or pompous. [C15: via Old French from Latin *magnificus* great in deeds, from *magnus* great + *facere* to do] ► **mag'nifically** *adv*

Magnificat (mæg'nɪfɪˌkæt) *n Christianity.* the hymn of the Virgin Mary (Luke

1:46-55), used as a canticle. [from the opening phrase in the Latin version, *Magnificat anima mea Dominum* (my soul doth magnify the Lord)]

magnification (ˌmægnɪfɪˈkeɪʃən) *n* **1** the act of magnifying or the state of being magnified. **2** the degree to which something is magnified. **3** a copy, photograph, drawing, etc., of something magnified. **4** a measure of the ability of a lens or other optical instrument to magnify, expressed as the ratio of the size of the image to that of the object.

magnificence (mægˈnɪfɪsəns) *n* the quality of being magnificent. [C14: via French from Latin *magnificentia*]

magnificent (mægˈnɪfɪsᵊnt) *adj* **1** splendid or impressive in appearance. **2** superb or very fine. **3** (esp. of ideas) noble or elevated. **4** *Archaic.* great or exalted in rank or action. [C16: from Latin *magnificentio* more splendid; irregular comparative of *magnificus* great in deeds; see MAGNIFIC] ▸ **magˈnificently** *adv* ▸ **magˈnificentness** *n*

magnifico (mægˈnɪfɪˌkəʊ) *n, pl* **-coes.** a magnate; grandee. [C16: Italian from Latin *magnificus;* see MAGNIFIC]

magnify (ˈmægnɪˌfaɪ) *vb* **-fies, -fying, -fied. 1** to increase, cause to increase, or be increased in apparent size, as through the action of a lens, microscope, etc. **2** to exaggerate or become exaggerated in importance: *don't magnify your troubles.* **3** (*tr*) *Rare.* to increase in actual size. **4** (*tr*) *Archaic.* to glorify. [C14: via Old French from Latin *magnificāre* to praise; see MAGNIFIC] ▸ **ˈmagniˌfiable** *adj*

magnifying glass *or* **magnifier** *n* a convex lens used to produce an enlarged image of an object.

magniloquent (mægˈnɪləkwənt) *adj* (of speech) lofty in style; grandiloquent. [C17: from Latin *magnus* great + *loquī* to speak] ▸ **magˈniloquence** *n* ▸ **magˈniloquently** *adv*

Magnitogorsk (*Russian* məgnitaˈgɔrsk) *n* a city in central Russia, on the Ural River: founded in 1930 to exploit local magnetite ores; site of one of the world's largest, but outdated, metallurgical plants. Pop.: 427 000 (1995 est.).

magnitude (ˈmægnɪˌtjuːd) *n* **1** relative importance or significance: *a problem of the first magnitude.* **2** relative size or extent: *the magnitude of the explosion.* **3** *Maths.* a number assigned to a quantity, such as weight, and used as a basis of comparison for the measurement of similar quantities. **4** Also called: **apparent magnitude.** *Astronomy.* the apparent brightness of a celestial body expressed on a numerical scale on which bright stars have a low value. Values are measured by eye (**visual magnitude**) or more accurately by photometric or photographic methods, and range from –26.7 (the sun), through 1.5 (Sirius), down to about +30. Each integral value represents a brightness 2.512 times greater than the next highest integral value. See also **absolute magnitude. 5** Also called: **earthquake magnitude.** *Geology.* a measure of the size of an earthquake based on the quantity of energy released: specified on the Richter scale. See **Richter scale.** [C14: from Latin *magnitūdō* size, from *magnus* great] ▸ **ˌmagniˈtudinous** *adj*

magnolia (mægˈnəʊlɪə) *n* **1** any tree or shrub of the magnoliaceous genus *Magnolia* of Asia and North America: cultivated for their white, pink, purple, or yellow showy flowers. **2** the flower of any of these plants. **3** a very pale pinkish-white or purplish-white colour. [C18: New Latin, named after Pierre *Magnol* (1638–1715), French botanist]

magnoliaceous (mægˌnəʊlɪˈeɪʃəs) *adj* of, relating to, or belonging to the *Magnoliaceae,* a family of trees and shrubs, including magnolias and the tulip tree, having large showy flowers.

magnolia metal *n Engineering.* an alloy used for bearings, consisting largely of lead (up to 80 per cent) and antimony, with the addition of smaller quantities of iron and tin.

magnox (ˈmægnɒks) *n* an alloy consisting mostly of magnesium with small amounts of aluminium and other metals, used in fuel elements of nuclear reactors. [C20: from *mag*(*nesium*) *n*(*o*) *ox*(*idation*)]

magnox reactor *n* a nuclear reactor using carbon dioxide as the coolant, graphite as the moderator, and uranium cased in magnox as the fuel.

magnum (ˈmægnəm) *n, pl* **-nums.** a wine bottle holding the equivalent of two normal bottles (approximately 52 fluid ounces). [C18: from Latin: a big thing, from *magnus* large]

magnum opus *n* a great work of art or literature, esp. the greatest single work of an artist. [Latin]

magnus hitch (ˈmægnəs) *n* a knot similar to a clove hitch but having one more turn. [C19 *magnus,* of unknown origin]

Magog (ˈmeɪgɒg) *n* See **Gog and Magog.**

magot (mɑːˈgəʊ, ˈmægət) *n* **1** a Chinese or Japanese figurine in a crouching position, usually grotesque. **2** a less common name for **Barbary ape.** [C17: from French: grotesque figure, after the Biblical giant MAGOG]

magpie (ˈmægˌpaɪ) *n* **1** any of various passerine birds of the genus *Pica,* esp. *P. pica,* having a black-and-white plumage, long tail, and a chattering call: family *Corvidae* (crows, etc.). **2** any of various similar birds of the Australian family *Cracticidae.* See also **butcherbird** (sense 2). **3** any of various other similar or related birds. **4** (*often cap.*) a variety of domestic fancy pigeon typically having black-and-white markings. **5** *Brit.* a person who hoards small objects. **6** a person who chatters. **7a** the outmost ring but one on a target. **7b** a shot that hits this ring. [C17: from *Mag* diminutive of *Margaret,* used to signify a chatterbox + PIE[2]]

magpie goose *n* a large black-and-white goose, *Anseranas semipalmata,* of N Australia and adjacent islands.

magpie lark *n* a common black-and-white bird of Australia, *Grallina cyanoleuca,* that builds a mud nest. Also called: **peewee.**

magpie moth *n* **1** a geometrid moth, *Abraxas grossulariata,* showing variable patterning in black on white or yellow, whose looper larvae attack currant and gooseberry bushes. The paler **clouded magpie** is *A. sylvata.* **2 small magpie.** an unrelated micro, *Eurrhypara hortulata.*

MAgr *abbrev. for* Master of Agriculture.

Magritte (*French* magrit) *n* **René** (rəne). 1898–1967, Belgian surrealist painter. By juxtaposing incongruous objects, depicted with meticulous realism, his works create a bizarre and disturbing impression.

mag tape *n Informal.* short for **magnetic tape.**

maguey (ˈmægweɪ) *n* **1** any of various tropical American agave plants of the genera *Agave* or *Furcraea,* esp. one that yields a fibre or is used in making an alcoholic beverage. **2** the fibre from any of these plants, used esp. for rope. [C16: Spanish, from Taino]

magus (ˈmeɪgəs) *n, pl* **magi** (ˈmeɪdʒaɪ). **1** a Zoroastrian priest. **2** an astrologer, sorcerer, or magician of ancient times. [C14: from Latin, from Greek *magos,* from Old Persian *magus* magician]

Magus (ˈmeɪgəs) *n* **Simon.** *New Testament.* a sorcerer who tried to buy spiritual powers from the apostles (Acts 8:9-24).

Magyar (ˈmægjɑː) *n* **1** (*pl* **-yars**) a member of the predominant ethnic group of Hungary, also found in NW Siberia. **2** the Hungarian language. ◆ *adj* **3** of or relating to the Magyars or their language. **4** *Sewing.* of or relating to a style of sleeve cut in one piece with the bodice.

Magyarország (ˈmɔdjɔrorsaːg) *n* the Hungarian name for **Hungary.**

Mahabharata (məˌhɑːˈbɑːrətə), **Mahabharatam,** *or* **Mahabharatum** (məˌhɑːˈbɑːrətəm) *n* an epic Sanskrit poem of India, dealing chiefly with the struggle between two rival families. It contains many separate episodes, the most notable of which is the *Bhagavad-Gita.* [Sanskrit, from *mahā* great + *bhārata* story]

Mahajanga (ˌmæhəˈdʒæŋgə) *n* a port in NW Madagascar, on Bombetoka Bay. Pop.: 100 807 (1993). Former name: **Majunga.**

Mahalla el Kubra (məˈhɑːlə ɛl ˈkuːbrə) *n* a city in N Egypt, on the Nile delta: one of the largest diversified textile centres in Egypt. Pop.: 408 000 (1992 est.).

Mahanadi (məˈhɑːnədɪ) *n* a river in E India, rising in S Madhya Pradesh and flowing north, then south and east to the Bay of Bengal. Length: 885 km (550 miles).

maharajah *or* **maharaja** (ˌmɑːhəˈrɑːdʒə) *n* any of various Indian princes, esp. any of the rulers of the former native states. [C17: Hindi, from *mahā* great + RAJAH]

maharani *or* **maharanee** (ˌmɑːhəˈrɑːniː) *n* **1** the wife of a maharajah. **2** a woman holding the rank of maharajah. [C19: from Hindi, from *mahā* great + RANI]

Maharashtra (ˌmɑːhəˈræʃtrə) *n* a state of W central India, formed in 1960 from the Marathi-speaking S and E parts of former Bombay state: lies mainly on the Deccan plateau; mainly agricultural. Capital: Bombay. Pop.: 85 565 000 (1994 est.). Area: 307 690 sq. km (118 800 sq. miles).

maharishi (ˌmɑːhɑːˈriːʃɪ, məˈhɑːriːʃɪ) *n Hinduism.* a Hindu teacher of religious and mystical knowledge. [from Hindi, from *mahā* great + *rishi* sage, saint]

mahatma (məˈhɑːtmə, -ˈhæt-) *n* (*sometimes cap.*) **1** *Hinduism.* a Brahman sage. **2** *Theosophy.* an adept or sage. [C19: from Sanskrit *mahātman,* from *mahā* great + *ātman* soul] ▸ **maˈhatmaism** *n*

Mahavira (ˌmɑːhəˈvɪərə) *n* the title of **Vardhamana.** 599–527 B.C., Indian ascetic and religious teacher, regarded as the founder of Jainism.

Mahayana (ˌmɑːhəˈjɑːnə) *n* **a** a liberal Buddhist school of Tibet, China, and Japan, whose adherents aim to disseminate Buddhist doctrines, seeking enlightenment not for themselves alone, but for all sentient beings. **b** (*as modifier*): *Mahayana Buddhism.* [from Sanskrit, from *mahā* great + *yāna* vehicle] ▸ **ˌMahaˈyanist** *n*

Mahdi (ˈmɑːdɪ) *n* **1** the title assumed by *Mohammed Ahmed.* ?1843–85, Sudanese military leader, who led a revolt against Egypt (1881) and captured Khartoum (1885). **2** *Islam.* any of a number of Muslim messiahs expected to forcibly convert all mankind to Islam. [Arabic *mahdīy* one who is guided, from *madā* to guide aright] ▸ **ˈMahdism** *n* ▸ **ˈMahdist** *n, adj*

Mahé (mɑːˈheɪ) *n* an island in the Indian Ocean, the chief island of the Seychelles. Capital: Victoria. Pop.: 59 500 (1987). Area: 147 sq. km (57 sq. miles).

mahewu (maˈhewʊ, -ˈxe-) *n* (in South Africa) fermented liquid mealie-meal porridge, used as a stimulant, esp. by Black Africans. [from Xhosa *amarewu*]

Mahfouz *or* **Mahfuz** (mɑːˈfuːz) *n* **Naguib** (nɑːˈgiːb). born 1911, Egyptian novelist and writer, author of the trilogy of novels *Bain al-Kasrain* (1945–57). His novel *Children of Gebelawi* (1959) was banned by the Muslim authorities in Egypt. Nobel prize for literature 1988.

Mahican (məˈhiːkən) *n, pl* **-cans** *or* **-can.** a variant of **Mohican.**

mah jong *or* **mah-jongg** (ˌmɑːˈdʒɒŋ) *n* a game of Chinese origin, usually played by four people, in which tiles bearing various designs are drawn and discarded until one player has an entire hand of winning combinations. [from Chinese, literally: sparrows]

Mahler (ˈmɑːlə) *n* **Gustav** (ˈgʊstaf). 1860–1911, Austrian composer and conductor, whose music links the romantic tradition of the 19th century with the music of the 20th century. His works include nine complete symphonies for large orchestras, the symphonic song cycle *Das Lied von der Erde* (1908), and the song cycle *Kindertotenlieder* (1902).

mahlstick (ˈmɔːlˌstɪk) *n* a variant spelling of **maulstick.**

mahogany (məˈhɒgənɪ) *n, pl* **-nies. 1** any of various tropical American trees of the meliaceous genus *Swietenia,* esp. *S. mahagoni* and *S. macrophylla,* valued for their hard reddish-brown wood. **2** any of several trees with similar wood, such as African mahogany (genus *Khaya*) and Philippine mahogany (genus *Shorea*). **3a** the wood of any of these trees. See also **acajou** (sense 1). **3b** (*as modifier*): *a mahogany table.* **4** a reddish-brown colour. [C17: origin obscure]

Mahomet (məˈhɒmɪt) *n* a variant of **Mohammed.**

Mahometan (məˈhɒmɪtᵊn) *n, adj* a former word for **Muslim.** ▸ **Maˈhometanism** *n*

mahonia (məˈhəʊnɪə) *n* any evergreen berberidaceous shrub of the Asian and

American genus *Mahonia*, esp. *M. aquifolium:* cultivated for their ornamental spiny divided leaves and clusters of small yellow flowers. [C19: New Latin, named after Bernard *McMahon* (died 1816), American botanist]

Mahound (mə'haʊnd, -'hu:nd) *n* an archaic name for **Mohammed.** [C16: from Old French *Mahun*]

mahout (mə'haʊt) *n* (in India and the East Indies) an elephant driver or keeper. [C17: Hindi *mahāut,* from Sanskrit *mahāmātra* of great measure, originally a title]

Mahratta (mə'rɑ:tə) *n* a variant spelling of **Maratha.** ▸ **Mah'ratti** *n, adj*

Mähren ('mɛ:rən) *n* the German name for **Moravia**[1].

mahseer ('mɑ:sɪə) *n* any of various large freshwater Indian cyprinid fishes, such as *Barbus tor.* [from Hindi]

mahzor *Hebrew.* (max'zɔr; *English* mɑ:k'zɔ:) *n, pl* ***-zorim*** (-zɔ'ri:m; *English* -zə'ri:m). a variant spelling of **machzor.**

Maia ('maɪə) *n Greek myth.* the eldest of the seven Pleiades, mother by Zeus of Hermes.

maid (meɪd) *n* **1** *Archaic or literary.* a young unmarried girl; maiden. **2a** a female servant. **2b** (*in combination*): *a housemaid.* **3** a spinster. [C12: shortened form of MAIDEN] ▸ **'maidish** *adj* ▸ **'maidishness** *n*

maidan (mæ'dɑ:n) *n* (in Pakistan, India, etc.) an open space used for meetings, sports, etc. [Urdu, from Arabic]

maiden ('meɪdᵊn) *n* **1** *Archaic or literary.* **1a** a young unmarried girl, esp. when a virgin. **1b** (*as modifier*): *a maiden blush.* **2** *Horse racing.* **2a** a horse that has never won a race. **2b** (*as modifier*): *a maiden race.* **3** *Cricket.* See **maiden over. 4** Also called: **clothes maiden.** *Northern English dialect.* a frame on which clothes are hung to dry; clothes horse. **5** (*modifier*) of or relating to an older unmarried woman: *a maiden aunt.* **6** (*modifier*) of or involving an initial experience or attempt: *a maiden voyage; maiden speech.* **7** (*modifier*) (of a person or thing) untried; unused. **8** (*modifier*) (of a place) never trodden, penetrated, or captured. [Old English *mægden;* related to Old High German *magad,* Old Norse *mogr* young man, Old Irish *mug* slave] ▸ **'maidenish** *adj* ▸ **'maiden,like** *adj*

maidenhair fern *or* **maidenhair** ('meɪdᵊn,hɛə) *n* any fern of the genus *Adiantum,* esp. *A. capillis-veneris,* of tropical and warm regions, having delicate fan-shaped fronds with small pale-green leaflets: family *Polypodiaceae.* [C15: so called from the hairlike appearance of its fine fronds]

maidenhair tree *n* another name for **ginkgo.**

maidenhead ('meɪdᵊn,hɛd) *n* **1** a nontechnical word for the **hymen. 2** virginity; maidenhood. [C13: from *maiden* + *-hed,* variant of -HOOD]

Maidenhead ('meɪdᵊn,hɛd) *n* a town in S England, in Windsor and Maidenhead unitary authority on the River Thames. Pop.: 59 605 (1991).

maidenhood ('meɪdᵊn,hʊd) *n* **1** the time during which a woman is a maiden or a virgin. **2** the condition of being a maiden or virgin.

maidenly ('meɪdᵊnlɪ) *adj* of or befitting a maiden. ▸ **'maidenliness** *n*

maiden name *n* a woman's surname before marriage.

maiden over *n Cricket.* an over in which no runs are scored.

maiden voyage *n Nautical.* the first voyage of a vessel.

Maid Marian *n* **1** a character in morris dancing, played by a man dressed as a woman. **2** *Legend.* the sweetheart of Robin Hood.

maid of all work *n* **1** a maid who does all types of housework. **2** a general factotum.

maid of honour *n* **1** *U.S. and Canadian.* the principal unmarried attendant of a bride. Compare **bridesmaid, matron of honour. 2** *Brit.* a small tart with an almond-flavoured filling. **3** an unmarried lady attending a queen or princess.

Maid of Orléans *n* **the.** another name for **Joan of Arc.**

maidservant ('meɪd,sɜ:vənt) *n* a female servant.

Maidstone ('meɪdstən, -,stəʊn) *n* a town in SE England, administrative centre of Kent, on the River Medway. Pop.: 90 878 (1991).

Maiduguri (,maɪdʊ'gu:rɪ) *n* a city in NE Nigeria, capital of Bornu State; agricultural trade centre. Pop.: 320 000 (1996 est.). Also called: **Yerwa-Maiduguri.**

maieutic (meɪ'ju:tɪk) *or* **maieutical** *adj Philosophy.* of or relating to the Socratic method of eliciting knowledge by a series of questions and answers. [C17: from Greek *maieutikos* relating to midwifery (used figuratively by Socrates), from *maia* midwife]

maigre ('meɪgə) *adj R.C. Church.* **1** not containing flesh, and so permissible as food on days of religious abstinence: *maigre food.* **2** of or designating such a day. [C17: from French: thin; see MEAGRE]

maihem ('meɪhɛm) *n* a variant spelling of **mayhem.**

maik (mek) *n Scot.* an old halfpenny. Also called **meck.** [of obscure origin]

Maikop (*Russian* maj'kɔp) *n* a city in SW Russia, capital of the Adygei Republic: extensive oilfields to the southwest; mineral springs. Pop.: 165 000 (1995 est.).

mail[1] (meɪl) *n* **1** Also called (esp. Brit.): **post.** letters, packages, etc., that are transported and delivered by the post office. **2** the postal system. **3** a single collection or delivery of mail. **4** a train, ship, or aircraft that carries mail. **5** short for **electronic mail. 6** (*modifier*) of, involving, or used to convey mail: *a mail train.* ◆ *vb* (*tr*) **7** *Chiefly U.S. and Canadian.* to send by mail. Usual Brit. word: **post. 8** to contact (a person) by electronic mail. **9** to send (a message, document, etc.) by electronic mail. [C13: from Old French *male* bag, probably from Old High German *malha* wallet] ▸ **'mailable** *adj*

mail[2] (meɪl) *n* **1** a type of flexible armour consisting of riveted metal rings or links. **2** the hard protective shell of such animals as the turtle and lobster. ◆ *vb* **3** (*tr*) to clothe or arm with mail. [C14: from Old French *maille* mesh, from Latin *macula* spot] ▸ **'mail-less** *adj*

mail[3] (meɪl) *n Archaic, chiefly Scot.* a monetary payment, esp. of rent or taxes. [Old English *māl* terms, from Old Norse *māl* agreement]

mail[4] (meɪl) *n Austral. informal.* a rumour or report, esp. a racing tip.

mailbag ('meɪl,bæg), **mailsack,** *or U.S.* (*sometimes*) **mailpouch** *n* a large bag used for transporting or delivering mail.

mailbox ('meɪl,bɒks) *n* another name (esp. U.S. and Canadian) for **letter box.**

mailcoach ('meɪl,kəʊtʃ) *or U.S. and Canadian* **mailcar** *n* a railway coach specially constructed for the transportation of mail.

mail drop *n Chiefly U.S. and Canadian.* a receptacle or chute for mail.

mailer ('meɪlə) *n* **1** a person who addresses or mails letters, etc. **2** *U.S. and Canadian.* a machine used for stamping and addressing mail. **3** *U.S. and Canadian.* a container for mailing things.

Mailer ('meɪlə) *n* **Norman.** born 1923, U.S. author. His works, which are frequently critical of modern American society, include the war novel *The Naked and the Dead* (1948), *An American Dream* (1965), his account of the 1967 peace march on Washington *The Armies of the Night* (1968), *Why Are We In Vietnam* (1967) and *Harlot's Ghost* (1991).

mailing list *n* a register of names and addresses to which advertising matter, etc., is sent by post or electronic mail.

Maillol (*French* majɔl) *n* **Aristide** (aristid). 1861–1944, French sculptor, esp. of monumental female nudes.

maillot (mæ'jəʊ) *n* **1** tights worn for ballet, gymnastics, etc. **2** a woman's swimsuit. **3** a jersey. [from French]

mailman ('meɪl,mæn) *n, pl* **-men.** *Chiefly U.S. and Canadian.* another name for **postman.**

mail merging *n Computing.* a software facility that can produce a large number of personalized letters by combining a file containing a list of names and addresses with one containing a single standard document.

mail order *n* **1** an order for merchandise sent by post. **2a** a system of buying and selling merchandise through the post. **2b** (*as modifier*): *a mail-order firm.*

mailsack ('meɪl,sæk) *n* another name for a **mailbag.**

mailshot ('meɪl,ʃɒt) *n* a circular, leaflet, or other advertising material sent by post, or the posting of such material to a large group of people at one time.

maim (meɪm) *vb* (*tr*) **1** to mutilate, cripple, or disable a part of the body of (a person or animal). **2** to make defective. ◆ *n* **3** *Obsolete.* an injury or defect. [C14: from Old French *mahaignier* to wound, probably of Germanic origin] ▸ **maimedness** ('meɪmɪdnɪs) *n* ▸ **'maimer** *n*

mai mai ('maɪ maɪ) *n N.Z.* a duck-shooter's shelter; hide. [probably from Australian aboriginal *mia-mia* shelter]

Maimonides (maɪ'mɒnɪ,di:z) *n* also called Rabbi *Moses ben Maimon.* 1135–1204, Jewish philosopher, physician, and jurist, born in Spain. He codified Jewish law in *Mishneh Torah* (1180). ▸ **Mai,moni'dean** *adj, n*

main[1] (meɪn) *adj* (*prenominal*) **1** chief or principal in rank, importance, size, etc. **2** sheer or utmost (esp. in the phrase **by main force**). **3** *Nautical.* of, relating to, or denoting any gear, such as a stay or sail, belonging to the mainmast. **4** *Obsolete.* significant or important. ◆ *n* **5** a principal pipe, conduit, duct, or line in a system used to distribute water, electricity, etc. **6** (*pl*) **6a** the main distribution network for water, gas, or electricity. **6b** (*as modifier*): *mains voltage.* **7** the chief or most important part or consideration. **8** great strength or force (now chiefly in the phrase **(with) might and main**). **9** *Literary.* the open ocean. **10** *Archaic.* short for **Spanish Main. 11** *Archaic.* short for **mainland. 12 in** (*or* **for**) **the main.** on the whole; for the most part. [C13: from Old English *mægen* strength]

main[2] (meɪn) *n* **1** a throw of the dice in dice games. **2** a cockfighting contest. **3** a match in archery, boxing, etc. [C16: of unknown origin]

Main (meɪn; *German* main) *n* a river in central and W Germany, flowing west through Würzburg and Frankfurt to the Rhine. Length: about 515 km (320 miles).

mainbrace ('meɪn,breɪs) *n Nautical.* a brace attached to the main yard.

main clause *n Grammar.* a clause that can stand alone as a sentence. Compare **subordinate clause.**

main course *n* **1** the principal dish of a meal. **2** *Nautical.* a square mainsail.

main deck *n* the uppermost sheltered deck that runs the entire length of a vessel.

Maine (meɪn) *n* a state of the northeastern U.S., on the Atlantic: chiefly hilly, with many lakes, rivers, and forests. Capital: Augusta. Pop.: 1 242 051 (1997 est.). Area: 86 156 sq. km (33 265 sq. miles). Abbrev. (with zip code): **ME**

Maine-et-Loire (*French* mɛnelwar) *n* a department of W France, in Pays de la Loire region. Capital: Angers. Pop.: 721 200 (1995). Area: 7218 sq. km (2815 sq. miles).

mainframe ('meɪn,freɪm) *n* **1a** a high-speed general-purpose computer, usually with a large store capacity. **1b** (*as modifier*): *mainframe systems.* **2** the central processing unit of a computer.

mainland ('meɪnlənd) *n* **1** the main part of a land mass as opposed to an island or peninsula. **2 the mainland.** a particular landmass as viewed from a nearby island with which it has close links, such as Great Britain as viewed from Northern Ireland or continental Australia as viewed from Tasmania. ▸ **'mainlander** *n*

Mainland ('meɪnlənd) *n* **1** an island off N Scotland: the largest of the Shetland Islands. Chief town: Lerwick. Pop.: 17 596 (1991). Area: about 583 sq. km (225 sq. miles). **2** Also called: **Pomona.** an island off N Scotland: the largest of the Orkney Islands. Chief town: Kirkwall. Pop.: 15 128 (1991). Area: 492 sq. km (190 sq. miles). **3 the Mainland.** *N.Z.* a South Islanders' name for **South Island.**

main line *n* **1** *Railways.* **1a** the trunk route between two points, usually fed by branch lines. **1b** (*as modifier*): *a main-line station.* **2** *U.S.* a main road. ◆ *vb* **mainline. 3** (*intr*) *Slang.* to inject a drug into a vein. ◆ *adj* **mainline. 4** having an important position, esp. having responsibility for the main areas of activity. ▸ **'main,liner** *n*

mainly ('meɪnlɪ) *adv* **1** for the most part; to the greatest extent; principally. **2** *Obsolete.* strongly; very much.

main man *n Slang, chiefly U.S.* **1** one's best friend. **2** a boss or leader.

main market *n* the market for trading in the listed securities of companies on the London Stock Exchange. Compare **Third Market, unlisted securities market.**

mainmast ('meɪnˌmɑːst) *n Nautical.* the chief mast of a sailing vessel with two or more masts, being the foremast of a yawl, ketch, or dandy and the second mast from the bow of most others.

main memory *n* the central memory-storage facility in a computer.

main plane *n* **a** one of the principal supporting surfaces of an aircraft, esp. either of the wings. **b** both wings considered together.

mainsail ('meɪnˌseɪl; *Nautical* 'meɪnsᵊl) *n Nautical.* the largest and lowermost sail on the mainmast.

main sequence *n Astronomy.* **a** a diagonal band on the Hertzsprung Russell diagram containing about 90% of all known stars; stars evolve onto and then off the band during their lifetime. **b** (*as modifier*): *a main-sequence star.*

mainsheet ('meɪnˌʃiːt) *n Nautical.* the line used to control the angle of the mainsail to the wind.

mainspring ('meɪnˌsprɪŋ) *n* **1** the principal spring of a mechanism, esp. in a watch or clock. **2** the chief cause or motive of something.

mainstay ('meɪnˌsteɪ) *n* **1** *Nautical.* the forestay that braces the mainmast. **2** a chief support.

main store *n Computing.* another name for **memory** (sense 7).

mainstream ('meɪnˌstriːm) *n* **1a** the main current (of a river, cultural trend, etc.): *in the mainstream of modern literature.* **1b** (*as modifier*): *mainstream politics.* ◆ *adj* **2** of or relating to the style of jazz that lies between the traditional and the modern.

mainstream corporation tax *n* (in Britain) the balance of the corporation tax paid by a company for an accounting period after the advance corporation tax has been deducted.

mainstreeting ('meɪnˌstriːtɪŋ) *n Canadian.* the practice of a politician walking about the streets of a town or city to gain votes and greet supporters.

maintain (meɪn'teɪn) *vb* (*tr*) **1** to continue or retain; keep in existence. **2** to keep in proper or good condition: *to maintain a building.* **3** to support a style of living: *the money maintained us for a month.* **4** (*takes a clause as object*) to state or assert: *he maintained that Talbot was wrong.* **5** to defend against contradiction; uphold: *she maintained her innocence.* **6** to defend against physical attack. **[C13:** from Old French *maintenir,* ultimately from Latin *manū tenēre* to hold in the hand**]** ▸ **main'tainable** *adj* ▸ **main'tainer** *n*

maintained school *n* a school financially supported by the state.

maintenance ('meɪntɪnəns) *n* **1** the act of maintaining or the state of being maintained. **2** a means of support; livelihood. **3** (*modifier*) of or relating to the maintaining of buildings, machinery, etc.: *maintenance man.* **4** *Law.* (formerly unlawful) the interference in a legal action by a person having no interest in it, as by providing funds to continue the action. See also **champerty. 5** *Law.* a provision ordered to be made by way of periodical payments or a lump sum, as after a divorce for a spouse. **6** *Computer Technol.* **6a** the correction or prevention of faults in hardware by a programme of inspection and the replacement of parts. **6b** the removal of existing faults and the modification of software in response to changes in specification or environment. **[C14:** from Old French; see MAINTAIN**]**

Maintenon (*French* mɛ̃tnɔ̃) *n* **Marquise de,** title of *Françoise d'Aubigné.* 1635–1719, the mistress and, from about 1685, second wife of Louis XIV.

maintop ('meɪnˌtɒp) *n* a top or platform at the head of the mainmast.

main-topmast *n Nautical.* the mast immediately above the mainmast.

maintopsail (ˌmeɪn'tɒpseɪl; *Nautical* ˌmeɪn'tɒpsᵊl) *n Nautical.* a topsail set on the mainmast.

main yard *n Nautical.* a yard for a square mainsail.

Mainz (*German* maints) *n* a port in W Germany, capital of the Rhineland-Palatinate, at the confluence of the Main and Rhine: an archbishopric from about 780 until 1801; important in the 15th century for the development of printing (by Johann Gutenberg). Pop.: 183 720 (1996 est.). French name: **Mayence.**

maiolica (mə'jɒlɪkə) *n* a variant of **majolica.**

maisonette *or* **maisonnette** (ˌmeɪzə'nɛt) *n* self-contained living accommodation often occupying two floors of a larger house and having its own outside entrance. **[C19:** from French, diminutive of *maison* house**]**

maist (mest) *determiner* a Scot. word for **most.**

Maistre (*French* mɛstrə) *n* **Josephe de** (ʒozɛf də). 1753–1821, French writer and diplomat, noted for his extreme reactionary views, expounded in such works as *Les Soirées de St Petersbourg* (1821).

Maitland[1] ('meɪtlənd) *n* a town in SE Australia, in E New South Wales: industrial centre of an agricultural region. Pop.: 38 863 (1981).

Maitland[2] ('meɪtlənd) *n* **Frederic William.** 1850–1906, English legal historian.

maître d'hôtel (ˌmɛtrə dəʊ'tɛl; *French* mɛtrə dotɛl) *n, pl* **maîtres d'hôtel. 1** a head waiter or steward. **2** the manager or owner of a hotel. **[C16:** from French: master of (the) hotel**]**

maître d'hôtel butter *n* melted butter mixed with parsley and lemon juice.

Maitreya (mi'treːjə) *n* the future Buddha. **[**Sanskrit**]**

maize (meɪz) *n* **1** Also called: **Indian corn. 1a** a tall annual grass, *Zea mays,* cultivated for its yellow edible grains, which develop on a spike. **1b** the grain of this plant, used for food, fodder, and as a source of oil. Usual U.S. and Canadian name: **corn.** See also **sweet corn. 2** a yellow colour. **[C16:** from Spanish *maiz,* from Taino *mahiz***]**

Maj. *abbrev. for* Major.

majestic (mə'dʒɛstɪk) *or* (*less commonly*) **majestical** *adj* having or displaying majesty or great dignity; grand; lofty. ▸ **ma'jestically** *adv*

majesty ('mædʒɪstɪ) *n* **1** great dignity of bearing; loftiness; grandeur. **2** supreme power or authority. **3** an archaic word for **royalty. [C13:** from Old French, from Latin *mājestās;* related to Latin *major,* comparative of *magnus* great**]**

Majesty ('mædʒɪstɪ) *n, pl* **-ties.** (preceded by *Your, His, Her,* or *Their*) a title used to address or refer to a sovereign or the wife or widow of a sovereign.

Maj. Gen. *abbrev. for* Major General.

Majlis ('mædʒlɪs) *n* **1** the parliament of Iran. **2** (in various N African and Middle Eastern countries) an assembly; council. **[**from Persian: assembly**]**

majolica (mə'dʒɒlɪkə, mə'jɒl-) *or* **maiolica** *n* a type of porous pottery glazed with bright metallic oxides that was originally imported into Italy via Majorca and was extensively made in Italy during the Renaissance. **[C16:** from Italian, from Late Latin *Mājorica* Majorca**]**

major ('meɪdʒə) *n* **1** *Military.* an officer immediately junior to a lieutenant colonel. **2** a person who is superior in a group or class. **3** (often preceded by *the*) *Music.* a major key, chord, mode, or scale. **4** *U.S., Canadian, Austral., and N.Z.* **4a** the principal field of study of a student at a university, etc.: *his major is sociology.* **4b** a student who is studying a particular subject as his principal field: *a sociology major.* **5** a person who has reached the age of legal majority. **6** *Logic.* a major term or premise. **7** (*pl*) **the.** *U.S. and Canadian.* the major leagues. ◆ *adj* **8** larger in extent, number, etc.: *the major part.* **9** of greater importance or priority. **10** very serious or significant: *a major disaster.* **11** main, chief, or principal. **12** of, involving, or making up a majority. **13** *Music.* **13a** (of a scale or mode) having notes separated by the interval of a whole tone, except for the third and fourth degrees, and seventh and eighth degrees, which are separated by a semitone. **13b** relating to or employing notes from the major scale: *a major key.* **13c** (*postpositive*) denoting a specified key or scale as being major: *C major.* **13d** denoting a chord or triad having a major third above the root. **13e** (in jazz) denoting a major chord with a major seventh added above the root. **14** *Logic.* constituting the major term or major premise of a syllogism. **15** *Chiefly U.S., Canadian, Austral., and N.Z.* of or relating to a student's principal field of study at a university, etc. **16** *Brit.* the elder: used after a schoolboy's surname if he has one or more younger brothers in the same school: *Price major.* **17** of full legal age. **18** (*postpositive*) *Change-ringing.* of, relating to, or denoting a method rung on eight bells. ◆ *vb* **19** (*intr;* usually foll. by *in*) *U.S., Canadian, Austral., and N.Z.* to do one's principal study (in a particular subject): *to major in English literature.* **[C15** (adj): from Latin, comparative of *magnus* great; **C17** (n, in military sense): from French, short for SERGEANT MAJOR**]** ▸ **'majorship** *n*

Major ('meɪdʒə) *n* **John.** born 1943, British Conservative politician: Chancellor of the Exchequer (1989–90); prime minister (1990–97).

major axis *n* the longer or longest axis of an ellipse or ellipsoid.

Majorca (mə'jɔːkə, -'dʒɔː-) *n* an island in the W Mediterranean: the largest of the Balearic Islands; tourism. Capital: Palma. Pop.: 605 512 (1987 est.). Area: 3639 sq. km (1465 sq. miles). Spanish name: **Mallorca.**

major-domo (ˌmeɪdʒə'dəʊməʊ) *n, pl* **-mos. 1** the chief steward or butler of a great household. **2** *Facetious.* a steward or butler. **[C16:** from Spanish *mayordomo,* from Medieval Latin *mājor domūs* head of the household**]**

majorette (ˌmeɪdʒə'rɛt) *n* See **drum majorette.**

major general *n Military.* an officer immediately junior to a lieutenant general. ▸ **'major-'generalship** *or* **'major-'generalcy** *n*

majority (mə'dʒɒrɪtɪ) *n, pl* **-ties. 1** the greater number or part of something: *the majority of the constituents.* **2** (in an election) the number of votes or seats by which the strongest party or candidate beats the combined opposition or the runner-up. See **relative majority, absolute majority. 3** the largest party or group that votes together in a legislative or deliberative assembly. **4** the time of reaching or state of having reached full legal age, when a person is held competent to manage his own affairs, exercise civil rights and duties, etc. **5** the rank, office, or commission of major. **6** *Euphemistic.* the dead (esp. in the phrases **join the majority, go** *or* **pass over to the majority**). **7** *Obsolete.* the quality or state of being greater; superiority. **8** (*modifier*) of, involving, or being a majority: *a majority decision; a majority verdict.* **9 in the majority.** forming or part of the greater number of something. **[C16:** from Medieval Latin *mājoritās,* from MAJOR (adj)**]**

USAGE *The majority of* can only refer to a number of things or people. When talking about an amount, *most of* should be used: *most of* (not *the majority of*) *the harvest was saved.*

majority carrier *n* the entity responsible for carrying the greater part of the current in a semiconductor. In n-type semiconductors the majority carriers are electrons; in p-type semiconductors they are positively charged holes. Compare **minority carrier.**

major league *n U.S. and Canadian.* a league of highest classification in baseball, football, hockey, etc.

majorly ('meɪdʒəlɪ) *adv Slang, chiefly U.S. and Canadian.* very; really; extremely: *it was majorly important for us to do that.*

Major Mitchell *n* an Australian cockatoo, *Kakatoe leadbeateri,* with a white-and-pink plumage. **[C19:** named after Major (later Sir) Thomas MITCHELL**]**

major orders *pl n R.C. Church.* the three higher degrees of holy orders: bishop, priest, and deacon.

major planet *n* a planet of the solar system, as opposed to an asteroid (minor planet).

major premise *n Logic.* the premise of a syllogism containing the predicate of its conclusion.

major seventh chord *n* a chord much used in modern music, esp. jazz and pop, consisting of a major triad with an added major seventh above the root. Compare **minor seventh chord.** Often shortened to **major seventh.**

major suit *n Bridge.* hearts or spades. Compare **minor suit.**

major term *n Logic.* the predicate of the conclusion of a syllogism, also occurring as the subject or predicate in the major premise.

Majunga (*French* maʒœ̃ga) *n* the former name of **Mahajanga.**

majuscule ('mædʒəˌskjuːl) *n* **1** a large letter, either capital or uncial, used in printing or writing. ◆ *adj* **2** relating to, printed, or written in such letters.

Compare **minuscule.** [C18: via French from Latin *mājusculus,* diminutive of *mājor* bigger, MAJOR] ► **majuscular** (mə'dʒʌskjulə) *adj*

mak (mæk) *vb* a Scot. word for **make**[1].

Makalu ('mʌkə,luː) *n* a massif in NE Nepal, on the border with Tibet in the Himalayas.

makar ('mækər) *n Scot.* a creative artist, esp. a poet. [a Scot. variant of *maker*]

Makarios III (mə'kɑːrɪ,ɒs) *n* original name *Mikhail Christodoulou Mouskos.* 1913–77, Cypriot archbishop, patriarch, and statesman; first president of the republic of Cyprus (1960–74; 1974–77).

Makasar, Makassar, *or* **Macassar** (mə'kæsə, -'kɑː-) *n* another name for **Ujung Pandang.**

make[1] (meɪk) *vb* **makes, making, made.** (*mainly tr*) **1** to bring into being by shaping, changing, or combining materials, ideas, etc.; form or fashion; create: *to make a chair from bits of wood; make a poem.* **2** to draw up, establish, or form: *to make a decision; make one's will.* **3** to cause to exist, bring about, or produce: *don't make a noise.* **4** to cause, compel, or induce: *please make him go away.* **5** to appoint or assign, as to a rank or position: *they made him chairman.* **6** to constitute: *one swallow doesn't make a summer.* **7** (*also intr*) to come or cause to come into a specified state or condition: *to make merry; make someone happy.* **8** (*copula*) to be or become through development: *he will make a good teacher.* **9** to cause or ensure the success of: *your news has made my day.* **10** to amount to: *twelve inches make a foot.* **11** to be part of or a member of: *did she make one of the party?* **12** to serve as or be suitable for: *that piece of cloth will make a coat.* **13** to prepare or put into a fit condition for use: *to make a bed.* **14** to be the essential element in or part of: *charm makes a good salesman.* **15** to carry out, effect, or do: *to make a gesture.* **16** (*intr;* foll. by *to, as if to,* or *as though to*) to act with the intention or with a show of doing something: *they made to go out; he made as if to hit her.* **17** to use for a specified purpose: *I will make this town my base.* **18** to deliver or pronounce: *to make a speech.* **19** to judge, reckon, or give one's own opinion or information as to: *what time do you make it?* **20** to cause to seem or represent as being: *that furniture makes the room look dark.* **21** to earn, acquire, or win for oneself: *to make friends; make a fortune.* **22** to engage in: *make love not war.* **23** to traverse or cover (distance) by travelling: *we can make a hundred miles by nightfall.* **24** to arrive in time for: *he didn't make the first act of the play.* **25** *Cards.* **25a** to win a trick with (a specified card). **25b** to shuffle (the cards). **25c** *Bridge.* to fulfil (a contract) by winning the necessary number of tricks. **26** *Cricket.* to score (runs). **27** *Electronics.* to close (a circuit) permitting a flow of current. Compare **break** (sense 44). **28** (*intr*) to increase in depth: *the water in the hold was making a foot a minute.* **29** (*intr*) (of hay) to dry and mature. **30** *Informal.* to gain a place or position on or in: *to make the headlines; make the first team.* **31** *Informal.* to achieve the rank of. **32** *Taboo slang.* to seduce. **33 make a book.** to take bets on a race or other contest. **34 make a day, night,** etc., **of it.** to cause an activity to last a day, night, etc. **35 make do.** See **do**[1] (sense 36). **36 make eyes at.** to flirt with or ogle. **37 make good.** See **good** (sense 44). **38 make heavy weather (of). 38a** *Nautical.* to roll and pitch in heavy seas. **38b** *Informal.* to carry out with great difficulty or unnecessarily great effort. **39 make it. 39a** *Informal.* to be successful in doing something. **39b** (foll. by *with*) *Taboo slang.* to have sexual intercourse. **39c** *Slang.* to inject a narcotic drug. **40 make like.** *Slang, chiefly U.S. and Canadian.* to imitate. **41 make love (to). 41a** to have sexual intercourse (with). **41b** *Now archaic.* to engage in courtship (with). **42 make or break.** to bring success or ruin. **43 make time.** See **time** (sense 45). **44 make water. 44a** another term for **urinate. 44b** (of a boat, hull, etc.) to let in water. ◆ *n* **45** brand, type, or style: *what make of car is that?* **46** the manner or way in which something is made. **47** disposition or character; make-up. **48** the act or process of making. **49** the amount or number made. **50** *Bridge.* the contract to be played. **51** *Cards.* a player's turn to shuffle. **52 on the make. 52a** *Informal.* out for profit or conquest. **52b** *Slang.* in search of a sexual partner. ◆ See also **make after, make away, make for, make of, make off, make out, make over, make-up, make with.** [Old English *macian;* related to Old Frisian *makia* to construct, Dutch *maken,* German *machen* to make] ► **'makable** *adj*

make[2] (meɪk) *n Archaic.* **1** a peer or consort. **2** a mate or spouse. [Old English *gemaca* mate; related to MATCH[1]] ► **'makeless** *adj*

make after *vb* (*intr, prep*) *Archaic.* to set off in pursuit of; chase.

make away *vb* (*intr, adv*) **1** to depart in haste. **2 make away with. 2a** to steal or abduct. **2b** to kill, destroy, or get rid of.

make believe *vb* **1** to pretend or enact a fantasy: *the children made believe they were doctors.* ◆ *n* **make-believe. 2a** a fantasy, pretence, or unreality. **2b** (*as modifier*): *a make-believe world.* **3** a person who pretends.

Makedhonia (,makeðə'nia) *n* transliteration of the Modern Greek name for **Macedonia** (sense 2).

makefast ('meɪk,fɑːst) *n* a strong support to which a vessel is secured.

make for *vb* (*intr, prep*) **1** to head towards, esp. in haste. **2** to prepare to attack. **3** to help to bring about: *your cooperation will make for the success of our project.*

make of *vb* (*tr, prep*) **1** to interpret as the meaning of: *what do you make of this news?* **2** to produce or construct from: *houses made of brick.* **3 make little, nothing,** etc., **of. 3a** not to understand. **3b** to attribute little, no, etc., importance to. **3c** to gain little or no benefit from. **4 make much, a lot,** etc., **of. 4a** (*used with a negative*) to make sense of: *he couldn't make much of her babble.* **4b** to give importance to. **4c** to gain benefit from. **4d** to pay flattering attention to: *the reporters made much of the film star.*

make off *vb* **1** (*intr, adv*) to go or run away in haste. **2 make off with.** to steal or abduct.

make out *vb* (*adv*) **1** (*tr*) to discern or perceive: *can you make out that house in the distance?* **2** (*tr*) to understand or comprehend: *I can't make out this letter.* **3** (*tr*) to write out: *he made out a cheque.* **4** (*tr*) to attempt to establish or prove: *he made me out to be a liar.* **5** (*intr*) to pretend: *he made out that he could cook.* **6** (*intr*) to manage or fare: *how did you make out in the contest?* **7** (*intr;* often foll. by *with*) *Informal, chiefly U.S. and Canadian.* to engage in necking or petting: *Alan is making out with Jane.*

make over *vb* (*tr, adv*) **1** to transfer the title or possession of (property, etc.). **2** to renovate or remodel: *she made over the dress to fit her sister.* ◆ *n* **makeover** ('meɪk,əuvə). **3** a complete remodelling. **4** a series of alterations, including beauty treatments and new clothes, intended to make a noticeable improvement in a person's appearance.

maker ('meɪkə) *n* **1** a person who makes (something); fabricator; constructor. **2** a person who executes a legal document, esp. one who signs a promissory note. **3** *Archaic, Scot.* Also called (esp. Scot.): **makar.** a poet.

Maker ('meɪkə) *n* **1** a title given to **God** (as Creator). **2 (go to) meet one's Maker.** to die.

make-ready *n Printing.* the process of preparing the forme and the cylinder or platen packing to achieve the correct impression all over the forme.

makeshift ('meɪk,ʃɪft) *adj* **1** serving as a temporary or expedient means, esp. during an emergency. ◆ *n* **2** something serving in this capacity.

make-up *n* **1** cosmetics, such as powder, lipstick, etc., applied to the face to improve its appearance. **2a** the cosmetics, false hair, etc., used by an actor to highlight his features or adapt his appearance. **2b** the art or result of applying such cosmetics. **3** the manner of arrangement of the parts or qualities of someone or something. **4** the arrangement of type matter and illustrations on a page or in a book. **5** mental or physical constitution. ◆ *vb* **make up.** (*adv*) **6** (*tr*) to form or constitute: *these arguments make up the case for the defence.* **7** (*tr*) to devise, construct, or compose, sometimes with the intent to deceive: *to make up a song; to make up an excuse.* **8** (*tr*) to supply what is lacking or deficient in; complete: *these extra people will make up our total.* **9** (*tr*) to put in order, arrange, or prepare: *to make up a bed.* **10** (*intr;* foll. by *for*) to compensate or atone (for): *his kindness now makes up for his rudeness yesterday.* **11** to settle (differences) amicably (often in the phrase **make it up**). **12** to apply cosmetics to (the face) to enhance one's appearance or so as to alter the appearance for a theatrical role. **13** to assemble (type and illustrations) into (columns or pages). **14** (*tr*) to surface (a road) with tarmac, concrete, etc. **15** (*tr*) **15a** to set in order and balance (accounts). **15b** to draw up (accounting statements). **16 make up one's mind.** to decide (about something or to do something): *he made up his mind to take vengeance.* **17 make up to.** *Informal.* **17a** to make friendly overtures to. **17b** to flirt with.

makeweight ('meɪk,weɪt) *n* **1** something put on a scale to make up a required weight. **2** an unimportant person or thing added to make up a lack.

make with *vb* (*intr, prep*) *Slang, chiefly U.S.* to proceed with the doing, showing, etc., of: *make with the music.*

Makeyevka (*Russian* ma'kjejɪfkə) *n* a city in the SE Ukraine: coal-mining centre. Pop.: 409 000 (1996 est.).

Makhachkala (*Russian* məxətʃka'la) *n* a port in SW Russia, capital of the Dagestan Republic, on the Caspian Sea: fishing fleet; oil refining. Pop.: 339 000 (1995 est.). Former name (until 1921): **Petrovsk.**

making ('meɪkɪŋ) *n* **1a** the act of a person or thing that makes or the process of being made. **1b** (*in combination*): *watchmaking.* **2 be the making of.** to cause the success of. **3 in the making.** in the process of becoming or being made: *a politician in the making.* **4** something made or the quantity of something made at one time. **5** make-up; composition.

makings ('meɪkɪŋz) *pl n* **1** potentials, qualities, or materials: *he had the makings of a leader.* **2** Also called: **rollings.** *Slang.* the tobacco and cigarette paper used for rolling a cigarette. **3** profits; earnings.

Makkah *or* **Makah** ('mækə, -kɑː) *n* transliteration of the Arabic name for **Mecca.**

mako[1] ('mɑːkəu) *n, pl* **-kos. 1** any shark of the genus *Isurus,* esp. *I. glaucus* of Indo-Pacific and Australian seas: family *Isuridae.* **2** *N.Z.* the teeth of the mako worn as a decoration by early Maoris. [from Maori]

mako[2] ('mɑːkəu) *or* **mako-mako** ('mɑːkəu,mɑːkəu) *n, pl* **-kos. 1** Also called: **wineberry.** a small evergreen New Zealand tree, *Aristotelia serrata:* family *Elaeocarpaceae.* **2** *N.Z.* another name for the **bellbird,** *Anthornis melanura.* [from Maori]

Makurdi (mə'kɜːdɪ) *n* a port in E central Nigeria, capital of Benue State on the Benue River: agricultural trade centre. Pop.: 123 100 (1996 est.).

makuta (mɑː'kuːtɑː) *n* the plural of **likuta.**

MAL *international car registration for* Malaysia.

Mal. *abbrev. for:* **1** *Bible.* Malachi. **2** Malay(an).

mal- *combining form.* bad or badly; wrong or wrongly; imperfect or defective: *maladjusted; malfunction.* [Old French, from Latin *malus* bad, *male* badly]

mala ('mɑːlɑː) *n Hinduism.* a string of beads or knots, used in praying and meditating.

Malabar Coast *or* **Malabar** ('mælə,bɑː) *n* a region along the SW coast of India, extending from Goa to Cape Comorin: includes most of Kerala state.

Malabo (mə'lɑːbəu) *n* the capital and chief port of Equatorial Guinea, on the island of Bioko in the Gulf of Guinea. Pop.: 58 040 (1991 est.). Former name (until 1973): **Santa Isabel.**

malabsorption (mæləb'sɔːpʃən) *n* a failure of absorption, esp. by the small intestine in coeliac disease, cystic fibrosis, etc.

malacca *or* **malacca cane** (mə'lækə) *n* **1** the stem of the rattan palm. **2** a walking stick made from this stem.

Malacca (mə'lækə) *n* a state of SW Peninsular Malaysia: rubber plantations. Capital: Malacca. Pop.: 583 400 (1993 est.). Area: 1650 sq. km (637 sq. miles).

Malachi ('mælə,kaɪ) *n Old Testament.* **1** a Hebrew prophet of the 5th century B.C. **2** the book containing his oracles. Douay spelling: **Malachias** (,mælə'kaɪəs).

malachite ('mælə,kaɪt) *n* a bright green mineral, found in veins and in association with copper deposits. It is a source of copper and is used as an ornamental stone. Composition: hydrated copper carbonate. Formula: $Cu_2CO_3(OH)_2$. Crystal structure: monoclinic. [C16: via Old French from Latin *molochītēs,* from Greek *molokhitis* mallow-green stone, from *molokhē* mallow]

Malachy (ˈmæləˌkaɪ) *n* **Saint.** 1094–1148, Irish prelate; he became Archbishop of Armagh (1132) and founded (1142) the first Cistercian abbey in Ireland. Feast day: Nov. 3.

malacia (məˈleɪʃɪə) *n* the pathological softening of an organ or tissue, such as bone.

malaco- *or before a vowel* **malac-** *combining form.* denoting softness: *malacology; malacostracan.* [from Greek *malakos*]

malacology (ˌmæləˈkɒlədʒɪ) *n* the branch of zoology concerned with the study of molluscs. ▸ **malacological** (ˌmæləkəˈlɒdʒɪkᵊl) *adj* ▸ ˌ**malaˈcologist** *n*

malacophily (ˌmæləˈkɒfɪlɪ) *n Botany.* pollination of plants by snails. ▸ ˌ**malaˈcophilous** *adj*

malacophyllous (ˌmæləˈkɒfɪləs) *adj* (of plants living in dry regions) having fleshy leaves in which water is stored.

malacopterygian (ˌmæləˌkɒptəˈrɪdʒɪən) *adj* **1** of, relating to, or belonging to the *Malacopterygii,* a group of teleost fishes, including herrings and salmon, having soft fin rays. ◆ *n* **2** any malacopterygian fish; a soft-finned fish. ◆ Compare **acanthopterygian.** [C19: from New Latin *Malacopterygii,* from MALACO- + Greek *pterux* wing, fin]

malacostracan (ˌmæləˈkɒstrəkᵊn) *n* **1** any crustacean of the subclass or group *Malacostraca,* including lobsters, crabs, woodlice, sand hoppers, and opossum shrimps. ◆ *adj also* **malacostracous. 2** of, relating to, or belonging to the *Malacostraca.* [C19: from New Latin, from Greek *malakōstrakos,* from MALACO- + *ostrakon* shell]

maladaptive (ˌmæləˈdæptɪv) *adj* **1** unsuitably adapted or adapting poorly to (a situation, purpose, etc.). **2** not encouraging adaptation. ▸ ˌ**malaˈdapted** *adj* ▸ ˌ**malaˈdaptively** *adv*

maladdress (ˌmæləˈdres) *n* awkwardness; tactlessness.

maladjusted (ˌmæləˈdʒʌstɪd) *adj* **1** *Psychol.* suffering from maladjustment. **2** badly adjusted.

maladjustment (ˌmæləˈdʒʌstmənt) *n* **1** *Psychol.* a failure to meet the demands of society, such as coping with problems and social relationships: usually reflected in emotional instability. **2** faulty or bad adjustment.

maladminister (ˌmælədˈmɪnɪstə) *vb* (*tr*) to administer badly, inefficiently, or dishonestly. ▸ ˌ**maladˌminisˈtration** *n* ▸ ˌ**maladˈminisˌtrator** *n*

maladroit (ˌmæləˈdrɔɪt) *adj* **1** showing or characterized by clumsiness; not dexterous. **2** tactless and insensitive in behaviour or speech. [C17: from French, from *mal* badly + ADROIT] ▸ ˌ**malaˈdroitly** *adv* ▸ ˌ**malaˈdroitness** *n*

malady (ˈmælədɪ) *n, pl* **-dies. 1** any disease or illness. **2** any unhealthy, morbid, or desperate condition: *a malady of the spirit.* [C13: from Old French, from Vulgar Latin *male habitus* (unattested) in poor condition, from Latin *male* badly + *habitus,* from *habēre* to have]

mala fide (ˈmælə ˈfaɪdɪ) *adj* undertaken in bad faith. [from Latin]

Málaga (ˈmæləgə; *Spanish* ˈmalaɣa) *n* **1** a port and resort in S Spain, in Andalusia on the Mediterranean. Pop.: 532 425 (1995 est.). **2** a sweet fortified dessert wine from Málaga.

Malagasy (ˌmæləˈgæzɪ) *n* **1** (*pl* **-gasy** *or* **-gasies**) a native or inhabitant of Madagascar. **2** the official language of Madagascar belonging to the Malayo-Polynesian family. ◆ *adj* **3** of or relating to Madagascar, its people, or their language.

Malagasy Republic *n* the former name (1958–75) of **Madagascar.**

malagueña (ˌmæləˈgeɪnjə) *n* a Spanish dance similar to the fandango. [Spanish: of MÁLAGA]

malaise (mæˈleɪz) *n* **1** a feeling of unease or depression. **2** a mild sickness, not symptomatic of any disease or ailment. **3** a complex of problems affecting a country, economy, etc.: *Bulgaria's economic malaise.* [C18: from Old French, from *mal* bad + *aise* EASE]

malam (ˈmælæm, -əm) *n* a variant spelling of **mallam.**

Malamud (ˈmæləməd, -mud) *n* **Bernard.** 1914–86, U.S. novelist and short-story writer. His works include *The Fixer* (1966) and *Dubin's Lives* (1979).

malamute *or* **malemute** (ˈmæləˌmuːt) *n* an Alaskan Eskimo dog of the spitz type, having a dense usually greyish coat. [from the name of an Eskimo tribe]

malanders, mallanders, *or* **mallenders** (ˈmæləndəz) *pl n* (*functioning as sing*) a disease of horses characterized by an eczematous inflammation behind the knee. [C15: via Old French from Latin *malandria* sore on the neck of a horse]

Malang (ˈmælæŋ) *n* a city in S Indonesia, on E Java: commercial centre. Pop.: 763 400 (1995 est.).

malapert (ˈmæləˌpɜːt) *Archaic or literary.* ◆ *adj* **1** saucy or impudent. ◆ *n* **2** a saucy or impudent person. [C15: from Old French: unskilful (see MAL-, EXPERT); meaning in English influenced by *apert* frank, from Latin *apertus* open] ▸ ˈ**malaˌpertly** *adv* ▸ ˈ**malaˌpertness** *n*

malapropism (ˈmæləprɒpˌɪzəm) *n* **1** the unintentional misuse of a word by confusion with one of similar sound, esp. when creating a ridiculous effect, as in *I am not under the affluence of alcohol.* **2** the habit of misusing words in this manner. [C18: after Mrs *Malaprop* in Sheridan's play *The Rivals* (1775), a character who misused words, from MALAPROPOS] ▸ ˈ**malaprop** *or* ˌ**malaˈpropian** *adj*

malapropos (ˌmælæprəˈpəʊ) *adj* **1** of an inappropriate or misapplied nature or kind. ◆ *adv* **2** in an inappropriate way or manner. ◆ *n* **3** something inopportune or inappropriate. [C17: from French *mal à propos* not to the purpose]

malar (ˈmeɪlə) *adj* **1** of or relating to the cheek or cheekbone. ◆ *n* **2** Also called: **malar bone.** another name for **zygomatic bone.** [C18: from New Latin *mālāris,* from Latin *māla* jaw]

Mälar (ˈmeɪlə) *n* **Lake.** a lake in S Sweden, extending 121 km (75 miles) west from Stockholm, where it joins with an inlet of the Baltic Sea (the **Saltsjön**). Area: 1140 sq. km (440 sq. miles). Swedish name: **Mälaren** (ˈmelaren).

malaria (məˈlɛərɪə) *n* an infectious disease characterized by recurring attacks of chills and fever, caused by the bite of an anopheles mosquito infected with any of four protozoans of the genus *Plasmodium* (*P. vivax, P. falciparum, P. malariae,* or *P. ovale*). [C18: from Italian *mala aria* bad air, from the belief that the disease was caused by the unwholesome air in swampy districts] ▸ **maˈlarial, maˈlarian,** *or* **maˈlarious** *adj*

malariology (məˌlɛərɪˈɒlədʒɪ) *n* the study of malaria. ▸ **maˌlariˈologist** *n*

malarkey *or* **malarky** (məˈlɑːkɪ) *n Slang.* nonsense; rubbish. [C20: of unknown origin]

malassimilation (ˌmæləˌsɪmɪˈleɪʃən) *n Pathol.* defective assimilation of nutrients.

malate (ˈmæleɪt, ˈmeɪ-) *n* any salt or ester of malic acid. [C18: from MALIC ACID]

Malatesta (*Italian* malaˈtesta) *n* an Italian family that ruled Rimini from the 13th to the 16th century.

Malathion (ˌmæləˈθaɪɒn) *n Trademark.* a yellow organophosphorus insecticide used as a dust or mist for the control of house flies and garden pests. Formula: $C_{10}H_{19}O_6PS_2$. [C20: from (*diethyl*) MAL(EATE) + THIO- + -ON]

Malatya (ˌmɑːlɑːˈtjɑː) *n* a city in E central Turkey: nearby is the ruined Roman and medieval city of Melitene (Old Malatya). Pop.: 314 539 (1995 est.).

Malawi (məˈlɑːwɪ) *n* **1** a republic in E central Africa: established as a British protectorate in 1891; became independent in 1964 and a republic, within the Commonwealth, in 1966; lies along the Great Rift Valley, with Lake Nyasa (Malawi) along the E border, the Nyika Plateau in the northwest, and the Shiré Highlands in the southeast. Official language: Chichewa; English and various other Bantu languages are also widely spoken. Religion: Christian majority, Muslim, and animist minorities. Currency: kwacha. Capital: Lilongwe. Pop.: 9 840 000 (1998 est.). Area: 118 484 sq. km (45 747 sq. miles). Former name: **Nyasaland. 2 Lake.** the Malawi name for (Lake) **Nyasa.**

Malay (məˈleɪ) *n* **1** a member of a people living chiefly in Malaysia and Indonesia who are descendants of Mongoloid immigrants. **2** the language of this people, belonging to the Malayo-Polynesian family. ◆ *adj* **3** of or relating to the Malays or their language.

Malaya (məˈleɪə) *n* **1 States of the Federation of.** part of Malaysia, in the S Malay Peninsula, constituting Peninsular Malaysia: consists of the former Federated Malay States, the former Unfederated Malay States, and the former Straits Settlements. Capital: Kuala Lumpur. Pop.: 14 127 556 (1990). Area: 131 587 sq. km (50 806 sq. miles). **2 Federation of.** a federation of the nine Malay States of the Malay Peninsula and two of the Straits Settlements (Malacca and Penang): formed in 1948: became part of the British Commonwealth in 1957 and joined Malaysia in 1963. ▸ **Maˈlayan** *adj, n*

Malayalam *or* **Malayalaam** (ˌmælɪˈɑːləm) *n* a language of SW India, belonging to the Dravidian family and closely related to Tamil: the state language of Kerala.

Malay Archipelago *n* a group of islands in the Indian and Pacific Oceans, between SE Asia and Australia: the largest group of islands in the world; includes over 3000 Indonesian islands, about 7000 islands of the Philippines, and, sometimes, New Guinea.

Malayo-Polynesian *n* **1** Also called: **Austronesian.** a family of languages extending from Madagascar to the central Pacific, including Malagasy, Malay, Indonesian, Tagalog, and Polynesian. See also **Austro-Asiatic.** ◆ *adj* **2** of or relating to this family of languages.

Malay Peninsula *n* a peninsula of SE Asia, extending south from the Isthmus of Kra in Thailand to Cape Tanjong Piai in Malaysia: consists of SW Thailand and the states of Malaya (Peninsular Malaysia). Ancient name: **Chersonesus Aurea** (ˌkɜːsəˈniːsəsˈɔːrɪə).

Malaysia (məˈleɪzɪə) *n* a federation in SE Asia (within the Commonwealth), consisting of **Peninsular Malaysia,** on the Malay Peninsula, and **East Malaysia** (Sabah and Sarawak), occupying the N part of the island of Borneo: formed in 1963 as a federation of Malaya, Sarawak, Sabah, and Singapore (the latter seceded in 1965); densely forested and mostly mountainous. Official language: Malay; English and various Chinese and Indian minority languages are also spoken. Official religion: Muslim. Currency: ringgit. Capital: Putrajaya (the transfer of government from Kuala Lumpur is scheduled for completion in 2000). Pop.: 22 083 000 (1998 est.). Area: 333 403 sq. km (128 727 sq. miles). ▸ **Maˈlaysian** *adj, n*

Malay States *pl n* the former states of the Malay Peninsula that, together with Penang and Malacca, formed the Union of Malaya (1946) and the Federation of Malaya (1948). Perak, Selangor, Negri Sembilan, and Pahang were established as the **Federated Malay States** by the British in 1895 and Perlis, Kedah, Kelantan, and Trengannu as the **Unfederated Malay States** in 1909 (joined by Johore in 1914).

Malcolm (ˈmælkəm) *n* **George.** born 1917, British harpsichordist.

Malcolm III *n* died 1093, king of Scotland (1057–93). He became king after Macbeth.

Malcolm X (ɛks) *n* original name *Malcolm Little.* 1925–65, U.S. Black civil-rights leader: assassinated.

malcontent (ˈmælkənˌtɛnt) *adj* **1** disgusted or discontented. ◆ *n* **2** a person who is malcontent. [C16: from Old French]

mal de mer *French.* (mal də mɛr) *n* seasickness.

maldistribution (ˌmældɪstrɪˈbjuːʃən) *n* faulty, unequal, or unfair distribution (as of wealth, business, etc.).

Maldives (ˈmɔːldaɪvz) *pl n* **Republic of.** a republic occupying an archipelago of 1087 coral islands in the Indian Ocean, southwest of Sri Lanka: came under British protection in 1887; became independent in 1965 and a republic in 1968; a member of the Commonwealth. Official language: Divehi. Official religion: (Sunni) Muslim. Currency: rufiyaa. Capital: Malé. Pop.: 270 000 (1998 est.).

Area: 298 sq. km (115 sq. miles). Also called: **Maldive Islands.** ▸ **Maldivian** (mɔːlˈdɪvɪən) *or* **Maldivan** (ˈmɔːldaɪvᵊn, -dɪ-) *adj, n*

Maldon (ˈmɔːldən) *n* a market town in SE England, in Essex; scene of a battle (991) between the East Saxons and the victorious Danes, celebrated in *The Battle of Maldon,* an Old English poem. Pop.: 15 841 (1991).

male (meɪl) *adj* **1** of, relating to, or designating the sex producing gametes (spermatozoa) that can fertilize female gametes (ova). **2** of, relating to, or characteristic of a man; masculine. **3** for or composed of men or boys: *a male choir.* **4** (of gametes) capable of fertilizing an egg cell in sexual reproduction. **5** (of reproductive organs, such as a testis or stamen) capable of producing male gametes. **6** (of flowers) bearing stamens but lacking a functional pistil. **7** *Electronics, mechanical engineering.* having a projecting part or parts that fit into a female counterpart: *a male plug.* ◆ *n* **8** a male person, animal, or plant. [C14: via Old French from Latin *masculus* MASCULINE] ▸ ˈ**maleness** *n*

Malé (ˈmɑːleɪ) *n* the capital of the Republic of Maldives, on Malé Island in the centre of the island group. Pop.: 62 973 (1995 est.).

maleate (ˈmælɪˌeɪt) *n* any salt or ester of maleic acid. [C19: from MALE(IC ACID) + -ATE[1]]

Malebranche (*French* malbrɑ̃ʃ) *n* **Nicolas** (nikɔla). 1638–1715, French philosopher. Originally a follower of Descartes, he developed the philosophy of occasionalism, esp. in *De la recherche de la vérité* (1674).

male chauvinism *n* the belief, held or alleged to be held by certain men, that men are inherently superior to women. ▸ **male chauvinist** *n, adj*

male chauvinist pig *n Informal, derogatory.* a man who exhibits male chauvinism. Abbrev.: **MCP.**

maledict (ˈmælɪdɪkt) *vb* **1** (*tr*) *Literary.* to utter a curse against. ◆ *adj* **2** *Archaic.* cursed or detestable.

malediction (ˌmælɪˈdɪkʃən) *n* **1** the utterance of a curse against someone or something. **2** slanderous accusation or comment. [C15: from Latin *maledictiō* a reviling, from *male* ill + *dīcere* to speak] ▸ ˌ**maleˈdictive** *or* ˌ**maleˈdictory** *adj*

malefactor (ˈmælɪˌfæktə) *n* a criminal; wrongdoer. [C15: via Old French from Latin, from *malefacere* to do evil] ▸ ˈ**maleˌfaction** *n* ▸ ˈ**maleˌfactress** *fem n*

male fern *n* a fern, *Dryopteris filix-mas,* having scaly stalks and pinnate fronds with kidney-shaped spore-producing bodies on the underside: family *Polypodiaceae.* [C16: so called because it was formerly believed to be the male of the lady fern]

maleficent (məˈlɛfɪsənt) *adj* causing or capable of producing evil or mischief; harmful or baleful. [C17: from Latin *maleficent-,* from *maleficus* wicked, prone to evil, from *malum* evil] ▸ **maˈlefic** *adj* ▸ **maˈleficence** *n*

maleic acid (məˈleɪɪk) *n* a colourless soluble crystalline substance used to synthesize other compounds. Formula: HOOCCH:CHCOOH. Systematic name: ***cis*-butanedioic acid.** [C19: from French *maléique,* altered form of *malique;* see MALIC ACID]

male menopause *n* a period in a man's later middle age in which he may experience an identity crisis as he feels age overtake his sexual powers.

malemute (ˈmæləˌmuːt) *n* a variant spelling of **malamute.**

Malenkov (*Russian* məlɪnˈkɔf) *n* **Georgi Maksimilianovich** (gɪˈɔrgij ˌməksjimɪlˈjɑnəvjɪtʃ). 1902–88, Soviet politician; prime minister (1953–55). He was removed from the party presidium (1957) for plotting against Khrushchev; expelled from the Communist Party (1961).

Malevich (*Russian* ˈmalɪvitʃ) *n* **Kasimir** (kəziˈmir). 1878–1935, Russian painter. He founded the abstract art movement known as Suprematism.

malevolent (məˈlɛvələnt) *adj* **1** wishing or appearing to wish evil to others; malicious. **2** *Astrology.* having an evil influence. [C16: from Latin *malevolens,* from *male* ill + *volens,* present participle of *velle* to wish] ▸ **maˈlevolence** *n* ▸ **maˈlevolently** *adv*

malfeasance (mælˈfiːzᵊns) *n Law.* the doing of a wrongful or illegal act, esp. by a public official. Compare **misfeasance, nonfeasance.** [C17: from Old French *mal faisant,* from *mal* evil + *faisant* doing, from *faire* to do, from Latin *facere*] ▸ **malˈfeasant** *n, adj*

malformation (ˌmælfɔːˈmeɪʃən) *n* **1** the condition of being faulty or abnormal in form or shape. **2** *Pathol.* a deformity in the shape or structure of a part, esp. when congenital. ▸ **malˈformed** *adj*

malfunction (mælˈfʌŋkʃən) *vb* **1** (*intr*) to function imperfectly or irregularly or fail to function. ◆ *n* **2** failure to function or defective functioning.

malgré lui *French.* (malgre lwi) *adv* in spite of himself.

Malherbe (*French* malɛrb) *n* **François de** (frɑ̃swa də). 1555–1628, French poet and critic. He advocated the classical ideals of clarity and concision of meaning.

Mali (ˈmɑːlɪ) *n* a landlocked republic in West Africa: conquered by the French by 1898 and incorporated (as French Sudan) into French West Africa; became independent in 1960; settled chiefly in the basins of the Rivers Senegal and Niger in the south. Official language: French. Religion: Muslim majority, also animist. Currency: franc. Capital: Bamako. Pop.: 10 109 000 (1998 est.). Area: 1 248 574 sq. km (482 077 sq. miles). Former name (1898–1959): **French Sudan.**

malibu board (ˈmælɪbuː) *n* a lightweight surfboard, usually having a fin. [C20: named after *Malibu* beach, California]

malic acid (ˈmælɪk, ˈmeɪ-) *n* a colourless crystalline compound occurring in apples and other fruits. Formula: $HOOCCH_2CH(OH)COOH$. [C18 *malic,* via French *malique* from Latin *mālum* apple]

malice (ˈmælɪs) *n* **1** the desire to do harm or mischief. **2** evil intent. **3** *Law.* the state of mind with which an act is committed and from which the intent to do wrong may be inferred. See also **malice aforethought.** [C13: via Old French from Latin *malitia,* from *malus* evil]

malice aforethought *n Criminal law.* **1** the predetermination to do an unlawful act, esp. to kill or seriously injure. **2** the intent with which an unlawful killing is effected, which must be proved for the crime to constitute murder. See also **murder, manslaughter.**

malicious (məˈlɪʃəs) *adj* **1** characterized by malice. **2** motivated by wrongful, vicious, or mischievous purposes. ▸ **maˈliciously** *adv* ▸ **maˈliciousness** *n*

malign (məˈlaɪn) *adj* **1** evil in influence, intention, or effect. ◆ *vb* **2** (*tr*) to slander or defame. [C14: via Old French from Latin *malīgnus* spiteful, from *malus* evil] ▸ **maˈligner** *n* ▸ **maˈlignly** *adv*

malignancy (məˈlɪgnənsɪ) *n, pl* **-cies. 1** the state or quality of being malignant. **2** *Pathol.* a cancerous growth.

malignant (məˈlɪgnənt) *adj* **1** having or showing desire to harm others. **2** tending to cause great harm; injurious. **3** *Pathol.* (of a tumour) uncontrollable or resistant to therapy; rapidly spreading. ◆ *n* **4** *History.* (in the English Civil War) a Parliamentarian term for a **royalist.** [C16: from Late Latin *malīgnāre* to behave spitefully, from Latin *malīgnus* MALIGN] ▸ **maˈlignantly** *adv*

malignity (məˈlɪgnɪtɪ) *n, pl* **-ties. 1** the condition or quality of being malign, malevolent, or deadly. **2** (*often pl*) a malign or malicious act or feeling.

malihini (ˌmɑːlɪˈhiːnɪ) *n, pl* **-nis.** (in Hawaii) a foreigner or stranger. [from Hawaiian]

malimprinted (ˌmælɪmˈprɪntɪd) *adj* (of an animal or person) suffering from a defect in the behavioural process of imprinting, resulting in attraction to members of other species, fetishism, etc. ▸ ˌ**malimˈprinting** *n*

malines (məˈliːn) *n* **1** a type of silk net used in dressmaking. **2** another name for **Mechlin lace.** [C19: from French *Malines* (Mechelen), where this lace was traditionally made]

Malines (malin) *n* the French name for **Mechelen.**

malinger (məˈlɪŋgə) *vb* (*intr*) to pretend or exaggerate illness, esp. to avoid work. [C19: from French *malingre* sickly, perhaps from *mal* badly + Old French *haingre* feeble] ▸ **maˈlingerer** *n*

Malinke (məˈlɪŋkɪ) *or* **Maninke** *n* **1** (*pl* **-ke** *or* **-kes**) a member of a Negroid people of W Africa, living chiefly in Guinea and Mali, noted for their use of cowry shells as currency. **2** the language of this people, belonging to the Mande branch of the Niger-Congo family.

Malinowski (ˌmælɪˈnɒfskɪ) *n* **Bronislaw Kasper** (brɔˈnislaf ˈkaspɛr). 1884–1942, Polish anthropologist in England and the U.S., who researched into the sexual behaviour of primitive people in New Guinea and Melanesia.

malison (ˈmælɪzᵊn, -sᵊn) *n* an archaic or poetic word for **curse.** [C13: via Old French from Latin *maledictiō* MALEDICTION]

malkin (ˈmɔːkɪn, ˈmɔːl-, ˈmæl-) *n* **1** an archaic or dialect name for a **cat**[1]. Compare **grimalkin. 2** a variant of **mawkin.** [C13: diminutive of *Maud*]

mall (mæl, mɔːl) *n* **1** a shaded avenue, esp. one that is open to the public. **2** *U.S., Canadian, Austral., and N.Z.* short for **shopping mall.** [C17: after *The Mall,* in St James's Park, London. See PALL-MALL]

mallam *or* **malam** (ˈmælæm, -əm) *n W African.* **1** (in Islamic W Africa) a man learned in Koranic studies. **2** (in N Nigeria) a title and form of address for a learned or educated man. [C20: from Hausa]

mallanders (ˈmæləndəz) *n* a variant spelling of **malanders.**

mallard (ˈmælɑːd) *n, pl* **-lard** *or* **-lards.** a duck, *Anas platyrhynchos,* common over most of the N hemisphere, the male of which has a dark green head and reddish-brown breast: the ancestor of all domestic breeds of duck. [C14: from Old French *mallart,* perhaps from *maslart* (unattested); see MALE, -ARD]

Mallarmé (*French* malarme) *n* **Stéphane** (stefan). 1842–98, French symbolist poet, noted for his free verse, in which he chooses words for their evocative qualities; his works include *L'Après-midi d'un Faune* (1876), *Vers et Prose* (1893), and *Divagations* (1897).

Malle (*French* mal) *n* **Louis.** 1932–95, French film director: his films include *Le Feu follet* (1963), *Au revoir les enfants* (1987), and *Vanya on 42nd Street* (1994).

malleable (ˈmælɪəbᵊl) *adj* **1** (esp. of metal) able to be worked, hammered, or shaped under pressure or blows without breaking. **2** able to be influenced; pliable or tractable. [C14: via Old French from Medieval Latin *malleābilis,* from Latin *malleus* hammer] ▸ ˌ**malleaˈbility** *or* (*less commonly*) ˈ**malleableness** *n* ▸ ˈ**malleably** *adv*

malleable iron *n* **1** Also called: **malleable cast iron.** cast iron that has been toughened by gradual heating or slow cooling. **2** a less common name for **wrought iron.**

mallee (ˈmæliː) *n* **1** any of several low shrubby eucalyptus trees that flourish in desert regions of Australia. **2** (usually preceded by *the*) *Austral. informal.* another name for the **bush** (sense 4). **3** See **mallee root.** [C19: native Australian name]

mallee fowl *n* an Australian megapode, *Leipoa ocellata,* that allows its eggs to incubate naturally in a sandy mound.

mallee root *n Austral.* the rootstock (rhizome) of a mallee tree, often used as fuel.

mallemuck (ˈmælɪˌmʌk) *n* any of various sea birds, such as the albatross, fulmar, or shearwater. [C17: from Dutch *mallemok* from *mal* silly + *mok* gull]

mallenders (ˈmæləndəz) *n* a less common spelling of **malanders.**

malleolus (məˈliːələs) *n, pl* **-li** (-ˌlaɪ). either of two rounded bony projections of the tibia and fibula on the sides of each ankle joint. [C17: diminutive of Latin *malleus* hammer] ▸ **malˈleolar** *adj*

mallet (ˈmælɪt) *n* **1** a tool resembling a hammer but having a large head of wood, copper, lead, leather, etc., used for driving chisels, beating sheet metal, etc. **2** a long stick with a head like a hammer used to strike the ball in croquet or polo. **3** *Chiefly U.S.* a very large powerful steam locomotive with a conventional boiler but with two separate articulated engine units. [C15: from Old French *maillet* wooden hammer, diminutive of *mail* MAUL (n)]

malleus (ˈmælɪəs) *n, pl* **-lei** (-lɪˌaɪ). the outermost and largest of the three small bones in the middle ear of mammals. Nontechnical name: **hammer.** See also **incus, stapes.** [C17: from Latin: hammer]

Mallorca (ma'ʎɔrka) *n* the Spanish name for **Majorca.**

mallow ('mæləʊ) *n* **1** any plant of the malvaceous genus *Malva,* esp. *M. sylvestris* of Europe, having purple, pink, or white flowers. See also **dwarf mallow, musk mallow. 2** any of various related plants, such as the marsh mallow, rose mallow, Indian mallow, and tree mallow. [Old English *mealuwe,* from Latin *malva;* probably related to Greek *malakhē* mallow]

malm (mɑːm) *n* **1** a soft greyish limestone that crumbles easily. **2** a chalky soil formed from this limestone. **3** an artificial mixture of clay and chalk used to make bricks. [Old English *mealm-* (in compound words); related to Old Norse *malmr* ore, Gothic *malma* sand]

Malmédy (*French* malmedi) *n* See **Eupen and Malmédy.**

Malmö ('mælməʊ; *Swedish* 'malmøː) *n* a port in S Sweden, on the Sound: part of Denmark until 1658; industrial centre. Pop.: 248 007 (1997 est.).

malmsey ('mɑːmzɪ) *n* a sweet Madeira wine. [C15: from Medieval Latin *Malmasia,* corruption of Greek *Monembasia,* Greek port from which the wine was shipped]

malnourished (mæl'nʌrɪʃt) *adj* undernourished.

malnutrition (ˌmælnjuː'trɪʃən) *n* lack of adequate nutrition resulting from insufficient food, unbalanced diet, or defective assimilation.

malocclusion (ˌmælə'kluːʒən) *n Dentistry.* a defect in the normal position of the upper and lower teeth when the mouth is closed, as from abnormal development of the jaw. ▸ **ˌmaloc'cluded** *adj*

malodorous (mæl'əʊdərəs) *adj* having a bad smell. ▸ **mal'odorously** *adv* ▸ **mal'odorousness** *n*

malonic acid (mə'ləʊnɪk, -'lɒn-) *n* another name for **propanedioic acid.** [C19: from French *malonique,* altered form of *malique;* see MALIC ACID]

malonylurea (ˌmælənɪlju'rɪə, -'jʊərɪə, -niːl-) *n* another name for **barbituric acid.**

Malory ('mælərɪ) *n* Sir **Thomas.** 15th-century English author of *Le Morte d'Arthur* (?1470), a prose collection of Arthurian legends, translated from the French.

Malpighi (*Italian* mal'piːgi) *n* **Marcello** (mar'tʃello). 1628–94, Italian physiologist. A pioneer in microscopic anatomy, he identified the capillary system (1661). ▸ **Malpighian** (mæl'pɪgɪən) *adj*

malpighiaceous (mælˌpɪgɪ'eɪʃəs) *adj* of, relating to, or belonging to the *Malpighiaceae,* a family of tropical plants many of which are lianas. [C19: from New Latin *Malpighia,* after Marcello MALPIGHI]

Malpighian corpuscle *or* **body** *n Anatomy.* an encapsulated cluster of capillaries at the end of each urine-secreting tubule of the kidney.

Malpighian layer *n Anatomy.* the innermost layer of the epidermis.

Malpighian tubules *or* **tubes** *pl n* organs of excretion in insects and many other arthropods: narrow tubules opening into the anterior part of the hindgut.

malposition (ˌmælpə'zɪʃən) *n* abnormal position of a bodily part. ▸ **malposed** (mæl'pəʊzd) *adj*

malpractice (mæl'præktɪs) *n* **1** immoral, illegal, or unethical professional conduct or neglect of professional duty. **2** any instance of improper professional conduct. ▸ **malpractitioner** (ˌmælpræk'tɪʃənə) *n*

Malraux (*French* malro) *n* **André** (ɑ̃dre). 1901–76, French writer and statesman. His novels include *La Condition humaine* (1933) on the Kuomintang revolution (1927–28) and *L'Espoir* (1937) on the Spanish Civil War, in both of which events he took part. He also wrote on art, notably in *Les Voix du silence* (1951).

malt (mɔːlt) *n* **1** cereal grain, such as barley, that is kiln-dried after it has germinated by soaking in water. **2** See **malt liquor. 3** short for **malt whisky.** ◆ *vb* **4** to make into or become malt. **5** to make (something, esp. liquor) with malt. [Old English *mealt;* related to Dutch *mout,* Old Norse *malt;* see also MELT]

Malta ('mɔːltə) *n* a republic occupying the islands of Malta, Gozo, and Comino, in the Mediterranean south of Sicily: governed by the Knights Hospitallers from 1530 until Napoleon's conquest in 1798; French driven out, with British help, 1800; became British dependency 1814; suffered severely in World War II; became independent in 1964 and a republic in 1974; a member of the Commonwealth. Official languages: Maltese and English. Official religion: Roman Catholic. Currency: Maltese lira. Capital: Valletta. Pop.: 377 000 (1998 est.). Area: 316 sq. km (122 sq. miles).

Malta fever *n* another name for **brucellosis.**

maltase ('mɔːlteɪz) *n* an enzyme that hydrolyses maltose and similar glucosides (α-glucosides) to glucose. Also called: **α-glu'cosiˌdase.** [C19: from MALT + -ASE]

malted milk *n* **1** a soluble powder made from dehydrated milk and malted cereals. **2** a drink made from this powder.

Maltese (mɔː'tiːz) *adj* **1** of or relating to Malta, its inhabitants, or their language. ◆ *n* **2** (*pl* **-tese**) a native or inhabitant of Malta. **3** the official language of Malta, a form of Arabic with borrowings from Italian, etc. **4** a breed of toy dog having a very long straight silky white coat. **5** a domestic fancy pigeon having long legs and a long neck.

Maltese cross *n* **1** a cross with triangular arms that taper towards the centre, sometimes having indented outer sides: formerly worn by the Knights of Malta. **2** (in a film projector) a cam mechanism of this shape that produces intermittent motion.

malt extract *n* a sticky substance obtained from an infusion of malt.

maltha ('mælθə) *n* **1** another name for **mineral tar. 2** any of various naturally occurring mixtures of hydrocarbons, such as ozocerite. [C15: via Latin from Greek: a mixture of wax and pitch]

Malthus ('mælθəs) *n* **Thomas Robert.** 1766–1834, English economist. He propounded his population theory in *An Essay on the Principle of Population* (1798).

Malthusian (mæl'θjuːzɪən) *adj* **1** of or relating to the theory of Malthus stating that increases in population tend to exceed increases in the means of subsistence and that therefore sexual restraint should be exercised. ◆ *n* **2** a supporter of this theory. ▸ **Mal'thusianism** *n*

malting ('mɔːltɪŋ) *n* a building in which malt is made or stored. Also called: **malt house.**

malt liquor *n* any alcoholic drink brewed from malt.

maltose ('mɔːltəʊz) *n* a disaccharide of glucose formed by the enzymic hydrolysis of starch: used in bacteriological culture media and as a nutrient in infant feeding. Formula: $C_{12}H_{22}O_{11}$. [C19: from MALT + -OSE[2]]

maltreat (mæl'triːt) *vb* (*tr*) to treat badly, cruelly, or inconsiderately. [C18: from French *maltraiter*] ▸ **mal'treater** *n* ▸ **mal'treatment** *n*

maltster ('mɔːltstə) *n* a person who makes or deals in malt.

malt whisky *n* whisky made from malted barley.

malty ('mɔːltɪ) *adj* **maltier, maltiest.** of, like, or containing malt. ▸ **'maltiness** *n*

Maluku (mɑː'luːkuː) *n* the Indonesian name for the **Moluccas.**

malvaceous (mæl'veɪʃəs) *adj* of, relating to, or belonging to the *Malvaceae,* a family of plants that includes mallow, cotton, okra, althaea, and abutilon. [C17: from Latin *malvāceus,* from *malva* MALLOW]

malvasia (ˌmælvə'sɪə) *n* **1** another word for **malmsey. 2** the type of grape used to make malmsey. [C19: from Italian, from Greek *Monembasia;* see MALMSEY] ▸ **ˌmalva'sian** *adj*

Malvern ('mɔːlvən) *n* a town and resort in W England, in S Worcestershire on the E slopes of the **Malvern Hills:** annual dramatic festival; mineral springs. Pop.: 31 537 (1991).

malversation (ˌmælvɜː'seɪʃən) *n Rare.* professional or public misconduct. [C16: from French, from *malverser* to behave badly, from Latin *male versārī*]

Malvinas (*Spanish* mal'βinas) *pl n* **Islas** ('izlas). the Argentine name for the **Falkland Islands.**

malvoisie ('mælvɔɪzɪ, -və-) *n* an amber dessert wine made in France, similar to malmsey. [C14: via Old French from Italian *Malvasia,* from Greek *Monembasia;* see MALMSEY]

malwa ('malwa) *n* a Ugandan drink brewed from millet. [from Rutooro, a language of W Uganda]

mam (mæm) *n Informal or dialect.* another word for **mother**[1].

mama (mə'mɑː) *n Old-fashioned.* an informal word for **mother**[1].

mamaguy ('mɑːməˌgaɪ) *Caribbean.* ◆ *vb* **1** (*tr*) to deceive or tease, either in jest or by deceitful flattery. ◆ *n* **2** an instance of such deception or flattery. [from Spanish *mamar el gallo,* literally: to feed the cock]

mamba ('mæmbə) *n* any aggressive partly arboreal tropical African venomous elapid snake of the genus *Dendroaspis,* esp. *D. angusticeps* (**green** and **black mambas**). [from Zulu *im-amba*]

mambo ('mæmbəʊ) *n, pl* **-bos. 1** a modern Latin American dance, resembling the rumba, derived from the ritual dance of voodoo. ◆ *vb* **2** (*intr*) to perform this dance. [American Spanish, probably from Haitian Creole: voodoo priestess]

mamelon ('mæməlᵊn) *n* a small rounded hillock. [C19: from French: nipple]

Mameluke *or* **Mamaluke** ('mæmɪˌluːk) *n* **1** a member of a military class, originally of Turkish slaves, ruling in Egypt from about 1250 to 1517 and remaining powerful until crushed in 1811. **2** (in Muslim countries) a slave. [C16: via French, ultimately from Arabic *mamlūk* slave, from *malaka* to possess]

Mamet ('mæmɪt) *n* **David.** born 1947, U.S. dramatist and film director. His plays include *Sexual Perversity in Chicago* (1974), *American Buffalo* (1976), *Glengarry Glen Ross* (1983), and *The Spanish Prisoner* (1998).

mamey, mammee, *or* **mammee apple** (mæ'miː) *n* **1** a tropical American tree, *Mammea americana,* cultivated for its large edible fruits: family *Guttiferae.* **2** the fruit of this tree, having yellow pulp and a red skin. **3** another name for the **marmalade tree.** [C16: from Spanish *mamey,* from Haitian]

mamilla *or U.S.* **mammilla** (mæ'mɪlə) *n, pl* **-lae** (-liː). **1** a nipple or teat. **2** any nipple-shaped part or prominence. [C17: from Latin, diminutive of *mamma* breast] ▸ **'mamillary** *or U.S.* **'mammillary** *adj*

mamillate ('mæmɪˌleɪt), **mamillated** *or U.S.* **mammillate, mammillated** *adj* having nipples or nipple-like protuberances.

mamma[1] *n Chiefly U.S.* **1** ('mɑːmə, mə'mɑː). Also: **momma.** another word for **mother**[1]. **2** ('mɑːmə). *Informal.* a buxom and voluptuous woman. [C16: reduplication of childish syllable *ma;* compare Welsh *mam,* French *maman,* Russian *mama*]

mamma[2] ('mæmə) *n, pl* **-mae** (-miː). **1** the milk-secreting organ of female mammals: the breast in women, the udder in cows, sheep, etc. **2** (*functioning as pl*) breast-shaped protuberances, esp. from the base of cumulonimbus clouds. [C17: from Latin: breast]

mammal ('mæməl) *n* any animal of the *Mammalia,* a large class of warm-blooded vertebrates having mammary glands in the female, a thoracic diaphragm, and a four-chambered heart. The class includes the whales, carnivores, rodents, bats, primates, etc. [C19: via New Latin from Latin *mamma* breast] ▸ **mammalian** (mæ'meɪlɪən) *adj, n* ▸ **'mammalˌlike** *adj*

mammalogy (mæ'mælədʒɪ) *n* the branch of zoology concerned with the study of mammals. ▸ **mammalogical** (ˌmæmə'lɒdʒɪkᵊl) *adj* ▸ **mam'malogist** *n*

mammary ('mæmərɪ) *adj* of, relating to, or like a mamma or breast.

mammary gland *n* any of the milk-producing glands in mammals. In higher mammals each gland consists of a network of tubes and cavities connected to the exterior by a nipple.

mammee (mæ'miː) *n* a variant spelling of **mamey.**

mammet ('mæmɪt) *n* another word for **maumet.**

mammiferous (mæ'mɪfərəs) *adj* having breasts or mammae.

mammilla (mæ'mɪlə) *n, pl* **-lae** (-liː). the U.S. spelling of **mamilla.** ▸ **'mammillary** *adj*

mammillate ('mæmɪˌleɪt) *or* **mammillated** *adj* the U.S. spellings of **mamillate, mamillated.**

mammock ('mæmək) *Dialect.* ◆ *n* **1** a fragment. ◆ *vb* **2** (*tr*) to tear or shred. [C16: of unknown origin]

mammography (mæ'mɒgrəfɪ) *n* the technique of using X-rays to examine the breast in the early detection of cancer. ► **'mammoˌgraph** *or* **'mammoˌgram** *n*

mammon ('mæmən) *n* **1** riches or wealth regarded as a source of evil and corruption. **2** avarice or greed. [C14: via Late Latin from New Testament Greek *mammōnas,* from Aramaic *māmōnā* wealth] ► **'mammonish** *adj* ► **'mammonism** *n* ► **'mammonist** *or* **'mammonite** *n* ► **ˌmammon'istic** *adj*

Mammon ('mæmən) *n New Testament.* the personification of riches and greed in the form of a false god.

mammoth ('mæməθ) *n* **1** any large extinct elephant of the Pleistocene genus *Mammuthus* (or *Elephas*), such as *M. primigenius* (**woolly mammoth**), having a hairy coat and long curved tusks. ◆ *adj* **2** of gigantic size or importance. [C18: from Russian *mamot,* from Tartar *mamont,* perhaps from *mamma* earth, because of a belief that the animal made burrows]

Mammoth Cave National Park *n* a national park in W central Kentucky: established in 1941 to protect a system of limestone caverns.

mammy *or* **mammie** ('mæmɪ) *n, pl* **-mies. 1** a child's word for **mother**[1]. **2** *Chiefly southern U.S.* a Black woman employed as a nurse or servant to a White family.

mammy wagon *n* a W African vehicle built on a lorry chassis, capable of carrying both passengers and goods.

Mamoré (*Spanish* mamo're) *n* a river in central Bolivia, flowing north to the Beni River to form the Madeira River. Length: about 1500 km (930 miles).

mampara (mam'pɑːrə) *n S. African informal.* a clumsy Black African. [of unknown origin]

mampoer (məm'pʊə) *n S. African.* a home-distilled brandy made from peaches, prickly pears, etc. [Afrikaans, possibly from Sotho *mampuru,* strong man]

mamzer ('mɑmzə) *n* **1** a Yiddish slang word for **bastard. 2** *Judaism.* a child of an incestuous or adulterous union. [from Hebrew]

man (mæn) *n, pl* **men** (mɛn). **1** an adult male human being, as distinguished from a woman. **2** (*modifier*) male; masculine: *a man child.* **3** a human being regardless of sex or age, considered as a representative of mankind; a person. **4** (*sometimes cap.*) human beings collectively; mankind: *the development of man.* **5** Also called: **modern man. 5a** a member of any of the living races of *Homo sapiens,* characterized by erect bipedal posture, a highly developed brain, and powers of articulate speech, abstract reasoning, and imagination. **5b** any extinct member of the species *Homo sapiens,* such as Cro-Magnon man. **6** a member of any of the extinct species of the genus *Homo,* such as Java man, Heidelberg man, and Solo man. **7** an adult male human being with qualities associated with the male, such as courage or virility: *be a man.* **8** manly qualities or virtues: *the man in him was outraged.* **9a** a subordinate, servant, or employee contrasted with an employer or manager. **9b** (*in combination*): *the number of man-days required to complete a job.* **10** (*usually pl*) a member of the armed forces who does not hold commissioned, warrant, or noncommissioned rank (as in the phrase **officers and men**). **11** a member of a group, team, etc. **12** a husband, boyfriend, etc.: *man and wife.* **13** an expression used parenthetically to indicate an informal relationship between speaker and hearer. **14** a movable piece in various games, such as draughts. **15** *S. African slang.* any person: used as a term of address. **16** a vassal of a feudal lord. **17 as one man.** with unanimous action or response. **18 be one's own man.** to be independent or free. **19 he's your man.** he's the person needed (for a particular task, role, job, etc.). **20 man and boy.** from childhood. **21 sort out** *or* **separate the men from the boys.** to separate the experienced from the inexperienced. **22 to a man. 22a** unanimously. **22b** without exception: *they were slaughtered to a man.* ◆ *interj* **23** *Informal.* an exclamation or expletive, often indicating surprise or pleasure. ◆ *vb* **mans, manning, manned.** (*tr*) **24** to provide with sufficient men for operation, defence, etc.: *to man a ship.* **25** to take one's place at or near in readiness for action. **26** *Falconry.* to induce (a hawk or falcon) to endure the presence of and handling by man, esp. strangers. [Old English *mann;* related to Old Frisian *man,* Old High German *man,* Dutch *man,* Icelandic *mathr*] ► **'manless** *adj*

Man[1] (mæn) *n* **the.** (*sometimes not cap.*) *U.S.* **1** *Black slang.* a White man or White men collectively, esp. when in authority, in the police, or held in contempt. **2** *Slang.* a drug peddler.

Man[2] (mæn) *n* **Isle of.** an island in the British Isles, in the Irish Sea between Cumbria and Northern Ireland: a Crown possession with its own parliament, the Court of Tynwald; a dependency of Norway until 1266, when it came under Scottish rule; its own language, Manx, is now almost extinct. Capital: Douglas. Pop.: 72 600 (1998 est.). Area: 588 sq. km (227 sq. miles).

Man. *abbrev. for:* **1** Manila (paper). **2** Manitoba.

-man *n combining form.* indicating a person who has a role, works in a place, or operates equipment as specified: *salesman, barman, cameraman.*

USAGE The use of words ending in *-man* is avoided as implying a male in job advertisements, where sexual discrimination is illegal, and in many other contexts where a term that is not gender-specific is available, such as *salesperson, barperson, camera operator.*

mana ('mɑːnə) *n Anthropol.* **1** (in Polynesia, Melanesia, etc.) a concept of a life force, believed to be seated in the head, and associated with high social status and ritual power. **2** any power achieved by ritual means; prestige; authority. [from Polynesian]

man about town *n* a fashionable sophisticate, esp. one in a big city.

manacle ('mænək°l) *n* **1** (*usually pl*) a shackle, handcuff, or fetter, used to secure the hands of a prisoner, convict, etc. ◆ *vb* (*tr*) **2** to put manacles on. **3** to confine or constrain. [C14: via Old French from Latin *manicula,* diminutive of *manus* hand]

Manado (mə'nɑːdəʊ) *n* a variant of **Menado.**

manage ('mænɪdʒ) *vb* (*mainly tr*) **1** (*also intr*) to be in charge (of); administer: *to manage one's affairs; to manage a shop.* **2** to succeed in being able (to do something) despite obstacles; contrive: *did you manage to go to sleep?* **3** to have room, time, etc., for: *can you manage dinner tomorrow?* **4** to exercise control or domination over, often in a tactful or guileful manner. **5** (*intr*) to contrive to carry on despite difficulties, esp. financial ones: *he managed quite well on very little money.* **6** to wield or handle (a weapon). **7** *Rare.* to be frugal in the use of. ◆ *n* **8** an archaic word for **manège.** [C16: from Italian *maneggiare* to control, train (esp. horses), ultimately from Latin *manus* hand]

manageable ('mænɪdʒəb°l) *adj* able to be managed or controlled. ► **ˌmanagea'bility** *or* (*less commonly*) **'manageableness** *n* ► **'manageably** *adv*

managed bonds *pl n* investment in a combination of fixed interest securities, equities, gilts, and property, in which an investment manager, acting on a client's behalf, varies the amount invested in each according to the returns expected.

managed currency *n* a currency that is subject to governmental control with respect to the amount in circulation and the rate of exchange with other currencies.

management ('mænɪdʒmənt) *n* **1** the members of the executive or administration of an organization or business. See also **line management, middle management, top management. 2** managers or employers collectively. **3** the technique, practice, or science of managing or controlling. **4** the skilful or resourceful use of materials, time, etc. **5** the specific treatment of a disease, disorder, etc.

management accounting *n* another name for **cost accounting.**

management buyout *n* the purchase of a company by its managers, usually with outside backing from a bank or other institution.

management company *n* a company that manages a unit trust.

management information system *n* an arrangement of equipment and procedures, often computerized, that is designed to provide managers with information.

management union *n* a union that represents managers in negotiations with their employers concerning terms and conditions of employment.

manager ('mænɪdʒə) *n* **1** a person who directs or manages an organization, industry, shop, etc. **2** a person who controls the business affairs of an actor, entertainer, etc. **3** a person who controls the training of a sportsman or team. **4** a person who has a talent for managing efficiently. **5** *Law.* a person appointed by a court to carry on a business during receivership. **6** (in Britain) a member of either House of Parliament appointed to arrange a matter in which both Houses are concerned. **7** a computer program that organizes a resource, such as a set of files or a database. ► **'managerˌship** *n*

manageress (ˌmænɪdʒə'rɛs, 'mænɪdʒəˌrɛs) *n* a woman who is in charge of a shop, department, canteen, etc.

managerial (ˌmænɪ'dʒɪərɪəl) *adj* of or relating to a manager or to the functions, responsibilities, or position of management. ► **ˌmana'gerially** *adv*

managerialism (ˌmænɪ'dʒɪərɪəˌlɪzəm) *n* the application of managerial techniques of businesses to the running of other organizations, such as the civil service or local authorities. ► **ˌmana'gerialist** *n*

managing ('mænɪdʒɪŋ) *adj* having administrative control or authority: *a managing director.*

Managua (mə'nægwə; *Spanish* ma'naɣwa) *n* **1** the capital of Nicaragua, on the S shore of Lake Managua: chosen as capital in 1857. Pop.: 1 195 000 (1995 est.). **2 Lake.** a lake in W Nicaragua: drains into Lake Nicaragua by the Tipitapa River. Length: 61 km (38 miles). Width: about 26 km (16 miles).

manakin ('mænəkɪn) *n* **1** any small South American passerine bird of the family *Pipridae,* having a colourful plumage, short bill, and elaborate courtship behaviour. **2** a variant of **manikin.**

Manama (mə'nɑːmə) *n* the capital of Bahrain, at the N end of Bahrain Island: transit port. Pop.: 148 000 (1995 est.).

mañana *Spanish.* (ma'ɲana; *English* mə'njɑːnə) *n, adv* **a** tomorrow. **b** some other and later time.

Manáos (*Portuguese* mə'naus) *n* a variant spelling of **Manaus.**

Manassas (mə'næsəs) *n* a town in NE Virginia, west of Alexandria: site of the victory of Confederate forces in the Battles of Bull Run, or First and Second Manassas (1861; 1862), during the American Civil War. Pop.: 27 957 (1990).

Manasseh (mə'næsɪ) *n Old Testament.* **1** the elder son of Joseph (Genesis 41:51). **2** the Israelite tribe descended from him. **3** the territory of this tribe, in the upper Jordan valley. Douay spelling: **Manases** (mə'næsiːz).

manat (mæ'næt) *n* **1** the standard monetary unit of Azerbaijan, divided into 100 gopik. **2** the standard monetary unit of Turkmenistan, divided into 100 tenesi.

man-at-arms *n, pl* **men-at-arms.** a soldier, esp. a heavily armed mounted soldier in medieval times.

manatee (ˌmænə'tiː) *n* any sirenian mammal of the genus *Trichechus,* occurring in tropical coastal waters of America, the Caribbean, and Africa: family *Trichechidae.* They resemble whales and have a prehensile upper lip and a broad flattened tail. [C16: via Spanish from Carib *Manattoui*] ► **'manaˌtoid** *adj*

Manaus *or* **Manáos** (*Portuguese* mə'naus) *n* a port in N Brazil, capital of Amazonas state, on the Rio Negro 19 km (12 miles) above its confluence with the Amazon: chief commercial centre of the Amazon basin. Pop. conurbation: 1 189 000 (1995).

Manche (*French* mɑ̃ʃ) *n* **1** a department of NW France, in Basse-Normandie region. Capital: St Lô. Pop.: 484 100 (1995). Area: 6412 sq. km (2501 sq. miles). **2** La. the French name for the **English Channel.**

manchester (ˈmæntʃɪstə) *n Austral. and N.Z.* **1** household linen or cotton goods, such as sheets and towels. **2** Also called: **manchester department.** a section of a store where such goods are sold. [from MANCHESTER, England]

Manchester (ˈmæntʃɪstə) *n* **1** a city in NW England, in Manchester unitary authority, Greater Manchester: linked to the Mersey estuary by the **Manchester Ship Canal**: commercial and industrial centre, esp. of the cotton and textile trades; university (1846). Pop.: 402 889 (1991). Latin name: **Manˈcunium. 2** a unitary authority in NW England, in Greater Manchester. Pop.: 432 600 (1995 est.). Area: 116 sq. km (45 sq. miles).

Manchester terrier *n* a breed of terrier with a glossy black-and-tan coat. Also called (less commonly): **black-and-tan terrier.**

manchineel (ˌmæntʃɪˈniːl) *n* a tropical American euphorbiaceous tree, *Hippomane mancinella,* having fruit and milky highly caustic poisonous sap, which causes skin blisters. [C17: via French from Spanish MANZANILLA]

Manchu (mænˈtʃuː) *n* **1** (*pl* **-chus** *or* **-chu**) a member of a Mongoloid people of Manchuria who conquered China in the 17th century, establishing an imperial dynasty that lasted until 1912. **2** the language of this people, belonging to the Tungusic branch of the Altaic family. ◆ *adj* **3** Also: **Ching.** of or relating to the dynasty of the Manchus. [from Manchu, literally: pure]

Manchukuo *or* **Manchoukuo** (ˈmænˈtʃuːˈkwəʊ) *n* a former state of E Asia (1932–45), consisting of the three provinces of old Manchuria and Jehol.

Manchuria (mænˈtʃʊərɪə) *n* a region of NE China, historically the home of the Manchus, rulers of China from 1644 to 1912: includes part of the Inner Mongolian AR and the provinces of Heilongjiang, Jilin, and Liaoning. Area: about 1 300 000 sq. km (502 000 sq. miles). ▸ **Manˈchurian** *adj, n*

manciple (ˈmænsɪpᵊl) *n* a steward who buys provisions, esp. in a college, Inn of Court, or monastery. [C13: via Old French from Latin *mancipium* purchase, from *manceps* purchaser, from *manus* hand + *capere* to take]

Mancunian (mæŋˈkjuːnɪən) *n* **1** a native or inhabitant of Manchester. ◆ *adj* **2** of or relating to Manchester. [from Medieval Latin *Mancunium* Manchester]

-mancy *n combining form.* indicating divination of a particular kind: *chiromancy.* [from Old French *-mancie,* from Latin *-mantia,* from Greek *manteia* soothsaying] ▸ **-mantic** *adj combining form.*

Mandaean *or* **Mandean** (mænˈdɪən) *n* **1** a member of a Gnostic sect of Iraq. **2** the form of Aramaic used by this sect. ◆ *adj* **3** of or relating to this sect. [C19: from Aramaic *mandaya* Gnostics, from *mandā* knowledge] ▸ **Manˈdaeanism** *or* **Manˈdeanism** *n*

mandala (ˈmændələ, mænˈdɑːlə) *n* **1** *Hindu and Buddhist art.* any of various designs symbolizing the universe, usually circular. **2** *Psychol.* such a symbol expressing a person's striving for unity of the self. [Sanskrit: circle]

Mandalay (ˌmændəˈleɪ) *n* a city in central Myanmar, on the Irrawaddy River: the second largest city in the country and former capital of Burma and of Upper Burma; Buddhist religious centre. Pop.: 677 000 (1995 est.).

mandamus (mænˈdeɪməs) *n, pl* **-muses.** *Law.* formerly a writ from, now an order of, a superior court commanding an inferior tribunal, public official, corporation, etc., to carry out a public duty. [C16: Latin, literally: we command, from *mandāre* to command]

mandarin (ˈmændərɪn) *n* **1** (in the Chinese Empire) a member of any of the nine senior grades of the bureaucracy, entered by examinations. **2** a high-ranking official whose powers are extensive and thought to be outside political control. **3** a person of standing and influence, as in literary or intellectual circles. **4a** a small citrus tree, *Citrus nobilis,* cultivated for its edible fruit. **4b** the fruit of this tree, resembling the tangerine. [C16: from Portuguese *mandarim,* via Malay *menteri* from Sanskrit *mantrin* counsellor, from *mantra* counsel] ▸ **ˈmandarinate** *n*

Mandarin Chinese *or* **Mandarin** *n* the official language of China since 1917; the form of Chinese spoken by about two thirds of the population and taught in schools throughout China. See also **Chinese, Pekingese.**

Mandarin collar *n* a high stiff round collar.

mandarin duck *n* an Asian duck, *Aix galericulata,* the male of which has a brightly coloured and patterned plumage and crest.

mandate *n* (ˈmændeɪt, -dɪt). **1** an official or authoritative instruction or command. **2** *Politics.* the support or commission given to a government and its policies or an elected representative and his policies through an electoral victory. **3** (*often cap.*) Also called: **mandated territory.** (formerly) any of the territories under the trusteeship of the League of Nations administered by one of its member states. **4a** *Roman law.* a contract by which one person commissions another to act for him gratuitously and the other accepts the commission. **4b** *Contract law.* a contract of bailment under which the party entrusted with goods undertakes to perform gratuitously some service in respect of such goods. **4c** *Scots Law.* a contract by which a person is engaged to act in the management of the affairs of another. ◆ *vb* (ˈmændeɪt). (*tr*) **5** *International law.* to assign (territory) to a nation under a mandate. **6** to delegate authority to. **7** *Obsolete.* to give a command to. [C16: from Latin *mandātum* something commanded, from *mandāre* to command, perhaps from *manus* hand + *dāre* to give] ▸ **ˈmanˌdator** *n*

mandatory (ˈmændətərɪ, -trɪ) *adj* **1** having the nature or powers of a mandate. **2** obligatory; compulsory. **3** (of a state) having received a mandate over some territory. ◆ *n, pl* **-ries. 4** Also called: **mandatary.** a person or state holding a mandate. ▸ **ˈmandatorily** *adv*

Mande (ˈmɑːndeɪ) *n, pl* **-de** *or* **-des. 1** a group of African languages, a branch of the Niger-Congo family, spoken chiefly in Mali, Guinea, and Sierra Leone. ◆ *adj* **2** of or relating to this group of languages.

Mandela (mænˈdelə) *n* **1 Nelson (Rolihlahla).** born 1918, Black South African statesman: president of South Africa (1994–99). Jailed in 1962 for 5 years and, in 1964, for life, he was released in 1990 after a long international campaign; deputy president of the African National Congress (1990–91) and president (1991–97); elected president of South Africa in 1994; Nobel peace prize jointly with F. W. de Klerk in 1993. **2 (Numzano) Winnie.** born 1934, Black South African political activist: campaigned for the release of her husband Nelson Mandela; they divorced in 1996.

Mandelbrot set (ˈmændəlˌbrɒt) *n Maths.* a set of points in the complex plane that is self-replicating according to some predetermined rule such that the boundary of the set has fractal dimensions, used in the study of fractal geometry and in producing patterns in computer graphics. [C20: after Benoît *Mandelbrot* (born 1924), French mathematician, born in Poland]

Mandelstam *or* **Mandelshtam** (ˈmændᵊlˌʃtɑːm) *n* **1 Nadezhda (Yakovlevna)** (næˈdeʃdə), born *Nadezhda Khazina.* 1899–1980, Soviet writer, wife of Osip Mandelstam: noted for her memoirs *Hope against Hope* (1971) and *Hope Abandoned* (1973) describing life in Stalin's Russia. **2 Osip (Emilyevich)** (ˈɒsiːp). 1891–?1938, Soviet poet and writer, born in Warsaw; he was persecuted by Stalin and died in a labour camp. His works include *Tristia* (1922), *Poems* (1928), and the autobiographical *Journey to Armenia* (1933).

Mandeville (ˈmændəvɪl) *n* **1 Bernard de.** ?1670–1733, English author, born in Holland, noted for his satire *The Fable of the Bees* (1723). **2** Sir **John.** 14th century, English author of *The Travels of Sir John Mandeville.* The book claims to be an account of the author's journeys in the East but is largely a compilation from other works.

mandi (ˈmʌndɪ) *n* (in India) a big market. [Hindi]

mandible (ˈmændɪbᵊl) *n* **1** the lower jawbone in vertebrates. See **jaw** (sense 1). **2** either of a pair of mouthparts in insects and other arthropods that are usually used for biting and crushing food. **3** *Ornithol.* either the upper or the lower part of the bill, esp. the lower part. [C16: via Old French from Late Latin *mandibula* jaw, from *mandere* to chew] ▸ **mandibular** (mænˈdɪbjʊlə) *adj* ▸ **mandibulate** (mænˈdɪbjʊlɪt, -ˌleɪt) *n, adj*

Mandingo (mænˈdɪŋgəʊ) *n, pl* **-gos** *or* **-goes.** a former name for **Mande** or **Malinke.**

mandir (ˈmʌndɪə) *n* a Hindu or Jain temple. [Hindi, from Sanskrit *mandira*]

mandola (ˈmændələ) *n* an early type of mandolin. [from Italian]

mandolin *or* **mandoline** (ˌmændəˈlɪn) *n* a plucked stringed instrument related to the lute, having four pairs of strings tuned in ascending fifths stretched over a small light body with a fretted fingerboard. It is usually played with a plectrum, long notes being sustained by the tremolo. [C18: via French from Italian *mandolino,* diminutive of *mandora* lute, ultimately from Greek *pandoura* musical instrument with three strings] ▸ **ˌmandoˈlinist** *n*

mandorla (mænˈdɔːlə) *n* (in painting, sculpture, etc.) an almond-shaped area of light, usually surrounding the resurrected Christ or the Virgin at the Assumption. Also called: **vesica.** [from Italian, literally: almond, from Late Latin *amandula;* see ALMOND]

mandrake (ˈmændreɪk) *or* **mandragora** (mænˈdrægərə) *n* **1** a Eurasian solanaceous plant, *Mandragora officinarum,* with purplish flowers and a forked root. It was formerly thought to have magic powers and a narcotic was prepared from its root. **2** another name for the **May apple.** [C14: probably via Middle Dutch from Latin *mandragoras* (whence Old English *mandragora*), from Greek. The form *mandrake* was probably adopted through folk etymology, because of the allegedly human appearance of the root and because *drake* (dragon) suggested magical powers]

mandrel *or* **mandril** (ˈmændrəl) *n* **1** a spindle on which a workpiece is supported during machining operations. **2** a shaft or arbor on which a machining tool is mounted. **3** the driving spindle in the headstock of a lathe. **4** *Brit.* a miner's pick. [C16: perhaps related to French *mandrin* lathe]

mandrill (ˈmændrɪl) *n* an Old World monkey, *Mandrillus sphinx,* of W Africa. It has a short tail and brown hair, and the ridged muzzle, nose, and hindquarters are red and blue. [C18: from MAN + DRILL[4]]

manducate (ˈmændjʊˌkeɪt) *vb* (*tr*) *Literary.* to eat or chew. [C17: from Latin *mandūcāre* to chew] ▸ **ˌmanduˈcation** *n* ▸ **ˌmanduˈcatory** *adj*

mane (meɪn) *n* **1** the long coarse hair that grows from the crest of the neck in such mammals as the lion and horse. **2** long thick human hair. [Old English *manu;* related to Old High German *mana,* Old Norse *mǫn,* and perhaps to Old English *mene* and Old High German *menni* necklace] ▸ **maned** *adj* ▸ **ˈmaneless** *adj*

man-eater *n* **1** an animal, such as a tiger, that has become accustomed to eating human flesh. **2** any of various sharks that feed on human flesh, esp. the great white shark (*Carcharodon carcharias*). **3** a human cannibal. **4** *Informal.* a woman with many lovers. ▸ **ˈman-ˌeating** *adj*

manège *or* **manege** (mæˈneɪʒ) *n* **1** the art of training horses and riders. Compare **dressage. 2** a riding school. [C17: via French from Italian *maneggio,* from *maneggiare* to MANAGE]

manes (ˈmɑːneɪz; *Latin* ˈmɑːnes) *pl n* (*sometimes cap.*) (in Roman legend) **1** the spirits of the dead, often revered as minor deities. **2** (*functioning as sing*) the shade of a dead person. [C14: from Latin, probably: the good ones, from Old Latin *mānus* good]

Manes (ˈmeɪniːz) *n* See **Mani.**

Manet (*French* manɛ) *n* **Édouard** (edwar). 1832–83, French painter. His painting *Le Déjeuner sur l'herbe* (1863), which was condemned by the Parisian establishment, was acclaimed by the impressionists, whom he decisively influenced.

maneuver (məˈnuːvə) *n, vb* the usual U.S. spelling of **manoeuvre.** ▸ **maˈneuverable** *adj* ▸ **maˌneuveraˈbility** *n* ▸ **maˈneuverer** *n* ▸ **maˈneuvering** *n*

man Friday *n* a loyal male servant or assistant. [after the native in Daniel Defoe's novel *Robinson Crusoe* (1719)]

manful (ˈmænfʊl) *adj* a less common word for **manly.** ▸ **ˈmanfully** *adv* ▸ **ˈmanfulness** *n*

manga ('mæŋgə) *n, pl* **manga. a** a type of Japanese comic book with an adult theme. **b** (*as modifier*): *manga videos.*

mangabey ('mæŋgə,beɪ) *n* any of several large agile arboreal Old World monkeys of the genus *Cercocebus,* of central Africa, having long limbs and tail and white upper eyelids. [C18: after the name of a region in Madagascar]

Mangalore (,mæŋgə'lɔː) *n* a port in S India, in Karnataka on the Malabar Coast. Pop.: 273 304 (1991).

manganate ('mæŋgə,neɪt) *n* a salt of manganic acid.

manganese ('mæŋgə,niːz) *n* a brittle greyish-white metallic element that exists in four allotropic forms, occurring principally in pyrolusite and rhodonite: used in making steel and ferromagnetic alloys. Symbol: Mn; atomic no.: 25; atomic wt.: 54.93805; valency: 1, 2 ,3, 4, 6, or 7; relative density: 7.21–7.44; melting pt.: 1246±3°C; boiling pt.: 2062°C. [C17: via French from Italian *manganese,* probably altered form of Medieval Latin MAGNESIA]

manganese bronze *n* any of various alloys containing copper (55–60 per cent), zinc (35–42 per cent), and manganese (about 3.5 per cent).

manganese nodule *n Geology.* a small irregular concretion found on deep ocean floors having high concentrations of certain metals, esp. manganese.

manganese steel *n* any very hard steel containing manganese (11–14 per cent), used in dredger buckets, rock-crushers, railway points, etc.

manganic (mæn'gænɪk) *adj* of or containing manganese in the trivalent state.

manganic acid *n* a hypothetical dibasic acid known only in solution and in the form of manganate salts. Formula: H_2MnO_4.

Manganin ('mæŋgənɪn) *n Trademark.* an alloy of copper containing manganese (13–18 per cent) and nickel (1–4 per cent): it has a high electrical resistance that does not vary greatly with temperature and is used in resistors.

manganite ('mæŋgə,naɪt) *n* a blackish mineral consisting of basic manganese oxide in monoclinic crystalline form: a source of manganese. Formula: MnO(OH).

manganous ('mæŋgənəs, mæn'gænəs) *adj* of or containing manganese in the divalent state.

mange (meɪndʒ) *n* an infectious disorder mainly affecting domestic animals, characterized by itching, formation of papules and vesicles, and loss of hair: caused by parasitic mites. [C14: from Old French *mangeue* itch, literally: eating, from *mangier* to eat]

mangelwurzel ('mæŋgᵊl,wɜːzᵊl) *or* **mangoldwurzel** ('mæŋgəʊld,wɜːzᵊl) *n* a Eurasian variety of the beet plant, *Beta vulgaris,* cultivated as a cattle food, having a large yellowish root. Often shortened to **mangel, mangold.** [C18: from German *Mangoldwurzel,* from *Mangold* beet + *Wurzel* root]

manger ('meɪndʒə) *n* **1** a trough or box in a stable, barn, etc., from which horses or cattle feed. **2** *Nautical.* a basin-like construction in the bows of a vessel for catching water draining from an anchor rode or coming in through the hawseholes. [C14: from Old French *maingeure* food trough, from *mangier* to eat, ultimately from Latin *mandūcāre* to chew]

mangetout ('mɑ̃ʒ'tuː) *n* a variety of garden pea in which the pod is also edible. Also called: **sugar pea.** [C20: from French: eat all]

mangey ('meɪndʒɪ) *adj* **-gier, -giest.** a variant spelling of **mangy.**

mangle[1] ('mæŋgᵊl) *vb* (*tr*) **1** to mutilate, disfigure, or destroy by cutting, crushing, or tearing. **2** to ruin, spoil, or mar. [C14: from Norman French *mangler,* probably from Old French *mahaignier* to maim] ► **'mangler** *n* ► **'mangled** *adj*

mangle[2] ('mæŋgᵊl) *n* **1** Also called: **wringer.** a machine for pressing or drying wet textiles, clothes, etc., consisting of two heavy rollers between which the cloth is passed. ♦ *vb* (*tr*) **2** to press or dry in a mangle. [C18: from Dutch *mangel,* ultimately from Late Latin *manganum.* See MANGONEL]

mango ('mæŋgəʊ) *n, pl* **-goes** *or* **-gos. 1** a tropical Asian anacardiaceous evergreen tree, *Mangifera indica,* cultivated in the tropics for its fruit. **2** the ovoid edible fruit of this tree, having a smooth rind and sweet juicy orange-yellow flesh. [C16: via Portuguese from Malay *mangā,* from Tamil *mānkāy* from *mān* mango tree + *kāy* fruit]

mangonel ('mæŋgə,nɛl) *n History.* a war engine for hurling stones. [C13: via Old French from Medieval Latin *manganellus,* ultimately from Greek *manganon*]

mangosteen ('mæŋgəʊ,stiːn) *n* **1** an East Indian tree, *Garcinia mangostana,* with thick leathery leaves and edible fruit: family *Guttiferae.* **2** the fruit of this tree, having a sweet juicy pulp and a hard skin. [C16: from Malay *mangustan*]

mangrove ('mæŋgrəʊv, 'mæn-) *n* **1a** any tropical evergreen tree or shrub of the genus *Rhizophora,* having stiltlike intertwining aerial roots and forming dense thickets along coasts: family *Rhizophoraceae.* **1b** (*as modifier*): *mangrove swamp.* **2** any of various similar trees or shrubs of the genus *Avicennia:* family *Avicenniaceae.* [C17 *mangrow* (changed through influence of *grove*), from Portuguese *mangue,* ultimately from Taino]

mangy *or* **mangey** ('meɪndʒɪ) *adj* **-gier, -giest. 1** having or caused by mange: *a mangy dog.* **2** scruffy or shabby: *a mangy carpet.* **3** *Irish informal.* stingy or miserly: *a mangy reward.* ► **'mangily** *adv* ► **'manginess** *n*

manhandle ('mæn,hændᵊl, ,mæn'hændᵊl) *vb* (*tr*) **1** to handle or push (someone) about roughly. **2** to move or do by manpower rather than by machinery. [C19: from MAN + HANDLE; sense 1 perhaps also influenced by Devon dialect *manangle* to mangle]

Manhattan (mæn'hætᵊn, mən-) *n* **1** an island at the N end of New York Bay, between the Hudson, East, and Harlem Rivers: administratively (with adjacent islets) a borough of New York City; a major financial, commercial, and cultural centre. Pop.: 1 487 536 (1990). Area: 47 sq. km (22 sq. miles). **2** a mixed drink consisting of four parts whisky, one part vermouth, and a dash of bitters.

Manhattan District *n* (during World War II) the code name for a unit of U.S. army engineers established in 1942 to produce the atomic bomb in secret. Also called: **Manhattan Project.**

manhole ('mæn,həʊl) *n* **1** Also called: **inspection chamber.** a shaft with a removable cover that leads down to a sewer or drain. **2** a hole, usually with a detachable cover, through which a man can enter a boiler, tank, etc.

manhood ('mænhʊd) *n* **1** the state or quality of being a man or being manly. **2** men collectively. **3** the state of being human.

manhood suffrage *n* the right of adult male citizens to vote.

man-hour *n* a unit for measuring work in industry, equal to the work done by one man in one hour.

manhunt ('mæn,hʌnt) *n* an organized search, usually by police, for a wanted man or fugitive. ► **'man,hunter** *n*

Mani ('mɑːnɪ) *n* ?216–?276 A.D., Persian prophet who founded Manichaeism. Also called: **Manes, Manichaeus.**

mania ('meɪnɪə) *n* **1** a mental disorder characterized by great excitement and occasionally violent behaviour. See also **manic-depressive. 2** an obsessional enthusiasm or partiality: *a mania for mushrooms.* [C14: via Late Latin from Greek: madness]

-mania *n combining form.* indicating extreme desire or pleasure of a specified kind or an abnormal excitement aroused by something: *kleptomania; nymphomania; pyromania.* [from MANIA] ► **-maniac** *n and adj combining form.*

maniac ('meɪnɪ,æk) *n* **1** a wild disorderly person. **2** a person who has a great craving or enthusiasm for something: *a football maniac.* **3** *Psychiatry, obsolete.* a person afflicted with mania. [C17: from Late Latin *maniacus* belonging to madness, from Greek]

maniacal (mə'naɪəkᵊl) *or* **maniac** ('meɪnɪæk) *adj* **1** affected with or characteristic of mania. **2** characteristic of or befitting a maniac: *maniacal laughter.* ► **ma'niacally** *adv*

manic ('mænɪk) *adj* **1** characterizing, denoting, or affected by mania. ♦ *n* **2** a person afflicted with mania. [C19: from Greek, from MANIA]

manic-depressive *Psychiatry.* ♦ *adj* **1** denoting a mental disorder characterized either by an alternation between extreme euphoria and deep depression (bipolar manic-depressive disorder or syndrome) or by depression on its own or (rarely) by elation on its own (unipolar disorder). ♦ *n* **2** a person afflicted with this disorder. Compare **cyclothymia.**

Manichaeism *or* **Manicheism** ('mænɪkiː,ɪzəm) *n* **1** the system of religious doctrines, including elements of Gnosticism, Zoroastrianism, Christianity, Buddhism, etc., taught by the Persian prophet Mani about the 3rd century A.D. It was based on a supposed primordial conflict between light and darkness or goodness and evil. **2** *Chiefly R.C. Church.* any similar heretical philosophy involving a radical dualism. [C14: from Late Latin *Manichaeus,* from Late Greek *Manikhaios* of Mani] ► **,Mani'chaean** *or* **,Mani'chean** *adj, n* ► **'Manichee** *n*

Manichaeus *or* **Manicheus** (,mænɪ'kiːəs) *n* See **Mani.**

manicotti (,mænɪ'kɒtɪ) *pl n* large tubular noodles, usually stuffed with ricotta cheese and baked in a tomato sauce. [Italian: sleeves, plural of *manicotto,* diminutive of *manica* sleeve]

manicure ('mænɪ,kjʊə) *n* **1** care of the hands and fingernails, involving shaping the nails, removing cuticles, etc. **2** another word for **manicurist.** ♦ *vb* **3** to care for (the hands and fingernails) in this way. **4** (*tr*) to trim neatly. [C19: from French, from Latin *manus* hand + *cūra* care]

manicurist ('mænɪ,kjʊərɪst) *n* a person who gives manicures, esp. as a profession.

manifest ('mænɪ,fɛst) *adj* **1** easily noticed or perceived; obvious; plain. **2** *Psychoanal.* of or relating to the ostensible elements of a dream: *manifest content.* Compare **latent** (sense 5). ♦ *vb* **3** (*tr*) to show plainly; reveal or display: *to manifest great emotion.* **4** (*tr*) to prove beyond doubt. **5** (*intr*) (of a disembodied spirit) to appear in visible form. **6** (*tr*) to list in a ship's manifest. ♦ *n* **7** a customs document containing particulars of a ship, its cargo, and its destination. **8a** a list of cargo, passengers, etc., on an aeroplane. **8b** a list of railway trucks or their cargo. **8c** *Chiefly U.S. and Canadian.* a fast freight train carrying perishables. [C14: from Latin *manifestus* plain, literally: struck with the hand, from *manū* with the hand + *-festus* struck] ► **'mani,festable** *adj* ► **'mani,festly** *adv* ► **'mani,festness** *n*

manifestation (,mænɪfɛ'steɪʃən) *n* **1** the act of demonstrating; display: *a manifestation of solidarity.* **2** the state of being manifested. **3** an indication or sign. **4** a public demonstration of feeling. **5** the materialization of a disembodied spirit. ► **,manifes'tational** *adj* ► **,mani'festative** *adj*

Manifest Destiny *n* (esp. in the 19th-century U.S.) the belief that the U.S. was a chosen land that had been allotted the entire North American continent by God.

manifesto (,mænɪ'fɛstəʊ) *n, pl* **-tos** *or* **-toes.** a public declaration of intent, policy, aims, etc., as issued by a political party, government, or movement. [C17: from Italian, from *manifestare* to MANIFEST]

manifold ('mænɪ,fəʊld) *adj Formal.* **1** of several different kinds; multiple: *manifold reasons.* **2** having many different forms, features, or elements: *manifold breeds of dog.* ♦ *n* **3** something having many varied parts, forms, or features. **4** a copy of a page, book, etc. **5** a chamber or pipe with a number of inlets or outlets used to collect or distribute a fluid. In an internal-combustion engine the **inlet manifold** carries the vaporized fuel from the carburettor to the inlet ports and the **exhaust manifold** carries the exhaust gases away. **6** *Maths.* **6a** a collection of objects or a set. **6b** a topological space having specific properties. **7** (in the philosophy of Kant) the totality of the separate elements of sensation which are then organized by the active mind and conceptualized as a perception of an external object. ♦ *vb* **8** (*tr*) to duplicate (a page, book, etc.). **9** to make manifold; multiply. [Old English *manigfeald.* See MANY, -FOLD] ► **'mani,folder** *n* ► **'mani,foldly** *adv* ► **'mani,foldness** *n*

manikin, mannikin ('mænɪkɪn) *or* (*formerly*) **manakin** *n* **1** a little man; dwarf or child. **2a** an anatomical model of the body or a part of the body, esp. for use in medical or art instruction. **2b** Also called: **phantom.** an anatomical model of a fully developed fetus, for use in teaching midwifery or obstetrics. **3** variant spellings of **mannequin.** [C17: from Dutch *manneken,* diminutive of MAN]

Manila (məˈnɪlə) *n* **1** the chief port of the Philippines, on S Luzon on Manila Bay: capital of the republic until 1948 and from 1976; seat of the Far Eastern University and the University of Santo Tomas (1611). Pop.: 1 894 667 (1991 est.), with a conurbation of 8 594 150 (1994 est.). **2** a type of cigar made in this city. **3** (*often not cap.*) short for **Manila hemp, Manila paper.**

Manila Bay *n* an almost landlocked inlet of the South China Sea in the Philippines, in W Luzon: mostly forms Manila harbour. Area: 1994 sq. km (770 sq. miles).

Manila hemp *or* **Manilla hemp** *n* a fibre obtained from the plant abaca, used for rope, paper, etc.

Manila paper *or* **Manilla paper** *n* a strong usually brown paper made from Manila hemp or similar fibres.

Manila rope *or* **Manilla rope** *n* rope of Manila hemp.

manilla (məˈnɪlə) *n* an early form of currency in W Africa in the pattern of a small bracelet. [from Spanish: bracelet, diminutive of *mano* hand, from Latin *manus*]

manille (mæˈnɪl) *n* (in ombre and quadrille) the second best trump. [C17: from French, from Spanish *malilla,* diminutive of *mala* bad]

Maninke (məˈnɪŋkə) *n, pl* **-ke** *or* **-kes.** a variant of **Malinke.**

man in the moon *n* **1** the moon when considered to resemble the face of a man. **2** (in folklore and nursery rhyme) a character dwelling in the moon.

man in the street *n* the typical or ordinary person, esp. as a hypothetical unit in statistics.

manioc (ˈmænɪˌɒk) *or* **manioca** (ˌmænɪˈəʊkə) *n* another name for **cassava** (sense 1). [C16: from Tupi *mandioca;* earlier form *manihot* from French, from Guarani *mandio*]

maniple (ˈmænɪpᵊl) *n* **1** (in ancient Rome) a unit of 120 to 200 foot soldiers. **2** *Christianity.* an ornamental band formerly worn on the left arm by the celebrant at the Eucharist. [C16: from Medieval Latin *manipulus* (the Eucharistic vestment), from Latin, literally: a handful, from *manus* hand]

manipular (məˈnɪpjʊlə) *adj* **1** of or relating to an ancient Roman maniple. **2** of or relating to manipulation.

manipulate (məˈnɪpjʊˌleɪt) *vb* **1** (*tr*) to handle or use, esp. with some skill, in a process or action: *to manipulate a pair of scissors.* **2** to negotiate, control, or influence (something or someone) cleverly, skilfully, or deviously. **3** to falsify (a bill, accounts, etc.) for one's own advantage. **4** (in physiotherapy) to examine or treat manually, as in loosening a joint. [C19: back formation from *manipulation,* from Latin *manipulus* handful] ▸ **manipulability** (məˌnɪpjʊləˈbɪlɪtɪ) *n* ▸ **maˈnipuˌlatable** *or* **maˈnipulable** *adj* ▸ **maˌnipuˈlation** *n* ▸ **maˈnipulative** *adj* ▸ **maˈnipulatively** *adv* ▸ **maˈnipuˌlator** *n* ▸ **maˈnipulatory** *adj*

Manipur (ˌmʌnɪˈpʊə) *n* a state in NE India: largely densely forested mountains. Capital: Imphal. Pop.: 2 010 000 (1994 est.). Area: 22 327 sq. km (8621 sq. miles).

Manisa (ˈmɑːnɪˌsɑː) *n* a city in W Turkey: the Byzantine seat of government (1204–1313). Pop.: 1 191 287 (1995 est.).

Manitoba (ˌmænɪˈtəʊbə) *n* **1** a province of W Canada: consists of prairie in the southwest, with extensive forests in the north and tundra near Hudson Bay in the northeast. Capital: Winnipeg. Pop.: 1 145 200 (1997 est.). Area: 650 090 sq. km (251 000 sq. miles). Abbrev.: **MB. 2 Lake.** a lake in W Canada, in S Manitoba: fed by the outflow from Lake Winnipegosis; drains into Lake Winnipeg. Area: 4706 sq. km (1817 sq. miles). ▸ ˌ**Maniˈtoban** *n, adj*

manitou, manitu (ˈmænɪˌtuː), *or* **manito** (ˈmænɪˌtəʊ) *n, pl* **-tous, -tus, -tos** *or* **-tou, -tu, -to.** (among the Algonquian Indians) a deified spirit or force. [C17: from Algonquian; related to Ojibwa *manito* spirit]

Manitoulin Island (ˌmænɪˈtuːlɪn) *n* an island in N Lake Huron in Ontario: the largest freshwater island in the world. Length: 129 km (80 miles). Width: up to 48 km (30 miles).

Manizales (ˌmænɪˈzɑːlɛs; *Spanish* maniˈθales) *n* a city in W Colombia, in the Cordillera Central of the Andes at an altitude of 2100 m (7000 ft.): commercial centre of a rich coffee-growing area. Pop.: 358 194 (1997 est.).

man jack *n Informal.* a single individual (in the phrases **every man jack, no man jack**).

mankind (ˌmænˈkaɪnd) *n* **1** human beings collectively; humanity. **2** men collectively, as opposed to womankind.

USAGE Some people object to the use of *mankind* to refer to all human beings and prefer the term *humankind.*

manky (ˈmæŋkɪ) *adj* **mankier, mankiest.** *Slang.* **1** worthless, rotten, or in bad taste. **2** dirty, filthy, or bad. [via Polari from Italian *mancare* to be lacking]

Manley (ˈmænlɪ) *n* **Michael Norman.** 1924–97, Jamaican statesman; prime minister of Jamaica (1972–80; 1989–92).

manlike (ˈmænˌlaɪk) *adj* resembling or befitting a man.

man lock *n Civil engineering.* an airlock that allows workmen to pass in and out of spaces with differing air pressures.

manly (ˈmænlɪ) *adj* **-lier, -liest. 1** possessing qualities, such as vigour or courage, generally regarded as appropriate to or typical of a man; masculine. **2** characteristic of or befitting a man: *a manly sport.* ▸ **ˈmanliness** *n*

man-made *adj* made or produced by man; artificial.

Mann (*German* man) *n* **1 Heinrich** (ˈhainrɪç). 1871–1950, German novelist: works include *Professor Unrat* (1905), which was filmed as *The Blue Angel* (1928), and *Man of Straw* (1918). **2** his brother, **Thomas** (ˈtoːmas). 1875–1955, German novelist, in the U.S. after 1937. His works deal mainly with the problem of the artist in bourgeois society and include the short story *Death in Venice* (1913) and the novels *Buddenbrooks* (1900), *The Magic Mountain* (1924), and *Doctor Faustus* (1947): Nobel prize for literature 1929.

manna (ˈmænə) *n* **1** *Old Testament.* the miraculous food which sustained the Israelites in the wilderness (Exodus 16:14–36). **2** any spiritual or divine nourishment. **3** a windfall; an unexpected gift (esp. in the phrase **manna from heaven**). **4** a sweet substance obtained from various plants, esp. from an ash tree, *Fraxinus ornus* (**manna** or **flowering ash**) of S Europe, used as a mild laxative. [Old English via Late Latin from Greek, from Hebrew *mān*]

Mannar (məˈnɑː) *n* **Gulf of.** the part of the Indian Ocean between SE India and the island of Sri Lanka: pearl fishing.

manned (mænd) *adj* **1** supplied or equipped with men, esp. soldiers. **2** (of spacecraft, aircraft, etc.) having a human crew.

mannequin (ˈmænɪkɪn) *n* **1** a woman who wears the clothes displayed at a fashion show; model. **2** a life-size dummy of the human body used to fit or display clothes. **3** *Arts.* another name for **lay figure.** [C18: via French from Dutch *manneken* MANIKIN]

manner (ˈmænə) *n* **1** a way of doing or being. **2** a person's bearing and behaviour: *she had a cool manner.* **3** the style or customary way of doing or accomplishing something: *sculpture in the Greek manner.* **4** type or kind: *what manner of man is this?* **5** mannered style, as in art; mannerism. **6 by all manner of means.** certainly; of course. **7 by no manner of means.** definitely not: *he was by no manner of means a cruel man.* **8 in a manner of speaking.** in a way; so to speak. **9 to the manner born.** naturally fitted to a specified role or activity. ◆ See also **manners.** [C12: via Norman French from Old French *maniere,* from Vulgar Latin *manuāria* (unattested) a way of handling something, noun use of Latin *manuārius* belonging to the hand, from *manus* hand]

mannered (ˈmænəd) *adj* **1** having idiosyncrasies or mannerisms; affected: *mannered gestures.* **2** of or having mannerisms of style, as in art or literature. **3** (*in combination*) having manners as specified: *ill-mannered.*

Mannerheim (ˈmænəˌheɪm) *n* Baron **Carl Gustaf Emil.** 1867–1951, Finnish soldier and statesman; president of Finland (1944–46).

mannerism (ˈmænəˌrɪzəm) *n* **1** a distinctive and individual gesture or trait; idiosyncrasy. **2** (*often cap.*) a principally Italian movement in art and architecture between the High Renaissance and Baroque periods (1520–1600) that sought to represent an ideal of beauty rather than natural images of it, using characteristic distortion and exaggeration of human proportions, perspective, etc. **3** adherence to a distinctive or affected manner, esp. in art or literature. ▸ **ˈmannerist** *n* ▸ ˌ**mannerˈistic** *or* ˌ**mannerˈistical** *adj* ▸ ˌ**mannerˈistically** *adv*

mannerless (ˈmænəlɪs) *adj* having bad manners; boorish. ▸ **ˈmannerlessness** *n*

mannerly (ˈmænəlɪ) *adj* **1** well-mannered; polite; courteous. ◆ *adv* **2** *Now rare.* with good manners; politely; courteously. ▸ **ˈmannerliness** *n*

manners (ˈmænəz) *pl n* **1** social conduct: *he has the manners of a pig.* **2** a socially acceptable way of behaving.

Mannheim[1] (ˈmænhaɪm; *German* ˈmanhaɪm) *n* a city in SW Germany, in Baden-Württemberg at the confluence of the Rhine and Neckar: one of Europe's largest inland harbours; a cultural and musical centre. Pop.: 311 292 (1996 est.).

Mannheim[2] (*Hungarian* ˈmanhaɪm) *n* **Karl** (karl). 1893–1947, Hungarian sociologist, living in Britain from 1933: author of *Ideology and Utopia* (1929) and *Man and Society in an Age of Reconstruction* (1941).

Mannheim School *n Music.* a group of musicians and composers connected with the court orchestra at Mannheim during the mid-18th century, who evolved the controlled orchestral crescendo as well as a largely homophonic musical style.

mannikin (ˈmænɪkɪn) *n* a variant spelling of **manikin.**

Manning (ˈmænɪŋ) *n* **1 Henry Edward.** 1808–92, British churchman. Originally an Anglican, he was converted to Roman Catholicism (1851) and made archbishop of Westminster (1865) and cardinal (1875). **2 Olivia.** 1908–80, British novelist and short-story writer, best known for her novel sequence *Fortunes of War,* comprising the *Balkan Trilogy* (1960–65) and the *Levant Trilogy* (1977–80).

mannish (ˈmænɪʃ) *adj* **1** (of a woman) having or displaying qualities regarded as typical of a man. **2** of or resembling a man. ▸ **ˈmannishly** *adv* ▸ **ˈmannishness** *n*

mannitol (ˈmænɪˌtɒl) *or* **mannite** (ˈmænaɪt) *n* a white crystalline water-soluble sweet-tasting alcohol, found in plants and used in diet sweets and as a dietary supplement (**E421**). Formula: $C_6H_8(OH)_6$. [from MANNOSE + -ITE[2] + -OL[1]] ▸ **mannitic** (məˈnɪtɪk) *adj*

mannose (ˈmænəʊs, -nəʊz) *n* a hexose sugar found in mannitol and many polysaccharides. Formula: $C_6H_{12}O_6$. [C20: from MANNA + -OSE[2]]

Mann-Whitney test (ˈmænˈwɪtnɪ) *n* a statistical test of the difference between the distributions of data collected in two experimental conditions applied to unmatched groups of subjects but comparing the distributions of the ranks of the scores. Also called: **Wilcoxon Mann-Whitney test.**

manoeuvre *or U.S.* **maneuver** (məˈnuːvə) *n* **1** a contrived, complicated, and possibly deceptive plan or action: *political manoeuvres.* **2** a movement or action requiring dexterity and skill. **3a** a tactic or movement of one or a number of military or naval units. **3b** (*pl*) tactical exercises, usually on a large scale. **4** a planned movement of an aircraft in flight. **5** any change from the straight steady course of a ship. ◆ *vb* **6** (*tr*) to contrive or accomplish with skill or cunning. **7** (*intr*) to manipulate situations, etc., in order to gain some end: *to manoeuvre for the leadership.* **8** (*intr*) to perform a manoeuvre or manoeuvres. **9** to move or deploy or be moved or deployed, as military units, etc. [C15: from French, from Medieval Latin *manuopera* manual work, from Latin *manū operāre* to work with the hand] ▸ **maˈnoeuvrable** *or U.S.* **maˈneuverable** *adj* ▸ **maˌnoeuvraˈbility** *or U.S.* **maˌneuveraˈbility** *n* ▸ **maˈnoeuvrer** *or U.S.* **maˈneuverer** *n* ▸ **maˈnoeuvring** *or U.S.* **maˈneuvering** *n*

man of God *n* **1** a saint or prophet. **2** a clergyman.

man of straw *n* 1 a person of little substance. 2 Also called: **straw man.** *Chiefly U.S.* a person used as a cover for some dubious plan or enterprise; front man.

man-of-war *or* **man o' war** *n, pl* **men-of-war, men o' war.** 1 a warship. 2 See **Portuguese man-of-war.**

man-of-war bird *or* **man-o'-war bird** *n* another name for **frigate bird.**

Manolete (*Spanish* mano'lete) *n* original name *Manuel Rodriguez y Sánchez.* 1917–47, Spanish bullfighter.

manometer (mə'nɒmɪtə) *n* an instrument for comparing pressures; typically a glass U-tube containing mercury, in which pressure is indicated by the difference in levels in the two arms of the tube. [C18: from French *manomètre,* from Greek *manos* sparse + *metron* measure] ▸ **manometric** (ˌmænəʊ'metrɪk) *or* ˌ**mano'metrical** *adj* ▸ ˌ**mano'metrically** *adv* ▸ **ma'nometry** *n*

manor ('mænə) *n* 1 (in medieval Europe) the manor house of a lord and the lands attached to it. 2 (before 1776 in some North American colonies) a tract of land granted with rights of inheritance by royal charter. 3 a manor house. 4 a landed estate. 5 *Brit. slang.* a geographical area of operation, esp. of a local police force. [C13: from Old French *manoir* dwelling, from *maneir* to dwell, from Latin *manēre* to remain] ▸ **manorial** (mə'nɔːrɪəl) *adj*

man orchid *n* an orchid, *Aceras anthropophorum,* having greenish or reddish flowers in a loose spike, with a deeply lobed dark brown lip thought to resemble the silhouette of a man.

manor house *n* (esp. formerly) the house of the lord of a manor.

manoscopy (mə'nɒskəpɪ) *n Chem.* the measurement of the densities of gases.

manpower ('mænˌpaʊə) *n* 1 power supplied by men. 2 a unit of power based on the rate at which a man can work; approximately 75 watts. 3 available or suitable power: *the manpower of a battalion.*

manpower planning *n* a procedure used in organizations to balance future requirements for all levels of employee with the availability of such employees.

Manpower Services Commission *n Brit.* the former name of the **Training Agency.**

manqué *French.* (mɑ̃ke; *English* 'mɒŋkeɪ) *adj* (*postpositive*) unfulfilled; potential; would-be: *the manager is an actor manqué.* [C19: literally: having missed]

Manresa (*Spanish* man'rɛsa) *n* a city in NE Spain: contains a cave used as the spiritual retreat of St Ignatius Loyola. Pop.: 65 607 (1988 est.).

manrope ('mænˌrəʊp) *n Nautical.* a rope railing.

mansard ('mænsɑːd, -səd) *n* 1 Also called: **mansard roof.** a roof having two slopes on both sides and both ends, the lower slopes being steeper than the upper. Compare **gambrel roof.** 2 an attic having such a roof. [C18: from French *mansarde,* after François MANSART]

Mansart (*French* mɑ̃sar) *n* 1 **François** (frɑ̃swa). 1598–1666, French architect, who established the classical style in French architecture. 2 his great-nephew, **Jules Hardouin** (ʒyl ardwɛ̃). 1646–1708, French architect and town planner, who completed the Palace of Versailles.

manse (mæns) *n* (in certain religious denominations) the house provided for a minister. [C15: from Medieval Latin *mansus* dwelling, from the past participle of Latin *manēre* to stay]

Mansell ('mænsəl) *n* **Nigel.** born 1953, English motor-racing driver: world champion in 1992.

manservant ('mænˌsɜːvənt) *n, pl* **menservants.** a male servant, esp. a valet.

Mansfield[1] ('mænsˌfiːld) *n* a town in central England, in W Nottinghamshire: former coal-mining and cotton-textiles industries. Pop.: 71 858 (1991).

Mansfield[2] ('mænsˌfiːld) *n* **Katherine,** real name *Kathleen Mansfield Beauchamp.* 1888–1923, British writer, born in New Zealand, noted for her short stories, such as those in *Bliss* (1920) and *The Garden Party* (1922).

Mansholt (*Dutch* 'mɑnshɔlt) *n* **Sicco Leendert** ('sɪko 'leːndərt). 1908–95, Dutch economist and politician; vice president (1958–72) and president (1972–73) of the European Economic Community Commission. He was the author of the Mansholt Plan for the agricultural organization of the European Economic Community.

mansion ('mænʃən) *n* 1 Also called: **mansion house.** a large and imposing house. 2 a less common word for **manor house.** 3 *Archaic.* any residence. 4 *Brit.* (*pl*) a block of flats. 5 *Astrology.* any of 28 divisions of the zodiac each occupied on successive days by the moon. [C14: via Old French from Latin *mansio* a remaining, from *mansus;* see MANSE]

Mansion House *n* **the.** 1 the residence of the Lord Mayor of London. 2 the residence of the Lord Mayor of Dublin.

man-sized *adj* 1 of a size appropriate for or convenient for a man. 2 *Informal.* big; large.

manslaughter ('mænˌslɔːtə) *n* 1 *Law.* the unlawful killing of one human being by another without malice aforethought. Compare **murder.** See also **homicide, malice aforethought.** 2 (loosely) the killing of a human being.

Manson ('mænsən) *n* Sir **Patrick.** 1844–1922, British physician, who established that mosquitoes transmit certain parasites responsible for human diseases.

mansuetude ('mænswɪˌtjuːd) *n Archaic.* gentleness or mildness. [C14: from Latin *mansuētūdō,* from *mansuētus,* past participle of *mansuēscere* to make tame by handling, from *manus* hand + *suescere* to train]

Mansur (mæn'sʊə) *n* **Abu Ja'far al-** ('æbuː 'dʒæfə 'æl). 712–75 A.D., 2nd caliph of the Abbasid dynasty (754–75). He founded Baghdad (762) and made it the Islamic capital.

Mansûra (mæn'sʊərə) *n* See **El Mansûra.**

manta ('mæntə; *Spanish* 'manta) *n* 1 Also called: **manta ray, devilfish, devil ray.** any large ray (fish) of the family *Mobulidae,* having very wide winglike pectoral fins and feeding on plankton. 2 a rough cotton cloth made in Spain and Spanish America. 3 a piece of this used as a blanket or shawl. 4 another word for **mantelet** (sense 2). [Spanish: cloak, from Vulgar Latin; see MANTLE. The manta ray is so called because it is caught in a trap resembling a blanket]

manteau ('mæntəʊ; *French* mɑ̃to) *n, pl* **-teaus** (-təʊz) *or* **-teaux** (*French* -to). a cloak or mantle. [C17: via French from Latin *mantellum* MANTLE]

Mantegna (*Italian* man'teɲɲa) *n* **Andrea** (an'drɛːa). 1431–1506, Italian painter and engraver, noted esp. for his frescoes, such as those in the Ducal Palace, Mantua.

mantel *or* (*less commonly*) **mantle** ('mænt[ə]l) *n* 1 a wooden or stone frame around the opening of a fireplace, together with its decorative facing. 2 Also called: **mantel shelf.** a shelf above this frame. [C15: from French, variant of MANTLE]

mantelet ('mænt[ə]ˌlɛt) *or* **mantlet** *n* 1 a woman's short mantle, often lace-trimmed, worn in the mid-19th century. 2 a portable bulletproof screen or shelter. [C14: from Old French, diminutive of *mantel* MANTLE]

mantelletta (ˌmæntɪ'lɛtə) *n R.C. Church.* a sleeveless knee-length vestment, worn by cardinals, bishops, etc. [Italian, from Old French *mantelet* or Medieval Latin *mantelletum,* diminutive of Latin *mantellum* MANTLE]

mantelpiece ('mænt[ə]lˌpiːs) *n* 1 Also called: **mantel shelf, chimneypiece.** a shelf above a fireplace often forming part of the mantel. 2 another word for **mantel** (sense 1).

manteltree *or* **mantletree** ('mænt[ə]lˌtriː) *n* a beam made of stone or wood that forms the lintel over a fireplace.

mantic ('mæntɪk) *adj* 1 of or relating to divination and prophecy. 2 having divining or prophetic powers. [C19: from Greek *mantikos* prophetic, from *mantis* seer] ▸ **'mantically** *adv*

-mantic *adj combining form.* forming adjectives corresponding to nouns ending in **-mancy:** *necromantic.*

mantilla (mæn'tɪlə) *n* 1 a woman's lace or silk scarf covering the shoulders and head, often worn over a comb in the hair, esp. in Spain. 2 a similar covering for the shoulders only. [C18: Spanish, diminutive of *manta* cloak]

Mantinea *or* **Mantineia** (ˌmæntɪ'nɪə) *n* (in ancient Greece) a city in E Arcadia; site of several battles.

mantis ('mæntɪs) *n, pl* **-tises** *or* **-tes** (-tiːz). any carnivorous typically green insect of the family *Mantidae,* of warm and tropical regions, having a long body and large eyes and resting with the first pair of legs raised as if in prayer: order *Dictyoptera.* Also called: **praying mantis.** See also **cockroach.** [C17: New Latin, from Greek: prophet, alluding to its praying posture]

mantissa (mæn'tɪsə) *n* the fractional part of a common logarithm representing the digits of the associated number but not its magnitude: *the mantissa of 2.4771 is .4771.* Compare **characteristic** (sense 2a). [C17: from Latin: something added, of Etruscan origin]

mantis shrimp *or* **crab** *n* any of various burrowing marine shrimplike crustaceans of the order *Stomatopoda* that have a pair of large grasping appendages: subclass *Malacostraca.* See also **squilla.**

mantle ('mænt[ə]l) *n* 1 *Archaic.* a loose wrap or cloak. 2 such a garment regarded as a symbol of someone's power or authority: *he assumed his father's mantle.* 3 anything that covers completely or envelops: *a mantle of snow.* 4 a small dome-shaped or cylindrical mesh impregnated with cerium or thorium nitrates, used to increase illumination in a gas or oil lamp. 5 Also called: **pallium.** *Zoology.* 5a a protective layer of epidermis in molluscs that secretes a substance forming the shell. 5b a similar structure in brachiopods. 6 *Ornithol.* the feathers of the folded wings and back, esp. when these are of a different colour from the remaining feathers. 7 *Geology.* the part of the earth between the crust and the core, accounting for more than 82% of the earth's volume (but only 68% of its mass) and thought to be composed largely of peridotite. See also **asthenosphere.** 8 a less common spelling of **mantel.** 9 *Anatomy.* another word for **pallium** (sense 3). 10 a clay mould formed around a wax model which is subsequently melted out. ◆ *vb* 11 (*tr*) to envelop or supply with a mantle. 12 to spread over or become spread over: *the trees were mantled with snow.* 13 (*tr*) (of the face, cheeks) to become suffused with blood; flush. 14 (*intr*) *Falconry.* (of a hawk or falcon) to spread the wings and tail over food. [C13: via Old French from Latin *mantellum,* diminutive of *mantum* cloak]

mantling ('mæntlɪŋ) *n Heraldry.* the drapery or scrollwork around a shield. [C16: from MANTLE]

man-to-man *adj* characterized by directness or candour: *a man-to-man discussion.*

Mantoux test (mæn'tuː; *French* mɑ̃tu) *n Med.* a test for determining the presence of a tubercular infection by injecting tuberculin into the skin. [C19: named after C. *Mantoux,* French physician (1877–1956)]

Mantova ('mantova) *n* the Italian name for **Mantua.**

mantra ('mæntrə, 'mʌn-) *n* 1 *Hinduism.* any of those parts of the Vedic literature which consist of the metrical psalms of praise. 2 *Hinduism, Buddhism.* any sacred word or syllable used as an object of concentration and embodying some aspect of spiritual power. [C19: from Sanskrit, literally: speech, instrument of thought, from *man* to think]

mantrap ('mænˌtræp) *n* a snare for catching people, esp. trespassers.

mantua ('mæntjʊə) *n* a loose gown of the 17th and 18th centuries, worn open in front to show the underskirt. [C17: changed from MANTEAU, through the influence of MANTUA]

Mantua ('mæntjʊə) *n* a city in N Italy, in E Lombardy, surrounded by lakes: birthplace of Virgil. Pop.: 54 808 (1990). Italian name: **Mantova.**

manual ('mænjʊəl) *adj* 1 of or relating to a hand or hands. 2 operated or done by hand: *manual controls.* 3 physical, as opposed to mental or mechanical: *manual labour.* 4 by human labour rather than automatic or computer-aided means. 5 of, relating to, or resembling a manual. ◆ *n* 6 a book, esp. of instructions or information: *a car manual.* 7 *Music.* one of the keyboards played by hand on an organ. 8 *Military.* the prescribed drill with small arms. [C15: via Old French from Latin *manuālis,* from *manus* hand] ▸ **'manually** *adv*

manubrium (məˈnjuːbrɪəm) *n, pl* **-bria** (-brɪə) *or* **-briums. 1** *Anatomy.* any handle-shaped part, esp. the upper part of the sternum. **2** *Zoology.* the tubular mouth that hangs down from the centre of a coelenterate medusa such as a jellyfish. [C17: from New Latin, from Latin: handle, from *manus* hand] ▸ **maˈnubrial** *adj*

Manuel I (*Portuguese* maˈnwel) *n* called *the Fortunate.* 1469–1521, king of Portugal (1495–1521); his reign saw the discovery of Brazil and the beginning of Portuguese trade with India and the East.

manuf. *or* **manufac.** *abbrev. for:* **1** manufacture. **2** manufactured. **3** manufacturer. **4** manufacturing.

manufactory (ˌmænjuˈfæktərɪ, -trɪ) *n, pl* **-ries.** an obsolete word for **factory.** [C17: from obsolete *manufact;* see MANUFACTURE]

manufacture (ˌmænjuˈfæktʃə) *vb* **1** to process or make (a product) from a raw material, esp. as a large-scale operation using machinery. **2** (*tr*) to invent or concoct: *to manufacture an excuse.* ◆ *n* **3** the production of goods, esp. by industrial processes. **4** a manufactured product. **5** the creation or production of anything. [C16: from obsolete *manufact* hand-made, from Late Latin *manūfactus,* from Latin *manus* hand + *facere* to make] ▸ **ˌmanuˈfacturable** *adj* ▸ **ˌmanuˈfacturing** *n, adj*

manufacturer (ˌmænjuˈfæktʃərə) *n* a person or business concern that manufactures goods or owns a factory.

manuka (ˈmɑːnuːkə) *n* a New Zealand myrtaceous tree, *Leptospermum scoparium,* with strong elastic wood and aromatic leaves. Also called: **tea tree.**

Manukau (ˈmɑːnʊˌkaʊ) *n* a city in New Zealand, on **Manukau Harbour** (an inlet of the Tasman Sea) near Auckland on NW North Island. Pop.: 254 577 (1996).

manumit (ˌmænjuˈmɪt) *vb* **-mits, -mitting, -mitted.** (*tr*) to free from slavery, servitude, etc.; emancipate. [C15: from Latin *manūmittere* to release, from *manū* from one's hand + *ēmittere* to send away] ▸ **manumission** (ˌmænjuˈmɪʃən) *n* ▸ **ˌmanuˈmitter** *n*

manure (məˈnjʊə) *n* **1** animal excreta, usually with straw, used to fertilize land. **2** *Chiefly Brit.* any material, esp. chemical fertilizer, used to fertilize land. ◆ *vb* **3** (*tr*) to spread manure upon (fields or soil). [C14: from Medieval Latin *manuopera;* manual work; see MANOEUVRE] ▸ **maˈnurer** *n*

manus (ˈmeɪnəs) *n, pl* **-nus. 1** *Anatomy.* the wrist and hand. **2** the corresponding part in other vertebrates. **3** *Roman law.* the authority of a husband over his wife. **4** *English law.* (formerly) an oath or the person taking an oath. [C19: Latin: hand]

manuscript (ˈmænjʊˌskrɪpt) *n* **1** a book or other document written by hand. **2** the original handwritten or typed version of a book, article, etc., as submitted by an author for publication. **3a** handwriting, as opposed to printing. **3b** (*as modifier*): *a manuscript document.* [C16: from Medieval Latin *manūscriptus,* from Latin *manus* hand + *scribere* to write]

Manutius (məˈnjuːʃɪəs) *n* See **Aldus Manutius.**

Manx (mæŋks) *adj* **1** of, relating to, or characteristic of the Isle of Man, its inhabitants, their language, or their dialect of English. ◆ *n* **2** an almost extinct language of the Isle of Man, belonging to the N Celtic branch of the Indo-European family and closely related to Scottish Gaelic. **3** (*functioning as pl*) the people of the Isle of Man. [C16: earlier *Maniske,* from Scandinavian, from *Mana* Isle of Man + *-iske* -ISH]

Manx cat *n* a short-haired tailless variety of cat, believed to originate on the Isle of Man.

Manxman (ˈmæŋksmən) *or* (*fem*) **Manxwoman** (ˈmæŋkswʊmən) *n, pl* **-men** *or* **-women.** a native or inhabitant of the Isle of Man.

Manx shearwater *n* a European oceanic bird, *Puffinus puffinus,* with long slender wings and black-and-white plumage: family *Procellariidae* (shearwaters).

many (ˈmɛnɪ) *determiner* **1** (sometimes preceded by *a great* or *a good*) **1a** a large number of: *many coaches; many times.* **1b** (*as pronoun; functioning as pl*): *many are seated already.* **2** (foll. by *a, an,* or *another,* and a sing noun) each of a considerable number of: *many a man.* **3** (preceded by *as, too, that,* etc.) **3a** a great number of: *as many apples as you like; too many clouds to see.* **3b** (*as pronoun; functioning as pl*): *I have as many as you.* ◆ *n* **4 the many.** the majority of mankind, esp. the common people: *the many are kept in ignorance while the few prosper.* Compare **few** (sense 7). ◆ See also **more, most.** [Old English *manig;* related to Old Frisian *manich,* Middle Dutch *menech,* Old High German *manag*]

many-one *adj Maths, logic.* (of a function) associating a single element of a range with more than one member of the domain.

manyplies (ˈmɛnɪˌplaɪz) *n* (*functioning as sing*) another name for **psalterium.** [C18: from the large number of plies or folds of its membrane]

many-sided *adj* having many sides, aspects, etc.: *a many-sided personality.* ▸ **ˌmany-ˈsidedness** *n*

many-valued logic *n* **a** the study of logical systems in which the truth-values that a proposition may have are not restricted to two, representing only truth and falsity. **b** such a logical system.

manzanilla (ˌmænzəˈnɪlə) *n* a very dry pale sherry. [C19: from Spanish: camomile (referring to its bouquet)]

Manzoni (*Italian* manˈdzoːni) *n* **Alessandro** (alesˈsandro). 1785–1873, Italian romantic novelist and poet, famous for his historical novel *I Promessi sposi* (1825–27).

Maoism (ˈmaʊɪzəm) *n* **1** Marxism-Leninism as interpreted by Mao Tse-tung: distinguished by its theory of guerrilla warfare and its emphasis on the revolutionary potential of the peasantry. **2** adherence to or reverence for Mao Tse-tung and his teachings. ▸ **ˈMaoist** *n, adj*

Maori (ˈmaʊrɪ) *n* **1** (*pl* **-ri** *or* **-ris**) a member of the people living in New Zealand and the Cook Islands since before the arrival of European settlers. They are descended from Polynesian voyagers who migrated in successive waves from the ninth century onwards. **2** the language of this people, belonging to the Malayo-Polynesian family. ◆ *adj* **3** of or relating to this people or their language.

Maori Battalion *n* the Maori unit of the 2nd New Zealand Expeditionary Force in World War II.

Maori bug *n* a large shining black wingless cockroach of New Zealand, *Platyzosteria novae-zelandiae.*

Maori bunk *n N.Z.* a raised sleeping platform.

Maori hen *n N.Z.* another name for **weka.**

Maoriland (ˈmaʊrɪˌlænd) *n* an obsolete name for **New Zealand.** ▸ **ˈMaoriˌlander** *n*

Maori oven *n* another name for **hangi** (sense 1).

Maori rat *n* a small brown rat, *Rattus exulans* Peale, native to New Zealand.

Maoritanga (ˈmaʊrɪˌtʌŋə) *n N.Z.* the Maori culture; Maori way of life. [Maori]

Maori warden *n* a person appointed to exercise advisory and minor disciplinary powers in Maori communities.

Mao suit (maʊ) *n* a simple style of clothing, traditionally made of cotton and commonly worn in Communist China, consisting of loose trousers and a straight jacket with a close-fitting stand-up collar. [C20: named after MAO TSE-TUNG, who popularized the style]

Mao Tse-tung (ˈmaʊ tseɪˈtʊŋ) *or* **Mao Ze Dong** *n* 1893–1976, Chinese Marxist theoretician and statesman. The son of a peasant farmer, he helped to found the Chinese Communist Party (1921) and established a soviet republic in SE China (1931–34). He led the retreat of Communist forces to NW China known as the Long March (1935–36), emerging as leader of the party. In opposing the Japanese in World War II, he united with the Kuomintang regime, which he then defeated in the ensuing civil war. He founded the People's Republic of China (1949) of which he was chairman until 1959. As party chairman until his death, he instigated the Cultural Revolution in 1966.

map (mæp) *n* **1** a diagrammatic representation of the earth's surface or part of it, showing the geographical distributions, positions, etc., of natural or artificial features such as roads, towns, relief, rainfall, etc. **2** a diagrammatic representation of the distribution of stars or of the surface of a celestial body: *a lunar map.* **3** a maplike drawing of anything. **4** *Maths.* another name for **function** (sense 4). **5** a slang word for **face** (sense 1). **6 off the map.** no longer important or in existence (esp. in the phrase **wipe off the map**). **7 put on the map.** to make (a town, company, etc.) well-known. ◆ *vb* **maps, mapping, mapped.** (*tr*) **8** to make a map of. **9** *Maths.* to represent or transform (a function, figure, set, etc.). [C16: from Medieval Latin *mappa* (*mundi*) map (of the world), from Latin *mappa* cloth] ▸ **ˈmappable** *adj* ▸ **ˈmapless** *adj* ▸ **ˈmapper** *n*

Map (mæp) *or* **Mapes** (mæps, ˈmeɪpiːz) *n* **Walter.** ?1140–?1209, Welsh ecclesiastic and satirical writer. His chief work is the miscellany *De Nugis curialium.*

maple (ˈmeɪpᵊl) *n* **1** any tree or shrub of the N temperate genus *Acer,* having winged seeds borne in pairs and lobed leaves: family *Aceraceae.* **2** the hard close-grained wood of any of these trees, used for furniture and flooring. **3** the flavour of the sap of the sugar maple. ◆ See also **sugar maple, silver maple, Norway maple, sycamore.** [C14: from Old English *mapel-,* as in *mapeltrēow* maple tree]

maple sugar *n U.S. and Canadian.* sugar made from the sap of the sugar maple.

maple syrup *n* a very sweet syrup made from the sap of the sugar maple.

map out *vb* (*tr, adv*) to plan or design: *to map out a route.*

mapping (ˈmæpɪŋ) *n Maths.* another name for **function** (sense 4).

map projection *n* a means of representing or a representation of the globe or celestial sphere or part of it on a flat map, using a grid of lines of latitude and longitude.

Maputo (məˈpuːtəʊ) *n* the capital and chief port of Mozambique, in the south on Delagoa Bay: became capital in 1907; the nearest port to the Rand gold-mining and industrial region of South Africa. Pop.: 931 591 (1991 est.). Former name (until 1975): **Lourenço Marques.**

maquette (mæˈkɛt) *n* a sculptor's small preliminary model or sketch. [C20: from French, from Italian *macchietta* a little sketch, from *macchia,* from *macchiare,* from Latin *maculāre* to stain, from *macula* spot, blemish]

maquillage *French.* (makijaʒ) *n* **1** make-up; cosmetics. **2** the application of make-up. [from *maquiller* to make up]

maquis (mɑːˈkiː) *n, pl* **-quis** (-ˈkiː). **1** Also called: **garrigue.** shrubby mostly evergreen vegetation found in coastal regions of the Mediterranean: includes myrtles, heaths, arbutus, cork oak, and ilex. **2** (*often cap.*) **2a** the French underground movement that fought against the German occupying forces in World War II. **2b** a member of this movement. [C20: from French, from Italian *macchia* thicket, from Latin *macula* spot]

mar (mɑː) *vb* **mars, marring, marred. 1** (*tr*) to cause harm to; spoil or impair. ◆ *n* **2** a disfiguring mark; blemish. [Old English *merran;* compare Old Saxon *merrian* to hinder, Old Norse *merja* to bruise] ▸ **ˈmarrer** *n*

mar. *abbrev. for:* **1** maritime. **2** married.

Mar. *abbrev. for* March.

mara (məˈrɑː) *n* a harelike South American rodent, *Dolichotis patagonum,* inhabiting the pampas of Argentina: family *Caviidae* (cavies). [from American Spanish *mará,* perhaps of Araucanian origin]

marabi (ˌmaˈrɑːbɪ) *n S. African.* a kind of music popular in townships in the 1930s. [of uncertain origin, possibly from Sotho]

marabou (ˈmærəˌbuː) *n* **1** a large black-and-white African carrion-eating stork, *Leptoptilos crumeniferus,* with a very short naked neck and a straight heavy bill. See also **adjutant bird. 2** a down feather of this bird, used to trim garments. **3a** a fine white raw silk. **3b** fabric made of this. [C19: from French, from Arabic *murābit* MARABOUT, so called because the stork is considered a holy bird in Islam]

marabout ('mærə,buː) *n* **1** a Muslim holy man or hermit of North Africa. **2** a shrine of the grave of a marabout. [C17: via French and Portuguese *marabuto,* from Arabic *murābit*]

marabunta ('mærə,bʌntə) *n Caribbean.* **1** any of several social wasps. **2** *Slang.* an ill-tempered woman. [C19: perhaps of W African origin]

maraca (mə'rækə) *n* a percussion instrument, usually one of a pair, consisting of a gourd or plastic shell filled with dried seeds, pebbles, etc. It is used chiefly in Latin American music. [C20: Brazilian Portuguese, from Tupi]

Maracaibo (,mærə'kaɪbəʊ; *Spanish* mara'kaiβo) *n* **1** a port in NW Venezuela, on the channel from Lake Maracaibo to the Gulf of Venezuela: the second largest city in the country; University of Zulia (1891); major oil centre. Pop.: 1 249 670 (1990). **2 Lake.** a lake in NW Venezuela, linked with the Gulf of Venezuela by a dredged channel: centre of the Venezuelan and South American oil industry. Area: about 13 000 sq. km (500 sq. miles).

Maracanda (,mærə'kændə) *n* the ancient name for **Samarkand.**

Maracay (*Spanish* mara'kai) *n* a city in N central Venezuela: developed greatly as the headquarters of Juan Vicente Gómez during his dictatorship; textile industries. Pop.: 354 196 (1990).

Maradona (,mærə'dɒnə) *n* **Diego Armando** (dɪ'eɪgəʊ). born 1960, Argentinian footballer.

marae (mə'raɪ) *n* **1** *N.Z.* a traditional Maori tribal meeting place, originally one in the open air, now frequently a purpose-built building. **2** (in Polynesia) an open-air place of worship. [Maori]

maraging steel ('mɑː,reɪdʒɪŋ) *n* a strong low-carbon steel containing nickel and small amounts of titanium, aluminium, and niobium, produced by transforming to a martensitic structure and heating at 500°C. [C20 *maraging,* from MAR(TENSITE) + *aging*]

Marajó (*Portuguese* mara'ʒɔ) *n* an island in N Brazil, at the mouth of the Amazon. Area: 38 610 sq. km (15 444 sq. miles).

Maranhão (*Portuguese* marə'ɲɐ̃u) *n* a state of NE Brazil, on the Atlantic: forested and humid in the northwest, with high plateaus in the east and south. Capital: São Luís. Pop.: 5 231 300 (1995 est.). Area: 328 666 sq. km (128 179 sq. miles).

Marañón (*Spanish* mara'ɲɔn) *n* a river in NE Peru, rising in the Andes and flowing northwest into the Ucayali River, forming the Amazon. Length: about 1450 km (900 miles).

maranta (mə'ræntə) *n* any plant of the tropical American rhizomatous genus *Maranta,* some species of which are grown as pot plants for their showy leaves in variegated shades of green: family *Marantaceae.* [named after Bartolomea *Maranti,* died 1571, Venetian botanist]

marari ('mɑːrɑːriː) *n N.Z.* a Maori name for **butterfish** (sense 2).

Maraş (mæ'ræʃ) *n* a town in S Turkey: noted formerly for the manufacture of weapons but now for carpets and embroidery. Pop.: 228 129 (1985).

marasca (mə'ræskə) *n* a European cherry tree, *Prunus cerasus marasca,* with red acid-tasting fruit from which maraschino is made. [C19: from Italian, variant of *amarasca* from *amaro,* from Latin *amārus* bitter]

maraschino (,mærə'skiːnəʊ, -'ʃiːnəʊ) *n* a liqueur made from marasca cherries and flavoured with the kernels, having a taste like bitter almonds. [C18: from Italian; see MARASCA]

maraschino cherry *n* a cherry preserved in maraschino or an imitation of this liqueur, used as a garnish.

marasmus (mə'ræzməs) *n Pathol.* general emaciation and wasting, esp. of infants, thought to be associated with severe malnutrition or impaired utilization of nutrients. [C17: from New Latin, from Greek *marasmos,* from *marainein* to waste] ▸ **ma'rasmic** *adj*

Marat (*French* mara) *n* **Jean Paul** (ʒɑ̃ pɔl). 1743–93, French revolutionary leader and journalist. He founded the radical newspaper *L'Ami du peuple* and was elected to the National Convention (1792). He was instrumental in overthrowing the Girondists (1793); he was stabbed to death in his bath by Charlotte Corday.

Maratha *or* **Mahratta** (mə'rɑːtə) *n* a member of a people of India living chiefly in Maharashtra.

Marathi *or* **Mahratti** (mə'rɑːtɪ) *adj* **1** of or relating to Maharashtra state in India, its people, or their language. ◆ *n* **2** the state language of Maharashtra, belonging to the Indic branch of the Indo-European family.

marathon ('mærəθən) *n* **1** a race on foot of 26 miles 385 yards (42.195 kilometres): an event in the modern Olympics. **2a** any long or arduous task, assignment, etc. **2b** (*as modifier*): *a marathon effort.* [referring to the feat of the messenger who ran more than 20 miles from Marathon to Athens to bring the news of victory in 490 B.C.]

Marathon ('mærəθən) *n* a plain in Attica northeast of Athens: site of a victory of the Athenians and Plataeans over the Persians (490 B.C.).

marathon group *n* (in psychotherapy) an encounter group that lasts for many hours or days.

maraud (mə'rɔːd) *vb* **1** to wander or raid in search of plunder. ◆ *n* **2** an archaic word for **foray.** [C18: from French *marauder* to prowl, from *maraud* vagabond] ▸ **ma'rauder** *n* ▸ **ma'rauding** *adj*

maravedi (,mærə'veɪdɪ) *n, pl* **-dis.** any of various Spanish coins of copper or gold. [C15: from Spanish, from Arabic *Murābitīn* (plural of *murābit* MARABOUT), the Moorish dynasty in Córdoba, 1087–1147]

marble ('mɑːbᵊl) *n* **1a** a hard crystalline metamorphic rock resulting from the recrystallization of a limestone: takes a high polish and is used for building and sculpture. **1b** (*as modifier*): *a marble bust.* Related adj: **marmoreal. 2** a block or work of art of marble. **3** a small round glass or stone ball used in playing marbles. **4 make one's marble good.** *Austral. and N.Z. informal.* to succeed or do the right thing. **5 pass in one's marble.** *Austral. informal.* to die. ◆ *vb* **6** (*tr*) to mottle with variegated streaks in imitation of marble. ◆ *adj* **7** cold, hard, or unresponsive. **8** white like some kinds of marble. ◆ See also **marbles.** [C12: via Old French from Latin *marmor,* from Greek *marmaros,* related to Greek *marmairein* to gleam] ▸ **'marbled** *adj* ▸ **'marbler** *n* ▸ **'marbly** *adj*

marble cake *n* a cake with a marbled appearance obtained by incompletely mixing dark and light mixtures.

marbled white *n* any butterfly of the satyrid genus *Melanargia,* with panelled black-and-white wings, but technically a brown butterfly; found in grassland.

marbles ('mɑːbᵊlz) *n* **1** (*functioning as sing*) a game in which marbles are rolled at one another, similar to bowls. **2** (*functioning as pl*) *Informal.* wits: *to lose one's marbles.*

marblewood ('mɑːbᵊl,wʊd) *n* **1** a Malaysian tree, *Diospyros marmorata*: family *Ebenaceae.* **2** the distinctively marked wood of this tree, having black bands on a lighter background.

marbling ('mɑːblɪŋ) *n* **1** a mottled effect or pattern resembling marble. **2** such an effect obtained by transferring floating colours from a bath of gum solution. **3** the streaks of fat in lean meat.

Marburg ('mɑː,bɜːg; *German* 'maːrbʊrk) *n* **1** a city in W central Germany, in Hesse: famous for the religious debate between Luther and Zwingli in 1529; Europe's first Protestant university (1527). Pop.: 75 400 (1995 est.). **2** the German name for **Maribor.**

Marburg disease *n* a severe, sometimes fatal, viral disease of the green monkey, which may be transmitted to humans. Symptoms include fever, vomiting, and internal bleeding. Also called: **green monkey disease.**

marc (mɑːk; *French* mar) *n* **1** the remains of grapes or other fruit that have been pressed for wine-making. **2** a brandy distilled from these. [C17: from French, from Old French *marchier* to trample (grapes), MARCH[1]]

Marc (*German* mark) *n* **Franz** (frants). 1880–1916, German expressionist painter; cofounder with Kandinsky of the *Blaue Reiter* group (1911). He is noted for his symbolic compositions of animals.

marcasite ('mɑːkə,saɪt) *n* **1** a metallic pale yellow mineral consisting of iron pyrites in orthorhombic crystalline form used in jewellery. **2** a cut and polished form of steel or any white metal used for making jewellery. [C15: from Medieval Latin *marcasīta,* from Arabic *marqashītā,* perhaps from Persian] ▸ **marcasitical** (,mɑːkə'sɪtɪkᵊl) *adj*

marcato (mɑː'kɑːtəʊ) *Music.* ◆ *adj* **1** (of notes) heavily accented. ◆ *adv* **2** with each note heavily accented. [C19: from Italian: marked]

Marceau (*French* marso) *n* **Marcel** (marsɛl). born 1923, French mime artist.

marcel (mɑː'sɛl) *n* **1** Also called: **marcel wave.** a hairstyle characterized by repeated regular waves, popular in the 1920s. ◆ *vb* **-cels, -celling, -celled. 2** (*tr*) to make such waves in (the hair) with special hot irons. [C20: after *Marcel* Grateau (1852–1936), French hairdresser] ▸ **mar'celler** *n*

Marcel (*French* marsɛl) *n* **Gabriel (Honoré)** (gabriɛl). 1889–1973, French Christian existentialist philosopher and dramatist, whose philosophical works include *Being and Having* (1949) and *The Mystery of Being* (1951).

Marcellus (mɑː'sɛləs) *n* **Marcus Claudius** ('mɑːkəs 'klɔːdɪəs). ?268–208 B.C., Roman general and consul, who captured Syracuse (212) in the Second Punic War.

marcescent (mɑː'sɛsənt) *adj* (of the parts of certain plants) remaining attached to the plant when withered. [C18: from Latin *marcescere* to grow weak, from *marcēre* to wither] ▸ **mar'cescence** *n*

march[1] (mɑːtʃ) *vb* **1** (*intr*) to walk or proceed with stately or regular steps, usually in a procession or military formation. **2** (*tr*) to make (a person or group) proceed: *he marched his army to the town.* **3** (*tr*) to traverse or cover by marching: *to march a route.* ◆ *n* **4** the act or an instance of marching. **5** a regular stride: *a slow march.* **6** a long or exhausting walk. **7** advance; progression (of time, etc.). **8** a distance or route covered by marching. **9** a piece of music, usually in four beats to the bar, having a strongly accented rhythm. **10 steal a march on.** to gain an advantage over, esp. by a secret or underhand enterprise. [C16: from Old French *marchier* to tread, probably of Germanic origin; compare Old English *mearcian* to MARK[1]] ▸ **'marcher** *n*

march[2] (mɑːtʃ) *n* **1** Also called: **marchland.** a frontier, border, or boundary or the land lying along it, often of disputed ownership. ◆ *vb* **2** (*intr; often foll. by upon* or *with*) to share a common border (with). [C13: from Old French *marche,* from Germanic; related to MARK[1]]

March[1] (mɑːtʃ) *n* the third month of the year, consisting of 31 days. [from Old French, from Latin *Martius* (month) of Mars]

March[2] (març) *n* the German name for the **Morava** (sense 1).

MArch *abbrev. for* Master of Architecture.

March. *abbrev. for* Marchioness.

march brown *n* an angler's name for the dun and spinner of various mayflies or an artificial fly imitating one of these.

Marche (*French* marʃ) *n* a former province of central France.

marcher ('mɑːtʃə) *n* **1** an inhabitant of any of the Marches. **2** (formerly) **2a** a lord governing and defending such a borderland. **2b** (*as modifier*): *the marcher lords.*

Marches ('mɑːtʃɪz) *n* **the. 1** the border area between England and Wales or Scotland, both characterized by continual feuding (13th–16th centuries). **2** a region of central Italy. Capital: Ancona. Pop.: 1 443 172 (1996 est.). Area: 9692 sq. km (3780 sq. miles). Italian name: **Le Marche** (le 'marke). **3** any of various other border regions.

marchesa *Italian.* (mar'keːza) *n, pl* **-se** (-ze). (in Italy) the wife or widow of a marchese; marchioness.

marchese *Italian.* (mar'keːze) *n, pl* **-si** (-zi). (in Italy) a nobleman ranking below a prince and above a count; marquis.

Marcheshvan *Hebrew.* (marxeʃ'van) *n* another word for ***Cheshvan.*** [from Hebrew *mar* bitter (because it contains no festivals) + CHESHVAN]

March hare *n* a hare during its breeding season in March, noted for its wild and excitable behaviour (esp. in the phrase **mad as a March hare**).

marching girl *n* (*often pl*) *Austral. and N.Z.* one of a team of girls dressed in fancy uniform who perform marching formations.

marching orders *pl n* **1** military orders, esp. to infantry, giving instructions about a march, its destination, etc. **2** *Informal.* notice of dismissal, esp. from employment. **3** *Informal.* the instruction to proceed with a task.

marchioness ('mɑːʃənɪs, ˌmɑːʃə'nɛs) *n* **1** the wife or widow of a marquis. **2** a woman who holds the rank of marquis. [C16: from Medieval Latin *marchionissa,* feminine of *marchiō* MARQUIS]

marchland ('mɑːtʃˌlænd, -lənd) *n* a less common word for **borderland** *or* **march**[2].

marchpane ('mɑːtʃˌpeɪn) *n* an archaic word for **marzipan.** [C15: from French]

march past *n* the marching of troops on parade past a person who is reviewing them.

Marciano (ˌmɑːsɪ'ænəʊ, -'ɑːnəʊ) *n* **Rocky.** original name *Rocco Francis Marchegiano.* 1923–69, U.S. heavyweight boxer; world heavyweight champion, 1952–56.

Marcionism ('mɑːʃəˌnɪzəm) *n* a Gnostic movement of the 2nd and 3rd centuries A.D. [C16: after *Marcion* of Sinope, 2nd-century Gnostic]

Marconi (mɑː'kəʊnɪ) *n* **Guglielmo** (guʎ'ʎɛlmo). 1874–1937, Italian physicist, who developed radiotelegraphy and succeeded in transmitting signals across the Atlantic (1901): Nobel prize for physics 1909.

Marconi rig *n Nautical.* a fore-and-aft sailing boat rig with triangular sails. [C20: from MARCONI, from its resemblance to some types of radio aerial] ▸ **Mar'coni-ˌrigged** *adj*

Marco Polo ('mɑːkəʊ 'pəʊləʊ) *n* See (Marco) **Polo.**

Marcos ('mɑːkɒs) *n* **Ferdinand (Edralin).** 1917–89, Filipino statesman; president of the Philippines from 1965; deposed and exiled in 1986.

Marcus Aurelius Antoninus ('mɑːkəs ɔː'riːlɪəs ˌæntə'naɪnəs) *n* original name *Marcus Annius Verus.* 121–180 A.D., Roman emperor (161–180) noted particularly for his *Meditations,* propounding his stoic view of life.

Marcuse (mɑː'kuːzə) *n* **Herbert.** 1898–1979, U.S. philosopher, born in Germany. In his later works he analysed the situation of man under monopoly capitalism and the dehumanizing effects of modern technology. His works include *Eros and Civilization* (1958) and *One Dimensional Man* (1964).

Mar del Plata (*Spanish* 'mar ðel 'plata) *n* a city and resort in E Argentina, on the Atlantic: fishing port. Pop.: 512 880 (1991).

Mardi Gras ('mɑːdɪ 'grɑː) *n* the festival of Shrove Tuesday, celebrated in some cities with great revelry. [French: fat Tuesday]

Marduk ('mɑːdʊk) *n* the chief god of the Babylonian pantheon.

mardy ('mɑːdɪ) *adj Dialect.* **1** (of a child) spoilt. **2** irritable. [from *marred,* past participle of MAR]

mare[1] (mɛə) *n* the adult female of a horse or zebra. [C12: from Old English, of Germanic origin; related to Old High German *mariha,* Old Norse *merr* mare]

mare[2] ('mɑːreɪ, -rɪ) *n, pl* **maria** ('mɑːrɪə). **1** (*cap. when part of a name*) any of a large number of huge dry plains on the surface of the moon, visible as dark markings and once thought to be seas: *Mare Imbrium* (*Sea of Showers*). **2** a similar area on the surface of Mars, such as *Mare Sirenum.* [from Latin: sea]

mare clausum ('mɑːreɪ 'klaʊsʊm) *n Law.* a sea coming under the jurisdiction of one nation and closed to all others. Compare **mare liberum.** [Latin: closed sea]

mare liberum ('mɑːreɪ 'liːbərʊm) *n Law.* a sea open to navigation by shipping of all nations. Compare **mare clausum.** [Latin: free sea]

maremma (mə'rɛmə) *n, pl* **-me** (-miː). a marshy unhealthy region near the shore, esp. in Italy. [C19: from Italian, from Latin *maritima* MARITIME]

Marengo[1] (mə'rɛŋgəʊ) *adj* (*postpositive*) browned in oil and cooked with tomatoes, mushrooms, garlic, wine, etc.: *chicken Marengo.* [C19: after a dish prepared for Napoleon after the battle of Marengo]

Marengo[2] (mə'rɛŋgəʊ; *Italian* ma'reŋgo) *n* a village in NW Italy: site of a major battle in which Napoleon decisively defeated the Austrians (1800).

mare nostrum *Latin.* ('mɑːreɪ 'nɒstrʊm) *n* the Latin name for the **Mediterranean.** [literally: our sea]

Marenzio (*Italian* ma'rɛntsjo) *n* **Luca** ('luːka). 1553–99, Italian composer of madrigals.

mare's-nest *n* **1** a discovery imagined to be important but proving worthless. **2** a disordered situation.

mare's-tail *n* **1** a wisp of trailing cirrus cloud, indicating strong winds at high levels. **2** an erect pond plant, *Hippuris vulgaris,* with minute flowers and crowded whorls of narrow leaves: family *Hippuridaceae.*

Mareva injunction (mə'riːvə) *n Law.* an order enabling the court to freeze the assets of a defendant, esp. to prevent him from taking them abroad. [C20: named after *Mareva Companai Naviera SA,* the plaintiff in an early case (1975) in which such an order was made]

marg (mɑːdʒ) *n Brit. informal.* short for **margarine.**

marg. *abbrev. for* margin(al).

Margaret ('mɑːgrət) *n* **1** called the *Maid of Norway.* ?1282–90, queen of Scotland (1286–90); daughter of Eric II of Norway. Her death while sailing to England to marry the future Edward II led Edward I to declare dominion over Scotland. **2** 1353–1412, queen of Sweden (1388–1412) and regent of Norway and Denmark (1380–1412), who united the three countries under her rule. **3** **Princess.** born 1930, younger sister of Queen Elizabeth II of Great Britain and Northern Ireland.

Margaret of Anjou *n* 1430–82, queen of England. She married the mentally unstable Henry VI of England in 1445 to confirm the truce with France during the Hundred Years' War. She became a leader of the Lancastrians in the Wars of the Roses and was defeated at Tewkesbury (1471) by Edward IV.

Margaret of Navarre *n* Also called: **Margaret of Angoulême.** 1492–1549, queen of Navarre (1544–49) by marriage to Henry II of Navarre; sister of Francis I of France. She was a poet, a patron of humanism, and author of the *Heptaméron* (1558).

Margaret of Scotland *n* **Saint.** 1045–93, queen consort of Malcolm III of Scotland. Her piety and benefactions to the church led to her canonization (1250). Feast days: June 10, Nov. 16.

Margaret of Valois *n* 1553–1615, daughter of Henry II of France and Catherine de' Medici; queen of Navarre (1572) by marriage to Henry of Navarre. The marriage was dissolved (1599) after his accession as Henry IV of France: noted for her *Mémoires.*

margaric (mɑː'gærɪk) *or* **margaritic** *adj* of or resembling pearl. [C19: from Greek *margaron* pearl]

margaric acid *n* another name for **heptadecanoic acid.**

margarine (ˌmɑːdʒə'riːn, ˌmɑːgə-) *n* a substitute for butter, prepared from vegetable and animal fats by emulsifying them with water and adding small amounts of milk, salt, vitamins, colouring matter, etc. [C19: from MARGARIC]

margarita (ˌmɑːgə'riːtə) *n* a mixed drink consisting of tequila and lemon juice. [C20: from the woman's name]

Margarita (ˌmɑːgə'riːtə) *n* an island in the Caribbean, off the NE coast of Venezuela: pearl fishing. Capital: La Asunción.

margarite ('mɑːgəˌraɪt) *n* **1** a pink pearly micaceous mineral consisting of hydrated calcium aluminium silicate. Formula: $CaAl_4Si_2O_{10}(OH)_2$. **2** an aggregate of minute beadlike masses occurring in some glassy igneous rocks. [C19: via German from Greek *margaron* pearl]

Margate ('mɑːgeɪt) *n* a town and resort in SE England, in E Kent on the Isle of Thanet. Pop.: 56 734 (1991).

Margaux (*French* margo) *n* a red wine produced in the region around the village of Margaux near Bordeaux.

margay ('mɑːˌgeɪ) *n* a feline mammal, *Felis wiedi,* of Central and South America, having a dark-striped coat. [C18: from French, from Tupi *mbaracaiá*]

marge[1] (mɑːdʒ) *n Brit. informal.* short for **margarine.**

marge[2] (mɑːdʒ) *n Archaic.* a margin. [C16: from French]

margin ('mɑːdʒɪn) *n* **1** an edge or rim, and the area immediately adjacent to it; border. **2** the blank space surrounding the text on a page. **3** a vertical line on a page, esp. one on the left-hand side, delineating this space. **4** an additional amount or one beyond the minimum necessary: *a margin of error.* **5** *Chiefly Austral.* a payment made in addition to a basic wage, esp. for special skill or responsibility. **6** a bound or limit. **7** the amount by which one thing differs from another: *a large margin separated the parties.* **8** *Commerce.* the profit on a transaction. **9** *Economics.* the minimum return below which an enterprise becomes unprofitable. **10** *Finance.* **10a** collateral deposited by a client with a broker as security. **10b** the excess of the value of a loan's collateral over the value of the loan. ◆ Also (archaic): **margent** ('mɑːdʒənt). ◆ *vb* (*tr*) **11** to provide with a margin; border. **12** *Finance.* to deposit a margin upon. [C14: from Latin *margō* border; related to MARCH[2], MARK[1]]

marginal ('mɑːdʒɪnᵊl) *adj* **1** of, in, on, or constituting a margin. **2** close to a limit, esp. a lower limit: *marginal legal ability.* **3** not considered central or important; insignificant, minor, small. **4** *Economics.* relating to goods or services produced and sold at the margin of profitability: *marginal cost.* **5** *Politics, chiefly Brit. and N.Z.* of or designating a constituency in which elections tend to be won by small margins: *a marginal seat.* **6** designating agricultural land on the margin of cultivated zones. **7** *Economics.* relating to a small change in something, such as total cost, revenue, or consumer satisfaction. ▸ **marginality** (ˌmɑːdʒɪ'nælɪtɪ) *n* ▸ **'marginally** *adv*

marginal costing *n* a method of cost accounting and decision making used for internal reporting in which only marginal costs are charged to cost units and fixed costs are treated as a lump sum. Compare **absorption costing.**

marginalia (ˌmɑːdʒɪ'neɪlɪə) *pl n* notes in the margin of a book, manuscript, or letter. [C19: New Latin, noun (neuter plural) from *marginālis* marginal]

marginalize *or* **marginalise** ('mɑːdʒɪnᵊˌlaɪz) *vb* (*tr*) to relegate to the fringes, out of the mainstream; make seem unimportant: *various economic assumptions marginalize women.* ▸ **ˌmarginali'zation** *or* **ˌmarginali'sation** *n*

marginal probability *n Statistics.* (in a multivariate distribution) the probability of one variable taking a specific value irrespective of the values of the others.

marginate ('mɑːdʒɪˌneɪt) *vb* **1** (*tr*) to provide with a margin or margins. ◆ *adj* **2** *Biology.* having a margin of a distinct colour or form: *marginate leaves.* [C18: from Latin *margināre*] ▸ **ˌmargin'ation** *n*

margravate ('mɑːgrəvɪt) *or* **margraviate** (mɑː'greɪvɪɪt) *n* the domain of a margrave.

margrave ('mɑːˌgreɪv) *n* a German nobleman ranking above a count. Margraves were originally counts appointed to govern frontier provinces, but all had become princes of the Holy Roman Empire by the 12th century. [C16: from Middle Dutch *markgrave,* literally: count of the MARCH[2]]

margravine ('mɑːgrəˌviːn) *n* **1** the wife or widow of a margrave. **2** a woman who holds the rank of margrave. [C17: from Middle Dutch, feminine of MARGRAVE]

Margrethe II (*Danish* mar'greːdə) *n* born 1940, queen of Denmark from 1972.

marguerite (ˌmɑːgə'riːt) *n* **1** a cultivated garden plant, *Chrysanthemum frutescens,* whose flower heads have white or pale yellow rays around a yellow disc: family *Compositae* (composites). **2** any of various related plants with daisy-like flowers, esp. *C. leucanthemum.* [C19: from French: daisy, pearl, from Latin *margarīta,* from Greek *margaritēs,* from *margaron*]

Marheshvan *or* ***Marcheshvan*** *Hebrew.* (marxɛʃ'van) *n* another word for **Cheshvan.**

Mari ('mɑːrɪ) *n, pl* **Mari** *or* **Maris.** another name for **Cheremiss.**

maria ('mɑːrɪə) *n* the plural of **mare**[2].

mariachi (ˌmɑːrɪ'ɑːtʃɪ) *n* a small ensemble of street musicians in Mexico. [C20: from Mexican Spanish]

Maria de' Medici (*Italian* ma'ri:a de 'mɛ:ditʃi) *n* French name *Marie de Médicis*. 1573–1642, queen of France (1600–10) by marriage to Henry IV of France; daughter of Francesco, grand duke of Tuscany. She became regent for her son (later Louis XIII) but continued to wield power after he came of age (1614). She was finally exiled from France in 1631 after plotting to undermine Richelieu's influence at court.

mariage blanc *French* (marjaʒ blɑ̃) *n, pl* ***mariages blancs*** (marjaʒ blɑ̃). unconsummated marriage. **[C20:** literally: white marriage**]**

mariage de convenance *French.* (marjaʒ də kɔ̃vənɑ̃s) *n, pl* ***mariages de convenance.*** another term for **marriage of convenience.**

Marian ('mɛərɪən) *adj* **1** of or relating to the Virgin Mary. **2** of or relating to some other Mary, such as Mary Queen of Scots or Mary I of England. ◆ *n* **3** a person who has a special devotion to the Virgin Mary. **4** a supporter of some other Mary.

Mariana Islands (ˌmærɪ'ɑ:nə) *pl n* a chain of volcanic and coral islands in the W Pacific, east of the Philippines and north of New Guinea: divided politically into Guam (a U.S. unincorporated territory) and the islands north of Guam constituting the Commonwealth of the Northern Mariana Islands (a U.S. commonwealth territory). Pop.: (Guam) 148 000 (1998 est.); (Northern Marianas) 66 600 (1998 est.). Area: 958 sq. km (370 sq. miles). Former name (1521–1668): **Ladrone Islands.**

Marianao (*Spanish* marja'nao) *n* a city in NW Cuba, adjacent to W Havana city: the chief Cuban military base. Pop.: 133 016 (1989 est).

Marianne (*French* marjan) *n* a female figure personifying the French republic after the Revolution (1789).

Mariánské Lázně (*Czech* 'marjanske: 'la:znjɛ) *n* a town in the W Czech Republic: a fashionable spa in the 18th and 19th centuries. Pop.: 15 380 (1991). German name: **Marienbad.**

Maria Theresa (mə'ri:ə tə'reɪzə) *n* 1717–80, archduchess of Austria and queen of Hungary and Bohemia (1740–80); the daughter and heiress of Emperor Charles VI of Austria; the wife of Emperor Francis I; the mother of Emperor Joseph II. In the War of the Austrian Succession (1740–48) she was confirmed in all her possessions except Silesia, which she attempted unsuccessfully to regain in the Seven Years' War (1756–63).

Mari El Republic ('mɑ:rɪ) *n* a constituent republic of W central Russia, in the middle Volga basin. Capital: Yoshkar-Ola. Pop.: 766 000 (1995 est.). Area: 23 200 sq. km (8955 sq. miles).

Maribor ('mærɪbɔ:) *n* an industrial city in N Slovenia on the Drava River: a flourishing Hapsburg trading centre in the 13th century; resort. Pop.: 134 289 (1996 est.). German name: **Marburg.**

mariculture ('mærɪˌkʌltʃə) *n* the cultivation of marine plants and animals in their natural environment. **[C20:** from Latin *mari-, mare* sea + CULTURE**]**

Marie (mə'ri:) *n* 1875–1938, queen consort of Ferdinand I of Romania. A granddaughter of Queen Victoria, she secured Romania's support for the Allies in World War I.

Marie Antoinette (*French* mari ɑ̃twanɛt) *n* 1755–93, queen of France (1774–93) by marriage to Louis XVI of France. Her opposition to reform during the Revolution contributed to the overthrow of the monarchy; guillotined.

Marie Byrd Land ('mɑ:rɪ 'bɜ:d) *n* the former name of **Byrd Land.**

Marie de France (*French* mari də frɑ̃s) *n* 12th century A.D., French poet, who probably lived in England; noted for her *lais* (verse narratives) based on Celtic tales.

Marie Galante (*French* mari galɑ̃t) *n* an island in the E Caribbean southeast of Guadeloupe, of which it is a dependency. Chief town: Grand Bourg. Pop.: 13 463 (1990). Area: 155 sq. km (60 sq. miles).

Mariehamn (mariə'hamn) *n* a city in SW Finland, chief port of the Åland Islands. Pop.: 10 260 (1990). Finnish name: **Maarianhamina.**

Marie Louise (*French* mari lwiz) *n* 1791–1847, empress of France (1811–15) as the second wife of Napoleon I; daughter of Francis I of Austria. On Napoleon's abdication (1815) she became Duchess of Parma.

Marienbad ('mærɪənˌbæd; *German* ma'ri:ənba:t) *n* the German name for **Mariánské Lázně.**

marigold ('mærɪˌgəʊld) *n* **1** any of various tropical American plants of the genus *Tagetes*, esp. *T. erecta* (**African marigold**) and *T. patula* (**French marigold**), cultivated for their yellow or orange flower heads and strongly scented foliage: family *Compositae* (composites). **2** any of various similar or related plants, such as the marsh marigold, pot marigold, bur marigold, and fig marigold. **[C14:** from *Mary* (the Virgin) + GOLD**]**

marigram ('mærɪˌgræm) *n* a graphic record of the tide levels at a particular coastal station. **[**from Latin *mare* sea + -GRAM**]**

marigraph ('mærɪˌgræf, -ˌgrɑ:f) *n* a gauge for recording the levels of the tides. **[**from Latin *mare* sea + -GRAPH**]**

marijuana *or* **marihuana** (ˌmærɪ'hwɑ:nə) *n* **1** the dried leaves and flowers of the hemp plant, used for its euphoric effects, esp. in the form of cigarettes. See also **cannabis. 2** another name for **hemp** (the plant). **[C19:** from Mexican Spanish**]**

marimba (mə'rɪmbə) *n* a Latin American percussion instrument consisting of a set of hardwood plates placed over tuned metal resonators, played with two soft-headed sticks in each hand. **[C18:** of West African origin**]**

Marin ('mɑ:rɪn) *n* **John.** 1870–1953, U.S. painter, noted esp. for his watercolour landscapes and seascapes.

marina (mə'ri:nə) *n* an elaborate docking facility for pleasure boats. **[C19:** via Italian and Spanish from Latin: MARINE**]**

marinade *n* (ˌmærɪ'neɪd). **1** a spiced liquid mixture of oil, wine, vinegar, herbs, etc., in which meat or fish is soaked before cooking. **2** meat or fish soaked in this liquid. ◆ *vb* ('mærɪˌneɪd). **3** a variant of **marinate. [C17:** from French, from Spanish *marinada,* from *marinar* to pickle in brine, MARINATE**]**

marinate ('mærɪˌneɪt) *vb* to soak in marinade. **[C17:** probably from Italian *marinato,* from *marinare* to pickle, ultimately from Latin *marīnus* MARINE**]** ▸ ˌ**mari'nation** *n*

Marinduque (ˌmɑ:rɪn'du:keɪ) *n* an island of the central Philippines, east of Mindoro: forms, with offshore islets, a province of the Philippines. Capital: Boac. Pop.: 173 715 (1980). Area: 960 sq. km (370 sq. miles).

marine (mə'ri:n) *adj (usually prenominal)* **1** of, found in, or relating to the sea. **2** of or relating to shipping, navigation, etc. **3** of or relating to a body of seagoing troops: *marine corps.* **4** of or relating to a government department concerned with maritime affairs. **5** used or adapted for use at sea: *a marine camera.* ◆ *n* **6** shipping and navigation in general: *the merchant marine.* **7** *(cap. when part of a name)* a member of a marine corps or similar body. **8** a picture of a ship, seascape, etc. **9 tell it to the marines.** *Informal.* an expression of disbelief. **[C15:** from Old French *marin,* from Latin *marīnus,* from *mare* sea**]**

marine borer *n* any mollusc or crustacean that lives usually in warm seas and destroys wood by boring into and eating it. The gribble and shipworm are the best known since they penetrate any wood in favourable water. See also **piddock.**

marine engineer *n* an engineer responsible for all heavy machinery on a ship or an offshore structure.

marine insurance *n* insurance covering damage to or loss of ship, passengers, or cargo caused by the sea.

mariner ('mærɪnə) *n* a formal or literary word for **seaman. [C13:** from Anglo-French, ultimately from Latin *marīnus* MARINE**]**

Mariner ('mærɪnə) *n* any of a series of U.S. space probes launched between 1962 and 1971 that sent back photographs and information concerning the surface of Mars and Venus and also studied interplanetary matter.

marine railway *n* another term for **slipway** (sense 2).

Marinetti (*Italian* mari'netti) *n* **Filippo Tommaso** (fi'lippo tom'ma:zo). 1876–1944, Italian poet; founder of futurism (1909).

Mariolatry *or* **Maryolatry** (ˌmɛərɪ'ɒlətrɪ) *n Derogatory.* exaggerated veneration of the Virgin Mary. ▸ ˌ**Mari'olater** *or* ˌ**Mary'olater** *n* ▸ ˌ**Mari'olatrous** *or* ˌ**Mary'olatrous** *adj*

Mariology *or* **Maryology** (ˌmɛərɪ'ɒlədʒɪ) *n R.C. Church.* the study of the traditions and doctrines concerning the Virgin Mary. ▸ ˌ**Mari'ologist** *or* ˌ**Mary'ologist** *n*

marionette (ˌmærɪə'nɛt) *n* an articulated puppet or doll whose jointed limbs are moved by strings. **[C17:** from French, from *Marion,* diminutive of *Marie* Mary + -ETTE**]**

mariposa (ˌmærɪ'pəʊzə, -sə) *n* any of several liliaceous plants of the genus *Calochortus,* of the southwestern U.S. and Mexico, having brightly coloured tulip-like flowers. Also called: **mariposa lily** or **tulip. [C19:** from Spanish: butterfly; from the likeness of the blooms to butterflies**]**

marish ('mærɪʃ) *adj Obsolete.* marshy; swampy. **[C14:** from Old French *marais* MARSH**]**

Marist ('mɛərɪst) *R.C. Church.* ◆ *n* **1** a member of the Society of Mary, a religious congregation founded in 1824. **2** *N.Z.* a teacher or pupil in a school belonging to the Marist Order. ◆ *adj* **3** of a Marist. **[C19:** from French *Mariste,* from *Marie* Mary (the virgin)**]**

maritage ('mærɪtɪdʒ) *n Feudal history.* **1** the right of a lord to choose the spouses of his wards. **2** a sum paid to a lord in lieu of his exercising this right. **[C16:** from Medieval Latin *marītāgium,* a Latinized form of French *mariage* marriage**]**

Maritain (*French* maritɛ̃) *n* **Jacques** (ʒak). 1882–1973, French neo-Thomist Roman Catholic philosopher.

marital ('mærɪtᵊl) *adj* **1** of or relating to marriage: *marital status.* **2** of or relating to a husband. **[C17:** from Latin *marītālis,* from *marītus* married (adj), husband (n); related to *mās* male**]** ▸ '**maritally** *adv*

maritime ('mærɪˌtaɪm) *adj* **1** of or relating to navigation, shipping, etc.; seafaring. **2** of, relating to, near, or living near the sea. **3** (of a climate) having small temperature differences between summer and winter; equable. **[C16:** from Latin *maritimus* from *mare* sea**]**

Maritime Alps *pl n* a range of the W Alps in SE France and NW Italy. Highest peak: Argentera, 3297 m (10 817 ft.).

Maritime Provinces *or* **Maritimes** *pl n* **the.** another name for the **Atlantic Provinces,** but often excluding Newfoundland.

Maritimer ('mærɪˌtaɪmə) *n* a native or inhabitant of the Maritime Provinces of Canada.

Maritsa (*Bulgarian* ma'ritsa) *n* a river in S Europe, rising in S Bulgaria and flowing east into Turkey, then south from Edirne as part of the border between Turkey and Greece to the Aegean. Length: 483 km (300 miles). Turkish name: **Meriç.** Greek name: **Évros.**

Mariupol (*Russian* məri'upəlj) *n* a port in SE Ukraine, on an estuary leading to the Sea of Azov. Pop.: 510 000 (1996 est.). Former name (1948–91): **Zhdanov.**

Marius ('mɛərɪəs, 'mærɪəs) *n* **Gaius** ('gaɪəs). ?155–86 B.C., Roman general and consul. He defeated Jugurtha, the Cimbri, and the Teutons (107–101), but his rivalry with Sulla caused civil war (88). He was exiled but returned (87) and took Rome.

Marivaux (*French* marivo) *n* **Pierre Carlet de Chamblain de** (pjɛr karlɛ də ʃɑ̃blɛ̃ də). 1688–1763, French dramatist and novelist, noted particularly for his comedies, such as *Le jeu de l'amour et du hasard* (1730) and *La Vie de Marianne* (1731–41).

marjoram ('mɑ:dʒərəm) *n* **1** Also called: **sweet marjoram.** an aromatic Mediterranean plant, *Origanum* (or *Marjorana*) *hortensis,* with small pale purple flowers and sweet-scented leaves, used for seasoning food and in salads: family *Labiatae* (labiates). **2** Also called: **wild marjoram, pot marjoram, origan.** a similar and related European plant, *Origanum vulgare.* See also **oregano, origanum. [C14:** via Old French *majorane,* from Medieval Latin *marjorana***]**

mark[1] (mɑ:k) *n* **1** a visible impression, stain, etc., on a surface, such as a spot or scratch. **2** a sign, symbol, or other indication that distinguishes something: *an owner's mark.* **3** a cross or other symbol made instead of a signature. **4** a written or printed sign or symbol, as for punctuation: *a question mark.* **5** a letter, number, or percentage used to grade academic work. **6** a thing that indicates position or directs; marker. **7** a desired or recognized standard: *he is not up to the mark.* **8** an indication of some quality, feature, or prowess: *he has the mark of an athlete.* **9** quality or importance; note: *a person of little mark.* **10** a target or goal. **11** impression or influence: *he left his mark on German literature.* **12** one of the temperature settings on a gas oven: *gas mark 5.* **13** (*often cap.*) (in trade names) **13a** model, brand, or type: *the car is a Mark 4.* **13b** a variation on a particular model: *a Mark 3 Cortina.* **14** *Slang.* a suitable victim, esp. for swindling. **15** *Nautical.* one of the intervals distinctively marked on a sounding lead. Compare **deep** (sense 21). **16** *Bowls.* another name for the **jack. 17** *Rugby Union.* an action in which a player standing inside his own 22m line catches a forward kick by an opponent and shouts "mark", entitling himself to a free kick. **18** *Australian Rules football.* a catch of the ball from a kick of at least 10 yards, after which a free kick is taken. **19 the mark.** *Boxing.* the middle of the stomach at or above the line made by the boxer's trunks. **20** (in medieval England and Germany) a piece of land held in common by the free men of a community. **21** an obsolete word for **frontier. 22** *Statistics.* See **class mark. 23 make one's mark.** to succeed or achieve recognition. **24 on your mark** *or* **marks.** a command given to runners in a race to prepare themselves at the starting line. ♦ *vb* **25** to make or receive (a visible impression, trace, or stain) on (a surface). **26** (*tr*) to characterize or distinguish: *his face was marked by anger.* **27** (often foll. by *off* or *out*) to set boundaries or limits (on): *to mark out an area for negotiation.* **28** (*tr*) to select, designate, or doom by or as if by a mark: *to mark someone as a criminal.* **29** (*tr*) to put identifying or designating labels, stamps, etc., on, esp. to indicate price: *to mark the book at one pound.* **30** (*tr*) to pay heed or attention to: *mark my words.* **31** to observe; notice. **32** to grade or evaluate (scholastic work): *she marks fairly.* **33** *Brit., football, etc.* to stay close to (an opponent) to hamper his play. **34** to keep (score) in some games. **35 mark time. 35a** to move the feet alternately as in marching but without advancing. **35b** to act in a mechanical and routine way. **35c** to halt progress temporarily, while awaiting developments. ♦ *interj* **36** *Rugby Union.* the shout given by a player when calling for a mark. ♦ See also **markdown, mark-up.** [Old English *mearc* mark; related to Old Norse *mörk* boundary land, Old High German *marha* boundary, Latin *margō* MARGIN]

mark[2] (mɑːk) *n* **1** See **Deutschmark, markka, Reichsmark, Ostmark. 2** a former monetary unit and coin in England and Scotland worth two thirds of a pound sterling. **3** a silver coin of Germany until 1924. [Old English *marc* unit of weight of precious metal, perhaps from the marks on metal bars; apparently of Germanic origin and related to MARK[1]]

Mark (mɑːk) *n New Testament.* **1** one of the four Evangelists. Feast day: April 25. **2** the second Gospel, traditionally ascribed to him.

marka (ˈmɑːkə) *n* a unit of currency introduced as an interim currency in Bosnia-Herzegovina.

Mark Antony *n* See (Mark) **Antony.**

markdown (ˈmɑːkˌdaʊn) *n* **1** a price reduction. ♦ *vb* **mark down. 2** (*tr, adv*) to reduce in price.

marked (mɑːkt) *adj* **1** obvious, evident, or noticeable. **2** singled out, esp. for punishment, killing, etc.: *a marked man.* **3** *Linguistics.* distinguished by a specific feature, as in phonology. For example, of the two phonemes /t/ and /d/, the /d/ is marked because it exhibits the feature of voice. ▸ **markedly** (ˈmɑːkɪdlɪ) *adv* ▸ ˈ**markedness** *n*

marker (ˈmɑːkə) *n* **1a** something used for distinguishing or marking. **1b** (*as modifier*): *a marker buoy.* **2** a person or thing that marks. **3** a person or object that keeps or shows scores in a game.

market (ˈmɑːkɪt) *n* **1a** an event or occasion, usually held at regular intervals, at which people meet for the purpose of buying and selling merchandise. **1b** (*as modifier*): *market day.* **2** a place, such as an open space in a town, at which a market is held. **3** a shop that sells a particular merchandise: *an antique market.* **4 the market.** business or trade in a commodity as specified: *the sugar market.* **5** the trading or selling opportunities provided by a particular group of people: *the foreign market.* **6** demand for a particular product or commodity: *there is no market for furs here.* **7** See **stock market. 8** See **market price, market value. 9 at market.** at the current price. **10 be in the market for.** to wish to buy or acquire. **11 on the market.** available for purchase. **12 play the market. 12a** to speculate on a stock exchange. **12b** to act aggressively or unscrupulously in one's own commercial interests. **13 seller's** (*or* **buyer's**) **market.** a market characterized by excess demand (or supply) and thus favourable to sellers (or buyers). ♦ *vb* **-kets, -keting, -keted. 14** (*tr*) to offer or produce for sale. **15** (*intr*) to buy or deal in a market. [C12: from Latin *mercātus;* from *mercāri* to trade, from *merx* merchandise] ▸ ˈ**marketer** *n*

marketable (ˈmɑːkɪtəbᵊl) *adj* **1** (of commodities, assets, etc.) **1a** being in good demand; saleable. **1b** suitable for sale. **2** of or relating to buying or selling on a market: *marketable value.* ▸ ˌ**marketaˈbility** *or* ˈ**marketableness** *n* ▸ ˈ**marketably** *adv*

market forces *pl n* the effect of supply and demand on trading within a free market.

market garden *n Chiefly Brit.* an establishment where fruit and vegetables are grown for sale. ▸ **market gardener** *n*

market gardening *n Chiefly Brit.* the business of growing fruit and vegetables on a commercial scale. Also called (in the U.S. and Canada): **truck farming, trucking.**

marketing (ˈmɑːkɪtɪŋ) *n* the provision of goods or services to meet customer or consumer needs.

marketing mix *n* the variables, such as price, promotion, and service, managed by an organization to influence demand for a product or service.

market maker *n* a dealer in securities on the London Stock Exchange who buys and sells as a principal and since 1986 can also deal with the public as a broker.

market order *n* an instruction to a broker to sell or buy at the best price currently obtainable on the market.

marketplace (ˈmɑːkɪtˌpleɪs) *n* **1** a place where a public market is held. **2** any centre where ideas, opinions, etc., are exchanged. **3** the commercial world of buying and selling.

market price *n* the prevailing price, as determined by supply and demand, at which goods, services, etc., may be bought or sold.

market rent *n* (in Britain) the rent chargeable for accommodation, allowing for the scarcity of that kind of property and the willingness of tenants to pay.

market research *n* the study of influences upon customer and consumer behaviour and the analysis of market characteristics and trends.

market segment *n* a part of a market identifiable as having particular customers with specific buying characteristics.

market segmentation *n* the division of a market into identifiable groups, esp. to improve the effectiveness of a marketing strategy.

market share *n* the percentage of a total market, in terms of either value or volume, accounted for by the sales of a specific brand.

market-test *vb* (*tr*) to put (a section of a public-sector enterprise) out to tender, often as a prelude to full-scale privatization.

market town *n Chiefly Brit.* a town that holds a market, esp. an agricultural centre in a rural area.

market value *n* the amount obtainable on the open market for the sale of property, financial assets, or goods and services. Compare **par value, book value.**

Markham (ˈmɑːkəm) *n* **Mount.** a mountain in Antarctica, in Victoria Land. Height: 4350 m (14 272 ft.).

markhor (ˈmɑːkɔː) *or* **markhoor** (ˈmɑːkʊə) *n, pl* **-khors, -khor** *or* **-khoors, -khoor.** a large wild Himalayan goat, *Capra falconeri,* with a reddish-brown coat and large spiralled horns. [C19: from Persian, literally: snake-eater, from *mār* snake + *-khōr* eating]

Markiewicz (mɑːˈkjeɪvɪtʃ) *n* **Constance,** Countess, original name *Constance Gore-Booth.* 1868–1927, Irish nationalist, married to a Polish count. She fought in the Easter Rising (1916) and was sentenced to death but reprieved. The first woman elected to the British parliament (1918), she refused to take her seat.

marking (ˈmɑːkɪŋ) *n* **1** a mark or series of marks. **2** the arrangement of colours on an animal, plant, etc. **3** assessment and correction of school children's or students' written work by teaching staff.

marking ink *n* indelible ink used for marking linen, clothes, etc.

markka (ˈmɑːkɑː, -kə) *n, pl* **-kaa** (-kɑː). the standard monetary unit of Finland, divided into 100 penniä. [Finnish. See MARK[2]]

Markova (mɑːˈkəʊvə) *n* Dame **Alicia.** real name *Lilian Alicia Marks.* born 1910, English ballerina.

Markov chain (ˈmɑːkɒf) *n Statistics.* a sequence of events the probability for each of which is dependent only on the event immediately preceding it. [C20: named after Andrei *Markov* (1856–1922), Russian mathematician]

marksman (ˈmɑːksmən) *n, pl* **-men. 1** a person skilled in shooting. **2** a serviceman selected for his skill in shooting, esp. for a minor engagement. **3** a qualification awarded in certain armed services for skill in shooting. ▸ ˈ**marksmanˌship** *n* ▸ ˈ**marksˌwoman** *fem n*

mark-up *n* **1** a percentage or amount added to the cost of a commodity to provide the seller with a profit and to cover overheads, costs, etc. **2a** an increase in the price of a commodity. **2b** the amount of this increase. ♦ *vb* **mark up.** (*tr, adv*) **3** to add a percentage for profit, overheads, etc., to the cost of (a commodity). **4** to increase the price of.

marl[1] (mɑːl) *n* **1** a fine-grained sedimentary rock consisting of clay minerals, calcite or aragonite, and silt: used as a fertilizer. ♦ *vb* **2** (*tr*) to fertilize (land) with marl. [C14: via Old French, from Late Latin *margila,* diminutive of Latin *marga*] ▸ **marlacious** (mɑːˈleɪʃəs) *or* ˈ**marly** *adj*

marl[2] (mɑːl) *vb Nautical.* to seize (a rope) with marline, using a hitch at each turn. [C15 *marlyn* to bind; related to Dutch *marlen* to tie, Old English *mārels* cable]

Marlborough[1] (ˈmɑːlbərə, -brə, ˈmɔːl-) *n* a town in S England, in Wiltshire: besieged and captured by Royalists in the Civil War (1642); site of Marlborough College, a public school founded in 1843. Pop.: 6429 (1991).

Marlborough[2] (ˈmɑːlbərə, -brə, ˈmɔːl-) *n* **1st Duke of,** title of *John Churchill.* 1650–1722, English general; commander of British forces in the War of the Spanish Succession (1701-14), in which he won victories at Blenheim (1704), Ramillies (1706), Oudenaarde (1708), and Malplaquet (1709).

Marley (ˈmɑːlɪ) *n* **Bob,** full name *Robert Nesta Marley.* 1945–81, Jamaican reggae singer, guitarist, and songwriter. With his group, the Wailers, his albums included *Burnin'* (1973), *Natty Dread* (1975), *Rastaman Vibration* (1976), and *Exodus* (1977).

marlin (ˈmɑːlɪn) *n, pl* **-lin** *or* **-lins.** any of several large scombroid food and game fishes of the genera *Makaira, Istiompax,* and *Tetrapturus,* of warm and tropical seas, having a very long upper jaw: family *Istiophoridae.* Also called: **spearfish.** [C20: from MARLINESPIKE; with allusion to the shape of the beak]

marline, marlin (ˈmɑːlɪn), *or* (*less commonly*) **marling** (ˈmɑːlɪŋ) *n Nautical.* a light rope, usually tarred, made of two strands laid left-handed. [C15: from Dutch *marlijn,* from *marren* to tie + *lijn* line]

marlinespike, marlinspike (ˈmɑːlɪnˌspaɪk), *or* (*less commonly*) **marlingspike** (ˈmɑːlɪŋˌspaɪk) *n Nautical.* a pointed metal tool used as a fid, spike, and for various other purposes.

marlite (ˈmɑːlaɪt) *or* **marlstone** (ˈmɑːlˌstəʊn) *n* a type of marl that contains clay and calcium carbonate and is resistant to the decomposing action of air.

Marlowe (ˈmɑːləʊ) *n* **Christopher.** 1564–93, English dramatist and poet, who established blank verse as a creative form of dramatic expression. His plays include *Tamburlaine the Great* (1590), *Edward II* (?1592), and *Dr Faustus* (1604). He was stabbed to death in a tavern brawl.

marmalade (ˈmɑːməˌleɪd) *n* **1** a preserve made by boiling the pulp and rind of citrus fruits, esp. oranges, with sugar. ♦ *adj* **2** (of cats) streaked orange or yellow and brown. **[C16:** via French from Portuguese *marmelada,* from *marmelo* quince, from Latin, from Greek *melimēlon,* from *meli* honey + *mēlon* apple**]**

marmalade tree *n* a tropical American sapotaceous tree, *Calocarpum sapota,* with durable wood: its fruit is used to make preserves. Also called: **mamey.**

Marmara *or* **Marmora** (ˈmɑːmərə) *n* **Sea of.** a deep inland sea in NW Turkey, linked with the Black Sea by the Bosporus and with the Aegean by the Dardanelles: separates Turkey in Europe from Turkey in Asia. Area: 11 471 sq. km (4429 sq. miles). Ancient name: **Propontis.**

marmite (ˈmɑːmaɪt) *n* **1** a large cooking pot. **2** soup cooked in such a pot. **3** an individual covered casserole for serving soup. **[**from French: pot**]**

Marmite (ˈmɑːmaɪt) *n Brit. trademark.* a yeast and vegetable extract used as a spread, flavouring, etc.

Marmolada (*Italian* marmoˈlaːda) *n* a mountain in NE Italy: highest peak in the Dolomites. Height: 3342 m (10 965 ft.).

marmoreal (mɑːˈmɔːrɪəl) *or* (*less commonly*) **marmorean** *adj* of, relating to, or resembling marble: *a marmoreal complexion.* **[C18:** from Latin *marmoreus,* from *marmor* marble**]** ▸ **marˈmoreally** *adv*

marmoset (ˈmɑːməˌzɛt) *n* **1** any small South American monkey of the genus *Callithrix* and related genera, having long hairy tails, clawed digits, and tufts of hair around the head and ears: family *Callithricidae.* **2 pygmy marmoset.** a related form, *Cebuella pygmaea:* the smallest monkey, inhabiting tropical forests of the Amazon. **[C14:** from Old French *marmouset* grotesque figure, of obscure origin**]**

marmot (ˈmɑːmət) *n* **1** any burrowing sciurine rodent of the genus *Marmota,* of Europe, Asia, and North America. They are heavily built, having short legs, a short furry tail, and coarse fur. **2 prairie marmot.** another name for **prairie dog.** **[C17:** from French *marmotte,* perhaps ultimately from Latin *mūr-* (stem of *mūs*) mouse + *montis* of the mountain**]**

Marne (*French* marn) *n* **1** a department of NE France, in Champagne-Ardenne region. Capital: Châlons-sur-Marne. Pop.: 567 300 (1995). Area: 8205 sq. km (3200 sq. miles). **2** a river in NE France, rising on the plateau of Langres and flowing north, then west to the River Seine, north of Paris: linked by canal with the Rivers Saône, Rhine, and Aisne; scene of two unsuccessful German offensives (1914, 1918) during World War I. Length: 525 km (326 miles).

Maroc (marɔk) *n* the French name for **Morocco.**

marocain (ˈmærəˌkeɪn) *n* **1** a fabric of ribbed crepe. **2** a garment made from this fabric. **[C20:** from French *maroquin* Moroccan**]**

Maronite (ˈmærəˌnaɪt) *n Christianity.* a member of a body of Uniats of Syrian origin, now living chiefly in Lebanon. **[C16:** from Late Latin *Marōnīta,* after *Maro,* 5th-century Syrian monk**]**

maroon[1] (məˈruːn) *vb* (*tr*) **1** to leave ashore and abandon, esp. on an island. **2** to isolate without resources. ♦ *n* **3** a descendant of a group of runaway slaves living in the remoter areas of the Caribbean or Guyana. **[C17** (applied to fugitive slaves): from American Spanish *cimarrón* wild, literally: dwelling on peaks, from Spanish *cima* summit**]**

maroon[2] (məˈruːn) *n* **1a** a dark red to purplish-red colour. **1b** (*as adj*): *a maroon carpet.* **2** an exploding firework, esp. one used as a warning signal. **[C18:** from French, literally: chestnut, MARRON[1]**]**

maroquin (ˌmærəˈkiːn; ˈmærəkɪn, -kwɪn) *n Tanning.* morocco leather. **[C16:** from French: Moroccan**]**

Maros (ˈmɔrɔʃ) *n* the Hungarian name for the **Mureş.**

Marprelate (ˈmɑːprɛlɪt) *n* **Martin,** the pen name of the anonymous author or authors of a series of satirical Puritan tracts (1588–89), attacking the bishops of the Church of England.

Marq. *abbrev. for* Marquis.

Marquand (mɑːˈkwɒnd) *n* **J(ohn) P(hillips).** 1893–1960, U.S. novelist, noted for his stories featuring the Japanese detective Mr Moto and for his satirical comedies of New England life, such as *The Late George Apley* (1937).

marque (mɑːk) *n* **1** a brand of product, esp. of a car. **2** an emblem or nameplate used to identify a product, esp. a car. **3** See **letter of marque.** **[**from French, from *marquer* to MARK[1]**]**

marquee (mɑːˈkiː) *n* **1** a large tent used for entertainment, exhibition, etc. **2** Also called: **marquise.** *Chiefly U.S. and Candian.* a canopy over the entrance to a theatre, hotel, etc. **[C17** (originally an officer's tent): invented singular form of MARQUISE, erroneously taken to be plural**]**

Marquesan (mɑːˈkeɪzᵊn, -sᵊn) *adj* **1** of or relating to the Marquesas Islands or their inhabitants. ♦ *n* **2** a native or inhabitant of the Marquesas Islands.

Marquesas Islands (mɑːˈkeɪsæs) *pl n* a group of volcanic islands in the S Pacific, in French Polynesia. Pop.: 7538 (1988). Area: 1287 sq. km (497 sq. miles). French name: **Îles Marquises** (il markiz).

marquess (ˈmɑːkwɪs) *n* **1** (in the British Isles) a nobleman ranking between a duke and an earl. **2** See **marquis.**

marquessate (ˈmɑːkwɪzɪt) *n* (in the British Isles) the dignity, rank, or position of a marquess; marquisate.

marquetry *or* **marqueterie** (ˈmɑːkɪtrɪ) *n, pl* **-quetries** *or* **-queteries.** a pattern of inlaid veneers of wood, brass, ivory, etc., fitted together to form a picture or design, used chiefly as ornamentation in furniture. Compare **parquetry.** **[C16:** from Old French, from *marqueter* to inlay, from *marque* MARK[1]**]**

Marquette (mɑːˈkɛt) *n* **Jacques** (ʒak), known as *Père Marquette.* 1637–75, French Jesuit missionary and explorer, with Louis Jolliet, of the Mississippi river.

Márquez (ˈmɑːkɛz) *n* **Gabriel García.** See (Gabriel) **García Márquez.**

marquis (ˈmɑːkwɪs, mɑːˈkiː; *French* marki) *n, pl* **-quises** *or* **-quis.** (in various countries) a nobleman ranking above a count, corresponding to a British marquess. The title of marquis is often used in place of that of marquess. **[C14:** from Old French *marchis,* literally: count of the march, from *marche* MARCH[2]**]**

Marquis (ˈmɑːkwɪs) *n* **Don(ald Robert Perry).** 1878–1937, U.S. humorist; author of *archy and mehitabel* (1927).

marquisate (ˈmɑːkwɪzɪt) *n* **1** the rank or dignity of a marquis. **2** the domain of a marquis.

marquise (mɑːˈkiːz; *French* markiz) *n* **1** (in various countries) another word for **marchioness. 2a** a gemstone, esp. a diamond, cut in a pointed oval shape and usually faceted. **2b** a piece of jewellery, esp. a ring, set with such a stone or with an oval cluster of stones. **3** another name for **marquee** (sense 2). **[C18:** from French, feminine of MARQUIS**]**

marquisette (ˌmɑːkɪˈzɛt, -kwɪ-) *n* a leno-weave fabric of cotton, silk, etc. **[C20:** from French, diminutive of MARQUISE**]**

Marrakech *or* **Marrakesh** (məˈrækɛʃ, ˌmærəˈkɛʃ) *n* a city in W central Morocco: several times capital of Morocco; tourist centre. Pop.: 621 914 (1994).

marram grass (ˈmærəm) *n* any of several grasses of the genus *Ammophila* (or *Psamma*), esp. *A. arenaria,* that grow on sandy shores and can withstand drying: often planted to stabilize sand dunes. **[C17** *marram,* from Old Norse *marálmr,* from *marr* sea + *hálmr* HAULM**]**

Marrano (məˈrɑːnəʊ) *n, pl* **-nos.** a Spanish or Portuguese Jew of the late Middle Ages who was converted to Christianity, esp. one forcibly converted but secretly adhering to Judaism. **[**from Spanish, literally: pig, with reference to the Jewish prohibition against eating pig meat**]**

marri (ˈmærɪ) *n, pl* **-ris.** a species of eucalyptus, *Eucalyptus calophylla,* of Western Australia, widely cultivated for its coloured flowers. **[C19:** from a native Australian language**]**

marriage (ˈmærɪdʒ) *n* **1** the state or relationship of being husband and wife. **2a** the legal union or contract made by a man and woman to live as husband and wife. **2b** (*as modifier*): *marriage licence; marriage certificate.* **3** the religious or legal ceremony formalizing this union; wedding. **4** a close or intimate union, relationship, etc.: *a marriage of ideas.* **5** (in certain card games, such as bezique, pinochle) the king and queen of the same suit. ♦ Related adjs.: **conjugal, marital, nuptial.** **[C13:** from Old French; see MARRY[1], -AGE**]**

marriageable (ˈmærɪdʒəbᵊl) *adj* (esp. of women) suitable for marriage, usually with reference to age. ▸ **ˌmarriageaˈbility** *or* **ˈmarriageableness** *n*

marriage bureau *n* an agency that provides introductions to single people seeking a marriage partner.

marriage guidance *n* **a** advice given to couples who have problems in their married life. **b** (*as modifier*): *a marriage guidance counsellor.*

marriage of convenience *n* a marriage based on expediency rather than on love.

married (ˈmærɪd) *adj* **1** having a husband or wife. **2** joined in marriage: *a married couple.* **3** of or involving marriage or married persons. **4** closely or intimately united. ♦ *n* **5** (*usually pl*) a married person (esp. in the phrase **young marrieds**).

Marriner (ˈmærɪnə) *n* Sir **Neville.** born 1924, British conductor and violinist; founder (1956) and director of the Academy of St Martin in the Fields, which specializes in baroque music.

marron[1] (ˈmærən; *French* marɔ̃) *n* a large edible sweet chestnut. **[**from French, of obscure origin**]**

marron[2] (ˈmærən) *n* a large freshwater crayfish of Western Australia, *Cherax tenuimanus.* **[**from a native Australian language**]**

marrons glacés *French.* (marɔ̃ glase) *pl n* chestnuts cooked in syrup and glazed.

marrow[1] (ˈmærəʊ) *n* **1** the fatty network of connective tissue that fills the cavities of bones. **2** the vital part; essence. **3** vitality. **4** rich food. **5** *Brit.* short for **vegetable marrow.** **[**Old English *mærg;* related to Old Frisian *merg,* Old Norse *mergr***]** ▸ **ˈmarrowy** *adj*

marrow[2] (ˈmærəʊ, -rə) *n Northeastern English dialect, chiefly Durham.* a companion, esp. a workmate. **[C15** *marwe* fellow worker, perhaps of Scandinavian origin; compare Icelandic *margr* friendly**]**

marrowbone (ˈmærəʊˌbəʊn) *n* **a** a bone containing edible marrow. **b** (*as modifier*): *marrowbone jelly.*

marrowbones (ˈmærəʊˌbəʊnz) *pl n* **1** *Facetious.* the knees. **2** a rare word for **crossbones.**

marrowfat (ˈmærəʊˌfæt) *or* **marrow pea** *n* **1** any of several varieties of pea plant that have large seeds. **2** the seed of such a plant.

marrow squash *n U.S. and Canadian.* any of several oblong squashes that have a hard smooth rind, esp. the vegetable marrow.

marry[1] (ˈmærɪ) *vb* **-ries, -rying, -ried. 1** to take (someone as one's husband or wife) in marriage. **2** (*tr*) to join or give in marriage. **3** (*tr*) to acquire (something) by marriage: *marry money.* **4** to unite closely or intimately. **5** (*tr; sometimes foll. by up*) to fit together or align (two things); join. **6** (*tr*) *Nautical.* **6a** to match up (the strands) of unlaid ropes before splicing. **6b** to seize (two ropes) together at intervals along their lengths. **[C13:** from Old French *marier,* from Latin *marītāre,* from *marītus* married (man), perhaps from *mās* male**]** ▸ **ˈmarrier** *n*

marry[2] (ˈmærɪ) *interj Archaic.* an exclamation of surprise, anger, etc. **[C14:** euphemistic for the Virgin *Mary***]**

Marryat (ˈmærɪət) *n* **Frederick,** known as *Captain Marryat.* 1792–1848, English novelist and naval officer; author of novels of sea life, such as *Mr Midshipman Easy* (1836), and children's stories, such as *The Children of the New Forest* (1847).

marry into *vb* (*intr, prep*) to become a member of (a family) by marriage.

marry off *vb* (*tr, adv*) to find a husband or wife for (a person, esp. one's son or daughter).

Mars[1] (mɑːz) *n* the Roman god of war, the father of Romulus and Remus. Greek counterpart: **Ares**.

Mars[2] (mɑːz) *n* **1** Also called: the **Red Planet**. the fourth planet from the sun, having a reddish-orange surface with numerous dark patches and two white polar caps. It has a thin atmosphere, mainly carbon dioxide, and low surface temperatures. Spacecraft encounters have revealed a history of volcanic activity and running surface water. The planet has two tiny satellites, Phobos and Deimos. Mean distance from sun: 228 million km; period of revolution around sun: 686.98 days; period of axial rotation: 24.6225 hours; diameter and mass: 53.2 and 10.7 per cent that of earth respectively. **2** the alchemical name for **iron**.

Marsala (mɑːˈsɑːlə) *n* **1** a port in W Sicily: landing place of Garibaldi at the start of his Sicilian campaign (1860). Pop.: 80 760 (1990). **2** (*sometimes not caps.*) a dark sweet dessert wine made in Sicily.

Marsalis (mɑːˈsɑːlɪs) *n* **Wynton**. born 1962, U.S. jazz and classical trumpeter.

Marseillaise (ˌmɑːsəˈleɪz; *French* marsejez) *n* **the**. the French national anthem. Words and music were composed in 1792 by C. J. Rouget de Lisle as a war song for the Rhine army of revolutionary France. [**C18**: from French (*chanson*) *Marseillaise* song of Marseille (it was first sung in Paris by the battalion of Marseille)]

marseille (mɑːˈseɪl) *or* **marseilles** (mɑːˈseɪlz) *n* a strong cotton fabric with a raised pattern, used for bedspreads, etc. [**C18**: from *Marseille quilting*, made in Marseille]

Marseille (*French* marsej) *n* a port in SE France, on the Gulf of Lions: second largest city in the country and a major port; founded in about 600 B.C. by Greeks from Phocaea; oil refining. Pop.: 807 726 (1990). Ancient name: **Mas'silia**. English name: **Marseilles** (mɑːˈseɪ, -ˈseɪlz).

marsh (mɑːʃ) *n* low poorly drained land that is sometimes flooded and often lies at the edge of lakes, streams, etc. Related adj: **paludal**. Compare **swamp** (sense 1). [Old English *merisc*; related to German *Marsch*, Dutch *marsk*; related to MERE[2]] ► **'marsh,like** *adj*

Marsh (mɑːʃ) *n* **1** Dame (**Edith**) **Ngaio** (ˈnaɪəʊ). 1899–1981, New Zealand crime writer, living in Britain (from 1928). Her many detective novels include *Final Curtain* (1947) and *Last Ditch* (1977). **2 Rodney** (**William**). born 1947, Australian cricketer. He finished his career with a world record of 355 Test match dismissals.

marshal (ˈmɑːʃəl) *n* **1** (in some armies and air forces) an officer of the highest rank. **2** (in England) an officer, usually a junior barrister, who accompanies a judge on circuit and performs miscellaneous secretarial duties. **3** (in the U.S.) **3a** a Federal court officer assigned to a judicial district whose functions are similar to those of a sheriff. **3b** (in some states) the chief police or fire officer. **4** an officer who organizes or conducts ceremonies, parades, etc. **5** Also called: **knight marshal**. (formerly in England) an officer of the royal family or court, esp. one in charge of protocol. **6** an obsolete word for **ostler**. ◆ *vb* **-shals, -shalling, -shalled** *or U.S.* **-shals, -shaling, -shaled**. (*tr*) **7** to arrange in order: *to marshal the facts*. **8** to assemble and organize (troops, vehicles, etc.) prior to onward movement. **9** to arrange (assets, mortgages, etc.) in order of priority. **10** to guide or lead, esp. in a ceremonious way. **11** to combine (two or more coats of arms) on one shield. [**C13**: from Old French *mareschal*; related to Old High German *marahscalc* groom, from *marah* horse + *scalc* servant] ► **'marshalcy** *or* **'marshal,ship** *n* ► **'marshaller** *or U.S.* **'marshaler** *n*

Marshall (ˈmɑːʃəl) *n* **1 Alfred**. 1842–1924, English economist, author of *Principles of Economics* (1890). **2 George Catlett**. 1880–1959, U.S. general and statesman. He was chief of staff of the U.S. army (1939–45) and, as secretary of state (1947–49), he proposed the Marshall Plan (1947), later called the European Recovery Programme: Nobel peace prize 1953. **3 John**. 1755–1835, U.S. jurist and statesman. As chief justice of the Supreme Court (1801–35), he established the principles of U.S. constitutional law. **4** Sir **John Ross**. 1912–88, New Zealand politician; prime minister (1972).

marshalling yard *n Railways*. a place or depot where railway wagons are shunted and made up into trains and where engines, carriages, etc., are kept when not in use.

Marshall Islands *pl n* a republic, consisting of a group of 34 coral islands in the W central Pacific: administratively part of the Trust Territory of the Pacific Islands (1947–87); status of free association with the U.S. from 1986; consists of two parallel chains, Ralik and Ratak. Official languages: Marshallese and English. Religion: Roman Catholic majority. Currency: U.S. dollar. Capital: Majuro. Pop.: 62 800 (1998 est.). Area: (land) 181 sq. km (70 sq. miles); (lagoon) 11 655 sq. km (4500 sq. miles).

Marshall Plan *n* a programme of U.S. economic aid for the reconstruction of post-World War II Europe (1948–52). Official name: **European Recovery Programme**.

Marshal of the Royal Air Force *n* a rank in the Royal Air Force comparable to that of Field Marshal in the British army.

Marshalsea (ˈmɑːʃəlˌsiː) *n* **1** (formerly in England) a court held before the knight marshal: abolished 1849. **2** a prison for debtors and others, situated in Southwark, London: abolished in 1842. [**C14**: see MARSHAL, -CY]

marsh andromeda *n* a low-growing pink-flowered ericaceous evergreen shrub, *Andromeda polifolia*, that grows in peaty bogs of northern regions. Also called: **moorwort**.

marshbuck (ˈmɑːʃˌbʌk) *n* an antelope of the central African swamplands, *Strepsiceros spekei*, with spreading hoofs adapted to boggy ground; an important vector of the tsetse fly. Also called: **sitatunga**.

marsh elder *n* any of several North American shrubs of the genus *Iva*, growing in salt marshes: family *Compositae* (composites). Compare **elder**[2].

marsh fern *n* a fern of marshy woodlands, *Thelypteris palustris*, having pale green pinnate leaves and an underground rootstock.

marsh fever *n* another name for **malaria**.

marsh gas *n* a hydrocarbon gas largely composed of methane formed when organic material decays in the absence of air.

marsh harrier *n* **1** a European harrier, *Circus aeruginosus*, that frequents marshy regions. **2** a U.S. and Canadian name for **hen harrier**.

marsh hawk *n* the usual U.S. and Canadian name for the **hen harrier**.

marsh hen *n* any bird that frequents marshes and swamps, esp. a rail, coot, or gallinule.

marshland (ˈmɑːʃlənd) *n* land consisting of marshes.

marshmallow (ˌmɑːʃˈmæləʊ) *n* **1** a sweet of a spongy texture containing gum arabic or gelatine, sugar, etc. **2** a sweetened paste or confection made from the root of the marsh mallow. ► **ˌmarsh'mallowy** *adj*

marsh mallow *n* **1** a malvaceous plant, *Althaea officinalis*, that grows in salt marshes and has pale pink flowers. The roots yield a mucilage formerly used to make marshmallows. **2** *U.S. and Canadian*. another name for **rose mallow** (sense 1).

marsh marigold *n* a yellow-flowered ranunculaceous plant, *Caltha palustris*, that grows in swampy places. Also called: **kingcup, May blobs**, and (U.S.) **cowslip**.

marsh orchid *n* any of various orchids of the genus *Dactylorchis*, growing in damp places and having mostly purplish flowers.

marsh tit *n* a small European songbird, *Parus palustris*, with a black head and greyish-brown body: family *Paridae* (tits).

marshwort (ˈmɑːʃˌwɜːt) *n* a prostrate creeping aquatic perennial umbelliferous plant, *Apium inundatum*, having small white flowers: related to wild celery.

marshy (ˈmɑːʃɪ) *adj* **marshier, marshiest**. of, involving, or like a marsh. ► **'marshiness** *n*

Marsilius of Padua (mɑːˈsɪlɪəs) *n* Italian name *Marsiglio dei Mainardini*. ?1290–?1343, Italian political philosopher, best known as the author of the *Defensor pacis* (1324), which upheld the power of the temporal ruler over that of the church.

marsipobranch (ˈmɑːsɪpəʊˌbræŋk) *n, adj* another word for **cyclostome**. [**C19**: from New Latin *Marsipobranchia*, from Greek *marsipos* pouch + *branchia* gills]

Marston (ˈmɑːstən) *n* **John**. ?1576–1634, English dramatist and satirist. His works include the revenge tragedies *Antonio and Mellida* (1602) and *Antonio's Revenge* (1602) and the satirical comedy *The Malcontent* (1604).

Marston Moor *n* a flat low-lying area in NE England, west of York: scene of a battle (1644) in which the Parliamentarians defeated the Royalists.

marsupial (mɑːˈsjuːpɪəl, -ˈsuː-) *n* **1** any mammal of the order *Marsupialia*, in which the young are born in an immature state and continue development in the marsupium. The order occurs mainly in Australia and South and Central America and includes the opossums, bandicoots, koala, wombats, and kangaroos. ◆ *adj* **2** of, relating to, or belonging to the *Marsupialia*. **3** of or relating to a marsupium. [**C17**: see MARSUPIUM] ► **marsupialian** (mɑːˌsjuːpɪˈeɪlɪən, -ˌsuː-) *or* **mar'supian** *n, adj*

marsupial mole *n* any molelike marsupial of the family *Notoryctidae*.

marsupial mouse *n* any mouselike insectivorous marsupial of the subfamily *Phascogalinae*: family *Dasyuridae*.

marsupium (mɑːˈsjuːpɪəm, -ˈsuː-) *n, pl* **-pia** (-pɪə). an external pouch in most female marsupials within which the newly born offspring are suckled and complete their development. [**C17**: New Latin, from Latin: purse, from Greek *marsupion*, diminutive of *marsipos*]

mart (mɑːt) *n* a market or trading centre. [**C15**: from Middle Dutch *mart* MARKET]

Martaban (ˌmɑːtɑːˈbɑːn) *n* **Gulf of**. an inlet of the Bay of Bengal in Myanmar.

martagon *or* **martagon lily** (ˈmɑːtəgən) *n* a Eurasian lily plant, *Lilium martagon*, cultivated for its mottled purplish-red flowers with reflexed petals. Also called: **Turk's-cap lily**. [**C15**: from French, from Turkish *martagān* a type of turban]

Martel (mɑːˈtel) *n* See **Charles Martel**.

martellato (ˌmɑːtəˈlɑːtəʊ) *or* **martellando** *n* (in string playing) the practice of bowing the string with a succession of short sharp blows. [Italian: hammered]

Martello tower *or* **Martello** (mɑːˈteləʊ) *n* a small circular tower for coastal defence, formerly much used in Europe. [**C18**: after Cape *Mortella* in Corsica, where the British navy captured a tower of this type in 1794]

marten (ˈmɑːtɪn) *n, pl* **-tens** *or* **-ten**. **1** any of several agile arboreal musteline mammals of the genus *Martes*, of Europe, Asia, and North America, having bushy tails and golden brown to blackish fur. See also **pine marten**. **2** the highly valued fur of these animals, esp. that of *M. americana*. ◆ See also **sable** (sense 1). [**C15**: from Middle Dutch *martren*, from Old French (*peau*) *martrine* skin of a marten, from *martre*, probably of Germanic origin]

martensite (ˈmɑːtɪnˌzaɪt) *n* a constituent formed in steels by rapid quenching, consisting of a supersaturated solid solution of carbon in iron. It is formed by the breakdown of austenite when the rate of cooling is large enough to prevent pearlite forming. [**C20**: named after Adolf *Martens* (died 1914), German metallurgist] ► **martensitic** (ˌmɑːtɪnˈzɪtɪk) *adj*

Martha (ˈmɑːθə) *n* **Saint**. *New Testament*. a sister of Mary and Lazarus, who lived at Bethany and ministered to Jesus (Luke 10:38–42). Feast day: July 29 or June 4.

martial (ˈmɑːʃəl) *adj* of, relating to, or characteristic of war, soldiers, or the military life. [**C14**: from Latin *martiālis* of MARS[1]] ► **'martialism** *n* ► **'martialist** *n* ► **'martially** *adv* ► **'martialness** *n*

Martial[1] (ˈmɑːʃəl) *adj* of or relating to Mars.

Martial[2] (ˈmɑːʃəl) *n* full name *Marcus Valerius Martialis*. ?40–?104 A.D., Latin epigrammatist and poet, born in Spain.

martial art *n* any of various philosophies of self-defence and techniques of single combat, such as judo or karate, originating in the Far East.

martial law *n* the rule of law established and maintained by the military in the absence of civil law.

Martian ('mɑːʃən) *adj* **1** of, occurring on, or relating to the planet Mars. ◆ *n* **2** an inhabitant of Mars, esp. in science fiction.

martin ('mɑːtɪn) *n* any of various swallows of the genera *Progne, Delichon, Riparia,* etc., having a square or slightly forked tail. See also **house martin.** [C15: perhaps from St MARTIN, because the birds were believed to migrate at the time of Martinmas]

Martin ('mɑːtɪn) *n* **1 Archer John Porter.** born 1910, British biochemist; Nobel prize for chemistry 1952 (with Richard Synge; 1914–94) for developing paper chromatography (1944). He subsequently developed gas chromatography (1953). **2** (*French* martɛ̃) **Frank.** 1890–1974, Swiss composer. He used a modified form of the twelve-note technique in some of his works, which include *Petite Symphonie Concertante* (1946) and the oratorio *Golgotha* (1949). **3 John.** 1789–1854, British painter, noted for his visionary landscapes and large-scale works with biblical subjects. **4 Saint,** called *Saint Martin of Tours.* ?316–?397 A.D., bishop of Tours (?371–?397); a patron saint of France. He furthered monasticism in Gaul. Feast day: Nov. 11 or 12.

Martin V *n* original name *Oddone Colonna.* 1368–1431, pope (1417–31). His election at the Council of Constance brought to an end the Great Schism.

Martin du Gard (*French* martɛ̃ dy gar) *n* **Roger** (rɔʒe). 1881–1958, French novelist, noted for his series of novels, *Les Thibault* (1922–40): Nobel prize for literature 1937.

Martineau ('mɑːtɪˌnəʊ) *n* **1 Harriet.** 1802–76, English author of books on political economy and of novels and children's stories. **2** her brother, **James.** 1805–1900, English Unitarian theologian and minister.

martinet (ˌmɑːtɪ'nɛt) *n* a person who maintains strict discipline, esp. in a military force. [C17: from French, from the name of General *Martinet,* drillmaster under Louis XIV] ▸ ˌ**marti'netish** *adj* ▸ ˌ**marti'netism** *n*

martingale ('mɑːtɪnˌgeɪl) *n* **1** a strap from the reins to the girth of a horse preventing it from carrying its head too high. **2** any gambling system in which the stakes are raised, usually doubled, after each loss. **3** Also called: **martingale boom.** *Nautical.* **3a** a chain or cable running from a jib boom to the dolphin striker, serving to counteract strain. **3b** another term for **dolphin striker.** [C16: from French, of uncertain origin]

martini (mɑː'tiːnɪ) *n, pl* **-nis. 1** (*often cap.*) *Trademark.* an Italian vermouth. **2** a cocktail of gin and vermouth. [C19 (sense 2): perhaps from the name of the inventor]

Martini (*Italian* mar'tiːni) *n* **Simone** (si'moːne). ?1284–1344, Sienese painter.

Martinique (ˌmɑːtɪ'niːk) *n* an island in the E Caribbean, in the Windward Islands of the Lesser Antilles: administratively an overseas region of France. Capital: Fort-de-France. Pop.: 398 000 (1998 est.). Area: 1090 sq. km (420 sq. miles). ▸ ˌ**Marti'nican** *n, adj*

Martinmas ('mɑːtɪnməs) *n* the feast of St Martin on Nov. 11; one of the four quarter days in Scotland.

Martinů ('mɑːtɪˌnuː; *Czech* 'martjinuː) *n* **Bohuslav** ('bɔhuslaf). 1890–1959, Czech composer.

martlet ('mɑːtlɪt) *n* **1** an archaic name for a **martin. 2** *Heraldry.* a footless bird often found in coats of arms, standing for either a martin or a swallow. [C16: from French *martelet,* variant of *martinet,* diminutive of MARTIN]

martyr ('mɑːtə) *n* **1** a person who suffers death rather than renounce his religious beliefs. **2** a person who suffers greatly or dies for a cause, belief, etc. **3** a person who suffers from poor health, misfortune, etc.: *he's a martyr to rheumatism.* **4** *Facetious or derogatory.* a person who feigns suffering to gain sympathy, help, etc. ◆ *vb also* '**martyrˌize** *or* '**martyrˌise.** (*tr*) **5** to kill as a martyr. **6** to make a martyr of. [Old English *martir,* from Church Latin *martyr,* from Late Greek *martur-, martus* witness] ▸ ˌ**martyri'zation** *or* ˌ**martyri'sation** *n*

martyrdom ('mɑːtədəm) *n* **1** the sufferings or death of a martyr. **2** great suffering or torment.

martyrology (ˌmɑːtə'rɒlədʒɪ) *n, pl* **-gies. 1** an official list of martyrs. **2** *Christianity.* the study of the lives of the martyrs. **3** a historical account of the lives of martyrs. ▸ **martyrological** (ˌmɑːtərə'lɒdʒɪkᵊl) *or* ˌ**martyro'logic** *adj* ▸ ˌ**martyr'ologist** *n*

martyry ('mɑːtərɪ) *n, pl* **-tyries.** a shrine or chapel erected in honour of a martyr.

MARV (mɑːv) *n acronym for* manoeuvrable re-entry vehicle: a missile that has one or more warheads that may be controlled so as to avoid enemy defences.

marvel ('mɑːvᵊl) *vb* **-vels, -velling, -velled** *or U.S.* **-vels, -veling, -veled. 1** (when *intr,* often foll. by *at* or *about;* when *tr, takes a clause as object*) to be filled with surprise or wonder. ◆ *n* **2** something that causes wonder. **3** *Archaic.* astonishment. [C13: from Old French *merveille,* from Late Latin *mīrābilia,* from Latin *mīrābilis,* from *mīrārī* to wonder at]

Marvell ('mɑːvᵊl) *n* **Andrew.** 1621–78, English poet and satirist. He is noted for his lyrical poems and verse and prose satires attacking the government after the Restoration.

marvellous *or U.S.* **marvelous** ('mɑːvᵊləs) *adj* **1** causing great wonder, surprise, etc.; extraordinary. **2** improbable or incredible. **3** excellent; splendid. ▸ '**marvellously** *or U.S.* '**marvelously** *adv* ▸ '**marvellousness** *or U.S.* '**marvelousness** *n*

marvel-of-Peru *n, pl* **marvels-of-Peru.** another name for **four-o'clock** (the plant). [C16: first found in Peru]

Marx (mɑːks) *n* **Karl** (karl). 1818–83, German founder of modern communism, in England from 1849. With Engels, he wrote *The Communist Manifesto* (1848). He developed his theories of the class struggle and the economics of capitalism in *Das Kapital* (1867; 1885; 1895). He was one of the founders of the International Workingmen's Association (First International) (1864).

Marx Brothers (mɑːks) *n* **the.** a U.S. family of film comedians, esp. **Arthur Marx,** known as *Harpo* (1888–1964), **Herbert Marx,** known as *Zeppo* (1901–79), **Julius Marx,** known as *Groucho* (1890–1977), and **Leonard Marx,** known as *Chico* (1886–1961). Their films include *Animal Crackers* (1930), *Monkey Business* (1931), *Horsefeathers* (1932), *Duck Soup* (1933), and *A Day at the Races* (1937).

Marxian ('mɑːksɪən) *adj* of or relating to Karl Marx and his theories. ▸ '**Marxianism** *n*

Marxism ('mɑːksɪzəm) *n* the economic and political theory and practice originated by Karl Marx and Friedrich Engels that holds that actions and human institutions are economically determined, that the class struggle is the basic agency of historical change, and that capitalism will ultimately be superseded by communism.

Marxism-Leninism *n* the modification of Marxism by Lenin stressing that imperialism is the highest form of capitalism. ▸ '**Marxist-'Leninist** *n, adj*

Marxist ('mɑːksɪst) *n* **1** a follower of Marxism. ◆ *adj* **2** (of an economic or political theory) analogous to or derived from the doctrines of Marx. **3** of or relating to Marx, Marxism, or Marxists and their theories.

Mary ('mɛərɪ) *n* **1** *New Testament.* **1a Saint.** Also called: the **Virgin Mary.** the mother of Jesus, believed to have conceived and borne him while still a virgin; she was married to Joseph (Matthew 1:18–25). Major feast days: Feb. 2, Mar. 25, May 31, Aug. 15, Sept. 8. **1b** the sister of Martha and Lazarus (Luke 10:38–42; John 11:1–2). **2** original name *Princess Mary of Teck.* 1867–1953, queen of Great Britain and Northern Ireland (1910–36) by marriage to George V. **3** (*pl* '**Maries**) *Austral. derogatory slang. Obsolete.* an Aboriginal woman or girl.

Mary I *n* family name *Tudor,* known as *Bloody Mary.* 1516–58, queen of England (1553–58). The daughter of Henry VIII and Catherine of Aragon, she married Philip II of Spain in 1554. She restored Roman Catholicism to England and about 300 Protestants were burnt at the stake as heretics.

Mary II *n* 1662–94, queen of England, Scotland, and Ireland (1689–94), ruling jointly with her husband William III. They were offered the crown by parliament, which objected to the arbitrary rule of her father James II.

mary jane *n U.S. and Canadian.* a slang term for **marijuana.**

Maryland ('mɛərɪˌlænd, 'mɛrɪlənd) *n* a state of the eastern U.S., on the Atlantic: divided into two unequal parts by Chesapeake Bay: mostly low-lying, with the Alleghenies in the northwest. Capital: Annapolis. Pop.: 5 094 289 (1997 est.). Area: 31 864 sq. km (12 303 sq. miles). Abbrevs.: **Md.** or (with zip code) **MD**

Mary Magdalene *n New Testament.* **Saint.** a woman of **Magdala** ('mægdələ) in Galilee whom Jesus cured of evil spirits (Luke 8:2) and who is often identified with the sinful woman of Luke 7:36–50. In Christian tradition she is usually taken to have been a prostitute. See **magdalen.** Feast day: July 22.

Maryolatry (ˌmɛərɪ'ɒlətrɪ) *n* a variant spelling of **Mariolatry.**

Maryology (ˌmɛərɪ'ɒlədʒɪ) *n* a variant spelling of **Mariology.**

Mary, Queen of Scots *n* family name *Stuart.* 1542–87, queen of Scotland (1542–67); daughter of James V of Scotland and Mary of Guise. She was married to Francis II of France (1558–60), her cousin Lord Darnley (1565–67), and the Earl of Bothwell (1567–71), who was commonly regarded as Darnley's murderer. She was forced to abdicate in favour of her son (later James VI of Scotland) and fled to England. Imprisoned by Elizabeth I until 1587, she was beheaded for plotting against the English crown.

marzipan ('mɑːzɪˌpæn) *n* **1** a paste made from ground almonds, sugar, and egg whites, used to coat fruit cakes or moulded into sweets. Also called (esp. formerly): **marchpane.** ◆ *modifier.* **2** *Informal.* of or relating to the stratum of middle managers in a financial institution or other business: *marzipan layer job losses.* [C19: via German from Italian *marzapane.* See MARCHPANE]

-mas *n combining form.* indicating a Christian festival: *Christmas; Michaelmas.* [from MASS]

Masaccio (*Italian* ma'zattʃo) *n* original name *Tommaso Guidi.* 1401–28, Florentine painter. He was the first to apply to painting the laws of perspective discovered by Brunelleschi. His chief work is the frescoes in the Brancacci chapel in the church of Sta. Maria del Carmine, Florence.

Masada (mə'sɑːdə) *n* an ancient mountaintop fortress in Israel, 400 m (1300 ft.) above the W shore of the Dead Sea: the last Jewish stronghold during a revolt in Judaea (66–73 A.D.). Besieged by the Romans for a year, almost all of the inhabitants killed themselves rather than surrender. The site is an Israeli national monument.

Masai ('mɑːsaɪ, mɑː'saɪ, 'mæsaɪ) *n* **1** (*pl* **-sais** *or* **-sai**) a member of a Nilotic people, formerly noted as warriors, living chiefly in Kenya and Tanzania. **2** the language of this people, belonging to the Nilotic group of the Nilo-Saharan family.

Masakhane (ˌmasa'kanɪ) *n S. African.* a political slogan of solidarity. [C20: Nguni, literally: let us build together]

Masan ('mɑːˌsɑːn) *n* a port in SE South Korea, on an inlet of the Korea Strait: first opened to foreign trade in 1899. Pop.: 441 358 (1995).

Masaryk ('mæsərɪk; *Czech* 'masarik) *n* **1 Jan** (jan). 1886–1948, Czech statesman; foreign minister (1941–48). He died in mysterious circumstances after the Communists took control of the government. **2** his father, **Tomáš Garrigue** ('tɔmaːʃ 'garik). 1850–1937, Czech philosopher and statesman; a founder of Czechoslovakia (1918) and its first president (1918–35).

Masbate (mæs'bɑːtɪ) *n* **1** an island in the central Philippines, between Negros and SE Luzon: agricultural, with resources of gold, copper, and manganese. Pop.: 599 355 (1990). Area: 4045 sq. km (1562 sq. miles). **2** the capital of this island, a port in the northeast. Pop.: 52 944 (1980).

masc. *abbrev. for* masculine.

Mascagni (*Italian* mas'kaɲɲi) *n* **Pietro** ('pjɛːtro). 1863–1945, Italian composer of operas, including *Cavalleria rusticana* (1890).

mascara (mæ'skɑːrə) *n* a cosmetic substance for darkening, colouring, and thickening the eyelashes, applied with a brush or rod. [C20: from Spanish: mask]

Mascarene Islands (ˌmæskəˈriːn) *pl n* a group of volcanic islands in the W Indian Ocean, east of Madagascar: consists of the islands of Réunion, Mauritius, and Rodrigues. French name: **Îles Mascareignes.**

mascarpone (ˌmæskəˈpəunɪ) *n* a soft Italian cream cheese. [from Italian, from dialect (Lombardy) *mascherpa* ricotta]

mascle (ˈmɑːskᵊl) *n Heraldry.* a charge consisting of a lozenge with a lozenge-shaped hole in the middle. Also called: **voided lozenge.** [C14: from Old French *macle,* perhaps from Latin *macula* spot]

mascon (ˈmæskɒn) *n* any of several lunar regions of high gravity. [C20: from MAS(S) + CON(CENTRATION)]

mascot (ˈmæskət) *n* a person, animal, or thing considered to bring good luck. [C19: from French *mascotte,* from Provençal *mascotto* charm, from *masco* witch]

masculine (ˈmæskjʊlɪn) *adj* **1** possessing qualities or characteristics considered typical of or appropriate to a man; manly. **2** unwomanly. **3** *Grammar.* **3a** denoting a gender of nouns, occurring in many inflected languages, that includes all kinds of referents as well as some male animate referents. **3b** *(as n): German "Weg" is a masculine.* [C14: via French from Latin *masculīnus,* from *masculus* male, from *mās* a male] ▸ **ˈmasculinely** *adv* ▸ **ˌmascuˈlinity** *or (less commonly)* **ˈmasculineness** *n*

masculine ending *n Prosody.* a stressed syllable at the end of a line of verse. Compare **feminine ending.**

masculine rhyme *n Prosody.* a rhyme between stressed monosyllables or between the final stressed syllables of polysyllabic words: *book, cook; collect, direct.* Compare **feminine rhyme.**

masculinist (ˈmæskjʊlɪnɪst) *or* **masculist** (ˈmæskjʊlɪst) *n* **1** an advocate of the rights of men. ◆ *adj* **2** of, characterized by, or relating to men's rights.

masculinize *or* **masculinise** (ˈmæskjʊlɪˌnaɪz) *vb* to make or become masculine, esp. to cause (a woman) to show male secondary sexual characteristics as a result of taking steroids. ▸ **ˌmasculiniˈzation** *or* **ˌmasculiniˈsation** *n*

Masefield (ˈmeɪsˌfiːld) *n* **John.** 1878–1967, English poet, novelist, and critic; poet laureate (1930–67).

maser (ˈmeɪzə) *n* a device for amplifying microwaves, working on the same principle as a laser. [C20: *m(icrowave) a(mplification by) s(timulated) e(mission of) r(adiation)*]

Maseru (məˈseəruː) *n* the capital of Lesotho, in the northwest near the W border with South Africa; established as capital of Basutoland in 1869. Pop.: 297 000 (1995 est.).

mash (mæʃ) *n* **1** a soft pulpy mass or consistency. **2** *Agriculture.* a feed of bran, meal, or malt mixed with water and fed to horses, cattle, or poultry. **3** (esp. in brewing) a mixture of mashed malt grains and hot water, from which malt is extracted. **4** *Brit., informal.* mashed potatoes. **5** *Northern English dialect.* a brew of tea. ◆ *vb (tr)* **6** to beat or crush into a mash. **7** to steep (malt grains) in hot water in order to extract malt, esp. for making malt liquors. **8** *Northern English dialect.* to brew (tea). **9** *Archaic.* to flirt with. [Old English *mǣsc-* (in compound words); related to Middle Low German *mēsch*] ▸ **mashed** *adj* ▸ **ˈmasher** *n*

MASH (mæʃ) *n* (in the U.S.) *acronym for* Mobile Army Surgical Hospital.

Masham (ˈmæsəm) *n* a crossbreed of large sheep having a black and white face and a long curly fleece: kept for lamb production. [C20: named after *Masham,* town in N Yorkshire]

Masharbrum *or* **Masherbrum** (ˈmʌʃəˌbrʊm) *n* a mountain in N India, in N Kashmir in the Karakoram Range of the Himalayas. Height: 7822 m (25 660 ft.).

Mashhad (mæʃˈhæd) *or* **Meshed** *n* a city in NE Iran: the holy city of Shi'ite Muslims; carpet manufacturing. Pop.: 1 964 489 (1994 est.).

mashiach (məˈʃiɑx) *n Judaism.* the messiah. [Hebrew, literally: anointed; compare MESSIAH]

mashie *or* **mashy** (ˈmæʃɪ) *n, pl* **mashies.** *Golf.* (formerly) a club, corresponding to the modern No. 5 or No. 6 iron, used for approach shots. [C19: perhaps from French *massue* club, ultimately from Latin *mateola* mallet]

Mashona (məˈʃəunə) *n, pl* **-na** *or* **-nas.** another name for the **Shona** (sense 1).

Masinissa *or* **Massinissa** (ˌmæsɪˈnɪsə) *n* ?238–?149 B.C., king of Numidia (?210–149), who fought as an ally of Rome against Carthage in the Second Punic War.

masjid *or* **musjid** (ˈmʌsdʒɪd) *n* a mosque in an Arab country. [Arabic; see MOSQUE]

mask (mɑːsk) *n* **1** any covering for the whole or a part of the face worn for amusement, protection, disguise, etc. **2** a fact, action, etc., that conceals something: *his talk was a mask for his ignorance.* **3** another name for **masquerade.** **4** a likeness of a face or head, either sculpted or moulded, such as a death mask. **5** an image of a face worn by an actor, esp. in ancient Greek and Roman drama, in order to symbolize the character being portrayed. **6** a variant spelling of **masque.** **7** *Surgery.* a sterile gauze covering for the nose and mouth worn esp. during operations to minimize the spread of germs. **8** *Sport.* a protective covering for the face worn for fencing, ice hockey, etc. **9** a carving in the form of a face or head, used as an ornament. **10** a natural land feature or artificial object which conceals troops, etc., from view. **11** a device placed over the nose and mouth to facilitate or prevent inhalation of a gas. **12** *Photog.* a shield of paper, paint, etc., placed over an area of unexposed photographic surface to stop light falling on it. **13** *Electronics.* a thin sheet of material from which a pattern has been cut, placed over a semiconductor chip so that an integrated circuit can be formed on the exposed areas. **14** *Computing.* a bit pattern which, by convolution with a second pattern in a logical operation, can be used to isolate a specific subset of the second pattern for examination. **15** *Entomol.* a large prehensile mouthpart (labium) of the dragonfly larva. **16** the face or head of an animal, such as a fox, or the dark coloration of the face of some animals, such as Siamese cats and certain dogs. **17** another word for **face pack.** **18** *Now rare.* a person wearing a mask. ◆ *vb* **19** to cover with or put on a mask. **20** *(tr)* to conceal; disguise: *to mask an odour.* **21** *(tr) Photog.* to shield a particular area of (an unexposed photographic surface) in order to prevent or reduce the action of light there. **22** *(tr)* to shield a particular area of (a surface to be painted) with masking tape. **23** *(tr)* to cover (cooked food, esp. meat) with a savoury sauce or glaze. [C16: from Italian *maschera,* ultimately from Arabic *maskharah* clown, from *sakhira* mockery] ▸ **ˈmaskˌlike** *adj*

maskanonge (ˈmæskəˌnɒndʒ), **maskinonge** (ˈmæskɪˌnɒndʒ), *or* **maskalonge** (ˈmæskəˌlɒndʒ) *n, pl* **-nonges, -nonge** *or* **-longes, -longe.** variants of **muskellunge.**

masked (mɑːskt) *adj* **1** disguised or covered by or as if by a mask. **2** *Botany.* another word for **personate**[2].

masked ball *n* a ball at which masks are worn.

masker *or* **masquer** (ˈmɑːskə) *n* a person who wears a mask or takes part in a masque.

masking (ˈmɑːskɪŋ) *n* **1** the act or practice of masking. **2** *Psychol.* the process by which a stimulus (usually visual or auditory) is obscured by the presence of another almost simultaneous stimulus.

masking tape *n* an adhesive tape used to mask and protect surfaces surrounding an area to be painted.

masochism (ˈmæsəˌkɪzəm) *n* **1** *Psychiatry.* an abnormal condition in which pleasure, esp. sexual pleasure, is derived from pain or from humiliation, domination, etc., by another person. **2** *Psychoanal.* the directing towards oneself of any destructive tendencies. **3** a tendency to take pleasure from one's own suffering. Compare **sadism.** [C19: named after Leopold von Sacher *Masoch* (1836–95), Austrian novelist, who described it] ▸ **ˈmasochist** *n, adj* ▸ **ˌmasoˈchistic** *adj* ▸ **ˌmasoˈchistically** *adv*

mason (ˈmeɪsᵊn) *n* **1** a person skilled in building with stone. **2** a person who dresses stone. ◆ *vb* **3** *(tr)* to construct or strengthen with masonry. [C13: from Old French *masson,* of Frankish origin; perhaps related to Old English *macian* to make]

Mason (ˈmeɪsᵊn) *n* short for **Freemason.**

mason bee *n* any bee of the family *Megachilidae* that builds a hard domelike nest of sand, clay, etc., held together with saliva.

Mason-Dixon Line *or* **Mason and Dixon Line** (ˈdɪksən) *n* the state boundary between Maryland and Pennsylvania: surveyed between 1763 and 1767 by Charles Mason and Jeremiah Dixon; popularly regarded as the dividing line between North and South, esp. between the free and the slave states before the American Civil War.

masonic (məˈsɒnɪk) *adj* **1** *(often cap.)* of, characteristic of, or relating to Freemasons or Freemasonry. **2** of or relating to masons or masonry. ▸ **maˈsonically** *adv*

Masonite (ˈmeɪsəˌnaɪt) *n Austral. and N.Z. trademark.* a kind of dark brown hardboard used for partitions, lining, etc.

masonry (ˈmeɪsənrɪ) *n, pl* **-ries.** **1** the craft of a mason. **2** work that is built by a mason; stonework or brickwork. **3** *(often cap.)* short for **Freemasonry.**

mason wasp *n* a solitary wasp of the genus *Odynerus* that excavates its nest in sand or the mortar of old walls.

Masora, Masorah, Massora, *or* **Massorah** (məˈsɔːrə) *n* **1** the text of the Hebrew Bible as officially revised by the Masoretes from the 6th to the 10th centuries A.D., with critical notes and commentary. **2** the collection of these notes, commentaries, etc. [C17: from Hebrew: tradition]

Masorete, Massorete (ˈmæsəˌriːt), *or* **Masorite** (ˈmæsəˌraɪt) *n* **1** a member of the school of rabbis that produced the Masora. **2** a Hebrew scholar who is expert in the Masora. [C16: from Hebrew *māsōreth* MASORA]

Masoretic, Massoretic (ˌmæsəˈrɛtɪk) *or* **Masoretical, Massoretical** *adj* of or relating to the Masora, the Masoretes, or the system of textual criticism and explanation evolved by them.

Masqat (ˈmʌskət, -kæt) *n* a transliteration of the Arabic name for **Muscat.**

masque *or* **mask** (mɑːsk) *n* **1** a dramatic entertainment of the 16th to 17th centuries in England, consisting of pantomime, dancing, dialogue, and song, often performed at court. **2** the words and music written for a masque. **3** short for **masquerade.** [C16: variant of MASK]

masquer (ˈmɑːskə) *n* a variant spelling of **masker.**

masquerade (ˌmæskəˈreɪd) *n* **1** a party or other gathering to which the guests wear masks and costumes. **2** the disguise worn at such a function. **3** a pretence or disguise. ◆ *vb (intr)* **4** to participate in a masquerade; disguise oneself. **5** to dissemble. [C16: from Spanish *mascarada,* from *mascara* MASK] ▸ **ˌmasquerˈader** *n*

mass (mæs) *n* **1** a large coherent body of matter without a definite shape. **2** a collection of the component parts of something. **3** a large amount or number, such as a great body of people. **4** the main part or majority: *the mass of the people voted against the government's policy.* **5** **in the mass.** in the main; collectively. **6** the size of a body; bulk. **7** *Physics.* a physical quantity expressing the amount of matter in a body. It is a measure of a body's resistance to changes in velocity (**inertial mass**) and also of the force experienced in a gravitational field (**gravitational mass**): according to the theory of relativity, inertial and gravitational masses are equal. **8** (in painting, drawing, etc.) an area of unified colour, shade, or intensity, usually denoting a solid form or plane. **9** *Pharmacol.* a pastelike composition of drugs from which pills are made. **10** *Mining.* an irregular deposit of ore not occurring in veins. ◆ *(modifier)* **11** done or occurring on a large scale: *mass hysteria; mass radiography.* **12** consisting of a mass or large number, esp. of people: *a mass meeting.* ◆ *vb* **13** to form (people or things) or (of people or things) to join together into a mass: *the crowd massed outside the embassy.* ◆ See also **masses, mass in.** [C14: from Old French *masse,* from Latin *massa* that which forms a lump, from Greek *maza* barley cake; perhaps related to Greek *massein* to knead] ▸ **massed** *adj* ▸ **massedly** ('mæsɪdlɪ, 'mæstlɪ) *adv*

Mass (mæs, mɑːs) *n* **1** (in the Roman Catholic Church and certain Protestant Churches) the celebration of the Eucharist. See also **High Mass, Low Mass. 2** a musical setting of those parts of the Eucharistic service sung by choir or congregation. [Old English *mæsse,* from Church Latin *missa,* ultimately from Latin *mittere* to send away; perhaps derived from the concluding dismissal in the Roman Mass, *Ite, missa est,* Go, it is the dismissal]

Mass. *abbrev. for* Massachusetts.

Massa (*Italian* 'massa) *n* a town in W Italy, in NW Tuscany. Pop.: 67 780 (1990).

Massachuset (,mæsə'tʃuːsɪt) *or* **Massachusetts** *n* **1** (*pl* **-sets, -set,** *or* **-setts**) a member of a North American Indian people formerly living around Massachusetts Bay. **2** the language of this people, belonging to the Algonquian family. [probably from Algonquian, literally: at the big hill]

Massachusetts (,mæsə'tʃuːsɪts) *n* a state of the northeastern U.S., on the Atlantic: a centre of resistance to English colonial policy during the War of American Independence; consists of a coastal plain rising to mountains in the west. Capital: Boston. Pop.: 6 117 520 (1997 est.). Area: 20 269 sq. km (7826 sq. miles). Abbrevs.: **Mass.** or (with zip code) **MA**

Massachusetts Bay *n* an inlet of the Atlantic on the E coast of Massachusetts.

massacre ('mæsəkə) *n* **1** the wanton or savage killing of large numbers of people, as in battle. **2** *Informal.* an overwhelming defeat, as in a game. ◆ *vb* (*tr*) **3** to kill indiscriminately or in large numbers. **4** *Informal.* to defeat overwhelmingly. [C16: from Old French, of unknown origin] ▸ **massacrer** ('mæsəkrə) *n*

Massacre of the Innocents *n* the slaughter of all the young male children of Bethlehem at Herod's command in an attempt to destroy Jesus (Matthew 2:16–18).

massage ('mæsɑːʒ, -sɑːdʒ) *n* **1** the act of kneading, rubbing, etc., parts of the body to promote circulation, suppleness, or relaxation. ◆ *vb* (*tr*) **2** to give a massage to. **3** to treat (stiffness, aches, etc.) by a massage. **4** to manipulate (statistics, data, etc.) so that they appear to support a particular interpretation or to be better than they are; doctor. **5 massage (someone's) ego.** to boost (someone's) sense of self-esteem by flattery. [C19: from French, from *masser* to rub; see MASS] ▸ **'massager** *or* **'massagist** *n*

massage parlour *n* **1** a business providing massage services. **2** *Euphemistic.* a brothel.

massasauga (,mæsə'sɔːgə) *n* a North American venomous snake, *Sistrurus catenatus,* that has a horny rattle at the end of the tail: family *Crotalidae* (pit vipers). [C19: named after the *Missisauga* River, Ontario, Canada, where it was first found]

Massasoit ('mæsə,sɔɪt) *n* died 1661, Wampanoag Indian chief, who negotiated peace with the Pilgrim Fathers (1621).

Massawa *or* **Massaua** (mə'sɑːwə) *n* a port in E central Eritrea, on the Red Sea: capital of Eritrea during Italian occupation, from 1885 until 1900. Pop.: 40 000 (1992).

mass defect *n Physics.* the amount by which the mass of a particular nucleus is less than the total mass of its constituent particles. See also **binding energy.**

massé *or* **massé shot** ('mæsɪ) *n Billiards.* a stroke made by hitting the cue ball off centre with the cue held nearly vertically, esp. so as to make the ball move in a curve around another ball before hitting the object ball. [C19: from French, from *masser* to hit from above with a hammer, from *masse* sledgehammer, from Old French *mace* MACE[1]]

massed practice *n Psychol.* learning with no intervals or short intervals between successive bouts of learning. Compare **distributed practice.**

Masséna (*French* masena) *n* **André** (ɑ̃dre), Prince d'Essling. 1758–1817, French marshal under Napoleon I: victories at Saorgio (1794), Loano (1795), Rivoli (1797), Zürich (1799), and Caldiero (1805): defeated by Wellington in the Peninsular War (1810–11).

mass-energy *n* mass and energy considered as equivalent and interconvertible, according to the theory of relativity.

Massenet ('mæsə,neɪ; *French* masnɛ) *n* **Jules Émile Frédéric** (ʒyl emil frederik). 1842–1912, French composer of operas, including *Manon* (1884), *Werther* (1892), and *Thaïs* (1894).

masses ('mæsɪz) *pl n* **1** (preceded by *the*) the body of common people. **2** (often foll. by *of*) *Informal, chiefly Brit.* great numbers or quantities: *masses of food.*

masseter (mæ'siːtə) *n Anatomy.* a muscle of the cheek used in moving the jaw, esp. in chewing. [C17: from New Latin from Greek *masētēr* one who chews, from *masāsthai* to chew] ▸ **masseteric** (,mæsɪ'tɛrɪk) *adj*

masseur (mæ'sɜː) *or* (*fem*) **masseuse** (mæ'sɜːz) *n* a person who gives massages, esp. as a profession. [C19: from French *masser* to MASSAGE]

Massey ('mæsɪ) *n* **1 Raymond.** 1896–1983, Canadian actor and film star. His films include *The Scarlet Pimpernel* (1934) and *East of Eden* (1955). He also appeared in the television series *Dr Kildare* (1961–65). **2 Vincent.** 1887–1967, Canadian statesman: first Canadian governor general of Canada (1952–59). **3 William Ferguson.** 1856–1925, New Zealand statesman, born in Ireland: prime minister of New Zealand (1912–25).

massicot ('mæsɪ,kɒt) *n* a yellow earthy secondary mineral consisting of lead oxide. Formula: PbO. [C15: via French from Italian *marzacotto* ointment, perhaps from Arabic *shabb qubti* Egyptian alum]

massif ('mæsiːf; *French* masif) *n* **1** a mass of rock or a series of connected masses forming the peaks of a mountain range. **2** a part of the earth's crust that is bounded by faults and may be shifted by tectonic movements. [C19: from French, noun use of *massif* MASSIVE]

Massif Central (*French* masif sɑ̃tral) *n* a mountainous plateau region of S central France, occupying about one sixth of the country: contains several extinct volcanic cones, notably Puy de Dôme, 1465 m (4806 ft.). Highest point: Puy de Sancy, 1886 m (6188 ft.). Area: about 85 000 sq. km (33 000 sq. miles).

mass in *vb* (*adv*) to fill or block in (the areas of unified colour, shade, etc.) in a painting or drawing.

Massine (mɑː'siːn) *n* **Léonide** (leɔnid). 1896–1979, U.S. ballet dancer and choreographer, born in Russia.

Massinger ('mæsɪndʒə) *n* **Philip.** 1583–?1640, English dramatist, noted esp. for his comedy *A New Way to pay Old Debts* (1633).

Massinissa (,mæsɪ'nɪsə) *n* a variant spelling of **Masinissa.**

massive ('mæsɪv) *adj* **1** (of objects) large in mass; bulky, heavy, and usually solid. **2** impressive or imposing in quality, degree, or scope: *massive grief.* **3** relatively intensive or large; considerable: *a massive dose.* **4** *Pathol.* affecting a large area of the body: *a massive cancer.* **5** *Geology.* **5a** (of igneous rocks) having no stratification, cleavage, etc.; homogeneous. **5b** (of sedimentary rocks) arranged in thick poorly defined strata. **6** *Mineralogy.* without obvious crystalline structure. [C15: from French *massif,* from *masse* MASS] ▸ **'massively** *adv* ▸ **'massiveness** *n*

mass leave *n* (in India) leave taken by a large number of employees at the same time, as a form of protest.

mass-market *adj* of, for, or appealing to a large number of people; popular: *mass-market paperbacks.*

mass media *pl n* the means of communication that reach large numbers of people in a short time, such as television, newspapers, magazines, and radio.

mass noun *n* a noun that refers to an extended substance rather than to each of a set of isolable objects, as, for example, *water* as opposed to *lake.* In English when used indefinitely they are characteristically preceded by *some* rather than *a* or *an;* they do not have normal plural forms. Compare **count noun.**

mass number *n* the total number of neutrons and protons in the nucleus of a particular atom. Symbol: *A* Also called: **nucleon number.**

mass observation *n Chiefly Brit.* (*sometimes caps.*) the study of the social habits of people through observation, interviews, etc.

Massorete ('mæsə,riːt) *n* a variant spelling of **Masorete.**

massotherapy (,mæsəʊ'θɛrəpɪ) *n* medical treatment by massage. [C20: from MASS(AGE) + THERAPY] ▸ **massotherapeutic** (,mæsəʊ,θɛrə'pjuːtɪk) *adj* ▸ **,masso'therapist** *n*

mass-produce *vb* (*tr*) to manufacture (goods) to a standardized pattern on a large scale by means of extensive mechanization and division of labour. ▸ **,mass-pro'duced** *adj* ▸ **,mass-pro'ducer** *n* ▸ **mass production** *n*

mass ratio *n* the ratio of the mass of a fully-fuelled rocket at liftoff to the mass of the rocket without fuel.

mass spectrograph *n* a mass spectrometer that produces a photographic record of the mass spectrum.

mass spectrometer *or* **spectroscope** *n* an analytical instrument in which ions, produced from a sample, are separated by electric or magnetic fields according to their ratios of charge to mass. A record is produced (**mass spectrum**) of the types of ion present and their relative amounts.

massy ('mæsɪ) *adj* **massier, massiest.** a literary word for **massive.** ▸ **'massiness** *n*

Massys (*Flemish* 'masaɪs), **Matsys,** *or* **Metsys** *n* **Quentin** ('kventin). 1466–1530, Flemish painter, based in Antwerp; noted for his portraits and scenes of everyday life.

mast[1] (mɑːst) *n* **1** *Nautical.* any vertical spar for supporting sails, rigging, flags, etc., above the deck of a vessel or any components of such a composite spar. **2** any sturdy upright pole used as a support. **3** Also called: **captain's mast.** *Nautical.* a hearing conducted by the captain of a vessel into minor offences of the crew. **4 before the mast.** *Nautical.* as an apprentice seaman. ◆ *vb* **5** (*tr*) *Nautical.* to equip with a mast or masts. [Old English *mæst;* related to Middle Dutch *mast* and Latin *mālus* pole] ▸ **'mastless** *adj* ▸ **'mast,like** *adj*

mast[2] (mɑːst) *n* the fruit of forest trees, such as beech, oak, etc., used as food for pigs. [Old English *mæst;* related to Old High German *mast* food, and perhaps to MEAT]

mast- *combining form.* a variant of **masto-** before a vowel.

mastaba *or* **mastabah** ('mæstəbə) *n* a mudbrick superstructure above tombs in ancient Egypt from which the pyramid developed. [from Arabic: bench]

mast cell *n* a type of granular basophil cell in connective tissue that releases heparin, histamine, and serotonin during inflammation and allergic reactions. [C19: from MAST[2], on the model of German *Mastzelle*]

mastectomy (mæ'stɛktəmɪ) *n, pl* **-mies.** the surgical removal of a breast.

-masted *adj* (*in combination*) *Nautical.* having a mast or masts of a specified kind or number: *three-masted; tall-masted.*

master ('mɑːstə) *n* **1** the man in authority, such as the head of a household, the employer of servants, or the owner of slaves or animals. Related adj: **magistral. 2a** a person with exceptional skill at a certain thing: *a master of the violin.* **2b** (*as modifier*): *a master thief.* **3** (*often cap.*) a great artist, esp. an anonymous but influential artist. **4a** a person who has complete control of a situation. **4b** an abstract thing regarded as having power or influence: *they regarded fate as the master of their lives.* **5a** a workman or craftsman fully qualified to practise his trade and to train others in it. **5b** (*as modifier*): *master carpenter.* **6a** an original copy, stencil, tape, etc., from which duplicates are made. **6b** (*as modifier*): *master copy.* **7** a player of a game, esp. chess or bridge, who has won a specified number of tournament games. **8** the principal of some colleges. **9** a highly regarded teacher or leader whose religion or philosophy is accepted by followers. **10** a graduate holding a master's degree. **11** the chief executive officer aboard a merchant ship. **12** a person presiding over a function, organization, or institution. **13** *Chiefly Brit.* a male teacher. **14** an officer of the Supreme Court of Judicature subordinate to a judge. **15** the superior person or side in a contest. **16** a machine or device that operates to control a similar one. **17** (*often cap.*) the heir apparent of a Scottish viscount or baron. ◆ (*modifier*) **18**

overall or controlling: *master plan.* **19** designating a device or mechanism that controls others: *master switch.* **20** main; principal: *master bedroom.* ◆ *vb (tr)* **21** to become thoroughly proficient in: *to master the art of driving.* **22** to overcome; defeat: *to master your emotions.* **23** to rule or control as master. [Old English *magister* teacher, from Latin; related to Latin *magis* more, to a greater extent] ► **'masterdom** *n* ► **'master,hood** *n* ► **'masterless** *adj* ► **'mastership** *n*

Master ('mɑːstə) *n* **1** a title of address placed before the first name or surname of a boy. **2** a respectful term of address, esp. as used by disciples when addressing or referring to a religious teacher. **3** an archaic equivalent of **Mr.**

master aircrew *n* a warrant rank in the Royal Air Force, equal to but before a warrant officer.

master-at-arms *n, pl* **masters-at-arms.** the senior rating, of Chief Petty Officer rank, in a naval unit responsible for discipline, administration, and police duties.

master builder *n* **1** a person skilled in the design and construction of buildings, esp. before the foundation of the profession of architecture. **2** a self-employed builder who employs labour.

masterclass ('mɑːstə,klɑːs) *n* a session of tuition by an expert, esp. a musician, for exceptional students, usually given in public or on television.

master corporal *n* a noncommissioned officer in the Canadian forces senior to a corporal and junior to a sergeant.

master cylinder *n* a large cylinder in a hydraulic system in which the working fluid is compressed by a piston. See also **slave cylinder.**

masterful ('mɑːstəfʊl) *adj* **1** having or showing mastery. **2** fond of playing the master; imperious. **3** masterly. ► **'masterfully** *adv* ► **'masterfulness** *n*

USAGE The use of *masterful* to mean masterly as in *a masterful performance*, although common, is considered incorrect by many people.

master key *n* a key that opens all the locks of a set, the individual keys of which are not interchangeable. Also called: **pass key.**

masterly ('mɑːstəlɪ) *adj* of the skill befitting a master: *a masterly performance.* ► **'masterliness** *n*

mastermind ('mɑːstə,maɪnd) *vb* **1** *(tr)* to plan and direct (a complex undertaking): *he masterminded the robbery.* ◆ *n* **2** a person of great intelligence or executive talent, esp. one who directs an undertaking.

Master of Arts *n* a degree, usually postgraduate and in a nonscientific subject, or the holder of this degree. Abbrev.: **MA.**

master of ceremonies *n* a person who presides over a public ceremony, formal dinner, or entertainment, introducing the events, performers, etc. Abbrev.: **MC.**

master of foxhounds *n* a person responsible for the maintenance of a pack of foxhounds and the associated staff, equipment, hunting arrangements, etc. Abbrev.: **MFH.**

Master of Science *n* a postgraduate degree, usually in science, or the holder of this degree. Abbrev.: **MSc.**

Master of the Horse *n* (in England) the third official of the royal household.

Master of the Queen's Music *n* (in Britain when the sovereign is female) a court post dating from the reign of Charles I. It is an honorary title and normally held by an established English composer. Also called (when the sovereign is male): **Master of the King's Music.**

Master of the Rolls *n* (in England) a judge of the court of appeal: the senior civil judge in the country and the Keeper of the Records at the Public Record Office.

masterpiece ('mɑːstə,piːs) *or (less commonly)* **masterwork** ('mɑːstə,wɜːk) *n* **1** an outstanding work, achievement, or performance. **2** the most outstanding piece of work of a creative artist, craftsman, etc. [C17: compare Dutch *meesterstuk,* German *Meisterstück,* a sample of work submitted to a guild by a craftsman in order to qualify for the rank of master]

master race *n* a race, nation, or group, such as the Germans or Nazis as viewed by Hitler, believed to be superior to other races. German name: **Herrenvolk.**

Masters ('mɑːstəz) *n* **Edgar Lee.** 1868–1950, U.S. poet; best known for *Spoon River Anthology* (1915).

master sergeant *n* a senior noncommissioned officer in the U.S. Army, Air Force, and Marine Corps and certain other military forces, ranking immediately below the most senior noncommissioned rank.

mastersinger ('mɑːstə,sɪŋə) *n* an English spelling of **Meistersinger.**

masterstroke ('mɑːstə,strəʊk) *n* an outstanding piece of strategy, skill, talent, etc.: *your idea is a masterstroke.*

master warrant officer *n* a noncommissioned officer in the Canadian forces junior to a chief warrant officer.

mastery ('mɑːstərɪ) *n, pl* **-teries. 1** full command or understanding of a subject. **2** outstanding skill; expertise. **3** the power of command; control. **4** victory or superiority.

masthead ('mɑːst,hɛd) *n* **1** *Nautical.* **1a** the head of a mast. **1b** *(as modifier): masthead sail.* **2** Also called: **flag.** the name of a newspaper or periodical, its proprietors, staff, etc., printed in large type at the top of the front page. ◆ *vb (tr)* **3** to send (a sailor) to the masthead as a punishment. **4** to raise (a sail) to the masthead.

mastic ('mæstɪk) *n* **1** an aromatic resin obtained from the mastic tree and used as an astringent and to make varnishes and lacquers. **2 mastic tree. 2a** a small Mediterranean anacardiaceous evergreen tree, *Pistacia lentiscus,* that yields the resin mastic. **2b** any of various similar trees, such as the pepper tree. **3** any of several sticky putty-like substances used as a filler, adhesive, or seal in wood, plaster, or masonry. **4** a liquor flavoured with mastic gum. [C14: via Old French from Late Latin *mastichum,* from Latin, from Greek *mastikhē* resin used as chewing gum; from *mastikhan* to grind the teeth]

masticate ('mæstɪ,keɪt) *vb* **1** to chew (food). **2** to reduce (materials such as rubber) to a pulp by crushing, grinding, or kneading. [C17: from Late Latin *masticāre,* from Greek *mastikhan* to grind the teeth] ► **'masticable** *adj* ► **,masti'cation** *n* ► **'masti,cator** *n*

masticatory ('mæstɪkətərɪ, -trɪ) *adj* **1** of, relating to, or adapted to chewing. ◆ *n, pl* **-tories. 2** a medicinal substance chewed to increase the secretion of saliva.

mastiff ('mæstɪf) *n* an old breed of large powerful short-haired dog, usually fawn or brindle with a dark mask. [C14: from Old French, ultimately from Latin *mansuētus* tame; see MANSUETUDE]

mastigophoran (,mæstɪ'gɒfərən) *n also* **mastigophore** ('mæstɪgə,fɔː). **1** any protozoan having one or more flagella. ◆ *adj also* **mastigophorous. 2** of or relating to flagellated protozoans. ◆ Also: **flagellate.** [C19 *mastigophore* whip-bearer, from Greek *mastigophoros,* from *mastix* whip + *-phoros* -PHORE]

mastitis (mæ'staɪtɪs) *n* inflammation of a breast or an udder.

masto- *or before a vowel* **mast-** *combining form.* indicating the breast, mammary glands, or something resembling a breast or nipple: *mastodon; mastoid.* [from Greek *mastos* breast]

mastodon ('mæstə,dɒn) *n* any extinct elephant-like proboscidean mammal of the genus *Mammut* (or *Mastodon*), common in Pliocene times. [C19: from New Latin, literally: breast-tooth, referring to the nipple-shaped projections on the teeth] ► **,masto'dontic** *adj*

mastoid ('mæstɔɪd) *adj* **1** shaped like a nipple or breast. **2** designating or relating to a nipple-like process of the temporal bone behind the ear. ◆ *n* **3** the mastoid process. **4** *Informal.* mastoiditis.

mastoidectomy (,mæstɔɪ'dektəmɪ) *n, pl* **-mies.** surgical removal of the mastoid process.

mastoiditis (,mæstɔɪ'daɪtɪs) *n* inflammation of the mastoid process.

Mastroianni ('mæstrɔɪ'jɑːnɪ) *n* **Marcello** (mɑː'tʃeləʊ). 1924–96, Italian film actor; his films include *Le notti bianche* (1957), *La dolce vita* (1960), *Ginger and Fred* (1985), and *Prêt à Porter* (1995).

masturbate ('mæstə,beɪt) *vb* to stimulate the genital organs of (oneself or another) to achieve sexual pleasure. [C19: from Latin *masturbārī,* of unknown origin; formerly thought to be derived from *manus* hand + *stuprāre* to defile] ► **,mastur'bation** *n* ► **'mastur,bator** *n* ► **masturbatory** ('mæstə,beɪtərɪ) *adj*

Masuria (mə'sjʊərɪə) *n* a region of NE Poland: until 1945 part of East Prussia: includes the **Masurian Lakes,** scene of Russian defeats by the Germans (1914, 1915) during World War I. ► **Ma'surian** *adj, n*

masurium (mə'sʊərɪəm) *n* the former name for **technetium.** [C20: New Latin, after MASURIA, where it was discovered]

mat[1] (mæt) *n* **1** a thick flat piece of fabric used as a floor covering, a place to wipe one's shoes, etc. **2** a smaller pad of material used to protect a surface from the heat, scratches, etc., of an object placed upon it. **3** a large piece of thick padded material put on the floor as a surface for wrestling, judo, or gymnastic sports. **4** *N.Z.* a Maori cloak. **5 go back to the mat.** *N.Z.* to abandon urban civilization. **6** any surface or mass that is densely interwoven or tangled: *a mat of grass and weeds.* **7** the solid part of a lace design. **8** a heavy net of cable or rope laid over a blasting site to prevent the scatter of debris. **9** *Civil engineering.* short for **mattress** (sense 3). ◆ *vb* **mats, matting, matted. 10** to tangle or weave or become tangled or woven into a dense mass. **11** *(tr)* to cover with a mat or mats. [Old English *matte;* related to Old High German *matta*] ► **'matless** *adj*

mat[2] (mæt) *n* **1** a border of cardboard, cloth, etc., placed around a picture to act as a frame or as a contrast between picture and frame. **2** a surface, as on metal or paint. ◆ *adj* **3** having a dull, lustreless, or roughened surface. ◆ *vb* **mats, matting, matted.** *(tr)* **4** to furnish (a picture) with a mat. **5** to give (a surface) a mat finish. ◆ Also (for senses 2, 3, 5): **matt.** [C17: from French, literally: dead; see CHECKMATE]

mat[3] (mæt) *n Printing, informal.* short for **matrix** (sense 5).

mat. *abbrev. for* matinée.

Matabele (,mætə'biːlɪ, -'beɪlɪ) *n* **1** *(pl* **-les** *or* **-le)** a member of a formerly warlike people of southern Africa, now living in Zimbabwe: driven out of the Transvaal by the Boers in 1837. Now known as **Ndebele. 2** the language of this people, belonging to the Bantu group of the Niger-Congo family.

Matabeleland (,mætə'biːlɪ,lænd, -'beɪlɪ-) *n* a region of W Zimbabwe, between the Rivers Limpopo and Zambezi, comprises three provinces, Matabeleland North, Matabeleland South, and Bulawayo: rich gold deposits. Chief town: Bulawayo. Area: 181 605 sq. km (70 118 sq. miles).

Matadi (mə'tɑːdɪ) *n* the chief port of the Democratic Republic of the Congo (formerly Zaïre), in the west at the mouth of the River Congo. Pop.: 172 730 (1994 est.).

matador ('mætədɔː) *n* **1** the principal bullfighter who is appointed to kill the bull. **2** (in some card games such as skat) one of the highest ranking cards. **3** a game played with dominoes in which the dots on adjacent halves must total seven. [C17: from Spanish, from *matar* to kill]

matagouri (,mætə'guːrɪ) *n, pl* **-ris.** a thorny bush of New Zealand, *Discaria toumatou,* that forms thickets in open country. Also called: **wild Irishman.** [from Maori *tumatakuru*]

Mata Hari ('mɑːtə 'hɑːrɪ) *n* real name *Gertrud Margarete Zelle.* 1876–1917, Dutch dancer in France, who was executed as a German spy in World War I.

matai ('mɑːtaɪ) *n, pl* **-tais.** a coniferous evergreen tree of New Zealand, *Podocarpus spicatus,* having a bluish bark and small linear leaves arranged in two rows: timber used for flooring and weatherboards. Also called: **black pine.** [Maori]

mata-mata ('mata'mata) *n* (in Malaysia) a former name for **police.** [from Malay, reduplicated plural of *mata* eye]

Matamoros (,mætə'mɔːrəs; *Spanish* mata'morɔs) *n* a port in NE Mexico, on the Río Grande: scene of bitter fighting during the U.S.–Mexican War; centre of a cotton-growing area. Pop.: 266 055 (1990).

Matanzas (mə'tænzəs; *Spanish* ma'tanθas) *n* a port in W central Cuba:

founded in 1693 and developed into the second city of Cuba in the mid-19th century; exports chiefly sugar. Pop.: 123 843 (1994 est.).

Matapan ('mætə,pæn, ,mætə'pæn) *n* **Cape.** a cape in S Greece, at the S central tip of the Peloponnese: the southern point of the mainland of Greece. Modern Greek name: **Taínaron.**

match[1] (mætʃ) *n* **1** a formal game or sports event in which people, teams, etc., compete to win. **2** a person or thing able to provide competition for another: *she's met her match in talking ability.* **3** a person or thing that resembles, harmonizes with, or is equivalent to another in a specified respect: *that coat is a good match for your hat.* **4** a person or thing that is an exact copy or equal of another. **5a** a partnership between a man and a woman, as in marriage. **5b** an arrangement for such a partnership. **6** a person regarded as a possible partner, as in marriage. ♦ *vb (mainly tr)* **7** to fit (parts) together: *to match the tongue and groove of boards.* **8** (*also intr;* sometimes foll. by *up*) to resemble, harmonize with, correspond to, or equal (one another or something else): *the skirt matches your shoes well.* **9** (sometimes foll. by *with* or *against*) to compare in order to determine which is the superior: *they matched wits.* **10** (often foll. by *to* or *with*) to adapt so as to correspond with: *to match hope with reality.* **11** (often foll. by *with* or *against*) to arrange a competition between. **12** to find a match for. **13** *Electronics.* to connect (two circuits) so that their impedances are equal or are equalized by a coupling device, to produce a maximum transfer of energy. [Old English *gemæcca* spouse; related to Old High German *gimmaha* wife, Old Norse *maki* mate] ▸ **'matchable** *adj* ▸ **'matcher** *n* ▸ **'matching** *adj*

match[2] (mætʃ) *n* **1** a thin strip of wood or cardboard tipped with a chemical that ignites by friction when rubbed on a rough surface or a surface coated with a suitable chemical (see **safety match**). **2** a length of cord or wick impregnated with a chemical so that it burns slowly. It is used to fire cannons, explosives, etc. [C14: from Old French *meiche,* perhaps from Latin *myxa* wick, from Greek *muxa* lamp nozzle]

matchboard ('mætʃ,bɔːd) *n* a long thin board with a tongue along one edge and a corresponding groove along the other, used with similar boards to line walls, ceilings, etc.

matchbox ('mætʃ,bɒks) *n* a small box for holding matches.

matched-pairs design *n (modifier) Statistics.* (of an experiment) concerned with measuring the values of the dependent variables for pairs of subjects that have been matched to eliminate individual differences and that are respectively subjected to the control and the experimental condition. Compare **between-subjects design, within-subjects design.**

matched sample *n Statistics.* a sample in which the individuals selected for analysis share all properties except that under investigation.

matchet ('mætʃət) *n* an earlier name for **machete.**

match-fit *adj* in good physical condition for competing in a match.

matchless ('mætʃlɪs) *adj* unequalled; incomparable; peerless. ▸ **'matchlessly** *adv* ▸ **'matchlessness** *n*

matchlock ('mætʃ,lɒk) *n* **1** an obsolete type of gunlock igniting the powder by means of a slow match. **2** a gun having such a lock.

matchmaker[1] ('mætʃ,meɪkə) *n* **1** a person who brings together suitable partners for marriage. **2** a person who arranges competitive matches. ▸ **'match,making** *n, adj*

matchmaker[2] ('mætʃ,meɪkə) *n* a person who makes matches (for igniting). ▸ **'match,making** *n, adj*

matchmark ('mætʃ,mɑːk) *n* **1** a mark made on mating components of an engine, machine, etc., to ensure that the components are assembled in the correct relative positions. ♦ *vb* **2** (*tr*) to stamp (an object) with matchmarks.

match play *n Golf.* **a** scoring according to the number of holes won and lost. **b** (*as modifier*): *a matchplay tournament.* ♦ Compare **Stableford, stroke play.** ▸ **match player** *n*

match point *n* **1** *Tennis, squash, etc.* the final point needed to win a match. **2** *Bridge.* the unit used for scoring in tournaments.

matchstick ('mætʃ,stɪk) *n* **1** the wooden part of a match. ♦ *adj* **2** made with or as if with matchsticks: *a matchstick model.* **3** (esp. of figures drawn with single strokes) thin and straight: *matchstick men.*

matchwood ('mætʃ,wʊd) *n* **1** wood suitable for making matches. **2** splinters or fragments: *the bomb blew the house to matchwood.*

mate[1] (meɪt) *n* **1** the sexual partner of an animal. **2** a marriage partner. **3a** *Informal, chiefly Brit., Austral., and N.Z.* a friend, usually of the same sex: often used between males in direct address. **3b** (*in combination*) an associate, colleague, fellow sharer, etc.: *a classmate; a flatmate.* **4** one of a pair of matching items. **5** *Nautical.* **5a** short for **first mate. 5b** any officer below the master on a commercial ship. **5c** a warrant officer's assistant on a ship. **6** (in some trades) an assistant: *a plumber's mate.* **7** *Archaic.* a suitable associate. ♦ *vb* **8** to pair (a male and female animal) or (of animals) to pair for reproduction. **9** to marry or join in marriage. **10** (*tr*) to join as a pair; match. [C14: from Middle Low German; related to Old English *gemetta* table-guest, from *mete* MEAT] ▸ **'mateless** *adj*

mate[2] (meɪt) *n, vb Chess.* See **checkmate.**

maté *or* **mate** ('mɑːteɪ, 'mæteɪ) *n* **1** an evergreen tree, *Ilex paraguariensis,* cultivated in South America for its leaves, which contain caffeine: family *Aquifoliaceae.* **2** a stimulating milky beverage made from the dried leaves of this tree. ♦ Also called: **Paraguay tea, yerba, yerba maté.** [C18: from American Spanish (originally referring to the vessel in which the drink was brewed), from Quechua *máti* gourd]

matelassé (mæt'læseɪ) *adj* (in textiles) having a raised design, as quilting; embossed. [C19: from French *matelasser* to quilt, from *matelas* MATTRESS]

matelot, matlo, *or* **matlow** ('mætləʊ) *n Slang, chiefly Brit.* a sailor. [C20: from French]

matelote *or* **matelotte** ('mætᵊ,ləʊt; *French* matlɔt) *n* fish served with a sauce of wine, onions, seasonings, and fish stock. [C18: from French, feminine of *matelot* sailor]

mater ('meɪtə) *n Brit. public school slang.* a word for **mother**[1]: often used facetiously. [C16: from Latin]

mater dolorosa (,dɒlə'rəʊsə) *n* the Virgin Mary sorrowing for the dead Christ, esp. as depicted in art. [Latin: sorrowful mother]

materfamilias (,meɪtəfə'mɪlɪ,æs) *n, pl* **matresfamilias** (,meɪtreɪzfə'mɪlɪ,æs) the mother of a family or the female head of a family. [C18: from Latin]

material (mə'tɪərɪəl) *n* **1** the substance of which a thing is made or composed; component or constituent matter: *raw material.* **2** facts, notes, etc., that a finished work may be based on or derived from: *enough material for a book.* **3** cloth or fabric. **4** a person who has qualities suitable for a given occupation, training, etc.: *that boy is not university material.* ♦ *adj* **5** of, relating to, or composed of physical substance; corporeal. **6** *Philosophy.* composed of or relating to physical as opposed to mental or spiritual substance: *the material world.* **7** of, relating to, or affecting economic or physical wellbeing: *material ease.* **8** of or concerned with physical rather than spiritual interests. **9** of great import or consequence: *of material benefit to the workers.* **10** (often foll. by *to*) relevant. **11** *Philosophy.* of or relating to matter as opposed to form. **12** *Law.* relevant to the issue before court: applied esp. to facts or testimony of much significance: *a material witness.* ♦ See also **materials.** [C14: via French from Late Latin *māteriālis,* from Latin *māteria* MATTER] ▸ **ma'terialness** *n*

material implication *n Logic.* **1** the truth-functional connective that forms a compound sentence from two given sentences and assigns the value false to it only when its antecedent is true and its consequent false, without consideration of relevance; loosely corresponds to the English *if ... then.* **2** a compound sentence formed with this connective.

materialism (mə'tɪərɪə,lɪzəm) *n* **1** interest in and desire for money, possessions, etc., rather than spiritual or ethical values. **2** *Philosophy.* the monist doctrine that matter is the only reality and that the mind, the emotions, etc., are merely functions of it. Compare **idealism** (sense 3), **dualism** (sense 2). See also **identity theory. 3** *Ethics.* the rejection of any religious or supernatural account of things. ▸ **ma'terialist** *n, adj* ▸ **ma,terial'istic** *adj* ▸ **ma,terial'istically** *adv*

materiality (mə,tɪərɪ'ælɪtɪ) *n* **1** the state or quality of being physical or material. **2** substance; matter.

materialize *or* **materialise** (mə'tɪərɪə,laɪz) *vb* **1** (*intr*) to become fact; actually happen: *our hopes never materialized.* **2** to invest or become invested with a physical shape or form. **3** to cause (a spirit, as of a dead person) to appear in material form or (of a spirit) to appear in such form. **4** (*intr*) to take shape; become tangible: *after hours of discussion, the project finally began to materialize.* **5** *Physics.* to form (material particles) from energy, as in pair production. ▸ **ma,teriali'zation** *or* **ma,teriali'sation** *n* ▸ **ma'terial,izer** *or* **ma'terial,iser** *n*

materially (mə'tɪərɪəlɪ) *adv* **1** to a significant extent; considerably: *his death alters the situation materially.* **2** with respect to material objects. **3** *Philosophy.* with respect to substance as distinct from form.

material mode *n Philosophy.* the normal use of language that refers to extra-linguistic subjects without explicit mention of the words themselves. *Fido is a dog* is in the material mode, while *"Fido" is a dog's name* is in the formal mode. See also **use** (sense 18).

materials (mə'tɪərɪəlz) *pl n* the equipment necessary for a particular activity.

materia medica (mə'tɪərɪə 'mɛdɪkə) *n* **1** the branch of medical science concerned with the study of drugs used in the treatment of disease: includes pharmacy, pharmacology, and the history and physical and chemical properties of drugs. **2** the drugs used in the treatment of disease. [C17: from Medieval Latin: medical matter]

materiel *or* **matériel** (mə,tɪərɪ'ɛl) *n* the materials and equipment of an organization, esp. of a military force. Compare **personnel.** [C19: from French: MATERIAL]

maternal (mə'tɜːnᵊl) *adj* **1** of, relating to, derived from, or characteristic of a mother. **2** related through the mother's side of the family: *his maternal uncle.* [C15: from Medieval Latin *māternālis,* from Latin *māternus,* from *māter* mother] ▸ **ma'ternalism** *n* ▸ **ma,ternal'istic** *adj* ▸ **ma'ternally** *adv*

maternity (mə'tɜːnɪtɪ) *n* **1** motherhood. **2** the characteristics associated with motherhood; motherliness. **3** (*modifier*) relating to pregnant women or women at the time of childbirth: *a maternity ward.*

maternity benefit *n* (in the British National Insurance scheme) a payment (**maternity allowance**) made to a woman having a child, normally from 11 weeks before confinement for a period of 18 weeks, in addition to a flat-rate benefit (**maternity grant**).

maternity leave *n* a period of paid absence from work, in Britain currently six months, to which a woman is legally entitled during the months immediately before and after childbirth.

mateship ('meɪtʃɪp) *n Austral.* the comradeship of friends, usually male, viewed as an institution.

mate's rates *pl n N.Z. informal.* preferential rates of payment offered to a friend.

matey *or* **maty** ('meɪtɪ) *Brit. informal.* ♦ *adj* **1** friendly or intimate; on good terms. ♦ *n* **2** friend or fellow: usually used in direct address. ▸ **'mateyness** *or* **'matiness** *n*

mat grass *n* a widespread perennial European grass, *Nardus stricta,* with dense tufts of bristly leaves, characteristic of peaty moors.

math (mæθ) *n U.S. and Canadian informal.* short for **mathematics.** Brit. equivalent: **maths.**

math. *U.S. and Canadian abbrev. for* mathematics.

mathematical (,mæθə'mætɪkᵊl, ,mæθ'mæt-) *or* (*less commonly*) **mathematic** *adj* **1** of, used in, or relating to mathematics. **2** characterized by or using the precision of mathematics; exact. **3** using, determined by, or in accordance with the principles of mathematics. ► **,mathe'matically** *adv*

mathematical expectation *n Statistics.* another name for **expected value.**

mathematical logic *n* symbolic logic, esp. that branch concerned with the foundations of mathematics.

mathematical probability *n Statistics.* **1** the probability of an event consisting of *n* out of *m* possible equally likely occurrences, defined to be $^{n}/_{m}$. See also **principle of indifference. 2** the study of such probabilities. ◆ Also called: **classical probability.**

mathematician (ˌmæθəmə'tɪʃən, ˌmæθmə-) *n* an expert or specialist in mathematics.

mathematics (ˌmæθə'mætɪks, ˌmæθ'mæt-) *n* **1** (*functioning as sing*) a group of related sciences, including algebra, geometry, and calculus, concerned with the study of number, quantity, shape, and space and their interrelationships by using a specialized notation. **2** (*functioning as sing or pl*) mathematical operations and processes involved in the solution of a problem or study of some scientific field. **[C14** *mathematik* (n), via Latin from Greek (adj), from *mathēma* a science, *mathēmatikos* (adj); related to *manthanein* to learn**]**

maths (mæθs) *n* (*functioning as sing*) *Brit. informal.* short for **mathematics.** U.S. and Canadian equivalent: **math.**

maths. *Brit. abbrev. for* mathematics.

Mathura ('mʌtʊərə, mʌ'θʊərə) *n* a city in N India, in W Uttar Pradesh on the Jumna River: a place of Hindu pilgrimage, revered as the birthplace of Krishna. Pop.: 226 691 (1991). Former name: **Muttra.**

Matilda[1] (mə'tɪldə) *n Austral. informal.* **1** a bushman's swag. **2 walk** *or* **waltz Matilda.** to travel the road carrying one's swag. **[C20:** from the Christian name**]**

Matilda[2] (mə'tɪldə) *n* known as *the Empress Maud.* 1102–67, only daughter of Henry I of England and wife of Geoffrey of Anjou. After her father's death (1135) she unsuccessfully waged a civil war with Stephen for the English throne; her son succeeded as Henry II.

matin, mattin ('mætɪn), *or* **matinal** *adj* of or relating to matins. **[C14:** see MATINS**]**

matinée ('mætɪˌneɪ) *n* a daytime, esp. afternoon, performance of a play, concert, etc. **[C19:** from French; see MATINS**]**

matinée coat *or* **jacket** *n* a short coat for a baby.

matinée idol *n* (esp. in the 1930s and 1940s) an actor popular as a romantic figure among women.

matins *or* **mattins** ('mætɪnz) *n* (*functioning as sing or pl*) **1a** *Chiefly R.C. Church.* the first of the seven canonical hours of prayer, originally observed at night but now often recited with lauds at daybreak. **1b** the service of morning prayer in the Church of England. **2** *Literary.* a morning song, esp. of birds. **[C13:** from Old French, ultimately from Latin *mātūtīnus* of the morning, from *Mātūta* goddess of dawn**]**

Matisse (*French* matis) *n* **Henri** (ɑ̃ri). 1869–1954, French painter and sculptor; leader of Fauvism.

matlo *or* **matlow** ('mætləʊ) *n* variant spellings of **matelot.**

Matlock ('mætˌlɒk) *n* a town in England, on the River Derwent, administrative centre of Derbyshire: mineral springs. Pop.: 14 680 (1991).

Mato Grosso *or* **Matto Grosso** ('mætəʊ 'grɒsəʊ; *Portuguese* 'matu 'grosu) *n* **1** a high plateau of SW Brazil: forms the watershed separating the Amazon and Plata river systems. **2** a state of W central Brazil: mostly on the Mato Grosso Plateau, with the Amazon basin to the north; valuable mineral resources. Capital: Cuiabá. Pop.: 2 313 600 (1995 est.). Area: 881 001 sq. km (340 083 sq. miles).

Mato Grosso do Sul ('duː sul) *n* a state of W central Brazil: formed in 1979 from part of Mato Grosso state. Capital: Campo Grande. Pop.: 1 912 800 (1995 est.). Area: 350 548 sq. km (135 318 sq. miles).

matoke (mа'tɔkɛ) *n* (in Uganda) the flesh of bananas, boiled and mashed as a food. **[C20:** from Luganda**]**

Matopo Hills (mə'təʊpə) *or* **Matopos** *pl n* the granite hills south of Bulawayo, Zimbabwe, where Cecil Rhodes chose to be buried.

Matozinhos (*Portuguese* mətu'ziɲuʃ) *n* a port in N Portugal, on the estuary of the Leça River north of Oporto: fishing industry. Pop.: 26 500 (latest est.).

matrass *or* **mattrass** ('mætrəs) *n Chem., obsolete.* a long-necked glass flask, used for distilling, dissolving substances, etc. **[C17:** from French, perhaps related to Latin *mētiri* to measure**]**

matri- *combining form.* mother or motherhood: *matriarchy.* **[**from Latin *māter* mother**]**

matriarch ('meɪtrɪˌɑːk) *n* **1** a woman who dominates an organization, community, etc. **2** the female head of a tribe or family, esp. in a matriarchy. **3** a very old or venerable woman. **[C17:** from MATRI- + -ARCH, by false analogy with PATRIARCH**]** ► **'matriˌarchal** *or* (*less commonly*) **'matriˌarchic** *adj* ► **ˌmatri'archalism** *n*

matriarchate ('meɪtrɪˌɑːkɪt, -keɪt) *n Rare.* a family or people under female domination or government.

matriarchy ('meɪtrɪˌɑːkɪ) *n, pl* **-chies. 1** a form of social organization in which a female is head of the family or society, and descent and kinship are traced through the female line. **2** any society dominated by women.

matric (mə'trɪk) *n Brit.* short for **matriculation** (sense 2).

matrices ('meɪtrɪˌsiːz, 'mæ-) *n* a plural of **matrix.**

matricide ('mætrɪˌsaɪd, 'meɪ-) *n* **1** the act of killing one's own mother. **2** a person who kills his mother. **[C16:** from Latin *mātrīcīdium* (the act), *mātrīcīda* (the agent). See MATRI-, -CIDE**]** ► **ˌmatri'cidal** *adj*

matriclinous (ˌmætrɪ'klaɪnəs), **matroclinous,** *or* **matroclinal** *adj* (of an animal or plant) showing the characters of the female parent. Compare **patriclinous. [C20:** from MATRI- + Greek *klīnein* to lean**]**

matriculate *vb* (mə'trɪkjʊˌleɪt). **1** to enrol or be enrolled in an institution, esp. a college or university. **2** (*intr*) to attain the academic standard required for a course at such an institution. ◆ *n* (mə'trɪkjʊlɪt). **3** Also called: **ma'triculant.** a person who has matriculated. **[C16:** from Medieval Latin *mātrīculāre* to register, from *mātrīcula,* diminutive of *matrix* list, MATRIX**]** ► **ma'tricuˌlator** *n*

matriculation (məˌtrɪkjʊ'leɪʃən) *n* **1** the process of matriculating. **2** (in Britain, except Scotland) a former school examination, which was replaced by the General Certificate of Education (Ordinary Level), now superseded by the General Certificate of Secondary Education.

matrilineal (ˌmætrɪ'lɪnɪəl, ˌmeɪ-) *adj* relating to descent or kinship through the female line. ► **ˌmatri'lineally** *adv*

matrilocal ('mætrɪˌləʊkᵊl, 'meɪ-) *adj* denoting, having, or relating to a marriage pattern in which the couple live with the wife's family. ► **matrilocality** (ˌmætrɪləʊ'kælɪtɪ, ˌmeɪ-) *n* ► **ˌmatri'locally** *adv*

matrimonial (ˌmætrɪ'məʊnɪəl) *adj* relating to marriage: *matrimonial troubles.* ► **ˌmatri'monially** *adv*

matrimony ('mætrɪmənɪ) *n, pl* **-nies. 1** the state or condition of being married. **2** the ceremony or sacrament of marriage. **3a** a card game in which the king and queen together are a winning combination. **3b** such a combination. **[C14:** via Norman French from Latin *mātrimōnium* wedlock, from *māter* mother**]**

matrimony vine *n* any of various shrubs of the solanaceous genus *Lycium,* cultivated for their purple flowers and colourful berries. Also called: **boxthorn.**

matrix ('meɪtrɪks, 'mæ-) *n, pl* **matrices** ('meɪtrɪˌsiːz, 'mæ-) *or* **matrixes. 1** a substance, situation, or environment in which something has its origin, takes form, or is enclosed. **2** *Anatomy.* the thick tissue at the base of a nail from which a fingernail or toenail develops. **3** the intercellular substance of bone, cartilage, connective tissue, etc. **4a** the rock material in which fossils, pebbles, etc., are embedded. **4b** the material in which a mineral is embedded; gangue. **5** *Printing.* **5a** a metal mould for casting type. **5b** a papier-mâché or plastic mould impressed from the forme and used for stereotyping. Sometimes shortened to **mat. 6** a mould used in the production of gramophone records. It is obtained by electrodeposition onto the master. **7** a bed of perforated material placed beneath a workpiece in a press or stamping machine against which the punch operates. **8** *Metallurgy.* **8a** the shaped cathode used in electroforming. **8b** the metal constituting the major part of an alloy. **8c** the soft metal in a plain bearing in which the hard particles of surface metal are embedded. **9** *Maths.* a rectangular array of elements set out in rows and columns, used to facilitate the solution of problems, such as the transformation of coordinates. Usually indicated by parentheses: $\left(\begin{smallmatrix} a & b & c \\ d & e & f \end{smallmatrix}\right)$. Compare **determinant** (sense 3). **10** *Linguistics.* the main clause of a complex sentence. **11** *Computing.* a rectangular array of circuit elements usually used to generate one set of signals from another. **12** *Obsolete.* the womb. **[C16:** from Latin: womb, female animal used for breeding, from *māter* mother**]**

matroclinous (ˌmætrə'klaɪnəs) *adj* a variant of **matriclinous.**

matron ('meɪtrən) *n* **1** a married woman regarded as staid or dignified, esp. a middle-aged woman with children. **2** a woman in charge of the domestic or medical arrangements in an institution. **3** *U.S.* a wardress in a prison. **4** Official name: **nursing officer.** *Brit.* the administrative head of the nursing staff in a hospital. **[C14:** via Old French from Latin *mātrōna,* from *māter* mother**]** ► **'matronal** *adj* ► **'matronˌhood** *or* **'matronˌship** *n* ► **'matron-ˌlike** *adj*

matronage ('meɪtrənɪdʒ) *n* **1** the state of being a matron. **2** supervision or care by a matron. **3** matrons collectively.

matronly ('meɪtrənlɪ) *adj* of, characteristic of, or suitable for a matron; staid and dignified in a manner associated with a middle-aged, usually plump, woman. ► **'matronliness** *n*

matron of honour *n, pl* **matrons of honour. 1** a married woman serving as chief attendant to a bride. Compare **bridesmaid, maid of honour. 2** a married woman, usually a member of the nobility, who attends a queen or princess.

matronymic (ˌmætrə'nɪmɪk) *adj, n* a less common word for **metronymic.**

Matsu *or* **Mazu** (mæt'suː) *n* an island group in Formosa Strait, off the SE coast of mainland China: belongs to Taiwan. Pop.: 3145 (1990 est.). Area: 44 sq. km (17 sq. miles).

Matsuo Basho ('mætzuːəʊ bɑː'ʃɔː) *n* See **Basho.**

Matsuyama (ˌmætsʊ'jɑːmə) *n* a port in SW Japan, on NW Shikoku: textile and chemical industries; Ehime University (1949). Pop.: 460 870 (1995).

Matsys (*Flemish* 'matsaɪs) *n* a variant spelling of (Quentin) **Massys.**

matt *or* **matte** (mæt) *adj, n, vb* variant spellings of **mat**[2] (senses 2, 3, 5).

Matt. *Bible. abbrev. for* Matthew.

mattamore ('mætəˌmɔː) *n* a subterranean storehouse or dwelling. **[C17:** from French, from Arabic *matmurā,* from *tamara* to store, bury**]**

matte[1] (mæt) *n* an impure fused material consisting of metal sulphides produced during the smelting of a sulphide ore. **[C19:** from French**]**

matte[2] (mæt) *n Films, television.* a mask used to blank out part of an image so that another image can be superimposed.

matted ('mætɪd) *adj* **1** tangled into a thick mass: *matted hair.* **2** covered with or formed of matting.

matter ('mætə) *n* **1** that which makes up something, esp. a physical object; material. **2** substance that occupies space and has mass, as distinguished from substance that is mental, spiritual, etc. **3** substance of a specified type: *vegetable matter; reading matter.* **4** (sometimes foll. by *of* or *for*) thing; affair; concern; question: *a matter of taste; several matters to attend to; no laughing matter.* **5** a quantity or amount: *a matter of a few pence.* **6** the content of written or verbal material as distinct from its style or form. **7** (*used with a negative*) importance; consequence. **8** *Philosophy.* (in the writings of Aristotle and the Scholastics) that which is itself formless but can receive form and become substance. **9** *Philosophy.* (in the Cartesian tradition) one of two basic modes of existence, the other being **mind:** matter being extended in space as well as time. **10** *Printing.* **10a** type set up, either standing or for use. **10b** copy to be set in type. **11** a secretion or discharge, such as pus. **12** *Law.* **12a** something to be proved. **12b** statements or allegations to be considered by a court. **13 for that matter.** as regards that. **14** See **grey matter. 15 no matter. 15a** regardless of; irrespective of: *no matter what the excuse, you must not be late.* **15b** (*sentence substitute*) it is unimportant. **16 the matter.** wrong; the trouble: *there's nothing the matter.* ◆ *vb* (*intr*) **17** to be of consequence or importance. **18** to form and discharge pus. [C13 (n), C16 (vb): from Latin *māteria* cause, substance, esp. wood, or a substance that produces something else; related to *māter* mother]

Matterhorn ('mætəˌhɔːn) *n* a mountain on the border between Italy and Switzerland, in the Pennine Alps. Height: 4477 m (14 688 ft.). French name: **Mont Cervin.** Italian name: **Monte Cervino** ('monte tʃer'viːno).

matter of course *n* **1** an event or result that is natural or inevitable. ◆ *adj* **matter-of-course. 2** (*usually postpositive*) occurring as a matter of course. **3** accepting things as inevitable or natural: *a matter-of-course attitude.*

matter of fact *n* **1** a fact that is undeniably true. **2** *Law.* a statement of facts the truth of which the court must determine on the basis of the evidence before it: contrasted with **matter of law. 3** *Philosophy.* a proposition that is amenable to empirical testing, as contrasted with the truths of logic or mathematics. **4 as a matter of fact.** actually; in fact. ◆ *adj* **matter-of-fact. 5** unimaginative or emotionless: *he gave a matter-of-fact account of the murder.*

matter of law *n Law.* an issue requiring the court's interpretation of the law or relevant principles of the law: contrasted with **matter of fact.**

matter of opinion *n* a point open to question; a debatable statement.

matter waves *pl n* See **de Broglie waves.**

mattery ('mætərɪ) *adj* discharging pus.

Matthew ('mæθjuː) *n New Testament.* **1 Saint.** Also called: **Levi.** a tax collector of Capernaum called by Christ to be one of the 12 apostles (Matthew 9:9–13; 10:3). Feast day: Sept. 21 or Nov. 16. **2** the first Gospel, traditionally ascribed to him.

Matthew Paris *n* See (Matthew) **Paris**[2] (sense 2).

Matthews ('mæθjuːz) *n* Sir **Stanley.** born 1915, English footballer.

Matthew Walker *n* a knot made at the end of a rope by unlaying the strands and passing them up through the loops formed in the next two strands. [C19: probably named after the man who introduced it]

Matthias (mə'θaɪəs) *n* **1** 1557–1619, Holy Roman Emperor (1612–19); king of Hungary (1608–18) and Bohemia (1611–17). **2 Saint.** *New Testament.* the disciple chosen by lot to replace Judas as one of the 12 apostles (Acts 1:15–26). Feast day: May 14 or Aug. 9.

Matthias I Corvinus (kɔː'vaɪnəs) *n* ?1440–90, king of Hungary (1458–90): built up the most powerful kingdom in Central Europe. A patron of Renaissance art, he founded the Corvina library, one of the finest in Europe. Hungarian name: **Mátyás Hollós** ('maːtjaːʃ 'holoʃ).

matting[1] ('mætɪŋ) *n* **1** a coarsely woven fabric, usually made of a natural fibre such as straw or hemp and used as a floor covering, packing material, etc. **2** the act or process of making mats. **3** material for mats.

matting[2] ('mætɪŋ) *n* **1** another word for **mat**[2] (sense 1). **2** the process of producing a mat finish.

mattins ('mætɪnz) *n* a variant spelling of **matins.**

mattock ('mætək) *n* a type of large pick that has one end of its blade shaped like an adze, used for loosening soil, cutting roots, etc. [Old English *mattuc,* of unknown origin; related to Latin *mateola* club, mallet]

Matto Grosso ('mætəʊ 'grɒsəʊ) *n* a variant spelling of **Mato Grosso.**

mattoid ('mætɔɪd) *n Rare.* a person displaying eccentric behaviour and mental characteristics that approach the psychotic. [C19: from Italian, from *matto* insane]

mattrass ('mætrəs) *n* a variant spelling of **matrass.**

mattress ('mætrɪs) *n* **1** a large flat pad with a strong cover, filled with straw, foam rubber, etc., and often incorporating coiled springs, used as a bed or as part of a bed. **2** Also called: **Dutch mattress.** a woven mat of brushwood, poles, etc., used to protect an embankment, dyke, etc., from scour. **3** a concrete or steel raft or slab used as a foundation or footing. Sometimes shortened to **mat. 4** a network of reinforcing rods or expanded metal sheeting, used in reinforced concrete. **5** *Civil engineering.* another name for **blinding** (sense 3). [C13: via Old French from Italian *materasso,* from Arabic *almatrah* place where something is thrown]

maturate ('mætjʊˌreɪt, 'mætʃʊ-) *vb* **1** to mature or bring to maturity. **2** a less common word for **suppurate.** ▸ **maturative** (mə'tjʊərətɪv, mə'tʃʊə-) *adj*

maturation (ˌmætjʊ'reɪʃən, ˌmætʃʊ-) *n* **1** the process of maturing or ripening. **2** *Zoology.* the development of ova and spermatozoa from precursor cells in the ovary and testis, involving meiosis. **3** a less common word for **suppuration.** ▸ **ˌmatu'rational** *adj*

mature (mə'tjʊə, -'tʃʊə) *adj* **1** relatively advanced physically, mentally, emotionally, etc.; grown-up. **2** (of plans, theories, etc.) fully considered; perfected. **3** due or payable: *a mature debenture.* **4** *Biology.* **4a** fully developed or differentiated: *a mature cell.* **4b** fully grown; adult: *a mature animal.* **5** (of fruit, wine, cheese, etc.) ripe or fully aged. **6** (of a river valley or land surface) in the middle stage of the cycle of erosion, characterized by meanders, maximum relief, etc. See also **youthful** (sense 4), **old** (sense 18). ◆ *vb* **7** to make or become mature. **8** (*intr*) (of notes, bonds, etc.) to become due for payment or repayment. [C15: from Latin *mātūrus* early, developed] ▸ **ma'turely** *adv* ▸ **ma'tureness** *n*

mature student *n* a student at a college or university who has passed the usual age for formal education.

maturity (mə'tjʊərɪtɪ, -'tʃʊə-) *n* **1** the state or quality of being mature; full development. **2** *Finance.* **2a** the date upon which a bill of exchange, bond, note, etc., becomes due for repayment. **2b** the state of a bill, note, etc., when due.

matutinal (ˌmætjʊ'taɪnᵊl) *adj* of, occurring in, or during the morning. [C17: from Late Latin *mātūtīnālis,* from Latin *mātūtīnus,* from *Mātūta* goddess of the dawn] ▸ **ˌmatu'tinally** *adv*

maty ('meɪtɪ) *n, adj* **matier, matiest.** a variant of **matey.**

matzo, matzoh ('mætsəʊ) *or* **matza, matzah** ('mætsə) *n, pl* **matzos, matzohs, matzas, matzahs,** *or* **matzoth** (*Hebrew* ma'tsɔt). a brittle very thin biscuit of unleavened bread, traditionally eaten during Passover. [from Hebrew *matsāh*]

matzoon (mɑːt'suːn) *or* **madzoon** (mɑːd'zuːn) *n* a fermented milk product similar to yogurt. [from Armenian *madzun*]

Maubeuge (*French* mobøʒ) *n* an industrial town in N France, near the border with Belgium. Pop.: 35 225 (1990).

mauby ('mɑːbɪ, 'mɔː-) *n, pl* **-bies.** (in the E Caribbean) a bittersweet drink made from the bark of a rhamnaceous tree. [C20: of uncertain origin]

maud (mɔːd) *n* a shawl or rug of grey wool plaid formerly worn in Scotland. [C18: of unknown origin]

maudlin ('mɔːdlɪn) *adj* foolishly tearful or sentimental, as when drunk. [C17: from Middle English *Maudelen* Mary Magdalene, typically portrayed as a tearful penitent] ▸ **'maudlinism** *n* ▸ **'maudlinly** *adv* ▸ **'maudlinness** *n*

Maugham ('mɔːm) *n* **W(illiam) Somerset.** 1874–1965, English writer. His works include the novels *Of Human Bondage* (1915) and *Cakes and Ale* (1930), short stories, and comedies.

maugre *or* **mauger** ('mɔːgə) *prep Obsolete.* in spite of. [C13 (meaning: ill will): from Old French *maugre,* literally: bad pleasure]

Maui ('maʊɪ) *n* a volcanic island in S central Hawaii: the second largest of the Hawaiian Islands. Pop.: 91 361 (1990). Area: 1885 sq. km (728 sq. miles).

maul (mɔːl) *vb* (*tr*) **1** to handle clumsily; paw. **2** to batter or lacerate. ◆ *n* **3** a heavy two-handed hammer suitable for driving piles, wedges, etc. **4** *Rugby.* a loose scrum that forms around a player who is holding the ball and on his feet. [C13: from Old French *mail,* from Latin *malleus* hammer. See MALLET] ▸ **'mauler** *n*

Maulana (mɔː'lɑːnɑː) *n* (in Pakistan, India, etc.) a title used for a scholar of Persian and Arabic. [Urdu, from Arabic *mawlānā*]

maulers ('mɔːləz) *pl n Brit. slang.* the hands.

Maulmain (maʊl'meɪn) *n* a variant spelling of **Moulmein.**

maulstick *or* **mahlstick** ('mɔːlˌstɪk) *n* a long stick used by artists to steady the hand holding the brush. [C17: partial translation of Dutch *maalstok,* from obsolete *malen* to paint + *stok* STICK[1]]

Mau Mau ('maʊ ˌmaʊ) *n, pl* **Mau Maus** *or* **Mau Mau. 1** a secret political society consisting chiefly of Kikuyu tribesmen that was founded in 1952 to drive European settlers from Kenya by acts of terrorism. **2** *E African slang.* a Ugandan motorcycle policeman who directs traffic.

maumet ('mɔːmɪt) *or* **mammet** ('mæmɪt) *n Obsolete.* a false god; idol. [C13: from Old French *mahomet* idol, literally: the prophet *Mohammed,* from the belief that his image was worshipped] ▸ **'maumetry** *n*

maun, man (mɑːn, mɔːn), *or* **mun** (mʌn) *vb* a dialect word for **must**[1]. [C14: from Old Norse *man* must, will]

Mauna Kea ('maʊnɑː 'keɪɑː) *n* an extinct volcano in Hawaii, on N central Hawaii Island: the highest island mountain in the world. Height: 4206 m (13 799 ft.).

Mauna Loa ('maʊnɑː 'ləʊɑː) *n* an active volcano in Hawaii, on S central Hawaii Island. Height: 4171 m (13 684 ft.).

maund (mɔːnd) *n* a unit of weight used in Asia, esp. India, having different values in different localities. A common value in India is 82 pounds or 37 kilograms. [C17: from Hindi *man,* from Sanskrit *manā*]

maunder ('mɔːndə) *vb* (*intr*) to move, talk, or act aimlessly or idly. [C17: perhaps from obsolete *maunder* to beg, from Latin *mendīcāre;* see MENDICANT] ▸ **'maunderer** *n* ▸ **'maundering** *adj*

maundy ('mɔːndɪ) *n, pl* **maundies.** *Christianity.* the ceremonial washing of the feet of poor persons in commemoration of Jesus' washing of his disciples' feet (John 13:4–34) re-enacted in some churches on Maundy Thursday. [C13: from Old French *mandé* something commanded, from Latin *mandatum* commandment, from the words of Christ: *Mandātum novum dō vōbīs* A new commandment give I unto you]

Maundy money *n* specially minted coins distributed by the British sovereign on Maundy Thursday.

Maundy Thursday *n Christianity.* the Thursday before Easter observed as a commemoration of the Last Supper.

maungy ('mɔːndʒɪ) *adj* **-gier, -giest.** *West Yorkshire dialect.* (esp. of a child) sulky, bad-tempered, or peevish. [variant of MANGY, in extended sense: restless, dissatisfied]

Maupassant (*French* mopɑsɑ̃) *n* (**Henri René Albert**) **Guy de** (gi də). 1850–93, French writer, noted esp. for his short stories, such as *Boule de suif* (1880), *La Maison Tellier* (1881), and *Mademoiselle Fifi* (1883). His novels include *Bel Ami* (1885) and *Pierre et Jean* (1888).

Maupertuis (*French* mopɛrtɥi) *n* **Pierre Louis Moreau de** (pjɛr lwi mɔro də). 1698–1759, French mathematician, who originated the principle of least action (or Maupertuis principle).

Mauretania (ˌmɒrɪ'teɪnɪə) *n* an ancient region of N Africa, corresponding approximately to the N parts of modern Algeria and Morocco. ▸ **ˌMaure'tanian** *adj, n*

Mauriac (*French* mɔrjak) *n* **François** (frɑ̃swa). 1885–1970, French novelist, noted esp. for his psychological studies of the conflict between religious belief and human desire. His works include *Le désert de l'amour* (1925), *Thérèse Desqueyroux* (1927), and *Le nœud de vipères* (1932): Nobel prize for literature 1952.

Maurice ('mɒrɪs) *n* **1** 1521–53, duke of Saxony (1541–53) and elector of Saxony (1547–53). He was instrumental in gaining recognition of Protestantism in Germany. **2** known as *Maurice of Nassau.* 1567–1625, prince of Orange and count of Nassau; the son of William the Silent, after whose death he led the United Provinces of the Netherlands in their struggle for independence from Spain (achieved by 1609). **3 Frederick Denison.** 1805–72, English Anglican theologian and pioneer of Christian socialism.

Maurist (ˈmɔːrɪst) *n* a member of a congregation of French Benedictine monks founded in 1621 and noted for its scholarly work. [C19: named after *St Maurus*, 6th-century disciple of St Benedict]

Mauritania (ˌmɒrɪˈteɪnɪə) *n* a republic in NW Africa, on the Atlantic: established as a French protectorate in 1903 and a colony in 1920; gained independence in 1960; lies in the Sahara; contains rich resources of iron ore. Official language: Arabic; Fulani, Soninke, Wolof, and French are also spoken. Official religion: Muslim. Currency: ouguiya. Capital: Nouakchott. Pop.: 2 511 000 (1998 est.). Area: 1 030 700 sq. km (398 000 sq. miles). Official name: **Islamic Republic of Mauritania.** ▸ **ˌMauriˈtanian** *adj, n*

Mauritius (məˈrɪʃəs) *n* an island and state in the Indian Ocean, east of Madagascar: originally uninhabited, it was settled by the Dutch (1638–1710) then abandoned; taken by the French in 1715 and the British in 1810; became an independent member of the Commonwealth in 1968. It is economically dependent on sugar. Official language: English; a French creole is widely spoken. Religion: Hindu majority, large Christian minority. Currency: rupee. Capital: Port Louis. Pop.: 1 157 000 (1998 est.). Area: 1865 sq. km (720 sq. miles). Former name (1715–1810): **Île-de-France.** ▸ **Mauˈritian** *adj, n*

Maurois (*French* mɔrwa) *n* **André** (ɑ̃dre), pen name of *Émile Herzog.* 1885–1967, French writer, best known for his biographies, such as those of Shelley, Byron, and Proust.

Maurras (*French* mɔra) *n* **Charles** (ʃarl). 1868–1952, French writer and political theorist, who founded (1899) the extreme right-wing group L'Action Français: sentenced (1945) to life imprisonment for supporting Pétain during World War II.

Maury (ˈmɔːrɪ) *n* **Matthew Fontaine.** 1806–73, U.S. pioneer hydrographer and oceanographer.

Maurya (ˈmaurjə) *n* a dynasty (?321–?185 B.C.) that united most of the Indian subcontinent and presided over a great flowering of Indian civilization.

Mauser (ˈmauzə) *n Trademark.* **1** a high-velocity magazine rifle. **2** a type of automatic pistol. [C19: named after P. P. von *Mauser* (1838–1914), German firearms inventor]

mausoleum (ˌmɔːsəˈlɪəm) *n, pl* **-leums** *or* **-lea** (-ˈlɪə). a large stately tomb. [C16: via Latin from Greek *mausōleion,* the tomb of *Mausolus,* king of Caria; built at Halicarnassus in the 4th century B.C.] ▸ **ˌmausoˈlean** *adj*

mauvaise foi *French.* (movɛz fwa) *n* (in the philosophy of Sartre) the expression usually rendered as *bad faith:* see **bad faith** (sense 2).

mauvais pas (ˈməuvɛ ˈpɑː) *n, pl* **mauvais pas** (-ˈpɑː, -ˈpɑːz). *Mountaineering.* a place that presents a particular difficulty on a climb or walk. [C19: from French: bad step]

mauvais quart d'heure *French.* (movɛ kar dœr) *n Brit.* a brief unpleasant experience. [literally: (a) bad quarter of an hour]

mauve (məuv) *n* **1a** any of various pale to moderate pinkish-purple or bluish-purple colours. **1b** (*as adj*): *a mauve flower.* **2** Also called: **Perkin's mauve, mauveine** (ˈməuviːn, -vɪn). a reddish-purple aniline dye. [C19: from French, from Latin *malva* MALLOW]

maven *or* **mavin** (ˈmeɪvən) *n U.S.* an expert or connoisseur. [C20: from Yiddish, from Hebrew *mevin* understanding]

maverick (ˈmævərɪk) *n* **1** (in U.S. and Canadian cattle-raising regions) an unbranded animal, esp. a stray calf. **2a** a person of independent or unorthodox views. **2b** (*as modifier*): *a maverick politician.* [C19: after Samuel A. *Maverick* (1803–70), Texas rancher, who did not brand his cattle]

mavis (ˈmeɪvɪs) *n* a popular name for the **song thrush.** [C14: from Old French *mauvis* thrush; origin obscure]

mavourneen *or* **mavournin** (məˈvuəniːn) *n Irish.* my darling. [C18: from Irish, from *mo* my + *muirnīn* love]

maw (mɔː) *n* **1** the mouth, throat, crop, or stomach of an animal, esp. of a voracious animal. **2** *Informal.* the mouth or stomach of a greedy person. [Old English *maga;* related to Middle Dutch *maghe,* Old Norse *magi*]

mawger (ˈmɔːgə) *adj Caribbean.* (of persons or animals) thin or lean. [from Dutch *mager* thin, MEAGRE]

mawkin (ˈmɔːkɪn) *n* **1** a variant of **malkin. 2** *Brit. dialect.* **2a** a slovenly woman. **2b** a scarecrow.

mawkish (ˈmɔːkɪʃ) *adj* **1** falsely sentimental, esp. in a weak or maudlin way. **2** nauseating or insipid in flavour, smell, etc. [C17: from obsolete *mawk* MAGGOT + -ISH] ▸ **ˈmawkishly** *adv* ▸ **ˈmawkishness** *n*

Mawson (ˈmɔːsən) *n* Sir **Douglas.** 1882–1958, Australian Antarctic explorer, born in England.

max (mæks) *n Informal.* **1** the most significant, highest, furthest, or greatest thing. **2 to the max.** to the ultimate extent.

max. *abbrev. for* maximum.

maxi (ˈmæksɪ) *adj* **1a** (of a garment) reaching the ankle. **1b** (*as n*): *she wore a maxi.* **1c** (*in combination*): *a maxidress.* ♦ *n* **2** a type of large racing yacht. [C20: shortened from MAXIMUM]

maxilla (mækˈsɪlə) *n, pl* **-lae** (-liː). **1** the upper jawbone in vertebrates. See **jaw** (sense 1). **2** any member of one or two pairs of mouthparts in insects and other arthropods used as accessory jaws. [C17: New Latin, from Latin: jaw] ▸ **maxillar** (mækˈsɪlə) *or* **maxˈillary** *adj*

maxilliped (mækˈsɪlɪˌpɛd) *n* any member of three pairs of appendages in crustaceans, behind the maxillae: specialized for feeding. [C19: *maxilli-,* from MAXILLA + -PED] ▸ **maxˌilliˈpedary** *adj*

maxillofacial (mækˌsɪləuˈfeɪʃəl, ˌmæksɪləu-) *adj* of, relating to, or affecting the upper jawbone and face: *maxillofacial surgery.* [C20: from MAXILLA + -O- + FACIAL]

maxim (ˈmæksɪm) *n* a brief expression of a general truth, principle, or rule of conduct. [C15: via French from Medieval Latin, from *maxima,* in the phrase *maxima prōpositio* basic axiom (literally: greatest proposition); see MAXIMUM]

Maxim (ˈmæksɪm) *n* Sir **Hiram Stevens.** 1840–1916, British inventor of the first automatic machine gun (1884), born in the U.S.

maxima (ˈmæksɪmə) *n* a plural of **maximum.**

maximal (ˈmæksɪməl) *adj* **1** of, relating to, or achieving a maximum; being the greatest or best possible. **2** *Maths.* (of a member of an ordered set) being preceded, in order, by all other members of the set. ▸ **ˈmaximally** *adv*

maximalist (ˈmæksɪməlɪst) *n* a person who favours direct action to achieve all his goals and rejects compromise.

Maximalist (ˈmæksɪməlɪst) *n* (in early 20th-century Russia) **1** a member of the radical faction of Social Revolutionaries that supported terrorism against the tsarist regime and advocated a short period of postrevolutionary working-class dictatorship. **2** a less common name for a **Bolshevik.** ♦ Compare **Minimalist.** [C20: from French, a translation of Russian; see BOLSHEVIK]

Maxim gun *n* an obsolete water-cooled machine gun having a single barrel and utilizing the recoil force of each shot to maintain automatic fire. [C19: named after Sir Hiram MAXIM]

Maximilian (ˌmæksɪˈmɪlɪən) *n* full name *Ferdinand Maximilian Joseph.* 1832–67, archduke of Austria and emperor of Mexico (1864–67). After the French had partially conquered Mexico, he was offered the throne but was defeated and shot by the Mexicans under Juárez.

Maximilian I *n* 1459–1519, king of Germany (1486–1519) and Holy Roman Emperor (1493–1519).

maximin (ˈmæksɪˌmɪn) *n* **1** *Maths.* the highest of a set of minimum values. **2** (in game theory, etc.) the procedure of choosing the strategy that most benefits the least advantaged member of a group. Compare **minimax.** [C20: from MAXI(MUM) + MIN(IMUM)]

maximize *or* **maximise** (ˈmæksɪˌmaɪz) *vb* **1** (*tr*) to make as high or great as possible; increase to a maximum. **2** *Maths.* to find the maximum of (a function). ▸ **ˌmaximiˈzation, ˌmaximiˈsation,** *or* **ˌmaxiˈmation** *n* ▸ **ˈmaxiˌmizer** *or* **ˈmaxiˌmiser** *n*

maximum (ˈmæksɪməm) *n, pl* **-mums** *or* **-ma** (-mə). **1** the greatest possible amount, degree, etc. **2** the highest value of a variable quantity. **3** *Maths.* **3a** a value of a function that is greater than any neighbouring value. **3b** a stationary point on a curve at which the tangent changes from a positive value on the left of this point to a negative value on the right. Compare **minimum** (sense 4). **3c** the largest number in a set. **4** *Astronomy.* **4a** the time at which the brightness of a variable star has its greatest value. **4b** the magnitude of the star at that time. ♦ *adj* **5** of, being, or showing a maximum or maximums. ♦ Abbrev.: **max.** [C18: from Latin: greatest (the neuter form used as noun), from *magnus* great]

maximum likelihood *n Statistics.* **1** the probability of randomly drawing a given sample from a population maximized over the possible values of the population parameters. **2** the non-Bayesian rule that, given an experimental observation, one should utilize as point estimates of parameters of a distribution those values which give the highest conditional probability to that observation, irrespective of the prior probability assigned to the parameters.

maximum-minimum thermometer *n* a thermometer that records the highest and lowest temperatures since it was last set.

maximus (ˈmæksɪməs) *n Change-ringing.* a method rung on twelve bells. [from Latin: superlative of *magnus* great]

maxixe (məˈʃiːʃ, mækˈsiːks, məˈʃiːʃeɪ) *n* a Brazilian dance in duple time, a precursor of the tango. [from Brazilian Portuguese]

Max Müller (*German* maks ˈmylər) *n* See (Friedrich Max) **Müller.**

maxwell (ˈmækswəl) *n* the cgs unit of magnetic flux equal to the flux through one square centimetre normal to a field of one gauss. It is equivalent to 10^{-8} weber. Symbol: Mx [C20: named after J. C. MAXWELL]

Maxwell (ˈmækswəl) *n* **1 James Clerk.** 1831–79, Scottish physicist. He made major contributions to the electromagnetic theory, developing the equations (**Maxwell equations**) upon which classical theory is based. He also contributed to the kinetic theory of gases, and colour vision. **2 (Ian) Robert,** original name *Robert Hoch.* 1923–91, British publisher, born in Slovakia: founder (1949) of Pergamon Press; chairman of Mirror Group Newspapers Ltd. (1984–91); theft from his employees' pension funds and other frauds discovered after his death led to the collapse of his business.

may[1] (meɪ) *vb past* **might.** (takes an infinitive without *to* or an implied infinitive) used as an auxiliary **1** to indicate that permission is requested by or granted to someone: *he may go to the park tomorrow if he behaves himself.* **2** (often foll. by *well*) to indicate possibility: *the rope may break; he may well be a spy.* **3** to indicate ability or capacity, esp. in questions: *may I help you?* **4** to express a strong wish: *long may she reign.* **5** to indicate result or purpose: used only in clauses introduced by *that* or *so that: he writes so that the average reader may understand.* **6** another word for **might**[1]. **7** to express courtesy in a question: *whose child may this little girl be?* **8 be that as it may.** in spite of that: a sentence connector conceding the possible truth of a previous statement and introducing an adversative clause: *be that as it may, I still think he should come.* **9 come what may.** whatever happens. **10 that's as may be.** (foll. by a clause introduced by *but*) that may be so. [Old English *mæg,* from *magan:* compare Old High German *mag,* Old Norse *mā*]

USAGE It was formerly considered correct to use *may* rather than *can* when referring to permission as in: *you may use the laboratory for your experiments*, but this use of *may* is now almost entirely restricted to polite questions such as: *may I open the window?* The use of *may* with *if* in constructions such as *your analysis may have been more credible if . . .* is generally regarded as incorrect, *might* being preferred: *your analysis might have been more credible if . . .*

may[2] (meɪ) *n* an archaic word for **maiden.** [Old English *mæg;* related to Old High German *māg* kinsman, Old Norse *māgr* a relative by marriage]

may[3] (meɪ) *n* **1** Also: **may tree.** a Brit. name for **hawthorn. 2** short for **may blossom.** [C16: from the month of MAY, when it flowers]

May[1] (meɪ) *n* the fifth month of the year, consisting of 31 days. [from Old French, from Latin *Maius,* probably from *Maia,* Roman goddess, identified with the Greek goddess MAIA]

May[2] (meɪ) *n* Sir **Robert McCredie.** born 1936, Australian biologist and ecologist.

maya ('maɪə, 'mɑːjə, 'mɑːjɑː) *n Hinduism.* illusion, esp. the material world of the senses regarded as illusory. [C19: from Sanskrit] ► **'mayan** *adj*

Maya[1] ('maɪə, 'mɑːjə, 'mɑːjɑː) *n* the Hindu goddess of illusion, the personification of the idea that the material world is illusory. ► **'Mayan** *adj*

Maya[2] ('maɪə) *n* **1** (*pl* **-ya** *or* **-yas**) Also called: **Mayan.** a member of an American Indian people of Yucatan, Belize, and N Guatemala, having an ancient culture once characterized by outstanding achievements in architecture, astronomy, chronology, painting, and pottery. **2** the language of this people. See also **Mayan.**

Mayagüez (*Spanish* maja'ɣweθ) *n* a port in W Puerto Rico; needlework industry. Pop.: 100 937 (1996 est.).

Mayakovski *or* **Mayakovsky** (*Russian* məjɪ'kɔfskij) *n* **Vladimir Vladimirovich** (vla'dimir vla'dimirəvitʃ). 1893–1930, Russian Futurist poet and dramatist. His poems include *150 000 000* (1921) and *At the Top of my Voice* (1930); his plays include *Vladimir Mayakovsky —a Tragedy* (1913) and *The Bedbug* (1929).

Mayan ('maɪən) *adj* **1** of, relating to, or characteristic of the Maya or any of their languages. ◆ *n* **2** a family of Central American Indian languages, including Maya, possibly a member of the Penutian phylum. **3** another name for a **Maya**[2].

May apple *n* **1** an American plant, *Podophyllum peltatum,* with edible yellowish egg-shaped fruit: family *Podophyllaceae.* **2** the fruit of this plant.

maybe ('meɪˌbiː) *adv* **1a** perhaps. **1b** (*as sentence modifier*): *maybe I'll come tomorrow.* ◆ *sentence substitute.* **2** possibly; neither yes nor no.

May beetle *or* **bug** *n* another name for **cockchafer** and **June bug.**

May blobs *n* (*functioning as sing*) another name for **marsh marigold.**

may blossom *or* **may** *n* the blossom of the may tree or hawthorn.

Mayday ('meɪˌdeɪ) *n* the international radiotelephone distress signal. [C20: phonetic spelling of French *m'aidez* help me]

May Day *n* **a** the first day of May, traditionally a celebration of the coming of spring: in some countries now observed as a holiday in honour of workers. **b** (*as modifier*): *May-Day celebrations.*

Mayence (majɑ̃s) *n* the French name for **Mainz.**

Mayenne (*French* majɛn) *n* a department of NW France, in Pays de la Loire region. Capital: Laval. Pop.: 281 900 (1995). Area: 5212 sq. km (2033 sq. miles).

Mayer *n* **1** (*German* 'maiər). **Julius Robert von** ('juːlius'roːbert fɔn). 1814–78, German physicist whose research in thermodynamics (1842) contributed to the discovery of the law of conservation of energy. **2** ('meɪə). **Louis B(urt).** 1885–1957, U.S. film producer, born in Russia; founder (with S. Goldwyn) and first head (1924–48) of the Metro-Goldwyn-Mayer (MGM) film company.

mayest ('meɪɪst) *vb* a variant of **mayst.**

Mayfair ('meɪˌfɛə) *n* a fashionable district of west central London.

mayflower ('meɪˌflaʊə) *n* **1** any of various plants that bloom in May. **2** *U.S. and Canadian.* another name for **trailing arbutus. 3** *Brit.* another name for **hawthorn, cowslip,** or **marsh marigold.**

Mayflower ('meɪˌflaʊə) *n* **the.** the ship in which the Pilgrim Fathers sailed from Plymouth to Massachusetts in 1620.

mayfly ('meɪˌflaɪ) *n, pl* **-flies. 1** Also called: **dayfly.** any insect of the order *Ephemeroptera* (or *Ephemerida*). The short-lived adults, found near water, have long tail appendages and large transparent wings; the larvae are aquatic. **2** *Angling.* an artificial fly resembling this.

mayhap ('meɪˌhæp) *adv* an archaic word for **perhaps.** [C16: shortened from *it may hap*]

mayhem *or* **maihem** ('meɪhɛm) *n* **1** *Law.* the wilful and unlawful infliction of injury upon a person, esp. (formerly) the injuring or removing of a limb rendering him less capable of defending himself against attack. **2** any violent destruction or confusion. [C15: from Anglo-French *mahem* injury, from Germanic; related to Icelandic *meitha* to hurt. See MAIM]

Mayhew ('meɪhjuː) *n* **Henry.** 1812–87, British social commentator, journalist, and writer; a founder of *Punch* (1841): best known for *London Labour and the London Poor* (1851–62).

Maying ('meɪɪŋ) *n* the traditional celebration of May Day.

mayn't ('meɪənt, meɪnt) *vb contraction of* may not.

Mayo[1] ('meɪəʊ) *n* a county of NW Republic of Ireland, in NW Connacht province, on the Atlantic: has many offshore islands and several large lakes. County town: Castlebar. Pop.: 111 000 (1996). Area: 5397 sq. km (2084 sq. miles).

Mayo[2] ('meɪəʊ) *n* a family of U.S. medical practitioners. They pioneered group practice and established (1903) the **Mayo Clinic** in Rochester, Minnesota. Foremost among them were **William Worrall Mayo** (1819–1911), his sons **William James Mayo** (1861–1939) and **Charles Horace Mayo** (1865–1939), and Charles's son, **Charles William Mayo** (1898–1968).

Mayon (mɑː'jɔːn) *n* a volcano in the Philippines, on SE Luzon: Height: 2421 m (7943 ft.).

mayonnaise (ˌmeɪə'neɪz) *n* a thick creamy sauce made from egg yolks, oil, and vinegar or lemon juice, eaten with salads, eggs, etc. [C19: from French, perhaps from *Mahonnais* of *Mahón,* a port in Minorca]

mayor (mɛə) *n* the chairman and civic head of a municipal corporation in many countries. Scottish equivalent: **provost.** [C13: from Old French *maire,* from Latin *maior* greater. See MAJOR] ► **'mayoral** *adj* ► **'mayorˌship** *n*

mayoralty ('mɛərəltɪ) *n, pl* **-ties.** the office or term of office of a mayor. [C14: from Old French *mairalté*]

mayoress ('mɛərɪs) *n* **1** *Chiefly Brit.* the wife of a mayor. **2** a female mayor.

Mayotte (*French* majɔt) *n* an island in the Indian Ocean, northwest of Madagascar; administered by France. Pop. (including Pamanzi): 134 000 (1998 est.). Area: 374 sq. km (146 sq. miles).

maypole ('meɪˌpəʊl) *n* a tall pole fixed upright in an open space during May-Day celebrations, around which people dance holding streamers attached at its head.

May queen *n* a girl chosen, esp. for her beauty, to preside over May-Day celebrations.

mayst (meɪst) *or* **mayest** *vb Archaic or dialect.* (used with the pronoun *thou* or its relative equivalent) a singular form of the present tense of **may.**

may tree *n* a Brit. name for **hawthorn.**

mayweed ('meɪˌwiːd) *n* **1** Also called: **dog fennel, stinking mayweed.** a widespread Eurasian weedy plant, *Anthemis cotula,* having evil-smelling leaves and daisy-like flower heads: family *Compositae* (composites). **2 scentless mayweed.** a similar and related plant, *Tripleurospermum maritimum,* with scentless leaves. [C16: changed from Old English *mægtha* mayweed + WEED[1]]

mazard *or* **mazzard** ('mæzəd) *n* **1** an obsolete word for the **head** or **skull. 2** another word for **mazer.** [C17: altered from MAZER]

Mazarin ('mæzərɪn; *French* mazarɛ̃) *n* **Jules** (ʒyl), original name *Giulio Mazarini.* 1602–61, French cardinal and statesman, born in Italy. He succeeded Richelieu (1642) as chief minister to Louis XIII and under the regency of Anne of Austria (1643–61). Despite the disturbances of the Fronde (1648–53), he strengthened the power of France in Europe.

Mazatlán (*Spanish* maθa'tlan) *n* a port in W Mexico, in S Sinaloa on the Pacific: situated opposite the tip of the peninsula of Lower California, for which it is the chief link with the mainland. Pop.: 262 705 (1990).

Mazdaism *or* **Mazdeism** ('mæzdəˌɪzəm) *n* another word for **Zoroastrianism.**

maze (meɪz) *n* **1** a complex network of paths or passages, esp. one with high hedges in a garden, designed to puzzle those walking through it. Compare **labyrinth** (sense 1). **2** a similar system represented diagrammatically as a pattern of lines. **3** any confusing network of streets, pathways, etc.: *a maze of paths.* **4** a state of confusion. ◆ *vb* **5** an archaic or dialect word for **amaze.** [C13: see AMAZE] ► **'mazeˌlike** *adj* ► **'mazement** *n*

mazer ('meɪzə), **mazard,** *or* **mazzard** ('mæzəd) *n Obsolete.* a large hardwood drinking bowl. [C12: from Old French *masere,* of Germanic origin; compare Old Norse *mösurr* maple]

Mazu ('mæ'zuː) *n* the Pinyin transliteration of the Chinese name for **Matsu.**

mazuma (mə'zuːmə) *n Slang, chiefly U.S.* money. [C20: from Yiddish]

mazurka *or* **mazourka** (mə'zɜːkə) *n* **1** a Polish national dance in triple time. **2** a piece of music composed for this dance. [C19: from Polish: (dance) of *Mazur* (Mazovia) province in Poland]

mazy ('meɪzɪ) *adj* **mazier, maziest.** of or like a maze; perplexing or confused. ► **'mazily** *adv* ► **'maziness** *n*

mazzard *or* **mazard** ('mæzəd) *n* a wild sweet cherry tree, *Prunus avium,* often used as a grafting stock for cultivated cherries. [C16: perhaps related to MAZER]

Mazzini (*Italian* mat'tsiːni) *n* **Giuseppe** (dʒu'zeppe). 1805–72, Italian nationalist. In 1831, in exile, he established the Young Italy association in Marseille, which sought to unite Italy as a republic. In 1849 he was one of the triumvirate that ruled the short-lived Roman republic.

mb *symbol for* millibar.

Mb *Computing. abbrev. for* megabyte.

MB *abbrev. for:* **1** Bachelor of Medicine. **2** maternity benefit. **3** Manitoba. **4** (in Canada) Medal of Bravery.

MBA *abbrev. for* Master of Business Administration.

Mbabane (ᵊmbɑː'bɑːnɪ) *n* the capital of Swaziland, in the northwest: administrative and financial centre, with a large iron mine nearby. Pop.: 47 000 (1990 est.).

mbaqanga (ᵊmbɑː'kæŋgə) *n* a style of Black popular music of urban South Africa. [C20: perhaps from Zulu *umbaqanga* mixture]

MBE *abbrev. for* Member of the Order of the British Empire (a Brit. title).

Mbeki (ᵊm'bɛkɪ) *n* **Thabo (Mvuyelwa)** ('tɑːbəʊ). born 1942, South African politician: a member of the African National Congress (ANC); president of South Africa from 1999; deputy president of South Africa (1994–99).

mbira (ᵊm'biːrə) *n* an African musical instrument consisting of tuned metal strips attached to a resonating box, which are plucked with the thumbs. Also called: **thumb piano.** [Shona]

Mbujimayi (ᵊm'buːdʒɪˌmaiː) *n* a city in S Democratic Republic of the Congo (formerly Zaïre): diamond mining. Pop.: 806 475 (1994 est.).

mbyte *Computing. abbrev. for* megabyte.

MC *abbrev. for:* **1** Master of Ceremonies. **2** *Astrology.* Medium Coeli. [Latin: Midheaven]. **3** (in the U.S.) Member of Congress. **4** (in Britain) Military Cross. ◆ **5** *international car registration for* Monaco.

Mc- *prefix* a variant of **Mac-.** For names beginning with this prefix, see under **Mac-.**

MCB *abbrev. for* miniature circuit breaker; a small trip switch operated by an overload and used to protect an electric circuit, esp. a domestic circuit as an alternative to a fuse.

MCC (in Britain) *abbrev. for* Marylebone Cricket Club.

MCh *abbrev. for* Master of Surgery. [Latin *Magister Chirurgiae*]

McJob (mək'dʒɒb) *n Informal.* a job that is poorly paid and menial. [C20: a humorous corruption of *McDonald's,* a major American fast-food enterprise]

MCom *abbrev. for* Master of Commerce.

MCP *Informal. abbrev. for* male chauvinist pig.

MCPS *abbrev. for* Mechanical Copyright Protection Society.

Md *the chemical symbol for* mendelevium.
MD *abbrev. for:* **1** Doctor of Medicine. [from Latin *Medicinae Doctor*] **2** Maryland. **3** Medical Department. **4** mentally deficient. **5** Managing Director.
Md. *abbrev. for* Maryland.
MDMA *abbrev. for* 3,4-methylenedioxymethamphetamine. Also called (informal): **ecstasy.**
MDS *abbrev. for* Master of Dental Surgery.
mdse *abbrev. for* merchandise.
me[1] (miː; *unstressed* mɪ) *pron* (*objective*) **1** refers to the speaker or writer: *that shocks me; he gave me the glass.* **2** *Chiefly U.S.* a dialect word for **myself** when used as an indirect object: *I want to get me a car.* ◆ *n* **3** *Informal.* the personality of the speaker or writer or something that expresses it: *the real me comes out when I'm happy.* [Old English *mē* (dative); compare Dutch, German *mir,* Latin *mē* (accusative), *mihi* (dative)]

USAGE It was formerly regarded as correct to use *I, he, she,* etc. rather than *me, him, her,* after the verb *to be* , as in: *it is I who told him.* Since both *I* and *me* can sound strange in a sentence like this, it is better to use a different construction: *I am the one who told him.* The use of a possessive before an *-ing* form of a verb was formerly thought to be preferable to using *me* , etc., but now both forms are acceptable: *he didn't like my/me having a job of my own.*

me[2] (miː) *n* a variant spelling of **mi.**
Me *chemical symbol for* the methyl group.
ME *abbrev. for:* **1** Maine. **2** Marine Engineer. **3** Mechanical Engineer. **4** Methodist Episcopal. **5** Mining Engineer. **6** Middle English. **7** (in titles) Most Excellent. **8** myalgic encephalomyelitis.
Me. *abbrev. for:* **1** Maine. **2** Maître.
mea culpa *Latin.* ('meɪɑː 'kʊlpɑː) an acknowledgment of guilt. [literally: my fault]
mead[1] (miːd) *n* an alcoholic drink made by fermenting a solution of honey, often with spices added. [Old English *meodu;* related to Old High German *metu,* Greek *methu,* Welsh *medd*]
mead[2] (miːd) *n* an archaic or poetic word for **meadow.** [Old English *mæd*]
Mead[1] (miːd) *n* **Lake.** a reservoir in NW Arizona and SE Nevada, formed by the Hoover Dam across the Colorado River: one of the largest man-made lakes in the world. Area: 588 sq. km (227 sq. miles).
Mead[2] (miːd) *n* **Margaret.** 1901–78, U.S. anthropologist. Her works include *Coming of Age in Samoa* (1928) and *Male and Female* (1949).
Meade (miːd) *n* **George Gordon.** 1815–72, Union general in the American Civil War. He commanded the Army of the Potomac, defeating the Confederates at Gettysburg (1863).
meadow ('mɛdəʊ) *n* **1** an area of grassland, often used for hay or for grazing of animals. **2** a low-lying piece of grassland, often boggy and near a river. [Old English *mædwe,* from *mæd* MEAD[2]; related to *māwan* to MOW[1]] ▸ **'meadowy** *adj*
meadow fescue *n* an erect Eurasian perennial grass, *Festuca pratensis,* with lustrous leaves and stem bases surrounded by dark brown sheaths.
meadow grass *n* a perennial grass, *Poa pratensis,* that has erect hairless leaves and grows in meadows and similar places in N temperate regions.
meadowlark ('mɛdəʊ,lɑːk) *n* either of two North American yellow-breasted songbirds, *Sturnella magna* (**eastern meadowlark**) or *S. neglecta* (**western meadowlark**): family *Icteridae* (American orioles).
meadow lily *n* another name for **Canada lily.**
meadow mouse *n U.S.* another name for **vole**[1].
meadow mushroom *n* a saprotrophic agaricaceous edible fungus, *Agaricus* (or *Psalliota*) *campestris,* having a white cap with pink or brown gills on the underside.
meadow pipit *n* a common European songbird, *Anthus pratensis,* with a pale brown speckled plumage: family *Motacillidae* (pipits and wagtails).
meadow rue *n* any ranunculaceous plant of the N temperate genus *Thalictrum,* esp. *T. flavum,* having clusters of small yellowish-green, white, or purple flowers.
meadow saffron *n* another name for **autumn crocus.**
meadowsweet ('mɛdəʊ,swiːt) *n* **1** a Eurasian rosaceous plant, *Filipendula ulmaria,* with dense heads of small fragrant cream-coloured flowers. See also **dropwort** (sense 1). **2** any of several North American rosaceous plants of the genus *Spiraea,* having pyramid-shaped sprays of small flowers.
Meads (miːdz) *n* **Colin.** born 1935, New Zealand Rugby Union footballer. A forward, he played for the All Blacks (1957–71).
meagre *or U.S.* **meager** ('miːgə) *adj* **1** deficient in amount, quality, or extent. **2** thin or emaciated. **3** lacking in richness or strength. [C14: from Old French *maigre,* from Latin *macer* lean, poor] ▸ **'meagrely** *or U.S.* **'meagerly** *adv* ▸ **'meagreness** *or U.S.* **'meagerness** *n*
meal[1] (miːl) *n* **1a** any of the regular occasions, such as breakfast, lunch, dinner, etc., when food is served and eaten. **1b** (*in combination*): *mealtime.* Related adj: **prandial. 2** the food served and eaten. **3 make a meal of.** *Informal.* to perform (a task) with unnecessarily great effort. [Old English *mǣl* measure, set time, meal; related to Old High German *māl* mealtime]
meal[2] (miːl) *n* **1** the edible part of a grain or pulse (excluding wheat) ground to a coarse powder, used chiefly as animal food. **2** *Scot.* oatmeal. **3** *Chiefly U.S.* maize flour. [Old English *melu;* compare Dutch *meel,* Old High German *melo,* Old Norse *mjöl*] ▸ **'mealless** *adj*
mealie *or* **mielie** ('miːlɪ) *n S. African.* an ear of maize. See also **mealies.** [C19: from Afrikaans *milie,* from Portuguese *milho,* from Latin *milium* millet]
mealie meal *or* **mielie meal** *n S. African.* finely ground maize.
mealie pap *or* **mielie pap** *n S. African.* mealie porridge. [Afrikaans]
mealies *or* **mielies** ('miːlɪz) *n* (*functioning as sing*) a South African word for **maize.**
meal moth *n* a small pyralid moth, *Pyralis farinalis,* whose larvae are an important pest of stored cereals. The **Indian meal moth** (*Plodia interpunctella*) and the **Mediterranean flour moth** (*Ephestia kuehniella*) are other pyralids with similar habits.
meals on wheels *or* **meals-on-wheels** *n* (*functioning as sing*) *Social welfare, Brit.* a service, usually subsidized, and run by a social services department or voluntary body, which delivers hot meals to elderly or housebound people who might otherwise be unable to have them.
meal ticket *n Slang.* a person, situation, etc., providing a source of livelihood or income. [from original U.S. sense of ticket entitling holder to a meal]
mealworm ('miːl,wɜːm) *n* the larva of various beetles of the genus *Tenebrio,* esp. *T. molitor,* feeding on meal, flour, and similar stored foods: family *Tenebrionidae.*
mealy ('miːlɪ) *adj* **mealier, mealiest. 1** resembling meal; powdery. **2** containing or consisting of meal or grain. **3** sprinkled or covered with meal or similar granules. **4** (esp. of horses) spotted; mottled. **5** pale in complexion. **6** short for **mealy-mouthed.** ▸ **'mealiness** *n*
mealy bug *n* any plant-eating homopterous insect of the genus *Pseudococcus* and related genera, coated with a powdery waxy secretion: some species are pests of citrus fruits and greenhouse plants: family *Pseudococcidae.*
mealy-mouthed *adj* hesitant or afraid to speak plainly; not outspoken. [C16: from MEALY (in the sense: soft, soft-spoken)] ▸ **,mealy-'mouthedness** *n*
mean[1] (miːn) *vb* **means, meaning, meant.** (*mainly tr*) **1** (*may take a clause as object or an infinitive*) to intend to convey or express. **2** (*may take a clause as object or an infinitive*) intend: *she didn't mean to hurt it.* **3** (*may take a clause as object*) to say or do in all seriousness: *the boss means what he says about strikes.* **4** (*often passive;* often foll. by *for*) to destine or design (for a certain person or purpose): *she was meant for greater things.* **5** (*may take a clause as object or an infinitive*) to denote or connote; signify; represent: *examples help show exactly what a word means.* **6** (*may take a clause as object*) to produce; cause: *the weather will mean long traffic delays.* **7** (*may take a clause as object*) to foretell; portend: *those dark clouds mean rain.* **8** to have the importance of: *money means nothing to him.* **9** (*intr*) to have the intention of behaving or acting (esp. in the phrases **mean well** *or* **mean ill**). **10 mean business.** to be in earnest. [Old English *mænan;* compare Old Saxon *mēnian* to intend, Dutch *meenen*]

USAGE In standard English, *mean* should not be followed by *for* when expressing intention: *I didn't mean this to happen* (not *I didn't mean for this to happen*).

mean[2] (miːn) *adj* **1** *Chiefly Brit.* miserly, ungenerous, or petty. **2** humble, obscure, or lowly: *he rose from mean origins to high office.* **3** despicable, ignoble, or callous: *a mean action.* **4** poor or shabby: *mean clothing; a mean abode.* **5** *Informal, chiefly U.S. and Canadian.* bad-tempered; vicious. **6** *Informal.* ashamed: *he felt mean about not letting the children go to the zoo.* **7** *Informal, chiefly U.S.* unwell; in low spirits. **8** *Slang.* excellent; skilful: *he plays a mean trombone.* **9 no mean. 9a** of high quality: *no mean performer.* **9b** difficult: *no mean feat.* [C12: from Old English *gemǣne* common; related to Old High German *gimeini,* Latin *communis* common, at first with no pejorative sense] ▸ **'meanly** *adv* ▸ **'meanness** *n*
mean[3] (miːn) *n* **1** the middle point, state, or course between limits or extremes. **2** moderation. **3** *Maths.* **3a** the second and third terms of a proportion, as *b* and *c* in $a/b = c/d$. **3b** another name for **average** (sense 2). See also **geometric mean. 4** *Statistics.* a statistic obtained by multiplying each possible value of a variable by its probability and then taking the sum or integral over the range of the variable. ◆ *adj* **5** intermediate or medium in size, quantity, etc. **6** occurring halfway between extremes or limits; average. ◆ See also **means.** [C14: via Anglo-Norman from Old French *moien,* from Late Latin *mediānus* MEDIAN]
meander (mɪ'ændə) *vb* (*intr*) **1** to follow a winding course. **2** to wander without definite aim or direction. ◆ *n* **3** (*often pl*) a curve or bend, as in a river. **4** (*often pl*) a winding course or movement. **5** an ornamental pattern, esp. as used in ancient Greek architecture. [C16: from Latin *maeander,* from Greek *Maiandros* the River Maeander; see MENDERES (sense 1)] ▸ **me'anderer** *n* ▸ **me'andering** *adj* ▸ **me'anderingly** *adv* ▸ **me'androus** *adj*
Meander (miː'ændə) *n* a variant spelling of **Maeander.**
mean deviation *n Statistics.* **1** the difference between an observed value of a variable and its mean. **2** Also called: **mean deviation from the mean** (*or* **median**), **average deviation.** a measure of dispersion derived by computing the mean of the absolute values of the differences between observed values of a variable and the variable's mean.
mean distance *n* the average of the greatest and least distances of a celestial body from its primary.
mean free path *n* the average distance travelled by a particle, atom, etc., between collisions.
meanie *or* **meany** ('miːnɪ) *n, pl* **meanies.** *Informal.* **1** *Chiefly Brit.* a miserly or stingy person. **2** *Chiefly U.S.* a nasty ill-tempered person.
meaning ('miːnɪŋ) *n* **1** the sense or significance of a word, sentence, symbol, etc.; import; semantic or lexical content. **2** the purpose underlying or intended by speech, action, etc. **3** the inner, symbolic, or true interpretation, value, or message: *the meaning of a dream.* **4** valid content; efficacy: *a law with little or no meaning.* **5** *Philosophy.* **5a** the sense of an expression; its connotation. **5b** the reference of an expression; its denotation. In recent philosophical writings meaning can be used in both the above senses. See also **sense** (sense 13). ◆ *adj* **6** expressive of some sense, intention, criticism, etc.: *a meaning look.* ◆ See also **well-meaning.**
meaningful ('miːnɪŋfʊl) *adj* **1** having great meaning or validity. **2** eloquent, expressive: *a meaningful silence.* ▸ **'meaningfully** *adv* ▸ **'meaningfulness** *n*
meaningless ('miːnɪŋlɪs) *adj* futile or empty of meaning. ▸ **'meaninglessly** *adv* ▸ **'meaninglessness** *n*

mean lethal dose *n* another term for **median lethal dose.**

mean life *n Physics.* the average time of existence of an unstable or reactive entity, such as a nucleus, elementary particle, charge carrier, etc.; lifetime. It is equal to the half-life divided by 0.693 15. Symbol: τ

means (mi:nz) *n* **1** (*functioning as sing or pl*) the medium, method, or instrument used to obtain a result or achieve an end: *a means of communication.* **2** (*functioning as pl*) resources or income. **3** (*functioning as pl*) considerable wealth or income: *a man of means.* **4 by all means.** without hesitation or doubt; certainly: *come with us by all means.* **5 by means of.** with the use or help of. **6 by no manner of means.** definitely not: *he was by no manner of means a cruel man.* **7 by no** (*or* **not by any**) **means.** on no account; in no way: *by no means come!*

mean sea level *n* (in the UK) the sea level used by the Ordnance Survey as a datum level, determined at Newlyn in Cornwall. See **sea level.**

means of production *pl n* (in Marxist theory) the raw materials and means of labour (tools, machines, etc.) employed in the production process.

mean solar day *n* the time between two successive passages of the mean sun across the meridian at noon. It equals the earth's rotation period, which is not precisely constant at 24 hours when checked against atomic time.

means test *n* a test involving the checking of a person's income to determine whether he qualifies for financial or social aid from a government. Compare **needs test.** ▸ **'means-tested** *adj*

mean sun *n* an imaginary sun moving along the celestial equator at a constant speed and completing its annual course in the same time as the sun takes to move round the ecliptic at a varying speed. It is used in the measurement of mean solar time.

meant (mɛnt) *vb* the past tense and past participle of **mean**[1].

mean time *or* **mean solar time** *n* the time, at a particular place, measured in terms of the passage of the mean sun; the timescale is not precisely constant. See **mean solar day.**

meantime ('mi:nˌtaɪm) *n* **1** the intervening time or period, as between events (esp. in the phrase **in the meantime**). ◆ *adv* **2** another word for **meanwhile.**

mean-tone tuning *n* See **temperament** (sense 4).

meanwhile ('mi:nˌwaɪl) *adv* **1** during the intervening time or period. **2** at the same time, esp. in another place. ◆ *n* **3** another word for **meantime.**

meany ('mi:nɪ) *n Informal.* a variant spelling of **meanie.**

Mearns (mɛənz) *n* **the.** another name for **Kincardineshire.**

meas. *abbrev. for* measure.

measled ('mi:zəld) *adj* (of cattle, sheep, or pigs) infested with tapeworm larvae; measly.

measles ('mi:zəlz) *n* (*functioning as sing or pl*) **1** a highly contagious viral disease common in children, characterized by fever, profuse nasal discharge of mucus, conjunctivitis, and a rash of small red spots spreading from the forehead down to the limbs. Technical names: **morbilli, rubeola.** See also **German measles. 2** a disease of cattle, sheep, and pigs, caused by infestation with tapeworm larvae. [C14: from Middle Low German *masele* spot on the skin; influenced by Middle English *mesel* leper, from Latin *misellus,* diminutive of *miser* wretched]

measly ('mi:zlɪ) *adj* **-slier, -sliest. 1** *Informal.* meagre in quality or quantity. **2** (of meat) measled. **3** having or relating to measles. [C17: see MEASLES]

measurable ('mɛʒərəbᵊl, 'mɛʒrə-) *adj* able to be measured; perceptible or significant. ▸ **ˌmeasura'bility** *or* **'measurableness** *n* ▸ **'measurably** *adv*

measure ('mɛʒə) *n* **1** the extent, quantity, amount, or degree of something, as determined by measurement or calculation. **2** a device for measuring distance, volume, etc., such as a graduated scale or container. **3** a system of measurement: *give the size in metric measure.* **4** a standard used in a system of measurements: *the international prototype kilogram is the measure of mass in SI units.* **5** a specific or standard amount of something: *a measure of grain; short measure; full measure.* **6** a basis or standard for comparison: *his work was the measure of all subsequent attempts.* **7** reasonable or permissible limit or bounds: *we must keep it within measure.* **8** degree or extent (often in phrases such as **in some measure, in a measure,** etc.): *they gave him a measure of freedom.* **9** (*often pl*) a particular action intended to achieve an effect: *they took measures to prevent his leaving.* **10** a legislative bill, act, or resolution: *to bring in a measure.* **11** *Music.* another word for **bar**[1] (sense 15a). **12** *Prosody.* poetic rhythm or cadence; metre. **13** a metrical foot. **14** *Poetic.* a melody or tune. **15** the act of measuring; measurement. **16** *Archaic.* a dance. **17** *Printing.* the width of a page or column of type. **18 for good measure.** as an extra precaution or beyond requirements. **19 get the measure of** *or* **get someone's measure.** to assess the nature, character, quality, etc., of someone or something. **20 made to measure.** (of clothes) made to fit an individual purchaser. ◆ *vb* **21** (*tr;* often foll. by *up*) to determine the size, amount, etc., of by measurement. **22** (*intr*) to make a measurement or measurements. **23** (*tr*) to estimate or determine: *I measured his strength to be greater than mine.* **24** (*tr*) to function as a measurement of: *the ohm measures electrical resistance.* **25** (*tr*) to bring into competition or conflict: *he measured his strength against that of his opponent.* **26** (*intr*) to be as specified in extent, amount, etc.: *the room measures six feet.* **27** (*tr*) to travel or move over as if measuring. **28** (*tr*) to adjust or choose: *he measured his approach to suit the character of his client.* **29** (*intr*) to allow or yield to measurement. ◆ See also **measure off, measure out, measures, measure up.** [C13: from Old French, from Latin *mēnsūra* measure, from *mēnsus,* past participle of *mētīrī* to measure] ▸ **'measurer** *n*

measured ('mɛʒəd) *adj* **1** determined by measurement. **2** slow, stately, or leisurely. **3** carefully considered; deliberate. ▸ **'measuredly** *adv* ▸ **'measuredness** *n*

measured daywork ('deɪˌwɜ:k) *n* a system of wage payment, usually determined by work-study techniques, whereby the wage of an employee is fixed on the understanding that a specific level of work performance will be maintained.

measureless ('mɛʒəlɪs) *adj* limitless, vast, or infinite. ▸ **'measurelessly** *adv* ▸ **'measurelessness** *n*

measurement ('mɛʒəmənt) *n* **1** the act or process of measuring. **2** an amount, extent, or size determined by measuring. **3** a system of measures based on a particular standard.

measurement ton *n* the full name for **ton**[1] (sense 5).

measure off *or* **out** *vb* (*tr, adv*) to determine the limits of; mark out: *to measure off an area.*

measure out *vb* (*tr, adv*) **1** to pour or dole out: *they measure out a pint of fluid.* **2** to administer; mete out: *they measured out harsh punishments.*

measures ('mɛʒəz) *pl n* rock strata that are characterized by a particular type of sediment or deposit: *coal measures.*

measure up *vb* **1** (*adv*) to determine the size of (something) by measurement. **2 measure up to.** to fulfil (expectations, standards, etc.).

measuring jug *n* a graduated jug used in cooking to measure ingredients.

measuring worm *n* the larva of a geometrid moth: it has legs on its front and rear segments only and moves in a series of loops. Also called: **looper, inchworm.**

meat (mi:t) *n* **1** the flesh of mammals used as food, as distinguished from that of birds and fish. **2** anything edible, esp. flesh with the texture of meat: *crab meat.* **3** food, as opposed to drink. **4** the essence or gist. **5** an archaic word for **meal**[1]. **6 meat and drink.** a source of pleasure. **7 have one's meat and one's manners.** *Irish informal.* to lose nothing because one's offer is not accepted. [Old English *mete;* related to Old High German *maz* food, Old Saxon *meti,* Gothic *mats*] ▸ **'meatless** *adj*

meataxe ('mi:tˌæks) *n* **1** a cleaver. **2 mad as a meataxe.** *Austral. and N.Z. informal.* raving.

meatball ('mi:tˌbɔ:l) *n* **1** minced beef, shaped into a ball before cooking. **2** *U.S. and Canadian slang.* a stupid or boring person.

Meath (mi:ð, mi:θ) *n* a county of E Republic of Ireland, in Leinster province on the Irish Sea: formerly a kingdom much larger than the present county; livestock farming. County town: Trim. Pop.: 109 000 (1996). Area: 2338 sq. km (903 sq. miles).

meatus (mɪ'eɪtəs) *n, pl* **-tuses** *or* **-tus.** *Anatomy.* a natural opening or channel, such as the canal leading from the outer ear to the eardrum. [C17: from Latin: passage, from *meāre* to pass]

meaty ('mi:tɪ) *adj* **meatier, meatiest. 1** of, relating to, or full of meat: *a meaty stew.* **2** heavily built; fleshy or brawny. **3** full of import or interest: *a meaty discussion.* **4** *Judaism.* another word for **fleishik.** ▸ **'meatily** *adv* ▸ **'meatiness** *n*

mecamylamine (ˌmɛkə'mɪləˌmi:n) *n* a drug administered orally to lower high blood pressure. Formula: $C_{11}H_{21}N.HCl$. [C20: from ME(THYL) + *cam(phane)* (a former name of bornane) + -YL + AMINE]

Mecca *or* **Mekka** ('mɛkə) *n* **1** a city in W Saudi Arabia, joint capital (with Riyadh) of Saudi Arabia: birthplace of Mohammed; the holiest city of Islam, containing the Kaaba. Pop.: 630 000 (1991 est.). Arabic name: **Makkah. 2** (*sometimes not cap.*) a place that attracts many visitors: *Athens is a Mecca for tourists.*

Meccano (mɪ'kɑ:nəʊ) *n Trademark.* a construction set consisting of miniature metal or plastic parts from which mechanical models can be made.

mech. *abbrev. for:* **1** mechanical. **2** mechanics. **3** mechanism.

mechanic (mɪ'kænɪk) *n* **1** a person skilled in maintaining or operating machinery, motors, etc. **2** *Archaic.* a common labourer. [C14: from Latin *mēchanicus,* from Greek *mēkhanikos,* from *mēkhanē* MACHINE]

mechanical (mɪ'kænɪkᵊl) *adj* **1** made, performed, or operated by or as if by a machine or machinery: *a mechanical process.* **2** concerned with machines or machinery. **3** relating to or controlled or operated by physical forces. **4** of or concerned with mechanics. **5** (of a gesture, etc.) automatic; lacking thought, feeling, etc. **6** *Philosophy.* accounting for phenomena by physically determining forces. **7** (of paper, such as newsprint) made from pulp that has been mechanically ground and contains impurities. ◆ *n* **8** *Printing.* another name for **camera-ready copy. 9** *Archaic.* another word for **mechanic** (sense 2). ▸ **me'chanicalism** *n* ▸ **me'chanically** *adv* ▸ **me'chanicalness** *n*

mechanical advantage *n* the ratio of the working force exerted by a mechanism to the applied effort.

mechanical drawing *n* a drawing to scale of a machine, machine component, architectural plan, etc., from which dimensions can be taken.

mechanical engineering *n* the branch of engineering concerned with the design, construction, and operation of machines and machinery. ▸ **mechanical engineer** *n*

mechanical equivalent of heat *n Physics.* a factor for converting units of energy into heat units. It has the value 4.1855 joules per calorie. Symbol: *J*

mechanical instrument *n* a musical instrument, such as a barrel organ or music box, that plays a preselected piece of music by mechanical means.

mechanician (ˌmɛkə'nɪʃən) *or* **mechanist** *n* a person skilled in making machinery and tools; technician.

mechanics (mɪ'kænɪks) *n* **1** (*functioning as sing*) the branch of science, divided into statics, dynamics, and kinematics, concerned with the equilibrium or motion of bodies in a particular frame of reference. See also **quantum mechanics, wave mechanics, statistical mechanics. 2** (*functioning as sing*) the science of designing, constructing, and operating machines. **3** the working parts of a machine. **4** the technical aspects of something: *the mechanics of poetic style.*

mechanism ('mɛkəˌnɪzəm) *n* **1** a system or structure of moving parts that performs some function, esp. in a machine. **2** something resembling a machine in the arrangement and working of its parts: *the mechanism of the ear.* **3** any form of mechanical device or any part of such a device. **4** a process or technique, esp. of execution: *the mechanism of novel writing.* **5** *Philosophy.* **5a** the doctrine that human action can be explained in purely physical terms, whether mechanical or biological. **5b** the explanation of phenomena in causal rather than teleological or essentialist terms. **5c** the view that the task of science is to seek such explanations. **5d** strict determinism. ◆ Compare **dynamism, vitalism. 6** *Psychoanal.* **6a** the ways in which psychological forces interact and operate. **6b** a structure having an influence on the behaviour of a person, such as a defence mechanism.

mechanist ('mɛkənɪst) *n* **1** a person who accepts a mechanistic philosophy. **2** another name for a **mechanician.**

mechanistic (ˌmɛkə'nɪstɪk) *adj* **1** *Philosophy.* of or relating to the theory of mechanism. **2** *Maths.* of or relating to mechanics. ▸ ˌ**mecha'nistically** *adv*

mechanize *or* **mechanise** ('mɛkəˌnaɪz) *vb (tr)* **1** to equip (a factory, industry, etc.) with machinery. **2** to make mechanical, automatic, or monotonous. **3** to equip (an army, etc.) with motorized or armoured vehicles. ▸ ˌ**mechani'zation** *or* ˌ**mechani'sation** *n* ▸ '**mechaˌnizer** *or* '**mechaˌniser** *n*

mechanoreceptor (ˌmɛkənəʊrɪ'sɛptə) *n Physiol.* a sensory receptor, as in the skin, that is sensitive to a mechanical stimulus, such as pressure.

mechanotherapy (ˌmɛkənəʊ'θɛrəpɪ) *n* the treatment of disorders or injuries by means of mechanical devices, esp. devices that provide exercise for bodily parts.

mechatronics (ˌmɛkə'trɒnɪks) *n (functioning as sing)* the combination of mechanical engineering and electronics, as used in the design and development of new manufacturing techniques. [C20: from MECHA(NICS) + (ELEC)TRONICS]

Mechelen ('mɛxələn) *n* a city in N Belgium, in Antwerp province: capital of the Netherlands from 1507 to 1530; formerly famous for lace-making; now has an important vegetable market. Pop.: 75 718 (1995 est.). French name: **Malines.** English name: **Mechlin.**

Mechlin ('mɛklɪn) *n* the English name for **Mechelen.**

Mechlin lace *n* bobbin lace made at Mechlin, characterized by patterns outlined by a heavier flat thread. Also called: **malines.**

meck (mɛk) *n Northeastern Scot. dialect.* a variant of **maik.**

Mecklenburg ('mɛklənˌbɜːg; *German* 'meːklənbʊrk) *n* a historic region and former state of NE Germany, along the Baltic coast; now part of Mecklenburg-West Pomerania: formerly (1949–90) in East Germany.

Mecklenburg-West Pomerania (ˌpɒmə'reɪnɪə) *n* a state of NE Germany, along the Baltic coast: consists of the former state of Mecklenburg and those parts of W Pomerania not incorporated into Poland after World War II: part of East Germany until 1990. Pop.: 1 823 100 (1996 est.).

MEcon *abbrev. for* Master of Economics.

meconium (mɪ'kəʊnɪəm) *n* **1** the dark green mucoid material that forms the first faeces of a newborn infant. **2** opium or the juice from the opium poppy. [C17: from New Latin, from Latin: poppy juice (used also of infant's excrement because of similarity in colour), from Greek *mēkōneion,* from *mēkōn* poppy]

meconopsis (ˌmɛkə'nɒpsɪs) *n* any plant of the mostly Asiatic papaveraceous genus *Meconopsis,* esp. *M. betonicifolia* (the Tibetan or blue poppy), grown for its showy sky-blue flowers. *M. cambrica* is the Welsh poppy. [New Latin, from Greek *mēkōn* poppy + -OPSIS]

Med (mɛd) *n* **the.** *Informal.* the Mediterranean region.

MEd *abbrev. for* Master of Education.

MED (in New Zealand) *abbrev. for* Municipal Electricity Department.

med. *abbrev. for:* **1** medical. **2** medicine. **3** medieval. **4** medium.

médaillons (medaɪ'jɔ̃) *pl n Cookery.* small round thin pieces of meat, fish, vegetables, etc. Also called: **medallions.** [C20: French: medallions]

medal ('mɛdᵊl) *n* **1** a small flat piece of metal bearing an inscription or image, given as an award or commemoration of some outstanding action, event, etc. ◆ *vb* **-als, -alling, -alled** *or U.S.* **-als, -aling, -aled. 2** *(tr)* to honour with a medal. [C16: from French *médaille,* probably from Italian *medaglia,* ultimately from Latin *metallum* METAL] ▸ **medallic** (mɪ'dælɪk) *adj*

medallion (mɪ'dæljən) *n* **1** a large medal. **2** an oval or circular decorative device resembling a medal, usually bearing a portrait or relief moulding, used in architecture and textile design. [C17: from French, from Italian *medaglione,* from *medaglia* MEDAL]

medallist *or U.S.* **medalist** ('mɛdᵊlɪst) *n* **1** a designer, maker, or collector of medals. **2** *Chiefly sport.* a winner or recipient of a medal or medals.

Medal of Bravery *n* a Canadian award for courage. Abbrev.: **MB.**

Medal of Honor *n* the highest U.S. military decoration, awarded by Congress for conspicuous bravery in action: instituted in 1861 (Navy), 1862 (Army).

medal play *n Golf.* another name for **stroke play.**

Medan ('mɛdɑːn) *n* a city in Indonesia, in NE Sumatra: seat of the University of North Sumatra (1952) and the Indonesian Islam University (1952). Pop.: 1 909 700 (1995 est.).

Medawar ('mɛdəwə) *n* Sir **Peter Brian.** 1915–87, English zoologist, who shared the Nobel prize for physiology or medicine (1960) with Sir Macfarlane Burnet for work on immunology.

meddle ('mɛdᵊl) *vb (intr)* **1** (usually foll. by *with*) to interfere officiously or annoyingly. **2** (usually foll. by *in*) to involve oneself unwarrantedly: *to meddle in someone's private affairs.* [C14: from Old French *medler,* ultimately from Latin *miscēre* to mix] ▸ '**meddler** *n* ▸ '**meddling** *adj* ▸ '**meddlingly** *adv*

meddlesome ('mɛdᵊlsəm) *adj* intrusive or meddling. ▸ '**meddlesomely** *adv* ▸ '**meddlesomeness** *n*

Mede (miːd) *n* a member of an Indo-European people of West Iranian speech who established an empire in SW Asia in the 7th and 6th centuries B.C. ▸ '**Median** *n, adj*

Medea (mɪ'dɪə) *n Greek myth.* a princess of Colchis, who assisted Jason in obtaining the Golden Fleece from her father.

Medellín (*Spanish* meðe'ʎin) *n* a city in W Colombia, at an altitude of 1554 m (5100 ft.): the second largest city in the country, with three universities; important coffee centre, with large textile mills; dominated by drug cartels in recent years. Pop.: 1 970 691 (1997 est.).

medevac ('mɛdəˌvæk) *n Military.* the evacuation of casualties from forward areas to the nearest hospital or base. [C20: from *med(ical) evac(uation)*]

medfly ('mɛdˌflaɪ) *n, pl* **-fly** *or* **-flies.** another name for **Mediterranean fruit fly.**

media[1] ('miːdɪə) *n* **1** a plural of **medium. 2** the means of communication that reach large numbers of people, such as television, newspapers, and radio. ◆ *adj* **3** of or relating to the mass media: *media hype.*

USAGE When *media* refers to the mass media, it is sometimes treated as a singular form, as in: *the media has shown great interest in these events.* Many people think this use is incorrect and that *media* should always be treated as a plural form: *the media have shown great interest in these events.*

media[2] ('mɛdɪə) *n, pl* **-diae** (-dɪˌiː). **1** the middle layer of the wall of a blood or lymph vessel. **2** one of the main veins in the wing of an insect. **3** *Phonetics.* **3a** a consonant whose articulation lies midway between that of a voiced and breathed speech sound. **3b** a consonant pronounced with weak voice, as *c* in French *second.* [C19: from Latin *medius* middle]

Media ('miːdɪə) *n* an ancient country of SW Asia, south of the Caspian Sea: inhabited by the Medes; overthrew the Assyrian Empire in 612 B.C. in alliance with Babylonia; conquered by Cyrus the Great in 550 B.C.; corresponds to present-day NW Iran.

mediacy ('miːdɪəsɪ) *n* **1** the quality or state of being mediate. **2** a less common word for **mediation.**

mediad ('miːdɪæd) *adj Anatomy, zoology.* situated near the median line or plane of an organism.

mediaeval (ˌmɛdɪ'iːvᵊl) *adj* a variant spelling of **medieval.**

media event *n* an event that is staged for or exploited by the mass media, whose attention lends it an apparent importance.

medial ('miːdɪəl) *adj* **1** of or situated in the middle. **2** ordinary or average in size. **3** *Maths.* relating to an average. **4** another word for **median** (senses 1, 2, 3). **5** *Zoology.* of or relating to a media. ◆ *n* **6** *Phonetics.* a speech sound between being fortis and lenis; media. [C16: from Late Latin *mediālis,* from *medius* middle] ▸ '**medially** *adv*

median ('miːdɪən) *adj* **1** of, relating to, situated in, or directed towards the middle. **2** *Biology.* of or relating to the plane that divides an organism or organ into symmetrical parts. **3** *Statistics.* of or relating to the median. ◆ *n* **4** a middle point, plane, or part. **5** *Geometry.* **5a** a straight line joining one vertex of a triangle to the midpoint of the opposite side. See also **centroid. 5b** a straight line joining the midpoints of the nonparallel sides of a trapezium. **6** *Statistics.* the middle value in a frequency distribution, below and above which lie values with equal total frequencies. **7** *Statistics.* the middle number or average of the two middle numbers in an ordered sequence of numbers: *7 is the median of both 1, 7, 31 and 2, 5, 9, 16.* **8** the Canadian word for **central reserve.** [C16: from Latin *mediānus,* from *medius* middle] ▸ '**medianly** *adv*

median lethal dose *or* **mean lethal dose** *n* **1** the amount of a drug or other substance that, when administered to a group of experimental animals, will kill 50 per cent of the group in a specified time. **2** the amount of ionizing radiation that will kill 50 per cent of a population in a specified time. ◆ Abbrev.: $\mathbf{LD_{50}}$.

median strip *n* the U.S. term for **central reserve.**

mediant ('miːdɪənt) *n Music.* **a** the third degree of a major or minor scale. **b** (*as modifier*): *a mediant chord.* [C18: from Italian *mediante,* from Late Latin *mediāre* to be in the middle]

mediastinum (ˌmiːdɪə'staɪnəm) *n, pl* **-na** (-nə). *Anatomy.* **1** a membrane between two parts of an organ or cavity such as the pleural tissue between the two lungs. **2** the part of the thoracic cavity that lies between the lungs, containing the heart, trachea, etc. [C16: from medical Latin, neuter of Medieval Latin *mediastīnus* median, from Latin: low grade of servant, from *medius* mean] ▸ ˌ**medias'tinal** *adj*

mediate *vb* ('miːdɪˌeɪt). **1** (*intr;* usually foll. by *between* or *in*) to intervene (between parties or in a dispute) in order to bring about agreement. **2** to bring about (an agreement). **3** to bring about (an agreement) between parties in a dispute. **4** to resolve (differences) by mediation. **5** (*intr*) to be in a middle or intermediate position. **6** (*tr*) to serve as a medium for causing (a result) or transferring (objects, information, etc.). ◆ *adj* ('miːdɪɪt). **7** occurring as a result of or dependent upon mediation. **8** a rare word for **intermediate. 9** *Logic.* (of an inference) having more than one premise, esp., being syllogistic in form. [C16: from Late Latin *mediāre* to be in the middle] ▸ '**mediately** *adv* ▸ '**mediateness** *n* ▸ '**mediative, 'mediatory,** *or* ˌ**media'torial** *adj* ▸ '**mediˌator** *n* ▸ ˌ**media'torially** *adv*

mediation (ˌmiːdɪ'eɪʃən) *n* **1** the act of mediating; intercession. **2** *International law.* an attempt to reconcile disputed matters arising between states, esp. by the friendly intervention of a neutral power. **3** a method of resolving an industrial dispute whereby a third party consults with those involved and recommends a solution which is not, however, binding on the parties.

mediatize *or* **mediatise** ('miːdɪəˌtaɪz) *vb (tr)* to annex (a state) to another state, allowing the former ruler to retain his title and some authority. [C19: from French *médiatiser;* see MEDIATE, -IZE] ▸ ˌ**mediati'zation** *or* ˌ**mediati'sation** *n*

medic[1] ('mɛdɪk) *n Informal.* a doctor, medical orderly, or medical student. [C17: from MEDICAL]

medic[2] ('mɛdɪk) *n* the usual U.S. spelling of **medick.**

medicable ('mɛdɪkəbᵊl) *adj* potentially able to be treated or cured medically. ▸ '**medicably** *adv*

Medicaid ('mɛdɪˌkeɪd) *n U.S.* a health assistance programme financed by federal, state, and local taxes to help pay hospital and medical costs for persons of low income. [C20: MEDIC(AL) + AID]

medical ('mɛdɪkᵊl) *adj* **1** of or relating to the science of medicine or to the treatment of patients by drugs, etc., as opposed to surgery. **2** a less common word for **medicinal.** ◆ *n* **3** *Informal.* a medical examination. [C17: from Medieval Latin *medicālis,* from Latin *medicus* physician, surgeon, from *medērī* to heal] ► **'medically** *adv*

medical audit *n* a review of the professional standards of doctors, usually within a hospital, conducted by a medical committee.

medical certificate *n* **1** a document stating the result of a satisfactory medical examination. **2** a doctor's certificate giving evidence of a person's unfitness for work.

medical examination *n* an examination carried out to determine the physical fitness of an applicant for a job, life insurance, etc.

medical examiner *n* **1** *Chiefly U.S.* a medical expert, usually a physician, employed by a state or local government to determine the cause of sudden death in cases of suspected violence, suicide, etc. Compare **coroner. 2** a physician who carries out medical examinations.

medical jurisprudence *n* another name for **forensic medicine.**

medicament (mɪ'dɪkəmənt, 'mɛdɪ-) *n* a medicine or remedy. [C16: via French from Latin *medicāmentum,* from *medicāre* to cure] ► **medicamental** (ˌmɛdɪkə'mɛntᵊl) *or* **ˌmedica'mentary** *adj*

Medicare ('mɛdɪˌkɛə) *n* **1** (in the U.S.) a federally sponsored health insurance programme for persons of 65 or older. **2** (*often not cap.*) (in Canada) a similar programme covering all citizens. **3** (in Australia) a government-controlled general health-insurance scheme. [C20: MEDI(CAL) + CARE]

medicate ('mɛdɪˌkeɪt) *vb* (*tr*) **1** to cover or impregnate (a wound, etc.) with an ointment, cream, etc. **2** to treat (a patient) with a medicine. **3** to add a medication to (a bandage, shampoo, etc.). [C17: from Latin *medicāre* to heal] ► **'mediˌcated** *adj* ► **'medicative** *adj*

medication (ˌmɛdɪ'keɪʃən) *n* **1** treatment with drugs or remedies. **2** a drug or remedy.

Medici ('mɛdɪtʃɪ, mə'di:tʃɪ; *Italian* 'mɛ:ditʃi) *n* **1** an Italian family of bankers, merchants, and rulers of Florence and Tuscany, prominent in Italian political and cultural history in the 15th, 16th, and 17th centuries, including: **2 Catherine de'** (ka'tri:n de). See **Catherine de' Medici. 3 Cosimo I** ('kɔ:zimo), known as *Cosimo the Great.* 1519–74, duke of Florence and first grand duke of Tuscany (1569–74). **4 Cosimo de',** known as *Cosimo the Elder.* 1389–1464, Italian banker, statesman, and patron of arts, who established the political power of the family in Florence (1434). **5 Giovanni de',** (dʒo'vanni de). See **Leo X. 6 Giulio de'** ('dʒu:ljo de). See **Clement VII. 7 Lorenzo de'** (lo'rɛntso de), known as *Lorenzo the Magnificent.* 1449–92, Italian statesman, poet, and scholar; ruler of Florence (1469–92) and first patron of Michelangelo. **8 Maria de'** (ma'ri:a de). See **Maria de' Medici.** ◆ French name: **Médicis** (medisis). ► **Medicean** (ˌmɛdɪ'si:ən, -'tʃi:-) *adj*

medicinal (mɛ'dɪsɪnᵊl) *adj* **1** relating to or having therapeutic properties. ◆ *n* **2** a medicinal substance. ► **me'dicinally** *adv*

medicinal leech *n* a large European freshwater leech, *Hirudo medicinalis,* formerly used in medical bloodletting.

medicine ('mɛdɪsɪn, 'mɛdsɪn) *n* **1** any drug or remedy for use in treating, preventing, or alleviating the symptoms of disease. **2** the science of preventing, diagnosing, alleviating, or curing disease. **3** any nonsurgical branch of medical science. **4** the practice or profession of medicine: *he's in medicine.* Related adjs.: **Aesculapian, iatric. 5** something regarded by primitive people as having magical or remedial properties. **6 take one's medicine.** to accept a deserved punishment. **7 a taste** (*or* **dose**) **of one's own medicine.** an unpleasant experience in retaliation for and by similar methods to an unkind or aggressive act. [C13: via Old French from Latin *medicīna* (*ars*) (art of) healing, from *medicus* doctor, from *medērī* to heal]

medicine ball *n* a heavy ball used for physical training.

medicine chest *n* a small chest or cupboard for storing medicines, bandages, etc.

medicine lodge *n* a wooden structure used for magical and religious ceremonies among certain North American Indian peoples.

medicine man *n* (among certain peoples, esp. North American Indians) a person believed to have supernatural powers of healing; a magician or sorcerer.

medicine shop *n* (in Malaysia) a Chinese chemist's shop where traditional herbs are sold as well as modern drugs. It is not, however, a dispensary for prescribed medicines.

medick *or U.S.* **medic** ('mɛdɪk) *n* any small papilionaceous plant of the genus *Medicago,* such as black medick or sickle medick, having yellow or purple flowers and trifoliate leaves. [C15: from Latin *mēdica,* from Greek *mēdikē* (*poa*) Median (grass), a type of clover]

medico ('mɛdɪˌkəʊ) *n, pl* **-cos.** *Informal.* a doctor or medical student. [C17: via Italian from Latin *medicus*]

medico- *combining form.* medical: *medicolegal.*

medieval *or* **mediaeval** (ˌmɛdɪ'i:vᵊl) *adj* **1** of, relating to, or in the style of the Middle Ages. **2** *Informal.* old-fashioned; primitive. [C19: from New Latin *medium aevum* the middle age. See MEDIUM, AGE] ► **ˌmedi'evally** *or* **ˌmedi'aevally** *adv*

Medieval Greek *n* the Greek language from the 7th century A.D. to shortly after the sacking of Constantinople in 1204. Also called: **Middle Greek, Byzantine Greek.** Compare **Koine, Late Greek, Ancient Greek.**

medievalism *or* **mediaevalism** (ˌmɛdɪ'i:vəˌlɪzəm) *n* **1** the beliefs, life, or style of the Middle Ages or devotion to those. **2** a belief, custom, or point of style copied or surviving from the Middle Ages.

medievalist *or* **mediaevalist** (ˌmɛdɪ'i:vəlɪst) *n* a student or devotee of the Middle Ages. ► **ˌmediˌeval'istic** *or* **ˌmediˌaeval'istic** *adj*

Medieval Latin *n* the Latin language as used throughout Europe in the Middle Ages. It had many local forms incorporating Latinized words from other languages.

medina (mɛ'di:nə) *n* (*sometimes cap.*) the ancient quarter of any of various North African cities. Compare **kasbah.** [C20: Arabic, literally: town]

Medina (mɛ'di:nə) *n* a city in W Saudi Arabia: the second most holy city of Islam (after Mecca), with the tomb of Mohammed; university (1960). Pop.: 400 000 (1991 est.). Arabic name: **Al Madinah.** Ancient Arabic name: **Yathrib.**

mediocre (ˌmi:dɪ'əʊkə, 'mi:dɪˌəʊkə) *adj Often derogatory.* average or ordinary in quality: *a mediocre book.* [C16: via French from Latin *mediocris* moderate, literally: halfway up the mountain, from *medius* middle + *ocris* stony mountain]

mediocrity (ˌmi:dɪ'ɒkrɪtɪ, ˌmɛd-) *n, pl* **-ties. 1** the state or quality of being mediocre. **2** a mediocre person or thing.

Medit. *abbrev. for* Mediterranean.

meditate ('mɛdɪˌteɪt) *vb* **1** (*intr;* foll. by *on* or *upon*) to think about something deeply. **2** (*intr*) to reflect deeply on spiritual matters, esp. as a religious act. **3** (*tr*) to plan, consider, or think of doing (something). [C16: from Latin *meditārī* to reflect upon] ► **'meditative** *adj* ► **'meditatively** *adv* ► **'meditativeness** *n* ► **'mediˌtator** *n*

meditation (ˌmɛdɪ'teɪʃən) *n* **1** the act of meditating; contemplation; reflection. **2** contemplation of spiritual matters, esp. as a religious practice.

Mediterranean (ˌmɛdɪtə'reɪnɪən) *n* **1** short for the **Mediterranean Sea. 2** a native or inhabitant of a Mediterranean country. ◆ *adj* **3** of, relating to, situated or dwelling on or near the Mediterranean Sea. **4** denoting a postulated subdivision of the Caucasoid race, characterized by slender build and dark complexion. **5** *Meteorol.* (of a climate) characterized by hot summers and relatively warm winters when most of the annual rainfall occurs. **6** (*often not cap.*) *Obsolete.* situated in the middle of a landmass; inland. [C16: from Latin *mediterrāneus,* from *medius* middle + *-terrāneus,* from *terra* land, earth]

Mediterranean fever *n* another name for **brucellosis.**

Mediterranean fruit fly *n* a species of dipterous fly, *Ceratitis capitata,* having marbled wings, whose maggots tunnel into fruits such as citrus, peach, and vine in the Mediterranean area, South Africa, and elsewhere: family *Trypetidae.* Also called: **medfly.**

Mediterranean Sea *n* a large inland sea between S Europe, N Africa, and SW Asia: linked with the Atlantic by the Strait of Gibraltar, with the Red Sea by the Suez Canal, and with the Black Sea by the Dardanelles, Sea of Marmara, and Bosporus; many ancient civilizations developed around its shores. Greatest depth: 4770 m (15 900 ft.). Length: (west to east) over 3700 km (2300 miles). Greatest width: about 1368 km (850 miles). Area: (excluding the Black Sea) 2 512 300 sq. km (970 000 sq. miles). Ancient name: **'Mare In'ternum.**

medium ('mi:dɪəm) *adj* **1** midway between extremes; average: *a medium size.* **2** (of a colour) reflecting or transmitting a moderate amount of light: *a medium red.* Compare **light**[1] (sense 29), **dark** (sense 2). ◆ *n, pl* **-dia** (-dɪə) *or* **-diums. 3** an intermediate or middle state, degree, or condition; mean: *the happy medium.* **4** an intervening substance or agency for transmitting or producing an effect; vehicle: *air is a medium for sound.* **5** a means or agency for communicating or diffusing information, news, etc., to the public: *television is a powerful medium.* **6** a person supposedly used as a spiritual intermediary between the dead and the living. **7** the substance in which specimens of animals and plants are preserved or displayed. **8** *Biology.* short for **culture medium. 9** the substance or surroundings in which an organism naturally lives or grows. **10** *Art.* **10a** the category of a work of art, as determined by its materials and methods of production: *the medium of wood engraving.* **10b** the materials used in a work of art. **11** any solvent in which pigments are mixed and thinned. **12** any one of various sizes of writing or printing paper, esp. 18½ by 23½ inches or 17½ by 22 inches (**small medium**). ◆ See also **mediums.** [C16: from Latin: neuter singular of *medius* middle]

USAGE See at **media.**

medium-dated *adj* (of a gilt-edged security) having between five and fifteen years to run before redemption. Compare **long-dated, short-dated.**

medium frequency *n* a radio-frequency band or radio frequency lying between 3000 and 300 kilohertz. Abbrev.: **MF.**

medium of exchange *n* anything acceptable as a measure of value and a standard of exchange for goods and services in a particular country, region, etc.

medium-range ballistic missile *n* a missile that can carry a nuclear weapon with a range of 800 to 2400 km. Abbrev.: **MRBM.**

mediums ('mi:dɪəmz) *pl n* medium-dated gilt-edged securities.

medium wave *n* **a** a radio wave with a wavelength between 100 and 1000 metres. **b** (*as modifier*): *a medium-wave broadcast.*

medlar ('mɛdlə) *n* **1** a small Eurasian rosaceous tree, *Mespilus germanica.* **2** the fruit of this tree, which resembles the crab apple and is not edible until it has begun to decay. **3** any of several other rosaceous trees or their fruits. [C14: from Old French *medlier,* from Latin *mespilum* medlar fruit, from Greek *mespilon*]

medley ('mɛdlɪ) *n* **1** a mixture of various types or elements. **2** a musical composition consisting of various tunes arranged as a continuous whole. **3** Also called: **medley relay. 3a** *Swimming.* a race in which a different stroke is used for each length. **3b** *Athletics.* a relay race in which each leg has a different distance. **4** an archaic word for **melee.** ◆ *adj* **5** of, being, or relating to a mixture or variety. [C14: from Old French *medlee,* from *medler* to mix, quarrel]

Médoc (meɪ'dɒk, 'mɛdɒk; *French* medɔk) *n* **1** a district of SW France, on the left bank of the Gironde estuary: famous vineyards. **2** a fine red wine from this district.

medulla (mɪ'dʌlə) *n, pl* **-las** *or* **-lae** (-li:). **1** *Anatomy.* **1a** the innermost part of an organ or structure. **1b** short for **medulla oblongata. 2** *Botany.* another name for **pith** (sense 4). [C17: from Latin: marrow, pith, probably from *medius* middle] ► **me'dullary** *or* **me'dullar** *adj*

medulla oblongata (ˌɒblɒŋˈgɑːtə) *n, pl* **medulla oblongatas** *or* **medullae oblongatae** (mɪˈdʌliː ˌɒblɒŋˈgɑːtiː). the lower stalklike section of the brain, continuous with the spinal cord, containing control centres for the heart and lungs. [C17: New Latin: oblong-shaped medulla]

medullary ray *n* any of the sheets of conducting tissue that run radially through the vascular tissue of some higher plants.

medullary sheath *n* **1** *Anatomy.* a myelin layer surrounding and insulating certain nerve fibres. **2** a layer of thick-walled cells surrounding the pith of the stems of some higher plants.

medullated (ˈmɛdəˌleɪtɪd, mɪˈdʌl-) *adj* **1** *Anatomy.* encased in a myelin sheath. **2** having a medulla.

medulloblastoma (mɪˌdʌləʊblæsˈtəʊmə) *n* a rapidly growing brain tumour that develops in children and is responsive to radiotherapy.

medusa (mɪˈdjuːzə) *n, pl* **-sas** *or* **-sae** (-ziː). **1** another name for **jellyfish** (senses 1, 2). **2** one of the two forms in which a coelenterate exists. It has a jelly-like umbrella-shaped body, is free swimming, and produces gametes. Also called: **medusoid, medusan.** Compare **polyp.** [C18: from the likeness of its tentacles to the snaky locks of Medusa] ► **meˈdusan** *adj*

Medusa (mɪˈdjuːzə) *n Greek myth.* a mortal woman who was transformed by Athena into one of the three Gorgons. Her appearance was so hideous that those who looked directly at her were turned to stone. Perseus eventually slew her. See also **Pegasus**[1]. ► **Meˈdusan** *adj*

medusoid (mɪˈdjuːzɔɪd) *adj* **1** of, relating to, or resembling a medusa. ◆ *n* **2** another name for **medusa** (sense 2).

Medway (ˈmɛdˌweɪ) *n* **1** a river in SE England, flowing through Kent and the **Medway towns** (Rochester, Chatham, and Gillingham) to the Thames estuary. Length: 110 km (70 miles). **2** a unitary authority in SE England, in Kent. Pop.: 239 500 (1996 est.). Area: 204 sq. km (79 sq. miles).

mee (miː) *n* (in Malaysia) noodles or a dish containing noodles. [from Chinese (Cantonese) *mien* noodles]

Meech Lake Accord (miːtʃ) *n* the agreement reached in 1987 at Meech Lake, Quebec, at a Canadian federal-provincial conference that accepted Quebec's conditions for signing the Constitution Act of 1982. The Accord lapsed when the legislatures of two provinces, Newfoundland and Quebec, failed to ratify it by the deadline of June 23, 1990.

meed (miːd) *n Archaic.* a recompense; reward. [Old English: wages; compare Old High German *mēta* pay]

meek (miːk) *adj* **1** patient, long-suffering, or submissive in disposition or nature; humble. **2** spineless or spiritless; compliant. **3** an obsolete word for **gentle.** [C12: related to Old Norse *mjūkr* amenable; compare Welsh *mwytho* to soften] ► **ˈmeekly** *adv* ► **ˈmeekness** *n*

meerkat (ˈmɪəˌkæt) *n* any of several South African mongooses, esp. *Suricata suricatta* (**slender-tailed meerkat** or **suricate**), which has a lemur-like face and four-toed feet. [C19: from Dutch: sea-cat]

meerschaum (ˈmɪəʃəm) *n* **1** Also called: **sepiolite.** a white, yellowish, or pink compact earthy mineral consisting of hydrated magnesium silicate: used to make tobacco pipes and as a building stone. Formula: $Mg_2Si_3O_6(OH)_4$. **2** a tobacco pipe having a bowl made of this mineral. [C18: German, literally: sea foam]

Meerut (ˈmɪərət) *n* an industrial city in N India, in W Uttar Pradesh: founded as a military base by the British in 1806 and scene of the first uprising (1857) of the Indian Mutiny. Pop.: 753 778 (1991).

meet[1] (miːt) *vb* **meets, meeting, met. 1** (sometimes foll. by *up* or (*U.S.*) *with*) to come together (with), either by design or by accident; encounter: *I met him unexpectedly; we met at the station.* **2** to come into or be in conjunction or contact with (something or each other): *the roads meet in the town; the sea meets the sky.* **3** (*tr*) to come to or be at the place of arrival of: *to meet a train.* **4** to make the acquaintance of or be introduced to (someone or each other): *have you two met?* **5** to gather in the company of (someone or each other): *the board of directors meets on Tuesday.* **6** to come into the presence of (someone or each other) as opponents: *Joe meets Fred in the boxing match.* **7** (*tr*) to cope with effectively; satisfy: *to meet someone's demands.* **8** (*tr*) to be apparent to (esp. in the phrase **meet the eye**). **9** (*tr*) to return or counter: *to meet a blow with another.* **10** to agree with (someone or each other): *we met him on the price he suggested.* **11** (*tr;* sometimes foll. by *with*) to experience; suffer: *he met his death in a road accident.* **12** to occur together: *courage and kindliness met in him.* **13** (*tr*) *Caribbean.* to find (a person, situation, etc.) in a specified condition: *I met the door open.* ◆ *n* **14** the assembly of hounds, huntsmen, etc., prior to a hunt. **15** a meeting, esp. a sports meeting. **16** *U.S.* the place where the paths of two railway trains meet or cross. [Old English *mētan;* related to Old Norse *mœta,* Old Saxon *mōtian*] ► **ˈmeeter** *n*

meet[2] (miːt) *adj Archaic.* proper, fitting, or correct. [C13: from variant of Old English *gemǣte;* related to Old High German *māza* suitability, Old Norse *mǣtr* valuable] ► **ˈmeetly** *adv*

meeting (ˈmiːtɪŋ) *n* **1** an act of coming together; encounter. **2** an assembly or gathering. **3** a conjunction or union. **4** a sporting competition, as of athletes, or of horse racing.

meeting house *n* **1** the place in which certain religious groups, esp. Quakers, hold their meetings for worship. **2** Also called: **wharepuni.** *N.Z.* a large Maori tribal hall.

mefloquine (ˈmɛfləʊˌkwiːn) *n* a synthetic drug administered orally to prevent or treat malaria. [C20]

meg (mɛg) *n Informal.* short for **megabyte.**

mega (ˈmɛgə) *adj Slang.* extremely good, great, or successful. [C20: probably independent use of MEGA-]

mega- *combining form.* **1** denoting 10^6: *megawatt.* Symbol: M **2** (in computer technology) denoting 2^{20} (1 048 576): *megabyte.* **3** large or great: *megalith.* **4** *Informal.* greatest: *megastar.* [from Greek *megas* huge, powerful]

megabit (ˈmɛgəˌbɪt) *n Computing.* **1** one million bits. **2** 2^{20} bits.

megabuck (ˈmɛgəˌbʌk) *n U.S. and Canadian slang.* **a** a million dollars. **b** (*as modifier*): *a megabuck movie.*

megabyte (ˈmɛgəˌbaɪt) *n Computing.* 2^{20} or 1 048 576 bytes. Abbrevs.: **MB, mbyte.** See also **mega-** (sense 2).

megacephaly (ˌmɛgəˈsɛfəlɪ) *or* **megalocephaly** *n* the condition of having an unusually large head or cranial capacity. It can be of congenital origin or result from an abnormal overgrowth of the facial bones. Compare **microcephaly.** ► **megacephalic** (ˌmɛgəsɪˈfælɪk), **ˌmegaˈcephalous, ˌmegaloceˈphalic,** *or* **ˌmegaloˈcephalous** *adj*

megadeath (ˈmɛgəˌdɛθ) *n* the death of a million people, esp. in a nuclear war or attack.

megadose (ˈmɛgəˌdəʊs) *n* a very large dose, as of a medicine, vitamin, etc.

Megaera (mɪˈdʒɪərə) *n Greek myth.* one of the three Furies; the others are Alecto and Tisiphone.

megafauna (ˈmɛgəˌfɔːnə) *n* the component of the fauna of a region or period that comprises the larger terrestrial animals.

megaflop (ˈmɛgəˌflɒp) *n Computing.* a measure of processing speed, consisting of a million floating-point operations a second. [C20: from MEGA- + *flo(ating) p(oint)*]

megagamete (ˌmɛgəgæˈmiːt) *n* another name for **macrogamete.**

megahertz (ˈmɛgəˌhɜːts) *n, pl* **-hertz.** one million hertz; one million cycles per second. Symbol: **MHz.** Former name: **megacycle.**

megalith (ˈmɛgəlɪθ) *n* a stone of great size, esp. one forming part of a prehistoric monument. See also **alignment** (sense 6), **circle** (sense 11). ► **ˌmegaˈlithic** *adj*

megalithic tomb *n* a burial chamber constructed of large stones, either underground or covered by a mound and usually consisting of long transepted corridors (**gallery graves**) or of a distinct chamber and passage (**passage graves**). The tombs may date from the 4th millennium B.C.

megalo- *or before a vowel* **megal-** *combining form.* indicating greatness, or abnormal size: *megalopolis; megaloblast.* [from Greek *megas* great]

megaloblast (ˈmɛgələʊˌblɑːst) *n* an abnormally large red blood cell present in certain types of anaemia. ► **megaloblastic** (ˌmɛgələʊˈblæstɪk) *adj*

megaloblastic anaemia *n* any anaemia, esp. pernicious anaemia, characterized by the presence of megaloblasts in the blood or bone marrow.

megalocardia (ˌmɛgələʊˈkɑːdɪə) *n Pathol.* abnormal increase in the size of the heart. Also called: **cardiomegaly.**

megalocephaly (ˌmɛgələʊˈsɛfəlɪ) *n* another word for **megacephaly.**

megalomania (ˌmɛgələʊˈmeɪnɪə) *n* **1** a mental illness characterized by delusions of grandeur, power, wealth, etc. **2** *Informal.* a lust or craving for power. ► **ˌmegaloˈmaniac** *adj, n* ► **megalomaniacal** (ˌmɛgələʊməˈnaɪəkᵊl) *adj*

megalopolis (ˌmɛgəˈlɒpəlɪs) *n* an urban complex, usually comprising several large towns. [C20: MEGALO- + Greek *polis* city] ► **megalopolitan** (ˌmɛgələˈpɒlɪtᵊn) *adj, n*

megalosaur (ˈmɛgələʊˌsɔː) *n* any very large Jurassic or Cretaceous bipedal carnivorous dinosaur of the genus *Megalosaurus,* common in Europe: suborder *Theropoda* (theropods). [C19: from New Latin *megalosaurus,* from MEGALO- + Greek *sauros* lizard] ► **ˌmegaloˈsaurian** *adj, n*

megaphanerophyte (ˌmɛgəˈfænərəʊˌfaɪt) *n Botany.* any tree with a height over 30 metres.

megaphone (ˈmɛgəˌfəʊn) *n* a funnel-shaped instrument used to amplify the voice. See also **loud-hailer.** ► **megaphonic** (ˌmɛgəˈfɒnɪk) *adj* ► **ˌmegaˈphonically** *adv*

megaphyll (ˈmɛgəfɪl) *n Botany.* the relatively large type of leaf produced by ferns and seed plants. Compare **microphyll.**

megapode (ˈmɛgəˌpəʊd) *n* any ground-living gallinaceous bird of the family *Megapodiidae,* of Australia, New Guinea, and adjacent islands. Their eggs incubate in mounds of sand, rotting vegetation, etc., by natural heat. Also called: **mound-builder.** See also **brush turkey, mallee fowl.**

Megara (ˈmɛgərə) *n* a town in E central Greece: an ancient trading city, founding many colonies in the 7th and 8th centuries B.C. Pop.: 26 562 (1991 est.).

megaron (ˈmɛgəˌrɒn) *n, pl* **-ra** (-rə). a tripartite rectangular room containing a central hearth surrounded by four pillars, found in Bronze Age Greece and Asia Minor. [from Greek, literally: hall, from *megas* large]

megascopic (ˌmɛgəˈskɒpɪk) *adj* another word for **macroscopic.**

megasporangium (ˌmɛgəspɔːˈrændʒɪəm) *n, pl* **-gia** (-dʒɪə). the structure in certain ferns in which the megaspores are formed: corresponds to the ovule in seed plants. Compare **microsporangium.**

megaspore (ˈmɛgəˌspɔː) *n* **1** Also called: **macrospore.** the larger of the two types of spore produced by some ferns, which develops into the female gametophyte. Compare **microspore** (sense 1). **2** the embryo sac of flowering plants. ► **ˌmegaˈsporic** *adj*

megasporophyll (ˌmɛgəˈspɔːrəfɪl) *n* a leaf on which the megaspores are formed: corresponds to the carpel of a flowering plant. Compare **microsporophyll.** [C20: from MEGA- + SPOROPHYLL]

megass *or* **megasse** (məˈgæs) *n* another name for **bagasse** (sense 2). [C19: of obscure origin]

megastar (ˈmɛgəˌstɑː) *n* a very well-known personality in the entertainment business.

megathere (ˈmɛgəˌθɪə) *n* any of various gigantic extinct American sloths of the genus *Megatherium* and related genera, common in late Cenozoic times. [C19: from New Latin *megathērium,* from MEGA- + *-there,* from Greek *thērion* wild beast] ► **ˌmegaˈtherian** *adj*

megaton (ˈmɛgəˌtʌn) *n* **1** one million tons. **2** an explosive power, esp. of a nuclear weapon, equal to the power of one million tons of TNT. Abbrev.: **mt.** ► **megatonic** (ˌmɛgəˈtɒnɪk) *adj*

megavolt (ˈmɛgəˌvəʊlt) *n* one million volts. Symbol: MV

megawatt ('mɛgə,wɒt) *n* one million watts. Symbol: MW

Me generation *n* the generation, originally in the 1970s, characterized by self-absorption; in the 1980s, characterized by material greed.

Megger ('mɛgə) *n Trademark.* an instrument that generates a high voltage in order to test the resistance of insulation, etc.

Meghalaya (,meɪgə'leɪə) *n* a state of NE India, created in 1969 from part of Assam. Capital: Shillong. Pop.: 1 960 000 (1994 est.). Area: 22 429 sq. km (7800 sq. miles).

Megiddo (mə'gɪdəʊ) *n* an ancient town in N Palestine, strategically located on a route linking Egypt to Mesopotamia: site of many battles, including an important Egyptian victory over rebel chieftains in 1469 or 1468 B.C. See also **Armageddon.**

megillah (mə'gɪlə; *Hebrew* migi'la) *n, pl* **-lahs** *or* **-loth** (*Hebrew* -'lɔt). *Judaism.* **1** a scroll of the Book of Esther, read on the festival of Purim. **2** a scroll of the Book of Ruth, Song of Songs, Lamentations, or Ecclesiastes. **3** *Slang.* anything, such as a story or letter, that is too long or unduly drawn out. **[**Hebrew: scroll, from *galal* to roll**]**

megilp *or* **magilp** (mə'gɪlp) *n* an oil-painting medium of linseed oil mixed with mastic varnish or turpentine. **[C18:** of unknown origin**]**

megohm ('mɛg,əʊm) *n* one million ohms. Symbol: MΩ

megrim[1] ('mi:grɪm) *n Archaic.* **1** (*often pl*) a caprice. **2** a migraine. **[C14:** see MIGRAINE**]**

megrim[2] ('mi:grɪm) *n* a flatfish, *Lepidorhombus whiffiagonis,* of the turbot family, having a yellowish translucent body up to 50 cm (20 in.) in length, found in European waters, and caught for food. **[C19:** of uncertain origin**]**

megrims ('mi:grɪmz) *n (functioning as sing)* **1** *Now rare.* a fit of depression. **2** a disease of horses and cattle; staggers.

Mehemet Ali (mɪ'hɛmɪt 'ɑ:lɪ) *or* **Mohammed Ali** *n* 1769–1849, Albanian commander in the service of Turkey. He was made viceroy of Egypt (1805) and its hereditary ruler (1841), founding a dynasty that ruled until 1952.

meibomian cyst (maɪ'bəʊmɪən) *n* another name for **chalazion.** **[C19:** named after H. *Meibom* (1638–1700), German anatomist**]**

meibomian gland *n* any of the small sebaceous glands in the eyelid, beneath the conjunctiva.

Meiji ('meɪ'dʒi:) *n* **1** *Japanese history.* the reign of Emperor Mutsuhito (1867–1912), during which Japan began a rapid process of Westernization, industrialization, and expansion in foreign affairs. **2** the throne name of **Mutsuhito** (,mu:tsʊ'hi:təʊ). 1852–1912, emperor of Japan (1867–1912). **[**Japanese, from Chinese *ming* enlightened + *dji* government**]**

Meilhac (*French* mɛjak) *n* **Henri** (ɑ̃ri). 1831–97, French dramatist, who collaborated with Halévy on opera libretti, esp. Offenbach's *La Belle Hélène* (1865) and *La Vie parisienne* (1867).

meiny *or* **meinie** ('meɪnɪ) *n, pl* **meinies.** *Obsolete.* **1** a retinue or household. **2** *Scot.* a crowd. **[C13:** from Old French *mesnie,* from Vulgar Latin *mansiōnāta* (unattested), from Latin *mansiō* a lodging; see MANSION**]**

meiocyte ('maɪəʊ,saɪt) *n Botany.* a cell that divides by meiosis to produce four haploid spores (**meiospores**).

meiofauna ('maɪəʊ,fɔ:nə) *n* the component of the fauna of a sea or lake bed comprising small (but not microscopic) animals, such as tiny worms and crustaceans. **[C20:** from Greek *meiōn* less + FAUNA**]** ▸ **,meio'faunal** *adj*

meiosis (maɪ'əʊsɪs) *n, pl* **-ses** (-,si:z). **1** a type of cell division in which a nucleus divides into four daughter nuclei, each containing half the chromosome number of the parent nucleus: occurs in all sexually reproducing organisms in which haploid gametes or spores are produced. Compare **mitosis.** See also **prophase** (sense 2). **2** *Rhetoric.* another word for **litotes.** **[C16:** via New Latin from Greek: a lessening, from *meioun* to diminish, from *meiōn* less**]** ▸ **meiotic** (maɪ'ɒtɪk) *adj* ▸ **mei'otically** *adv*

Meir (meɪ'ɪə) *n* **Golda** ('gəʊldə) 1898–1978, Israeli stateswoman, born in Russia; prime minister (1969–74).

Meissen (*German* 'maisən) *n* a town in E Germany, in Saxony, in Dresden district on the River Elbe: famous for its porcelain (Dresden china), first made here in 1710. Pop.: 38 100 (1989 est.).

Meissner effect ('maɪsnə) *n Physics.* the phenomenon in which magnetic flux is excluded from a substance when it is in a superconducting state, except for a thin layer at the surface. **[C20:** named after Fritz Walther *Meissner* (1882–1974), German physicist**]**

Meistersinger ('maɪstə,sɪŋə) *n, pl* **-singer** *or* **-singers.** a member of one of the various German guilds of workers or craftsmen organized to compose and perform poetry and music. These flourished in the 15th and 16th centuries. **[C19:** German: master singer**]**

Meitner (*German* 'maitnər) *n* **Lise** ('li:zə). 1878–1968, Austrian nuclear physicist. With Hahn, she discovered protactinium (1918), and they demonstrated with F. Strassmann the fission of uranium.

meitnerium ('maɪtnɪərɪəm) *n* a synthetic element produced in small quantities by high-energy ion bombardment. Symbol: Mt; atomic no.: 109. **[C20:** after Lise MEITNER**]**

Méjico ('mɛxiko) *n* the Spanish name for **Mexico.**

Mekka ('mɛkə) *n* a variant spelling of **Mecca.**

Meknès (mɛk'nɛs) *n* a city in N central Morocco, in the Middle Atlas Mountains: noted for the making of carpets. Pop.: 188 224 (1994).

Mekong (,mi:'kɒŋ) *n* a river in SE Asia, rising in SW China in Qinghai province: flows southeast forming the border between Laos and Myanmar, and part of the border between Laos and Thailand, then continues south across Cambodia and Vietnam to the South China Sea by an extensive delta, one of the greatest rice-growing areas in Asia. Length: about 4025 km (2500 miles).

mel (mɛl) *n Pharmacol.* a pure form of honey used in pharmaceutical products. **[**from Latin**]**

mela ('mi:lə, 'mɛlə) *n* an Asian cultural or religious fair or festival. **[C19:** Hindi, from Sanskrit *mēlā* an assembly, from *mil* to meet**]**

melaleuca (,mɛlə'lu:kə) *n* any shrub or tree of the mostly Australian myrtaceous genus *Melaleuca,* found in sandy or swampy regions. **[C19:** New Latin, from Greek *melas* black + *leukos* white, from its black trunk and white branches**]**

melamine ('mɛlə,mi:n) *n* **1** a colourless crystalline compound used in making synthetic resins; 2,4,6-triamino-1,3,5-triazine. Formula: $C_3H_6N_6$. **2** melamine resin or a material made from this resin. **[C19:** from German *Melamin,* from *Melam* distillate of ammonium thiocyanate, with *-am* representing *ammonia***]**

melamine resin *n* a thermosetting amino resin, stable to heat and light, produced from melamine and used for moulded products, adhesives, and surface coatings.

melancholia (,mɛlən'kəʊlɪə) *n* a former name for **depression.** ▸ **,melan'choli,ac** *adj, n*

melancholic (,mɛlən'kɒlɪk) *adj* **1** relating to or suffering from melancholy or melancholia. ◆ *n* **2** a person who suffers from melancholia. ▸ **,melan'cholically** *adv*

melancholy ('mɛlənkəlɪ) *n, pl* **-cholies.** **1** a constitutional tendency to gloominess or depression. **2** a sad thoughtful state of mind; pensiveness. **3** *Archaic.* **3a** a gloomy character, thought to be caused by too much black bile. **3b** one of the four bodily humours; black bile. See **humour** (sense 8). ◆ *adj* **4** characterized by, causing, or expressing sadness, dejection, etc. **[C14:** via Old French from Late Latin *melancholia,* from Greek *melankholia,* from *melas* black + *kholē* bile**]** ▸ **melancholily** ('mɛlən,kɒlɪlɪ) *adv* ▸ **'melan,choliness** *n*

Melanchthon (mə'læŋkθən; *German* me'lançtɔn) *n* **Philipp** ('fi:lɪp). original surname *Schwarzerd.* 1497–1560, German Protestant reformer. His *Loci Communes* (1521) was the first systematic presentation of Protestant theology and in the Augsburg Confession (1530) he stated the faith of the Lutheran churches. He also reformed the German educational system.

Melanesia (,mɛlə'ni:zɪə) *n* one of the three divisions of islands in the Pacific (the others being Micronesia and Polynesia); the SW division of Oceania: includes Fiji, New Caledonia, Vanuatu, the Bismarck Archipelago, and the Louisiade, Solomon, Santa Cruz, and Loyalty Islands, which all lie northeast of Australia. **[C19:** from Greek *melas* black + *nēsos* island; with reference to the dark skins of the inhabitants; on the model of *Polynesia***]**

Melanesian (,mɛlə'ni:zɪən) *adj* **1** of or relating to Melanesia, its people, or their languages. ◆ *n* **2** a native or inhabitant of Melanesia: generally Negroid with frizzy hair and small stature. **3** a group or branch of languages spoken in Melanesia, belonging to the Malayo-Polynesian family. **4** See also **Neo-Melanesian.**

melange *or* **mélange** (meɪ'lɑ:nʒ) *n* **1** a mixture; confusion. **2** *Geology.* a totally disordered mixture of rocks of different shapes, sizes, ages, and origins. **[C17:** from French *mêler* to mix. See MEDLEY**]**

melanic (mə'lænɪk) *adj* relating to melanism or melanosis.

melanin ('mɛlənɪn) *n* any of a group of black or dark brown pigments present in the hair, skin, and eyes of man and animals: produced in excess in certain skin diseases and in melanomas.

melanism ('mɛlə,nɪzəm) *n* **1** the condition in man and animals of having dark-coloured or black skin, feathers, etc. **Industrial melanism** is the occurrence of dark varieties of animals, esp. moths, in smoke-blackened industrial regions, in which they are well camouflaged. **2** another name for **melanosis.** ▸ **,mela'nistic** *adj*

melanite ('mɛlə,naɪt) *n* a black variety of andradite garnet.

melano- *or before a vowel* **melan-** *combining form.* black or dark: *melanin; melanism; melanocyte; melanoma.* **[**from Greek *melas* black**]**

Melanochroi (,mɛlə'nɒkrəʊ,aɪ) *pl n* a postulated subdivision of the Caucasoid race, characterized by dark hair and pale complexion. **[C19:** New Latin (coined by T. H. Huxley), from Greek, from *melas* dark + *ōchros* pale**]** ▸ **Melanochroid** (,mɛlə'nɒkrɔɪd) *adj*

melanocyte ('mɛlənəʊ,saɪt) *n Anatomy, zoology.* a cell, usually in the epidermis, that contains melanin.

melanoid ('mɛlə,nɔɪd) *adj* **1** resembling melanin; dark coloured. **2** characterized by or resembling melanosis.

melanoma (,mɛlə'nəʊmə) *n, pl* **-mas** *or* **-mata** (-mətə). *Pathol.* a malignant tumour composed of melanocytes, occurring esp. in the skin, often as a result of excessive exposure to sunlight.

melanosis (,mɛlə'nəʊsɪs) *or* **melanism** ('mɛlə,nɪzəm) *n Pathol.* a skin condition characterized by excessive deposits of melanin. ▸ **melanotic** (,mɛlə'nɒtɪk) *adj*

melanous ('mɛlənəs) *adj* having a dark complexion and black hair. ▸ **melanosity** (,mɛlə'nɒsɪtɪ) *n*

melaphyre ('mɛlə,faɪə) *n Geology, obsolete.* a type of weathered amygdaloidal basalt or andesite. **[C19:** via French from Greek *melas* black + *(por)phura* purple**]**

melatonin (,mɛlə'təʊnɪn) *n* the hormone-like secretion of the pineal gland, causing skin colour changes in some animals and thought to be involved in reproductive function. **[C20:** probably from MELA(NOCYTE) + (SERO)TONIN**]**

Melba ('mɛlbə) *n* **1** Dame **Nellie,** stage name of *Helen Porter Mitchell.* 1861–1931, Australian operatic soprano. **2** **do a Melba.** *Austral slang.* to make repeated farewell appearances.

Melba sauce *n* a sweet sauce made from fresh raspberries and served with peach melba, fruit sundaes, etc. **[C20:** named after Dame Nellie MELBA**]**

Melba toast *n* very thin crisp toast. **[C20:** named after Dame Nellie MELBA**]**

Melbourne[1] ('mɛlbən) *n* a port in SE Australia, capital of Victoria, on Port Phillip Bay: the second largest city in the country; settled in 1835 and developed rapidly with the discovery of rich goldfields in 1851; three universities. Pop.: 3 218 100 (1995 est.). ▸ **Melburnian** (mɛl'bɜ:nɪən) *n, adj*

Melbourne[2] ('mɛlbən) *n* **William Lamb,** 2nd Viscount. 1779–1848; Whig prime minister (1834; 1835–41). He was the chief political adviser to the young Queen Victoria.

Melchior ('mɛlkɪ,ɔː) *n* **1** (in Christian tradition) one of the Magi, the others being Balthazar and Caspar. **2 Lauritz** ('laurɪts). 1890–1973, U.S. operatic tenor, born in Denmark.

Melchite ('mɛlkaɪt) *Eastern Churches.* ◆ *adj* **1** of or relating to the Uniat Greek Catholic Church in Syria, Egypt, and Israel. ◆ *n* **2** a member of this Church. [C17: from Church Latin *Melchīta,* from Medieval Greek *Melkhītēs,* literally: royalist, from Syriac *malkā* king]

Melchizedek (mɛl'kɪzə,dɛk) *n Old Testament.* the priest-king of Salem who blessed Abraham (Genesis 14:18-19) and was taken as a prototype of Christ's priesthood (Hebrews 7). Douay spelling: **Melchisedech.**

meld[1] (mɛld) *vb* **1** (in some card games) to declare or lay down (cards), which then score points. ◆ *n* **2** the act of melding. **3** a set of cards for melding. [C19: from German *melden* to announce; related to Old English *meldian*]

meld[2] (mɛld) *vb* to blend or become blended; combine. [C20: blend of MELT + WELD[1]]

Meleager (,mɛlɪ'eɪgə) *n Greek myth.* one of the Argonauts, slayer of the Calydonian boar.

melee *or* **mêlée** ('mɛleɪ) *n* a noisy riotous fight or brawl. [C17: from French *mêlée.* See MEDLEY]

meliaceous (,miːlɪ'eɪʃɪəs) *adj* of, relating to, or belonging to the *Meliaceae,* a family of tropical and subtropical trees, including mahogany, some of which yield valuable timber. [C19: from New Latin *Melia* type genus, from Greek: ash]

melic ('mɛlɪk) *adj* (of poetry, esp. ancient Greek lyric poems) intended to be sung. [C17: via Latin from Greek *melikos,* from *melos* song]

melick ('mɛlɪk) *n* either of two pale green perennial grasses of the genus *Melica,* related to fescue, esp. **wood melick** (*M. uniflora*) having branching flower heads, that are common in woodlands. [New Latin *melica,* of unknown origin]

Méliès (*French* meljɛs) *n* **Georges** (ʒɔrʒ). 1861–1938, French pioneer film director.

Melilla (*French* melija) *n* the chief town of a Spanish enclave in Morocco, on the Mediterranean coast: founded by the Phoenicians; exports iron ore. Pop.: 59 576 (1996 est.).

melilot ('mɛlɪ,lɒt) *n* any papilionaceous plant of the Old World genus *Melilotus,* having narrow clusters of small white or yellow fragrant flowers. Also called: **sweet clover.** [C15: via Old French from Latin *melilōtos,* from Greek: sweet clover, from *meli* honey + *lōtos* LOTUS]

melinite ('mɛlɪ,naɪt) *n* a high explosive made from picric acid. [C19: via French from Greek *mēlinos* (colour) of a quince, from *mēlon* fruit, quince]

meliorate ('miːlɪə,reɪt) *vb* a variant of **ameliorate.** ▶ **'meliorable** *adj* ▶ **meliorative** ('miːlɪərətɪv) *adj, n* ▶ **'melio,rator** *n*

melioration (,miːlɪə'reɪʃən) *n* the act or an instance of improving or the state of being improved.

meliorism ('miːlɪə,rɪzəm) *n* the notion that the world can be improved by human effort. [C19: from Latin *melior* better] ▶ **'meliorist** *adj, n* ▶ **,melio'ristic** *adj*

melisma (mɪ'lɪzmə) *n, pl* **-mata** (-mətə) *or* **-mas.** *Music.* an expressive vocal phrase or passage consisting of several notes sung to one syllable. [C19: from Greek: melody] ▶ **melismatic** (,mɛlɪz'mætɪk) *adj*

Melitopol (*Russian* mɪli'tɔpəlj) *n* a city in the SE Ukraine. Pop.: 174 000 (1996 est.).

Melk (mɛlk) *n* a town in N Austria, on the River Danube: noted for its baroque Benedictine abbey. Pop.: 5163 (1991).

melliferous (mɪ'lɪfərəs) *or* **mellific** (mɪ'lɪfɪk) *adj* forming or producing honey. [C17: from Latin *mellifer,* from *mel* honey + *ferre* to bear]

mellifluous (mɪ'lɪfluəs) *or* **mellifluent** *adj* (of sounds or utterances) smooth or honeyed; sweet. [C15: from Late Latin *mellifluus* flowing with honey, from Latin *mel* honey + *fluere* to flow] ▶ **mel'lifluously** *or* **mel'lifluently** *adv* ▶ **mel'lifluousness** *or* **mel'lifluence** *n*

melliphagous (mɪ'lɪfəgəs) *or* **mellivorous** (mɪ'lɪvərəs) *adj Zoology.* (of an animal) feeding on honey. [C19: from Latin *mel* honey + Greek *-phagos,* from *phagein* to consume]

mellophone ('mɛlə,fəun) *n Music.* a brass band instrument similar in tone to a French horn. [C20: from MELLOW + -PHONE]

mellow ('mɛləu) *adj* **1** (esp. of fruits) full-flavoured; sweet; ripe. **2** (esp. of wines) well-matured. **3** (esp. of colours or sounds) soft or rich. **4** kind-hearted, esp. through maturity or old age. **5** genial, as through the effects of alcohol. **6** (of soil) soft and loamy. ◆ *vb* **7** to make or become mellow; soften; mature. **8** (foll. by *out*) to become calm and relaxed or (esp. of a drug) to have a calming or relaxing effect on (someone). [C15: perhaps from Old English *meru* soft (as through ripeness)] ▶ **'mellowly** *adv* ▶ **'mellowness** *n*

melodeon *or* **melodion** (mɪ'ləudɪən) *n Music.* **1** a type of small accordion. **2** a type of keyboard instrument similar to the harmonium. [C19: from German, from *Melodie* melody]

melodic (mɪ'lɒdɪk) *adj* **1** of or relating to melody. **2** of or relating to a part in a piece of music. **3** tuneful or melodious. ▶ **me'lodically** *adv*

melodic minor scale *n Music.* a minor scale modified from the natural by the sharpening of the sixth and seventh when taken in ascending order and the restoration of their original pitches when taken in descending order. See **minor** (sense 4a). Compare **harmonic minor scale.**

melodious (mɪ'ləudɪəs) *adj* **1** having a tune that is pleasant to the ear. **2** of or relating to melody; melodic. ▶ **me'lodiously** *adv* ▶ **me'lodiousness** *n*

melodist ('mɛlədɪst) *n* **1** a composer of melodies. **2** a singer.

melodize *or* **melodise** ('mɛlə,daɪz) *vb* **1** (*tr*) to provide with a melody. **2** (*tr*) to make melodious. **3** (*intr*) to sing or play melodies. ▶ **'melo,dizer** *or* **'melo,diser** *n*

melodrama ('mɛlə,drɑːmə) *n* **1** a play, film, etc., characterized by extravagant action and emotion. **2** (formerly) a romantic drama characterized by sensational incident, music, and song. **3** overdramatic emotion or behaviour. **4** a poem or part of a play or opera spoken to a musical accompaniment. [C19: from French *mélodrame,* from Greek *melos* song + *drame* DRAMA] ▶ **melodramatist** (,mɛlə'dræmətɪst) *n* ▶ **melodramatic** (,mɛlədrə'mætɪk) *adj* ▶ **,melodra'matically** *adv*

melodramatize *or* **melodramatise** (,mɛləu'dræmə,taɪz) *vb* (*tr*) to make melodramatic.

melody ('mɛlədɪ) *n, pl* **-dies. 1** *Music.* **1a** a succession of notes forming a distinctive sequence; tune. **1b** the horizontally represented aspect of the structure of a piece of music. Compare **harmony** (sense 4b). **2** sounds that are pleasant because of tone or arrangement, esp. words of poetry. [C13: from Old French, from Late Latin *melōdia,* from Greek *melōidia* singing, from *melos* song + *-ōidia,* from *aoidein* to sing]

meloid ('mɛlɔɪd) *n* **1** any long-legged beetle of the family *Meloidae,* which includes the blister beetles and oil beetles. ◆ *adj* **2** of, relating to, or belonging to the *Meloidae.* [C19: from New Latin *Meloē* name of genus]

melon ('mɛlən) *n* **1** any of several varieties of two cucurbitaceous vines (see **muskmelon, watermelon**), cultivated for their edible fruit. **2** the fruit of any of these plants, which has a hard rind and juicy flesh. **3 cut a melon.** *U.S. and Canadian slang.* to declare an abnormally high dividend to shareholders. [C14: via Old French from Late Latin *mēlo,* shortened form of *mēlopepō,* from Greek *mēlopepōn,* from *mēlon* apple + *pepōn* gourd]

Melos ('miːlɒs) *n* an island in the SW Aegean Sea, in the Cyclades: of volcanic origin, with hot springs; centre of early Aegean civilization, where the Venus de Milo was found. Pop.: 5000 (latest est.). Area: 132 sq. km (51 sq. miles). Modern Greek name: **Mílos.**

Melpomene (mɛl'pɒmɪnɪ) *n Greek myth.* the Muse of tragedy.

Melrose Abbey ('mɛlrəuz) *n* a ruined Cistercian abbey in Melrose in Scottish Borders: founded in 1136 and sacked by the English in 1385 and 1547: repaired in 1822 by Sir Walter Scott.

melt (mɛlt) *vb* **melts, melting, melted; melted** *or* **molten** ('məultən). **1** to liquefy (a solid) or (of a solid) to become liquefied, as a result of the action of heat. **2** to become or make liquid; dissolve: *cakes that melt in the mouth.* **3** (often foll. by *away*) to disappear; fade. **4** (foll. by *down*) to melt (metal scrap) for reuse. **5** (often foll. by *into*) to blend or cause to blend gradually. **6** to make or become emotional or sentimental; soften. ◆ *n* **7** the act or process of melting. **8** something melted or an amount melted. [Old English *meltan* to digest; related to Old Norse *melta* to malt (beer), digest, Greek *meldein* to melt] ▶ **'meltable** *adj* ▶ **,melta'bility** *n* ▶ **'melter** *n* ▶ **'meltingly** *adv* ▶ **'meltingness** *n*

meltage ('mɛltɪdʒ) *n* the process or result of melting or the amount melted: *rapid meltage of ice.*

meltdown ('mɛlt,daun) *n* **1** (in a nuclear reactor) the melting of the fuel rods as a result of a defect in the cooling system, with the possible escape of radiation into the environment. **2** *Informal.* a sudden disastrous failure with potential for widespread harm, as a stock-exchange crash. **3** *Informal.* the process or state of irreversible breakdown or decline: *the community is slowly going into meltdown.*

meltemi (mɛl'tɛmɪ) *n* a northerly wind in the northeast Mediterranean; etesian wind. [C20: from Modern Greek, from Turkish *meltem*]

melting point *n* the temperature at which a solid turns into a liquid. It is equal to the freezing point.

melting pot *n* **1** a pot in which metals or other substances are melted, esp. in order to mix them. **2** an area in which many races, ideas, etc., are mixed.

melton ('mɛltən) *n* a heavy smooth woollen fabric with a short nap, used esp. for overcoats. Also called: **melton cloth.** [C19: from MELTON MOWBRAY, Leicestershire, a former centre for making this cloth]

Melton Mowbray ('mɛltən 'məubrɪ) *n* a town in central England, in Leicestershire: pork pies and Stilton cheese. Pop.: 24 348 (1991).

meltwater ('mɛlt,wɔːtə) *n* melted snow or ice.

melungeon (mə'lʌndʒən) *n* any of a dark-skinned group of people of the Appalachians in E Tennessee, of mixed Indian, White, and Black ancestry. [C20: of unknown origin]

Melville ('mɛlvɪl) *n* **Herman.** 1819–91, U.S. novelist and short-story writer. Among his works, *Moby Dick* (1851) and *Billy Budd* (written 1891, published 1924) are outstanding.

Melville Island *n* **1** an island in the Arctic Ocean, north of Victoria Island: administratively part of the Northwest Territories of Canada. Area: 41 865 sq. km (16 164 sq. miles). **2** an island in the Arafura Sea, off the N central coast of Australia, separated from the mainland by Clarence Strait. Area: 6216 sq. km (2400 sq. miles).

Melville Peninsula *n* a peninsula of N Canada, in the Northwest Territories, between the Gulf of Boothia and Foxe Basin.

mem (mɛm) *n* the 13th letter in the Hebrew alphabet (מ or, at the end of a word, ם), transliterated as *m.* [Hebrew, literally: water]

mem. *abbrev. for:* **1** member. **2** memoir. **3** memorandum. **4** memorial.

member ('mɛmbə) *n* **1** a person who belongs to a club, political party, etc. **2** any individual plant or animal in a taxonomic group: *a member of the species.* **3** any part of an animal body, such as a limb. **4** another word for **penis. 5** any part of a plant, such as a petal, root, etc. **6** *Maths.* any individual object belonging to a set or logical class. **7** a distinct part of a whole, such as a proposition in a syllogism. **8** a component part of a building or construction. [C13: from Latin *membrum* limb, part] ▶ **'memberless** *adj*

Member ('mɛmbə) *n* (*sometimes not cap.*) **1** short for **Member of Parlia-**

ment. 2 short for **Member of Congress. 3** a member of some other legislative body.

Member of Congress *n* a member of the U.S. Congress, esp. of the House of Representatives.

Member of Parliament *n* a member of the House of Commons or similar legislative body, as in many Commonwealth countries. Abbrev.: **MP.**

membership ('mɛmbə,ʃɪp) *n* **1** the members of an organization collectively. **2** the state of being a member.

membrane ('mɛmbreɪn) *n* **1** any thin pliable sheet of material. **2** a pliable sheetlike usually fibrous tissue that covers, lines, or connects plant and animal organs or cells. **3** *Biology.* a double layer of lipid, containing some proteins, that surrounds biological cells and some of their internal structures. **4** *Physics.* a two-dimensional entity postulated as a fundamental constituent of matter in some theories of particle physics. **5** a skin of parchment forming part of a roll. [C16: from Latin *membrāna* skin covering a part of the body, from *membrum* MEMBER]

membrane bone *n* any bone that develops within membranous tissue, such as the clavicle and bones of the skull, without cartilage formation. Compare **cartilage bone.**

membrane transport *n* the process by which physiologically important substances, such as calcium ions, sugars, etc., are conveyed across a biological membrane.

membranous ('mɛmbrənəs, mɛm'breɪnəs), **membraneous** (mɛm'breɪnɪəs), *or* **membranaceous** (,mɛmbrə'neɪʃəs) *adj* of or relating to a membrane. ▸ **'membranously** *adv*

Memel ('meːməl) *n* **1** the German name for **Klaipeda. 2** the lower course of the Neman River.

memento (mɪ'mɛntəʊ) *n, pl* **-tos** *or* **-toes. 1** something that reminds one of past events; souvenir. **2** *R.C. Church.* either of two prayers occurring during the Mass. [C15: from Latin, imperative of *meminisse* to remember]

memento mori ('mɔːriː) *n* an object, such as a skull, intended to remind people of the inevitability of death. [C16: Latin: remember you must die]

Memling ('mɛmlɪŋ) *or* **Memlinc** ('mɛmlɪŋk) *n* **Hans** (hɑns). ?1430–94, Flemish painter of religious works and portraits.

Memnon ('mɛmnɒn) *n* **1** *Greek myth.* a king of Ethiopia, son of Eos: slain by Achilles in the Trojan War. **2** a colossal statue of Amenhotep III at Thebes in ancient Egypt, which emitted a sound thought by the Greeks to be the voice of Memnon. ▸ **Memnonian** (mɛm'nəʊnɪən) *adj*

memo ('mɛməʊ, 'miːməʊ) *n, pl* **memos.** short for **memorandum.**

memoir ('mɛmwɑː) *n* **1** a biography or historical account, esp. one based on personal knowledge. **2** an essay or monograph, as on a specialized topic. **3** *Obsolete.* a memorandum. [C16: from French, from Latin *memoria* MEMORY] ▸ **'memoirist** *n*

memoirs ('mɛmwɑːz) *pl n* **1** a collection of reminiscences about a period, series of events, etc., written from personal experience or special sources. **2** an autobiographical record. **3** a collection or record, as of transactions of a society, etc.

memorabilia (,mɛmərə'bɪlɪə) *pl n, sing* **-rabile** (-'ræbɪlɪ). **1** memorable events or things. **2** objects connected with famous people or events. [C17: from Latin, from *memorābilis* MEMORABLE]

memorable ('mɛmərəbᵊl, 'mɛmrə-) *adj* worth remembering or easily remembered; noteworthy. [C15: from Latin *memorābilis,* from *memorāre* to recall, from *memor* mindful] ▸ **,memora'bility** *or* **'memorableness** *n* ▸ **'memorably** *adv*

memorandum (,mɛmə'rændəm) *n, pl* **-dums** *or* **-da** (-də). **1** a written statement, record, or communication such as within an office. **2** a note of things to be remembered. **3** an informal diplomatic communication, often unsigned: often summarizing the point of view of a government. **4** *Law.* a short written summary of the terms of a transaction. ◆ Often (esp. for senses 1 and 2) shortened to **memo.** [C15: from Latin: (something) to be remembered]

memorial (mɪ'mɔːrɪəl) *adj* **1** serving to preserve the memory of the dead or a past event. **2** of or involving memory. ◆ *n* **3** something serving as a remembrance. **4** a written statement of facts submitted to a government, authority, etc., in conjunction with a petition. **5** an informal diplomatic paper. [C14: from Late Latin *memoriāle* a reminder, neuter of *memoriālis* belonging to remembrance] ▸ **me'morially** *adv*

Memorial Day *n* a holiday in the United States, May 30th in most states, commemorating the servicemen killed in all American wars.

memorialist (mɪ'mɔːrɪəlɪst) *n* **1** a person who writes or presents a memorial. **2** a writer of a memoir or memoirs.

memorialize *or* **memorialise** (mɪ'mɔːrɪə,laɪz) *vb (tr)* **1** to honour or commemorate. **2** to present or address a memorial to. ▸ **me,moriali'zation** *or* **me,moriali'sation** *n* ▸ **me'morial,izer** *or* **me'morial,iser** *n*

memoria technica (mɪ'mɔːrɪə 'tɛknɪkə) *n* a method or device for assisting the memory. [C18: New Latin: artificial memory]

memorize *or* **memorise** ('mɛmə,raɪz) *vb (tr)* to commit to memory; learn so as to remember. ▸ **'memo,rizable** *or* **'memo,risable** *adj* ▸ **,memori'zation** *or* **,memori'sation** *n* ▸ **'memo,rizer** *or* **'memo,riser** *n*

memory ('mɛmərɪ) *n, pl* **-ries. 1a** the ability of the mind to store and recall past sensations, thoughts, knowledge, etc.: *he can do it from memory.* **1b** the part of the brain that appears to have this function. **2** the sum of everything retained by the mind. **3** a particular recollection of an event, person, etc. **4** the time over which recollection extends: *within his memory.* **5** commemoration or remembrance: *in memory of our leader.* **6** the state of being remembered, as after death. **7** Also called: **RAM, main store, store.** a part of a computer in which information is stored for immediate use by the central processing unit. See also **backing store, virtual storage. 8** the tendency for a material, system, etc., to show effects that depend on its past treatment or history. **9** the ability of a material, etc., to return to a former state after a constraint has been removed. [C14: from Old French *memorie,* from Latin *memoria,* from *memor* mindful]

memory mapping *n* a technique whereby computer peripherals may be addressed as though they formed part of the main memory of the computer.

memory span *n Psychol.* the capacity of short-term memory, usually between 5 and 10 items.

memory trace *n Psychol.* the hypothetical structural alteration in brain cells following learning. See also **engram.**

Memphian ('mɛmfɪən) *adj* **1** of or relating to ancient Memphis or its inhabitants. ◆ *n* **2** an inhabitant or native of ancient Memphis.

Memphis ('mɛmfɪs) *n* **1** a port in SW Tennessee, on the Mississippi River: the largest city in the state; a major cotton and timber market; Memphis State University (1909). Pop.: 596 725 (1996 est.). **2** a ruined city in N Egypt, the ancient centre of Lower Egypt, on the Nile: administrative and artistic centre, sacred to the worship of Ptah.

Memphremagog (,mɛmfriː'meɪgɒg) *n* **Lake.** a lake on the border between the U.S. and Canada, in N Vermont and S Quebec. Length: about 43 km (27 miles). Width: up to 6 km (4 miles).

memsahib ('mɛm,sɑːɪb, -hɪb) *n* (formerly in India) a term of respect used of a European married woman. [C19: from MA'AM + SAHIB]

men (mɛn) *n* the plural of **man.**

menace ('mɛnɪs) *vb* **1** to threaten with violence, danger, etc. ◆ *n* **2** *Literary.* a threat or the act of threatening. **3** something menacing; a source of danger. **4** *Informal.* a nuisance. [C13: ultimately related to Latin *minax* threatening, from *minārī* to threaten] ▸ **'menacer** *n* ▸ **'menacing** *adj* ▸ **'menacingly** *adv*

menad ('miːnæd) *n* a variant spelling of **maenad.**

menadione (,mɛnə'daɪəʊn) *n* a yellow crystalline compound used in fungicides and as an additive to animal feeds. Also called: **vitamin K_3.** Formula: $C_{11}H_8O_2$. [C20: from ME(THYL) + NA(PHTHA) + DI-[1] + -ONE]

Menado (me'nɑːdəʊ) *or* **Manado** *n* a port in NE Indonesia, on NE Sulawesi: founded by the Dutch in 1657. Pop.: 398 900 (1995 est.).

ménage (meɪ'nɑːʒ; *French* menaʒ) *n* the persons of a household. [C17: from French, from Vulgar Latin *mansiōnāticum* (unattested) household; see MANSION]

ménage à trois *French.* (menaʒ a trwɑ) *n, pl* ***ménages à trois*** (menaʒ a trwɑ). a sexual arrangement involving a married couple and the lover of one of them. [literally: household of three]

menagerie (mɪ'nædʒərɪ) *n* **1** a collection of wild animals kept for exhibition. **2** the place where such animals are housed. [C18: from French: household management, which formerly included care of domestic animals. See MÉNAGE]

Menai Strait ('menaɪ) *n* a channel of the Irish Sea between the island of Anglesey and the mainland of NW Wales: famous suspension bridge (1819–26) designed by Thomas Telford and tubular bridge (1846–50) by Robert Stephenson. Length: 24 km (15 miles). Width: up to 3 km (2 miles).

Menam (miː'næm) *n* another name for the **Chao Phraya.**

Menander (mə'nændə) *n* **1** ?160 B.C.–?120 B.C., Greek king of the Punjab. A Buddhist convert, he reigned over much of NW India. **2** ?342–?292 B.C., Greek comic dramatist. The *Dyskolos* is his only complete extant comedy but others survive in adaptations by Terence and Plautus.

menaquinone (,mɛnəkwɪ'nəʊn) *n* a form of vitamin K synthesized by bacteria in the intestine or in putrefying organic matter. Also called: **vitamin K_2.** [C20: from *me(thyl)-na(phtho)quinone*]

menarche (mɛ'nɑːkɪ) *n* the first occurrence of menstruation in a woman's life. [C20: New Latin, from Greek *mēn* month + *arkhē* beginning] ▸ **men'archeal** *or* **men'archial** *adj*

Mencius ('mɛnʃɪəs, -ʃəs) *n* Chinese name *Mengzi* or *Meng-tze.* ?372–?289 B.C., Chinese philosopher, who propounded the ethical system of Confucius.

Mencken ('mɛŋkən) *n* **H(enry) L(ouis).** 1880–1956, U.S. journalist and literary critic, noted for *The American Language* (1919): editor of the *Smart Set* and the *American Mercury,* which he founded (1924).

mend (mɛnd) *vb* **1** *(tr)* to repair (something broken or unserviceable). **2** to improve or undergo improvement; reform (often in the phrase **mend one's ways**). **3** *(intr)* to heal or recover. **4** (of conditions) to improve; become better. ◆ *n* **5** the act of repairing. **6** a mended area, esp. on a garment. **7 on the mend.** becoming better, esp. in health. [C12: shortened from AMEND] ▸ **'mendable** *adj* ▸ **'mender** *n*

mendacity (mɛn'dæsɪtɪ) *n, pl* **-ties. 1** the tendency to be untruthful. **2** a falsehood. [C17: from Late Latin *mendācitās,* from Latin *mendāx* untruthful] ▸ **mendacious** (mɛn'deɪʃəs) *adj* ▸ **men'daciously** *adv* ▸ **men'daciousness** *n*

Mendel ('mɛndᵊl) *n* **Gregor Johann** ('greːgɔr jo'han). 1822–84, Austrian monk and botanist; founder of the science of genetics. He developed his theory of organic inheritance from his experiments on the hybridization of green peas. His findings were published (1865) but remained unrecognized until 1900. See **Mendel's laws.**

mendelevium (,mɛndɪ'liːvɪəm) *n* a transuranic element artificially produced by bombardment of einsteinium. Symbol: Md; atomic no.: 101; half-life of most stable isotope, ^{258}Md: 60 days (approx.); valency: 2 or 3. [C20: named after D. I. MENDELEYEV]

Mendeleyev *or* **Mendeleev** (*Russian* mɪndɪ'ljejɪf) *n* **Dmitri Ivanovich** ('dmitrij i'vanəvitʃ). 1834–1907, Russian chemist. He devised the original periodic table of the elements (1869).

Mendelian (mɛn'diːlɪən) *adj* of or relating to Mendel's laws.

Mendelism ('mɛndə,lɪzəm) *or* **Mendelianism** (mɛn'diːlɪə,nɪzəm) *n* the science of heredity based on Mendel's laws with some modifications in the light of more recent knowledge.

Mendel's laws *pl n* the principles of heredity proposed by Gregor Mendel. The

Law of Segregation states that each hereditary character is determined by a pair of units in the reproductive cells: the pairs separate during meiosis so that each gamete carries only one unit of each pair. The **Law of Independent Assortment** states that the separation of the units of each pair is not influenced by that of any other pair.

Mendelssohn ('mɛndᵊlsən; *German* 'mɛndəlzo:n) *n* **1 Felix** ('fe:lɪks), full name *Jacob Ludwig Felix Mendelssohn-Bartholdy*. 1809–47, German romantic composer. His works include the overtures *A Midsummer Night's Dream* (1826) and *Fingal's Cave* (1832), five symphonies, the oratorio *Elijah* (1846), piano pieces, and songs. He was instrumental in the revival of the music of J. S. Bach in the 19th century. **2** his grandfather, **Moses** ('mo:zəs). 1729–86, German Jewish philosopher. His best-known work is *Jerusalem* (1783), in which he defends Judaism and appeals for religious toleration.

Menderes (ˌmɛndɛ'rɛs) *n* **1** a river in SW Turkey flowing southwest, then west to the Aegean. Length: about 386 km (240 miles). Ancient name: **Maeander. 2** a river in NW Turkey flowing west and northwest to the Dardanelles. Length: 104 km (65 miles). Ancient name: **Scamander.**

Mendès-France (*French* mɛ̃dɛsfrɑ̃s) *n* **Pierre** (pjɛr). 1907–82, French statesman; prime minister (1954–55). He concluded the war in Indochina and granted independence to Tunisia.

mendicant ('mɛndɪkənt) *adj* **1** begging. **2** (of a member of a religious order) dependent on alms for sustenance: *mendicant friars.* **3** characteristic of a beggar. ◆ *n* **4** a mendicant friar. **5** a less common word for **beggar.** [C16: from Latin *mendīcāre* to beg, from *mendīcus* beggar, from *mendus* flaw] ▸ **'mendicancy** *or* **mendicity** (mɛn'dɪsɪtɪ) *n*

mending ('mɛndɪŋ) *n* something to be mended, esp. clothes.

Mendips ('mɛndɪps) *pl n* a range of limestone hills in SW England, in N Somerset: includes the Cheddar Gorge and numerous caves. Highest point: 325 m (1068 ft.). Also called: **Mendip Hills.**

Mendoza[1] (mɛn'dəʊzə; *Spanish* men'doθa) *n* a city in W central Argentina, in the foothills of the Sierra de los Paramillos: largely destroyed by an earthquake in 1861; commercial centre of an intensively cultivated irrigated region; University of Cuyo (1939). Pop.: 773 113 (1991).

Mendoza[2] (*Spanish* men'doθa) *n* **Pedro de** ('peðro de). died 1537, Spanish soldier and explorer; founder of Buenos Aires (1536).

meneer (mə'nɪə) *n* a South African title of address equivalent to *sir* when used alone or *Mr* when placed before a name. [Afrikaans]

Menelaus (ˌmɛnɪ'leɪəs) *n Greek myth.* a king of Sparta and the brother of Agamemnon. He was the husband of Helen, whose abduction led to the Trojan War.

Menelik II ('mɛnɪlɪk) *n* 1844–1913, emperor of Abyssinia (1889–1910). He defeated the Italians at Aduwa (1896), maintaining the independence of Abyssinia in an era of European expansion in Africa.

mene, mene, tekel, upharsin ('mi:ni: 'mi:ni: 'tɛkəl ju:'fɑ:sɪn) *n Old Testament.* the words that appeared on the wall during Belshazzar's Feast (Daniel 5:25), interpreted by Daniel to mean that God had doomed the kingdom of Belshazzar. [Aramaic: numbered, numbered, weighed, divided]

Menes ('mi:ni:z) *n* the first king of the first dynasty of Egypt (?3100 B.C.). He is said to have united Upper and Lower Egypt and founded Memphis.

menfolk ('mɛnˌfəʊk) *or U.S.* (*sometimes*) **menfolks** *pl n* men collectively, esp. the men of a particular family.

Mengelberg ('mɛŋgᵊlˌbɜ:g; *Dutch* 'mɛŋəlbɛrx) *n* (**Josef**) **Willem** ('wɪləm). 1871–1951, Dutch orchestral conductor, noted for his performances of the music of Mahler.

Mengistu Haile Mariam (mɛŋ'gɪstu: 'haɪlɪ 'mɑ:rɪəm) *n* born 1937, Ethiopian soldier and statesman; head of state from 1977 until 1991 when rebels seized power and he fled into exile.

Mengzi *or* **Meng-tze** ('mɛŋ'tseɪ) *n* the Chinese name for **Mencius.**

menhaden (mɛn'heɪdᵊn) *n, pl* **-den.** a marine North American fish, *Brevoortia tyrannus:* source of fishmeal, fertilizer, and oil: family *Clupeidae* (herrings, etc.). [C18: from Algonquian; probably related to Narragansett *munnawhatteaûg* fertilizer, menhaden]

menhir ('mɛnhɪə) *n* a single standing stone, often carved, dating from the middle Bronze Age in the British Isles and from the late Neolithic Age in W Europe. [C19: from Breton *men* stone + *hir* long]

menial ('mi:nɪəl) *adj* **1** consisting of or occupied with work requiring little skill, esp. domestic duties such as cleaning. **2** of, involving, or befitting servants. **3** servile. ◆ *n* **4** a domestic servant. **5** a servile person. [C14: from Anglo-Norman *meignial,* from Old French *meinie* household. See MEINY] ▸ **'menially** *adv*

Ménière's syndrome *or* **disease** (meɪn'jɛəz) *n* a disorder of the inner ear characterized by a ringing or buzzing in the ear, dizziness, and impaired hearing. [C19: named after Prosper *Ménière* (1799–1862), French physician]

menilite ('mɛnɪˌlaɪt) *n* another name for **liver opal,** esp. a brown or grey variety.

Meninga (mɪn'ɪŋgə) *n* **Mal.** born 1960, Australian rugby league player.

meninges (mɪ'nɪndʒi:z) *pl n, sing* **meninx** ('mi:nɪŋks). the three membranes (**dura mater, arachnoid, pia mater**) that envelop the brain and spinal cord. [C17: from Greek, pl of *meninx* membrane] ▸ **meningeal** (mɪ'nɪndʒɪəl) *adj*

meningitis (ˌmɛnɪn'dʒaɪtɪs) *n* inflammation of the membranes that surround the brain or spinal cord, caused by infection. ▸ **meningitic** (ˌmɛnɪn'dʒɪtɪk) *adj*

meningocele (me'nɪŋgəʊˌsi:l) *n Pathol.* protrusion of the meninges through the skull or backbone. [C19: from *meningo-* (see MENINGES) + -CELE]

meningococcus (meˌnɪŋgəʊ'kɒkəs) *n, pl* **-cocci** (-'kɒksaɪ). the bacterium that causes cerebrospinal meningitis. ▸ **meˌningo'coccal** *adj*

meniscus (mɪ'nɪskəs) *n, pl* **-nisci** (-'nɪsaɪ) *or* **-niscuses. 1** the curved upper surface of a liquid standing in a tube, produced by the surface tension. **2** a crescent or half-moon-shaped body or design. **3** a crescent-shaped fibrous cartilage between the bones at certain joints, esp. at the knee. **4** a crescent-shaped lens; a concavo-convex or convexo-concave lens. [C17: from New Latin, from Greek *mēniskos* crescent, diminutive of *mēnē* moon] ▸ **me'niscoid** *adj*

menispermaceous (ˌmɛnɪspɜ:'meɪʃəs) *adj* of, relating to, or belonging to the *Menispermaceae,* a family of mainly tropical and subtropical plants, most of which are woody climbers with small flowers. [C19: from New Latin *Mēnispermum* name of genus, from Greek *mēnē* moon + *sperma* seed]

Mennonite ('mɛnəˌnaɪt) *n* a member of a Protestant sect that rejects infant baptism, Church organization, and the doctrine of transubstantiation and in most cases refuses military service, public office, and the taking of oaths. [C16: from German *Mennonit,* after *Menno* Simons (1496–1561), Frisian religious leader] ▸ **'MennoˌnitismC** *n*

meno ('mɛnəʊ) *adv Music.* **1** (esp. preceding a dynamic or tempo marking) to be played less quickly, less softly, etc. **2** short for **meno mosso.** [from Italian, from Latin *minus* less]

meno- *combining form.* menstruation: *menorrhagia.* [from Greek *mēn* month]

menology (mɪ'nɒlədʒɪ) *n, pl* **-gies. 1** an ecclesiastical calendar of the months. **2** *Eastern Churches.* a liturgical book containing the lives of the saints arranged by months. [C17: from New Latin *mēnologium,* from Late Greek *mēnologion,* from Greek *mēn* month + *logos* word, account]

Menomini *or* **Menominee** (mə'nɒmənɪ) *n* **1** (*pl* **-ni, -nis** *or* **-nee, -nees**) a member of a North American Indian people formerly living between Lake Michigan and Lake Superior. **2** the language of this people, belonging to the Algonquian family.

meno mosso ('mɛnəʊ 'mɒsəʊ) *adv Music.* to be played at reduced speed. Often shortened to **meno.** [Italian: less rapid]

Menon ('mɛnən) *n* **Vengalil Krishnan Krishna** ('vɛŋgəlɪl 'kri:ʃnən 'kri:ʃnə). 1897–1974, Indian diplomat and politician, who was a close associate of Nehru and played a key role in the Indian nationalist movement.

menopause ('mɛnəʊˌpɔ:z) *n* the period during which a woman's menstrual cycle ceases, normally occurring at an age of 45 to 50. Nontechnical name: **change of life.** [C19: from French, from Greek *mēn* month + *pausis* halt] ▸ ˌ**meno'pausal** *or* (*rarely*) ˌ**meno'pausic** *adj*

menorah (mɪ'nɔ:rə; *Hebrew* mə'nɑʊrɔ) *n Judaism.* **1** a seven-branched candelabrum used in the Temple and now an emblem of Judaism and the badge of the state of Israel. **2** a candelabrum having eight branches and a shammes that is lit during the festival of Hanukkah. [from Hebrew: candlestick]

Menorca (me'nɔrka) *n* the Spanish name for **Minorca** (sense 1).

menorrhagia (ˌmɛnɔ:'reɪdʒɪə) *n* excessive bleeding during menstruation. ▸ **menorrhagic** (ˌmɛnə'rædʒɪk) *adj*

menorrhoea (ˌmɛnə'rɪə) *n* normal bleeding in menstruation.

Menotti (mə'nɒtɪ; *Italian* me'nɔtti) *n* **Gian Carlo** (dʒan 'karlo). born 1911, Italian composer, in the U.S. from 1928. His works include the operas *The Medium* (1946), *The Consul* (1950), *Amahl and the Night Visitors* (1951), and *Giorno di Nozze* (1988).

Mensa[1] ('mɛnsə) *n, Latin genitive* **Mensae** ('mɛnsi:). a faint constellation in the S hemisphere lying between Hydrus and Volans and containing part of the Large Magellanic Cloud. [Latin, literally: the table]

Mensa[2] ('mɛnsə) *n* an international society, membership of which is restricted to people whose intelligence test scores exceed those expected of 98 per cent of the population.

mensal[1] ('mɛnsᵊl) *adj Rare.* monthly. [C15: from Latin *mensis* month]

mensal[2] ('mɛnsᵊl) *adj Rare.* relating to or used at the table. [C15: from Latin *mensālis,* from *mensa* table]

mens sana in corpore sano *Latin.* (mɛnz 'sænə ɪn 'kɔ:pɔ:reɪ 'sænəʊ) *n* a sound mind in a sound body. [Latin]

menses ('mɛnsi:z) *n, pl* **menses. 1** another name for **menstruation. 2** the period of time, usually from three to five days, during which menstruation occurs. **3** the matter discharged during menstruation. [C16: from Latin, pl of *mensis* month]

Menshevik ('mɛnʃɪvɪk) *or* **Menshevist** *n* a member of the moderate wing of the Russian Social Democratic Party, advocating gradual reform to achieve socialism. Compare **Bolshevik.** [C20: from Russian, literally: minority, from *menshe* less, from *malo* few] ▸ **'Menshevism** *n*

mens rea ('mɛnz 'reɪə) *n Law.* a criminal intention or knowledge that an act is wrong. It is assumed to be an ingredient of all criminal offences although some minor statutory offences are punishable irrespective of it. [Latin, literally: guilty mind]

men's room *n Chiefly U.S. and Canadian.* a public lavatory for men.

menstrual ('mɛnstrʊəl) *adj* of or relating to menstruation or the menses.

menstruate ('mɛnstrʊˌeɪt) *vb* (*intr*) to undergo menstruation. [C17: from Latin *menstruāre,* from *mensis* month]

menstruation (ˌmɛnstrʊ'eɪʃən) *n* the approximately monthly discharge of blood and cellular debris from the uterus by nonpregnant women from puberty to the menopause. Also called: **menses.** Nontechnical name: **period.** ▸ **menstruous** ('mɛnstrʊəs) *adj*

menstruum ('mɛnstrʊəm) *n, pl* **-struums** *or* **-strua** (-strʊə). a solvent, esp. one used in the preparation of a drug. [C17 (meaning: solvent), C14 (menstrual discharge): from Medieval Latin, from Latin *mēnstruus* monthly, from *mēnsis* month; from an alchemical comparison between a base metal being transmuted into gold and the supposed action of the menses]

mensurable ('mɛnsjʊrəbᵊl, -ʃə-) *adj* a less common word for **measurable.** [C17: from Late Latin *mēnsūrābilis,* from *mēnsūra* MEASURE] ▸ ˌ**mensura'bility** *n*

mensural ('mɛnʃərəl) *adj* **1** of or involving measure. **2** *Music.* of or relating to music in which notes have fixed values in relation to each other. [C17: from Late Latin *mēnsūrālis,* from *mēnsūra* MEASURE]

mensuration (ˌmɛnʃəˈreɪʃən) *n* **1** the study of the measurement of geometric magnitudes such as length. **2** the act or process of measuring; measurement. ▸ ˌ**mensuˈrational** *adj* ▸ **mensurative** (ˈmɛnʃərətɪv) *adj*

menswear (ˈmɛnzˌwɛə) *n* clothing for men.

-ment *suffix forming nouns, esp. from verbs.* **1** indicating state, condition, or quality: *enjoyment.* **2** indicating the result or product of an action: *embankment.* **3** indicating process or action: *management.* [from French, from Latin *-mentum*]

mental[1] (ˈmɛntᵊl) *adj* **1** of or involving the mind or an intellectual process. **2** occurring only in the mind: *mental calculations.* **3** affected by mental illness: *a mental patient.* **4** concerned with care for persons with mental illness: *a mental hospital.* **5** *Slang.* insane. [C15: from Late Latin *mentālis,* from Latin *mēns* mind] ▸ ˈ**mentally** *adv*

mental[2] (ˈmɛntᵊl) *adj Anatomy.* of or relating to the chin. Also: **genial.** [C18: from Latin *mentum* chin]

mental age *n Psychol.* the mental ability of a child, expressed in years and based on a comparison of his test performance with the performance of children with a range of chronological ages. See also **intelligence quotient.**

mental block *n* See **block** (sense 21).

mental cruelty *n* behaviour that causes distress to another person but that does not involve physical assault.

mental deficiency *n Psychiatry.* a less common term for **mental retardation.**

mental disorder *n Law.* (in England, according to the Mental Health Act 1983) mental illness, arrested or incomplete development of mind, psychopathic disorder, or any other disorder or disability of the mind. ▸ **mentally disordered** *adj*

mental handicap *n* a general or specific intellectual disability, resulting directly or indirectly from injury to the brain or from abnormal neurological development. ▸ **mentally handicapped** *adj*

mental healing *n* the healing of a disorder by mental concentration or suggestion. ▸ **mental healer** *n*

mental home, hospital, *or* **institution** *n* a home, hospital, or institution for people who are mentally ill.

mental illness *n* any of various disorders in which a person's thoughts, emotions, or behaviour are so abnormal as to cause suffering to himself, herself, or other people.

mental impairment *n Law.* (in England, according to the Mental Health Act 1983) a state of arrested or incomplete development of mind, which includes significant impairment of intelligence and social functioning and is associated with abnormally aggressive or seriously irresponsible conduct. ▸ **mentally impaired** *adj*

mentalism (ˈmɛntᵊˌlɪzəm) *n Philosophy.* the doctrine that mind is the fundamental reality and that objects of knowledge exist only as aspects of the subject's consciousness. Compare **physicalism, idealism** (sense 3). See also **monism** (sense 1), **materialism** (sense 2). ▸ ˈ**mentalist** *n* ▸ ˌ**mentalˈistic** *adj* ▸ ˌ**mentalˈistically** *adv*

mentality (mɛnˈtælɪtɪ) *n, pl* **-ties. 1** the state or quality of mental or intellectual ability. **2** a way of thinking; mental inclination or character: *his weird mentality.*

mental lexicon *n* the store of words in a person's mind.

mental reservation *n* a tacit withholding of full assent or an unexpressed qualification made when one is taking an oath, making a statement, etc.

mental retardation *n Psychiatry.* the condition of having a low intelligence quotient (below 70).

mentation (mɛnˈteɪʃən) *n* the process or result of mental activity.

menthaceous (mɛnˈθeɪʃɪəs) *adj* of, relating to, or belonging to the labiate plant genus *Mentha* (mints, etc.) the members of which have scented leaves. [from New Latin, from Latin *mentha* MINT[1]]

menthol (ˈmɛnθɒl) *n* an optically active organic compound found in peppermint oil and used as an antiseptic, in inhalants, and as an analgesic. Formula: $C_{10}H_{20}O$. [C19: from German, from Latin *mentha* MINT[1]]

mentholated (ˈmɛnθəˌleɪtɪd) *adj* containing, treated, or impregnated with menthol.

mention (ˈmɛnʃən) *vb* (*tr*) **1** to refer to or speak about briefly or incidentally. **2** to acknowledge or honour. **3 not to mention (something).** to say nothing of (something too obvious to mention). ◆ *n* **4** a recognition or acknowledgment. **5** a slight reference or allusion: *he only got a mention in the article; the author makes no mention of that.* **6** the act of mentioning. **7** *Philosophy, logic, linguistics.* the occurrence (of an expression) in such a context that it is itself referred to rather than performing its own linguistic function. In *"Fido" names Fido,* the word *Fido* is first mentioned and then used to refer to the dog. Compare **use** (sense 18). See also **formal mode.** [C14: via Old French from Latin *mentiō* a calling to mind, naming, from *mēns* mind] ▸ ˈ**mentionable** *adj* ▸ ˈ**mentioner** *n*

Mentmore (ˈmɛntˌmɔː) *n* a mansion in Mentmore in Buckinghamshire: built by Sir Joseph Paxton in the 19th century for the Rothschild family; now owned by the Maharishi University of Natural Law.

Menton (mɛnˈtəʊn; *French* mɑ̃tɔ̃) *n* a town and resort in SE France, on the Mediterranean: belonged to Monaco from the 14th century until 1848, then an independent republic until purchased by France in 1860. Pop.: 25 500 (latest est.).

mentor (ˈmɛntɔː) *n* a wise or trusted adviser or guide. [C18: from MENTOR] ▸ **menˈtorial** *adj*

Mentor (ˈmɛntɔː) *n* the friend whom Odysseus put in charge of his household when he left for Troy. He was the adviser of the young Telemachus.

mentoring (ˈmɛntərɪŋ) *n* (in business) the practice of assigning a junior member of staff to the care of a more experienced person who assists him in his career.

menu (ˈmɛnjuː) *n* **1** a list of dishes served at a meal or that can be ordered in a restaurant. **2** a list of options displayed on a visual display unit from which the operator selects an action to be carried out by positioning the cursor or by depressing the appropriate key. [C19: from French *menu* small, detailed (list), from Latin *minūtus* MINUTE[2]]

menu-driven *adj* (of a computer system) operated through menus.

Menuhin (ˈmɛnjʊɪn) *n* **Yehudi** (jɛˈhuːdɪ), Baron. 1916–99, British violinist, born in the U.S.

Menzies (ˈmɛnzɪz) *n* Sir **Robert Gordon.** 1894–1978, Australian statesman; prime minister (1939–41; 1949–66).

meow, miaou, miaow (mɪˈaʊ, mjaʊ), *or* **miaul** (mɪˈaʊl, mjaʊl) *vb* **1** (*intr*) (of a cat) to make a characteristic crying sound. ◆ *interj* **2** an imitation of this sound.

MEP (in Britain) *abbrev. for* Member of the European Parliament.

mepacrine (ˈmɛpəkrɪn) *n Brit.* a drug, mepacrine dihydrochloride, one of the first synthetic substitutes for quinine, formerly widely used to treat malaria but now largely replaced by chloroquine. Formula: $C_{23}H_{30}ClN_3O.2HCl.2H_2O$. U.S. name: **quinacrine.** [C20: from ME(THYL) + PA(LUDISM + A)CR(ID)INE]

meperidine (məˈpɛrɪˌdiːn, -dɪn) *n* a white crystalline water-soluble drug used as an analgesic. Formula: $C_{15}H_{21}NO_2.HCl$. Also called: **meperidine hydrochloride.** [C20: from METHYL + PIPERIDINE]

Mephistopheles (ˌmɛfɪˈstɒfɪˌliːz) *or* **Mephisto** (məˈfɪstəʊ) *n* a devil in medieval mythology and the one to whom Faust sold his soul in the Faust legend. ▸ **Mephistophelean** *or* **Mephistophelian** (ˌmɛfɪstəˈfiːlɪən) *adj*

mephitic (mɪˈfɪtɪk) *or* **mephitical** *adj* **1** poisonous; foul. **2** foul-smelling; putrid. [C17: from Late Latin *mephīticus* pestilential. See MEPHITIS] ▸ **meˈphitically** *adv*

mephitis (mɪˈfaɪtɪs) *n* **1** a foul or poisonous stench. **2** a poisonous or unpleasant gas emitted from the earth. [C18: from Latin: unwholesome smell, origin obscure]

meprobamate (məˈprəʊbəˌmeɪt, ˌmɛprəʊˈbæmeɪt) *n* a white bitter powder used as a tranquillizer. Formula: $C_9H_{18}N_2O_4$. [ME(THYL) + PRO(PYL + CAR)BAMATE]

mer. *abbrev. for* meridian.

-mer *suffix forming nouns. Chem.* denoting a substance of a particular class: *monomer; polymer.* [from Greek *meros* part]

Merano (məˈrɑːnəʊ; *Italian* meˈraːno) *n* a town and resort in NE Italy, in the foothills of the central Alps: capital of the Tyrol (12th–15th century); under Austrian rule until 1919. Pop.: 33 638 (1993 est.). German name: **Meran** (meˈraːn).

meranti (mɪˈræntɪ) *n* wood from any of several Malaysian trees of the dipterocarpaceous genus *Shorea.* [C18: from Malay]

merbromin (məˈbrəʊmɪn) *n* a green iridescent crystalline compound that forms a red solution in water: used in medicine as an antiseptic. Formula: $C_{20}H_8Br_2HgNa_2O_6$. See also **Mercurochrome.** [C20: blend of MERCURIC + *dibromofluorescein*]

Merca (ˈmɛəkə) *n* a port in S Somalia on the Indian Ocean. Pop.: 100 000 (1987 est.).

Mercalli scale (mɜːˈkælɪ) *n* a 12-point scale for expressing the intensity of an earthquake, ranging from 1 (not felt, except by few under favourable circumstances) to 12 (total destruction). Compare **Richter scale.** See also **intensity** (sense 4). [C20: named after Giuseppe *Mercalli* (1850–1914), Italian volcanologist and seismologist]

mercantile (ˈmɜːkənˌtaɪl) *adj* **1** of, relating to, or characteristic of trade or traders; commercial. **2** of or relating to mercantilism. [C17: from French, from Italian, from *mercante* MERCHANT]

mercantile agency *n* an enterprise that collects and supplies information about the financial credit standing of individuals and enterprises.

mercantile paper *n* another name for **commercial paper.**

mercantilism (ˈmɜːkəntɪˌlɪzəm) *n* **1** Also called: **mercantile system.** *Economics.* a theory prevalent in Europe during the 17th and 18th centuries asserting that the wealth of a nation depends on its possession of precious metals and therefore that the government of a nation must maximize the foreign trade surplus, and foster national commercial interests, a merchant marine, the establishment of colonies, etc. **2** a rare word for **commercialism** (sense 1). ▸ ˈ**mercanˌtilist** *n, adj*

mercaptan (mɜːˈkæptæn) *n* another name (not in technical usage) for **thiol.** [C19: from German, from Medieval Latin *mercurium captans,* literally: seizing quicksilver]

mercaptide (məˈkæptaɪd, mɜː-) *n* a salt of a mercaptan, containing the ion RS^-, where R is an alkyl or aryl group.

mercapto- (mɜːˈkæptəʊ) *combining form.* (in chemical compounds) indicating the presence of an HS- group.

mercaptopurine (məˌkæptəˈpjʊəriːn) *n* a drug used in the treatment of leukaemia. Formula: $C_5H_4N_4S$.

mercat (ˈmɛrkət) *n* a Scot. word for **market.**

Mercator (mɜːˈkeɪtə) *n* **Gerardus** (dʒəˈrɑːdəs). Latinized name of *Gerhard Kremer.* 1512–94, Flemish cartographer and mathematician.

Mercator projection *n* an orthomorphic map projection on which parallels and meridians form a rectangular grid, scale being exaggerated with increasing distance from the equator. Also called: **Mercator's projection.** [C17: named after G. MERCATOR]

mercenary (ˈmɜːsɪnərɪ, -sɪnrɪ) *adj* **1** influenced by greed or desire for gain. **2** of or relating to a mercenary or mercenaries. ◆ *n, pl* **-naries. 3** a man hired to fight for a foreign army, etc. **4** *Rare.* any person who works solely for pay.

[C16: from Latin *mercēnārius,* from *mercēs* wages] ▸ **'mercenarily** *adv* ▸ **'mercenariness** *n*

mercer ('mɜːsə) *n Brit.* a dealer in textile fabrics and fine cloth. [C13: from Old French *mercier* dealer, from Vulgar Latin *merciārius* (unattested), from Latin *merx* goods, wares] ▸ **'mercery** *n*

Mercer ('mɜːsə) *n* **Johnny,** full name *John Herndon Mercer.* 1909–76, U.S. popular songwriter and singer. His most popular songs include "Blues in the Night" (1941) and "Moon River" (1961).

mercerize *or* **mercerise** ('mɜːsəˌraɪz) *vb (tr)* to treat (cotton yarn) with an alkali to increase its strength and reception to dye and impart a lustrous silky appearance. [C19: named after John *Mercer* (1791–1866), English maker of textiles] ▸ **ˌmerceri'zation** *or* **ˌmerceri'sation** *n*

merchandise *n* ('mɜːtʃənˌdaɪs, -ˌdaɪz). **1** commercial goods; commodities. ◆ *vb* ('mɜːtʃənˌdaɪz). **2** to engage in the commercial purchase and sale of (goods or services); trade. [C13: from Old French. See MERCHANT] ▸ **'merchanˌdiser** *n*

merchandising ('mɜːtʃənˌdaɪzɪŋ) *n* **1** the selection and display of goods in a retail outlet. **2** commercial goods, esp. ones issued to exploit the popularity of a pop group, sporting event, etc.

merchant ('mɜːtʃənt) *n* **1** a person engaged in the purchase and sale of commodities for profit, esp. on international markets; trader. **2** *Chiefly U.S. and Canadian.* a person engaged in retail trade. **3** (esp. in historical contexts) any trader. **4** *Derogatory.* a person dealing or involved in something undesirable: *a gossip merchant.* **5** *(modifier)* **5a** of the merchant navy: *a merchant sailor.* **5b** of or concerned with trade: *a merchant ship.* ◆ *vb* **6** *(tr)* to conduct trade in; deal in. [C13: from Old French, probably from Vulgar Latin *mercātāre* (unattested), from Latin *mercārī* to trade, from *merx* goods, wares] ▸ **'merchant-ˌlike** *adj*

Merchant ('mɜːtʃənt) *n* **Ismail** ('ɪzmeɪəl). born 1936, Indian film producer, noted for his collaboration with James Ivory on such films as *Shakespeare Wallah* (1965), *The Europeans* (1979), *A Room with a View* (1986), *Howard's End* (1992), and *The Remains of the Day* (1993).

merchantable ('mɜːtʃəntəbᵊl) *adj* suitable for trading.

merchant bank *n* (in Britain) a financial institution engaged primarily in accepting foreign bills, advising companies on flotations and takeovers, underwriting new issues, hire-purchase finance, making long-term loans to companies, and managing investment portfolios, funds, and trusts. ▸ **merchant banker** *n*

merchantman ('mɜːtʃəntmən) *n, pl* **-men.** a merchant ship.

merchant navy *or* **marine** *n* the ships or crew engaged in a nation's commercial shipping.

merchant prince *n* a very wealthy merchant.

merchet ('mɜːtʃɪt) *n* (in feudal England) a fine paid by a tenant, esp. a villein, to his lord for allowing the marriage of his daughter. [C13: from Anglo-French, literally: MARKET]

Mercia ('mɜːʃɪə) *n* a kingdom and earldom of central and S England during the Anglo-Saxon period that reached its height under King Offa (757–96).

Mercian ('mɜːʃɪən) *adj* **1** of or relating to Mercia or the dialect spoken there. ◆ *n* **2** the dialect of Old and Middle English spoken in the Midlands of England south of the River Humber. See also **Anglian, Northumbrian.**

merciful ('mɜːsɪful) *adj* showing or giving mercy; compassionate. ▸ **'mercifully** *adv* ▸ **'mercifulness** *n*

merciless ('mɜːsɪlɪs) *adj* without mercy; pitiless, cruel, or heartless. ▸ **'mercilessly** *adv* ▸ **'mercilessness** *n*

Merckx ('mɛrks) *n* **Eddy.** born 1945, Belgian professional cyclist: five times winner of the Tour de France, including four consecutive victories (1969–72).

Mercouri (mɜː'kuːrɪ) *n* **Melina** (mə'liːnə). 1925–94, Greek actress and politician: her films include *Never on Sunday* (1960); minister of culture (1981–85 and 1993–94).

mercurate ('mɜːkjuˌreɪt) *vb* **1** *(tr)* to treat or mix with mercury. **2** to undergo or cause to undergo a chemical reaction in which a mercury atom is added to a compound. ▸ **ˌmercu'ration** *n*

mercurial (mɜː'kjuərɪəl) *adj* **1** of, like, containing, or relating to mercury. **2** volatile; lively: *a mercurial temperament.* **3** *(sometimes cap.)* of, like, or relating to the god or the planet Mercury. ◆ *n* **4** *Med.* any salt of mercury for use as a medicine. [C14: from Latin *mercuriālis*] ▸ **mer'curially** *adv* ▸ **mer'curialness** *or* **merˌcuri'ality** *n*

mercurialism (mɜː'kjuərɪəˌlɪzᵊm) *n* poisoning caused by chronic ingestion of mercury.

mercurialize *or* **mercurialise** (mɜː'kjuərɪəˌlaɪz) *vb (tr)* **1** to make mercurial. **2** to treat with mercury or a mercury compound. ▸ **merˌcuriali'zation** *or* **merˌcuriali'sation** *n*

mercuric (mɜː'kjuərɪk) *adj* of or containing mercury in the divalent state; denoting a mercury(II) compound.

mercuric chloride *n* a white poisonous soluble crystalline substance used as a pesticide, antiseptic, and preservative for wood. Formula: $HgCl_2$. Systematic name: **mercury(II) chloride.** Also called: **bichloride of mercury, corrosive sublimate.**

mercuric oxide *n* a soluble poisonous substance existing in red and yellow powdered forms: used as pigments. Formula: HgO. Systematic name: **mercury(II) oxide.**

mercuric sulphide *n* a compound of mercury, usually existing as a black solid (**metacinnabarite**) or a red solid (**cinnabar** or **vermilion**), which is used as a pigment. Formula: HgS. Systematic name: **mercury(II) sulphide.**

Mercurochrome (mə'kjuərəˌkrəum) *n Trademark.* a solution of merbromin, used as topical antibacterial agent.

mercurous ('mɜːkjurəs) *adj* of or containing mercury in the monovalent state; denoting a mercury(I) compound. Mercurous salts contain the divalent ion Hg_2^{2+}.

mercurous chloride *n* a white tasteless insoluble powder used as a fungicide and formerly as a medical antiseptic, cathartic, and diuretic. Formula: Hg_2Cl_2. Systematic name: **mercury(I) chloride.** Also called: **calomel.**

mercury ('mɜːkjurɪ) *n, pl* **-ries. 1** Also called: **quicksilver, hydrargyrum.** a heavy silvery-white toxic liquid metallic element occurring principally in cinnabar: used in thermometers, barometers, mercury-vapour lamps, and dental amalgams. Symbol: Hg; atomic no.: 80; atomic wt.: 200.59; valency: 1 or 2; relative density: 13.546; melting pt.: –38.842°C; boiling pt.: 357°C. **2** any plant of the euphorbiaceous genus *Mercurialis.* See **dog's mercury. 3** *Archaic.* a messenger or courier. [C14: from Latin *Mercurius* messenger of Jupiter, god of commerce; related to *merx* merchandise]

Mercury[1] ('mɜːkjurɪ) *n Roman myth.* the messenger of the gods. Greek counterpart: **Hermes.**

Mercury[2] ('mɜːkjurɪ) *n* the second smallest planet and the nearest to the sun. Mean distance from sun: 57.9 million km; period of revolution around sun: 88 days; period of axial rotation: 59 days; diameter and mass: 38 and 5.4 per cent that of earth respectively.

mercury arc *n* **a** an electric discharge through ionized mercury vapour, producing a brilliant bluish-green light containing ultraviolet radiation. **b** *(as modifier): a mercury-arc rectifier.* See also **ignitron.**

mercury chloride *n* See **mercurous chloride, mercuric chloride.**

mercury switch *n Electrical engineering.* a switch in which a circuit is completed between two terminals by liquid mercury when the switch is tilted.

mercury-vapour lamp *n* a lamp in which an electric discharge through a low pressure of mercury vapour is used to produce a greenish-blue light. It is used for street lighting and is also a source of ultraviolet radiation.

mercy ('mɜːsɪ) *n, pl* **-cies. 1** compassionate treatment of or attitude towards an offender, adversary, etc., who is in one's power or care; clemency; pity. **2** the power to show mercy: *to throw oneself on someone's mercy.* **3** a relieving or welcome occurrence or state of affairs: *his death was a mercy after weeks of pain.* **4 at the mercy of.** in the power of. [C12: from Old French, from Latin *mercēs* wages, recompense, price, from *merx* goods]

mercy flight *n* an aircraft flight to bring a seriously ill or injured person to hospital from an isolated community.

mercy killing *n* another term for **euthanasia.**

mercy seat *n* **1** *Old Testament.* the gold platform covering the Ark of the Covenant and regarded as the throne of God where he accepted sacrifices and gave commandments (Exodus 25:17, 22). **2** *Christianity.* the throne of God.

mere[1] (mɪə) *adj superlative* **merest.** being nothing more than something specified: *she is a mere child.* [C15: from Latin *merus* pure, unmixed] ▸ **'merely** *adv*

mere[2] (mɪə) *n* **1** *Dialect or archaic.* a lake or marsh. **2** *Obsolete.* the sea or an inlet of it. [Old English *mere* sea, lake; related to Old Saxon *meri* sea, Old Norse *marr,* Old High German *mari;* compare Latin *mare*]

mere[3] (mɪə) *n Archaic.* a boundary or boundary marker. [Old English *gemǣre*]

mere[4] ('mɛrɪ) *n N.Z.* a short flat striking weapon. [Maori]

-mere *n combining form.* indicating a part or division: *blastomere.* [from Greek *meros* part, portion] ▸ **-meric** *adj combining form.*

Meredith ('mɛrɪdɪθ) *n* **George.** 1828–1909, English novelist and poet. His works, notable for their social satire and analysis of character, include the novels *Beauchamp's Career* (1876) and *The Egoist* (1879) and the long tragic poem *Modern Love* (1862).

merengue (mə'rɛŋgeɪ) *n* **1** a type of lively dance music originating in the Dominican Republic, which combines African and Spanish elements. **2** a Caribbean dance in duple time with syncopated rhythm performed to such music. [from American Spanish and Haitian Creole]

mereology (ˌmiːrɪ'ɒlədʒɪ) *n* the formal study of the logical properties of the relation of part and whole. [C20: via French from Greek *meros* part + -LOGY] ▸ **ˌmereo'logical** *adj*

meretricious (ˌmɛrɪ'trɪʃəs) *adj* **1** superficially or garishly attractive. **2** insincere: *meretricious praise.* **3** *Archaic.* of, like, or relating to a prostitute. [C17: from Latin *merētrīcius,* from *merētrix* prostitute, from *merēre* to earn money] ▸ **ˌmere'triciously** *adv* ▸ **ˌmere'triciousness** *n*

merganser (mɜː'gænsə) *n, pl* **-sers** *or* **-ser.** any of several typically crested large marine diving ducks of the genus *Mergus,* having a long slender hooked bill with serrated edges. Also called: **sawbill.** See also **goosander.** [C18: from New Latin, from Latin *mergus* waterfowl, from *mergere* to plunge + *anser* goose]

merge (mɜːdʒ) *vb* **1** to meet and join or cause to meet and join. **2** to blend or cause to blend; fuse. [C17: from Latin *mergere* to plunge] ▸ **'mergence** *n*

merger ('mɜːdʒə) *n* **1** *Commerce.* the combination of two or more companies, either by the creation of a new organization or by absorption by one of the others. Often called (Brit.): **amalgamation. 2** *Law.* the extinguishment of an estate, interest, contract, right, offence, etc., by its absorption into a greater one. **3** the act of merging or the state of being merged.

Mergui Archipelago (mɜː'gwiː) *n* a group of over 200 islands in the Andaman Sea, off the Tenasserim coast of S Myanmar: mountainous and forested.

Meriç (mə'riːtʃ) *n* the Turkish name for the **Maritsa.**

Mérida (*Spanish* 'meriða) *n* **1** a city in SE Mexico, capital of Yucatán state: founded in 1542 on the site of the ancient Mayan city of T'ho; centre of the henequen industry; university. Pop.: 523 422 (1990). **2** a city in W Venezuela: founded in 1558 by Spanish conquistadores; University of Los Andes (1785). Pop.: 167 990 (1991). **3** a market town in W Spain, in Estremadura, on the Guadiana River: founded in 25 B.C.; became the capital of Lusitania and one of the chief cities of Iberia. Pop.: 49 830 (1991). Latin name: **Au'gusta E'merita.**

meridian (mə'rɪdɪən) *n* **1a** one of the imaginary lines joining the north and south poles at right angles to the equator, designated by degrees of longitude from 0° at Greenwich to 180°. **1b** the great circle running through both poles. See **prime meridian. 2** *Astronomy.* **2a** the great circle on the celestial sphere passing through the north and south celestial poles and the zenith and nadir of the observer. **2b** (*as modifier*): *a meridian instrument.* **3** Also called: **meridian section.** *Maths.* a section of a surface of revolution, such as a paraboloid, that contains the axis of revolution. **4** the peak; zenith: *the meridian of his achievements.* **5** (in acupuncture, etc.) any of the channels through which vital energy is believed to circulate round the body. **6** *Obsolete.* noon. ♦ *adj* **7** along or relating to a meridian. **8** of or happening at noon. **9** relating to the peak of something. [C14: from Latin *merīdiānus* of midday, from *merīdiēs* midday, from *medius* MID[1] + *diēs* day]

meridian circle *n* an instrument used in astronomy for determining the declination and right ascension of stars. It consists of a telescope attached to a graduated circle.

meridional (məˈrɪdɪənᵊl) *adj* **1** along, relating to, or resembling a meridian. **2** characteristic of or located in the south, esp. of Europe. ♦ *n* **3** an inhabitant of the south, esp. of France. [C14: from Late Latin *merīdiōnālis* southern; see MERIDIAN; for form, compare *septentriōnālis* SEPTENTRIONAL] ► **meˈridionally** *adv*

Mérimée (*French* merime) *n* **Prosper** (prɔspɛr). 1803–70, French novelist, dramatist, and short-story writer, noted particularly for his short novels *Colomba* (1840) and *Carmen* (1845), on which Bizet's opera was based.

mering (ˈmɪərɪŋ) *n Chiefly Irish.* **a** another word for **mere**[3]. **b** (*as modifier*): *the mering wall.* [C16: from MERE[3]]

meringue (məˈræŋ) *n* **1** stiffly beaten egg whites mixed with sugar and baked, often as a topping for pies, cakes, etc. **2** a small cake or shell of this mixture, often filled with cream. [C18: from French, origin obscure]

merino (məˈriːnəʊ) *n, pl* **-nos. 1** a breed of sheep, originating in Spain. **2** the long fine wool of this sheep. **3** the yarn made from this wool, often mixed with cotton. **4 pure merino.** *Austral. informal.* **4a** *History.* a free settler rather than a convict. **4b** an affluent and socially prominent person. **4c** (*as modifier*): *a pure merino cricketer.* ♦ *adj* **5** made from merino wool. [C18: from Spanish, origin uncertain]

Merionethshire (ˌmɛrɪˈɒnɪθˌʃɪə, -ʃə) *n* (until 1974) a county of N Wales, now part of Gwynedd.

meristem (ˈmɛrɪˌstɛm) *n* a plant tissue responsible for growth, whose cells divide and differentiate to form the tissues and organs of the plant. Meristems occur within the stem (see **cambium**) and leaves and at the tips of stems and roots. [C19: from Greek *meristos* divided, from *merizein* to divide, from *meris* portion] ► **meristematic** (ˌmɛrɪstɪˈmætɪk) *adj*

meristic (məˈrɪstɪk) *adj Biology.* **1** of or relating to the number of organs or parts in an animal or plant body: *meristic variation.* **2** segmented: *meristic worms.*

merit (ˈmɛrɪt) *n* **1** worth or superior quality; excellence: *work of great merit.* **2** (*often pl*) a deserving or commendable quality or act: *judge him on his merits.* **3** *Christianity.* spiritual credit granted or received for good works. **4** the fact or state of deserving; desert. **5** an obsolete word for **reward.** ♦ *vb* **-its, -iting, -ited. 6** (*tr*) to be worthy of; deserve: *he merits promotion.* ♦ See also **merits.** [C13: via Old French from Latin *meritum* reward, desert, from *merēre* to deserve] ► **ˈmerited** *adj* ► **ˈmeritless** *adj*

meritocracy (ˌmɛrɪˈtɒkrəsɪ) *n, pl* **-cies. 1** rule by persons chosen not because of birth or wealth, but for their superior talents or intellect. **2** the persons constituting such a group. **3** a social system formed on such a basis. ► **ˈmeritocrat** *n* ► **meritocratic** (ˌmɛrɪtəˈkrætɪk) *adj*

meritorious (ˌmɛrɪˈtɔːrɪəs) *adj* praiseworthy; showing merit. [C15: from Latin *meritōrius* earning money] ► **ˌmeriˈtoriously** *adv* ► **ˌmeriˈtoriousness** *n*

merits (ˈmɛrɪts) *pl n* **1** the actual and intrinsic rights and wrongs of an issue, esp. in a law case, as distinct from extraneous matters and technicalities. **2 on its (his, her,** etc.) **merits.** on the intrinsic qualities or virtues.

merit system *n U.S.* the system of employing and promoting civil servants solely on the basis of ability rather than patronage. Compare **spoils system.**

merkin (ˈmɜːkɪn) *n* **1** an artificial hairpiece for the pudendum; a pubic wig. **2** *Obsolete.* the pudendum itself. [C16: of unknown origin]

merle[1] *or* **merl** (mɜːl; *Scot.* mɛrl) *n Scot.* another name for the (European) **blackbird.** [C15: via Old French from Latin *merula*]

merle[2] (mɜːl) *adj* (of a dog, esp. a collie) having a bluish-grey coat with speckles or streaks of black. Often **blue merle.** [C20: from dialect *mirlet, mirly* speckled]

Merleau-Ponty (*French* mɛrlopɔ̃ti) *n* **Maurice** (mɔris). 1908–61, French phenomenological philosopher.

merlin (ˈmɜːlɪn) *n* a small falcon, *Falco columbarius,* that has a dark plumage with a black-barred tail: used in falconry. See also **pigeon hawk.** [C14: from Old French *esmerillon,* from *esmeril,* of Germanic origin]

Merlin (ˈmɜːlɪn) *n* (in Arthurian legend) a wizard and counsellor to King Arthur eternally imprisoned in a tree by a woman to whom he revealed his secret craft.

merlon (ˈmɜːlən) *n Fortifications.* the solid upright section in a crenellated battlement. [C18: from French, from Italian *merlone,* from *merlo* battlement]

Merlot (ˈmɜːləʊ) *n* (*sometimes not cap.*) **1** a black grape grown in France, Hungary, Bulgaria, etc., used, often in a blend, for making wine. **2** any of various wines made from this grape. [from French *merlot,* literally: young blackbird, diminutive of *merle* MERLE[1], probably alluding to the colour of the grape]

mermaid (ˈmɜːˌmeɪd) *n* an imaginary sea creature fabled to have a woman's head and upper body and a fish's tail. [C14: from *mere* lake, inlet + MAID]

mermaid's purse *n* another name for **sea purse.**

merman (ˈmɜːˌmæn) *n, pl* **-men.** a male counterpart of the mermaid. [C17: see MERMAID]

mero- *combining form.* part or partial: *merocrine.* [from Greek *meros* part, share]

meroblastic (ˌmɛrəʊˈblæstɪk) *adj Embryol.* of or showing cleavage of only the nonyolky part of the zygote, as in birds' eggs. Compare **holoblastic.** ► **ˌmeroˈblastically** *adv*

merocrine (ˈmɛrəˌkraɪn, -krɪn) *adj* (of the secretion of glands) characterized by formation of the product without undergoing disintegration. Compare **holocrine, apocrine.** [C20: from MERO- + Greek *krinein* to separate]

Meroë (ˈmɛrəʊˌiː) *n* an ancient city in N Sudan, on the Nile; capital of a kingdom that flourished from about 700 B.C. to about 350 A.D.

meroplankton (ˌmɛrəʊˈplæŋktən) *n* plankton consisting of organisms at a certain stage of their life cycles, esp. larvae, the other stages not being spent as part of the plankton community. Compare **holoplankton.**

-merous *adj combining form.* (in biology) having a certain number or kind of parts: *dimerous.* [from Greek *meros* part, division]

Merovingian (ˌmɛrəʊˈvɪndʒɪən) *adj* **1** of or relating to a Frankish dynasty founded by Clovis I, which ruled Gaul and W Germany from about 500 to 751 A.D. ♦ *n* **2** a member or supporter of this dynasty. [C17: from French, from Medieval Latin *Merovingi* offspring of *Merovaeus,* Latin form of *Merowig,* traditional founder of the line]

merozoite (ˌmɛrəʊˈzəʊaɪt) *n* any of the cells formed by fission of a schizont during the life cycle of sporozoan protozoans, such as the malaria parasite. Compare **trophozoite.** [C20: from MERO- + ZO(O) + -ITE[1]]

merriment (ˈmɛrɪmənt) *n* gaiety, fun, or mirth.

merry (ˈmɛrɪ) *adj* **-rier, -riest. 1** cheerful; jolly. **2** very funny; hilarious. **3** *Brit. informal.* slightly drunk. **4** *Archaic.* delightful. **5 make merry.** to revel; be festive. **6 play merry hell with.** *Informal.* to disturb greatly; disrupt. [Old English *merige* agreeable] ► **ˈmerrily** *adv* ► **ˈmerriness** *n*

merry-andrew *n* a joker, clown, or buffoon. [C17: original reference of *Andrew* unexplained]

merry dancers *pl n Scot.* the aurora borealis.

merry-go-round *n* **1** another name for **roundabout** (sense 1). **2** a whirl of activity or events: *the merry-go-round of the fashion world.*

merrymaking (ˈmɛrɪˌmeɪkɪŋ) *n* fun, revelry, or festivity. ► **ˈmerryˌmaker** *n*

merry men *pl n Facetious.* a person's assistants or followers. [C19: originally, the companions of a knight, outlaw, etc.]

merrythought (ˈmɛrɪˌθɔːt) *n Brit.* a less common word for **wishbone.**

merse (mɜːs; *Scot.* mɛrs) *n Scot.* **1** low level ground by a river or shore, often alluvial and fertile. **2** a marsh. [Old English *merse* marsh]

Merse (mɜːs; *Scot.* mɛrs) *n* **the.** a fertile lowland area of SE Scotland, in Scottish Borders, north of the Tweed.

Merseburg (*German* ˈmɛrzəburk) *n* a city in E Germany, on the Saale River, in Saxony-Anhalt: residence of the dukes of Saxe-Merseburg (1656–1738); chemical industry. Pop.: 46 250 (1989 est.).

Mersey (ˈmɜːzɪ) *n* a river in W England, rising in N Derbyshire and flowing northwest and west to the Irish Sea through a large estuary on which is situated the port of Liverpool. Length: about 112 km (70 miles).

Mersey beat *n* **a** the characteristic pop music of the Beatles and other groups from Liverpool in the 1960s. **b** (*as modifier*): *the Merseybeat years.*

Merseyside (ˈmɜːzɪˌsaɪd) *n* a metropolitan county of NW England, administered since 1986 by the unitary authorities of Sefton, Liverpool, St Helens, Knowsley, and Wirral. Area: 652 sq. km (252 sq. miles).

Mersin (mɛəˈsiːn) *n* a port in S Turkey, on the Mediterranean: oil refinery. Pop.: 523 000 (1994 est.). Also called: **Içel.**

Merthyr Tydfil (ˈmɜːθə ˈtɪdvɪl) *n* **1** a town in SE Wales, in Merthyr Tydfil county borough: formerly an important centre for the mining industry. Pop.: 39 482 (1991). **2** a county borough in SE Wales, created from part of N Mid Glamorgan in 1996. Pop.: 59 500 (1996 est.). Area: 111 sq. km (43 sq. miles).

Merton[1] (ˈmɜːtᵊn) *n* a borough in SW Greater London. Pop.: 177 200 (1994 est.). Area: 38 sq. km (15 sq. miles).

Merton[2] (ˈmɜːtᵊn) *n* **Thomas (Feverel).** 1915–68, U.S. writer, monk, and mystic; noted esp. for his autobiography *The Seven Storey Mountain* (1948).

mes- *combining form.* a variant of **meso-** before a vowel: *mesarch; mesencephalon; mesenteron.*

mesa (ˈmeɪsə) *n* a flat tableland with steep edges, common in the southwestern U.S. [from Spanish: table]

mésalliance (meˈzælɪəns; *French* mezaljɑ̃s) *n* marriage with a person of lower social status. [C18: from French: MISALLIANCE]

mesarch (ˈmɛsɑːk) *adj Botany.* (of a xylem strand) having the first-formed xylem surrounded by that formed later, as in fern stems. Compare **exarch**[2], **endarch.** [C19: from MES(O)- + Greek *arkhē* beginning]

Mesa Verde (ˈmeɪsə ˈvɜːd) *n* a high plateau in SW Colorado: remains of numerous prehistoric cliff dwellings, inhabited by the Pueblo Indians.

mescal (mɛˈskæl) *n* **1** Also called: **peyote.** a spineless globe-shaped cactus, *Lophophora williamsii,* of Mexico and the southwestern U.S. Its button-like tubercles (**mescal buttons**) contain mescaline and are chewed by certain Indian tribes for their hallucinogenic effects. **2** a colourless alcoholic spirit distilled from the fermented juice of certain agave plants. [C19: from American Spanish, from Nahuatl *mexcalli* the liquor, from *metl* MAGUEY + *ixcalli* stew]

mescaline *or* **mescalin** (ˈmɛskəˌliːn, -lɪn) *n* a hallucinogenic drug derived from mescal buttons. Formula: $C_{11}H_{17}NO_3$.

mesdames (ˈmeɪˌdæm; *French* medam) *n* the plural of **madame** and **madam** (sense 1).

mesdemoiselles (ˌmeɪdmwəˈzɛl; *French* medmwazɛl) *n* the plural of **mademoiselle.**

meseems (mɪˈsiːmz) *vb past* **meseemed.** (*tr; takes a clause as object*) *Archaic.* it seems to me.

mesembryanthemum (mɪzˌɛmbrɪˈænθɪməm) *n* any plant of a South African genus (*Mesembryanthemum*) of succulent-leaved prostrate or erect plants widely grown in gardens and greenhouses: family *Aizoaceae.* See **fig marigold, ice plant, Livingstone daisy.** [C18: New Latin, from Greek *mesēmbria* noon + *anthemon* flower]

mesencephalon (ˌmɛsɛnˈsɛfəˌlɒn) *n* the part of the brain that develops from the middle portion of the embryonic neural tube. Compare **prosencephalon, rhombencephalon.** Nontechnical name: **midbrain.** ▸ **mesencephalic** (ˌmɛsɛnsɪˈfælɪk) *adj*

mesenchyme (ˈmɛsɛŋˌkaɪm) *n Embryol.* the part of the mesoderm that develops into connective tissue, cartilage, lymph, blood, etc. [C19: New Latin, from MESO- + -ENCHYMA] ▸ **mesenchymal** (mɛsˈɛŋkɪməl) *or* **mesenchymatous** (ˌmɛsɛŋˈkɪmətəs) *adj*

mesenteritis (mɛsˌɛntəˈraɪtɪs) *n* inflammation of the mesentery.

mesenteron (mɛsˈɛntəˌrɒn) *n, pl* **-tera** (-tərə). a former name for **midgut** (sense 1). ▸ **mesˌenterˈonic** *adj*

mesentery (ˈmɛsəntərɪ, ˈmɛz-) *n, pl* **-teries.** the double layer of peritoneum that is attached to the back wall of the abdominal cavity and supports most of the small intestine. [C16: from New Latin *mesenterium;* see MESO- + ENTERON] ▸ **ˌmesenˈteric** *adj*

mesh (mɛʃ) *n* **1** a network; net. **2** an open space between the strands of a network. **3** (*often pl*) the strands surrounding these spaces. **4** anything that ensnares, or holds like a net: *the mesh of the secret police.* **5** the engagement of teeth on interacting gearwheels: *the gears are in mesh.* **6** a measure of spacing of the strands of a mesh or grid, expressed as the distance between strands for coarse meshes or a number of strands per unit length for fine meshes. ◆ *vb* **7** to entangle or become entangled. **8** (of gear teeth) to engage or cause to engage. **9** (*intr;* often foll. by *with*) to coordinate (with): *to mesh with a policy.* **10** to work or cause to work in harmony. [C16: probably from Dutch *maesche;* related to Old English *masc,* Old High German *masca*] ▸ **ˈmeshy** *adj*

Meshach (ˈmiːʃæk) *n Old Testament.* one of Daniel's three companions who, together with Shadrach and Abednego, was miraculously saved from destruction in Nebuchadnezzar's fiery furnace (Daniel 3:12-30).

mesh connection *n Electrical engineering.* (in a polyphase system) an arrangement in which the end of each phase is connected to the beginning of the next, forming a ring, each junction being connected to a terminal. See also **delta connection, star connection.**

Meshed (mɛˈʃɛd) *n* a variant of **Mashhad.**

meshuga (mɪˈʃugə) *adj Yiddish.* crazy. [from Hebrew]

mesiad (ˈmiːzɪæd) *adj Anatomy, zoology.* relating to or situated at the middle or centre.

mesial (ˈmiːzɪəl) *adj Anatomy.* another word for **medial** (sense 1). [C19: from MESO- + -IAL] ▸ **ˈmesially** *adv*

mesic (ˈmiːzɪk) *adj* **1** of, relating to, or growing in conditions of medium water supply: *mesic plants.* **2** of or relating to a meson. ▸ **ˈmesically** *adv*

mesitylene (mɪˈsɪtɪˌliːn, ˈmɛsɪtɪˌliːn) *n* a colourless liquid that occurs in crude petroleum; 1,3,5-trimethylbenzene. Formula: $C_6H_3(CH_3)_3$. [C19: from *mesityl,* from *mesite,* from New Latin *mesita,* from Greek *mesitēs* mediator + -ENE]

mesmerism (ˈmɛzməˌrɪzəm) *n Psychol.* **1** a hypnotic state induced by the operator's imposition of his will on that of the patient. **2** an early doctrine concerning this. [C19: named after F. A. *Mesmer* (1734–1815), Austrian physician] ▸ **mesmeric** (mɛzˈmɛrɪk) *adj* ▸ **mesˈmerically** *adv* ▸ **ˈmesmerist** *n*

mesmerize *or* **mesmerise** (ˈmɛzməˌraɪz) *vb* (*tr*) **1** a former word for **hypnotize. 2** to hold (someone) as if spellbound. ▸ **ˌmesmeriˈzation** *or* **ˌmesmeriˈsation** *n* ▸ **ˈmesmerˌizer** *or* **ˈmesmerˌiser** *n*

mesnalty (ˈmiːnəltɪ) *n, pl* **-ties.** *History.* the lands of a mesne lord. [C16: from legal French, from MESNE]

mesne (miːn) *adj Law.* **1** intermediate or intervening: used esp. of any assignment of property before the last: *a mesne assignment.* **2 mesne profits.** rents or profits accruing during the rightful owner's exclusion from his land. [C15: from legal French *meien* in the middle, MEAN[3]]

mesne lord *n* (in feudal society) a lord who held land from a superior lord and kept his own tenants on it.

meso- *or before a vowel* **mes-** *combining form.* middle or intermediate: *mesomorph.* [from Greek *misos* middle]

Mesoamerica *or* **Meso-America** (ˌmɛsəʊəˈmɛrɪkə) *n* another name for **Central America.** ▸ **ˌMesoaˈmerican** *or* **ˌMeso-Aˈmerican** *adj, n*

mesobenthos (ˌmɛzəˈbɛnθɒs, ˌmɛsə-) *n* flora and fauna living at the bottom of seas 182 to 914 metres deep. [from MESO- + Greek *benthos* depth of the sea]

mesoblast (ˈmɛsəʊˌblæst) *n* another name for **mesoderm.** ▸ **ˌmesoˈblastic** *adj*

mesocarp (ˈmɛsəʊˌkɑːp) *n* the middle layer of the pericarp of a fruit, such as the flesh of a peach.

mesocephalic (ˌmɛsəʊsɪˈfælɪk) *Anatomy.* ◆ *adj* **1** having a medium-sized head, esp. one with a cephalic index between 75 and 80. ◆ *n* **2** an individual with such a head. ◆ Compare **brachycephalic, dolichocephalic.** ▸ **mesocephaly** (ˌmɛsəʊˈsɛfəlɪ) *n*

mesocratic (ˌmɛsəˈkrætɪk) *adj* (of igneous rocks) containing 30–60 per cent of ferromagnesian minerals. [C20: from MESO- + -CRAT, with allusion to the moderately dark colour of the rock. Compare LEUCOCRATIC]

mesoderm (ˈmɛsəʊˌdɜːm) *n* the middle germ layer of an animal embryo, giving rise to muscle, blood, bone, connective tissue, etc. See also **ectoderm, endoderm.** ▸ **ˌmesoˈdermal** *or* **ˌmesoˈdermic** *adj*

mesogastrium (ˌmɛsəʊˈgæstrɪəm) *n* the mesentery supporting the embryonic stomach. ▸ **ˌmesoˈgastric** *adj*

mesoglea *or* **mesogloea** (ˌmɛsəʊˈgliːə) *n* the gelatinous material between the outer and inner cellular layers of jellyfish and other coelenterates. [C19: New Latin, from MESO- + Greek *gloia* glue]

mesognathous (mɪˈsɒgnəθəs) *adj Anthropol.* having slightly projecting jaws. ▸ **meˈsognathism** *or* **meˈsognathy** *n*

mesokurtic (ˌmɛsəʊˈkɜːtɪk) *adj Statistics.* (of a distribution) having kurtosis $B_2 = 3$, concentrated around its mean like a normal distribution. Compare **leptokurtic, platykurtic.** [C20: from MESO- + Greek *kurtos* arched, bulging + -IC]

Mesolithic (ˌmɛsəʊˈlɪθɪk) *n* **1** the period between the Palaeolithic and the Neolithic, in Europe from about 12 000 to 3000 B.C., characterized by the appearance of microliths. ◆ *adj* **2** of or relating to the Mesolithic.

Mesolonghi (ˌmɛsəˈlɔːŋgɪ) *n* a variant of **Missolonghi.**

Mesolóngion (ˌmɛsəˈlɒŋgɪˌɒn) *n* transliteration of the Modern Greek name for **Missolonghi.**

mesomorph (ˈmɛsəʊˌmɔːf) *n* a person with a muscular body build: said to be correlated with somatotonia. Compare **ectomorph, endomorph** (sense 1).

mesomorphic (ˌmɛsəʊˈmɔːfɪk) *adj also* **mesomorphous. 1** *Chem.* existing in or concerned with an intermediate state of matter between a true liquid and a true solid. See also **liquid crystal, smectic, nematic. 2** relating to or being a mesomorph. ▸ **ˌmesoˈmorphism** *n* ▸ **ˈmesoˌmorphy** *n*

meson (ˈmiːzɒn) *n* any of a group of elementary particles, such as a pion or kaon, that has a rest mass between those of an electron and a proton, and an integral spin. They are responsible for the force between nucleons in the atomic nucleus. Former name: **mesotron.** See also **muon.** [C20: from MESO- + -ON] ▸ **meˈsonic** *or* **ˈmesic** *adj*

mesonephros (ˌmɛsəʊˈnɛfrɒs) *n* the middle part of the embryonic kidney in vertebrates, becoming the adult kidney in fishes and amphibians and the epididymis in reptiles, birds, and mammals. See also **pronephros, metanephros.** [C19: New Latin, from MESO- + Greek *nephros* kidney] ▸ **ˌmesoˈnephric** *adj*

mesopause (ˈmɛsəʊˌpɔːz) *n Meteorol.* the zone of minimum temperature between the mesosphere and the thermosphere.

mesopelagic (ˌmɛsəʊpəˈlædʒɪk) *adj* of, relating to, or inhabiting the intermediate depths of the ocean between approximately 100 and 1000 metres.

mesophilic (ˌmɛsəʊˈfɪlɪk) *adj Biology.* (esp. of bacteria) having an ideal growth temperature of 20–45°C. ▸ **mesophile** (ˈmɛsəʊˌfaɪl) *n*

mesophyll (ˈmɛsəʊˌfɪl) *n* the soft chlorophyll-containing tissue of a leaf between the upper and lower layers of epidermis: involved in photosynthesis. ▸ **ˌmesoˈphyllic** *or* **ˌmesoˈphyllous** *adj*

mesophyte (ˈmɛsəʊˌfaɪt) *n* any plant that grows in surroundings receiving an average supply of water. ▸ **mesophytic** (ˌmɛsəʊˈfɪtɪk) *adj*

Mesopotamia (ˌmɛsəpəˈteɪmɪə) *n* a region of SW Asia between the lower and middle reaches of the Tigris and Euphrates rivers: site of several ancient civilizations. [Latin from Greek *mesopotamia* (*khora*) (the land) between rivers] ▸ **ˌMesopoˈtamian** *n, adj*

mesosphere (ˈmɛsəʊˌsfɪə) *n* **1** the atmospheric layer lying between the stratosphere and the thermosphere, characterized by a rapid decrease in temperature with height. **2** the solid part of the earth's mantle lying between the asthenosphere and the core. ▸ **mesospheric** (ˌmɛsəʊˈsfɛrɪk) *adj*

mesothelioma (ˌmɛzəʊˌθiːlɪˈəʊmə) *n, pl* **-mata** (-mətə) *or* **-mas.** a tumour of the epithelium lining the lungs, abdomen, or heart: often associated with exposure to asbestos dust. [C20: from MESOTHELI(UM) + -OMA]

mesothelium (ˌmɛsəʊˈθiːlɪəm) *n, pl* **-liums** *or* **-lia** (-lɪə). epithelium, derived from embryonic mesoderm lining body cavities. [from New Latin, from MESO- + (EPI)THELIUM] ▸ **ˌmesoˈthelial** *adj*

mesothorax (ˌmɛsəʊˈθɔːræks) *n, pl* **-raxes** *or* **-races** (-rəˌsiːz). the middle segment of the thorax of an insect, bearing the second pair of walking legs and the first pair of wings. See also **prothorax, metathorax.** ▸ **mesothoracic** (ˌmɛsəʊθɔːˈræsɪk) *adj*

mesothorium (ˌmɛsəʊˈθɔːrɪəm) *n Physics, obsolete.* either of two radioactive elements. **Mesothorium I** is now called radium-228. **Mesothorium II** is now called actinium-228.

mesotron (ˈmɛsəˌtrɒn) *n* a former name for **meson.**

Mesozoic (ˌmɛsəʊˈzəʊɪk) *adj* **1** of, denoting, or relating to an era of geological time that began 225 000 000 years ago with the Triassic period and lasted about 155 000 000 years until the end of the Cretaceous period. ◆ *n* **2 the.** the Mesozoic era.

mesquite *or* **mesquit** (mɛˈskiːt, ˈmɛskiːt) *n* any small mimosaceous tree of the genus *Prosopis,* esp. the tropical American *P. juliflora,* whose sugary pods (**mesquite beans**) are used as animal fodder. Also called: **algarroba, honey locust, honey mesquite.** [C19: from Mexican Spanish, from Nahuatl *mizquitl*]

mess (mɛs) *n* **1** a state of confusion or untidiness, esp. if dirty or unpleasant: *the house was in a mess.* **2** a chaotic or troublesome state of affairs; muddle: *his life was a mess.* **3** *Informal.* a dirty or untidy person or thing. **4** *Archaic.* a portion of food, esp. soft or semiliquid food. **5** a place where service personnel eat or take recreation: *an officers' mess.* **6** a group of people, usually servicemen, who eat together. **7** the meal so taken. **8 mess of pottage.** a material gain involving the sacrifice of a higher value. ◆ *vb* **9** (*tr;* often foll. by *up*) to muddle or dirty. **10** (*intr*) to make a mess. **11** (*intr*) (often foll. by *with*) to interfere; meddle. **12** (*intr*) (often foll. by *with* or *together*) *Military.* to group together, esp. for eating. [C13: from Old French *mes* dish of food, from Late Latin *missus* course (at table), from Latin *mittere* to send forth, set out]

mess about *or* **around** *vb* (*adv*) **1** (*intr*) to occupy oneself trivially; potter. **2** (when *intr,* often foll. by *with*) to interfere or meddle (with). **3** (*intr;* sometimes foll. by *with*) *Chiefly U.S.* to engage in adultery.

message (ˈmɛsɪdʒ) *n* **1** a communication, usually brief, from one person or group to another. **2** an implicit meaning or moral, as in a work of art. **3** a formal communiqué. **4** an inspired communication of a prophet or religious leader. **5** a mission; errand. **6** (*pl*) *Scot.* shopping: *going for the messages.* **7 get the message.** *Informal.* to understand what is meant. ◆ *vb* **8** (*tr*) to send as a message, esp. to signal (a plan, etc.). [C13: from Old French, from Vulgar Latin *missāticum* (unattested) something sent, from Latin *missus*, past participle of *mittere* to send]

Messager (*French* mɛsaʒe) *n* **André** (**Charles Prosper**) (ɑ̃dre). 1853–1929, French composer and conductor.

message stick *n* a stick bearing carved symbols, carried by a native Australian as identification.

message switching *n Computing.* the maintenance of a telecommunication link between two devices for the duration of a message.

Messalina (ˌmɛsəˈliːnə) *n* **Valeria** (vəˈlɪərɪə). died 48 A.D., wife of the Roman emperor Claudius, notorious for her debauchery and cruelty.

messaline (ˌmɛsəˈliːn, ˈmɛsəˌliːn) *n* a light lustrous twilled-silk fabric. [C20: from French, origin obscure]

Messapian (məˈseɪpɪən) *or* **Messapic** (məˈseɪpɪk, -ˈsæpɪk) *n* a scantily recorded language of an ancient people of Calabria (the **Messapii**), thought by some to be related to ancient Illyrian.

Messeigneurs *French.* (mesɛɲœr) *n* the plural of **Monseigneur.**

Messene (mɛˈsiːnɪ) *n* an ancient Greek city in the SW Peloponnese: founded in 369 B.C. as the capital of Messenia.

messenger (ˈmɛsɪndʒə) *n* **1** a person who takes messages from one person or group to another or others. **2** a person who runs errands or is employed to run errands. **3** a carrier of official dispatches; courier. **4** *Nautical.* **4a** a light line used to haul in a heavy rope. **4b** an endless belt of chain, rope, or cable, used on a powered winch to take off power. **5** *Archaic.* a herald. [C13: from Old French *messagier,* from MESSAGE]

messenger RNA *n Biochem.* a form of RNA, transcribed from a single strand of DNA, that carries genetic information required for protein synthesis from DNA to the ribosomes. Sometimes shortened to **m-RNA.** See also **transfer RNA, genetic code.**

Messenia (məˈsiːnɪə) *n* the southwestern area of the Peloponnese in S Greece.

Messerschmitt (*German* ˈmɛsərˌʃmɪt) *n* **Willy** (ˈvɪlɪ). 1898–1978, German aeronautical engineer. His military planes figured prominently in World War II, including the Me-262, the first jet fighter.

mess hall *n* a military dining room, usually large.

Messiaen (*French* mɛsjɑ̃) *n* **Olivier** (ɔlivje). 1908–92, French composer and organist. His music is distinguished by its rhythmic intricacy; he was influenced by Hindu and Greek rhythms and bird song.

Messiah (mɪˈsaɪə) *n* **1** *Judaism.* the awaited redeemer of the Jews, to be sent by God to free them. **2** Jesus Christ, when regarded in this role. **3** an exceptional or hoped for liberator of a country or people. [C14: from Old French *Messie,* ultimately from Hebrew *māshīach* anointed] ▸ **Mesˈsiahˌship** *n*

messianic (ˌmɛsɪˈænɪk) *adj* **1** (*sometimes cap.*) *Bible.* **1a** of or relating to the Messiah, his awaited deliverance of the Jews, or the new age of peace expected to follow this. **1b** of or relating to Jesus Christ or the salvation believed to have been brought by him. **2a** of or relating to any popular leader promising deliverance or an ideal era of peace and prosperity. **2b** of or relating to promises of this kind or to an ideal era of this kind. ▸ ˌ**messiˈanically** *adv* ▸ **messianism** (mɛˈsaɪənɪzəm) *n*

Messidor *French.* (mesidɔr) *n* the month of harvest: the tenth month of the French revolutionary calendar, extending from June 20 to July 19. [C19: from French, from Latin *messis* harvest + Greek *dōron* gift]

Messier catalogue (ˈmɛsɪeɪ) *n Astronomy.* a catalogue of 103 nonstellar objects, such as nebulae and galaxies, prepared in 1781–86. An object is referred to by its number in this catalogue, for example the Andromeda Galaxy is referred to as *M*31. [C18: named after Charles *Messier* (1730–1817), French astronomer]

messieurs (ˈmɛsəz; *French* mesjø) *n* the plural of **monsieur.**

Messina (mɛˈsiːnə) *n* a port in NE Sicily, on the **Strait of Messina:** colonized by Greeks around 730 B.C.; under Spanish rule (1282–1676 and 1678–1713); university (1549). Pop.: 263 092 (1996 est.).

mess jacket *n* a waist-length jacket tapering to a point at the back, worn by officers in the mess for formal dinners.

mess kit *n Military.* **1** *Brit.* formal evening wear for officers. **2** Also called: **mess gear.** eating utensils used esp. in the field.

messmate (ˈmɛsˌmeɪt) *n* **1** a person with whom one shares meals in a mess, esp. in the army. **2** *Austral.* any of various eucalyptus trees that grow amongst other species.

Messrs (ˈmɛsəz) *n* the plural of **Mr.** [C18: abbreviation from French *messieurs*]

messuage (ˈmɛswɪdʒ) *n Property law.* a dwelling house together with its outbuildings, curtilage, and the adjacent land appropriated to its use. [C14: from Norman French: household, perhaps through misspelling of Old French *mesnage* MÉNAGE]

messy (ˈmɛsɪ) *adj* **messier, messiest.** dirty, confused, or untidy. ▸ ˈ**messily** *adv* ▸ ˈ**messiness** *n*

mestee (mɛˈstiː) *n* a variant of **mustee.**

mester (ˈmɛstə) *n South Yorkshire dialect.* **1** master: used as a term of address for a man who is the head of a house. **2 bad mester.** a term for the devil, used when speaking to children.

mestizo (mɛˈstiːzəʊ, mɪ-) *n, pl* **-zos** *or* **-zoes.** a person of mixed parentage, esp. the offspring of a Spanish American and an American Indian. [C16: from Spanish, ultimately from Latin *miscēre* to mix] ▸ **mestiza** (mɛˈstiːzə) *fem n*

mestome (ˈmɛstəʊm) *or* **mestom** *n Botany.* **a** conducting tissue associated with parenchyma. **b** (*as modifier*): *a mestome sheath.* [C19: from Greek *mestōma* filling up]

mestranol (ˈmɛstrəˌnɒl, -ˌnəʊl) *n* a synthetic oestrogen used in combination with progesterones as an oral contraceptive. Formula: $C_{21}H_{26}O_2$. [C20: from M(ETHYL) + (O)ESTR(OGEN) + (*pregn*)*an*(*e*) ($C_{21}H_{36}$) + -OL]

Meštrović (*Serbo-Croat* ˈmɛʃtrɔvitʃ) *n* **Ivan** (ˈivan). 1883–1962, U.S. sculptor, born in Austria: his works include portraits of Sir Thomas Beecham and Pope Pius XI.

met (mɛt) *vb* the past tense and past participle of **meet.**

met. *abbrev. for:* **1** metaphor. **2** metaphysics. **3** meteorological: *the met. office weather report.* **4** meteorology. **5** metropolitan.

Meta (ˈmeɪtə; *Spanish* ˈmeta) *n* a river in Colombia, rising in the Andes and flowing northeast and east, forming part of the border between Colombia and Venezuela, to join the Orinoco River. Length: about 1000 km (620 miles).

meta- *or sometimes before a vowel* **met-** *prefix* **1** indicating change, alteration, or alternation: *metabolism; metamorphosis.* **2** (of an academic discipline, esp. philosophy) concerned with the concepts and results of the named discipline: *metamathematics; meta-ethics.* See also **metatheory. 3** occurring or situated behind or after: *metaphase.* **4** (*often in italics*) denoting that an organic compound contains a benzene ring with substituents in the 1,3-positions: *metadinitrobenzene; meta*-cresol. Abbrev.: *m*-. Compare **ortho-** (sense 4), **para-**[1] (sense 6). **5** denoting an isomer, polymer, or compound related to a specified compound (often differing from similar compounds that are prefixed by *para-*): *metaldehyde.* **6** denoting an oxyacid that is a lower hydrated form of the anhydride or a salt of such an acid: *metaphosphoric acid.* Compare **ortho-** (sense 5). [Greek, from *meta* with, after, between, among. Compare Old English *mid, mith* with, Old Norse *meth* with, between]

metabolic pathway *n* any of the sequences of biochemical reactions, catalysed by enzymes, that occur in all living cells: concerned mainly with the exchange of energy and chemicals. See also **Krebs cycle.**

metabolism (mɪˈtæbəˌlɪzəm) *n* **1** the sum total of the chemical processes that occur in living organisms, resulting in growth, production of energy, elimination of waste material, etc. See **anabolism, basal metabolism, catabolism. 2** the sum total of the chemical processes affecting a particular substance in the body: *carbohydrate metabolism; iodine metabolism.* [C19: from Greek *metabolē* change, from *metaballein* to change, from META- + *ballein* to throw] ▸ **metabolic** (ˌmɛtəˈbɒlɪk) *adj* ▸ ˌ**metaˈbolically** *adv*

metabolite (mɪˈtæbəˌlaɪt) *n* a substance produced during or taking part in metabolism. [C19: METABOL(ISM) + -ITE[1]]

metabolize *or* **metabolise** (mɪˈtæbəˌlaɪz) *vb* to produce or be produced by metabolism. ▸ **meˈtaboˌlizable** *or* **meˈtaboˌlisable** *adj*

metaboly (mɪˈtæbəlɪ) *n Biology.* the ability of some cells, esp. protozoans, to alter their shape.

metacarpal (ˌmɛtəˈkɑːpᵊl) *Anatomy.* ◆ *adj* **1** of or relating to the metacarpus. ◆ *n* **2** a metacarpal bone.

metacarpus (ˌmɛtəˈkɑːpəs) *n, pl* **-pi** (-paɪ). **1** the skeleton of the hand between the wrist and the fingers, consisting of five long bones. **2** the corresponding bones in other vertebrates.

metacentre *or U.S.* **metacenter** (ˈmɛtəˌsɛntə) *n* the intersection of a vertical line through the centre of buoyancy of a floating body at equilibrium with a vertical line through the centre of buoyancy when the body is tilted. ▸ ˌ**metaˈcentric** *adj*

metachromatic (ˌmɛtəkrəʊˈmætɪk) *adj* **1** (of tissues and cells stained for microscopical examination) taking a colour different from that of the dye solution. **2** (of dyes) capable of staining tissues or cells a colour different from that of the dye solution. **3** of or relating to metachromatism.

metachromatism (ˌmɛtəˈkrəʊməˌtɪzəm) *n* a change in colour, esp. when caused by a change in temperature. [C19: from META- + CHROMATO- + -ISM]

metachrosis (ˌmɛtəˈkrəʊsɪs) *n Zoology.* the ability of some animals, such as chameleons, to change their colour. [C19: from META- + Greek *khrōs* colour]

metacinnabarite (ˌmɛtəsɪˈnæbəˌraɪt) *n* the black solid form of mercuric sulphide.

metacognition (ˌmɛtəkɒgˈnɪʃən) *n Psychol.* thinking about one's own mental processes.

meta-ethics *n* (*functioning as sing*) the philosophical study of questions about the nature of ethical judgment as distinct from questions of normative ethics, for example, whether ethical judgments state facts or express attitudes, whether there are objective standards of morality, and how moral judgments can be justified. ▸ ˌ**meta-ˈethical** *adj*

metafemale (ˌmɛtəˈfiːmeɪl) *n Genetics.* a sterile female organism, esp. a fruit fly (*Drosophila*) that has three X chromosomes. Former name: **superfemale.**

metagalaxy (ˌmɛtəˈgæləksɪ) *n, pl* **-axies.** the total system of galaxies and intergalactic space making up the universe. ▸ **metagalactic** (ˌmɛtəgəˈlæktɪk) *adj*

metage (ˈmiːtɪdʒ) *n* **1** the official measuring of weight or contents. **2** a charge for this. [C16: from METE[1]]

metagenesis (ˌmɛtəˈdʒɛnɪsɪs) *n* another name for **alternation of generations.** ▸ metagenetic (ˌmɛtədʒɪˈnɛtɪk) *or* ˌ**metaˈgenic** *adj* ▸ ˌ**metageˈnetically** *adv*

metagnathous (mɪˈtægnəθəs) *adj* (of the beaks of birds such as the crossbill) having crossed tips. [C19: from META- + -GNATHOUS] ▸ **meˈtagnaˌthism** *n*

metal (ˈmɛtᵊl) *n* **1a** any of a number of chemical elements, such as iron or copper, that are often lustrous ductile solids, have basic oxides, form positive ions, and are good conductors of heat and electricity. **1b** an alloy, such as brass or steel, containing one or more of these elements. **2** *Printing.* type made of metal. **3** the substance of glass in a molten state or as the finished product. **4** short for **road metal. 5** *Informal.* short for **heavy metal** (sense 1). **6** *Navy.* **6a** the total weight of projectiles that can be shot by a ship's guns at any one time. **6b** the total weight or number of a ship's guns. **7** *Astronomy.* any element heavier than helium. Also called: **heavy element. 8** *Heraldry.* gold or silver. **9** (*pl*) the rails of a railway. ◆ *adj* **10** made of metal. ◆ *vb* **-als, -alling, -alled** *or U.S.* **-als, -aling, -aled.** (*tr*) **11** to fit or cover with metal. **12** to make or mend (a road) with **road metal.** [C13: from Latin *metallum* mine, product of a mine, from Greek *metallon*] ▸ ˈ**metalled** *adj* ▸ ˈ**metal-ˌlike** *adj*

metal. *or* **metall.** *abbrev. for:* **1** metallurgical. **2** metallurgy.

metalanguage ('mɛtə,læŋgwɪdʒ) *n* a language or system of symbols used to discuss another language or system. See also **formal language, natural language.** Compare **object language.**

metal detector *n* a device that gives an audible or visual signal when its search head comes close to a metallic object embedded in food, buried in the ground, etc.

metallic (mɪ'tælɪk) *adj* **1** of, concerned with, or consisting of metal or a metal. **2** suggestive of a metal: *a metallic click; metallic lustre.* **3** *Chem.* (of a metal element) existing in the free state rather than in combination: *metallic copper.* ▸ **me'tallically** *adv*

metallic bond *n Chem.* the covalent bonding between atoms in metals, in which the valence electrons are free to move through the crystal.

metallic lens *n* an arrangement of louvres used to direct and focus electromagnetic or sound waves.

metallic soap *n* any one of a number of colloidal stearates, palmitates, or oleates of various metals, including aluminium, calcium, magnesium, iron, and zinc. They are used as bases for ointments, fungicides, fireproofing and waterproofing agents, and dryers for paints and varnishes.

metalliferous (,mɛtᵊ'lɪfərəs) *adj* containing a metallic element: *a metalliferous ore.* **[C17:** from Latin *metallifer* yielding metal, from *metallum* metal + *ferre* to bear**]**

metalline ('mɛtə,laɪn) *adj* **1** of, resembling, or relating to metals. **2** containing metals or metal ions.

metallist *or U.S.* **metalist** ('mɛtᵊlɪst) *n* **1** a person who works with metals. **2** a person who advocates a system of currency based on a metal, such as gold or silver.

metallize, metallise, *or U.S.* **metalize** ('mɛtə,laɪz) *vb* (*tr*) to make metallic or to coat or treat with metal. ▸ **,metalli'zation, ,metalli'sation,** *or U.S.* **,metali'zation** *n*

metallo- *combining form.* denoting metal: *metallography; metalloid; metallurgy.* **[**from Greek *metallon***]**

metallocene (mɪ'tæləʊ,siːn) *n Chem.* any one of a class of organometallic sandwich compounds of the general formula $M(C_5H_5)_2$, where M is a metal atom. See **ferrocene. [C20:** from METALLO- + *-cene,* as in FERROCENE**]**

metallography (,mɛtə'lɒgrəfɪ) *n* **1** the branch of metallurgy concerned with the composition and structure of metals and alloys. **2** a lithographic process using metal plates instead of stone; metal lithography. ▸ **,metal'lographer** *or* **,metal'lographist** *n* ▸ **metallographic** (mɪ,tælə'græfɪk) *adj* ▸ **me,tallo'graphically** *adv*

metalloid ('mɛtə,lɔɪd) *n* **1** a nonmetallic element, such as arsenic or silicon, that has some of the properties of a metal. ◆ *adj also* **metalloidal** (,mɛtə'lɔɪdᵊl). **2** of or being a metalloid. **3** resembling a metal.

metallophone (mɛ'tælə,fəʊn) *n* any of various musical instruments consisting of tuned metal bars struck with a hammer, such as the glockenspiel.

metallurgy (mɛ'tælədʒɪ; *U.S.* 'mɛtᵊ,lɜːdʒɪ) *n* the scientific study of the extraction, refining, alloying, and fabrication of metals and of their structure and properties. ▸ **,metal'lurgic** *or* **,metal'lurgical** *adj* ▸ **,metal'lurgically** *adv* ▸ **metallurgist** (mɛ'tælədʒɪst, 'mɛtə,lɜːdʒɪst) *n*

metal spraying *n* a process in which a layer of one metal is sprayed onto another in the molten state.

metal tape *n* a magnetic recording tape coated with pure iron rather than iron oxide or chromedioxide: it gives enhanced recording quality.

metalwork ('mɛtᵊl,wɜːk) *n* **1** the craft of working in metal. **2** work in metal or articles made from metal.

metalworking ('mɛtᵊl,wɜːkɪŋ) *n* the processing of metal to change its shape, size, etc., as by rolling, forging, etc., or by making metal articles. ▸ **'metal,worker** *n*

metamale ('mɛtə,meɪl) *n Genetics.* a sterile male organism, esp. a fruit fly (*Drosophila*) that has one X chromosome and three sets of autosomes. Former name: **supermale.**

metamathematics (,mɛtə,mæθɪ'mætɪks) *n* (*functioning as sing*) the logical analysis of the reasoning, principles, and rules that control the use and combination of mathematical symbols, numbers, etc. ▸ **,meta,mathe'matical** *adj* ▸ **,meta,mathema'tician** *n*

metamer ('mɛtəmə) *n* any of two or more isomeric compounds exhibiting metamerism.

metamere ('mɛtə,mɪə) *n* one of the similar body segments into which earthworms, crayfish, and similar animals are divided longitudinally. Also called: **somite. [C19:** from META- + -MERE**]** ▸ **metameral** (mɪ'tæmərəl) *adj*

metameric (,mɛtə'mɛrɪk) *adj* **1** divided into or consisting of metameres. See also **metamerism** (sense 1). **2** of or concerned with metamerism. ▸ **,meta'merically** *adv*

metamerism (mɪ'tæmə,rɪzəm) *n* **1** Also called: (**metameric**) **segmentation.** the division of an animal into similar segments (metameres). In many vertebrates it is confined to the embryonic nervous and muscular systems. **2** *Chem.* a type of isomerism in which molecular structures differ by the attachment of different groups to the same atom, as in $CH_3OC_3H_7$ and $C_2H_5OC_2H_5$.

metamict ('mɛtə,mɪkt) *adj* of or denoting the amorphous state of a substance that has lost its crystalline structure as a result of the radioactivity of uranium or thorium within it: *metamict minerals.* **[C19:** from Danish *metamikt,* from META- + Greek *miktos* mixed**]** ▸ **,metamicti'zation** *or* **,metamicti'sation** *n*

metamorphic (,mɛtə'mɔːfɪk) *or* **metamorphous** *adj* **1** relating to or resulting from metamorphosis or metamorphism. **2** (of rocks) altered considerably from the original structure and composition by pressure and heat. Compare **igneous, sedimentary.**

metamorphism (,mɛtə'mɔːfɪzəm) *n* **1** the process by which metamorphic rocks are formed. **2** a variant of **metamorphosis.**

metamorphose (,mɛtə'mɔːfəʊz) *vb* to undergo or cause to undergo metamorphosis or metamorphism.

metamorphosis (,mɛtə'mɔːfəsɪs) *n, pl* **-ses** (-,siːz). **1** a complete change of physical form or substance. **2** a complete change of character, appearance, etc. **3** a person or thing that has undergone metamorphosis. **4** *Zoology.* the rapid transformation of a larva into an adult that occurs in certain animals, for example the stage between tadpole and frog or between chrysalis and butterfly. **[C16:** via Latin from Greek: transformation, from META- + *morphē* form**]**

metanephros (,mɛtə'nɛfrɒs) *n, pl* **-roi** (-rɔɪ). the last-formed posterior part of the embryonic kidney in reptiles, birds, and mammals, which remains functional in the adult. See also **pronephros, mesonephros. [C19:** New Latin, from META- + Greek *nephros* kidney**]**

metaph. *abbrev. for:* **1** metaphor(ical). **2** metaphysics.

metaphase ('mɛtə,feɪz) *n* **1** *Biology.* the second stage of mitosis during which a body of longitudinally arranged threads (see **spindle** (sense 7)) is formed within the cell. See also **prophase** (sense 1), **anaphase** (sense 1), **telophase** (sense 1). **2** the corresponding stage of the first division of meiosis.

metaphor ('mɛtəfə, -,fɔː) *n* a figure of speech in which a word or phrase is applied to an object or action that it does not literally denote in order to imply a resemblance, for example *he is a lion in battle.* Compare **simile. [C16:** from Latin, from Greek *metaphora,* from *metapherein* to transfer, from META- + *pherein* to bear**]** ▸ **metaphoric** (,mɛtə'fɒrɪk) *or* **,meta'phorical** *adj* ▸ **,meta'phorically** *adv* ▸ **,meta'phoricalness** *n*

metaphosphate (,mɛtə'fɒsfeɪt) *n* any salt of metaphosphoric acid.

metaphosphoric acid (,mɛtəfɒs'fɒrɪk) *n* a glassy deliquescent highly polymeric solid, used as a dehydrating agent. Formula: $(HPO_3)_x$. See also **polyphosphoric acid.**

metaphrase ('mɛtə,freɪz) *n* **1** a literal translation. Compare **paraphrase.** ◆ *vb* (*tr*) **2** to alter or manipulate the wording of. **3** to translate literally. **[C17:** from Greek *metaphrazein* to translate**]**

metaphrast ('mɛtə,fræst) *n* a person who metaphrases, esp. one who changes the form of a text, as by rendering verse into prose. **[C17:** from Medieval Greek *metaphrastēs* translator**]** ▸ **,meta'phrastic** *or* **,meta'phrastical** *adj* ▸ **,meta'phrastically** *adv*

metaphysic (,mɛtə'fɪzɪk) *n* **1** the system of first principles and assumptions underlying an enquiry or philosophical theory. **2** an obsolete word for **metaphysician.** ◆ *adj* **3** *Rare.* another word for **metaphysical.**

metaphysical (,mɛtə'fɪzɪkᵊl) *adj* **1** relating to or concerned with metaphysics. **2** (of a statement or theory) having the form of an empirical hypothesis, but in fact immune from empirical testing and therefore (in the view of the logical positivists) literally meaningless. **3** (popularly) abstract, abstruse, or unduly theoretical. **4** incorporeal; supernatural. ▸ **,meta'physically** *adv*

Metaphysical (,mɛtə'fɪzɪkᵊl) *adj* **1** denoting or relating to certain 17th-century poets who combined intense feeling with ingenious thought and often used elaborate imagery and conceits. Notable among them were Donne, Herbert, and Marvell. ◆ *n* **2** a poet of this group.

metaphysicize *or* **metaphysicise** (,mɛtə'fɪzɪ,saɪz) *vb* **1** (*intr*) to think, write, etc., metaphysically. **2** (*tr*) to treat (a subject) metaphysically.

metaphysics (,mɛtə'fɪzɪks) *n* (*functioning as sing*) **1** the branch of philosophy that deals with first principles, esp. of being and knowing. **2** the philosophical study of the nature of reality, concerned with such questions as the existence of God, the external world, etc. **3** See **descriptive metaphysics. 4** (popularly) abstract or subtle discussion or reasoning. **[C16:** from Medieval Latin, from Greek *ta meta ta phusika* the things after the physics, from the arrangement of the subjects treated in the works of Aristotle**]** ▸ **metaphysician** (,mɛtəfɪ'zɪʃən) *or* **metaphysicist** (,mɛtə'fɪzɪsɪst) *n*

metaplasia (,mɛtə'pleɪzɪə) *n* the transformation of one kind of tissue into a different kind.

metaplasm ('mɛtə,plæzəm) *n* the nonliving constituents, such as starch and pigment granules, of the cytoplasm of a cell. ▸ **,meta'plasmic** *adj*

metapolitics (,mɛtə'pɒlɪtɪks) *n* (*functioning as sing*) political theory (often used derogatorily). ▸ **metapolitical** (,mɛtəpə'lɪtɪkᵊl) *adj*

metapsychology (,mɛtəsaɪ'kɒlədʒɪ) *n Psychol.* **1** the study of philosophical questions, such as the relation between mind and body, that go beyond the laws of experimental psychology. **2** any attempt to state the general laws of psychology. **3** another word for **parapsychology.** ▸ **metapsychological** (,mɛtə,saɪkə'lɒdʒɪkᵊl) *adj*

metarchon (mɪ'tɑːkɒn) *n* a nontoxic substance, such as a chemical to mask pheromones, that reduces the persistence of a pest.

metasoma (,mɛtə'səʊmə) *n Zoology.* the posterior part of an arachnid's abdomen (opisthosoma) that never carries appendages.

metasomatism (,mɛtə'səʊmə,tɪzəm) *or* **metasomatosis** (,mɛtə,səʊmə'təʊsɪs) *n* change in the composition of a rock or mineral by the addition or replacement of chemicals. **[C19:** from New Latin; see META-, SOMATO-**]**

metastable (,mɛtə'steɪbᵊl) *Physics.* ◆ *adj* **1** (of a body or system) having a state of apparent equilibrium although capable of changing to a more stable state. **2** (of an atom, molecule, ion, or atomic nucleus) existing in an excited state with a relatively long lifetime. ◆ *n* **3** a metastable atom, ion, molecule, or nucleus. ▸ **,metasta'bility** *n*

Metastasio (*Italian* metas'taːzjo) *n* **Pietro** ('pjɛːtro), original name *Pietro Antonio Domenico Trapassi.* 1698–1782, Italian poet and librettist; Viennese court poet (from 1730). His works include *La clemenza di Tito* (1732).

metastasis (mɪ'tæstəsɪs) *n, pl* **-ses** (-,siːz). **1** *Pathol.* the spreading of a disease, esp. cancer cells, from one part of the body to another. **2** a transformation or change, as in rhetoric, from one point to another. **3** a rare word for **metabolism. [C16:** via Latin from Greek: transition**]** ▸ **metastatic** (,mɛtə'stætɪk) *adj* ▸ **,meta'statically** *adv*

metastasize *or* **metastasise** (mɪˈtæstəˌsaɪz) *vb* (*intr*) *Pathol.* (esp. of cancer cells) to spread to a new site in the body via blood or lymph vessels.

metatarsal (ˌmetəˈtɑːsᵊl) *Anatomy.* ♦ *adj* **1** of or relating to the metatarsus. ♦ *n* **2** any bone of the metatarsus.

metatarsus (ˌmetəˈtɑːsəs) *n, pl* **-si** (-saɪ). **1** the skeleton of the human foot between the toes and the tarsus, consisting of five long bones. **2** the corresponding skeletal part in other vertebrates.

metatheory (ˈmɛtəˌθɪərɪ) *n* **1** philosophical discussion of the foundations, structure, or results of some theory, such as metamathematics. **2** a formal system that describes the structure of some other system. See also **metalanguage.** ► **metatheoretical** (ˌmɛtəθɪəˈrɛtɪkᵊl) *adj*

metatherian (ˌmɛtəˈθɪərɪən) *adj* **1** of, relating to, or belonging to the *Metatheria,* a subclass of mammals comprising the marsupials. ♦ *n* **2** any metatherian mammal; a marsupial. ♦ Compare **eutherian, prototherian.** [C19: from New Latin, from META- + Greek *thērion* animal]

metathesis (mɪˈtæθəsɪs) *n, pl* **-ses** (-ˌsiːz). **1** the transposition of two sounds or letters in a word. **2** *Chem.* another name for **double decomposition.** [C16: from Late Latin, from Greek, from *metatithenai* to transpose] ► **metathetic** (ˌmɛtəˈθɛtɪk) *or* ˌ**meta**ˈ**thetical** *adj*

metathesize *or* **metathesise** (mɪˈtæθɪˌsaɪz) *vb* to change or cause to change by metathesis.

metathorax (ˌmetəˈθɔːræks) *n, pl* **-raxes** *or* **-races** (-rəˌsiːz). the third and last segment of an insect's thorax, which bears the third pair of walking legs and the second pair of wings. See also **prothorax, mesothorax.** ► **metathoracic** (ˌmɛtəθɔːˈræsɪk) *adj*

metaxylem (ˌmetəˈzaɪlɛm) *n* xylem tissue that consists of rigid thick-walled cells and occurs in parts of the plant that have finished growing. Compare **protoxylem.**

metazoan (ˌmetəˈzəʊən) *n* **1** any multicellular animal of the group *Metazoa*: includes all animals except sponges. ♦ *adj also* **metazoic. 2** of, relating to, or belonging to the *Metazoa.* [C19: from New Latin *Metazoa;* see META-, -ZOA]

Metchnikoff (*French* mɛtʃnikɔf; *Russian* ˈmjetʃnikəf) *n* **Élie** (eli). 1845–1916, Russian bacteriologist in France. He formulated the theory of phagocytosis and shared the Nobel prize for physiology or medicine 1908.

mete[1] (miːt) *vb* (*tr*) **1** (usually foll. by *out*) *Formal.* to distribute or allot (something, often unpleasant). ♦ *vb, n* **2** *Poetic, dialect.* (to) measure. [Old English *metan;* compare Old Saxon *metan,* Old Norse *meta,* German *messen* to measure]

mete[2] (miːt) *n Rare.* a mark, limit, or boundary (esp. in the phrase **metes and bounds**). [C15: from Old French, from Latin *mēta* goal, turning post (in race)]

metecdysis (ˌmetɛkˈdaɪsɪs) *n, pl* **-ses** (-ˌsiːz) the period following the moult (ecdysis) of an arthropod, when the new cuticle is forming.

metempirical (ˌmetɛmˈpɪrɪkᵊl) *or* **metempiric** *adj* **1** beyond the realm of experience. **2** of or relating to metempirics. ► ˌ**metem**ˈ**pirically** *adv*

metempirics (ˌmetɛmˈpɪrɪks) *n* (*functioning as sing*) the branch of philosophy that deals with things existing beyond the realm of experience. ► ˌ**metem**ˈ**piricist** *n*

metempsychosis (ˌmetəmsaɪˈkəʊsɪs) *n, pl* **-ses** (-siːz). **1** the migration of a soul from one body to another. **2** the entering of a soul after death upon a new cycle of existence in a new body either of human or animal form. [C16: via Late Latin from Greek, from *metempsukhousthai,* from META- + *-em-* in + *psukhē* soul] ► ˌ**metempsy**ˈ**chosist** *n*

metencephalon (ˌmetɛnˈsɛfəˌlɒn) *n, pl* **-lons** *or* **-la** (-lə). the part of the embryonic hindbrain that develops into the cerebellum and pons Varolii. ► **metencephalic** (ˌmetɛnsɪˈfælɪk) *adj*

meteor (ˈmiːtɪə) *n* **1** a very small meteoroid that has entered the earth's atmosphere. Such objects have speeds approaching 70 kilometres per second. **2** Also called: **shooting star, falling star.** the bright streak of light appearing in the sky due to the incandescence of such a body heated by friction at its surface. [C15: from Medieval Latin *meteōrum,* from Greek *meteōron* something aloft, from *meteōros* lofty, from *meta-* (intensifier) + *aeirein* to raise]

meteoric (ˌmiːtɪˈɒrɪk) *adj* **1** of, formed by, or relating to meteors. **2** like a meteor in brilliance, speed, or transience. **3** *Rare.* of or relating to the weather; meteorological. ► ˌ**mete**ˈ**orically** *adv*

meteoric water *n Geology.* ground water that has recently originated from the atmosphere.

meteorism (ˈmiːtɪəˌrɪzəm) *n Med.* another name for **tympanites.**

meteorite (ˈmiːtɪəˌraɪt) *n* a rocklike object consisting of the remains of a meteoroid that has fallen on earth. It may be stony (see **aerolite**) or metallic (see **siderite**). ► **meteoritic** (ˌmiːtɪəˈrɪtɪk) *adj*

meteoritics (ˌmiːtɪəˈrɪtɪks) *n* (*functioning as sing*) the branch of science concerned with meteors and meteorites. ► ˌ**meteor**ˈ**iticist** *n*

meteorograph (ˈmiːtɪərəˌgrɑːf, -ˌgræf) *n* an instrument that records various meteorological conditions. ► ˌ**meteoro**ˈ**graphic** *or* ˌ**meteoro**ˈ**graphical** *adj*

meteoroid (ˈmiːtɪəˌrɔɪd) *n* any of the small celestial bodies that are thought to orbit the sun, possibly as the remains of comets. When they enter the earth's atmosphere, they become visible as meteors. ► ˌ**meteor**ˈ**oidal** *adj*

meteorol. *or* **meteor.** *abbrev. for:* **1** meteorological. **2** meteorology.

meteorology (ˌmiːtɪəˈrɒlədʒɪ) *n* the study of the earth's atmosphere, esp. of weather-forming processes and weather forecasting. [C17: from Greek *meteorologia,* from *meteōron* something aloft + *-logia* -LOGY. See METEOR] ► **meteorological** (ˌmiːtɪərəˈlɒdʒɪkᵊl) *or* ˌ**meteoro**ˈ**logic** *adj* ► ˌ**meteoro**ˈ**logically** *adv* ► ˌ**meteor**ˈ**ologist** *n*

meteor shower *n* a transient rain of meteors, such as the Perseids, occurring at regular intervals and coming from a particular region in the sky. It is caused by the earth passing through a large number of meteoroids (a **meteor swarm**).

meter[1] (ˈmiːtə) *n* the U.S. spelling of **metre**[1].

meter[2] (ˈmiːtə) *n* the U.S. spelling of **metre**[2].

meter[3] (ˈmiːtə) *n* **1** any device that measures and records the quantity of a substance, such as gas, that has passed through it during a specified period. **2** any device that measures and sometimes records an electrical or magnetic quantity, such as current, voltage, etc. **3** See **parking meter.** ♦ *vb* (*tr*) **4** to measure (a rate of flow) with a meter. **5** to print with stamps by means of a postage meter. [C19: see METE[1]]

-meter *n combining form.* **1** indicating an instrument for measuring: *barometer.* **2** *Prosody.* indicating a verse having a specified number of feet: *pentameter.* [from Greek *metron* measure]

metered mail *n* mail franked privately, under licence, with a machine bearing special markings (**meter marks**).

meter maid *n Informal.* a female traffic warden.

metestrus (metˈestrəs, -ˈiːstrəs) *n* the U.S. spelling of **metoestrus.** ► **met**ˈ**estrous** *adj*

Meth. *abbrev. for* Methodist.

meth- *combining form.* indicating a chemical compound derived from methane or containing methyl groups: *methacrylate resin.*

methacrylate (meθˈækrɪˌleɪt) *n* **1** any ester of methacrylic acid. **2** See **methacrylate resin.**

methacrylate resin *n* any acrylic resin derived from methacrylic acid.

methacrylic acid (ˌmɛθəˈkrɪlɪk) *n* a colourless crystalline water-soluble substance used in the manufacture of acrylic resins; 2-methylpropenoic acid. Formula: CH_2:C(CH_3)COOH.

methadone (ˈmɛθəˌdəʊn) *or* **methadon** (ˈmɛθəˌdɒn) *n* a narcotic analgesic drug similar to morphine and formerly thought to be less habit-forming. Formula: $C_{21}H_{27}NO$. [C20: from (*di*)*meth*(*yl*) + A(MINO) + D(IPHENYL) + -ONE]

methaemoglobin (metˌhiːməˈgləʊbɪn, mɛˌθiːmə-) *n* a brown compound of oxygen and haemoglobin formed in the blood by the action of certain drugs.

methamphetamine (ˌmeθæmˈfɛtəmɪn) *n* a variety of amphetamine used for its stimulant action. [C20: from METH- + AMPHETAMINE]

methanal (ˈmɛθəˌnæl) *n* the systematic name for **formaldehyde.**

methane (ˈmiːθeɪn) *n* a colourless odourless flammable gas, the simplest alkane and the main constituent of natural gas: used as a fuel. Formula: CH_4. See also **marsh gas, firedamp.** [C19: from METH(YL) + -ANE]

methane series *n* another name for the **alkane series.** See **alkane.**

methanoic acid (ˈmeθəˌnəʊɪk) *n* the systematic name for **formic acid.**

methanol (ˈmɛθəˌnɒl) *n* a colourless volatile poisonous liquid compound used as a solvent and fuel. Formula: CH_3OH. Also called: **methyl alcohol, wood alcohol.** [C20: from METHANE + -OL[1]]

metheglin (məˈθɛglɪn) *n* (esp. formerly) spiced or medicated mead. [C16: from Welsh *meddyglyn,* from *meddyg* healer (from Latin *medicus* MEDICAL) + *llyn* liquor]

methenamine (meˈθiːnəˌmiːn, -ˌmaɪn) *n* another name for **hexamethylenetetramine.** [C20: METH- + -ENE + AMINE]

methinks (mɪˈθɪŋks) *vb past* **methought.** (*tr*) (*takes a clause as object*) *Archaic.* it seems to me.

methionine (meˈθaɪəˌniːn, -ˌnaɪn) *n* an essential amino acid containing sulphur, which occurs in many proteins: important in methylating reactions. [C20: METH- + THIONINE]

metho (ˈmɛθəʊ) *n Austral.* an informal name for **methylated spirits.**

method (ˈmɛθəd) *n* **1** a way of proceeding or doing something, esp. a systematic or regular one. **2** orderliness of thought, action, etc. **3** (*often pl*) the techniques or arrangement of work for a particular field or subject. **4** *Bell-ringing.* any of several traditional sets of changes. See **major** (sense 18), **minor** (sense 8). [C16: via French from Latin *methodus,* from Greek *methodos,* literally: a going after, from *meta-* after + *hodos* way]

Method (ˈmɛθəd) *n* (*sometimes not cap.*) **a** a technique of acting based on the theories of Stanislavsky, in which the actor bases his role on the inner motivation of the character he plays. **b** (*as modifier*): *a Method actor.*

methodical (mɪˈθɒdɪkᵊl) *or* (*less commonly*) **methodic** *adj* characterized by method or orderliness; systematic. ► **me**ˈ**thodically** *adv* ► **me**ˈ**thodicalness** *n*

Methodism (ˈmɛθəˌdɪzəm) *n* the system and practices of the Methodist church, developed by John Wesley and his followers.

Methodist (ˈmɛθədɪst) *n* **1** a member of any of the Nonconformist denominations that derive from the system of faith and practice initiated by John Wesley and his followers. ♦ *adj also* **Methodistic** *or* **Methodistical. 2** of or relating to Methodism or the Church embodying it (the **Methodist Church**). ► ˌ**Meth-od**ˈ**istically** *adv*

Methodius (meˈθəʊdɪəs) *n* **Saint,** with his younger brother Saint Cyril called *the Apostles of the Slavs.* 815–885 A.D., Greek Christian theologian sent as a missionary to the Moravians. Feast day: Feb. 14 or May 11.

methodize *or* **methodise** (ˈmeθəˌdaɪz) *vb* (*tr*) to organize according to a method; systematize. ► ˌ**methodi**ˈ**zation** *or* ˌ**methodi**ˈ**sation** *n* ► ˈ**meth-od**ˌ**izer** *or* ˈ**method**ˌ**iser** *n*

methodology (ˌmɛθəˈdɒlədʒɪ) *n, pl* **-gies. 1** the system of methods and principles used in a particular discipline. **2** the branch of philosophy concerned with the science of method and procedure. ► **methodological** (ˌmɛθədəˈlɒdʒɪkᵊl) *adj* ► ˌ**methodo**ˈ**logically** *adv* ► ˌ**method**ˈ**ologist** *n*

methotrexate (ˌmɛθəʊˈtrekseɪt, ˌmiːθəʊ-) *n* a drug used in the treatment of certain cancers. Formula: $C_{20}H_{22}N_8O_5$.

methought (mɪˈθɔːt) *vb Archaic.* the past tense of **methinks.**

methoxide (meθˈɒksaɪd) *n* a saltlike compound in which the hydrogen atom in the hydroxyl group of methanol has been replaced by a metal atom, usually an alkali metal atom as in sodium methoxide, $NaOCH_3$. Also called: **methylate.**

meths (mɛθs) *n Chiefly Brit., Austral., and N.Z.* an informal name for **methylated spirits.**
Methuselah[1] (mə'θju:zələ) *n* a wine bottle holding the equivalent of eight normal bottles.
Methuselah[2] (mɪ'θju:zələ) *n Old Testament.* a patriarch supposed to have lived 969 years (Genesis 5:21–27) who has come to be regarded as epitomizing longevity. Douay spelling: **Mathusala.**
methyl ('mi:θaɪl, 'mɛθɪl) *n* **1** (*modifier*) of, consisting of, or containing the monovalent group of atoms CH_3. **2** an organometallic compound in which methyl groups are bound directly to a metal atom. [C19: from French *méthyle,* back formation from METHYLENE] ▸ **methylic** (mə'θɪlɪk) *adj*
methyl acetate *n* a colourless volatile flammable liquid ester with a fragrant odour, used as a solvent, esp. in paint removers. Formula: CH_3COOCH_3.
methylal ('mɛθɪ,læl) *n* a colourless volatile flammable liquid with an odour resembling that of chloroform, used as a solvent and in the manufacture of perfumes and adhesives. Formula: $(CH_3O)_2CH_2$. Also called: **formal.**
methyl alcohol *n* another name for **methanol.**
methylamine (mi:'θaɪlə,mi:n) *n* a colourless flammable water-soluble gas, used in the manufacture of herbicides, dyes, and drugs. Formula: CH_3NH_2.
methylate ('mɛθɪ,leɪt) *vb* **1** (*tr*) to mix with methanol. **2** to undergo or cause to undergo a chemical reaction in which a methyl group is introduced into a molecule. ◆ *n* **3** another name for **methoxide.** ▸ **,methyl'ation** *n* ▸ **'methyl,ator** *n*
methylated spirits *or* **spirit** *n* (*functioning as sing or pl*) alcohol that has been denatured by the addition of methanol and pyridine and a violet dye. Also called: **metho, meths.**
methyl bromide *n* a colourless poisonous gas or volatile liquid with an odour resembling that of chloroform, used as a solvent, and extinguishant. Formula: CH_3Br.
methyl chloride *n* a colourless gas with an ether-like odour, used as a refrigerant and anaesthetic. Formula: CH_3Cl. Systematic name: **chloromethane.**
methyl chloroform *n* the traditional name for **trichloroethane.**
methyldopa (,mi:θaɪl'dəʊpə) *n* a catecholamine drug used to treat hypertension. Formula: $C_{10}H_{13}NO_4$. [C20: from *methyl* + *d(ihydr)o(xy)p(henyl)-a(lanine)*]
methylene ('mɛθɪ,li:n) *n* (*modifier*) of, consisting of, or containing the divalent group of atoms $=CH_2$: *a methylene group or radical.* [C19: from French *méthylène,* from Greek *methu* wine + *hulē* wood + -ENE: originally referring to a substance distilled from wood]
methylene blue *n* a dark-green crystalline compound forming a blue aqueous solution, used as a mild antiseptic and biological stain. Formula: $C_{16}H_{18}N_3SCl.3H_2O$. Also called: **methylthionine chloride.**
methylene chloride *n* another name for **dichloromethane.**
methyl ethyl ketone *n* another name for **butanone.**
methyl isobutyl ketone (,aɪsəʊ'bju:taɪl, -tɪl) *n* a colourless insoluble liquid ketone used as a solvent for organic compounds, esp. nitrocellulose; 4-methylpentan-2-one. Formula: $CH_3COC_4H_9$. Also called: **hexone.**
methyl methacrylate *n* a colourless liquid compound, used in the manufacture of certain methacrylate resins. Formula: $CH_2C(CH_3)COOCH_3$.
methylnaphthalene (,mi:θaɪl'næpθə,li:n) *n* either of two isomeric derivatives of naphthalene: a liquid (1-methylnaphthalene), used in standardizing diesel fuels, or a solid (2-methylnaphthalene), an insecticide.
methylthionine chloride (,mi:θaɪl'θaɪə,ni:n) *n* another name for **methylene blue.**
metic ('mɛtɪk) *n* (in ancient Greece) an alien having some rights of citizenship in the city in which he lives. [C19: from Greek *metoikos,* from META- (indicating change) + *-oikos* dwelling]
meticulous (mɪ'tɪkjʊləs) *adj* very precise about details, even trivial ones; painstaking. [C16 (meaning: timid): from Latin *meticulōsus* fearful, from *metus* fear] ▸ **me'ticulously** *adv* ▸ **me'ticulousness** *n*
métier ('mɛtɪeɪ) *n* **1** a profession or trade, esp. that to which one is well suited. **2** a person's strong point or speciality. [C18: from French, ultimately from Latin *ministerium* service]
Métis (me'ti:s) *n, pl* **-tis** (-'ti:s, -'ti:z). **1** a person of mixed parentage. **2** *Canadian.* **2a** the offspring or a descendant of a French Canadian and a North American Indian. **2b** a member or descendant of a group of such people, who established themselves in Manitoba and Saskatchewan as a distinct political and cultural force during the nineteenth century. **3** *U.S.* a person having one eighth Black ancestry; octoroon. [C19: from French, from Vulgar Latin *mixtīcius* (unattested) of mixed race; compare MESTIZO] ▸ **Métisse** (me'ti:s) *fem n*
metoestrus (mɛt'i:strəs, -'ɛstrəs) *or U.S.* **metestrus** *n Zoology.* the period in the oestrous cycle following oestrus, characterized by lack of sexual activity. ▸ **met'oestrous** *or U.S.* **met'estrous** *adj*
metol ('mi:tɒl) *n* a colourless soluble organic substance used, in the form of its sulphate, as a photographic developer; *p*-methylaminophenol. See also **aminophenol.** [C20: from German, an arbitrary coinage]
Metonic cycle (mɪ'tɒnɪk) *n* a cycle of 235 synodic months after which the phases of the moon recur on the same day of the month. See also **golden number.** [C17: named after *Meton,* 5th-century B.C. Athenian astronomer]
metonym ('mɛtənɪm) *n* a word used in a metonymy. For example *the bottle* is a metonym for *alcoholic drink.*
metonymy (mɪ'tɒnɪmɪ) *n, pl* **-mies.** the substitution of a word referring to an attribute for the thing that is meant, as for example the use of *the crown* to refer to a monarch. Compare **synecdoche.** [C16: from Late Latin from Greek: a changing of name, from *meta-* (indicating change) + *onoma* name] ▸ **metonymical** (,mɛtə'nɪmɪk°l) *or* **,meto'nymic** *adj* ▸ **,meto'nymically** *adv*
metope ('mɛtəʊp, 'mɛtəpɪ) *n Architect.* a square space between two triglyphs in a Doric frieze. [C16: via Latin from Greek *metopē,* from *meta* between + *opē* one of the holes for the beam-ends]
metopic (mɪ'tɒpɪk) *adj* of or relating to the forehead.
metralgia (mɪ'trældʒɪə) *n* pain in the uterus. [C20: from METRO-[1] + -ALGIA]
metre[1] *or U.S.* **meter** ('mi:tə) *n* **1** a metric unit of length equal to approximately 1.094 yards. **2** the basic SI unit of length; the length of the path travelled by light in free space during a time interval of 1/299 792 458 of a second. In 1983 this definition replaced the previous one based on krypton-86, which in turn had replaced the definition based on the platinum-iridium metre bar kept in Paris. Symbol: m [C18: from French; see METRE[2]]
metre[2] *or U.S.* **meter** ('mi:tə) *n* **1** *Prosody.* the rhythmic arrangement of syllables in verse, usually according to the number and kind of feet in a line. **2** *Music.* another word (esp. U.S.) for **time** (sense 22). [C14: from Latin *metrum,* from Greek *metron* measure]
metre-kilogram-second *n* See **mks units.**
metric ('mɛtrɪk) *adj* **1** of or relating to the metre or metric system. **2** *Maths.* denoting or relating to a set containing pairs of points for each of which a non-negative real number $\rho(x, y)$ (the distance) can be defined, satisfying specific conditions. ◆ *n* **3** *Maths.* the function $\rho(x, y)$ satisfying the conditions of membership of such a set (a **metric space**).
metrical ('mɛtrɪk°l) *or* **metric** ('mɛtrɪk) *adj* **1** of or relating to measurement. **2** of or in poetic metre. ▸ **'metrically** *adv*
metrical psalm *n* a translation of one of the psalms into rhyming strict-metre verse usually sung as a hymn.
metricate ('mɛtrɪ,keɪt) *vb* to convert (a measuring system, instrument, etc.) from nonmetric to metric units. ▸ **,metri'cation** *n*
metric hundredweight *n* See **hundredweight** (sense 3).
metrics ('mɛtrɪks) *n* (*functioning as sing*) *Prosody.* the art of using poetic metre.
metric system *n* any decimal system of units based on the metre. For scientific purposes the Système International d'Unités (SI units) is used.
metric ton *n* another name (not in technical use) for **tonne.**
metrify ('mɛtrɪ,faɪ) *vb* **-fies, -fying, -fied.** (*tr*) *Prosody.* to render into poetic metre. ▸ **'metri,fier** *n*
metrist ('mɛtrɪst) *n Prosody.* a person skilled in the use of poetic metre.
metritis (mɪ'traɪtɪs) *n* inflammation of the uterus.
metro ('mɛtrəʊ) *or* **métro** (*French* metro) *n, pl* **-ros.** an underground, or largely underground, railway system in certain cities, esp. in Europe, such as that in Paris. [C20: from French, short for *chemin de fer métropolitain* metropolitan railway]
metro-[1] *or before a vowel* **metr-** *combining form.* indicating the uterus: *metrorrhagia.* [from Greek *mētra* womb]
metro-[2] *combining form.* indicating a measure: *metronome.* [from Greek *metron* measure]
metrology (mɪ'trɒlədʒɪ) *n, pl* **-gies. 1** the science of weights and measures; the study of units of measurement. **2** a particular system of units. [C19: from Greek *metron* measure] ▸ **metrological** (,mɛtrə'lɒdʒɪk°l) *adj* ▸ **,metro'logically** *adv* ▸ **me'trologist** *n*
metronidazole (,mɛtrə'naɪdə,zəʊl) *n* a pale yellow crystalline compound used to treat vaginal trichomoniasis. Formula: $C_6H_9N_3O_3$. [C20: from ME(THYL) + (NI)TRO- + *-n-* + (IM)ID(E) + AZOLE]
metronome ('mɛtrə,nəʊm) *n* a mechanical device which indicates the exact tempo of a piece of music by producing a clicking sound from a pendulum with an adjustable period of swing. [C19: from Greek *metron* measure + *nomos* rule, law] ▸ **metronomic** (,mɛtrə'nɒmɪk) *adj*
metronymic (,mɛtrə'nɪmɪk) *or* (*less commonly*) **matronymic** *adj* **1** (of a name) derived from the name of its bearer's mother or another female ancestor. ◆ *n* **2** a metronymic name. [C19: from Greek *mētronumikos,* from *mētēr* mother + *onoma* name]
metropolis (mɪ'trɒpəlɪs) *n, pl* **-lises. 1** the main city, esp. of a country or region; capital. **2** a centre of activity. **3** the chief see in an ecclesiastical province. [C16: from Late Latin from Greek: mother city or state, from *mētēr* mother + *polis* city]
metropolitan (,mɛtrə'pɒlɪtən) *adj* **1** of or characteristic of a metropolis. **2** constituting a city and its suburbs: *the metropolitan area.* **3** of, relating to, or designating an ecclesiastical metropolis. **4** of or belonging to the home territories of a country, as opposed to overseas territories: *metropolitan France.* ◆ *n* **5a** *Eastern Churches.* the head of an ecclesiastical province, ranking between archbishop and patriarch. **5b** *Church of England.* an archbishop. **5c** *R.C. Church.* an archbishop or bishop having authority in certain matters over the dioceses in his province. ▸ **,metro'politanism** *n*
metropolitan county *n* (in England) any of the six conurbations established as administrative units in the new local government system in 1974; the metropolitan county councils were abolished in 1986.
metropolitan district *n* any of the districts making up the metropolitan counties of England: since 1986 they have functioned as unitary authorities, forming the sole principal tier of local government. Each metropolitan district has an elected council responsible for education, social services, etc. See also **district** (sense 4).
Metropolitan Museum of Art *n* the principal museum in New York City: founded in 1870 and housed in its present premises in Central Park since 1880.
metrorrhagia (,mi:trə:'reɪdʒɪə, ,mɛt-) *n* abnormal bleeding from the uterus.
-metry *n combining form.* indicating the process or science of measuring: *anthropometry; geometry.* [from Old French *-metrie,* from Latin *-metria,* from Greek, from *metron* measure] ▸ **-metric** *adj combining form.*
Metsys (*Flemish* 'mɛtsaɪs) *n* a variant spelling of (Quentin) **Massys.**
Metternich (*German* 'mɛtərnɪç) *n* **Klemens** ('kle:məns). 1773–1859, Austrian statesman. He became foreign minister (1809) and made a significant contribution to the Congress of Vienna (1815). From 1821 to 1848 he was both foreign

minister and chancellor of Austria and is noted for his defence of autocracy in Europe.

mettle ('mɛtᵊl) *n* **1** courage; spirit. **2** inherent character. **3 on one's mettle.** roused to putting forth one's best efforts. **[C16:** originally variant spelling of METAL**]**

mettled ('mɛtᵊld) *or* **mettlesome** ('mɛtᵊlsəm) *adj* spirited, courageous, or valiant.

Metz (mɛts; *French* mɛs) *n* a city in NE France on the River Moselle: a free imperial city in the 13th century; annexed by France in 1552; part of Germany (1871–1918); centre of the Lorraine iron-mining region. Pop.: 123 920 (1990).

meu (mjuː) *n* another name for **spignel. [C16:** from Latin *mēum,* from Greek *mēon***]**

meum et tuum *Latin.* ('meɪum ɛt 'tuːum) mine and thine: used to express rights to property. **[C16:** neuter of *mēus* mine and *tuus* yours**]**

Meung (*French* mœ̃) *n* See **Jean de Meung.**

meunière (mən'jɛə; *French* mønjɛr) *adj* (of fish) dredged with flour, fried in butter, and served with butter, lemon juice, and parsley. **[**French, literally: miller's wife**]**

Meurthe-et-Moselle (*French* mœrtemozɛl) *n* a department of NE France, in Lorraine region. Capital: Nancy. Pop.: 716 200 (1995). Area: 5280 sq. km (2059 sq. miles).

Meuse (mɜːz; *French* møz) *n* **1** a department of N France, in Lorraine region: heavy fighting occurred here in World War I. Capital: Bar-le-Duc. Pop.: 194 000 (1995). Area: 6241 sq. km (2434 sq. miles). **2** a river in W Europe, rising in NE France and flowing north across E Belgium and the S Netherlands to join the Waal River before entering the North Sea. Length: 926 km (575 miles). Dutch name: **Maas.**

MeV *symbol for* million electronvolts (10^6 electronvolts).

mevrou (mə'frəʊ) *n* a South African title of address equivalent to *Mrs* when placed before a surname or *madam* when used alone. **[**Afrikaans**]**

mew[1] (mjuː) *vb* **1** (*intr*) (esp. of a cat) to make a characteristic high-pitched cry. ◆ *n* **2** such a sound. **[C14:** imitative**]**

mew[2] (mjuː) *n* any seagull, esp. the common gull, *Larus canus.* Also called: **mew gull, sea mew. [**Old English *mǣw;* compare Old Saxon *mēu,* Middle Dutch *mēwe***]**

mew[3] (mjuː) *n* **1** a room or cage for hawks, esp. while moulting. ◆ *vb* **2** (*tr;* often foll. by *up*) to confine (hawks or falcons) in a shelter, cage, etc., usually by tethering them to a perch. **3** to confine, conceal. **[C14:** from Old French *mue,* from *muer* to moult, from Latin *mūtāre* to change**]**

mew[4] (mjuː) *vb* **1** (*intr*) (of hawks or falcons) to moult. **2** (*tr*) *Obsolete.* to shed (one's covering, clothes, etc.). **[C14:** from Old French *muer* to moult, from Latin *mūtāre* to change**]**

Mewar (mɛ'wɑː) *n* another name for **Udaipur** (sense 1).

mewl (mjuːl) *vb* **1** (*intr*) (esp. of a baby) to cry weakly; whimper (often in the phrase **mewl and puke**). ◆ *n* **2** such a cry. **[C17:** imitative**]** ▸ **'mewler** *n*

mews (mjuːz) *n* (*functioning as sing or pl*) *Chiefly Brit.* **1** a yard or street lined by buildings originally used as stables but now often converted into dwellings. **2** the buildings around a mews. **3** *Informal.* an individual residence in a mews. **[C14:** pl of MEW[3], originally referring to royal stables built on the site of hawks' mews at Charing Cross in London**]**

MEX *international car registration for* Mexico.

Mex. *abbrev. for:* **1** Mexican. **2** Mexico.

Mexicali (ˌmɛksɪ'kɑːlɪ; *Spanish* mexi'kali) *n* a city in NW Mexico, capital of Baja California Norte state, on the border with the U.S. adjoining Calexico, California: centre of a rich irrigated agricultural region. Pop.: 438 377 (1990).

Mexican hairless *n* a breed of small hairless dog with mottled skin.

Mexican War *n* the war fought between the U.S. and Mexico (1846–48), through which the U.S. acquired the present-day Southwest.

Mexican wave *n* the rippling effect produced when the spectators in successive sections of a sports stadium stand up while raising their arms and then sit down. **[C20:** so called because it was first demonstrated at the World Cup in Mexico in 1986**]**

Mexico ('mɛksɪˌkəʊ) *n* **1** a republic in North America, on the Gulf of Mexico and the Pacific: early Mexican history includes the Maya, Toltec, and Aztec civilizations; conquered by the Spanish between 1519 and 1525 and achieved independence in 1821; lost Texas to the U.S. in 1836 and California and New Mexico in 1848. It is generally mountainous with three ranges of the Sierra Madre (east, west, and south) and a large central plateau. Official language: Spanish. Religion: Roman Catholic majority. Currency: peso. Capital: Mexico City. Pop.: 95 830 000 (1998 est.). Area: 1 967 183 sq. km (761 530 sq. miles). Official name: **United Mexican States.** Spanish name: **Méjico. 2** a state of Mexico, on the central plateau surrounding Mexico City, which is not administratively part of the state. Capital: Toluca. Pop.: 11 704 934 (1995 est.). Area: 21 460 sq. km (8287 sq. miles). **3 Gulf of.** an arm of the Atlantic, bordered by the U.S., Cuba, and Mexico: linked with the Atlantic by the Straits of Florida and with the Caribbean by the Yucatán Channel. Area: about 1 600 000 sq. km (618 000 sq. miles). ▸ **Mexican** ('mɛksɪkən) *adj, n*

Mexico City *n* the capital of Mexico, on the central plateau at an altitude of 2240 m (7350 ft.): founded as the Aztec capital (Tenochtitlán) in about 1300; conquered and rebuilt by the Spanish in 1521; forms, with its suburbs, the federal district of Mexico; the largest industrial complex in the country. Pop.: 9 815 795 (1990).

Meyerbeer (*German* 'maiərbeːr) *n* **Giacomo** ('dʒaːkomo), real name *Jakob Liebmann Beer.* 1791–1864, German composer, esp. of operas, such as *Robert le diable* (1831) and *Les Huguenots* (1836).

Meyerhof (*German* 'maiərhoːf) *n* **Otto (Fritz)** ('ɔto). 1884–1951, German physiologist, noted for his work on the metabolism of muscles. He shared the Nobel prize for physiology or medicine 1922.

Meyerhold ('maɪəhəʊlt) *n* **Vsevolod Emilievich,** original name *Karl Theodor Kasimir.* 1874–*c.* 1940, Russian theatre director, noted for his experimental nonrealistic productions. He was arrested in 1939 and died in custody.

MEZ *abbrev. for* Central European Time. **[**from German *Mitteleuropäische Zeit***]**

mezcal (mɛ'skæl) *n* a variant spelling of **mescal.**

mezcaline ('mɛskəˌliːn) *n* a variant spelling of **mescaline.**

meze ('mɛzɛ) *n* a type of hors d'oeuvre eaten esp. with an apéritif or other drink in Greece and the Near East. **[C20:** from Turkish *meze* snack, appetizer**]**

mezereon (mɛ'zɪərɪən) *n* **1** a Eurasian thymelaeaceous shrub, *Daphne mezereum,* with fragrant early-blooming purplish-pink flowers and small scarlet fruits. **2** another name for **mezereum. [C15:** via Medieval Latin from Arabic *māzaryūn***]**

mezereum (mɪ'zɪərɪəm) *or* **mezereon** *n* the dried bark of certain shrubs of the genus *Daphne,* esp. mezereon, formerly used as a vesicant and to treat arthritis.

Mézières (*French* mezjɛr) *n* a town in NE France, on the River Meuse opposite Charleville. See **Charleville-Mézières.**

mezuzah (mə'zuzə, -'zuː-; *Hebrew* məzu'zɑ; *Yiddish* mə'zuzə) *n, pl* **-zuzahs** *or* **-zuzoth** (*Hebrew* -zu'zɔt). *Judaism.* **1** a piece of parchment inscribed with biblical passages and fixed to the doorpost of the rooms of a Jewish house. **2** a metal case for such a parchment, sometimes worn as an ornament. **[**from Hebrew, literally: doorpost**]**

mezzanine ('mɛzəˌniːn, 'mɛtsəˌniːn) *n* **1** Also called: **mezzanine floor, entresol.** an intermediate storey, esp. a low one between the ground and first floor of a building. **2** *Theatre, U.S. and Canadian.* the first balcony. **3** *Theatre, Brit.* a room or floor beneath the stage. ◆ *adj* **4** often shortened to **mezz.** of or relating to an intermediate stage in a financial process: *mezzanine funding.* **[C18:** from French, from Italian, diminutive of *mezzano* middle, from Latin *mediānus* MEDIAN**]**

mezza voce ('mɛtsə 'vəʊtʃɪ; *Italian* 'mɛddza 'votʃe) *adv Music.* (in singing) softly; quietly. **[**Italian, literally: half voice**]**

mezzo ('mɛtsəʊ) *Music.* ◆ *adv* **1** moderately; quite: *mezzo forte; mezzo piano.* ◆ *n, pl* **-zos. 2** See **mezzo-soprano** (sense 1). **[C19:** from Italian, literally: half, from Latin *medius* middle**]**

mezzo-relievo *or* **mezzo-rilievo** (ˌmɛtsəʊrɪ'liːvəʊ) *n* carving in which the depth of the relief is halfway between that of high relief and low relief. **[**from Italian: half relief**]**

mezzo-soprano *n, pl* **-nos. 1** a female voice intermediate between a soprano and contralto and having a range from the A below middle C to the F an eleventh above it. Sometimes shortened to **mezzo. 2** a singer with such a voice.

mezzotint ('mɛtsəʊˌtɪnt) *n* **1** a method of engraving a copper plate by scraping and burnishing the roughened surface. **2** a print made from a plate so treated. ◆ *vb* **3** (*tr*) to engrave (a copper plate) in this fashion. **[C18:** from Italian *mezzotinto* half tint**]** ▸ **'mezzoˌtinter** *n*

mf *Music. abbrev. for* mezzo forte. **[**Italian: moderately loud**]**

MF *abbrev. for:* **1** *Radio.* medium frequency. **2** Middle French.

mfd *abbrev. for* manufactured.

mfg *abbrev. for* manufacturing.

MFH *Hunting. abbrev. for* Master of Foxhounds.

mfr *abbrev. for:* **1** manufacture. **2** manufacturer.

mg *symbol for* milligram.

Mg *the chemical symbol for* magnesium.

MG *abbrev. for* machine gun.

MGB *abbrev. for* Ministry of State Security; the Soviet secret police from 1946 to 1954. **[**from Russian *Ministerstvo gosudarstvennoi bezopasnosti***]**

M. Glam *abbrev. for* Mid Glamorgan.

Mgr *abbrev. for:* **1** manager. **2** Monseigneur. **3** Monsignor.

MHA (in Australia and Newfoundland, Canada) *abbrev. for* Member of the House of Assembly.

MHD *abbrev. for* magnetohydrodynamics.

MHG *abbrev. for* Middle High German.

mho (məʊ) *n, pl* **mhos.** the former name for **siemens. [C19:** formed by reversing the letters of OHM (first used by Lord Kelvin)**]**

MHR (in the U.S. and Australia) *abbrev. for* Member of the House of Representatives.

MHz *symbol for* megahertz.

mi *or* **me** (miː) *n Music.* (in tonic sol-fa) the third degree of any major scale; mediant. **[C16:** see GAMUT**]**

MI *abbrev. for:* **1** Michigan. **2** Military Intelligence.

mi. *abbrev. for* mile.

MI5 *abbrev. for* Military Intelligence, section five; a former official and present-day popular name for the counterintelligence agency of the British Government.

MI6 *abbrev. for* Military Intelligence, section six; a former official and present-day popular name for the intelligence and espionage agency of the British Government.

MIA *abbrev. for:* **1** *Military, chiefly U.S.* missing in action: officially unaccounted for following combat. **2** (in Australia) Murrumbidgee Irrigation Area.

Miami (maɪ'æmɪ) *n* a city and resort in SE Florida, on Biscayne Bay: developed chiefly after 1896, esp. with the Florida land boom of the 1920s; centre of an extensive tourist area. Pop.: 365 127 (1996 est.).

mia mia ('miːə 'miːə) *n* a native Australian's hut. **[**from a native Australian language**]**

Miami Beach *n* a resort in SE Florida, on an island separated from Miami by Biscayne Bay. Pop.: 94 540 (1996 est.).

miaou *or* **miaow** (mɪ'aʊ, mjaʊ) *vb, interj* variant spellings of **meow.**

miasma (mɪ'æzmə) *n, pl* **-mata** (-mətə) *or* **-mas. 1** an unwholesome or foreboding atmosphere. **2** pollution in the atmosphere, esp. noxious vapours from decomposing organic matter. [C17: New Latin, from Greek: defilement, from *miainein* to defile] ▸ **mi'asmal, miasmatic** (ˌmiːəz'mætɪk), **ˌmias'matical,** *or* **mi'asmic** *adj*

miaul (mɪ'aʊl) *vb* (*intr*) another word for **meow.**

mic (maɪk) *n Informal.* short for **microphone.**

Mic. *Bible abbrev. for* Micah.

mica ('maɪkə) *n* any of a group of lustrous rock-forming minerals consisting of hydrous silicates of aluminium, potassium, etc., in monoclinic crystalline form, occurring in igneous and metamorphic rock. Because of their resistance to electricity and heat they are used as dielectrics, in heating elements, etc. Also called: **isinglass.** [C18: from Latin: grain, morsel] ▸ **micaceous** (maɪ'keɪʃəs) *adj*

Micah ('maɪkə) *n Old Testament.* **1** a Hebrew prophet of the late 8th century B.C. **2** the book containing his prophecies. Douay spelling: **Micheas** (maɪ'kiːəs).

Micawber (mɪ'kɔːbə) *n* a person who idles and trusts to fortune. [C19: after a character in Dickens' novel *David Copperfield*] ▸ **Mi'cawberish** *adj* ▸ **Mi'cawberism** *n*

mice (maɪs) *n* the plural of **mouse.**

micelle, micell (mɪ'sɛl), *or* **micella** (mɪ'sɛlə) *n Chem.* **a** a charged aggregate of molecules of colloidal size in a solution. **b** any molecular aggregate of colloidal size, such as a particle found in coal. [C19: from New Latin *micella*, diminutive of Latin *mīca* crumb] ▸ **mi'cellar** *adj*

mich (mɪtʃ) *vb* (*intr*) a variant spelling of **mitch.**

Mich. *abbrev. for:* **1** Michaelmas. **2** Michigan.

Michael ('maɪkᵊl) *n* **1** 1596–1645, tsar of Russia (1613–45); founder of the Romanov dynasty. **2** born 1921, king of Romania (1927–30, as part of a three-part regency; 1940–47), who relinquished the throne (1930–40) in favour of his father, Carol II. He led the coup d'état that overthrew (1944) Antonescu but was forced to abdicate (1947) by the Communists. **3 Saint.** *Bible.* one of the archangels. Feast day: Sept. 29 or Nov. 8.

Michael VIII *n* surnamed *Palaeologus* ('pælɪəˌləʊgəs). 1224–82, Byzantine emperor (1259–82); founder of the Palaeologan dynasty. His reign saw the recovery of Constantinople from the Latins (1261) and the reunion (1274) of the Greek and Roman churches.

Michaelmas ('mɪkᵊlməs) *n* Sept. 29, the feast of St Michael the archangel; in England, Ireland, and Wales, one of the four quarter days.

Michaelmas daisy *n Brit.* any of various plants of the genus *Aster* that have small autumn-blooming purple, pink, or white flowers: family *Compositae* (composites).

Michaelmas term *n* the autumn term at Oxford and Cambridge Universities, the Inns of Court, and some other educational establishments.

Michelangelo (ˌmaɪkᵊl'ændʒɪˌləʊ) *n* full name *Michelangelo Buonarroti.* 1475–1564, Florentine sculptor, painter, architect, and poet; one of the outstanding figures of the Renaissance. Among his creations are the sculptures of *David* (1504) and of *Moses* which was commissioned for the tomb of Julius II, for whom he also painted the ceiling of the Sistine Chapel (1508–12). *The Last Judgment* (1533–41), also in the Sistine, includes a torturous vision of Hell and a disguised self-portrait. His other works include the design of the Laurentian Library (1523–29) and of the dome of St Peter's, Rome.

Michelet (*French* miʃəle) *n* **Jules** (ʒyl). 1798–1874, French historian, noted esp. for his *Histoire de France* (17 vols, 1833–67).

Michelin (*French* miʃəlɛ̃) *n* **André** (ɑ̃dre). 1853–1931, French industrialist; founder, with his brother **Édouard Michelin** (1859–1940), of the Michelin Tyre Company (1888): the first to use demountable pneumatic tyres on motor vehicles.

Michelozzo (*Italian* mike'lɔttso) *n* full name *Michelozzo di Bartolommeo.* 1396–1472, Italian architect and sculptor. His most important design was the Palazzo Riccardo for the Medici family in Florence (1444–59).

Michelson ('maɪkᵊlsᵊn) *n* **Albert Abraham.** 1852–1931, U.S. physicist, born in Germany: noted for his part in the Michelson-Morley experiment: Nobel prize for physics 1907.

Michelson-Morley experiment *n* an experiment first performed in 1887 by A. A. Michelson and E. W. Morley, in which an interferometer was used to attempt to detect a difference in the velocities of light in directions parallel and perpendicular to the earth's motion. The negative result was explained by the special theory of relativity.

michigan ('mɪʃɪgən) *n* the U.S. name for **newmarket** (sense 2).

Michigan ('mɪʃɪgən) *n* **1** a state of the N central U.S., occupying two peninsulas between Lakes Superior, Huron, Michigan, and Erie: generally low-lying. Capital: Lansing. Pop.: 9 773 892 (1997 est.). Area: 147 156 sq. km (56 817 sq. miles). Abbrevs.: **Mich.** or (with zip code) **MI** **2 Lake.** a lake in the N central U.S. between Wisconsin and Michigan: the third largest of the five Great Lakes and the only one wholly in the U.S.; linked with Lake Huron by the Straits of Mackinac. Area: 58 000 sq. km (22 400 sq. miles). ▸ **Michigander** (ˌmɪʃɪ'gændə) *n* ▸ **'Michiganˌite** *adj, n*

Michoacán (*Spanish* mitʃoa'kan) *n* a state of SW Mexico, on the Pacific: rich mineral resources. Capital: Morelia. Pop.: 3 869 133 (1995 est.). Area: 59 864 sq. km (23 114 sq. miles).

micht (mɪxt) *vb, n* a Scot. word for **might**[1] and **might**[2].

Mick (mɪk) *or* **Mickey** ('mɪkɪ) *n* (*sometimes not cap.*) *Derogatory.* a slang name for an Irishman or a Roman Catholic. [C19: from the nickname for *Michael*]

mickey[1] *or* **micky** ('mɪkɪ) *n* **take the mickey** (**out of**). *Informal.* to tease. [C20: of unknown origin]

mickey[2] *or* **micky** ('mɪkɪ) *n Austral. informal.* a young bull, esp. one that is wild and unbranded.

Mickey Finn *n Slang.* **a** a drink containing a drug to make the drinker unconscious, usually formed by the combination of chloral hydrate and alcohol. It can be poisonous. **b** the drug itself. ◆ Often shortened to **Mickey.** [C20: of unknown origin]

Mickey Mouse *adj* (*sometimes not caps.*) *Slang.* **1** ineffective; trivial; insignificant: *he settled for a Mickey Mouse job instead of something challenging.* **2** *Chiefly U.S. and Canadian.* (of music, esp. that of dance bands) mechanical or spiritless. [C20: from the name of a cartoon character created by Walt Disney, known for his simple-minded attitudes]

Mickiewicz (*Polish* mits'kjɛvitʃ) *n* **Adam** ('adam). 1798–1855, Polish poet, whose epic *Thaddeus* (1834) is regarded as a masterpiece of Polish literature.

mickle ('mɪkᵊl) *or* **muckle** ('mʌkᵊl) *Archaic or Scot. and northern English dialect.* ◆ *adj* **1** great or abundant. ◆ *adv* **2** much; greatly. ◆ *n* **3** a great amount, esp. in the proverb, *mony a little makes a mickle.* **4** *Scot.* a small amount, esp. in the proverb, *many a mickle maks a muckle.* [C13 *mikel*, from Old Norse *mikell*, replacing Old English *micel* MUCH]

Micmac ('mɪkmæk) *n* **1** (*pl* **-macs** *or* **-mac**) a member of a North American Indian people formerly living in the Maritime Provinces of Canada. **2** the language of this people, belonging to the Algonquian family.

MICR *abbrev. for* magnetic ink character recognition.

micra ('maɪkrə) *n* a plural of **micron.**

micro ('maɪkrəʊ) *adj* **1** very small. ◆ *n, pl* **-cros. 2** short for **microcomputer, microlepidoptera, microprocessor, microwave oven.**

micro- *or* **micr-** *combining form.* **1** small or minute: *microspore.* **2** involving the use of a microscope: *micrography.* **3** indicating a method or instrument for dealing with small quantities: *micrometer.* **4** (in pathology) indicating abnormal smallness or underdevelopment: *microcephaly; microcyte.* Compare **macro-** (sense 2). **5** denoting 10^{-6}: *microsecond.* Symbol: μ [from Greek *mikros* small]

microaerophile (ˌmaɪkrəʊ'ɛərəʊˌfaɪl) *n* an organism, esp. a bacterium, that thrives in an environment low in oxygen. ▸ **microaerophilic** (ˌmaɪkrəʊˌɛərəʊ'fɪlɪk) *adj*

microanalysis (ˌmaɪkrəʊə'nælɪsɪs) *n, pl* **-ses** (-ˌsiːz). the qualitative or quantitative chemical analysis of very small amounts of substances. ▸ **microanalyst** (ˌmaɪkrəʊ'ænəlɪst) *n* ▸ **microanalytic** (ˌmaɪkrəʊˌænə'lɪtɪk) *or* **ˌmicroˌana'lytical** *adj*

microbalance ('maɪkrəʊˌbæləns) *n* a precision balance designed to weigh quantities between 10^{-6} and 10^{-9} kilogram.

microbarograph (ˌmaɪkrəʊ'bærəˌgrɑːf, -ˌgræf) *n* a barograph that records minute changes in atmospheric pressure.

microbe ('maɪkrəʊb) *n* any microscopic organism, esp. a disease-causing bacterium. [C19: from French, from MICRO- + Greek *bios* life] ▸ **mi'crobial, mi'crobic,** *or* (*less commonly*) **mi'crobian** *adj*

microbiology (ˌmaɪkrəʊbaɪ'ɒlədʒɪ) *n* the branch of biology involving the study of microorganisms and their effects on man. ▸ **microbiological** (ˌmaɪkrəʊˌbaɪə'lɒdʒɪkᵊl) *or* **ˌmicroˌbio'logic** *adj* ▸ **ˌmicroˌbio'logically** *adv* ▸ **ˌmicrobi'ologist** *n*

microburst ('maɪkrəʊˌbɜːst) *n* another name for **downburst.**

microcephaly (ˌmaɪkrəʊ'sɛfəlɪ) *n* the condition of having an abnormally small head or cranial capacity. Compare **megacephaly.** ▸ **microcephalic** (ˌmaɪkrəʊsɪ'fælɪk) *adj, n* ▸ **ˌmicro'cephalous** *adj*

microchemistry (ˌmaɪkrəʊ'kɛmɪstrɪ) *n* chemical experimentation with minute quantities of material. ▸ **ˌmicro'chemical** *adj*

microchip ('maɪkrəʊˌtʃɪp) *n* a small piece of semiconductor material carrying many integrated circuits.

microcircuit ('maɪkrəʊˌsɜːkɪt) *n* a miniature electronic circuit, esp. one in which a number of permanently connected components are contained in one small chip of semiconducting material. See **integrated circuit.** ▸ **ˌmicro'circuitry** *n*

microclimate ('maɪkrəʊˌklaɪmɪt) *n Ecology.* **1** the atmospheric conditions affecting an individual or a small group of organisms, esp. when they differ from the climate of the rest of the community. **2** the entire environment of an individual or small group of organisms. ▸ **microclimatic** (ˌmaɪkrəʊklaɪ'mætɪk) *adj* ▸ **ˌmicrocli'matically** *adv*

microclimatology (ˌmaɪkrəʊˌklaɪmə'tɒlədʒɪ) *n* the study of climate on a small scale, as of a city. ▸ **microclimatologic** (ˌmaɪkrəʊˌklaɪmətə'lɒdʒɪk) *or* **ˌmicroˌclimato'logical** *adj* ▸ **ˌmicroˌclima'tologist** *n*

microcline ('maɪkrəʊˌklaɪn) *n* a white, creamy yellow, red, or green mineral of the feldspar group, found in igneous, sedimentary, and metamorphic rocks: used in the manufacture of glass and ceramics. Composition: potassium aluminium silicate. Formula: $KAlSi_3O_8$. Crystal structure: triclinic [C19: from German *mikroklin*, from *mikro-* MICRO- + Greek *klinein* to lean; so called because its cleavage plane is slightly different from 90°]

micrococcus (ˌmaɪkrəʊ'kɒkəs) *n, pl* **-cocci** (-'kɒksaɪ). **1** any spherical Gram-positive bacterium of the genus *Micrococcus*, causing fermentation of milk: family *Micrococcaceae.* **2** any other bacterium of the family *Micrococcaceae.*

microcomputer ('maɪkrəʊkəmˌpjuːtə) *n* a small computer in which the central processing unit is contained in one or more silicon chips. Sometimes shortened to **micro.**

microcopy ('maɪkrəʊˌkɒpɪ) *n, pl* **-copies.** a greatly reduced photographic copy of a printed page, drawing, etc., on microfilm or microfiche. Sometimes called **microphotograph.**

microcosm ('maɪkrəʊˌkɒzəm) *or* **microcosmos** (ˌmaɪkrəʊ'kɒzmɒs) *n* **1** a miniature representation of something, esp. a unit, group, or place regarded as a copy of a larger one. **2** man regarded as epitomizing the universe. ◆ Compare **macrocosm.** [C15: via Medieval Latin from Greek *mikros kosmos* little world] ▸ **ˌmicro'cosmic** *or* **ˌmicro'cosmical** *adj*

microcosmic salt *n* a white soluble solid obtained from human urine; ammonium sodium hydrogen phosphate. It is used as a flux in bead tests on metal oxides.

microcrystalline (ˌmaɪkrəʊ'krɪstəˌlaɪn) *adj* (of a solid) composed of microscopic crystals.
microcyte ('maɪkrəʊˌsaɪt) *n* an unusually small red blood cell. ▸ **microcytic** (ˌmaɪkrəʊ'sɪtɪk) *adj*
microdetector (ˌmaɪkrəʊdɪ'tɛktə) *n* any instrument for measuring small quantities or detecting small effects, esp. a sensitive galvanometer.
microdont ('maɪkrəʊˌdɒnt) *or* **microdontous** (ˌmaɪkrəʊ'dɒntəs) *adj* having unusually small teeth.
microdot ('maɪkrəʊˌdɒt) *n* **1** a microcopy about the size of a pinhead, used esp. in espionage. **2** a tiny tablet containing LSD.
microeconomics (ˌmaɪkrəʊˌi:kə'nɒmɪks, -ˌɛkə-) *n* (*functioning as sing*) the branch of economics concerned with particular commodities, firms, or individuals and the economic relationships between them. Compare **macroeconomics.** ▸ **ˌmicroˌeco'nomic** *adj*
microelectronics (ˌmaɪkrəʊɪlɛk'trɒnɪks) *n* (*functioning as sing*) the branch of electronics concerned with microcircuits. ▸ **ˌmicroelec'tronic** *adj*
microenvironment ('maɪkrəʊɪnˌvaɪrənmənt) *n Ecology.* the environment of a small area, such as that around a leaf or plant.
microfarad ('maɪkrəʊˌfærəd) *n* one millionth of a farad; 10^{-6} farad. Symbol: μF
microfiche ('maɪkrəʊˌfi:ʃ) *n* a sheet of film, usually the size of a filing card, on which books, newspapers, documents, etc., can be recorded in miniaturized form. Sometimes shortened to **fiche.** See also **ultrafiche. [C20:** from French, from MICRO- + *fiche* small card, from Old French *fichier* to fix**]**
microfilament (ˌmaɪkrəʊ'fɪləmənt) *n* thin filament, composed of the protein actin and associated proteins, that occurs abundantly in muscle and in the cytoplasm of other cells.
microfilaria (ˌmaɪkrəʊfɪ'lɛərɪə) *n, pl* **-iae** (-ɪˌi:). *Zoology.* the early larval stage of certain parasitic nematodes (filariae), found in the blood of infected individuals.
microfilm ('maɪkrəʊˌfɪlm) *n* **1** a strip of film of standard width on which books, newspapers, documents, etc., can be recorded in miniaturized form. ◆ *vb* **2** to photograph (a page, document, etc.) on microfilm. ◆ See also **microfiche.**
microfilm plotter *n Computing.* a type of incremental plotter that has a film rather than a paper output.
microform ('maɪkrəʊˌfɔ:m) *n Computing.* a method of storing symbolic information by using photographic reduction techniques, such as microfilm, microfiche, etc.
microfossil ('maɪkrəʊˌfɒsəl) *n* a fossil generally less than 0.5 millimetre in size, such as a protozoan, bacterium, or pollen grain.
microgamete (ˌmaɪkrəʊ'gæmi:t) *n* the smaller and apparently male of two gametes in conjugating protozoans. Compare **macrogamete.**
microglia (ˌmaɪkrəʊ'glɪə) *n* one of the two types of non-nervous tissue (glia) found in the central nervous system, having macrophage activity. Compare **macroglia.**
micrograph ('maɪkrəʊˌgræf, -ˌgrɑ:f) *n* **1** a photograph or drawing of an object as viewed through a microscope. **2** an instrument or machine for producing very small writing or engraving.
micrography (maɪ'krɒgrəfɪ) *n* **1** the description, study, drawing, or photography of microscopic objects. **2** the technique of using a microscope. **3** the art or practice of writing in minute characters. ▸ **mi'crographer** *n* ▸ **micrographic** (ˌmaɪkrəʊ'græfɪk) *adj* ▸ **ˌmicro'graphically** *adv*
microgravity ('maɪkrəʊˌgrævɪtɪ) *n* gravitational effects operating, or apparently operating, in a localized region, as in a spacecraft under conditions of weightlessness.
microgroove ('maɪkrəʊˌgru:v) *n* **a** the narrow groove in a long-playing gramophone record. **b** (*as modifier*): *a microgroove record.*
microhabitat (ˌmaɪkrəʊ'hæbɪtæt) *n Ecology.* the smallest part of the environment that supports a distinct flora and fauna, such as a fallen log in a forest.
microinstruction ('maɪkrəʊɪnˌstrʌkʃən) *n Computing.* an instruction produced within an arithmetic and logic unit in accordance with a microprogram, that activates a particular circuit to perform part of the operation specified by a machine instruction.
microlepidoptera (ˌmaɪkrəʊˌlɛpɪ'dɒptərə) *pl n* a collector's name for the smaller moths: a term without taxonomic significance. Compare **macrolepidoptera.**
microlight *or* **microlite** ('maɪkrəʊˌlaɪt) *n* a small private aircraft carrying no more than two people, with an empty weight of not more than 150 kg and a wing area not less than 10 square metres: used in pleasure flying and racing.
microlith ('maɪkrəʊˌlɪθ) *n Archaeol.* a small Mesolithic flint tool which was made from a blade and formed part of hafted tools. ▸ **ˌmicro'lithic** *adj*
micromarketing (ˌmaɪkrəʊ'mɑ:kɪtɪŋ) *n* the marketing of products or services designed to meet the needs of a very small section of the market.
micromere ('maɪkrəʊˌmɪə) *n Embryol.* any of the small cells formed by unequal cleavage of a fertilized ovum.
micrometeorite (ˌmaɪkrəʊ'mi:tɪəˌraɪt) *n* a tiny meteorite having a diameter of 10–40 micrometres, found esp. in rainwater and seawater, having entered the atmosphere as a **micrometeoroid** (extremely small meteoroid).
micrometeorology (ˌmaɪkrəʊˌmi:tɪə'rɒlədʒɪ) *n* the study of the layer of air immediately above the earth and of small-scale meteorological processes.
micrometer (maɪ'krɒmɪtə) *n* **1** any of various instruments or devices for the accurate measurement of distances or angles. **2** Also called: **micrometer gauge, micrometer calliper.** a type of gauge for the accurate measurement of small distances, thicknesses, diameters, etc. The gap between its measuring faces is adjusted by a fine screw, the rotation of the screw giving a sensitive measure of the distance moved by the face. ▸ **mi'crometry** *n* ▸ **micrometric** (ˌmaɪkrəʊ'mɛtrɪk) *or* **ˌmicro'metrical** *adj*
micrometer screw *n* a screw with a fine thread of definite pitch, such as that of a micrometer gauge.
micrometre ('maɪkrəʊˌmi:tə) *n* a unit of length equal to 10^{-6} metre. Symbol μm Former name: **micron.**
microminiaturization *or* **microminiaturisation** (ˌmaɪkrəʊˌmɪnɪtʃəraɪ'zeɪʃən) *n* the production and application of very small semiconductor components and the circuits and equipment in which they are used.
micron ('maɪkrɒn) *n, pl* **-crons** *or* **-cra** (-krə). a unit of length equal to 10^{-6} metre. It is being replaced by the micrometre, the equivalent SI unit. **[C19:** New Latin, from Greek *mikros* small**]**
Micronesia (ˌmaɪkrəʊ'ni:zɪə) *n* **1** one of the three divisions of islands in the Pacific (the others being Melanesia and Polynesia); the NW division of Oceania: includes the Mariana, Caroline, Marshall, and Kiribati island groups, and Nauru Island. **2 Federated States of.** an island group in the W Pacific, formerly within the United States Trust Territory of the Pacific Islands: comprises the islands of Truk, Yap, Ponape, and Kosrae: formed in 1979 when the islands became self-governing: status of free association with the U.S. from 1982. Languages: English and Micronesian languages. Religion: Christian majority. Currency: U.S. dollar. Capital: Palikir. Pop.: 108 000 (1998 est.). **[C19:** from MICRO- + Greek *nēsos* island; so called from the small size of many of the islands; on the model of *Polynesia***]**
Micronesian (ˌmaɪkrəʊ'ni:zɪən) *adj* **1** of or relating to Micronesia, its inhabitants, or their languages. ◆ *n* **2** a native or inhabitant of Micronesia, more akin to the Polynesians than the Melanesians, but having Mongoloid traces. **3** a group of languages spoken in Micronesia, belonging to the Malayo-Polynesian family.
micronucleus (ˌmaɪkrəʊ'nju:klɪəs) *n, pl* **-clei** (-klɪˌaɪ) *or* **-cleuses.** the smaller of two nuclei in ciliated protozoans, involved in reproduction. Compare **macronucleus.**
micronutrient (ˌmaɪkrəʊ'nju:trɪənt) *n* any substance, such as a vitamin or trace element, essential for healthy growth and development but required only in minute amounts.
microorganism (ˌmaɪkrəʊ'ɔ:gəˌnɪzəm) *n* any organism, such as a bacterium, protozoan, or virus, of microscopic size.
micropalaeontology (ˌmaɪkrəʊˌpælɪɒn'tɒlədʒɪ) *n* the branch of palaeontology concerned with the study of microscopic fossils. ▸ **micropalaeontological** (ˌmaɪkrəʊˌpælɪɒntə'lɒdʒɪkəl) *or* **ˌmicroˌpalaeonto'logic** *adj* ▸ **ˌmicroˌpalaeon'tologist** *n*
microparasite (ˌmaɪkrəʊ'pærəˌsaɪt) *n* any parasitic microorganism. ▸ **microparasitic** (ˌmaɪkrəʊˌpærə'sɪtɪk) *adj*
microphagous (maɪ'krɒfəgəs) *adj Zoology.* (of an animal) feeding on small particles of food.
microphanerophyte (ˌmaɪkrəʊ'fænərəʊˌfaɪt) *n Botany.* any shrub or tree having a height of 2 to 8 metres.
microphone ('maɪkrəˌfəʊn) *n* a device used in sound-reproduction systems for converting sound into electrical energy, usually by means of a ribbon or diaphragm set into motion by the sound waves. The vibrations are converted into the equivalent audio-frequency electric currents. Informal name: **mike.** See also **carbon microphone.** Compare **loudspeaker.**
microphonic (ˌmaɪkrə'fɒnɪk) *adj* **1** of or relating to microphones. **2** (of valves or other electronic components) unusually sensitive to incident sound or mechanical shock.
microphotograph (ˌmaɪkrəʊ'fəʊtəˌgrɑ:f, -ˌgræf) *n* **1** a photograph in which the image is greatly reduced and therefore requires optical enlargement for viewing purposes. **2** a less common name for **microcopy** or **photomicrograph** (sense 1). ▸ **ˌmicroˌphoto'graphic** *adj* ▸ **microphotography** (ˌmaɪkrəʊfə'tɒgrəfɪ) *n*
microphyll ('maɪkrəʊfɪl) *n Botany.* the relatively small type of leaf produced by club mosses and horsetails. Compare **megaphyll.**
microphysics (ˌmaɪkrəʊ'fɪzɪks) *n* (*functioning as sing*) the branch of physics concerned with small objects and systems, such as atoms, molecules, nuclei, and elementary particles. ▸ **ˌmicro'physical** *adj*
microphyte ('maɪkrəʊˌfaɪt) *n* any microscopic plant, esp. a parasite. ▸ **microphytic** (ˌmaɪkrəʊ'fɪtɪk) *adj*
microprint ('maɪkrəʊˌprɪnt) *n* a microphotograph reproduced on paper and read by a magnifying device. It is used in order to reduce the size of large books, etc.
microprism ('maɪkrəʊˌprɪzəm) *n Photog.* a small prism incorporated in the focusing screen of many single-lens reflex cameras. The prism stops shimmering when the subject is in focus.
microprocessor (ˌmaɪkrəʊ'prəʊsɛsə) *n Computing.* a single integrated circuit performing the basic functions of the central processing unit in a small computer.
microprogram ('maɪkrəʊˌprəʊgræm) *n Computing.* a sequence of microinstructions that controls the operation of an arithmetic and logic unit so that machine code instructions are executed.
micropropagation (ˌmaɪkrəʊˌprɒpə'geɪʃən) *n Botany.* the production of a large number of individual plants from a small piece of plant tissue cultured in a nutrient medium.
micropsia (maɪ'krɒpsɪə) *n* a defect of vision in which objects appear to be smaller than they appear to a person with normal vision.
micropterous (maɪ'krɒptərəs) *adj* (of certain animals, esp. some types of ant) having small reduced wings.
micropyle ('maɪkrəʊˌpaɪl) *n* **1** a small opening in the integuments of a plant ovule through which the male gametes pass. **2** a small pore in the shell of an insect's eggs through which the sperm passes. **[C19:** from MICRO- + Greek *pulē* gate**]** ▸ **ˌmicro'pylar** *adj*
micropyrometer (ˌmaɪkrəʊpaɪ'rɒmɪtə) *n* a pyrometer for measuring the temperature of very small objects.

microreader (ˈmaɪkrəʊˌriːdə) *n* an apparatus that produces an enlarged image of a microphotograph.

microscope (ˈmaɪkrəˌskəʊp) *n* **1** an optical instrument that uses a lens or combination of lenses to produce a magnified image of a small, close object. Modern optical microscopes have magnifications of about 1500 to 2000. See also **simple microscope, compound microscope, ultramicroscope. 2** any instrument, such as the electron microscope, for producing a magnified visual image of a small object.

microscopic (ˌmaɪkrəˈskɒpɪk) *or* (*less commonly*) **microscopical** *adj* **1** not large enough to be seen with the naked eye but visible under a microscope. Compare **macroscopic. 2** very small; minute. **3** of, concerned with, or using a microscope. **4** characterized by or done with great attention to detail. ► ˌ**micro'scopically** *adv*

Microscopium (ˌmaɪkrəˈskəʊpɪəm) *n, Latin genitive* **Microscopii** (ˌmaɪkrəˈskəʊpɪˌaɪ). a faint constellation in the S hemisphere lying near Sagittarius and Capricornus.

microscopy (maɪˈkrɒskəpɪ) *n* **1** the study, design, and manufacture of microscopes. **2** investigation by use of a microscope. ► **microscopist** (maɪˈkrɒskəpɪst) *n*

microsecond (ˈmaɪkrəʊˌsɛkənd) *n* one millionth of a second. Symbol: µs

microseism (ˈmaɪkrəʊˌsaɪzəm) *n* a very slight tremor of the earth's surface, thought not to be caused by an earthquake. ► **microseismic** (ˌmaɪkrəʊˈsaɪzmɪk) *or* ˌ**micro'seismical** *adj*

microsleep (ˈmaɪkrəʊˌsliːp) *n* a period of sleep which is so momentary as to be imperceptible.

microsmatic (ˌmaɪkrɒzˈmætɪk) *adj* (of humans and certain animals) having a poor sense of smell. **[**from MICRO- + Greek *osmē* smell**]**

microsome (ˈmaɪkrəʊˌsəʊm) *n* any of the small particles consisting of ribosomes and fragments of attached endoplasmic reticulum that can be isolated from cells by centrifugal action. ► ˌ**micro'somal** *adj*

microsporangium (ˌmaɪkrəʊspɔːˈrændʒɪəm) *n, pl* **-gia** (-dʒɪə). the structure in certain ferns in which the microspores are formed: corresponds to the pollen sac in seed plants. Compare **megasporangium.**

microspore (ˈmaɪkrəʊˌspɔː) *n* **1** the smaller of two types of spore produced by some ferns, which develops into the male gametophyte. Compare **megaspore** (sense 1). **2** the pollen grain of seed plants. ► ˌ**micro'sporic** *or* ˌ**micro'sporous** *adj*

microsporophyll (ˌmaɪkrəʊˈspɔːrəfɪl) *n* a leaf on which the microspores are formed: corresponds to the stamen of a flowering plant. Compare **megasporophyll. [**C19: from MICRO- + SPOROPHYLL**]**

microstomatous (ˌmaɪkrəʊˈstɒmətəs) *or* **microstomous** (maɪˈkrɒstəməs) *adj Anatomy.* having an unusually small mouth.

microstructure (ˈmaɪkrəʊˌstrʌktʃə) *n* structure on a microscopic scale, esp. the structure of an alloy as observed by etching, polishing, and observation under a microscope.

microsurgery (ˌmaɪkrəʊˈsɜːdʒərɪ) *n* intricate surgery performed on cells, tissues, etc., using a specially designed operating microscope and miniature precision instruments. ► ˌ**micro'surgical** *adj*

microswitch (ˈmaɪkrəʊˌswɪtʃ) *n Electrical engineering.* a switch that operates by small movements of a lever.

microtechnology (ˌmaɪkrəʊtɛkˈnɒlədʒɪ) *n* technology that uses microelectronics.

microtome (ˈmaɪkrəʊˌtəʊm) *n* an instrument used for cutting thin sections, esp. of biological material, for microscopical examination.

microtomy (maɪˈkrɒtəmɪ) *n, pl* **-mies.** the cutting of sections with a microtome. ► **microtomic** (ˌmaɪkrəʊˈtɒmɪk) *or* ˌ**micro'tomical** *adj* ► **mi'crotomist** *n*

microtone (ˈmaɪkrəʊˌtəʊn) *n* any musical interval smaller than a semitone. ► ˌ**micro'tonal** *adj* ► ˌ**microto'nality** *n* ► ˌ**micro'tonally** *adv*

microtubule (ˌmaɪkrəʊˈtjuːbjuːl) *n Biology.* a tubular aggregate of protein subunits that forms structures, such as the mitotic spindle or the cilia of animal cells or of protozoans, in which the protein interacts with other proteins to generate various cellular movements.

microvillus (ˌmaɪkrəʊˈvɪləs) *n, pl* **-li** (-laɪ). *Physiol.* a thin protuberance present in great abundance at the surface of some epithelial cells, notably in the gut, thus increasing the surface area available for absorption.

microwave (ˈmaɪkrəʊˌweɪv) *n* **1a** electromagnetic radiation in the wavelength range 0.3 to 0.001 metres: used in radar, cooking, etc. **1b** (*as modifier*): *microwave generator.* **2** short for **microwave oven.** ◆ *vb* (*tr*) **3** to cook in a microwave oven.

microwave background *n* a background of microwave electromagnetic radiation discovered in space in 1965, believed to have emanated from the big bang with which the universe began.

microwave detector *n* a device for recording the speed of a motorist.

microwave oven *n* an oven in which food is cooked by microwaves. Often shortened to **micro, microwave.**

microwave spectroscopy *n* a type of spectroscopy in which information is obtained on the structure and chemical bonding of molecules and crystals by measurements of the wavelengths of microwaves emitted or absorbed by the sample. ► **microwave spectroscope** *n*

microwriter (ˈmaɪkrəʊˌraɪtə) *n* a small device with six keys for creating text that can be printed or displayed on a visual display unit.

micrurgy (ˈmaɪkrɜːdʒɪ) *n Biology.* the manipulation and examination of single cells under a microscope. **[**C20: from MICRO- + Greek *-ourgia* work**]**

micturate (ˈmɪktjʊˌreɪt) *vb* (*intr*) a less common word for **urinate. [**C19: from Latin *micturīre* to desire to urinate, from *mingere* to urinate**]** ► **micturition** (ˌmɪktjʊˈrɪʃən) *n*

mid[1] (mɪd) *adj* **1** *Phonetics.* of, relating to, or denoting a vowel whose articulation lies approximately halfway between high and low, such as *e* in English *bet.* ◆ *n* **2** an archaic word for **middle. [**C12 *midre* (inflected form of *midd,* unattested); related to Old Norse *mithr,* Gothic *midjis***]**

mid[2] *or* **'mid** (mɪd) *prep* a poetic word for **amid.**

mid. *abbrev. for* middle.

Mid. *abbrev. for* Midshipman.

mid- *combining form.* indicating a middle part, point, time, or position: *midday; mid-April; mid-Victorian.* **[**Old English; see MIDDLE, MID[1]**]**

midair (ˌmɪdˈɛə) *n* **a** some point above ground level, in the air. **b** (*as modifier*): *a midair collision of aircraft.*

Midas (ˈmaɪdəs) *n* **1** *Greek legend.* a king of Phrygia given the power by Dionysus of turning everything he touched to gold. **2 the Midas touch.** ability to make money.

MIDAS (ˈmaɪdəs) *n acronym for* Missile Defence Alarm System.

mid-Atlantic *adj* characterized by a blend of British and American styles, elements, etc.: *a disc jockey's mid-Atlantic accent.*

midbrain (ˈmɪdˌbreɪn) *n* the nontechnical name for **mesencephalon.**

midday (ˈmɪdˈdeɪ) *n* **a** the middle of the day; noon. **b** (*as modifier*): *a midday meal.*

Middelburg (ˈmɪdᵊlˌbɜːg; *Dutch* ˈmɪdəlbyrx) *n* a city in the SW Netherlands, capital of Zeeland province, on Walcheren Island: an important trading centre in the Middle Ages and member of the Hanseatic League; 12th-century abbey; market town. Pop.: 40 118 (1994).

midden (ˈmɪdᵊn) *n* **1a** *Archaic or dialect.* a dunghill or pile of refuse. **1b** *Dialect.* a dustbin. **1c** *Northern English dialect.* an earth closet. **2** See **kitchen midden. [**C14: from Scandinavian; compare Danish *mödding* from *mög* MUCK + *dynge* pile**]**

middle (ˈmɪdᵊl) *adj* **1** equally distant from the ends or periphery of something; central. **2** intermediate in status, situation, etc. **3** located between the early and late parts of a series, time sequence, etc. **4** not extreme, esp. in size; medium. **5** (esp. in Greek and Sanskrit grammar) denoting a voice of verbs expressing reciprocal or reflexive action. Compare **active** (sense 5), **passive** (sense 5). **6** (*usually cap.*) (of a language) intermediate between the earliest and the modern forms: *Middle English.* ◆ *n* **7** an area or point equal in distance from the ends or periphery or in time between the early and late parts. **8** an intermediate part or section, such as the waist. **9** *Grammar.* the middle voice. **10** *Logic.* See **middle term. 11** the ground between rows of growing plants. **12** a discursive article in a journal, placed between the leading articles and the book reviews. ◆ *vb* (*tr*) **13** to place in the middle. **14** *Nautical.* to fold in two. **15** *Football.* to return (the ball) from the wing to midfield. **16** *Cricket.* to hit (the ball) with the middle of the bat. **[**Old English *middel;* compare Old Frisian *middel,* Dutch *middel,* German *mittel***]**

middle age *n* the period of life between youth and old age, usually (in man) considered to occur approximately between the ages of 40 and 60. ► ˌ**middle-'aged** *adj*

Middle Ages *n* **the.** *European history.* **1** (broadly) the period from the end of classical antiquity (or the deposition of the last W Roman emperor in 476 A.D.) to the Italian Renaissance (or the fall of Constantinople in 1453). **2** (narrowly) the period from about 1000 A.D. to the 15th century. Compare **Dark Ages.**

middle-age spread *or* **middle-aged spread** *n* the fat that appears round many people's waist during middle age.

Middle America *n* **1** the territories between the U.S. and South America: Mexico, Central America, Panama, and the Greater and Lesser Antilles. **2** the U.S. middle class, esp. those groups that are politically conservative. ► **Middle American** *adj, n*

Middle Atlantic States *or* **Middle States** *pl n* the states of New York, Pennsylvania, and New Jersey.

middlebreaker (ˈmɪdᵊlˌbreɪkə) *or* **middlebuster** *n* a type of plough that cuts a furrow with the soil heaped on each side, often used for sowing. Also called: **lister.**

middlebrow (ˈmɪdᵊlˌbraʊ) *Disparaging.* ◆ *n* **1** a person with conventional tastes and limited cultural appreciation. ◆ *adj also* **middlebrowed. 2** of or appealing to middlebrows: *middlebrow culture.* ► **'middleˌbrowism** *n*

middle C *n Music.* the note graphically represented on the first ledger line below the treble staff or the first ledger line above the bass staff and corresponding in pitch to an internationally standardized fundamental frequency of 261.63 hertz.

middle class *n* **1** Also called: **bourgeoisie.** a social stratum that is not clearly defined but is positioned between the lower and upper classes. It consists of businessmen, professional people, etc., along with their families, and is marked by bourgeois values. Compare **lower class, upper class, working class.** ◆ *adj* **middle-class. 2** of, relating to, or characteristic of the middle class.

middle common room *n* (in certain universities and colleges) a common room for the use of postgraduate students. Compare **junior common room, senior common room.**

Middle Congo *n* one of the four territories of former French Equatorial Africa, in W central Africa: became an autonomous member of the French Community, as the Republic of the Congo, in 1958.

middle-distance *adj* **1** *Athletics.* relating to or denoting races of a length between the sprints and the distance events, esp. the 800 metres and the 1500 metres. ◆ *n* **middle distance. 2** part of a painting, esp. a landscape between the foreground and far distance.

Middle Dutch *n* the Dutch language from about 1100 to about 1500. Abbrev.: **MD.**

middle ear *n* the sound-conducting part of the ear, containing the malleus, incus, and stapes.

Middle East *n* **1** (loosely) the area around the E Mediterranean, esp. Israel and the Arab countries from Turkey to North Africa and eastwards to Iran. **2** (formerly) the area extending from the Tigris and Euphrates to Myanmar. ▸ **Middle Eastern** *adj*

middle eight *n* the third contrasting eight-bar section of a 32-bar pop song.

Middle England *n* a characterization of a predominantly middle-class, middle-income section of British society living mainly in suburban and rural England.

Middle English *n* the English language from about 1100 to about 1450: main dialects are Kentish, Southwestern (West Saxon), East Midland (which replaced West Saxon as the chief literary form and developed into Modern English), West Midland, and Northern (from which the Scots of Lowland Scotland and other modern dialects developed). Compare **Old English, Modern English.** Abbrev.: **ME.**

middle game *n Chess.* the central phase between the opening and the endgame.

Middle Greek *n* another name for **Medieval Greek.**

middle ground *n* **1** another term for **middle distance. 2** a position of compromise between two opposing views, parties, etc.

Middle High German *n* High German from about 1200 to about 1500. Abbrev.: **MHG.**

Middle Irish *n* Irish Gaelic from about 1100 to about 1500.

Middle Kingdom *n* **1** a period of Egyptian history extending from the late 11th to the 13th dynasty (?2040–?1670 B.C.). **2a** the former Chinese empire (from the belief that it lay at the centre of the earth). **2b** the original 18 provinces of China; China proper.

Middle Low German *n* Low German from about 1200 to about 1500. Abbrev.: **MLG.**

middleman ('mɪdəl,mæn) *n, pl* **-men. 1** an independent trader engaged in the distribution of goods from producer to consumer. **2** an intermediary. **3** *Theatre.* the interlocutor in minstrel shows.

middle management *n* a level of management in an organization or business consisting of executives or senior supervisory staff in charge of the detailed running of an organization or business and reporting to top management. Compare **top management.** ▸ **middle manager** *n*

middlemost ('mɪdəl,məʊst) *adj* another word for **midmost.**

middle name *n* **1** a name between a person's first name and surname. **2** a characteristic quality for which a person is known: *caution is my middle name.*

middle-of-the-road *adj* **1** not extreme, esp. in political views; moderate. **2** of, denoting, or relating to popular music having a wide general appeal. ▸ **'middle-of-the-'roader** *n*

Middle Palaeolithic *n* **1** the period between the Lower and the Upper Palaeolithic, usually taken as equivalent to the Mousterian. ◆ *adj* **2** of or relating to this period.

middle passage *n* **the.** *History.* the journey across the Atlantic Ocean from the W coast of Africa to the Caribbean: the longest part of the journey of the slave ships sailing to the Caribbean or the Americas.

Middle Persian *n* the classical form of modern Persian, spoken from about 300 A.D. to about 900. See also **Pahlavi**[2].

Middlesbrough ('mɪdəlzbrə) *n* **1** an industrial town in NE England, in Middlesbrough unitary authority, North Yorkshire: on the Tees estuary. Pop.: 145 800 (1994 est.). **2** a unitary authority in NE England, in North Yorkshire: formerly (1974–96) part of Cleveland county. Pop.: 146 000 (1996 est.). Area: 54 sq. km (21 sq. miles).

middle school *n* (in England and Wales) a school for children aged between 8 or 9 and 12 or 13. Compare **first school.**

Middlesex ('mɪdəl,sɛks) *n* a former county of SE England: became mostly part of N and W Greater London in 1965. Abbrev.: **Middx.**

Middle States *pl n* another name for the **Middle Atlantic States.**

Middle Temple *n* (in England) one of the four legal societies in London which together form the Inns of Court.

middle term *n Logic.* the term that appears in both the major and minor premises of a syllogism, but not in the conclusion. Also called: **mean, middle.**

Middleton[1] ('mɪdəltən) *n* a town in NW England, in Oldham unitary authority, Greater Manchester. Pop.: 45 621 (1991).

Middleton[2] ('mɪdəltən) *n* **Thomas.** ?1570–1627, English dramatist. His plays include the tragedies *Women beware Women* (1621) and, in collaboration with William Rowley (?1585–?1642), *The Changeling* (1622) and the political satire *A Game at Chess* (1624).

middle watch *n Nautical.* the watch between midnight and 4 a.m.

middleweight ('mɪdəl,weɪt) *n* **1a** a professional boxer weighing 154–160 pounds (70–72.5 kg). **1b** an amateur boxer weighing 71–75 kg (157–165 pounds). **1c** (*as modifier*): *a middleweight contest.* **2** a wrestler in a similar weight category (usually 172–192 pounds (78–87 kg)).

Middle West *n* another name for the **Midwest.** ▸ **Middle Western** *adj* ▸ **Middle Westerner** *n*

middling ('mɪdlɪŋ) *adj* **1** mediocre in quality, size, etc.; neither good nor bad, esp. in health (often in the phrase **fair to middling**). ◆ *adv* **2** *Informal.* moderately: *middling well.* [C15 (northern English and Scottish): from MID[1] + -LING[2]] ▸ **'middlingly** *adv*

middlings ('mɪdlɪŋz) *pl n* **1** the poorer or coarser part of flour or other products. **2** commodities of intermediate grade, quality, size, or price. **3** *Chiefly U.S.* the part of a pig between the ham and shoulder.

Middx *abbrev. for* Middlesex.

middy ('mɪdɪ) *n, pl* **-dies. 1** *Informal.* See **midshipman** (sense 1). **2** See **middy blouse. 3** *Austral.* a middle-sized glass of beer.

middy blouse *n* a blouse with a sailor collar, worn by women and children, esp. formerly.

Mideast (,mɪd'iːst) *n Chiefly U.S.* another name for **Middle East.**

midfield (,mɪd'fiːld) *n Soccer.* **a** the general area between the two opposing defences. **b** (*as modifier*): *a midfield player.*

Midgard ('mɪdgɑːd), **Midgarth** ('mɪdgɑːð), *or* **Mithgarthr** ('mɪðgɑːðə) *n Norse myth.* the dwelling place of mankind, formed from the body of the giant Ymir and linked by the bridge Bifrost to Asgard, home of the gods. [C19: from Old Norse *mithgarthr;* see MID[1], YARD[2]]

midge (mɪdʒ) *n* **1** any fragile mosquito-like dipterous insect of the family *Chironomidae,* occurring in dancing swarms, esp. near water. **2** any similar or related insect, such as the biting midge and gall midge. **3** a small or diminutive person or animal. [Old English *mycge;* compare Old High German *mucca,* Danish *myg*] ▸ **'midgy** *adj*

midget ('mɪdʒɪt) *n* **1** a dwarf whose skeleton and features are of normal proportions. **2a** something small of its kind. **2b** (*as modifier*): *a midget car.* [C19: from MIDGE + -ET]

Mid Glamorgan *n* a former county of S Wales, formed in 1974 from parts of Breconshire, Glamorgan, and Monmouthshire: replaced in 1996 by the county boroughs of Bridgend, Rhondda Cynon Taff, Merthyr Tydfil, and part of Caerphilly.

midgut ('mɪd,gʌt) *n* **1** the middle part of the digestive tract of vertebrates, including the small intestine. **2** the middle part of the digestive tract of arthropods. ◆ See also **foregut, hindgut.**

Midheaven ('mɪd'hɛvən) *n Astrology.* **1** the point on the ecliptic, measured in degrees, that crosses the meridian of a particular place at a particular time. On a person's birth chart it relates to the time of birth. Abbrev.: **MC. 2** the sign of the zodiac containing this point. [C16: initials *MC* represent Latin *medium caeli* middle of the sky]

midi ('mɪdɪ) *adj* **a** (of a skirt, coat, etc.) reaching to below the knee or midcalf. **b** (*as n*): *she wore her new midi.* [C20: from MID-; on the model of MAXI and MINI]

Midi (*French* midi) *n* **1** the south of France. **2 Canal du.** a canal in S France, extending from the River Garonne at Toulouse to the Mediterranean at Sète and providing a link between the Mediterranean and Atlantic coasts: built between 1666 and 1681. Length: 181 km (150 miles).

MIDI ('mɪdɪ) *n* (*modifier*) a generally accepted specification for the external control of electronic musical instruments: *a MIDI synthesizer; a MIDI system.* [C20: from *m(usical) i(nstrument) d(igital) i(nterface)*]

Midian ('mɪdɪən) *n Old Testament.* **1** a son of Abraham (Genesis 25:1–2). **2** a nomadic nation claiming descent from him. ▸ **'Midian,ite** *n, adj* ▸ **'Midian,itish** *adj*

midinette (,mɪdɪ'nɛt; *French* midinɛt) *n, pl* **-nettes** (-'nɛts; *French* -nɛt). a Parisian seamstress or salesgirl in a clothes shop. [C20: from French, from *midi* noon + *dinette* light meal, since the girls had time for no more than a snack at midday]

Midi-Pyrénées (*French* midipirene) *n* a region of SW France: consists of N slopes of the Pyrenees in the south, a fertile lowland area in the west crossed by the River Garonne, and the edge of the Massif Central in the north and east.

midiron ('mɪd,aɪən) *n Golf.* a club, usually a No. 5, 6, or 7 iron, used for medium-length approach shots.

midi system *n* a complete set of hi-fi sound equipment designed as a single unit that is more compact than the standard equipment.

midland ('mɪdlənd) *n* **a** the central or inland part of a country. **b** (*as modifier*): *a midland region.*

Midlands ('mɪdləndz) *n* (*functioning as pl or sing*) **the.** the central counties of England, including Warwickshire, Northamptonshire, Leicestershire, Nottinghamshire, Derbyshire, Staffordshire, the unitary authorities in the area of the former West Midlands metropolitan county, and Worcestershire: characterized by manufacturing industries. ▸ **'Midlander** *n*

midlife crisis ('mɪd,laɪf) *n* a crisis that may be experienced in middle age involving frustration, panic, and feelings of pointlessness, sometimes resulting in radical and often ill-advised changes of lifestyle.

Midlothian (mɪd'ləʊðɪən) *n* a council area of SE central Scotland: the historical county of Midlothian (including Edinburgh) became part of Lothian region in 1975; separate unitary authorities were created for Midlothian and City of Edinburgh in 1996; mainly agricultural. Administrative centre: Dalkeith. Pop.: 79 910 (1996 est.). Area: 356 sq. km (137 sq. miles).

midmost ('mɪd,məʊst) *adj, adv* in the middle or midst.

midnight ('mɪd,naɪt) *n* **1a** the middle of the night; 12 o'clock at night. **1b** (*as modifier*): *the midnight hour.* **2 burn the midnight oil.** to work or study late into the night. ▸ **'mid,nightly** *adj, adv*

midnight blue *n* **a** a very dark blue colour; bluish black. **b** (*as adj*): *a midnight-blue suit.*

midnight sun *n* the sun visible at midnight during the summer inside the Arctic and Antarctic circles.

mid-off *n Cricket.* **1** the fielding position on the off side closest to the bowler. **2** a fielder in this position.

mid-on *n Cricket.* **1** the fielding position on the on side closest to the bowler. **2** a fielder in this position.

midpoint ('mɪd,pɔɪnt) *n* **1** the point on a line that is at an equal distance from either end. **2** a point in time halfway between the beginning and end of an event.

midrash ('mɪdræʃ; *Hebrew* mi'draʃ) *n, pl* **midrashim** (mɪ'drɔʃɪm; *Hebrew* midra'ʃim). *Judaism.* **1** a homily on a scriptural passage derived by traditional Jewish exegetical methods and consisting usually of embellishment of the scriptural narrative. **2** one of a number of collections of such homilies composed between 400 and 1200 A.D. [C17: from Hebrew: commentary, from *darash* to search] ▸ **midrashic** (mɪd'ræʃɪk) *adj*

midrib ('mɪd,rɪb) *n* the main vein of a leaf, running down the centre of the blade.

midriff (ˈmɪdrɪf) *n* **1a** the middle part of the human body, esp. between waist and bust. **1b** (*as modifier*): *midriff bulge.* **2** *Anatomy.* another name for the **diaphragm** (sense 1). **3** the part of a woman's garment covering the midriff. **4** *U.S.* a woman's garment which exposes the midriff. [Old English *midhrif,* from MID[1] + *hrif* belly]
midsection (ˈmɪdˌsɛkʃən) *n* **1** the middle of something. **2** the middle region of the human body; midriff.
midship (ˈmɪdˌʃɪp) *Nautical.* ◆ *adj* **1** in, of, or relating to the middle of a vessel. ◆ *n* **2** the middle of a vessel.
midshipman (ˈmɪdˌʃɪpmən) *n, pl* **-men. 1** a probationary rank held by young naval officers under training, or an officer holding such a rank. **2** any of several American toadfishes of the genus *Porichthys,* having small light-producing organs on the undersurface of their bodies.
midships (ˈmɪdˌʃɪps) *adv, adj Nautical.* See **amidships.**
midst[1] (mɪdst) *n* **1 in the midst of.** surrounded or enveloped by; at a point during, esp. a climactic one. **2 in our midst.** among us. **3** *Archaic.* the centre. [C14: back formation from *amiddes* AMID]
midst[2] (mɪdst) *prep Poetic.* See **amid.**
midstream (ˈmɪdˌstriːm) *n* **1** the middle of a stream or river. **2** the middle of a process or action: *they tried to change the rules in midstream.* ◆ *adv, adj* **3** in or towards the middle of a stream or river: *moored midstream.*
midsummer (ˈmɪdˈsʌmə) *n* **1a** the middle or height of the summer. **1b** (*as modifier*): *a midsummer carnival.* **2** another name for **summer solstice.**
midsummer madness *n* foolish or extravagant behaviour, supposed to occur during the summer.
midsummer-men *n* (*functioning as sing or pl*) another name for **rose-root.**
Midsummer's Day *or* **Midsummer Day** *n* June 24, the feast of St John the Baptist; in England, Ireland, and Wales, one of the four quarter days. See also **summer solstice.**
midterm (ˈmɪdˈtɜːm) *n* **1a** the middle of a term in a school, university, etc. **1b** (*as modifier*): *midterm exam.* **2** *U.S. Politics.* **2a** the middle of a term of office, esp. of a presidential term, when congressional and local elections are held. **2b** (*as modifier*): *midterm elections.* **3a** the middle of the gestation period. **3b** (*as modifier*): *midterm checkup.* See **term** (sense 6).
midtown (ˈmɪdˌtaʊn) *n U.S. and Eastern Canadian.* the centre of a town. See also **downtown, uptown.**
mid-Victorian *adj* **1** *British history.* of or relating to the middle period of the reign of Queen Victoria (1837–1901). ◆ *n* **2** a person of the mid-Victorian era.
midway (ˈmɪdˌweɪ) *adj, adv* **1** in or at the middle of the distance; halfway. ◆ *n* **2** *U.S. and Canadian.* a place in a fair, carnival, etc., where sideshows are located. **3** *Obsolete.* a middle place, way, etc.
Midway Islands *pl n* an atoll in the central Pacific, about 2100 km (1300 miles) northwest of Honolulu: annexed by the U.S. in 1867: scene of a decisive battle (June, 1942), in which the U.S. combined fleets destroyed Japan's carrier fleet. Pop.: 450 (1995 est.). Area: 5 sq. km (2 sq. miles).
midweek (ˈmɪdˈwiːk) *n* **a** the middle of the week. **b** (*as modifier*): *a midweek holiday.* ▸ ˌ**midˈweekly** *adj*
Midwest (ˈmɪdˈwest) *or* **Middle West** *n* the N central part of the U.S.; the region consisting of the states from Ohio westwards that border on the Great Lakes, often extended to include the upper Mississippi and Missouri valleys. ▸ ˈ**Midˈwestern** *adj* ▸ ˈ**Midˈwesterner** *n*
mid-wicket *n Cricket.* **1** the fielding position on the on side, approximately midway between square leg and mid-on. **2** a fielder in this position.
midwife (ˈmɪdˌwaɪf) *n, pl* **-wives** (-ˌwaɪvz). a person qualified to deliver babies and to care for women before, during, and after childbirth. [C14: from Old English *mid* with + *wif* woman]
midwifery (ˈmɪdˌwɪfərɪ) *n* the art or practice of a midwife; obstetrics.
midwife toad *n* a European toad, *Alytes obstetricans,* the male of which carries the fertilized eggs on its hind legs until they hatch: family *Discoglossidae.*
midwinter (ˈmɪdˈwɪntə) *n* **1a** the middle or depth of the winter. **1b** (*as modifier*): *a midwinter festival.* **2** another name for **winter solstice.**
midyear (ˈmɪdˈjɪə) *n* **a** the middle of the year. **b** (*as modifier*): *a midyear examination.*
mielie (ˈmiːlɪ) *n* a variant of **mealie.**
mien (miːn) *n Literary.* a person's manner, bearing, or appearance, expressing personality or mood: *a noble mien.* [C16: probably variant of obsolete *demean* appearance; related to French *mine* aspect]
Mieres (*Spanish* ˈmjeres) *n* a city in N Spain, south of Oviedo: steel and chemical industries; iron and coal mines. Pop.: 26 500 (1987 est.).
Mies van der Rohe (ˈmiːz væn də ˈrəʊə) *n* **Ludwig.** 1886–1969, U.S. architect, born in Germany. He directed the Bauhaus (1929–33) and developed a functional style, characterized by geometrical design. His works include the Seagram building, New York (1958).
mifepristone (mɪˈfɛprɪˌstəʊn) *n* See **abortion pill.**
miff (mɪf) *Informal.* ◆ *vb* **1** to take offence or offend. ◆ *n* **2** a petulant mood. **3** a petty quarrel. [C17: perhaps an imitative expression of bad temper]
miffy (ˈmɪfɪ) *adj* **-fier, -fiest.** *Informal.* easily upset; oversensitive. ▸ ˈ**miffily** *adv* ▸ ˈ**miffiness** *n*
MiG (mɪg) *n* any of various types of Soviet fighter aircraft. [from *Mi(koyan)* and *G(urevich),* names of designers]
might[1] (maɪt) *vb* (takes an implied infinitive or an infinitive without *to*) used as an auxiliary: **1** making the past tense or subjunctive mood of **may**[1]: *he might have come last night.* **2** (often foll. by *well*) expressing theoretical possibility: *he might well come.* In this sense *might* looks to the future and functions as a weak form of *may.* See **may**[1] (sense 2).
USAGE See at **may**[1].
might[2] (maɪt) *n* **1** power, force, or vigour, esp. of a great or supreme kind. **2** physical strength. **3** (**with**) **might and main.** See **main**[1] (sense 8). [Old English *miht;* compare Old High German *maht,* Dutch *macht*]
mightily (ˈmaɪtɪlɪ) *adv* **1** to a great extent, amount, or degree. **2** with might; powerfully or vigorously.
mighty (ˈmaɪtɪ) *adj* **mightier, mightiest. 1a** having or indicating might; powerful or strong. **1b** (*as collective n; preceded by the*): *the mighty.* **2** very large; vast. **3** very great in extent, importance, etc. ◆ *adv* **4** *Informal, chiefly U.S. and Canadian.* (intensifier): *he was mighty tired.* ▸ ˈ**mightiness** *n*
migmatite (ˈmɪgməˌtaɪt) *n* a composite rock body containing two types of rock that have interacted with each other but are nevertheless still distinguishable. [C20: alteration of Swedish *migmatit,* from Greek *migma* mixture + -ITE[1]]
mignon (ˈmɪnjɒn; *French* miɲɔ̃) *adj* small and pretty; dainty. [C16: from French, from Old French *mignot* dainty] ▸ **mignonne** (ˈmɪnjɒn; *French* miɲɔn) *fem n*
mignonette (ˌmɪnjəˈnɛt) *n* **1** any of various mainly Mediterranean plants of the resedaceous genus *Reseda,* such as *R. odorata* (**garden mignonette**), that have spikes of small greenish-white flowers with prominent anthers. **2** a type of fine pillow lace. ◆ *adj* **3** of a greyish-green colour; reseda. [C18: from French, diminutive of MIGNON]
migraine (ˈmiːgreɪn, ˈmaɪ-) *n* a throbbing headache usually affecting only one side of the head and commonly accompanied by nausea and visual disturbances. [C18: (earlier form, C14 *mygrame* MEGRIM[1]): from French, from Late Latin *hēmicrānia* pain in half of the head, from Greek *hēmikrania,* from HEMI- + *kranion* CRANIUM] ▸ ˈ**migrainous** *adj*
migrant (ˈmaɪgrənt) *n* **1** a person or animal that moves from one region, place, or country to another. **2** an itinerant agricultural worker who travels from one district to another. **3** *Chiefly Austral.* **3a** an immigrant, esp. a recent one. **3b** (*as modifier*): *a migrant hostel.* ◆ *adj* **4** moving from one region, place, or country to another; migratory. [C17: from Latin *migrāre* to change one's abode]
migrate (maɪˈgreɪt) *vb* (*intr*) **1** to go from one region, country, or place of abode to settle in another, esp. in a foreign country. **2** (of birds, fishes, etc.) to journey between different habitats at specific times of the year. [C17: from Latin *migrāre* to change one's abode] ▸ **miˈgrator** *n*
migration (maɪˈgreɪʃən) *n* **1** the act or an instance of migrating. **2** a group of people, birds, etc., migrating in a body. **3** *Chem.* a movement of atoms, ions, or molecules, such as the motion of ions in solution under the influence of electric fields. ▸ **miˈgrational** *adj*
migratory (ˈmaɪgrətərɪ, -trɪ) *adj* **1** of, relating to, or characterized by migration. **2** nomadic; itinerant.
MIG welding (mɪg) *n* metal inert gas welding: a method of welding in which the filler metal wire supplies the electric current to maintain the arc, which is shielded from the access of air by an inert gas, usually argon. Compare **TIG welding.**
mihrab (ˈmiːræb, -rəb) *n Islam.* the niche in a mosque showing the direction of Mecca. [from Arabic]
mikado (mɪˈkɑːdəʊ) *n, pl* **-dos.** (*often cap.*) *Archaic.* the Japanese emperor. Compare **tenno.** [C18: from Japanese, from *mi-* honourable + *kado* gate]
mike (maɪk) *n Informal.* short for **microphone.**
Mike (maɪk) *n Communications.* a code word for the letter *m.*
Míkonos (*Greek* ˈmikonos) *n* transliteration of the modern Greek name for **Mykonos.**
mikvah *or* **mikveh** (mikˈvɑ, ˈmikvə) *n Judaism.* a pool used esp. by women for ritual purification after their monthly period. [from Hebrew]
mil (mɪl) *n* **1** a unit of length equal to one thousandth of an inch. **2** an obsolete pharmaceutical unit of volume equal to one millilitre. **3** a unit of angular measure, used in gunnery, equal to one sixty-four-hundredth of a circumference. [C18: short for Latin *millēsimus* thousandth]
mil. *abbrev. for:* **1** military. **2** militia.
milady *or* **miladi** (mɪˈleɪdɪ) *n, pl* **-dies.** (formerly) a continental title used for an English gentlewoman.
milage (ˈmaɪlɪdʒ) *n* a variant spelling of **mileage.**
Milan (mɪˈlæn) *n* a city in N Italy, in central Lombardy: Italy's second largest city and chief financial and industrial centre; a centre of the Renaissance under the Visconti and Sforza families. Pop.: 1 306 494 (1996 est.). Italian name: **Milano** (miˈlaːno).
Milanese (ˌmɪləˈniːz) *adj* **1** of or relating to Milan, its people, culture, etc. **2** of a fine lightweight knitted fabric of silk, rayon, etc. ◆ *n* **3** the Italian dialect spoken in Milan. **4** (*pl* **-ese**) a native or inhabitant of Milan.
Milazzo (*Italian* miˈlattso) *n* a port in NE Sicily: founded in the 8th century B.C.; scene of a battle (1860), in which Garibaldi defeated the Bourbon forces. Pop.: 32 000 (1987 est.). Ancient name: **Mylae** (ˈmaɪˌliː).
milch (mɪltʃ) *n* **1** (*modifier*) (esp. of cattle) yielding milk. **2 milch cow.** *Informal.* a source of easy income, esp. a person. [C13: from Old English *-milce* (in compounds); related to Old English *melcan* to milk]
milchik *or* **milchig** (ˈmɪlxɪk) *adj Judaism.* containing or used in the preparation of milk products and so not to be used with meat products. Also called: **milky.** Compare **fleishik.** See also **kashruth.** [Yiddish, from *milch* milk, ultimately from Old High German; compare MILCH; see also MILK]
mild (maɪld) *adj* **1** (of a taste, sensation, etc.) not powerful or strong; bland: *a mild curry.* **2** gentle or temperate in character, climate, behaviour, etc. **3** not extreme; moderate: *a mild rebuke.* **4** feeble; unassertive. ◆ *n* **5** *Brit.* draught beer, of darker colour than bitter and flavoured with fewer hops. [Old English *milde;* compare Old Saxon *mildi,* Old Norse *mildr*] ▸ ˈ**mildly** *adv* ▸ ˈ**mildness** *n*
milden (ˈmaɪldən) *vb* to make or become mild or milder.
mildew (ˈmɪlˌdjuː) *n* **1** any of various diseases of plants that affect mainly the leaves and are caused by parasitic fungi. See also **downy mildew, powdery**

mildew. 2 any fungus causing this kind of disease. 3 another name for **mould**[2]. ◆ *vb* 4 to affect or become affected with mildew. [Old English *mildēaw,* from *mil-* honey (compare Latin *mel,* Greek *mēli*) + *dēaw* DEW] ▸ **ˈmilˌdewy** *adj*

mild steel *n* any of a class of strong tough steels that contain a low quantity of carbon (0.1–0.25 per cent).

mile (maɪl) *n* 1 Also called: **statute mile.** a unit of length used in the U.K., the U.S., and certain other countries, equal to 1760 yards. 1 mile is equivalent to 1.609 34 kilometres. 2 See **nautical mile.** 3 See **Swedish mile.** 4 any of various units of length used at different times and places, esp. the Roman mile, equivalent to 1620 yards. 5 (*often pl*) *Informal.* a great distance; great deal: *he missed by a mile.* 6 a race extending over a mile. ◆ *adv* 7 **miles.** (intensifier): *he likes his new job miles better.* [Old English *mīl,* from Latin *mīlia* (*passuum*) a thousand (paces)]

mileage *or* **milage** (ˈmaɪlɪdʒ) *n* 1 a distance expressed in miles. 2 the total number of miles that a motor vehicle has travelled. 3 allowance for travelling expenses, esp. as a fixed rate per mile. 4 the number of miles a motor vehicle will travel on one gallon of fuel. 5 *Informal.* use, benefit, or service provided by something: *this scheme has a lot of mileage left.* 6 *Informal.* grounds, substance, or weight: *some mileage in the objectors' arguments.*

mileometer *or* **milometer** (maɪˈlɒmɪtə) *n* a device that records the number of miles that a bicycle or motor vehicle has travelled. Usual U.S. and Canadian name: **odometer.**

milepost (ˈmaɪlˌpəʊst) *n* 1 *Horse racing.* a marking post on a racecourse a mile before the finishing line. 2 Also called (esp. Brit.): **milestone.** *Chiefly U.S. and Canadian.* a signpost that shows the distance in miles to or from a place.

miler (ˈmaɪlə) *n* an athlete, horse, etc., that runs or specializes in races of one mile.

Miles (maɪlz) *n* **Bernard,** Baron Miles of Blackfriars. 1907–91, British actor and theatre manager. He founded the Mermaid Theatre in London, and was known as a character actor.

miles gloriosus *Latin.* (ˈmiːleɪs ˌɡlɔːrɪˈəʊsʊs) *n, pl* ***milites gloriosi*** (ˈmiːlɪˌteɪs ˌɡlɔːrɪˈəʊsaɪ). a braggart soldier, esp. as a stock figure in comedy. [from the title of a comedy by Plautus]

Milesian[1] (maɪˈliːzɪən) *adj* 1 of or relating to Miletus. ◆ *n* 2 an inhabitant of Miletus. [via Latin from Greek *Milēsios*]

Milesian[2] (maɪˈliːzɪən) *Facetious.* ◆ *adj* 1 Irish. ◆ *n* 2 an Irishman. [C16: from *Milesius,* a fictitious king of Spain whose sons were supposed to have conquered Ireland]

milestone (ˈmaɪlˌstəʊn) *n* 1 a stone pillar that shows the distance in miles to or from a place. 2 a significant event in life, history, etc.

Miletus (mɪˈliːtəs) *n* an ancient city on the W coast of Asia Minor: a major Ionian centre of trade and learning in the ancient world.

milfoil (ˈmɪlˌfɔɪl) *n* 1 another name for **yarrow.** 2 See **water milfoil.** [C13: from Old French, from Latin *milifolium,* from *mille* thousand + *folium* leaf]

Milford Haven (ˈmɪlfəd) *n* a port in SW Wales, in Pembrokeshire on **Milford Haven** (a large inlet of St George's Channel): major oil port. Pop.: 13 194 (1991).

Milhaud (*French* mijo) *n* **Darius** (darjys). 1892–1974, French composer; member of Les Six. A notable exponent of polytonality, his large output includes operas, symphonies, ballets, string quartets, and songs.

miliaria (ˌmɪlɪˈɛərɪə) *n* an acute itching eruption of the skin, caused by blockage of the sweat glands. Nontechnical names: **heat rash, prickly heat.** [C19: from New Latin, from Latin *miliārius* MILIARY]

miliary (ˈmɪljərɪ) *adj* 1 resembling or relating to millet seeds. 2 (of a disease or skin eruption) characterized by small lesions resembling millet seeds: *miliary tuberculosis.* [C17: from Latin *miliārius,* from *milium* MILLET]

miliary fever *n* an acute infectious fever characterized by profuse sweating and the formation on the skin of minute fluid-filled vesicles. Nontechnical name: **sweating sickness.**

milieu (ˈmiːljɜː; *French* miljø) *n, pl* **-lieux** (-ljɜː, -ljɜːz; *French* -ljø) *or* **-lieus.** surroundings, location, or setting. [C19: from French, from *mi-* MID[1] + *lieu* place]

milit. *abbrev. for* military.

militant (ˈmɪlɪtənt) *adj* 1 aggressive or vigorous, esp. in the support of a cause: *a militant protest.* 2 warring; engaged in warfare. ◆ *n* 3 a militant person. [C15: from Latin *mīlitāre* to be a soldier, from *mīles* soldier] ▸ **ˈmilitancy** *or* (*less commonly*) **ˈmilitantness** *n* ▸ **ˈmilitantly** *adv*

Militant (ˈmɪlɪtənt) *n* 1 short for **Militant Tendency.** 2 a member of Militant Tendency.

Militant Tendency *n* a Trotskyist group formerly operating within the Labour Party.

militaria (ˌmɪlɪˈtɛərɪə) *pl n* items of military interest, such as weapons, uniforms, medals, etc., esp. from the past.

militarism (ˈmɪlɪtəˌrɪzəm) *n* 1 military spirit; pursuit of military ideals. 2 domination by the military in the formulation of policies, ideals, etc., esp. on a political level. 3 a policy of maintaining a strong military organization in aggressive preparedness for war.

militarist (ˈmɪlɪtərɪst) *n* 1 a supporter of or believer in militarism. 2 a devotee of military history, strategy, etc. ▸ **ˌmilitaˈristic** *adj* ▸ **ˌmilitaˈristically** *adv*

militarize *or* **militarise** (ˈmɪlɪtəˌraɪz) *vb* (*tr*) 1 to convert to military use. 2 to imbue with militarism. ▸ **ˌmilitariˈzation** *or* **ˌmilitariˈsation** *n*

military (ˈmɪlɪtərɪ, -trɪ) *adj* 1 of or relating to the armed forces (esp. the army), warlike matters, etc. 2 of, characteristic of, or about soldiers. ◆ *n, pl* **-taries** *or* **-tary.** 3 (preceded by *the*) the armed services (esp. the army). [C16: via French from Latin *mīlitāris,* from *mīles* soldier] ▸ **ˈmilitarily** *adv*

military academy *n* a training establishment for young officer cadets entering the army.

military engineering *n* the design, construction, etc., of military fortifications and communications.

military honours *pl n* ceremonies performed by troops in honour of royalty, at the burial of an officer, etc.

military-industrial complex *n* (in the U.S.) the combined interests of the military establishment and industries involved in producing military material considered as exerting influence on U.S. foreign and economic policy.

military law *n* articles or regulations that apply to those belonging to the armed services. Compare **martial law.**

military orchid *n* another name for **soldier orchid.**

military pace *n* the pace of a single step in marching, taken to be 30 inches for quick time (120 paces to the minute) in both the British and U.S. armies.

military police *n* a corps within an army that performs police and disciplinary duties. ▸ **military policeman** *n*

militate (ˈmɪlɪˌteɪt) *vb* (*intr;* usually foll. by *against* or *for*) (of facts, actions, etc.) to have influence or effect: *the evidence militated against his release.* [C17: from Latin *mīlitātus,* from *mīlitāre* to be a soldier] ▸ **ˌmiliˈtation** *n*

USAGE See at **mitigate.**

militia (mɪˈlɪʃə) *n* 1 a body of citizen (as opposed to professional) soldiers. 2 an organization containing men enlisted for service in emergency only. [C16: from Latin: soldiery, from *mīles* soldier]

militiaman (mɪˈlɪʃəmən) *n, pl* **-men.** a man serving with the militia.

milium (ˈmɪlɪəm) *n, pl* **-ia** (-ɪə). *Pathol.* a small whitish nodule on the skin, usually resulting from a clogged sebaceous gland. [C19: from Latin: millet]

milk (mɪlk) *n* **1a** a whitish nutritious fluid produced and secreted by the mammary glands of mature female mammals and used for feeding their young until weaned. **1b** the milk of cows, goats, or other animals used by man as a food or in the production of butter, cheese, etc. Related adjs.: **lacteal, lactic.** 2 any similar fluid in plants, such as the juice of a coconut. 3 any of various milklike pharmaceutical preparations, such as milk of magnesia. 4 **cry over spilt milk.** to lament something that cannot be altered. ◆ *vb* 5 to draw milk from the udder of (a cow, goat, or other animal). 6 (*intr*) (of cows, goats, or other animals) to yield milk. 7 (*tr*) to draw off or tap in small quantities: *to milk the petty cash.* 8 (*tr*) to extract as much money, help, etc., as possible from: *to milk a situation of its news value.* 9 (*tr*) to extract venom, sap, etc., from. [Old English *milc;* compare Old Saxon *miluk,* Old High German *miluh,* Old Norse *mjolk*]

milk-and-water *adj* (**milk and water** *when postpositive*). weak, feeble, or insipid.

milk bar *n* 1 a snack bar at which milk drinks and light refreshments are served. 2 (in Australia) a shop selling, in addition to milk, basic provisions and other items.

milk cap *n* any of a large genus (*Lactarius*) of basidiomycetous fungi that are brittle to touch and exude a milky liquid when crushed. Some are funnel-shaped and some parasol-shaped, and most, except for *L. deliciosus,* are inedible.

milk chocolate *n* chocolate that has been made with milk, having a creamy taste. Compare **plain chocolate.**

milker (ˈmɪlkə) *n* 1 a cow, goat, etc., that yields milk, esp. of a specified quality or amount: *a poor milker.* 2 a person who milks. 3 another name for **milking machine.**

milk fever *n* 1 a fever that sometimes occurs shortly after childbirth, once thought to result from engorgement of the breasts with milk but now thought to be caused by infection. 2 *Vet. science.* a disease of cows, goats, etc., occurring shortly after parturition, characterized by low blood calcium levels, paralysis, and loss of consciousness.

milkfish (ˈmɪlkˌfɪʃ) *n, pl* **-fish** *or* **-fishes.** a large silvery tropical clupeoid food and game fish, *Chanos chanos:* family *Chanidae.*

milk float *n Brit.* a small motor vehicle used to deliver milk to houses.

milk glass *n* opaque white glass, originally produced in imitation of Chinese porcelain.

milking machine *n* an apparatus for milking cows.

milking shed *n* a building in which a herd of cows is milked. Compare **milking parlour** (see **parlour** (sense 6)).

milking stool *n* a low three-legged stool.

milk leg *n* inflammation and thrombosis of the femoral vein following childbirth, characterized by painful swelling of the leg. Also called: **white leg.** Technical name: **phlegmasia alba dolens.**

milkmaid (ˈmɪlkˌmeɪd) *n* a girl or woman who milks cows.

milkman (ˈmɪlkmən) *n, pl* **-men.** 1 a man who delivers or sells milk. 2 a man who milks cows; dairyman.

milko (ˈmɪlkəʊ) *n, pl* **milkos.** *Austral.* an informal name for **milkman** (sense 1).

milk of magnesia *n* a suspension of magnesium hydroxide in water, used as an antacid and laxative.

milk pudding *n Chiefly Brit.* a hot or cold pudding made by boiling or baking milk with a grain, esp. rice.

milk punch *n* a spiced drink made of milk and spirits.

milk round *n Brit.* 1 a route along which a milkman regularly delivers milk. **2a** a regular series of visits, esp. as made by recruitment officers from industry to universities. **2b** (*as modifier*): *milk-round recruitment.*

milk run *n Aeronautics, informal.* a routine and uneventful flight, esp. on a dangerous mission. [C20: referring to the regular and safe routine of a milkman's round]

milk shake *n* a cold frothy drink made of milk, flavouring, and sometimes ice cream, whisked or beaten together.

milk sickness *n* 1 an acute disease characterized by weakness, vomiting, and constipation, caused by ingestion of the flesh or dairy products of cattle affected with trembles. 2 *Vet. science.* another name for **trembles** (sense 1).

milk snake *n* a nonvenomous brown-and-grey North American colubrid snake *Lampropeltis doliata,* related to the king snakes.

milksop (ˈmɪlk,sɒp) *n* **1** a feeble or ineffectual man or youth. **2** *Brit.* a dish of bread soaked in warm milk, given esp. to infants and invalids. ► **ˈmilk,soppy** *or* **ˈmilk,sopping** *adj* ► **ˈmilk,sopism** *n*

milk stout *n Brit.* a rich mellow stout lacking a bitter aftertaste. [C20: so called because its ingredients include LACTOSE]

milk sugar *n* another name for **lactose.**

milk thistle *n* another name for **sow thistle.**

milk tooth *n* any of the first teeth to erupt; a deciduous tooth. Also called: **baby tooth.** See also **dentition.**

milk vetch *n* any of various papilionaceous plants of the genus *Astragalus,* esp. *A. glycyphyllos,* with clusters of purple, white, or yellowish flowers: formerly reputed to increase milk production in goats.

milkweed (ˈmɪlk,wiːd) *n* **1** Also called: **silkweed.** any plant of the mostly North American genus *Asclepias,* having milky sap and pointed pods that split open to release tufted seeds: family *Asclepiadaceae.* See also **asclepias. 2** any of various other plants having milky sap. **3 orange milkweed.** another name for **butterfly weed. 4** another name for **monarch** (the butterfly).

milkwort (ˈmɪlk,wɜːt) *n* any of several plants of the genus *Polygala,* having small blue, pink, or white flowers with two petal-like sepals: family *Polygalaceae.* They were formerly believed to increase milk production in nursing women. See also **senega.**

milky (ˈmɪlkɪ) *adj* **milkier, milkiest. 1** resembling milk, esp. in colour or cloudiness. **2** of or containing milk. **3** spiritless or spineless. **4** *Judaism.* another word for **milchik.** ► **ˈmilkily** *adv* ► **ˈmilkiness** *n*

Milky Way *n* **the. 1** the diffuse band of light stretching across the night sky that consists of millions of faint stars, nebulae, etc., and forms part of the Galaxy. **2** another name for the **Galaxy.** [C14: translation of Latin *via lactea*]

mill[1] (mɪl) *n* **1** a building in which grain is crushed and ground to make flour. **2** a factory, esp. one which processes raw materials: *a steel mill.* **3** any of various processing or manufacturing machines, esp. one that grinds, presses, or rolls. **4** any of various small hand mills used for grinding pepper, salt, or coffee for domestic purposes. See also **coffee mill, pepper mill. 5** a machine that tools or polishes metal. **6** a hard roller for impressing a design, esp. in a textile-printing machine or in a machine for printing banknotes. **7** a system, institution, etc., that influences people or things in the manner of a factory: *going through the educational mill.* **8** an unpleasant experience; ordeal (esp. in the phrases **go** *or* **be put through the mill**). **9** a fist fight. **10 run of the mill.** ordinary or routine. ◆ *vb* **11** (*tr*) to grind, press, or pulverize in or as if in a mill. **12** (*tr*) to process or produce in or with a mill. **13** to cut or roll (metal) with or as if with a milling machine. **14** (*tr*) to groove or flute the edge of (a coin). **15** (*intr;* often foll. by *about* or *around*) to move about in a confused manner. **16** (*usually tr*) *Now rare.* to beat (chocolate, etc.). **17** *Archaic slang.* to fight, esp. with the fists. [Old English *mylen* from Late Latin *molīna* a mill, from Latin *mola* mill, millstone, from *molere* to grind] ► **ˈmillable** *adj*

mill[2] (mɪl) *n* a U.S. and Canadian monetary unit used in calculations, esp. for property taxes, equal to one thousandth of a dollar. [C18: short for Latin *millēsimum* a thousandth (part)]

Mill (mɪl) *n* **1 James.** 1773–1836, Scottish philosopher, historian, and economist. He expounded Bentham's utilitarian philosophy in *Elements of Political Economy* (1821) and *Analysis of the Phenomena of the Human Mind* (1829) and also wrote a *History of British India* (1817–18). **2** his son, **John Stuart.** 1806–73, English philosopher and economist. He modified Bentham's utilitarian philosophy in *Utilitarianism* (1861) and in his treatise *On Liberty* (1859) he defended the rights and freedom of the individual. Other works include *A System of Logic* (1843) and *Principles of Political Economy* (1848).

Millais (ˈmɪleɪ) *n* Sir **John Everett.** 1829–96, English painter, who was a founder of the Pre-Raphaelite Brotherhood. His works include *The Order of Release* (1853) and *The Blind Girl* (1856).

Millay (mɪˈleɪ) *n* **Edna St Vincent.** 1892–1950, U.S. poet, noted esp. for her sonnets; her collections include *The Buck in the Snow* (1928) and *Fatal Interview* (1931).

millboard (ˈmɪl,bɔːd) *n* strong pasteboard, used esp. in book covers. [C18: changed from *milled board*]

milldam (ˈmɪl,dæm) *n* a dam built in a stream to raise the water level sufficiently for it to turn a millwheel.

milled (mɪld) *adj* **1** (of coins, etc.) having a grooved or fluted edge. **2** made or treated in a mill.

millefeuille *French.* (milfœj) *n Brit.* a small iced cake made of puff pastry filled with jam and cream. U.S. name: **napoleon.** [literally: thousand leaves]

millefiori (,mɪlɪˈfjɔːrɪ) *n* **a** decorative glassware in which coloured glass rods are fused and cut to create flower patterns: an ancient technique revived in Venice in the sixteenth century and in France and England in the nineteenth century. **b** (*as modifier*): *a millefiori paperweight.* [C19: from Italian: thousand flowers]

millefleurs (ˈmiːl,flɜː) *n* a design of stylized floral patterns, used in textiles, tapestries, etc. [French: thousand flowers]

millenarian (,mɪlɪˈnɛərɪən) *or* **millenary** *adj* **1** of or relating to a thousand or to a thousand years. **2** of or relating to the millennium or millenarianism. ◆ *n* **3** an adherent of millenarianism.

millenarianism (,mɪlɪˈnɛərɪə,nɪzəm) *n* **1** *Christianity.* the belief in a future millennium following the Second Coming of Christ during which he will reign on earth in peace: based on Revelation 20:1–5. **2** any belief in a future period of ideal peace and happiness.

millenary (mɪˈlɛnərɪ) *n, pl* **-naries. 1** a sum or aggregate of one thousand, esp. one thousand years. **2** another word for a **millennium.** ◆ *adj, n* **3** another word for **millenarian.** [C16: from Late Latin *millēnārius* containing a thousand, from Latin *mille* thousand]

millennium (mɪˈlɛnɪəm) *n, pl* **-nia** (-nɪə) *or* **-niums. 1 the.** *Christianity.* the period of a thousand years of Christ's awaited reign upon earth. **2** a period or cycle of one thousand years. **3** a time of peace and happiness, esp. in the distant future. **4** a thousandth anniversary. [C17: from New Latin, from Latin *mille* thousand + *annus* year; for form, compare QUADRENNIUM] ► **milˈlennial** *adj* ► **milˈlennialist** *n* ► **milˈlennially** *adv*

millennium bug *n Computing.* any software problem arising from the change in date at the start of the 21st century.

millepede (ˈmɪlɪ,piːd) *or* **milleped** (ˈmɪlɪ,pɛd) *n* variants of **millipede.**

millepore (ˈmɪlɪ,pɔː) *n* any tropical colonial coral-like medusoid hydrozoan of the order *Milleporina,* esp. of the genus *Millepora,* having a calcareous skeleton. [C18: from New Latin, from Latin *mille* thousand + *porus* hole]

miller (ˈmɪlə) *n* **1** a person who keeps, operates, or works in a mill, esp. a corn mill. **2** another name for **milling machine. 3** a person who operates a milling machine. **4** any of various pale coloured or white moths, especially the medium-sized noctuid *Apatele leporina.* **5** an edible basidiomycetous fungus, *Clitopilus prunulus,* with a white funnel-shaped cap and pinkish spores, often forming rings in grass.

Miller (ˈmɪlə) *n* **1 Arthur.** born 1915, U.S. dramatist. His plays include *Death of a Salesman* (1949), *The Crucible* (1953), *A View from the Bridge* (1955), and *Mr Peters' Connections* (1998). **2 Glenn.** 1904–44, U.S. composer, trombonist, and band leader. His popular compositions include "Moonlight Serenade". During World War II he was leader of the U.S. Air Force band in Europe. He disappeared without trace on a flight between England and France. **3 Henry.** 1891–1980, U.S. novelist, author of *Tropic of Cancer* (1934) and *Tropic of Capricorn* (1938). **4 Hugh** 1802–56, Scottish geologist and writer. **5 Jonathan (Wolfe).** born 1934, British doctor, actor, and theatre director. His productions include Shakespeare, Ibsen, and Chekhov as well as several operas. He has also presented many television medical programmes.

millerite (ˈmɪlə,raɪt) *n* a yellow mineral consisting of nickel sulphide in hexagonal crystalline form: a minor ore of nickel. Formula: NiS. [C19: named after W. H. *Miller* (1801–1880), English mineralogist]

miller's thumb *n* any of several small freshwater European fishes of the genus *Cottus,* esp. *C. gobio,* having a flattened body: family *Cottidae* (bullheads, etc.). [C15: from the alleged likeness of the fish's head to a thumb]

millesimal (mɪˈlɛsɪməl) *adj* **1a** denoting a thousandth. **1b** (*as n*): *a millesimal.* **2** of, consisting of, or relating to a thousandth. [C18: from Latin *millēsimus*]

millet (ˈmɪlɪt) *n* **1** a cereal grass, *Setaria italica,* cultivated for grain and animal fodder. **2a** an East Indian annual grass, *Panicum miliaceum,* cultivated for grain and forage, having pale round shiny seeds. **2b** the seed of this plant. **3** any of various similar or related grasses, such as pearl millet and Indian millet. Related adj: **miliary.** [C14: via Old French from Latin *milium;* related to Greek *melinē* millet]

Millet (*French* milɛ) *n* **Jean François** (ʒɑ̃ frɑ̃swa). 1814–75, French painter of the Barbizon school, noted for his studies of peasants at work.

Millett (ˈmɪlɪt) *n* **Kate.** full name *Katherine Murray Millett.* born 1934, U.S. feminist writer and artist; books include *Sexual Politics* (1969) and *The Politics of Cruelty* (1994).

milli- *prefix* denoting 10^{-3}: *millimetre.* Symbol: m [from French, from Latin *mille* thousand, this meaning being maintained in words borrowed from Latin (*millipede*)]

milliard (ˈmɪlɪ,ɑːd, ˈmɪljɑːd) *n Brit.* (no longer in technical use) a thousand million. U.S. and Canadian equivalent: **billion.** [C19: from French]

milliary (ˈmɪljərɪ) *adj* relating to or marking a distance equal to an ancient Roman mile of a thousand paces. [C17: from Latin *milliārius* containing a thousand, from *mille* thousand]

millibar (ˈmɪlɪ,bɑː) *n* a cgs unit of atmospheric pressure equal to 10^{-3} bar, 100 newtons per square metre or 0.7500617 millimetre of mercury.

millieme (miːlˈjɛm) *n* a Tunisian monetary unit worth one thousandth of a dinar. Also called: **millime.** [from French *millième* thousandth]

Milligan (ˈmɪlɪgən) *n* **Spike,** real name *Terence Alan Milligan.* born 1918, British radio, stage, and film comedian and author, born in India. He appeared in *The Goon Show* (with Peter Sellers and Harry Secombe; BBC Radio, 1952–60) and his films include *Postman's Knock* (1962), *Adolf Hitler, My Part in his Downfall* (1972), *The Three Musketeers* (1974), *The Last Remake of Beau Geste* (1977), and *Yellowbeard* (1982).

milligram *or* **milligramme** (ˈmɪlɪ,græm) *n* one thousandth of a gram. Symbol: mg [C19: from French]

Millikan (ˈmɪlɪkən) *n* **Robert Andrews.** 1868–1953, U.S. physicist. He measured the charge of an electron (1910), verified Einstein's equation for the photoelectric effect (1916), and studied cosmic rays; Nobel prize for physics 1923.

millilitre *or U.S.* **milliliter** (ˈmɪlɪ,liːtə) *n* one thousandth of a litre. Symbol: ml

millimetre *or U.S.* **millimeter** (ˈmɪlɪ,miːtə) *n* one thousandth of a metre. Symbol: mm

millimicron (ˈmɪlɪ,maɪkrɒn) *n* an obsolete name for a nanometre; one millionth of a millimetre.

milliner (ˈmɪlɪnə) *n* a person who makes or sells women's hats. [C16: originally *Milaner,* a native of *Milan,* at that time famous for its fancy goods]

millinery (ˈmɪlɪnərɪ, -nrɪ) *n* **1** hats, trimmings, etc., sold by a milliner. **2** the business or shop of a milliner.

milling (ˈmɪlɪŋ) *n* **1** the act or process of grinding, pressing, or crushing in a mill. **2** the vertical grooves or fluting on the edge of a coin, etc. **3** (in W North America) a method of halting a stampede of cattle by turning the leaders in a wide arc until the herd turns in upon itself in a tightening spiral.

milling machine *n* a machine tool in which a horizontal arbor or vertical spindle rotates a cutting tool above a horizontal table.

million ('mɪljən) *n, pl* **-lions** *or* **-lion. 1** the cardinal number that is the product of 1000 multiplied by 1000. See also **number** (sense 1). **2** a numeral, 1 000 000, 10^6, M, etc., representing this number. **3** (*often pl*) *Informal.* an extremely large but unspecified number, quantity, or amount: *I have millions of things to do.* ◆ *determiner* **4** (preceded by *a* or by a numeral) **4a** amounting to a million: *a million light years away.* **4b** (*as pronoun*): *I can see a million under the microscope.* **5 gone a million.** *Austral. informal.* done for; sunk. ◆ Related prefix: **mega-**. [C17: via Old French from early Italian *millione,* from *mille* thousand, from Latin]

millionaire *or* **millionnaire** (ˌmɪljə'nɛə) *n* a person whose assets are worth at least a million of the standard monetary units of his country. ▸ **ˌmillion'airess** *or* **ˌmillion'nairess** *fem n*

millionth ('mɪljənθ) *n* **1a** one of 1 000 000 approximately equal parts of something. **1b** (*as modifier*): *a millionth part.* **2** one of 1 000 000 equal divisions of a particular scientific quantity. Related prefix: **micro-**. **3** the fraction equal to one divided by 1 000 000. ◆ *adj* **4** (*usually prenominal*) **4a** being the ordinal number of 1 000 000 in numbering or counting order, etc. **4b** (*as n*): *the millionth to be manufactured.*

millipede, millepede ('mɪlɪˌpiːd), *or* **milleped** *n* any terrestrial herbivorous arthropod of the class *Diplopoda,* having a cylindrical body made up of many segments, each of which bears two pairs of walking legs. See also **myriapod.** [C17: from Latin, from *mille* thousand + *pēs* foot]

millisecond ('mɪlɪˌsɛkənd) *n* one thousandth of a second. Symbol: ms

millpond ('mɪlˌpɒnd) *n* **1** a pool formed by damming a stream to provide water to turn a millwheel. **2** any expanse of calm water: *the sea was a millpond.*

millrace ('mɪlˌreɪs) *or* **millrun** *n* **1** the current of water that turns a millwheel. **2** the channel for this water.

mill-rind *n* an iron support fitted across an upper millstone.

millrun ('mɪlˌrʌn) *n* **1** another name for **millrace. 2** *Mining.* **2a** the process of milling an ore or rock in order to determine the content or quality of the mineral. **2b** the mineral so examined. ◆ *adj* **mill-run. 3** *Chiefly U.S.* (of commodities) taken straight from the production line; unsorted as to quality.

Mills (mɪlz) *n* **1 Hayley.** born 1946, British actress. Her films include *Pollyanna* (1960) and *The Parent Trap* (1961). **2** her father, Sir **John.** born 1908, British actor. His films include *This Happy Breed* (1944), *Ryan's Daughter* (1971), and *Appointment with Death* (1987).

Mills bomb (mɪlz) *n* a type of high-explosive hand grenade. [C20: named after Sir William *Mills* (1856–1932), English inventor]

millstone ('mɪlˌstəʊn) *n* **1** one of a pair of heavy flat disc-shaped stones that are rotated one against the other to grind grain. **2** a heavy burden, such as a responsibility or obligation: *his debts were a millstone round his neck.*

millstream ('mɪlˌstriːm) *n* a stream of water used to turn a millwheel.

millwheel ('mɪlˌwiːl) *n* a wheel, esp. a waterwheel, that drives a mill.

millwork ('mɪlˌwɜːk) *n* work done in a mill.

millwright ('mɪlˌraɪt) *n* a person who designs, builds, or repairs grain mills or mill machinery.

Milne (mɪln) *n* **A**(**lan**) **A**(**lexander**). 1882–1956, English writer, noted for his books and verse for children, including *When We Were Very Young* (1924) and *Winnie the Pooh* (1926).

milo ('maɪləʊ) *n, pl* **-los.** any of various early-growing cultivated varieties of sorghum with heads of yellow or pinkish seeds resembling millet. [C19: from Sotho *maili*]

milometer (maɪ'lɒmɪtə) *n* a variant spelling of **mileometer.**

milord (mɪ'lɔːd) *n* (formerly) a continental title used for an English gentleman. [C19: via French from English *my lord*]

Mílos ('milɔs) *n* transliteration of the Modern Greek name for **Melos.**

Milošević (miː'lɒsɛˌvɪtʃ) *n* **Slobodan** ('slɒbədæn). born 1941, Serbian politician, president of Serbia (1989–97) and of the Federal Republic of Yugoslavia from 1997. He supported military action against Slovenia and Croatia in 1991–92 and ethnic cleansing in Bosnia-Herzegovina (1992–95) and Kosovo (1998–99). He was indicted in 1999 for war crimes committed in Kosovo.

Miłosz ('miːlɒʃ; *Polish* 'miwɔʃ) *n* **Czeslaw** ('tʃɛslɔː; 'tʃɛswaf). born 1911, U.S. poet and writer, born in Lithuania, writing in Polish; author of *The Captive Mind* (1953). Nobel prize for literature 1980.

milquetoast ('mɪlkˌtəʊst) *n U.S. and Canadian.* a meek, submissive, or timid person. [C20: from Caspar *Milquetoast,* a cartoon character invented by H. T. Webster (1885–1952)]

milreis ('mɪlˌreɪs; *Portuguese* mil'rɐiʃ) *n, pl* **-reis.** a former monetary and currency unit of Portugal and Brazil, divided into 1000 reis. [C16: from Portuguese, from *mil* thousand + *réis,* pl. of *real* royal]

Milstein ('mɪlstaɪn) *n* **Nathan.** 1904–92, U.S. violinist, born in the Ukraine.

milt (mɪlt) *n* **1** the testis of a fish. **2** the spermatozoa and seminal fluid produced by a fish. **3** *Rare.* the spleen of certain animals, esp. fowls and pigs. ◆ *vb* **4** to fertilize (the roe of a female fish) with milt, esp. artificially. [Old English *milte* spleen; in the sense: fish sperm, probably from Middle Dutch *milte*]

milter ('mɪltə) *n* a male fish that is mature and ready to breed.

Miltiades (mɪl'taɪəˌdiːz) *n* ?540–?489 B.C., Athenian general, who defeated the Persians at Marathon (490).

Milton ('mɪltən) *n* **John.** 1608–74, English poet. His early works, notably *L'Allegro* and *Il Penseroso* (1632), the masque *Comus* (1634), and the elegy *Lycidas* (1637), show the influence of his Christian humanist education and his love of Italian Renaissance poetry. A staunch Parliamentarian and opponent of episcopacy, he published many pamphlets during the Civil War period, including *Areopagitica* (1644), which advocated freedom of the press. His greatest works were the epic poems *Paradise Lost* (1667; 1674), and *Paradise Regained* (1671) and the verse drama *Samson Agonistes* (1671).

Miltonic (mɪl'tɒnɪk) *or* **Miltonian** (mɪl'təʊnɪən) *adj* characteristic of or resembling Milton's literary style, esp. in being sublime and majestic.

Milton Keynes ('mɪltən 'kiːnz) *n* **1** a new town in central England, in Milton Keynes unitary authority, N Buckinghamshire: founded in 1967: electronics, clothing, machinery. Pop.: 156 148 (1991). **2** a unitary authority in central England, in Buckinghamshire. Pop.: 188 400 (1994 est.). Area: 310 sq. km (119 sq. miles).

Milton Work count *n Bridge.* a system of hand valuation in which aces count 4, kings 3, queens 2, and jacks 1. [C20: named after *Milton Work,* authority on auction bridge]

Milwaukee (mɪl'wɔːkiː) *n* a port in SE Wisconsin, on Lake Michigan: the largest city in the state; established as a trading post in the 18th century; an important industrial centre. Pop.: 590 503 (1996 est.). ▸ **Mil'waukeean** *adj, n*

mim (mɪm) *adj Dialect.* prim, modest, or demure. [C17: perhaps imitative of lip-pursing]

Mimas ('maɪməs, -mæs) *n* a satellite of the planet Saturn.

mime (maɪm) *n* **1** the theatrical technique of expressing an idea or mood or portraying a character entirely by gesture and bodily movement without the use of words. **2** Also called: **mime artist.** a performer specializing in such a technique, esp. a comic actor. **3** a dramatic presentation using such a technique. **4** (in the classical theatre) **4a** a comic performance depending for effect largely on exaggerated gesture and physical action. **4b** an actor in such a performance. ◆ *vb* **5** to express (an idea) in actions or gestures without speech. **6** (of singers or musicians) to perform as if singing (a song) or playing (a piece of music) that is actually prerecorded. [Old English *mīma,* from Latin *mīmus* mimic actor, from Greek *mimos* imitator] ▸ **'mimer** *n*

Mimeograph ('mɪmɪəˌgrɑːf, -ˌgræf) *n* **1** *Trademark.* an office machine for printing multiple copies of text or line drawings from an inked drum to which a cut stencil is fixed. **2** a copy produced by this machine. ◆ *vb* **3** to print copies from (a prepared stencil) using this machine.

mimesis (mɪ'miːsɪs) *n* **1** *Art, literature.* the imitative representation of nature or human behaviour. **2a** any disease that shows symptoms of another disease. **2b** a condition in a hysterical patient that mimics an organic disease. **3** *Biology.* another name for **mimicry** (sense 2). **4** *Rhetoric.* representation of another person's alleged words in a speech. [C16: from Greek, from *mimeisthai* to imitate]

mimetic (mɪ'mɛtɪk) *adj* **1** of, resembling, or relating to mimesis or imitation, as in art, etc. **2** *Biology.* of or exhibiting mimicry. ▸ **mi'metically** *adv*

mimetite ('mɪmɪˌtaɪt, 'maɪmɪ-) *n* a rare secondary mineral consisting of a chloride and arsenate of lead in the form of white or yellowish needle-like hexagonal crystals. Formula: $Pb_5Cl(AsO_4)_3$. [C19: from German, from Greek *mimētēs* imitator (of pyromorphite)]

mimic ('mɪmɪk) *vb* **-ics, -icking, -icked.** (*tr*) **1** to imitate (a person, a manner, etc.), esp. for satirical effect; ape. **2** to take on the appearance of; resemble closely: *certain flies mimic wasps.* **3** to copy closely or in a servile manner. ◆ *n* **4** a person or an animal, such as a parrot, that is clever at mimicking. **5** an animal that displays mimicry. ◆ *adj* **6** of, relating to, or using mimicry; imitative. **7** simulated, make-believe, or mock. [C16: from Latin *mīmicus,* from Greek *mimikos,* from *mimos* MIME] ▸ **'mimicker** *n*

mimic panel *n* a panel simulating the geographical layout of a television studio, railway points system, traffic interchange, etc., in which small indicator lamps display the selected state of the lighting circuits, signalling, traffic lights, etc.

mimicry ('mɪmɪkrɪ) *n, pl* **-ries. 1** the act or art of copying or imitating closely; mimicking. **2** the resemblance shown by one animal species, esp. an insect, to another, which protects it from predators.

MIMinE *abbrev. for* Member of the Institute of Mining Engineers.

miminy-piminy (ˌmɪmɪnɪ'pɪmɪnɪ) *adj* a variant of **niminy-piminy.**

Mimir ('miːmɪə) *n Norse myth.* a giant who guarded the well of wisdom near the roots of Yggdrasil.

mimosa (mɪ'məʊsə, -zə) *n* **1** any tropical shrubs or trees of the Mimosaceous genus *Mimosa,* having ball-like clusters of typically yellow flowers and compound leaves that are often sensitive to touch or light. See also **sensitive plant. 2** any similar or related tree. [C18: from New Latin, probably from Latin *mīmus* MIME, because the plant's sensitivity to touch imitates the similar reaction of animals]

mimosaceous (ˌmɪmə'seɪʃəs, ˌmaɪmə-) *adj* of, relating to, or belonging to the *Mimosaceae,* a family of tropical and temperate leguminous plants with tiny ball-like clusters: includes acacia, mimosa, and the fever tree.

mimulus ('mɪmjʊləs) *n* See **monkey flower.** [New Latin, from Greek *mimō* ape (from the shape of the corolla)]

MIMunE *abbrev. for* Member of the Institution of Municipal Engineers.

min *symbol for* minim (liquid measure).

Min (mɪn) *n* any of the dialects or forms of Chinese spoken in Fukien province. Also called: **Fukien.**

min. *abbrev. for:* **1** mineralogy *or* mineralogical. **2** minimum. **3** mining. **4** minute *or* minutes.

Min. *abbrev. for:* **1** Minister. **2** Ministry.

mina ('maɪnə) *n, pl* **-nae** (-niː) *or* **-nas.** an ancient unit of weight and money, used in Asia Minor, equal to one sixtieth of a talent. [C16: via Latin from Greek *mnā,* of Semitic origin; related to Hebrew *māneh* mina]

minacious (mɪ'neɪʃəs) *adj* threatening. [C17: from Latin *minax,* from *minārī* to threaten] ▸ **mi'naciously** *adv* ▸ **minacity** (mɪ'næsɪtɪ) *n*

Mina Hassan Tani ('miːnə hɑː'sɑːn 'tɑːnɪ) *n* a port in NW Morocco, on the Sebou River 16 km (10 miles) from the Atlantic. Pop.: 234 000 (1993 est.). Also called: **Kénitra.** Former name (1932–56): **Port Lyautey.**

Minamoto Yoritomo ('mɪnəˌməʊtəʊ ˌjɒrɪ'təʊməʊ) *n* 1147–99, Japanese nobleman; the first shogun (1192–99) of the feudal era.

minaret (ˌmɪnə'rɛt, 'mɪnəˌrɛt) *n* **1** a slender tower of a mosque having one or more balconies from which the muezzin calls the faithful to prayer. **2** any structure resembling this. [C17: from French, from Turkish, from Arabic *manārat* lamp, from *nār* fire] ► ˌminaˈreted *adj*

Minas Basin (ˈmaɪnəs) *n* a bay in E Canada, in central Nova Scotia: the NE arm of the Bay of Fundy, with which it is linked by **Minas Channel.**

Minas Gerais (*Portuguese* ˈminaʒ ʒəˈraiʒ) *n* an inland state of E Brazil: situated on the high plateau of the Brazilian Highlands; large reserves of iron ore and manganese. Capital: Belo Horizonte. Pop.: 16 505 300 (1995 est.). Area: 587 172 sq. km (226 707 sq. miles).

minatory (ˈmɪnətərɪ, -trɪ) *or* **minatorial** *adj* threatening or menacing. [C16: from Late Latin *minātōrius*, from Latin *minārī* to threaten] ► **ˈminatorily** *or* **ˌminaˈtorially** *adv*

mince (mɪns) *vb* **1** (*tr*) to chop, grind, or cut into very small pieces. **2** (*tr*) to soften or moderate, esp. for the sake of convention or politeness: *I didn't mince my words.* **3** (*intr*) to walk or speak in an affected dainty manner. ◆ *n* **4** *Chiefly Brit.* minced meat. [C14: from Old French *mincier*, from Vulgar Latin *minūtiāre* (unattested), from Late Latin *minūtia* smallness; see MINUTIAE] ► **ˈmincer** *n*

mincemeat (ˈmɪnsˌmiːt) *n* **1** a mixture of dried fruit, spices, etc., used esp. for filling pies. **2** minced meat. **3 make mincemeat of.** *Informal.* to defeat completely.

mince pie *n* a small round pastry tart filled with mincemeat.

Minch (mɪntʃ) *n* **the.** a channel of the Atlantic divided into the **North Minch**, between the mainland of Scotland and the Isle of Lewis, and the **Little Minch**, between the Isle of Skye and Harris and North Uist.

Mincha *Hebrew* (*Hebrew* minˈxɑː; *Yiddish* ˈminxa) *n Judaism.* the afternoon service.

mincing (ˈmɪnsɪŋ) *adj* (of a person) affectedly elegant in gait, manner, or speech. ► **ˈmincingly** *adv*

mind (maɪnd) *n* **1** the human faculty to which are ascribed thought, feeling, etc.; often regarded as an immaterial part of a person. **2** intelligence or the intellect, esp. as opposed to feelings or wishes. **3** recollection or remembrance; memory: *it comes to mind.* **4** the faculty of original or creative thought; imagination: *it's all in the mind.* **5** a person considered as an intellectual being: *the great minds of the past.* **6** opinion or sentiment: *we are of the same mind; to change one's mind; to have a mind of one's own; to know one's mind; to speak one's mind.* **7** condition, state, or manner of feeling or thought: *no peace of mind; his state of mind.* **8** an inclination, desire, or purpose: *I have a mind to go.* **9** attention or thoughts: *keep your mind on your work.* **10** a sound mental state; sanity (esp. in the phrase **out of one's mind**). **11** intelligence, as opposed to material things: *the mind of the universe.* **12** (in Cartesian philosophy) one of two basic modes of existence, the other being matter. **13 blow someone's mind.** *Slang.* **13a** to cause someone to have a psychedelic experience. **13b** to astound or surprise someone. **14 give** (**someone**) **a piece of one's mind.** to criticize or censure (someone) frankly or vehemently. **15 in** *or* **of two minds.** undecided; wavering: *he was in two minds about marriage.* **16 make up one's mind.** to decide (something or to do something): *he made up his mind to go.* **17 on one's mind.** in one's thoughts. **18 put** (**one**) **in mind of.** to remind (one) of. ◆ *vb* **19** (when *tr, may take a clause as object*) to take offence at: *do you mind if I smoke? I don't mind.* **20** to pay attention to (something); heed; notice: *to mind one's own business.* **21** (*tr; takes a clause as object*) to make certain; ensure: *mind you tell her.* **22** (*tr*) to take care of; have charge of: *to mind the shop.* **23** (when *tr, may take a clause as object*) to be cautious or careful about (something): *mind how you go; mind your step.* **24** (*tr*) to obey (someone or something); heed: *mind your father!* **25** to be concerned (about); be troubled (about); *never mind your hat; never mind about your hat; never mind.* **26** (*tr; passive; takes an infinitive*) to be intending or inclined (to do something): *clearly he was not minded to finish the story.* **27** (*tr*) *Scot. and English dialect.* to remember: *do ye mind his name?* **28** (*tr*) *Scot.* to remind: *that minds me of another story.* **29 mind you.** an expression qualifying a previous statement: *Dogs are nice. Mind you, I don't like all dogs.* ◆ Related adjs.: **mental, noetic, phrenic.** ◆ See also **mind out.** [Old English *gemynd* mind; related to Old High German *gimunt* memory]

Mindanao (ˌmɪndəˈnaʊ) *n* the second largest island of the Philippines, in the S part of the archipelago: mountainous and volcanic. Chief towns: Davao, Zamboanga. Pop.: 14 298 000 (1990 est.). Area: (including offshore islands) 94 631 sq. km (36 537 sq. miles).

mind-bending *adj Informal.* **1** very difficult to understand; complex. **2** altering one's state of consciousness: *mind-bending drugs.* **3** reaching the limit of credibility: *they offered a mind-bending salary.* ◆ *n* **4** the process of brainwashing.

mind-blowing *adj Informal.* producing euphoria; psychedelic.

mind-body problem *n* the traditional philosophical problem concerning the nature of mind, body, and the relationship between them. See **dualism** (sense 2), **interactionism, parallelism** (sense 3), **monism** (sense 1), **idealism** (sense 3), **materialism** (sense 2), **identity theory, behaviourism** (sense 2).

mind-boggling *adj Informal.* astonishing; bewildering.

minded (ˈmaɪndɪd) *adj* **1** having a mind, inclination, intention, etc., as specified: *politically minded.* **2** (*in combination*): *money-minded.*

Mindel (ˈmɪndᵊl) *n* the second major Pleistocene glaciation of Alpine Europe. See also **Günz, Riss, Würm.** [C20: named after the River *Mindel*, in Bavaria, Germany]

minder (ˈmaɪndə) *n* **1** someone who looks after someone or something. **2** short for **child minder. 3** *Slang.* an aide to someone in public life, esp. a politician or political candidate, who keeps control of press and public relations. **4** *Slang.* someone acting as a bodyguard, guard, or assistant, esp. in the criminal underworld.

mind-expanding *adj* (of a drug such as LSD) causing a sensation of heightened consciousness; psychedelic.

mindful (ˈmaɪndfʊl) *adj* (usually *postpositive* and foll. by *of*) keeping aware; heedful: *mindful of your duties.* ► **ˈmindfully** *adv* ► **ˈmindfulness** *n*

mindless (ˈmaɪndlɪs) *adj* **1** stupid or careless. **2** requiring little or no intellectual effort: *a mindless task.* ► **ˈmindlessly** *adv* ► **ˈmindlessness** *n*

mind-numbing *adj* extremely boring and uninspiring. ► **ˈmind-ˌnumbingly** *adv*

Mindoro (mɪnˈdɔːrəʊ) *n* a mountainous island in the central Philippines, south of Luzon. Pop.: 912 000 (1995 est.). Area: 9736 sq. km (3759 sq. miles).

mind out *vb* (*intr, adv*) *Brit.* to be careful or pay attention.

mind-reader *n* a person seemingly able to discern the thoughts of another. ► **ˈmind-ˌreading** *n*

mind-set *n* the ideas and attitudes with which a person approaches a situation, esp. when these are seen as being difficult to alter.

mind's eye *n* the visual memory or the imagination.

Mindszenty (ˈmɪndsɛntɪ) *n* **Joseph.** 1892–1975, Hungarian cardinal. He was sentenced to life imprisonment on a charge of treason (1949) but released during the 1956 Revolution.

mind-your-own-business *n* a Mediterranean urticaceous plant, *Helxine soleirolii*, with small dense leaves: used for cover.

mine[1] (maɪn) *pron* **1** something or someone belonging to or associated with me: *mine is best.* **2 of mine.** belonging to or associated with me. ◆ *determiner* **3** (*preceding a vowel*) an archaic word for **my:** *mine eyes; mine host.* [Old English *mīn*; compare Old High German, Old Norse *mīn*, Dutch *mijn*]

mine[2] (maɪn) *n* **1** a system of excavations made for the extraction of minerals, esp. coal, ores, or precious stones. **2** any deposit of ore or minerals. **3** a lucrative source or abundant supply: *she was a mine of information.* **4** a device containing an explosive designed to destroy ships, vehicles, or personnel, usually laid beneath the ground or in water. **5** a tunnel or sap dug to undermine a fortification. **6** a groove or tunnel made by certain insects, esp. in a leaf. ◆ *vb* **7** to dig into (the earth) for (minerals). **8** to make (a hole, tunnel, etc.) by digging or boring. **9** to place explosive mines in position below the surface of (the sea or land). **10** to undermine (a fortification) by digging mines or saps. **11** another word for **undermine.** [C13: from Old French, probably of Celtic origin; compare Irish *mein*, Welsh *mwyn* ore, mine] ► **ˈminable** *or* **ˈmineable** *adj*

mine detector *n* an instrument designed to detect explosive mines. ► **mine detection** *n*

mine dump *n S. African.* a large mound of residue, esp. from gold-mining operations.

minefield (ˈmaɪnˌfiːld) *n* **1** an area of ground or water containing explosive mines. **2** a subject, situation, etc., beset with hidden problems.

minehunter (ˈmaɪnˌhʌntə) *n* a naval vessel that searches for mines by electronic means.

minelayer (ˈmaɪnˌleɪə) *n* a warship or aircraft designed for the carrying and laying of mines.

miner (ˈmaɪnə) *n* **1** a person who works in a mine. **2** Also called: **continuous miner.** a large machine for the automatic extraction of minerals, esp. coal, from a mine. **3** any of various insects or insect larvae that bore into and feed on plant tissues. See also **leaf miner. 4** *Austral.* any of several honey-eaters of the genus *Manorina*, esp. *M. melanocephala* (**noisy miner**), of scrub regions.

mineral (ˈmɪnərəl, ˈmɪnrəl) *n* **1** any of a class of naturally occurring solid inorganic substances with a characteristic crystalline form and a homogeneous chemical composition. **2** any inorganic matter. **3** any substance obtained by mining, esp. a metal ore. **4** (*often pl*) *Brit.* short for **mineral water. 5** *Brit.* a soft drink containing carbonated water and flavourings. Usual U.S. word: **soda.** ◆ *adj* **6** of, relating to, containing, or resembling minerals. [C15: from Medieval Latin *minerāle* (n), from *minerālis* (adj); related to *minera* mine, ore, of uncertain origin]

mineral. *abbrev. for* mineralogy *or* mineralogical.

mineralize *or* **mineralise** (ˈmɪnərəˌlaɪz, ˈmɪnrə-) *vb* (*tr*) **1a** to impregnate (organic matter, water, etc.) with a mineral substance. **1b** to convert (such matter) into a mineral; petrify. **2** (of gases, vapours, etc., in magma) to transform (a metal) into an ore. ► **ˌmineraliˈzation** *or* **ˌmineraliˈsation** *n*

mineralizer *or* **mineraliser** (ˈmɪnərəˌlaɪzə) *n* **1** any of various gases dissolved in magma that affect the crystallization of igneous rocks and the formation of minerals when the magma cools. **2** an element, such as oxygen, that combines with a metal to form an ore.

mineral jelly *n* another name for **petrolatum.**

mineral kingdom *n* all nonliving material, esp. rocks and minerals. Compare **animal kingdom, plant kingdom.**

mineralocorticoid (ˌmɪnərələʊˈkɔːtɪˌkɔɪd) *n* any corticosteroid that controls electrolyte and water balance, esp. by promoting retention of sodium by the kidney tubules.

mineralogy (ˌmɪnəˈrælədʒɪ) *n* the branch of geology concerned with the study of minerals. ► **mineralogical** (ˌmɪnərəˈlɒdʒɪkᵊl) *or* **ˌmineralˈogic** *adj* ► **ˌmineralˈogically** *adv* ► **ˌminerˈalogist** *n*

mineral oil *n* **1** *Brit.* any oil of mineral origin, esp. petroleum. **2** a U.S. and Canadian name for **liquid paraffin.**

mineral pitch *n* another name for **asphalt.**

mineral spring *n* a spring of water that contains a high proportion of dissolved mineral salts.

mineral tar *n* a natural black viscous tar intermediate in properties between petroleum and asphalt. Also called: **maltha.**

mineral water *n* water containing dissolved mineral salts or gases, usually having medicinal properties.

mineral wax *n* another name for **ozocerite.**

mineral wool *n* a fibrous material made by blowing steam or air through molten slag and used for packing and insulation. Also called: **rock wool.**

miner's right *n Austral. and N.Z. history.* a licence to prospect for minerals, esp. gold. [C19]

Minerva (mɪ'nɜ:və) *n* the Roman goddess of wisdom. Greek counterpart: **Athena.**

minestrone (ˌmɪnɪ'strəʊnɪ) *n* a soup made from a variety of vegetables and pasta. [from Italian, from *minestrare* to serve]

minesweeper ('maɪnˌswi:pə) *n* a naval vessel equipped to detect and clear mines. ▸ **'mineˌsweeping** *n*

Ming (mɪŋ) *n* **1** the imperial dynasty of China from 1368 to 1644. ◆ *adj* **2** of or relating to Chinese porcelain produced during the Ming dynasty, characterized by the use of brilliant colours and a fine-quality body.

minge (mɪndʒ) *n Brit. taboo slang.* **1** the female genitals. **2** women collectively considered as sexual objects. [C20: from Romany; of obscure origin]

mingle ('mɪŋgᵊl) *vb* **1** to mix or cause to mix. **2** (*intr;* often foll. by *with*) to come into close association. [C15: from Old English *mengan* to mix; related to Middle Dutch *mengen,* Old Frisian *mengja*] ▸ **'mingler** *n*

Mingrelian (mɪŋ'gri:lɪən) *or* **Mingrel** ('mɪŋgrəl) *n* **1** a member of a people of Georgia living in the mountains northeast of the Black Sea. **2** the language of this people, belonging to the South Caucasian family and closely related to Georgian. ◆ *adj* **3** of or relating to the Mingrelians or their language.

ming tree *n* an artificial plant resembling a bonsai plant. [perhaps from MING]

Mingus ('mɪŋgəs) *n* **Charles,** known as *Charlie Mingus.* 1922–79, U.S. jazz double bassist, composer, and band leader.

mingy ('mɪndʒɪ) *adj* **-gier, -giest.** *Brit. informal.* miserly, stingy, or niggardly. [C20: probably a blend of MEAN[2] + STINGY[1]]

Minho ('mi:ɲu) *n* the Portuguese name for the **Miño.**

mini ('mɪnɪ) *adj* **1** (of a woman's dress, skirt, etc.) very short; thigh-length. **2** (*prenominal*) small; miniature. ◆ *n, pl* **minis. 3** something very small of its kind, esp. a small car or a miniskirt.

mini- *combining form.* smaller or shorter than the standard size: *minibus; miniskirt.* [C20: from MINIATURE and MINIMUM]

miniature ('mɪnɪtʃə) *n* **1** a model, copy, or similar representation on a very small scale. **2** anything that is very small of its kind. **3** a very small painting, esp. a portrait, showing fine detail on ivory or vellum. **4** a very small bottle of whisky or other spirits, which can hold 50 millilitres. **5** an illuminated letter or other decoration in a manuscript. **6 in miniature.** on a small scale: *games are real life in miniature.* ◆ *adj* **7** greatly reduced in size. **8** on a small scale; minute. [C16: from Italian, from Medieval Latin *miniātūra,* from *miniāre* to paint red, (in illuminating manuscripts); from MINIUM]

miniature camera *n* a small camera using 35 millimetre film.

miniaturist ('mɪnɪtʃərɪst) *n* a person who paints miniature portraits.

miniaturize *or* **miniaturise** ('mɪnɪtʃəˌraɪz) *vb* (*tr*) to make or construct (something, esp. electronic equipment) on a very small scale; reduce in size. ▸ **ˌminiaturi'zation** *or* **ˌminiaturi'sation** *n*

minibar ('mɪnɪˌbɑ:) *n* a selection of drinks and confectionery provided in a hotel bedroom and charged to the guest's bill if used.

minibus ('mɪnɪˌbʌs) *n* a small bus able to carry approximately ten passengers.

minicab ('mɪnɪˌkæb) *n Brit.* a small saloon car used as a taxi.

minicom ('mɪnɪˌkɒm) *n* a device used by deaf and hard-of-hearing people, allowing typed telephone messages to be sent and received.

minicomputer (ˌmɪnɪkəm'pju:tə) *n* a small comparatively cheap digital computer.

minidress ('mɪnɪˌdrɛs) *n* a very short dress, at least four inches above the knee. Often shortened to **mini.**

Minié ball ('mɪnɪˌeɪ; *French* miɲe) *n* a conical rifle bullet, used in the 19th century, manufactured with a hollow base designed to expand when fired to fit the rifling. [C19: named after Capt. C. E. *Minié* (1814–1879), French army officer who invented it]

minify ('mɪnɪˌfaɪ) *vb* **-fies, -fying, -fied.** (*tr*) *Rare.* to minimize or lessen the size or importance of (something). [C17: from Latin *minus* less; for form, compare MAGNIFY] ▸ **minification** (ˌmɪnɪfɪ'keɪʃən) *n*

minikin ('mɪnɪkɪn) *Obsolete.* ◆ *n* **1** a small, dainty, or affected person or thing. ◆ *adj* **2** dainty, prim, or affected. [C16: from Dutch *minneken,* diminutive of *minne* love]

minim ('mɪnɪm) *n* **1** a unit of fluid measure equal to one sixtieth of a drachm. It is approximately equal to one drop. Symbol: M, ♏ **2** *Music.* a note having the time value of half a semibreve. Usual U.S. and Canadian name: **half-note. 3** a small or insignificant person or thing. **4** a downward stroke in calligraphy. ◆ *adj* **5** *Rare.* very small; tiny. [C15 (in its musical meaning): from Latin *minimus* smallest]

minima ('mɪnɪmə) *n* a plural of **minimum.**

minimal ('mɪnɪməl) *adj* of the least possible; minimum or smallest. ▸ **'minimally** *adv*

minimal art *n* abstract painting or sculpture in which expressiveness and illusion are minimized by the use of simple geometric shapes, flat colour, and arrangements of ordinary objects. ▸ **minimal artist** *n*

minimalism ('mɪnɪməˌlɪzəm) *n* **1** another name for **minimal art. 2** a type of music based on simple elements and avoiding elaboration or embellishment. **3** design or style in which the simplest and fewest elements are used to create the maximum effect.

minimalist ('mɪnɪməlɪst) *n* **1** a person advocating a minimal policy, style, technique, action, etc. **2** a minimal artist. ◆ *adj* **3** of or relating to minimal art or artists.

Minimalist ('mɪnɪməlɪst) *n* (in early 20th-century Russia) **1** a member of the faction of the Social Revolutionaries that advocated immediate postrevolutionary democracy. **2** a less common name for a **Menshevik.** ◆ Compare **Maximalist.**

minimally *or* **minimal invasive** *adj* (of surgery) involving as little incision into the body as possible, through the use of techniques such as keyhole surgery and laser treatment.

minimal pair *n Linguistics.* a pair of speech elements in a given language differing in only one respect and thus serving to identify minimum units such as phonemes, morphemes, etc. For example, *tin* and *din* constitute a minimal pair in English.

minimax ('mɪnɪˌmæks) *n* **1** *Maths.* the lowest of a set of maximum values. **2** (in game theory, etc.) the procedure of choosing the strategy that least benefits the most advantaged member of a group. Compare **maximin.** [C20: from MINI(MUM) + MAX(IMUM)]

minimize *or* **minimise** ('mɪnɪˌmaɪz) *vb* (*tr*) **1** to reduce to or estimate at the least possible degree or amount: *to minimize a risk.* **2** to rank or treat at less than the true worth; belittle: *to minimize someone's achievements.* ▸ **ˌminimi'zation** *or* **ˌminimi'sation** *n* ▸ **'miniˌmizer** *or* **'miniˌmiser** *n*

minimum ('mɪnɪməm) *n, pl* **-mums** *or* **-ma** (-mə). **1** the least possible amount, degree, or quantity. **2** the least amount recorded, allowed, or reached: *the minimum in our temperature record this month was 50°.* **3** (*modifier*) being the least possible, recorded, allowed, etc.: *minimum age.* **4** *Maths.* a value of a function that is less than any neighbouring value. ◆ *adj* **5** of or relating to a minimum or minimums. [C17: from Latin: smallest thing, from *minimus* least]

minimum lending rate *n* (in Britain) the minimum rate at which the Bank of England would lend to discount houses between 1971 and 1981, after which it was replaced by the less formal base rate. Abbrev.: **MLR.**

minimum wage *n* the lowest wage that an employer is permitted to pay by law or union contract.

minimus ('mɪnɪməs) *adj* (*immediately postpositive*) *Brit.* the youngest: sometimes used after the surname of a schoolboy having elder brothers at the same school: *Hunt minimus.*

mining ('maɪnɪŋ) *n* **1** the act, process, or industry of extracting coal, ores, etc., from the earth. **2** *Military.* the process of laying mines.

mining bee *n* a solitary bee of the genera *Andrena* and *Halictus,* which sometimes resemble honey bees. [named from their burrowing habits]

minion ('mɪnjən) *n* **1** a favourite or dependant, esp. a servile or fawning one. **2** a servile agent: *the minister's minions.* **3** a size of printer's type, approximately equal to 7 point. ◆ *adj* **4** dainty, pretty, or elegant. [C16: from French *mignon,* from Old French *mignot,* of Gaulish origin]

minipill ('mɪnɪˌpɪl) *n* a low-dose oral contraceptive containing progesterone only.

miniseries ('mɪnɪˌsɪəri:z) *n* a television programme in several parts that is shown on consecutive days or weeks for a short period.

miniskirt ('mɪnɪˌskɜ:t) *n* a very short skirt, originally in the 1960s one at least four inches above the knee. Often shortened to **mini.** ▸ **'miniˌskirted** *adj*

minister ('mɪnɪstə) *n* **1** (esp. in Presbyterian and some Nonconformist Churches) a member of the clergy. **2** a person appointed to head a government department. **3** any diplomatic agent accredited to a foreign government or head of state. **4** short for **minister plenipotentiary** or **envoy extraordinary and minister plenipotentiary.** See **envoy**[1] (sense 1). **5** Also called (in full): **minister resident.** a diplomat ranking after an envoy extraordinary and minister plenipotentiary. **6** a person who attends to the needs of others, esp. in religious matters. **7** a person who acts as the agent or servant of a person or thing. ◆ *vb* **8** (*intr;* often foll. by *to*) to attend to the needs (of); take care (of). **9** (*tr*) *Archaic.* to provide; supply. [C13: via Old French from Latin: servant; related to *minus* less] ▸ **'ministerˌship** *n*

ministerial (ˌmɪnɪ'stɪərɪəl) *adj* **1** of or relating to a minister of religion or his office. **2** of or relating to a government minister or ministry: *a ministerial act.* **3** (*often cap.*) of or supporting the ministry or government against the opposition. **4** *Law.* relating to or possessing delegated executive authority. **5** *Law.* (of an office, duty, etc.) requiring the following of instructions, without power to exercise any personal discretion in doing so. **6** acting as an agent or cause; instrumental. ▸ **ˌminis'terially** *adv*

ministerialist (ˌmɪnɪ'stɪərɪəlɪst) *n Brit.* a supporter of the governing ministry.

ministerium (ˌmɪnɪ'stɪərɪəm) *n, pl* **-ria** (-rɪə). the body of the Lutheran ministers in a district. [C19: Latin: MINISTRY]

minister of state *n* **1** (in the British Parliament) a minister, usually below cabinet rank, appointed to assist a senior minister with heavy responsibilities. **2** any government minister.

Minister of the Crown *n Brit.* any Government minister of cabinet rank.

minister plenipotentiary *n, pl* **ministers plenipotentiary.** See **envoy**[1] (sense 1).

ministrant ('mɪnɪstrənt) *adj* **1** ministering or serving as a minister. ◆ *n* **2** a person who ministers. [C17: from Latin *ministrans,* from *ministrāre* to wait upon]

ministration (ˌmɪnɪ'streɪʃən) *n* **1** the act or an instance of serving or giving aid. **2** the act or an instance of ministering religiously. [C14: from Latin *ministrātiō,* from *ministrāre* to wait upon] ▸ **ministrative** ('mɪnɪstrətɪv) *adj*

ministry ('mɪnɪstrɪ) *n, pl* **-tries. 1a** the profession or duties of a minister of religion. **1b** the performance of these duties. **2** ministers of religion or government ministers considered collectively. **3** the tenure of a minister. **4a** a government department headed by a minister. **4b** the buildings of such a department. [C14: from Latin *ministerium* service, from *minister* servant; see MINISTER]

Minitrack ('mɪnɪˌtræk) *n Trademark.* a system for tracking the course of rockets or satellites by radio signals received at ground stations.

minium ('mɪnɪəm) *n* another name for **red lead.** [C14 (meaning: vermilion): from Latin]

miniver ('mɪnɪvə) *n* white fur, used in ceremonial costumes. [C13: from Old French *menu vair,* from *menu* small + *vair* variegated fur, VAIR]

minivet ('mɪnɪvɛt) *n* any brightly coloured tropical Asian cuckoo shrike of the genus *Pericrocotus*. [C19: of unknown origin]

mink (mɪŋk) *n, pl* **mink** *or* **minks. 1** any of several semiaquatic musteline mammals of the genus *Mustela,* of Europe, Asia, and North America, having slightly webbed feet. **2** the highly valued fur of these animals, esp. that of the American mink (*M. vison*). **3** a garment made of this, esp. a woman's coat or stole. [C15: from Scandinavian; compare Danish *mink,* Swedish *mänk*]

minke whale ('mɪŋkə) *n* a type of small whalebone whale or rorqual, *Balaenoptera acutorostrata,* up to 10 metres long. Also called: **minke.** [C20: probably from Norwegian *minkehval,* from *minke* lesser + *hval* whale]

Minkowski (mɪŋ'kɒfskɪ) *n* **Hermann** ('hɜːmən). 1864–1909, German mathematician, born in Russia. His concept of a four-dimensional space-time continuum (1907) proved crucial for the general theory of relativity developed by Einstein.

Minkowski space-time *n* a four-dimensional space in which three coordinates specify the position of a point in space and the fourth represents the time at which an event occurred at that point. [C20: named after Hermann MINKOWSKI]

min min (mɪn mɪn) *n Austral.* will-o'-the-wisp. [from a native Australian language]

Minn. *abbrev. for* Minnesota.

Minna ('mɪnə) *n* a city in W central Nigeria, capital of Niger state. Pop.: 136 900 (1996 est.).

Minneapolis (ˌmɪnɪ'æpəlɪs) *n* a city in SE Minnesota, on the Mississippi River adjacent to St Paul: the largest city in the state; important centre for the grain trade. Pop.: 358 785 (1996 est.).

Minnelli (mɪ'nɛlɪ) *n* **Liza** ('laɪzə). born 1946, U.S. actress and singer, daughter of Judy Garland. Her films include *Charlie Bubbles* (1968), *Cabaret* (1972), *Arthur* (1981), and *Stepping Out* (1991).

minneola (ˌmɪnɪ'əʊlə) *n* a juicy citrus fruit that is a cross between a tangerine and a grapefruit. [C20: perhaps from *Mineola,* Texas]

minnesinger ('mɪnɪˌsɪŋə) *n* one of the German lyric poets and musicians of the 12th to 14th centuries. [C19: from German: love-singer]

Minnesota (ˌmɪnɪ'səʊtə) *n* **1** a state of the N central U.S.: chief U.S. producer of iron ore. Capital: St Paul. Pop.: 4 685 549 (1997 est.). Area: 218 600 sq. km (84 402 sq. miles). Abbrevs.: **Minn.** or (with zip code) **MN 2** a river in S Minnesota, flowing southeast and northeast to the Mississippi River near St Paul. Length: 534 km (332 miles). ▸ ˌ**Minne'sotan** *adj, n*

minnow ('mɪnəʊ) *n, pl* **-nows** *or* **-now. 1** a small slender European freshwater cyprinid fish, *Phoxinus phoxinus*. **2** any other small cyprinid. **3** *Angling.* a spinning lure imitating a minnow. **4** a small or insignificant person. [C15: related to Old English *myne* minnow; compare Old High German *muniwa* fish]

Miño (*Spanish* 'miɲo) *n* a river in SW Europe, rising in NW Spain and flowing southwest (as part of the border between Spain and Portugal) to the Atlantic. Length: 338 km (210 miles). Portuguese name: **Minho.**

Minoan (mɪ'nəʊən) *adj* **1** denoting the Bronze Age culture of Crete from about 3000 B.C. to about 1100 B.C. Compare **Mycenaean. 2** of or relating to the linear writing systems used in Crete and later in mainland Greece. See **Linear A, Linear B.** ◆ *n* **3** a Cretan belonging to the Minoan culture. [C19: named after MINOS, from the excavations at his supposed palace at Knossos]

minor ('maɪnə) *adj* **1** lesser or secondary in amount, extent, importance, or degree: *a minor poet; minor burns.* **2** of or relating to the minority. **3** below the age of legal majority. **4** *Music.* **4a** (of a scale) having a semitone between the second and third and fifth and sixth degrees (**natural minor**). See also **harmonic minor scale, melodic minor scale. 4b** (of a key) based on the minor scale. **4c** (*postpositive*) denoting a specified key based on the minor scale: *C minor.* **4d** (of an interval) reduced by a semitone from the major. **4e** (of a chord, esp. a triad) having a minor third above the root. **4f** (esp. in jazz) of or relating to a chord built upon a minor triad and containing a minor seventh: *a minor ninth.* See also **minor key, minor mode. 5** *Logic.* (of a term or premise) having less generality or scope than another term or proposition. **6** *U.S. education.* of or relating to an additional secondary subject taken by a student. **7** (*immediately postpositive*) *Brit.* the younger or junior: sometimes used after the surname of a schoolboy if he has an older brother in the same school: *Hunt minor.* **8** (*postpositive*) *Change-ringing.* of, relating to, or denoting a set of changes rung on six bells: *grandsire minor.* ◆ *n* **9** a person or thing that is lesser or secondary. **10** a person below the age of legal majority. **11** *U.S. and Canadian education.* a subsidiary subject in which a college or university student needs fewer credits than in his or her major. **12** *Music.* a minor key, chord, mode, or scale. **13** *Logic.* a minor term or premise. **14** *Maths.* **14a** a determinant associated with a particular element of a given determinant and formed by removing the row and column containing that element. **14b** Also called: **cofactor, signed minor.** the number equal to this reduced determinant. **15** (*cap.*) another name for **Minorite.** ◆ *vb* **16** (*intr;* usually foll. by *in*) *U.S. education.* to take a minor. ◆ Compare **major.** [C13: from Latin: less, smaller; related to Old High German *minniro* smaller, Gothic *minniza* least, Latin *minuere* to diminish, Greek *meiōn* less]

minor axis *n* the shorter or shortest axis of an ellipse or ellipsoid.

Minorca (mɪ'nɔːkə) *n* **1** an island in the W Mediterranean, northeast of Majorca: the second largest of the Balearic Islands. Chief town: Mahón. Pop.: 55 500 (1985). Area: 702 sq. km (271 sq. miles). Spanish name: **Menorca. 2** a breed of light domestic fowl with glossy white, black, or blue plumage. ▸ **Mi'norcan** *adj, n*

minor canon *n Church of England.* a clergyman who is attached to a cathedral to assist at daily services but who is not a member of the chapter.

Minorite ('maɪnəˌraɪt) *n* a member of the Franciscan Friars Minor. Also called: **Minor.** [C16: from Medieval Latin *frātrēs minōrēs* lesser brethren, name adopted by St Francis as a token of humility]

minority (maɪ'nɒrɪtɪ, mɪ-) *n, pl* **-ties. 1** the smaller in number of two parts, factions, or groups. **2** a group that is different racially, politically, etc., from a larger group of which it is a part. **3a** the state of being a minor. **3b** the period during which a person is below legal age. ◆ Compare **majority. 4** (*modifier*) relating to or being a minority: *a minority interest; a minority opinion.* [C16: from Medieval Latin *minōritās,* from Latin MINOR]

minority carrier *n* the entity responsible for carrying the lesser part of the current in a semiconductor. Compare **majority carrier.**

minor key *n Music.* a key based on notes taken from a corresponding minor scale.

minor league *n* **1** *U.S. and Canadian.* any professional league in baseball other than a major league. Compare **major league. 2** (*modifier*) of relatively little importance: *that firm is very minor league.*

minor mode *n Music.* any arrangement of notes present in or characteristic of a minor scale or key.

minor orders *pl n R.C. Church.* the four lower degrees of holy orders, namely porter, exorcist, lector, and acolyte. Compare **major orders.**

minor planet *n* another name for **asteroid** (sense 1).

minor premise *n Logic.* the premise of a syllogism containing the subject of its conclusion.

minor seventh chord *n* a chord consisting of a minor triad with an added minor seventh above the root. Compare **major seventh chord.** Often shortened to **minor seventh.**

minor suit *n Bridge.* diamonds or clubs. Compare **major suit.**

minor term *n Logic.* the subject of the conclusion of a syllogism, also occurring as the subject or predicate in the minor premise.

Minos ('maɪnɒs) *n Greek myth.* a king of Crete for whom Daedalus built the Labyrinth to contain the Minotaur.

Minotaur ('maɪnəˌtɔː) *n Greek myth.* a monster with the head of a bull and the body of a man. It was kept in the Labyrinth in Crete, feeding on human flesh, until destroyed by Theseus. [C14: via Latin from Greek *Minōtauros,* from MINOS + *tauros* bull]

Minsk (mɪnsk) *n* the capital of Belarus: an industrial city and educational and cultural centre, with a university (1921). Pop.: 1 700 000 (1996 est.).

minster ('mɪnstə) *n Brit.* any of certain cathedrals and large churches, usually originally connected to a monastery. [Old English *mynster,* probably from Vulgar Latin *monisterium* (unattested), variant of Church Latin *monastērium* MONASTERY]

minstrel ('mɪnstrəl) *n* **1** a medieval wandering musician who performed songs or recited poetry with instrumental accompaniment. **2** a performer in a minstrel show. **3** *Archaic or poetic.* any poet, musician, or singer. [C13: from Old French *menestral,* from Late Latin *ministeriālis* an official, from Latin MINISTER]

minstrel show *n* a theatrical entertainment consisting of songs, dances, comic turns, etc., performed by a troupe of actors wearing black face make-up.

minstrelsy ('mɪnstrəlsɪ) *n, pl* **-sies. 1** the art of a minstrel. **2** the poems, music, or songs of a minstrel. **3** a troupe of minstrels.

mint[1] (mɪnt) *n* **1** any N temperate plant of the genus *Mentha,* having aromatic leaves and spikes of small typically mauve flowers: family *Labiatae* (labiates). The leaves of some species are used for seasoning and flavouring. See also **peppermint, spearmint, horsemint, water mint. 2 stone mint.** another name for **dittany** (sense 2). **3** a sweet flavoured with mint. [Old English *minte,* from Latin *mentha,* from Greek *minthē;* compare Old High German *minza*] ▸ '**minty** *adj*

mint[2] (mɪnt) *n* **1** a place where money is coined by governmental authority. **2** a very large amount of money: *he made a mint in business.* **3 in mint condition.** in perfect condition; as if new. ◆ *adj* **4** (of coins, postage stamps, etc.) in perfect condition as issued. ◆ *vb* **5** to make (coins) by stamping metal. **6** (*tr*) to invent (esp. phrases or words). [Old English *mynet* coin, from Latin *monēta* money, mint, from the temple of Juno *Monēta,* used as a mint in ancient Rome] ▸ '**minter** *n*

mintage ('mɪntɪdʒ) *n* **1** the process of minting. **2** money minted. **3** a fee paid for minting a coin. **4** an official impression stamped on a coin.

mint bush *n* an aromatic shrub of the genus *Prostanthera* with a mintlike odour: family *Labiatae* (labiates): native to Australia.

mint julep *n Chiefly U.S.* a long drink consisting of bourbon whiskey, crushed ice, sugar, and sprigs of mint.

Minton ('mɪntən) *n* **a** fine-quality porcelain ware produced in Stoke-on-Trent since 1798. **b** (*as modifier*): *Minton plate.* [C19: named after Thomas *Minton* (1765–1836), English potter]

mint sauce *n* a sauce made from mint leaves, sugar, and vinegar, usually served with lamb.

minuend ('mɪnjʊˌɛnd) *n* the number from which another number, the **subtrahend,** is to be subtracted. [C18: from Latin *minuendus* (*numerus*) (the number) to be diminished]

minuet (ˌmɪnjʊ'ɛt) *n* **1** a stately court dance of the 17th and 18th centuries in triple time. **2** a piece of music composed for or in the rhythm of this dance, sometimes as a movement in a suite, sonata, or symphony. See also **scherzo.** [C17: from French *menuet* dainty (referring to the dance steps), from *menu* small]

minus ('maɪnəs) *prep* **1** reduced by the subtraction of: *four minus two* (written 4 – 2). **2** *Informal.* deprived of; lacking: *minus the trimmings, that hat would be ordinary.* ◆ *adj* **3a** indicating or involving subtraction: *a minus sign.* **3b** Also: **negative.** having a value or designating a quantity less than zero: *a minus number.* **4** on the negative part of a scale or coordinate axis: *a value of minus 40°C.* **5** involving a disadvantage, harm, etc.: *a minus factor.* **6** (*postpositive*) *Education.* slightly below the standard of a particular grade: *he received* *a B minus for his essay.* **7** *Botany.* designating the strain of a fungus that can only undergo sexual reproduction with a plus strain. **8** denoting a negative electric charge. ◆ *n* **9** short for **minus sign. 10** a negative quantity. **11** a disadvantage, loss, or deficit. **12** *Informal.* something detrimental or negative. ◆ Mathematical symbol: – [C15: from Latin, neuter of MINOR]

minuscule ('mɪnəˌskjuːl) *n* **1** a lower-case letter. **2** writing using such letters. **3** a small cursive 7th-century style of lettering derived from the uncial. ◆ *adj* **4** relating to, printed in, or written in small letters. Compare **majuscule. 5** very small. **6** (of letters) lower-case. [C18: from French, from Latin (*littera*) *minuscula* very small (letter), diminutive of MINOR] ▸ **minuscular** (mɪ'nʌskjʊlə) *adj*

minus sign *n* the symbol –, indicating subtraction or a negative quantity.

minute[1] ('mɪnɪt) *n* **1** a period of time equal to 60 seconds; one sixtieth of an hour. **2** a unit of angular measure equal to one sixtieth of a degree. Symbol: ′. Also called: **minute of arc. 3** any very short period of time; moment. **4** a short note or memorandum. **5** the distance that can be travelled in a minute: *it's only two minutes away.* **6 up to the minute** (**up-to-the-minute** *when prenominal*). very latest or newest. ◆ *vb* (*tr*) **7** to record in minutes: *to minute a meeting.* **8** to time in terms of minutes. ◆ See also **minutes.** [C14: from Old French from Medieval Latin *minūta,* n. use of Latin *minūtus* MINUTE[2]]

minute[2] (maɪ'njuːt) *adj* **1** very small; diminutive; tiny. **2** unimportant; petty. **3** precise or detailed: *a minute examination.* [C15: from Latin *minūtus,* past participle of *minuere* to diminish] ▸ **mi'nuteness** *n*

minute gun ('mɪnɪt) *n* a gun fired at one-minute intervals as a sign of distress or mourning.

minute hand ('mɪnɪt) *n* the pointer on a timepiece that indicates minutes, typically the longer hand of two. Compare **hour hand, second hand.**

minutely[1] (maɪ'njuːtlɪ) *adv* in great detail.

minutely[2] ('mɪnɪtlɪ) *adj* **1** occurring every minute. ◆ *adv* **2** every minute.

Minuteman ('mɪnɪtˌmæn) *n, pl* **-men. 1** (*sometimes not cap.*) (in the War of American Independence) a colonial militiaman who promised to be ready to fight at one minute's notice. **2** a U.S. three-stage intercontinental ballistic missile.

minute mark ('mɪnɪt) *n* the symbol ′ used for minutes of arc and linear feet.

minutes ('mɪnɪts) *pl n* an official record of the proceedings of a meeting, conference, convention, etc.

minute steak ('mɪnɪt) *n* a small thinly-cut piece of steak that can be cooked quickly.

minutiae (mɪ'njuːʃɪˌiː) *pl n, sing* **-tia** (-ʃɪə). small, precise, or trifling details. [C18: pl of Late Latin *minūtia* smallness, from Latin *minūtus* MINUTE[2]]

minx (mɪŋks) *n* a bold, flirtatious, or scheming woman. [C16: of unknown origin] ▸ **'minxish** *adj*

Minya ('mɪnjə) *n* See **El Minya.**

minyan *Hebrew.* (min'jan; *English* 'mɪnjən) *n, pl* ***minyanim*** (minja'nim) *or* ***minyans.*** the number of persons required by Jewish law to be present for a religious service, namely, at least ten males over thirteen years of age. [literally: number]

Miocene ('maɪəˌsiːn) *adj* **1** of, denoting, or formed in the fourth epoch of the Tertiary period, between the Oligocene and Pliocene epochs, which lasted for 14 million years. ◆ *n* **2 the.** this epoch or rock series. [C19: from Greek *meiōn* less + -CENE]

miombo (mɪ'ɔmbɔ) *n* (in E Africa) a dry wooded area with sparse deciduous growth. [C19: probably from a Niger-Congo language]

miosis *or* **myosis** (maɪ'əʊsɪs) *n, pl* **-ses** (-siːz). **1** excessive contraction of the pupil of the eye, as in response to drugs. **2** a variant spelling of **meiosis** (sense 1). [C20: from Greek *muein* to shut the eyes + -OSIS] ▸ **miotic** *or* **myotic** (maɪ'ɒtɪk) *adj, n*

MIP *abbrev. for:* **1** monthly investment plan. **2** maximum investment plan: an endowment assurance policy designed to produce maximum profits.

MIPS (mɪps) *n Computing. acronym for* million instructions per second.

Miquelon ('miːkəˌlɒn; *French* miklɔ̃) *n* a group of islands in the French territory of **Saint Pierre and Miquelon.**

mir *Russian.* (mir) *n, pl* ***miri*** ('miri). a peasant commune in prerevolutionary Russia. [literally: world]

Mir (mɪə) *n* a Soviet (now Russian) space station launched in February 1986 and designed as a habitable module for a permanently manned scientific station: in 1997 it collided with an unmanned cargo ship in the first crash in space. [C20: Russian: peace]

Mirabeau (*French* mirabo) *n* **Comte de,** title of *Honoré-Gabriel Riqueti.* 1749–91, French Revolutionary politician.

mirabile dictu *Latin.* (mɪ'ræbɪleɪ 'dɪktuː) wonderful to relate; amazing to say.

Mira Ceti ('maɪrə 'siːtaɪ) *n* a binary star one component of which, a red supergiant, is a long-period variable with an average period of 330 days.

miracidium (ˌmaɪrə'sɪdɪəm) *n, pl* **-ia** (-ɪə). the flat ciliated larva of flukes that hatches from the egg and gives rise asexually to other larval forms. [C20: New Latin, via Late Latin *miracidion,* from Greek *meirax* boy, girl] ▸ **ˌmira'cidial** *adj*

miracle ('mɪrək°l) *n* **1** an event that is contrary to the established laws of nature and attributed to a supernatural cause. **2** any amazing or wonderful event. **3** a person or thing that is a marvellous example of something: *the bridge was a miracle of engineering.* **4** short for **miracle play. 5** (*modifier*) being or seeming a miracle: *a miracle cure.* [C12: from Latin *mīrāculum,* from *mīrārī* to wonder at]

miracle play *n* a medieval play based on a biblical story or the life of a saint. Compare **mystery play.**

miraculous (mɪ'rækjʊləs) *adj* **1** of, like, or caused by a miracle; marvellous. **2** surprising. **3** having the power to work miracles. ▸ **mi'raculously** *adv* ▸ **mi'raculousness** *n*

mirador (ˌmɪrə'dɔː) *n* a window, balcony, or turret. [C17: from Spanish, from *mirar* to look]

Miraflores (ˌmɪrə'flɔːrəs; *Spanish* mira'flores) *n* **Lake.** an artificial lake in Panama, in the S Canal Zone of the Panama Canal.

mirage (mɪ'rɑːʒ) *n* **1** an image of a distant object or sheet of water, often inverted or distorted, caused by atmospheric refraction by hot air. **2** something illusory. [C19: from French, from (*se*) *mirer* to be reflected]

Miranda[1] (mɪ'rændə) *n* one of the larger satellites of the planet Uranus.

Miranda[2] (*Spanish* mi'randa) *n* **Francisco de** (fran'sisko de). 1750–1816, Venezuelan revolutionary, who planned to liberate South and Central America from Spain. A leader (1811–12) of the Venezuelan uprising, he surrendered to Spain and died in prison.

MIRAS ('maɪˌræs) *n* (in Britain) *acronym for* mortgage interest relief at source.

mire (maɪə) *n* **1** a boggy or marshy area. **2** mud, muck, or dirt. ◆ *vb* **3** to sink or cause to sink in a mire. **4** (*tr*) to make dirty or muddy. **5** (*tr*) to involve, esp. in difficulties. [C14: from Old Norse *mȳrr;* related to MOSS] ▸ **'miriness** *n* ▸ **'miry** *adj*

mirepoix (mɪə'pwɑː) *n* a mixture of sautéed root vegetables used as a base for braising meat or for various sauces. [French, probably named in honour of C. P. G. F. de Lévis, Duke of *Mirepoix,* 18th-century French general]

Miriam ('mɪrɪəm) *n Old Testament.* the sister of Moses and Aaron. (Numbers 12:1–15). Douay name: **Mary.**

mirk (mɜːk) *n* a variant spelling of **murk.** ▸ **'mirky** *adj* ▸ **'mirkily** *adv* ▸ **'mirkiness** *n*

Miró (*Spanish* mi'ro) *n* **Joan** (xwan). 1893–1983, Spanish surrealist painter.

mirror ('mɪrə) *n* **1** a surface, such as polished metal or glass coated with a metal film, that reflects light without diffusion and produces an image of an object placed in front of it. **2** such a reflecting surface mounted in a frame. **3** any reflecting surface. **4** a thing that reflects or depicts something else: *the press is a mirror of public opinion.* ◆ *vb* **5** (*tr*) to reflect, represent, or depict faithfully: *he mirrors his teacher's ideals.* [C13: from Old French from *mirer* to look at, from Latin *mīrārī* to wonder at] ▸ **'mirror-ˌlike** *adj*

mirror ball *n* a large revolving ball covered with small pieces of mirror glass so that it reflects light in changing patterns: used in discos and ballrooms.

mirror canon *n Music.* **1** a canon in which the parts are written as though seen in a mirror placed between them: one part or set of parts is the upside-down image of the other. **2** sometimes, less accurately, a piece that can be played backwards.

mirror carp *n* a variety of the common carp (*Cyprinus carpio*) with reduced scales, giving a smooth shiny body surface.

mirror finish *n* a smooth highly polished surface produced on metal by mechanical or electrolytic polishing or lapping.

mirror image *n* **1** an image as observed in a mirror. **2** an object that corresponds to another object in the same way as it would correspond to its image in a mirror.

mirror lens *n Photog.* a lens of long focal length in which some of the lens elements are replaced by mirrors in order to shorten its overall length and reduce its weight.

mirror symmetry *n* symmetry about a plane (**mirror plane**) that divides the object or system into two mutual mirror images.

mirror writing *n* backward writing that forms a mirror image of normal writing.

mirth (mɜːθ) *n* laughter, gaiety, or merriment. [Old English *myrgth;* compare MERRY] ▸ **'mirthful** *adj* ▸ **'mirthfully** *adv* ▸ **'mirthfulness** *n* ▸ **'mirthless** *adj* ▸ **'mirthlessly** *adv* ▸ **'mirthlessness** *n*

MIRV (mɜːv) *n acronym for* multiple independently targeted re-entry vehicle: **a** a missile that has several warheads, each one being directed to different enemy targets. **b** any of the warheads.

mirza ('mɜːzə, mɪə'zɑː) *n* (in Iran) **1** a title of respect placed before the surname of an official, scholar, or other distinguished man. **2** a royal prince: used as a title after a name. [C17: from Persian: son of a lord]

mis-[1] *prefix* **1** wrong, bad, or erroneous; wrongly, badly, or erroneously: *misunderstanding; misfortune; misspelling; mistreat; mislead.* **2** lack of; not: *mistrust.* [Old English *mis(se)-;* related to Middle English *mes-,* from Old French *mes-;* compare Old High German *missa-,* Old Norse *mis-*]

mis-[2] *prefix* a variant of **miso-** before a vowel.

misadventure (ˌmɪsəd'ventʃə) *n* **1** an unlucky event; misfortune. **2** *Law.* accidental death not due to crime or negligence.

misalliance (ˌmɪsə'laɪəns) *n* an unsuitable alliance or marriage.

misandry ('mɪsændrɪ) *n* hatred of men. [C20: from Greek, from MISO- + *-andria,* from *anēr* man] ▸ **mis'andrist** *n, adj* ▸ **mis'androus** *adj*

misanthrope ('mɪzənˌθrəʊp) *or* **misanthropist** (mɪ'zænθrəpɪst) *n* a person who dislikes or distrusts other people or mankind in general. [C17: from Greek *mīsanthrōpos,* from *misos* hatred + *anthrōpos* man] ▸ **misanthropic** (ˌmɪzən'θrɒpɪk) *or* **ˌmisan'thropical** *adj* ▸ **ˌmisan'thropically** *adv* ▸ **misanthropy** (mɪ'zænθrəpɪ) *n*

misapply (ˌmɪsə'plaɪ) *vb* **-plies, -plying, -plied.** (*tr*) **1** to apply wrongly or badly. **2** another word for **misappropriate.** ▸ **misapplication** (ˌmɪsæplɪ'keɪʃən) *n*

misapprehend (ˌmɪsæprɪ'hend) *vb* (*tr*) to misunderstand. ▸ **misapprehen-**

ˌ**misa'ligned** *adj* ˌ**misa'lignment** *n*

sion (ˌmɪsæprɪˈhɛnʃən) *n* ▸ ˌ**misappreˈhensive** *adj* ▸ ˌ**misappreˈhensively** *adv* ▸ ˌ**misappreˈhensiveness** *n*
misappropriate (ˌmɪsəˈprəʊprɪˌeɪt) *vb* (*tr*) to appropriate for a wrong or dishonest use; embezzle or steal. ▸ ˌ**misapˌpropriˈation** *n*
misbecome (ˌmɪsbɪˈkʌm) *vb* **-comes, -coming, -came.** (*tr*) to be unbecoming to or unsuitable for.
misbegotten (ˌmɪsbɪˈgɒtᵊn) *adj* **1** unlawfully obtained: *misbegotten gains.* **2** badly conceived, planned, or designed: *a misbegotten scheme.* **3** Also: **misbegot** (ˌmɪsbɪˈgɒt). *Literary and dialect.* illegitimate; bastard.
misbehave (ˌmɪsbɪˈheɪv) *vb* to behave (oneself) badly. ▸ ˌ**misbeˈhaver** *n* ▸ **misbehaviour** (ˌmɪsbɪˈheɪvjə) *n*
misbelief (ˌmɪsbɪˈliːf) *n* a false or unorthodox belief.
misc. *abbrev. for:* **1** miscellaneous. **2** miscellany.
miscalculate (ˌmɪsˈkælkjʊˌleɪt) *vb* (*tr*) to calculate wrongly. ▸ ˌ**miscalcuˈlation** *n* ▸ ˌ**misˈcalcuˌlator** *n*
miscall (ˌmɪsˈkɔːl) *vb* (*tr*) **1** to call by the wrong name. **2** *Dialect.* to abuse or malign. ▸ ˌ**misˈcaller** *n*
miscarriage (mɪsˈkærɪdʒ) *n* **1** (*also* ˈmɪskær-). spontaneous expulsion of a fetus from the womb, esp. prior to the 20th week of pregnancy. **2** an act of mismanagement or failure: *a miscarriage of justice.* **3** *Brit.* the failure of freight to reach its destination.
miscarry (mɪsˈkærɪ) *vb* **-ries, -rying, -ried.** (*intr*) **1** to expel a fetus prematurely from the womb; abort. **2** to fail: *all her plans miscarried.* **3** *Brit.* (of freight, mail, etc.) to fail to reach a destination.
miscast (ˌmɪsˈkɑːst) *vb* **-casts, -casting, -cast.** (*tr*) **1** to cast badly. **2** (*often passive*) **2a** to cast (a role or the roles) in (a play, film, etc.) inappropriately: *Falstaff was certainly miscast.* **2b** to assign an inappropriate role to: *he was miscast as Othello.*
miscegenation (ˌmɪsɪdʒɪˈneɪʃən) *n* interbreeding of races, esp. where differences of pigmentation are involved. **[C19:** from Latin *miscēre* to mingle + *genus* race**]** ▸ **miscegenetic** (ˌmɪsɪdʒɪˈnɛtɪk) *adj*
miscellanea (ˌmɪsəˈleɪnɪə) *pl n* a collection of miscellaneous items, esp. literary works. **[C16:** from Latin: neuter pl of *miscellāneus* MISCELLANEOUS**]**
miscellaneous (ˌmɪsəˈleɪnɪəs) *adj* **1** composed of or containing a variety of things; mixed; varied. **2** having varied capabilities, sides, etc. **[C17:** from Latin *miscellāneus,* from *miscellus* mixed, from *miscēre* to mix**]** ▸ ˌ**miscelˈlaneously** *adv* ▸ ˌ**miscelˈlaneousness** *n*
miscellanist (mɪˈsɛlənɪst) *n* a writer of miscellanies.
miscellany (mɪˈsɛlənɪ; *U.S.* ˈmɪsəˌleɪnɪ) *n, pl* **-nies. 1** a mixed assortment of items. **2** (*sometimes pl*) a miscellaneous collection of essays, poems, etc., by different authors in one volume. **[C16:** from French *miscellanées* (pl) MISCELLANEA**]**
mischance (mɪsˈtʃɑːns) *n* **1** bad luck. **2** a stroke of bad luck.
mischief (ˈmɪstʃɪf) *n* **1** wayward but not malicious behaviour, usually of children, that causes trouble, irritation, etc. **2** a playful inclination to behave in this way or to tease or disturb. **3** injury or harm caused by a person or thing. **4** a person, esp. a child, who is mischievous. **5** a source of trouble, difficulty, etc.: *floods are a great mischief to the farmer.* **[C13:** from Old French *meschief* disaster, from *meschever* to meet with calamity; from *mes-* MIS-[1] + *chever* to reach an end, from *chef* end, CHIEF**]**
mischievous (ˈmɪstʃɪvəs) *adj* **1** inclined to acts of mischief. **2** teasing; slightly malicious: *a mischievous grin.* **3** causing or intended to cause harm: *a mischievous plot.* ▸ ˈ**mischievously** *adv* ▸ ˈ**mischievousness** *n*
misch metal (mɪʃ) *n* an alloy of cerium and other rare earth metals, used esp. as a flint in cigarette lighters. **[C20:** from German *Mischmetall,* from *mischen* to mix**]**
miscible (ˈmɪsɪbᵊl) *adj* capable of mixing: *alcohol is miscible with water.* **[C16:** from Medieval Latin *miscibilis,* from Latin *miscēre* to mix**]** ▸ ˌ**misciˈbility** *n*
misconceive (ˌmɪskənˈsiːv) *vb* to have the wrong idea; fail to understand. ▸ ˌ**misconˈceiver** *n*
misconceived (ˌmɪskənˈsiːvd) *adj* faultily or wrongly planned or based.
misconception (ˌmɪskənˈsɛpʃən) *n* a false or mistaken view, opinion, or attitude.
misconduct *n* (mɪsˈkɒndʌkt). **1** behaviour, such as adultery or professional negligence, that is regarded as immoral or unethical. ◆ *vb* (ˌmɪskənˈdʌkt). (*tr*) **2** to conduct (oneself) in such a way. **3** to manage (something) badly.
misconstruction (ˌmɪskənˈstrʌkʃən) *n* **1** a false interpretation of evidence, facts, etc. **2** a faulty construction, esp. in grammar.
misconstrue (ˌmɪskənˈstruː) *vb* **-strues, -struing, -strued.** (*tr*) to interpret mistakenly.
miscount (ˌmɪsˈkaʊnt) *vb* **1** to count or calculate incorrectly. ◆ *n* **2** a false count or calculation.
miscreance (ˈmɪskrɪəns) *or* **miscreancy** *n Archaic.* lack of religious belief or faith.
miscreant (ˈmɪskrɪənt) *n* **1** a wrongdoer or villain. **2** *Archaic.* an unbeliever or heretic. ◆ *adj* **3** evil or villainous. **4** *Archaic.* unbelieving or heretical. **[C14:** from Old French *mescreant* unbelieving, from *mes-* MIS-[1] + *creant,* ultimately from Latin *credere* to believe**]**
miscreate *vb* (ˌmɪskrɪˈeɪt). **1** to create (something) badly or incorrectly. ◆ *adj* (ˈmɪskrɪɪt, -ˌeɪt). **2** *Archaic.* badly or unnaturally formed or made. ▸ ˌ**miscreˈation** *n*
miscue (ˌmɪsˈkjuː) *n* **1** *Billiards.* a faulty stroke in which the cue tip slips off the cue ball or misses it altogether. **2** *Informal.* a blunder or mistake. ◆ *vb* **-cues, -cuing, -cued. 3** (*intr*) *Billiards.* to make a miscue. **4** (*intr*) *Theatre.* to fail to answer one's own cue or answer the cue of another. **5** *Radio.* to start (a record or tape) at the wrong point. **6** (*intr*) *Informal.* to blunder.
miscue analysis *n Brit. Education.* analysis of the errors a pupil makes while reading.
misdate (mɪsˈdeɪt) *vb* (*tr*) to date (a letter, event, etc.) wrongly.
misdeal (ˌmɪsˈdiːl) *vb* **-deals, -dealing, -dealt. 1** (*intr*) to deal out cards incorrectly. ◆ *n* **2** a faulty deal. ▸ ˌ**misˈdealer** *n*
misdeed (ˌmɪsˈdiːd) *n* an evil or illegal action.
misdemean (ˌmɪsdɪˈmiːn) *vb* a rare word for **misbehave.**
misdemeanant (ˌmɪsdɪˈmiːnənt) *n Criminal law.* (formerly) a person who has committed or been convicted of a misdemeanour. Compare **felon**[1].
misdemeanour *or U.S.* **misdemeanor** (ˌmɪsdɪˈmiːnə) *n* **1** *Criminal law.* (formerly) an offence generally less heinous than a felony and which until 1967 involved a different form of trial. Compare **felony. 2** any minor offence or transgression.
misdirect (ˌmɪsdɪˈrɛkt) *vb* (*tr*) **1** to give (a person) wrong directions or instructions. **2** to address (a letter, parcel, etc.) wrongly. ▸ ˌ**misdiˈrection** *n*
misdoubt (mɪsˈdaʊt) *vb* an archaic word for **doubt** or **suspect.**
mise (miːz, maɪz) *n Law.* **1** the issue in the obsolete writ of right. **2** an agreed settlement. **[C15:** from Old French: action of putting, from *mettre* to put**]**
mise en scène *French.* (miz ɑ̃ sɛn) *n* **1a** the arrangement of properties, scenery, etc., in a play. **1b** the objects so arranged; stage setting. **2** the environment of an event.
Miseno (*Italian* miˈzɛːno) *n* a cape in SW Italy, on the N shore of the Bay of Naples: remains of the town of **Misenum,** a naval base constructed by Agrippa in 31 B.C.
miser[1] (ˈmaɪzə) *n* **1** a person who hoards money or possessions, often living miserably. **2** selfish person. **[C16:** from Latin: wretched**]**
miser[2] (ˈmaɪzə) *n Civil engineering.* a large hand-operated auger used for loose soils. **[C19:** origin unknown**]**
miserable (ˈmɪzərəbᵊl, ˈmɪzrə-) *adj* **1** unhappy or depressed; wretched. **2** causing misery, discomfort, etc.: *a miserable life.* **3** contemptible: *a miserable villain.* **4** sordid or squalid: *miserable living conditions.* **5** *Scot., Austral., and N.Z.* mean; stingy. **6** (pejorative intensifier): *you miserable wretch.* **[C16:** from Old French, from Latin *miserābilis* worthy of pity, from *miserārī* to pity, from *miser* wretched**]** ▸ ˈ**miserableness** *n* ▸ ˈ**miserably** *adv*
miserablist (ˈmɪzərəblɪst, ˈmɪzrə-) *n* **1** a person who appears to enjoy being depressed, esp. a performer of or listener to gloomy music. ◆ *adj* **2** of, resembling, or likely to be enjoyed by a miserablist or miserablists.
misère (mɪˈzɛə) *n* **1** a call in solo whist and other card games declaring a hand that will win no tricks. **2** a hand that will win no tricks. **[C19:** from French: misery**]**
miserere (ˌmɪzəˈrɛərɪ, -ˈrɪərɪ) *n* another word for **misericord** (sense 1).
Miserere (ˌmɪzəˈrɛərɪ, -ˈrɪərɪ) *n* the 51st psalm, the Latin version of which begins "Miserere mei, Deus" ("Have mercy on me, O God").
misericord *or* **misericorde** (mɪˈzɛrɪˌkɔːd) *n* **1** a ledge projecting from the underside of the hinged seat of a choir stall in a church, on which the occupant can support himself while standing. **2** *Christianity.* **2a** a relaxation of certain monastic rules for infirm or aged monks or nuns. **2b** a monastery where such relaxations can be enjoyed. **3** a small medieval dagger used to give the death stroke to a wounded foe. **[C14:** from Old French, from Latin *misericordia* compassion, from *miserēre* to pity + *cor* heart**]**
miserly (ˈmaɪzəlɪ) *adj* of or resembling a miser; avaricious. ▸ ˈ**miserliness** *n*
misery (ˈmɪzərɪ) *n, pl* **-eries. 1** intense unhappiness, discomfort, or suffering; wretchedness. **2** a cause of such unhappiness, discomfort, etc. **3** squalid or poverty-stricken conditions. **4** *Brit. informal.* a person who is habitually depressed: *he is such a misery.* **5** *Dialect.* a pain or ailment. **[C14:** via Anglo-Norman from Latin *miseria,* from *miser* wretched**]**
misfeasance (mɪsˈfiːzəns) *n Law.* the improper performance of an act that is lawful in itself. Compare **malfeasance, nonfeasance. [C16:** from Old French *mesfaisance,* from *mesfaire* to perform misdeeds**]** ▸ **misˈfeasor** *n*
misfile (ˌmɪsˈfaɪl) *vb* to file (papers, records, etc.) wrongly.
misfire (ˌmɪsˈfaɪə) *vb* (*intr*) **1** (of a firearm or its projectile) to fail to fire, explode, or ignite as or when expected. **2** (of a motor engine or vehicle, etc.) to fail to fire at the appropriate time, often causing a backfire. **3** to fail to operate or occur as intended. ◆ *n* **4** the act or an instance of misfiring.
misfit *n* (ˈmɪsˌfɪt). **1** a person not suited in behaviour or attitude to a particular social environment. **2** something that does not fit or fits badly. ◆ *vb* (ˌmɪsˈfɪt), **-fits, -fitting, -fitted.** (*intr*) **3** to fail to fit or be fitted.
misfortune (mɪsˈfɔːtʃən) *n* **1** evil fortune; bad luck. **2** an unfortunate or disastrous event; calamity.
misgive (mɪsˈgɪv) *vb* **-gives, -giving, -gave, -given.** to make or be apprehensive or suspicious.
misgiving (mɪsˈgɪvɪŋ) *n* (*often pl*) a feeling of uncertainty, apprehension, or doubt.
misgovern (ˌmɪsˈgʌvən) *vb* to govern badly. ▸ ˌ**misˈgovernment** *n* ▸ ˌ**misˈgovernor** *n*
misguide (ˌmɪsˈgaɪd) *vb* (*tr*) to guide or direct wrongly or badly. ▸ ˌ**misˈguidance** *n* ▸ ˌ**misˈguider** *n*
misguided (ˌmɪsˈgaɪdɪd) *adj* foolish or unreasonable, esp. in action or behaviour. ▸ ˌ**misˈguidedly** *adv*
mishandle (ˌmɪsˈhændᵊl) *vb* (*tr*) to handle or treat badly or inefficiently.
mishap (ˈmɪshæp) *n* **1** an unfortunate accident. **2** bad luck.

ˌ**misˈdiagˌnose** *vb*	ˌ**misdiagˈnosis** *n*	**misˈeduˌcate** *vb*	ˌ**miseduˈcation** *n*

mishear (ˌmɪsˈhɪə) *vb* **-hears, -hearing, -heard.** to fail to hear correctly.

Mishima (ˈmɪʃɪmə) *n* **Yukio** (ˈjuːkɪəʊ). 1925–70, Japanese novelist and short-story writer, whose works reflect a preoccupation with homosexuality and death. He committed harakiri in protest at the decline of traditional Japanese values.

mishit *Sport.* ◆ *n* (ˈmɪsˌhɪt). **1** a faulty shot or stroke. ◆ *vb* (ˌmɪsˈhɪt), **-hits, -hitting, -hit. 2** to hit (a ball) with a faulty stroke.

mishmash (ˈmɪʃˌmæʃ) *n* a confused collection or mixture; hotchpotch. [C15: reduplication of MASH]

Mishmi (ˈmɪʃmɪ) *n* **1** (*pl* **-mi** *or* **-mis**) a member of a Mongoloid hill people of the Brahmaputra area of NE India. **2** the language of this people, belonging to the Tibeto-Burman branch of the Sino-Tibetan family. ◆ *adj* **3** of or relating to this people or their language.

Mishna (ˈmɪʃnə; *Hebrew* miʃˈna) *n, pl* **Mishnayoth** (mɪʃˈnɑːjəʊt; *Hebrew* miʃnaˈjɔt) *Judaism.* a compilation of precepts passed down as an oral tradition and collected by Judah ha-Nasi in the late second century A.D. It forms the earlier part of the Talmud. See also **Gemara.** [C17: from Hebrew: instruction by repetition, from *shānāh* to repeat] ▸ **Mishnaic** (mɪʃˈneɪɪk), **ˈMishnic,** *or* **ˈMishnical** *adj*

misinform (ˌmɪsɪnˈfɔːm) *vb* (*tr*) to give incorrect information to. ▸ **ˌmisinˈformant** *or* **ˌmisinˈformer** *n* ▸ **misinformation** (ˌmɪsɪnfəˈmeɪʃən) *n*

misinterpret (ˌmɪsɪnˈtɜːprɪt) *vb* (*tr*) to interpret badly, misleadingly, or incorrectly. ▸ **ˌmisinˌterpreˈtation** *n* ▸ **ˌmisinˈterpreter** *n*

misjoinder (mɪsˈdʒɔɪndə) *n Law.* the improper joining of parties as coplaintiffs or codefendants or of different causes of action in one suit. Compare **nonjoinder.**

misjudge (ˌmɪsˈdʒʌdʒ) *vb* to judge (a person or persons) wrongly or unfairly. ▸ **ˌmisˈjudger** *n* ▸ **ˌmisˈjudgment** *or* **ˌmisˈjudgement** *n*

Miskolc (*Hungarian* ˈmiʃkolts) *n* a city in NE Hungary: the second most important industrial centre in Hungary; iron and steel industries. Pop.: 178 000 (1997 est.).

mislay (mɪsˈleɪ) *vb* **-lays, -laying, -laid.** (*tr*) **1** to lose (something) temporarily, esp. by forgetting where it is. **2** to lay (something) badly. ▸ **misˈlayer** *n*

mislead (mɪsˈliːd) *vb* **-leads, -leading, -led.** (*tr*) **1** to give false or misleading information to. **2** to lead or guide in the wrong direction. ▸ **misˈleader** *n*

misleading (mɪsˈliːdɪŋ) *adj* tending to confuse or mislead; deceptive. ▸ **misˈleadingly** *adv*

mislike (mɪsˈlaɪk) *Archaic.* ◆ *vb* (*tr*) **1** to dislike. ◆ *n also* **misliking. 2** dislike or aversion. ▸ **misˈliker** *n*

mismanage (ˌmɪsˈmænɪdʒ) *vb* (*tr*) to manage badly or wrongly. ▸ **ˌmisˈmanagement** *n* ▸ **ˌmisˈmanager** *n*

mismatch (ˌmɪsˈmætʃ) *vb* **1** to match badly, esp. in marriage. ◆ *n* **2** a bad or inappropriate match.

misnomer (ˌmɪsˈnəʊmə) *n* **1** an incorrect or unsuitable name or term for a person or thing. **2** the act of referring to a person by the wrong name. [C15: via Anglo-Norman from Old French *mesnommer* to misname, from Latin *nōmināre* to call by name]

miso (ˈmiːsəʊ) *n* a thick brown salty paste made from soya beans, used to flavour savoury dishes, esp. soups. [from Japanese]

miso- *or before a vowel* **mis-** *combining form.* indicating hatred: *misogyny.* [from Greek *misos* hatred]

misogamy (mɪˈsɒgəmɪ, maɪ-) *n* hatred of marriage. ▸ **miˈsogamist** *n*

misogyny (mɪˈsɒdʒɪnɪ, maɪ-) *n* hatred of women. [C17: from Greek, from MISO- + *gunē* woman] ▸ **miˈsogynist** *n, adj* ▸ **miˌsogyˈnistic** *or* **miˈsogynous** *adj*

misology (mɪˈsɒlədʒɪ, maɪ-) *n* hatred of reasoning or reasoned argument. [C19: from Greek *misologia,* from *misos* hatred + *logos* word, reasoning. See LOGOS] ▸ **miˈsologist** *n*

misoneism (ˌmɪsəʊˈniːˌɪzəm, ˌmaɪ-) *n* hatred of anything new. [C19: from Italian *misoneismo;* see MISO-, NEO-, -ISM] ▸ **ˌmisoˈneist** *n* ▸ **ˌmisoneˈistic** *adj*

mispickel (ˈmɪsˌpɪkᵊl) *n* another name for **arsenopyrite.** [C17: from German]

misplace (ˌmɪsˈpleɪs) *vb* (*tr*) **1** to put (something) in the wrong place, esp. to lose (something) temporarily by forgetting where it was placed; mislay. **2** (*often passive*) to bestow (trust, confidence, affection, etc.) unadvisedly. ▸ **ˌmisˈplacement** *n*

misplaced modifier *n Grammar.* a participle intended to modify a noun but having the wrong grammatical relationship to it as for example *having left* in the sentence *Having left Europe for good, Peter's future seemed bleak indeed.* Usual U.S. and Canadian name: **dangling participle.**

misplay (ˌmɪsˈpleɪ) *vb* **1** (*tr*) to play badly or wrongly in games or sports: *the batsman misplayed the ball.* ◆ *n* **2** a wrong or unskilful play.

misplead (mɪsˈpliːd) *vb* **-pleads, -pleading, -pleaded, -plead** (-ˈplɛd), *or* **-pled.** (*tr*) to plead incorrectly.

mispleading (mɪsˈpliːdɪŋ) *n Law.* an error or omission in pleading.

misprint *n* (ˈmɪsˌprɪnt). **1** an error in printing, made through damaged type, careless reading, etc. ◆ *vb* (ˌmɪsˈprɪnt). **2** (*tr*) to print (a letter) incorrectly.

misprision[1] (mɪsˈprɪʒən) *n* **a** a failure to inform the proper authorities of the commission of an act of treason. **b** the deliberate concealment of the commission of a felony. [C15: via Anglo-French from Old French *mesprision* error, from *mesprendre* to mistake, from *mes-* MIS-[1] + *prendre* to take]

misprision[2] (mɪsˈprɪʒən) *n Archaic.* **1** contempt. **2** failure to appreciate the value of something. [C16: from MISPRIZE]

misprize *or* **misprise** (mɪsˈpraɪz) *vb* to fail to appreciate the value of; undervalue or disparage. [C15: from Old French *mesprisier,* from *mes-* MIS-[1] + *prisier* to PRIZE[2]]

mispronounce (ˌmɪsprəˈnaʊns) *vb* to pronounce (a word) wrongly. ▸ **mispronunciation** (ˌmɪsprəˌnʌnsɪˈeɪʃən) *n*

misquote (ˌmɪsˈkwəʊt) *vb* to quote (a text, speech, etc.) inaccurately. ▸ **ˌmisquoˈtation** *n*

misread (ˌmɪsˈriːd) *vb* **-reads, -reading, -read** (-ˈrɛd). (*tr*) **1** to read incorrectly. **2** to misinterpret.

misreport (ˌmɪsrɪˈpɔːt) *vb* **1** (*tr*) to report falsely or inaccurately. ◆ *n* **2** an inaccurate or false report. ▸ **ˌmisreˈporter** *n*

misrepresent (ˌmɪsrɛprɪˈzɛnt) *vb* (*tr*) to represent wrongly or inaccurately. ▸ **ˌmisrepresenˈtation** *n* ▸ **ˌmisrepreˈsentative** *adj* ▸ **ˌmisrepreˈsenter** *n*

misrule (ˌmɪsˈruːl) *vb* **1** (*tr*) to govern inefficiently or without humanity or justice. ◆ *n* **2** inefficient or inhumane government. **3** disorder.

miss[1] (mɪs) *vb* **1** to fail to reach, hit, meet, find, or attain (some specified or implied aim, goal, target, etc.). **2** (*tr*) to fail to attend or be present for: *to miss a train; to miss an appointment.* **3** (*tr*) to fail to see, hear, understand, or perceive: *to miss a point.* **4** (*tr*) to lose, overlook, or fail to take advantage of: *to miss an opportunity.* **5** (*tr*) to leave out; omit: *to miss an entry in a list.* **6** (*tr*) to discover or regret the loss or absence of: *he missed his watch; she missed him.* **7** (*tr*) to escape or avoid (something, esp. a danger), usually narrowly: *he missed death by inches.* **8 miss the boat** *or* **bus.** to lose an opportunity. ◆ *n* **9** a failure to reach, hit, meet, find, etc. **10 give (something) a miss.** *Informal.* to avoid (something): *give the lecture a miss; give the pudding a miss.* ◆ See also **miss out.** [Old English *missan* (meaning: to fail to hit); related to Old High German *missan,* Old Norse *missa*] ▸ **ˈmissable** *adj*

miss[2] (mɪs) *n Informal.* an unmarried woman or girl, esp. a schoolgirl. [C17: shortened form of MISTRESS]

Miss (mɪs) *n* a title of an unmarried woman or girl, usually used before the surname or sometimes alone in direct address. [C17: shortened from MISTRESS]

Miss. *abbrev. for* Mississippi.

missal (ˈmɪsᵊl) *n R.C. Church.* a book containing the prayers, rites, etc., of the Masses for a complete year. [C14: from Church Latin *missale* (n), from *missālis* concerning the MASS]

missel thrush (ˈmɪsᵊl) *n* a variant spelling of **mistle thrush.**

misshape *vb* (ˌmɪsˈʃeɪp). **-shapes, -shaping, -shaped; -shaped** *or* **-shapen.** (*tr*) **1** to shape badly; deform. ◆ *n* (ˈmɪsˌʃeɪp). **2** something that is badly shaped.

misshapen (ˌmɪsˈʃeɪpᵊn) *adj* badly shaped; deformed. ▸ **ˌmisˈshapenly** *adv* ▸ **ˌmisˈshapenness** *n*

missile (ˈmɪsaɪl) *n* **1** any object or weapon that is thrown at a target or shot from an engine, gun, etc. **2a** a rocket-propelled weapon that flies either in a fixed trajectory (**ballistic missile**) or in a trajectory that can be controlled during flight (**guided missile**). **2b** (*as modifier*): *a missile carrier.* [C17: from Latin: *missilis,* from *mittere* to send]

missilery *or* **missilry** (ˈmɪsaɪlrɪ) *n* **1** missiles collectively. **2** the design, operation, or study of missiles.

missing (ˈmɪsɪŋ) *adj* **1** not present; absent or lost. **2** not able to be traced and not known to be dead: *nine men were missing after the attack.* **3 go missing.** to become lost or disappear.

missing fundamental *n* a tone, not present in the sound received by the ear, whose pitch is that of the difference between the two tones that are sounded.

missing link *n* **1** (*sometimes caps.;* usually preceded by *the*) a hypothetical extinct animal or animal group, formerly thought to be intermediate between the anthropoid apes and man. **2** any missing section or part in an otherwise complete series.

missiology (ˌmɪsɪˈɒlədʒɪ) *n Christian theol.* the study of the missionary function of the Christian Church.

mission (ˈmɪʃən) *n* **1** a specific task or duty assigned to a person or group of people: *their mission was to irrigate the desert.* **2** a person's vocation (often in the phrase **mission in life**). **3** a group of persons representing or working for a particular country, business, etc., in a foreign country. **4a** a special embassy sent to a foreign country for a specific purpose. **4b** *U.S.* a permanent legation. **5a** a group of people sent by a religious body, esp. a Christian church, to a foreign country to do religious and social work. **5b** the campaign undertaken by such a group. **6a** the work or calling of a missionary. **6b** a building or group of buildings in which missionary work is performed. **6c** the area assigned to a particular missionary. **7** the dispatch of aircraft or spacecraft to achieve a particular task. **8** a church or chapel that has no incumbent of its own. **9** a charitable centre that offers shelter, aid, or advice to the destitute or underprivileged. **10** (*modifier*) of or relating to an ecclesiastical mission: *a mission station.* **11** (*modifier*) *U.S.* (of furniture) in the style of the early Spanish missions of the southwestern U.S. ◆ *vb* **12** (*tr*) to direct a mission to or establish a mission in (a given region). [C16: from Latin *missiō,* from *mittere* to send]

missionary (ˈmɪʃənərɪ) *n, pl* **-aries. 1** a member of a religious mission. ◆ *adj* **2** of or relating to missionaries: *missionary work.* **3** resulting from a desire to convert people to one's own beliefs: *missionary zeal.*

missionary position *n Informal.* a position for sexual intercourse in which the man lies on top of the woman and they are face to face. [C20: from the

ˌmisiˌdentifiˈcation *n*
misˈname *vb,* **-names, -naming, -named.**
misˈnumber *vb*
ˌmisperˈception *n*
ˌmisproˈportion *n*

belief that missionaries advocated this as the proper position to primitive peoples among whom it was unknown]

Missionary Ridge *n* a ridge in NW Georgia and SE Tennessee: site of a battle (1863) during the Civil War: Northern victory leading to the campaign in Georgia.

missioner ('mɪʃənə) *n* **1** a less common name for **missionary. 2** a person heading a parochial mission in a Christian country.

mission statement *n* an official statement of the aims and objectives of a business or other organization.

missis ('mɪsɪz, -ɪs) *n* a variant spelling of **missus.**

Mississauga (ˌmɪsə'sɔːgə) *n* a town in SE Ontario: a SW suburb of Toronto. Pop.: 463 388 (1991).

Mississippi (ˌmɪsɪ'sɪpɪ) *n* **1** a state of the southeastern U.S., on the Gulf of Mexico: consists of a largely forested undulating plain, with swampy regions in the northwest and on the coast, the Mississippi river forming the W border; cotton, rice, and oil. Capital: Jackson. Pop.: 2 730 501 (1997 est.). Area: 122 496 sq. km (47 296 sq. miles). Abbrevs.: **Miss.** or (with zip code) **MS 2** a river in the central U.S., rising in NW Minnesota and flowing generally south to the Gulf of Mexico through several mouths, known as the Passes: the second longest river in North America (after its tributary, the Missouri), with the third largest drainage basin in the world (after the Amazon and the Congo). Length: 3780 km (2348 miles).

Mississippian (ˌmɪsɪ'sɪpɪən) *adj* **1** of or relating to the state of Mississippi or the Mississippi river. **2** (in North America) of, denoting, or formed in the lower of two subdivisions of the Carboniferous period (see also **Pennsylvanian** (sense 2)), which lasted for 50 million years. ◆ *n* **3** an inhabitant or native of the state of Mississippi. **4 the.** the Mississippian period or rock system equivalent to the lower Carboniferous of Europe.

missive ('mɪsɪv) *n* **1** a formal or official letter. **2** a formal word for **letter.** ◆ *adj* **3** *Rare.* sent or intended to be sent. [C15: from Medieval Latin *missivus,* from *mittere* to send]

Missolonghi (ˌmɪsə'lɒŋgɪ) *or* **Mesolonghi** *n* a town in W Greece, near the Gulf of Patras: famous for its defence against the Turks in 1822–23 and 1825–26 and for its association with Lord Byron, who died here in 1824. Pop.: 11 275 (1981). Modern Greek name: **Mesolóngion.**

Missouri (mɪ'zʊərɪ) *n* **1** a state of the central U.S.: consists of rolling prairies in the north, the Ozark Mountains in the south, and part of the Mississippi flood plain in the southeast, with the Mississippi forming the E border; chief U.S. producer of lead and barytes. Capital: Jefferson City. Pop.: 5 402 058 (1997 est.). Area: 178 699 sq. km (68 995 sq. miles). Abbrevs.: **Mo.** or (with zip code) **MO 2** a river in the W and central U.S., rising in SW Montana: flows north, east, and southeast to join the Mississippi above St Louis; the longest river in North America; chief tributary of the Mississippi. Length: 3970 km (2466 miles). ▸ **Mis'sourian** *n, adj*

miss out *vb* **1** (*tr, adv*) to leave out; overlook. **2** (*intr, adv; often foll. by on*) to fail to experience: *by leaving early you missed out on the celebrations.*

misspell (ˌmɪs'spel) *vb* **-spells, -spelling, -spelt** *or* **-spelled.** to spell (a word or words) wrongly.

misspelling (ˌmɪs'spelɪŋ) *n* a wrong spelling.

misspend (ˌmɪs'spend) *vb* **-spends, -spending, -spent.** to spend thoughtlessly or wastefully. ▸ **ˌmis'spender** *n*

misstate (ˌmɪs'steɪt) *vb* (*tr*) to state incorrectly. ▸ **ˌmis'statement** *n*

misstep (ˌmɪs'step) *n* **1** a false step. **2** an error.

missus *or* **missis** ('mɪsɪz, -ɪs) *n* **1** (usually preceded by *the*) *Informal.* one's wife or the wife of the person addressed or referred to. **2** an informal term of address for a woman. [C19: spoken version of MISTRESS]

missy ('mɪsɪ) *n, pl* **missies.** *Informal.* an affectionate or sometimes disparaging form of address to a young girl.

mist (mɪst) *n* **1** a thin fog resulting from condensation in the air near the earth's surface. **2** *Meteorol.* such an atmospheric condition with a horizontal visibility of 1–2 kilometres. **3** a fine spray of any liquid, such as that produced by an aerosol container. **4** *Chem.* a colloidal suspension of a liquid in a gas. **5** condensed water vapour on a surface that blurs the surface. **6** something that causes haziness or lack of clarity, such as a film of tears. ◆ *vb* **7** to cover or be covered with or as if with mist. [Old English; related to Middle Dutch, Swedish *mist,* Greek *omikhlē* fog]

mistakable *or* **mistakeable** (mɪ'steɪkəbᵊl) *adj* liable to be mistaken. ▸ **mis'takably** *or* **mis'takeably** *adv*

mistake (mɪ'steɪk) *n* **1** an error or blunder in action, opinion, or judgment. **2** a misconception or misunderstanding. ◆ *vb* **-takes, -taking, -took, -taken. 3** (*tr*) to misunderstand; misinterpret: *she mistook his meaning.* **4** (*tr; foll. by for*) to take (for), interpret (as), or confuse (with): *she mistook his direct manner for honesty.* **5** (*tr*) to choose badly or incorrectly: *he mistook his path.* **6** (*intr*) to make a mistake in action, opinion, judgment, etc. [C13 (meaning: to do wrong, err): from Old Norse *mistaka* to take erroneously] ▸ **mis'taker** *n*

mistaken (mɪ'steɪkən) *adj* **1** (*usually predicative*) wrong in opinion, judgment, etc.: *she is mistaken.* **2** arising from error in judgment, opinion, etc.: *a mistaken viewpoint.* ▸ **mis'takenly** *adv* ▸ **mis'takenness** *n*

mistal ('mɪstəl) *n Dialect.* a cow shed; byre. [C17: of uncertain origin]

Mistassini (ˌmɪstə'siːnɪ) *n* **Lake.** a lake in E Canada, in N Quebec: the largest lake in the province; drains through the Rupert River into James Bay. Area: 2175 sq. km (840 sq. miles). Length: about 160 km (100 miles).

mister ('mɪstə) (*sometimes cap.*) ◆ *n* **1** an informal form of address for a man. **2** *Naval.* **2a** the official form of address for subordinate or senior warrant officers. **2b** the official form of address for all officers in a merchant ship, other than the captain. **2c** *U.S. Navy.* the official form of address used by the commanding officer to his officers, esp. to the more junior. **3** *Brit.* the form of address for a surgeon. **4** the form of address for officials holding certain positions: *mister chairman.* ◆ *vb* **5** (*tr*) *Informal.* to call (someone) mister. [C16: variant of MASTER]

Mister ('mɪstə) *n* the full form of **Mr.**

Misti (*Spanish* 'misti) *n* See **El Misti.**

mistigris ('mɪstɪgriː) *n* **1** the joker or a blank card used as a wild card in a variety of draw poker. **2** the variety of draw poker using this card. [C19: from French *mistigris* jack of clubs, game in which this card was wild]

mistime (ˌmɪs'taɪm) *vb* (*tr*) to time (an action, utterance, etc.) wrongly.

Mistinguett (*French* mistɛ̃gɛt) *n* original name *Jeanne-Marie Bourgeois.* 1875–1956, French dancer, chanteuse, and entertainer.

mistle thrush *or* **missel thrush** ('mɪsᵊl) *n* a large European thrush, *Turdus viscivorus,* with a brown back and spotted breast, noted for feeding on mistletoe berries. [C18: from Old English *mistel* MISTLETOE]

mistletoe ('mɪsᵊlˌtəʊ) *n* **1** a Eurasian evergreen shrub, *Viscum album,* with leathery leaves, yellowish flowers, and waxy white berries: grows as a partial parasite on various trees: used as a Christmas decoration: family *Loranthaceae.* **2** any of several similar and related American plants, esp. *Phoradendron flavescens.* **3 mistletoe cactus.** an epiphytic cactus, *Rhipsalis cassytha,* that grows in tropical America. [Old English *misteltān, from mistel* mistletoe + *tān* twig; related to Old Norse *mistilteinn*]

mistook (mɪ'stʊk) *vb* the past tense of **mistake.**

mistral ('mɪstrəl, mɪ'strɑːl) *n* a strong cold dry wind that blows through the Rhône valley and S France to the Mediterranean coast, mainly in the winter. [C17: via French from Provençal, from Latin *magistrālis* MAGISTRAL, as in *magistrālis ventus* master wind]

Mistral *n* **1** (*French* mistral). **Frédéric** (frederik). 1830–1914, French Provençal poet, who led a movement to revive Provençal language and literature: shared the Nobel prize for literature 1904. **2** (*Spanish* mis'tral). **Gabriela** (ga'βrjela), pen name of *Lucila Godoy de Alcayaga.* 1889–1957, Chilean poet, educationalist, and diplomatist. Her poetry includes the collection *Desolación* (1922): Nobel prize for literature 1945.

mistreat (ˌmɪs'triːt) *vb* (*tr*) to treat badly. ▸ **ˌmis'treatment** *n*

mistress ('mɪstrɪs) *n* **1** a woman who has a continuing extramarital sexual relationship with a man. **2** a woman in a position of authority, ownership, or control, such as the head of a household. **3** a woman or female personification having control over something specified: *she was mistress of her own destiny.* **4** *Chiefly Brit.* short for **schoolmistress. 5** an archaic or dialect word for **sweetheart.** [C14: from Old French; see MASTER, -ESS]

Mistress ('mɪstrɪs) *n* an archaic or dialect title equivalent to **Mrs.**

Mistress of the Robes *n* (in Britain) a lady of high rank in charge of the Queen's wardrobe.

mistrial (mɪs'traɪəl) *n* **1** a trial made void because of some error, such as a defect in procedure. **2** (in the U.S.) an inconclusive trial, as when a jury cannot agree on a verdict.

mistrust (ˌmɪs'trʌst) *vb* **1** to have doubts or suspicions about (someone or something). ◆ *n* **2** distrust. ▸ **ˌmis'truster** *n* ▸ **ˌmis'trustful** *adj* ▸ **ˌmis'trustfully** *adv* ▸ **ˌmis'trustfulness** *n*

misty ('mɪstɪ) *adj* **mistier, mistiest. 1** consisting of or resembling mist. **2** obscured by or as if by mist. **3** indistinct; blurred: *the misty past.* ▸ **'mistily** *adv* ▸ **'mistiness** *n*

misunderstand (ˌmɪsʌndə'stænd) *vb* **-stands, -standing, -stood.** to fail to understand properly.

misunderstanding (ˌmɪsʌndə'stændɪŋ) *n* **1** a failure to understand properly. **2** a disagreement.

misunderstood (ˌmɪsʌndə'stʊd) *adj* not properly or sympathetically understood: *a misunderstood work of art; misunderstood adolescent.*

misuse *n* (ˌmɪs'juːs), *also* **misusage. 1** erroneous, improper, or unorthodox use: *misuse of words.* **2** cruel or inhumane treatment. ◆ *vb* (ˌmɪs'juːz). (*tr*) **3** to use wrongly. **4** to treat badly or harshly.

misuser (ˌmɪs'juːzə) *n Law.* an abuse of some right, privilege, office, etc., such as one that may lead to its forfeiture. [C17: from Old French *mesuser* (infinitive used as noun)]

MIT *abbrev. for* Massachusetts Institute of Technology.

mitch *or* **mich** (mɪtʃ) *vb* (*intr*) *Dialect.* to play truant from school. [C13: probably from Old French *muchier, mucier* to hide, lurk]

Mitchell ('mɪtʃəl) *n* **1 Joni,** original name *Roberta Joan Anderson.* born 1943, Canadian folk-rock singer and songwriter. Her albums include *Blue* (1971), *Court and Spark* (1974), *Mingus* (1979), and *Turbulent Indigo* (1994). **2 Margaret.** 1900–49, U.S. novelist; author of *Gone with the Wind* (1936). **3 Reginald Joseph.** 1895–1937, British aeronautical engineer; designer of the Spitfire fighter. **4** Sir **Thomas Livingstone,** known as *Major Mitchell.* 1792–1855, Australian explorer born in Scotland.

Mitchum ('mɪtʃəm) *n* **Robert.** 1917–97, U.S. film actor. His many films include *Night of the Hunter* (1955) and *Farewell my Lovely* (1975).

mite[1] (maɪt) *n* any of numerous small free-living or parasitic arachnids of the order *Acarina* (or *Acari*) that can occur in terrestrial or aquatic habitats. See also **gall mite, harvest mite, itch mite, spider mite.** Related adj: **acaroid.** Compare **tick**[2]. [Old English *mīte;* compare Old High German *mīza* gnat, Dutch *mijt*]

mite[2] (maɪt) *n* **1** a very small particle, creature, or object. **2** a very small contribu-

ˌ**mistrans'late** *vb*   **mis'type** *vb*

tion or sum of money. See also **widow's mite. 3** a former Flemish coin of small value. **4 a mite.** *Informal.* somewhat: *he's a mite foolish.* [C14: from Middle Low German, Middle Dutch *mīte;* compare MITE[1]]

miter ('maɪtə) *n, vb* the usual U.S. spelling of **mitre.**

miterwort ('maɪtə,wɜːt) *n* the U.S. spelling of **mitrewort.**

mither ('mɪðər) *n* a Scot. word for **mother**[1].

Mithgarthr ('mɪð,gɑːðə) *n* a variant of **Midgard.**

Mithraism ('mɪθreɪ,ɪzəm) *or* **Mithraicism** (mɪθ'reɪɪ,sɪzəm) *n* the ancient Persian religion of Mithras. It spread to the Roman Empire during the first three centuries A.D. ▸ **Mithraic** (mɪθ'reɪɪk) *or* ,**Mithra'istic** *adj* ▸ '**Mithraist** *n, adj*

Mithras ('mɪθræs) *or* **Mithra** ('mɪθrə) *n Persian myth.* the god of light, identified with the sun, who slew a primordial bull and fertilized the world with its blood.

mithridate ('mɪθrɪ,deɪt) *n Obsolete.* a substance believed to be an antidote to every poison and a cure for every disease. [C16: from Late Latin *mithradatium,* after MITHRIDATES VI, alluding to his legendary immunity to poisons]

Mithridates VI *or* **Mithradates VI** (,mɪθrɪ'deɪtiːz) *n* called *the Great.* ?132–63 B.C., king of Pontus (?120–63). He waged three wars against Rome (88–84; 83–81; 74–64) and was finally defeated by Pompey: committed suicide.

mithridatism ('mɪθrɪdeɪ,tɪzəm) *n* immunity to large doses of poison by prior ingestion of gradually increased doses. ▸ **mithridatic** (,mɪθrɪ'dætɪk, -'deɪ-) *adj*

miticide ('mɪtɪ,saɪd) *n* any drug or agent that destroys mites. ▸ ,**miti'cidal** *adj*

mitigate ('mɪtɪ,geɪt) *vb* to make or become less severe or harsh; moderate. [C15: from Latin *mītigāre,* from *mītis* mild + *agere* to make] ▸ **mitigable** ('mɪtɪgəbᵊl) *adj* ▸ ,**miti'gation** *n* ▸ '**miti,gative** *or* '**miti,gatory** *adj* ▸ '**miti,gator** *n*

USAGE *Mitigate* is sometimes wrongly used where *militate* is meant: *his behaviour militates* (not *mitigates*) *against his chances of promotion.*

mitigating circumstances *pl n* circumstances that may be considered to lessen the culpability of an offender.

Mitilíni (miti'lini) *n* transliteration of the Modern Greek name for **Mytilene** (sense 1).

mitis ('maɪtɪs, 'miː-) *or* **mitis metal** *n* a malleable iron, fluid enough for casting, made by adding a small amount of aluminium to wrought iron. [C19: from Latin: soft]

Mitnaged (,mitnɑ'ged) *or* **Misnaged** (mis'nɑged) *n, pl* **Mitnagdim** (,mitnɑg'dim) *or* **Misnagdim** (mis'nɑgdim) *Judaism.* an orthodox opponent of Chassidism. See **Chassid.** [from Hebrew, literally: opponent]

mitochondrion (,maɪtəʊ'kɒndrɪən) *n, pl* **-dria** (-drɪə). a small spherical or rodlike body, bounded by a double membrane, in the cytoplasm of most cells: contains enzymes responsible for energy production. Also called: **chondriosome.** [C19: New Latin, from Greek *mitos* thread + *khondrion* small grain] ▸ ,**mito'chondrial** *adj*

mitogen ('maɪtədʒən) *n* any agent that induces mitosis. ▸ **mitogenic** (,maɪtəʊ'dʒenɪk) *adj*

mitosis (maɪ'təʊsɪs, mɪ-) *n* a method of cell division, in which the nucleus divides into daughter nuclei, each containing the same number of chromosomes as the parent nucleus. See **prophase, metaphase, anaphase, telophase.** Compare **meiosis** (sense 1). [C19: from New Latin, from Greek *mitos* thread] ▸ **mitotic** (maɪ'tɒtɪk, mɪ-) *adj* ▸ **mi'totically** *adv*

mitrailleuse (,mɪtraɪ'ɜːz) *n* **1** an early form of breech-loading machine gun having several parallel barrels. **2** any French machine gun. [C19: from French, from *mitraille* small shot, from Old French *mistraille* pieces of money, from MITE[2]]

mitral ('maɪtrəl) *adj* **1** of or like a mitre. **2** *Anatomy.* of or relating to the mitral valve.

mitral valve *n* the valve between the left atrium and the left ventricle of the heart, consisting of two membranous flaps, that prevents regurgitation of blood into the atrium. Also called: **bicuspid valve.**

mitre *or U.S.* **miter** ('maɪtə) *n* **1** *Christianity.* the liturgical headdress of a bishop or abbot, in most western churches consisting of a tall pointed cleft cap with two bands hanging down at the back. **2** short for **mitre joint. 3** a bevelled surface of a mitre joint. **4** (in sewing) a diagonal join where the hems along two sides meet at a corner of the fabric. ◆ *vb* (*tr*) **5** to make a mitre joint between (two pieces of material, esp. wood). **6** to make a mitre in (a fabric). **7** to confer a mitre upon: *a mitred abbot.* [C14: from Old French, from Latin *mitra,* from Greek *mitra* turban]

mitre block *n* a block of wood with slots for cutting mitre joints with a saw.

mitre box *n* an open-ended box with sides having narrow slots to guide a saw in cutting mitre joints.

mitre gear *n* one of a pair of similar bevel gears having a pitch cone angle of 45°.

mitre joint *n* a corner joint formed between two pieces of material, esp. wood, by cutting bevels of equal angles at the ends of each piece. Sometimes shortened to **mitre.**

mitre square *n* a tool with two blades that are at a fixed angle to one another, used to bevel a mitre joint.

mitrewort *or U.S.* **miterwort** ('maɪtə,wɜːt) *n* any of several Asian and North American saxifragaceous plants of the genus *Mitella,* having clusters of small white flowers and capsules resembling a bishop's mitre. Also called: **bishop's-cap.**

mitt (mɪt) *n* **1** any of various glovelike hand coverings, such as one that does not cover the fingers. **2** short for **mitten** (sense 1). **3** *Baseball.* a large round thickly padded leather mitten worn by the catcher. See also **glove** (sense 2). **4** (*often pl*) a slang word for **hand. 5** *Slang.* a boxing glove. [C18: shortened from MITTEN]

Mittelland Canal (*German* 'mɪtəllant) *n* a canal in Germany, linking the Rivers Rhine and Elbe. Length: 325 km (202 miles).

mitten ('mɪtᵊn) *n* **1** a glove having one section for the thumb and a single section for the other fingers. Sometimes shortened to **mitt. 2** *Slang.* a boxing glove. [C14: from Old French *mitaine,* of uncertain origin]

Mitterrand (*French* mitɛrɑ̃) *n* **François Maurice Marie** (frɑ̃swa mɔris mari). 1916–96, French statesman; first secretary of the socialist party (1971–95); president (1981–95).

mittimus ('mɪtɪməs) *n, pl* **-muses.** *Law.* a warrant of commitment to prison or a command to a jailer directing him to hold someone in prison. [C15: from Latin: we send, the first word of such a command]

Mitty ('mɪtɪ) *n* **Walter. a** a fictional character given to grand and elaborate fantasies; daydreamer. **b** (*as modifier*): *a Walter Mitty character; a Mitty act.* [C20: from a short story *The Secret Life of Walter Mitty* (1939), by James THURBER] ▸ ,**Mitty'esque** *or* '**Mitty-,like** *adj*

mitzvah ('mɪtsvə; *Hebrew* mits'va) *n, pl* **-vahs** *or* **-voth** (*Hebrew* -'vɔt). *Judaism.* **1** a commandment or precept, esp. one found in the Bible. **2** a good deed. [from Hebrew: commandment]

mix (mɪks) *vb* **1** (*tr*) to combine or blend (ingredients, liquids, objects, etc.) together into one mass. **2** (*intr*) to become or have the capacity to become combined, joined, etc.: *some chemicals do not mix.* **3** (*tr*) to form (something) by combining two or more constituents: *to mix cement.* **4** (*tr;* often foll. by *in* or *into*) to add as an additional part or element (to a mass or compound): *to mix flour into a batter.* **5** (*tr*) to do at the same time; combine: *to mix study and pleasure.* **6** (*tr*) to consume (drinks or foods) in close succession. **7** to come or cause to come into association socially: *Pauline has never mixed well.* **8** (*intr;* often foll. by *with*) to go together; complement. **9** (*tr*) to crossbreed (differing strains of plants or breeds of livestock), esp. more or less at random. **10** (*tr*) *Electronics.* to combine (two or more signals). **11** *Music.* **11a** (in sound recording) to balance and adjust (the recorded tracks) on a multitrack tape machine. **11b** (in live performance) to balance and adjust (the output levels from microphones and pick-ups). **12** (*tr*) to merge (two lengths of film) so that the effect is imperceptible. **13 mix it.** *Informal.* **13a** to cause mischief or trouble, often for a person named: *she tried to mix it for John.* **13b** to fight. ◆ *n* **14** the act or an instance of mixing. **15** the result of mixing; mixture. **16** a mixture of ingredients, esp. one commercially prepared for making a cake, bread, etc. **17** *Music.* the sound obtained by mixing. **18** *Building trades, civil engineering.* the proportions of cement, sand, and aggregate in mortar, plaster, or concrete. **19** *Informal.* a state of confusion, bewilderment. ◆ See also **mix-up.** [C15: back formation from *mixt* mixed, via Old French from Latin *mixtus,* from *miscēre* to mix] ▸ '**mixable** *adj* ▸ ,**mixa'bility** *n*

mixdown ('mɪks,daʊn) *n* (in sound recording) the transfer of a multitrack master mix to two-track stereo tape.

mixed (mɪkst) *adj* **1** formed or blended together by mixing. **2** composed of different elements, races, sexes, etc.: *a mixed school.* **3** consisting of conflicting elements, thoughts, attitudes, etc.: *mixed feelings; mixed motives.* **4** (of a legal action) **4a** having the nature of both a real and a personal action, such as a demand for the return of wrongfully withheld property as well as for damages to compensate for the loss. **4b** having aspects or issues determinable by different persons or bodies: *a mixed question of law and fact.* **5** (of an inflorescence) containing cymose and racemose branches. **6** (of a nerve) containing both motor and sensory nerve fibres. **7** *Maths.* **7a** (of a number) consisting of the sum of an integer and a fraction, as 5½. **7b** (of a decimal) consisting of the sum of an integer and a decimal fraction, as 17.43. **7c** (of an algebraic expression) consisting of the sum of a polynomial and a rational fraction, such as $2x + 4x^2 + 2/3x$. ▸ **mixedly** ('mɪksɪdlɪ) *adv* ▸ **mixedness** ('mɪksɪdnɪs) *n*

mixed bag *n Informal.* something composed of diverse elements, characteristics, people, etc.

mixed blessing *n* an event, situation, etc., having both advantages and disadvantages.

mixed bud *n* a bud containing both rudimentary flowers and foliage leaves.

mixed crystal *n Chem.* a crystal consisting of a solid solution of two or more distinct compounds.

mixed doubles *pl n Tennis.* a doubles game with a man and a woman as partners on each side.

mixed economy *n* an economy in which some industries are privately owned and others are publicly owned or nationalized.

mixed farming *n* combined arable and livestock farming (on **mixed farms**).

mixed-flow turbine *n* a water turbine in which water flows radially and axially through the rotating vanes.

mixed grill *n* a dish made of several kinds of grilled meats, often served with grilled tomatoes and mushrooms.

mixed language *n* any language containing items of vocabulary or other linguistic characteristics borrowed from two or more existing languages. See also **pidgin, creole** (sense 1), **lingua franca.**

mixed marriage *n* a marriage between persons of different races or religions.

mixed metaphor *n* a combination of incongruous metaphors, as *when the Nazi jackboots sing their swan song.*

mixed-up *adj* in a state of mental confusion; perplexed.

mixer ('mɪksə) *n* **1** a person or thing that mixes. **2** *Informal.* **2a** a person considered in relation to his ability to mix socially. **2b** a person who creates trouble for others. **3** a kitchen appliance, usually electrical, used for mixing foods, etc. **4** a drink such as ginger ale, fruit juice, etc., used in preparing cocktails. **5** *Electronics.* a device in which two or more input signals are combined to give a single output signal. **6** short for **sound mixer, vision mixer.**

mixer tap *n* a tap in which hot and cold water supplies have a joint outlet but are controlled separately.

Mixe-Zoque ('mɪks'zɒk) *n* **1** a member of an American Indian people of Mexico. **2** any of the languages of this people.

mixolydian (ˌmɪksəʊ'lɪdɪən) *adj Music.* of, relating to, or denoting an authentic mode represented by the ascending natural diatonic scale from G to G. See **Hypo-**. [C16: from Greek *mixoludios* half-Lydian]

mixte ('mɪkstɪ) *adj* of or denoting a type of bicycle frame, usually for women, in which angled twin lateral tubes run back to the rear axle. [C20: from French]

Mixtec ('miːstɛk) *n* **1** (*pl* **-tecs** or **-tec**) a member of an American Indian people of Mexico. **2** the language of this people. ► **Mix'tecan** *adj, n*

mixter-maxter ('mɪkstər'mækstər) *Scot.* ◆ *adj* **1** chaotic or confused. ◆ *n* **2** a chaotic or confused mixture; jumble. [C19: reduplicated form based on MIX]

mixture ('mɪkstʃə) *n* **1** the act of mixing or state of being mixed. **2** something mixed; a result of mixing. **3** *Chem.* a substance consisting of two or more substances mixed together without any chemical bonding between them. **4** *Pharmacol.* a liquid medicine in which an insoluble compound is suspended in the liquid. **5** *Music.* an organ stop that controls several ranks of pipes sounding the upper notes in a harmonic series. **6** the mixture of petrol vapour and air in an internal-combustion engine. [C16: from Latin *mixtūra*, from *mixtus*, past participle of *miscēre* to mix]

mix-up *n* **1** a confused condition or situation. **2** *Informal.* a fight. ◆ *vb* **mix up.** (*tr, adv*) **3** to make into a mixture: *to mix up ingredients.* **4** to confuse or confound: *Tom mixes John up with Bill.* **5** (*often passive*) to put (someone) into a state of confusion: *I'm all mixed up.* **6** (foll. by *in* or *with;* usually passive) to involve (in an activity or group, esp. one that is illegal): *why did you get mixed up in that drugs racket?* **7 mix it up.** *U.S. and Canadian informal.* to fight.

Mizar ('maɪzɑː) *n* a multiple star having four components that lies in the Plough in the constellation Ursa Major and forms a visible binary with the star Alcor (period 300 years). Visual magnitude: 2.2; spectral type: A2. [from Arabic *mi'zar* cloak]

Mizoguchi (ˌmiːtsə'guːtʃɪ) *n* **Kenji** ('kɛndʒɪ). 1898–1956, Japanese film director. His films include *A Paper Doll's Whisper of Spring* (1925), *Woman of Osaka* (1940), and *Ugetsu Monogatari* (1952).

Mizoram (mɪ'zɔːrəm) *n* a state (since 1986) in NE India, created in 1972 from the former Mizo Hills District of Assam. Capital: Aijal. Pop.: 775 000 (1994 est.). Area: about 21 081 sq. km (8140 sq. miles).

mizzen *or* **mizen** ('mɪzᵊn) *Nautical.* ◆ *n* **1** a sail set on a mizzenmast. **2** short for **mizzenmast.** ◆ *adj* **3** of or relating to any kind of gear used with a mizzenmast: *a mizzen staysail.* [C15: from French *misaine*, from Italian *mezzana*, *mezzano* middle]

mizzenmast *or* **mizenmast** ('mɪzᵊnˌmɑːst; *Nautical* 'mɪzᵊnməst) *n Nautical.* **1** (on a yawl, ketch, or dandy) the after mast. **2** (on a vessel with three or more masts) the third mast from the bow.

mizzle[1] ('mɪzᵊl) *vb, n* a dialect word for **drizzle.** [C15: perhaps from Low German *miseln* to drizzle; compare Dutch dialect *miezelen* to drizzle] ► **'mizzly** *adj*

mizzle[2] ('mɪzᵊl) *vb* (*intr*) *Brit. slang.* to decamp. [C18: of unknown origin]

mk *Currency. symbol for:* **1** mark. **2** markka.

Mk *abbrev. for* mark (type of car).

MKSA system *n* another name for **Giorgi system.**

mks units *pl n* a metric system of units based on the metre, kilogram, and second as the units of length, mass, and time; it forms the basis of the SI units.

mkt *abbrev. for* market.

ml *symbol for:* **1** millilitre. **2** mile.

ML *abbrev. for* Medieval Latin.

MLA *abbrev. for:* **1** Member of the Legislative Assembly. **2** Modern Language Association (of America).

MLC (in India and Australia) *abbrev. for* Member of the Legislative Council.

MLD *abbrev. for* minimum lethal dose (the smallest amount of a drug or toxic agent that will kill a laboratory animal).

MLF *abbrev. for* multilateral (nuclear) force.

MLG *abbrev. for* Middle Low German.

MLitt *abbrev. for* Master of Letters. [Latin *Magister Litterarum*]

Mlle *pl* **Mlles** the French equivalent of **Miss.** [from French *Mademoiselle*]

MLR *abbrev. for* minimum lending rate.

mm 1 *symbol for* millimetre. **2** *abbrev. for* mutatis mutandis.

MM 1 *abbrev. for* Military Medal. **2** the French equivalent of **Messrs.** [from French *Messieurs*]

MMC (in Britain) *abbrev. for* Monopolies and Mergers Commission.

MMDS *abbrev. for* multipoint microwave distribution system: a radio alternative to cable television. Sometimes shortened to **MDS.**

Mme *pl* **Mmes** the French equivalent of **Mrs.** [from French *Madame, Mesdames*]

mmf *abbrev. for* magnetomotive force.

mmHg *abbrev. for* millimetre(s) of mercury (a unit of pressure equal to the pressure that can support a column of mercury 1 millimetre high).

MMM (in Canada) *abbrev. for* Member of the Order of Military Merit.

MMP *abbrev. for* mixed member proportional: a system of proportional representation, used in Germany and New Zealand.

MMR *n* a combined vaccine against measles, mumps, and rubella, given to young children.

MMus. *abbrev. for* Master of Music.

Mn *the chemical symbol for* manganese.

MN *abbrev. for:* **1** (in Britain) Merchant Navy. **2** Minnesota.

MNA (in Canada) *abbrev. for* Member of the National Assembly (of Quebec).

mnemonic (nɪ'mɒnɪk) *adj* **1** aiding or meant to aid one's memory. **2** of or relating to memory or mnemonics. ◆ *n* **3** something, such as a verse, to assist memory. [C18: from Greek *mnēmonikos*, from *mnēmōn* mindful, from *mnasthai* to remember] ► **mne'monically** *adv*

mnemonics (nɪ'mɒnɪks) *n* (*usually functioning as sing*) **1** the art or practice of improving or of aiding the memory. **2** a system of rules to aid the memory.

Mnemosyne (niː'mɒzɪˌniː, -'mɒs-) *n Greek myth.* the goddess of memory and mother by Zeus of the Muses.

mo (məʊ) *n Informal.* **1** *Chiefly Brit.* short for **moment** (sense 1) (esp. in the phrase **half a mo**). **2** *Chiefly Austral.* short for **moustache** (sense 1).

Mo *the chemical symbol for* molybdenum.

MO *abbrev. for:* **1** Missouri. **2** Medical Officer.

mo. *pl* **mos.** *abbrev. for* month.

Mo. *abbrev. for* Missouri.

m.o. *or* **MO** *abbrev. for:* **1** mail order. **2** money order.

-mo *suffix forming nouns.* (in bookbinding) indicating book size by specifying the number of leaves formed by folding one sheet of paper: *12mo, twelvemo,* or *duodecimo; 16mo* or *sixteenmo.* [abstracted from DUODECIMO]

moa ('məʊə) *n* any large flightless bird of the recently extinct order *Dinornithiformes* of New Zealand (see **ratite**). [C19: from Maori]

Moab ('məʊæb) *n Old Testament.* an ancient kingdom east of the Dead Sea, in what is now the SW part of Jordan: flourished mainly from the 9th to the 6th centuries B.C. ► **Moabite** ('məʊəˌbaɪt) *adj, n*

moa hunter *n* the name given by anthropologists to the early Maori inhabitants of New Zealand.

moan (məʊn) *n* **1** a low prolonged mournful sound expressive of suffering or pleading. **2** any similar mournful sound, esp. that made by the wind. **3** a grumble or complaint. ◆ *vb* **4** to utter (words) in a low mournful manner. **5** (*intr*) to make a sound like a moan. **6** (*usually intr*) to grumble or complain (esp. in the phrase **moan and groan**). [C13: related to Old English *mǣnan* to grieve over] ► **'moaner** *n* ► **'moanful** *adj* ► **'moaning** *n, adj* ► **'moaningly** *adv*

moat (məʊt) *n* **1** a wide water-filled ditch surrounding a fortified place, such as a castle. ◆ *vb* **2** (*tr*) to surround with or as if with a moat: *a moated grange.* [C14: from Old French *motte* mound]

mob (mɒb) *n* **1a** a riotous or disorderly crowd of people; rabble. **1b** (*as modifier*): *mob law; mob violence.* **2** *Often derogatory.* a group or class of people, animals, or things. **3** *Austral. and N.Z.* a flock (of sheep) or a herd (of cattle, esp. when droving). **4** *Often derogatory.* the masses. **5** *Slang.* a gang of criminals. ◆ *vb* **mobs, mobbing, mobbed.** (*tr*) **6** to attack in a group resembling a mob. **7** to surround, esp. in order to acclaim: *they mobbed the film star.* **8** to crowd into (a building, plaza, etc.). **9** (of a group of animals of a prey species) to harass (a predator). ◆ See also **mobs.** [C17: shortened from Latin *mōbile vulgus* the fickle populace; see MOBILE] ► **'mobber** *n* ► **'mobbish** *adj*

mobcap ('mɒbˌkæp) *n* a woman's large cotton cap with a pouched crown and usually a frill, worn esp. during the 18th century. Often shortened to **mob.** [C18: from obsolete *mob* woman, esp. a loose-living woman, + CAP]

mob-handed *adj, adv Informal.* in or with a large group of people: *the police turned up mob-handed.*

mobile ('məʊbaɪl) *adj* **1** having freedom of movement; movable. **2** changing quickly in expression: *a mobile face.* **3** *Sociol.* (of individuals or social groups) moving within and between classes, occupations, and localities: *upwardly mobile.* **4** (of military forces) able to move freely and quickly to any given area. **5** (*postpositive*) *Informal.* having transport available: *are you mobile tonight?* ◆ *n* **6a** a sculpture suspended in midair with delicately balanced parts that are set in motion by air currents. **6b** (*as modifier*): *mobile sculpture.* **7** short for **mobile phone.** [C15: via Old French from Latin *mōbilis*, from *movēre* to move]

Mobile ('məʊbiːl, məʊ'biːl) *n* a port in SW Alabama, on **Mobile Bay** (an inlet of the Gulf of Mexico): the state's only port and its first permanent settlement, made by French colonists in 1711. Pop.: 202 581 (1996 est.).

-mobile (məʊˌbiːl) *suffix forming nouns.* indicating a vehicle designed for a particular person or purpose: *Popemobile.*

mobile home *n* living quarters mounted on wheels and capable of being towed by a motor vehicle.

mobile library *n* a vehicle providing lending library facilities. U.S. and Canadian equivalent: **bookmobile.**

mobile phone *n* a portable telephone that works by means of a cellular radio system.

mobility (məʊ'bɪlɪtɪ) *n* **1** the ability to move physically: *a handicapped person's mobility may be limited; mobility is part of physical education.* **2** *Sociol.* (of individuals or social groups) movement within or between classes and occupations. See also **vertical mobility, horizontal mobility.**

mobility housing *n Social welfare.* houses designed or adapted for people who have difficulty in walking but are not necessarily chairbound. See also **wheelchair housing.**

mobilize *or* **mobilise** ('məʊbɪˌlaɪz) *vb* **1** to prepare for war or other emergency by organizing (national resources, the armed services, etc.). **2** (*tr*) to organize for a purpose; marshal. **3** (*tr*) to put into motion, circulation, or use. ► **'mobiˌlizable** *or* **'mobiˌlisable** *adj* ► **ˌmobili'zation** *or* **ˌmobili'sation** *n*

Möbius strip ('mɜːbɪəs; *German* 'møːbiʊs) *n Maths.* a one-sided continuous surface, formed by twisting a long narrow rectangular strip of material through 180° and joining the ends. [C19: named after August *Möbius* (1790–1868), German mathematician who invented it]

mobocracy (mɒ'bɒkrəsɪ) *n, pl* **-cies. 1** rule or domination by a mob. **2** the mob that rules. ► **mobocrat** ('mɒbəˌkræt) *n* ► **ˌmobo'cratic** *or* **ˌmobo'cratical** *adj*

mobs (mɒbz) *Informal.* ◆ *pl n* **1** (usually foll. by *of*) great numbers or quantities; lots: *mobs of people.* ◆ *adv* **2** *Austral. and N.Z.* a great deal: *mobs better.*

mobster ('mɒbstə) *n* a U.S. slang word for **gangster.**

Mobutu[1] (mə'bu:tu:) *n* **Lake.** the former name (until 1997) of **Lake Albert.**

Mobutu[2] (mə'bu:tu:) *n* **Sese Seko** ('sɛsɛ 'sɛkəʊ), original name *Joseph.* 1930–97, Zaïrese statesman; president of Zaïre (now the Democratic Republic of the Congo) (1970–97); accused of corruption and overthrown by rebels in 1997; died in exile.

MoC *abbrev. for* mother of the chapel.

Moçambique (musəm'bikə) *n* the Portuguese name for **Mozambique.**

moccasin ('mɒkəsɪn) *n* **1** a shoe of soft leather, esp. deerskin, worn by North American Indians. **2** any soft shoe resembling this. **3** *N.Z.* a sheepshearer's footgear, usually made of sacking. **4** short for **water moccasin.** [C17: from Algonquian; compare Narraganset *mocussin* shoe]

moccasin flower *n* any of several North American orchids of the genus *Cypripedium* with a pink solitary flower. See also **lady's-slipper, cypripedium** (sense 1).

moccasin telegraph *n Canadian informal.* the transmission of rumour or secret information; the grapevine.

mocha ('mɒkə) *n* **1** a strongly flavoured dark brown coffee originally imported from Arabia. **2** a flavouring made from coffee and chocolate. **3** a soft glove leather with a suede finish, made from goatskin or sheepskin. **4a** a dark brown colour. **4b** (*as adj*): *mocha shoes.*

Mocha *or* **Mokha** ('mɒkə) *n* a port in Yemen, on the Red Sea; in North Yemen until 1990: formerly important for the export of Arabian coffee. Pop.: about 2000 (1990 est.).

mocha stone *n* another name for **moss agate.**

mock (mɒk) *vb* **1** (when *intr,* often foll. by *at*) to behave with scorn or contempt (towards); show ridicule (for). **2** (*tr*) to imitate, esp. in fun; mimic. **3** (*tr*) to deceive, disappoint, or delude. **4** (*tr*) to defy or frustrate: *the team mocked the visitors' attempt to score.* ◆ *n* **5** the act of mocking. **6** a person or thing mocked. **7** a counterfeit; imitation. **8** (*often pl*) *Informal.* (in England and Wales) the school examinations taken as practice before public examinations. ◆ *adj* (*prenominal*) **9** sham or counterfeit. **10** serving as an imitation or substitute, esp. for practice purposes: *a mock battle; mock finals.* ◆ See also **mock-up.** [C15: from Old French *mocquer*] ▸ **'mockable** *adj* ▸ **'mocker** *n* ▸ **'mocking** *n, adj* ▸ **'mockingly** *adv*

mocker ('mɒkə) *n Austral. slang., old-fashioned.* **1** clothing. **2 all mockered up.** dressed up. [of unknown origin]

mockernut ('mɒkə,nʌt) *n* **1** Also called: **black hickory.** a species of smooth-barked hickory, *Carya tomentosa,* with fragrant foliage that turns bright yellow in autumn. **2** the nut of this tree. [so called because the nut is difficult to extract]

mockers ('mɒkəz) *pl n Informal.* **put the mockers on.** to ruin the chances of success of. Also (Austral.): **put the mock** (*or* **mocks**) **on.** [C20: perhaps from MOCK]

mockery ('mɒkərɪ) *n, pl* **-eries. 1** ridicule, contempt, or derision. **2** a derisive action or comment. **3** an imitation or pretence, esp. a derisive one. **4** a person or thing that is mocked. **5** a person, thing, or action that is inadequate or disappointing.

mock-heroic *adj* **1** (of a literary work, esp. a poem) imitating the style of heroic poetry in order to satirize an unheroic subject, as in Pope's *The Rape of the Lock.* ◆ *n* **2** burlesque imitation of the heroic style or of a single work in this style.

mockingbird ('mɒkɪŋ,bɜ:d) *n* any American songbird of the family *Mimidae,* having a long tail and grey plumage: noted for their ability to mimic the song of other birds.

mock moon *n* another name for **paraselene.**

mockney ('mɒknɪ) *n* **1** (*often cap.*) a person who affects a cockney accent. **2** an affected cockney accent. ◆ *adj* **3** denoting an affected cockney accent or a person who has one. [C20: MOCK + COCKNEY]

mock orange *n* **1** Also called: **syringa.** any shrub of the genus *Philadelphus,* esp. *P. coronarius,* with white fragrant flowers that resemble those of the orange: family *Philadelphaceae.* **2** any other shrub or tree that resembles the orange tree.

mock sun *n* another name for **parhelion.**

mock turtle soup *n* an imitation turtle soup made from a calf's head.

mock-up *n* **1** a working full-scale model of a machine, apparatus, etc., for testing, research, etc. **2** a layout of printed matter. ◆ *vb* **mock up. 3** (*tr, adv*) to build or make a mock-up of.

mod[1] (mɒd) *n Brit.* **a** a member of a group of teenagers in the mid-1960s, noted for their clothes-consciousness and opposition to the rockers. **b** a member of a revived group of this type in the late 1970s and early 1980s, noted for their clothes-consciousness and opposition to the skinheads. **c** (*as modifier*): *a mod haircut.* [C20: from MODERNIST]

mod[2] (mɒd) *n* an annual Highland Gaelic meeting with musical and literary competitions. [C19: from Gaelic *mōd* assembly, from Old Norse; related to MOOT]

mod[3] (mɒd) *Maths. abbrev. for* modulus.

MOD (in Britain) *abbrev. for* Ministry of Defence.

mod. *abbrev. for:* **1** moderate. **2** moderato. **3** modern.

modal ('məʊdᵊl) *adj* **1** of, relating to, or characteristic of mode or manner. **2** *Grammar.* (of a verb form or auxiliary verb) expressing a distinction of mood, such as that between possibility and actuality. The modal auxiliaries in English include *can, do, may, must, need, ought, shall, should, will,* and *would.* **3** *Philosophy, logic.* **3a** qualifying or expressing a qualification of the truth of some statement, for example, as necessary or contingent. **3b** relating to analogous qualifications such as that of rules as obligatory or permissive. **4** *Metaphysics.* of or relating to the form of a thing as opposed to its attributes, substance, etc. **5** *Music.* of or relating to a mode. **6** of or relating to a statistical mode. ▸ **'modally** *adv*

modality (məʊ'dælɪtɪ) *n, pl* **-ties. 1** the condition of being modal. **2** a quality, attribute, or circumstance that denotes mode, mood, or manner. **3** *Logic.* the property of a statement of being classified under one of the concepts studied by modal logic, esp. necessity or possibility. **4** any physical or electrical therapeutic method or agency. **5** any of the five senses.

modal logic *n* **1** the logical study of such philosophical concepts as necessity, possibility, contingency, etc. **2** the logical study of concepts whose formal properties resemble certain moral, epistemological, and psychological concepts. See also **alethic, deontic, epistemic, doxastic. 3** any formal system capable of being interpreted as a model for the behaviour of such concepts.

mod cons *pl n Informal.* modern conveniences; the usual installations of a modern house, such as hot water, heating, etc.

mode (məʊd) *n* **1** a manner or way of doing, acting, or existing. **2** the current fashion or style. **3** *Music.* **3a** any of the various scales of notes within one octave, esp. any of the twelve natural diatonic scales taken in ascending order used in plainsong, folk song, and art music until 1600. **3b** (in the music of classical Greece) any of the descending diatonic scales from which the liturgical modes evolved. **3c** either of the two main scale systems in music since 1600: *major mode; minor mode.* **4** *Logic, linguistics.* another name for **modality** (sense 3) or **mood**[2] (sense 2). **5** *Philosophy.* a complex combination of ideas the realization of which is not determined by the component ideas. **6** that one of a range of values that has the highest frequency as determined statistically. Compare **mean**[3] (sense 4), **median** (sense 6). **7** the quantitative mineral composition of an igneous rock. **8** *Physics.* one of the possible configurations of a travelling or stationary wave. **9** *Physics.* one of the fundamental vibrations. [C14: from Latin *modus* measure, manner]

model ('mɒdᵊl) *n* **1a** a representation, usually on a smaller scale, of a device, structure, etc. **1b** (*as modifier*): *a model train.* **2a** a standard to be imitated: *she was my model for good scholarship.* **2b** (*as modifier*): *a model wife.* **3** a representative form, style, or pattern. **4** a person who poses for a sculptor, painter, or photographer. **5** a person who wears clothes to display them to prospective buyers; mannequin. **6** a preparatory sculpture in clay, wax, etc., from which the finished work is copied. **7** a design or style, esp. one of a series of designs of a particular product: *last year's model.* **8** *Brit.* **8a** an original unique article of clothing. **8b** (*as modifier*): *a model coat.* **9** a simplified representation or description of a system or complex entity, esp. one designed to facilitate calculations and predictions. **10** *Logic.* **10a** an interpretation of a formal system under which the theorems derivable in that system are mapped onto truths. **10b** a theory in which a given sentence is true. ◆ *vb* **-els, -elling, -elled** *or U.S.* **-els, -eling, -eled. 11** to make a model of (something or someone). **12** to form in clay, wax, etc.; mould. **13** to display (clothing and accessories) as a mannequin. **14** to plan or create according to a model or models. **15** to arrange studio lighting so that highlights and shadows emphasize the desired features of a human form or an inanimate object. [C16: from Old French *modelle,* from Italian *modello,* from Latin *modulus,* diminutive of *modus* MODE] ▸ **'modeller** *or U.S.* **'modeler** *n*

modelling *or U.S.* **modeling** ('mɒdᵊlɪŋ) *n* **1** the act or an instance of making a model. **2** the practice or occupation of a person who models clothes. **3** a technique in psychotherapy in which the therapist encourages the patient to model his behaviour on his own.

model theory *n* the branch of logic that deals with the properties of models; the semantic study of formal systems. ▸ **'model-,theo'retic** *adj*

modem ('məʊdɛm) *n Computing.* a device for connecting two computers by a telephone line, consisting of a modulator that converts computer signals into audio signals and a corresponding demodulator. [C20: from *mo(dulator) dem(odulator)*]

Modena (*Italian* 'mɔ:dena) *n* **1** a city in N Italy, in Emilia-Romagna: ruled by the Este family (18th–19th century); university (1678). Pop.: 174 518 (1996 est.). Ancient name: **Mutina. 2** (*sometimes not cap.*) a popular variety of domestic fancy pigeon originating in Modena.

moderate *adj* ('mɒdərɪt, 'mɒdrɪt). **1** not extreme or excessive; within due or reasonable limits: *moderate demands.* **2** not violent; mild or temperate. **3** of average quality or extent: *moderate success.* ◆ *n* ('mɒdərɪt,'mɒdrɪt). **4** a person who holds moderate views, esp. in politics. ◆ *vb* ('mɒdə,reɪt). **5** to become or cause to become less extreme or violent. **6** (when *intr,* often foll. by *over*) to preside over a meeting, discussion, etc. **7** *Brit. and N.Z.* to act as an external moderator of the overall standards and marks for (some types of educational assessment). **8** *Physics.* to slow down (neutrons), esp. by using a moderator. [C14: from Latin *moderātus* observing moderation, from *moderārī* to restrain] ▸ **'moderately** *adv* ▸ **'moderateness** *n* ▸ **'moderatism** *n*

moderate breeze *n* a wind of force four on the Beaufort scale.

moderate gale *n* a gale of force seven on the Beaufort scale, capable of swaying trees.

moderation (,mɒdə'reɪʃən) *n* **1** the state or an instance of being moderate; mildness; balance. **2** the act of moderating. **3 in moderation.** within moderate or reasonable limits.

Moderations (,mɒdə'reɪʃənz) *pl n* short for **Honour Moderations.**

moderato (,mɒdə'rɑ:təʊ) *adv Music.* **1** at a moderate tempo. **2** (preceded by a tempo marking) a direction indicating that the tempo specified is to be used with restraint: *allegro moderato.* [C18: from Italian, from Latin *moderātus;* see MODERATE]

moderator ('mɒdə,reɪtə) *n* **1** a person or thing that moderates. **2** *Presbyterian Church.* a minister appointed to preside over a Church court, synod, or general assembly. **3** a presiding officer at a public or legislative assembly. **4** a material, such as heavy water or graphite, used for slowing down neutrons in the cores of nuclear reactors so that they have more chance of inducing nuclear fission. **5** an examiner at Oxford or Cambridge Universities in first public examinations.

6 (in Britain and New Zealand) one who is responsible for consistency of standards in the grading of some educational assessments. ▸ **'mode,ratorship** *n*

modern ('mɒdən) *adj* 1 of, involving, or befitting the present or a recent time; contemporary. 2 of, relating to, or characteristic of contemporary styles or schools of art, literature, music, etc., esp. those of an experimental kind. 3 belonging or relating to the period in history from the end of the Middle Ages to the present. ◆ *n* 4 a contemporary person. 5 *Printing.* a type style that originated around the beginning of the 19th century, characterized chiefly by marked contrast between thick and thin strokes. Compare **old face.** [C16: from Old French, from Late Latin *modernus,* from *modō* (adv) just recently, from *modus* MODE] ▸ **'modernly** *adv* ▸ **'modernness** *n*

modern apprenticeship *n* an arrangement that allows a school leaver to gain vocational qualifications while being trained in a job.

modern dance *n* a style of free and expressive theatrical dancing not bound by the classical rules of ballet.

moderne (mə'dɛən) *adj Chiefly U.S.* of or relating to the style of architecture and design, prevalent in Europe and the U.S. in the late 1920s and 1930s, typified by the use of straight lines, tubular chromed steel frames, contrasting inlaid woods, etc. Compare **Art Deco.**

Modern English *n* the English language since about 1450, esp. any of the standard forms developed from the S East Midland dialect of Middle English. See also **English, Middle English, Old English.**

modern greats *pl n* (at Oxford University) the Honour School of Philosophy, Politics, and Economics.

Modern Greek *n* the Greek language since about 1453 A.D. (the fall of Byzantium). Compare **Demotic, Katharevusa.**

Modern Hebrew *n* the official language of the state of Israel; a revived form of ancient Hebrew.

modernism ('mɒdə,nɪzəm) *n* 1 modern tendencies, characteristics, thoughts, etc., or the support of these. 2 something typical of contemporary life or thought. 3 a 20th-century divergence in the arts from previous traditions, esp. in architecture. See **International Style.** 4 *(cap.) R.C. Church.* the movement at the end of the 19th and beginning of the 20th centuries that sought to adapt doctrine to the supposed requirements of modern thought. ▸ **'modernist** *n, adj* ▸ **,modern'istic** *adj* ▸ **,modern'istically** *adv*

modernity (mɒ'dɜːnɪtɪ) *n, pl* **-ties.** 1 the quality or state of being modern. 2 something modern.

modernize *or* **modernise** ('mɒdə,naɪz) *vb* 1 *(tr)* to make modern in appearance or style: *to modernize a room.* 2 *(intr)* to adopt modern ways, ideas, etc. ▸ **,moderni'zation** *or* **,moderni'sation** *n* ▸ **'modern,izer** *or* **'modern,iser** *n*

modern jazz *n* any of the styles of jazz that evolved between the early 1940s and the later emergence of avant-garde jazz, characterized by a greater harmonic and rhythmic complexity than hitherto.

modern language *n* any of the languages spoken in present-day Europe, with the exception of English.

modern pentathlon *n* an athletic contest consisting of five different events: horse riding with jumps, fencing with electric épée, freestyle swimming, pistol shooting, and cross-country running.

modern sequence dancing *n* a form of dancing in which ballroom dance steps are used as the basis of a wide variety of different dances typically performed in a sequence.

modest ('mɒdɪst) *adj* 1 having or expressing a humble opinion of oneself or one's accomplishments or abilities. 2 reserved or shy: *modest behaviour.* 3 not ostentatious or pretentious. 4 not extreme or excessive; moderate. 5 decorous or decent. [C16: via Old French from Latin *modestus* moderate, from *modus* MODE] ▸ **'modestly** *adv*

modesty ('mɒdɪstɪ) *n, pl* **-ties.** the quality or condition of being modest.

modge (mɒdʒ) *vb (tr) Midland English dialect.* to do shoddily; make a mess of. [C20: perhaps a variant of *mudge* to crush (hops)]

modicum ('mɒdɪkəm) *n* a small amount or portion. [C15: from Latin: a little way, from *modicus* moderate]

modification (,mɒdɪfɪ'keɪʃən) *n* 1 the act of modifying or the condition of being modified. 2 something modified; the result of a modification. 3 a small change or adjustment. 4 *Grammar.* the relation between a modifier and the word or phrase that it modifies. ▸ **'modifi,catory** *or* **'modifi,cative** *adj*

modifier ('mɒdɪ,faɪə) *n* 1 Also called: **qualifier.** *Grammar.* a word or phrase that qualifies the sense of another word; for example, the noun *alarm* is a modifier of *clock* in *alarm clock* and the phrase *every day* is an adverbial modifier of *walks* in *he walks every day.* 2 a person or thing that modifies.

modify ('mɒdɪ,faɪ) *vb* **-fies, -fying, -fied.** *(mainly tr)* 1 to change the structure, character, intent, etc., of. 2 to make less extreme or uncompromising: *to modify a demand.* 3 *Grammar.* (of a word or group of words) to bear the relation of modifier to (another word or group of words). 4 *Linguistics.* to change (a vowel) by umlaut. 5 *(intr)* to be or become modified. [C14: from Old French *modifier,* from Latin *modificāre* to limit, control, from *modus* measure + *facere* to make] ▸ **'modi,fiable** *adj* ▸ **,modi,fia'bility** *or* **'modi,fiableness** *n*

Modigliani (*Italian* modiʎ'ʎaːni) *n* **Amedeo** (ame'dɛːo). 1884–1920, Italian painter and sculptor, noted esp. for the elongated forms of his portraits.

modillion (mə'dɪljən) *n Architect.* one of a set of ornamental brackets under a cornice, esp. as used in the Corinthian order. Compare **mutule.** [C16: via French from Italian *modiglione,* probably from Vulgar Latin *mutiliō* (unattested), from Latin *mūtulus* MUTULE]

modiolus (məʊ'daɪəʊləs, mə-) *n, pl* **-li** (-,laɪ). the central bony pillar of the cochlea. [C19: New Latin, from Latin: hub of a wheel, from *modus* a measure]

modish ('məʊdɪʃ) *adj* in the current fashion or style; contemporary. ▸ **'modishly** *adv* ▸ **'modishness** *n*

modiste (məʊ'diːst) *n* a fashionable dressmaker or milliner. [C19: from French, from *mode* fashion]

Modred ('məʊdrɪd) *or* **Mordred** ('mɔːdrɛd) *n* (in Arthurian legend) a knight of the Round Table who rebelled against and killed his uncle King Arthur.

Mods (mɒdz) *n* (at Oxford University) short for **Honour Moderations.**

modular ('mɒdjʊlə) *adj* of, consisting of, or resembling a module or modulus. ▸ **modularity** (,mɒdjʊ'lærɪtɪ) *n*

modulate ('mɒdjʊ,leɪt) *vb* 1 *(tr)* to change the tone, pitch, or volume of. 2 *(tr)* to adjust or regulate the degree of. 3 *Music.* 3a to subject to or undergo modulation in music. 3b (often foll. by *to*) to make or become in tune (with a pitch, key, etc.). 4 *(tr) Physics, electronics.* to cause to vary by a process of modulation. [C16: from Latin *modulātus* in due measure, melodious, from *modulārī* to regulate, from *modus* measure] ▸ **modulability** (,mɒdjʊlə'bɪlɪtɪ) *n* ▸ **'modulative** *or* **'modulatory** *adj* ▸ **'modu,lator** *n*

modulation (,mɒdjʊ'leɪʃən) *n* 1 the act of modulating or the condition of being modulated. 2 *Music.* the transition from one key to another. 3 *Grammar.* 3a another word for **intonation** (sense 1). 3b the grammatical expression of modality. 4 *Electrical engineering.* 4a the act or process of superimposing the amplitude, frequency, phase, etc., of a wave or signal onto another wave or signal or onto an electron beam. See also **amplitude modulation, frequency modulation, phase modulation, velocity modulation.** 4b the variation of the modulated signal.

module ('mɒdjuːl) *n* 1 a self-contained unit or item, such as an assembly of electronic components and associated wiring or a segment of computer software, which itself performs a defined task and can be linked with other such units to form a larger system. 2 a standard unit of measure, esp. one used to coordinate the dimensions of buildings and components; in classical architecture, half the diameter of a column at the base of the shaft. 3 a standardized unit designed to be added to or used as part of an arrangement of similar units, as in furniture. 4 *Astronautics.* any of several self-contained separable units making up a spacecraft or launch vehicle, each of which has one or more specified tasks: *command module; service module.* 5 *Education.* a short course of study, esp. of a vocational or technical subject, that together with other such completed courses can count towards a particular qualification. [C16: from Latin *modulus,* diminutive of *modus* MODE]

modulus ('mɒdjʊləs) *n, pl* **-li** (-,laɪ). 1 *Physics.* a coefficient expressing a specified property of a specified substance. See **bulk modulus, modulus of rigidity, Young's modulus.** 2 *Maths.* another name for the **absolute value** (sense 2) of a complex number. 3 *Maths.* the number by which a logarithm to one base is multiplied to give the corresponding logarithm to another base. 4 *Maths.* an integer that can be divided exactly into the difference between two other integers: *7 is a modulus of 25 and 11.* See also **congruence** (sense 2). [C16: from Latin, diminutive of *modus* measure]

modulus of elasticity *n* the ratio of the stress applied to a body or substance to the resulting strain within the elastic limit. Also called: **elastic modulus.** See also **Young's modulus, bulk modulus, modulus of rigidity.**

modulus of rigidity *n* a modulus of elasticity equal to the ratio of the tangential force per unit area to the resulting angular deformation. Symbol: G

modus operandi ('məʊdəs ,ɒpə'rændiː, -'rændaɪ) *n, pl* **modi operandi** ('məʊdiː ,ɒpə'rændiː,'məʊdaɪ ,ɒpə'rændaɪ). procedure; method of operating. [C17: from Latin]

modus ponens *Latin.* ('məʊdəs 'pəʊ,nɛnz) *n Logic.* the principle that whenever a conditional statement and its antecedent are given to be true its consequent may be validly inferred, as in *if it's Tuesday this must be Belgium* and *it's Tuesday so this must be Belgium.* [literally: mood that affirms]

modus tollens *Latin.* ('məʊdəs 'tɒl,ɛnz) *n Logic.* the principle that whenever a conditional statement and the negation of its consequent are given to be true, the negation of its antecedent may be validly inferred, as in *if it's Tuesday this must be Belgium* and *this isn't Belgium so it's not Tuesday.* [literally: mood that denies]

modus vivendi ('məʊdəs vɪ'vendiː, -'vɛndaɪ) *n, pl* **modi vivendi** ('məʊdiː vɪ'vendiː, 'məʊdaɪ vɪ'vɛndaɪ). a working arrangement between conflicting interests; practical compromise. [C19: from Latin: way of living]

Moers (*German* mœːrs) *n* a city in W Germany, in North Rhine-Westphalia: coalmining centre. Pop.: 107 095 (1996 est.).

mofette (məʊ'fɛt) *n* an opening in a region of nearly extinct volcanic activity, through which carbon dioxide, nitrogen, and other gases pass. [C19: from French, from Neapolitan Italian *mofeta;* compare dialect German *muffezen* to smell fetid]

moffie ('mɒfɪ) *S. African slang.* *n* 1 a homosexual. ◆ *adj* 2 homosexual. [C18: from *mophrodite,* a variant of HERMAPHRODITE]

Mogadishu (,mɒgə'dɪʃuː) *or* **Mogadiscio** (,mɒgə'dɪʃɪ,əʊ, -'dɪʃəʊ) *n* the capital and chief port of Somalia, on the Indian Ocean: founded by Arabs around the 10th century; taken by the Sultan of Zanzibar in 1871 and sold to Italy in 1905. Pop.: 997 000 (1995 est.).

Mogadon ('mɒgə,dɒn) *n Trademark.* a drug of the benzodiazepine group, a preparation of nitrazepam, used to treat insomnia.

Mogador (,mɒgə'dɔː; *French* mɔgadɔr) *n* the former name (until 1956) of **Essaouira.**

Mogen David ('məʊgən 'deɪvɪd) *n* another name for the **Star of David.**

moggy ('mɒgɪ) *n, pl* **moggies.** *Brit.* a slang name for **cat**[1] (sense 1). Sometimes shortened to **mog.** [C20: of dialect origin, originally a pet name for a cow]

Mogilev (*Russian* məgi'ljɔf) *or* **Mohilev** *n* an industrial city in E Belarus on the Dnieper River: passed to Russia in 1772 after Polish rule. Pop.: 367 000 (1996 est.).

mogul[1] ('məʊgʌl, məʊ'gʌl) *n* 1 an important or powerful person. 2 a type of steam locomotive with a wheel arrangement of two leading wheels, six driving wheels, and no trailing wheels. [C18: from MOGUL]

mogul[2] ('məʊgᵊl) *n* a mound of hard snow on a ski slope. [C20: perhaps from South German dialect *Mugl*]

Mogul ('məʊgʌl, məʊ'gʌl) *n* **1** a member of the Muslim dynasty of Indian emperors established by Baber in 1526. See **Great Mogul. 2** a Muslim Indian, Mongol, or Mongolian. ◆ *adj* **3** of or relating to the Moguls or their empire. [C16: from Persian *mughul* Mongol]

mogul skiing *n* a skiing event in which skiers descend a slope which is covered in mounds of snow, making two jumps during the descent.

MOH (in Britain) *abbrev. for* Medical Officer of Health.

mohair ('məʊˌhɛə) *n* **1** Also called: **angora.** the long soft silky hair that makes up the outer coat of the Angora goat. **2a** a fabric made from the yarn of this hair and cotton or wool. **2b** (*as modifier*): *a mohair suit.* [C16: variant (influenced by *hair*) of earlier *mocayare,* ultimately from Arabic *mukhayyar,* literally: choice, from *khayyara* to choose]

Moham. *abbrev. for* Mohammedan.

Mohammed (məʊ'hæmɪd) *or* **Muhammad** *n* ?570–632 A.D., the prophet believed by Muslims to be the channel for the final unfolding of God's revelation to mankind: popularly regarded as the founder of Islam. He began to teach in Mecca in 610 but persecution forced him to flee with his followers to Medina in 622. After several battles, he conquered Mecca (630), establishing the principles of Islam (embodied in the Koran) over all Arabia. Other names: **Mahomet,** (*archaic*) **Mahound.**

Mohammed II *n* ?1430–81, Ottoman sultan of Turkey (1451–81). He captured Constantinople (1453) and conquered large areas of the Balkans.

Mohammed Ahmed (məʊ'hæmɪd 'ɑːmɛd) *n* the original name of the **Mahdi.**

Mohammed Ali *n* **1** See **Mehemet Ali. 2** See **Muhammad Ali.**

Mohammedan (məʊ'hæmɪdᵊn) *n, adj* another word, formerly common in Western usage but never used among Muslims, for **Muslim.**

Mohammedanism (məʊ'hæmɪdᵊˌnɪzəm) *n* a name, formerly common in Western usage but never used among Muslims, for the Muslim religion; Islam. See **Islam.**

Mohammedanize *or* **Mohammedanise** (məʊ'hæmɪdᵊˌnaɪz) *vb* (*tr*) another word, formerly common in Western usage but never used among Muslims, for **Islamize.**

Mohammed Reza Pahlavi (məʊ'hæmɪd 'riːzə 'pɑːləvɪ) *n* See **Pahlavi**[1].

Moharram (məʊ'hærəm) *n* a variant of **Muharram.**

Mohave *or* **Mojave** (məʊ'hɑːvɪ) *n* **1** (*pl* **-ves** *or* **-ve**) a member of a North American Indian people formerly living along the Colorado River. **2** the language of this people, belonging to the Yuman family.

Mohave Desert *or* **Mojave Desert** *n* a desert in S California, south of the Sierra Nevada: part of the Great Basin. Area: 38 850 sq. km (15 000 sq. miles).

mohawk ('məʊhɔːk) *n Ice skating.* a half turn from either edge of either skate to the corresponding edge of the other skate. [C19: after MOHAWK[1]]

Mohawk[1] ('məʊhɔːk) *n* **1** (*pl* **-hawks** *or* **-hawk**) a member of a North American Indian people formerly living along the Mohawk River; one of the Iroquois peoples. **2** the language of this people, belonging to the Iroquoian family.

Mohawk[2] ('məʊhɔːk) *n* a river in E central New York State, flowing south and east to the Hudson River at Cohoes: the largest tributary of the Hudson. Length: 238 km (148 miles).

mohel ('məɛl, mɔɪl) *n Judaism.* a man qualified to conduct circumcisions. [from Hebrew]

Mohenjo-Daro (mə'hɛndʒəʊ'dɑːrəʊ) *n* an excavated city in SE Pakistan, southwest of Sukkur near the River Indus: flourished during the third millennium B.C.

mohican (məʊ'hiːkən) *n* **1** a punk hairstyle in which the head is shaved at the sides and the remaining strip of hair is worn stiffly erect and sometimes brightly coloured. **2** a person wearing such a hairstyle.

Mohican ('məʊɪkən, məʊ'hiːkən) *or* **Mahican** (mə'hiːkən) *n* **1** (*pl* **-cans** *or* **-can**) a member of a North American Indian people formerly living along the Hudson river and east of it. **2** the language of this people, belonging to the Algonquian family.

Moho ('məʊhəʊ) *n* short for **Mohorovičić discontinuity.**

Mohock ('məʊhɒk) *n* (in 18th-century London) one of a group of aristocratic ruffians, who attacked people in the streets at night. [C18: variant of MOHAWK[1]]

Mohole ('məʊˌhəʊl) *n* an abandoned research project to drill through the earth's crust down to the Mohorovičić discontinuity to obtain samples of mantle rocks. [C20: from *Moho(rovičić)* + HOLE. See MOHOROVIČIĆ DISCONTINUITY]

Moholy-Nagy (mə'həʊlɪ'nɒdʒ) *n* **Laszlo** ('læzləʊ) *or* **Ladislaus** ('lɑːdɪsˌlaʊs). 1895–1946, U.S. painter and teacher, born in Hungary. He worked at the Bauhaus (1923–29).

Mohorovičić discontinuity (ˌməʊhə'rəʊvɪtʃɪtʃ) *n* the boundary between the earth's crust and mantle, across which there is a sudden change in the velocity of seismic waves. Often shortened to **Moho.** [C20: named after Andrija *Mohorovičić* (1857–1936), Croatian geologist]

Mohs scale (məʊz) *n* a scale for expressing the hardness of solids by comparing them with ten standards ranging from talc, with a value of 1, to diamond, with a value of 10. [C19: named after Friedrich *Mohs* (1773–1839), German mineralogist]

mohur ('məʊhə) *n* a former Indian gold coin worth 15 rupees. [C17: from Hindi]

MOI *abbrev. for* Ministry of Information (now superseded by **COI**).

moidore ('mɔɪdɔː) *n* a former Portuguese gold coin. [C18: from Portuguese *moeda de ouro:* money of gold]

moiety ('mɔɪɪtɪ) *n, pl* **-ties. 1** a half. **2** one of two parts or divisions of something. [C15: from Old French *moitié,* from Latin *mediētās* middle, from *medius*]

moil (mɔɪl) *Archaic or dialect.* ◆ *vb* **1** to moisten or soil or become moist, soiled, etc. **2** (*intr*) to toil or drudge (esp. in the phrase **toil and moil**). ◆ *n* **3** toil; drudgery. **4** confusion; turmoil. [C14 (to moisten; later: to work hard in unpleasantly wet conditions) from Old French *moillier,* ultimately from Latin *mollis* soft] ► **'moiler** *n*

Moirai ('mɔɪriː) *pl n, sing* **Moira** ('mɔɪrə), **the.** the Greek goddesses of fate. Roman counterparts: the **Parcae.** See **Fates.**

moire (mwɑː) *n* a fabric, usually silk, having a watered effect. [C17: from French, earlier *mouaire,* from MOHAIR]

moiré ('mwɑːreɪ) *adj* **1** having a watered or wavelike pattern. ◆ *n* **2** such a pattern, impressed on fabrics by means of engraved rollers. **3** any fabric having such a pattern; moire. **4** Also: **moiré pattern.** a pattern seen when two geometrical patterns, such as grids, are visually superimposed. [C17: from French, from *moire* MOHAIR]

Moism ('məʊɪzəm) *n* the religious and ethical teaching of Mo-Zi and his followers, emphasizing universal love, ascetic self-discipline, and obedience to the will of Heaven.

moist (mɔɪst) *adj* **1** slightly damp or wet. **2** saturated with or suggestive of moisture. [C14: from Old French, ultimately related to Latin *mūcidus* musty, from *mūcus* MUCUS] ► **'moistly** *adv* ► **'moistness** *n*

moisten ('mɔɪsᵊn) *vb* to make or become moist. ► **'moistener** *n*

moisture ('mɔɪstʃə) *n* water or other liquid diffused as vapour or condensed on or in objects. ► **'moistureless** *adj*

moisturize *or* **moisturise** ('mɔɪstʃəˌraɪz) *vb* (*tr*) to add or restore moisture to (the air, the skin, etc.). ► **'moisturˌizer** *or* **'moisturˌiser** *n*

moither ('mɔɪðə) *or* **moider** ('mɔɪdə) *vb Dialect.* **1** (*tr; usually passive*) to bother or bewilder. **2** (*intr*) to talk in a rambling or confused manner. [C17: of obscure origin]

Mojave (məʊ'hɑːvɪ) *n* a variant spelling of **Mohave.**

mojo ('məʊdʒəʊ) *n, pl* **mojos** *or* **mojoes.** *U.S. slang.* **1a** an amulet, charm, or magic spell. **1b** (*as modifier*): *ancient mojo spells.* **2** the art of casting magic spells. [C20: of W African origin]

moke (məʊk) *n* **1** *Brit.* a slang name for **donkey** (sense 1). **2** *Austral. slang.* an inferior type of horse. [C19: origin obscure]

Mokha ('məʊkə, 'mɒk-) *n* a variant of **Mocha.**

moki ('məʊkɪ) *n, pl* **mokis** *or* **moki.** either of two edible sea fish of New Zealand, the blue cod (*Percis colias*) or the bastard trumpeter (*Latridopsis ciliaris*). [Maori]

moko ('məʊkəʊ) *n, pl* **mokos.** *N.Z.* a Maori tattoo or tattoo pattern. [Maori]

Mokpo (ˌməʊk'pəʊ) *n* a port in SW South Korea, on the Yellow Sea. Pop.: 247 524 (1995).

moksha ('mɒkʃə) *n Hinduism.* freedom from the endless cycle of transmigration into a state of bliss. [from Sanskrit *moksa* liberation]

mol *Chem. symbol for* mole[3].

mol. *abbrev. for:* **1** molecular. **2** molecule.

mola ('məʊlə) *n, pl* **-la** *or* **-las.** another name for **sunfish** (sense 1). [C17: from Latin, literally: millstone]

molal ('məʊləl) *adj Chem.* of or consisting of a solution containing one mole of solute per thousand grams of solvent. [C20: from MOLE[3] + -AL[1]]

molality (mɒ'lælɪtɪ) *n, pl* **-ties.** (not in technical usage) a measure of concentration equal to the number of moles of solute in a thousand grams of solvent.

molar[1] ('məʊlə) *n* **1** any of the 12 broad-faced grinding teeth in man. **2** a corresponding tooth in other mammals. ◆ *adj* **3** of, relating to, or designating any of these teeth. **4** used for or capable of grinding. [C16: from Latin *molāris* for grinding, from *mola* millstone]

molar[2] ('məʊlə) *adj* **1** (of a physical quantity) per unit amount of substance: *molar volume.* **2** (not recommended in technical usage) (of a solution) containing one mole of solute per litre of solution. [C19: from Latin *mōlēs* a mass]

molarity (mɒ'lærɪtɪ) *n* another name (not in technical usage) for **concentration** (sense 4).

molasse (mə'læs) *n* a soft sediment produced by the erosion of mountain ranges after the final phase of mountain building. [C18: from French, perhaps alteration of *mollasse,* from Latin *mollis* soft]

molasses (mə'læsɪz) *n* (*functioning as sing*) **1** the thick brown uncrystallized bitter syrup obtained from sugar during refining. **2** the U.S. and Canadian name for **treacle** (sense 1). [C16: from Portuguese *melaço,* from Late Latin *mellāceum* must, from Latin *mel* honey]

mold (məʊld) *n, vb* the U.S. spelling of **mould.**

Moldau ('mɔldaʊ) *n* **1** the German name for **Moldavia. 2** the German name for the **Vltava.**

Moldavia (mɒl'deɪvɪə) *n* **1** another name for **Moldova. 2** a former principality of E Europe, consisting of the basins of the Rivers Prut and Dniester: the E part (Bessarabia) became Moldova; the W part remains a province of Romania. Romanian name: **Moldova** (mol'dova). German name: **Moldau.** ► **Mol'davian** *adj, n*

moldavite ('mɒldəˌvaɪt) *n* a green tektite found in the Czech Republic, thought to be the product of an ancient meteorite impact in Germany. [C19: named after MOLDAVIA]

moldboard ('məʊldˌbɔːd) *n* the U.S. spelling of **mouldboard.**

molder ('məʊldə) *vb, n* the U.S. spelling of **moulder.**

molding ('məʊldɪŋ) *n* the U.S. spelling of **moulding.**

Moldova (mɒl'dəʊvə) *n* a republic in SE Europe: comprising the E part of the former principality of Moldavia, the E part of which (Bessarabia) was ceded to the Soviet Union in 1940 and formed the Moldavian Soviet Socialist Republic until it gained independence in 1991; an agricultural region with many vineyards. Official language: Romanian. Religion: nonreligious and Christian. Currency: leu. Capital: Kishinev. Pop.: 4 243 000 (1998 est.). Area: 33 670 sq. km (13 000 sq. miles). Also called: **Moldavia** (mɒl'deɪvɪə).

moldy ('məʊldɪ) *adj* **moldier, moldiest.** the U.S. spelling of **mouldy.** ▸ **'moldiness** *n*

mole[1] (məʊl) *n Pathol.* a nontechnical name for **naevus.** [Old English *māl;* related to Old High German *meil* spot]

mole[2] (məʊl) *n* **1** any small burrowing mammal, of the family *Talpidae,* of Europe, Asia, and North and Central America: order *Insectivora* (insectivores). They have velvety, typically dark fur and forearms specialized for digging. **2 golden mole.** any small African burrowing molelike mammal of the family *Chrysochloridae,* having copper-coloured fur: order *Insectivora* (insectivores). **3** *Informal.* a spy who has infiltrated an organization and, often over a long period, become a trusted member of it. [C14: from Middle Dutch *mol,* of Germanic origin; compare Middle Low German *mol*]

mole[3] (məʊl) *n* the basic SI unit of amount of substance; the amount that contains as many elementary entities as there are atoms in 0.012 kilogram of carbon-12. The entity must be specified and may be an atom, a molecule, an ion, a radical, an electron, a photon, etc. Symbol: mol [C20: from German *Mol,* short for *Molekül* MOLECULE]

mole[4] (məʊl) *n* **1** a breakwater. **2** a harbour protected by a breakwater. [C16: from French *môle,* from Latin *mōlēs* mass]

mole[5] (məʊl) *n Pathol.* a fleshy growth in the uterus formed by the degeneration of fetal tissues. [C17: medical use of Latin *mola* millstone]

Molech ('məʊlɛk) *n Old Testament.* a variant of **Moloch.**

mole cricket *n* any subterranean orthopterous insect of the family *Gryllotalpidae,* of Europe and North America, similar and related to crickets but having the first pair of legs specialized for digging.

molecular (məʊ'lɛkjʊlə, mə-) *adj* **1** of or relating to molecules: *molecular hydrogen.* **2** *Logic.* (of a sentence, formula, etc.) capable of analysis into atomic formulae of the appropriate kind. ▸ **molecularity** (məʊˌlɛkjʊ'lærɪtɪ) *n* ▸ **mo'lecularly** *adv*

molecular beam *or* **ray** *n Physics.* a parallel beam of atoms or molecules that are at low pressure and suffer no interatomic or intermolecular collisions.

molecular biology *n* the study of the structure and function of biological molecules, esp. nucleic acids and proteins.

molecular cloud *n* a cool dense interstellar region composed of a wide variety of molecules, mainly hydrogen, plus some dust, in which stars are forming.

molecular distillation *n* distillation in which a substance is heated under vacuum, the pressure being so low that no intermolecular collisions can occur before condensation.

molecular film *n* another name for **monolayer.**

molecular formula *n* a chemical formula indicating the numbers and types of atoms in a molecule: *H_2SO_4 is the molecular formula of sulphuric acid.* Compare **empirical formula, structural formula.**

molecular genetics *n* (*functioning as sing*) the study of the molecular constitution of genes and chromosomes.

molecular sieve *n Chem.* a material that can absorb large amounts of certain compounds while not absorbing others and is thus suitable for use in separating mixtures.

molecular volume *n* the volume occupied by one mole of a substance. Also called: **molar volume.**

molecular weight *n* the former name for **relative molecular mass.**

molecule ('mɒlɪˌkjuːl) *n* **1** the simplest unit of a chemical compound that can exist, consisting of two or more atoms held together by chemical bonds. **2** a very small particle. [C18: via French from New Latin *mōlēcula,* diminutive of Latin *mōlēs* mass, MOLE[4]]

mole drain *n* an underground cylindrical drainage channel cut by a special plough to drain heavy agricultural soil.

molehill ('məʊlˌhɪl) *n* **1** the small mound of earth thrown up by a burrowing mole. **2 make a mountain out of a molehill.** to exaggerate an unimportant matter out of all proportion.

mole rat *n* **1** any burrowing molelike African rodent of the family *Bathyergidae.* **2** any similar rodent, esp. any member of the genus *Spalax,* of Asia and North Africa: family *Spalacidae.* **3** another name for **bandicoot rat** (see **bandicoot** (sense 2)).

mole run *n* (*usually pl*) *Informal.* any part of a system of underground tunnels, rooms, etc., prepared for use in the event of nuclear war.

moleskin ('məʊlˌskɪn) *n* **1** the dark grey dense velvety pelt of a mole, used as a fur. **2** a hard-wearing cotton fabric of twill weave used for work clothes, etc. **3** (*modifier*) made from moleskin: *a moleskin waistcoat.*

moleskins ('məʊlˌskɪnz) *pl n* clothing of moleskin.

molest (mə'lɛst) *vb* (*tr*) **1** to disturb or annoy by malevolent interference. **2** to accost or attack, esp. with the intention of assaulting sexually. [C14: from Latin *molestāre* to annoy, from *molestus* troublesome, from *mōlēs* mass] ▸ **molestation** (ˌməʊlɛ'steɪʃən) *n* ▸ **mo'lester** *n*

Molière (*French* mɔljɛr) *n* real name *Jean-Baptiste Poquelin.* 1622–73, French dramatist, regarded as the greatest French writer of comedy. His works include *Tartuffe* (1664), *Le Misanthrope* (1666), *L'Avare* (1668), *Le Bourgeois gentilhomme* (1670), and *Le Malade imaginaire* (1673).

Molina (*Spanish* mo'lina) *n* See **Tirso de Molina.**

moline (mə'laɪn) *adj Heraldry.* (of a cross) having arms of equal length, forked and curved back at the ends. [C16: probably from Anglo-French *moliné,* from *molin* MILL[1], referring to the arms curved back like the ends of a mill-rind]

Molinism ('mɒlɪnɪzəm) *n R.C. Church.* a doctrine of grace that attempts to reconcile the efficacy of divine grace with human free will in responding to it. [C17: named after *Luis de Molina* (1535–1600), Spanish Jesuit who taught such a doctrine]

Molise (*Italian* mo'liːze) *n* a region of S central Italy, the second smallest of the regions: separated from **Abruzzi e Molise** in 1965. Capital: Campobasso. Pop.: 331 446 (1996 est.). Area: 4438 sq. km (1731 sq. miles).

moll (mɒl) *n Slang.* **1** the female accomplice of a gangster. **2** a prostitute. [C17: from *Moll,* familiar form of *Mary*]

mollah ('mɔːlə) *n* an older spelling of **mullah.**

mollify ('mɒlɪˌfaɪ) *vb* **-fies, -fying, -fied.** (*tr*) **1** to pacify; soothe. **2** to lessen the harshness or severity of. [C15: from Old French *mollifier,* via Late Latin, from Latin *mollis* soft + *facere* to make] ▸ **'molliˌfiable** *adj* ▸ **ˌmollifi'cation** *n* ▸ **'molliˌfier** *n*

mollusc *or U.S.* **mollusk** ('mɒləsk) *n* any invertebrate of the phylum *Mollusca,* having a soft unsegmented body and often a shell, secreted by a fold of skin (the mantle). The group includes the gastropods (snails, slugs, etc.), bivalves (clams, mussels, etc.), and cephalopods (cuttlefish, octopuses, etc.). [C18: via New Latin from Latin *molluscus,* from *mollis* soft] ▸ **molluscan** *or U.S.* **molluskan** (mɒ'lʌskən) *adj, n* ▸ **'mollusc-ˌlike** *or U.S.* **'mollusk-ˌlike** *adj*

molluscoid (mɒ'lʌskɔɪd) *or* **molluscoidal** (ˌmɒlʌs'kɔɪdᵊl) *adj* of, relating to, or belonging to the *Molluscoidea,* a former phylum including the brachiopods and bryozoans now classified separately. [C19: via New Latin from Latin *molluscus* soft]

Mollweide projection ('mɒlˌvaɪdə) *n* an equal-area map projection with the parallels and the central meridian being straight lines and the other meridians curved. It is often used to show world distributions of various phenomena. [C19: named after Karl B. *Mollweide* (1774–1825), German mathematician and astronomer]

molly[1] ('mɒlɪ) *n, pl* **-lies.** any brightly coloured tropical or subtropical American freshwater cyprinodont fish of the genus *Mollienisia.* [C19: from New Latin *Mollienisia,* from Comte F. N. *Mollien* (1758–1850), French statesman]

molly[2] ('mɒlɪ) *n, pl* **-lies.** *Irish informal.* an effeminate, weak, or cowardly boy or man. [C18: perhaps from *Molly,* pet name for *Mary*]

mollycoddle ('mɒlɪˌkɒdᵊl) *vb* **1** (*tr*) to treat with indulgent care; pamper. ◆ *n* **2** a pampered person. [C19: from MOLLY[2] + CODDLE] ▸ **'mollyˌcoddler** *n*

mollyhawk ('mɒlɪˌhɔːk) *n N.Z.* the juvenile of the southern black-backed gull (*Larus dominicanus*).

Molly Maguire ('mɒlɪ mə'gwaɪə) *n* **1** *Irish history.* a member of a secret society that terrorized law officers during the 1840s to prevent evictions. **2** (in Pennsylvania from about 1865 to 1877) a member of a society of miners that terrorized mine owners and their agents in an effort to obtain better pay. [C19: the name refers to the female disguise adopted by members of these societies]

mollymawk ('mɒlɪˌmɔːk) *n N.Z.* an informal name for **mallemuck.**

Molnár (*Hungarian* 'molnaːr) *n* **Ferenc** ('fɛrɛnts). 1878–1952, Hungarian dramatist and novelist. His plays include *Liliom* (1909).

moloch ('məʊlɒk) *n* a spiny Australian desert-living lizard, *Moloch horridus,* that feeds on ants: family *Agamidae* (agamas). Also called: **mountain devil, spiny lizard.**

Moloch ('məʊlɒk) *or* **Molech** ('məʊlɛk) *n Old Testament.* a Semitic deity to whom parents sacrificed their children.

Molokai (ˌməʊləʊ'kaːɪ) *n* an island in central Hawaii. Pop.: 6717 (1990). Area: 676 sq. km (261 sq. miles).

Molopo (mə'ləʊpəʊ) *n* a seasonal river rising in N South Africa and flowing west and southwest to the Orange river. Length: about 1000 km (600 miles).

Molotov[1] ('mɒləˌtɒf; *Russian* 'mɔlətəf) *n* the former name (1940–62) for **Perm.**

Molotov[2] ('mɒləˌtɒf; *Russian* 'mɔlətəf) *n* **Vyacheslav Mikhailovich** (vɪtʃɪ'slaf mi'xajləvitʃ), original surname *Skriabin.* 1890–1986, Soviet statesman. As commissar and later minister for foreign affairs (1939–49; 1953–56) he negotiated the nonaggression pact with Nazi Germany and attended the founding conference of the United Nations and the Potsdam conference (1945).

Molotov cocktail *n* an elementary incendiary weapon, usually a bottle of petrol with a short-delay fuse or wick; petrol bomb. [C20: named after V. M. MOLOTOV]

molt (məʊlt) *vb, n* the usual U.S. spelling of **moult.**

molten ('məʊltən) *adj* **1** liquefied; melted: *molten lead.* **2** made by having been melted: *molten casts.* ◆ *vb* **3** the past participle of **melt.**

Moltke (*German* 'mɔltkə) *n* **1** Count **Helmuth Johannes Ludwig von** ('hɛlmuːt jo'hanəs 'luːtvɪç fɔn). 1848–1916, German general; chief of the German general staff (1906–14). **2** his uncle Count **Helmuth Karl Bernhard von** ('hɛlmuːt karl 'bɛrnhart fɔn). 1800–91, German field marshal; chief of the Prussian general staff (1858–88).

molto ('mɒltəʊ) *adv Music.* (preceded or followed by a musical direction, esp. a tempo marking) very: *allegro molto; molto adagio.* [from Italian, from Latin *multum* (adv) much]

Moluccas (məʊ'lʌkəz, mə-) *or* **Molucca Islands** *pl n* a group of islands in the Malay Archipelago, between Sulawesi (Celebes) and New Guinea. Capital: Amboina. Pop.: 2 094 700 (1995 est.). Area: about 74 505 sq. km (28 766 sq. miles). Indonesian name: **Maluku.** Former name: **Spice Islands.**

mol. wt. *abbrev. for* molecular weight.

moly ('məʊlɪ) *n, pl* **-lies. 1** *Greek myth.* a magic herb given by Hermes to Odysseus to nullify the spells of Circe. **2** a liliaceous plant, *Allium moly,* that is native to S Europe and has yellow flowers in a dense cluster. [C16: from Latin *mōly,* from Greek *mōlu*]

molybdate (mɒ'lɪbdeɪt) *n* a salt or ester of a molybdic acid.

molybdenite (mɒ'lɪbdɪˌnaɪt) *n* a soft grey mineral consisting of molybdenum sulphide in hexagonal crystalline form with rhenium as an impurity: the main source of molybdenum and rhenium. Formula: MoS_2.

molybdenous (mɒ'lɪbdɪnəs) *adj* of or containing molybdenum in the divalent state.

molybdenum (mɒ'lɪbdɪnəm) *n* a very hard ductile silvery-white metallic element occurring principally in molybdenite: used mainly in alloys, esp. to harden and strengthen steels. Symbol: Mo; atomic no.: 42; atomic wt.: 95.94;

valency: 2–6; relative density: 10.22; melting pt.: 2623°C; boiling pt.: 4639°C. [C19: from New Latin, from Latin *molybdaena* galena, from Greek *molubdaina,* from *molubdos* lead]

molybdic (mɒ'lɪbdɪk) *adj* of or containing molybdenum in the trivalent or hexavalent state.

molybdous (mɒ'lɪbdəs) *adj* of or containing molybdenum, esp. in a low valence state.

mom (mɒm) *n Chiefly U.S. and Canadian.* an informal word for **mother**[1].

Mombasa (mɒm'bæsə) *n* a port in S Kenya, on a coral island in a bay of the Indian Ocean: the chief port for Kenya, Uganda, and NE Tanzania; became British in 1887, capital of the East African Protectorate until 1907. Pop.: 600 000 (1991 est.).

moment ('məʊmənt) *n* **1** a short indefinite period of time: *he'll be here in a moment.* **2** a specific instant or point in time: *at that moment the doorbell rang.* **3 the moment.** the present point of time: *at the moment it's fine.* **4** import, significance, or value: *a man of moment.* **5** *Physics.* **5a** a tendency to produce motion, esp. rotation about a point or axis. **5b** the product of a physical quantity, such as force or mass, and its distance from a fixed reference point. See also **moment of inertia. 6** *Statistics.* the mean of a specified power of the deviations of all the values of a variable in its frequency distribution. The power of the deviations indicates the order of the moment and the deviations may be from the origin (giving a **moment about the origin**) or from the mean (giving a **moment about the mean**). [C14: from Old French, from Latin *mōmentum,* from *movēre* to move]

momentarily ('məʊməntərəlɪ, -trɪlɪ) *adv* **1** for an instant; temporarily. **2** from moment to moment; every instant. **3** *U.S. and Canadian.* very soon. ◆ Also (for senses 1, 2): **momently** ('məʊməntlɪ).

momentary ('məʊməntərɪ, -trɪ) *adj* lasting for only a moment; temporary. ▸ **'momentariness** *n*

moment of inertia *n* the tendency of a body to resist angular acceleration, expressed as the sum of the products of the mass of each particle in the body and the square of its perpendicular distance from the axis of rotation. Symbol: *I*

moment of truth *n* **1** a moment when a person or thing is put to the test. **2** the point in a bullfight when the matador is about to kill the bull.

momentous (məʊ'mɛntəs) *adj* of great significance. ▸ **mo'mentously** *adv* ▸ **mo'mentousness** *n*

momentum (məʊ'mɛntəm) *n, pl* **-ta** (-tə) *or* **-tums. 1** *Physics.* the product of a body's mass and its velocity. Symbol: *p* See also **angular momentum. 2** the impetus of a body resulting from its motion. **3** driving power or strength. [C17: from Latin: movement; see MOMENT]

momma ('mɒmə) *n* a variant (esp. U.S. and Canadian) of **mamma**[1].

Mommsen (*German* 'mɔmzən) *n* **Theodor** ('teːodoːr). 1817–1903, German historian, noted esp. for *The History of Rome* (1854–56): Nobel prize for literature 1902.

Momus ('məʊməs) *n, pl* **-muses** *or* **-mi** (-maɪ). **1** *Greek myth.* the god of blame and mockery. **2** a cavilling critic.

Mon (məʊn) *n* **1** (*pl* **Mon** *or* **Mons**) a member of a people of Myanmar and Thailand related to the Khmer of Cambodia. **2** the language of this people, belonging to the Mon-Khmer family. ◆ Also called: **Talaing.**

mon. *abbrev. for* monetary.

Mon. *abbrev. for* Monday.

mon- *combining form.* a variant of **mono-** before a vowel.

mona ('məʊnə) *n* a W African guenon monkey, *Cercopithecus mona,* with dark fur on the back and white or yellow underparts. [C18: from Spanish or Portuguese: monkey]

monachal ('mɒnəkəl) *adj* a less common word for **monastic.** [C16: from Old French, from Church Latin *monachālis,* from *monachus* MONK] ▸ **'monachism** *n* ▸ **'monachist** *adj, n*

monacid (mɒn'æsɪd) *or* **monacidic** (ˌmɒnə'sɪdɪk) *adj* variants of **monoacid.**

Monaco ('mɒnəˌkəʊ, mə'nɑːkəʊ; *French* mɔnako) *n* a principality in SW Europe, on the Mediterranean and forming an enclave in SE France: the second smallest sovereign state in the world (after the Vatican); consists of **Monaco-Ville** (the capital) on a rocky headland, **La Condamine** (a business area and port), **Monte Carlo** (the resort centre), and **Fontvieille,** a light industrial area. Language: French. Religion: Roman Catholic. Currency: franc. Pop.: 32 000 (1998 est.). Area: 189 hectares (476 acres). Related adj: **Monegasque.** ▸ **Monacan** ('mɒnəkən, mə'nɑː-) *n, adj*

monad ('mɒnæd, 'məʊ-) *n* **1** (*pl* **-ads** *or* **-ades** (-əˌdiːz)) *Philosophy.* **1a** any fundamental singular metaphysical entity, esp. if autonomous. **1b** (in the metaphysics of Leibnitz) a simple indestructible nonspatial element regarded as the unit of which reality consists. **1c** (in the pantheistic philosophy of Giordano Bruno) a fundamental metaphysical unit that is spatially extended and psychically aware. **2** a single-celled organism, esp. a flagellate protozoan. **3** an atom, ion, or radical with a valency of one. ◆ Also called (for senses 1, 2): **monas.** [C17: from Late Latin *monas,* from Greek: unit, from *monos* alone] ▸ **mo'nadical** *adj* ▸ **mo'nadically** *adv*

monadelphous (ˌmɒnə'dɛlfəs) *adj* **1** (of stamens) having united filaments forming a tube around the style. **2** (of flowers) having monadelphous stamens. [C19: from MONO- + Greek *adelphos* brother, twin + -OUS]

monadic (mɒ'nædɪk) *adj* **1** being or relating to a monad. **2** *Logic, maths.* (of an operator, predicate, etc.) having only a single argument place.

monadism ('mɒnəˌdɪzəm, 'məʊ-) *or* **monadology** (ˌmɒnə'dɒlədʒɪ, ˌməʊ-) *n* (esp. in the writings of Leibnitz) the philosophical doctrine that monads are the ultimate units of reality. ▸ **ˌmonad'istic** *adj*

monadnock (mə'nædnɒk) *n* a residual hill that consists of hard rock in an otherwise eroded area. [C19: named after Mount *Monadnock,* in New Hampshire]

Monaghan ('mɒnəhən) *n* **1** a county of NE Republic of Ireland, in Ulster province: many small lakes. County town: Monaghan. Pop.: 51 000 (1996). Area: 1292 sq. km (499 sq. miles). **2** a town in NE Republic of Ireland, county town of Co. Monaghan. Pop.: 6200 (1995 est.).

monal *or* **monaul** ('mɒnɔːl) *n* any of several S Asian pheasants of the genus *Lophophorus,* the males of which have a brilliantly coloured plumage. [C18: from Hindi]

Mona Lisa ('məʊnə 'liːzə) *n* a portrait of a young woman painted by Leonardo da Vinci, admired for her enigmatic smile. Also called: **La Gioconda.**

monandrous (mɒ'nændrəs) *adj* **1** having or preferring only one male sexual partner over a period of time. **2** (of plants) having flowers with only one stamen. **3** (of flowers) having only one stamen. [C19: from MONO- + -ANDROUS] ▸ **mo'nandry** *n*

monanthous (mɒ'nænθəs) *adj* (of certain plants) having or producing only one flower. [C19: from MONO- + Greek *anthos* flower]

Mona Passage ('məʊnə) *n* a strait between Puerto Rico and the Dominican Republic, linking the Atlantic with the Caribbean.

monarch ('mɒnək) *n* **1** a sovereign head of state, esp. a king, queen, or emperor, who rules usually by hereditary right. **2** a supremely powerful or pre-eminent person or thing. **3** Also called: **milkweed.** a large migratory butterfly, *Danaus plexippus,* that has orange-and-black wings and feeds on the milkweed plant: family *Danaidae.* [C15: from Late Latin *monarcha,* from Greek; see MONO-, -ARCH] ▸ **monarchal** (mɒ'nɑːkəl) *or* **monarchial** (mɒ'nɑːkɪəl) *adj* ▸ **mo'narchally** *adv* ▸ **mo'narchical** *or* **mo'narchic** *adj* ▸ **mo'narchically** *adv* ▸ **'monarchism** *n* ▸ **'monarchist** *n, adj* ▸ **ˌmonar'chistic** *adj*

monarchy ('mɒnəkɪ) *n, pl* **-chies. 1** a form of government in which supreme authority is vested in a single and usually hereditary figure, such as a king, and whose powers can vary from those of an absolute despot to those of a figurehead. **2** a country reigned over by a king, prince, or other monarch.

monarda (mɒ'nɑːdə) *n* any mintlike North American plant of the genus *Monarda:* family *Labiatae* (labiates). See also **horsemint** (sense 2), **bergamot** (sense 4). [C19: from New Latin, named after N. *Monardés* (1493–1588), Spanish botanist]

monas ('mɒnæs, 'məʊ-) *n, pl* **monades** ('mɒnəˌdiːz). another word for **monad** (senses 1, 2).

monastery ('mɒnəstərɪ, -strɪ) *n, pl* **-teries.** the residence of a religious community, esp. of monks, living in seclusion from secular society and bound by religious vows. [C15: from Church Latin *monastērium,* from Late Greek *monastērion,* from Greek *monázein* to live alone, from *monos* alone] ▸ **monasterial** (ˌmɒnə'stɪərɪəl) *adj*

monastic (mə'næstɪk) *adj also* (*less commonly*) **monastical. 1** of or relating to monasteries or monks, nuns, etc. **2** resembling this sort of life; reclusive. ◆ *n* **3** a person who is committed to this way of life, esp. a monk. ▸ **mo'nastically** *adv*

monasticism (mə'næstɪˌsɪzəm) *n* the monastic system, movement, or way of life.

Monastral (mə'næstrəl) *adj Trademark.* denoting certain fast pigments used in paints and inks, derived from phthalocyanine.

monatomic (ˌmɒnə'tɒmɪk) *or* **monoatomic** (ˌmɒnəʊə'tɒmɪk) *adj Chem.* **1** (of an element) having or consisting of single atoms: *argon is a monatomic gas.* **2** (of a compound or molecule) having only one atom or group that can be replaced in a chemical reaction. **3** a less common word for **monovalent.**

monaul ('mɒnɔːl) *n* a variant spelling of **monal.**

monaural (mɒ'nɔːrəl) *adj* **1** relating to, having, or hearing with only one ear. **2** another word for **monophonic.** ▸ **mon'aurally** *adv*

monaxial (mɒ'næksɪəl) *adj* another word for **uniaxial.**

monazite ('mɒnəˌzaɪt) *n* a yellow to reddish-brown mineral consisting of a phosphate of thorium, cerium, and lanthanum in monoclinic crystalline form. [C19: from German, from Greek *monazein* to live alone, so called because of its rarity]

Mönchengladbach (*German* mœnçən'glatbax) *n* a city in W Germany, in W North Rhine-Westphalia: headquarters of NATO forces in N central Europe; textile industry. Pop.: 266 702 (1996 est.). Former name: **München-Gladbach.**

Monck (mʌŋk) *n* **George.** 1st Duke of Albemarle. 1608–70, English general. In the Civil War he was a Royalist until captured (1644) and persuaded to support the Commonwealth. After Cromwell's death he was instrumental in the restoration of Charles II (1660).

Moncton ('mɒŋktən) *n* a city in E Canada, in SE New Brunswick. Pop.: 80 744 (1991).

mondaine (*French* mɔ̃dɛn) *or* (*masc*) **mondain** (*French* mɔ̃dɛ̃) *n* **1** a woman or man who moves in fashionable society. ◆ *adj* **2** characteristic of fashionable society; worldly. [C19: from French; see MUNDANE]

Mondale ('mɒnˌdeɪl) *n* **Walter** (**Frederick**). born 1928, U.S. Democratic politician; vice president of the U.S. (1977–81).

Monday ('mʌndɪ) *n* the second day of the week; first day of the working week. [Old English *mōnandæg* moon's day, translation of Late Latin *lūnae diēs*]

Monday Club *n* (in Britain) a club made up of right-wing Conservatives who originally met together for lunch on Monday: founded in 1961.

Mondayize *or* **Mondayise** ('mʌndɪˌaɪz) *vb* (*tr*) *N.Z.* to move (a statutory holiday, such as the Queen's birthday) to the nearest Monday in order to secure a long weekend. ▸ **ˌMondayi'zation** *or* **ˌMondayi'sation** *n*

mondial ('mɒndɪəl) *adj* of or involving the whole world. [C20: from French, ultimately from Latin *mundus*]

Mond process (mɒnd; *German* mɔnt) *n* a process for obtaining nickel by heating the ore in carbon monoxide to produce nickel carbonyl vapour, which is then decomposed at a higher temperature to yield the metal. [C19: named after Ludwig *Mond* (1839–1909), German chemist and industrialist]

Mondrian (*Dutch* 'mɔndriːaːn) *n* **Piet** (piːt). 1872–1944, Dutch painter, noted esp. as an exponent of the abstract art movement De Stijl.

monecious (mɒ'niːʃəs) *adj* a variant spelling of **monoecious**. ▸ **mo'neciously** *adv*

Monegasque (ˌmɒnə'gæsk) *n* **1** a native or inhabitant of Monaco. ◆ *adj* **2** of or relating to Monaco or its inhabitants. [from French, from Provençal *mounegasc*, from *Mounegue* Monaco]

Monel metal *or* **Monell metal** (mɒ'nɛl) *n Trademark.* any of various silvery corrosion-resistant alloys containing copper (28 per cent), nickel (67 per cent), and smaller quantities of such metals as iron, manganese, and aluminium. [C20: named after A. *Monell* (died 1921), president of the International Nickel Co., New York, which introduced the alloys]

moneme ('məuniːm) *n Linguistics.* a less common word for **morpheme**. [C20: from MONO- + -EME]

Monet (*French* mɔnɛ) *n* **Claude** (klod). 1840–1926, French landscape painter; the leading exponent of impressionism. His interest in the effect of light on colour led him to paint series of pictures of the same subject at different times of day. These include *Haystacks* (1889–93), *Rouen Cathedral* (1892–94), the *Thames* (1899–1904), and *Water Lilies* (1899–1906).

monetarism ('mʌnɪtəˌrɪzəm) *n* **1** the theory that inflation is caused by an excess quantity of money in an economy. **2** an economic policy based on this theory and on a belief in the efficiency of free market forces, that gives priority to achieving price stability by monetary control, balanced budgets, etc., and maintains that unemployment results from excessive real wage rates and cannot be controlled by Keynesian demand management. ▸ **'monetarist** *n, adj*

monetary ('mʌnɪtərɪ, -trɪ) *adj* **1** of or relating to money or currency. **2** of or relating to monetarism: *a monetary policy.* [C19: from Late Latin *monētārius*, from Latin *monēta* MONEY] ▸ **'monetarily** *adv*

monetary unit *n* a unit of value and money of a country, esp. the major or standard unit.

monetize *or* **monetise** ('mʌnɪˌtaɪz) *vb* (*tr*) **1** to establish as the legal tender of a country. **2** to give a legal value to (a coin). ▸ **ˌmoneti'zation** *or* **ˌmoneti'sation** *n*

money ('mʌnɪ) *n* **1** a medium of exchange that functions as legal tender. **2** the official currency, in the form of banknotes, coins, etc., issued by a government or other authority. **3** a particular denomination or form of currency: *silver money.* **4** property or assets with reference to their realizable value. **5** (*Law or archaic pl* **moneys** *or* **monies**) a pecuniary sum or income. **6** an unspecified amount of paper currency or coins: *money to lend.* **7 for one's money.** in one's opinion. **8 in the money.** *Informal.* well-off; rich. **9 money for old rope.** *Informal.* profit obtained by little or no effort. **10 money to burn.** more money than one needs. **11 one's money's worth.** full value for the money one has paid for something. **12 put money into.** to invest money in. **13 put money on.** to place a bet on. **14 put one's money where one's mouth is.** See **mouth** (sense 19). ◆ Related adj: **pecuniary.** [C13: from Old French *moneie*, from Latin *monēta* coinage; see MINT[2]]

moneybags ('mʌnɪˌbægz) *n* (*functioning as sing*) *Informal.* a very rich person.

moneychanger ('mʌnɪˌtʃeɪndʒə) *n* **1** a person engaged in the business of exchanging currencies or money. **2** *Chiefly U.S.* a machine for dispensing coins.

money cowry *n* **1** a tropical marine gastropod, *Cypraea moneta.* **2** the shell of this mollusc, used as money in some parts of Africa and S Asia.

moneyed *or* **monied** ('mʌnɪd) *adj* **1** having a great deal of money; rich. **2** arising from or characterized by money.

moneyer ('mʌnɪə) *n* **1** *Archaic.* a person who coins money. **2** an obsolete word for **banker**[1].

money-grubbing *adj Informal.* seeking greedily to obtain money at every opportunity. ▸ **'money-ˌgrubber** *n*

moneylender ('mʌnɪˌlɛndə) *n* a person who lends money at interest as a living. ▸ **'moneyˌlending** *adj, n*

moneymaker ('mʌnɪˌmeɪkə) *n* **1** a person who is intent on accumulating money. **2** a person or thing that is or might be profitable. ▸ **'moneyˌmaking** *adj, n*

money market *n Finance.* the financial institutions dealing with short-term loans and capital and with foreign exchange. Compare **capital market.**

money of account *n* another name (esp. U.S. and Canadian) for **unit of account.**

money order *n* another name (esp. U.S. and Canadian) for **postal order.**

money spider *n* any of certain small shiny brownish spiders of the family *Linyphiidae.*

money-spinner *n Informal.* an enterprise, idea, person, or thing that is a source of wealth.

money supply *n* the total amount of money in a country's economy at a given time. See also **M0, M1, M2, M3, M3c, M4, M5.**

money wages *pl n Economics.* wages evaluated with reference to the money paid rather than the equivalent purchasing power. Also called: **nominal wages.** Compare **real wages.**

moneywort ('mʌnɪˌwɜːt) *n* a European and North American creeping primulaceous plant, *Lysimachia nummularia*, with round leaves and yellow flowers. Also called: **creeping Jennie.**

mong (mʌŋ) *n Austral. informal.* short for **mongrel.**

monger ('mʌŋgə) *n* **1** (*in combination except in archaic use*) a trader or dealer: *ironmonger.* **2** (*in combination*) a promoter of something unpleasant: *warmonger.* [Old English *mangere*, ultimately from Latin *mangō* dealer; compare Old High German *mangari*] ▸ **'mongering** *n, adj*

mongo[1] *or* **mongoe** ('mɒŋgəu) *n, pl* **-gos** *or* **-goes.** a Mongolian monetary unit worth one hundredth of a tugrik.

mongo[2] *or* **mongoe** ('mɒŋgəu) *n* a variant of **mungo.**

mongol ('mɒŋgᵊl) *n Offensive.* a person affected by Down's syndrome.

Mongol ('mɒŋgɒl, -gᵊl) *n* **1** a native or inhabitant of Mongolia, esp. a nomad. **2** the Mongolian language.

Mongolia (mɒŋ'gəulɪə) *n* **1** a republic in E central Asia: made a Chinese province in 1691; became autonomous in 1911 and a republic in 1924; multiparty democracy introduced in 1990. It consists chiefly of a high plateau, with the Gobi Desert in the south, a large lake district in the northwest, and the Altai and Khangai Mountains in the west. Official language: Khalkha. Religion: nonreligious majority. Currency: tugrik. Capital: Ulan Bator. Pop.: 2 413 000 (1998 est.). Area: 1 565 000 sq. km (604 095 sq. miles). Former names: (until 1924) **Outer Mongolia,** (1924–92) **Mongolian People's Republic. 2** a vast region of central Asia, inhabited chiefly by Mongols: now divided into the republic of Mongolia, the Inner Mongolian Autonomous Region of China, and the Tuva Republic of S Russia; at its height during the 13th century under Genghis Khan.

mongolian (mɒŋ'gəulɪən) *adj* (not in technical use) of, relating to, or affected by Down's syndrome.

Mongolian (mɒŋ'gəulɪən) *adj* **1** of or relating to Mongolia, its people, or their language. ◆ *n* **2** (*pl* **-lians**) a native of Mongolia. **3** the language of Mongolia: see **Khalkha.**

Mongolian People's Republic *n* the former name of **Mongolia** (sense 1).

Mongolic (mɒŋ'gɒlɪk) *n* **1** a branch or subfamily of the Altaic family of languages, including Mongolian, Kalmuck, and Buryat. **2** another word for **Mongoloid.**

mongolism ('mɒŋgəˌlɪzəm) *n Pathol.* a former name (not in technical use) for **Down's syndrome.** [C20: so named because Down's syndrome produces facial features similar to those of the Mongoloid peoples]

mongoloid ('mɒŋgəˌlɔɪd) (not in technical use) ◆ *adj* **1** relating to or characterized by Down's syndrome. ◆ *n* **2** a person affected by Down's syndrome.

Mongoloid ('mɒŋgəˌlɔɪd) *adj* **1** denoting, relating to, or belonging to one of the major racial groups of mankind, characterized by yellowish complexion, straight black hair, slanting eyes, short nose, and scanty facial hair, including most of the peoples of Asia, the Eskimos, and the North American Indians. ◆ *n* **2** a member of this group.

mongoose ('mɒŋˌguːs) *n, pl* **-gooses.** any small predatory viverrine mammal of the genus *Herpestes* and related genera, occurring in Africa and from S Europe to SE Asia, typically having a long tail and brindled coat. [C17: from Marathi *mangūs*, of Dravidian origin]

mongrel ('mʌŋgrəl) *n* **1** a plant or animal, esp. a dog, of mixed or unknown breeding; a crossbreed or hybrid. **2** *Derogatory.* a person of mixed race. ◆ *adj* **3** of mixed origin, breeding, character, etc. [C15: from obsolete *mong* mixture; compare Old English *gemong* a mingling] ▸ **'mongrelism** *n* ▸ **'mongrelly** *adj*

mongrelize *or* **mongrelise** ('mʌŋgrəˌlaɪz) *vb* (*tr*) to make mixed or mongrel in breed, race, character, kind, etc. ▸ **ˌmongreli'zation** *or* **ˌmongreli'sation** *n* ▸ **'mongrelˌizer** *or* **'mongrelˌiser** *n*

'mongst (mʌŋst) *prep Poetic.* short for **amongst.**

monied ('mʌnɪd) *adj* a less common spelling of **moneyed.**

monies ('mʌnɪz) *n Law, archaic.* a plural of **money.**

moniker *or* **monicker** ('mɒnɪkə) *n Slang.* a person's name or nickname. [C19: from Shelta *munnik*, altered from Irish *ainm* name]

monilial (mə'nɪlɪəl) *adj Pathol.* denoting a thrush infection, caused by the fungus *Candida* (formerly *Monilia*) *albicans.* [C20: from New Latin *monilia*, from Latin *monīle* necklace (referring to the beadlike form of the fungus)]

moniliform (mɒ'nɪlɪˌfɔːm) *adj Biology.* shaped like a string of beads: *moniliform fungi.* [C19: from New Latin *monīliformis*, from Latin *monīle* necklace + *forma* shape]

monism ('mɒnɪzəm) *n* **1** *Philosophy.* the doctrine that the person consists of only a single substance, or that there is no crucial difference between mental and physical events or properties. Compare **dualism** (sense 2). See also **materialism** (sense 2), **idealism** (sense 3). **2** *Philosophy.* the doctrine that reality consists of an unchanging whole in which change is mere illusion. Compare **pluralism** (sense 5). **3** the epistemological theory that the object and datum of consciousness are identical. **4** the attempt to explain anything in terms of one principle only. [C19: from Greek *monos* single + -ISM] ▸ **'monist** *n, adj* ▸ **mo'nistic** *adj* ▸ **mo'nistically** *adv*

monition (məu'nɪʃən) *n* **1** a warning or caution; admonition. **2** *Christianity.* a formal notice from a bishop or ecclesiastical court requiring a person to refrain from committing a specific offence. [C14: via Old French from Latin *monitiō*, from *monēre* to warn]

monitor ('mɒnɪtə) *n* **1** a person or piece of equipment that warns, checks, controls, or keeps a continuous record of something. **2** *Education.* **2a** a senior pupil with various supervisory duties. **2b** a pupil assisting a teacher in classroom organization, etc. **3** a television screen used to display certain kinds of information in a television studio, airport, etc. **4a** a loudspeaker used in a recording studio control room to determine quality or balance. **4b** a loudspeaker used on stage to enable musicians to hear themselves. **5** a device for controlling the direction of a water jet in fire fighting. **6** any large predatory lizard of the genus *Varanus* and family *Varanidae*, inhabiting warm regions of Africa, Asia, and Australia. See also **Komodo dragon. 7** Also called: **giant.** *Mining.* a nozzle for directing a high-pressure jet of water at the material to be excavated. **8** (formerly) a small heavily armoured shallow-draught warship used for coastal assault. ◆ *vb* (*tr*) **9** to act as a monitor of. **10** to observe or record (the activity or performance) of (an engine or other device). **11** to check (the technical quality of) (a radio or television broadcast). [C16: from Latin, from *monēre* to advise] ▸ **monitorial** (ˌmɒnɪ'tɔːrɪəl) *adj* ▸ **ˌmoni'torially** *adv* ▸ **'monitorˌship** *n* ▸ **'monitress** *fem n*

monitory ('mɒnɪtərɪ, -trɪ) *adj also* **monitorial. 1** warning or admonishing: *a monitory look.* ◆ *n, pl* **-ries. 2** *Rare.* a letter containing a monition.

monk (mʌŋk) *n* **1** a male member of a religious community bound by vows of poverty, chastity, and obedience. Related adj: **monastic. 2** (*sometimes cap.*) a fancy pigeon having a bald pate and often large feathered feet. [Old English *munuc,* from Late Latin *monachus,* from Late Greek: solitary (man), from Greek *monos* alone]

Monk (mʌŋk) *n* **1 Thelonious (Sphere)** (θə'ləʊnɪəs). 1920–82, U.S. jazz pianist and composer. **2** a variant spelling of (George) **Monck.**

monkery ('mʌŋkərɪ) *n, pl* **-eries.** *Derogatory.* **1** monastic life or practices. **2** a monastery or monks collectively.

monkey ('mʌŋkɪ) *n* **1** any of numerous long-tailed primates excluding the prosimians (lemurs, tarsiers, etc.): comprise the families *Cercopithecidae* (see **Old World monkey**), *Cebidae* (see **New World monkey**), and *Callithricidae* (marmosets). Related adj: **simian. 2** any primate except man. **3** a naughty or mischievous person, esp. a child. **4** the head of a pile-driver (**monkey engine**) or of some similar mechanical device. **5** (*modifier*) *Nautical.* denoting a small light structure or piece of equipment contrived to suit an immediate purpose: *a monkey foresail; a monkey bridge.* **6** *U.S. and Canadian slang.* an addict's dependence on a drug (esp. in the phrase **have a monkey on one's back**). **7** *Slang.* a butt of derision; someone made to look a fool (esp. in the phrase **make a monkey of**). **8** *Slang.* (esp. in bookmaking) £500. **9** *U.S. and Canadian slang.* $500. **10** *Austral. slang., archaic.* a sheep. **11 give a monkey's.** *Brit. slang.* to care about or regard as important: *who gives a monkey's what he thinks?* ◆ *vb* **12** (*intr;* usually foll. by *around, with,* etc.) to meddle, fool, or tinker. **13** (*tr*) *Rare.* to imitate; ape. [C16: perhaps from Low German; compare Middle Low German *Moneke* name of the ape's son in the tale of Reynard the Fox]

monkey bread *n* **1** the gourdlike fruit of the baobab tree. **2 monkey bread tree.** another name for **baobab.**

monkey business *n Informal.* mischievous, suspect, dishonest, or meddlesome behaviour or acts.

monkey climb *n* a wrestling throw in which a contestant seizes his opponent's arms or neck, places his feet on his opponent's stomach, and falls backwards, straightening his legs and throwing the opponent over his head.

monkey flower *n* any of various scrophulariaceous plants of the genus *Mimulus,* cultivated for their yellow or red flowers. See also **musk** (sense 3).

monkey jacket *n* a short close-fitting jacket, esp. a waist-length jacket similar to a mess jacket.

monkey nut *n Brit.* another name for a **peanut.**

monkey orchid *n* a European orchid, *Orchis simia,* rare in Britain, having a short dense flower spike that opens from the top downwards. The flowers are white streaked with pink or violet and have five spurs thought to resemble a monkey's arms, legs, and tail.

monkeypot ('mʌŋkɪˌpɒt) *n* **1** any of various tropical trees of the genus *Lecythis:* family *Lecythidaceae.* **2** the large urn-shaped pod of any of these trees, formerly used to catch monkeys by baiting it with sugar. **3** a melting pot used in making flint glass.

monkey puzzle *n* a South American coniferous tree, *Araucaria araucana,* having branches shaped like a candelabrum and stiff sharp leaves: family *Araucariaceae.* Also called: **Chile pine.** [so called because monkeys allegedly have difficulty climbing them]

monkey suit *n U.S. slang.* a man's evening dress.

monkey's wedding *n S. African informal.* a combination of sunshine and light rain.

monkey tricks *or U.S.* **monkey shines** *pl n Informal.* mischievous behaviour or acts, such as practical jokes.

monkey wrench *n* a wrench with adjustable jaws.

monkfish ('mʌŋkˌfɪʃ) *n, pl* **-fish** *or* **-fishes. 1** Also called (U.S.): **goosefish.** any of various anglers of the genus *Lophius.* **2** another name for the **angel shark.**

Mon-Khmer *n* **1** a family of languages spoken chiefly in Cambodia, Myanmar, and Assam; probably a member of the Austro-Asiatic phylum. ◆ *adj* **2** of or belonging to this family of languages.

monkhood ('mʌŋkhʊd) *n* **1** the condition of being a monk. **2** monks collectively.

monkish ('mʌŋkɪʃ) *adj* of, relating to, or resembling a monk or monks. ▸ **'monkishly** *adv* ▸ **'monkishness** *n*

monk's cloth *n* a heavy cotton fabric of basket weave, used mainly for bedspreads. [C19: so called because a similar material was used for making monks' habits]

monkshood ('mʌŋksˌhʊd) *n* any of several poisonous N temperate plants of the ranunculaceous genus *Aconitum,* esp. *A. napellus,* that have hooded blue-purple flowers.

Monmouth[1] ('mɒnməθ) *n* a market town in E Wales, in Monmouthshire: Norman castle, where Henry V was born in 1387. Pop.: 7246 (1991).

Monmouth[2] ('mɒnməθ) *n* **James Scott,** Duke of Monmouth. 1649–85, the illegitimate son of Charles II of England, he led a rebellion against James II in support of his own claim to the Crown; captured and beheaded.

Monmouthshire ('mɒnməθˌʃɪə, -ʃə) *n* a county of E Wales: administratively part of England for three centuries (until 1830); mainly absorbed into the county of Gwent in 1974; reinstated with reduced boundaries in 1996: chiefly agricultural, with the Black Mountains in the N. Administrative centre: Cwmbran. Pop.: 85 600 (1996 est.). Area: 851 sq. km (329 sq. miles).

Monnet (*French* mɔnɛ) *n* **Jean** (ʒɑ̃). 1888–1979, French economist and public servant, regarded as founding father of the European Economic Community. He was first president (1952–55) of the European Coal and Steel Community.

mono ('mɒnəʊ) *adj* **1** short for **monophonic.** ◆ *n* **2** monophonic sound; monophony.

mono- *or before a vowel* **mon-** *combining form.* **1** one; single: *monochrome; monorail.* **2** indicating that a chemical compound contains a single specified atom or group: *monoxide.* [from Greek *monos*]

monoacid (ˌmɒnəʊ'æsɪd), **monacid, monoacidic** (ˌmɒnəʊə'sɪdɪk), *or* **monacidic** *adj Chem.* (of a base) capable of reacting with only one molecule of a monobasic acid; having only one hydroxide ion per molecule.

monoamine (ˌmɒnəʊ'eɪmiːn) *n* a substance, such as adrenaline, noradrenaline, or serotonin, that contains a single amine group.

monoamine oxidase *n Biochem.* an enzyme present in nerve tissue that is responsible for the inactivation of neurotransmitters.

monoamine oxidase inhibitor *n Biochem.* an agent that inhibits the action of monoamine oxidase. Such inhibitors are used in the treatment of depression.

monoatomic (ˌmɒnəʊə'tɒmɪk) *adj* a variant of **monatomic.**

monobasic (ˌmɒnəʊ'beɪsɪk) *adj Chem.* (of an acid, such as hydrogen chloride) having only one replaceable hydrogen atom per molecule.

monocarp ('mɒnəʊˌkɑːp) *n* a plant that is monocarpic.

monocarpellary (ˌmɒnəʊ'kɑːpɪlərɪ) *or* **monocarpous** (ˌmɒnəʊ'kɑːpəs) *adj* **1** (of flowers) having only one carpel. **2** (of a plant gynoecium) consisting of one carpel.

monocarpic (ˌmɒnəʊ'kɑːpɪk) *or* **monocarpous** *adj* (of some flowering plants) producing fruit only once before dying. Also: **hapaxanthic.**

Monoceros (mə'nɒsərəs) *n, Latin genitive* **Monocerotis** (məˌnɒsə'rəʊtɪs). a faint constellation on the celestial equator crossed by the Milky Way and lying close to Orion and Canis Major. [C14: via Old French from Latin: unicorn, from Greek *monokeros* with a single horn, from MONO- + *keras* horn]

monochasium (ˌmɒnəʊ'keɪzɪəm) *n, pl* **-sia** (-zɪə). *Botany.* a cymose inflorescence in which each branch gives rise to one other branch only, as in the forget-me-not and buttercup. Compare **dichasium.** [C19: MONO- + *-chasium* as in DICHASIUM] ▸ ˌ**mono'chasial** *adj*

monochlamydeous (ˌmɒnəʊklə'mɪdɪəs) *adj* (of a flower) having a perianth of one whorl of members; not having a separate calyx and corolla. [C19: from Greek, from MONO- + *khlamus* a cloak + -EOUS]

monochloride (ˌmɒnə'klɔːraɪd) *n* a chloride containing one atom of chlorine per molecule.

monochord ('mɒnəʊˌkɔːd) *n* an instrument employed in acoustic analysis or investigation, consisting usually of one string stretched over a resonator of wood. Also called: **sonometer** (sə'nɒmɪtə). [C15: from Old French, from Late Latin, from Greek *monokhordon,* from MONO- + *khordē* string]

monochromat (ˌmɒnəʊ'krəʊmæt) *or* **monochromate** (ˌmɒnəʊ'krəʊmeɪt) *n* a person who perceives all colours as a single hue.

monochromatic (ˌmɒnəʊkrəʊ'mætɪk) *or* **monochroic** (ˌmɒnəʊ'krəʊɪk) *adj* **1** Also: **homochromatic.** (of light or other electromagnetic radiation) having only one wavelength. **2** *Physics.* (of moving particles) having only one kinetic energy. **3** of or relating to monochromatism. ◆ *n* **4** a person who is totally colour-blind. ▸ ˌ**monochro'matically** *adv*

monochromatism (ˌmɒnəʊ'krəʊməˌtɪzəm) *n* a visual defect in which all colours appear as variations of a single hue.

monochromator (ˌmɒnəʊ'krəʊmeɪtə) *n Physics.* a device that isolates a single wavelength of radiation.

monochrome ('mɒnəˌkrəʊm) *n* **1** a black-and-white photograph or transparency. **2** *Photog.* black and white. **3a** a painting, drawing, etc., done in a range of tones of a single colour. **3b** the technique or art of this. **4** (*modifier*) executed in or resembling monochrome: *a monochrome print.* ◆ *adj* **5** devoid of any distinctive or stimulating characteristics. ◆ Also called (for senses 3, 4): **monotint.** [C17: via Medieval Latin from Greek *monokhrōmos* of one colour] ▸ ˌ**mono'chromic** *or* ˌ**mono'chromical** *adj* ▸ **'monoˌchromist** *n*

monocle ('mɒnək^{ə}l) *n* a lens for correcting defective vision of one eye, held in position by the facial muscles. [C19: from French, from Late Latin *monoculus* one-eyed, from MONO- + *oculus* eye] ▸ **'monocled** *adj*

monocline ('mɒnəʊˌklaɪn) *n* a fold in stratified rocks in which the strata are inclined in the same direction from the horizontal. [C19: from MONO- + Greek *klīnein* to lean] ▸ ˌ**mono'clinal** *adj, n* ▸ ˌ**mono'clinally** *adv*

monoclinic (ˌmɒnəʊ'klɪnɪk) *adj Crystallog.* relating to or belonging to the crystal system characterized by three unequal axes, one pair of which are not at right angles to each other. [C19: from MONO- + Greek *klīnein* to lean + -IC]

monoclinous (ˌmɒnəʊ'klaɪnəs, 'mɒnəʊˌklaɪnəs) *adj* (of flowering plants) having the male and female reproductive organs on the same flower. Compare **diclinous.** [C19: from MONO- + Greek *klīnē* bed + -OUS] ▸ **'monoˌclinism** *n*

monoclonal antibody (ˌmɒnəʊ'kləʊn^{ə}l) *n* an antibody, produced by a single clone of cells grown in culture, that is both pure and specific and is capable of proliferating indefinitely to produce unlimited quantities of identical antibodies: used in diagnosis, therapy, and biotechnology.

monocoque ('mɒnəˌkɒk) *n* **1** a type of aircraft fuselage, car body, etc., in which all or most of the loads are taken by the skin. **2** a type of racing-car, racing-cycle, or powerboat design with no separate chassis and body. ◆ *adj* **3** of or relating to the design characteristic of a monocoque. [C20: from French, from MONO- + *coque* shell]

monocotyledon (ˌmɒnəʊˌkɒtɪ'liːd^{ə}n) *n* any flowering plant of the class *Monocotyledonae,* having a single embryonic seed leaf, leaves with parallel veins, and flowers with parts in threes: includes grasses, lilies, palms, and orchids. Often shortened to **monocot.** Compare **dicotyledon.** ▸ ˌ**monoˌcoty'ledonous** *adj*

monocracy (mɒ'nɒkrəsɪ) *n, pl* **-cies.** government by one person. ▸ **monocrat** ('mɒnəˌkræt) *n* ▸ ˌ**mono'cratic** *adj*

monocular (mɒ'nɒkjʊlə) *adj* **1** having to do with or using only one eye. ◆ *n* **2** a device for use with one eye, such as a field glass. [C17: from Late Latin *monoculus* one-eyed] ▸ **mo'nocularly** *adv*

monoculture ('mɒnəʊˌkʌltʃə) *n* the continuous growing of one type of crop.

monocycle ('mɒnəˌsaɪk^{ə}l) *n* another name for **unicycle.**

monocyclic (ˌmɒnəʊ'saɪklɪk) *adj* **1** Also: **mononuclear.** (of a chemical compound) containing only one ring of atoms. **2** (of sepals, petals, or stamens) arranged in a single whorl. **3** (of a plant) having a life cycle that is completed in one year.

monocyte ('mɒnəʊˌsaɪt) *n* a large phagocytic leucocyte with a spherical nucleus and clear cytoplasm. ▸ **monocytic** (ˌmɒnəˈsɪtɪk) *adj* ▸ ˌ**monoˈcytoid** *adj*

monodactylous (ˌmɒnəʊˈdæktɪləs) *adj* (of certain animals) having a single functional digit.

monodisperse (ˌmɒnəʊdɪsˈpɜːs) *adj Chem.* (of a colloidal system) having particles of similar size.

monodont ('mɒnəʊˌdɒnt) *adj* (of certain animals, esp. the male narwhal) having a single tooth throughout life.

monodrama ('mɒnəʊˌdrɑːmə) *n* a play or other dramatic piece for a single performer. ▸ ˌ**monodraˈmatic** *adj*

monody ('mɒnədɪ) *n, pl* **-dies. 1** (in Greek tragedy) an ode sung by a single actor. **2** any poem of lament for someone's death. **3** *Music.* a style of composition consisting of a single vocal part, usually with accompaniment. [C17: via Late Latin from Greek *monōidia,* from MONO- + *aeidein* to sing] ▸ **monodic** (mɒˈnɒdɪk) *or* **moˈnodical** *adj* ▸ **moˈnodically** *adv* ▸ **ˈmonodist** *n*

monoecious, monecious (mɒˈniːʃəs), *or* **monoicous** (mɒˈnɔɪkəs) *adj* **1** (of some flowering plants) having the male and female reproductive organs in separate flowers on the same plant. **2** (of some animals and lower plants) hermaphrodite. ◆ Compare **dioecious.** [C18: from New Latin *monoecia,* from MONO- + Greek *oikos* house] ▸ **moˈnoeciously** *or* **moˈneciously** *adv*

monofilament (ˌmɒnəˈfɪləmənt) *or* **monofil** ('mɒnəfɪl) *n* **1** synthetic thread or yarn composed of a single strand rather than twisted fibres. **2** a fishing line made of monofilaments.

monogamist (mɒˈnɒgəmɪst) *n* a person who advocates or practises monogamy. ▸ **moˌnogaˈmistic** *adj*

monogamy (mɒˈnɒgəmɪ) *n* **1** the state or practice of having only one husband or wife over a period of time. Compare **bigamy, polygamy** (sense 1), **digamy. 2** *Zoology.* the practice of having only one mate. [C17: via French from Late Latin *monogamia,* from Greek; see MONO- + -GAMY] ▸ **moˈnogamous** *adj* ▸ **moˈnogamously** *adv* ▸ **moˈnogamousness** *n*

monogenesis (ˌmɒnəʊˈdʒɛnɪsɪs) *or* **monogeny** (mɒˈnɒdʒɪnɪ) *n* **1** the hypothetical descent of all organisms from a single cell or organism. **2** asexual reproduction in animals. **3** the direct development of an ovum into an organism resembling the adult. **4** the hypothetical descent of all human beings from a single pair of ancestors. ◆ Compare **polygenesis.**

monogenetic (ˌmɒnəʊdʒɪˈnɛtɪk) *or* **monogenous** (mɒˈnɒdʒənəs) *adj* **1** of, relating to, or showing monogenesis. **2** of or relating to animals, such as some flukes, that complete their life cycle on only one host. **3** (of rocks and rock formations) formed from one source or by one process.

monogenic (ˌmɒnəʊˈdʒɛnɪk) *adj* **1** *Genetics.* of or relating to an inherited character difference that is controlled by one pair of genes. **2** (of animals) producing offspring of one sex.

monogram ('mɒnəˌgræm) *n* **1** a design of one or more letters, esp. initials, embroidered on clothing, printed on stationery, etc. ◆ *vb* **monograms, monogramming, monogrammed. 2** (*tr; usually passive*) to decorate (clothing, stationery, etc.) with a monogram. [C17: from Late Latin *monogramma,* from Greek; see MONO-, -GRAM] ▸ **monogrammatic** (ˌmɒnəgrəˈmætɪk) *adj*

monograph ('mɒnəˌgrɑːf, -ˌgræf) *n* **1** a paper, book, or other work concerned with a single subject or aspect of a subject. ◆ *vb* **2** (*tr*) to write a monograph on. ▸ **monographer** (mɒˈnɒgrəfə) *or* **moˈnographist** *n* ▸ ˌ**monoˈgraphic** *adj* ▸ ˌ**monoˈgraphically** *adv*

monogyny (mɒˈnɒdʒɪnɪ) *n* the custom of having only one female sexual partner over a period of time. ▸ **moˈnogynist** *n* ▸ **moˈnogynous** *adj*

monohull ('mɒnəʊˌhʌl) *n* a sailing vessel with a single hull. Compare **multihull.**

monohybrid (ˌmɒnəʊˈhaɪbrɪd) *n Genetics.* the offspring of two individuals that differ with respect to one pair of genes.

monohydrate (ˌmɒnəʊˈhaɪdreɪt) *n* a hydrate, such as ferrous sulphate monohydrate, $FeSO_4.H_2O$, containing one molecule of water per molecule of the compound. ▸ ˌ**monoˈhydrated** *adj*

monohydric (ˌmɒnəʊˈhaɪdrɪk) *adj* another word for **monohydroxy,** esp. when applied to alcohols.

monohydroxy (ˌmɒnəʊhaɪˈdrɒksɪ) *adj* (of a chemical compound) containing one hydroxyl group per molecule. Also: **monohydric.**

monoicous (mɒˈnɔɪkəs) *adj* a variant of **monoecious.** ▸ **moˈnoicously** *adv*

monolatry (mɒˈnɒlətrɪ) *n* the exclusive worship of one god without excluding the existence of others. ▸ **monolater** (mɒˈnɒlətə) *or* **moˈnolatrist** *n* ▸ **moˈnolatrous** *adj*

monolayer ('mɒnəʊˌleɪə) *n* a single layer of atoms or molecules adsorbed on a surface. Also called: **molecular film.**

monolingual (ˌmɒnəʊˈlɪŋgwəl) *adj* **1** knowing or expressed in only one language. ◆ *n* **2** a monolingual person. ◆ Compare **bilingual, multilingual.**

monolith ('mɒnəlɪθ) *n* **1** a large block of stone or anything that resembles one in appearance, intractability, etc. **2** a statue, obelisk, column, etc., cut from one block of stone. **3** a large hollow foundation piece sunk as a caisson and having a number of compartments that are filled with concrete when it has reached its correct position. [C19: via French from Greek *monolithos* made from a single stone]

monolithic (ˌmɒnəˈlɪθɪk) *adj* **1** of, relating to, or like a monolith. **2** characterized by hugeness, impenetrability, or intractability: *a monolithic government.* **3** *Electronics.* (of an integrated circuit) having all components manufactured into or on top of a single chip of silicon. Compare **hybrid** (sense 6). ▸ ˌ**monoˈlithically** *adv*

monologue ('mɒnəˌlɒg) *n* **1** a long speech made by one actor in a play, film, etc., esp. when alone. **2** a dramatic piece for a single performer. **3** any long speech by one person, esp. when interfering with conversation. [C17: via French from Greek *monologos* speaking alone] ▸ **monologic** (ˌmɒnəˈlɒdʒɪk) *or* ˌ**monoˈlogical** *adj* ▸ **monologist** ('mɒnəˌlɒgɪst, məˈnɒləgɪst) *n* ▸ **monology** (mɒˈnɒlədʒɪ) *n*

USAGE See at **soliloquy.**

monomania (ˌmɒnəʊˈmeɪnɪə) *n* an excessive mental preoccupation with one thing, idea, etc. ▸ ˌ**monoˈmaniˌac** *n, adj* ▸ **monomaniacal** (ˌmɒnəʊməˈnaɪək(ə)l) *adj*

monomark ('mɒnəmɑːk) *n Brit.* a series of letters or figures to identify goods, personal articles, etc.

monomer ('mɒnəmə) *n Chem.* a compound whose molecules can join together to form a polymer. ▸ **monomeric** (ˌmɒnəˈmɛrɪk) *adj*

monomerous (mɒˈnɒmərəs) *adj* (of flowers) having whorls consisting of only one member. [C19: from Greek *monomerēs* of one part; see MONO-, -MERE]

monometallic (ˌmɒnəʊmɪˈtælɪk) *adj* **1** (esp. of coins) consisting of one metal only. **2** relating to monometallism.

monometallism (ˌmɒnəʊˈmɛt(ə)ˌlɪzəm) *n* **1** the use of one metal, esp. gold or silver, as the sole standard of value and currency. **2** the economic policies supporting a monometallic standard. ▸ ˌ**monoˈmetallist** *n*

monometer (mɒˈnɒmɪtə) *n Prosody.* a line of verse consisting of one metrical foot. ▸ **monometrical** (ˌmɒnəʊˈmɛtrɪk(ə)l) *or* ˌ**monoˈmetric** *adj*

monomial (mɒˈnəʊmɪəl) *n* **1** *Maths.* an expression consisting of a single term, such as 5*ax.* ◆ *adj* **2** consisting of a single algebraic term. **3** *Biology.* of, relating to, or denoting a taxonomic name that consists of a single term. [C18: MONO- + (BIN)OMIAL]

monomode ('mɒnəʊˌməʊd) *adj* denoting or relating to a type of optical fibre with a core less than 10 micrometres in diameter.

monomolecular (ˌmɒnəʊməˈlɛkjʊlə) *adj* of, concerned with, or involving single molecules: *a monomolecular layer.*

monomorphic (ˌmɒnəʊˈmɔːfɪk) *or* **monomorphous** *adj* **1** (of an individual organism) showing little or no change in structure during the entire life history. **2** (of a species) existing or having parts that exist in only one form. **3** (of a chemical compound) having only one crystalline form. ▸ ˌ**monoˈmorphism** *n*

Monongahela (məˌnɒŋgəˈhiːlə) *n* a river in the northeastern U.S., flowing generally north to the Allegheny River at Pittsburgh, Pennsylvania, forming the Ohio River. Length: 206 km (128 miles).

mononuclear (ˌmɒnəʊˈnjuːklɪə) *adj* **1** (of a cell) having only one nucleus. **2** another word for **monocyclic** (sense 1).

mononucleosis (ˌmɒnəʊˌnjuːklɪˈəʊsɪs) *n* **1** *Pathol.* the presence of a large number of monocytes in the blood. **2** See **infectious mononucleosis.**

monopetalous (ˌmɒnəʊˈpɛt(ə)ləs) *adj* **1** another word for **gamopetalous. 2** (of flowers) having only one petal.

monophagous (məˈnɒfəgəs) *adj* feeding on only one type of food: *monophagous insects.* ▸ **moˈnophagy** *n*

monophobia (ˌmɒnəʊˈfəʊbɪə) *n* a strong fear of being alone. ▸ ˌ**monoˈphobic** *adj*

monophonic (ˌmɒnəʊˈfɒnɪk) *adj* **1** Also: **monaural.** (of a system of broadcasting, recording, or reproducing sound) using only one channel between source and loudspeaker. Sometimes shortened to **mono.** Compare **stereophonic. 2** *Music.* of or relating to a style of musical composition consisting of a single melodic line. See also **monody** (sense 3). ▸ **monophony** (mɒˈnɒfənɪ) *n*

monophthong ('mɒnəfˌθɒŋ) *n* a simple or pure vowel. [C17: from Greek *monophthongos,* from MONO- + *thongos* sound] ▸ **monophthongal** (ˌmɒnəfˈθɒŋg(ə)l) *adj*

monophyletic (ˌmɒnəʊfaɪˈlɛtɪk) *adj* **1** relating to or characterized by descent from a single ancestral group of animals or plants. **2** (of animals or plants) of or belonging to a single stock.

monophyllous (ˌmɒnəʊˈfɪləs) *adj Botany.* having or consisting of only one leaf or leaflike part.

Monophysite (mɒˈnɒfɪˌsaɪt) *Christianity.* ◆ *n* **1** a person who holds that there is only one nature in the person of Christ, which is primarily divine with human attributes. ◆ *adj* **2** of or relating to this belief. [C17: via Church Latin from Late Greek, from MONO- + *phusis* nature] ▸ **Monophysitic** (ˌmɒnəʊfɪˈsɪtɪk) *adj* ▸ **Moˈnophyˌsitism** *n*

monoplane ('mɒnəʊˌpleɪn) *n* an aeroplane with only one pair of wings. Compare **biplane.**

monoplegia (ˌmɒnəʊˈpliːdʒɪə) *n Pathol.* paralysis limited to one limb or a single group of muscles. ▸ **monoplegic** (ˌmɒnəʊˈpliːdʒɪk) *adj*

monoploid ('mɒnəˌplɔɪd) *adj, n* a less common word for **haploid.**

monopode ('mɒnəˌpəʊd) *n* **1** a member of a legendary one-legged race of Africa. **2** another word for **monopodium.** [C19: from Late Latin *monopodius*]

monopodium (ˌmɒnəˈpəʊdɪəm) *n, pl* **-dia** (-dɪə). the main axis of growth in the pine tree and similar plants: the main stem, which elongates from the tip and gives rise to lateral branches. Compare **sympodium.** [C19: New Latin, from Greek *monopous,* from MONO- + *pous* foot] ▸ ˌ**monoˈpodial** *adj* ▸ ˌ**monoˈpodially** *adv*

monopole ('mɒnəˌpəʊl) *n Physics.* **1** an electric charge or magnetic pole considered in isolation. **2** Also called: **magnetic monopole.** a hypothetical elementary particle postulated in certain theories of particle physics to exist as an isolated north or south magnetic pole.

monopolistic competition *n Economics.* the form of imperfect competition that exists when there are many producers or sellers of similar but differentiated goods or services.

monopolize *or* **monopolise** (məˈnɒpəˌlaɪz) *vb* (*tr*) **1** to have, control, or make use of fully, excluding others. **2** to obtain, maintain, or exploit a monopoly of (a market, commodity, etc.). ▸ **mo͵nopoli'zation** *or* **mo͵nopoli'sation** *n* ▸ **mo'nopo͵lizer** *or* **mo'nopo͵liser** *n*

monopoly (mə'nɒpəlɪ) *n, pl* **-lies. 1** exclusive control of the market supply of a product or service. **2a** an enterprise exercising this control. **2b** the product or service so controlled. **3** *Law.* the exclusive right or privilege granted to a person, company, etc., by the state to purchase, manufacture, use, or sell some commodity or to carry on trade in a specified country or area. **4** exclusive control, possession, or use of something. [C16: from Late Latin, from Greek *monopōlion*, from MONO- + *pōlein* to sell] ▸ **mo'nopolism** *n* ▸ **mo'nopolist** *n* ▸ **mo͵nopo'listic** *adj* ▸ **mo͵nopo'listically** *adv*

Monopoly (mə'nɒpəlɪ) *n Trademark.* a board game for two to six players who throw dice to advance their tokens around a board, the object being to acquire the property on which their tokens land.

monopropellant (͵mɒnəʊprə'pɛlənt) *n* a solid or liquid rocket propellant containing both the fuel and the oxidizer.

monopsony (mə'nɒpsənɪ) *n, pl* **-nies.** a situation in which the entire market demand for a product or service consists of only one buyer. [C20: MONO- + Greek *opsōnia* purchase, from *opsōnein* to buy] ▸ **mo͵nopso'nistic** *adj*

monopteros (mɒn'ɒptə͵rɒs) *or* **monopteron** *n, pl* **-teroi** (-tə͵rɔɪ) *or* **-tera** (-tərə). a circular classical building, esp. a temple, that has a single ring of columns surrounding it. [C18: Late Latin from Greek, from MONO- + *pteron* a wing] ▸ **mon'opteral** *adj*

monorail ('mɒnəʊ͵reɪl) *n* a single-rail railway, often elevated and with suspended cars.

monosaccharide (͵mɒnəʊ'sækə͵raɪd, -rɪd) *n* a simple sugar, such as glucose or fructose, that does not hydrolyse to yield other sugars.

monosemy ('mɒnəʊ͵siːmɪ) *n* the fact of having only a single meaning; absence of ambiguity in a word. Compare **polysemy.** [C20: from MONO- + (POLY)SEMY]

monosepalous (͵mɒnəʊ'sɛpələs) *adj* **1** another word for **gamosepalous. 2** (of flowers) having only one sepal.

monoski ('mɒnəʊ͵skiː) *n* a wide ski on which the skier stands with both feet. ▸ **'mono͵skier** *n* ▸ **'mono͵skiing** *n*

monosodium glutamate (͵mɒnəʊ'səʊdɪəm) *n* a white crystalline substance, the sodium salt of glutamic acid, that has little flavour itself but enhances the flavour of proteins either by increasing the amount of saliva produced in the mouth or by stimulating the taste buds: used as a food additive, esp. in Chinese foods. Formula: $NaC_5H_8O_4$. Also called: **sodium glutamate.** Abbrev.: **MSG.**

monosome ('mɒnə͵səʊm) *n* an unpaired chromosome, esp. an X-chromosome in an otherwise diploid cell. ▸ **monosomic** (͵mɒnə'səʊmɪk) *adj*

monospermous (͵mɒnəʊ'spɜːməs) *or* **monospermal** *adj* (of certain plants) producing only one seed.

monostable (͵mɒnəʊ'steɪbᵊl) *adj Physics.* (of an electronic circuit) having only one stable state but able to pass into a second state in response to an input pulse.

monostich ('mɒnə͵stɪk) *n* a poem of a single line. [C16: via Late Latin from Greek; see MONO-, STICH] ▸ **͵mono'stichic** *adj*

monostichous (͵mɒnəʊ'staɪkəs) *adj Botany.* (of parts) forming one row.

monostome ('mɒnə͵stəʊm) *or* **monostomous** (mɒ'nɒstəməs) *adj Zoology, botany.* having only one mouth, pore, or similar opening.

monostrophe (mɒ'nɒstrəfɪ, 'mɒnə͵strəʊf) *n* a poem in which all the stanzas or strophes are written in the same metre. ▸ **monostrophic** (͵mɒnə'strɒfɪk) *adj*

monostylous (͵mɒnəʊ'staɪləs) *adj Botany.* having only one style.

monosyllabic (͵mɒnəsɪ'læbɪk) *adj* **1** (of a word) containing only one syllable. **2** characterized by monosyllables; curt: *a monosyllabic answer.* ▸ **͵monosyl'labically** *adv*

monosyllable ('mɒnə͵sɪləbᵊl) *n* a word of one syllable, esp. one used as a sentence. ▸ **͵mono'sylla͵bism** *n*

monosymmetric (͵mɒnəsɪ'mɛtrɪk) *or* **monosymmetrical** *adj* **1** *Crystallog.* variants of **monoclinic. 2** *Biology.* variants of **zygomorphic.** ▸ **͵monosym'metrically** *adv* ▸ **monosymmetry** (͵mɒnə'sɪmɪtrɪ) *n*

monoterpene ('mɒnə͵tɜːpiːn) *n Chem.* an isoprene unit, C_5H_8, forming a terpene.

monotheism ('mɒnəʊθɪ͵ɪzəm) *n* the belief or doctrine that there is only one God. ▸ **'mono͵theist** *n, adj* ▸ **͵monothe'istic** *adj* ▸ **͵monothe'istically** *adv*

monotint ('mɒnə͵tɪnt) *n* another word for **monochrome** (senses 3, 4).

monotocous (ma'nɒtəkəs) *adj* (of certain animals) producing a single offspring at a birth. [from MONO- + Greek *tokos* birth]

monotone ('mɒnə͵təʊn) *n* **1** a single unvaried pitch level in speech, sound, etc. **2** utterance, etc., without change of pitch. **3** lack of variety in style, expression. etc. ◆ *adj* **4** unvarying or monotonous. **5** Also: **monotonic** (͵mɒnə'tɒnɪk). *Maths.* (of a sequence or function) consistently increasing or decreasing in value.

monotonize *or* **monotonise** (mə'nɒtə͵naɪz) *vb (tr)* to make monotonous.

monotonous (mə'nɒtənəs) *adj* **1** dull and tedious, esp. because of repetition. **2** unvarying in pitch or cadence. ▸ **mo'notonously** *adv* ▸ **mo'notonousness** *n*

monotony (mə'nɒtənɪ) *n, pl* **-nies. 1** wearisome routine; dullness. **2** lack of variety in pitch or cadence.

monotreme ('mɒnəʊ͵triːm) *n* any mammal of the primitive order *Monotremata*, of Australia and New Guinea: egg-laying toothless animals with a single opening (cloaca) for the passage of eggs or sperm, faeces, and urine. The group contains only the echidnas and the platypus. [C19: via New Latin from MONO- + Greek *trēma* hole] ▸ **monotrematous** (͵mɒnəʊ'triːmətəs) *adj*

monotrichous (mɒ'nɒtrɪkəs) *or* **monotrichic** (͵mɒnəʊ'trɪkɪk) *adj* (of bacteria) having a single flagellum.

monotype ('mɒnə͵taɪp) *n* **1** a single print made from a metal or glass plate on which a picture has been painted. **2** *Biology.* a monotypic genus or species.

Monotype ('mɒnə͵taɪp) *n* **1** *Trademark.* any of various typesetting systems, esp. originally one in which each character was cast individually from hot metal. **2** type produced by such a system.

monotypic (͵mɒnəʊ'tɪpɪk) *adj* **1** (of a genus or species) consisting of only one type of animal or plant. **2** of or relating to a monotype.

monounsaturated (͵mɒnəʊʌn'sætʃə͵reɪtɪd) *adj* of or relating to a class of vegetable oils, such as olive oil, the molecules of which have long chains of carbon atoms containing only one double bond. See also **polyunsaturated.**

monovalent (͵mɒnəʊ'veɪlənt) *adj Chem.* **a** having a valency of one. **b** having only one valency. ◆ Also: **univalent.** ▸ **͵mono'valence** *or* **͵mono'valency** *n*

monoxide (mɒ'nɒksaɪd) *n* an oxide that contains one oxygen atom per molecule: *carbon monoxide, CO.*

Monroe (mən'rəʊ) *n* **1 James.** 1758–1831, U.S. statesman; fifth president of the U.S. (1817–25). He promulgated the Monroe Doctrine (1823). **2 Marilyn,** real name *Norma Jean Baker* or *Mortenson.* 1926–62, U.S. film actress. Her films include *Niagara* (1952), *Gentlemen Prefer Blondes* (1953), and *Some Like It Hot* (1959).

Monroe doctrine *n* a principle of U.S. foreign policy that opposes the influence or interference of outside powers in the Americas.

Monrovia (mɒn'rəʊvɪə) *n* the capital and chief port of Liberia, on the Atlantic: founded in 1822 as a home for freed American slaves; University of Liberia (1862). Pop.: 962 000 (1995 est.).

Mons (*French* mɔ̃s) *n* a town in SW Belgium, capital of Hainaut province: scene of the first battle (1914) of the British Expeditionary Force during World War I. Pop.: 92 666 (1995 est.). Flemish name: **Bergen.**

Monseigneur *French.* (mɔ̃sɛɲœr) *n, pl* ***Messeigneurs*** (mesɛɲœr). a title given to French bishops, prelates, and princes. Abbrev.: **Mgr.** [literally: my lord]

monsieur (*French* məsjø; *English* məs'jɜː) *n, pl* **messieurs** (*French* mesjø; *English* 'mɛsəz). a French title of address equivalent to *sir* when used alone or *Mr* when placed before a name. [literally: my lord]

Monsignor (mɒn'siːnjə; *Italian* monsiɲ'ɲor) *n, pl* **Monsignors** *or* **Monsignori** (*Italian* monsiɲ'ɲoːri). *R.C. Church.* an ecclesiastical title attached to certain offices or distinctions usually bestowed by the Pope. Abbrevs.: **Mgr, Msgr.** [C17: from Italian, from French MONSEIGNEUR]

monsoon (mɒn'suːn) *n* **1** a seasonal wind of S Asia that blows from the southwest in summer, bringing heavy rains, and from the northeast in winter. **2** the rainy season when the SW monsoon blows, from about April to October. **3** any wind that changes direction with the seasons. [C16: from obsolete Dutch *monssoen*, from Portuguese *monção*, from Arabic *mawsim* season] ▸ **mon'soonal** *adj*

mons pubis ('mɒnz 'pjuːbɪs) *n, pl* **montes pubis** ('mɒntiːz). the fatty cushion of flesh in human males situated over the junction of the pubic bones. Compare **mons veneris.** [C17: New Latin: hill of the pubes]

monster ('mɒnstə) *n* **1** an imaginary beast, such as a centaur, usually made up of various animal or human parts. **2** a person, animal, or plant with a marked structural deformity. **3** a cruel, wicked, or inhuman person. **4a** a very large person, animal, or thing. **4b** (*as modifier*): *a monster cake.* [C13: from Old French *monstre*, from Latin *monstrum* portent, from *monēre* to warn]

monstera (mɒn'stɪərə) *n* any plant of the tropical climbing genus *Monstera*, some species of which are grown as greenhouse or pot plants for their unusual leathery perforated leaves: family *Araceae. M. deliciosa* is the Swiss cheese plant. [New Latin, perhaps because the leaves were regarded as an aberration]

monstrance ('mɒnstrəns) *n R.C. Church.* a receptacle, usually of gold or silver, with a transparent container in which the consecrated Host is exposed for adoration. [C16: from Medieval Latin *mōnstrantia*, from Latin *mōnstrāre* to show]

monstrosity (mɒn'strɒsɪtɪ) *n, pl* **-ties. 1** an outrageous or ugly person or thing; monster. **2** the state or quality of being monstrous.

monstrous ('mɒnstrəs) *adj* **1** abnormal, hideous, or unnatural in size, character, etc. **2** (of plants and animals) abnormal in structure. **3** outrageous, atrocious, or shocking: *it is monstrous how badly he is treated.* **4** huge: *a monstrous fire.* **5** of, relating to, or resembling a monster. ▸ **'monstrously** *adv* ▸ **'monstrousness** *n*

mons veneris ('mɒnz 'vɛnərɪs) *n, pl* **montes veneris** ('mɒntiːz). the fatty cushion of flesh in human females situated over the junction of the pubic bones. Compare **mons pubis.** [C17: New Latin: hill of Venus]

Mont. *abbrev. for* Montana.

montage (mɒn'tɑːʒ; *French* mɔ̃taʒ) *n* **1** the art or process of composing pictures by the superimposition or juxtaposition of miscellaneous elements, such as other pictures or photographs. **2** such a composition. **3** a method of film editing involving the juxtaposition or partial superimposition of several shots to form a single image. **4** a rapidly cut film sequence of this kind. [C20: from French, from *monter* to MOUNT[1]]

Montagnard (͵mɒntən'jɑːd, -'jɑː) *n, pl* **-gnards** *or* **-gnard. 1** a member of a hill people living on the border between Vietnam, Laos, and NE Cambodia. **2** a member of a North American Indian people living in the N Rocky Mountains. [C19: from French: mountaineer, from *montagne* MOUNTAIN]

Montagu ('mɒntə͵gjuː) *n* **1 Charles.** See (Earl of) **Halifax. 2** Lady **Mary Wortley.** 1689–1762, English writer, noted for her *Letters from the East* (1763).

Montague grammar ('mɒntə͵gjuː) *n Logic, linguistics.* a model-theoretic semantic theory for natural language that seeks to encompass indexical expressions and opaque contexts within an extensional theory by constructing set-theoretic representations of the intension of an expression in terms of functions of possible worlds. [named after Richard Merett *Montague* (1930–71), U.S. logician]

Montagu's harrier *n* a brownish European bird of prey, *Circus pygargus,* with long narrow wings and a long tail: family *Accipitridae* (hawks, harriers, etc.). [C19: named after Col. George *Montagu* (1751–1815), British naturalist]

Montaigne (*French* mɔ̃tɛɲ) *n* **Michel Eyquem de** (miʃɛl ikɛm də). 1533–92, French writer. His life's work, the *Essays* (begun in 1571), established the essay as a literary genre and record the evolution of his moral ideas.

Montale (*Italian* mon'taːle) *n* **Eugenio** (eu'dʒɛːnjo). 1896–1981, Italian poet: Nobel prize for literature 1975.

Montana[1] (mɒn'tænə) *n* a state of the western U.S.: consists of the Great Plains in the east and the Rocky Mountains in the west. Capital: Helena. Pop.: 878 810 (1997 est.). Area: 377 070 sq. km (145 587 sq. miles). Abbrevs.: **Mont.** or (with zip code) **MT** ▸ **Mon'tanan** *adj, n*

Montana[2] (mɒn'tænə) *n* **Joe.** born 1958, American football quarterback.

montane ('mɒnteɪn) *adj* of or inhabiting mountainous regions: *a montane flora.* [C19: from Latin *montānus,* from *mons* MOUNTAIN]

montan wax ('mɒntæn) *n* a hard wax obtained from lignite and peat, varying in colour from white to dark brown. It is used in polishes and candles. [C20: from Latin *montānus* of a mountain]

Montauban (*French* mɔ̃tobɑ̃) *n* a city in SW France: a stronghold in the 16th and 17th centuries, taken by Richelieu in 1629. Pop.: 53 280 (1990).

Montbéliard (*French* mɔ̃beljar) *n* an industrial town in E France: former capital of the duchy of Burgundy. Pop.: 30 639 (1990).

Mont Blanc (*French* mɔ̃ blɑ̃) *n* a massif in SW Europe, mainly between France and Italy: the highest mountain in the Alps; beneath it is **Mont Blanc Tunnel,** 12 km (7.5 miles) long. Highest peak (in France): 4807 m (15 771 ft.). Italian name: **Monte Bianco** ('monte 'bjaŋko).

montbretia (mɒn'briːʃə) *n* **1** any plant of the African iridaceous genus *Montbretia,* with ornamental orange or yellow flowers, grown mostly as pot plants. **2** See **crocosmia.** [C19: New Latin, named after A. F. E. Coquebert de *Montbret* (1780–1801), French botanist]

Montcalm (mɒnt'kɑːm; *French* mɔ̃kalm) *n* **Louis Joseph** (lwi ʒozɛf), Marquis de Montcalm de Saint-Véran. 1712–59, French general in Canada (1756); killed in Quebec by British forces under General Wolfe.

Mont Cenis (*French* mɔ̃səni) *n* See (Mont) **Cenis.**

Mont Cervin (mɔ̃ sɛrvɛ̃) *n* the French name for the **Matterhorn.**

mont-de-piété *French.* (mɔ̃dpjete) *n, pl* ***monts-de-piété*** (mɔ̃dpjete). (formerly) a public pawnshop. [from Italian *monte di pietà* bank of pity]

monte ('mɒntɪ) *n* **1** a gambling card game of Spanish origin. **2** *Austral. informal.* a certainty. [C19: from Spanish: mountain, hence pile of cards]

Monte Carlo ('mɒntɪ 'kɑːləʊ; *French* mɔ̃te karlo) *n* a town and resort forming part of the principality of Monaco, on the Riviera: famous casino and the destination of an annual car rally (the **Monte Carlo Rally**). Pop.: 12 000 (1985).

Monte Carlo method *n* a heuristic mathematical technique for evaluation or estimation of intractable problems by probabilistic simulation and sampling. [C20: named after the casino at Monte Carlo, where systems for winning at roulette, etc., are often tried]

Monte Cassino ('mɒntɪ kə'siːnəʊ; *Italian* 'monte kas'siːno) *n* a hill above Cassino in central Italy: site of Benedictine monastery (530 A.D.); in 1944 mistaken for German observation post and destroyed by the Allies.

Monte Corno (*Italian* 'monte 'korno) *n* See (Monte) **Corno.**

Montefeltro (*Italian* monte'feltro) *n* an Italian noble family who ruled Urbino from the 13th to the 16th century. **Federigo Montefeltro,** duke of Urbino (1422–82), was a noted patron of the arts and military leader.

Montego Bay (mɒn'tiːgəʊ) *n* a port and resort in NW Jamaica: the second largest town on the island. Pop.: 83 446 (1991).

monteith (mɒn'tiːθ) *n* a large ornamental bowl, usually of silver, for cooling wineglasses, which are suspended from the notched rim. [C17: said to be from the name of a Scot who wore a cloak with a scalloped edge]

Montenegro (ˌmɒntɪ'niːgrəʊ) *n* a constituent republic of Yugoslavia, bordering on the Adriatic: declared a kingdom in 1910 and united with Serbia, Croatia, and other territories in 1918 to form Yugoslavia; remained united with Serbia as the Federal Republic of Yugoslavia when the other Yugoslav constituent republics became independent in 1991–92. Capital: Podgorica. Pop.: 635 000 (1995 est.). Area: 13 812 sq. km (5387 sq. miles). ▸ **ˌMonte'negrin** *adj, n*

Monterey (ˌmɒntə'reɪ) *n* a city in W California: capital of Spain's Pacific empire from 1774 to 1825; taken by the U.S. (1846). Pop.: 31 954 (1990).

Monterey cypress *n* another name for **macrocarpa.**

montero (mɒn'tɛərəʊ; *Spanish* mon'tero) *n, pl* **-ros** (-rəʊz; *Spanish* -ros). a round cap with a flap at the back worn by hunters, esp. in Spain in the 17th and 18th centuries. [C17: from Spanish, literally: mountaineer]

Monterrey (ˌmɒntə'reɪ; *Spanish* mɔnte'rreɪ) *n* a city in NE Mexico, capital of Nuevo Léon state: the third largest city in Mexico; a major industrial centre, esp. for metals. Pop.: 1 068 996 (1990).

Montespan (*French* mɔ̃tɛspɑ̃) *n* **Marquise de,** title of *Françoise Athénaïs de Rochechouart.* 1641–1707, French noblewoman; mistress of Louis XIV of France.

Montesquieu (*French* mɔ̃tɛskjø) *n* **Baron de la Brède et de** (barɔ̃ də la brɛd e də), title of *Charles Louis de Secondat.* 1689–1755, French political philosopher. His chief works are the satirical *Lettres persanes* (1721) and *L'Esprit des lois* (1748), a comparative analysis of various forms of government, which had a profound influence on political thought in Europe and the U.S.

Montessori (ˌmɒntɪ'sɔːrɪ; *Italian* montes'sɔːri) *n* **Maria** (ma'riːa). 1870–1952, Italian educational reformer, who evolved the Montessori method of teaching children.

Montessori method *n* a method of nursery education in which children are provided with generous facilities for practical play and allowed to develop at their own pace.

Monteux (*French* mɔ̃tø) *n* **Pierre** (pjɛr). 1875–1964, U.S. conductor, born in France.

Monteverdi (ˌmɒntɪ'vɛədɪ) *n* **Claudio** ('klaʊdɪˌəʊ). ?1567–1643, Italian composer, noted esp. for his innovations in opera and for his expressive use of dissonance. His operas include *Orfeo* (1607) and *L'Incoronazione di Poppea* (1642) and he also wrote many motets and madrigals.

Montevideo (ˌmɒntɪvɪ'deɪəʊ; *Spanish* mɔnteβi'ðeo) *n* the capital and chief port of Uruguay, in the south on the Río de la Plata estuary: the largest city in the country: University of the Republic (1849); resort. Pop.: 1 378 707 (1996).

Montez (mɒn'tɛz) *n* **Lola** ('ləʊlə), original name *Marie Gilbert.* 1818–61, Irish dancer; mistress of Louis I of Bavaria (1786–1868; reigned 1825–48).

Montezuma II (ˌmɒntɪ'zuːmə) *n* 1466–1520, Aztec emperor of Mexico (?1502–20). He was overthrown and killed by the Spanish conquistador Cortés.

Montezuma's revenge *n Informal.* an acute attack of infectious diarrhoea, esp. when experienced in Mexico by tourists.

Montfort ('mɒntfət) *n* **Simon de,** Earl of Leicester. ?1208–65, English soldier, born in Normandy. He led the baronial rebellion against Henry III and ruled England from 1264 to 1265; he was killed at Evesham.

montgolfier (mɒnt'gɒlfɪə; *French* mɔ̃gɔlfje) *n* a hot-air balloon. [C18: see MONTGOLFIER]

Montgolfier (*French* mɔ̃gɔlfje) *n* **Jacques Étienne** (ʒak etjɛn), 1745–99, and his brother **Joseph Michel** (ʒozɛf miʃɛl), 1740–1810, French inventors, who built (1782) and ascended in (1783) the first practical hot-air balloon.

Montgomery[1] (mənt'gʌmərɪ) *n* a city in central Alabama, on the Alabama River: state capital; capital of the Confederacy (1861). Pop.: 196 363 (1996 est.).

Montgomery[2] (mənt'gʌmərɪ) *n* **Bernard Law,** 1st Viscount Montgomery of Alamein, nicknamed *Monty.* 1887–1976, British field marshal. As commander of the 8th Army in North Africa, he launched the offensive, beginning with the victory at El Alamein (1942), that drove Rommel's forces back to Tunis. He also commanded the ground forces in the invasion of Normandy (1944) and accepted Germany's surrender at Lüneburg Heath (May 7, 1945).

Montgomeryshire (mənt'gʌmərɪˌʃɪə, -ʃə) *n* (until 1974) a county of central Wales, now part of Powys.

month (mʌnθ) *n* **1** one of the twelve divisions (**calendar months**) of the calendar year. **2** a period of time extending from one date to a corresponding date in the next calendar month. **3** a period of four weeks or of 30 days. **4** the period of time (**solar month**) taken by the moon to return to the same longitude after one complete revolution around the earth; 27.321 58 days (approximately 27 days, 7 hours, 43 minutes, 4.5 seconds). **5** the period of time (**sidereal month**) taken by the moon to make one complete revolution around the earth, measured between two successive conjunctions with a particular star; 27.321 66 days (approximately 27 days, 7 hours, 43 minutes, 11 seconds). **6** Also called: **lunation.** the period of time (**lunar** or **synodic month**) taken by the moon to make one complete revolution around the earth, measured between two successive new moons; 29.530 59 days (approximately 29 days, 12 hours, 44 minutes, 3 seconds). **7 a month of Sundays.** *Informal.* a long unspecified period. ◆ Related adj: **mensal.** [Old English *mōnath;* related to Old High German *mānōd,* Old Norse *mānathr;* compare Gothic *mena* moon]

Montherlant (*French* mɔ̃tɛrlɑ̃) *n* **Henri** (**Millon**) **de** (ɑ̃ri də). 1896–1972, French novelist and dramatist: his novels include *Les Jeunes Filles* (1935–39) and *Le Chaos et la nuit* (1963).

monthly ('mʌnθlɪ) *adj* **1** occurring, done, appearing, payable, etc., once every month. **2** lasting or valid for a month: *a monthly subscription.* ◆ *adv* **3** once a month. ◆ *n, pl* **-lies. 4** a book, periodical, magazine, etc., published once a month. **5** *Informal.* a menstrual period.

month's mind *n R.C. Church.* a Mass celebrated in remembrance of a person one month after his death.

monticule ('mɒntɪˌkjuːl) *n* a small hill or mound, such as a secondary volcanic cone. [C18: via French from Late Latin *monticulus,* diminutive of Latin *mons* mountain]

Montluçon (*French* mɔ̃lysɔ̃) *n* an industrial city in central France, on the Cher River. Pop.: 56 434 (1983 est.).

Montmartre (*French* mɔ̃martrə) *n* a district of N Paris, on a hill above the Seine: the highest point in the city; famous for its associations with many artists.

montmorillonite (ˌmɒntmə'rɪləˌnaɪt) *n* a clay mineral consisting of hydrated aluminium silicate: an important component of bentonite. [C19: named after *Montmorillon,* French town where it was first found, + -ITE[1]]

Montparnasse (*French* mɔ̃parnas) *n* a district of S Paris, on the left bank of the Seine: noted for its cafés, frequented by artists, writers, and students.

Montpelier (mɒnt'piːljə) *n* a city in N central Vermont, on the Winooski River: the state capital. Pop.: 8254 (1990).

Montpellier (*French* mɔ̃pəlje) *n* a city in S France, the chief town of Languedoc: its university was founded by Pope Nicholas IV in 1289; wine trade. Pop.: 210 866 (1990).

Montreal (ˌmɒntrɪ'ɔːl) *n* a city and major port in central Canada, in S Quebec on **Montreal Island** at the junction of the Ottawa and St Lawrence Rivers. Pop.: 1 017 666 (1991), with a conurbation of 3 127 242 (1991). French name: **Montréal** (mɔ̃real).

Montreuil (*French* mɔ̃trœj) *n* an E suburb of Paris: formerly famous for peaches, but now increasingly industrialized. Pop.: 94 754 (1990).

Montreux (*French* mɔ̃trø) *n* a town and resort in W Switzerland, in Vaud canton on Lake Geneva: annual television festival. Pop.: 19 850 (1990).

Montrose (mɒn'trəʊz) *n* **James Graham,** 1st Marquess and 5th Earl of Montrose. 1612–50, Scottish general, noted for his victories in Scotland for Charles I in the Civil War. He was later captured and hanged.

Mont-Saint-Michel (*French* mɔ̃sɛ̃miʃɛl) *n* a rocky islet off the coast of NW France, accessible at low tide by a causeway, in the **Bay of St Michel** (an inlet of the Gulf of St Malo): Benedictine abbey (966), used as a prison from the Revolution until 1863; reoccupied by Benedictine monks since 1966. Area: 1 hectare (3 acres).

Montserrat *n* **1** (ˌmɒntsəˈræt). a volcanic island in the Caribbean, in the Leeward Islands: a UK Overseas Territory: much of the island rendered uninhabitable by volcanic eruptions in 1997. Capital: Plymouth. Pop.: 11 957 (1991). Area: 103 sq. km (40 sq. miles). **2** (*Spanish* mɔnseˈrrat). a mountain in NE Spain, northwest of Barcelona: famous Benedictine monastery. Height: 1235 m (4054 ft.). Ancient name: **Mons Serratus** (mɒnz səˈrætəs).

monument (ˈmɒnjʊmənt) *n* **1** an obelisk, statue, building, etc., erected in commemoration of a person or event or in celebration of something. **2** a notable building or site, esp. one preserved as public property. **3** a tomb or tombstone. **4** a literary or artistic work regarded as commemorative of its creator or a particular period. **5** *U.S.* a boundary marker. **6** an exceptional example: *his lecture was a monument of tedium.* **7** an obsolete word for **statue.** [C13: from Latin *monumentum,* from *monēre* to remind, advise]

Monument (ˈmɒnjʊmənt) *n* **the.** a tall columnar building designed (1671) by Sir Christopher Wren to commemorate the Fire of London (1666), which destroyed a large part of the medieval city.

monumental (ˌmɒnjʊˈmɛntᵊl) *adj* **1** like a monument, esp. in large size, endurance, or importance: *a monumental work of art.* **2** of, relating to, or being a monument. **3** *Informal.* (intensifier): *monumental stupidity.* ▸ **ˌmonumenˈtality** *n* ▸ **ˌmonuˈmentally** *adv*

mony (ˈmɒnɪ) *determiner* a Scot. word for **many.**

Monza (*Italian* ˈmontsa) *n* a city in N Italy, northeast of Milan: the ancient capital of Lombardy; scene of the assassination of King Umberto I in 1900; motor-racing circuit. Pop.: 119 658 (1996 est.).

monzonite (ˈmɒnzəˌnaɪt) *n* a coarse-grained plutonic igneous rock consisting of equal amounts of plagioclase and orthoclase feldspar, with ferromagnesian minerals. [C19: from German, named after *Monzoni,* Tyrolean mountain where it was found] ▸ **monzonitic** (ˌmɒnzəˈnɪtɪk) *adj*

moo (muː) *vb* **1** (*intr*) (of a cow, bull, etc.) to make a characteristic deep long sound; low. ◆ *interj* **2** an instance or imitation of this sound.

mooch (muːtʃ) *vb Slang.* **1** (*intr*) (often with *around*) to loiter or walk aimlessly. **2** (*intr*) to behave in an apathetic way. **3** (*intr*) to sneak or lurk; skulk. **4** (*tr*) to cadge **5** (*tr*) *Chiefly U.S. and Canadian.* to steal. [C17: perhaps from Old French *muchier* to skulk] ▸ **ˈmoocher** *n*

mood[1] (muːd) *n* **1** a temporary state of mind or temper: *a cheerful mood.* **2** a sullen or gloomy state of mind, esp. when temporary: *she's in a mood.* **3** a prevailing atmosphere or feeling. **4** **in the mood.** in a favourable state of mind (for something or to do something). [Old English *mōd* mind, feeling; compare Old Norse *mōthr* grief, wrath]

mood[2] (muːd) *n* **1** *Grammar.* a category of the verb or verbal inflections that expresses semantic and grammatical differences, including such forms as the indicative, subjunctive, and imperative. **2** *Logic.* one of the possible arrangements of the syllogism, classified solely by whether the component propositions are universal or particular and affirmative or negative. Compare **figure** (sense 18). ◆ Also called: **mode.** [C16: from MOOD[1], influenced in meaning by MODE]

moody (ˈmuːdɪ) *adj* **moodier, moodiest. 1** sullen, sulky, or gloomy. **2** temperamental or changeable. ▸ **ˈmoodily** *adv* ▸ **ˈmoodiness** *n*

Moody (ˈmuːdɪ) *n* **Dwight Lyman.** 1837–99, U.S. evangelist and hymnodist, noted for his revivalist campaigns in Britain and the U.S. with I. D. Sankey.

Moog (muːg, məʊg) *n Music, trademark.* a type of synthesizer. [C20: named after Robert *Moog* (born 1934), U.S. engineer]

mooi (mɔɪ) *adj S. African slang.* pleasing; nice. [Afrikaans]

moolah (ˈmuːlɑː) *n* a slang word for **money.**

mooli (ˈmuːlɪ) *n* a type of large white radish. [E African native name]

moolvie *or* **moolvi** (ˈmuːlviː) *n* (esp. in India) a Muslim doctor of the law, teacher, or learned man: also used as a title of respect. [C17: from Urdu, from Arabic *mawlawīy;* compare MULLAH]

Moomba (ˈmuːmbə) *n Austral.* **1** a festival held annually in Melbourne since 1954, named in the belief that *moomba* was an Aboriginal word meaning "Let's get together and have fun." **2** a natural gas field in South Australia. [from a native Australian language *moom* buttocks, anus]

moon (muːn) *n* **1** (*sometimes cap.*) the natural satellite of the earth. Diameter: 3476 km; mass: 7.4×10^{22} kg; mean distance from earth: 384 400 km; periods of rotation and revolution: 27.32 days. Related adj: **lunar. 2** the face of the moon as it is seen during its revolution around the earth, esp. at one of its phases: *new moon; full moon.* **3** any natural satellite of a planet. **4** moonlight; moonshine. **5** something resembling a moon. **6** a month, esp. a lunar one. **7** **once in a blue moon.** very seldom. **8** **over the moon.** *Informal.* extremely happy; ecstatic. **9** **reach for the moon.** to desire or attempt something unattainable or difficult to obtain. ◆ *vb* **10** (when *tr,* often foll. by *away;* when *intr,* often foll. by *around*) to be idle in a listless way, as if in love, or to idle (time) away. **11** (*intr*) *Slang.* to expose one's buttocks to passers-by. [Old English *mōna;* compare Old Frisian *mōna,* Old High German *māno*] ▸ **ˈmoonless** *adj*

Moon[1] (muːn) *n* a system of embossed alphabetical signs for blind readers, the fourteen basic characters of which can, by rotation, mimic most of the letters of the Roman alphabet, thereby making learning easier for those who learned to read before going blind. Compare **Braille**[1].

Moon[2] (muːn) *n* **William.** 1818–94, British inventor of the Moon writing system in 1847, who, himself blind, taught blind children in Brighton and printed mainly religious works from stereotyped plates of his own designing.

moonbeam (ˈmuːnˌbiːm) *n* a ray of moonlight.

moon blindness *n* **1** *Ophthalmol.* a nontechnical name for **nyctalopia. 2** Also called: **mooneye.** *Vet. science.* a disorder affecting horses, which causes inflammation of the eyes and sometimes blindness. ▸ **ˈmoon-ˌblind** *adj*

mooncalf (ˈmuːnˌkɑːf) *n, pl* **-calves** (-ˌkɑːvz). **1** a born fool; dolt. **2** a person who idles time away. **3** *Obsolete.* a freak or monster.

Moon Child *n* a euphemistic name for **Cancer** (sense 2b).

mooned (muːnd) *adj* decorated with a moon.

mooneye (ˈmuːnˌaɪ) *n* **1** any of several North American large-eyed freshwater clupeoid fishes of the family *Hiodontidae,* esp. *Hiodon tergisus.* See also **goldeye. 2** *Vet. science.* another name for **moon blindness** (sense 2).

moon-eyed *adj* **1** having the eyes open wide, as in awe. **2** *Vet. science.* affected with moon blindness.

moon-faced *adj* having a round face; full-faced.

moonfish (ˈmuːnˌfɪʃ) *n, pl* **-fishes** *or* **-fish. 1** any of several deep-bodied silvery carangid fishes, occurring in warm and tropical American coastal waters. **2** any of various other round silvery fishes, such as the Indo-Pacific *Monodactylus argenteus.* **3** another name for **opah.**

moonflower (ˈmuːnˌflaʊə) *n* **1** any of several night-blooming convolvulaceous plants, esp. the white-flowered *Calonyction* (or *Ipomoea*) *aculeatum.* **2** Also called: **angels' tears.** a Mexican solanaceous plant, *Datura suaveolens,* planted in the tropics for its white night-blooming flowers.

Moonie (ˈmuːnɪ) *n Informal.* **1** a member of the Unification Church. **2** (*pl;* preceded by *the*) the Unification Church. [C20: named after the founder Sun Myung *Moon* (born 1920), S Korean industrialist]

moonlight (ˈmuːnˌlaɪt) *n* **1** Also called: **moonshine.** light from the sun received on earth after reflection by the moon. **2** (*modifier*) illuminated by the moon: *a moonlight walk.* **3** short for **moonlight flit.** ◆ *vb* **-lights, -lighting, -lighted. 4** (*intr*) *Informal.* to work at a secondary job, esp. at night, and often illegitimately. ▸ **ˈmoonˌlighter** *n*

moonlight flit *n Brit. informal.* a hurried departure at night, esp. from rented accommodation to avoid payment of rent owed. Often shortened to **moonlight.**

moonlighting (ˈmuːnˌlaɪtɪŋ) *n* **1** working at a secondary job. **2** (in 19th-century Ireland) the carrying out of cattle-maiming, murders, etc., during the night in protest against the land-tenure system.

moonlit (ˈmuːnlɪt) *adj* illuminated by the moon.

moon pool *n* (in the oil industry) an open shaft in the centre of the hull of a ship engaged in deep-sea drilling through which drilling takes place.

moonquake (ˈmuːnˌkweɪk) *n* a light tremor of the moon, detected on the moon's surface.

moonraker (ˈmuːnˌreɪkə) *n Nautical.* a small square sail set above a skysail.

moon rat *n* a ratlike SE Asian nocturnal mammal, *Echinosorex gymnurus,* with greyish fur and an elongated snout: family *Erinaceidae* (hedgehogs): the largest living insectivore.

moonrise (ˈmuːnˌraɪz) *n* the moment when the moon appears above the horizon.

moonscape (ˈmuːnˌskeɪp) *n* the general surface of the moon or a representation of it.

moonseed (ˈmuːnˌsiːd) *n* any menispermaceous climbing plant of the genus *Menispermum* and related genera, having red or black fruits with crescent-shaped or ring-shaped seeds.

moonset (ˈmuːnˌsɛt) *n* the moment when the moon disappears below the horizon.

moonshine (ˈmuːnˌʃaɪn) *n* **1** another word for **moonlight** (sense 1). **2** *U.S. and Canadian.* illegally distilled or smuggled whisky or other spirit. **3** foolish talk or thought.

moonshiner (ˈmuːnˌʃaɪnə) *n U.S. and Canadian.* a person who illegally makes or smuggles distilled spirits.

moonshot (ˈmuːnˌʃɒt) *n* the launching of a spacecraft, rocket, etc., to the moon.

moonstone (ˈmuːnˌstəʊn) *n* a gem variety of orthoclase or albite that is white and translucent with bluish reflections.

moonstruck (ˈmuːnˌstrʌk) *or* **moonstricken** (ˈmuːnˌstrɪkən) *adj* deranged or mad.

moonwort (ˈmuːnˌwɜːt) *n* **1** Also called (U.S.): **grape fern.** any of various ferns of the genus *Botrychium,* esp. *B. lunaria,* which has crescent-shaped leaflets. **2** another name for **honesty** (sense 4).

moony (ˈmuːnɪ) *adj* **moonier, mooniest. 1** *Informal.* dreamy or listless. **2** of or like the moon. **3** *Brit. slang.* crazy or foolish. ▸ **ˈmoonily** *adv* ▸ **ˈmooniness** *n*

moor[1] (mʊə, mɔː) *n* a tract of unenclosed ground, usually having peaty soil covered with heather, coarse grass, bracken, and moss. [Old English *mōr;* related to Old Saxon *mōr,* Old High German *muor* swamp] ▸ **ˈmoory** *adj*

moor[2] (mʊə, mɔː) *vb* **1** to secure (a ship, boat, etc.) with cables or ropes. **2** (of a ship, boat, etc.) to be secured in this way. **3** (not in technical usage) a less common word for **anchor** (sense 11). [C15: of Germanic origin; related to Old English *mærelsrāp* rope for mooring]

Moor (mʊə, mɔː) *n* a member of a Muslim people of North Africa, of mixed Arab and Berber descent. In the 8th century they were converted to Islam and established power in North Africa and Spain, where they established a civilization (756–1492). [C14: via Old French from Latin *Maurus,* from Greek *Mauros,* possibly from Berber]

moorage (ˈmʊərɪdʒ, ˈmɔːrɪdʒ) *n* **1** a place for mooring a vessel. **2** a charge for mooring. **3** the act of mooring.

moorburn *or* **muirburn** (ˈmuːrˌbʌrn, ˈmʊəˌbɜːn) *n Scot.* the practice of burning off old growth on a heather moor to encourage new growth for grazing.

moorcock (ˈmʊəˌkɒk, ˈmɔː-) *n* the male of the red grouse.

Moore[1] (mʊə, mɔː) *n* **1** **Bobby,** full name *Robert Frederick Moore.* 1941–93, British footballer: captain of the England team that won the World Cup in

1966. **2 Dudley** (**Stuart John**). born 1935, British actor, comedian, and musician: noted for his comedy partnership (1960–73) with Peter Cook and such films as *10* (1979) and *Arthur* (1981). **3 George.** 1852–1933, Irish novelist. His works include *Esther Waters* (1894) and *The Brook Kerith* (1916). **4 G**(**eorge**) **E**(**dward**). 1873–1958, British philosopher, noted esp. for his *Principia Ethica* (1903). **5 Gerald.** 1899–1987, British pianist, noted as an accompanist esp. to lieder singers. **6 Henry.** 1898–1986, British sculptor. His works are characterized by monumental organic forms and include the *Madonna and Child* (1943) at St Matthew's Church, Northampton. **7** Sir **John.** 1761–1809, British general; commander of the British army (1808–09) in the Peninsular War: killed at Corunna. **8 Marianne** (**Craig**). 1887–1972, U.S. poet: her works include *Observations* (1924) and *Selected Poems* (1935). **9 Thomas.** 1779–1852, Irish poet, best known for *Irish Melodies* (1807–34).

Moore[2] ('mʊʊre) *n* another name for **Mossi.**

moorfowl ('mʊəˌfaʊl, 'mɔː-) *n* (in Brit. game laws) an archaic name for **red grouse.** Compare **heathfowl.**

moor grass *n* a grass characteristic of moors, especially **purple moor grass** (*Molinia caerulea*) of heath and fenland and **blue moor grass** (*Sesleria caerulea*) of limestone uplands.

moorhen ('mʊəˌhɛn, 'mɔː-) *n* **1** a bird, *Gallinula chloropus,* inhabiting ponds, lakes, etc., having a black plumage, red bill, and a red shield above the bill: family *Rallidae* (rails). **2** the female of the red grouse.

mooring ('mʊərɪŋ, 'mɔː-) *n* **1** a place for mooring a vessel. **2** a permanent anchor, dropped in the water and equipped with a floating buoy, to which vessels can moor. ♦ See also **moorings.**

mooring mast *n* a mast or tower to which a balloon or airship may be moored. Also called: **mooring tower.**

moorings ('mʊərɪŋz, 'mɔː-) *pl n* **1** *Nautical.* the ropes, anchors, etc., used in mooring a vessel. **2** (*sometimes sing*) something that provides security or stability.

Moorish ('mʊərɪʃ, 'mɔː-) *adj* **1** of or relating to the Moors. **2** denoting the style of architecture used in Spain from the 13th to 16th century, characterized by the horseshoe arch. ♦ Also: **Morisco** *or* **Moresco.**

Moorish idol *n* a tropical marine spiny-finned fish, *Zanclus canescens,* that is common around coral reefs: family *Zanclidae.* It has a deeply compressed body with yellow and black stripes, a beaklike snout, and an elongated dorsal fin.

moorland ('mʊələnd, 'mɔː-) *n Brit.* an area of moor.

moorwort ('mʊəˌwɜːt, 'mɔː-) *n* another name for **marsh andromeda.**

moose (muːs) *n, pl* **moose.** a large North American deer, *Alces alces,* having large flattened palmate antlers: also occurs in Europe and Asia where it is called an elk. **[C17:** from Algonquian; related to Narraganset *moos,* from *moosu* he strips, alluding to the moose's habit of stripping trees**]**

Moose Jaw *n* a city in W Canada, in S Saskatchewan. Pop.: 33 593 (1991).

moot (muːt) *adj* **1** subject or open to debate: *a moot point.* ♦ *vb* **2** (*tr*) to suggest or bring up for debate. **3** (*intr*) to plead or argue theoretical or hypothetical cases, as an academic exercise or as vocational training for law students. ♦ *n* **4** a discussion or debate of a hypothetical case or point, held as an academic activity. **5** (in Anglo-Saxon England) an assembly, mainly in a shire or hundred, dealing with local legal and administrative affairs. **[**Old English *gemōt;* compare Old Saxon *mōt,* Middle High German *muoze* meeting**]** ▸ **'mooter** *n*

moot court *n* a mock court trying hypothetical legal cases.

mop[1] (mɒp) *n* **1** an implement with a wooden handle and a head made of twists of cotton or a piece of synthetic sponge, used for polishing or washing floors, or washing dishes. **2** something resembling this, such as a tangle of hair. ♦ *vb* **mops, mopping, mopped. 3** (*tr;* often foll. by *up*) to clean or soak up with or as if with a mop. ♦ See also **mop up. [C15** *mappe,* from earlier *mappel,* from Medieval Latin *mappula* cloth, from Latin *mappa* napkin**]**

mop[2] (mɒp) *Rare.* ♦ *vb* **mops, mopping, mopped. 1** (*intr*) to make a grimace or sad expression (esp. in the phrase **mop and mow**). ♦ *n* **2** such a face or expression. **[C16:** perhaps from Dutch *moppen* to pour; compare Dutch *mop* pug dog**]**

mop[3] (mɒp) *n* (in various parts of England) an annual fair at which formerly servants were hired. **[C17:** from the practice of servants carrying a mop, broom, or flail, etc., to signify the job sought**]**

mopani *or* **mopane** (mɒ'pɑːnɪ) *n* a leguminous tree, *Colophospermum* (or *Copaifera*) *mopane,* native to southern Africa, that is highly resistant to drought and produces very hard wood. Also called: **ironwood. [C19:** from Setswana (a Bantu language) *mo-pane***]**

mopani worm *n* an edible caterpillar that feeds on mopani leaves.

mopboard ('mɒpˌbɔːd) *n* a U.S. word for **skirting board.**

mope (məʊp) *vb* (*intr*) **1** to be gloomy or apathetic. **2** to move or act in an aimless way. ♦ *n* **3** a gloomy person. ♦ See also **mopes. [C16:** perhaps from obsolete *mope* fool and related to MOP[2]**]** ▸ **'moper** *n* ▸ **'mopy** *adj*

moped ('məʊpɛd) *n Brit.* a light motorcycle, not over 50cc. **[C20:** from MOTOR + PEDAL[1], originally equipped with auxiliary pedals**]**

mopes (məʊps) *pl n* **the.** low spirits.

mopoke ('məʊˌpəʊk) *n* **1** Also called (N.Z.): **ruru.** a small spotted owl, *Ninox novaeseelandiae,* of Australia and New Zealand. In Australia the tawny frogmouth, *Podargus strigoides,* is very often wrongly identified as the mopoke. **2** *Austral. and N.Z. slang.* a slow or lugubrious person. ♦ Also called: **morepork. [C19:** imitative of the bird's cry**]**

moppet ('mɒpɪt) *n* a less common word for **poppet** (sense 1). **[C17:** from obsolete *mop* rag doll; of obscure origin**]**

mop up *vb* (*tr, adv*) **1** to clean with a mop. **2** *Informal.* to complete (a task, etc.). **3** *Military.* to clear (remaining enemy forces) after a battle, as by killing, taking prisoner, etc. ♦ *n* **mop-up. 4** the act or an instance of mopping up.

moquette (mɒ'kɛt) *n* a thick velvety fabric used for carpets, upholstery, etc. **[C18:** from French; of uncertain origin**]**

mor (mɔː) *n* a layer of acidic humus formed in cool moist areas where decomposition is slow. Compare **mull**[4]. **[**Danish**]**

MOR *abbrev. for* middle-of-the-road: used esp. in radio programming.

Mor. *abbrev. for* Morocco.

mora ('mɔːrə) *n, pl* **-rae** (-riː) *or* **-ras.** *Prosody.* the quantity of a short syllable in verse represented by the breve (˘). **[C16:** from Latin: pause**]**

moraceous (mɔː'reɪʃəs) *adj* of, relating to, or belonging to the *Moraceae,* a mostly tropical and subtropical family of trees and shrubs, including fig, mulberry, breadfruit, and hop, many of which have latex in the stems and heads enclosed in a fleshy receptacle. **[C20:** via New Latin from Latin *morus* mulberry tree**]**

Moradabad (ˌmɔːrədə'bæd) *n* a city in N India, in N Uttar Pradesh. Pop.: 429 214 (1991).

moraine (mɒ'reɪn) *n* a mass of debris, carried by glaciers and forming ridges and mounds when deposited. **[C18:** from French, from Savoy dialect *morena,* of obscure origin**]** ▸ **mo'rainal** *or* **mo'rainic** *adj*

moral ('mɒrəl) *adj* **1** concerned with or relating to human behaviour, esp. the distinction between good and bad or right and wrong behaviour: *moral sense.* **2** adhering to conventionally accepted standards of conduct. **3** based on a sense of right and wrong according to conscience: *moral courage; moral law.* **4** having psychological rather than tangible effects: *moral support.* **5** having the effects but not the appearance of (victory or defeat): *a moral victory; a moral defeat.* **6** having a strong probability: *a moral certainty.* **7** *Law.* (of evidence, etc.) based on a knowledge of the tendencies of human nature. ♦ *n* **8** the lesson to be obtained from a fable or event: *point the moral.* **9** a concise truth; maxim. **10** (*pl*) principles of behaviour in accordance with standards of right and wrong. **[C14:** from Latin *mōrālis* relating to morals or customs, from *mōs* custom**]** ▸ **'morally** *adv*

morale (mɒ'rɑːl) *n* the degree of mental or moral confidence of a person or group; spirit of optimism. **[C18:** morals, from French, n use of MORAL (adj)**]**

moral hazard *n Insurance.* a risk incurred by an insurance company with respect to the possible lack of honesty or prudence among policyholders.

moralism ('mɒrəˌlɪzəm) *n* **1** the habit or practice of moralizing. **2** a moral saying. **3** the practice of moral principles without reference to religion.

moralist ('mɒrəlɪst) *n* **1** a person who seeks to regulate the morals of others or to imbue others with a sense of morality. **2** a person who lives in accordance with moral principles. **3** a philosopher who is concerned with casuistic discussions of right action, or who seeks a general characterization of right action, often contrasted with a moral philosopher whose concern is with general philosophical questions about ethics. ▸ ˌ**moral'istic** *adj* ▸ ˌ**moral'istically** *adv*

morality (mə'rælɪtɪ) *n, pl* **-ties. 1** the quality of being moral. **2** conformity, or degree of conformity, to conventional standards of moral conduct. **3** a system of moral principles. **4** an instruction or lesson in morals. **5** short for **morality play.**

morality play *n* a type of drama written between the 14th and 16th centuries concerned with the conflict between personified virtues and vices.

moralize *or* **moralise** ('mɒrəˌlaɪz) *vb* **1** (*intr*) to make moral pronouncements. **2** (*tr*) to interpret or explain in a moral sense. **3** (*tr*) to improve the morals of. ▸ ˌ**morali'zation** *or* ˌ**morali'sation** *n* ▸ **'moralˌizer** *or* **'moralˌiser** *n*

moral majority *n* a presumed majority of people believed to be in favour of a stricter code of public morals. **[C20:** after *Moral Majority,* a right-wing U.S. religious organization, based on SILENT MAJORITY**]**

moral philosophy *n* the branch of philosophy dealing with both argument about the content of morality and meta-ethical discussion of the nature of moral judgment, language, argument, and value.

Moral Rearmament *n* a worldwide movement for moral and spiritual renewal founded by Frank Buchman in 1938. Also called: **Buchmanism.** Former name: **Oxford Group.**

moral theology *n* the branch of theology dealing with ethics.

Morar ('mɔːrə) *n* **Loch.** a lake in W Scotland, in the SW Highlands: the deepest in Scotland. Length: 18 km (11 miles). Depth: 296 m (987 ft.).

morass (mə'ræs) *n* **1** a tract of swampy low-lying land. **2** a disordered or muddled situation or circumstance, esp. one that impedes progress. **[C17:** from Dutch *moeras,* ultimately from Old French *marais* MARSH**]**

moratorium (ˌmɒrə'tɔːrɪəm) *n, pl* **-ria** (-rɪə) *or* **-riums. 1** a legally authorized postponement of the fulfilment of an obligation. **2** an agreed suspension of activity. **[C19:** New Latin, from Late Latin *morātōrius* dilatory, from *mora* delay**]** ▸ **moratory** ('mɒrətərɪ, -trɪ) *adj*

Morava (mə'rɑːvə) *n* **1** a river in central Europe, rising in the Sudeten Mountains, in the Czech Republic, and flowing south through Slovakia to the Danube: forms part of the border between the Czech Republic, Slovakia, and Austria. Length: 370 km (230 miles). German name: **March. 2** a river in E Yugoslavia, formed by the confluence of the Southern Morava and the Western Morava near Stalac: flows north to the Danube. Length: 209 km (130 miles). **3** ('mɔrava). the Czech name for **Moravia**[1].

Moravia[1] (mə'reɪvɪə, mɒ-) *n* a region of the Czech Republic around the Morava River, bounded by the Bohemian-Moravian Highlands, the Sudeten Mountains, and the W Carpathians: became a separate Austrian crownland in 1848; part of Czechoslovakia 1918–92; valuable mineral resources. Czech name: **Morava.** German name: **Mähren.**

Moravia[2] (*Italian* mo'raːvja) *n* **Alberto** (al'bɛrto), pen name of *Alberto Pincherle.* 1907–90, Italian novelist and short-story writer: his works include *The Time of Indifference* (1929), *The Woman of Rome* (1949), *The Lie* (1966), and *Erotic Tales* (1985).

Moravian (mə'reɪvɪən, mɒ-) *adj* **1** of or relating to Moravia, its people, or their dialect of Czech. **2** of or relating to the Moravian Church. ♦ *n* **3** the Moravian dialect. **4** a native or inhabitant of Moravia. **5** a member of the Moravian Church. ► **Mo'ravianism** *n*

Moravian Church *n* a Protestant Church originating in Moravia in 1722 as a revival of the sect of Bohemian Brethren. It has close links with the Lutheran Church.

Moravian Gate *n* a low mountain pass linking S Poland and Moravia (the Czech Republic), between the SE Sudeten Mountains and the W Carpathian Mountains.

moray (mɒ'reɪ) *n, pl* **-rays.** any voracious marine coastal eel of the family *Muraenidae,* esp. *Muraena helena,* marked with brilliant patterns and colours. [C17: from Portuguese *moréia,* from Latin *mūrēna,* from Greek *muraina*]

Moray[1] ('mʌrɪ) *n* a council area and historical county of NE Scotland: part of Grampian region from 1975 to 1996: mainly hilly, with the Cairngorm mountains in the S. Administrative centre: Elgin. Pop.: 86 250 (1996 est.). Area: 2238 sq. km (874 sq. miles). Former name: **Elgin.**

Moray[2] *or* **Murray** ('mʌrɪ) *n* **1st Earl of,** title of *James Stuart.* ?1531–70, regent of Scotland (1567–70) following the abdication of Mary, Queen of Scots, his half-sister. He defeated Mary and Bothwell at Langside (1568); assassinated by a follower of Mary.

Moray Firth *n* an inlet of the North Sea on the NE coast of Scotland. Length: about 56 km (35 miles).

morbid ('mɔːbɪd) *adj* **1** having an unusual interest in death or unpleasant events. **2** gruesome. **3** relating to or characterized by disease; pathologic: *a morbid growth.* [C17: from Latin *morbidus* sickly, from *morbus* illness] ► **'morbidly** *adv* ► **'morbidness** *n*

morbid anatomy *n* the branch of medical science concerned with the study of the structure of diseased organs and tissues.

morbidity (mɔː'bɪdɪtɪ) *n* **1** the state of being morbid. **2** Also called: **morbidity rate.** the relative incidence of a particular disease in a specific locality.

morbific (mɔː'bɪfɪk) *adj* causing disease; pathogenic. ► **mor'bifically** *adv*

Morbihan (*French* mɔrbiɑ̃) *n* a department of NW France, in S Brittany. Capital: Vannes. Pop.: 633 000 (1995). Area: 7092 sq. km (2766 sq. miles).

morbilli (mɔː'bɪlaɪ) *n* a technical name for **measles.** [C17: from Medieval Latin *morbillus* pustule, diminutive of Latin *morbus* illness]

morceau *French.* (mɔrso) *n, pl* ***-ceaux*** (-so). **1** a fragment or morsel. **2** a short composition, esp. a musical one. [C18: from Old French: MORSEL]

morcha ('mɔːtʃɑː) *n* (in India) a hostile demonstration against the government. [Hindi: entrenchment]

mordacious (mɔː'deɪʃəs) *adj* sarcastic, caustic, or biting. [C17: from Latin *mordax,* from *mordēre* to bite] ► **mor'daciously** *adv* ► **mordacity** (mɔː'dæsɪtɪ) *or* **mor'daciousness** *n*

mordant ('mɔːdᵊnt) *adj* **1** sarcastic or caustic. **2** having the properties of a mordant. **3** pungent. ◆ *n* **4** a substance used before the application of a dye, possessing the ability to fix colours in textiles, leather, etc. See also **lake**[2] (sense 1). **5** an acid or other corrosive fluid used to etch lines on a printing plate. ◆ *vb* **6** (*tr*) to treat (a fabric, yarn, etc.) with a mordant. [C15: from Old French: biting, from *mordre* to bite, from Latin *mordēre*] ► **'mordancy** *n* ► **'mordantly** *adv*

Mordecai (ˌmɔːdə'kaɪ, 'mɔːdəˌkaɪ) *n Old Testament.* the cousin of Esther who averted a massacre of the Jews (Esther 2–9).

mordent ('mɔːdᵊnt) *n Music.* a melodic ornament consisting of the rapid alternation of a note with a note one degree lower than it. Also called: **lower mordent.** [C19: from German, from Italian *mordente,* from *mordere* to bite]

Mordred ('mɔːdrɛd) *n* a variant of **Modred.**

Mordvin ('mɔːdvɪn) *n* **1** (*pl* **-vin** *or* **-vins**) a member of a Finnish people of the middle Volga region, living chiefly in the Mordvinian Republic. **2** the language of this people, belonging to the Finno-Ugric family.

Mordvinian Republic (mɔː'dvɪnɪən) *n* a constituent republic of W central Russia, in the middle Volga basin. Capital: Saransk. Pop.: 960 000 (1995 est.). Area: 26 200 sq. km (10 110 sq. miles). Also called: **Mordovian Republic** (mɔː'dəʊvɪən), **Mordovia.**

more (mɔː) *determiner* **1a** the comparative of **much** or **many:** *more joy than you know; more pork sausages.* **1b** (*as pronoun; functioning as sing or pl*): *he has more than she has; even more are dying every day.* **2a** additional; further: *no more bananas.* **2b** (*as pronoun; functioning as sing or pl*): *I can't take any more; more than expected.* **3 more of.** to a greater extent or degree: *we see more of Sue these days; more of a nuisance than it should be.* ◆ *adv* **4** used to form the comparative of some adjectives and adverbs: *a more believable story; more quickly.* **5** the comparative of **much:** *people listen to the radio more now.* **6** additionally; again: *I'll look at it once more.* **7 more or less. 7a** as an estimate; approximately. **7b** to an unspecified extent or degree: *the party was ruined, more or less.* **8 more so.** to a greater extent or degree. **9 neither more nor less than.** simply. **10 think more of.** to have a higher opinion of. **11 what is more.** moreover. [Old English *māra;* compare Old Saxon, Old High German *mēro,* Gothic *maiza.* See also MOST]

USAGE See at **most.**

More (mɔː) *n* **1 Hannah.** 1745–1833, English writer, noted for her religious tracts, esp. *The Shepherd of Salisbury Plain.* **2** Sir **Thomas.** 1478–1535, English statesman, humanist, and Roman Catholic Saint; Lord Chancellor to Henry VIII (1529–32). His opposition to the annulment of Henry's marriage to Catherine of Aragon and his refusal to recognize the Act of Supremacy resulted in his execution on a charge of treason. In *Utopia* (1516) he set forth his concept of the ideal state. Feast day: June 22 or July 6.

Morea (mɔː'rɪə) *n* the medieval name for the **Peloponnese.**

Moreau (*French* mɔro) *n* **1 Gustave** (gystav) 1826–98, French symbolist painter. **2 Jean Victor** (ʒɑ̃ viktɔr). 1763–1813, French general in the Revolutionary and Napoleonic Wars. **3 Jeanne** (ʒan). born 1928, French stage and film actress. Her films include *Jules et Jim* (1961) and *Viva Maria* (1965).

Morecambe[1] ('mɔːkəm) *n* a port and resort in NW England, in NW Lancashire on **Morecambe Bay** (an inlet of the Irish Sea). Pop. (with Heysham): 46 657 (1991).

Morecambe[2] ('mɔːkəm) *n* **Eric,** real name *John Eric Bartholomew.* 1926–84, British comedian and actor, noted esp. for his comedy partnership (from 1941) with Ernie Wise (real name Ernest Wiseman, 1925–99).

moreen (mɒ'riːn) *n* a heavy, usually watered, fabric of wool or wool and cotton, used esp. in furnishing. [C17: perhaps from MOIRE, influenced by VELVETEEN]

moreish *or* **morish** ('mɔːrɪʃ) *adj Informal.* (of food) causing a desire for more: *these cakes are very moreish.*

morel (mɒ'rɛl) *n* any edible saprotrophic ascomycetous fungus of the genus *Morchella,* in which the mushroom has a pitted cap: order *Pezizales.* [C17: from French *morille,* probably of Germanic origin; compare Old High German *morhila,* diminutive of *morha* carrot]

Morelia (*Spanish* mo'relia) *n* a city in central Mexico, capital of Michoacán state: a cultural centre during colonial times; two universities. Pop.: 428 486 (1990). Former name (until 1828): **Valladolid.**

morello (mə'rɛləʊ) *n, pl* **-los.** a variety of small very dark sour cherry, *Prunus cerasus austera.* [C17: perhaps from Medieval Latin *amārellum* diminutive of Latin *amārus* bitter, but also influenced by Italian *morello* blackish]

Morelos (*Spanish* mo'relɔs) *n* an inland state of S central Mexico, on the S slope of the great plateau. Capital: Cuernavaca. Pop.: 1 442 587 (1995 est.). Area: 4988 sq. km (1926 sq. miles).

moreover (mɔː'rəʊvə) *sentence connector.* in addition to what has already been said; furthermore.

morepork ('mɔːˌpɔːk) *n* another name (esp. N.Z.) for **mopoke.**

mores ('mɔːreɪz) *pl n Sociol.* the customs and conventions embodying the fundamental values of a group or society. [C20: from Latin, plural of *mōs* custom]

Moresco (mə'rɛskəʊ) *n, adj* a variant of **Morisco.**

Moresque (mɔː'rɛsk) *adj* **1** (esp. of decoration and architecture) of Moorish style. ◆ *n* **2a** Moorish design or decoration. **2b** a specimen of this. [C17: from French, from Italian *moresco,* from *Moro* MOOR]

Moreton Bay bug ('mɔːtᵊn) *n* a flattish edible shellfish, *Thenus orientalis,* of Northern Australian waters. [named after *Moreton Bay,* Queensland, Australia]

Moreton Bay fig ('mɔːtᵊn) *n* a large Australian fig tree, *Ficus macrophilla,* having glossy leaves and smooth bark. [named after *Moreton Bay,* Queensland, Australia]

Morgan[1] ('mɔːgən) *n* an American breed of small compact saddle horse. [C19: named after Justin *Morgan* (1747–98), American owner of the original sire]

Morgan[2] ('mɔːgən) *n* **1** Sir **Henry.** 1635–88, Welsh buccaneer, who raided Spanish colonies in the West Indies for the English. **2 John Pierpont.** 1837–1913, U.S. financier, philanthropist, and art collector. **3 Thomas Hunt.** 1866–1945, U.S. biologist. He formulated the chromosome theory of heredity. Nobel prize for physiology or medicine 1933.

morganatic (ˌmɔːgə'nætɪk) *adj* of or designating a marriage between a person of high rank and a person of low rank, by which the latter is not elevated to the higher rank and any issue have no rights to the succession of the higher party's titles, property, etc. [C18: from the Medieval Latin phrase *mātrimōnium ad morganāticum* marriage based on the morning-gift (a token present after consummation representing the husband's only liability); *morganātica,* ultimately from Old High German *morgan* morning; compare Old English *morgengiefu* morning-gift] ► **ˌmorga'natically** *adv*

morganite ('mɔːgəˌnaɪt) *n* a pink variety of beryl, used as a gemstone. [C20: named after J. P. MORGAN]

Morgan le Fay ('mɔːgən lə 'feɪ) *or* **Morgain le Fay** ('mɔːgaɪn, -gən) *n* a wicked sorceress of Arthurian legend, the half-sister of King Arthur.

morgen ('mɔːgən) *n* **1** a South African unit of area, equal to about two acres or 0.8 hectare. **2** a unit of area, formerly used in Prussia and Scandinavia, equal to about two thirds of an acre. [C17: from Dutch: morning, a morning's ploughing]

morgue (mɔːg) *n* **1** another word for **mortuary** (sense 1). **2** *Informal.* a room or file containing clippings, files, etc., used for reference in a newspaper. [C19: from French *le Morgue,* a Paris mortuary]

morgue *French.* (mɔrg) *n* superiority; haughtiness.

MORI ('mɔːrɪ) *n acronym for* Market and Opinion Research Institute: *a MORI poll.*

moribund ('mɒrɪˌbʌnd) *adj* **1** near death. **2** stagnant; without force or vitality. [C18: from Latin, from *morī* to die] ► **ˌmori'bundity** *n* ► **'moriˌbundly** *adv*

Mörike (*German* 'mœːrɪkə) *n* **Eduard** ('eːduart). 1804–75, German poet, noted for his lyrics, such as *On a Winter's Morning before Sunrise* and *At Midnight.*

morion[1] ('mɔːrɪən) *n* a 16th-century helmet with a brim and wide comb. [C16: via Old French from Spanish *morrión,* perhaps from *morra* crown of the head]

morion[2] ('mɔːrɪən) *n* a smoky brown, grey, or blackish variety of quartz, used as a gemstone. [C18: via French from Latin *mōrion,* a misreading of *mormorion*]

Moriori (ˌmɒrɪ'ɔːrɪ) *n* **1** a Polynesian people of New Zealand, esp. of the Chatham Islands, closely related to the mainland Maori: now racially intermixed. **2** (*pl* **-ri** *or* **-ris**) a member of this people. **3** the language of the Moriori, belonging to the Malayo-Polynesian family. ◆ *adj* **4** of or relating to the Moriori or their language.

Morisco (mə'rɪskəʊ) *or* **Moresco** (mə'rɛskəʊ) *n, pl* **-cos** *or* **-coes. 1** a Spanish Moor. **2** a morris dance. ◆ *adj* **3** another word for **Moorish.** [C16: from Spanish, from *Moro* MOOR]

morish ('mɔːrɪʃ) *adj* a variant spelling of **moreish.**

Morisot (*French* morizo) *n* **Berthe** (bertə). 1841–95, French impressionist painter; noted for her studies of women and children.

Morley[1] ('mɔːlɪ) *n* an industrial town in N England, in Leeds unitary authority, West Yorkshire. Pop.: 47 579 (1991).

Morley[2] ('mɔːlɪ) *n* **1 Edward Williams.** 1838–1923, U.S. chemist who collaborated with A. A. Michelson in the Michelson-Morley experiment. **2 John,** Viscount Morley of Blackburn. 1838–1923, British Liberal statesman and writer; secretary of state for India (1905–10). **3 Robert.** 1908–92, British actor. His many films include *Major Barbara* (1940), *Oscar Wilde* (1960), and *The Blue Bird* (1976). **4 Thomas.** ?1557–?1603, English composer and organist, noted for his madrigals and his textbook on music, *A Plaine and Easie Introduction to Practicall Musicke* (1597).

Mormon ('mɔːmən) *n* **1** a member of the Church of Jesus Christ of Latter-day Saints, founded in 1830 at La Fayette, New York, by Joseph Smith. **2** a prophet whose supposed revelations were recorded by Joseph Smith in the Book of Mormon. ◆ *adj* **3** of or relating to the Mormons, their Church, or their beliefs. ▸ **'Mormonism** *n*

morn (mɔːn) *n* **1** a poetic word for **morning. 2 the morn.** *Scot.* tomorrow. **3 the morn's nicht.** *Scot.* tomorrow night. [Old English *morgen;* compare Old High German *morgan,* Old Norse *morginn*]

mornay ('mɔːneɪ) *adj* (*often immediately postpositive*) denoting a cheese sauce used in several dishes: *eggs mornay.* [perhaps named after Philippe de MORNAY]

Mornay (*French* mɔrnɛ) *n* **Philippe de** (filip də), Seigneur du Plessis-Marly. 1549–1623, French Huguenot leader. Also called: **Duplessis-Mornay.**

morning ('mɔːnɪŋ) *n* **1** the first part of the day, ending at or around noon. **2** sunrise; daybreak; dawn. **3** the beginning or early period: *the morning of the world.* **4 the morning after.** *Informal.* the aftereffects of excess, esp. a hangover. **5** (*modifier*) of, used, or occurring in the morning: *morning coffee.* ◆ See also **mornings.** [C13 *morwening,* from MORN, formed on the model of EVENING]

morning-after pill *n* an oral contraceptive that is effective if taken some hours after intercourse.

morning coat *n* a cutaway frock coat, part of morning dress. Also called: **tail coat, swallow-tailed coat.**

morning dress *n* formal day dress for men, comprising a morning coat, usually with grey trousers and top hat.

morning-glory *n, pl* **-ries.** any of various mainly tropical convolvulaceous plants of the genus *Ipomoea* and related genera, with trumpet-shaped blue, pink, or white flowers, which close in late afternoon.

mornings ('mɔːnɪŋz) *adv Informal.* in the morning, esp. regularly, or during every morning.

morning sickness *n* nausea occurring shortly after rising: an early symptom of pregnancy.

morning star *n* a planet, usually Venus, seen just before sunrise during the time that the planet is west of the sun. Also called: **daystar.** Compare **evening star.**

morning tea *n Austral. and N.Z.* a mid-morning snack with a cup of tea. Brit. equivalent: **elevenses.**

morning watch *n Nautical.* the watch between 4 and 8 a.m.

Moro[1] ('mɔːrəʊ) *n* **1** (*pl* **-ros** *or* **-ro**) a member of a group of predominantly Muslim peoples of the S Philippines: noted for their manufacture of weapons. **2** the language of these peoples, belonging to the Malayo-Polynesian family. [C19: via Spanish from Latin *Maurus* MOOR]

Moro[2] (*Italian* 'mɔːro) *n* **Aldo** ('aldo). 1916–78, Italian Christian Democrat statesman; prime minister of Italy (1963–68; 1974–76) and minister of foreign affairs (1965–66; 1969–72; 1973–74). He negotiated the entry of the Italian Communist Party into coalition government before being kidnapped by the Red Brigades in 1978 and murdered.

morocco (mə'rɒkəʊ) *n* **a** a fine soft leather made from goatskins, used for bookbinding, shoes, etc. **b** (*as modifier*): *morocco leather.* [C17: after MOROCCO, where it was originally made]

Morocco (mə'rɒkəʊ) *n* a kingdom in NW Africa, on the Mediterranean and the Atlantic: conquered by the Arabs in about 683, who introduced Islam; at its height under Berber dynasties (11th–13th centuries); became a French protectorate in 1912 and gained independence in 1956. It is mostly mountainous, with the Atlas Mountains in the centre and the Rif range along the Mediterranean coast, with the Sahara in the south and southeast; an important exporter of phosphates. Official language: Arabic; Berber and French are also widely spoken. Official religion: (Sunni) Muslim. Currency: dirham. Capital: Rabat. Pop.: 27 772 000 (1998 est.). Area: 458 730 sq. km (177 117 sq. miles). French name: **Maroc.** ▸ **Moroccan** (mə'rɒkən) *adj, n*

moron ('mɔːrɒn) *n* **1** a foolish or stupid person. **2** a person having an intelligence quotient of between 50 and 70, able to work under supervision. [C20: from Greek *mōros* foolish] ▸ **moronic** (mɒ'rɒnɪk) *adj* ▸ **mo'ronically** *adv* ▸ **'moronism** *or* **mo'ronity** *n*

Moroni (mə'rəʊnɪ; *French* mɔrɔni) *n* the capital of Comoros, on the island of Njazídja (Grande Comore). Pop.: 30 000 (1991).

morose (mə'rəʊs) *adj* ill-tempered or gloomy. [C16: from Latin *mōrōsus* peevish, capricious, from *mōs* custom, will, caprice] ▸ **mo'rosely** *adv* ▸ **mo'roseness** *n*

Morpeth ('mɔːpəθ) *n* a town in NE England, the administrative centre of Northumberland. Pop.: 14 393 (1991).

morph[1] (mɔːf) *n Linguistics.* the phonological representation of a morpheme. [C20: shortened form of MORPHEME]

morph[2] (mɔːf) *n Biology.* any of the different forms of individual found in a polymorphic species. [C20: from Greek *morphē* shape]

morph[3] (mɔːf) *vb* **1** to cause or undergo morphing. ◆ *n* **2** a morphed image.

morph. *or* **morphol.** *abbrev. for:* **1** morphological. **2** morphology.

-morph *n combining form.* indicating shape, form, or structure of a specified kind: *ectomorph.* [from Greek *-morphos,* from *morphē* shape] ▸ **-morphic** *or* **-morphous** *adj combining form.* ▸ **-morphy** *n combining form.*

morphallaxis (ˌmɔːfə'læksɪs) *n, pl* **-laxes** (-'læksiːz). *Zoology.* the transformation of one part into another that sometimes occurs during regeneration of organs in certain animals. [C20: New Latin, from MORPHO- + Greek *allaxis* exchange, from *allassein* to exchange, from *allos* other]

morpheme ('mɔːfiːm) *n Linguistics.* a speech element having a meaning or grammatical function that cannot be subdivided into further such elements. [C20: from French, from Greek *morphē* form, coined on the model of PHONEME; see -EME] ▸ **mor'phemic** *adj* ▸ **mor'phemically** *adv*

Morpheus ('mɔːfɪəs, -fjuːs) *n Greek myth.* the god of sleep and dreams. ▸ **'Morphean** *adj*

morphine ('mɔːfiːn) *or* **morphia** ('mɔːfɪə) *n* an alkaloid extracted from opium: used in medicine as an anaesthetic and sedative although repeated use causes addiction. Formula: $C_{17}H_{19}NO_3$. [C19: from French, from MORPHEUS]

morphing ('mɔːfɪŋ) *n* a computer technique used for graphics and in films, in which one image is gradually transformed into another image without individual changes being noticeable in the process. [C20: from METAMORPHOSIS]

morphinism ('mɔːfɪˌnɪzəm) *n* morphine addiction.

morpho- *or before a vowel* **morph-** *combining form.* **1** indicating form or structure: *morphology.* **2** morpheme: *morphophonemics.* [from Greek *morphē* form, shape]

morphogenesis (ˌmɔːfəʊ'dʒɛnɪsɪs) *n* **1** the development of form and structure in an organism during its growth from embryo to adult. **2** the evolutionary development of form in an organism or part of an organism. ▸ **morphogenetic** (ˌmɔːfəʊdʒɪ'nɛtɪk) *or* ˌ**morpho'genic** *adj*

morphology (mɔː'fɒlədʒɪ) *n* **1** the branch of biology concerned with the form and structure of organisms. **2** the form and structure of words in a language, esp. the consistent patterns of inflection, combination, derivation and change, etc., that may be observed and classified. **3** the form and structure of anything. ▸ **morphologic** (ˌmɔːfə'lɒdʒɪk) *or* ˌ**morpho'logical** *adj* ▸ ˌ**morpho'logically** *adv* ▸ **mor'phologist** *n*

morphophoneme (ˌmɔːfəʊ'fəʊniːm) *n Linguistics.* the set of phonemes or sequences of phonemes that constitute the various allomorphs of a morpheme. [C20: from MORPHEME + PHONEME]

morphophonemics (ˌmɔːfəʊfəʊ'niːmɪks) *n* (*functioning as sing*) *Linguistics.* the study of the phonemic realization of the allomorphs of the morphemes of a language. ▸ ˌ**morphophonemic** *adj*

morphosis (mɔː'fəʊsɪs) *n, pl* **-ses** (-siːz). *Biology.* development in an organism or its parts characterized by structural change. [C17: via New Latin from Greek, from *morphoun* to form, from *morphē* form] ▸ **morphotic** (mɔː'fɒtɪk) *adj*

Morphy ('mɔːfɪ) *n* **Paul.** 1837–84, U.S. chess player, widely considered to have been the world's greatest player.

morrell (mə'rel) *n* a tall eucalyptus, *Eucalyptus longicornis,* of SW Australia, having pointed buds. [from a native Australian language]

Morris ('mɒrɪs) *n* **William.** 1834–96, English poet, designer, craftsman, and socialist writer. He founded the Kelmscott Press (1890).

Morris chair *n* an armchair with an adjustable back and large cushions. [C19: named after William MORRIS]

morris dance *n* any of various old English folk dances usually performed by men (**morris men**) to the accompaniment of violin, concertina, etc. The dancers are adorned with bells and often represent characters from folk tales. Often shortened to **morris.** [C15 *moreys daunce* Moorish dance. See MOOR] ▸ **morris dancing** *n*

Morrison ('mɒrɪsᵊn) *n* **1 Herbert Stanley,** Baron Morrison of Lambeth. 1888–1965, British Labour statesman, Home Secretary and Minister for Home Security in Churchill's War Cabinet (1942–45). **2 Jim,** full name *James Douglas Morrison.* 1943–71, U.S. rock singer and songwriter, lead vocalist with the Doors. **3 Toni,** full name *Chloe Anthony Morrison.* born 1931, U.S. novelist, whose works include *Sula* (1974), *Song of Solomon* (1977), *Beloved* (1987), *Jazz* (1992), and *Paradise* (1998): awarded the Nobel Prize for literature in 1993. **4 Van,** full name *George Ivan Morrison.* born 1945, Northern Irish rock singer and songwriter. His albums include *Astral Weeks* (1968), *Moondance* (1970), and *Too Long in Exile* (1993).

morro ('mɒrəʊ; *Spanish* 'morro) *n, pl* **-ros** (-rəʊz; *Spanish* -ros). a rounded hill or promontory. [from Spanish]

morrow ('mɒrəʊ) *n* (usually preceded by *the*) *Archaic or poetic.* **1** the next day. **2** the period following a specified event. **3** the morning. [C13 *morwe,* from Old English *morgen* morning; see MORN]

Mors (mɔːz) *n* the Roman god of death. Greek counterpart: **Thanatos.**

morse (mɔːs) *n* a clasp or fastening on a cope. [C15: from Old French *mors,* from Latin *morsus* clasp, bite, from *mordēre* to bite]

Morse (mɔːs) *n* **Samuel Finley Breese** ('fɪnlɪ briːz). 1791–1872, U.S. inventor and painter. He invented the first electric telegraph and the Morse code.

Morse code *n* a telegraph code formerly used internationally for transmitting messages; it was superseded by satellite technology in 1999. Letters, numbers, etc., are represented by groups of shorter dots and longer dashes, or by groups of the corresponding sounds, *dits* and *dahs,* the groups being separated by spaces. Also called: **international Morse code.** [C19: named after Samuel MORSE]

morsel ('mɔːsᵊl) *n* **1** a small slice or mouthful of food. **2** a small piece; bit. **3** *Irish informal.* a term of endearment for a child. [C13: from Old French, from *mors* a bite, from Latin *morsus,* from *mordēre* to bite]

Morse taper *n Trademark, engineering.* a taper that is one of a standard series used in the shank of tools to fit a matching taper in the mandrel of a machine tool. [probably named after the *Morse* Twist Drill Co., Massachusetts, U.S.]

mort[1] (mɔːt) *n* a call blown on a hunting horn to signify the death of the animal hunted. [C16: via Old French from Latin *mors* death]

mort[2] (mɔːt) *n* a great deal; a great many. [possibly a shortened form of MORTAL used as an intensifier]

mortal ('mɔːtᵊl) *adj* **1** (of living beings, esp. human beings) subject to death. **2** of or involving life or the world. **3** ending in or causing death; fatal: *a mortal blow.* **4** deadly or unrelenting: *a mortal enemy.* **5** of or like the fear of death; dire: *mortal terror.* **6** great or very intense: *mortal pain.* **7** possible: *there was no mortal reason to go.* **8** *Slang.* long and tedious: *for three mortal hours.* ◆ *n* **9** a mortal being. **10** *Informal.* a person: *a mean mortal.* [C14: from Latin *mortālis,* from *mors* death] ▸ **'mortally** *adv*

mortality (mɔː'tælɪtɪ) *n, pl* **-ties. 1** the condition of being mortal. **2** great loss of life, as in war or disaster. **3** the number of deaths in a given period. **4** mankind; humanity. **5** an obsolete word for **death.**

mortality rate *n* another term for **death rate.**

mortality table *n Insurance.* an actuarial table indicating life expectancy and death frequency for a given age, occupation, etc.

mortal sin *n Christianity.* a sin regarded as involving total loss of grace. Compare **venial sin.**

mortar ('mɔːtə) *n* **1** a mixture of cement or lime or both with sand and water, used as a bond between bricks or stones or as a covering on a wall. **2** a muzzle-loading cannon having a short barrel and relatively wide bore that fires low-velocity shells in high trajectories over a short range. **3** a similar device for firing lifelines, fireworks, etc. **4** a vessel, usually bowl-shaped, in which substances are pulverized with a pestle. **5** *Mining.* a cast-iron receptacle in which ore is crushed. ◆ *vb (tr)* **6** to join (bricks or stones) or cover (a wall) with mortar. **7** to fire on with mortars. [C13: from Latin *mortārium* basin in which mortar is mixed; in some senses, via Old French *mortier* substance mixed inside such a vessel]

mortarboard ('mɔːtə,bɔːd) *n* **1** a black tasselled academic cap with a flat square top covered with cloth. **2** Also called: **hawk.** a small square board with a handle on the underside for carrying mortar.

mortgage ('mɔːgɪdʒ) *n* **1** an agreement under which a person borrows money to buy property, esp. a house, and the lender may take possession of the property if the borrower fails to repay the money. **2** the deed effecting such an agreement. **3** the loan obtained under such an agreement: *a mortgage of £48000.* **4** a regular payment of money borrowed under such an agreement: *a mortgage of £247 per month.* ◆ *vb (tr)* **5** to pledge (a house or other property) as security for the repayment of a loan. ◆ *adj* **6** of or relating to a mortgage: *a mortgage payment.* [C14: from Old French, literally: dead pledge, from *mort* dead + *gage* security, GAGE[1]] ▸ **'mortgageable** *adj*

mortgagee (,mɔːgɪ'dʒiː) *n Law.* **1** the party to a mortgage who makes the loan. **2** a person who holds mortgaged property as security for repayment of a loan.

mortgage rate *n* the level of interest charged by building societies and banks on house-purchase loans.

mortgagor ('mɔːgɪdʒə, ,mɔːgɪ'dʒɔː) *or* **mortgager** *n Property law.* a person who borrows money by mortgaging his property to the lender as security.

mortician (mɔː'tɪʃən) *n Chiefly U.S.* another word for **undertaker.** [C19: from MORTUARY + *-ician,* as in *physician*]

mortification (,mɔːtɪfɪ'keɪʃən) *n* **1** a feeling of loss of prestige or self-respect; humiliation. **2** something causing this. **3** *Christianity.* the practice of mortifying the senses. **4** another word for **gangrene.**

mortify ('mɔːtɪ,faɪ) *vb* **-fies, -fying, -fied. 1** *(tr)* to humiliate or cause to feel shame. **2** *(tr) Christianity.* to subdue and bring under control by self-denial, disciplinary exercises, etc. **3** *(intr)* to undergo tissue death or become gangrenous. [C14: via Old French from Church Latin *mortificāre* to put to death, from Latin *mors* death + *facere* to do] ▸ **'morti,fier** *n* ▸ **'morti,fying** *adj* ▸ **'morti,fyingly** *adv*

Mortimer ('mɔːtɪmə) *n* **1** Sir **John (Clifford).** born 1923, British barrister, playwright, and novelist, best known for the television series featuring the barrister Horace Rumpole. His novels include *Paradise Postponed* (1985) and *The Sound of Trumpets* (1998). **2 Roger de,** 8th Baron of Wigmore and 1st Earl of March. 1287–1330, lover of Isabella, the wife of Edward II of England: they invaded England in 1326 and compelled the king to abdicate in favour of his son, Edward III; executed.

mortise *or* **mortice** ('mɔːtɪs) *n* **1** a slot or recess, usually rectangular, cut into a piece of wood, stone, etc., to receive a matching projection (tenon) of another piece, or a mortise lock. **2** *Printing.* a cavity cut into a letterpress printing plate into which type or another plate is inserted. ◆ *vb (tr)* **3** to cut a slot or recess in (a piece of wood, stone, etc.). **4** to join (two pieces of wood, stone, etc.) by means of a mortise and tenon. **5** to cut a cavity in (a letterpress printing plate) for the insertion of type, etc. [C14: from Old French *mortoise,* perhaps from Arabic *murtazza* fastened in position] ▸ **'mortiser** *n*

mortise lock *n* a lock set into a mortise in a door so that the mechanism of the lock is enclosed by the door.

mortmain ('mɔːt,meɪn) *n Law.* the state or condition of lands, buildings, etc., held inalienably, as by an ecclesiastical or other corporation. [C15: from Old French *mortemain,* from Medieval Latin *mortua manus* dead hand, inalienable ownership]

Morton ('mɔːtᵊn) *n* **1 4th Earl of,** title of *James Douglas.* 1516–81, regent of Scotland (1572–78) for the young James VI. He was implicated in the murders of Rizzio (1566) and Darnley (1567) and played a leading role in ousting Mary, Queen of Scots; executed. **2 Jelly Roll,** real name *Ferdinand Joseph La Menthe Morton.* 1885–1941, U.S. jazz pianist, singer, and songwriter; one of the creators of New Orleans jazz.

mortuary ('mɔːtʃʊərɪ) *n, pl* **-aries. 1** Also called: **morgue.** a building where dead bodies are kept before cremation or burial. ◆ *adj* **2** of or relating to death or burial. [C14 (as n, a funeral gift to a parish priest): via Medieval Latin *mortuārium* (n) from Latin *mortuārius* of the dead]

morula ('mɒrjʊlə) *n, pl* **-las** *or* **-lae** (-,liː). *Embryol.* a solid ball of cells resulting from cleavage of a fertilized ovum. [C19: via New Latin, diminutive of Latin *morum* mulberry, from Greek *moron*] ▸ **'morular** *adj*

morwong ('mɔː,wɒŋ) *n* a food fish of Australasian coastal waters belonging to the genus *Cheilodactylos:* family *Cirrhitidae* (or *Cheilodactylidae*). [from a native Australian language]

moryah (mɒr'jæ) *interj Irish.* an exclamation of annoyance, disbelief, etc. [from Irish Gaelic *Mar dhea* forsooth]

MOS *Electronics. abbrev. for* metal oxide silicon.

mos. *abbrev. for* months.

mosaic (mə'zeɪɪk) *n* **1** a design or decoration made up of small pieces of coloured glass, stone, etc. **2** the process of making a mosaic. **3a** a mottled yellowing that occurs in the leaves of plants affected with any of various virus diseases. **3b** Also called: **mosaic disease.** any of the diseases, such as **tobacco mosaic,** that produce this discoloration. **4** *Genetics.* another name for **chimera** (sense 4). **5** an assembly of aerial photographs forming a composite picture of a large area on the ground. **6** a light-sensitive surface on a television camera tube, consisting of a large number of granules of photoemissive material deposited on an insulating medium. [C16: via French and Italian from Medieval Latin *mōsaicus,* from Late Greek *mouseion* mosaic work, from Greek *mouseios* of the Muses, from *mousa* MUSE] ▸ **mosaicist** (mə'zeɪɪsɪst) *n*

Mosaic (məʊ'zeɪɪk) *or* **Mosaical** *adj* of or relating to Moses or the laws and traditions ascribed to him.

mosaic disease *n* a serious viral disease of plants, esp. tobacco, maize, and sugar cane, in which the leaves become mottled by discoloration.

mosaic gold (mə'zeɪɪk) *n* stannic sulphide, esp. when suspended in lacquer for use in gilding surfaces.

Mosaic law (məʊ'zeɪɪk) *n Old Testament.* the laws of the Hebrews ascribed to Moses and contained in the Pentateuch.

mosasaur ('məʊsə,sɔː) *or* **mosasaurus** (,məʊsə'sɔːrəs) *n, pl* **-saurs** *or* **-sauri** (-'sɔːraɪ). any of various extinct Cretaceous giant marine lizards of the genus *Mosasaurus* and related genera, typically having paddle-like limbs. [C18: from Latin *Mosa* the river MEUSE (near which remains were first found) + -SAUR]

moschatel (,mɒskə'tel) *n* a small N temperate plant, *Adoxa moschatellina,* with greenish-white musk-scented flowers: family *Adoxaceae.* Also called: **townhall clock, five-faced bishop.** [C18: via French from Italian *moscatella,* diminutive of *moscato* MUSK]

Moscow ('mɒskəʊ) *n* the capital of Russia and of the Moscow Autonomous Region, on the Moskva River: dates from the 11th century; capital of the grand duchy of Russia from 1547 to 1712; capital of the Soviet Union 1918–91; centres on the medieval Kremlin; chief political, cultural, and industrial centre of Russia, with two universities. Pop.: 8 717 000 (1995 est.). Russian name: **Moskva.** Related noun: **Muscovite.**

Moseley ('məʊzlɪ) *n* **Henry Gwyn-Jeffreys.** 1887–1915, English physicist. He showed that the wavelengths of X-rays emitted from the elements are related to their atomic numbers.

Moselle (məʊ'zel) *n* **1** a department of NE France, in Lorraine region. Capital: Metz. Pop.: 1 015 900 (1995). Area: 6253 sq. km (2439 sq. miles). **2** a river in W Europe, rising in NE France and flowing northwest, forming part of the border between Luxembourg and Germany, then northeast to the Rhine: many vineyards along its lower course. Length: 547 km (340 miles). German name: **Mosel** ('moːzᵊl). **3** *(sometimes not cap.)* a German white wine from the Moselle valley.

Moses ('məʊzɪz) *n* **1** *Old Testament.* the Hebrew prophet who led the Israelites out of Egypt to the Promised Land and gave them divinely revealed laws. **2 Ed.** born 1956, U.S. hurdler; winner of the 400 m hurdles in the 1976 and 1984 Olympic Games. **3 Grandma,** real name *Anna Mary Robertson Moses.* 1860–1961, U.S. painter of primitives, who began to paint at the age of 75.

Moses basket *n* a portable cradle for a baby, often made of straw or wicker. [C20: from Moses being left in a cradle of bulrushes (Exodus 2:3)]

mosey ('məʊzɪ) *vb (intr) Informal.* (often foll. by *along* or *on*) to walk in a leisurely manner; amble. [C19: origin unknown]

MOSFET ('mɒsfet) *n Electronics.* metal-oxide-silicon field-effect transistor; a type of IGFET.

mosh (mɒʃ) *n* **1** a type of dance, performed to loud rock music, in which people throw themselves about in a frantic and violent manner. ◆ *vb* **2** *(intr)* to dance in this manner. [C20: of uncertain origin]

moshav *Hebrew.* (mɔ'ʃav) *n, pl* **-shavim** (-ʃa'vim). a cooperative settlement in Israel, consisting of a number of small farms. [C20: from Hebrew *mōshābh* a dwelling]

Moshesh (mɒ'ʃeʃ) *or* **Moshoeshoe** (mɒ'ʃuʃu) *n* died 1870, African chief, who founded the Basotho nation, now Lesotho.

mosh pit *n Informal.* an area at a rock-music concert, usually in front of the stage, where members of the audience dance in a frantic and violent manner.

Moskva (*Russian* mas'kva) *n* **1** transliteration of the Russian name for **Moscow. 2** a river in W central Russia, rising in the Smolensk-Moscow upland, and flowing southeast through Moscow to the Oka River: linked with the River Volga by the Moscow Canal. Length: about 500 km (310 miles).

Moslem ('mɒzləm) *n, pl* **-lems** *or* **-lem,** *adj* a variant of **Muslim.** ▸ **Moslemic** (mɒz'lemɪk) *adj* ▸ **'Moslemism** *n*

Mosley ('məʊzlɪ) *n* Sir **Oswald Ernald.** 1896–1980, British politician; founder of the British Union of Fascists (1932).

Mosotho (mʊ'suːtuː) *n, pl* **-tho** *or* **-thos.** a member of the Basotho people. Former name: **Basuto.**

mosque (mɒsk) *n* a Muslim place of worship, usually having one or more minarets and often decorated with elaborate tracery and texts from the Koran. Also called: **masjid, musjid.** [C14: earlier *mosquee,* from Old French via Italian *moschea,* ultimately from Arabic *masjid* temple, place of prostration]

mosquito (məˈskiːtəʊ) *n, pl* **-toes** *or* **-tos.** any dipterous insect of the family *Culicidae:* the females have a long proboscis adapted for piercing the skin of man and animals to suck their blood. See also **aedes, anopheles, culex.** [C16: from Spanish, diminutive of *mosca* fly, from Latin *musca*]

mosquito boat *n* another name for **MTB.**

mosquito hawk *n* another name for **nighthawk** (sense 1).

mosquito net *or* **netting** *n* a fine curtain or net put in windows, around beds, etc., to keep mosquitoes out.

moss (mɒs) *n* **1** any bryophyte of the class *Musci,* typically growing in dense mats on trees, rocks, moist ground, etc. See also **peat moss. 2** a clump or growth of any of these plants. **3** any of various similar but unrelated plants, such as club moss, Spanish moss, Ceylon moss, rose moss, and reindeer moss. **4** *Scot. and northern English.* a peat bog or marsh. [Old English *mos* swamp; compare Middle Dutch, Old High German *mos* bog, Old Norse *mosi;* compare also Old Norse *mȳrr* MIRE] ▸ **ˈmossˌlike** *adj* ▸ **ˈmossy** *adj* ▸ **ˈmossiness** *n*

Moss (mɒs) *n* **Stirling.** born 1929, English racing driver.

Mossad (ˈmɒsæd) *n* the secret intelligence service of Israel. [C20: Hebrew *Mosad LeModi'in U-LeTafkidim Miyuhadim* establishment for information and special tasks]

moss agate *n* a variety of chalcedony with dark greenish mossy markings, used as a gemstone.

mossback (ˈmɒsˌbæk) *n U.S. and Canadian.* **1** an old turtle, shellfish, etc., that has a growth of algae on its back. **2** *Informal.* a provincial or conservative person. ▸ **ˈmossˌbacked** *adj*

Mössbauer effect (ˈmɒsˌbaʊə; *German* ˈmœsbauər) *n Physics.* the phenomenon in which an atomic nucleus in a crystal of certain substances emits a gamma ray without any recoil to the atom. The study of the emitted gamma rays (**Mössbauer spectroscopy**) is used to determine the energy levels in a nucleus, the structure of molecules, etc. [C20: named after Rudolf Ludwig *Mössbauer* (born 1929), German physicist]

mossbunker (ˈmɒsˌbʌŋkə) *n U.S.* another name for **menhaden.** [C18: from Dutch *marsbanker* scad, horse-mackerel]

moss-grown *adj* covered with moss.

Mossi (ˈmɒsɪ) *n* **1** (*pl* **-sis** *or* **-si**) a member of a Negroid people of W Africa, living chiefly in Burkina-Faso: noted for their use of cowry shells as currency and for their trading skill. **2** the language of this people, belonging to the Gur branch of the Niger-Congo family. ◆ Also called: **Moore.**

mossie[1] *or* **mozzie** (ˈmɒzɪ) *n Austral. and N.Z.* an informal name for **mosquito.**

mossie[2] (ˈmɒsɪ) *n* another name for the **Cape sparrow.** [Afrikaans]

moss layer *n* See **layer** (sense 2).

mosso (ˈmɒsəʊ) *adv Music.* to be performed with rapidity. See also **meno mosso.** [Italian, past participle of *muovere* to MOVE]

moss pink *n* a North American plant, *Phlox subulata,* forming dense mosslike mats: cultivated for its pink, white, or lavender flowers: family *Polemoniaceae.* Also called: **ground pink.**

moss rose *n* a variety of rose, *Rosa centifolia muscosa,* that has a mossy stem and calyx and fragrant pink flowers.

moss stitch *n* a knitting stitch made up of alternate plain and purl stitches.

mosstrooper (ˈmɒsˌtruːpə) *n* a raider in the border country of England and Scotland in the mid-17th century. [C17 *moss,* in northern English dialect sense: bog]

most (məʊst) *determiner* **1a** a great majority of; nearly all: *most people like eggs.* **1b** (*as pronoun; functioning as sing or pl*): *most of them don't know; most of it is finished.* **2 the most. 2a** the superlative of **many** and **much:** *you have the most money; the most apples.* **2b** (*as pronoun*): *the most he can afford is two pounds.* **3 at (the) most.** at the maximum: *that girl is four at the most.* **4 for the most part.** generally. **5 make the most of.** to use to the best advantage: *she makes the most of her accent.* **6 than most.** than most others: *the leaves are greener than most.* **7 the most.** *Slang, chiefly U.S.* wonderful: *that chick's the most.* ◆ *adv* **8 the most.** used to form the superlative of some adjectives and adverbs: *the most beautiful daughter of all.* **9** the superlative of **much:** *people welcome a drink most after work.* **10** (intensifier): *a most absurd story.* **11** *U.S. and Canadian informal or dialect.* almost: *most every town in this state.* [Old English *māst* or *mǣst,* whence Middle English *moste, mēst;* compare Old Frisian *maest,* Old High German *meist,* Old Norse *mestr*]

USAGE *More* and *most* should be distinguished when used in comparisons. *More* applies to cases involving two persons, objects, etc., *most* to cases involving three or more: *John is the more intelligent of the two; he is the most intelligent of the students.*

-most *suffix. forming the superlative degree of some adjectives and adverbs: hindmost; uppermost.* [Old English *-mǣst, -mest,* originally a superlative suffix, later mistakenly taken as derived from *mǣst* (adv) most]

Mostaganem (məˌstægəˈnɛm) *n* a port in NW Algeria, on the Mediterranean Sea: exports wine, fruit, and vegetables. Pop.: 107 000 (1987).

Most Honourable *n* a courtesy title applied to marquesses and members of the Privy Council and the Order of the Bath.

mostly (ˈməʊstlɪ) *adv* **1** almost entirely; chiefly. **2** on many or most occasions; usually.

Most Reverend *n* (in Britain) a courtesy title applied to Anglican and Roman Catholic archbishops.

Mosul (ˈməʊsəl) *n* a city in N Iraq, on the River Tigris opposite the ruins of Nineveh: an important commercial centre with nearby Ayn Zalah oilfield; university. Pop.: 664 221 (1987).

mot[1] (məʊ) *n* short for **bon mot.** [C16: via French from Vulgar Latin *mottum* (unattested) utterance, from Latin *muttum* a mutter, from *muttīre* to mutter]

mot[2] (mɒt) *n Dublin slang.* a girl or young woman, esp. one's girlfriend. [perhaps a variant of *mort,* obsolete slang for girl or woman, of unknown origin]

MOT *abbrev. for:* **1** (in Britain and New Zealand) Ministry of Transport (*Brit.,* now Department of Transport). **2** (in Britain) MOT test: a compulsory annual test for all road vehicles over a certain age, which require a valid **MOT certificate.**

mote[1] (məʊt) *n* a tiny speck. [Old English *mot;* compare Middle Dutch *mot* grit, Norwegian *mutt* speck]

mote[2] (məʊt) *vb past* **moste** (məʊst). (takes an infinitive without *to*) *Archaic.* may or might. [Old English *mōt,* first person singular present tense of *mōtan* to be allowed]

motel (məʊˈtɛl) *n* a roadside hotel for motorists, usually having direct access from each room or chalet to a parking space or garage. [C20: from *motor* + *hotel*]

motet (məʊˈtɛt) *n* a polyphonic choral composition used as an anthem in the Roman Catholic service. [C14: from Old French, diminutive of *mot* word; see MOT[1]]

moth (mɒθ) *n* any of numerous insects of the order *Lepidoptera* that typically have stout bodies with antennae of various shapes (but not clubbed), including large brightly coloured species, such as hawk moths, and small inconspicuous types, such as the clothes moths. Compare **butterfly** (sense 1). [Old English *moththe;* compare Middle Dutch *motte,* Old Norse *motti*]

mothball (ˈmɒθˌbɔːl) *n* **1** Also called: **camphor ball.** a small ball of camphor or naphthalene used to repel clothes moths in stored clothing, blankets, etc. **2 put in mothballs.** to postpone work on (a project, activity, etc.). ◆ *vb* (*tr*) **3** to prepare (a ship, aircraft, etc.) for a long period of storage by sealing all openings with plastic to prevent corrosion. **4** to take (a factory, plant, etc.) out of operation but maintain it so that it can be used in the future. **5** to postpone work on (a project, activity, etc.).

moth-eaten *adj* **1** decayed, decrepit, or outdated. **2** eaten away by or as if by moths.

mother[1] (ˈmʌðə) *n* **1a** a female who has given birth to offspring. **1b** (*as modifier*): *a mother bird.* **2** (*often cap., esp. as a term of address*) a person's own mother. **3** a female substituting in the function of a mother. **4** (*often cap.*) *Chiefly archaic.* a term of address for an old woman. **5a** motherly qualities, such as maternal affection: *it appealed to the mother in her.* **5b** (*as modifier*): *mother love.* **5c** (*in combination*): *mothercraft.* **6a** a female or thing that creates, nurtures, protects, etc., something. **6b** (*as modifier*): *mother church; mother earth.* **7** a title given to certain members of female religious orders: *mother superior.* **8** *Christian Science.* God as the eternal Principle. **9** (*modifier*) native or innate: *mother wit.* **10** *Offensive taboo slang, chiefly U.S.* short for **motherfucker. 11 be mother.** to pour the tea: *I'll be mother.* **12 the mother of all...** *Informal.* the greatest example of its kind: *the mother of all parties.* ◆ *vb* (*tr*) **13** to give birth to or produce. **14** to nurture, protect, etc. as a mother. ◆ Related adj: **maternal.** [Old English *mōdor;* compare Old Saxon *mōdar,* Old High German *muotar,* Latin *māter,* Greek *mētēr*] ▸ **ˈmothering** *n*

mother[2] (ˈmʌðə) *n* a stringy slime containing various bacteria that forms on the surface of liquids undergoing acetous fermentation. It can be added to wine, cider, etc. to promote vinegar formation. Also called: **mother of vinegar.** [C16: perhaps from MOTHER[1], but compare Spanish *madre* scum, Dutch *modder* dregs, Middle Low German *modder* decaying object, *mudde* sludge] ▸ **ˈmothery** *adj*

motherboard (ˈmʌðəˌbɔːd) *n* (in an electronic system) a printed circuit board through which signals between all other boards are routed.

Mother Carey's chicken (ˈkɛərɪz) *n* another name for **storm petrel.** [origin unknown]

mother country *n* **1** the original country of colonists or settlers. **2** another term for **fatherland.**

motherfucker (ˈmʌðəˌfʌkə) *n Offensive taboo slang, chiefly U.S.* a person or thing, esp. an exasperating or unpleasant one. Often shortened to **mother.**

Mother Goose *n* the imaginary author of the collection of nursery rhymes published in 1781 in London as *Mother Goose's Melody.* [C18: translated from French *Contes de ma mère l'Oye* (1697), title of a collection of tales by Charles PERRAULT]

motherhood (ˈmʌðəˌhʊd) *n* **1** the state of being a mother. **2** the qualities characteristic of a mother.

Mother Hubbard (ˈhʌbəd) *n* (*sometimes not caps.*) a woman's full-length unbelted dress. [C19: after *Mother Hubbard,* a character in a nursery rhyme]

Mothering Sunday (ˈmʌðərɪŋ) *n Brit.* the fourth Sunday in Lent, when mothers traditionally receive presents from their children. Also called: **Mother's Day.**

mother-in-law *n, pl* **mothers-in-law.** the mother of one's wife or husband.

mother-in-law's tongue *n* See **sansevieria.**

motherland (ˈmʌðəˌlænd) *n* another word for **fatherland.**

motherless (ˈmʌðələs) *adj* **1** not having a mother. ◆ *adv* **2** (intensifier) *Austral. informal.: motherless broke.*

mother lode *n Mining.* the principal lode in a system.

motherly (ˈmʌðəlɪ) *adj* of or resembling a mother, esp. in warmth, or protectiveness. ▸ **ˈmotherliness** *n*

Mother of God *n* a title given to the Virgin Mary: used in Orthodox and Roman Catholic churches to emphasize the belief that Jesus was God.

Mother of Parliaments *n* **the.** the British Parliament: the model and creator of many other Parliaments. [C19: first used of England in 1865 by John BRIGHT]

mother-of-pearl *n* a hard iridescent substance, mostly calcium carbonate, that forms the inner layer of the shells of certain molluscs, such as the oyster. It is used to make buttons, inlay furniture, etc. Also called: **nacre.** Related adj: **nacreous.**

mother-of-pearl moth *n* a pyralid moth, *Pleuroptya ruralis,* having a pale sheen, that is often seen around nettles, on which its green larvae feed.

mother of the chapel *n* (in British trade unions in the publishing and printing industries) a woman shop steward. Abbrev.: **MoC.**

mother-of-thousands *n* **1** a S European perennial creeping plant, *Linaria cymbalaria,* having small pale blue or lilac flowers. **2** a saxifragaceous plant, *Saxifraga sarmentosa* or *S. stolonifera,* having white flowers and creeping red runners.

Mother's Day *n* **1** *U.S. and Canadian.* the second Sunday in May, observed as a day in honour of mothers. **2** See **Mothering Sunday.**

mother ship *n* a ship providing facilities and supplies for a number of small vessels.

Mother Shipton ('ʃɪptᵊn) *n* a day-flying noctuid moth, *Callistege mi,* mottled brown in colour and named from a fancied resemblance between its darker marking and a haggish profile. [named after *Mother Shipton,* a legendary prophetess in 15th-century Yorkshire]

mother superior *n, pl* **mother superiors** *or* **mothers superior.** the head of a community of nuns.

mother tongue *n* **1** the language first learned by a child. **2** a language from which another has evolved.

Motherwell ('mʌðəwəl) *n* a town in S central Scotland, the administrative centre of North Lanarkshire on the River Clyde: industrial centre. Pop.: 30 717 (1991).

mother wit *n* native practical intelligence; common sense.

motherwort ('mʌðəˌwɜːt) *n* any of several plants of the Eurasian genus *Leonurus,* esp. *L. cardiaca,* having divided leaves and clusters of small purple or pink flowers: family *Labiatae* (labiates). [C14: so named because it was thought to be beneficial in uterine disorders]

mothproof ('mɒθˌpruːf) *adj* **1** (esp. of clothes) chemically treated so as to repel clothes moths. ◆ *vb* **2** (*tr*) to make (clothes, etc.) mothproof.

mothy ('mɒθɪ) *adj* **mothier, mothiest. 1** ragged; moth-eaten. **2** containing moths; full of moths.

motif (məʊ'tiːf) *n* **1** a distinctive idea, esp. a theme elaborated on in a piece of music, literature, etc. **2** Also: **motive.** a recurring form or shape in a design or pattern. **3** a single added piece of decoration, such as a symbol or name on a jumper, sweatshirt, etc. [C19: from French. See MOTIVE]

motile ('məʊtaɪl) *adj* **1** capable of moving spontaneously and independently. ◆ *n* **2** *Psychol.* a person whose mental imagery strongly reflects movement, esp. his own. [C19: from Latin *mōtus* moved, from *movēre* to move] ▸ **motility** (məʊ'tɪlɪtɪ) *n*

motion ('məʊʃən) *n* **1** the process of continual change in the physical position of an object; movement: *linear motion.* ◆ Related adj: **kinetic. 2** a movement or action, esp. of part of the human body; a gesture. **3a** the capacity for movement. **3b** a manner of movement, esp. walking; gait. **4** a mental impulse. **5** a formal proposal to be discussed and voted on in a debate, meeting, etc. **6** *Law.* an application made to a judge or court for an order or ruling necessary to the conduct of legal proceedings. **7** *Brit.* **7a** the evacuation of the bowels. **7b** excrement. **8a** part of a moving mechanism. **8b** the action of such a part. **9** *Music.* the upward or downward course followed by a part or melody. Parts whose progressions are in the same direction exhibit **similar motion,** while two parts whose progressions are in opposite directions exhibit **contrary motion.** See also **parallel** (sense 3). **10 go through the motions. 10a** to act or perform the task (of doing something) mechanically or without sincerity. **10b** to mimic the action (of something) by gesture. **11 in motion.** operational or functioning (often in the phrases **set in motion, set the wheels in motion**). ◆ *vb* **12** (when *tr, may take a clause as object or an infinitive*) to signal or direct (a person) by a movement or gesture. [C15: from Latin *mōtiō* a moving, from *movēre* to move] ▸ **'motional** *adj*

motionless ('məʊʃənlɪs) *adj* not moving; absolutely still. ▸ **'motionlessly** *adv* ▸ **'motionlessness** *n*

motion picture *n* a U.S. and Canadian term for **film** (sense 1).

motion sickness *n* the state or condition of being dizzy or nauseous from riding in a moving vehicle.

motion study *n* short for **time and motion study.**

motivate ('məʊtɪˌveɪt) *vb* (*tr*) to give incentive to.

motivation (ˌməʊtɪ'veɪʃən) *n* **1** the act or an instance of motivating. **2** desire to do; interest or drive. **3** incentive or inducement. **4** *Psychol.* the process that arouses, sustains and regulates human and animal behaviour. ▸ **ˌmoti'vational** *adj* ▸ **'motiˌvative** *adj*

motivational research *n* the application of psychology to the study of consumer behaviour, esp. the planning of advertising and sales campaigns. Also called: **motivation research.**

motive ('məʊtɪv) *n* **1** the reason for a certain course of action, whether conscious or unconscious. **2** a variant of **motif** (sense 2). ◆ *adj* **3** of or causing motion or action: *a motive force.* **4** of or acting as a motive; motivating. ◆ *vb* (*tr*) **5** to motivate. [C14: from Old French *motif,* from Late Latin *mōtīvus* (adj) moving, from Latin *mōtus,* past participle of *movēre* to move] ▸ **'motiveless** *adj* ▸ **'motivelessly** *adv* ▸ **'motivelessness** *n*

motive power *n* **1** any source of energy used to produce motion. **2** the means of supplying power to an engine, vehicle, etc. **3** any driving force.

motivity (məʊ'tɪvɪtɪ) *n* the power of moving or of initiating motion.

mot juste *French.* (mo ʒyst) *n, pl* ***mots justes*** (mo ʒyst). the appropriate word or expression.

motley ('mɒtlɪ) *adj* **1** made up of elements of varying type, quality, etc. **2** multicoloured. ◆ *n* **3** a motley collection or mixture. **4** the particoloured attire of a jester. **5** *Obsolete.* a jester. [C14: perhaps from *mot* speck, MOTE[1]]

motmot ('mɒtmɒt) *n* any tropical American bird of the family *Momotidae,* having a long tail and blue and brownish-green plumage: order *Coraciiformes* (kingfishers, etc.). [C19: from American Spanish, imitative of the bird's call]

motocross ('məʊtəˌkrɒs) *n* **1** a motorcycle race across very rough ground. **2** another name for **rallycross.** See also **autocross.** [C20: from MOTO(R) + CROSS(-COUNTRY)]

motoneuron (ˌməʊtəʊ'njʊərɒn) *n Anatomy.* an efferent nerve cell; motor neuron.

motor ('məʊtə) *n* **1a** the engine, esp. an internal-combustion engine, of a vehicle. **1b** (*as modifier*): *a motor scooter.* **2** Also called: **electric motor.** a machine that converts electrical energy into mechanical energy by means of the forces exerted on a current-carrying coil placed in a magnetic field. **3** any device that converts another form of energy into mechanical energy to produce motion. **4a** *Chiefly Brit.* a car or other motor vehicle. **4b** (*as modifier*): *motor spares.* ◆ *adj* **5** producing or causing motion. **6** *Physiol.* **6a** of or relating to nerves or neurons that carry impulses that cause muscles to contract. **6b** of or relating to movement or to muscles that induce movement. ◆ *vb* **7** (*intr*) to travel by car. **8** (*tr*) *Brit.* to transport by car. **9** (*intr*) *Informal.* to move fast; make good progress. [C16: from Latin *mōtor* a mover, from *movēre* to move]

motorable ('məʊtərəbᵊl) *adj* (of a road) suitable for use by motor vehicles.

motorbicycle ('məʊtəˌbaɪsɪkᵊl) *n* **1** a motorcycle. **2** a moped.

motorbike ('məʊtəˌbaɪk) *n* a less formal name for **motorcycle.**

motorboat ('məʊtəˌbəʊt) *n* any boat powered by a motor.

motorbus ('məʊtəˌbʌs) *n* a bus driven by an internal-combustion engine.

motorcade ('məʊtəˌkeɪd) *n* a parade of cars or other motor vehicles. [C20: from MOTOR + CAVALCADE]

motor camp *n N.Z.* a camp for motorists, tents, and caravans.

motorcar ('məʊtəˌkɑː) *n* **1** a more formal word for **car** (sense 1). **2** a self-propelled electric railway car.

motor caravan *n Brit.* a motor vehicle fitted with equipment for cooking, sleeping, etc., like that of a caravan.

motorcoach ('məʊtəˌkəʊtʃ) *n* a coach driven by an internal-combustion engine.

motorcycle ('məʊtəˌsaɪkᵊl) *n* **1** Also called: **motorbike.** a two-wheeled vehicle, having a stronger frame than a bicycle, that is driven by a petrol engine, usually with a capacity of between 125 cc and 1000 cc. ◆ *vb* (*intr*) **2** to ride on a motorcycle. ▸ **'motorˌcyclist** *n*

motor drive *n Photog.* a battery-operated motorized system to give fast film advance between exposures. Compare **autowinder.**

-motored *adj* (*in combination*) having a specified type of motor or number of motors.

motor generator *n* a generator driven by an electric motor, by means of which the voltage, frequency, or phases of an electrical power supply can be changed.

motorist ('məʊtərɪst) *n* a driver of a car, esp. when considered as a car-owner.

motorize *or* **motorise** ('məʊtəˌraɪz) *vb* (*tr*) **1** to equip with a motor. **2** to provide (military units) with motor vehicles. ▸ **ˌmotori'zation** *or* **ˌmotori'sation** *n*

motorman ('məʊtəmən) *n, pl* **-men. 1** the driver of an electric train. **2** the operator of a motor.

motor neurone disease *n* a progressively degenerative disease of the motor system causing muscle weakness and wasting.

motor park *n* a W African name for **car park.**

motor scooter *n* a light motorcycle with small wheels and an enclosed engine. Often shortened to **scooter.**

motor vehicle *n* a road vehicle driven by a motor or engine, esp. an internal-combustion engine.

motor vessel *or* **ship** *n* a ship whose main propulsion system is a diesel or other internal-combustion engine.

motorway ('məʊtəˌweɪ) *n Brit.* a main road for fast-moving traffic, having limited access, separate carriageways for vehicles travelling in opposite directions, and usually a total of four or six lanes. U.S. names: **superhighway,** (*also Canadian*) **expressway.**

Motown ('məʊˌtaʊn) *n Trademark.* music combining rhythm and blues and pop, or gospel rhythms and modern ballad harmony. [C20: from *Motown Records* of Detroit; from *Mo(tor)Town,* a nickname for Detroit, Michigan, centre of the U.S. car industry]

motser *or* **motza** ('mɒtsə) *n Austral. informal.* a large sum of money, esp. a gambling win. [of uncertain origin; possibly Yiddish]

motte (mɒt) *n History.* a natural or man-made mound on which a castle was erected. [C14: see MOAT]

MOT test *n* (in Britain) See **MOT** (sense 2).

mottle ('mɒtᵊl) *vb* **1** (*tr*) to colour with streaks or blotches of different shades. ◆ *n* **2** a mottled appearance, as of the surface of marble. **3** one streak or blotch of colour in a mottled surface. [C17: back formation from MOTLEY]

motto ('mɒtəʊ) *n, pl* **-toes** *or* **-tos. 1** a short saying expressing the guiding maxim or ideal of a family, organization, etc., esp. when part of a coat of arms. **2** a short explanatory phrase inscribed on or attached to something. **3** a verse or maxim contained in a paper cracker. **4** a quotation prefacing a book or chapter of a book. **5** a recurring musical phrase. [C16: via Italian from Latin *muttum* utterance]

motty ('mɒtɪ) *n Irish.* the target at which coins are aimed in pitch-and-toss.

Motu ('məʊtuː) *n* **1** (*pl* **-tu** *or* **-tus**) a member of an aboriginal people of S Papua. **2** the language of this people, belonging to the Malayo-Polynesian family. **3** Also called: **Hiri Motu** *or* (esp. formerly) **Police Motu.** a pidgin version of this language, widely used in Papua-New Guinea. Compare **Neo-Melanesian.**

motu proprio ('məʊtuː 'prəʊprɪˌəʊ) *n* an administrative papal bull. [Latin: of his own accord]

Mo-tzu ('məʊ'tsuː) *n* a variant transliteration of **Mo-Zi.**

moue *French.* (mu) *n* a disdainful or pouting look.

mouflon *or* **moufflon** ('mu:flɒn) *n* a wild short-fleeced mountain sheep, *Ovis musimon,* of Corsica and Sardinia. [C18: via French from Corsican *mufrone,* from Late Latin *mufrō*]

mouillé ('mwi:eɪ) *adj Phonetics.* palatalized, as in the sounds represented by Spanish *ll* or *ñ,* Italian *gl* or *gn* (pronounced as (ʎ) and (ɲ) respectively), or French *ll* (representing a (j) sound). [C19: from French, past participle of *mouiller* to moisten, from Latin *mollis* soft]

moujik ('mu:ʒɪk) *n* a variant spelling of **muzhik.**

mould[1] *or U.S.* **mold** (məʊld) *n* **1** a shaped cavity used to give a definite form to fluid or plastic material. **2** a frame on which something may be constructed. **3** something shaped in or made on a mould. **4** shape, form, design, or pattern. **5** specific nature, character, or type: *heroic mould.* ◆ *vb* (*tr*) **6** to make in a mould. **7** to shape or form, as by using a mould. **8** to influence or direct: *to mould opinion.* **9** to cling to: *the skirt moulds her figure.* **10** *Metallurgy.* [C13 (n): changed from Old French *modle,* from Latin *modulus* a small measure, MODULE] ▸ **'mouldable** *or U.S.* **'moldable** *adj* ▸ **,moulda'bility** *or U.S.* **,molda'bility** *n*

mould[2] *or U.S.* **mold** (məʊld) *n* **1** a coating or discoloration caused by various saprotrophic fungi that develop in a damp atmosphere on the surface of stored food, fabrics, wallpaper, etc. **2** any of the fungi that causes this growth. ◆ *vb* **3** to become or cause to become covered with this growth. ◆ Also called: **mildew.** [C15: dialect (Northern English) *mowlde* mouldy, from the past participle of *moulen* to become mouldy, probably of Scandinavian origin; compare Old Norse *mugla* mould]

mould[3] *or U.S.* **mold** (məʊld) *n* **1** loose soil, esp. when rich in organic matter. **2** *Poetic.* the earth. [Old English *molde;* related to Old High German *molta* soil, Gothic *mulde*]

mouldboard *or U.S.* **moldboard** ('məʊld,bɔ:d) *n* the curved blade of a plough, which turns over the furrow.

moulder[1] *or U.S.* **molder** ('məʊldə) *vb* (often foll. by *away*) to crumble or cause to crumble, as through decay. [C16: verbal use of MOULD[3]]

moulder[2] *or U.S.* **molder** ('məʊldə) *n* **1** a person who moulds or makes moulds. **2** *Printing.* one of the set of electrotypes used for making duplicates.

moulding *or U.S.* **molding** ('məʊldɪŋ) *n* **1** *Architect.* **1a** a shaped outline, esp. one used on cornices, etc. **1b** a shaped strip made of wood, stone, etc. **2** something moulded.

moulding board *n* a board on which dough is kneaded.

mouldwarp ('məʊld,wɔ:p) *or* **mouldywarp** ('məʊldɪ,wɔ:p) *n* an archaic or dialect name for a **mole**[1] (sense 1). [C14 *moldewarpe;* ultimately from Germanic *moldeworpon* (unattested) earth-thrower, from *moldā* MOULD[3] + *wurp, werp* to throw (both unattested)]

mouldy *or U.S.* **moldy** ('məʊldɪ) *adj* **mouldier, mouldiest** *or U.S.* **moldier, moldiest. 1** covered with mould. **2** stale or musty, esp. from age or lack of use. **3** *Slang.* boring; dull. ▸ **'mouldiness** *or U.S.* **'moldiness** *n*

mouldy fig *n Dated slang.* a rigid adherent to older jazz forms.

moulin ('mu:lɪn) *n* a vertical shaft in a glacier, maintained by a constant descending stream of water and debris. [C19: from French: a mill]

Moulin (*French* mulɛ̃) *n* **Jean** (ʒɑ̃). 1899–1943, French lawyer and Resistance hero; Chairman of the National Council of the Resistance (1943): tortured to death by the Nazis.

Moulins (*French* mulɛ̃) *n* a market town in central France, on the Allier River. Pop.: 23 350 (1990).

Moulmein *or* **Maulmain** (maʊl'meɪn) *n* a port in S Myanmar, near the mouth of the Salween River: exports teak and rice. Pop.: 202 967 (1983).

moult *or U.S.* **molt** (məʊlt) *vb* **1** (of birds, mammals, reptiles, and arthropods) to shed (feathers, hair, skin, or cuticle). ◆ *n* **2** the periodic process of moulting. See also **ecdysis.** [C14 *mouten,* from Old English *mūtian,* as in *bimūtian* to exchange for, from Latin *mūtāre* to change] ▸ **'moulter** *or U.S.* **'molter** *n*

mound[1] (maʊnd) *n* **1** a raised mass of earth, debris, etc. **2** any heap or pile: *a mound of washing.* **3** a small natural hill. **4** *Archaeol.* another word for **barrow**[2]. **5** an artificial ridge of earth, stone, etc., used for defence. ◆ *vb* **6** (often foll. by *up*) to gather into a mound; heap. **7** (*tr*) to cover or surround with a mound: *to mound a grave.* ◆ Related adj: **tumular.** [C16: earthwork, perhaps from Old English *mund* hand, hence defence: compare Middle Dutch *mond* protection]

mound[2] (maʊnd) *n Heraldry.* a rare word for **orb** (sense 1). [C13 (meaning: world, C16: orb): from French *monde,* from Latin *mundus* world]

Mound Builder *n* a member of a group of prehistoric inhabitants of the Mississippi region who built altar-mounds, tumuli, etc.

mound-builder *n* another name for **megapode.**

mount[1] (maʊnt) *vb* **1** to go up (a hill, stairs, etc.); climb. **2** to get up on (a horse, a platform, etc.). **3** (*intr;* often foll. by *up*) to increase; accumulate: *excitement mounted.* **4** (*tr*) to fix onto a backing, setting, or support: *to mount a photograph; to mount a slide.* **5** (*tr*) to provide with a horse for riding, or to place on a horse. **6** (of male animals) to climb onto (a female animal) for copulation. **7** (*tr*) to prepare (a play, musical comedy, etc.) for production. **8** (*tr*) to plan and organize (a compaign, an exhibition, etc.) **9** (*tr*) *Military.* to prepare or launch (an operation): *the Allies mounted an offensive.* **10** (*tr*) to prepare (a skeleton, dead animal, etc.) for exhibition as a specimen. **11** (*tr*) to place or carry (weapons) in such a position that they can be fired. **12 mount guard.** See **guard** (sense 26). ◆ *n* **13** a backing, setting, or support onto which something is fixed. **14** the act or manner of mounting. **15** a horse for riding. **16** a slide used in microscopy. **17** *Philately.* **17a** a small transparent pocket in an album for a postage stamp. **17b hinge** (sense 5). [C16: from Old French *munter,* from Vulgar Latin *montāre* (unattested) from Latin *mons* MOUNT[2]] ▸ **'mountable** *adj* ▸ **'mounter** *n*

mount[2] (maʊnt) *n* **1** a mountain or hill: used in literature and (when cap.) in proper names: *Mount Everest.* **2** (in palmistry) any of the seven cushions of flesh on the palm of the hand. [Old English *munt,* from Latin *mons* mountain, but influenced in Middle English by Old French *mont*]

mountain ('maʊntɪn) *n* **1a** a natural upward projection of the earth's surface, higher and steeper than a hill and often having a rocky summit. **1b** (*as modifier*): *mountain people; mountain scenery.* **1c** (*in combination*): *a mountaintop.* **2** a huge heap or mass: *a mountain of papers.* **3** anything of great quantity or size. **4** a surplus of a commodity, esp. in the European Union: *the butter mountain.* **5 a mountain to climb.** *Brit. informal.* a serious or considerable difficulty or obstruction to overcome. **6 make a mountain out of a molehill.** See **molehill** (sense 2). [C13: from Old French *montaigne,* from Vulgar Latin *montānea* (unattested) mountainous, from Latin *montānus,* from *mons* mountain]

Mountain ('maʊntɪn) *n* **the.** an extremist faction during the French Revolution led by Danton and Robespierre. [C18: so called because its members sat in the highest row of seats at the National Convention Hall in 1793]

mountain ash *n* **1** any of various trees of the rosaceous genus *Sorbus,* such as *S. aucuparia* (**European mountain ash** or **rowan**), having clusters of small white flowers and bright red berries. **2** any of several Australian eucalyptus trees, such as *Eucalyptus regnans.*

mountain avens *n* See **avens** (sense 2).

mountain bike a type of sturdy bicycle with at least 16 and up to 21 gears, straight handlebars, and heavy-duty tyres.

mountain cat *n* any of various wild feline mammals, such as the bobcat, lynx, or puma.

mountain chain *n* a series of ranges of mountains.

mountain devil *n* another name for **moloch.**

mountaineer (,maʊntɪ'nɪə) *n* **1** a person who climbs mountains. **2** a person living in a mountainous area. ◆ *vb* **3** (*intr*) to climb mountains. ▸ **,mountain'eering** *n*

mountain everlasting *n* another name for **cat's-foot.**

mountain goat *n* **1** short for **Rocky Mountain goat. 2** any wild goat inhabiting mountainous regions.

mountain laurel *n* any of various ericaceous shrubs or trees of the genus *Kalmia,* esp. *K. latifolia* of E North America, which has leathery poisonous leaves and clusters of pink or white flowers. Also called: **calico bush.**

mountain lion *n* another name for **puma.**

mountainous ('maʊntɪnəs) *adj* **1** of or relating to mountains: *a mountainous region.* **2** like a mountain, esp. in size or impressiveness. ▸ **'mountainously** *adv* ▸ **'mountainousness** *n*

mountain range *n* a series of adjoining mountains or of lines of mountains of similar origin.

mountain sheep *n* **1** another name for **bighorn. 2** any wild sheep inhabiting mountainous regions.

mountain sickness *n* nausea, headache, and shortness of breath caused by climbing to high altitudes (usually above 12 000 ft.). Also called: **altitude sickness.**

Mountain Standard Time *n* one of the standard times used in North America, seven hours behind Greenwich Mean Time. Abbrev.: **MST.**

Mountbatten (maʊnt'bætən) *n* **Louis** (**Francis Albert Victor Nicholas**), 1st Earl Mountbatten of Burma. 1900–79, British naval commander; great-grandson of Queen Victoria. During World War II he was supreme allied commander in SE Asia (1943–46). He was the last viceroy of India (1947) and governor general (1947–48); killed by an IRA bomb.

Mount Cook lily *n* a large white buttercup, *Ranunculus lyallii,* of the South Island alpine country of New Zealand. Also called: **great mountain buttercup.**

Mount Desert Island *n* an island off the coast of Maine: lakes and granite peaks. Area: 279 sq. km (108 sq. miles).

mountebank ('maʊntɪ,bæŋk) *n* **1** (formerly) a person who sold quack medicines in public places. **2** a charlatan; fake. ◆ *vb* **3** (*intr*) to play the mountebank. [C16: from Italian *montambanco* a climber on a bench, from *montare* to MOUNT[1] + *banco* BENCH (see also BANK[1])] ▸ **,mounte'bankery** *n*

mounted ('maʊntɪd) *adj* **1** equipped with or riding horses: *mounted police.* **2** provided with a support, backing, etc.

Mountie *or* **Mounty** ('maʊntɪ) *n, pl* **Mounties.** *Informal.* a member of the Royal Canadian Mounted Police. [nickname evolved from MOUNTED]

mounting ('maʊntɪŋ) *n* another word for **mount**[1] (sense 13).

mounting-block *n* a block of stone formerly used to aid a person when mounting a horse.

Mount Isa ('aɪzə) *n* a city in NE Australia in NW Queensland: mining of copper and other minerals. Pop.: 24 104 (1988 est.).

Mount McKinley National Park *n* a national park in S central Alaska: contains part of the Alaska Range. Area: 7847 sq. km (3030 sq. miles).

Mount Rainier National Park *n* a national park in W Washington, in the Cascade Range. Area: 976 sq. km (377 sq. miles).

mourn (mɔ:n) *vb* **1** to feel or express sadness for the death or loss of (someone or something). **2** (*intr*) to observe the customs of mourning, as by wearing black. **3** (*tr*) to grieve over (loss or misfortune). [Old English *murnan;* compare Old High German *mornēn* to be troubled, Gothic *maurnan* to grieve, Greek *mermeros* worried]

Mourne Mountains (mɔ:rn) *pl n* a mountain range in SE Northern Ireland. Highest peak: Slieve Donard, 853 m (2798 ft).

mourner ('mɔ:nə) *n* **1** a person who mourns, esp. at a funeral. **2** (at U.S. revivalist meetings) a person who repents publicly.

mournful ('mɔ:nfʊl) *adj* **1** evoking grief; sorrowful. **2** gloomy; sad. ▸ **'mournfully** *adv* ▸ **'mournfulness** *n*

mourning ('mɔ:nɪŋ) *n* **1** the act or feelings of one who mourns; grief. **2** the conventional symbols of grief, such as the wearing of black. **3** the period of time during which a death is officially mourned. **4 in mourning.** observing the conventions of mourning. ◆ *adj* **5** of or relating to mourning. ▸ **'mourningly** *adv*

mourning band *n* a piece of black material, esp. an armband, worn to indicate that the wearer is in mourning.

mourning cloak *n* the U.S. name for **Camberwell beauty.**

mourning dove *n* a brown North American dove, *Zenaidura macroura,* with a plaintive song.

mouse *n* (maʊs), *pl* **mice** (maɪs). **1** any of numerous small long-tailed rodents of the families *Muridae* and *Cricetidae* that are similar to but smaller than rats. See also **fieldmouse, harvest mouse, house mouse.** Related adj: **murine. 2** any of various related rodents, such as the jumping mouse. **3** a quiet, timid, or cowardly person. **4** *Computing.* a hand-held device used to control the cursor movement and select computing functions without keying. **5** *Slang.* a black eye. **6** *Nautical.* another word for **mousing.** ◆ *vb* (maʊz). **7** to stalk and catch (mice). **8** (*intr*) to go about stealthily. **9** (*tr*) *Nautical.* to secure (a hook) with mousing. [Old English *mūs;* compare Old Saxon *mūs,* German *maus,* Old Norse *mūs,* Latin *mūs,* Greek *mūs*] ▸ **'mouse,like** *adj*

mousebird ('maʊs,bɜːd) *n* another name for **coly.**

mouse deer *n* another name for **chevrotain.**

mouse-ear *n* short for **mouse-ear chickweed** (see **chickweed** (sense 2)).

mouser ('maʊzə, 'maʊsə) *n* a cat or other animal that is used to catch mice: usually qualified: *a good mouser.*

mousetail ('maʊs,teɪl) *n* any of various N temperate ranunculaceous plants of the genus *Myosurus,* esp. *M. minimus,* with tail-like flower spikes.

mousetrap ('maʊs,træp) *n* **1** any trap for catching mice, esp. one with a spring-loaded metal bar that is released by the taking of the bait. **2** *Brit. informal.* cheese of indifferent quality.

mousey ('maʊsɪ) *adj* **mousier, mousiest.** a variant spelling of **mousy.** ▸ **'mousily** *adv* ▸ **'mousiness** *n*

mousing ('maʊzɪŋ) *n Nautical.* a lashing, shackle, etc., for closing off a hook to prevent a load from slipping off.

moussaka *or* **mousaka** (mu'sɑːkə) *n* a dish originating in the Balkan States, consisting of meat, aubergines, and tomatoes, topped with cheese sauce. [C20: from Modern Greek]

mousse (muːs) *n* **1** a light creamy dessert made with eggs, cream, fruit, etc., set with gelatine. **2** a similar dish made from fish or meat. **3** short for **styling mousse.** [C19: from French: froth]

mousseline (*French* muslin) *n* **1** a fine fabric made of rayon or silk. **2** a type of fine glass. **3** short for **mousseline sauce.** [C17: French: MUSLIN]

mousseline de laine *French.* (muslin də lɛn) *n* a light woollen fabric. [literally: muslin of wool]

mousseline de soie *French.* (muslin də swa) *n* a thin gauzelike fabric of silk or rayon. [literally: muslin of silk]

mousseline sauce *n* a light sauce, made by adding whipped cream or egg whites to hollandaise sauce. [from French *mousseline,* literally: muslin]

Moussorgsky (mu'sɔːgskɪ; *Russian* 'musərkskij) *n* a variant spelling of (Modest Petrovich) **Mussorgsky.**

moustache *or U.S.* **mustache** (mə'stɑːʃ) *n* **1** the unshaved growth of hair on the upper lip, and sometimes down the sides of the mouth. **2** a similar growth of hair or bristles (in animals) or feathers (in birds). **3** a mark like a moustache. [C16: via French from Italian *mostaccio,* ultimately from Doric Greek *mustax* upper lip] ▸ **mous'tached** *or U.S.* **mus'tached** *adj*

moustache cup *n* a cup with a partial cover to protect a drinker's moustache.

Mousterian (muː'stɪərɪən) *n* **1** a culture characterized by flint flake tools and associated with Neanderthal man, found throughout Europe, North Africa, and the Near East, dating from before 70 000–32 000 B.C. ◆ *adj* **2** of or relating to this culture. [C20: from French *Moustérien* from archaeological finds of the same period in the cave of *Le Moustier,* Dordogne, France]

mousy *or* **mousey** ('maʊsɪ) *adj* **mousier, mousiest. 1** resembling a mouse, esp. in having a light brown or greyish hair colour. **2** shy or ineffectual: *a mousy little woman.* **3** infested with mice. ▸ **'mousily** *adv* ▸ **'mousiness** *n*

mouth *n* (maʊθ), *pl* **mouths** (maʊðz). **1** the opening through which many animals take in food and issue vocal sounds. **2** the system of organs surrounding this opening, including the lips, tongue, teeth, etc. **3** the visible part of the lips on the face. Related adjs.: **oral, oscular. 4** a person regarded as a consumer of food: *four mouths to feed.* **5** verbal expression (esp. in the phrase **give mouth to**). **6** a particular manner of speaking: *a foul mouth.* **7** *Informal.* boastful, rude, or excessive talk: *he is all mouth.* **8** the point where a river issues into a sea or lake. **9** the opening of a container, such as a jar. **10** the opening of or place leading into a cave, tunnel, volcano, etc. **11** that part of the inner lip of a horse on which the bit acts, esp. when specified as to sensitivity: *a hard mouth.* **12** *Music.* the narrow slit in an organ pipe. **13** the opening between the jaws of a vice or other gripping device. **14** a pout; grimace. **15 by word of mouth.** orally rather than by written means. **16 down in** *or* **at the mouth.** in low spirits. **17 have a big mouth** *or* **open one's big mouth.** *Informal.* to speak indiscreetly, loudly, or excessively. **18 keep one's mouth shut.** to keep a secret. **19 put one's money where one's mouth is.** to take appropriate action to support what one has said. **20 put words into someone's mouth. 20a** to represent, often inaccurately, what someone has said. **20b** to tell someone what to say. **21 run off at the mouth.** *Informal.* to talk incessantly, esp. about unimportant matters. ◆ *vb* (maʊð). **22** to speak or say (something) insincerely, esp. in public. **23** (*tr*) to form (words) with movements of the lips but without speaking. **24** (*tr*) to accustom (a horse) to wearing a bit. **25** (*tr*) to take (something) into the mouth or to move (something) around inside the mouth. **26** (*intr;* usually foll. by *at*) to make a grimace. [Old English *mūth;* compare Old Norse *muthr,* Gothic *munths,* Dutch *mond*] ▸ **mouther** ('maʊðə) *n*

mouthbrooder ('maʊθ,bruːdə) *or* **mouthbreeder** ('maʊθ,briːdə) *n* any of various African cichlid fishes of the genera *Tilapia Haplochromis* that carry their eggs and young around in the mouth.

mouthful ('maʊθ,fʊl) *n, pl* **-fuls. 1** as much as is held in the mouth at one time. **2** a small quantity, as of food. **3** a long word or phrase that is difficult to say. **4** *Brit. informal.* an abusive response. **5** *Informal, chiefly U.S. and Canadian.* an impressive remark (esp. in the phrase **say a mouthful**).

mouth organ *n* another name for **harmonica** (sense 1).

mouthpart ('maʊθ,pɑːt) *n* any of the paired appendages in arthropods that surround the mouth and are specialized for feeding.

mouthpiece ('maʊθ,piːs) *n* **1** the part of a wind instrument into which the player blows. **2** the part of a telephone receiver into which a person speaks. **3** the part of a container forming its mouth. **4** a person who acts as a spokesman, as for an organization. **5** a publication, esp. a periodical, expressing the official views of an organization. **6** *Boxing.* another name for **gumshield.**

mouth-to-mouth *adj* designating a method of artificial respiration involving blowing air rhythmically into the mouth of a person who has stopped breathing, to stimulate return of spontaneous breathing.

mouthwash ('maʊθ,wɒʃ) *n* a medicated aqueous solution, used for gargling and for cleansing the mouth.

mouthwatering ('maʊθ,wɔːtərɪŋ) *adj* whetting the appetite, as from smell, appearance, or description.

mouthy ('maʊðɪ) *adj* **mouthier, mouthiest.** bombastic; excessively talkative.

mouton ('muːtɒn) *n* sheepskin processed to resemble the fur of another animal, esp. beaver or seal. [from French: sheep. See MUTTON]

movable *or* **moveable** ('muːvəbᵊl) *adj* able to be moved or rearranged; not fixed. **2** (esp. of religious festivals such as Easter) varying in date from year to year. **3** (usually spelt **moveable**). *Law.* denoting or relating to personal property as opposed to realty. **4** *Printing.* (of type) cast singly so that each character is on a separate piece of type suitable for composition by hand, as founder's type. ◆ *n* **5** (*often pl*) a movable article, esp. a piece of furniture. ▸ **,mova'bility** *or* **'movableness** *n* ▸ **'movably** *adv*

move (muːv) *vb* **1** to go or take from one place to another; change in location or position. **2** (*usually intr*) to change (one's dwelling, place of business, etc.). **3** to be or cause to be in motion; stir. **4** (*intr*) (of machines, etc.) to work or operate. **5** (*tr*) to cause (to do something); prompt. **6** (*intr*) to begin to act: *move soon or we'll lose the order.* **7** (*intr*) to associate oneself with a specified social circle: *to move in exalted spheres.* **8** (*intr*) to make progress. **9** (*tr*) to arouse affection, pity, or compassion in; touch. **10** (in board games) to change the position of (a piece) or (of a piece) to change position. **11** (*intr*) (of merchandise) to be disposed of by being bought. **12** (when *tr, often takes a clause as object;* when *intr,* often foll. by *for*) to suggest (a proposal) formally, as in debating or parliamentary procedure. **13** (*intr;* usually foll. by *on* or *along*) to go away or to another place; leave. **14** to cause (the bowels) to evacuate or (of the bowels) to be evacuated. **15** (*intr*) *Informal.* to be exciting or active: *the party started moving at twelve.* **16 move heaven and earth.** to take every step possible (to achieve something). ◆ *n* **17** the act of moving; movement. **18** one of a sequence of actions, usually part of a plan; manoeuvre. **19** the act of moving one's residence, place of business, etc. **20** (in board games) **20a** a player's turn to move his piece or take other permitted action. **20b** a permitted manoeuvre of a piece. **21 get a move on.** *Informal.* **21a** to get started. **21b** to hurry up. **22 make a move.** (*usually used with a negative*) *Informal.* to take even the slightest action: *don't make a move without phoning me.* **23 make one's move.** to commit oneself to a position or course of action. **24 on the move. 24a** travelling from place to place. **24b** advancing; succeeding. **24c** very active; busy. [C13: from Anglo-French *mover,* from Latin *movēre*]

move in *vb* (*mainly adv*) **1** (*also prep*) Also (when *prep*): **move into.** to occupy or take possession of (a new residence, place of business, etc.) or help (someone) to do this. **2** (*intr;* often foll. by *on*) *Informal.* to creep close (to), as in preparing to capture. **3** (*intr;* often foll. by *on*) *Informal.* to try to gain power or influence (over) or interfere (with).

movement ('muːvmənt) *n* **1a** the act, process, or result of moving. **1b** an instance of moving. **2** the manner of moving. **3a** a group of people with a common ideology, esp. a political or religious one. **3b** the organized action of such a group. **4** a trend or tendency in a particular sphere. **5** the driving and regulating mechanism of a watch or clock. **6** (*often pl*) a person's location and activities during a specific time. **7a** the evacuation of the bowels. **7b** the matter evacuated. **8** *Music.* a principal self-contained section of a symphony, sonata, etc., usually having its own structure. **9** tempo or pace, as in music or literature. **10** *Fine arts.* the appearance of motion in painting, sculpture, etc. **11** *Prosody.* the rhythmic structure of verse. **12** a positional change by one or a number of military units. **13** a change in the market price of a security or commodity.

move out *vb* (*adv*) to vacate a residence, place of business, etc., or help (someone) to do this.

mover ('muːvə) *n* **1** *Informal.* a person, business, idea, etc., that is advancing or progressing. **2** a person who moves a proposal, as in a debate. **3** *U.S. and Canadian.* a removal firm or a person who works for one.

movers and shakers *pl n Informal.* the people with power and influence in a particular field of activity. [C20: perhaps from the line "We are the movers and shakers of the world for ever" in 'Ode' by Arthur O'Shaughnessy (1844–81), British poet]

movie ('muːvɪ) *n* **a** an informal word for **film** (sense 1). **b** (*as modifier*): *movie ticket.* [C20: from MOV(ING PICTURE) + -IE]

movie camera *n* the U.S. and Canadian term for **cine camera.**

movie film *n* the U.S. and Canadian term for **cine film.**

Movietone ('muːvɪ,təʊn) *n U.S. trademark.* the earliest technique of including a soundtrack on film.

moving ('mu:vɪŋ) *adj* **1** arousing or touching the emotions. **2** changing or capable of changing position. **3** causing motion. ▸ **'movingly** *adv*

moving average *n Statistics.* (of a sequence of values) a derived sequence of the averages of successive subsequences of a given number of members, often used in time series to even out short-term fluctuations and make a trend clearer: *the 3-term moving average of 4, 6, 8, 7, 9, 8 is 6, 7, 8.*

moving coil *adj* denoting an electromechanical device in which a suspended coil is free to move in a magnetic field. A current passing through the coil causes it to move, as in loudspeakers and electrical measuring instruments, or movement of the coil gives rise to induced currents, as in microphones and some record-player pick-ups.

moving picture *n* a U.S. and Canadian name for **film** (sense 1).

moving staircase *or* **stairway** *n* less common terms for **escalator** (sense 1).

Moviola (ˌmu:vɪ'əʊlə) *n Trademark.* a viewing machine used in cutting and editing film.

mow[1] (məʊ) *vb* **mows, mowing, mowed, mowed** *or* **mown. 1** to cut down (grass, crops, etc.) with a hand implement or machine. **2** (*tr*) to cut the growing vegetation of (a field, lawn, etc.). [Old English *māwan;* related to Old High German *māen,* Middle Dutch *maeyen* to mow, Latin *metere* to reap, Welsh *medi*] ▸ **'mower** *n*

mow[2] (maʊ) *n* **1** the part of a barn where hay, straw, etc., is stored. **2** the hay, straw, etc., stored. [Old English *mūwa;* compare Old Norse *mūgr* heap, Greek *mukōn*]

mow[3] (maʊ) *n, vb* an archaic word for **grimace.** [C14: from Old French *moe* a pout, or Middle Dutch *mouwe*]

MOW (in New Zealand) *abbrev. for* Ministry of Works.

mowburnt ('məʊˌbɜ:nt) *adj* (of hay, straw, etc.) damaged by overheating in a mow.

mowdie ('maʊdɪ) *or* **mowdiewart** ('maʊdɪˌwært) *n* Scot. words for **mole**[2]. [C18: a Scot. variant of MOULDWARP]

mow down *vb* (*tr, adv*) to kill in large numbers, esp. by gunfire.

Mowlam ('məʊlæm) *n* **Mo,** full name *Marjorie Mowlam.* born 1949, British Labour politician; secretary of state for Northern Ireland from 1997.

mown (məʊn) *vb* a past participle of **mow**[1].

moxa ('mɒksə) *n* **1** a downy material obtained from various plants and used in Oriental medicine by being burned on the skin as a cauterizing agent or counterirritant for the skin. **2** any of various plants yielding this material, such as the wormwood *Artemisia chinensis.* [C17: anglicized version of Japanese *mogusa,* contraction of *moe gusa* burning herb]

moxibustion (ˌmɒksɪ'bʌstʃən) *n* a method of treatment, originally in Chinese medicine, in which a moxa is burned on the skin. [C20: from MOXA + (COM)BUSTION]

moxie ('mɒksɪ) *n U.S. and Canadian slang.* courage, nerve, or vigour. [from the trademark *Moxie,* a soft drink]

Moya ('mɔɪjə) *n* **(John) Hidalgo.** 1920–94, British architect: in partnership with Philip Powell, his designs include Skylon, Festival of Britain (1950), Wolfson College, Oxford (1974), and the Queen Elizabeth Conference Centre, Westminster (1986).

Moyle (mɔɪl) *n* a district of NE Northern Ireland, in Co. Antrim. Pop.: 14 789 (1991). Area: 494 sq. km (191 sq. miles).

moz *or* **mozz** (mɒz) *n Austral. slang., obsolete.* **1** a hoodoo; hex. **2 put the moz on.** to jinx. [short for *mozzle,* from Hebrew *mazzal* luck]

Mozambique (ˌməʊzəm'bi:k) *n* a republic in SE Africa: colonized by the Portuguese from 1505 onwards and a slave-trade centre until 1878; made an overseas province of Portugal in 1951; became an independent republic in 1975; became a member of the Commonwealth in 1995. Official language: Portuguese. Religion: animist majority. Currency: metical. Capital: Maputo. Pop.: 18 641 000 (1998 est.). Area: 812 379 sq. km (313 661 sq. miles). Portuguese name: **Moçambique.** Also called (until 1975): **Portuguese East Africa.**

Mozambique Channel *n* a strait between Mozambique and Madagascar. Length: about 1600 km (1000 miles). Width: 400 km (250 miles).

Mozarab (məʊ'zærəb) *n* (formerly) a Christian of Moorish Spain. [C18: via Spanish from Arabic *musta'rib* a would-be Arab] ▸ **Moz'arabic** *adj*

Mozart ('məʊtsɑ:t) *n* **Wolfgang Amadeus** ('vɔlfgaŋ ama'de:ʊs). 1756–91, Austrian composer. A child prodigy and prolific genius, his works include operas, such as *The Marriage of Figaro* (1786), *Don Giovanni* (1787), and *The Magic Flute* (1791), symphonies, concertos for piano, violin, clarinet, and French horn, string quartets and quintets, sonatas, songs, and Masses, such as the unfinished *Requiem* (1791). ▸ **Mo'zartean** *or* **Mo'zartian** *adj*

Mo-Zi ('məʊ'tsi:) *or* **Mo-tzu** *n* ?470–?391 B.C., Chinese religious philosopher; his teaching, expounded in the book *Mo-Zi,* emphasizes love, frugality, avoidance of aggressive war, and submission to Heaven.

mozzarella (ˌmɒtsə'rɛlə) *n* a moist white Italian curd cheese made originally from buffalo milk. [from Italian, diminutive of *mozza* a type of cheese, from *mozzare* to cut off]

mozzetta (məʊ'zɛtə; *Italian* mot'tsetta) *or* **mozetta** *n R.C. Church.* a short hooded cape worn by the pope, cardinals, etc. [C18: from Italian, shortened from *almozzetta,* from Medieval Latin *almutia* ALMUCE]

mozzie ('mɒzɪ) *n* a variant spelling of **mossie**[1].

mp *abbrev. for:* **1** melting point. **2** *Music.* mezzo piano. [Italian: moderately soft]

MP *abbrev. for:* **1** (in Britain) Member of Parliament. **2** (in Britain) Metropolitan Police. **3** Military Police. **4** Mounted Police.

mpg *abbrev. for* miles per gallon.

MPG (in Britain) *abbrev. for* main professional grade: the basic salary scale for classroom teachers.

mph *abbrev. for* miles per hour.

MPhil *or* **MPh** *abbrev. for* Master of Philosophy.

MPLA *abbrev. for* Movimento Popular de Libertacão de Angola. [Portuguese: Popular Movement for the Liberation of Angola]

MP/M *n Computing.* a multiuser operating system that resembles a CP/M.

MPP (in Canada) *abbrev. for* Member of the Provincial Parliament (of Ontario).

MPS *abbrev. for:* **1** Member of the Pharmaceutical Society. **2** Member of the Philological Society. **3** Member of the Physical Society.

Mpumalanga (m'pʌmɑ:ˌlɑ:ngə) *n* a province of E South Africa; formed in 1994 from part of the former province of Transvaal: agriculture and service industries. Capital: Nelspruit. Pop.: 3 007 100 (1995 est.). Area: 78 370 sq. km (30 259 sq. miles).

MPV *abbrev. for* multipurpose vehicle.

Mr ('mɪstə) *n, pl* **Messrs** ('mɛsəz). **1** a title used before a man's name or names or before some office that he holds: *Mr Jones; Mr President.* **2** (in military contexts) a title used in addressing a warrant officer, officer cadet, or junior naval officer. **3** a title placed before the surname of a surgeon. [C17: abbreviation of MISTER]

MR *abbrev. for:* **1** (in Britain) Master of the Rolls. **2** motivation(al) research.

MRA *abbrev. for* Moral Rearmament.

Mr Big *n Slang, chiefly U.S.* the head of an organization, esp. of a criminal organization.

MRBM *abbrev. for* medium-range ballistic missile.

MRC (in Britain) *abbrev. for* Medical Research Council.

MRCA *abbrev. for* multirole combat aircraft.

MRI *abbrev. for* magnetic resonance imaging.

MRIA *abbrev. for* Member of the Royal Irish Academy.

mridang (mrɪ'dʌŋg) *n* a drum used in Indian music. [Hindi]

m-RNA *abbrev. for* messenger RNA.

MRP *abbrev. for* manufacturers' recommended price.

Mr Right *n Informal.* the man considered by a woman to be her perfect marriage partner.

Mrs ('mɪsɪz) *n, pl* **Mrs** *or* **Mesdames.** a title used before the name or names of a married woman. [C17: originally an abbreviation of MISTRESS]

MRSA *abbrev. for* methicillin-resistant *Staphylococcus aureus*: a bacterium that enters the skin through open wounds to cause septicaemia and is extremely resistant to most antibiotics. It has been responsible for outbreaks of untreatable infections among patients in hospitals.

MRSC *abbrev. for* Member of the Royal Society of Chemistry.

Mrs Mop *n Informal.* a cleaning lady.

Ms (mɪz, məs) *n* a title substituted for **Mrs** or **Miss** before a woman's name to avoid making a distinction between married and unmarried women.

MS *abbrev. for:* **1** Master of Surgery. **2** (on gravestones) memoriae sacrum. [Latin: sacred to the memory of] **3** Mississippi. **4** motor ship. **5** multiple sclerosis. ◆ **6** *international car registration for* Mauritius.

MS. *or* **ms.** *pl* **MSS.** *or* **mss.** *abbrev. for* manuscript.

msb *Computing. abbrev. for* most significant bit; the bit of binary number with the greatest numerical value or the bit in some other binary pattern which occupies this position.

MSc *abbrev. for* Master of Science.

MS-DOS (ɛm'ɛs'dɒs) *n Trademark, computing.* a type of disk operating system. [C20: from *M(icro)s(oft),* the company that developed it, + DOS]

MSF (in Britain) *abbrev. for* Manufacturing, Science, Finance (a trade union).

MSG *abbrev. for* monosodium glutamate.

Msgr *abbrev. for* Monsignor.

MSI *Electronics. abbrev. for* medium scale integration.

msl *or* **MSL** *abbrev. for* mean sea level.

MSS *or* **mss** *abbrev. for* manuscripts.

MST *abbrev. for* Mountain Standard Time.

Ms-Th *Physics. symbol for* mesothorium.

Mt *or* **mt** *abbrev. for:* **1** mount: *Mt Everest.* **2** Also: **mtn.** mountain.

MT *abbrev. for* Montana.

mt. *abbrev. for* megaton.

MTB *n Brit.* a motor torpedo boat.

MTBE *abbrev. for* methyl tertiary-butyl ether: a lead-free antiknock petrol additive.

MTBF *abbrev. for* mean time between failures.

MTech *abbrev. for* Master of Technology.

mtg *abbrev. for* meeting.

mtg. *or* **mtge** *abbrev. for* mortgage.

Mt Rev. *abbrev. for* Most Reverend.

MTV *abbrev. for* music television: a U.S. music channel that operates 24 hours a day.

mu (mju:) *n* the 12th letter in the Greek alphabet (Μ, μ), a consonant, transliterated as *m.*

MU *abbrev. for* Musicians' Union.

Mu'awiyah I (ˌmu:ə'wi:jə) *n* ?602–680 A.D., first caliph (661–80) of the Omayyad dynasty of Damascus; regarded as having secularized the caliphate.

Mubarak (mʊ'bɑ:rək) *n* **(Muhammad) Hosni** ('hʊsnɪ). born 1928, Egyptian statesman; president of Egypt from 1981.

muc- *combining form.* a variant of **muco-** before a vowel.

much (mʌtʃ) *determiner* **1a** (*usually used with a negative*) a great quantity or degree of: *there isn't much honey left.* **1b** (*as pronoun*): *much has been learned from this.* **2 a bit much.** *Informal.* rather excessive. **3 as much.** exactly that: *I suspected as much when I heard.* **4 make much of.** See **make of** (sense 4). **5 not much of.** not to any appreciable degree or extent: *he's not much of an actor really.* **6 not up to much.** *Informal.* of a low standard: *this beer is not up to much.* **7 think much of.** (*used with a negative*) to have a high opinion of: *I don't think much of his behaviour.* ◆ *adv* **8** considerably: *they're much better now.* **9** practically; nearly (esp. in the phrase **much the same**). **10** (*usually* *used with a negative*) often; a great deal: *it doesn't happen much in this country.* **11** (**as**) **much as.** even though; although: *much as I'd like to, I can't come.* ◆ *adj* **12** (*predicative; usually used with a negative*) impressive or important: *this car isn't much.* ◆ See also **more, most.** [Old English *mycel;* related to Old English *micel* great, Old Saxon *mikil,* Gothic *mikils;* compare also Latin *magnus,* Greek *megas*]

muchness (ˈmʌtʃnɪs) *n* **1** *Archaic or informal.* magnitude. **2** **much of a muchness.** *Brit.* very similar.

mucic acid (ˈmjuːsɪk) *n* a colourless crystalline solid carboxylic acid found in milk sugar and used in the manufacture of pyrrole. Formula: $C_4H_4(OH)_4(COOH)_2$. [C19: *mucic,* from French *mucique;* see MUCUS, -IC]

mucid (ˈmjuːsɪd) *adj Rare.* mouldy, musty, or slimy. [C17: from Latin *mūcidus,* from *mucēre* to be mouldy] ▸ **muˈcidity** *or* **ˈmucidness** *n*

mucigen (ˈmjuːsɪdʒən) *n* a substance present in mucous cells that is converted into mucin.

mucilage (ˈmjuːsɪlɪdʒ) *n* **1** a sticky preparation, such as gum or glue, used as an adhesive. **2** a complex glutinous carbohydrate secreted by certain plants. [C14: via Old French from Late Latin *mūcilāgo* mouldy juice; see MUCID] ▸ **mucilaginous** (ˌmjuːsɪˈlædʒɪnəs) *adj* ▸ **ˌmuciˈlaginously** *adv* ▸ **ˌmuciˈlaginousness** *n*

mucin (ˈmjuːsɪn) *n Biochem.* any of a group of nitrogenous mucoproteins occurring in saliva, skin, tendon, etc., that produce a very viscous solution in water. [C19: via French from Latin MUCUS] ▸ **ˈmucinous** *adj*

muck (mʌk) *n* **1** farmyard dung or decaying vegetable matter. **2** Also called: **muck soil.** an organic soil rich in humus and used as a fertilizer. **3** dirt or filth. **4** earth, rock material, etc., removed during mining excavations. **5** *Slang, chiefly Brit.* rubbish. **6** See **Lord Muck, Lady Muck.** **7** **make a muck of.** *Slang, chiefly Brit.* to ruin or spoil. ◆ *vb* (*tr*) **8** to spread manure upon (fields, gardens, etc.). **9** to soil or pollute. **10** (often foll. by *out*) to clear muck from. ◆ See also **muck about, muck in, muck up.** [C13: probably of Scandinavian origin; compare Old Norse *myki* dung, Norwegian *myk*]

muck about *vb Brit. slang.* **1** (*intr*) to waste time; misbehave. **2** (when *intr,* foll. by *with*) to interfere with, annoy, or waste the time of.

muckamuck (ˈmʌkəˌmʌk) *Canadian W coast.* ◆ *n* **1** food. ◆ *vb* **2** (*intr*) to consume food; eat. [Chinook Jargon]

mucker (ˈmʌkə) *n* **1** *Mining.* a person who shifts broken rock or waste. **2** *Brit. slang.* **2a** a friend; mate. **2b** a coarse person. ▸ **ˈmuckerish** *adj*

muck in *vb* (*intr, adv*) *Brit. slang.* to share something, such as duties, work, etc. (with other people).

muckle (ˈmʌkᵊl) *Scot.* ◆ *adj* **1** large; much. ◆ *adv* **2** much; greatly. [dialect variant of MICKLE]

muckrake (ˈmʌkˌreɪk) *n* **1** an agricultural rake for spreading manure. ◆ *vb* **2** (*intr*) to seek out and expose scandal, esp. concerning public figures. ▸ **ˈmuckˌraker** *n* ▸ **ˈmuckˌraking** *n*

mucksweat (ˈmʌkˌswɛt) *n Brit. informal.* profuse sweat or a state of profuse sweating.

muck up *vb* (*adv*) *Informal.* **1** (*tr*) *Brit. and Austral.* to ruin or spoil; make a mess of. **2** (*intr*) *Austral.* to misbehave.

muck-up day *n Austral. slang.* the last day of school before the annual examinations, marked by practical jokes and other student pranks.

muckworm (ˈmʌkˌwɜːm) *n* **1** any larva or worm that lives in mud. **2** *Informal.* a miser.

mucky (ˈmʌkɪ) *adj* **muckier, muckiest. 1** dirty. **2** of or like muck. ▸ **ˈmuckily** *adv* ▸ **ˈmuckiness** *n*

muco- *or before a vowel* **muc-** *combining form.* mucus or mucous: *mucoprotein; mucin.*

mucoid (ˈmjuːkɔɪd) *or* **mucoidal** *adj* of the nature of or resembling mucin.

mucopolysaccharide (ˌmjuːkəʊˌpɒlɪˈsækəraɪd) *n Biochem.* any of a group of complex polysaccharides composed of repeating units of two sugars, one of which contains an amino group.

mucoprotein (ˌmjuːkəʊˈprəʊtiːn) *n* any of a group of conjugated proteins containing small quantities of mucopolysaccharides; glycoprotein.

mucopurulent (ˌmjuːkəʊˈpjʊərələnt) *adj Pathol.* composed of or containing both mucus and pus.

mucor (ˈmjuːkɔː) *n* any fungus belonging to the genus *Mucor,* which comprises many common moulds. [C20: New Latin, from Latin: mould]

mucosa (mjuːˈkəʊsə) *n, pl* **-sae** (-siː). another word for **mucous membrane.** [C19: New Latin, from Latin *mūcōsus* slimy] ▸ **muˈcosal** *adj*

mucous (ˈmjuːkəs) *or* **mucose** (ˈmjuːkəʊs, -kəʊz) *adj* of, resembling, or secreting mucus. [C17: from Latin *mūcōsus* slimy, from MUCUS] ▸ **mucosity** (mjuːˈkɒsɪtɪ) *n*

USAGE The noun *mucus* is often misspelled *mucous. Mucous* can only be correctly used as an adjective.

mucous membrane *n* a mucus-secreting membrane that lines body cavities or passages that are open to the external environment. Also called: **mucosa.** ▸ **mucomembranous** (ˌmjuːkəʊˈmɛmbrənəs) *adj*

mucro (ˈmjuːkrəʊ) *n, pl* **mucrones** (mjuːˈkrəʊniːz). *Biology.* a short pointed projection from certain parts or organs, as from the tip of a leaf. [C17: from Latin *mūcrō* point]

mucronate (ˈmjuːkrəʊnɪt, -ˌneɪt) *or* **mucronated** *adj* terminating in a sharp point. [C18: from Latin *mūcrōnātus* pointed, from MUCRO] ▸ **ˌmucroˈnation** *n*

mucus (ˈmjuːkəs) *n* the slimy protective secretion of the mucous membranes, consisting mainly of mucin. [C17: from Latin: nasal secretions; compare *mungere* to blow the nose; related to Greek *muxa* mucus, *muktēr* nose]

USAGE See at **mucous.**

mud (mʌd) *n* **1** a fine-grained soft wet deposit that occurs on the ground after rain, at the bottom of ponds, lakes, etc. **2** *Informal.* slander or defamation. **3** **clear as mud.** *Informal.* not at all clear. **4** **drag** (**someone's**) **name in the mud.** to disgrace or defame (someone). **5** **here's mud in your eye.** *Informal.* a humorous drinking toast. **6** (**someone's**) **name is mud.** *Informal.* (someone) is disgraced. **7** **throw** (*or* **sling**) **mud at.** *Informal.* to slander; vilify. ◆ *vb* **muds, mudding, mudded. 8** (*tr*) to soil or cover with mud. [C14: probably from Middle Low German *mudde;* compare Middle High German *mot* swamp, mud, Swedish *modd* slush]

mud bath *n* **1** a medicinal bath in heated mud. **2** a dirty or muddy occasion, state, etc.

mudcat (ˈmʌdˌkæt) *n* any of several large North American catfish living in muddy rivers, esp. in the Mississippi valley.

mud dauber *n* any of various wasps of the family *Sphecidae,* that construct cells of mud or clay in which they lay their eggs and store live insects as food for the developing larvae. See also **digger wasp.**

muddle (ˈmʌdᵊl) *vb* (*tr*) **1** (often foll. by *up*) to mix up (objects, items, etc.); jumble. **2** to confuse. **3** to make (water) muddy or turbulent. **4** *U.S.* to mix or stir (alcoholic drinks, etc.). ◆ *n* **5** a state of physical or mental confusion. [C16: perhaps from Middle Dutch *moddelen* to make muddy] ▸ **ˈmuddled** *adj* ▸ **ˈmuddledness** *or* **ˈmuddlement** *n* ▸ **ˈmuddling** *adj, n* ▸ **ˈmuddlingly** *adv* ▸ **ˈmuddly** *adj*

muddle along *or* **on** *vb* (*intr, adv*) to proceed in a disorganized way.

muddleheaded (ˌmʌdᵊlˈhɛdɪd) *adj* mentally confused or vague. ▸ **ˌmuddleˈheadedness** *n*

muddler (ˈmʌdlə) *n* **1** a person who muddles or muddles through. **2** *U.S.* an instrument for mixing drinks thoroughly.

muddle through *vb* (*intr, adv*) *Chiefly Brit.* to succeed in some undertaking in spite of lack of organization.

muddy (ˈmʌdɪ) *adj* **-dier, -diest. 1** covered or filled with mud. **2** not clear or bright: *muddy colours.* **3** cloudy: *a muddy liquid.* **4** (esp. of thoughts) confused or vague. ◆ *vb* **-dies, -dying, -died. 5** to become or cause to become muddy. ▸ **ˈmuddily** *adv* ▸ **ˈmuddiness** *n*

Mudéjar *Spanish.* (muˈðexar) *n, pl* **-jares** (-xares). **1** *Medieval history.* a Spanish Moor, esp. one permitted to stay in Spain after the Christian reconquest. ◆ *adj* **2** of or relating to a style of architecture orginated by Mudéjares. [from Arabic *mudajjan* one permitted to remain]

mudfish (ˈmʌdˌfɪʃ) *n, pl* **-fish** *or* **-fishes.** any of various fishes, such as the bowfin and cichlids, that live at or frequent the muddy bottoms of rivers, lakes, etc.

mud flat *n* a tract of low muddy land, esp. near an estuary, that is covered at high tide and exposed at low tide.

mudflow (ˈmʌdˌfləʊ) *n Geology.* a flow of soil mixed with water down a steep unstable slope.

mudguard (ˈmʌdˌgɑːd) *n* a curved part of a motorcycle, bicycle, etc., attached above the wheels to reduce the amount of water or mud thrown up by them. U.S. and Canadian name: **fender.**

mud hen *n* any of various birds that frequent marshes or similar places, esp. the coots, rails, etc.

mudir (muːˈdɪə) *n* a local governor. [C19: via Turkish, from Arabic, from *adāra* to administrate]

mudlark (ˈmʌdˌlɑːk) *n* **1** *Slang, now rare.* a street urchin. **2** (formerly) one who made a living by picking up odds and ends in the mud of tidal rivers. **3** *Austral. slang.* a racehorse that runs well on a wet or muddy course.

mud map *n Austral. informal.* a map drawn on the ground with a stick, or any other roughly drawn map.

mudpack (ˈmʌdˌpæk) *n* a cosmetic astringent paste containing fuller's earth, used to improve the complexion.

mud pie *n* a mass of mud moulded into a pie-like shape by a child.

mud puppy *n* any aquatic North American salamander of the genus *Necturus,* esp. *N. maculosus,* having red feathery external gills and other persistent larval features: family *Proteidae.* See also **neoteny.**

mudra (məˈdrɑː) *n* any of various ritual hand movements in Hindu religious dancing. [Sanskrit, literally: sign, token]

mudskipper (ˈmʌdˌskɪpə) *n* any of various gobies of the genus *Periophthalmus* and related genera that occur in tropical coastal regions of Africa and Asia and can move on land by means of their strong pectoral fins.

mudslinging (ˈmʌdˌslɪŋɪŋ) *n* casting malicious slurs on an opponent, esp. in politics. ▸ **ˈmudˌslinger** *n*

mudstone (ˈmʌdˌstəʊn) *n* a dark grey clay rock similar to shale but with the lamination less well developed.

mud turtle *n* any of various small turtles of the genus *Kinosternon* and related genera that inhabit muddy rivers in North and Central America: family *Kinosternidae.*

mud volcano *n* a cone-shaped mound formed from fine mud ejected, with gases and water, from hot springs, geysers, etc., in volcanic regions.

muenster (ˈmʊnstə) *n* a whitish-yellow semihard whole milk cheese, often flavoured with caraway or aniseed. [after *Muenster,* Haut-Rhin, France]

muesli (ˈmjuːzlɪ) *n* a mixture of rolled oats, nuts, fruit, etc., eaten with milk. [Swiss German, from German *Mus* mush, purée + *-li,* diminutive suffix]

muezzin (muːˈɛzɪn) *n Islam.* the official of a mosque who calls the faithful to prayer five times a day from the minaret. [C16: changed from Arabic *mu'adhdhin*]

muff[1] (mʌf) *n* **1** an open-ended cylinder of fur or cloth into which the hands are placed for warmth. **2** the tuft on either side of the head of certain fowls. [C16: probably from Dutch *mof,* ultimately from French *mouffle* MUFFLE[1]]

muff[2] (mʌf) *vb* **1** to perform (an action) awkwardly. **2** (*tr*) to bungle (a shot, catch, etc.) in a game. ◆ *n* **3** any unskilful play in a game, esp. a dropped catch. **4** any clumsy or bungled action. **5** a bungler. [C19: of uncertain origin]

muffin (ˈmʌfɪn) *n* **1** *Brit.* a thick round baked yeast roll, usually toasted and served with butter. **2** *U.S. and Canadian.* a small cup-shaped sweet bread roll, usually eaten hot with butter. [C18: perhaps from Low German *muffen,* cakes]

muffin man *n Brit.* (formerly) an itinerant seller of muffins.

muffle[1] ('mʌfᵊl) *vb* (*tr*) **1** (often foll. by *up*) to wrap up (the head) in a scarf, cloak, etc., esp. for warmth. **2** to deaden (a sound or noise), esp. by wrapping. **3** to prevent (the expression of something) by (someone). ◆ *n* **4** something that muffles. **5** a kiln with an inner chamber for firing porcelain, enamel, etc., at a low temperature. [C15: probably from Old French; compare Old French *moufle* mitten, *emmouflé* wrapped up]

muffle[2] ('mʌfᵊl) *n* the fleshy hairless part of the upper lip and nose in ruminants and some rodents. [C17: from French *mufle,* of unknown origin]

muffler ('mʌflə) *n* **1** a thick scarf, collar, etc. **2** the U.S. and Canadian name for **silencer** (sense 1). **3** something that muffles.

mufti[1] ('mʌftɪ) *n, pl* **-tis. 1** a Muslim legal expert and adviser on the law of the Koran. **2** (in the former Ottoman empire) the leader of the religious community. [C16: from Arabic *muftī,* from *aftā* to give a (legal) decision]

mufti[2] ('mʌftɪ) *n, pl* **-tis.** civilian dress, esp. as worn by a person who normally wears a military uniform. [C19: perhaps from MUFTI[1]]

Mufulira (ˌmu:fu:'lɪərə) *n* a mining town in the Copper Belt of Zambia. Pop.: 152 944 (1990).

mug[1] (mʌg) *n* **1** a drinking vessel with a handle, usually cylindrical and made of earthenware. **2** Also called: **mugful.** the quantity held by a mug or its contents. [C16: probably from Scandinavian; compare Swedish *mugg*]

mug[2] (mʌg) *n* **1** *Slang.* a person's face or mouth: *get your ugly mug out of here!* **2** *Slang.* a grimace. **3** *Brit. slang.* a gullible person, esp. one who is swindled easily. **4 a mug's game.** a worthless activity. ◆ *vb* **mugs, mugging, mugged. 5** (*tr*) *Informal.* to attack or rob (someone) violently. **6** (*intr*) *Brit. slang.* to pull faces or overact, esp. in front of a camera. ◆ See also **mug up.** [C18: perhaps from MUG[1], since drinking vessels were sometimes modelled into the likeness of a face]

Mugabe (mʊ'gɑ:bɪ) *n* **Robert.** born 1925, Zimbabwean politician; leader of one wing of the Patriotic Front against the government of Ian Smith of Rhodesia, and of the Zanu party; prime minister (1980–87); president from 1988.

mugger[1] ('mʌgə) *n* **1** *Informal.* a person who commits robbery with violence, esp. in the street. **2** *Chiefly U.S. and Canadian.* a person who overacts.

mugger[2], **muggar,** *or* **muggur** ('mʌgə) *n* a large freshwater crocodile, *Crocodylus niloticus,* inhabiting marshes and pools of India and Ceylon. Also called: **marsh crocodile.** [C19: from Hindi *magar*]

muggins ('mʌgɪnz) *n* **1** *Brit. slang.* **1a** a simpleton; silly person. **1b** a title used humorously to refer to oneself. **2** a variation on the game of dominoes. **3** a card game. [C19: probably from the surname *Muggins*]

muggy ('mʌgɪ) *adj* **-gier, -giest.** (of weather, air, etc.) unpleasantly warm and humid. [C18: dialect *mug* drizzle, probably from Scandinavian; compare Old Norse *mugga* mist] ▸ **'muggily** *adv* ▸ **'mugginess** *n*

mug up *vb* (*adv*) *Brit. slang.* to study (a subject) hard, esp. for an exam. [C19: of unknown origin]

mugwort ('mʌgˌwɜ:t) *n* **1** a N temperate perennial herbaceous plant, *Artemisia vulgaris,* with aromatic leaves and clusters of small greenish-white flowers: family *Compositae* (composites). **2** another name for **crosswort.** [Old English *mucgwyrt,* perhaps from Old English *mycg* MIDGE]

mugwump ('mʌgˌwʌmp) *n U.S.* a neutral or independent person, esp. in politics. [C19: from Algonquian: great chief, from *mogki* great + *-omp* man] ▸ **'mugˌwumpery** *or* **'mugˌwumpism** *n* ▸ **'mugˌwumpish** *adj*

Muhammad (mʊ'hæməd) *n* a variant of **Mohammed.**

Muhammad Ali *or* **Muhammed Ali** *or* **Mohammed Ali** ('ɑ:lɪ, ɑ:'li:, 'ælɪ) *n* original name *Cassius* (*Marcellus*) *Clay.* born 1942, U.S. boxer, who was world heavyweight champion three times (1964–67; 1974–78; 1978).

Muhammadan *or* **Muhammedan** (mʊ'hæmədᵊn) *n, adj* another word (not in Muslim use) for **Muslim.**

Muharram (mu:'hærəm) *or* **Moharram** *n* the first month of the Islamic year. [from Arabic: sacred]

Mühlhausen (my:l'hauzən) *n* the German name for **Mulhouse.**

muir (mu:r, mju:r, myr) *n* **a** a Scot. word for **moor**[1]. **b** (*in place names*): *Sheriffmuir.*

Muir (mjʊə) *n* **Edwin.** 1887–1959, Scottish poet, novelist, and critic.

muirburn ('mu:rˌbʌrn, 'mju:r-, 'myr-) *n Scot.* a variant of **moorburn.**

Muir Glacier *n* a glacier in SE Alaska, in the St Elias Mountains, flowing south-east from Mount Fairweather. Area: about 900 sq. km (350 sq. miles).

mujaheddin, mujahedeen *or* **mujahideen** ('mu:dʒəhə'di:n) *pl n* (preceded by *the; sometimes cap.*) (in Afghanistan and Iran) fundamentalist Muslim guerrillas; in Afghanistan in 1992 the mujaheddin overthrew the government but were unable to agree on a constitution due to factional conflict and in 1996 Taliban forces seized power. [C20: from Arabic *mujāhidīn* fighters, ultimately from JIHAD]

mujik ('mu:ʒɪk) *n* a variant spelling of **muzhik.**

Mukden ('mʊkdən) *n* a former name of **Shenyang.**

mukluk ('mʌklʌk) *n* a soft boot, usually of sealskin, worn by Eskimos. [from Eskimo *muklok* large seal]

mulatto (mju:'lætəʊ) *n, pl* **-tos** *or* **-toes. 1** a person having one Black and one White parent. ◆ *adj* **2** of a light brown colour. [C16: from Spanish *mulato* young mule, variant of *mulo* MULE[1]]

mulberry ('mʌlbərɪ, -brɪ) *n, pl* **-ries. 1** any moraceous tree of the temperate genus *Morus,* having edible blackberry-like fruit, such as *M. alba* (**white mulberry**), the leaves of which are used to feed silkworms. **2** the fruit of any of these trees. **3** any of several similar or related trees, such as the paper mulberry and Indian mulberry. **4a** a dark purple colour. **4b** (*as adj*): *a mulberry dress.* [C14: from Latin *mōrum,* from Greek *moron;* related to Old English *mōrberie;* compare Dutch *moerbezie,* Old High German *mūrberi*]

Mulberry Harbour *n* either of two prefabricated floating harbours towed across the English Channel to the French coast for the Allied invasion of Normandy in 1944. [from the code name Operation *Mulberry*]

mulch (mʌltʃ) *n* **1** half-rotten vegetable matter, peat, etc., used to prevent soil erosion or enrich the soil. ◆ *vb* **2** (*tr*) to cover (the surface of land) with mulch. [C17: from obsolete *mulch* soft; related to Old English *mylisc* mellow; compare dialect German *molsch* soft, Latin *mollis* soft]

Mulciber ('mʌlsɪbə) *n* another name for **Vulcan**[1].

mulct (mʌlkt) *vb* (*tr*) **1** to cheat or defraud. **2** to fine (a person). ◆ *n* **3** a fine or penalty. [C15: via French from Latin *multa* a fine]

Muldoon (mʌl'du:n) *n* Sir **Robert David.** 1921–92, New Zealand statesman; prime minister of New Zealand (1975–84).

mule[1] (mju:l) *n* **1** the sterile offspring of a male donkey and a female horse, used as a beast of burden. Compare **hinny**[1]. **2** any hybrid animal: *a mule canary.* **3** Also called: **spinning mule.** a machine invented by Samuel Crompton that spins cotton into yarn and winds the yarn on spindles. **4** *Informal.* an obstinate or stubborn person. **5** *Slang.* a person who is paid to transport illegal drugs for a dealer. [C13: from Old French *mul,* from Latin *mūlus* ass, mule]

mule[2] (mju:l) *n* a backless shoe or slipper. [C16: from Old French from Latin *mulleus* a magistrate's shoe]

mule deer *n* a W North American deer, *Odocoileus hemionus,* with long ears and a black-tipped tail.

mules (mju:lz) *vb* (*tr*) *Austral.* to perform the Mules operation on (a sheep).

mule skinner *n U.S. and Canadian.* an informal term for **muleteer.**

Mules operation (mju:lz) *n Austral.* the surgical removal of folds of skin in the breech of a sheep to reduce blowfly strike. [named after J. H. W. *Mules* (died 1946), Australian grazier who first suggested it]

muleta (mju:'letə) *n* the small cape attached to a stick used by the matador during the final stages of a bullfight. [Spanish: small mule, crutch, from *mula* MULE[1]]

muleteer (ˌmju:lɪ'tɪə) *n* a person who drives mules.

muley ('mju:lɪ) *or* **mulley** ('mʌlɪ) *adj* **1** (of cattle) having no horns. ◆ *n* **2** any hornless cow. [C16: variant of dialect *moiley,* from Gaelic *maol,* Welsh *moel* bald]

mulga ('mʌlgə) *n Austral.* **1** any of various Australian acacia shrubs, esp. *Acacia aneura,* which grows in the central desert regions and has leaflike leafstalks. **2** scrub comprised of a dense growth of acacia. **3** the outback; bush. [from a native Australian language]

Mulhacén (*Spanish* mula'θen) *n* a mountain in S Spain, in the Sierra Nevada: the highest peak in Spain. Height: 3478 m (11 410 ft.).

Mülheim an der Ruhr (*German* 'my:lhaim an der 'ru:r) *or* **Mülheim** *n* an industrial city in W Germany, in North Rhine-Westphalia on the River Ruhr: river port. Pop.: 176 530 (1996 est.).

Mulhouse (*French* myluz) *n* a city in E France, on the Rhône–Rhine canal: under German rule (1871–1918); textiles. Pop.: 109 905 (1990). German name: **Mühlhausen.**

muliebrity (ˌmju:lɪ'ɛbrɪtɪ) *n* **1** the condition of being a woman. **2** femininity. [C16: via Late Latin from Latin *muliēbris* womanly, from *mulier* woman]

mulish ('mju:lɪʃ) *adj* stubborn; obstinate; headstrong. ▸ **'mulishly** *adv* ▸ **'mulishness** *n*

Mulki ('mʊlkɪ) *n* a native or inhabitant of the former Hyderabad State in India. [Urdu, from *mulk* country]

mull[1] (mʌl) *vb* (*tr*) (often foll. by *over*) to study or ponder. [C19: probably from MUDDLE]

mull[2] (mʌl) *vb* (*tr*) to heat (wine, ale, etc.) with sugar and spices to make a hot drink. [C17: of unknown origin]

mull[3] (mʌl) *n* a light muslin fabric of soft texture. [C18: earlier *mulmull,* from Hindi *malmal*]

mull[4] (mʌl) *n* a layer of nonacidic humus formed in well drained and aerated soils. Compare **mor.** [C20: from Danish *muld;* see MOULD[3]]

mull[5] (mʌl) *n Scot.* a promontory. [C14: related to Gaelic *maol,* Icelandic *múli*]

Mull (mʌl) *n* a mountainous island off the west coast of Scotland, in the Inner Hebrides, separated from the mainland by the **Sound of Mull.** Chief town: Tobermory. Pop.: 2605 (latest est.). Area: 909 sq. km (351 sq. miles).

mullah, mulla ('mʌlə, 'mʊlə), *or* **mollah** ('mɒlə) *n* (formerly) a Muslim scholar, teacher, or religious leader: also used as a title of respect. [C17: from Turkish *molla,* Persian and Hindi *mulla,* from Arabic *mawlā* master]

mullein *or* **mullen** ('mʌlɪn) *n* any of various Mediterranean herbaceous plants of the scrophulariaceous genus *Verbascum,* such as *V. thapsus* (**common mullein** or **Aaron's rod**), typically having tall spikes of yellow flowers and broad hairy leaves. [C15: from Old French *moleine,* probably from Old French *mol* soft, from Latin *mollis*]

muller ('mʌlə) *n* a flat heavy implement of stone or iron used to grind material against a slab of stone. [C15: probably from *mullen* to grind to powder; compare Old English *myl* dust]

Muller ('mʌlə) *n* **Hermann Joseph.** 1890–1967, U.S. geneticist, noted for his work on the transmutation of genes by X-rays: Nobel prize for physiology or medicine 1946.

Müller (*German* 'mylər) *n* **1 Friedrich Max** ('fri:drɪç maks). 1823–1900, British Sanskrit scholar born in Germany. **2 Johann** (jo'han). See **Regiomontanus. 3 Johannes Peter** (jo'hanəs 'pe:tər). 1801–58, German physiologist, anatomist, and experimental psychologist. **4 Paul Hermann** (paul 'hɛrman). 1899–1965, Swiss chemist. He synthesized DDT (1939) and discovered its use as an insecticide: Nobel prize for physiology or medicine 1948.

Müllerian mimicry (mu:'lɪərɪən) *n Zoology.* mimicry in which two or more harmful or inedible species resemble each other, so that predators tend to avoid them. [C19: named after J.F.T. *Müller* (1821–97), German zoologist who first described it]

Müller-Lyer illusion ('mu:lə'laɪə) *n* an optical illusion in which a line with inward pointing arrowheads is seen as longer than an equal line with outward pointing arrowheads. [C19: named after Franz *Müller-Lyer* (1857–1916), German sociologist and psychiatrist]

mullet ('mʌlɪt) *n* **1** any of various teleost food fishes belonging to the families *Mugilidae* (see **grey mullet**) or *Mullidae* (see **red mullet**). **2** the U.S. name for **grey mullet.** [C15: via Old French from Latin *mullus*, from Greek *mullos*]

mulley ('mʌlɪ) *adj, n* a variant of **muley.**

mulligan ('mʌlɪgən) *n U.S. and Canadian.* a stew made from odds and ends of food. [C20: perhaps from the surname]

mulligatawny (ˌmʌlɪgə'tɔ:nɪ) *n* a curry-flavoured soup of Anglo-Indian origin, made with meat stock. [C18: from Tamil *milakutanni*, from *milaku* pepper + *tanni* water]

Mulliken ('mʌlɪkən) *n* **Robert Sanderson.** 1896–1986, U.S. physicist and chemist, who won the Nobel prize for chemistry (1966) for his work on bonding and the electronic structure of molecules.

Mullingar (ˌmʌlɪn'gɑ:) *n* a town in N central Republic of Ireland, the county town of Co. Westmeath; site of cathedral; cattle raised. Pop.: 11 800 (1995 est.).

mullion ('mʌlɪən) *n* **1** a vertical member between the casements or panes of a window or the panels of a screen. **2** one of the ribs on a rock face. ◆ *vb* **3** (*tr*) to furnish (a window, screen, etc.) with mullions. [C16: variant of Middle English *munial*, from Old French *moinel*, of unknown origin]

mullite ('mʌlaɪt) *n* a colourless mineral consisting of aluminium silicate in orthorhombic crystalline form: used as a refractory. Formula: $Al_6Si_2O_{13}$. [from island of MULL]

mullock ('mʌlək) *n* **1** *Austral.* waste material from a mine. **2** *Dialect.* a mess or muddle. **3 poke mullock at.** *Austral. informal.* to ridicule. [C14: related to Old English *myl* dust, Old Norse *mylja* to crush; see MULLER] ▸ **'mullocky** *adj*

mulloway ('mʌləˌweɪ) *n* a large Australian marine sciaenid fish, *Sciaena antarctica*, valued for sport and food. [C19: of unknown origin]

Mulroney (mʌl'rəʊnɪ) *n* **(Martin) Brian.** born 1939, Canadian statesman; Conservative prime minister (1984–93).

Multan (ˌmʊl'tɑ:n) *n* a city in central Pakistan, near the Chenab River. Pop.: 1 257 000 (1995 est.).

multangular (mʌl'tæŋgjʊlə) *or* **multiangular** *adj* having many angles.

multeity (mʌl'ti:ɪtɪ) *n* manifoldness. [C19: from Latin *multus* many, perhaps formed by analogy with HAECCEITY]

multi- *combining form.* **1** many or much: *multiflorous; multimillion.* **2** more than one: *multiparous; multistorey.* [from Latin *multus* much, many]

multiaccess (ˌmʌltɪ'æksɛs) *n Computing.* a system in which several users are permitted to have apparently simultaneous access to a computer.

multichannel analyser (ˌmʌltɪ'tʃænᵊl) *n* an electronic instrument, such as a pulse height analyser, that splits an input waveform into a large number of channels in accordance with a particular parameter of the input.

multicide ('mʌltɪˌsaɪd) *n* mass murder.

multicollinearity (ˌmʌltɪkəʊˌlɪnɪ'ærɪtɪ) *n Statistics.* the condition occurring when two or more of the independent variables in a regression equation are correlated.

multicoloured ('mʌltɪˌkʌləd) *adj* having many colours.

multicultural (ˌmʌltɪ'kʌltʃərəl) *adj* consisting of, relating to, or designed for the cultures of several different races.

multiculturalism (ˌmʌltɪ'kʌltʃərəˌlɪzəm) *n* **1** the state or condition of being multicultural. **2** the policy of maintaining a diversity of ethnic cultures within a community.

multidisciplinary (ˌmʌltɪ'dɪsɪˌplɪnərɪ) *adj* of or relating to the study of one topic, involving several subject disciplines.

multiethnic (ˌmʌltɪ'eθnɪk) *adj* consisting of, relating to, or designed for various different races.

multifaceted (ˌmʌltɪ'fæsɪtɪd) *adj* **1** (of a gem) having many facets. **2** having many aspects, abilities, etc.

multifactorial (ˌmʌltɪfæk'tɔ:rɪəl) *adj* **1** *Genetics.* of or designating inheritance that depends on more than one gene. **2** involving or including a number of elements or factors.

multifarious (ˌmʌltɪ'fɛərɪəs) *adj* having many parts of great variety. [C16: from Late Latin *multifārius* manifold, from Latin *multifāriam* on many sides] ▸ ˌ**multi'fariously** *adv* ▸ ˌ**multi'fariousness** *n*

multifid ('mʌltɪfɪd) *or* **multifidous** (mʌl'tɪfɪdəs) *adj* having or divided into many lobes or similar segments: *a multifid leaf.* [C18: from Latin *multifidus*, from *multus* many + *findere* to split] ▸ **'multifidly** *adv*

multiflora rose (ˌmʌltɪ'flɔ:rə) *n* an Asian climbing shrubby rose, *Rosa multiflora*, having clusters of small fragrant flowers: the source of many cultivated roses.

multifoil ('mʌltɪˌfɔɪl) *n* an ornamental design having a large number of foils. See also **trefoil** (sense 4), **quatrefoil** (sense 2), **cinquefoil** (sense 2).

multifold ('mʌltɪˌfəʊld) *adj* many times doubled; manifold.

multifoliate (ˌmʌltɪ'fəʊlɪɪt, -ˌeɪt) *adj Botany.* having many leaves or leaflets: *a multifoliate compound leaf.*

multiform ('mʌltɪˌfɔ:m) *adj* having many forms or kinds. ▸ **multiformity** (ˌmʌltɪ'fɔ:mɪtɪ) *n*

multigravida (ˌmʌltɪ'grævɪdə) *n* a woman who is pregnant for at least the third time. Compare **multipara.** [C20: New Latin; see MULTI-, GRAVID]

multigym ('mʌltɪˌdʒɪm) *n* an exercise apparatus incorporating a variety of weights, used for toning the muscles.

multihull ('mʌltɪˌhʌl) *n* a sailing vessel with two or more hulls. Compare **monohull.**

multilateral (ˌmʌltɪ'lætərəl, -'lætrəl) *adj* **1** of or involving more than two nations or parties: *a multilateral pact.* **2** having many sides. ▸ ˌ**multi'laterally** *adv*

multilingual (ˌmʌltɪ'lɪŋgwəl) *adj* **1** able to speak more than two languages. **2** written or expressed in more than two languages. Compare **bilingual, monolingual.**

multimedia (ˌmʌltɪ'mi:dɪə) *pl n* **1** the combined use of media such as television, slides, etc., esp. in education. ◆ *adj* **2** of or relating to the use of a combination of media: *multimedia teaching aids.* **3** *Computing.* of or relating to any of various systems which can manipulate data in a variety of forms, such as sound, graphics, or text.

multimeter ('mʌltɪˌmi:tə) *n* an electrical test instrument offering measurement of several values, usually voltage, current, and resistance.

multimillionaire (ˌmʌltɪˌmɪljə'nɛə) *n* a person with a fortune of several million pounds, dollars, etc.

multinational (ˌmʌltɪ'næʃənᵊl) *adj* **1** (of a large business company) operating in several countries. ◆ *n* **2** such a company.

multinomial (ˌmʌltɪ'nəʊmɪəl) *n* another name for **polynomial** (sense 2b). [C17: from MULTI- + *-nomial* as in BINOMIAL]

multinuclear (ˌmʌltɪ'nju:klɪə) *or* **multinucleate** (ˌmʌltɪ'nju:klɪɪt, -ˌeɪt) *adj* (of a cell, microorganism, etc.) having more than two nuclei.

multipack ('mʌltɪˌpæk) *n* a form of packaging of foodstuffs, etc., that contains several units and is offered at a price below that of the equivalent number of units.

multipara (mʌl'tɪpərə) *n, pl* **-rae** (-ˌri:). a woman who has given birth to more than one viable fetus or living child. Compare **multigravida.** [C19: New Latin, feminine of *multiparus* MULTIPAROUS]

multiparous (mʌl'tɪpərəs) *adj* **1** (of certain species of mammal) producing many offspring at one birth. **2** of, relating to, or designating a multipara. [C17: from New Latin *multiparus*] ▸ **multiparity** (ˌmʌltɪ'pærɪtɪ) *n*

multipartite (ˌmʌltɪ'pɑ:taɪt) *adj* **1** divided into many parts or sections. **2** *Government.* a less common word for **multilateral.**

multi-part stationery *n Computing.* continuous stationery comprising two or more sheets, either carbonless or with carbon paper between the sheets.

multiparty (ˌmʌltɪ'pɑ:tɪ) *adj* of or relating to a state, political system, etc., in which more than one political party is permitted: *multiparty democracy.*

multipath ('mʌltɪˌpɑ:θ) *adj* relating to television or radio signals that travel by more than one route from a transmitter and arrive at slightly different times, causing ghost images or audio distortion.

multiped ('mʌltɪˌpɛd) *or* **multipede** ('mʌltɪˌpi:d) *Rare.* ◆ *adj* **1** having many feet. ◆ *n* **2** an insect or animal having many feet. [C17: from Latin *multipēs*]

multiphase ('mʌltɪˌfeɪz) *adj* another word for **polyphase** (sense 1).

multiplane ('mʌltɪˌpleɪn) *n* an aircraft that has more than one pair of wings. Compare **monoplane.**

multiple ('mʌltɪpᵊl) *adj* **1** having or involving more than one part, individual, etc. **2** *Electronics, U.S. and Canadian.* (of a circuit) having a number of conductors in parallel. ◆ *n* **3** the product of a given number or polynomial and any other one: *6 is a multiple of 2.* **4** *Telephony.* an electrical circuit accessible at a number of points to any one of which a connection can be made. **5** short for **multiple store.** [C17: via French from Late Latin *multiplus*, from Latin MULTIPLEX] ▸ **'multiply** *adv*

multiple alleles *pl n* a group of three or more alleles produced by mutation of the gene. Only two of them are present in a normal diploid cell at the same time. ▸ **multiple allelism** *n*

multiple-choice *adj* having a number of possible given answers out of which the correct one must be chosen.

multiple factors *pl n Genetics.* two or more pairs of genes that act as a unit, producing cumulative effects in the phenotype.

multiple fission *n Zoology.* asexual reproduction in unicellular organisms, esp. sporozoans, in which the nucleus divides a number of times, followed by division of the cytoplasm, to form daughter cells.

multiple fruit *n* a fruit, such as a pineapple, formed from the ovaries of individual flowers in an inflorescence.

multiple personality *n Psychiatry.* a mental disorder in which an individual's personality appears to have become separated into two or more distinct personalities, each with its own complex organization. Nontechnical name: **split personality.**

multiplepoinding (ˌmʌltɪpᵊl'pɪndɪŋ) *n Scots Law.* an action to determine the division of a property or fund between several claimants, brought by or on behalf of the present holder.

multiple sclerosis *n* a chronic progressive disease of the central nervous system characterized by loss of some of the myelin sheath surrounding certain nerve fibres and resulting in speech and visual disorders, tremor, muscular incoordination, partial paralysis, etc. Also called: **disseminated sclerosis.**

multiple star *n* a system of three or more stars associated by gravitation. See also **binary star.**

multiple store *n* one of several retail enterprises under the same ownership and management. Also called: **multiple shop.**

multiplet ('mʌltɪˌplɛt, -plɪt) *n Physics.* **1** a line in a spectrum formed of two or more closely spaced lines, resulting from small differences in energy level of atoms or molecules. **2** a group of related elementary particles that differ only in electric charge. [from MULTIPLE; on the model of DOUBLET]

multiple voting *n* the practice of voting in more than one constituency in the same election.

multiplex ('mʌltɪˌplɛks) *n* **1** *Telecomm.* **1a** the use of a common communications channel for sending two or more messages or signals. In **frequency-division multiplex** the frequency band transmitted by the common channel is split into narrower bands each of which constitutes a distinct channel. In

time-division multiplex different channels are established by intermittent connections to the common channel. **1b** (*as modifier*): *a multiplex transmitter.* **2a** a purpose-built complex containing a number of cinemas and usually a restaurant or bar. **2b** (*as modifier*): *a multiplex cinema.* ◆ *adj* **3** designating a method of map-making using three cameras to produce a stereoscopic effect. **4** a less common word for **multiple.** ◆ *vb* **5** to send (messages or signals) or (of messages or signals) be sent by multiplex. [C16: from Latin: having many folds, from MULTI- + *plicāre* to fold] ▸ **'multi,plexer** *n*

multiplicand (,mʌltɪplɪ'kænd) *n* a number to be multiplied by another number, the **multiplier.** [C16: from Latin *multiplicandus,* gerund of *multiplicāre* to MULTIPLY]

multiplicate ('mʌltɪplɪ,keɪt) *adj Rare.* manifold.

multiplication (,mʌltɪplɪ'keɪʃən) *n* **1** an arithmetical operation, defined initially in terms of repeated addition, usually written $a \times b$, $a.b$, or ab, by which the product of two quantities is calculated: to multiply a by positive integral b is to add a to itself b times. Multiplication by fractions can then be defined in the light of the associative and commutative properties; multiplication by $1/n$ is equivalent to multiplication by 1 followed by division by n: for example $0.3 \times 0.7 = 0.3 \times 7/10 = (0.3 \times 7)/10 = 2.1/10 = 0.21$. **2** the act of multiplying or state of being multiplied. **3** the act or process in animals, plants, or people of reproducing or breeding. ▸ **,multipli'cational** *adj*

multiplication sign *n* the symbol ×, placed between numbers to be multiplied, as in $3 \times 4 \times 5 = 60$.

multiplication table *n* one of a group of tables giving the results of multiplying two numbers together.

multiplicative ('mʌltɪplɪ,keɪtɪv, ,mʌltɪ'plɪkətɪv) *adj* **1** tending or able to multiply. **2** *Maths.* involving multiplication. ▸ **'multipli,catively** *adv*

multiplicity (,mʌltɪ'plɪsɪtɪ) *n, pl* **-ties. 1** a large number or great variety. **2** the state of being multiple. **3** *Physics.* **3a** the number of levels into which the energy of an atom, molecule, or nucleus splits as a result of coupling between orbital angular momentum and spin angular momentum. **3b** the number of elementary particles in a multiplet.

multiplier ('mʌltɪ,plaɪə) *n* **1** a person or thing that multiplies. **2** the number by which another number, the **multiplicand,** is multiplied. **3** *Physics.* any device or instrument, such as a photomultiplier, for increasing an effect. **4** *Economics.* **4a** the ratio of the total change in income (resulting from successive rounds of spending) to an initial autonomous change in expenditure. **4b** (*as modifier*): *multiplier effects.*

multiply ('mʌltɪ,plaɪ) *vb* **-plies, -plying, -plied. 1** to increase or cause to increase in number, quantity, or degree. **2** (*tr*) to combine (two numbers or quantities) by multiplication. **3** (*intr*) to increase in number by reproduction. [C13: from Old French *multiplier,* from Latin *multiplicāre* to multiply, from *multus* much, many + *plicāre* to fold] ▸ **'multi,pliable** *or* **'multi,plicable** *adj*

multiprocessor (,mʌltɪ'prəʊsesə) *n Computing.* a number of central processing units linked together to enable parallel processing to take place.

multiprogramming (,mʌltɪ'prəʊgræmɪŋ) *n* a time-sharing technique by which several computer programs are each run for a short period in rotation.

multipurpose (,mʌltɪ'pɜːpəs) *adj* able to be used for many purposes: *a multipurpose gadget.*

multipurpose vehicle *n* a large car, similar to a van, designed to carry up to eight passengers. Abbrev.: **MPV.**

multiracial (,mʌltɪ'reɪʃəl) *adj* comprising people of many races. ▸ **,multi'racialism** *n*

multirole ('mʌltɪ,rəʊl) *adj* having a number of roles, functions, etc.

multiseriate (,mʌltɪ'sɪərɪeɪt) *adj Botany.* arranged in rows or composed of more than one cell layer.

multiskilling ('mʌltɪ,skɪlɪŋ) *n* the practice of training employees to do a number of different tasks.

multistage ('mʌltɪ,steɪdʒ) *adj* **1** (of a rocket or missile) having several stages, each of which can be jettisoned after it has burnt out. **2** (of a turbine, compressor, or supercharger) having more than one rotor. **3** (of any process or device) having more than one stage.

multistorey (,mʌltɪ'stɔːrɪ) *adj* **1** (of a building) having many storeys. ◆ *n* **2** a multistorey car park.

multitasking (,mʌltɪ'tɑːskɪŋ) *n Computing.* the execution of various diverse tasks simultaneously.

multitrack ('mʌltɪ,træk) *adj* (in sound recording) using tape containing two or more tracks, usually four to twenty-four.

multitude ('mʌltɪ,tjuːd) *n* **1** a large gathering of people. **2 the.** the common people. **3** a large number. **4** the state or quality of being numerous. [C14: via Old French from Latin *multitūdō*]

multitudinous (,mʌltɪ'tjuːdɪnəs) *adj* **1** very numerous. **2** *Rare.* great in extent, variety, etc. **3** *Poetic.* crowded. ▸ **,multi'tudinously** *adv* ▸ **,multi'tudinousness** *n*

multi-user *adj* (of a computer) capable of being used by several people at once.

multivalent (,mʌltɪ'veɪlənt) *adj* another word for **polyvalent.** ▸ **,multi'valency** *n*

multivariate (,mʌltɪ'vɛərɪɪt) *adj Statistics.* (of a distribution) involving a number of distinct, though not usually independent, random variables.

multiversity (,mʌltɪ'vɜːsɪtɪ) *n Chiefly U.S. and Canadian.* a university with many constituent and affiliated institutions. [C20: MULTI- + UNIVERSITY]

multivibrator (,mʌltɪvaɪ'breɪtə) *n* an electronic oscillator consisting of two transistors or other electronic devices, coupled so that the input of each is derived from the output of the other.

multivocal (,mʌltɪ'vəʊkᵊl) *adj* having many meanings. [C19: from Latin *multus* many + *vocare* to call; on the model of EQUIVOCAL]

multiwindow (,mʌltɪ'wɪndəʊ) *n* a visual display unit screen that can be divided to show a number of different documents simultaneously.

multum in parvo ('mʊltʊm ɪn 'pɑːvəʊ) much in a small space. [Latin]

multure ('mʌltʃə) *n Archaic or Scot.* **1** a fee formerly paid to a miller for grinding grain. **2** the right to receive such a fee. [C13: from Old French *moulture,* from Medieval Latin *molitūra* a grinding, from Latin *molere*]

mum[1] (mʌm) *n Chiefly Brit.* an informal word for **mother**[1]. [C19: a child's word]

mum[2] (mʌm) *adj* **1** keeping information to oneself; silent. ◆ *n* **2 mum's the word.** silence or secrecy is to be observed. [C14: suggestive of closed lips]

mum[3] *or* **mumm** (mʌm) *vb* **mums, mumming, mummed.** (*intr*) to act in a mummer's play. [C16: verbal use of MUM[2]]

mum[4] (mʌm) *n Brit., obsolete.* a type of beer made from cereals, beans, etc. [C17: from German *Mumme,* perhaps from the name of its original brewer]

Mumbai (mʊm'baɪ) *n* the Hindi name for **Bombay.**

mumble ('mʌmbᵊl) *vb* **1** to utter indistinctly, as with the mouth partly closed; mutter. **2** *Rare.* to chew (food) ineffectually or with difficulty. ◆ *n* **3** an indistinct or low utterance or sound. [C14 *momelen,* from MUM[2]] ▸ **'mumbler** *n* ▸ **'mumbling** *adj* ▸ **'mumblingly** *adv*

mumbo jumbo ('mʌmbəʊ) *n, pl* **mumbo jumbos. 1** foolish religious reverence, ritual, or incantation. **2** meaningless or unnecessarily complicated language. **3** an object of superstitious awe or reverence. [C18: probably from Mandingo *mama dyumbo,* name of a tribal god]

mumchance ('mʌm,tʃɑːns) *adj* silent; struck dumb. [C16 (masquerade, dumb show): from Middle Low German *mummenschanze* masked serenade; from *mummen* (see MUMMER) + *schanze* CHANCE]

mu meson (mjuː) *n* a former name for **muon.**

Mumford ('mʌmfəd) *n* **Lewis.** 1895–1990, U.S. sociologist, whose works are chiefly concerned with the relationship between man and his environment. They include *The City in History* (1962) and *Roots of Contemporary Architecture* (1972).

mummer ('mʌmə) *n* **1** one of a group of masked performers in folk play or mime. **2** a mime artist. **3** *Humorous or derogatory.* an actor. [C15: from Old French *momeur,* from *momer* to mime; related to *momon* mask]

Mummerset ('mʌməsɪt, -,set) *n* an imitation West Country accent used in drama. [C20: from MUMMER + (SOMER)SET]

mummery ('mʌmərɪ) *n, pl* **-meries. 1** a performance by mummers. **2** hypocritical or ostentatious ceremony.

mummify ('mʌmɪ,faɪ) *vb* **-fies, -fying, -fied. 1** (*tr*) to preserve the body of (a human or animal) as a mummy. **2** (*intr*) to dry up; shrivel. **3** (*tr*) to preserve (an outdated idea, institution, etc.) while making lifeless. ▸ **,mummifi'cation** *n*

mummy[1] ('mʌmɪ) *n, pl* **-mies. 1** an embalmed or preserved body, esp. as prepared for burial in ancient Egypt. **2** *Obsolete.* the substance of such a body used medicinally. **3** a mass of pulp. **4** a dark brown pigment. [C14: from Old French *momie,* from Medieval Latin *mumia,* from Arabic *mūmiyah* asphalt, from Persian *mūm* wax]

mummy[2] ('mʌmɪ) *n, pl* **-mies.** *Chiefly Brit.* a child's word for **mother**[1]. [C19: variant of MUM[1]]

mump[1] (mʌmp) *vb* (*intr*) *Archaic.* to be silent. [C16 (to grimace, sulk, be silent): of imitative origin, alluding to the shape of the mouth when mumbling or chewing]

mump[2] (mʌmp) *vb* (*intr*) *Archaic.* to beg. [C17: perhaps from Dutch *mompen* to cheat]

mumps (mʌmps) *n* (*functioning as sing or pl*) an acute contagious viral disease of the parotid salivary glands, characterized by swelling of the affected parts, fever, and pain beneath the ear: usually affects children. Also called: **epidemic parotitis.** [C16: from MUMP[1] (to grimace)] ▸ **'mumpish** *adj*

mumsy ('mʌmzɪ) *adj* **-sier, -siest.** out of fashion; homely or drab.

mun. *abbrev. for* municipal.

munch (mʌntʃ) *vb* to chew (food) steadily, esp. with a crunching noise. [C14 *monche,* of imitative origin; compare CRUNCH] ▸ **'muncher** *n*

Munch (mʊŋk) *n* **Edvard** ('ɛdvard). 1863–1944, Norwegian painter and engraver, whose works, often on the theme of death, include *The Scream* (1893); a major influence on the expressionists, esp. on *die Brücke.*

Munchausen (*German* 'mynçhauzən) *n* **1** an exaggerated story. **2** a person who tells such a story. [C19: after Baron *Münchhausen,* subject of a series of exaggerated adventure tales written in English by R. E. Raspe (1737–94)]

Munchausen's syndrome *n* a mental disorder in which a patient feigns illness to obtain hospital treatment.

Munchausen's syndrome by proxy *or* **Munchausen by proxy** *n* a mental disorder in which an individual derives emotional satisfaction from inflicting injury on others and then subjecting them to medical treatment.

München ('mynçən) *n* the German name for **Munich.**

München-Gladbach (mynçən'glatbax) *n* the former name of **Mönchengladbach.**

munchies ('mʌntʃɪz) *pl n Slang.* **1 the.** a craving for food, induced by alcohol or drugs. **2** snacks or food collectively.

munchkin ('mʌntʃkɪn) *n Informal, chiefly U.S.* an undersized person or a child, esp. an appealing one. [C20: from the *Munchkins,* a dwarfish race of people in L. Frank Baum's *The Wonderful Wizard of Oz* (1900)]

Munda ('mʊndə) *n* **1** a family of languages spoken by scattered peoples throughout central India. **2** (*pl* **-das**) a member of any of these peoples.

mundane ('mʌndeɪn, mʌn'deɪn) *adj* **1** everyday, ordinary, or banal. **2** relating to the world or worldly matters. [C15: from French *mondain,* via Late Latin, from Latin *mundus* world] ▸ **'mundanely** *adv* ▸ **mun'danity** *or* **'mundaneness** *n*

munga ('mʌŋgə) *n N.Z. informal.* an army canteen. [C20: perhaps from French *manger* to eat or from Maori *manga* food remains]

mung bean (mʌŋ) *n* **1** an E Asian bean plant, *Phaseolus aureus,* grown for forage and as the source of bean sprouts used in oriental cookery. **2** the seed of this plant. [C20 *mung,* changed from *mungo,* from Tamil *mūngu,* ultimately from Sanskrit *mudga*]

mungo ('mʌŋgəʊ), **mongo,** *or* **mongoe** *n, pl* **-gos** *or* **-goes.** a cheap felted fabric made from waste wool. [C19: of unknown origin]

Munich ('mjuːnɪk) *n* a city in SW Germany, capital of the state of Bavaria, on the Isar River: became capital of Bavaria in 1508; headquarters of the Nazi movement in the 1920s; a major financial, commercial, and manufacturing centre. Pop.: 1 236 370 (1996 est.). German name: **München.**

Munich Pact *or* **Agreement** *n* the pact signed by Germany, the United Kingdom, France, and Italy on Sept. 29, 1938, to settle the crisis over Czechoslovakia, by which the Sudetenland was ceded to Germany.

municipal (mjuː'nɪsɪpᵊl) *adj* of or relating to a town, city, or borough or its local government. [C16: from Latin *mūnicipium* a free town, from *mūniceps* citizen from *mūnia* responsibilities + *capere* to take] ▸ **mu'nicipalism** *n* ▸ **mu'nicipalist** *n* ▸ **mu'nicipally** *adv*

municipality (mjuːˌnɪsɪ'pælɪtɪ) *n, pl* **-ties. 1** a city, town, or district enjoying some degree of local self-government. **2** the governing body of such a unit.

municipalize *or* **municipalise** (mjuː'nɪsɪpəˌlaɪz) *vb (tr)* **1** to bring under municipal ownership or control. **2** to make a municipality of. ▸ **muˌnicipali'zation** *or* **muˌnicipali'sation** *n*

munificent (mjuː'nɪfɪsənt) *adj* **1** (of a person) very generous; bountiful. **2** (of a gift) generous; liberal. [C16: back formation from Latin *mūnificentia* liberality, from *mūnificus,* from *mūnus* gift + *facere* to make] ▸ **mu'nificence** *or* **mu'nificentness** *n* ▸ **mu'nificently** *adv*

muniment ('mjuːnɪmənt) *n Rare.* a means of defence. [C15: via Old French, from Latin *munīre* to defend]

muniments ('mjuːnɪmənts) *pl n* **1** *Law.* the title deeds and other documentary evidence relating to the title to land. **2** *Archaic.* furnishings or supplies.

munition (mjuː'nɪʃən) *vb (tr)* to supply with munitions. [C16: via French from Latin *mūnītiō* fortification, from *mūnīre* to fortify. See AMMUNITION] ▸ **mu'nitioner** *n*

munitions (mjuː'nɪʃənz) *pl n (sometimes sing)* military equipment and stores, esp. ammunition.

Munnings ('mʌnɪŋz) *n* Sir **Alfred.** 1878–1959, British painter, best known for his horse paintings.

munnion ('mʌnjən) *n* an archaic word for **mullion.** [C16: from *monial* mullion]

Munro[1] (mʌn'rəʊ) *n, pl* **Munros.** *Mountaineering.* any separate mountain peak over 3000 feet high: originally used of Scotland only but now sometimes extended to other parts of the British Isles. [C20: named after Hugh Thomas *Munro* (1856–1919), who published a list of these in 1891]

Munro[2] (mʌn'rəʊ) *n* **H(ector) H(ugh),** pen name *Saki.* 1870–1916, Scottish author, born in Burma (now Myanmar), noted for his collections of satirical short stories, such as *Reginald* (1904) and *Beasts and Superbeasts* (1914).

Munsell scale ('mʌnsᵊl) *n* a standard chromaticity scale used in specifying colour. It gives approximately equal changes in visual hue. [C20: named after A. H. *Munsell* (1858–1918), U.S. inventor]

münster ('mynstə) *n* a variant of **muenster.**

Munster ('mʌnstə) *n* a province of SW Republic of Ireland: the largest of the four provinces and historically a kingdom; consists of the counties of Clare, Cork, Kerry, Limerick, Tipperary, and Waterford. Capital: Cork. Pop.: 1 033 000 (1996). Area: 24 125 sq. km (9315 sq. miles).

Münster (*German* 'mynstər) *n* a city in NW Germany, in North Rhine-Westphalia on the Dortmund–Ems Canal: one of the treaties comprising the Peace of Westphalia (1648) was signed here; became capital of Prussian Westphalia in 1815. Pop.: 265 061 (1996 est.).

Münsterberg ('mʊnstəˌbɜːg) *n* **Hugo.** 1863–1916, German psychologist, in the U.S. from 1897, noted for his pioneering work in applied psychology.

munt (mʊnt) *n S. African and Zimbabwean slang, derogatory.* a Black African. [from Zulu *umuntu* person]

muntin ('mʌntɪn) *n* another name (esp. U.S.) for **glazing-bar.** [C17: variant of C15 *mountant,* from Old French *montant,* present participle of *monter* to MOUNT[1]]

muntjac *or* **muntjak** ('mʌntˌdʒæk) *n* any small Asian deer of the genus *Muntiacus,* typically having a chestnut-brown coat, small antlers, and a barklike cry. Also called: **barking deer.** [C18: probably changed from Javanese *mindjangan* deer]

Müntzer ('muntzə; *German* 'myntzər) *n* **Thomas.** c. 1490–1525, German radical religious and political reformer; executed for organizing the Peasants' War (1524–25).

Muntz metal (mʌnts) *n* a type of brass consisting of three parts copper and two parts zinc, used in casting and extrusion. [C19: named after G. F. *Muntz* (1794–1857), English metallurgist]

muon ('mjuːɒn) *n* a positive or negative elementary particle with a mass 207 times that of an electron and spin ½. It was originally called the **mu meson** but is now classified as a lepton. [C20: short for MU MESON] ▸ **muonic** (mjuː'ɒnɪk) *adj*

muon-catalysed fusion *n Physics.* an experimental form of nuclear fusion in which hydrogen and deuterium muonic atoms are formed. Because the mass of the muon is much larger than that of the electron, the atoms are smaller, and the nuclei are close enough for fusion to occur.

muonic atom *n Physics.* an atom in which an orbiting electron has been replaced by a muon.

murage ('mjʊərɪdʒ) *n Brit., archaic.* a tax levied for the construction or maintenance of town walls. [C13: from Old French, ultimately from Latin *mūrus* wall]

mural ('mjʊərəl) *n* **1** a large painting or picture on a wall. ◆ *adj* **2** of or relating to a wall. [C15: from Latin *mūrālis,* from *mūrus* wall] ▸ **'muralist** *n*

Murasaki Shikibu (ˌmʊərɑː'sɑːkiː 'ʃiːkiːˌbuː) *n* 11th-century Japanese court lady, author of *The Tale of Genji,* perhaps the world's first novel.

Murat (*French* myra) *n* **Joachim** (ʒɔaʃɛ̃). 1767?–1815, French marshal, during the Napoleonic Wars; king of Naples (1808–15).

Murchison ('mɜːtʃɪsᵊn) *n* Sir **Roderick Impey.** 1792–1871, Scottish geologist: played a major role in establishing parts of the geological time scale, esp. the Silurian, Permian, and Devonian periods.

Murcia (*Spanish* 'murθja) *n* **1** a region and ancient kingdom of SE Spain, on the Mediterranean: taken by the Moors in the 8th century; an independent Muslim kingdom in the 11th and 12th centuries. **2** a city in SE Spain, capital of Murcia province: trading centre for a rich agricultural region; silk industry; university (1915). Pop.: 344 904 (1995 est.).

murdabad ('mʊədɑːˌbɑːd) *vb (tr) Indian.* down with; death to: used as part of a slogan in India, Pakistan, etc. Compare **zindabad.** [from Urdu, from Persian *murda* dead]

murder ('mɜːdə) *n* **1** the unlawful premeditated killing of one human being by another. Compare **manslaughter, homicide. 2** *Informal.* something dangerous, difficult, or unpleasant: *driving around London is murder.* **3 cry blue murder.** *Informal.* to make an outcry. **4 get away with murder.** *Informal.* to escape censure; do as one pleases. ◆ *vb (mainly tr)* **5** *(also intr)* to kill (someone) unlawfully with premeditation or during the commission of a crime. **6** to kill brutally. **7** *Informal.* to destroy; ruin: *he murdered her chances of happiness.* **8** *Informal.* to defeat completely; beat decisively: *the home team murdered their opponents.* ◆ Also (archaic or dialect): **murther.** [Old English *morthor;* related to Old English *morth,* Old Norse *morth,* Latin *mors* death; compare French *meurtre*] ▸ **'murderer** *n* ▸ **'murderess** *fem n*

murderous ('mɜːdərəs) *adj* **1** intending, capable of, or guilty of murder. **2** *Informal.* very dangerous, difficult, or unpleasant: *a murderous road.* ▸ **'murderously** *adv* ▸ **'murderousness** *n*

Murdoch ('mɜːdɒk) *n* **1** Dame **(Jean) Iris.** 1919–99, British writer. Her books include *The Bell* (1958), *A Severed Head* (1961), *The Sea, The Sea* (1978), which won the Booker Prize, *The Philosopher's Pupil* (1983), and *Existentialists and Mystics* (1997). **2 (Keith) Rupert.** born 1931, U.S. publisher and media entrepreneur, born in Australia; chairman of News International Ltd. and Times Newspapers Ltd.

mure (mjʊə) *vb (tr)* an archaic or literary word for **immure.** [C14: from Old French *murer,* from Latin *mūrus* wall]

Mureş ('mʊəreʃ) *n* a river in SE central Europe, rising in central Romania in the Carpathian Mountains and flowing west to the Tisza River at Szeged, Hungary. Length: 885 km (550 miles). Hungarian name: **Maros.**

murex ('mjʊəreks) *n, pl* **murices** ('mjʊərɪˌsiːz). any of various spiny-shelled marine gastropods of the genus *Murex* and related genera: formerly used as a source of the dye Tyrian purple. [C16: from Latin *mūrex* purple fish; related to Greek *muax* sea mussel]

muriate ('mjʊərɪɪt, -ˌeɪt) *n* an obsolete name for a **chloride.** [C18: back formation from *muriatic;* see MURIATIC ACID]

muriatic acid (ˌmjʊərɪ'ætɪk) *n* a former name for **hydrochloric acid.** [C17: from Latin *muriāticus* pickled, from *muria* brine]

muricate ('mjʊərɪˌkeɪt) *or* **muricated** *adj Biology.* having a surface roughened by numerous short points: *muricate stems.* [C17: from Latin *mūricātus* pointed like a MUREX]

Murillo (mjʊə'rɪləʊ; *Spanish* mu'riʎo) *n* **Bartolomé Esteban** (bartolo'me es'teβan). 1618–82, Spanish painter, esp. of religious subjects and beggar children.

murine ('mjʊəraɪn, -rɪn) *adj* **1** of, relating to, or belonging to the *Muridae,* an Old World family of rodents, typically having long hairless tails: includes rats and mice. **2** resembling a mouse or rat. ◆ *n* **3** any animal belonging to the *Muridae.* [C17: from Latin *mūrīnus* of mice, from *mūs* MOUSE]

murk *or* **mirk** (mɜːk) *n* **1** gloomy darkness. ◆ *adj* **2** an archaic variant of **murky.** [C13: probably from Old Norse *myrkr* darkness; compare Old English *mirce* dark]

murky *or* **mirky** ('mɜːkɪ) *adj* **murkier, murkiest** *or* **mirkier, mirkiest. 1** gloomy or dark. **2** cloudy or impenetrable as with smoke or fog. ▸ **'murkily** *or* **'mirkily** *adv* ▸ **'murkiness** *or* **'mirkiness** *n*

Murman Coast ('mʊəmən) *or* **Murmansk Coast** *n* a coastal region of NW Russia, in the north of the Kola Peninsula: within the Arctic Circle, but ice-free.

Murmansk (*Russian* 'murmənsk) *n* a port in NW Russia, on the Kola Inlet of the Barents Sea: founded in 1915; the world's largest town north of the Arctic Circle, with a large fishing fleet. Pop.: 407 000 (1995 est.).

murmur ('mɜːmə) *n* **1** a continuous low indistinct sound, as of distant voices. **2** an indistinct utterance: *a murmur of satisfaction.* **3** a complaint; grumble: *he made no murmur at my suggestion.* **4** *Med.* any abnormal soft blowing sound heard within the body, usually over the chest. See also **heart murmur.** ◆ *vb* **-murs, -muring, -mured. 5** to utter (something) in a murmur. **6** *(intr)* to complain in a murmur. [C14: as n, from Latin *murmur;* vb. via Old French *murmurer* from Latin *murmurāre* to rumble] ▸ **'murmurer** *n* ▸ **'murmuring** *n, adj* ▸ **'murmuringly** *adv* ▸ **'murmurous** *adj*

murphy ('mɜːfɪ) *n, pl* **-phies.** a dialect or informal word for **potato.** [C19: from the common Irish surname *Murphy*]

Murphy ('mɜːfɪ) *n* **1 Alex.** born 1939, British rugby league player and coach. **2 William Parry.** 1892–1987, U.S. physician: with G. R. Minot, he discovered the liver treatment for anaemia and they shared, with G. H. Whipple, the Nobel prize for physiology or medicine in 1934.

Murphy bed *n U.S. and Canadian.* a bed designed to be folded or swung into a cabinet when not in use. [C20: named after William *Murphy,* U.S. inventor]

Murphy's Law *n Informal.* another term for **Sod's law.** [C20: of uncertain origin]

murra ('mʌrə) *n* See **murrhine** (sense 2).

murragh ('mʌrə) *n* an angler's name for the **great red sedge,** a large caddis fly, *Phryganea grandis,* of still and running water, esteemed by trout. [perhaps from MURREY]

murrain ('mʌrɪn) *n* **1** any plaguelike disease in cattle. **2** *Archaic.* a plague. [C14: from Old French *morine, from morir* to die, from Latin *morī*]

Murray[1] ('mʌrɪ) *n* a river in SE Australia, rising in New South Wales and flowing northwest into SE South Australia, then south into the sea at Encounter Bay: the main river of Australia, important for irrigation and power. Length: 2590 km (1609 miles).

Murray[2] ('mʌrɪ) *n* **1 1st Earl of.** See (1st Earl of) **Moray. 2** Sir **(George) Gilbert (Aimé).** 1866–1957, British classical scholar, born in Australia: noted for his verse translations of Greek dramatists, esp. Euripides. **3** Sir **James Augustus Henry.** 1837–1915, Scottish lexicographer; one of the original editors (1879–1915) of what became the *Oxford English Dictionary.* **4 Murray of Epping Forest,** Baron, title of *Lionel Murray,* known as *Len.* born 1922, British trades union leader; general secretary of the Trades Union Congress (1973–84).

murre (mɜː) *n U.S. and Canadian.* any guillemot of the genus *Uria.* [C17: origin unknown]

murree *or* **murri** ('mʌrɪ) *n, pl* **-rees** *or* **-ris.** *Austral.* a native Australian. [C19: from a native Australian language]

murrelet ('mɜːlɪt) *n* any of several small diving birds of the genus *Brachyramphus* and related genera, similar and related to the auks: family *Alcidae,* order *Charadriiformes.* [C19: from MURRE + -LET]

murrey ('mʌrɪ) *adj Brit., archaic.* mulberry-coloured. [C14: from Old French *moré,* ultimately from Latin *mōrum* mulberry]

murrhine *or* **murrine** ('mʌraɪn, -ɪn) *adj* **1** of or relating to an unknown substance used in ancient Rome to make vases, cups, etc. ◆ *n* **2** Also called: **murra.** the substance so used. [C16: from Latin *murr(h)inus* belonging to *murra*]

murrhine glass *n* a type of Eastern glassware made from fluorspar and decorated with pieces of coloured metal.

Murrumbidgee (ˌmʌrəm'bɪdʒɪ) *n* a river in SE Australia, rising in S New South Wales and flowing north and west to the Murray River: important for irrigation. Length: 1690 km (1050 miles).

murther ('mɜːðə) *n, vb* an archaic word for **murder.** ► **'murtherer** *n*

murti ('muːrtɪ) *n Hinduism.* an image of a deity, which itself is considered divine once consecrated. [from Sanskrit, literally: embodiment]

mus. *abbrev. for:* **1** museum. **2** music. **3** musical.

musaceous (mjuː'zeɪʃəs) *adj* of, relating to, or belonging to the *Musaceae,* a family of tropical flowering plants having large leaves and clusters of elongated berry fruits: includes the banana, plantain, and Manila hemp. [C19: from New Latin *Mūsāceae,* from *Mūsa* genus name, from Arabic *mawzah* banana]

Musaf *Hebrew.* (*Hebrew* mu'sɑf; *Yiddish* 'mʊsəf) *n Judaism.* the additional prayers added to the morning service on Sabbaths, festivals, and Rosh Chodesh. [literally: addition]

musar *Hebrew.* (*Hebrew* mu'sɑː; *Yiddish* 'mʊsə) *n Judaism.* **1** rabbinic literature concerned with ethics, right conduct, etc. **2** any moralizing speech, esp. one which is critical. [literally: instruction]

MusB *or* **MusBac** *abbrev. for* Bachelor of Music.

Musca ('mʌskə) *n, Latin genitive* **Muscae** ('mʌskiː). a small constellation in the S hemisphere lying between the Southern Cross and Chamaeleon. [Latin: a fly]

muscadel *or* **muscadelle** (ˌmʌskə'dɛl) *n* another name for **muscatel.**

Muscadet ('mʌskəˌdeɪ; *French* myskadɛ) *n* (*sometimes not cap.*) **1** a white grape, grown esp. in the Loire valley, used for making wine. **2** any of various dry white wines made from this grape. [C20: from the region of Brittany where the grape was first grown]

muscadine ('mʌskədɪn, -ˌdaɪn) *n* **1** a woody climbing vitaceous plant, *Vitis rotundifolia,* of the southeastern U.S. **2** Also called: **scuppernong, bullace grape.** the thick-skinned musk-scented purple grape produced by this plant: used to make wine. [C16: from MUSCADEL]

muscae volitantes ('mʌsiː vɒlɪ'tæntiːz) *pl n Pathol.* moving black specks or threads seen before the eyes, caused by opaque fragments floating in the vitreous humour or a defect in the lens. [C18: New Latin: flying flies]

muscarine ('mʌskərɪn, -ˌriːn) *n* a poisonous alkaloid occurring in certain mushrooms. Formula: $C_8H_{19}NO_3$. [C19: from Latin *muscārius* of flies, from *musca* fly]

muscat ('mʌskət, -kæt) *n* **1** any of various grapevines that produce sweet white grapes used for making wine or raisins. **2** another name for **muscatel** (sense 1). [C16: via Old French from Provençal *muscat,* from *musc* MUSK]

Muscat ('mʌskət, -kæt) *n* the capital of the Sultanate of Oman, a port on the Gulf of Oman: a Portuguese port from the early 16th century; controlled by Persia (1650–1741). Pop.: 51 969 (1993). Arabic name: **Masqat.**

Muscat and Oman *n* the former name (until 1970) of (the Sultanate of) **Oman.**

muscatel (ˌmʌskə'tɛl), **muscadel,** *or* **muscadelle** *n* **1** Also called: **muscat.** a rich sweet wine made from muscat grapes. **2** the grape or raisin from a muscat vine. [C14: from Old French *muscadel,* from Old Provençal, from *moscadel,* from *muscat* musky. See MUSK]

muscid ('mʌsɪd) *n* **1** any fly of the dipterous family *Muscidae,* including the housefly and tsetse fly. ◆ *adj* **2** of, relating to, or belonging to the *Muscidae.* [C19: via New Latin from Latin *musca* fly]

muscle ('mʌsᵊl) *n* **1** a tissue composed of bundles of elongated cells capable of contraction and relaxation to produce movement in an organ or part. **2** an organ composed of muscle tissue. **3** strength or force. ◆ *vb* **4** (*intr;* often foll. by *in, on,* etc.) *Informal.* to force one's way (in). [C16: from medical Latin *musculus* little mouse, from the imagined resemblance of some muscles to mice, from Latin *mūs* mouse] ► **'muscly** *adj*

muscle-bound *adj* **1** having overdeveloped and inelastic muscles. **2** lacking flexibility.

muscle fibre *n* any of the numerous elongated contractile cells that contain many nuclei and make up striated muscle.

muscleman ('mʌsᵊlˌmæn) *n, pl* **-men. 1** a man with highly developed muscles. **2** a henchman employed by a gangster to intimidate or use violence upon victims.

muscle sense *n* another name for **kinaesthesia.**

muscovado *or* **muscavado** (ˌmʌskə'vɑːdəʊ) *n* raw sugar obtained from the juice of sugar cane by evaporating the molasses. [C17: from Portuguese *açúcar mascavado* separated sugar; *mascavado* from *mascavar* to separate, probably from Latin]

muscovite ('mʌskəˌvaɪt) *n* a pale brown, green, or colourless mineral of the mica group, found in plutonic rocks such as granite and in sedimentary rocks. It is used in the manufacture of lubricants, insulators, paints, and Christmas "snow". Composition: potassium aluminium silicate. Formula: $KAl_2(AlSi_3)O_{10}(OH)_2$. Crystal structure: monoclinic. See also **mica.** [C19: from the phrase *Muscovy glass,* an early name for mica]

Muscovite ('mʌskəˌvaɪt) *n* **1** a native or inhabitant of Moscow. ◆ *adj* **2** an archaic word for **Russian.**

Muscovy ('mʌskəvɪ) *n* **1** a Russian principality (13th to 16th centuries), of which Moscow was the capital. **2** an archaic name for **Russia** and **Moscow.**

Muscovy duck *or* **musk duck** *n* a large crested widely domesticated South American duck, *Cairina moschata,* having a greenish-black plumage with white markings and a large red caruncle on the bill. [C17: originally *musk duck,* a name later mistakenly associated with MUSCOVY]

muscular ('mʌskjʊlə) *adj* **1** having well-developed muscles; brawny. **2** of, relating to, or consisting of muscle. [C17: from New Latin *muscularis,* from *musculus* MUSCLE] ► **muscularity** (ˌmʌskjʊ'lærɪtɪ) *n* ► **'muscularly** *adv*

muscular dystrophy *n* a genetic disease characterized by progressive deterioration and wasting of muscle fibres, causing difficulty in walking.

musculature ('mʌskjʊlətʃə) *n* **1** the arrangement of muscles in an organ or part. **2** the total muscular system of an organism.

musculocutaneous (ˌmʌskjʊləʊkjuː'teɪnɪəs) *adj* of, relating to, or supplying the muscles and skin: *musculocutaneous nerve.*

MusD *or* **MusDoc** *abbrev. for* Doctor of Music.

muse[1] (mjuːz) *vb* **1** (when *intr,* often foll. by *on* or *about*) to reflect (about) or ponder (on), usually in silence. **2** (*intr*) to gaze thoughtfully. ◆ *n* **3** *Archaic.* a state of abstraction. [C14: from Old French *muser,* perhaps from *mus* snout, from Medieval Latin *mūsus*] ► **'muser** *n* ► **'museful** *adj* ► **'musefully** *adv*

muse[2] (mjuːz) *n* (often preceded by *the*) a goddess that inspires a creative artist, esp. a poet. [C14: from Old French, from Latin *Mūsa,* from Greek *Mousa* a Muse]

Muse (mjuːz) *n Greek myth.* any of nine sister goddesses, each of whom was regarded as the protectress of a different art or science. Daughters of Zeus and Mnemosyne, the nine are Calliope, Clio, Erato, Euterpe, Melpomene, Polyhymnia, Terpsichore, Thalia, and Urania.

museology (ˌmjuːzɪ'ɒlədʒɪ) *n* the science of museum organization. ► **ˌmuseo'logical** *adj* ► **ˌmuse'ologist** *n*

musette (mjuː'zɛt; *French* myzɛt) *n* **1** a type of bagpipe with a bellows popular in France during the 17th and 18th centuries. **2** a dance, with a drone bass originally played by a musette. [C14: from Old French, diminutive of *muse* bagpipe]

musette bag *n U.S.* an army officer's haversack.

museum (mjuː'zɪəm) *n* a place or building where objects of historical, artistic, or scientific interest are exhibited, preserved, or studied. [C17: via Latin from Greek *Mouseion* home of the Muses, from *Mousa* MUSE]

museum beetle *n* See **dermestid.**

museum piece *n* **1** an object of sufficient age or interest to be kept in a museum. **2** *Informal.* a person or thing regarded as antiquated or decrepit.

Museveni (ˌmʊsə'veɪnɪ) *n* **Yoweri.** born 1944, Ugandan politician; president of Uganda from 1986.

Musgrave ('mʌzgreɪv) *n* **Thea.** born 1928, Scottish composer, noted esp. for her operas.

mush[1] (mʌʃ) *n* **1** a soft pulpy mass or consistency. **2** *U.S.* a thick porridge made from corn meal. **3** *Informal.* cloying sentimentality. **4** *Radio.* interference in reception, esp. a hissing noise. [C17: from obsolete *moose* porridge; probably related to MASH; compare Old English *mōs* food]

mush[2] (mʌʃ) *Canadian.* ◆ *interj* **1** an order to dogs in a sled team to start up or go faster. ◆ *vb* **2** to travel by or drive a dog sled. **3** (*intr*) to travel on foot, esp. with snowshoes. ◆ *n* **4** a journey with a dogsled. [C19: perhaps from French *marchez* or *marchons,* imperatives of *marcher* to advance] ► **'musher** *n*

mush[3] (mʊʃ) *n Brit.* a slang word for **face** (sense 1). [C19: from MUSH[1], alluding to the softness of the face]

mush[4] (mʊʃ) *n Brit. slang.* a familiar or contemptuous term of address. [C19: probably from Gypsy *moosh* a man]

mush area *n* a region where signals from two or more radio transmitters overlap, causing fading and distortion.

mushroom ('mʌʃruːm, -rʊm) *n* **1a** the fleshy spore-producing body of any of various basidiomycetous fungi, typically consisting of a cap (see **pileus**) at the end of a stem arising from an underground mycelium. Some species, such as the field mushroom, are edible. Compare **toadstool. 1b** (*as modifier*): *mushroom soup.* **2** the fungus producing any of these structures. **3a** something resembling a mushroom in shape or rapid growth. **3b** (*as modifier*): *mushroom expansion.* ◆ *vb* (*intr*) **4** to grow rapidly: *demand mushroomed overnight.* **5** to assume a mushroom-like shape. **6** to gather mushrooms. [C15: from Old French *mousseron,* from Late Latin *mussiriō,* of obscure origin]

mushroom cloud *n* the large mushroom-shaped cloud of dust, debris, etc. produced by a nuclear explosion.

mushy ('mʌʃɪ) *adj* **mushier, mushiest. 1** soft and pulpy. **2** *Informal.* excessively sentimental or emotional. ▸ **'mushily** *adv* ▸ **'mushiness** *n*

music ('mjuːzɪk) *n* **1** an art form consisting of sequences of sounds in time, esp. tones of definite pitch organized melodically, harmonically, rhythmically and according to tone colour. **2** such an art form characteristic of a particular people, culture, or tradition: *Indian music; rock music; baroque music.* **3** the sounds so produced, esp. by singing or musical instruments. **4** written or printed music, such as a score or set of parts. **5** any sequence of sounds perceived as pleasing or harmonious. **6** *Rare.* a group of musicians: *the Queen's music.* **7 face the music.** *Informal.* to confront the consequences of one's actions. **8 music to one's ears.** something that is very pleasant to hear: *his news is music to my ears.* [C13: via Old French from Latin *mūsica,* from Greek *mousikē* (*tekhnē*) (art) belonging to the Muses, from *Mousa* MUSE]

musical ('mjuːzɪkᵊl) *adj* **1** of, relating to, or used in music: *a musical instrument.* **2** harmonious; melodious: *musical laughter.* **3** talented in or fond of music. **4** involving or set to music: *a musical evening.* ◆ *n* **5** short for **musical comedy.** ▸ **'musically** *adv* ▸ **'musicalness** *or* **ˌmusi'cality** *n*

musical chairs *n* (*functioning as sing*) **1** a party game in which players walk around chairs while music is played, there being one fewer chair than players. Whenever the music stops, the player who fails to find a chair is eliminated. **2** any situation involving a number of people in a series of interrelated changes.

musical comedy *n* **1** a play or film, usually having a light romantic story, that consists of dialogue interspersed with singing and dancing. **2** such plays and films collectively.

musicale (ˌmjuːzɪ'kɑːl) *n U.S. and Canadian.* a party or social evening with a musical programme. [C19: shortened from French *soirée musicale* musical evening]

musical glasses *pl n* another term for **glass harmonica.**

music box *or* **musical box** *n* a mechanical instrument that plays tunes by means of pins on a revolving cylinder striking the tuned teeth of a comblike metal plate, contained in a box.

music centre *n* a single hi-fi unit containing a turntable, amplifier, radio, cassette player, and compact disc player.

music drama *n* **1** an opera in which the musical and dramatic elements are of equal importance and strongly interfused. **2** the genre of such operas. [C19: translation of German *Musikdrama,* coined by Wagner to describe his later operas]

music hall *n Chiefly Brit.* **1a** a variety entertainment consisting of songs, comic turns, etc. U.S. and Canadian name: **vaudeville. 1b** (*as modifier*): *a music-hall song.* **2** a theatre at which such entertainments are staged.

musician (mjuː'zɪʃən) *n* a person who plays or composes music, esp. as a profession. ▸ **mu'sicianly** *adj*

musicianship (mjuː'zɪʃənʃɪp) *n* skill or artistry in performing music.

music of the spheres *n* the celestial music supposed by Pythagoras to be produced by the regular movements of the stars and planets.

musicology (ˌmjuːzɪ'kɒlədʒɪ) *n* the scholarly study of music. ▸ **musicological** (ˌmjuːzɪkə'lɒdʒɪkᵊl) *adj* ▸ **ˌmusico'logically** *adv* ▸ **ˌmusi'cologist** *n*

music paper *n* paper ruled or printed with a stave for writing music.

music roll *n* a roll of perforated paper for use in a mechanical instrument such as a player piano.

music stand *n* a frame, usually of wood or metal, upon which a musical score or orchestral part is supported.

Musil (*German* 'muːzɪl) *n* **Robert** ('roːbɛrt). 1880–1942, Austrian novelist, whose novel *The Man Without Qualities* (1930–42) is an ironic examination of contemporary ills.

musique concrète *French.* (myzik kõkrɛt) *n* another term for **concrete music.**

musjid ('mʌsdʒɪd) *n* a variant spelling of **masjid.**

musk (mʌsk) *n* **1** a strong-smelling glandular secretion of the male musk deer, used in perfumery. **2** a similar substance produced by certain other animals, such as the civet and otter, or manufactured synthetically. **3** any of several scrophulariaceous plants of the genus *Mimulus,* esp. the North American *M. moschatus,* which has yellow flowers and was formerly cultivated for its musky scent. See also **monkey flower. 4** the smell of musk or a similar heady smell. **5** (*modifier*) containing or resembling musk: *musk oil; a musk flavour.* [C14: from Late Latin *muscus,* from Greek *moskhos,* from Persian *mushk,* probably from Sanskrit *mushká* scrotum (from the appearance of the musk deer's musk bag), diminutive of *mūsh* MOUSE]

musk deer *n* a small central Asian mountain deer, *Moschus moschiferus.* The male has long tusklike canine teeth and secretes musk.

musk duck *n* **1** another name for **Muscovy duck. 2** a duck, *Biziura lobata,* inhabiting swamps, lakes, and streams in Australia. The male has a leathery pouch beneath the bill and emits a musky odour.

muskeg ('mʌsˌkɛg) *n Chiefly Canadian.* **1** undrained boggy land characterized by sphagnum moss vegetation: *vast areas of muskeg.* **2** a bog or swamp of this nature. [C19: from Algonquian: grassy swamp]

muskellunge ('mʌskəˌlʌndʒ), **maskalonge** ('mæskəˌlɒndʒ), *or* **maskanonge** ('mæskəˌnɒndʒ) *n, pl* **-lunges, -longes, -nonges** *or* **-lunge, -longe, -nonge.** a large North American freshwater game fish, *Esox masquinongy:* family *Esocidae* (pikes, etc.). Often shortened (informally) to **musky** or **muskie.** [C18 *maskinunga,* of Algonquian origin; compare Ojibwa *mashkinonge* big pike]

musket ('mʌskɪt) *n* a long-barrelled muzzle-loading shoulder gun used between the 16th and 18th centuries by infantry soldiers. [C16: from French *mousquet,* from Italian *moschetto* arrow, earlier: sparrow hawk, from *moscha* a fly, from Latin *musca*]

musketeer (ˌmʌskɪ'tɪə) *n* (formerly) a soldier armed with a musket.

musketry ('mʌskɪtrɪ) *n* **1** muskets or musketeers collectively. **2** the technique of using small arms.

muskie ('mʌskɪ) *n Canadian.* an informal name for the **muskellunge.**

Muskie ('mʌskɪ) *n* **Edmund** (**Sixtus**). 1914–96, U.S. Democratic politician: Governor of Maine (1955–59): senator for Maine (1959–80): Secretary of State (1980–81).

musk mallow *n* **1** a malvaceous plant, *Malva moschata,* of Europe and N Africa, with purple-spotted stems, pink flowers, and a faint scent of musk. **2** another name for **abelmosk.**

muskmelon ('mʌskˌmɛlən) *n* **1** any of several varieties of the melon *Cucumis melo,* such as the cantaloupe and honeydew. **2** the fruit of any of these melons, having ribbed or warty rind and sweet yellow, white, or green flesh with a musky aroma.

Muskogean *or* **Muskhogean** (mʌs'kəʊgɪən) *n* a family of North American Indian languages, probably distantly related to the Algonquian family.

musk orchid *n* a small Eurasian orchid, *Herminium monorchis,* with dense spikes of musk-scented greenish-yellow flowers.

musk ox *n* a large bovid mammal, *Ovibos moschatus,* which has a dark shaggy coat, short legs, and widely spaced downward-curving horns and emits a musky smell: now confined to the tundras of Canada and Greenland.

muskrat ('mʌskˌræt) *n, pl* **-rats** *or* **-rat. 1** a North American beaver-like amphibious rodent, *Ondatra zibethica,* closely related to but larger than the voles: family *Cricetidae.* **2** the brown fur of this animal. **3** either of two closely related rodents, *Ondatra obscurus* or *Neofiber alleni* (**round-tailed muskrat**). ◆ Also called: **musquash.** [C17: by folk etymology, from the same source as MUSQUASH]

musk rose *n* a prickly shrubby Mediterranean rose, *Rosa moschata,* cultivated for its white musk-scented flowers.

musk turtle *n* any of several small turtles of the genus *Sternotherus,* esp. *S. odoratus* (**common musk turtle** or **stinkpot**), that emit a strong unpleasant odour: family *Kinosternidae.*

musky[1] ('mʌskɪ) *adj* **muskier, muskiest.** resembling the smell of musk; having a heady or pungent sweet aroma. ▸ **'muskiness** *n*

musky[2] ('mʌskɪ) *n, pl* **muskies.** an informal name for the **muskellunge.**

Muslim ('mʊzlɪm, 'mʌz-) *or* **Moslem** *n, pl* **-lims** *or* **-lim. 1** a follower of the religion of Islam. ◆ *adj* **2** of or relating to Islam, its doctrines, culture, etc. ◆ Also (but not in Muslim use): **Muhammadan, Muhammedan, Mohammedan.** [C17: from Arabic, literally: one who surrenders] ▸ **'Muslimism** *or* **'Moslemism** *n*

muslin ('mʌzlɪn) *n* a fine plain-weave cotton fabric. [C17: from French *mousseline,* from Italian *mussolina,* from Arabic *mawṣilīy* of Mosul, from *Mawṣil* Mosul, Iraq, where it was first produced]

MusM *abbrev. for* Master of Music.

muso ('mjuːzəʊ) *n, pl* **musos.** *Slang.* **1** *Brit. derogatory.* a musician, esp. a pop musician, regarded as being overconcerned with technique rather than musical content or expression. **2** *Austral.* any musician, esp. a professional one.

musquash ('mʌskwɒʃ) *n* another name for **muskrat,** esp. the fur. [C17: from Algonquian: compare Natick *musquash,* Abnaki *muskwessu*]

muss (mʌs) *U.S. and Canadian informal.* ◆ *vb* **1** (*tr;* often foll. by *up*) to make untidy; rumple. ◆ *n* **2** a state of disorder; muddle. [C19: probably a blend of MESS + FUSS] ▸ **'mussy** *adj* ▸ **'mussily** *adv* ▸ **'mussiness** *n*

mussel ('mʌsᵊl) *n* **1** any of various marine bivalves of the genus *Mytilus* and related genera, esp. *M. edulis* (**edible mussel**), having a dark slightly elongated shell and living attached to rocks, etc., **2** any of various freshwater bivalves of the genera *Anodonta, Unio,* etc., attached to rocks, sand, etc. having a flattened oval shell (a source of mother-of-pearl). The **zebra mussel,** *Dreissena polymorpha,* can be a serious nuisance in water mains. [Old English *muscle,* from Vulgar Latin *muscula* (unattested), from Latin *musculus,* diminutive of *mūs* mouse]

Musset (*French* mysɛ) *n* **Alfred de** (alfrɛd də). 1810–57, French romantic poet and dramatist: his works include the play *Lorenzaccio* (1834) and the lyrics *Les Nuits* (1835–37), tracing his love affair with George Sand.

Mussolini (ˌmʊsə'liːnɪ; *Italian* musso'liːni) *n* **Benito** (be'niːto) known as *il Duce.* 1883–1945, Italian Fascist dictator. After the Fascist march on Rome, he was appointed prime minister by King Victor Emmanuel III (1922) and assumed dictatorial powers. He annexed Abyssinia and allied Italy with Germany (1936), entering World War II in 1940. He was forced to resign following the Allied invasion of Sicily (1943) and was eventually shot by Italian partisans.

Mussorgsky *or* **Moussorgsky** (mʊ'sɔːgskɪ; *Russian* 'musərkskij) *n* **Modest Petrovich** (ma'dɛst pɪ'trɔvitʃ). 1839–81, Russian composer. He translated inflections of speech into melody in such works as the song cycle *Songs and Dances of Death* (1875–77) and the opera *Boris Godunov* (1874). His other works include *Pictures at an Exhibition* (1874) for piano.

Mussulman *or* **Mussalman** ('mʌsᵊlmən) *n, pl* **-mans.** an archaic word for **Muslim.** [C16: from Persian *Musulmān* (pl) from Arabic *Muslimūn,* pl. of MUSLIM]

must[1] (mʌst; *unstressed* məst, məs) *vb* (takes an infinitive without *to* or an implied infinitive) used as an auxiliary: **1** to express obligation or compulsion: *you must pay your dues.* In this sense, *must* does not form a negative. If used with a negative infinitive it indicates obligatory prohibition. **2** to indicate necessity: *I must go to the bank tomorrow.* **3** to indicate the probable correctness of a statement: *he must be there by now.* **4** to indicate inevitability: *all good things must come to an end.* **5** to express resolution: **5a** on the part of the speaker when used with *I* or *we: I must finish this.* **5b** on the part of another or others as imputed to them by the speaker, when used with *you, he, she, they,* etc.: *let him get drunk if he must.* **6** (used emphatically) to express conviction or certainty on the part of the speaker: *he must have reached the town by now, surely; you must be joking.* **7** (foll. by *away*) used with an implied verb of motion to express compelling haste: *I must away.* ◆ *n* **8** an essential or necessary thing: *strong shoes are a must for hill walking.* [Old English *mōste* past tense of *mōtan* to be allowed, be obliged to; related to Old Saxon *mōtan,* Old High German *muozan,* German *müssen*]

must[2] (mʌst) *n* the newly pressed juice of grapes or other fruit ready for fermentation. [Old English, from Latin *mustum* new wine, must, from *mustus* (adj) newborn]

must[3] (mʌst) *n* mustiness or mould. [C17: back formation from MUSTY]

must[4] (mʌst) *n* a variant spelling of **musth.**

mustache (mə'stɑːʃ) *n* the U.S. spelling of **moustache.** ▸ **mus'tached** *adj*

mustachio (mə'stɑːʃɪˌəʊ) *n, pl* **-chios.** (*often pl when considered as two halves*) *Often humorous.* a moustache, esp. when bushy or elaborately shaped. [C16: from Spanish *mostacho* and Italian *mostaccio*] ▸ **mus'tachioed** *adj*

Mustafa Kemal ('mʊstəfə kə'mɑːl) *n* See (Kemal) **Atatürk.**

mustang ('mʌstæŋ) *n* a small breed of horse, often wild or half wild, found in the southwestern U.S. [C19: from Mexican Spanish *mestengo,* from *mesta* a group of stray animals]

mustard ('mʌstəd) *n* **1** any of several Eurasian plants of the cruciferous genus *Brassica,* esp. black mustard and white mustard, having yellow flowers and slender pods: cultivated for their pungent seeds. See also **charlock. 2** a paste made from the powdered seeds of any of these plants and used as a condiment. **3a** a brownish yellow colour. **3b** (*as adj*): *a mustard carpet.* **4** *Slang, chiefly U.S.* zest or enthusiasm. **5 cut the mustard.** *Slang.* to come up to expectations. [C13: from Old French *moustarde,* from Latin *mustum* MUST[2], since the original condiment was made by adding must]

mustard and cress *n* seedlings of white mustard and garden cress, used in salads.

mustard gas *n* an oily liquid vesicant compound used in chemical warfare. Its vapour causes blindness and burns. Formula: $(ClCH_2CH_2)_2S$.

mustard oil *n* an oil that is obtained from mustard seeds and used in making soap.

mustard plaster *n Med.* a mixture of powdered black mustard seeds and an adhesive agent applied to the skin for its relaxing, stimulating, or counterirritant effects.

mustee (mʌ'stiː, 'mʌstiː) *or* **mestee** (mɛ'stiː) *n* **1** the offspring of a White and a quadroon. **2** any person of mixed ancestry. [C17: shortened from MESTIZO]

musteline ('mʌstɪˌlaɪn, -lɪn) *adj* **1** of, relating to, or belonging to the *Mustelidae,* a family of typically predatory mammals including weasels, ferrets, minks, polecats, badgers, skunks, and otters: order *Carnivora* (carnivores). ◆ *n* **2** any musteline animal. [C17: from Latin *mustēlīnus,* from *mustēla* weasel, from *mūs* mouse + *-tēla,* of unknown origin]

muster ('mʌstə) *vb* **1** to call together (numbers of men) for duty, inspection, etc., or (of men) to assemble in this way. **2 muster in** *or* **out.** *U.S.* to enlist into or discharge from military service. **3** (*tr*) *Austral. and N.Z.* to round up (livestock). **4** (*tr;* sometimes foll. by *up*) to summon or gather: *to muster one's arguments; to muster up courage.* ◆ *n* **5** an assembly of military personnel for duty, inspection, etc. **6** a collection, assembly, or gathering. **7** *Austral. and N.Z.* the rounding up of livestock. **8** a flock of peacocks. **9 pass muster.** to be acceptable. [C14: from old French *moustrer,* from Latin *monstrāre* to show, from *monstrum* portent, omen]

muster roll *n* a list of the officers and men in a regiment, ship's company, etc.

musth *or* **must** (mʌst) *n* (often preceded by *in*) a state of frenzied sexual excitement in the males of certain large mammals, esp. elephants, associated with discharge from a gland between the ear and eye. [C19: from Urdu *mast,* from Persian: drunk]

musty ('mʌstɪ) *adj* **-tier, -tiest. 1** smelling or tasting old, stale, or mouldy. **2** old-fashioned, dull, or hackneyed: *musty ideas.* [C16: perhaps a variant of obsolete *moisty,* influenced by MUST[3]] ▸ **'mustily** *adv* ▸ **'mustiness** *n*

mut (mʌt) *n Printing.* another word for **em** (sense 1). [C20: shortened from MUTTON]

mutable ('mjuːtəbᵊl) *adj* **1** able to or tending to change. **2** *Astrology.* of or relating to four of the signs of the zodiac, Gemini, Virgo, Sagittarius, and Pisces, which are associated with the quality of adaptability. Compare **cardinal** (sense 9), **fixed** (sense 10). [C14: from Latin *mūtābilis* fickle, from *mūtāre* to change] ▸ **ˌmuta'bility** *or* (*less commonly*) **'mutableness** *n* ▸ **'mutably** *adv*

mutagen ('mjuːtədʒən) *n* a substance or agent that can induce genetic mutation. [C20: from MUTATION + -GEN] ▸ **mutagenic** (ˌmjuːtə'dʒɛnɪk) *adj* ▸ **ˌmutagen'icity** *n*

mutagenesis (ˌmjuːtə'dʒɛnɪsɪs) *n Genetics.* the origin and devlopment of a mutation. [C20: from MUTATION + -GENESIS]

mutant ('mjuːtᵊnt) *n* **1** Also called: **mutation.** an animal, organism, or gene that has undergone mutation. ◆ *adj* **2** of, relating to, undergoing, or resulting from change or mutation. [C20: from Latin *mutāre* to change]

Mutare (muː'tɑːrɪ) *n* a city in E Zimbabwe, near the Mozambique border: rail and trade centre in a mining and tobacco-growing region. Pop.: 131 808 (1992). Former name (until 1982): **Umtali.**

mutate (mjuː'teɪt) *vb* to undergo or cause to undergo mutation. [C19: from Latin *mūtātus* changed, from *mūtāre* to change] ▸ **mutative** ('mjuːtətɪv, mjuː'teɪtɪv) *adj*

mutation (mjuː'teɪʃən) *n* **1** the act or process of mutating; change; alteration. **2** a change or alteration. **3** a change in the chromosomes or genes of a cell. When this change occurs in the gametes the structure and development of the resultant offspring may be affected. See also **inversion** (sense 11). **4** another word for **mutant** (sense 1). **5** a physical characteristic of an individual resulting from this type of chromosomal change. **6** *Phonetics.* **6a** (in Germanic languages) another name for **umlaut. 6b** (in Celtic languages) a phonetic change in certain initial consonants caused by a preceding word. ▸ **mu'tational** *adj* ▸ **mu'tationally** *adv*

mutation stop *n* an organ pipe sounding the harmonic of the note normally produced.

mutatis mutandis *Latin.* (muː'tɑːtɪs muː'tændɪs) the necessary changes having been made.

Mutazilite (muː'tɑːzɪˌlaɪt) *n* a member of an 8th-century liberal Muslim sect, later merged into the Shiahs. [from Arabic *mu'tazilah* body of seceders + -ITE[1]]

mutch[1] (mʌtʃ) *n* a close-fitting linen cap formerly worn by women and children in Scotland. [C15: from Middle Dutch *mutse* cap, from Medieval Latin *almucia* ALMUCE]

mutch[2] (mʌtʃ) *vb Dialect.* **1** (*tr*) to cadge; beg. **2** (*intr*) another word for **mitch.**

mutchkin ('mʌtʃkɪn) *n* a Scottish unit of liquid measure equal to slightly less than one pint. [C15: from Middle Dutch *mudseken,* from Latin *modius* measure for grain]

mute[1] (mjuːt) *adj* **1** not giving out sound or speech; silent. **2** unable to speak; dumb. **3** unspoken or unexpressed: *mute dislike.* **4** *Law.* (of a person arraigned on indictment) refusing to answer a charge. **5** *Phonetics.* another word for **plosive. 6** (of a letter in a word) silent. ◆ *n* **7** a person who is unable to speak. **8** *Law.* a person who refuses to plead when arraigned on indictment for an offence. **9** any of various devices used to soften the tone of stringed or brass instruments. **10** *Phonetics.* a plosive consonant; stop. **11** a silent letter. **12** an actor in a dumb show. **13** a hired mourner at a funeral. ◆ *vb* (*tr*) **14** to reduce the volume of (a musical instrument) by means of a mute, soft pedal, etc. **15** to subdue the strength of (a colour, tone, lighting, etc.). [C14 *muwet* from Old French *mu,* from Latin *mūtus* silent] ▸ **'mutely** *adv* ▸ **'muteness** *n*

mute[2] (mjuːt) *Archaic.* ◆ *vb* **1** (of birds) to discharge (faeces). ◆ *n* **2** birds' faeces. [C15: from Old French *meutir,* variant of *esmeltir,* of Germanic origin; probably related to SMELT[1] and MELT]

muted ('mjuːtɪd) *adj* **1** (of a sound or colour) softened: *a muted pink shirt.* **2** (of an emotion or action) subdued or restrained: *his response was muted.* **3** (of a musical instrument) being played while fitted with a mute: *muted trumpet.*

mute swan *n* a Eurasian swan, *Cygnus olor,* with a pure white plumage, an orange-red bill with a black base, and a curved neck. Compare **whistling swan.**

muti ('mʊtɪ) *n S. African informal.* medicine, esp. herbal medicine. [from Zulu *umuthi* tree, medicine]

Muti ('mʊtɪ) *n* **Riccardo** (rɪ'kɑːdəʊ). born 1941, Italian conductor: musical director of Philharmonia Orchestra, London (1979–82), Philadelphia Orchestra (1980–92), and La Scala, Milan (from 1986).

muticous ('mjuːtɪkəs) *adj Botany.* lacking an awn, spine, or point. Also: **muticate.** [C19: from Latin *muticus* awnless, curtailed]

mutilate ('mjuːtɪˌleɪt) *vb* (*tr*) **1** to deprive of a limb, essential part, etc.; maim; dismember. **2** to mar, expurgate, or damage (a text, book, etc). [C16: from Latin *mutilāre* to cut off; related to *mutilus* maimed] ▸ **ˌmuti'lation** *n* ▸ **'mutiˌlative** *adj* ▸ **'mutiˌlator** *n*

mutineer (ˌmjuːtɪ'nɪə) *n* a person who mutinies.

mutinous ('mjuːtɪnəs) *adj* **1** openly rebellious or disobedient: *a mutinous child.* **2** characteristic or indicative of mutiny. ▸ **'mutinously** *adv* ▸ **'mutinousness** *n*

mutiny ('mjuːtɪnɪ) *n, pl* **-nies. 1** open rebellion against constituted authority, esp. by seamen or soldiers against their officers. ◆ *vb* **-nies, -nying, -nied. 2** (*intr*) to engage in mutiny. [C16: from obsolete *mutine,* from Old French *mutin* rebellious, from *meute* mutiny, ultimately from Latin *movēre* to move]

mutism ('mjuːtɪzəm) *n* **1** the state of being mute. **2** *Psychiatry.* **2a** a refusal to speak although the mechanism of speech is not damaged. **2b** the lack of development of speech, due usually to early deafness.

Mutsuhito (ˌmuːtsʊ'hiːtəʊ) *n* See **Meiji.**

mutt (mʌt) *n Slang.* **1** an inept, ignorant, or stupid person. **2** a mongrel dog; cur. [C20: shortened from MUTTONHEAD]

mutter ('mʌtə) *vb* **1** to utter (something) in a low and indistinct tone. **2** (*intr*) to grumble or complain. **3** (*intr*) to make a low continuous murmuring sound. ◆ *n* **4** a muttered sound or complaint. [C14 *moteren;* related to Norwegian (dialect) *mutra,* Old High German *mutilōn;* compare Old English *mōtian* to speak] ▸ **'mutterer** *n* ▸ **'muttering** *n, adj* ▸ **'mutteringly** *adv*

Mutter ('mʊtə) *n* **Anne-Sophie.** born 1963, German violinist.

mutton ('mʌtᵊn) *n* **1** the flesh of sheep, esp. of mature sheep, used as food. **2 mutton dressed as lamb.** an older woman dressed up to look young. **3** *Printing.* another word for **em** (sense 1). Compare **nut** (sense 12). [C13 *moton* sheep, from Old French, from Medieval Latin *multō,* of Celtic origin; the term was adopted in printing to distinguish the pronunciation of *em quad* from *en quad*] ▸ **'muttony** *adj*

mutton bird *n* any of several shearwaters, having a dark plumage with greyish underparts, esp. the sooty shearwater (*Puffinus griseus*) of New Zealand, which is collected for food by Maoris. It inhabits the Pacific Ocean and in summer nests in Australia and New Zealand. [C19: so named because their cooked flesh is claimed to taste like mutton]

mutton-birder *n N.Z.* a person who hunts mutton birds.

mutton chop *n* a piece of mutton from the loin.

muttonchops ('mʌtᵊnˌtʃɒps) *pl n* side whiskers trimmed in the shape of chops, widening out from the temples.

muttonhead ('mʌtᵊnˌhɛd) *n Slang.* a stupid or ignorant person; fool. ▸ **'muttonˌheaded** *adj*

Muttra ('mʌtrə) *n* the former name of **Mathura.**

mutual ('mjuːtʃʊəl) *adj* **1** experienced or expressed by each of two or more people or groups about the other; reciprocal: *mutual distrust.* **2** common to or shared by both or all of two or more parties: *a mutual friend; mutual interests.* **3** denoting an insurance company, etc., in which the policyholders share the profits and expenses and there are no shareholders. [C15: from Old French *mutuel,* from Latin *mūtuus* reciprocal (originally: borrowed); related to *mūtāre* to change] ▸ **mutuality** (ˌmjuːtjʊˈælɪtɪ) *or* **ˈmutualness** *n* ▸ **ˈmutually** *adv*

USAGE The use of *mutual* to mean *common to or shared by two or more parties* was formerly considered incorrect, but is now acceptable. Tautologous use of *mutual* should be avoided: *cooperation* (not *mutual cooperation*) *between the two countries.*

mutual fund *n* the U.S. and Canadian name for **unit trust.**

mutual inductance *n* a measure of the mutual induction between two magnetically linked circuits, given as the ratio of the induced electromotive force to the rate of change of current producing it. It is usually measured in henries. Symbol: M or L_{12} Also called: **coefficient of mutual induction.**

mutual induction *n* the production of an electromotive force in a circuit by a current change in a second circuit magnetically linked to the first. See also **mutual inductance.** Compare **self-induction.**

mutual insurance *n* a system of insurance by which all policyholders become company members under contract to pay premiums into a common fund out of which claims are paid. See also **mutual** (sense 3).

mutualism (ˈmjuːtjʊəˌlɪzəm) *n* another name for **symbiosis.** ▸ **ˈmutualist** *n, adj* ▸ **ˌmutualˈistic** *adj*

mutualize *or* **mutualise** (ˈmjuːtjʊəˌlaɪz) *vb* **1** to make or become mutual. **2** (*tr*) *U.S.* to organize or convert (a business enterprise) so that customers or employees own a majority of shares. ▸ **ˌmutualiˈzation** *or* **ˌmutualiˈsation** *n*

mutual savings bank *n Chiefly U.S.* a savings bank having no subscribed capital stock and distributing all available net profit to depositors who, however, remain creditors without voting power.

mutuel (ˈmjuːtjʊəl) *n* short for **pari-mutuel.**

mutule (ˈmjuːtjuːl) *n Architect.* one of a set of flat blocks below the corona of a Doric cornice. Compare **modillion.** [C16: via French from Latin *mūtulus* modillion]

muu-muu (ˈmuːˌmuː) *n* a loose brightly-coloured dress worn by women in Hawaii. [from Hawaiian]

Muybridge (ˈmaɪbrɪdʒ) *n* **Eadweard** (ˈɛdwəd), original name *Edward James Muggeridge.* 1830–1904, U.S. photographer, born in England; noted for his high-speed photographic studies of animals and people in motion.

Muzak (ˈmjuːzæk) *n Trademark.* recorded light music played in shops, restaurants, factories, etc., to entertain, increase sales or production, etc.

muzhik, moujik, *or* **mujik** (ˈmuːʒɪk) *n* a Russian peasant, esp. under the tsars. [C16: from Russian: peasant]

Muzorewa (ˌmuzəˈreɪwə) *n* **Abel (Tendekayi)** (ˈeɪbᵊl). born 1925, Zimbabwean Methodist bishop and politician; president of the African National Council (1971–85). He was one of the negotiators of an internal settlement (1978–79); prime minister of Rhodesia (1979).

muzz (mʌz) *vb* (*tr*) *Brit. informal.* to make (something) muzzy.

muzzle (ˈmʌzᵊl) *n* **1** the projecting part of the face, usually the jaws and nose, of animals such as the dog and horse. **2** a guard or strap fitted over an animal's nose and jaws to prevent it biting or eating. **3** the front end of a gun barrel. ◆ *vb* (*tr*) **4** to prevent from being heard or noticed: *to muzzle the press.* **5** to put a muzzle on (an animal). **6** to take in (a sail). [C15 *mosel,* from Old French *musel,* diminutive of *muse* snout, from Medieval Latin *mūsus,* of unknown origin] ▸ **ˈmuzzler** *n*

muzzle-loader *n* a firearm receiving its ammunition through the muzzle. ▸ **ˈmuzzle-ˌloading** *adj*

muzzle velocity *n* the velocity of a projectile as it leaves a firearm's muzzle.

muzzy (ˈmʌzɪ) *adj* **-zier, -ziest. 1** blurred, indistinct, or hazy. **2** confused, muddled, or befuddled. [C18: origin obscure] ▸ **ˈmuzzily** *adv* ▸ **ˈmuzziness** *n*

mv *Music. abbrev. for* mezzo voce.

MV *abbrev. for:* **1** motor vessel. **2** muzzle velocity. ◆ **3** *symbol for* megavolt.

MVD *abbrev. for* Ministry of Internal Affairs; the police organization in the former Soviet Union, formed in 1946. [from Russian *Ministerstvo vnutrennikh del*]

MVO (in Britain) *abbrev. for* Member of the Royal Victorian Order.

MVS *abbrev. for* Master of Veterinary Surgery.

MVSc *abbrev. for* Master of Veterinary Science.

MW 1 *symbol for* megawatt. **2** *Radio. abbrev. for* medium wave. **3** *international car registration for* Malawi.

mwalimu (mwɑːˈliːmuː) *n E African.* a teacher. [Swahili]

Mweru (ˈmwɛəruː) *n* a lake in central Africa, on the border between Zambia and the Democratic Republic of the Congo (formerly Zaïre). Area: 4196 sq. km (1620 sq. miles).

Mx *Physics. symbol for* maxwell.

MX *U.S. abbrev. for* missile-experimental: an intercontinental ballistic missile with up to ten nuclear warheads.

my (maɪ) *determiner* **1** of, belonging to, or associated with the speaker or writer (me): *my own ideas; do you mind my smoking?* **2** used in various forms of address: *my lord; my dear boy.* **3** used in various exclamations: *my goodness!* ◆ *interj* **4** an exclamation of surprise, awe, etc.: *my, how you've grown!* [C12 *mī,* variant of Old English *mīn* when preceding a word beginning with a consonant]

USAGE See at **me.**

MY *abbrev. for* motor yacht.

my- *combining form.* a variant of **myo-** before a vowel.

myalgia (maɪˈældʒɪə) *n* pain in a muscle or a group of muscles. [C19: from MYO- + -ALGIA] ▸ **myˈalgic** *adj*

myalgic encephalomyelitis (maɪˈældʒɪk ɛnˌsɛfələʊˌmaɪɪˈlaɪtɪs) *n* another name for **chronic fatigue syndrome.** Abbrev.: **ME.**

myalism (ˈmaɪəˌlɪzəm) *n* a kind of witchcraft, similar to obi, practised esp. in the Caribbean. [C19: from *myal,* probably of West African origin] ▸ **ˈmyalist** *n*

myall (ˈmaɪəl) *n* **1** any of several Australian acacias, esp. *Acacia pendula,* having hard scented wood used for fences. **2** a native Australian living independently of society. [C19: from a native Australian name]

Myanmar *or* **Myanma** (ˈmaɪænmɑː, ˈmjænmɑː) *n* a republic in SE Asia, on the Bay of Bengal and the Andaman Sea: unified from small states in 1752; annexed by Britain (1823–85) and made a province of India in 1886; became independent in 1948. It is generally mountainous, with the basins of the Chindwin and Irrawaddy Rivers in the central part and the Irrawaddy delta in the south. Official language: Burmese. Religion: Buddhist majority. Currency: kyat. Capital: Yangon. Pop.: 47 305 000 (1998 est.). Area: 676 577 sq. km (261 228 sq. miles). Official name: **the Union of Myanmar.** Former name (until 1989): **Burma.**

myasthenia (ˌmaɪəsˈθiːnɪə) *n* **1** any muscular weakness. **2** short for **myasthenia gravis.** [C19: from MYO- + ASTHENIA] ▸ **myasthenic** (ˌmaɪəsˈθɛnɪk) *adj*

myasthenia gravis (ˈgrɑːvɪs) *n* a chronic progressive disease in which the muscles, esp. those of the head and face, become weak and easily fatigued.

myc- *combining form.* a variant of **myco-** before a vowel.

mycelium (maɪˈsiːlɪəm) *n, pl* **-lia** (-lɪə). the vegetative body of fungi: a mass of branching filaments (hyphae) that spread throughout the nutrient substratum. [C19 (literally: nail of fungus): from MYCO- + Greek *hēlos* nail] ▸ **myˈcelial** *adj* ▸ **myceloid** (ˈmaɪsɪˌlɔɪd) *adj*

mycella (maɪˈsɛlə) *n* a blue-veined Danish cream cheese, less strongly flavoured than Danish blue. [C20: New Latin, from Greek *mukēs* fungus]

Mycenae (maɪˈsiːniː) *n* an ancient Greek city in the NE Peloponnesus on the plain of Argos.

Mycenaean (ˌmaɪsɪˈniːən) *adj* **1** of or relating to ancient Mycenae or its inhabitants. **2** of or relating to the Aegean civilization of Mycenae (1400 to 1100 B.C.).

-mycete *n combining form.* indicating a fungus: *ascomycete.* [from New Latin *-mycetes,* from Greek *mukētes,* plural of *mukēs* fungus]

myceto- *or before a vowel* **mycet-** *combining form.* fungus: *mycetophagous.* [from Greek *mukēs* fungus]

mycetoma (ˌmaɪsɪˈtəʊmə) *n, pl* **-mas** *or* **-mata** (-mətə). a chronic fungal infection, esp. of the foot, characterized by swelling, usually resulting from a wound.

mycetophagous (ˌmaɪsɪˈtɒfəgəs) *adj Zoology.* feeding on fungi.

mycetozoan (maɪˌsiːtəʊˈzəʊən) *n* a former name for a **slime mould.**

-mycin *n combining form.* indicating an antibiotic compound derived from a fungus: *streptomycin.* [from Greek *mukēs* fungus + -IN]

myco- *or before a vowel* **myc-** *combining form.* indicating fungus: *mycology.* [from Greek *mukēs* fungus]

mycobacterium (ˌmaɪkəʊbækˈtɪərɪəm) *n, pl* **-ria** (-rɪə). any rod-shaped Gram-positive bacterium of the genus *Mycobacterium,* esp. the tubercle bacillus: family *Mycobacteriaceae.*

mycobiont (ˌmaɪkəʊˈbaɪɒnt) *n Botany.* the fungal constituent of a lichen. Compare **phycobiont.**

mycol. *abbrev. for:* **1** mycological. **2** mycology.

mycology (maɪˈkɒlədʒɪ) *n* **1** the branch of biology concerned with the study of fungi. **2** the fungi of a particular region. ▸ **mycological** (ˌmaɪkəˈlɒdʒɪkᵊl) *or* **ˌmycoˈlogic** *adj* ▸ **myˈcologist** *n*

mycoplasma (ˌmaɪkəʊˈplæzmə) *n* any prokaryotic microorganism of the genus *Mycoplasma,* some species of which cause disease (**mycoplasmosis**) in animals and humans.

mycorrhiza *or* **mycorhiza** (ˌmaɪkəˈraɪzə) *n, pl* **-zae** (-ziː) *or* **-zas.** an association of a fungus and a plant in which the fungus lives within or on the outside of the plant's roots forming a symbiotic or parasitic relationship. See **ectotrophic, endotrophic.** [C19: from MYCO- + Greek *rhiza* root] ▸ **ˌmycorˈrhizal** *or* **ˌmycoˈrhizal** *adj*

mycosis (maɪˈkəʊsɪs) *n* any infection or disease caused by fungus. ▸ **mycotic** (maɪˈkɒtɪk) *adj*

Mycostatin (ˌmaɪkəʊˈstætɪn) *n* (in the U.S. and Australia) *Trademark.* a brand of **nystatin.**

mycotoxin (ˌmaɪkəˈtɒksɪn) *n* any of various toxic substances produced by fungi some of which may affect food and others of which are alleged to have been used in warfare. See also **aflatoxin, yellow rain.** ▸ **ˌmycotoxˈology** *n*

mycotrophic (ˌmaɪkəʊˈtrɒfɪk) *adj Botany.* (of a plant) symbiotic with a fungus, esp. a mycorrhizal fungus.

mydriasis (mɪˈdraɪəsɪs, maɪ-) *n* abnormal dilation of the pupil of the eye, produced by drugs, coma, etc. [C17: via Late Latin from Greek; origin obscure]

mydriatic (ˌmɪdrɪˈætɪk) *adj* **1** relating to or causing mydriasis. ◆ *n* **2** a mydriatic drug.

myel- *or before a consonant* **myelo-** *combining form.* the spinal cord or bone marrow: *myeloid.* [from Greek *muelos* marrow, spinal cord, from *mus* muscle]

myelencephalon (ˌmaɪɪlɛnˈsɛfəˌlɒn) *n, pl* **-lons** *or* **-la** (-lə). the part of the embryonic hindbrain that develops into the medulla oblongata. Nontechnical name: **afterbrain.** ▸ **myelencephalic** (ˌmaɪɪlɛnsəˈfælɪk) *adj*

myelin (ˈmaɪɪlɪn) *or* **myeline** (ˈmaɪɪˌliːn) *n* a white tissue forming an insulating sheath (**myelin sheath**) around certain nerve fibres. Damage to the myelin sheath causes neurological disease, as in multiple sclerosis. ▸ **ˌmyeˈlinic** *adj*

myelinated (ˈmaɪɪlɪˌneɪtɪd) *adj* (of a nerve fibre) having a myelin sheath.

myelitis (ˌmaɪɪˈlaɪtɪs) *n* inflammation of the spinal cord or of the bone marrow.

myeloblast (ˈmaɪələʊˌblɑːst) *n* a cell that gives rise to a granulocyte, normally occurring in the bone marrow but detected in the blood in certain diseases, esp. leukaemia. ▸ **myeloblastic** (ˌmaɪələʊˈblæstɪk) *adj*

myelocyte (ˈmaɪələʊˌsaɪt) *n* an immature granulocyte, normally occurring in the bone marrow but detected in the blood in certain diseases. ▸ **myelocytic** (ˌmaɪələʊˈsɪtɪk) *adj*

myelogram (maɪˈɛləˌgræm) *n* an X-ray of the spinal cord, after injection with a radio-opaque medium. ▸ ˌ**myeˈlography** *n*
myeloid (ˈmaɪɪˌlɔɪd) *adj* of or relating to the spinal cord or the bone marrow.
myeloma (ˌmaɪɪˈləʊmə) *n, pl* **-mas** *or* **-mata** (-mətə). a usually malignant tumour of the bone marrow or composed of cells normally found in bone marrow. ▸ ˌ**myeˈlomaˌtoid** *adj*
Myers (ˈmaɪəz) *n* **L(eopold) H(amilton).** 1881–1944, British novelist, best known for his novel sequence *The Near and the Far* (1929–40).
myiasis (ˈmaɪəsɪs) *n, pl* **-ses** (-ˌsiːz). **1** infestation of the body by the larvae of flies. **2** any disease resulting from such infestation. [C19: New Latin, from Greek *muia* a fly]
Mykonos (ˈmɪkənɒs, -əʊs, ˈmiːkɔ-) *n* a Greek island in the S Aegean Sea, one of the Cyclades: a popular tourist resort with many churches. Pop.: 5500 (latest est.). Greek name: **Míkonos.**
My Lai (ˈmaɪ ˈlaɪ, ˈmiː) *n* a village in S Vietnam where in 1968 U.S. troops massacred over 400 civilians.
mylonite (ˈmaɪləˌnaɪt, ˈmɪlə-) *n* a fine-grained metamorphic rock, often showing banding and micaceous fracture, formed by the crushing, grinding, or rolling of the original structure. [C19: from Greek *mulōn* mill]
mynah *or* **myna** (ˈmaɪnə) *n* any of various tropical Asian starlings of the genera *Acridotheres, Gracula,* etc., esp. *G. religiosa* (see **hill mynah**), some of which can mimic human speech. [C18: from Hindi *mainā*, from Sanskrit *madana*]
Mynheer (məˈnɪə) *n* a Dutch title of address equivalent to *Sir* when used alone or to *Mr* when placed before a name. [C17: from Dutch *mijnheer,* my lord]
myo- *or before a vowel* **my-** *combining form.* muscle: *myocardium.* [from Greek *mus* MUSCLE]
myocardial infarction *n* destruction of an area of heart muscle as the result of occlusion of a coronary artery. Compare **coronary thrombosis.**
myocardiograph (ˌmaɪəʊˈkɑːdɪəˌgræf, -ˌgrɑːf) *n* an instrument for recording the movements of heart muscle.
myocarditis (ˌmaɪəʊkɑːˈdaɪtɪs) *n* inflammation of the heart muscle.
myocardium (ˌmaɪəʊˈkɑːdɪəm) *n, pl* **-dia** (-dɪə). the muscular tissue of the heart. [C19: *myo-* + *cardium,* from Greek *kardia* heart] ▸ ˌ**myoˈcardial** *adj*
myoelectric (ˌmaɪəʊɪˈlɛktrɪk) *adj* denoting a type of powered artificial hand or limb that detects electrical changes in the muscles of the stump and converts these into movements.
myogenic (ˌmaɪəˈdʒɛnɪk) *adj* originating in or forming muscle tissue.
myoglobin (ˌmaɪəʊˈgləʊbɪn) *n* a protein that is the main oxygen-carrier of muscle.
myograph (ˈmaɪəˌgræf, -ˌgrɑːf) *n* an instrument for recording tracings (**myograms**) of muscular contractions. ▸ ˌ**myoˈgraphic** *adj* ▸ ˌ**myoˈgraphically** *adv* ▸ **myography** (maɪˈɒgrəfɪ) *n*
myology (maɪˈɒlədʒɪ) *n* the branch of medical science concerned with the structure and diseases of muscles. ▸ **myologic** (ˌmaɪəˈlɒdʒɪk) *or* ˌ**myoˈlogical** *adj* ▸ **myˈologist** *n*
myoma (maɪˈəʊmə) *n, pl* **-mas** *or* **-mata** (-mətə). a benign tumour composed of muscle tissue. ▸ **myˈomatous** *adj*
myomectomy (ˌmaɪəˈmɛktəmɪ) *n, pl* **-mies.** surgical removal of a myoma, especially in the uterus.
myopathy (maɪˈɒpəθɪ) *n* any disease affecting muscles or muscle tissue.
myope (ˈmaɪəʊp) *n* any person afflicted with myopia. [C18: via French from Greek *muōps;* see MYOPIA]
myophily *or* **myiophily** (maɪˈɒfɪlɪ) *n* pollination of plants by flies. [from Greek *muia* fly + *philos* loving] ▸ **myˈophilous** or **myiˈophilous** *adj*
myopia (maɪˈəʊpɪə) *n* inability to see distant objects clearly because the images are focused in front of the retina; short-sightedness. [C18: via New Latin from Greek *muōps* short-sighted, from *muein* to close (the eyes), blink + *ōps* eye] ▸ **myopic** (maɪˈɒpɪk) *adj* ▸ **myˈopically** *adv*
myosin (ˈmaɪəsɪn) *n* the chief protein of muscle that interacts with actin to form actomyosin during muscle contraction; it is also present in many other cell types. [C19: from MYO- + -OSE[2] + -IN]
myosis (maɪˈəʊsɪs) *n, pl* **-ses** (-siːz). a variant spelling of **miosis.**
myosotis (ˌmaɪəˈsəʊtɪs) *or* **myosote** (ˈmaɪəˌsəʊt) *n* any plant of the boraginaceous genus *Myosotis.* See **forget-me-not.** [C18: New Latin from Greek *muosōtis* mouse-ear (referring to its furry leaves), from *muos,* genitive of *mus* mouse + *-ōt-,* stem of *ous* ear]
myotome (ˈmaɪəˌtəʊm) *n* **1** any segment of embryonic mesoderm that develops into skeletal muscle in the adult. **2** any of the segmentally arranged blocks of muscle in lower vertebrates such as fishes.
myotonia (ˌmaɪəˈtəʊnɪə) *n* lack of muscle tone, frequently including muscle spasm or rigidity. Also called: **amyotonia.** ▸ **myotonic** (ˌmaɪəˈtɒnɪk) *adj*
myria- *combining form.* indicating a very great number: *myriapod.* [from Greek *murios* countless]
myriad (ˈmɪrɪəd) *adj* **1** innumerable. ◆ *n* **2** (*also used in pl*) a large indefinite number. **3** *Archaic.* ten thousand. [C16: via Late Latin from Greek *murias* ten thousand]
myriapod (ˈmɪrɪəˌpɒd) *n* **1** any terrestrial arthropod of the group *Myriapoda,* having a long segmented body and many walking limbs: includes the centipedes and millipedes. ◆ *adj* **2** of, relating to, or belonging to the *Myriapoda.* [C19: from New Latin *Myriapoda.* See MYRIAD, -POD] ▸ **myriapodan** (ˌmɪrɪˈæpədᵊn) *adj* ▸ ˌ**myriˈapodous** *adj*
myrica (mɪˈraɪkə) *n* the dried root bark of the wax myrtle, used as a tonic and to treat diarrhoea. [C18: via Latin from Greek *murikē* the tamarisk]
myrmeco- *combining form.* ant: *myrmecology; myrmecophile.* [from Greek *murmēx*]
myrmecochory (ˌmɜːmɪkəʊˈkɔːrɪ) *n* the dispersal of fruits and seeds by ants.
myrmecology (ˌmɜːmɪˈkɒlədʒɪ) *n* the branch of zoology concerned with the study of ants. ▸ **myrmecological** (ˌmɜːmɪkəˈlɒdʒɪkᵊl) *adj* ▸ ˌ**myrmeˈcologist** *n*
myrmecophagous (ˌmɜːmɪˈkɒfəgəs) *adj* **1** (of jaws) specialized for feeding on ants. **2** feeding on ants.
myrmecophile (ˈmɜːmɪkəʊˌfaɪl) *n* an animal that lives in a colony of ants. ▸ **myrmecophilous** (ˌmɜːmɪˈkɒfɪləs) *adj*
myrmecophily (ˌmɜːmɪˈkɒfɪlɪ) *n Biology.* **1** symbiosis with ants. **2** pollination of plants by ants.
Myrmidon (ˈmɜːmɪˌdɒn, -dᵊn) *n, pl* **Myrmidons** *or* **Myrmidones** (mɜːˈmɪdᵊˌniːz). **1** *Greek myth.* one of a race of people whom Zeus made from a nest of ants. They settled in Thessaly and were led against Troy by Achilles. **2** (*often not cap.*) a follower or henchman.
myrobalan (maɪˈrɒbələn, mɪ-) *n* **1** the dried plumlike fruit of various tropical trees of the genus *Terminalia,* used in dyeing, tanning, ink, and medicine. **2** a dye extracted from this fruit. **3** another name for **cherry plum.** [C16: via Latin from Greek *murobalanos,* from *muron* ointment + *balanos* acorn]
Myron (ˈmaɪərən) *n* 5th century B.C., Greek sculptor. He worked mainly in bronze and introduced a greater variety of pose into Greek sculpture, as in his *Discobolus.*
myrrh (mɜː) *n* **1** any of several burseraceous trees and shrubs of the African and S Asian genus *Commiphora,* esp. *C. myrrha,* that exude an aromatic resin. Compare **balm of Gilead** (sense 1). **2** the resin obtained from such a plant, used in perfume, incense, and medicine. **3** another name for **sweet cicely** (sense 1). [Old English *myrre,* via Latin from Greek *murrha,* ultimately from Akkadian *murrū;* compare Hebrew *mōr,* Arabic *murr*]
myrtaceous (mɜːˈteɪʃəs) *adj* of, relating to, or belonging to the *Myrtaceae,* a family of mostly tropical and subtropical trees and shrubs having oil glands in the leaves: includes eucalyptus, clove, myrtle, and guava. [C19: via New Latin from Latin *myrtus* myrtle, from Greek *murtos*]
myrtle (ˈmɜːtᵊl) *n* **1** any evergreen shrub or tree of the myrtaceous genus *Myrtus,* esp. *M. communis,* a S European shrub with pink or white flowers and aromatic blue-black berries. **2** short for **crape myrtle. 3 creeping** *or* **trailing myrtle.** *U.S. and Canadian.* another name for **periwinkle** (the plant). [C16: from Medieval Latin *myrtilla,* from Latin *myrtus,* from Greek *murtos*]
myself (maɪˈsɛlf) *pron* **1a** the reflexive form of *I* or *me.* **1b** (intensifier): *I myself know of no answer.* **2** (*preceded by a copula*) my usual self: *I'm not myself today.* **3** *Not standard.* used instead of *I* or *me* in compound noun phrases: *John and myself are voting together.*
Mysia (ˈmɪsɪə) *n* an ancient region in the NW corner of Asia Minor. ▸ ˈ**Mysian** *adj, n*
Mysore (maɪˈsɔː) *n* **1** a city in S India, in S Karnataka state: former capital of the state of Mysore; manufacturing and trading centre; university (1916). Pop.: 480 692 (1991). **2** the former name (until 1973) of **Karnataka.**
mystagogue (ˈmɪstəˌgɒg) *n* (in Mediterranean mystery religions) a person who instructs those who are preparing for initiation into the mysteries. [C16: via Latin from Greek *mustagōgos,* from *mustēs* candidate for initiation + *agein* to lead. See MYSTIC] ▸ **mystagogic** (ˌmɪstəˈgɒdʒɪk) *or* ˌ**mystaˈgogical** *adj* ▸ ˌ**mystaˈgogically** *adv* ▸ **mystagogy** (ˈmɪstəˌgɒdʒɪ) *n*
mysterious (mɪˈstɪərɪəs) *adj* **1** characterized by or indicative of mystery. **2** puzzling, curious, or enigmatic. ▸ **mysˈteriously** *adv* ▸ **mysˈteriousness** *n*
mystery[1] (ˈmɪstərɪ, -trɪ) *n, pl* **-teries. 1** an unexplained or inexplicable event, phenomenon, etc. **2** a person or thing that arouses curiosity or suspense because of an unknown, obscure, or enigmatic quality. **3** the state or quality of being obscure, inexplicable, or enigmatic. **4** a story, film, etc., which arouses suspense and curiosity because of facts concealed. **5** *Christianity.* any truth that is divinely revealed but otherwise unknowable. **6** *Christianity.* a sacramental rite, such as the Eucharist, or (*when pl*) the consecrated elements of the Eucharist. **7** (*often pl*) any of various rites of certain ancient Mediterranean religions. **8** short for **mystery play.** [C14: via Latin from Greek *mustērion* secret rites. See MYSTIC]
mystery[2] (ˈmɪstərɪ) *n, pl* **-teries.** *Archaic.* **1** a trade, occupation, or craft. **2** a guild of craftsmen. [C14: from Medieval Latin *mistērium,* from Latin *ministerium* occupation, from *minister* official]
mystery play *n* (in the Middle Ages) a type of drama based on the life of Christ. Compare **miracle play.**
mystery tour *n* an excursion to an unspecified destination.
mystic (ˈmɪstɪk) *n* **1** a person who achieves mystical experience or an apprehension of divine mysteries. ◆ *adj* **2** another word for **mystical.** [C14: via Latin from Greek *mustikos,* from *mustēs* mystery initiate; related to *muein* to initiate into sacred rites]
mystical (ˈmɪstɪkᵊl) *adj* **1** relating to or characteristic of mysticism. **2** *Christianity.* having a divine or sacred significance that surpasses natural human apprehension. **3** having occult or metaphysical significance, nature, or force. **4** a less common word for **mysterious.** ▸ ˈ**mystically** *adv* ▸ ˈ**mysticalness** *n*
mysticism (ˈmɪstɪˌsɪzəm) *n* **1** belief in or experience of a reality surpassing normal human understanding or experience, esp. a reality perceived as essential to the nature of life. **2** a system of contemplative prayer and spirituality aimed at achieving direct intuitive experience of the divine. **3** obscure or confused belief or thought.
mystify (ˈmɪstɪˌfaɪ) *vb* **-fies, -fying, -fied.** (*tr*) **1** to confuse, bewilder, or puzzle. **2** to make mysterious or obscure. [C19: from French *mystifier,* from *mystère* MYSTERY[1] or *mystique* MYSTIC] ▸ ˌ**mystifiˈcation** *n* ▸ ˈ**mystiˌfier** *n* ▸ ˈ**mystiˌfying** *adj* ▸ ˈ**mystiˌfyingly** *adv*
mystique (mɪˈstiːk) *n* an aura of mystery, power, and awe that surrounds a person or thing: *the mystique of the theatre; the mystique of computer programming.* [C20: from French (adj): MYSTIC]
myth (mɪθ) *n* **1a** a story about superhuman beings of an earlier age taken by preliterate society to be a true account, usually of how natural phenomena, social

customs, etc., came into existence. **1b** another word for **mythology** (senses 1, 3). **2** a person or thing whose existence is fictional or unproven. **3** (in modern literature) a theme or character type embodying an idea: *Hemingway's myth of the male hero.* **4** *Philosophy.* (esp. in the writings of Plato) an allegory or parable. **[C19:** via Late Latin from Greek *muthos* fable, word**]**

myth. *abbrev. for:* **1** mythological. **2** mythology.

mythical ('mɪθɪkᵊl) *or* **mythic** ('mɪθɪk) *adj* **1** of or relating to myth. **2** imaginary or fictitious. ► **'mythically** *adv*

mythicize *or* **mythicise** ('mɪθɪˌsaɪz) *vb* (*tr*) to make into or treat as a myth. ► **ˌmythiciˈzation** *or* **ˌmythiciˈsation** *n* ► **'mythicist, 'mythiˌcizer,** *or* **'mythiˌciser** *n*

mytho- *combining form.* myth: *mythogenesis; mythography.*

mythological (ˌmɪθəˈlɒdʒɪkᵊl) *adj* **1** of or relating to mythology. **2** mythical. ► **ˌmythoˈlogically** *adv*

mythologist (mɪˈθɒlədʒɪst) *n* **1** an expert in or student of mythology. **2** a writer or editor of myths.

mythologize *or* **mythologise** (mɪˈθɒləˌdʒaɪz) *vb* **1** to tell, study, or explain (myths). **2** (*intr*) to create or make up myths. **3** (*tr*) to convert into a myth. ► **myˌthologiˈzation** *or* **myˌthologiˈsation** *n* ► **myˈthologer, myˈtholoˌgizer,** *or* **myˈtholoˌgiser** *n*

mythology (mɪˈθɒlədʒɪ) *n, pl* **-gies. 1** a body of myths, esp. one associated with a particular culture, institution, person, etc. **2** a body of stories about a person, institution, etc.: *the mythology of Hollywood.* **3** myths collectively. **4** the study or collecting of myths.

mythomania (ˌmɪθəʊˈmeɪnɪə) *n Psychiatry.* the tendency to lie, exaggerate, or relate incredible imaginary adventures as if they had really happened, occurring in some mental disorders. ► **mythomaniac** (ˌmɪθəʊˈmeɪnɪˌæk) *n, adj*

mythopoeia (ˌmɪθəʊˈpiːə) *or* **mythopoesis** (ˌmɪθəpəʊˈiːsɪs) *n* the composition or making of myths. **[C19:** from Greek, from *muthopoiein,* from *muthos* myth + *poiein* to make**]**

mythopoeic (ˌmɪθəʊˈpiːɪk) *adj* of or relating to the composition of myths; productive of myths. ► **ˌmythoˈpoeism** *n* ► **ˌmythoˈpoeist** *n*

mythos ('maɪθɒs, 'mɪθɒs) *n, pl* **-thoi** (-θɔɪ). **1** the complex of beliefs, values, attitudes, etc., characteristic of a specific group or society. **2** another word for **myth** or **mythology.**

Mytilene (ˌmɪtɪˈliːnɪ) *n* **1** a port on the Greek island of Lesbos: Roman remains; Byzantine fortress. Pop.: 25 000 (latest est.). Modern Greek name: **Mitilíni. 2** a former name for **Lesbos.**

myxo ('mɪksəʊ) *n Austral. slang.* short for **myxomatosis.**

myxo- *or before a vowel* **myx-** *combining form.* mucus or slime: *myxomycete.* [from Greek *muxa* slime, mucus]

myxoedema *or U.S.* **myxedema** (ˌmɪksɪˈdiːmə) *n* a disease resulting from underactivity of the thyroid gland characterized by puffy eyes, face, and hands and mental sluggishness. See also **cretinism.** ► **myxoedemic** (ˌmɪksɪˈdɛmɪk), **myxoedematous** (ˌmɪksɪˈdɛmətəs, -ˈdiː-) *or U.S.* **ˌmyxeˈdemic, ˌmyxeˈdematous** *adj*

myxoma (mɪkˈsəʊmə) *n, pl* **-mas** *or* **-mata** (-mətə). a tumour composed of mucous connective tissue, usually situated in subcutaneous tissue. ► **myxomatous** (mɪkˈsɒmətəs) *adj*

myxomatosis (ˌmɪksəməˈtəʊsɪs) *n* an infectious and usually fatal viral disease of rabbits characterized by swelling of the mucous membranes and formation of skin tumours.

myxomycete (ˌmɪksəʊmaɪˈsiːt) *n* a slime mould, esp. a slime mould of the phylum *Myxomycota* (division *Myxomycetes* in traditional classifications). ► **ˌmyxomyˈcetous** *adj*

myxovirus ('mɪksəʊˌvaɪərəs) *n* any of a group of viruses that cause influenza, mumps, and certain other diseases.

mzee (ᵊmˈzeɪ) *E African.* ♦ *n* **1** an old person. ♦ *adj* **2** advanced in years. **[C19:** from Swahili**]**

Nn

n *or* **N** (ɛn) *n, pl* **n's, N's,** *or* **Ns. 1** the 14th letter and 11th consonant of the modern English alphabet. **2** a speech sound represented by this letter, usually an alveolar nasal, as in *nail.*

n[1] *symbol for:* **1** neutron. **2** *Optics.* index of refraction. **3** nano-.

n[2] (ɛn) *determiner* an indefinite number (of): *there are n objects in a box.*

N *symbol for:* **1** Also: **kt.** *Chess.* knight. **2** neper. **3** neutral. **4** newton(s). **5** *Chem.* nitrogen. **6** North. **7** Avogadro's number. **8** noun. ◆ **9** *international car registration for* Norway.

n. *abbrev. for:* **1** natus. [Latin: born] **2** neuter. **3** new. **4** nominative. **5** noon. **6** note. **7** noun. **8** number.

N. *abbrev. for:* **1** National(ist). **2** Navy. **3** New. **4** Norse.

n- *prefix Chem.* short for **normal** (sense 6).

na (nɑː) a variant of **nae.**

Na *the chemical symbol for* sodium. [Latin *natrium*]

NA 1 *abbrev. for* North America. **2** *international car registration for* Netherlands Antilles.

n/a *abbrev. for* not applicable.

NAACP (in the U.S.) *abbrev. for* National Association for the Advancement of Colored People.

NAAFI *or* **Naafi** ('næfɪ) *n* **1** *acronym for* Navy, Army, and Air Force Institutes: an organization providing canteens, shops, etc., for British military personnel at home or overseas. **2** a canteen, shop, etc., run by this organization.

naan (nɑːn) *n* another name for **nan bread.**

naartjie ('nɑːtʃɪ) *n S. African.* a tangerine. [Afrikaans]

nab (næb) *vb* **nabs, nabbing, nabbed.** *(tr) Informal.* **1** to arrest. **2** to catch (someone) in wrongdoing. **3** to seize suddenly; snatch. [C17: perhaps of Scandinavian origin; compare Danish *nappe,* Swedish *nappa* to snatch. See KIDNAP]

Nabataean *or* **Nabatean** (ˌnæbə'tiːən) *n* **1** a member of an Arab trading people who flourished southeast of Palestine, around Petra, in the Hellenistic and Roman periods. **2** the extinct form of Aramaic spoken by this people.

Nabis (*French* nabi) *pl n, sing* **-bi** (-bi). a group of French artists much influenced by Gauguin, including Bonnard and Vuillard, who reacted against the naturalism of the impressionists. See also **synthetism.** [C19: French, from Hebrew *nābhi* prophet]

nabla ('næblə) *n Maths.* another name for **del.** [C19: from Greek *nabla* stringed instrument, because it is shaped like a harp]

Nablus ('nɑːbləs) *n* a town west of the River Jordan: near the site of ancient Shechem. Pop.: 98 000 (1989 est.).

nabob ('neɪbɒb) *n* **1** *Informal.* a rich, powerful, or important man. **2** (formerly) a European who made a fortune in the Orient, esp. in India. **3** another name for a **nawab.** [C17: from Portuguese *nababo,* from Hindi *nawwāb;* see NAWAB] ▸ **nabobery** ('neɪbɒbərɪ, neɪ'bɒbərɪ) *or* '**nabobism** *n* ▸ '**nabobish** *adj*

Nabokov (nə'bɒkɒf, 'næbəˌkɒf) *n* **Vladimir Vladimirovich** (vla'dimir vla'dimirəvitʃ). 1899–1977, U.S. novelist, born in Russia. His works include *Lolita* (1955), *Pnin* (1957), *Pale Fire* (1962), and *Ada* (1969). ▸ **Nabokovian** (ˌnæbə'kəʊvɪən) *adj*

Nabonidus (ˌnæbə'naɪdəs) *n Old Testament.* the father of Belshazzar; last king of Babylon before it was captured by Cyrus in 539 B.C.

Naboth ('neɪbɒθ) *n Old Testament.* an inhabitant of Jezreel, murdered by King Ahab at the instigation of his wife Jezebel for refusing to sell his vineyard (I Kings 21).

NAC *abbrev. for* National Advisory Council.

nacelle (nə'sɛl) *n* a streamlined enclosure on an aircraft, not part of the fuselage, to accommodate an engine, passengers, crew, etc. [C20: from French: small boat, from Late Latin *nāvicella,* a diminutive of Latin *nāvis* ship]

nacho ('nɑːtʃəʊ) *n, pl* **nachos.** *Mexican cookery.* a snack consisting of a piece of tortilla topped with cheese, hot peppers, etc., and grilled.

NACODS ('neɪkɒdz) *n acronym for* National Association of Colliery Overmen, Deputies, and Shotfirers.

nacre ('neɪkə) *n* the technical name for **mother-of-pearl.** [C16: via French from Old Italian *naccara,* from Arabic *naqqārah* shell, drum] ▸ '**nacred** *adj*

nacreous ('neɪkrɪəs) *adj* **1** relating to or consisting of mother-of-pearl. **2** having the lustre of mother-of-pearl: *nacreous minerals.*

NACRO *or* **Nacro** ('nækrəʊ) *n acronym for* National Association for the Care and Resettlement of Offenders.

NAD *n Biochem.* nicotinamide adenine dinucleotide; a coenzyme that is a hydrogen carrier in metabolic reactions, esp. in tissue respiration. Former name: **DPN.**

Nadar (*French* nadar) *n* real name *Gaspard Félix Tournachon.* 1820–1910, French photographer, writer, and caricaturist: noted for his portrait photographs of artists and writers and for taking the first aerial photographs (1858).

Na-Dene *or* **Na-Déné** (nɑː'deɪnɪ, nə'diːn) *n* a phylum of North American Indian languages including Athapascan, Tlingit, and Haida. [from Haida *na* to dwell + Athapascan *dene* people; coined by Edward Sapir (1884–1939), American anthropologist]

Nader ('neɪdə) *n* **Ralph.** born 1934, U.S. lawyer and campaigner for consumer rights.

NADH *n Biochem.* the chemically reduced form of NAD.

nadir ('neɪdɪə, 'næ-) *n* **1** the point on the celestial sphere directly below an observer and diametrically opposite the zenith. **2** the lowest or deepest point; depths: *the nadir of despair.* [C14: from Old French, from Arabic *nazīr assamt,* literally: opposite the zenith]

nadors ('nɑːˌdɔːz) *n S. African.* a thirst brought on by excessive consumption of alcohol. [from Afrikaans *na* after + *dors* thirst]

NADP *n Biochem.* nicotinamide adenine dinucleotide phosphate; a coenzyme with functions similar to those of NAD. Former name: **TPN.**

NADPH *n Biochem.* the chemically reduced form of NADP.

nae (neɪ) *or* **na** (nɑː) a Scot. word for **no** or **not.**

naevus *or U.S.* **nevus** ('niːvəs) *n, pl* **-vi** (-vaɪ). any congenital growth or pigmented blemish on the skin; birthmark or mole. [C19: from Latin; related to (*g*)*natus* born, produced by nature] ▸ '**naevoid** *or U.S.* '**nevoid** *adj*

naff (næf) *adj Brit. slang.* inferior; in poor taste. [C19: perhaps back slang for *fan,* short for FANNY] ▸ '**naffness** *n*

naff off *sentence substitute. Brit. slang.* a forceful expression of dismissal or contempt.

NAFTA ('næftə) *n acronym for* North American Free Trade Agreement.

nag[1] (næg) *vb* **nags, nagging, nagged. 1** to scold or annoy constantly. **2** (when *intr,* often foll. by *at*) to be a constant source of discomfort or worry (to): *toothache nagged him all day.* ◆ *n* **3** a person, esp. a woman, who nags. [C19: of Scandinavian origin; compare Swedish *nagga* to GNAW, irritate, German *nagen*] ▸ '**nagger** *n* ▸ '**naggingly** *adv*

nag[2] (næg) *n* **1** *Often derogatory.* a horse. **2** a small riding horse. [C14: of Germanic origin; related to NEIGH]

Naga ('nɑːgə) *n* **1** (*pl* **Nagas** *or* **Naga**) a member of a people of NE India and W Myanmar: until the early 20th century they practised head-hunting. **2** the language of this people, belonging to the Sino-Tibetan family of languages and having many dialects.

Nagaland ('nɑːgəˌlænd) *n* a state of NE India: formed in 1962 from parts of Assam and the North-East Frontier Agency; inhabited chiefly by Naga tribes; consists of almost inaccessible forested hills and mountains (the **Naga Hills**); shifting cultivation predominates. Capital: Kohima. Pop.: 1 410 000 (1994 est.). Area: 16 579 sq. km (6401 sq. miles).

nagana (nə'gɑːnə) *n* a disease of hoofed animals of central and southern Africa, caused by parasitic protozoa of the genus *Trypanosoma* that is transmitted by tsetse flies. [from Zulu *u-nakane*]

Nagano (nə'gɑːnəʊ) *n* a city in central Japan, on central Honshu: Buddhist shrine; two universities. Pop.: 358 512 (1995).

Nagari ('nɑːgərɪ) *n* **1** a set of scripts, including Devanagari, used as the writing systems for several languages of India. **2** another word for **Devanagari.**

Nagarjuna (ˌnægɑː'dʒuːnə) *n c.* 150–*c.* 250 A.D., Indian Buddhist monk, founder of the Madhyamika (Middle Path) school of Mahayana Buddhism: noted for his philosophical writings.

Nagasaki (ˌnɑːgə'sɑːkɪ) *n* a port in SW Japan, on W Kyushu: almost completely destroyed in 1945 by the second atomic bomb dropped on Japan by the U.S.; shipbuilding industry. Pop.: 438 724 (1995).

nagor ('neɪgɔː) *n* another name for **reedbuck.** [C18: from French, arbitrarily named by Buffon, from earlier *nanguer*]

Nagorno-Karabakh Autonomous Region (nə'gɔːnəʊkərʌ'bɑːk) *n* an administrative division in S Azerbaijan. In 1990 violent unrest caused by Armenian claims to the region culminated in the declaration of a state of emergency. Capital: Stepanakert. Pop.: 193 300 (1991 est.). Area: 4400 sq. km (1700 sq. miles).

Nagoya ('nɑːgəujə) *n* a city in central Japan, on S Honshu on Ise Bay: a major industrial centre. Pop.: 2 152 258 (1995).

Nagpur (næg'pʊə) *n* a city in central India, in NE Maharashtra state: became capital of the kingdom of Nagpur (1743); capital of the Central Provinces (later Madhya Pradesh) from 1861 to 1956. Pop.: 1 624 752 (1991).

Nagy (*Hungarian* nɒdj) *n* **Imre** ('imrɛ). 1896–1958, Hungarian statesman; prime minister (1953–55; 1956). He was removed from office and later executed when Soviet forces suppressed the revolution of 1956; reburied with honours in 1989.

Nagyszeben ('nɒdjsɛːˌbɛn) *n* the Hungarian name for **Sibiu.**

Nagyvárad ('nɒdjvaːrɒd) *n* the Hungarian name for **Oradea.**

Nah. *Bible. abbrev. for* Nahum.

Naha ('nɑːhə) *n* a port in S Japan, on the SW coast of Okinawa Island: chief city of the Ryukyu Islands. Pop.: 301 928 (1995).

Nahal (nə'hɑːl) *n* **1** (in Israel) a military youth organization. **2** (*not cap.*) an agricultural settlement, esp. in a border area, set up or manned by Nahal members. [C20: from Hebrew acronym for *No'ar Halutzi Lohem* Pioneer and Military Youth]

NAHT (in Britain) *abbrev. for* National Association of Head Teachers.

Nahuatl ('nɑːwɑːtᵊl, nɑː'wɑːtᵊl) *n* **1** (*pl* **-tl** *or* **-tls**) a member of one of a group of Central American and Mexican Indian peoples including the Aztecs. **2** the language of these peoples, belonging to the Uto-Aztecan family. ◆ Also: **Na'huatlan.**

Nahum (ˈneɪhəm) *n Old Testament.* **1** a Hebrew prophet of the 7th century B.C. **2** the book containing his oracles.

NAI (in Britain) *abbrev. for* nonaccidental injury.

naiad (ˈnaɪæd) *n, pl* **-ads** *or* **-ades** (-əˌdiːz). **1** *Greek myth.* a nymph dwelling in a lake, river, spring, or fountain. **2** the aquatic larva of the dragonfly, mayfly, and related insects. **3** Also called: **water nymph.** any monocotyledonous submerged aquatic plant of the genus *Naias* (or *Najas*), having narrow leaves and small flowers: family *Naiadaceae* (or *Najadaceae*). **4** any of certain freshwater mussels of the genus *Unio.* See **mussel** (sense 2). **[C17:** via Latin from Greek *nāias* water nymph; related to *náein* to flow**]**

naïf (nɑːˈiːf) *adj, n* a less common word for **naive.**

nail (neɪl) *n* **1** a fastening device usually made from round or oval wire, having a point at one end and a head at the other. **2** anything resembling such a fastening device, esp. in function or shape. **3** the horny plate covering part of the dorsal surface of the fingers or toes. See **fingernail, toenail.** Related adjs.: **ungual, ungular.** **4** the claw of a mammal, bird, or reptile. **5** *Slang.* a hypodermic needle, used for injecting drugs. **6** a unit of length, formerly used for measuring cloth, equal to two and a quarter inches. **7 a nail in one's coffin.** an experience or event that tends to shorten life or hasten the end of something. **8 bite one's nails. 8a** to chew off the ends of one's fingernails. **8b** to be worried or apprehensive. **9 hard as nails. 9a** in tough physical condition. **9b** without sentiment or feelings. **10 hit the nail on the head.** to do or say something correct or telling. **11 on the nail.** (of payments) at once (esp. in the phrase **pay on the nail**). ◆ *vb (tr)* **12** to attach with or as if with nails. **13** *Informal.* to arrest or seize. **14** *Informal.* to hit or bring down, as with a shot: *I nailed the sniper.* **15** *Informal.* to expose or detect (a lie or liar). **16** to fix or focus (one's eyes, attention, etc.) on an object. **17** to stud with nails. ◆ See also **nail down, nail up.** **[**Old English *nægl;* related to Old High German *nagal* nail, Latin *unguis* fingernail, claw, Greek *onux***]** ► **ˈnailer** *n* ► **ˈnail-less** *adj*

nail-biting *n* **1** the act or habit of biting one's fingernails. **2a** anxiety or tension. **2b** *(as modifier): nail-biting suspense.*

nail bomb *n* an explosive device containing nails, used by terrorists to cause serious injuries in crowded situations.

nailbrush (ˈneɪlˌbrʌʃ) *n* a small stiff-bristled brush for cleaning the fingernails.

nail down *vb (tr, adv)* **1** to fasten down with or as if with nails. **2** *Informal.* to extort a definite promise or consent from: *I nailed him down on the deadline.* **3** *Informal.* to settle in a definite way: *they nailed down the agreement.*

nailfile (ˈneɪlˌfaɪl) *n* a small file, chiefly either of metal or of board coated with emery, used to trim the nails.

nailhead (ˈneɪlˌhed) *n* a decorative device, as on tooled leather, resembling the round head of a nail.

nail polish *or* **varnish** *or U.S.* **enamel** *n* a quick-drying lacquer applied to colour the nails or make them shiny or esp. both.

nail set *or* **punch** *n* a punch for driving the head of a nail below or flush with the surrounding surface.

nail up *vb (tr, adv)* to shut in or fasten tightly with or as if with nails.

nainsook (ˈneɪnsʊk, ˈnæn-) *n* a light soft plain-weave cotton fabric, used esp. for babies' wear. **[C19:** from Hindi *nainsukh,* literally: delight to the eye, from *nain* eye + *sukh* delight, from Sanskrit *sukha***]**

Naipaul (naɪˈpɔːl) *n* Sir **V**(**idiadhar**) **S**(**urajprasad**). born 1932, Trinidadian novelist of Indian descent, living in Britain. His works include *A House for Mr Biswas* (1961), *In a Free State* (1971), which won the Booker Prize, *A Bend in the River* (1979), *The Enigma of Arrival* (1987), and *A Way in the World* (1994).

naira (ˈnaɪrə) *n* the standard monetary unit of Nigeria, divided into 100 kobo. **[C20:** altered from NIGERIA**]**

NAI register *n Social welfare.* (in Britain) a list of children deemed to be at risk of abuse or injury from their parents or guardians, compiled and held by a local authority, area health authority, or NSPCC Special Unit. Also called: **child abuse register.**

Nairnshire (ˈnɛənˌʃɪə, -ʃə) *n* (until 1975) a county of NE Scotland, now part of Highland.

Nairobi (naɪˈrəʊbɪ) *n* the capital of Kenya, in the southwest at an altitude of 1650 m (5500 ft.): founded in 1899; became capital in 1905; commercial and industrial centre; the **Nairobi National Park** (a game reserve) is nearby. Pop.: 2 000 000 (1991 est.).

NAIRU (ˈnaɪruː) *n Economics. acronym for* non-accelerating inflation rate of unemployment: the rate of unemployment at which inflation is neither accelerating nor decelerating. Also called: **natural rate of unemployment.**

Naismith's rule (ˈneɪsmɪθs) *n Mountaineering.* a rule of thumb for calculating the time needed for a climbing expedition, allowing 1 hour for every 3 miles of distance plus 1 hour for every 2000 feet of height. **[C19:** named after W. W. *Naismith* (1856–1935), Scottish climber, who formulated it**]**

naissant (ˈneɪsᵊnt) *adj Heraldry.* (of a beast) having only the forepart shown above a horizontal division of a shield. **[C16:** from Old French, literally: being born. See NASCENT**]**

naive, naïve (nɑːˈiːv, naɪˈiːv), *or* **naïf** *adj* **1a** having or expressing innocence and credulity; ingenuous. **1b** *(as collective n;* preceded by *the): only the naive believed him.* **2** artless or unsophisticated. **3** lacking developed powers of analysis, reasoning, or criticism: *a naive argument.* **4** another word for **primitive** (sense 5). ◆ *n* **5** *Rare.* a person who is naive, esp. in artistic style. See **primitive** (sense 10). **[C17:** from French, feminine of *naïf,* from Old French *naif* native, spontaneous, from Latin *nātīvus* NATIVE, from *nasci* to be born**]** ► **naˈively, naˈïvely,** *or* **naˈïfly** *adv* ► **naˈiveness, naˈïveness,** *or* **naˈïfness** *n*

naive realism *n Philosophy.* the doctrine that in perception of physical objects what is before the mind is the object itself and not a representation of it. Compare **representationalism** (sense 1).

naivety (naɪˈiːvtɪ), **naiveté,** *or* **naïveté** (ˌnɑːiːvˈteɪ) *n, pl* **-ties** *or* **-tés. 1** the state or quality of being naive; ingenuousness; simplicity. **2** a naive act or statement.

naked (ˈneɪkɪd) *adj* **1** having the body completely unclothed; undressed. Compare **bare**[1]. **2** having no covering; bare; exposed: *a naked flame.* **3** with no qualification or concealment; stark; plain: *the naked facts.* **4** unaided by any optical instrument, such as a telescope or microscope (esp. in the phrase **the naked eye**). **5** with no defence, protection, or shield. **6** (usually foll. by *of*) stripped or destitute: *naked of weapons.* **7** (of the seeds of gymnosperms) not enclosed in a pericarp. **8** (of flowers) lacking a perianth. **9** (of stems) lacking leaves and other appendages. **10** (of animals) lacking hair, feathers, scales, etc. **11** *Law.* **11a** unsupported by authority or financial or other consideration: *a naked contract.* **11b** lacking some essential condition to render valid; incomplete. **[**Old English *nacod;* related to Old High German *nackot* (German *nackt*), Old Norse *noktr,* Latin *nudus***]** ► **ˈnakedly** *adv* ► **ˈnakedness** *n*

naked ladies *n (functioning as sing)* another name for **autumn crocus.**

naked lady *n* a leafless pink orchid found in Australia and New Zealand.

naked singularity *n Astronomy.* a hypothetical location at which there would be a discontinuity in the space-time continuum as a result of the gravitational collapse of a spherical mass. See also **black hole.**

naker (ˈneɪkə, ˈnæk-) *n* one of a pair of small kettledrums used in medieval music. **[C14:** from Old French *nacre,* via Medieval Greek *anakara,* from Arabic *naqāra***]**

nakfa (ˈnækfə) *n* the standard currency unit of Eritrea.

Nakhichevan *(Russian* nəxitʃɪˈvanj) *n* a city in W Azerbaijan, capital of the Nakhichevan Autonomous Republic: an ancient trading town; ceded to Russia in 1828. Pop.: 66 800 (1994). Ancient name: **Naxuana** (ˌnækˈswɑːnə).

Nakhichevan Autonomous Republic (nəˌkɪtʃɛˈvɑːn) *n* a region belonging to Azerbaijan, from which it is separated by part of Armenia; annexed by Russia in 1828; unilaterally declared secession from the Soviet Union in 1990. Capital: Nakhichevan. Pop.: 315 000 (1994). Area: 5500 sq. km (2120 sq. miles).

Nakuru (nəˈkuːruː) *n* a town in W Kenya, on Lake Nakuru: commercial centre of an agricultural region. Pop.: 124 200 (1991 est.).

Nalchik *(Russian* ˈnaljtʃik) *n* a city in SW Russia, capital of the Kabardino-Balkar Republic, in a valley of the Greater Caucasus: health resort. Pop.: 239 000 (1995 est.).

NALGO (ˈnælgəʊ) *n* (formerly, in Britain) *acronym for* National and Local Government Officers' Association.

naloxone (nəˈlɒksəʊn) *n* a chemical substance that counteracts the effects of opiates by binding to opiate receptors on cells. **[C20:** from *N-al(lyl-nor)ox(ymorph)one,* the chemical name**]**

Nam *or* **'Nam** (næm) *n Chiefly U.S. informal.* Vietnam.

Nama (ˈnɑːmə) *or* **Namaqua** (nəˈmɑːkwə) *n* **1** *(pl* **-ma, -mas** *or* **-qua, -quas)** a member of a Khoikhoi people living chiefly in Namaqualand. **2** the Khoikhoi language spoken by this people, belonging to the Khoisan family. See also **Damara.** ► **ˈNaman** *or* **Naˈmaquan** *n, adj*

Namangan *(Russian* nəmanˈgan) *n* a city in E Uzbekistan. Pop.: 341 000 (1996).

Namaqualand (nəˈmɑːkwəˌlænd) *n* a semiarid coastal region of SW Africa, extending from near Windhoek, Namibia, into W South Africa: divided by the Orange River into **Little Namaqualand** in South Africa, and **Great Namaqualand** in Namibia; rich mineral resources. Area: 47 961 sq. km (18 518 sq. miles). Also called: **Namaland** (ˈnɑːməˌlænd).

namas kar (nəˈmʌs kɑː) *n* a salutation used in India. **[**Sanskrit, from *namas* salutation, bow + *kara* doing**]**

namby-pamby (ˌnæmbɪˈpæmbɪ) *adj* **1** sentimental or prim in a weak insipid way: *namby-pamby manners.* **2** clinging, feeble, or spineless: *a namby-pamby child.* ◆ *n, pl* **-bies. 3** a person who is namby-pamby. **[C18:** a nickname of Ambrose Phillips (died 1749), whose pastoral verse was ridiculed for being insipid**]**

Nam Co (ˈnɑːm ˈkɔː) *or* **Nam Tso** *n* a salt lake in SW China, in SE Tibet at an altitude of 4629 m (15 186 ft.). Area: about 1800 sq. km (700 sq. miles). Also called: **Tengri Nor.**

name (neɪm) *n* **1** a word or term by which a person or thing is commonly and distinctively known. Related adj: **nominal. 2** mere outward appearance or form as opposed to fact (esp. in the phrase **in name**): *he was a ruler in name only.* **3** a word, title, or phrase descriptive of character, usually abusive or derogatory: *to call a person names.* **4** reputation, esp., if unspecified, good reputation: *he's made quite a name for himself.* **5a** a famous person or thing: *a name in the advertising world.* **5b** *Chiefly U.S. and Canadian. (as modifier): a name product.* **6** a member of Lloyd's who provides part of the capital of a syndicate and shares in its profits or losses but does not arrange its business. **7 in** *or* **under the name of.** using as a name. **8 in the name of. 8a** for the sake of. **8b** by the sanction or authority of. **9 know by name.** to have heard of without having met. **10 name of the game. 10a** anything that is essential, significant, or important. **10b** expected or normal conditions, circumstances, etc.: *in gambling, losing money's the name of the game.* **11 to one's name.** belonging to one: *I haven't a penny to my name.* ◆ *vb (tr)* **12** to give a name to; call by a name: *she named the child Edward.* **13** to refer to by name; cite: *he named three French poets.* **14** to determine, fix, or specify: *they have named a date for the meeting.* **15** to appoint to or cite for a particular title, honour, or duty; nominate: *he was named Journalist of the Year.* **16** to ban (an MP) from the House of Commons by mentioning him formally by name as being guilty of disorderly conduct. **17 name names.** to cite people, esp. in order to blame or accuse them. **18 name the day.** to choose the day for one's wedding. **19 you name it.** whatever you need, mention, etc. **[**Old English *nama,* related to Latin *nomen,* Greek *noma,* Old High German *namo,* German *namen***]** ► **ˈnamable** *or* **ˈnameable** *adj*

name-calling *n* verbal abuse, esp. as a crude form of argument.

namecheck (ˈneɪmˌtʃek) *vb (tr)* **1** to mention (someone) specifically by name.

◆ *n* **2** a specific mention of someone's name, for example on a radio programme.

name day *n* **1** *R.C. Church.* the feast day of a saint whose name one bears. **2** another name for **ticket day.**

name-dropping *n Informal.* the practice of referring frequently to famous or fashionable people, esp. as though they were intimate friends, in order to impress others. ► **'name-,dropper** *n*

nameless ('neɪmlɪs) *adj* **1** without a name; anonymous. **2** incapable of being named; indescribable: *a nameless horror seized him.* **3** too unpleasant or disturbing to be mentioned: *nameless atrocities.* **4** having no legal name; illegitimate: *a nameless child.* ► **'namelessly** *adv* ► **'namelessness** *n*

namely ('neɪmlɪ) *adv* that is to say: *it was another colour, namely green.*

Namen ('nɑːmə) *n* the Flemish name for **Namur.**

name part *n* another name for **title role.**

nameplate ('neɪm,pleɪt) *n* a small panel on or next to the door of a room or building, bearing the occupant's name and profession.

namesake ('neɪm,seɪk) *n* **1** a person or thing named after another. **2** a person or thing with the same name as another. **[**C17: probably a shortening of the phrase describing people connected *for the name's sake***]**

nametape ('neɪm,teɪp) *n* a narrow cloth tape bearing the owner's name and attached to an article.

Namhoi ('nɑːm'hɔɪ) *n* another name for **Foshan.**

Namibe (næ'miːb) *n* a port in SW Angola: fishing industry. Pop.: 77 000 (1987).

Namibia (nɑː'mɪbɪə, nə-) *n* a country in southern Africa bordering on South Africa: annexed by Germany in 1884 and mandated by the League of Nations to South Africa in 1920. The mandate was terminated by the UN in 1966 but this was ignored by South Africa, as was the 1971 ruling by the International Court of Justice that the territory be surrendered. Independence was achieved in 1990 and Namibia became a member of the Commonwealth; Walvis Bay remained a South African enclave until 1994 when it was returned to Namibia. Official language: English; Afrikaans and German also spoken. Religion: mostly animist, with some Christians. Currency: dollar. Capital: Windhoek. Pop.: 1 622 000 (1998 est.). Area: 823 328 sq. km (317 887 sq. miles). Also called: **South West Africa.** Former name (1885–1919): **German Southwest Africa.** ► **Na'mibian** *adj, n*

Namier ('neɪmɪə) *n* Sir **Lewis Bernstein**, original name *Ludwik Bernsztajn vel Niemirowski.* 1888–1960, British historian, born in Poland: noted esp. for his studies of 18th-century British politics.

namma hole ('næmə) *n Austral.* a natural well in a rock. **[**C19: from a native Australian language**]**

Nam Tso ('nɑːm 'tsɔː) *n* a variant transliteration of the Chinese name for **Nam Co.**

Namur (næ'mʊə; *French* namyr) *n* **1** a province of S Belgium. Capital: Namur. Pop.: 435 677 (1996 est.). Area: 3660 sq. km (1413 sq. miles). **2** a town in S Belgium, capital of Namur province: strategically situated on a promontory between the Sambre and Meuse Rivers, besieged and captured many times. Pop.: 105 059 (1996 est.). Flemish name: **Namen.**

nan (næn), **nana,** *or* **nanna** ('nænə) *n* a child's words for **grandmother.** [see NANNY; compare Greek *nanna* aunt, Medieval Latin *nonna* old woman]

nana ('nɑːnə) *n* **1** *Slang.* a fool. **2** *Austral. slang.* the head. **3 do one's nana.** *Austral. slang.* to become very angry. **4 off one's nana.** *Austral. slang.* mad; insane. **[**C19: probably from BANANA**]**

Nanak ('nɑːnək) *n* 1469–1538, Indian religious leader; founder and first guru of Sikhism.

Nana Sahib ('nænə 'sɑːhɪb) *n* real name *Dandhu Panth.* ?1825–?1860, Indian nationalist, who led the uprising at Cawnpore during the Indian Mutiny.

nan bread *or* **naan** (nɑːn) *n* (in Indian cookery) a slightly leavened bread in a large flat leaf shape. **[**from Hindi**]**

Nanchang *or* **Nan-ch'ang** ('næn'tʃæŋ) *n* a walled city in SE China, capital of Jiangxi province, on the Kan River: largest city in the Poyang basin. Pop.: 1 350 000 (1991 est.).

Nan-ching ('næn'tʃɪŋ) *n* a variant spelling of **Nanjing.**

nancy ('nænsɪ) *n, pl* **-cies. a** an effeminate or homosexual boy or man. **b** (*as modifier*): *his nancy ways.* ◆ Also called: **nancy boy. [**C20: from the girl's name *Nancy***]**

Nancy ('nænsɪ; *French* nɑ̃si) *n* a city in NE France: became the capital of the dukes of Lorraine in the 12th century, becoming French in 1766; administrative and financial centre. Pop.: 102 410 (1990).

Nanda Devi ('nʌndə 'diːvɪ) *n* a mountain in N India, in N Uttar Pradesh in the Himalayas. Height: 7817 m (25 645 ft.).

NAND circuit *or* **gate** (nænd) *n Electronics.* a computer logic circuit having two or more input wires and one output wire that has an output signal if one or more of the input signals are at a low voltage. Compare **OR circuit. [**C20: from *not* + AND; see NOT CIRCUIT, AND CIRCUIT**]**

nane (nen) *pron* a Scot. word for **none**[1].

Nanga Parbat ('nʌŋgə 'pɑːbʌt) *n* a mountain in N India, in NW Kashmir in the W Himalayas. Height: 8126 m (26 660 ft.).

Nanhai ('nɑːn'haɪ) *n* the Chinese name for the **South China Sea.**

Nanjing ('næn'dʒɪŋ), **Nanking** ('næn'kɪŋ) *or* **Nan-ching** *n* a port in E central China, capital of Jiangsu province, on the Yangtze River: capital of the Chinese empire and a literary centre from the 14th to 17th centuries; capital of Nationalist China (1928–37); site of a massacre of about 300 000 civilians by the invading Japanese army in 1937; university (1928). Pop.: 2 500 000 (1991 est.).

nankeen (næŋ'kiːn) *or* **nankin** ('nænkɪn) *n* **1** a hard-wearing buff-coloured cotton fabric. **2a** a pale greyish-yellow colour. **2b** (*as adj*): *a nankeen carpet.* **[**C18: named after *Nanking,* China, where it originated**]**

Nanning *or* **Nan-ning** ('næn'nɪŋ) *n* a port in S China, capital of Guanxi Zhuang AR, on the Xiang River: rail links with North Vietnam. Pop.: 1 070 000 (1991 est.).

nanny ('nænɪ) *n, pl* **-nies. 1** a nurse or nursemaid for children. **2a** any person or thing regarded as treating people like children, esp. by being patronizing or overprotective. **2b** (*as modifier*): *the nanny state.* **3** a child's word for **grandmother.** ◆ *vb* **nannies, nannying, nannied. 4** (*intr*) to nurse or look after someone else's children. **5** (*tr*) to be overprotective towards. **[**C19: child's name for a nurse**]**

nannygai ('nænɪ,gaɪ) *n, pl* **-gais.** an edible sea fish, *Centroberyx affinis,* of Australia which is red in colour and has large prominent eyes. Also called: **red fish. [**C19: from a native Australian language**]**

nanny goat *n* a female goat. Compare **billy goat.**

nano- *combining form.* **1** denoting 10^{-9}: *nanosecond.* Symbol: n **2** indicating extreme smallness: *nanoplankton.* **[**from Latin *nānus* dwarf, from Greek *nanos***]**

nanometre ('nænəʊ,miːtə) *n* one thousand-millionth of a metre. Symbol: nm

nanook ('nænuːk) *n N Canadian.* the polar bear. **[**from Eskimo *nanug***]**

nanoplankton *or* **nannoplankton** ('nænəʊ,plæŋktən) *n* microscopic organisms in plankton.

nanosecond ('nænəʊ,sekənd) *n* one thousand-millionth of a second. Symbol: ns

nanotechnology (,nænəʊtek'nɒlədʒɪ) *n* a branch of technology dealing with the manufacture of objects with dimensions of less than 100 nanometres and the manipulation of individual molecules and atoms.

Nansen ('nænsən) *n* **Fridtjof** ('fridjɔf). 1861–1930, Norwegian arctic explorer, statesman, and scientist. He crossed Greenland (1888–89) and attempted to reach the North Pole (1893–96), attaining a record 86° 14′ N (1895). He was the League of Nations' high commissioner for refugees (1920–22): Nobel peace prize 1922.

Nansen bottle *n* an instrument used by oceanographers for obtaining samples of sea water from a desired depth. **[**C19: named after F. NANSEN**]**

Nansen passport *n* a passport issued to stateless persons by the League of Nations after World War I. **[**C20: named after F. NANSEN**]**

Nan Shan ('næn 'ʃæn) *pl n* a mountain range in N central China, mainly in Qinghai province, with peaks over 6000 m (20 000 ft.).

Nanterre (*French* nɑ̃tɛr) *n* a town in N France, on the Seine: an industrial suburb of Paris. Pop.: 84 565 (1990).

Nantes (*French* nɑ̃t) *n* **1** a port in W France, at the head of the Loire estuary: scene of the signing of the Edict of Nantes and of the Noyades (drownings) during the French Revolution; extensive shipyards, and large metallurgical and food processing industries. Pop.: 264 857 (1990). **2** *History.* See **Edict of Nantes.**

Nantong *or* **Nantung** ('næn'tʌŋ) *n* a city in E China, in Jiangsu province on the Yangtze estuary. Pop.: 343 341 (1990 est.).

Nantucket (næn'tʌkɪt) *n* an island off SE Massachusetts: formerly a centre of the whaling industry; now a resort. Length: nearly 24 km (15 miles). Width: 5 km (3 miles). Pop.: 6012 (1990).

Naoise ('niːʃə) *n Irish myth.* the husband of Deirdre, killed by his uncle Conchobar. See also **Deirdre.**

Naomi ('neɪəmɪ) *n Old Testament.* the mother-in-law of Ruth (Ruth 1:2). Douay spelling: **Noemi.**

naos ('neɪɒs) *n, pl* **naoi** ('neɪɔɪ). **1** *Rare.* an ancient classical temple. **2** *Architect.* another name for **cella. [**C18: from Greek: inner part of temple**]**

nap[1] (næp) *vb* **naps, napping, napped.** (*intr*) **1** to sleep for a short while; doze. **2** to be unaware or inattentive; be off guard (esp. in the phrase **catch someone napping**). ◆ *n* **3** a short light sleep; doze. **[**Old English *hnappian;* related to Middle High German *napfen***]**

nap[2] (næp) *n* **1a** the raised fibres of velvet or similar cloth. **1b** the direction in which these fibres lie when smoothed down. **2** any similar downy coating. **3** *Austral. informal.* blankets, bedding. ◆ *vb* **naps, napping, napped. 4** (*tr*) to raise the nap of (cloth, esp. velvet) by brushing or similar treatment. **[**C15: probably from Middle Dutch *noppe;* related to Old English *hnoppian* to pluck**]**

nap[3] (næp) *n* **1** Also called: **napoleon.** a card game similar to whist, usually played for stakes. **2** a call in this card game, undertaking to win all five tricks. **3** *Horse racing.* a tipster's choice for an almost certain winner. **4 go nap. 4a** to undertake to win all five tricks at nap. **4b** to risk everything on one chance. **5 not to go nap on.** *Austral. slang.* to hold in disfavour. **6 nap hand.** a position in which there is a very good chance of success if a risk is taken. ◆ *vb* **naps, napping, napped. 7** (*tr*) *Horse racing.* to name (a horse) as likely to win a race. **[**C19: short for NAPOLEON, the original name of the card game**]**

napalm ('neɪpɑːm, 'næ-) *n* **1** a thick and highly incendiary liquid, usually consisting of petrol gelled with aluminium soaps, used in firebombs, flamethrowers, etc. ◆ *vb* **2** (*tr*) to attack with napalm. **[**C20: from NA(PHTHENE) + PALM(ITATE)**]**

nape (neɪp) *n* the back of the neck. Related adj: **nuchal. [**C13: of unknown origin**]**

napery ('neɪpərɪ) *n Rare.* household linen, esp. table linen. **[**C14: from Old French *naperie, from nape* tablecloth, from Latin *mappa.* See NAPKIN**]**

Naphtali ('næftə,laɪ) *n Old Testament.* **1** Jacob's sixth son, whose mother was Rachel's handmaid (Genesis 30:7–8). **2** the tribe descended from him. **3** the territory of this tribe, between the Sea of Galilee and the mountains of central Galilee. Douay spelling: **Nephtali.**

naphtha ('næfθə, 'næp-) *n* **1** a distillation product from coal tar boiling in the approximate range 80–170°C and containing aromatic hydrocarbons. **2** a distillation product from petroleum boiling in the approximate range 100–200°C and containing aliphatic hydrocarbons: used as a solvent and in petrol. **3** an obsolete name for **petroleum. [**C16: via Latin from Greek, of Iranian origin; related to Persian *neft* naphtha**]**

naphthalene, naphthaline ('næfθəˌliːn, 'næp-), *or* **naphthalin** ('næfθəlɪn, 'næp-) *n* a white crystalline volatile solid with a characteristic penetrating odour: an aromatic hydrocarbon used in mothballs and in the manufacture of dyes, explosives, etc. Formula: $C_{10}H_8$. [C19: from NAPHTHA + ALCOHOL + -ENE] ▸ **naphthalic** (næf'θælɪk, næp-) *adj*

naphthene ('næfθiːn, 'næp-) *n* any of a class of cycloalkanes, mainly derivatives of cyclopentane, found in petroleum. [C20: from NAPHTHA + -ENE]

naphthol ('næfθɒl, 'næp-) *n* a white crystalline solid having two isomeric forms, **alpha-naphthol,** used in dyes, and **beta-naphthol,** used in dyes and as an antioxidant. Formula: $C_{10}H_7OH$. [C19: from NAPHTHA + -OL[1]]

naphthyl ('næfθaɪl, -θɪl, 'næp-) *n* (*modifier*) of, consisting of, or containing either of two forms of the monovalent group $C_{10}H_7$–. [C19: from NAPHTHA + -YL]

Napier[1] ('neɪpɪə) *n* a port in New Zealand, on E North Island on Hawke Bay: wool trade centre. Pop.: 53 500 (1995 est.).

Napier[2] ('neɪpɪə) *n* **1** Sir **Charles James.** 1782–1853, British general and colonial administrator: conquered Sind (1843): governor of Sind (1843–47). **2** **John.** 1550–1617, Scottish mathematician: invented logarithms and pioneered the decimal notation used today. **3** **Robert** (**Cornelis**), 1st Baron Napier of Magdala. 1810–90, British field marshal, who commanded in India during the Sikh Wars (1845, 1848–49) and the Indian Mutiny (1857–59). He captured Magdala (1868) while rescuing British diplomats from Ethiopia.

Napierian logarithm (nə'pɪərɪən, neɪ-) *n* another name for **natural logarithm.**

Napier's bones *pl n* a set of graduated rods formerly used for multiplication and division. [C17: based on a method invented by John NAPIER]

napiform ('neɪpɪˌfɔːm) *adj Botany.* shaped like a turnip. [C19: from Latin *nāpus* turnip]

napkin ('næpkɪn) *n* **1** Also called: **table napkin.** a usually square piece of cloth or paper used while eating to protect the clothes, wipe the mouth, etc.; serviette. **2** *Rare.* a similar piece of cloth used for example as a handkerchief or headscarf. **3** a more formal name for **nappy**[1]. **4** a less common term for **sanitary towel.** [C15: from Old French, from *nape* tablecloth, from Latin *mappa* small cloth, towel; see MAP]

Naples ('neɪpəlz) *n* **1** a port in SW Italy, capital of Campania region, on the Bay of Naples: the third largest city in the country; founded by Greeks in the 6th century B.C.; incorporated into the Kingdom of the Two Sicilies in 1140 and its capital (1282–1503); university (1224). Pop.: 1 050 234 (1996 est.). Ancient name: **Ne'apolis.** Italian name: **Napoli.** Related adj: **Neapolitan.** **2** **Bay of.** an inlet of the Tyrrhenian Sea in the SW coast of Italy.

Naples yellow *n* **1** a yellow pigment, used by artists; lead antimonate. **2** a similar pigment consisting of a mixture of zinc oxide with yellow colouring matter. **3** the colour of either of these pigments.

napoleon (nə'pəʊlɪən) *n* **1** a former French gold coin worth 20 francs bearing a portrait of either Napoleon I or Napoleon III. **2** *Cards.* the full name for **nap**[3] (sense 1). **3** the U.S. name for ***millefeuille.*** [C19: from French *napoléon,* after NAPOLEON I]

Napoleon I (nə'pəʊlɪən) *n* full name *Napoleon Bonaparte.* 1769–1821, Emperor of the French (1804–15). He came to power as the result of a coup in 1799 and established an extensive European empire. A brilliant general, he defeated every European coalition against him until, irreparably weakened by the Peninsular War and the Russian campaign (1812), his armies were defeated at Leipzig (1813). He went into exile but escaped and ruled as emperor during the Hundred Days. He was finally defeated at Waterloo (1815). As an administrator, his achievements were of lasting significance and include the *Code Napoléon,* which remains the basis of French law.

Napoleon II *n* Duke of Reichstadt. 1811–32, son of Napoleon Bonaparte and Marie Louise. He was known as the *King of Rome* during the first French empire and was entitled Napoleon II by Bonapartists after Napoleon I's death (1821).

Napoleon III *n* full name *Charles Louis Napoleon Bonaparte,* known as *Louis-Napoleon.* 1808–73, Emperor of the French (1852–70); nephew of Napoleon I. He led two abortive Bonapartist risings (1836; 1840) and was elected president of the Second Republic (1848), establishing the Second Empire in 1852. Originally successful in foreign affairs, he was deposed after the disastrous Franco-Prussian War.

Napoleonic (nəˌpəʊlɪ'ɒnɪk) *adj* relating to or characteristic of Napoleon I or his era.

Napoleonic Code *n* the English name for the ***Code Napoléon.***

Napoleonic Wars *pl n* the series of wars fought between France, under Napoleon Bonaparte, and (principally) Great Britain, Prussia, Russia, and Austria either alone or in alliances (1799–1815).

Napoli ('naːpoli) *n* the Italian name for **Naples.**

nappa ('næpə) *n* a soft leather, used in gloves and clothes, made from sheepskin, lambskin, or kid. [C19: named after *Napa,* California, where it was originally made]

nappe (næp) *n* **1** a large sheet or mass of rock, originally a recumbent fold, that has been thrust from its original position by earth movements. **2** the sheet of water that flows over a dam or weir. **3** *Geometry.* either of the two parts into which a cone (sense 2) is divided by the vertex. [C20: from French: tablecloth]

napper[1] ('næpə) *n* a person or thing that raises the nap on cloth.

napper[2] ('næpə) *n Brit.* a slang or dialect word for **head** (sense 1). [C18: from NAP[1]]

nappy[1] ('næpɪ) *n, pl* **-pies.** *Brit.* a piece of soft material, esp. towelling or a disposable material, wrapped around a baby in order to absorb its excrement. Also called: **napkin.** U.S. and Canadian name: **diaper.** [C20: changed from NAPKIN]

nappy[2] ('næpɪ) *adj* **-pier, -piest.** **1** having a nap; downy; fuzzy. **2** (of alcoholic drink, esp. beer) **2a** having a head; frothy. **2b** strong or heady. **3** *Dialect, chiefly Brit.* slightly intoxicated; tipsy. **4** (of a horse) jumpy or irritable; nervy. ♦ *n* **5** any strong alcoholic drink, esp. heady beer. ▸ **'nappiness** *n*

nappy rash *n Brit.* (in babies) any irritation to the skin around the genitals, anus, or buttocks, usually caused by contact with urine or excrement. Formal name: **napkin rash.** U.S. and Canadian name: **diaper rash.**

Nara ('nɑːrə) *n* a city in central Japan, on S Honshu: the first permanent capital of Japan (710–784). Pop.: 359 234 (1995).

Narayan (nə'raɪjən) *n* **R(asipuram) K(rishnaswamy).** born 1906, Indian novelist writing in English. His books include *Swami and Friends* (1938), *The Man-Eater of Malgudi* (1961), *Under the Banyan Tree* (1985), and *The World of Nagaraj* (1990).

Narayanganj (nə'rɑːjənˌgʌndʒ) *n* a city in central Bangladesh, on the Ganges delta just southeast of Dhaka. Pop.: 296 000 (1991).

Narbada (nə'bʌdə) *n* another name for the **Narmada.**

Narbonne (*French* narbɔn) *n* a city in S France: capital of the Roman province of **Gallia Narbonensis;** harbour silted up in the 14th century. Pop.: 47 090 (1990).

narc (nɑːk) *n U.S. slang.* a narcotics agent.

narceine *or* **narceen** ('nɑːsiːn) *n* a narcotic alkaloid that occurs in opium. Formula: $C_{23}H_{27}O_8N$. [C19: via French from Greek *narkē* numbness]

narcissism ('nɑːsɪˌsɪzəm) *or* **narcism** ('nɑːˌsɪzəm) *n* **1** an exceptional interest in or admiration for oneself, esp. one's physical appearance. **2** sexual satisfaction derived from contemplation of one's own physical or mental endowments. [C19: from NARCISSUS] ▸ **'narcissist** *n* ▸ **ˌnarcis'sistic** *adj*

narcissus (nɑː'sɪsəs) *n, pl* **-cissuses** *or* **-cissi** (-'sɪsaɪ, -'sɪsiː). any amaryllidaceous plant of the Eurasian genus *Narcissus,* esp. *N. poeticus,* whose yellow, orange, or white flowers have a crown surrounded by spreading segments. [C16: via Latin from Greek *nárkissos,* perhaps from *narkē* numbness, because of narcotic properties attributed to species of the plant]

Narcissus (nɑː'sɪsəs) *n Greek myth.* a beautiful youth who fell in love with his reflection in a pool and pined away, becoming the flower that bears his name.

narco- *or sometimes before a vowel* **narc-** *combining form.* **1** indicating numbness or torpor: *narcolepsy.* **2** connected with or derived from illicit drug production: *narcoeconomies.* [from Greek *narkē* numbness]

narcoanalysis (ˌnɑːkəʊə'nælɪsɪs) *n* psychoanalysis of a patient in a trance induced by a narcotic drug.

narcolepsy ('nɑːkəˌlɛpsɪ) *n Pathol.* a rare condition characterized by sudden and uncontrollable episodes of deep sleep. ▸ **ˌnarco'leptic** *adj*

narcosis (nɑː'kəʊsɪs) *n* unconsciousness induced by narcotics or general anaesthetics.

narcotic (nɑː'kɒtɪk) *n* **1** any of a group of drugs, such as opium and morphine, that produce numbness and stupor. They are used medicinally to relieve pain but are sometimes also taken for their pleasant effects; prolonged use may cause addiction. **2** anything that relieves pain or induces sleep, mental numbness, etc. **3** any illegal drug. ♦ *adj* **4** of, relating to, or designating narcotics. **5** of or relating to narcotics addicts or users. **6** of or relating to narcosis. [C14: via Medieval Latin from Greek *narkōtikós,* from *narkoūn* to render numb, from *narkē* numbness] ▸ **nar'cotically** *adv*

narcotism ('nɑːkəˌtɪzəm) *n* stupor or addiction induced by narcotic drugs.

narcotize *or* **narcotise** ('nɑːkəˌtaɪz) *vb* (*tr*) to place under the influence of a narcotic drug. ▸ **ˌnarcoti'zation** *or* **ˌnarcoti'sation** *n*

nard (nɑːd) *n* **1** another name for **spikenard** (senses 1, 2). **2** any of several plants, such as certain valerians, whose aromatic roots were formerly used in medicine. [C14: via Latin from Greek *nárdos,* perhaps ultimately from Sanskrit *nalada* Indian spikenard, perhaps via Semitic (Hebrew *nērd,* Arabic *nārdīn*)]

nardoo ('nɑːduː) *n* **1** any of certain cloverlike ferns of the genus *Marsilea,* which grow in swampy areas. **2** the spores of such a plant, used as food in Australia. [C19: from a native Australian language]

nares ('nɛəriːz) *pl n, sing* **naris** ('nɛərɪs). *Anatomy.* the nostrils. [C17: from Latin; related to Old English *nasu,* Latin *nāsus* nose]

narghile, nargile, *or* **nargileh** ('nɑːgɪlɪ, -ˌleɪ) *n* another name for **hookah.** [C19: from French *narguilé,* from Persian *nārgīleh* a pipe having a bowl made of coconut shell, from *nārgīl* coconut]

narial ('nɛərɪəl) *or* **narine** ('nɛərɪn, -raɪn) *adj Anatomy.* of or relating to the nares. [C19: from Latin *nāris* nostril]

nark (nɑːk) *Slang.* ♦ *n* **1** *Brit., Austral., and N.Z.* an informer or spy, esp. one working for the police (**copper's nark**). **2** *Brit.* a person who complains irritatingly: *an old nark.* **3** *Austral. and N.Z.* a spoilsport. ♦ *vb* **4** *Brit., Austral., and N.Z.* to annoy, upset, or irritate: *he was narked by her indifference.* **5** (*intr*) *Brit., Austral., and N.Z.* to inform or spy, esp. for the police. **6** (*intr*) *Brit.* to complain irritatingly. **7** **nark at** (**someone**). *N.Z.* to nag (someone). **8** **nark it.** *Brit.* stop it! [C19: probably from Romany *nāk* nose]

narky ('nɑːkɪ) *adj* **narkier, narkiest.** *Slang.* irritable, complaining, or sarcastic.

Narmada (nə'mʌdə) *or* **Narbada** *n* a river in central India, rising in Madhya Pradesh and flowing generally west to the Gulf of Cambay in a wide estuary: the second most sacred river in India. Length: 1290 km (801 miles).

Narraganset *or* **Narragansett** (ˌnærə'gænsɪt) *n* **1** (*pl* **-set, -sets** *or* **-sett, -setts**) a member of a North American Indian people formerly living in Rhode Island. **2** the language of this people, belonging to the Algonquian family.

Narragansett Bay *n* an inlet of the Atlantic in SE Rhode Island: contains several islands, including Rhode Island, Prudence Island, and Conanicut Island.

narrate (nə'reɪt) *vb* **1** to tell (a story); relate. **2** to speak in accompaniment of (a film, television programme, etc.). [C17: from Latin *narrāre* to recount, from *gnārus* knowing] ▸ **nar'ratable** *adj* ▸ **nar'rator** *n*

narration (nə'reɪʃən) *n* **1** the act or process of narrating. **2** a narrated account or story; narrative. **3** (in traditional rhetoric) the third step in making a speech, the putting forward of the question.

narrative ('nærətɪv) *n* **1** an account, report, or story, as of events, experiences, etc. **2** (sometimes preceded by *the*) the part of a literary work that relates events. **3** the process or technique of narrating. ◆ *adj* **4** telling a story: *a narrative poem.* **5** of or relating to narration: *narrative art.* ▸ **'narratively** *adv*

narrow ('nærəʊ) *adj* **1** small in breadth, esp. in comparison to length. **2** limited in range or extent. **3** limited in outlook; lacking breadth of vision. **4** limited in means or resources; meagre: *narrow resources.* **5** barely adequate or successful (esp. in the phrase **a narrow escape**). **6** painstakingly thorough; minute: *a narrow scrutiny.* **7** *Finance.* denoting an assessment of liquidity as including notes and coin in circulation with the public, banks' till money, and banks' balances: *narrow money.* Compare **broad** (sense 14). **8** *Dialect.* overcareful with money; parsimonious. **9** *Phonetics.* **9a** another word for **tense**[1] (sense 4). **9b** relating to or denoting a transcription used to represent phonetic rather than phonemic distinctions. **9c** another word for **close**[1] (sense 21). **10** (of agricultural feeds) especially rich in protein. **11** **narrow squeak.** *Informal.* an escape only just managed. ◆ *vb* **12** to make or become narrow; limit; restrict. ◆ *n* **13** a narrow place, esp. a pass or strait. ◆ See also **narrows.** [Old English *nearu;* related to Old Saxon *naru*] ▸ **'narrowly** *adv* ▸ **'narrowness** *n*

narrow boat *n* a long narrow bargelike boat with a beam of 2.1 metres (7 feet) or less, used on canals.

narrowcast ('nærəʊ,kɑːst) *vb* **-casts, -casting, -cast** *or* **-casted.** **1** (*tr*) to supply (television programmes) to a small area by cable television. **2** (*intr*) (of programmers or advertisers) to target a specialized audience on radio or television. ◆ Compare **broadcast.** ▸ **'narrow,casting** *n*

narrow gauge *n* **1** a railway track with a smaller distance between the lines than the standard gauge of 56½ inches. ◆ *adj* **narrow-gauge** *or* **narrow-gauged. 2** of, relating to, or denoting a railway with a narrow gauge.

narrow-minded *adj* having a biased or illiberal viewpoint; bigoted, intolerant, or prejudiced. ▸ **,narrow-'mindedly** *adv* ▸ **,narrow-'mindedness** *n*

narrows ('nærəʊz) *pl n* a narrow part of a strait, river, current, etc.

narrow seas *pl n* the channels between Great Britain and the Continent and Great Britain and Ireland.

narthex ('nɑːθɛks) *n* **1** a portico at the west end of a basilica or church, esp. one that is at right angles to the nave. **2** a rectangular entrance hall between the porch and nave of a church. [C17: via Latin from Medieval Greek: enclosed porch, enclosure (earlier: box), from Greek *narthēx* giant fennel, the stems of which were used to make boxes]

Narva (*Russian* 'narvə) *n* a port in Estonia on the Narva River near the Gulf of Finland: developed around a Danish fortress in the 13th century; textile centre. Pop.: 77 770 (1995).

Narvik ('nɑːvɪk; *Norwegian* 'narvik) *n* a port in N Norway: scene of two naval battles in 1940; exports iron ore from Kiruna and Gällivare (Sweden). Pop.: 18 500 (1990).

narwhal, narwal ('nɑːwəl), *or* **narwhale** ('nɑː,weɪl) *n* an arctic toothed whale, *Monodon monoceros,* having a black-spotted whitish skin and, in the male, a long spiral tusk: family *Monodontidae.* [C17: of Scandinavian origin; compare Danish, Norwegian *narhval,* from Old Norse *nāhvalr,* from *nār* corpse + *hvalr* whale, from its white colour, supposed to resemble a human corpse]

nary ('nɛərɪ) *adv Dialect.* not; never: *nary a man was left.* [C19: variant of *ne'er a* never a]

NASA ('næsə) *n* (in the U.S.) *acronym for* National Aeronautics and Space Administration.

nasal ('neɪz(ə)l) *adj* **1** of or relating to the nose. **2** *Phonetics.* pronounced with the soft palate lowered allowing air to escape via the nasal cavity instead of or as well as through the mouth. ◆ *n* **3** a nasal speech sound, such as English *m, n,* or *ng.* **4** another word for **nosepiece** (sense 1). [C17: from French from Late Latin *nāsālis,* from Latin *nāsus* nose] ▸ **nasality** (neɪ'zælɪtɪ) *n* ▸ **'nasally** *adv*

nasal index *n* the ratio of the widest part of the nose to its length multiplied by 100.

nasalize *or* **nasalise** ('neɪz(ə),laɪz) *vb* (*tr*) to pronounce nasally. ▸ **,nasali'zation** *or* **,nasali'sation** *n*

nascent ('næs(ə)nt, 'neɪ-) *adj* **1** starting to grow or develop; being born. **2** *Chem.* (of an element or simple compound, esp. hydrogen) created within the reaction medium in the atomic form and having a high activity. [C17: from Latin *nascēns* present participle of *nāscī* to be born] ▸ **'nascence** *or* **'nascency** *n*

naseberry ('neɪz,bɛrɪ) *n, pl* **-berries.** another name for **sapodilla.** [C17: from Spanish *néspera* medlar + BERRY]

Naseby ('neɪzbɪ) *n* a village in Northamptonshire: site of a major Parliamentarian victory (1645) in the Civil War, when Cromwell routed Prince Rupert's force.

Nash (næʃ) *n* **1 John.** 1752–1835, English town planner and architect. He designed Regent's Park, Regent Street, and the Marble Arch in London. **2 Ogden.** 1902–71, U.S. humorous poet. **3 Paul.** 1889–1946, English painter, noted esp. as a war artist in both World Wars and for his landscapes. **4 Richard,** known as *Beau Nash.* 1674–1762, English dandy. **5** See (Thomas) **Nashe. 6** Sir **Walter.** 1882–1968, New Zealand Labour statesman, born in England: prime minister of New Zealand (1957–60).

Nashe *or* **Nash** (næʃ) *n* **Thomas.** 1567–1601, English pamphleteer, satirist, and novelist, author of the first picaresque novel in English, *The Unfortunate Traveller, or the Life of Jack Wilton* (1594).

nashi ('næʃɪ) *n, pl* **nashi** *or* **nashis.** another name for **Asian pear.** [Japanese: pear]

Nasho ('næʃəʊ) *n Obsolete Austral. slang.* **1** compulsory military training; conscription. **2** (*pl* **Nashos**) a conscript. [C20: shortening and alteration of *national service*]

Nashville ('næʃvɪl) *n* a city in central Tennessee, the state capital, on the Cumberland River: an industrial and commercial centre, noted for its recording industry. Pop.: 511 263 (1996 est.).

nasi goreng ('nɑːsɪ gə'rɛŋ) *n* a dish, originating in Malaysia, consisting of rice fried with a selection of other ingredients. [C20: from Malay *nasi* (cooked) rice + *goreng* fry]

Nasik ('nɑːsɪk) *n* a city in W India, in Maharashtra: a centre for Hindu pilgrims. Pop.: 656 925 (1991).

nasion ('neɪzɪən) *n* a craniometric point where the top of the nose meets the ridge of the forehead. [C20: New Latin, from Latin *nāsus* nose] ▸ **'nasial** *adj*

Nasmyth ('neɪsmɪθ) *n* **James.** 1808–90, British engineer; inventor of the steam hammer (1839).

naso- *combining form.* nose: *nasopharynx.* [from Latin *nāsus* nose]

nasofrontal (,neɪzəʊ'frʌnt(ə)l) *adj Anatomy.* of or relating to the nasal and frontal bones.

nasogastric (,neɪzəʊ'gæstrɪk) *adj Anatomy.* of or relating to the nose and stomach: *a nasogastric tube.*

nasopharynx (,neɪzəʊ'færɪŋks) *n, pl* **-pharynges** (-fə'rɪndʒiːz) *or* **-pharynxes.** the part of the pharynx situated above and behind the soft palate. ▸ **nasopharyngeal** (,neɪzəʊfə'rɪndʒɪəl, -,færɪn'dʒɪəl) *adj*

Nassau *n* **1** (*German* 'nasau). a region of W central Germany: formerly a duchy (1816–66), from which a branch of the House of Orange arose (represented by the present rulers of the Netherlands and Luxembourg); annexed to the Prussian province of Hesse-Nassau in 1866; corresponds to present-day W Hesse and NE Rhineland-Palatinate states; formerly (1949–90) part of West Germany. **2** ('næsɔː). the capital and chief port of the Bahamas, on the NE coast of New Providence Island: resort. Pop.: 172 196 (1990).

Nasser ('nɑːsə, 'næsə) *n* **Gamal Abdel** (gə'mɑːl 'æbdɛl). 1918–70, Egyptian soldier and statesman; president of Egypt (1956–70). He was one of the leaders of the coup that deposed King Farouk (1952) and became premier (1954). His nationalization of the Suez Canal (1956) led to an international crisis, and during his presidency Egypt was twice defeated by Israel (1956; 1967).

Nastase (nə'stɑːsɪ) *n* **Ilie** (iːliː). born 1946, Romanian tennis player.

nastic movement ('næstɪk) *n* a response of plant parts that is independent of the direction of the external stimulus, such as the opening of buds caused by an alteration in light intensity. [C19 *nastic,* from Greek *nastos* close-packed, from *nassein* to press down]

nasturtium (nə'stɜːʃəm) *n* any of various plants of the genus *Tropaeolum,* esp. *T. major,* having round leaves and yellow, red, or orange trumpet-shaped spurred flowers: family *Tropaeolaceae.* [C17: from Latin: kind of cress, from *nāsus* nose + *tortus* twisted, from *torquēre* to twist, distort; so called because the pungent smell causes one to wrinkle one's nose]

nasty ('nɑːstɪ) *adj* **-tier, -tiest. 1** unpleasant, offensive, or repugnant. **2** (of an experience, condition, etc.) unpleasant, dangerous, or painful: *a nasty wound.* **3** spiteful, abusive, or ill-natured. **4** obscene or indecent. **5** **nasty piece of work.** *Brit. informal.* a cruel or mean person. ◆ *n, pl* **-ties. 6** an offensive or unpleasant person or thing: *a video nasty.* [C14: origin obscure; probably related to Swedish dialect *nasket* and Dutch *nestig* dirty] ▸ **'nastily** *adv* ▸ **'nastiness** *n*

-nasty *n combining form.* indicating a nastic movement to a certain stimulus: *nyctinasty.* [from Greek *nastos* pressed down, close-pressed] ▸ **-nastic** *adj combining form.*

NAS/UWT (in Britain) *abbrev. for* National Association of Schoolmasters/Union of Women Teachers.

Nat (næt) *n Informal.* **1** a member or supporter of the Scottish National Party. **2** *N.Z.* a member of the National Party. **3** *N.Z.* a Member of Parliament for the National Party.

nat. *abbrev. for:* **1** national. **2** native. **3** natural.

natal[1] ('neɪt(ə)l) *adj* **1** of or relating to birth. **2** a rare word for **native:** *natal instincts.* [C14: from Latin *nātālis* of one's birth, from *nātus,* from *nascī* to be born]

natal[2] ('neɪt(ə)l) *adj Anatomy.* of or relating to the buttocks. [from New Latin *nates* buttocks]

Natal *n* **1** (nə'tæl). a former province of E South Africa, between the Drakensberg and the Indian Ocean: set up as a republic by the Boers in 1838; became a British colony in 1843; joined South Africa in 1910; replaced by KwaZulu/Natal in 1994. Capital: Pietermaritzburg. **2** (*Portuguese* na'tal). a port in NE Brazil, capital of Rio Grande do Norte state, near the mouth of the Potengi River. Pop.: 459 827 (1991).

natality (neɪ'tælɪtɪ) *n, pl* **-ties.** another name (esp. U.S.) for **birth rate.**

natant ('neɪt(ə)nt) *adj* **1** (of aquatic plants) floating on the water. **2** *Rare.* floating or swimming. [C18: from Latin *natāns,* present participle of *natāre* to swim]

natation (nə'teɪʃən) *n* a formal or literary word for **swimming.** [C16: from Latin *natātiō* a swimming, from *natāre* to swim] ▸ **na'tational** *adj*

natatorium (,neɪtə'tɔːrɪəm) *n, pl* **-riums** *or* **-ria** (-rɪə). *Rare.* a swimming pool, esp. an indoor pool. [C20: from Late Latin: swimming place, pool]

natatory (nə'teɪtərɪ) *or* **natatorial** (,nætə'tɔːrɪəl) *adj* of or relating to swimming. [C18: from Late Latin *natātōrius,* from *natāre* to swim]

natch (nætʃ) *sentence substitute. Informal.* short for **naturally** (sense 3).

nates ('neɪtiːz) *n, pl, sing* **-tis** (-tɪs). a technical word for the **buttocks.** [C17: from Latin; compare Greek *nōton* back, *nosthi* buttocks]

NATFHE *abbrev. for* National Association of Teachers in Further and Higher Education.

Nathan ('neɪθən) *n Old Testament.* a prophet at David's court (II Samuel 7:1–17; 12:1–15).

Nathanael (nə'θænjəl) *n New Testament.* a Galilean who is perhaps to be identified with Bartholomew among the apostles (John 1:45–51; 21:1).

natheless ('neɪθlɪs) *or* **nathless** ('næθlɪs) *Archaic.* ◆ *sentence connector.* **1** another word for **nonetheless.** ◆ *prep* **2** notwithstanding; despite. [Old English *nāthylǣs,* from *nā* never + *thȳ* for that + *lǣs* less]

nation ('neɪʃən) *n* **1** an aggregation of people or peoples of one or more cultures, races, etc., organized into a single state: *the Australian nation.* **2** a community of persons not constituting a state but bound by common descent, language, history, etc.: *the French-Canadian nation.* **3a** a federation of tribes, esp. American Indians. **3b** the territory occupied by such a federation. [C13: via Old French from Latin *nātiō* birth, tribe, from *nascī* to be born] ▸ **'nation,hood** *n* ▸ **'nationless** *adj*

national ('næʃənᵊl) *adj* **1** of, involving, or relating to a nation as a whole. **2** of, relating to, or characteristic of a particular nation: *the national dress of Poland.* **3** *Rare.* nationalistic or patriotic. ◆ *n* **4** a citizen or subject. **5** a national newspaper. ▸ **'nationally** *adv*

National ('næʃənᵊl) *n* **the.** short for the **Grand National.**

national accounting *n* another name for **social accounting.**

national agreement *n* written formal agreements covering rates of pay and other terms and conditions of employment that are the result of collective bargaining at national level between one or more trade unions and employers in a sector of the economy.

national anthem *n* a patriotic hymn or other song adopted by a nation for use on public or state occasions.

National Assembly *n French history.* the body constituted by the French third estate in June 1789 after the calling of the Estates General. It was dissolved in Sept. 1791 to be replaced by the new Legislative Assembly.

national assistance *n* (in Britain) formerly a weekly allowance paid to certain people by the state to bring their incomes up to minimum levels established by law. Now replaced by **income support.**

national bank *n* **1** (in the U.S.) a commercial bank incorporated under a Federal charter and legally required to be a member of the Federal Reserve System. Compare **state bank. 2** a bank owned and operated by a government.

National Bureau of Standards *n U.S.* an organization, founded in 1901, whose function is to establish and maintain standards for units of measurements. Compare **British Standards Institution, International Standards Organization.**

national code *n* another term for **Australian Rules.**

National Convention *n* **1** a convention held every four years by each major U.S. political party to choose its presidential candidate. **2** *French history.* the longest lasting of the revolutionary assemblies, lasting from Sept. 1792 to Oct. 1795, when it was replaced by the Directory.

National Country Party *n* (in Australia) a former name for **National Party.** Abbrev.: **NCP.**

National Covenant *n* See **Covenant.**

National Curriculum *n* (in England and Wales) the curriculum of subjects taught in state schools progressively from 1989. There are ten foundation subjects: English, maths, and science (the core subjects); art, design and technology, geography, history, music, physical education, and a foreign language. Pupils are assessed according to specified attainment targets throughout each of four key stages. Schools must also provide religious education and from 1999 lessons in citizenship.

national debt *n* the total outstanding borrowings of a nation's central government. Also called (esp. U.S.): **public debt.**

National Economic Development Council *n* an advisory body on general economic policy in Britain, composed of representatives of government, management, and trade unions: established in 1962; abolished in 1992. Abbrevs.: **NEDC,** (informal) **Neddy.**

National Enterprise Board *n* a public corporation established in 1975 to help the economy of the UK. In 1981 it merged with the National Research and Development Council to form the British Technology Group. Abbrev.: **NEB.**

National Front *n* (in Britain) a small political party of the right with racist and other extremist policies. Abbrev.: **NF.**

National Gallery *n* a major art gallery in London, in Trafalgar Square. Founded in 1824, it contains the largest collection of paintings in Britain.

national grid *n* **1** *Brit.* a network of high-voltage power lines connecting major power stations. **2** a grid of metric coordinates used by the Ordnance Survey in Britain and Ireland and in New Zealand by the New Zealand Lands and Survey Department and printed on their maps.

National Guard *n* **1** (*sometimes not caps.*) the armed force, first commanded by Lafayette, that was established in France in 1789 and existed intermittently until 1871. **2** (in the U.S.) a state military force that can be called into federal service by the president.

National Health Service *n* (in Britain) the system of national medical services since 1948, financed mainly by taxation.

national hunt *n Brit.* (*often cap.*) **a** the racing of horses on racecourses with jumps. **b** (*as modifier*): *a National Hunt jockey.*

national income *n Economics.* the total of all incomes accruing over a specified period to residents of a country and consisting of wages, salaries, profits, rent, and interest.

national insurance *n* (in Britain) state insurance based on weekly contributions from employees and employers and providing payments to the unemployed, the sick, the retired, etc., as well as medical services. See also **social security.**

nationalism ('næʃənə,lɪzəm, 'næʃnə-) *n* **1** a sentiment based on common cultural characteristics that binds a population and often produces a policy of national independence or separatism. **2** loyalty or devotion to one's country; patriotism. **3** exaggerated, passionate, or fanatical devotion to a national community. See also **chauvinism.** ▸ **'nationalist** *n, adj* ▸ **,national'istic** *adj*

Nationalist China *n* an unofficial name for (the Republic of) **China.**

nationality (,næʃə'nælɪtɪ) *n, pl* **-ties. 1** the state or fact of being a citizen of a particular nation. **2** a body of people sharing common descent, history, language, etc.; a nation. **3** a national group: *30 different nationalities are found in this city.* **4** national character or quality. **5** the state or fact of being a nation; national status.

nationalize *or* **nationalise** ('næʃənə,laɪz,'næʃnə-) *vb* (*tr*) **1** to put (an industry, resources, etc.) under state control or ownership. **2** to make national in scope, character, or status. **3** a less common word for **naturalize.** ▸ **,nationali'zation** *or* **,nationali'sation** *n*

National Liberation Front *n* **1** (*sometimes not caps.*) a revolutionary movement that seeks the national independence of a country, usually by guerrilla warfare. **2** Also called: **National Liberation Front of South Vietnam.** a political organization formed in South Vietnam in 1960 by the Vietcong.

national park *n* an area of countryside for public use designated by a national government as being of notable scenic, environmental, or historical importance.

National Park *n* a mountainous volcanic region in New Zealand, in the central North Island: ski resort.

National Party *n* **1** (in New Zealand) the more conservative of the two main political parties. **2** (in Australia) a political party drawing its main support from rural areas. Former name: **National Country Party. 3** (in South Africa) a political party composed mainly of centre-to-right-wing Afrikaners. It ruled from 1948 until the country's first multiracial elections in 1994 when it was defeated by the African National Congress. See also **Progressive Federal Party, United Party.**

National Physical Laboratory *n* a UK establishment founded in 1900 at Teddington to carry out research in physics and monitor standards of measurement. Abbrev.: **NPL.**

National Portrait Gallery *n* an art gallery in London, established in 1856, displaying portraits and photographs of eminent figures in British history.

National Savings Bank *n* (in Britain) a government savings bank, run through the post office, esp. for small savers.

National School *n* **1** (in Ireland) a state primary school. **2** (in England in the 19th century) a school run by the Church of England for the children of the poor.

national service *n Chiefly Brit.* compulsory military service.

National Socialism *n German history.* the doctrines and practices of the Nazis, involving the supremacy of Hitler as Führer, anti-Semitism, state control of the economy, and national expansion. Also called: **Nazism, Naziism.** ▸ **National Socialist** *n, adj*

national superannuation *n N.Z.* a means-related pension paid to elderly people.

National Theatre *n* the former name of the **Royal National Theatre.**

National Trust *n* **1** (in Britain) an organization concerned with the preservation of historic buildings and monuments and areas of the countryside of great beauty in England, Wales, and Northern Ireland. It was founded in 1895 and incorporated by act of parliament in 1907. The **National Trust for Scotland** was founded in 1931. **2** (in Australia) a similar organization in each of the states.

nation-state *n* an independent state inhabited by all the people of one nation and one nation only.

nationwide ('neɪʃən,waɪd) *adj* covering or available to the whole of a nation; national: *a nationwide survey.*

native ('neɪtɪv) *adj* **1** relating or belonging to a person or thing by virtue of conditions existing at the time of birth: *a native language.* **2** inherent, natural, or innate: *a native strength.* **3** born in a specified place: *a native Indian.* **4** (when *postpositive,* foll. by *to*) originating in a specific place or area: *kangaroos are native to Australia.* **5** characteristic of or relating to the indigenous inhabitants of a country or area: *the native art of the New Guinea Highlands.* **6** (of chemical elements, esp. metals) found naturally in the elemental form. **7** unadulterated by civilization, artifice, or adornment; natural. **8** *Archaic.* related by birth or race. **9 go native.** (of a settler) to adopt the lifestyle of the local population, esp. when it appears less civilized. ◆ *n* **10** (usually foll. by *of*) a person born in a particular place: *a native of Geneva.* **11** (usually foll. by *of*) a species originating in a particular place or area: *the kangaroo is a native of Australia.* **12** a member of an indigenous people of a country or area, esp. a non-White people, as opposed to colonial settlers and immigrants. **13** *Derogatory, rare.* any non-White. [C14: from Latin *nātīvus* innate, natural, from *nascī* to be born] ▸ **'natively** *adv* ▸ **'nativeness** *n*

Native American *n* another name for an **American Indian.**

native bear *n* an Australian name for **koala.**

native-born *adj* born in the country or area indicated.

native bush *n N.Z.* indigenous forest.

native companion *n Austral.* another name for the **brolga.** [C19: so called because the birds were observed in pairs]

native dog *n Austral.* a dingo.

native oak *n Austral.* another name for **casuarina.**

native speaker *n* a person having a specified native language: *a native speaker of Cree.*

Native States *pl n* the former 562 semi-independent states of India, ruled by Indians but subject to varying degrees of British authority: merged with provinces by 1948; largest states were Hyderabad, Gwalior, Baroda, Mysore, Cochin, Jammu and Kashmir, Travancore, Sikkim, and Indore. Also called: **Indian States and Agencies.**

nativism ('neɪtɪ,vɪzəm) *n* **1** *Chiefly U.S.* the policy of favouring the natives of a country over the immigrants. **2** *Anthropol.* the policy of protecting and reaffirming native tribal cultures in reaction to acculturation. **3** the doctrine that the mind and its capacities are innately structured and that much knowledge is innate. ▸ **'nativist** *n, adj* ▸ **,nativ'istic** *adj*

nativity (nəˈtɪvɪtɪ) *n, pl* **-ties.** birth or origin, esp. in relation to the circumstances surrounding it. [C14: via Old French from Late Latin *nātīvitas* birth: see NATIVE]

Nativity (nəˈtɪvɪtɪ) *n* **1** the birth of Jesus Christ. **2** the feast of Christmas as a commemoration of this. **3a** an artistic representation of the circumstances of the birth of Christ. **3b** (*as modifier*): *a Nativity play.*

natl *abbrev. for* national.

NATO *or* **Nato** (ˈneɪtəʊ) *n acronym for* North Atlantic Treaty Organization, an international organization composed of the U.S., Canada, Britain, and a number of European countries: established by the **North Atlantic Treaty** (1949) for purposes of collective security. In 1994 it launched the partnerships for peace initiative, in order to forge alliances with former Warsaw Pact countries; in 1997 a treaty of cooperation with Russia was signed and in 1999 Hungary, Poland, and the Czech Republic became full NATO members.

natrium (ˈneɪtrɪəm) *n* an obsolete name for **sodium.** [C19: New Latin; see NATRON]

natrolite (ˈnætrəˌlaɪt, ˈneɪ-) *n* a colourless, white, or yellow zeolite mineral consisting of sodium aluminium silicate in the form of needle-like orthorhombic crystals. Formula: $Na_2Al_2Si_3O_{10}.2H_2O$. [C19: from NATRON + -LITE]

natron (ˈneɪtrən) *n* a whitish or yellow mineral that consists of hydrated sodium carbonate and occurs in saline deposits and salt lakes. Formula: $Na_2CO_3.10H_2O$. [C17: via French and Spanish from Arabic *natrūn,* from Greek *nitron*]

NATSOPA (nætˈsəʊpə) *n* (formerly, in Britain) *acronym for* National Society of Operative Printers, Graphical and Media Personnel.

natter (ˈnætə) *Chiefly Brit.* ◆ *vb* **1** (*intr*) to talk idly and at length; chatter or gossip. ◆ *n* **2** prolonged idle chatter or gossip. [C19: changed from *gnatter* to grumble, of imitative origin; compare Low German *gnatteren*] ▸ **ˈnatterer** *n*

natterjack (ˈnætəˌdʒæk) *n* a European toad, *Bufo calamita,* of sandy regions, having a greyish-brown body marked with reddish warty processes: family *Bufonidae.* [C18: of unknown origin]

natty (ˈnætɪ) *adj* **-tier, -tiest.** *Informal.* smart in appearance or dress; spruce; dapper: *a natty outfit.* [C18: perhaps from obsolete *netty,* from *net* NEAT[1]; compare Old French *net* trim] ▸ **ˈnattily** *adv* ▸ **ˈnattiness** *n*

natural (ˈnætʃrəl, -tʃərəl) *adj* **1** of, existing in, or produced by nature: *natural science; natural cliffs.* **2** in accordance with human nature: *it is only natural to want to be liked.* **3** as is normal or to be expected; ordinary or logical: *the natural course of events.* **4** not acquired; innate: *a natural gift for sport.* **5** being so through innate qualities: *a natural leader.* **6** not supernatural or strange: *natural phenomena.* **7** not constrained or affected; genuine or spontaneous. **8** not artificially dyed or coloured: *a natural blonde.* **9** following or resembling nature or life; lifelike: *she looked more natural without her make-up.* **10** not affected by man or civilization; uncultivated; wild: *in the natural state this animal is not ferocious.* **11** illegitimate; born out of wedlock. **12** not adopted but rather related by blood: *her natural parents.* **13** *Music.* **13a** not sharp or flat. **13b** (*postpositive*) denoting a note that is neither sharp nor flat: *B natural.* **13c** (of a key or scale) containing no sharps or flats. Compare **flat**[1] (sense 23), **sharp** (sense 12). **14** *Music.* of or relating to a trumpet, horn, etc., without valves or keys, on which only notes of the harmonic series of the keynote can be obtained. **15** determined by inborn conviction: *natural justice; natural rights.* **16** *Cards.* **16a** (of a card) not a joker or wild card. **16b** (of a canasta or sequence) containing no wild cards. **16c** (of a bid in bridge) describing genuine values; not conventional. **17** based on the principles and findings of human reason and what is to be learned of God from nature rather than on revelation: *natural religion.* ◆ *n* **18** *Informal.* a person or thing regarded as certain to qualify for success, selection, etc.: *the horse was a natural for first place.* **19** *Music.* **19a** Also called (U.S.): **cancel.** an accidental cancelling a previous sharp or flat. Usual symbol: ♮ **19b** a note affected by this accidental. Compare **flat**[1] (sense 35), **sharp** (sense 19). **20** *Pontoon.* the combination of an ace with a ten or court card when dealt to a player as his or her first two cards. **21** *Obsolete.* an imbecile; idiot. ▸ **ˈnaturally** *adv* ▸ **ˈnaturalness** *n*

natural-born *adj* being as specified through one's birth: *a natural-born Irishman.*

natural childbirth *n* a method of childbirth characterized by the absence of anaesthetics, in which the expectant mother is given special breathing and relaxing exercises.

natural classification *n Biology.* classification of organisms according to relationships based on descent from a common ancestor.

natural deduction *n* a system of formal logic that has no axioms but permits the assumption of premises of an argument. Such a system uses sequents to record which assumptions are operative at any stage. Compare **axiomatic** (sense 3).

natural frequency *n Physics.* the frequency at which a system vibrates when set in free vibration. Compare **forcing frequency.**

natural gas *n* a gaseous mixture consisting mainly of methane trapped below ground; used extensively as a fuel.

natural gender *n* grammatical gender that reflects, as in English, the sex or animacy of the referent of a noun rather than the form or any other feature of the word.

natural history *n* **1** the study of animals and plants in the wild state. **2** the study of all natural phenomena. **3** the sum of these phenomena in a given place or at a given time: *the natural history of Iran.* ▸ **natural historian** *n*

natural immunity *n* immunity with which an individual is born, which has a genetic basis.

naturalism (ˈnætʃrəˌlɪzəm, -tʃərə-) *n* **1a** a movement, esp. in art and literature, advocating detailed realistic and factual description, esp. that in 19th-century France in the writings of Zola, Flaubert, etc. **1b** the characteristics or effects of this movement. **2** a school of painting or sculpture characterized by the faithful imitation of appearances for their own sake. **3** the belief that all religious truth is based not on revelation but rather on the study of natural causes and processes. **4** *Philosophy.* **4a** a scientific account of the world in terms of causes and natural forces that rejects all spiritual, supernatural, or teleological explanations. **4b** the meta-ethical thesis that moral properties are reducible to natural ones, or that ethical judgments are derivable from nonethical ones. See **naturalistic fallacy.** Compare **descriptivism.** **5** action or thought caused by natural desires and instincts. **6** devotion to that which is natural.

naturalist (ˈnætʃrəlɪst, -tʃərəl-) *n* **1** a person who is versed in or interested in botany or zoology. **2** a person who advocates or practises naturalism, esp. in art or literature.

naturalistic (ˌnætʃrəˈlɪstɪk, -tʃərə-) *adj* **1** of, imitating, or reproducing nature in effect or characteristics. **2** of or characteristic of naturalism, esp. in art or literature. **3** of or relating to naturalists. **4** (of an ethical theory) permitting the inference of ethical judgments from statements of nonethical fact. See **Hume's law.** ▸ **ˌnaturalˈistically** *adv*

naturalistic fallacy *n* the supposed fallacy of inferring evaluative conclusions from purely factual premises. See **Hume's law.** Compare **non-naturalism.**

naturalize *or* **naturalise** (ˈnætʃrəˌlaɪz, -tʃərə-) *vb* **1** (*tr*) to give citizenship to (a person of foreign birth). **2** to be or cause to be adopted in another place, as a word, custom, etc. **3** (*tr*) to introduce (a plant or animal from another region) and cause it to adapt to local conditions. **4** (*intr*) (of a plant or animal) to adapt successfully to a foreign environment. **5** (*tr*) to explain (something unusual) with reference to nature, excluding the supernatural. **6** (*tr*) to make natural or more lifelike. ▸ **ˌnaturaliˈzation** *or* **ˌnaturaliˈsation** *n*

natural justice *n* the principles and procedures that govern the adjudication of disputes between persons or organizations, chief among which are that the adjudication should be unbiased and given in good faith, and that each party should have equal access to the tribunal and should be aware of arguments and documents adduced by the other.

natural language *n* **1** a language that has evolved naturally as a means of communication among people. Compare **artificial language, formal language.** **2** languages of this kind considered collectively.

natural law *n* **1** an ethical belief or system of beliefs supposed to be inherent in human nature and discoverable by reason rather than revelation. **2** a nonlogically necessary truth; law of nature. See also **nomological** (sense 2). **3** the philosophical doctrine that the authority of the legal system or of certain laws derives from their justifiability by reason, and indeed that a legal system which cannot be so justified has no authority.

natural logarithm *n* a logarithm to the base e (see **e** (sense 1)). Usually written $\log_e$ or ln. Also called: **Napierian logarithm.** Compare **common logarithm.**

naturally (ˈnætʃrəlɪ, -tʃərə-) *adv* **1** in a natural or normal way. **2** through nature; inherently; instinctively. ◆ *adv, sentence substitute.* **3** of course; surely.

natural number *n* any of the numbers 0,1,2,3,4,... that can be used to count the members of a set; the nonnegative integers.

natural philosophy *n* (now only used in Scottish universities) physical science, esp. physics. ▸ **natural philosopher** *n*

natural rate of unemployment *n* another name for **NAIRU.**

natural resources *pl n* naturally occurring materials such as coal, fertile land, etc., that can be used by man.

natural science *n* **1** the sciences collectively that are involved in the study of the physical world and its phenomena, including biology, physics, chemistry, and geology, but excluding social sciences, abstract or theoretical sciences, such as mathematics, and applied sciences. **2** any one of these sciences. ▸ **natural scientist** *n*

natural selection *n* a process resulting in the survival of those individuals from a population of animals or plants that are best adapted to the prevailing environmental conditions. The survivors tend to produce more offspring than those less well adapted, so that the composition of the population is changed.

natural slope *n Civil engineering.* the maximum angle at which soil will lie in a bank without slipping.

natural theology *n* the attempt to derive theological truth, and esp. the existence of God, from empirical facts by reasoned argument. Compare **revealed religion, fideism, revelation** (sense 3). ▸ **natural theologian** *n*

natural virtues *pl n* (esp. among the scholastics) those virtues of which man is capable without direct help from God, specifically justice, temperance, prudence, and fortitude. Compare **theological virtues.**

natural wastage *n* another term for **attrition** (sense 3).

nature (ˈneɪtʃə) *n* **1** the fundamental qualities of a person or thing; identity or essential character. **2** (*often cap., esp. when personified*) the whole system of the existence, arrangement, forces, and events of all physical life that are not controlled by man. **3** all natural phenomena and plant and animal life, as distinct from man and his creations. **4** a wild primitive state untouched by man or civilization. **5** natural unspoilt scenery or countryside. **6** disposition or temperament. **7** tendencies, desires, or instincts governing behaviour. **8** the normal biological needs or urges of the body. **9** sort; kind; character. **10** the real appearance of a person or thing: *a painting very true to nature.* **11** accepted standards of basic morality or behaviour. **12** *Biology.* the complement of genetic material that partly determines the structure of an organism; genotype. Compare **nurture** (sense 3). **13** *Irish.* sympathy and fondness for one's own people or native place: *she is full of nature.* **14 against nature.** unnatural or immoral. **15 by nature.** essentially or innately. **16 call of nature.** *Informal, euphemistic or humorous.* the need to urinate or defecate. **17 from nature.** using natural models in drawing, painting, etc. **18 in** (*or* **of**) **the nature of.** essentially the same as; by way of. [C13: via Old French from Latin *nātūra,* from *nātus,* past participle of *nascī* to be born]

Nature Conservancy Council *n* (in Britain) a body set up by act of parliament in 1973 to establish and manage nature reserves, identify SSSIs, and provide information and advice about nature conservation. In 1991–92 it was replaced by English Nature, Scottish National Heritage, and the Countryside Council for Wales. Abbrev.: **NCC.**

nature reserve *n* an area of land that is protected and managed in order to preserve a particular type of habitat and its flora and fauna which are often rare or endangered.

nature strip *n Austral. informal.* a grass strip in front of a house between a fence or footpath and a roadway.

nature study *n* the study of the natural world, esp. animals and plants, by direct observation at an elementary level.

nature trail *n* a path through countryside designed and usually signposted to draw attention to natural features of interest.

naturism ('neɪtʃə,rɪzəm) *n* another name for **nudism.** ▸ **'naturist** *n, adj*

naturopathy (,neɪtʃə'rɒpəθɪ) *n* a method of treating disorders, involving the use of herbs and other naturally grown foods, sunlight, fresh air, etc. Also called: **nature cure.** ▸ **naturopath** ('neɪtʃərə,pæθ) *n* ▸ **naturopathic** (,neɪtʃərə'pæθɪk) *adj*

nauch (nɔːtʃ) *n* a variant spelling of **nautch.**

Naucratis ('nɔːkrətɪs) *n* an ancient Greek city in N Egypt, in the Nile delta: founded in the 7th century B.C.

naught (nɔːt) *n* **1** *Archaic or literary.* nothing or nothingness; ruin or failure. **2** a variant spelling (esp. U.S.) of **nought. 3 set at naught.** to have disregard or scorn for; disdain. ◆ *adv* **4** *Archaic or literary.* not at all: *it matters naught.* ◆ *adj* **5** *Obsolete.* worthless, ruined, or wicked. **[**Old English *nāwiht,* from *nā* NO[1] + *wiht* thing, person; see WIGHT[1], WHIT**]**

naughty ('nɔːtɪ) *adj* **-tier, -tiest. 1** (esp. of children or their behaviour) mischievous or disobedient; bad. **2** mildly indecent; titillating. ◆ *n, pl* **-ties. 3** *Austral. and N.Z. slang.* an act of sexual intercourse. **[C14** (originally: needy, of poor quality): from NAUGHT**]** ▸ **'naughtily** *adv* ▸ **'naughtiness** *n*

naughty nineties *n* **the.** (in Britain) the 1890s, considered to be a period of fun loving and laxity, esp. in sexual morals.

naumachia (nɔː'meɪkɪə) *or* **naumachy** ('nɔːməkɪ) *n, pl* **-chiae** (-kɪ,iː), **-chias,** *or* **-chies.** (in ancient Rome) **1** a mock sea fight performed as an entertainment. **2** an artificial lake used in such a spectacle. **[C16:** via Latin from Greek *naumakhia,* from *naus* ship + *makhē* battle**]**

nauplius ('nɔːplɪəs) *n, pl* **-plii** (-plɪ,aɪ). the larva of many crustaceans, having a rounded unsegmented body with three pairs of limbs. **[C19:** from Latin: type of shellfish, from Greek *Nauplios,* one of the sons of Poseidon**]**

Nauru (nɑː'uːruː) *n* an island republic in the SW Pacific, west of Kiribati: administered jointly by Australia, New Zealand, and Britain as a UN trust territory before becoming independent in 1968 as a special member of the Commonwealth (not represented at meetings of Commonwealth heads of state). The economy is based on export of phosphates. Languages: Nauruan (a Malayo-Polynesian language) and English. Religion: Christian. Currency: Australian dollar. Pop.: 10 500 (1998 est.). Area: 2130 hectares (5263 acres). Former name: **Pleasant Island.** ▸ **Na'uruan** *adj, n*

nausea ('nɔːzɪə, -sɪə) *n* **1** the sensation that precedes vomiting. **2** a feeling of disgust or revulsion. **[C16:** via Latin from Greek: seasickness, from *naus* ship**]**

nauseate ('nɔːzɪ,eɪt, -sɪ-) *vb* **1** (*tr*) to arouse feelings of disgust or revulsion in. **2** to feel or cause to feel sick. ▸ **'nause,ating** *adj* ▸ **,nause'ation** *n*

nauseous ('nɔːzɪəs, -sɪəs) *adj* **1** feeling sick. **2** causing nausea. **3** distasteful to the mind or senses; repulsive. ▸ **'nauseously** *adv* ▸ **'nauseousness** *n*

Nausicaä (nɔː'sɪkɪə) *n Greek myth.* a daughter of Alcinous, king of the Phaeacians, who assisted the shipwrecked Odysseus after discovering him on a beach.

naut. *abbrev. for* nautical.

-naut *n combining form.* indicating a person engaged in the navigation of a vehicle, esp. one used for scientific investigation: *astronaut.*

nautch *or* **nauch** (nɔːtʃ) *n* **a** an intricate traditional Indian dance performed by professional dancing girls. **b** (*as modifier*): *a nautch girl.* **[C18:** from Hindi *nāc,* from Sanskrit *nṛtya,* from *nṛtyati* he acts or dances**]**

nautical ('nɔːtɪk^əl) *adj* of, relating to, or involving ships, navigation, or seamen. **[C16:** from Latin *nauticus,* from Greek *nautikos,* from *naus* ship**]** ▸ **'nautically** *adv*

nautical mile *n* **1** Also called **international nautical mile, air mile.** a unit of length, used esp. in navigation, equivalent to the average length of a minute of latitude, and corresponding to a latitude of 45°, i.e. 1852 m (6076.12 ft.). **2** a former British unit of length equal to 1853.18 m (6080 ft.), which was replaced by the international nautical mile in 1970. Former name: **geographical mile.** Compare **sea mile.**

nautiloid ('nɔːtɪ,lɔɪd) *n* **1** any mollusc of the *Nautiloidea,* a group of cephalopods that includes the pearly nautilus and many extinct forms. ◆ *adj* **2** of, relating to, or belonging to the *Nautiloidea.*

nautilus ('nɔːtɪləs) *n, pl* **-luses** *or* **-li** (-,laɪ). **1** any cephalopod mollusc of the genus *Nautilus,* esp. the pearly nautilus. **2** short for **paper nautilus. [C17:** via Latin from Greek *nautilos* sailor, from *naus* ship**]**

NAV *abbrev. for* net asset value.

nav. *abbrev. for:* **1** naval. **2** navigable. **3** navigation. **4** navigator.

Navaho *or* **Navajo** ('nævə,həʊ, 'nɑː-) *n* **1** (*pl* **-ho, -hos, -hoes** *or* **-jo, -jos, -joes**) a member of a North American Indian people of Arizona, New Mexico, and Utah. **2** the language of this people, belonging to the Athapascan group of the Na-Dene phylum. **[C18:** from Spanish *Navajó* pueblo, from Tena *Navahu* large planted field**]**

naval ('neɪv^əl) *adj* **1** of, relating to, characteristic of, or having a navy. **2** of or relating to ships; nautical. **[C16:** from Latin *nāvālis,* from *nāvis* ship; related to Greek *naus,* Old Norse *nōr* ship, Sanskrit *nau***]**

naval architecture *n* the designing of ships. ▸ **naval architect** *n*

navar ('nævɑː) *n* a system of air navigation in which a ground radar station relays signals to each aircraft indicating the relative positions of neighbouring aircraft. **[C20:** from *nav(igational and traffic control rad)ar***]**

Navaratri (nævə'rɑːtrɪ) *n* an annual Hindu festival celebrated over nine days in September–October. Observed throughout India, it commemorates the slaying of demons by Rama and the goddess Durga; in some places it is dedicated to all female deities. Also called **Durga Puja. [**from Sanskrit *navaratri* nine nights**]**

navarin ('nævərɪn; *French* navarɛ̃) *n* a stew of mutton or lamb with root vegetables. **[**from French**]**

Navarino (nava'riːno) *n* **1** the Italian name for **Pylos. 2** a sea battle (Oct. 20, 1827) in which the defeat of the Turkish-Egyptian fleet by a combined British, French, and Russian fleet decided Greek independence.

Navarre (nə'vɑː) *n* a former kingdom of SW Europe: established in the 9th century by the Basques; the parts south of the Pyrenees joined Spain in 1515 and the N parts passed to France in 1589. Capital: Pamplona. Spanish name: **Navarra** (na'βarra).

nave[1] (neɪv) *n* the central space in a church, extending from the narthex to the chancel and often flanked by aisles. **[C17:** via Medieval Latin from Latin *nāvis* ship, from the similarity of shape**]**

nave[2] (neɪv) *n* the central block or hub of a wheel. **[**Old English *nafu, nafa;* related to Old High German *naba***]**

navel ('neɪv^əl) *n* **1** the scar in the centre of the abdomen, usually forming a slight depression, where the umbilical cord was attached. Technical name: **umbilicus.** Related adj: **umbilical. 2** a central part, location, or point; middle. **3** short for **navel orange. [**Old English *nafela;* related to Old Frisian *navla,* Old High German *nabulo* (German *Nabel*), Latin *umbilīcus***]**

navel orange *n* a sweet orange that is usually seedless and has at its apex a navel-like depression enclosing an underdeveloped secondary fruit.

navelwort ('neɪv^əl,wɜːt) *n* another name for **pennywort** (sense 1).

navew ('neɪvjuː) *n* another name for **turnip** (senses 1, 2). **[C16:** from Old French *navel,* from Latin *nāpus***]**

navicert ('nævɪ,sɜːt) *n* a certificate specifying the contents of a neutral ship's cargo, issued esp. in time of war by a blockading power. **[C20:** from Latin *nāvi(s)* ship + CERT(IFICATE)**]**

navicular (nə'vɪkjʊlə) *Anatomy.* ◆ *adj* **1** shaped like a boat. ◆ *n also* **naviculare** (nə,vɪkjʊ'lɑːrɪ). **2** a small boat-shaped bone of the wrist or foot. **[C16:** from Late Latin *nāviculāris,* from Latin *nāvicula,* diminutive of *nāvis* ship**]**

navig. *abbrev. for* navigation.

navigable ('nævɪgəb^əl) *adj* **1** wide, deep, or safe enough to be sailed on or through: *a navigable channel.* **2** capable of being steered or controlled: *a navigable raft.* ▸ **,naviga'bility** *or* **'navigableness** *n* ▸ **'navigably** *adv*

navigate ('nævɪ,geɪt) *vb* **1** to plan, direct, or plot the path or position of (a ship, an aircraft, etc.). **2** (*tr*) to travel over, through, or on (water, air, or land) in a boat, aircraft, etc. **3** *Informal.* to direct (oneself, one's way, etc.) carefully or safely: *he navigated his way to the bar.* **4** (*intr*) (of a passenger in a motor vehicle) to give directions to the driver; point out the route. **5** (*intr*) *Rare.* to voyage in a ship; sail. **[C16:** from Latin *nāvigāre* to sail, from *nāvis* ship + *agere* to drive**]**

navigation (,nævɪ'geɪʃən) *n* **1** the skill or process of plotting a route and directing a ship, aircraft, etc., along it. **2** the act or practice of navigating: *dredging made navigation of the river possible.* **3** *U.S., rare.* ship traffic; shipping. **4** *Midland English dialect.* an inland waterway; canal. ▸ **,navi'gational** *adj*

Navigation Acts *pl n* a series of acts of Parliament, the first of which was passed in 1381, that attempted to restrict to English ships the right to carry goods to and from England and its colonies. The attempt to enforce the acts helped cause the War of American Independence.

navigator ('nævɪ,geɪtə) *n* **1** a person who is skilled in or performs navigation, esp. on a ship or aircraft. **2** (esp. formerly) a person who explores by ship. **3** an instrument or device for assisting a pilot to navigate an aircraft.

Návpaktos (*Greek* 'nafpaktos) *n* the Greek name for **Lepanto.**

Navratilova (næ,vrætɪ'ləʊvə) *n* **Martina.** born 1956, Czech-born U.S. tennis player: Wimbledon champion 1978, 1979, 1982–87, 1990; world champion 1980 and 1984.

navvy ('nævɪ) *n, pl* **-vies.** *Brit. informal.* a labourer on a building site, excavations, etc. **[C19:** shortened from *navigator,* builder of a navigation (sense 4)**]**

navy ('neɪvɪ) *n, pl* **-vies. 1** the warships and auxiliary vessels of a nation or ruler. **2** (*often cap.*; usually preceded by *the*) the branch of a country's armed services comprising such ships, their crews, and all their supporting services and equipment. **3** short for **navy blue. 4** *Archaic or literary.* a fleet of ships. **5** (*as modifier*): *a navy custom.* **[C14:** via Old French from Vulgar Latin *nāvia* (unattested) ship, from Latin *nāvis* ship**]**

navy blue *n* **a** a dark greyish-blue colour. **b** (*as adj*): *a navy-blue suit.* ◆ Sometimes shortened to **navy. [C19:** from the colour of the British naval uniform**]**

navy cut *n* tobacco finely cut from a block.

Navy List *n* (in Britain) an official list of all serving commissioned officers of the Royal Navy and reserve officers liable for recall.

navy yard *n* a naval shipyard, esp. in the U.S.

nawab (nə'wɑːb) *n* (formerly) a Muslim ruling prince or powerful landowner in India. Also called: **nabob. [C18:** from Hindi *nawwāb,* from Arabic *nuwwāb,* plural of *na'ib* viceroy, governor**]**

Naxalite ('nʌksə,laɪt) *n* a member of an extreme Maoist group in India that originated in 1967 in West Bengal and which employs tactics of agrarian terrorism and direct action. **[C20:** named after *Naxalbari,* a town in West Bengal where the movement started**]**

Naxos ('næksɒs) *n* a Greek island in the S Aegean, the largest of the Cyclades: ancient centre of the worship of Dionysius. Pop.: 14 000 (latest est.). Area: 438 sq. km (169 sq. miles).

nay (neɪ) *sentence substitute.* **1** a word for **no**[1]: archaic or dialectal except in voting by voice. ◆ *n* **2a** a person who votes in the negative. **2b** a negative vote.

♦ *adv* **3** (*sentence modifier*) *Archaic.* an emphatic form of **no**[1]. ♦ Compare **aye**[1]. [C12: from Old Norse *nei,* from *ne* not + *ei* ever, AY[1]]

Nayarit (*Spanish* naja'rit) *n* a state of W Mexico, on the Pacific: includes the offshore Tres Marías Islands. Capital: Tepic. Pop.: 895 975 (1995 est.). Area: 27 621 sq. km (10 772 sq. miles).

Nazarene (ˌnæzəˈriːn) *n also* **Nazarite. 1** an early name for a **Christian** (Acts 24:5) or (when preceded by *the*) for **Jesus Christ. 2** a member of one of several groups of Jewish-Christians found principally in Syria. **3** a member of an association of German artists called the Nazarenes or Brotherhood of St Luke, including Friedrich Overbeck (1789–1869) and Peter von Cornelius (1783–1867), founded (1809) in Vienna to revive German religious art after the examples of the Middle Ages and early Renaissance. ♦ *adj* **4** of or relating to Nazareth or the Nazarenes.

Nazareth (ˈnæzərɪθ) *n* a town in N Israel, in Lower Galilee: the home of Jesus in his youth. Pop.: 51 000 (1989).

Nazarite[1] (ˈnæzəˌraɪt) *n* another word for **Nazarene** (senses 1, 2).

Nazarite[2] *or* **Nazirite** (ˈnæzəˌraɪt) *n* a religious ascetic of ancient Israel. [C16: from Latin *Nazaraeus,* from Hebrew *nāzīr,* from *nāzar* to consecrate + -ITE[1]]

Naze (neɪz) *n* **the. 1** a flat marshy headland in SE England, in Essex on the North Sea coast. **2** another name for **Lindesnes.**

Nazi (ˈnɑːtsɪ) *n, pl* **Nazis. 1** a member of the fascist National Socialist German Workers' Party, which was founded in 1919 and seized political control in Germany in 1933 under Adolf Hitler. **2** *Derogatory.* anyone who thinks or acts like a Nazi, esp. showing racism, brutality, etc. ♦ *adj* **3** of, characteristic of, or relating to the Nazis. [C20: from German, phonetic spelling of the first two syllables of *Nationalsozialist* National Socialist] ▸ **Nazism** (ˈnɑːtˌsɪzəm) *or* **Naziism** (ˈnɑːtsɪˌɪzəm) *n*

Nazify (ˈnɑːtsɪˌfaɪ) *vb* **-fies, -fying, -fied.** (*tr*) to make Nazi in character. ▸ **ˌNazifiˈcation** *n*

nb *Cricket. abbrev. for* no ball.

Nb *the chemical symbol for* niobium.

NB *abbrev. for* New Brunswick.

NB, N.B., nb, *or* **n.b.** *abbrev. for* nota bene. [Latin: note well]

NBA *abbrev. for* Net Book Agreement.

NBC *abbrev. for:* **1** (in the U.S.) National Broadcasting Company. **2** (of weapons or warfare) nuclear, biological, and chemical.

NBG *Informal. abbrev. for* no bloody good. Also: **nbg.**

NC *or* **N.C.** *abbrev. for:* **1** North Carolina. **2** *Brit. education.* National Curriculum.

NCB *abbrev. for* National Coal Board.

NCC (in Britain) *abbrev. for* Nature Conservancy Council.

NCCL *abbrev. for* National Council for Civil Liberties.

NCO *abbrev. for* noncommissioned officer.

NCVO (in Britain) *abbrev. for* National Council for Voluntary Organizations.

nd *abbrev. for* no date.

Nd *the chemical symbol for* neodymium.

ND, N.D., *or* **N. Dak.** *abbrev. for* North Dakota.

NDE *abbrev. for* near-death experience.

Ndebele (ᵊnˈdɛbɛle) *n* **1** (*pl* **Ndebele**) a member of a Negroid people of Zimbabwe. See also **Matabele. 2** the language of this people, belonging to the Bantu grouping of the Niger-Congo family.

Ndjamena *or* **N'djamena** (ᵊndʒɑːˈmeɪnə) *n* the capital of Chad, in the southwest, at the confluence of the Shari and Logone Rivers: trading centre for livestock. Pop.: 530 965 (1993). Former name (until 1973): **Fort Lamy.**

Ndola (ᵊnˈdəʊlə) *n* a city in N Zambia: copper, cobalt, and sugar refineries. Pop.: 376 311 (1990).

NDP *abbrev. for:* **1** net domestic product. **2** (in Canada) New Democratic Party.

NDT *abbrev. for* nondestructive testing.

Ne *the chemical symbol for* neon.

NE 1 *symbol for* northeast(ern). **2** *abbrev. for* Nebraska.

NE *or* **N.E.** *abbrev. for* New England.

ne- *combining form.* a variant of **neo-,** esp. before a vowel: *Nearctic.*

Neagh (neɪ) *n* **Lough.** a lake in Northern Ireland, in SW Co. Antrim: the largest lake in the British Isles. Area: 388 sq. km (150 sq. miles).

Neanderthal (nɪˈændəˌtɑːl) (*sometimes not cap.*) ♦ *adj* **1** relating to or characteristic of Neanderthal man. **2** primitive; uncivilized. **3** *Informal.* ultraconservative; reactionary. ♦ *n* **4** a person showing any such characteristics.

Neanderthal man (nɪˈændəˌtɑːl) *n* a type of primitive man, *Homo neanderthalensis,* or *H. sapiens neanderthalensis,* occurring throughout much of Europe in late Palaeolithic times: it is thought that they did not interbreed with other early humans and are not the ancestors of modern humans. [C19: from the anthropological findings (1857) in the Neandertal, a valley near Düsseldorf, Germany]

neanic (nɪˈænɪk) *adj Zoology.* of or relating to the early stages in the life cycle of an organism, esp. the pupal stage of an insect. [C19: from Greek *neanikus* youthful]

neap (niːp) *adj* **1** of, relating to, or constituting a neap tide. ♦ *n* **2** short for **neap tide.** [Old English, as in *nēpflōd* neap tide, of uncertain origin]

Neapolitan (ˌnɪəˈpɒlɪtᵊn) *n* **1** a native or inhabitant of Naples. ♦ *adj* **2** of or relating to Naples. [C15: from Latin *Neāpolītānus,* ultimately from Greek *Neapolis* new town]

Neapolitan ice cream *n* ice cream, usually in brick form, with several layers of different colours and flavours.

Neapolitan sixth *n* (in musical harmony) a chord composed of the subdominant of the key, plus a minor third and a minor sixth. Harmonically it is equivalent to the first inversion of a major chord built upon the flattened supertonic.

neap tide *n* either of the two tides that occur at the first or last quarter of the moon when the tide-generating forces of the sun and moon oppose each other and produce the smallest rise and fall in tidal level. Compare **spring tide** (sense 1).

near (nɪə) *prep* **1** at or to a place or time not far away from; close to. ♦ *adv* **2** at or to a place or time not far away; close by. **3 near to.** not far from; near. **4** short for **nearly** (esp. in phrases such as **damn near**): *I was damn near killed.* ♦ *adj* **5** (*postpositive*) at or in a place not far away. **6** (*prenominal*) only just successful or only just failing: *a near escape.* **7** (*postpositive*) *Informal.* miserly, mean. **8** (*prenominal*) closely connected or intimate: *a near relation.* ♦ *vb* **9** to come or draw close (to). ♦ *n* **10** Also called: **nearside. 10a** the left side of a horse, team of animals, vehicle, etc. **10b** (*as modifier*): *the near foreleg.* [Old English *nēar* (adv), comparative of *nēah* close, NIGH; related to Old Frisian *niār,* Old Norse *nǣr,* Old High German *nāhōr*] ▸ **ˈnearness** *n*

near- *combining form.* nearly; almost: *a near-perfect landing.*

nearby *adj* (ˈnɪəˌbaɪ), *adv* (ˌnɪəˈbaɪ). not far away; close at hand.

Nearctic (nɪˈɑːktɪk) *adj* of or denoting a zoogeographical region consisting of North America, north of the tropic of Cancer, and Greenland.

near-death experience *n* an experience, instances of which have been widely reported, in which a person near death is apparently outside his body and aware of it and the attendant circumstances as separate from him. Abbrev.: **NDE.**

Near East *n* **1** another term for the **Middle East. 2** (formerly) the Balkan States and the area of the Ottoman Empire.

near gale *n Meteorol.* a wind of force seven on the Beaufort scale or from 32–38 mph.

nearly (ˈnɪəlɪ) *adv* **1** not quite; almost; practically. **2 not nearly.** nowhere near; not at all: *not nearly enough money.* **3** closely: *the person most nearly concerned.*

near-market research *n* scientific research that, while not linked to the development of a specific product, is likely to be commercially exploitable.

near miss *n* **1** a bomb, shell, etc., that does not exactly hit the target. **2** any attempt or shot that just fails to be successful. **3** an incident in which two vehicles narrowly avoid collision.

near money *n* liquid assets that can be converted to cash very quickly, such as a bank deposit or bill of exchange.

near point *n Optics.* the nearest point to the eye at which an object remains in focus.

near rhyme *n Prosody.* another term for **half-rhyme.**

nearside (ˈnɪəˌsaɪd) *n* **1** (usually preceded by *the*) *Chiefly Brit.* **1a** the side of a vehicle normally nearer the kerb (in Britain, the left side). **1b** (*as modifier*): *the nearside door.* ♦ Compare **offside. 2a** the left side of an animal, team of horses, etc. **2b** (*as modifier*): *the nearside flank.*

near-sighted (ˌnɪəˈsaɪtɪd) *adj* relating to or suffering from myopia. ▸ **ˌnear-ˈsightedly** *adv* ▸ **ˌnear-ˈsightedness** *n*

near thing *n Informal.* an event or action whose outcome is nearly a failure, success, disaster, etc.

nearthrosis (ˌniːɑːˈθrəʊsɪs) *n, pl* **-ses** (-siːz). another name for **pseudoarthrosis.**

neat[1] (niːt) *adj* **1** clean, tidy, and orderly. **2** liking or insisting on order and cleanliness; fastidious. **3** smoothly or competently done; efficient: *a neat job.* **4** pat or slick: *his excuse was suspiciously neat.* **5** (of alcoholic drinks) without added water, lemonade, etc.; undiluted. **6** a less common word for **net**[2]: *neat profits.* **7** *Slang, chiefly U.S. and Canadian.* good; pleasing; admirable. [C16: from Old French *net,* from Latin *nitidus* clean, shining, from *nitēre* to shine; related to Middle Irish *niam* beauty, brightness, Old Persian *naiba-* beautiful] ▸ **ˈneatly** *adv* ▸ **ˈneatness** *n*

neat[2] (niːt) *n, pl* **neat.** *Archaic or dialect.* a domestic bovine animal. [Old English *neat*]

neaten (ˈniːtᵊn) *vb* (*tr*) to make neat; tidy.

neath *or* **'neath** (niːθ) *prep Archaic.* short for **beneath.**

Neath Port Talbot (ˈniːθ ˈpɔːt ˈtɔːlbət, ˈtæl-) *n* a county borough in S Wales, created from part of West Glamorgan in 1996. Administrative centre: Port Talbot. Pop.: 106 307 (1996 est.). Area: 439 sq. km (169 sq. miles).

neat's-foot oil *n* a yellow fixed oil obtained by boiling the feet and shinbones of cattle and used esp. to dress leather.

neb (nɛb) *n Archaic or dialect.* **1** *Chiefly Scot. and northern English.* the peak of a cap. **2** the beak of a bird or the nose or snout of an animal. **3** a person's mouth or nose. **4** the projecting part or end of anything. **5a** a peak, esp. in N England. **5b** a prominent gritstone overhang. [Old English *nebb;* related to Old Norse *nef,* Old High German *snabul* (German *Schnabel*)]

NEB *abbrev. for:* **1** New English Bible. **2** National Enterprise Board.

Nebo (ˈniːbəʊ) *n* **Mount.** a mountain in Jordan, northeast of the Dead Sea: the highest point of a ridge known as Pisgah, from which Moses viewed the Promised Land just before his death (Deuteronomy 34:1). Height: 802 m (2631 ft.).

Nebr. *abbrev. for* Nebraska.

Nebraska (nɪˈbræskə) *n* a state of the western U.S.: consists of an undulating plain. Capital: Lincoln. Pop.: 1 656 870 (1997 est.). Area: 197 974 sq. km (76 483 sq. miles). Abbrevs.: **Nebr.** or (with zip code) **NE** ▸ **Neˈbraskan** *adj, n*

Nebuchadnezzar[1] (ˌnɛbjʊkədˈnɛzə) *n* a wine bottle, used esp. for display, holding the equivalent of twenty normal bottles (approximately 520 ounces). [C20: named after NEBUCHADNEZZAR[2], from the custom of naming large wine bottles after Old Testament figures; compare JEROBOAM]

Nebuchadnezzar[2] (ˌnɛbjʊkədˈnɛzə) *or* **Nebuchadrezzar** *n Old Testament.* a king of Babylon, 605–562 B.C., who conquered and destroyed Jerusalem and exiled the Jews to Babylon (II Kings 24–25).

nebula (ˈnɛbjʊlə) *n, pl* **-lae** (-ˌliː) *or* **-las. 1** *Astronomy.* a diffuse cloud of particles and gases (mainly hydrogen) that is visible either as a hazy patch of light (either an **emission** or a **reflection nebula**) or an irregular dark region (**dark nebula**). Compare **planetary nebula. 2** *Pathol.* **2a** opacity of the cornea. **2b** cloudiness of the urine. **3** any substance for use in an atomizer spray. [C17: from Latin: mist, cloud; related to Greek *nephétē* cloud, Old High German *nebul* cloud, Old Norse *njól* night] ▸ **'nebular** *adj*

nebular hypothesis *n* the theory that the solar system evolved from nebular matter.

nebulize *or* **nebulise** ('nɛbju,laɪz) *vb* (*tr*) to convert (a liquid) into a mist or fine spray; atomize. ▸ **,nebuli'zation** *or* **,nebuli'sation**

nebulizer *or* **nebuliser** ('nɛbju,laɪzə) *n* a device for converting a drug in liquid form into a mist or fine spray which is inhaled through a mask to provide medication for the respiratory system.

nebulosity (,nɛbju'lɒsɪtɪ) *n, pl* **-ties. 1** the state or quality of being nebulous. **2** *Astronomy.* a nebula.

nebulous ('nɛbjuləs) *adj* **1** lacking definite form, shape, or content; vague or amorphous: *nebulous reasons.* **2** of, characteristic of, or resembling a nebula. **3** *Rare.* misty or hazy. ▸ **'nebulously** *adv* ▸ **'nebulousness** *n*

NEC *abbrev. for* National Executive Committee.

necessaries ('nɛsɪsərɪz) *pl n* **1** (*sometimes sing*) what is needed; essential items: *the necessaries of life.* **2** *Law.* food, clothing, etc., essential for the maintenance of a dependant in the condition of life to which he or she is accustomed.

necessarily ('nɛsɪsərɪlɪ, ,nɛsɪ'sɛrɪlɪ) *adv* **1** as an inevitable or natural consequence: *girls do not necessarily like dolls.* **2** as a certainty: *he won't necessarily come.*

necessary ('nɛsɪsərɪ) *adj* **1** needed to achieve a certain desired effect or result; required. **2** resulting from necessity; inevitable: *the necessary consequences of your action.* **3** *Logic.* **3a** (of a statement, formula, etc.) true under all interpretations or in all possible circumstances. **3b** (of a proposition) determined to be true by its meaning, so that its denial would be self-contradictory. **3c** (of a property) essential, so that without it its subject would not be the entity it is. **3d** (of an inference) always yielding a true conclusion when its premises are true; valid. **3e** (of a condition) entailed by the truth of some statement or the obtaining of some state of affairs. ◆ Compare **sufficient** (sense 2). **4** *Philosophy.* (in a nonlogical sense) expressing a law of nature, so that if it is in this sense necessary that all As are B, even although it is not contradictory to conceive of an A which is not B, we are licensed to infer that if something were an A it would have to be B. **5** *Rare.* compelled, as by necessity or law; not free. ◆ *n* **6** *Informal.* (preceded by *the*) the money required for a particular purpose. **7 do the necessary.** *Informal.* to do something that is necessary in a particular situation. ◆ See also **necessaries.** [C14: from Latin *necessārius* indispensable, from *necesse* unavoidable]

necessitarianism (nɪ,sɛsɪ'tɛərɪə,nɪzəm) *or* **necessarianism** (,nɛsɪ'sɛərɪə,nɪzəm) *n Philosophy.* another word for **determinism.** Compare **libertarian.** ▸ **ne,cessi'tarian** *or* **,neces'sarian** *n, adj*

necessitate (nɪ'sɛsɪ,teɪt) *vb* (*tr*) **1** to cause as an unavoidable and necessary result. **2** (*usually passive*) to compel or require (someone to do something). ▸ **ne,cessi'tation** *n* ▸ **ne'cessitative** *adj*

necessitous (nɪ'sɛsɪtəs) *adj* very needy; destitute; poverty-stricken. ▸ **ne'cessitously** *adv*

necessity (nɪ'sɛsɪtɪ) *n, pl* **-ties. 1** (*sometimes pl*) something needed for a desired result; prerequisite: *necessities of life.* **2** a condition or set of circumstances, such as physical laws or social rules, that inevitably requires a certain result: *it is a matter of necessity to wear formal clothes when meeting the Queen.* **3** the state or quality of being obligatory or unavoidable. **4** urgent requirement, as in an emergency or misfortune: *in time of necessity we must all work together.* **5** poverty or want. **6** *Rare.* compulsion through laws of nature; fate. **7** *Philosophy.* **7a** a condition, principle, or conclusion that cannot be otherwise. **7b** the constraining force of physical determinants on all aspects of life. Compare **freedom** (sense 8). **8** *Logic.* **8a** the property of being necessary. **8b** a statement asserting that some property is essential or statement is necessarily true. **8c** the operator that indicates that the expression it modifies is true in all possible worlds. Usual symbol: □ or L **9 of necessity.** inevitably; necessarily.

neck (nɛk) *n* **1** the part of an organism connecting the head with the rest of the body. Related adjs.: **cervical, jugular. 2** the part of a garment around or nearest the neck. **3** something resembling a neck in shape or position: *the neck of a bottle.* **4** *Anatomy.* a constricted portion of an organ or part, such as the cervix of the uterus. **5** a narrow or elongated projecting strip of land; a peninsula or isthmus. **6** a strait or channel. **7** the part of a violin, cello, etc., that extends from the body to the tuning pegs and supports the fingerboard. **8** a solid block of lava from the opening of an extinct volcano, exposed after erosion of the surrounding rock. **9** *Botany.* the upper, usually tubular, part of the archegonium of mosses, ferns, etc. **10** the length of a horse's head and neck taken as an approximate distance by which one horse beats another in a race: *to win by a neck.* **11** *Informal.* a short distance, amount, or margin: *he is always a neck ahead in new techniques.* **12** *Informal.* impudence; audacity: *he had the neck to ask for a rise.* **13** *Architect.* the narrow band at the top of the shaft of a column between the necking and the capital, esp. as used in the Tuscan order. **14** another name for **beard** (on printer's type). **15 break one's neck.** *Informal.* to exert oneself greatly, esp. by hurrying, in order to do something. **16 by the neck.** *Irish and Scot. slang.* (of a bottle of beer) served unpoured: *give me two bottles of stout by the neck.* **17 get it in the neck.** *Informal.* to be reprimanded or punished severely. **18 neck and neck.** absolutely level or even in a race or competition. **19 neck of the woods.** *Informal.* an area or locality: *a quiet neck of the woods.* **20 risk one's neck.** to take a great risk. **21 save one's** *or* **someone's neck.** *Informal.* to escape from or help someone else to escape from a difficult or dangerous situation. **22 stick one's neck out.** *Informal.* to risk criticism, ridicule, failure, etc., by speaking one's mind. **23 up to one's neck (in).** deeply involved (in). ◆ *vb* **24** (*intr*) *Informal.* to kiss, embrace, or fondle someone or one another passionately. [Old English *hnecca;* related to Old High German *hnack,* Old Irish *cnocc* hill] ▸ **'necker** *n*

Neckar ('nɛkɑː) *n* a river in SW Germany, rising in the Black Forest and flowing generally north into the Rhine at Mannheim. Length: 394 km (245 miles).

neckband ('nɛk,bænd) *n* a band around the neck of a garment as finishing, decoration, or a base for a collar.

neckcloth ('nɛk,klɒθ) *n* a large ornamental usually white cravat worn formerly by men.

Necker ('nɛkə; *French* nɛkɛr) *n* **Jacques** (ʒak). 1732–1804, French financier and statesman, born in Switzerland; finance minister of France (1777–81; 1788–90). He attempted to reform the fiscal system and in 1789 he recommended summoning the States General. His subsequent dismissal was one of the causes of the storming of the Bastille (1789).

neckerchief ('nɛkətʃɪf, -,tʃiːf) *n* a piece of ornamental cloth, often square, worn around the neck. [C14: from NECK + KERCHIEF]

Necker cube *n* a line drawing showing the 12 edges of a transparent cube, so that it can be seen alternately facing in two different directions: an example of an ambiguous figure. [C19: named after Louis Albert *Necker* (1786–1861), Swiss mineralogist]

necking ('nɛkɪŋ) *n* **1** *Informal.* the activity of kissing and embracing passionately. **2** Also called: **gorgerin.** *Architect.* one or more mouldings at the top of a column between the shaft and the capital.

necklace ('nɛklɪs) *n* **1** a chain, band, or cord, often bearing beads, pearls, jewels, etc., worn around the neck as an ornament, esp. by women. **2** (in South Africa) a tyre soaked in petrol, placed round a person's neck, and set on fire in order to burn the person to death. ◆ *vb* **3** (*tr*) *S. African.* to kill (someone) by placing a burning tyre round his or her neck.

necklet ('nɛklɪt) *n* an ornament worn round the neck.

neckline ('nɛk,laɪn) *n* the shape or position of the upper edge of a dress, blouse, etc.: *a plunging neckline.*

neckpiece ('nɛk,piːs) *n* a piece of fur, cloth, etc., worn around the neck or neckline.

necktie ('nɛk,taɪ) *n* the U.S. name for **tie** (sense 11).

neckwear ('nɛk,wɛə) *n* articles of clothing, such as ties, scarves, etc., worn around the neck.

necro- *or before a vowel* **necr-** *combining form.* indicating death, a dead body, or dead tissue: *necrology; necrophagous; necrosis.* [from Greek *nekros* corpse]

necrobiosis (,nɛkrəubaɪ'əusɪs) *n Physiol.* the normal degeneration and death of cells. Compare **necrosis.** ▸ **necrobiotic** (,nɛkrəubaɪ'ɒtɪk) *adj*

necrolatry (nɛ'krɒlətrɪ) *n* the worship of the dead.

necrology (nɛ'krɒlədʒɪ) *n, pl* **-gies. 1** a list of people recently dead. **2** a less common word for **obituary.** ▸ **necrological** (,nɛkrə'lɒdʒɪkᵊl) *adj* ▸ **ne'crologist** *n*

necromancy ('nɛkrəu,mænsɪ) *n* **1** the art or practice of supposedly conjuring up the dead, esp. in order to obtain from them knowledge of the future. **2** black magic; sorcery. [C13: (as in sense 1) ultimately from Greek *nekromanteia,* from *nekros* corpse; (as in sense 2) from Medieval Latin *nigromantia,* from Latin *niger* black, which replaced *necro-* through folk etymology] ▸ **'necro,mancer** *n* ▸ **,necro'mantic** *adj*

necromania (,nɛkrəu'meɪnɪə) *n* another word for **necrophilia.** ▸ **,necro'mani,ac** *n*

necrophagous (nə'krɒfəgəs) *adj* (of an animal, bird, etc.) feeding on carrion.

necrophilia (,nɛkrəu'fɪlɪə) *n* sexual attraction for or sexual intercourse with dead bodies. Also called: **necromania, necrophilism.** ▸ **,necro'phili,ac** *or* **necrophile** ('nɛkrəu,faɪl) *n* ▸ **,necro'philic** *adj*

necrophilism (nɛ'krɒfɪ,lɪzəm) *n* **1** another word for **necrophilia. 2** a strong desire to be dead.

necrophobia (,nɛkrəu'fəubɪə) *n* an abnormal fear of death or dead bodies. ▸ **'necro,phobe** *n* ▸ **,necro'phobic** *adj*

necrophorous (nɪ'krɒfərəs) *adj* denoting animals, such as certain beetles, that carry away the bodies of dead animals.

necropolis (nɛ'krɒpəlɪs) *n, pl* **-lises** *or* **-leis** (-,leɪs). a burial site or cemetery. [C19: Greek, from *nekros* dead + *polis* city]

necropsy ('nɛkrɒpsɪ) *or* **necroscopy** (nɛ'krɒskəpɪ) *n, pl* **-sies** *or* **-pies.** another name for **autopsy.** [C19: from Greek *nekros* dead body + *opsis* sight]

necrose (nɛ'krəus, 'nɛkrəus) *vb* (*intr*) to cause or undergo necrosis. [C19: back formation from NECROSIS]

necrosis (nɛ'krəusɪs) *n* **1** the death of one or more cells in the body, usually within a localized area, as from an interruption of the blood supply to that part. **2** death of plant tissue due to disease, frost, etc. [C17: New Latin from Greek *nekrōsis,* from *nekroun* to kill, from *nekros* corpse] ▸ **necrotic** (nɛ'krɒtɪk) *adj*

necrotomy (nɛ'krɒtəmɪ) *n, pl* **-mies. 1** dissection of a dead body. **2** surgical excision of dead tissue from a living organism.

necrotroph ('nɛkrəu,trəuf) *n* a parasitic organism that kills the living cells of its host and then feeds on the dead matter. ▸ **necrotrophic** (,nɛkrəu'trɒfɪk) *adj*

nectar ('nɛktə) *n* **1** a sugary fluid produced in the nectaries of flowers and collected by bees and other insects. **2** *Classical myth.* the drink of the gods. Compare **ambrosia** (sense 1). **3** any delicious drink, esp. a sweet one. **4** something very pleasant or welcome: *your words are nectar to me.* **5** *Chiefly U.S.* **5a** the undiluted juice of a fruit. **5b** a mixture of fruit juices. [C16: via Latin from Greek *néktar,* perhaps *nek-* death (related to *nekros* corpse) + *-tar,* related to Sanskrit *tarati* he overcomes; compare Latin *nex* death and *trans* across] ▸ **nectareous** (nɛk'tɛərɪəs) *or* **'nectarous** *adj*

nectarine ('nɛktərɪn) *n* **1** a variety of peach tree, *Prunus persica nectarina.* **2** the fruit of this tree, which has a smooth skin. [C17: apparently from NECTAR]

nectarivorous (,nɛktə'rɪvərəs) *adj Zoology.* feeding on nectar.

nectary ('nɛktərɪ) *n, pl* **-ries. 1** any of various glandular structures secreting nectar that occur in the flowers, leaves, stipules, etc., of a plant. **2** any of the abdominal tubes in aphids through which honeydew is secreted. [C18: from New Latin *nectarium*, from NECTAR] ▸ **nectarial** (nɛk'tɛərɪəl) *adj*

NEDC *abbrev. for* National Economic Development Council. Also (informal): **Neddy** ('nɛdɪ).

neddy ('nɛdɪ) *n, pl* **-dies. 1** a child's word for a **donkey. 2** *Informal.* a silly person; fool. **3** *Austral. informal.* a horse, esp. a racehorse: *he lost his money on the neddies.* [C18: from *Ned,* pet form of *Edward*]

Nederland ('ne:dərlɑnt) *n* the Dutch name for the **Netherlands.**

née *or* **nee** (neɪ) *adj* indicating the maiden name of a married woman: *Mrs Bloggs née Blandish.* [C19: from French: past participle (fem) of *naître* to be born, from Latin *nascī*]

need (ni:d) *vb* **1** (*tr*) to be in want of: *to need money.* **2** (*tr*) to require or be required of necessity (to be or do something); be obliged: *to need to do more work.* **3** (takes an infinitive without *to*) used as an auxiliary in negative and interrogative sentences to express necessity or obligation and does not add *-s* when used with *he, she, it,* and singular nouns: *need he go?* **4** (*intr*) *Archaic.* to be essential or necessary to: *there needs no reason for this.* ◆ *n* **5** the fact or an instance of feeling the lack of something: *he has need of a new coat.* **6** a requirement: *the need for vengeance.* **7** necessity or obligation resulting from some situation: *no need to be frightened.* **8** distress or extremity: *a friend in need.* **9** extreme poverty or destitution; penury. ◆ See also **needs.** [Old English *nēad, nied;* related to Old Frisian *nēd,* Old Saxon *nōd,* Old High German *nōt*]

needful ('ni:dfʊl) *adj* **1** necessary; needed; required. **2** *Archaic.* needy; poverty-stricken. ◆ *n Informal.* **3** money or funds: *do you have the needful?* **4 do the needful.** to perform a necessary task. ▸ **'needfully** *adv* ▸ **'needfulness** *n*

neediness ('ni:dɪnɪs) *n* the state of being needy; poverty.

needle ('ni:dᵊl) *n* **1** a pointed slender piece of metal, usually steel, with a hole or eye in it through which thread is passed for sewing. **2** a somewhat larger rod with a point at one or each end, used in knitting. **3** a similar instrument with a hook at one end for crocheting. **4a** another name for **stylus** (sense 3). **4b** a small thin pointed device, esp. one made of stainless steel, used to transmit the vibrations from a gramophone record to the pick-up. **5** *Med.* **5a** the long hollow pointed part of a hypodermic syringe, which is inserted into the body. **5b** an informal name for **hypodermic syringe. 6** *Surgery.* a pointed steel instrument, often curved, for suturing, puncturing, or ligating. **7** a long narrow stiff leaf in which water loss is greatly reduced: *pine needles.* **8** any slender sharp spine, such as the spine of a sea urchin. **9** any slender pointer for indicating the reading on the scale of a measuring instrument. **10** short for **magnetic needle. 11** a crystal resembling a needle in shape. **12** a sharp pointed metal instrument used in engraving and etching. **13** anything long and pointed, such as an obelisk: *a needle of light.* **14** a short horizontal beam passed through a wall and supported on vertical posts to take the load of the upper part of the wall. **15** *Informal.* **15a** anger or intense rivalry, esp. in a sporting encounter. **15b** (*as modifier*): *a needle match.* **16 have** *or* **get the needle (to).** *Brit. informal.* to feel dislike, distaste, nervousness, or annoyance (for): *she got the needle after he had refused her invitation.* ◆ *vb* **17** (*tr*) *Informal.* to goad or provoke, as by constant criticism. **18** (*tr*) to sew, embroider, or prick (fabric) with a needle. **19** (*tr*) *U.S.* to increase the alcoholic strength of (beer or other beverages). **20** (*intr*) (of a substance) to form needle-shaped crystals. [Old English *nǣdl;* related to Gothic *nēthla,* German *Nadel*]

needle bearing *n Engineering.* an antifriction roller bearing in which long rollers of very small diameter fill the race without a cage to provide spacers between them.

needlecord ('ni:dᵊl,kɔ:d) *n* a corduroy fabric with narrow ribs.

needlecraft ('ni:dᵊl,krɑ:ft) *n* the art or practice of needlework.

needle exchange *n* a centre where drug users can exchange used hypodermic syringes for new ones.

needlefish ('ni:dᵊl,fɪʃ) *n, pl* **-fish** *or* **-fishes. 1** any ferocious teleost fish of the family *Belonidae* of warm and tropical regions, having an elongated body and long toothed jaws. **2** another name for **pipefish.**

needle fly *n* a small stonefly of the genus *Leuctra,* whose rolled-up wings at rest give it a slender pointed appearance.

needleful ('ni:dᵊlfʊl) *n* a length of thread cut for use in a needle.

needlepoint ('ni:dᵊl,pɔɪnt) *n* **1** embroidery done on canvas with the same stitch throughout so as to resemble tapestry. **2** another name for **point lace.**

needless ('ni:dlɪs) *adj* not required or desired; unnecessary. ▸ **'needlessly** *adv* ▸ **'needlessness** *n*

needle time *n* the limited time allocated by a radio channel to the broadcasting of music from records.

needle valve *n* a valve with a needle-like part that can be moved to control the flow of a fluid.

needlewoman ('ni:dᵊl,wʊmən) *n, pl* **-women.** a woman who does needlework; seamstress.

needlework ('ni:dᵊl,wɜ:k) *n* **1** work done with a needle, esp. sewing and embroidery. **2** the result of such work.

needs (ni:dz) *adv* **1** (preceded or foll. by *must*) of necessity: *we must needs go; we will go, if needs must.* ◆ *pl n* **2** what is required; necessities: *the needs of the third world; his needs are modest.*

needs test *n Social welfare.* an examination of a person's physical or social, rather than financial, circumstances, to determine whether he is eligible for a particular welfare benefit or service. Compare **means test.**

needy ('ni:dɪ) *adj* **needier, neediest. a** in need of practical or emotional support; distressed. **b** (*as collective n;* preceded by *the*): *the needy.*

Néel (neel) *n* **Louis** (lwi). born 1904, French physicist, noted for his research on magnetism; shared the Nobel prize for physics in 1970.

Néel point *or* **temperature** *n* the temperature above which an antiferromagnetic substance loses its antiferromagnetism and becomes paramagnetic.

neem (ni:m) *n* a large tree of India, *Azadirachta indica,* all parts of which are useful to man: the leaves act as a natural pesticide, the fruit and seeds yield a medicinal oil, the bark is used to make a tonic, and the trunk exudes a gum. [C19: from Hindi *nīm,* from Sanskrit *nimba*]

neep (ni:p) *n Brit.* a dialect name for a **turnip.** [Old English *nǣp,* from Latin *nāpus* turnip]

ne'er (nɛə) *adv* a poetic contraction of **never.**

Ne'erday ('nerde) *n Scot.* New Year's Day.

ne'er-do-well *n* **1** an improvident, irresponsible, or lazy person. ◆ *adj* **2** useless; worthless: *your ne'er-do-well schemes.*

nefarious (nɪ'fɛərɪəs) *adj* evil; wicked; sinful. [C17: from Latin *nefārius,* from *nefās* unlawful deed, from *nē* not + *fās* divine law] ▸ **ne'fariously** *adv* ▸ **ne'fariousness** *n*

Nefertiti (,nɛfə'ti:tɪ) *or* **Nofretete** *n* 14th century B.C., Egyptian queen; wife of Akhenaton.

NEG (in transformational grammar) *abbrev. for* negative.

neg. *abbrev. for* negative(ly).

negate (nɪ'geɪt) *vb* (*tr*) **1** to make ineffective or void; nullify; invalidate. **2** to deny or contradict. [C17: from Latin *negāre,* from *neg-,* variant of *nec* not + *aio* I say] ▸ **ne'gator** *or* **ne'gater** *n*

negation (nɪ'geɪʃən) *n* **1** the opposite or absence of something. **2** a negative thing or condition. **3** the act or an instance of negating. **4** *Logic.* **4a** the operator that forms one sentence from another and corresponds to the English *not.* **4b** a sentence so formed. It is usually written $-p$, $\sim p$, $\bar{p}$, or $\neg p$, where p is the given sentence, and is false when the given sentence is true, and true when it is false.

negative ('nɛgətɪv) *adj* **1** expressing or meaning a refusal or denial: *a negative answer.* **2** lacking positive or affirmative qualities, such as enthusiasm, interest, or optimism. **3** showing or tending towards opposition or resistance. **4a** measured in a direction opposite to that regarded as positive. **4b** having the same magnitude but opposite sense to an equivalent positive quantity. **5** *Biology.* indicating movement or growth away from a particular stimulus: *negative geotropism.* **6** *Med.* (of the results of a diagnostic test) indicating absence of the disease or condition for which the test was made. **7** another word for **minus** (senses 3b, 5). **8** *Physics.* **8a** (of an electric charge) having the same polarity as the charge of an electron. **8b** (of a body, system, ion, etc.) having a negative electric charge; having an excess of electrons. **8c** (of a point in an electric circuit) having a lower electrical potential than some other point with an assigned zero potential. **9** short for **electronegative. 10** (of a lens) capable of causing divergence of a parallel beam of light. **11** of or relating to a photographic negative. **12** *Logic.* (of a categorial proposition) denying the satisfaction by the subject of the predicate, as in *some men are irrational; no pigs have wings.* **13** *Astrology.* of, relating to, or governed by the signs of the zodiac of the earth and water classifications, which are thought to be associated with a receptive passive nature. **14** short for **Rh negative.** ◆ *n* **15** a statement or act of denial, refusal, or negation. **16** a negative person or thing. **17** *Photog.* a piece of photographic film or a plate, previously exposed and developed, showing an image that, in black-and-white photography, has a reversal of tones. In colour photography the image is in complementary colours to the subject so that blue sky appears yellow, green grass appears purple, etc. **18** *Physics.* a negative object, such as a terminal or a plate in a voltaic cell. **19** a sentence or other linguistic element with a negative meaning, as the English word *not.* **20** a quantity less than zero or a quantity to be subtracted. **21** *Logic.* a negative proposition. **22** *Archaic.* the right of veto. **23 in the negative.** indicating denial or refusal. ◆ *sentence substitute.* **24** (esp. in military communications) a signal code word for **no**[1]. ◆ *vb* (*tr*) **25** to deny or nullify; negate. **26** to show to be false; disprove. **27** to refuse consent to or approval of: *the proposal was negatived.* ◆ Compare **positive, affirmative.** ▸ **'negatively** *adv* ▸ **'negativeness** *or* **,nega'tivity** *n*

negative equity *n* the state of holding a property the value of which is less than the amount of mortgage still unpaid.

negative feedback *n* See **feedback.**

negative hallucination *n Psychol.* an apparent abnormal inability to perceive an object.

negative polarity *n Grammar.* the grammatical character of a word or phrase, such as *ever* or *any,* that may normally only be used in a semantically or syntactically negative or interrogative context.

negative-raising *n Transformational grammar.* a rule that moves a negative element out of the complement clause of certain verbs, such as *think,* into the main clause, as in the derivation of *He doesn't think that he'll finish.*

negative reinforcement *n Psychol.* the reinforcing of a response by giving an aversive stimulus when the response is not made and omitting the aversive stimulus when the response is made.

negative resistance *n* a characteristic of certain electronic components in which an increase in the applied voltage increases the resistance, producing a proportional decrease in current.

negative sign *n* the symbol (−) used to indicate a negative quantity or a subtraction; minus sign.

negative tax *n* a payment by the State to a person with a low income, the magnitude of the payment increasing as the income decreases. It is regarded as a form of social welfare. Also called: **negative income tax.**

negativism ('nɛgətɪv,ɪzəm) *n* **1** a tendency to be or a state of being unconstructively critical. **2** any sceptical or derisive system of thought. **3** *Psychiatry.* refusal to do what is expected or suggested or the tendency to do the opposite. ▸ **'negativist** *n, adj* ▸ **,negativ'istic** *adj*

negator (nɪ'geɪtə) *n Electronics.* another name for **NOT circuit.**

negatron ('nɛgə,trɒn) *n* an obsolete word for **electron.** [C20: from NEGA(TIVE + ELEC)TRON]

Negev ('nɛgɛv) *or* **Negeb** ('nɛgɛb) *n* the S part of Israel, on the Gulf of Aqaba: a triangular-shaped semidesert region, with large areas under irrigation; scene of fighting between Israeli and Egyptian forces in 1948. Chief town: Beersheba. Area: 12 820 sq. km (4950 sq. miles).

neglect (nɪ'glɛkt) *vb* (*tr*) **1** to fail to give due care, attention, or time to: *to neglect a child.* **2** to fail (to do something) through thoughtlessness or carelessness: *he neglected to tell her.* **3** to ignore or disregard: *she neglected his frantic signals.* ◆ *n* **4** lack of due care or attention; negligence: *the child starved through neglect.* **5** the act or an instance of neglecting or the state of being neglected. [C16: from Latin *neglegere* to neglect, from *nec* not + *legere* to select] ▸ **ne'glecter** *or* **ne'glector** *n*

neglectful (nɪ'glɛktfʊl) *adj* (when *postpositive,* foll. by *of*) not giving due care and attention (to); careless; heedless. ▸ **ne'glectfully** *adv* ▸ **ne'glectfulness** *n*

negligee *or* **negligée** ('nɛglɪˌʒeɪ) *n* **1** a woman's light dressing gown, esp. one that is lace-trimmed. **2** any informal attire. [C18: from French *négligée,* past participle (fem) of *négliger* to NEGLECT]

negligence ('nɛglɪdʒəns) *n* **1** the state or quality of being negligent. **2** a negligent act. **3** *Law.* a civil wrong whereby the defendant is in breach of a legal duty of care, resulting in injury to the plaintiff.

negligent ('nɛglɪdʒənt) *adj* **1** habitually neglecting duties, responsibilities, etc.; lacking attention, care, or concern; neglectful. **2** careless or nonchalant. ▸ **'negligently** *adv*

negligible ('nɛglɪdʒəbᵊl) *adj* so small, unimportant, etc., as to be not worth considering; insignificant. ▸ **ˌnegligi'bility** *or* **'negligibleness** *n* ▸ **'negligibly** *adv*

negotiable (nɪ'gəʊʃəbᵊl) *adj* **1** able to be negotiated. **2** (of a bill of exchange, promissory note, etc.) legally transferable in title from one party to another. ▸ **neˌgotia'bility** *n*

negotiable instrument *n* a legal document, such as a cheque or bill of exchange, that is freely negotiable.

negotiant (nɪ'gəʊʃɪənt) *n* a person, nation, organization, etc. involved in a negotiation.

negotiate (nɪ'gəʊʃɪˌeɪt) *vb* **1** to work or talk (with others) to achieve (a transaction, an agreement, etc.). **2** (*tr*) to succeed in passing through, around, or over: *to negotiate a mountain pass.* **3** (*tr*) *Finance.* **3a** to transfer (a negotiable commercial paper) by endorsement to another in return for value received. **3b** to sell (financial assets). **3c** to arrange for (a loan). [C16: from Latin *negōtiārī* to do business, from *negōtium* business, from *nec* not + *ōtium* leisure] ▸ **ne'goti,ator** *n*

negotiation (nɪˌgəʊʃɪ'eɪʃən) *n* **1** a discussion set up or intended to produce a settlement or agreement. **2** the act or process of negotiating.

Negress ('ni:grɪs) *n* a female Black person.

Negrillo (nɪ'grɪləʊ) *n, pl* **-los** *or* **-loes.** a member of a dwarfish Negroid race of central and southern Africa. [C19: from Spanish, diminutive of *negro* black]

Negri Sembilan ('nɛgrɪ sɛm'bi:lən) *n* a state of S Peninsular Malaysia: mostly mountainous, with large areas under paddy and rubber. Capital: Seremban. Pop.: 723 900 (1993 est.). Area: 6643 sq. km (2565 sq. miles).

Negritic (nɪ'grɪtɪk) *adj* relating to the Negroes or the Negritos.

Negrito (nɪ'gri:təʊ) *n, pl* **-tos** *or* **-toes.** a member of any of various dwarfish Negroid peoples of SE Asia and Melanesia. [C19: from Spanish, diminutive of *negro* black]

negritude ('ni:grɪˌtju:d, 'nɛg-) *n* **1** the fact of being a Negro. **2** awareness and cultivation of the Negro heritage, values, and culture. [C20: from French, from *nègre* NEGRO¹]

Negro¹ ('ni:grəʊ) *Old-fashioned.* ◆ *n, pl* **-groes. 1** a member of any of the dark-skinned indigenous peoples of Africa and their descendants elsewhere. ◆ *adj* **2** relating to or characteristic of Negroes. [C16: from Spanish or Portuguese: black, from Latin *niger* black] ▸ **'Negroˌism** *n*

Negro² ('neɪgrəʊ, 'nɛg-) *n* **Río. 1** a river in NW South America, rising in E Colombia (as the Guainía) and flowing east, then south as part of the border between Colombia and Venezuela, entering Brazil and continuing southeast to join the Amazon at Manáus. Length: about 2250 km (1400 miles). **2** a river in S central Argentina, formed by the confluence of the Neuquén and Limay Rivers and flowing east and southeast to the Atlantic. Length: about 1014 km (630 miles). **3** a river in central Uruguay, rising in S Brazil and flowing southwest into the Uruguay River. Length: about 467 km (290 miles).

Negroid ('ni:grɔɪd) *adj* **1** denoting, relating to, or belonging to one of the major racial groups of mankind, characterized by brown-black skin, tightly-curled hair, a short nose, and full lips. This group includes the indigenous peoples of Africa south of the Sahara, their descendants elsewhere, and some Melanesian peoples. ◆ *n* **2** a member of this racial group.

Negrophil ('ni:grəʊfɪl) *or* **Negrophile** ('ni:grəʊˌfaɪl) *n* a person who admires Negroes and their culture. ▸ **Negrophilism** (ni:'grɒfɪˌlɪzəm) *n*

Negrophobe ('ni:grəʊˌfəʊb) *n* a person who dislikes or fears Negroes. ▸ **ˌNegro'phobia** *n* ▸ **ˌNegro'phobic** *adj*

Negropont ('nɛgrəʊˌpɒnt) *n* **1** the former English name for **Euboea. 2** the medieval English name for **Chalcis.**

Negros ('neɪgrəʊs; *Spanish* 'neɣrɔs) *n* an island of the central Philippines, one of the Visayan Islands. Capital: Bacolod. Pop.: 3 168 000 (1990 est.). Area: 13 670 sq. km (5278 sq. miles).

Negro spiritual ('ni:grəʊ) *n* a type of religious song originating among Black slaves in the American South.

negus ('ni:gəs) *n, pl* **-guses.** a hot drink of port and lemon juice, usually spiced and sweetened. [C18: named after Col. Francis *Negus* (died 1732), its English inventor]

Negus ('ni:gəs) *n, pl* **-guses.** a title of the emperor of Ethiopia. [from Amharic: king]

Neh. *Bible. abbrev. for* Nehemiah.

Nehemiah (ˌni:ɪ'maɪə) *n Old Testament.* **1** a Jewish official at the court of Artaxerxes, king of Persia, who in 444 B.C. became a leader in the rebuilding of Jerusalem after the Babylonian captivity. **2** the book recounting the acts of Nehemiah.

Nehru ('nɛəru:) *n* **1 Jawaharlal** (dʒəwəhə'lɑ:l). 1889–1964, Indian statesman and nationalist leader. He spent several periods in prison for his nationalist activities and practised a policy of noncooperation with Britain during World War II. He was the first prime minister of the republic of India (1947–64). **2** his father, **Motilal** (məʊtɪ'lɑ:l), known as *Pandit Nehru.* 1861–1931, Indian nationalist, lawyer, and journalist; first president of the reconstructed Indian National Congress.

neigh (neɪ) *n* **1** the high-pitched cry of a horse; whinny. ◆ *vb* **2** (*intr*) to make a neigh or a similar noise. **3** (*tr*) to utter with a sound like a neigh. [Old English *hnǣgan;* related to Old Saxon *hnēgian*]

neighbour *or U.S.* **neighbor** ('neɪbə) *n* **1** a person who lives near or next to another. **2a** a person or thing near or next to another. **2b** (*as modifier*): *neighbour states.* ◆ *vb* **3** (when *intr,* often foll. by *on*) to be or live close (to a person or thing). [Old English *nēahbūr,* from *nēah* NIGH + *būr, gebūr* dweller; see BOOR] ▸ **'neighbouring** *or U.S.* **'neighboring** *adj*

neighbourhood *or U.S.* **neighborhood** ('neɪbəˌhʊd) *n* **1** the immediate environment; surroundings; vicinity. Related adj: **vicinal. 2** a district where people live. **3** the people in a particular area; neighbours. **4** neighbourly feeling. **5** *Maths.* the set of all points whose distance from a given point is less than a specified value. **6** (*modifier*) of or for a neighbourhood: *a neighbourhood community worker.* **7 in the neighbourhood of.** approximately (a given number).

neighbourhood watch *n* a scheme under which members of a community agree together to take responsibility for keeping an eye on each other's property, as a way of preventing crime.

neighbourly *or U.S.* **neighborly** ('neɪbəlɪ) *adj* kind, friendly, or sociable, as befits a neighbour. ▸ **'neighbourliness** *or U.S.* **'neighborliness** *n*

Neill (ni:l) *n* **A(lexander) S(utherland).** 1883–1973, Scottish educationalist and writer, who put his progressive educational theories into practice at Summerhill school (founded 1921).

Neisse ('naɪsə) *n* **1** Also called: **Glatzer Neisse** ('glɑ:tsə). Polish name: **Nysa.** a river in SW Poland, rising on the northern Czech border, and flowing northeast to join the Oder near Brzeg. Length: about 193 km (120 miles). **2** Also called: **Lusatian Neisse.** a river in E Europe, rising near Liberec in the Czech Republic and flowing north to join the Oder: forms part of the German-Polish border. Length: 225 km (140 miles).

neither ('naɪðə, 'ni:ðə) *determiner* **1a** not one nor the other (of two); not either: *neither foot is swollen.* **1b** (*as pronoun*): *neither can win.* ◆ *conj* **2** (*coordinating*) **2a** (used preceding alternatives joined by *nor*) not: *neither John nor Mary nor Joe went.* **2b** another word for **nor** (sense 2). ◆ *adv* **3** (*sentence modifier*) *Not standard.* another word for **either** (sense 4). [C13 (literally, *ne either* not either): changed from Old English *nāwther,* from *nāhwæther,*from *nā* not + *hwæther* which of two; see WHETHER]

USAGE A verb following a compound subject that uses *neither...(nor)* should be in the singular if both subjects are in the singular: *neither Jack nor John has done the work.*

Nejd (nɛʒd, neɪd) *n* a region of central Saudi Arabia: formerly an independent sultanate of Arabia; united with Hejaz to form the kingdom of Saudi Arabia (1932).

nek (nɛk) *n* (*cap. when part of name*) *S. African.* a mountain pass: *Lundeans Nek.*

Nekrasov (*Russian* nɪ'krasəf) *n* **Nikolai Alekseyevich** (nika'laj alɪk'sjejɪvitʃ). 1821–77, Russian poet, who wrote chiefly about the sufferings of the peasantry.

nekton ('nɛktɒn) *n* the population of free-swimming animals that inhabits the middle depths of a sea or lake. Compare **plankton.** [C19: via German from Greek *nēkton* a swimming thing, from *nēkhein* to swim] ▸ **nek'tonic** *adj*

nelly ('nɛlɪ) *n* **not on your nelly.** (*sentence substitute*). *Brit. slang.* not under any circumstances; certainly not.

nelson ('nɛlsən) *n* any wrestling hold in which a wrestler places his arm or arms under his opponent's arm or arms from behind and exerts pressure with his palms on the back of his opponent's neck. See **full nelson, half-nelson.** [C19: from a proper name]

Nelson¹ ('nɛlsən) *n* **1** a town in NW England, in E Lancashire: textile industry. Pop.: 29 120 (1991). **2** a port in New Zealand, on N South Island on Tasman Bay. Pop.: 51 200 (1995 est.). **3 River.** a river in central Canada, in N central Manitoba, flowing from Lake Winnipeg northeast to Hudson Bay. Length: about 650 km (400 miles).

Nelson² ('nɛlsən) *n* **1 Horatio,** Viscount Nelson. 1758–1805, British naval commander during the Revolutionary and Napoleonic Wars. He became rear admiral in 1797 after the battle of Cape St Vincent and in 1798 almost destroyed the French fleet at the battle of the Nile. He was killed at Trafalgar (1805) after defeating Villeneuve's fleet. **2 Willie.** born 1933, U.S. country singer and songwriter.

nelumbo (nɪ'lʌmbəʊ) *n, pl* **-bos.** either of the two aquatic plants of the genus *Nelumbo:* family *Nelumbonaceae.* See **lotus** (sense 4), **water chinquapin.** [C19: New Latin, from Sinhalese *nelumbu* lotus]

Neman *or* **Nyeman** (*Russian* 'njemən) *n* a river in NE Europe, rising in Belarus and flowing northwest through Lithuania to the Baltic. Length: 937 km (582 miles). Polish name: **Niemen.**

nemathelminth (ˌnɛmə'θɛlmɪnθ) *n* any unsegmented worm of the group *Nemathelminthes,* including the nematodes, nematomorphs, and acanthocephalans.

nematic (nɪ'mætɪk) *adj Chem.* (of a substance) existing in or having a mesomorphic state in which a linear orientation of the molecules causes anisotropic properties. Compare **smectic.** See also **liquid crystal.** [C20: NEMAT(O)- (referring to the threadlike chains of molecules in liquid) + -IC]

nemato- *or before a vowel* **nemat-** *combining form.* indicating a threadlike form: *nematocyst.* [from Greek *nēma* thread]

nematocyst ('nɛmətəˌsɪst, nɪ'mætə-) *n* a structure in coelenterates, such as jellyfish, consisting of a capsule containing a hollow coiled thread that can be everted to sting or paralyse prey and enemies. ► **ˌnemato'cystic** *adj*

nematode ('nɛməˌtəʊd) *n* any unsegmented worm of the phylum (or class) *Nematoda,* having a tough outer cuticle. The group includes free-living forms and disease-causing parasites, such as the hookworm and filaria. Also called: **nematode worm, roundworm.**

Nembutal ('nɛmbjʊˌtɑːl) *n* a trademark for **pentobarbitone sodium.**

nem. con. *abbrev. for* nemine contradicente. [Latin: no-one contradicting; unanimously]

Nemea (nɪ'miːə) *n* (in ancient Greece) a valley in N Argolis in the NE Peloponnese; site of the **Nemean Games,** a Panhellenic festival and athletic competition held every other year. ► **Ne'mean** *adj*

Nemean lion *n Greek myth.* an enormous lion that was strangled by Hercules as his first labour.

nemertean (nɪ'mɜːtɪən) *or* **nemertine** ('nɛməˌtaɪn) *n* **1** Also called: **ribbon worm.** any soft flattened ribbon-like marine worm of the phylum (or class) *Nemertea* (or *Nemertina*), having an eversible threadlike proboscis. ◆ *adj* **2** of, relating to, or belonging to the *Nemertea.* [C19: via New Latin from Greek *Nēmertēs* a NEREID[1]]

nemesia (nɪ'miːʒə) *n* any plant of the southern African scrophulariaceous genus *Nemesia:* cultivated for their brightly coloured (often reddish) flowers. [C19: New Latin, from Greek *nemesion,* name of a plant resembling this]

Nemesis ('nɛmɪsɪs) *n, pl* **-ses** (-ˌsiːz). **1** *Greek myth.* the goddess of retribution and vengeance. **2** (*sometimes not cap.*) any agency of retribution and vengeance. [C16: via Latin from Greek: righteous wrath, from *némein* to distribute what is due]

nemophila (nə'mɒfɪlə) *n* any of a genus, *Nemophila,* of low-growing hairy annual plants, esp. *N. menziesii,* grown for its blue or white flowers: family *Hydrophyllaceae.* [New Latin, from Greek *nemos* a grove + *philein* to love]

nene ('neɪˌneɪ) *n* a rare black-and-grey short-winged Hawaiian goose, *Branta sandvicensis,* having partly webbed feet. [from Hawaiian]

neo- *or sometimes before a vowel* **ne-** *combining form.* **1** (*sometimes cap.*) new, recent, or a new or modern form or development: *neoclassicism; neocolonialism.* **2** (*usually cap.*) the most recent subdivision of a geological period: *Neogene.* [from Greek *neos* new]

neoanthropic (ˌniːəʊæn'θrɒpɪk) *adj Anthropol.* of, relating to, or resembling modern man.

neoarsphenamine (ˌniːəʊɑːs'fɛnəˌmiːn, -fɪ'næmɪn) *n* a derivative of arsenic used in treating syphilis.

Neocene ('niːəˌsiːn) *adj, n* a former word for **Neogene.**

neoclassicism (ˌniːəʊ'klæsɪˌsɪzəm) *n* **1** a late 18th- and early 19th-century style in architecture, decorative art, and fine art, based on the imitation of surviving classical models and types. **2** *Music.* a movement of the 1920s, involving Hindemith, Stravinsky, etc., that sought to avoid the emotionalism of late romantic music by reviving the use of counterpoint, forms such as the classical suite, and small instrumental ensembles. ► **neoclassical** (ˌniːəʊ'klæsɪk°l) *or* **ˌneo'classic** *adj* ► **ˌneo'classicist** *n*

neocolonialism (ˌniːəʊkə'ləʊnɪəˌlɪzəm) *n* (in the modern world) political control by an outside power of a country that is in theory sovereign and independent, esp. through the domination of its economy. ► **ˌneoco'lonial** *adj* ► **ˌneoco'lonialist** *n*

Neo-Darwinism (ˌniːəʊ'dɑːwɪnˌɪzəm) *n* a modern theory of evolution that relates Darwinism to the occurrence of inheritable variation by genetic mutation. ► **ˌNeo-Dar'winian** *adj, n*

neodymium (ˌniːəʊ'dɪmɪəm) *n* a toxic silvery-white metallic element of the lanthanide series, occurring principally in monazite: used in colouring glass. Symbol: Nd; atomic no.: 60; atomic wt.: 144.24; valency: 3; relative density: 6.80 and 7.00 (depending on allotrope); melting pt.: 1024°C; boiling pt.: 3127°C. [C19: New Latin; see NEO- + DIDYMIUM]

Neogaea (ˌniːəʊ'dʒiːə) *n* a zoogeographical area comprising the Neotropical region. Compare **Arctogaea, Notogaea.** [C19: New Latin, from NEO- + GAEA, from Greek *gaia* earth] ► **ˌNeo'gaean** *adj*

Neogene ('niːəˌdʒiːn) *adj* **1** of, denoting, or formed during the Miocene and Pliocene epochs. ◆ *n* **2 the.** the Neogene period or system.

neogothic (ˌnɪəʊ'gɒθɪk) *n* another name for **Gothic Revival.**

neoimpressionism (ˌniːəʊɪm'prɛʃəˌnɪzəm) *n* a movement in French painting initiated mainly by Seurat in the 1880s and combining his vivid colour technique with strictly formal composition. See also **pointillism.** ► **ˌneoim'pressionist** *n, adj*

Neo-Lamarckism (ˌniːəʊlə'mɑːkɪzəm) *n* a modern theory of evolution based on Lamarckism and emphasizing the influence of environmental factors on genetic changes. ► **ˌNeo-La'marckian** *adj, n*

Neo-Latin (ˌniːəʊ'lætɪn) *n* **1** another term for **New Latin.** ◆ *adj* **2** denoting or relating to New Latin. **3** denoting or relating to language that developed from Latin; Romance.

neolith ('niːəʊlɪθ) *n* a Neolithic stone implement.

Neolithic (ˌniːəʊ'lɪθɪk) *n* **1** the cultural period that lasted in SW Asia from about 9000 to 6000 B.C. and in Europe from about 4000 to 2400 B.C. and was characterized by primitive crop growing and stock rearing and the use of polished stone and flint tools and weapons. ◆ *adj* **2** relating to this period. ◆ See also **Mesolithic, Palaeolithic.**

neologism (nɪ'ɒləˌdʒɪzəm) *or* **neology** *n, pl* **-gisms** *or* **-gies. 1** a newly coined word, or a phrase or familiar word used in a new sense. **2** the practice of using or introducing neologisms. **3** *Rare.* a tendency towards adopting new views, esp. rationalist views, in matters of religion. [C18: via French from NEO- + *-logism,* from Greek *logos* word, saying] ► **ne'ologist** *n* ► **neˌolo'gistic, neˌolo'gistical,** *or* **neological** (ˌnɪə'lɒdʒɪk°l) *adj* ► **neˌolo'gistically** *or* **ˌneo'logically** *adv*

neologize *or* **neologise** (nɪ'ɒləˌdʒaɪz) *vb* (*intr*) to invent or use neologisms.

Neo-Melanesian *n* an English-based creole language widely spoken in the SW Pacific, with borrowings from other languages, esp. Motu. Also called: **Beach-la-Mar.**

neomycin (ˌniːəʊ'maɪsɪn) *n* an antibiotic obtained from the bacterium *Streptomyces fradiae,* administered locally in the treatment of skin and eye infections or orally for bowel infections. Formula: $C_{12}H_{26}N_4O_6$. [C20: from NEO- + Greek *mukēs* fungus + -IN]

neon ('niːɒn) *n* **1** a colourless odourless rare gaseous element, an inert gas occurring in trace amounts in the atmosphere: used in illuminated signs and lights. Symbol: Ne; atomic no.: 10; atomic wt.: 20.1797; valency: 0; density: 0.89990 kg/m^3; melting pt.: –248.59°C; boiling pt.: –246.08°C. **2** (*modifier*) of or illuminated by neon or neon lamps: *neon sign.* [C19: via New Latin from Greek *neon* new]

neonate ('niːəʊˌneɪt) *n* a newborn child, esp. in the first week of life and up to four weeks old. ► **ˌneo'natal** *adj* ► **ˌneo'natally** *adv*

neonatology (ˌniːəʊnə'tɒlədʒɪ) *n* the branch of medicine concerned with the development and disorders of newborn babies. ► **ˌneona'tologist** *n*

neon lamp *n* a glass bulb or tube containing neon at low pressure that gives a pink or red glow when a voltage is applied.

neo-orthodoxy (ˌniːəʊ'ɔːθəˌdɒksɪ) *n* a movement in 20th-century Protestantism, reasserting certain older traditional Christian doctrines. ► **ˌneo-'orthodox** *adj*

neophilia (ˌniːəʊ'fɪlɪə) *n* a tendency to like anything new; love of novelty. ► **'neoˌphiliac** *n*

neophobia (ˌniːəʊ'fəʊbɪə) *n* a tendency to dislike anything new; fear of novelty. ► **'neoˌphobe** *n* ► **ˌneo'phobic** *adj*

neophyte ('niːəʊˌfaɪt) *n* **1** a person newly converted to a religious faith. **2** *R.C. Church.* a novice in a religious order. **3** a novice or beginner. [C16: via Church Latin from New Testament Greek *neophutos* recently planted, from *neos* new + *phuton* a plant] ► **neophytic** (ˌniːəʊ'fɪtɪk) *adj*

neoplasm ('niːəʊˌplæzəm) *n Pathol.* any abnormal new growth of tissue; tumour. ► **neoplastic** (ˌniːəʊ'plæstɪk) *adj*

neoplasticism (ˌniːəʊ'plæstɪˌsɪzəm) *n* the style of abstract painting evolved by Mondrian and the Dutch de Stijl movement, characterized by the use of horizontal and vertical lines and planes and by black, white, grey, and primary colours.

neoplasty ('niːəʊˌplæstɪ) *n* the surgical formation of new tissue structures or repair of damaged structures.

Neo-Platonism *or* **Neoplatonism** (ˌniːəʊ'pleɪtəˌnɪzəm) *n* a philosophical system which was first developed in the 3rd century A.D. as a synthesis of Platonic, Pythagorean, and Aristotelian elements, and which, although originally opposed to Christianity, later incorporated it. It dominated European thought until the 13th century and re-emerged during the Renaissance. ► **Neo-Platonic** (ˌniːəʊplə'tɒnɪk) *adj* ► **ˌNeo-'Platonist** *n, adj*

neoprene ('niːəʊˌpriːn) *n* a synthetic rubber obtained by the polymerization of chloroprene. It is resistant to oil and ageing and is used in waterproof products, such as diving suits, paints, and adhesives. [C20: from NEO- + PR(OPYL) + -ENE]

Neoptolemus (ˌniːɒp'tɒləməs) *n Greek myth.* a son of Achilles and slayer of King Priam of Troy. Also called: **Pyrrhus.**

neorealism (ˌniːəʊ'rɪːəlɪzəm) *n Films.* a movement to depict directly the poor in society: originating in postwar Italy. ► **ˌneo'realist** *n, adj*

neoteny (nɪ'ɒtənɪ) *n* the persistence of larval or fetal features in the adult form of an animal. For example, the adult axolotl, a salamander, retains larval external gills. See also **paedogenesis.** [C19: from New Latin *neotenia,* from Greek NEO- + *teinein* to stretch] ► **ne'otenous** *adj*

neoteric (ˌniːəʊ'tɛrɪk) *Rare.* ◆ *adj* **1** belonging to a new fashion or trend; modern: *a neoteric genre.* ◆ *n* **2** a new writer or philosopher. [C16: via Late Latin from Greek *neōterikos* young, fresh, from *neoteros* younger, more recent, from *neos* new, recent] ► **ˌneo'terically** *adv*

Neotropical (ˌniːəʊ'trɒpɪk°l) *adj* of or denoting a zoogeographical region consisting of South America and North America south of the tropic of Cancer.

neotype ('niːəʊˌtaɪp) *n Biology.* a specimen selected to replace a type specimen that has been lost or destroyed.

Neozoic (ˌniːəʊ'zəʊɪk) *adj* of or formed at any time after the end of the Mesozoic era.

NEP *abbrev. for* New Economic Policy.

Nepal (nɪ'pɔːl) *n* a kingdom in S Asia: the world's only Hindu kingdom; united in 1768 by the Gurkhas; consists of swampy jungle in the south and great massifs, valleys, and gorges of the Himalayas over the rest of the country, with many peaks over 8000 m (26 000 ft.) (notably Everest and Kangchenjunga). A multiparty democracy was instituted in 1990. Official language: Nepali. Official religion: Hinduism; Mahayana Buddhist minority. Currency: rupee. Capital: Katmandu. Pop.: 21 959 000 (1998 est.). Area: 147 181 sq. km (56 815 sq. miles). ► **Nepalese** (ˌnɛpə'liːz) *adj, n*

Nepali (nɪ'pɔːlɪ) *n* **1** the official language of Nepal, also spoken in Sikkim and parts of India. It forms the E group of Pahari and belongs to the Indic branch of Indo-European. **2** (*pl* **-pali** *or* **-palis**) a native or inhabitant of Nepal; a Nepalese. ◆ *adj* **3** of or relating to Nepal, its inhabitants, or their language; Nepalese.

nepenthe (nɪ'pɛnθɪ) *n* **1** a drug, or the plant providing it, that ancient writers referred to as a means of forgetting grief or trouble. **2** anything that produces sleep, forgetfulness, or pleasurable dreaminess. [C16: via Latin from Greek *nēpenthes* sedative made from a herb, from *nē-* not + *penthos* grief] ▸ **ne'penthean** *adj*

neper ('neɪpə, 'ni:-) *n* a unit expressing the ratio of two quantities, esp. amplitudes in telecommunications, equal to the natural logarithm of the ratio of the two quantities. Symbol: Np, N [C20: named after John NAPIER (1550–1617); the name was approved in 1928]

nepeta ('nɛpətə) *n* See **catmint.** [Latin: catmint]

nepheline ('nɛfɪlɪn, -ˌli:n) *or* **nephelite** ('nɛfɪˌlaɪt) *n* a whitish mineral consisting of sodium potassium aluminium silicate in hexagonal crystalline form: used in the manufacture of glass and ceramics. Formula: $(Na,K)(AlSi)_2O_4$. [C19: from French *néphéline,* from Greek *nephelē* cloud, so called because pieces of it become cloudy if dipped in nitric acid]

nephelinite ('nɛfɪlɪˌnaɪt) *n* a fine-grained basic laval rock consisting of pyroxene and nepheline.

nephelometer (ˌnɛfɪ'lɒmɪtə) *n Chem.* an instrument for measuring the size or density of particles suspended in a fluid. [C19 (in the sense: an instrument for measuring the cloudiness of the sky): from Greek *nephelē* cloud + -O- + -METER] ▸ **nephelometric** (ˌnɛfɪləʊ'mɛtrɪk) *adj* ▸ **ˌnephe'lometry** *n*

nephew ('nɛvju:, 'nɛf-) *n* a son of one's sister or brother. [C13: from Old French *neveu,* from Latin *nepōs;* related to Old English *nefa,* Old High German *nevo* relative]

nepho- *combining form.* concerning cloud or clouds. [from Greek *nephos* cloud]

nephogram ('nɛfəˌgræm) *n Meteorol.* a photograph of a cloud.

nephograph ('nɛfəˌgrɑ:f, -ˌgræf) *n* an instrument for photographing clouds.

nephology (nɪ'fɒlədʒɪ) *n* the study of clouds. ▸ **nephological** (ˌnɛfə'lɒdʒɪkᵊl) *adj* ▸ **ne'phologist** *n*

nephoscope ('nɛfəˌskəʊp) *n* an instrument for measuring the altitude, velocity, and direction of movement of clouds.

nephralgia (nɪ'frældʒɪə) *n* pain in a kidney. ▸ **ne'phralgic** *adj*

nephrectomy (nɪ'frɛktəmɪ) *n, pl* **-mies.** surgical removal of a kidney.

nephridium (nɪ'frɪdɪəm) *n, pl* **-ia** (-ɪə). a simple excretory organ of many invertebrates, consisting of a tube through which waste products pass to the exterior. [C19: New Latin: little kidney] ▸ **ne'phridial** *adj*

nephrite ('nɛfraɪt) *n* a tough fibrous amphibole mineral: a variety of jade consisting of calcium magnesium silicate in monoclinic crystalline form. Formula: $Ca_2Mg_5Si_8O_{22}(OH)_2$. Also called: **kidney stone.** [C18: via German *Nephrit* from Greek *nephrós* kidney, so called because it was thought to be beneficial in kidney disorders]

nephritic (nɪ'frɪtɪk) *adj* **1** of or relating to the kidneys. **2** relating to or affected with nephritis.

nephritis (nɪ'fraɪtɪs) *n* inflammation of a kidney.

nephro- *or before a vowel* **nephr-** *combining form.* kidney or kidneys: *nephrotomy.* [from Greek *nephros*]

nephrolepis (ˌnɛfrə'li:pɪs) *n* any fern of the tropical genus *Nephrolepis,* some species of which are grown as ornamental greenhouse or house plants for their handsome deeply-cut drooping fronds: family *Polypodiaceae.* Also called **ladder fern, Boston fern.** [New Latin, from Greek *nephros* kidney + *lepsis* scale (from the shape of the indusium)]

nephrology (nɪ'frɒlədgɪ) *n* the branch of medicine concerned with diseases of the kidney. ▸ **ne'phrologist** *n*

nephron ('nɛfrɒn) *n* any of the minute urine-secreting tubules that form the functional unit of the kidneys.

nephroscope ('nɛfrəˌskəʊp) *n* a tubular medical instrument inserted through an incision in the skin to enable examination of a kidney. ▸ **nephroscopy** (nɪ'frɒskəpɪ) *n*

nephrosis (nɪ'frəʊsɪs) *n* any noninflammatory degenerative kidney disease. ▸ **nephrotic** (nɪ'frɒtɪk) *adj*

nephrotomy (nɪ'frɒtəmɪ) *n, pl* **-mies.** surgical incision into a kidney.

nepionic (ˌnɛpɪ'ɒnɪk) *adj Zoology.* of or relating to the juvenile period in the life cycle of an organism.

nepit ('ni:pɪt) *n* another word for **nit**[4].

ne plus ultra *Latin.* ('neɪ 'plʊs 'ʊltrɑ:) *n* the extreme or perfect point or state. [literally: not more beyond (that is, go no further), allegedly a warning to sailors inscribed on the Pillars of Hercules at Gibraltar]

Nepos ('ni:pɒs) *n* **Cornelius.** ?100–?25 B.C., Roman historian and biographer; author of *De Viris illustribus.*

nepotism ('nɛpəˌtɪzəm) *n* favouritism shown to relatives or close friends by those with power or influence. [C17: from Italian *nepotismo,* from *nepote* NEPHEW, from the former papal practice of granting special favours to nephews or other relatives] ▸ **nepotic** (nɪ'pɒtɪk) *or* **ˌnepo'tistic** *adj* ▸ **'nepotist** *n*

Neptune[1] ('nɛptju:n) *n* the Roman god of the sea. Greek counterpart: **Poseidon.**

Neptune[2] ('nɛptju:n) *n* the eighth planet from the sun, having eight satellites, the largest being Triton and Nereid, and a faint planar system of rings or ring fragments. Mean distance from sun: 4497 million km; period of revolution around sun: 164.8 years; period of rotation: 14 to 16 hours; diameter and mass: 4.0 and 17.2 times that of earth respectively.

Neptunian (nɛp'tju:nɪən) *adj* **1** of or relating to the Roman god Neptune or the sea. **2** of, occurring on, or relating to the planet Neptune. **3** *Geology.* (of sedimentary rock formations such as dykes) formed under water.

neptunium (nɛp'tju:nɪəm) *n* a silvery metallic transuranic element synthesized in the production of plutonium and occurring in trace amounts in uranium ores. Symbol: Np; atomic no.: 93; half-life of most stable isotope, ^{237}Np: 2.14×10^6 years; valency: 3, 4, 5, or 6; relative density: 20.25; melting pt.: 639±1°C; boiling pt.: 3902°C (est.). [C20: from NEPTUNE[2], the planet beyond Uranus, because neptunium is the element beyond uranium in the periodic table]

neptunium series *n* a radioactive series that starts with plutonium-241 and ends with bismuth-209. Neptunium-237 is the longest-lived member of the series. The series does not occur in nature.

neral ('nɪəræl) *n Chem.* the *trans-* isomer of citral. [C20: from *nerol* (an alcohol from NEROLI OIL) + -AL[3]]

NERC *abbrev. for* Natural Environment Research Council.

nerd *or* **nurd** (nɜ:d) *n Slang.* **1** a boring or unpopular person, esp. one obsessed with something specified: *a computer nerd* **2** a stupid and feeble person. ▸ **'nerdish** *or* **'nurdish** *adj* ▸ **'nerdy** *or* **'nurdy** *adj*

Nereid[1] ('nɪərɪɪd) *n, pl* **Nereides** (nə'ri:əˌdi:z). *Greek myth.* any of the 50 sea nymphs who were the daughters of the sea god Nereus. [C17: via Latin from Greek *Nērēid,* from NEREUS; compare Latin *nāre* to swim]

Nereid[2] ('nɪərɪɪd) *n* a satellite of the planet Neptune, in a large and highly eccentric orbit.

nereis ('nɪərɪɪs) *n* any polychaete worm of the genus *Nereis.* See **ragworm.** [C18: from Latin; see NEREID[1]]

Nereus ('nɪərɪˌu:s) *n Greek myth.* a sea god who lived in the depths of the sea with his wife Doris and their daughters the Nereides.

Neri ('nɪərɪ) *n* **Saint Philip.** Italian name *Filippo de' Neri.* 1515–95, Italian priest; founder of the Congregation of the Oratory (1564). Feast day: May 26.

nerine (nə'ri:nɪ) *n* any plant of the bulbous S. African genus *Nerine,* related to the amaryllis; several species are grown as garden or pot plants for their beautiful pink, orange, red, or white flowers. *N. sarniensis* is the pink-flowered Guernsey lily family *Amaryllidaceae.* [Latin, from Greek *nērēis* a sea nymph]

neritic (nɛ'rɪtɪk) *adj* of or formed in the region of shallow seas near a coastline. [C20: perhaps from Latin *nērīta* sea mussel, from Greek *nērítēs,* from NEREUS]

Nernst (*German* nɛrnst) *n* **Walther Hermann** ('valtər'hɛrman). 1864–1941, German physical chemist who formulated the third law of thermodynamics: Nobel prize for chemistry 1920.

Nernst heat theorem (nɛənst) *n* the principle that reactions in crystalline solids involve changes in entropy that tend to zero as the temperature approaches absolute zero. See **law of thermodynamics** (sense 1).

Nero ('nɪərəʊ) *n* full name *Nero Claudius Caesar Drusus Germanicus;* original name *Lucius Domitius Ahenobarbus.* 37–68 A.D., Roman emperor (54–68). He became notorious for his despotism and cruelty, and was alleged to have started the fire (64) that destroyed a large part of Rome.

neroli oil *or* **neroli** ('nɪərəlɪ) *n* a brown oil distilled from the flowers of various orange trees, esp. the Seville orange: used in perfumery. [C17: named after Anne Marie de la Tremoïlle of *Neroli,* French-born Italian princess believed to have discovered it]

Neruda (*Spanish* ne'ruða) *n* **Pablo** ('paβlo), real name *Neftali Ricardo Reyes.* 1904–73, Chilean poet. His works include *Veinte poemas de amor y una canción desesperada* (1924) and *Canto general* (1950), an epic history of the Americas: Nobel prize for literature 1971.

Nerva ('nɜ:və) *n* full name *Marcus Cocceius Nerva.* ?30–98 A.D., Roman emperor (96–98), who introduced some degree of freedom after the repressive reign of Domitian. He adopted Trajan as his son and successor.

Nerval (*French* nɛrval) *n* **Gérard de** (ʒerar də), real name *Gérard Labrunie.* 1808–55, French poet, noted esp. for the sonnets of mysticism, myth, and private passion in *Les Chimères* (1854).

nervate ('nɜ:veɪt) *adj* (of leaves) having veins.

nervation (nɜ:'veɪʃən) *or* **nervature** ('nɜ:vətʃə) *n* a less common word for **venation.**

nerve (nɜ:v) *n* **1** any of the cordlike bundles of fibres that conduct sensory or motor impulses between the brain or spinal cord and another part of the body. Related adj: **neural. 2** courage, bravery, or steadfastness. **3 lose one's nerve.** to become timid, esp. failing to perform some audacious act. **4** *Informal.* boldness or effrontery; impudence: *he had the nerve to swear at me.* **5** muscle or sinew (often in the phrase **strain every nerve**). **6** a large vein in a leaf. **7** any of the veins of an insect's wing. **8 touch, hit,** *or* **strike a** (**raw**) **nerve.** to mention or bring to mind a sensitive issue or subject. ◆ *vb* (*tr*) **9** to give courage to (oneself); steel (oneself). **10** to provide with nerve or nerves. ◆ See also **nerves.** [C16: from Latin *nervus;* related to Greek *neuron;* compare Sanskrit *snāvan* sinew]

nerve block *n* induction of anaesthesia in a specific part of the body by injecting a local anaesthetic close to the sensory nerves that supply it.

nerve cell *n* another name for **neurone.**

nerve centre *n* **1** a group of nerve cells associated with a specific function. **2** a principal source of control over any complex activity: *Wall Street is the financial nerve centre of America.*

nerve fibre *n* a threadlike extension of a nerve cell; axon.

nerve gas *n* (esp. in chemical warfare) any of various poisonous gases that have a paralysing effect on the central nervous system that can be fatal.

nerve impulse *n* the electrical wave transmitted along a nerve fibre, usually following stimulation of the nerve-cell body. See also **action potential.**

nerveless ('nɜ:vlɪs) *adj* **1** calm and collected. **2** listless or feeble. ▸ **'nervelessly** *adv* ▸ **'nervelessness** *n*

nerve-racking *or* **nerve-wracking** *adj* very distressing, exhausting, or harrowing.

nerves (nɜ:vz) *pl n Informal.* **1** the imagined source of emotional control: *my nerves won't stand it.* **2** anxiety, tension, or imbalance: *she's all nerves.* **3 bundle of nerves.** a very nervous person. **4 get on one's nerves.** to irritate, annoy, or upset one.

Nervi (*Italian* 'nɛrvi) *n* **Pier Luigi** (pjɛ:r lu'i:dʒi). 1891–1979, Italian engineer and architect; noted for his pioneering use of reinforced concrete as a decorative material. He codesigned the UNESCO building in Paris (1953).

nervine ('nɜ:vi:n) *adj* **1** having a soothing or calming effect upon the nerves.

◆ *n* **2** a nervine drug or agent. [C17: from New Latin *nervīnus,* from Latin *nervus* NERVE]

nerving ('nɜːvɪŋ) *n Vet. science.* surgical removal of part of a nerve trunk, usually because of chronic and disabling inflammation.

nervous ('nɜːvəs) *adj* **1** very excitable or sensitive; highly strung. **2** (often foll. by *of*) apprehensive or worried: *I'm nervous of traffic.* **3** of, relating to, or containing nerves; neural: *nervous tissue.* **4** affecting the nerves or nervous tissue: *a nervous disease.* **5** *Archaic.* active, vigorous, or forceful. ▸ **'nervously** *adv* ▸ **'nervousness** *n*

nervous breakdown *n* any mental illness not primarily of organic origin, in which the patient ceases to function properly, often accompanied by severely impaired concentration, anxiety, insomnia, and lack of self-esteem; used esp. of episodes of depression.

nervous system *n* the sensory and control apparatus of all multicellular animals above the level of sponges, consisting of a network of nerve cells (see **neurone**). See also **central nervous system.**

nervure ('nɜːvjʊə) *n* **1** *Entomol.* any of the stiff chitinous rods that form the supporting framework of an insect's wing; vein. **2** *Botany.* any of the veins or ribs of a leaf. [C19: from French; see NERVE, -URE]

nervy ('nɜːvɪ) *adj* **nervier, nerviest. 1** *Brit. informal.* tense or apprehensive. **2** having or needing bravery or endurance. **3** *U.S. and Canadian informal.* brash or cheeky. **4** *Archaic.* muscular; sinewy. ▸ **'nervily** *adv* ▸ **'nerviness** *n*

Nesbit ('nɛzbɪt) *n* **E(dith).** 1858–1924, British writer of children's books, including *The Phoenix and the Carpet* (1904) and *The Railway Children* (1906).

nescience ('nɛsɪəns) *n* a formal or literary word for **ignorance.** [C17: from Late Latin *nescientia,* from Latin *nescīre* to be ignorant of, from *ne* not + *scīre* to know; compare SCIENCE] ▸ **'nescient** *adj*

nesh (nɛʃ) *adj Dialect.* **1** sensitive to the cold. **2** timid or cowardly. [from Old English *hnesce;* related to Gothic *hnasqus* tender, soft; of obscure origin]

ness (nɛs) *n* **a** *Archaic.* a promontory or headland. **b** (*cap. as part of a name*): *Orford Ness.* [Old English *næs* headland; related to Old Norse *nes,* Old English *nasu* NOSE]

Ness (nɛs) *n* **Loch.** a lake in NW Scotland, in the Great Glen: said to be inhabited by a legendary aquatic monster. Length: 36 km (22.5 miles). Depth: 229 m (754 ft.).

-ness *suffix forming nouns chiefly from adjectives and participles.* indicating state, condition, or quality, or an instance of one of these: *greatness; selfishness; meaninglessness; a kindness.* [Old English *-nes,* of Germanic origin; related to Gothic *-nassus*]

nesselrode ('nɛsᵊlˌrəʊd) *n* a rich frozen pudding, made of chestnuts, eggs, cream, etc. [C19: named after Count NESSELRODE, whose chef invented the dish]

Nesselrode ('nɛsᵊlˌrəʊd; *Russian* nɪsɪl'rɔdə) *n* Count **Karl Robert.** 1780–1862, Russian diplomat: as foreign minister (1822–56), he negotiated the Treaty of Paris after the Crimean War (1856).

Nessus ('nɛsəs) *n Greek myth.* a centaur that killed Hercules. A garment dipped in its blood fatally poisoned Hercules, who had been given it by Deianira who thought it was a love charm.

nest (nɛst) *n* **1** a place or structure in which birds, fishes, insects, reptiles, mice, etc., lay eggs or give birth to young. **2** a number of animals of the same species and their young occupying a common habitat: *an ants' nest.* **3** a place fostering something undesirable: *a nest of thievery.* **4** the people in such a place: *a nest of thieves.* **5** a cosy or secluded place. **6** a set of things, usually of graduated sizes, designed to fit together: *a nest of tables.* **7** *Military.* a weapon emplacement: *a machine-gun nest.* ◆ *vb* **8** (*intr*) to make or inhabit a nest. **9** (*intr*) to hunt for birds' nests. **10** (*tr*) to place in a nest. [Old English; related to Latin *nīdus* (nest) and to BENEATH, SIT] ▸ **'nester** *n* ▸ **'nest,like** *adj*

nest box *or* **nesting box** *n* **1** a box in a henhouse in which domestic chickens lay eggs. **2** a box designed as a nesting place for wild birds and positioned in a garden, park, or reserve to encourage them to breed there.

nest egg *n* **1** a fund of money kept in reserve; savings. **2** a natural or artificial egg left in a nest to induce hens to lay their eggs in it.

nestle ('nɛsᵊl) *vb* **1** (*intr;* often foll. by *up* or *down*) to snuggle, settle, or cuddle closely. **2** (*intr*) to be in a sheltered or protected position; lie snugly. **3** (*tr*) to shelter or place snugly or partly concealed, as in a nest. [Old English *nestlian.* See NEST] ▸ **'nestler** *n*

nestling ('nɛstlɪŋ, 'nɛslɪŋ) *n* **1a** a young bird not yet fledged. **1b** (*as modifier*): *a nestling thrush.* **2** any young person or animal. [C14: from NEST + -LING[1]]

Nestor ('nɛstɔː) *n* **1** *Greek myth.* the oldest and wisest of the Greeks in the Trojan War. **2** (*sometimes not cap.*) a wise old man; sage.

Nestorianism (nɛ'stɔːrɪəˌnɪzəm) *n* the doctrine that Christ was two distinct persons, divine and human, implying a denial that the Virgin Mary was the mother of God. It is attributed to Nestorius and survives in the Iraqi Church. ▸ **Nes'torian** *n, adj*

Nestorius (nɛ'stɔːrɪəs) *n* died ?451 A.D., Syrian churchman; patriarch of Constantinople (428–431); deposed for heresy by the Council of Ephesus.

net[1] (nɛt) *n* **1** an openwork fabric of string, rope, wire, etc.; mesh. Related adj: **retiary. 2** a device made of net, used to protect or enclose things or to trap animals. **3a** a thin light mesh fabric of cotton, nylon, or other fibre, used for curtains, dresses, etc. **3b** (*as modifier*): *net curtains.* **4** a plan, strategy, etc., intended to trap or ensnare: *the murderer slipped through the police net.* **5** *Tennis, badminton, etc.* **5a** a strip of net that divides the playing area into two equal parts. **5b** a shot that hits the net, whether or not it goes over. **6** the goal in soccer, hockey, etc. **7** (*often pl*) *Cricket.* **7a** a pitch surrounded by netting, used for practice. **7b** a practice session in a net. **8** *Informal.* short for **Internet. 9** another word for **network** (sense 2). ◆ *vb* **nets, netting, netted. 10** (*tr*) to catch with or as if with a net; ensnare. **11** (*tr*) to shelter or surround with a net. **12** (*intr*) *Tennis, badminton, etc.* to hit a shot into the net. **13** to make a net out of (rope, string, etc.). [Old English *net;* related to Gothic *nati,* Dutch *net*]

net[2] *or* **nett** (nɛt) *adj* **1** remaining after all deductions, as for taxes, expenses, losses, etc.: *net profit.* Compare **gross** (sense 2). **2** (of weight) after deducting tare. **3** ultimate; final; conclusive (esp. in the phrase **net result**). ◆ *n* **4** net income, profits, weight, etc. ◆ *vb* **nets, netting, netted. 5** (*tr*) to yield or earn as clear profit. [C14: clean, neat, from French *net* NEAT[1]; related to Dutch *net,* German *nett*]

Netaji ('neɪtɑːdʒɪ) *n* the title for (Subhash Chandra) **Bose.** [Hindi, from *neta* leader + -JI]

Netanyahu (nɛtᵊn'jɑːhuː) *n* **Benjamin** ('bɪnjæˌmiːn). born 1949, Israeli politician: leader of the Likud party (1993–1999); prime minister (1996–99).

net asset value *n* the total value of the assets of an organization less its liabilities and capital charges. Abbrev.: **NAV.**

netball ('nɛtˌbɔːl) *n* a team game similar to basketball, played mainly by women. ▸ **'net,baller** *n*

Net Book Agreement *n* a former agreement between U.K. publishers and booksellers that until 1995 prohibited booksellers from undercutting the price of books sold in bookshops. Abbrev.: **NBA.**

net domestic product *n Economics.* the gross domestic product minus an allowance for the depreciation of capital goods. Abbrev.: **NDP.**

Neth. *abbrev. for* Netherlands.

nether ('nɛðə) *adj* placed or situated below, beneath, or underground: *nether regions; a nether lip.* [Old English *niothera, nithera,* literally: further down, from *nither* down. Related to Old Irish *nitaram,* German *nieder*]

Netherlands ('nɛðələndz) *n* (*functioning as sing or pl*) **the. 1** Also called: **Holland.** a kingdom in NW Europe, on the North Sea: declared independence from Spain in 1581 as the United Provinces; became a major maritime and commercial power in the 17th century, gaining many overseas possessions; a member of the European Union. It is mostly flat and low-lying, with about 40 per cent of the land being below sea level, much of it on polders protected by dykes. Official language: Dutch. Religion: Christian majority, Protestant and Roman Catholic, large nonreligious minority. Currency: euro and guilder. Capital: Amsterdam, with the seat of government at The Hague. Pop.: 15 691 000 (1998 est.). Area: 41 526 sq. km (16 033 sq. miles). Dutch name: **Nederland. 2** the kingdom of the Netherlands together with the Flemish-speaking part of Belgium, esp. as ruled by Spain and Austria before 1581; the Low Countries. ▸ **Netherlander** ('nɛðəˌlændə) *n*

Netherlands Antilles *pl n* **the.** two groups of islands in the Caribbean, in the Lesser Antilles: overseas division of the Netherlands, consisting of the S group of Curaçao, Aruba, and Bonaire, and the N group of Saint Eustatius, Saba, and the S part of Saint Martin; economy based on refining oil from Venezuela. Capital: Willemstad (on Curaçao). Pop.: 213 000 (1998 est.). Area: 996 sq. km (390 sq. miles). Former names: **Curaçao** (until 1949), **Dutch West Indies, Netherlands West Indies.**

Netherlands East Indies *pl n* **the.** a former name (1798–1945) for **Indonesia.**

Netherlands Guiana *n* a former name for **Surinam.**

Netherlands West Indies *pl n* **the.** a former name for the **Netherlands Antilles.**

nethermost ('nɛðəˌməʊst) *adj* **the.** farthest down; lowest.

nether world *n* **1** the world after death; the underworld. **2** hell. ◆ Also called: **nether regions.**

netiquette ('nɛtɪˌkɛt) *n* the informal code of behaviour on the Internet. [C20: from NET(WORK) + (ET)IQUETTE]

net national product *n* gross national product minus an allowance for the depreciation of capital goods. Abbrev.: **NNP.**

net present value *n Accounting.* an assessment of the long-term profitability of a project made by adding together all the revenue it can be expected to achieve over its whole life and deducting all the costs involved, discounting both future costs and revenue at an appropriate rate. Abbrev.: **NPV.**

net profit *n* gross profit minus all operating costs not included in the calculation of gross profit, esp. wages, overheads, and depreciation.

net realizable value *n* the net value of an asset if it were to be sold, taking into account the cost of making the sale and of bringing the asset into a saleable state. Abbrev.: **NRV.**

netsuke ('nɛtsʊkɪ) *n* (in Japan) a carved toggle, esp. of wood or ivory, originally used to tether a medicine box, purse, etc., worn dangling from the waist. [C19: from Japanese]

nett (nɛt) *adj, n, vb* a variant spelling of **net**[2].

netting ('nɛtɪŋ) *n* any netted fabric or structure.

nettle ('nɛtᵊl) *n* **1** any weedy plant of the temperate urticaceous genus *Urtica,* such as *U. dioica* (**stinging nettle**), having serrated leaves with stinging hairs and greenish flowers. **2** any of various other urticaceous plants with stinging hairs or spines. **3** any of various plants that resemble urticaceous nettles, such as the dead-nettle, hemp nettle, and horse nettle. **4 grasp the nettle.** to attempt or approach something with boldness and courage. ◆ *vb* (*tr*) **5** to bother; irritate. **6** to sting as a nettle does. [Old English *netele;* related to Old High German *nazza* (German *Nessel*)] ▸ **'nettle-,like** *adj* ▸ **'nettly** *adj*

nettle rash *n* a nontechnical name for **urticaria.**

nettlesome ('nɛtᵊlsəm) *adj* causing or susceptible to irritation.

net ton *n* the full name for **ton**[1] (sense 2).

netty ('nɛtɪ) *n, pl* **-ties.** *Northeast English dialect.* a lavatory, originally an earth closet. [of obscure origin]

Neturei Karta (nə'tʊreɪ 'kɑrtɑ) *n* a small ultra-orthodox Jewish group living mainly in Jerusalem and New York who oppose the establishment of a Jewish state by temporal means. [Aramaic: guardians of the walls]

network ('nɛtˌwɜːk) *n* **1** an interconnected group or system: *a network of shops.*

2 Also: **net.** a system of intersecting lines, roads, veins, etc. **3** another name for **net**[1] (sense 1) or **netting. 4** *Radio, television.* a group of broadcasting stations that all transmit the same programme simultaneously. **5** *Electronics.* a system of interconnected components or circuits. **6** *Computing.* a system of interconnected computer systems, terminals, and other equipment allowing information to be exchanged. ◆ *vb* **7** (*tr*) *Radio, television.* to broadcast on stations throughout the country: *the Scotland-England match was networked.* **8** *Computing.* (of computers, terminals, etc.) to connect or be connected. **9** (*intr*) to form business contacts through informal social meetings.

networking ('nɛtˌwɜːkɪŋ) *n* **1** *Computing.* the interconnection of two or more networks in different places, as in working at home with a link to a central computer in an office. **2** forming business connections and contacts through informal social meetings. ◆ *adj* **3** of or for networking: *networking systems.* ▸ **'netˌworker** *n*

Neubrandenburg (*German* nɔy'brandənbʊrk) *n* a city in NE Germany, in Mecklenburg-West Pomerania: 14th-century city walls. Pop.: 87 880 (1991).

Neuchâtel (*French* nøʃɑtɛl) *n* **1** a canton in the Jura Mountains of W Switzerland. Capital: Neuchâtel. Pop.: 165 258 (1996 est.). Area: 798 sq. km (308 sq. miles). **2** a town in W Switzerland, capital of Neuchâtel canton, on Lake Neuchâtel: until 1848 the seat of the last hereditary rulers in Switzerland. Pop.: 32 509 (1990). **3 Lake.** a lake in W Switzerland: the largest lake wholly in Switzerland. Area: 216 sq. km (83 sq. miles). ◆ German name (for senses 1, 2): **Neuenburg** ('nɔyənbʊrk).

Neufchâtel (*French* nøʃɑtɛl) *n* a soft creamy whole milk cheese, similar to cream cheese. [named after *Neufchâtel,* town in N France where it is made]

Neuilly-sur-Seine (*French* nœjisyrsɛn) *n* a town in N France, on the Seine: a suburb of NW Paris. Pop.: 61 768 (1990).

neuk (njuːk) *n* a Scot. word for **nook.**

Neumann *n* **1** (*German* 'nɔyman). **Johann Balthasar** (jo'han 'baltazar). 1687–1753, German rococo architect. His masterpiece is the church of Vierzehnheiligen in Bavaria. **2** ('njuːmən). See (John) **von Neumann.**

neume *or* **neum** (njuːm) *n Music.* one of a series of notational symbols used before the 14th century. [C15: from Medieval Latin *neuma* group of notes sung on one breath, from Greek *pneuma* breath] ▸ **'neumic** *adj*

Neumünster (*German* nɔy'mynstər) *n* a town in N Germany, in Schleswig-Holstein: manufacturing of textiles and machinery. Pop.: 81 175 (1991).

neural ('njʊərəl) *adj* of or relating to a nerve or the nervous system. ▸ **'neurally** *adv*

neural chip *n* another name for **neurochip.**

neural computer *n* another name for **neurocomputer.**

neuralgia (njʊ'rældʒə) *n* severe spasmodic pain caused by damage to or malfunctioning of a nerve and often following the course of the nerve. ▸ **neu'ralgic** *adj*

neural network *n* **1** an interconnected system of neurons, as in the brain or other parts of the nervous system. **2** Also called: **neural net.** an analogous network of electronic components, esp. one in a computer designed to mimic the operation of the human brain.

neural tube *n* the structure in mammalian embryos that develops into the brain and spinal cord. Incomplete development results in **neural-tube defects,** such as spina bifida, in a newborn baby.

neuraminidase (ˌnjʊərə'mɪnɪdeɪz) *n* any of various enzymes, found esp. in viruses, that catalyse the breakdown of glucosides containing neuraminic acid, an amino sugar. [C20: from *neuramin(ic acid)* (from NEURO- + AMINE + -IC) + -IDE + -ASE]

neurasthenia (ˌnjʊərəs'θiːnɪə) *n* an obsolete technical term for a neurosis characterized by extreme lassitude and inability to cope with any but the most trivial tasks. ▸ **neurasthenic** (ˌnjʊərəs'θɛnɪk) *adj* ▸ **ˌneuras'thenically** *adv*

neurectomy (njʊ'rɛktəmɪ) *n, pl* **-mies.** the surgical removal of a nerve segment.

neurilemma (ˌnjʊərɪ'lɛmə) *n* a variant of **neurolemma.** [C19: from French *névrilème,* from Greek *neuron* nerve + *eilēma* covering, but influenced also by Greek *lemma* husk]

neuritis (njʊ'raɪtɪs) *n* inflammation of a nerve or nerves, often accompanied by pain and loss of function in the affected part. ▸ **neuritic** (njʊ'rɪtɪk) *adj*

neuro- *or before a vowel* **neur-** *combining form.* indicating a nerve or the nervous system: *neuroblast; neurology.* [from Greek *neuron* nerve; related to Latin *nervus*]

neuroanatomy (ˌnjʊərəʊə'nætəmɪ) *n* the study of the structure of the nervous system. ▸ **ˌneuroa'natomist** *n*

neurobiology (ˌnjʊərəʊbaɪ'ɒlədʒɪ) *n* the study of the anatomy, physiology, and biochemistry of the nervous system. ▸ **ˌneurobi'ologist** *n*

neuroblast ('njʊərəʊˌblæst) *n* an embryonic nerve cell.

neurochip ('njʊərəʊˌtʃɪp) *n Computing.* a semiconductor chip designed for use in an electronic neural network. Also called: **neural chip.**

neurocoele ('njʊərəˌsiːl) *n Embryol.* a cavity in the embryonic brain and spinal cord that develops into the ventricles and central canal respectively. [C19: from NEURO- + Greek *koilos* hollow]

neurocomputer ('njʊərəʊˌkəmpjuːtə) *n* a type of computer designed to mimic the action of the human brain by use of an electronic neural network. Also called: **neural computer.**

neuroendocrine (ˌnjʊərəʊ'ɛndəʊˌkraɪn) *adj* of, relating to, or denoting the dual control of certain body functions by both nervous and hormonal stimulation: *neuroendocrine system.*

neuroendocrinology (ˌnjʊərəʊˌɛndəʊkrɪ'nɒlədʒɪ) *n* the study of neuroendocrine systems and neurohormones.

neurofibril (ˌnjʊərəʊ'faɪbrɪl) *n* any of the delicate threads within the body of a nerve cell that extend into the axon and dendrites. ▸ **ˌneuro'fibrilar, ˌneurofi'brillar,** *or* **ˌneurofi'brillary** *adj*

neurofibromatosis (ˌnjʊərəʊˌfaɪbrəmə'təʊsɪs) *n* a condition characterized by the formation of benign tumours on the fibrous coverings of the peripheral nerves and the development of areas of brown pigmentation on the skin.

neurogenic (ˌnjʊərəʊ'dʒɛnɪk) *adj* originating in or stimulated by the nervous system or nerve impulses.

neuroglia (njʊ'rɒglɪə) *n* another name for **glia.**

neurohormone ('njʊərəʊˌhɔːməʊn) *n* a hormone, such as noradrenaline, oxytocin, or vasopressin, that is produced by specialized nervous tissue rather than by endocrine glands.

neurohypophysis (ˌnjʊərəʊhaɪ'pɒfɪsɪs) *n, pl* **-ses** (-ˌsiːz). the posterior lobe of the pituitary gland. Compare **adenohypophysis.**

neurol. *abbrev. for* neurology.

neurolemma (ˌnjʊərəʊ'lɛmə) *n* the thin membrane that forms a sheath around nerve fibres. Also: **neurilemma.** [C19: New Latin, from NEURO- + Greek *eilēma* covering]

neuroleptic (ˌnjʊərəʊ'lɛptɪk) *adj* **1** capable of affecting the brain, esp. by reducing the intensity of nerve function; tranquillizing. ◆ *n* **2** a neuroleptic drug; major tranquillizer: used in the treatment of psychosis.

neurolinguistics (ˌnjʊərəʊlɪŋ'gwɪstɪks) *n* (*functioning as sing*) the branch of linguistics that deals with the encoding of the language faculty in the brain.

neurology (njʊ'rɒlədʒɪ) *n* the study of the anatomy, physiology, and diseases of the nervous system. ▸ **neurological** (ˌnjʊərə'lɒdʒɪk°l) *adj* ▸ **neu'rologist** *n*

neuroma (njʊ'rəʊmə) *n, pl* **-mata** (-mətə) *or* **-mas.** any tumour composed of nerve tissue. ▸ **neuromatous** (njʊ'rɒmətəs) *adj*

neuromuscular (ˌnjʊərəʊ'mʌskjʊlə) *adj* of, relating to, or affecting nerves and muscles.

neurone ('njʊərəʊn) *or* **neuron** ('njʊərɒn) *n* a cell specialized to conduct nerve impulses: consists of a cell body, axon, and dendrites. Also called: **nerve cell.** ▸ **neu'ronal** *adj* ▸ **neuronic** (njʊ'rɒnɪk) *adj*

neuropath ('njʊərəʊˌpæθ) *n* a person suffering from or predisposed to a disorder of the nervous system.

neuropathology (ˌnjʊərəʊpə'θɒlədʒɪ) *n* the study of diseases of the nervous system. ▸ **neuropathological** (ˌnjʊərəʊˌpæθə'lɒdʒɪk°l) *adj* ▸ **ˌneuropa'thologist** *n*

neuropathy (njʊ'rɒpəθɪ) *n* any disease of the nervous system. ▸ **neuropathic** (ˌnjʊərəʊ'pæθɪk) *adj* ▸ **ˌneuro'pathically** *adv*

neuropeptide (ˌnjʊərəʊ'pɛptaɪd) *n* a peptide produced by neural tissue, esp. one with hormonal activity.

neurophysiology (ˌnjʊərəʊˌfɪzɪ'ɒlədʒɪ) *n* the study of the functions of the nervous system. ▸ **neurophysiological** (ˌnjʊərəʊˌfɪzɪə'lɒdʒɪk°l) *adj* ▸ **ˌneuroˌphysio'logically** *adv* ▸ **ˌneuroˌphysi'ologist** *n*

neuropil ('njʊərəʊpɪl) *n* a dense network of neurons and glia in the central nervous system. [from NEURO- + Greek *pilos* hair]

neuropsychiatry (ˌnjʊərəʊsaɪ'kaɪətrɪ) *n* the branch of psychiatry that investigates the links between mental illness and organic disease of the brain. ▸ **neuropsychiatric** (ˌnjʊərəʊˌsaɪkɪ'ætrɪk) *adj* ▸ **ˌneuropsy'chiatrist** *n*

neuropsychology (ˌnjʊərəʊsaɪ'kɒlədʒɪ) *n* the study of the effects of brain damage on behaviour and the mind. ▸ **ˌneuropsy'chologist** *n*

neuropteran *or* **neuropteron** (njʊ'rɒptərən) *n, pl* **-terans** *or* **-tera** (-tərə). any neuropterous insect.

neuropterous (njʊ'rɒptərəs) *or* **neuropteran** *adj* of, relating to, or belonging to the *Neuroptera,* an order of insects having two pairs of large much-veined wings and biting mouthparts: includes the lacewings and antlions. [C18: from New Latin *Neuroptera;* see NEURO-, -PTEROUS]

neuroscience ('njʊərəʊˌsaɪəns) *n* the study of the anatomy, physiology, and biochemistry of the nervous system.

neurosis (njʊ'rəʊsɪs) *n, pl* **-ses** (-siːz). a relatively mild mental disorder, characterized by symptoms such as hysteria, anxiety, depression, or obsessive behaviour. Also called: **psychoneurosis.**

neurosurgery (ˌnjʊərəʊ'sɜːdʒərɪ) *n* the branch of surgery concerned with the nervous system. ▸ **ˌneuro'surgeon** *n* ▸ **ˌneuro'surgical** *adj* ▸ **ˌneuro'surgically** *adv*

neurotic (njʊ'rɒtɪk) *adj* **1** of, relating to, or afflicted by neurosis. ◆ *n* **2** a person who is afflicted with a neurosis or who tends to be emotionally unstable or unusually anxious. ▸ **neu'rotically** *adv*

neuroticism (njʊ'rɒtɪˌsɪzəm) *n* a personality trait characterized by instability, anxiety, aggression, etc.

neurotomy (njʊ'rɒtəmɪ) *n, pl* **-mies.** the surgical cutting of a nerve, esp. to relieve intractable pain. ▸ **neu'rotomist** *n*

neurotoxin (ˌnjʊərəʊ'tɒksɪn) *n* any of several natural substances that interfere with the electrical activities of nerves, thus preventing them from functioning. ▸ **ˌneuro'toxic** *adj*

neurotransmitter (ˌnjʊərəʊtrænz'mɪtə) *n* a chemical by which a nerve cell communicates with another nerve cell or with a muscle.

neurovascular (ˌnʊərəʊ'væskjʊlə) *adj* of, relating to, or affecting both the nerves and the blood vessels.

Neusatz ('nɔyzats) *n* the German name for **Novi Sad.**

Neuss (*German* nɔys) *n* an industrial city in W Germany, in North Rhine-Westphalia west of Düsseldorf: founded as a Roman fortress in the 1st century A.D. Pop.: 148 796 (1996 est.). Latin name: **No'vaesium.**

neuston ('njuːst°n) *n* **1** organisms, similar to plankton, that float on the surface film of open water. **2** the ecosystem of the surface film of open water in which such organisms as copepods graze on tiny flagellates, bacteria, etc. [C20: via German from Greek *neustos* swimming, from *nein* to swim] ▸ **neus'tonic** *adj*

Neustria ('njuːstrɪə) *n* the western part of the kingdom of the Merovingian Franks formed in 561 A.D. in what is now N France. ▸ **'Neustrian** *adj*

neut. *abbrev. for* neuter.

neuter ('nju:tə) *adj* **1** *Grammar.* **1a** denoting or belonging to a gender of nouns which for the most part have inanimate referents or do not specify the sex of their referents. **1b** (*as n*): *German "Mädchen" (meaning "girl") is a neuter.* **2** (of animals and plants) having nonfunctional, underdeveloped, or absent reproductive organs. **3** sexless or giving no indication of sex: *a neuter sort of name.* ◆ *n* **4** a sexually underdeveloped female insect, such as a worker bee. **5** a castrated animal, esp. a domestic animal. **6** a flower in which the stamens and pistil are absent or nonfunctional. ◆ *vb* **7** (*tr*) to castrate (an animal). [C14: from Latin, from *ne* not + *uter* either (of two)]

neutral ('nju:trəl) *adj* **1** not siding with any party to a war or dispute. **2** of, belonging to, or appropriate to a neutral party, country, etc.: *neutral land.* **3** of no distinctive quality, characteristics, or type; indifferent. **4** (of a colour such as white or black) having no hue; achromatic. **5** (of a colour) dull, but harmonizing with most other colours. **6** a less common term for **neuter** (sense 2). **7** *Chem.* neither acidic nor alkaline. **8** *Physics.* having zero charge or potential. **9** *Rare.* having no magnetism. **10** *Phonetics.* (of a vowel) articulated with the tongue relaxed in mid-central position and the lips midway between spread and rounded: *the word "about" begins with a neutral vowel.* ◆ *n* **11** a neutral person, nation, etc. **12** a citizen of a neutral state. **13** the position of the controls of a gearbox that leaves the transmission disengaged. [C16: from Latin *neutrālis*; see NEUTER] ► **'neutrally** *adv*

neutral axis *n Engineering.* the line or plane through the section of a beam or plate which does not suffer extension or compression when the beam or plate bends.

neutral density *n* **a** black, white, or a shade of grey; a colourless tone. **b** (*as modifier*): *a neutral-density filter.*

neutralism ('nju:trəˌlɪzəm) *n* (in international affairs) the policy, practice, or attitude of neutrality, noninvolvement, or nonalignment with power blocs. ► **'neutralist** *n, adj*

neutrality (nju:'trælɪtɪ) *n* **1** the state or character of being neutral, esp. in a dispute, contest, etc. **2** the condition of being chemically or electrically neutral.

neutralize *or* **neutralise** ('nju:trəˌlaɪz) *vb* (*mainly tr*) **1** (*also intr*) to render or become ineffective or neutral by counteracting, mixing, etc.; nullify. **2** (*also intr*) to make or become electrically or chemically neutral. **3** to exclude (a country) from the sphere of warfare or alliances by international agreement: *the great powers neutralized Belgium in the 19th century.* **4** to render (an army) incapable of further military action. ► **ˌneutraliˈzation** *or* **ˌneutraliˈsation** *n* ► **'neutralˌizer** *or* **'neutralˌiser** *n*

neutral monism *n* the philosophical doctrine that mind and body are both constructs of the same elements which cannot themselves be classified either as mental or physical. See also **monism** (sense 1).

neutral spirits *n* (*functioning as sing or pl*) *U.S.* ethanol of more than 190° proof.

neutretto (nju:'tretəʊ) *n, pl* **-tos.** *Physics.* **1** the neutrino associated with the muon. **2** (formerly) any of various hypothetical neutral particles. [C20: from NEUTR(INO) + diminutive suffix *-etto*]

neutrino (nju:'tri:nəʊ) *n, pl* **-nos.** *Physics.* a stable leptonic neutral elementary particle with zero rest mass and spin ½ that travels at the speed of light. Three types exist, associated with the electron, the muon, and the tau particle. [C20: from Italian, diminutive of *neutrone* NEUTRON]

neutrino astronomy *n* the detection of neutrinos emitted by the sun from which information about the solar interior can be obtained.

neutron ('nju:trɒn) *n Physics.* a neutral elementary particle with a rest mass of $1.674\,82 \times 10^{-27}$ kilogram and spin ½; classified as a baryon. In the nucleus of an atom it is stable but when free it decays. [C20: from NEUTRAL, on the model of ELECTRON]

neutron bomb *n* a type of nuclear weapon designed to provide a high yield of neutrons but to cause little blast or long-lived radioactive contamination. The neutrons destroy all life in the target area, which theoretically can be entered relatively soon after the attack. Technical name: **enhanced radiation weapon.**

neutron gun *n Physics.* a device used for producing a beam of fast neutrons.

neutron number *n* the number of neutrons in the nucleus of an atom. Symbol: *N*

neutron poison *n Physics.* a nonfissionable material used to absorb neutrons and thus to control nuclear reactions.

neutron star *n* a star that has collapsed under its own gravity to a diameter of about 10 to 15 kilometres. It is composed solely of neutrons, has a mass of between 1.4 and about 3 times that of the sun, and a density in excess of 10^{17} kilograms per cubic metre.

neutropenia (ˌnju:trə'pi:nɪə) *n* an abnormal reduction in the number of neutrophils in the blood, as seen in certain anaemias and leukaemias.

neutrophil ('nju:trəˌfɪl) *or* **neutrophile** ('nju:trəˌfaɪl) *n* **1** Also called: **polymorph.** a leucocyte having a lobed nucleus and a fine granular cytoplasm, which stains with neutral dyes. ◆ *adj* **2** (of cells and tissues) readily stainable by neutral dyes.

Nev. *abbrev. for* Nevada.

Neva ('ni:və; *Russian* nɪ'va) *n* a river in NW Russia, flowing west to the Gulf of Finland by the delta on which Saint Petersburg stands. Length: 74 km (46 miles).

Nevada (nɪ'vɑ:də) *n* a state of the western U.S.: lies almost wholly within the Great Basin, a vast desert plateau; noted for production of gold and copper. Capital: Carson City. Pop.: 1 676 809 (1997 est.). Area: 284 612 sq. km (109 889 sq. miles). Abbrevs.: **Nev.** or (with zip code) **NV**

névé ('neveɪ) *n* **1** Also called: **firn.** a mass of porous ice, formed from snow, that has not yet become frozen into glacier ice. **2** a snowfield at the head of a glacier that becomes transformed to ice. [C19: from Swiss French *névé* glacier, from Late Latin *nivātus* snow-cooled, from *nix* snow]

never ('nevə) *adv, sentence substitute.* **1** at no time; not ever. **2** certainly not; by no means; in no case. ◆ *interj* **3** Also: **well I never!** surely not! [Old English *nǣfre,* from *ne* not + *ǣfre* EVER]

USAGE In informal speech and writing, *never* can be used instead of *not* with the simple past tenses of certain verbs, for emphasis (*I never said that; I never realized how clever he was*), but this usage should be avoided in serious writing.

never-ending *adj* having or seeming to have no end; interminable.

nevermore (ˌnevə'mɔ:) *adv Literary.* never again.

never-never *Informal.* ◆ *n* **1** the hire-purchase system of buying. **2** *Austral.* remote desert country, as that of W Queensland and central Australia. ◆ *adj* **3** imaginary; idyllic (esp. in the phrase **never-never land**).

Nevers (*French* nəvɛr) *n* a city in central France: capital of the former duchy of Nivernais; engineering industry. Pop.: 43 890 (1990).

nevertheless (ˌnevəðə'les) *sentence connector.* in spite of that; however; yet.

Nevis *n* **1** ('ni:vɪs, 'nevɪs). an island in the Caribbean, part of St Kitts-Nevis; the volcanic cone of **Nevis Peak,** which rises to 1002 m (3287 ft.), lies in the centre of the island. Capital: Charlestown. Pop.: 8794 (1991). Area: 129 sq. km (50 sq. miles). **2** ('nevɪs). See **Ben Nevis.**

Nevski ('nefskɪ; *Russian* 'njefskij) *n* See **Alexander Nevski.**

nevus ('ni:vəs) *n, pl* **-vi** (-vaɪ). the usual U.S. spelling of **naevus.**

new (nju:) *adj* **1a** recently made or brought into being: *a new dress; our new baby.* **1b** (*as collective n;* preceded by *the*): *the new.* **2** of a kind never before existing; novel: *a new concept in marketing.* **3** having existed before but only recently discovered: *a new comet.* **4** markedly different from what was before: *the new liberalism.* **5** fresh and unused; not second-hand: *a new car.* **6** (*prenominal*) having just or recently become: *a new bride.* **7** (often foll. by *to* or *at*) recently introduced (to); inexperienced (in) or unaccustomed (to): *new to this neighbourhood.* **8** (*cap. in names or titles*) more or most recent of two or more things with the same name: *the New Testament.* **9** (*prenominal*) fresh; additional: *I'll send some new troops.* **10** (often foll. by *to*) unknown; novel: *this is new to me.* **11** (of a cycle) beginning or occurring again: *a new year.* **12** (*prenominal*) (of crops) harvested early: *new carrots.* **13** changed, esp. for the better: *she returned a new woman from her holiday.* **14** up-to-date; fashionable. **15** (*cap. when part of a name*) (*prenominal*) being the most recent, usually living, form of a language: *New High German.* **16 turn over a new leaf.** to reform; make a fresh start. ◆ *adv* (*usually in combination*) **17** recently, freshly: *new-laid eggs.* **18** anew; again. ◆ See also **news.** ◆ Related prefix: **neo-.** [Old English *nīowe*; related to Gothic *niujis,* Old Norse *naujas,* Latin *novus*] ► **'newness** *n*

New Age *n* **1a** a philosophy, originating in the late 1980s, characterized by a belief in alternative medicine, astrology, spiritualism, etc. **1b** (*as modifier*): *New Age therapies.* **2** short for **New Age music.**

New Age music *or* **New Age** *n* a type of gentle melodic popular music originating in the U.S. in the late 1980s, which takes in elements of jazz, folk, and classical music and is played largely on synthesizers and acoustic instruments.

New Amsterdam *n* the Dutch settlement established on Manhattan (1624–26); capital of New Netherlands; captured by the English and renamed New York in 1664.

Newark ('nju:ək) *n* **1** a town in N central England, in Nottinghamshire. Pop.: 35 129 (1991). Official name: **Newark-on-Trent. 2** a port in NE New Jersey, just west of New York City, on Newark Bay and the Passaic River: the largest city in the state; founded in 1666 by Puritans from Connecticut; industrial and commercial centre. Pop.: 268 510 (1996 est.).

New Australia *n* the colony on socialist principles founded by William Lane in Paraguay in 1893.

New Australian *n* an immigrant to Australia, esp. one whose native tongue is not English.

New Bedford *n* a port and resort in SE Massachusetts, near Buzzards Bay: settled by Plymouth colonists in 1652; a leading whaling port (18th–19th centuries). Pop.: 96 903 (1996 est.).

newborn ('nju:ˌbɔ:n) *adj* **1a** recently or just born. **1b** (*as collective n;* preceded by *the*): *the newborn.* **2** (of hope, faith, etc.) reborn.

New Britain *n* an island in the S Pacific, northeast of New Guinea: the largest island of the Bismarck Archipelago; part of Papua New Guinea; mountainous, with several active volcanoes. Capital: Rabaul. Pop.: 312 955 (1990). Area: 36 519 sq. km (14 100 sq. miles).

new broom *n* a newly appointed person eager to make changes.

New Brunswick *n* a province of SE Canada on the Gulf of St Lawrence and the Bay of Fundy: extensively forested. Capital: Fredericton. Pop.: 762 000 (1997 est.). Area: 72 092 sq. km (27 835 sq. miles). Abbrev.: **NB.** ► **New Brunswicker** ('brʌnzwɪkə) *n*

new brutalism *n* another name for **brutalism.**

Newburg ('nju:bɜ:g) *adj* (*immediately postpositive*) (of shellfish, esp. lobster) cooked in a rich sauce of butter, cream, sherry, and egg yolks. [of unknown origin]

Newbury ('nju:bərɪ) *n* a market town in West Berkshire unitary authority, S England: scene of a Parliamentarian victory (1643) and a Royalist victory (1644) during the Civil War; racecourse. Pop.: 33 273 (1991).

Newby Hall ('nju:bɪ) *n* a mansion near Ripon in Yorkshire: built in 1705 and altered (1770–76) by Robert Adam.

New Caledonia *n* an island in the SW Pacific, east of Australia: forms, with its dependencies, an overseas territory of France; discovered by Captain Cook in 1774; rich mineral resources. Capital: Nouméa. Pop.: 204 000 (1998 est.). Area: 19 103 sq. km (7374 miles). French name: **Nouvelle-Calédonie.**

New Castile *n* a region and former province of central Spain. Chief town: Toledo.

Newcastle[1] ('nju:ˌkɑ:sᵊl) *n* a port in SE Australia, in E New South Wales near the mouth of the Hunter River: important industrial centre, with extensive steel, metalworking, engineering, shipbuilding, and chemical industries. It suffered Australia's first fatal earthquake in 1989. Pop.: 466 000 (1995 est.).

Newcastle[2] ('nju:ˌkɑ:sᵊl) *n* **Duke of,** the title of *Thomas Pelham Holles.* 1693–1768, English Whig prime minister (1754–56; 1757–62): brother of Henry Pelham.

Newcastle disease *n* an acute viral disease of birds, esp. poultry, characterized by pneumonia and inflammation of the central nervous system. **[**C20: named after NEWCASTLE UPON TYNE, where it was recorded in 1926**]**

Newcastle-under-Lyme *n* a town in W central England, in Staffordshire. Pop.: 73 731 (1991). Often shortened to **Newcastle.**

Newcastle upon Tyne *n* **1** a port in NE England in Newcastle upon Tyne unitary authority, Tyne and Wear, near the mouth of the River Tyne opposite Gateshead: Roman remains; engineering industries, including ship repairs; two universities. Pop.: 189 150 (1991). Often shortened to **Newcastle. 2** a unitary authority in NE England, in Tyne and Wear. Pop.: 283 100 (1995 est.). Area: 112 sq. km (43 sq. miles).

new chum *n* **1** *Austral. and N.Z. archaic informal.* a recent British immigrant. **2** *Austral.* a novice in any activity. **3** *Austral.* (in the 19th century) a new arrival in a hulk.

New Church *n* another name for the **New Jerusalem Church.**

Newcomb ('nju:kəm) *n* **Simon.** 1835–1909, U.S. astronomer, noted for his tables of celestial bodies and astronomical constants.

Newcomen ('nju:ˌkʌmən) *n* **Thomas.** 1663–1729, English engineer who invented a steam engine, which James Watt later modified and developed.

newcomer ('nju:ˌkʌmə) *n* a person who has recently arrived or started to participate in something.

New Country *n* a style of country music of the late 1980s characterized by down-to-earth rather than sentimental lyrics.

new criticism *n* an approach to literary criticism through close analysis of the text. ► **new critic** *n* ► **new critical** *adj*

New Deal *n* **1** the domestic policies of Franklin D. Roosevelt for economic and social reform. **2** the period of the implementation of these policies (1933–40). ► **New Dealer** *n*

New Delhi *n* See **Delhi.**

New Democratic Party *n* the Canadian social democratic party formed in 1961. Abbrev.: **NDP.**

New Economic Policy *n* an economic programme in the former Soviet Union from 1921 to 1928, that permitted private ownership of industries, etc. Abbrev.: **NEP.**

newel ('nju:əl) *n* **1** the central pillar of a winding staircase, esp. one that is made of stone. **2** See **newel post. [**C14: from Old French *nouel* knob, from Medieval Latin *nōdellus,* diminutive of *nōdus* NODE**]**

newel post *n* the post at the top or bottom of a flight of stairs that supports the handrail. Sometimes shortened to **newel.**

New England *n* **1** the NE part of the U.S., consisting of the states of Maine, New Hampshire, Vermont, Massachusetts, Rhode Island, and Connecticut: settled originally chiefly by Puritans in the mid-17th century. **2** a region in SE Australia, in the northern tablelands of New South Wales. ► **New Englander** *n*

New England Range *n* a mountain range in SE Australia, in NE New South Wales: part of the Great Dividing Range. Highest peak: Ben Lomond, 1520 m (4986 ft.).

New English Bible *n* a new Modern English version of the Bible and Apocrypha, published in full in 1970.

newfangled ('nju:'fæŋᵍᵊld) *adj* **1** newly come into existence or fashion, esp. excessively modern. **2** *Rare.* excessively fond of new ideas, fashions, etc. **[**C14 *newefangel* liking new things, from *new* + *-fangel,* from Old English *fōn* to take**]** ► **'new'fangledness** *n*

new-fashioned *adj* of or following a recent design, trend, etc.

Newfie ('nju:fɪ) *n Informal.* **1** a native or inhabitant of Newfoundland. **2** the province or island of Newfoundland.

New Forest *n* a region of woodland and heath in S England, in SW Hampshire: a hunting ground of the West Saxon kings; tourist area, noted for its ponies. Area: 336 sq. km (130 sq. miles).

new-found *adj* newly or recently discovered: *new-found confidence.*

Newfoundland ('nju:fəndlənd, -fənlənd, -ˌlænd; nju:'faʊndlənd) *n* **1** an island of E Canada, separated from the mainland by the Strait of Belle Isle: with the Coast of Labrador forms the province of Newfoundland; consists of a rugged plateau with the Long Range Mountains in the west. Area: 110 681 sq. km (42 734 sq. miles). **2** a province of E Canada, consisting of the island of Newfoundland and the Coast of Labrador. Capital: St John's. Pop.: 563 600 (1997 est.). Area: 404 519 sq. km (156 185 sq. miles). Abbrevs.: **Nfld** *or* **NF. 3** a large heavy breed of dog similar to a Saint Bernard with a flat coarse usually black coat. ► **Newfoundlander** (nju:'faʊndləndə) *n*

New France *n* the former French colonies and possessions in North America, most of which were lost to England and Spain by 1763: often restricted to the French possessions in Canada.

Newgate ('nju:gɪt, -ˌgeɪt) *n* a famous London prison, in use from the Middle Ages: demolished in 1902.

New Georgia *n* **1** a group of islands in the SW Pacific, in the Solomon Islands. **2** the largest island in this group. Area: about 1300 sq. km (500 sq. miles).

New Granada *n* **1** a former Spanish presidency and later viceroyalty in South America. At its greatest extent it consisted of present-day Panama, Colombia, Venezuela, and Ecuador. **2** the name of Colombia when it formed, with Panama, part of Great Colombia (1819–30).

New Guinea *n* **1** an island in the W Pacific, north of Australia: divided politically into Irian Jaya (a province of Indonesia) in the west and Papua New Guinea in the east. There is a central chain of mountains and a lowland area of swamps in the south and along the Sepik River in the north. Area: 775 213 sq. km (299 310 sq. miles). **2 Trust Territory of.** (until 1975) an administrative division of the former Territory of Papua and New Guinea, consisting of the NE part of the island of New Guinea together with the Bismarck Archipelago; now part of Papua New Guinea.

New Guinea macrophylum (ˌmækrəʊ'faɪləm) *n* the older term for **Trans-New Guinea phylum.**

New Guinea Pidgin *n* the variety of Neo-Melanesian spoken in Papua New Guinea and neighbouring islands.

Newham ('nju:əm) *n* a borough of E Greater London, on the River Thames: established in 1965. Pop.: 226 800 (1994 est.). Area: 36 sq. km (14 sq. miles).

New Hampshire *n* a state of the northeastern U.S.: generally hilly. Capital: Concord. Pop.: 1 172 709 (1997 est.). Area: 23 379 sq. km (9027 sq. miles). Abbrevs.: **N.H.** or (with zip code) **NH**

New Harmony *n* a village in SW Indiana, on the Wabash River: scene of two experimental cooperative communities, the first founded in 1815 by George Rapp, a German religious leader, and the second by Robert Owen in 1825.

Newhaven ('nju:ˌheɪvᵊn) *n* a ferry port and resort on the S coast of England, in East Sussex. Pop.: 11 208 (1991).

New Haven *n* an industrial city and port in S Connecticut, on Long Island Sound: settled in 1638 by English Puritans, who established it as a colony in 1643; seat of Yale University (1701). Pop.: 124 665 (1996 est.).

New Hebrides *pl n* the former name (until 1980) of **Vanuatu.**

Ne Win ('neɪ 'wɪn) *n* **U** (u:). born 1911, Burmese statesman and general; prime minister (1958–60), head of the military government (1962–74), and president (1974–81).

New Ireland *n* an island in the S Pacific, in the Bismarck Archipelago, separated from New Britain by St George's Channel: part of Papua New Guinea. Chief town and port: Kavieng. Pop.: 87 194 (1990.). Area (including adjacent islands): 9850 sq. km (3800 sq. miles).

newish ('nju:ɪʃ) *adj* fairly new. ► **'newishly** *adv* ► **'newishness** *n*

new issue *n Stock Exchange.* an issue of shares being offered to the public for the first time.

New Jersey *n* a state of the eastern U.S., on the Atlantic and Delaware Bay: mostly low-lying, with a heavy industrial area in the northeast and many coastal resorts. Capital: Trenton. Pop.: 8 052 849 (1997 est.). Area: 19 479 sq. km (7521 sq. miles). Abbrevs.: **N.J.** or (with zip code) **NJ**

New Jerusalem *n Christianity.* heaven regarded as the prototype of the earthly Jerusalem; the heavenly city.

New Jerusalem Church *n* a sect founded in 1787 on the teachings of Swedenborg. Often shortened to **New Church.**

New Journalism *n* a style of journalism originating in the U.S. in the 1960s, which uses techniques borrowed from fiction to portray a situation or event as vividly as possible.

New Kingdom *n* a period of Egyptian history, extending from the 18th to the 20th dynasty (?1570–?1080 B.C.).

Newlands ('nju:ləndz) *n* **John Alexander.** 1838–98, British chemist: classified the elements in order of their atomic weight, noticing similarities in every eighth and thus discovering his law of octaves.

New Latin *n* the form of Latin used since the Renaissance, esp. for scientific nomenclature. Also called: **Neo-Latin.**

New Learning *n* the classical and Biblical studies of Renaissance Europe in the 15th and 16th centuries.

New Left *n* a loose grouping of left-wing radicals, esp. among students, that arose in many countries after 1960.

New Look *n* **the.** a fashion in women's clothes introduced in 1947, characterized by long full skirts.

newly ('nju:lɪ) *adv* **1** recently; lately or just: *a newly built shelf.* **2** again; afresh; anew: *newly raised hopes.* **3** in a new manner; differently: *a newly arranged hairdo.*

Newlyn datum ('nju:lɪn) *n* another name for **ordnance datum. [**named after *Newlyn,* Cornwall, where the observations were taken**]**

newlywed ('nju:lɪˌwɛd) *n* (*often pl*) a recently married person.

Newman ('nju:mən) *n* **1 Barnet.** 1905–70, U.S. painter, a founder of Abstract Expressionism: his paintings include the series *Stations of the Cross* (1965–66). **2 John Henry.** 1801–90, British theologian and writer. Originally an Anglican minister, he was a prominent figure in the Oxford Movement. He became a Roman Catholic (1845) and a priest (1847) and was made a cardinal (1879). His writings include the spiritual autobiography, *Apologia pro vita sua* (1864), a treatise on the nature of belief, *The Grammar of Assent* (1870), and hymns. **3 Paul.** born 1925, U.S. film actor and director, who appeared in such films as *Hud* (1963), *Butch Cassidy and the Sundance Kid* (1969), *The Sting* (1973), *The Verdict* (1982), *Blaze* (1990), and *Twilight* (1998).

New Man *n* **the.** a type of modern man who allows the caring side of his nature to show by being supportive and by sharing child care and housework.

newmarket ('nju:ˌmɑ:kɪt) *n* **1** a double-breasted waisted coat with a full skirt worn, esp. for riding, in the 19th century. **2** a simple gambling card game.

Newmarket ('nju:ˌmɑ:kɪt) *n* a town in SE England, in W Suffolk: a famous horse-racing centre since the reign of James I. Pop.: 18 430 (1991).

new maths *n* (*functioning as sing*) *Brit.* an approach to mathematics in which the basic principles of set theory are introduced at an elementary level.

New Mexico *n* a state of the southwestern U.S.: has high semiarid plateaus and mountains, crossed by the Rio Grande and the Pecos River; large Spanish-American and Indian populations; contains over two-thirds of U.S. uranium reserves. Capital: Santa Fé. Pop.: 1 729 751 (1997 est.). Area: 314 451 sq. km

(121 412 sq. miles). Abbrevs.: **N. Mex, N.M.**, or (with zip code) **NM** ▸ **New Mexican** *adj, n*

New Model Army *n* the army established (1645) during the Civil War by the English parliamentarians, which exercised considerable political power under Cromwell.

new moon *n* **1** the moon when it appears as a narrow waxing crescent. **2** the time at which this occurs. **3** *Astronomy*. one of the four principal phases of the moon, occurring when it lies between the earth and the sun.

New Netherland ('nɛðələnd) *n* a Dutch North American colony of the early 17th century, centred on the Hudson valley. Captured by the English in 1664, it was divided into New York and New Jersey.

New Orleans ('ɔ:li:ənz, -lənz; ɔ:'li:nz) *n* a port in SE Louisiana, on the Mississippi River about 172 km (107 miles) from the sea: the largest city in the state and the second most important port in the U.S.; founded by the French in 1718; belonged to Spain (1763–1803). It is largely below sea level, built around the Vieux Carré (French quarter); famous for its annual Mardi Gras festival and for its part in the history of jazz; a major commercial, industrial, and transportation centre. Pop.: 476 625 (1996 est.).

New Orleans jazz *n* the jazz originating in New Orleans from about 1914; traditional jazz.

new penny *n* another name for **penny** (sense 1).

new planets *pl n* the outer planets Uranus, Neptune, and Pluto, only discovered comparatively recently.

New Plymouth *n* a port in New Zealand, on W North Island: founded in 1841. Pop.: 49 800 (1995 est.).

Newport ('nju:ˌpɔ:t) *n* **1** a port in SE Wales, in Newport county borough on the River Usk: electronics. Pop.: 129 900 (1991). **2** a county borough in SE Wales, created from part of Gwent in 1996. Pop.: 133 318 (1996 est.). Area: 190 sq. km (73 sq. miles). **3** a port in SE Rhode Island: founded in 1639, it became one of the richest towns of colonial America; centre of a large number of U.S. naval establishments. Pop.: 28 227 (1990). **4** a town in S England, administrative centre of the Isle of Wight. Pop.: 20 574 (1991).

Newport News *n* (*functioning as sing*) a port in SE Virginia, at the mouth of the James River: an industrial centre, with one of the world's largest shipyards. Pop.: 176 122 (1996 est.).

New Providence *n* an island in the Atlantic, in the Bahamas. Chief town: Nassau. Pop.: 172 196 (1990). Area: 150 sq. km (58 sq. miles).

New Quebec *n* a region of E Canada, formerly the Ungava district of Northwest Territories (1895–1912), extending from the line of the Eastmain and Hamilton Rivers north between Hudson Bay and Labrador: absorbed by Quebec in 1912: contains extensive iron deposits. Area: about 777 000 sq. km (300 000 sq. miles).

New Right *n* a range of radical right-wing groups and ideologies which advocate laissez-faire economic policies, anti-welfarism, and the belief in the rights of the individual over the common good.

New Romney *n* a market town in SE England, in Kent on Romney Marsh: of early importance as one of the Cinque Ports, but is now over 1.6 km (1 mile) inland. Pop.: 4563 (latest est.). Former name (until 1563): **Romney.**

Newry ('njʊərɪ) *n* a port in Northern Ireland, in Newry and Mourne district, Co. Down: close to the border with the Republic of Ireland, it has been the scene of sectarian violence in recent years. Pop.: 22 975 (1991).

Newry and Mourne ('mɔ:n) *n* a district of SE Northern Ireland, in Co. Down. Pop.: 82 943 (1991). Area: 909 sq. km (351 sq. miles).

news (nju:z) *n* (*functioning as sing*) **1** current events; important or interesting recent happenings. **2** information about such events, as in the mass media. **3a the.** a presentation, such as a radio broadcast, of information of this type: *the news is at six.* **3b** (*in combination*): *a newscaster.* **4** interesting or important information not previously known or realized: *it's news to me.* **5** a person, fashion, etc., widely reported in the mass media: *she is no longer news in the film world.* [C15: from Middle English *newes,* plural of *newe* new (*adj*) on model of Old French *noveles* or Medieval Latin *nova* new things] ▸ **'newsless** *adj*

newsagency ('nju:zˌeɪdʒənsɪ) *n Austral.* a newsagent's shop.

news agency *n* an organization that collects news reports for newspapers, periodicals, etc. Also called: **press agency.**

newsagent ('nju:zˌeɪdʒənt) *or U.S.* **newsdealer** ('nju:zˌdi:lə) *n* a shopkeeper who sells newspapers, stationery, etc.

newsboy ('nju:zˌbɔɪ) *or* (*fem*) **newsgirl** ('nju:zˌgɜ:l) *n* a boy or girl who sells or delivers newspapers.

newscast ('nju:zˌkɑ:st) *n* a radio or television broadcast of the news. [C20: from NEWS + (BROAD)CAST] ▸ **'newsˌcaster** *n*

news conference *n* another name for **press conference.**

newsflash ('nju:zˌflæʃ) *n* a brief item of important news, often interrupting a radio or television programme.

newsgroup ('nju:zˌgru:p) *n Computing.* a forum where subscribers exchange information about a specific subject by electronic mail.

newshawk ('nju:zˌhɔ:k) *n U.S. and Canadian informal.* a newspaper reporter. Also called: **newshound** ('nju:zˌhaʊnd).

New Siberian Islands *pl n* an archipelago in the Arctic Ocean, off the N mainland of Russia, in the Sakha Republic. Area: about 37 555 sq. km (14 500 sq. miles).

newsletter ('nju:zˌlɛtə) *n* **1** Also called: **news-sheet.** a printed periodical bulletin circulated to members of a group. **2** *History.* a written or printed account of the news.

newsmonger ('nju:zˌmʌŋgə) *n Old-fashioned.* a gossip.

new sol (sɒl) *n* the standard monetary unit of Peru, divided into 100 céntimos. Spanish name: **nuevo sol.**

New South *n Austral. informal.* See **New South Wales.**

New South Wales *n* a state of SE Australia: originally contained over half the continent, but was reduced by the formation of other states (1825–1911); consists of a narrow coastal plain, separated from extensive inland plains by the Great Dividing Range; the most populous state; mineral resources. Capital: Sydney. Pop.: 6 173 000 (1996 est.). Area: 801 428 sq. km (309 433 sq. miles).

New Spain *n* a Spanish viceroyalty of the 16th to 19th centuries, composed of Mexico, Central America north of Panama, the Spanish West Indies, the southwestern U.S., and the Philippines.

newspaper ('nju:zˌpeɪpə) *n* **1a** a weekly or daily publication consisting of folded sheets and containing articles on the news, features, reviews, and advertisements. Often shortened to **paper. 1b** (*as modifier*): *a newspaper article.* **2** a less common name for **newsprint.**

newspaperman ('nju:zˌpeɪpəˌmæn) *or* (*fem*) **newspaperwoman** *n, pl* **-men** *or* **-women. 1** a person who works for a newspaper as a reporter or editor. **2** the owner or proprietor of a newspaper.

newspeak ('nju:ˌspi:k) *n* the language of bureaucrats and politicians, regarded as deliberately ambiguous and misleading. [C20: from *1984,* a novel by George Orwell]

newsprint ('nju:zˌprɪnt) *n* an inexpensive wood-pulp paper used for newspapers.

newsreader ('nju:zˌri:də) *n* a news announcer on radio or television.

newsreel ('nju:zˌri:l) *n* a short film with a commentary presenting current events.

newsroom ('nju:zˌru:m, -ˌrʊm) *n* a room in a newspaper office or television or radio station, where news is received and prepared for publication or broadcasting.

newsstand ('nju:zˌstænd) *n* a portable stand or stall in the street, from which newspapers are sold.

New Stone Age *n* (not now in technical use) another term for **Neolithic.**

New Style *n* the present method of reckoning dates using the Gregorian calendar.

news vendor *n* a person who sells newspapers.

newsworthy ('nju:zˌwɜ:ðɪ) *adj* sufficiently interesting to be reported in a news bulletin. ▸ **'newsˌworthiness** *n*

newsy ('nju:zɪ) *adj* **newsier, newsiest.** full of news, esp. gossipy or personal news: *a newsy letter.* ▸ **'newsiness** *n*

newt (nju:t) *n* **1** any of various small semiaquatic urodele amphibians, such as *Triturus vulgaris* (**common newt**) of Europe, having a long slender body and tail and short feeble legs. **2** *Chiefly Brit.* any other urodele amphibian, including the salamanders. [C15: from *a newt,* a mistaken division of *an ewt; ewt,* from Old English *eveta* EFT[1]]

New Test. *abbrev. for* New Testament.

New Testament *n* the collection of writings consisting of the Gospels, Acts of the Apostles, Pauline and other Epistles, and the book of Revelation, composed soon after Christ's death and added to the Jewish writings of the Old Testament to make up the Christian Bible.

New Thought *n* a movement interested in spiritual healing and the power of constructive thinking.

newton ('nju:t^{ə}n) *n* the derived SI unit of force that imparts an acceleration of 1 metre per second per second to a mass of 1 kilogram; equivalent to 10^5 dynes or 7.233 poundals. Symbol: N [C20: named after Sir Isaac NEWTON]

Newton[1] ('nju:t^{ə}n) *n* one of the deepest craters on the moon, over 7300 metres deep and about 112 kilometres in diameter, situated in the SE quadrant.

Newton[2] ('nju:t^{ə}n) *n* Sir **Isaac.** 1642–1727, English mathematician, physicist, astronomer, and philosopher, noted particularly for his law of gravitation, his three laws of motion, his theory that light is composed of corpuscles, and his development of calculus independently of Leibnitz. His works include *Principia Mathematica* (1687) and *Opticks* (1704). ▸ **Newtonian** (nju:'təʊnɪən) *adj*

Newtonian mechanics *n* (*functioning as sing*) a system of mechanics based on Newton's laws of motion.

Newtonian telescope *n* a type of astronomical reflecting telescope in which light is reflected from a large concave mirror, onto a plane mirror, and through a hole in the side of the body of the telescope to form an image.

Newton's cradle *n* an ornamental puzzle consisting of a frame in which five metal balls are suspended in such a way that when one is moved it sets all the others in motion in turn.

Newton's law of gravitation *n* the principle that two particles attract each other with forces directly proportional to the product of their masses divided by the square of the distance between them.

Newton's laws of motion *pl n* three laws of mechanics describing the motion of a body. **The first law** states that a body remains at rest or in uniform motion in a straight line unless acted upon by a force. **The second law** states that a body's rate of change of momentum is proportional to the force causing it. **The third law** states that when a force acts on a body an equal and opposite force acts simultaneously on another body.

Newtown ('nju:taʊn) *n* a new town in central Wales, in Powys. Pop.: 10 548 (1991).

new town *n* (in Britain) a town that has been planned as a complete unit and built with government sponsorship, esp. to accommodate overspill population.

Newtownabbey (ˌnju:t^{ə}n'æbɪ) *n* **1** a town in Northern Ireland, in Newtownabbey district, Co. Antrim on Belfast Lough: the third largest town in Northern Ireland, formed in 1958 by the amalgamation of seven villages; light industrial centre, esp. for textiles. Pop.: 57 103 (1991). **2** a district of E Northern Ireland, in Co. Antrim. Pop.: 74 035 (1991). Area: 151 sq. km (58 sq. miles).

Newtown St Boswells ('nju:taʊn sənt 'bɒzwəlz) *n* a village in SE Scotland, administrative centre of Scottish Borders: agricultural centre. Pop.: 1108 (1991).

new wave *n* a movement in art, film-making, politics, etc., that consciously breaks with traditional ideas.

New Wave[1] *n* **the.** a movement in the French cinema of the 1960s, led by such directors as Godard, Truffaut, and Resnais, and characterized by a fluid use of the camera and an abandonment of traditional editing techniques. Also called: **Nouvelle Vague.**

New Wave[2] *n* rock music of the late 1970s, related to punk but more complex: sometimes used to include punk.

New Windsor *n* the official name of **Windsor**[1] (sense 1).

new wool *n* wool that is being processed or woven for the first time. Usual U.S. term: **virgin wool.**

New World *n* **the.** the Americas; the western hemisphere.

New World monkey *n* any monkey of the family *Cebidae,* of Central and South America, having widely separated nostrils: many are arboreal and have a prehensile tail. Compare **Old World monkey.**

New Year *n* the first day or days of the year in various calendars, usually celebrated as a holiday.

New Year's Day *n* January 1, celebrated as a holiday in many countries. Often shortened to (U.S. and Canadian informal) **New Year's.**

New Year's Eve *n* the evening of Dec. 31, often celebrated with parties. See also **Hogmanay.**

New York *n* **1** Also called: **New York City.** a city in SE New York State, at the mouth of the Hudson River: the largest city and chief port of the U.S.; settled by the Dutch as New Amsterdam in 1624 and captured by the British in 1664, when it was named New York; consists of five boroughs (Manhattan, the Bronx, Queens, Brooklyn, and Richmond) and many islands, with its commercial and financial centre in Manhattan; the country's leading commercial and industrial city. Pop.: 7 380 906 (1996 est.). Abbrevs.: **N.Y.C., NYC. 2** a state of the northeastern U.S.: consists chiefly of a plateau with the Finger Lakes in the centre, the Adirondack Mountains in the northeast, the Catskill Mountains in the southeast, and Niagara Falls in the west. Capital: Albany. Pop.: 18 137 226 (1997 est.). Area: 123 882 sq. km (47 831 sq. miles). Abbrevs.: **N.Y.** or (with zip code) **NY** ► **New Yorker** *n*

New York Bay *n* an inlet of the Atlantic at the mouth of the Hudson River: forms the harbour of the port of New York.

New York State Barge Canal *n* a system of inland waterways in New York State, connecting the Hudson River with Lakes Erie and Ontario and, via Lake Champlain, with the St Lawrence. Length: 845 km (525 miles).

New Zealand ('zi:lənd) *n* an independent dominion within the Commonwealth, occupying two main islands (the North Island and the South Island), Stewart Island, the Chatham Islands, and a number of minor islands in the SE Pacific: original Maori inhabitants ceded sovereignty to the British government in 1840; became a dominion in 1907; a major world exporter of dairy products, wool, and meat. Official languages: English and Maori. Religion: Christian majority, nonreligious and Maori minorities. Currency: New Zealand dollar. Capital: Wellington. Pop.: 3 801 000 (1998 est.). Area: 270 534 sq. km (104 454 sq. miles). ► **New Zealander** *n*

New Zealand greenstone *n* a variety of nephrite from New Zealand, used as a gemstone.

Nexø (*Danish* 'nɛgsø:) *n* **Martin Andersen** ('martən). 1869–1954, Danish novelist. His chief works are the novels *Pelle the Conqueror* (1906–10), which deals with the labour movement, and *Ditte, Daughter of Man* (1917–21).

next (nɛkst) *adj* **1** immediately following: *the next patient to be examined; do it next week.* **2** immediately adjoining: *the next room.* **3** closest to in degree: *the tallest boy next to James; the next-best thing.* **4 the next (Sunday) but one.** the (Sunday) after the next. ◆ *adv* **5** at a time or on an occasion immediately to follow: *the patient to be examined next; next, he started to unscrew the telephone receiver.* **6 next to. 6a** adjacent to; at or on one side of: *the house next to ours.* **6b** following in degree: *next to your mother, who do you love most?* **6c** almost: *next to impossible.* ◆ *prep* **7** *Archaic.* next to. [Old English *nēhst,* superlative of *nēah* NIGH; compare NEAR, NEIGHBOUR]

next door *adj* (**next-door** *when prenominal*), *adv* at, in, or to the adjacent house, flat, building, etc.: *we live next door to the dentist; the next-door house.*

next friend *n Law.* a person acting on behalf of an infant or other person under legal disability.

next of kin *n* a person's closest relative or relatives.

nexus ('nɛksəs) *n, pl* **nexus. 1** a means of connection between members of a group or things in a series; link; bond. **2** a connected group or series. [C17: from Latin: a binding together, from *nectere* to bind]

Ney (neɪ; *French* nɛ) *n* **Michel** (miʃɛl), Duc d'Elchingen. 1769–1815, French marshal, who earned the epithet *Bravest of the Brave* at the battle of Borodino (1812) in the Napoleonic Wars. He rallied to Napoleon on his return from Elba and was executed for treason (1815).

Nez Percé ('nɛz 'pɜ:s; *French* ne pɛrse) *n* **1** (*pl* **Nez Percés** ('pɜ:sɪz; *French* pɛrse) *or* **Nez Percé**) a member of a North American Indian people of the Pacific coast, a tribe of the Sahaptino. **2** the Sahaptin language of this people. [French, literally: pierced nose]

NF *abbrev. for:* **1** Norman French (language). **2** (in Britain) National Front.

N/F *or* **NF** *Banking. abbrev. for* no funds.

NFA *abbrev. for:* **1** (in the U.S.) National Futures Association. **2** (in Britain) no fixed abode.

NFL (in the U.S. and Canada) *abbrev. for* National Football League.

Nfld *or* **NF** *abbrev. for* Newfoundland.

NFS (in Britain) *abbrev. for* National Fire Service.

NFT *abbrev. for* National Film Theatre.

NFU (in Britain) *abbrev. for* National Farmers' Union.

NFWI (in Britain) *abbrev. for* National Federation of Women's Institutes.

NG *abbrev. for:* **1** (in the U.S.) National Guard. **2** New Guinea. **3** Also: **ng** no good.

NGA (formerly, in Britain) *abbrev. for* National Graphical Association.

ngaio ('naɪəʊ) *n, pl* **ngaios.** a small New Zealand tree, *Myoporum laetum,* yielding useful timber: family *Myoporaceae.* [from Maori]

Ngaliema Mountain (ᵊŋgɑ:'ljeɪmə) *n* the Congolese name for (Mount) **Stanley.**

ngati ('nɑ:ti:) *n N.Z.* (occurring as part of the name of a tribe) tribe or clan. [Maori]

NGC *abbrev. for* New General Catalogue of Nebulae and Clusters of Stars; a catalogue in which over 8000 nebulae, galaxies, and clusters are listed numerically.

NGk *abbrev. for* New Greek.

NGL *abbrev. for* natural gas liquids: liquid hydrocarbons derived from natural gas.

NGO *abbrev. for:* **1** Non-Governmental Organization. **2** (in India) nongazetted officer.

ngoma (ᵊŋ'gəʊmə, ᵊŋ'gɒm-) *n E African.* a type of drum. [Swahili]

ngultrum (ᵊŋ'gu:ltrəm) *n* the standard monetary unit of Bhutan, divided into 100 chetrum.

Nguni (ᵊŋ'gu:nɪ) *n* a group of Bantu languages of southern Africa, consisting chiefly of Zulu, Xhosa, and Swazi.

Nguyen Kao Ky (ᵊŋ'gu:jɛn 'kau 'ki:) *n* See (Nguyen Kao) **Ky.**

ngwee (ᵊŋ'gweɪ) *n* a Zambian monetary unit worth one hundredth of a kwacha.

NH *or* **N.H.** *abbrev. for* New Hampshire.

Nha Trang ('njɑ: 'træŋ) *n* a port in SE Vietnam, on the South China Sea: nearby temples of the Cham civilization; fishing industry. Pop.: 221 331 (1992 est.).

NHI (in Britain) *abbrev. for* National Health Insurance.

NHS (in Britain) *abbrev. for* National Health Service.

Ni *the chemical symbol for* nickel.

NI *abbrev. for:* **1** (in Britain) National Insurance. **2** Northern Ireland. **3** *N.Z.* North Island.

niacin ('naɪəsɪn) *n* another name for **nicotinic acid.** [C20: from NI(COTINIC) AC(ID) + -IN]

Niagara (naɪ'ægrə, -'ægərə) *n* **1** a river in NE North America, on the border between W New York State and Ontario, Canada, flowing from Lake Erie to Lake Ontario. Length: 45 km (28 miles). **2** a torrent.

Niagara Falls *n* **1** (*functioning as pl*) the falls of the Niagara River, on the border between the U.S. and Canada: divided by Goat Island into the American Falls, 50 m (167 ft.) high, and the Horseshoe or Canadian Falls, 47 m (158 ft.) high. **2** (*functioning as sing*) a city in W New York State, situated at the falls of the Niagara River. Pop.: 61 840 (1990). **3** (*functioning as sing*) a city in S Canada, in SE Ontario on the Niagara River just below the falls: linked to the city of Niagara Falls in the U.S. by three bridges. Pop.: 75 399 (1991).

Niamey (njɑ:'meɪ) *n* the capital of Niger, in the southwest on the River Niger: became capital in 1926; airport and land route centre. Pop.: 495 000 (1995 est.).

Niarchos (nɪ'ɑ:kɒs) *n* **Stavros Spyro** ('stævrɒs 'spɪərəʊ). 1909–96, Greek shipowner. He pioneered the use of supertankers in the 1950s.

nib (nɪb) *n* **1** the writing point of a pen, esp. an insertable tapered metal part with a split tip. **2** a point, tip, or beak. **3** (*pl*) crushed cocoa beans. ◆ *vb* **nibs, nibbing, nibbed.** (*tr*) **4** to provide with a nib. **5** to prepare or sharpen the nib of. [C16 (in the sense: beak): origin obscure; compare Northern German *nibbe* tip. See NEB, NIBBLE] ► **'nib,like** *adj*

nibble ('nɪbᵊl) *vb* (when *intr,* often foll. by *at*) **1** (esp. of animals, such as mice) to take small repeated bites (of). **2** to take dainty or tentative bites: *to nibble at a cake.* **3** to bite (at) gently or caressingly. **4** (*intr*) to make petty criticisms. **5** (*intr*) to consider tentatively or cautiously: *to nibble at an idea.* ◆ *n* **6** a small mouthful. **7** an instance or the act of nibbling. [C15: related to Low German *nibbelen.* Compare NIB, NEB]

nibbler ('nɪblə) *n* **1** a person, animal, or thing that nibbles. **2** *Engineering.* a tool that cuts sheet material by a series of small rapidly reciprocating cuts.

Nibelung ('ni:bə,lʊŋ) *n, pl* **-lungs** *or* **-lungen** (-,lʊŋən). *German myth.* **1** any of the race of dwarfs who possessed a treasure hoard stolen by Siegfried. **2** one of Siegfried's companions or followers. **3** (in the *Nibelungenlied*) a member of the family of Gunther, king of Burgundy.

Nibelungenlied *German.* ('ni:bəlʊŋənli:t) *n* a medieval High German heroic epic of unknown authorship based on German history and legend and written about 1200. [literally: song of the Nibelungs]

niblick ('nɪblɪk) *n Golf.* (formerly) a club, a No. 9 iron, giving a great deal of lift. [C19: of unknown origin]

nibs (nɪbz) *pl n* **his nibs.** *Slang.* a mock title used of someone in authority. [C19: of unknown origin]

NIC *international car registration for* Nicaragua.

Nicaea (naɪ'si:ə) *n* an ancient city in NW Asia Minor, in Bithynia: site of the **first council of Nicaea** (325 A.D.), which composed the Nicene Creed. Modern Turkish name: **Iznik.** ► **Nicene** ('naɪsi:n) *or* **Ni'caean** *adj*

NICAM *acronym for* near-instantaneous companding system: a technique for coding audio signals into digital form.

Nicaragua (,nɪkə'rægjʊə, -gwə; *Spanish* nika'raɣwa) *n* **1** a republic in Central America, on the Caribbean and the Pacific: colonized by the Spanish from the 1520s; gained independence in 1821 and was annexed by Mexico, becoming a republic in 1838. Official language: Spanish. Religion: Roman Catholic majority. Currency: córdoba. Capital: Managua. Pop.: 4 763 000 (1998 est.). Area: 131 812 sq. km (50 893 sq. miles). **2 Lake.** a lake in SW Nicaragua, separated from the Pacific by an isthmus 19 km (12 miles) wide: the largest lake in Central America. Area: 8264 sq. km (3191 sq. miles). ► **,Nica'raguan** *adj, n*

niccolite ('nɪkə,laɪt) *n* a copper-coloured mineral consisting of nickel arsenide in hexagonal crystalline form, occurring associated with copper and silver ores:

a source of nickel. Formula: NiAs. [C19: from New Latin *niccolum* NICKEL + -ITE[1]]

nice (naɪs) *adj* **1** pleasant or commendable: *a nice day.* **2** kind or friendly: *a nice gesture of help.* **3** good or satisfactory: *they made a nice job of it.* **4** subtle, delicate, or discriminating: *a nice point in the argument.* **5** precise; skilful: *a nice fit.* **6** *Now rare.* fastidious; respectable: *he was not too nice about his methods.* **7** *Obsolete.* **7a** foolish or ignorant. **7b** delicate. **7c** shy; modest. **7d** wanton. **8** **nice and.** pleasingly: *it's nice and cool.* [C13 (originally: foolish): from Old French *nice* simple, silly, from Latin *nescius* ignorant, from *nescīre* to be ignorant; see NESCIENCE] ▸ **'nicely** *adv* ▸ **'niceness** *n* ▸ **'nicish** *adj*

Nice (*French* nis) *n* a city in SE France, on the Mediterranean: a leading resort of the French Riviera; founded by Phocaeans from Marseille in about the 3rd century B.C. Pop.: 345 674 (1990).

nice-looking *adj Informal.* attractive in appearance; pretty or handsome.

Nicene Council *n* **1** the first council of Nicaea, the first general council of the Church, held in 325 A.D. to settle the Arian controversy. **2** the second council of Nicaea, the seventh general council of the Church, held in 787 A.D. to settle the question of images.

Nicene Creed *n* **1** the formal summary of Christian beliefs promulgated at the first council of Nicaea in 325 A.D. **2** a longer formulation of Christian beliefs authorized at the council of Constantinople in 381, and now used in most Christian liturgies.

nicety ('naɪsɪtɪ) *n, pl* **-ties. 1** a subtle point of delicacy or distinction: *a nicety of etiquette.* **2** (*usually pl*) a refinement or delicacy: *the niceties of first-class travel.* **3** subtlety, delicacy, or precision. **4** excessive refinement; fastidiousness. **5 to a nicety.** with precision.

niche (nɪtʃ, ni:ʃ) *n* **1** a recess in a wall, esp. one that contains a statue. **2** any similar recess, such as one in a rock face. **3** a position particularly suitable for the person occupying it: *he found his niche in politics.* **4** (*modifier*) relating to or aimed at a small specialized group or market. **5** *Ecology.* the status of a plant or animal within its community, which determines its activities, relationships with other organisms, etc. ◆ *vb* **6** (*tr*) to place (a statue) in a niche; ensconce (oneself). [C17: from French, from Old French *nichier* to nest, from Vulgar Latin *nīdicāre* (unattested) to build a nest, from Latin *nīdus* NEST]

Nichiren (ni:tʃi:rɛn) *n* a Buddhist sect of Japan based on the teachings of the Buddhist priest Nichiren (1222–82), who claimed that the Lotus Sutra contained the only way to salvation.

Nicholas ('nɪkələs) *n* **Saint.** 4th-century A.D. bishop of Myra, in Asia Minor; patron saint of Russia and of children, sailors, merchants, and pawnbrokers. Feast day: Dec. 6. See also **Santa Claus.**

Nicholas I *n* **1 Saint,** called *the Great.* died 867 A.D., Italian ecclesiastic; pope (858–867). He championed papal supremacy. Feast day: Nov. 13. **2** 1796–1855, tsar of Russia (1825–55). He gained notoriety for his autocracy and his emphasis on military discipline and bureaucracy.

Nicholas II *n* 1868–1918, tsar of Russia (1894–1917). After the disastrous Russo-Japanese War (1904–05), he was forced to summon a representative assembly, but his continued autocracy and incompetence precipitated the Russian Revolution (1917): he abdicated and was shot.

Nicholas V *n* original name *Tommaso Parentucelli.* 1397–1455, Italian ecclesiastic; pope (1447–55). He helped to found the Vatican Library.

Nicholas of Cusa ('kju:zə) *n* 1401–64, German cardinal, philosopher, and mathematician: anticipated Copernicus in asserting that the earth revolves around the sun.

Nichols ('nɪkəlz) *n* **Peter (Richard).** born 1927, British dramatist, whose works include *A Day in the Death of Joe Egg* (1967), the musical *Privates on Parade* (1977), and *Blue Murder* (1995).

Nicholson ('nɪkəlsən) *n* **1 Ben.** 1894–1982, English painter, noted esp. for his abstract geometrical works. **2 Jack.** born 1937, U.S. film actor. His films include *Easy Rider* (1969), *One Flew Over the Cuckoo's Nest* (1974), *Terms of Endearment* (1983), *Batman* (1989), and *As Good As It Gets* (1998). **3 John.** 1821–57, British general and administrator, born in Ireland: deputy commissioner in the Punjab (1851–56), where he became the object of hero-worship among the natives and kept the Punjab loyal during the Indian Mutiny: played a major role in the capture of Delhi.

Nichrome ('naɪkrəum) *n Trademark.* any of various alloys containing nickel, iron, and chromium, with smaller amounts of other components. It is used in electrical heating elements, furnaces, etc.

nicht (nɪxt) *n* a Scot. word for **night.**

Nicias ('nɪsɪəs) *n* died 414 B.C., Athenian statesman and general. He ended the first part of the Peloponnesian War by making peace with Sparta (421).

nick (nɪk) *n* **1** a small notch or indentation on an edge or surface. **2** a groove on the shank of a printing type, used to orientate type and often to distinguish the fount. **3** *Brit.* a slang word for **prison** or **police station. 4 in good nick.** *Informal.* in good condition. **5 in the nick of time.** at the last possible moment; at the critical moment. ◆ *vb* **6** (*tr*) to chip or cut. **7** (*tr*) *Slang, chiefly Brit.* **7a** to steal. **7b** to take into legal custody; arrest. **8** (*intr*; often foll. by *off*) *Informal.* to move or depart rapidly. **9** to divide and reset (certain of the tail muscles of a horse) to give the tail a high carriage. **10** (*tr*) to guess, catch, etc., exactly. **11** (*intr*) (of breeding stock) to mate satisfactorily. **12 nick (someone) for.** *U.S. and Canadian slang.* to defraud (someone) to the extent of. [C15: perhaps changed from C14 *nocke* NOCK]

nickel ('nɪk^{ə}l) *n* **1** a malleable ductile silvery-white metallic element that is strong and corrosion-resistant, occurring principally in pentlandite and niccolite: used in alloys, esp. in toughening steel, in electroplating, and as a catalyst in organic synthesis. Symbol: Ni; atomic no.: 28; atomic wt.: 58.6934; valency: 0, 1, 2, or 3; relative density: 8.902; melting pt.: 1455°C; boiling pt.: 2914°C. **2** a U.S. and Canadian coin and monetary unit worth five cents. ◆ *vb* **-els, -elling, -elled** *or U.S.* **-els, -eling, -eled. 3** (*tr*) to plate with nickel. [C18: shortened form of German *Kupfernickel* NICCOLITE, literally: copper demon, so called by miners because it was mistakenly thought to contain copper]

nickel bloom *n* another name for **annabergite.**

nickelic (nɪ'kɛlɪk) *adj* **1** of or containing metallic nickel. **2** of or containing nickel in the trivalent state.

nickeliferous (ˌnɪkə'lɪfərəs) *adj* containing nickel.

nickelodeon (ˌnɪkə'ləudɪən) *n U.S.* **1** an early form of jukebox. **2** (formerly) a cinema charging five cents for admission. **3** (formerly) a Pianola, esp. one operated by inserting a five-cent piece. [C20: from NICKEL + (MEL)ODEON]

nickelous ('nɪkələs) *adj* of or containing nickel, esp. in the divalent state.

nickel plate *n* a thin layer of nickel deposited on a surface, usually by electrolysis.

nickel silver *n* any of various white alloys containing copper (46–63 per cent), zinc (18–36 per cent), and nickel (6–30 per cent): used in making tableware, etc. Also called: **German silver, pakthong.**

nickel steel *n Engineering.* steel containing between 0.5 and 6.0 per cent nickel to increase its strength.

nicker[1] ('nɪkə) *vb* (*intr*) **1** (of a horse) to neigh softly. **2** to laugh quietly; snigger. [C18: perhaps from NEIGH]

nicker[2] ('nɪkə) *n, pl* **-er.** *Brit. slang.* a pound sterling. [C20: of unknown origin]

Nicklaus ('nɪklaus) *n* **Jack.** born 1940, U.S. professional golfer: won the British Open Championship (1966; 1970; 1978) and the U.S. Open Championship (1962; 1967; 1972; 1980).

nick-nack ('nɪkˌnæk) *n* a variant spelling of **knick-knack.**

nickname ('nɪkˌneɪm) *n* **1** a familiar, pet, or derisory name given to a person, animal, or place: *his nickname was Lefty because he was left-handed.* **2** a shortened or familiar form of a person's name: *Joe is a nickname for Joseph.* ◆ *vb* **3** (*tr*) to call by a nickname; give a nickname to. [C15 *a nekename,* mistaken division of *an ekename* an additional name, from *eke* addition + NAME]

nickpoint ('nɪkˌpɔɪnt) *n* a variant spelling (esp. U.S.) of **knickpoint.**

nicky-tam ('nɪkɪ'tæm) *n Scot.* a strap or string secured round a trouser leg below the knee, formerly worn esp. by farm workers to keep the trouser bottoms clear of dirt. [C20: from *knicker* + *tam, taum* a fishing line or string]

Nicobar Islands ('nɪkəˌbɑ:) *pl n* a group of 19 islands in the Indian Ocean, south of the Andaman Islands, with which they form a territory of India. Area: 1645 sq. km (635 sq. miles).

Nicodemus (ˌnɪkə'di:məs) *n New Testament.* a Pharisee and a member of the Sanhedrin, who supported Jesus against the other Pharisees (John 8:50–52).

Nicolai (*German* niko'laɪ) *n* **Carl Otto Ehrenfried** (karl 'ɔto 'e:rənfri:t). 1810–49, German composer: noted for his opera *The Merry Wives of Windsor* (1849).

Nicol prism ('nɪk^{ə}l) *n* a device composed of two prisms of Iceland spar or calcite cut at specified angles and cemented together with Canada balsam. It is used for producing plane-polarized light. [C19: named after William *Nicol* (?1768–1851), Scottish physicist, its inventor]

Nicolson ('nɪkəlsən) *n* Sir **Harold (George).** 1886–1968, British diplomat, politician, and author: married to Vita Sackville-West.

Nicosia (ˌnɪkə'si:ə, -'sɪə) *n* the capital of Cyprus, in the central part on the Pedieos River: capital since the 10th century. Pop. (Greek and Turkish): 228 215 (1994 est.). Greek name: **Levkosia** *or* **Leukosia.** Turkish name: **Lefkoşa.**

nicotiana (nɪˌkəuʃɪ'ɑ:nə, -'eɪnə) *n* any solanaceous plant of the American and Australian genus *Nicotiana,* such as tobacco, having white, yellow, or purple fragrant flowers. [C16: see NICOTINE]

nicotinamide (ˌnɪkə'tɪnəˌmaɪd, -'ti:n-) *n* the amide of nicotinic acid: a component of the vitamin B complex and essential in the diet for the prevention of pellagra. Formula: $C_6H_6ON_2$.

nicotine ('nɪkəˌti:n) *n* a colourless oily acrid toxic liquid that turns yellowish-brown in air and light: the principal alkaloid in tobacco, used as an agricultural insecticide. Formula: $C_{10}H_{14}N_2$. [C19: from French, from New Latin *herba nicotiana* Nicot's plant, named after J. *Nicot* (1530-1600), French diplomat who introduced tobacco into France] ▸ **'nicoˌtined** *adj* ▸ **nicotinic** (ˌnɪkə'tɪnɪk) *adj*

nicotinic acid *n* a vitamin of the B complex that occurs in milk, liver, yeast, etc. Lack of it in the diet leads to the disease pellagra. Formula: $(C_5H_4N)COOH$. Also called: **niacin.**

nicotinism ('nɪkəti:ˌnɪzəm) *n Pathol.* a toxic condition of the body or a bodily organ or part caused by nicotine.

Nictheroy (*Portuguese* nite'rɔi) *n* another name for **Niterói.**

nictitate ('nɪktɪˌteɪt) *or* **nictate** ('nɪkteɪt) *vb* technical words for **blink** (sense 1). [C19: from Medieval Latin *nictitāre* to wink repeatedly, from Latin *nictāre* to wink, from *nicere* to beckon] ▸ **ˌnicti'tation** *or* **nic'tation** *n*

nictitating membrane *n* (in reptiles, birds, and some mammals) a thin fold of skin beneath the eyelid that can be drawn across the eye. Also called: **third eyelid, haw.**

Nidaros (*Norwegian* 'ni:darɔ:s) *n* the former name (1930–31) of **Trondheim.**

nidation (naɪ'deɪʃən) *n Physiol.* another name for **implantation** (sense 2). [from Latin *nīdus* nest]

niddering *or* **nidering** ('nɪdərɪŋ) *Archaic.* ◆ *n* **1** a coward. ◆ *adj* **2** cowardly. [C16: a mistaken reading of Old English *nithing* coward; related to *nīth* malice]

niddle-noddle ('nɪd^{ə}lˌnɒd^{ə}l) *adj* **1** nodding. ◆ *vb* **2** to nod rapidly or unsteadily. [C18: reduplication of NOD]

nide (naɪd) *n* another word for **nye.** [C17: from Latin *nīdus* nest]

nidicolous (nɪ'dɪkələs) *adj* (of young birds) remaining in the nest for some time after hatching. [C19: from Latin *nīdus* nest + *colere* to inhabit]

nidifugous (nɪ'dɪfjugəs) *adj* (of young birds) leaving the nest very soon after hatching. [C19: from Latin *nīdus* nest + *fugere* to flee]

nidify ('nɪdɪˌfaɪ) *or* **nidificate** ('nɪdɪfɪˌkeɪt) *vb* **-fies, -fying, -fied.** (*intr*) (of a bird) to make or build a nest. [C17: from Latin *nīdificāre*, from *nīdus* a nest + *facere* to make] ▸ ˌ**nidifiˈcation** *n*

nid-nod (ˈnɪdˌnɒd) *vb* **-nods, -nodding, -nodded.** to nod repeatedly. [C18: reduplication of NOD]

nidus (ˈnaɪdəs) *n, pl* **-di** (-daɪ). **1** the nest in which insects or spiders deposit their eggs. **2** *Pathol.* a focus of infection. **3** a cavity in which plant spores develop. [C18: from Latin: NEST] ▸ ˈ**nidal** *adj*

Niebuhr (ˈniːbʊə) *n* **1 Barthold Georg** (ˈbartɔltˈgeːɔrk). 1776–1831, German historian, noted for his critical approach to sources, esp. in *History of Rome* (1811–32). **2 Reinhold** (ˈraɪnˌhəʊld). 1892–1971, U.S. Protestant theologian. His works include *Moral Man and Immoral Society* (1932) and *The Nature and Destiny of Man* (1941–43).

niece (niːs) *n* a daughter of one's sister or brother. [C13: from Old French: niece, granddaughter, ultimately from Latin *neptis* granddaughter]

Niederösterreich (ˈniːdərøːstəraɪç) *n* the German name for **Lower Austria.**

Niedersachsen (ˈniːdərzaksən) *n* the German name for **Lower Saxony.**

niello (nɪˈɛləʊ) *n, pl* **-li** (-lɪ) *or* **-los. 1** a black compound of sulphur and silver, lead, or copper used to incise a design on a metal surface. **2** the process of decorating surfaces with niello. **3** a surface or object decorated with niello. ◆ *vb* **-los, -loing, -loed. 4** (*tr*) to decorate or treat with niello. [C19: from Italian from Latin *nigellus* blackish, from *niger* black] ▸ **niˈellist** *n*

Nielsen (ˈniːlsən; *Danish* ˈnelsən) *n* **Carl (August)** (karl). 1865–1931, Danish composer. His works include six symphonies and the opera *Masquerade* (1906).

Niemen (ˈnjɛmɛn) *n* the Polish name for the **Neman.**

Niemeyer (ˈniːˌmaɪə) *n* **Oscar.** born 1907, Brazilian architect. His work includes many buildings in Brasília, esp. the president's palace (1959) and the cathedral (1964).

Niemöller (*German* ˈniːmœlər) *n* **Martin** (ˈmartiːn). 1892–1984, German Protestant theologian, who was imprisoned (1938–45) for his opposition to Hitler.

Niepce (*French* njɛps) *n* **Joseph-Nicéphore** (ʒozɛfnisefor). 1765–1833, French inventor. He produced the first photographic image (1816) and the first permanent camera photograph (1826).

Niersteiner (*German* ˈniːrʃtaɪnər) *n* a white wine from the region around Nierstein, Germany.

Nietzsche (ˈniːtʃə) *n* **Friedrich Wilhelm** (ˈfriːdrɪç ˈvɪlhɛlm). 1844–1900, German philosopher, poet, and critic, noted esp. for his concept of the superman and his rejection of traditional Christian values. His chief works are *The Birth of Tragedy* (1872), *Thus Spake Zarathustra* (1883–91), and *Beyond Good and Evil* (1886). ▸ **Nietzschean** (ˈniːtʃɪən) *n, adj* ▸ ˈ**Nietzscheˌism** *or* ˈ**Nietzscheanˌism** *n*

nieve (niːv) *n Scot. and northern English dialect.* the closed hand; fist. [C14: from Old Norse *hnefi*]

Nièvre (*French* njɛvrə) *n* a department of central France, in Burgundy region. Capital: Nevers. Pop.: 230 400 (1995). Area: 6888 sq. km (2686 sq. miles).

nife (naɪf, ˈnaɪfɪ) *n* the earth's core, thought to be composed of nickel and iron. [C20: from the chemical symbols *Ni* (nickel) and *Fe* (iron)]

nifedipine (naɪˈfɛdɪpiːn) *n Med.* a calcium antagonist used in the treatment of hypertension and angina pectoris.

niff (nɪf) *Brit. slang.* ◆ *n* **1** a bad smell. ◆ *vb* (*intr*) **2** to smell badly; stink. [C20: perhaps from SNIFF] ▸ ˈ**niffy** *adj*

Niflheim (ˈnɪvəlˌheɪm) *n Norse myth.* the abode of the dead. [Old Norse, literally: mist home]

nifty (ˈnɪftɪ) *adj* **-tier, -tiest.** *Informal.* **1** pleasing, apt, or stylish. **2** quick, agile: *he's nifty on his feet.* [C19: of uncertain origin] ▸ ˈ**niftily** *adv* ▸ ˈ**niftiness** *n*

nigella (naɪˈdʒɛlə) *n* any plant of the ranunculaceous genus *Nigella*, from the Mediterranean and W Asia, esp. *N. damascena:* see **love-in-a-mist.** [New Latin, diminutive of Latin *niger* black, from the colour of the seeds]

Niger *n* **1** (niːˈʒɛə, ˈnaɪdʒə). a landlocked republic in West Africa: important since earliest times for its trans-Saharan trade routes; made a French colony in 1922 and became fully independent in 1960; exports peanuts and livestock. Official language: French. Religion: Muslim majority. Currency: franc. Capital: Niamey. Pop.: 9 672 000 (1998 est.). Area: 1 267 000 sq. km (489 000 sq. miles). **2** (ˈnaɪdʒə). a river in West Africa, rising in S Guinea and flowing in a great northward curve through Mali, then southwest through Niger and Nigeria to the Gulf of Guinea: the third longest river in Africa, with the largest delta, covering an area of 36 260 sq. km (14 000 sq. miles). Length: 4184 km (2600 miles). **3** (ˈnaɪdʒə). a state of W central Nigeria, formed in 1976 from part of North-Western State. Capital: Minna. Pop.: 2 775 526 (1995 est.). Area: 76 363 sq. km (29 476 sq. miles). ▸ **Nigerien** (niːˈʒɛərɪən) *adj, n*

Niger-Congo *n* **1** a family of languages of Africa consisting of the Bantu languages together with most of the languages of the coastal regions of West Africa. The chief branches are Benue-Congo (including Bantu), Kwa, Mande, and West Atlantic. ◆ *adj* **2** relating to or belonging to this family of languages.

Nigeria (naɪˈdʒɪərɪə) *n* a republic in West Africa, on the Gulf of Guinea: Lagos annexed by the British in 1861; protectorates of Northern and Southern Nigeria formed in 1900 and united as a colony in 1914; gained independence as a member of the Commonwealth in 1960 (membership suspended from 1995 to 1999 following human rights violations); Eastern Region seceded as the Republic of Biafra for the duration of the severe civil war (1967–70); ruled by military governments from 1966; in 1993 the annulment of democratic elections by the military government precipitated a political and social crisis. It consists of a belt of tropical rain forest in the south, with semidesert in the extreme north and highlands in the east; the main export is petroleum. Official language: English; Hausa, Ibo, and Yoruba are the chief regional languages. Religion: animist, Muslim, and Christian. Currency: naira. Capital: Abuja. Pop.: 110 532 000 (1998 est.). Area: 923 773 sq. km (356 669 sq. miles). ▸ **Niˈgerian** *adj, n*

Niger seed *n* another name for **ramtil** (sense 2).

niggard (ˈnɪgəd) *n* **1** a stingy person. ◆ *adj* **2** *Archaic.* miserly. [C14: perhaps of Scandinavian origin; related to Swedish dialect *nygg* and Old English *hnēaw* stingy]

niggardly (ˈnɪgədlɪ) *adj* **1** stingy or ungenerous. **2** meagre: *a niggardly salary.* ◆ *adv* **3** stingily; grudgingly. ▸ ˈ**niggardliness** *n*

nigger (ˈnɪgə) *n* **1** *Offensive.* **1a** another name for a Negro. **1b** (*as modifier*): *nigger minstrels.* **2** *Offensive.* a member of any dark-skinned race. **3 nigger in the woodpile.** a hidden snag or hindrance. [C18: from C16 dialect *neeger*, from French *nègre*, from Spanish NEGRO[1]]

niggle (ˈnɪgəl) *vb* **1** (*intr*) to find fault continually. **2** (*intr*) to be preoccupied with details; fuss. **3** (*tr*) to irritate; worry. ◆ *n* **4** a slight or trivial objection or complaint. **5** a slight feeling as of misgiving, uncertainty, etc. [C16: from Scandinavian; related to Norwegian *nigla.* Compare NIGGARD] ▸ ˈ**niggler** *n* ▸ ˈ**niggly** *adj*

niggling (ˈnɪglɪŋ) *adj* **1** petty. **2** fussy. **3** irritating. **4** requiring painstaking work. ◆ *n* **5** an act or instance of niggling. ▸ ˈ**nigglingly** *adv*

nigh (naɪ) *adj, adv, prep* an archaic, poetic, or dialect word for **near.** [Old English *nēah, nēh;* related to German *nah*, Old Frisian *nei.* Compare NEAR, NEXT]

night (naɪt) *n* **1** the period of darkness each 24 hours between sunset and sunrise, as distinct from day. **2** (*modifier*) of, occurring, working, etc., at night: *a night nurse.* **3** the occurrence of this period considered as a unit: *four nights later they left.* **4** the period between sunset and retiring to bed; evening. **5** the time between bedtime and morning: *she spent the night alone.* **6** the weather conditions of the night: *a clear night.* **7** the activity or experience of a person during a night. **8** (*sometimes cap.*) any evening designated for a special observance or function. **9** nightfall or dusk. **10** a state or period of gloom, ignorance, etc. **11 make a night of it.** to go out and celebrate for most of the night. **12 night and day.** continually: *that baby cries night and day.* ◆ Related adj: **nocturnal.** [Old English *niht;* compare Dutch *nacht*, Latin *nox*, Greek *nux*] ▸ ˈ**nightless** *adj* ▸ ˈ**nightˌlike** *adj*

night blindness *n Pathol.* a nontechnical term for **nyctalopia.** ▸ ˈ**nightˌblind** *adj*

night-blooming cereus *n* any of several cacti of the genera *Hylocereus, Selenicereus,* etc., having large fragrant flowers that open at night.

nightcap (ˈnaɪtˌkæp) *n* **1** a bedtime drink, esp. an alcoholic or hot one. **2** a soft cap formerly worn in bed.

nightclothes (ˈnaɪtˌkləʊðz) *pl n* clothes worn in bed.

nightclub (ˈnaɪtˌklʌb) *n* a place of entertainment open until late at night, usually offering food, drink, a floor show, dancing, etc. ▸ ˈ**nightˌclubber** *n*

night dancer *n* (in Uganda) a person believed to employ the help of the dead in destroying other people.

nightdress (ˈnaɪtˌdrɛs) *n Brit.* a loose dress worn in bed by women. Also called: **nightgown, nightie.**

nightfall (ˈnaɪtˌfɔːl) *n* the approach of darkness; dusk.

night fighter *n* an interceptor aircraft used for operations at night.

nightgown (ˈnaɪtˌgaʊn) *n* **1** another name for **nightdress. 2** a man's nightshirt.

nighthawk (ˈnaɪtˌhɔːk) *n* **1** Also called: **bullbat, mosquito hawk.** any American nightjar of the genus *Chordeiles* and related genera, having a dark plumage and, in the male, white patches on the wings and tail. **2** *Informal.* another name for **night owl.**

night heron *n* any nocturnal heron of the genus *Nycticorax* and related genera, having short legs and neck, a heavy body, and a short heavy bill.

nightie *or* **nighty** (ˈnaɪtɪ) *n, pl* **nighties.** *Informal.* short for **nightdress.**

nightingale (ˈnaɪtɪŋˌgeɪl) *n* **1** a brownish European songbird, *Luscinia megarhynchos*, with a broad reddish-brown tail: well known for its musical song, usually heard at night. **2** any of various similar or related birds, such as *Luscinia luscinia* (**thrush nightingale**). [Old English *nihtegale*, literally: night-singer, from NIGHT + *galan* to sing]

Nightingale (ˈnaɪtɪŋˌgeɪl) *n* **Florence,** known as *the Lady with the Lamp.* 1820–1910, English nurse, famous for her work during the Crimean War. She helped to raise the status and quality of the nursing profession and founded a training school for nurses in London (1860).

Nightingale ward *n* a long hospital ward with beds on either side and the nurses' station in the middle.

nightjar (ˈnaɪtˌdʒɑː) *n* any nocturnal bird of the family *Caprimulgidae*, esp. *Caprimulgus europaeus* (**European nightjar**): order *Caprimulgiformes.* They have a cryptic plumage and large eyes and feed on insects. [C17: NIGHT + JAR[2], so called from its discordant cry]

night latch *n* a door lock that is operated by means of a knob on the inside and a key on the outside.

night letter *n* (formerly, in the U.S. and Canada) a telegram sent for delivery the next day at a cheaper rate than a regular telegram.

nightlife (ˈnaɪtˌlaɪf) *n* social life or entertainment taking place in the late evening or night, as in nightclubs.

night-light *n* a dim light burning at night, esp. for children.

nightlong (ˈnaɪtˌlɒŋ) *adj, adv* throughout the night.

nightly (ˈnaɪtlɪ) *adj* **1** happening or relating to each night. **2** happening at night. ◆ *adv* **3** at night or each night.

nightmare (ˈnaɪtˌmɛə) *n* **1** a terrifying or deeply distressing dream. **2a** an event or condition resembling a terrifying dream: *the nightmare of shipwreck.* **2b** (*as modifier*): *a nightmare drive.* **3** a thing that is feared. **4** (formerly) an evil spirit supposed to harass or suffocate sleeping people. [C13 (meaning: incubus; C16: bad dream): from NIGHT + Old English *mare, mære* evil spirit, from Germanic; compare Old Norse *mara* incubus, Polish *zmora*, French *cauchemar* nightmare] ▸ ˈ**nightˌmarish** *adj* ▸ ˈ**nightˌmarishly** *adv* ▸ ˈ**nightˌmarishness** *n*

night-night *sentence substitute.* an informal word for **good night.**
night nurse *n* a nurse whose duty is to look after a patient or patients during the night.
night owl *or* **hawk** *n Informal.* a person who is or prefers to be up and about late at night.
night raven *n Poetic.* any bird, esp. the night heron, that is most active at night.
nightrider ('naɪt,raɪdə) *n* a member of a band of mounted and usually masked Whites in the southern U.S. who carried out acts of revenge and intimidation at night after the Civil War. ► **'night,riding** *n*
night robe *n* a U.S. and Canadian name for **nightdress.**
nights (naɪts) *adv Informal.* at night, esp. regularly: *he works nights.*
night safe *n* a safe built into the outside wall of a bank, in which customers can deposit money at times when the bank is closed.
night school *n* an educational institution that holds classes in the evening for those who are not free during the day.
nightshade ('naɪt,ʃeɪd) *n* **1** any of various solanaceous plants, such as deadly nightshade, woody nightshade, and black nightshade. **2** See **enchanter's nightshade.** [Old English *nihtscada,* apparently NIGHT + SHADE, referring to the poisonous or soporific qualities of these plants]
night shift *n* **1** a group of workers who work a shift during the night in an industry or occupation where a day shift or a back shift are also worked. **2** the period worked. ◆ See also **back shift.**
nightshirt ('naɪt,ʃɜːt) *n* a loose knee-length or longer shirtlike garment worn in bed by men.
night soil *n* human excrement collected at night from cesspools, privies, etc., and sometimes used as a fertilizer.
nightspot ('naɪt,spɒt) *n* an informal word for **nightclub.**
night stick *n* a U.S. and Canadian name for **truncheon.**
night terrors *pl n* a condition in which a person, usually a child, suddenly starts from sleep in a state of extreme fear but cannot later remember the incident.
night-time *n* **a** the time from sunset to sunrise; night as distinct from day. **b** (*as modifier*): *a night-time prowler.*
night watch *n* **1** a watch or guard kept at night, esp. for security. **2** the period of time the watch is kept. **3** a person who keeps such a watch; night watchman.
night watchman *n* **1** Also called: **night watch.** a person who keeps guard at night on a factory, public building, etc. **2** *Cricket.* a batsman sent in to bat to play out time when a wicket has fallen near the end of a day's play.
nightwear ('naɪt,wɛə) *n* apparel worn in bed or before retiring to bed; pyjamas, nightdress, dressing gown, etc.
nigrescent (naɪ'grɛsᵊnt) *adj* blackish; dark. [C18: from Latin *nigrescere* to grow black, from *niger* black; see NEGRO[1]] ► **ni'grescence** *n*
nigritude ('nɪgrɪ,tjuːd) *n Rare.* blackness; darkness. [C17: from Latin *nigritūdō,* from *niger* black]
nigrosine ('nɪgrə,siːn, -sɪn) *or* **nigrosin** ('nɪgrəsɪn) *n* any of a class of black pigments and dyes obtained from aniline: used in inks and shoe polishes and for dyeing textiles. [C19: from Latin *niger* black + -OSE[1] + -INE[1]]
NIHE (in Ireland) *abbrev. for* National Institute for Higher Education.
nihil *Latin.* ('naɪhɪl, 'niːhɪl) *n* nil; nothing.
nihilism ('naɪɪ,lɪzəm) *n* **1** a complete denial of all established authority and institutions. **2** *Philosophy.* an extreme form of scepticism that systematically rejects all values, belief in existence, the possibility of communication, etc. **3** a revolutionary doctrine of destruction for its own sake. **4** the practice or promulgation of terrorism. [C19: from Latin *nihil* nothing + -ISM, on the model of German *Nihilismus*] ► **'nihilist** *n, adj* ► **,nihil'istic** *adj*
Nihilism ('naɪɪ,lɪzəm) *n* (in tsarist Russia) any of several revolutionary doctrines that upheld terrorism.
nihility (naɪ'hɪlɪtɪ) *n* the state or condition of being nothing; nothingness; nullity.
nihil obstat ('ɒbstæt) the phrase used by a Roman Catholic censor to declare publication inoffensive to faith or morals. [Latin, literally: nothing hinders]
Nihon ('niː'hɒn) *n* transliteration of a Japanese name for **Japan.**
NII (in Britain) *abbrev. for* nuclear installations inspectorate.
Niigata ('niːɪ,gɑːtə) *n* a port in central Japan, on NW Honshu at the mouth of the Shinano River: the chief port on the Sea of Japan. Pop.: 494 785 (1995).
Nijinsky (nɪ'dʒɪnskɪ) *n* **Waslaw** *or* **Vaslaw** (vats'laf). 1890–1950, Russian ballet dancer and choreographer, who was associated with Diaghilev. His creations include settings of Stravinsky's *Petrushka* and *The Rite of Spring.*
Nijmegen ('naɪ,meɪgən; *Dutch* 'neimeːxə) *n* an industrial town in the E Netherlands, in Gelderland province on the Waal River: the oldest town in the country; scene of the signing (1678) of the peace treaty between Louis XIV, the Netherlands, Spain, and the Holy Roman Empire. Pop.: 147 600 (1996 est.). Latin name: **,Novio'magus.** German name: **Nimwegen.**
-nik *suffix forming nouns.* denoting a person associated with a specified state, belief, or quality: *beatnik; refusenik.* [C20: from Russian *-nik,* as in SPUTNIK, and influenced by Yiddish *-nik* (agent suffix)]
Nikaria (nɪ'kɛərɪə, naɪ-) *n* another name for **Icaria.**
nikau *or* **nikau palm** ('niːkaʊ) *n* a palm tree of the genus *Rhopalostylis,* esp. *R. sapida,* native to New Zealand. The leaves were used by the Maoris to build their whares and the top of the stem is sometimes eaten. [Maori]
Nike ('naɪkiː) *n Greek myth.* the winged goddess of victory. Roman counterpart: **Victoria.** [from Greek: victory]
Nikkei Stock Average ('nɪkeɪ) *n* an index of prices on the Tokyo Stock Exchange. [C20: from *Nik(on) Kei(zai Shimbun),* a Japanese newspaper group]
Nikko ('niːkəʊ) *n* a town in central Japan, on NE Honshu: a major pilgrimage centre, with a 4th-century Shinto shrine, a Buddhist temple (767), and the shrines and mausoleums of the Tokugawa shoguns. Pop.: 20 128 (1990).
Nikolainkaupunki (*Finnish* ,nikəlaɪn'kaupuŋki) *n* the former name of **Vaasa.**
Nikolayev (*Russian* nika'lajɪf) *n* a city in the S Ukraine on the Southern Bug about 64 km (40 miles) from the Black Sea: founded as a naval base in 1788; one of the leading Black Sea ports. Pop.: 508 000 (1996 est.). Former name: **Vernoleninsk.**
nil (nɪl) *n* another word for nothing: used esp. in the scoring of certain games. [C19: from Latin]
nil desperandum ('nɪl ,dɛspə'rændəm) *sentence substitute.* never despair. [from Latin, literally: nothing to be despaired of]
Nile (naɪl) *n* a river in Africa, rising in S central Burundi in its remotest headstream, the **Luvironza:** flows into Lake Victoria and leaves the lake as the **Victoria Nile,** flowing to Lake Albert, which is drained by the **Albert Nile,** becoming the White Nile on the border between Uganda and the Sudan; joined by its chief tributary, the **Blue Nile** (which rises near Lake Tana, Ethiopia) at Khartoum, and flows north to its delta on the Mediterranean; the longest river in the world. Length: (from the source of the Luvironza to the Mediterranean) 6741 km (4187 miles).
Nile blue *n* **a** a pale greenish-blue colour. **b** (*as adj*): *a Nile-blue carpet.*
Nile green *n* **a** a pale bluish-green colour. **b** (*as adj*): *a Nile-green dress.*
nilgai ('nɪlgaɪ), **nilghau,** *or* **nylghau** ('nɪlgɔː) *n, pl* **-gai, -gais** *or* **-ghau, -ghaus.** a large Indian antelope, *Boselaphus tragocamelus.* The male is blue-grey with white markings and has small horns; the female is brownish and has no horns. [C19: from Hindi *nīlgāw* blue bull, from Sanskrit *nīla* dark blue + *go* bull]
Nilgiri Hills ('nɪlgɪrɪ) *or* **Nilgiris** *pl n* a plateau in S India, in Tamil Nadu. Average height: 2000 m (6500 ft.), reaching 2635 m (8647 ft.) in Doda Betta.
Nilometer (naɪ'lɒmɪtə) *n* a graduated pillar by which the rise and fall of the Nile can be measured.
Nilo-Saharan (,naɪləʊsə'hɑːrən) *n* **1** a family of languages of Africa, spoken chiefly by Nilotic peoples in a region extending from the Sahara to Kenya and Tanzania, including the Chari-Nile, Saharan, Songhai, and other branches. Classification is complicated by the fact that many languages spoken in this region belong to the unrelated Afro-Asiatic, Kordofanian, and Niger-Congo families. ◆ *adj* **2** relating to or belonging to this family of languages.
Nilotic (naɪ'lɒtɪk) *adj* **1** of or relating to the Nile. **2** of, relating to, or belonging to a tall Negroid pastoral people inhabiting the S Sudan, parts of Kenya and Uganda, and neighbouring countries. **3** relating to or belonging to the group of languages spoken by the Nilotic peoples. ◆ *n* **4** a group of languages of E Africa, including Luo, Dinka, and Masai, now generally regarded as belonging to the Chari-Nile branch of the Nilo-Saharan family. [C17: via Latin from Greek *Neilotikós,* from *Neilos* the NILE]
nil return *n* a reply of zero to a request for a quantified reply.
Nilsson (*Swedish* 'nilsɔn) *n* **Birgit** ('birgit). born 1918, Swedish operatic soprano.
nim (nɪm) *n* a game in which two players alternately remove one or more small items, such as matchsticks, from one of several rows or piles, the object being to take (or avoid taking) the last item remaining on the table. [C20: perhaps from archaic *nim* to take, from Old English *niman*]
nimble ('nɪmbᵊl) *adj* **1** agile, quick, and neat in movement: *nimble fingers.* **2** alert; acute: *a nimble intellect.* [Old English *næmel* quick to grasp, and *numol* quick at seizing, both from *niman* to take] ► **'nimbleness** *n* ► **'nimbly** *adv*
nimblewit ('nɪmbəl,wɪt) *n Chiefly U.S. and Canadian.* an alert, bright, and clever person. ► **'nimble,witted** *adj*
nimbostratus (,nɪmbəʊ'streɪtəs, -'strɑːtəs) *n, pl* **-ti** (-taɪ). a dark-coloured rain-bearing stratus cloud.
nimbus ('nɪmbəs) *n, pl* **-bi** (-baɪ) *or* **-buses. 1a** a dark grey rain-bearing cloud. **1b** (*in combination*): *cumulonimbus clouds.* **2a** an emanation of light surrounding a saint or deity. **2b** a representation of this emanation. **3** a surrounding aura or atmosphere. [C17: from Latin: cloud, radiance] ► **'nimbused** *adj*
NIMBY ('nɪmbɪ) *n acronym for* not in my back yard: a person who objects to the occurrence of something if it will affect them or take place in their locality.
Nîmes (*French* nim) *n* a city in S France: Roman remains including an amphitheatre and the Pont du Gard aqueduct. Pop.: 133 607 (1990).
nimiety (nɪ'maɪɪtɪ) *n, pl* **-ties.** a rare word for **excess.** [C16: from Late Latin *nimietās,* from Latin *nimis* too much]
niminy-piminy ('nɪmɪnɪ'pɪmɪnɪ) *adj* excessively refined; prim. [C19: imitative of a prim affected enunciation]
Nimitz ('nɪmɪts) *n* **Chester William.** 1885–1966, U.S. admiral; commander in chief of the U.S. Pacific fleet in World War II (1941–45).
nimonic alloy (nɪ'mɒnɪk) *n* any of various nickel-based alloys used at high temperatures, as in gas turbine blades. [C20: from NI(CKEL) + MO(LYBDENUM) + -IC]
n'importe *French.* (nɛ̃pɔrt) no matter.
Nimrod ('nɪmrɒd) *n* **1** *Old Testament.* a hunter, who was famous for his prowess (Genesis 10:8–9). **2** a person who is dedicated to or skilled in hunting. Douay spelling: **Nemrod.** ► **Nim'rodian** *or* **Nim'rodic** *adj*
Nimrud (nɪm'ruːd) *n* an ancient city in Assyria, near the present-day city of Mosul (Iraq): founded in about 1250 B.C. and destroyed by the Medes in 612 B.C.; excavated by Sir Austen Henry Layard.
Nimwegen ('nɪmveːgən) *n* the German name for **Nijmegen.**
Nimzowitsch ('nɪmzə,vɪtʃ) *n* **Aaron Isayevich** (ɪ'zaɪjevɪtʃ) 1886–1935, Latvian chess player and theorist; influential in enunciating the principles of the hypermodern school, of which he was the main instigator.
Niña ('niːnə; *Spanish* 'niɲa) *n* **the.** one of the three ships commanded by Columbus in 1492.
nincompoop ('nɪnkəm,puːp, 'nɪŋ-) *n* a stupid person; fool; idiot. [C17: of unknown origin]

nine (naɪn) *n* **1** the cardinal number that is the sum of one and eight. See also **number** (sense 1). **2** a numeral, 9, IX, etc., representing this number. **3** something representing, represented by, or consisting of nine units, such as a playing card with nine symbols on it. **4** Also: **nine o'clock.** nine hours after noon or midnight: *the play starts at nine.* **5 dressed (up) to the nines.** *Informal.* elaborately dressed. **6 999** (in Britain) the telephone number of the emergency services. **7 nine to five.** normal office hours: *he works nine to five; a nine-to-five job.* ◆ *determiner* **8a** amounting to nine: *nine days.* **8b** (*as pronoun*): *nine of the ten are ready.* ◆ Related prefix: **nona-**. [Old English *nigon;* related to Gothic *niun,* Latin *novem*]

nine-days wonder *n* something that arouses great interest, but only for a short period.

ninefold ('naɪn,fəʊld) *adj* **1** equal to or having nine times as many or as much. **2** composed of nine parts. ◆ *adv* **3** by or up to nine times as many or as much.

ninepins ('naɪn,pɪnz) *n* **1** (*functioning as sing*) another name for **skittles. 2** (*sing*) one of the pins used in this game.

nineteen (,naɪn'tiːn) *n* **1** the cardinal number that is the sum of ten and nine and is a prime number. See also **number** (sense 1). **2** a numeral, 19, XIX, etc., representing this number. **3** something represented by, representing, or consisting of 19 units. **4 talk nineteen to the dozen.** to talk incessantly. ◆ *determiner* **5a** amounting to nineteen: *nineteen pictures.* **5b** (*as pronoun*): *only nineteen voted.* [Old English *nigontīne*]

nineteenth (,naɪn'tiːnθ) *adj* **1** (*usually prenominal*) **1a** coming after the eighteenth in numbering or counting order, position, time, etc., being the ordinal number of *nineteen.* Often written: 19th. **1b** (*as n*): *the nineteenth was rainy.* ◆ *n* **2a** one of 19 approximately equal parts of something. **2b** (*as modifier*): *a nineteenth part.* **3** the fraction that is equal to one divided by 19 (1/19).

nineteenth hole *n Golf, slang.* the bar in a golf clubhouse. [C20: from its being the next objective after a standard 18-hole round]

nineteenth man *n* **1** *Australian Rules football.* the first reserve in a team. **2** any person acting as a reserve or substitute.

ninetieth ('naɪntɪɪθ) *adj* **1** (*usually prenominal*) **1a** being the ordinal number of *ninety* in numbering or counting order, position, time, etc. Often written: 90th. **1b** (*as n*): *the ninetieth in succession.* ◆ *n* **2a** one of 90 approximately equal parts of something. **2b** (*as modifier*): *a ninetieth part.* **3** the fraction equal to one divided by 90 (1/90).

ninety ('naɪntɪ) *n, pl* **-ties. 1** the cardinal number that is the product of ten and nine. See also **number** (sense 1). **2** a numeral, 90, XC, etc., representing this number. **3** something represented by, representing, or consisting of 90 units. ◆ *determiner* **4a** amounting to ninety: *ninety times out of a hundred.* **4b** (*as pronoun*): *at least ninety are thought to be missing.* [Old English *nigontig*]

Nineveh ('nɪnɪvə) *n* the ancient capital of Assyria, on the River Tigris opposite the present-day city of Mosul (N Iraq): at its height in the 8th and 7th centuries B.C.; destroyed in 612 B.C. by the Medes and Babylonians. ▸ **'Ninevite** *n*

Ningbo *or* **Ningpo** ('nɪŋ'pəʊ) *n* a port in E China, in NE Zhejiang, on the Yung River, about 20 km (12 miles) from its mouth at Hangzhou Bay: one of the first sites of European settlement in China. Pop.: 1 090 000 (1991 est.).

Ningsia *or* **Ninghsia** ('nɪŋ'ʃjɑː) *n* **1** a former province of NW China: mostly included in the Inner Mongolian AR in 1956, with the smaller part constituted as the Ningxia Hui AR in 1958. **2** the former name of **Yinchuan.**

Ningxia Hui Autonomous Region ('nɪŋ'ʃjɑː 'huːɪ) *n* an administrative division of NW China, south of the Inner Mongolian AR. Capital: Yinchuan. Pop.: 5 130 000 (1996 est.). Area: 66 400 sq. km (25 896 sq. miles).

ninhydrin (nɪn'haɪdrɪn) *n* a chemical reagent used for the detection and analysis of primary amines, esp. amino acids, with which it forms a derivative with an intense purple colour. [C20: from the chemical name *triketo hydrindene*]

Ninian ('nɪnjən) *n* **Saint.** ?360–?432 A.D., the first known apostle of Scotland; built a stone church (*candida casa*) at Whithorn on his native Solway; preached to the Picts. Feast day: Sept. 16.

ninja ('nɪndʒə) *n, pl* **-ja** *or* **-jas.** (*sometimes cap.*) a person skilled in **ninjutsu**, a Japanese martial art characterized by stealthy movement and camouflage. [Japanese]

ninny ('nɪnɪ) *n, pl* **-nies.** a dull-witted person. [C16: perhaps from *an innocent* simpleton] ▸ **'ninnyish** *adj*

ninon ('niːnɒn, 'naɪnɒn; *French* ninɔ̃) *n* a fine strong silky fabric. [C20: from French]

ninth (naɪnθ) *adj* **1** (*usually prenominal*) **1a** coming after the eighth in counting order, position, time, etc.; being the ordinal number of *nine.* Often written: 9th. **1b** (*as n*): *he came on the ninth; ninth in line.* ◆ *n* **2a** one of nine equal or nearly equal parts of an object, quantity, measurement, etc. **2b** (*as modifier*): *a ninth part.* **3** the fraction equal to one divided by nine (1/9). **4** *Music.* **4a** an interval of one octave plus a second. **4b** one of two notes constituting such an interval. **4c** See **ninth chord.** ◆ *adv* **5** Also: **'ninthly.** after the eighth person, position, event, etc. ◆ *sentence connector.* **6** Also: **ninthly.** as the ninth point: linking what follows to the previous statement. [Old English *nigotha;* related to Old High German *niunto,* Old Norse *nīundi*]

ninth chord *n* a chord much used in jazz and pop, consisting of a major or minor triad with the seventh and ninth added above the root. Often shortened to **ninth.**

Ninus ('naɪnəs) *n* a king of Assyria and the legendary founder of Nineveh, husband of Semiramis.

Niobe ('naɪəbɪ) *n Greek myth.* a daughter of Tantalus, whose children were slain after she boasted of them: although turned into stone, she continued to weep. ▸ **Niobean** (naɪ'əʊbɪən) *adj*

niobic (naɪ'əʊbɪk, -'ɒbɪk) *adj* of or containing niobium in the pentavalent state. Also: **columbic.**

niobite ('naɪə,baɪt) *n* another name for **columbite.** [C19: NIOBIUM + -ITE[1]]

niobium (naɪ'əʊbɪəm) *n* a ductile white superconductive metallic element that occurs principally in columbite and tantalite: used in steel alloys. Symbol: Nb; atomic no.: 41; atomic wt.: 92.90638; valency: 2, 3, or 5; relative density: 8.57; melting pt.: 2469±10°C; boiling pt.: 4744°C. Former name: **columbium.** [C19: from New Latin, from NIOBE (daughter of Tantalus), so named because it occurred in TANTALITE]

niobous (naɪ'əʊbəs) *adj* of or containing niobium in the trivalent state. Also: **columbous.**

Niort (*French* njɔr) *n* a market town in W France. Pop.: 58 660 (1990).

nip[1] (nɪp) *vb* **nips, nipping, nipped.** (*mainly tr*) **1** to catch or tightly compress, as between a finger and the thumb; pinch. **2** (often foll. by *off*) to remove by clipping, biting, etc. **3** (when *intr*, often foll. by *at*) to give a small sharp bite (to): *the dog nipped at his heels.* **4** (esp. of the cold) to affect with a stinging sensation. **5** to harm through cold: *the frost nipped the young plants.* **6** to check or destroy the growth of (esp. in the phrase **nip in the bud**). **7** *Slang.* to steal. **8** (*intr;* foll. by *along, up, out,* etc.) *Brit. informal.* to hurry; dart. **9** *Slang, chiefly U.S. and Canadian.* to snatch. ◆ *n* **10** the act of nipping; a pinch, snip, etc. **11a** a frosty or chilly quality. **11b** severe frost or cold: *the first nip of winter.* **12** a small piece or quantity: *he went out for a nip of fresh air.* **13** a sharp flavour or tang. **14** *Archaic.* a taunting remark. **15 nip and tuck. 15a** *Chiefly U.S. and Canadian.* neck and neck. **15b** *Informal.* plastic surgery performed for cosmetic reasons. **16 put the nips in.** *Austral. and N.Z. slang.* to exert pressure on someone, esp. in order to extort money. [C14: of Scandinavian origin; compare Old Norse *hnippa* to prod]

nip[2] (nɪp) *n* **1** a small drink of spirits; dram. **2** *Chiefly Brit.* a measure of spirits usually equal to one sixth of a gill. ◆ *vb* **nips, nipping, nipped. 3** to drink (spirits), esp. habitually in small amounts. [C18: shortened from *nipperkin* a vessel holding a half-pint or less, of uncertain origin; compare Dutch *nippen* to sip]

Nip (nɪp) *n Slang.* a derogatory word for a **Japanese.** [C20: short for *Nipponese*]

nipa ('niːpə, 'naɪ-) *n* **1** a palm tree, *Nipa fruticans,* of S and SE Asia, having feathery leaves, used for thatching, and edible fruit. **2** the fruit or thatch obtained from this tree. **3** the sap of this tree, used to make a liquor. [C16: from Malay *nīpah*]

Nipigon ('nɪpəgɒn) *n* **Lake.** a lake in central Canada, in NW Ontario, draining into Lake Superior via the **Nipigon River.** Area: 4843 sq. km (1870 sq. miles).

Nipissing ('nɪpɪsɪŋ) *n* **Lake.** a lake in central Canada, in E Ontario between the Ottawa River and Georgian Bay. Area: 855 sq. km (330 sq. miles).

nipper ('nɪpə) *n* **1** a person or thing that nips. **2** the large pincer-like claw of a lobster, crab, or similar crustacean. **3** *Informal.* a small child. **4** *Austral.* a type of small prawn used as bait.

nippers ('nɪpəz) *pl n* an instrument or tool, such as a pair of pliers, for snipping, pinching, or squeezing.

nipping ('nɪpɪŋ) *adj* **1** sharp and biting: *a nipping wind.* **2** sarcastic; bitter. ▸ **'nippingly** *adv*

nipple ('nɪpᵊl) *n* **1** Also called: **mamilla, papilla, teat.** the small conical projection in the centre of the areola of each breast, which in women contains the outlet of the milk ducts. Related adj: **mamillary. 2** something resembling a nipple in shape or function. **3** Also called: **grease nipple.** a small drilled bush, usually screwed into a bearing, through which grease is introduced. **4** *U.S. and Canadian.* an informal word for **dummy** (sense 11). [C16: from earlier *neble, nible,* perhaps from NEB, NIB]

nipplewort ('nɪpᵊl,wɜːt) *n* an annual Eurasian plant, *Lapsana communis,* with pointed oval leaves and small yellow flower heads: family *Compositae* (composites).

Nippon ('nɪpɒn) *n* transliteration of a Japanese name for **Japan.** ▸ **Nipponese** (,nɪpə'niːz) *adj, n*

Nippur (nɪ'pʊə) *n* an ancient Sumerian and Babylonian city, the excavated site of which is in SE Iraq: an important religious centre, abandoned in the 12th or 13th century.

nippy ('nɪpɪ) *adj* **-pier, -piest. 1** (of weather) chilly, keen, or frosty. **2** *Brit. informal.* **2a** quick; nimble; active. **2b** (of a motor vehicle) small and relatively powerful. **3** (of the taste of food) biting, sharp, or pungent. **4** (of a dog) inclined to bite. ▸ **'nippily** *adv* ▸ **'nippiness** *n*

NIRC *abbrev. for* National Industrial Relations Court.

Nirenberg ('naɪrənbɜːg) *n* **Marshall Warren.** born 1927, U.S. biochemist; shared the Nobel prize for physiology or medicine (1968) for his role in deciphering the genetic code.

NIREX ('naɪreks) *n acronym for* Nuclear Industry Radioactive Waste Executive.

nirvana (nɪə'vɑːnə, nɜː-) *n Buddhism, Hinduism.* final release from the cycle of reincarnation attained by extinction of all desires and individual existence, culminating (in Buddhism) in absolute blessedness, or (in Hinduism) in absorption into Brahman. [C19: from Sanskrit: extinction, literally: a blowing out, from *nir-* out + *vāti* it blows] ▸ **nir'vanic** *adj*

Niš *or* **Nish** (niːʃ) *n* an industrial town in E Yugoslavia, in SE Serbia: situated on routes between central Europe and the Aegean. Pop.: 175 391 (1991).

Nisan (niː'san) *n* (in the Jewish calendar) the first month of the year according to biblical reckoning and the seventh month of the civil year, usually falling within March and April. [from Hebrew]

Nisei ('niːseɪ) *n* a native-born citizen of the United States or Canada whose parents were Japanese immigrants. [Japanese, literally: second generation]

Nishapur (,niːʃɑː'pʊə) *n* a town in NE Iran, at an altitude of 1195 m (3920 ft.): birthplace and burial place of Omar Khayyám. Pop.: 154 511 (1994 est.).

Nishinomiya (,niːʃɪ'nɒmɪjə) *n* an industrial city in central Japan, on S Honshu, northwest of Osaka. Pop.: 390 388 (1995).

nisi ('naɪsaɪ) *adj* (*postpositive*) *Law.* (of a court order) coming into effect on a specified date unless cause is shown within a certain period why it should not: *a decree nisi.* [C19: from Latin: unless, if not]

nisi prius ('praɪəs) *n* **1** *English legal history.* **1a** a direction that a case be brought up to Westminster for trial before a single judge and a jury. **1b** the writ giving this direction. **1c** trial before the justices taking the assizes. **2** (in the U.S.) a court where civil actions are tried by a single judge sitting with a jury as distinguished from an appellate court. **[C15:** from Latin: unless previously**]**

Nissen hut ('nɪsᵊn) *n* a military shelter of semicircular cross section, made of corrugated steel sheet. U.S. and Canadian equivalent: **Quonset hut. [C20:** named after Lt Col. Peter *Nissen* (1871–1930), British mining engineer, its inventor**]**

nisus ('naɪsəs) *n, pl* **-sus.** an impulse towards or striving after a goal. **[C17:** from Latin: effort, from *nītī* to strive**]**

nit[1] (nɪt) *n* **1** the egg of a louse, usually adhering to human hair. **2** the larva of a louse or similar insect. **[**Old English *hnitu;* related to Dutch *neet,* Old High German *hniz***]**

nit[2] (nɪt) *n* a unit of luminance equal to 1 candela per square metre. **[C20:** from Latin *nitor* brightness**]**

nit[3] (nɪt) *n Informal, chiefly Brit.* short for **nitwit.**

nit[4] (nɪt) *n* a unit of information equal to 1.44 bits. Also called: **nepit. [C20:** from *N(apierian dig)it***]**

nit[5] (nɪt) *n* **keep nit.** *Austral. informal.* to keep watch, esp. during illegal activity. **[C19:** from NIX[1]**]**

niter ('naɪtə) *n* the usual U.S. spelling of **nitre.**

niterie ('naɪtərɪ, -trɪ) *n Slang.* a nightclub.

Niterói (*Portuguese* nite'rɔi) *n* a port in SE Brazil, on Guanabara Bay opposite Rio de Janeiro: contains Brazil's chief shipyards. Pop.: 400 586 (1991). Also called: **Nictheroy.**

nitid ('nɪtɪd) *adj Poetic.* bright; glistening. **[C17:** from Latin *nitidus,* from *nitēre* to shine**]**

niton ('naɪtɒn) *n* a less common name for **radon. [C20:** from Latin *nitēre* to shine**]**

nit-picking *Informal.* ◆ *n* **1** a concern with insignificant details, esp. with the intention of finding fault. ◆ *adj* **2** showing such a concern; fussy. **[C20:** from NIT[1] + PICK[1]**]** ▸ **'nit-,picker** *n*

nitramine ('naɪtrə,miːn) *n* another name for **tetryl.**

nitrate ('naɪtreɪt) *n* **1** any salt or ester of nitric acid, such as sodium nitrate, $NaNO_3$. **2** a fertilizer consisting of or containing nitrate salts. ◆ *vb* **3** (*tr*) to treat with nitric acid or a nitrate. **4** to convert or be converted into a nitrate. **5** to undergo or cause to undergo the chemical process in which a nitro group is introduced into a molecule. ▸ **ni'tration** *n*

nitrazepam (naɪ'treɪzɪ,pæm) *n* a synthetic chemical compound belonging to the benzodiazepine group of drugs; a minor tranquillizer used mainly in sleeping pills such as Mogadon. Formula $C_{15}H_{11}N_3O_3$. **[C20:** from NITRO- + *-azepam;* see DIAZEPAM**]**

nitre *or U.S.* **niter** ('naɪtə) *n* another name for **potassium nitrate** *or* **sodium nitrate. [C14:** via Old French from Latin *nitrum,* from Greek *nitron* NATRON**]**

nitric ('naɪtrɪk) *adj* of or containing nitrogen, esp. in the pentavalent state.

nitric acid *n* a colourless or yellowish fuming corrosive liquid usually used in aqueous solution. It is an oxidizing agent and a strong monobasic acid: important in the manufacture of fertilizers, explosives, and many other chemicals. Formula: HNO_3. Former name: **aqua fortis.**

nitric bacteria *pl n* bacteria that convert nitrites to nitrates in the soil. See also **nitrobacteria.**

nitric oxide *n* a colourless slightly soluble gas forming red fumes of nitrogen dioxide in air. Formula: NO. Systematic name: **nitrogen monoxide.**

nitride ('naɪtraɪd) *n* a compound of nitrogen with a more electropositive element, for example magnesium nitride, Mg_3N_2.

nitriding ('naɪtraɪdɪŋ) *n* a type of case-hardening in which steel is heated for long periods in ammonia vapour so that nitrogen produced by dissociation on the surface enters the steel.

nitrification (,naɪtrɪfɪ'keɪʃən) *n* **1** the oxidation of the ammonium compounds in dead organic material into nitrites and nitrates by soil nitrobacteria, making nitrogen available to plants. See also **nitrogen cycle. 2a** the addition of a nitro group to an organic compound. **2b** the substitution of a nitro group for another group in an organic compound.

nitrify ('naɪtrɪ,faɪ) *vb* **-fies, -fying, -fied.** (*tr*) **1** to treat or cause to react with nitrogen or a nitrogen compound. **2** to treat (soil) with nitrates. **3** (of nitrobacteria) to convert (ammonium compounds) into nitrates by oxidation. ▸ **'nitri,fiable** *adj*

nitrile ('naɪtrɪl, -traɪl) *n* any one of a class of organic compounds containing the monovalent group, -CN. Also called (not in technical usage): **cyanide.**

nitrite ('naɪtraɪt) *n* any salt or ester of nitrous acid.

nitro ('naɪtrəʊ) *n Slang.* short for **nitroglycerine.**

nitro- *or before a vowel* **nitr-** *combining form.* **1** indicating that a chemical compound contains a nitro group, $-NO_2$: *nitrobenzene.* **2** indicating that a chemical compound is a nitrate ester: *nitrocellulose.* **[**from Greek *nitron* NATRON**]**

nitrobacteria (,naɪtrəʊbæk'tɪərɪə) *pl n, sing* **-terium** (-'tɪərɪəm). soil bacteria of the order *Pseudomonadales* that are involved in nitrification, including species of *Nitrosomonas* and *Nitrobacter.*

nitrobenzene (,naɪtrəʊ'benziːn) *n* a yellow oily toxic water-insoluble liquid compound, used as a solvent and in the manufacture of aniline. Formula: $C_6H_5NO_2$.

nitrocellulose (,naɪtrəʊ'seljʊ,ləʊs) *n* another name (not in chemical usage) for **cellulose nitrate.**

Nitro-chalk *n Trademark.* a chemical fertilizer containing calcium carbonate and ammonium nitrate.

nitrochloroform (,naɪtrəʊ'klɒrə,fɔːm) *n* another name for **chloropicrin.**

nitro compound ('naɪtrəʊ) *n* any one of a class of usually organic compounds that contain the monovalent group, $-NO_2$ (**nitro group** or **radical**), linked to a carbon atom. The commonest example is nitrobenzene, $C_6H_5NO_2$.

nitrogen ('naɪtrədʒən) *n* **a** a colourless odourless relatively unreactive gaseous element that forms 78 per cent (by volume) of the air, occurs in many compounds, and is an essential constituent of proteins and nucleic acids: used in the manufacture of ammonia and other chemicals and as a refrigerant. Symbol: N; atomic no.: 7; atomic wt.: 14.00674; valency: 3 or 5; density: 1/2506 kg/m^3; melting pt.: –210.00°C; boiling pt.: –195.8°C. **b** (*as modifier*): *nitrogen cycle.*

nitrogen cycle *n* the natural circulation of nitrogen by living organisms. Nitrates in the soil, derived from dead organic matter by bacterial action (see **nitrification, nitrogen fixation**), are absorbed and synthesized into complex organic compounds by plants and reduced to nitrates again when the plants and the animals feeding on them die and decay.

nitrogen dioxide *n* a red-brown poisonous irritating gas that, at ordinary temperatures, exists in equilibrium with dinitrogen tetroxide. It is an intermediate in the manufacture of nitric acid, a nitrating agent, and an oxidizer for rocket fuels. Formula: NO_2.

nitrogen fixation *n* **1** the conversion of atmospheric nitrogen into nitrogen compounds by certain bacteria, such as *Rhizobium* in the root nodules of legumes. **2** a process, such as the Haber process, in which atmospheric nitrogen is converted into a nitrogen compound, used esp. for the manufacture of fertilizer. ▸ **'nitrogen-,fixing** *adj*

nitrogenize *or* **nitrogenise** (naɪ'trɒdʒɪ,naɪz) *vb* to combine or treat with nitrogen or a nitrogen compound. ▸ **ni,trogeni'zation** *or* **ni,trogeni'sation** *n*

nitrogen monoxide *n* the systematic name for **nitric oxide.**

nitrogen mustard *n* any of a class of organic compounds resembling mustard gas in their molecular structure. General formula: $RN(CH_2CH_2Cl)_2$, where R is an organic group: important in the treatment of cancer.

nitrogenous (naɪ'trɒdʒɪnəs) *adj* containing nitrogen or a nitrogen compound: *a nitrogenous fertilizer.*

nitrogen peroxide *n* **1** an obsolete name for **nitrogen dioxide. 2** the equilibrium mixture of nitrogen dioxide and dinitrogen tetroxide.

nitrogen tetroxide *n* **1** another name for **dinitrogen tetroxide. 2** a brown liquefied mixture of nitrogen dioxide and dinitrogen tetroxide, used as a nitrating, bleaching, and oxidizing agent.

nitroglycerine (,naɪtrəʊ'glɪsə,riːn) *or* **nitroglycerin** (,naɪtrəʊ'glɪsərɪn) *n* a pale yellow viscous explosive liquid substance made from glycerol and nitric and sulphuric acids and used in explosives and in medicine as a vasodilator. Formula: $CH_2NO_3CHNO_3CH_2NO_3$. Also called: **trinitroglycerine.**

nitrohydrochloric acid (,naɪtrəʊ,haɪdrəʊ'klɒrɪk) *n* another name for **aqua regia.**

nitrometer (naɪ'trɒmɪtə) *n* an instrument for measuring the amount of nitrogen in a substance. ▸ **nitrometric** (,naɪtrəʊ'metrɪk) *adj*

nitromethane (,naɪtrəʊ'miːθeɪn) *n* an oily colourless liquid obtained from methane and used as a solvent and rocket fuel and in the manufacture of synthetic resins. Formula: CH_3NO_2.

nitroparaffin (,naɪtrəʊ'pærəfɪn) *n* any of a class of colourless toxic compounds with the general formula $C_nH_{2n+1}NO_2$.

nitrophilous (naɪ'trɒfɪləs) *adj* (of plants) growing in soil well supplied with nitrogen.

nitrosamine (,naɪtrəʊsə'miːn, ,naɪtrəʊs'æmiːn) *n* any one of a class of neutral, usually yellow oily compounds containing the divalent group =NNO.

nitroso (naɪ'trəʊsəʊ) *n* (*modifier*) of, consisting of, or containing the monovalent group O:N-: *a nitroso compound.* **[C19:** from Latin *nitrōsus* full of natron; see NITRE**]**

nitrosyl ('naɪtrəsɪl, -,saɪl) *n* (*modifier*) another word for **nitroso,** esp. when applied to inorganic compounds: *nitrosyl chloride.* **[C19:** see NITROSO**]**

nitrous ('naɪtrəs) *adj* of, derived from, or containing nitrogen, esp. in a low valency state. **[C17:** from Latin *nitrōsus* full of natron**]**

nitrous acid *n* a weak monobasic acid known only in solution and in the form of nitrite salts. Formula: HNO_2. Systematic name: **dioxonitric(III) acid.**

nitrous bacteria *pl n* bacteria that convert ammonia to nitrites in the soil. See also **nitrobacteria.**

nitrous oxide *n* a colourless nonflammable slightly soluble gas with a sweet smell: used as an anaesthetic in dentistry and surgery. Formula: N_2O. Systematic name: **dinitrogen oxide.** Also called: **laughing gas.**

nitty[1] ('nɪtɪ) *adj* **-tier, -tiest.** infested with nits.

nitty[2] ('nɪtɪ) *adj* **-tier, -tiest.** *Informal.* foolish; stupid. **[C20:** from NITWIT**]**

nitty-gritty ('nɪtɪ'grɪtɪ) *n* **the.** *Informal.* the basic facts of a matter, situation, etc.; the core. **[C20:** perhaps rhyming compound formed from GRIT**]**

nitwit ('nɪt,wɪt) *n Informal.* a foolish or dull person. **[C20:** perhaps from NIT[1] + WIT[1]**]**

Niue ('njuːeɪ) *n* an island in the S Pacific, between Tonga and the Cook Islands: annexed by New Zealand (1901); achieved full internal self-government in 1974. Chief town and port: Alofi. Pop.: 1977 (1993 est.). Area: 260 sq. km (100 sq. miles). Also called: **Savage Island.** ▸ **Niuean** (njuː'ɪən) *n, adj*

nival ('naɪvᵊl) *adj* of or growing in or under snow. **[C17:** from Latin *nivālis,* from *nix* snow**]**

nivation (naɪ'veɪʃən) *n* the weathering of rock around a patch of snow by alternate freezing and thawing. **[C19:** from Latin *nix,* stem *niv-* snow**]**

Niven ('nɪvᵊn) *n* **David.** 1909–83, British film actor and author. His films include *The Prisoner of Zenda* (1937), *Around the World in 80 Days* (1956), *Casino Royale* (1967), and *Paper Tiger* (1975). He wrote the autobiographical *The Moon's a Balloon* (1972) and *Bring on the Empty Horses* (1975).

niveous ('nɪvɪəs) *adj* resembling snow, esp. in colour. **[C17:** from Latin *niveus,* from *nix* snow**]**

Nivernais (*French* nivɛrnɛ) *n* a former province of central France, around Nevers.

Nivôse *French.* (nivoz) *n* the fourth month of the French revolutionary calendar, extending from Dec. 22 to Jan. 20. [C18: via French from Latin *nivōsus* snowy, from *nix* snow]

nix[1] (nɪks) *U.S. and Canadian informal.* ◆ *sentence substitute.* **1** another word for **no**[1] (sense 1). **2** be careful! watch out! ◆ *n* **3** a rejection or refusal. **4** nothing at all. ◆ *vb* **5** (*tr*) to veto, deny, reject, or forbid (plans, suggestions, etc.). [C18: from German, colloquial form of *nichts* nothing]

nix[2] (nɪks) *or* (*fem*) **nixie** (ˈnɪksɪ) *n Germanic myth.* a water sprite, usually unfriendly to humans. [C19: from German *Nixe* nymph or water spirit, from Old High German *nihhus;* related to Old English *nicor* sea monster]

nixer (ˈnɪksə) *n Dublin dialect.* a spare-time job. [from NIX[1], (in the sense), no (tax or insurance) + -ER[1]]

Nixie tube (ˈnɪksɪ) *n Electronics.* another name for **digitron.**

Nixon (ˈnɪksən) *n* **Richard M(ilhous).** 1913–94, U.S. Republican politician; 37th president from 1969 until he resigned in 1974.

nizam (naɪˈzæm) *n* (formerly) a Turkish regular soldier. [C18: ultimately from Arabic *nizām* order, arrangement]

Nizam (nɪˈzɑːm) *n* the title of the ruler of Hyderabad, India, from 1724 to 1948.

Nizam al-Mulk (ælˈmʊlk) *n* title of *Abu Ali Hasan Ibn Ali.* ?1018–92, Persian statesman; vizier of Persia (1063–92) for the Seljuk sultans: assassinated.

Nizhni Novgorod (*Russian* ˈniʒnij ˈnɔvgərət) *n* an industrial city and port in central Russia, at the confluence of the Volga and Oka Rivers: situated on the Volga route from the Baltic to central Asia; birthplace of Maxim Gorki. Pop.: 1 383 000 (1995 est.). Former name (1932–91): **Gorki.**

Nizhni Tagil (*Russian* ˈniʒnij taˈgil) *n* a city in central Russia, on the E slopes of the Ural Mountains: a major metallurgical centre. Pop.: 409 000 (1995 est.).

NJ *or* **N.J.** *abbrev. for* New Jersey.

Njord (njɔːd) *or* **Njorth** (njɔːθ) *n Norse myth.* the god of the sea, fishing, and prosperity.

NKGB *abbrev. for* (formerly) People's Commissariat of State Security: the Soviet secret police from 1943 to 1946. [from Russian *Narodny komissariat gosudarstvennoi bezopasnosti*]

Nkomo (ᵊŋˈkəʊməʊ) *n* **Joshua.** 1917–99, Zimbabwean politician; coleader, with Robert Mugabe, of the Patriotic Front (1976–80) against the government of Ian Smith in Rhodesia; minister (1980–82; 1988–99) and vice-president (1990–96).

nkosi (ᵊŋˈkɔːsɪ) *n S. African.* a term of address to a superior; master; chief. [Nguni *inkosi* chief, lord]

Nkrumah (ᵊŋˈkruːmə) *n* **Kwame** (ˈkwɑːmɪ). 1909–72, Ghanaian statesman, prime minister (1957-60) and president (1960-66). He led demands for self-government in the 1950s, achieving Ghanaian independence in 1957. He was overthrown by a military coup (1966).

NKVD *abbrev.* (formerly) the Soviet police and secret police from 1934 to 1943: the police from 1943–46. [from Russian *Narodny komissariat vnutrennikh del* People's Commissariat of Internal Affairs]

nl *abbrev. for:* **1** non licet. [Latin: it is not permitted] **2** non liquet. [Latin: it is not clear]

NL *abbrev. for:* **1** New Latin. **2** (in Australia) no liability: denoting a public limited company. **3** *international car registration for* the Netherlands.

NLC *abbrev. for* National Liberal Club.

NLF *abbrev. for* National Liberation Front.

NLLST *abbrev. for* National Lending Library for Science and Technology.

NLS *abbrev. for* National Library of Scotland.

NLW *abbrev. for* National Library of Wales.

nm *abbrev. for:* **1** nautical mile. **2** nanometre.

NM *or* **N. Mex.** *abbrev. for* New Mexico.

NMR *abbrev. for* nuclear magnetic resonance.

NNE *symbol for* north-northeast.

NNP *abbrev. for* net national product.

NNW *symbol for* north-northwest.

no[1] (nəʊ) *sentence substitute.* **1** used to express denial, disagreement, refusal, disapproval, disbelief, or acknowledgment of negative statements. **2** used with question intonation to query a previous negative statement, as in disbelief: *Alfred isn't dead yet. No?* ◆ *n, pl* **noes** *or* **nos. 3** an answer or vote of *no.* **4** (*often pl*) a person who votes in the negative. **5 the noes have it.** there is a majority of votes in the negative. Compare (for senses 3–5) **aye**[1]. **6 not take no for an answer.** to continue in a course of action despite refusals. ◆ Compare **yes,** (for senses 3–5) **aye**[1]. [Old English *nā,* from *ne* not, no + *ā* ever; see AY[1]]

no[2] (nəʊ) *determiner* **1** not any, not a, or not one: *there's no money left; no card in the file.* **2** not by a long way; not at all: *she's no youngster.* **3** (foll. by comparative adjectives and adverbs) not: *no less than forty men; no more quickly than before.* **4 no go.** See **go** (sense 74). [Old English *nā,* changed from *nān* NONE[1]]

No[1] *or* **Noh** (nəʊ) *n, pl* **No** *or* **Noh.** the stylized classic drama of Japan, developed in the 15th century or earlier, using music, dancing, chanting, elaborate costumes, and themes from religious stories or myths. [from Japanese *nō* talent, from Chinese *neng*]

No[2] *the chemical symbol for* nobelium.

No[3] (nəʊ) *n* **Lake.** a lake in the S central Sudan, where the Bahr el Jebel (White Nile) is joined by the Bahr el Ghazal. Area: about 103 sq. km (40 sq. miles).

No. *abbrev. for:* **1** north(ern). **2** (*pl* **Nos.** *or* **nos.**) Also: **no.** number. [from French *numéro*]

n.o. *Cricket. abbrev. for* not out.

no' (no, nəʊ) *adv Scots.* not.

no-account *adj* **1** worthless; good-for-nothing. ◆ *n* **2** a worthless person.

Noachian (nəʊˈeɪkɪən) *or* **Noachic** (nəʊˈækɪk, -ˈeɪkɪk) *adj Old Testament.* of or relating to the patriarch Noah.

noah (ˈnəʊə) *n Austral.* a shark. [from Australian rhyming slang *Noah's Ark*]

Noah (ˈnəʊə) *n Old Testament.* a Hebrew patriarch, who saved himself, his family, and specimens of each species of animal and bird from the Flood by building a ship (**Noah's Ark**) in which they all survived (Genesis 6–8).

Noahide Laws (ˈnəʊəˌhaɪd) *pl n Judaism.* the seven laws given to Noah after the Flood, which decree the establishment of a fair system of justice in society, and prohibit idolatry, blasphemy, murder, adultery and incest, robbery, and the eating of flesh taken from a living animal.

nob[1] (nɒb) *n Cribbage.* **1** the jack of the suit turned up. **2 one for his nob.** the call made with this jack, scoring one point. [C19: of uncertain origin]

nob[2] (nɒb) *n Slang, chiefly Brit.* a person of social distinction. [C19: of uncertain origin] ▸ **'nobby** *adj* ▸ **'nobbily** *adv*

nob[3] (nɒb) *n Slang.* the head. [C17: perhaps a variant of KNOB]

nob[4] (nɒb) *n* a variant spelling of **knob** (sense 4).

no-ball *n* **1** *Cricket.* an illegal ball, as for overstepping the crease, throwing, etc., for which the batting side scores a run, and from which the batsman can be out only by being run out. **2** *Rounders.* an illegal ball, esp. one bowled too high or too low. ◆ *sentence substitute.* **3** *Cricket, rounders.* a call by the umpire indicating a no-ball.

nobble (ˈnɒbᵊl) *vb* (*tr*) *Brit. slang.* **1** to disable (a racehorse), esp. with drugs. **2** to win over or outwit (a person) by underhand means. **3** to suborn (a person, esp. a juror) by threats, bribery, etc. **4** to steal; filch. **5** to get hold of; grab. **6** to kidnap. [C19: back formation from *nobbler,* from false division of *an hobbler* (one who hobbles horses) as *a nobbler*] ▸ **'nobbler** *n*

nobbut (ˈnɒbət) *adv Dialect.* nothing but; only. [C14: from NO[2] + BUT[1]]

Nobel (nəʊˈbɛl) *n* **Alfred Bernhard** (ˈalfreːdˈbæːrnhard). 1833–96, Swedish chemist and philanthropist, noted for his invention of dynamite (1866) and his bequest founding the Nobel prizes.

nobelium (nəʊˈbiːlɪəm) *n* a transuranic element produced artificially from curium. Symbol: No; atomic no.: 102; half-life of most stable isotope, ^{255}No: 180 seconds (approx.); valency: 2 or 3. [C20: New Latin, named after *Nobel* Institute, Stockholm, where it was discovered]

Nobel prize *n* a prize for outstanding contributions to chemistry, physics, physiology or medicine, literature, economics, and peace that may be awarded annually. It was established in 1901; the prize for economics being added in 1969. The recipients are chosen by an international committee centred in Sweden, except for the peace prize which is awarded in Oslo by a committee of the Norwegian parliament.

Nobile (*Italian* nɔbile) *n* **Umberto.** 1885–1978, Italian aeronautical engineer and aviator. He flew his *Norge* airship over the North Pole (1926) with Amundsen and his *Italia* airship over the Pole in 1928, crashing on the return.

nobiliary (nəˈbɪlɪərɪ) *adj* of or relating to the nobility. [C18: from French *nobiliaire;* see NOBLE, -ARY]

nobiliary particle *n* a preposition, such as French *de* or German *von,* occurring as part of a title or surname: *Marquis de Sade.*

nobility (nəʊˈbɪlɪtɪ) *n, pl* **-ties. 1** a socially or politically privileged class whose titles are conferred by descent or by royal decree. **2** the state or quality of being morally or spiritually good; dignity: *the nobility of his mind.* **3** (in the British Isles) the class of people holding the title of dukes, marquesses, earls, viscounts, or barons and their feminine equivalents collectively; peerage.

noble (ˈnəʊbᵊl) *adj* **1** of or relating to a hereditary class with special social or political status, often derived from a feudal period. **2** of or characterized by high moral qualities; magnanimous: *a noble deed.* **3** having dignity or eminence; illustrious. **4** grand or imposing; magnificent: *a noble avenue of trees.* **5** of superior quality or kind; excellent: *a noble strain of horses.* **6** *Chem.* **6a** (of certain elements) chemically unreactive. **6b** (of certain metals, esp. copper, silver, and gold) resisting oxidation. **7** *Falconry.* **7a** designating long-winged falcons that capture their quarry by stooping on it from above. Compare **ignoble. 7b** designating the type of quarry appropriate to a particular species of falcon. ◆ *n* **8** a person belonging to a privileged social or political class whose status is usually indicated by a title conferred by sovereign authority or descent. **9** (in the British Isles) a person holding the title of duke, marquess, earl, viscount, or baron, or a feminine equivalent. **10** a former Brit. gold coin having the value of one third of a pound. [C13: via Old French from Latin *nōbilis,* originally, capable of being known, hence well-known, noble, from *noscere* to know] ▸ **'nobleness** *n* ▸ **'nobly** *adv*

noble art *or* **science** *n* **the.** boxing.

noble gas *n* another name for **inert gas** (sense 1).

nobleman (ˈnəʊbᵊlmən) *or* (*fem*) **noblewoman** *n, pl* **-men** *or* **-women.** a person of noble rank, title, or status; peer; aristocrat.

noble rot *n Winemaking.* a condition in which grapes are deliberately affected by *Botrytis cinerea,* resulting in the shrivelling of the ripened grapes, which in turn leads to an increased sugar content. [C20: translation of French *pourriture noble*]

noble savage *n* (in romanticism) an idealized view of primitive man.

noblesse (nəʊˈblɛs) *n Literary.* **1** noble birth or condition. **2** the noble class. [C13: from Old French; see NOBLE]

noblesse oblige (nəʊˈblɛs əʊˈbliːʒ; *French* nɔblɛs ɔbliʒ) *n Often ironic.* the supposed obligation of nobility to be honourable and generous. [French, literally: nobility obliges]

nobody (ˈnəʊbədɪ) *pron* **1** no person; no-one. ◆ *n, pl* **-bodies. 2** an insignificant person.

USAGE See at **everyone.**

Nobunaga (ˈnɒbuːˌnɑːgə) *n* See **Oda Nobunaga.**

nociceptive (ˌnəʊsɪˈsɛptɪv) *adj* causing or reacting to pain. [C20: from Latin *nocēre* to injure + RECEPTIVE]

nocireceptor (ˈnəʊsɪrɪˌsɛptə) *n Physiol.* a receptor sensitive to pain.

nock (nɒk) *n* **1** a notch on an arrow that fits on the bowstring. **2** either of the grooves at each end of a bow that hold the bowstring. ◆ *vb* (*tr*) **3** to fit (an arrow) on a bowstring. **4** to put a groove or notch in (a bow or arrow). [C14: related to Swedish *nock* tip]

nocking point *n* a marked part of the bowstring where the arrow is placed.

no-claims bonus *n* a reduction on an insurance premium, esp. one covering a motor vehicle, if no claims have been made within a specified period. Also called: **no-claim bonus.**

noctambulism (nɒk'tæmbjʊˌlɪzəm) *or* **noctambulation** *n* another word for **somnambulism.** [C19: from Latin *nox* night + *ambulāre* to walk] ▸ **noc'tambulist** *n*

nocti- *or before a vowel* **noct-** *combining form.* night: *noctilucent.* [from Latin *nox, noct-*]

noctiluca (ˌnɒktɪ'lu:kə) *n, pl* **-cae** (-si:). any bioluminescent marine dinoflagellate of the genus *Noctiluca.* [C17: from Latin, from *nox* night + *lūcēre* to shine]

noctilucent (ˌnɒktɪ'lu:s^{ə}nt) *adj* shining at night, usu. of very thin high altitude clouds observable in the summer twilight sky. ▸ **ˌnocti'lucence** *n*

noctuid ('nɒktjʊɪd) *n* **1** any nocturnal moth of the family *Noctuidae:* includes the underwings and antler moth. See also **cutworm, army worm.** ◆ *adj* **2** of, relating to, or belonging to the *Noctuidae.* [C19: via New Latin from Latin *noctua* night owl, from *nox* night]

noctule ('nɒktju:l) *n* any of several large Old World insectivorous bats of the genus *Nyctalus,* esp. *N. noctula:* family *Vespertilionidae.* [C18: probably from Late Latin *noctula* small owl, from Latin *noctua* night owl]

nocturn ('nɒktɜ:n) *n R.C. Church.* any of the main sections of the office of matins. [C13: from Medieval Latin *nocturna* (n), from Latin *nocturnus* nocturnal, from *nox* night]

nocturnal (nɒk'tɜ:n^{ə}l) *adj* **1** of, used during, occurring in, or relating to the night. **2** (of animals) active at night. **3** (of plants) having flowers that open at night and close by day. ◆ Compare **diurnal.** [C15: from Late Latin *nocturnālis,* from Latin *nox* night] ▸ **ˌnoctur'nality** *n* ▸ **noc'turnally** *adv*

nocturne ('nɒktɜ:n) *n* **1** a short, lyrical piece of music, esp. one for the piano. **2** a painting or tone poem of a night scene.

nocuous ('nɒkjʊəs) *adj Rare.* harmful; noxious. [C17: from Latin *nocuus,* from *nocēre* to hurt] ▸ **'nocuously** *adv* ▸ **'nocuousness** *n*

nod (nɒd) *vb* **nods, nodding, nodded. 1** to lower and raise (the head) briefly, as to indicate agreement, invitation, etc. **2** (*tr*) to express or indicate by nodding: *she nodded approval.* **3** (*tr*) to bring or direct by nodding: *she nodded me towards the manager's office.* **4** (*intr*) (of flowers, trees, etc.) to sway or bend forwards and back. **5** (*intr*) to let the head fall forward through drowsiness; be almost asleep: *the old lady sat nodding by the fire.* **6** (*intr*) to be momentarily inattentive or careless: *even Homer sometimes nods.* ◆ *n* **7** a quick down-and-up movement of the head, as in assent, command, etc.: *she greeted him with a nod.* **8** a short sleep; nap. See also **land of Nod. 9** a swaying motion, as of flowers, etc., in the wind. **10 nodding acquaintance.** a slight, casual, or superficial knowledge (of a subject or a person). **11 on the nod.** *Informal.* **11a** agreed, as in a committee meeting, without any formal procedure. **11b** (formerly) on credit. **12 the nod.** *Boxing, informal.* the award of a contest to a competitor on the basis of points scored. ◆ See also **nod off, nod out.** [C14 *nodde,* of obscure origin] ▸ **'nodding** *adj, n*

nodal ('nəʊd^{ə}l) *adj* of or like a node. ▸ **no'dality** *n* ▸ **'nodally** *adv*

nodding donkey *n Informal.* (in the oil industry) a type of reciprocating pump used to extract oil from an inland well. [C20: so called from its shape and movement]

noddle[1] ('nɒd^{ə}l) *n Informal, chiefly Brit.* the head or brains: *use your noddle!* [C15: origin obscure]

noddle[2] ('nɒd^{ə}l) *vb Informal, chiefly Brit.* to nod (the head), as through drowsiness. [C18: from NOD]

noddy[1] ('nɒdɪ) *n, pl* **-dies. 1** any of several tropical terns of the genus *Anous,* esp. *A. stolidus* (**common noddy**), typically having a dark plumage. **2** a fool or dunce. [C16: perhaps noun use of obsolete *noddy* foolish, drowsy, perhaps from NOD (vb); the bird is so called because it allows itself to be caught by hand]

noddy[2] ('nɒdɪ) *n, pl* **-dies.** (*usually pl*) *Television.* film footage of an interviewer's reactions to comments made by an interviewee, used in editing the interview after it has been recorded. [C20: from NOD]

node (nəʊd) *n* **1** a knot, swelling, or knob. **2** the point on a plant stem from which the leaves or lateral branches grow. **3** *Physics.* a point at which the amplitude of one of the two kinds of displacement in a standing wave has zero or minimum value. Generally the other kind of displacement has its maximum value at this point. See also **standing wave.** Compare **antinode. 4** Also called: **crunode.** *Maths.* a point at which two branches of a curve intersect, each branch having a distinct tangent. **5** *Maths, linguistics.* one of the objects of which a graph or a tree consists; vertex. **6** *Astronomy.* either of the two points at which the orbit of a body intersects the plane of the ecliptic. When the body moves from the south to the north side of the ecliptic it passes the **ascending node** and from the north to the south side it passes the **descending node. 7** *Anatomy.* **7a** any natural bulge or swelling of a structure or part, such as those that occur along the course of a lymphatic vessel (**lymph node**). **7b** a finger joint or knuckle. **8** *Computing.* an interconnection point on a computer network. [C16: from Latin *nōdus* knot]

node house *n* a prefabricated shelter used by welders during the construction of an oil rig.

node of Ranvier ('rɑ:nvɪˌeɪ) *n* any of the gaps that occur at regular intervals along the length of the sheath of a myelinated nerve fibre, at which the axon is exposed. [C19: named after Louis-Antoine *Ranvier* (1835–1922), French histologist]

nodical ('nəʊdɪk^{ə}l, 'nɒdɪ-) *adj* of or relating to the nodes of a celestial body, esp. of the moon.

nod off *vb* (*intr, adv*) *Informal.* to fall asleep.

nodose ('nəʊdəʊs, nəʊ'dəʊs) *or* **nodous** ('nəʊdəs) *adj* having nodes or knot-like swellings: *nodose stems.* [C18: from Latin *nōdōsus* knotty] ▸ **nodosity** (nəʊ'dɒsɪtɪ) *n*

nod out *vb* (*intr, adv*) *Slang.* to lapse into stupor, esp. on heroin.

nodule ('nɒdju:l) *n* **1** a small knot, lump, or node. **2** Also called: **root nodule.** any of the knoblike outgrowths on the roots of clover and many other legumes: contain bacteria involved in nitrogen fixation. **3** *Anatomy.* any small node or knoblike protuberance. **4** a small rounded lump of rock or mineral substance, esp. in a matrix of different rock material. [C17: from Latin *nōdulus,* from *nōdus* knot] ▸ **'nodular, 'nodulose,** *or* **'nodulous** *adj*

nodus ('nəʊdəs) *n, pl* **-di** (-daɪ). **1** a problematic idea, situation, etc. **2** another word for **node.** [C14: from Latin: knot]

Noel *or* **Noël** (nəʊ'ɛl) *n* **1** (esp. in carols) another word for **Christmas. 2** (*often not cap.*) *Rare.* a Christmas carol. [C19: from French, from Latin *nātālis* a birthday; see NATAL[1]]

noesis (nəʊ'i:sɪs) *n* **1** *Philosophy.* the exercise of reason, esp. in the apprehension of universal forms. Compare **dianoia. 2** *Psychol.* the mental process used in thinking and perceiving; the functioning of the intellect. See also **cognition.** [C19: from Greek *noēsis* thought, from *noein* to think]

noetic (nəʊ'ɛtɪk) *adj* of or relating to the mind, esp. to its rational and intellectual faculties. [C17: from Greek *noētikos,* from *noein* to think, from *nous* the mind]

Nofretete (ˌnɒfre'ti:tɪ) *n* a variant of **Nefertiti.**

nog[1] *or* **nogg** (nɒg) *n* **1** Also called: **flip.** a drink, esp. an alcoholic one, containing beaten egg. **2** *East Anglian dialect.* strong local beer. [C17 (originally: a strong beer): of obscure origin]

nog[2] (nɒg) *n* **1** a wooden peg or block built into a masonry or brick wall to provide a fixing for nails. **2** short for **nogging** (sense 1). [C17: origin unknown]

noggin ('nɒgɪn) *n* **1** a small quantity of spirits, usually 1 gill. **2** a small mug or cup. **3** an informal word for **head** (sense 1). [C17: of obscure origin]

nogging ('nɒgɪŋ) *n* **1** Also called: **nog,** (Scot. and N.Z.) **dwang.** a short horizontal timber member used between the studs of a framed partition. **2** masonry or brickwork between the timber members of a framed construction. **3** a number of wooden pieces fitted between the timbers of a half-timbered wall.

no-go area *n* **1** a district in a town that is barricaded off, usually by a paramilitary organization, within which the police, army, etc., can only enter by force. **2** an area that is barred to certain individuals, groups, etc.

Noguchi (nɔ:'gu:tʃɪ) *n* **Hideyo** ('hi:deˌjɔ:). 1876–1928, Japanese bacteriologist, active in the U.S. He made important discoveries in the treatment of syphilis.

Noh (nəʊ) *n* a variant spelling of **No**[1].

no-hoper *n Informal.* a useless person; failure.

nohow ('nəʊˌhaʊ) *adv Not standard.* (*in negative constructions*) **a** under any conditions. **b** in any manner.

noil (nɔɪl) *n Textiles.* the short or knotted fibres that are separated from the long fibres, or staple, by combing. [C17: of unknown origin]

noir (nwɑ:) *adj* (of a film) showing characteristics of a *film noir,* in plot or style.

noise (nɔɪz) *n* **1** a sound, esp. one that is loud or disturbing. **2** loud shouting; clamour; din. **3** any undesired electrical disturbance in a circuit, degrading the useful information in a signal. See also **signal-to-noise ratio. 4** undesired or irrelevant elements in a visual image: *removing noise from pictures.* **5** talk or interest: *noise about strikes.* **6** (*pl*) conventional comments or sounds conveying a reaction, attitude, feeling, etc.: *she made sympathetic noises.* **7 make a noise.** to talk a great deal or complain. **8 make noises about.** *Informal.* to give indications of one's intentions: *the government is making noises about new social security arrangements.* **9 noises off.** *Theatre.* sounds made offstage intended for the ears of the audience: used as a stage direction. ◆ *vb* **10** (*tr;* usually foll. by *abroad* or *about*) to spread (news, gossip, etc.). **11** (*intr*) *Rare.* to talk loudly or at length. **12** (*intr*) *Rare.* to make a din or outcry; be noisy. [C13: from Old French, from Latin: NAUSEA]

noise generator *n* a device used in synthesizers to produce high-frequency sound effects.

noiseless ('nɔɪzlɪs) *adj* making little or no sound; silent. ▸ **'noiselessly** *adv* ▸ **'noiselessness** *n*

noisemaker ('nɔɪzˌmeɪkə) *n U.S. and Canadian.* something, such as a clapper or bell, used to make a loud noise at football matches, celebrations, etc. ▸ **'noiseˌmaking** *n, adj*

noise pollution *n* annoying or harmful noise in an environment.

noisette (nwɑ:'zet) *adj* **1** flavoured or made with hazelnuts. ◆ *n* **2** a small round boneless slice of lamb from the fillet or leg. **3** a chocolate made with hazelnuts. [from French: hazelnut]

noisome ('nɔɪsəm) *adj* **1** (esp. of smells) offensive. **2** harmful or noxious. [C14: from obsolete *noy,* variant of ANNOY + -SOME[1]] ▸ **'noisomely** *adv* ▸ **'noisomeness** *n*

noisy ('nɔɪzɪ) *adj* **noisier, noisiest. 1** making a loud or constant noise. **2** full of or characterized by noise. ▸ **'noisily** *adv* ▸ **'noisiness** *n*

noisy miner *n* a honey-eater, *Manorina melanocephala,* of eastern Australia, having a grey-white plumage and brown wings and noted for its raucous cries.

Nolan ('nəʊlən) *n* Sir **Sidney.** 1917–92, Australian painter, whose works explore themes in Australian folklore.

Nolde (*German* 'nɔldə) *n* **Emil** ('e:mi:l). 1867–1956, German painter and engraver, noted particularly for his violent use of colour and the primitive mask-like quality of his figures.

nolens volens *Latin.* ('nəʊlenz 'vəʊlenz) *adv* whether willing or unwilling.

noli-me-tangere ('nəʊlɪˌmeɪ'tæŋgərɪ) *n* **1** a warning against interfering or against touching a person or thing. **2** a work of art depicting Christ appearing to Mary Magdalene after His Resurrection. **3** another name for **touch-me-not. 4** a cancerous ulcer affecting soft tissue and bone. [from Latin: do not touch me, the words spoken by Christ to Mary Magdalene (Vulgate, John 20:17)]

Nollekens ('nɒləkɪnz) *n* **Joseph.** 1737–1823, British neoclassical sculptor of portrait busts, tombs, and mythological subjects.

nolle prosequi ('nɒlɪ 'prɒsɪˌkwaɪ) *n Law.* an entry made on the court record when the plaintiff in a civil suit or prosecutor in a criminal prosecution undertakes not to continue the action or prosecution. Compare **non prosequitur.** [Latin: do not pursue (prosecute)]

nolo contendere ('nəʊləʊ kɒn'tendərɪ) *n Law, chiefly U.S.* a plea made by a defendant to a criminal charge having the same effect in those proceedings as a plea of guilty but not precluding him from denying the charge in a subsequent action. [Latin: I do not wish to contend]

nol. pros. *or* **nolle pros.** *abbrev. for* nolle prosequi.

nom. *abbrev. for:* **1** nominal. **2** nominative.

noma ('nəʊmə) *n* a gangrenous inflammation of the mouth, esp. one affecting malnourished children. [C19: New Latin, from Latin *nomē* ulcer, from Greek *nomē* feeding; related to Greek *nemein* to feed]

nomad ('nəʊmæd) *n* **1** a member of a people or tribe who move from place to place to find pasture and food. **2** a person who continually moves from place to place; wanderer. [C16: via French from Latin *nomas* wandering shepherd, from Greek; related to *nemein* to feed, pasture] ▸ **'nomadism** *n*

nomadic (nəʊ'mædɪk) *adj* relating to or characteristic of nomads or their way of life. ▸ **no'madically** *adv*

nomadize *or* **nomadise** ('nəʊmædˌaɪz) *vb* **1** (*intr*) to live as nomads. **2** (*tr*) to make into nomads. **3** (*tr*) to people (a place) with nomads.

no-man's-land *n* **1** land between boundaries, esp. an unoccupied zone between opposing forces. **2** an unowned or unclaimed piece of land. **3** an ambiguous area of activity or thought.

nomarch ('nɒmɑːk) *n* **1** the head of an ancient Egyptian nome. **2** the senior administrator in a Greek nomarchy. [C17: from Greek *nomarkhēs*]

nomarchy ('nɒmɑːkɪ, -əkɪ) *n, pl* **-chies.** any of the provinces of modern Greece; nome. [C19: from Greek; see NOME, -ARCHY]

nombles ('nʌmbᵊlz) *pl n* a variant spelling of **numbles.**

nombril ('nɒmbrɪl) *n Heraldry.* a point on a shield between the fesse point and the lowest point. [C16: from French, literally: navel]

nom de guerre ('nɒm də 'gɛə) *n, pl* **noms de guerre** ('nɒm də 'gɛə). an assumed name; pseudonym. [French, literally: war name]

nom de plume ('nɒm də 'pluːm) *n, pl* **noms de plume** ('nɒm də 'pluːm). another term for **pen name.**

nome (nəʊm) *n* **1** any of the former provinces of modern Greece; nomarchy. **2** an administrative division of ancient Egypt. [C18: from Greek *nomos* pasture, region]

nomen ('nəʊmɛn) *n, pl* **nomina** ('nɒmɪnə). an ancient Roman's second name, designating his gens or clan. See also **agnomen, cognomen, praenomen.** [Latin: a name]

nomenclator ('nəʊmɛnˌkleɪtə) *n* a person who invents or assigns names, as in scientific classification. [C16: from Latin, from *nōmen* name + *calāre* to call]

nomenclature (nəʊ'mɛnklətʃə; *U.S.* 'nəʊmənˌkleɪtʃər) *n* the terminology used in a particular science, art, activity, etc. [C17: from Latin *nōmenclātūra* list of names; see NOMENCLATOR]

nomenklatura (ˌnəʊmɛnklə'tʃuːrə) *n* (formerly, in the USSR and E Europe) a list of individuals drawn up by the Communist Party from which were selected candidates for vacant senior positions in the state, party, and other important organizations. [C20: Russian, from Latin *nōmenclātūra* list of names]

nominal ('nɒmɪnᵊl) *adj* **1** in name only; theoretical: *the nominal leader.* **2** minimal in comparison with real worth or what is expected; token: *a nominal fee.* **3** of, relating to, constituting, bearing, or giving a name. **4** *Grammar.* of or relating to a noun or noun phrase. ◆ *n* **5** *Grammar.* a nominal element; a noun, noun phrase, or syntactically similar structure. **6** *Bell-ringing.* the harmonic an octave above the strike tone of a bell. [C15: from Latin *nōminālis* of a name, from *nōmen* name] ▸ **'nominally** *adv*

nominal aphasia *n* aphasia in which the primary symptom is an inability to recognize words and to speak the right word.

nominalism ('nɒmɪnᵊˌlɪzəm) *n* the philosophical theory that the variety of objects to which a single general word, such as *dog,* applies have nothing in common but the name. Compare **conceptualism, realism.** ▸ **'nominalist** *n, adj* ▸ **ˌnominal'istic** *adj*

nominal scale *n Statistics.* a discrete classification of data, in which data are neither measured nor ordered but subjects are merely allocated to distinct categories: *a record of students' course choices constitutes nominal data which could be correlated with school results.* Compare **ordinal scale, interval scale, ratio scale.**

nominal value *n* another name for **par value.**

nominal wages *pl n* another name for **money wages.**

nominate *vb* ('nɒmɪˌneɪt). (*mainly tr*) **1** to propose as a candidate, esp. for an elective office. **2** to appoint to an office or position. **3** to name (someone) to act on one's behalf, esp. to conceal one's identity. **4** (*intr*) *Austral.* to stand as a candidate in an election. **5** *Archaic.* to name, entitle, or designate. ◆ *adj* ('nɒmɪnɪt). **6** *Rare.* having a particular name. [C16: from Latin *nōmināre* to call by name, from *nōmen* name] ▸ **'nomiˌnator** *n*

nomination (ˌnɒmɪ'neɪʃən) *n* the act of nominating or state of being nominated, esp. as an election candidate.

nominative ('nɒmɪnətɪv, 'nɒmnə-) *adj* **1** *Grammar.* denoting a case of nouns and pronouns in inflected languages that is used esp. to identify the subject of a finite verb. See also **subjective** (sense 6). **2** appointed rather than elected to a position, office, etc. **3** bearing the name of a person. ◆ *n* **4** *Grammar.* **4a** the nominative case. **4b** a word or speech element in the nominative case. [C14: from Latin *nōminātīvus* belonging to naming, from *nōmen* name] ▸ **nominatival** (ˌnɒmɪnə'taɪvᵊl, ˌnɒmnə-) *adj* ▸ **'nominatively** *adv*

nominee (ˌnɒmɪ'niː) *n* **1** a person who is nominated to an office or as a candidate. **2a** a person or organization named to act on behalf of someone else, esp. to conceal the identity of the nominator. **2b** (*as modifier*): *nominee shareholder.* [C17: from NOMINATE + -EE]

nomism ('nəʊmɪzəm) *n* adherence to a law or laws as a primary exercise of religion. [C20: from Greek *nomos* law, custom] ▸ **no'mistic** *adj*

nomo- *combining form.* indicating law or custom: *nomology.* [from Greek *nomos* law, custom]

nomocracy (nɒ'mɒkrəsɪ, nəʊ-) *n, pl* **-cies.** government based on the rule of law rather than arbitrary will, terror, etc. [C19: from Greek, from *nomos* law + -CRACY]

nomogram ('nɒməˌgræm, 'nəʊmə-) *or* **nomograph** *n* **1** an arrangement of two linear or logarithmic scales such that an intersecting straight line enables intermediate values or values on a third scale to be read off. **2** any graphic representation of numerical relationships. [C20: from Greek *nomos* law + -GRAM, on the model of French *nomogramme*]

nomography (nɒ'mɒgrəfɪ) *n, pl* **-phies.** the science of constructing nomographs. See **nomogram.** ▸ **no'mographer** *n* ▸ **nomographic** (ˌnɒmə'græfɪk) *or* **ˌnomo'graphical** *adj* ▸ **ˌnomo'graphically** *adv*

nomological (ˌnɒmə'lɒdʒɪkᵊl) *adj* **1** of or relating to nomology. **2** stating or relating to a nonlogical necessity or law of nature. The difference between a nomological and a merely universal statement is that from the universal *all As are Bs* one cannot, but from the nomological *all As must be Bs* one can, infer the counterfactual *if this were an A it would (have to) be a B.* ▸ **ˌnomo'logically** *adv*

nomology (nəʊ'mɒlədʒɪ) *n* **1** the science of law and law-making. **2** the branch of science concerned with the formulation of laws explaining natural phenomena. ▸ **no'mologist** *n*

nomothetic (ˌnɒmə'θɛtɪk) *or* **nomothetical** *adj* **1** giving or enacting laws; legislative. **2** *Psychol.* of or relating to the search for general laws or traits, esp. in personality theory. Compare **idiographic.** [C17: from Greek *nomothetikos,* from *nomothetēs* lawgiver]

-nomy *n combining form.* indicating a science or the laws governing a certain field of knowledge: *agronomy; economy.* [from Greek *-nomia* law; related to *nemein* to distribute, control] ▸ **-nomic** *adj combining form.*

non- *prefix* **1** indicating negation: *nonexistent.* **2** indicating refusal or failure: *noncooperation.* **3** indicating exclusion from a specified class of persons or things: *nonfiction.* **4** indicating lack or absence, esp. of a quality associated with what is specified: *nonobjective; nonevent.* [from Latin *nōn* not]

nona- *or before a vowel* **non-** *combining form.* nine: *nonagon.* [from Latin *nōnus*]

nonaccidental injury (ˌnɒnæksɪ'dɛntᵊl) *n Social welfare.* damage, such as a bruise, burn, or fracture, deliberately inflicted on a child or an old person. Abbrev.: **NAI.** See also **child abuse.**

nonage ('nəʊnɪdʒ) *n* **1** *Law.* the state of being under any of various ages at which a person may legally enter into certain transactions, such as the making of binding contracts, marrying, etc. **2** any period of immaturity.

nonagenarian (ˌnəʊnədʒɪ'nɛərɪən) *n* **1** a person who is from 90 to 99 years old. ◆ *adj* **2** of, relating to, or denoting a nonagenarian. [C19: from Latin *nōnāgēnārius,* from *nōnāginta* ninety]

nonaggression (ˌnɒnə'grɛʃən) *n* **a** restraint of aggression, esp. between states. **b** (*as modifier*): *a nonaggression pact.*

nonagon ('nɒnəˌgɒn) *n* a polygon having nine sides. Also called: **enneagon.** ▸ **nonagonal** (nɒn'ægənᵊl) *adj*

nonaligned (ˌnɒnə'laɪnd) *adj* (of states) not part of a major alliance or power bloc, esp. not allied to the U.S., China, or formerly the Soviet Union. ▸ **ˌnona'lignment** *n*

nonanoic acid (ˌnɒnə'nəʊɪk) *n* a colourless oily fatty acid with a rancid odour: used in making pharmaceuticals, lacquers, and plastics. Formula: $CH_3(CH_2)_7COOH$. Also called: **pelargonic acid.** [C19: from *nonane* a paraffin, ninth in the methane series, from Latin *nōnus* ninth + -ANE]

non-A, non-B hepatitis *n* a form of viral hepatitis, not caused by the agents responsible for hepatitis A and hepatitis B, that is commonly transmitted by infected blood transfusions. The causative virus has been isolated. Also called **hepatitis C.**

nonappearance (ˌnɒnə'pɪərəns) *n* failure to appear or attend, esp. as a defendant or witness in court.

nonbeing (nɒn'biːɪŋ) *n* the philosophical problem arising from the fact that the ability to refer appears to presuppose the existence of whatever is referred to, and yet we can talk intelligibly about nonexistent objects. See also **subsistence** (sense 5).

nonce[1] (nɒns) *n* the present time or occasion (now only in the phrase **for the nonce**). [C12: from the phrase *for the nonce,* a mistaken division of *for then anes,* literally: for the once, from *then* dative singular of *the* + *anes* ONCE]

ˌnonaca'demic *adj*
ˌnonac'ceptance *n*
ˌnonad'dictive *adj*
ˌnonagri'cultural *adj*
ˌnonalco'holic *adj*
ˌnonat'tendance *n*
ˌnonat'tributable *adj*
ˌnonauto'matic *adj*
ˌnonbe'liever *n*
ˌnonbel'ligerent *adj*
ˌnonbio'logical *adj*
non-'Catholic *adj, n*
non'causal *adj*

nonce[2] (nɒns) *n Prison slang.* a rapist or child molester; a sexual offender. [C20: of unknown origin]

nonce word *n* a word coined for a single occasion.

nonchalant ('nɒnʃələnt) *adj* casually unconcerned or indifferent; uninvolved. [C18: from French, from *nonchaloir* to lack warmth, from NON- + *chaloir,* from Latin *calēre* to be warm] ▸ **'nonchalance** *n* ▸ **'nonchalantly** *adv*

noncognitivism (nɒn'kɒgnɪtɪˌvɪzəm) *n Philosophy.* the semantic meta-ethical thesis that moral judgments do not express facts and so do not have a truth value thus excluding both naturalism and non-naturalism. See **emotivism, prescriptivism.**

non-com ('nɒnˌkɒm) *n* short for **noncommissioned officer.**

noncombatant (nɒn'kɒmbətənt) *n* **1** a civilian in time of war. **2** a member of the armed forces whose duties do not include fighting, such as a chaplain or surgeon.

noncommissioned officer (ˌnɒnkə'mɪʃənd) *n* (in the armed forces) a person, such as a sergeant or corporal, who is appointed from the ranks as a subordinate officer.

noncommittal (ˌnɒnkə'mɪtᵊl) *adj* **1** not involving or revealing commitment to any particular opinion or course of action: *a noncommittal reply.* **2** *Rare.* having no outstanding quality, meaning, etc.

non compos mentis *Latin.* ('nɒn 'kɒmpəs 'mɛntɪs) *adj* mentally incapable of managing one's own affairs; of unsound mind. [Latin: not in control of one's mind]

nonconductor (ˌnɒnkən'dʌktə) *n* a substance that is a poor conductor of heat, electricity, or sound.

nonconformist (ˌnɒnkən'fɔːmɪst) *n* **1** a person who does not conform to generally accepted patterns of behaviour or thought. ◆ *adj* **2** of or characterized by behaviour that does not conform to generally accepted patterns. ▸ **ˌnoncon'formism** *n*

Nonconformist (ˌnɒnkən'fɔːmɪst) *n* **1** a member of a Protestant denomination that dissents from an Established Church, esp. the Church of England. ◆ *adj* **2** of, relating to, or denoting Nonconformists. ▸ **ˌNoncon'formity** *or* **ˌNoncon'formism** *n*

nonconformity (ˌnɒnkən'fɔːmɪtɪ) *n* **1** failure or refusal to conform. **2** absence of agreement or harmony.

noncontributory (ˌnɒnkən'trɪbjʊtərɪ, -trɪ) *adj* **1a** denoting an insurance or pension scheme for employees, the premiums of which are paid entirely by the employer. **1b** (of a state benefit) not dependent on national insurance contributions. **2** not providing contribution; noncontributing.

noncooperation (ˌnɒnkəʊˌɒpə'reɪʃən) *n* **1** failure or refusal to cooperate. **2** refusal to pay taxes, obey government decrees, etc., as a protest. ▸ **noncooperative** (ˌnɒnkəʊ'ɒpərətɪv) *adj* ▸ **ˌnonco'operˌator** *n*

nondescript ('nɒndɪˌskrɪpt) *adj* **1** lacking distinct or individual characteristics; having no outstanding features. ◆ *n* **2** a nondescript person or thing. [C17: from NON- + Latin *dēscriptus,* past participle of *dēscribere* to copy, DESCRIBE]

nondestructive testing (ˌnɒndɪ'strʌktɪv) *n* any of several methods of detecting flaws in metals without causing damage. The most common techniques involve the use of X-rays, gamma rays, and ultrasonic vibrations. Abbrev.: **NDT.**

nondirective therapy *n Psychiatry.* another name for **client-centred therapy.**

nondisjunction (ˌnɒndɪs'dʒʌŋkʃən) *n* the failure of paired homologous chromosomes to move to opposite poles of the cell during meiosis.

nondomiciled (nɒn'dɒmɪsaɪld) *adj* of, relating to, or denoting a person who is not domiciled in his country of origin.

nondrip (nɒn'drɪp) *adj* (of paint) specially formulated to minimize dripping during application.

none[1] (nʌn) *pron* **1** not any of a particular class: *none of my letters has arrived.* **2** no-one; nobody: *there was none to tell the tale.* **3** no part (of a whole); not any (of): *none of it looks edible.* **4 none other.** no other person: *none other than the Queen herself.* **5 none the.** (*foll. by a comparative adj*) in no degree: *she was none the worse for her ordeal.* **6 none too.** not very: *he was none too pleased with his car.* [Old English *nān,* literally: not one]

USAGE *None* is a singular pronoun and should be used with a singular form of a verb: *none of the students has* (not *have*) *a car.*

none[2] (nəʊn) *n* another word for **nones.**

noneffective (ˌnɒnɪ'fɛktɪv) *Chiefly U.S.* ◆ *adj* **1** not effective. **2** unfit for or incapable of active military service. ◆ *n* **3** *Military.* a noneffective person.

nonego (nɒn'iːgəʊ, -'ɛgəʊ) *n Philosophy.* everything that is outside one's conscious self, such as one's environment.

nonentity (nɒn'ɛntɪtɪ) *n, pl* **-ties. 1** an insignificant person or thing. **2** a nonexistent thing. **3** the state of not existing; nonexistence.

nonequivalence (ˌnɒnɪ'kwɪvələns) *n* **1** the relationship of being unequal or incomparable. **2** *Logic.* **2a** the relation between two statements only one of which can be true in any circumstances. **2b** a function of two statements that takes the value true only when one but not both of its arguments is true. **2c** a compound statement asserting that just one of its components is true. ◆ Also called: **exclusive or.**

nones (nəʊnz) *n* (*functioning as sing or pl*) **1** (in the Roman calendar) the ninth day before the ides of each month: the seventh day of March, May, July, and October, and the fifth of each other month. See also **calends. 2** *Chiefly R.C. Church.* the fifth of the seven canonical hours of the divine office, originally fixed at the ninth hour of the day, about 3 p.m. [Old English *nōn,* from Latin *nōna hora* ninth hour, from *nōnus* ninth]

nonessential (ˌnɒnɪ'sɛnʃəl) *adj* **1** not essential; not necessary. **2** *Biochem.* (of an amino acid in a particular organism) able to be synthesized from other substances. ◆ *n* **3** a nonessential person or thing.

nonesuch *or* **nonsuch** ('nʌnˌsʌtʃ) *n* **1** *Archaic.* a matchless person or thing; nonpareil. **2** another name for **black medick.**

nonet (nɒ'nɛt) *n* **1** a piece of music composed for a group of nine instruments. **2** an instrumental group of nine players. [C19: from Italian *nonetto,* from *nono* ninth, from Latin *nōnus*]

nonetheless (ˌnʌnðə'lɛs) *sentence connector.* despite that; however; nevertheless.

non-Euclidean geometry *n* the branch of modern geometry in which certain axioms of Euclidean geometry are restated. It introduces fundamental changes into the concept of space.

nonevent (ˌnɒnɪ'vɛnt) *n* a disappointing or insignificant occurrence, esp. one predicted to be important.

nonexecutive director *n* a director of a commercial company who is not a full-time member of the company but is brought in to advise the other directors.

nonfeasance (nɒn'fiːzᵊns) *n Law.* a failure to act when under an obligation to do so. Compare **malfeasance, misfeasance.** [C16: from NON- + *feasance* (obsolete) performing or doing, from French *faisance,* from *faire* to do, from Latin *facere*]

nonferrous (nɒn'fɛrəs) *adj* **1** denoting any metal other than iron. **2** not containing iron: *a nonferrous alloy.*

nonfiction (nɒn'fɪkʃən) *n* **1** writing dealing with facts and events rather than imaginative narration. **2** (*modifier*) relating to or denoting nonfiction. ▸ **non'fictional** *adj* ▸ **non'fictionally** *adv*

nonflammable (nɒn'flæməbᵊl) *adj* incapable of burning or not easily set on fire; not flammable.

nong (nɒŋ) *n Austral. slang.* a stupid or incompetent person. [C19: perhaps alteration of obsolete English dialect *nigmenog* silly fellow, of unknown origin]

nonharmonic (ˌnɒnhɑː'mɒnɪk) *adj Music.* not relating to the harmony formed by a chord or chords.

non-Hodgkin's lymphoma *n* any form of lymphoma other than Hodgkin's disease.

nonillion (nəʊ'nɪljən) *n* **1** (in Britain, France, and Germany) the number represented as one followed by 54 zeros (10^{54}). **2** (in the U.S. and Canada) the number represented as one followed by 30 zeros (10^{30}). Brit. word: **quintillion.** [C17: from French, from Latin *nōnus* ninth, on the model of MILLION] ▸ **no'nillionth** *adj, n*

non-impact printer *n Computing.* any printing device in which the images are created without being struck on to the paper, such as a laser printer or ink-jet printer.

nonintervention (ˌnɒnɪntə'vɛnʃən) *n* refusal to intervene, esp. the abstention by a state from intervening in the affairs of other states or in its own internal disputes. ▸ **ˌnoninter'ventional** *adj* ▸ **ˌnoninter'ventionist** *n, adj*

noninvasive (ˌnɒnɪn'veɪsɪv) *adj* (of medical treatment) not involving the making of a relatively large incision in the body or the insertion of instruments, etc., into the patient.

noniron (nɒn'aɪən) *adj* (of a fabric) composed of any of various man-made fibres that are crease-resistant and do not require ironing.

nonjoinder (nɒn'dʒɔɪndə) *n Law.* the failure to join as party to a suit a person who should have been included either as a plaintiff or as a defendant. Compare **misjoinder.**

nonjudgmental *or* **nonjudgemental** (ˌnɒndʒʌdʒ'mɛntᵊl) *adj* of, relating to, or denoting an attitude, approach, etc., that is open and not incorporating a judgment one way or the other.

nonjuror (nɒn'dʒʊərə) *n* a person who refuses to take an oath, as of allegiance.

Nonjuror (nɒn'dʒʊərə) *n* any of a group of clergy in England and Scotland who declined to take the oath of allegiance to William and Mary in 1689.

non licet ('nɒn 'laɪsɪt) *adj* not permitted; unlawful. [C17: Latin, literally: it is not allowed]

non liquet ('nɒn 'laɪkwɪt) *adj Roman law.* (of a cause, evidence, etc.) not clear. [C17: Latin, literally: it is not clear]

non-'Christian *adj, n*
ˌnoncom'bustible *adj*
ˌnoncom'mercial *adj*
ˌnoncom'missioned *adj*
non'communist *adj, n*
ˌnoncom'petitive *adj*
ˌnoncom'pliance *n*
ˌnoncon'secutive *adj*
ˌnoncon'tributing *adj*
ˌnoncontro'versial *adj*
ˌnoncon'ventional *adj*
ˌnoncon'vertible *adj*
ˌnoncor'roding *adj*
non'critical *adj*
ˌnondemo'cratic *adj*
ˌnondeˌnomi'national *adj*
ˌnondiplo'matic *adj*
non'drinker *n*
non'earning *adj*
ˌnoneco'nomic *adj*
ˌnone'lection *n*
ˌnone'quivalent *adj*
non'ethical *adj*
ˌnonex'clusive *adj*
ˌnonex'ecutive *adj*
ˌnonex'istence *n*
ˌnonex'istent *adj*
ˌnonex'plosive *adj*
non'fatal *adj*
non'fattening *adj*
non'finite *adj*
non'functional *adj*
ˌnongovern'mental *adj*
non'greasy *adj*
ˌnonhe'reditary *adj*
non'human *adj*
ˌnoni'dentical *adj*
ˌnonin'dictable *adj*
ˌnonin'dustrial *adj*
ˌnonin'heritable *adj*
ˌnonintel'lectual *adj*
ˌnoninter'changeable *adj*
ˌnonin'volvement *n*
non'irritant *adj, n*
non'lethal *adj*
non'linear *adj*

nonmetal (nɒn'met^{ə}l) *n* any of a number of chemical elements that form negative ions, have acidic oxides, and are generally poor conductors of heat and electricity.

nonmetallic (ˌnɒnmɪ'tælɪk) *adj* **1** not of metal. **2** of, concerned with, or being a nonmetal.

nonmonetary advantages (nɒn'mʌnɪtərɪ) *pl n* the beneficial aspects of an employment, such as the stimulation of the work, attractiveness of the workplace, or its nearness to one's home, that do not reflect its financial remuneration.

nonmoral (nɒn'mɒrəl) *adj* not involving or related to morality or ethics; neither moral nor immoral.

non-naturalism *n* the meta-ethical doctrine that moral properties exist but are not reducible to "natural", empirical, or supernatural ones, and that moral judgments therefore state a special kind of fact. Compare **naturalistic fallacy.** See also **descriptivism.**

Nonne's syndrome (nɒnz) *n* another name for **cerebellar syndrome.**

Nono (*Italian* 'nɔːno) *n* **Luigi** (lu'iːdʒi). 1924–90, Italian composer of 12-tone music.

nonobjective (ˌnɒnəb'dʒɛktɪv) *adj* of or designating an art movement in which things are depicted in an abstract or purely formalized way, not as they appear in reality.

no-nonsense (ˌnəʊ'nɒnsəns) *adj* sensible, practical, straightforward; without nonsense of any kind: *a businesslike no-nonsense approach; a severe no-nonsense look.*

nonparametric statistics (ˌnɒnpærə'mɛtrɪk) *n* (*functioning as sing*) the branch of statistics that studies data measurable on an ordinal or nominal scale, to which arithmetic operations cannot be applied.

nonpareil ('nɒnpərəl, ˌnɒnpə'reɪl) *n* **1** a person or thing that is unsurpassed or unmatched; peerless example. **2** (formerly) a size of printers' type equal to 6 point. **3** *U.S.* a small bead of coloured sugar used to decorate cakes, biscuits, etc. **4** *Chiefly U.S.* a flat round piece of chocolate covered with this sugar. ◆ *adj* **5** having no match or equal; peerless. **[C15:** from French, from NON- + *pareil* similar**]**

nonparous (nɒn'pærəs) *adj* never having given birth.

nonparticipating (ˌnɒnpɑː'tɪsɪˌpeɪtɪŋ) *adj* **1** not participating. **2** (of an assurance policy, share, etc.) not carrying the right to share in a company's profit.

nonpartisan *or* **nonpartizan** (ˌnɒnpɑːtɪ'zæn) *adj* not partisan or aligned, esp. not affiliated to, influenced by, or supporting any one political party. ▸ **ˌnonpartiˈsanˌship** *or* **ˌnonpartiˈzanˌship** *n*

nonparty (nɒn'pɑːtɪ) *adj* not connected with any one political party.

nonpersistent (ˌnɒnpə'sɪstənt) *adj* (of pesticides) breaking down rapidly after application; not persisting in the environment.

non-person *n* a person regarded as nonexistent or unimportant; a nonentity.

nonplus (nɒn'plʌs) *vb* **-plusses, -plussing, -plussed** *or U.S.* **-pluses, -plusing, -plused. 1** (*tr*) to put at a loss; confound: *he was nonplussed by the sudden announcement.* ◆ *n, pl* **-pluses. 2** a state of utter perplexity prohibiting action or speech. **[C16:** from Latin *nōn plūs* no further (that is, nothing further can be said or done)**]**

nonproductive (ˌnɒnprə'dʌktɪv) *adj* **1** (of workers) not directly responsible for producing goods. **2** having disappointing results; unproductive. ▸ **ˌnonproˈductiveness** *n* ▸ **nonproductivity** (ˌnɒnprɒdʌk'tɪvɪtɪ) *n*

non-profit-making *or U.S.* (*often*) **nonprofit** (nɒn'prɒfɪt) *adj* not yielding a profit, esp. because organized or established for some other reason: *a non-profit-making organization.*

nonproliferation (ˌnɒnprəˌlɪfə'reɪʃən) *n* **1a** limitation of the production or spread of something, esp. nuclear or chemical weapons. **1b** (*as modifier*): *a nonproliferation treaty.* **2** failure or refusal to proliferate.

non pros. *Law. abbrev. for* non prosequitur.

non-pros (ˌnɒn'prɒs) *n* **1** short for **non prosequitur.** ◆ *vb* **-prosses, -prossing, -prossed. 2** (*tr*) to enter a judgment of non prosequitur against (a plaintiff).

non prosequitur ('nɒn prəʊ'sɛkwɪtə) *n Law.* (formerly) a judgment in favour of a defendant when the plaintiff failed to take the necessary steps in an action within the time allowed. Compare **nolle prosequi.** **[**Latin, literally: he does not prosecute**]**

nonreflexive (ˌnɒnrɪ'flɛksɪv) *adj Logic.* (of a relation) neither reflexive nor irreflexive; holding between some members of its domain and themselves, and failing to hold between others.

nonrepresentational (ˌnɒnrɛprɪzɛn'teɪʃən^{ə}l) *adj Art.* another word for **abstract** (sense 4).

nonresident (nɒn'rɛzɪdənt) *n* **1** a person who is not residing in the place implied or specified: *the hotel restaurant is open to nonresidents.* **2** a British person employed abroad on a contract for a minimum of one year, who is exempt from UK income tax provided that he does not spend more than 90 days in the UK during that tax year. ◆ *adj* **3** not residing in the place specified. ▸ **nonˈresidence** *or* **nonˈresidency** *n*

nonresistant (ˌnɒnrɪ'zɪstənt) *adj* **1** incapable of resisting something, such as a disease; susceptible. **2** *History.* (esp. in 17th-century England) practising passive obedience to royal authority even when its commands were unjust. ▸ **ˌnonreˈsistance** *n*

nonrestrictive (ˌnɒnrɪ'strɪktɪv) *adj* **1** not restrictive or limiting. **2** *Grammar.* denoting a relative clause that is not restrictive. Compare **restrictive** (sense 2).

nonreturn (ˌnɒnrɪ'tɜːn) *adj* denoting a mechanism that permits flow in a pipe, tunnel, etc., in one direction only: *a nonreturn valve.*

nonreturnable (ˌnɒnrɪ'tɜːnəb^{ə}l) *adj* denoting a container, esp. a bottle, on which no returnable deposit is paid on purchase of the contents.

nonreturn valve *n* another name for **check valve.**

nonrhotic (nɒn'rəʊtɪk) *adj Phonetics.* denoting or speaking a dialect of English in which preconsonantal *r*s are not pronounced. ▸ **ˌnonrhoˈticity** *n*

nonrigid (nɒn'rɪdʒɪd) *adj* **1** not rigid; flexible. **2** (of the gas envelope of an airship) flexible and held in shape only by the internal gas pressure.

nonscheduled (nɒn'ʃɛdjuːld; *also, esp. U.S.* nɒn'skɛdʒʊəld) *adj* **1** not according to a schedule or plan; unscheduled. **2** (of an airline) operating without published flight schedules.

nonsense ('nɒnsəns) *n* **1** something that has or makes no sense; unintelligible language; drivel. **2** conduct or action that is absurd. **3** foolish or evasive behaviour or manners: *she'll stand no nonsense.* **4** See **no-nonsense. 5** things of little or no value or importance; trash. ◆ *interj* **6** an exclamation of disagreement. ▸ **nonsensical** (nɒn'sɛnsɪk^{ə}l) *adj* ▸ **nonˈsensically** *adv* ▸ **nonˈsensicalness** *or* **nonˌsensiˈcality** *n*

nonsense correlation *n Statistics.* a correlation supported by data but having no basis in reality, as between incidence of the common cold and ownership of televisions.

nonsense syllable *n Psychol.* a syllable, like *bik,* having no meaning. Lists of such syllables have been used to investigate memory and learning.

nonsense verse *n* verse in which the sense is nonexistent or absurd, such as that of Edward Lear.

non seq. *abbrev. for* non sequitur.

non sequitur ('nɒn 'sɛkwɪtə) *n* **1** a statement having little or no relevance to what preceded it. **2** *Logic.* a conclusion that does not follow from the premises. Abbrev.: **non seq.** **[**Latin, literally: it does not follow**]**

nonslip (nɒn'slɪp) *adj* designed to reduce or prevent slipping.

nonsmoker (nɒn'sməʊkə) *n* **1** a person who does not smoke. **2** a train compartment in which smoking is forbidden. ▸ **nonˈsmoking** *adj*

nonspecific urethritis *n* inflammation of the urethra as a result of a venereal infection that cannot be traced to a specific cause. Abbrev.: **NSU.**

nonspecular reflection (nɒn'spɛkjʊlə) *n Physics.* the diffuse reflection of sound or light waves.

nonstandard (nɒn'stændəd) *adj* **1** denoting or characterized by idiom, vocabulary, etc., that is not regarded as correct and acceptable by educated native speakers of a language; not standard. **2** deviating from a given standard.

nonstarter (nɒn'stɑːtə) *n* **1** a horse that fails to run in a race for which it has been entered. **2** a person or thing that is useless, has little chance of success, etc.

nonstative (nɒn'steɪtɪv) *Grammar.* ◆ *adj* **1** denoting a verb describing an action rather than a state, as for example *throw* or *thank* as opposed to *know* or *hate.* Compare **stative.** ◆ *n* **2** a nonstative verb. ◆ Also: **active.**

nonstick ('nɒn'stɪk) *adj* (of saucepans, frying pans, etc.) coated with a substance such as polytetrafluoroethylene (PTFE) that prevents food sticking to them.

nonstoichiometric (nɒnˌstɔɪkɪə'mɛtrɪk) *adj Chem.* (of a solid compound) having a composition in which the ratio of the atoms present is not a simple integer. An example is titanium(IV) oxide, $TiO_{1.8}$.

nonstop ('nɒn'stɒp) *adj, adv* done without pause or interruption: *a nonstop flight.*

nonstriated (nɒn'straɪeɪtɪd) *adj* (esp. of certain muscle fibres) having no striations.

non-striker *n Cricket.* the batsman who is not facing the bowling.

nonsuch ('nʌnˌsʌtʃ) *n* a variant spelling of **nonesuch.**

Nonsuch Palace ('nʌnˌsʌtʃ) *n* a former royal palace in Cuddington in Lon-

nonˈliterary *adj*
nonˈlocal *adj*
nonˈlogical *adj*
nonˈluminous *adj*
ˌnonmagˈnetic *adj*
ˌnonmaˈlignant *adj*
nonˈmarried *adj*
ˌnonmaˌterialˈistic *adj*
ˌnonmatheˈmatical *adj*
nonˈmedical *adj*
nonˈmember *n*
nonˈmetric *adj*
nonˈmilitant *adj*
non-ˈnational *adj*
non-ˈnative *adj*
non-ˈnatural *adj*
non-neˈgotiable *adj*
ˌnon-ˈnervous *adj*
non-ˈnuclear *adj*
ˌnonofˈficial *adj*
ˌnonoperˈational *adj*
ˌnonorˈganic *adj*
nonˈorthoˌdox *adj*
nonˈparaˌlel *adj*
ˌnonparliaˈmentary *adj*
nonˈpaying *adj*
nonˈpayment *n*
nonˈpermanent *adj*
nonˈphysical *adj*
nonˈplaying *adj*
nonˈpoisonous *adj*
ˌnonpoˈlitical *adj*
ˌnonpolˈluting *adj*
nonˈporous *adj*
nonˈpractising *adj*
ˌnonproˈfessional *adj*
ˌnonproˈgressive *adj*
nonˈracial *adj*
ˌnonradioˈactive *adj*
nonˈrational *adj*
ˌnonrealˈistic *adj*
ˌnonrecogˈnition *n*
ˌnonreˈligious *adj*
ˌnonreˈnewable *adj*
ˌnonresiˈdential *adj*
ˌnonscienˈtific *adj*
ˌnonsecˈtarian *adj*
nonˈsegreˌgated *adj*
ˌnonseˈlective *adj*
nonˈsexist *adj*
nonˈsexual *adj*
ˌnonsigˈnificant *adj*
nonˈskilled *adj*
nonˈsocial *adj*
nonˈspeaking *adj*
nonˈspecialist *n*
ˌnonspeˈcific *adj*
nonˈsporting *adj*
nonˈstaining *adj*
nonˈstellar *adj*
ˌnonstraˈtegic *adj*

don: built in 1538 for Henry VIII; later visited by Elizabeth I, James I, Charles I, and Charles II; demolished (1682–1702).

nonsuit (nɒnˈsuːt, -ˈsjuːt) *Law.* ♦ *n* **1** an order of a judge dismissing a suit when the plaintiff fails to show he has a good cause of action or fails to produce any evidence. ♦ *vb* **2** (*tr*) to order the dismissal of the suit of (a person).

nonsymmetric (ˌnɒnsɪˈmɛtrɪk) *adj Logic, maths.* (of a relation) not symmetric, asymmetric, or antisymmetric; holding between some pairs of arguments *x* and *y* and failing to hold for some other pairs when it holds between *y* and *x*.

nontransitive (nɒnˈtrænsɪtɪv) *adj Logic.* (of a relation) neither transitive nor intransitive.

non troppo (ˈnɒn ˈtrɒpəʊ) *adv Music.* (preceded by a musical direction, esp. a tempo marking) not to be observed too strictly (esp. in the phrases **allegro ma non troppo, adagio ma non troppo**).

non-U (nɒnˈjuː) *adj Brit. informal.* (esp. of language) not characteristic of or used by the upper class. Compare **U**[1].

nonunion (nɒnˈjuːnjən) *adj* **1** not belonging or related to a trade union: *nonunion workers.* **2** not favouring or employing union labour: *a nonunion shop.* **3** not produced by union labour: *nonunion shirts.* ♦ *n* **4** *Pathol.* failure of broken bones or bone fragments to heal.

nonunionism (nɒnˈjuːnjəˌnɪzəm) *n Chiefly U.S.* opposition to trade unionism. ► **nonˈunionist** *n, adj*

nonverbal communication (nɒnˈvɜːbᵊl) *n Psychol.* those aspects of communication, such as gestures and facial expressions, that do not involve verbal communication but which may include nonverbal aspects of speech itself (accent, tone of voice, speed of speaking, etc.).

nonviolence (nɒnˈvaɪələns) *n* abstention from the use of physical force to achieve goals. ► **nonˈviolent** *adj*

nonvoter (nɒnˈvəʊtə) *n* **1** a person who does not vote. **2** a person not eligible to vote.

nonvoting (nɒnˈvəʊtɪŋ) *adj* **1** of or relating to a nonvoter. **2** *Finance.* (of shares) not entitling the holder to vote at company meetings.

non-White *n* a person not of the Caucasoid or White race.

noodle[1] (ˈnuːdᵊl) *n* (*often pl*) a ribbon-like strip of pasta: noodles are often served in soup or with a sauce. **[C18:** from German *Nudel,* origin obscure**]**

noodle[2] (ˈnuːdᵊl) *n* **1** *U.S. and Canadian.* a slang word for **head** (sense 1). **2** a simpleton. **[C18:** perhaps a blend of NODDLE[1] and NOODLE[1]**]**

noodle[3] (ˈnuːdᵊl) *vb* (*intr*) *Slang.* to improvise aimlessly on a musical instrument.

Noogoora burr (nəˈguːrə) *n Austral.* a European cocklebur, *Xanthium pungens,* that is poisonous to stock. **[**from *Noogoora* a sheep station in Queensland**]**

nook (nʊk) *n* **1** a corner or narrow recess, as in a room. **2** a secluded or sheltered place; retreat. **[C13:** origin obscure; perhaps related to Norwegian dialect *nok* hook**]**

nooky *or* **nookie** (ˈnʊkɪ) *n Slang.* sexual intercourse. **[C20:** of uncertain origin; perhaps from NOOK**]**

noon (nuːn) *n* **1a** the middle of the day; 12 o'clock in the daytime or the time or point at which the sun crosses the local meridian. **1b** (*as modifier*): *the noon sun.* **2** *Poetic.* the highest, brightest, or most important part; culmination. **[**Old English *nōn,* from Latin *nōna* (*hōra*) ninth hour (originally 3 p.m., the ninth hour from sunrise)**]**

noonday (ˈnuːnˌdeɪ) *n* **a** the middle of the day; noon. **b** (*as modifier*): *the noonday sun.*

no-one *or* **no one** *pron* no person; nobody.

USAGE See at **everyone.**

nooning (ˈnuːnɪŋ) *n Dialect, chiefly U.S.* **1** a midday break for rest or food. **2** midday; noon.

noontime (ˈnuːnˌtaɪm) *or* **noontide** *n* **a** the middle of the day; noon. **b** (*as modifier*): *a noontime drink.*

Noordbrabant (noːrdˈbraːbɑnt) *n* the Dutch name for **North Brabant.**

Noordholland (noːrtˈhɔlɑnt) *n* the Dutch name for **North Holland.**

noose (nuːs) *n* **1** a loop in the end of a rope or cord, such as a lasso, snare, or hangman's halter, usually tied with a slipknot. **2** something that restrains, binds, or traps. **3 put one's head in a noose.** to bring about one's own downfall. ♦ *vb* (*tr*) **4** to secure or catch in or as if in a noose. **5** to make a noose of or in. **[C15:** perhaps from Provençal *nous,* from Latin *nōdus* NODE**]**

Nootka (ˈnʊtkə, ˈnuːt-) *n* **1** (*pl* **-ka** *or* **-kas**) a member of a North American Indian people living in British Columbia and Vancouver Island. **2** the language of this people, belonging to the Wakashan family.

nopal (ˈnəʊpᵊl) *n* **1** any of various cactuses of the genus *Nopalea,* esp. the red-flowered *N. cochinellifera,* which is a host plant of the cochineal insect. **2** a cactus, *Opuntia lindheimeri,* having yellow flowers and purple fruits. See also **prickly pear. [C18:** from Spanish, from Nahuatl *nopálli* cactus**]**

no-par *adj* (of securities) without a par value.

nope (nəʊp) *sentence substitute.* an informal word for **no**[1]. **[C19:** originally U.S., a variant of NO[1]**]**

nor (nɔː; *unstressed* nə) *conj* (*coordinating*), *prep* **1** (used to join alternatives, the first of which is preceded by *neither*) and not: *neither measles nor mumps.* **2** (foll. by an auxiliary verb or *have, do,* or *be* used as main verbs) (and) not...either: *they weren't talented—nor were they particularly funny.* **3** *Dialect.* than: *better nor me.* **4** *Poetic.* neither: *nor wind nor rain.* **[C13:** contraction of Old English *nōther,* from *nāhwæther* NEITHER**]**

Nor. *abbrev. for:* **1** Norman. **2** north. **3** Norway. **4** Norwegian.

nor- *combining form.* **1** indicating that a chemical compound is derived from a specified compound by removal of a group or groups: *noradrenaline.* **2** indicating that a chemical compound is a normal isomer of a specified compound. **[**by shortening from NORMAL**]**

noradrenaline (ˌnɔːrəˈdrɛnəlɪn, -liːn) *or* **noradrenalin** *n* a hormone secreted by the adrenal medulla, increasing blood pressure and heart rate, and by the endings of sympathetic nerves, when it acts as a neurotransmitter both centrally and peripherally. Formula: $C_8H_{11}NO_3$. U.S. name: **norepinephrine.**

Noraid (ˈnɔːrˌeɪd) *n* an American organization that supports the Republicans in Northern Ireland.

NOR circuit *or* **gate** (nɔː) *n Computing.* a logic circuit having two or more input wires and one output wire that has a high-voltage output signal only if all input signals are at a low voltage. Compare **AND circuit. [C20:** from NOR, so named because the action performed is similar to the operation of the conjunction *nor* in logic**]**

Nord (*French* nɔr) *n* a department of N France, in Nord-Pas-de-Calais region. Capital: Lille. Pop.: 2 556 800 (1995 est.). Area: 5774 sq. km (2252 sq. miles).

Nordau (*German* ˈnɔrdau) *n* **Max Simon** (maks ˈziːmɔn), original name *Max Simon Südfeld.* 1849–1923, German author, born in Hungary; a leader of the Zionist movement.

Nordenskjöld (*Swedish* ˈnuːrdənʃœld) *n* Baron **Nils Adolf Erik** (nils ˈɑːdɔlf ˈeːrik). 1832–1901, Swedish Arctic explorer and geologist, born in Finland. He was the first to navigate the Northeast Passage (1878–79).

Nordenskjöld Sea *n* the former name of the **Laptev Sea. [**named after N. A. E. NORDENSKJÖLD**]**

nordic (ˈnɔːdɪk) *adj Skiing.* of or relating to competitions in cross-country racing and ski-jumping. Compare **alpine** (sense 4).

Nordic (ˈnɔːdɪk) *adj* of, relating to, or belonging to a subdivision of the Caucasoid race typified by the tall blond blue-eyed long-headed inhabitants of N Britain, Scandinavia, N Germany, and the Netherlands. **[C19:** from French *nordique,* from *nord* NORTH**]**

Nordkyn Cape (*Norwegian* ˈnuːrçyːn) *n* a cape in N Norway: the northernmost point of the European mainland.

Nord-Pas-de-Calais (*French* nɔrpɑdəkalɛ) *n* a region of N France, on the Straits of Dover (the **Pas de Calais**): coal-mining, textile, and metallurgical industries.

Nordrhein-Westfalen (ˈnɔrtrainvɛstˈfaːlən) *n* the German name for **North Rhine-Westphalia.**

norepinephrine (ˌnɔːrɛpɪˈnɛfrɪn, -riːn) *n* the U.S. name for **noradrenaline.**

Norfolk (ˈnɔːfək) *n* **1** a county of E England, on the North Sea and the Wash: low-lying, with large areas of fens in the west and the Broads in the east; rich agriculturally. Administrative centre: Norwich. Pop.: 768 500 (1994 est.). Area: 5368 sq. km (2072 sq. miles). **2** a port in SE Virginia, on the Elizabeth River and Hampton Roads: headquarters of the U.S. Atlantic fleet; shipbuilding. Pop.: 233 430 (1996 est.).

Norfolk Island *n* an island in the S Pacific, between New Caledonia and N New Zealand: an Australian external territory; discovered by Captain Cook in 1774; a penal settlement in early years. Pop.: 2665 (1993). Area: 36 sq. km (14 sq. miles).

Norfolk jacket *n* a man's single-breasted belted jacket with one or two chest pockets and a box pleat down the back. **[C19:** worn in NORFOLK for duck shooting**]**

Norfolk terrier *n* a small wiry-coated breed of terrier having a short tail and pendent ears.

Norge (ˈnɔrgə) *n* the Norwegian name for **Norway.**

noria (ˈnɔːrɪə) *n* a water wheel with buckets attached to its rim for raising water from a stream into irrigation canals: common in Spain and the Orient. **[C18:** via Spanish from Arabic *nā'ūra,* from *na'ara* to creak**]**

Noricum (ˈnɒrɪkəm) *n* an Alpine kingdom of the Celts, south of the Danube: comprises present-day central Austria and parts of Bavaria; a Roman province from about 16 B.C.

norite (ˈnɔːraɪt) *n* a variety of gabbro that has hypersthene as the main ferromagnesian mineral. **[C19:** from Norwegian *norit,* from NORGE Norway + *-it* -ITE[1]**]**

nork (nɔːk) *n* (*usually pl*) *Austral. slang.* a female breast. **[C20:** of unknown origin**]**

norland (ˈnɔːlənd) *n Archaic.* the north part of a country or the earth. **[C17:** contraction of NORTH + LAND**]**

norm (nɔːm) *n* **1** an average level of achievement or performance, as of a group or person. **2** a standard of achievement or behaviour that is required, desired, or designated as normal. **3** *Sociol.* an established standard of behaviour shared by members of a social group to which each member is expected to conform. **4** *Maths.* **4a** the length of a vector expressed as the square root of the sum of the square of its components. **4b** another name for **mode** (sense 6). **5** *Geology.* the theoretical standard mineral composition of an igneous rock. **[C19:** from Latin *norma* carpenter's rule, square**]**

Norm (nɔːm) *n* a stereotype of the unathletic Australian male. **[**from a cartoon figure in the government-sponsored *Life, Be In It* campaign**]**

nonˈsurgical *adj*	**nonˈteaching** *adj*	**ˌnontraˈditional** *adj*	**nonˈverbal** *adj*
nonˈswimmer *n*	**nonˈtechnical** *adj*	**nonˈuniˌform** *adj*	**nonˈvintage** *adj*
ˌnonsystemˈatic *adj*	**ˌnonterriˈtorial** *adj*	**nonˈuse** *n*	**nonˈvolaˌtile** *adj*
nonˈtaxable *adj*	**nonˈtoxic** *adj*	**nonˈvenomous** *adj*	**nonˈworking** *adj*

norm. *abbrev. for* normal.

Norm. *abbrev. for* Norman.

Norma ('nɔːmə) *n, Latin genitive* **Normae** ('nɔːmiː). a constellation in the S hemisphere crossed by the Milky Way lying near Scorpius and Ara.

normal ('nɔːm°l) *adj* **1** usual; regular; common; typical: *the normal way of doing it; the normal level.* **2** constituting a standard: *if we take this as normal.* **3** *Psychol.* **3a** being within certain limits of intelligence, educational success or ability, etc. **3b** conforming to the conventions of one's group. **4** *Biology, med.* (of laboratory animals) maintained in a natural state for purposes of comparison with animals treated with drugs, etc. **5** *Chem.* (of a solution) containing a number of grams equal to the equivalent weight of the solute in each litre of solvent. Symbol: *N* **6** *Chem.* denoting a straight-chain hydrocarbon: *a normal alkane.* Prefix: ***n*-**, e.g. *n*-octane. **7** *Geometry.* another word for **perpendicular** (sense 1). ◆ *n* **8** the usual, average, or typical state, degree, form, etc. **9** anything that is normal. **10** *Geometry.* a line or plane perpendicular to another line or plane or to the tangent of a curved line or plane at the point of contact. [C16: from Latin *normālis* conforming to the carpenter's square, from *norma* NORM] ▸ **normality** (nɔː'mælɪtɪ) *or esp. U.S.* **'normalcy** *n*

normal curve *n Statistics.* a symmetrical bell-shaped curve representing the probability density function of a normal distribution. The area of a vertical section of the curve represents the probability that the random variable lies between the values which delimit the section.

normal distribution *n Statistics.* a continuous distribution of a random variable with its mean, median, and mode equal, the probability density function of which is given by $(exp[(x-\mu)^2/2\sigma^2]/\sigma\sqrt{(2\pi)})$ *where* μ is the mean and σ^2 the variance. Also called: **Gaussian distribution.**

normalization *or* **normalisation** (ˌnɔːməlaɪ'zeɪʃən) *n* **1** the act or process of normalizing. **2** *Social welfare.* the policy of offering mentally or physically handicapped people patterns, conditions, and experiences of everyday life as close as possible to those of nonhandicapped people, by not segregating them physically, socially, and administratively from the rest of society.

normalize *or* **normalise** ('nɔːməˌlaɪz) *vb (tr)* **1** to bring or make into the normal state. **2** to bring into conformity with a standard. **3** to heat (steel) above a critical temperature and allow it to cool in air to relieve internal stresses; anneal.

normally ('nɔːməlɪ) *adv* **1** as a rule; usually; ordinarily. **2** in a normal manner.

normal matrix *n* a square matrix *A* for which *AA** = *A*A*, where *A** is the Hermitian conjugate of *A*.

normal school *n* (in France, and formerly England, the U.S., and Canada) a school or institution for training teachers. [C19: from French *école normale:* the first French school so named was intended as a model for similar institutions]

Norman[1] ('nɔːmən) *n* **1** (in the Middle Ages) a member of the people of Normandy descended from the 10th-century Scandinavian conquerors of the country and the native French. **2** a native or inhabitant of Normandy. **3** another name for **Norman French.** ◆ *adj* **4** of, relating to, or characteristic of the Normans, esp. the Norman kings of England, the Norman people living in England, or their dialect of French. **5** of, relating to, or characteristic of Normandy or its inhabitants. **6** denoting, relating to, or having the style of Romanesque architecture used in Britain from the Norman Conquest until the 12th century. It is characterized by the rounded arch, the groin vault, massive masonry walls, etc.

Norman[2] ('nɔːmən) *n* **1 Greg.** born 1955, Australian golfer. **2 Jessye** ('dʒɛsɪ). born 1945, U.S. Black soprano.

Norman arch *n Chiefly Brit.* a semicircular arch, esp. one in the Romanesque style of architecture developed by the Normans in England. Also called: **Roman arch.**

Norman Conquest *n* the invasion and settlement of England by the Normans, following the Battle of Hastings (1066).

Normandy ('nɔːməndɪ) *n* a former province of N France, on the English Channel: settled by Vikings under Rollo in the 10th century; scene of the Allied landings in 1944. Chief town: Rouen. French name: **Normandie** (nɔrmɑ̃di).

Norman English *n* the dialect of English used by the Norman conquerors of England.

Norman French *n* the medieval Norman and English dialect of Old French. See also **Anglo-French** (sense 3).

Normanize *or* **Normanise** ('nɔːməˌnaɪz) *vb* to make or become Norman in character, style, customs, etc. ▸ **ˌNormani'zation** *or* **ˌNormani'sation** *n*

normative ('nɔːmətɪv) *adj* **1** implying, creating, or prescribing a norm or standard, as in language: *normative grammar.* **2** expressing value judgments or prescriptions as contrasted with stating facts: *normative economics.* **3** of, relating to, or based on norms. ▸ **'normatively** *adv* ▸ **'normativeness** *n*

normotensive (ˌnɔːməʊ'tɛnsɪv) *adj* having or denoting normal blood pressure.

Norn[1] (nɔːn) *n Norse myth.* any of the three virgin goddesses of fate, who predestine the lives of the gods and men. [C18: Old Norse]

Norn[2] (nɔːn) *n* the medieval Norse language of the Orkneys, Shetlands, and parts of N Scotland. It was extinct by 1750. [C17: from Old Norse *norrœna* Norwegian, from *northr* north]

Norodom Sihanouk (ˌnɒrə'dɒm 'siːənʊk) *n* See (Norodom) **Sihanouk.**

Norrköping (*Swedish* 'nɔrtçøːpiŋ) *n* a port in SE Sweden, near the Baltic. Pop.: 123 531 (1997 est.).

Norroy ('nɒrɔɪ) *n* the third King-of-Arms in England: since 1943, called **Norroy and Ulster.** [C15: Old French *nor* north + *roy* king]

Norse (nɔːs) *adj* **1** of, relating to, or characteristic of ancient and medieval Scandinavia or its inhabitants. **2** of, relating to, or characteristic of Norway. ◆ *n* **3a** the N group of Germanic languages, spoken in Scandinavia; Scandinavian. **3b** any one of these languages, esp. in their ancient or medieval forms. See also **Proto-Norse, Old Norse. 4 the Norse.** (*functioning as pl*) **4a** the Norwegians. **4b** the Vikings.

Norseman ('nɔːsmən) *n, pl* **-men.** another name for a **Viking.**

north (nɔːθ) *n* **1** one of the four cardinal points of the compass, at 0° or 360°, that is 90° from east and west and 180° from south. **2** the direction along a meridian towards the North Pole. **3** the direction in which a compass needle points; magnetic north. **4 the north.** (*often cap.*) any area lying in or towards the north. Related adjs.: **arctic, boreal. 5** *Cards.* (*usually cap.*) the player or position at the table corresponding to north on the compass. ◆ *adj* **6** situated in, moving towards, or facing the north. **7** (esp. of the wind) from the north. ◆ *adv* **8** in, to, or towards the north. **9** *Archaic.* (of the wind) from the north. ◆ Symbol.: **N** [Old English; related to Old Norse *northr,* Dutch *noord,* Old High German *nord*]

North[1] (nɔːθ) *n* **the. 1** the northern area of England, generally regarded as reaching approximately the southern boundaries of Yorkshire, Derbyshire, and Cheshire. **2** (in the U.S.) the area approximately north of Maryland and the Ohio River, esp. those states north of the Mason-Dixon Line that were known as the Free States during the Civil War. **3** the northern part of North America, esp. the area consisting of Alaska, the Yukon, and the Northwest Territories; the North Country. **4** the countries of the world that are economically and technically advanced. **5** *Poetic.* the north wind. ◆ *adj* **6a** of or denoting the northern part of a specified country, area, etc. **6b** (*as part of a name*): *North Africa.*

North[2] (nɔːθ) *n* **1 Frederick,** 2nd Earl of Guildford, called *Lord North.* 1732–92, British statesman; prime minister (1770–82), dominated by George III. He was held responsible for the loss of the American colonies. **2 Sir Thomas.** ?1535–?1601, English translator of Plutarch's *Lives* (1579), which was the chief source of Shakespeare's Roman plays.

North Africa *n* the part of Africa between the Mediterranean and the Sahara: consists chiefly of Morocco, Algeria, Tunisia, Libya, and N Egypt. ▸ **North African** *adj, n*

Northallerton (nɔː'θælət°n) *n* a market town in N England, administrative centre of North Yorkshire. Pop.: 13 774 (1991).

North America *n* the third largest continent, linked with South America by the Isthmus of Panama and bordering on the Arctic Ocean, the N Pacific, the N Atlantic, the Gulf of Mexico, and the Caribbean. It consists generally of a great mountain system (the Western Cordillera) extending along the entire W coast, actively volcanic in the extreme north and south, with the Great Plains to the east and the Appalachians still further east, separated from the Canadian Shield by an arc of large lakes (Great Bear, Great Slave, Winnipeg, Superior, Michigan, Huron, Erie, Ontario); reaches its greatest height of 6194 m (20 320 ft.) in Mount McKinley, Alaska, and its lowest point of 85 m (280 ft.) below sea level in Death Valley, California, and ranges from snowfields, tundra, and taiga in the north to deserts in the southwest and tropical forests in the extreme south. Pop.: 421 006 000 (1996 est.). Area: over 24 000 000 sq. km (9 500 000 sq. miles). ▸ **North American** *adj, n*

Northampton (nɔː'θæmptən, nɔːθ'hæmp-) *n* **1** a town in central England, administrative centre of Northamptonshire, on the River Nene: footwear and engineering industries. Pop.: 179 596 (1991). **2** short for **Northamptonshire.**

Northamptonshire (nɔː'θæmptənˌʃɪə, -ʃə, nɔːθ'hæmp-) *n* a county of central England: agriculture, food processing, engineering, and footwear industries. Administrative centre: Northampton. Pop.: 594 800 (1994 est.). Area: 2367 sq. km (914 sq. miles). Abbrev.: **Northants.**

Northants (nɔː'θænts) *abbrev. for* Northamptonshire.

North Atlantic Drift *or* **Current** *n* the warm ocean current flowing northeast, under the influence of prevailing winds, from the Gulf of Mexico towards NW Europe and warming its climate. Also called: **Gulf Stream.**

North Atlantic Treaty Organization *n* the full name of **NATO.**

North Ayrshire ('ɛəʃɪə, -ʃə) *n* A council area of W central Scotland, on the Firth of Clyde: comprises the N part of the historical county of Ayrshire, including the Isle of Arran; formerly part of Strathclyde Region (1975–96): chiefly agricultural, with fishing and tourism. Administrative centre: Irvine. Pop.: 139 020 (1996 est.). Area: 884 sq. km (341 sq. miles).

North Borneo *n* the former name (until 1963) of **Sabah.**

northbound ('nɔːθˌbaʊnd) *adj* going or leading towards the north.

North Brabant *n* a province of the S Netherlands: formed part of the medieval duchy of Brabant. Capital: 's Hertogenbosch. Pop.: 2 290 400 (1996 est.). Area: 4965 sq. km (1917 sq. miles). Dutch name: **Noordbrabant.**

north by east *n* **1** one point on the compass east of north, 11° 15′ clockwise from north. ◆ *adj, adv* **2** in, from, or towards this direction.

north by west *n* **1** one point on the compass west of north, 348° 45′ clockwise from north. ◆ *adj, adv* **2** in, from, or towards this direction.

North Cape *n* **1** a cape on N Magerøy Island, in the Arctic Ocean off the N coast of Norway. **2** a cape on N North Island, New Zealand.

North Carolina *n* a state of the southeastern U.S., on the Atlantic: consists of a coastal plain rising to the Piedmont Plateau and the Appalachian Mountains in the west. Capital: Raleigh. Pop.: 7 425 183 (1997 est.). Area: 126 387 sq. km (48 798 sq. miles). Abbrevs.: **N.C.** or (with zip code) **NC** ▸ **North Carolinian** *adj, n*

North Channel *n* a strait between NE Ireland and SW Scotland, linking the North Atlantic with the Irish Sea.

Northcliffe ('nɔːθklɪf) *n* **Viscount.** title of *Alfred Charles William Harmsworth.* 1865–1922, British newspaper proprietor. With his brother, 1st Viscount Rothermere, he built up a vast chain of newspapers. He founded the *Daily Mail* (1896), the *Daily Mirror* (1903), and acquired *The Times* (1908).

North Country *n* (usually preceded by *the*) **1** another name for **North**[1] (sense 1). **2** the geographic region formed by Alaska, the Yukon, and the Northwest Territories.

northcountryman (ˌnɔːθˈkʌntrɪmən) *n, pl* **-men.** a native or inhabitant of the North of England.

Northd *abbrev. for* Northumberland.

North Dakota *n* a state of the western U.S.: mostly undulating prairies and plains, rising from the Red River valley in the east to the Missouri plateau in the west, with the infertile Bad Lands in the extreme west. Capital: Bismarck. Pop.: 640 883 (1997 est.). Area: 183 019 sq. km (70 664 sq. miles). Abbrevs.: **N.Dak., N.D.,** or (with zip code) **ND** ▸ **North Dakotan** *adj, n*

North Down *n* a district of E Northern Ireland, in Co. Down. Pop.: 71 832 (1991). Area: 82 sq. km (32 sq. miles).

northeast (ˌnɔːθˈiːst; *Nautical* ˌnɔːrˈiːst) *n* **1** the point of the compass or direction midway between north and east, 45° clockwise from north. **2** (*often cap.; usually preceded by the*) any area lying in or towards this direction. ◆ *adj also* **northeastern. 3** (*sometimes cap.*) of or denoting the northeastern part of a specified country, area, etc.: *northeast Lincolnshire.* **4** situated in, proceeding towards, or facing the northeast. **5** (esp. of the wind) from the northeast. ◆ *adv* **6** in, to, towards, or (esp. of the wind) from the northeast. ◆ Symbol: **NE** ▸ **ˌnorthˈeasternmost** *adj*

Northeast (ˌnɔːθˈiːst) *n* (usually preceded by *the*) the northeastern part of England, esp. Northumberland, Durham, and the Tyneside area.

northeast by east *n* **1** one point on the compass east of northeast, 56° 15′ clockwise from north. ◆ *adj, adv* **2** in, from, or towards this direction.

northeast by north *n* **1** one point on the compass north of northeast, 33° 45′ clockwise from north. ◆ *adj, adv* **2** in, from, or towards this direction.

northeaster (ˌnɔːθˈiːstə; *Nautical* ˌnɔːrˈiːstə) *n* a strong wind or storm from the northeast.

northeasterly (ˌnɔːθˈiːstəlɪ; *Nautical* ˌnɔːrˈiːstəlɪ) *adj, adv* **1** in, towards, or (esp. of a wind) from the northeast. ◆ *n, pl* **-lies. 2** a wind or storm from the northeast.

North East Frontier Agency *n* the former name (until 1972) of **Arunachal Pradesh.**

North East Lincolnshire (ˈlɪŋkənˌʃɪə, -ʃə) *n* a unitary authority in NE England, in Lincolnshire: formerly (1974–96) part of the county of Humberside. Pop.: 164 000 (1996 est.). Area: 192 sq. km (74 sq. miles).

Northeast Passage *n* a shipping route along the Arctic coasts of Europe and Asia, between the Atlantic and Pacific: first navigated by Nordenskjöld (1878–79).

northeastward (ˌnɔːθˈiːstwəd; *Nautical* ˌnɔːrˈiːstwəd) *adj* **1** towards or (esp. of a wind) from the northeast. ◆ *n* **2** a direction towards or area in the northeast. ▸ **ˌnorthˈeastwardly** *adj, adv*

northeastwards (ˌnɔːθˈiːstwədz; *Nautical* ˌnɔːrˈiːstwədz) *or* **northeastward** *adv* to the northeast.

norther (ˈnɔːðə) *n Chiefly southern U.S.* a wind or storm from the north.

northerly (ˈnɔːðəlɪ) *adj* **1** of, relating to, or situated in the north. ◆ *adv, adj* **2** towards or in the direction of the north. **3** from the north: *a northerly wind.* ◆ *n, pl* **-lies. 4** a wind from the north. ▸ **ˈnortherliness** *n*

northern (ˈnɔːðən) *adj* **1** situated in or towards the north: *northern towns.* **2** directed or proceeding towards the north: *a northern flow of traffic.* **3** (esp. of winds) proceeding from the north. **4** (*sometimes cap.*) of, relating to, or characteristic of the north or North. **5** (*sometimes cap.*) *Astronomy.* north of the celestial equator.

Northern Cross *n* a group of the five brightest stars that form a large cross in the constellation Cygnus.

Northern Dvina *n* See **Dvina** (sense 1).

Northerner (ˈnɔːðənə) *n* (*sometimes not cap.*) a native or inhabitant of the north of any specified region, esp. England or the U.S.

northern hemisphere *n* (*often caps.*) **1** that half of the globe lying north of the equator. **2** *Astronomy.* that half of the celestial sphere north of the celestial equator. ◆ Abbrev.: **N hemisphere.**

Northern Ireland *n* that part of the United Kingdom occupying the NE part of Ireland: separated from the rest of Ireland, which became independent in law in 1920; it remained part of the United Kingdom, with a separate Parliament (Stormont), inaugurated in 1921, and limited self-government: scene of severe conflict between Catholics and Protestants, including terrorist bombing from 1969: direct administration from Westminster from 1972. Capital: Belfast. Pop.: 1 575 200 (1987 est.). Area: 14 121 sq. km (5452 sq. miles).

Northern Isles *pl n* the Orkneys and Shetland.

northern lights *pl n* another name for **aurora borealis.**

northernmost (ˈnɔːðənˌməʊst) *adj* situated or occurring farthest north.

Northern Rhodesia *n* the former name (until 1964) of **Zambia.**

Northern Sotho *n* another name for **Pedi** (the language).

Northern Territories *pl n* a former British protectorate in W Africa, established in 1897; attached to the Gold Coast in 1901; now constitutes the Northern Region of Ghana (since 1957).

Northern Territory *n* an administrative division of N central Australia, on the Timor and Arafura Seas: includes Ashmore and Cartier Islands; the Arunta Desert lies in the east, the Macdonnell Ranges in the south, and Arnhem Land in the north (containing Australia's largest Aboriginal reservation). Capital: Darwin. Pop.: 177 500 (1996 est.). Area: 1 347 525 sq. km (520 280 sq. miles).

North Germanic *n* a subbranch of the Germanic languages that consists of Danish, Norwegian, Swedish, Icelandic, and their associated dialects. See also **Old Norse.**

North Holland *n* a province of the NW Netherlands, on the peninsula between the North Sea and IJsselmeer: includes the West Frisian Island of Texel. Capital: Haarlem. Pop.: 2 468 400 (1996 est.). Area: 2663 sq. km (1029 sq. miles). Dutch name: **Noordholland.**

northing (ˈnɔːθɪŋ, -ðɪŋ) *n* **1** *Navigation.* movement or distance covered in a northerly direction, esp. as expressed in the resulting difference in latitude. **2** *Astronomy.* a north or positive declination. **3** *Cartography.* **3a** the distance northwards of a point from a given parallel indicated by the second half of a map grid reference. **3b** a latitudinal grid line. Compare **easting** (sense 2).

North Island *n* **the.** the northernmost of the two main islands of New Zealand. Pop.: 2 733 083 (1996). Area: 114 729 sq. km (44 297 sq. miles).

North Korea *n* a republic in NE Asia, on the Sea of Japan and the Yellow Sea: established in 1948 as a people's republic; mostly rugged and mountainous, with fertile lowlands in the west. Language: Korean. Currency: won. Capital: Pyongyang. Pop.: 21 234 000 (1998 est.). Area: 122 313 sq. km (47 225 sq. miles). Official name: **Democratic People's Republic of Korea.** Korean name: **Chosŏn.** ▸ **North Korean** *adj, n*

North Lanarkshire (ˈlænəkˌʃɪə, -ʃə) *n* a council area of central Scotland: consists mainly of the NE part of the historical county of Lanarkshire; formerly (1974–96) part of Strathclyde Region: engineering and metalworking industries. Administrative centre: Motherwell. Pop.: 307 100 (1996 est.). Area: 1771 sq. km (684 sq. miles).

Northland (ˈnɔːθlənd) *n* **1** the peninsula containing Norway and Sweden. **2** (in Canada) the far north. ▸ **ˈNorthlander** *n*

North Lincolnshire (ˈlɪŋkənˌʃɪə, -ʃə) *n* a unitary authority of NE England, in Lincolnshire: formerly (1975–96) part of the county of Humberside. Pop.: 153 000 (1996 est.). Area: 1497 sq. km (578 sq. miles).

Northman (ˈnɔːθmən) *n, pl* **-men.** another name for a **Viking.**

north-northeast *n* **1** the point on the compass or the direction midway between north and northeast, 22° 30′ clockwise from north. ◆ *adj, adv* **2** in, from, or towards this direction. ◆ Symbol: **NNE**

north-northwest *n* **1** the point on the compass or the direction midway between northwest and north, 337° 30′ clockwise from north. ◆ *adj, adv* **2** in, from, or towards this direction. ◆ Symbol: **NNW**

North Ossetian Republic (əˈsiːʃən) *n* a constituent republic of S Russia, on the N slopes of the central Caucasus Mountains. Capital: Vladikavkaz. Pop.: 658 000 (1995 est.). Area: about 8000 sq. km (3088 sq. miles). Also called: **North Ossetia, Alania.**

North Pole *n* **1** the northernmost point on the earth's axis, at a latitude of 90°N, characterized by very low temperatures. **2** Also called: **north celestial pole.** *Astronomy.* the point of intersection of the earth's extended axis and the northern half of the celestial sphere, lying about 1° from Polaris. **3** (*usually not caps.*) the pole of a freely suspended magnet, which is attracted to the earth's magnetic North Pole.

North Rhine-Westphalia *n* a state of W Germany: formed in 1946 by the amalgamation of the Prussian province of Westphalia with the N part of the Prussian Rhine province and later with the state of Lippe; part of West Germany until 1990: highly industrialized. Capital: Düsseldorf. Pop.: 17 893 000 (1996 est.). Area: 34 039 sq. km (13 142 sq. miles). German name: **Nordrhein-Westfalen.**

North Riding *n* (until 1974) an administrative division of Yorkshire, now constituting most of North Yorkshire.

North Saskatchewan *n* a river in W Canada, rising in W Alberta and flowing northeast, east, and southeast to join the South Saskatchewan River and form the Saskatchewan River. Length: 1223 km (760 miles).

North Sea *n* an arm of the Atlantic between Great Britain and the N European mainland. Area: about 569 800 sq. km (220 000 sq. miles). Former name: **German Ocean.**

North-Sea gas *n* (in Britain) natural gas obtained from deposits below the North Sea.

North Somerset (ˈsʌməsɛt) *n* a unitary authority of SW England, in Somerset: formerly (1974–96) part of the county of Avon. Pop.: 177 000 (1996 est.). Area: 375 sq. km (145 sq. miles).

North Star *n* **the.** another name for **Polaris** (sense 1).

North Tyneside (ˈtaɪnsaɪd) *n* a unitary authority of NE England, in Tyne and Wear. Pop.: 194 100 (1996 est.). Area: 84 sq. km (32 sq. miles).

Northumberland[1] (nɔːˈθʌmbələnd) *n* the northernmost county of England, on the North Sea: hilly in the north (the Cheviots) and west (the Pennines), with many Roman remains, notably Hadrian's Wall; shipbuilding, coal mining. Administrative centre: Morpeth. Pop.: 307 700 (1994 est.). Area: 5032 sq. km (1943 sq. miles). Abbrev.: **Northd**

Northumberland[2] (nɔːˈθʌmbələnd) *n* **1st Duke of,** title of *John Dudley.* 1502–53, English statesman and soldier, who governed England (1549–53) during the minority of Edward VI. His attempt (1553) to gain the throne for his daughter-in-law, Lady Jane Grey, led to his execution.

Northumbria (nɔːˈθʌmbrɪə) *n* **1** (in Anglo-Saxon Britain) a region that stretched from the Humber to the Firth of Forth: formed in the 7th century A.D., it became an important intellectual centre; a separate kingdom until 876 A.D. **2** an area of NE England roughly corresponding to the Anglo-Saxon region of Northumbria.

Northumbrian (nɔːˈθʌmbrɪən) *adj* **1** of or relating to the English county of Northumberland, its inhabitants, or their dialect of English. **2** of or relating to ancient Northumbria, its inhabitants, or their dialect. ◆ *n* **3a** the dialect of Old and Middle English spoken north of the River Humber. See also **Anglian, Mercian. 3b** the dialect of Modern English spoken in Northumberland.

North Vietnam *n* a region of N Vietnam, on the Gulf of Tonkin: an independent Communist state from 1954 until 1976. Area: 164 061 sq. km (63 344 sq. miles).

northward (ˈnɔːθwəd; *Nautical* ˈnɔːðəd) *adj* **1** moving, facing, or situated towards the north. ◆ *n* **2** the northward part, direction, etc.; the north. ◆ *adv* **3** a variant of **northwards.** ▸ **ˈnorthwardly** *adj, adv*

northwards (ˈnɔːθwədz) *or* **northward** *adv* towards the north.

northwest (ˌnɔːθˈwɛst; *Nautical* ˌnɔːˈwɛst) *n* **1** the point of the compass or direction midway between north and west, clockwise 315° from north. **2** (*often* *cap.;* usually preceded by *the*) any area lying in or towards this direction. ◆ *adj also* **northwestern**. 3 (*sometimes cap.*) of or denoting the northwestern part of a specified country, area, etc.: *northwest Greenland.* ◆ *adj, adv* 4 in, to, towards, or (esp. of the wind) from the northwest. ◆ Symbol: **NW** ▸ **,north'westernmost** *adj*

Northwest (,nɔːθ'wɛst) *n* (usually preceded by *the*) 1 the northwestern part of England, esp. Lancashire and the Lake District. 2 the northwestern part of the U.S., consisting of the states of Washington, Oregon, and sometimes Idaho. 3 (in Canada) the region north and west of the Great Lakes.

northwest by north *n* 1 one point on the compass north of northwest, 326° 15′ clockwise from north. ◆ *adj, adv* 2 in, from, or towards this direction.

northwest by west *n* 1 one point on the compass south of northwest, 303° 45′ clockwise from north. ◆ *adj, adv* 2 in, from, or towards this direction.

northwester (,nɔːθ'wɛstə; *Nautical* ,nɔː'wɛstə) *n* a strong wind or storm from the northwest.

northwesterly (,nɔːθ'wɛstəlɪ; *Nautical* ,nɔː'wɛstəlɪ) *adj, adv* 1 in, towards, or (esp. of a wind) from the northwest. ◆ *n, pl* **-lies**. 2 a wind or storm from the northwest.

North-West Frontier Province *n* a province in N Pakistan between Afghanistan and Jammu and Kashmir: part of British India from 1901 until 1947; of strategic importance, esp. for the Khyber Pass. Capital: Peshawar. Pop.: 12 287 000 (1985 est.). Area: 74 522 sq. km (28 773 sq. miles).

Northwest Passage *n* the passage by sea from the Atlantic to the Pacific along the N coast of America: attempted for over 300 years by Europeans seeking a short route to the Far East, before being successfully navigated by Amundsen (1903–06).

Northwest Territories *pl n* the part of Canada north of the provinces and east of the Yukon Territory, including the islands of the Arctic, Hudson Bay, James Bay, and Ungava Bay; comprised over a third of Canada's total area until Nunavut became a separate territory in 1999: rich mineral resources. Pop.: 45 500 (1999 est.). Area: 1 224 920 sq. km (477 950 sq. miles). Abbrev.: **NWT.**

Northwest Territory *n* See **Old Northwest.**

northwestward (,nɔːθ'wɛstwəd; *Nautical* ,nɔː'wɛstwəd) *adj* 1 towards or (esp. of a wind) from the northwest. ◆ *n* 2 a direction towards or area in the northwest. ▸ **,north'westwardly** *adj, adv*

northwestwards (,nɔːθ'wɛstwədz; *Nautical* ,nɔː'wɛstwədz) *or* **northwestward** *adv* towards or (esp. of a wind) from the northwest.

Northwich ('nɔːθwɪtʃ) *n* a town in NW England, in Cheshire: salt and chemical industries. Pop.: 34 520 (1991).

North Yemen *n* a former republic in SW Arabia, on the Red Sea; now part of Yemen: declared a republic in 1962: united with South Yemen in 1990. Official name: **Yemen Arab Republic.** See also **Yemen, South Yemen.**

North Yorkshire *n* a county in N England, formed in 1974 from most of the North Riding of Yorkshire and parts of the East and West Ridings: the geographical and ceremonial county includes the unitary authorities of Middlesbrough, Redcar and Cleveland, and part of Stockton on Tees (all within Cleveland until 1996), and York (created in 1997). Administrative centre: Northallerton. Pop. (including unitary authorities): 1 016 100 (1996 est.). Area (including unitary authorities): 8603 sq. km (3322 sq. miles).

Norw. *abbrev. for:* 1 Norway. 2 Norwegian.

Norway ('nɔː,weɪ) *n* a kingdom in NW Europe, occupying the W part of the Scandinavian peninsula: first united in the Viking age (800–1050); under the rule of Denmark (1523–1814) and Sweden (1814–1905); became an independent monarchy in 1905. Its coastline is deeply indented by fjords and fringed with islands, rising inland to plateaus and mountains. Norway has a large fishing fleet and its merchant navy is among the world's largest. Official language: Norwegian. Official religion: Evangelical Lutheran. Currency: krone. Capital: Oslo. Pop.: 4 429 000 (1998 est.). Area: 323 878 sq. km (125 050 sq. miles). Norwegian name: **Norge.**

Norway lobster *n* a European lobster, *Nephrops norvegicus,* fished for food.

Norway maple *n* a large Eurasian maple tree, *Acer platanoides,* with broad five-lobed pale green leaves.

Norway rat *n* another name for **brown rat.**

Norway spruce *n* a European spruce tree, *Picea abies,* planted for timber and ornament, having drooping branches and dark green needle-like leaves.

Norwegian (nɔː'wiːdʒən) *adj* 1 of, relating to, or characteristic of Norway, its language, or its people. ◆ *n* 2 any of the various North Germanic languages of Norway. See also **Nynorsk, Bokmål.** Compare **Norse.** 3 a native, citizen, or inhabitant of Norway.

Norwegian Sea *n* part of the Arctic Ocean between Greenland and Norway.

nor'wester (,nɔː'wɛstə) *n* 1 a less common name for **sou'wester.** 2 a drink of strong liquor. 3 a strong northwest wind. 4 *N.Z.* a hot dry wind from the Southern Alps. [C18 (in the sense: storm from the northwest): a contraction of NORTHWESTER]

Norwich ('nɒrɪdʒ) *n* a city in E England, administrative centre of Norfolk: cathedral (founded 1096); University of East Anglia (1963); footwear industry. Pop.: 171 304 (1991).

Norwich terrier *n* a small wiry-coated breed of terrier having either erect or pendent ears.

Nos. *or* **nos.** *abbrev. for* numbers.

nose (nəuz) *n* 1 the organ of smell and entrance to the respiratory tract, consisting of a prominent structure divided into two hair-lined air passages by a median septum. Related adjs: **nasal, rhinal.** 2 the sense of smell itself: in hounds and other animals, the ability to follow trails by scent (esp. in the phrases **a good nose, a bad nose**). 3 another word for **bouquet** (sense 2). 4 instinctive skill or facility, esp. in discovering things (sometimes in the phrase **follow one's nose**): *he had a nose for good news stories.* 5 any part regarded as resembling a nose in form or function, such as a nozzle or spout. 6 the forward part of a vehicle, aircraft, etc., esp. the front end of an aircraft. 7 narrow margin of victory (in the phrase (**win**) **by a nose**). 8 **cut off one's nose to spite one's face.** to carry out a vengeful action that hurts oneself more than another. 9 **get up (someone's) nose.** *Informal.* to annoy or irritate (someone). 10 **keep one's nose clean.** to stay out of trouble; behave properly. 11 **keep one's nose to the grindstone.** to work hard and continuously. 12 **lead (someone) by the nose.** to make (someone) do unquestioningly all one wishes; dominate (someone). 13 **look down one's nose at.** *Informal.* to be contemptuous or disdainful of. 14 **nose to tail.** (of vehicles) moving or standing very close behind one another. 15 **on the nose.** *Slang.* 15a (in horse-race betting) to win only: *I bet twenty pounds on the nose on that horse.* 15b *Chiefly U.S. and Canadian.* precisely; exactly. 15c *Austral.* bad or bad-smelling. 16 **pay through the nose.** *Informal.* to pay an exorbitant price. 17 **poke, stick,** etc., **one's nose into.** *Informal.* to pry into or interfere in. 18 **put someone's nose out of joint.** *Informal.* to thwart or offend someone, esp. by supplanting him or gaining something he regards as his. 19 **rub someone's nose in it.** *Informal.* to remind someone unkindly of his failing or error. 20 **see no further than (the end of) one's nose.** *Informal.* 20a to be short-sighted; suffer from myopia. 20b to lack insight or foresight. 21 **turn up one's nose (at).** *Informal.* to behave disdainfully (towards). 22 **under one's nose.** 22a directly in front of one. 22b without one noticing. 23 **with one's nose in the air.** haughtily. ◆ *vb* 24 (*tr*) (esp. of horses, dogs, etc.) to rub, touch, or sniff with the nose; nuzzle. 25 to smell or sniff (wine, etc.). 26 (*intr;* usually foll. by *after* or *for*) to search (for) by or as if by scent. 27 to move or cause to move forwards slowly and carefully: *the car nosed along the cliff top; we nosed the car into the garage.* 28 (*intr;* foll. by *into, around, about,* etc.) to pry or snoop (into) or meddle (in). ◆ See also **nose out.** [Old English *nosu;* related to Old Frisian *nose,* Norwegian *nosa* to smell and *nus* smell] ▸ **'noseless** *adj* ▸ **'nose,like** *adj*

nosebag ('nəuz,bæg) *n* a bag, fastened around the head of a horse and covering the nose, in which feed is placed.

noseband ('nəuz,bænd) *n* the detachable part of a horse's bridle that goes around the nose. Also called: **nosepiece.** ▸ **'nose,banded** *adj*

nosebleed ('nəuz,bliːd) *n* bleeding from the nose, as the result of injury, etc. Technical name: **epistaxis.**

nose cone *n* the conical forward section of a missile, spacecraft, etc., designed to withstand high temperatures, esp. during re-entry into the earth's atmosphere.

nose dive *n* 1 a sudden plunge with the nose or front pointing downwards, esp. of an aircraft. 2 *Informal.* a sudden drop or sharp decline: *prices took a nose dive.* ◆ *vb* **nose-dive.** 3 to perform or cause to perform a nose dive. 4 (*intr*) *Informal.* to drop suddenly.

nose flute *n* (esp. in the South Sea Islands) a type of flute blown through the nose.

nosegay ('nəuz,geɪ) *n* a small bunch of flowers; posy. [C15: from NOSE + archaic *gay* a toy]

nose job *n Slang.* a surgical remodelling of the nose for cosmetic reasons.

nose out *vb* (*tr, adv*) 1 to discover by smelling. 2 to discover by cunning or persistence: *the reporter managed to nose out a few facts.* 3 *Informal.* to beat by a narrow margin: *he was nosed out of first place by the champion.*

nosepiece ('nəuz,piːs) *n* 1 Also called: **nasal.** a piece of armour, esp. part of a helmet, that serves to protect the nose. 2 the connecting part of a pair of spectacles that rests on the nose; bridge. 3 the part of a microscope to which one or more objective lenses are attached. 4 a less common word for **noseband.**

nose rag *n Slang.* a handkerchief.

nose ring *n* a ring fixed through the nose, as for leading a bull.

nose wheel *n* a wheel fitted to the forward end of a vehicle, esp. the landing wheel under the nose of an aircraft.

nosey ('nəuzɪ) *adj* a variant spelling of **nosy.**

nosh (nɒʃ) *Slang.* ◆ *n* 1 food or a meal. ◆ *vb* 2 to eat. [C20: from Yiddish; compare German *naschen* to nibble] ▸ **'nosher** *n*

no-show *n* a person who fails to take up a reserved seat, place, etc., without having cancelled it.

nosh-up *n Brit. slang.* a large and satisfying meal.

no-side *n Rugby.* the end of a match, signalled by the referee's whistle.

nosing ('nəuzɪŋ) *n* 1 the edge of a step or stair tread that projects beyond the riser. 2 a projecting edge of a moulding, esp. one that is half-round. [C18: from NOSE + -ING[1]]

noso- *or before a vowel* **nos-** *combining form.* disease: *nosology.* [from Greek *nosos*]

nosocomial (,nɒsə'kəumɪəl) *adj Medicine.* originating in hospital: *nosocomial disease.* [C19: New Latin *nosocomialis,* via Late Latin from Greek, from *nosokomos* one that tends the sick, from *nosos* (see NOSO-) + *komein* to tend]

nosography (nɒ'sɒgrəfɪ) *n* a written classification and description of various diseases. ▸ **no'sographer** *n* ▸ **nosographic** (,nɒsə'græfɪk) *adj*

nosology (nɒ'sɒlədʒɪ) *n* the branch of medicine concerned with the classification of diseases. ▸ **nosological** (,nɒsə'lɒdʒɪkəl) *adj* ▸ **,noso'logically** *adv* ▸ **no'sologist** *n*

nosophobia (,nɒsə'fəubɪə) *n* the morbid dread of contracting disease.

nostalgia (nɒ'stældʒə, -dʒɪə) *n* 1 a yearning for the return of past circumstances, events, etc. 2 the evocation of this emotion, as in a book, film, etc. 3 longing for home or family; homesickness. [C18: New Latin (translation of German *Heimweh* homesickness), from Greek *nostos* a return home + -ALGIA] ▸ **nos'talgic** *adj* ▸ **nos'talgically** *adv*

nostoc ('nɒstɒk) *n* any cyanobacterium of the genus *Nostoc,* occurring in moist places as rounded colonies consisting of coiled filaments in a gelatinous substance. [C17: New Latin, coined by Paracelsus]

nostology (nɒ'stɒlədʒɪ) *n Med.* another word for **gerontology.** [C20: from

Greek *nostos* a return home (with reference to ageing or second childhood) + -LOGY] ► **nostologic** (ˌnɒstəˈlɒdʒɪk) *adj*

Nostradamus (ˌnɒstrəˈdɑːməs) *n* Latinized name of *Michel de Notredame.* 1503–66, French physician and astrologer; author of a book of prophecies in rhymed quatrains, *Centuries* (1555).

nostril (ˈnɒstrɪl) *n* either of the two external openings of the nose. Related adjs.: **narial, narine.** [Old English *nosthyrl,* from *nosu* NOSE + *thyrel* hole]

nostro account (ˈnɒstrəʊ) *n* a bank account conducted by a British bank with a foreign bank, usually in the foreign currency. Compare **vostro account.**

nostrum (ˈnɒstrəm) *n* **1** a patent or quack medicine. **2** a favourite remedy, as for political or social problems. [C17: from Latin: our own (make), from *noster* our]

nosy *or* **nosey** (ˈnəʊzɪ) *adj* **nosier, nosiest.** *Informal.* prying or inquisitive. ► ˈ**nosily** *adv* ► ˈ**nosiness** *n*

nosy parker *n Informal.* a prying person. [C20: apparently arbitrary use of surname *Parker*]

not (nɒt) *adv* **1a** used to negate the sentence, phrase, or word that it modifies: *I will not stand for it.* **1b** (*in combination*): *they cannot go.* **2 not that.** (*conj*) Also (archaic): **not but what.** which is not to say or suppose that: *I expect to lose the game—not that I mind.* ♦ *sentence substitute.* **3** used to indicate denial, negation, or refusal: *certainly not.* [C14 *not,* variant of *nought* nothing, from Old English *nāwiht,* from *nā* no +*wiht* creature, thing. See NAUGHT, NOUGHT]

not- *combining form.* a variant of **noto-** before a vowel.

nota (ˈnəʊtə) *n* the plural of **notum.**

nota bene *Latin.* (ˈnəʊtə ˈbiːnɪ) note well; take note. Abbrevs.: **NB, N.B., nb, nb.**

notability (ˌnəʊtəˈbɪlɪtɪ) *n, pl* **-ties. 1** the state or quality of being notable. **2** a distinguished person; notable.

notable (ˈnəʊtəbᵊl) *adj* **1** worthy of being noted or remembered; remarkable; distinguished. ♦ *n* **2** a notable person. [C14: via Old French from Latin *notābilis,* from *notāre* to NOTE] ► ˈ**notableness** *n* ► ˈ**notably** *adv*

notarize *or* **notarise** (ˈnəʊtəˌraɪz) *vb* (*tr*) to attest to or authenticate (a document, contract, etc.), as a notary.

notary (ˈnəʊtərɪ) *n, pl* **-ries. 1** a notary public. **2** (formerly) a clerk licensed to prepare legal documents. **3** *Archaic.* a clerk or secretary. [C14: from Latin *notārius* clerk, from *nota* a mark, note] ► **notarial** (nəʊˈtɛərɪəl) *adj* ► **noˈtarially** *adv* ► ˈ**notaryship** *n*

notary public *n, pl* **notaries public.** a public official, usually a solicitor, who is legally authorized to administer oaths, attest and certify certain documents, etc.

notate (nəʊˈteɪt) *vb* to write (esp. music) in notation. [C20: back formation from NOTATION]

notation (nəʊˈteɪʃən) *n* **1** any series of signs or symbols used to represent quantities or elements in a specialized system, such as music or mathematics. **2** the act or process of notating. **3a** the act of noting down. **3b** a note or record. [C16: from Latin *notātiō* a marking, from *notāre* to NOTE] ► **noˈtational** *adj*

notch (nɒtʃ) *n* **1** a V-shaped cut or indentation; nick. **2** a cut or nick made in a tally stick or similar object. **3** *U.S. and Canadian.* a narrow pass or gorge. **4** *Informal.* a step or level (esp. in the phrase **a notch above**). ♦ *vb* (*tr*). **5** to cut or make a notch in. **6** to record with or as if with a notch. **7** (usually foll. by *up*) *Informal.* to score or achieve: *the team notched up its fourth win.* [C16: from incorrect division of *an otch* (as *a notch*), from Old French *oche* notch, from Latin *obsecāre* to cut off, from *secāre* to cut] ► ˈ**notchy** *adj*

notch effect *n Metallurgy, building trades.* the increase in stress in an area of a component near a crack, depression, etc., or a change in section, such as a sharp angle: can be enough to cause failure of the component although the calculated average stress may be quite safe.

NOT circuit *or* **gate** (nɒt) *n Computing.* a logic circuit that has a high-voltage output signal if the input signal is low, and vice versa: used extensively in computers. Also called: **inverter, negator.** [C20: so named because the action performed on electrical signals is similar to the operation of *not* in logical constructions]

note (nəʊt) *n* **1** a brief summary or record in writing, esp. a jotting for future reference. **2** a brief letter, usually of an informal nature. **3** a formal written communication, esp. from one government to another. **4** a short written statement giving any kind of information. **5** a critical comment, explanatory statement, or reference in the text of a book, often preceded by a number. **6** short for **banknote. 7** a characteristic element or atmosphere: *a note of sarcasm.* **8** a distinctive vocal sound, as of a species of bird or animal: *the note of the nightingale.* **9** any of a series of graphic signs representing a musical sound whose pitch is indicated by position on the stave and whose duration is indicated by the sign's shape. **10** Also called (esp. U.S. and Canadian): **tone.** a musical sound of definite fundamental frequency or pitch. **11** a key on a piano, organ, etc. **12** a sound, as from a musical instrument, used as a signal or warning: *the note to retreat was sounded.* **13** short for **promissory note. 14** *Archaic or poetic.* a tune or melody. **15 of note. 15a** distinguished or famous: *an athlete of note.* **15b** worth noticing or paying attention to; important: *nothing of note.* **16 strike the right** (*or* **a false**) **note.** to behave appropriately (or inappropriately). **17 take note.** (often foll. by *of*) to observe carefully; pay close attention (to). ♦ *vb* (*tr; may take a clause as object*) **18** to notice; perceive: *he noted that there was a man in the shadows.* **19** to pay close attention to; observe: *they noted every movement.* **20** to make a written note or memorandum of: *she noted the date in her diary.* **21** to make particular mention of; remark upon: *I note that you do not wear shoes.* **22** to write down (music, a melody, etc.) in notes. **23** to take (an unpaid or dishonoured bill of exchange) to a notary public to re-present the bill and if it is still unaccepted or unpaid to note the circumstances in a register. See **protest** (sense 12). **24** a less common word for **annotate.** ♦ See also **notes.** [C13: via Old French from Latin *nota* sign, indication] ► ˈ**noteless** *adj*

notebook (ˈnəʊtˌbʊk) *n* **1** a book for recording notes or memoranda. **2** a book for registering promissory notes.

notebook computer *n* a portable computer smaller than a laptop model, often approximately the size of a sheet of A4 paper.

notecase (ˈnəʊtˌkeɪs) *n* a less common word for **wallet** (sense 1).

noted (ˈnəʊtɪd) *adj* **1** distinguished; celebrated; famous. **2** of special note or significance; noticeable: *a noted increase in the crime rate.* ► ˈ**notedly** *adv*

notelet (ˈnəʊtlɪt) *n* a folded card with a printed design on the front, for writing a short informal letter.

note of hand *n* another name for **promissory note.**

notepaper (ˈnəʊtˌpeɪpə) *n* paper for writing letters; writing paper.

note row (rəʊ) *n Music.* another name for **tone row.**

notes (nəʊts) *pl n* **1** short descriptive or summarized jottings taken down for future reference. **2** a record of impressions, reflections, etc., esp. as a literary form.

notes inégales *French.* (nɔts inegal) *pl n* **1** (esp. in French baroque music) notes written down evenly but executed as if they were divided into pairs of long and short notes. **2** the style of playing in this manner. [literally: unequal notes]

note value *n* another term for **time value.**

noteworthy (ˈnəʊtˌwɜːðɪ) *adj* worthy of notice; notable. ► ˈ**noteˌworthily** *adv* ► ˈ**noteˌworthiness** *n*

nothing (ˈnʌθɪŋ) *pron* **1** (*indefinite*) no thing; not anything, as of an implied or specified class of things: *I can give you nothing.* **2** no part or share: *to have nothing to do with this crime.* **3** a matter of no importance or significance: *it doesn't matter, it's nothing.* **4** indicating the absence of anything perceptible; nothingness. **5** indicating the absence of meaning, value, worth, etc.: *to amount to nothing.* **6** zero quantity; nought. **7 be nothing to. 7a** not to concern or be significant to (someone). **7b** to be not nearly as good as. **8 have** *or* **be nothing to do with.** to have no connection with. **9 have** (**got**) **nothing on. 9a** to have no engagements to keep. **9b** to be undressed or naked. **9c** *Informal.* to compare unfavourably with. **10 in nothing flat.** *Informal.* in almost no time; very quickly or soon. **11 nothing but.** not something other than; only. **12 nothing doing.** *Informal.* an expression of dismissal, disapproval, lack of compliance with a request, etc. **13 nothing if not.** at the very least; certainly. **14 nothing less than** *or* **nothing short of.** downright; truly. **15** (**there's**) **nothing for it.** (there's) no choice; no other course. **16 there's nothing like.** a general expression of praise: *there's nothing like a good cup of tea.* **17 there's nothing to it.** it is very simple, easy, etc. **18 think nothing of. 18a** to regard as routine, easy, or natural. **18b** to have no compunction or hesitation about. **18c** to have a very low opinion of. **19 to say nothing of.** as well as; even disregarding: *he was warmly dressed in a shirt and heavy jumper, to say nothing of his thick overcoat.* **20 stop at nothing.** to be prepared to do anything; be unscrupulous or ruthless. ♦ *adv* **21** in no way; not at all: *he looked nothing like his brother.* ♦ *n* **22** *Informal.* a person or thing of no importance or significance. **23 sweet nothings.** words of endearment or affection. [Old English *nāthing, nān thing,* from *nān* NONE[1] + THING[1]]

USAGE *Nothing* normally takes a singular verb, but when *nothing but* is followed by a plural form of a noun, a plural verb is usually used: *it was a large room where nothing but souvenirs were sold.*

nothingness (ˈnʌθɪŋnɪs) *n* **1** the state or condition of being nothing; nonexistence. **2** absence of consciousness or life. **3** complete insignificance or worthlessness. **4** something that is worthless or insignificant.

notice (ˈnəʊtɪs) *n* **1** the act of perceiving; observation; attention: *to escape notice.* **2 take notice.** to pay attention; attend. **3 take no notice of.** to ignore or disregard. **4** information about a future event; warning; announcement. **5** a displayed placard or announcement giving information. **6** advance notification of intention to end an arrangement, contract, etc., as of renting or employment (esp. in the phrase **give notice**). **7 at short, two hours', etc., notice.** with notification only a little, two hours, etc., in advance. **8** *Chiefly Brit.* dismissal from employment. **9** favourable, interested, or polite attention: *she was beneath his notice.* **10** a theatrical or literary review: *the play received very good notices.* ♦ *vb* (*tr*) **11** to become conscious or aware of; perceive; note. **12** to point out or remark upon. **13** to pay polite or interested attention to. **14** to recognize or acknowledge (an acquaintance). [C15: via Old French from Latin *notitia* fame, from *nōtus* known, celebrated]

noticeable (ˈnəʊtɪsəbᵊl) *adj* easily seen or detected; perceptible: *the stain wasn't noticeable.* ► ˌ**noticeaˈbility** *n* ► ˈ**noticeably** *adv*

notice board *n Brit.* a board on which notices, advertisements, bulletins, etc., are displayed. U.S. and Canadian name: **bulletin board.**

notifiable (ˈnəʊtɪˌfaɪəbᵊl) *adj* **1** denoting certain infectious diseases of humans, such as smallpox and tuberculosis, outbreaks of which must be reported to the public health authorities. **2** denoting certain infectious diseases of animals, such as BSE, foot-and-mouth disease, and rabies, outbreaks of which must be reported to the appropriate veterinary authority.

notification (ˌnəʊtɪfɪˈkeɪʃən) *n* **1** the act of notifying. **2** a formal announcement. **3** something that notifies; a notice.

notify (ˈnəʊtɪˌfaɪ) *vb* **-fies, -fying, -fied.** (*tr*) **1** to inform; tell. **2** *Chiefly Brit.* to draw attention to; make known; announce. [C14: from Old French *notifier,* from Latin *notificāre* to make known, from *nōtus* known + *facere* to make] ► ˈ**notiˌfier** *n*

no-tillage *n* a system of farming in which planting is done in a narrow trench, without tillage, and weeds are controlled with herbicide.

notion (ˈnəʊʃən) *n* **1** a vague idea; impression. **2** an idea, concept, or opinion. **3** an inclination or whim. ♦ See also **notions.** [C16: from Latin *nōtiō* a becoming acquainted (with), examination (of), from *noscere* to know]

notional (ˈnəʊʃənᵊl) *adj* **1** relating to, expressing, or consisting of notions or ideas. **2** not evident in reality; hypothetical or imaginary: *a notional tax credit.*

3 characteristic of a notion or concept, esp. in being speculative or imaginary; abstract. **4** *Grammar.* **4a** (of a word) having lexical meaning. **4b** another word for **semantic.** ► **'notionally** *adv*

notions ('nəʊʃənz) *pl n Chiefly U.S. and Canadian.* pins, cotton, ribbon, and similar wares used for sewing; haberdashery.

notitia (nəʊ'tɪʃɪə) *n* a register or list, esp. of ecclesiastical districts. **[C18:** Latin, literally: knowledge, from *notus* known**]**

noto- *or before a vowel* **not-** *combining form.* the back: *notochord.* **[**from Greek *nōton* the back**]**

notochord ('nəʊtəˌkɔːd) *n* a fibrous longitudinal rod in all embryo and some adult chordate animals, immediately above the gut, that supports the body. It is replaced in adult vertebrates by the vertebral column. ► ˌ**noto'chordal** *adj*

Notogaea (ˌnəʊtə'dʒiːə) *n* a zoogeographical area comprising the Australasian region. Compare **Arctogaea, Neogaea. [C19:** from Greek *notos* south wind + *gaia* land**]** ► ˌ**Noto'gaean** *n, adj*

notorious (nəʊ'tɔːrɪəs) *adj* **1** well-known for some bad or unfavourable quality, deed, etc.; infamous. **2** *Rare.* generally known or widely acknowledged. **[C16:** from Medieval Latin *notōrius* well-known, from *nōtus* known, from *noscere* to know**]** ► **notoriety** (ˌnəʊtə'raɪɪtɪ) *or* **no'toriousness** *n* ► **no'toriously** *adv*

notornis (nəʊ'tɔːnɪs) *n* a rare flightless rail of the genus *Notornis,* of New Zealand. See **takahe. [C19:** New Latin, from Greek *notos* south + *ornis* bird**]**

nototherium (ˌnəʊtəʊ'θɪərɪəm) *n* an extinct Pleistocene rhinoceros-sized marsupial of the genus *Nototherium,* related to the wombats. **[C19:** New Latin, from Greek *notos* south (referring to their discovery in the S hemisphere) + *thērion* beast**]**

notour ('nəʊtə) *adj* (in Scots Law) short for **notorious.** A **notour bankrupt** is one who has failed to discharge his debts within the days of grace allowed by the court.

not proven ('prəʊvᵊn) *adj* (*postpositive*) a third verdict available to Scottish courts, returned when there is evidence against the defendant but insufficient to convict.

Notre Dame ('nəʊtrə 'dɑːm, 'nɒtrə; *French* nɔtrə dam) *n* the early Gothic cathedral of Paris, on the Île de la Cité: built between 1163 and 1257.

no-trump *Bridge.* ♦ *n also* **no-trumps. 1** a bid or contract to play without trumps. ♦ *adj also* **no-trumper. 2** (of a hand) of balanced distribution suitable for playing without trumps.

Nottingham ('nɒtɪŋəm) *n* a city and from 1998 a unitary authority in N central England, administrative centre of Nottinghamshire, on the River Trent: scene of the outbreak of the Civil War (1642); famous for its associations with the Robin Hood legend; university (1881). Pop.: 283 800 (1995 est.).

Nottinghamshire ('nɒtɪŋəmˌʃɪə, -ʃə) *n* an inland county of central England: generally low-lying, with part of the S Pennines and the remnant of Sherwood Forest in the east. Administrative centre: Nottingham. Pop.: 1 030 900 (1994 est.). Area: 2164 sq. km (835 sq. miles). Abbrev.: **Notts.**

Nottm *abbrev. for* Nottingham.

Notts (nɒts) *abbrev. for* Nottinghamshire.

notum ('nəʊtəm) *n, pl* **-ta** (-tə). a cuticular plate covering the dorsal surface of a thoracic segment of an insect. **[C19:** New Latin, from Greek *nōton* back**]** ► **'notal** *adj*

Notus ('nəʊtəs) *n Classical myth.* a personification of the south or southwest wind.

notwithstanding (ˌnɒtwɪθ'stændɪŋ, -wɪð-) *prep* **1** (*often immediately postpositive*) in spite of; despite. ♦ *conj* **2** (*subordinating*) despite the fact that; although. ♦ *sentence connector.* **3** in spite of that; nevertheless. **[C14:** NOT + *withstanding,* from Old English *withstandan,* on the model of Medieval Latin *non obstante,* Old French *non obstant***]**

Nouakchott (*French* nwakʃɔt) *n* the capital of Mauritania, near the Atlantic coast: replaced St Louis as capital in 1957; situated on important caravan routes. Pop.: 480 395 (1992 est.).

nougat ('nuːgɑː, 'nʌgət) *n* a hard chewy pink or white sweet containing chopped nuts, cherries, etc. **[C19:** via French from Provençal *nogat,* from *noga* nut, from Latin *nux* nut**]**

nought (nɔːt) *n also* **naught, ought, aught. 1** another name for **zero:** used esp. in counting or numbering. ♦ *n, adj, adv* **2** a variant spelling of **naught. [**Old English *nōwiht,* from *ne* not, no + *ōwiht* something; see WHIT**]**

noughts and crosses *n* (*functioning as sing*) a game in which two players, one using a nought, "O", the other a cross, "X", alternately mark one square out of nine formed by two pairs of crossed lines, the winner being the first to get three of his symbols in a row. U.S. and Canadian term: **tick-tack-toe,** (U.S.) **crisscross.**

Nouméa (ˌnuː'meɪə; *French* numea) *n* the capital and chief port of the French Overseas Territory of New Caledonia. Pop.: 65 000 (1994 est.).

noumenon ('nuːmɪnən, 'naʊ-) *n, pl* **-na** (-nə). **1** (in the philosophy of Kant) a thing as it is in itself, not perceived or interpreted, incapable of being known, but only inferred from the nature of experience. Compare **phenomenon** (sense 3). See also **thing-in-itself. 2** the object of a purely intellectual intuition. **[C18:** via German from Greek: thing being thought of, from *noein* to think, perceive; related to *nous* mind**]** ► **'noumenal** *adj* ► **'noumenalism** *n* ► **'noumenalist** *n, adj* ► ˌ**noume'nality** *n* ► **'noumenally** *adv*

noun (naʊn) *n* **a** a word or group of words that refers to a person, place, or thing or any syntactically similar word. **b** (*as modifier*)*: a noun phrase.* Abbrevs.: **N, n** Related adj: **nominal. [C14:** via Anglo-French from Latin *nōmen* NAME**]** ► **'nounal** *adj* ► **'nounally** *adv* ► **'nounless** *adj*

noun phrase *n Grammar.* a constituent of a sentence that consists of a noun and any modifiers it may have, a noun clause, or a word, such as a pronoun, that takes the place of a noun. Abbrev.: **NP.**

nourish ('nʌrɪʃ) *vb* (*tr*) **1** to provide with the materials necessary for life and growth. **2** to support or encourage (an idea, feeling, etc.); foster: *to nourish resentment.* **[C14:** from Old French *norir,* from Latin *nūtrīre* to feed, care for**]** ► **'nourisher** *n* ► **'nourishing** *adj* ► **'nourishingly** *adv*

nourishment ('nʌrɪʃmənt) *n* **1** the act or state of nourishing. **2** a substance that nourishes; food; nutriment.

nous (naʊs) *n* **1** *Metaphysics.* mind or reason, esp. when regarded as the principle governing all things. **2** *Brit. slang.* common sense; intelligence. **[C17:** from Greek, literally: mind**]**

nouveau *or before a plural noun* **nouveaux** ('nuːvəʊ) *adj* (*prenominal*) *Facetious or derogatory.* having recently become the thing specified: *a nouveau hippy.* **[C20:** French, literally: new; on the model of NOUVEAU RICHE**]**

nouveau riche (ˌnuːvəʊ 'riːʃ; *French* nuvo riʃ) *n, pl* **nouveaux riches** (ˌnuːvəʊ 'riːʃ; *French* nuvo riʃ). **1** (often *pl* and preceded by *the*) a person who has acquired wealth recently and is regarded as vulgarly ostentatious or lacking in social graces. ♦ *adj* **2** of or characteristic of the nouveaux riches. **[**French, literally: new rich**]**

nouveau roman *French.* (nuvo rɔmɑ̃) *n, pl* ***nouveaux romans*** (nuvo rɔmɑ̃). another term for **anti-roman.** See **antinovel. [**literally: new novel**]**

Nouvelle-Calédonie (nuvelkaledɔ'ni) *n* the French name for **New Caledonia.**

nouvelle cuisine ('nuːvel kwiː'ziːn) *n* a style of preparing and presenting food, often raw or only lightly cooked, with light sauces, and unusual combinations of flavours and garnishes. **[C20:** French, literally: new cookery**]**

Nouvelle Vague *French.* (nuvel vag) *n Films.* another term for **New Wave**[1].

Nov. *abbrev. for* November.

nova ('nəʊvə) *n, pl* **-vae** (-viː) *or* **-vas.** a variable star that undergoes a cataclysmic eruption, observed as a sudden large increase in brightness with a subsequent decline over months or years; it is a close binary system with one component a white dwarf. Compare **supernova. [C19:** New Latin *nova* (*stella*) new (star), from Latin *novus* new**]**

novaculite (nəʊ'vækjʊˌlaɪt) *n* a fine-grained dense hard rock containing quartz and feldspar: used as a whetstone. **[C18:** from Latin *novācula* sharp knife, razor, from *novāre* to renew**]**

Novalis (*German* no'vaːlɪs) *n* real name *Friedrich von Hardenberg.* 1772–1801, German romantic poet. His works include the mystical *Hymnen an die Nacht* (1797; published 1800) and *Geistliche Lieder* (1799).

Nova Lisboa (*Portuguese* 'nɔvə liʒ'βoə) *n* the former name (1928–73) of **Huambo.**

Novara (*Italian* no'vaːra) *n* a city in NW Italy, in NE Piedmont: scene of the Austrian defeat of the Piedmontese in 1849. Pop.: 102 219 (1996 est.).

Nova Scotia ('nəʊvə 'skəʊʃə) *n* **1** a peninsula in E Canada, between the Gulf of St Lawrence and the Bay of Fundy. **2** a province of E Canada, consisting of the Nova Scotia peninsula and Cape Breton Island: first settled by the French as Acadia. Capital: Halifax. Pop.: 947 900 (1997 est.). Area: 52 841 sq. km (20 402 sq. miles). Abbrev.: **NS.** ► **Nova Scotian** *n, adj*

novation (nəʊ'veɪʃən) *n* **1** *Law.* the substitution of a new obligation for an old one by mutual agreement between the parties, esp. of one debtor or creditor for another. **2** an obsolete word for **innovation. [C16:** from Late Latin *novātio* a renewing, from Latin *novāre* to renew**]**

Novaya Zemlya (*Russian* 'nɔvəjə zɪm'lja) *n* an archipelago in the Arctic Ocean, off the NE coast of Russia: consists of two large islands and many islets. Area: about 81 279 sq. km (31 382 sq. miles).

novel[1] ('nɒvᵊl) *n* **1** an extended work in prose, either fictitious or partly so, dealing with character, action, thought, etc., esp. in the form of a story. **2 the.** the literary genre represented by novels. **3** (*usually pl*) *Obsolete.* a short story or novella, as one of those in the *Decameron* of Boccaccio. **[C15:** from Old French *novelle,* from Latin *novella* (*narrātiō*) new (story); see NOVEL[2]**]**

novel[2] ('nɒvᵊl) *adj* of a kind not seen before; fresh; new; original: *a novel suggestion.* **[C15:** from Latin *novellus* new, diminutive of *novus* new**]**

novel[3] ('nɒvᵊl) *n Roman law.* a new decree or an amendment to an existing statute. See also **Novels.**

novelese (ˌnɒvə'liːz) *n Derogatory.* a style of writing characteristic of poor novels.

novelette (ˌnɒvə'lɛt) *n* **1** an extended prose narrative story or short novel. **2** a novel that is regarded as being slight, trivial, or sentimental. **3** a short piece of lyrical music, esp. one for the piano.

novelettish (ˌnɒvə'lɛtɪʃ) *adj* characteristic of a novelette; trite or sentimental.

novelist ('nɒvəlɪst) *n* a writer of novels.

novelistic (ˌnɒvə'lɪstɪk) *adj* of or characteristic of novels, esp. in style or method of treatment: *his novelistic account annoyed other historians.*

novelize *or* **novelise** ('nɒvəˌlaɪz) *vb* to convert (a true story, film, etc.) into a novel. ► ˌ**noveli'zation** *or* ˌ**noveli'sation** *n*

novella (nəʊ'vɛlə) *n, pl* **-las** *or* **-le** (-leɪ). **1** (formerly) a short narrative tale, esp. a popular story having a moral or satirical point, such as those in Boccaccio's *Decameron.* **2** a short novel; novelette. **[C20:** from Italian; see NOVEL[1]**]**

Novello (nə'vɛləʊ) *n* **Ivor,** real name *Ivor Novello Davies.* 1893–1951, Welsh actor, composer, songwriter, and dramatist.

Novels ('nɒvᵊlz) *pl n Roman law.* the new statutes of Justinian and succeeding emperors supplementing the Institutes, Digest, and Code: now forming part of the Corpus Juris Civilis. **[**Latin *Novellae* (*constitūtiōnēs*) new (laws)**]**

novelty ('nɒvᵊltɪ) *n, pl* **-ties. 1a** the quality of being new and fresh and interesting. **1b** (*as modifier*)*: novelty value.* **2** a new or unusual experience or occurrence. **3** (*often pl*) a small usually cheap new toy, ornament, or trinket. **[C14:** from Old French *novelté;* see NOVEL[2]**]**

November (nəʊ'vɛmbə) *n* **1** the eleventh month of the year, consisting of 30 days. **2** *Communications.* a code word for the letter *n* **[C13:** via Old French from Latin: ninth month, from *novem* nine**]**

novena (nəʊ'viːnə) *n, pl* **-nas** *or* **-nae** (-niː). *R.C. Church.* a devotion consisting of prayers or services on nine consecutive days. [C19: from Medieval Latin, from Latin *novem* nine]

novercal (nəʊ'vɜːkᵊl) *adj Rare.* stepmotherly. [C17: from Latin *novercālis,* from *noverca* stepmother]

Novgorod (*Russian* 'nɔvgərət) *n* a city in NW Russia, on the Volkhov River; became a principality in 862 under Rurik, an event regarded as the founding of the Russian state; a major trading centre in the Middle Ages; destroyed by Ivan the Terrible in 1570. Pop.: 233 000 (1995 est.).

novice ('nɒvɪs) *n* **1a** a person who is new to or inexperienced in a certain task, situation, etc.; beginner; tyro. **1b** (*as modifier*): *novice driver.* **2** a probationer in a religious order. **3** a sportsman, esp. an oarsman, who has not won a recognized prize, performed to an established level, etc. **4** a racehorse, esp. a steeplechaser or hurdler, that has not won a specified number of races. [C14: via Old French from Latin *novīcius,* from *novus* new]

Novi Sad (*Serbo-Croat* 'nɔviː 'saːd) *n* a port in NE Yugoslavia, in Serbia, on the River Danube: founded in 1690 as the seat of the Serbian patriarch; university (1960). Pop.: 179 626 (1991). German name: **Neusatz.**

novitiate *or* **noviciate** (nəʊ'vɪʃɪɪt, -ˌeɪt) *n* **1** the state of being a novice, esp. in a religious order, or the period for which this lasts. **2** the part of a religious house where the novices live. **3** a less common word for **novice.** [C17: from French *noviciat,* from Latin *novīcius* NOVICE]

Novocaine ('nəʊvəˌkeɪn) *n* a trademark for **procaine hydrochloride.** See **procaine.**

Novokuznetsk (*Russian* nɔvəkuz'njɛtsk) *n* a city in S central Russia: iron and steel works. Pop.: 572 000 (1995 est.). Former name (1932–61): **Stalinsk.**

Novosibirsk (*Russian* nəvəsi'birsk) *n* a city in W central Russia, on the River Ob: the largest town in Siberia; developed with the coming of the Trans-Siberian railway in 1893; important industrial centre. Pop.: 1 369 000 (1995 est.).

now (naʊ) *adv* **1** at or for the present time or moment. **2** at this exact moment; immediately. **3** in these times; nowadays. **4** given the present circumstances: *now we'll have to stay to the end.* **5** (preceded by *just*) very recently: *he left just now.* **6** (often preceded by *just*) very soon: *he is leaving just now.* **7** (**every**) **now and again** *or* **then.** occasionally; on and off. **8 for now.** for the time being. **9 now now!** (*interj*) an exclamation used to rebuke or pacify someone. **10 now then. 10a** (*sentence connector*) used to preface an important remark, the next step in an argument, etc. **10b** (*interj*) an expression of mild reproof: *now then, don't tease!* ◆ *conj* **11** (*subordinating;* often foll. by *that*) seeing that; since it has become the case that: *now you're in charge, things will be better.* ◆ *sentence connector.* **12a** used as a transitional particle or hesitation word: *now, I can't really say.* **12b** used for emphasis: *now listen to this.* **12c** used at the end of a command, esp. in dismissal: *run along, now.* ◆ *n* **13** the present moment or time: *now is the time to go.* ◆ *adj* **14** *Informal.* of the moment; fashionable: *the now look is street fashion.* [Old English *nū;* compare Old Saxon *nū,* German *nun,* Latin *nunc,* Greek *nu*]

nowadays ('naʊəˌdeɪz) *adv* in these times. [C14: from NOW + *adays* from Old English *a* on + *daeges* genitive of day]

noway ('nəʊˌweɪ) *adv* **1** Also in the U.S. (not standard): **'noways.** in no manner; not at all; nowise. ◆ *sentence substitute.* **no way. 2** used to make an emphatic refusal, denial etc.

Nowel *or* **Nowell** (nəʊ'ɛl) *n* archaic spellings of **Noel.**

nowhence ('nəʊˌwɛns) *adv Archaic.* from no place; from nowhere.

nowhere ('nəʊˌwɛə) *adv* **1** in, at, or to no place; not anywhere. **2 get nowhere (fast).** *Informal.* to fail completely to make any progress. **3 nowhere near.** far from; not nearly. ◆ *n* **4** a nonexistent or insignificant place. **5 middle of nowhere.** a completely isolated, featureless, or insignificant place.

nowhither ('nəʊˌwɪðə) *adv Archaic.* to no place; to nowhere. [Old English *nāhwider.* See NEITHER]

no-win *adj* offering no possibility of a favourable outcome (esp. in the phrase **a no-win situation**).

nowise ('nəʊˌwaɪz) *adv* another word for **noway.**

nowt[1] (naʊt) *n Northern English.* a dialect word for **nothing.** [from NAUGHT]

nowt[2] (naʊt) *n Scot. and northern English.* a dialect word for **bullock** and **cattle.** [C13: from Old Norse *naut;* see NEAT[2]]

Nox (nɒks) *n* the Roman goddess of the night. Greek counterpart: **Nyx.**

noxious ('nɒkʃəs) *adj* **1** poisonous or harmful. **2** harmful to the mind or morals; corrupting. [C17: from Latin *noxius* harmful, from *noxa* injury] ► **'noxiously** *adv* ► **'noxiousness** *n*

noyade (nwɑː'jɑːd; *French* nwajad) *n French history.* execution by drowning, esp. as practised during the Reign of Terror at Nantes from 1793 to 1794. [C19: from French, from *noyer* to drown, from Late Latin *necāre* to drown, from Latin: to put to death]

noyau ('nwaɪəʊ) *n* a liqueur made from brandy flavoured with nut kernels. [C18: from French: kernel, from Latin *nux* nut]

Noyon (*French* nwajɔ̃) *n* a town in N France: scene of the coronations of Charlemagne (768) and Hugh Capet (987); birthplace of John Calvin. Pop.: 14 426 (1990).

nozzle ('nɒzᵊl) *n* **1** a projecting pipe or spout from which fluid is discharged. **2** Also called: **propelling nozzle.** a pipe or duct, esp. in a jet engine or rocket, that directs the effluent and accelerates or diffuses the flow to generate thrust. **3** a socket, such as the part of a candlestick that holds the candle. [C17 *nosle, nosel,* diminutive of NOSE]

np *abbrev. for:* **1** *Printing.* new paragraph. **2** *Law.* nisi prius. **3** no place of publication.

Np 1 *symbol for* neper. **2** *the chemical symbol for* neptunium.

NP *abbrev. for* **1** neuropsychiatric. **2** neuropsychiatry. **3** Also: **np.** Notary Public. **4** noun phrase.

NPA *abbrev. for* Newspaper Publishers' Association.

NPD *Commerce. abbrev. for* new product development.

NPL *abbrev. for* National Physical Laboratory.

NPV *abbrev. for:* **1** net present value. **2** no par value.

nr *abbrev. for* near.

NRA (in Britain) *abbrev. for:* **1** National Rifle Association. **2** National Rivers Authority.

NRV *abbrev. for* net realizable value.

ns *abbrev. for:* **1** new series. **2** not specified.

NS *abbrev. for:* **1** New Style (method of reckoning dates). **2** not sufficient *or* not satisfactory. **3** Nova Scotia. **4** nuclear ship.

NSAID *abbrev. for* nonsteroidal anti-inflammatory drug: any of a class of drugs, including aspirin and ibuprofen, used for reducing inflammation and pain in rheumatic diseases. Possible adverse effects include gastric ulceration.

NSB *abbrev. for* National Savings Bank.

NSC *abbrev. for* National Safety Council.

NSF *or* **N/S/F** *Banking. abbrev. for* not sufficient funds.

NSG *Brit. Education. abbrev. for* nonstatutory guidelines: practical nonmandatory advice and information on the implementation of the National Curriculum.

NSPCC *abbrev. for* National Society for the Prevention of Cruelty to Children.

NSU *abbrev. for* nonspecific urethritis.

NSW *abbrev. for* New South Wales.

NT *abbrev. for:* **1** National Trust. **2** New Testament. **3** Northern Territory. **4** no-trump. **5** (in Ireland) National Teacher (teacher in a National School).

-n't *contraction of* not: used as an enclitic after *be* and *have* when they function as main verbs and after auxiliary verbs or verbs operating syntactically as auxiliaries: *can't; don't; shouldn't; needn't; daren't; isn't.*

nth (ɛnθ) *adj* **1** *Maths.* of or representing an unspecified ordinal number, usually the greatest in a series of values: *the nth power.* **2** *Informal.* being the last, most recent, or most extreme of a long series: *for the nth time, eat your lunch!* **3 to the nth degree.** *Informal.* to the utmost extreme; as much as possible.

Nth *abbrev. for* North.

NTP *abbrev. for* normal temperature and pressure: standard conditions of 0°C temperature and 101.325 kPa (760 mmHg) pressure. Also: **STP.**

NTS *abbrev. for* National Trust for Scotland.

n-tuple *n Logic, maths.* an ordered set of *n* elements.

nt. wt. *or* **nt wt** *abbrev. for* net weight.

n-type *adj* **1** (of a semiconductor) having more conduction electrons than mobile holes. **2** associated with or resulting from the movement of electrons in a semiconductor: *n-type conductivity.* ◆ Compare **p-type.**

nu (njuː) *n* the 13th letter in the Greek alphabet (Ν, ν), a consonant, transliterated as *n* [from Greek, of Semitic origin; compare NUN[2]]

Nu (njuː) *n* **U** (uː), original name *Thakin Nu.* 1907–95, Burmese statesman and writer; prime minister (1948–56, 1957–58, 1960–62). He attempted to establish parliamentary democracy, but was ousted (1962) by Ne Win.

NUAAW (in Britain) *abbrev. for* National Union of Agricultural and Allied Workers.

nuance (njuː'ɑːns, 'njuːɑːns) *n* **1** a subtle difference in colour, meaning, tone, etc.; a shade or graduation. ◆ *vb* (*tr; passive*) **2** to give subtle differences to: *carefully nuanced words.* [C18: from French, from *nuer* to show light and shade, ultimately from Latin *nūbēs* a cloud]

nub (nʌb) *n* **1** a small lump or protuberance. **2** a small piece or chunk. **3** the point or gist: *the nub of a story.* **4** a small fibrous knot in yarn. [C16: variant of *knub,* from Middle Low German *knubbe* KNOB] ► **'nubbly** *or* **'nubby** *adj*

Nuba ('njuːbə) *n* **1** (*pl* **-bas** *or* **-ba**) a member of a formerly warlike Nilotic people living chiefly in the hills of S central Sudan. **2** the language or group of related dialects spoken by this people, belonging to the Chari-Nile branch of the Nilo-Saharan family.

nubbin ('nʌbɪn) *n U.S. and Canadian.* something small or undeveloped, esp. a fruit or ear of corn. [C19: diminutive of NUB]

nubble ('nʌbᵊl) *n* a small lump. [C19: diminutive of NUB]

nubecula (njuː'bɛkjʊlə) *n, pl* **-lae** (-liː). See **Magellanic Cloud.** [C19: from Latin, diminutive of *nubes* cloud]

Nubia ('njuːbɪə) *n* an ancient region of NE Africa, on the Nile, extending from Aswan to Khartoum. ► **'Nubian** *n, adj*

Nubian Desert *n* a desert in the NE Sudan, between the Nile valley and the Red Sea: mainly a sandstone plateau.

nubile ('njuːbaɪl) *adj* (of a girl or woman) **1** ready or suitable for marriage by virtue of age or maturity. **2** sexually attractive. [C17: from Latin *nūbilis,* from *nūbere* to marry] ► **nubility** (njuː'bɪlɪtɪ) *n*

nucellus (njuː'sɛləs) *n, pl* **-li** (-laɪ). the central part of a plant ovule containing the embryo sac. [C19: New Latin, from Latin *nucella,* from *nux* nut] ► **nu'cellar** *adj*

nucha ('njuːkə) *n, pl* **-chae** (-kiː). *Zoology, anatomy.* the back or nape of the neck. [C14: from Medieval Latin, from Arabic *nukhā'* spinal marrow] ► **'nuchal** *adj*

nucivorous (njuː'sɪvərəs) *adj* (of animals) feeding on nuts. [from Latin *nux* nut + -VOROUS]

nuclear ('njuːklɪə) *adj* **1** of, concerned with, or involving the nucleus of an atom: *nuclear fission.* **2** *Biology.* of, relating to, or contained within the nucleus of a cell: *a nuclear membrane.* **3** of, relating to, forming, or resembling any other kind of nucleus. **4** of, concerned with, or operated by energy from fission or fusion of atomic nuclei: *a nuclear weapon.* **5** involving, concerned with, or possessing nuclear weapons: *nuclear war; a nuclear strike.*

nuclear bomb *n* a bomb whose force is due to uncontrolled nuclear fusion or nuclear fission.

nuclear chemistry *n* the branch of chemistry concerned with nuclear reactions.

nuclear energy *n* energy released during a nuclear reaction as a result of fission or fusion. Also called: **atomic energy.**

nuclear family *n Sociol., anthropol.* a primary social unit consisting of parents and their offspring. Compare **extended family.**

nuclear fission *n* the splitting of an atomic nucleus into approximately equal parts, either spontaneously or as a result of the impact of a particle usually with an associated release of energy. Sometimes shortened to **fission.** Compare **nuclear fusion.**

nuclear-free zone *n* an area barred, esp. by local authorities, to the storage or deployment of nuclear weapons.

nuclear fuel *n* a fuel that provides nuclear energy, used in nuclear power stations, nuclear submarines, etc.

nuclear fusion *n* a reaction in which two nuclei combine to form a nucleus with the release of energy. Sometimes shortened to **fusion.** Compare **nuclear fission.** See also **thermonuclear reaction.**

nuclear isomer *n* the more formal name for **isomer** (sense 2). ► **nuclear isomerism** *n*

nuclear magnetic resonance *n* a technique for determining the magnetic moments of nuclei by subjecting a substance to high-frequency radiation and a large magnetic field. The technique is used as a method of determining structure. Abbrev.: **NMR.** See also **electron spin resonance.**

nuclear magnetic resonance scanner *n* a machine for the medical technique in which changes in the constituent atoms of the body under the influence of a powerful electromagnet are used to generate computed images of the internal organs.

nuclear medicine *n* the branch of medicine concerned with the use of radionuclides in the diagnosis and treatment of disease.

nuclear physics *n (functioning as sing)* the branch of physics concerned with the structure and behaviour of the nucleus and the particles of which it consists. ► **nuclear physicist** *n*

nuclear power *n* power, esp. electrical or motive, produced by a nuclear reactor. Also called: **atomic power.**

nuclear reaction *n* a process in which the structure and energy content of an atomic nucleus is changed by interaction with another nucleus or particle.

nuclear reactor *n* a device in which a nuclear reaction is maintained and controlled for the production of nuclear energy. Sometimes shortened to **reactor.** Former name: **atomic pile.** See also **fission reactor, fusion reactor.**

nuclear threshold *n* the point in war at which a combatant brings nuclear weapons into use.

nuclear waste *n* another name for **radioactive waste.**

nuclear winter *n* a period of extremely low temperatures and little light that has been suggested would occur as a result of a nuclear war.

nuclease ('nju:klɪˌeɪz) *n* any of a group of enzymes that hydrolyse nucleic acids to simple nucleotides.

nucleate ('nju:klɪɪt, -ˌeɪt) *adj* **1** having a nucleus. ◆ *vb (intr)* **2** to form a nucleus. ► ˌ**nucle'ation** *n* ► '**nucleˌator** *n*

nucleating agent *n Meteorology.* a substance used to seed clouds to control rainfall and fog formation.

nuclei ('nju:klɪˌaɪ) *n* a plural of **nucleus.**

nucleic acid (nju:'kli:ɪk, -'kleɪ-) *n Biochem.* any of a group of complex compounds with a high molecular weight that are vital constituents of all living cells. See also **RNA, DNA.**

nuclein ('nju:klɪɪn) *n* any of a group of proteins, containing phosphorus, that occur in the nuclei of living cells.

nucleo- *or before a vowel* **nucle-** *combining form.* **1** nucleus or nuclear: *nucleoplasm.* **2** nucleic acid: *nucleoprotein.*

nucleolus (ˌnju:klɪ'əʊləs) *n, pl* **-li** (-laɪ). a small rounded body within a resting nucleus that contains RNA and proteins and is involved in protein synthesis. Also called: '**nucleole.** [C19: from Latin, diminutive of NUCLEUS] ► ˌ**nucle'olar,** '**nucleoˌlate,** *or* '**nucleoˌlated** *adj*

nucleon ('nju:klɪˌɒn) *n* a proton or neutron, esp. one present in an atomic nucleus. [C20: from NUCLE(US) + -ON]

nucleonics (ˌnju:klɪ'ɒnɪks) *n (functioning as sing)* the branch of physics concerned with the applications of nuclear energy. ► ˌ**nucle'onic** *adj* ► ˌ**nucle'onically** *adv*

nucleon number *n* another name for **mass number.**

nucleophilic (ˌnju:klɪəʊ'fɪlɪk) *adj Chem.* having or involving an affinity for positive charge. Nucleophilic reagents (**nucleophiles**) are molecules, atoms, and ions that behave as electron donors. Compare **electrophilic.**

nucleoplasm ('nju:klɪəˌplæzəm) *n* the protoplasm constituting the nucleus of a plant or animal cell. Also called: **karyoplasm.** ► ˌ**nucleo'plasmic** *or* ˌ**nucleoplas'matic** *adj*

nucleoprotein (ˌnju:klɪəʊ'prəʊti:n) *n* a compound within a cell nucleus that consists of a protein bound to a nucleic acid.

nucleoside ('nju:klɪəˌsaɪd) *n Biochem.* a compound containing a purine or pyrimidine base linked to a sugar (usually ribose or deoxyribose). [C20: from NUCLEO- + -OSE[2] + -IDE]

nucleosome ('nju:klɪəˌsəʊm) *n* a repeating structural unit of chromatin that contains DNA and histones.

nucleosynthesis (ˌnju:klɪəʊ'sɪnθɪsɪs) *n Astronomy.* the formation of heavier elements from lighter elements by nuclear fusion in stars.

nucleotide ('nju:klɪəˌtaɪd) *n Biochem.* a compound consisting of a nucleoside linked to phosphoric acid. Nucleic acids are made up of long chains (polynucleotides) of such compounds. [C20: from NUCLEO- + *t* (added for ease of pronunciation) + -IDE]

nucleus ('nju:klɪəs) *n, pl* **-clei** (-klɪˌaɪ) *or* **-cleuses. 1** a central or fundamental part or thing around which others are grouped; core. **2** a centre of growth or development; basis; kernel: *the nucleus of an idea.* **3** *Biology.* the spherical or ovoid compartment of a cell, bounded by a membrane, that contains the chromosomes and associated molecules that control the characteristics and growth of the cell. **4** *Anatomy.* any of various groups of nerve cells in the central nervous system. **5** *Astronomy.* the central portion in the head of a comet, consisting of small solid particles of ice and frozen gases, which vaporize on approaching the sun to form the coma and tail. **6** *Physics.* the positively charged dense region at the centre of an atom, composed of protons and neutrons, about which electrons orbit. **7** *Chem.* a fundamental group of atoms in a molecule serving as the base structure for related compounds and remaining unchanged during most chemical reactions: *the benzene nucleus.* **8** *Botany.* **8a** the central point of a starch granule. **8b** a rare name for **nucellus. 9** *Phonetics.* the most sonorous part of a syllable, usually consisting of a vowel or frictionless continuant. **10** *Logic.* the largest individual that is a mereological part of every member of a given class. [C18: from Latin: kernel, from *nux* nut]

nuclide ('nju:klaɪd) *n* a species of atom characterized by its atomic number and its mass number. See also **isotope.** [C20: from NUCLEO- + *-ide,* from Greek *eidos* shape]

nuddy ('nʌdɪ) *n* **in the nuddy.** *Informal, chiefly Brit. and Austral.* in the nude; naked. [C20: originally Australian, a variant of NUDE]

nude (nju:d) *adj* **1** completely unclothed; undressed. **2** having no covering; bare; exposed. **3** *Law.* **3a** lacking some essential legal requirement, esp. supporting evidence. **3b** (of a contract, agreement, etc.) made without consideration and void unless under seal. ◆ *n* **4** the state of being naked (esp. in the phrase **in the nude**). **5** a naked figure, esp. in painting, sculpture, etc. [C16: from Latin *nūdus*] ► '**nudely** *adv* ► '**nudeness** *n*

nudge (nʌdʒ) *vb (tr)* **1** to push or poke (someone) gently, esp. with the elbow, to get attention; jog. **2** to push slowly or lightly: *as I drove out, I just nudged the gatepost.* **3** to give (someone) a gentle reminder or encouragement. ◆ *n* **4** a gentle poke or push. [C17: perhaps from Scandinavian; compare Icelandic *nugga* to push] ► '**nudger** *n*

nudi- *combining form.* naked or bare: *nudibranch.* [from Latin *nūdus*]

nudibranch ('nju:dɪˌbræŋk) *n* any marine gastropod of the order *Nudibranchia,* characterized by a shell-less, often beautifully coloured, body bearing external gills and other appendages. Also called: **sea slug.** [C19: from NUDI- + *branche,* from Latin *branchia* gills]

nudicaudate (ˌnju:dɪ'kɔ:deɪt) *adj* (of such animals as rats) having a hairless tail.

nudicaul ('nju:dɪˌkɔ:l) *or* **nudicaulous** (ˌnju:dɪ'kɔ:ləs) *adj* (of plants) having stems without leaves. [C20: from NUDI- + *caul,* from Latin *caulis* stem]

nudism ('nju:dɪzəm) *n* the practice of nudity, esp. for reasons of health, religion, etc. ► '**nudist** *n, adj*

nudity ('nju:dɪtɪ) *n, pl* **-ties. 1** the state or fact of being nude; nakedness. **2** *Rare.* a nude figure, esp. in art.

nudum pactum ('nju:dʊm 'pæktʊm) *n Law.* an agreement made without consideration and void unless made under seal. [Latin: nude (sense 3b) agreement]

nuée ardente ('nʊeɪ ɑ:'dɑ̃t) *n* a rapidly moving turbulent incandescent cloud of gas, ash, and rock fragments flowing close to the ground after violent ejection from a volcano. See also **ignimbrite.** [C20: from French, literally: burning cloud]

Nuevo Laredo (*Spanish* 'nweβo la'reðo) *n* a city and port of entry in NE Mexico, in Tamaulipas state on the Rio Grande opposite Laredo, Texas: oil industries. Pop.: 218 413 (1990).

Nuevo León ('nweɪvəʊ leɪ'əʊn, nu:'eɪ-; *Spanish* 'nweβo le'ɔn) *n* a state of NE Mexico: the first centre of heavy industry in Latin America. Capital: Monterrey. Pop.: 3 549 273 (1995 est.). Area: 64 555 sq. km (24 925 sq. miles).

nuevo sol ('nweɪvəʊ sɒl) *n* the Spanish name for **new sol.**

Nuffield ('nʌfi:ld) *n* **William Richard Morris,** 1st Viscount Nuffield. 1877–1963, English motorcar manufacturer and philanthropist. He endowed Nuffield College at Oxford (1937) and the Nuffield Foundation (1943), a charitable trust for the furtherance of medicine and education.

Nuffield teaching project *n* (in Britain) a complete school programme in mathematics, science, languages, etc., with suggested complementary theory and practical work.

nugatory ('nju:gətərɪ, -trɪ) *adj* **1** of little value; trifling. **2** not valid: *a nugatory law.* [C17: from Latin *nūgātōrius,* from *nūgārī* to jest, from *nūgae* trifles]

nuggar ('nʌgə) *n* a sailing boat used to carry cargo on the Nile. [from Arabic]

nugget ('nʌgɪt) *n* **1** a small piece or lump, esp. of gold in its natural state. **2** something small but valuable or excellent. **3** *N.Z. trademark.* shoe polish. ◆ *vb (tr)* **4** *N.Z. informal.* to shine (shoes). [C19: origin unknown]

nuggety ('nʌgɪtɪ) *adj* **1** of or resembling a nugget. **2** *Austral. and N.Z. informal.* (of a person) thickset; stocky.

nuisance ('nju:səns) *n* **1a** a person or thing that causes annoyance or bother. **1b** *(as modifier): nuisance calls.* **2** *Law.* something unauthorized that is obnoxious or injurious to the community at large (**public nuisance**) or to an individual, esp. in relation to his ownership or occupation of property (**private nuisance**). **3** **nuisance value.** the usefulness of a person's or thing's capacity to cause difficulties or irritation. [C15: via Old French from *nuire* to injure, from Latin *nocēre*]

Nuits-Saint-Georges (*French* nɥisɛ̃ʒɔrʒ) *n* a fine red wine produced near the town of Nuits-Saint-Georges in Burgundy.

NUJ (in Britain) *abbrev. for* National Union of Journalists.

Nu Jiang ('nu: 'dʒjæŋ) *n* the Chinese name for the **Salween.**

nuke (nju:k) *Slang.* ◆ *vb (tr)* **1** to attack or destroy with nuclear weapons. ◆ *n* **2** a nuclear bomb. **3** a military strike with nuclear weapons. **4** nuclear power. **5** *Chiefly U.S.* a nuclear power plant.

Nuku'alofa (ˌnu:ku:ə'lɔ:fə) *n* the capital of Tonga, a port on the N coast of Tongatapu Island. Pop.: 34 000 (1990 est.).

Nukus (*Russian* nu'kus) *n* a city in Uzbekistan, capital of the Kara-Kalpak Autonomous Republic, on the Amu Darya River. Pop.: 185 000 (1993 est.).

null (nʌl) *adj* **1** without legal force; invalid; (esp. in the phrase **null and void**). **2** without value or consequence; useless. **3** lacking distinction; characterless: *a null expression.* **4** nonexistent; amounting to nothing. **5** *Maths.* **5a** quantitatively zero. **5b** relating to zero. **5c** (of a set) having no members. **5d** (of a sequence) having zero as a limit. **6** *Physics.* involving measurement in which an instrument has a zero reading, as with a Wheatstone bridge. **[C16:** from Latin *nullus* none, from *ne* not + *ullus* any**]**

nullah ('nʌlɑː) *n* a stream or drain. **[C18:** from Hindi *nālā***]**

nulla-nulla (ˌnʌlə'nʌlə) *n Austral.* a wooden club used by native Australians. **[**from a native Australian language**]**

Nullarbor Plain ('nʌləˌbɔː) *n* a vast low plateau of S Australia: extends north from the Great Australian Bight to the Great Victoria Desert; has no surface water or trees. Area: 260 000 sq. km (100 000 sq. miles).

null hypothesis *n Statistics.* the residual hypothesis if the alternative hypothesis tested against it fails to achieve a predetermined significance level. See **hypothesis testing.** Compare **alternative hypothesis.**

nullifidian (ˌnʌlɪ'fɪdɪən) *n* **1** a person who has no faith or belief; sceptic; disbeliever. ◆ *adj* **2** having no faith or belief. **[C16:** from Latin, from *nullus* no + *fidēs* faith**]**

nullify ('nʌlɪˌfaɪ) *vb* **-fies, -fying, -fied.** *(tr)* **1** to render legally void or of no effect. **2** to render ineffective or useless; cancel out. **[C16:** from Late Latin *nullificāre* to despise, from Latin *nullus* of no account + *facere* to make**]** ► **ˌnullifi'cation** *n* ► **'nulliˌfier** *n*

nullipara (nʌ'lɪpərə) *n, pl* **-rae** (-ˌriː). a woman who has never borne a child. **[C19:** New Latin, from *nullus* no, not any + *-para,* from *parere* to bring forth; see -PAROUS**]** ► **nul'liparous** *adj*

nullipore ('nʌlɪˌpɔː) *n* any of several red seaweeds that secrete and become encrusted with calcium carbonate: family *Rhodophyceae.* **[C19:** from Latin, from *nullus* no + PORE[2]**]**

nulli secundus *Latin.* ('nʊliː sə'kʊndʊs) *adj* second to none.

nullity ('nʌlɪtɪ) *n, pl* **-ties. 1** the state of being null. **2** a null or legally invalid act or instrument. **3** something null, ineffective, characterless, etc. **[C16:** from Medieval Latin *nullitās,* from Latin *nullus* no, not any**]**

NUM (in Britain) *abbrev. for* National Union of Mineworkers.

num. *abbrev. for:* **1** number. **2** numeral.

Num. *Bible. abbrev. for* Numbers.

Numantia (njuː'mæntɪə) *n* an ancient city in N Spain: a centre of Celtic resistance to Rome in N Spain: captured by Scipio the Younger in 133 B.C. ► **Nu'mantian** *adj, n*

Numa Pompilius ('njuːmə pɒm'pɪlɪəs) *n* the legendary second king of Rome (?715–?673 B.C.), said to have instituted religious rites.

numb (nʌm) *adj* **1** deprived of feeling through cold, shock, etc. **2** unable to move; paralysed. **3** characteristic of or resembling numbness: *a numb sensation.* ◆ *vb* **4** *(tr)* to make numb; deaden, shock, or paralyse. **[C15** *nomen,* literally: taken (with paralysis), from Old English *niman* to take; related to Old Norse *nema,* Old High German *niman***]** ► **'numbly** *adv* ► **'numbness** *n*

numbat ('nʌmˌbæt) *n* a small Australian marsupial, *Myrmecobius fasciatus,* having a long snout and tongue and strong claws for hunting and feeding on termites: family *Dasyuridae.* Also called: **banded anteater. [C20:** from a native Australian language**]**

number ('nʌmbə) *n* **1** a concept of quantity that is or can be derived from a single unit, the sum of a collection of units, or zero. Every number occupies a unique position in a sequence, enabling it to be used in counting. It can be assigned to one or more sets that can be arranged in a hierarchical classification: every number is a **complex number;** a complex number is either an **imaginary number** or a **real number,** and the latter can be a **rational number** or an **irrational number;** a rational number is either an **integer** or a **fraction,** while an irrational number can be a **transcendental number** or an **algebraic number.** See also **cardinal number, ordinal number. 2** the symbol used to represent a number; numeral. **3** a numeral or string of numerals used to identify a person or thing, esp. in numerical order: *a telephone number.* **4** the person or thing so identified or designated: *she was number seven in the race.* **5** the sum or quantity of equal or similar units or things: *a large number of people.* **6** one of a series, as of a magazine or periodical; issue. **7a** a self-contained piece of pop or jazz music. **7b** a self-contained part of an opera or other musical score, esp. one for the stage. **8** a group or band of people, esp. an exclusive group: *he was not one of our number.* **9** *Slang.* a person, esp. a woman: *who's that nice little number?* **10** *Informal.* an admired article, esp. an item of clothing for a woman: *that little number is by Dior.* **11** *Slang.* a cannabis cigarette: *roll another number.* **12** a grammatical category for the variation in form of nouns, pronouns, and any words agreeing with them, depending on how many persons or things are referred to, esp. as singular or plural in number and in some languages dual or trial. **13 any number of.** several or many. **14 by numbers.** *Military.* (of a drill procedure, etc.) performed step by step, each move being made on the call of a number. **15 do a number on (someone).** *U.S. slang.* to manipulate or trick (someone). **16 get** *or* **have someone's number.** *Informal.* to discover someone's true character or intentions. **17 in numbers.** in large numbers; numerously. **18 one's number is up.** *Brit. informal.* one is finished; one is ruined or about to die. **19 without** *or* **beyond number.** of too great a quantity to be counted; innumerable. ◆ *vb (mainly tr)* **20** to assign a number to. **21** to add up to; total. **22** *(also intr)* to list (items) one by one; enumerate. **23** *(also intr)* to put or be put into a group, category, etc.: *they were numbered among the worst hit.* **24** to limit the number of: *his days were numbered.* **[C13:** from Old French *nombre,* from Latin *numerus***]**

number crunching *n Computing.* the large-scale processing of numerical data. ► **number cruncher** *n*

numbered account *n Banking.* an account identified only by a number, esp. one in a Swiss bank that could contain funds illegally obtained.

number eight wire *n N.Z.* **1** a standard gauge of fencing wire. **2** this wire or something similar used for emergency repairs.

numberless ('nʌmbəlɪs) *adj* **1** too many to be counted; countless. **2** not containing or consisting of numbers. ► **'numberlessly** *adv* ► **'numberlessness** *n*

number line *n* an infinite line on which points represent the real numbers by their distance from a reference point.

number off *vb (adv)* to call out or cause to call out one's number or place in a sequence, esp. in a rank of soldiers: *the sergeant numbered his men off from the right.*

number one *n* **1** the first in a series or sequence. **2** an informal phrase for **oneself, myself,** etc.: *to look after number one.* **3** *Informal.* the most important person; leader, chief: *he's number one in the organization.* **4** *Informal.* the bestselling pop record in any one week. ◆ *adj* **5** first in importance, urgency, quality, etc.: *number one priority.* **6** *Informal.* (of a pop record) having reached the top of the charts.

numberplate ('nʌmbəˌpleɪt) *n* a plate mounted on the front and back of a motor vehicle bearing the registration number. Usual U.S. term: **license plate,** (Canadian) **licence plate.**

Numbers ('nʌmbəz) *n (functioning as sing)* the fourth book of the Old Testament, recording the numbers of the Israelites who followed Moses out of Egypt.

numbers game *or* **racket** *n U.S.* an illegal lottery in which money is wagered on a certain combination of digits appearing at the beginning of a series of numbers published in a newspaper, as in share prices or sports results. Often shortened to **numbers.**

Number Ten *n* 10 Downing Street, the British prime minister's official London residence.

number theory *n* the study of integers, their properties, and the relationship between integers.

number work *n* simple arithmetic and similar mathematical procedures as used and studied at primary level. Also called (esp. formerly): **sums.**

numbfish ('nʌmˌfɪʃ) *n, pl* **-fish** *or* **-fishes.** any of several electric rays, such as *Narcine tasmaniensis* (**Australian numbfish**). **[C18:** so called because it numbs its victims**]**

numbles ('nʌmbᵊlz) *pl n Archaic.* the heart, lungs, liver, etc., of a deer or other animal, cooked for food. **[C14:** from Old French *nombles,* plural of *nomble* thigh muscle of a deer, changed from Latin *lumbulus* a little loin, from *lumbus* loin; see HUMBLE PIE**]**

numbskull *or* **numskull** ('nʌmˌskʌl) *n* a stupid person; dolt; blockhead. **[C18:** from NUMB + SKULL**]**

numdah ('nʌmdɑː) *n* **1** a coarse felt made esp. in India. **2** a saddle pad made from this. **3** an embroidered rug made from this. ◆ Also called (for senses 1, 2): **numnah. [C19:** from Urdu *namdā***]**

numen ('njuːmɛn) *n, pl* **-mina** (-mɪnə). **1** (esp. in ancient Roman religion) a deity or spirit presiding over a thing or place. **2** a guiding principle, force, or spirit. **[C17:** from Latin: a nod (indicating a command), divine power; compare *nuere* to nod**]**

numerable ('njuːmərəbᵊl) *adj* able to be numbered or counted. ► **'numerably** *adv*

numeral ('njuːmərəl) *n* **1** a symbol or group of symbols used to express a number: for example, *6 (Arabic), VI (Roman), 110 (binary).* ◆ *adj* **2** of, consisting of, or denoting a number. **[C16:** from Late Latin *numerālis* belonging to number, from Latin *numerus* number**]**

numerary ('njuːmərərɪ) *adj* of or relating to numbers.

numerate *adj* ('njuːmərɪt). **1** able to use numbers, esp. in arithmetical operations. Compare **literate.** ◆ *vb* ('njuːməˌreɪt). *(tr)* **2** to read (a numerical expression). **3** a less common word for **enumerate. [C18** (vb): from Latin *numerus* number + -ATE[1], by analogy with *literate***]** ► **numeracy** ('njuːmərəsɪ) *n*

numeration (ˌnjuːmə'reɪʃən) *n* **1** the act or process of writing, reading, or naming numbers. **2** a system of numbering or counting. ► **'numerative** *adj*

numerator ('njuːməˌreɪtə) *n* **1** *Maths.* the dividend of a fraction: *the numerator of* ⅞ is 7. Compare **denominator. 2** a person or thing that numbers; enumerator.

numerical (njuː'mɛrɪkᵊl) *or* **numeric** *adj* **1** of, relating to, or denoting a number or numbers. **2** measured or expressed in numbers: *numerical value.* **3** *Maths.* **3a** containing or using constants, coefficients, terms, or elements represented by numbers: $3x^2 + 4y = 2$ is a numerical equation. Compare **literal** (sense 6). **3b** another word for **absolute** (sense 11a). ► **nu'merically** *adv*

numerical analysis *n* a branch of mathematics concerned with methods, usually iterative, for obtaining solutions to problems by means of a computer.

numerical control *n Engineering.* a form of computer control applied to machine tools, by which an operation is directed from numerical data stored on tape or punched on cards.

numerical identity *n Logic.* the relation that holds between two relata when they are the selfsame entity, that is, when the terms designating them have the same reference. Compare **qualitative identity.** See also **Leibnitz's law.**

numerology (ˌnjuːmə'rɒlədʒɪ) *n* the study of numbers, such as the figures in a birth date, and of their supposed influence on human affairs. ► **numerological** (ˌnjuːmərə'lɒdʒɪkᵊl) *adj* ► **ˌnumer'ologist** *n*

numerous ('njuːmərəs) *adj* **1** being many. **2** consisting of many units or parts: *a numerous collection.* ► **'numerously** *adv* ► **'numerousness** *n*

Numidia (njuː'mɪdɪə) *n* an ancient country of N Africa, corresponding roughly to present-day Algeria: flourished until its invasion by Vandals in 429; chief towns were Cirta and Hippo Regius. ► **Nu'midian** *n, adj*

Numidian crane *n* another name for **demoiselle crane** (see **demoiselle** (sense 1)).

numina ('nju:mɪnə) *n* the plural of **numen.**
numinous ('nju:mɪnəs) *adj* **1** denoting, being, or relating to a numen; divine. **2** arousing spiritual or religious emotions. **3** mysterious or awe-inspiring. **[C17:** from Latin *numin-*, NUMEN + -OUS**]**
numis. *or* **numism.** *abbrev. for* numismatic(s).
numismatics (ˌnju:mɪz'mætɪks) *n* (*functioning as sing*) the study or collection of coins, medals, etc. Also called: ˌ**numisma'tology. [C18:** from French *numismatique,* from Latin *nomisma,* from Greek: piece of currency, from *nomizein* to have in use, from *nōmos* use**]** ▸ ˌ**numis'matic** *adj* ▸ ˌ**numis'matically** *adv*
numismatist (nju:'mɪzmətɪst) *or* **numismatologist** (nju:ˌmɪzmə'tɒlədʒɪst) *n* a person who studies or collects coins, medals, etc.
nummary ('nʌmərɪ) *adj* of or relating to coins. **[C17:** from Latin *nummārius***]**
nummular ('nʌmjʊlə) *adj* shaped like a coin; disc-shaped; circular. **[C19:** from Latin *nummulus* a small coin**]**
nummulite ('nʌmjʊˌlaɪt) *n* any of various large fossil protozoans of the family *Nummulitidae,* common in Tertiary times: phylum *Foraminifera* (foraminifers). **[C19:** from New Latin *Nummulites* genus name, from Latin *nummulus,* from *nummus* coin**]** ▸ **nummulitic** (ˌnʌmjʊ'lɪtɪk) *adj*
numnah ('nʌmnɑ:) *n* another word for **numdah** (senses 1, 2).
numskull ('nʌmˌskʌl) *n* a variant spelling of **numbskull.**
nun[1] (nʌn) *n* **1** a female member of a religious order. **2** (*sometimes cap.*) a variety of domestic fancy pigeon having a black-and-white plumage with a ridged peak or cowl of short white feathers. **[**Old English *nunne,* from Church Latin *nonna,* from Late Latin: form of address used for an elderly woman**]** ▸ **'nunlike** *adj*
nun[2] (nʊn) *n* the 14th letter in the Hebrew alphabet (נ or, at the end of a word, ן), transliterated as *n*
nunatak ('nʌnəˌtæk) *n* an isolated mountain peak projecting through the surface of surrounding glacial ice and supporting a distinct fauna and flora after recession of the ice. **[C19:** via Danish from Eskimo**]**
Nunavut ('nʌnəvʌt) *n* a territory of NW Canada, formed in 1999 from part of the Northwest Territories as a semiautonomous region for the Inuit. Capital: Iqaluit. Pop.: 25 000 (1999 est.). Area: 2 201 400 sq. km (844 960 sq. miles).
nun buoy (nʌn) *n Nautical.* a buoy, conical at the top, marking the right side of a channel leading into a harbour: green in British waters but red in U.S. waters. Compare **can buoy. [C18:** from obsolete *nun* a child's spinning top + BUOY**]**
Nunc Dimittis ('nʌŋk dɪ'mɪtɪs, 'nʊŋk) *n* **1** the Latin name for the Canticle of Simeon (Luke 2:29–32). **2** a musical setting of this. **[**from the opening words (Vulgate): now let depart**]**
nunciature ('nʌnsɪətʃə) *n* the office or term of office of a nuncio. **[C17:** from Italian *nunziatura;* see NUNCIO**]**
nuncio ('nʌnʃɪˌəʊ, -sɪ-) *n, pl* **-cios.** *R.C. Church.* a diplomatic representative of the Holy See, ranking above an internuncio and esp. having ambassadorial status. **[C16:** via Italian from Latin *nuntius* messenger**]**
nuncle ('nʌŋkᵊl) *n* an archaic or dialect word for **uncle. [C16:** from division of *mine uncle* as *my nuncle***]**
nuncupative ('nʌŋkjʊˌpeɪtɪv, nʌŋ'kju:pətɪv) *adj* (of a will) declared orally by the testator and later written down. **[C16:** from Late Latin *nuncupātīvus* nominal, from Latin *nuncupāre* to name**]**
Nuneaton (nʌn'i:tᵊn) *n* a town in central England, in Warwickshire. Pop.: 66 715 (1991).
nunhood ('nʌnhʊd) *n* **1** the condition, practice, or character of a nun. **2** nuns collectively.
Nunn (nʌn) *n* **Trevor (Robert).** born 1940, British theatre director; artistic director (1968–86) and chief executive (1968–86) of the Royal Shakespeare Company; artistic director of the Royal National Theatre from 1997. His productions include *Nicholas Nickleby* (1980), *Cats* (1981), and *Sunset Boulevard* (1993).
nunnery ('nʌnərɪ) *n, pl* **-neries.** the convent or religious house of a community of nuns.
nunny bag ('nʌnɪ) *n Canadian.* a small sealskin haversack, used chiefly in Newfoundland. **[C19** *nunny,* probably from Scottish dialect *noony* luncheon, from NOON**]**
nun's cloth *or* **veiling** (nʌnz) *n* a thin soft plain-weave silk or worsted fabric used for veils, dresses, etc.
Nupe ('nu:peɪ) *n* **1** (*pl* **-pe** *or* **-pes**) a member of a Negroid people of Nigeria, noted as fishermen, who live near the confluence of the Niger and Benue Rivers. **2** the language of this people, belonging to the Kwa branch of the Niger-Congo family.
NUPE ('nju:pɪ) *n* (formerly, in Britain) *acronym for* National Union of Public Employees.
nuptial ('nʌpʃəl, -tʃəl) *adj* **1** relating to marriage; conjugal: *nuptial vows.* **2** *Zoology.* of or relating to mating: *the nuptial flight of a queen bee.* **[C15:** from Latin *nuptiālis,* from *nuptiae* marriage, from *nubere* to marry**]** ▸ **'nuptially** *adv*
nuptials ('nʌpʃəlz, -tʃəlz) *pl n* (*sometimes sing*) a marriage ceremony; wedding.
NUR (in Britain) *abbrev. for* National Union of Railwaymen.
nurd (nɜ:d) *n* a variant spelling of **nerd.**
Nuremberg ('njʊərəmˌbɜ:g) *n* a city in S Germany, in N Bavaria: scene of annual Nazi rallies (1933–38), the anti-Semitic Nuremberg decrees (1935), and the trials of Nazi leaders for their war crimes (1945–46); important metalworking and electrical industries. Pop.: 492 425 (1996 est.). German name: **Nürnberg.**
Nureyev ('njʊərɪɛf, njʊ'reɪ-) *n* **Rudolf.** 1938–93, Austrian ballet dancer, born in the Soviet Union: he lived in England (1961–83) and France (1983–89). He became an Austrian citizen in 1982.
Nurhachi (ˌnʊə'hɑ:tʃɪ) *n* 1559–1626, Manchurian leader, who unified the Manchurian state and began (1618) the Manchurian conquest of China.
Nuri ('nʊərɪ) *n* **1** (*pl* **-ris** *or* **-ri**) Also called: **Kafir.** a member of an Indo-European people of Nuristan and neighbouring parts of Pakistan. **2** Also called: **'Kafiri.** the Indo-Iranian language of this people.
Nuri as-Said ('nju:rɪ æssaɪ'i:d) *n* 1888–1958, Iraqi soldier and statesman: prime minister of Iraq 14 times between 1930 and 1958: he died during a military coup.
Nuristan (ˌnʊərɪ'stɑ:n) *n* a region of E Afghanistan: consists mainly of high mountains (including part of the Hindu Kush), steep narrow valleys, and forests. Area: about 13 000 sq. km (5000 sq. miles). Former name: **Kafiristan.**
Nurmi ('nɜ:mɪ; *Finnish* 'nurmi) *n* **Paavo** ('pɑ:vɔ), known as *The Flying Finn.* 1897–1973, Finnish runner, winner of the 1500, 5000, and 10 000 metres' races at the 1924 Olympic Games in Paris.
Nürnberg ('nyrnbɛrk) *n* the German name for **Nuremberg.**
nurse (nɜ:s) *n* **1** a person, usually a woman, who tends the sick, injured, or infirm. **2** short for **nursemaid. 3** a woman employed to breast-feed another woman's child; wet nurse. **4** a worker in a colony of social insects that takes care of the larvae. ◆ *vb* (*mainly tr*) **5** (*also intr*) to tend (the sick). **6** (*also intr*) to feed (a baby) at the breast; suckle. **7** to try to cure (an ailment). **8** to clasp carefully or fondly: *she nursed the crying child in her arms.* **9** (*also intr*) (of a baby) to suckle at the breast (of). **10** to look after (a child) as one's employment. **11** to attend to carefully; foster, cherish: *he nursed the magazine through its first year; having a very small majority he nursed the constituency diligently.* **12** to harbour; preserve: *to nurse a grudge.* **13** *Billiards.* to keep (the balls) together for a series of cannons. **[C16:** from earlier *norice,* Old French *nourice,* from Late Latin *nūtrīcia* nurse, from Latin *nūtrīcius* nourishing, from *nūtrīre* to nourish**]**
nursehound ('nɜ:sˌhaʊnd) *n* a species of European dogfish, *Scyliorrhinus caniculus.* **[C20:** NURSE (SHARK) + HOUND[1]**]**
nursemaid ('nɜ:sˌmeɪd) *or* **nurserymaid** ('nɜ:srɪˌmeɪd) *n* a woman or girl employed to look after someone else's children. Often shortened to **nurse.**
nursery ('nɜ:srɪ) *n, pl* **-ries. 1a** a room in a house set apart for use by children. **1b** (*as modifier*): *nursery wallpaper.* **2** a place where plants, young trees, etc., are grown commercially. **3** an establishment providing residential or day care for babies and very young children; crèche. **4** short for **nursery school. 5** anywhere serving to foster or nourish new ideas, etc. **6** Also called: **nursery cannon.** *Billiards.* **6a** a series of cannons with the three balls adjacent to a cushion, esp. near a corner pocket. **6b** a cannon in such a series.
nurseryman ('nɜ:srɪmən) *n, pl* **-men.** a person who owns or works in a nursery in which plants are grown.
nursery rhyme *n* a short traditional verse or song for children, such as *Little Jack Horner.*
nursery school *n* a school for young children, usually from three to five years old.
nursery slopes *pl n* gentle slopes used by beginners in skiing.
nursery stakes *pl n* a race for two-year-old horses.
nurse shark *n* any of various sharks of the family *Orectolobidae,* such as *Ginglymostoma cirratum* of the Atlantic Ocean, having an external groove on each side of the head between the mouth and nostril. **[C15** *nusse fisshe* (later influenced in spelling by NURSE), perhaps from division of obsolete *an huss* shark, dogfish (of uncertain origin) as *a nuss***]**
nursing ('nɜ:sɪŋ) *n* **1a** the practice or profession of caring for the sick and injured. **1b** (*as modifier*): *a nursing home.*
nursing bottle *n* another term (esp. U.S.) for **feeding bottle.**
nursing father *n* a biblical name for **foster father.**
nursing home *n* **1** a private hospital or residence staffed and equipped to care for aged or infirm persons. **2** *Brit.* a private maternity home.
nursing mother *n* **1** a mother who is breast-feeding her baby. **2** a biblical name for **foster mother.**
nursing officer *n* (in Britain) the official name for **matron** (sense 4).
nursling *or* **nurseling** ('nɜ:slɪŋ) *n* a child or young animal that is being suckled, nursed, or fostered.
nurture ('nɜ:tʃə) *n* **1** the act or process of promoting the development, etc., of a child. **2** something that nourishes. **3** *Biology.* the environmental factors that partly determine the structure of an organism. See also **nature** (sense 12). ◆ *vb* (*tr*) **4** to feed or support. **5** to educate or train. **[C14:** from Old French *norriture,* from Latin *nutrīre* to nourish**]** ▸ **'nurturable** *adj* ▸ **'nurturer** *n*
NUS (in Britain) *abbrev. for:* **1** National Union of Seamen. **2** National Union of Students.
Nusa Tenggara ('nu:sə tɛŋ'gɑ:rə) *n* an island chain of Indonesia, east of Java: the main islands are Bali, Lombok, Sumbawa, Sumba, Flores, Alor, and Timor. Pop.: 7 237 600 (1995 est.). Area: 73 144 sq. km (28 241 sq. miles). Former name: **Lesser Sunda Islands.**
nut (nʌt) *n* **1** a dry one-seeded indehiscent fruit that usually possesses a woody wall. **2** (*not in technical use*) any similar fruit, such as the walnut, having a hard shell and an edible kernel. **3** the edible kernel of such a fruit. **4** *Slang.* **4a** an eccentric person. **4b** a person who is mentally disturbed. **5** a slang word for **head** (sense 1). **6 do one's nut.** *Brit. slang.* to be extremely angry; go into a rage. **7 off one's nut.** *Slang.* mad, crazy, or foolish. **8** a person or thing that presents difficulties (esp. in the phrase **a tough** *or* **hard nut to crack**). **9** a small square or hexagonal block, usu. metal, with a threaded hole through the middle for screwing on the end of a bolt. **10** *Mountaineering.* a variously shaped small metal block, usually a wedge or hexagonal prism (originally an ordinary engineer's nut) with a wire or rope loop attached, for jamming into a crack to provide security. Also called; **chock. 11** Also called (U.S. and Canadian): **frog.** *Music.* **11a** the ledge or ridge at the upper end of the fingerboard of a violin, cello, etc., over which the strings pass to the tuning pegs. **11b** the end of a vio-

lin bow that is held by the player. **12** *Printing.* another word for **en. 13** a small usually gingery biscuit. **14** *Brit.* a small piece of coal. ◆ *vb* **nuts, nutting, nutted. 15** (*intr*) to gather nuts. **16** (*tr*) *Slang.* to butt (someone) with the head. ◆ See also **nuts.** [Old English *hnutu;* related to Old Norse *hnot,* Old High German *hnuz* (German *Nuss*)] ▸ **'nut,like** *adj*

NUT (in Britain) *abbrev. for* National Union of Teachers.

nutant ('nju:tᵊnt) *adj Botany.* having the apex hanging down: *nutant flowers.* [C18: from Latin *nūtāre* to nod]

nutation (nju:'teɪʃən) *n* **1** *Astronomy.* a periodic variation in the precession of the earth's axis causing the earth's poles to oscillate about their mean position. **2** *Physics.* a periodic variation in the precession of the axis of any spinning body, such as a gyroscope, about the horizontal. **3** the spiral growth of a shoot, tendril, or similar plant organ, caused by variation in the growth rate in different parts. **4** the act or an instance of nodding the head. [C17: from Latin *nutātiō,* from *nūtāre* to nod] ▸ **nu'tational** *adj*

nutbrown ('nʌt'braʊn) *adj* of a brownish colour, esp. a reddish-brown: *nutbrown hair.*

nutcase ('nʌt,keɪs) *n Slang.* an insane or very foolish person.

nutcracker ('nʌt,krækə) *n* **1** (*often pl*) a device for cracking the shells of nuts. **2** either of two birds, *Nucifraga caryocatactes* of the Old World or *N. columbianus* (**Clark's nutcracker**) of North America, having speckled plumage and feeding on nuts, seeds, etc.: family *Corvidae* (crows).

nutgall ('nʌt,gɔ:l) *n* a nut-shaped gall caused by gall wasps on the oak and other trees.

nuthatch ('nʌt,hætʃ) *n* any songbird of the family *Sittidae,* esp. *Sitta europaea,* having strong feet and bill, and feeding on insects, seeds, and nuts. [C14 *notehache,* from *note* nut + *hache* hatchet, from the bird's habit of splitting nuts; see NUT, HACK[1]]

nuthouse ('nʌt,haʊs) *n Slang.* a mental hospital or asylum.

nut key *n Mountaineering.* a tool for extracting a nut, chock, etc., from a crack after use.

nutlet ('nʌtlɪt) *n* **1** any of the one-seeded portions of a fruit, such as a labiate fruit, that fragments when mature. **2** the stone of a drupe, such as a plum. **3** a small nut.

nutmeg ('nʌtmɛg) *n* **1** an East Indian evergreen tree, *Myristica fragrans,* cultivated in the tropics for its hard aromatic seed: family *Myristicaceae.* See also **mace**[2]. **2** the seed of this tree, used as a spice. **3** any of several similar trees or their fruit. **4** a greyish-brown colour. ◆ *vb* **-megs, -megging, -megged.** (*tr*) **5** *Brit. sport informal.* to kick or hit the ball between the legs of (an opposing player). [C13: from Old French *nois muguede,* from Old Provençal *noz muscada* musk-scented nut, from Latin *nux* NUT + *muscus* MUSK]

nut oil *n* oil obtained from walnuts, hazelnuts, etc., used in paints and varnishes and in cooking.

nut pine *n* either of two varieties of the pine tree *Pinus cembroides,* of Mexico, Arizona, and California, having edible nuts.

nutria ('nju:trɪə) *n* **1** another name for **coypu,** esp. the fur. **2** a brown colour with a grey tinge. [C19: from Spanish: otter, variant of *lutria,* ultimately from Latin *lūtra* otter]

nutrient ('nju:trɪənt) *n* **1** any of the mineral substances that are absorbed by the roots of plants for nourishment. **2** any substance that nourishes an animal. ◆ *adj* **3** providing or contributing to nourishment: *a nutrient solution.* [C17: from Latin *nūtrīre* to nourish]

nutriment ('nju:trɪmənt) *n* any material providing nourishment. [C16: from Latin *nūtrīmentum,* from *nūtrīre* to nourish] ▸ **nutrimental** (,nju:trɪ'mɛntᵊl) *adj*

nutrition (nju:'trɪʃən) *n* **1** a process in animals and plants involving the intake of nutrient materials and their subsequent assimilation into the tissues. Related adjs.: **alimentary, trophic. 2** the act or process of nourishing. **3** the study of nutrition, esp. in humans. [C16: from Late Latin *nūtrītiō,* from *nūtrīre* to nourish] ▸ **nu'tritional** *or* (less commonly) **nu'tritionary** *adj* ▸ **nu'tritionally** *adv*

nutritionist (nju:'trɪʃənɪst) *n* a person who specializes in nutrition and the nutritive value of various foods.

nutritious (nju:'trɪʃəs) *adj* nourishing, sometimes to a high degree. [C17: from Latin *nūtrīcius* nourishing, from *nūtrix* a NURSE] ▸ **nu'tritiously** *adv* ▸ **nu'tritiousness** *n*

nutritive ('nju:trɪtɪv) *adj* **1** providing nourishment. **2** of, concerning, or promoting nutrition. ◆ *n* **3** a nutritious food. ▸ **'nutritively** *adv*

nuts (nʌts) *adj* **1** a slang word for **insane. 2** (foll. by *about* or *on*) *Slang.* extremely fond (of) or enthusiastic (about). ◆ *interj* **3** *Slang.* an expression of disappointment, contempt, refusal, or defiance. ◆ *pl n* **4** a taboo slang word for **testicles.**

nuts and bolts *pl n Informal.* the essential or practical details.

nutshell ('nʌt,ʃɛl) *n* **1** the shell around the kernel of a nut. **2 in a nutshell.** in essence; briefly.

nutter ('nʌtə) *n Brit. slang.* a mad or eccentric person.

nutting ('nʌtɪŋ) *n* the act or pastime of gathering nuts.

nutty ('nʌtɪ) *adj* **-tier, -tiest. 1** containing or abounding in nuts. **2** resembling nuts, esp. in taste. **3** a slang word for **insane. 4** (foll. by *over* or *about*) *Informal.* extremely fond (of) or enthusiastic (about). ▸ **'nuttily** *adv* ▸ **'nuttiness** *n*

nutwood ('nʌt,wʊd) *n* **1** any of various nut-bearing trees, such as walnut. **2** the wood of any of these trees.

Nuuk (nu:k) *n* the capital of Greenland, in the southwest: the oldest Danish settlement in Greenland, founded in 1721. Pop.: 12 181 (1993). Former name (until 1979): **Godthaab.**

nux vomica ('nʌks 'vɒmɪkə) *n* **1** an Indian spiny loganiaceous tree, *Strychnos nux-vomica,* with orange-red berries containing poisonous seeds. **2** any of the seeds of this tree, which contain strychnine and other poisonous alkaloids. **3** a medicine manufactured from the seeds of this tree, formerly used as a heart stimulant. [C16: from Medieval Latin: vomiting nut]

nuzzle ('nʌzᵊl) *vb* **1** to push or rub gently against the nose or snout. **2** (*intr*) to nestle; lie close. **3** (*tr*) to dig out with the snout. [C15 *nosele,* from NOSE (n)]

NV *abbrev. for* Nevada.

NVQ (in Britain) *abbrev. for* national vocational qualification: a qualification which rewards competence in a specified type of employment.

NW *Symbol for* northwest(ern).

NWT *abbrev. for* Northwest Territories (of Canada).

NY *or* **N.Y.** *abbrev. for* New York (city or state).

nyaff (njæf) *n Scot.* a small or contemptible person. [C19: perhaps imitative of the bark of a small dog]

nyala ('njɑ:lə) *n, pl* **-la** *or* **-las. 1** a spiral-horned southern African antelope, *Tragelaphus angasi,* with a fringe of white hairs along the length of the back and neck. **2 mountain nyala.** a similar and related Ethiopian animal, *T. buxtoni,* lacking the white crest. [from Zulu]

Nyanja ('njændʒə) *n* **1** (*pl* **-ja** *or* **-jas**) a member of a Negroid people of central Africa, living chiefly in Malawi. **2** the language of this people, belonging to the Bantu group of the Niger-Congo family. Nyanja forms the basis of a pidgin used as a lingua franca in central Africa.

nyanza ('njænzə, nɪ'ænzə) *n* (*cap. when part of a name*) (in E Africa) a lake. [from Bantu]

Nyasa *or* **Nyassa** (nɪ'æsə, naɪ'æsə) *n* **Lake.** a lake in central Africa at the S end of the Great Rift Valley: the third largest lake in Africa, drained by the Shiré River into the Zambezi. Area: about 28 500 sq. km (11 000 sq. miles). Malawi name: **Lake Malawi.**

Nyasaland (nɪ'æsə,lænd, naɪ'æsə-) *n* the former name (until 1964) of **Malawi.**

NYC *abbrev. for* New York City.

nyctaginaceous (,nɪktədʒɪ'neɪʃəs) *adj* of, relating to, or belonging to the *Nyctaginaceae,* a family of mostly tropical plants, including bougainvillea, having large coloured bracts surrounding each flower. [from New Latin, from *Nyctago* type genus, from Greek *nukt-, nux* night]

nyctalopia (,nɪktə'ləʊpɪə) *n* inability to see normally in dim light. Nontechnical name: **night blindness.** Compare **hemeralopia.** [C17: via Late Latin from Greek *nuktálōps,* from *nux* night + *alaos* blind + *ōps* eye]

nyctanthous (nɪk'tænθəs) *adj* (of plants) flowering at night.

nyctinasty ('nɪktɪ,næstɪ) *n Botany.* a nastic movement, such as the closing of petals, that occurs in response to the alternation of day and night. [C20: from Greek *nukt-, nux* night + -NASTY] ▸ **,nycti'nastic** *adj*

nyctitropism (nɪk'tɪtrə,pɪzəm) *n* a tendency of some plant parts to assume positions at night that are different from their daytime positions. [C19: *nyct-,* from Greek *nukt-, nux* night + -TROPISM] ▸ **nyctitropic** (,nɪktɪ'trɒpɪk) *adj*

nyctophobia (,nɪktəʊ'fəʊbɪə) *n Psychiatry.* an abnormal dread of night or darkness. [*nyct-,* from Greek *nukt-, nux* night + -PHOBIA] ▸ **,nycto'phobic** *adj*

nye (naɪ) *n* a flock of pheasants. Also called: **nide, eye.** [C15: from old French *ni,* from Latin *nīdus* nest]

Nyeman (*Russian* 'njɛmən) *n* a variant spelling of **Neman.**

Nyerere (njə'rɛrɪ, nɪ-) *n* **Julius Kambarage** (kæm'bɑ:rɑ:gə). born 1922, Tanzanian statesman; president (1964–85). He became prime minister of Tanganyika in 1961 and president in 1962, negotiating the union of Tanganyika and Zanzibar to form Tanzania (1964).

Nyíregyháza (*Hungarian* 'nji:rɛtjhɑ:zɔ) *n* a market town in NE Hungary. Pop.: 113 000 (1997 est.).

Nykøbing (*Danish* 'nykø:bɛŋ) *n* a port in Denmark, on the W coast of Falster Island. Pop.: 64 428 (1987).

nylghau ('nɪlgɔ:) *n, pl* **-ghau** *or* **-ghaus.** another name for **nilgai.**

nylon ('naɪlɒn) *n* **1** a class of synthetic polyamide materials made by copolymerizing dicarboxylic acids with diamines. They can be moulded into a variety of articles, such as combs and machine parts. Nylon monofilaments are used for bristles, etc., and nylon fibres can be spun into yarn. **2a** yarn or cloth made of nylon, used for clothing, stockings, etc. **2b** (*as modifier*): *a nylon dress.* [C20: originally a trademark]

nylons ('naɪlənz) *pl n* stockings made of nylon or other man-made material.

nymph (nɪmf) *n* **1** *Myth.* a spirit of nature envisaged as a beautiful maiden. **2** *Chiefly poetic.* a beautiful young woman. **3** the larva of insects such as the dragonfly and mayfly. It resembles the adult, apart from having underdeveloped wings and reproductive organs, and develops into the adult without a pupal stage. [C14: via Old French from Latin, from Greek *numphē* nymph; related to Latin *nūbere* to marry] ▸ **'nymphal** *or* **nymphean** ('nɪmfɪən) *adj* ▸ **'nymphlike** *adj*

nympha ('nɪmfə) *n, pl* **-phae** (-fi:). *Anatomy.* either one of the labia minora. Also called **'labium 'minus pu'dendi.** [C17: from Latin: bride, NYMPH]

nymphaeaceous (,nɪmfɪ'eɪʃəs) *adj* of, relating to, or belonging to the *Nymphaeaceae,* a family of plants, including the water lilies, that grow in water or marshes and have typically floating leaves and showy flowers. [from New Latin, from Latin *nymphaea* water lily, ultimately from Greek *numphaios* sacred to nymphs]

nymphalid ('nɪmfəlɪd) *n* **1** any butterfly of the family *Nymphalidae,* typically having brightly coloured wings: includes the fritillaries, tortoiseshells, red admirals, and peacock. ◆ *adj* **2** of, relating to, or belonging to the *Nymphalidae.* [C19: from New Latin, from *Nymphālis* genus name, from Latin; see NYMPH]

nymphet ('nɪmfɪt) *n* a young girl who is sexually precocious and desirable. [C17 (meaning: a young nymph): diminutive of NYMPH]

nympho ('nɪmfəʊ) *n, pl* **-phos.** *Informal.* a nymphomaniac.

nympholepsy ('nɪmfə,lɛpsɪ) *n, pl* **-sies.** a state of violent emotion, esp. when associated with a desire for something one cannot have. [C18: from NYMPHOLEPT, on the model of *epilepsy*] ▸ ˌ**nympho'leptic** *adj*

nympholept ('nɪmfəˌlɛpt) *n* a person afflicted by nympholepsy. [C19: from Greek *numpholēptos* caught by nymphs, from *numphē* nymph + *lambanein* to seize]

nymphomania (ˌnɪmfə'meɪnɪə) *n* a neurotic condition in women in which the symptoms are a compulsion to have sexual intercourse with as many men as possible and an inability to have lasting relationships with them. Compare **satyriasis.** [C18: New Latin, from Greek *numphē* nymph + -MANIA] ▸ ˌ**nympho'maniac** *n, adj* ▸ **nymphomaniacal** (ˌnɪmfəʊmə'naɪək°l) *adj*

Nynorsk (*Norwegian* 'nyːnɔːsk; *English* 'niːnɔːsk) *n* one of the two mutually intelligible official forms of written Norwegian: it also exists in spoken form and is derived from the dialect of W and N Norway. Also called: **Landsmål.** Compare **Bokmål.** [Norwegian: new Norse]

Nyoro ('njɔːrəʊ) *n* **1** (*pl* **-ro** *or* **-ros**) a member of a Negroid people of W Uganda. **2** the language of this people, belonging to the Bantu group of the Niger-Congo family.

Nysa ('nɪsə) *n* the Polish name for the **Neisse** (sense 1).

nystagmus (nɪ'stægməs) *n* involuntary movement of the eye comprising a smooth drift followed by a flick back, occurring in several situations, for example after the body has been rotated.

nystatin ('nɪstətɪn) *n* an antibiotic obtained from the bacterium *Streptomyces noursei:* used in the treatment of infections caused by certain fungi, esp. *Candida albicans.* [C20: from *New York State,* where it was originated + -IN]

Nyx (nɪks) *n Greek myth.* the goddess of the night, daughter of Chaos. Roman counterpart: **Nox.**

NZ *international car registration for* New Zealand.

NZ *or* **N. Zeal.** *abbrev. for* New Zealand.

NZBC *abbrev. for* New Zealand Broadcasting Commission.

NZCER *abbrev. for* New Zealand Council for Educational Research.

NZEF *abbrev. for* New Zealand Expeditionary Force, the New Zealand army that served 1914–18. **2NZEF** is used to refer to the Second New Zealand Expeditionary Force, in World War II.

NZEFIP *abbrev. for* New Zealand Expeditionary Force in the Pacific, the 3rd division of the New Zealand Expeditionary Force serving in the Pacific campaign in World War II.

NZEI *abbrev. for* New Zealand Educational Institute.

NZLR *abbrev. for* New Zealand Law Reports.

NZMA *abbrev. for* New Zealand Medical Association.

NZR *abbrev. for* New Zealand Railways.

NZRFU *abbrev. for* New Zealand Rugby Football Union.

NZRN *abbrev. for* New Zealand Registered Nurse.

Oo

o *or* **O** (əʊ) *n, pl* **o's, O's,** *or* **Os. 1** the 15th letter and fourth vowel of the modern English alphabet. **2** any of several speech sounds represented by this letter, in English as in *code, pot, cow, move,* or *form.* **3** another name for **nought.**

O[1] *symbol for:* **1** *Chem.* oxygen. **2** a human blood type of the ABO group. See **universal donor. 3** *Logic.* a particular negative categorial proposition, such as *some men are not married:* often symbolized as **SoP.** Compare **A, E, I**[2]. [from Latin (*neg*)*o* I deny]

O[2] (əʊ) *interj* **1** a variant spelling of **oh. 2** an exclamation introducing an invocation, entreaty, wish, etc.: *O God! O for the wings of a dove!*

o. *abbrev. for:* **1** octavo. **2** old. **3** only. **4** order. **5** *Pharmacol.* pint. [from Latin *octarius*]

O. *abbrev. for:* **1** Ocean. **2** octavo. **3** old.

o- *prefix* short for **ortho-** (sense 4).

o' (ə) *prep Informal or archaic.* shortened form of **of:** *a cup o' tea.*

O'- *prefix* (in surnames of Irish Gaelic origin) descendant of: *O'Corrigan.* [from Irish Gaelic *ó, ua* descendant]

-o *suffix.* forming informal and slang variants and abbreviations, esp. of nouns: *wino; lie doggo; Jacko.* [probably special use of OH]

-o- *connective vowel.* used to connect elements in a compound word: *chromosome; filmography.* Compare **-i-.** [from Greek, stem vowel of many nouns and adjectives in combination]

oaf (əʊf) *n* a stupid or loutish person. [C17: variant of Old English *ælf* ELF] ▸ **'oafish** *adj* ▸ **'oafishly** *adv* ▸ **'oafishness** *n*

Oahu (əʊ'ɑːhuː) *n* an island in central Hawaii: the third largest of the Hawaiian Islands. Chief town: Honolulu. Pop.: 836 231 (1990). Area: 1574 sq. km (608 sq. miles).

oak (əʊk) *n* **1** any deciduous or evergreen tree or shrub of the fagaceous genus *Quercus,* having acorns as fruits and lobed leaves. See also **holm oak, cork oak, red oak, Turkey oak, durmast.** Related adj: **quercine. 2a** the wood of any of these trees, used esp. as building timber and for making furniture. **2b** (*as modifier*): *an oak table.* **3** any of various trees that resemble the oak, such as the poison oak, silky oak, and Jerusalem oak. **4** the leaves of an oak tree, worn as a garland. **5** the dark brownish colour of oak wood. **6** *Austral.* any of various species of casuarina, such as desert oak, swamp oak, or she-oak. [Old English *āc;* related to Old Norse *eik,* Old High German *eih,* Latin *aesculus*]

oak apple *or* **gall** *n* any of various brownish round galls on oak trees, containing the larva of certain wasps.

Oak-apple Day *n* (in Britain) May 29, the anniversary of the Restoration (1660), formerly commemorated by the wearing of oak apples or oak leaves, recalling the **Boscobel oak** in which Charles II hid after the battle of Worcester.

oaken ('əʊkən) *adj* made of the wood of the oak.

oak fern *n* a graceful light green polypody fern, *Thelypteris dryopteris,* having a creeping rhizome, found in acid woodlands of the northern hemisphere.

Oakham ('əʊkəm) *n* a market town in E central England, the administrative centre of Rutland. Pop.: 8691 (1991).

Oakland ('əʊklənd) *n* a port and industrial centre in W California, on San Francisco Bay; damaged by earthquake in 1989. Pop.: 367 230 (1996 est.).

oak-leaf cluster *n U.S.* an insignia consisting of oak leaves and acorns awarded to holders of certain military decorations to indicate a further award of the same decoration.

Oakley ('əʊklɪ) *n* **Annie,** real name *Phoebe Anne Oakley Mozee.* 1860–1926, U.S. markswoman.

Oaks (əʊks) *n* (*functioning as sing*) **the. 1** a horse race for fillies held annually at Epsom since 1779: one of the classics of English flat racing. **2** any of various similar races. [named after an estate near Epsom]

oakum ('əʊkəm) *n* loose fibre obtained by unravelling old rope, used esp. for caulking seams in wooden ships. [Old English *ācuma,* variant of *ācumba,* literally: off-combings, from *ā-* off + *-cumba,* from *cemban* to COMB]

Oakville ('əʊkvɪl) *n* a city in SE Canada, in SE Ontario on Lake Ontario southwest of Toronto: motor-vehicle industry. Pop.: 114 670 (1991).

Oamaru stone ('ɒməruː) *n* a kind of limestone, of building quality, found at Oamaru on South Island, New Zealand.

O & M *abbrev. for* organization and method (in studies of working methods).

oanshagh ('oːnʃəx) *n Irish.* a foolish girl or woman. [from Irish Gaelic *óinseach*]

OAP (in Britain) *abbrev. for* old age pension *or* pensioner.

OAPEC (əʊ'eɪpek) *n acronym for* Organization of Arab Petroleum Exporting Countries.

oar (ɔː) *n* **1** a long shaft of wood for propelling a boat by rowing, having a broad blade that is dipped into and pulled against the water. Oars were also used for steering certain kinds of ancient sailing boats. **2** short for **oarsman. 3 put one's oar in.** to interfere or interrupt. ◆ *vb* **4** to row or propel with or as if with oars: *the two men were oaring their way across the lake.* [Old English *ār,* of Germanic origin; related to Old Norse *ār*] ▸ **'oarless** *adj* ▸ **'oar,like** *adj*

oared (ɔːd) *adj* **1** equipped with oars. **2** (*in combination*) having oars as specified: *two-oared.*

oarfish ('ɔː,fɪʃ) *n, pl* **-fish** *or* **-fishes.** a very long ribbonfish, *Regalecus glesne,* with long slender ventral fins. Also called: **king of the herrings.** [C19: referring to the flattened oarlike body]

oarlock ('ɔː,lɒk) *n* the usual U.S. and Canadian word for **rowlock.**

oarsman ('ɔːzmən) *n, pl* **-men.** a man who rows, esp. one who rows in a racing boat. ▸ **'oarsman,ship** *n*

oarweed ('ɔː,wiːd) *n* any of various brown seaweeds, especially a kelp of the genus *Laminaria,* with long broad fronds, common below the low-water mark. [from earlier *oreweed,* from *wore,* from Old English *wár* seaweed + WEED[1]]

OAS *abbrev. for:* **1** Organization of American States. **2** *Organisation de l'Armée Secrète;* an organization of European settlers in Algeria who opposed Algerian independence by acts of terrorism (1961–63).

oasis (əʊ'eɪsɪs) *n, pl* **-ses** (-siːz). **1** a fertile patch in a desert occurring where the water table approaches or reaches the ground surface. **2** a place of peace, safety, or happiness in the midst of trouble or difficulty. [C17: via Latin from Greek, probably of Egyptian origin]

Oasis (əʊ'eɪsɪs) *n Trademark.* a block of light porous material, used as a base for flower arrangements.

oast (əʊst) *n Chiefly Brit.* **1** a kiln for drying hops. **2** Also called: **oast house.** a building containing such kilns, usually having a conical or pyramidal roof. [Old English *āst;* related to Old Norse *eisa* fire]

Oastler ('əʊstlə) *n* **Richard.** 1789–1861, British social reformer; he campaigned against child labour and helped achieve the ten-hour day (1847).

oat (əʊt) *n* **1** an erect annual grass, *Avena sativa,* grown in temperate regions for its edible seed. **2** (*usually pl*) the seeds or fruits of this grass. **3** any of various other grasses of the genus *Avena,* such as the wild oat. **4** *Poetic.* a flute made from an oat straw. **5 feel one's oats.** *U.S. and Canadian informal.* **5a** to feel exuberant. **5b** to feel self-important. **6 get one's oats.** *Slang.* to have sexual intercourse. **7 sow one's (wild) oats.** to indulge in adventure or promiscuity during youth. [Old English *āte,* of obscure origin]

oatcake ('əʊt,keɪk) *n* a brittle unleavened oatmeal biscuit.

oaten ('əʊtᵊn) *adj* made of oats or oat straw.

Oates (əʊts) *n* **1** Captain **Lawrence Edward Grace.** 1880–1912, English explorer. He died on Scott's second Antarctic expedition. **2 Titus** ('taɪtəs). 1649–1705, English conspirator. He fabricated the Popish Plot (1678), a supposed Catholic conspiracy to kill Charles II, burn London, and massacre Protestants. His perjury caused the execution of many innocent Catholics.

oat grass *n* any of various oatlike grasses, esp. of the genera *Arrhenatherum* and *Danthonia,* of Eurasia and N. Africa.

oath (əʊθ) *n, pl* **oaths** (əʊðz). **1** a solemn pronouncement to affirm the truth of a statement or to pledge a person to some course of action, often involving a sacred being or object as witness. Related adj: **juratory. 2** the form of such a pronouncement. **3** an irreverent or blasphemous expression, esp. one involving the name of a deity; curse. **4 on, upon,** *or* **under oath. 4a** under the obligation of an oath. **4b** *Law.* having sworn to tell the truth, usually with one's hand on the Bible. **5 take an oath.** to declare formally with an oath or pledge, esp. before giving evidence. [Old English *āth;* related to Old Saxon, Old Frisian *ēth,* Old High German *eid*]

oatmeal ('əʊt,miːl) *n* **1** meal ground from oats, used for making porridge, oatcakes, etc. **2a** a greyish-yellow colour. **2b** (*as adj*): *an oatmeal coat.*

OAU *abbrev. for* Organization of African Unity; an association of African states, established in 1963 to fight colonialism and promote unity among African nations.

Oaxaca (wə'hɑːkə; *Spanish* oa'xaka) *n* **1** a state of S Mexico, on the Pacific: includes most of the Isthmus of Tehuantepec; inhabited chiefly by Indians. Capital: Oaxaca de Juárez. Pop.: 3 224 270 (1995 est.). Area: 95 363 sq. km (36 820 sq. miles). **2** a city in S Mexico, capital of Oaxaca state: founded in 1486 by the Aztecs and conquered by Spain in 1521. Pop.: 212 818 (1990). Official name: **Oaxaca de Juárez** (de 'xwareθ).

Ob (*Russian* ɔpj) *n* a river in N central Russia, formed at Bisk by the confluence of the Biya and Katun Rivers and flowing generally north to the **Gulf of Ob** (an inlet of the Arctic Ocean): one of the largest rivers in the world, with a drainage basin of about 2 930 000 sq. km (1 131 000 sq. miles). Length: 3682 km (2287 miles).

OB *Brit. abbrev. for:* **1** Old Boy. **2** outside broadcast.

ob. *abbrev. for:* **1** (on tombstones) obiit. [Latin: he (or she) died] **2** obiter. [Latin: incidentally; in passing] **3** oboe.

o.b. *N.Z. abbrev. for* ordinary building (grade) (of timber not from the heart of a log).

ob- *prefix* inverse or inversely: *obovate.* [from Old French, from Latin *ob.* In compound words of Latin origin, *ob-* (and *oc-, of-, op-*) indicates: to, towards (*object*); against (*oppose*); away from (*obsolete*); before (*obstetric*); down, over (*obtect*); for the sake of (*obsecrate*); and is used as an intensifier (*oblong*)]

oba ('ɔːbɑː, -bə) *n* (in W Africa) a Yoruba chief or ruler.

Obad. *Bible. abbrev. for* Obadiah.

Obadiah (,əʊbə'daɪə) *n Old Testament.* **1** a Hebrew prophet. **2** the book containing his oracles, chiefly directed against Edom. Douay spelling: **Abdias** (æb'daɪəs).

Oban ('əʊbᵊn) *n* a small port and resort in W Scotland, in Argyll and Bute on the Firth of Lorne. Pop.: 8203 (1991).

obb. *abbrev. for* obbligato.

obbligato *or* **obligato** (ˌɒblɪ'gɑːtəʊ) *Music.* ◆ *adj* **1** not to be omitted in performance. ◆ *n, pl* **-tos** *or* **-ti** (-tiː). **2** an essential part in a score: *with oboe obbligato.* ◆ See **ad-lib.** [C18: from Italian, from *obbligare* to OBLIGE]

obconic (ɒb'kɒnɪk) *or* **obconical** *adj Botany.* (of a fruit or similar part) shaped like a cone and attached at the pointed end.

obcordate (ɒb'kɔːdeɪt) *adj Botany.* heart-shaped and attached at the pointed end: *obcordate leaves.*

obdt *abbrev. for* obedient.

obdurate ('ɒbdjʊrɪt) *adj* **1** not easily moved by feelings or supplication; hard-hearted. **2** impervious to persuasion, esp. to moral persuasion. [C15: from Latin *obdūrāre* to make hard, from *ob-* (intensive) + *dūrus* hard; compare ENDURE] ▸ **'obduracy** *or* **'obdurateness** *n* ▸ **'obdurately** *adv*

OBE *abbrev. for* **1** Officer of the Order of the British Empire (a Brit. title). **2** out-of-the-body experience.

obeah ('əʊbɪə) *n* another word for **obi**².

obedience (ə'biːdɪəns) *n* **1** the condition or quality of being obedient. **2** the act or an instance of obeying; dutiful or submissive behaviour. **3** the authority vested in a Church or similar body. **4** the collective group of persons submitting to this authority. See also **passive obedience.**

obedient (ə'biːdɪənt) *adj* obeying or willing to obey. [C13: from Old French, from Latin *oboediens,* present participle of *oboedīre* to OBEY] ▸ **o'bediently** *adv*

obedientiary (əʊˌbiːdɪ'ɛnʃərɪ) *n, pl* **-ries.** *Christianity.* the holder of any monastic office under the superior. [C18: from Medieval Latin *obedientiarius;* see OBEDIENT, -ARY]

obeisance (əʊ'beɪsəns, əʊ'biː-) *n* **1** an attitude of deference or homage. **2** a gesture expressing obeisance. [C14: from Old French *obéissant,* present participle of *obéir* to OBEY] ▸ **o'beisant** *adj* ▸ **o'beisantly** *adv*

obelisk ('ɒbɪlɪsk) *n* **1** a stone pillar having a square or rectangular cross section and sides that taper towards a pyramidal top, often used as a monument in ancient Egypt. **2** *Printing.* another name for **dagger** (sense 2). [C16: via Latin from Greek *obeliskos* a little spit, from *obelos* spit] ▸ **ˌobe'liscal** *adj* ▸ **ˌobe'liskoid** *adj*

obelize *or* **obelise** ('ɒbɪˌlaɪz) *vb* (*tr*) to mark (a word or passage) with an obelus. [C17: from Greek *obelizein*]

obelus ('ɒbɪləs) *n, pl* **-li** (-ˌlaɪ). **1** a mark (— or ÷) used in editions of ancient documents to indicate spurious words or passages. **2** another name for **dagger** (sense 2). [C14: via Late Latin from Greek *obelos* spit]

Oberammergau (*German* oːbər'amərgau) *n* a village in S Germany, in Bavaria in the foothills of the Alps: famous for its Passion Play, performed by the villagers every ten years (except during the World Wars) since 1634, in thanksgiving for the end of the Black Death. Pop.: 4740 (1989 est.).

Oberhausen (*German* 'oːbərhauzən) *n* an industrial city in W Germany, in North Rhine-Westphalia on the Rhine-Herne Canal: site of the first ironworks in the Ruhr. Pop.: 224 397 (1996 est.).

Oberland ('əʊbəˌlænd) *n* the lower parts of the Bernese Alps in central Switzerland, mostly in S Bern canton.

Oberon¹ ('əʊbəˌrɒn) *n* (in medieval folklore) the king of the fairies, husband of Titania.

Oberon² ('əʊbəˌrɒn) *n* the outermost of the satellites of Uranus.

Oberösterreich ('oːbərˌøːstəraɪç) *n* the German name for **Upper Austria.**

obese (əʊ'biːs) *adj* excessively fat or fleshy; corpulent. [C17: from Latin *obēsus,* from *ob-* (intensive) + *edere* to eat] ▸ **o'besity** *or* **o'beseness** *n*

obey (ə'beɪ) *vb* **1** to carry out (instructions or orders); comply with (demands). **2** to behave or act in accordance with (one's feelings, whims, etc.). [C13: from Old French *obéir,* from Latin *oboedīre,* from *ob-* to, towards + *audīre* to hear] ▸ **o'beyer** *n*

obfuscate ('ɒbfʌsˌkeɪt) *vb* (*tr*) **1** to obscure or darken. **2** to perplex or bewilder. [C16: from Latin *ob-* (intensive) + *fuscāre* to blacken, from *fuscus* dark] ▸ **ˌobfus'cation** *n* ▸ **ˌobfus'catory** *adj*

obi¹ ('əʊbɪ) *n, pl* **obis** *or* **obi. 1** a broad sash tied in a large flat bow at the back, worn by Japanese women and children as part of the national costume. **2** a narrow sash worn by Japanese men. [C19: from Japanese]

obi² ('əʊbɪ) *or* **obeah** *n, pl* **obis** *or* **obeahs. 1** a kind of witchcraft originating in Africa and practised by some West Indians. **2** a charm or amulet used in this. [of West African origin; compare Edo *obi* poison] ▸ **'obiism** *n*

obit ('ɒbɪt, 'əʊbɪt) *n Informal.* **1** short for **obituary. 2** a memorial service.

obiter dictum ('ɒbɪtə 'dɪktəm, 'əʊ-) *n, pl* **obiter dicta** ('dɪktə). **1** *Law.* an observation by a judge on some point of law not directly in issue in the case before him and thus neither requiring his decision nor serving as a precedent, but nevertheless of persuasive authority. **2** any comment, remark, or observation made in passing. [Latin: something said in passing]

obituary (ə'bɪtjʊərɪ) *n, pl* **-aries.** a published announcement of a death, often accompanied by a short biography of the dead person. [C18: from Medieval Latin *obituārius,* from Latin *obīre* to fall, from *ob-* down + *īre* to go] ▸ **o'bituarist** *n*

obj. *abbrev. for:* **1** *Grammar.* object(ive). **2** objection.

object¹ ('ɒbdʒɪkt) *n* **1** a tangible and visible thing. **2** a person or thing seen as a focus or target for feelings, thought, etc.: *an object of affection.* **3** an aim, purpose, or objective. **4** *Informal.* a ridiculous or pitiable person, spectacle, etc. **5** *Philosophy.* that towards which cognition is directed, as contrasted with the thinking subject; anything regarded as external to the mind, esp. in the external world. **6** *Grammar.* a noun, pronoun, or noun phrase whose referent is the recipient of the action of a verb. See also **direct object, indirect object. 7** *Grammar.* a noun, pronoun, or noun phrase that is governed by a preposition. **8 no object.** not a hindrance or obstacle: *money is no object.* **9** *Computing.* a self-contained identifiable component of a software system or design: *object-oriented programming.* [C14: from Late Latin *objectus* something thrown before (the mind), from Latin *obicere;* see OBJECT²]

object² (əb'dʒɛkt) *vb* **1** (*tr; takes a clause as object*) to state as an objection: *he objected that his motives had been good.* **2** (*intr;* often foll. by *to*) to raise or state an objection (to); present an argument (against). [C15: from Latin *obicere,* from *ob-* against + *jacere* to throw]

object ball *n Billiards, etc.* any ball except the cue ball, esp. one which the striker aims to hit with the cue ball.

object glass *n Optics.* another name for **objective** (sense 11).

objectify (əb'dʒɛktɪˌfaɪ) *vb* **-fies, -fying, -fied.** (*tr*) to represent concretely; present as an object. ▸ **obˌjectifi'cation** *n*

objection (əb'dʒɛkʃən) *n* **1** an expression, statement, or feeling of opposition or dislike. **2** a cause for such an expression, statement, or feeling. **3** the act of objecting.

objectionable (əb'dʒɛkʃənəbᵊl) *adj* unpleasant, offensive, or repugnant. ▸ **obˌjectiona'bility** *or* **ob'jectionableness** *n* ▸ **ob'jectionably** *adv*

objective (əb'dʒɛktɪv) *adj* **1** existing independently of perception or an individual's conceptions: *are there objective moral values?* **2** undistorted by emotion or personal bias. **3** of or relating to actual and external phenomena as opposed to thoughts, feelings, etc. **4** *Med.* (of disease symptoms) perceptible to persons other than the individual affected. **5** *Grammar.* denoting a case of nouns and pronouns, esp. in languages having only two cases, that is used to identify the direct object of a finite verb or preposition and for various other purposes. In English the objective case of pronouns is also used in many elliptical constructions (as in *Poor me! Who, him?*), as the subject of a gerund (as in *It was me helping him*), informally as a predicate complement (as in *It's me*), and in nonstandard use as part of a compound subject (as in *John, Larry, and me went fishing*). See also **accusative. 6** of, or relating to a goal or aim. ◆ *n* **7** the object of one's endeavours; goal; aim. **8** Also called: **objective point.** *Military.* a place or position towards which forces are directed. **9** an actual phenomenon; reality. **10** *Grammar.* **10a** the objective case. **10b** a word or speech element in the objective case. **11** Also called: **object glass.** *Optics.* **11a** the lens or combination of lenses nearest to the object in an optical instrument. **11b** the lens or combination of lenses forming the image in a camera or projector. ◆ Abbrev.: **obj.** Compare **subjective.** ▸ **objectival** (ˌɒbdʒɛk'taɪvəl) *adj* ▸ **ob'jectively** *adv* ▸ **ˌobjec'tivity** *or* (*less commonly*) **ob'jectiveness** *n*

objective danger *n Mountaineering.* a danger, such as a stone fall or avalanche, to which climbing skill is irrelevant.

objective genitive *n Grammar.* a use of the genitive case to express an objective relationship, as in Latin *timor mortis* (fear of death).

objective point *n Military.* another term for **objective** (sense 8).

objective test *n* a test, such as one using multiple-choice questions, in which the feelings or opinions of the person marking it cannot affect the marks given.

objectivism (əb'dʒɛktɪˌvɪzəm) *n* **1** the tendency to stress what is objective. **2** *Philosophy.* **2a** the meta-ethical doctrine that there are certain moral truths that are independent of the attitudes of any individuals. **2b** the philosophical doctrine that reality is objective, and that sense data correspond with it. ▸ **ob'jectivist** *n, adj* ▸ **obˌjectiv'istic** *adj* ▸ **obˌjectiv'istically** *adv*

object language *n* a language described by or being investigated by another language. Compare **metalanguage.**

object lesson *n* **1** a convincing demonstration of some principle or ideal. **2** (esp. formerly) a lesson in which a material object forms the basis of the teaching and is available to be inspected.

object program *n* a computer program translated from the equivalent source program into machine language by the compiler or assembler.

object relations theory *n* a form of psychoanalytic theory postulating that people relate to others in order to develop themselves.

objet d'art *French.* (ɔbʒɛ dar) *n, pl* ***objets d'art*** (ɔbʒɛ dar). a small object considered to be of artistic worth. [French: object of art]

objet de vertu (ɒb'ʒeɪ də vɜː'tuː) *n, pl* **objets de vertu** (ɒb'ʒeɪ də vɜː'tuː). another name for **object of virtu:** see **virtu.** [French, coined by the British as a translation of *object of virtu* but literally meaning only "object of virtue"]

objet trouvé *French.* (ɔbʒɛ truve) *n, pl* ***objets trouvés*** (ɔbʒɛ truve). any ordinary object considered from an aesthetic viewpoint. [C20: French: found object]

objure (ɒb'dʒʊə) *vb Rare.* **1** (*tr*) to put on oath. **2** (*intr*) to swear. [C17: from Latin *objūrāre* to bind by oath] ▸ **ˌobju'ration** *n*

objurgate ('ɒbdʒəˌgeɪt) *vb* (*tr*) to scold or reprimand. [C17: from Latin *ob - jurgāre,* from *ob-* against + *jurgāre* to scold] ▸ **ˌobjur'gation** *n* ▸ **'objurˌgator** *n* ▸ **objurgatory** (ɒb'dʒɜːgətərɪ, -trɪ) *or* **ob'jurgative** *adj*

obl. *abbrev. for:* **1** oblique. **2** oblong.

oblanceolate (ɒb'lɑːnsɪəlɪt, -ˌleɪt) *adj Botany.* (esp. of leaves) having a broad rounded apex and a tapering base.

oblast ('ɒblɑːst) *n* **1** an administrative division of the constituent republics of Russia. **2** an administrative and territorial division in some republics of the former Soviet Union. [from Russian, from Old Slavonic, *vlast* government]

oblate¹ ('ɒbleɪt) *adj* having an equatorial diameter of greater length than the polar diameter: *the earth is an oblate sphere.* Compare **prolate.** [C18: from New Latin *oblātus* lengthened, from Latin *ob-* towards + *lātus,* past participle of *ferre* to bring] ▸ **'oblately** *adv*

oblate² ('ɒbleɪt) *n* a person dedicated to a monastic or religious life. [C19: from French *oblat,* from Medieval Latin *oblātus,* from Latin *offerre* to OFFER]

oblation (ɒ'bleɪʃən) *n Christianity.* **1** the offering of the bread and wine of the Eucharist to God. **2** any offering made for religious or charitable purposes. [C15: from Church Latin *oblātiō;* see OBLATE²] ▸ **oblatory** ('ɒblətərɪ, -trɪ) *or* **ob'lational** *adj*

obligate ('ɒblɪˌgeɪt) *vb* **1** to compel, constrain, or oblige morally or legally. **2**

(in the U.S.) to bind (property, funds, etc.) as security. ◆ *adj* **3** compelled, bound, or restricted. **4** *Biology.* able to exist under only one set of environmental conditions: *an obligate parasite cannot live independently of its host.* Compare **facultative** (sense 4). [C16: from Latin *obligāre* to OBLIGE] ▸ **'obligable** *adj* ▸ **ob'ligative** *adj* ▸ **'obli,gator** *n*

obligation (ˌɒblɪˈɡeɪʃən) *n* **1** a moral or legal requirement; duty. **2** the act of obligating or the state of being obligated. **3** *Law.* a legally enforceable agreement to perform some act, esp. to pay money, for the benefit of another party. **4** *Law.* **4a** a written contract containing a penalty. **4b** an instrument acknowledging indebtedness to secure the repayment of money borrowed. **5** a person or thing to which one is bound morally or legally. **6** something owed in return for a service or favour. **7** a service or favour for which one is indebted. ▸ **ˌobli'gational** *adj*

obligato (ˌɒblɪˈɡɑːtəʊ) *adj, n Music.* a variant spelling of **obbligato.**

obligatory (ɒˈblɪɡətərɪ, -trɪ) *adj* **1** required to be done, obtained, possessed, etc. **2** of the nature of or constituting an obligation. ▸ **ob'ligatorily** *adv*

oblige (əˈblaɪdʒ) *vb* **1** (*tr; often passive*) to bind or constrain (someone to do something) by legal, moral, or physical means. **2** (*tr; usually passive*) to make indebted or grateful (to someone) by doing a favour or service: *we are obliged to you for dinner.* **3** to do a service or favour to (someone): *she obliged the guest with a song.* [C13: from Old French *obliger,* from Latin *obligāre,* from *ob-* to, towards + *ligāre* to bind] ▸ **o'bliger** *n*

obligee (ˌɒblɪˈdʒiː) *n* **1** a person in whose favour an obligation, contract, or bond is created; creditor. **2** a person who receives a bond.

obligement (əˈblaɪdʒmənt) *n Now chiefly Scot.* a kind helpful action; favour.

obliging (əˈblaɪdʒɪŋ) *adj* ready to do favours; agreeable; kindly. ▸ **o'bligingly** *adv* ▸ **o'bligingness** *n*

obligor (ˌɒblɪˈɡɔː) *n* **1** a person who binds himself by contract to perform some obligation; debtor. **2** a person who gives a bond.

oblique (əˈbliːk) *adj* **1** at an angle; slanting; sloping. **2** *Geometry.* **2a** (of lines, planes, etc.) neither perpendicular nor parallel to one another or to another line, plane, etc. **2b** not related to or containing a right angle. **3** indirect or evasive. **4** *Grammar.* denoting any case of nouns, pronouns, etc., other than the nominative and vocative. **5** *Biology.* having asymmetrical sides or planes: *an oblique leaf.* **6** (of a map projection) constituting a type of zenithal projection in which the plane of projection is tangential to the earth's surface at some point between the equator and the poles. ◆ *n* **7** something oblique, esp. a line. **8** another name for **solidus** (sense 1). **9** *Navigation.* the act of changing course by less than 90°. **10** an aerial photograph taken at an oblique angle. ◆ *vb* (*intr*) **11** to take or have an oblique direction. **12** (of a military formation) to move forward at an angle. [C15: from Old French, from Latin *oblīquus,* of obscure origin] ▸ **o'bliquely** *adv* ▸ **o'bliqueness** *n*

oblique angle *n* an angle that is not a right angle or any multiple of a right angle.

oblique fault *n* a fault that runs obliquely to, rather than parallel to or perpendicular to, the strike of the affected rocks.

oblique sailing *n* a ship's movement on a course that is not due north, south, east, or west.

oblique-slip fault *n* a fault on which the movement is along both the strike and the dip of the fault.

obliquity (əˈblɪkwɪtɪ) *n, pl* **-ties. 1** the state or condition of being oblique. **2** a deviation from the perpendicular or horizontal. **3** a moral or mental deviation. **4** Also called: **obliquity of the ecliptic.** *Astronomy.* the angle between the plane of the earth's orbit and that of the celestial equator, equal to approximately 23° 27′ at present. ▸ **o'bliquitous** *adj*

obliterate (əˈblɪtəˌreɪt) *vb* (*tr*) to destroy every trace of; wipe out completely. [C16: from Latin *oblitterāre* to erase, from *ob-* out + *littera* letter] ▸ **oˌblite'ration** *n* ▸ **o'bliterative** *adj* ▸ **o'bliterˌator** *n*

oblivion (əˈblɪvɪən) *n* **1** the condition of being forgotten or disregarded. **2** the state of being mentally withdrawn or blank. **3** *Law.* an intentional overlooking, esp. of political offences; amnesty; pardon. [C14: via Old French from Latin *oblīviō* forgetfulness, from *oblīviscī* to forget]

oblivious (əˈblɪvɪəs) *adj* (foll. by *to* or *of*) unaware or forgetful. ▸ **ob'liviously** *adv* ▸ **ob'liviousness** *n*

USAGE It was formerly considered incorrect to use *oblivious* to mean *unaware,* but this use is now acceptable.

oblong (ˈɒbˌlɒŋ) *adj* **1** having an elongated, esp. rectangular, shape. ◆ *n* **2** a figure or object having this shape. [C15: from Latin *oblongus,* from *ob-* (intensive) + *longus* LONG¹]

obloquy (ˈɒbləkwɪ) *n, pl* **-quies. 1** defamatory or censorious statements, esp. when directed against one person. **2** disgrace brought about by public abuse. [C15: from Latin *obloquium* contradiction, from *ob-* against + *loquī* to speak]

obmutescence (ˌɒbmjuːˈtɛsəns) *n Archaic.* persistent silence. [C17: from Latin *obmūtescere* to become mute] ▸ **ˌobmu'tescent** *adj*

obnoxious (əbˈnɒkʃəs) *adj* **1** extremely unpleasant. **2** *Obsolete.* exposed to harm, injury, etc. [C16: from Latin *obnoxius,* from *ob-* to + *noxa* injury, from *nocēre* to harm] ▸ **ob'noxiously** *adv* ▸ **ob'noxiousness** *n*

obnubilate (ɒbˈnjuːbɪˌleɪt) *vb* (*tr*) *Literary.* to darken or obscure. [C16: ultimately from Latin *obnūbilāre* to cover with clouds, from *nubes* cloud]

oboe (ˈəʊbəʊ) *n* **1** a woodwind instrument of the family that includes the bassoon and cor anglais, consisting of a conical tube fitted with a mouthpiece having a double reed. It has a penetrating nasal tone. Range: about two octaves plus a sixth upwards from B flat below middle C. **2** a person who plays this instrument in an orchestra: *second oboe.* ◆ Archaic form: **hautboy.** [C18: via Italian *oboe,* phonetic approximation to French *haut bois,* literally: high wood (referring to its pitch)] ▸ **'oboist** *n*

oboe da caccia (də ˈkætʃə) *n* a member of the oboe family; the predecessor of the cor anglais. [Italian: hunting oboe]

oboe d'amore (dɑːˈmɔːreɪ) *n* a type of oboe pitched a minor third lower than the oboe itself. It is used chiefly in the performance of baroque music.

obolus (ˈɒbələs) *or* **obol** (ˈɒbɒl) *n, pl* **-li** (-ˌlaɪ) *or* **-ols. 1** a modern Greek unit of weight equal to one tenth of a gram. **2** a silver coin of ancient Greece worth one sixth of a drachma. [C16: via Latin from Greek *obolos* small coin, nail; related to *obelos* spit, variant of OBELUS]

Obote (ɒˈbəʊteɪ, -tɪ) *n* (**Apollo**) **Milton.** born 1924, Ugandan politician; prime minister of Uganda (1962–66) and president (1966–71; 1980–85). He was deposed by Amin in 1971 and remained in exile until 1980; deposed again in 1985 by the Acholi army.

obovate (ɒbˈəʊveɪt) *adj* (of a leaf or similar flat part) shaped like the longitudinal section of an egg with the narrower end at the base; inversely ovate.

obovoid (ɒbˈəʊvɔɪd) *adj* (of a fruit or similar solid part) egg-shaped with the narrower end at the base. Compare **ovoid** (sense 2).

obreption (ɒˈbrɛpʃən) *n Now rare.* the obtaining of something, such as a gift, in Scots Law esp. a grant from the Crown, by giving false information. Compare **subreption** (sense 1). [C17: from Latin *obreptio,* from *obrepere* to creep up to]

O'Brien (əˈbraɪən) *n* **1 Conor Cruise.** born 1917, Irish diplomat and writer. As an Irish Labour MP he served in the coalition government of 1973–77, becoming a senator (1977–79). He edited the *Observer* (1978–81). **2 Edna.** born 1936, Irish novelist. Her books include *The Country Girls* (1960), *House of Splendid Isolation* (1994), and *Down by the River* (1997). She has also written plays, film scripts, and short stories. **3 Flann,** real name *Brian O'Nolan.* 1911–66, Irish novelist and journalist. His novels include *At Swim-Two-Birds* (1939) and the posthumously published *The Third Policeman* (1967). As Myles na Gopaleen he wrote a satirical column for the *Irish Times.*

obs. *abbrev. for:* **1** obscure. **2** observation. **3** Also: **Obs.** observatory. **4** obsolete.

obscene (əbˈsiːn) *adj* **1** offensive or outrageous to accepted standards of decency or modesty. **2** *Law.* (of publications) having a tendency to deprave or corrupt. **3** disgusting; repellent: *an obscene massacre.* [C16: from Latin *obscēnus* inauspicious, perhaps related to *caenum* filth] ▸ **ob'scenely** *adv*

obscenity (əbˈsɛnɪtɪ) *n, pl* **-ties. 1** the state or quality of being obscene. **2** an obscene act, statement, work, etc.

obscurant (əbˈskjʊərənt) *n* **1** an opposer of reform and enlightenment. ◆ *adj* **2** of or relating to an obscurant. **3** causing obscurity. ▸ **ˌobscu'rantism** *n* ▸ **ˌobscu'rantist** *n, adj*

obscure (əbˈskjʊə) *adj* **1** unclear or abstruse. **2** indistinct, vague, or indefinite. **3** inconspicuous or unimportant. **4** hidden, secret, or remote. **5** (of a vowel) reduced to or transformed into a neutral vowel (ə). **6** gloomy, dark, clouded, or dim. ◆ *vb* (*tr*) **7** to make unclear, vague, or hidden. **8** to cover or cloud over. **9** *Phonetics.* to pronounce (a vowel) with articulation that causes it to become a neutral sound represented by (ə). ◆ *n* **10** a rare word for **obscurity.** [C14: via Old French from Latin *obscūrus* dark] ▸ **obscuration** (ˌɒbskjʊˈreɪʃən) *n* ▸ **ob'scurely** *adv* ▸ **ob'scureness** *n*

obscurity (əbˈskjʊərɪtɪ) *n, pl* **-ties. 1** the state or quality of being obscure. **2** an obscure person or thing.

obscurum per obscurius (əbˈskjʊərəm pɜː əbˈskjʊərɪəs) *n* another term for **ignotum per ignotius.** [Latin: the obscure by the more obscure]

obsecrate (ˈɒbsɪˌkreɪt) *vb* (*tr*) a rare word for **beseech.** [C16: from Latin *obsecrāre* to entreat (in the name of the gods), from *ob-* for the sake of + *sacrāre*to hold in reverence; see SACRED] ▸ **ˌobse'cration** *n*

obsequent (ˈɒbsɪkwənt) *adj* (of a river) flowing into a subsequent stream in the opposite direction to the original slope of the land. [C16 (in the obsolete sense: yielding): from Latin *obsequī,* from *sequī* to follow]

obsequies (ˈɒbsɪkwɪz) *pl n, sing* **-quy.** funeral rites. [C14: via Anglo-Norman from Medieval Latin *obsequiae* (influenced by Latin *exsequiae*), from *obsequium* compliance] ▸ **obsequial** (ɒbˈsiːkwɪəl) *adj*

obsequious (əbˈsiːkwɪəs) *adj* **1** obedient or attentive in an ingratiating or servile manner. **2** *Now rare.* submissive or compliant. [C15: from Latin *obsequiōsus* compliant, from *obsequium* compliance, from *obsequi* to follow, from *ob-* to + *sequi* to follow] ▸ **ob'sequiously** *adv* ▸ **ob'sequiousness** *n*

observance (əbˈzɜːvəns) *n* **1** recognition of or compliance with a law, custom, practice, etc. **2** the act of such recognition. **3** a ritual, ceremony, or practice, esp. of a religion. **4** observation or attention. **5** the degree of strictness of a religious order or community in following its rule. **6** *Archaic.* respectful or deferential attention.

observant (əbˈzɜːvənt) *adj* **1** paying close attention to detail; watchful or heedful. **2** adhering strictly to rituals, ceremonies, laws, etc. ▸ **ob'servantly** *adv*

observation (ˌɒbzəˈveɪʃən) *n* **1** the act of observing or the state of being observed. **2** a comment or remark. **3** detailed examination of phenomena prior to analysis, diagnosis, or interpretation: *the patient was under observation.* **4** the facts learned from observing. **5** an obsolete word for **observance. 6** *Navigation.* **6a** a sight taken with an instrument to determine the position of an observer relative to that of a given heavenly body. **6b** the data so taken. ▸ **ˌobser'vational** *adj* ▸ **ˌobser'vationally** *adv*

observation car *n* a railway carriage fitted with large expanses of glass to provide a good view of the scenery.

observation post *n Military.* a position from which observations can be made or from which fire can be directed.

observatory (əbˈzɜːvətərɪ, -trɪ) *n, pl* **-ries. 1** an institution or building specially designed and equipped for observing meteorological and astronomical phenomena. **2** any building or structure providing an extensive view of its surroundings.

observe (əbˈzɜːv) *vb* **1** (*tr; may take a clause as object*) to see; perceive; notice: *we have observed that you steal.* **2** (when *tr, may take a clause as object*) to watch (something) carefully; pay attention to (something). **3** to make observations of (something), esp. scientific ones. **4** (when *intr,* usually foll. by *on* or *upon;* when *tr, may take a clause as object*) to make a comment or remark: *the speaker observed that times had changed.* **5** (*tr*) to abide by, keep, or follow (a custom, tradition, law, holiday, etc.). [C14: via Old French from Latin *ob - servāre,* from *ob-* to + *servāre* to watch] ▸ **ob'servable** *adj* ▸ **ob'servableness** *or* **ob,serva'bility** *n* ▸ **ob'servably** *adv*

observer (əb'zɜːvə) *n* **1** a person or thing that observes. **2** a person who attends a conference solely to note the proceedings. **3** a person trained to identify aircraft, esp., formerly, a member of an aircrew.

obsess (əb'sɛs) *vb* **1** (*tr;* when passive, foll. by *with* or *by*) to preoccupy completely; haunt. **2** (*intr,* usually foll. by *on* or *over*) to brood obsessively. [C16: from Latin *obsessus* besieged, past participle of *obsidēre,* from *ob-* in front of + *sedēre* to sit] ▸ **ob'sessive** *adj, n* ▸ **ob'sessively** *adv* ▸ **ob'sessiveness** *n*

obsession (əb'sɛʃən) *n* **1** *Psychiatry.* a persistent idea or impulse that continually forces its way into consciousness, often associated with anxiety and mental illness. **2** a persistent preoccupation, idea, or feeling. **3** the act of obsessing or the state of being obsessed. ▸ **ob'sessional** *adj* ▸ **ob'sessionally** *adv*

obsessive-compulsive disorder *n Psychiatry.* an anxiety disorder in which patients are driven to repeat the same act, such as washing their hands, over and over again, usually for many hours. Abbrev.: **OCD.**

obsidian (ɒb'sɪdɪən) *n* a dark glassy volcanic rock formed by very rapid solidification of lava. Also called: **Iceland agate.** [C17: from Latin *obsidiānus,* erroneous transcription of *obsiānus* (*lapis*) (stone of) *Obsius,* the name (in Pliny) of the discoverer of a stone resembling obsidian]

obsolesce (,ɒbsə'lɛs) *vb* (*intr*) to become obsolete.

obsolescent (,ɒbsə'lɛsᵊnt) *adj* becoming obsolete or out of date. [C18: from Latin *obsolescere;* see OBSOLETE] ▸ **,obso'lescence** *n* ▸ **,obso'lescently** *adv*

obsolete ('ɒbsə,liːt, ,ɒbsə'liːt) *adj* **1** out of use or practice; not current. **2** out of date; unfashionable or outmoded. **3** *Biology.* (of parts, organs, etc.) vestigial; rudimentary. [C16: from Latin *obsolētus* worn out, past participle of *obsolēre* (unattested), from *ob-* opposite to + *solēre* to be used] ▸ **'obso,letely** *adv* ▸ **'obso,leteness** *n*

USAGE The word *obsoleteness* is hardly ever used, *obsolescence* standing as the noun form for both *obsolete* and *obsolescent.*

obstacle ('ɒbstəkᵊl) *n* **1** a person or thing that opposes or hinders something. **2** *Brit.* a fence or hedge used in showjumping. [C14: via Old French from Latin *obstāculum,* from *obstāre,* from *ob-* against + *stāre* to stand]

obstacle race *n* a race in which competitors have to negotiate various obstacles.

obstet. *abbrev. for* obstetric(s).

obstetric (ɒb'stɛtrɪk) *or* **obstetrical** *adj* of or relating to childbirth or obstetrics. [C18: via New Latin from Latin *obstetrīcius,* from *obstetrix* a midwife, literally: woman who stands opposite, from *obstāre* to stand in front of; see OBSTACLE] ▸ **ob'stetrically** *adv*

obstetrician (,ɒbstɛ'trɪʃən) *n* a physician who specializes in obstetrics.

obstetrics (ɒb'stɛtrɪks) *n* (*functioning as sing*) the branch of medicine concerned with childbirth and the treatment of women before and after childbirth.

obstinacy ('ɒbstɪnəsɪ) *n, pl* **-cies. 1** the state or quality of being obstinate. **2** an obstinate act, attitude, etc.

obstinate ('ɒbstɪnɪt) *adj* **1** adhering fixedly to a particular opinion, attitude, course of action, etc. **2** self-willed or headstrong. **3** difficult to subdue or alleviate; persistent: *an obstinate fever.* [C14: from Latin *obstinātus,* past participle of *obstināre* to persist in, from *ob-* (intensive) + *stin-,* variant of *stare* to stand] ▸ **'obstinately** *adv*

obstipation (,ɒbstɪ'peɪʃən) *n Pathol.* a severe form of constipation, usually resulting from obstruction of the intestinal tract. [C16: from Latin *obstīpātiō,* from *ob-* (intensive) + *stīpāre* to press together]

obstreperous (əb'strɛpərəs) *adj* noisy or rough, esp. in resisting restraint or control. [C16: from Latin, from *obstrepere,* from *ob-* against + *strepere* to roar] ▸ **ob'streperously** *adv* ▸ **ob'streperousness** *n*

obstruct (əb'strʌkt) *vb* (*tr*) **1** to block (a road, passageway, etc.) with an obstacle. **2** to make (progress or activity) difficult. **3** to impede or block a clear view of. [C17: Latin *obstructus* built against, past participle of *obstruere,* from *ob-* against + *struere* to build] ▸ **ob'structor** *n* ▸ **ob'structive** *adj, n* ▸ **ob'structively** *adv* ▸ **ob'structiveness** *n*

obstruction (əb'strʌkʃən) *n* **1** a person or thing that obstructs. **2** the act or an instance of obstructing. **3** delay of business, esp. in a legislature by means of procedural devices. **4** *Sport.* the act of unfairly impeding an opposing player. **5** the state or condition of being obstructed. ▸ **ob'structional** *adj* ▸ **ob'structionally** *adv*

obstructionist (əb'strʌkʃənɪst) *n* **a** a person who deliberately obstructs business, esp. in a legislature. **b** (*as modifier*): *obstructionist tactics.* ▸ **ob'structionism** *n*

obstruent ('ɒbstrʊənt) *Med.* ◆ *adj* **1** causing obstruction, esp. of the intestinal tract. ◆ *n* **2** anything that causes obstruction. [C17: from Latin *obstruere* to OBSTRUCT]

obtain (əb'teɪn) *vb* **1** (*tr*) to gain possession of; acquire; get. **2** (*intr*) to be customary, valid, or accepted: *a new law obtains in this case.* **3** (*tr*) *Archaic.* to arrive at. **4** (*intr*) *Archaic.* to win a victory; succeed. [C15: via Old French from Latin *obtinēre* to take hold of, from *ob-* (intensive) + *tenēre* to hold] ▸ **ob'tainable** *adj* ▸ **ob,taina'bility** *n* ▸ **ob'tainer** *n* ▸ **ob'tainment** *n*

obtaining by deception *n Law.* the offence of dishonestly obtaining the property of another by some deception or misrepresentation of facts.

obtect (ɒb'tɛkt) *adj* (of a pupa) encased in a hardened secretion so that the wings, legs, etc., are held immovably to the body, as in butterflies. Also: **ob'tected.** [C19: from Latin *obtectus* covered, past participle of *obtegere,* from *ob-* (intensive) + *tegere* to cover]

obtemper (ɒb'tɛmpə) *vb Scots Law.* to comply (with). [C15: from Latin *obtemperāre* to obey, from *ob-* towards + *temperāre* to temper]

obtest (ɒb'tɛst) *vb Rare.* **1** (*tr; may take a clause as object or an infinitive*) to beg (someone) earnestly. **2** (when *tr, takes a clause as object;* when *intr,* may be foll. by *with* or *against*) to object; protest. **3** (*tr*) to call (a supernatural power) to witness. [C16: from Latin *obtestārī* to protest, from *ob-* to + *testārī* to bear or call as witness] ▸ **,obtes'tation** *n*

obtrude (əb'truːd) *vb* **1** to push (oneself, one's opinions, etc.) on others in an unwelcome way. **2** (*tr*) to push out or forward. [C16: from Latin *obtrūdere,* from *ob-* against + *trūdere* to push forward] ▸ **ob'truder** *n* ▸ **obtrusion** (əb'truːʒən) *n*

obtrusive (əb'truːsɪv) *adj* **1** obtruding or tending to obtrude. **2** sticking out; protruding; noticeable. ▸ **ob'trusively** *adv* ▸ **ob'trusiveness** *n*

obtund (ɒb'tʌnd) *vb* (*tr*) *Rare.* to deaden or dull. [C14: from Latin *obtundere* to beat against, from *ob-* against + *tundere* to belabour] ▸ **ob'tundent** *adj, n*

obturate ('ɒbtjʊə,reɪt) *vb* (*tr*) to stop up (an opening, esp. the breech of a gun). [C17: from Latin *obtūrāre* to block up, of obscure origin] ▸ **,obtu'ration** *n* ▸ **'obtu,rator** *n*

obtuse (əb'tjuːs) *adj* **1** mentally slow or emotionally insensitive. **2** *Maths.* **2a** (of an angle) lying between 90° and 180°. **2b** (of a triangle) having one interior angle greater than 90°. **3** not sharp or pointed. **4** indistinctly felt, heard, etc.; dull: *obtuse pain.* **5** (of a leaf or similar flat part) having a rounded or blunt tip. [C16: from Latin *obtūsus* dulled, past participle of *obtundere* to beat down; see OBTUND] ▸ **ob'tusely** *adv* ▸ **ob'tuseness** *n*

obverse ('ɒbvɜːs) *adj* **1** facing or turned towards the observer. **2** forming or serving as a counterpart. **3** (of certain plant leaves) narrower at the base than at the top. ◆ *n* **4** a counterpart or complement. **5** the side of a coin that bears the main design or device. Compare **reverse** (sense 15). **6** *Logic.* a categorial proposition derived from another by replacing the original predicate by its negation and changing the proposition from affirmative to negative or vice versa, as *no sum is correct* from *every sum is incorrect.* [C17: from Latin *obversus* turned towards, past participle of *obvertere,* from *ob-* to + *vertere* to turn] ▸ **ob'versely** *adv*

obvert (ɒb'vɜːt) *vb* (*tr*) **1** *Logic.* to deduce the obverse of (a proposition). **2** *Rare.* to turn so as to show the main or other side. [C17: from Latin *obvertere* to turn towards; see OBVERSE] ▸ **ob'version** *n*

obviate ('ɒbvɪ,eɪt) *vb* (*tr*) to do away with or counter. [C16: from Late Latin *obviātus* prevented, past participle of *obviāre;* see OBVIOUS] ▸ **,obvi'ation** *n*

USAGE Only things which have not yet occurred can be *obviated.* For example, one can *obviate* a possible future difficulty, but not one which already exists.

obvious ('ɒbvɪəs) *adj* **1** easy to see or understand; evident. **2** exhibiting motives, feelings, intentions, etc., clearly or without subtlety. **3** naive or unsubtle: *the play was rather obvious.* **4** *Obsolete.* being or standing in the way. [C16: from Latin *obvius,* from *obviam* in the way, from *ob-* against + *via* way] ▸ **'obviously** *adv* ▸ **'obviousness** *n*

obvolute ('ɒbvə,luːt) *adj* **1** (of leaves or petals in the bud) folded so that the margins overlap each other. **2** turned in or rolled. [C18: from Latin *obvolūtus* past participle of *obvolvere,* from *ob-* to, over + *volvere* to roll] ▸ **,obvo'lution** *n* ▸ **'obvo,lutive** *adj*

OC *abbrev. for* Officer Commanding.

Oc. *abbrev. for* Ocean.

o/c *abbrev. for* overcharge.

oca ('əʊkə) *n* any of various South American herbaceous plants of the genus *Oxalis,* cultivated for their edible tubers: family *Oxalidaceae.* [C20: via Spanish from Quechua *okka*]

OCAM *abbrev. for* Organisation commune africaine et malgache: an association of the 14 principal Francophone states of Africa, established in 1965 to further political cooperation and economic and social development.

ocarina (,ɒkə'riːnə) *n* an egg-shaped wind instrument with a protruding mouthpiece and six to eight finger holes, producing an almost pure tone. Also called (U.S. informal): **sweet potato.** [C19: from Italian: little goose, from *oca* goose, ultimately from Latin *avis* bird]

O'Casey (əʊ'keɪsɪ) *n* **Sean** (ʃɔːn). 1880–1964, Irish dramatist. His plays include *Juno and the Paycock* (1924) and *The Plough and the Stars* (1926), which are realistic pictures of Dublin slum life.

Occam ('ɒkəm) *n* a variant spelling of (William of) **Ockham.**

Occam's razor *n* a variant spelling of **Ockham's razor.**

occas. *abbrev. for* occasional(ly).

occasion (ə'keɪʒən) *n* **1** (sometimes foll. by *of*) the time of a particular happening or event. **2** (sometimes foll. by *for*) a reason or cause (to do or be something); grounds: *there was no occasion to complain.* **3** an opportunity (to do something); chance. **4** a special event, time, or celebration: *the party was quite an occasion.* **5 on occasion.** every so often. **6 rise to the occasion.** to have the courage, wit, etc., to meet the special demands of a situation. **7 take occasion.** to avail oneself of an opportunity (to do something). ◆ *vb* **8** (*tr*) to bring about, esp. incidentally or by chance. ◆ See also **occasions.** [C14: from Latin *occāsiō* a falling down, from *occidere,* from *ob-* down + *cadere* to fall]

occasional (ə'keɪʒənᵊl) *adj* **1** taking place from time to time; not frequent or regular. **2** of, for, or happening on special occasions. **3** serving as an occasion (for something).

occasionalism (ə'keɪʒənə,lɪzəm) *n* the post-Cartesian theory that the seeming interconnection of mind and matter is effected by God.

occasional licence *n Brit.* a licence granted to sell alcohol only at specified times.

occasionally (ə'keɪʒənəlɪ) *adv* from time to time.

occasional table *n* a small table with no regular use.

occasions (ə'keɪʒənz) *pl n Archaic.* **1** (*sometimes sing*) needs; necessities. **2** personal or business affairs.

occident ('ɒksɪdənt) *n* a literary or formal word for **west.** Compare **orient.**

[C14: via Old French from Latin *occidere* to fall, go down (with reference to the setting sun); see OCCASION]

Occident ('ɒksɪdənt) *n* (usually preceded by *the*) **1** the countries of Europe and America. **2** the western hemisphere.

occidental (ˌɒksɪ'dɛntᵊl) *adj* a literary or formal word for **western**. Compare **oriental**.

Occidental (ˌɒksɪ'dɛntᵊl) (*sometimes not cap.*) ◆ *adj* **1** of or relating to the Occident. ◆ *n* **2** an inhabitant, esp. a native, of the Occident. ▸ **ˌOcci'dentalism** *n* ▸ **ˌOcci'dentalist** *n, adj* ▸ **ˌOcci'dentally** *adv*

Occidentalize *or* **Occidentalise** (ˌɒksɪ'dɛntəˌlaɪz) *vb* to make or become Occidental. ▸ **ˌOcciˌdentali'zation** *or* **ˌOcciˌdentali'sation** *n*

occipital (ɒk'sɪpɪtᵊl) *adj* **1** of or relating to the back of the head or skull. ◆ *n* **2** short for **occipital bone.**

occipital bone *n* the saucer-shaped bone that forms the back part of the skull and part of its base.

occipital lobe *n* the posterior portion of each cerebral hemisphere, concerned with the interpretation of visual sensory impulses.

occiput ('ɒksɪˌpʌt, -pət) *n, pl* **occiputs** *or* **occipita** (ɒk'sɪpɪtə). the back part of the head or skull. [C14: from Latin, from *ob-* at the back of + *caput* head]

occlude (ə'klu:d) *vb* **1** (*tr*) to block or stop up (a passage or opening); obstruct. **2** (*tr*) to prevent the passage of. **3** (*tr*) *Chem.* (of a solid) to incorporate (a substance) by absorption or adsorption. **4** *Meteorol.* to form or cause to form an occluded front. **5** *Dentistry.* to produce or cause to produce occlusion, as in chewing. [C16: from Latin *occlūdere,* from *ob-* (intensive) + *claudere* to close] ▸ **oc'cludent** *adj*

occluded front *n Meteorol.* the line or plane occurring where the cold front of a depression has overtaken the warm front, raising the warm sector from ground level. Also called: **occlusion.**

occlusion (ə'klu:ʒən) *n* **1** the act or process of occluding or the state of being occluded. **2** *Meteorol.* another term for **occluded front. 3** *Dentistry.* the normal position of the teeth when the jaws are closed. **4** *Phonetics.* the complete closure of the vocal tract at some point, as in the closure prior to the articulation of a plosive. ▸ **occlusal** (ə'klu:səl) *adj*

occlusive (ə'klu:sɪv) *adj* **1** of or relating to the act of occlusion. ◆ *n* **2** *Phonetics.* an occlusive speech sound. ▸ **oc'clusiveness** *n*

occult *adj* (ɒ'kʌlt, 'ɒkʌlt). **1a** of or characteristic of magical, mystical, or supernatural arts, phenomena, or influences. **1b** (*as n*): *the occult.* **2** beyond ordinary human understanding. **3** secret or esoteric. ◆ *vb* (ɒ'kʌlt). **4** *Astronomy.* (of a celestial body) to hide (another celestial body) from view by occultation or (of a celestial body) to become hidden by occultation. **5** to hide or become hidden or shut off from view. **6** (*intr*) (of lights, esp. in lighthouses) to shut off at regular intervals. [C16: from Latin *occultus,* past participle of *occulere,* from *ob-* over, up + *-culere,* related to *celāre* to conceal] ▸ **oc'cultly** *adv* ▸ **oc'cultness** *n*

occultation (ˌɒkʌl'teɪʃən) *n* **1** the temporary disappearance of one celestial body as it moves out of sight behind another body. **2** the act of occulting or the state of being occulted.

occultism ('ɒkʌlˌtɪzəm) *n* belief in and the study and practice of magic, astrology, etc. ▸ **'occultist** *n, adj*

occupancy ('ɒkjupənsɪ) *n, pl* **-cies. 1** the act of occupying; possession of a property. **2** *Law.* the possession and use of property by or without agreement and without any claim to ownership. **3** *Law.* the act of taking possession of unowned property, esp. land, with the intent of thus acquiring ownership. **4** the condition or fact of being an occupant, esp. a tenant. **5** the period of time during which one is an occupant, esp. of property.

occupant ('ɒkjupənt) *n* **1** a person, thing, etc., holding a position or place. **2** *Law.* a person who has possession of something, esp. an estate, house, etc.; tenant. **3** *Law.* a person who acquires by occupancy the title to something previously without an owner.

occupation (ˌɒkju'peɪʃən) *n* **1** a person's regular work or profession; job or principal activity. **2** any activity on which time is spent by a person. **3** the act of occupying or the state of being occupied. **4** the control of a country by a foreign military power. **5** the period of time that a nation, place, or position is occupied. **6** (*modifier*) for the use of the occupier of a particular property: *occupation road; occupation bridge.*

occupational (ˌɒkju'peɪʃənᵊl) *adj* of, relating to, or caused by an occupation: *an occupational pension scheme; an occupational disease.* ▸ **ˌoccu'pationally** *adv*

occupational pension *n* a pension derived from a private pension scheme organized by the employer or employers for whom the recipient used to work: distinguished from a state pension financed from national insurance.

occupational pension scheme *n* a pension scheme provided for the members of a particular occupation or employed by a specific employer or group of employers.

occupational psychology *n Psychol.* the study of human behaviour at work, including ergonomics, selection procedures, and the effects of stress.

occupational therapy *n Med.* treatment of people with physical, emotional, or social problems, using purposeful activity to help them overcome or learn to deal with their problems. ▸ **occupational therapist** *n*

occupation franchise *n Brit.* the right of a tenant to vote in national and local elections.

occupation groupings *pl n* a system of classifying people according to occupation, based originally on information obtained by government census and subsequently developed by market research. The classifications are used by the advertising industry to identify potential markets. The groups are **A, B, C1, C2, D,** and **E.**

occupier ('ɒkjuˌpaɪə) *n* **1** *Brit.* a person who is in possession or occupation of a house or land. **2** a person or thing that occupies.

occupy ('ɒkjuˌpaɪ) *vb* **-pies, -pying, -pied.** (*tr*) **1** to live or be established in (a house, flat, office, etc.). **2** (*often passive*) to keep (a person) busy or engrossed; engage the attention of. **3** (*often passive*) to take up (a certain amount of time or space). **4** to take and hold possession of, esp. as a demonstration: *students occupied the college buildings.* **5** to fill or hold (a position or rank). [C14: from Old French *occuper,* from Latin *occupāre* to seize hold of, from *ob-* (intensive) + *capere* to take]

occur (ə'kɜ:) *vb* **-curs, -curring, -curred.** (*intr*) **1** to happen; take place; come about. **2** to be found or be present; exist. **3** (foll. by *to*) to be realized or thought of (by); suggest itself (to). [C16: from Latin *occurrere* to run up to, from *ob-* to + *currere* to run]

USAGE It is usually regarded as incorrect to talk of pre-arranged events *occurring* or *happening: the wedding took place* (not *occurred* or *happened*) *in the afternoon.*

occurrence (ə'kʌrəns) *n* **1** something that occurs; a happening; event. **2** the act or an instance of occurring: *a crime of frequent occurrence.*

occurrent (ə'kʌrənt) *adj Philosophy.* (of a property) relating to some observable feature of its bearer. Compare **disposition** (sense 4).

OCD *abbrev. for* obsessive-compulsive disorder.

ocean ('əuʃən) *n* **1** a very large stretch of sea, esp. one of the five oceans of the world, the Atlantic, Pacific, Indian, Arctic, and Antarctic. **2** the body of salt water covering approximately 70 per cent of the earth's surface. **3** a huge quantity or expanse: *an ocean of replies.* **4** *Literary.* the sea. [C13: via Old French from Latin *ōceanus,* from Greek *ōkeanos* OCEANUS]

oceanarium (ˌəuʃə'nɛərɪəm) *n, pl* **-iums** *or* **-ia** (-ɪə). a large saltwater aquarium for marine life.

ocean floor spreading *n* another term for **seafloor spreading.**

ocean-going *adj* (of a ship, boat, etc.) suited for travel on the open ocean.

ocean greyhound *n* a fast ship, esp. a liner.

Oceania (ˌəuʃɪ'ɑ:nɪə) *n* the islands of the central and S Pacific, including Melanesia, Micronesia, and Polynesia: sometimes also including Australasia and the Malay Archipelago. ▸ **ˌOce'anian** *adj, n*

oceanic (ˌəuʃɪ'ænɪk) *adj* **1** of or relating to the ocean. **2** living in the depths of the ocean beyond the continental shelf at a depth exceeding 200 metres: *oceanic fauna.* **3** huge or overwhelming. **4** (of geological formations) of volcanic origin, arising from the ocean: *oceanic islands.*

Oceanic (ˌəuʃɪ'ænɪk) *n* **1** a branch, group, or subfamily of the Malayo-Polynesian family of languages, comprising Polynesian and Melanesian. ◆ *adj* **2** of, relating to, or belonging to this group of languages. **3** of or relating to Oceania.

oceanic ridge *n* any section of the narrow, largely continuous range of submarine mountains that extends into all the major oceans and at which new oceanic lithosphere is created by the rise of magma from the earth's interior. See also **seafloor spreading.**

oceanic trench *n* a long narrow steep-sided depression in the earth's oceanic crust, usually lying above a Benioff zone.

Oceanid (əu'sɪənɪd) *n, pl* **Oceanids** *or* **Oceanides** (ˌəusɪ'ænɪˌdi:z). *Greek myth.* any of the ocean nymphs born of Oceanus and Tethys.

Ocean of Storms *n* the largest of the dark plains (maria) on the surface of the moon, situated in the second and third quadrant. Also called: **Oceanus Procellarum** (ˌəuʃɪ'ænəs ˌprəusɛ'lærəm).

oceanog. *abbrev. for* oceanography.

oceanography (ˌəuʃə'nɒgrəfɪ, ˌəuʃɪə-) *n* the branch of science dealing with the physical, chemical, geological, and biological features of the oceans and ocean basins. ▸ **ˌocean'ographer** *n* ▸ **oceanographic** (ˌəuʃənə'græfɪk, ˌəuʃɪə-) *or* **ˌoceano'graphical** *adj* ▸ **ˌoceano'graphically** *adv*

oceanology (ˌəuʃə'nɒlədʒɪ, ˌəuʃɪə-) *n* the study of the sea, esp. of its economic geography.

Oceanus (əu'sɪənəs) *n Greek myth.* a Titan, divinity of the stream believed to flow around the earth.

ocellus (ɒ'sɛləs) *n, pl* **-li** (-laɪ). **1** the simple eye of insects and some other invertebrates, consisting basically of light-sensitive cells. **2** any eyelike marking in animals, such as the eyespot on the tail feather of a peacock. **3** *Botany.* **3a** an enlarged discoloured cell in a leaf. **3b** a swelling on the sporangium of certain fungi. [C19: via New Latin from Latin: small eye, from *oculus* eye] ▸ **o'cellar** *adj* ▸ **ocellate** ('ɒsɪˌleɪt) *or* **ocellated** ('ɒsɪˌleɪtɪd) *adj* ▸ **ˌocel'lation** *n*

ocelot ('ɒsɪˌlɒt, 'əu-) *n* a feline mammal, *Felis pardalis,* inhabiting the forests of Central and South America and having a dark-spotted buff-brown coat. [C18: via French from Nahuatl *ocelotl* jaguar]

och (ɒx) *Scot. and Irish.* ◆ *interj* **1** an expression of surprise, contempt, annoyance, impatience, or disagreement. ◆ *sentence connector.* **2** an expression used to preface a remark, gain time, etc.: *och, I suppose so.* ◆ Also: **ach.**

oche ('ɒkɪ) *n Darts.* the mark or ridge on the floor behind which a player must stand to throw. [of unknown origin; perhaps connected with obsolete *oche* to chop off, from Old French *ocher* to cut a notch in]

ocher ('əukə) *n, adj, vb* the U.S. spelling of **ochre.** ▸ **'ocherous** *or* **'ochery** *adj* ▸ **ochroid** ('əukrɔɪd) *adj*

ochlocracy (ɒk'lɒkrəsɪ) *n, pl* **-cies.** rule by the mob; mobocracy. [C16: via French, from Greek *okhlokratia,* from *okhlos* mob + *kratos* power] ▸ **ochlocrat** ('ɒkləˌkræt) *n* ▸ **ˌochlo'cratic** *adj*

ochlophobia (ˌɒklə'fəubɪə) *n Psychol.* the fear of crowds. [C19: from New Latin, from Greek *okhlos* mob + -PHOBIA]

ochone (ɒ'xəun) *interj Scot. and Irish.* an expression of sorrow or regret. [from Gaelic *ochóin*]

ochre *or U.S.* **ocher** ('əukə) *n* **1** any of various natural earths containing ferric oxide, silica, and alumina: used as yellow or red pigments. **2a** a moderate yellow-orange to orange colour. **2b** (*as adj*): *an ochre dress.* ◆ *vb* **3** (*tr*) to colour with ochre. [C15: from Old French *ocre,* from Latin *ōchra,* from Greek *ōkhra,* from *ōkhros* pale yellow] ▸ **ochreous** ('əukrɪəs, 'əukərəs), **ochrous** ('əukrəs), **ochry** ('əukərɪ, 'əukrɪ) *or U.S.* **'ocherous, 'ochery** *adj* ▸ **ochroid** ('əukrɔɪd) *adj*

ochrea ('ɒkrɪə) *n, pl* **-reae** (-rɪ,iː). a variant spelling of **ocrea.**

-ock *suffix forming nouns.* indicating smallness: *hillock.* [Old English *-oc, -uc*]

Ockeghem *or* **Okeghem** ('ɒkə,gɛm; *Dutch* 'ɔkəxəm) *n* **Johannes** (joː'hanəs), **Jean d'** (ʒɑ̃ d), or **Jan van** (jɑn vɑn). ?1430–?95, Flemish composer. Also: **Ockenheim** ('ɒkən,haɪm).

ocker ('ɒkə) *Austral. slang.* ◆ *n* **1** (*often cap.*) an uncultivated or boorish Australian. ◆ *adj, adv* **2** typical of such a person. [C20: of uncertain origin]

Ockham *or* **Occam** ('ɒkəm) *n* **William of.** died ?1349, English nominalist philosopher, who contested the temporal power of the papacy and ended the conflict between nominalism and realism. See **Ockham's razor.**

Ockham's razor *or* **Occam's razor** *n* a maxim, attributed to William of Ockham, stating that in explaining something assumptions must not be needlessly multiplied. Also called: **the principle of economy.**

o'clock (ə'klɒk) *adv* **1** used after a number from one to twelve to indicate the hour of the day or night. **2** used after a number to indicate direction or position relative to the observer, twelve o'clock being directly ahead or overhead and other positions being obtained by comparisons with a clock face. [C18: abbreviation for *of the clock*]

O'Connell (əu'kɒnᵊl) *n* **Daniel.** 1775–1847, Irish nationalist leader and orator, whose election to the British House of Commons (1828) forced the acceptance of Catholic emancipation (1829).

O'Connor (əu'kɒnə) *n* **1 Feargus.** 1794–1855, Irish politician and journalist, a leader of the Chartist movement. **2 (Mary) Flannery.** 1925–64, U.S. novelist and short-story writer, author of *Wise Blood* (1952) and *The Violent Bear it Away* (1960). **3 Frank,** real name *Michael O'Donovan.* 1903–66, Irish short-story writer and critic. **4 Thomas Power,** known as *Tay Pay.* 1848–1929, Irish journalist and nationalist leader.

ocotillo (,əukə'tiːljəu) *n, pl* **-los.** a cactus-like tree, *Fouquieria splendens,* of Mexico and the southwestern U.S., with scarlet tubular flowers: used for hedges and candlewood: family *Fouquieriaceae.* [Mexican Spanish: diminutive of *ocote* pine, from Nahuatl *ocotl* torch]

OCR *abbrev. for* optical character reader *or* recognition.

ocrea *or* **ochrea** ('ɒkrɪə) *n, pl* **-reae** (-rɪ,iː). a cup-shaped structure that sheathes the stems of certain plants, formed from united stipules or leaf bases. [C19: from Latin: greave, legging, of obscure origin]

ocreate ('ɒkrɪɪt, -,eɪt) *adj* **1** *Botany.* possessing an ocrea; sheathed. **2** *Ornithol.* another word for **booted** (sense 2).

OCS *abbrev. for* Officer Candidate School.

Oct. *abbrev. for* October.

oct- *combining form.* a variant of **octo-** before a vowel.

octa ('ɒktə) *n* a variant spelling of **okta.**

octa- *combining form.* a variant of **octo-.**

octachord ('ɒktə,kɔːd) *n* **1** an eight-stringed musical instrument. **2** a series of eight notes, esp. a scale.

octad ('ɒktæd) *n* **1** a group or series of eight. **2** *Chem.* an element or group with a valency of eight. [C19: from Greek *oktás,* from *oktō* eight] ▸ **oc'tadic** *adj*

octagon ('ɒktəgən) *or* (*less commonly*) **octangle** *n* a polygon having eight sides. [C17: via Latin from Greek *oktagōnos,* having eight angles]

octagonal (ɒk'tægənᵊl) *adj* **1** having eight sides and eight angles. **2** of or relating to an octagon. ▸ **oc'tagonally** *adv*

octahedral (,ɒktə'hiːdrəl) *adj* **1** having eight plane surfaces. **2** shaped like an octahedron.

octahedrite (,ɒktə'hiːdraɪt) *n* another name for **anatase.**

octahedron (,ɒktə'hiːdrən) *n, pl* **-drons** *or* **-dra** (-drə). a solid figure having eight plane faces.

octal notation *or* **octal** ('ɒktəl) *n* a number system having a base 8: often used in computing, one octal digit being equivalent to a group of three bits.

octamerous (ɒk'tæmərəs) *adj* consisting of eight parts, esp. (of flowers) having the parts arranged in groups of eight.

octameter (ɒk'tæmɪtə) *n Prosody.* a verse line consisting of eight metrical feet.

octane ('ɒkteɪn) *n* a liquid alkane hydrocarbon found in petroleum and existing in 18 isomeric forms, esp. the isomer *n*-octane. Formula: C_8H_{18}. See also **isooctane.**

octanedioic acid (,ɒkteɪndaɪ'əuɪk) *n* a colourless crystalline dicarboxylic acid found in suberin and castor oil and used in the manufacture of synthetic resins. Formula: $HOOC(CH_2)_6COOH$. Also called: **suberic acid.** [C20: from OCTANE + DIOL]

octane number *or* **rating** *n* a measure of the quality of a petrol expressed as the percentage of isooctane in a mixture of isooctane and *n*-heptane that gives a fuel with the same antiknock qualities as the given petrol.

octangle ('ɒktæŋgᵊl) *n* a less common name for **octagon.**

octangular (ɒk'tæŋgjulə) *adj* having eight angles.

Octans ('ɒktænz) *n, Latin genitive* **Octantis** (ɒk'tæntɪs). a faint constellation in the S hemisphere in which the S celestial pole is situated.

octant ('ɒktənt) *n* **1** *Maths.* **1a** any of the eight parts into which the three planes containing the Cartesian coordinate axes divide space. **1b** an eighth part of a circle. **2** *Astronomy.* the position of a celestial body when it is at an angular distance of 45° from another body. **3** an instrument used for measuring angles, similar to a sextant but having a graduated arc of 45°. [C17: from Latin *octans* half quadrant, from *octo* eight]

octarchy ('ɒktɑːkɪ) *n, pl* **-chies. 1** government by eight rulers. **2** a confederacy of eight kingdoms, tribes, etc.

octaroon (,ɒktə'ruːn) *n* a variant spelling of **octoroon.**

octavalent (,ɒktə'veɪlənt) *adj Chem.* having a valency of eight.

octave ('ɒktɪv) *n* **1a** the interval between two musical notes one of which has twice the pitch of the other and lies eight notes away from it counting inclusively along the diatonic scale. **1b** one of these two notes, esp. the one of higher pitch. **1c** (*as modifier*): *an octave leap.* ◆ See also **perfect** (sense 9), **diminished** (sense 2), **interval** (sense 5). **2** *Prosody.* a rhythmic group of eight lines of verse. **3** ('ɒkteɪv). **3a** a feast day and the seven days following. **3b** the final day of this period. **4** the eighth of eight basic positions in fencing. **5** any set or series of eight. ◆ *adj* **6** consisting of eight parts. [C14: (originally: eighth day) via Old French from Medieval Latin *octāva diēs* eighth day (after a festival), from Latin *octo* eight]

octave coupler *n* a mechanism on an organ and on some harpsichords that enables keys or pedals an octave apart to be played simultaneously.

Octavia (ɒk'teɪvɪə) *n* died 11 B.C., wife of Mark Antony; sister of Augustus.

Octavian (ɒk'teɪvɪən) *n* the name of **Augustus** before he became emperor (27 B.C.).

octavo (ɒk'teɪvəu) *n, pl* **-vos. 1** Also called: **eightvo.** a book size resulting from folding a sheet of paper of a specified size to form eight leaves: *demi-octavo.* Often written: **8vo, 8°. 2** a book of this size. **3** (formerly) a size of cut paper 8 inches by 5 inches (20.3 cm by 12.7 cm). [C16: from New Latin phrase *in octavo* in an eighth (of a whole sheet)]

octennial (ɒk'tenɪəl) *adj* **1** occurring every eight years. **2** lasting for eight years. [C17: from Latin *octennium* eight years, from *octo* eight + *annus* year] ▸ **oc'tennially** *adv*

octet (ɒk'tɛt) *n* **1** any group of eight, esp. eight singers or musicians. **2** a piece of music composed for such a group. **3** *Prosody.* another word for **octave** (sense 2). **4** *Chem.* a group of eight electrons forming a stable shell in an atom. ◆ Also (for senses 1, 2, 3): **oc'tette.** [C19: from Latin *octo* eight, on the model of DUET]

octillion (ɒk'tɪljən) *n* **1** (in Britain and Germany) the number represented as one followed by 48 zeros (10^{48}). **2** (in the U.S., Canada, and France) the number represented as one followed by 27 zeros (10^{27}). [C17: from French, on the model of MILLION] ▸ **oc'tillionth** *adj*

octo-, octa-, *or before a vowel* **oct-** *combining form.* eight: *octosyllabic; octagon.* [from Latin *octo,* Greek *oktō*]

October (ɒk'təubə) *n* the tenth month of the year, consisting of 31 days. [Old English, from Latin, from *octo* eight, since it was the eighth month in Roman reckoning]

October Revolution *n* another name for the **Russian Revolution** (sense 2).

Octobrist (ɒk'təubrɪst) *n* a member of a Russian political party favouring the constitutional reforms granted in a manifesto issued by Nicholas II in Oct. 1905.

octocentenary (,ɒktəusɛn'tiːnərɪ) *n, pl* **-naries.** an eight-hundredth anniversary.

octodecimo (,ɒktəu'dɛsɪməu) *n, pl* **-mos.** *Bookbinding.* another word for **eighteenmo.** [C18: from New Latin phrase *in octodecimo* in an eighteenth (of a whole sheet)]

octogenarian (,ɒktəudʒɪ'nɛərɪən) *or* (*less commonly*) **octogenary** (ɒk'tɒdʒɪnərɪ) *n, pl* **-narians** *or* **-naries. 1** a person who is from 80 to 89 years old. ◆ *adj* **2** of or relating to an octogenarian. [C19: from Latin *octōgēnārius* containing eighty, from *octōgēnī* eighty each]

octonary ('ɒktənərɪ) *Rare.* ◆ *adj* **1** relating to or based on the number eight. ◆ *n, pl* **-naries. 2** *Prosody.* a stanza of eight lines. **3** a group of eight. [C16: from Latin *octōnārius,* from *octōnī* eight at a time]

octopod ('ɒktə,pɒd) *n* **1** any cephalopod mollusc of the order *Octopoda,* including octopuses and the paper nautilus, having eight tentacles, and lacking an internal shell. ◆ *adj* **2** of, relating to, or belonging to the *Octopoda.*

octopus ('ɒktəpəs) *n, pl* **-puses. 1** any cephalopod mollusc of the genera *Octopus, Eledone,* etc., having a soft oval body with eight long suckered tentacles and occurring at the sea bottom: order *Octopoda* (octopods). **2** a powerful influential organization with far-reaching effects, esp. harmful ones. **3** another name for **spider** (sense 8). [C18: via New Latin from Greek *oktōpous* having eight feet]

octoroon *or* **octaroon** (,ɒktə'ruːn) *n* a person having one quadroon and one White parent and therefore having one-eighth Black blood. Compare **quadroon.** [C19: OCTO- + *-roon* as in QUADROON]

octosyllable ('ɒktə,sɪləbᵊl) *n* **1** a line of verse composed of eight syllables. **2** a word of eight syllables. ▸ **octosyllabic** (,ɒktəsɪ'læbɪk) *adj*

octroi ('ɒktrwɑː) *n* **1** (in some European countries, esp. France) a duty on various goods brought into certain towns or cities. **2** the place where such a duty is collected. **3** the officers responsible for its collection. [C17: from French *octroyer* to concede, from Medieval Latin *auctorizāre* to AUTHORIZE]

octuple ('ɒktjupᵊl) *n* **1** a quantity or number eight times as great as another. ◆ *adj* **2** eight times as much or as many. **3** consisting of eight parts. ◆ *vb* **4** (*tr*) to multiply by eight. [C17: from Latin *octuplus,* from *octo* eight + *-plus* as in *duplus* double]

ocular ('ɒkjulə) *adj* **1** of or relating to the eye. ◆ *n* **2** another name for **eyepiece.** [C16: from Latin *oculāris* from *oculus* eye] ▸ **'ocularly** *adv*

ocularist ('ɒkjulərɪst) *n* a person who makes artificial eyes.

oculate ('ɒkju,leɪt) *adj Zoology.* **1** possessing eyes. **2** relating to or resembling eyes: *oculate markings.*

oculist ('ɒkjulɪst) *n Med.* a former term for **ophthalmologist.** [C17: via French from Latin *oculus* eye]

oculo- *or sometimes before a vowel* **ocul-** *combining form.* indicating the eye: *oculomotor.* [from Latin *oculus*]

oculomotor (,ɒkjuləu'məutə) *adj* relating to or causing eye movements. [C19: from Latin *oculus* eye + MOTOR]

oculomotor nerve *n* the third cranial nerve, which supplies most of the eye muscles.

od (ɒd, əʊd), **odyl,** *or* **odyle** *n Archaic.* a hypothetical force formerly thought to be responsible for many natural phenomena, such as magnetism, light, and hypnotism. [C19: coined arbitrarily by Baron Karl von Reichenbach (1788–1869), German scientist] ► **'odic** *adj*

Od, 'Od, *or* **Odd** (ɒd) *n Euphemistic.* (used in mild oaths) an archaic word for **God.**

OD[1] (,əʊ'diː) *Informal.* ◆ *n* **1** an overdose of a drug. ◆ *vb* (*intr*) **OD'ing, OD'd. 2** to take an overdose of a drug. [C20: from *o(ver)d(ose)*]

OD[2] *abbrev. for:* **1** Officer of the Day. **2** Old Dutch. **3** ordnance datum. **4** outside diameter. **5** Also: **o.d.** *Military.* olive drab. **6** Also: **O/D.** *Banking.* **6a** on demand. **6b** overdraft. **6c** overdrawn.

ODA (in Britain) *abbrev. for* Overseas Development Administration.

odalisque *or* **odalisk** ('əʊdəlɪsk) *n* a female slave or concubine. [C17: via French, changed from Turkish *ōdalik,* from *ōdah* room + *-lik* n. suffix]

Oda Nobunaga ('əʊdə ,nɒbjuː'nɑːgə) *n* 1534–82, Japanese general and feudal leader, who unified much of Japan under his control: assassinated.

odd (ɒd) *adj* **1** unusual or peculiar in appearance, character, etc. **2** occasional, incidental, or random: *odd jobs.* **3** leftover or additional: *odd bits of wool.* **4a** not divisible by two. **4b** represented or indicated by a number that is not divisible by two: *graphs are on odd pages.* Compare **even**[1] (sense 7). **5** being part of a matched pair or set when the other or others are missing: *an odd sock; odd volumes.* **6** (*in combination*). used to designate an indefinite quantity more than the quantity specified in round numbers: *fifty-odd pounds.* **7** out-of-the-way or secluded: *odd corners.* **8** *Maths.* (of a function) changing sign but not absolute value when the sign of the independent variable is changed, as in $y=x^3$. Compare **even**[1] (sense 13). **9 odd man out.** a person or thing excluded from others forming a group, unit, etc. ◆ *n* **10** *Golf.* **10a** one stroke more than the score of one's opponent. **10b** an advantage or handicap of one stroke added to or taken away from a player's score. **11** a thing or person that is odd in sequence or number. ◆ See also **odds.** [C14: *odde:* from Old Norse *oddi* point, angle, triangle, third or odd number. Compare Old Norse *oddr* point, spot, place; Old English *ord* point, beginning] ► **'oddly** *adv* ► **'oddness** *n*

oddball ('ɒd,bɔːl) *Informal.* ◆ *n* **1** Also called: **odd bod, odd fish.** a strange or eccentric person. ◆ *adj* **2** strange or peculiar.

Oddfellow ('ɒd,fɛləʊ) *n* a member of the **Independent Order of Oddfellows,** a secret benevolent and fraternal association founded in England in the 18th century.

oddity ('ɒdɪtɪ) *n, pl* **-ties. 1** an odd person or thing. **2** an odd quality or characteristic. **3** the condition of being odd.

odd-jobman *or* **odd-jobber** *n, pl* **-men** *or* **-bers.** a person who does casual work, esp. domestic repairs.

odd lot *n* **1** a batch of merchandise that contains less than or more than the usual number of units. **2** *Stock Exchange.* a number of securities less than the standard trading unit of 100.

oddment ('ɒdmənt) *n* **1** (*often pl*) an odd piece or thing; leftover. **2** (*pl*) *N.Z.* pieces of wool, such as belly wool or neck wool, removed from a fleece and sold separately.

odd-pinnate *adj* (of a plant leaf) pinnate with a single leaflet at the apex.

odds (ɒdz) *pl n* **1** (foll. by *on* or *against*) the probability, expressed as a ratio, that a certain event will take place: *the odds against the outsider are a hundred to one.* **2** the amount, expressed as a ratio, by which the wager of one better is greater than that of another: *he was offering odds of five to one.* **3** the likelihood that a certain state of affairs will be found to be so: *the odds are that he is drunk.* **4** the chances or likelihood of success in a certain undertaking: *their odds were very poor after it rained.* **5** an equalizing allowance, esp. one given to a weaker side in a contest. **6** the advantage that one contender is judged to have over another: *the odds are on my team.* **7** *Brit.* a significant difference (esp. in the phrase **it makes no odds**). **8 at odds. 8a** on bad terms. **8b** appearing not to correspond or match: *the silvery hair was at odds with her youthful shape.* **9 give** *or* **lay odds.** to offer a bet with favourable odds. **10 take odds.** to accept such a bet. **11 over the odds. 11a** more than is expected, necessary, etc.: *he got two pounds over the odds for this job.* **11b** unfair or excessive. **12 what's the odds?** *Brit. informal.* what difference does it make?

odds and ends *pl n* miscellaneous items or articles.

odds and sods *pl n Brit. informal.* miscellaneous people or things.

odds-on *adj* **1** (of a chance, horse, etc.) rated at even money or less to win. **2** regarded as more or most likely to win, succeed, happen, etc.

ode (əʊd) *n* **1** a lyric poem, typically addressed to a particular subject, with lines of varying lengths and complex rhythms. See also **Horatian ode, Pindaric ode. 2** (formerly) a poem meant to be sung. [C16: via French from Late Latin *ōda,* from Greek *ōidē,* from *aeidein* to sing]

-ode[1] *n combining form.* denoting resemblance: *nematode.* [from Greek *-ōdēs,* from *eidos* shape, form]

-ode[2] *n combining form.* denoting a path or way: *electrode.* [from Greek *-odos,* from *hodos* a way]

odea ('əʊdɪə) *n* the plural of **odeum.**

Odelsting *or* **Odelsthing** ('əʊdəlsˌtɪŋ) *n* the lower chamber of the Norwegian parliament. See also **Lagting, Storting.**

Odense (*Danish* 'oːðənsə) *n* a port in S Denmark, on Funen Island: cathedral founded by King Canute in the 11th century. Pop.: 183 564 (1996 est.).

Oder ('əʊdə) *n* a river in central Europe, rising in the NE Czech Republic and flowing north and west, forming part of the border between Germany and Poland to the Baltic. Length: 913 km (567 miles). Czech and Polish name: **Odra.**

Oder-Neisse Line ('əʊdə'naɪsə) *n* the present-day boundary between Germany and Poland along the Rivers Oder and Neisse. Established in 1945, it originally separated the Soviet Zone of Germany from the regions under Polish administration.

Odessa (əʊ'dɛsə; *Russian* a'djesə) *n* a port in the S Ukraine on the Black Sea: the chief Russian grain port in the 19th century; university (1865); industrial centre and important naval base. Pop.: 1 046 000 (1996 est.).

Odets (əʊ'dɛts) *n* **Clifford.** 1906–63, U.S. dramatist; founder member of the Group Theatre. His plays include *Waiting for Lefty* (1935) and *Golden Boy* (1937).

odeum ('əʊdɪəm) *n, pl* **odea** ('əʊdɪə). (esp. in ancient Greece and Rome) a building for musical performances. Also called: **'odeon.** [C17: from Latin, from Greek *ōideion,* from *ōidē* ODE]

Odin ('əʊdɪn) *or* **Othin** *n Norse myth.* the supreme creator god; the divinity of wisdom, culture, war, and the dead. Germanic counterpart: **Wotan, Woden.**

odious ('əʊdɪəs) *adj* offensive; repugnant. [C17: from Latin; see ODIUM] ► **'odiously** *adv* ► **'odiousness** *n*

odium ('əʊdɪəm) *n* **1** the dislike accorded to a hated person or thing. **2** hatred; repugnance. [C17: from Latin; related to *ōdī* I hate, Greek *odussasthai* to be angry]

ODM *abbrev. for* Ministry of Overseas Development.

Odoacer (,ɒdə'eɪsə) *or* **Odovacar** (,əʊdə'vɑːkə) *n* ?434–493 A.D., barbarian ruler of Italy (476–493); assassinated by Theodoric.

odometer (ɒ'dɒmɪtə, əʊ-) *n* the usual U.S. and Canadian name for **mileometer.** [C18 *hodometer,* from Greek *hodos* way + -METER] ► **o'dometry** *n*

-odont *adj and n combining form.* having teeth of a certain type; -toothed: *acrodont.* [from Greek *odōn* tooth]

odontalgia (,ɒdɒn'tældʒɪə) *n* a technical name for **toothache.** ► **,odon'talgic** *adj*

odonto- *or before a vowel* **odont-** *combining form.* indicating a tooth or teeth: *odontology.* [from Greek *odōn* tooth]

odontoblast (ɒ'dɒntə,blæst) *n* any of a layer of cells lining the pulp cavity of a tooth and giving rise to the dentine. ► **o,donto'blastic** *adj*

odontoglossum (ɒ,dɒntə'glɒsəm) *n* any epiphytic orchid of the tropical American genus *Odontoglossum,* having clusters of brightly coloured flowers.

odontoid (ɒ'dɒntɔɪd) *adj* **1** toothlike. **2** of or relating to the odontoid process.

odontoid process *n Anatomy.* the toothlike upward projection at the back of the second vertebra of the neck.

odontolite (ɒ'dɒntə,laɪt) *n* another name for **bone turquoise.**

odontology (,ɒdɒn'tɒlədʒɪ) *n* the branch of science concerned with the anatomy, development, and diseases of teeth and related structures. ► **odontological** (ɒ,dɒntə'lɒdʒɪkəl) *adj* ► **,odon'tologist** *n*

odontophore (ɒ'dɒntə,fɔː) *n* an oral muscular protrusible structure in molluscs that supports the radula. ► **odontophoral** (,ɒdɒn'tɒfərəl) *or* **,odon'tophorous** *adj*

odontorhynchous (ɒ,dɒntə'rɪŋkəs) *adj* (of birds) having toothlike ridges inside the beak. [C19: from ODONTO- + Greek *rhunkhos* snout + -OUS]

odor ('əʊdə) *n* the U.S. spelling of **odour.** ► **'odorless** *adj*

odoriferous (,əʊdə'rɪfərəs) *adj* having or emitting an odour, esp. a fragrant one. ► **,odor'iferously** *adv* ► **,odor'iferousness** *n*

odorimetry (,əʊdə'rɪmɪtrɪ) *n Chem.* the measurement of the strength and permanence of odours. Also called: **olfactometry.**

odoriphore (əʊ'dɒrɪ,fɔː) *n Chem.* the group of atoms in an odorous molecule responsible for its odour.

odorous ('əʊdərəs) *adj* having or emitting a characteristic smell or odour. ► **'odorously** *adv* ► **'odorousness** *n*

odour *or U.S.* **odor** ('əʊdə) *n* **1** the property of a substance that gives it a characteristic scent or smell. **2** a pervasive quality about something: *an odour of dishonesty.* **3** repute or regard (in the phrases **in good odour, in bad odour**). [C13: from Old French *odur,* from Latin *odor;* related to Latin *olēre* to smell, Greek *ōzein*] ► **'odourless** *or U.S.* **'odorless** *adj*

odour of sanctity *n Derogatory.* sanctimoniousness. [C18: originally, the sweet smell said to be exhaled by the bodies of dead saints]

Odovacar (,əʊdə'vɑːkə) *n* a variant of **Odoacer.**

Odra ('ɔdra) *n* the Czech and Polish name for the **Oder.**

odyl *or* **odyle** ('ɒdɪl) *n* other words for **od.**

Odysseus (ə'diːsɪəs) *n Greek myth.* one of the foremost of the Greek heroes at the siege of Troy, noted for his courage and ingenuity. His return to his kingdom of Ithaca was fraught with adventures in which he lost all his companions and he was acknowledged by his wife Penelope only after killing her suitors. Roman name: **Ulysses.**

Odyssey ('ɒdɪsɪ) *n* **1** a Greek epic poem, attributed to Homer, describing the ten-year homeward wanderings of Odysseus after the fall of Troy. **2** (*often not cap.*) any long eventful journey. ► **Odyssean** (,ɒdɪ'siːən) *adj*

Oe *symbol for* oersted.

OE *abbrev. for* Old English (language).

o.e. *Commerce. abbrev. for* omissions excepted.

OECD *abbrev. for* Organization for Economic Cooperation and Development; an association of 21 nations to promote growth and trade, set up in 1961 to supersede the OEEC.

oecology (iː'kɒlədʒɪ) *n* a less common spelling of **ecology.** ► oecological (,ɛkə'lɒdʒɪkəl,,iː-) *adj* ► **,oeco'logically** *adv* ► **oe'cologist** *n*

oecumenical (,iːkjʊ'mɛnɪkəl) *adj* a less common spelling of **ecumenical.**

OED *abbrev. for* Oxford English Dictionary.

oedema *or* **edema** (ɪ'diːmə) *n, pl* **-mata** (-mətə). **1** *Pathol.* an excessive accumulation of serous fluid in the intercellular spaces of tissue. **2** *Plant pathol.* an abnormal swelling in a plant caused by a large mass of parenchyma or an accumulation of water in the tissues. [C16: via New Latin from Greek *oidēma,* from *oidein* to swell] ► **oedematous, edematous** (ɪ'dɛmətəs) *or* **oe'dema,tose, e'dema,tose** *adj*

Oedipus ('iːdɪpəs) *n Greek myth.* the son of Laius and Jocasta, the king and queen of Thebes, who killed his father, being unaware of his identity, and unwittingly married his mother, by whom he had four children. When the truth was revealed, he put out his eyes and Jocasta killed herself.

Oedipus complex *n Psychoanal.* a group of emotions, usually unconscious, involving the desire of a child, esp. a male child, to possess sexually the parent of the opposite sex while excluding the parent of the same sex. Compare **Electra complex.** ▸ **'oedipal** *or* **,oedi'pean** *adj*

oedometer (iː'dɒmɪtə) *n Civil engineering.* an instrument for measuring the rate and amount of consolidation of a soil specimen under pressure. [C20: from Greek *oidēma* (see OEDEMA) + -METER]

OEEC *abbrev. for* Organization for European Economic Cooperation; an organization of European nations set up in 1948 to allocate postwar U.S. aid and to stimulate trade and cooperation. It was superseded by the OECD in 1961.

Oehlenschläger *or* **Öhlenschläger** (*Danish* 'øːlənslɛːgər) *n* **Adam Gottlob** ('adam 'gɔtlɔp). 1779–1850, Danish romantic poet and dramatist.

oeil-de-boeuf *French.* (œjdəbœf) *n, pl* ***oeils-de-boeuf*** (œjdəbœf). a circular window, esp. in 17th- and 18th-century French architecture. [literally: bull's eye]

oeillade (ɜː'jɑːd; *French* œjad) *n Literary.* an amorous or suggestive glance; ogle. [C16: from French, from *oeil* eye, from Latin *oculus* + *-ade* as in FUSILLADE]

OEM *abbrev. for* original equipment manufacturer: a computer company whose products are made by customizing basic parts supplied by others.

oenology *or* **enology** (iː'nɒlədʒɪ) *n* the study of wine. [C19: from Greek *oinos* wine + -LOGY] ▸ **oenological** *or* **enological** (ˌiːnə'lɒdʒɪkᵊl) *adj* ▸ **oe'nologist** *or* **e'nologist** *n*

oenomel ('iːnəˌmɛl) *n* **1** a drink made of wine and honey. **2** *Literary.* a source of strength and sweetness. [C16: via Latin from Greek *oinos* wine + *meli* honey]

Oenone (iː'nəunɪ) *n Greek myth.* a nymph of Mount Ida, whose lover Paris left her for Helen.

oenophile ('iːnəˌfaɪl) *n* a lover or connoisseur of wines. [C20: from Greek *oinos* wine + -PHILE]

oenothera (ˌiːnə'θɪərə) *n* any plant of the large taxonomically complicated American genus *Oenothera,* typically having yellow flowers that open in the evening: family *Onagraceae.* See **evening primrose.**

o'er (ɔː, əuə) *prep, adv* a poetic contraction of **over.**

oersted ('ɜːstɛd) *n* the cgs unit of magnetic field strength; the field strength that would cause a unit magnetic pole to experience a force of 1 dyne in a free space. It is equivalent to 79.58 amperes per metre. Symbol: Oe [C20: named after H. C. *Oersted* (1777–1851), Danish physicist, who discovered electromagnetism]

oesophagoscope *or U.S.* **esophagoscope** (iː'sɒfəgəuˌskəup) *n Med.* an instrument for examining the oesophagus. ▸ **oesophagoscopy** (iːˌsɒfə'gɒskəpɪ) *n*

oesophagus *or U.S.* **esophagus** (iː'sɒfəgəs) *n, pl* **-gi** (-ˌgaɪ). the part of the alimentary canal between the pharynx and the stomach; gullet. [C16: via New Latin from Greek *oisophagos, from oisein,* future infinitive of *pherein* to carry + *-phagos,* from *phagein* to eat] ▸ **oesophageal** *or U.S.* **esophageal** (iːˌsɒfə'dʒiːəl) *adj*

oestradiol (ˌiːstrə'daɪɒl, ˌɛstrə-) *or U.S.* **estradiol** *n* the most potent oestrogenic hormone secreted by the mammalian ovary: synthesized and used to treat oestrogen deficiency and cancer of the breast. Formula: $C_{18}H_{24}O_2$. [C20: from New Latin, from OESTRIN + DI-[1] + -OL[1]]

oestrin ('iːstrɪn, 'ɛstrɪn) *or U.S.* **estrin** *n* an obsolete term for **oestrogen.** [C20: from OESTR(US) + -IN]

oestriol ('iːstrɪˌɒl, 'ɛstrɪ-) *or U.S.* **estriol** *n* a weak oestrogenic hormone secreted by the mammalian ovary: a synthetic form is used to treat oestrogen deficiency. Formula: $C_{18}H_{24}O_3$. [C20: from OESTRIN + TRI- + -OL[1]]

oestrogen ('iːstrədʒən, 'ɛstrə-) *or U.S.* **estrogen** *n* any of several steroid hormones, that are secreted chiefly by the ovaries and placenta, that induce oestrus, stimulate changes in the female reproductive organs during the oestrous cycle, and promote development of female secondary sexual characteristics. [C20: from OESTRUS + -GEN] ▸ **oestrogenic** (ˌiːstrə'dʒɛnɪk, ˌɛstrə-) *or U.S.* **estrogenic** (ˌɛstrə'dʒɛnɪk, ˌiːstrə-) *adj* ▸ **,oestro'genically** *or U.S.* **,estro'genically** *adv*

oestrone ('iːstrəun, 'ɛstrəun) *or U.S.* **estrone** *n* a weak oestrogenic hormone secreted by the mammalian ovary and having the same medical uses as oestradiol. Formula: $C_{18}H_{22}O_2$. [C20: from OESTR(US) + -ONE]

oestrous cycle *n* a hormonally controlled cycle of activity of the reproductive organs in many female mammals. The follicular stage (growth of the Graafian follicles, thickening of the lining of the uterus, secretion of oestrogen, and ovulation (see **oestrus**)), is succeeded by the luteal phase (formation of the corpus luteum and secretion of progesterone), followed by regression and a return to the first stage.

oestrus ('iːstrəs, 'ɛstrəs) *or U.S.* **estrus, estrum** ('iːstrəm, 'ɛstrəm) *n* a regularly occurring period of sexual receptivity in most female mammals, except humans, during which ovulation occurs and copulation can take place; heat. [C17: from Latin *oestrus* gadfly, hence frenzy, from Greek *oistros*] ▸ **'oestrous, 'oestral** *or U.S.* **'estrous, 'estral** *adj*

oeuvre *French.* (œvrə) *n* **1** a work of art, literature, music, etc. **2** the total output of a writer, painter, etc. [ultimately from Latin *opera,* plural of *opus* work]

of (ɒv; *unstressed* əv) *prep* **1** used with a verbal noun or gerund to link it with a following noun that is either the subject or the object of the verb embedded in the gerund: *the breathing of a fine swimmer* (subject); *the breathing of clean air* (object). **2** used to indicate possession, origin, or association: *the house of my sister; to die of hunger.* **3** used after words or phrases expressing quantities: *a pint of milk.* **4** constituted by, containing, or characterized by: *a family of idiots; a rod of iron; a man of some depth.* **5** used to indicate separation, as in time or space: *within a mile of the town; within ten minutes of the beginning of the concert.* **6** used to mark apposition: *the city of Naples; a speech on the subject of archaeology.* **7** about; concerning: *speak to me of love.* **8** used in passive constructions to indicate the agent: *he was beloved of all.* **9** *Informal.* used to indicate a day or part of a period of time when some activity habitually occurs: *I go to the pub of an evening.* **10** *U.S.* before the hour of: *a quarter of nine.* [Old English (as prep and adv); related to Old Norse *af,* Old High German *aba,* Latin *ab,* Greek *apo*]

USAGE See at **off.**

OF *abbrev. for* Old French (language).

ofay ('əufeɪ) *n U.S. slang.* a derogatory term for a White person. [C20: origin unknown]

off (ɒf) *prep* **1** used to indicate actions in which contact is absent or rendered absent, as between an object and a surface: *to lift a cup off the table.* **2** used to indicate the removal of something that is or has been appended to or in association with something else: *to take the tax off potatoes.* **3** out of alignment with: *we are off course.* **4** situated near to or leading away from: *just off the High Street.* **5** not inclined towards: *I'm off work; I've gone off you.* ◆ *adv* **6** (*particle*) so as to be deactivated or disengaged: *turn off the radio.* **7** (*particle*) **7a** so as to get rid of: *sleep off a hangover.* **7b** so as to be removed from, esp. as a reduction: *he took ten per cent off.* **8** spent away from work or other duties: *take the afternoon off.* **9a** on a trip, journey, or race: *I saw her off at the station.* **9b** (*particle*) so as to be completely absent, used up, or exhausted: *this stuff kills off all vermin.* **10** out from the shore or land: *the ship stood off.* **11a** out of contact; at a distance: *the ship was 10 miles off.* **11b** out of the present location: *the girl ran off.* **12** away in the future: *August is less than a week off.* **13** (*particle*) so as to be no longer taking place: *the match has been rained off.* **14** (*particle*) removed from contact with something, as clothing from the body: *the girl took all her clothes off.* **15** offstage: *noises off.* **16** *Commerce.* (used with a preceding number) indicating the number of items required or produced: *please supply 100 off.* **17 off and on** *or* **on and off.** occasionally; intermittently: *he comes here off and on.* **18 off with.** (*interj*) a command, often peremptory, or an exhortation to remove or cut off (something specified): *off with his head; off with that coat, my dear.* ◆ *adj* **19** not on; no longer operative: *the off position on the dial.* **20** (*postpositive*) not or no longer taking place; cancelled or postponed: *the meeting is off.* **21** in a specified condition regarding money, provisions, etc.: *well off; how are you off for bread?* **22** unsatisfactory or disappointing: *his performance was rather off; an off year for good tennis.* **23** (*postpositive*) in a condition as specified: *I'd be better off without this job.* **24** (*postpositive*) no longer on the menu; not being served at the moment: *sorry, love, haddock is off.* **25** (*postpositive*) (of food or drink) having gone bad, sour, etc.: *this milk is off.* ◆ *n* **26** *Cricket.* **26a** the part of the field on that side of the pitch to which the batsman presents his bat when taking strike: thus for a right-hander, off is on the right-hand side. Compare **leg** (sense 13). **26b** (*in combination*): a fielding position in this part of the field: *mid-off.* **26c** (*as modifier*): *the off stump.* [originally variant of OF; fully distinguished from it in the 17th century]

USAGE In standard English, *off* is not followed by *of: he stepped off* (not *off of*) *the platform.*

off. *abbrev. for:* **1** offer. **2** office. **3** officer. **4** official.

Offa ('ɒfə) *n* died 796 A.D., king of Mercia (757–796), who constructed an earthwork (**Offa's Dyke**) between Wales and Mercia.

off-air *adj, adv* **1** obtained by reception of a radiated broadcasting signal rather than by line feed: *an off-air recording.* **2** connected with a radio or television programme but not broadcast: *an off-air phone-in.*

offal ('ɒfᵊl) *n* **1** the edible internal parts of an animal, such as the heart, liver, and tongue. **2** dead or decomposing organic matter. **3** refuse; rubbish. [C14: from OFF + FALL, referring to parts fallen or cut off; compare German *Abfall* rubbish]

Offaly ('ɒfəlɪ) *n* an inland county of E central Republic of Ireland, in Leinster province: formerly an ancient kingdom, which also included parts of Tipperary, Leix, and Kildare. County town: Tullamore. Pop.: 59 000 (1996). Area: 2000 sq. km (770 sq. miles).

off-balance sheet reserve *n Accounting.* a sum of money or an asset that should appear on a company's balance but does not; hidden reserve.

offbeat ('ɒfˌbiːt) *n* **1** *Music.* any of the normally unaccented beats in a bar, such as the second and fourth beats in a bar of four-four time. They are stressed in most rock and some jazz and dance music, such as the bossa nova. ◆ *adj* **2a** unusual, unconventional, or eccentric. **2b** (*as n*): *he liked the offbeat in fashion.*

off break *n Cricket.* a bowled ball that spins from off to leg on pitching.

off-Broadway *adj* **1** designating the kind of experimental, low-budget, or noncommercial productions associated with theatre outside the Broadway area in New York. **2** (of theatres) not located in Broadway. ◆ Compare **off-off-Broadway.**

off-centre *adj* **1** displaced from a centre point or axis. **2** slightly eccentric or unconventional; not completely sound or balanced.

off chance *n* **1** a slight possibility. **2 on the off chance.** with the hope: *on the off chance of getting the job.*

off colour *adj* (**off-colour** *when prenominal*). **1** *Chiefly Brit.* slightly ill; unwell. **2** indecent or indelicate; risqué.

offcut ('ɒfˌkʌt) *n* a piece of paper, plywood, fabric, etc., remaining after the main pieces have been cut; remnant.

Offenbach[1] (*German* 'ɔfənbax) *n* a city in central Germany, on the River Main in Hesse opposite Frankfurt am Main: leather-goods industry. Pop.: 116 533 (1996 est.).

Offenbach[2] ('ɒfənˌbɑːk; *French* ɔfənbak) *n* **Jacques** (ʒak). 1819–80, German-born French composer of many operettas, including *Orpheus in the Underworld* (1858), and of the opera *The Tales of Hoffmann* (1881).

offence *or U.S.* **offense** (ə'fɛns) *n* **1** a violation or breach of a law, custom, rule, etc. **2a** any public wrong or crime. **2b** a nonindictable crime punishable on summary conviction. 3 annoyance, displeasure, or resentment. **4 give offence (to).** to cause annoyance or displeasure (to). **5 take offence.** to feel injured, humiliated, or offended. 6 a source of annoyance, displeasure, or anger. 7 attack; assault. 8 *Archaic.* injury or harm. 9 ('ɒfɛns). *American football.* (usually preceded by *the*) **9a** the team that has possession of the ball. **9b** the members of a team that play in such circumstances. ▸ **of'fenceless** *or U.S.* **of'fenseless** *adj*

offend (ə'fɛnd) *vb* **1** to hurt the feelings, sense of dignity, etc., of (a person). **2** (*tr*) to be disagreeable to; disgust: *the smell offended him.* **3** (*intr except in archaic uses*) to break (a law or laws in general). [C14: via Old French *offendre* to strike against, from Latin *offendere,* from *ob-* against + *fendere* to strike] ▸ **of'fender** *n* ▸ **of'fending** *adj*

offensive (ə'fɛnsɪv) *adj* **1** unpleasant or disgusting, as to the senses. **2** causing anger or annoyance; insulting. **3** for the purpose of attack rather than defence. ◆ *n* **4** (usually preceded by *the*) an attitude or position of aggression. **5** an assault, attack, or military initiative, esp. a strategic one. ▸ **of'fensively** *adv* ▸ **of'fensiveness** *n*

offer ('ɒfə) *vb* **1** to present or proffer (something, someone, oneself, etc.) for acceptance or rejection. **2** (*tr*) to present as part of a requirement: *she offered English as a second subject.* **3** (*tr*) to provide or make accessible: *this stream offers the best fishing.* **4** (*intr*) to present itself: *if an opportunity should offer.* **5** (*tr*) to show or express willingness or the intention (to do something). **6** (*tr*) to put forward (a proposal, opinion, etc.) for consideration. **7** (*tr*) to present for sale. **8** (*tr*) to propose as payment; bid or tender. **9** (when *tr,* often foll. by *up*) to present (a prayer, sacrifice, etc.) as or during an act of worship. **10** (*tr*) to show readiness for: *to offer battle.* **11** (*intr*) *Archaic.* to make a proposal of marriage. **12** (*tr;* sometimes foll. by *up* or *to*) *Engineering.* to bring (a mechanical piece) near to or in contact with another, and often to proceed to fit the pieces together. ◆ *n* **13** something, such as a proposal or bid, that is offered. **14** the act of offering or the condition of being offered. **15** *Contract law.* a proposal made by one person that will create a binding contract if accepted unconditionally by the person to whom it is made. See also **acceptance. 16** a proposal of marriage. **17** short for **offer price. 18 on offer.** for sale at a reduced price. [Old English, from Latin *offerre* to present, from *ob-* to + *ferre* to bring] ▸ **'offerer** *or* **'offeror** *n*

Offer ('ɒfə) *n* (in Britain) *acronym for* Office of Electricity Regulation: a government body set up in 1989 to supervise the activities of the electricity companies and to protect the interests of the consumers.

offer document *n* a document sent by a person or firm making a takeover bid to the shareholders of the target company, giving details of the offer that has been made and, usually, reasons for accepting it.

offering ('ɒfərɪŋ) *n* **1** something that is offered. **2** a contribution to the funds of a religious organization. **3** a sacrifice, as of an animal, to a deity.

offer price *n Stock Exchange.* the price at which a market maker is prepared to sell a specific security. Often shortened to **offer.** Compare **bid price.**

offertory ('ɒfətərɪ) *n, pl* **-tories.** *Christianity.* **1** the oblation of the bread and wine at the Eucharist. **2** the offerings of the worshippers at this service. **3** the prayers said or sung while the worshippers' offerings are being received. [C14: from Church Latin *offertōrium* place appointed for offerings, from Latin *offerre* to OFFER]

off-glide *n Phonetics.* a glide caused by the movement of the articulators away from their position in articulating the previous speech sound. Compare **on-glide.**

offhand (ˌɒf'hænd) *adj also* **offhanded,** *adv* **1** without care, thought, or consideration; sometimes, brusque or ungracious: *an offhand manner.* **2** without preparation or warning; impromptu. ▸ **ˌoff'handedly** *adv* ▸ **ˌoff'handedness** *n*

office ('ɒfɪs) *n* **1a** a room or set of rooms in which business, professional duties, clerical work, etc., are carried out. **1b** (*as modifier*): *office furniture; an office boy.* **2** (*often pl*) the building or buildings in which the work of an organization, such as a business or government department, is carried out. **3** a commercial or professional business: *the architect's office approved the plans.* **4** the group of persons working in an office: *it was a happy office until she came.* **5** (*cap. when part of a name*) (in Britain) a department of the national government: *the Home Office.* **6** (*cap. when part of a name*) (in the U.S.) **6a** a governmental agency, esp. of the Federal government. **6b** a subdivision of such an agency or of a department: *Office of Science and Technology.* **7a** a position of trust, responsibility, or duty, esp. in a government or organization: *the office of president; to seek office.* **7b** (*in combination*): *an office-holder.* **8** duty or function: *the office of an administrator.* **9** (*often pl*) a minor task or service: *domestic offices.* **10** (*often pl*) an action performed for another, usually a beneficial action: *through his good offices.* **11** a place where tickets, information, etc., can be obtained: *a ticket office.* **12** *Christianity.* **12a** (*often pl*) a ceremony or service, prescribed by ecclesiastical authorities, esp. one for the dead. **12b** the order or form of these. **12c** *R.C. Church.* the official daily service. **12d** short for **divine office. 13** (*pl*) the parts of a house or estate where work is done, goods are stored, etc. **14** (*usually pl*) *Brit., euphemistic.* a lavatory (esp. in the phrase **usual offices**). **15 in** (*or* **out of**) **office.** (of a government) in (or out of) power. **16 the office.** *Slang.* a hint or signal. [C13: via Old French from Latin *officium* service, duty, from *opus* work, service + *facere* to do]

office bearer *n* a person who holds an office, as in a society, company, club, etc.; official.

office block *n* a large building designed to provide office accommodation.

office boy *n* a former name for **office junior.**

office hours *pl n* **1** the hours during which an office is open for business. **2** the number of hours worked in an office.

office junior *n* a young person, esp. a school-leaver, employed in an office for running errands and doing other minor jobs.

officer ('ɒfɪsə) *n* **1** a person in the armed services who holds a position of responsibility, authority, and duty, esp. one who holds a commission. **2** See **police officer. 3** (on a non-naval ship) any person including the captain and mate, who holds a position of authority and responsibility: *radio officer; engineer officer.* **4** a person appointed or elected to a position of responsibility or authority in a government, society, etc. **5** a government official: *a customs officer.* **6** (in the Order of the British Empire) a member of the grade below commander. ◆ *vb* (*tr*) **7** to furnish with officers. **8** to act as an officer over (some section, group, organization, etc.).

officer of arms *n Heraldry.* a pursuivant or herald.

officer of the day *n* a military officer whose duty is to take charge of the security of the unit or camp for a day. Also called: **orderly officer.**

officer of the guard *n* a junior officer whose duty is to command a ceremonial guard. Abbrev.: **OG.**

official (ə'fɪʃəl) *adj* **1** of or relating to an office, its administration, or its duration. **2** sanctioned by, recognized by, or derived from authority: *an official statement.* **3** appointed by authority, esp. for some special duty. **4** having a formal ceremonial character: *an official dinner.* ◆ *n* **5** a person who holds a position in an organization, government department, etc., esp. a subordinate position. ▸ **of'ficially** *adv*

Official (ə'fɪʃəl) *adj* **1** of or relating to one of the two factions of the IRA and Sinn Féin, which have existed since a split in 1969. The Official movement emphasizes political rather than guerrilla activity. ◆ *n* **2** a member of the Official IRA and Sinn Féin. Compare **Provisional.**

officialdom (ə'fɪʃəldəm) *n* **1** the outlook or behaviour of officials, esp. those rigidly adhering to regulations; bureaucracy. **2** officials or bureaucrats collectively.

officialese (əˌfɪʃə'liːz) *n* language characteristic of official documents, esp. when verbose or pedantic.

Official Receiver *n* an officer appointed by the Department of Trade and Industry to receive the income and manage the estate of a bankrupt pending the appointment of a trustee in bankruptcy. See also **receiver** (sense 2).

Official Referee *n Law.* (in England) a circuit judge attached to the High Court who is empowered to try certain cases, esp. where a detailed examination of accounts or other documents is involved.

Official Solicitor *n* an officer of the Supreme Court of Judicature with special responsibilities for protecting the interests of persons under disability.

official strike *n* a collective stoppage of work by part or all of the workforce of an organization with the approval of the trade union concerned. The stoppage may be accompanied by the payment of strike pay by the trade union concerned.

officiant (ə'fɪʃɪənt) *n* a person who presides and officiates at a religious ceremony.

officiary (ə'fɪʃɪərɪ) *n, pl* **-aries. 1** a body of officials. ◆ *adj* **2** of, relating to, or derived from office.

officiate (ə'fɪʃɪˌeɪt) *vb* (*intr*) **1** to hold the position, responsibility, or function of an official. **2** to conduct a religious or other ceremony. [C17: from Medieval Latin *officiāre,* from Latin *officium;* see OFFICE] ▸ **ofˌfici'ation** *n* ▸ **of'ficiˌator** *n*

officinal (ɒ'fɪsɪnᵊl, ˌɒfɪ'saɪnᵊl) *Pharmacol., obsolete.* ◆ *adj* **1** (of pharmaceutical products) available without prescription. **2** (of a plant) having pharmacological properties. ◆ *n* **3** an officinal preparation or plant. [C17: from Medieval Latin *officīnālis,* from Latin *officīna* workshop; see OFFICE] ▸ **of'ficinally** *adv*

officious (ə'fɪʃəs) *adj* **1** unnecessarily or obtrusively ready to offer advice or services. **2** marked by such readiness. **3** *Diplomacy.* informal or unofficial. **4** *Obsolete.* attentive or obliging. [C16: from Latin *officiōsus* kindly, from *officium* service; see OFFICE] ▸ **of'ficiously** *adv* ▸ **of'ficiousness** *n*

offing ('ɒfɪŋ) *n* **1** the part of the sea that can be seen from the shore. **2 in the offing.** likely to occur soon.

offish ('ɒfɪʃ) *adj Informal.* aloof or distant in manner. ▸ **'offishly** *adv* ▸ **'offishness** *n*

off key *adj* (**off-key** *when prenominal*), *adv* **1** *Music.* **1a** not in the correct key. **1b** out of tune. **2** out of keeping; discordant.

off-licence *n Brit.* **1** a shop, or a counter in a pub or hotel, where alcoholic drinks are sold for consumption elsewhere. U.S. equivalents: **package store, liquor store. 2** a licence permitting such sales.

off limits *adj* (**off-limits** *when prenominal*). **1** not to be entered; out of bounds. ◆ *adv* **2** in or into an area forbidden by regulations.

off line *adj* (**off-line** *when prenominal*). **1** of, relating to, or concerned with a part of a computer system not connected to the central processing unit but controlled by a computer storage device. Compare **on line. 2** disconnected from a computer; switched off. **3** extra to or not involving a continuous sequence of operations, such as a production line. **4** *Radio, television.* (of processes, such as editing) not carried out on the actual transmission medium.

off-load *vb* (*tr*) to get rid of (something unpleasant or burdensome), as by delegation to another.

off-off-Broadway *adj* of or relating to highly experimental informal small-scale theatrical productions in New York, usually taking place in cafés, small halls, etc. Compare **off-Broadway.**

off-peak *adj* of or relating to services as used outside periods of intensive use or electricity supplied at cheaper rates during the night.

off-piste *adj* of or relating to skiing on virgin snow off the regular runs.

offprint ('ɒfˌprɪnt) *n* **1** Also called (U.S.): **separate.** a separate reprint of an article that originally appeared in a larger publication. ◆ *vb* **2** (*tr*) to reprint (an article taken from a larger publication) separately.

off-putting *adj Brit. informal.* disconcerting or disturbing.

off-road *adj* (of a motor vehicle) designed or built for use away from public roads, esp. on rough terrain.

off-sales *pl n Brit.* sales of alcoholic drink for consumption off the premises by a pub or an off-licence attached to a pub.

offscourings ('ɒfˌskaʊərɪŋz) *pl n* scum; dregs.

off season *adj* (**off-season** *when prenominal*). **1** denoting or occurring during a period of little activity in a trade or business. ◆ *n* **2** such a period. ◆ *adv* **3** in an off-season period.

offset *n* ('ɒfˌsɛt). **1** something that counterbalances or compensates for something else. **2** an allowance made to counteract some effect. **3a** a printing method in which the impression is made onto an intermediate surface, such as a rubber blanket, which transfers it to the paper. **3b** (*modifier*) relating to, involving, or printed by offset: *offset letterpress; offset lithography*. **4** another name for **set-off.** **5** *Botany.* **5a** a short runner in certain plants, such as the houseleek, that produces roots and shoots at the tip. **5b** a plant produced from such a runner. **6** a ridge projecting from a range of hills or mountains. **7** a narrow horizontal or sloping surface formed where a wall is reduced in thickness towards the top. **8** a person or group descended collaterally from a particular group or family; offshoot. **9** *Surveying.* a measurement of distance to a point at right angles to a survey line. ◆ *vb* (ˌɒf'sɛt), **-sets, -setting, -set. 10** (*tr*) to counterbalance or compensate for. **11** (*tr*) to print (pictures, text, etc.) using the offset process. **12** (*tr*) to construct an offset in (a wall). **13** (*intr*) to project or develop as an offset.

offshoot ('ɒfˌʃuːt) *n* **1** a shoot or branch growing from the main stem of a plant. **2** something that develops or derives from a principal source or origin.

offshore (ˌɒf'ʃɔː) *adj, adv* **1** from, away from, or at some distance from the shore. ◆ *adj* **2** sited or conducted at sea as opposed to on land: *offshore industries*. **3** based or operating abroad in places where the tax system is more advantageous than that of the home country: *offshore banking; offshore fund*.

offside ('ɒf'saɪd) *adj, adv* **1** *Sport.* (in football, hockey, etc.) in a position illegally ahead of the ball or puck when it is played, usually when within one's opponents' half or the attacking zone. ◆ *n* **2** (usually preceded by *the*) *Chiefly Brit.* **2a** the side of a vehicle nearest the centre of the road (in Britain, the right side). **2b** (*as modifier*): *the offside passenger door*. ◆ Compare **nearside.**

offsider (ˌɒf'saɪdə) *n Austral. and N.Z.* a partner or assistant.

offspring ('ɒfˌsprɪŋ) *n* **1** the immediate descendant or descendants of a person, animal, etc.; progeny. **2** a product, outcome, or result.

offstage ('ɒf'steɪdʒ) *adj, adv* out of the view of the audience; off the stage.

off-street *adj* located away from a street: *off-street parking*.

off the record *adj* (**off-the-record** *when prenominal*). **1** not intended for publication or disclosure; confidential. ◆ *adv* **2** with such an intention; unofficially.

off the shelf *adv* **1** from stock and readily available: *you can have this model off the shelf*. ◆ *adj* (**off-the-shelf** *when prenominal*). **2** of or relating to a product that is readily available: *an off-the-shelf model*. **3** of or denoting a company that has been registered with the Registrar of Companies for the sole purpose of being sold.

off-the-wall *adj* (**off the wall** *when postpositive*). *Slang.* new or unexpected in an unconventional or eccentric way: *an off-the-wall approach to humour*. [C20: possibly from the use of the phrase in handball and squash to describe a shot that is unexpected]

off-white *n* **1** a colour, such as cream or bone, consisting of white mixed with a tinge of grey or with a pale hue. ◆ *adj* **2** of such a colour: *an off-white coat*.

off-year election *n* (in the U.S.) an election held in a year when a presidential election does not take place.

Ofgas ('ɒfˌgæs) *n* (in Britain) *acronym for* Office of Gas Supply: a government body set up in 1986 to monitor the activities of British Gas, and to protect the interests of its consumers.

oflag ('ɒfˌlɑːg) *n* a German prisoner-of-war camp for officers in World War II. [German, short for *Offizierslager* officers' camp]

Oflot ('ɒfˌlɒt) *n* (in Britain) *acronym for* Office of the National Lottery: a government body set up in 1993 to oversee the running of the National Lottery.

O'Flaherty (əʊ'flæhətɪ) *n* **Liam** ('lɪəm). 1897–1984, Irish novelist and short-story writer. His novels include *The Informer* (1925) and *Famine* (1937).

OFM *abbrev. for* Ordo Fratrum Minorum (the Franciscans). [Latin: Order of Minor Friars]

OFris *abbrev. for* Old Frisian.

OFS *abbrev. for* Orange Free State.

Ofsted ('ɒfˌstɛd) *n* (in Britain) *acronym for* Office for Standards in Education: a government body set up in 1993 to inspect and assess the educational standards of schools and colleges in England and Wales.

oft (ɒft) *adv* short for **often** (archaic or poetic except in combinations such as **oft-repeated** and **oft-recurring**). [Old English *oft*; related to Old High German *ofto*]

OFT (in Britain) *abbrev. for* Office of Fair Trading.

Oftel ('ɒfˌtɛl) *n* (in Britain) *acronym for* Office of Telecommunications: a government body set up in 1984 to supervise telecommunications activities in the UK, and to protect the interests of the consumers.

often ('ɒfᵊn, 'ɒftᵊn) *adv* **1** frequently or repeatedly; much of the time. Archaic equivalents: **'oftenˌtimes, 'oftˌtimes. 2 as often as not.** quite frequently. **3 every so often.** at intervals. **4 more often than not.** in more than half the instances. ◆ *adj* **5** *Archaic.* repeated; frequent. [C14: variant of OFT before vowels and *h*]

Ofwat ('ɒfˌwɒt) *n* (in Britain) *acronym for* Office of Water Services: a government body set up in 1989 to regulate the activities of the water companies in England and Wales, and to protect the interests of their consumers.

OG *abbrev. for:* **1** officer of the guard. **2** Also: **o.g.** *Philately.* original gum.

o.g. *abbrev. for* own goal.

Ogaden (ˌɒgə'dɛn) *n* **the.** an autonomous region of SE Ethiopia, bordering on Somalia: consists of a desert plateau, inhabited by Somali nomads; a secessionist movement, supported by Somalia, has existed within the region since the early 1960s and led to bitter fighting between Ethiopia and Somalia (1977–78).

Ogasawara Gunto (ˌɒgəsə'wɑːrə 'gʌntəʊ) *n* transliteration of the Japanese name for the **Bonin Islands.**

Ogbomosho (ˌɒgbə'məʊʃəʊ) *n* a city in SW Nigeria: the third largest town in Nigeria; trading centre for an agricultural region. Pop.: 730 000 (1996 est.).

Ogden ('ɒgdən) *n* **C(harles) K(ay).** 1889–1957, English linguist, who, with I. A. Richards, devised Basic English.

ogdoad ('ɒgdəʊˌæd) *n* a group of eight. [C17: via Late Latin from Greek *ogdoos* eighth, from *oktō* eight]

Ogdon ('ɒgdən) *n* **John (Andrew Howard).** 1937–89, British pianist and composer.

ogee ('əʊdʒiː) *n Architect.* **1** Also called: **talon.** a moulding having a cross section in the form of a letter S. **2** short for **ogee arch.** [C15: probably variant of OGIVE]

ogee arch *n Architect.* a pointed arch having an S-shaped curve on both sides. Sometimes shortened to **ogee.** Also called: **keel arch.**

Ogen melon ('əʊgen) *n* a variety of small melon having a green skin and sweet pale green flesh. [C20: named after a kibbutz in Israel where it was first developed]

ogham *or* **ogam** ('ɒgəm, ɔːm) *n* an ancient alphabetical writing system used by the Celts in Britain and Ireland, consisting of straight lines drawn or carved perpendicular to or at an angle to another long straight line. [C17: from Old Irish *ogom,* of uncertain origin but associated with the name *Ogma,* legendary inventor of this alphabet]

ogive ('əʊdʒaɪv, əʊ'dʒaɪv) *n* **1** a diagonal rib or groin of a Gothic vault. **2** another name for **lancet arch. 3** *Statistics.* a graph the ordinates of which represent cumulative frequencies of the values indicated by the corresponding abscissas. **4** the conical head of a missile or rocket that protects the payload during its passage through the atmosphere. [C17: from Old French, of uncertain origin] ▸ **o'gival** *adj*

ogle ('əʊgᵊl) *vb* **1** to look at (someone) amorously or lustfully. **2** (*tr*) to stare or gape at. ◆ *n* **3** a flirtatious or lewd look. [C17: probably from Low German *oegeln,* from *oegen* to look at] ▸ **'ogler** *n*

Oglethorpe ('əʊgᵊlˌθɔːp) *n* **James Edward.** 1696–1785, English general and colonial administrator; founder of the colony of Georgia (1733).

Ogooué *or* **Ogowe** (ɒ'gəʊweɪ) *n* a river in W central Africa, rising in the SW Congo Republic and flowing generally northwest and north through Gabon to the Atlantic. Length: about 970 km (683 miles).

Ogpu ('ɒgpuː) *n* the Soviet police and secret police from 1923 to 1934. [C20: from Russian *O(byedinyonnoye) g(osudarstvennoye) p(oliticheskoye) u(pravleniye)* United State Political Administration]

O grade *n* (formerly in Scotland) **1a** the basic level of the Scottish Certificate of Education, now replaced by **Standard Grade. 1b** (*as modifier*): *O grade history*. **2** a pass in a particular subject at O grade: *she has ten O grades*. ◆ Formal name: **Ordinary grade.**

ogre ('əʊgə) *n* **1** (in folklore) a giant, usually given to eating human flesh. **2** any monstrous or cruel person. [C18: from French, perhaps from Latin *Orcus* god of the infernal regions] ▸ **'ogreish** *adj* ▸ **'ogress** *fem n*

Ogun (əʊ'gʊn) *n* a state of SW Nigeria, formed in 1976 from part of Western State. Capital: Abeokuta. Pop.: 2 614 747 (1995 est.). Area: 16 762 sq. km (6472 sq. miles).

Ogygian (əʊ'dʒɪdʒɪən) *adj* of very great age; prehistoric. [C19: from Greek *ōgugios* relating to *Ogyges,* the most ancient king of Greece, mythical ruler of Boeotia or Attica]

oh (əʊ) *interj* **1** an exclamation expressive of surprise, pain, pleasure, etc. ◆ *sentence connector.* **2** an expression used to preface a remark, gain time, etc.: *oh, I suppose so*.

OH *abbrev. for* Ohio.

O. Henry (əʊ 'hɛnrɪ) *n* pen name of *William Sidney Porter.* 1862–1910, U.S. short-story writer. His collections of stories, characterized by his use of caricature and surprising endings, include *Cabbages and Kings* (1904) and *The Four Million* (1906).

OHG *abbrev. for* Old High German.

O'Higgins (əʊ'hɪgɪnz; *Spanish* o'iɣins) *n* **1 Ambrosio** (æm'brəʊzɪˌəʊ). ?1720–1801, Irish soldier, who became viceroy of Chile (1789–96) and of Peru (1796–1801). **2** his son, **Bernardo** (bɛr'narðo). 1778–1842, Chilean revolutionary. He was one of the leaders in the struggle for independence from Spain and was Chile's first president (1817–23).

Ohio (əʊ'haɪəʊ) *n* **1** a state of the central U.S., in the Midwest on Lake Erie: consists of prairies in the W and the Allegheny plateau in the E, the Ohio River forming the S and most of the E borders. Capital: Columbus. Pop.: 11 186 331 (1997 est.). Area: 107 044 sq. km (41 330 sq. miles). Abbrev. (with zip code): **OH 2** a river in the eastern U.S., formed by the confluence of the Allegheny and Monongahela Rivers at Pittsburgh: flows generally W and SW to join the Mississippi at Cairo, Illinois, as its chief E tributary. Length: 1570 km (975 miles).

Öhlenschläger *Danish.* ('øːlənslɛːyər) *n* a variant spelling of **Oehlenschläger.**

ohm (əʊm) *n* the derived SI unit of electrical resistance; the resistance between two points on a conductor when a constant potential difference of 1 volt between them produces a current of 1 ampere. Symbol: Ω [C19: named after Georg Simon OHM]

Ohm (əʊm) *n* **Georg Simon** ('geːɔrk 'ziːmɔn). 1787–1854, German physicist, who formulated the law named after him.

ohmage ('əʊmɪdʒ) *n* electrical resistance in ohms.

ohmic ('əʊmɪk) *adj* of or relating to a circuit element, the electrical resistance of which obeys Ohm's law.

ohmmeter ('əʊmˌmiːtə) *n* an instrument for measuring electrical resistance.

OHMS (in Britain and the dominions of the Commonwealth) *abbrev. for* On Her (*or* His) Majesty's Service.

Ohm's law *n* the principle that the electric current passing through a conductor is directly proportional to the potential difference across it, provided that the temperature remains constant. The constant of proportionality is the resistance of the conductor.

oho (əʊ'həʊ) *interj* an exclamation expressing surprise, exultation, or derision.

ohv *abbrev. for* overhead valve.

-oid *suffix forming adjectives and associated nouns.* indicating likeness, resemblance, or similarity: *anthropoid.* [from Greek *-oeidēs* resembling form of, from *eidos* form]

-oidea *suffix forming plural proper nouns.* forming the names of zoological classes or superfamilies: *Crinoidea; Canoidea.* [from New Latin, from Latin *-oīdēs* -OID]

oidium (əʊ'ɪdɪəm) *n, pl* **-ia** (-ɪə). *Botany.* any of various fungal spores produced in the form of a chain by the development of septa in a hypha. [New Latin: from OO- + *-idium* diminutive suffix]

oik (ɔɪk) *n Brit. derogatory, slang.* a person regarded as inferior because ignorant, ill-educated, or lower-class.

oil (ɔɪl) *n* **1** any of a number of viscous liquids with a smooth sticky feel. They are usually flammable, insoluble in water, soluble in organic solvents, and are obtained from plants and animals, from mineral deposits, and by synthesis. They are used as lubricants, fuels, perfumes, foodstuffs, and raw materials for chemicals. See also **essential oil, fixed oil. 2a** another name for **petroleum. 2b** (*as modifier*): *an oil engine; an oil rig.* **3a** Also called: **lubricating oil.** any of a number of substances usually derived from petroleum and used for lubrication. **3b** (*in combination*): *an oilcan; an oilstone.* **3c** (*as modifier*): *an oil pump.* **4** Also called: **fuel oil.** a petroleum product used as a fuel in domestic heating, industrial furnaces, marine engines, etc. **5** *Brit.* **5a** paraffin, esp. when used as a domestic fuel. **5b** (*as modifier*): *an oil lamp; an oil stove.* **6** any substance of a consistency resembling that of oil: *oil of vitriol.* **7** the solvent, usually linseed oil, with which pigments are mixed to make artists' paints. **8a** (*often pl*) oil colour or paint. **8b** (*as modifier*): *an oil painting.* **9** an oil painting. **10 the good (dinkum) oil.** *Austral. and N.Z. slang.* facts or news. **11 strike oil. 11a** to discover petroleum while drilling for it. **11b** *Informal.* to become very rich or successful. ◆ *vb* (*tr*) **12** to lubricate, smear, polish, etc., with oil or an oily substance. **13** *Informal.* to bribe (esp. in the phrase **oil someone's palm**). **14 oil the wheels.** to make things run smoothly. **15** See **well-oiled.** [C12: from Old French *oile,* from Latin *oleum* (olive) oil, from *olea* olive tree, from Greek *elaia* OLIVE] ▸ **'oil-ˌlike** *adj*

oil beetle *n* any of various beetles of the family *Meloidae* that exude an oily evil-smelling blood from their joints, which deters enemies.

oilbird ('ɔɪlˌbɜːd) *n* a nocturnal gregarious cave-dwelling bird, *Steatornis caripensis,* of N South America and Trinidad, having a hooked bill and dark plumage: family *Steatornithidae,* order *Caprimulgiformes.* Also called: **guacharo.**

oil cake *n* stock feed consisting of compressed cubes made from the residue of the crushed seeds of oil-bearing crops such as linseed.

oilcan ('ɔɪlˌkæn) *n* a container with a long nozzle for applying lubricating oil to machinery.

oilcloth ('ɔɪlˌklɒθ) *n* **1** waterproof material made by treating one side of a cotton fabric with a drying oil, or a synthetic resin. **2** another name for **linoleum.**

oil-cooled *adj Engineering, etc.* (of an engine, apparatus, etc.) having its heat removed by the circulation of oil. ▸ **oil cooler** *n*

oilcup ('ɔɪlˌkʌp) *n* a cup-shaped oil reservoir in a machine providing continuous lubrication for a bearing.

oil drum *n* a metal drum used to contain or transport oil.

oiled silk *n* silk treated with oil to make it waterproof.

oiler ('ɔɪlə) *n* **1** a person, device, etc., that lubricates or supplies oil. **2** an oil tanker. **3** an oil well.

oilfield ('ɔɪlˌfiːld) *n* an area containing reserves of petroleum, esp. one that is already being exploited.

oilfired ('ɔɪlˌfaɪəd) *adj* (of central heating) using oil as fuel.

oilgas ('ɔɪlˌgæs) *n* a gaseous mixture of hydrocarbons used as a fuel, obtained by the destructive distillation of mineral oils.

oil hardening *n* a process of hardening high-carbon or alloy steels by heating and cooling in oil. Compare **air hardening.**

oilman ('ɔɪlmən) *n, pl* **-men. 1** a person who owns or operates oil wells. **2** a person who makes or sells oil.

oil of turpentine *n* another name for **turpentine** (sense 3).

oil of vitriol *n* another name for **sulphuric acid.**

oil paint *or* **colour** *n* paint made of pigment ground in oil, usually linseed oil, used for oil painting.

oil painting *n* **1** a picture painted with oil paints. **2** the art or process of painting with oil paints. **3 he's** *or* **she's no oil painting.** *Informal.* he or she is not good-looking.

oil palm *n* a tropical African palm tree, *Elaeis guineensis,* the fruits of which yield palm oil.

oil rig *n* See **rig** (sense 6).

Oil Rivers *pl n* the delta of the Niger River in S Nigeria.

oil sand *n* a sandstone impregnated with hydrocarbons, esp. such deposits in Alberta, Canada.

oil-seed rape *n* another name for **rape**[2].

oil shale *n* a fine-grained shale containing oil, which can be extracted by heating.

oilskin ('ɔɪlˌskɪn) *n* **1a** a cotton fabric treated with oil and pigment to make it waterproof. **1b** (*as modifier*): *an oilskin hat.* **2** (*often pl*) a protective outer garment of this fabric.

oil slick *n* a mass of floating oil covering an area of water, esp. oil that has leaked or been discharged from a ship.

oilstone ('ɔɪlˌstəʊn) *n* a stone with a fine grain lubricated with oil and used for sharpening cutting tools. See also **whetstone.**

oil varnish *n* another name for **varnish** (sense 1).

oil well *n* a boring into the earth or sea bed for the extraction of petroleum.

oily ('ɔɪlɪ) *adj* **oilier, oiliest. 1** soaked in or smeared with oil or grease. **2** consisting of, containing, or resembling oil. **3** flatteringly servile or obsequious. ▸ **'oilily** *adv* ▸ **'oiliness** *n*

oink (ɔɪŋk) *interj* an imitation or representation of the grunt of a pig.

ointment ('ɔɪntmənt) *n* **1** a fatty or oily medicated preparation applied to the skin to heal or protect. **2** a similar substance used as a cosmetic. [C14: from Old French *oignement,* from Latin *unguentum* UNGUENT]

Oireachtas ('ɛrəkθəs; *Gaelic* 'ɛrəxtəs) *n* the parliament of the Republic of Ireland, consisting of the president, the Dáil Éireann, and the Seanad Éireann. See also **Dáil Éireann, Seanad Éireann.** [Irish: assembly, from Old Irish *airech* nobleman]

Oise (*French* waz) *n* **1** a department of N France, in Picardy region. Capital: Beauvais. Pop.: 762 700 (1995). Area: 5887 sq. km (2296 sq. miles). **2** a river in N France, rising in Belgium, in the Ardennes, and flowing southwest to join the Seine at Conflans. Length: 302 km (188 miles).

Oistrakh ('ɔɪstrɑːk; *Russian* 'ɔjstrəx) *n* **1 David** (da'vit). 1908–74, Russian violinist. **2** his son, **Igor** ('igərj). born 1931, Russian violinist.

Oita ('ɔɪtə) *n* an industrial city in SW Japan, on NE Kyushu: dominated most of Kyushu in the 16th century. Pop.: 426 981 (1995).

Ojibwa (əʊ'dʒɪbwə) *n* **1** (*pl* **-was** *or* **-wa**) a member of a North American Indian people living in a region west of Lake Superior. **2** the language of this people, belonging to the Algonquian family. ◆ Also called: **Chippewa.**

OK *abbrev. for* Oklahoma.

O.K. (ˌəʊ'keɪ) *Informal.* ◆ *sentence substitute.* **1** an expression of approval, agreement, etc. ◆ *adj* (*usually postpositive*), *adv* **2** in good or satisfactory condition. ◆ *vb* **O.K.s, O.K.ing** (ˌəʊ'keɪɪŋ), **O.K.ed** (ˌəʊ'keɪd). **3** (*tr*) to approve or endorse. ◆ *n, pl* **O.K.s. 4** approval or agreement. ◆ Also: **OK, o.k., o'kay.** [C19: perhaps from *o(ll) k(orrect),* jocular alteration of *all correct*]

oka ('əʊkə) *or* **oke** (əʊk) *n* **1** a unit of weight used in Turkey, equal to about 2.75 pounds or 1.24 kilograms. **2** a unit of liquid measure used in Turkey, equal to about 1.3 pints or 0.75 litres. [C17: from Turkish *ōqah,* from Arabic *ūqiyah,* probably from Greek *ounkia;* perhaps related to Latin *uncia* one twelfth; see OUNCE[1]]

Oka ('əʊkə) *n* a brine-cured Canadian cheese. [named after *Oka,* Quebec, where it is made at a monastery]

Okanagan (ˌəʊkə'nɑːgən) *n* **1** Also (U.S.): ˌ**Oka'nogan.** a river in North America that flows south from Okanagan Lake in Canada into the Columbia River in NE Washington, U.S. Length: about 483 km (300 miles). **2** Also: ˌ**Oka'nogan,** ˌ**Oki'nagan.** a member of a North American Indian people living in the Okanagan River valley in British Columbia and Washington. **3** Also: ˌ**Oka'nogan,** ˌ**Oki'nagan.** the language of this people, belonging to the Salish family.

Okanagan Lake *n* a lake in SW Canada, in S British Columbia: drained by the Okanagan River into the Columbia River. Length: about 111 km (69 miles). Width: from 3.2–6.4 km (2–4 miles).

okapi (əʊ'kɑːpɪ) *n, pl* **-pis** *or* **-pi.** a ruminant mammal, *Okapia johnstoni,* of the forests of central Africa, having a reddish-brown coat with horizontal white stripes on the legs and small horns: family *Giraffidae.* [C20: from a Central African word]

Okavango *or* **Okovango** (ˌəʊkə'vɑːŋgəʊ) *n* a river in SW central Africa, rising in central Angola and flowing southeast, then east as part of the border between Angola and Namibia, then southeast across the Caprivi Strip into Botswana to form a great marsh known as the **Okavango Basin.** Length: about 1600 km (1000 miles).

okay (ˌəʊ'keɪ) *sentence substitute, adj, vb, n* a variant of **O.K.**

Okayama (ˌɒkə'jɑːmə) *n* a city in SW Japan, on W Honshu on the Inland Sea. Pop.: 616 056 (1995).

oke[1] (əʊk) *n* another name for **oka.**

oke[2] (əʊk) *adj, adv Informal.* another term for **O.K.**

Okeechobee (ˌəʊkɪ'tʃəʊbɪ) *n* **Lake.** a lake in S Florida, in the Everglades: second largest freshwater lake wholly within the U.S. Area: 1813 sq. km (700 sq. miles).

O'Keeffe (əʊ'kiːf) *n* **Georgia.** 1887–1986, U.S. painter, best known for her semiabstract still lifes, esp. of flowers: married the photographer Alfred Stieglitz.

Okefenokee Swamp (ˌəʊkɪfɪ'nəʊkɪ) *n* a swamp in the U.S., in SE Georgia and N Florida: protected flora and fauna. Area: 1554 sq. km (600 sq. miles).

Okeghem ('ɒkəˌgem; *Dutch* 'ɔkəxəm) *n* a variant spelling of **Ockeghem.**

okey-doke ('əʊkɪ'dəʊk) *or* **okey-dokey** ('əʊkɪ'dəʊkɪ) *sentence substitute, adj, adv Informal.* another term for **O.K.**

Okhotsk ('əʊkɒtsk; *Russian* a'xɔtsk) *n* **Sea of.** part of the NW Pacific, surrounded by the Kamchatka Peninsula, the Kurile Islands, Sakhalin Island, and the E coast of Siberia. Area: 1 589 840 sq. km (613 838 sq. miles).

Okie ('əʊkɪ) *n U.S. slang, sometimes considered offensive.* **1** an inhabitant of Oklahoma. **2** an impoverished migrant farm worker, esp. one who left Oklahoma during the Depression of the 1930s to work elsewhere in the U.S.

Okinawa (ˌəʊkɪ'nɑːwə) *n* a coral island of SW Japan, the largest of the Ryukyu Islands in the N Pacific: scene of heavy fighting in World War II; administered by the U.S. (1945–72); agricultural. Chief town: Naha City. Pop.: 1 273 508 (1995). Area: 1176 sq. km (454 sq. miles).

Okla. *abbrev. for* Oklahoma.

Oklahoma (ˌəʊklə'həʊmə) *n* a state in the S central U.S.: consists of plains in the west, rising to mountains in the southwest and east; important for oil.

Capital: Oklahoma City. Pop.: 3 317 091 (1997 est.). Area: 181 185 sq. km (69 956 sq. miles). Abbrevs.: **Okla.** or (with zip code) **OK** ▸ **ˌOklaˈhoman** *adj, n*

Oklahoma City *n* a city in central Oklahoma: the state capital and a major agricultural and industrial centre. Pop.: 469 852 (1996 est.).

Okovango (ˌəukəˈvɑːŋgəu) *n* a variant spelling of **Okavango.**

okra (ˈəukrə) *n* **1** Also called: **ladies' fingers.** an annual malvaceous plant, *Hibiscus esculentus,* of the Old World tropics, with yellow-and-red flowers and edible oblong sticky green pods. **2** the pod of this plant, eaten in soups, stews, etc. See also **gumbo** (sense 1). [C18: of W African origin]

Okri (ˈɒkrɪ) *n* **Ben.** born 1959, Nigerian writer; his books include *The Famished Road* (1991).

okta *or* **octa** (ˈɒktə) *n* a unit used in meteorology to measure cloud cover, equivalent to a cloud cover of one eighth of the sky. [C20: from Greek *okta-, oktō* eight]

-ol[1] *suffix forming nouns.* denoting an organic chemical compound containing a hydroxyl group, esp. alcohols and phenols: *ethanol; quinol.* [from ALCOHOL]

-ol[2] *n combining form.* (*not used systematically*) a variant of **-ole**[1].

Olaf I (ˈəuləf) *or* **Olav I** (ˈəuləv) *n* known as *Olaf Tryggvesson.* ?965–?1000 A.D., king of Norway (995–?1000). He began the conversion of Norway to Christianity.

Olaf II *or* **Olav II** *n* **Saint.** 995–1030 A.D., king of Norway (1015–28), who worked to complete the conversion of Norway to Christianity; deposed by Canute; patron saint of Norway. Feast day: July 29.

Olaf V *or* **Olav V** *n* 1903–91, king of Norway 1957–91; son of Haakon VII.

Öland (*Swedish* ˈøːland) *n* an island in the Baltic Sea, separated from the mainland of SE Sweden by Kalmar Sound: the second largest Swedish island. Chief town: Borgholm. Pop.: 24 100 (1988 est.). Area: 1347 sq. km (520 sq. miles).

old (əuld) *adj* **1** having lived or existed for a relatively long time: *an old man; an old tradition; old wine; an old house; an old country.* **2a** of or relating to advanced years or a long life: *old age.* **2b** (*as collective n;* preceded by *the*): *the old.* **2c old and young.** people of all ages. **3** decrepit or senile. **4** worn with age or use: *old clothes; an old car.* **5a** (*postpositive*) having lived or existed for a specified period: *a child who is six years old.* **5b** (*in combination*): *a six-year-old child.* **5c** (*as n in combination*): *a six-year-old.* **6** (*cap. when part of a name or title*) earlier or earliest of two or more things with the same name: *the old edition; the Old Testament; old Norwich.* **7** (*cap. when part of a name*) designating the form of a language in which the earliest known records are written: *Old English.* **8** (*prenominal*) familiar through long acquaintance or repetition: *an old friend; an old excuse.* **9** practised; hardened: *old in cunning.* **10** (*prenominal*) (often preceded by *good*) cherished; dear: used as a term of affection or familiarity: *good old George.* **11** *Informal.* (with any of several nouns) used as a familiar form of address to a person: *old thing; old bean; old stick; old fellow.* **12** skilled through long experience (esp. in the phrase **an old hand**). **13** out-of-date; unfashionable. **14** remote or distant in origin or time of origin: *an old culture.* **15** (*prenominal*) former; previous: *my old house was small.* **16a** (*prenominal*) established for a relatively long time: *an old member.* **16b** (*in combination*): *old-established.* **17** sensible, wise, or mature: *old beyond one's years.* **18** (of a river, valley, or land surface) in the final stage of the cycle of erosion, characterized by flat extensive flood plains and minimum relief. See also **youthful** (sense 4), **mature** (sense 6). **19** (intensifier) (esp. in phrases such as **a good old time, any old thing, any old how,** etc.). **20** (of crops) harvested late. **21 good old days.** an earlier period of time regarded as better than the present. **22 little old.** *Informal.* indicating affection, esp. humorous affection: *my little old wife.* **23 the old one** (*or* **gentleman**). *Informal.* a jocular name for **Satan.** ◆ *n* **24** an earlier or past time (esp. in the phrase **of old**): *in days of old.* [Old English *eald;* related to Old Saxon *ald,* Old High German, German *alt,* Latin *altus* high] ▸ **ˈoldish** *adj* ▸ **ˈoldness** *n*

old age pension *n* a former name for the state **retirement pension.** ▸ **old age pensioner** *n*

Old Bailey *n* the chief court exercising criminal jurisdiction in London; the Central Criminal Court of England.

Old Bill *n Brit. slang.* **1** a policeman. **2** (*functioning as pl;* preceded by *the*) policemen collectively or in general. [C20: of uncertain origin: perhaps derived from the World War I cartoon of a soldier with a drooping moustache]

old bird *n Jocular.* a wary and astute person.

old boy *n* **1** (*sometimes caps.*) *Brit.* a male ex-pupil of a school. **2** *Informal, chiefly Brit.* **2a** a familiar name used to refer to a man. **2b** an old man.

old boy network *n Brit. informal.* the appointment to power of former pupils of the same small group of public schools or universities.

Old Bulgarian *n* another name for **Old Church Slavonic.**

Old Castile *n* a region of N Spain, on the Bay of Biscay: formerly a province. Spanish name: **Castilla la Vieja.**

Oldcastle (ˈəuldˌkɑːsᵊl) *n* Sir **John,** Baron Cobham. ?1378–1417, Lollard leader. In 1411 he led an English army in France but in 1413 he was condemned as a heretic and later hanged and burnt. He is thought to have been a model for Shakespeare's character Falstaff in *Henry IV.*

Old Catholic *adj* **1** of or relating to several small national Churches which have broken away from the Roman Catholic Church on matters of doctrine. ◆ *n* **2** a member of one of these Churches.

old chum *n Austral. informal.* (formerly) **1** a person who is experienced, esp. in life in colonial Australia. **2** an experienced convict.

Old Church Slavonic *or* **Slavic** *n* the oldest recorded Slavonic language: the form of Old Slavonic into which the Bible was translated in the ninth century, preserved as a liturgical language of various Orthodox Churches: belonging to the South Slavonic subbranch of languages.

old clothes man *n* a person who deals in second-hand clothes.

Old Contemptibles *pl n* the British expeditionary force to France in 1914. [so named from the Kaiser's alleged reference to them as a "contemptible little army"]

old country *n* the country of origin of an immigrant or an immigrant's ancestors.

Old Dart *n* **the.** *Austral. slang.* England. [C19: of unknown origin]

Old Delhi *n* See **Delhi.**

Old Dutch *n* the Dutch language up to about 1100, derived from the Low Franconian dialect of Old Low German. See also **Franconian.** Abbrev.: **OD.**

olden (ˈəuldᵊn) *adj* an archaic or poetic word for **old** (often in phrases such as **in olden days** and **in olden times**).

Oldenbarneveldt (ˌɒldənˈbɑːnəˌvelt) *n* **Johan van.** 1547–1619, Dutch statesman, regarded as a founder of Dutch independence; the leading figure (from 1586) in the United Provinces of the Netherlands: executed by Maurice of Nassau.

Oldenburg[1] (ˈəuldᵊnˌbɜːg; *German* ˈɔldənburk) *n* **1** a city in NW Germany, in Lower Saxony: former capital of Oldenburg state. Pop.: 151 382 (1996 est.). **2** a former state of NW Germany: became part of Lower Saxony in 1946.

Oldenburg[2] (ˈəuldᵊnˌbɜːg) *n* **Claes** (klɔːs). born 1929, U.S. pop sculptor and artist, born in Sweden.

Old English *n* **1** Also called: **Anglo-Saxon.** the English language from the time of the earliest settlements in the fifth century A.D. to about 1100. The main dialects were West Saxon (the chief literary form), Kentish, and Anglian. Compare **Middle English, Modern English.** Abbrev.: **OE.** **2** *Printing.* a Gothic typeface commonly used in England up until the 18th century.

Old English sheepdog *n* a breed of large bobtailed sheepdog with a profuse shaggy coat.

older (ˈəuldə) *adj* **1** the comparative of **old. 2** Also (of people, esp. members of the same family): **elder.** having lived or existed longer; of greater age.

old-established *adj* established for a long time.

olde-worlde (ˈəuldɪˈwɜːldɪ) *adj Sometimes facetious.* old-world or quaint.

old face *n Printing.* a type style that originated in the 18th century, characterized by little contrast between thick and thin strokes. Compare **modern** (sense 5).

oldfangled (ˈəuldˈfæŋgᵊld) *adj Derogatory.* out-of-date; old-fashioned. [C20: formed on analogy with NEWFANGLED]

old-fashioned *adj* **1** belonging to, characteristic of, or favoured by former times; outdated: *old-fashioned ideas.* **2** favouring or adopting the dress, manners, fashions, etc., of a former time. **3** quizzically doubtful or disapproving: *she did not reply, but gave him an old-fashioned look.* **4** *Scot. and northern English dialect.* old for one's age: *an old-fashioned child.* ◆ *n* **5** a cocktail containing spirit, bitters, fruit, etc. ▸ **ˌold-ˈfashionedly** *adv*

Oldfield (ˈəuldˌfiːld) *n* **Bruce.** born 1950, British fashion designer.

Old French *n* the French language in its earliest forms, from about the 9th century up to about 1400. Abbrev.: **OF.**

Old Frisian *n* the Frisian language up to about 1400. Abbrev.: **OFris.**

old girl *n* **1** (*sometimes caps.*) *Brit.* a female ex-pupil of a school. **2** *Informal, chiefly Brit.* **2a** a familiar name used to refer to a woman. **2b** an old woman.

Old Glory *n* a nickname for the flag of the United States of America.

old gold *n* **a** a dark yellow colour, sometimes with a brownish tinge. **b** (*as adj*): *an old-gold carpet.*

old guard *n* **1** a group that works for a long-established or old-fashioned cause or principle. **2** the conservative element in a political party or other group. [C19: from OLD GUARD]

Old Guard *n* the French imperial guard created by Napoleon in 1804.

Oldham (ˈəuldəm) *n* **1** a town in NW England, in Oldham unitary authority, Greater Manchester. Pop.: 103 931 (1991). **2** a unitary authority in NW England, in Greater Manchester. Pop.: 220 000 (1995 est.). Area: 141 sq. km (54 sq. miles).

old hand *n* **1** a person who is skilled at something through long experience. **2** *Austral. informal.* (in the nineteenth century) an ex-convict. **3** *Austral. informal.* a person who is long established in a place.

Old Harry *n Informal.* a jocular name for **Satan.**

old hat *adj* (*postpositive*) old-fashioned or trite.

Old High German *n* a group of West Germanic dialects that eventually developed into modern German; High German up to about 1200: spoken in the Middle Ages on the upper Rhine, in Bavaria, Alsace, and elsewhere, including Alemannic, Bavarian, Langobardic, and Upper Franconian. Abbrev.: **OHG.**

Old Icelandic *n* the dialect of Old Norse spoken and written in Iceland; the Icelandic language up to about 1600.

old identity *n N.Z.* a person known for a long time in the one locality.

oldie (ˈəuldɪ) *n Informal.* an old person or thing.

Old Irish *n* the Celtic language of Ireland up to about 900 A.D., introduced to Scotland by Irish settlers about 500 A.D.

Old Kingdom *n* a period of Egyptian history: usually considered to extend from the third to the sixth dynasty (?2700–?2150 B.C.).

old lady *n* **1** an informal term for **mother**[1] or **wife** (sense 1). **2** a large noctuid moth, *Mormo maura,* that has drab patterned wings originally thought to resemble an elderly Victorian lady's shawl.

Old Latin *n* the Latin language before the classical period, up to about 100 B.C.

old-line *adj* **1** *U.S. and Canadian.* conservative; old-fashioned. **2** well-established; traditional. ▸ **ˌold-ˈliner** *n*

Old Low German *n* the Saxon and Low Franconian dialects of German up to about 1200; the old form of modern Low German and Dutch. Abbrev.: **OLG.**

old maid *n* **1** a woman regarded as unlikely ever to marry; spinster. **2** *Informal.* a prim, fastidious, or excessively cautious person. **3** a card game using a pack from which one card has been removed, in which players try to avoid holding the unpaired card at the end of the game. ▸ **ˌold-ˈmaidish** *adj*

old man *n* **1** an informal term for **father** or **husband** (sense 1). **2** (*sometimes caps.*) *Informal.* a man in command, such as an employer, foreman, or captain of a ship. **3** *Sometimes facetious.* an affectionate term used in addressing a man. 4 another name for **southernwood.** 5 *Austral. informal.* **5a** an adult male kangaroo. **5b** (*modifier*) very large. 6 *Christianity.* the unregenerate aspect of human nature.

old man's beard *n* any of various plants having white feathery seed heads, esp. traveller's joy and Spanish moss.

old master *n* **1** one of the great European painters of the period 1500 to 1800. **2** a painting by one of these.

old moon *n* **1** a phase of the moon lying between last quarter and new moon, when it appears as a waning crescent. **2** the moon when it appears as a waning crescent. **3** the time at which this occurs.

Old Nick *n Informal.* a jocular name for **Satan.**

Old Norse *n* the language or group of dialects of medieval Scandinavia and Iceland from about 700 to about 1350, forming the North Germanic branch of the Indo-European family of languages. See also **Proto-Norse, Old Icelandic.** Abbrev.: **ON.**

Old North French *n* any of the dialects of Old French spoken in N France, such as Norman French.

Old Northwest *n* (in the early U.S.) the land between the Great Lakes, the Mississippi, and the Ohio River. Awarded to the U.S. in 1783, it was organized into the **Northwest Territory** in 1787 and now forms the states of Ohio, Indiana, Illinois, Wisconsin, Michigan, and part of Minnesota.

Old Persian *n* an ancient language belonging to the West Iranian branch of the Indo-European family, recorded in cuneiform inscriptions of the 6th to the 4th centuries B.C. See also **Middle Persian.**

Old Pretender *n* See (James Francis Edward) **Stuart.**

Old Prussian *n* the former language of the non-German Prussians, belonging to the Baltic branch of the Indo-European family: extinct by 1700.

Old Red Sandstone *n* **1** a thick sequence of sedimentary rock (generally, but not always, red) deposited in Britain and NW Europe during the Devonian period. **2** (in Britain) another term for **Devonian.** ◆ Abbrev.: **ORS.**

old rose *n* **a** a greyish-pink colour. **b** (*as adj*): *old-rose gloves.*

Old Saxon *n* the Saxon dialect of Low German up to about 1200, from which modern Low German is derived. Abbrev.: **OS.**

old school *n* **1** *Chiefly Brit.* a school formerly attended by a person. **2** a group of people favouring traditional ideas or conservative practices.

old school tie *n* **1** *Brit.* a distinctive tie that indicates which school the wearer attended. **2** the attitudes, loyalties, values, etc., associated with British public schools.

Old Slavonic *or* **Slavic** *n* the South Slavonic language up to about 1400: the language of the Macedonian Slavs that developed into Serbo-Croat and Bulgarian. See also **Old Church Slavonic.**

old sod *n Informal.* one's native country: *back to the old sod.*

old soldier *n* **1** a former soldier or veteran. **2** an experienced or practised person.

Old South *n* the American South before the Civil War.

old squaw *n U.S. and Canadian.* a long-tailed northern sea duck, *Clangula hyemalis,* having dark wings and a white-and-brown head and body. Also called: **oldwife.**

old stager *n* a person with experience; old hand.

oldster ('əʊldstə) *n* **1** *Informal.* an older person. **2** *Brit. Navy.* a person who has been a midshipman for four years.

Old Stone Age *n* (*not now in technical usage*) another term for **Palaeolithic.**

old style *n Printing.* a type style reviving the characteristics of old face.

Old Style *n* the former method of reckoning dates using the Julian calendar. Compare **New Style.**

old sweat *n Brit. informal.* **1** an old soldier; veteran. **2** a person who has a great deal of experience in some activity.

old talk *Caribbean.* ◆ *n* **1** superficial chatting. ◆ *vb* **old-talk. 2** (*intr*) to indulge in such chatting.

Old Test. *abbrev. for* Old Testament.

Old Testament *n* the collection of books comprising the sacred Scriptures of the Hebrews and essentially recording the history of the Hebrew people as the chosen people of God; the first part of the Christian Bible.

old-time *adj* (*prenominal*) of or relating to a former time; old-fashioned: *old-time dancing.*

old-time dance *n Brit.* a formal or formation dance, such as the lancers. ▸ **old-time dancing** *n*

old-timer *n* **1** a person who has been in a certain place, occupation, etc., for a long time. **2** *U.S.* an old man.

Olduvai Gorge ('ɒldʊˌvaɪ) *n* a gorge in N Tanzania, north of the Ngorongoro Crater: fossil evidence of early man and other closely related species, together with artefacts.

oldwife ('əʊldˌwaɪf) *n, pl* **-wives. 1** another name for **old squaw. 2** any of various fishes, esp. the menhaden or the alewife.

old wives' tale *n* a belief, usually superstitious or erroneous, passed on by word of mouth as a piece of traditional wisdom.

old woman *n* **1** an informal term for **mother**[1] or **wife** (sense 1). **2** a timid, fussy, or cautious person. ▸ **old womanish** *adj*

Old World *n* that part of the world that was known before the discovery of the Americas, comprising Europe, Asia, and Africa; the eastern hemisphere.

old-world *adj* of or characteristic of former times, esp., in Europe, quaint or traditional. ▸ ˌ**old-'worldly** *adv*

Old World monkey *n* any monkey of the family *Cercopithecidae,* including macaques, baboons, and mandrills. They are more closely related to anthropoid apes than are the New World monkeys, having nostrils that are close together and nonprehensile tails.

olé (əʊ'leɪ) *interj* **1** an exclamation of approval or encouragement customary at bullfights, flamenco dancing, and other Spanish or Latin American events. ◆ *n* **2** a cry of olé. [Spanish, from Arabic *wa-llāh,* from *wa* and + *allāh* God]

-ole[1] *or* **-ol** *n combining form.* **1** denoting an organic unsaturated compound containing a 5-membered ring: *thiazole.* **2** denoting an aromatic organic ether: *anisole.* [from Latin *oleum* oil, from Greek *elaion,* from *elaia* olive]

-ole[2] *suffix of nouns.* indicating something small: *arteriole.* [from Latin *-olus,* diminutive suffix]

olea ('əʊlɪə) *n* a plural of **oleum.**

oleaceous (ˌəʊlɪ'eɪʃəs) *adj* of, relating to, or belonging to the *Oleaceae,* a family of trees and shrubs, including the ash, jasmine, privet, lilac, and olive. [C19: via New Latin from Latin *olea* OLIVE; see also OIL]

oleaginous (ˌəʊlɪ'ædʒɪnəs) *adj* **1** resembling or having the properties of oil. **2** containing or producing oil. [C17: from Latin *oleāginus,* from *olea* OLIVE; see also OIL]

oleander (ˌəʊlɪ'ændə) *n* a poisonous evergreen Mediterranean apocynaceous shrub or tree, *Nerium oleander,* with fragrant white, pink, or purple flowers. Also called: **rosebay.** [C16: from Medieval Latin, variant of *arodandrum,* perhaps from Latin RHODODENDRON]

oleaster (ˌəʊlɪ'æstə) *n* **1** any of several shrubs of the genus *Elaeagnus,* esp. *E. angustifolia,* of S Europe, Asia, and North America, having silver-white twigs, yellow flowers, and an olive-like fruit: family *Elaeagnaceae.* **2** Also called: **wild olive.** a wild specimen of the cultivated olive. [Latin: from *olea;* see OLIVE, OIL]

oleate ('əʊlɪˌeɪt) *n* any salt or ester of oleic acid, containing the ion $C_{17}H_{33}COO^-$ or the group $C_{17}H_{33}COO$-: common components of natural fats.

olecranon (əʊ'lekrəˌnɒn, ˌəʊlɪ'kreɪnɒn) *n Anatomy.* the bony projection of the ulna behind the elbow joint. [C18: from Greek, shortened from *ōlenokrānon,* from *ōlenē* elbow + *krānion* head] ▸ **olecranal** (əʊ'lekrənᵊl, ˌəʊlɪ'kreɪnᵊl) *adj*

olefine *or* **olefin** ('əʊlɪˌfiːn, -fɪn, 'ɒl-) *n* other names for **alkene.** [C19: from French *oléfiant,* ultimately from Latin *oleum* oil + *facere* to make] ▸ ˌ**ole'finic** *adj*

oleic acid (əʊ'liːɪk) *n* a colourless oily liquid unsaturated acid occurring, as the glyceride, in almost all natural fats used in making soaps, ointments, cosmetics, and lubricating oils. Formula: $CH_3(CH_2)_7CH{:}CH(CH_2)_7COOH$. Systematic name: ***cis*-9-octadecenoic acid.** [C19 *oleic,* from Latin *oleum* oil + -IC]

olein ('əʊlɪɪn) *n* another name for **triolein.** [C19: from French *oléine,* from Latin *oleum* oil + -IN]

oleo- *combining form.* oil: *oleomargarine.* [from Latin *oleum* OIL]

oleograph ('əʊlɪəˌgrɑːf, -ˌgræf) *n* **1** a chromolithograph printed in oil colours to imitate the appearance of an oil painting. **2** the pattern formed by a drop of oil spreading on water. ▸ **oleographic** (ˌəʊlɪə'græfɪk) *adj* ▸ **oleography** (ˌəʊlɪ'ɒgrəfɪ) *n*

oleomargarine (ˌəʊlɪəʊˌmɑːdʒə'riːn) *or* **oleomargarin** (ˌəʊlɪəʊ'mɑːdʒərɪn) *n* other names (esp. U.S.) for **margarine.**

oleo oil ('əʊlɪəʊ) *n* an oil extracted from beef fat, consisting mainly of a mixture of olein and palmitin. It is used in the manufacture of margarine.

oleoresin (ˌəʊlɪəʊ'rezɪn) *n* **1** a semisolid mixture of a resin and essential oil, obtained from certain plants. **2** *Pharmacol.* a liquid preparation of resins and oils, obtained by extraction from plants. ▸ ˌ**oleo'resinous** *adj*

oleum ('əʊlɪəm) *n, pl* **olea** ('əʊlɪə) *or* **oleums.** another name for **fuming sulphuric acid.** [from Latin: oil, referring to its oily consistency]

O level *n* (formerly in Britain) **1a** the basic level of the General Certificate of Education, now replaced by **GCSE. 1b** (*as modifier*): *O level maths.* **2** a pass in a particular subject at O level: *he has eight O levels.* ◆ Formal name: **Ordinary level.**

olfaction (ɒl'fækʃən) *n* **1** the sense of smell. **2** the act or function of smelling.

olfactometry (ˌɒlfæk'tɒmɪtrɪ) *n Chem.* another name for **odorimetry.**

olfactory (ɒl'fæktərɪ, -trɪ) *adj* **1** of or relating to the sense of smell. ◆ *n, pl* **-ries. 2** (*usually pl*) an organ or nerve concerned with the sense of smell. [C17: from Latin *olfactus,* past participle of *olfacere,* from *olere* to smell + *facere* to make]

olfactory bulb *n* the anterior and slightly enlarged end of the olfactory tract, from which the cranial nerves concerned with the sense of smell originate.

olfactory nerve *n* either one of the first pair of cranial nerves, supplying the mucous membrane of the nose.

olfactory tract *n* a long narrow triangular band of white tissue originating in the olfactory bulb and extending back to the point at which its fibres enter the base of the cerebrum.

OLG *abbrev. for* Old Low German.

olibanum (ɒ'lɪbənəm) *n* another name for **frankincense.** [C14: from Medieval Latin, from Greek *libanos*]

olid ('ɒlɪd) *adj* foul-smelling. [C17: from Latin *olidus,* from *olēre* to smell]

oligaemia *or U.S.* **oligemia** (ˌɒlɪ'giːmɪə) *n Med.* a reduction in the volume of the blood, as occurs after haemorrhage. ▸ ˌ**oli'gaemic** *or U.S.* ˌ**oli'gemic** *adj*

oligarch ('ɒlɪˌgɑːk) *n* a member of an oligarchy.

oligarchy ('ɒlɪˌgɑːkɪ) *n, pl* **-chies. 1** government by a small group of people. **2** a state or organization so governed. **3** a small body of individuals ruling such a state. **4** *Chiefly U.S.* a small clique of private citizens who exert a strong influence on government. [C16: via Medieval Latin from Greek *oligarkhia,* from *olígos* few + -ARCHY] ▸ ˌ**oli'garchic** *or* ˌ**oli'garchical** *adj* ▸ ˌ**oli'garchically** *adv*

oligo- *or before a vowel* **olig-** *combining form.* indicating a few or little: *oligopoly.* [from Greek *oligos* little, few]

Oligocene ('ɒlɪgəʊˌsiːn, ɒ'lɪg-) *adj* **1** of, denoting, or formed in the third epoch of the Tertiary period, which lasted for 15 000 000 years. ◆ *n* **2 the.** the Oligocene epoch or rock series. [C19: OLIGO- + -CENE]

oligochaete ('ɒlɪgəʊˌkiːt) *n* **1** any freshwater or terrestrial annelid worm of the class *Oligochaeta,* having bristles (chaetae) borne singly along the length of the body: includes the earthworms. ◆ *adj* **2** of, relating to, or belonging to the class *Oligochaeta.* [C19: from New Latin; see OLIGO-, CHAETA]

oligoclase ('ɒlɪgəʊˌkleɪs) *n* a white, bluish, or reddish-yellow feldspar mineral of the plagioclase series, consisting of aluminium silicates of sodium and calcium. Formula: $NaAlSi_3O_8.CaAl_2Si_2O_8$. [C19: from OLIGO- + -CLASE]

oligomer (ɒ'lɪgəmə) *n* a compound of relatively low molecular weight containing up to five monomer units. Compare **polymer, copolymer.** [C20: from OLIGO- + *-mer,* as in *polymer*]

oligomerous (ˌɒlɪ'gɒmərəs) *adj Biology.* having a small number of component parts.

oligonucleotide (ˌɒlɪgəʊ'nju:klɪəˌtaɪd) *n* a polymer consisting of a small number of nucleotides.

oligopeptide (ˌɒlɪgəʊ'peptaɪd) *n Biochem.* a peptide comprising less than ten amino acids.

oligopoly (ˌɒlɪ'gɒpəlɪ) *n, pl* **-lies.** *Economics.* a market situation in which control over the supply of a commodity is held by a small number of producers each of whom is able to influence prices and thus directly affect the position of competitors. [C20: from OLIGO- + Greek *pōlein* to sell, on the model of MONOPOLY] ▶ **ˌoliˌgopo'listic** *adj*

oligopsony (ˌɒlɪ'gɒpsənɪ) *n, pl* **-nies.** a market situation in which the demand for a commodity is represented by a small number of purchasers. [C20: from OLIGO- + *-opsony,* from Greek *opsōnia* purchase of food] ▶ **ˌoliˌgopso'nistic** *adj*

oligosaccharide (ˌɒlɪgəʊ'sækəˌraɪd, -rɪd) *n* any one of a class of carbohydrates consisting of a few monosaccharide units linked together. Compare **polysaccharide.**

oligospermia (ˌɒlɪgəʊ'spɜ:mɪə) *n* the condition of having less than the normal number of spermatozoa in the semen: a cause of infertility in men.

oligotrophic (ˌɒlɪgəʊ'trɒfɪk) *adj* (of lakes and similar habitats) poor in nutrients and plant life and rich in oxygen. Compare **eutrophic.** [C20: from OLIGO- + Greek *trophein* to nourish + -IC] ▶ **oligotrophy** (ˌɒlɪ'gɒtrəfɪ) *n*

oliguria (ˌɒlɪ'gjʊərɪə) *or* **oliguresis** (ˌɒlɪgjʊ'ri:sɪs) *n* excretion of an abnormally small volume of urine, often as the result of a kidney disorder. Compare **anuria.** [C19: from OLIGO- + -URIA] ▶ **oliguretic** (ˌɒlɪgjʊ'retɪk) *adj*

Ólimbos ('ɔlimbɔs) *n* transliteration of the Modern Greek name for (Mount) **Olympus** (sense 1).

olio ('əʊlɪˌəʊ) *n, pl* **olios.** **1** a dish of many different ingredients. **2** a miscellany or potpourri. [C17: from Spanish *olla* stew, from Latin: jar]

Oliphant ('ɒlɪfənt) *n* Sir **Mark Laurence Elwin.** born 1901, British nuclear physicist, born in Australia.

olivaceous (ˌɒlɪ'veɪʃəs) *adj* of an olive colour.

Olivares (ˌəʊlɪ'vɑ:reɪs) *n* **Conde-Ducque de,** title of *Gaspar de Guzmán y Pimental.* 1587–1645, Spanish statesman: court favourite and prime minister (1621–43) of Philip IV. His attempts to establish Hapsburg domination of Europe ended in failure.

olivary ('ɒlɪvərɪ) *adj* **1** shaped like an olive. **2** *Anatomy.* of or relating to either of two masses of tissue (**olivary bodies**) on the forward portion of the medulla oblongata. [C16: from Latin *olivārius,* from *oliva* OLIVE]

olive ('ɒlɪv) *n* **1** an evergreen oleaceous tree, *Olea europaea,* of the Mediterranean region but cultivated elsewhere, having white fragrant flowers, and edible shiny black fruits. **2** the fruit of this plant, eaten as a relish and used as a source of olive oil. **3** the wood of the olive tree, used for ornamental work. **4** any of various trees or shrubs resembling the olive. **5a** a yellow-green colour. **5b** (*as adj*): *an olive coat.* **6** an angler's name for the dun of various mayflies or an artificial fly in imitation of this. ◆ *adj* **7** of, relating to, or made of the olive tree, its wood, or its fruit. [C13: via Old French from Latin *oliva,* related to Greek *elaia* olive tree; compare Greek *elaion* oil]

olive branch *n* **1** a branch of an olive tree used to symbolize peace. **2** any offering of peace or conciliation.

olive brown *n* **a** a dull yellowish-brown to yellowish-green colour. **b** (*as adj*): *an olive-brown coat.*

olive crown *n* (esp. in ancient Greece and Rome) a garland of olive leaves awarded as a token of victory.

olive drab *n U.S.* **1a** a dull but fairly strong greyish-olive colour. **1b** (*as adj*): *an olive-drab jacket.* **2** cloth or clothes in this colour, esp. the uniform of the U.S. Army.

olive green *n* **a** a colour that is greener, stronger, and brighter than olive; deep yellowish-green. **b** (*as adj*): *an olive-green coat.*

olivenite (ɒ'lɪvɪˌnaɪt) *n* a green to black rare secondary mineral consisting of hydrated basic copper arsenate in orthorhombic crystalline form. Formula: $Cu_2(AsO_4)(OH)$. [C19: from German *Oliven(erz)* olive (ore) + -ITE[1]]

olive oil *n* a pale yellow oil pressed from ripe olive fruits and used in cooking, medicines, soaps, etc.

Oliver ('ɒlɪvə) *n* **1** one of Charlemagne's 12 paladins. See also **Roland.** **2 Isaac.** ?1556–1617, English portrait miniaturist, born in France: he studied under Hilliard and worked at James I's court. **3 Joseph,** known as *King Oliver.* 1885–1938, U.S. pioneer jazz cornetist.

Olives ('ɒlɪvz) *n* **Mount of.** a hill to the east of Jerusalem: in New Testament times the village Bethany (Mark 11:11) was on its eastern slope and Gethsemane on its western one.

Olivier (ə'lɪvɪˌeɪ) *n* **Laurence** (**Kerr**), Baron Olivier of Brighton. 1907–89, English stage, film, and television actor and director: director of the National Theatre Company (1961–73): films include the Shakespeare adaptations *Henry V* (1944), *Hamlet* (1948), and *Richard III* (1956).

olivine ('ɒlɪˌvi:n, ˌɒlɪ'vi:n) *n* **1** an olive-green mineral of the olivine group, found in igneous and metamorphic rocks. The clear-green variety (peridot) is used as a gemstone. Composition: magnesium iron silicate. Formula: $(MgFe)_2SiO_4$. Crystal structure: orthorhombic. **2** any mineral in the group having the general formula $(Mg,Fe,Mn,Ca)_2SiO_4$. [C18: from German, named after its colour]

olla ('ɒlə; *Spanish* 'oʎa) *n* **1** a cooking pot. **2** short for **olla podrida.** [Spanish, from Latin *olla,* variant of *aulla* pot]

olla podrida (pɒ'dri:də; *Spanish* po'ðriða) *n* **1** a Spanish dish, consisting of a stew with beans, sausages, etc. **2** an assortment; miscellany. [literally: rotten pot]

olm (əʊlm, ɒlm) *n* a pale blind eel-like salamander, *Proteus anguinus,* of underground streams in SE Europe, that retains its larval form throughout its life: family *Proteidae.* See also **mud puppy.** [C20: from German]

Olmec ('ɒlmɛk) *n, pl* **-mecs** *or* **-mec.** **1** a member of an ancient Central American Indian people who inhabited the southern Gulf Coast of Mexico and flourished between about 1200 and 400 B.C. ◆ *adj* **2** of or relating to these people or their civilization or culture.

Olmütz ('ɔlmyts) *n* the German name for **Olomouc.**

ologoan (ˌʌlə'go:n) *vb* (*intr*) *Irish.* to complain loudly without reason: *she's always ologoaning about something.* [from Irish Gaelic *olagón* lament]

ology ('ɒlədʒɪ) *n, pl* **-gies.** *Informal.* a science or other branch of knowledge. [C19: abstracted from words with this ending, such as *theology, biology,* etc.; see -LOGY]

Olomouc (*Czech* 'ɔlɔmɔuts) *n* a city in the Czech Republic, in North Moravia on the Morava River: capital of Moravia until 1640; university (1576). Pop.: 104 845 (1996 est.). German name: **Olmütz.**

oloroso (ˌɒlə'rəʊsəʊ) *n* a full-bodied golden-coloured sweet sherry. [from Spanish: fragrant]

Olsztyn (*Polish* 'ɔlʃtin) *n* a town in NE Poland: founded in 1334 by the Teutonic Knights; communications centre. Pop.: 167 400 (1996 est.).

Olympia (ə'lɪmpɪə) *n* **1** a plain in Greece, in the NW Peloponnese: in ancient times a major sanctuary of Zeus and site of the original Olympic Games. **2** a port in W Washington, the state capital, on Puget Sound. Pop.: 33 840 (1990).

Olympiad (ə'lɪmpɪˌæd) *n* **1** a staging of the modern Olympic Games. **2** the four-year period between consecutive celebrations of the Olympic Games; a unit of ancient Greek chronology dating back to 776 B.C. **3** an international contest in chess, bridge, etc.

Olympian (ə'lɪmpɪən) *adj* **1** of or relating to Mount Olympus or to the classical Greek gods. **2** majestic or godlike in manner or bearing. **3** superior to mundane considerations, esp. when impractical. **4** of or relating to ancient Olympia or its inhabitants. ◆ *n* **5** a god of Olympus. **6** an inhabitant or native of ancient Olympia. **7** *Chiefly U.S.* a competitor in the Olympic Games.

Olympic (ə'lɪmpɪk) *adj* **1** of or relating to the Olympic Games. **2** of or relating to ancient Olympia.

Olympic Games *n* (*functioning as sing or pl*) **1** the greatest Panhellenic festival, held every fourth year in honour of Zeus at ancient Olympia. From 472 B.C., it consisted of five days of games, sacrifices, and festivities. **2** Also called: **the Olympics.** the modern revival of these games, consisting of international athletic and sporting contests held every four years in a selected country since their inception in Athens in 1896. See also **Winter Olympic Games.**

Olympic Mountains *pl n* a mountain range in NW Washington: part of the Coast Range. Highest peak: Mount Olympus, 2427 m (7965 ft.).

Olympic Peninsula *n* a large peninsula of W Washington.

Olympus (əʊ'lɪmpəs) *n* **1 Mount.** a mountain in NE Greece: the highest mountain in Greece, believed in Greek mythology to be the dwelling place of the greater gods. Height: 2911 m (9550 ft.). Modern Greek name: **Ólimbos.** **2 Mount.** a mountain in NW Washington: highest peak of the Olympic Mountains. Height: 2427 m (7965 ft.). **3** a poetic word for **heaven.**

Olympus Mons *n* the highest of the giant shield volcanoes on Mars, lying 18°N of the equator. Height: 26 km; base diameter: over 600 km.

Olynthus (əʊ'lɪnθəs) *n* an ancient city in N Greece: the centre of Chalcidice.

Om (əʊm) *n Hinduism.* a sacred syllable typifying the three gods Brahma, Vishnu, and Siva, who are concerned in the threefold operation of integration, maintenance, and disintegration. [from Sanskrit]

OM **1** *abbrev. for* Order of Merit (a Brit. title). ◆ **2** *Currency. symbol for* Ostmark.

Om. *abbrev. for* Ostmark.

-oma *n combining form.* indicating a tumour: *carcinoma.* [from Greek *-ōma*]

omadhaun ('ɒmədɑ:n) *n Irish.* a foolish man or boy. [C19: from Irish Gaelic *amadán*]

Omagh (əʊ'mɑ:, 'əʊmə) *n* **1** a market town in Northern Ireland. Pop.: 17 280 (1991). **2** a district of W Northern Ireland, in Co. Tyrone. Pop.: 45 809 (1991). Area: 1130 sq. km (436 sq. miles).

Omaha ('əʊməˌhɑ:) *n* a city in E Nebraska, on the Missouri River opposite Council Bluffs, Iowa: the largest city in the state; the country's largest livestock market and meat-packing centre. Pop.: 364 253 (1996 est.).

Oman (əʊ'mɑ:n) *n* a sultanate in SE Arabia, on the **Gulf of Oman** and the Arabian Sea: the most powerful state in Arabia in the 19th century, ruling Zanzibar, much of the Persian coast, and part of Pakistan. Official language: Arabic. Official religion: Muslim. Currency: rial. Capital: Muscat. Pop.: 2 364 000 (1998 est.). Area: about 306 000 sq. km (118 150 sq. miles). Former name (until 1970): **Muscat and Oman.** ▶ **O'mani** *adj, n*

OMAN *international car registration for* Oman.

Omar ('əʊmɑ:) *or* **Umar** *n* died 644 A.D., the second caliph of Islam (634–44). During his reign Islamic armies conquered Syria and Mesopotamia: murdered.

Omar Khayyám ('əʊmɑ: kaɪ'ɑ:m) *n* ?1050–?1123, Persian poet, mathematician, and astronomer, noted for the *Rubáiyát,* a collection of quatrains, popularized in the West by Edward Fitzgerald's version (1859).

omasum (əʊ'meɪsəm) *n, pl* **-sa** (-sə). another name for **psalterium.** [C18: from Latin: bullock's tripe]

Omayyad *or* **Ommiad** (əʊ'maɪæd) *n, pl* **-yads, -yades** (-əˌdi:z) *or* **-ads, -ades** (-əˌdi:z). **1** a caliph of the dynasty ruling (661–750 A.D.) from its capital at Damascus. 2 an emir (756–929 A.D.) or caliph (929–1031 A.D.) of the Omayyad dynasty in Spain.

ombre *or U.S.* **omber** ('ɒmbə) *n* an 18th-century card game. [C17: from Spanish *hombre* man, referring to the player who attempts to win the stakes]

ombro- *combining form.* indicating rain: *ombrogenous; ombrophilous.* [from Greek *ombros* shower of rain]

ombrogenous (ɒm'brɒdʒɪnəs) *adj* (of plants) able to flourish in wet conditions.

ombrophilous (ɒm'brɒfɪləs) *adj* (of plants) tolerant of wet conditions.

ombrophobous (ɒm'brɒfəbəs) *adj* (of plants) not able to tolerate wet conditions.

ombudsman ('ɒmbʊdzmən) *n, pl* **-men. 1** a commissioner who acts as independent referee between individual citizens and their government or its administration. **2** (in Britain) an official, without power of sanction or mechanism of appeal, who investigates complaints of maladministration by members of the public against national or local government or its servants. Formal names: **Commissioner for Local Administration, Health Service Commissioner, Parliamentary Commissioner.** See also **Financial Ombudsman.** [C20: from Swedish: commissioner]

Omdurman (ˌɒmdɜː'mɑːn) *n* a city in the central Sudan, on the White Nile, opposite Khartoum: the largest town in the Sudan; scene of the **Battle of Omdurman** (1898), in which the Mahdi's successor was defeated by Lord Kitchener's forces. Pop.: 1 267 077 (1993).

-ome *n combining form.* denoting a mass or part of a specified kind: *rhizome.* [variant of -OMA]

omega ('əʊmɪgə) *n* **1** the 24th and last letter of the Greek alphabet (Ω, ω), a long vowel, transliterated as *o* or *ō*. **2** the ending or last of a series. [C16: from Greek *ō mega* big o; see MEGA-, OMICRON]

omega minus *n* an unstable negatively charged elementary particle, classified as a baryon, that has a mass 3276 times that of the electron.

omelette *or esp. U.S.* **omelet** ('ɒmlɪt) *n* a savoury or sweet dish of beaten eggs cooked in fat. [C17: from French *omelette,* changed from *alumette,* from *alumelle* sword blade, changed by mistaken division from *la lemelle,* from Latin (see LAMELLA); apparently from the flat shape of the omelette]

omen ('əʊmən) *n* **1** a phenomenon or occurrence regarded as a sign of future happiness or disaster. **2** prophetic significance. ◆ *vb* **3** (*tr*) to portend. [C16: from Latin]

omentum (əʊ'mɛntəm) *n, pl* **-ta** (-tə). *Anatomy.* a double fold of peritoneum connecting the stomach with other abdominal organs. [C16: from Latin: membrane, esp. a caul, of obscure origin]

omer ('əʊmə) *n* an ancient Hebrew unit of dry measure equal to one tenth of an ephah. [C17: from Hebrew *'ōmer* a measure]

Omer ('əʊmə) *n Judaism.* a period of seven weeks extending from the second day of Passover to the first day of Shavuoth, and observed as a period of semi-mourning. [named because sacrifices of an OMER of grain were made]

omertà *Italian.* (omer'ta) *n* a conspiracy of silence.

omicron (əʊ'maɪkrɒn, 'ɒmɪkrɒn) *n* the 15th letter in the Greek alphabet (Ο, ο), a short vowel, transliterated as *o*. [from Greek *ō mikron* small o; see MICRO-, OMEGA]

ominous ('ɒmɪnəs) *adj* **1** foreboding evil. **2** serving as or having significance as an omen. [C16: from Latin *ōminōsus,* from OMEN] ▸ **'ominously** *adv* ▸ **'ominousness** *n*

omission (əʊ'mɪʃən) *n* **1** something that has been omitted or neglected. **2** the act of omitting or the state of having been omitted. [C14: from Latin *omissiō,* from *omittere* to OMIT] ▸ **o'missive** *adj* ▸ **o'missiveness** *n*

omit (əʊ'mɪt) *vb* **omits, omitting, omitted.** (*tr*) **1** to neglect to do or include. **2** to fail (to do something). [C15: from Latin *omittere,* from *ob-* away + *mittere* to send] ▸ **omissible** (əʊ'mɪsɪbᵊl) *adj* ▸ **o'mitter** *n*

OMM (in Canada) *abbrev. for* Officer of the Order of Military Merit.

ommatidium (ˌɒmə'tɪdɪəm) *n, pl* **-tidia** (-'tɪdɪə). any of the numerous cone-shaped units that make up the compound eyes of some arthropods. [C19: via New Latin from Greek *ommatidion,* from *omma* eye] ▸ **ˌomma'tidial** *adj*

ommatophore (ɒ'mætəˌfɔː) *n Zoology.* a movable stalk or tentacle bearing an eye, occurring in lower animals such as crabs and snails. [C19: from Greek *omma* eye + -PHORE] ▸ **ommatophorous** (ˌɒmə'tɒfərəs) *adj*

Ommiad (əʊ'maɪæd) *n, pl* **-ads** *or* **-ades** (-əˌdiːz). a variant spelling of **Omayyad.**

omni- *combining form.* all or everywhere: *omnipresent.* [from Latin *omnis* all]

omnia vincit amor *Latin.* ('ɒmnɪə 'vɪnsɪt 'æmɔː) love conquers all things. [from Virgil's Eclogues 10:69]

omnibus ('ɒmnɪˌbʌs, -bəs) *n, pl* **-buses. 1** a less common word for **bus** (sense 1). **2** Also called: **omnibus volume.** a collection of works by one author or several works on a similar topic, reprinted in one volume. **3** Also called: **omnibus edition.** a television or radio programme consisting of two or more programmes broadcast earlier in the week. ◆ *adj* **4** (*prenominal*) of, dealing with, or providing for many different things or cases. [C19: from Latin, literally: for all, from *omnis* all]

omnicompetent (ˌɒmnɪ'kɒmpɪtənt) *adj* able to judge or deal with all matters. ▸ **ˌomni'competence** *n*

omnidirectional (ˌɒmnɪdɪ'rɛkʃənᵊl, -daɪ-) *adj* **1** (of an antenna) capable of transmitting and receiving radio signals equally in any direction in the horizontal plane. **2** (of a microphone) equally sensitive in all directions.

omnifarious (ˌɒmnɪ'fɛərɪəs) *adj* of many or all varieties or forms. [C17: from Late Latin *omnifārius,* from Latin *omnis* all + *-farius* doing, related to *facere* to do] ▸ **ˌomni'fariously** *adv* ▸ **ˌomni'fariousness** *n*

omnific (ɒm'nɪfɪk) *or* **omnificent** (ɒm'nɪfɪsᵊnt) *adj Rare.* creating all things. [C17: via Medieval Latin from Latin *omni-* + *-ficus,* from *facere* to do] ▸ **om'nificence** *n*

omnipotent (ɒm'nɪpətənt) *adj* **1** having very great or unlimited power. ◆ *n* **2 the Omnipotent.** an epithet for God. [C14: via Old French from Latin *omnipotens* all-powerful, from OMNI- + *potens,* from *posse* to be able] ▸ **om'nipotence** *n* ▸ **om'nipotently** *adv*

omnipresent (ˌɒmnɪ'prɛzᵊnt) *adj* (esp. of a deity) present in all places at the same time. ▸ **ˌomni'presence** *n*

omnirange ('ɒmnɪˌreɪndʒ) *n* a very-high-frequency ground radio navigational system to assist a pilot in plotting his exact position.

omniscient (ɒm'nɪsɪənt) *adj* **1** having infinite knowledge or understanding. **2** having very great or seemingly unlimited knowledge. [C17: from Medieval Latin *omnisciens,* from Latin OMNI- + *scīre* to know] ▸ **om'niscience** *n* ▸ **om'nisciently** *adv*

omnium-gatherum ('ɒmnɪəm'gæðərəm) *n Often facetious.* a miscellaneous collection; assortment. [C16: from Latin *omnium* of all, from *omnis* all + Latinized form of English *gather*]

omnivore ('ɒmnɪˌvɔː) *n* an omnivorous person or animal.

omnivorous (ɒm'nɪvərəs) *adj* **1** eating food of both animal and vegetable origin, or any type of food indiscriminately. **2** taking in or assimilating everything, esp. with the mind. [C17: from Latin *omnivorus* all-devouring, from OMNI- + *vorāre* to eat greedily] ▸ **om'nivorously** *adv* ▸ **om'nivorousness** *n*

omophagia (ˌəʊmə'feɪdʒɪə) *or* **omophagy** (əʊ'mɒfədʒɪ) *n* the eating of raw food, esp. meat. [C18: via New Latin from Greek *ōmophagia,* from *ōmos* raw + *-phagia;* see -PHAGY] ▸ **omophagic** (ˌəʊmə'fædʒɪk) *or* **omophagous** (əʊ'mɒfəgəs) *adj*

Omphale ('ɒmfəˌliː) *n Greek myth.* a queen of Lydia, whom Hercules was required to serve as a slave to atone for the murder of Iphitus.

omphalos ('ɒmfəˌlɒs) *n* **1** (in the ancient world) a sacred conical object, esp. a stone. The most famous omphalos at Delphi was assumed to mark the centre of the earth. **2** the central point. **3** *Literary.* another word for **navel.** [Greek: navel]

OMS *abbrev. for* Organisation Mondiale de la Santé. [French: World Health Organization]

Omsk (ɒmsk) *n* a city in W central Russia, at the confluence of the Irtysh and Om Rivers: a major industrial centre, with pipelines from the second Baku oilfield. Pop.: 1 163 000 (1995 est.).

Omuta ('əʊmuːˌtɑː) *n* a city in SW Japan, on W Kyushu on Ariake Bay: former coal-mining centre; chemical industries and manufacturing. Pop.: 146 691 (1996).

on (ɒn) *prep* **1** in contact or connection with the surface of; at the upper surface of: *an apple on the ground; a mark on the table cloth.* **2** attached to: *a puppet on a string.* **3** carried with: *I've no money on me.* **4** in the immediate vicinity of; close to or along the side of: *a house on the sea; this verges on the ridiculous!* **5** within the time limits of a day or date: *he arrived on Thursday.* **6** being performed upon or relayed through the medium of: *what's on the television?* **7** at the occasion of: *on his retirement.* **8** used to indicate support, subsistence, contingency, etc.: *he lives on bread; it depends on what you want.* **9a** regularly taking (a drug): *she's on the pill.* **9b** addicted to: *he's on heroin.* **10** by means of (something considered as a mode of transport) (esp. in such phrases as **on foot, on wheels, on horseback,** etc.). **11** in the process or course of: *on a journey; on strike.* **12** concerned with or relating to: *a tax on potatoes; a programme on archaeology.* **13** used to indicate the basis, grounds, or cause, as of a statement or action: *I have it on good authority.* **14** against: used to indicate opposition: *they marched on the city at dawn.* **15** used to indicate a meeting or encounter: *he crept up on her.* **16** (used with an adj preceded by *the*) indicating the manner or way in which an action is carried out: *on the sly; on the cheap.* **17** *Informal or dialect.* to the loss or disadvantage of: *the old car gave out on us.* ◆ *adv* (*often used as a particle*) **18** in the position or state required for the commencement or sustained continuation, as of a mechanical operation: *the radio's been on all night.* **19a** attached to, surrounding, or placed in contact with something: *the girl had nothing on.* **19b** taking place: *what's on tonight?* **20** in a manner indicating continuity, persistence, concentration, etc.: *don't keep on about it; the play went on all afternoon.* **21** in a direction towards something, esp. forwards; so as to make progress: *we drove on towards London; march on!* **22 on and off** *or* **off and on.** intermittently; from time to time. **23 on and on.** without ceasing; continually. ◆ *adj* **24** functioning; operating: *the on position on a radio control.* **25** (*postpositive*) *Informal.* **25a** staked or wagered as a bet: *ten pounds on that horse.* **25b** performing, as on stage: *I'm on in five minutes.* **25c** definitely taking place: *the match is on for Friday; their marriage is still on.* **25d** charged to: *the drinks are on me.* **25e** tolerable, practicable, acceptable, etc.: *your plan just isn't on.* **25f** (of a person) willing to do something. **26 on at.** *Informal.* nagging: *she was always on at her husband.* **27 on it.** *Austral. informal.* drinking alcoholic liquor. **28** *Cricket.* (of a bowler) bowling. ◆ *n* **29** *Cricket.* **29a** (*modifier*) relating to or denoting the leg side of a cricket field or pitch: *the on side; an on drive.* **29b** (*in combination*) used to designate certain fielding positions on the leg side: *long-on; mid-on.* [Old English *an, on;* related to Old Saxon *an,* Old High German, Gothic *ana*]

On (ɒn) *n* the ancient Egyptian and biblical name for **Heliopolis.**

ON *abbrev. for* **1** Old Norse. **2** Ontario.

-on *suffix forming nouns.* **1** indicating a chemical substance: *interferon; parathion.* **2** (in physics) indicating an elementary particle or quantum: *electron; photon.* **3** (in chemistry) indicating an inert gas: *neon; radon.* **4** (in biochemistry) a molecular unit: *codon; operon.* [from ION]

onager ('ɒnədʒə) *n, pl* **-gri** (-ˌgraɪ) *or* **-gers. 1** a Persian variety of the wild ass, *Equus hemionus.* Compare **kiang. 2** an ancient war engine for hurling stones.

[C14: from Late Latin: military engine for stone throwing, from Latin: wild ass, from Greek *onagros,* from *onos* ass + *agros* field]

onagraceous (ˌɒnəˈɡreɪʃəs) *adj* of, relating to, or belonging to the *Onagraceae,* a family of flowering plants including fuchsia and willowherb. [C19: via New Latin *Onagrāceae,* from Latin *onager;* see ONAGER]

onanism (ˈəʊnəˌnɪzəm) *n* another name for **masturbation** or **coitus interruptus.** [C18: after *Onan,* son of Judah; see Genesis 38:9] ▸ **ˈonanist** *n, adj* ▸ **ˌonanˈistic** *adj*

Onassis (əʊˈnæsɪs) *n* **Aristotle** (**Socrates**). 1906–75, Argentinian (formerly Greek) shipowner, born in Turkey. In 1968 he married **Jacqueline,** 1929–94, the widow of U.S. President John F. Kennedy.

onbeat (ˈɒnˌbiːt) *n Music.* the first and third beats in a bar of four-four time.

ONC (in Britain) *abbrev. for* Ordinary National Certificate; a qualification recognized by many national technical and professional institutions, roughly equivalent to GCE A Level.

once (wʌns) *adv* **1** one time; on one occasion or in one case. **2** at some past time; formerly: *I could speak French once.* **3** by one step or degree (of relationship): *a cousin once removed.* **4** (*in conditional clauses, negatives, etc.*) ever; at all: *if you once forget it.* **5** multiplied by one. **6 once and away. 6a** conclusively. **6b** occasionally. **7 once and for all.** conclusively; for the last time. **8 once in a while.** occasionally; now and then. **9 once or twice** *or* **once and again.** a few times. **10 once upon a time.** used to begin fairy tales and children's stories. ◆ *conj* **11** (*subordinating*) as soon as; if ever or whenever: *once you begin, you'll enjoy it.* ◆ *n* **12** one occasion or case: *you may do it, this once.* **13 all at once. 13a** suddenly or without warning. **13b** simultaneously. **14 at once. 14a** immediately. **14b** simultaneously. **15 for once.** this time, if (or but) at no other time. [C12 *ones, anes,* adverbial genitive of *on, an* ONE]

once-over *n Informal.* **1** a quick examination or appraisal. **2** a quick but comprehensive piece of work. **3** a violent beating or thrashing (esp. in the phrase **give (a person** or **thing) the** (or **a**) **once-over**).

oncer (ˈwʌnsə) *n* **1** *Brit. slang.* (formerly) a one-pound note. **2** *Austral. slang.* a person elected to Parliament who can only expect to serve one term. **3** *N.Z.* something that happens on only one occasion. [C20: from ONCE]

onchocerciasis (ˌɒŋkəʊsəˈkaɪəsɪs) *n, pl* **-ses.** a disease found in parts of Africa and tropical America that is caused by a parasitic worm, *Onchocerca volvulus,* and transmitted to humans by various species of black fly. It results in inflammation of the skin and in some cases blindness. Also called: **river blindness.** [C20: from *Onchocerc(a),* the genus of worms + -IASIS]

onco- *combining form.* denoting a tumour: *oncology.* [from Greek *onkos*]

oncogene (ˈɒŋkəʊˌdʒiːn) *n* any of several genes, first identified in viruses but present in all cells, that when abnormally activated can cause cancer.

oncogenic (ˌɒŋkəʊˈdʒɛnɪk) *or* **oncogenous** (ɒŋˈkɒdʒənəs) *adj* causing the formation of a tumour: *an oncogenic virus.* ▸ **ˌoncoˈgenesis** *n*

oncology (ɒŋˈkɒlədʒɪ) *n* the branch of medicine concerned with the study, classification, and treatment of tumours. ▸ **oncological** (ˌɒŋkəˈlɒdʒɪkᵊl) *adj* ▸ **onˈcologist** *n*

oncoming (ˈɒnˌkʌmɪŋ) *adj* **1** coming nearer in space or time; approaching. ◆ *n* **2** the approach or onset: *the oncoming of winter.*

oncost (ˈɒnˌkɒst) *n Brit.* **1** another word for **overhead** (sense 7). **2** (*sometimes pl*) another word for **overheads.**

OND (in Britain) *abbrev. for* Ordinary National Diploma; a nationally recognized qualification in technical subjects, reached after a two-year full-time or sandwich course.

Ondaatje (ɒnˈdɑːtjɛ) *n* **Michael.** born 1943, Sri Lankan-born Canadian writer: his works include the poetry collection *There's a Trick with a Knife I'm Learning to Do* (1979) and the Booker-prizewinning novel *The English Patient* (1992), which was made into a highly successful film (1997).

ondes Martenot (ɔ̃d mɑːtəˈnəʊ) *n Music.* an electronic keyboard instrument in which the frequency of an oscillator is varied to produce separate musical notes. [C20: French, literally: Martenot waves, invented by Maurice *Martenot* (1898–1980)]

on dit *French* (ɔ̃ di) *n, pl* ***on dits*** (ɔ̃ di). a rumour; piece of gossip. [literally: it is said, they say]

Ondo (ˈɒndəʊ) *n* a state of SW Nigeria, on the Bight of Benin: formed in 1976 from part of Western State. Capital: Akure. Pop.: 4 343 230 (1995 est.). Area: 20 959 sq. km (8092 sq. miles).

ondograph (ˈɒndəʊˌɡrɑːf, -ˌɡræf) *n* an instrument for producing a graphical recording of an alternating current by measuring the charge imparted to a capacitor at different points in the cycle. [C20: from French, from *onde* wave + -GRAPH]

one (wʌn) *determiner* **1a** single; lone; not two or more: *one car.* **1b** (*as pronoun*): *one is enough for now; one at a time.* **1c** (*in combination*): *one-eyed; one-legged.* **2a** distinct from all others; only; unique: *one girl in a million.* **2b** (*as pronoun*): *one of a kind.* **3a** a specified (person, item, etc.) as distinct from another or others of its kind: *raise one hand and then the other.* **3b** (*as pronoun*): *which one is correct?* **4** a certain, indefinite, or unspecified (time); some: *one day you'll be sorry.* **5** *Informal.* an emphatic word for **a**[1] or **an**[1]: *it was one hell of a fight.* **6** a certain (person): *one Miss Jones was named.* **7** (**all**) **in one.** combined; united. **8 all one. 8a** all the same. **8b** of no consequence: *it's all one to me.* **9 at one.** (often foll. by *with*) in a state of agreement or harmony. **10 be made one.** (of a man and a woman) to become married. **11 many a one.** many people. **12 neither one thing nor the other.** indefinite, undecided, or mixed. **13 never a one.** none. **14 one and all.** everyone, without exception. **15 one by one.** one at a time; individually. **16 one or two.** a few. **17 one way and another.** on balance. **18 one with another.** on average. ◆ *pron* **19** an indefinite person regarded as typical of every person: *one can't say any more than that.* **20** any indefinite person: used as the subject of a sentence to form an alternative grammatical construction to that of the passive voice: *one can catch fine trout in this stream.* **21** *Archaic.* an unspecified person: *one came to him.* ◆ *n* **22** the smallest whole number and the first cardinal number; unity. See also **number** (sense 1). **23** a numeral (1, I, i, etc.) representing this number. **24** *Music.* the numeral 1 used as the lower figure in a time signature to indicate that the beat is measured in semibreves. **25** something representing, represented by, or consisting of one unit. **26** Also called: **one o'clock.** one hour after noon or midnight. **27** a blow or setback (esp. in the phrase **one in the eye for**). **28 the one.** (in Neo-Platonic philosophy) the ultimate being. **29 the Holy One** *or* **the One above.** God. **30 the Evil one.** Satan; the devil. ◆ Related prefixes: **mono-, uni-.** Related adj: **single.** [Old English *ān,* related to Old French *ān, ēn,* Old High German *ein,* Old Norse *einn,* Latin *unus,* Greek *oinē* ace]

-one *suffix forming nouns.* indicating that a chemical compound is a ketone: *acetone.* [arbitrarily from Greek *-ōnē,* feminine patronymic suffix, but perhaps influenced by *-one* in OZONE]

one another *pron* the reflexive form of plural pronouns when the action, attribution, etc., is reciprocal: *they kissed one another; knowing one another.* Also: **each other.**

one-armed bandit *n* a fruit machine operated by pulling down a lever at one side.

Onega (*Russian* aˈnjɛɡə) *n* a lake in NW Russia, mostly in the Karelian Republic: the second largest lake in Europe. Area: 9891 sq. km (3819 sq. miles).

one-horse *adj* **1** drawn by or using one horse. **2** (*prenominal*) *Informal.* small or obscure: *a one-horse town.*

Oneida (əʊˈnaɪdə) *n, pl* **-das** *or* **-da. 1 Lake.** a lake in central New York State: part of the New York State Barge Canal system. Length: about 35 km (22 miles). Greatest width: 9 km (6 miles). **2** (preceded by *the; functioning as pl*) a North American Indian people formerly living east of Lake Ontario; one of the Iroquois peoples. **3** a member of this people. **4** the language of this people, belonging to the Iroquoian family. [from Iroquois *onēyóte',* literally: standing stone]

O'Neill (əʊˈniːl) *n* **Eugene** (**Gladstone**). 1888–1953, U.S. dramatist. His works, which are notable for their emotional power and psychological analysis, include *Desire under the Elms* (1924), *Strange Interlude* (1928), *Mourning becomes Elektra* (1931), *Long Day's Journey into Night* (1941), and *The Iceman Cometh* (1946): Nobel prize for literature 1936.

oneiric (əʊˈnaɪərɪk) *adj* of or relating to dreams.

oneiro- *combining form.* indicating a dream: *oneirocritic.* [from Greek *oneiros* dream]

oneirocritic (əʊˌnaɪərəʊˈkrɪtɪk) *n* a person who interprets dreams. [C17: from Greek *oneirokritikos*] ▸ **oˌneiroˈcritical** *adj* ▸ **oˌneiroˈcritically** *adv*

oneiromancy (əʊˈnaɪərəʊˌmænsɪ) *n Rare.* divination by the interpretation of dreams. [C17: from Greek *oneiros* dream + -MANCY] ▸ **oˈneiroˌmancer** *n*

one-liner *n Informal.* a short joke or witty remark or riposte.

one-man *adj* consisting of or done by or for one man: *a one-man band; a one-man show.*

one-many *adj Maths, logic.* (of a relation) holding between more than one ordered pair of elements with the same first member.

oneness (ˈwʌnnɪs) *n* **1** the state or quality of being one; singleness. **2** the state of being united; agreement. **3** uniqueness. **4** sameness.

one-night stand *n* **1** a performance given only once at any one place. **2** *Informal.* **2a** a sexual encounter lasting only one evening or night. **2b** a person regarded as being only suitable for such an encounter.

one-off *n Brit.* **a** something that is carried out or made only once. **b** (*as modifier*): *a one-off job.* Also: **one-shot.** [See OFF (sense 15)]

one-on-one *adj* denoting a relationship or encounter in which someone is involved with only one other person: *a one-on-one meeting.*

one-parent family *n* a household consisting of at least one dependent child and the mother or father, the other parent being dead or permanently absent.

one-piece *adj* **1** (of a garment, esp. a bathing costume) made in one piece. ◆ *n* **2** a garment, esp. a bathing costume, made in one piece.

oner (ˈwʌnə) *n Brit. informal.* **1** a single continuous action (esp. in the phrase **down it in a oner**). **2** an outstanding person or thing. **3** a heavy blow. [C20: from ONE]

onerous (ˈɒnərəs, ˈəʊ-) *adj* **1** laborious or oppressive. **2** *Law.* (of a contract, lease, etc.) having or involving burdens or obligations that counterbalance or outweigh the advantages. [C14: from Latin *onerōsus* burdensome, from *onus* load] ▸ **ˈonerously** *adv* ▸ **ˈonerousness** *n*

oneself (wʌnˈsɛlf) *pron* **1a** the reflexive form of *one.* **1b** (intensifier): *one doesn't do that oneself.* **2** (*preceded by a copula*) one's normal or usual self: *one doesn't feel oneself after such an experience.*

one-sided *adj* **1** considering or favouring only one side of a matter, problem, etc. **2** having all the advantage on one side. **3** larger or more developed on one side. **4** having, existing on, or occurring on one side only. **5** another term for **unilateral. 6** denoting a surface on which any two points can be joined without crossing an edge. See **Möbius strip.** ▸ **ˌone-ˈsidedly** *adv* ▸ **ˌone-ˈsidedness** *n*

one-step *n* **1** an early 20th-century ballroom dance with long quick steps, the precursor of the foxtrot. **2** a piece of music composed for or in the rhythm of this dance.

one-stop *adj* having or providing a range of related services or goods in one place: *a one-stop shop.*

one-tailed *adj Statistics.* (of a significance test) concerned with the hypothesis that an observed value of a sampling statistic either significantly exceeds or falls significantly below a given value, where the error is relevant only in one direction: for instance, in testing whether scales are fair a customer does not regard overweight goods as a relevant error. Compare **two-tailed.**

One Thousand Guineas *n* See **Thousand Guineas.**

one-time *adj* **1** (*prenominal*) at some time in the past; former. ◆ *adv* **2** *Caribbean informal.* at once.

one-to-one *adj* **1** (of two or more things) corresponding exactly. **2** denoting a relationship or encounter in which someone is involved with only one other person: *one-to-one tuition.* **3** *Maths.* characterized by or involving the pairing of each member of one set with only one member of another set, without remainder.

one-track *adj* **1** *Informal.* obsessed with one idea, subject, etc. **2** having or consisting of a single track.

one-two *n* **1** *Boxing.* a jab with the leading hand followed by a cross with the other hand. **2** *Soccer.* another term for **wall pass.**

one-up *adj Informal.* having or having scored an advantage or lead over someone or something.

one-upmanship (wʌnˈʌpmənʃɪp) *n Informal.* the art or practice of achieving or maintaining an advantage over others, often by slightly unscrupulous means.

one-way *adj* **1** moving or allowing travel in one direction only: *one-way traffic; a one-way ticket.* **2** entailing no reciprocal obligation, action, etc.: *a one-way agreement.*

one-way ticket *n* the U.S. and Canadian name for **single ticket.**

on-glide *n Phonetics.* a glide immediately preceding a speech sound, for which the articulators are taking position. Compare **off-glide.**

ongoing (ˈɒnˌgəʊɪŋ) *adj* **1** actually in progress: *ongoing projects.* **2** continually moving forward; developing. **3** remaining in existence; continuing.

ongoings (ˈɒngəʊɪŋz) *pl n* a Scot. word for **goings-on.**

onie (ˈɒnɪ) *determiner Scot.* a variant spelling of **ony.**

onion (ˈʌnjən) *n* **1** an alliaceous plant, *Allium cepa,* having greenish-white flowers: cultivated for its rounded edible bulb. **2** the bulb of this plant, consisting of concentric layers of white succulent leaf bases with a pungent odour and taste. **3** any of several related plants similar to *A. cepa,* such as *A. fistulosum* (Welsh onion). **4 know one's onions.** *Brit. slang.* to be fully acquainted with a subject. [C14: via Anglo-Norman from Old French *oignon,* from Latin *unio* onion, related to UNION] ► ˈ**oniony** *adj*

onion dome *n* a bulb-shaped dome characteristic of Byzantine and Russian church architecture.

onion fly *n* a small grey dipterous insect, *Delia antiqua,* that is a serious pest of onions. The larvae destroy the bulbs.

Onions (ˈʌnjənz) *n* **Charles Talbut.** 1873–1965, English lexicographer; an editor of the *Oxford English Dictionary.*

onionskin (ˈʌnjənˌskɪn) *n* a glazed translucent paper.

onion weed *n* a plant of Australia and New Zealand, *Nuthoscordum inodorum,* having a strong onion-like smell and reproducing from bulbs and seeds.

Onitsha (əˈnɪtʃə) *n* a port in S Nigeria, in Anambra State on the Niger River: industrial centre. Pop.: 371 900 (1996 est.).

onium compound *or* **salt** (ˈəʊnɪəm) *n Chem.* any salt in which the positive ion (**onium ion**) is formed by the attachment of a proton to a neutral compound, as in ammonium, oxonium, and sulphonium compounds. [C20: from (AMM)ONIUM]

on key *adj* (**on-key** *when prenominal*), *adv* **1** in the right key. **2** in tune.

on line *adj* (**on-line** *when prenominal*). **1** of, relating to, or concerned with a peripheral device that is directly connected to and controlled by the central processing unit of a computer. **2** occurring as part of, or involving, a continuous sequence of operations, such as a production line. ◆ Compare **off line.**

onlooker (ˈɒnˌlʊkə) *n* a person who observes without taking part. ► ˈ**onˌlooking** *adj*

only (ˈəʊnlɪ) *adj* (*prenominal*) **1 the.** being single or very few in number: *the only men left in town were too old to bear arms.* **2** (of a child) having no siblings. **3** unique by virtue of being superior to anything else; peerless. **4 one and only. 4a** (*adj*) incomparable; unique. **4b** (*as n*) the object of all one's love: *you are my one and only.* ◆ *adv* **5** without anyone or anything else being included; alone: *you have one choice only; only a genius can do that.* **6** merely or just: *it's only Henry.* **7** no more or no greater than: *we met only an hour ago.* **8** *Irish.* (intensifier): *she was only marvellous; it was only dreadful.* **9** used in conditional clauses introduced by *if* to emphasize the impossibility of the condition ever being fulfilled: *if I had only known, this would never have happened.* **10** not earlier than; not...until: *I only found out yesterday.* **11 if only** *or* **if...only.** an expression used to introduce a wish, esp. one felt to be unrealizable. **12 only if.** never...except when. **13 only too. 13a** (intensifier): *he was only too pleased to help.* **13b** most regrettably (esp. in the phrase **only too true**). ◆ *sentence connector.* **14** but; however: used to introduce an exception or condition: *play outside: only don't go into the street.* [Old English *ānlīc,* from *ān* ONE + *-līc* -LY[2]]

USAGE In informal English, *only* is often used as a sentence connector: *I would have phoned you, only I didn't know your number.* This use should be avoided in formal writing: *I would have phoned you if I'd known your number.* In formal speech and writing, *only* is placed directly before the word or words that it modifies: *she could interview only three applicants in the morning.* In all but the most formal contexts, however, it is generally regarded as acceptable to put *only* before the verb: *she could only interview three applicants in the morning.* Care must be taken not to create ambiguity, esp. in written English, in which intonation will not, as it does in speech, help to show to which item in the sentence *only* applies. A sentence such as *she only drinks tea in the afternoon* is capable of two interpretations and is therefore better rephrased either as *she drinks only tea in the afternoon* (i.e. no other drink) or *she drinks tea only in the afternoon* (i.e. at no other time).

only-begotten *adj Archaic.* (of a child) being the only offspring of its father.

o.n.o. (*Brit., Austral., and N.Z.* in advertisements) *abbrev. for* or near(est) offer: *£50 o.n.o.*

onomasiology (ˌɒnəʊˌmeɪsɪˈɒlədʒɪ) *n* **1** another name for **onomastics** (sense 1). **2** the branch of semantics concerned with the meanings of and meaning relations between individual words.

onomastic (ˌɒnəˈmæstɪk) *adj* **1** of or relating to proper names. **2** *Law.* denoting a signature in a different handwriting from that of the document to which it is attached. [C17: from Greek *onomastikos,* from *onomazein* to name, from *onoma* NAME]

onomastics (ˌɒnəˈmæstɪks) *n* **1** (*functioning as sing*) the study of proper names, esp. of their origins. **2** (*functioning as sing or pl*) a systematization of the facts about how proper names are formed in a given language.

onomatopoeia (ˌɒnəˌmætəˈpiːə) *n* **1** the formation of words whose sound is imitative of the sound of the noise or action designated, such as *hiss, buzz,* and *bang.* **2** the use of such words for poetic or rhetorical effect. [C16: via Late Latin from Greek *onoma* name + *poiein* to make] ► ˌ**onoˌmatoˈpoeic** *or* **onomatopoetic** (ˌɒnəˌmætəpəʊˈetɪk) *adj* ► ˌ**onoˌmatoˈpoeically** *or* ˌ**onoˌmatopoˈetically** *adv*

Onondaga (ˌɒnənˈdɑːgə) *n* **1 Lake.** a salt lake in central New York State. Area: about 13 sq. km (5 sq. miles). **2** (*pl* **-gas** *or* **-ga**) a member of a North American Indian Iroquois people formerly living between Lake Champlain and the St Lawrence River. **3** the language of this people, belonging to the Iroquoian family. [from Iroquois *onõtáge',* literally: on the top of the hill (the name of their principal village)] ► ˌ**Ononˈdagan** *adj*

onrush (ˈɒnˌrʌʃ) *n* a forceful forward rush or flow.

onset (ˈɒnˌset) *n* **1** an attack; assault. **2** a start; beginning.

onshore (ˈɒnˈʃɔː) *adj, adv* **1** towards the land: *an onshore gale.* **2** on land; not at sea.

onside (ˌɒnˈsaɪd) *adj, adv Football, hockey, etc.* (of a player) in a legal position, as when behind the ball or with a required number of opponents between oneself and the opposing team's goal line. Compare **offside.**

onslaught (ˈɒnˌslɔːt) *n* a violent attack. [C17: from Middle Dutch *aenslag,* from *aan* ON + *slag* a blow, related to SLAY]

Ont. *abbrev. for* Ontario.

Ontario (ɒnˈtɛərɪəʊ) *n* **1** a province of central Canada: lies mostly on the Canadian Shield and contains the fertile plain of the lower Great Lakes and the St Lawrence River, one of the world's leading industrial areas; the second largest and the most populous province. Capital: Toronto. Pop.: 11 407 700 (1997 est.). Area: 891 198 sq. km (344 092 sq. miles). Abbrevs.: **Ont.** *or* **ON. 2 Lake.** a lake between the U.S. and Canada, bordering on New York State and Ontario province: the smallest of the Great Lakes; linked with Lake Erie by the Niagara River and Welland Canal; drained by the St Lawrence. Area: 19 684 sq. km (7600 sq. miles). ► **Onˈtarian** *or* **Ontarioan** (ɒnˈtɛərɪˌəʊən) *n, adj*

onto *or* **on to** (ˈɒntʊ; *unstressed* ˈɒntə) *prep* **1** to a position that is on: *step onto the train as it passes.* **2** having become aware of (something illicit or secret): *the police are onto us.* **3** into contact with: *get onto the factory.*

USAGE *Onto* is now generally accepted as a word in its own right. *On to* is still used, however, where *on* is considered to be part of the verb: *he moved on to a different town* as contrasted with *he jumped onto the stage.*

onto- *combining form.* existence or being: *ontogeny; ontology.* [from Late Greek, from *ōn* (stem *ont-*) being, present participle of *einai* to be]

ontogeny (ɒnˈtɒdʒənɪ) *or* **ontogenesis** (ˌɒntəˈdʒenɪsɪs) *n* the entire sequence of events involved in the development of an individual organism. Compare **phylogeny.** ► **ontogenic** (ˌɒntəˈdʒenɪk) *or* **ontogenetic** (ˌɒntədʒɪˈnetɪk) *adj* ► ˌ**ontoˈgenically** *or* ˌ**ontogeˈnetically** *adv*

ontological argument *n Philosophy.* **1** the traditional a priori argument for the existence of God on the grounds that the concept itself necessitates existence. Compare **cosmological argument, teleological argument. 2** any analogous argument from the nature of some concept to the existence of whatever instantiates it.

ontology (ɒnˈtɒlədʒɪ) *n* **1** *Philosophy.* the branch of metaphysics that deals with the nature of being. **2** *Logic.* the set of entities presupposed by a theory. ► ˌ**ontoˈlogical** *adj* ► ˌ**ontoˈlogically** *adv*

onus (ˈəʊnəs) *n, pl* **onuses.** a responsibility, task, or burden. [C17: from Latin: burden]

onus probandi (ˈəʊnəs prəʊˈbændɪ) *n Law.* the Latin phrase for **burden of proof.**

onward (ˈɒnwəd) *adj* **1** directed or moving forwards, onwards, etc. ◆ *adv* **2** a variant of **onwards.**

onwards (ˈɒnwədz) *or* **onward** *adv* at or towards a point or position ahead, in advance, etc.

ony (ˈɒnɪ) *determiner* a Scot. word for **any.**

onychophoran (ˌɒnɪˈkɒfərən) *n* any wormlike invertebrate of the phylum *Onychophora,* having a segmented body, short unjointed limbs, and breathing by means of tracheae: intermediate in structure and evolutionary development between annelids and arthropods. [from New Latin *Onychophora,* from Greek *onukh-* nail, claw + -PHORE]

-onym *n combining form.* indicating a name or word: *acronym; pseudonym.* [from Greek *-onumon,* from *onuma,* Doric variant of *onoma* name]

onymous (ˈɒnɪməs) *adj* (of a book) bearing its author's name. [C18: back formation from ANONYMOUS]

onyx (ˈɒnɪks) *n* **1** a variety of chalcedony with alternating black and white parallel bands, used as a gemstone. Formula: SiO_2. **2** a compact variety of calcite used as an ornamental stone; onyx marble. Formula: $CaCO_3$. [C13: from Latin from Greek: fingernail (so called from its veined appearance)]

ONZ *abbrev. for* Order of New Zealand (a N.Z. title).

oo- *or* **oö-** *combining form.* egg or ovum: *oosperm.* [from Greek *ōion* EGG[1]]

oocyst (ˈəʊəˌsɪst) *n* an encysted zygote of sporozoan protozoans that undergoes sporogony to produce infective sporozoites.

oocyte (ˈəʊəˌsaɪt) *n* an immature female germ cell that gives rise to an ovum after two meiotic divisions.

oodles (ˈuːdᵊlz) *pl n Informal.* great quantities: *oodles of money.* [C20: of uncertain origin]

oof (uːf) *n Slang.* money. [C19: from Yiddish *ooftisch,* from German *auf dem Tische* on the table (referring to gambling stakes)] ▸ **ˈoofy** *adj*

oogamy (əʊˈɒgəmɪ) *n* sexual reproduction involving a small motile male gamete and a large much less motile female gamete: occurs in all higher animals and some plants. ▸ **oˈogamous** *adj*

oogenesis (ˌəʊəˈdʒɛnɪsɪs) *n* the formation and maturation of ova from undifferentiated cells in the ovary. See also **oocyte.** ▸ **oogenetic** (ˌəʊədʒɪˈnɛtɪk) *adj*

oogonium (ˌəʊəˈgəʊnɪəm) *n, pl* **-nia** (-nɪə) *or* **-niums. 1** an immature female germ cell forming oocytes by repeated divisions. **2** a female sex organ of some algae and fungi producing female gametes (oospheres). ▸ **ooˈgonial** *adj*

ooh (uː) *interj* an exclamation of surprise, pleasure, pain, etc.

Ookpik (ˈuːkpɪk) *n Canadian trademark.* a sealskin doll resembling an owl, first made in 1963 by an Inuit and used abroad as a symbol of Canadian handicrafts. [from Eskimo *ukpik* a snowy owl]

oolite (ˈəʊəˌlaɪt) *n* any sedimentary rock, esp. limestone, consisting of tiny spherical concentric grains within a fine matrix. [C18: from French from New Latin *oolītēs,* literally: egg stone; probably a translation of German *Rogenstein* roe stone] ▸ **oolitic** (ˌəʊəˈlɪtɪk) *adj*

oolith (ˈəʊəˌlɪθ) *n* any of the tiny spherical grains of sedimentary rock of which oolite is composed.

oology (əʊˈɒlədʒɪ) *n* the branch of ornithology concerned with the study of birds' eggs. ▸ **oological** (ˌəʊəˈlɒdʒɪkᵊl) *adj* ▸ **oˈologist** *n*

oolong (ˈuːˌlɒŋ) *n* a kind of dark tea, grown in China, that is partly fermented before being dried. [C19: from Chinese *wu lung,* from *wu* black + *lung* dragon]

oom ˈuːəm) *n S. African.* a title of respect used to address an elderly man. [Afrikaans: literally, uncle]

oomiak *or* **oomiac** (ˈuːmɪˌæk) *n* other words for **umiak.**

oompah (ˈuːmˌpɑː) *n* a representation of the sound made by a deep brass instrument, esp. in military band music.

oomph (ʊmf) *n Informal.* **1** enthusiasm, vigour, or energy. **2** sex appeal. [C20: perhaps imitative of the bellow of a mating bull]

oont (ʊnt) *n Anglo-Indian dialect.* a camel. [C19: from Hindi *unt*]

oophorectomy (ˌəʊəfəˈrɛktəmɪ) *n, pl* **-mies.** surgical removal of an ovary or ovarian tumour. Also called: **ovariectomy.** Compare **ovariotomy.** [C19: from New Latin *ōophoron* ovary, from Greek *ōion* egg + *phoros* bearing, + -ECTOMY]

oophoritis (ˌəʊəfəˈraɪtɪs) *n* inflammation of an ovary; ovaritis. ▸ **oophoritic** (ˌəʊəfəˈrɪtɪk) *adj*

oophyte (ˈəʊəˌfaɪt) *n* the gametophyte in mosses, liverworts, and ferns. ▸ **oophytic** (ˌəʊəˈfɪtɪk) *adj*

oops (ʊps, uːps) *interj* an exclamation of surprise or of apology as when someone drops something or makes a mistake.

Oort (ɔːt) *n* **Jan Hendrick.** 1900–92, Dutch astronomer, who confirmed (1927) and developed the theory of galactic rotation. He was the first to propose (1950) the existence of a mass of comets orbiting the sun far beyond the orbit of Pluto (the **Oort cloud**).

oose (uːs) *n Scot. dialect.* dust; fluff. [of unknown origin] ▸ **ˈoosy** *adj*

oosperm (ˈəʊəˌspɜːm) *n* a fertilized ovum; zygote.

oosphere (ˈəʊəˌsfɪə) *n* a large female gamete produced in the oogonia of algae and fungi.

oospore (ˈəʊəˌspɔː) *n* a thick-walled sexual spore that develops from a fertilized oosphere in some algae and fungi. ▸ **ˌooˈsporic** *or* **ˌooˈsporous** *adj*

Oostende (oːstˈɛndə) *n* the Flemish name for **Ostend.**

ootheca (ˌəʊəˈθiːkə) *n, pl* **-cae** (-siː). a capsule containing eggs that is produced by some insects and molluscs. [C19: New Latin, from OO- + *thēkē* case] ▸ **ˌooˈthecal** *adj*

ootid (ˈəʊətɪd) *n Zoology.* an immature female gamete that develops into an ovum. [C20: from OO- + (SPERMA)TID]

ooze[1] (uːz) *vb* **1** (*intr*) to flow or leak out slowly, as through pores or very small holes. **2** to exude or emit (moisture, gas, etc.). **3** (*tr*) to overflow with: *to ooze charm.* **4** (*intr;* often foll. by *away*) to disappear or escape gradually. ◆ *n* **5** a slow flowing or leaking. **6** an infusion of vegetable matter, such as sumach or oak bark, used in tanning. [Old English *wōs* juice]

ooze[2] (uːz) *n* **1** a soft thin mud found at the bottom of lakes and rivers. **2** a fine-grained calcareous or siliceous marine deposit consisting of the hard parts of planktonic organisms. **3** muddy ground, esp. of bogs. [Old English *wāse* mud; related to Old French *wāse,* Old Norse *veisa*]

ooze leather *n* a very soft leather with a suedelike finish. [C19: from OOZE[1] (sense 6)]

oozy[1] (ˈuːzɪ) *adj* **oozier, ooziest.** moist or dripping.

oozy[2] (ˈuːzɪ) *adj* **oozier, ooziest.** of, resembling, or containing mud; slimy. ▸ **ˈoozily** *adv* ▸ **ˈooziness** *n*

OP *abbrev. for:* **1** *Military.* observation post. **2** Ordo Praedictatorum (the Dominicans). **3** organophosphate. [Latin: Order of Preachers]

op. *abbrev. for:* **1** opera. **2** operation. **3** opposite. **4** opus. **5** operator. **6** optical.

o.p. *or* **O.P.** *abbrev. for* out of print.

opacity (əʊˈpæsɪtɪ) *n, pl* **-ties. 1** the state or quality of being opaque. **2** the degree to which something is opaque. **3** an opaque object or substance. **4** obscurity of meaning; unintelligibility. **5** *Physics, photog.* the ratio of the intensity of light incident on a medium, such as a photographic film, to that transmitted through the medium. **6** *Logic, philosophy.* the property of being an opaque context.

opah (ˈəʊpə) *n* a large soft-finned deep-sea teleost fish, *Lampris regius* (or *luna*), of the Atlantic and Pacific Oceans and the Mediterranean Sea, having a deep, brilliantly coloured body: family *Lampridae.* Also called: **moonfish, kingfish.** [C18: of West African origin]

opal (ˈəʊpᵊl) *n* an amorphous, usually iridescent, mineral that can be of almost any colour, found in igneous rocks and around hot springs. It is used as a gemstone. Composition: hydrated silica. Formula: $SiO_2.nH_2O$. [C16: from Latin *opalus,* from Greek *opallios,* from Sanskrit *upala* precious stone] ▸ **ˈopal-ˌlike** *adj*

opalesce (ˌəʊpəˈlɛs) *vb* (*intr*) to exhibit a milky iridescence.

opalescent (ˌəʊpəˈlɛsᵊnt) *adj* having or emitting an iridescence like that of an opal. ▸ **ˌopalˈescence** *n*

opal glass *n* glass that is opalescent or white, made by the addition of fluorides.

opaline (ˈəʊpəˌlaɪn) *adj* **1** opalescent. ◆ *n* **2** an opaque or semiopaque whitish glass.

opaque (əʊˈpeɪk) *adj* **1** not transmitting light; not transparent or translucent. **2** not reflecting light; lacking lustre or shine; dull. **3** not transmitting radiant energy, such as electromagnetic or corpuscular radiation, or sound. **4** hard to understand; unintelligible. **5** unintelligent; dense. ◆ *n* **6** *Photog.* an opaque pigment used to block out particular areas on a negative. ◆ *vb* **opaques, opaquing, opaqued.** (*tr*) **7** to make opaque. **8** *Photog.* to block out particular areas, such as blemishes, on (a negative), using an opaque. [C15: from Latin *opācus* shady] ▸ **oˈpaquely** *adv* ▸ **oˈpaqueness** *n*

opaque context *n Philosophy, logic.* an expression in which the replacement of a term by another with the same reference may change the truth-value of the whole. *John believes that Cicero was a Roman* is opaque, since even though Cicero and Tully are the same person John may know that the given statement is true but not that Tully was a Roman. Compare **transparent context.** See also **intensional, Electra paradox.**

opaque projector *n* the U.S. and Canadian name for **episcope.**

op art (ɒp) *n* a style of abstract art chiefly concerned with the exploitation of optical effects such as the illusion of movement. [C20 *op,* short for *optical*]

OPC *or* **opc** *abbrev. for* ordinary Portland cement.

op. cit. (in textual annotations) *abbrev. for* opere citato. [Latin: in the work cited]

ope (əʊp) *vb, adj* an archaic or poetic word for **open.**

OPEC (ˈəʊˌpɛk) *n acronym for* Organization of Petroleum-Exporting Countries: an organization formed in 1961 to administer a common policy for the sale of petroleum. Its members are Algeria, Indonesia, Iran, Iraq, Kuwait, Libya, Nigeria, Qatar, Saudi Arabia, the United Arab Emirates, and Venezuela. Ecuador and Gabon were members but withdrew in 1992 and 1995 respectively.

open (ˈəʊpᵊn) *adj* **1** not closed or barred: *the door is open.* **2** affording free passage, access, view, etc.; not blocked or obstructed: *the road is open for traffic.* **3** not sealed, fastened, or wrapped: *an open package.* **4** having the interior part accessible: *an open drawer.* **5** extended, expanded, or unfolded: *an open newspaper; an open flower.* **6** ready for business: *the shops are open.* **7** able to be obtained; available: *the position advertised last week is no longer open.* **8** unobstructed by buildings, trees, etc.: *open countryside.* **9** free to all to join, enter, use, visit, etc.: *an open competition.* **10** unengaged or unoccupied: *the doctor has an hour open for you to call.* **11** See **open season. 12** not decided or finalized: *an open question.* **13** ready to entertain new ideas; not biased or prejudiced: *an open mind.* **14** unreserved or candid: *she was very open in her description.* **15** liberal or generous: *an open hand.* **16** extended or eager to receive (esp. in the phrase **with open arms**). **17** exposed to view; blatant: *open disregard of the law.* **18** liable or susceptible: *you will leave yourself open to attack if you speak.* **19** (of climate or seasons) free from frost; mild. **20** free from navigational hazards, such as ice, sunken ships, etc.: *open water.* **21** *U.S.* without legal restrictions or enforceable regulations, esp. in relation to gambling, vice, etc.: *an open town.* **22** without barriers to prevent absconding: *an open prison.* **23** having large or numerous spacing or apertures: *open ranks.* **24** full of small openings or gaps; porous: *an open texture.* **25** *Printing.* (of type matter) generously leaded or widely spaced. **26** *Music.* **26a** (of a violin or guitar string) not stopped with the finger. **26b** (of a pipe, such as an organ pipe) not closed at either end. **26c** (of a note) played on such a string or pipe. **27** *Commerce.* **27a** in operation; active: *an open account.* **27b** unrestricted; unlimited: *open credit; open insurance cover.* **28** See **open cheque. 29** (of a return ticket) not specifying a date for travel. **30** *Sport.* **30a** (of a goal, court, etc.) unguarded or relatively unprotected: *the forward missed an open goal.* **30b** (of a stance, esp. in golf) characterized by the front of the body being turned forward. **31** (of a wound) exposed to the air. **32** (esp. of the large intestine) free from obstruction. **33** undefended and of no military significance: *an open city.* **34** *Phonetics.* **34a** denoting a vowel pronounced with the lips relatively wide apart. **34b** denoting a syllable that does not end in a consonant, as in *pa.* **35** *Chess.* (of a file) having no pawns on it. **36** *Maths.* (of a set) containing points whose neighbourhood consists of other points of the same set: *points inside a circle are an open set.* **37** *Computing.* (of software or a computer system) designed to an internationally agreed standard in order to allow communication between computers, irrespective of size, maufacturer, etc. ◆ *vb* **38** to move or cause to move from a closed or fastened position: *to open a window.* **39** (when *intr,* foll. by *on* or *onto*) to render, be, or become accessible or unobstructed: *to open a road; to open a parcel; the door opens into the hall.* **40** (*intr*) to come into or appear in view: *the lake opened before us.* **41** (*tr*) to puncture (a boil) so as to permit drainage. **42** to extend or unfold or cause to extend or unfold: *to open a newspaper.* **43** to disclose or uncover or be disclosed or uncovered: *to open one's heart.* **44** to cause (the mind) to become receptive or (of the mind) to become receptive. **45** to operate or cause to operate: *to open a shop.* **46** (when *intr,* sometimes foll. by *out*) to make or become less compact or dense in structure: *to open ranks.* **47** to set or be set in action; start: *to open a discussion; to open the batting.* **48** (*tr*) to arrange for (a bank account, savings account, etc.)

usually by making an initial deposit. **49** to turn to a specified point in (a book, magazine, etc.): *open at page one.* **50** *Law.* to make the opening statement in (a case before a court of law). **51** (*intr*) *Cards.* to bet, bid, or lead first on a hand. ◆ *n* **52** (often preceded by *the*) any wide or unobstructed space or expanse, esp. of land or water. **53** See **open air.** **54** *Sport.* a competition which anyone may enter. **55** **bring** (*or* **come**) **into the open.** to make (or become) evident or public. ◆ See also **open up.** [Old English; related to Old French *open, epen,* Old Saxon *opan,* Old High German *offan*] ► **'openable** *adj* ► **'openly** *adv* ► **'openness** *n*

open air *n* **a** the place or space where the air is unenclosed; the outdoors. **b** (*as modifier*): *an open-air concert.*

open-and-shut *adj* easily decided or solved; obvious: *an open-and-shut case.*

open book *n* a person or thing without secrecy or concealment that can be easily known or interpreted.

Open Brethren *n* one of the two main divisions of the Plymouth Brethren that, in contrast to the Exclusive Brethren, permits contacts with members outside the sect.

opencast mining ('əʊpᵊnˌkɑːst) *n Brit.* mining by excavating from the surface. Also called: (esp. U.S.) **strip mining,** (Austral. and N.Z.) **open-cut mining.** [C18: from OPEN + archaic *cast* ditch or cutting]

open chain *n* a chain of atoms in a molecule that is not joined at its ends into the form of a ring.

open cheque *n* an uncrossed cheque that can be cashed at the drawee bank.

open circuit *n* an incomplete electrical circuit in which no current flows. Compare **closed circuit.**

Open College *n* **the.** (in Britain) a college of art founded in 1987 for mature students studying foundation courses in arts and crafts by television programmes, written materials, and tutorials.

open court *n* a court or trial to which members of the public are freely admitted.

open cut *n Civil engineering.* an excavation made in the open rather than in a tunnel. See **cut-and-cover.**

open-cut mining *n* the Austral. and N.Z. name for **opencast mining.**

open day *n* an occasion on which an institution, such as a school, is open for inspection by the public. Also called: **at-home.** U.S. and Canadian name: **open house.**

open door *n* **1** a policy or practice by which a nation grants opportunities for trade to all other nations equally. **2** free and unrestricted admission. ◆ *adj* **open-door. 3** open to all; accessible. **4** (in industrial relations) designating a policy of management being prepared to talk to workers in the office at any time.

open-ended *adj* **1** without definite limits, as of duration or amount: *an open-ended contract.* **2** denoting a question, esp. one on a questionnaire, that cannot be answered "yes", "no", or "don't know".

opener ('əʊpənə) *n* **1** an instrument used to open sealed containers such as tins or bottles: *a bottle opener.* **2** a person who opens, esp. the player who makes the first bid or play. **3** the first or opening section or episode in a series. **4** *U.S.* the first song, act, etc., in a variety show. **5** (*pl*) a start; beginning (esp. in the phrase **for openers**).

open-eyed *adj* **1** with the eyes wide open, as in amazement. **2** watchful; alert.

open-faced *adj* **1** having an ingenuous expression. **2** (of a watch) having no lid or cover other than the glass.

open-field *adj* (*prenominal*) *Medieval history.* of or denoting the system in which an arable area was divided into unenclosed strips, esp. cultivated by different tenants.

open game *n Chess.* a relatively simple game involving open ranks and files, permitting tactical play, and usually following symmetrical development. Compare **closed game.**

open-handed *adj* generous; liberal. ► ˌ**open-'handedly** *adv* ► ˌ**open-'handedness** *n*

open-hearted *adj* **1** kindly and warm. **2** disclosing intentions and thoughts clearly; candid. ► ˌ**open-'heartedly** *adv* ► ˌ**open-'heartedness** *n*

open-hearth furnace *n* (esp. formerly) a steel-making reverbatory furnace in which pig iron and scrap are contained in a shallow hearth and heated by producer gas.

open-hearth process *n* a process for making steel using an open-hearth furnace.

open-heart surgery *n* surgical repair of the heart during which the blood circulation is often maintained mechanically.

open house *n* **1** a U.S. and Canadian name for **at-home** or **open day. 2 keep open house.** to be always ready to provide hospitality. **3** *U.S. and N.Z.* a house available for inspection by prospective buyers.

opening ('əʊpənɪŋ) *n* **1** the act of making or becoming open. **2** a vacant or unobstructed space, esp. one that will serve as a passageway; gap. **3** *Chiefly U.S.* a tract in a forest in which trees are scattered or absent. **4** the first part or stage of something. **5a** the first performance of something, esp. a theatrical production. **5b** (*as modifier*): *the opening night.* **6** a specific or formal sequence of moves at the start of any of certain games, esp. chess or draughts. **7** an opportunity or chance, esp. for employment or promotion in a business concern. **8** *Law.* the preliminary statement made by counsel to the court or jury before adducing evidence in support of his case.

opening time *n Brit.* the time at which public houses can legally start selling alcoholic drinks.

open learning *n* a system of further education on a flexible part-time basis.

open letter *n* a letter, esp. one of protest, addressed to a person but also made public, as through the press.

open market *n* **a** a market in which prices are determined by supply and demand, there are no barriers to entry, and trading is not restricted to a specific area. **b** (*as modifier*): *open-market value.*

open market operations *pl n Finance.* the purchase and sale on the open market of government securities by the Bank of England for the purpose of regulating the supply of money and credit to the economy.

open marriage *n* a marriage in which the partners are free to pursue their own social and sexual lives.

open-minded *adj* having a mind receptive to new ideas, arguments, etc.; unprejudiced. ► ˌ**open-'mindedly** *adv* ► ˌ**open-'mindedness** *n*

open-mouthed *adj* **1** having an open mouth, esp. in surprise. **2** greedy or ravenous. **3** clamorous or vociferous.

open order *n Military.* a formation that allows additional space between the ranks of a guard or inspected unit to allow the inspecting officer to pass.

open-plan *adj* having no or few dividing walls between areas: *an open-plan office floor.*

open policy *n* an insurance policy in which the amount payable in the event of a claim is settled after the loss or damage has occurred. Compare **valued policy.**

open position *n Commerce.* a situation in which a dealer in commodities, securities, or currencies has either unsold stock or uncovered sales.

open primary *n U.S. government.* a primary in which any registered voter may participate. Compare **closed primary.**

open prison *n* a penal establishment in which the prisoners are trusted to serve their sentences and so do not need to be locked up, thus extending the range of work and occupation they can safely undertake.

open punctuation *n* punctuation characterized by sparing use of stops, esp. of the comma. Compare **close punctuation.**

open question *n* **1** a matter which is undecided. **2** a question that cannot be answered with yes or no but requires a developed answer.

open-reel *adj* another term for **reel-to-reel.**

open sandwich *n* a slice of bread covered with a spread or filling but without a top.

open season *n* **1** a specified period of time in the year when it is legal to hunt or kill game or fish protected at other times by law. **2** (often foll. by *on*) a time when criticism or mistreatment is common: *open season on women employees.*

open secret *n* something that is supposed to be secret but is widely known.

open sentence *n Logic.* an expression containing a free variable that can be replaced by a name to yield a sentence, as *x is wise.* Also called: **propositional function, sentential function.**

open sesame *n* a very successful means of achieving a result. [from the magical words used by Ali Baba in *The Arabian Nights' Entertainments* to open the door of the robbers' den]

open set *n Maths.* **1** a set which is not a closed set. **2** an interval on the real line excluding its end points, as]0, 1[, the set of reals between, but excluding, 0 and 1.

open shop *n* an establishment in which persons are hired and employed irrespective of their membership or nonmembership of a trade union. Compare **closed shop, union shop.**

open slather *n* See **slather** (sense 2).

open texture *n Philosophy.* the failure of natural languages to determine future usage, particularly the ability of predicates to permit the construction of borderline cases.

Open University *n* **the.** (in Britain) a university founded in 1969 for mature students studying by television and radio lectures, correspondence courses, local counselling, and summer schools.

open up *vb* (*adv*) **1** (*intr*) to start firing a gun or guns. **2** (*intr*) to speak freely or without restraint. **3** (*intr*) *Informal.* (of a motor vehicle) to accelerate. **4** (*tr*) to render accessible: *the motorway opened up the remoter areas.* **5** to make or become more exciting or lively: *the game opened up after half-time.*

open verdict *n* a finding by a coroner's jury of death without stating the cause.

openwork ('əʊpᵊnˌwɜːk) *n* ornamental work, as of metal or embroidery, having a pattern of openings or holes.

opera[1] ('ɒpərə, 'ɒprə) *n* **1** an extended dramatic work in which music constitutes a dominating feature, either consisting of separate recitatives, arias, and choruses, or having a continuous musical structure. **2** the branch of music or drama represented by such works. **3** the score, libretto, etc., of an opera. **4** a theatre where opera is performed. [C17: via Italian from Latin: work, a work, plural of *opus* work]

opera[2] ('ɒpərə) *n* a plural of **opus.**

operable ('ɒpərəbᵊl, 'ɒprə-) *adj* **1** capable of being treated by a surgical operation. **2** capable of being operated. **3** capable of being put into practice. ► ˌ**opera'bility** *n* ► **'operably** *adv*

opéra bouffe ('ɒpərə 'buːf; *French* ɔpera buf) *n, pl* **opéras bouffes** (*French* ɔpera buf). a type of light or satirical opera common in France during the 19th century. [from French: comic opera]

opera buffa ('buːfə; *Italian* 'opera 'buffa) *n, pl* **opera buffas** *or* **opere buffe** (*Italian* 'opere'buffe). comic opera, esp. that originating in Italy during the 18th century. [from Italian: comic opera]

opera cloak *n* a large cloak worn over evening clothes. Also called: **opera hood.**

opéra comique (kɒ'miːk; *French* ɔpera kɔmik) *n, pl* **opéras comiques** (*French* ɔpera kɔmik). a type of opera, not necessarily comic, current in France during the 19th century and characterized by spoken dialogue. It originated in satirical parodies of grand opera.

opera glasses *pl n* small low-powered binoculars used by audiences in theatres and opera houses.

opera hat *n* a collapsible top hat operated by a spring. Also called: **gibus.**

opera house *n* a theatre designed for opera.

operand ('ɒpə,rænd) *n* a quantity or function upon which a mathematical or logical operation is performed. [C19: from Latin *operandum* (something) to be worked upon, from *operārī* to work]

operant ('ɒpərənt) *adj* **1** producing effects; operating. ◆ *n* **2** a person or thing that operates. **3** *Psychol.* any response by an organism that is not directly caused by a stimulus.

operant learning *n Psychol.* another name for **instrumental learning**.

opera seria ('sɪərɪə; *Italian* 'opera 'sɛːrja) *n, pl* **opere serie** (*Italian* 'opere 'sɛːrje). a type of opera current in 18th century Italy based on a serious plot, esp. a mythological tale. [from Italian: serious opera]

operate ('ɒpə,reɪt) *vb* **1** to function or cause to function. **2** (*tr*) to control the functioning of: *operate a machine.* **3** to manage, direct, run, or pursue (a business, system, etc.). **4** (*intr*) to perform a surgical operation (upon a person or animal). **5** (*intr*) to produce a desired or intended effect. **6** (*tr; usually foll. by on*) to treat or process in a particular or specific way. **7** (*intr*) to conduct military or naval operations. **8** (*intr*) to deal in securities on a stock exchange. [C17: from Latin *operārī* to work]

operatic (,ɒpə'rætɪk) *adj* **1** of or relating to opera. **2** histrionic or exaggerated. ▸ **,oper'atically** *adv*

operating budget *n Account.* a forecast of the sales revenue, production costs, overheads, cash flow, etc., of an organization, used to monitor its trading activities, usually for one year.

operating system *n* the set of software that controls the overall operation of a computer system, typically by performing such tasks as memory allocation, job scheduling, and input/output control.

operating table *n* the table on which the patient lies during a surgical operation.

operating theatre *n* a room in which surgical operations are performed.

operation (,ɒpə'reɪʃən) *n* **1** the act, process, or manner of operating. **2** the state of being in effect, in action, or operative (esp. in the phrases **in** *or* **into operation**). **3** a process, method, or series of acts, esp. of a practical or mechanical nature. **4** *Surgery.* any manipulation of the body or one of its organs or parts to repair damage, arrest the progress of a disease, remove foreign matter, etc. **5a** a military or naval action, such as a campaign, manoeuvre, etc. **5b** (*cap. and prenominal when part of a name*): *Operation Crossbow.* **6** *Maths.* **6a** any procedure, such as addition, multiplication, involution, or differentiation, in which one or more numbers or quantities are operated upon according to specific rules. **6b** a function from a set onto itself. **7** a commercial or financial transaction.

operational (,ɒpə'reɪʃənᵊl) *adj* **1** of or relating to an operation or operations. **2** in working order and ready for use. **3** *Military.* capable of, needed in, or actually involved in operations. ▸ **,oper'ationally** *adv*

operational amplifier *n* a high-gain direct-coupled amplifier, the response of which may be controlled by negative-feedback circuits externally connected.

operationalism (,ɒpə'reɪʃənə,lɪzəm) *or* **operationism** (,ɒpə'reɪʃə,nɪzəm) *n Philosophy.* the theory that scientific terms are defined by the experimental operations which determine their applicability. ▸ **,oper,ational'istic** *adj*

Operation Barbarossa *n* the codename for Hitler's invasion (1941) of Russia.

Operation Desert Storm *n* the codename for the U.S.-led UN operation to liberate Kuwait from Iraq (1991).

Operation Overlord *n* the codename for the Allied invasion (June 1944) of northern France.

Operation Sealion *n* the codename for Hitler's proposed invasion (1940) of Great Britain.

operations research *n* the analysis of problems in business and industry involving the construction of models and the application of linear programming, critical path analysis, and other quantitative techniques. Also: **operational research.**

operations room *n* a room from which all the operations of a military, police, or other disciplined activity are controlled.

operative ('ɒpərətɪv) *adj* **1** in force, effect, or operation. **2** exerting force or influence. **3** producing a desired effect; significant: *the operative word.* **4** of or relating to a surgical procedure. ◆ *n* **5** a worker, esp. one with a special skill. **6** *U.S.* a private detective. ▸ **'operatively** *adv* ▸ **'operativeness** *or* **,opera'tivity** *n*

operatize *or* **operatise** ('ɒpərə,taɪz) *vb* (*tr*) to turn (a play, novel, etc.) into an opera.

operator ('ɒpə,reɪtə) *n* **1** a person who operates a machine, instrument, etc., esp., a person who makes connections on a telephone switchboard or at an exchange. **2** a person who owns or operates an industrial or commercial establishment. **3** a speculator, esp. one who operates on currency or stock markets. **4** *Informal.* a person who manipulates affairs and other people. **5** *Maths.* any symbol, term, letter, etc., used to indicate or express a specific operation or process, such as ∫ (the integral operator), or Δ (the differential operator).

operculum (əʊ'pɜːkjʊləm) *n, pl* **-la** (-lə) *or* **-lums.** **1** *Zoology.* **1a** the hard bony flap covering the gill slits in fishes. **1b** the bony plate in certain gastropods covering the opening of the shell when the body is withdrawn. **2** *Botany.* the covering of the spore-bearing capsule of a moss. **3** *Biology.* any other covering or lid in various organisms. [C18: via New Latin from Latin: lid, from *operīre* to cover] ▸ **o'percular** *or* **operculate** (əʊ'pɜːkjʊlɪt, -,leɪt) *adj*

operetta (,ɒpə'rɛtə) *n* a type of comic or light-hearted opera. [C18: from Italian: a small OPERA[1]] ▸ **,oper'ettist** *n*

operon ('ɒpə,rɒn) *n Genetics.* a group of adjacent genes functioning as a unit under the control of another gene (the **operator gene**). [C20: from OPERATE]

operose ('ɒpə,rəʊs) *adj Rare.* **1** laborious. **2** industrious; busy. [C17: from Latin *operōsus* painstaking, from *opus* work] ▸ **'oper,osely** *adv* ▸ **'oper,oseness** *n*

ophicleide ('ɒfɪ,klaɪd) *n Music.* an obsolete keyed wind instrument of bass pitch. [C19: from French *ophicléide,* from Greek *ophis* snake + *kleis* key]

ophidian (əʊ'fɪdɪən) *adj* **1** snakelike. **2** of, relating to, or belonging to the *Ophidia,* a suborder of reptiles that comprises the snakes. ◆ *n* **3** any reptile of the suborder *Ophidia;* a snake. [C19: from New Latin *Ophidia* name of suborder, from Greek *ophidion,* from *ophis* snake]

ophiology (,ɒfɪ'ɒlədʒɪ) *n* the branch of zoology that is concerned with the study of snakes. [C19: from Greek *ophis* snake + -LOGY] ▸ **ophiological** (,ɒfɪə'lɒdʒɪkᵊl) *adj* ▸ **,ophi'ologist** *n*

Ophir ('əʊfə) *n Bible.* a region, probably situated on the SW coast of Arabia on the Red Sea, renowned, esp. in King Solomon's reign, for its gold and precious stones (I Kings 9:28; 10:10).

ophite ('əʊfaɪt) *n* any of several greenish mottled rocks with ophitic texture, such as dolerite and diabase. [C17: from Latin *ophītēs,* from Greek, from *ophis* snake: because the mottled appearance resembles the markings of a snake]

ophitic (əʊ'fɪtɪk) *adj* (of the texture of rocks such as dolerite) having small elongated unorientated feldspar crystals embedded in the ferromagnesian matrix.

Ophiuchus (ɒ'fjuːkəs) *n, Latin genitive* **Ophiuchi** (ɒ'fjuːkaɪ). a large constellation lying on the celestial equator between Hercules and Scorpius and containing the dark nebula, **Ophiuchus Nebula.** [C17: via Latin from Greek *Ophioukhos,* from *ophis* snake + *ekhein* to hold]

ophthalmia (ɒf'θælmɪə) *n* inflammation of the eye, often including the conjunctiva. [C16: via Late Latin from Greek, from *ophthalmos* eye; see OPTIC]

ophthalmic (ɒf'θælmɪk) *adj* of or relating to the eye.

ophthalmic optician *n* See **optician.**

ophthalmitis (,ɒfθæl'maɪtɪs) *n* inflammation of the eye.

ophthalmo- *or before a vowel* **ophthalm-** *combining form.* indicating the eye or the eyeball: *ophthalmoscope.* [from Greek *ophthalmos* EYE[1]]

ophthalmol. *or* **ophthal.** *abbrev. for* ophthalmology.

ophthalmologist (,ɒfθæl'mɒlədʒɪst) *n* a medical practitioner specializing in the diagnosis and treatment of eye diseases.

ophthalmology (,ɒfθæl'mɒlədʒɪ) *n* the branch of medicine concerned with the eye and its diseases. ▸ **ophthalmological** (ɒf,θælmə'lɒdʒɪkᵊl) *adj*

ophthalmoscope (ɒf'θælmə,skəʊp) *n* an instrument for examining the interior of the eye. ▸ **ophthalmoscopic** (ɒf,θælmə'skɒpɪk) *adj*

ophthalmoscopy (,ɒfθæl'mɒskəpɪ) *n* examination of the interior of the eye with an ophthalmoscope.

Ophüls ('ɔːfəls; *German* 'ɔphyls) *n* **Max** (maks). 1902–57, German film director, whose films include *Liebelei* (1932), *La Signora di tutti* (1934), *La Ronde* (1950), *Le Plaisir* (1952), and *Lola Montes* (1955).

-opia *n combining form.* indicating a visual defect or condition: *myopia.* [from Greek, from *ōps* eye] ▸ **-opic** *adj combining form.*

opiate *n* ('əʊpɪɪt). **1** any of various narcotic drugs containing opium or an alkaloid of opium. **2** any other narcotic or sedative drug. **3** something that soothes, deadens, or induces sleep. ◆ *adj* ('əʊpɪɪt). **4** containing or consisting of opium. **5** inducing relaxation; soporific. ◆ *vb* ('əʊpɪ,eɪt). (*tr*) *Rare.* **6** to treat with an opiate. **7** to dull or deaden. [C16: from Medieval Latin *opiātus;* from Latin *opium* poppy juice, OPIUM]

opine (əʊ'paɪn) *vb* (when *tr, usually takes a clause as object*) to hold or express an opinion: *he opined that it was all a sad mistake.* [C16: from Latin *opīnārī*]

opinion (ə'pɪnjən) *n* **1** judgment or belief not founded on certainty or proof. **2** the prevailing or popular feeling or view: *public opinion.* **3** evaluation, impression, or estimation of the value or worth of a person or thing. **4** an evaluation or judgment given by an expert: *a medical opinion.* **5** the advice given by counsel on a case submitted to him for his view on the legal points involved. **6 a matter of opinion.** a point open to question. **7 be of the opinion (that).** to believe (that). [C13: via Old French from Latin *opīniō* belief, from *opīnārī* to think; see OPINE]

opinionated (ə'pɪnjə,neɪtɪd) *adj* holding obstinately and unreasonably to one's own opinions; dogmatic. ▸ **o'pinion,atedly** *adv* ▸ **o'pinion,atedness** *n*

opinionative (ə'pɪnjənətɪv) *adj Rare.* **1** of or relating to opinion. **2** another word for **opinionated.** ▸ **o'pinionatively** *adv* ▸ **o'pinionativeness** *n*

opinion poll *n* another term for a **poll** (sense 3).

opioid ('əʊpɪ,ɔɪd) *n* any of a group of substances that resemble morphine in their physiological or pharmacological effects, esp. in their pain-relieving properties.

opisthobranch (ə'pɪsθə,bræŋk) *n* any marine gastropod of the class *Opisthobranchia* (or *Opisthobranchiata*), in which the shell is reduced or absent: includes the pteropods, sea hares, and nudibranchs. [via New Latin from Greek *opisthen* behind + -BRANCH]

opisthognathous (,ɒpɪs'θɒgnəθəs) *adj* (of a person or animal) having receding jaws. [C19: from Greek *opisthen* behind + -GNATHOUS] ▸ **,opis'thognathism** *n*

opisthosoma (ɒ,pɪsθə'səʊmə) *n Zoology.* the abdomen of a spider or other arachnid. [C19: from Greek *opisthen* behind + SOMA[1]]

opium ('əʊpɪəm) *n* **1** an addictive narcotic drug extracted from the unripe seed capsules of the opium poppy and containing alkaloids such as morphine and codeine: used in medicine as an analgesic and hypnotic. **2** something having a tranquillizing or stupefying effect. [C14: from Latin: poppy juice, from Greek *opion,* diminutive of *opos* juice of a plant]

opium den *n* a place where opium is sold and used.

opiumism ('əʊpɪə,mɪzəm) *n Pathol.* addiction to opium or a condition resulting from prolonged use of opium.

opium poppy *n* a poppy, *Papaver somniferum,* of SW Asia, with greyish-green leaves and typically white or reddish flowers: widely cultivated as a source of opium.

Opium Wars *pl n* two wars (1839–42; 1856–60) between China and Britain resulting from the Chinese refusal to allow the importation of opium from India. China ceded Hong Kong after the British victory in 1842. The British and French victory in the second war established free trade in Chinese ports and the legalization of the opium trade.

Oporto (əˈpɔːtəʊ) *n* a port in NW Portugal, near the mouth of the Douro River: the second largest city in Portugal, famous for port wine (begun in 1678). Pop.: 309 485 (1991). Portuguese name: **Pôrto.**

opossum (əˈpɒsəm) *n, pl* **-sums** *or* **-sum. 1** any thick-furred marsupial, esp. *Didelphis marsupialis* (**common opossum**), of the family *Didelphidae* of S North, Central, and South America, having an elongated snout and a hairless prehensile tail. Sometimes (informal) shortened to **possum. 2** Also called (Austral. and N.Z.): **possum.** any of various similar animals, esp. the phalanger, *Trichosurus vulpecula,* of the New Zealand bush. [C17: from Algonquian *aposoum;* related to Delaware *apässum,* literally: white beast]

opossum block *n* (in New Zealand) a block of bush allocated to a licensed opossum trapper.

opossum shrimp *n* any of various shrimplike crustaceans of the genera *Mysis, Praunus,* etc., of the order *Mysidacea,* in which the females carry the eggs and young around in a ventral brood pouch.

opp. *abbrev. for:* **1** opposed. **2** opposite.

Oppenheimer (ˈɒpən,haɪmə) *n* **J(ulius) Robert.** 1904–67, U.S. nuclear physicist. He was director of the Los Alamos laboratory (1943–45), which produced the first atomic bomb. He opposed the development of the hydrogen bomb (1949) and in 1953 was alleged to be a security risk. He was later exonerated.

oppidan (ˈɒpɪdən) *Rare.* ◆ *adj* **1** of a town; urban. ◆ *n* **2** a person living in a town. [C16: from Latin *oppidānus,* from *oppidum* town]

oppilate (ˈɒpɪ,leɪt) *vb* (*tr*) *Pathol.* to block (the pores, bowels, etc.). [C16: from Latin *oppīlāre,* from *ob-* against + *pīlāre* to pack closely] ▸ **,oppiˈlation** *n*

opponent (əˈpəʊnənt) *n* **1** a person who opposes another in a contest, battle, etc. **2** *Anatomy.* an opponent muscle. ◆ *adj* **3** opposite, as in position. **4** *Anatomy.* (of a muscle) bringing two parts into opposition. **5** opposing; contrary. [C16: from Latin *oppōnere* to oppose, from *ob-* against + *pōnere* to place] ▸ **opˈponency** *n*

opportune (ˈɒpə,tjuːn) *adj* **1** occurring at a time that is suitable or advantageous. **2** fit or suitable for a particular purpose or occurrence. [C15: via Old French from Latin *opportūnus,* from *ob-* to + *portus* harbour (originally: coming to the harbour, obtaining timely protection)] ▸ **ˈoppor,tunely** *adv* ▸ **ˈoppor,tuneness** *n*

opportunist (,ɒpəˈtjuːnɪst) *n* **1** a person who adapts his actions, responses, etc., to take advantage of opportunities, circumstances, etc. ◆ *adj* **2** taking advantage of opportunities and circumstances in this way. ▸ **,opporˈtunism** *n*

opportunistic (,ɒpətjuˈnɪstɪk) *adj* **1** of or characterized by opportunism. **2** *Medicine.* (of an infection) caused by any microorganism that is harmless to a healthy person but debilitates a person whose immune system has been weakened by disease or drug treatment. ▸ **,opportuˈnistically** *adv*

opportunity (,ɒpəˈtjuːnɪtɪ) *n, pl* **-ties. 1** a favourable, appropriate, or advantageous combination of circumstances. **2** a chance or prospect.

opportunity cost *n Economics.* the benefit that could have been gained from an alternative use of the same resource.

opportunity shop *n Austral. and N.Z.* a shop selling second-hand goods for charitable funds. Also called: **op-shop.**

opposable (əˈpəʊzəbᵊl) *adj* **1** capable of being opposed. **2** Also: **apposable.** (of the thumb of primates, esp. man) capable of being moved into a position facing the other digits so as to be able to touch the ends of each. **3** capable of being placed opposite something else. ▸ **opˈposably** *adv* ▸ **op,posaˈbility** *n*

oppose (əˈpəʊz) *vb* **1** (*tr*) to fight against, counter, or resist strongly. **2** (*tr*) to be hostile or antagonistic to; be against. **3** (*tr*) to place or set in opposition; contrast or counterbalance. **4** (*tr*) to place opposite or facing. **5** (*intr*) to be or act in opposition. [C14: via Old French from Latin *oppōnere,* from *ob-* against + *pōnere* to place] ▸ **opˈposer** *n* ▸ **opˈposing** *adj* ▸ **opˈposingly** *adv* ▸ **oppositive** (əˈpɒzɪtɪv) *adj*

opposed-cylinder *adj* (of an internal-combustion engine) having cylinders on opposite sides of the crankcase in the same plane.

opposite (ˈɒpəzɪt, -sɪt) *adj* **1** situated or being on the other side or at each side of something between: *their houses were at opposite ends of the street.* **2** facing or going in contrary directions: *opposite ways.* **3** diametrically different in character, tendency, belief, etc.: *opposite views.* **4** *Botany.* **4a** (of leaves, flowers, etc.) arranged in pairs on either side of the stem. **4b** (of parts of a flower) arranged opposite the middle of another part. **5** *Maths.* **5a** (of two vertices or sides in an even-sided polygon) separated by the same number of vertices or sides in both a clockwise and anticlockwise direction. **5b** (of a side in a triangle) facing a specified angle. Abbrev.: **opp.** ◆ *n* **6** a person or thing that is opposite; antithesis. **7** *Maths.* the side facing a specified angle in a right-angled triangle. **8** a rare word for **opponent.** ◆ *prep* **9** Also: **opposite to.** facing; corresponding to (something on the other side of a division): *the house opposite ours.* **10** as a co-star with: *she played opposite Olivier in "Hamlet".* ◆ *adv* **11** on opposite sides: *she lives opposite.* ▸ **ˈoppositely** *adv* ▸ **ˈoppositeness** *n*

opposite number *n* a person holding an equivalent and corresponding position on another side or situation.

opposite prompt *n Theatre.* another name for **stage right.** See **prompt.**

opposite sex *n* **the.** women in relation to men or men in relation to women.

opposition (,ɒpəˈzɪʃən) *n* **1** the act of opposing or the state of being opposed. **2** hostility, unfriendliness, or antagonism. **3** a person or group antagonistic or opposite in aims to another. **4a** (usually preceded by *the*) a political party or group opposed to the ruling party or government. **4b** (*cap. as part of a name, esp. in Britain and other Commonwealth countries*): *Her Majesty's Loyal Opposition.* **4c in opposition.** (of a political party) opposing the government. **5** a position facing or opposite another. **6** the act of placing something facing or opposite something else. **7** something that acts as an obstacle to some course or progress. **8** *Astronomy.* **8a** the position of an outer planet or the moon when it is in line or nearly in line with the earth as seen from the sun and is approximately at its nearest to the earth. **8b** the position of two celestial bodies when they appear to be diametrically opposite each other on the celestial sphere. **9** *Astrology.* an exact aspect of 180° between two planets, etc., an orb of 8° being allowed. Compare **conjunction** (sense 5), **square** (sense 10), **trine** (sense 1). **10** *Logic.* **10a** the relation between propositions having the same subject and predicate but differing in quality, quantity, or both, as with *all men are wicked; no men are wicked; some men are not wicked.* **10b square of opposition.** a diagram representing these relations with the contradictory propositions at diagonally opposite corners. **11 the opposition.** *Chess.* a relative position of the kings in the endgame such that the player who has the move is at a disadvantage: *his opponent has the opposition.* ▸ **,oppoˈsitional** *adj* ▸ **,oppoˈsitionist** *n* ▸ **,oppoˈsitionless** *adj*

oppress (əˈprɛs) *vb* (*tr*) **1** to subjugate by cruelty, force, etc. **2** to afflict or torment. **3** to lie heavy on (the mind, imagination, etc.). **4** an obsolete word for **overwhelm.** [C14: via Old French from Medieval Latin *oppressāre,* from Latin *opprimere,* from *ob-* against + *premere* to press] ▸ **opˈpressingly** *adv* ▸ **opˈpression** *n* ▸ **opˈpressor** *n*

oppressive (əˈprɛsɪv) *adj* **1** cruel, harsh, or tyrannical. **2** heavy, constricting, or depressing. ▸ **opˈpressively** *adv* ▸ **opˈpressiveness** *n*

opprobrious (əˈprəʊbrɪəs) *adj* **1** expressing scorn, disgrace, or contempt. **2** shameful or infamous. ▸ **opˈprobriously** *adv* ▸ **opˈprobriousness** *n*

opprobrium (əˈprəʊbrɪəm) *n* **1** the state of being abused or scornfully criticized. **2** reproach or censure. **3** a cause of disgrace or ignominy. [C17: from Latin *ob-* against + *probrum* a shameful act]

oppugn (əˈpjuːn) *vb* (*tr*) to call into question; dispute. [C15: from Latin *oppugnāre,* from *ob-* against + *pugnāre* to fight, from *pugnus* clenched fist; see PUGNACIOUS] ▸ **opˈpugner** *n*

oppugnant (əˈpʌgnənt) *adj Rare.* combative, antagonistic, or contrary. ▸ **opˈpugnancy** *n* ▸ **opˈpugnantly** *adv*

Ops (ɒps) *n* the Roman goddess of abundance and fertility, wife of Saturn. Greek counterpart: **Rhea.**

ops. *abbrev. for* operations.

opsimath (ˈɒpsɪ,mæθ) *n* a person who learns late in life. [C19: from Greek *opsimathēs,* from *opse* late + *math-* learn] ▸ **opsimathy** (ɒpˈsɪməθɪ) *n*

opsin (ˈɒpsɪn) *n* the protein that together with retinene makes up the purple visual pigment rhodopsin. [C20: back formation from RHODOPSIN]

-opsis *n combining form.* indicating a specified appearance or resemblance: *coreopsis.* [from Greek *opsis* sight]

opsonic index *n* the ratio of the number of bacteria destroyed by phagocytes in the blood of a test patient to the number destroyed in the blood of a normal individual.

opsonin (ˈɒpsənɪn) *n* a constituent of blood serum that renders invading bacteria more susceptible to ingestion by phagocytes in the serum. [C20: from Greek *opsōnion* victuals] ▸ **opsonic** (ɒpˈsɒnɪk) *adj*

opsonize, opsonise (ˈɒpsə,naɪz), *or* **opsonify** (ɒpˈsɒnɪ,faɪ) *vb* (*tr*) to subject (bacteria) to the action of opsonins. ▸ **,opsoniˈzation, ,opsoniˈsation,** *or* **op,sonifiˈcation** *n*

opt (ɒpt) *vb* (when *intr,* foll. by *for*) to show preference (for) or choose (to do something). See also **opt out.** [C19: from French *opter,* from Latin *optāre* to choose]

opt. *abbrev. for:* **1** *Grammar.* optative. **2** optical. **3** optician. **4** optics. **5** optimum. **6** optional.

optative (ˈɒptətɪv) *adj* **1** indicating or expressing choice, preference, or wish. **2** *Grammar.* denoting a mood of verbs in Greek, Sanskrit, etc., expressing a wish. ◆ *n* **3** *Grammar.* **3a** the optative mood. **3b** a verb in this mood. [C16: via French *optatif,* from Late Latin *optātīvus,* from Latin *optāre* to desire]

optic (ˈɒptɪk) *adj* **1** of or relating to the eye or vision. **2** a less common word for **optical.** ◆ *n* **3** an informal word for **eye**[1]. **4** *Brit., trademark.* a device attached to an inverted bottle for dispensing measured quantities of liquid, such as whisky, gin, etc. [C16: from Medieval Latin *opticus,* from Greek *optikos,* from *optos* visible, seen; related to *ōps* eye]

optical (ˈɒptɪkᵊl) *adj* **1** of, relating to, producing, or involving light. **2** of or relating to the eye or to the sense of sight; optic. **3** (esp. of a lens) aiding vision or correcting a visual disorder. ▸ **ˈoptically** *adv*

optical activity *n* the ability of substances that are optical isomers to rotate the plane of polarization of a transmitted beam of plane-polarized light.

optical bench *n* an apparatus for experimentation in optics, typically consisting of an adjustable arrangement of light source, lenses, prisms, etc.

optical character reader *n* a computer peripheral device enabling letters, numbers, or other characters usually printed on paper to be optically scanned and input to a storage device, such as magnetic tape. The device uses the process of **optical character recognition.** Abbrev. (for both *reader* and *recognition*): **OCR.**

optical crown *n* an optical glass of low dispersion and relatively low refractive index. It is used in the construction of lenses.

optical density *n Physics.* the former name for **reflection density** or **transmission density.**

optical disc *n Computers.* an inflexible disc on which information is stored in digital form by laser technology. Also called: **video disc.**

optical double star *n* two stars that appear close together when viewed through a telescope but are not physically associated and are often separated by a great distance. Compare **binary star.**

optical fibre *n* a communications cable consisting of a thin glass fibre in a protective sheath. Light transmitted along the fibre may be modulated with vision, sound, or data signals. See also **fibre optics.**

optical flint *n* an optical glass of high dispersion and high refractive index containing lead oxide. They are used in the manufacture of lenses, artificial gems, and cut glass. Also called: **flint glass.**

optical glass *n* any of several types of clear homogeneous glass of known refractive index used in the construction of lenses, etc. See **optical flint, optical crown.**

optical illusion *n* **1** an object causing a false visual impression. **2** an instance of deception by such an object.

optical isomerism *n* isomerism of chemical compounds in which the two isomers differ only in that their molecules are mirror images of each other. See also **dextrorotation, laevorotatory, racemize.** ► **optical isomer** *n*

optical mark reading *n* the reading of marks by an optical device whereby the information can be stored in machine-readable form.

optical pyrometer *n* See **pyrometer.**

optical rotation *n* the angle through which plane-polarized light is rotated in its passage through a substance exhibiting optical activity.

optical scanner *n* a computer peripheral device enabling printed material, including characters and diagrams, to be scanned and converted into a form that can be stored in a computer. See also **optical character reader.**

optical sound *n* sound recorded in the form of a photographic image on cinematograph films.

optic axis *n* the direction in a uniaxial crystal or one of the two directions in a biaxial crystal along which a ray of unpolarized light may pass without undergoing double refraction.

optic disc *n* a small oval-shaped area on the retina marking the site of entrance into the eyeball of the optic nerve. See **blind spot** (sense 1).

optician (ɒp'tɪʃən) *n* a general name used to refer to: **a ophthalmic optician.** Also called: **optometrist.** a person qualified to examine the eyes and prescribe and supply spectacles and contact lenses. **b dispensing optician.** a person who supplies and fits spectacle frames but is not qualified to prescribe lenses. ◆ See also **optometrist.** Compare **ophthalmologist.**

optic nerve *n* the second cranial nerve, which provides a sensory pathway from the retina to the brain.

optics ('ɒptɪks) *n* (*functioning as sing*) the branch of science concerned with vision and the generation, nature, propagation, and behaviour of electromagnetic light.

optic thalamus *n Anatomy.* an older term for **thalamus** (senses 1, 2).

optimal ('ɒptɪməl) *adj* another word for **optimum** (sense 2). ► ,**opti'mality** *n* ► '**optimally** *adv*

optimism ('ɒptɪ,mɪzəm) *n* **1** the tendency to expect the best and see the best in all things. **2** hopefulness; confidence. **3** the doctrine of the ultimate triumph of good over evil. **4** the philosophical doctrine that this is the best of all possible worlds. ◆ Compare **pessimism.** [C18: from French *optimisme,* from Latin *optimus* best, superlative of *bonus* good] ► '**optimist** *n* ► ,**opti'mistic** *or* ,**opti'mistical** *adj* ► ,**opti'mistically** *adv*

optimize *or* **optimise** ('ɒptɪ,maɪz) *vb* **1** (*tr*) to take the full advantage of. **2** (*tr*) to plan or carry out (an economic activity) with maximum efficiency. **3** (*intr*) to be optimistic. **4** (*tr*) to write or modify (a computer program) to achieve maximum efficiency in storage capacity, time, cost, etc. **5** (*tr*) to find the best compromise among several often conflicting requirements, as in engineering design. ► ,**optimi'zation** *or* ,**optimi'sation** *n*

optimum ('ɒptɪməm) *n, pl* **-ma** (-mə) *or* **-mums. 1** a condition, degree, amount or compromise that produces the best possible result. ◆ *adj* **2** most favourable or advantageous; best: *optimum conditions.* [C19: from Latin: the best (thing), from *optimus* best; see OPTIMISM]

optimum population *n Economics.* a population that is sufficiently large to provide an adequate workforce with minimal unemployment.

option ('ɒpʃən) *n* **1** the act or an instance of choosing or deciding. **2** the power or liberty to choose. **3** an exclusive opportunity, usually for a limited period, to buy something at a future date: *he has a six month option on the Canadian rights to this book.* **4** *Commerce.* the right to buy (**call option**) or sell (**put option**) a fixed quantity of a commodity, security, foreign exchange, etc., at a fixed price at a specified date in the future. See also **traded option. 5** something chosen; choice. **6** *N.Z.* short for **local option. 7 keep** (*or* **leave**) **one's options open.** not to commit oneself. **8** See **soft option.** ◆ *vb* **9** (*tr*) to obtain or grant an option on: *the BBC have optioned her latest novel.* [C17: from Latin *optiō* free choice, from *optāre* to choose]

optional ('ɒpʃənᵊl) *adj* possible but not compulsory; left to personal choice. ► '**optionally** *adv*

option money *n Commerce.* the price paid for buying an option.

optoelectronics (,ɒptəʊɪlɛk'trɒnɪks) *n* (*functioning as sing*) the study or use of devices in which an optical input produces an electrical output, or in which electrical stimulation produces visible or infrared output. ► ,**optoelec'tronic** *adj*

optometer (ɒp'tɒmɪtə) *n* any of various instruments for measuring the refractive power of the eye.

optometrist (ɒp'tɒmɪtrɪst) *n* a person who is qualified to examine the eyes and prescribe and supply spectacles and contact lenses. Also called (esp. Brit.): **ophthalmic optician.** Compare **optician, ophthalmologist.**

optometry (ɒp'tɒmɪtrɪ) *n* the science or practice of testing visual acuity and prescribing corrective lenses. ► **optometric** (,ɒptə'mɛtrɪk) *adj*

optophone ('ɒptə,fəʊn) *n* a device for blind people that converts printed words into sounds.

opt out *vb* **1** (*intr, adv;* often foll. by *of*) to choose not to be involved (in) or part (of). ◆ *n* **opt-out. 2** the act of opting out, esp. of local-authority administration: *opt-outs by hospitals and schools.*

opulent ('ɒpjʊlənt) *adj* **1** having or indicating wealth. **2** abundant or plentiful. [C17: from Latin *opulens,* from *opēs* (pl) wealth] ► '**opulence** *or* (*less commonly*) '**opulency** *n* ► '**opulently** *adv*

opuntia (ɒ'pʌnʃɪə) *n* any cactus of the genus *Opuntia,* esp. prickly pear, having fleshy branched stems and green, red, or yellow flowers. [C17: New Latin, from Latin *Opuntia* (*herba*) the Opuntian (plant), from *Opus,* ancient town of Locris, Greece]

opus ('əʊpəs, 'ɒp-) *n, pl* **opuses** *or* **opera** ('ɒpərə). **1** an artistic composition, esp. a musical work. **2** (*often cap.*) (usually followed by a number) a musical composition by a particular composer, generally catalogued in order of publication: *Beethoven's opus 61 is his violin concerto.* Abbrev.: **op.** [C18: from Latin: a work; compare Sanskrit *apas* work]

opus anglicanum *Latin.* ('əʊpəs æŋglɪ'kɑːnəm) *n* fine embroidery, esp. of church vestments, produced in England *c.* 1200–*c.*1350; characterized by the rich materials used, esp. silver gilt thread. [literally: English work]

opuscule (ɒ'pʌskjuːl) *n Rare.* a small or insignificant artistic work. [C17: via French from Latin *opusculum,* from *opus* work] ► **o'puscular** *adj*

Opus Dei ('əʊpəs 'deɪɪ) *n* **1** another name for **divine office. 2** an international Roman Catholic organization of lay people and priests founded in Spain in 1928 by Josemaria Escrivá de Balaguer (1902–75), with the aim of spreading Christian principles.

or[1] (ɔː; *unstressed* ə) *conj* (*coordinating*) **1** used to join alternatives: *apples or pears; apples or pears or cheese; apples, pears, or cheese.* **2** used to join rephrasings of the same thing: *to serve in the army, or rather to fight in the army; twelve, or a dozen.* **3** used to join two alternatives when the first is preceded by *either* or *whether: whether it rains or not we'll be there; either yes or no.* **4 one or two, four or five,** etc. a few. **5 or else.** See **else** (sense 3). **6** a poetic word for **either** or **whether,** as the first element in correlatives, with *or* also preceding the second alternative. ◆ See also **exclusive or** and **inclusive or.** [C13: contraction of *other,* used to introduce an alternative, changed (through influence of EITHER) from Old English *oththe;* compare Old High German *odar* (German *oder*)]

or[2] (ɔː) *Archaic.* ◆ *conj* **1** (*subordinating;* foll. by *ever* or *ere*) before; when. ◆ *prep* **2** before. [Old English *ār* soon; related to Old Norse *ār* early, Old High German *ēr*]

or[3] (ɔː) *adj* (*usually postpositive*) *Heraldry.* of the metal gold. [C16: via French from Latin *aurum* gold]

OR *abbrev. for:* **1** operational research. **2** Oregon. **3** *Military.* other ranks.

o.r. *Commerce. abbrev. for* owner's risk.

-or[1] *suffix forming nouns from verbs.* a person or thing that does what is expressed by the verb: *actor; conductor; generator; sailor.* [via Old French *-eur, -eor,* from Latin *-or* or *-ātor*]

-or[2] *suffix forming nouns.* **1** indicating state, condition, or activity: *terror; error.* **2** the U.S. spelling of **-our.**

ora ('ɔːrə) *n* the plural of **os**[2].

orache *or esp. U.S.* **orach** ('ɒrɪtʃ) *n* any of several herbaceous plants or small shrubs of the chenopodiaceous genus *Atriplex,* esp. *A. hortensis* (**garden orache**), which is cultivated as a vegetable. They have typically greyish-green lobed leaves and inconspicuous flowers. [C15: from Old French *arache,* from Latin *atriplex,* from Greek *atraphaxus,* of obscure origin]

oracle ('ɒrəkᵊl) *n* **1** a prophecy, often obscure or allegorical, revealed through the medium of a priest or priestess at the shrine of a god. **2** a shrine at which an oracular god is consulted. **3** an agency through which a prophecy is transmitted. **4** any person or thing believed to indicate future action with infallible authority. **5** a statement believed to be infallible and authoritative. **6** *Bible.* **6a** a message from God. **6b** the holy of holies in the Israelite temple. ◆ See also **oracles.** [C14: via Old French from Latin *ōrāculum,* from *ōrāre* to request]

oracles ('ɒrəkᵊlz) *pl n* another term for **Scripture** (sense 1).

oracular (ɒ'rækjʊlə) *adj* **1** of or relating to an oracle. **2** wise and prophetic. **3** mysterious or ambiguous. ► **o'racularly** *adv*

oracy ('ɔːrəsɪ) *n* the capacity to express oneself in and understand speech. [C20: from Latin *or-, os* mouth, by analogy with *literacy*]

Oradea (*Romanian* o'radea) *n* an industrial city in NW Romania, in Transylvania: ceded by Hungary (1919). Pop.: 221 885 (1994 est.). German name: **Grosswardein.** Hungarian name: **Nagyvárad.**

ora et labora *Latin.* ('ɔːrɑː ɛt 'læbɔː,rɑː) pray and work.

oral ('ɔːrəl, 'ɒrəl) *adj* **1** spoken or verbal: *an oral agreement.* **2** relating to, affecting, or for use in the mouth: *an oral thermometer.* **3** of or relating to the surface of an animal, such as a jellyfish, on which the mouth is situated. **4** denoting a drug to be taken by mouth: *an oral contraceptive.* Compare **parenteral. 5** of, relating to, or using spoken words. **6** *Phonetics.* pronounced with the soft palate in a raised position completely closing the nasal cavity and allowing air to pass out only through the mouth. **7** *Psychoanal.* **7a** relating to a stage of psychosexual development during which the child's interest is concentrated on the mouth. **7b** denoting personality traits, such as dependence, selfishness, and aggression, resulting from fixation at the oral stage. Compare **anal** (sense 2), **genital** (sense 2), **phallic** (sense 2). ◆ *n* **8** an examination in which the questions and answers are spoken rather than written. [C17: from Late Latin *ōrālis,* from Latin *ōs* face] ► '**orally** *adv*

oral eroticism *n Psychoanal.* libidinal pleasure derived from the lips and mouth, for example by kissing.

oral history *n* the memories of living people about events or social conditions which they experienced in their earlier lives taped and preserved as historical evidence.

oral hygiene *n* another name for **dental hygiene.**

oral hygienist *n* another name for **dental hygienist.**

Oral Law *n Judaism.* the traditional body of religious law believed to have been revealed to Moses as an interpretation of the Torah and passed on orally until it was codified and recorded, principally in the Mishna and Gemara.

oral society *n* a society that has not developed literacy.

Oran (ə'ræn, ə'rɑːn; *French* ɔrɑ̃) *n* a port in NW Algeria: the second largest city in the country; scene of the destruction by the British of most of the French fleet in the harbour in 1940 to prevent its capture by the Germans. Pop.: 609 823 (1987).

orang (ɔː'ræŋ, 'ɔːræŋ) *n* short for **orang-utan.**

orange ('ɒrɪndʒ) *n* **1** any of several citrus trees, esp. *Citrus sinensis* (**sweet orange**) and the Seville orange, cultivated in warm regions for their round edible fruit. See also **tangerine** (sense 1). **2a** the fruit of any of these trees, having a yellowish-red bitter rind and segmented juicy flesh. See also **navel orange. 2b** (*as modifier*): *orange peel.* **3** the hard wood of any of these trees. **4** any of a group of colours, such as that of the skin of an orange, that lie between red and yellow in the visible spectrum in the approximate wavelength range 620–585 nanometres. **5** a dye or pigment producing these colours. **6** orange cloth or clothing: *dressed in orange.* **7** any of several trees or herbaceous plants that resemble the orange, such as mock orange. ◆ *adj* **8** of the colour orange. [C14: via Old French from Old Provençal *auranja,* from Arabic *nāranj,* from Persian *nārang,* from Sanskrit *nāranga,* probably of Dravidian origin]

Orange[1] *n* **1** ('ɒrɪndʒ) a river in S Africa, rising in NE Lesotho and flowing generally west across the South African plateau to the Atlantic: the longest river in South Africa. Length: 2093 km (1300 miles). **2** (*French* ɔrɑ̃ʒ). a town in SE France: a small principality in the Middle Ages, the descendants of which formed the House of Orange. Pop.: 28 136 (1990). Ancient name: **Arausio** (ə'raʊsɪəʊ).

Orange[2] ('ɒrɪndʒ) *n* **1** a princely family of Europe. Its possessions, originally centred in S France, passed in 1544 to the count of Nassau, who became William I of Orange and helped to found the United Provinces of the Netherlands. Since 1815 it has been the name of the reigning house of the Netherlands. It was the ruling house of Great Britain and Ireland under William III and Mary (1689–94) and under William III as sole monarch (1694–1702). **2** (*modifier*) of or relating to the Orangemen. **3** (*modifier*) of or relating to the royal dynasty of Orange.

orangeade (ˌɒrɪndʒ'eɪd) *n* an effervescent or still orange-flavoured drink.

orange blossom *n* the flowers of the orange tree, traditionally worn by brides.

orange chromide ('krəʊmaɪd) *n* an Asian cichlid fish, *Etropus maculatus,* with a brownish-orange spotted body.

orange flower water *n* a distilled infusion of orange blossom, used in cakes, confectionery, etc.

Orange Free State *n* a former province of central South Africa, between the Orange and Vaal rivers: settled by Boers in 1836 after the Great Trek; annexed by Britain in 1848; became a province of South Africa in 1910; replaced in 1994 by the new province of Free State; economy based on agriculture and mineral resources (esp. gold and uranium). Capital: Bloemfontein.

Orangeism ('ɒrɪndʒˌɪzəm) *n* the practices or principles of Orangemen, esp. Protestant supremacy in the Republic of Ireland, Northern Ireland, or Canada.

Orangeman ('ɒrɪndʒmən) *n, pl* **-men.** a member of a society founded in Ireland (1795) to uphold the Protestant religion, the Protestant dynasty, and the Protestant constitution. **Orange Lodges** have since spread to many parts of the former British Empire. [C18: after William, prince of *Orange* (king of England as William III)]

Orangeman's Day *n* the 12th of July, celebrated by Protestants in Northern Ireland to commemorate the anniversary of the Battle of the Boyne (1690).

orange peel *n* **1** the thick pitted rind of an orange. **2** anything resembling this in surface texture, such as skin or porcelain.

orange-peel fungus *n* See **elf-cup.**

orange pekoe *n* a superior grade of black tea made from the small leaves at the tips of the plant stems and growing in India and Sri Lanka.

orange roughy ('rʌfɪ) *n* a marine food fish, *Hoplosthenus atlanticus,* of S Pacific waters.

orangery ('ɒrɪndʒərɪ, -dʒrɪ) *n, pl* **-eries.** a building, such as a greenhouse, in which orange trees are grown.

orange stick *n* a small stick used to clean the fingernails and cuticles, having one pointed and one rounded end.

orange-tip *n* a European butterfly, *Anthocharis cardamines,* having whitish wings with orange-tipped forewings: family *Pieridae.*

orangewood ('ɒrɪndʒˌwʊd) *n* **a** the hard fine-grained yellowish wood of the orange tree. **b** (*as modifier*): *an orangewood table.*

orang-utan (ɔːˌræŋuː'tæn, ˌɔːræŋ'uːtæn) *or* **orang-utang** (ɔːˌræŋuː'tæŋ, ˌɔːræŋ'uːtæŋ) *n* a large anthropoid ape, *Pongo pygmaeus,* of the forests of Sumatra and Borneo, with shaggy reddish-brown hair and strong arms. Sometimes shortened to **orang.** [C17: from Malay *orang hutan,* from *ōrang* man + *hūtan* forest]

ora pro nobis *Latin.* ('ɔːrɑː prəʊ 'nəʊbɪs) *R.C. Church.* a Latin invocation meaning *pray for us.*

orate (ɔː'reɪt) *vb* (*intr*) **1** to make or give an oration. **2** to speak pompously and lengthily.

oration (ɔː'reɪʃən) *n* **1** a formal public declaration or speech. **2** any rhetorical, lengthy, or pompous speech. **3** an academic exercise or contest in public speaking. [C14: from Latin *ōrātiō* speech, harangue, from *ōrāre* to plead, pray]

orator ('ɒrətə) *n* **1** a public speaker, esp. one versed in rhetoric. **2** a person given to lengthy or pompous speeches. **3** *Obsolete.* the plaintiff in a cause of action in chancery.

Oratorian (ˌɒrə'tɔːrɪən) *n* a member of the religious congregation of the Oratory.

oratorio (ˌɒrə'tɔːrɪəʊ) *n, pl* **-rios.** a dramatic but unstaged musical composition for soloists, chorus, and orchestra, based on a religious theme. [C18: from Italian, literally: ORATORY[2], referring to the Church of the Oratory at Rome where musical services were held]

oratory[1] ('ɒrətərɪ, -trɪ) *n* **1** the art of public speaking. **2** rhetorical skill or style. [C16: from Latin (*ars*) *ōrātōria* (the art of) public speaking] ▸ **ˌora'torical** *adj* ▸ **ˌora'torically** *adv*

oratory[2] ('ɒrətərɪ, -trɪ) *n, pl* **-ries.** a small room or secluded place, set apart for private prayer. [C14: from Anglo-Norman, from Church Latin *ōrātōrium* place of prayer, from *ōrāre* to plead, pray]

Oratory ('ɒrətərɪ, -trɪ) *n R.C. Church.* **1** Also called: **Congregation of the Oratory.** the religious society of secular priests (**Oratorians**) living in a community founded by St Philip Neri. **2** any church belonging to this society: *the Brompton Oratory.*

orb (ɔːb) *n* **1** (in royal regalia) an ornamental sphere surmounted by a cross, representing the power of a sovereign. **2** a sphere; globe. **3** *Poetic.* another word for **eye**[1]. **4** *Obsolete or poetic.* **4a** a celestial body, esp. the earth or sun. **4b** the orbit of a celestial body. **5** an archaic word for **circle.** ◆ *vb* **6** to make or become circular or spherical. **7** (*tr*) an archaic word for **encircle.** [C16: from Latin *orbis* circle, disc]

orbicular (ɔː'bɪkjʊlə), **orbiculate,** *or* **orbiculated** *adj* **1** circular or spherical. **2** (of a leaf or similar flat part) circular or nearly circular. **3** *Rare.* rounded or total. ▸ **orbicularity** (ɔːˌbɪkjʊ'lærɪtɪ) *n* ▸ **or'bicularly** *adv*

Orbison ('ɔːbɪsən) *n* **Roy (Kelton).** 1936–89, U.S. pop singer and songwriter. His records include the singles "Only the Lonely" (1960) and "Oh Pretty Woman" (1964) and the album *Mystery Girl* (1989).

orbit ('ɔːbɪt) *n* **1** *Astronomy.* the curved path, usually elliptical, followed by a planet, satellite, comet, etc., in its motion around another celestial body under the influence of gravitation. **2** a range or field of action or influence; sphere: *he is out of my orbit.* **3** *Anatomy.* the bony cavity containing the eyeball. Nontechnical name: **eye socket. 4** *Zoology.* **4a** the skin surrounding the eye of a bird. **4b** the hollow in which lies the eye or eyestalk of an insect or other arthropod. **5** *Physics.* the path of an electron in its motion around the nucleus of an atom. ◆ *vb* **6** to move around (a body) in a curved path, usually circular or elliptical. **7** (*tr*) to send (a satellite, spacecraft, etc.) into orbit. **8** (*intr*) to move in or as if in an orbit. [C16: from Latin *orbita* course, from *orbis* circle, ORB] ▸ **'orbitally** *adv*

orbital ('ɔːbɪtᵊl) *adj* **1** of or denoting an orbit. ◆ *n* **2** a region surrounding an atomic nucleus in which the distribution of electrons is given by a wave function.

orbital velocity *n* the velocity required by a spacecraft, satellite, etc., to enter and maintain a given orbit.

orbiter ('ɔːbɪtə) *n* a spacecraft or satellite designed to orbit a planet or other body without landing on it.

orc (ɔːk) *n* **1** any of various whales, such as the killer and grampus. **2** a mythical monster. [C16: via Latin *orca,* perhaps from Greek *orux* whale]

Orcadian (ɔː'keɪdɪən) *n* **1** a native or inhabitant of the Orkneys. ◆ *adj* **2** of or relating to the Orkneys. [from Latin *Orcades* the Orkney Islands]

Orcagna (*Italian* or'kaɲa) *n* **Andrea** (an'drɛːa), original name *Andrea di Cione.* ?1308–68, Florentine painter, sculptor, and architect.

orcein ('ɔːsɪɪn) *n* a brown crystalline material formed by the action of ammonia on orcinol and present in orchil: used as a dye, biological stain, and antiseptic. Formula: $C_{28}H_{24}O_7N_2$. [C19: see ORCINOL]

orch. *abbrev. for:* **1** orchestra(l). **2** orchestrated by.

orchard ('ɔːtʃəd) *n* **1** an area of land devoted to the cultivation of fruit trees. **2** a collection of fruit trees especially cultivated. [Old English *orceard, ortigeard,* from *ort-,* from Latin *hortus* garden + *geard* YARD[2]]

orchard bush *n W African.* open savanna country with occasional trees and scrub, as found north of the W African forest belt.

orchardman ('ɔːtʃədmən) *n, pl* **-men.** a person who grows and sells orchard fruits.

orchestra ('ɔːkɪstrə) *n* **1** a large group of musicians, esp. one whose members play a variety of different instruments. See also **symphony orchestra, string orchestra, chamber orchestra. 2** a group of musicians, each playing the same type of instrument: *a balalaika orchestra.* **3** Also called: **orchestra pit.** the space reserved for musicians in a theatre, immediately in front of or under the stage. **4** *Chiefly U.S. and Canadian.* the stalls in a theatre. **5** (in the ancient Greek theatre) the semicircular space in front of the stage. [C17: via Latin from Greek: the space in the theatre reserved for the chorus, from *orkheisthai* to dance] ▸ **orchestral** (ɔː'kɛstrəl) *adj* ▸ **or'chestrally** *adv*

orchestrate ('ɔːkɪˌstreɪt) *vb* (*tr*) **1** to score or arrange (a piece of music) for orchestra. **2** to arrange, organize, or build up for special or maximum effect. ▸ **ˌorches'tration** *n* ▸ **'orchesˌtrator** *n*

orchestrina (ˌɔːkɪs'triːnə) or **orchestrion** (ɔː'kɛstrɪən) *n* any of various types of mechanical musical instrument designed to imitate the sound of an orchestra.

orchid ('ɔːkɪd) *n* any terrestrial or epiphytic plant of the family *Orchidaceae,* having flowers of unusual shapes and beautiful colours, specialized for pollination by certain insects. See **bee orchid, burnt-tip orchid, fly orchid, frog orchid, lady orchid, lizard orchid, man orchid, monkey orchid, purple-fringed orchid, pyramidal orchid, scented orchid, spider orchid, spotted orchid.** [C19: from New Latin *Orchideae;* see ORCHIS]

orchidaceous (ˌɔːkɪ'deɪʃəs) *adj* of, relating to, or belonging to the *Orchidaceae,* a family of flowering plants including the orchids.

orchidectomy (ˌɔːkɪ'dɛktəmɪ) *n, pl* **-mies.** the surgical removal of one or both testes. [C19: from Greek *orkhis* testicle + -ECTOMY]

orchil ('ɔːkɪl, -tʃɪl) *or* **archil** *n* **1** any of various lichens, esp. any of the genera *Roccella, Dendrographa,* and *Lecanora.* **2** Also called: **cudbear.** a purplish dye obtained by treating these lichens with aqueous ammonia: contains orcinol, orcein, and litmus. **[**C15: from Old French *orcheil,* of uncertain origin**]**

orchis ('ɔːkɪs) *n* **1** any terrestrial orchid of the N temperate genus *Orchis,* having fleshy tubers and spikes of typically pink flowers. **2** any of various temperate or tropical orchids of the genus *Habenaria,* such as the fringed orchis. **[**C16: via Latin from Greek *orkhis* testicle; so called from the shape of its roots**]**

orchitis (ɔː'kaɪtɪs) *n* inflammation of one or both testicles. **[**C18: from New Latin, from Greek *orkhis* testicle + -ITIS**]** ▸ **orchitic** (ɔː'kɪtɪk) *adj*

orcinol ('ɔːsɪˌnɒl) *or* **orcin** ('ɔːsɪn) *n* a colourless crystalline water-soluble solid that occurs in many lichens and from which the dyes found in litmus are derived. Formula: $CH_3C_6H_3(OH)_2$. **[**C20: from New Latin *orcina,* from Italian *orcello* ORCHIL**]**

OR circuit *or* **gate** (ɔː) *n Computing.* a logic circuit having two or more input wires and one output wire that gives a high-voltage output signal if one or more input signals are at a high voltage: used extensively as a basic circuit in computers. Compare **AND circuit, NAND circuit. [**C20: so named from its similarity to the function of *or* in logical constructions**]**

Orcus ('ɔːkəs) *n* another name for **Dis** (sense 1).

Orczy ('ɔːtsɪ) *n* Baroness **Emmuska** ('ɛmʊʃkə). 1865–1947, British novelist, born in Hungary; author of *The Scarlet Pimpernel* (1905).

Ord (ɔːd) *n* a river in NE Western Australia, rising on the Kimberley Plateau and flowing generally north to the Timor Sea: subject of a major irrigation scheme. Length: about 500 km (300 miles).

ord. *abbrev. for:* **1** order. **2** ordinal. **3** ordinance. **4** ordnance. **5** ordinary.

ordain (ɔː'deɪn) *vb (tr)* **1** to consecrate (someone) as a priest; confer holy orders upon. **2** (*may take a clause as object*) to decree, appoint, or predestine irrevocably. **3** (*may take a clause as object*) to order, establish, or enact with authority. **4** *Obsolete.* to select for an office. **[**C13: from Anglo-Norman *ordeiner,* from Late Latin *ordināre,* from Latin *ordo* ORDER**]** ▸ **or'dainer** *n* ▸ **or'dainment** *n*

ordeal (ɔː'diːl) *n* **1** a severe or trying experience. **2** *History.* a method of trial in which the guilt or innocence of an accused person was determined by subjecting him to physical danger, esp. by fire or water. The outcome was regarded as an indication of divine judgment. **[**Old English *ordāl, ordēl;* related to Old Frisian *ordēl,* Old High German *urteili* (German *Urteil*) verdict. See DEAL[1], DOLE[1]**]**

order ('ɔːdə) *n* **1** a state in which all components or elements are arranged logically, comprehensibly, or naturally. **2** an arrangement or disposition of things in succession; sequence: *alphabetical order.* **3** an established or customary method or state, esp. of society. **4** a peaceful or harmonious condition of society: *order reigned in the streets.* **5** (*often pl*) a class, rank, or hierarchy: *the lower orders.* **6** *Biology.* any of the taxonomic groups into which a class is divided and which contains one or more families. *Carnivora, Primates,* and *Rodentia* are three orders of the class *Mammalia.* **7** an instruction that must be obeyed; command. **8** a decision or direction of a court or judge entered on the court record but not included in the final judgment. **9a** a commission or instruction to produce or supply something in return for payment. **9b** the commodity produced or supplied. **9c** (*as modifier*): *order form.* **10** a procedure followed by an assembly, meeting, etc. **11** (*cap. when part of a name*) a body of people united in a particular aim or purpose. **12** Also called: **religious order.** (*usually cap.*) a group of persons who bind themselves by vows in order to devote themselves to the pursuit of religious aims. **13** *History.* a society of knights constituted as a fraternity, such as the Knights Templars. **14a** a group of people holding a specific honour for service or merit, conferred on them by a sovereign or state. **14b** the insignia of such a group. **15a** any of the five major classical styles of architecture classified by the style of columns and entablatures used. See also **Doric, Ionic, Corinthian, Tuscan, Composite. 15b** any style of architecture. **16** *Christianity.* **16a** the sacrament by which bishops, priests, etc., have their offices conferred upon them. **16b** any of the degrees into which the ministry is divided. **16c** the office of an ordained Christian minister. **17** a form of Christian Church service prescribed to be used on specific occasions. **18** *Judaism.* one of the six sections of the Mishna or the corresponding tractates of the Talmud. **19** *Maths.* **19a** the number of times a function must be differentiated to obtain a given derivative. **19b** the order of the highest derivative in a differential equation. **19c** the number of rows or columns in a determinant or square matrix. **19d** the number of members of a finite group. **20** short for **order of magnitude. 21** *Military.* (often preceded by *the*) the dress, equipment, or formation directed for a particular purpose or undertaking: *drill order; battle order.* **22 a tall order.** something difficult, demanding, or exacting. **23 in order. 23a** in sequence. **23b** properly arranged. **23c** appropriate or fitting. **24 in order to.** (*prep;* foll. by an infinitive) so that it is possible to: *to eat in order to live.* **25 in order that.** (*conj*) with the purpose that; so that. **26 keep order.** to maintain or enforce order. **27 of** *or* **in the order of.** having an approximately specified size or quantity. **28 on order.** having been ordered or commissioned but not having been delivered. **29 out of order. 29a** not in sequence. **29b** not working. **29c** not following the rules or customary procedure. **30 to order. 30a** according to a buyer's specifications. **30b** on request or demand. ◆ *vb* **31** (*tr*) to give a command to (a person or animal to do or be something). **32** to request (something) to be supplied or made, esp. in return for payment: *he ordered a hamburger.* **33** (*tr*) to instruct or command to move, go, etc. (to a specified place): *they ordered her into the house.* **34** (*tr; may take a clause as object*) to authorize; prescribe: *the doctor ordered a strict diet.* **35** (*tr*) to arrange, regulate, or dispose (articles) in their proper places. **36** (of fate or the gods) to will; ordain. **37** (*tr*) *Rare.* to ordain. ◆ *interj* **38** an exclamation of protest against an infringement of established procedure. **39** an exclamation demanding that orderly behaviour be restored. ◆ See also **orders.** **[**C13: from Old French *ordre,* from Latin *ordō***]** ▸ **'orderer** *n* ▸ **'orderless** *adj*

order about *or* **around** *vb (tr)* to bully or domineer.

order arms *interj, n Military.* the order in drill to hold the rifle close to the right side with the butt resting on the ground.

order-driven *adj* denoting an electronic market system, esp. for stock exchanges, in which prices are determined by the publication of orders to buy or sell. Compare **quote-driven.**

ordered set *n Logic, maths.* a sequence of elements that is distinguished from the other sequences of the same element by the order of the elements. Thus <a, b> is not identical with <b, a>.

order in council *n* (in Britain and various other Commonwealth countries) a decree of the Cabinet, usually made under the authority of a statute: in theory a decree of the sovereign and Privy Council.

ordering ('ɔːdərɪŋ) *n Logic.* any of a number of categories of relations that permit at least some members of their domain to be placed in order. A **linear** or **simple ordering** is reflexive, antisymmetric, transitive, and connected, as *less than or equal to* on the integers. A **partial ordering** is reflexive, antisymmetric, and transitive, as set inclusion. Either of these orderings is called *strict* if it is asymmetric instead of reflexive and antisymmetric. It is a *well-ordering* if every nonempty subset has a least member under the relation.

orderly ('ɔːdəlɪ) *adj* **1** in order, properly arranged, or tidy. **2** obeying or appreciating method, system, and arrangement. **3** harmonious or peaceful. **4** *Military.* of or relating to orders: *an orderly book.* ◆ *adv* **5** *Now rare.* according to custom or rule. ◆ *n, pl* **-lies. 6** *Med.* a male hospital attendant. **7** *Military.* a junior rank detailed to carry orders or perform minor tasks for a more senior officer. ▸ **'orderliness** *n*

orderly officer *n* another name for **officer of the day.**

orderly room *n Military.* a room in the barracks of a battalion or company used for general administrative purposes.

Order of Canada *n* an order awarded to Canadians for outstanding achievement; established in 1967.

order of magnitude *n* the approximate size of something, esp. measured in powers of 10: *the order of magnitude of the deficit was as expected; their estimates differ by an order of magnitude.* Also called: **order.**

Order of Merit *n Brit.* an order conferred on civilians and servicemen for eminence in any field.

Order of Military Merit *n* an order awarded to members of the Canadian Forces for conspicuous merit; established in 1972.

order of the day *n* **1** the general directive of a commander in chief or the specific instructions of a commanding officer. **2** *Informal.* the prescribed or only thing offered or available: *prunes were the order of the day.* **3** (in Parliament and similar legislatures) any item of public business ordered to be considered on a specific day. **4** an agenda or programme.

Order of the Garter *n* the highest order of British knighthood (but see also **Order of the Thistle**) open to women since 1987. It consists of the sovereign, 24 knight companions, and extra members created by statute. Also called: the **Garter.**

Order of the Thistle *n* an ancient Scottish order of knighthood revived by James VII of Scotland in 1687. It consists of the sovereign, 16 knights brethren, and extra members created by statute. It is the equivalent of the Order of the Garter, and is usually conferred on Scots. Also called: the **Thistle.**

order paper *n* a list indicating the order in which business is to be conducted, esp. in Parliament.

orders ('ɔːdəz) *pl n* **1** short for **holy orders. 2 in (holy) orders.** ordained. **3 take (holy) orders.** to become ordained. **4** short for **major orders** or **minor orders.**

ordinal ('ɔːdɪnᵊl) *adj* **1** denoting a certain position in a sequence of numbers. **2** of, relating to, or characteristic of an order in biological classification. ◆ *n* **3** short for **ordinal number. 4** a book containing the forms of services for the ordination of ministers. **5** *R.C. Church.* a service book. **[**C14 (in the sense: orderly): from Late Latin *ordinalis* denoting order or place in a series, from Latin *ordō* ORDER**]**

ordinal number *n* **1** a number denoting relative position in a sequence, such as *first, second, third.* Sometimes shortened to **ordinal. 2** *Logic, maths.* a measure of not only the size of a set but also the order of its elements. ◆ Compare **cardinal number.**

ordinal scale *n Statistics.* a scale on which data is shown simply in order of magnitude since there is no standard of measurement of differences: for instance, a squash ladder is an ordinal scale since one can say only that one person is better than another, but not by how much. Compare **interval scale, ratio scale, nominal scale.**

ordinance ('ɔːdɪnəns) *n* an authoritative regulation, decree, law, or practice. **[**C14: from Old French *ordenance,* from Latin *ordināre* to set in order**]**

ordinand ('ɔːdɪˌnænd) *n Christianity.* a candidate for ordination.

ordinarily ('ɔːdᵊnrɪlɪ, 'ɔːdᵊˌnɛrɪlɪ) *adv* in ordinary, normal, or usual practice; usually; normally.

ordinary ('ɔːdᵊnrɪ) *adj* **1** of common or established type or occurrence. **2** familiar, everyday, or unexceptional. **3** uninteresting or commonplace. **4** having regular or ex officio jurisdiction: *an ordinary judge.* **5** *Maths.* (of a differential equation) containing two variables only and derivatives of one of the variables with respect to the other. ◆ *n, pl* **-naries. 6** a common or average situation, amount, or degree (esp. in the phrase **out of the ordinary**). **7** a normal or commonplace person or thing. **8** *Civil law.* a judge who exercises jurisdiction in his own right. **9** (*usually cap.*) an ecclesiastic, esp. a bishop, holding an office to which certain jurisdictional powers are attached. **10** *R.C. Church.* **10a** the parts of the Mass that do not vary from day to day. Compare **proper** (sense 13). **10b** a prescribed form of divine service, esp. the Mass. **11** the U.S. name for penny-farthing. 12 *Heraldry.* any of several conventional figures, such as the bend, the fesse, and the cross, commonly charged upon shields. 13 *History.* a clergyman who visited condemned prisoners before their death. 14 *Brit. obsolete.* 14a a meal provided regularly at a fixed price. 14b the inn providing such meals. 15 **in ordinary.** *Brit.* (used esp. in titles) in regular service or attendance: *physician in ordinary to the sovereign.* [C16 (adj) and C13 (some n senses): ultimately from Latin *ordinārius* orderly, from *ordō* order]

Ordinary grade *n* (in Scotland) the formal name for **O grade.**

ordinary lay *n* the form of lay found in a cable-laid rope.

Ordinary level *n* (in Britain) the formal name for **O level.**

ordinary rating *n* a rank in the Royal Navy comparable to that of a private in the army.

ordinary ray *n* the plane-polarized ray of light that obeys the laws of refraction in a doubly-refracting crystal. See **double refraction.** Compare **extraordinary ray.**

ordinary seaman *n* a seaman of the lowest rank, being insufficiently experienced to be an able-bodied seaman.

ordinary shares *pl n Brit.* shares representing part of the capital issued by a company and entitling their holders to a dividend that varies according to the prosperity of the company, to vote at all meetings of members, and to a claim on the net assets of the company, after the holders of preference shares have been paid. U.S. equivalent: **common stock.** Compare **preference shares.** See also **A shares.**

ordinate ('ɔːdɪnɪt) *n* the vertical or *y*-coordinate of a point in a two-dimensional system of Cartesian coordinates. Compare **abscissa.** [C16: from New Latin phrase (*linea*) *ordināte* (*applicāta*) (line applied) in an orderly manner, from *ordināre* to arrange in order]

ordination (ˌɔːdɪ'neɪʃən) *n* 1a the act of conferring holy orders. 1b the reception of holy orders. 2 the condition of being ordained or regulated. 3 an arrangement or order.

ordn. *abbrev. for* ordnance.

ordnance ('ɔːdnəns) *n* 1 cannon or artillery. 2 military supplies; munitions. 3 **the.** a department of an army or government dealing with military supplies. [C14: variant of ORDINANCE]

ordnance datum *n* mean sea level calculated from observation taken at Newlyn, Cornwall, and used as the official basis for height calculation on British maps. Abbrev.: **OD.**

Ordnance Survey *n* the official map-making body of the British or Irish government.

ordonnance ('ɔːdənəns; *French* ɔrdɔnɑ̃s) *n* 1 the proper disposition of the elements of a building or an artistic or literary composition. 2 an ordinance, law, or decree, esp. in French law. [C17: from Old French *ordenance* arrangement, influenced by *ordonner* to order]

Ordovician (ˌɔːdəʊ'vɪʃɪən) *adj* 1 of, denoting, or formed in the second period of the Palaeozoic era, between the Cambrian and Silurian periods, which lasted for 60 000 000 years during which marine invertebrates flourished. ◆ *n* 2 **the.** the Ordovician period or rock system. [C19: from Latin *Ordovices* ancient Celtic tribe in N Wales]

ordure ('ɔːdjʊə) *n* 1 excrement; dung. 2 something regarded as being morally offensive. [C14: via Old French, from *ord* dirty, from Latin *horridus* shaggy]

Ordzhonikidze *or* **Orjonikidze** (*Russian* ardʒəni'kidzɪ) *n* the former name (until 1991) of **Vladikavkaz.**

ore (ɔː) *n* any naturally occurring mineral or aggregate of minerals from which economically important constituents, esp. metals, can be extracted. [Old English *ār, ōra;* related to Gothic *aiz,* Latin *aes,* Dutch *oer*]

öre ('ørə) *n, pl* **öre.** a Scandinavian monetary unit worth one hundredth of a Swedish krona and (**øre**) one hundredth of a Danish and Norwegian krone.

oread ('ɔːrɪˌæd) *n Greek myth.* a mountain nymph. [C16: via Latin from Greek *Oreias,* from *oros* mountain]

Örebro (*Swedish* œːrə'bruː) *n* a town in S Sweden: one of Sweden's oldest towns; scene of the election of Jean Bernadotte as heir to the throne in 1810. Pop.: 120 774 (1997 est.).

orectic (ɒ'rɛktɪk) *adj* of or relating to the desires. [C18: from Greek *orektikos* causing desire, from *oregein* to desire]

ore dressing *n* the first stage in the extraction of a metal from an ore in which as much gangue as possible is removed and the ore is prepared for smelting, refining, etc. Also called: **mineral dressing, mineral processing.**

Oreg. *abbrev. for* Oregon.

oregano (ˌɒrɪ'gɑːnəʊ) *n* 1 a Mediterranean variety of wild marjoram (*Origanum vulgare*), with pungent leaves. 2 the dried powdered leaves of this plant, used to season food. ◆ See also **origanum.** [C18: American Spanish, from Spanish, from Latin *orīganum,* from Greek *origanon* an aromatic herb, perhaps marjoram]

Oregon ('ɒrɪgən) *n* a state of the northwestern U.S., on the Pacific: consists of the Coast and Cascade Ranges in the west and a plateau in the east; important timber production. Capital: Salem. Pop.: 3 243 487 (1997 est.). Area: 251 418 sq. km (97 073 sq. miles). Abbrevs.: **Oreg.** or (with zip code) **OR**

Oregon fir *or* **pine** *n* other names for **Douglas fir.**

Oregon grape *n* 1 an evergreen berberidaceous shrub, *Mahonia aquifolium,* of NW North America, having yellow fragrant flowers and small blue edible berries. 2 the berry of this shrub.

Oregon trail *n* an early pioneering route across the central U.S., from Independence, W Missouri, to the Columbia River country of N Oregon: used chiefly between 1804 and 1860. Length: about 3220 km (2000 miles).

Orel *or* **Oryol** (*Russian* a'rjɔl) *n* a city in W Russia; founded in 1564 but damaged during World War II. Pop.: 348 000 (1995 est.).

Ore Mountains (ɔː) *pl n* another name for the **Erzgebirge.**

Orenburg ('ɒrənˌbɜːg; *Russian* arɪn'burk) *n* a city in W Russia, on the Ural River. Pop.: 532 000 (1995 est.). Former name (1938–57): **Chkalov.**

Orense (*Spanish* o'rense) *n* a city in NW Spain, in Galicia on the Miño River: warm springs. Pop.: 110 796 (1995 est.).

Oresme (*French* ɔrɛm) *n* **Nicole d'** (nikɔl). ?1320–82, French economist, mathematician, and cleric: bishop of Lisieux (1378–82).

Orestes (ɒ'rɛstiːz) *n Greek myth.* the son of Agamemnon and Clytemnestra, who killed his mother and her lover Aegisthus in revenge for their murder of his father.

Øresund (œːrə'sʊnd) *n* the Swedish and Danish name for the **Sound.**

orfe (ɔːf) *n* a small slender European cyprinoid fish, *Idus idus,* occurring in two colour varieties, namely the **silver orfe** and the **golden orfe,** popular aquarium fishes. Compare **goldfish.** [C17: from German; related to Latin *orphus,* Greek *orphos* the sea perch]

Orff (ɔːf) *n* **Carl** (karl). 1895–1982, German composer. His works include the secular oratorio *Carmina Burana* (1937) and the opera *Antigone* (1949).

orfray ('ɔːfrɪ) *n* a less common spelling of **orphrey.**

org. *abbrev. for:* 1 organic. 2 organization. 3 organized.

organ ('ɔːgən) *n* 1a Also called: **pipe organ.** a large complex musical keyboard instrument in which sound is produced by means of a number of pipes arranged in sets or stops, supplied with air from a bellows. The largest instruments possess three or more manuals and one pedal keyboard and have the greatest range of any instrument. 1b (*as modifier*): *organ pipe; organ stop; organ loft.* 2 any instrument, such as a harmonium, in which sound is produced in this way. See also **reed organ, harmonica.** 3 short for **electric organ** (sense 1a), **electronic organ.** 4 a fully differentiated structural and functional unit, such as a kidney or a root, in an animal or plant. 5 an agency or medium of communication, esp. a periodical issued by a specialist group or party. 6 an instrument with which something is done or accomplished. 7 a euphemistic word for **penis.** [C13: from Old French *organe,* from Latin *organum* implement, from Greek *organon* tool; compare Greek *ergein* to work]

organa ('ɔːgənə) *n* a plural of **organon** and **organum.**

organdie *or esp. U.S.* **organdy** ('ɔːgəndɪ, ɔː'gæn-) *n, pl* **-dies.** a fine and slightly stiff cotton fabric used esp. for dresses. [C19: from French *organdi,* of unknown origin]

organelle (ˌɔːgə'nɛl) *n* a structural and functional unit, such as a mitochondrion, in a cell or unicellular organism. [C20: from New Latin *organella,* from Latin *organum:* see ORGAN]

organ-grinder *n* a street musician playing a hand organ for money.

organic (ɔː'gænɪk) *adj* 1 of, relating to, derived from, or characteristic of living plants and animals. 2 of or relating to animal or plant constituents or products having a carbon basis. 3 of or relating to one or more organs of an animal or plant. 4 of, relating to, or belonging to the class of chemical compounds that are formed from carbon: *an organic compound.* Compare **inorganic** (sense 2). 5 constitutional in the structure of something; fundamental; integral. 6 of or characterized by the coordination of integral parts; organized. 7 of or relating to the essential constitutional laws regulating the government of a state: *organic law.* 8 of, relating to, or grown with the use of fertilizers or pesticides deriving from animal or vegetable matter, rather than from chemicals. ◆ *n* 9 any substance, such as a fertilizer or pesticide, that is derived from animal or vegetable matter. ▸ **or'ganically** *adv*

organic chemistry *n* the branch of chemistry concerned with the compounds of carbon: originally confined to compounds produced by living organisms but now extended to include man-made substances based on carbon, such as plastics. Compare **inorganic chemistry.**

organic disease *n* any disease in which there is a physical change in the structure of an organ or part. Compare **functional disease.**

organicism (ɔː'gænɪˌsɪzəm) *n* 1 the theory that the functioning of living organisms is determined by the working together of all organs as an integrated system. 2 the theory that all symptoms are caused by organic disease. 3 the theory that each organ of the body has its own peculiar constitution. ▸ **or'ganicist** *n, adj* ▸ **orˌgani'cistic** *adj*

organic psychosis *n* a severe mental illness produced by damage to the brain, as a result of poisoning, alcoholism, disease, etc. Compare **functional** (sense 4b).

organism ('ɔːgəˌnɪzəm) *n* 1 any living animal or plant, including any bacterium or virus. 2 anything resembling a living creature in structure, behaviour, etc. ▸ **ˌorgan'ismal** *or* **ˌorgan'ismic** *adj* ▸ **ˌorgan'ismally** *adv*

organist ('ɔːgənɪst) *n* a person who plays the organ.

organization *or* **organisation** (ˌɔːgənaɪ'zeɪʃən) *n* 1 the act of organizing or the state of being organized. 2 an organized structure or whole. 3 a business or administrative concern united and constructed for a particular end. 4 a body of administrative officials, as of a political party, a government department, etc. 5 order or system; method. ▸ **ˌorgani'zational** *or* **ˌorgani'sational** *adj* ▸ **ˌorgani'zationally** *or* **ˌorgani'sationally** *adv*

organizational culture *n* the customs, rituals, and values shared by the members of an organization that have to be accepted by new members.

organizational psychology *n* the study of the structure of an organization and of the ways in which the people in it interact, usually undertaken in order to improve the organization.

organization chart *n* a diagram representing the management structure of a company, showing the responsibilities of each department, the relationships of the departments to each other, and the hierarchy of management.

organization man *n* 1 a person who subordinates his personal life to the demands of the organization he works for. 2 a person who specializes in or is good at organization.

Organization of African Unity *n* See **OAU.**

Organization of American States *n* an association consisting of the U.S.

and other republics in the W hemisphere, founded at Bogotá in 1948 to promote military, economic, social, and cultural cooperation among the member states. Abbrev.: **OAS**. See also **Pan American Union.**

organize *or* **organise** ('ɔːgəˌnaɪz) *vb* **1** to form (parts or elements of something) into a structured whole; coordinate. **2** (*tr*) to arrange methodically or in order. **3** (*tr*) to provide with an organic structure. **4** (*tr*) to enlist (the workers) of (a factory, concern, or industry) in a trade union. **5** (*intr*) to join or form an organization or trade union. **6** (*tr*) *Informal.* to put (oneself) in an alert and responsible frame of mind. **[C15:** from Medieval Latin *organizare,* from Latin *organum* ORGAN**]**

organized *or* **organised** ('ɔːgəˌnaɪzd) *adj* **1** planned and controlled on a large scale and involving many people: *organized crime.* **2** orderly and efficient: *a highly organized campaign.* **3** (of the workers in a factory or office) belonging to a trade union: *organized labour.*

organizer *or* **organiser** ('ɔːgəˌnaɪzə) *n* **1** a person who organizes or is capable of organizing. **2** a container with a number of compartments for storage: *hanging organizers to keep your clothes smart.* **3** *Embryol.* any part of an embryo or any substance produced by it that induces specialization of undifferentiated cells.

organo- *combining form.* **1** (in biology or medicine) indicating an organ or organs: *organogenesis.* **2** (in chemistry) indicating a compound containing an organic group: *organometallic; organochlorine; organophosphate.*

organ of Corti ('kɔːtɪ) *n* the sense organ of the cochlea by which sounds are converted into nerve impulses. **[**named after Alfonso *Corti* (died 1876), Italian anatomist**]**

organogenesis (ˌɔːgənəʊ'dʒɛnɪsɪs) *n* **1** the formation and development of organs in an animal or plant. **2** Also called: **organogeny** (ˌɔːgən'ɒdʒənɪ). the study of this process. ► **organogenetic** (ˌɔːgənəʊdʒɪ'nɛtɪk) *adj* ► **ˌorganoge'netically** *adv*

organography (ˌɔːgə'nɒgrəfɪ) *n* the description of the organs and major structures of animals and plants. ► **organographic** (ˌɔːgənəʊ'græfɪk) *or* **ˌorgano'graphical** *adj* ► **ˌorgan'ographist** *n*

organoleptic (ˌɔːgənəʊ'lɛptɪk) *adj Physiol.* **1** able to stimulate an organ, esp. a special sense organ. **2** able to perceive a sensory stimulus.

organology (ˌɔːgə'nɒlədʒɪ) *n* the study of the structure and function of the organs of animals and plants. ► **organological** (ˌɔːgənəʊ'lɒdʒɪkᵊl) *adj* ► **ˌorgan'ologist** *n*

organometallic (ɔːˌgænəʊmɪ'tælɪk) *adj* of, concerned with, or being an organic compound with one or more metal atoms in its molecules: *an organometallic compound.*

organon ('ɔːgəˌnɒn) *or* **organum** *n, pl* **organa** ('ɔːgənə), **-nons** *or* **-na, -nums.** *Epistemology.* **1** a system of logical or scientific rules, esp. that of Aristotle. **2** *Archaic.* a sense organ, regarded as an instrument for acquiring knowledge. **[C16:** from Greek: implement; see ORGAN**]**

organophosphate (ɔːˌgænəʊ'fɒsfeɪt) *n* any of a group of organic compounds containing phosphate groups and used as a pesticide.

organotherapy (ˌɔːgənəʊ'θɛrəpɪ) *n* the treatment of disease with extracts of animal endocrine glands. ► **organotherapeutic** (ˌɔːgənəʊˌθɛrə'pjuːtɪk) *adj*

organotin (ˌɔːgænəʊ'tɪn) *adj* of, concerned with, or being an organic compound with one or more tin atoms in its molecules: used as a pesticide, hitherto considered to decompose safely, now found to be toxic in the food chain.

organ screen *n* a wooden or stone screen that supports the organ in a cathedral or church and divides the choir from the nave.

organum ('ɔːgənəm) *n, pl* **-na** (-nə) *or* **-nums. 1** a form of polyphonic music originating in the ninth century, consisting of a plainsong melody with parts added at the fourth and fifth. **2** a variant of **organon. [C17:** via Latin from Greek; see ORGAN**]**

organza (ɔː'gænzə) *n* a thin stiff fabric of silk, cotton, nylon, rayon, etc. **[C20:** perhaps related to ORGANZINE**]**

organzine ('ɔːgənˌziːn, ɔː'gænziːn) *n* **1** a strong thread made of twisted strands of raw silk. **2** fabric made of such threads. **[C17:** from French *organsin,* from Italian *organzino,* probably from *Urgench,* a town in Uzbekistan where the fabric was originally produced**]**

orgasm ('ɔːgæzəm) *n* **1** the most intense point during sexual excitement, characterized by extremely pleasurable sensations and in the male accompanied by ejaculation of semen. **2** *Rare.* intense or violent excitement. **[C17:** from New Latin *orgasmus,* from Greek *orgasmos,* from *organ* to mature, swell**]** ► **or'gasmic** *or* **or'gastic** *adj*

orgeat ('ɔːʒɑː; *French* ɔrʒa) *n* a drink made from barley or almonds, and orange flower water. **[C18:** via French, from *orge* barley, from Latin *hordeum***]**

orgone ('ɔːgəʊn) *n* a substance postulated by Wilhelm Reich, who thought it was present everywhere and needed to be incorporated in people for sexual activity and mental health. **[C20:** from ORG(ASM) + (HORM)ONE**]**

orgulous ('ɔːgjʊləs) *adj Archaic.* proud. **[C13:** from Old French, from *orgueil* pride, from Frankish *urgōli* (unattested)**]**

orgy ('ɔːdʒɪ) *n, pl* **-gies. 1** a wild gathering marked by promiscuous sexual activity, excessive drinking, etc. **2** an act of immoderate or frenzied indulgence. **3** (*often pl*) secret religious rites of Dionysus, Bacchus, etc., marked by drinking, dancing, and songs. **[C16:** from French *orgies,* from Latin *orgia,* from Greek: nocturnal festival**]** ► **ˌorgi'astic** *adj*

oribi ('ɒrɪbɪ) *n, pl* **-bi** *or* **-bis.** a small African antelope, *Ourebia ourebi,* of grasslands and bush south of the Sahara, with fawn-coloured coat and, in the male, ridged spikelike horns. **[C18:** from Afrikaans, probably from Khoikhoi *arab***]**

oriel window ('ɔːrɪəl) *n* a bay window, esp. one that is supported by one or more brackets or corbels. Sometimes shortened to **oriel. [C14:** from Old French *oriol* gallery, perhaps from Medieval Latin *auleolum* niche**]**

orient *n* ('ɔːrɪənt). **1** *Poetic.* another word for **east.** Compare **occident. 2** *Archaic.* the eastern sky or the dawn. **3a** the iridescent lustre of a pearl. **3b** (*as modifier*): *orient pearls.* **4** a pearl of high quality. ◆ *adj* ('ɔːrɪənt). **5** *Now chiefly poetic.* eastern. **6** *Archaic.* (of the sun, stars, etc.) rising. ◆ *vb* ('ɔːrɪˌɛnt). **7** to adjust or align (oneself or something else) according to surroundings or circumstances. **8** (*tr*) to position, align, or set (a map, surveying instrument, etc.) with reference to the points of the compass or other specific directions. **9** (*tr*) to set or build (a church) in an easterly direction. **[C18:** via French from Latin *oriēns* rising (sun), from *orīrī* to rise**]**

Orient ('ɔːrɪənt) *n* (usually preceded by *the*) **1** the countries east of the Mediterranean. **2** the eastern hemisphere.

oriental (ˌɔːrɪ'ɛntᵊl) *adj* another word for **eastern.** Compare **occidental.**

Oriental (ˌɔːrɪ'ɛntᵊl) *adj* **1** (*sometimes not cap.*) of or relating to the Orient. **2** of or denoting a zoogeographical region consisting of southeastern Asia from India to Borneo, Java, and the Philippines. ◆ *n* **3** (*sometimes not cap.*) an inhabitant, esp. a native, of the Orient.

Oriental almandine *n* a variety of corundum resembling almandine in colour and used as a gemstone.

Oriental emerald *n* a green variety of corundum used as a gemstone.

Orientalism (ˌɔːrɪ'ɛntəˌlɪzəm) *n* **1** knowledge of or devotion to the Orient. **2** an Oriental quality, style, or trait. ► **ˌOri'entalist** *n* ► **ˌOriˌental'istic** *adj*

Orientalize *or* **Orientalise** (ˌɔːrɪ'ɛntəˌlaɪz) *vb* to make, become, or treat as Oriental. ► **ˌOriˌentali'zation** *or* **ˌOriˌentali'sation** *n*

Oriental topaz *n* a variety of corundum resembling topaz in colour and used as a gemstone.

orientate ('ɔːrɪɛnˌteɪt) *vb* a variant of **orient.**

orientation (ˌɔːrɪɛn'teɪʃən) *n* **1** the act or process of orienting or the state of being oriented. **2** position or positioning with relation to the points of the compass or other specific directions. **3** the adjustment or alignment of oneself or one's ideas to surroundings or circumstances. **4** Also called: **orientation course.** *Chiefly U.S. and Canadian.* **4a** a course, programme, lecture, etc., introducing a new situation or environment. **4b** (*as modifier*): *an orientation talk.* **5** *Psychol.* the knowledge of one's own temporal, social, and practical circumstances in life. **6** basic beliefs or preferences: *sexual orientation.* **7** *Biology.* the change in position of the whole or part of an organism in response to a stimulus, such as light. **8** *Chem.* the relative dispositions of atoms, ions, or groups in molecules or crystals. **9** the siting of a church on an east-west axis, usually with the altar at the E end. ► **ˌorien'tational** *adj*

-oriented *suffix forming adjectives.* designed for, directed towards, motivated by, or concerned with: *computer-oriented courses; managers who are profit-oriented.*

orienteer (ˌɔːrɪən'tɪə) *vb* (*intr*) **1** to take part in orienteering. ◆ *n* **2** a person who takes part in orienteering.

orienteering (ˌɔːrɪɛn'tɪərɪŋ) *n* a sport in which contestants race on foot over a course consisting of checkpoints found with the aid of a map and a compass. **[C20:** from Swedish *orientering;* compare ORIENT**]**

orifice ('ɒrɪfɪs) *n Chiefly technical.* an opening or mouth into a cavity; vent; aperture. **[C16:** via French from Late Latin *ōrificium,* from Latin *ōs* mouth + *facere* to make**]**

orifice meter *n Engineering.* a plate having a central hole that is placed across the flow of a liquid, usually between flanges in a pipeline. The pressure difference generated by the flow velocity through the hole enables the flow quantity to be measured.

oriflamme ('ɒrɪˌflæm) *n* a scarlet flag, originally of the abbey of St. Denis in N France, adopted as the national banner of France in the Middle Ages. **[C15:** via Old French, from Latin *aurum* gold + *flamma* flame**]**

orig. *abbrev. for:* **1** origin. **2** original(ly).

origami (ˌɒrɪ'gɑːmɪ) *n* the art or process, originally Japanese, of paper folding. **[**from Japanese, from *ori* a folding + *kami* paper**]**

origan ('ɒrɪgən) *n* another name for **marjoram** (sense 2). **[C16:** from Latin *orīganum,* from Greek *origanon* an aromatic herb, perhaps marjoram; compare OREGANO**]**

origanum (ə'rɪgənəm) *n* any plant of the herbaceous aromatic Mediterranean genus *Origanum: family Labiatae.* See **oregano, marjoram, dittany** (sense 1). **[**New Latin, from Greek *origanon* wild marjoram**]**

Origen ('ɒrɪˌdʒɛn) *n* ?185–?254 A.D., Christian theologian, born in Alexandria. His writings include *Hexapla,* a synopsis of the Old Testament, *Contra Celsum,* a defence of Christianity, and *De principiis,* a statement of Christian theology.

origin ('ɒrɪdʒɪn) *n* **1** a primary source; derivation. **2** the beginning of something; first stage or part. **3** (*often pl*) ancestry or parentage; birth; extraction. **4** *Anatomy.* **4a** the end of a muscle, opposite its point of insertion. **4b** the beginning of a nerve or blood vessel or the site where it first starts to branch out. **5** *Maths.* **5a** the point of intersection of coordinate axes or planes. **5b** the point whose coordinates are all zero. See also **pole**[2] (sense 8). **6** *Commerce.* the country from which a commodity or product originates: *shipment from origin.* **[C16:** from French *origine,* from Latin *orīgō* beginning, birth, from *orīrī* to rise, spring from**]**

original (ə'rɪdʒɪnᵊl) *adj* **1** of or relating to an origin or beginning. **2** fresh and unusual; novel. **3** able to think of or carry out new ideas or concepts. **4** being that from which a copy, translation, etc., is made. ◆ *n* **5** the first and genuine form of something, from which others are derived. **6** a person or thing used as a model in art or literature. **7** a person whose way of thinking is unusual or creative. **8** an unconventional or strange person. **9** the first form or occurrence of something. **10** an archaic word for **originator,** see **originate.**

originality (əˌrɪdʒɪ'nælɪtɪ) *n, pl* **-ties. 1** the quality or condition of being original. **2** the ability to create or innovate. **3** something original.

originally (ə'rɪdʒɪnəlɪ) *adv* **1** in the first place. **2** in an original way. **3** with reference to the origin or beginning.

original sin *n* a state of sin held to be innate in mankind as the descendants of Adam.

originate (əˈrɪdʒɪˌneɪt) *vb* **1** to come or bring into being. **2** (*intr*) *U.S. and Canadian.* (of a bus, train, etc.) to begin its journey at a specified point. ► **oˌrigiˈnation** *n* ► **oˈrigiˌnator** *n*

orinasal (ˌɔːrɪˈneɪzᵊl) *Phonetics.* ◆ *adj* **1** pronounced with simultaneous oral and nasal articulation, such as the French nasalized vowels œ̃ (as in *un*), ɔ̃ (as in *bon*), and ɑ̃ (as in *blanc*). ◆ *n* **2** an orinasal speech sound. [C19: from Latin *ōr-* (from *ōs* mouth) + NASAL] ► ˌ**oriˈnasally** *adv*

O-ring *n* a rubber ring used in machinery as a seal against oil, air, etc.

Orinoco (ˌɒrɪˈnəʊkəʊ) *n* a river in N South America, rising in S Venezuela and flowing west, then north as part of the border between Colombia and Venezuela, then east to the Atlantic by a great delta: the third largest river system in South America, draining an area of 945 000 sq. km (365 000 sq. miles); reaches a width of 22 km (14 miles) during the rainy season. Length: about 2575 km (1600 miles).

oriole (ˈɔːrɪˌəʊl) *n* **1** any songbird of the mainly tropical Old World family *Oriolidae,* such as *Oriolus oriolus* (**golden oriole**), having a long pointed bill and a mostly yellow-and-black plumage. **2** any American songbird of the family *Icteridae,* esp. those of the genus *Icterus,* such as the Baltimore oriole, with a typical male plumage of black with either orange or yellow. [C18: from Medieval Latin *oryolus,* from Latin *aureolus,* diminutive of *aureus,* from *aurum* gold]

Orion[1] (əˈraɪən) *n Greek myth.* a Boeotian giant famed as a great hunter, who figures in several tales.

Orion[2] (əˈraɪən) *n, Latin genitive* **Orionis** (ˌɔːrɪˈəʊnɪs). a conspicuous constellation near Canis Major containing two first magnitude stars (Betelgeuse and Rigel) and a distant bright emission nebula (the **Orion Nebula**).

orison (ˈɒrɪzᵊn) *n Literary.* another word for **prayer**[1]. [C12: from Old French *oreison,* from Late Latin *ōrātiō,* from Latin: speech, from *ōrāre* to speak]

Orissa (ɒˈrɪsə) *n* a state of E India, on the Bay of Bengal: part of the province of Bihar and Orissa (1912–36); enlarged by the addition of 25 native states in 1949. Capital: Bhubaneswar. Pop.: 33 795 000 (1994 est.). Area: 155 707 sq. km (60 119 sq. miles).

Oriya (ɒˈriːə) *n* **1** (*pl* **-ya**) a member of a people of India living chiefly in Orissa and neighbouring states. **2** the state language of Orissa, belonging to the Indic branch of the Indo-European family.

Orizaba (ˌɔːrɪˈzɑːbə; *Spanish* oriˈθaβa) *n* **1** a city and resort in SE Mexico, in Veracruz state. Pop.: 114 216 (1990). **2 Pico de.** the Spanish name for **Citlaltépetl.**

Orjonikidze (*Russian* ardʒəniˈkidzɪ) *n* a variant spelling of **Ordzhonikidze.**

Orkneys (ˈɔːknɪz), **Orkney** (ˈɔːknɪ), *or* **Orkney Islands** *pl n* a group of over 70 islands off the N coast of Scotland, separated from the mainland by the Pentland Firth: constitutes an island authority of Scotland; low-lying and treeless; prehistoric remains. Administrative centre: Kirkwall. Pop.: 19 800 (1996 est.). Area: 974 sq. km (376 sq. miles). Related word: **Orcadian.** ► ˈ**Orkneyman** *n*

Orlando (ɔːˈlændəʊ) *n* a city in the U.S., in Florida: site of Walt Disney World. Pop.: 173 902 (1996 est.).

orle (ɔːl) *n Heraldry.* a border around a shield. [C16: from French, from *ourler* to hem]

Orléanais (*French* ɔrleanɛ) *n* a former province of N central France, centred on Orléans.

Orleanist (ɔːˈlɪənɪst) *n* an adherent of the Orléans branch of the French Bourbons.

Orléans[1] (ɔːˈlɪənz; *French* ɔrleɑ̃) *n* a city in N central France, on the River Loire: famous for its deliverance by Joan of Arc from the long English siege in 1429; university (1305); an important rail and road junction. Pop.: 107 965 (1990).

Orléans[2] (*French* ɔrleɑ̃) *n* **1 Charles** (Jarl), Duc d'Orléans. 1394–1465, French poet; noted for the poems written during his imprisonment in England; father of Louis XII. **2 Louis Philippe Joseph** (lwi filip ʒozɛf), Duc d'Orléans, known as *Philippe Égalité* (after 1792). 1747–93, French nobleman, who supported the French Revolution and voted for the death of his cousin, Louis XVI, but was executed after his son, the future king Louis-Philippe, defected to the Austrians.

Orlon (ˈɔːlɒn) *n Trademark.* a crease-resistant acrylic fibre or fabric used for clothing, furnishings, etc.

orlop *or* **orlop deck** (ˈɔːlɒp) *n Nautical.* (in a vessel with four or more decks) the lowest deck. [C15: from Dutch *overloopen* to run over, spill. See OVER, LEAP]

Orlov (ˈɔːlɒf) *n* Count **Grigori Grigorievich.** 1734–83, Russian soldier and a lover of Catherine II. He led (with his brother, Count **Aleksey Grigorievich Orlov**, 1737–1808) the coup that brought Catherine to power.

Orly (ˈɔːlɪː; *French* ɔrli) *n* a suburb of SE Paris, France, with an international airport.

Ormandy (ˈɔːməndɪ) *n* **Eugene.** 1899–1985, U.S. conductor, born in Hungary.

Ormazd *or* **Ormuzd** (ˈɔːməzd) *n Zoroastrianism.* the creative deity, embodiment of good and opponent of Ahriman. Also called: **Ahura Mazda.** [from Persian, from Avestan *Ahura-Mazda,* from *ahura* spirit + *mazdā* wise]

ormer (ˈɔːmə) *n* **1** Also called: **sea-ear.** an edible marine gastropod mollusc, *Haliotis tuberculata,* that has an ear-shaped shell perforated with holes and occurs near the Channel Islands. **2** any other abalone. [C17: from French (Guernsey dialect), apparently from Latin *auris* ear + *mare* sea]

ormolu (ˈɔːməˌluː) *n* **1a** a gold-coloured alloy of copper, tin, or zinc used to decorate furniture, mouldings, etc. **1b** (*as modifier*): *an ormolu clock.* **2** gold prepared to be used for gilding. [C18: from French *or moulu* ground gold]

Ormonde (ˈɔːmənd) *n* **1st Duke of,** title of *James Butler.* 1610–88, Anglo-Irish general; commander (1641–50) of the royalist forces in Ireland; Lord Lieutenant of Ireland (1661–69; 1677–84).

Ormuz (ˈɔːmʌz) *n* a variant spelling of **Hormuz.**

ornament *n* (ˈɔːnəmənt). **1** anything that enhances the appearance of a person or thing. **2** decorations collectively: *she was totally without ornament.* **3** a small decorative object. **4** something regarded as a source of pride or beauty. **5** *Music.* any of several decorations, such as the trill, mordent, etc., occurring chiefly as improvised embellishments in baroque music. ◆ *vb* (ˈɔːnəˌmɛnt). (*tr*) **6** to decorate with or as if with ornaments. **7** to serve as an ornament to. [C14: from Latin *ornāmentum,* from *ornāre* to adorn] ► ˌ**ornamenˈtation** *n*

ornamental (ˌɔːnəˈmɛntᵊl) *adj* **1** of value as an ornament; decorative. **2** (of a plant) used to decorate houses, gardens, etc. ◆ *n* **3** a plant cultivated for show or decoration. ► ˌ**ornaˈmentally** *adv*

ornate (ɔːˈneɪt) *adj* **1** heavily or elaborately decorated. **2** (of style in writing) overembellished; flowery. [C15: from Latin *ornāre* to decorate] ► **orˈnately** *adv* ► **orˈnateness** *n*

Orne (*French* ɔrn) *n* a department of NW France, in Basse-Normandie. Capital: Alençon. Pop.: 294 700 (1995). Area: 6144 sq. km (2396 sq. miles).

ornery (ˈɔːnərɪ) *adj U.S. and Canadian dialect or informal.* **1** stubborn or vile-tempered. **2** low; treacherous: *an ornery trick.* **3** ordinary. [C19: alteration of ORDINARY] ► ˈ**orneriness** *n*

ornis (ˈɔːnɪs) *n* a less common word for **avifauna.** [C19: from Greek: bird]

ornithic (ɔːˈnɪθɪk) *adj* of or relating to birds or a bird fauna. [C19: from Greek *ornithikos,* from *ornis* bird]

ornithine (ˈɔːnɪˌθiːn) *n* an amino acid produced from arginine by hydrolysis: involved in the formation of urea in the liver; diaminopentanoic acid. Formula: $NH_2(CH_2)_3CHNH_2COOH$. [C19: from *ornithuric* (*acid*) secreted in the urine of birds, from ORNITHO- + URIC]

ornithischian (ˌɔːnɪˈθɪskɪən) *adj* **1** of, relating to, or belonging to the *Ornithischia,* an order of dinosaurs that included the ornithopods, stegosaurs, ankylosaurs, and triceratops. ◆ *n* **2** any dinosaur of the order *Ornithischia.* [C20: from ORNITHO- + Greek *ischion* hip joint]

ornitho- *or before a vowel* **ornith-** *combining form.* bird or birds: *ornithology; ornithomancy; ornithopter; ornithoscopy; ornithosis.* [from Greek *ornis, ornith-* bird]

ornithol. *or* **ornith.** *abbrev. for:* **1** ornithological. **2** ornithology.

ornithology (ˌɔːnɪˈθɒlədʒɪ) *n* the study of birds, including their physiology, classification, ecology, and behaviour. ► **ornithological** (ˌɔːnɪθəˈlɒdʒɪkᵊl) *adj* ► ˌ**ornithoˈlogically** *adv* ► ˌ**orniˈthologist** *n*

ornithomancy (ˈɔːnɪθəʊˌmænsɪ) *n* divination from the flight and cries of birds.

ornithophily (ˌɔːnɪˈθɒfɪlɪ) *n* pollination of flowers by birds. ► ˌ**orniˈthophilous** *adj*

ornithopod (ˈɔːnɪθəˌpɒd) *n* any herbivorous typically bipedal ornithischian dinosaur of the suborder *Ornithopoda,* including the iguanodon.

ornithopter (ˈɔːnɪˌθɒptə) *n* a heavier-than-air craft sustained in and propelled through the air by flapping wings. Also called: **orthopter.**

ornithorhynchus (ˌɔːnɪθəʊˈrɪŋkəs) *n* the technical name for **duck-billed platypus.** [C19: New Latin, from ORNITHO- + Greek *rhunkhos* bill]

ornithoscopy (ˌɔːnɪˈθɒskəpɪ) *n* divination from the observation of birds.

ornithosis (ˌɔːnɪˈθəʊsɪs) *n* a disease identical to psittacosis that occurs in birds other than parrots and can be transmitted to man.

oro-[1] *combining form.* mountain: *orogeny; orography.* [from Greek *oros*]

oro-[2] *combining form.* oral; mouth: *oromaxillary.* [from Latin, from *ōs*]

orobanchaceous (ˌɔːrəʊbæŋˈkeɪʃəs) *adj* of, relating to, or belonging to the *Orobanchaceae,* a family of flowering plants all of which are root parasites, including broomrape and toothwort. [via Latin from Greek *orobankhē* broomrape]

orogeny (ɒˈrɒdʒɪnɪ) *or* **orogenesis** (ˌɒrəʊˈdʒɛnɪsɪs) *n* the formation of mountain ranges by intense upward displacement of the earth's crust. ► **orogenic** (ˌɒrəʊˈdʒɛnɪk) *or* **orogenetic** (ˌɒrəʊdʒɪˈnɛtɪk) *adj* ► ˌ**oroˈgenically** *or* ˌ**orogeˈnetically** *adv*

orography (ɒˈrɒgrəfɪ) *or* **orology** (ɒˈrɒlədʒɪ) *n* the study or mapping of relief, esp. of mountains. ► **oˈrographer** *or* **oˈrologist** *n* ► **orographic** (ˌɒrəʊˈgræfɪk) *or* **orological** (ˌɒrəʊˈlɒdʒɪkᵊl) *adj* ► ˌ**oroˈgraphically** *or* ˌ**oroˈlogically** *adv*

oroide (ˈɔːrəʊˌaɪd) *n* an alloy containing copper, tin, and other metals, used as imitation gold. [C19: from French *or* gold + -OID]

orometer (ɒˈrɒmɪtə) *n* an aneroid barometer with an altitude scale. [C19: from ORO-[1] (mountain, altitude) + -METER]

oronasal (ˌɔːrəʊˈneɪzᵊl) *adj Anatomy.* of or relating to the mouth and nose.

Orontes (ɒˈrɒntiːz) *n* a river in SW Asia, rising in Lebanon and flowing north through Syria into Turkey, where it turns west to the Mediterranean. Length: 571 km (355 miles). Arabic name: **'Asi.**

orotund (ˈɒrəʊˌtʌnd) *adj* **1** (of the voice) resonant; booming. **2** (of speech or writing) bombastic; pompous. [C18: from Latin phrase *ore rotundo* with rounded mouth]

Orozco (*Spanish* oˈrɔθko) *n* **José Clemente** (xoˈse kleˈmente). 1883–1949, Mexican painter, noted for his monumental humanistic murals.

orphan (ˈɔːfən) *n* **1a** a child, one or (more commonly) both of whose parents are dead. **1b** (*as modifier*): *an orphan child.* ◆ *vb* **2** (*tr*) to deprive of one or both parents. **3** *Printing.* the first line of a paragraph separated from the rest of the paragraph by occurring at the foot of a page. [C15: from Late Latin *orphanus,* from Greek *orphanos;* compare Latin *orbus* bereaved]

orphanage (ˈɔːfənɪdʒ) *n* **1** an institution for orphans and abandoned children. **2** the state of being an orphan.

orpharion (ɔːˈfærɪən) *n* a large lute in use during the 16th and 17th centuries. [C16: from ORPH(EUS) + *Arion,* musicians of Greek mythology]

Orphean (ˈɔːfɪən) *adj* **1** of or relating to Orpheus. **2** melodious or enchanting.

Orpheus (ˈɔːfɪəs, -fjuːs) *n Greek myth.* a poet and lyre-player credited with the authorship of the poems forming the basis of Orphism. He married Eurydice and sought her in Hades after her death. He failed to win her back and was killed by a band of bacchantes.

Orphic ('ɔːfɪk) *adj* **1** of or relating to Orpheus or Orphism. **2** (*sometimes not cap.*) mystical or occult. ► **'Orphically** *adv*

Orphism ('ɔːfɪzəm) *n* a mystery religion of ancient Greece, widespread from the 6th century B.C. onwards, combining pre-Hellenic beliefs, the Thracian cult of (Dionysius) Zagreus, etc. ► **Or'phistic** *adj*

orphrey *or* (*less commonly*) **orfray** ('ɔːfrɪ) *n* a richly embroidered band or border, esp. on an ecclesiastical vestment. **[**C13 *orfreis,* from Old French, from Late Latin *aurifrisium, auriphrygium,* from Latin *aurum* gold + *Phrygius* Phrygian**]**

orpiment ('ɔːpɪmənt) *n* a yellow mineral consisting of arsenic trisulphide in monoclinic crystalline form occurring in association with realgar: it is an ore of arsenic. Formula: As_2S_3. **[**C14: via Old French from Latin *auripigmentum* gold pigment**]**

orpine ('ɔːpaɪn) *or* **orpin** ('ɔːpɪn) *n* a succulent perennial N temperate crassulaceous plant, *Sedum telephium,* with toothed leaves and heads of small purplish-white flowers. Also called: **livelong** (Brit.), **live-forever** (U.S.). **[**C14: from Old French, apparently from ORPIMENT (perhaps referring to the yellow flowers of a related species)**]**

Orpington[1] ('ɔːpɪŋtən) *n* **1** a heavy breed of domestic fowl of various single colours, laying brown eggs. **2** a breed of brown duck with an orange bill.

Orpington[2] ('ɔːpɪŋtən) *n* a district of SE London, part of the Greater London borough of Bromley from 1965.

orra ('ɒrə) *adj Scot.* **1** odd or unmatched; supernumerary. **2** occasional or miscellaneous. **3 orra man** *or* **orraman.** an odd-jobman. **[**C18: of unknown origin**]**

orrery ('ɒrərɪ) *n, pl* **-ries.** a mechanical model of the solar system in which the planets can be moved at the correct relative velocities around the sun. **[**C18: originally made for Charles Boyle, Earl of *Orrery***]**

orris[1] *or* **orrice** ('ɒrɪs) *n* **1** any of various irises, esp. *Iris florentina,* that have fragrant rhizomes. **2** Also called: **'orrisroot.** the rhizome of such a plant, prepared and used as perfume. **[**C16: variant of IRIS**]**

orris[2] ('ɒrɪs) *n* a kind of lace made of gold or silver, used esp. in the 18th century. **[**from Old French *orfreis,* from L *auriphrygium* Phrygian gold**]**

Orsini (*Italian* or'siːni) *n* an Italian aristocratic family that was prominent in Rome from the 12th to the 18th century.

Orsk (*Russian* ɔrsk) *n* a city in W Russia, on the Ural River: a major railway and industrial centre, with an oil refinery linked by pipeline with the Emba field (on the Caspian). Pop.: 275 000 (1995 est.).

ortanique (ˌɔːtə'niːk) *n* a hybrid between an orange and a tangerine. **[**C20: from OR(ANGE) + TAN(GERINE) + (UN)IQUE**]**

Ortega (ɔː'teɪgə) *n* **Daniel**, full surname *Ortega Saavedra.* born 1945, Nicaraguan politician and former resistance leader; president of Nicaragua (1985–90).

Ortegal (*Spanish* ɔrte'ɣal) *n* **Cape.** a cape in NW Spain, projecting into the Bay of Biscay.

Ortega y Gasset (*Spanish* ɔr'teɣa i ga'sɛt) *n* **José** (xo'se). 1883–1955, Spanish essayist and philosopher. His best-known work is *The Revolt of the Masses* (1930).

Orth. *abbrev. for* Orthodox (religion).

orthicon ('ɔːθɪˌkɒn) *n* a television camera tube in which an optical image produces a corresponding electrical charge pattern on a mosaic surface that is scanned from behind by an electron beam. The resulting discharge of the mosaic provides the output signal current. See also **image orthicon. [**C20: from ORTHO- + ICON(OSCOPE)**]**

ortho- *or before a vowel* **orth-** *combining form.* **1** straight or upright: *orthotropous.* **2** perpendicular or at right angles: *orthoclastic.* **3** correct or right: *orthodontics; orthodox; orthography; orthoptics.* **4** (*often in italics*) denoting an organic compound containing a benzene ring with substituents attached to adjacent carbon atoms (the 1,2- positions): *orthodinitrobenzene.* Abbrev.: **o-**. Compare **para-**[1] (sense 6), **meta-** (sense 4). **5** denoting an oxyacid regarded as the highest hydrated form of the anhydride or a salt of such an acid: *orthophosphoric acid.* Compare **meta-** (sense 6). **6** denoting a diatomic substance in which the spins of the two atoms are parallel: *orthohydrogen.* Compare **para-**[1] (sense 8). **[**from Greek *orthos* straight, right, upright**]**

orthoboric acid (ˌɔːθəʊ'bɔːrɪk) *n* the more formal name for **boric acid** (sense 1).

orthocentre *or U.S.* **orthocenter** ('ɔːθəʊˌsɛntə) *n* the point of intersection of any two altitudes of a triangle.

orthocephalic (ˌɔːθəʊsɪ'fælɪk) *or* **orthocephalous** (ˌɔːθəʊ'sɛfələs) *adj* having a skull whose breadth is between 70 and 75 per cent of its length. ► **ˌortho'cephaly** *n*

orthochromatic (ˌɔːθəʊkrəʊ'mætɪk) *adj Photog.* of or relating to an emulsion giving a rendering of relative light intensities of different colours that corresponds approximately to the colour sensitivity of the eye, esp. one that is insensitive to red light. Sometimes shortened to **ortho.** Compare **panchromatic.** ► orthochromatism (ˌɔːθəʊ'krəʊməˌtɪzəm) *n*

orthoclase ('ɔːθəʊˌkleɪs, -ˌkleɪz) *n* a white to pale yellow, red, or green mineral of the feldspar group, found in igneous, sedimentary, and metamorphic rocks. It is used in the manufacture of glass and ceramics. Composition: potassium aluminium silicate. Formula: $KAlSi_3O_8$. Crystal structure: monoclinic.

orthodontics (ˌɔːθəʊ'dɒntɪks) *or* **orthodontia** (ˌɔːθəʊ'dɒntɪə) *n* (*functioning as sing*) the branch of dentistry concerned with preventing or correcting irregularities of the teeth. Also called: **dental orthopaedics.** ► **ˌortho'dontic** *adj* ► **ˌortho'dontist** *n*

orthodox ('ɔːθəˌdɒks) *adj* **1** conforming with established or accepted standards, as in religion, behaviour, or attitudes. **2** conforming to the Christian faith as established by the early Church. **[**C16: via Church Latin from Greek *orthodoxos,* from *orthos* correct + *doxa* belief**]** ► **'orthoˌdoxly** *adv*

Orthodox ('ɔːθəˌdɒks) *adj* **1** of or relating to the Orthodox Church of the East. **2** (*sometimes not cap.*) **2a** of or relating to Orthodox Judaism. **2b** (of an individual Jew) strict in the observance of Talmudic law and in personal devotions.

Orthodox Church *n* **1** Also called: **Byzantine Church, Eastern Orthodox Church, Greek Orthodox Church.** the collective body of those Eastern Churches that were separated from the western Church in the 11th century and are in communion with the Greek patriarch of Constantinople. **2** any of these Churches.

Orthodox Judaism *n* the form of Judaism characterized by allegiance to the traditional interpretation and to strict observance of the Mosaic Law as interpreted in the Talmud, etc., and regarded as divinely revealed. Compare **Conservative Judaism, Reform Judaism.**

orthodoxy ('ɔːθəˌdɒksɪ) *n, pl* **-doxies. 1** orthodox belief or practice. **2** the quality of being orthodox.

orthoepy ('ɔːθəʊˌɛpɪ) *n* the study of correct or standard pronunciation. **[**C17: from Greek *orthoepeia,* from ORTHO- straight + *epos* word**]** ► **orthoepic** (ˌɔːθəʊ'ɛpɪk) *adj* ► **ˌortho'epically** *adv*

orthogenesis (ˌɔːθəʊ'dʒɛnɪsɪs) *n* **1** *Biology.* **1a** evolution of a group of organisms in a particular direction, which is generally predetermined. **1b** the theory that proposes such a development. **2** the theory that there is a series of stages through which all cultures pass in the same order. ► **orthogenetic** (ˌɔːθəʊdʒɪ'nɛtɪk) *adj* ► **ˌorthoge'netically** *adv*

orthogenic (ˌɔːθəʊ'dʒɛnɪk) *adj* **1** *Med.* relating to corrective procedures designed to promote healthy development. **2** of or relating to orthogenesis. ► **ˌortho'genically** *adv*

orthognathous (ɔː'θɒgnəθəs) *adj Anatomy.* having normally aligned jaws. ► **or'thognaˌthism** *or* **or'thognathy** *n*

orthogonal (ɔː'θɒgənᵊl) *adj* **1** relating to, consisting of, or involving right angles; perpendicular. **2** *Maths.* **2a** (of a pair of vectors) having a defined scalar product equal to zero. **2b** (of a pair of functions) having a defined product equal to zero. ► **or'thogonally** *adv*

orthogonal matrix *n Maths.* a matrix that is the inverse of its transpose so that any two rows or any two columns are orthogonal vectors. Compare **symmetric matrix.**

orthogonal projection *n Engineering.* the method used in engineering drawing of projecting views of the object being described, such as plan, elevation, side view, etc., at right angles to each other.

orthographic (ˌɔːθəʊ'græfɪk) *or* **orthographical** *adj* of or relating to spelling. ► **ˌortho'graphically** *adv*

orthographic projection *n* **1** a style of engineering drawing in which true dimensions are represented as if projected from infinity on three planes perpendicular to each other, avoiding the effects of perspective. **2** a type of zenithal map projection in which the area is mapped as if projected from infinity, with resulting distortion of scale away from the centre.

orthography (ɔː'θɒgrəfɪ) *n, pl* **-phies. 1** a writing system. **2a** spelling considered to be correct. **2b** the principles underlying spelling. **3** the study of spelling. **4** orthographic projection. ► **or'thographer** *or* **or'thographist** *n*

orthohydrogen (ˌɔːθəʊ'haɪdrədʒən) *n Chem.* the form of molecular hydrogen, constituting about 75 per cent of the total at normal temperatures, in which the nuclei of the atoms spin in the same direction. Compare **parahydrogen.**

orthomorphic (ˌɔːθəʊ'mɔːfɪk) *adj Geography.* another word for **conformal** (sense 2).

orthopaedics *or U.S.* **orthopedics** (ˌɔːθəʊ'piːdɪks) *n* (*functioning as sing*) **1** the branch of surgery concerned with disorders of the spine and joints and the repair of deformities of these parts. **2 dental orthopaedics.** another name for **orthodontics.** ► **ˌortho'paedic** *or U.S.* **ˌortho'pedic** *adj* ► **ˌortho'paedist** *or U.S.* **ˌortho'pedist** *n*

orthophosphate (ˌɔːθəʊ'fɒsfeɪt) *n* any salt or ester of orthophosphoric acid.

orthophosphoric acid (ˌɔːθəʊfɒs'fɒrɪk) *n* a colourless soluble solid tribasic acid used in the manufacture of fertilizers and soaps. Formula: H_3PO_4. Also called: **phosphoric acid.**

orthophosphorous acid (ˌɔːθəʊ'fɒsfərəs) *n* a white or yellowish hygroscopic crystalline dibasic acid. Formula: H_3PO_3. Also called: **phosphorous acid.**

orthopraxy ('ɔːθəˌpræksɪ) *n Theology.* the belief that right action is as important as religious faith. **[**from Greek *orthos* correct + *praxis* deed, action**]**

orthopsychiatry (ˌɔːθəʊsaɪ'kaɪətrɪ) *n* the study and treatment of mental disorders with emphasis on prevention during childhood. ► **orthopsychiatric** (ˌɔːθəʊˌsaɪkɪ'ætrɪk) *adj* ► **ˌorthopsy'chiatrist** *n*

orthopter ('ɔːθɒptə) *n* another name for **ornithopter.**

orthopteran (ɔː'θɒptərən) *n, pl* **-terans. 1** Also: **orthopteron** (*pl* **-tera** (-tərə)) any orthopterous insect. ♦ *adj* **2** another word for **orthopterous.**

orthopterous (ɔː'θɒptərəs) *or* **orthopteran** *adj* of, relating to, or belonging to the *Orthoptera,* a large order of insects, including crickets, locusts, and grasshoppers, having leathery forewings and membranous hind wings, hind legs adapted for leaping, and organs of stridulation.

orthoptic (ɔː'θɒptɪk) *adj* relating to normal binocular vision.

orthoptics (ɔː'θɒptɪks) *n* (*functioning as sing*) the science or practice of correcting defective vision, as by exercises to strengthen weak eye muscles.

orthoptist (ɔː'θɒptɪst) *n* a person who is qualified to practise orthoptics.

orthopyroxene (ˌɔːθəʊpaɪ'rɒksiːn) *n* a member of the pyroxene group of minerals having an orthorhombic crystal structure, such as enstatite and hypersthene.

orthorhombic (ˌɔːθəʊ'rɒmbɪk) *adj Crystallog.* relating to the crystal system characterized by three mutually perpendicular unequal axes. Also: **rhombic, trimetric.**

orthoscope ('ɔːθəʊˌskəʊp) *n Med., obsolete.* a 19th-century instrument for viewing the fundus of the eye through a layer of water, which eliminates distortion caused by the cornea.

orthoscopic (ˌɔːθəʊˈskɒpɪk) *adj* **1** of, relating to, or produced by normal vision. **2** yielding an undistorted image.

orthosis (ɔːˈθəʊsɪs) *n, pl* **-ses** (-siːz). an artificial or mechanical aid, such as a brace, to support or assist movement of a weak or injured part of the body.

orthostichy (ɔːˈθɒstɪkɪ) *n, pl* **-chies. 1** an imaginary vertical line that connects a row of leaves on a stem. **2** an arrangement of leaves so connected. ◆ Compare **parastichy.** [C19: from ORTHO- + Greek *stikhos*] ► **orˈthostichous** *adj*

orthotics (ɔːˈθɒtɪks) *n* (*functioning as sing*) the provision and use of artificial or mechanical aids, such as braces, to prevent or assist movement of weak or injured joints or muscles.

orthotist (ɔːˈθɒtɪst) *n* a person who is qualified to practise orthotics.

orthotone (ˈɔːθəʊˌtəʊn) *adj* **1** (of a word) having an independent accent. ◆ *n* **2** an independently accented word.

orthotropic (ˌɔːθəʊˈtrɒpɪk) *adj* **1** *Botany.* relating to or showing growth that is in direct line with the stimulus. **2** (of a material) having different elastic properties in different planes. ► **orthotropism** (ɔːˈθɒtrəˌpɪzəm) *n*

orthotropous (ɔːˈθɒtrəpəs) *adj* (of a plant ovule) growing straight during development so that the micropyle is at the apex. Compare **anatropous.**

Ortles (*Italian* ˈɔrtles) *pl n* a range of the Alps in N Italy. Highest peak: 3899 m (12 792 ft.). Also called: **Ortler** (ˈɔːtlə).

ortolan (ˈɔːtələn) *n* **1** Also called: **ortolan bunting.** a brownish Old World bunting, *Emberiza hortulana,* regarded as a delicacy. **2** any of various other small birds eaten as delicacies, esp. the bobolink. [C17: via French from Latin *hortulānus,* from *hortulus,* diminutive of *hortus* garden]

Orton (ˈɔːtᵊn) *n* **Joe** (**Kingsley**). 1933–67, British dramatist, noted for his black comedies: these include *Entertaining Mr Sloane* (1964), *Loot* (1966), and *What the Butler Saw* (1969).

orts (ɔːts) *pl n* (*sometimes sing*) *Archaic or dialect.* scraps or leavings. [C15: of Germanic origin; related to Dutch *oorete,* from *oor-* remaining + *ete* food]

Oruro (*Spanish* oˈruro) *n* a city in W Bolivia: a former silver-mining centre; university (1892); tin, copper, and tungsten. Pop.: 201 831 (1993 est.).

Orvieto (*Italian* orˈvjɛːto) *n* **1** a market town in central Italy, in Umbria: Etruscan remains. Pop.: 21 575 (1990). Latin name: **Urbs Vetus** (ˈʊəbz ˈviːtəs). **2** a light white wine from this region.

Orwell (ˈɔːwəl, -wɛl) *n* **George,** real name *Eric Arthur Blair.* 1903–50, English novelist and essayist, born in India. He is notable for his social criticism, as in *The Road to Wigan Pier* (1932); his account of his experiences of the Spanish Civil War *Homage to Catalonia* (1938); and his satirical novels *Animal Farm* (1945), an allegory on the Russian Revolution, and *1984* (1949), in which he depicts an authoritarian state of the future. ► **Orwellian** (ɔːˈwɛlɪən) *adj*

-ory[1] *suffix forming nouns.* **1** indicating a place for: *observatory.* **2** something having a specified use: *directory.* [via Old French *-orie,* from Latin *-ōrium, -ōria*]

-ory[2] *suffix forming adjectives.* of or relating to; characterized by; having the effect of: *contributory; promissory.* [via Old French *-orie,* from Latin *-ōrius*]

Oryol (*Russian* aˈrjɔl) *n* a variant spelling of **Orel.**

oryx (ˈɒrɪks) *n, pl* **-yxes** *or* **-yx.** any large African antelope of the genus *Oryx,* typically having long straight nearly upright horns. [C14: via Latin from Greek *orux* stonemason's axe, used also of the pointed horns of an antelope]

os[1] (ɒs) *n, pl* **ossa** (ˈɒsə). *Anatomy.* the technical name for **bone.** [C16: from Latin: bone; compare Greek *osteon*]

os[2] (ɒs) *n, pl* **ora** (ˈɔːrə). *Anatomy, zoology.* a mouth or mouthlike part or opening. [C18: from Latin]

os[3] (əʊs) *n, pl* **osar** (ˈəʊsɑː). another name for **esker.** [C19 *osar* (pl), from Swedish *ås* (sing) ridge]

Os *the chemical symbol for* osmium.

OS *abbrev. for:* **1** Old School. **2** Old Style (method of reckoning dates). **3** Ordinary Seaman. **4** (in Britain) Ordnance Survey. **5** outsize. **6** Old Saxon (language).

o.s. *abbrev. for:* **1** old series. **2** only son. **3** Also: **OS, O/S** out of stock. **4** Also: **OS, O/S** *Banking.* outstanding.

OSA *abbrev. for* Order of Saint Augustine.

Osage (əʊˈseɪdʒ, ˈəʊseɪdʒ) *n* **1** (*pl* **Osages** *or* **Osage**) a member of a North American Indian people formerly living in an area between the Missouri and Arkansas Rivers. **2** the language of this people, belonging to the Siouan family.

Osage orange *n* **1** a North American moraceous tree, *Maclura pomifera,* grown for hedges and ornament. **2** the warty orange-like fruit of this plant.

Osaka (əʊˈsɑːkə) *n* a port in S Japan, on S Honshu on **Osaka Bay** (an inlet of the Pacific): the third largest city in Japan (the chief commercial city during feudal times); university (1931); an industrial and commercial centre. Pop.: 2 602 352 (1995).

OSB *abbrev. for* Order of Saint Benedict.

Osborne (ˈɒzbən, -ˌbɔːn) *n* **John** (**James**). 1929–94, British dramatist. His plays include *Look Back in Anger* (1956), containing the prototype of the angry young man, Jimmy Porter, *The Entertainer* (1957), and *Inadmissible Evidence* (1964).

Osborne House (ˈɒzˌbɔːn) *n* a house near Cowes on the Isle of Wight: the favourite residence of Queen Victoria, who died there; now a convalescent home.

Oscan (ˈɒskən) *n* **1** an extinct language of ancient S Italy belonging to the Italic branch of the Indo-European family. See also **Osco-Umbrian. 2** a speaker of this language; Samnite. ◆ *adj* **3** of or relating to this language.

oscar (ˈɒskə) *n Austral. slang, rare.* cash; money. [C20: rhyming slang, from *Oscar* Asche (1871–1936), Australian actor]

Oscar (ˈɒskə) *n* **1** any of several small gold statuettes awarded annually in the United States by the Academy of Motion Picture Arts and Sciences for outstanding achievements in films. Official name: **Academy Award. 2** *Communications.* a code word for the letter *o.* [C20: sense 1 said to have been named after a remark made by an official on first seeing the statuette, that it reminded her of her uncle Oscar]

Oscar II *n* 1829–1907, king of Sweden (1872–1907) and of Norway (1872–1905).

OSCE *abbrev. for* Organization for Cooperation and Security in Europe.

oscillate (ˈɒsɪˌleɪt) *vb* **1** (*intr*) to move or swing from side to side regularly. **2** (*intr*) to waver between opinions, courses of action, etc. **3** *Physics.* to undergo or produce or cause to undergo or produce oscillation. [C18: from Latin *oscillāre* to swing, from *oscillum* a swing]

oscillating universe theory *n* the theory that the universe is oscillating between periods of expansion and contraction.

oscillation (ˌɒsɪˈleɪʃən) *n* **1** *Physics, statistics.* **1a** regular fluctuation in value, position, or state about a mean value, such as the variation in an alternating current or the regular swinging of a pendulum. **1b** a single cycle of such a fluctuation. **2** the act or process of oscillating. ► **oscillatory** (ˈɒsɪlətərɪ, -trɪ) *adj*

oscillator (ˈɒsɪˌleɪtə) *n* **1** a circuit or instrument for producing an alternating current or voltage of a required frequency. **2** any instrument for producing oscillations. **3** a person or thing that oscillates.

oscillogram (ɒˈsɪləˌɡræm) *n* the recording obtained from an oscillograph or the trace on an oscilloscope screen.

oscillograph (ɒˈsɪləˌɡrɑːf, -ˌɡræf) *n* a device for producing a graphical record of the variation of an oscillating quantity, such as an electric current. ► **oscillographic** (ɒˌsɪləˈɡræfɪk) *adj* ► **oscillography** (ˌɒsɪˈlɒɡrəfɪ) *n*

oscilloscope (ɒˈsɪləˌskəʊp) *n* an instrument for producing a representation of a rapidly changing quantity on the screen of a cathode-ray tube. The rapid changes are converted into electric signals, which are applied to plates in the cathode-ray tube. Changes in the magnitude of the potential across the plates deflect the electron beam and thus produce a trace on the screen.

oscine (ˈɒsaɪn, ˈɒsɪn) *adj* of, relating to, or belonging to the *Oscines,* a suborder of passerine birds that includes most of the songbirds. [C17: via New Latin from Latin *oscen* singing bird]

oscitancy (ˈɒsɪtənsɪ) *or* **oscitance** *n, pl* **-tancies** *or* **-tances. 1** the state of being drowsy, lazy, or inattentive. **2** the act of yawning. ◆ Also called: **ˌosciˈtation.** [C17: from Latin *oscitāre* to gape, yawn] ► **ˈoscitant** *adj*

Osco-Umbrian (ˌɒskəʊˈʌmbrɪən) *n* **1** a group of extinct languages of ancient Italy, including Oscan, Umbrian, and Sabellian, which were displaced by Latin. ◆ *adj* **2** relating to or belonging to this group of languages.

osculant (ˈɒskjʊlənt) *adj* **1** *Biology.* (of an organism or group of organisms) possessing some of the characteristics of two different taxonomic groups. **2** *Zoology.* closely joined or adhering. [C19: from Latin *ōsculārī* to kiss; see OSCULUM]

oscular (ˈɒskjʊlə) *adj* **1** *Zoology.* of or relating to an osculum. **2** of or relating to the mouth or to kissing.

osculate (ˈɒskjʊˌleɪt) *vb* **1** *Usually humorous.* to kiss. **2** (*intr*) (of an organism or group of organisms) to be intermediate between two taxonomic groups. **3** *Geometry.* to touch in osculation. [C17: from Latin *ōsculārī* to kiss; see OSCULUM]

osculation (ˌɒskjʊˈleɪʃən) *n* **1** Also called: **tacnode.** *Maths.* a point at which two branches of a curve have a common tangent, each branch extending in both directions of the tangent. **2** *Rare.* the act or an instance of kissing. ► **osculatory** (ˈɒskjʊlətərɪ, -trɪ) *adj*

osculum (ˈɒskjʊləm) *n, pl* **-la** (-lə). *Zoology.* a mouthlike aperture, esp. the opening in a sponge out of which water passes. [C17: from Latin: a kiss, little mouth, diminutive of *ōs* mouth]

OSD *abbrev. for* Order of Saint Dominic.

-ose[1] *suffix forming adjectives.* possessing; resembling: *verbose; grandiose.* [from Latin *-ōsus;* see -OUS]

-ose[2] *suffix forming nouns.* **1** indicating a carbohydrate, esp. a sugar: *lactose.* **2** indicating a decomposition product of protein: *albumose.* [from GLUCOSE]

OSF *abbrev. for* Order of Saint Francis.

Oshawa (ˈɒʃəwə) *n* a city in central Canada, in SE Ontario on Lake Ontario: motor-vehicle industry. Pop.: 129 344 (1991).

Oshogbo (əˈʃɒɡbəʊ) *n* a city in SW Nigeria: trade centre. Pop.: 476 800 (1996 est.).

OSI *abbrev. for* open systems interconnection; an international standardization model to facilitate communications among computers with different protocols.

osier (ˈəʊzɪə) *n* **1** any of various willow trees, esp. *Salix viminalis,* whose flexible branches or twigs are used for making baskets, etc. **2** a twig or branch from such a tree. **3** any of several North American dogwoods, esp. the red osier. [C14: from Old French, probably from Medieval Latin *ausēria,* perhaps of Gaulish origin; compare Breton *aoz*]

Osijek (*Serbo-Croat* ˈɔsijek) *n* a town in NE Croatia on the Drava River: under Turkish rule from 1526 to 1687. Pop.: 129 792 (1991). Ancient name: **Mursa** (ˈmʊəsə).

Osiris (əʊˈsaɪrɪs) *n* an ancient Egyptian god, ruler of the underworld and judge of the dead. ► **Oˈsirian** *adj*

-osis *suffix forming nouns.* **1** indicating a process or state: *metamorphosis.* **2** indicating a diseased condition: *tuberculosis.* Compare **-iasis. 3** indicating the formation or development of something: *fibrosis.* [from Greek, suffix used to form nouns from verbs with infinitives in *-oein* or *-oun*]

Oslo (ˈɒzləʊ; *Norwegian* ˈuslu) *n* the capital and chief port of Norway, in the southeast at the head of **Oslo Fjord** (an inlet of the Skagerrak): founded in about 1050; university (1811); a major commercial and industrial centre, producing about a quarter of Norway's total output. Pop.: 493 973 (1997 est.). Former names: **Christiania** (1624–1877), **ˌKristiˈania** (1877–1924).

Osman I (ˈɒzmən, ɒzˈmɑːn) *or* **Othman I** *n* 1259–1326, Turkish sultan; founder of the Ottoman Empire.

Osmanli (ɒzˈmænlɪ) *adj* **1** of or relating to the Ottoman Empire. ◆ *n* **2** (*pl* **-lis**) (formerly) a subject of the Ottoman Empire. **3** the Turkish language, esp. as written in Arabic letters under the Ottoman Empire. [C19: from Turkish, from OSMAN I]

osmic ('ɒzmɪk) *adj* of or containing osmium in a high valence state, esp. the tetravalent state.

osmious ('ɒzmɪəs) *adj* another word for **osmous.**

osmiridium (ˌɒzmɪ'rɪdɪəm) *n* a very hard corrosion-resistant white or grey natural alloy of osmium and iridium in variable proportions, often containing smaller amounts of platinum, ruthenium, and rhodium: used esp. in pen nibs. Also: **iridosmine.** [C19: from OSM(IUM) + IRIDIUM]

osmium ('ɒzmɪəm) *n* a very hard brittle bluish-white metal, the heaviest known element, occurring with platinum and alloyed with iridium in osmiridium: used to produce platinum alloys, mainly for pen tips and instrument pivots, as a catalyst, and in electric-light filaments. Symbol: Os; atomic no.: 76; atomic wt.: 190.2; valency: 0 to 8; relative density: 22.57; melting pt.: 3033±30°C; boiling pt.: 5012±100°C. [C19: from Greek *osmē* smell, so called from its penetrating odour]

osmium tetroxide *n* a yellowish poisonous water-soluble crystalline substance with a penetrating odour, used as a reagent and catalyst in organic synthesis. Formula: OsO_4.

osmometer (ɒz'mɒmɪtə) *n* an instrument for measuring osmotic pressure. [C20: from OSMO(SIS) + -METER] ▸ **osmometric** (ˌɒzmə'mɛtrɪk) *adj* ▸ **ˌosmo'metrically** *adv* ▸ **os'mometry** *n*

osmoregulation (ˌɒzməʊˌrɛgjʊ'leɪʃən) *n Zoology.* the adjustment of the osmotic pressure of a cell or organism in relation to the surrounding fluid.

osmose ('ɒzməʊs, -məʊz, 'ɒs-) *vb* **1** to undergo or cause to undergo osmosis. ◆ *n* **2** a former name for **osmosis.** [C19 (n): abstracted from the earlier terms *endosmose* and *exosmose;* related to Greek *ōsmos* push]

osmosis (ɒz'məʊsɪs, ɒs-) *n* **1** the passage of a solvent through a semipermeable membrane from a less concentrated to a more concentrated solution until both solutions are of the same concentration. **2** diffusion through any membrane or porous barrier, as in dialysis. **3** gradual or unconscious assimilation or adoption, as of ideas. [C19: Latinized form from OSMOSE (n), from Greek *ōsmos* push, thrust] ▸ **osmotic** (ɒz'mɒtɪk, ɒs-) *adj* ▸ **os'motically** *adv*

osmotic pressure *n* the pressure necessary to prevent osmosis into a given solution when the solution is separated from the pure solvent by a semipermeable membrane.

osmous ('ɒzməs) *adj* of or containing osmium in a low valence state, esp. the divalent state. Also: **osmious.**

osmunda (ɒz'mʌndə) *or* **osmund** ('ɒzmənd) *n* any fern of the genus *Osmunda,* such as the royal fern, having large spreading fronds: family *Osmundaceae.* [C13: from Old French *osmonde,* of unknown origin]

Osnabrück (*German* ɔsna'bryk) *n* an industrial city in NW Germany, in Lower Saxony: a member of the Hanseatic League in the Middle Ages; one of the treaties comprising the Peace of Westphalia (1648) was signed here. Pop.: 168 618 (1996 est.).

osnaburg ('ɒznəˌbɜːg) *n* a coarse plain-woven cotton used for sacks, furnishings, etc. [C16: corruption of OSNABRÜCK, where it was originally made]

osprey ('ɒsprɪ, -preɪ) *n* **1** a large broad-winged fish-eating diurnal bird of prey, *Pandion haliaetus,* with a dark back and whitish head and underparts: family *Pandioridae.* Often called (U.S. and Canadian): **fish hawk. 2** any of the feathers of various other birds, used esp. as trimming for hats. [C15: from Old French *ospres,* apparently from Latin *ossifraga,* literally: bone-breaker, from *os* bone + *frangere* to break]

ossa ('ɒsə) *n* the plural of **os**[1].

Ossa ('ɒsə) *n* a mountain in NE Greece, in E Thessaly: famous in mythology for the attempt of the twin giants, Otus and Ephialtes, to reach heaven by piling Ossa on Olympus and Pelion on Ossa. Height: 1978 m (6489 ft.).

ossein ('ɒsɪɪn) *n* a protein that forms the organic matrix of bone, constituting about 40 per cent of its matter. [C19: from Latin *osseus* bony, from *os* bone]

osseous ('ɒsɪəs) *adj* consisting of or containing bone, bony. [C17: from Latin *osseus,* from *os* bone] ▸ **'osseously** *adv*

Osset ('ɒsɪt) *n* a member of an Iranian people living in S Russia and N Georgia, chiefly in Ossetia in the Caucasus.

Ossetia (ɒ'siːʃə) *n* a region of central Asia, in the Caucasus: consists administratively of the North Ossetian Republic in Russia and the South Ossetian Autonomous Region in Georgia.

Ossetic (ɒ'sɛtɪk) *or* **Ossetian** (ɒ'siːʃən) *adj* **1** of or relating to Ossetia, its people, or their language. ◆ *n* **2** the language of the Ossets, belonging to the East Iranian branch of the Indo-European family.

Ossi ('ɒsɪ; *German* 'ɔsi) *n Informal.* a native, inhabitant, or citizen of that part of Germany that was formerly East Germany. [C20: from German *ostdeutsch* East German]

Ossian ('ɒsɪən) *n* a legendary Irish hero and bard of the 3rd century A.D. See also (James) **Macpherson.** ▸ **ˌOssi'anic** *adj*

ossicle ('ɒsɪkᵊl) *n* a small bone, esp. one of those in the middle ear. [C16: from Latin *ossiculum,* from *os* bone] ▸ **ossicular** (ɒ'sɪkjʊlə) *adj*

Ossie ('ɒzɪ) *adj, n* a variant spelling of **Aussie.**

Ossietzky (ˌɒsɪ'ɛtskɪ) *n* **Carl von** (karl fɔn). 1889–1938, German pacifist leader. He was imprisoned for revealing Germany's secret rearmament (1931–32) and again under Hitler (1933–36): Nobel peace prize 1935.

ossiferous (ɒ'sɪfərəs) *adj Geology.* containing or yielding bones: *ossiferous caves.*

ossification (ˌɒsɪfɪ'keɪʃən) *n* **1** the formation of or conversion into bone. **2** the process of ossifying or the state of being ossified.

ossifrage ('ɒsɪfrɪdʒ, -ˌfreɪdʒ) *n* an archaic name for the **lammergeier** and **osprey** (sense 1). [C17: from Latin *ossifraga* sea eagle; see OSPREY]

ossify ('ɒsɪˌfaɪ) *vb* **-fies, -fying, -fied. 1** to convert or be converted into bone. **2** (*intr*) (of habits, attitudes, etc.) to become inflexible. [C18: from French *ossifier,* from Latin *os* bone + *facere* to make] ▸ **'ossiˌfier** *n*

osso bucco ('ɒsəʊ 'bʊkəʊ) *n* a stew, originally from Italy, made with knuckle of veal, cooked in tomato sauce. [C20: from Italian: marrowbone]

ossuary ('ɒsjʊərɪ) *n, pl* **-aries.** any container for the burial of human bones, such as an urn or vault. [C17: from Late Latin *ossuārium,* from Latin *os* bone]

OST (in the U.S.) *abbrev. for* Office of Science and Technology.

osteal ('ɒstɪəl) *adj* **1** of or relating to bone or to the skeleton. **2** composed of bone; osseous. [C19: from Greek *osteon* bone]

osteichthyan (ˌɒstɪ'ɪkθɪən) *n Zool.* a technical name for a **bony fish.** [New Latin, from Greek *osteon* bone + *ikhthus* fish]

osteitis (ˌɒstɪ'aɪtɪs) *n* inflammation of a bone. ▸ **osteitic** (ˌɒstɪ'ɪtɪk) *adj*

osteitis deformans (dɪ'fɔːmənz) *n* another name for **Paget's disease** (sense 1).

Ostend (ɒs'tɛnd) *n* a port and resort in NW Belgium, in West Flanders on the North Sea. Pop.: 68 858 (1995 est.). French name: **Ostende** (ɔstɑ̃d). Flemish name: **Oostende.**

ostensible (ɒ'stɛnsɪbᵊl) *adj* **1** apparent; seeming. **2** pretended. [C18: via French from Medieval Latin *ostensibilis,* from Latin *ostendere* to show, from *ob-* before + *tendere* to extend] ▸ **osˌtensi'bility** *n* ▸ **os'tensibly** *adv*

ostensive (ɒ'stɛnsɪv) *adj* **1** obviously or manifestly demonstrative. **2** a less common word for **ostensible. 3** *Philosophy.* (of a definition) given by demonstrative means, esp. by pointing. [C17: from Late Latin *ostentīvus,* from Latin *ostendere* to show; see OSTENSIBLE] ▸ **os'tensively** *adv*

ostensory (ɒs'tɛnsərɪ) *n, pl* **-sories. R.C. Church.** another word for **monstrance.** [C18: from Medieval Latin *ostensorium;* see OSTENSIBLE]

ostentation (ˌɒstɛn'teɪʃən) *n* pretentious, showy, or vulgar display. ▸ **ˌosten'tatious** *adj* ▸ **ˌosten'tatiously** *adv*

osteo- *or before a vowel* **oste-** *combining form.* indicating bone or bones: *osteopathy.* [from Greek *osteon*]

osteoarthritis (ˌɒstɪəʊɑː'θraɪtɪs) *n* chronic inflammation of the joints, esp. those that bear weight, with pain and stiffness. Also called: **degenerative joint disease.** ▸ **osteoarthritic** (ˌɒstɪəʊɑː'θrɪtɪk) *adj, n*

osteoblast ('ɒstɪəʊˌblæst) *n* a bone-forming cell. ▸ **ˌosteo'blastic** *adj*

osteoclasis (ˌɒstɪ'ɒkləsɪs) *n* **1** surgical fracture of a bone to correct deformity. **2** absorption of bone tissue.

osteoclast ('ɒstɪəʊˌklæst) *n* **1** a surgical instrument for fracturing bone. **2** a large multinuclear cell formed in bone marrow that is associated with the normal absorption of bone. ▸ **ˌosteo'clastic** *adj*

osteogenesis (ˌɒstɪəʊ'dʒɛnɪsɪs) *n* the formation of bone. ▸ **ˌosteo'genic** *adj*

osteogenesis imperfecta (ˌɪmpə'fɛktə) *n* a hereditary disease caused by a collagen abnormality, causing fragility of the skeleton which results in fractures and deformities. Also called: **brittle bone syndrome.**

osteoid ('ɒstɪˌɔɪd) *adj* of or resembling bone; bony.

osteology (ˌɒstɪ'ɒlədʒɪ) *n* the study of the structure and function of bones. ▸ **osteological** (ˌɒstɪə'lɒdʒɪkᵊl) *adj* ▸ **ˌosteo'logically** *adv* ▸ **ˌoste'ologist** *n*

osteoma (ˌɒstɪ'əʊmə) *n, pl* **-mata** (-mətə) *or* **-mas.** a benign tumour composed of bone or bonelike tissue.

osteomalacia (ˌɒstɪəʊmə'leɪʃɪə) *n* a disease in adults characterized by softening of the bones, resulting from a deficiency of vitamin D and of calcium and phosphorus. [C19: from New Latin, from OSTEO- + Greek *malakia* softness] ▸ **ˌosteoma'lacial** *or* **osteomalacic** (ˌɒstɪəʊmə'læsɪk) *adj*

osteomyelitis (ˌɒstɪəʊˌmaɪɪ'laɪtɪs) *n* inflammation of bone marrow, caused by infection.

osteopath ('ɒstɪəˌpæθ) *or (less commonly)* **osteopathist** (ˌɒstɪ'ɒpəθɪst) *n* a person who practises osteopathy.

osteopathy (ˌɒstɪ'ɒpəθɪ) *n* a system of healing based on the manipulation of bones or other parts of the body. ▸ **osteopathic** (ˌɒstɪə'pæθɪk) *adj* ▸ **ˌosteo'pathically** *adv*

osteophyte ('ɒstɪəˌfaɪt) *n* a small abnormal bony outgrowth. ▸ **osteophytic** (ˌɒstɪə'fɪtɪk) *adj*

osteoplastic (ˌɒstɪə'plæstɪk) *adj* **1** of or relating to osteoplasty. **2** of or relating to the formation of bone.

osteoplasty ('ɒstɪəˌplæstɪ) *n, pl* **-ties.** the branch of surgery concerned with bone repair or bone grafting.

osteoporosis (ˌɒstɪəʊpɔː'rəʊsɪs) *n* porosity and brittleness of the bones due to loss of calcium from the bone matrix. [C19: from OSTEO- + PORE[2] + -OSIS] ▸ **ˌosteopo'rotic** *adj*

osteotome ('ɒstɪəˌtəʊm) *n* a surgical instrument for cutting bone, usually a special chisel.

osteotomy (ˌɒstɪ'ɒtəmɪ) *n, pl* **-mies.** the surgical cutting or dividing of bone, usually to correct a deformity.

Österreich ('øːstəraɪç) *n* the German name for **Austria.**

Ostia ('ɒstɪə) *n* an ancient town in W central Italy, originally at the mouth of the Tiber but now about 6 km (4 miles) inland: served as the port of ancient Rome; harbours built by Claudius and Trajan; ruins excavated since 1854.

ostiary ('ɒstɪərɪ) *n, pl* **-aries.** *R.C. Church.* another word for **porter**[2] (sense 4). [C15: from Latin *ostiārius* doorkeeper, from *ostium* door]

ostinato (ˌɒstɪ'nɑːtəʊ) *n* **a** a continuously reiterated musical phrase. **b** (*as modifier*): *an ostinato passage.* [Italian: from Latin *obstinātus* OBSTINATE]

ostiole ('ɒstɪˌəʊl) *n Biology.* **1** the pore in the reproductive bodies of certain algae and fungi through which spores pass. **2** any small pore. [C19: from Latin *ostiolum,* diminutive of *ostium* door] ▸ **ostiolar** ('ɒstɪələ) *or* **'ostioˌlate** *adj*

ostium ('ɒstɪəm) *n, pl* **-tia** (-tɪə). *Biology.* **1** any of the pores in sponges through which water enters the body. **2** any of the openings in the heart of an arthropod through which blood enters. **3** any similar opening. [C17: from Latin: door, entrance]

ostler *or* **hostler** ('ɒslə) *n Archaic.* a stableman, esp. one at an inn. [C15: variant of *hostler,* from HOSTEL]

Ostmark ('ɒst,mɑːk; *German* 'ɔstmark) *n* (formerly) the standard monetary unit of East Germany, divided into 100 pfennigs. [German, literally: east mark]

ostosis (ɒs'təʊsɪs) *n* the formation of bone; ossification.

Ostpreussen ('ɔstprɔysən) *n* the German name for **East Prussia.**

ostracize *or* **ostracise** ('ɒstrə,saɪz) *vb (tr)* **1** to exclude or banish (a person) from a particular group, society, etc. **2** (in ancient Greece) to punish by temporary exile. [C17: from Greek *ostrakizein* to select someone for banishment by voting on potsherds; see OSTRACON] ► **'ostracism** *n* ► **'ostra,cizable** *or* **'ostra,cisable** *adj* ► **'ostra,cizer** *or* **'ostra,ciser** *n*

ostracod ('ɒstrə,kɒd) *n* any minute crustacean of the mainly freshwater subclass *Ostracoda,* in which the body is enclosed in a transparent two-valved carapace. [C19: via New Latin from Greek *ostrakōdēs* having a shell, from *ostrakon* shell] ► **ostracodan** (,ɒstrə'kəʊdən) *or* **,ostra'codous** *adj*

ostracoderm ('ɒstrəkə,dɜːm, ɒs'trækə-) *n* any extinct Palaeozoic fishlike jawless vertebrate of the group *Ostracodermi,* characterized by a heavily armoured body. [C19: via New Latin from Greek *ostrakon* shell + -DERM]

ostracon ('ɒstrə,kɒn) *n* (in ancient Greece) a potsherd used for ostracizing. [from Greek]

Ostrava (*Czech* 'ɔstrava) *n* an industrial city in the E Czech Republic, on the River Oder: the chief coal-mining area in the Czech Republic, in Upper Silesia. Pop.: 324 813 (1996 est.).

ostrich ('ɒstrɪtʃ) *n, pl* **-triches** *or* **-trich. 1** a fast-running flightless African bird, *Struthio camelus,* that is the largest living bird, with stout two-toed feet and dark feathers, except on the naked head, neck, and legs: order *Struthioniformes* (see **ratite**). Related adj: **struthious. 2 American ostrich.** another name for **rhea. 3** a person who refuses to recognize the truth, reality, etc.: a reference to the ostrich's supposed habit of burying its head in the sand. [C13: from Old French *ostrice,* from Latin *avis* bird + Late Latin *struthio* ostrich, from Greek *strouthion*]

Ostrogoth ('ɒstrə,gɒθ) *n* a member of the eastern group of the Goths, who formed a kingdom in Italy from 493 to 552. [C17: from Late Latin *Ostrogothī,* from *ostro-* east, eastward + GOTH] ► **,Ostro'gothic** *adj*

Ostrovsky (ɒs'trɒfskɪ) *n* **Aleksandr Nikolayevich.** 1823–86, Russian dramatist, noted for his satirical comedies about the bourgeoisie. His plays include *The Bankrupt* (1849) and *The Storm* (1859), a tragedy.

Ostwald (*German* 'ɔstvalt) *n* **Wilhelm** ('vɪlhɛlm). 1853–1932, German chemist, noted for his pioneering work in catalysis. He also invented a process for making nitric acid from ammonia and developed a new theory of colour: Nobel prize for chemistry 1909.

Ostyak ('ɒstɪ,æk) *n* **1** (*pl* **-aks** *or* **-ak**) a member of an Ugrian people living in NW Siberia E of the Urals. **2** the language of this people, belonging to the Finno-Ugric family: related to Hungarian.

Osun (əʊ'sʌn) *n* a state of SW Nigeria. Capital: Oshogbo. Pop.: 2 463 185 (1995 est.). Area: 9251 sq. km (3570 sq. miles).

Oswald ('ɒzwəld) *n* **1 Lee Harvey.** 1939–63, presumed assassin (1963) of U.S. president John F. Kennedy; murdered by Jack Ruby two days later. **2 Saint.** ?605–41 A.D., king of Northumbria (634–41); with St Aidan he restored Christianity to the region. He was killed in battle by Penda of Mercia. Feast day: Aug. 5.

Oświęcim (*Polish* ɔʃ'fjɛntʃim) *n* the Polish name for **Auschwitz.**

OT *abbrev. for:* **1** occupational therapy. **2** occupational therapist. **3** Old Testament. **4** overtime.

ot- *combining form.* a variant of **oto-** before a vowel: *otalgia.*

Otago (ɒ'tɑːgəʊ) *n* a council region of New Zealand, formerly a province, founded by Scottish settlers in the south of South Island. The University of Otago (1869) in Dunedin is the oldest university in New Zealand. Chief town: Dunedin. Pop. (urban area): 191 684 (1996).

otalgia (əʊ'tældʒɪə, -dʒə) *n* the technical name for **earache.**

OTC *abbrev. for:* **1** (in Britain) Officers' Training Corps. **2** over-the-counter. **3** oxytetracycline.

OTE *abbrev. for* on-target earnings: referring to the salary a salesperson should be able to achieve.

O tempora! O mores! *Latin.* (əʊ 'tempɔːrɑː əʊ 'mɔːreɪz) *sentence substitute.* oh the times! oh the customs!: an exclamation at the evil of them.

other ('ʌðə) *determiner* **1a** (when used before a singular noun, usually preceded by *the*) the remaining (one or ones in a group of which one or some have been specified): *I'll read the other sections of the paper later.* **1b the other.** (*as pronoun; functioning as sing*): *one walks while the other rides.* **2** (a) different (one or ones from that or those already specified or understood): *he found some other house; no other man but you; other days were happier.* **3** additional; further: *there are no other possibilities.* **4** (preceded by *every*) alternate; two: *it buzzes every other minute.* **5 other than. 5a** apart from; besides: *a lady other than his wife.* **5b** different from: *he couldn't be other than what he is.* Archaic form: **other from. 6 no other.** *Archaic.* nothing else: *I can do no other.* **7 or other.** (preceded by a phrase or word with *some*) used to add vagueness to the preceding pronoun, noun, noun phrase, or adverb: *some dog or other bit him; he's somewhere or other.* **8 other things being equal.** conditions being the same or unchanged. **9 the other day, night,** etc. a few days, nights, etc., ago. **10 the other thing.** an unexpressed alternative. ◆ *pron* **11** another: *show me one other.* **12** (*pl*) additional or further ones: *the police have found two and are looking for others.* **13** (*pl*) other people or things. **14 the others.** the remaining ones (of a group): *take these and leave the others.* **15** (*pl*) different ones (from those specified or understood): *they'd rather have others, not these.* See also **each other, one another.** ◆ *adv* **16** (usually used with a negative and foll. by *than*) otherwise; differently: *they couldn't behave other than they do.* [Old English *ōther;* related to Old Saxon *āthar, ōthar,* Old High German *andar*]

USAGE See at **otherwise.**

other-directed *adj* guided by values derived from external influences. Compare **inner-directed.**

otherness ('ʌðənɪs) *n* the quality of being different or distinct in appearance, character, etc.

other ranks *pl n* (*rarely used in sing*) *Chiefly Brit.* (in the armed forces) all those who do not hold a commissioned rank.

otherwhere ('ʌðə,wɛə) *adv Archaic, poetic.* elsewhere.

otherwise ('ʌðə,waɪz) *sentence connector.* **1** or else; if not, then: *go home — otherwise your mother will worry.* ◆ *adv* **2** differently: *I wouldn't have thought otherwise.* **3** in other respects: *an otherwise hopeless situation.* ◆ *adj* **4** (*predicative*) of an unexpected nature; different: *the facts are otherwise.* ◆ *pron* **5** something different in outcome: *success or otherwise.* [C14: from Old English *on ōthre wīsan* in other manner]

USAGE The expression *otherwise than* means *in any other way than* and should not be followed by an adjective: *no-one taught by this method can be other than* (not *otherwise than*) *successful; you are not allowed to use the building otherwise than as a private dwelling.*

other world *n* the spirit world or afterlife.

otherworldly (,ʌðə'wɜːldlɪ) *adj* **1** of or relating to the spiritual or imaginative world. **2** impractical or unworldly. ► **,other'worldliness** *n*

Othin ('əʊðɪn) *n* a variant of **Odin.**

Othman ('ɒθmən, ɒθ'mɑːn) *adj, n* a variant of **Ottoman.**

Othman I *n* a variant of **Osman I.**

Otho I ('əʊθəʊ) *n* a variant of **Otto I.**

otic ('əʊtɪk, 'ɒtɪk) *adj* of or relating to the ear. [C17: from Greek *ōtikos,* from *ous* ear]

-otic *suffix forming adjectives.* **1** relating to or affected by: *sclerotic.* **2** causing: *narcotic.* [from Greek *-ōtikos*]

otiose ('əʊtɪ,əʊs, -,əʊz) *adj* **1** serving no useful purpose: *otiose language.* **2** *Rare.* indolent; lazy. [C18: from Latin *ōtiōsus* leisured, from *ōtium* leisure] ► **otiosity** (,əʊtɪ'ɒsɪtɪ) *or* **'otioseness** *n*

otitis (əʊ'taɪtɪs) *n* inflammation of the ear, esp. the middle ear (**otitis media**), with pain, impaired hearing, etc. See also **labyrinthitis.**

oto- *or before a vowel* **ot-** *combining form.* indicating the ear: *otitis; otolith.* [from Greek *ous, ōt-* ear]

otocyst ('əʊtəʊ,sɪst) *n* **1** another name for **statocyst. 2** the embryonic structure in vertebrates that develops into the inner ear in the adult. ► **,oto'cystic** *adj*

otolaryngology (,əʊtəʊ,lærɪŋ'gɒlədʒɪ) *n* the branch of medicine concerned with the ear, nose, and throat and their diseases. Sometimes called: **,oto,rhino,laryn'gology.** ► **otolaryngological** (,əʊtəʊlə,rɪŋgə'lɒdʒɪkᵊl) *adj* ► **,oto,laryn'gologist** *n*

otolith ('əʊtəʊ,lɪθ) *n* **1** any of the granules of calcium carbonate in the inner ear of vertebrates. Movement of otoliths, caused by a change in position of the animal, stimulates sensory hair cells, which convey the information to the brain. **2** another name for **statolith** (sense 1). ► **,oto'lithic** *adj*

otology (əʊ'tɒlədʒɪ) *n* the branch of medicine concerned with the ear. ► **otological** (,əʊtə'lɒdʒɪkᵊl) *adj* ► **o'tologist** *n*

O'Toole (əʊ'tuːl) *n* (**Seamus**) ('ʃeɪməs) **Peter.** born 1932, British actor, born in Ireland. His films include *Lawrence of Arabia* (1962), *The Lion in Winter* (1968), *High Spirits* (1988), and *Fairytale* (1998); stage appearances include *Jeffrey Bernard is Unwell* (1989).

otoscope ('əʊtəʊ,skəʊp) *n* a medical instrument for examining the external ear. ► **otoscopic** (,əʊtəʊ'skɒpɪk) *adj*

Otranto (*Italian* 'ɔːtranto) *n* a small port in SE Italy, in Apulia on the **Strait of Otranto:** the most easterly town in Italy; dates back to Greek times and was an important Roman port; its ruined castle was the setting of Horace Walpole's *Castle of Otranto.* Pop.: 5075 (1987 est.).

OTT *Slang abbrev. for* over the top: see **top**[1] (sense 19b).

ottar ('ɒtə) *n* a variant of **attar.**

ottava (əʊ'tɑːvə) *n* an interval of an octave. See **all'ottava.** [Italian: OCTAVE]

ottava rima ('riːmə) *n Prosody.* a stanza form consisting of eight iambic pentameter lines, rhyming a b a b a b c c. [Italian: eighth rhyme]

Ottawa ('ɒtəwə) *n* **1** the capital of Canada, in E Ontario on the Ottawa River: name changed from Bytown to Ottawa in 1854. Pop.: 313 987 (1991). **2** a river in central Canada, rising in W Quebec and flowing west, then southeast to join the St Lawrence River as its chief tributary at Montreal; forms the border between Quebec and Ontario for most of its length. Length: 1120 km (696 miles).

otter ('ɒtə) *n, pl* **-ters** *or* **-ter. 1** any freshwater carnivorous musteline mammal of the subfamily *Lutrinae,* esp. *Lutra lutra* (**Eurasian otter**), typically having smooth fur, a streamlined body, and webbed feet. **2** the fur of any of these animals. **3** Also called: **otter board.** a type of fishing tackle consisting of a weighted board to which hooked and baited lines are attached. ◆ *vb* **4** to fish using an otter. [Old English *otor;* related to Old Norse *otr,* Old High German *ottar*]

Otterburn ('ɒtə,bɜːn) *n* a village in NE England, in central Northumberland: scene of a battle (1388) in which the Scots, led by the earl of Douglas, defeated the English, led by Hotspur.

otter hound *n* a dog used for otter hunting, esp. one of a breed, now rare, that stands about 60 cm (24 in.) high and has a harsh thick coat, often greyish with tan markings.

otter shell *n* See **gaper** (sense 2).

otter shrew *n* any small otter-like amphibious mammal, esp. *Potamogale velox,* of the family *Potamogalidae* of W and central Africa: order *Insectivora* (insectivores).

otto ('ɒtəʊ) *n* another name for **attar.**
Otto (*German* 'ɔto) *n* **Rudolf** ('ru:dɔlf). 1869–1937, German theologian: his best-known work is *The Idea of the Holy* (1923).
Otto I ('ɒtəʊ) *or* **Otho I** *n* called *the Great.* 912–73 A.D., king of Germany (936–73); Holy Roman Emperor (962–73).
Otto IV *n* ?1175–1218. German king and Holy Roman Emperor (1198–1215): invaded S Italy (1210) but was later (1214) defeated by France and deposed.
Otto cycle *n* an engine cycle used on four-stroke petrol engines (**Otto engines**) in which, ideally, combustion and rejection of heat both take place at constant volume. Compare **diesel cycle.** [C19: named after Nikolaus August *Otto* (1832–91), German engineer]
ottoman ('ɒtəmən) *n, pl* **-mans. 1a** a low padded seat, usually armless, sometimes in the form of a chest. **1b** a cushioned footstool. **2** a corded fabric. [C17: from French *ottomane,* feminine of OTTOMAN]
Ottoman ('ɒtəmən) *or* **Othman** *adj* **1** *History.* of or relating to the Ottomans or the Ottoman Empire. **2** denoting or relating to the Turkish language. ◆ *n, pl* **-mans. 3** a member of a Turkish people who invaded the Near East in the late 13th century. [C17: from French, via Medieval Latin, from Arabic *Othmānī* Turkish, from Turkish *Othman* OSMAN I]
Ottoman Empire *n* the former Turkish empire in Europe, Asia, and Africa, which lasted from the late 13th century until the end of World War I. Also called: **Turkish Empire.**
Otway ('ɒtweɪ) *n* **Thomas.** 1652–85, English dramatist, noted for *The Orphan* (1680) and *Venice Preserv'd* (1682).
ou (əʊ) *n S. African slang.* a man, bloke, or chap. [Afrikaans]
OU *abbrev. for:* **1** the Open University. **2** Oxford University.
ouabain ('wɑ:bɑ:ɪn) *n* a poisonous white crystalline glycoside extracted from certain trees and used as a heart stimulant and, by some African tribes, on poison darts. Formula: $C_{29}H_{44}O_{12}.8H_2O$. [C19: from French *ouabaïo,* from Somali *waba yo* native name of tree]
Ouachita *or* **Washita** ('wɒʃɪ,tɔ:) *n* a river in the S central U.S., rising in the **Ouachita Mountains** and flowing east, south, and southeast into the Red River in E Louisiana. Length: 974 km (605 miles).
Ouagadougou (,wɑ:gə'du:gu:) *n* the capital of Burkina-Faso, on the central plateau: terminus of the railway from Abidjan (Côte d'Ivoire). Pop.: 690 000 (1993 est.).
ouananiche (,wɑ:nə'ni:ʃ) *n* a landlocked variety of the Atlantic salmon, *Salmo salar,* found in lakes in SE Canada. [from Canadian French, from Montagnais *wananish,* diminutive of *wanans* salmon]
oubaas ('əʊ,bɑ:s) *n S. African.* a person who is senior in years or rank. [Afrikaans]
Oubangui (u:'bɑ:ŋgi:, ju:'bæŋgɪ) *n* the French name for **Ubangi.**
oubliette (,u:blɪ'ɛt) *n* a dungeon the only entrance to which is through the top. [C19: from French, from *oublier* to forget]
ouch[1] (aʊtʃ) *interj* an exclamation of sharp sudden pain.
ouch[2] (aʊtʃ) *n Archaic.* **1** a brooch or clasp set with gems. **2** the setting of a gem. [C15 *an ouch,* mistaken division of C14 *a nouche,* from Old French *nouche,* of Germanic origin; compare Old High German *nusca* buckle]
oud (u:d) *n* an Arabic stringed musical instrument resembling a lute or mandolin. [from Arabic *al 'ūd,* literally: the wood. Compare LUTE[1]]
Oudh (aʊd) *n* **1** a region of N India, in central Uttar Pradesh: annexed by Britain in 1856 and a centre of the Indian Mutiny (1857–58); joined with Agra in 1877, becoming the United Provinces of Agra and Oudh in 1902, which were renamed Uttar Pradesh in 1950. **2** another name for **Ayodha.**
Oudry (*French* udri) *n* **Jean-Baptiste** (ʒɑ̃batist). 1686–1755, French rococo painter and tapestry designer, noted esp. for animal and hunting scenes.
Ouessant (wesɑ̃) *n* the French name for **Ushant.**
ought[1] (ɔ:t) *vb* (foll. by *to; takes an infinitive or implied infinitive*) used as an auxiliary **1** to indicate duty or obligation: *you ought to pay your dues.* **2** to express prudent expediency: *you ought to be more careful with your money.* **3** (usually with reference to future time) to express probability or expectation: *you ought to finish this work by Friday.* **4** to express a desire or wish on the part of the speaker: *you ought to come next week.* [Old English *āhte,* past tense of *āgan* to OWE; related to Gothic *aihta*]
USAGE In correct English, *ought* is not used with *did* or *had. I ought not to do it,* not *I didn't ought to do it; I ought not to have done it,* not *I hadn't ought to have done it.*
ought[2] (ɔ:t) *pron, adv* a variant spelling of **aught**[1].
ought[3] (ɔ:t) *n* a less common word for **nought** (zero). [C19: mistaken division of *a nought* as *an ought;* see NOUGHT]
ouguiya (u:'gi:jə) *n* the standard monetary unit of Mauritania, divided into 5 khoums.
Ouida ('wi:də) *n* real name *Marie Louise de la Ramée.* 1839–1908, British popular novelist, best known for *Under Two Flags* (1867).
Ouija board ('wi:dʒə) *n Trademark.* a board on which are marked the letters of the alphabet. Answers to questions are spelt out by a pointer or glass held by the fingertips of the participants, and are supposedly formed by spiritual forces. [C19: from French *oui* yes + German *ja* yes]
Oujda (u:dʒ'dɑ:) *n* a city in NE Morocco, near the border with Algeria: frontier post. Pop.: 146 142 (1994).
Oulu ('əulu) *n* an industrial city and port in W Finland, on the Gulf of Bothnia: university (1959). Pop.: 111 556 (1997 est.). Swedish name: **Uleåborg.**
ouma ('əʊmɑ:) *n S. African.* **1** grandmother, esp. in titular use with surname. **2** *Slang.* any elderly woman. [Afrikaans]
ounce[1] (aʊns) *n* **1** a unit of weight equal to one sixteenth of a pound (avoirdupois); 1 ounce is equal to 437.5 grains or 28.349 grams. Abbrev.: **oz. 2** a unit of weight equal to one twelfth of a Troy or Apothecaries' pound; 1 ounce is equal to 480 grains or 31.103 grams. **3** short for **fluid ounce. 4** a small portion or amount. [C14: from Old French *unce,* from Latin *uncia* a twelfth; from *ūnus* one]
ounce[2] (aʊns) *n* another name for **snow leopard.** [C18: from Old French *once,* by mistaken division of *lonce* as if *l'once,* from Latin LYNX]
oupa ('əʊpɑ:) *n S. African.* **1** grandfather, esp. in titular use with surname. **2** *Slang.* any elderly man. [Afrikaans]
our (aʊə) *determiner* **1** of, belonging to, or associated in some way with us: *our best vodka; our parents are good to us.* **2** belonging to or associated with all people or people in general: *our nearest planet is Venus.* **3** a formal word for *my* used by editors or other writers, and monarchs. **4** *Informal.* (often sarcastic) used instead of *your: are our feet hurting?* **5** *Dialect.* belonging to the family of the speaker: *it's our Sandra's birthday tomorrow.* [Old English *ūre* (genitive plural), from US; related to Old French, Old Saxon *ūser,* Old High German *unsēr,* Gothic *unsara*]
-our *suffix forming nouns.* indicating state, condition, or activity: *behaviour; labour.* [in Old French *-eur,* from Latin *-or,* noun suffix]
Our Father *n* another name for the **Lord's Prayer,** taken from its opening words.
Our Lady *n* a title given to the **Virgin Mary.**
ours (aʊəz) *pron* **1** something or someone belonging to or associated with us: *ours have blue tags.* **2 of ours.** belonging to or associated with us.
ourself (aʊə'sɛlf) *pron Archaic.* a variant of **myself,** formerly used by monarchs or editors in formal contexts.
ourselves (aʊə'sɛlvz) *pron* **1a** the reflexive form of *we* or *us.* **1b** (intensifier): *we ourselves will finish it.* **2** (*preceded by a copula*) our usual selves: *we are ourselves when we're together.* **3** *Not standard.* used instead of *we* or *us* in compound noun phrases: *other people and ourselves.*
-ous *suffix forming adjectives.* **1** having, full of, or characterized by: *dangerous; spacious; languorous.* **2** (in chemistry) indicating that an element is chemically combined in the lower of two possible valency states: *ferrous; stannous.* Compare **-ic** (sense 2). [from Old French, from Latin *-ōsus* or *-us,* Greek *-os,* adj. suffixes]
Ouse (u:z) *n* **1** Also called: **Great Ouse.** a river in E England, rising in Northamptonshire and flowing northeast to the Wash near King's Lynn; for the last 56 km (35 miles) follows mainly artificial channels. Length: 257 km (160 miles). **2** a river in NE England, in Yorkshire, formed by the confluence of the Swale and Ure Rivers: flows southeast to the Humber. Length: 92 km (57 miles). **3** a river in S England, rising in Sussex and flowing south to the English Channel. Length: 48 km (30 miles).
ousel ('u:zᵊl) *n* a variant spelling of **ouzel.**
oust (aʊst) *vb (tr)* **1** to force out of a position or place; supplant or expel. **2** *Property law.* to deprive (a person) of the possession of land. [C16: from Anglo-Norman *ouster,* from Latin *obstāre* to withstand, from *ob-* against + *stāre* to stand]
ouster ('aʊstə) *n Property law.* the act of dispossessing of freehold property; eviction; ejection.
out (aʊt) *adv* **1** (*often used as a particle*) at or to a point beyond the limits of some location; outside: *get out at once.* **2** (*particle*) out of consciousness: *she passed out at the sight of blood.* **3** (*particle*) used to indicate a burst of activity as indicated by the verb: *fever broke out.* **4** (*particle*) used to indicate obliteration of an object: *the graffiti were painted out.* **5** (*particle*) used to indicate an approximate drawing or description: *sketch out; chalk out.* **6** (*often used as a particle*) away from one's custody or ownership, esp. on hire: *to let out a cottage.* **7** on sale or on view to the public: *the book is being brought out next May.* **8** (of a young woman) in or into polite society: *Lucinda had a fabulous party when she came out.* **9** (of a jury) withdrawn to consider a verdict in private. **10** (*particle*) used to indicate exhaustion or extinction: *the sugar's run out; put the light out.* **11** (*particle*) used to indicate a goal or object achieved at the end of the action specified by the verb: *he worked it out; let's fight it out, then!* **12** (*preceded by a superlative*) existing: *the friendliest dog out.* **13** an expression in signalling, radio, etc., to indicate the end of a transmission. **14** *Austral. and N.Z. archaic.* in or to Australia or New Zealand: *he came out last year.* **15 out of. 15a** at or to a point outside: *out of his reach.* **15b** away from; not in: *stepping out of line; out of focus.* **15c** because of, motivated by: *doing it out of jealousy.* **15d** from (a material or source): *made out of plastic.* **15e** not or no longer having any of (a substance, material, etc.): *we're out of sugar.* ◆ *adj (postpositive).* **16** not or not any longer worth considering: *that plan is out because of the weather.* **17** not allowed: *smoking on duty is out.* **18** (*also prenominal*) not in vogue; unfashionable: *that sort of dress is out these days.* **19** (of a fire or light) no longer burning or providing illumination: *the fire is out.* **20** not working: *the radio's out.* **21** unconscious: *he was out for two minutes.* **22 out to it.** *Austral. and N.Z. informal.* asleep or unconscious, esp. because drunk. **23** not in; not at home: *call back later, they're out now.* **24** desirous of or intent on (something or doing something): *I'm out for as much money as I can get.* **25** Also: **out on strike.** on strike: *the machine shop is out.* **26** (in several games and sports) denoting the state in which a player is caused to discontinue active participation, esp. in some specified role. **27** used up; exhausted: *our supplies are completely out.* **28** worn into holes: *this sweater is out at the elbows.* **29** inaccurate, deficient, or discrepant: *out by six pence.* **30** not in office or authority: *his party will be out at the election.* **31** completed or concluded, as of time: *before the year is out.* **32** in flower: *the roses are out now.* **33** in arms, esp., in rebellion: *one of his ancestors was out in the Forty-Five.* **34** (*also prenominal*) being out: *the out position on the dial.* **35** *Informal.* not concealing one's homosexuality. ◆ *prep* **36** out of; out through: *he ran out the door.* **37** *Archaic or dialect.* outside; beyond: *he comes from out our domain.* ◆ *interj* **38a** an exclamation, usually peremptory, of dismissal, reproach, etc. **38b** (in wireless telegraphy) an expression used to signal that the speaker is signing off. **39 out with it.** a command to make something known immediately, without missing any details. ◆ *n* **40** *Chiefly U.S.* a method of escape from a place, difficult

situation, punishment, etc. **41** *Baseball.* an instance of the putting out of a batter; putout. **42** *Printing.* **42a** the omission of words from a printed text; lacuna. **42b** the words so omitted. **43 ins and outs.** See **in** (sense 29). ♦ *vb* **44** (*tr*) to put or throw out. **45** (*intr*) to be made known or effective despite efforts to the contrary (esp. in the phrase **will out**): *the truth will out.* **46** (*tr*) *Informal.* (of homosexuals) to expose (a public figure) as being a fellow homosexual. **47** (*tr*) *Informal.* to expose something secret, embarrassing, or unknown about (a person): *he was eventually outed as a talented goal scorer.* [Old English *ūt;* related to Old Saxon, Old Norse *ūt,* Old High German *ūz,* German *aus*]

USAGE The use of *out* as a preposition, though common in American English, is regarded as incorrect in British English: *he climbed out of* (not *out*) *a window; he went out through the door.*

out- *prefix* **1** excelling or surpassing in a particular action: *outlast; outlive.* **2** indicating an external location or situation away from the centre: *outpost; outpatient.* **3** indicating emergence, an issuing forth, etc.: *outcrop; outgrowth.* **4** indicating the result of an action: *outcome.*

outage ('aʊtɪdʒ) *n* **1** a quantity of goods missing or lost after storage or shipment. **2** a period of power failure, machine stoppage, etc.

out and about *adj* regularly going out of the house to work, take part in social activity, etc., esp. after an illness.

out and away *adv* by far.

out-and-out *adj* (*prenominal*) thoroughgoing; complete.

out-and-outer *n Slang.* **1** a thorough or thoroughgoing person or thing. **2** a person or thing that is excellent of its kind. **3** an extremist.

outasight (ˌaʊtə'saɪt) *or* **out-of-sight** *adj, interj Slang.* another term for **far-out.**

outback ('aʊtˌbæk) *n* **a** the remote bush country of Australia. **b** (*as modifier*): *outback life.*

outbalance (ˌaʊt'bæləns) *vb* another word for **outweigh.**

outbid (ˌaʊt'bɪd) *vb* **-bids, -bidding, -bid, -bidden** *or* **-bid.** (*tr*) to bid higher than; outdo in bidding.

outboard ('aʊtˌbɔːd) *adj* **1** (of a boat's engine) portable, with its own propeller, and designed to be attached externally to the stern. Compare **inboard** (sense 1). **2** in a position away from, or further away from, the centre line of a vessel or aircraft, esp. outside the hull or fuselage. ♦ *adv* **3** away from the centre line of a vessel or aircraft, esp. outside the hull or fuselage. ♦ *n* **4** an outboard motor. **5** a boat fitted with an outboard motor.

outbound ('aʊtˌbaʊnd) *adj* going out; outward bound.

outbrave (ˌaʊt'breɪv) *vb* (*tr*) **1** to surpass in bravery. **2** to confront defiantly.

outbreak ('aʊtˌbreɪk) *n* a sudden, violent, or spontaneous occurrence, esp. of disease or strife.

outbreed (ˌaʊt'briːd) *vb* **-breeds, -breeding, -bred.** **1** (*intr*) *Anthropol.* to produce offspring through sexual relations outside a particular family or tribe. **2** to breed (animals that are not closely related) or (of such animals) to be bred. ► ˌ**out'breeding** *n*

outbuilding ('aʊtˌbɪldɪŋ) *n* a building subordinate to but separate from a main building; outhouse.

outburst ('aʊtˌbɜːst) *n* **1** a sudden and violent expression of emotion. **2** an explosion or eruption.

outcast ('aʊtˌkɑːst) *n* **1** a person who is rejected or excluded from a social group. **2** a vagabond or wanderer. **3** anything thrown out or rejected. ♦ *adj* **4** rejected, abandoned, or discarded; cast out.

outcaste ('aʊtˌkɑːst) *n* **1** a person who has been expelled from a caste. **2** a person having no caste. ♦ *vb* **3** (*tr*) to cause (someone) to lose his caste.

outclass (ˌaʊt'klɑːs) *vb* (*tr*) **1** to surpass in class, quality, etc. **2** to defeat easily.

outcome ('aʊtˌkʌm) *n* something that follows from an action, dispute, situation, etc.; result; consequence.

outcrop *n* ('aʊtˌkrɒp). **1** part of a rock formation or mineral vein that appears at the surface of the earth. **2** an emergence; appearance. ♦ *vb* (ˌaʊt'krɒp), **-crops, -cropping, -cropped.** (*intr*) **3** (of rock strata, mineral veins, etc.) to protrude through the surface of the earth. **4** another word for **crop out.**

outcross *vb* (ˌaʊt'krɒs). **1** to breed (animals or plants of the same breed but different strains). ♦ *n* ('aʊtˌkrɒs). **2** an animal or plant produced as a result of outcrossing. **3** an act of outcrossing.

outcry *n* ('aʊtˌkraɪ), *pl* **-cries.** **1** a widespread or vehement protest. **2** clamour; uproar. **3** *Commerce.* a method of trading in which dealers shout out bids and offers at a prearranged meeting: *sale by open outcry.* ♦ *vb* (ˌaʊt'kraɪ), **-cries, -crying, -cried.** **4** (*tr*) to cry louder or make more noise than (someone or something).

outdate (ˌaʊt'deɪt) *vb* (*tr*) (of something new) to cause (something else) to become old-fashioned or obsolete.

outdated (ˌaʊt'deɪtɪd) *adj* old-fashioned or obsolete.

outdistance (ˌaʊt'dɪstəns) *vb* (*tr*) to leave far behind.

outdo (ˌaʊt'duː) *vb* **-does, -doing, -did, -done.** (*tr*) to surpass or exceed in performance or execution.

outdoor ('aʊt'dɔː) *adj* (*prenominal*) taking place, existing, or intended for use in the open air: *outdoor games; outdoor clothes.* Also: **out-of-door.**

outdoor relief *n* another name for **out-relief.**

outdoors (ˌaʊt'dɔːz) *adv* **1** Also: **out-of-doors.** in the open air; outside. ♦ *n* **2** the world outside or far away from human habitation: *the great outdoors.*

outer ('aʊtə) *adj* (*prenominal*) **1** being or located on the outside; external. **2** further from the middle or central part. ♦ *n* **3** *Archery.* **3a** the white outermost ring on a target. **3b** a shot that hits this ring. **4** *Austral.* the unsheltered part of the spectator area at a sports ground. **5 on the outer.** *Austral. and N.Z. informal.* excluded or neglected.

outer bar *n* (in England) a collective name for junior barristers who plead from outside the bar of the court. Compare **Queen's Counsel.**

outer garments *pl n* the garments that are worn over a person's other clothes.

Outer Hebrides *pl n* See **Hebrides.**

Outer Mongolia *n* the former name (until 1924) of the republic of **Mongolia.**

outermost ('aʊtəˌməʊst) *adj* furthest from the centre or middle; outmost.

outer planet *n* any of the planets Jupiter, Saturn, Uranus, Neptune, and Pluto, whose orbit lies outside the asteroid belt.

outer space *n* (*not in technical usage*) any region of space beyond the atmosphere of the earth.

outface (ˌaʊt'feɪs) *vb* (*tr*) **1** to face or stare down. **2** to confront boldly or defiantly.

outfall ('aʊtˌfɔːl) *n* the end of a river, sewer, drain, etc., from which it discharges.

outfield ('aʊtˌfiːld) *n* **1** *Cricket.* the area of the field relatively far from the pitch; the deep. Compare **infield** (sense 1). **2** *Baseball.* **2a** the area of the playing field beyond the lines connecting first, second, and third bases. **2b** the positions of the left fielder, centre fielder, and right fielder taken collectively. Compare **infield** (sense 2). **3** *Agriculture.* farmland most distant from the farmstead. ► **'outˌfielder** *n*

outfighting ('aʊtˌfaɪtɪŋ) *n* fighting at a distance and not at close range.

outfit ('aʊtˌfɪt) *n* **1** a set of articles or equipment for a particular task, occupation, etc. **2** a set of clothes, esp. a carefully selected one. **3** *Informal.* any group or association regarded as a cohesive unit, such as a military company, business house, etc. **4** the act of fitting out. **5** *Canadian.* (formerly) the annual shipment of trading goods and supplies sent by a fur company to its trading posts. ♦ *vb* **-fits, -fitting, -fitted.** **6** to furnish or be furnished with an outfit, equipment, etc.

outfitter ('aʊtˌfɪtə) *n Chiefly Brit.* **1** a shop that sells men's clothes. **2** a person who provides outfits.

outflank (ˌaʊt'flæŋk) *vb* (*tr*) **1** to go around the flank of (an opposing army). **2** to get the better of.

outflow ('aʊtˌfləʊ) *n* **1** anything that flows out, such as liquid, money, ideas, etc. **2** the amount that flows out. **3** the act or process of flowing out.

outfoot (ˌaʊt'fʊt) *vb* (*tr*) **1** (of a boat) to go faster than (another boat). **2** to surpass in running, dancing, etc.

outfox (ˌaʊt'fɒks) *vb* (*tr*) to surpass in guile or cunning.

outgas (ˌaʊt'gæs) *vb* **-gases** *or* **-gasses, -gassing, -gassed.** to undergo or cause to undergo the removal of adsorbed or absorbed gas from solids, often by heating in free space.

outgeneral (ˌaʊt'dʒenərəl) *vb* **-als, -alling, -alled** *or U.S.* **-als, -aling, -aled.** (*tr*) to surpass in generalship.

outgo *vb* (ˌaʊt'gəʊ), **-goes, -going, -went, -gone.** **1** (*tr*) to exceed or outstrip. ♦ *n* ('aʊtˌgəʊ). **2** cost; outgoings; outlay. **3** something that goes out; outflow.

outgoing ('aʊtˌgəʊɪŋ) *adj* **1** departing; leaving. **2** leaving or retiring from office: *the outgoing chairman.* **3** friendly and sociable. ♦ *n* **4** the act of going out.

outgoings ('aʊtˌgəʊɪŋz) *pl n* expenditure.

out-group *n Sociol.* persons excluded from an in-group.

outgrow (ˌaʊt'grəʊ) *vb* **-grows, -growing, -grew, -grown.** (*tr*) **1** to grow too large for (clothes, shoes, etc.). **2** to lose (a habit, idea, reputation, etc.) in the course of development or time. **3** to grow larger or faster than.

outgrowth ('aʊtˌgrəʊθ) *n* **1** a thing growing out of a main body. **2** a development, result, or consequence. **3** the act of growing out.

outgun (ˌaʊt'gʌn) *vb* (*tr*) **-guns, -gunning, -gunned.** **1** to surpass in fire power. **2** to surpass in shooting. **3** *Informal.* to surpass or excel.

outhaul ('aʊtˌhɔːl) *n Nautical.* a line or cable for tightening the foot of a sail by hauling the clew out along the boom or yard. Also: **'outˌhauler.**

out-Herod *vb* (*tr*) to surpass in evil, excesses, or cruelty. [C17: originally *out-Herod Herod,* from Shakespeare's *Hamlet* (act 3, scene 2); see also HEROD: portrayed in medieval mystery plays as a ranting tyrant]

outhouse ('aʊtˌhaʊs) *n* **1** a building near to, but separate from, a main building; outbuilding. **2** *U.S.* an outside lavatory.

outing ('aʊtɪŋ) *n* **1** a short outward and return journey; trip; excursion. **2** *Informal.* the naming by homosexuals of other prominent homosexuals, often against their will.

outjockey (ˌaʊt'dʒɒkɪ) *vb* (*tr*) to outwit by deception.

outland *adj* ('aʊtˌlænd, -lənd). **1** outlying or distant. **2** *Archaic.* foreign; alien. ♦ *n* ('aʊtˌlænd). **3** (*usually pl*) the outlying areas of a country or region.

outlander ('aʊtˌlændə) *n* a foreigner or stranger.

outlandish (aʊt'lændɪʃ) *adj* **1** grotesquely unconventional in appearance, habits, etc. **2** *Archaic.* foreign. ► **out'landishly** *adv* ► **out'landishness** *n*

outlaw ('aʊtˌlɔː) *n* **1** (formerly) a person excluded from the law and deprived of its protection. **2** any fugitive from the law, esp. a habitual transgressor. **3** a wild or untamed beast. ♦ *vb* (*tr*) **4** to put (a person) outside the law and deprive of its protection. **5** (in the U.S.) to deprive (a contract) of legal force. **6** to ban.

ˌ**out'box** *vb*
ˌ**out'dance** *vb*
ˌ**out'fight** *vb,* **-'fights, -'fighting, -'fought.**
ˌ**out'fly** *vb,* **-'flies, -'flying, -'flew, -'flown.**
ˌ**out'guess** *vb*
ˌ**out'hit** *vb,* **-'hits, -'hitting, -'hit.**
ˌ**out'last** *vb*

outlawry ('aʊtˌlɔːrɪ) *n, pl* **-ries.** 1 the act of outlawing or the state of being outlawed. 2 disregard for the law.

outlay *n* ('aʊtˌleɪ). 1 an expenditure of money, effort, etc. ◆ *vb* (ˌaʊt'leɪ), **-lays, -laying, -laid.** 2 (*tr*) to spend (money).

outlet ('aʊtlɛt, -lɪt) *n* 1 an opening or vent permitting escape or release. 2 a means for release or expression of emotion, creative energy, etc. **3a** a market for a product or service. **3b** a commercial establishment retailing the goods of a particular producer or wholesaler. **4a** a channel that drains a body of water. **4b** the mouth of a river. 5 a point in a wiring system from which current can be taken to supply electrical devices. 6 *Anatomy.* the beginning or end of a passage, esp. the lower opening of the pelvis (**pelvic outlet**).

outlier ('aʊtˌlaɪə) *n* 1 an outcrop of rocks that is entirely surrounded by older rocks. 2 a person, thing, or part situated away from a main or related body. 3 a person who lives away from his place of work, duty, etc. 4 *Statistics.* a point in a sample widely separated from the main cluster of points in the sample. See **scatter diagram.**

outline ('aʊtˌlaɪn) *n* 1 a preliminary or schematic plan, draft, account, etc. 2 (*usually pl*) the important features of an argument, theory, work, etc. 3 the line by which an object or figure is or appears to be bounded. **4a** a drawing or manner of drawing consisting only of external lines. **4b** (*as modifier*): *an outline map.* ◆ *vb* (*tr*) 5 to draw or display the outline of. 6 to give the main features or general idea of.

outlive (ˌaʊt'lɪv) *vb* (*tr*) 1 to live longer than (someone). 2 to live beyond (a date or period): *he outlived the century.* 3 to live through (an experience).

outlook ('aʊtˌlʊk) *n* 1 a mental attitude or point of view. 2 the probable or expected condition or outcome of something: *the weather outlook.* 3 the view from a place. 4 view or prospect. 5 the act or state of looking out.

outlying ('aʊtˌlaɪɪŋ) *adj* distant or remote from the main body or centre, as of a town or region.

outman (ˌaʊt'mæn) *vb* **-mans, -manning, -manned.** (*tr*) 1 to surpass in manpower. 2 to surpass in manliness.

outmanoeuvre *or U.S.* **outmaneuver** (ˌaʊtmə'nuːvə) *vb* (*tr*) to secure a strategic advantage over by skilful manoeuvre.

outmoded (ˌaʊt'məʊdɪd) *adj* 1 no longer fashionable or widely accepted. 2 no longer practical or usable. ▸ **ˌout'modedly** *adv* ▸ **ˌout'modedness** *n*

outmost ('aʊtˌməʊst) *adj* another word for **outermost.**

outness ('aʊtnɪs) *n* 1 the state or quality of being external. 2 outward expression.

outnumber (ˌaʊt'nʌmbə) *vb* (*tr*) to exceed in number.

out of bounds *adj* (*postpositive*), *adv* 1 (often foll. by *to*) not to be entered (by); barred (to): *out of bounds to civilians.* 2 outside specified or prescribed limits.

out of date *adj* (**out-of-date** *when prenominal*), *adv* no longer valid, current, or fashionable; outmoded.

out-of-door *adj* (*prenominal*) another term for **outdoor.**

out-of-doors *adv, adj* (*postpositive*) in the open air; outside. Also: **outdoors.**

out of pocket *adj* (**out-of-pocket** *when prenominal*). 1 (*postpositive*) having lost money, as in a commercial enterprise. 2 without money to spend. 3 (*prenominal*) (of expenses) unbudgeted and paid for in cash.

out-of-the-body experience *n* a vivid feeling of being detached from one's body, usually involving observing it and its environment from nearby. Abbrev.: **OBE** *or* **OOBE.** Compare **near-death experience.**

out-of-the-way *adj* (*prenominal*) 1 distant from more populous areas. 2 uncommon or unusual.

outpatient ('aʊtˌpeɪʃənt) *n* a nonresident hospital patient. Compare **inpatient.**

outplacement ('aʊtˌpleɪsmənt) *n* a service that offers counselling and careers advice, esp. to redundant executives, which is paid for by their previous employer.

outpoint (ˌaʊt'pɔɪnt) *vb* (*tr*) 1 to score more points than. 2 *Nautical.* to sail closer to the wind (point higher) than (another sailing vessel).

outport ('aʊtˌpɔːt) *n* 1 *Chiefly Brit.* a subsidiary port built in deeper water than the original port. 2 *Canadian.* one of the many isolated fishing villages located in the bays and other indentations of the Newfoundland coast.

outporter ('aʊtˌpɔːtə) *n Canadian.* an inhabitant or native of a Newfoundland outport.

outpost ('aʊtˌpəʊst) *n* 1 *Military.* **1a** a position stationed at a distance from the area occupied by a major formation. **1b** the troops assigned to such a position. 2 an outlying settlement or position. 3 a limit or frontier.

outpour *n* ('aʊtˌpɔː). 1 the act of flowing or pouring out. 2 something that pours out. ◆ *vb* (ˌaʊt'pɔː). 3 to pour or cause to pour out freely or rapidly.

outpouring ('aʊtˌpɔːrɪŋ) *n* 1 a passionate or exaggerated outburst; effusion. 2 another word for **outpour** (senses 1, 2).

output ('aʊtˌpʊt) *n* 1 the act of production or manufacture. 2 Also called: **outturn.** the amount produced, as in a given period: *a high weekly output.* 3 the material produced, manufactured, yielded, etc. 4 *Electronics.* **4a** the power, voltage, or current delivered by a circuit or component. **4b** the point at which the signal is delivered. 5 the power, energy, or work produced by an engine or a system. 6 *Computing.* **6a** the information produced by a computer. **6b** the operations and devices involved in producing this information. See also **input/output.** 7 (*modifier*) of or relating to electronic, computer, or other output: *output signal; output device; output tax.* ◆ *vb* **-puts, -putting, -putted** *or* **-put.** (*tr*) 8 *Computing.* to cause (data) to be emitted as output.

outrage ('aʊtˌreɪdʒ) *n* 1 a wantonly vicious or cruel act. 2 a gross violation of decency, morality, honour, etc. 3 profound indignation, anger, or hurt, caused by such an act. ◆ *vb* (*tr*) 4 to cause profound indignation, anger, or resentment in. 5 to offend grossly (feelings, decency, human dignity, etc.). 6 to commit an act of wanton viciousness, cruelty, or indecency on. 7 a euphemistic word for **rape**[1]. [C13 (meaning: excess): via French from *outré* beyond, from Latin *ultrā*]

outrageous (aʊt'reɪdʒəs) *adj* 1 being or having the nature of an outrage. 2 grossly offensive to decency, authority, etc. 3 violent or unrestrained in behaviour or temperament. 4 extravagant or immoderate. ▸ **out'rageously** *adv* ▸ **out'rageousness** *n*

Outram ('uːtrəm) *n* Sir **James.** 1803–63, British soldier and administrator in India; he participated in the relief of Lucknow (1857) during the Indian Mutiny.

outrank (ˌaʊt'ræŋk) *vb* (*tr*) 1 to be of higher rank than. 2 to take priority over.

outré ('uːtreɪ) *adj* deviating from what is usual or proper. [C18: from French past participle of *outrer* to pass beyond]

outreach *vb* (ˌaʊt'riːtʃ). 1 (*tr*) to surpass in reach. 2 (*tr*) to go beyond. 3 to reach or cause to reach out. ◆ *n* ('aʊtˌriːtʃ). 4 the act or process of reaching out. 5 the length or extent of reach. 6 *Social Welfare.* any systematic effort to provide unsolicited and predefined help to groups or individuals deemed to need it. 7 (*modifier*) (of welfare work or workers) propagating take-up of a service by seeking out appropriate people and persuading them to accept what is judged good for them. Compare **detached** (sense 3).

out-relief *n English history.* money given to poor people not living in a workhouse. Also called: **outdoor relief.**

outride *vb* (ˌaʊt'raɪd), **-rides, -riding, -rode, -ridden.** (*tr*) 1 to outdo by riding faster, farther, or better than. 2 (of a vessel) to ride out (a storm). ◆ *n* ('aʊtˌraɪd). 3 *Prosody, rare.* an extra unstressed syllable within a metrical foot.

outrider ('aʊtˌraɪdə) *n* 1 a person who goes ahead of a car, group of people, etc., to ensure a clear passage. 2 a person who goes in advance to investigate, discover a way, etc.; scout. 3 a person who rides in front of or beside a carriage, esp. as an attendant or guard. 4 *U.S.* a mounted herdsman.

outrigger ('aʊtˌrɪgə) *n* 1 a framework for supporting a pontoon outside and parallel to the hull of a boat to provide stability. 2 a boat equipped with such a framework, esp. one of the canoes of the South Pacific. 3 any projecting framework attached to a boat, aircraft, building, etc., to act as a support. 4 *Rowing.* another name for **rigger** (sense 2). [C18: from OUT- + RIG[1] + -ER[1]; perhaps influenced by archaic *outligger* outlier]

outright *adj* ('aʊtˌraɪt). (*prenominal*) 1 without qualifications or limitations: *outright ownership.* 2 complete; total: *an outright lie.* 3 straightforward; direct: *an outright manner.* ◆ *adv* (ˌaʊt'raɪt). 4 without restrictions: *buy outright.* 5 without reservation or concealment: *ask outright.* 6 instantly: *he was killed outright.* 7 *Obsolete.* straight ahead or out.

outrun (ˌaʊt'rʌn) *vb* **-runs, -running, -ran, -run.** (*tr*) 1 to run faster, farther, or better than. 2 to escape from by or as if by running. 3 to go beyond; exceed.

outrunner ('aʊtˌrʌnə) *n* 1 an attendant who runs in front of a carriage, etc. 2 the leading dog in a sled team.

outrush ('aʊtˌrʌʃ) *n* a flowing or rushing out.

outsell (ˌaʊt'sɛl) *vb* **-sells, -selling, -sold.** (*tr*) to sell or be sold in greater quantities than.

outsert ('aʊtˌsɜːt) *n* another word for **wrapround** (sense 5). [C20: based on INSERT]

outset ('aʊtˌsɛt) *n* a start; beginning (esp. in the phrase **from** (*or* **at**) **the outset**).

outshine (ˌaʊt'ʃaɪn) *vb* **-shines, -shining, -shone.** 1 (*tr*) to shine more brightly than. 2 (*tr*) to surpass in excellence, beauty, wit, etc. 3 (*intr*) *Rare.* to emit light.

outshoot *vb* (ˌaʊt'ʃuːt), **-shoots, -shooting, -shot.** 1 (*tr*) to surpass or excel in shooting. 2 to go or extend beyond (something). ◆ *n* ('aʊtˌʃuːt). 3 a thing that projects or shoots out. 4 the act or state of shooting out or protruding.

outside *prep* (ˌaʊt'saɪd). 1 (sometimes foll. by *of*) on or to the exterior of: *outside the house.* 2 beyond the limits of: *outside human comprehension.* 3 apart from; other than: *no-one knows outside you and me.* ◆ *adj* ('aʊtˌsaɪd). 4 (*prenominal*) situated on the exterior: *an outside lavatory.* 5 remote; unlikely: *an outside chance.* 6 not a member of. 7 the greatest possible or probable (prices, odds, etc.). ◆ *adv* (ˌaʊt'saɪd). 8 outside a specified thing or place; out of doors. 9 *Slang.* not in prison. ◆ *n* ('aʊt'saɪd). 10 the external side or surface: *the outside of the garage.* 11 the external appearance or aspect. 12 the exterior or outer part of something. 13 (of a path, pavement, etc.) the side nearest the road or away from a wall or building. 14 *Sport.* an outside player, as in football. 15 (*pl*) the outer sheets of a ream of paper. 16 *Canadian.* (in the north) the settled parts of Canada. 17 **at the outside.** *Informal.* at the most or at the greatest extent: *two days at the outside.* 18 **outside in.** another term for **inside out.** See **inside** (sense 5).

USAGE The use of *outside of* and *inside of*, although fairly common, is generally thought to be incorrect or non-standard: *she waits outside* (not *outside of*) *the school.*

outside broadcast *n Radio, television.* a broadcast not made from a studio.

outside director *n* a director of a company who is not employed by that company but is often employed by a holding or associated company.

outsider (ˌaʊt'saɪdə) *n* 1 a person or thing excluded from or not a member of a set, group, etc. 2 a contestant, esp. a horse, thought unlikely to win in a race. 3 *Canadian.* (in the north) a person who does not live in the Arctic regions.

ˌout'match *vb*
ˌout'matched *adj*
ˌout'pace *vb*
ˌoutper'form *vb*
ˌout'play *vb*

outside work *n* work done off the premises of a business.
out sister *n* a member of a community of nuns who performs tasks in the outside world on behalf of the community.
outsize ('aʊt,saɪz) *adj* **1** Also: **'out,sized.** very large or larger than normal: *outsize tomatoes.* ◆ *n* **2** something outsize, such as a garment or person. **3** (*modifier*) relating to or dealing in outsize clothes: *an outsize shop.*
outskirts ('aʊt,skɜːts) *pl n* (*sometimes sing*) outlying or bordering areas, districts, etc., as of a city.
outsmart (,aʊt'smɑːt) *vb* (*tr*) *Informal.* to get the better of; outwit.
outsole ('aʊt,səʊl) *n* the outermost sole of a shoe.
outsource (,aʊt'sɔːs) *vb* (*tr*) (of a manufacturer) **1** to subcontract (work) to another company. **2** to buy in (components for a product) rather than manufacture them.
outspan *S. African.* ◆ *n* ('aʊt,spæn). **1** an area on a farm kept available for travellers to rest and refresh animals. **2** the act of unharnessing or unyoking. ◆ *vb* (,aʊt'spæn), **-spans, -spanning, -spanned. 3** to unharness or unyoke (animals). [C19: partial translation of Afrikaans *uitspan,* from *uit* out + *spannen* to stretch]
outspoken (,aʊt'spəʊkən) *adj* **1** candid or bold in speech. **2** said or expressed with candour or boldness. ► **out'spokenness** *adj*
outspread *vb* (,aʊt'sprɛd), **-spreads, -spreading, -spread. 1** to spread out or cause to spread out. ◆ *adj* ('aʊt'sprɛd). **2** spread or stretched out. **3** scattered or diffused widely. ◆ *n* ('aʊt,sprɛd). **4** a spreading out.
outstand (,aʊt'stænd) *vb* **-stands, -standing, -stood. 1** (*intr*) to be outstanding or excel. **2** (*intr*) *Nautical.* to stand out to sea. **3** (*tr*) *Archaic.* to last beyond.
outstanding (,aʊt'stændɪŋ) *adj* **1** superior; excellent; distinguished. **2** prominent, remarkable, or striking. **3** still in existence; unsettled, unpaid, or unresolved. **4** (of shares, bonds, etc.) issued and sold. **5** projecting or jutting upwards or outwards. ► **,out'standingly** *adv*
outstation ('aʊt,steɪʃən) *n* **1** a station or post in a remote region. **2** in a radio network, any station other than the base station. **3** *Austral.* a station set up independently of the head station of a large sheep or cattle farm. **4 outstation movement.** *Austral.* the programme to resettle native Australians on their tribal lands. ◆ *adv* **5** (in Malaysia) away from (the speaker's) town or area.
outstay (,aʊt'steɪ) *vb* (*tr*) **1** to stay longer than. **2** to stay beyond (a limit). **3 outstay one's welcome.** See **overstay** (sense 4).
outstretch (,aʊt'strɛtʃ) *vb* (*tr*) **1** to extend or expand; stretch out. **2** to stretch or extend beyond.
outstrip (,aʊt'strɪp) *vb* **-strips, -stripping, -stripped.** (*tr*) **1** to surpass in a sphere of activity, competition, etc. **2** to be or grow greater than. **3** to go faster than and leave behind.
outswing ('aʊt,swɪŋ) *n Cricket.* the movement of a ball from leg to off through the air. Compare **inswing.** ► **'out,swinger** *n*
outtake ('aʊt,teɪk) *n* an unreleased take from a recording session, film, or television programme.
outthink (,aʊt'θɪŋk) *vb* **-thinks, -thinking, -thought.** (*tr*) **1** to outdo in thinking. **2** to outwit.
out-tray *n* (in an office) a tray for outgoing correspondence, documents, etc.
outturn ('aʊt,tɜːn) *n* **1** another word for **output** (sense 2). **2** outcome; result.
outvote (,aʊt'vəʊt) *vb* (*tr*) to defeat by a majority of votes.
outward ('aʊtwəd) *adj* **1** of or relating to what is apparent or superficial. **2** of or relating to the outside of the body. **3** belonging or relating to the external, as opposed to the mental, spiritual, or inherent. **4** of, relating to, or directed towards the outside or exterior. **5** (of a ship, part of a voyage, etc.) leaving for a particular destination. **6 the outward man. 6a** the body as opposed to the soul. **6b** *Facetious.* clothing. ◆ *adv* **7** (of a ship) away from port. **8** a variant of **outwards.** ◆ *n* **9** the outward part; exterior. ► **'outwardness** *n*
Outward Bound *n Trademark.* (in Britain) a scheme to provide adventure training for young people.
outwardly ('aʊtwədlɪ) *adv* **1** in outward appearance. **2** with reference to the outside or outer surface; externally.
outwards ('aʊtwədz) *or* **outward** *adv* towards the outside; out.
outwash ('aʊt,wɒʃ) *n* a mass of gravel, sand, etc., carried and deposited by the water derived from melting glaciers.
outwear (,aʊt'wɛə) *vb* **-wears, -wearing, -wore, -worn.** (*tr*) **1** to use up or destroy by wearing. **2** to last or wear longer than. **3** to outlive, outgrow, or develop beyond. **4** to deplete or exhaust in strength, determination, etc.
outweigh (,aʊt'weɪ) *vb* (*tr*) **1** to prevail over; overcome: *his desire outweighed his discretion.* **2** to be more important or significant than. **3** to be heavier than.
outwit (,aʊt'wɪt) *vb* **-wits, -witting, -witted.** (*tr*) **1** to get the better of by cunning or ingenuity. **2** *Archaic.* to be of greater intelligence than.
outwith (,aʊt'wɪθ) *prep Scot.* outside; beyond.
outwork *n* ('aʊt,wɜːk). **1** (*often pl*) defences which lie outside main defensive works. **2** work performed away from the factory, office, etc., by which it has been commissioned. ◆ *vb* (,aʊt'wɜːk), **-works, -working, -worked** *or* **-wrought.** (*tr*) **3** to work better, harder, etc., than. **4** to work out to completion. ► **'out,worker** *n*
outworn ('aʊtwɔːn, ,aʊt'wɔːn) *adj* no longer accepted, used, believed, etc.; obsolete or outmoded.
ouzel *or* **ousel** ('uːzᵊl) *n* **1** short for **ring ouzel** or **water ouzel** (see **dipper**). **2** an archaic name for the (European) **blackbird.** [Old English *ōsle,* related to Old High German *amsala* (German *Amsel*), Latin *merula* MERLE¹]
ouzo ('uːzəʊ) *n* a strong aniseed-flavoured spirit from Greece. [Modern Greek *ouzon,* of obscure origin]

ova ('əʊvə) *n* the plural of **ovum.**
oval ('əʊvᵊl) *adj* **1** having the shape of an ellipse or ellipsoid. ◆ *n* **2** anything that is oval in shape, such as a sports ground. [C16: from Medieval Latin *ōvālis,* from Latin *ōvum* egg] ► **'ovally** *adv* ► **'ovalness** *or* **ovality** (əʊ'vælɪtɪ) *n*
Oval ('əʊvᵊl) *n* **the.** a cricket ground in south London, in the borough of Lambeth.
Oval Office *n* **the. 1** the private office of the president of the U.S., a large oval room in the White House. **2** the U.S. presidency.
ovals of Cassini (kə'siːnɪ) *pl n Maths.* the locus of a point *x,* whose distance from two fixed points, *a* and *b,* is such that |*x*–*a*| |*x*–*b*| is a constant. [C18: named after J. D. *Cassini* (1625–1712), Italian-French astronomer and mathematician]
Ovambo (əʊ'væmbəʊ, ɔː'vambɔː) *n* **1** (*pl* **-bo** *or* **-bos**) a member of a mixed Khoikhoi and Negroid people of southern Africa, living chiefly in N Namibia: noted for their skill in metal work. **2** the language of this people, belonging to the Bantu group of the Niger-Congo family.
ovariectomy (əʊ,vɛərɪ'ɛktəmɪ) *n, pl* **-mies.** *Surgery.* another name for **oophorectomy.**
ovariotomy (əʊ,vɛərɪ'ɒtəmɪ) *n, pl* **-mies.** surgical incision into an ovary. Compare **oophorectomy.**
ovaritis (,əʊvə'raɪtɪs) *n* inflammation of an ovary; oophoritis.
ovary ('əʊvərɪ) *n, pl* **-ries. 1** either of the two female reproductive organs, which produce ova and secrete oestrogen hormones. **2** the corresponding organ in vertebrate and invertebrate animals. **3** *Botany.* the hollow basal region of a carpel containing one or more ovules. In some plants the carpels are united to form a single compound ovary. [C17: from New Latin *ōvārium,* from Latin *ōvum* egg] ► **ovarian** (əʊ'vɛərɪən) *adj*
ovate ('əʊveɪt) *adj* **1** shaped like an egg. **2** (esp. of a leaf) shaped like the longitudinal section of an egg, with the broader end at the base. Compare **obovate.** [C18: from Latin *ōvātus* egg-shaped; see OVUM] ► **'ovately** *adv*
ovation (əʊ'veɪʃən) *n* **1** an enthusiastic reception, esp. one of prolonged applause: *a standing ovation.* **2** a victory procession less glorious than a triumph awarded to a Roman general. [C16: from Latin *ovātiō* rejoicing, from *ovāre* to exult] ► **o'vational** *adj*
ovel ('ɒvəl) *n Judaism.* a mourner, esp. during the first seven days after a death. See also **shivah.** [from Hebrew]
oven ('ʌvᵊn) *n* **1** an enclosed heated compartment or receptacle for baking or roasting food. **2** a similar device, usually lined with a refractory material, used for drying substances, firing ceramics, heat-treating, etc. ◆ *vb* **3** (*tr*) to cook in an oven. [Old English *ofen;* related to Old High German *ofan,* Old Norse *ofn*] ► **'oven-,like** *adj*
ovenable ('ʌvᵊnəbᵊl) *adj* **1** (of food) suitable for cooking in an oven. **2** (of a container) suitable for use in an oven.
ovenbird ('ʌvᵊn,bɜːd) *n* **1** any of numerous small brownish South American passerine birds of the family *Furnariidae* that build oven-shaped clay nests. **2** a common North American warbler, *Seiurus aurocapillus,* that has an olive-brown striped plumage with an orange crown and builds a cup-shaped nest on the ground.
oven-ready *adj* (of various foods) bought already prepared so that they are ready to be cooked in the oven.
ovenware ('ʌvᵊn,wɛə) *n* heat-resistant dishes in which food can be both cooked and served.
over ('əʊvə) *prep* **1** directly above; on the top of; via the top or upper surface of: *over one's head.* **2** on or to the other side of: *over the river.* **3** during; through, or throughout (a period of time). **4** in or throughout all parts of: *to travel over England.* **5** throughout the whole extent of: *over the racecourse.* **6** above; in preference to: *I like that over everything else.* **7** by the agency of (an instrument of telecommunication): *we heard it over the radio.* **8** more than: *over a century ago.* **9** on the subject of; about: *an argument over nothing.* **10** while occupied in: *discussing business over golf.* **11** having recovered from the effects of: *she's not over that last love affair yet.* **12 over and above.** added to; in addition to: *he earns a large amount over and above his salary.* ◆ *adv* **13** in a state, condition, situation, or position that is or has been placed or put over something: *to climb over.* **14** (*particle*) so as to cause to fall: *knocking over a policeman.* **15** at or to a point across intervening space, water, etc.: *come over and see us; over in America.* **16** throughout a whole area: *the world over.* **17** (*particle*) from beginning to end, usually cursorily: *to read a document over.* **18** throughout a period of time: *stay over for this week.* **19** (esp. in signalling and radio) it is now your turn to speak, act, etc. **20** more than is expected or usual: *not over well.* **21 over again.** once more. **22 over against. 22a** opposite to. **22b** contrasting with. **23 over and over.** (often foll. by *again*) repeatedly. **24 over the odds. 24a** in addition, esp. when not expected. **24b** unfair or excessive. ◆ *adj* **25** (*postpositive*) finished; no longer in progress: *is the concert over yet?* ◆ *adv, adj* **26** remaining; surplus (often in the phrase **left over**). ◆ *n* **27** *Cricket.* **27a** a series of six balls bowled by a bowler from the same end of the pitch. **27b** the play during this. [Old English *ofer;* related to Old High German *ubir, obar,* Old Norse *yfir,* Latin *super,* Greek *huper*]
over- *prefix* **1** excessive or excessively; beyond an agreed or desirable limit: *overcharge; overdue; oversimplify.* **2** indicating superior rank: *overseer.* **3** indicating location or movement above: *overhang.* **4** indicating movement downwards: *overthrow.*
overachieve (,əʊvərə'tʃiːv) *vb* (*intr*) to perform (for example, in examinations) better than would be expected on the basis of one's age or talents. ► **,over-a'chiever** *n*

,out'sprint *vb* **,out'stare** *vb* **,out'talk** *vb*

overact (ˌəʊvərˈækt) *vb* to act or behave in an exaggerated manner, as in a theatrical production. Also: **overplay.**

overage (ˌəʊvərˈeɪdʒ) *adj* beyond a specified age.

overall *adj* (ˈəʊvərˌɔːl) (*prenominal*) **1** from one end to the other. **2** including or covering everything: *the overall cost.* ◆ *adv* (ˌəʊvərˈɔːl). **3** in general; on the whole. ◆ *n* (ˈəʊvərˌɔːl). **4** *Brit.* a protective work garment usually worn over ordinary clothes. **5** (*pl*) hard-wearing work trousers with a bib and shoulder straps or jacket attached.

overarch (ˌəʊvərˈɑːtʃ) *vb* (*tr*) to form an arch over.

overarm (ˈəʊvərˌɑːm) *adj* **1** *Sport, esp. cricket.* bowled, thrown, or performed with the arm raised above the shoulder. ◆ *adv* **2** with the arm raised above the shoulder.

overawe (ˌəʊvərˈɔː) *vb* (*tr*) to subdue, restrain, or overcome by affecting with a feeling of awe.

overbalance *vb* (ˌəʊvəˈbæləns). **1** to lose or cause to lose balance. **2** (*tr*) another word for **outweigh.** ◆ *n* (ˈəʊvəˌbæləns). **3** excess of weight, value, etc.

overbear (ˌəʊvəˈbɛə) *vb* **-bears, -bearing, -bore, -borne. 1** (*tr*) to dominate or overcome: *to overbear objections.* **2** (*tr*) to press or bear down with weight or physical force. **3** to produce or bear (fruit, progeny, etc.) excessively.

overbearing (ˌəʊvəˈbɛərɪŋ) *adj* **1** domineering or dictatorial in manner or action. **2** of particular or overriding importance or significance. ▸ **ˌoverˈbearingly** *adv*

overbid *vb* (ˌəʊvəˈbɪd), **-bids, -bidding, -bid, -bidden** *or* **-bid. 1** (*intr*) *Bridge.* to bid for more tricks than one can expect to win. **2** to bid more than the value of (something). ◆ *n* (ˈəʊvəˌbɪd). **3** a bid higher than someone else's bid.

overbite (ˈəʊvəˌbaɪt) *n Dentistry.* an extension of the upper front teeth over the lower front teeth when the mouth is closed. Also called: **vertical overlap.**

overblouse (ˈəʊvəˌblaʊz) *n* a blouse designed to be worn not tucked into trousers or a skirt but to fit loosely over the waist or hips.

overblow (ˌəʊvəˈbləʊ) *vb* **-blows, -blowing, -blew, -blown. 1** *Music.* to blow into (a wind instrument) with greater force than normal in order to obtain a harmonic or overtone instead of the fundamental tone. **2** to blow (a wind instrument) or (of a wind instrument) to be blown too hard. **3** to blow over, away, or across.

overblown (ˌəʊvəˈbləʊn) *adj* **1** overdone or excessive. **2** bombastic; turgid: *overblown prose.* **3** (of flowers, such as the rose) past the stage of full bloom.

overboard (ˈəʊvəˌbɔːd) *adv* **1** from on board a vessel into the water. **2 go overboard.** *Informal.* **2a** to be extremely enthusiastic. **2b** to go to extremes. **3 throw overboard.** to reject or abandon.

overboot (ˈəʊvəˌbuːt) *n* a protective boot worn over an ordinary boot or shoe.

overbuild (ˌəʊvəˈbɪld) *vb* **-builds, -building, -built.** (*tr*) **1** to build over or on top of. **2** to erect too many buildings in (an area). **3** to build too large or elaborately.

overburden *vb* (ˌəʊvəˈbɜːdᵊn). **1** (*tr*) to load with excessive weight, work, etc. ◆ *n* (ˈəʊvəˌbɜːdᵊn). **2** an excessive burden or load. **3** *Geology.* the sedimentary rock material that covers coal seams, mineral veins, etc. ▸ **ˌoverˈburdensome** *adj*

overcall *Bridge.* ◆ *n* (ˈəʊvəˌkɔːl). **1** a bid higher than the preceding one. ◆ *vb* (ˌəʊvəˈkɔːl). **2** to bid higher than (an opponent).

overcapitalize *or* **overcapitalise** (ˌəʊvəˈkæpɪtəˌlaɪz) *vb* (*tr*) **1** to provide or issue capital for (an enterprise) in excess of profitable investment opportunities. **2** to estimate the capital value of (a company) at an unreasonably or unlawfully high level. **3** to overestimate the market value of (property). ▸ **ˌoverˌcapitaliˈzation** *or* **ˌoverˌcapitaliˈsation** *n*

overcast *adj* (ˈəʊvəˌkɑːst). **1** covered over or obscured, esp. by clouds. **2** *Meteorol.* (of the sky) more than 95 per cent cloud-covered. **3** gloomy or melancholy. **4** sewn over by overcasting. ◆ *vb* (ˌəʊvəˈkɑːst). **5** to make or become overclouded or gloomy. **6** to sew (an edge, as of a hem) with long stitches passing successively over the edge. ◆ *n* (ˈəʊvəˌkɑːst). **7** a covering, as of clouds or mist. **8** *Meteorol.* the state of the sky when more than 95 per cent of it is cloud-covered. **9** *Mining.* a crossing of two passages without an intersection.

overcharge *vb* (ˌəʊvəˈtʃɑːdʒ). **1** to charge too much. **2** (*tr*) to fill or load beyond capacity. **3** *Literary.* another word for **exaggerate.** ◆ *n* (ˈəʊvəˌtʃɑːdʒ). **4** an excessive price or charge. **5** an excessive load.

overcheck (ˈəʊvəˌtʃɛk) *n* **1** a thin leather strap attached to a horse's bit to keep its head up. **2** (in textiles) **2a** a checked pattern laid over another checked pattern. **2b** a fabric patterned in such a way.

overcloud (ˌəʊvəˈklaʊd) *vb* **1** to make or become covered with clouds. **2** to make or become dark or dim.

overcoat (ˈəʊvəˌkəʊt) *n* a warm heavy coat worn over the outer clothes in cold weather.

overcome (ˌəʊvəˈkʌm) *vb* **-comes, -coming, -came, -come. 1** (*tr*) to get the better of in a conflict. **2** (*tr; often passive*) to render incapable or powerless by laughter, sorrow, exhaustion, etc.: *he was overcome by fumes.* **3** (*tr*) to surmount (obstacles, objections, etc.). **4** (*intr*) to be victorious.

overcommit (ˌəʊvəkəˈmɪt) *vb* **-mits, -mitting, -mitted.** (*tr*) to promise, undertake, or allocate more than the available resources justify.

overcompensate (ˌəʊvəˈkɒmpɛnˌseɪt) *vb* **1** to compensate (a person or thing) excessively. **2** (*intr*) *Psychol.* to engage in overcompensation. ▸ **ˌoverˈcompenˌsatory** *adj*

overcompensation (ˌəʊvəˌkɒmpɛnˈseɪʃən) *n Psychol.* an attempt to make up for a character trait by overexaggerating its opposite.

overcrop (ˌəʊvəˈkrɒp) *vb* **-crops, -cropping, -cropped.** (*tr*) to exhaust (land) by excessive cultivation.

overcrowd (ˌəʊvəˈkraʊd) *vb* (*tr*) to fill (a room, vehicle, city, etc.) with more people or things than is desirable. ▸ **ˌoverˈcrowding** *n*

overdevelop (ˌəʊvədɪˈvɛləp) *vb* (*tr*) **1** to develop too much or too far. **2** *Photog.* to process (a film, plate, or print) in developer for more than the required time, at too great a concentration, etc. ▸ **ˌoverdeˈvelopment** *n*

overdeviate (ˌəʊvəˈdiːvɪˌeɪt) *vb* to cause (a frequency-modulated radio transmitter) to exceed its specified frequency excursion from the rest frequency.

overdo (ˌəʊvəˈduː) *vb* **-does, -doing, -did, -done.** (*tr*) **1** to take or carry too far; do to excess. **2** to exaggerate, overelaborate, or overplay. **3** to cook or bake too long. **4 overdo it** *or* **things.** to overtax one's strength, capacity, etc.

overdose *n* (ˈəʊvəˌdəʊs). **1** (esp. of drugs) an excessive dose. ◆ *vb* (ˌəʊvəˈdəʊs). **2** to take an excessive dose or give an excessive dose to. ▸ **ˌoverˈdosage** *n*

overdraft (ˈəʊvəˌdrɑːft) *n* **1** a draft or withdrawal of money in excess of the credit balance on a bank or building-society cheque account. **2** the amount of money drawn or withdrawn thus.

overdraught (ˈəʊvəˌdrɑːft) *n* a current of air passed above a fire, as in a furnace.

overdraw (ˌəʊvəˈdrɔː) *vb* **-draws, -drawing, -drew, -drawn. 1** to draw on (a bank account) in excess of the credit balance. **2** (*tr*) to strain or pull (a bow) too far. **3** (*tr*) to exaggerate in describing or telling.

overdress *vb* (ˌəʊvəˈdrɛs). **1** to dress (oneself or another) too elaborately or finely. ◆ *n* (ˈəʊvəˌdrɛs). **2** a dress that may be worn over a jumper, blouse, etc.

overdrive *n* (ˈəʊvəˌdraɪv). **1** a very high gear in a motor vehicle used at high speeds to reduce wear and save fuel. **2 in** *or* **into overdrive.** in *or* into a state of intense activity. ◆ *vb* (ˌəʊvəˈdraɪv), **-drives, -driving, -drove, -driven. 3** (*tr*) to drive too hard or too far; overwork or overuse.

overdub (in multitrack recording) ◆ *vb* (ˌəʊvəˈdʌb), **-dubs, -dubbing, -dubbed. 1** to add (new sound) on a spare track or tracks. ◆ *n* (ˈəʊvəˌdʌb). **2** the addition of new sound to a recording; the blending of various layers of sound in one recording.

overdue (ˌəʊvəˈdjuː) *adj* past the time specified, required, or preferred for arrival, occurrence, payment, etc.

overdye (ˌəʊvəˈdaɪ) *vb* (*tr*) **1** to dye (a fabric, yarn, etc.) excessively. **2** to dye for a second or third time with a different colour.

overestimate *vb* (ˌəʊvərˈɛstɪˌmeɪt). **1** (*tr*) to value or estimate too highly. ◆ *n* (ˌəʊvərˈɛstɪmɪt). **2** an estimate that is too high. ▸ **ˌoverˌestiˈmation** *n*

overexpose (ˌəʊvərɪksˈpəʊz) *vb* (*tr*) **1** to expose too much or for too long. **2** *Photog.* to expose (a film, plate, or paper) for too long a period or with too bright a light. ▸ **ˌoverexˈposure** *n*

overfall (ˈəʊvəˌfɔːl) *n* **1** a turbulent stretch of water caused by marine currents over an underwater ridge. **2** a mechanism that allows excess water to escape from a dam or lock.

overflight (ˈəʊvəˌflaɪt) *n* the flight of an aircraft over a specific area or territory.

overflow *vb* (ˌəʊvəˈfləʊ), **-flows, -flowing, -flowed** *or* (*formerly*) **-flown. 1** to flow or run over (a limit, brim, bank, etc.). **2** to fill or be filled beyond capacity so as to spill or run over. **3** (*intr*; usually foll. by *with*) to be filled with happiness, tears, etc. **4** (*tr*) to spread or cover over; flood or inundate. ◆ *n* (ˈəʊvəˌfləʊ). **5** overflowing matter, esp. liquid. **6** any outlet that enables surplus liquid to be discharged or drained off, esp. one just below the top of a tank or cistern. **7** the amount by which a limit, capacity, etc., is exceeded. **8** *Computing.* a condition that occurs when numeric operations produce results too large to store in the register available.

overfly (ˌəʊvəˈflaɪ) *vb* **-flies, -flying, -flew, -flown.** (*tr*) to fly over (a territory) or past (a point).

overfold (ˈəʊvəˌfəʊld) *n Geology.* a fold in the form of an anticline in which one limb is more steeply inclined than the other.

ˌoveraˈbundance *n*
ˌoverˈactive *adj*
ˌoveragˈgressive *adj*
ˌoveramˈbitious *adj*
ˌoverˈanxious *adj*
ˌoverasˈsertive *adj*
ˌoverasˈsertiveness *n*
ˌoveratˈtentive *adj*
ˌoverˈbook *vb*
ˌovercaˈpacity *n*
ˌoverˈcareful *adj*
ˌoverˈcautious *adj*
ˌoverˈcivil *adj*
ˌoverˈcommon *adj*
ˌovercomˈplacency *n*
ˌovercomˈplacent *adj*
ˌoverˈcomplex *adj*
ˌoverˈcompliˌcate *vb*
ˌoverconˈcern *n*
ˌoverˈconfidence *n*
ˌoverˈconfident *adj*
ˌoverˌconsciˈentious *adj*
ˌoverconˈservative *adj*
ˌoverconˈsumption *n*
ˌoverˈcook *vb*
ˌoverˈcritical *adj*
ˌoverˈdecoˌrate *vb*
ˌoverdeˈpendence *n*
ˌoverdeˈpendent *adj*
ˌoverdraˈmatic *adj*
ˌoverˈdramaˌtize *or* **ˌoverˈdramaˌtise** *vb*
ˌoverˈeager *adj*
ˌoverˈearnest *adj*
ˌoverˈeat *vb*, **-ˈeats, -ˈeating, -ˈate, -ˈeaten.**
ˌoverefˈfusive *adj*
ˌovereˈlaborate *adj, vb*
ˌovereˌlaboˈration *n*
ˌoveremˈbellish *vb*
ˌovereˈmotional *adj*
ˌoverˈemphasis *n*
ˌoverˈemphaˌsize *or* **ˌoverˈemphaˌsise** *vb*
ˌoveremˈphatic *adj*
ˌoverenˈthusiˌasm *n*
ˌoverenˌthusiˈastic *adj*
ˌoverexˈcitable *adj*
ˌoverexˈcited *adj*
ˌoverˈexerˌcise *vb*
ˌoverexˈert *vb*
ˌoverexˈpansion *n*
ˌoverexˈtend *vb*
ˌoverfaˈmiliar *adj*
ˌoverfaˌmiliˈarity *n*
ˌoverˈfar *adj, adv*
ˌoverˈfeed *vb*, **-ˈfeeds, -ˈfeeding, -ˈfed.**
ˌoverˈfill *vb*
ˌoverˈfish *vb*

overfunding ('əʊvəˌfʌndɪŋ) *n* (in Britain) a government policy in which it sells more of its securities than would be required to finance public spending, with the object of absorbing surplus funds to curb inflation.

overgarment ('əʊvəˌgɑːmənt) *n* any garment worn over other clothes, esp. to protect them from wear or dirt.

overgear (ˌəʊvə'gɪə) *vb* (*tr; usually passive*) to cause (a company) to have too high a proportion of loan stock and preference shares in comparison to its ordinary share capital.

overglaze ('əʊvəˌgleɪz) *adj* (of decoration or colours) applied to porcelain or pottery above the glaze.

overgraze (ˌəʊvə'greɪz) *vb* (*tr*) to graze (land) beyond its capacity to sustain stock.

overground ('əʊvəˌgraʊnd) *adj* on or above the surface of the ground: *an overground railway.*

overgrow (ˌəʊvə'grəʊ) *vb* **-grows, -growing, -grew, -grown. 1** (*tr*) to grow over or across (an area, path, lawn, etc.). **2** (*tr*) to choke or supplant by a stronger growth. **3** (*tr*) to grow too large for. **4** (*intr*) to grow beyond normal size. ► **'overˌgrowth** *n*

overhand ('əʊvəˌhænd) *adj* **1** thrown or performed with the hand raised above the shoulder. **2** sewn with thread passing over two edges in one direction. ◆ *adv* **3** with the hand above the shoulder; overarm. **4** with shallow stitches passing over two edges. ◆ *vb* **5** to sew (two edges) overhand.

overhand knot *n* a knot formed by making a loop in a piece of cord and drawing one end through it. Also called: **thumb knot.**

overhang *vb* (ˌəʊvə'hæŋ), **-hangs, -hanging, -hung. 1** to project or extend beyond (a surface, building, etc.). **2** (*tr*) to hang or be suspended over. **3** (*tr*) to menace, threaten, or dominate. ◆ *n* ('əʊvəˌhæŋ). **4** a formation, object, part of a structure, etc., that extends beyond or hangs over something, such as an outcrop of rock overhanging a mountain face. **5** the amount or extent of projection. **6** *Aeronautics.* **6a** half the difference in span of the main supporting surfaces of a biplane or other multiplane. **6b** the distance from the outer supporting strut of a wing to the wing tip. **7** *Finance.* the shares, collectively, that the underwriters have to buy when a new issue has not been fully taken up by the market.

overhaul *vb* (ˌəʊvə'hɔːl). (*tr*) **1** to examine carefully for faults, necessary repairs, etc. **2** to make repairs or adjustments to (a car, machine, etc.). **3** to overtake. ◆ *n* ('əʊvəˌhɔːl). **4** a thorough examination and repair.

overhead *adj* ('əʊvəˌhɛd). **1** situated or operating above head height or some other reference level. **2** (*prenominal*) inclusive: *the overhead price included meals.* ◆ *adv* (ˌəʊvə'hɛd). **3** over or above head height, esp. in the sky. ◆ *n* ('əʊvəˌhɛd). **4a** a stroke in racket games played from above head height. **4b** (*as modifier*): *an overhead smash.* **5** *Nautical.* the interior lining above one's head below decks in a vessel. **6** short for **overhead door. 7** (*modifier*) of, concerned with, or resulting from overheads: *overhead costs.* ◆ See also **overheads.**

overhead camshaft *n* a type of camshaft situated above the cylinder head in an internal-combustion engine. It is usually driven by a chain or a toothed belt from the crankshaft and the cams bear directly onto the valve stems or rocker arms.

overhead door *n* a door that rotates on a horizontal axis and is supported horizontally when open. Sometimes shortened to **overhead.**

overhead projector *n* a projector that throws an enlarged image of a transparency onto a surface above and behind the person using it. Alterations and additions can be made to the material on the transparency while the projector is in use.

overheads ('əʊvəˌhɛdz) *pl n* business expenses, such as rent, that are not directly attributable to any department or product and can therefore be assigned only arbitrarily. Also called: **burden, fixed costs, indirect costs, oncost.** Compare **prime cost.**

overhead-valve engine *n* a type of internal-combustion engine in which the inlet and exhaust valves are in the cylinder head above the pistons. U.S. name: **valve-in-head engine.** Compare **side-valve engine.**

overhear (ˌəʊvə'hɪə) *vb* **-hears, -hearing, -heard.** (*tr*) to hear (a person, remark, etc.) without the knowledge of the speaker.

overheat (ˌəʊvə'hiːt) *vb* **1** to make or become excessively hot. **2** (*tr; often passive*) to make very agitated, irritated, etc. **3** (*intr*) (of an economy) to tend towards inflation, often as a result of excessive growth in demand. **4** (*tr*) to cause (an economy) to tend towards inflation. ◆ *n* **5** the condition of being overheated.

Overijssel (*Dutch* oːvər'eisəl) *n* a province of the E Netherlands: generally lowlying. Capital: Zwolle. Pop.: 1 054 000 (1996 est.). Area: 3929 sq. km (1517 sq. miles).

overindulge (ˌəʊvərɪn'dʌldʒ) *vb* **1** to indulge (in something, esp. food or drink) immoderately; binge. **2** (*tr*) to yield excessively to the wishes of; spoil. ► **ˌoverin'dulgence** *n* ► **ˌoverin'dulgent** *adj*

overissue ('əʊvərˌɪsjuː, -ˌɪʃuː) *vb* **-sues, -suing, -sued.** (*tr*) **1** to issue (shares, banknotes, etc.) in excess of demand or ability to pay. ◆ *n* **2** shares, banknotes, etc., thus issued.

overjoy (ˌəʊvə'dʒɔɪ) *vb* (*tr*) to give great delight to. ► **ˌover'joyed** *adj*

overkill ('əʊvəˌkɪl) *n* **1** the capability to deploy more weapons, esp. nuclear weapons, than is necessary to ensure military advantage. **2** any capacity or treatment that is greater than that required or appropriate.

overland ('əʊvəˌlænd) *adj* (*prenominal*), *adv* **1** over or across land. ◆ *vb* **2** *Austral. history.* to drive (cattle or sheep) overland. ► **'overˌlander** *n*

overlap *vb* (ˌəʊvə'læp), **-laps, -lapping, -lapped. 1** (of two things) to extend or lie partly over (each other). **2** to cover and extend beyond (something). **3** (*intr*) to coincide partly in time, subject, etc. ◆ *n* ('əʊvəˌlæp). **4** a part that overlaps or is overlapped. **5** the amount, length, etc., overlapping. **6** the act or fact of overlapping. **7** a place of overlapping. **8** *Geology.* the horizontal extension of the lower beds in a series of rock strata beyond the upper beds, usually caused by submergence of the land.

overlay *vb* (ˌəʊvə'leɪ), **-lays, -laying, -laid.** (*tr*) **1** to lay or place something over or upon (something else). **2** (often foll. by *with*) to cover, overspread, or conceal (with). **3** (foll. by *with*) to cover (a surface) with an applied decoration: *ebony overlaid with silver.* **4** to achieve the correct printing pressure all over (a forme or plate) by adding to the appropriate areas of the packing. ◆ *n* ('əʊvəˌleɪ). **5** something that is laid over something else; covering. **6** an applied decoration or layer, as of gold leaf. **7** a transparent sheet giving extra details to a map or diagram over which it is designed to be placed. **8** *Printing.* material, such as paper, used to overlay a forme or plate.

overleaf (ˌəʊvə'liːf) *adv* on the other side of the page. Also: **ˌover'page.**

overlie (ˌəʊvə'laɪ) *vb* **-lies, -lying, -lay, -lain.** (*tr*) **1** to lie or rest upon. Compare **overlay. 2** to kill (a baby or newborn animal) by lying upon it.

overlive (ˌəʊvə'lɪv) *vb* **1** to live longer than (another person). **2** to survive or outlive (an event).

overload *vb* (ˌəʊvə'ləʊd). **1** (*tr*) to put too large a load on or in. ◆ *n* ('əʊvəˌləʊd). **2** an excessive load.

overlong (ˌəʊvə'lɒŋ) *adj, adv* too or excessively long.

overlook *vb* (ˌəʊvə'lʊk). (*tr*) **1** to fail to notice or take into account. **2** to disregard deliberately or indulgently. **3** to look at or over from above: *the garden is overlooked by the prison.* **4** to afford a view of from above: *the house overlooks the bay.* **5** to rise above. **6** to look after. **7** to look at carefully. **8** to bewitch or cast the evil eye upon (someone). ◆ *n* ('əʊvəˌlʊk). *U.S.* **9** a high place affording a view. **10** an act of overlooking.

overlooker ('əʊvəˌlʊkə) *n* another word (less common) for **overseer** (sense 1).

overlord ('əʊvəˌlɔːd) *n* a supreme lord or master. ► **'overˌlordship** *n*

overly ('əʊvəlɪ) *adv* too; excessively.

overman *vb* (ˌəʊvə'mæn), **-mans, -manning, -manned. 1** (*tr*) to supply with an excessive number of men. ◆ *n* ('əʊvəˌmæn), *pl* **-men. 2** a man who oversees others. **3** the Nietzschean superman.

overmantel ('əʊvəˌmæntᵊl) *n* an ornamental shelf over a mantelpiece, often with a mirror.

overmaster (ˌəʊvə'mɑːstə) *vb* (*tr*) to overpower.

overmatch *Chiefly U.S.* ◆ *vb* (ˌəʊvə'mætʃ). (*tr*) **1** to be more than a match for. **2** to match with a superior opponent. ◆ *n* ('əʊvəˌmætʃ). **3** a person superior in ability. **4** a match in which one contestant is superior.

overmatter ('əʊvəˌmætə) *n Printing.* type that has been set but cannot be used for printing owing to lack of space. Also called: **overset.**

overmuch (ˌəʊvə'mʌtʃ) *adv, adj* **1** too much; very much. ◆ *n* **2** an excessive amount.

overnice (ˌəʊvə'naɪs) *adj* too fastidious, precise, etc.

overnight *adv* (ˌəʊvə'naɪt). **1** for the duration of the night: *we stopped overnight.* **2** in or as if in the course of one night; suddenly: *the situation changed overnight.* ◆ *adj* ('əʊvəˌnaɪt). (*usually prenominal*) **3** done in, occurring in, or lasting the night: *an overnight stop.* **4** staying for one night: *overnight guests.* **5** lasting one night: *an overnight trip; an overnight bank loan.* **6** for use during a single night: *overnight clothes.* **7** occurring in or as if in the course of one night; sudden: *an overnight victory.* ◆ *vb* (*intr*) **8** to stay the night.

overpage (ˌəʊvə'peɪdʒ) *adv* another word for **overleaf.**

overpass *n* ('əʊvəˌpɑːs). **1** another name for **flyover** (sense 1). ◆ *vb* (ˌəʊvə'pɑːs), **-passes, -passing, -passed, -past.** (*tr*) *Now rare.* **2** to pass over, through, or across. **3** to exceed. **4** to get over. **5** to ignore.

overpay (ˌəʊvə'peɪ) *vb* **-pays, -paying, -paid. 1** to pay (someone) at too high a rate. **2** to pay (someone) more than is due, as by an error.

overpersuade (ˌəʊvəpə'sweɪd) *vb* (*tr*) to persuade (someone) against his inclination or judgment.

overpitch (ˌəʊvə'pɪtʃ) *vb Cricket.* to bowl (a ball) so that it pitches too close to the stumps.

overplay (ˌəʊvə'pleɪ) *vb* **1** (*tr*) to exaggerate the importance of. **2** another word for **overact. 3 overplay one's hand.** to overestimate the worth or strength of one's position.

overplus ('əʊvəˌplʌs) *n* surplus or excess quantity.

overpower (ˌəʊvə'paʊə) *vb* (*tr*) **1** to conquer or subdue by superior force. **2** to have such a strong effect on as to make helpless or ineffective. **3** to supply with more power than necessary.

overpowering (ˌəʊvə'paʊərɪŋ) *adj* **1** so strong or intense as to be unbearable. **2** so powerful as to crush or conquer. ► **ˌover'poweringly** *adv*

overpressure ('əʊvəˌprɛʃə) *n* the blast effect of a nuclear weapon expressed as an amount of pressure greater than normal barometric pressure.

overprint *vb* (ˌəʊvə'prɪnt). **1** (*tr*) to print (additional matter or another colour) on a sheet of paper. ◆ *n* ('əʊvəˌprɪnt). **2** additional matter or another colour printed onto a previously printed sheet. **3** additional matter, other than a

ˌover'fond *adj*
ˌover'full *adj*
ˌover'generous *adj*
ˌover'hasty *adj*
ˌover'interest *n*
ˌover'laden *adj*
ˌover'large *adj*
ˌover'many *adj*
ˌover'optiˌmism *n*
ˌover'optimist *n*
ˌoverˌopti'mistic *adj*
ˌover'peopled *adj*
ˌoverˌpessi'mistic *adj*
ˌover'popuˌlated *adj*
ˌoverˌpopu'lation *n*
ˌover'powerful *adj*
ˌover'price *vb*
ˌover'priced *adj*

change in face value, applied to a finished postage stamp by printing, stamping, etc. See also **surcharge** (sense 5), **provisional** (sense 2).

overprotect (ˌəʊvəprəˈtɛkt) *vb* (*tr*) to protect more than necessary, esp. to shield a child excessively so as to inhibit its development. ▸ **ˌoverproˈtective** *adj*

overqualified (ˌəʊvəˈkwɒlɪˌfaɪd) *adj* having more managerial experience or academic qualifications than required for a particular job.

overrate (ˌəʊvəˈreɪt) *vb* (*tr*) to assess too highly.

overreach (ˌəʊvəˈriːtʃ) *vb* **1** (*tr*) to defeat or thwart (oneself) by attempting to do or gain too much. **2** (*tr*) to aim for but miss by going too far or attempting too much. **3** to get the better of (a person) by trickery. **4** (*tr*) to reach or extend beyond or over. **5** (*intr*) to reach or go too far. **6** (*intr*) (of a horse) to strike the back of a forefoot with the edge of the opposite hind foot.

overreact (ˌəʊvərɪˈækt) *vb* (*intr*) to react excessively to something. ▸ **ˌoverreˈaction** *n*

overrefine (ˌəʊvərɪˈfaɪn) *vb* **1** to refine (something) to excess. **2** (*intr*) to make excessively fine distinctions. ▸ **ˌoverreˈfinement** *n*

override (ˌəʊvəˈraɪd) *vb* **-rides, -riding, -rode, -ridden.** (*tr*) **1** to set aside or disregard with superior authority or power. **2** to supersede or annul. **3** to dominate or vanquish by or as if by trampling down. **4** to take manual control of (a system that is usually under automatic control). **5** to extend or pass over, esp. to overlap. **6** to ride (a horse) too hard. **7** to ride over or across. ◆ *n* **8** a device or system that can override an automatic control.

overrider (ˈəʊvəˌraɪdə) *n* either of two metal or rubber attachments fitted to the bumper of a motor vehicle to prevent the bumpers interlocking with those of another vehicle.

overriding (ˌəʊvəˈraɪdɪŋ) *adj* taking precedence.

overrule (ˌəʊvəˈruːl) *vb* (*tr*) **1** to disallow the arguments of (a person) by the use of authority. **2** to rule or decide against (an argument, decision, etc.). **3** to prevail over, dominate, or influence. **4** to exercise rule over.

overrun *vb* (ˌəʊvəˈrʌn), **-runs, -running, -ran, -run. 1** (*tr*) to attack or invade and defeat conclusively. **2** (*tr*) to swarm or spread over rapidly. **3** to run over (something); overflow. **4** to extend or run beyond a limit. **5** (*intr*) (of an engine) to run with a closed throttle at a speed dictated by that of the vehicle it drives, as on a decline. **6** (*tr*) **6a** to print (a book, journal, etc.) in a greater quantity than ordered. **6b** to print additional copies of (a publication). **7** (*tr*) *Printing.* to transfer (set type and other matter) from one column, line, or page, to another. **8** (*tr*) *Archaic.* to run faster than. ◆ *n* (ˈəʊvəˌrʌn). **9** the act or an instance of overrunning. **10** the amount or extent of overrunning. **11** the number of copies of a publication in excess of the quantity ordered. **12** the cleared level area at the end of an airport runway.

overrun brake *n* a brake fitted to a trailer or other towed vehicle that prevents the towed vehicle travelling faster than the towing vehicle when slowing down or descending an incline.

oversaturated (ˌəʊvəˈsætʃəˌreɪtɪd) *adj* (of igneous rocks) containing excess silica.

overscore (ˌəʊvəˈskɔː) *vb* (*tr*) to cancel or cross out by drawing a line or lines over or through.

overseas *adv* (ˌəʊvəˈsiːz). **1** beyond the sea; abroad. ◆ *adj* (ˈəʊvəˈsiːz). **2** of, to, in, from, or situated in countries beyond the sea. **3** Also: **oversea** (ˌəʊvəˈsiː). of or relating to passage over the sea. ◆ *n* (ˌəʊvəˈsiːz). **4** (*functioning as sing*) *Informal.* a foreign country or foreign countries collectively.

overseas *or* **international telegram** *n Brit.* another name for **cable** (sense 5).

oversee (ˌəʊvəˈsiː) *vb* **-sees, -seeing, -saw, -seen.** (*tr*) **1** to watch over and direct; supervise. **2** to watch secretly or accidentally.

overseer (ˈəʊvəˌsiːə) *n* **1** Also called (less commonly): **overlooker.** a person who oversees others, esp. workmen. **2** *British history.* short for **overseer of the poor;** a minor official of a parish attached to the workhouse or poorhouse.

oversell (ˌəʊvəˈsɛl) *vb* **-sells, -selling, -sold. 1** (*tr*) to sell more of (a commodity) than can be supplied. **2** to use excessively aggressive methods in selling (commodities). **3** (*tr*) to exaggerate the merits of.

overset *vb* (ˌəʊvəˈsɛt), **-sets, -setting, -set.** (*tr*) **1** to disturb or upset. **2** *Printing.* to set (type or copy) in excess of the space available. ◆ *n* (ˈəʊvəˌsɛt). **3** another name for **overmatter.**

oversew (ˈəʊvəˌsəʊ, ˌəʊvəˈsəʊ) *vb* **-sews, -sewing, -sewed, -sewn.** to sew (two edges) with close stitches that pass over them both.

oversexed (ˌəʊvəˈsɛkst) *adj* having an excessive preoccupation with or need for sexual activity.

overshadow (ˌəʊvəˈʃædəʊ) *vb* (*tr*) **1** to render insignificant or less important in comparison. **2** to cast a shadow or gloom over.

overshoe (ˈəʊvəˌʃuː) *n* a protective shoe worn over an ordinary shoe.

overshoot (ˌəʊvəˈʃuːt) *vb* **-shoots, -shooting, -shot. 1** to shoot or go beyond (a mark or target). **2** to cause (an aircraft) to fly or taxi too far along (a runway) during landing or taking off, or (of an aircraft) to fly or taxi too far along a runway. **3** (*tr*) to pass swiftly over or down over, as water over a wheel. ◆ *n* **4** an act or instance of overshooting. **5** the extent of such overshooting. **6** a momentary excessive response of an electrical or mechanical system.

overshot (ˈəʊvəˌʃɒt) *adj* **1** having or designating an upper jaw that projects beyond the lower jaw, esp. when considered as an abnormality. **2** (of a water wheel) driven by a flow of water that passes over the wheel rather than under it. Compare **undershot.**

overside (ˈəʊvəˌsaɪd) *adv* over the side (of a ship).

oversight (ˈəʊvəˌsaɪt) *n* **1** an omission or mistake, esp. one made through failure to notice something. **2** supervision.

oversimplify (ˌəʊvəˈsɪmplɪˌfaɪ) *vb* **-fies, -fying, -fied.** to simplify (something) to the point of distortion or error. ▸ **ˌoverˌsimplifiˈcation** *n*

oversize *adj* (ˌəʊvəˈsaɪz). **1** Also: **ˌoverˈsized.** larger than the usual size. ◆ *n* (ˈəʊvəˌsaɪz). **2** a size larger than the usual or proper size. **3** something that is oversize.

overskirt (ˈəʊvəˌskɜːt) *n* an outer skirt, esp. one that reveals a decorative underskirt.

overslaugh (ˈəʊvəˌslɔː) *n* **1** *Military.* the passing over of one duty for another that takes precedence. ◆ *vb* **2** (*tr*) *U.S.* to pass over; ignore. [**C18:** from Dutch *overslaan* to pass over]

oversleep (ˌəʊvəˈsliːp) *vb* **-sleeps, -sleeping, -slept.** (*intr*) to sleep beyond the intended time for getting up.

oversleeve (ˈəʊvəˌsliːv) *n* a protective sleeve covering an ordinary sleeve.

overspend *vb* (ˌəʊvəˈspend). **-spends, -spending, -spent. 1** to spend in excess of (one's desires or what one can afford or is allocated). **2** (*tr; usually passive*) to wear out; exhaust. ◆ *n* (ˈəʊvəˌspend). **3** the amount by which someone or something is overspent.

overspill *n* (ˈəʊvəˌspɪl). **1a** something that spills over or is in excess. **1b** (*as modifier*): *overspill population.* ◆ *vb* (ˌəʊvəˈspɪl), **-spills, -spilling, -spilt** *or* **-spilled. 2** (*intr*) to overflow.

overstaff (ˌəʊvəˈstɑːf) *vb* (*tr*) to provide an excessive number of staff for (a factory, hotel, etc.).

overstate (ˌəʊvəˈsteɪt) *vb* (*tr*) to state too strongly; exaggerate or overemphasize. ▸ **ˌoverˈstatement** *n*

overstay (ˌəʊvəˈsteɪ) *vb* (*tr*) **1** to stay beyond the time, limit, or duration of. **2** *Finance.* to delay a transaction in (a market) until after the point at which the maximum profit would have been made. **3** *N.Z.* to stay in New Zealand beyond (the period sanctioned by the immigration authorities or the period of a visitor's permit). **4 overstay** *or* **outstay one's welcome.** to stay (at a party, on a visit, etc.), longer than pleases the host or hostess.

overstayer (ˈəʊvəˌsteɪə) *n* a person who illegally remains in a country after the period of the permitted visit has expired.

oversteer (ˌəʊvəˈstɪə) *vb* (*intr*) (of a vehicle) to turn more sharply, for a particular turn of the steering wheel, than is desirable or anticipated.

overstep (ˌəʊvəˈstɛp) *vb* **-steps, -stepping, -stepped.** (*tr*) to go beyond (a certain or proper limit).

overstock (ˌəʊvəˈstɒk) *vb* (*tr*) **1** to hold or supply (a commodity) in excess of requirements. **2** to run more farm animals on (a piece of land) than it is capable of maintaining.

overstrung (ˌəʊvəˈstrʌŋ) *adj* **1** too highly strung; tense. **2** (of a piano) having two sets of strings crossing each other at an oblique angle.

overstuff (ˌəʊvəˈstʌf) *vb* (*tr*) **1** to force too much into. **2** to cover (furniture) entirely with upholstery.

oversubscribe (ˌəʊvəsəbˈskraɪb) *vb* (*tr; often passive*) to subscribe or apply for in excess of available supply. ▸ **ˌoversubˈscription** *n*

overt (ˈəʊvɜːt, əʊˈvɜːt) *adj* **1** open to view; observable. **2** *Law.* open; deliberate. Criminal intent may be inferred from an overt act. [**C14:** via Old French, from *ovrir* to open, from Latin *aperīre*] ▸ **oˈvertly** *adv* ▸ **oˈvertness** *n*

overtake (ˌəʊvəˈteɪk) *vb* **-takes, -taking, -took, -taken. 1** *Chiefly Brit.* to move past (another vehicle or person) travelling in the same direction. **2** (*tr*) to pass or do better than, after catching up with. **3** (*tr*) to come upon suddenly or unexpectedly: *night overtook him.* **4** (*tr*) to catch up with; draw level with.

overtask (ˌəʊvəˈtɑːsk) *vb* (*tr*) to impose too heavy a task upon.

overtax (ˌəʊvəˈtæks) *vb* (*tr*) **1** to tax too heavily. **2** to impose too great a strain on.

over-the-counter *adj* **1a** (of securities) not listed or quoted on a stock exchange. **1b** (of a security market) dealing in such securities. **1c** (of security transactions) conducted through a broker's office directly between purchaser and seller and not on a stock exchange. **2** (of medicinal drugs) able to be sold without a prescription. Abbrev.: **OTC.**

overthrow *vb* (ˌəʊvəˈθrəʊ), **-throws, -throwing, -threw, -thrown. 1** (*tr*) to effect the downfall or destruction of (a ruler, institution, etc.), esp. by force. **2** (*tr*) to throw or turn over. **3** (*tr*) to throw (something, esp. a ball) too far. ◆ *n* (ˈəʊvəˌθrəʊ). **4** an act of overthrowing. **5** downfall; destruction. **6** *Cricket.* **6a** a ball thrown back too far by a fielder. **6b** a run scored because of this.

overthrust (ˈəʊvəˌθrʌst) *n Geology.* a reverse fault in which the rocks on the upper surface of a fault plane have moved over the rocks on the lower surface. Compare **underthrust.**

overtime *n* (ˈəʊvəˌtaɪm). **1a** work at a regular job done in addition to regular working hours. **1b** (*as modifier*): *overtime pay.* **2** the rate of pay established for such work. **3** time in excess of a set period. **4** *Sport, U.S. and Canadian.* extra time. ◆ *adv* (ˈəʊvəˌtaɪm). **5** beyond the regular or stipulated time. ◆ *vb* (ˌəʊvəˈtaɪm). **6** (*tr*) to exceed the required time for (a photographic exposure).

ˌoverproˈduce *vb*
ˌoverproˈduction *n*
ˌoverreˈliance *n*
ˌoverˈrich *adj*
ˌoverˈripe *adj*
ˌoverˈroast *vb*
ˌoverˈsensitive *adj*
ˌoverˈsmart *adj*
ˌoverˌspecialiˈzation *or* **ˌoverˌspecialiˈsation** *n*
ˌoverˈspecialˌize *or* **ˌoverˈspecialˌise** *vb*
ˌoverˈspread *vb,* **-ˈspreads, -ˈspreading, -ˈspread.**
ˌoverˈstimuˌlate *vb*
ˌoverˈstrain *vb*
ˌoverˈstretch *vb*
ˌoverˈstrict *adj*
ˌoverˈsubtle *adj*
ˌoversupˈply *n, vb,* **-ˈplies, -ˈplying, -ˈplied.**

overtone ('əʊvə,təʊn) *n* **1** (*often pl*) additional meaning or nuance: *overtones of despair.* **2** *Music, acoustics.* any of the tones, with the exception of the fundamental, that constitute a musical sound and contribute to its quality, each having a frequency that is a multiple of the fundamental frequency. See also **harmonic** (sense 7), **partial** (sense 6).

overtop (,əʊvə'tɒp) *vb* **-tops, -topping, -topped.** (*tr*) **1** to exceed in height. **2** to surpass; excel. **3** to rise over the top of.

overtrade (,əʊvə'treɪd) *vb* (*intr*) (of an enterprise) to trade in excess of capacity or working capital.

overtrick ('əʊvə,trɪk) *n Bridge.* a trick by which a player exceeds his contract.

overtrump (,əʊvə'trʌmp) *vb Cards.* to play a trump higher than (one previously played to the trick).

overture ('əʊvə,tjʊə) *n* **1** *Music.* **1a** a piece of orchestral music containing contrasting sections that is played at the beginning of an opera or oratorio, often containing the main musical themes of the work. **1b** a similar piece preceding the performance of a play. **1c** Also called: **concert overture.** a one-movement orchestral piece, usually having a descriptive or evocative title. **1d** a short piece in three movements (**French overture** or **Italian overture**) common in the 17th and 18th centuries. **2** (*often pl*) a proposal, act, or gesture initiating a relationship, negotiation, etc. **3** something that introduces what follows. ◆ *vb* (*tr*) **4** to make or present an overture to. **5** to introduce with an overture. **[C14:** via Old French, from Late Latin *apertūra* opening, from Latin *aperīre* to open; see OVERT**]**

overturn *vb* (,əʊvə'tɜːn). **1** to turn or cause to turn from an upright or normal position. **2** (*tr*) to overthrow or destroy. **3** (*tr*) to invalidate; reverse: *the bill was passed in the Commons but overturned in the Lords.* ◆ *n* ('əʊvə,tɜːn). **4** the act of overturning or the state of being overturned.

over-under *U.S.* ◆ *adj* **1** (of a two-barrelled firearm) having one barrel on top of the other. ◆ *n* **2** an over-under firearm.

over-use *vb* (,əʊvə'juːz). (*tr*) **1** to use excessively. ◆ *n* (,əʊvə'juːs) **2** excessive use.

overview ('əʊvə,vjuː) *n* a general survey.

overvoltage ('əʊvə,vəʊltɪdʒ) *n* a voltage above the normal level.

overwatch (,əʊvə'wɒtʃ) *vb* (*tr*) **1** to watch over. **2** *Archaic.* to fatigue with long watching or lack of sleep.

overweening (,əʊvə'wiːnɪŋ) *adj* **1** (of a person) excessively arrogant or presumptuous. **2** (of opinions, appetites, etc.) excessive; immoderate. **[C14:** OVER- + *weening,* from Old English *wēnan:* see WEEN**]** ▸ **,over'weeningly** *adv* ▸ **,over'weeningness** *n*

overweigh (,əʊvə'weɪ) *vb* (*tr*) **1** to exceed in weight; overbalance. **2** to weigh down; oppress.

overweight *adj* (,əʊvə'weɪt). **1** weighing more than is usual, allowed, or healthy. ◆ *n* ('əʊvə,weɪt). **2** extra or excess weight. **3** *Archaic.* greater importance or effect. ◆ *vb* (,əʊvə'weɪt). (*tr*) **4** to give too much emphasis or consideration to. **5** to add too much weight to. **6** to weigh down.

overwhelm (,əʊvə'wɛlm) *vb* (*tr*) **1** to overpower the thoughts, emotions, or senses of. **2** to overcome with irresistible force. **3** to overcome, as with a profusion or concentration of something. **4** to cover over or bury completely. **5** to weigh or rest upon overpoweringly. **6** *Archaic.* to overturn.

overwhelming (,əʊvə'wɛlmɪŋ) *adj* overpowering in effect or force. ▸ **,over'whelmingly** *adv*

overwind (,əʊvə'waɪnd) *vb* **-winds, -winding, -wound.** (*tr*) to wind (a watch) beyond the proper limit.

overwinter (,əʊvə'wɪntə) *vb* **1** (*intr*) to spend winter (in or at a particular place). **2** (*tr*) to keep (animals or plants) alive through the winter. **3** (*intr*) (of an animal or plant) to remain alive throughout the winter.

overword ('əʊvə,wɜːd) *n* a repeated word or phrase.

overwork *vb* (,əʊvə'wɜːk). (*mainly tr*) **1** (*also intr*) to work or cause to work too hard or too long. **2** to use too much: *to overwork an excuse.* **3** to decorate the surface of. **4** to work up. ◆ *n* ('əʊvə,wɜːk). **5** excessive or excessively tiring work. ▸ **,over'worked** *adj*

overwrite (,əʊvə'raɪt) *vb* **-writes, -writing, -wrote, -written. 1** to write (something) in an excessively ornate or prolix style. **2** to write too much about (someone or something). **3** to write on top of (other writing). **4** to record on a storage medium, such as a magnetic disk, thus destroying what was originally recorded there.

overwrought (,əʊvə'rɔːt) *adj* **1** full of nervous tension; agitated. **2** too elaborate; fussy: *an overwrought style.* **3** (*often postpositive* and foll. by *with*) with the surface decorated or adorned.

Ovett ('əʊvɛt) *n* **Steve.** born 1955, British middle-distance runner: winner of the 800 metres in the 1980 Olympic Games.

ovi- *or* **ovo-** *combining form.* egg or ovum: *oviform; ovotestis.* **[**from Latin *ōvum***]**

Ovid ('ɒvɪd) *n* Latin name *Publius Ovidius Naso.* 43 B.C.–?17 A.D., Roman poet. His verse includes poems on love, *Ars Amatoria,* on myths, *Metamorphoses,* and on his sufferings in exile, *Tristia.* ▸ **Ovidian** (ɒ'vɪdɪən) *adj*

oviduct ('ɒvɪ,dʌkt, 'əʊ-) *n* the tube through which ova are conveyed from an ovary. Also called (in mammals): **Fallopian tube.** ▸ **oviducal** (,ɒvɪ'djuːkᵊl, ,əʊ-) *or* **,ovi'ductal** *adj*

Oviedo (*Spanish* o'βjeðo) *n* a city in NW Spain: capital of Asturias from 810 until 1002; centre of a coal- and iron-mining area. Pop.: 202 421 (1995 est.).

oviferous (əʊ'vɪfərəs) *or* **ovigerous** (əʊ'vɪdʒərəs) *adj Zoology.* carrying or producing eggs or ova: *the oviferous legs of certain spiders.*

oviform ('əʊvɪ,fɔːm) *adj Biology.* shaped like an egg.

ovine ('əʊvaɪn) *adj* of, relating to, or resembling a sheep. **[C19:** from Late Latin *ovīnus,* from Latin *ovis* sheep**]**

oviparous (əʊ'vɪpərəs) *adj* (of fishes, reptiles, birds, etc.) producing eggs that hatch outside the body of the mother. Compare **ovoviviparous, viviparous** (sense 1). ▸ **oviparity** (,əʊvɪ'pærɪtɪ) *n* ▸ **o'viparously** *adv*

oviposit (,əʊvɪ'pɒzɪt) *vb* (*intr*) (of insects and fishes) to deposit eggs through an ovipositor. **[C19:** OVI- + *positus,* past participle of Latin *pōnere* to place**]** ▸ **oviposition** (,əʊvɪpə'zɪʃən) *n*

ovipositor (,əʊvɪ'pɒzɪtə) *n* **1** the egg-laying organ of most female insects, consisting of a pair of specialized appendages at the end of the abdomen. **2** a similar organ in certain female fishes, formed by an extension of the edges of the genital opening.

ovisac ('əʊvɪ,sæk) *n* a capsule or sac, such as an ootheca, in which egg cells are produced.

ovo- *combining form.* a variant of **ovi-**.

ovoid ('əʊvɔɪd) *adj* **1** egg-shaped. **2** *Botany.* (of a fruit or similar part) egg-shaped with the broader end at the base. Compare **obovoid.** ◆ *n* **3** something that is ovoid.

ovolo ('əʊvə,ləʊ) *n, pl* **-li** (-,laɪ). *Architect.* a convex moulding having a cross section in the form of a quarter of a circle or ellipse. Also called: **quarter round, thumb.** Compare **congé** (sense 3), **echinus** (sense 1). **[C17:** from Italian: a little egg, from *ovo* egg, from Latin *ōvum***]**

ovotestis (,əʊvəʊ'tɛstɪs) *n, pl* **-tes** (-tiːz). the reproductive organ of snails, which produces both ova and spermatozoa.

ovoviviparous (,əʊvəʊvaɪ'vɪpərəs) *adj* (of certain reptiles, fishes, etc.) producing eggs that hatch within the body of the mother. Compare **oviparous, viviparous** (sense 1). ▸ **ovoviviparity** (,əʊvəʊ,vaɪvɪ'pærɪtɪ) *n*

ovulate ('ɒvjʊ,leɪt) *vb* (*intr*) to produce or discharge eggs from an ovary. **[C19:** from OVULE**]** ▸ **,ovu'lation** *n*

ovulation method *n* another name for **Billings method.**

ovule ('ɒvjuːl) *n* **1** a small body in seed-bearing plants that contains the egg cell and develops into the seed after fertilization. **2** *Zoology.* an immature ovum. **[C19:** via French from Medieval Latin *ōvulum* a little egg, from Latin *ōvum* egg**]** ▸ **'ovular** *adj*

ovum ('əʊvəm) *n, pl* **ova** ('əʊvə). an unfertilized female gamete; egg cell. **[**from Latin: egg**]**

ow (aʊ) *interj* an exclamation of pain.

owe (əʊ) *vb* (*mainly tr*) **1** to be under an obligation to pay (someone) to the amount of. **2** (*intr*) to be in debt: *he still owes for his house.* **3** (often foll. by *to*) to have as a result (of): *he owes his success to chance.* **4** to feel the need or obligation to do, give, etc.: *to owe somebody thanks; to owe it to oneself to rest.* **5** to hold or maintain in the mind or heart (esp. in the phrase **owe a grudge**). **[**Old English *āgan* to have (C12: to have to); related to Old Saxon *ēgan,* Old High German *eigan***]**

owelty ('əʊəltɪ) *n, pl* **-ties.** *Law.* equality, esp. in financial transactions. **[C16:** from Anglo-French *owelté,* ultimately from Latin *aequalitas,* from *aequalis* EQUAL**]**

Owen ('əʊɪn) *n* **1 David** (**Anthony Llewellyn**), Baron. born 1938, British politician: Labour foreign secretary (1977–79); cofounder of the Social Democratic Party (1981) and its leader (1983–87): leader (1988–92) of the section of the Social Democratic Party that did not merge with the Liberal Party in 1988; peace envoy to Bosnia-Herzegovina (1992–94). **2** Sir **Richard.** 1804–92, English comparative anatomist and palaeontologist. **3 Robert.** 1771–1858, Welsh industrialist and social reformer. He formed a model industrial community at New Lanark, Scotland, and pioneered cooperative societies. His books include *New View of Society* (1813). **4 Wilfred.** 1893–1918, English poet of World War I, who was killed in action.

Owen gun *n* a type of simple recoil-operated sub-machine-gun first used by Australian forces in World War II. **[**named after E. E. *Owen* (1915–49), its Australian inventor**]**

Owens ('əʊɪnz) *n* **Jesse,** real name *John Cleveland Owens.* 1913–80, U.S. Black athlete: won four gold medals at the Berlin Olympics (1936).

Owen Stanley Range *n* a mountain range in SE New Guinea. Highest peak: Mount Victoria, 4073 m (13 363 ft.).

ower *or* **owre** ('aʊər) *prep, adv, adj* a Scot. word for **over.**

Owerri (ə'wɛrɪ) *n* a market town in S Nigeria, capital of Imo state. Pop.: 35 010 (latest est.).

owing ('əʊɪŋ) *adj* **1** (*postpositive*) owed; due. **2 owing to.** (*prep*) because of or on account of.

owl (aʊl) *n* **1** any nocturnal bird of prey of the order *Strigiformes,* having large front-facing eyes, a small hooked bill, soft feathers, and a short neck. **2** any of various breeds of owl-like fancy domestic pigeon (esp. the **African owl, Chinese owl,** and **English owl**). **3** a person who looks or behaves like an owl, esp. in having a solemn manner. **[**Old English *ūle;* related to Dutch *uil,* Old High German *ūwila,* Old Norse *ugla***]** ▸ **'owl-,like** *adj*

owlet ('aʊlɪt) *n* a young or nestling owl.

owlish ('aʊlɪʃ) *adj* **1** like an owl. **2** solemn and wise in appearance. ▸ **'owlishly** *adv* ▸ **'owlishness** *n*

own (əʊn) *determiner* (*preceded by a possessive*) **1a** (intensifier): *John's own idea; your own mother.* **1b** (*as pronoun*): *I'll use my own.* **2** on behalf of oneself or in relation to oneself: *he is his own worst enemy.* **3 come into one's own.**

,over'tire *vb*
,over'tired *adj*
,over'train *vb*
,over'value *vb,* **-ues, -uing, -ued.**
,over'water *vb*
,over'zealous *adj*
,over'zealously *adv*

3a to become fulfilled: *she really came into her own when she got divorced.* **4 get one's own back.** *Informal.* to have revenge. **5 hold one's own.** to maintain one's situation or position, esp. in spite of opposition or difficulty. **6 on one's own. 6a** without help. **6b** by oneself; alone. ◆ *vb* **7** (*tr*) to have as one's possession. **8** (when *intr*, often foll. by *up, to,* or *up to*) to confess or admit; acknowledge. **9** (*tr; takes a clause as object*) *Now rare.* to concede: *I own that you are right.* [Old English *āgen,* originally past participle of *āgan* to have; related to Old Saxon *ēgan,* Old Norse *eiginn.* See OWE]

own brand *n* **a** an item packaged and marketed under the brand name of a particular retailer, usually a large supermarket chain, rather than that of the manufacturer. **b** (*as modifier*): *own-brand products.* ◆ Also **own label.**

owner ('əʊnə) *n* a person who owns; legal possessor.

owner-occupier *n Brit.* a person who owns or is in the process of buying the house or flat he lives in. ► ˌ**owner-'occuˌpied** *adj* ► **'owner-ˌoccu'pation** *n*

ownership ('əʊnəʃɪp) *n* **1** the state or fact of being an owner. **2** legal right of possession; proprietorship.

own goal *n* **1** *Soccer.* a goal scored by a player accidentally kicking the ball into his own team's net. Abbrev.: **o.g. 2** *Informal.* any action that results in disadvantage to the person who took it or to a party, group, etc. with which that person is associated.

owt (aʊt) *pron Northern English.* a dialect word for **anything.** [a variant of AUGHT[1]]

ox (ɒks) *n, pl* **oxen** ('ɒksən). **1** an adult castrated male of any domesticated species of cattle, esp. *Bos taurus,* used for draught work and meat. **2** any bovine mammal, esp. any of the domestic cattle. [Old English *oxa;* related to Old Saxon, Old High German *ohso,* Old Norse *oxi*]

oxa- *or before a vowel* **ox-** *combining form.* indicating that a chemical compound contains oxygen, used esp. to denote that a heterocyclic compound is derived from a specified compound by replacement of a carbon atom with an oxygen atom: *oxalic acid; oxazine.*

oxalate ('ɒksəˌleɪt) *n* a salt or ester of oxalic acid.

oxalic acid (ɒk'sælɪk) *n* a colourless poisonous crystalline dicarboxylic acid found in many plants: used as a bleach and a cleansing agent for metals. Formula: $(COOH)_2$. Systematic name: **ethanedioic acid.** [C18: from French *oxalique,* from Latin *oxalis* garden sorrel; see OXALIS]

oxalis ('ɒksəlɪs, ɒk'sælɪs) *n* any plant of the genus *Oxalis,* having clover-like leaves which contain oxalic acid and white, pink, red, or yellow flowers: family *Oxalidaceae.* See also **wood sorrel.** [C18: via Latin from Greek: sorrel, sour wine, from *oxus* acid, sharp]

oxazine ('ɒksəˌziːn) *n* any of 13 heterocyclic compounds with the formula C_4H_5NO. [from OXY-[2] + AZINE]

oxblood ('ɒksˌblʌd) *or* **oxblood red** *adj* of a dark reddish-brown colour.

oxbow ('ɒksˌbəʊ) *n* **1** a U-shaped piece of wood fitted under and around the neck of a harnessed ox and attached to the yoke. **2** Also called: **oxbow lake, cutoff.** a small curved lake lying on the flood plain of a river and constituting the remnant of a former meander.

Oxbridge ('ɒksˌbrɪdʒ) *n* **a** the British universities of Oxford and Cambridge, esp. considered as ancient and prestigious academic institutions, bastions of privilege and superiority, etc. **b** (*as modifier*): *Oxbridge graduates.*

oxen ('ɒksən) *n* the plural of **ox.**

Oxenstierna *or* **Oxenstjerna** (*Swedish* 'uksənʃæːrna) *n* **Count Axel** ('aksəl). 1583–1654, Swedish statesman. He was chancellor (1612–54) and successfully directed Swedish foreign policy for most of the Thirty Years' War.

oxeye ('ɒksˌaɪ) *n* **1** any Eurasian plant of the genus *Buphthalmum,* having daisy-like flower heads with yellow rays and dark centres: family *Compositae* (composites). **2** any of various North American plants of the related genus *Heliopsis,* having daisy-like flowers. **3 oxeye daisy.** another name for **daisy** (sense 2).

ox-eyed *adj* having large round eyes, like those of an ox.

OXFAM *or* **Oxfam** ('ɒksfæm) *n acronym for* Oxford Committee for Famine Relief.

Oxford[1] ('ɒksfəd) *n* **1** a city in S England, administrative centre of Oxfordshire, at the confluence of the Rivers Thames and Cherwell: Royalist headquarters during the Civil War; university, consisting of 40 separate colleges, the oldest being University College (1249); motor-vehicle industry. Pop.: 118 795 (1991). Related word: **Oxonian. 2** Also called: **Oxford Down.** a breed of sheep with short wool and a dark brown face and legs. **3** a type of stout laced shoe with a low heel. **4** a lightweight fabric of plain or twill weave used esp. for men's shirts.

Oxford[2] ('ɒksfəd) *n* **1st Earl of.** title of (Robert) **Harley.**

Oxford accent *n* the accent associated with Oxford English.

Oxford bags *pl n* trousers with very wide baggy legs, originally popular in the 1920s. Often shortened to **bags.**

Oxford blue *n* **1a** a dark blue colour. **1b** (*as adj*): *an Oxford-blue scarf.* **2** a person who has been awarded a blue from Oxford University.

Oxford English *n* that form of the received pronunciation of English supposed to be typical of Oxford University and regarded by many as affected or pretentious.

Oxford frame *n* a type of picture frame in which the sides of the frame cross each other and project outwards.

Oxford Group *n* an early name for **Moral Rearmament.**

Oxford Movement *n* a movement within the Church of England that began at Oxford in 1833 and was led by Pusey, Newman, and Keble. It affirmed the continuity of the Church with early Christianity and strove to restore the High-Church ideals of the 17th century. Its views were publicized in a series of tracts (**Tracts for the Times**) 1833–41. The teaching and practices of the Movement are maintained in the High-Church tradition within the Church of England. Also called: **Tractarianism.**

Oxfordshire ('ɒksfədˌʃɪə, -ʃə) *n* an inland county of S central England: situated mostly in the basin of the Upper Thames, with the Cotswolds in the west and the Chilterns in the southeast. Administrative centre: Oxford. Pop.: 590 200 (1994 est.). Area: 2608 sq. km (1007 sq. miles). Abbrev.: **Oxon.**

oxhide ('ɒksˌhaɪd) *n* leather made from the hide of an ox.

oxidant ('ɒksɪdənt) *n* a substance that acts or is used as an oxidizing agent. Also called (esp. in rocketry): **oxidizer.**

oxidase ('ɒksɪˌdeɪs, -ˌdeɪz) *n* any of a group of enzymes that bring about biological oxidation.

oxidate ('ɒksɪˌdeɪt) *vb* another word for **oxidize.**

oxidation (ˌɒksɪ'deɪʃən) *n* **a** the act or process of oxidizing. **b** (*as modifier*): *an oxidation state; an oxidation potential.* ► ˌ**oxi'dational** *adj* ► **'oxiˌdative** *adj*

oxidation-reduction *n* **a** a reversible chemical process usually involving the transfer of electrons, in which one reaction is an oxidation and the reverse reaction is a reduction. **b** Also: **redox.** (*as modifier*): *an oxidation-reduction reaction.*

oxidative phosphorylation *n* the process by which the energy liberated by oxidation of metabolites is used to synthesize the energy-rich molecule ATP.

oxide ('ɒksaɪd) *n* **1** any compound of oxygen with another element. **2** any organic compound in which an oxygen atom is bound to two alkyl or aryl groups; an ether. [C18: from French, from *ox(ygène)* + *(ac)ide;* see OXYGEN, ACID]

oxidimetry (ˌɒksɪ'dɪmɪtrɪ) *n Chem.* a branch of volumetric analysis in which oxidizing agents are used in titrations. [C20: from OXID(ATION) + -METRY] ► **oxidimetric** (ˌɒksɪdɪ'metrɪk) *adj*

oxidize *or* **oxidise** ('ɒksɪˌdaɪz) *vb* **1** to undergo or cause to undergo a chemical reaction with oxygen, as in formation of an oxide. **2** to form or cause to form a layer of metal oxide, as in rusting. **3** to lose or cause to lose hydrogen atoms. **4** to undergo or cause to undergo a decrease in the number of electrons. Compare **reduce** (sense 12c). ► ˌ**oxidi'zation** *or* ˌ**oxidi'sation** *n*

oxidizer *or* **oxidiser** ('ɒksɪˌdaɪzə) *n* an oxidant, esp. a substance that combines with the fuel in a rocket engine.

oxidizing agent *n Chem.* a substance that oxidizes another substance, being itself reduced in the process. Common oxidizing agents are oxygen, hydrogen peroxide, and ferric salts. Compare **reducing agent.**

oxime ('ɒksiːm) *n* any of a class of compounds with the general formula RR′NOH, where R is an organic group and R′ is either an organic group (**ketoxime**) or hydrogen atom (**aldoxime**): used in the chemical analysis of carbonyl compounds. [C19: from OX(YGEN) + IM(ID)E]

oxlip ('ɒksˌlɪp) *n* **1** Also called: **paigle.** a primulaceous Eurasian woodland plant, *Primula elatior,* with small drooping pale yellow flowers. **2** a similar and related plant that is a natural hybrid between the cowslip and primrose. [Old English *oxanslyppe,* literally: ox's slippery dropping; see SLIP[3], compare COWSLIP]

Oxo ('ɒksəʊ) *n Trademark.* extract of beef in the shape of small cubes which are mixed with boiling water and used for flavouring, as stock, a drink, etc. [C20: from OX + -O]

oxo- *or before a vowel* **ox-** *combining form.* indicating that a chemical compound contains oxygen linked to another atom by a double bond, used esp. to denote that a compound is derived from a specified compound by replacement of a methylene group with a carbonyl group: *oxobutanoic acid.*

oxo acid ('ɒksəʊ) *n* another name for **oxyacid.**

Oxon *abbrev. for* Oxfordshire. [from Latin *Oxonia*]

Oxon. ('ɒksən) *abbrev. for* (in degree titles) of Oxford. [from Latin *Oxoniensis*]

Oxonian (ɒk'səʊnɪən) *adj* **1** of or relating to Oxford or Oxford University. ◆ *n* **2** a member of Oxford University. **3** an inhabitant or native of Oxford.

oxonium compound *or* **salt** (ɒk'səʊnɪəm) *n Chem.* any of a class of salts derived from certain organic ethers or alcohols by adding a proton to the oxygen atom and thus producing a positive ion (**oxonium ion**).

oxpecker ('ɒksˌpekə) *n* either of two African starlings, *Buphagus africanus* or *B. erythrorhynchus,* having flattened bills with which they obtain food from the hides of cattle. Also called: **tick-bird.**

oxtail ('ɒksˌteɪl) *n* the skinned tail of an ox, used esp. in soups and stews.

oxter ('ɒkstə) *n Scot., Irish, and northern English dialect.* the armpit. [C16: from Old English *oxta;* related to Old High German *Ahsala,* Latin *axilla*]

oxtongue ('ɒksˌtʌŋ) *n* **1** any of various Eurasian plants of the genus *Picris,* having oblong bristly leaves and clusters of dandelion-like flowers: family *Compositae* (composites). **2** any of various other plants having bristly tongue-shaped leaves, such as alkanet. **3** the tongue of an ox, braised or boiled as food.

Oxus ('ɒksəs) *n* the ancient name for the **Amu Darya.**

oxy-[1] *combining form.* denoting something sharp; acute: *oxytone.* [from Greek, from *oxus*]

oxy-[2] *combining form.* **1** containing or using oxygen: *oxyacetylene.* **2** a former equivalent of **hydroxy-.**

oxyacetylene (ˌɒksɪə'setɪˌliːn) *n* **a** a mixture of oxygen and acetylene; used in a blowpipe for cutting or welding metals at high temperatures. **b** (*as modifier*): *an oxyacetylene burner.*

oxyacid (ˌɒksɪ'æsɪd) *n* any acid that contains oxygen. Also called: **oxo acid.**

oxycephaly (ˌɒksɪ'sefəlɪ) *n Pathol.* the condition of having a conical skull. [C20: from Greek *oxys* sharp + -CEPHALY] ► **oxycephalic** (ˌɒksɪsɪ'fælɪk) *or* ˌ**oxy'cephalous** *adj*

oxygen ('ɒksɪdʒən) *n* **a** a colourless odourless highly reactive gaseous element: the most abundant element in the earth's crust (49.2 per cent). It is essential for aerobic respiration and almost all combustion and is widely used in industry. Symbol: O; atomic no.: 8; atomic wt.: 15.9994; valency: 2; density: 1.429

kg/m^3; melting pt.: –218.79°C; boiling pt.: –182.97°C. **b** *(as modifier): an oxygen mask.* ▸ **oxygenic** (ˌɒksɪˈdʒɛnɪk) *or* **oxygenous** (ɒkˈsɪdʒɪnəs) *adj*

oxygen acid *n* another name for **oxyacid.**

oxygenate (ˈɒksɪdʒɪˌneɪt), **oxygenize,** *or* **oxygenise** *vb* to enrich or be enriched with oxygen: *to oxygenate blood.* ▸ **ˌoxygenˈation** *n* ▸ **ˈoxygeˌnizer** *or* **ˈoxygeˌniser** *n*

oxygenator (ˈɒksɪdʒɪˌneɪtə) *n* an apparatus that oxygenates the blood, esp. while a patient is undergoing an operation.

oxygen effect *n Biology.* the increased sensitivity to radiation of living organisms, tissues, etc., when they are exposed in the presence of oxygen.

oxygen mask *n* a device, worn over the nose and mouth, to which oxygen is supplied from a cylinder or other source: used to aid breathing.

oxygen tent *n Med.* a transparent enclosure covering a bedridden patient, into which oxygen is released to help maintain respiration.

oxygen weed *n N.Z.* another name for **water hyacinth.**

oxyhaemoglobin *or U.S.* **oxyhemoglobin** (ˌɒksɪˌhiːməʊˈgləʊbɪn, -ˌhɛm-) *n Biochem.* the bright red product formed when oxygen from the lungs combines with haemoglobin in the blood.

oxyhydrogen (ˌɒksɪˈhaɪdrədʒən) *n* **a** a mixture of hydrogen and oxygen used to provide an intense flame for welding. **b** *(as modifier): an oxyhydrogen blowpipe.*

oxymoron (ˌɒksɪˈmɔːrɒn) *n, pl* **-mora** (-ˈmɔːrə). *Rhetoric.* an epigrammatic effect, by which contradictory terms are used in conjunction: *living death; fiend angelical.* [C17: via New Latin from Greek *oxumōron,* from *oxus* sharp + *mōros* stupid]

oxyntic (ɒkˈsɪntɪk) *adj Physiol.* secreting acid: *oxyntic cells.* [C19: from Greek *oxus* acid, sharp]

oxysalt (ˌɒksɪˈsɔːlt) *n* any salt of an oxyacid.

oxysulphide (ˌɒksɪˈsʌlfaɪd) *n Chem.* a compound containing an element combined with oxygen and sulphur.

oxytetracycline (ˌɒksɪˌtɛtrəˈsaɪklɪn) *n* a broad-spectrum antibiotic, obtained from the bacterium *Streptomyces rimosus,* used in treating various infections. Formula: $C_{22}H_{24}N_2O_9$. Abbrev.: **OTC.**

oxytocic (ˌɒksɪˈtəʊsɪk) *adj* **1** accelerating childbirth by stimulating uterine contractions. ◆ *n* **2** an oxytocic drug or agent. [C19: from Greek, from OXY-[1] + *tokos* childbirth]

oxytocin (ˌɒksɪˈtəʊsɪn) *n* a polypeptide hormone, secreted by the pituitary gland, that stimulates contractions of the uterus or oviduct and ejection of milk in mammals; alphahypophame: used therapeutically for aiding childbirth. Formula: $C_{43}H_{66}N_{12}O_{12}S_2$. Compare **vasopressin.**

oxytone (ˈɒksɪˌtəʊn) (in the classical Greek language) ◆ *adj* **1** (of a word) having an accent on the final syllable. ◆ *n* **2** an oxytone word. ◆ Compare **paroxytone, proparoxytone.** [C18: from Greek *oxytonos,* from *oxys* sharp + *tonos* tone]

oyer (ɔɪə) *n* **1** *English legal history.* (in the 13th century) an assize. **2** (formerly) the reading out loud of a document in court. **3** See **oyer and terminer.**

oyer and terminer (ˈtɜːmɪnə) *n* **1** *English law.* (formerly) a commission issued to judges to try cases on assize. It became obsolete with the abolition of assizes and the setting up of crown courts in 1972. **2** the court in which such a hearing was held. **3** (in the U.S.) a court exercising higher criminal jurisdiction. [C15: from Anglo-Norman, from *oyer* to hear + *terminer* to judge]

oyez *or* **oyes** (əʊˈjɛs, -ˈjɛz) *interj* **1** a cry, usually uttered three times, by a public crier or court official for silence and attention before making a proclamation. ◆ *n* **2** such a cry. [C15: via Anglo-Norman from Old French *oiez!* hear!]

-oyl *suffix of nouns* (in chemistry) indicating an acyl group or radical: *ethanoyl, methanoyl.* [C20: from O(XYGEN) + -YL]

Oyo (ˈəʊjəʊ) *n* a state of SW Nigeria, formed in 1976 from part of Western State. Capital: Ibadan. Pop.: 3 900 803 (1995 est.). Area: 28 454 sq. km (10 986 sq. miles).

oyster (ˈɔɪstə) *n* **1a** any edible marine bivalve mollusc of the genus *Ostrea,* having a rough irregularly shaped shell and occurring on the sea bed, mostly in coastal waters. **1b** *(as modifier): oyster farm; oyster knife.* **2** any of various similar and related molluscs, such as the pearl oyster and the **saddle oyster** *(Anomia ephippium).* **3** the oyster-shaped piece of dark meat in the hollow of the pelvic bone of a fowl. **4** something from which advantage, delight, profit, etc., may be derived: *the world is his oyster.* **5** *Informal.* a very uncommunicative person. ◆ *vb* **6** *(intr)* to dredge for, gather, or raise oysters. [C14 *oistre,* from Old French *uistre,* from Latin *ostrea,* from Greek *ostreon;* related to Greek *osteon* bone, *ostrakon* shell]

oyster bed *n* a place, esp. on the sea bed, where oysters breed and grow naturally or are cultivated for food or pearls. Also called: **oyster bank, oyster park.**

oystercatcher (ˈɔɪstəˌkætʃə) *n* any shore bird of the genus *Haematopus* and family *Haematopodidae,* having a black or black-and-white plumage and a long stout laterally compressed red bill.

oyster crab *n* any of several small soft-bodied crabs of the genus *Pinnotheres,* esp. *P. ostreum,* that live as commensals in the mantles of oysters.

oysterman (ˈɔɪstəmən) *n, pl* **-men.** *Chiefly U.S.* **1** a person who gathers, cultivates, or sells oysters. **2** a boat used in gathering oysters.

oyster pink *n* **a** a delicate pinkish-white colour, sometimes with a greyish tinge. **b** *(as adj): oyster-pink shoes.*

oyster plant *n* another name for **salsify** (sense 1) and **sea lungwort** (see **lungwort** (sense 2)).

oyster white *n* **a** a greyish-white colour. **b** *(as adj): oyster-white walls.*

oz *or* **oz.** *abbrev. for* ounce. [from Italian *onza*]

Oz (ɒz) *n Austral. slang.* Australia.

Özal (əʊˈzɑːl) *n* **Turgut** (ˈtɜːgʊt). 1927–93, Turkish statesman: prime minister of Turkey (1983–89); president (1989–93).

Ozalid (ˈɒzəlɪd) *n* **1** *Trademark.* a method of duplicating typematter, illustrations, etc., when printed on translucent paper. It is used for proofing. **2** a reproduction produced by this method. [C20: formed by reversing DIAZO and inserting *l*]

Ozark Plateau (ˈəʊzɑːk) *n,* **Ozark Mountains,** *or* **Ozarks** *pl n* an eroded plateau in S Missouri, N Arkansas, and NE Oklahoma. Area: about 130 000 sq. km (50 000 sq. miles).

ozocerite *or* **ozokerite** (əʊˈzəʊkəˌraɪt) *n* a brown or greyish wax that occurs associated with petroleum and is used for making candles and wax paper. Also called: **earth wax, mineral wax.** [C19: from German *ozokerit,* from Greek *ozein* odour + *kēros* beeswax]

ozone (ˈəʊzəʊn, əʊˈzəʊn) *n* **1** a colourless gas with a chlorine-like odour, formed by an electric discharge in oxygen: a strong oxidizing agent, used in bleaching, sterilizing water, purifying air, etc. Formula: O_3; density: 2.14 kg/m^3; melting pt.: –192°C; boiling pt.: –110.51. Technical name: **trioxygen. 2** *Informal.* clean bracing air, as found at the seaside. [C19: from German *ozon,* from Greek: smell] ▸ **ozonic** (əʊˈzɒnɪk) *or* **ˈozonous** *adj*

ozone-friendly *adj* not harmful to the ozone layer; using substances that do not produce gases harmful to the ozone layer: *an ozone-friendly refrigerator.*

ozone layer *n* the region of the stratosphere with the highest concentration of ozone molecules, which by absorbing high-energy solar ultraviolet radiation protects organisms on earth. Also called: **ozonosphere.**

ozonide (əʊˈzəʊnaɪd) *n* any of a class of unstable explosive compounds produced by the addition of ozone to a double bond in an organic compound.

ozoniferous (ˌəʊzəʊˈnɪfərəs) *adj* containing ozone.

ozonize *or* **ozonise** (ˈəʊzəʊˌnaɪz) *vb (tr)* **1** to convert (oxygen) into ozone. **2** to treat (a substance) with ozone. ▸ **ˌozoniˈzation** *or* **ˌozoniˈsation** *n* ▸ **ˈozoˌnizer** *or* **ˈozoˌniser** *n*

ozonolysis (ˌəʊzəʊˈnɒlɪsɪs) *n Chem.* the process of treating an organic compound with ozone to form an ozonide: used to locate double bonds in molecules.

ozonosphere (əʊˈzəʊnəˌsfɪə, -ˈzɒnə-) *n* another name for **ozone layer.**

ozs *or* **ozs.** *abbrev. for* ounces.

Pp

p *or* **P** (piː) *n, pl* **p's, P's,** or **Ps. 1** the 16th letter and 12th consonant of the modern English alphabet. **2** a speech sound represented by this letter, usually a voiceless bilabial stop, as in *pig.* **3 mind one's p's and q's.** to be careful to behave correctly and use polite or suitable language.

p *symbol for:* **1** (in Britain) penny *or* pence. **2** *Music.* piano: an instruction to play quietly. **3** pico-. **4** *Physics.* **4a** momentum. **4b** proton. **4c** pressure.

P *symbol for:* **1** *Chem.* phosphorus. **2** *Physics.* **2a** pressure. **2b** power. **2c** parity. **2d** poise. **3** (on road signs) parking. **4** *Chess.* pawn. **5** *Currency.* **5a** peseta. **5b** peso. **5c** pataca. **5d** pula. ◆ *abbrev. for:* **6** pharmacy only: used on medicines that can be obtained without a prescription, but only at a shop, such as a chemist's, where there is a pharmacist. ◆ **7** *international car registration for* Portugal.

p. *abbrev. for:* **1** (*pl* **pp.**) page. **2** part. **3** participle. **4** past. **5** per. **6** pint. **7** pipe. **8** population. **9** post [Latin: after] **10** pro [Latin: in favour of; for]

P. *abbrev. for:* **1** Pastor. **2** President. **3** Priest. **4** Prince.

p- *prefix* short for **para-**[1] (sense 6).

pa[1] (pɑː) *n* an informal word for **father.**

pa[2] *or* **pah** (pɑː) *n N.Z.* **1** a Maori village or settlement. **2** *History.* a Maori defensive position and settlement on a hilltop. **3 go back to the pa.** to abandon city life in favour of rural life. [Maori]

Pa 1 *the chemical symbol for* protactinium. **2** *symbol for* pascal.

PA *abbrev. for:* **1** Pennsylvania. **2** personal appearance. **3** personal assistant. **4** *Military.* Post Adjutant. **5** power of attorney. **6** press agent. **7** Press Association. **8** *Banking.* private account. **9** public-address system. **10** publicity agent. **11** Publishers Association. **12** purchasing agent. **13** *Insurance.* particular average. ◆ **14** *international car registration for* Panama.

Pa. *abbrev. for* Pennsylvania.

p.a. *abbrev. for* per annum. [Latin: yearly]

paal (pɑːl) *n Caribbean.* a stake driven into the ground. [from Dutch: a pile, stake]

pa'anga (pɑːˈɑːŋgə) *n* the standard monetary unit of Tonga, divided into 100 seniti.

PABA (ˈpɑːbə) *n acronym for* para-aminobenzoic acid.

Pabst (*German* paːpst) *n* **G(eorge) W(ilhelm).** 1885–1967, German film director, whose films include *Joyless Street* (1925), *Pandora's Box* (1929), and *The Last Act* (1954).

pabulum (ˈpæbjʊləm) *n Rare.* **1** food. **2** food for thought, esp. when bland or dull. [C17: from Latin, from *pascere* to feed]

PABX (in Britain) *abbrev. for* private automatic branch exchange. See also **PBX.**

Pac. *abbrev. for* Pacific.

paca (ˈpɑːkə, ˈpækə) *n* a large burrowing hystricomorph rodent, *Cuniculus paca,* of Central and South America, having white-spotted brown fur and a large head: family *Dasyproctidae.* [C17: from Spanish, from Tupi]

pace[1] (peɪs) *n* **1a** a single step in walking. **1b** the distance covered by a step. **2** a measure of length equal to the average length of a stride, approximately 3 feet. See also **Roman pace, geometric pace, military pace. 3** speed of movement, esp. of walking or running. **4** rate or style of proceeding at some activity: *to live at a fast pace.* **5** manner or action of stepping, walking, etc.; gait. **6** any of the manners in which a horse or other quadruped walks or runs, the three principal paces being the walk, trot, and canter (or gallop). **7** a manner of moving, natural to the camel and sometimes developed in the horse, in which the two legs on the same side of the body are moved and put down at the same time. **8** *Architect.* a step or small raised platform. **9 keep pace with.** to proceed at the same speed as. **10 put (someone) through his paces.** to test the ability of (someone). **11 set the pace.** to determine the rate at which a group runs or walks or proceeds at some other activity. **12 stand** *or* **stay the pace.** to keep up with the speed or rate of others. ◆ *vb* **13** (*tr*) to set or determine the pace for, as in a race. **14** (often foll. by *about, up and down,* etc.) to walk with regular slow or fast paces, as in boredom, agitation, etc.: *to pace the room.* **15** (*tr;* often foll. by *out*) to measure by paces: *to pace out the distance.* **16** (*intr*) to walk with slow regular strides: *to pace along the street.* **17** (*intr*) (of a horse) to move at the pace (the specially developed gait). [C13: via Old French from Latin *passūs* step, from *pandere* to spread, unfold, extend (the legs as in walking)]

pace[2] (ˈpeɪsɪ; *Latin* ˈpɑːkɛ) *prep* with due deference to: used to acknowledge politely someone who disagrees with the speaker or writer. [C19: from Latin, from *pāx* peace]

PACE (peɪs) *n* (in England and Wales) *acronym for* Police and Criminal Evidence Act.

pace bowler *n Cricket.* a bowler who characteristically delivers the ball rapidly.

pacemaker (ˈpeɪsˌmeɪkə) *n* **1** a person, horse, vehicle, etc., used in a race or speed trial to set the pace. **2** a person, an organization, etc., regarded as being the leader in a particular field of activity. **3** Also called: **cardiac pacemaker.** a small area of specialized tissue within the wall of the right atrium of the heart whose spontaneous electrical activity initiates and controls the beat of the heart. **4** Also called: **artificial pacemaker.** an electronic device for use in certain cases of heart disease to assume the functions of the natural cardiac pacemaker.

pacer (ˈpeɪsə) *n* **1** a horse trained to move at a special gait, esp. for racing. **2** another word for **pacemaker** (sense 1).

pacesetter (ˈpeɪsˌsɛtə) *n* another word for **pacemaker** (senses 1, 2).

paceway (ˈpeɪsˌweɪ) *n Austral.* a racecourse for trotting and pacing.

pacey *or* **pacy** (ˈpeɪsɪ) *adj* **pacier, paciest.** fast-moving, quick, lively: *a pacey story.*

pacha (ˈpɑːʃə, ˈpæʃə) *n* a variant spelling of **pasha.**

pachalic (ˈpɑːʃəlɪk) *n* a variant spelling of **pashalik.**

Pachelbel (*German* ˈpaxəlbɛl) *n* **Johann** (ˈjohan). 1653–1706, German organist and composer, noted esp. for his popular *Canon in D Major.*

pachisi (pəˈtʃiːzɪ, pɑː-) *n* an Indian game somewhat resembling backgammon, played on a cruciform board using six cowries as dice. [C18: from Hindi *pacīsī,* from *pacīs* twenty-five (the highest score possible in one throw)]

Pachomius (pəˈkəʊmɪəs) *n* **Saint.** ?290–346 A.D., Egyptian hermit; founder of the first Christian monastery (318). Feast day: May 14 or 15.

pachouli (ˈpætʃʊlɪ, pəˈtʃuːlɪ) *n* a variant spelling of **patchouli.**

Pachuca (*Spanish* paˈtʃuka) *n* a city in central Mexico, capital of Hidalgo state, in the Sierra Madre Oriental: silver mines; university (1961). Pop.: 174 013 (1990).

Pachuco (pəˈtʃuːkəʊ) *n, pl* **-cos.** *U.S.* a young Mexican living in the U.S., esp. one of low social status who belongs to a street gang. [C20: from Mexican Spanish]

pachyderm (ˈpækɪˌdɜːm) *n* any very large thick-skinned mammal, such as an elephant, rhinoceros, or hippopotamus. [C19: from French *pachyderme,* from Greek *pakhudermos* thick-skinned, from *pakhus* thick + *derma* skin] ▸ **ˌpachyˈdermatous** *adj*

pachytene (ˈpækɪˌtiːn) *n* the third stage of the prophase of meiosis during which the chromosomes become shorter and thicker and divide into chromatids. [from Greek *pakhus* thick + *tainia* band]

pacific (pəˈsɪfɪk) *adj* **1** tending or conducive to peace; conciliatory. **2** not aggressive; opposed to the use of force. **3** free from conflict; peaceful. [C16: from Old French *pacifique,* from Latin *pācificus,* from *pāx* peace + *facere* to make] ▸ **paˈcifically** *adv*

Pacific (pəˈsɪfɪk) *n* **1 the.** short for **Pacific Ocean.** ◆ *adj* **2** of or relating to the Pacific Ocean or its islands.

pacification (ˌpæsɪfɪˈkeɪʃən) *n* the act, process, or policy of pacifying. ▸ **ˈpacifiˌcatory** *adj*

Pacific Islands *pl n* a former Trust Territory; an island group in the W Pacific Ocean, mandated to Japan after World War I and assigned to the U.S. by the United Nations in 1947: comprised 2141 islands (96 inhabited) of the Caroline, Marshall, and Mariana groups (excluding Guam). In 1978 the Northern Marianas became a commonwealth in union with the U.S. The three remaining entities consisting of the Marshall Islands, the Republic of Belau (formerly Palau), and the Federated States of Micronesia became self-governing during the period 1979–80. In 1982 they signed agreements of free association with the U.S. Administrative centre: Saipan (Mariana Islands). Land area: about 1800 sq. km (700 sq. miles), scattered over about 7 500 000 sq. km (3 000 000 sq. miles) of ocean.

Pacific Northwest *n* the region of North America lying north of the Columbia River and west of the Rockies.

Pacific Ocean *n* the world's largest and deepest ocean, lying between Asia and Australia and North and South America: almost landlocked in the north, linked with the Arctic Ocean only by the Bering Strait, and extending to Antarctica in the south; has exceptionally deep trenches, and a large number of volcanic and coral islands. Area: about 165 760 000 sq. km (64 000 000 sq. miles). Average depth: 4215 m (14 050 ft.). Greatest depth: Challenger Deep (in the Marianas Trench), 11 033 m (37 073 ft.). Greatest width: (between Panama and Mindanao, Philippines) 17 066 km (10 600 miles).

Pacific rim *n* the regions, countries, etc., that lie on the western shores of the Pacific Ocean, esp. in the context of their developing manufacturing capacity and consumer markets.

Pacific Standard Time *n* one of the standard times used in North America, based on the local time of the 120° meridian, eight hours behind Greenwich Mean Time. Abbrev.: **PST.**

pacifier (ˈpæsɪˌfaɪə) *n* **1** a person or thing that pacifies. **2** *U.S. and Canadian.* a baby's dummy or teething ring.

pacifism (ˈpæsɪˌfɪzəm) *n* **1** the belief that violence of any kind is unjustifiable and that one should not participate in war. **2** the belief that international disputes can be settled by arbitration rather than war.

pacifist (ˈpæsɪfɪst) *n* **1** a person who supports pacifism. **2** a person who refuses military service. ◆ *adj* **3** advocating, relating to, or characterized by pacifism.

pacify (ˈpæsɪˌfaɪ) *vb* **-fies, -fying, -fied.** (*tr*) **1** to calm the anger or agitation of; mollify. **2** to restore to peace or order, esp. by the threat or use of force. [C15: from Old French *pacifier;* see PACIFIC] ▸ **ˈpaciˌfiable** *adj*

Pacino (pəˈtʃiːnəʊ) *n* **Al,** full name *Alfredo James Pacino.* born 1940, U.S. film actor; his films include *The Godfather* (1972), *Dog Day Afternoon* (1975), *Scent of a Woman* (1992), for which he won an Oscar, and *Heat* (1995).

pack[1] (pæk) *n* **1a** a bundle or load, esp. one carried on the back. **1b** (*as* *modifier): a pack animal.* **2** a collected amount of anything. **3** a complete set of similar things, esp. a set of 52 playing cards. **4** a group of animals of the same kind, esp. hunting animals: *a pack of hounds.* **5** any group or band that associates together, esp. for criminal purposes. **6** *Rugby.* the forwards of a team or both teams collectively, as in a scrum or in rucking. **7** the basic organizational unit of Cub Scouts and Brownie Guides. **8a** a small package, carton, or container, used to retail commodities, esp. foodstuffs, cigarettes, etc. **8b** (*in combination*): *pack-sealed.* **9** a U.S. and Canadian word for **packet** (sense 1). **10** short for **pack ice.** **11** the quantity of something, such as food, packaged for preservation. **12** *Med.* **12a** a sheet or blanket, either damp or dry, for wrapping about the body, esp. for its soothing effect. **12b** a material such as cotton or gauze for temporarily filling a bodily cavity, esp. to control bleeding. **13** short for **backpack** or **rucksack.** **14** *Mining.* a roof support, esp. one made of rubble. **15** short for **face pack.** **16** a parachute folded and ready for use. **17** *Computing.* another name for **deck** (sense 5). **18 go to the pack.** *Austral. and N.Z. informal.* to fall into a lower state or condition. ◆ *vb* **19** to place or arrange (articles) in (a container), such as clothes in a suitcase. **20** (*tr*) to roll up into a bundle. **21** (when *passive,* often foll. by *out*) to press tightly together; cram: *the audience packed into the foyer; the hall was packed out.* **22** (*tr;* foll. by *in* or *into*) to fit (many things, experiences, etc.) into a limited space or time: *she packed a lot of theatre visits into her holiday.* **23** to form (snow, ice, etc.) into a hard compact mass or (of snow, ice, etc.) to become compacted. **24** (*tr*) to press in or cover tightly: *to pack a hole with cement.* **25** (*tr*) to load (a horse, donkey, etc.) with a burden. **26** (often foll. by *off* or *away*) to send away or go away, esp. hastily. **27** (*tr*) to seal (a joint) by inserting a layer of compressible material between the faces. **28** (*tr*) to fill (a bearing or gland) with grease to lubricate it. **29** (*tr*) to separate (two adjoining components) so that they have a predetermined gap between them, by introducing shims, washers, plates, etc. **30** (*tr*) *Med.* to treat with a pack. **31** (*tr*) *Slang.* to be capable of inflicting (a blow): *he packs a mean punch.* **32** (*tr*) *U.S. informal.* to carry or wear habitually: *he packs a gun.* **33** (*intr;* often foll. by *down*) *Rugby.* to form a scrum. **34** (*tr;* often foll. by *into, to,* etc.) *U.S., Canadian, and N.Z.* to carry (goods), esp. on the back: *will you pack your camping equipment into the mountains?* **35 pack one's bags.** *Informal.* to get ready to leave. **36 send packing.** *Informal.* to dismiss peremptorily. ◆ See also **pack in, pack up.** [C13: related to Middle Low German *pak,* of obscure origin] ► **'packable** *adj*

pack[2] (pæk) *vb* (*tr*) to fill (a legislative body, committee, etc.) with one's own supporters: *to pack a jury.* [C16: perhaps changed from PACT]

package ('pækɪdʒ) *n* **1** any wrapped or boxed object or group of objects. **2a** a proposition, offer, or thing for sale in which separate items are offered together as a single or inclusive unit. **2b** (*as modifier*): *a package holiday; a package deal.* **3** a complete unit consisting of a number of component parts sold separately. **4** the act or process of packing or packaging. **5** *Computing.* a set of programs designed for a specific type of problem in statistics, production control, etc., making it unnecessary for a separate program to be written for each problem. **6** a U.S. and Canadian word for **packet** (sense 1). ◆ *vb* (*tr*) **7** to wrap in or put into a package. **8** to design and produce a package for (retail goods). **9** to group (separate items) together as a single unit. **10** to compile (complete books) for a publisher to market.

packager ('pækɪdʒə) *n* an independent firm specializing in design and production, as of illustrated books or television programmes which are sold to publishers or television companies as finished products.

package store *n U.S.* a store where alcoholic drinks are sold for consumption elsewhere. Canadian name (also sometimes used in the U.S.): **liquor store.** Brit. equivalent: **off-licence.**

packaging ('pækɪdʒɪŋ) *n* **1a** the box or wrapping in which a product is offered for sale. **1b** the design of such a box or wrapping, esp. with reference to its ability to attract customers. **2** the presentation of a person, product, television programme, etc., to the public in a way designed to build up a favourable image. **3** the work of a packager.

pack animal *n* an animal, such as a donkey, used to transport goods, equipment, etc.

pack drill *n* a military punishment by which the offender is made to march about carrying a full pack of equipment.

packed (pækt) *adj* **1** completely filled; full: *a packed theatre.* **2** (of a picnic type of meal) prepared and put in a container or containers beforehand; prepacked: *a packed lunch.*

packer ('pækə) *n* **1** a person or company whose business is to pack goods, esp. food: *a meat packer.* **2** a person or machine that packs.

packet ('pækɪt) *n* **1** a small or medium-sized container of cardboard, paper, etc., often together with its contents: *a packet of biscuits.* Usual U.S. and Canadian word: **package, pack.** **2** a small package; parcel. **3** Also called: **packet boat.** a boat that transports mail, passengers, goods, etc., on a fixed short route. **4** *Slang.* a large sum of money: *to cost a packet.* **5** *Computing.* a unit into which a larger piece of data is broken down for more efficient transmission. See also **packet switching.** ◆ *vb* **6** (*tr*) to wrap up in a packet or as a packet. [C16: from Old French *pacquet,* from *pacquer* to pack, from Old Dutch *pak* a pack]

packet switching *n Computing.* the concentration of data into units that are allocated an address prior to transmission.

packframe ('pæk,freɪm) *n Mountaineering.* a light metal frame with shoulder straps, used for carrying heavy or awkward loads.

packhorse ('pæk,hɔːs) *n* a horse used to transport goods, equipment, etc.

pack ice *n* a large area of floating ice, usually occurring in polar seas, consisting of separate pieces that have become massed together. Also called: **ice pack.**

pack in *vb* (*tr, adv*) **1** *Brit. and N.Z. informal.* to stop doing (something) (esp. in the phrase **pack it in**). **2** to carry (something) to base camp, etc. by pack.

packing ('pækɪŋ) *n* **1a** material used to cushion packed goods. **1b** (*as modifier*): *a packing needle.* **2** the packaging of foodstuffs. **3** *Med.* **3a** the application of a medical pack. **3b** gauze or other absorbent material for packing a wound. **4** *Printing.* sheets of material, esp. paper, used to cover the platen or impression cylinder of a letterpress machine. **5** any substance or material used to make watertight or gastight joints, esp. in a stuffing box. **6** *Engineering.* pieces of material of various thicknesses used to adjust the position of a component or machine before it is secured in its correct position or alignment.

packing box *n* another name for **stuffing box.**

packing density *n Computing.* a measure of the amount of data that can be held by unit length of a storage medium, such as magnetic tape.

packing fraction *n* a measure of the stability of a nucleus, equal to the difference between its mass in amu and its mass number, divided by the mass number.

pack of lies *n* a completely false story, account, etc.

pack rat *n* any rat of the genus *Neotoma,* of W North America, having a long tail that is furry in some species: family *Cricetidae.* Also called: **wood rat.**

packsack ('pæk,sæk) *n* a U.S. and Canadian word for **knapsack.**

packsaddle ('pæk,sædᵊl) *n* a saddle hung with packs, equipment, etc., used on a pack animal.

packthread ('pæk,θrɛd) *n* a strong twine for sewing or tying up packages.

pack up *vb* (*adv*) **1** to put (things) away in a proper or suitable place. **2** *Informal.* to give up (an attempt) or stop doing (something): *if you don't do your work better, you might as well pack up.* **3** (*intr*) (of an engine, machine, etc.) to fail to operate; break down. **4** *Engineering.* to use packing to adjust the height of a component or machine before it is secured in its correct position or alignment.

pact (pækt) *n* an agreement or compact between two or more parties, nations, etc., for mutual advantage. [C15: from Old French *pacte,* from Latin *pactum,* from *pacīscī* to agree]

pacy ('peɪsɪ) *adj* a variant spelling of **pacey.**

pad[1] (pæd) *n* **1** a thick piece of soft material used to make something comfortable, give it shape, or protect it. **2** a guard made of flexible resilient material worn in various sports to protect parts of the body. **3** Also called: **stamp pad, ink pad.** a block of firm absorbent material soaked with ink for transferring to a rubber stamp. **4** Also called: **'notepad, writing pad.** a number of sheets of paper fastened together along one edge. **5** a flat piece of stiff material used to back a piece of blotting paper. **6a** the fleshy cushion-like underpart of the foot of a cat, dog, etc. **6b** any of the parts constituting such a structure. **7** any of various level surfaces or flat-topped structures, such as a launch pad. **8** *Entomol.* a nontechnical name for **pulvillus.** **9** the large flat floating leaf of the water lily. **10** *Electronics.* a resistive attenuator network inserted in the path of a signal to reduce amplitude or to match one circuit to another. **11** *Slang.* a person's residence. **12** *Slang.* a bed or bedroom. ◆ *vb* **pads, padding, padded.** (*tr*) **13** to line, stuff, or fill out with soft material, esp. in order to protect or give shape to. **14** (often foll. by *out*) to inflate with irrelevant or false information: *to pad out a story.* [C16: origin uncertain; compare Low German *pad* sole of the foot]

pad[2] (pæd) *vb* **pads, padding, padded.** **1** (*intr;* often foll. by *along, up,* etc.) to walk with a soft or muffled tread. **2** (when *intr,* often foll. by *around*) to travel (a route) on foot, esp. at a slow pace; tramp: *to pad around the country.* ◆ *n* **3** a dull soft sound, esp. of footsteps. **4** *Archaic.* short for **footpad.** **5** *Archaic or dialect.* a slow-paced horse; nag. **6** *Dialect and Austral.* a path or track: *a cattle pad.* [C16: perhaps from Middle Dutch *paden,* from *pad* PATH]

padang ('pædæŋ) *n* (in Malaysia) a playing field. [from Malay: plain]

Padang ('pɑːdɑːŋ) *n* a port in W Indonesia, in W Sumatra at the foot of the **Padang Highlands** on the Indian Ocean. Pop.: 721 500 (1995 est.).

padauk *or* **padouk** (pə'daʊk, -'dɔːk) *n* **1** any of various tropical African or Asian papilionaceous trees of the genus *Pterocarpus* that have reddish wood. **2** the wood of any of these trees, used in decorative cabinetwork. ◆ See also **amboyna.** [from a native Burmese word]

padded cell *n* a room, esp. one in a mental hospital, with padded surfaces in which violent inmates are placed.

padding ('pædɪŋ) *n* **1** any soft material used to pad clothes, furniture, etc. **2** superfluous material put into a speech or written work to pad it out; waffle. **3** inflated or false entries in a financial account, esp. an expense account.

paddle[1] ('pædᵊl) *n* **1** a short light oar with a flat blade at one or both ends, used without a rowlock to propel a canoe or small boat. **2** Also called: **float.** a blade of a water wheel or paddle wheel. **3** a period of paddling: *to go for a paddle upstream.* **4a** a paddle wheel used to propel a boat. **4b** (*as modifier*): *a paddle steamer.* **5** the sliding panel in a lock or sluicegate that regulates the level or flow of water. **6** any of various instruments shaped like a paddle and used for beating, mixing, etc. **7** a table-tennis bat. **8** the flattened limb of a seal, turtle, or similar aquatic animal, specialized for swimming. ◆ *vb* **9** to propel (a canoe, small boat, etc.) with a paddle. **10 paddle one's own canoe.** **10a** to be self-sufficient. **10b** to mind one's own business. **11** (*tr*) to convey by paddling: *we paddled him to the shore.* **12** (*tr*) to stir or mix with or as if with a paddle. **13** to row (a boat) steadily, esp. (of a racing crew) to row firmly but not at full pressure. **14** (*intr*) (of steamships) to be propelled by paddle wheels. **15** (*intr*) to swim with short rapid strokes, like a dog. **16** (*tr*) *U.S. and Canadian informal.* to spank. [C15: of unknown origin] ► **'paddler** *n*

paddle[2] ('pædᵊl) *vb* (*mainly intr*) **1** to walk or play barefoot in shallow water, mud, etc. **2** to dabble the fingers, hands, or feet in water. **3** to walk unsteadily, like a baby. **4** (*tr*) *Archaic.* to fondle with the fingers. ◆ *n* **5** the act of paddling in water. [C16: of uncertain origin] ► **'paddler** *n*

paddlefish ('pædᵊl,fɪʃ) *n, pl* **-fish** *or* **-fishes.** **1** a primitive bony fish, *Polyodon spathula,* of the Mississippi River, having a long paddle-like projection to the snout: family *Polyodontidae.* **2** a similar and related Chinese fish, *Psephurus gladius,* of the Yangtze River.

paddle wheel *n* a large wheel fitted with paddles, turned by an engine to propel a vessel on the water.

paddle worm *n* any of a family of green-blue faintly iridescent active marine polychaete worms of the genus *Phyllodoce,* having paddle-shaped swimming lobes, found under stones on the shore.

paddock[1] ('pædək) *n* **1** a small enclosed field, often for grazing or training horses, usually near a house or stable. **2** (in horse racing) the enclosure in which horses are paraded and mounted before a race, together with the accompanying rooms. **3** (in motor racing) an area near the pits where cars are worked on before races. **4** *Austral. and N.Z.* any area of fenced land. **5** *Austral. and N.Z.* a playing field. **6 the long paddock.** *Austral. informal.* a stockroute or roadside area offering feed to sheep and cattle in dry times. ◆ *vb* **7** (*tr*) to confine (horses, etc.) in a paddock. [C17: variant of dialect *parrock,* from Old English *pearruc* enclosure, of Germanic origin. See PARK]

paddock[2] ('pædək) *n Archaic or dialect.* a frog or toad. Also called (Scot.): **puddock.** [C12: from *pad* toad, probably from Old Norse *padda;* see -OCK]

paddy[1] ('pædɪ) *n, pl* **-dies. 1** Also called: **paddy field.** a field planted with rice. **2** rice as a growing crop or when harvested but not yet milled. [from Malay *pādī*]

paddy[2] ('pædɪ) *n, pl* **-dies.** *Brit. informal.* a fit of temper. [C19: from PADDY]

Paddy ('pædɪ) *n, pl* **-dies.** (*sometimes not cap.*) an informal, often derogatory, name for an Irishman. [from *Patrick*]

paddy-last *n Irish.* the last person in a race or competition: *she was paddy-last.*

paddy wagon *n U.S., Austral., and N.Z.* an informal word for **patrol wagon.**

paddywhack *or* **paddywack** ('pædɪˌwæk) *n Informal.* **1** *Brit.* another word for **paddy**[2]. **2** a spanking or smack.

pademelon *or* **paddymelon** ('pædɪˌmɛlən) *n* a small wallaby of the genus *Thylogale,* of coastal scrubby regions of Australia. [C19: from a native Australian name]

Paderborn (*German* paːdər'bɔrn) *n* a market town in NW Germany, in North Rhine-Westphalia: scene of the meeting between Charlemagne and Pope Leo III (799 A.D.) that led to the foundation of the Holy Roman Empire. Pop.: 133 717 (1996 est.).

Paderewski (*Polish* padɛ'rɛfski) *n* **Ignace Jan** (iɲas jan). 1860–1941, Polish pianist, composer, and statesman; prime minister (1919).

Padishah ('pɑːdɪˌʃɑː) *n* a title of the shah of Iran. [from Persian *pādi* lord + SHAH]

padkos ('padˌkɒs) *pl n S. African.* snacks and provisions for a journey. [Afrikaans, literally: road food]

padlock ('pædˌlɒk) *n* **1** a detachable lock having a hinged or sliding shackle, which can be used to secure a door, lid, etc., by passing the shackle through rings or staples. ◆ *vb* **2** (*tr*) to fasten with or as if with a padlock. [C15 *pad,* of obscure origin]

Padma Shri ('pʌdmə 'ʃriː) *n* (in India) an award for distinguished service in any field. [Hindi: lotus decoration]

padouk (pə'daʊk, -'dɔːk) *n* a variant spelling of **padauk.**

Padova ('paːdova) *n* the Italian name for **Padua.**

padre ('pɑːdrɪ) *n Informal.* (*sometimes cap.*) **1** father: used to address or refer to a clergyman, esp. a priest. **2** a chaplain to the armed forces. [via Spanish or Italian from Latin *pater* father]

padrone (pə'drəʊnɪ) *n, pl* **-nes** *or* **-ni** (-niː). **1** the owner or proprietor of an inn, esp. in Italy. **2** *U.S.* an employer who completely controls his workers, esp. a man who exploits Italian immigrants in the U.S. [C17: from Italian; see PATRON[1]]

padsaw ('pædˌsɔː) *n* a small narrow saw used for cutting curves. [C19: from PAD[1] (in the sense: a handle that can be fitted to various tools) + SAW[1]]

Padua ('pædʒʊə, 'pædjʊə) *n* a city in NE Italy, in Veneto: important in Roman and Renaissance times; university (1222); botanical garden (1545). Pop.: 212 713 (1996 est.). Latin name: **Patavium** (pə'teɪvɪəm). Italian name: **Padova.**

paduasoy ('pædjʊəˌsɔɪ) *n* **1** a rich strong silk fabric used for hangings, vestments, etc. **2** a garment made of this. [C17: changed (through influence of PADUA) from earlier *poudesoy,* from French *pou-de-soie,* of obscure origin]

Padus ('peɪdəs) *n* the Latin name for the **Po**[2].

paean *or U.S.* (*sometimes*) **pean** ('piːən) *n* **1** a hymn sung in ancient Greece in invocation of or thanksgiving to a deity. **2** any song of praise. **3** enthusiastic praise: *the film received a paean from the critics.* [C16: via Latin from Greek *paiān* hymn to Apollo, from his title *Paiān,* denoting the physician of the gods]

paederast ('pɛdəˌræst) *n* a less common spelling of **pederast.** ► **ˌpaeder'astic** *adj* ► **'paederˌasty** *n*

paediatrician *or chiefly U.S.* **pediatrician** (ˌpiːdɪə'trɪʃən) *n* a medical practitioner who specializes in paediatrics.

paediatrics *or chiefly U.S.* **pediatrics** (ˌpiːdɪ'ætrɪks) *n* (*functioning as sing*) the branch of medical science concerned with children and their diseases. ► **ˌpaedi'atric** *or chiefly U.S.* **ˌpedi'atric** *adj*

paedo-, *before a vowel* **paed-** *or esp. U.S.* **pedo-, ped-** *combining form.* indicating a child or children: *paedology.* [from Greek *pais, paid-* child]

paedogenesis (ˌpiːdəʊ'dʒɛnɪsɪs) *n* sexual reproduction in an animal that retains its larval features. See also **neoteny.** ► **paedogenetic** (ˌpiːdəʊdʒə'nɛtɪk) *or* **ˌpaedo'genic** *adj*

paedology *or U.S.* **pedology** (piː'dɒlədʒɪ) *n* the study of the character, growth, and development of children. ► **paedological** *or U.S.* **pedological** (ˌpiːdəˈlɒdʒɪkəl) *adj* ► **pae'dologist** *or U.S.* **pe'dologist** *n*

paedomorphosis (ˌpiːdə'mɔːfəsɪs) *n* the resemblance of adult animals to the young of their ancestors: seen in the evolution of modern man, who shows resemblances to the young stages of australopithecines.

paedophilia *or esp. U.S.* **pedophilia** (ˌpiːdəʊ'fɪlɪə) *n* the condition of being sexually attracted to children. ► **paedophile** *or esp. U.S.* **pedophile** ('piːdəʊˌfaɪl) *or* **ˌpaedo'philiˌac** *or esp. U.S.* **ˌpedo'philiˌac** *n, adj*

paella (paɪ'ɛlə; *Spanish* pa'eʎa) *n, pl* **-las** (-ləz; *Spanish* -ʎas). **1** a Spanish dish made from rice, shellfish, chicken, and vegetables. **2** the large flat frying pan in which a paella is cooked. [from Catalan, from Old French *paelle,* from Latin *patella* small pan]

paeon ('piːən) *n Prosody.* a metrical foot of four syllables, with one long one and three short ones in any order. [C17: via Latin *paeon* from Greek *paiōn;* variant of PAEAN] ► **pae'onic** *adj*

paeony ('piːənɪ) *n, pl* **-nies.** a variant spelling of **peony.**

Paestum ('pɛstəm) *n* an ancient Greek colony on the coast of Lucania in S Italy.

Páez (*Spanish* 'paes) *n* **José Antonio** (xo'se an'tonjo). 1790–1873, Venezuelan revolutionary leader; first president (1831–46) of independent Venezuela.

pagan ('peɪgən) *n* **1** a member of a group professing a polytheistic religion or any religion other than Christianity, Judaism, or Islam. **2** a person without any religion; heathen. ◆ *adj* **3** of or relating to pagans or their faith or worship. **4** heathen; irreligious. [C14: from Church Latin *pāgānus* civilian (hence, not a soldier of Christ), from Latin: countryman, villager, from *pāgus* village] ► **'pagandom** *n* ► **'paganish** *adj* ► **'paganism** *n* ► **'paganist** *adj, n* ► **ˌpagan'istic** *adj* ► **ˌpagan'istically** *adv*

Paganini (*Italian* paga'niːni) *n* **Niccolò** (nikko'lɔ). 1782–1840, Italian violinist and composer.

paganize *or* **paganise** ('peɪgəˌnaɪz) *vb* to become pagan, render pagan, or convert to paganism. ► **ˌpagani'zation** *or* **ˌpagani'sation** *n* ► **'paganˌizer** *or* **'paganˌiser** *n*

page[1] (peɪdʒ) *n* **1** one side of one of the leaves of a book, newspaper, letter, etc. or the written or printed matter it bears. Abbrev.: **p.** (*pl* **pp.**). **2** such a leaf considered as a unit: *insert a new page.* **3** a screenful of information from a website, teletext service, etc., displayed on a television monitor or visual display unit. **4** an episode, phase, or period: *a glorious page in the revolution.* **5** *Printing.* the type as set up for printing a page. ◆ *vb* **6** another word for **paginate. 7** (*intr; foll. by through*) to look through (a book, report, etc.); leaf through. [C15: via Old French from Latin *pāgina*]

page[2] (peɪdʒ) *n* **1** a boy employed to run errands, carry messages, etc., for the guests in a hotel, club, etc. **2** a youth in attendance at official functions or ceremonies, esp. weddings. **3** *Medieval history.* **3a** a boy in training for knighthood in personal attendance on a knight. **3b** a youth in the personal service of a person of rank, esp. in a royal household: *page of the chamber.* **4** (in the U.S.) an attendant at Congress or other legislative body. **5** *Canadian.* a boy or girl employed in the debating chamber of the House of Commons, the Senate, or a legislative assembly to carry messages for members. ◆ *vb* (*tr*) **6** to call out the name of (a person), esp. by a loudspeaker system, so as to give him a message. **7** to call (a person) by an electronic device, such as a bleep. **8** to act as a page to or attend as a page. [C13: via Old French from Italian *paggio,* probably from Greek *paidion* boy, from *pais* child]

Page (peɪdʒ) *n* **1** Sir **Earle** (**Christmas Grafton**). 1880–1961, Australian statesman; co-leader, with S. M. Bruce, of the federal government of Australia (1923–29). **2** Sir **Frederick Handley.** 1885–1962, English pioneer in the design and manufacture of aircraft.

pageant ('pædʒənt) *n* **1** an elaborate colourful parade or display portraying scenes from history, esp. one involving rich costume. **2** any magnificent or showy display, procession, etc. [C14: from Medieval Latin *pāgina* scene of a play, from Latin: PAGE[1]]

pageantry ('pædʒəntrɪ) *n, pl* **-ries. 1** spectacular display or ceremony. **2** *Archaic.* pageants collectively.

pageboy ('peɪdʒˌbɔɪ) *n* **1** a smooth medium-length hairstyle with the ends of the hair curled under and a long fringe falling onto the forehead from the crown. **2** a less common word for **page**[2] (sense 1). **3** another word for **page**[2] (sense 2).

pager ('peɪdʒə) *n* a small electronic device, capable of receiving short messages; usually carried by people who need to be contacted urgently (e.g. doctors).

Paget's disease ('pædʒɪts) *n* **1** Also called: **osteitis deformans.** a chronic disease of the bones characterized by inflammation and deformation. **2** Also called: **Paget's cancer.** cancer of the nipple and surrounding tissue. [C19: named after Sir James *Paget* (1814–99), British surgeon and pathologist, who described these diseases]

page-turner *n* an exciting novel, such as a thriller, with a fast-moving story.

paginal ('pædʒɪnəl) *adj* **1** page-for-page: *paginal facsimile.* **2** of, like, or consisting of pages. [C17: from Late Latin *pāginālis,* from Latin *pāgina* page]

paginate ('pædʒɪˌneɪt) *vb* (*tr*) to number the pages of (a book, manuscript, etc.) in sequence. Compare **foliate.** ► **ˌpagi'nation** *n*

Pagnol (*French* paɲɔl) *n* **Marcel** (**Paul**) (marsɛl). 1895–1974, French dramatist, film director, and novelist, noted for his depiction of Provençal life in such films as *Manon des Sources* (1952; remade 1986).

pagoda (pə'gəʊdə) *n* an Indian or Far Eastern temple, esp. a tower, usually pyramidal and having many storeys. [C17: from Portuguese *pagode,* ultimately from Sanskrit *bhagavatī* divine]

pagoda tree *n* a Chinese leguminous tree, *Sophora japonica,* with ornamental white flowers and dark green foliage.

Pago Pago ('pɑːŋgəʊ 'pɑːŋgəʊ) *n* a port in American Samoa, on SE Tutuila Island. Pop.: 4000 (1990). Former name: **Pango Pango.**

pagurian (pə'gjʊərɪən) *or* **pagurid** (pə'gjʊərɪd, 'pægjʊrɪd) *n* **1** any decapod crustacean of the family *Paguridae,* which includes the hermit crabs. ◆ *adj* **2** of, relating to, or belonging to the *Paguridae.* [C19: from Latin *pagurus,* from Greek *pagouros* kind of crab]

pah (pɑː) *interj* an exclamation of disgust, disbelief, etc.

Pahang (pə'hʌŋ) *n* a state of Peninsular Malaysia, on the South China Sea: the largest Malayan state; mountainous and heavily forested. Capital: Kuantan. Pop.: 1 056 100 (1993 est.). Area: 35 964 sq. km (13 886 sq. miles).

Pahari (pəˈhɑːrɪ) *n* a group of Indo-European languages spoken in the Himalayas, divided into **Eastern Pahari** (Nepali) and **Western Pahari** (consisting of many dialects).

Pahlavi[1] (ˈpɑːləvɪ) *n* **1 Mohammed Reza** (ˈriːzə). 1919–80, shah of Iran (1941–79); forced into exile (1979) during civil unrest following which an Islamic republic was established led by the Ayatollah Khomeini. **2** his father, **Reza.** 1877–1944, shah of Iran (1925–41). Originally an army officer, he gained power by a coup d'état (1921) and was chosen shah by the National Assembly. He reorganized the army and did much to modernize Iran.

Pahlavi[2] (ˈpɑːləvɪ) *or* **Pehlevi** *n* the Middle Persian language, esp. as used in classical Zoroastrian and Manichean literature. [C18: from Persian *pahlavī*, from Old Persian *Parthava* PARTHIA]

Pahsien (ˈpɑːˈʃjɛn) *n* another name for **Chongqing.**

paid (peɪd) *vb* **1** the past tense and past participle of **pay**[1]. **2 put paid to.** *Chiefly Brit. and N.Z.* to end or destroy: *breaking his leg put paid to his hopes of running in the Olympics.*

paid-up *adj* **1** having paid the due, full, or required fee to be a member of an organization, club, political party, etc. **2** denoting a security in which all the instalments have been paid; fully paid: *a paid-up share.* **3** denoting all the money that a company has received from its shareholders: *the paid-up capital.* **4** denoting an endowment assurance policy on which the payment of premiums has stopped and the surrender value has been used to purchase a new single-premium policy.

paigle (ˈpeɪgᵊl) *n* another name for the **cowslip** and **oxlip.** [C16: of uncertain origin]

Paignton (ˈpeɪntən) *n* a town and resort in SW England, in Devon: administratively part of Torbay since 1968.

pail (peɪl) *n* **1** a bucket, esp. one made of wood or metal. **2** Also called: **ˈpailful.** the quantity that fills a pail. [Old English *pægel;* compare Catalan *paella* frying pan, PAELLA]

paillasse (ˈpælɪˌæs, ˌpælɪˈæs) *n* a variant spelling (esp. U.S.) of **palliasse.**

paillette (pælˈjɛt; *French* pajɛt) *n* **1** a sequin or spangle sewn onto a costume. **2** a small piece of metal or foil, used in enamelling for decoration. [C19: from French, diminutive of *paille* straw, from Latin *palea*]

pain (peɪn) *n* **1** the sensation of acute physical hurt or discomfort caused by injury, illness, etc. **2** emotional suffering or mental distress. **3 on pain of.** subject to the penalty of. **4** Also called: **pain in the neck** *or* (*taboo*) **arse.** *Informal.* a person or thing that is a nuisance. ♦ *vb* (*tr*) **5** to cause (a person) distress, hurt, grief, anxiety, etc. **6** *Informal.* to annoy; irritate. ♦ See also **pains.** [C13: from Old French *peine,* from Latin *poena* punishment, grief, from Greek *poinē* penalty]

Paine (peɪn) *n* **Thomas.** 1737–1809, American political pamphleteer, born in England. His works include the pamphlets *Common Sense* (1776) and *Crisis* (1776–83), supporting the American colonists' fight for independence; *The Rights of Man* (1791–92), a justification of the French Revolution; and *The Age of Reason* (1794–96), a defence of deism.

pained (peɪnd) *adj* having or expressing pain or distress, esp. mental or emotional distress: *a pained expression.*

painful (ˈpeɪnfʊl) *adj* **1** causing pain; distressing: *a painful duty.* **2** affected with pain: *a painful leg.* **3** tedious or difficult. **4** *Informal.* extremely bad: *a painful performance.* ▸ **ˈpainfully** *adv* ▸ **ˈpainfulness** *n*

painkiller (ˈpeɪnˌkɪlə) *n* **1** an analgesic drug or agent. **2** anything that relieves pain.

painless (ˈpeɪnlɪs) *adj* **1** not causing pain or distress. **2** not affected by pain. ▸ **ˈpainlessly** *adv* ▸ **ˈpainlessness** *n*

pains (peɪnz) *pl n* **1** care, trouble, or effort (esp. in the phrases **take pains, be at pains to**). **2** painful sensations experienced during contractions in childbirth; labour pains.

painstaking (ˈpeɪnzˌteɪkɪŋ) *adj* extremely careful, esp. as to fine detail: *painstaking research.* ▸ **ˈpainsˌtakingly** *adv* ▸ **ˈpainsˌtakingness** *n*

paint (peɪnt) *n* **1** a substance used for decorating or protecting a surface, esp. a mixture consisting of a solid pigment suspended in a liquid, that when applied to a surface dries to form a hard coating. **2** a dry film of paint on a surface. **3** the solid pigment of a paint before it is suspended in liquid. **4** *Informal.* face make-up, such as rouge. **5** short for **greasepaint.** ♦ *vb* **6** to make (a picture) of (a figure, landscape, etc.) with paint applied to a surface such as canvas. **7** to coat (a surface) with paint, as in decorating. **8** (*tr*) to apply (liquid) onto (a surface): *her mother painted the cut with antiseptic.* **9** (*tr*) to apply make-up onto (the face, lips, etc.). **10** (*tr*) to describe vividly in words. **11 paint the town red.** *Informal.* to celebrate uninhibitedly; go on a spree. [C13: from Old French *peint* painted, from *peindre* to paint, from Latin *pingere* to paint, adorn] ▸ **ˈpainty** *adj*

paintball game (ˈpeɪntˌbɔːl) *n* a game in which teams of players simulate a military skirmish, shooting each other with paint pellets that explode on impact, marking the players who have been shot.

paintbox (ˈpeɪntˌbɒks) *n* a box containing a tray of dry watercolour paints.

paintbrush (ˈpeɪntˌbrʌʃ) *n* a brush used to apply paint.

Painted Desert *n* a section of the high plateau country of N central Arizona, along the N side of the Little Colorado River Valley: brilliant-coloured rocks; occupied largely by Navaho and Hopi Indians. Area: about 20 000 sq. km (7500 sq. miles).

painted lady *n* a migratory nymphalid butterfly, *Vanessa cardui,* with pale brownish-red mottled wings.

painted woman *n* a woman of low moral character.

painter[1] (ˈpeɪntə) *n* **1** a person who paints surfaces as a trade. **2** an artist who paints pictures.

painter[2] (ˈpeɪntə) *n* a line attached to the bow of a boat for tying it up. [C15: probably from Old French *penteur* strong rope]

painterly (ˈpeɪntəlɪ) *adj* **1** having qualities peculiar to painting, esp. the depiction of shapes by means of solid masses of colour, rather than by lines. Compare **linear** (sense 5). **2** of or characteristic of a painter; artistic.

painter's colic *n Pathol.* another name for **lead colic.** [C19: so called because it frequently affected people who worked with lead-based paints or similar substances]

painting (ˈpeɪntɪŋ) *n* **1** the art or process of applying paints to a surface such as canvas, to make a picture or other artistic composition. **2** a composition or picture made in this way. **3** the act of applying paint to a surface with a brush.

paint stripper *or* **remover** *n* a liquid, often caustic, used to remove paint from a surface.

paintwork (ˈpeɪntˌwɜːk) *n* a surface, such as wood or a car body, that is painted.

pair[1] (pɛə) *n, pl* **pairs** *or* (*functioning as sing or pl*) **pair. 1** two identical or similar things matched for use together: *a pair of socks.* **2** two persons, animals, things, etc., used or grouped together: *a pair of horses; a pair of scoundrels.* **3** an object considered to be two identical or similar things joined together: *a pair of trousers.* **4** two people joined in love or marriage. **5** a male and a female animal of the same species, esp. such animals kept for breeding purposes. **6** *Parliamentary procedure.* **6a** two opposed members who both agree not to vote on a specified motion or for a specific period of time. **6b** the agreement so made. **7** two playing cards of the same rank or denomination: *a pair of threes.* **8** one member of a matching pair: *I can't find the pair to this glove.* **9** *Rowing.* See **pair-oar. 10** *Brit. and U.S. dialect.* a group or set of more than two. **11** *Logic, maths.* **11a** a set with two members. **11b** an ordered set with two members. ♦ *vb* **12** (often foll. by *off*) to arrange or fall into groups of twos. **13** to group or be grouped in matching pairs: *to pair socks.* **14** to join or be joined in marriage; mate or couple. **15** (when *tr, usually passive*) *Parliamentary procedure.* to form or cause to form a pair: *18 members were paired for the last vote.* ♦ See also **pairs.** [C13: from Old French *paire,* from Latin *paria* equal (things), from *pār* equal]

USAGE Like other collective nouns, *pair* takes a singular or a plural verb according to whether it is seen as a unit or as a collection of two things: *the pair are said to dislike each other; a pair of good shoes is essential.*

pair[2] (per) *adj* a Scot. word for **poor.**

pair bond *n* the exclusive relationship formed between a male and a female, esp. in some species of animals and birds during courtship and breeding. ▸ **pair bonding** *n*

pair-oar *n Rowing.* a racing shell in which two oarsmen sit one behind the other and pull one oar each. Also called: **pair.** Compare **double scull.**

pair production *n* the production of an electron and a positron from a gamma-ray photon that passes close to an atomic nucleus.

pair royal *n* (in some card games) a set of three cards of the same denomination.

pairs (pɛəz) *pl n* another name for **Pelmanism** (sense 2).

pair trawling *n* the act or practice of using two boats to trawl for fish.

paisa (ˈpaɪsɑː) *n, pl* **-se** (-seɪ). a monetary unit of India, Nepal, and Pakistan worth one hundredth of a rupee. [from Hindi]

paisano (paɪˈsɑːnəʊ; *Spanish* paiˈsano) *n, pl* **-nos** (-nəʊz; *Spanish* -nos). *Southwestern U.S.* (often a term of address) **1** *Informal.* a friend; pal. **2** a fellow countryman. [C20: via Spanish from French *paysan* PEASANT]

paisley (ˈpeɪzlɪ) *n* **1** a pattern of small curving shapes with intricate detailing, usually printed in bright colours. **2** a soft fine wool fabric traditionally printed with this pattern. **3** a garment made of this fabric, esp. a shawl popular in the late 19th century. **4** (*modifier*) of or decorated with this pattern: *a paisley scarf.* [C19: named after PAISLEY[1]]

Paisley[1] (ˈpeɪzlɪ) *n* an industrial town in SW Scotland, the administrative centre of Renfrewshire: one of the world's chief centres for the manufacture of thread, linen, and gauze in the 19th century. Pop.: 75 526 (1991).

Paisley[2] (ˈpeɪzlɪ) *n* **1 Bob.** 1919–96, English footballer and manager. **2** Rev. **Ian (Richard Kyle).** born 1926, Northern Ireland politician and Presbyterian minister; cofounder (1972) and leader of the Ulster Democratic Unionist Party.

paitrick (ˈpetrɪk) *n* a Scot. word for **partridge.**

Paiute *or* **Piute** (ˈpaɪˌuːt, paɪˈjuːt) *n* **1** (*pl* **-utes** *or* **-ute**) a member of either of two North American Indian peoples (**Northern Paiute** and **Southern Paiute**) of the Southwestern U.S., related to the Aztecs. **2** the language of either of these peoples, belonging to the Shoshonean subfamily of the Uto-Aztecan family.

pajamas (pəˈdʒɑːməz) *pl n* the U.S. spelling of **pyjamas.**

pakahi (ˈpɑːkəhiː) *n N.Z.* **a** acid land that is unsuitable for cultivation. **b** (*as modifier*): *pakahi soil.* [C19: from Maori]

pakapoo (ˈpækəpuː) *n, pl* **-poos.** *Austral. and N.Z.* **1** a Chinese lottery with betting slips marked with Chinese characters. **2 like a pakapoo ticket.** untidy, incomprehensible. [C19: from Chinese]

pak-choi cabbage (ˈpɑːkˈtʃɔɪ) *n* another name for **Chinese cabbage** (sense 2). [from Chinese (Cantonese dialect), literally: white vegetable]

pakeha (ˈpɑːkɪˌhɑː) *n* (in New Zealand) a person who is not of Maori ancestry, esp. a White person. [from Maori]

pakeha Maori *n* (in the 19th century) a European who adopted the Maori way of life.

Paki (ˈpækɪ) *Brit. slang, offensive.* ♦ *n, pl* **Pakis. 1** a Pakistani or person of Pakistani descent. **2** (loosely) a person from any part of the Indian subcontinent. ♦ *adj* **3** Pakistani or of Pakistani descent. **4** (loosely) denoting a person from the Indian subcontinent.

Paki-bashing *n Brit. slang.* the activity of making vicious and unprovoked physical assaults upon Pakistani immigrants or people of Pakistani descent. ▸ **ˈPaki-ˌbasher** *n*

pakirikiri (ˈpɑːkɪriːˌkɪriː) *n N.Z.* another name for **blue cod.**

Pakistan (ˌpɑːkɪˈstɑːn) *n* **1** a republic in S Asia, on the Arabian Sea: the Union of Pakistan, formed in 1947, comprised West and East Pakistan; East Pakistan gained independence as Bangladesh in 1971 and West Pakistan became Pakistan; a member of the Commonwealth from 1947, it withdrew from 1972 until 1989; contains the fertile plains of the Indus valley rising to mountains in the north and west. Official language: Urdu. Official religion: Muslim. Currency: rupee. Capital: Islamabad. Pop.: 141 900 000 (1998 est.). Area: 801 508 sq. km (309 463 sq. miles). **2** a former republic in S Asia consisting of the provinces of West Pakistan and East Pakistan (now Bangladesh), 1500 km (900 miles) apart: formed in 1947 from the predominantly Muslim parts of India. ► **ˌPakiˈstani** *n, adj*

pakoko (ˈpɑːkəʊkəʊ) *n N.Z.* another name for **bully**[2].

pakora (pəˈkɔːrə) *n* an Indian dish consisting of pieces of vegetable, chicken, etc., dipped in a spiced batter and deep-fried: served with a piquant sauce. [C20: from Hindi]

pakthong (pækˈθɒŋ) *n* another name for **nickel silver.**

pal (pæl) *Informal.* ♦ *n* **1** a close friend; comrade. **2** an accomplice. ♦ *vb* **pals, palling, palled. 3** (*intr;* usually foll. by *with* or *about*) to associate as friends. ♦ See also **pal up.** [C17: from English Gypsy: brother, ultimately from Sanskrit *bhrātar* BROTHER]

PAL (pæl) *n acronym for* phase alternation line: a colour-television broadcasting system used generally in Europe.

Pal. *abbrev. for* Palestine.

palace (ˈpælɪs) *n* (*cap. when part of a name*) **1** the official residence of a reigning monarch or member of a royal family: *Buckingham Palace.* **2** the official residence of various high-ranking church dignitaries or members of the nobility, as of an archbishop. **3** a large and richly furnished building resembling a royal palace. ♦ Related adjs.: **palatial, palatine.** [C13: from Old French *palais,* from Latin *Palātium* PALATINE[2], the site of the palace of the emperors]

palace revolution *n* a coup d'état made by those already in positions of power, usually with little violence.

Palacio Valdés (*Spanish* paˈlaθjo balˈdes) *n* **Armando** (arˈmando). 1853–1938, Spanish novelist and critic.

paladin (ˈpælədɪn) *n* **1** one of the legendary twelve peers of Charlemagne's court. **2** a knightly champion. [C16: via French from Italian *paladino,* from Latin *palātīnus* imperial official, from *Palātium* PALATINE[2]]

palaeanthropic (ˌpælɪænˈθrɒpɪk) *adj* relating to or denoting the earliest variety of man.

Palaearctic (ˌpælɪˈɑːktɪk) *adj* of or denoting a zoogeographical region consisting of Europe, Africa north of the Sahara, and most of Asia north of the Himalayas.

palaeethnology (ˌpælɪeθˈnɒlədʒɪ) *n* the study of prehistoric man. ► **palaeethnological** (ˌpælɪˌeθnəˈlɒdʒɪkᵊl) *adj* ► **ˌpalaeethˈnologist** *n*

palaeo-, *before a vowel* **palae-** *or esp. U.S.* **paleo-, pale-** *combining form.* old, ancient, or prehistoric: *palaeography.* [from Greek *palaios* old]

palaeoanthropology (ˌpælɪəʊˌænθrəˈpɒlədʒɪ) *n* the branch of anthropology concerned with primitive man.

palaeobotany (ˌpælɪəʊˈbɒtənɪ) *n* the study of fossil plants. ► **palaeobotanical** (ˌpælɪəʊbəˈtænɪkᵊl) *or* **ˌpalaeoboˈtanic** *adj* ► **ˌpalaeoˈbotanist** *n*

Palaeocene (ˈpælɪəʊˌsiːn) *adj* **1** of, denoting, or formed in the first epoch of the Tertiary period, which lasted for 10 million years. ♦ *n* **2 the.** the Palaeocene epoch or rock series. [C19: from French from *paléo-* PALAEO- + Greek *kainos* new, recent]

palaeoclimatology (ˌpælɪəʊˌklaɪməˈtɒlədʒɪ) *n* the study of climates of the geological past. ► **ˌpalaeoˌclimaˈtologist** *n*

palaeocurrent (ˈpælɪəʊˌkʌrənt) *n Geology.* an ancient current, esp. of water, evidence of which has been preserved in sedimentary rocks as fossilized ripple marks, etc.

palaeoecology (ˌpælɪəʊɪˈkɒlədʒɪ) *n* the study of fossil animals and plants in order to deduce their ecology and the environmental conditions in which they lived. ► **ˌpalaeoˌecoˈlogical** *adj* ► **ˌpalaeoeˈcologist** *n*

palaeoethnobotany (ˌpælɪəʊˌeθnəʊˈbɒtənɪ) *n* the study of fossil seeds and grains to further archaeological knowledge, esp. of the domestication of cereals.

Palaeogene (ˈpælɪəˌdʒiːn) *adj* **1** of or formed in the Palaeocene, Eocene, and Oligocene epochs. ♦ *n* **2 the.** the Palaeogene period or system.

palaeogeography (ˌpælɪəʊdʒɪˈɒgrəfɪ) *n* the study of geographical features of the geological past. ► **ˌpalaeogeˈographer** *n* ► **palaeogeographical** (ˌpælɪəʊˌdʒiːəʊˈgræfɪkᵊl) *or* **ˌpalaeoˌgeoˈgraphic** *adj* ► **ˌpalaeoˌgeoˈgraphically** *adv*

palaeography (ˌpælɪˈɒgrəfɪ) *n* **1** the study of the handwritings of the past, and often the manuscripts as well, so that they may be dated, read, etc., and may serve as historical and literary sources. **2** a handwriting of the past. ► **palaeˈographer** *n* ► **palaeographic** (ˌpælɪəʊˈgræfɪk) *or* **ˌpalaeoˈgraphical** *adj*

palaeolith (ˈpælɪəʊˌlɪθ) *n* a stone tool dating to the Palaeolithic.

Palaeolithic (ˌpælɪəʊˈlɪθɪk) *n* **1** the period of the emergence of primitive man and the manufacture of unpolished chipped stone tools, about 2.5 million to 3 million years ago until about 12 000 B.C. See also **Lower Palaeolithic, Middle Palaeolithic, Upper Palaeolithic.** ♦ *adj* **2** (*sometimes not cap.*) of or relating to this period.

Palaeolithic man *n* any of various primitive types of man, such as Neanderthal man and Java man, who lived in the Palaeolithic.

palaeomagnetism (ˌpælɪəʊˈmægnɪˌtɪzəm) *n* the study of the fossil magnetism in rocks, used to determine the past configurations of the continents and to investigate the past shape and magnitude of the earth's magnetic field. ► **ˌpalaeomagˈnetic** *adj*

palaeontography (ˌpælɪɒnˈtɒgrəfɪ) *n* the branch of palaeontology concerned with the description of fossils. [C19: from PALAEO- + ONTO- + -GRAPHY] ► **palaeontographic** (ˌpælɪˌɒntəˈgræfɪk) *or* **ˌpalaeˌontoˈgraphical** *adj*

palaeontol. *abbrev. for* palaeontology.

palaeontology (ˌpælɪɒnˈtɒlədʒɪ) *n* **1** the study of fossils to determine the structure and evolution of extinct animals and plants and the age and conditions of deposition of the rock strata in which they are found. See also **palaeobotany, palaeozoology. 2** another name for **palaeozoology.** [C19: from PALAEO- + ONTO- + -LOGY] ► **palaeontological** (ˌpælɪˌɒntəˈlɒdʒɪkᵊl) *adj* ► **ˌpalaeˌontoˈlogically** *adv* ► **ˌpalaeonˈtologist** *n*

palaeopathology (ˌpælɪəʊpəˈθɒlədʒɪ) *n* the study of diseases of ancient man. ► **ˈpalaeoˌpathoˈlogical** *adj* ► **ˌpalaeopaˈthologist** *n*

Palaeozoic (ˌpælɪəʊˈzəʊɪk) *adj* **1** of, denoting, or relating to an era of geological time that began 600 million years ago with the Cambrian period and lasted about 375 million years until the end of the Permian period. ♦ *n* **2 the.** the Palaeozoic era. [C19: from PALAEO- + Greek *zōē* life + -IC]

palaeozoology (ˌpælɪəʊzuːˈɒlədʒɪ) *n* the study of fossil animals. Also called: **palaeontology.** ► **palaeozoological** (ˌpælɪəʊˌzuəˈlɒdʒɪkᵊl) *adj* ► **ˌpalaeozoˈologist** *n*

palaestra *or esp. U.S.* **palestra** (pəˈlɛstrə, -ˈliː-) *n, pl* **-tras** *or* **-trae** (-triː). (in ancient Greece or Rome) a public place devoted to the training of athletes. [C16: via Latin from Greek *palaistra,* from *palaiein* to wrestle]

palagi (pəˈlæŋɪ) *n, pl* **-gis.** *N.Z.* a Samoan name for a **European.**

palais de danse *French.* (palɛ də dɑ̃s) *n* a dance hall.

palais glide (ˈpæleɪ) *n* a dance with high kicks and gliding steps in which performers link arms in a row. [C20: from PALAIS DE DANSE]

palanquin *or* **palankeen** (ˌpælənˈkiːn) *n* a covered litter, formerly used in the Orient, carried on the shoulders of four men. [C16: from Portuguese *palanquim,* from Prakrit *pallanka,* from Sanskrit *paryanka* couch]

palatable (ˈpælətəbᵊl) *adj* **1** pleasant to taste. **2** acceptable or satisfactory: *a palatable suggestion.* ► **ˌpalataˈbility** *or* **ˈpalatableness** *n* ► **ˈpalatably** *adv*

palatal (ˈpælətᵊl) *adj* **1** Also: **palatine.** of or relating to the palate. **2** *Phonetics.* of, relating to, or denoting a speech sound articulated with the blade of the tongue touching the hard palate. ♦ *n* **3** Also called: **palatine.** the bony plate that forms the palate. **4** *Phonetics.* a palatal speech sound, such as the semivowel (j). ► **ˈpalatally** *adv*

palatalize *or* **palatalise** (ˈpælətəˌlaɪz) *vb* (*tr*) to pronounce (a speech sound) with the blade of the tongue touching the palate. ► **ˌpalataliˈzation** *or* **ˌpalataliˈsation** *n*

palate (ˈpælɪt) *n* **1** the roof of the mouth, separating the oral and nasal cavities. See **hard palate, soft palate.** Related adj: **palatine. 2** the sense of taste: *she had no palate for the wine.* **3** relish or enjoyment. **4** *Botany.* (in some two-lipped corollas) the projecting part of the lower lip that closes the opening of the corolla. [C14: from Latin *palātum,* perhaps of Etruscan origin]

USAGE Avoid confusion with **palette,** or **pallet.**

palatial (pəˈleɪʃəl) *adj* of, resembling, or suitable for a palace; sumptuous. ► **paˈlatially** *adv* ► **paˈlatialness** *n*

palatinate (pəˈlætɪnɪt) *n* a territory ruled by a palatine prince or noble or count palatine.

Palatinate (pəˈlætɪnɪt) *n* **1 the.** either of two territories in SW Germany, once ruled by the counts palatine. **Upper Palatinate** is now in Bavaria; **Lower** or **Rhine Palatinate** is now in Rhineland-Palatinate, Baden-Württemberg, and Hesse. German name: **Pfalz. 2** a native or inhabitant of the Palatinate.

palatine[1] (ˈpæləˌtaɪn) *adj* **1** (of an individual) possessing royal prerogatives in a territory. **2** of, belonging to, characteristic of, or relating to a count palatine, county palatine, palatinate, or palatine. **3** of or relating to a palace. ♦ *n* **4** *Feudal history.* the lord of a palatinate. **5** any of various important officials at the late Roman, Merovingian, or Carolingian courts. **6** (in Colonial America) any of the proprietors of a palatine colony, such as Carolina. [C15: via French from Latin *palātīnus* belonging to the palace, from *palātium;* see PALACE]

palatine[2] (ˈpæləˌtaɪn) *adj* **1** of or relating to the palate. ♦ *n* **2** either of two bones forming the hard palate. [C17: from French *palatin,* from Latin *palātum* palate]

Palatine[1] (ˈpæləˌtaɪn) *adj* **1** of or relating to the Palatinate. ♦ *n* **2** a Palatinate.

Palatine[2] (ˈpæləˌtaɪn) *n* **1** one of the Seven Hills of Rome: traditionally the site of the first settlement of Rome. ♦ *adj* **2** of, relating to, or designating this hill.

Palau Islands (pɑːˈlaʊ) *pl n* a former name (until 1981) of the (Republic of) **Belau.**

palaver (pəˈlɑːvə) *n* **1** tedious or time-consuming business, esp. when of a formal nature: *all the palaver of filling in forms.* **2** loud and confused talk and activity; hubbub. **3** (often used humorously) a conference. **4** *Now rare.* talk intended to flatter or persuade. **5** *W African.* **5a** an argument. **5b** trouble arising from an argument. ♦ *vb* **6** (*intr*) (often used humorously) to have a conference. **7** (*intr*) to talk loudly and confusedly. **8** (*tr*) to flatter or cajole. [C18: from Portuguese *palavra* talk, from Latin *parabola* PARABLE]

Palawan (*Spanish* paˈlavan) *n* an island of the SW Philippines between the South China Sea and the Sulu Sea: the westernmost island in the country; mountainous and forested. Capital: Puerto Princesa. Pop.: 311 548 (1980). Area: 11 785 sq. km (4550 sq. miles).

palazzo pants (pəˈlætsəʊ) *pl n* women's trousers with very wide legs. [C20: *palazzo* from Italian, literally: PALACE]

pale[1] (peɪl) *adj* **1** lacking brightness of colour; whitish: *pale morning light.* **2** (of a colour) whitish; produced by a relatively small quantity of colouring agent. **3** dim or wan: *the pale stars.* **4** feeble: *a pale effort.* ♦ *vb* **5** to make or become pale or paler; blanch. **6** (*intr;* often foll. by *before*) to lose superiority or importance (in comparison to): *her beauty paled before that of her hostess.* [C13: from Old French *palle,* from Latin *pallidus* pale, from *pallēre* to look wan] ► **ˈpalely** *adv* ► **ˈpaleness** *n*

pale[2] (peɪl) *n* **1** a wooden post or strip used as an upright member in a fence. **2** an enclosing barrier, esp. a fence made of pales. **3** an area enclosed by a pale. **4** a sphere of activity within which certain restrictions are applied. **5** *Heraldry.* an ordinary consisting of a vertical stripe, usually in the centre of a shield. **6 be-**

yond the pale. outside the limits of social convention. ◆ *vb* **7** (*tr*) to enclose with pales. [C14: from Old French *pal,* from Latin *pālus* stake; compare POLE[1]]

palea ('peɪlɪə) *or* **pale** *n, pl* **paleae** ('peɪlɪˌiː) *or* **pales.** *Botany.* **1** the scalelike membranous bract that partly encloses a grass flower. **2** any small membranous bract or scale. [C18: from Latin: straw, chaff; see PALLET[1]] ► **paleaceous** (ˌpeɪlɪ'eɪʃəs) *adj*

paleface ('peɪlˌfeɪs) *n* a derogatory term for a White person, said to have been used by North American Indians.

Palembang (pɑː'lɛmbɑːŋ) *n* a port in W Indonesia, in S Sumatra; oil refineries; university (1955). Pop.: 1 352 300 (1995 est.).

Palencia (*Spanish* pa'lenθia) *n* a city in N central Spain: earliest university in Spain (1208); seat of Castilian kings (12th–13th centuries); communications centre. Pop.: 77 752 (1991).

Palenque (*Spanish* pa'leŋke) *n* the site of an ancient Mayan city in S Mexico famous for its architectural ruins.

paleo- *or before a vowel* **pale-** *combining form.* variants (esp. U.S.) of **palaeo-.**

Palermo (pə'lɛəməʊ, -'lɜː-; *Italian* pa'lermo) *n* the capital of Sicily, on the NW coast: founded by the Phoenicians in the 8th century B.C. Pop.: 689 301 (1996 est.).

Palestine ('pælɪˌstaɪn) *n* **1** Also called: the **Holy Land, Canaan.** the area between the Jordan River and the Mediterranean Sea in which most of the biblical narrative is located. **2** the province of the Roman Empire in this region. **3** the former British mandatory territory created by the League of Nations in 1922 (but effective from 1920), and including all of the present territories of Israel and Jordan between whom it was partitioned by the UN in 1948.

Palestine Liberation Organization *n* an organization founded in 1964 with the aim of creating a state for Palestinians; it recognized the state of Israel in 1993 and Israel granted Palestinians autonomy in the Gaza Strip and West Bank. Abbrev.: **PLO.**

Palestinian (ˌpælɪ'stɪnɪən) *adj* **1** of or relating to Palestine. ◆ *n* **2** a native or inhabitant of the former British mandate, or their descendants, esp. such Arabs now living in the Palestinian Administered Territories, Jordan, Lebanon, or Israel, or as refugees from Israeli-occupied territory.

Palestinian Administered Territories *n* the Gaza Strip and the West Bank in Israel: these areas were granted autonomous status under the control of the Palestinian National Authority following the 1993 peace agreement between Israel and the Palestine Liberation Organization. Also called: **Palestinian Autonomous Areas.**

Palestinian National Authority *n* the authority formed in 1994 to govern the Palestinian Administered Territories: it controls policy on health, education, social welfare, direct taxation, tourism, and culture and manages elections to the Palestinian Council. Abbrev.: **PNA.**

palestra (pə'lɛstrə, -'liː-) *n, pl* **-tras** *or* **-trae** (-triː). the usual U.S. spelling of **palaestra.**

Palestrina (ˌpælɛ'striːnə) *n* **Giovanni Pierluigi da** (dʒo'vanni pier'luiːdʒi da). ?1525–94, Italian composer and master of counterpoint. His works, nearly all for unaccompanied choir and religious in nature, include the *Missa Papae Marcelli* (1555).

paletot ('pæltəʊ) *n* **1** a loose outer garment. **2** a woman's fitted coat often worn over a crinoline or bustle. [C19: from French]

palette ('pælɪt) *n* **1** Also: **pallet.** a flat piece of wood, plastic, etc., used by artists as a surface on which to mix their paints. **2** the range of colours characteristic of a particular artist, painting, or school of painting: *a restricted palette.* **3** the available range of colours or patterns that can be displayed by a computer on a visual display unit. **4** either of the plates of metal attached by a strap to the cuirass in a suit of armour to protect the armpits. [C17: from French, diminutive of *pale* shovel, from Latin *pala* spade]

USAGE Avoid confusion with **palate** or **pallet.**

palette *or* **pallet knife** *n* **1** a round-ended spatula with a thin flexible blade used esp. by artists for mixing, applying, and scraping off paint, esp. oil paint. **2** a knife with a round-ended flexible blade used in cookery for scraping out a mixture from a bowl, spreading icing, etc.

Paley ('peɪlɪ) *n* **William.** 1743–1805, English theologian and utilitarian philosopher. His chief works are *The Principles of Moral and Political Philosophy* (1785), *Horae Paulinae* (1790), *A View of the Evidences of Christianity* (1794), and *Natural Theology* (1802).

palfrey ('pɔːlfrɪ) *n Archaic.* a light saddle horse, esp. ridden by women. [C12: from Old French *palefrei,* from Medieval Latin *palafredus,* from Late Latin *paraverēdus,* from Greek *para* beside + Latin *verēdus* light fleet horse, of Celtic origin]

Palgrave ('pɔːlgreɪv, 'pæl-) *n* **Francis Turner.** 1824–97, British critic and poet, editor of the poetry anthology *The Golden Treasury* (1861).

Pali ('pɑːlɪ) *n* an ancient language of India derived from Sanskrit; the language of the Buddhist scriptures. [C19: from Sanskrit *pāli-bhāsa,* from *pāli* canon + *bhāsa* language, of Dravidian origin]

palikar ('pælɪˌkɑː) *n* a Greek soldier in the war of independence against Turkey (1821–28). [C19: from Modern Greek *palikari* youth]

palilalia (ˌpælɪ'leɪlɪə) *n* a speech disorder in which a word or phrase is rapidly repeated. [C20: from Greek *palin* again + *lalein* to babble]

palimony ('pælɪmənɪ) *n U.S.* alimony awarded to a nonmarried partner after the break-up of a long-term relationship. [C20: from a blend of *pal* + *alimony*]

palimpsest ('pælɪmpˌsɛst) *n* **1** a manuscript on which two or more successive texts have been written, each one being erased to make room for the next. ◆ *adj* **2** (of a text) written on a palimpsest. **3** (of a document) used as a palimpsest. [C17: from Latin *palimpsestus* parchment cleaned for reuse, from Greek *palimpsēstos,* from *palin* again + *psēstos* rubbed smooth, from *psēn* to scrape]

palindrome ('pælɪnˌdrəʊm) *n* a word or phrase the letters of which, when taken in reverse order, give the same word or phrase, such as *able was I ere I saw Elba.* [C17: from Greek *palindromos* running back again, from *palin* again + -DROME] ► **palindromic** (ˌpælɪn'drɒmɪk) *adj*

paling ('peɪlɪŋ) *n* **1** a fence made of pales. **2** pales collectively. **3** a single pale. **4** the act of erecting pales.

palingenesis (ˌpælɪn'dʒɛnɪsɪs) *n, pl* **-ses** (-ˌsiːz). **1** *Christianity.* spiritual rebirth through metempsychosis of Christian baptism. **2** *Biology.* another name for **recapitulation** (sense 2). [C19: from Greek *palin* again + *genesis* birth, GENESIS] ► **palingenetic** (ˌpælɪndʒə'nɛtɪk) *adj* ► ˌ**palinge'netically** *adv*

palinode ('pælɪˌnəʊd) *n* **1** a poem in which the poet recants something he has said in a former poem. **2** *Rare.* a recantation. [C16: from Latin *palinōdia* repetition of a song, from Greek, from *palin* again + *ōidē* song, ODE]

palinopsia (ˌpælɪ'nɒpsɪə) *or* **palinopia** (ˌpælɪ'nəʊpɪə) *n* a visual disorder in which the patient perceives a prolonged afterimage. [from Greek *palin* again + *ōps* eye]

palisade (ˌpælɪ'seɪd) *n* **1** a strong fence made of stakes driven into the ground, esp. for defence. **2** one of the stakes used in such a fence. **3** *Botany.* a layer of elongated mesophyll cells containing many chloroplasts, situated below the outer epidermis of a leaf blade. ◆ *vb* **4** (*tr*) to enclose with a palisade. [C17: via French, from Old Provençal *palissada,* ultimately from Latin *pālus* stake; see PALE[2], POLE[1]]

palisades (ˌpælɪ'seɪdz, 'pælɪˌseɪdz) *pl n U.S. and Canadian.* high cliffs in a line, often along a river, resembling a palisade.

palish ('peɪlɪʃ) *adj* rather pale.

Palissy (*French* palisi) *n* **Bernard** (bernar). 1510–89, French Huguenot potter and writer on natural history, noted for his rustic glazed earthenware: died in the Bastille.

Palk Strait (pɔːk, pɔːlk) *n* a channel between SE India and N Ceylon. Width: about 64 km (40 miles).

pall[1] (pɔːl) *n* **1** a cloth covering, usually black, spread over a coffin or tomb. **2** a coffin, esp. during the funeral ceremony. **3** a dark heavy covering; shroud: *the clouds formed a pall over the sky.* **4** a depressing or oppressive atmosphere: *her bereavement cast a pall on the party.* **5** *Heraldry.* an ordinary consisting of a Y-shaped bearing. **6** *Christianity.* **6a** a small square linen cloth with which the chalice is covered at the Eucharist. **6b** an archaic word for **pallium** (sense 2). **7** an obsolete word for **cloak.** ◆ *vb* **8** (*tr*) to cover or depress with a pall. [Old English *pæll,* from Latin: PALLIUM]

pall[2] (pɔːl) *vb* **1** (*intr;* often foll. by *on*) to become or appear boring, insipid, or tiresome (to): *history classes palled on me.* **2** to cloy or satiate, or become cloyed or satiated. [C14: variant of APPAL]

Palladian[1] (pə'leɪdɪən) *adj* denoting, relating to, or having the style of architecture created by Andrea Palladio. [C18: after Andrea PALLADIO] ► **Pal'ladianˌism** *n*

Palladian[2] (pə'leɪdɪən) *adj* **1** of or relating to the goddess Pallas Athena. **2** *Literary.* wise or learned. [C16: from Latin *Palladius,* from Greek *Pallas,* an epithet applied to Athena, meaning perhaps "(spear) brandisher" or perhaps "virgin"]

palladic (pə'lædɪk, -'leɪ-) *adj* of or containing palladium in the trivalent or tetravalent state.

Palladio (*Italian* pal'laːdio) *n* **Andrea** (an'drɛːa). 1508–80, Italian architect who revived and developed classical architecture, esp. the ancient Roman ideals of symmetrical planning and harmonic proportions. His treatise *Four Books on Architecture* (1570) and his designs for villas and palaces profoundly influenced 18th-century domestic architecture in England and the U.S.

palladium[1] (pə'leɪdɪəm) *n* a ductile malleable silvery-white element of the platinum metal group occurring principally in nickel-bearing ores: used as a hydrogenation catalyst and, alloyed with gold, in jewellery. Symbol: Pd; atomic no.: 46; atomic wt.: 106.42; valency: 2, 3, or 4; relative density: 1202; melting pt.: 1555°C; boiling pt.: 2964°C. [C19: named after the asteroid PALLAS, at the time (1803) a recent discovery]

palladium[2] (pə'leɪdɪəm) *n* something believed to ensure protection; safeguard. [C17: after the PALLADIUM]

Palladium (pə'leɪdɪəm) *n* a statue of Pallas Athena, esp. the one upon which the safety of Troy depended.

palladous (pə'leɪdəs, 'pælədəs) *adj* of or containing palladium in the divalent state.

Pallas ('pæləs) *n Astronomy.* the second largest asteroid (diameter 520 km), revolving around the sun in a period of 4.62 years.

Pallas Athena *or* **Pallas** *n* another name for **Athena.**

pallbearer ('pɔːlˌbɛərə) *n* a person who carries or escorts the coffin at a funeral.

pallescent (pæ'lɛsənt) *adj Botany.* becoming paler in colour with increasing age.

pallet[1] ('pælɪt) *n* **1** a straw-filled mattress or bed. **2** any hard or makeshift bed. [C14: from Anglo-Norman *paillet,* from Old French *paille* straw, from Latin *palea* straw]

USAGE Avoid confusion with **palate** or **palette.**

pallet[2] ('pælɪt) *n* **1** an instrument with a handle and a flat, sometimes flexible, blade used by potters for shaping. **2** a standard-sized platform of box section open at two ends on which goods may be stacked. The open ends allow the entry of the forks of a lifting truck so that the palletized load can be raised and moved about easily. **3** *Horology.* the locking lever that engages and disengages alternate end pawls with the escape wheel to give impulses to the balance. **4** a variant spelling of **palette** (sense 1). **5** *Music.* a flap valve of wood faced with leather that opens to allow air from the wind chest to enter an organ pipe, causing it to sound. [C16: from Old French *palette* a little shovel, from *pale* spade, from Latin *pala* spade]

palletize *or* **palletise** ('pælɪˌtaɪz) *vb* (*tr*) to stack or transport on a pallet or pallets. ► ˌ**palleti'zation** *or* ˌ**palleti'sation** *n*

pallet knife *n* a variant spelling of **palette knife.**

pallet truck *n* a powered truck with a mast, sometimes telescopic, on which slides a carriage which can be raised and lowered hydraulically. The carriage has extended forks which can be passed under a palletized load for stacking or moving to a new position. Also called: **stacking truck.**

palliasse *or esp. U.S.* **paillasse** ('pælɪˌæs, ˌpælɪ'æs) *n* a straw-filled mattress; pallet. [C18: from French *paillasse,* from Italian *pagliaccio,* ultimately from Latin *palea* PALLET[1]]

palliate ('pælɪˌeɪt) *vb (tr)* **1** to lessen the severity of (pain, disease, etc.) without curing or removing; alleviate; mitigate. **2** to cause (an offence) to seem less serious by concealing evidence; extenuate. [C16: from Late Latin *palliāre* to cover up, from Latin *pallium* a cloak, PALLIUM] ▸ ˌ**palli'ation** *n* ▸ '**palliˌator** *n*

palliative ('pælɪətɪv) *adj* **1** serving to palliate; relieving without curing. ◆ *n* **2** something that palliates, such as a sedative drug or agent. ▸ '**palliatively** *adv*

pallid ('pælɪd) *adj* **1** lacking colour or brightness; wan: *a pallid complexion.* **2** lacking vigour; vapid: *a pallid performance.* [C17: from Latin *pallidus,* from *pallēre* to be PALE[1]] ▸ '**pallidly** *adv* ▸ '**pallidness** *or* **pal'lidity** *n*

pallium ('pælɪəm) *n, pl* **-lia** (-lɪə) *or* **-liums. 1** a garment worn by men in ancient Greece or Rome, made by draping a large rectangular cloth about the body. **2** *Chiefly R.C. Church.* a woollen vestment consisting of a band encircling the shoulders with two lappets hanging from it front and back: worn by the pope, all archbishops, and (as a mark of special honour) some bishops. **3** Also called: **mantle.** *Anatomy.* the cerebral cortex and contiguous white matter. **4** *Zoology.* another name for **mantle** (sense 5). [C16: from Latin: cloak; related to Latin *palla* mantle]

pall-mall ('pæl'mæl) *n Obsolete.* **1** a game in which a ball is driven by a mallet along an alley and through an iron ring. **2** the alley itself. [C17: from obsolete French, from Italian *pallamaglio,* from *palla* ball + *maglio* mallet]

Pall Mall ('pæl 'mæl) *n* a street in London, noted for its many clubs.

pallor ('pælə) *n* a pale condition, esp. when unnatural: *fear gave his face a deathly pallor.* [C17: from Latin: whiteness (of the skin), from *pallēre* to be PALE[1]]

pally ('pælɪ) *adj* **-lier, -liest.** *Informal.* on friendly or familiar terms

palm[1] (pɑːm) *n* **1** the inner part of the hand from the wrist to the base of the fingers. Related adjs.: **thenar, volar. 2** a corresponding part in animals, esp. apes and monkeys. **3** a linear measure based on the breadth or length of a hand, equal to three to four inches or seven to ten inches respectively. **4** the part of a glove that covers the palm. **5** a hard leather shield worn by sailmakers to protect the palm of the hand. **6a** the side of the blade of an oar that faces away from the direction of a boat's movement during a stroke. **6b** the face of the fluke of an anchor. **7** a flattened or expanded part of the antlers of certain deer. **8 in the palm of one's hand.** at one's mercy or command. ◆ *vb (tr)* **9** to conceal in or about the hand, as in sleight-of-hand tricks. **10** to touch or soothe with the palm of the hand. ◆ See also **palm off.** [C14 *paume,* via Old French from Latin *palma;* compare Old English *folm* palm of the hand, Greek *palamē*]

palm[2] (pɑːm) *n* **1** any treelike plant of the tropical and subtropical monocotyledonous family *Palmaceae* (or *Palmae*), having a straight unbranched trunk crowned with large pinnate or palmate leaves. **2** a leaf or branch of any of these trees, a symbol of victory, success, etc. **3** merit or victory. **4** an emblem or insignia representing a leaf or branch worn on certain military decorations. [Old English, from Latin *palma,* from the likeness of its spreading fronds to a hand; see PALM[1]]

Palma[1] (*Spanish* 'palma) *n* the capital of the Balearic Islands, on the SW coast of Majorca: a tourist centre. Pop.: 296 754 (1991). Official name: **Palma de Mallorca.**

Palma[2] (*Italian* 'palma) *n* **Jacopo** (ja'kopo), known as *Palma Vecchio,* original name *Jacopo Negretti.* ?1480–1528, Venetian painter, noted esp. for his portraits of women.

palmaceous (pæl'meɪʃəs) *adj* of, relating to, or belonging to the palm family, *Palmaceae* (or *Palmae*).

palmar ('pælmə) *adj* of or relating to the palm of the hand.

palmary ('pælmərɪ) *adj Rare.* worthy of praise. [C17: from Latin *palmārius* relating to the palm of victory; see PALM[2]]

Palmas ('pælməs) *n* a city in N Brazil, capital of Tocantins state. Pop.: 5750 (1990).

palmate ('pælmeɪt, -mɪt) *or* **palmated** *adj* **1** shaped like an open hand: *palmate antlers.* **2** *Botany.* having five lobes or segments that spread out from a common point: *palmate leaves.* **3** (of the feet of most water birds) having three toes connected by a web.

palmation (pæl'meɪʃən) *n* **1** the state of being palmate. **2** a projection or division of a palmate structure.

Palm Beach *n* a town in SE Florida, on an island between Lake Worth (a lagoon) and the Atlantic: major resort and tourist centre. Pop.: 9814 (1990).

palm civet *n* any of various small civet-like arboreal viverrine mammals of the genera *Paradoxurus, Hemigalus,* etc., of Africa and S and SE Asia.

palmcorder ('pɑːmˌkɔːdə) *n* a small camcorder which can be held in the palm of the hand.

Palme (*Swedish* 'palmə) *n* **(Sven) Olof (Joachim)** ('uːlof). 1927–86, Swedish Social Democratic statesman; prime minister (1969–76, 1982–86); assassinated.

palmer ('pɑːmə) *n* **1** (in Medieval Europe) a pilgrim bearing a palm branch as a sign of his visit to the Holy Land. **2** (in Medieval Europe) an itinerant monk. **3** (in Medieval Europe) any pilgrim. **4** any of various artificial angling flies characterized by hackles around the length of the body. [C13: from Old French *palmier,* from Medieval Latin *palmārius,* from Latin *palma* palm]

Palmer ('pɑːmə) *n* **1 Arnold.** born 1929, U.S. professional golfer: won the U.S. Open Championship (1960) and the British Open Championship (1961; 1962). **2 Samuel.** 1805–81, English painter of visionary landscapes, influenced by William Blake.

Palmer Archipelago *n* a group of islands between South America and Antarctica: part of the British colony of Falkland Islands and Dependencies. Former name: **Antarctic Archipelago.**

Palmer Land *n* the S part of the Antarctic Peninsula.

Palmer Peninsula *n* the former name (until 1964) for the **Antarctic Peninsula.**

Palmerston[1] ('pɑːməstən) *n* the former name (1869–1911) of **Darwin**[1].

Palmerston[2] ('pɑːməstən) *n* **Henry John Temple,** 3rd Viscount Palmerston. 1784–1865, British statesman; foreign secretary (1830–34; 1835–41; 1846–51); prime minister (1855–58; 1859–65). His talent was for foreign affairs, in which he earned a reputation as a British nationalist and for high-handedness and gunboat diplomacy.

Palmerston North *n* a city in New Zealand, in the S North Island on the Manawatu River. Pop. (urban area): 76 300 (1995 est.).

palmer worm *n* the hairy black and white caterpillar of the goldtail moth. [C16: originally applied to various destructive caterpillars of migratory habits]

palmette (pæl'mɛt) *n Archaeol.* an ornament or design resembling the palm leaf. [C19: from French: a little PALM[2]]

palmetto (pæl'mɛtəʊ) *n, pl* **-tos** *or* **-toes. 1** any of several small chiefly tropical fan palms, esp. any of the genus *Sabal,* of the southeastern U.S. See also **cabbage palmetto, saw palmetto. 2** any of various other fan palms such as palms of the genera *Serenoa, Thrinax,* and *Chamaerops.* [C16: from Spanish *palmito* a little PALM[2]]

Palmira (*Spanish* pal'mira) *n* a city in W Colombia: agricultural trading centre. Pop.: 256 823 (1995 est.).

palmistry ('pɑːmɪstrɪ) *n* the process or art of interpreting character, telling fortunes, etc., by the configuration of lines, marks, and bumps on a person's hand. Also called: **chiromancy.** [C15 *pawmestry,* from *paume PALM*[1]; the second element is unexplained] ▸ '**palmist** *n*

palmitate ('pælmɪˌteɪt) *n* any salt or ester of palmitic acid.

palmitic acid (pæl'mɪtɪk) *n* a white crystalline solid that is a saturated fatty acid: used in the manufacture of soap and candles. Formula: $(C_{15}H_{31})COOH$. Systematic name: **hexadecanoic acid.** [C19: from French *palmitique;* see PALM[2], -ITE[2], -IC]

palmitin ('pælmɪtɪn) *n* the colourless glyceride of palmitic acid, occurring in many natural oils and fats. Formula: $(C_{15}H_{31}COO)_3C_3H_5$. Also called: **tripalmitin.** [C19: from French *palmitine,* probably from *palmite* pith of the palm tree; see PALM[2]]

palm off *vb (tr, adv;* often foll. by *on)* **1** to offer, sell, or spend fraudulently: *to palm off a counterfeit coin.* **2** to divert in order to be rid of: *I palmed the unwelcome visitor off on John.*

palm oil *n* a yellow butter-like oil obtained from the fruit of the oil palm, used as an edible fat and in soap.

palm-oil chop *n* a W African dish made with meat and palm oil.

Palm Springs *n* a city in the U.S., in California: a popular tourist resort. Pop.: 40 181 (1990).

palm sugar *n* sugar obtained from the sap of certain species of palm trees.

Palm Sunday *n* the Sunday before Easter commemorating Christ's triumphal entry into Jerusalem.

palmtop computer ('pɑːmˌtɒp) *n* a computer that has a small screen and compressed keyboard and is small enough to be held in the hand, often used as a personal organizer. Often shortened to **palmtop.** Compare **laptop computer.**

palm vaulting *n* a less common name for **fan vaulting.**

palm wine *n* (esp. in W Africa) the sap drawn from the palm tree, esp. when allowed to ferment.

palmy ('pɑːmɪ) *adj* **palmier, palmiest. 1** prosperous, flourishing, or luxurious: *a palmy life.* **2** covered with, relating to, or resembling palms: *a palmy beach.*

palmyra (pæl'maɪrə) *n* a tall tropical Asian palm, *Borassus flabellifer* with large fan-shaped leaves used for thatching and weaving; grown also for its edible seedlings. [C17: from Portuguese *palmeira* palm tree (see PALM[2]); perhaps influenced by PALMYRA, city in Syria]

Palmyra (pæl'maɪrə) *n* **1** an ancient city in central Syria: said to have been built by Solomon. Biblical name: **Tadmor. 2** an island in the central Pacific, in the Line Islands: under U.S. administration.

Palo Alto *n* **1** ('pæləʊ 'æltəʊ). a city in W California, southeast of San Francisco: founded in 1891 as the seat of Stanford University. Pop.: 55 900 (1990). **2** (*Spanish* 'palo 'alto). a battlefield in E Mexico, northwest of Monterrey, where the first battle (1846) of the Mexican War took place, in which the Mexicans under General Mariano Arista were defeated by the Americans under General Zachary Taylor.

palolo worm (pə'ləʊləʊ) *n* any of several polychaete worms of the family *Eunicidae,* esp. *Eunice viridis,* of the S Pacific Ocean: reproductive segments are shed from the posterior end of the body when breeding. [C20 *palolo,* from Samoan or Tongan]

Palomar ('pæləˌmɑː) *n* **Mount.** a mountain in S California, northeast of San Diego: site of **Mount Palomar Observatory,** which has a large (200-inch) reflecting telescope. Height: 1871 m (6140 ft.).

palomino (ˌpælə'miːnəʊ) *n, pl* **-nos.** a golden horse with a cream or white mane and tail. [American Spanish, from Spanish: dovelike, from Latin *palumbīnus,* from *palumbēs* ring dove]

palooka (pə'luːkə) *n U.S. slang.* a stupid or clumsy boxer or other person. [C20: origin uncertain]

Palos (*Spanish* 'palɔs) *n* a village and former port in SW Spain: starting point of Columbus' voyage of discovery to America (1492).

palp (pælp) *or* **palpus** ('pælpəs) *n, pl* **palps** *or* **palpi** ('pælpaɪ). **1** either of a pair of sensory appendages that arise from the mouthparts of crustaceans and insects. **2** either of a pair of tactile organs arising from the head or anterior end of certain annelids and molluscs. [C19: from French, from Latin *palpus* a touching] ▸ **ˈpalpal** *adj*

palpable (ˈpælpəbᵊl) *adj* **1** (*usually prenominal*) easily perceived by the senses or the mind; obvious: *the excuse was a palpable lie.* **2** capable of being touched; tangible. **3** *Med.* capable of being discerned by the sense of touch: *a palpable tumour.* [C14: from Late Latin *palpābilis* that may be touched, from Latin *palpāre* to stroke, touch] ▸ **ˌpalpaˈbility** *or* **ˈpalpableness** *n* ▸ **ˈpalpably** *adv*

palpate[1] (ˈpælpeɪt) *vb* (*tr*) *Med.* to examine (an area of the body) by the sense of touch and pressure. [C19: from Latin *palpāre* to stroke] ▸ **palˈpation** *n*

palpate[2] (ˈpælpeɪt) *adj Zoology.* of, relating to, or possessing a palp or palps.

palpebral (ˈpælpɪbrəl) *adj* of or relating to the eyelid. [C19: from Late Latin *palpebrālis,* from Latin *palpebra* eyelid; probably related to *palpāre* to stroke]

palpebrate *adj* (ˈpælpɪbrɪt, -ˌbreɪt). **1** having eyelids. ◆ *vb* (ˈpælpɪˌbreɪt). **2** (*intr*) to wink or blink, esp. repeatedly.

palpitate (ˈpælpɪˌteɪt) *vb* (*intr*) **1** (of the heart) to beat with abnormal rapidity. **2** to flutter or tremble. [C17: from Latin *palpitāre* to throb, from *palpāre* to stroke] ▸ **ˈpalpitant** *adj* ▸ **ˌpalpiˈtation** *n*

palsgrave (ˈpɔːlzgreɪv) *n Archaic.* a German count palatine. [C16: from Dutch, from Middle Dutch *paltsgrave,* from *palts* estate of a palatine + *grave* count] ▸ **palsgravine** (ˈpɔːlzgrəˌviːn) *fem n*

palstave (ˈpɔːlˌsteɪv) *n Archaeol.* a kind of celt, usually of bronze, made to fit into a split wooden handle rather than having a socket for the handle. [C19: from Danish *paalstav,* from Old Norse, from *páll* spade + *stafr* STAFF[1]]

palsy (ˈpɔːlzɪ) *Pathol.* ◆ *n, pl* **-sies. 1** paralysis, esp. of a specified type: *cerebral palsy.* ◆ *vb* **-sies, -sying, -sied.** (*tr*) **2** to paralyse. [C13 *palesi,* from Old French *paralisie,* from Latin PARALYSIS] ▸ **ˈpalsied** *adj*

palter (ˈpɔːltə) *vb* (*intr*) **1** to act or talk insincerely. **2** to haggle. [C16: of unknown origin] ▸ **ˈpalterer** *n*

paltry (ˈpɔːltrɪ) *adj* **-trier, -triest. 1** insignificant; meagre. **2** worthless or petty. [C16: from Low Germanic *palter, paltrig* ragged] ▸ **ˈpaltrily** *adv* ▸ **ˈpaltriness** *n*

paludal (pəˈljuːdᵊl, ˈpæljudᵊl) *adj Rare.* **1** of, relating to, or produced by marshes. **2** malarial. [C19: from Latin *palus* marsh; related to Sanskrit *palvala* pond]

paludism (ˈpæljuˌdɪzəm) *n Pathol.* a rare word for **malaria.** [C19: from Latin *palus* marsh]

Paludrine (ˈpæljudrɪn) *n Trademark.* proguanil hydrochloride, a synthetic antimalarial drug first produced in 1944.

pal up *vb* (*intr, adv;* often foll. by *with*) *Informal.* to become friends (with): *he palled up with the other boys.*

paly (ˈpeɪlɪ) *adj* (*usually postpositive*) *Heraldry.* vertically striped. [C15: from Old French *palé,* from Latin *pālus* stake; see PALE[2]]

palynology (ˌpælɪˈnɒlədʒɪ) *n* the study of living and fossil pollen grains and plant spores. [C20: from Greek *palunein* to scatter + -LOGY] ▸ **palynological** (ˌpælɪnəˈlɒdʒɪkᵊl) *adj* ▸ **ˌpalyˈnologist** *n*

pam. *or* **pamph.** *abbrev. for* pamphlet.

Pama-Nyungan (ˈpɑːməˈnjuŋgən) *adj* **1** of or relating to the largest superfamily of languages within the phylum of languages spoken by the native Australians. ◆ *n* **2** this phylum.

Pamirs (pəˈmɪəz) *pl n* **the.** a mountainous area of central Asia, mainly in Tajikistan and partly in Kyrgyzstan, extending into China and Afghanistan: consists of a complex of high ranges, from which the Tian Shan projects to the north, the Kunlun and Karakoram to the east, and the Hindu Kush to the west; Kommunizma Peak is situated in the Tajik Pamirs. Highest peak: Kongur Shan, 7719 m (25 326 ft.). Also called: **Paˈmir.**

Pamlico Sound (ˈpæmlɪkəu) *n* an inlet of the Atlantic between the E coast of North Carolina and its chain of offshore islands. Length: 130 km (80 miles).

pampas (ˈpæmpəz) *n* (*functioning as sing or more often pl*) **a** the extensive grassy plains of temperate South America, esp. in Argentina. **b** (*as modifier*): *pampas dwellers.* [C18: from American Spanish *pampa* (sing), from Quechua *bamba* plain] ▸ **pampean** (ˈpæmpɪən, pæmˈpiːən) *adj*

pampas grass (ˈpæmpəs, -pəz) *n* any of various large grasses of the South American genus *Cortaderia* and related genera, widely cultivated for their large feathery silver-coloured flower branches.

Pampeluna (ˌpæmpəˈluːnə) *n* the former name of **Pamplona.**

pamper (ˈpæmpə) *vb* (*tr*) **1** to treat with affectionate and usually excessive indulgence; coddle; spoil. **2** *Archaic.* to feed to excess. [C14: of Germanic origin; compare German dialect *pampfen* to gorge oneself] ▸ **ˈpamperer** *n*

pampero (pæmˈpeərəu; *Spanish* pamˈpero) *n, pl* **-ros** (-rəuz; *Spanish* -ros). a dry cold wind in South America blowing across the pampas from the south or southwest. [C19: from American Spanish: (wind) of the PAMPAS]

pamphlet (ˈpæmflɪt) *n* **1** a brief publication generally having a paper cover; booklet. **2** a brief treatise, often on a subject of current interest, published in pamphlet form. [C14 *pamflet,* from Anglo-Latin *panfletus,* from Medieval Latin *Pamphilus* title of a popular 12th-century amatory poem from Greek *Pamphilos* masculine proper name]

pamphleteer (ˌpæmflɪˈtɪə) *n* **1** a person who writes or issues pamphlets, esp. of a controversial nature. ◆ *vb* **2** (*intr*) to write or issue pamphlets.

pamphrey (ˈpæmfrɪ) *n Ulster dialect.* a cabbage. [of unknown origin]

Pamphylia (pæmˈfɪlɪə) *n* an area on the S coast of ancient Asia Minor.

Pamplona (pæmˈpləunə; *Spanish* pamˈplona) *n* a city in N Spain in the foothills of the Pyrenees: capital of the kingdom of Navarre from the 11th century until 1841. Pop.: 181 776 (1995 est.). Former name: **Pampeluna.**

pampoen (ˌpamˈpun) *n S. African.* **1** a pumpkin. **2** *Informal.* a fool.

pampootie (ˌpæmˈpuːtiː) *n* a rawhide slipper worn by men in the Aran Islands. [C19: of uncertain origin]

pan[1] (pæn) *n* **1a** a wide metal vessel used in cooking. **1b** (*in combination*): *saucepan.* **2** Also called: **ˈpanful.** the amount such a vessel will hold. **3** any of various similar vessels used esp. in industry, as for boiling liquids. **4** a dish used by prospectors, esp. gold prospectors, for separating a valuable mineral from the gravel or earth containing it by washing and agitating. **5** either of the two dishlike receptacles on a balance. **6** Also called: **lavatory pan.** *Brit.* the bowl of a lavatory. **7a** a natural or artificial depression in the ground where salt can be obtained by the evaporation of brine. **7b** a natural depression containing water or mud. **8** *Caribbean.* the indented top from an oil drum used as the treble drum in a steel band. **9** See **hardpan, brainpan. 10** a small ice floe. **11** a slang word for **face** (sense 1a). **12** a small cavity containing priming powder in the locks of old guns. **13** a hard substratum of soil. **14** short for **pan loaf.** ◆ *vb* **pans, panning, panned. 15** (when *tr,* often foll. by *off* or *out*) to wash (gravel) in a pan to separate particles of (valuable minerals) from it. **16** (*intr;* often foll. by *out*) (of gravel) to yield valuable minerals by this process. **17** (*tr*) *Informal.* to criticize harshly: *the critics panned his new play.* ◆ See also **pan out.** [Old English *panne;* related to Old Saxon, Old Norse *panna,* Old High German *pfanna*]

pan[2] (pæn) *n* **1** the leaf of the betel tree. **2** a preparation of this leaf which is chewed, together with betel nuts and lime, in India and the East Indies. [C17: from Hindi, from Sanskrit *parna* feather, wing, leaf]

pan[3] (pæn) *vb* **pans, panning, panned. 1** to move (a film camera) or (of a film camera) to be moved so as to follow a moving object or obtain a panoramic effect. ◆ *n* **2a** the act of panning. **2b** (*as modifier*): *a pan shot.* [C20: shortened from *panoramic*]

Pan (pæn) *n Greek myth.* the god of fields, woods, shepherds, and flocks, represented as a man with a goat's legs, horns, and ears. Related adjs.: **Pandean, Panic.**

Pan. *abbrev. for* Panama.

pan- *combining form.* **1** all or every: *panchromatic.* **2** including or relating to all parts or members: *Pan-African; pantheistic.* [from Greek *pan,* neuter of *pas* all]

panacea (ˌpænəˈsɪə) *n* a remedy for all diseases or ills. [C16: via Latin from Greek *panakeia* healing everything, from *pan* all + *akēs* remedy] ▸ **ˌpanaˈcean** *adj*

panache (pəˈnæʃ, -ˈnɑːʃ) *n* **1** a dashing manner; style; swagger: *he rides with panache.* **2** a feathered plume on a helmet. [C16: via French from Old Italian *pennacchio,* from Late Latin *pinnāculum* feather, from Latin *pinna* feather; compare Latin *pinnāculum* PINNACLE]

panada (pəˈnɑːdə) *n* a mixture of flour, water, etc., or of breadcrumbs soaked in milk, used as a thickening. [C16: from Spanish, from *pan* bread, from Latin *pānis*]

Pan-African *adj* **1** of or relating to all African countries or the advocacy of political unity among African countries. ◆ *n* **2** a supporter of the Pan-African movement. ▸ **ˈPan-ˈAfricanˌism** *n*

Panaji (pɑːˈnɑːdʒiː) *n* a variant of **Panjim.**

Panama (ˌpænəˈmɑː, ˈpænəˌmɑː) *n* **1** a republic in Central America, occupying the Isthmus of Panama: gained independence from Spain in 1821 and joined Greater Colombia; became independent in 1903, with the immediate area around the canal forming the Canal Zone under U.S. jurisdiction; in 1979 Panama assumed sovereignty over the Canal Zone. Official language: Spanish; English is also widely spoken. Religion: Roman Catholic majority. Currency: balboa. Capital: Panama City. Pop.: 2 767 000 (1998 est.). Area: 75 650 sq. km (29 201 sq. miles). **2 Isthmus of.** an isthmus linking North and South America, between the Pacific and the Caribbean. Length: 676 km (420 miles). Width (at its narrowest point): 50 km (31 miles). Former name: (Isthmus of) **Darien. 3 Gulf of.** a wide inlet of the Pacific in Panama. ▸ **Panamanian** (ˌpænəˈmeɪnɪən) *adj, n*

Panama Canal *n* a canal across the Isthmus of Panama, linking the Atlantic and Pacific Oceans: extends from Colón on the Caribbean Sea southeast to Balboa on the Gulf of Panama; built by the U.S. (1904–14), after an unsuccessful previous attempt (1880–89) by the French under de Lesseps. Length: 64 km (40 miles).

Panama Canal Zone *n* See **Canal Zone.**

Panama City *n* the capital of Panama, near the Pacific entrance of the Panama Canal: developed rapidly with the building of the Panama Canal; seat of the University of Panama (1935). Pop.: 452 041 (1995 est.).

Panama hat *n* (*sometimes not cap.*) a hat made of the plaited leaves of the jipijapa plant of Central and South America. Often shortened to **panama** or **Panama.**

Pan-American *adj* of, relating to, or concerning North, South, and Central America collectively or the advocacy of political or economic unity among American countries. ▸ **ˈPan-Aˈmericanˌism** *n*

Pan American Union *n* the secretariat and major official agency of the Organization of American States.

pan and tilt head *n Films, television.* a mounting device on which a camera may be rotated in a horizontal plane (pan) or in a vertical plane (tilt).

Pan-Arabism (ˈærəˌbɪzəm) *n* the principle of, support for, or the movement towards Arab political union or cooperation. ▸ **ˈPan-ˈArab** *adj, n* ▸ **ˈPan-ˈArabic** *adj*

panatella (ˌpænəˈtɛlə) *n* a long slender cigar. [American Spanish *panetela* long slim biscuit, from Italian *panatella* small loaf, from *pane* bread, from Latin *pānis*]

Panathenaea (pæˌnæθɪˈniːə) *n* (in ancient Athens) a summer festival on the traditional birthday of Athena.

Panay (pɑːˈnaɪ) *n* an island in the central Philippines, the westernmost of the Visayan Islands. Pop.: 2 595 314 (1980). Area: 12 300 sq. km (4750 sq. miles).
pancake (ˈpænˌkeɪk) *n* **1a** a thin flat cake made from batter and fried on both sides, often served rolled and filled with a sweet or savoury mixture. **1b** (*as modifier*): *pancake mix*. **2** a Scot. name for **drop scone**. **3** a stick or flat cake of compressed make-up. **4** Also called: **pancake landing**. an aircraft landing made by levelling out a few feet from the ground and then dropping onto it. ◆ *vb* **5** to cause (an aircraft) to make a pancake landing or (of an aircraft) to make a pancake landing.
Pancake Day *n* another name for **Shrove Tuesday**.
pancake ice *n* thin slabs of newly formed ice in polar seas.
pancetta (pænˈtʃetə; *Italian* panˈtʃetta) *n* a lightly spiced cured bacon from Italy. [Italian, literally: little belly]
panchax (ˈpænˌtʃæks) *n* any of several brightly coloured tropical Asian cyprinodont fishes of the genus *Aplocheilus*, such as *A. panchax* (**blue panchax**). [C19: from New Latin (former generic name), of obscure origin]
Panchayat (pənˈtʃɑːjət) *n* a village council in India. [Hindi, from Sanskrit *panch* five, because such councils originally consisted of five members]
Panchen Lama (ˈpɑːntʃən) *n* one of the two Grand Lamas of Tibet, ranking below the Dalai Lama. Also called: **Tashi Lama**. [from Tibetan *panchen*, literally: great jewel, from the title of the lama (in full: great jewel among scholars)]
panchromatic (ˌpænkrəʊˈmætɪk) *adj Photog.* (of an emulsion or film) made sensitive to all colours by the addition of suitable dyes to the emulsion. Compare **orthochromatic**. ▸ **panchromatism** (pænˈkrəʊməˌtɪzəm) *n*
pancosmism (pænˈkɒzˌmɪzəm) *n* the philosophical doctrine that the material universe is all that exists. [C19: see PAN-, COSMOS, -ISM]
pancratium (pænˈkreɪʃɪəm) *n, pl* **-tia** (-ʃɪə). (in ancient Greece) a wrestling and boxing contest. [C17: via Latin from Greek *pankration*, from PAN- + *kratos* strength] ▸ **pancratic** (pænˈkrætɪk) *adj*
pancreas (ˈpæŋkrɪəs) *n* a large elongated glandular organ, situated behind the stomach, that secretes insulin and pancreatic juice. [C16: via New Latin from Greek *pankreas*, from PAN- + *kreas* flesh] ▸ **pancreatic** (ˌpæŋkrɪˈætɪk) *adj*
pancreatic juice *n* the clear alkaline secretion of the pancreas that is released into the duodenum and contains several digestive enzymes.
pancreatin (ˈpæŋkrɪətɪn) *n* the powdered extract of the pancreas of certain animals, such as the pig, used in medicine as an aid to the digestion.
pancreatitis (ˌpæŋkrɪəˈtaɪtɪs) *n* inflammation of the pancreas.
pancreozymin (ˌpæŋkrɪəʊˈzaɪmɪn) *n* another name for **cholecystokinin**.
panda (ˈpændə) *n* **1** Also called: **giant panda**. a large black-and-white herbivorous bearlike mammal, *Ailuropoda melanoleuca*, related to the raccoons and inhabiting the high mountain bamboo forests of China: family *Procyonidae*. **2** **lesser** *or* **red panda**. a closely related smaller animal resembling a raccoon, *Ailurus fulgens*, of the mountain forests of S Asia, having a reddish-brown coat and ringed tail. [C19: via French from a native Nepalese word]
panda car *n Brit.* a police patrol car, esp. a blue and white one. [C20: so called because it was originally white with black or blue markings, supposedly resembling the markings of the giant panda]
pandanaceous (ˌpændəˈneɪʃəs) *adj* of, relating to, or belonging to the *Pandanaceae*, an Old World tropical family of monocotyledonous plants including the screw pines.
pandanus (pænˈdeɪnəs) *n, pl* **-nuses**. any of various Old World tropical palmlike plants of the genus *Pandanus*, having large aerial prop roots and leaves that yield a fibre used for making mats, etc.: family *Pandanaceae*. See also **screw pine**. [C19: via New Latin from Malay *pandan*]
Pandarus (ˈpændərəs) *n* **1** *Greek myth.* the leader of the Lycians, allies of the Trojans in their war with the Greeks. He broke the truce by shooting Menelaus with an arrow and was killed in the ensuing battle by Diomedes. **2** (in medieval legend) the procurer of Cressida on behalf of Troilus.
Pandean (pænˈdiːən) *adj* of or relating to the god Pan.
pandect (ˈpændɛkt) *n* **1** a treatise covering all aspects of a particular subject. **2** (*often pl*) the complete body of laws of a country; legal code. [C16: via Late Latin from Greek *pandektēs* containing everything, from PAN- + *dektēs* receiver, from *dekhesthai* to receive]
Pandects of Justinian *pl n* another name for **Digest**.
pandemic (pænˈdɛmɪk) *adj* **1** (of a disease) affecting persons over a wide geographical area; extensively epidemic. ◆ *n* **2** a pandemic disease. [C17: from Late Latin *pandēmus*, from Greek *pandēmos* general, from PAN- + *demos* the people]
pandemonium (ˌpændɪˈməʊnɪəm) *n* **1** wild confusion; uproar. **2** a place of uproar and chaos. [C17: coined by Milton to designate the capital of hell in *Paradise Lost*, from PAN- + Greek *daimōn* DEMON] ▸ ˌ**pandeˈmoniˌac** *or* **pandemonic** (ˌpændɪˈmɒnɪk) *adj*
pander (ˈpændə) *vb* **1** (*intr*; foll. by *to*) to give gratification (to weaknesses or desires). **2** (archaic when *tr*) to act as a go-between in a sexual intrigue (for). ◆ *n also* ˈ**panderer**. **3** a person who caters for vulgar desires, esp. in order to make money. **4** a person who procures a sexual partner for another; pimp. [C16 (n): from *Pandare* PANDARUS]
pandit (ˈpʌndɪt; *spelling pron* ˈpændɪt) *n Hinduism.* a variant of **pundit** (sense 3).
Pandit (ˈpʌndɪt) *n* **Vijaya Lakshmi** (vɪˈjaɪə ˈlɑːkʃmɪ). 1900–90, Indian politician and diplomat; sister of Jawaharlal Nehru.
P & L *abbrev. for* profit and loss.
P & O *abbrev. for* the Peninsular and Oriental Steam Navigation Company.
pandora (pænˈdɔːrə) *n* **1** a handsome red sea bream, *Pagellus erythrinus*, of European coastal waters, caught for food in the Mediterranean. **2** a marine bivalve mollusc of the genus *Pandora* that lives on the surface of sandy shores and has thin equal valves. **3** *Music.* another word for **bandore**. [after PANDORA]
Pandora (pænˈdɔːrə) *or* **Pandore** (pænˈdɔː, ˈpændɔː) *n Greek myth.* the first woman, made out of earth as the gods' revenge on man for obtaining fire from Prometheus. Given a box (**Pandora's box**) that she was forbidden to open, she disobeyed out of curiosity and released from it all the ills that beset man, leaving only hope within. [from Greek, literally: all-gifted]
pandore (ˈpændɔː) *n Music.* another word for **bandore**.
pandour (ˈpænduə) *n* one of an 18th-century force of Croatian soldiers in the Austrian service, notorious for their brutality. [C18: via French from Hungarian *pandur*, from Croat: guard, probably from Medieval Latin *banderius* summoner, from *bannum* BAN[1]]
pandowdy (pænˈdaʊdɪ) *n, pl* **-dies**. *U.S.* a deep-dish pie made from fruit, esp. apples, with a cake topping: *apple pandowdy*. [C19: of unknown origin]
p & p *Brit. abbrev. for* postage and packing.
pandurate (ˈpændjʊˌreɪt) *or* **panduriform** (pænˈdjʊərɪˌfɔːm) *adj* (of plant leaves) shaped like the body of a fiddle. [C19: from Late Latin *pandūra* BANDORE]
pandy (ˈpændɪ) *Chiefly Scot. and Irish.* ◆ *n, pl* **-dies**. **1** (in schools) a stroke on the hand with a strap as a punishment. ◆ *vb* **-dies, -dying, -died**. **2** (*tr*) to punish with such strokes. [C19: from Latin *pande* (*manum*) stretch out (the hand), from *pandere* to spread or extend]
pane[1] (peɪn) *n* **1** a sheet of glass in a window or door. **2** a panel of a window, door, wall, etc. **3** a flat section or face, as of a cut diamond. **4** *Philately.* **4a** any of the rectangular marked divisions of a sheet of stamps made for convenience in selling. **4b** a single page in a stamp booklet. See also **tête-bêche, se tenant**. [C13: from Old French *pan* portion, from Latin *pannus* rag]
pane[2] (peɪn) *n, vb* a variant of **peen**.
pané *French.* (pane) *adj* (of fish, meat, etc.) dipped or rolled in breadcrumbs before cooking.
panegyric (ˌpænɪˈdʒɪrɪk) *n* a formal public commendation; eulogy. [C17: via French and Latin from Greek, from *panēguris* public gathering, from PAN- + *aguris* assembly] ▸ ˌ**paneˈgyrical** *adj* ▸ ˌ**paneˈgyrically** *adv* ▸ ˌ**paneˈgyrist** *n*
panegyrize *or* **panegyrise** (ˈpænɪdʒɪˌraɪz) *vb* to make a eulogy or eulogies (about).
panel (ˈpænᵊl) *n* **1** a flat section of a wall, door, etc. **2** any distinct section or component of something formed from a sheet of material, esp. of a car body, the spine of a book, etc. **3** a piece of material inserted in a skirt, dress, etc. **4a** a group of persons selected to act as a team in a quiz, to judge a contest, to discuss a topic before an audience, etc. **4b** (*as modifier*): *a panel game*. **5** a public discussion by such a group: *a panel on public health*. **6** *Law.* **6a** a list of persons summoned for jury service. **6b** the persons on a specific jury. **7** *Scots Law.* a person indicted or accused of crime after appearing in court. **8a** a thin board used as a surface or backing for an oil painting. **8b** a painting done on such a surface. **9** any picture with a length much greater than its breadth. **10** See **instrument panel**. **11** (in Britain) (formerly) **11a** a list of patients insured under the National Health Insurance Scheme. **11b** a list of medical practitioners within a given area available for consultation by these patients. **12 on the panel**. *Brit. informal.* receiving sickness benefit, esp. from the government. ◆ *vb* **-els, -elling, -elled** *or U.S.* **-els, -eling, -eled**. (*tr*) **13** to furnish or decorate with panels. **14** to divide into panels. **15** *Law.* **15a** to empanel (a jury). **15b** (in Scotland) to bring (a person) to trial; indict. [C13: from Old French: portion, from *pan* piece of cloth, from Latin *pannus*; see PANE[1]]
panel beater *n* a person who beats out the bodywork of motor vehicles.
panel heating *n* a system of space heating with panels that contain heating pipes or electrical conductors.
panelling *or U.S.* **paneling** (ˈpænᵊlɪŋ) *n* **1** panels collectively, as on a wall or ceiling. **2** material used for making panels.
panellist *or U.S.* **panelist** (ˈpænᵊlɪst) *n* a member of a panel, esp. on a radio or television programme.
panel pin *n* a light slender nail with a narrow head.
panel saw *n* a saw with a long narrow blade for cutting thin wood.
panel truck *n* the U.S. and Canadian name for **delivery van**.
panel van *n* **1** *Austral.* a small van with two rear doors, esp. one having windows and seats in the rear. **2** *N.Z.* a small enclosed delivery van.
panettone (pænəˈtəʊnɪ; *Italian* panetˈtoːne) *n, pl* **-nes** *or* **-ni** (-ni). a kind of Italian spiced brioche containing sultanas: traditionally eaten at Christmas in Italy. [Italian, from *panetto* small loaf, from *pane* bread, from Latin *pānis*]
Pan-European *adj* of or relating to all European countries or the advocacy of political or economic unity among European countries.
pang (pæŋ) *n* a sudden brief sharp feeling, as of loneliness, physical pain, or hunger. [C16: variant of earlier *prange*, of Germanic origin]
panga (ˈpæŋgə) *n* a broad heavy knife of E Africa, used as a tool or weapon. [from a native E African word]
Pangaea *or* **Pangea** (pænˈdʒiːə) *n* the ancient supercontinent, comprising all the present continents joined together, which began to break up about 200 million years ago. See also **Laurasia, Gondwanaland**. [C20: from Greek, literally: all-earth]
pangenesis (pænˈdʒɛnɪsɪs) *n* a former theory of heredity, that each body cell produces hereditary particles that circulate in the blood before collecting in the reproductive cells. See also **blastogenesis** (sense 1). ▸ **pangenetic** (ˌpændʒəˈnɛtɪk) *adj* ▸ ˌ**pangeˈnetically** *adv*
Pan-Germanism *n* (esp. in the 19th century) the movement for the unification of Germany.
Pang-fou (ˈpæŋˈfuː) *n* a variant transliteration of the Chinese name for **Bengbu**.
pangolin (pæŋˈgəʊlɪn) *n* any mammal of the order *Pholidota* found in tropical Africa, S Asia, and Indonesia, having a body covered with overlapping horny scales and a long snout specialized for feeding on ants and termites. Also called:

scaly anteater. [C18: from Malay *peng-gōling,* from *gōling* to roll over; from its ability to roll into a ball]

Pango Pango ('pɑːŋgəʊ 'pɑːŋgəʊ) *n* the former name of **Pago Pago.**

Pan Gu ('pæn'guː) *or* **P'an Ku** *n* 32–92 A.D., Chinese historian and court official, noted for his history of the Han dynasty: died in prison.

panhandle[1] ('pæn,hændᵊl) *n* **1** (*sometimes cap.*) (in the U.S.) a narrow strip of land that projects from one state into another. **2** (in a South African city) a plot of land without street frontage.

panhandle[2] ('pæn,hændᵊl) *vb U.S. and Canadian informal.* to accost and beg from (passers-by), esp. on the street. [C19: probably a back formation from *panhandler* a person who begs with a pan] ▸ **'pan,handler** *n*

Panhellenic (,pænhe'lenɪk) *adj* of or relating to all the Greeks, all Greece, or Panhellenism.

Panhellenism (ˌpæn'helɪ,nɪzəm) *n* the principle of or support for the union of all Greeks or all Greece. ▸ **,Pan'hellenist** *n* ▸ **,Pan,hellen'istic** *adj*

panic ('pænɪk) *n* **1** a sudden overwhelming feeling of terror or anxiety, esp. one affecting a whole group of people. **2** (*modifier*) of or resulting from such terror: *panic measures.* ◆ *vb* **-ics, -icking, -icked. 3** to feel or cause to feel panic. [C17: from French *panique,* from New Latin *pānicus,* from Greek *panikos* emanating from PAN, considered as the source of irrational fear] ▸ **'panicky** *adj*

Panic ('pænɪk) *adj* of or relating to the god Pan.

panic attack *n* an episode of acute and disabling anxiety associated with such physical symptoms as hyperventilation and sweating. See also **panic disorder.**

panic bolt *n* a bolt on the inside esp. of double doors that is released by pressure on a waist-high bar: used for emergency exits in theatres, shops, etc.

panic button *n* **1** a button or switch that operates any of various safety devices, for use in an emergency. **2 hit** *or* **press the panic button.** *Informal.* to react to a situation by demanding emergency action; become excited; panic.

panic buying *n* the buying up of large quantities of a commodity which, it is feared, is likely to be in short supply.

panic disorder *n Psychiatry.* a condition in which a person experiences recurrent panic attacks.

panic grass *n* any of various grasses of the genus *Panicum,* such as millet, grown in warm and tropical regions for fodder and grain. [C15 *panic,* from Latin *pānicum,* probably a back formation from *pānicula* PANICLE]

panicle ('pænɪkᵊl) *n* a compound raceme, as in the oat. [C16: from Latin *pānicula* tuft, diminutive of *panus* thread, ultimately from Greek *penos* web; related to *penion* bobbin] ▸ **'panicled** *adj*

panicmonger ('pænɪk,mʌŋgə) *n* a person who spreads panic.

panic stations *pl n Informal.* a state of alarm; panicky reaction: *when he realized he'd lost the keys it was panic stations.*

panic-stricken *or* **panic-struck** *adj* affected by panic.

paniculate (pə'nɪkjʊ,leɪt, -lɪt) *or* **paniculated** *adj Botany.* growing or arranged in panicles: *a paniculate inflorescence.* ▸ **pa'nicu,lately** *adv*

panidiomorphic (pæ,nɪdɪəʊ'mɔːfɪk) *adj* (of igneous rocks) having well-developed crystals. [C19: from PAN- + IDIOMORPHIC]

Panjabi (pʌn'dʒɑːbɪ) *n, adj* a variant spelling of **Punjabi.**

panjandrum (pæn'dʒændrəm) *n* a pompous self-important official or person of rank. [C18: after a character, the *Grand Panjandrum,* in a nonsense work (1755) by Samuel Foote, English playwright and actor]

Panjim ('pɑːn,ʒɪm) *or* **Panaji** *n* the capital of the Indian union territory of Goa, Daman, and Diu: a port on the Arabian Sea on the coast of Goa. Pop.: 85 515 (1991).

Pankhurst ('pæŋkhɜːst) *n* **1** Dame **Christabel.** 1880–1958, English suffragette. **2** her mother, **Emmeline.** 1858–1928, English suffragette leader, who founded the militant Women's Social and Political Union (1903). **3 Sylvia,** daughter of Emmeline Pankhurst. 1882–1960, English suffragette and pacifist.

pan loaf *n Irish and Scot. dialect.* a loaf of bread with a light crust all the way round. Often shortened to **pan.** Compare **batch**[1] (sense 4).

panmixia (pæn'mɪksɪə) *or* **panmixis** (pæn'mɪksɪs) *n* (in population genetics) random mating within an interbreeding population. [C20: from New Latin, from Greek PAN- + *mixis* act of mating]

Panmunjom ('pɑːn'mʊn'dʒɒm) *n* a village in the demilitarized zone of Korea: site of truce talks leading to the end of the Korean War (1950–53).

pannage ('pænɪdʒ) *n Archaic.* **1** pasturage for pigs, esp. in a forest. **2** the right to pasture pigs in a forest. **3** payment for this. **4** acorns, beech mast, etc., on which pigs feed. [C13: from Old French *pasnage,* ultimately from Latin *pastion-, pastiō* feeding, from *pascere* to feed]

panne (pæn) *n* a lightweight velvet fabric. [C19: via Old French, from Latin *pinna* wing, feather]

pannier ('pænɪə) *n* **1** a large basket, esp. one of a pair slung over a beast of burden. **2** one of a pair of bags slung either side of the back wheel of a motorcycle, bicycle, etc. **3** (esp. in the 18th century) **3a** a hooped framework to distend a woman's skirt. **3b** one of two puffed-out loops of material worn drawn back onto the hips to reveal the underskirt. [C13: from Old French *panier,* from Latin *pānārium* basket for bread, from *pānis* bread]

pannikin ('pænɪkɪn) *n Chiefly Brit.* a small metal cup or pan. [C19: from PAN[1] + -KIN]

pannikin boss *n Austral. informal.* a person in charge of a few fellow workers.

Pannonia (pə'nəʊnɪə) *n* a region of the ancient world south and west of the Danube: made a Roman province in 6 A.D.

panocha (pə'nəʊtʃə) *or* **penuche** *n* **1** a coarse grade of sugar made in Mexico. **2** (in the U.S.) a sweet made from brown sugar and milk, often with chopped nuts. [Mexican Spanish, diminutive of Spanish *pan* bread, from Latin *pānis*]

panoply ('pænəplɪ) *n, pl* **-plies. 1** a complete or magnificent array. **2** the entire equipment of a warrior. [C17: via French from Greek *panoplia* complete armour, from PAN- + *hopla* armour, pl of *hoplon* tool] ▸ **'panoplied** *adj*

panoptic (pæn'ɒptɪk) *or* **panoptical** *adj* taking in all parts, aspects, etc., in a single view; all-embracing: *a panoptic survey.* [C19: from Greek *panoptēs* seeing everything, from PAN- + *optos* visible] ▸ **pan'optically** *adv*

panorama (,pænə'rɑːmə) *n* **1** an extensive unbroken view, as of a landscape, in all directions. **2** a wide or comprehensive survey: *a panorama of the week's events.* **3** a large extended picture or series of pictures of a scene, unrolled before spectators a part at a time so as to appear continuous. **4** another name for **cyclorama.** [C18: from PAN- + Greek *horāma* view] ▸ **panoramic** (,pænə'ræmɪk) *adj* ▸ **,pano'ramically** *adv*

panoramic sight *n* a type of artillery sight with a large field of view.

pan out *vb* (*intr, adv*) *Informal.* to work out; turn out; result.

panpipes ('pæn,paɪps) *pl n* (*often sing; often cap.*) a number of reeds or whistles of graduated lengths bound together to form a musical wind instrument. Also called: **pipes of Pan, syrinx.**

pan potentiometer *n* a control on a stereo sound mixing desk by means of which the relative levels in right- and left-hand channels can be adjusted and hence the apparent position of the recorded or broadcast sound source within the stereo panorama can be controlled. Often shortened to **pan pot.** [C20: from PAN(ORAMIC) + POTENTIOMETER]

panradiometer (,pænreɪdɪ'ɒmɪtə) *n Physics.* an instrument used for measuring radiant heat independently of wavelength.

Pan-Slavism *n* (esp. in the 19th century) the movement for the union of the Slavic peoples, esp. under the hegemony of tsarist Russia. ▸ **'Pan-'Slavic** *adj*

pansophy ('pænsəfɪ) *n* universal knowledge. [C17: from New Latin *pansophia;* see PAN-, -SOPHY] ▸ **pansophic** (pæn'sɒfɪk) *or* **pan'sophical** *adj* ▸ **pan'sophically** *adv*

pansy ('pænzɪ) *n, pl* **-sies. 1** any violaceous garden plant that is a variety of *Viola tricolor,* having flowers with rounded velvety petals, white, yellow, or purple in colour. See also **wild pansy. 2** *Slang.* an effeminate or homosexual man or boy. **3a** a strong violet colour. **3b** (*as adj*)*: a pansy carpet.* [C15: from Old French *pensée* thought, from *penser* to think, from Latin *pensāre*]

pant (pænt) *vb* **1** to breathe with noisy deep gasps, as when out of breath from exertion or excitement. **2** to say (something) while breathing thus. **3** (*intr; often foll. by for*) to have a frantic desire (for); yearn. **4** (*intr*) to pulsate; throb rapidly. ◆ *n* **5** the act or an instance of panting. **6** a short deep gasping noise; puff. [C15: from Old French *pantaisier,* from Greek *phantasioun* to have visions, from *phantasia* FANTASY]

Pantagruel (pæn'tægruːel) *n* a gigantic prince, noted for his ironical buffoonery, in Rabelais's satire *Gargantua and Pantagruel* (1534). ▸ **,Pantagru'elian** *or* **,Pantagru'elic** *adj* ▸ **,Panta'gruel,ism** *n* ▸ **,Panta'gruelist** *n*

pantalets *or* **pantalettes** (,pæntə'lets) *pl n* **1** long drawers, usually trimmed with ruffles, extending below the skirts: worn during the early and mid 19th century. **2** a pair of ruffles for the ends of such drawers. [C19: diminutive of PANTALOONS]

pantaloon (,pæntə'luːn) *n Theatre.* **1** (in pantomime) an absurd old man, the butt of the clown's tricks. **2** (*usually cap.*) (in commedia dell'arte) a lecherous old merchant dressed in pantaloons. [C16: from French *Pantalon,* from Italian *Pantalone,* local nickname for a Venetian, probably from *San Pantaleone,* a fourth-century Venetian saint]

pantaloons (,pæntə'luːnz) *pl n* **1a** *History.* men's tight-fitting trousers, esp. those fastening under the instep worn in the late 18th and early 19th centuries. **1b** children's trousers resembling these. **2** *Informal or facetious.* any trousers, esp. baggy ones.

pantechnicon (pæn'teknɪkən) *n Brit.* **1** a large van, esp. one used for furniture removals. **2** a warehouse where furniture is stored. [C19: from PAN- + Greek *tekhnikon* relating to the arts, from *tekhnē* art; originally the name of a London bazaar, the building later being used as a furniture warehouse]

Pantelleria (*Italian* pantelle'riːa) *n* an Italian island in the Mediterranean, between Sicily and Tunisia: of volcanic origin; used by the Romans as a place of banishment. Pop.: 7316 (1991 est.). Area: 83 sq. km (32 sq. miles). Ancient name: **Cossyra** (kə'saɪrə).

Pan-Teutonism *n* another name for **Pan-Germanism.**

Panth (pʌnθ) *n* the Sikh community. [from Punjabi: path]

pantheism ('pænθɪ,ɪzəm) *n* **1** the doctrine that God is the transcendent reality of which man, nature, and the material universe are manifestations. **2** any doctrine that regards God as identical with the material universe or the forces of nature. **3** readiness to worship all or a large number of gods. ▸ **'pantheist** *n* ▸ **,panthe'istic** *or* **,panthe'istical** *adj* ▸ **,panthe'istically** *adv*

pantheon (pæn'θiːən, 'pænθɪən) *n* **1** (esp. in ancient Greece or Rome) a temple to all the gods. **2** all the gods collectively of a religion. **3** a monument or building commemorating a nation's dead heroes. [C14: via Latin from Greek *Pantheion,* from PAN- + *-theios* divine, from *theos* god]

Pantheon (pæn'θiːən, 'pænθɪən) *n* a circular temple in Rome dedicated to all the gods, built by Agrippa in 27 B.C., rebuilt by Hadrian 120–24 A.D., and used since 609 A.D. as a Christian church.

panther ('pænθə) *n, pl* **-thers** *or* **-ther. 1** another name for **leopard** (sense 1), esp. the black variety (**black panther**). **2** *U.S. and Canadian.* any of various related animals, esp. the puma. [C14: from Old French *pantère,* from Latin *panthēra,* from Greek *panthēr;* perhaps related to Sanskrit *pundarīka* tiger]

panties ('pæntɪz) *pl n* a pair of women's or children's underpants.

pantihose ('pæntɪ,həʊz) *pl n* another name (esp. U.S. and Austral.) for **tights** (sense 1). [C20: from PANTIES + HOSE[2]]

pantile ('pæn,taɪl) *n* **1** a roofing tile, with an S-shaped cross section, laid so that the downward curve of one tile overlaps the upward curve of the adjoining tile. **2** a tapering roofing tile with a semicircular cross section, laid alternately so that the convex side of one tile overlaps the concave side of adjoining tiles. [C17: from PAN[1] + TILE]

pantisocracy (,pæntɪ'sɒkrəsɪ) *n* a community, social group, etc., in which all have rule and everyone is equal. [C18 (coined by Robert SOUTHEY): from Greek, from PANTO- + *isos* equal + -CRACY]

panto ('pæntəʊ) *n, pl* **-tos.** *Brit. informal.* short for **pantomime** (sense 1).

panto- *or before a vowel* **pant-** *combining form.* all: *pantisocracy; pantofle; pantograph; pantomime.* [from Greek *pant-, pas*]

pantofle, pantoffle (pæn'tɒfᵊl), *or* **pantoufle** (pæn'tu:fᵊl) *n Archaic.* a kind of slipper. [C15: from French *pantoufle,* from Old Italian *pantofola,* perhaps from Medieval Greek *pantophellos* shoe made of cork, from PANTO- + *phellos* cork]

pantograph ('pæntəˌgrɑ:f) *n* **1** an instrument consisting of pivoted levers for copying drawings, maps, etc., to any desired scale. **2** a sliding type of current collector, esp. a diamond-shaped frame mounted on a train roof in contact with an overhead wire. **3** a device consisting of a parallelogram of jointed rods used to suspend a studio lamp so that its height can be adjusted. ▸ **pantographer** (pæn'tɒgrəfə) *n* ▸ **pantographic** (ˌpæntə'græfɪk) *adj* ▸ **ˌpanto'graphically** *adv* ▸ **pan'tography** *n*

pantomime ('pæntəˌmaɪm) *n* **1** (in Britain) **1a** a kind of play performed at Christmas time characterized by farce, music, lavish sets, stock roles, and topical jokes. Sometimes shortened to **panto. 1b** (*as modifier*): *a pantomime horse.* **2** a theatrical entertainment in which words are replaced by gestures and bodily actions. **3** action without words as a means of expression. **4** (in ancient Rome) an actor in a dumb show. **5** *Informal, chiefly Brit.* a confused or farcical situation. ◆ *vb* **6** another word for **mime** (sense 5). [C17: via Latin from Greek *pantomīmos;* see PANTO-, MIME] ▸ **pantomimic** (ˌpæntə'mɪmɪk) *adj* ▸ **pantomimist** ('pæntəˌmaɪmɪst) *n*

pantothenic acid (ˌpæntə'θenɪk) *n* an oily acid that is a vitamin of the B complex: occurs widely in animal and vegetable foods and is essential for cell growth. Formula: $C_{19}H_{17}NO_5$. [C20: from Greek *pantothen* from every side]

pantoum (pæn'tu:m) *n Prosody.* a verse form consisting of a series of quatrains in which the second and fourth lines of each verse are repeated as the first and third lines of the next. [C19: via French from Malay *pantun*]

pantry ('pæntrɪ) *n, pl* **-tries.** a small room or cupboard in which provisions, cooking utensils, etc., are kept; larder. [C13: via Anglo-Norman, from Old French *paneterie* store for bread, ultimately from Latin *pānis* bread]

pants (pænts) *pl n* **1** *Brit.* an undergarment reaching from the waist to the thighs or knees. **2** the usual U.S. and Canadian name for **trousers. 3 bore, scare,** etc., **the pants off.** *Informal.* to bore, scare, etc., extremely. [C19: shortened from *pantaloons;* see PANTALOON]

pantsuit ('pæntˌsju:t, -ˌsu:t) *n* the U.S. and Canadian term for **trouser suit.**

panty girdle ('pæntɪ) *n* a foundation garment with a crotch, often of lighter material than a girdle.

pantyhose ('pæntɪˌhəʊz) *n* the N.Z. spelling of **pantihose.**

pantywaist ('pæntɪˌweɪst) *n U.S. informal.* a man or boy considered as childish, lacking in courage, etc. [C20: originally a child's garment of trousers buttoned to a jacket at the waist]

Panufnik (pæ'nu:fnɪk) *n* Sir **Andrzej** (ændreɪ). 1914–91, British composer and conductor, born in Poland. His works include nine symphonies, the cantata *Winter Solstice* (1972), Polish folk-song settings, and ballet music.

panzer ('pænzə; *German* 'pantsər) *n* **1** (*modifier*) of, relating to, or characteristic of the fast mechanized armoured units employed by the German army in World War II: *a panzer attack.* **2** a vehicle belonging to a panzer unit, esp. a tank. **3** (*pl*) armoured troops. [C20: from German, from Middle High German, from Old French *panciere* coat of mail, from Latin *pantex* PAUNCH]

Pão de Açúcar (pɐ̃un di a'sukar) *n* the Portuguese name for the **Sugar Loaf Mountain.**

Paolozzi (paʊ'lɒtsɪ) *n* Sir **Eduardo** (**Luigi**). born 1924, British sculptor and designer, noted esp. for his semiabstract metal figures.

Paoting *or* **Pao-ting** ('paʊ'tɪŋ) *n* a variant transliteration of the Chinese name for **Baoding.**

Paotow ('paʊ'taʊ) *n* a variant transliteration of the Chinese name for **Baotou.**

pap[1] (pæp) *n* **1** any soft or semiliquid food, such as bread softened with milk, esp. for babies or invalids; mash. **2** *S. African.* porridge made from maize. **3** worthless or oversimplified ideas; drivel: *intellectual pap.* [C15: from Middle Low German *pappe,* via Medieval Latin from Latin *pappāre* to eat; compare Dutch *pap,* Italian *pappa*]

pap[2] (pæp) *n* **1** *Archaic or Scot. and northern English dialect.* a nipple or teat. **2a** something resembling a breast or nipple, such as (formerly) one of a pair of rounded hilltops. **2b** (*cap. as part of a name*): *the Pap of Glencoe.* [C12: of Scandinavian origin, imitative of a sucking sound; compare Latin *papilla* nipple, Sanskrit *pippalaka*]

papa[1] (pə'pɑ:) *n Old-fashioned.* an informal word for **father** (sense 1). [C17: from French, a children's word for father; compare Late Latin *pāpa,* Greek *pappa*]

papa[2] ('pɑ:pɑ:) *n R.C. Church.* another name for the **pope**[1] (sense 1). [C16: from Italian]

papa[3] ('pɑ:pa) *n N.Z.* a soft blue-grey clay of marine siltstone or sandstone. [Maori]

Papa ('pɑ:pɑ:) *n Communications.* a code word for the letter *p.*

papacy ('peɪpəsɪ) *n, pl* **-cies. 1** the office or term of office of a pope. **2** the system of government in the Roman Catholic Church that has the pope as its head. [C14: from Medieval Latin *pāpātia,* from *pāpa* POPE[1]]

Papadopoulos (ˌpæpə'dɒpələs; *Greek* papa'ðɔpulɔs) *n* **Georgios.** 1919–99, Greek army officer and statesman; prime minister (1967–73) and president (1973) in Greece's military government.

papain (pə'peɪɪn, -'paɪɪn) *n* a proteolytic enzyme occurring in the unripe fruit of the papaya tree, *Carica papaya:* used as a meat tenderizer and in medicine as an aid to protein digestion. [C19: from PAPAYA]

papal ('peɪpᵊl) *adj* of or relating to the pope or the papacy. ▸ **'papally** *adv*

papal cross *n* a cross with three crosspieces.

Papal States *pl n* the temporal domain of the popes in central Italy from 756 A.D. until the unification of Italy in 1870. Also called: **States of the Church.**

Papandreou (ˌpæpən'dreɪu:; *Greek* papan'ðrɛu) *n* **Andreas** (**George**) (an'drɛas). 1919–96, Greek economist and socialist politician; prime minister (1981–89; 1993–96).

Papanicolaou test *or* **smear** (ˌpæpə'nɪkəlu:) *n* the full name for **Pap test.**

paparazzo (ˌpæpə'rætsəʊ) *n, pl* **-razzi** (-'rætsi:). a freelance photographer who specializes in candid camera shots of famous people and often invades their privacy to obtain such photographs. [C20: from Italian]

papaveraceous (pəˌpeɪvə'reɪʃəs) *adj* of, relating to, or belonging to the *Papaveraceae,* a family of plants having large showy flowers and a cylindrical seed capsule with pores beneath the lid: includes the poppies and greater celandine. [C19: from New Latin, from Latin *papāver* POPPY]

papaverine (pə'peɪvəˌri:n, -rɪn) *n* a white crystalline almost insoluble alkaloid found in opium and used as an antispasmodic to treat coronary spasms and certain types of colic. Formula: $C_{20}H_{21}NO_4$. [C19: from Latin *papāver* POPPY]

papaw (pə'pɔ:) *or* **pawpaw** *n* **1** Also called: **custard apple. 1a** a bush or small tree, *Asimina triloba,* of central North America, having small fleshy edible fruit: family *Annonaceae.* **1b** the fruit of this tree. **2** another name for **papaya.** [C16: from Spanish PAPAYA]

papaya (pə'paɪə) *n* **1** a Caribbean evergreen tree, *Carica papaya,* with a crown of large dissected leaves and large green hanging fruit: family *Caricaceae.* **2** the fruit of this tree, having a yellow sweet edible pulp and small black seeds. ◆ Also called: **papaw, pawpaw.** [C15 *papaye,* from Spanish *papaya,* from an American Indian language; compare Carib *ababai*] ▸ **pa'payan** *adj*

Papeete (ˌpɑ:pɪ'i:tɪ) *n* the capital of French Polynesia, on the NW coast of Tahiti: one of the largest towns in the S Pacific. Pop.: 78 814 (1988).

Papen (*German* 'pa:pən) *n* **Franz von** (frants fɔn). 1879–1969, German statesman; chancellor (1932) and vice chancellor (1933–34) under Hitler, whom he was instrumental in bringing to power.

paper ('peɪpə) *n* **1** a substance made from cellulose fibres derived from rags, wood, etc., often with other additives, and formed into flat thin sheets suitable for writing on, decorating walls, wrapping, etc. Related adj: **papyraceous. 2** a single piece of such material, esp. if written or printed on. **3** (*usually pl*) documents for establishing the identity of the bearer; credentials. **4** (*pl*) Also called: **ship's papers.** official documents relating to the ownership, cargo, etc., of a ship. **5** (*pl*) collected diaries, letters, etc. **6** See **newspaper** or **wallpaper. 7** *Government.* See **white paper, green paper, command paper. 8** a lecture or short published treatise on a specific subject. **9** a short essay, as by a student. **10a** a set of written examination questions. **10b** the student's answers. **11** *Commerce.* See **commercial paper. 12** *Theatre slang.* a free ticket. **13 on paper.** in theory, as opposed to fact: *it was a good idea on paper, but failed in practice.* ◆ *adj* **14** made of paper: *paper cups do not last long.* **15** thin like paper: *paper walls.* **16** (*prenominal*) existing only as recorded on paper but not yet in practice: *paper profits; paper expenditure.* **17** taking place in writing: *paper battles.* ◆ *vb* **18** to cover (walls) with wallpaper. **19** (*tr*) to cover or furnish with paper. **20** (*tr*) *Theatre slang.* to fill (a performance) by giving away free tickets (esp. in the phrase **paper the house**). ◆ See also **paper over.** [C14: from Latin PAPYRUS] ▸ **'paperer** *n* ▸ **'papery** *adj* ▸ **'paperiness** *n*

paperback ('peɪpəˌbæk) *n* **1** a book or edition with covers made of flexible card, sold relatively cheaply. Compare **hardback.** ◆ *adj also* **'paperˌbound, soft-cover. 2** of or denoting a paperback or publication of paperbacks. ◆ *vb* (*tr*) **3** to publish in paperback. ▸ **'paperˌbacker** *n*

paperbark ('peɪpəˌbɑ:k) *n* any of several Australian myrtaceous trees of the genus *Melaleuca,* esp. *M. quinquenervia,* of swampy regions, having spear-shaped leaves and papery bark that can be peeled off in thin layers.

paperboard ('peɪpəˌbɔ:d) *n* **a** a thick cardboard made of compressed layers of paper pulp; pasteboard. **b** (*as modifier*): *a paperboard box.*

paperboy ('peɪpəˌbɔɪ) *n* a boy employed to deliver newspapers, magazines, etc. ▸ **'paperˌgirl** *fem n*

paper chase *n* a former type of cross-country run in which a runner laid a trail of paper for others to follow.

paperclip ('peɪpəˌklɪp) *n* a clip for holding sheets of paper together, esp. one made of bent wire.

paper-cutter *n* a machine for cutting paper, usually a blade mounted over a table on which paper can be aligned.

paper filigree *n* another name for **rolled paperwork.**

paperhanger ('peɪpəˌhæŋə) *n* **1** a person who hangs wallpaper as an occupation. **2** *U.S. slang.* a counterfeiter. ▸ **'paperˌhanging** *n*

paperknife ('peɪpəˌnaɪf) *n, pl* **-knives.** a knife with a comparatively blunt blade, esp. one of wood, bone, etc., for opening sealed envelopes.

paperless ('peɪpəlɪs) *adj* of, relating to, or denoting a means of communication, record keeping, etc., esp. electronic, that does not use paper: *the paperless office.*

paper money *n* paper currency issued by the government or the central bank as legal tender and which circulates as a substitute for specie.

paper mulberry *n* a small moraceous E Asian tree, *Broussonetia papyrifera,* the inner bark of which was formerly used for making paper in Japan. See also **tapa.**

paper nautilus *n* any cephalopod mollusc of the genus *Argonauta,* esp. *A. argo,* of warm and tropical seas, having a papery external spiral shell: order *Octopoda* (octopods). Also called: **argonaut.** Compare **pearly nautilus.**

paper over *vb* (*tr, adv*) to conceal (something controversial or unpleasant).

paper tape *n* a strip of paper for recording information in the form of rows of either six or eight holes, some or all of which are punched to produce a combination used as a discrete code symbol, formerly used in computers, telex machines, etc. U.S. equivalent: **perforated tape.**

paper tiger *n* a nation, institution, etc., that appears powerful but is in fact weak or insignificant. [C20: translation of a Chinese phrase first applied to the U.S.]

paperweight ('peɪpəˌweɪt) *n* a small heavy object placed on loose papers to prevent them from scattering.

paperwork ('peɪpəˌwɜːk) *n* clerical work, such as the completion of forms or the writing of reports or letters.

papeterie ('pæpətrɪ; *French* papetri) *n* a box or case for papers and other writing materials. [C19: from French, from *papetier* maker of paper, from *papier* PAPER]

Paphian ('peɪfɪən) *adj* **1** of or relating to Paphos. **2** of or relating to Aphrodite. **3** *Literary.* of sexual love.

Paphlagonia (ˌpæfləˈgəʊnɪə) *n* an ancient country and Roman province in N Asia Minor, on the Black Sea.

Paphos[1] ('peɪfɒs) *n* a village in SW Cyprus, near the sites of two ancient cities: famous as the centre of Aphrodite worship and traditionally the place at which she landed after her birth among the waves. Pop.: 32 575 (1992 est.).

Paphos[2] ('peɪfɒs) *or* **Paphus** ('peɪfəs) *n Greek myth.* the son of Pygmalion and Galatea, who succeeded his father on the throne of Cyprus.

Papiamento (*Spanish* papjaˈmento) *n* a creolized Spanish spoken in the Netherlands Antilles. [Spanish, from *papia* talk]

papier collé (*French* papje kɔle) *n* a type of collage, usually of an abstract design. [French, literally: glued paper]

papier-mâché (ˌpæpjeɪˈmæʃeɪ; *French* papjemɑʃe) *n* **1** a hard strong substance suitable for painting on, made of paper pulp or layers of paper mixed with paste, size, etc., and moulded when moist. ◆ *adj* **2** made of papier-mâché. [C18: from French, literally: chewed paper]

papilionaceous (pəˌpɪlɪəˈneɪʃəs) *adj* of, relating to, or belonging to the *Papilionaceae,* a family of leguminous plants having irregular flowers: includes peas, beans, clover, alfalfa, gorse, and broom. [C17: from New Latin, from Latin *pāpiliō* butterfly]

papilla (pəˈpɪlə) *n, pl* **-lae** (-liː). **1** the small projection of tissue at the base of a hair, tooth, or feather. **2** any other similar protuberance. **3** any minute blunt hair or process occurring in plants. [C18: from Latin: nipple; related to Latin *papula* pimple] ▸ **paˈpillary, ˈpapillate,** *or* **ˈpapillose** *adj*

papilloma (ˌpæpɪˈləʊmə) *n, pl* **-mata** (-mətə) *or* **-mas.** *Pathol.* a benign tumour derived from epithelial tissue and forming a rounded or lobulated mass. [C19: from PAPILLA + -OMA] ▸ **ˌpapilˈlomatous** *adj* ▸ **ˌpapilˌlomaˈtosis** *n*

papillon ('pæpɪˌlɒn) *n* a breed of toy spaniel with large ears. [French: butterfly, from Latin *pāpiliō*]

papillote ('pæpɪˌləʊt) *n* **1** a paper frill around cutlets, etc. **2 en papillote** (ɑ̃ papijɔt). (of food) cooked in oiled greaseproof paper or foil. [C18: from French PAPILLON]

papist ('peɪpɪst) *n, adj* (*often cap.*) *Usually disparaging.* another term for **Roman Catholic.** [C16: from French *papiste,* from Church Latin *pāpa* POPE[1]] ▸ **paˈpistical** *or* **paˈpistic** *adj* ▸ **ˈpapistry** *n*

papoose *or* **pappoose** (pəˈpuːs) *n* **1** an American Indian baby or child. **2** a pouchlike bag used for carrying a baby, worn on the back. [C17: from Algonquian *papoos*]

pappus ('pæpəs) *n, pl* **pappi** ('pæpaɪ). a ring of fine feathery hairs surrounding the fruit in composite plants, such as the thistle; aids dispersal of the fruits by the wind. [C18: via New Latin, from Greek *pappos* grandfather, old man, old man's beard, hence: pappus, down] ▸ **ˈpappose** *or* **ˈpappous** *adj*

Pappus of Alexandria ('pæpəs) *n* 3rd century B.C., Greek mathematician, whose eight-volume *Synagoge* is a valuable source of information about Greek mathematics.

pappy[1] ('pæpɪ) *adj* **-pier, -piest.** resembling pap; mushy.

pappy[2] ('pæpɪ) *n, pl* **-pies.** *U.S.* an informal word for **father.**

paprika ('pæprɪkə, pæˈpriː-) *n* **1** a mild powdered seasoning made from a sweet variety of red pepper. **2** the fruit or plant from which this seasoning is obtained. [C19: via Hungarian from Serbian, from *papar* PEPPER]

Pap test *or* **smear** (pæp) *n Med.* **1** another name for **cervical smear. 2** a similar test for precancerous cells in other organs. ◆ Also called: **Papanicolaou smear.** [C20: named after George *Papanicolaou* (1883–1962), U.S. anatomist, who devised it]

Papua ('pæpjʊə) *n* **1 Territory of.** a former territory of Australia, consisting of SE New Guinea and adjacent islands: now part of Papua New Guinea. Former name (1888–1906): **British New Guinea. 2 Gulf of.** an inlet of the Coral Sea in the SE coast of New Guinea.

Papuan ('pæpjʊən) *adj* **1** of or relating to Papua or any of the languages spoken there. ◆ *n* **2** a native or inhabitant of Papua New Guinea. **3** any of several languages of Papua New Guinea that apparently do not belong to the Malayo-Polynesian family.

Papua New Guinea *n* a country in the SW Pacific; consists of the E half of New Guinea, the Bismarck Archipelago, the W Solomon Islands, Trobriand Islands, D'Entrecasteaux Islands, Woodlark Island, and the Louisiade Archipelago; administered by Australia from 1949 until 1975, when it became an independent member of the Commonwealth. Official language: English; Tok Pisin (English Creole) and Motu are widely spoken. Religion: Christian majority. Currency: kina. Capital: Port Moresby. Pop.: 4 600 000 (1998 est.). Area: 461 693 sq. km (178 260 sq. miles).

papule ('pæpjuːl) *or* **papula** ('pæpjʊlə) *n, pl* **-ules** *or* **-ulae** (-jʊˌliː). *Pathol.* a small solid usually round elevation of the skin. [C19: from Latin *papula* pustule, pimple] ▸ **ˈpapular** *adj* ▸ **ˌpapuˈliferous** *adj*

papyraceous (ˌpæpɪˈreɪʃəs) *adj* of, relating to, made of, or resembling paper. [C18: from PAPYRUS + -ACEOUS. See PAPER]

papyrology (ˌpæpɪˈrɒlədʒɪ) *n* the study of ancient papyri. ▸ **papyrological** (ˌpæpɪrəˈlɒdʒɪkᵊl) *adj* ▸ **ˌpapyˈrologist** *n*

papyrus (pəˈpaɪrəs) *n, pl* **-ri** (-raɪ) *or* **-ruses. 1** a tall aquatic cyperaceous plant, *Cyperus papyrus,* of S Europe and N and central Africa with small green-stalked flowers arranged like umbrella spokes around the stem top. **2** a kind of paper made from the stem pith of this plant, used by the ancient Egyptians, Greeks, and Romans. **3** an ancient document written on this paper. [C14: via Latin from Greek *papūros* reed used in making paper]

par (pɑː) *n* **1** an accepted level or standard, such as an average (esp. in the phrase **up to par**). **2** a state of equality (esp. in the phrase **on a par with**). **3** *Finance.* the established value of the unit of one national currency in terms of the unit of another where both are based on the same metal standard. **4** *Commerce.* **4a** See **par value. 4b** the condition of equality between the current market value of a share, bond, etc., and its face value (the **nominal par**). This equality is indicated by **at par,** while **above** (*or* **below**) **par** indicates that the market value is above (or below) face value. **5** *Golf.* an estimated standard score for a hole or course that a good player should make: *par for the course was 72.* **6 below** *or* **under par.** not feeling or performing as well as normal. **7 par for the course.** an expected or normal occurrence or situation. ◆ *adj* **8** average or normal. **9** (*usually prenominal*) *Commerce.* of or relating to par: *par value.* [C17: from Latin *pār* equal, on a level; see PEER[1]]

par. *abbrev. for:* **1** paragraph. **2** parallel. **3** parenthesis. **4** parish.

Par. *abbrev. for* Paraguay.

par- *prefix* a variant of **para-**[1] before a vowel.

para[1] ('pɑːrə) *n, pl* **-ras** *or* **-ra.** a Yugoslavian monetary unit worth one hundredth of a dinar. [C17: Serbo-Croat, via Turkish from Persian *pārah* piece, portion]

para[2] ('pærə) *n Informal.* **1a** a soldier in an airborne unit. **1b** an airborne unit. **2** a paragraph.

Pará (*Portuguese* paˈra) *n* **1** a state of N Brazil, on the Atlantic: mostly dense tropical rainforest. Capital: Belém. Pop.: 5 448 600 (1995 est.). Area: 1 248 042 sq. km (474 896 sq. miles). **2** another name for **Belém. 3** an estuary in N Brazil into which flow the Tocantins River and a branch of the Amazon. Length: about 320 km (200 miles).

para-[1] *or before a vowel* **par-** *prefix* **1** beside; near: *parameter; parathyroid.* **2** beyond: *parapsychology.* **3** resembling: *paramnesia.* **4** defective; abnormal: *paraesthesia.* **5** subsidiary to: *paraphysis.* **6** (*usually in italics*) denoting that an organic compound contains a benzene ring with substituents attached to atoms that are directly opposite across the ring (the 1,4- positions): *paradinitrobenzene; para-*cresol. Abbrev.: *p-*. Compare **ortho-** (sense 4), **meta-** (sense 4). **7** denoting an isomer, polymer, or compound related to a specified compound: *paraldehyde; paracasein.* **8** denoting the form of a diatomic substance in which the spins of the two constituent atoms are antiparallel: *parahydrogen.* Compare **ortho-** (sense 6). [from Greek *para* (prep) alongside, beyond]

para-[2] *combining form.* indicating an object that acts as a protection against something: *parachute; parasol.* [via French from Italian *para-,* from *parare* to defend, shield against, ultimately from Latin *parāre* to prepare]

para-aminobenzoic acid *n Biochem.* an acid present in yeast and liver: used in the manufacture of dyes and pharmaceuticals. Formula: $C_6H_4(NH_2)COOH$.

parabasis (pəˈræbəsɪs) *n, pl* **-ses** (-ˌsiːz). (in classical Greek comedy) an address from the chorus to the audience. [C19: from Greek, from *parabanein* to step forward]

parabiosis (ˌpærəbaɪˈəʊsɪs) *n* **1** the natural union of two individuals, such as Siamese twins, so that they share a common circulation of the blood. **2** a similar union induced for experimental or therapeutic purposes. [C20: from PARA-[1] + Greek *biōsis* manner of life, from *bios* life] ▸ **parabiotic** (ˌpærəbaɪˈɒtɪk) *adj*

parablast ('pærəˌblæst) *n* the yolk of an egg, such as a hen's egg, that undergoes meroblastic cleavage. [C19: from PARA-[1] + -BLAST] ▸ **ˌparaˈblastic** *adj*

parable ('pærəbᵊl) *n* **1** a short story that uses familiar events to illustrate a religious or ethical point. Related adjs.: **parabolic, parabolical. 2** any of the stories of this kind told by Jesus Christ. [C14: from Old French *parabole,* from Latin *parabola* comparison, from Greek *parabolē* analogy, from *paraballein* to throw alongside, from PARA-[1] + *ballein* to throw] ▸ **parabolist** (pəˈræbəlɪst) *n*

parabola (pəˈræbələ) *n* a conic section formed by the intersection of a cone by a plane parallel to its side. Standard equation: $y^2 = 4ax$, where $2a$ is the distance between focus and directrix. [C16: via New Latin from Greek *parabolē* a setting alongside; see PARABLE]

parabolic[1] (ˌpærəˈbɒlɪk) *adj* **1** of, relating to, or shaped like a parabola. **2** shaped like a paraboloid: *a parabolic mirror.*

parabolic[2] (ˌpærəˈbɒlɪk) *or* **parabolical** *adj* of or resembling a parable. ▸ **ˌparaˈbolically** *adv*

parabolic aerial *n* a formal name for **dish aerial.**

parabolize[1] *or* **parabolise** (pəˈræbəˌlaɪz) *vb* (*tr*) to explain by a parable.

parabolize[2] *or* **parabolise** (pəˈræbəˌlaɪz) *vb* (*tr*) to shape like a parabola or paraboloid. ▸ **paˌraboliˈzation** *or* **paˌraboliˈsation** *n*

paraboloid (pəˈræbəˌlɔɪd) *n* a geometric surface whose sections parallel to two coordinate planes are parabolic and whose sections parallel to the third plane are either elliptical or hyperbolic. Equations: $x^2/a^2 \pm y^2/b^2 = 2cz$ ▸ **paˌraboˈloidal** *adj*

parabrake ('pærəˌbreɪk) *n* another name for **brake parachute.**

paracasein (ˌpærəˈkeɪsɪɪn, -siːn) *n U.S.* another name for **casein.**

Paracelsus (ˌpærəˈsɛlsəs) *n* **Philippus Aureolus** ('fɪlɪpəs ɔːˈrɪˈəʊləs), real name *Theophrastus Bombastus von Hohenheim.* 1493–1541, Swiss physician and alchemist, who pioneered the use of specific treatment, based on observation and experience, to remedy particular diseases.

paracentesis (ˌpærəsɛnˈtiːsɪs) *n Med.* the surgical puncture of a body cavity in order to draw off excess fluid.

paracetamol (ˌpærəˈsiːtəˌmɒl, -ˈsɛtə-) *n* a mild analgesic drug used as an alternative to aspirin. [C20: from *para-acetamidophenol*]

parachronism (pəˈrækrəˌnɪzəm) *n* an error in dating, esp. by giving too late a date. Compare **prochronism.** [C17: from PARA-[1] + *-chronism,* as in ANACHRONISM]

parachute ('pærə,ʃu:t) *n* **1a** a device used to retard the fall of a man or package from an aircraft, consisting of a large fabric canopy connected to a harness. **1b** (*as modifier*): *parachute troops.* Sometimes shortened to **chute.** See also **brake parachute.** ◆ *vb* **2** (of troops, supplies, etc.) to land or cause to land by parachute from an aircraft. **3** *Canadian.* (in an election) to bring in (a candidate, esp. someone well known) from outside the constituency. [C18: from French, from PARA-[2] + *chute* fall] ▸ **'para,chutist** *n*

paraclete ('pærə,kli:t) *n Rare.* a mediator or advocate.

Paraclete ('pærə,kli:t) *n Christianity.* the Holy Ghost as comforter or advocate. [C15: via Old French from Church Latin *Paraclētus,* from Late Greek *Paraklētos* advocate, from Greek *parakalein* to summon as a helper, from PARA-[1] + *kalein* to call]

parade (pə'reɪd) *n* **1** an ordered, esp. ceremonial, march, assembly, or procession, as of troops being reviewed: *on parade.* **2** Also called: **parade ground.** a place where military formations regularly assemble. **3** a visible show or display: *to make a parade of one's grief.* **4** a public promenade or street of shops. **5** a successive display of things or people. **6** the interior area of a fortification. **7** a parry in fencing. **8 on parade. 8a** on display. **8b** showing oneself off. ◆ *vb* **9** (when *intr,* often foll. by *through* or *along*) to walk or march, esp. in a procession (through): *to parade the streets.* **10** (*tr*) to exhibit or flaunt: *he was parading his medals.* **11** (*tr*) to cause to assemble in formation, as for a military parade. **12** (*intr*) to walk about in a public place. [C17: from French: a making ready, a setting out, a boasting display; compare Italian *parata,* Spanish *parada,* all ultimately from Latin *parāre* to prepare] ▸ **pa'rader** *n*

paradiddle ('pærə,dɪdᵊl) *n* a group of four drum beats produced by using alternate sticks in the pattern right-left-right-right or left-right-left-left. [C20: of imitative origin]

paradigm ('pærə,daɪm) *n* **1** *Grammar.* the set of all the inflected forms of a word or a systematic arrangement displaying these forms. **2** a pattern or model. **3** a typical or stereotypical example (esp. in the phrase **paradigm case**). **4** (in the philosophy of science) a very general conception of the nature of scientific endeavour within which a given enquiry is undertaken. [C15: via French and Latin from Greek *paradeigma* pattern, from *paradeiknunai* to compare, from PARA-[1] + *deiknunai* to show] ▸ **paradigmatic** (,pærədɪg'mætɪk) *adj*

paradisal (,pærə'daɪsᵊl), **paradisiacal** (,pærədɪ'saɪəkᵊl), *or* **paradisiac** (,pærə'dɪsɪ,æk) *adj* of, relating to, or resembling paradise.

paradise ('pærə,daɪs) *n* **1** heaven as the ultimate abode or state of the righteous. **2** *Islam.* the sensual garden of delights that the Koran promises the faithful after death. **3** Also called: **limbo.** (according to some theologians) the intermediate abode or state of the just prior to the Resurrection of Jesus, as in Luke 23:43. **4** the place or state of happiness enjoyed by Adam before the first sin; the Garden of Eden. **5** any place or condition that fulfils all one's desires or aspirations. **6** a park in which foreign animals are kept. [Old English, from Church Latin *paradīsus,* from Greek *paradeisos* garden, of Persian origin; compare Avestan *pairidaēza* enclosed area, from *pairi-* around + *daēza* wall]

paradise duck *n* a large duck, *Casarca variegata,* of New Zealand, having a brightly coloured plumage.

paradise fish *n* any of several beautifully coloured labyrinth fishes of the genus *Macropodus,* esp. *M. opercularis,* of S and SE Asia.

parador ('pærədɔ:; *Spanish* 'paraðor) *n, pl* **-dors** *or* **-dores.** a state-run hotel in Spain. [Spanish]

parados ('pærə,dɒs) *n* a bank behind a trench or other fortification, giving protection from being fired on from the rear. [C19: from French, from PARA-[2] + *dos* back, from Latin *dorsum;* compare PARASOL, PARAPET]

paradox ('pærə,dɒks) *n* **1** a seemingly absurd or self-contradictory statement that is or may be true: *religious truths are often expressed in paradox.* **2** a self-contradictory proposition, such as *I always tell lies.* **3** a person or thing exhibiting apparently contradictory characteristics. **4** an opinion that conflicts with common belief. [C16: from Late Latin *paradoxum,* from Greek *paradoxos* opposed to existing notions, from PARA-[1] + *doxa* opinion] ▸ **,para'doxical** *adj* ▸ **,para'doxically** *adv*

paradoxical intention *n* (in psychotherapy) the deliberate practice of a neurotic habit or thought, undertaken in order to remove it.

paradoxical sleep *n Physiol.* sleep that appears to be deep but that is characterized by a brain wave pattern similar to that of wakefulness, rapid eye movements, and heavier breathing.

paradrop ('pærə,drɒp) *n* the delivery of personnel or equipment from an aircraft by parachute.

paraesthesia *or U.S.* **paresthesia** (,pæres'θi:zɪə) *n Pathol.* an abnormal or inappropriate sensation in an organ, part, or area of the skin, as of burning, prickling, tingling, etc. ▸ **paraesthetic** *or U.S.* **paresthetic** (,pæres'θetɪk) *adj*

paraffin ('pærəfɪn) *or* (*less commonly*) **paraffine** ('pærə,fi:n) *n* **1** Also called: **paraffin oil,** (esp. U.S. and Canadian) **kerosene.** a liquid mixture consisting mainly of alkane hydrocarbons with boiling points in the range 150°–300°C, used as an aircraft fuel, in domestic heaters, and as a solvent. **2** another name for **alkane. 3** See **paraffin wax. 4** See **liquid paraffin.** ◆ *vb* (*tr*) **5** to treat with paraffin or paraffin wax. [C19: from German, from Latin *parum* too little + *affinis* adjacent; so called from its chemical inertia]

paraffin wax *n* a white insoluble odourless waxlike solid consisting mainly of alkane hydrocarbons with melting points in the range 50°–60°C, used in candles, waterproof paper, and as a sealing agent. Also called: **paraffin.**

paraformaldehyde (,pærəfɔ:'mældɪ,haɪd) *or* **paraform** *n* a white amorphous solid polymeric form of formaldehyde: used as a convenient source of formaldehyde and as a fumigant. Formula: $(CH_2O)n$, where *n* lies between 6 and 50.

paragenesis (,pærə'dʒenɪsɪs) *or* **paragenesia** (,pærədʒɪ'ni:zɪə) *n* the order in which the constituent minerals of a rock mass have been formed. ▸ **paragenetic** (,pærədʒɪ'netɪk) *adj* ▸ **,parage'netically** *adv*

paragliding ('pærə,glaɪdɪŋ) *n* the sport of cross-country gliding using a specially designed parachute shaped like flexible wings. The parachutist glides from an aeroplane to a predetermined landing area. ▸ **'para,glider** *n*

paragnathous (,pæræg'neɪθəs) *adj* (of certain vertebrates) having the upper and lower jaws of equal length.

paragoge (,pærə'gəʊdʒɪ) *or* **paragogue** ('pærə,gɒg) *n* the addition of a sound or a syllable to the end of a word, such as *st* in *amongst.* [C17: via Late Latin from Greek *paragōgē* an alteration, ultimately from *paragein* to lead past, change] ▸ **paragogic** (,pærə'gɒdʒɪk) *or* **,para'gogical** *adj* ▸ **,para'gogically** *adv*

paragon ('pærəgən) *n* **1** a model of excellence; pattern: *a paragon of virtue.* **2** a size of printer's type, approximately equal to 20 point. ◆ *vb* (*tr*) **3** *Archaic.* **3a** to equal or surpass. **3b** to compare. **3c** to regard as a paragon. [C16: via French from Old Italian *paragone* comparison, from Medieval Greek *parakonē* whetstone, from Greek *parakonan* to sharpen against, from PARA-[1] + *akonan* to sharpen, from *akonē* whetstone]

paragraph ('pærə,grɑ:f, -,græf) *n* **1** (in a piece of writing) one of a series of subsections each usually devoted to one idea and each usually marked by the beginning of a new line, indentation, increased interlinear space, etc. **2** *Printing.* the character ¶, used as a reference mark or to indicate the beginning of a new paragraph. **3** a short article in a newspaper. ◆ *vb* (*tr*) **4** to form into paragraphs. **5** to express or report in a paragraph. [C16: from Medieval Latin *paragraphus,* from Greek *paragraphos* line drawing attention to part of a text, from *paragraphein* to write beside, from PARA-[1] + *graphein* to write] ▸ **paragraphic** (,pærə'græfɪk) *or* **,para'graphical** *adj* ▸ **,para'graphically** *adv*

paragraphia (,pærə'grɑ:fɪə) *n Psychiatry.* the habitual writing of a different word or letter from the one intended, often the result of a mental disorder or brain injury. [C20: from New Latin; see PARA-[1], -GRAPH]

Paraguay ('pærə,gwaɪ) *n* **1** an inland republic in South America: colonized by the Spanish from 1537, gaining independence in 1811; lost 142 500 sq. km (55 000 sq. miles) of territory and over half its population after its defeat in the war against Argentina, Brazil, and Uruguay (1865–70). It is divided by the Paraguay River into a sparsely inhabited semiarid region (Chaco) in the west, and a central region of wooded hills, tropical forests, and rich grasslands, rising to the Paraná plateau in the east. Official languages: Spanish and Guarani. Religion: Roman Catholic majority. Currency: guarani. Capital: Asunción. Pop.: 5 223 000 (1998 est.). Area: 406 750 sq. km (157 047 sq. miles). **2** a river in South America flowing south through Brazil and Paraguay to the Paraná River. Length: about 2400 km (1500 miles). ▸ **,Para'guayan** *adj, n*

Paraguay tea *n* another name for **maté.**

parahydrogen (,pærə'haɪdrədʒən) *n Chem.* the form of molecular hydrogen (constituting about 25 per cent of the total at normal temperatures) in which the nuclei of the two atoms in each molecule spin in opposite directions. Compare **orthohydrogen.**

Paraíba (*Portuguese* para'iba) *n* **1** a state of NE Brazil, on the Atlantic: consists of a coastal strip, with hills and plains inland; irrigated agriculture. Capital: João Pessoa. Pop.: 3 340 000 (1995 est.). Area: 56 371 sq. km (21 765 sq. miles). **2** Also called: **Paraíba do Sul** ('du: sul). a river in SE Brazil, flowing southwest and then northeast to the Atlantic near Campos. Length: 1060 km (660 miles). **3** Also called: **Paraíba do Norte** ('du: 'nɔrtə). a river in NE Brazil, in Paraíba state, flowing northeast and east to the Atlantic. Length: 386 km (240 miles). **4** the former name (until 1930) of **João Pessoa.**

para-influenza virus *n* any of a group of viruses that cause respiratory infections with influenza-like symptoms, esp. in children.

parakeet *or* **parrakeet** ('pærə,ki:t) *n* any of numerous small usually brightly coloured long-tailed parrots, such as *Psittacula krameri* (**ring-necked parakeet**), of Africa. [C16: from Spanish *periquito* and Old French *paroquet* parrot, of uncertain origin]

parakelia *or* **parakeelya** (,pærə'ki:ljə) *n* a succulent herb of the genus *Calandrinia,* with purple flowers, that thrives in inland Australia. [from a native Australian language]

paralalia (,pærə'leɪlɪə) *n* any of various speech disorders, esp. the production of a sound different from that intended.

paralanguage ('pærə,læŋgwɪdʒ) *n Linguistics.* nonverbal elements in speech, such as intonation, that may affect the meaning of an utterance.

paraldehyde (pə'rældɪ,haɪd) *n* a colourless liquid substance that is a cyclic trimer of acetaldehyde: used in making dyestuffs and as a hypnotic and anticonvulsant drug. Formula: $(C_2H_4O)_3$.

paralegal (,pærə'li:gᵊl) *n* **1** a person trained to assist lawyers but not qualified to practise law. ◆ *adj* **2** of or designating such a person.

paralexia (,pærə'leksɪə) *n* a disorder of the ability to read in which words and syllables are meaninglessly transposed. ▸ **,para'lexic** *adj*

paralimnion (,pærə'lɪmnɪɒn) *n Ecology.* the region of a lake floor between the shoreline or water's edge and the zone of rooted vegetation. [from PARA-[1] + Greek *limnē* lake]

paralinguistics (,pærəlɪŋ'gwɪstɪks) *n* (*functioning as sing*) the study of paralanguage. ▸ **,paralin'guistic** *adj*

paralipomena (,pærəlaɪ'pɒmənə) *pl n* **1** things added in a supplement to a work. **2** *Old Testament.* another name for the Books of **Chronicles.** [C14: via late Latin from Greek *paraleipomena,* from PARA-[1] (on one side) + *leipein* to leave]

paralipsis (,pærə'lɪpsɪs) *or* **paraleipsis** (,pærə'laɪpsɪs) *n, pl* **-ses** (-si:z). a rhetorical device in which an idea is emphasized by the pretence that it is too obvious to discuss, as in *there are many drawbacks to your plan, not to mention the* *cost.* [C16: via Late Latin from Greek: neglect, from *paraleipein* to leave aside, from PARA-[1] + *leipein* to leave]

parallax (ˈpærəˌlæks) *n* **1** an apparent change in the position of an object resulting from a change in position of the observer. **2** *Astronomy.* the angle subtended at a celestial body, esp. a star, by the radius of the earth's orbit. **Annual** or **heliocentric parallax** is the apparent displacement of a nearby star resulting from its observation from the earth. **Diurnal** or **geocentric parallax** results from the observation of a planet, the sun, or the moon from the surface of the earth. [C17: via French from New Latin *parallaxis,* from Greek: change, from *parallassein* to change, from PARA-[1] + *allassein* to alter] ▸ **parallactic** (ˌpærəˈlæktɪk) *adj* ▸ **ˌparalˈlactically** *adv*

parallel (ˈpærəˌlɛl) *adj* (when *postpositive,* usually foll. by *to*) **1** separated by an equal distance at every point; never touching or intersecting: *parallel walls.* **2** corresponding; similar: *parallel situations.* **3** *Music.* **3a** Also: **consecutive.** (of two or more parts or melodies) moving in similar motion but keeping the same interval apart throughout: *parallel fifths.* **3b** denoting successive chords in which the individual notes move in parallel motion. **4** *Grammar.* denoting syntactic constructions in which the constituents of one construction correspond to those of the other. **5** *Computing.* operating on several items of information, instructions, etc., simultaneously. Compare **serial** (sense 6). ◆ *n* **6** *Maths.* one of a set of parallel lines, planes, etc. **7** an exact likeness. **8** a comparison. **9** Also called: **parallel of latitude.** any of the imaginary lines around the earth parallel to the equator, designated by degrees of latitude ranging from 0° at the equator to 90° at the poles. **10a** a configuration of two or more electrical components connected between two points in a circuit so that the same voltage is applied to each (esp. in the phrase **in parallel**). **10b** (*as modifier*): *a parallel circuit.* ◆ Compare **series** (sense 6). **11** *Printing.* the character (‖) used as a reference mark. **12** a trench or line lying in advance of and parallel to other defensive positions. ◆ *vb* **-lels, -leling, -leled.** (*tr*) **13** to make parallel. **14** to supply a parallel to. **15** to be a parallel to or correspond with: *your experience parallels mine.* [C16: via French and Latin from Greek *parallēlos* alongside one another, from PARA-[1] + *allēlos* one another]

parallel bars *pl n Gymnastics.* **a** (*functioning as pl*) a pair of wooden bars on uprights, sometimes at different heights, for various exercises. **b** (*functioning as sing*) an event in a gymnastic competition in which competitors exercise on such bars.

parallelepiped, parallelopiped (ˌpærəˌlɛləˈpaɪpɛd), *or* **parallelepipedon** (ˌpærəˌlɛləˈpɪpɪdən) *n* a geometric solid whose six faces are parallelograms. [C16: from Greek *parallēlepipedon;* from *parallēlos* PARALLEL + *epipedon* plane surface, from EPI- + *pedon* ground]

parallel importing *n* the importing of certain goods, esp. pharmaceutical drugs, by dealers who undersell local manufacturers.

paralleling (ˈpærəˌlɛlɪŋ) *n* a form of trading in which companies buy highly priced goods in a market in which the prices are low in order to be able to sell them in a market in which the prices are higher.

parallelism (ˈpærəlɛˌlɪzəm) *n* **1** the state of being parallel. **2** *Grammar.* the repetition of a syntactic construction in successive sentences for rhetorical effect. **3** *Philosophy.* the dualistic doctrine that mental and physical processes are regularly correlated but are not causally connected, so that, for example, pain always accompanies, but is not caused by, a pin-prick. Compare **interactionism, occasionalism.** ▸ **ˈparalˌlelist** *n, adj*

parallelogram (ˌpærəˈlɛləˌɡræm) *n* a quadrilateral whose opposite sides are parallel and equal in length. See also **rhombus, rectangle, trapezium, trapezoid.** [C16: via French from Late Latin, from Greek *parallēlogrammon,* from *parallēlos* PARALLEL + *grammē* line, related to *graphein* to write]

parallelogram rule *n Maths, physics.* a rule for finding the resultant of two vectors by constructing a parallelogram with two adjacent sides representing the magnitudes and directions of the vectors, the diagonal through the point of intersection of the vectors representing their resultant.

parallel processing *n* the performance by a computer system of two or more simultaneous operations.

parallel resonance *n* the resonance that results when circuit elements are connected with their inductance and capacitance in parallel, so that the impedance of the combination rises to a maximum at the resonant frequency. Compare **series resonance.**

parallel ruler *n Engineering.* a drawing instrument in which two parallel edges are connected so that they remain parallel, although the distance between them can be varied.

parallel turn *n Skiing.* a turn, executed by shifting one's weight, in which the skis stay parallel.

paralogism (pəˈræləˌdʒɪzəm) *n* **1** *Logic, psychology.* an argument that is unintentionally invalid. Compare **sophism.** **2** any invalid argument or conclusion. [C16: via Late Latin from Greek *paralogismos,* from *paralogizesthai* to argue fallaciously, from PARA-[1] + *-logizesthai,* ultimately from *logos* word] ▸ **paˈralogist** *n* ▸ **paˌraloˈgistic** *adj*

Paralympian (ˌpærəˈlɪmpɪən) *n* a competitor in the Paralympics.

Paralympic (ˌpærəˈlɪmpɪk) *adj* of or relating to the Paralympics.

Paralympics (ˌpærəˈlɪmpɪks) *pl n* **the.** a sporting event, modelled on the Olympic Games, held solely for disabled competitors. Also called: **the Parallel Olympics.** [C20: PARALLEL + OLYMPICS]

paralyse *or U.S.* **paralyze** (ˈpærəˌlaɪz) *vb* (*tr*) **1** *Pathol.* to affect with paralysis. **2** *Med.* to render (a part of the body) insensitive to pain, touch, etc., esp. by injection of an anaesthetic. **3** to make immobile; transfix. [C19: from French *paralyser,* from *paralysie* PARALYSIS] ▸ **ˌparalyˈsation** *or U.S.* **ˌparalyˈzation** *n* ▸ **ˈparaˌlyser** *or U.S.* **ˈparaˌlyzer** *n*

paralysis (pəˈrælɪsɪs) *n, pl* **-ses** (-ˌsiːz). **1** *Pathol.* **1a** impairment or loss of voluntary muscle function or of sensation (**sensory paralysis**) in a part or area of the body, usually caused by a lesion or disorder of the muscles or the nerves supplying them. **1b** a disease characterized by such impairment or loss; palsy. **2** cessation or impairment of activity: *paralysis of industry by strikes.* [C16: via Latin from Greek *paralusis;* see PARA-[1], -LYSIS]

paralysis agitans (ˈædʒɪˌtænz) *n* another name for **Parkinson's disease.**

paralytic (ˌpærəˈlɪtɪk) *adj* **1** of, relating to, or of the nature of paralysis. **2** afflicted with or subject to paralysis. **3** *Brit. informal.* very drunk. ◆ *n* **4** a person afflicted with paralysis. ▸ **ˌparaˈlytically** *adv*

paramagnetism (ˌpærəˈmæɡnɪˌtɪzəm) *n Physics.* the phenomenon exhibited by substances that have a relative permeability slightly greater than unity and a positive susceptibility. The effect is due to the alignment of unpaired spins of electrons in atoms of the material. Compare **diamagnetism, ferromagnetism.** ▸ **paramagnetic** (ˌpærəmæɡˈnɛtɪk) *adj*

Paramaribo (ˌpærəˈmærɪˌbəʊ; *Dutch* paːraːˈmaːriːboː) *n* the capital and chief port of Surinam, 27 km (17 miles) from the Atlantic on the Surinam River: the only large town in the country. Pop.: 200 970 (1993 est.).

paramatta *or* **parramatta** (ˌpærəˈmætə) *n* a lightweight twill-weave fabric of wool formerly with silk or cotton, used for dresses, etc., now used esp. for rubber-proofed garments. [C19: named after *Parramatta,* New South Wales, Australia, where it was originally produced]

paramecium (ˌpærəˈmiːsɪəm) *n, pl* **-cia** (-sɪə). any freshwater protozoan of the genus *Paramecium,* having an oval body covered with cilia and a ventral ciliated groove for feeding: phylum *Ciliophora* (ciliates). [C18: New Latin, from Greek *paramēkēs* elongated, from PARA-[1] + *mēkos* length]

paramedic (ˌpærəˈmɛdɪk) *or* **paramedical** *n* **1** a person, such as a laboratory technician, who supplements the work of the medical profession. **2** a member of an ambulance crew trained in a number of life-saving skills, including infusion and cardiac care. ◆ *adj* **3** of or designating such a person.

parament (ˈpærəmənt) *n, pl* **paraments** *or* **paramenta** (ˌpærəˈmɛntə). (*often pl*) an ecclesiastical vestment or decorative hanging. [C14: from Old French *parament,* from Medieval Latin *paramentum,* from Latin *parāre* to prepare]

parameter (pəˈræmɪtə) *n* **1** one of a number of auxiliary variables in terms of which all the variables in an implicit functional relationship can be explicitly expressed. See **parametric equations.** **2** a variable whose behaviour is not being considered and which may for present purposes be regarded as a constant, as *y* in the partial derivative $\partial f(x,y)/\partial x$. **3** *Statistics.* a characteristic of the distribution of a population, such as its mean, as distinct from that of a sample. Compare **statistic.** **4** *Informal.* any constant or limiting factor: *a designer must work within the parameters of budget and practicality.* [C17: from New Latin; see PARA-[1], -METER] ▸ **parametric** (ˌpærəˈmɛtrɪk) *or* **ˌparaˈmetrical** *adj*

parametric amplifier *n* a type of high-frequency amplifier in which energy from a pumping oscillator is transferred to the input signal through a circuit with a varying parameter, usually a varying reactance.

parametric equalizer *n* an electronic device for cutting or boosting selected frequencies by continuous narrowing or widening of the frequencies to be filtered. Compare **graphic equalizer.**

parametric equations *pl n* a set of equations expressing a number of quantities as explicit functions of the same set of independent variables and equivalent to some direct functional relationship of these quantities: *a circle* $x^2+y^2=r^2$ *has parametric equations* $x=r\cos\theta$ *and* $y=r\sin\theta$ *in terms of the parameters* r *and* θ.

parametric statistics *n* (*functioning as sing*) the branch of statistics concerned with data measurable on interval or ratio scales, so that arithmetic operations are applicable to them, enabling parameters such as the mean of the distribution to be defined.

paramilitary (ˌpærəˈmɪlɪtərɪ, -trɪ) *adj* **1** denoting or relating to a group of personnel with military structure functioning either as a civil force or in support of military forces. **2** denoting or relating to a force with military structure conducting armed operations against a ruling or occupying power. ◆ *n* **3a** a paramilitary force. **3b** a member of such a force.

paramnesia (ˌpæræmˈniːzɪə) *n Psychiatry.* a disorder of the memory or the faculty of recognition in which dreams may be confused with reality.

paramo (ˈpærəˌməʊ) *n, pl* **-mos.** a high plateau in the Andes between the tree line and the permanent snow line. [C18: American Spanish, from Spanish: treeless plain]

paramorph (ˈpærəˌmɔːf) *n* **1** a mineral that has undergone paramorphism. **2** a plant or animal that is classified on the basis of inadequate data and differs taxonomically from other members of the species in which it has been placed. ▸ **ˌparaˈmorphic** *or* **ˌparaˈmorphous** *adj*

paramorphine (ˌpærəˈmɔːfiːn) *n* another name for **thebaine.**

paramorphism (ˌpærəˈmɔːˌfɪzəm) *n* a process by which the crystalline structure of a mineral alters without any change in its chemical composition.

paramount (ˈpærəˌmaʊnt) *adj* **1** of the greatest importance or significance; pre-eminent. ◆ *n* **2** *Rare.* a supreme ruler. [C16: via Anglo-Norman from Old French *paramont,* from *par* by + *-amont* above, from Latin *ad montem* to the mountain] ▸ **ˈparaˌmountcy** *n* ▸ **ˈparaˌmountly** *adv*

paramour (ˈpærəˌmʊə) *n* **1** *Now usually derogatory.* a lover, esp. an adulterous woman. **2** an archaic word for **beloved** (sense 2). [C13: from Old French, literally: through love]

Paraná *n* **1** (parəˈna). a state of S Brazil, on the Atlantic: consists of a coastal plain and a large rolling plateau with extensive forests. Capital: Curitiba. Pop.: 8 712 800 (1995 est.). Area: 199 555 sq. km (77 048 sq. miles). **2** (paraˈna). a city in E Argentina, on the Paraná River opposite Santa Fe: capital of Argentina (1853–1862). Pop.: 211 936 (1991). **3** (*Portuguese* parəˈna; *Spanish* paraˈna). a river in central South America, formed in S Brazil by the confluence of the Rio Grande and the Paranaíba River and flowing generally south to the Atlantic through the Río de la Plata estuary. Length: 2900 km (1800 miles).

Paraná pine (pəˈrɑːnə) *n* **1** a large pine tree, *Araucaria angustifolia,* of South America yielding softwood timber: family *Pinaceae.* **2** the wood of this tree.

parang ('pɑːræŋ) *n* a short stout straight-edged knife used by the Dyaks of Borneo. [C19: from Malay]

paranoia (ˌpærəˈnɔɪə) *n* **1** a form of schizophrenia characterized by a slowly progressive deterioration of the personality, involving delusions and often hallucinations. **2** a mental disorder characterized by any of several types of delusions, in which the personality otherwise remains relatively intact. **3** *Informal.* intense fear or suspicion, esp. when unfounded. [C19: via New Latin from Greek: frenzy, from *paranoos* distraught, from PARA-[1] + *noos* mind] ▸ **paranoiac** (ˌpærəˈnɔɪɪk) *or* **paranoic** (ˌpærəˈnəʊɪk) *adj, n*

paranoid ('pærəˌnɔɪd) *adj* **1** of, characterized by, or resembling paranoia. **2** *Informal.* exhibiting undue suspicion, fear of persecution, etc. ◆ *n* **3** a person who shows the behaviour patterns associated with paranoia.

paranormal (ˌpærəˈnɔːməl) *adj* **1** beyond normal explanation. ◆ *n* **2 the.** paranormal happenings generally.

paranymph ('pærəˌnɪmf) *n Archaic.* a bridesmaid or best man. [C16: via Late Latin from Greek *paranumphos,* from PARA-[1] + *numphē* bride (literally: person beside the bride)]

paraparesis (ˌpærəpəˈriːsɪs) *n* muscle weakness, esp. of the legs, allowing limited movement; partial paralysis. ▸ **paraparetic** (ˌpærəpəˈrɛtɪk) *adj*

parapente ('pærəˌpɛntɪ) *n* **1** another name for **paraskiing. 2** the form of parachute used in this sport.

parapet ('pærəpɪt, -ˌpɛt) *n* **1** a low wall or railing along the edge of a balcony, roof, etc. **2** Also called: **breastwork.** a rampart, mound of sandbags, bank, etc., in front of a trench, giving protection from fire from the front. [C16: from Italian *parapetto,* literally: chest-high wall, from PARA-[2] + *petto,* from Latin *pectus* breast]

paraph ('pærəf) *n* a flourish after a signature, originally to prevent forgery. [C14: via French from Medieval Latin *paraphus,* variant of *paragraphus* PARAGRAPH]

paraphasia (ˌpærəˈfeɪzɪə) *n* a defect of speech in which the normal flow of words is interrupted by inappropriate words and phrases. [C20: from Greek PARA-[1] + *-phasia,* from *phanai* to speak]

paraphernalia (ˌpærəfəˈneɪlɪə) *pl n* (*sometimes functioning as sing*) **1** miscellaneous articles or equipment. **2** *Law.* (formerly) articles of personal property given to a married woman by her husband before or during marriage and regarded in law as her possessions over which she has some measure of control. [C17: via Medieval Latin from Latin *parapherna* personal property of a married woman, apart from her dowry, from Greek, from PARA-[1] + *phernē* dowry, from *pherein* to carry]

paraphilia (ˌpærəˈfɪlɪə) *n* any abnormal sexual behaviour; sexual anomaly or deviation. [C20: from PARA-[1] + *-philia,* from Greek *philos* loving]

paraphrase ('pærəˌfreɪz) *n* **1** an expression of a statement or text in other words, esp. in order to clarify. **2** the practice of making paraphrases. ◆ *vb* **3** to put (something) into other words; restate (something). [C16: via French from Latin *paraphrasis,* from Greek, from *paraphrazein* to recount] ▸ **paraphrastic** (ˌpærəˈfræstɪk) *adj*

paraphysis (pəˈræfɪsɪs) *n, pl* **-ses** (-ˌsiːz). any of numerous sterile cells occurring between the sex organs of mosses and algae and between the spore-producing bodies of basidiomycetous and ascomycetous fungi. [C19: New Latin from Greek: subsidiary growth, from PARA-[1] + *phusis* growth] ▸ **paˈraphysate** *adj*

paraplegia (ˌpærəˈpliːdʒə) *n Pathol.* paralysis of the lower half of the body, usually as the result of disease or injury of the spine. Compare **hemiplegia, quadriplegia.** [C17: via New Latin from Greek: a blow on one side, from PARA-[1] + *plēssein* to strike] ▸ **ˌparaˈplegic** *adj, n*

parapodium (ˌpærəˈpəʊdɪəm) *n, pl* **-dia** (-dɪə). **1** any of the paired unjointed lateral appendages of polychaete worms, used in locomotion, respiration, etc. **2** any of various similar appendages of other invertebrates, esp. certain molluscs. [New Latin: from PARA-[1] + -PODIUM]

parapraxis (ˌpærəˈpræksɪs) *n Psychoanal.* a minor error in action, such as slips of the tongue, supposedly the result of repressed impulses. See also **Freudian slip.** [C20: from PARA-[1] + Greek *praxis* a doing, deed]

parapsychology (ˌpærəsaɪˈkɒlədʒɪ) *n* the study of mental phenomena, such as telepathy, which are beyond the scope of normal physical explanation. ▸ **parapsychological** (ˌpærəsaɪkəˈlɒdʒɪkᵊl) *adj* ▸ **ˌparapsyˈchologist** *n*

Paraquat ('pærəˌkwɒt) *n Trademark.* a yellow extremely poisonous soluble solid used in solution as a weedkiller.

Pará rubber (pəˈrɑː, ˈpɑːrə) *n* a South American rubber obtained from any of various euphorbiaceous trees of the genus *Hevea,* esp. *H. brasiliensis.* See also **rubber tree.** [C19: from PARÁ]

parasailing ('pærəˌseɪlɪŋ) *n* a sport in which a water-skier wearing a parachute is towed by a speedboat, becomes airborne, and sails along in the air.

parasang ('pærəˌsæŋ) *n* a Persian unit of distance equal to about 5.5 km or 3.4 miles. [C16: via Latin and Greek from a Persian word related to modern Persian *farsang*]

parascending ('pærəˌsɛndɪŋ) *n* a sport in which a participant wears a parachute and becomes airborne by being towed by a vehicle into the wind and then descends by parachute.

parascience ('pærəˌsaɪəns) *n* the study of subjects that are outside the scope of traditional science because they cannot be explained by accepted scientific theory or tested by conventional scientific methods.

paraselene (ˌpærəsɪˈliːnɪ) *n, pl* **-nae** (-niː). *Meteorol.* a bright image of the moon on a lunar halo. Also called: **mock moon.** Compare **parhelion.** [C17: New Latin, from PARA-[1] + Greek *selēnē* moon] ▸ **ˌparaseˈlenic** *adj*

Parashah ('pærəˌʃɑː; *Hebrew* paraˈʃa) *n, pl* **-shoth** (-ˌʃəʊt; *Hebrew* -ˈʃɔt). *Judaism.* **1** any of the sections of the Torah read in the synagogue. **2** any of the subsections of the weekly lessons read on Sabbaths in the synagogue. ◆ Also called (Yiddish): **Parsha.** [from Hebrew, from *pārāsh* to divide, separate]

parasite ('pærəˌsaɪt) *n* **1** an animal or plant that lives in or on another (the host) from which it obtains nourishment. The host does not benefit from the association and is often harmed by it. **2** a person who habitually lives at the expense of others; sponger. **3** (formerly) a sycophant. [C16: via Latin from Greek *parasitos* one who lives at another's expense, from PARA-[1] + *sitos* grain] ▸ **parasitic** (ˌpærəˈsɪtɪk) *or* **ˌparaˈsitical** *adj* ▸ **ˌparaˈsitically** *adv*

parasite drag *n* the part of the drag on an aircraft that is contributed by non-lifting surfaces, such as fuselage, nacelles, etc. Also called: **parasite resistance.**

parasiticide (ˌpærəˈsɪtɪˌsaɪd) *n* **1** any substance capable of destroying parasites. ◆ *adj* **2** destructive to parasites. ▸ **ˌparaˌsitiˈcidal** *adj*

parasitic male *n Zoology.* a male animal that is much smaller than the female and is totally dependent on the female for its nutrition, such as the male of some species of deep-sea angler fish.

parasitic oscillation *n* (in an electronic circuit) oscillation at any undesired frequency. Sometimes shortened to **parasitic.**

parasitism ('pærəsaɪˌtɪzəm) *n* **1** the relationship between a parasite and its host. **2** the state of being infested with parasites. **3** the state of being a parasite.

parasitize *or* **parasitise** ('pærəsɪˌtaɪz, -saɪ-) *vb* (*tr*) **1** to infest or infect with parasites. **2** to live on (another organism) as a parasite.

parasitoid ('pærəsɪˌtɔːd) *n Zoology.* an animal, esp. an insect, that is parasitic during the larval stage of its life cycle but becomes free-living when adult.

parasitology (ˌpærəsaɪˈtɒlədʒɪ) *n* the branch of biology that is concerned with the study of parasites. ▸ **parasitological** (ˌpærəˌsaɪtᵊˈlɒdʒɪkᵊl) *adj* ▸ **ˌparasitˈologist** *n*

paraskiing ('pærəˌskiːɪŋ) *n* the sport of jumping off high mountains wearing skis and a light parachute composed of inflatable fabric tubes that form a semirigid wing. Also called: **parapente.**

parasol ('pærəˌsɒl) *n* an umbrella used for protection against the sun; sunshade. [C17: via French from Italian *parasole,* from PARA-[2] + *sole* sun, from Latin *sōl*]

parasol mushroom *n* any of several fungi of the basidiomycetous genus *Lepiota,* having an umbrella-shaped cap, white gills, and a slender brownish stem with a prominent white ring.

parastatal (ˌpærəˈsteɪtᵊl) *n* **1** a state-owned organization, esp. in Africa. ◆ *adj* **2** of or relating to such an organization.

parastichy (pəˈræstɪkɪ) *n, pl* **-chies. 1** a hypothetical spiral line connecting the bases of a series of leaves on a stem. **2** an arrangement of leaves so connected. ◆ Compare **orthostichy.** [C19: from PARA-[1] + Greek *stikhia,* from *stikhos* row, rank] ▸ **paˈrastichous** *adj*

parasuicide (ˌpærəˈsuːɪˌsaɪd) *n* **1** the deliberate infliction of injury on oneself or the taking of a drug overdose as an attempt at suicide which may not be intended to be successful. **2** a person who commits such an act.

parasymbiosis (ˌpærəˌsɪmbɪˈəʊsɪs) *n* the symbiotic relationship that occurs between certain species of fungi and lichens (which are themselves symbiotic associations between a fungus and an alga). ▸ **ˌparaˈsymbiont** *n* ▸ **ˌparaˌsymbiˈotic** *adj*

parasympathetic (ˌpærəˌsɪmpəˈθɛtɪk) *adj Anatomy, physiol.* of or relating to the division of the autonomic nervous system that acts in opposition to the sympathetic system by slowing the heartbeat, constricting the bronchi of the lungs, stimulating the smooth muscles of the digestive tract, etc. Compare **sympathetic** (sense 4).

parasynapsis (ˌpærəsɪˈnæpsɪs) *n* another name for **synapsis** (sense 1). ▸ **ˌparasynˈaptic** *adj*

parasynthesis (ˌpærəˈsɪnθɪsɪs) *n* formation of words by means of compounding a phrase and adding an affix, as for example *light-headed,* which is *light* + *head* with the affix *-ed.* ▸ **parasynthetic** (ˌpærəsɪnˈθɛtɪk) *adj*

parasyntheton (ˌpærəˈsɪnθətɒn) *n, pl* **-ta** (-tə). a word formed by parasynthesis; for example, *kind-hearted.* [from Greek]

parataxis (ˌpærəˈtæksɪs) *n* the juxtaposition of clauses in a sentence without the use of a conjunction, as for example *None of my friends stayed —they all left early.* [C19: New Latin from Greek, from *paratassein,* literally: to arrange side by side, from PARA-[1] + *tassein* to arrange] ▸ **paratactic** (ˌpærəˈtæktɪk) *adj* ▸ **ˌparaˈtactically** *adv*

parathion (ˌpærəˈθaɪɒn) *n* a slightly water-soluble toxic oil, odourless and colourless when pure, used as an insecticide. Formula: $C_{10}H_{14}NO_5PS$. [C20: from PARA-[1] + THIO- + -ON]

parathyroid (ˌpærəˈθaɪrɔɪd) *adj* **1** situated near the thyroid gland. **2** of or relating to the parathyroid glands. ◆ *n* **3** See **parathyroid gland.**

parathyroid gland *n* any one of the small egg-shaped endocrine glands situated near or embedded within the thyroid gland: they secrete parathyroid hormone.

parathyroid hormone *n* the hormone secreted by the parathyroid glands that controls the level of calcium in the blood: a deficiency of the hormone often results in tetany. Also called: **parathormone** (ˌpærəˈθɔːməʊn).

paratonic (ˌpærəˈtɒnɪk) *adj Botany.* (of a plant movement) occurring in response to an external stimulus.

paratroops ('pærəˌtruːps) *pl n* troops trained and equipped to be dropped by parachute into a battle area. Also called: **ˈparatroopers, parachute troops.**

paratyphoid (ˌpærəˈtaɪfɔɪd) *Pathol.* ◆ *adj* **1** resembling typhoid fever or its causative agent. **2** of or relating to paratyphoid fever. ◆ *n* **3** See **paratyphoid fever.**

paratyphoid fever *n Pathol.* a disease resembling but less severe than typhoid fever, characterized by chills, headache, nausea, vomiting, and diarrhoea, caused by bacteria of the genus *Salmonella.*

paravane ('pærəˌveɪn) *n* a torpedo-shaped device towed from the bow of a vessel so that the cables will cut the anchors of any moored mines. [C20: from PARA-[2] + VANE]

par avion *French.* (par avjɔ̃) *adv* by aeroplane: used in labelling mail sent by air.

paraxial (pæˈræksɪəl) *adj Physics.* (of a light ray) parallel to the axis of an optical system.

parazoan (ˌpærəˈzəʊən) *n, pl* **-zoa** (-ˈzəʊə). any multicellular invertebrate of the group *Parazoa,* which consists of the sponges (phylum *Porifera*). Compare **metazoan.** [C19: from *parazoa,* formed on the model of *protozoa* and *metazoa,* from PARA-[1] + Greek *zōon* animal]

parboil (ˈpɑːˌbɔɪl) *vb* (*tr*) **1** to boil until partially cooked, often before further cooking. **2** to subject to uncomfortable heat. [C15: from Old French *parboillir,* from Late Latin *perbullīre* to boil thoroughly (see PER-, BOIL[1]); modern meaning due to confusion of *par-* with *part*]

parbuckle (ˈpɑːˌbʌkᵊl) *n* **1** a rope sling for lifting or lowering a heavy cylindrical object, such as a cask or tree trunk. ◆ *vb* **2** (*tr*) to raise or lower (an object) with such a sling. [C17 *parbunkel:* of uncertain origin]

Parcae (ˈpɑːsiː) *pl n, sing* **Parca** (ˈpɑːkə). **the.** the Roman goddesses of fate. Greek counterparts: The **Moirai.**

parcel (ˈpɑːsᵊl) *n* **1** something wrapped up; package. **2** a group of people or things having some common characteristic. **3** a quantity of some commodity offered for sale; lot. **4** a distinct portion of land. **5** an essential part of something (esp. in the phrase **part and parcel**). ◆ *vb* **-cels, -celling, -celled** *or U.S.* **-cels, -celing, -celed.** (*tr*) **6** (often foll. by *up*) to make a parcel of; wrap up. **7** (often foll. by *out*) to divide (up) into portions. **8** *Nautical.* to bind strips of canvas around (a rope). ◆ *adv* **9** an archaic word for **partly.** [C14: from Old French *parcelle,* from Latin *particula* PARTICLE]

parcel-gilt *adj* partly gilded, esp. (of an item of silverware) having the inner surface gilded. [C15: from *parcel* (in the obsolete adv sense: partly)+GILT[1]]

parcenary (ˈpɑːsɪnərɪ) *n* joint heirship. Also called: **coparcenary.** [C16: from Old French *parçonerie,* from *parçon* distribution; see PARCENER]

parcener (ˈpɑːsɪnə) *n* a person who takes an equal share with another or others; coheir. Also called: **coparcener.** [C13: from Old French *parçonier,* from *parçon* distribution, from Latin *partītiō* a sharing, from *partīre* to divide]

parch (pɑːtʃ) *vb* **1** to deprive or be deprived of water; dry up: *the sun parches the fields.* **2** (*tr; usually passive*) to make very thirsty: *I was parched after the run.* **3** (*tr*) to roast (corn, etc.) lightly. [C14: of obscure origin]

Parcheesi (pɑːˈtʃiːzɪ) *n Trademark.* a modern board game derived from the ancient game of pachisi.

parchment (ˈpɑːtʃmənt) *n* **1** the skin of certain animals, such as sheep, treated to form a durable material, as for bookbinding, or (esp. formerly) manuscripts. **2** a manuscript, bookbinding, etc., made of or resembling this material. **3** a type of stiff yellowish paper resembling parchment. [C13: from Old French *parchemin,* via Latin from Greek *pergamēnē,* from *Pergamēnos* of Pergamum (where parchment was made); the form of Old French *parchemin* was influenced by *parche* leather, from Latin *Parthica* (*pellis*) Parthian (leather)] ▸ ˈ**parchmenty** *adj*

parclose (ˈpɑːˌkləʊz) *n* a screen or railing in a church separating off an altar, chapel, etc. [C14: from Old French, noun use of past participle of *parclore* to close off; see PER-, CLOSE[1]]

pard[1] (pɑːd) *n U.S.* short for **pardner.**

pard[2] (pɑːd) *n Archaic.* a leopard or panther. [C13: via Old French from Latin *pardus,* from Greek *pardos*]

pardalote (ˈpɑːdəˌləʊt) *n* another name for **diamond bird.** [C19: from New Latin, from Greek *pardalōtos* spotted like a leopard; see PARD[2]]

pardner (ˈpɑːdnə) *n U.S. dialect.* friend or partner: used as a term of address.

pardon (ˈpɑːdᵊn) *vb* (*tr*) **1** to excuse or forgive (a person) for (an offence, mistake, etc.): *to pardon someone; to pardon a fault.* ◆ *n* **2** forgiveness; allowance. **3a** release from punishment for an offence. **3b** the warrant granting such release. **4** a Roman Catholic indulgence. ◆ *sentence substitute.* **5** Also: **pardon me; I beg your pardon. 5a** sorry; excuse me. **5b** what did you say? [C13: from Old French, from Medieval Latin *perdōnum,* from *perdōnāre* to forgive freely, from Latin *per* (intensive) + *dōnāre* to grant] ▸ ˈ**pardonable** *adj* ▸ ˈ**pardonably** *adv* ▸ ˈ**pardonless** *adj*

pardoner (ˈpɑːdᵊnə) *n* (before the Reformation) a person licensed to sell ecclesiastical indulgences.

Pardubice (*Czech* ˈpardubitse) *n* a city in the central Czech Republic, on the Elbe River: 13th-century cathedral; oil refinery. Pop.: 163 000 (1993).

pare (pɛə) *vb* (*tr*) **1** to peel or cut (the outer layer) from (something). **2** to cut the edges from (the nails); trim. **3** to decrease bit by bit. [C13: from Old French *parer* to adorn, from Latin *parāre* to make ready] ▸ ˈ**parer** *n*

Paré (*French* pare) *n* **Ambroise** (ɑ̃brwaz). 1510–90, French surgeon. He reintroduced ligature of arteries following amputation instead of cauterization.

paregoric (ˌpærəˈɡɒrɪk) *n* a medicine consisting of opium, benzoic acid, camphor, and anise oil, formerly widely used to relieve diarrhoea and coughing in children. [C17 (meaning: relieving pain): via Late Latin from Greek *parēgorikos* soothing, from *parēgoros* relating to soothing speech, from PARA-[1] (beside, alongside of) + *-ēgor-,* from *agoreuein* to speak in assembly, from *agora* assembly]

pareira (pəˈrɛərə) *n* the root of a South American menispermaceous climbing plant, *Chondrodendron tomentosum,* used as a diuretic, tonic, and as a source of curare. [C18: from Portuguese *pareira brava,* literally: wild vine]

paren. *abbrev. for* parenthesis.

parenchyma (pəˈrɛŋkɪmə) *n* **1** a soft plant tissue consisting of simple thin-walled cells with intervening air spaces: constitutes the greater part of fruits, stems, roots, etc. **2** animal tissue that constitutes the essential or specialized part of an organ as distinct from the blood vessels, connective tissue, etc., associated with it. **3** loosely-packed tissue filling the spaces between the organs in lower animals such as flatworms. [C17: via New Latin from Greek *parenkhuma* something poured in beside, from PARA-[1] + *enkhuma* infusion] ▸ **parenchymatous** (ˌpærɛŋˈkɪmətəs) *adj*

parent (ˈpɛərənt) *n* **1** a father or mother. **2** a person acting as a father or mother; guardian. **3** *Rare.* an ancestor. **4** a source or cause. **5a** an organism or organization that has produced one or more organisms or organizations similar to itself. **5b** (*as modifier*): *a parent organism.* **6** *Physics, chem.* **6a** a precursor, such as a nucleus or compound, of a derived entity. **6b** (*as modifier*): *a parent nucleus; a parent ion.* [C15: via Old French from Latin *parens* parent, from *parere* to bring forth] ▸ ˈ**parenthood** *n*

parentage (ˈpɛərəntɪdʒ) *n* **1** ancestry. **2** derivation from a particular origin. **3** a less common word for **parenthood.**

parental (pəˈrɛntᵊl) *adj* **1** of or relating to a parent or parenthood. **2** *Genetics.* designating the first generation in a line, which gives rise to all succeeding (filial) generations. ▸ **paˈrentally** *adv*

parent company *n* a company that owns more than half the shares of another company.

parenteral (pæˈrɛntərəl) *adj Med.* **1** (esp. of the route by which a drug is administered) by means other than through the digestive tract, esp. by injection. **2** designating a drug to be injected. [C20: from PARA-[1] + ENTERO- + -AL[1]] ▸ **parˈenterally** *adv*

parenthesis (pəˈrɛnθɪsɪs) *n, pl* **-ses** (-ˌsiːz). **1** a phrase, often explanatory or qualifying, inserted into a passage with which it is not grammatically connected, and marked off by brackets, dashes, etc. **2** Also called: **bracket.** either of a pair of characters, (), used to enclose such a phrase or as a sign of aggregation in mathematical or logical expressions. **3** an intervening occurrence; interlude; interval. **4 in parenthesis.** inserted as a parenthesis. [C16: via Late Latin from Greek: something placed in besides, from *parentithenai,* from PARA-[1] + EN-[2] + *tithenai* to put] ▸ **parenthetic** (ˌpærənˈθɛtɪk) *or* ˌ**parenˈthetical** *adj* ▸ ˌ**parenˈthetically** *adv*

parenthesize *or* **parenthesise** (pəˈrɛnθɪˌsaɪz) *vb* (*tr*) **1** to place in parentheses. **2** to insert as a parenthesis. **3** to intersperse (a speech, writing, etc.) with parentheses.

parenting (ˈpɛərəntɪŋ) *n* the care and upbringing of a child.

parent metal *n Engineering, metallurgy.* the metal of components that are being welded by a molten filler metal.

Parents Anonymous *n* (in Britain) an association of local voluntary self-help groups offering help through an anonymous telephone service to parents who fear they will injure their children, or who have other problems in managing their children.

parent teacher association *n* a social group of the parents of children at a school and their teachers formed in order to foster better understanding between them and to organize activities on behalf of the school. Abbrev.: **PTA.**

parergon (pəˈrɛəɡɒn) *n, pl* **-ga** (-ɡə). work that is not one's main employment. [C17: from Latin, from Greek, from PARA-[1] + *ergon* work]

paresis (pəˈriːsɪs, ˈpærɪsɪs) *n, pl* **-ses** (-ˌsiːz). *Pathol.* **1** incomplete or slight paralysis of motor functions. **2** short for **general paresis.** See **general paralysis of the insane.** [C17: via New Latin from Greek: a relaxation, from *parienai* to let go, from PARA-[1] + *hienai* to release] ▸ **paretic** (pəˈrɛtɪk) *adj*

paresthesia (ˌpærɛsˈθiːzɪə) *n Pathol.* the usual U.S. spelling of **paraesthesia.** ▸ **paresthetic** (ˌpærɛsˈθɛtɪk) *adj*

Pareto (*Italian* paˈrɛːto) *n* **1 Vilfredo** (vilˈfreːdo). 1848–1923, Italian sociologist and economist. He anticipated Fascist principles of government in his *Mind and Society* (1916). **2** (*modifier*) denoting a law, mathematical formula, etc., originally used by Pareto to express the frequency distribution of incomes in a society.

pareu (ˈpɑːreɪˌuː) *n* a rectangle of fabric worn by Polynesians as a skirt or loincloth. [from Tahitian]

parev, pareve, *or* **parve** (ˈpɑrvə, ˈpɑrəv) *adj Judaism.* containing neither meat nor milk products and so fit for use with either meat or milk dishes. Compare **milchik, fleishik.** See also **kashruth.**

par excellence *French.* (par ɛkselɑ̃s; *English* pɑːrˈɛksələns) *adv* to a degree of excellence; beyond comparison: *she is the charitable lady par excellence.* [French, literally: by (way of) excellence]

parfait (pɑːˈfeɪ) *n* a rich frozen dessert made from eggs and cream with ice cream, fruit, etc. [from French: PERFECT]

parfleche (ˈpɑːflɛʃ) *n U.S. and Canadian.* **1** a sheet of rawhide that has been dried after soaking in lye and water to remove the hair. **2** an object, such as a case, made of this. [C19: from Canadian French, from French *parer* to ward off, protect + *flèche* arrow]

parget (ˈpɑːdʒɪt) *n* **1** Also called: ˈ**pargeting. 1a** plaster, mortar, etc., used to line chimney flues or cover walls. **1b** plasterwork that has incised ornamental patterns. **2** another name for **gypsum** (esp. when used in building). ◆ *vb* (*tr*) **3** to cover or decorate with parget. [C14: from Old French *pargeter* to throw over, from *par* PER- + *geter,* from Medieval Latin *jactāre* to throw]

parhelic circle *n Meteorol.* a luminous band at the same altitude as the sun, parallel to the horizon, caused by reflection of the sun's rays by ice crystals in the atmosphere.

parhelion (pɑːˈhiːlɪən) *n, pl* **-lia** (-lɪə). one of several bright spots on the parhelic circle or solar halo, caused by the diffraction of light by ice crystals in the atmosphere, esp. around sunset. Also called: **mock sun, sundog.** Compare **anthelion.** [C17: via Latin from Greek *parēlion,* from PARA-[1] (beside) + *hēlios* sun] ▸ **parhelic** (pɑːˈhiːlɪk, -ˈhɛlɪk) *or* **parheliacal** (ˌpɑːhɪˈlaɪəkᵊl) *adj*

pari- *combining form.* equal or equally; even (in number): *parisyllabic; paripinnate.* [from Latin *par*]

pariah (pəˈraɪə, ˈpærɪə) *n* **1** a social outcast. **2** (formerly) a member of a low caste in South India. [C17: from Tamil *paraiyan* drummer, from *parai* drum; so called because members of the caste were the drummers at festivals]

pariah dog *n* another term for **pye-dog.**

Parian (ˈpɛərɪən) *adj* **1** denoting or relating to a fine white marble mined in classical times in Paros. **2** denoting or relating to a fine biscuit porcelain used mainly for statuary. **3** of or relating to Paros. ◆ *n* **4** a native or inhabitant of Paros. **5** Parian marble. **6** Parian porcelain.

Paricutín (*Spanish* parikuˈtin) *n* a volcano in W central Mexico, in Michoacán state, formed in 1943 after a week of earth tremors; grew to a height of 2500 m (8200 ft.) in a year and buried the village of Paricutin.

paries ('pɛərɪ,iːz) *n, pl* **parietes** (pəˈraɪɪ,tiːz). the wall of an organ or bodily cavity. [C18: from Latin: wall]

parietal (pəˈraɪɪtᵊl) *adj* **1** *Anatomy, biology.* of, relating to, or forming the walls or part of the walls of a bodily cavity or similar structure: *the parietal bones of the skull.* **2** of or relating to the side of the skull. **3** (of plant ovaries) having ovules attached to the walls. **4** *U.S.* living or having authority within a college. ◆ *n* **5** a parietal bone. [C16: from Late Latin *parietālis,* from Latin *pariēs* wall]

parietal bone *n* either of the two bones forming part of the roof and sides of the skull.

parietal cell *n* any one of the cells in the lining of the stomach that produce hydrochloric acid.

parietal lobe *n* the portion of each cerebral hemisphere concerned with the perception and interpretation of sensations of touch, temperature, and taste and with muscular movements.

pari-mutuel (,pærɪˈmjuːtjʊəl) *n, pl* **pari-mutuels** *or* **paris-mutuels** (,pærɪˈmjuːtjʊəlz). **a** a system of betting in which those who have bet on the winners of a race share in the total amount wagered less a percentage for the management. **b** (*as modifier*): *the pari-mutuel machine.* [C19: from French, literally: mutual wager]

paring ('pɛərɪŋ) *n* (*often pl*) something pared or cut off.

pari passu *Latin.* (,pærɪ ˈpæsuː, ˈpɑːrɪ) *adv Usually legal.* with equal speed or progress; equably: often used to refer to the right of creditors to receive assets from the same source without one taking precedence.

paripinnate (,pærɪˈpɪneɪt) *adj* (of pinnate leaves) having an even number of leaflets and no terminal leaflet. Compare **imparipinnate.**

Paris[1] ('pærɪs; *French* pari) *n* **1** the capital of France, in the north on the River Seine: constitutes a department; dates from the 3rd century B.C., becoming capital of France in 987; centre of the French Revolution; centres around its original site on an island in the Seine, the **Île de la Cité**, containing Notre Dame; university (1150). Pop.: 2 130 900 (1995). Ancient name: **Lutetia. 2 Treaty of Paris. 2a** a treaty of 1783 between the U.S., Britain, France, and Spain, ending the War of American Independence. **2b** a treaty of 1763 signed by Britain, France, and Spain that ended their involvement in the Seven Years' War. **2c** a treaty of 1898 between Spain and the U.S. bringing to an end the Spanish-American War. [via French and Old French, from Late Latin (*Lūtētia*) *Parisiōrum* (marshes) of the *Parisii,* a tribe of Celtic Gaul] ▶ **Parisian** (pəˈrɪzɪən) *n, adj*

Paris[2] ('pærɪs) *n* **1** *Greek myth.* a prince of Troy, whose abduction of Helen from her husband Menelaus started the Trojan War. **2 Matthew.** ?1200–59, English chronicler, whose principal work is the *Chronica Majora.*

Paris Club *n* another name for **Group of Ten.**

Paris Commune *n French history.* the council established in Paris in the spring of 1871 in opposition to the National Assembly and esp. to the peace negotiated with Prussia following the Franco-Prussian War. Troops of the Assembly crushed the Commune with great bloodshed.

Paris green *n* an emerald-green poisonous insoluble substance used as a pigment and insecticide. It is a double salt of copper arsenite and copper acetate. Formula: $3Cu(AsO_2)_2.Cu(C_2H_3O_2)_2$.

parish ('pærɪʃ) *n* **1** a subdivision of a diocese, having its own church and a clergyman. Related adj: **parochial. 2** the churchgoers of such a subdivision. **3** (in England and, formerly, Wales) the smallest unit of local government in rural areas. **4** (in Louisiana) a unit of local government corresponding to a county in other states of the U.S. **5** the people living in a parish. **6 on the parish.** *History.* receiving parochial relief. [C13: from Old French *paroisse,* from Church Latin *parochia,* from Late Greek *paroikia,* from *paroikos* Christian, sojourner, from Greek: neighbour, from PARA-[1] (beside) + *oikos* house]

Parishad ('pʌrɪʃəd) *n* (in India) an assembly. [Hindi]

parish clerk *n* a person designated to assist in various church duties.

parish council *n* (in England and, formerly, Wales) the administrative body of a parish. See **parish** (sense 3).

parishioner (pəˈrɪʃənə) *n* a member of a particular parish.

parish pump *adj* of only local interest; parochial.

parish register *n* a book in which the births, baptisms, marriages, and deaths in a parish are recorded.

parison ('pærɪsᵊn) *n* an unshaped mass of glass before it is moulded into its final form. [C19: from French *paraison,* from *parer* to prepare]

parisyllabic (,pærɪsɪˈlæbɪk) *adj* (of a noun or verb, in inflected languages) containing the same number of syllables in all or almost all inflected forms. Compare **imparisyllabic.**

parity[1] ('pærɪtɪ) *n, pl* **-ties. 1** equality of rank, pay, etc. **2** close or exact analogy or equivalence. **3** *Finance.* **3a** the amount of a foreign currency equivalent at the established exchange rate to a specific sum of domestic currency. **3b** a similar equivalence between different forms of the same national currency, esp. the gold equivalent of a unit of gold-standard currency. **4** equality between prices of commodities or securities in two separate markets. **5** *Physics.* **5a** a property of a physical system characterized by the behaviour of the sign of its wave function when reflected in space. The wave function either remains unchanged (**even parity**) or changes in sign (**odd parity**). **5b** a quantum number describing this property, equal to +1 for even parity systems and −1 for odd parity systems. Symbol: *P.* See also **conservation of parity. 6** *Maths.* a relationship between two integers. If both are odd or both even they have the same parity; if one is odd and one even they have different parity. **7** (in the U.S.) a system of government support for farm products. [C16: from Late Latin *pāritās;* see PAR]

parity[2] ('pærɪtɪ) *n* **1** the condition or fact of having given birth. **2** the number of children to which a woman has given birth. [C19: from Latin *parere* to bear]

parity check *n* a check made of computer data to ensure that the total number of bits of value 1 (or 0) in each unit of information remains odd or even after transfer between a peripheral device and the memory or vice versa.

park (pɑːk) *n* **1** a large area of land preserved in a natural state for recreational use by the public. See also **national park. 2** a piece of open land in a town with public amenities. **3** *N.Z.* an area, esp. of mountain country, reserved for recreational purposes. **4** a large area of land forming a private estate. **5** *English law.* an enclosed tract of land where wild beasts are protected, acquired by a subject by royal grant or prescription. Compare **forest** (sense 5). **6** an area designed and landscaped to accommodate a group of related enterprises, businesses, research establishments, etc.: *science park.* **7** *U.S. and Canadian.* See **amusement park. 8** *U.S., Canadian, and N.Z.* See **car park. 9** *U.S. and Canadian.* a playing field or sports stadium. **10 the park.** *Brit. informal.* a soccer pitch. **11** a gear selector position on the automatic transmission of a motor vehicle that acts as a parking brake. **12** the area in which the equipment and supplies of a military formation are assembled. **13** a high valley surrounded by mountains in the western U.S. ◆ *vb* **14** to stop and leave (a vehicle) temporarily. **15** to manoeuvre (a motor vehicle) into a space for it to be left: *try to park without hitting the kerb.* **16** *Stock Exchange.* to register (securities) in the name of another or of nominees in order to conceal their real ownership. **17** (*tr*) *Informal.* to leave or put somewhere: *park yourself in front of the fire.* **18** (*intr*) *Military.* to arrange equipment in a park. **19** (*tr*) to enclose in or as a park. [C13: from Old French *parc,* from Medieval Latin *parricus* enclosure, from Germanic; compare Old High German *pfarrih* pen, Old English *pearruc* PADDOCK[1]] ▶ **ˈpark,like** *adj*

Park (pɑːk) *n* **1 Mungo** ('mʌŋgəʊ). 1771–1806, Scottish explorer. He led two expeditions (1795–97; 1805–06) to trace the course of the Niger in Africa. He was drowned during the second expedition. **2 Chung Hee** ('tʃʊŋ ˈhiː). 1917–79, South Korean politician; president of the Republic of Korea (1963–79); assassinated.

parka ('pɑːkə) *n* a warm hip-length weatherproof coat with a hood, originally worn by Eskimos. [C19: from Aleutian: skin]

Parker ('pɑːkə) *n* **1 Charlie.** nickname *Bird* or *Yardbird.* 1920–55, U.S. jazz alto saxophonist and composer; the leading exponent of early bop. **2 Dorothy** (**Rothschild**). 1893–1967, U.S. writer, noted esp. for the ironical humour of her short stories. **3 Matthew.** 1504–75, English prelate. As archbishop of Canterbury (1559–75), he supervised Elizabeth I's religious settlement.

Parker Morris standard *n* (*often pl*) (in Britain) a set of minimum criteria for good housing construction, design, and facilities, recommended by the 1961 report of the Central Housing Advisory Committee chaired by Sir Parker Morris. Subsequent governments have urged private and local authority house-builders to achieve these standards.

Parkes (pɑːks) *n* Sir **Henry.** 1815–96, Australian journalist and politician born in England, five times premier of New South Wales, advocate of free trade and Federation, and a founder of the public education system.

parkin ('pɑːkɪn) *or* **perkin** *n* (in Britain and New Zealand) a moist spicy ginger cake usually containing oatmeal. [C19: of unknown origin]

parking disc *n* See **disc** (sense 7a).

parking lot *n* the U.S. and Canadian term for **car park.**

parking meter *n* a timing device, usually coin-operated, that indicates how long a vehicle may be left parked.

parking orbit *n* an orbit around the earth or moon in which a spacecraft can be placed temporarily in order to prepare for the next step in its programme.

parking ticket *n* a summons served for a parking offence.

Parkinson's disease ('pɑːkɪnsənz) *n* a progressive chronic disorder of the central nervous system characterized by impaired muscular coordination and tremor. Often shortened to **Parkinson's.** Also called: **ˈParkinson,ism, Parkinson's syndrome, paralysis agitans, shaking palsy.** [C19: named after James *Parkinson* (1755–1824), British surgeon, who first described it]

Parkinson's law *n* the notion, expressed facetiously as a law of economics, that work expands to fill the time available for its completion. [C20: named after C. N. *Parkinson* (1909–93), British historian and writer, who formulated it]

park keeper *n* (in Britain) an official employed by a local authority to patrol and supervise a public park.

parkland ('pɑːk,lænd) *n* grassland with scattered trees.

park savanna *n* savanna grassland scattered with trees.

parkway ('pɑːk,weɪ) *n* (in the U.S. and Canada) a wide road planted with trees, turf, etc.

parky ('pɑːkɪ) *adj* **parkier, parkiest.** (*usually postpositive*) *Brit. informal.* (of the weather) chilly; cold. [C19: perhaps from PERKY]

Parl. *abbrev. for:* **1** Parliament. **2** Also: **parl.** parliamentary.

parlance ('pɑːləns) *n* **1** a particular manner of speaking, esp. when specialized; idiom: *political parlance.* **2** *Archaic.* any discussion, such as a debate. [C16: from Old French, from *parler* to talk, via Medieval Latin from Late Latin *parabola* speech, PARABLE; compare PARLEY]

parlando (pɑːˈlændəʊ) *adj, adv Music.* to be performed as though speaking. [Italian: speaking, from *parlare* to speak]

parlay ('pɑːlɪ) *U.S. and Canadian.* ◆ *vb* (*tr*) **1** to stake (winnings from one bet) on a subsequent wager. Brit. equivalent: **double up. 2** to exploit (one's talent) to achieve worldly success. ◆ *n* **3** a bet in which winnings from one wager are staked on another, or a series of such bets. [C19: variant of *paroli,* via French from Neapolitan Italian *parolo,* from *paro* a pair, from Latin *pār* equal, PAR]

parley ('pɑːlɪ) *n* **1** a discussion, esp. between enemies under a truce to decide terms of surrender, etc. ◆ *vb* **2** (*intr*) to discuss, esp. with an enemy under a truce. **3** (*tr*) to speak (a foreign language). [C16: from French, from *parler* to talk, from Medieval Latin *parabolāre,* from Late Latin *parabola* speech, PARABLE] ▶ **ˈparleyer** *n*

parleyvoo (ˌpɑːlɪˈvuː) *Informal.* ◆ *vb (intr)* **1** to speak French. ◆ *n* **2** the French language. **3** a Frenchman. [C20: jocular respelling of *parlez-vous (français)*? do you speak (French)?]

parliament (ˈpɑːləmənt) *n* **1** an assembly of the representatives of a political nation or people, often the supreme legislative authority. **2** any legislative or deliberative assembly, conference, etc. **3** Also: **ˈparlement.** (in France before the Revolution) any of several high courts of justice in which royal decrees were registered. [C13: from Anglo-Latin *parliamentum,* from Old French *parlement,* from *parler* to speak; see PARLEY]

Parliament (ˈpɑːləmənt) *n* **1** the highest legislative authority in Britain, consisting of the House of Commons, which exercises effective power, the House of Lords, and the sovereign. **2** a similar legislature in another country. **3** the two chambers of a Parliament. **4** the lower chamber of a Parliament. **5** any of the assemblies of such a body created by a general election and royal summons and dissolved before the next election.

parliamentarian (ˌpɑːləmenˈtɛərɪən) *n* **1** an expert in parliamentary procedures, etc. **2** *(sometimes cap.) Brit.* a Member of Parliament. ◆ *adj* **3** of or relating to a parliament or parliaments.

Parliamentarian (ˌpɑːləmenˈtɛərɪən) *n* **1** a supporter of Parliament during the Civil War. ◆ *adj* **2** of or relating to Parliament or its supporters during the Civil War.

parliamentarianism (ˌpɑːləmenˈtɛərɪəˌnɪzəm) *or* **parliamentarism** (ˌpɑːləˈmentəˌrɪzəm) *n* the system of parliamentary government.

parliamentary (ˌpɑːləˈmentərɪ, -trɪ) *adj (sometimes cap.)* **1** of or characteristic of a parliament or Parliament. **2** proceeding from a parliament or Parliament: *a parliamentary decree.* **3** conforming to or derived from the procedures of a parliament or Parliament: *parliamentary conduct.* **4** having a parliament or Parliament. **5** of or relating to Parliament or its supporters during the Civil War.

parliamentary agent *n* (in Britain) a person who is employed to manage the parliamentary business of a private group.

Parliamentary Commissioner *or in full* **Parliamentary Commissioner for Administration** *n* (in Britain) the official name for **ombudsman** (sense 2).

parliamentary private secretary *n* (in Britain) a backbencher in Parliament who assists a minister, esp. in liaison with backbenchers. Abbrev.: **PPS.**

parliamentary secretary *n* a Member of Parliament appointed, usually as a junior minister, to assist a Minister of the Crown with departmental responsibilities.

parlor car *n* (in the U.S. and Canada) a comfortable railway coach with individual reserved seats.

parlour *or U.S.* **parlor** (ˈpɑːlə) *n* **1** *Old-fashioned.* a living room, esp. one kept tidy for the reception of visitors. **2** a reception room in a priest's house, convent, etc. **3** a small room for guests away from the public rooms in an inn, club, etc. **4** *Chiefly U.S., Canadian, and N.Z.* a room or shop equipped as a place of business: *a billiard parlor.* **5** *Caribbean.* a small shop, esp. one selling cakes and nonalcoholic drinks. **6** Also called: **milking parlour.** a building equipped for the milking of cows. [C13: from Anglo-Norman *parlur,* from Old French *parleur* room in convent for receiving guests, from *parler* to speak; see PARLEY]

parlour game *n* an informal indoor game.

parlous (ˈpɑːləs) *Archaic or humorous.* ◆ *adj* **1** dangerous or difficult. **2** cunning. ◆ *adv* **3** extremely. [C14 *perlous,* variant of PERILOUS] ▸ **ˈparlously** *adv* ▸ **ˈparlousness** *n*

parl. proc. *abbrev. for* parliamentary procedure.

Parma *n* **1** *(Italian* ˈparma). a city in N Italy, in Emilia-Romagna: capital of the duchy of Parma and Piacenza from 1545 until it became part of Italy in 1860; important food industry (esp. Parmesan cheese). Pop.: 167 516 (1996 est.). **2** (ˈpɑːmə). a city in NE Ohio, south of Cleveland. Pop.: 85 006 (1996 est.). ▸ **Parmesan** (ˌpɑːmɪˈzæn, ˈpɑːmɪˌzæn) *adj, n*

Parmenides (pɑːˈmenɪˌdiːz) *n* 5th century B.C., Greek Eleatic philosopher, born in Italy. He held that the universe is single and unchanging and denied the existence of change and motion. His doctrines are expounded in his poem *On Nature,* of which only fragments are extant.

Parmentier (ˈpɑːmənˌtjeɪ; *French* parmɑ̃tje) *adj* (of soups, etc.) containing or garnished with potatoes. [C19: named after A. *Parmentier* (1737–1813), French horticulturist]

Parmesan *or* **Parmesan cheese** *n* a hard dry cheese made from skimmed milk, used grated, esp. on pasta dishes and soups.

Parmigianino *(Italian* parmidʒaˈnino) *n* real name *Girolamo Francesco Maria Mazzola.* 1503–40, Italian painter, one of the originators of mannerism. Also called: **Parmigiano** (parmiˈdʒano).

Parnaíba *or* **Parnahiba** *(Portuguese* parnaˈiba) *n* a river in NE Brazil, rising in the Serra das Mangabeiras and flowing generally northeast, to the Atlantic. Length: about 1450 km (900 miles).

Parnassian[1] (pɑːˈnæsɪən) *adj* of or relating to Mount Parnassus or poetry.

Parnassian[2] (pɑːˈnæsɪən) *n* **1** one of a school of French poets of the late 19th century who wrote verse that emphasized metrical form and restricted emotion. ◆ *adj* **2** of or relating to the Parnassians or their poetry. [C19: from French *parnassien,* from *Parnasse* PARNASSUS; from *Le Parnasse contemporain,* title of an anthology produced by these poets] ▸ **Parˈnassianˌism** *or* **Parˈnasˌsism** *n*

Parnassus (pɑːˈnæsəs) *n* **1** Mount. a mountain in central Greece, in NW Boeotia: in ancient times sacred to Dionysus, Apollo, and the Muses, with the Castalian Spring and Delphi on its slopes. Height: 2457 m (8061 ft.). Modern Greek names: **Parnassós** (ˌparnaˈsɔs), **Liákoura. 2a** the world of poetry. **2b** a centre of poetic or other creative activity. **3** a collection of verse or belles-lettres.

Parnell (ˈpɑːnᵊl, pɑːˈnel) *n* **Charles Stewart.** 1846–91, Irish nationalist, who led the Irish Home Rule movement in Parliament (1880–90) with a calculated policy of obstruction. Although Gladstone was converted to Home Rule (1886), Parnell's career was ruined by the scandal over his adultery with Mrs O'Shea. ▸ **ˈParnelˌlism** *n* ▸ **ˈParnellite** *n, adj*

parochial (pəˈrəʊkɪəl) *adj* **1** narrow in outlook or scope; provincial. **2** of or relating to a parish or parishes. [C14: via Old French from Church Latin *parochiālis;* see PARISH] ▸ **paˈrochialˌism** *n* ▸ **paˌrochiˈality** *n* ▸ **paˈrochially** *adv*

parochial church council *n Church of England.* an elected body of lay representatives of the members of a parish that administers the affairs of the parish.

parody (ˈpærədɪ) *n, pl* **-dies. 1** a musical, literary, or other composition that mimics the style of another composer, author, etc., in a humorous or satirical way. **2** mimicry of someone's individual manner in a humorous or satirical way. **3** something so badly done as to seem an intentional mockery; travesty. ◆ *vb* **-dies, -dying, -died. 4** *(tr)* to make a parody of. [C16: via Latin from Greek *paroidiā* satirical poem, from PARA-[1] + *ōidē* song] ▸ **parodic** (pəˈrɒdɪk) *or* **paˈrodical** *adj* ▸ **ˈparodist** *n*

paroicous (pəˈrɔɪkəs) *or* **paroecious** (pəˈriːʃəs) *adj* (of mosses and related plants) having the male and female reproductive organs at different levels on the same stem. [C19: from Greek *paroikos* living nearby, from PARA-[1] (beside) + *oikos* house; compare PARISH]

parol (ˈpærəl, pəˈrəʊl) *Law.* ◆ *n* **1** (formerly) the pleadings in an action when presented by word of mouth. **2** an oral statement; word of mouth (now only in the phrase **by parol**). ◆ *adj* **3a** (of a contract, lease, etc.) made orally or in writing but not under seal. **3b** expressed or given by word of mouth: *parol evidence.* [C15: from Old French *parole* speech; see PAROLE]

parole (pəˈrəʊl) *n* **1a** the freeing of a prisoner before his sentence has expired, on the condition that he is of good behaviour. **1b** the duration of such conditional release. **2** a promise given by a prisoner, as to be of good behaviour if granted liberty or partial liberty. **3** a variant spelling of **parol. 4** *U.S. military.* a password. **5** *Linguistics.* language as manifested in the individual speech acts of particular speakers. Compare **langue, performance** (sense 7), **competence** (sense 5). **6 on parole. 6a** conditionally released from detention. **6b** *Informal.* (of a person) under scrutiny, esp. for a recurrence of an earlier shortcoming. ◆ *vb (tr)* **7** to place (a person) on parole. [C17: from Old French, from the phrase *parole d'honneur* word of honour; *parole* from Late Latin *parabola* speech] ▸ **paˈrolable** *adj* ▸ **parolee** (pəˌrəʊˈliː) *n*

paronomasia (ˌpærənəʊˈmeɪzɪə) *n Rhetoric.* a play on words, esp. a pun. [C16: via Latin from Greek: a play on words, from *paronomazein* to make a change in naming, from PARA-[1] (beside) + *onomazein* to name, from *onoma* a name] ▸ **paronomastic** (ˌpærənəʊˈmæstɪk) *adj* ▸ **ˌparonoˈmastically** *adv*

paronym (ˈpærənɪm) *n Linguistics.* a cognate word. [C19: via Late Latin from Greek *paronumon,* from PARA-[1] (beside) + *onoma* a name] ▸ **ˌparoˈnymic** *or* **paronymous** (pəˈrɒnɪməs) *adj* ▸ **paˈronymously** *adv*

Páros (ˈpærɒs) *n* a Greek island in the S Aegean Sea, in the Cyclades: site of the discovery (1627) of the Parian Chronicle, a marble tablet outlining Greek history from before 1000 B.C. to about 354 B.C. (now at Oxford University). Pop.: 8000 (latest est.). Area: 166 sq. km (64 sq. miles).

parosmia (pæˈrɒzmɪə) *n* any disorder of the sense of smell. [C19: from PARA-[1] + Greek *osmē* smell]

parotic (pəˈrɒtɪk) *adj* situated near the ear. [C19: from New Latin *paroticus,* from Greek PARA-[1] (near) + *-oticus,* from *ous* ear]

parotid (pəˈrɒtɪd) *adj* **1** relating to or situated near the parotid gland. ◆ *n* **2** See **parotid gland.** [C17: via French, via Latin from Greek *parōtis,* from PARA-[1] (near) + *-ōtis,* from *ous* ear]

parotid gland *n* a large salivary gland, in man situated in front of and below each ear.

parotitis (ˌpærəˈtaɪtɪs) *or* **parotiditis** (pəˌrɒtɪˈdaɪtɪs) *n* inflammation of the parotid gland. See also **mumps.** ▸ **parotitic** (ˌpærəˈtɪtɪk) *or* **parotiditic** (pəˌrɒtɪˈdɪtɪk) *adj*

parotoid (pəˈrɒtɔɪd) *n* **1** Also called: **parotoid gland.** any of various warty poison glands on the head and back of certain toads and salamanders. ◆ *adj* **2** resembling a parotid gland. [C19: from Greek *parot(is)* (see PAROTID) + -OID]

-parous *adj combining form.* giving birth to: *oviparous.* [from Latin *-parus,* from *parere* to bring forth]

parousia (pəˈruːsɪə) *n Christianity.* another term for the **Second Coming.** [C19: from Greek: presence]

paroxetine (pæˈrɒksətiːn) *n* an antidepressant drug that acts by preventing the uptake of serotonin in the brain, thereby prolonging its action: used for treating depression, obsessive-compulsive disorders, and panic disorder.

paroxysm (ˈpærəkˌsɪzəm) *n* **1** an uncontrollable outburst: *a paroxysm of giggling.* **2** *Pathol.* **2a** a sudden attack or recurrence of a disease. **2b** any fit or convulsion. [C17: via French from Medieval Latin *paroxysmus* annoyance, from Greek *paroxusmos,* from *paroxunein* to goad, from PARA-[1] (intensifier) + *oxunein* to sharpen, from *oxus* sharp] ▸ **ˌparoxˈysmal** *or* **ˌparoxˈysmic** *adj* ▸ **ˌparoxˈysmally** *adv*

paroxytone (pəˈrɒksɪˌtəʊn) *adj* **1** (in the classical Greek language) of, relating to, or denoting words having an acute accent on the next to last syllable. ◆ *n* **2** a paroxytone word. ◆ Compare **oxytone.** [C18: via New Latin from Greek *paroxutonos,* from PARA-[1] (beside) + *-oxutonos* OXYTONE] ▸ **paroxytonic** (ˌpærɒksɪˈtɒnɪk) *adj*

parpend (ˈpɑːpənd) *or U.S.* **parpen** (ˈpɑːpən) *n* other names for **perpend**[1].

parquet (ˈpɑːkeɪ, -kɪ) *n* **1** a floor covering of pieces of hardwood fitted in a decorative pattern; parquetry. **2** Also called: **parquet floor.** a floor so covered. **3** *U.S.* the stalls of a theatre. **4** the main part of the Paris Bourse, where officially listed securities are traded. Compare **coulisse** (sense 3). **5** (in France) the department of government responsible for the prosecution of crimes. ◆ *vb (tr)* **6** to cover (a floor) with parquet. [C19: from Old French: small enclosure, from *parc* enclosure; see PARK]

parquet circle *n U.S.* the seating area of the main floor of a theatre that lies to the rear of the auditorium and underneath the balcony. Also called: **parterre.**

parquetry ('pɑːkɪtrɪ) *n* a geometric pattern of inlaid pieces of wood, often of different kinds, esp. as used to cover a floor or to ornament furniture. Compare **marquetry.**

parr (pɑː) *n, pl* **parrs** *or* **parr.** a salmon up to two years of age, with dark spots and transverse bands. [C18: of unknown origin]

Parr (pɑː) *n* **Catherine.** 1512–48, sixth wife of Henry VIII of England.

parrakeet ('pærəˌkiːt) *n* a variant spelling of **parakeet.**

parramatta (ˌpærə'mætə) *n* a variant spelling of **paramatta.**

parrel *or* **parral** ('pærəl) *n Nautical.* a ring that holds the jaws of a boom to the mast but lets it slide up and down. [C15: probably from obsolete *aparail* equipment, a variant of APPAREL]

parricide ('pærɪˌsaɪd) *n* **1** the act of killing either of one's parents. **2** a person who kills his parent. [C16: from Latin *parricīdium* murder of a parent or relative, and from *parricīda* one who murders a relative, from *parri-* (element related to Greek *pēos* kinsman) + *-cīdium, -cīda* -CIDE] ► ˌ**parri'cidal** *adj*

parritch ('pærɪtʃ, 'pɑːr-) *n* a Scot. word for **porridge.**

parrot ('pærət) *n* **1** any bird of the tropical and subtropical order *Psittaciformes,* having a short hooked bill, compact body, bright plumage, and an ability to mimic sounds. Related adj: **psittacine. 2** a person who repeats or imitates the words or actions of another unintelligently. **3 sick as a parrot.** *Usually facetious.* extremely disappointed. ◆ *vb* **-rots, -roting, -roted. 4** (*tr*) to repeat or imitate mechanically without understanding. [C16: probably from French *paroquet;* see PARAKEET] ► **'parrotry** *n*

parrot-fashion *adv Informal.* without regard for meaning; by rote: *she learned it parrot-fashion.*

parrot fever *or* **disease** *n* another name for **psittacosis.**

parrotfish ('pærətˌfɪʃ) *n, pl* **-fish** *or* **-fishes. 1** any brightly coloured tropical marine percoid fish of the family *Scaridae,* having parrot-like jaws. **2** any of various similar fishes.

parrot toadstool *n* See **wax cap.**

parry ('pærɪ) *vb* **-ries, -rying, -ried. 1** to ward off (an attack) by blocking or deflecting, as in fencing. **2** (*tr*) to evade (questions), esp. adroitly. ◆ *n, pl* **-ries. 3** an act of parrying, esp. (in fencing) using a stroke or circular motion of the blade. **4** a skilful evasion, as of a question. [C17: from French *parer* to ward off, from Latin *parāre* to prepare]

Parry ('pærɪ) *n* **1** Sir **(Charles) Hubert (Hastings).** 1848–1918, English composer, noted esp. for his choral works. **2** Sir **William Edward.** 1790–1855, English arctic explorer, who searched for the Northwest Passage (1819–25) and attempted to reach the North Pole (1827).

parse (pɑːz) *vb Grammar.* **1** to assign constituent structure to (a sentence or the words in a sentence). **2** (*intr*) (of a word or linguistic element) to play a specified role in the structure of a sentence. [C16: from Latin *pars* (*ōrātionis*) part (of speech)] ► **'parsable** *adj*

parsec ('pɑːˌsɛk) *n* a unit of astronomical distance equal to the distance from earth at which stellar parallax would be 1 second of arc; equivalent to 3.0857×10^{16} m or 3.262 light years. [C20: from PARALLAX + SECOND[2]]

Parsee *or* **Parsi** ('pɑːsiː) *n* **1** an adherent of a monotheistic religion of Zoroastrian origin, the practitioners of which were driven out of Persia by the Muslims in the eighth century A.D. It is now found chiefly in western India. ◆ *adj* **2** of or relating to the Parsees or their religion. [C17: from Persian *Pārsī* a Persian, from Old Persian *Pārsa* PERSIA] ► **'Parseeˌism** *n*

parser ('pɑːzə) *n Computing.* a program or part of a program that interprets input to a computer by recognizing key words or analysing sentence structure.

Parsha ('pɑːʃə; *Yiddish* 'parʃə) *n* the Yiddish word for **Parashah.**

Parsifal ('pɑːsɪf[ə]l, -ˌfɑːl) *or* **Parzival** *n German myth.* the hero of a medieval cycle of legends about the Holy Grail. English eqivalent: **Percival.**

parsimony ('pɑːsɪmənɪ) *n* extreme care or reluctance in spending; frugality; niggardliness. [C15: from Latin *parcimōnia,* from *parcere* to spare] ► **parsimonious** (ˌpɑːsɪ'məʊnɪəs) *adj* ► ˌ**parsi'moniously** *adv*

parsley ('pɑːslɪ) *n* **1** a S European umbelliferous plant, *Petroselinum crispum,* widely cultivated for its curled aromatic leaves, which are used in cooking. **2** any of various similar and related plants, such as fool's-parsley, stone parsley, and cow parsley. [C14 *persely,* from Old English *petersilie* + Old French *persil, peresil,* both ultimately from Latin *petroselīnum* rock parsley, from Greek *petroselinon,* from *petra* rock + *selinon* parsley]

parsley fern *n* **1** any of several plants with crisped foliage, resembling that of parsley. **2** a small bright green tufted European fern, *Cryptogramma crispa,* that grows on acid scree and rock in uplands.

parsley piert (pɪət) *n* a small N temperate rosaceous plant, *Aphanes arvensis,* having fan-shaped leaves and small greenish flowers. [C17: from French *perce pierre,* literally: break stone]

parsnip ('pɑːsnɪp) *n* **1** a strong-scented umbelliferous plant, *Pastinaca sativa,* cultivated for its long whitish root. **2** the root of this plant, eaten as a vegetable. **3** any of several similar plants, esp. the cow parsnip. [C14: from Old French *pasnaie,* from Latin *pastināca,* from *pastināre* to dig, from *pastinum* two-pronged tool for digging; also influenced by Middle English *nepe* TURNIP]

parson ('pɑːs[ə]n) *n* **1** a parish priest in the Church of England, formerly applied only to those who held ecclesiastical benefices. **2** any clergyman. [C13: from Medieval Latin *persōna* parish priest, representative of the parish, from Latin: personage; see PERSON] ► **parsonic** (pɑː'sɒnɪk) *or* **par'sonical** *adj*

parsonage ('pɑːs[ə]nɪdʒ) *n* the residence of a parson who is not a rector or vicar, as provided by the parish.

parson bird *n* another name for **tui.** [C19: so called because of its dark plumage with white neck feathers]

Parsons ('pɑːsənz) *n* **1** Sir **Charles Algernon.** 1854–1931, English engineer, who developed the steam turbine. **2 Talcott.** 1902–79, U.S. sociologist, author of *The Structure of Social Action* (1937) and *The Social System* (1951).

parson's nose *n* the fatty extreme end portion of the tail of a fowl when cooked. Also called: **pope's nose.**

part (pɑːt) *n* **1** a piece or portion of a whole. **2** an integral constituent of something: *dancing is part of what we teach.* **3a** an amount less than the whole; bit: *they only recovered part of the money.* **3b** (*as modifier*): *an old car in part exchange for a new one.* **4** one of several equal or nearly equal divisions: *mix two parts flour to one part water.* **5a** an actor's role in a play. **5b** the speech and actions which make up such a role. **5c** a written copy of these. **6** a person's proper role or duty: *everyone must do his part.* **7** (*often pl*) region; area: *you're well known in these parts.* **8** *Anatomy.* any portion of a larger structure. **9** a component that can be replaced in a machine, engine, etc.: *spare parts.* **10** the U.S., Canadian, and Austral. word for **parting** (sense 1). **11** *Music.* **11a** one of a number of separate melodic lines making up the texture of music. **11b** one of such melodic lines, which is assigned to one or more instrumentalists or singers: *the viola part; the soprano solo part.* **11c** such a line performed from a separately written or printed copy. See **part song. 12 for the most part.** generally. **13 for one's part.** as far as one is concerned. **14 in part.** to some degree; partly. **15 of many parts.** having many different abilities. **16 on the part of.** on behalf of. **17 part and parcel.** an essential ingredient. **18 play a part. 18a** to pretend to be what one is not. **18b** (foll. by *in*) to have something to do (with); be instrumental (in): *to play a part in the king's downfall.* **19 take in good part.** to respond to (teasing) with good humour. **20 take part in.** to participate in. **21 take someone's part.** to support someone in an argument. ◆ *vb* **22** to divide or separate from one another; take or come apart: *to part the curtains; the seams parted when I washed the dress.* **23** to go away or cause to go away from one another; stop or cause to stop seeing each other: *the couple parted amicably.* **24** (*intr;* foll. by *from*) to leave; say goodbye (to). **25** (*intr;* foll. by *with*) to relinquish, esp. reluctantly: *I couldn't part with my teddy bear.* **26** (*tr;* foll. by *from*) to cause to relinquish, esp. reluctantly: *he's not easily parted from his cash.* **27** (*intr*) to split; separate: *the path parts here.* **28** (*tr*) to arrange (the hair) in such a way that a line of scalp is left showing. **29** (*intr*) a euphemism for **die**[1] (sense 1). **30** (*intr*) *Archaic.* to depart. **31 part company. 31a** to end a friendship or association, esp. as a result of a quarrel; separate: *they were in partnership, but parted company last year.* **31b** (foll. by *with*) to leave; go away from; be separated from. ◆ *adv* **32** to some extent; partly. ◆ See also **parts.** [C13: via Old French from Latin *partīre* to divide, from *pars* a part]

part. *abbrev. for:* **1** participle. **2** particular.

partake (pɑː'teɪk) *vb* **-takes, -taking, -took, -taken.** (*mainly intr*) **1** (foll. by *in*) to have a share; participate: *to partake in the excitement.* **2** (foll. by *of*) to take or receive a portion, esp. of food or drink: *each partook of the food offered to him.* **3** (foll. by *of*) to suggest or have some of the quality (of): *music partaking of sadness.* **4** (*tr*) *Archaic.* to share in. [C16: back formation from *partaker,* earlier *part taker,* based on Latin *particeps* participant; see PART, TAKE] ► **par'taker** *n*

USAGE *Partake of* is sometimes wrongly used as if it were a synonym of *eat* or *drink.* Correctly, one can only *partake of* food or drink which is available for several people to share.

partan ('pɑːt[ə]n; *Scot.* 'part[ə]n) *n* a Scots word for **crab**[1] (senses 1 and 2). [C15: of Celtic origin]

parted ('pɑːtɪd) *adj* **1** *Botany.* divided almost to the base: *parted leaves.* **2** *Heraldry.* showing two coats of arms divided by a vertical central line.

parterre (pɑː'tɛə) *n* **1** a formally patterned flower garden. **2** *Brit., Irish.* the pit in a theatre. **3** *U.S.* another name for **parquet circle.** [C17: from French, from *par* along + *terre* ground]

part exchange *n* a transaction in which used goods are taken as partial payment for more expensive ones of the same type.

parthenocarpy (pɑː'θiːnəʊˌkɑːpɪ) *n* the development of fruit without fertilization or formation of seeds. [C20: from Greek *parthenos* virgin + *karpos* fruit] ► **parˌtheno'carpic** *or* **parˌtheno'carpous** *adj*

parthenogenesis (ˌpɑːθɪnəʊ'dʒɛnɪsɪs) *n* **1** a type of reproduction, occurring in some insects and flowers, in which the unfertilized ovum develops directly into a new individual. **2** human conception without fertilization by a male; virgin birth. [C19: from Greek *parthenos* virgin + *genesis* birth] ► **parthenogenetic** (ˌpɑːθɪˌnəʊdʒɪ'nɛtɪk) *adj* ► ˌ**partheˌnoge'netically** *adv*

Parthenon ('pɑːθəˌnɒn, -nən) *n* the temple on the Acropolis in Athens built in the 5th century B.C. and regarded as the finest example of the Greek Doric order.

Parthenopaeus (ˌpɑːθənəʊ'piːəs) *n Greek myth.* one of the Seven against Thebes, son of Atalanta.

Parthenope (pɑː'θɛnəpɪ) *n Greek myth.* a siren, who drowned herself when Odysseus evaded the lure of the sirens' singing. Her body was said to have been cast ashore at what became Naples.

Parthenos ('pɑːθɪˌnɒs) *n* an epithet meaning "Virgin", applied by the Greeks to several goddesses, esp. Athena.

parthenospore (pɑː'θiːnəʊˌspɔː) *n* another name for **azygospore.**

Parthia ('pɑːθɪə) *n* a country in ancient Asia, southeast of the Caspian Sea, that expanded into a great empire dominating SW Asia in the 2nd century B.C. It was destroyed by the Sassanids in the 3rd century A.D. ► **'Parthian** *n, adj*

Parthian shot *n* a hostile remark or gesture delivered while departing. [alluding to the custom of Parthian archers who shot their arrows backwards while retreating]

partial ('pɑːʃəl) *adj* **1** relating to only a part; not general or complete: *a partial eclipse.* **2** biased: *a partial judge.* **3** (*postpositive;* foll. by *to*) having a particular liking (for). **4** *Botany.* **4a** constituting part of a larger structure: *a partial umbel.* **4b** used for only part of the life cycle of a plant: *a partial habitat.* **4c** (of a parasite) not exclusively parasitic. **5** *Maths.* designating or relating to an operation in which only one of a set of independent variables is considered at a time. ◆ *n* 6 Also called: **partial tone.** *Music, acoustics.* any of the component tones of a single musical sound, including both those that belong to the harmonic series of the sound and those that do not. 7 *Maths.* a partial derivative. [C15: from Old French *parcial,* from Late Latin *partiālis* incomplete, from Latin *pars* PART] ▸ **'partially** *adv* ▸ **'partialness** *n*

USAGE See at **partly.**

partial derivative *n* the derivative of a function of two or more variables with respect to one of the variables, the other or others being considered constant. Written $\partial f/\partial x$.

partial eclipse *n* an eclipse, esp. of the sun, in which the body is only partially hidden. Compare **total eclipse, annular eclipse.**

partial fraction *n Maths.* one of a set of fractions into which a more complicated fraction can be resolved.

partiality (ˌpɑːʃɪ'ælɪtɪ) *n, pl* **-ties.** 1 favourable prejudice or bias. 2 (usually foll. by *for*) liking or fondness. 3 the state or condition of being partial.

partially sighted *adj* **a** unable to see properly so that even with corrective aids normal activities are prevented or seriously hindered. **b** (*as collective n; preceded by the*): *the partially sighted.* ▸ **partial sight** *n*

partial pressure *n* the pressure that a gas, in a mixture of gases, would exert if it alone occupied the whole volume occupied by the mixture.

partial product *n* the result obtained when a number is multiplied by one digit of a multiplier.

partial reinforcement *n Psychol.* the process of randomly rewarding an organism for making a response on only some of the occasions it makes it.

partible ('pɑːtəbᵊl) *adj* (esp. of property or an inheritance) divisible; separable. [C16: from Late Latin *partibilis,* from *part-, pars* PART]

Participaction (pɑːˌtɪsɪ'pækʃən) *n* (in Canada) a non-profit-making organization set up to promote physical fitness. [from PARTICIP(ATION) + ACTION]

participate (pɑː'tɪsɪˌpeɪt) *vb* (*intr;* often foll. by *in*) to take part, be or become actively involved, or share (in). [C16: from Latin *participāre,* from *pars* PART + *capere* to take] ▸ **par'ticipant** *adj, n* ▸ **parˌtici'pation** *n* ▸ **par'ticiˌpator** *n* ▸ **par'ticipatory** *adj*

participating insurance *n* a system of insurance by which policyholders receive dividends from the company's profit or surplus.

participle ('pɑːtɪsɪpᵊl, pɑː'tɪsɪpᵊl) *n* a nonfinite form of verbs, in English and other languages, used adjectivally and in the formation of certain compound tenses. See also **present participle, past participle.** [C14: via Old French from Latin *participium,* from *particeps* partaker, from *pars* PART + *capere* to take] ▸ **participial** (ˌpɑːtɪ'sɪpɪəl) *adj, n* ▸ **ˌparti'cipially** *adv*

particle ('pɑːtɪkᵊl) *n* 1 an extremely small piece of matter; speck. 2 a very tiny amount; iota: *it doesn't make a particle of difference.* 3 a function word, esp. (in certain languages) a word belonging to an uninflected class having suprasegmental or grammatical function: *the Greek particles "mēn" and "de" are used to express contrast; questions in Japanese are indicated by the particle "ka"; English "up" is sometimes regarded as an adverbial particle.* 4 a common affix, such as *re-, un-,* or *-ness.* 5 *Physics.* a body with finite mass that can be treated as having negligible size, and internal structure. 6 See **elementary particle.** 7 *R.C. Church.* a small piece broken off from the Host at Mass. 8 *Archaic.* a section or clause of a document. [C14: from Latin *particula* a small part, from *pars* PART]

particle accelerator *n* a machine for accelerating charged elementary particles to very high energies, used for research in nuclear physics. See also **linear accelerator, cyclotron, betatron, synchrotron, synchrocyclotron.**

particle beam *n* 1 a stream of energized particles produced by a particle accelerator. 2 such a stream emitted by a particle beam weapon.

particle beam weapon *n* a weapon that fires particle beams into the atmosphere or space.

particle board *n* another name for **chipboard.**

particle physics *n* the study of fundamental particles and their properties. Also called: **high-energy physics.**

particle separation *n Transformational grammar.* a rule that moves the particle of a phrasal verb, thus deriving a sentence like *He looked the answer up* from a structure that also underlies *He looked up the answer.*

parti-coloured *or* **party-coloured** ('pɑːtɪˌkʌləd) *adj* having different colours in different parts; variegated. [C16 *parti,* from (obsolete) *party* of more than one colour, from Old French: striped, from Latin *partīre* to divide]

particular (pə'tɪkjʊlə) *adj* 1 (*prenominal*) of or belonging to a single or specific person, thing, category, etc.; specific; special: *the particular demands of the job; no particular reason.* 2 (*prenominal*) exceptional or marked: *a matter of particular importance.* 3 (*prenominal*) relating to or providing specific details or circumstances: *a particular account.* 4 exacting or difficult to please, esp. in details; fussy. 5 (of the solution of a differential equation) obtained by giving specific values to the arbitrary constants in a general equation. 6 *Logic.* (of a proposition) affirming or denying something about only some members of a class of objects, as in *some men are not wicked.* Compare **universal** (sense 10). 7 *Property law.* denoting an estate that precedes the passing of the property into ultimate ownership. See also **remainder** (sense 3), **reversion** (sense 4). ◆ *n* 8 a separate distinct item that helps to form a generalization: opposed to *general.* 9 (*often pl*) an item of information; detail: *complete in every particular.* 10 *Logic.* another name for **individual** (sense 7a). 11 *Philosophy.* an individual object, as contrasted with a universal. See **universal** (sense 12b). 12 **in particular.** especially, particularly, or exactly. [C14: from Old French *particuler,* from Late Latin *particulāris* concerning a part, from Latin *particula* PARTICLE] ▸ **par'ticularly** *adv*

particular average *n Insurance.* partial damage to or loss of a ship or its cargo affecting only the shipowner or one cargo owner. Abbrev.: **PA.** Compare **general average.**

particularism (pə'tɪkjʊləˌrɪzəm) *n* 1 exclusive attachment to the interests of one group, class, sect, etc., esp. at the expense of the community as a whole. 2 the principle of permitting each state or minority in a federation the right to further its own interests or retain its own laws, traditions, etc. 3 *Theol.* the doctrine that divine grace is restricted to the elect. ▸ **par'ticularist** *n, adj* ▸ **parˌticular'istic** *adj*

particularity (pəˌtɪkjʊ'lærɪtɪ) *n, pl* **-ties.** 1 (*often pl*) a specific circumstance: *the particularities of the affair.* 2 great attentiveness to detail; fastidiousness. 3 the quality of being precise: *a description of great particularity.* 4 the state or quality of being particular as opposed to general; individuality: *the particularity of human situations.*

particularize *or* **particularise** (pə'tɪkjʊləˌraɪz) *vb* 1 to treat in detail; give details (about). 2 (*intr*) to go into detail. ▸ **parˌticulari'zation** *or* **parˌticulari'sation** *n* ▸ **par'ticularˌizer** *or* **par'ticularˌiser** *n*

Particulars of Claim *pl n Law.* (in England) the first reading made by the plaintiff in a county court action, showing the facts upon which he relies in support of his claim and the relief asked for.

particulate (pɑː'tɪkjʊlɪt, -ˌleɪt) *n* 1 a substance consisting of separate particles. ◆ *adj* 2 of or made up of separate particles. 3 *Genetics.* of, relating to, or designating inheritance of characteristics, esp. with emphasis on the role of genes.

parting ('pɑːtɪŋ) *n* 1 *Brit.* the line of scalp showing when sections of hair are combed in opposite directions. U.S., Canadian, and Austral. equivalent: **part.** 2 the act of separating or the state of being separated. 3a a departure or leave-taking, esp. one causing a final separation. 3b (*as modifier*): *a parting embrace.* 4 a place or line of separation or division. 5 *Chem.* a division of a crystal along a plane that is not a cleavage plane. 6 a euphemism for **death.** ◆ *adj* (*prenominal*) 7 *Literary.* departing: *the parting day.* 8 serving to divide or separate.

parting strip *n* a thin strip of wood, metal, etc., used to separate two adjoining materials.

parti pris *French.* (parti pri) *n* a preconceived opinion. [C19: literally: side taken]

Parti Québecois (*French* parti) *n* (in Canada) a political party in Quebec, formed in 1968 and originally advocating the separation of Quebec from the rest of the country. Abbrev.: **PQ.**

partisan[1] *or* **partizan** (ˌpɑːtɪ'zæn, 'pɑːtɪˌzæn) *n* 1 an adherent or devotee of a cause, party, etc. 2a a member of an armed resistance group within occupied territory. 2b (*as modifier*): *partisan forces.* ◆ *adj* 3 of, relating to, or characteristic of a partisan. 4 relating to or excessively devoted to one party, faction, etc.; one-sided: *partisan control.* [C16: via French, from Old Italian *partigiano,* from *parte* faction, from Latin *pars* PART] ▸ **ˌparti'sanship** *or* **ˌparti'zanship** *n*

partisan[2] *or* **partizan** ('pɑːtɪzᵊn) *n* a spear or pike with two opposing axe blades or spikes. [C16: from French *partizane,* from Old Italian *partigiana,* from *partigiano* PARTISAN[1]]

partita (pɑː'tiːtə) *n, pl* **-te** (-teɪ) *or* **-tas.** *Music.* a type of suite. [Italian: divided (piece), from Latin *partīre* to divide]

partite ('pɑːtaɪt) *adj* 1 (*in combination*) composed of or divided into a specified number of parts: *bipartite.* 2 (esp. of plant leaves) divided almost to the base to form two or more parts. [C16: from Latin *partīre* to divide]

partition (pɑː'tɪʃən) *n* 1 a division into parts; separation. 2 something that separates, such as a large screen dividing a room in two. 3 a part or share. 4 a division of a country into two or more separate nations. 5 *Property law.* a division of property, esp. realty, among joint owners. 6 *Maths.* any of the ways by which an integer can be expressed as a sum of integers. 7 *Logic, maths.* 7a the division of a class into a number of disjoint and exhaustive subclasses. 7b such a set of subclasses. 8 *Biology.* a structure that divides or separates. 9 *Rhetoric.* the second part of a speech where the chief lines of thought are announced. ◆ *vb* (*tr*) 10 (often foll. by *off*) to separate or apportion into sections: *to partition a room off with a large screen.* 11 to divide (a country) into two or more separate nations. 12 *Property law.* to divide (property, esp. realty) among joint owners, by dividing either the property itself or the proceeds of sale. [C15: via Old French from Latin *partītiō,* from *partīre* to divide] ▸ **par'titioner** *or* **par'titionist** *n*

partition coefficient *n Chem.* the ratio of the concentrations of a substance in two heterogenous phases in equilibrium with each other.

partitive ('pɑːtɪtɪv) *adj* 1 *Grammar.* indicating that a noun involved in a construction refers only to a part or fraction of what it otherwise refers to. The phrase *some of the butter* is a partitive construction; in some inflected languages it would be translated by the genitive case of the noun. 2 serving to separate or divide into parts. ◆ *n* 3 *Grammar.* a partitive linguistic element or feature. [C16: from Medieval Latin *partītīvus* serving to divide, from Latin *partīre* to divide] ▸ **'partitively** *adv*

partlet ('pɑːtlɪt) *n* a woman's garment covering the neck and shoulders, worn esp. during the 16th century. [C16: a variant of Middle English *patelet* strip of cloth, from Middle French *patelette*]

partly ('pɑːtlɪ) *adv* to some extent; not completely.

USAGE *Partly* and *partially* are to some extent interchangeable, but *partly* should be used when referring to a part or parts of something: *the building is partly* (not *partially*) *of stone,* while *partially* is preferred for the meaning *to some extent: his mother is partially* (not *partly*) *sighted.*

partner ('pɑːtnə) *n* 1 an ally or companion: *a partner in crime.* 2 a member of a partnership. 3 one of a pair of dancers or players on the same side in a game: *my bridge partner.* 4 either member of a couple in a relationship. ◆ *vb* 5 to be or cause to be a partner (of). [C14: variant (influenced by PART) of PARCENER] ▸ **'partnerless** *adj*

partners ('pɑːtnəz) *pl n Nautical.* a wooden construction around an opening in a deck, as to support a mast.

partnership ('pɑːtnəʃɪp) *n* **1a** a contractual relationship between two or more persons carrying on a joint business venture with a view to profit, each incurring liability for losses and the right to share in the profits. **1b** the deed creating such a relationship. **1c** the persons associated in such a relationship. **2** the state or condition of being a partner.

partnerships for peace *n* a subsidiary organization of NATO, comprising former Warsaw Pact countries that wish to be allied with NATO but have not been granted full NATO membership: established in 1994.

part-off *n Caribbean.* a screen used to divide off part of a room, such as the eating place of a parlour.

part of speech *n* a class of words sharing important syntactic or semantic features; a group of words in a language that may occur in similar positions or fulfil similar functions in a sentence. The chief parts of speech in English are noun, pronoun, adjective, determiner, adverb, verb, preposition, conjunction, and interjection.

parton ('pɑːˌtɒn) *n Physics.* a hypothetical elementary particle postulated as a constituent of neutrons and protons. **[**from PART + -ON**]**

Parton ('pɑːtən) *n* **Dolly.** born 1946, U.S. country and pop singer and songwriter.

partook (pɑː'tʊk) *vb* the past tense of **partake.**

partridge ('pɑːtrɪdʒ) *n, pl* **-tridges** *or* **-tridge. 1** any of various small Old World gallinaceous game birds of the genera *Perdix, Alectoris,* etc., esp. *P. perdix* (**common** or **European partridge**): family *Phasianidae* (pheasants). **2** *U.S. and Canadian.* any of various other gallinaceous birds, esp. the bobwhite and ruffed grouse. **[C13:** from Old French *perdriz,* from Latin *perdix,* from Greek**]**

Partridge ('pɑːtrɪdʒ) *n* **Eric** (**Honeywood**). 1894–1979, British lexicographer, born in New Zealand; author of works on English usage, idiom, slang, and etymology.

partridgeberry ('pɑːtrɪdʒˌberɪ) *n, pl* **-ries. 1** Also called: **boxberry, twinberry.** a creeping woody rubiaceous plant, *Mitchella repens,* of E North America with small white fragrant flowers and scarlet berries. **2** the berry of the wintergreen. **3** another name for **wintergreen** (sense 1).

partridge-wood *n* the dark striped wood of the tropical American papilionaceous tree, *Andira inermis,* used for cabinetwork.

parts (pɑːts) *pl n* **1** personal abilities or talents: *a man of many parts.* **2** short for **private parts.**

Parts of Holland *n* See **Holland**[1] (sense 3).

Parts of Kesteven *n* See (Parts of) **Kesteven.**

Parts of Lindsey *n* See (Parts of) **Lindsey.**

part song *n* **1** a song composed in harmonized parts. **2** (*in more technical usage*) a piece of homophonic choral music in which the topmost part carries the melody.

part-time *adj* **1** for less than the entire time appropriate to an activity: *a part-time job; a part-time waitress.* ◆ *adv* **part time. 2** on a part-time basis: *he works part time.* ◆ Compare **full-time.** ► ˌ**part-'timer** *n*

parturient (pɑː'tjʊərɪənt) *adj* **1** of or relating to childbirth. **2** giving birth. **3** producing or about to produce a new idea, etc. **[C16:** via Latin *parturīre,* from *parere* to bring forth**]** ► **par'turiency** *n*

parturifacient (pɑːˌtjʊərɪ'feɪʃənt) *adj, n* a medical word for **oxytocic. [C19:** from Latin *parturīre* to be in travail + *facere* to make**]**

parturition (ˌpɑːtjʊ'rɪʃən) *n* the act or process of giving birth. **[C17:** from Late Latin *parturītiō,* from *parturīre* to be in labour**]**

partway ('pɑːtˌweɪ) *adv* some of the way; partly: *I stopped reading partway through the chapter.*

part work *n Brit.* a series of magazines issued as at weekly or monthly intervals, which are designed to be bound together to form a complete course or book.

part-writing *n Music.* the aspect of composition concerned with the writing of parts, esp. counterpoint.

party ('pɑːtɪ) *n, pl* **-ties. 1a** a social gathering for pleasure, often held as a celebration. **1b** (*as modifier*): *party spirit.* **1c** (*in combination*): *partygoer.* **2** a group of people associated in some activity: *a rescue party.* **3a** (*often cap.*) a group of people organized together to further a common political aim, such as the election of its candidates to public office. **3b** (*as modifier*): *party politics.* **4** the practice of taking sides on public issues. **5** a person, esp. one who participates in some activity such as entering into a contract. **6** the person or persons taking part in legal proceedings, such as plaintiff or prosecutor: *a party to the action.* **7** *Informal, humorous.* a person: *he's an odd old party.* ◆ *vb* **-ties, -tying, -tied.** (*intr*) **8** *Informal.* to celebrate; revel. ◆ *adj* **9** *Heraldry.* (of a shield) divided vertically into two colours, metals, or furs. **[C13:** from Old French *partie* part, faction, from Latin *partīre* to divide; see PART**]**

party line *n* **1** a telephone line serving two or more subscribers. **2** the policies or dogma of a political party, to which all members are expected to subscribe. **3** *Chiefly U.S.* the boundary between adjoining property.

party list *n* (*modifier*) of or relating to a system of voting in which people vote for a party rather than for a candidate. Parties are assigned the number of seats which reflects their share of the vote. See **proportional representation.**

party man *n* a loyal member of a political party, esp. one who is extremely loyal or devoted.

party politics *pl n* politics conducted through, by, or for parties, as opposed to other interests or the public good.

party pooper ('puːpə) *n Informal.* a person whose behaviour or personality spoils other people's enjoyment. **[C20:** originally U.S.**]**

party wall *n Property law.* a wall separating two properties or pieces of land and over which each of the adjoining owners has certain rights.

parulis (pə'ruːlɪs) *n, pl* **-lides** (-lɪˌdiːz). *Pathol.* another name for **gumboil. [C19:** from PARA-[1] + Greek *oulon* gum**]**

parure (pə'rʊə) *n* a set of jewels or other ornaments. **[C15:** from Old French *pareure* adornment, from *parer* to embellish, from Latin *parāre* to arrange**]**

par value *n* the value imprinted on the face of a share certificate or bond and used to assess dividend, capital ownership, or interest. Also called: **face value.** Compare **market value, book value** (sense 2).

Parvati ('pʌrvətɪ) *n Hinduism.* goddess consort of the god Siva, associated with mountains. **[**from Sanskrit: the mountain-dwelling one**]**

parve ('pɑrvə) *adj* a variant of **parev.**

parvenu *or* (*fem*) **parvenue** ('pɑːvəˌnjuː) *n* **1** a person who, having risen socially or economically, is considered to be an upstart or to lack the appropriate refinement for his new position. ◆ *adj* **2** of or characteristic of a parvenu. **[C19:** from French, from *parvenir* to attain, from Latin *pervenīre,* from *per* through + *venīre* to come**]**

parvifoliate (ˌpɑːvɪ'fəʊlɪˌeɪt) *adj* (of plants) having small leaves in comparison with the size of the stem.

parvis *or* **parvise** ('pɑːvɪs) *n* a court or portico in front of a building, esp. a church. **[C14:** via Old French from Late Latin *paradīsus* PARADISE**]**

parvovirus ('pɑːvəʊˌvaɪrəs) *n* any of a group of viruses characterized by their very small size, each of which is specific to a particular species, as for example canine parvovirus. **[C20:** New Latin from Latin *parvus* little + VIRUS**]**

Parzival (*German* 'partsifal) *n* a variant of **Parsifal.**

pas (pɑː; *French* pa) *n, pl* **pas** (pɑːz; *French* pa). **1** a dance step or movement, esp. in ballet. **2** *Rare.* the right to precede; precedence. **[C18:** French, literally: step**]**

PA's *pl n Mountaineering.* a type of rock boot. **[C20:** named after Pierre Allain, French climber**]**

Pasadena (ˌpæsə'diːnə) *n* a city in SW California, east of Los Angeles. Pop.: 134 116 (1996 est.).

Pasargadae (pæ'sɑːgəˌdiː) *n* an ancient city in Persia, northeast of Persepolis in present-day Iran: built by Cyrus the Great.

Pasay ('pɑːsaɪ) *n* a city in the Philippines, on central Luzon just south of Manila, on Manila Bay. Pop.: 374 000 (1990). Also called: **Rizal.**

pascal ('pæsk^{ə}l) *n* the derived SI unit of pressure; the pressure exerted on an area of 1 square metre by a force of 1 newton; equivalent to 10 dynes per square centimetre or 1.45×10^{-4} pound per square inch. Symbol: Pa **[C20:** named after B. PASCAL**]**

Pascal[1] (*French* paskal) *n* **Blaise** (blɛz). 1623–62, French philosopher, mathematician, and physicist. As a scientist, he made important contributions to hydraulics and the study of atmospheric pressure and, with Fermat, developed the theory of probability. His chief philosophical works are *Lettres provinciales* (1656–57), written in defence of Jansenism and against the Jesuits, and *Pensées* (1670), fragments of a Christian apologia.

Pascal[2] ('pæsˌkæl, -k^{ə}l) *n* a high-level computer programming language developed as a teaching language: used for general-purpose programming.

Pascal's triangle *n* a triangle consisting of rows of numbers; the apex is 1 and each row starts and ends with 1, other numbers being obtained by adding together the two numbers on either side in the row above: used to calculate probabilities. **[C17:** named after B. PASCAL**]**

Pascal's wager *n Philosophy.* the argument that it is in one's rational self-interest to act as if God exists, since the infinite punishments of hell, provided they have a positive probability, however small, outweigh any countervailing advantage.

Pasch (pɑːsk, pæsk) *n* an archaic name for **Passover** (sense 1) or **Easter. [C12:** from Old French *pasche,* via Church Latin and Greek from Hebrew *pesakh* PESACH**]**

paschal ('pæsk^{ə}l) *adj* **1** of or relating to Passover. **2** of or relating to Easter.

paschal flower *n* another name for **pasqueflower.**

Paschal Lamb *n* **1** (*sometimes not caps.*) *Old Testament.* the lamb killed and eaten on the first day of the Passover. **2** Christ regarded as this sacrifice.

pas de basque (ˌpɑː də 'bɑːsk; *French* pa də bask) *n, pl* **pas de basque.** a dance step performed usually on the spot, consisting of one long and two short movements during which the weight is transferred from one foot to the other: used esp. in reels and jigs. **[**from French, literally: Basque step**]**

Pas-de-Calais (*French* padkalɛ) *n* a department of N France, in Nord-Pas-de-Calais region, on the Straits of Dover (the **Pas de Calais**): the part of France closest to the British Isles. Capital: Arras. Pop.: 1 438 000 (1995). Area: 6752 sq. km (2633 sq. miles).

pas de chat (*French* padʃa) *n, pl* **pas de chat.** *Ballet.* a catlike leap. **[**French: cat's step**]**

pas de deux (*French* paddø) *n, pl* **pas de deux.** *Ballet.* a sequence for two dancers. **[**French: step for two**]**

pase ('pɑːseɪ) *n Bullfighting.* a movement of the cape or muleta by a matador to attract the bull's attention and guide its attack. **[**from Spanish, literally: pass**]**

pash[1] (pæʃ) *n Slang.* infatuation. **[C20:** from PASSION**]**

pash[2] (pæʃ) *Obsolete or dialect.* ◆ *vb* **1** to throw or be thrown and break or be broken to bits; smash. ◆ *n* **2** a crushing blow. **[C17 (n):** from earlier *passhen* to throw with violence, probably of imitative origin**]**

pasha *or* **pacha** ('pɑːʃə, 'pæʃə) *n* (formerly) a provincial governor or other high official of the Ottoman Empire or the modern Egyptian kingdom: placed after a name when used as a title. **[C17:** from Turkish *paşa***]**

pashalik *or* **pashalic** ('pɑːʃəlɪk) *n* the province or jurisdiction of a pasha. **[C18:** from Turkish**]**

pashka ('pæʃkə) *n* a rich Russian dessert made of cottage cheese, cream, almonds, currants, etc., set in a special wooden mould and traditionally eaten at Easter.

pashm ('pæʃəm) *n* the underfur of various Tibetan animals, esp. goats, used for cashmere shawls. **[**from Persian, literally: wool**]**

Pashto, Pushto ('pʌʃtəʊ), *or* **Pushtu** *n* **1** a language of Afghanistan and NW

Pakistan, belonging to the East Iranian branch of the Indo-European family: since 1936 the official language of Afghanistan. 2 (*pl* **-to** *or* **-tos, -tu** *or* **tus**) a speaker of the Pashto language; a Pathan. ◆ *adj* 3 denoting or relating to this language or a speaker of it.

Pašić (pɑː'ʃɪtʃ) *n* **Nicola.** 1845–1926, Serbian statesman; prime minister of Serbia (1891–92; 1904–05; 1906–08; 1909–11; 1912–18) and of the Kingdom of Serbs, Croats, and Slovenes (1921–24; 1924–26).

Pasionaria (*Spanish* pasjo'narja) *n* **La** (la), real name *Dolores Ibarruri.* 1895–1989, Spanish Communist leader, who lived in exile in the Soviet Union (1939–75).

Pasiphaë[1] (pə'sɪfɪiː) *n Greek myth.* the wife of Minos and mother (by a bull) of the Minotaur.

Pasiphaë[2] (pə'sɪfɪiː) *n Astronomy.* a small outer satellite of the planet Jupiter.

Pasmore ('pæsˌmɔː) *n* **Victor.** 1908–98, British artist. Originally influenced by cubism, he devoted himself to abstract paintings and reliefs after 1947.

paso doble ('pæsəʊ 'dəʊbleɪ; *Spanish* 'paso 'doβle) *n, pl* **paso dobles** *or* **pasos dobles** (*Spanish* 'pasos 'doβles). 1 a modern ballroom dance in fast duple time. 2 a piece of music composed for or in the rhythm of this dance. [Spanish: double step]

PASOK ('pæsɒk) *n acronym for* Panhellenic Socialist Movement. [C20: Modern Greek *Pa(nhellenion) So(sialistiko) K(enema)*]

Pasolini (*Italian* pazo'lini) *n* **Pier Paolo** (pjɛr 'paːolo). 1922–75, Italian film director. His films include *The Gospel according to St. Matthew* (1964), *Oedipus Rex* (1967), *Theorem* (1968), *Pigsty* (1969), and *Decameron* (1970).

pas op ('pɑːs ˌɒp) *interj S. African.* beware. [Afrikaans]

paspalum (pæs'peɪləm) *n* any of various grasses of the genus *Paspalum* of Australia and New Zealand having wide leaves.

pasqueflower ('pɑːskˌflaʊə, 'pæsk-) *n* 1 a small purple-flowered ranunculaceous plant, *Anemone pulsatilla* (or *Pulsatilla vulgaris*), of N and Central Europe and W Asia. 2 any of several related North American plants, such as *A. patens.* ◆ Also called: **paschal flower, pulsatilla.** [C16: from French *passefleur,* from *passer* to excel + *fleur* flower; changed to *pasqueflower* Easter flower, because it blooms at Easter]

pasquinade (ˌpæskwɪ'neɪd) *or* **pasquil** ('pæskwɪl) *n* 1 an abusive lampoon or satire, esp. one posted in a public place. ◆ *vb* **-ades, -ading, -aded** *or* **-quils, -quilling, -quilled.** 2 (*tr*) to ridicule with pasquinade. [C17: from Italian *Pasquino* name given to an ancient Roman statue disinterred in 1501, which was annually posted with satirical verses] ▸ ˌ**pasquin'ader** *n*

pass (pɑːs) *vb* 1 to go onwards or move by or past (a person, thing, etc.). 2 to run, extend, or lead through, over, or across (a place): *the route passes through the city.* 3 to go through or cause to go through (an obstacle or barrier): *to pass a needle through cloth.* 4 to move or cause to move onwards or over: *he passed his hand over her face.* 5 (*tr*) to go beyond or exceed: *this victory passes all expectation.* 6 to gain or cause to gain an adequate or required mark, grade, or rating in (an examination, course, etc.): *the examiner passed them all.* 7 (often foll. by *away* or *by*) to elapse or allow to elapse: *we passed the time talking.* 8 **pass the time of day (with).** to spend time amicably (with), esp. in chatting, with no particular purpose. 9 (*intr*) to take place or happen: *what passed at the meeting?* 10 to speak or exchange or be spoken or exchanged: *angry words passed between them.* 11 to spread or cause to spread: *we passed the news round the class.* 12 to transfer or exchange or be transferred or exchanged: *the bomb passed from hand to hand.* 13 (*intr*) to undergo change or transition: *to pass from joy to despair.* 14 (when *tr,* often foll. by *down*) to transfer or be transferred by inheritance: *the house passed to the younger son.* 15 to agree to or sanction or to be agreed to or receive the sanction of a legislative body, person of authority, etc.: *the assembly passed 10 resolutions.* 16 (*tr*) (of a legislative measure) to undergo (a procedural stage) and be agreed: *the bill passed the committee stage.* 17 (when *tr,* often foll. by *on* or *upon*) to pronounce or deliver (judgment, findings, etc.): *the court passed sentence.* 18 to go or allow to go without comment or censure: *the intended insult passed unnoticed.* 19 (*intr*) to opt not to exercise a right, as by not answering a question or not making a bid or a play in card games. 20 *Physiol.* to discharge (urine, faeces, etc.) from the body. 21 **pass water.** to urinate. 22 (*intr*) to come to an end or disappear: *his anger soon passed.* 23 (*intr;* usually foll. by *for* or *as*) to be likely to be mistaken for or accepted as (someone or something else): *you could easily pass for your sister.* 24 (*intr;* foll. by *away, on,* or *over*) a euphemism for **die**[1] (sense 1). 25 (*tr*) *Chiefly U.S.* to fail to declare (a dividend). 26 (*intr;* usually foll. by *on* or *upon*) *Chiefly U.S.* (of a court, jury, etc.) to sit in judgment; adjudicate. 27 *Sport.* to hit, kick, or throw (the ball) to another player. 28 **bring to pass.** *Archaic.* to cause to happen. 29 **come to pass.** to happen. ◆ *n* 30 the act of passing. 31a a route through a range of mountains where the summit is lower or where there is a gap between peaks. 31b (*cap. as part of a name*): *the Simplon Pass.* 32 a way through any difficult region. 33 a permit, licence, or authorization to do something without restriction: *she has a pass to visit the museum on Sundays.* 34a a document allowing entry to and exit from a military installation. 34b a document authorizing leave of absence. 35 *Brit.* 35a the passing of a college or university examination to a satisfactory standard but not as high as honours. 35b (*as modifier*): *a pass degree.* ◆ Compare **honours** (sense 2). 36 a dive, sweep, or bombing or landing run by an aircraft. 37 a motion of the hand or of a wand as a prelude to or part of a conjuring trick. 38 *Informal.* an attempt, in words or action, to invite sexual intimacy (esp. in the phrase **make a pass at**). 39 a state of affairs or condition, esp. a bad or difficult one (esp. in the phrase **a pretty pass**). 40 *Sport.* the transfer of a ball from one player to another. 41 *Fencing.* a thrust or lunge with a sword. 42 *Bridge, etc.* the act of passing (making no bid). 43 *Bullfighting.* a variant of **pase.** 44 *Archaic.* a witty sally or remark. ◆ *interj* 45 *Bridge, etc.* a call indicating that a player has no bid to make. ◆ See also **pass by, pass off, pass out, pass over, pass up.** [C13: from Old French *passer* to pass, surpass, from Latin *passūs* step, PACE[1]]

pass. *abbrev. for:* 1 passive. 2 passenger. 3 passage.

passable ('pɑːsəbəl) *adj* 1 adequate, fair, or acceptable: *a passable but not outstanding speech.* 2 (of an obstacle) capable of being passed or crossed. 3 (of currency) valid for general circulation. 4 (of a proposed law) able to be ratified or enacted. ▸ '**passableness** *n*

passably ('pɑːsəblɪ) *adv* 1 fairly; somewhat. 2 acceptably; well enough: *she sings passably.*

passacaglia (ˌpæsə'kɑːljə) *n* 1 an old Spanish dance in slow triple time. 2 a slow instrumental piece characterized by a series of variations on a particular theme played over a repeated bass part. See also **chaconne** (sense 1). [C17: earlier *passacalle,* from Spanish *pasacalle* street dance, from *paso* step + *calle* street; the ending *-alle* was changed to *-aglia* to suggest an Italian origin]

passade (pæ'seɪd) *n Dressage.* the act of moving back and forth in the same place. [C17: via French from Italian *passata,* from *passare* to PASS]

passage[1] ('pæsɪdʒ) *n* 1 a channel, opening, etc., through or by which a person or thing may pass. 2 *Music.* a section or division of a piece, movement, etc. 3 a way, as in a hall or lobby. 4 a section of a written work, speech, etc., esp. one of moderate length. 5 a journey, esp. by ship: *the outward passage took a week.* 6 the act or process of passing from one place, condition, etc., to another: *passage of a gas through a liquid.* 7 the permission, right, or freedom to pass: *to be denied passage through a country.* 8 the enactment of a law or resolution by a legislative or deliberative body. 9 an evacuation of the bowels. 10 *Rare.* an exchange or interchange, as of blows, words, etc. (esp. in the phrase **passage of arms**). [C13: from Old French from *passer* to PASS]

passage[2] ('pæsɪdʒ, 'pæsɑːʒ) *Dressage.* ◆ *n* 1 a sideways walk in which diagonal pairs of feet are lifted alternately. 2 a cadenced lofty trot, the moment of suspension being clearly defined. ◆ *vb* 3 to move or cause to move at a passage. [C18: from French *passager,* variant of *passéger,* from Italian *passeggiare* to take steps, ultimately from Latin *passūs* step, PACE[1]]

passage hawk *or* **passager hawk** ('pæsɪdʒə) *n* a young hawk or falcon caught while on migration. Compare **eyas, haggard**[1] (sense 4).

passageway ('pæsɪdʒˌweɪ) *n* a way, esp. one in or between buildings; passage.

passage work *n Music.* scales, runs, etc., in a piece of music which have no structural significance but provide an opportunity for virtuoso display.

Passamaquoddy Bay (ˌpæsəmə'kwɒdɪ) *n* an inlet of the Bay of Fundy between New Brunswick (Canada) and Maine (U.S.) at the mouth of the St Croix River.

passant ('pæsənt) *adj* (*usually postpositive*) *Heraldry.* (of a beast) walking, with the right foreleg raised. [C14: from Old French, present participle of *passer* to PASS]

pass band *n* the band of frequencies that is transmitted with maximum efficiency through a circuit, filter, etc.

passbook ('pɑːsˌbʊk) *n* 1 a book for keeping a record of withdrawals from and payments into a building society. 2 another name for **bankbook.** 3 a customer's book in which is recorded by a trader a list of credit sales to that customer. 4 (formerly in South Africa) an official document serving to identify the bearer, his race, his residence, and his employment.

pass by *vb* 1 (*intr*) to go or move past. 2 (*tr, adv*) to overlook or disregard: *to pass by difficult problems.*

Passchendaele ('pæʃənˌdeɪl) *n* a village in NW Belgium, in West Flanders province: the scene of heavy fighting during the third battle of Ypres in World War I during which 245 000 British troops were lost.

passé ('pɑːseɪ, 'pæseɪ; *French* pɑse) *adj* 1 out-of-date: *passé ideas.* 2 past the prime; faded: *a passé society beauty.* [C18: from French, past participle of *passer* to PASS]

passel ('pæsəl) *n Informal or dialect, chiefly U.S.* a group or quantity of no fixed number. [variant of PARCEL]

passementerie (pæs'mɛntrɪ; *French* pɑsmɑ̃tri) *n* a decorative trimming of gimp, cord, beads, braid, etc. [C16: from Old French *passement,* from *passer* to trim, PASS]

passenger ('pæsɪndʒə) *n* 1a a person travelling in a car, train, boat, etc., not driven by him. 1b (*as modifier*): *a passenger seat.* 2 *Chiefly Brit.* a member of a group or team who is a burden on the others through not participating fully in the work. [C14: from Old French *passager* passing, from PASSAGE[1]]

passenger pigeon *n* a gregarious North American pigeon, *Ectopistes migratorius:* became extinct at the beginning of the 20th century.

passe-partout (ˌpæspɑː'tuː; *French* pɑspartu) *n* 1 a mounting for a picture in which strips of strong gummed paper are used to bind together the glass, picture, and backing. 2 the gummed paper used for this. 3 a mat, often decorated, on which a picture is mounted. 4 something that secures entry everywhere, esp. a master key. [C17: from French, literally: pass everywhere]

passepied (pɑːs'pjeɪ) *n, pl* **-pieds** (-'pjeɪ). 1 a lively minuet of Breton origin, in triple time, popular in the 17th century. 2 a piece of music composed for or in the rhythm of this dance. [C17: from French: pass the foot]

passer-by *n, pl* **passers-by.** a person that is passing or going by, esp. on foot.

passerine ('pæsəˌraɪn, -ˌriːn) *adj* 1 of, relating to, or belonging to the *Passeriformes,* an order of birds characterized by the perching habit: includes the larks, finches, crows, thrushes, starlings, etc. ◆ *n* 2 any bird belonging to the order *Passeriformes.* [C18: from Latin *passer* sparrow]

pas seul (*French* pɑ sœl) *n, pl* **pas seuls** (*French.* pɑ sœl). a dance sequence for one person. [French, literally: step on one's own]

passible ('pæsɪbəl) *adj* susceptible to emotion or suffering; able to feel. [C14: from Medieval Latin *passibilis,* from Latin *patī* to suffer; see PASSION] ▸ ˌ**pas'si'bility** *n*

passifloraceous (ˌpæsɪflɔː'reɪʃəs) *adj* of, relating to, or belonging to the *Passifloraceae,* a tropical and subtropical family of climbing plants including the passionflowers: the flowers have five petals and threadlike parts forming a dense mass (corona) around the central disc. [C19: from New Latin *Passiflora,* the type genus (passionflower)]

passim *Latin.* ('pæsɪm) *adv* here and there; throughout: used to indicate that what is referred to occurs frequently in the work cited.

passing ('pɑːsɪŋ) *adj* **1** transitory or momentary: *a passing fancy.* **2** cursory or casual in action or manner: *a passing reference.* ◆ *adv, adj* **3** *Archaic.* to an extreme degree: *the events were passing strange.* ◆ *n* **4** a place where or means by which one may pass, cross, ford, etc. **5** a euphemism for **death. 6 in passing.** by the way; incidentally: *he mentioned your visit in passing.*

passing bell *n* a bell rung to announce a death or a funeral. Also called: **death bell, death knell.**

passing note *or U.S.* **passing tone** *n Music.* a nonharmonic note through which a melody passes from one harmonic note to the next. Compare **auxiliary note.**

passing shot *n Tennis.* a winning shot hit outside an opponent's reach.

passion ('pæʃən) *n* **1** ardent love or affection. **2** intense sexual love. **3** a strong affection or enthusiasm for an object, concept, etc.: *a passion for poetry.* **4** any strongly felt emotion, such as love, hate, envy, etc. **5** a state or outburst of extreme anger: *he flew into a passion.* **6** the object of an intense desire, ardent affection, or enthusiasm. **7** an outburst expressing intense emotion: *he burst into a passion of sobs.* **8** *Philosophy.* **8a** any state of the mind in which it is affected by something external, such as perception, desire, etc., as contrasted with action. **8b** feelings, desires or emotions, as contrasted with reason. **9** the sufferings and death of a Christian martyr. [C12: via French from Church Latin *passiō* suffering, from Latin *patī* to suffer]

Passion ('pæʃən) *n* **1** the sufferings of Christ from the Last Supper to his death on the cross. **2** any of the four Gospel accounts of this. **3** a musical setting of this: *the St Matthew Passion.*

passional ('pæʃənᵊl) *adj* **1** of, relating to, or due to passion or the passions. ◆ *n* **2** a book recounting the sufferings of Christian martyrs or saints.

passionate ('pæʃənɪt) *adj* **1** manifesting or exhibiting intense sexual feeling or desire: *a passionate lover.* **2** capable of, revealing, or characterized by intense emotion: *a passionate plea.* **3** easily roused to anger; quick-tempered. ► **'passionately** *adv* ► **'passionateness** *n*

passionflower ('pæʃən,flaʊə) *n* any passifloraceous plant of the tropical American genus *Passiflora,* cultivated for their red, yellow, greenish, or purple showy flowers: some species have edible fruit. See also **granadilla.** [C17: so called from the alleged resemblance between parts of the flower and the instruments of Christ's crucifixion]

passion fruit *n* the edible fruit of any of various passionflowers, esp. granadilla.

passionless ('pæʃənlɪs) *adj* **1** empty of emotion or feeling: *a passionless marriage.* **2** calm and detached; dispassionate. ► **'passionlessly** *adv* ► **'passionlessness** *n*

Passion play *n* a play depicting the Passion of Christ.

Passion Sunday *n* the fifth Sunday in Lent (the second Sunday before Easter), when Passiontide begins.

Passiontide ('pæʃən,taɪd) *n* the last two weeks of Lent, extending from Passion Sunday to Holy Saturday.

Passion Week *n* **1** the week between Passion Sunday and Palm Sunday. **2** (formerly) Holy Week; the week before Easter.

passivate ('pæsɪ,veɪt) *vb (tr)* to render (a metal) less susceptible to corrosion by coating the surface with a substance, such as an oxide.

passive ('pæsɪv) *adj* **1** not active or not participating perceptibly in an activity, organization, etc. **2** unresisting and receptive to external forces; submissive. **3** not working or operating. **4** affected or acted upon by an external object or force. **5** *Grammar.* denoting a voice of verbs in sentences in which the grammatical subject is not the logical subject but rather the recipient of the action described by the verb, as *was broken* in the sentence *The glass was broken by a boy.* Compare **active** (sense 5a). **6** *Chem.* (of a substance, esp. a metal) apparently chemically unreactive, usually as a result of the formation of a thin protective layer that prevents further reaction. **7** *Electronics, telecomm.* **7a** containing no source of power and therefore capable only of attenuating a signal: *a passive network.* **7b** not capable of amplifying a signal or controlling a function: *a passive communications satellite.* **8** *Finance.* (of a bond, share, debt, etc.) yielding no interest. ◆ *n* **9** *Grammar.* **9a** the passive voice. **9b** a passive verb. [C14: from Latin *passīvus* susceptible of suffering, from *patī* to undergo] ► **'passively** *adv* ► **pas'sivity** *or* **'passiveness** *n*

passive obedience *n* **1** unquestioning obedience to authority. **2** the surrender of a person's will to another person.

passive resistance *n* resistance to a government, law, etc., made without violence, as by fasting, demonstrating peacefully, or refusing to cooperate.

passive smoking *n* the inhalation of smoke from other people's cigarettes by a nonsmoker. ► **passive smoker** *n*

passive vocabulary *n* all the words, collectively, that a person can understand. Compare **active vocabulary.**

passivism ('pæsɪ,vɪzəm) *n* **1** the theory, belief, or practice of passive resistance. **2** the quality, characteristics, or fact of being passive. ► **'passivist** *n, adj*

passkey ('pɑːs,kiː) *n* **1** any of various keys, esp. a latchkey. **2** another term for **master key** or **skeleton key.**

pass law *n* (formerly, in South Africa) a law restricting the movement of Black Africans, esp. from rural to urban areas.

pass off *vb (adv)* **1** to be or cause to be accepted or circulated in a false character or identity: *he passed the fake diamonds off as real.* **2** *(intr)* to come to a gradual end; disappear: *eventually the pain passed off.* **3** to emit (a substance) as a gas or vapour, or (of a substance) to be emitted in this way. **4** *(intr)* to take place: *the meeting passed off without disturbance.* **5** *(tr)* to set aside or disregard: *I managed to pass off his insult.*

pass out *vb (adv)* **1** *(intr) Informal.* to become unconscious; faint. **2** *(intr) Brit.* (esp. of an officer cadet) to qualify for a military commission; complete a course of training satisfactorily: *General Smith passed out from Sandhurst in 1933.* **3** *(tr)* to distribute.

pass over *vb* **1** *(tr, adv)* to take no notice of; disregard: *they passed me over in the last round of promotions.* **2** *(intr, prep)* to disregard (something bad or embarrassing): *we shall pass over your former faults.*

Passover ('pɑːs,əʊvə) *n* **1** Also called: **Pesach, Pesah, Feast of the Unleavened Bread.** an eight-day Jewish festival beginning on Nisan 15 and celebrated in commemoration of the passing over or sparing of the Israelites in Egypt, when God smote the firstborn of the Egyptians (Exodus 12). Related adj: **Paschal. 2** another term for the **Paschal Lamb.** [C16: from *pass over,* translation of Hebrew *pesah,* from *pāsah* to pass over]

passport ('pɑːspɔːt) *n* **1** an official document issued by a government, identifying an individual, granting him permission to travel abroad, and requesting the protection of other governments for him. **2** a licence granted by a state to a foreigner, allowing the passage of his person or goods through the country. **3** another word for **sea letter** (sense 1). **4** a quality, asset, etc., that gains a person admission or acceptance. [C15: from French *passeport,* from *passer* to PASS + PORT[1]]

pass up *vb (tr, adv)* **1** *Informal.* to let go by; ignore: *I won't pass up this opportunity.* **2** to take no notice of (someone).

passus ('pæsəs) *n, pl* **-sus** *or* **-suses.** (esp. in medieval literature) a division or section of a poem, story, etc. [C16: from Latin: step, PACE[1]]

password ('pɑːs,wɜːd) *n* **1** a secret word, phrase, etc., that ensures admission or acceptance by proving identity, membership, etc. **2** an action, quality, etc., that gains admission or acceptance. **3** a sequence of characters used to gain access to a computer system.

Passy (*French* pasi) *n* **Frédéric** (frederik). 1822–1912, French politician and economist, who campaigned for international arbitration to prevent war: shared the first Nobel peace prize 1901.

past (pɑːst) *adj* **1** completed, finished, and no longer in existence: *past happiness.* **2** denoting or belonging to all or a segment of the time that has elapsed at the present moment: *the past history of the world.* **3** denoting a specific unit of time that immediately precedes the present one: *the past month.* **4** *(prenominal)* denoting a person who has held and relinquished an office or position; former: *a past president.* **5** *Grammar.* denoting any of various tenses of verbs that are used in describing actions, events, or states that have been begun or completed at the time of utterance. Compare **aorist, imperfect** (sense 4), **perfect** (sense 8). ◆ *n* **6 the past.** the period of time or a segment of it that has elapsed: *forget the past.* **7** the history, experience, or background of a nation, person, etc.: *a soldier with a distinguished past.* **8** an earlier period of someone's life, esp. one that contains events kept secret or regarded as disreputable. **9** *Grammar.* **9a** a past tense. **9b** a verb in a past tense. ◆ *adv* **10** at a specified or unspecified time before the present; ago: *three years past.* **11** on or onwards: *I greeted him but he just walked past.* ◆ *prep* **12** beyond in time: *it's past midnight.* **13** beyond in place or position: *the library is past the church.* **14** moving beyond; in a direction that passes: *he walked past me.* **15** beyond or above the reach, limit, or scope of: *his foolishness is past comprehension.* **16** beyond or above in number or amount: *to count past ten.* **17 past it.** *Informal.* unable to perform the tasks one could do when one was younger. **18 not put it past someone.** to consider someone capable of (the action specified). [C14: from *passed,* past participle of PASS]

USAGE The past participle of *pass* is sometimes wrongly spelt *past: the time for recriminations has passed* (not *past*).

pasta ('pæstə) *n* any of several variously shaped edible preparations made from a flour and water dough, such as spaghetti. [Italian, from Late Latin: PASTE[1]]

paste[1] (peɪst) *n* **1** a mixture or material of a soft or malleable consistency, such as toothpaste. **2** an adhesive made from water and flour or starch, used esp. for joining pieces of paper. **3** a preparation of food, such as meat, that has been powdered to a creamy mass, for spreading on bread, crackers, etc. **4** any of various sweet doughy confections: *almond paste.* **5** dough, esp. when prepared with shortening, as for making pastry. **6a** Also called: **strass.** a hard shiny glass used for making imitation gems. **6b** an imitation gem made of this glass. **7** the combined ingredients of porcelain. See also **hard paste, soft paste.** ◆ *vb (tr)* **8** (often foll. by *on* or *onto*) to attach by or as if by using paste: *he pasted posters onto the wall.* **9** (usually foll. by *with*) to cover (a surface) with paper, usually attached with an adhesive: *he pasted the wall with posters.* [C14: via Old French from Late Latin *pasta* dough, from Greek *pastē* barley porridge, from *pastos,* from *passein* to sprinkle]

paste[2] (peɪst) *vb (tr) Slang.* to hit, esp. with the fists; punch or beat soundly. [C19: variant of BASTE[3]]

pasteboard ('peɪst,bɔːd) *n* **1a** a stiff board formed from layers of paper or pulp pasted together, esp. as used in bookbinding. **1b** *(as modifier): a pasteboard book cover.* **2** *Slang.* a card or ticket. ◆ *adj* **3** flimsy; insubstantial. **4** sham; fake.

pastel ('pæstᵊl, pæ'stɛl) *n* **1a** a substance made of ground pigment bound with gum, used for making sticks for drawing. **1b** a crayon of this. **1c** a drawing done in such crayons. **2** the medium or technique of pastel drawing. **3** a pale delicate colour. **4** a light prose work, esp. a poetic one. **5** another name for **woad.** ◆ *adj* **6** (of a colour) pale; delicate: *pastel blue.* [C17: via French from Italian *pastello,* from Late Latin *pastellus* woad compounded into a paste, diminutive of *pasta* PASTE[1]] ► **'pastelist** *or* **'pastellist** *n*

pastern ('pæstən) *n* **1** the part of a horse's foot between the fetlock and the hoof. **2** Also called: **fetter bone.** either of the two bones that constitute this part. [C14: from Old French *pasturon,* from *pasture* a hobble, from Latin *pāstōrius* of a shepherd, from PASTOR]

Pasternak ('pæstə,næk; *Russian* pastɪr'nak) *n* **Boris Leonidovich** (ba'ris lɪa'nidəvitʃ). 1890–1960, Russian lyric poet, novelist, and translator, noted particularly for his novel of the Russian Revolution, *Dr. Zhivago* (1957). He was awarded the Nobel prize for literature in 1958, but was forced to decline it.

paste-up *n Printing.* **1** an assembly of typeset matter, illustrations, etc., pasted on a sheet of paper or board and used as a guide or layout in the production of a publication. **2** a sheet of paper or board on which are pasted artwork, typeset matter, etc., for photographing prior to making a printing plate; another name for **camera-ready copy. 3** another name for **collage** (senses 1, 2).

Pasteur (*French* pastœr) *n* **Louis** (lwi). 1822–95, French chemist and bacteriologist. His discovery that the fermentation of milk and alcohol was caused by microorganisms resulted in the process of pasteurization. He also devised methods of immunization against anthrax and rabies and pioneered stereochemistry.

pasteurism ('pæstəˌrɪzəm, -stjə-, 'pɑː-) *n Med.* **1** a method of securing immunity from rabies in a person who has been bitten by a rabid animal, by daily injections of progressively more virulent suspensions of the infected spinal cord of a rabbit that died of rabies. **2** a similar method of treating patients with other viral infections by the serial injection of progressively more virulent suspensions of the causative virus. ◆ Also called: **Pasteur treatment.**

pasteurization *or* **pasteurisation** (ˌpæstəraɪ'zeɪʃən, -stjə-, ˌpɑː-) *n* the process of heating beverages, such as milk, beer, wine, or cider, or solid foods, such as cheese or crab meat, to destroy harmful or undesirable microorganisms or to limit the rate of fermentation by the application of controlled heat.

pasteurize *or* **pasteurise** ('pæstəˌraɪz, -stjə-,'pɑː-) *vb (tr)* **1** to subject (milk, beer, etc.) to pasteurization. **2** *Rare.* to subject (a patient) to pasteurism.

pasteurizer *or* **pasteuriser** ('pæstəˌraɪzə, -stjə-, 'pɑː-) *n* **1** an apparatus for pasteurizing substances (esp. milk). **2** a person who carries out pasteurization.

pastiche (pæ'stiːʃ) *or* **pasticcio** (pæ'stɪtʃəʊ) *n* **1** a work of art that mixes styles, materials, etc. **2** a work of art that imitates the style of another artist or period. **[C19:** French *pastiche,* Italian *pasticcio,* literally: piecrust (hence, something blended), from Late Latin *pasta* PASTE[1]**]**

pastille *or* **pastil** ('pæstɪl) *n* **1** a small flavoured or medicated lozenge for chewing. **2** an aromatic substance burnt to fumigate the air. **3** *Med.* a small coated paper disc formerly used to estimate the dose or intensity of radiation (esp. of X-rays): it changes colour when exposed. **4** a variant of **pastel** (sense 1). **[C17:** via French from Latin *pastillus* small loaf, from *pānis* bread**]**

pastime ('pɑːsˌtaɪm) *n* an activity or entertainment which makes time pass pleasantly: *golf is my favourite pastime.* **[C15:** from PASS + TIME, on the model of French *passe-temps***]**

pasting ('peɪstɪŋ) *n Slang.* a thrashing; heavy defeat.

pastis (pæ'stɪs, -'stiːs) *n* an anise-flavoured alcoholic drink. **[**from French, of uncertain origin**]**

pastitsio (pæs'tɪtsɪəʊ) *n* a Greek dish consisting of minced meat and macaroni topped with béchamel sauce. **[C20:** from Modern Greek**]**

past master *n* **1** a person with talent for, or experience in, a particular activity: *a past master of tact.* **2** a person who has held the office of master in a Freemasons' lodge, guild, etc.

Pasto (*Spanish* 'pasto) *n* a city in SE Colombia, at an altitude of 2590 m (8500 ft.). Pop.: 362 227 (1997 est.).

pastor ('pɑːstə) *n* **1** a clergyman or priest in charge of a congregation. **2** a person who exercises spiritual guidance over a number of people. **3** an archaic word for **shepherd** (sense 1). **4** Also called: **rosy pastor.** a S Asian starling, *Sturnus roseus,* having glossy black head and wings and a pale pink body. **[C14:** from Latin: shepherd, from *pascere* to feed**]** ▸ **'pastorˌship** *n*

pastoral ('pɑːstərəl) *adj* **1** of, characterized by, or depicting rural life, scenery, etc. **2** (of a literary work) dealing with an idealized form of rural existence in a conventional way. **3** (of land) used for pasture. **4** denoting or relating to the branch of theology dealing with the duties of a clergyman or priest to his congregation. **5** of or relating to a clergyman or priest in charge of a congregation or his duties as such. **6** of or relating to shepherds, their work, etc. ◆ *n* **7** a literary work or picture portraying rural life, esp. the lives of shepherds in an idealizing way. See also **eclogue. 8** *Music.* a variant of **pastorale. 9** *Christianity.* **9a** a letter from a clergyman to the people under his charge. **9b** the letter of a bishop to the clergy or people of his diocese. **9c** Also called: **pastoral staff.** the crosier or staff carried by a bishop as a symbol of his pastoral responsibilities. **[C15:** from Latin, from PASTOR**]** ▸ **'pastoralˌism** *n* ▸ **'pastorally** *adv*

pastorale (ˌpæstə'rɑːl) *n, pl* **-rales.** *Music.* **1** a composition evocative of rural life, characterized by moderate compound duple or quadruple time and sometimes a droning accompaniment. **2** a musical play based on a rustic story, popular during the 16th century. **[C18:** Italian, from Latin: PASTORAL**]**

pastoralist ('pɑːstərəlɪst) *n Austral.* a grazier or land-holder raising sheep, cattle, etc., on a large scale.

pastorate ('pɑːstərɪt) *n* **1** the office or term of office of a pastor. **2** a body of pastors; pastors collectively.

past participle *n* a participial form of verbs used to modify a noun that is logically the object of a verb, also used in certain compound tenses and passive forms of the verb in English and other languages.

past perfect *Grammar.* ◆ *adj* **1** denoting a tense of verbs used in relating past events where the action had already occurred at the time of the action of a main verb that is itself in a past tense. In English this is a compound tense formed with *had* plus the past participle. ◆ *n* **2a** the past perfect tense. **2b** a verb in this tense.

pastrami (pə'strɑːmɪ) *n* highly seasoned smoked beef, esp. prepared from a shoulder cut. **[**from Yiddish, from Romanian *pastramă,* from *păstra* to preserve**]**

pastry ('peɪstrɪ) *n, pl* **-tries. 1** a dough of flour, water, shortening, and sometimes other ingredients. **2** baked foods, such as tarts, made with this dough. **3** an individual cake or pastry pie. **[C16:** from PASTE[1]**]**

pastry cream *n* a creamy custard, often flavoured, used as a filling for éclairs, flans, etc. Also called: **pastry custard.**

pasturage ('pɑːstʃərɪdʒ) *n* **1** the right to graze or the business of grazing cattle. **2** another word for **pasture.**

pasture ('pɑːstʃə) *n* **1** land covered with grass or herbage and grazed by or suitable for grazing by livestock. **2** a specific tract of such land. **3** the grass or herbage growing on it. ◆ *vb* **4** *(tr)* to cause (livestock) to graze or (of livestock) to graze (a pasture). **[C13:** via Old French from Late Latin *pā-stūra,* from *pascere* to feed**]**

pasty[1] ('peɪstɪ) *adj* **pastier, pastiest. 1** of or like the colour, texture, etc., of paste. **2** (esp. of the complexion) pale or unhealthy-looking. ◆ *n, pl* **pasties. 3** either one of a pair of small round coverings for the nipples used by striptease dancers. ▸ **'pastily** *adv* ▸ **'pastiness** *n*

pasty[2] ('pæstɪ) *n, pl* **pasties.** a round of pastry folded over a filling of meat, vegetables, etc.: *Cornish pasty.* **[C13:** from Old French *pastée,* from Late Latin *pasta* dough**]**

PA system *n* See **public-address system.**

pat[1] (pæt) *vb* **pats, patting, patted. 1** to hit (something) lightly with the palm of the hand or some other flat surface: *to pat a ball.* **2** to slap (a person or animal) gently, esp. on the back, as an expression of affection, congratulation, etc. **3** *(tr)* to shape, smooth, etc., with a flat instrument or the palm. **4** *(intr)* to walk or run with light footsteps. **5 pat (someone) on the back.** *Informal.* to congratulate or encourage (someone). ◆ *n* **6** a light blow with something flat. **7** a gentle slap. **8** a small mass of something: *a pat of butter.* **9** the sound made by a light stroke or light footsteps. **10 pat on the back.** *Informal.* a gesture or word indicating approval or encouragement. **[C14:** perhaps imitative**]**

pat[2] (pæt) *adv* **1** Also: **off pat.** exactly or fluently memorized or mastered: *he recited it pat.* **2** opportunely or aptly. **3 stand pat. 3a** *Chiefly U.S. and Canadian.* to refuse to abandon a belief, decision, etc. **3b** (in poker, etc.) to play without adding new cards to the hand dealt. ◆ *adj* **4** exactly right for the occasion; apt: *a pat reply.* **5** too exactly fitting; glib: *a pat answer to a difficult problem.* **6** exactly right: *a pat hand in poker.* **[C17:** perhaps adverbial use ("with a light stroke") of PAT[1]**]**

pat[3] (pæt) *n* **on one's pat.** *Austral. informal.* alone; on one's own. **[C20:** rhyming slang, from *Pat* Malone**]**

Pat (pæt) *n* an informal name for an Irishman. **[**from *Patrick***]**

pat. *abbrev. for* patent(ed).

patagium (pə'teɪdʒɪəm) *n, pl* **-gia** (-dʒɪə). **1** a web of skin between the neck, limbs, and tail in bats and gliding mammals that functions as a wing. **2** a membranous fold of skin connecting margins of a bird's wing to the shoulder. **[C19:** New Latin from Latin, from Greek *patageion* gold border on a tunic**]**

Patagonia (ˌpætə'gəʊnɪə) *n* **1** the southernmost region of South America, in Argentina and Chile extending from the Andes to the Atlantic. Area: about 777 000 sq. km (300 000 sq. miles). **2** an arid tableland in the southernmost part of Argentina, rising towards the Andes in the west. ▸ **ˌPata'gonian** *adj*

patch (pætʃ) *n* **1a** a piece of material used to mend a garment or to make patchwork, a sewn-on pocket, etc. **1b** *(as modifier): a patch pocket.* **2** a small piece, area, expanse, etc. **3a** a small plot of land. **3b** its produce: *a patch of cabbages.* **4** a district for which particular officials, such as social workers or policemen, have responsibility: *he's a problem that's on your patch, John.* **5** *Pathol.* any discoloured area on the skin, mucous membranes, etc., usually being one sign of a specific disorder. **6** *Med.* **6a** a protective covering for an injured eye. **6b** any protective dressing. **7** an imitation beauty spot, esp. one made of black or coloured silk, worn by both sexes, esp. in the 18th century. **8** Also called: **flash.** an identifying piece of fabric worn on the shoulder of a uniform, on a vehicle, etc. **9** a small contrasting section or stretch: *a patch of cloud in the blue sky.* **10** a scrap; remnant. **11** a small set of instructions to correct or improve a computer program. **12 a bad patch.** a difficult or troubled time. **13 not a patch on.** *Informal.* not nearly as good as. ◆ *vb (tr)* **14** to mend or supply (a garment, etc.) with a patch or patches. **15** to put together or produce with patches. **16** (of material) to serve as a patch to. **17** (often foll. by *up*) to mend hurriedly or in a makeshift way. **18** (often foll. by *up*) to make (up) or settle (a quarrel). **19** to connect (electric circuits) together temporarily by means of a patch board. **20** (usually foll. by *through*) to connect (a telephone call) by means of a patch board. **21** *Computing.* to correct or improve (a program) by adding a small set of instructions. **[C16** *pacche,* perhaps from French *pieche* PIECE**]** ▸ **'patchable** *adj* ▸ **'patcher** *n*

patch board *or* **panel** *n* a device with a large number of sockets into which electrical plugs can be inserted to form many different temporary circuits: used in telephone exchanges, computer systems, etc. Also called: **plugboard.**

patchouli, pachouli, *or* **patchouly** ('pætʃʊlɪ, pə'tʃuːlɪ) *n* **1** any of several Asiatic trees of the genus *Pogostemon,* the leaves of which yield a heavy fragrant oil: family *Labiatae* (labiates). **2** the perfume made from this oil. **[C19:** from Tamil *paccilai,* from *paccu* green + *ilai* leaf**]**

patch pocket *n* a pocket on the outside of a garment.

patch quilt *n Irish.* a patchwork quilt.

patch test *n Med.* a test to detect an allergic reaction by applying small amounts of a suspected substance to the skin and then examining the area for signs of irritation.

patchwork ('pætʃˌwɜːk) *n* **1** needlework done by sewing pieces of different materials together. **2** something, such as a theory, made up of various parts: *a patchwork of cribbed ideas.*

patchy ('pætʃɪ) *adj* **patchier, patchiest. 1** irregular in quality, occurrence, intensity, etc.: *a patchy essay.* **2** having or forming patches. ▸ **'patchily** *adv* ▸ **'patchiness** *n*

patd *abbrev. for* patented.

pate (peɪt) *n* the head, esp. with reference to baldness or (in facetious use) intelligence. **[C14:** of unknown origin**]**

pâté ('pæteɪ; *French* pɑte) *n* **1** a spread of very finely minced liver, poultry, etc., served usually as an hors d'oeuvre. **2** a savoury pie of meat or fish. [from French: PASTE[1]]

pâté de foie gras (pɑte də fwa grɑ) *n, pl* **pâtés de foie gras** (pɑte də fwa grɑ). a smooth rich paste made from the liver of a specially fattened goose, considered a great delicacy. [French: pâté of fat liver]

patella (pəˈtɛlə) *n, pl* **-lae** (-liː). **1** *Anatomy.* a small flat triangular bone in front of and protecting the knee joint. Nontechnical name: **kneecap**. **2** *Biology.* a cuplike structure, such as the spore-producing body of certain ascomycetous fungi. **3** *Archaeol.* a small pan. [C17: from Latin, from *patina* shallow pan] ▸ **paˈtellar** *adj*

patellate (pəˈtɛlɪt, -ˌleɪt) *adj* having the shape of a patella. Also: **patelliform** (pəˈtɛlɪˌfɔːm).

paten (ˈpætᵊn), **patin,** *or* **patine** (ˈpætɪn) *n* a plate, usually made of silver or gold, esp. the plate on which the bread is placed in the Eucharist. [C13: from Old French *patene,* from Medieval Latin, from Latin *patina* pan]

patency (ˈpeɪtᵊnsɪ) *n* **1** the condition of being obvious. **2** the state of a bodily passage, duct, etc., of being open or unobstructed. **3** *Phonetics.* the degree to which the vocal tract remains unobstructed in the articulation of a speech sound. See also **closure** (sense 6).

Patenier *n* **Joachim.** See (Joachim) **Patinir.**

patent (ˈpeɪtᵊnt, ˈpætᵊnt) *n* **1a** a government grant to an inventor assuring him the sole right to make, use, and sell his invention for a limited period. **1b** a document conveying such a grant. **2** an invention, privilege, etc., protected by a patent. **3a** an official document granting a right. **3b** any right granted by such a document. **4** (in the U.S.) **4a** a grant by the government of title to public lands. **4b** the instrument by which such title is granted. **4c** the land so granted. **5** a sign that one possesses a certain quality. ◆ *adj* **6** open or available for inspection (esp. in the phrases **letters patent, patent writ**). **7** (ˈpeɪtᵊnt). obvious: *their scorn was patent to everyone.* **8** concerning protection, appointment, etc., of or by a patent or patents. **9** proprietary. **10** (esp. of a bodily passage or duct) being open or unobstructed. **11** *Biology.* spreading out widely: *patent branches.* **12** (of plate glass) ground and polished on both sides. ◆ *vb* (*tr*) **13** to obtain a patent for. **14** (in the U.S.) to grant (public land or mineral rights) by a patent. **15** *Metallurgy.* to heat (a metal) above a transformation temperature and cool it at a rate that allows cold working. [C14: via Old French from Latin *patēre* to lie open; n use, short for *letters patent,* from Medieval Latin *litterae patentes* letters lying open (to public inspection)] ▸ **ˈpatentable** *adj* ▸ **ˌpatentaˈbility** *n*

USAGE The pronunciation "ˈpætᵊnt" is heard in *letters patent* and *Patent Office* and is the usual U.S. pronunciation for all senses. In Britain "ˈpætᵊnt" is sometimes heard for senses 1, 2 and 3, but "ˈpeɪtᵊnt" is commoner and is regularly used in collocations like *patent leather.*

patentee (ˌpeɪtᵊnˈtiː, ˌpæ-) *n* a person, group, company, etc., that has been granted a patent.

patent fastener *n* (in Ireland) another name for **press stud.**

patent leather *n* leather or imitation leather processed with lacquer to give a hard glossy surface.

patent log *n Nautical.* any of several mechanical devices for measuring the speed of a vessel and the distance travelled, consisting typically of a trailing rotor that registers its rotations on a meter. Compare **chip log.**

patently (ˈpeɪtᵊntlɪ) *adv* obviously: *he was patently bored.*

patent medicine *n* a medicine, usually of low potency, protected by a patent and available without a doctor's prescription.

Patent Office (ˈpætᵊnt) *n* a government department that issues patents. Abbrev.: **Pat. Off.**

patentor (ˌpeɪtᵊnˈtɔː, ˌpæ-) *n* a person who or official body that grants a patent or patents.

patent right *n* the exclusive right granted by a patent.

Patent Rolls *pl n* (in Britain) the register of patents issued.

patent still *n* a type of still in which the distillation is continuous. [so called because a still of this type was patented in 1830]

pater (ˈpeɪtə) *n Brit.* a public school slang word for **father**: now chiefly used facetiously. [from Latin]

Pater (ˈpeɪtə) *n* **Walter** (**Horatio**). 1839–94, English essayist and critic, noted for his prose style and his advocation of the "love of art for its own sake". His works include the philosophical romance *Marius the Epicurean* (1885), *Studies in the History of the Renaissance* (1873), and *Imaginary Portraits* (1887).

paterfamilias (ˌpeɪtəfəˈmɪlɪˌæs) *n, pl* **patresfamilias** (ˌpɑːtreɪzfəˈmɪlɪˌæs). **1** the male head of a household. **2** *Roman law.* **2a** the head of a household having authority over its members. **2b** the parental or other authority of another person. [Latin: father of the family]

paternal (pəˈtɜːnᵊl) *adj* **1** relating to or characteristic of a father, esp. in showing affection, encouragement, etc.; fatherly. **2** (*prenominal*) related through the father: *his paternal grandfather.* **3** inherited or derived from the male parent. [C17: from Late Latin *paternālis,* from Latin *pater* father] ▸ **paˈternally** *adv*

paternalism (pəˈtɜːnəˌlɪzəm) *n* the attitude or policy of a government or other authority that manages the affairs of a country, company, community, etc., in the manner of a father, esp. in usurping individual responsibility and the liberty of choice. ▸ **paˈternalist** *n, adj* ▸ **paˌternalˈistic** *adj* ▸ **paˌternalˈistically** *adv*

paternity (pəˈtɜːnɪtɪ) *n* **1a** the fact or state of being a father. **1b** (*as modifier*): *a paternity suit was filed against the man.* **2** descent or derivation from a father. **3** authorship or origin: *the paternity of the theory is disputed.* [C15: from Late Latin *paternitās,* from Latin *pater* father]

paternity suit *n Law.* the U.S. (and in Britain a nontechnical) term for **affiliation proceedings.**

paternoster (ˌpætəˈnɒstə) *n* **1** *R.C. Church.* the beads at the ends of each decade of the rosary marking the points at which the Paternoster is recited. **2** any fixed form of words used as a prayer or charm. **3** Also called: **paternoster line.** a type of fishing tackle in which short lines and hooks are attached at intervals to the main line. **4** a type of lift in which platforms are attached to continuous chains. The lift does not stop at each floor but passengers enter while it is moving. [Latin, literally: our father (from the opening of the Lord's Prayer)]

Paternoster (ˌpætəˈnɒstə) *n* (*sometimes not cap.*) *R.C. Church.* **1** the Lord's Prayer, esp. in Latin. **2** the recital of this as an act of devotion. [see PATERNOSTER]

Paterson[1] (ˈpætəsᵊn) *n* a city in NE New Jersey: settled by the Dutch in the late 17th century. Pop.: 150 270 (1996 est.).

Paterson[2] (ˈpætəsᵊn) *n* **1 Andrew Barton,** known as *Banjo Paterson.* 1864–1941, Australian poet. His works include "Waltzing Matilda" and "The Man from Snowy River". **2 William.** 1658–1719, Scottish merchant and banker: founded the Bank of England (1694).

Paterson's curse *n* an Australian name for **viper's bugloss** (sense 2).

path (pɑːθ) *n, pl* **paths** (pɑːðz). **1** a road or way, esp. a narrow trodden track. **2** a surfaced walk, as through a garden. **3** the course or direction in which something moves: *the path of a whirlwind.* **4** a course of conduct: *the path of virtue.* [Old English *pæth;* related to Old High German, German *Pfad*] ▸ **ˈpathless** *adj*

path. (pæθ) *abbrev. for:* **1** pathological. **2** pathology.

-path *n combining form.* **1** denoting a person suffering from a specified disease or disorder: *neuropath.* **2** denoting a practitioner of a particular method of treatment: *osteopath.* [back formation from -PATHY]

Pathan (pəˈtɑːn) *n* a member of the Pashto-speaking people of Afghanistan, NW Pakistan, and elsewhere, most of whom are Muslim in religion. [C17: from Hindi]

pathetic (pəˈθɛtɪk) *adj* **1** evoking or expressing pity, sympathy, etc. **2** distressingly inadequate: *the old man sat huddled in front of a pathetic fire.* **3** *Brit. informal.* ludicrously or contemptibly uninteresting or worthless: *the standard of goalkeeping in amateur football today is pathetic.* **4** *Obsolete.* of or affecting the feelings. ◆ *pl n* **5** pathetic sentiments. [C16: from French *pathétique,* via Late Latin from Greek *pathetikos* sensitive, from *pathos* suffering; see PATHOS] ▸ **paˈthetically** *adv*

pathetic fallacy *n* (in literature) the presentation of inanimate objects in nature as possessing human feelings.

pathfinder (ˈpɑːθˌfaɪndə) *n* **1** a person who makes or finds a way, esp. through unexplored areas or fields of knowledge. **2** an aircraft or parachutist who indicates a target area by dropping flares, etc. **3** a radar device used for navigation or homing onto a target. ▸ **ˈpathˌfinding** *n*

pathfinder prospectus *n* a prospectus regarding the flotation of a new company that contains only sufficient details to test the market reaction.

pathic (ˈpæθɪk) *n* **1** a catamite. **2** a person who suffers; victim. ◆ *adj* **3** of or relating to a catamite. **4** of or relating to suffering. [C17: via Latin from Greek *pathikos* passive; see PATHOS]

patho- *or before a vowel* **path-** *combining form.* disease: *pathology.* [from Greek *pathos* suffering; see PATHOS]

pathogen (ˈpæθəˌdʒɛn) *or* **pathogene** (ˈpæθəˌdʒiːn) *n* any agent that can cause disease.

pathogenesis (ˌpæθəˈdʒɛnɪsɪs) *or* **pathogeny** (pəˈθɒdʒɪnɪ) *n* the origin, development, and resultant effects of a disease. ▸ **pathogenetic** (ˌpæθəudʒɪˈnɛtɪk) *adj*

pathogenic (ˌpæθəˈdʒɛnɪk) *adj* able to cause or produce disease: *pathogenic bacteria.*

pathognomonic (ˌpæθəgnəˈmɒnɪk) *adj Pathol.* characteristic or indicative of a particular disease. [C17: from Greek *pathognōmonikos* expert in judging illness, from PATHO- + *gnōmōn* judge] ▸ **ˌpathognoˈmonically** *adv*

pathognomy (pəˈθɒgnəmɪ) *n* study or knowledge of the passions or emotions or their manifestations. [C18: from PATHO- + *-gnomy,* as in PHYSIOGNOMY]

pathol. *abbrev. for:* **1** pathological. **2** pathology.

pathological (ˌpæθəˈlɒdʒɪkᵊl) *or* (*less commonly*) **pathologic** *adj* **1** of or relating to pathology. **2** relating to, involving, or caused by disease. **3** *Informal.* compulsively motivated: *a pathological liar.* ▸ **ˌpathoˈlogically** *adv*

pathology (pəˈθɒlədʒɪ) *n, pl* **-gies.** **1** the branch of medicine concerned with the cause, origin, and nature of disease, including the changes occurring as a result of disease. **2** the manifestations of disease, esp. changes occurring in tissues or organs. **3** any variant or deviant condition from normal. ▸ **paˈthologist** *n*

pathos (ˈpeɪθɒs) *n* **1** the quality or power, esp. in literature or speech, of arousing feelings of pity, sorrow, etc. **2** a feeling of sympathy or pity: *a stab of pathos.* [C17: from Greek: suffering; related to *penthos* sorrow]

pathway (ˈpɑːθˌweɪ) *n* **1** another word for **path** (senses 1, 2). **2** *Biochem.* a chain of reactions associated with a particular metabolic process.

-pathy *n combining form.* **1** indicating feeling, sensitivity, or perception: *telepathy.* **2** indicating disease or a morbid condition: *psychopathy.* **3** indicating a method of treating disease: *osteopathy.* [from Greek *patheia* suffering; see PATHOS] ▸ **-pathic** *adj combining form.*

Patiala (ˌpʌtɪˈɑːlə) *n* a city in N India, in E Punjab: seat of the Punjabi University (1962). Pop.: 238 368 (1991).

patience (ˈpeɪʃəns) *n* **1** tolerant and even-tempered perseverance. **2** the capacity for calmly enduring pain, trying situations, etc. **3** *Chiefly Brit.* any of various card games for one player only, in which the cards may be laid out in various combinations as the player tries to use up the whole pack. U.S. equivalent: **solitaire.** **4** *Obsolete.* permission; sufferance. [C13: via Old French from Latin *patientia* endurance, from *patī* to suffer]

patient (ˈpeɪʃənt) *adj* **1** enduring trying circumstances with even temper. **2** tolerant; understanding. **3** capable of accepting delay with equanimity. **4** persevering or diligent: *a patient worker.* **5** *Archaic.* admitting of a certain interpretation. ◆ *n* **6** a person who is receiving medical care. **7** *Rare.* a person or thing that is the recipient of some action. [C14: see PATIENCE] ▸ **'patiently** *adv*

patin *or* **patine** ('pætɪn) *n* variants of **paten.**

patina[1] ('pætɪnə) *n, pl* **-nas. 1** a film of oxide formed on the surface of a metal, esp. the green oxidation of bronze or copper. See also **verdigris** (sense 1). **2** any fine layer on a surface: *a patina of frost.* **3** the sheen on a surface that is caused by much handling. [C18: from Italian: coating, from Latin: PATINA[2]]

patina[2] ('pætɪnə) *n, pl* **-nae** (-ˌniː). a broad shallow dish used in ancient Rome. [from Latin, from Greek *patanē* platter]

Patinir *or* **Patenier** (ˌpɑːtɪ'nɪə) *n* **Joachim** ('jəʊəkɪm). ?1485–1524, Flemish painter, noted esp. for the landscapes in his paintings on religious themes.

patio ('pætɪˌəʊ) *n, pl* **-os. 1** an open inner courtyard, esp. one in a Spanish or Spanish-American house. **2** an area adjoining a house, esp. one that is paved and used for outdoor activities. [C19: from Spanish: courtyard]

patisserie (pə'tiːsərɪ) *n* **1** a shop where fancy pastries are sold. **2** such pastries. [C18: French, from *pâtissier* pastry cook, ultimately from Late Latin *pasta* PASTE[1]]

Patmore ('pætmɔː) *n* **Coventry** (**Kersey Dighton**). 1823–96, English poet. His works, celebrating both conjugal and divine love, include *The Angel in the House* (1854–62) and *The Unknown Eros* (1877).

Patmos ('pætmɒs) *n* a Greek island in the Aegean, in the NW Dodecanese: St John's place of exile (about 95 A.D.), where he wrote the Apocalypse. Pop.: 2650 (1995 est.). Area: 34 sq. km (13 sq. miles).

Patna ('pætnə) *n* a city in NE India, capital of Bihar state, on the River Ganges: founded in the 5th century B.C.; university (1917); centre of a rice-growing region. Pop.: 917 243 (1991).

Patna rice *n* a variety of long-grain rice, used for savoury dishes.

Pat. Off. *abbrev. for* Patent Office.

patois ('pætwɑː; *French* patwa) *n, pl* **patois** ('pætwɑːz; *French* patwa). **1** an unwritten regional dialect of a language, esp. of French, usually considered substandard. **2** the jargon of particular group. [C17: from Old French: rustic speech, perhaps from *patoier* to handle awkwardly, from *patte* paw]

Paton ('peɪtᵊn) *n* **Alan** (**Stewart**). 1903–88, South African writer, noted esp. for his novel dealing with racism and apartheid in South Africa, *Cry, the Beloved Country* (1965).

pat. pend. *abbrev. for* patent pending.

Patras (pə'træs, 'pætrəs) *n* a port in W Greece, in the NW Peloponnese on the **Gulf of Patras** (an inlet of the Ionian Sea): one of the richest cities in Greece until the 3rd century B.C.; under Turkish rule from 1458 to 1687 and from 1715 until the War of Greek Independence, which began here in 1821. Pop.: 155 180 (1991). Modern Greek name: **Pátrai** ('patrɛ).

patri- *combining form.* father: *patricide; patrilocal.* [from Latin *pater*, Greek *patēr* FATHER]

patrial ('peɪtrɪəl) *n* (in Britain formerly) a person having by statute the right of abode in the United Kingdom, and so not subject to immigration control. [C20: from Latin *patria* native land]

patriarch ('peɪtrɪˌɑːk) *n* **1** the male head of a tribe or family. Compare **matriarch** (sense 2). **2** a very old or venerable man. **3** *Old Testament.* any of a number of persons regarded as the fathers of the human race, divided into the antediluvian patriarchs, from Adam to Noah, and the postdiluvian, from Noah to Abraham. **4** *Old Testament.* any of the three ancestors of the Hebrew people: Abraham, Isaac, or Jacob. **5** *Old Testament.* any of Jacob's twelve sons, regarded as the ancestors of the twelve tribes of Israel. **6** *Early Christian Church.* the bishop of one of several principal sees, esp. those of Rome, Antioch, and Alexandria. **7** *Eastern Orthodox Church.* the bishops of the four ancient principal sees of Constantinople, Antioch, Alexandria, and Jerusalem, and also of Russia, Romania, and Serbia, the bishop of Constantinople (the **ecumenical Patriarch**) being highest in dignity among these. **8** *R.C. Church.* **8a** a title given to the pope. **8b** a title given to a number of bishops, esp. of the Uniat Churches, indicating their rank as immediately below that of the pope. **9** *Mormon Church.* another word for **Evangelist** (sense 2). **10** *Eastern Christianity.* the head of the Coptic, Armenian, Syrian Jacobite, or Nestorian Churches, and of certain other non-Orthodox Churches in the East. **11** the oldest or most venerable member of a group, community, etc.: *the patriarch of steam engines.* **12** a person regarded as the founder of a community, tradition, etc. [C12: via Old French from Church Latin *patriarcha*] ▸ **ˌpatri'archal** *adj* ▸ **ˌpatri'archally** *adv*

patriarchal cross *n* a cross with two high horizontal bars, the upper one shorter than the lower.

patriarchate ('peɪtrɪˌɑːkɪt) *n* **1** the office, jurisdiction, province, or residence of a patriarch. **2** a family or people under male domination or government.

patriarchy ('peɪtrɪˌɑːkɪ) *n, pl* **-chies. 1** a form of social organization in which a male is the head of the family and descent, kinship, and title are traced through the male line. **2** any society governed by such a system.

patrician (pə'trɪʃən) *n* **1** a member of the hereditary aristocracy of ancient Rome. In the early republic the patricians held almost all the higher offices. Compare **plebs** (sense 2). **2** a high nonhereditary title awarded by Constantine and his eastern Roman successors for services to the empire. **3** (in medieval Europe) **3a** a title borne by numerous princes including several emperors from the 8th to the 12th centuries. **3b** a member of the upper class in numerous Italian republics and German free cities. **4** an aristocrat. **5** a person of refined conduct, tastes, etc. ◆ *adj* **6** (esp. in ancient Rome) of, relating to, or composed of patricians. **7** aristocratic. **8** oligarchic and often antidemocratic or nonpopular: *patrician political views.* [C15: from Old French *patricien*, from Latin *patricius* noble, from *pater* father]

patriciate (pə'trɪʃɪɪt, -ˌeɪt) *n* **1** the dignity, position, or rank of a patrician. **2** the class or order of patricians.

patricide ('pætrɪˌsaɪd) *n* **1** the act of killing one's father. **2** a person who kills his father. ▸ **ˌpatri'cidal** *adj*

Patrick ('pætrɪk) *n* **Saint.** 5th century A.D., Christian missionary in Ireland, probably born in Britain; patron saint of Ireland. Feast day: March 17.

patriclinous (ˌpætrɪ'klaɪnəs), **patroclinous,** *or* **patroclinal** (ˌpætrə'klaɪnᵊl) *adj* (of animals and plants) showing the characters of the male parent. Compare **matriclinous.** [C20: from Latin *pater* father + *clīnāre* to incline]

patrilineal (ˌpætrɪ'lɪnɪəl) *or* **patrilinear** *adj* tracing descent, kinship, or title through the male line. ▸ **ˌpatri'lineally** *or* **ˌpatri'linearly** *adv*

patrilocal (ˌpætrɪ'ləʊkᵊl) *adj* having or relating to a marriage pattern in which the couple lives with the husband's family. ▸ **ˌpatri'locally** *adv*

patrimony ('pætrɪmənɪ) *n, pl* **-nies. 1** an inheritance from one's father or other ancestor. **2** the endowment of a church. [C14 *patrimoyne*, from Old French, from Latin *patrimonium* paternal inheritance] ▸ **patrimonial** (ˌpætrɪ'məʊnɪəl) *adj* ▸ **ˌpatri'monially** *adv*

patriot ('peɪtrɪət, 'pæt-) *n* a person who vigorously supports his country and its way of life. [C16: via French from Late Latin *patriōta*, from Greek *patriōtēs*, from *patris* native land; related to Greek *patēr* father; compare Latin *pater* father, *patria* fatherland] ▸ **patriotic** (ˌpætrɪ'ɒtɪk) *adj* ▸ **ˌpatri'otically** *adv*

Patriot ('peɪtrɪət) *n* a U.S. surface-to-air missile system with multiple launch stations and the capability to track multiple targets by radar.

patriotism ('pætrɪəˌtɪzəm) *n* devotion to one's own country and concern for its defence. Compare **nationalism.**

patristic (pə'trɪstɪk) *or* **patristical** *adj* of or relating to the Fathers of the Church, their writings, or the study of these. ▸ **pa'tristically** *adv* ▸ **pa'tristics** *n* (*functioning as sing*)

Patroclus (pə'trɒkləs) *n Greek myth.* a friend of Achilles, killed in the Trojan War by Hector. His death made Achilles return to the fight after his quarrel with Agamemnon.

patrol (pə'trəʊl) *n* **1** the action of going through or around a town, neighbourhood, etc., at regular intervals for purposes of security or observation. **2** a person or group that carries out such an action. **3** a military detachment with the mission of security, gathering information, or combat with enemy forces. **4** a division of a troop of Scouts or Guides. ◆ *vb* **-trols, -trolling, -trolled. 5** to engage in a patrol of (a place). [C17: from French *patrouiller*, from *patouiller* to flounder in mud, from *patte* paw] ▸ **pa'troller** *n*

patrol car *n* a police car with a radio telephone used for patrolling streets and motorways. See also **panda car.**

patrolman (pə'trəʊlmən) *n, pl* **-men. 1** *Chiefly U.S.* a man, esp. a policeman, who patrols a certain area. **2** *Brit.* a man employed to patrol an area to help motorists in difficulty.

patrology (pə'trɒlədʒɪ) *n* **1** the study of the writings of the Fathers of the Church. **2** a collection of such writings. [C17: from Greek *patr-*, *patēr* father + -LOGY] ▸ **patrological** (ˌpætrə'lɒdʒɪkᵊl) *adj* ▸ **pa'trologist** *n*

patrol wagon *n* the usual U.S., Austral., and N.Z. term for **Black Maria.** Also called (U.S.): **police wagon.**

patron[1] ('peɪtrən) *n* **1** a person who sponsors or aids artists, charities, etc.; protector or benefactor. **2** a customer of a shop, hotel, etc., esp. a regular one. **3** See **patron saint. 4** (in ancient Rome) the protector of a dependant or client, often the former master of a freedman still retaining certain rights over him. **5** *Church of England, etc.* a person or body having the right to present a clergyman to a benefice. [C14: via Old French from Latin *patrōnus* protector, from *pater* father] ▸ **patronal** (pə'trəʊnᵊl) *adj* ▸ **'patroness** *fem n* ▸ **'patronly** *adj*

patron[2] *French.* (patrɔ̃) *or* (*fem*) **patronne** (patrɔn) *n* a person who owns or manages a hotel, restaurant, or bar.

patron[3] ('pætərn) *n Irish.* a variant spelling of **pattern**[2].

patronage ('pætrənɪdʒ) *n* **1a** the support given or custom brought by a patron. **1b** the position of a patron. **2** (in politics) **2a** the practice of making appointments to office, granting contracts, etc. **2b** the favours so distributed. **3a** a condescending manner. **3b** any kindness done in a condescending way. **4** *Church of England, etc.* the right to present a clergyman to a benefice.

patronize *or* **patronise** ('pætrəˌnaɪz) *vb* **1** to behave or treat in a condescending way. **2** (*tr*) to act as a patron by sponsoring or bringing trade to. ▸ **'patronˌizer** *or* **'patronˌiser** *n*

patronizing *or* **patronising** ('pætrəˌnaɪzɪŋ) *adj* having a superior manner; condescending. ▸ **'patronˌizingly** *or* **'patronˌisingly** *adv*

patron saint *n* a saint regarded as the particular guardian of a country, church, trade, person, etc.

patronymic (ˌpætrə'nɪmɪk) *adj* **1** (of a name) derived from the name of its bearer's father or ancestor. In Western cultures, many surnames are patronymic in origin, as for example Irish names beginning with *O'* and English names ending with *-son;* in other cultures, such as Russian, a special patronymic name is used in addition to the surname. ◆ *n* **2** a patronymic name. [C17: via Late Latin from Greek *patrōnumikos*, from *patēr* father + *onoma* NAME]

patroon (pə'truːn) *n* (in the U.S.) a Dutch land-holder in New Netherland and New York with manorial rights in the colonial era. [C18: from Dutch: PATRON[1]] ▸ **pa'troonˌship** *n*

patsy ('pætsɪ) *n, pl* **-sies.** *Slang, chiefly U.S. and Canadian.* **1** a person who is easily cheated, victimized, etc. **2** a scapegoat. [C20: of unknown origin]

pattée ('pæteɪ, 'pætɪ) *adj* (*often postpositive*) (of a cross) having triangular arms widening outwards. [from French *patte* paw]

patten ('pætᵊn) *n* a wooden clog or sandal on a raised wooden platform or metal ring. [C14: from Old French *patin*, probably from *patte* paw]

patter[1] ('pætə) *vb* **1** (*intr*) to walk or move with quick soft steps. **2** to strike with or make a quick succession of light tapping sounds. **3** (*tr*) *Rare.* to cause to patter. ◆ *n* **4** a quick succession of light tapping sounds, as of feet: *the patter of mice.* [C17: from PAT[1]]

patter[2] (ˈpætə) *n* **1** the glib rapid speech of comedians, salesmen, etc. **2** quick idle talk; chatter. **3** the jargon of a particular group; lingo. ◆ *vb* **4** (*intr*) to speak glibly and rapidly. **5** to repeat (prayers) in a mechanical or perfunctory manner. [C14: from Latin *pater* in *Pater Noster* Our Father]

pattern[1] (ˈpætᵊn) *n* **1** an arrangement of repeated or corresponding parts, decorative motifs, etc.: *although the notes seemed random, a careful listener could detect a pattern.* **2** a decorative design: *a paisley pattern.* **3** a style: *various patterns of cutlery.* **4** a plan or diagram used as a guide in making something: *a paper pattern for a dress.* **5** a standard way of moving, acting, etc.: *traffic patterns.* **6** a model worthy of imitation: *a pattern of kindness.* **7** a representative sample. **8** a wooden or metal shape or model used in a foundry to make a mould. **9a** the arrangement of marks made in a target by bullets. **9b** a diagram displaying such an arrangement. ◆ *vb* (*tr*) **10** (often foll. by *after* or *on*) to model. **11** to arrange as or decorate with a pattern. [C14 *patron,* from Medieval Latin *patrōnus* example, from Latin: PATRON[1]]

pattern[2] *or* **patron** (ˈpætərn) *n Irish.* an outdoor assembly with religious practices, traders' stalls, etc. on the feast day of a patron saint. [C18: variant of PATRON[1]; see PATTERN[1]]

patter song *n Music.* a humorous song or aria, the text of which consists of rapid strings of words.

Patti (ˈpætɪ) *n* **Adelina** (adeˈliːna). 1843–1919, Italian operatic coloratura soprano, born in Spain.

Patton (ˈpætᵊn) *n* **George Smith.** 1885–1945, U.S. general, who successfully developed tank warfare as an extension of cavalry tactics in World War II: captured Palermo, Sicily (1942) and much of France (1944).

patty (ˈpætɪ) *n, pl* **-ties. 1** a small flattened cake of minced food. **2** a small pie. [C18: from French PÂTÉ]

patu (ˈpɑːtuː) *n, pl* **patus.** *N.Z.* a short Maori club, now used ceremonially. [Maori]

patulous (ˈpætjʊləs) *adj* **1** *Botany.* spreading widely or expanded: *patulous branches.* **2** *Rare.* gaping. [C17: from Latin *patulus* open, from *patēre* to lie open] ▸ ˈ**patulously** *adv* ▸ ˈ**patulousness** *n*

patutuki (ˈpɑːtuːˌtuːkɪ) *n N.Z.* another name for **blue cod.**

Pau (*French* po) *n* a city in SW France: residence of the French kings of Navarre; tourist centre for the Pyrenees. Pop.: 82 157 (1990).

PAU *abbrev. for* Pan American Union.

paua (ˈpɑːʊɑ) *n* an edible abalone, *Haliotis iris,* of New Zealand, having an iridescent shell used esp. for jewellery. [from Maori]

paucal (ˈpɔːkᵊl) *Grammar.* ◆ *n* **1** a grammatical number occurring in some languages for words in contexts where a few of their referents are described or referred to. ◆ *adj* **2** relating to or inflected for this number. [from Latin *paucus* few]

paucity (ˈpɔːsɪtɪ) *n* **1** smallness of quantity; insufficiency; dearth. **2** smallness of number; fewness. [C15: from Latin *paucitās* scarcity, from *paucus* few]

Paul (pɔːl) *n* **1 Saint.** Also called: **Paul the Apostle, Saul of Tarsus.** original name *Saul.* died ?67 A.D., one of the first Christian missionaries to the Gentiles, who died a martyr in Rome. Until his revelatory conversion he had assisted in persecuting the Christians. He wrote many of the Epistles in the New Testament. Feast day: June 29. Related adj: **Pauline. 2 Jean.** See **Jean Paul. 3 Les,** real name *Lester Polfuss.* born 1915, U.S. guitarist: creator of the solid-body electric guitar and pioneer in multitrack recording.

Paul I *n* **1** 1754–1801, tsar of Russia (1796–1801); son of Catherine II; assassinated. **2** 1901–64, king of the Hellenes (1947–64); son of Constantine I.

Paul III *n* original name *Alessandro Farnese.* 1468–1549, Italian ecclesiastic; pope (1534–49). He excommunicated Henry VIII of England (1538) and inaugurated the Counter-Reformation by approving the establishment of the Jesuits (1540), instituting the Inquisition in Italy, and convening the Council of Trent (1545).

Paul VI *n* original name *Giovanni Battista Montini.* 1897–1978, Italian ecclesiastic; pope (1963–1978).

pauldron (ˈpɔːldrən) *n* either of two metal plates worn with armour to protect the shoulders. [C15: from French *espauleron,* from *espaule* shoulder; see EPAULETTE]

Pauli (ˈpɔːlɪ, ˈpaʊlɪ) *n* **Wolfgang** (ˈvɒlfˌgæŋ). 1900–58, U.S. physicist, born in Austria. He formulated the exclusion principle (1924) and postulated the existence of the neutrino (1931), later confirmed by Fermi: Nobel prize for physics 1945.

Pauli exclusion principle *n Physics.* the principle that two identical fermions cannot occupy the same quantum state in a body such as an atom; sometimes shortened to **exclusion principle.**

Pauline (ˈpɔːlaɪn) *adj* relating to Saint Paul or his doctrines.

Pauling (ˈpɔːlɪŋ) *n* **Linus Carl** (ˈlaɪnəs). 1901–94, U.S. chemist, noted particularly for his work on the nature of the chemical bond and his opposition to nuclear tests: Nobel prize for chemistry 1954; Nobel peace prize 1962.

Paulinus (pɔːˈlaɪnəs) *n* **Saint.** died 644 A.D., Roman missionary to England; first bishop of York and archbishop of Rochester. Feast day: Oct. 10.

Paulinus of Nola (ˈnəʊlə) *n* **Saint.** ?353–431 A.D., Roman consul and Christian poet; bishop of Nola (409–431). Feast day: June 22.

Paul Jones *n* an old-time dance in which partners are exchanged. [C19: named after John Paul JONES]

paulownia (pɔːˈləʊnɪə) *n* any scrophulariaceous tree of the Japanese genus *Paulownia,* esp. *P. tomentosa,* having large heart-shaped leaves and clusters of purplish or white flowers. [C19: New Latin, named after Anna *Paulovna,* daughter of Paul I of Russia]

Paul Pry *n* a nosy person. [C19: from a character in the play *Paul Pry* by John Poole (1825)]

Paumotu Archipelago (pauˈməʊtuː) *n* another name for the **Tuamotu Archipelago.**

paunch (pɔːntʃ) *n* **1** the belly or abdomen, esp. when protruding. **2** another name for **rumen. 3** *Nautical.* a thick mat that prevents chafing. ◆ *vb* (*tr*) **4** to stab in the stomach; disembowel. [C14: from Anglo-Norman *paunche,* from Old French *pance,* from Latin *panticēs* (pl) bowels] ▸ ˈ**paunchy** *adj* ▸ ˈ**paunchiness** *n*

pauper (ˈpɔːpə) *n* **1** a person who is extremely poor. **2** (formerly) a destitute person supported by public charity. [C16: from Latin: poor] ▸ ˈ**pauperˌism** *n*

pauperize *or* **pauperise** (ˈpɔːpəˌraɪz) *vb* (*tr*) to make a pauper of; impoverish.

pauropod (ˈpɔːrəˌpɒd) *n* a member of the *Pauropoda,* a class of minute myriapods less than 2 mm (1/20 in.) in size, having 8 to 10 pairs of legs and branched antennae.

Pausanias (pɔːˈseɪnɪəs) *n* 2nd century A.D., Greek geographer and historian. His *Description of Greece* gives a valuable account of the topography of ancient Greece.

pause (pɔːz) *vb* (*intr*) **1** to cease an action temporarily; stop. **2** to hesitate; delay: *she replied without pausing.* ◆ *n* **3** a temporary stop or rest, esp. in speech or action; short break. **4** *Prosody.* another word for **caesura. 5** Also called: **fermata.** *Music.* a continuation of a note or rest beyond its normal length. Usual symbol: 𝄐 **6 give pause to.** to cause to hesitate. [C15: from Latin *pausa* pause, from Greek *pausis,* from *pauein* to halt] ▸ ˈ**pausal** *adj* ▸ ˈ**pauser** *n* ▸ ˈ**pausing** *n, adj*

pav (pæv) *n Austral. and N.Z. informal.* short for **pavlova.**

pavage (ˈpeɪvɪdʒ) *n* **1** *History.* a tax towards paving streets, or the right to levy such a tax. **2** the act of paving.

pavane *or* **pavan** (pəˈvɑːn, -ˈvæn, ˈpævᵊn) *n* **1** a slow and stately dance of the 16th and 17th centuries. **2** a piece of music composed for or in the rhythm of this dance, usually characterized by a slow stately triple time. [C16 *pavan,* via French from Spanish *pavana,* from Old Italian *padovana* Paduan (dance), from *Padova* Padua]

Pavarotti (*Italian* pavaˈrɔtti) *n* **Luciano.** born 1935, Italian operatic tenor, specializing in works by Verdi and Puccini.

pave (peɪv) *vb* (*tr*) **1** to cover (a road, path, etc.) with a firm surface suitable for travel, as with paving stones or concrete. **2** to serve as the material for a pavement or other hard layer: *bricks paved the causeway.* **3** (often foll. by *with*) to cover with a hard layer (of): *shelves paved with marble.* **4** to prepare or make easier (esp. in the phrase **pave the way**): *to pave the way for future development.* [C14: from Old French *paver,* from Latin *pavīre* to ram down] ▸ ˈ**paver** *n*

pavé (ˈpæveɪ) *n* **1** a paved surface, esp. an uneven one. **2** a style of setting gems so closely that no metal shows.

pavement (ˈpeɪvmənt) *n* **1** a hard-surfaced path for pedestrians alongside and a little higher than a road. U.S. and Canadian word: **sidewalk. 2** a paved surface, esp. one that is a thoroughfare. **3** the material used in paving. **4** *Civil engineering.* the hard layered structure that forms a road carriageway, airfield runway, vehicle park, or other paved areas. **5** *Geology.* a level area of exposed rock. See **limestone pavement.** [C13: from Latin *pavīmentum* a hard floor, from *pavīre* to beat hard]

Pavese (*Italian* paˈveːse) *n* **Cesare** (ˈtʃeːzare). 1908–50, Italian writer and translator. His works include collections of poems, such as *Verrà la morte e avra i tuoi occhi* (1953), short stories, such as the collection *Notte di festa* (1953), and the novel *La Luna e i falò* (1950).

Pavia (ˈpɑːvɪə) *n* a town in N Italy, in Lombardy: noted for its Roman and medieval remains, including the tomb of St Augustine. Pop.: 80 650 (1990). Latin name: **Ticinum.**

pavid (ˈpævɪd) *adj Rare.* fearful; timid. [C17: from Latin *pavidus* fearful, from *pavēre* to tremble with fear]

pavilion (pəˈvɪljən) *n* **1** *Brit.* a building at a sports ground, esp. a cricket pitch, in which players change. **2** a summerhouse or other decorative shelter. **3** a building or temporary structure, esp. one that is open and ornamental, for housing exhibitions. **4** a large ornate tent, esp. one with a peaked top, as used by medieval armies. **5** one of a set of buildings that together form a hospital or other large institution. **6** one of four main facets on a brilliant-cut stone between the girdle and the culet. ◆ *vb* (*tr*) *Literary.* **7** to place or set in or as if in a pavilion: *pavilioned in splendour.* **8** to provide with a pavilion or pavilions. [C13: from Old French *pavillon* canopied structure, from Latin *pāpiliō* butterfly, tent]

paving (ˈpeɪvɪŋ) *n* **1** a paved surface; pavement. **2** material used for a pavement. ◆ *adj* **3** of or for a paved surface or pavement. **4** preparatory, facilitating, enabling: *paving legislation.*

paving stone *n* a concrete or stone slab for paving.

paviour *or U.S.* **pavior** (ˈpeɪvjə) *n* **1** a person who lays paving. **2** a machine for ramming down paving. **3** material used for paving. [C15: from *paver,* from PAVE]

pavis *or* **pavise** (ˈpævɪs) *n* a large square shield, developed in the 15th century, at first portable but later heavy and set up in a permanent position. [C14: from Old French *pavais,* from Italian *pavese* of *Pavia,* Italian city where these shields were originally made]

Pavlodar (*Russian* pəvlaˈdar) *n* a port in NE Kazakhstan on the Irtysh River: major industrial centre with an oil refinery. Pop.: 340 700 (1995 est.).

Pavlov (ˈpævlɒv; *Russian* ˈpavləf) *n* **Ivan Petrovich** (iˈvan pɪˈtrɔvitʃ). 1849–1936, Russian physiologist. His study of conditioned reflexes in dogs influenced behaviourism. He also made important contributions to the study of digestion: Nobel prize for physiology or medicine 1904.

pavlova (pævˈləʊvə) *n* a meringue cake topped with whipped cream and fruit. [C20: named after Anna PAVLOVA]

Pavlova (pævˈləʊvə; *Russian* ˈpavləvə) *n* **Anna** (ˈannə). 1885–1931, Russian ballerina.

Pavlovian (pæv'ləuvɪən) *adj* **1** of or relating to the work of Ivan Pavlov. **2** (of a reaction or response) automatic; involuntary.

Pavo ('pɑːvəu) *n, Latin genitive* **Pavonis** (pə'vəunɪs). a small constellation near the South Pole lying between Tucana and Ara. [Latin: peacock]

pavonine ('pævəˌnaɪn) *adj* of or resembling a peacock or the colours, design, or iridescence of a peacock's tail. [C17: from Latin *pāvōnīnus*, from *pāvō* peacock]

paw (pɔː) *n* **1** any of the feet of a four-legged mammal, bearing claws or nails. **2** *Informal.* a hand, esp. one that is large, clumsy, etc. ◆ *vb* **3** to scrape or contaminate with the paws or feet. **4** (*tr*) *Informal.* to touch or caress in a clumsy, rough, or overfamiliar manner; maul. [C13: via Old French from Germanic; related to Middle Dutch *pōte*, German *Pfote*]

pawky ('pɔːkɪ) *adj* **pawkier, pawkiest.** *Dialect or Scot.* having or characterized by a dry wit. [C17: from Scottish *pawk* trick, of unknown origin] ▸ **'pawkily** *adv* ▸ **'pawkiness** *n*

pawl (pɔːl) *n* a pivoted lever shaped to engage with a ratchet wheel to prevent motion in a particular direction. [C17: perhaps from Dutch *pal* pawl]

pawn[1] (pɔːn) *vb* (*tr*) **1** to deposit (an article) as security for the repayment of a loan, esp. from a pawnbroker. **2** to stake: *to pawn one's honour.* ◆ *n* **3** an article deposited as security. **4** the condition of being so deposited (esp. in the phrase **in pawn**). **5** a person or thing that is held as a security, esp. a hostage. **6** the act of pawning. [C15: from Old French *pan* security, from Latin *pannus* cloth, apparently because clothing was often left as a surety; compare Middle Flemish *paen* pawn, German *Pfand* pledge] ▸ **'pawnage** *n*

pawn[2] (pɔːn) *n* **1** a chessman of the lowest theoretical value, limited to forward moves of one square at a time with the option of two squares on its initial move: it captures with a diagonal move only. Abbrev.: **P.** Compare **piece** (sense 12). **2** a person, group, etc., manipulated by another. [C14: from Anglo-Norman *poun*, from Old French *pehon*, from Medieval Latin *pedō* infantryman, from Latin *pēs* foot]

pawnbroker ('pɔːnˌbrəukə) *n* a dealer licensed to lend money at a specified rate of interest on the security of movable personal property, which can be sold if the loan is not repaid within a specified period. ▸ **'pawnˌbroking** *n*

Pawnee (pɔː'niː) *n* **1** (*pl* **-nees** *or* **-nee**) a member of a confederacy of related North American Indian peoples, formerly living in Nebraska and Kansas, now chiefly in Oklahoma. **2** the language of these peoples, belonging to the Caddoan family.

pawnshop ('pɔːnˌʃɒp) *n* the premises of a pawnbroker.

pawn ticket *n* a receipt for goods pawned.

pawpaw ('pɔːˌpɔː) *n* a variant of **papaw** or **papaya.**

pax (pæks) *n* **1** *Chiefly R.C. Church.* **1a** a greeting signifying Christian love transmitted from one to another of those assisting at the Eucharist; kiss of peace. **1b** a small metal or ivory plate, often with a representation of the Crucifixion, formerly used to convey the kiss of peace from the celebrant at Mass to those attending it, who kissed the plate in turn. ◆ *interj* **2** *Brit. school slang.* a call signalling an end to hostilities or claiming immunity from the rules of a game: usually accompanied by a crossing of the fingers. [Latin: peace]

Pax (pæks) *n* **1** the Roman goddess of peace. Greek counterpart: **Irene. 2** a period of general peace, esp. one in which there is one dominant nation. [Latin: peace]

PAX *abbrev. for* private automatic exchange.

Pax Romana ('pæks rəu'mɑːnə) *n* the Roman peace; the long period of stability under the Roman Empire.

Paxton ('pækstən) *n* Sir **Joseph.** 1801–65, English architect, who designed Crystal Palace (1851), the first large structure of prefabricated glass and iron parts.

pax vobiscum *Latin.* (pæks vəu'bɪskum) peace be with you.

paxwax ('pæksˌwæks) *n Dialect.* a strong ligament in the neck of many mammals, which supports the head. [C15: changed from C14 *fax wax*, probably from Old English *feax* hair of the head, *wax* growth]

pay[1] (peɪ) *vb* **pays, paying, paid. 1** to discharge (a debt, obligation, etc.) by giving or doing something: *he paid his creditors.* **2** (when *intr*, often foll. by *for*) to give (money) to (a person) in return for goods or services: *they pay their workers well; they pay by the hour.* **3** to give or afford (a person) a profit or benefit: *it pays one to be honest.* **4** (*tr*) to give or bestow (a compliment, regards, attention, etc.). **5** (*tr*) to make (a visit or call). **6** (*intr;* often foll. by *for*) to give compensation or make amends. **7** (*tr*) to yield a return of: *the shares pay 15 per cent.* **8** to give or do (something equivalent) in return; pay back: *he paid for the insult with a blow.* **9** (*tr; past tense and past participle* **paid** *or* **payed**) *Nautical.* to allow (a vessel) to make leeway. **10** *Austral. informal.* to acknowledge or accept (something) as true, just, etc. **11 pay one's way. 11a** to contribute one's share of expenses. **11b** to remain solvent without outside help. ◆ *n* **12a** money given in return for work or services; a salary or wage. **12b** (*as modifier*): *a pay slip; pay claim.* **13** paid employment (esp. in the phrase **in the pay of**). **14** (*modifier*) requiring the insertion of money or discs before or during use: *a pay phone; a pay toilet.* **15** (*modifier*) rich enough in minerals to be profitably mined or worked: *pay gravel.* ◆ See also **pay back, pay down, pay for, pay in, pay off, pay out, pay up.** [C12: from Old French *payer*, from Latin *pācāre* to appease (a creditor), from *pāx* PEACE]

pay[2] (peɪ) *vb* **pays, paying, payed.** (*tr*) *Nautical.* to caulk (the seams of a wooden vessel) with pitch or tar. [C17: from Old French *peier*, from Latin *picāre*, from *pix* pitch]

payable ('peɪəbᵊl) *adj* **1** (often foll. by *on*) to be paid: *payable on the third of each month.* **2** that is capable of being paid. **3** capable of being profitable. **4** (of a debt) imposing an obligation on the debtor to pay, esp. at once.

pay-and-display *adj* denoting a car-parking system in which a motorist buys a permit to park for a specified period from a coin-operated machine and displays the permit on or near the windscreen of his or her car so that it can be seen by a parking attendant.

pay back *vb* (*tr, adv*) **1** to retaliate against: *to pay someone back for an insult.* **2** to give or do (something equivalent) in return for a favour, insult, etc. **3** to repay (a loan). ◆ *n* **payback. 4a** the return on an investment. **4b** Also called: **payback period.** the time taken for a project to cover its outlay.

pay bed *n* an informal name for **amenity bed** or **private pay bed.**

payday ('peɪˌdeɪ) *n* the day on which wages or salaries are paid.

pay dirt *n* **1** a deposit rich enough in minerals to be worth mining. **2 strike** *or* **hit pay dirt.** *Informal.* to achieve one's objective.

pay down *vb* (*adv*) to pay (a sum of money) at the time of purchase as the first of a series of instalments.

PAYE (in Britain and New Zealand) *abbrev. for* pay as you earn; a system by which income tax levied on wage and salary earners is paid by employers directly to the government.

payee (peɪ'iː) *n* **1** the person to whom a cheque, money order, etc., is made out. **2** a person to whom money is paid or due.

payer ('peɪə) *n* **1** a person who pays. **2** the person named in a commercial paper as responsible for its payment on redemption.

pay for *vb* (*prep*) **1** to make payment (of) for. **2** (*intr*) to suffer or be punished, as for a mistake, wrong decision, etc.: *in his old age he paid for the laxity of his youth.*

pay in *vb* (*tr, adv*) to hand (money, a cheque, etc.) to a cashier for depositing in a bank, etc.

paying guest *n* a euphemism for **lodger.** Abbrev.: **PG.**

payload ('peɪˌləud) *n* **1** that part of a cargo earning revenue. **2a** the passengers, cargo, or bombs carried by an aircraft. **2b** the equipment carried by a rocket, satellite, or spacecraft. **3** the explosive power of a warhead, bomb, etc., carried by a missile or aircraft: *a missile carrying a 50-megaton payload.*

paymaster ('peɪˌmɑːstə) *n* an official of a government, business, etc., responsible for the payment of wages and salaries.

payment ('peɪmənt) *n* **1** the act of paying. **2** a sum of money paid. **3** something given in return; punishment or reward.

payment by results *n* a system of wage payment whereby all or part of the wage varies systematically according to the level of work performance of an employee.

paynim ('peɪnɪm) *n Archaic.* **1** a heathen or pagan. **2** a Muslim. [C13: from Old French *paienime*, from Late Latin *pāgānismus* paganism, from *pāgānus* PAGAN]

pay off *vb* **1** (*tr, adv*) to pay all that is due in wages, etc., and discharge from employment. **2** (*tr, adv*) to pay the complete amount of (a debt, bill, etc.). **3** (*intr, adv*) to turn out to be profitable, effective, etc.: *the gamble paid off.* **4** (*tr, adv* or *intr, prep*) to take revenge on (a person) or for (a wrong done): *to pay someone off for an insult.* **5** (*tr, adv*) *Informal.* to give a bribe to. **6** (*intr, adv*) *Nautical.* (of a vessel) to make leeway. ◆ *n* **payoff. 7** the final settlement, esp. in retribution: *the payoff came when the gang besieged the squealer's house.* **8** *Informal.* the climax, consequence, or outcome of events, a story, etc., esp. when unexpected or improbable. **9** the final payment of a debt, salary, etc. **10** the time of such a payment. **11** *Informal.* a bribe.

payola (peɪ'əulə) *n Informal, chiefly U.S.* **1** a bribe given to secure special treatment, esp. to a disc jockey to promote a commercial product. **2** the practice of paying or receiving such bribes. [C20: from PAY[1] + *-ola*, as in *Pianola*]

pay out *vb* (*adv*) **1** to distribute (money); disburse. **2** (*tr*) to release (a rope) gradually, hand over hand. **3** (*tr*) to retaliate against. ◆ *n* **payout. 4** a sum of money paid out.

pay-per-view *n* **a** a system of television broadcasting by which subscribers pay for each programme they wish to receive. **b** (*as modifier*): *a pay-per-view channel.*

payphone ('peɪˌfəun) *n* a public telephone operated by coins or a phonecard.

payroll ('peɪˌrəul) *n* **1** a list of employees, specifying the salary or wage of each. **2a** the total of these amounts or the actual money equivalent. **2b** (*as modifier*): *a payroll tax.*

Paysandú (*Spanish* paisan'du) *n* a port in W Uruguay, on the Uruguay River: the third largest city in the country. Pop.: 75 200 (1985).

Pays de la Loire (*French* pei də la lwar) *n* a region of W France, on the Bay of Biscay: generally low-lying, drained by the River Loire and its tributaries; agricultural.

payt *abbrev. for* payment.

pay television *n* a system by which television programmes are transmitted in scrambled form, unintelligible except to those who have paid for descrambling equipment. Also called: **subscription television.**

Payton ('peɪtᵊn) *n* **Walter.** born 1954, American footballer and sports administrator.

pay up *vb* (*adv*) to pay (money) promptly, in full, or on demand.

Paz (*Spanish* pas) *n* **Octavio** (ɔk'taβjo). 1914–98, Mexican poet and essayist. His poems include the cycle *Piedra de Sol* (1957) and *Blanco* (1967). Nobel prize for literature 1990.

pazzazz *or* **pazazz** (pə'zæz) *n Informal.* variants of **pizzazz.**

Pb *the chemical symbol for* lead. [from New Latin *plumbum*]

PB *abbrev. for:* **1** British Pharmacopoeia. **2** Prayer Book. **3** *Athletics.* personal best.

PBX (in Britain) *abbrev. for* private branch exchange; a telephone system that handles the internal and external calls of a building, firm, etc.

pc *abbrev. for:* **1** per cent. **2** postcard. **3** (in prescriptions) post cibum. [Latin: after meals]

PC *abbrev. for:* **1** personal computer. **2** Parish Council(lor). **3** Past Commander. **4** (in Britain) Police Constable. **5** politically correct. **6** Prince Consort. **7** (in Britain) Privy Council(lor). **8** (in Canada) Progressive Conservative.

pc. *abbrev. for:* **1** (*pl* **pcs.**) piece. **2** price.
P/C, p/c, *or* **p.c.** *abbrev. for:* **1** petty cash. **2** price current.
PCB *abbrev. for* polychlorinated biphenyl.
PCC (in Britain) *abbrev. for* Press Complaints Commission.
pcm *abbrev. for* pulse code modulation.
PCP *n* **1** *Trademark.* phencyclidine; a depressant drug used illegally as a hallucinogen. Informal name: **angel dust.** ◆ *abbrev. for* **2** *Pneumocystis carinii* pneumonia. See **pneumocystis.**
PCR *abbrev. for* polymerase chain reaction: a technique for rapidly producing many copies of a fragment of DNA for diagnostic or research purposes.
pct *U.S. abbrev. for* per cent.
PCV (in Britain) *abbrev. for* passenger carrying vehicle.
pd *abbrev. for:* **1** paid. **2** Also: **PD.** per diem. **3** potential difference.
Pd *the chemical symbol for* palladium.
PD (in the U.S.) *abbrev. for* Police Department.
pdq *Slang. abbrev. for* pretty damn quick.
PDR *abbrev. for* price-dividend ratio.
P-D ratio *n* short for price-dividend ratio.
PDSA (in Britain) *abbrev. for* People's Dispensary for Sick Animals.
pe (peɪ; *Hebrew* pe) *n* the 17th letter in the Hebrew alphabet (פ or, at the end of a word, ף) transliterated as *p* or, when final, *ph.* [from Hebrew *peh* mouth]
PE *abbrev. for:* **1** physical education. **2** potential energy. **3** Presiding Elder. **4** (esp. in addresses) Prince Edward Island (Canadian Province). **5** Also: **p.e.** printer's error. **6** *Statistics.* probable error. **7** Protestant Episcopal. ◆ **8** *international car registration for* Peru.
pea (piː) *n* **1** an annual climbing papilionaceous plant, *Pisum sativum,* with small white flowers and long green pods containing edible green seeds: cultivated in temperate regions. **2a** the seed of this plant, eaten as a vegetable. **2b** (*as modifier*): *pea soup.* **3** any of several other leguminous plants, such as the sweet pea, chickpea, and cowpea. [C17: from PEASE (incorrectly assumed to be a plural)] ▸ **'pea,like** *adj*
Peabody ('piː,bɒdɪ) *n* **George.** 1795–1869, U.S. merchant, banker, and philanthropist in the U.S. and England.
peace (piːs) *n* **1a** the state existing during the absence of war. **1b** (*as modifier*): *peace negotiations.* **2** (*modifier*) denoting a person or thing symbolizing support for international peace: *peace women.* **3** (*often cap.*) a treaty marking the end of a war. **4** a state of harmony between people or groups; freedom from strife. **5** law and order within a state; absence of violence or other disturbance: *a breach of the peace.* **6** absence of mental anxiety (often in the phrase **peace of mind**). **7** a state of stillness, silence, or serenity. **8 at peace. 8a** in a state of harmony or friendship. **8b** in a state of serenity. **8c** dead: *the old lady is at peace now.* **9 hold** *or* **keep one's peace.** to keep silent. **10 keep the peace.** to maintain or refrain from disturbing law and order. **11 make one's peace with.** to become reconciled with. **12 make peace.** to bring hostilities to an end. ◆ *vb* **13** (*intr*) *Obsolete except as an imperative.* to be or become silent or still. [C12: from Old French *pais,* from Latin *pāx*]
peaceable ('piːsəbᵊl) *adj* **1** inclined towards peace. **2** tranquil; calm. ▸ **'peaceableness** *n* ▸ **'peaceably** *adv*
Peace Corps *n* an agency of the U.S. government that sends American volunteers to developing countries, where they work on educational and other projects: established in 1961.
peace dividend *n* additional money available to a government from cuts in defence expenditure because of the end of a period of hostilities.
peaceful ('piːsfʊl) *adj* **1** not in a state of war or disagreement. **2** tranquil; calm. **3** not involving violence: *peaceful picketing.* **4** of, relating to, or in accord with a time of peace: *peaceful uses of atomic energy.* **5** inclined towards peace. ▸ **'peacefully** *adv* ▸ **'peacefulness** *n*
peacekeeping ('piːs,kiːpɪŋ) *n* **a** the maintenance of peace, esp. the prevention of further fighting between hostile forces in an area. **b** (*as modifier*): *a UN peacekeeping force.* ▸ **'peace,keeper** *n*
peacemaker ('piːs,meɪkə) *n* a person who establishes peace, esp. between others. ▸ **'peace,making** *n*
peace offering *n* **1** something given to an adversary in the hope of procuring or maintaining peace. **2** *Judaism.* a sacrificial meal shared between the offerer and Jehovah to intensify the union between them.
peace pipe *n* a long decorated pipe smoked by North American Indians on ceremonial occasions, esp. as a token of peace. Also called: **calumet, pipe of peace.**
Peace River *n* a river in W Canada, rising in British Columbia as the Finlay River and flowing northeast into the Slave River. Length: 1715 km (1065 miles).
peace sign *n* a gesture made with the palm of the hand outwards and the index and middle fingers raised in a V. See also **V-sign** (sense 2).
peacetime ('piːs,taɪm) *n* **a** a period without war; time of peace. **b** (*as modifier*): *a peacetime agreement.*
peach[1] (piːtʃ) *n* **1** a small rosaceous tree, *Prunus persica,* with pink flowers and rounded edible fruit: cultivated in temperate regions. See also **nectarine** (sense 1). **2** the soft juicy fruit of this tree, which has a downy reddish-yellow skin, yellowish-orange sweet flesh, and a single stone. See also **nectarine** (sense 2). **3a** a pinkish-yellow to orange colour. **3b** (*as adj*): *a peach dress.* **4** *Informal.* a person or thing that is especially pleasing. [C14 *peche,* from Old French, from Medieval Latin *persica,* from Latin *Persicum mālum* Persian apple]
peach[2] (piːtʃ) *vb* (*intr except in obsolete uses*) *Slang.* to inform against an accomplice. [C15: variant of earlier *apeche,* from French, from Late Latin *impedicāre* to entangle; see IMPEACH] ▸ **'peacher** *n*
peach-blow *n* **1a** a delicate purplish-pink colour. **1b** (*as adj*): *a peach-blow vase.* **2** a glaze of this colour on Oriental porcelain. [C19: from PEACH[1] + BLOW[3]]
peach brandy *n* (esp. in S. Africa) a brandy made from fermented peaches.
peach Melba *n* a dessert made of halved peaches, vanilla ice cream, and Melba sauce. [C20: named after Dame Nellie MELBA]
peachy ('piːtʃɪ) *adj* **peachier, peachiest. 1** of or like a peach, esp. in colour or texture. **2** *Informal.* excellent; fine. ▸ **'peachily** *adv* ▸ **'peachiness** *n*
peacock ('piː,kɒk) *n, pl* **-cocks** *or* **-cock. 1** a male peafowl, having a crested head and a very large fanlike tail marked with blue and green eyelike spots. Related adj: **pavonine. 2** another name for **peafowl. 3** a vain strutting person. ◆ *vb* **4** to display (oneself) proudly. **5** *Obsolete slang, Austral.* to acquire (the best pieces of land) in such a way that the surrounding land is useless to others. [C14 *pecok, pe-* from Old English *pāwa* (from Latin *pāvō* peacock) + COCK[1]] ▸ **'pea,cockish** *adj* ▸ **'pea,hen** *fem n*
Peacock ('piː,kɒk) *n* **Thomas Love.** 1785–1866, English novelist and poet, noted for his satirical romances, including *Headlong Hall* (1816) and *Nightmare Abbey* (1818).
peacock blue *n* **a** a greenish-blue colour. **b** (*as adj*): *a peacock-blue car.*
peacock butterfly *n* a European nymphalid butterfly, *Inachis io,* having reddish-brown wings each marked with a purple eyespot.
peacock ore *n* another name for **bornite.**
peacock's tail *n* a handsome brown seaweed, *Padina pavonia* (though coloured yellow-olive, red, and green) whose fan-shaped fronds have concentric bands of iridescent hairs.
pea crab *n* any of various globular soft-bodied crabs of the genus *Pinnotheres* and related genera that live commensally in the mantles of certain bivalves.
peafowl ('piː,faʊl) *n, pl* **-fowls** *or* **-fowl. 1** either of two large pheasants, *Pavo cristatus* (**blue peafowl**) of India and Ceylon and *P. muticus* (**green peafowl**) of SE Asia. The males (see **peacock** (sense 1)) have a characteristic bright plumage. **2** a rare closely related African species, *Afropavo congensis* (**Congo peafowl**), both sexes of which are brightly coloured.
peag *or* **peage** (piːg) *n* less common words for **wampum.** [shortened from Narraganset *wampompeag* WAMPUM]
pea green *n* **a** a yellowish-green colour. **b** (*as adj*): *a pea-green teapot.*
pea jacket *or* **peacoat** ('piː,kəʊt) *n* a sailor's short heavy double-breasted overcoat of navy wool. [C18: from Dutch *pijjekker,* from *pij* coat of coarse cloth + *jekker* jacket]
peak (piːk) *n* **1** a pointed end, edge, or projection: *the peak of a roof.* **2** the pointed summit of a mountain. **3** a mountain with a pointed summit. **4** the point of greatest development, strength, etc.: *the peak of his career.* **5a** a sharp increase in a physical quantity followed by a sharp decrease: *a voltage peak.* **5b** the maximum value of this quantity. **5c** (*as modifier*): *peak voltage.* **6** Also called: **visor.** a projecting piece on the front of some caps. **7a** See **widow's peak. 7b** the pointed end of a beard. **8** *Nautical.* **8a** the extreme forward (**forepeak**) or aft (**afterpeak**) part of the hull. **8b** (of a fore-and-aft quadrilateral sail) the after uppermost corner. **8c** the after end of a gaff. ◆ *vb* **9** (*tr*) *Nautical.* to set (a gaff) or tilt (oars) vertically. **10** to form or reach or cause to form or reach a peak or maximum. ◆ *adj* **11** of or relating to a period of highest use or demand, as for watching television, commuting, etc.: *peak viewing hours; peak time.* [C16: perhaps from PIKE[2], influenced by BEAK[1]; compare Spanish *pico,* French *pic,* Middle Low German *pēk*] ▸ **'peaky** *adj*
Peak District *n* a region of N central England, mainly in N Derbyshire at the S end of the Pennines: consists of moors in the north and a central limestone plateau; many caves. Highest point: 727 m (2088 ft.).
Peake (piːk) *n* **Mervyn.** 1911–68, English novelist, poet, and illustrator. In his trilogy *Gormenghast* (1946–59), he creates, with vivid imagination, a grotesque Gothic world.
peaked (piːkt) *adj* having a peak; pointed.
peak load *n* the maximum load on an electrical power-supply system. Compare **base load.**
peak programme meter *n* an instrument for assessing the maximum levels of an electrical sound signal. Abbrevs.: **PPM, ppm.**
peaky ('piːkɪ) *adj* **-kier, -kiest.** wan, emaciated, or sickly. [C16: of uncertain origin]
peal[1] (piːl) *n* **1** a loud prolonged usually reverberating sound, as of bells, thunder, or laughter. **2** *Bell-ringing.* a series of changes rung in accordance with specific rules, consisting of not less than 5000 permutations in a ring of eight bells. **3** (*not in technical usage*) the set of bells in a belfry. ◆ *vb* **4** (*intr*) to sound with a peal or peals. **5** (*tr*) to give forth loudly and sonorously. **6** (*tr*) to ring (bells) in peals. [C14 *pele,* variant of *apele* APPEAL]
peal[2] (piːl) *n* a dialect name for a grilse or a young sea trout.
pean[1] ('piːən) *n* a less common U.S. spelling of **paean.**
pean[2] (piːn) *n Heraldry.* a fur of sable spotted with or. [C16: of uncertain origin]
Peano's axioms (pɪ'ɑːnəʊz) *pl n* a set of axioms that yield the arithmetic of the natural numbers. [named after Giuseppe *Peano* (1858–1932), Italian mathematician]
peanut ('piː,nʌt) *n* Also called: **goober, goober pea** and, in Britain, **groundnut, monkey nut. a** a leguminous plant, *Arachis hypogaea,* of tropical America: widely cultivated for its edible seeds. The seed pods are forced underground where they ripen. See also **hog peanut. b** the edible nutlike seed of this plant, used for food and as a source of oil. ◆ See also **peanuts.**
peanut butter *n* a brownish oily paste made from peanuts.
peanut oil *n* oil that is made from peanut seeds and used for cooking, in soaps, and in pharmaceutical products.
peanuts ('piː,nʌts) *n Slang.* a trifling amount of money.
pear (peə) *n* **1** a widely cultivated rosaceous tree, *Pyrus communis,* having white flowers and edible fruits. **2** the sweet gritty-textured juicy fruit of this tree, which has a globular base and tapers towards the apex. **3** the wood of this tree, used for making furniture. **4 go pear-shaped.** *Informal.* to go wrong: *the plan started to go pear-shaped.* [Old English *pere,* ultimately from Latin *pirum*]

pea rifle *n* a small rifle.

pearl[1] (pɜːl) *n* **1** a hard smooth lustrous typically rounded structure occurring on the inner surface of the shell of a clam or oyster: consists of calcium carbonate secreted in layers around an invading particle such as a sand grain; much valued as a gem. Related adjs.: **margaric, margaritic. 2** any artificial gem resembling this. **3** See **mother-of-pearl. 4** a person or thing that is like a pearl, esp. in beauty or value. **5** a pale greyish-white colour, often with a bluish tinge. **6** a size of printer's type, approximately equal to 5 point. ◆ *adj* **7** of, made of, or set with pearl or mother-of-pearl. **8** having the shape or colour of a pearl. ◆ *vb* **9** (*tr*) to set with or as if with pearls. **10** to shape into or assume a pearl-like form or colour. **11** (*intr*) to dive or search for pearls. [C14: from Old French, from Vulgar Latin *pernula* (unattested), from Latin *perna* sea mussel]

pearl[2] (pɜːl) *n, vb* a variant spelling of **purl**[1] (senses 2, 3, 5).

pearl ash *n* the granular crystalline form of potassium carbonate.

pearl barley *n* barley ground into small round grains, used in cooking, esp. in soups and stews.

pearler ('pɜːlə) *n* **1** a person who dives for or trades in pearls. **2** a boat used while searching for pearls.

pearl grey *n* **a** a light bluish-grey colour. **b** (*as adj*): *pearl-grey shoes.*

Pearl Harbor *n* an almost landlocked inlet of the Pacific on the S coast of the island of Oahu, Hawaii: site of a U.S. naval base attacked by the Japanese in 1941, resulting in the U.S. entry into World War II.

pearlite ('pɜːlaɪt) *n* **1** the lamellar structure in carbon steels and some cast irons that consists of alternate plates of pure iron and iron carbide. **2** a variant spelling of **perlite.** ► **pearlitic** (pɜː'lɪtɪk) *adj*

pearlized *or* **pearlised** ('pɜːlaɪzd) *adj* having or given a pearly lustre: *a pearlized lipstick.*

pearl millet *n* a tall grass, *Pennisetum glaucum,* cultivated in Africa, E Asia, and the southern U.S. as animal fodder and for its pearly white seeds, which are used as grain.

pearl oyster *n* any of various tropical marine bivalves of the genus *Pinctada* and related genera: a major source of pearls.

Pearl River *n* **1** a river in central Mississippi, flowing southwest and south to the Gulf of Mexico. Length: 789 km (490 miles). **2** the English name for the **Zhu Jiang.**

pearlwort ('pɜːl,wɜːt) *n* any caryophyllaceous plant of the genus *Sagina,* having small white flowers that are spherical in bud.

pearly ('pɜːlɪ) *adj* **pearlier, pearliest. 1** resembling a pearl, esp. in lustre. **2** of the colour pearl; pale bluish-grey. **3** decorated with pearls or mother-of-pearl. ◆ *n, pl* **pearlies.** (in Britain) **4** a London costermonger or his wife who wear on ceremonial occasions a traditional dress of dark clothes covered with pearl buttons. **5** (*pl*) the clothes or the buttons themselves. ► **'pearliness** *n*

Pearly Gates *pl n* **1** *Informal.* the entrance to heaven. **2** (*not caps.*) *Brit. slang.* teeth.

pearly king *or* (*fem*) **pearly queen** *n* the London costermonger whose ceremonial clothes display the most lavish collection of pearl buttons. See also **pearly** (sense 4).

pearly nautilus *n* any of several cephalopod molluscs of the genus *Nautilus,* esp. *N. pompilius,* of warm and tropical seas, having a partitioned pale pearly external shell with brown stripes. Also called: **chambered nautilus.** Compare **paper nautilus.**

pearmain ('peə,meɪn) *n* any of several varieties of apple having a red skin. [C15: from Old French *permain* a type of pear, perhaps from Latin *Parmēnsis* of Parma]

Pears (pɪəz) *n* Sir **Peter.** 1910–86, British tenor, associated esp. with the works of Benjamin Britten.

Pearse (pɪəs) *n* **Patrick (Henry),** Irish name *Pádraic.* 1879–1916, Irish nationalist, who planned and led the Easter Rising (1916): executed by the British.

Pearson ('pɪəsən) *n* **1 Karl.** 1857–1936, British mathematician, noted for his work in statistics, esp. as applied to biological problems. **2 Lester B(owles).** 1897–1972, Canadian Liberal statesman; prime minister (1963–68): Nobel peace prize 1957 for helping to resolve the Suez crisis (1956).

Pearson's correlation coefficient *n* a statistic measuring the linear relationship between two variables in a sample and used as an estimate of the correlation in the whole population, given by $r = Cov(X, Y)/\sqrt{(Var(X).Var(Y))}$. In full: **Pearson's product moment correlation coefficient.** [named after Karl PEARSON]

peart (pɪət) *adj Dialect.* lively; spirited; brisk. [C15: variant of PERT] ► **'peartly** *adv* ► **'peartness** *n*

Peary ('pɪərɪ) *n* **Robert Edwin.** 1856–1920, U.S. arctic explorer, generally regarded as the first man to reach the North Pole (1909).

peasant ('pɛzᵊnt) *n* **1a** a member of a class of low social status that depends on either cottage industry or agricultural labour as a means of subsistence. **1b** (*as modifier*): *peasant dress.* **2** *Informal.* a person who lives in the country; rustic. **3** *Informal.* an uncouth or uncultured person. [C15: from Anglo-French, from Old French *païsant,* from *païs* country, from Latin *pāgus* rural area; see PAGAN]

peasantry ('pɛzᵊntrɪ) *n* **1** peasants as a class. **2** conduct characteristic of peasants. **3** the status of a peasant.

pease (piːz) *n, pl* **pease.** an archaic or dialect word for **pea.** [Old English *peose,* via Late Latin from Latin *pisa* peas, pl of *pisum,* from Greek *pison*]

pease-brose ('piːz'broz, -'brəuz) *n Scot.* brose made from a meal of dried peas.

peasecod *or* **peascod** ('piːz,kɒd) *n Archaic.* the pod of a pea plant. [C14: from PEASE + COD[2]]

pease pudding *n* (esp. in Britain) a dish of split peas that have been soaked and boiled, served with ham or pork.

peashooter ('piː,ʃuːtə) *n* a tube through which pellets such as dried peas are blown, used as a toy weapon.

peasouper (,piː'suːpə) *n* **1** *Informal, chiefly Brit.* dense dirty yellowish fog. **2** *Canadian.* a disparaging name for a **French Canadian.**

peat[1] (piːt) *n* **1a** a compact brownish deposit of partially decomposed vegetable matter saturated with water: found in uplands and bogs in temperate and cold regions and used as a fuel (when dried) and as a fertilizer. **1b** (*as modifier*): *peat bog.* **2** a piece of dried peat for use as fuel. [C14: from Anglo-Latin *peta,* perhaps from Celtic; compare Welsh *peth* thing] ► **'peaty** *adj*

peat[2] (piːt) *n* **1** *Archaic, derogatory.* a person, esp. a woman. **2** *Obsolete.* a term of endearment for a girl or woman. [C16: of uncertain origin]

peatland ('piːt,lænd) *n* an area of land consisting of peat bogs, usually containing many species of flora and fauna.

peat moss *n* any of various mosses, esp. sphagnum, that grow in wet places in dense masses and decay to form peat. Also called: **bog moss.** See also **sphagnum.**

peat reek *n* **1** the smoke of a peat fire. **2** whisky distilled over a peat fire.

peau de soie ('pəu də swɑː; *French* po də swa) *n* a rich reversible silk or rayon fabric. [literally: skin of silk]

peavey *or* **peavy** ('piːvɪ) *n, pl* **-veys** *or* **-vies.** *U.S. and Canadian.* a wooden lever with a metal pointed end and a hinged hook, used for handling logs. Compare **cant hook.** [C19: named after Joseph *Peavey,* American who invented it]

pebble ('pɛbᵊl) *n* **1a** a small smooth rounded stone, esp. one worn by the action of water. **1b** *Geology.* a rock fragment, often rounded, with a diameter of 4–64 mm and thus smaller than a cobble but larger than a granule. **2a** a transparent colourless variety of rock crystal, used for making certain lenses. **2b** such a lens. **3** (*modifier*) *Informal.* (of a lens or of spectacles) thick, with a high degree of magnification or distortion. **4a** a grainy irregular surface, esp. on leather. **4b** leather having such a surface. **5** *Informal, chiefly Austral.* a troublesome or obstinate person or animal. ◆ *vb* (*tr*) **6** to pave, cover, or pelt with pebbles. **7** to impart a grainy surface to (leather). [Old English *papolstān,* from *papol-* (perhaps of imitative origin) + *stān* stone] ► **'pebbly** *adj*

pebble dash *n Brit.* a finish for external walls consisting of small stones embedded in plaster.

pebble garden *n N.Z.* a small ornamental garden mainly composed of an arrangement of pebbles.

pebbling ('pɛblɪŋ) *n Curling.* the act of spraying the rink with drops of hot water to slow down the stone.

pec (pɛk) *n* (*usu. pl*) *Informal.* short for **pectoral muscle.**

pecan (pɪ'kæn, 'piːkən) *n* **1** a hickory tree, *Carya pecan* (or *C. illinoensis*), of the southern U.S., having deeply furrowed bark and edible nuts. **2** the smooth oval nut of this tree, which has a sweet oily kernel. [C18: from Algonquian *paccan;* related to Ojibwa *pagân* nut with a hard shell, Cree *pakan*]

peccable ('pɛkəbᵊl) *adj* liable to sin; susceptible to temptation. [C17: via French from Medieval Latin *peccābilis,* from Latin *peccāre* to sin] ► **,pecca'bility** *n*

peccadillo (,pɛkə'dɪləu) *n, pl* **-loes** *or* **-los.** a petty sin or trifling fault. [C16: from Spanish *pecadillo,* from *pecado* sin, from Latin *peccātum,* from *peccāre* to transgress]

peccant ('pɛkənt) *adj Rare.* **1** guilty of an offence; corrupt. **2** violating or disregarding a rule; faulty. **3** producing disease; morbid. [C17: from Latin *peccans,* from *peccāre* to sin] ► **'peccancy** *n* ► **'peccantly** *adv*

peccary ('pɛkərɪ) *n, pl* **-ries** *or* **-ry.** either of two piglike artiodactyl mammals, *Tayassu tajacu* (**collared peccary**) or *T. albirostris* (**white-lipped peccary**) of forests of southern North America, Central and South America: family *Tayassuidae.* [C17: from Carib]

peccavi (pɛ'kɑːviː) *n, pl* **-vis.** a confession of guilt. [C16: from Latin, literally: I have sinned, from *peccāre*]

pech (pɛx) *vb, n* a Scot. word for **pant.** [C15: of imitative origin]

Pechora (*Russian* pɪ'tʃɔrə) *n* a river in N Russia, rising in the Ural Mountains and flowing north in a great arc to the **Pechora Sea** (the SE part of the Barents Sea). Length: 1814 km (1127 miles).

peck[1] (pɛk) *n* **1** a unit of dry measure equal to 8 quarts or one quarter of a bushel. **2** a container used for measuring this quantity. **3** a large quantity or number. [C13: from Anglo-Norman, of uncertain origin]

peck[2] (pɛk) *vb* **1** (when *intr,* sometimes foll. by *at*) to strike with the beak or with a pointed instrument. **2** (*tr;* sometimes foll. by *out*) to dig (a hole) by pecking. **3** (*tr*) (of birds) to pick up (corn, worms, etc.) by pecking. **4** (*intr;* often foll. by *at*) to nibble or pick (at one's food). **5** *Informal.* to kiss (a person) quickly and lightly. **6** (*intr;* foll. by *at*) to nag. ◆ *n* **7** a quick light blow, esp. from a bird's beak. **8** a mark made by such a blow. **9** *Informal.* a quick light kiss. [C14: of uncertain origin; compare PICK[1], Middle Low German *pekken* to jab with the beak]

Peck (pɛk) *n* **Gregory.** born 1916, U.S. film actor; his films include *Keys of the Kingdom* (1944), *The Gunfighter* (1950), *The Big Country* (1958), *To Kill a Mockingbird* (1963), *The Omen* (1976), and *Other People's Money* (1991).

pecker ('pɛkə) *n* **1** *Brit. slang.* spirits (esp. in the phrase **keep one's pecker up**). **2** *Informal.* short for **woodpecker. 3** *U.S. and Canadian slang.* a taboo word for **penis.**

pecking order *n* **1** Also called: **peck order.** a natural hierarchy in a group of gregarious birds, such as domestic fowl. **2** any hierarchical order, as among people in a particular group.

Peckinpah ('pɛkɪn,pɑː) *n* **Sam(uel David).** 1926–84, U.S. film director, esp. of Westerns, such as *The Wild Bunch* (1969). Among his other films are *Straw Dogs* (1971), *Bring me the Head of Alfredo Garcia* (1974), and *Cross of Iron* (1977).

peckish ('pɛkɪʃ) *adj Informal, chiefly Brit.* feeling slightly hungry; having an appetite. [C18: from PECK[2]]

Pecksniffian (pɛk'snɪfɪən) *adj* affecting benevolence or high moral principles.

[C19: after Seth *Pecksniff,* character in *Martin Chuzzlewit* (1843), a novel by Dickens]

Pecos ('peɪkəs; *Spanish* 'pekos) *n* a river in the southwestern U.S., rising in N central New Mexico and flowing southeast to the Rio Grande. Length: about 1180 km (735 miles).

Pécs (*Hungarian* pe:tʃ) *n* an industrial city in SW Hungary: university (1367). Pop.: 161 000 (1997 est.).

pectase ('pɛkteɪs) *n* an enzyme occurring in certain ripening fruits: involved in transforming pectin into a soluble form. [C19: from PECTIN + -ASE]

pectate ('pɛkteɪt) *n* a salt or ester of pectic acid. [C19: from PECTIC ACID + -ATE[1]]

pecten ('pɛktɪn) *n, pl* **-tens** *or* **-tines** (-tɪˌni:z). **1** a comblike structure in the eye of birds and reptiles, consisting of a network of blood vessels projecting inwards from the retina, which it is thought to supply with oxygen. **2** any other comblike part or organ. **3** any scallop of the genus *Pecten,* which swim by expelling water from their shell valves in a series of snapping motions. [C18: from Latin: a comb, from *pectere,* related to Greek *pekein* to comb]

pectic acid *n* a complex acid containing arabinose and galactose that occurs in ripe fruit, beets, and other vegetables. Formula: $C_{35}H_{50}O_{33}$.

pectin ('pɛktɪn) *n Biochem.* any of the acidic hemicelluloses that occur in ripe fruit and vegetables: used in the manufacture of jams because of their ability to solidify to a gel when heated in a sugar solution (may be referred to on food labels as **E440(a)**). [C19: from Greek *pēktos* congealed, from *pegnuein* to set] ▸ **'pectic** *or* **'pectinous** *adj*

pectinate ('pɛktɪˌneɪt) *or* **pectinated** *adj* shaped like a comb: *pectinate antennae.* [C18: from Latin *pectinātus* combed; see PECTEN] ▸ **ˌpecti'nation** *n*

pectize *or* **pectise** ('pɛktaɪz) *vb* to change into a jelly; gel. [C19: from Greek *pēktos* solidified; see PECTIN] ▸ **'pectizable** *or* **'pectisable** *adj* ▸ **ˌpecti'zation** *or* **ˌpecti'sation** *n*

pectoral ('pɛktərəl) *adj* **1** of or relating to the chest, breast, or thorax: *pectoral fins.* **2** worn on the breast or chest: *a pectoral medallion.* **3** *Rare.* heartfelt or sincere. ◆ *n* **4** a pectoral organ or part, esp. a muscle or fin. **5** a medicine or remedy for disorders of the chest or lungs. **6** anything worn on the chest or breast for decoration or protection. [C15: from Latin *pectorālis,* from *pectus* breast] ▸ **'pectorally** *adv*

pectoral fin *n* either of a pair of fins, situated just behind the head in fishes, that help to control the direction of movement during locomotion.

pectoral girdle *or* **arch** *n* a skeletal support to which the front or upper limbs of a vertebrate are attached.

pectoral muscle *n* either of two large chest muscles (**pectoralis major** and **pectoralis minor**), that assist in movements of the shoulder and upper arm.

pectose ('pɛkˌtəʊz) *n* an insoluble carbohydrate found in the cell walls of unripe fruit that is converted to pectin by enzymic processes.

peculate ('pɛkjuˌleɪt) *vb* to appropriate or embezzle (public money). [C18: from Latin *pecūlārī,* from *pecūlium* private property (originally, cattle); see PECULIAR] ▸ **ˌpecu'lation** *n* ▸ **'pecuˌlator** *n*

peculiar (pɪ'kju:lɪə) *adj* **1** strange or unusual; odd: *a peculiar individual; a peculiar idea.* **2** distinct from others; special. **3** (*postpositive;* foll. by *to*) belonging characteristically or exclusively (to): *peculiar to North America.* ◆ *n* **4** Also called: **arbitrary.** *Printing.* a special sort, esp. an accented letter. **5** *Church of England.* a church or parish that is exempt from the jurisdiction of the ordinary in whose diocese it lies. [C15: from Latin *pecūliāris* concerning private property, from *pecūlium,* literally: property in cattle, from *pecus* cattle] ▸ **pe'culiarly** *adv*

peculiarity (pɪˌkju:lɪ'ærɪtɪ) *n, pl* **-ties.** **1** a strange or unusual habit or characteristic. **2** a distinguishing trait, etc. that is characteristic of a particular person; idiosyncrasy. **3** the state or quality of being peculiar.

peculiar people *pl n* **1** (*sometimes caps.*) a small sect of faith healers founded in London in 1838, having no ministers or external organization. **2** the Jews considered as God's elect.

peculium (pɪ'kju:lɪəm) *n Roman law.* property that a father or master allowed his child or slave to hold as his own. [C17: from Latin; see PECULIAR]

pecuniary (pɪ'kju:nɪərɪ) *adj* **1** consisting of or relating to money. **2** *Law.* (of an offence) involving a monetary penalty. [C16: from Latin *pecūniāris,* from *pecūnia* money] ▸ **pe'cuniarily** *adv*

pecuniary advantage *n Law.* financial advantage that is dishonestly obtained by deception and that constitutes a criminal offence.

ped. *abbrev. for:* **1** pedal. **2** pedestal.

ped- *combining form.* a variant (esp. U.S.) of **paedo-.**

-ped *or* **-pede** *n combining form.* foot or feet: *quadruped; centipede.* [from Latin *pēs, ped-* foot]

pedagogics (ˌpɛdə'gɒdʒɪks, -'gəʊ-) *n* (*functioning as sing*) another word for **pedagogy.**

pedagogue *or U.S.* (*sometimes*) **pedagog** ('pɛdəˌgɒg) *n* **1** a teacher or educator. **2** a pedantic or dogmatic teacher. [C14: from Latin *paedagōgus,* from Greek *paidagōgos* slave who looked after his master's son, from *pais* boy + *agōgos* leader] ▸ **ˌpeda'gogic** *or* **ˌpeda'gogical** *adj* ▸ **ˌpeda'gogically** *adv* ▸ **'pedaˌgogism** *or* **'pedaˌgoguism** *n*

pedagogy ('pɛdəˌgɒgɪ, -ˌgɒdʒɪ, -ˌgəʊdʒɪ) *n* the principles, practice, or profession of teaching.

pedal[1] ('pɛd[ə]l) *n* **1a** any foot-operated lever or other device, esp. one of the two levers that drive the chain wheel of a bicycle, the foot brake, clutch control, or accelerator of a car, one of the levers on an organ controlling deep bass notes, or one of the levers on a piano used to create a muted effect or sustain tone. **1b** (*as modifier*): *a pedal cycle; a pianist's pedal technique.* ◆ *vb* **-als, -alling, -alled** *or U.S.* **-als, -aling, -aled.** **2** to propel (a bicycle, boat, etc.) by operating the pedals. **3** (*intr*) to operate the pedals of an organ, piano, etc., esp. in a certain way. **4** to work (pedals of any kind). [C17: from Latin *pedālis;* see PEDAL[2]]

pedal[2] ('pi:d[ə]l) *adj* of or relating to the foot or feet. [C17: from Latin *pedālis,* from *pēs* foot]

pedalfer (pɪ'dælfə) *n* a type of zonal soil deficient in lime but containing deposits of aluminium and iron, found in wet areas, esp. those with high temperatures. Compare **pedocal.** [C20: PEDO-[2] + ALUM + *-fer,* from Latin *ferrum* iron]

pedalo ('pɛd[ə]ləʊ) *n, pl* **-los** *or* **-loes.** a pleasure craft driven by pedal-operated paddle wheels. [C20: from PEDAL[1]]

pedal point ('pɛd[ə]l) *n Music.* a sustained bass note, over which the other parts move bringing about changing harmonies. Often shortened to **pedal.**

pedal pushers *pl n* calf-length trousers or jeans worn by women.

pedal steel guitar *n* a floor-mounted, multineck, lap steel guitar with each set of strings tuned to a different open chord and foot pedals to raise or lower the pitch.

pedant ('pɛd[ə]nt) *n* **1** a person who relies too much on academic learning or who is concerned chiefly with insignificant detail. **2** *Archaic.* a schoolmaster or teacher. [C16: via Old French from Italian *pedante* teacher; perhaps related to Latin *paedagōgus* PEDAGOGUE] ▸ **pedantic** (pɪ'dæntɪk) *adj* ▸ **pe'dantically** *adv*

pedantry ('pɛd[ə]ntrɪ) *n, pl* **-ries.** the habit or an instance of being a pedant, esp. in the display of useless knowledge or minute observance of petty rules or details.

pedate ('pɛdeɪt) *adj* **1** (of a plant leaf) deeply divided into several lobes with the lateral lobes divided into smaller lobes. **2** *Zoology.* having or resembling a foot: *a pedate appendage.* [C18: from Latin *pedātus* equipped with feet, from *pēs* foot] ▸ **'pedately** *adv*

pedatifid (pɪ'dætɪfɪd, -'deɪ-) *adj* (of a plant leaf) pedately divided, with the divisions less deep than in a pedate leaf.

peddle ('pɛd[ə]l) *vb* **1** to go from place to place selling (goods, esp. small articles). **2** (*tr*) to sell (illegal drugs, esp. narcotics). **3** (*tr*) to advocate (ideas) persistently or importunately: *to peddle a new philosophy.* **4** (*intr*) *Archaic.* to trifle. [C16: back formation from PEDLAR]

peddler ('pɛdlə) *n* **1** a person who sells illegal drugs, esp. narcotics. **2** the usual U.S. spelling of **pedlar.**

-pede *n combining form.* a variant of **-ped.**

pederast *or* (*sometimes*) **paederast** ('pɛdəˌræst) *n* a man who practises pederasty.

pederasty *or* (*sometimes*) **paederasty** ('pɛdəˌræstɪ) *n* homosexual relations between men and boys. [C17: from New Latin *paederastia,* from Greek, from *pais* boy + *erastēs* lover, from *eran* to love] ▸ **ˌpeder'astic** *or* (*sometimes*) **ˌpaeder'astic** *adj*

pedes ('pɛdi:z) *n* the plural of **pes.**

pedestal ('pɛdɪst[ə]l) *n* **1** a base that supports a column, statue, etc., as used in classical architecture. **2** a position of eminence or supposed superiority (esp. in the phrases **place, put,** *or* **set on a pedestal**). **3a** either of a pair of sets of drawers used as supports for a writing surface. **3b** (*as modifier*): *a pedestal desk.* [C16: from French *piédestal,* from Old Italian *piedestallo,* from *pie* foot + *di* of + *stallo* a stall]

pedestrian (pɪ'dɛstrɪən) *n* **1a** a person travelling on foot; walker. **1b** (*as modifier*): *a pedestrian precinct.* ◆ *adj* **2** dull; commonplace: *a pedestrian style of writing.* [C18: from Latin *pedester,* from *pēs* foot]

pedestrian crossing *n Brit.* a path across a road marked as a crossing for pedestrians. See also **zebra crossing, pelican crossing.** U.S. and Canadian name: **crosswalk.**

pedestrianize *or* **pedestrianise** (pɪ'dɛstrɪəˌnaɪz) *vb* (*tr*) to convert (a street) into an area for the use of pedestrians only, by excluding all motor vehicles. ▸ **peˌdestriani'zation** *or* **peˌdestriani'sation** *n*

Pedi ('pɛdɪ) *n* **1** Also called: **Northern Sotho.** a member of a subgroup of the Sotho people resident in the Transvaal. **2** the dialect of Sotho spoken by this people.

pedi- *combining form.* indicating the foot: *pedicure.* [from Latin *pēs, ped-* foot]

pediatrician (ˌpi:dɪə'trɪʃən) *n* the U.S. spelling of **paediatrician.**

pediatrics (ˌpi:dɪ'ætrɪks) *n* the U.S. spelling of **paediatrics.**

pedicab ('pɛdɪˌkæb) *n* a pedal-operated tricycle, available for hire in some Asian countries, with an attached seat for one or two passengers.

pedicel ('pɛdɪˌsɛl) *n* **1** the stalk bearing a single flower of an inflorescence. **2** Also called: **peduncle.** *Biology.* any short stalk bearing an organ or organism. **3** the second segment of an insect's antenna. [C17: from New Latin *pedicellus,* from Latin *pedīculus,* from *pēs* foot] ▸ **pedicellate** (pɪ'dɪsɪˌleɪt) *adj*

pedicle ('pɛdɪk[ə]l) *n Biology.* any small stalk; pedicel; peduncle. [C17: from Latin *pedīculus* small foot; see PEDICEL]

pedicular (pɪ'dɪkjulə) *adj* **1** relating to, infested with, or caused by lice. **2** *Biology.* of or relating to a stem, stalk, or pedicle. [C17: from Latin *pedīculāris,* from *pedīculus,* diminutive of *pedis* louse]

pediculate (pɪ'dɪkjulɪt, -ˌleɪt) *adj* **1** of, relating to, or belonging to the *Pediculati,* a large order of teleost fishes containing the anglers. ◆ *n* **2** any fish belonging to the order *Pediculati.* [C19: from Latin *pedīculus* little foot; see PEDICEL]

pediculosis (pɪˌdɪkju'ləʊsɪs) *n Pathol.* the state of being infested with lice. [C19: via New Latin from Latin *pedīculus* louse; see PEDICULAR] ▸ **pediculous** (pɪ'dɪkjuləs) *adj*

pedicure ('pɛdɪˌkjʊə) *n* professional treatment of the feet, either by a medical expert or a cosmetician. [C19: via French from Latin *pēs* foot + *curāre* to care for]

pediform ('pɛdɪˌfɔ:m) *adj* shaped like a foot.

pedigree ('pɛdɪˌgri:) *n* **1a** the line of descent of a purebred animal. **1b** (*as modifier*): *a pedigree bull.* **2** a document recording this. **3** a genealogical table, esp. one indicating pure ancestry. **4** derivation or background: *the pedigree of* *an idea.* [C15: from Old French *pie de grue* crane's foot, alluding to the spreading lines used in a genealogical chart] ▸ **'pedi,greed** *adj*

pediment ('pɛdɪmənt) *n* **1** a low-pitched gable, esp. one that is triangular, as used in classical architecture. **2** a gently sloping rock surface, formed through denudation under arid conditions. [C16: from obsolete *periment,* perhaps workman's corruption of PYRAMID] ▸ **,pedi'mental** *adj*

pedipalp ('pɛdɪ,pælp) *n* either member of the second pair of head appendages of arachnids: specialized for feeding, locomotion, etc. [C19: from New Latin *pedipalpi,* from Latin *pēs* foot + *palpus* palp]

pedlar *or esp. U.S.* **peddler, pedler** ('pɛdlə) *n* a person who peddles; hawker. [C14: changed from *peder,* from *ped, pedde* basket, of obscure origin]

pedo-[1] *or before a vowel* **ped-** *combining form.* variants (esp. U.S.) of **paedo-**.

pedo-[2] *combining form.* indicating soil: *pedocal.* [from Greek *pedon*]

pedocal ('pɛdə,kæl) *n* a type of zonal soil that is rich in lime and characteristic of relatively dry areas. Compare **pedalfer.** [from PEDO-[2] + CAL(CIUM)]

pedology[1] (pɪ'dɒlədʒɪ) *n* a U.S. spelling of **paedology.**

pedology[2] (pɪ'dɒlədʒɪ) *n* the study of the formation, characteristics, and distribution of soils. ▸ **pedological** (,pi:də'lɒdʒɪkᵊl) *adj* ▸ **pe'dologist** *n*

pedometer (pɪ'dɒmɪtə) *n* a device containing a pivoted weight that records the number of steps taken in walking and hence the distance travelled.

pedophilia (,pi:dəʊ'fɪlɪə) *n* a variant spelling (esp. U.S.) of **paedophilia.**

Pedro I ('pɛdrəʊ) *n* 1798–1834, first emperor of Brazil (1822–31); son of John VI of Portugal: declared Brazilian independence (1822).

Pedro II *n* 1825–91, last emperor of Brazil (1831–89); son of Pedro I. He was deposed when Brazil became a republic (1889).

peduncle (pɪ'dʌŋkᵊl) *n* **1** the stalk of a plant bearing an inflorescence or solitary flower. **2** *Anatomy.* a stalklike structure, esp. a large bundle of nerve fibres within the brain. **3** *Pathol.* a slender process of tissue by which a polyp or tumour is attached to the body. **4** *Biology.* another name for **pedicel** (sense 2). [C18: from New Latin *pedunculus,* from Latin *pedīculus* little foot; see PEDICLE] ▸ **pe'duncled** *or* **peduncular** (pɪ'dʌŋkjʊlə) *adj*

pedunculate (pɪ'dʌŋkjʊlɪt, -,leɪt) *or* **pedunculated** *adj* having, supported on, or growing from a peduncle. ▸ **pe,duncu'lation** *n*

pedunculate oak *n* a large deciduous oak tree, *Quercus robur,* of Eurasia, having lobed leaves and stalked acorns. Also called: **common oak.**

pee (pi:) *Informal.* ◆ *vb* **pees, peeing, peed. 1** (*intr*) to urinate. ◆ *n* **2** urine. **3** the act of urinating. [C18: a euphemism for PISS, based on the initial letter]

Peebles ('pi:bᵊlz) *n* a town in SE Scotland, in Scottish Borders. Pop.: 7065 (1991).

Peeblesshire ('pi:bᵊlz,ʃɪə, -ʃə) *n* (until 1975) a county of SE Scotland, now part of Scottish Borders. Also called: **Tweeddale.**

peek (pi:k) *vb* **1** (*intr*) to glance quickly or furtively; peep. ◆ *n* **2** a quick or furtive glance. [C14 *pike,* related to Middle Dutch *kiken* to peek]

peekaboo ('pi:kə,bu:) *n* **1** a game for young children, in which one person hides his face and suddenly reveals it and cries "peekaboo." ◆ *adj* **2** (of a garment) made of fabric that is almost transparent or patterned with small holes. [C16: from PEEK + BOO]

peel[1] (pi:l) *vb* **1** (*tr*) to remove (the skin, rind, outer covering, etc.) of (a fruit, egg, etc.). **2** (*intr*) (of paint, etc.) to be removed from a surface, esp. through weathering. **3** (*intr*) (of a surface) to lose its outer covering of paint, etc. esp. through weathering. **4** (*intr*) (of a person or part of the body) to shed skin in flakes or (of skin) to be shed in flakes, esp. as a result of sunburn. **5** *Croquet.* to put (another player's ball) through a hoop or hoops. **6 keep one's eyes peeled** (*or* **skinned**). to watch vigilantly. ◆ *n* **7** the skin or rind of a fruit, etc. ◆ See also **peel off.** [Old English *pilian* to strip off the outer layer, from Latin *pilāre* to make bald, from *pilus* a hair]

peel[2] (pi:l) *n* a long-handled shovel used by bakers for moving bread, in an oven. [C14 *pele,* from Old French, from Latin *pāla* spade, from *pangere* to drive in; see PALETTE]

peel[3] (pi:l) *n* (in Britain) a fortified tower of the 16th century on the borders between England and Scotland, built to withstand raids. [C14 (fence made of stakes): from Old French *piel* stake, from Latin *pālus;* see PALE[2], PALING]

Peel (pi:l) *n* Sir **Robert.** 1788–1850, British statesman; Conservative prime minister (1834–35; 1841–46). As Home Secretary (1828–30) he founded the Metropolitan Police and in his second ministry carried through a series of free-trade budgets culminating in the repeal of the Corn Laws (1846), which split the Tory party. ▸ **'Peelite** *n*

Peele (pi:l) *n* **George.** ?1556–?96, English dramatist and poet. His works include the pastoral drama *The Arraignment of Paris* (1584) and the comedy *The Old Wives' Tale* (1595).

peeler[1] ('pi:lə) *n* **1** a special knife or mechanical device for peeling vegetables, fruit, etc.: *a potato peeler.* **2** *U.S. slang.* a striptease dancer.

peeler[2] ('pi:lə) *n Irish and obsolete Brit. slang.* another word for **policeman.** [C19: from the founder of the police force, Sir Robert PEEL]

peeling ('pi:lɪŋ) *n* a strip of skin, rind, bark, etc., that has been peeled off: *a potato peeling.*

peel off *vb* (*adv*) **1** to remove or be removed by peeling. **2** (*intr*) *Slang.* to undress. **3** (*intr*) (of an aircraft) to turn away as by banking, and leave a formation. **4** *Slang.* to go away or cause to go away.

peely-wally *or* **peelie-wallie** ('pi:lɪ'wælɪ) *adj Scot. urban dialect.* off colour; pale and ill-looking: *he's a wee bit peely-wally this morning.* [apparently a reduplicated form of WALLY[2] in the sense: faded]

peen (pi:n) *n* **1** the end of a hammer head opposite the striking face, often rounded or wedge-shaped. ◆ *vb* **2** (*tr*) to strike with the peen of a hammer or with a stream of metal shot in order to bend or shape (a sheet of metal). [C17: variant of *pane,* perhaps from French *panne,* ultimately from Latin *pinna* point]

Peenemünde (,pi:nə'mʊndə) *n* a village in N Germany, in Mecklenburg-West Pomerania on the Baltic coast: site of a German rocket-development centre in World War II.

peep[1] (pi:p) *vb* (*intr*) **1** to look furtively or secretly, as through a small aperture or from a hidden place. **2** to appear partially or briefly: *the sun peeped through the clouds.* ◆ *n* **3** a quick or furtive look. **4** the first appearance: *the peep of dawn.* [C15: variant of PEEK]

peep[2] (pi:p) *vb* (*intr*) **1** (esp. of young birds) to utter shrill small noises. **2** to speak in a thin shrill voice. ◆ *n* **3** a peeping sound. **4** *U.S.* any of various small sandpipers of the genus *Calidris* (or *Erolia*) and related genera, such as the pectoral sandpiper. [C15: of imitative origin]

peeper ('pi:pə) *n* **1** a person who peeps. **2** (*often pl*) a slang word for **eye**[1] (sense 1).

peephole ('pi:p,həʊl) *n* a small aperture, such as one in the door of a flat for observing callers before opening.

Peeping Tom *n* a man who furtively observes women undressing; voyeur. [C19: after the tailor who, according to legend, peeped at Lady Godiva when she rode naked through Coventry]

peepshow ('pi:p,ʃəʊ) *n* **1** Also called: **raree show.** a small box with a peephole through which a series of pictures, esp. of erotic poses, can be seen. **2** a booth from which a viewer can see a live nude model for a fee.

peep sight *n* an adjustable rear gun sight with a narrow aperture through which the target and the front sight are aligned when aiming.

peepul ('pi:pᵊl) *or* **pipal** *n* an Indian moraceous tree, *Ficus religiosa,* resembling the banyan: regarded as sacred by Buddhists. Also called: **bo tree.** [C18: from Hindi *pīpal,* from Sanskrit *pippala*]

peer[1] (pɪə) *n* **1** a member of a nobility; nobleman. **2** a person who holds any of the five grades of the British nobility: duke, marquess, earl, viscount, and baron. See also **life peer. 3** a person who is an equal in social standing, rank, age, etc.: *to be tried by one's peers.* **4** *Archaic.* a companion; mate. [C14 (in sense 3): from Old French *per,* from Latin *pār* equal]

peer[2] (pɪə) *vb* (*intr*) **1** to look intently with or as if with difficulty: *to peer into the distance.* **2** to appear partially or dimly: *the sun peered through the fog.* [C16: from Flemish *pieren* to look with narrowed eyes]

peerage ('pɪərɪdʒ) *n* **1** the whole body of peers; aristocracy. **2** the position, rank, or title of a peer. **3** (esp. in the British Isles) a book listing the peers and giving genealogical and other information about them.

peeress ('pɪərɪs) *n* **1** the wife or widow of a peer. **2** a woman holding the rank of a peer in her own right.

peer group *n* a social group composed of individuals of approximately the same age.

peerie[1] ('pi:rɪ) *n Scot.* a spinning top. [C19: perhaps from *peir* a Scot. variant of *pear,* alluding to the top's shape]

peerie[2] ('pi:rɪ) *adj Orkney and Shetland dialect.* small. [C19: of uncertain origin; perhaps from Norwegian dialect *piren* niggardly, thin]

peerless ('pɪəlɪs) *adj* having no equals; matchless.

peer of the realm *n, pl* **peers of the realm.** (in Great Britain and Northern Ireland) any member of the nobility entitled to sit in the House of Lords.

peetweet ('pi:t,wi:t) *n U.S.* another name for the **spotted sandpiper.** [C19: imitative of its cry]

peeve (pi:v) *Informal.* ◆ *vb* **1** (*tr*) to irritate; vex; annoy. ◆ *n* **2** something that irritates; vexation: *it was a pet peeve of his.* [C20: back formation from PEEVISH] ▸ **peeved** *adj*

peevers ('pi:vərz) *or* **peever** *n* (*functioning as sing*) *Scot. dialect.* hopscotch. [from *peever* (the stone used in the game), of obscure origin]

peevish ('pi:vɪʃ) *adj* **1** fretful or irritable: *a peevish child.* **2** *Obsolete.* perverse. [C14: of unknown origin] ▸ **'peevishly** *adv* ▸ **'peevishness** *n*

peewee ('pi:wi:) *n* **1** a variant spelling of **pewee. 2** a variant (esp. Scot.) of **peewit. 3** *Austral.* another name for **magpie lark.**

peewit ('pi:wɪt) *n* another name for **lapwing.** [C16: imitative of its call]

peg (pɛg) *n* **1** a small cylindrical pin or dowel, sometimes slightly tapered, used to join two parts together. **2** a pin pushed or driven into a surface: used to mark scores, define limits, support coats, etc. **3** *Music.* any of several pins passing through the head (**peg box**) of a stringed instrument, which can be turned so as to tune strings wound around them. See also **pin** (sense 11). **4** Also called: **clothes peg.** *Brit.* a split or hinged pin for fastening wet clothes to a line to dry. U.S. and Canadian equivalent: **clothespin. 5** *Brit.* a small drink of wine or spirits, esp. of brandy or whisky and soda. **6** an opportunity or pretext for doing something: *a peg on which to hang a theory.* **7** a mountaineering piton. **8** *Croquet.* a post that a player's ball must strike to win the game. **9** *Angling.* a fishing station allotted to an angler in a competition, marked by a peg in the ground. **10** *Informal.* a level of self-esteem, importance, etc. (esp. in the phrases **bring** *or* **take down a peg**). **11** *Informal.* See **peg leg. 12 off the peg.** *Chiefly Brit.* (of clothes) ready to wear, as opposed to tailor-made. ◆ *vb* **pegs, pegging, pegged. 13** (*tr*) to knock or insert a peg into or pierce with a peg. **14** (*tr;* sometimes foll. by *down*) to secure with pegs: *to peg a tent.* **15** *Mountaineering.* to insert or use pitons. **16** (*tr*) to mark (a score) with pegs, as in some card games. **17** (*tr*) *Informal.* to aim and throw (missiles) at a target. **18** (*intr;* foll. by *away, along,* etc.) *Chiefly Brit.* to work steadily: *he pegged away at his job for years.* **19** (*tr*) to stabilize (the price of a commodity, an exchange rate, etc.) by legislation or market operations. ◆ See also **peg down, peg out.** [C15: from Low Germanic *pegge*]

Pegasus[1] ('pɛgəsəs) *n Greek myth.* an immortal winged horse, which sprang from the blood of the slain Medusa and enabled Bellerophon to achieve many great deeds as his rider.

Pegasus[2] ('pɛgəsəs) *n, Latin genitive* **Pegasi** ('pɛgə,saɪ). a constellation in the N hemisphere lying close to Andromeda and Pisces.

pegboard ('pɛg,bɔ:d) *n* **1** a board having a pattern of holes into which small pegs can be fitted, used for playing certain games or keeping a score. **2** another name for **solitaire** (sense 1). **3** hardboard perforated by a pattern of holes in which articles may be pegged or hung, as for display.

peg climbing *n* another name for **aid climbing.**

peg down *vb (tr, adv)* to make (a person) committed to a course of action or bound to follow rules: *you won't peg him down to any decision.*

pegging ('pɛgɪŋ) *n* another name for **aid climbing.**

peg leg *n Informal.* **1** an artificial leg, esp. one made of wood. **2** a person with an artificial leg.

pegmatite ('pɛgməˌtaɪt) *n* any of a class of coarse-grained intrusive igneous rocks consisting chiefly of quartz and feldspar: usually occur as dykes among igneous rocks of finer grain. [C19: from Greek *pegma* something joined together] ▸ **pegmatitic** (ˌpɛgmə'tɪtɪk) *adj*

peg out *vb (adv)* **1** *(intr) Informal.* to collapse or die. **2** *Croquet.* **2a** *(intr)* to win a game by hitting the peg. **2b** *(tr)* to cause (an opponent's ball) to hit the peg, rendering it out of the game. **3** *(intr) Cribbage.* to score the point that wins the game. **4** *(tr)* to mark or secure with pegs: *to peg out one's claims to a piece of land.*

peg top *n* a child's spinning top, usually made of wood with a metal centre pin.

peg-top *adj* (of skirts, trousers, etc.) wide at the hips then tapering off towards the ankle.

Pegu (pɛ'gu:) *n* a city in S Myanmar: capital of a united Burma (16th century). Pop.: 150 447 (latest est.).

Péguy *(French* pegi) *n* **Charles** (ʃarl). 1873–1914, French poet and essayist, whose works include *Le Mystère de la charité de Jeanne d'Arc* (1910); founder of the journal *Cahiers de la quinzaine* (1900–14): killed in World War I.

Pehlevi ('peɪləvɪ) *n* a variant of **Pahlavi**[2].

Pei (peɪ) *n* **I(eoh) M(ing).** born 1917, U.S. architect, born in China. His buildings include the E wing of the National Museum of Art, Washington DC (1978), a glass and steel pyramid at the Louvre, Paris (1989), and the Rock and Roll Hall of Fame, Cleveland, U.S.A. (1995).

PEI *abbrev. for* Prince Edward Island.

peignoir ('peɪnwɑ:) *n* a woman's dressing gown or negligee. [C19: from French, from *peigner* to comb, since the garment was worn while the hair was combed]

Peipus ('paɪpəs) *n* a lake in W Russia, on the boundary with Estonia: drains into the Gulf of Finland. Area: 3512 sq. km (1356 sq. miles). Russian name: **Chudskoye Ozero.**

Peiraeus (paɪ'ri:əs, pɪ'reɪ-) *n* a variant spelling of **Piraeus.**

Peirce (pɪəs) *n* **Charles Sanders.** 1839–1914, U.S. logician, philosopher, and mathematician; pioneer of pragmatism.

pejoration (ˌpi:dʒə'reɪʃən) *n* **1** *Linguistics.* semantic change whereby a word acquires unfavourable connotations: *the English word "silly" changed its meaning from "holy" or "happy" by pejoration.* Compare **amelioration** (sense 3). **2** the process of worsening; deterioration.

pejorative (pɪ'dʒɒrətɪv, 'pi:dʒər-) *adj* **1** (of words, expressions, etc.) having an unpleasant or disparaging connotation. ◆ *n* **2** a pejorative word, expression, etc. [C19: from French *péjoratif,* from Late Latin *pējōrātus,* past participle of *pējōrāre* to make worse, from Latin *pēior* worse] ▸ **pe'joratively** *adv*

pekan ('pɛkən) *n* another name for **fisher** (sense 2). [C18: from Canadian French *pékan,* of Algonquian origin; compare Abnaki *pékané*]

peke (pi:k) *n Informal.* a Pekingese dog.

Pekin (pi:'kɪn) *n* a breed of white or cream duck with a bright orange bill. [C18: via French from PEKING]

Peking ('pi:'kɪŋ) *n* the former English name of **Beijing.**

Pekingese (ˌpi:kɪŋ'i:z) *or* **Pekinese** (ˌpi:kə'ni:z) *n* **1** *(pl* **-ese)** a small breed of pet dog with a profuse straight coat, curled plumed tail, and short wrinkled muzzle. **2** the dialect of Mandarin Chinese spoken in Beijing (formerly Peking), the pronunciation of which serves as a standard for the language. **3** *(pl* **-ese)** a native or inhabitant of Beijing (formerly Peking). ◆ *adj* **4** of or relating to Beijing (formerly Peking) or its inhabitants.

Peking man *n* an early type of man, *Homo erectus,* remains of which, of the Lower Palaeolithic age, were found in a cave near Peking (now Beijing), China, in 1927.

pekoe ('pi:kəʊ) *n* a high-quality tea made from the downy tips of the young buds of the tea plant. [C18: from Chinese (Amoy) *peh ho,* from *peh* white + *ho* down]

pelage ('pɛlɪdʒ) *n* the coat of a mammal, consisting of hair, wool, fur, etc. [C19: via French from Old French *pel* animal's coat, from Latin *pilus* hair]

pelagian (pɛ'leɪdʒɪən) *adj* of or inhabiting the open sea. [C18: from Latin *pelagius,* from Greek *pelagios* of the sea, from *pelagos* sea]

Pelagian (pɛ'leɪdʒɪən) *adj* **1** of or relating to Pelagius or his doctrines. ◆ *n* **2** an adherent of the doctrines of Pelagius. ◆ See **Pelagius, Pelagianism.**

Pelagian Islands (pɛ'leɪdʒɪən) *pl n* a group of Italian islands (Lampedusa, Linosa, and Lampione) in the Mediterranean, between Tunisia and Malta. Pop.: 4500 (latest est.). Area: about 27 sq. km (11 sq. miles). Italian name: **Isole Pelagie** ('i:zole pe'ladʒe).

Pelagianism (pɛ'leɪdʒɪəˌnɪzəm) *n Christianity.* a heretical doctrine, first formulated by Pelagius, that rejected the concept of original sin and maintained that the individual takes the initial steps towards salvation by his own efforts and not by the help of divine grace.

pelagic (pɛ'lædʒɪk) *adj* **1** of or relating to the open sea: *pelagic whaling.* **2** (of marine life) living or occurring in the upper waters of open sea. **3** (of geological formations) derived from material that has fallen to the bottom from the upper waters of the sea. [C17: from Latin *pelagicus,* from *pelagus,* from Greek *pelagos* sea]

Pelagius (pɛ'leɪdʒɪəs) *n* ?360–?420 A.D., British monk, who originated the body of doctrines known as Pelagianism and was condemned for heresy (417).

pelargonic acid (ˌpɛlə'gɒnɪk) *n* another name for **nonanoic acid.** [C19: so named because it was originally derived from PELARGONIUM leaves]

pelargonium (ˌpɛlə'gəʊnɪəm) *n* any plant of the chiefly southern African geraniaceous genus *Pelargonium,* having circular or lobed leaves and red, pink, or white aromatic flowers: includes many cultivated geraniums. [C19: via New Latin from Greek *pelargos* stork, on the model of GERANIUM; from the likeness of the seed vessels to a stork's bill]

Pelasgian (pɛ'læzdʒɪən) *n* **1** a member of any of the pre-Hellenic peoples (the **Pelasgi**) who inhabited Greece and the islands and coasts of the Aegean Sea before the arrival of the Bronze Age Greeks. ◆ *adj also* **Pelasgic. 2** of or relating to these peoples.

Pelé ('peleɪ) *n* real name *Edson Arantes do Nascimento.* born 1940, Brazilian footballer. He was awarded an honorary knighthood in 1997.

pelecypod (pɪ'lɛsɪˌpɒd) *n, adj* another word for **bivalve** (senses 1, 2). [C19: from Greek *pelekus* hatchet + -POD]

Pelée (pə'leɪ) *n* **Mount.** a volcano in the Caribbean, in N Martinique: erupted in 1902, killing every person but one in the town of Saint Pierre. Height: 1463 m (4800 ft.).

pelerine ('pɛləˌri:n) *n* a woman's narrow cape with long pointed ends in front. [C18: from French *pèlerine,* feminine of *pèlerin* PILGRIM, that is, a pilgrim's cape]

Pele's hair ('peɪleɪz, 'pi:li:z) *n* fine threads of volcanic rock material formed from molten lava by the action of wind, explosion, etc. [C20: translation of Hawaiian *lauoho-o Pele,* from Pele, name of the goddess of volcanoes]

Peleus ('pelɪəs, 'pi:lɪəs) *n Greek myth.* a king of the Myrmidons; father of Achilles.

Pelew Islands (pi:'lu:) *pl n* a former name of (the Republic of) **Belau.**

pelf (pɛlf) *n Contemptuous.* money or wealth, esp. if dishonestly acquired; lucre. [C14: from Old French *pelfre* booty; related to Latin *pilāre* to despoil]

pelham ('pɛləm) *n* a horse's bit for a double bridle, less severe than a curb but more severe than a snaffle. [probably from the proper name *Pelham*]

Pelham ('pɛləm) *n* **Henry.** 1696–1754, British statesman: prime minister (1743–54); brother of Thomas Pelham Holles, 1st Duke of Newcastle.

Pelham Holles ('pɛləm 'hɒlɪs) *n* **Thomas.** See (1st Duke of) **Newcastle.**

Pelias ('pi:lɪˌæs) *n Greek myth.* a son of Poseidon and Tyro. He feared his nephew Jason and sent him to recover the Golden Fleece, hoping he would not return.

pelican ('pɛlɪkən) *n* any aquatic bird of the tropical and warm water family *Pelecanidae,* such as *P. onocrotalus* **(white pelican)**: order *Pelecaniformes.* They have a long straight flattened bill, with a distensible pouch for engulfing fish. [Old English *pellican,* from Late Latin *pelicānus,* from Greek *pelekān;* perhaps related to Greek *pelekus* axe, perhaps from the shape of the bird's bill; compare Greek *pelekas* woodpecker]

pelican crossing *n* a type of road crossing marked by black-and-white stripes or by two rows of metal studs and consisting of a pedestrian-operated traffic-light system. [C20: from *pe(destrian) li(ght) con(trolled) crossing,* with *-con* adapted to *-can* of *pelican*]

Pelion ('pi:lɪən) *n* a mountain in NE Greece, in E Thessaly. In Greek mythology it was the home of the centaurs. Height: 1548 m (5079 ft.). Modern Greek name: **Pílion.**

pelisse (pɛ'li:s) *n* **1** a fur-trimmed cloak. **2** a high-waisted loose coat, usually fur-trimmed, worn esp. by women in the early 19th century. [C18: via Old French from Medieval Latin *pellicia* cloak, from Latin *pellis* skin]

pelite ('pi:laɪt) *n* any argillaceous rock such as shale. [C19: from Greek *pēlos* mud] ▸ **pelitic** (pɪ'lɪtɪk) *adj*

Pella ('pɛlə) *n* an ancient city in N Greece: the capital of Macedonia under Philip II.

pellagra (pə'leɪgrə, -'læ-) *n Pathol.* a disease caused by a dietary deficiency of nicotinic acid, characterized by burning or itching often followed by scaling of the skin, inflammation of the mouth, diarrhoea, mental impairment, etc. [C19: via Italian from *pelle* skin + *-agra,* from Greek *agra* paroxysm] ▸ **pel'lagrous** *adj*

Pelles ('pɛli:z) *n* (in Arthurian legend) the father of Elaine and one of the searchers for the Holy Grail.

pellet ('pɛlɪt) *n* **1** a small round ball, esp. of compressed matter: *a wax pellet.* **2a** an imitation bullet used in toy guns. **2b** a piece of small shot. **3** a stone ball formerly used as a catapult or cannon missile. **4** Also called: **cast, casting.** *Ornithol.* a mass of undigested food, including bones, fur, feathers, etc., that is regurgitated by certain birds, esp. birds of prey. **5** a small pill. **6** a raised area on coins and carved or moulded ornaments. ◆ *vb (tr)* **7** to strike with pellets. **8** to make or form into pellets. [C14: from Old French *pelote,* from Vulgar Latin *pilota* (unattested), from Latin *pila* ball]

Pelletier *(French* pɛltje) *n* **Pierre Joseph** (pjɛr ʒozɛf). 1788–1842, French chemist, who isolated quinine, chlorophyll, and other chemical substances.

pellicle ('pɛlɪkᵊl) *n* **1** a thin skin or film. **2** the hard protective outer layer of certain protozoans, such as those of the genus *Paramecium.* **3** *Botany.* **3a** the thin outer layer of a mushroom cap. **3b** a growth on the surface of a liquid culture. **4** *Photog.* the thin layer of emulsion covering a plate, film, or paper. [C16: via French from Latin *pellicula,* from *pellis* skin] ▸ **pellicular** (pɛ'lɪkjʊlə) *adj*

pellitory ('pɛlɪtərɪ, -trɪ) *n, pl* **-ries. 1** any of various urticaceous plants of the S and W European genus *Parietaria,* esp. *P. diffusa* **(pellitory-of-the-wall** or **wall pellitory)**, that grow in crevices and have long narrow leaves and small pink flowers. **2 pellitory of Spain.** a small Mediterranean plant, *Anacyclus pyrethrum,* the root of which contains an oil formerly used to relieve toothache: family *Compositae* (composites). [C16 *peletre,* from Old French *piretre,* from Latin *pyrethrum,* from Greek *purethron,* from *pur* fire, from the hot pungent taste of the root]

pell-mell ('pɛl'mɛl) *adv* **1** in a confused headlong rush: *the hounds ran pell-*

mell into the yard. **2** in a disorderly manner: *the things were piled pell-mell in the room.* ◆ *adj* **3** disordered; tumultuous: *a pell-mell rush for the exit.* ◆ *n* **4** disorder; confusion. [C16: from Old French *pesle-mesle,* jingle based on *mesler* to MEDDLE]

pellucid (pɛˈluːsɪd) *adj* **1** transparent or translucent. **2** extremely clear in style and meaning; limpid. [C17: from Latin *pellūcidus,* variant of *perlūcidus,* from *perlūcēre* to shine through, from *per* through + *lūcēre* to shine] ► **pelˈlucidly** *adv* ► ˌ**pelluˈcidity** *or* **pelˈlucidness** *n*

Pelmanism (ˈpɛlməˌnɪzəm) *n* **1** a system of training to improve the memory. **2** (*often not cap.*) Also called: **pairs,** (esp. U.S.) **concentration.** a memory card game in which a pack of cards is spread out face down and players try to turn up pairs with the same number. [named after the *Pelman* Institute, founded in London in 1898]

pelmet (ˈpɛlmɪt) *n* an ornamental drapery or board fixed above a window to conceal the curtain rail. [C19: probably from French *palmette* palm-leaf decoration on cornice moulding; see PALMETTE]

Peloponnese (ˌpɛləpəˈniːs) *n* **the.** the S peninsula of Greece, joined to central Greece by the Isthmus of Corinth: chief cities in ancient times were Sparta and Corinth, now Patras. Pop.: 607 428 (1991). Area: 21 439 sq. km (8361 sq. miles). Medieval name: **Morea.** Modern Greek name: **Peloponnesos.** Also called: **Peloponnesus.** ► **Peloponnesian** (ˌpɛləpəˈniːʃən) *adj*

Peloponnesian War *n* a war fought for supremacy in Greece from 431 to 404 B.C., in which Athens and her allies were defeated by the league centred on Sparta.

Pelops (ˈpiːlɒps) *n Greek myth.* the son of Tantalus, who as a child was killed by his father and served up as a meal for the gods.

peloria (pɛˈlɔːrɪə) *n* the abnormal production of regular flowers in a plant of a species that usually produces irregular flowers. [C19: via New Latin from Greek *pelōros,* from *pelōr* monster] ► **peloric** (pɛˈlɔːrɪk, -ˈlɒ-) *adj*

pelorus (pɪˈlɔːrəs) *n, pl* **-ruses.** a sighting device used in conjunction with a magnetic compass or a gyrocompass for measuring the relative bearings of observed points. [of uncertain origin, perhaps from Latin *Pelōrus* a dangerous Sicilian promontory]

pelota (pəˈlɒtə) *n* any of various games played in Spain, Spanish America, SW France, etc., by two players who use a basket strapped to their wrists or a wooden racket to propel a ball against a specially marked wall. [C19: from Spanish: ball, from Old French *pelote;* see PELLET]

Pelotas (*Portuguese* peˈlɔtas) *n* a port in S Brazil, in Rio Grande do Sul on the Canal de São Gonçalo. Pop.: 260 510 (1991).

peloton (ˈpɛləˌtɒn) *n Cycle racing.* the main field of riders in a road race. [C20: French, literally: pack]

pelt[1] (pɛlt) *vb* **1** (*tr*) to throw (missiles) at (a person). **2** (*tr*) to hurl (insults) at (a person). **3** (*intr;* foll. by *along, over,* etc.) to move rapidly; hurry. **4** (*intr;* often foll. by *down*) to rain heavily. ◆ *n* **5** a blow. **6** speed (esp. in the phrase **at full pelt**). [C15: of uncertain origin, perhaps from PELLET] ► **ˈpelter** *n*

pelt[2] (pɛlt) *n* **1** the skin of a fur-bearing animal, such as a mink, esp. when it has been removed from the carcass. **2** the hide of an animal, stripped of hair and ready for tanning. [C15: perhaps back formation from PELTRY]

peltast (ˈpɛltæst) *n* (in ancient Greece) a lightly armed foot soldier. [C17: from Latin *peltasta,* from Greek *peltastēs* soldier equipped with a *pelta,* a small leather shield]

peltate (ˈpɛlteɪt) *adj* (of leaves) having the stalk attached to the centre of the lower surface. [C18: from Latin *peltātus* equipped with a *pelta,* a small shield; see PELTAST] ► **ˈpeltately** *adv* ► **pelˈtation** *n*

Peltier effect (ˈpɛltɪˌeɪ) *n Physics.* the production of heat at one junction and the absorption of heat at the other junction of a thermocouple when a current is passed around the thermocouple circuit. The heat produced is additional to the heat arising from the resistance of the wires. Compare **Seebeck effect.** [C19: named after Jean *Peltier* (1785–1845), French physicist, who discovered it]

Peltier element *n* an electronic device consisting of metal strips between which alternate strips of n-type and p-type semiconductors are connected. Passage of a current causes heat to be absorbed from one set of metallic strips and emitted from the other by the Peltier effect.

Pelton wheel (ˈpɛltən) *n* a type of impulse turbine in which specially shaped buckets mounted on the perimeter of a wheel are struck by a fast-flowing water jet. [C19: named after L. A. *Pelton* (1829–1908), U.S. engineer who invented it]

peltry (ˈpɛltrɪ) *n, pl* **-ries.** the pelts of animals collectively. [C15: from Old French *peleterie* collection of pelts, from Latin *pilus* hair]

pelvic (ˈpɛlvɪk) *adj* of, near, or relating to the pelvis.

pelvic fin *n* either of a pair of fins attached to the pelvic girdle of fishes that help to control the direction of movement during locomotion.

pelvic girdle *or* **arch** *n* the skeletal structure to which the lower limbs in man, and the hind limbs or corresponding parts in other vertebrates, are attached.

pelvic inflammatory disease *n* inflammation of a woman's womb, Fallopian tubes, or ovaries as a result of infection with one of a group of bacteria. Abbrev.: **PID.**

pelvimetry (pɛlˈvɪmɪtrɪ) *n Obstetrics.* measurement of the dimensions of the female pelvis.

pelvis (ˈpɛlvɪs) *n, pl* **-vises** *or* **-ves** (-viːz). **1** the large funnel-shaped structure at the lower end of the trunk of most vertebrates: in man it is formed by the hipbones and sacrum. **2** the bones that form this structure. **3** any anatomical cavity or structure shaped like a funnel or cup. **4** short for **renal pelvis.** [C17: from Latin: basin, laver]

pelycosaur (ˈpɛlɪkəʊˌsɔː) *n* any extinct mammal-like reptile of the order *Pelycosauria,* of Upper Carboniferous to Lower Permian times, from which the therapsids are thought to have evolved. [C19: from New Latin *Pelycosauria,* from Greek *pelyx* bowl, PELVIS, + -SAUR]

Pemba (ˈpɛmbə) *n* an island in the Indian Ocean, off the E coast of Africa north of Zanzibar: part of Tanzania; produces most of the world's cloves. Chief town: Chake Chake. Pop.: 265 039 (1988). Area: 984 sq. km (380 sq. miles).

Pembroke (ˈpɛmbrʊk) *n* **1** a town in SW Wales, in Pembrokeshire on Milford Haven: 11th-century castle where Henry VII was born. Pop. (with Pembroke Dock): 15 424 (1991). **2** the smaller variety of corgi, usually having a docked or short tail.

Pembrokeshire (ˈpɛmbrʊkˌʃɪə, -ʃə) *n* a county of SW Wales, on the Irish Sea and the Bristol Channel: formerly (1974–96) part of Dyfed: a hilly peninsula with a deeply indented coast: tourism, agriculture, oil refining. Administrative centre: Haverfordwest. Pop.: 113 500 (1996 est.). Area: 1589 sq. km (614 sq. miles).

Pembroke table *n* a small table with drop leaves and often one or more drawers. [perhaps named after Mary Herbert, Countess of *Pembroke* (1561–1621), who originally ordered its design]

pemmican *or* **pemican** (ˈpɛmɪkən) *n* a small pressed cake of shredded dried meat, pounded into paste with fat and berries or dried fruits, used originally by American Indians and now chiefly for emergency rations. [C19: from Cree *pimikân,* from *pimii* fat, grease]

pemphigus (ˈpɛmfɪgəs, pɛmˈfaɪ-) *n Pathol.* any of a group of blistering skin diseases, esp. a potentially fatal form (**pemphigus vulgaris**) characterized by large blisters on the skin, mucous membranes of the mouth, genitals, intestines, etc., which eventually rupture and form painful denuded areas from which critical amounts of bodily protein, fluid, and blood may be lost. [C18: via New Latin from Greek *pemphix* bubble]

pen[1] (pɛn) *n* **1** an implement for writing or drawing using ink, formerly consisting of a sharpened and split quill, and now of a metal nib attached to a holder. See also **ballpoint, fountain pen. 2** the writing end of such an implement; nib. **3** style of writing. **4 the pen. 4a** writing as an occupation. **4b** the written word: *the pen is mightier than the sword.* **5** the long horny internal shell of a squid. ◆ *vb* **pens, penning, penned. 6** (*tr*) to write or compose. [Old English *pinne,* from Late Latin *penna* (quill) pen, from Latin: feather]

pen[2] (pɛn) *n* **1** an enclosure in which domestic animals are kept: *sheep pen.* **2** any place of confinement. **3** a dock for servicing submarines, esp. one having a bombproof roof. ◆ *vb* **pens, penning, penned** *or* **pent. 4** (*tr*) to enclose or keep in a pen. [Old English *penn,* perhaps related to PIN]

pen[3] (pɛn) *n U.S. and Canadian informal.* short for **penitentiary** (sense 1).

pen[4] (pɛn) *n* a female swan. [C16: of unknown origin]

PEN (pɛn) *n acronym for* International Association of Poets, Playwrights, Editors, Essayists, and Novelists.

Pen. *abbrev. for* Peninsula.

penal (ˈpiːnᵊl) *adj* **1** of, relating to, constituting, or prescribing punishment. **2** payable as a penalty: *a penal sum.* **3** used or designated as a place of punishment: *a penal institution.* [C15: from Late Latin *poenālis* concerning punishment, from *poena* penalty] ► **ˈpenally** *adv*

penal code *n* the codified body of the laws in any legal system that relate to crime and its punishment.

penalize *or* **penalise** (ˈpiːnəˌlaɪz) *vb* (*tr*) **1** to impose a penalty on (someone), as for breaking a law or rule. **2** to inflict a handicap or disadvantage on. **3** *Sport.* to award a free stroke, point, or penalty against (a player or team). **4** to declare (an act) legally punishable; make subject to a penalty. ► ˌ**penaliˈzation** *or* ˌ**penaliˈsation** *n*

penal servitude *n English criminal law.* (formerly) the imprisonment of an offender and his subjection to hard labour. It was substituted for transportation in 1853 and abolished in 1948. Compare **hard labour.**

penalty (ˈpɛnᵊltɪ) *n, pl* **-ties. 1** a legal or official punishment, such as a term of imprisonment. **2** some other form of punishment, such as a fine or forfeit for not fulfilling a contract. **3** loss, suffering, or other unfortunate result of one's own action, error, etc. **4** *Sport, games, etc.* a handicap awarded against a player or team for illegal play, such as a free shot at goal by the opposing team, loss of points, etc. [C16: from Medieval Latin *poenālitās* penalty; see PENAL]

penalty area *n Soccer.* a rectangular area in front of the goal, within which the goalkeeper may handle the ball and within which a penalty is awarded for a foul by the defending team.

penalty box *n* **1** *Soccer.* another name for **penalty area. 2** *Ice hockey.* a bench for players serving time penalties.

penalty corner *n Hockey.* a free hit from the goal line taken by the attacking side. Also called: **short corner.**

penalty kick *n* **1** *Soccer.* a free kick at the goal from a point (**penalty spot**) within the penalty area and 12 yards (about 11 m) from the goal, with only the goalkeeper allowed to defend it: awarded to the attacking team after a foul within the penalty area by a member of the defending team. **2** *Rugby Union.* a kick awarded after a serious foul that can be aimed straight at the goal to score three points.

penalty killer *n Ice hockey.* a good player who, when his team is short-handed because of a penalty, is sent onto the ice to prevent the other side from scoring.

penalty rates *pl n Austral. and N.Z.* rates of pay, such as double time, paid to employees working outside normal working hours.

penalty shoot-out *n* **1** *Soccer.* a method of deciding the winner of a drawn match, in which players from each team attempt to score with a penalty kick. **2** a similar method of resolving a tie in hockey, ice hockey, polo, etc.

penance (ˈpɛnəns) *n* **1** voluntary self-punishment to atone for a sin, crime, etc. **2** a feeling of regret for one's wrongdoings. **3** *Christianity.* **3a** a punishment usually consisting of prayer, fasting, etc., undertaken voluntarily as an expression of penitence for sin. **3b** a punishment of this kind imposed by church authority as a condition of absolution. ◆ *vb* **4** (*tr*) (of ecclesiastical authorities) to impose a penance upon (a sinner). [C13: via Old French from Latin *paenitentia* repentance; related to Latin *poena* penalty]

Penang (pɪ'næŋ) *n* **1** a state of Peninsular Malaysia: consists of the island of Penang and the province Wellesley on the mainland, which first united administratively in 1798 as a British colony. Capital: George Town. Pop.: 1 141 500 (1993 est). Area: 1031 sq. km (398 sq. miles). Also called: **Pulau Pinang. 2** a forested island off the NW coast of Malaya, in the Strait of Malacca. Area: 293 sq. km (113 sq. miles). Former name (until about 1867): **Prince of Wales Island. 3** another name for **George Town.**

penannular (pen'ænjʊlə) *adj* of or forming an almost complete ring. [C19: from PENE- + ANNULAR]

penates (pə'nɑ:ti:z) *pl n* See **lares and penates.** [Latin]

pence (pens) *n* a plural of **penny.**

USAGE Since the decimalization of British currency and the introduction of the abbreviation **p**, as in *10p, 85p*, etc., the abbreviation has tended to replace *pence* in speech, as in *4p* (ˌfɔ:'pi:), *12p* (ˌtwɛlv'pi:), etc.

pencel, pensel, *or* **pensil** ('pensᵊl) *n* a small pennon, originally one carried by a knight's squire. [C13: via Anglo-French from Old French *penoncel* a little PENNON]

penchant ('pɒŋʃɒŋ) *n* a strong inclination or liking; bent or taste. [C17: from French, from *pencher* to incline, from Latin *pendēre* to be suspended]

Penchi ('pen'tʃi:) *n* a variant transliteration of the Chinese name for **Benxi.**

pencil ('pensᵊl) *n* **1a** a thin cylindrical instrument used for writing, drawing, etc., consisting of a rod of graphite or other marking substance, usually either encased in wood and sharpened or held in a mechanical metal device. **1b** (*as modifier*): *a pencil drawing.* **2** something similar in shape or function: *a styptic pencil; an eyebrow pencil.* **3** a narrow set of lines or rays, such as light rays, diverging from or converging to a point. **4** *Archaic.* an artist's fine paintbrush. **5** *Rare.* an artist's individual style or technique in drawing. ◆ *vb* **-cils, -cilling, -cilled** *or U.S.* **-cils, -ciling, -ciled.** (*tr*) **6** to draw, colour, or write with a pencil. **7** to mark with a pencil. **8 pencil in.** to note, arrange, include, etc. provisionally or tentatively. [C14: from Old French *pincel*, from Latin *pēnicillus* painter's brush, from *pēniculus* a little tail, from *pēnis* tail] ▸ **'penciller** *or U.S.* **'penciler** *n*

pend (pend) *vb* (*intr*) **1** to await judgment or settlement. **2** *Dialect.* to hang; depend. ◆ *n* **3** *Scot.* an archway or vaulted passage. [C15: from Latin *pendēre* to hang; related to Latin *pendere* to suspend]

Penda ('pendə) *n* died 655 A.D., king of Mercia (?634–55).

pendant ('pendənt) *n* **1a** an ornament that hangs from a piece of jewellery. **1b** a necklace with such an ornament. **2** a hanging light, esp. a chandelier. **3** a carved ornament that is suspended from a ceiling or roof. **4** something that matches or complements something else. **5** Also called: **pennant.** *Nautical.* a length of wire or rope secured at one end to a mast or spar and having a block or other fitting at the lower end. ◆ *adj* **6** a variant spelling of **pendent.** [C14: from Old French, from *pendre* to hang, from Latin *pendēre* to hang down; related to Latin *pendere* to hang, *pondus* weight, Greek *span* to pull]

pendent ('pendənt) *adj* **1** dangling. **2** jutting. **3** (of a grammatical construction) incomplete: *a pendent nominative is a construction having no verb.* **4** a less common word for **pending** (senses 2, 3). ◆ *n* **5** a variant spelling of **pendant.** [C15: from Old French *pendant*, from *pendre* to hang; see PENDANT] ▸ **'pendency** *n* ▸ **'pendently** *adv*

pendente lite (pen'dentɪ 'laɪtɪ) *adj Law.* while a suit is pending. [Latin, literally: with litigation pending]

pendentive (pen'dentɪv) *n* any of four triangular sections of vaulting with concave sides, positioned at a corner of a rectangular space to support a circular or polygonal dome. [C18: from French *pendentif*, from Latin *pendens* hanging, from *pendere* to hang]

Penderecki (*Polish* pende'retski) *n* **Krzystof** ('kʃiʃtɔf). born 1933, Polish composer, noted for his highly individual orchestration. His works include *Threnody for the Victims of Hiroshima* for strings (1960), *Stabat Mater* (1962), *Polish Requiem* (1983–84), and the opera *Ubu Rex* (1991).

pending ('pendɪŋ) *prep* **1** while waiting for or anticipating. ◆ *adj* (*postpositive*) **2** not yet decided, confirmed, or finished: *what are the matters pending?* **3** imminent: *these developments have been pending for some time.*

pendragon (pen'drægən) *n* a supreme war chief or leader of the ancient Britons. [Welsh, literally: head dragon] ▸ **pen'dragon,ship** *n*

pendule ('pɒndjul, 'pen-) *n Mountaineering.* a manoeuvre by which a climber on a rope from above swings in a pendulum-like series of movements to reach another line of ascent. Also called: **pendulum.**

pendulous ('pendjʊləs) *adj* hanging downwards, esp. so as to swing from side to side. [C17: from Latin *pendulus*, from *pendēre* to hang down] ▸ **'pendulously** *adv* ▸ **'pendulousness** *n*

pendulum ('pendjʊləm) *n* **1** a body mounted so that it can swing freely under the influence of gravity. It is either a bob hung on a light thread (**simple pendulum**) or a more complex structure (**compound pendulum**). **2** such a device used to regulate a clockwork mechanism. **3** something that changes its position, attitude, etc. fairly regularly: *the pendulum of public opinion.* [C17: from Latin *pendulus* PENDULOUS]

pene- *or before a vowel* **pen-** *prefix* almost: *peneplain.* [from Latin *paene*]

Penelope (pə'neləpɪ) *n Greek myth.* the wife of Odysseus, who remained true to him during his long absence despite the importunities of many suitors.

peneplain *or* **peneplane** ('pi:nɪˌpleɪn, ˌpi:nɪ'pleɪn) *n* a relatively flat land surface produced by a long period of erosion. [C19: from PENE- + PLAIN[1]] ▸ **ˌpenepla'nation** *n*

penetralia (ˌpenɪ'treɪlɪə) *pl n* **1** the innermost parts. **2** secret matters. [C17: from Latin, from *penetrālis* inner, from *penetrāre* to PENETRATE] ▸ **ˌpene'tralian** *adj*

penetrance ('penɪtrəns) *n Genetics.* the percentage frequency with which a gene exhibits its effect. [C20: from PENETR(ANT) + -ANCE, on the model of German *penetranz*]

penetrant ('penɪtrənt) *adj* **1** sharp; penetrating. ◆ *n* **2** *Chem.* a substance that lowers the surface tension of a liquid and thus causes it to penetrate or be absorbed more easily. **3** a person or thing that penetrates.

penetrate ('penɪˌtreɪt) *vb* **1** to find or force a way into or through (something); pierce; enter. **2** to diffuse through (a substance); permeate. **3** (*tr*) to see through: *their eyes could not penetrate the fog.* **4** (*tr*) (of a man) to insert the penis into the vagina of (a woman). **5** (*tr*) to grasp the meaning of (a principle, etc.). **6** (*intr*) to be understood: *his face lit up as the new idea penetrated.* [C16: from Latin *penetrāre;* related to *penitus* inner, and *penus* the interior of a house] ▸ **'penetrable** *adj* ▸ **ˌpenetra'bility** *n* ▸ **'penetrably** *adv* ▸ **'penetrative** *adj* ▸ **'pene,trator** *n*

penetrating ('penɪˌtreɪtɪŋ) *adj* tending to or able to penetrate: *a penetrating mind; a penetrating voice.* ▸ **'pene,tratingly** *adv*

penetration (ˌpenɪ'treɪʃən) *n* **1** the act or an instance of penetrating. **2** the ability or power to penetrate. **3** keen insight or perception. **4** *Military.* an offensive manoeuvre that breaks through an enemy's defensive position. **5** Also called: **market penetration.** the proportion of the total number of potential purchasers of a product or service who either are aware of its existence or actually buy it. **6** another name for **depth of field.**

penetrometer (ˌpenɪ'trɒmɪtə) *n Physics.* an instrument used to measure the penetrating power of radiation, such as X-rays.

Peneus (pɪ'ni:əs) *n* the ancient name for the **Salambria.**

pen friend *n* another name for **pen pal.**

Penghu *or* **P'eng-hu** ('peŋ'hu:) *n* transliteration of the Chinese name for the **Pescadores.**

pengö ('peŋgɜ:) *n, pl* **-gös.** (formerly) the standard monetary unit of Hungary, replaced by the forint in 1946. [from Hungarian, from *pengeni* to sound]

Pengpu ('peŋ'pu:) *n* a variant transliteration of the Chinese name for **Bengbu.**

penguin ('peŋgwɪn) *n* **1** any flightless marine bird, such as *Aptenodytes patagonica* (king penguin) and *Pygoscelis adeliae* (**Adélie penguin**), of the order *Sphenisciformes* of cool southern, esp. Antarctic, regions: they have wings modified as flippers, webbed feet, and feathers lacking barbs. See also **emperor penguin, king penguin. 2** an obsolete name for **great auk.** [C16: perhaps from Welsh *pen gwyn*, from *pen* head + *gwyn* white]

penicillate (ˌpenɪ'sɪlɪt, -eɪt) *adj Biology.* having or resembling one or more tufts of fine hairs: *a penicillate caterpillar.* [C19: from Latin *pēnicillus* brush, PENCIL] ▸ **ˌpeni'cillately** *adv* ▸ **ˌpenicil'lation** *n*

penicillin (ˌpenɪ'sɪlɪn) *n* an antibiotic with powerful bacteriostatic action, used to treat pneumonia, gonorrhoea, and infections caused by streptococci and staphylococci: originally obtained from the fungus *Penicillium*, esp. *P. notatum*. Formula: $R\text{-}C_9H_{11}N_2O_4S$ where R is one of several side chains. [C20: from PENICILLIUM]

penicillium (ˌpenɪ'sɪlɪəm) *n, pl* **-cilliums** *or* **-cillia** (-'sɪlɪə). any ascomycetous saprophytic fungus of the genus *Penicillium*, which commonly grow as a green or blue mould on stale food: some species are used in cheese-making and others as a source of penicillin. [C19: New Latin, from Latin *pēnicillus* tuft of hairs; named from the tufted appearance of the sporangia of this fungus]

penile ('pi:naɪl) *adj* of or relating to the penis.

penillion *or* **pennillion** (pɪ'nɪlɪən) *pl n, sing* **penill** (pɪ'nɪl). the Welsh art or practice of singing poetry in counterpoint to a traditional melody played on the harp. [from Welsh: verses, plural of *penill* verse, stanza]

peninsula (pɪ'nɪnsjʊlə) *n* a narrow strip of land projecting into a sea or lake from the mainland. [C16: from Latin, literally: almost an island, from *paene* PENE- + *insula* island] ▸ **pen'insular** *adj*

USAGE The noun *peninsula* is sometimes confused with the adjective *peninsular: the Iberian peninsula* (not *peninsular*).

Peninsula *n* **the.** short for the **Iberian Peninsula.**

Peninsular War *n* the war (1808–14) fought in the Iberian Peninsula by British, Portuguese, and Spanish forces against the French, resulting in the defeat of the French: part of the Napoleonic Wars.

peninsulate (pɪ'nɪnsjʊˌleɪt) *vb* (*tr*) to cause (land) to become peninsular.

penis ('pi:nɪs) *n, pl* **-nises** *or* **-nes** (-ni:z). the male organ of copulation in higher vertebrates, also used for urine excretion in many mammals. [C17: from Latin]

penis envy *n Psychoanal.* a Freudian concept in which envy of the penis is postulated as the cause for some of the characteristics found in women.

penitent ('penɪtənt) *adj* **1** feeling regret for one's sins; repentant. ◆ *n* **2** a person who is penitent. **3** *Christianity.* **3a** a person who repents his sins and seeks forgiveness for them. **3b** *R.C. Church.* a person who confesses his sins to a priest and submits to a penance imposed by him. [C14: from Church Latin *paenitēns* regretting, from *paenitēre* to repent, of obscure origin] ▸ **'penitence** *n* ▸ **'penitently** *adv*

penitential (ˌpenɪ'tenʃəl) *adj* **1** of, showing, or constituting penance. ◆ *n* **2** *Chiefly R.C. Church.* a book or compilation of instructions for confessors. **3** a less common word for **penitent** (senses 2, 3). ▸ **ˌpeni'tentially** *adv*

penitentiary (ˌpenɪ'tenʃərɪ) *n, pl* **-ries. 1** (in the U.S. and Canada) a state or federal prison: in Canada, esp. a federal prison for offenders convicted of serious crimes. Sometimes shortened to **pen. 2** *R.C. Church.* **2a** a cleric appointed to supervise the administration of the sacrament of penance in a particular area. **2b** a priest who has special faculties to absolve particularly grave sins. **2c** a cardinal who presides over a tribunal that decides all matters affecting the sacrament of penance. **2d** this tribunal itself. ◆ *adj* **3** another word for **penitential** (sense 1). **4** *U.S. and Canadian.* (of an offence) punishable by imprisonment in a penitentiary. [C15 (meaning also: an officer dealing with penances): from Medieval Latin *poenitentiārius*, from Latin *paenitēns* PENITENT]

Penki ('pen'tʃi:) *n* a variant transliteration of the Chinese name for **Benxi.**

penknife ('pɛnˌnaɪf) *n, pl* **-knives.** a small knife with one or more blades that fold into the handle; pocketknife. [C15: so called because it was originally used for making and repairing quill pens]

penman ('pɛnmən) *n, pl* **-men. 1** a person skilled in handwriting. **2** a person who writes by hand in a specified way: *a bad penman.* **3** an author.

penmanship ('pɛnmənʃɪp) *n* style or technique of writing by hand. Also called: **calligraphy.**

Penn (pɛn) *n* **1 Irving.** born 1917, U.S. photographer, noted for his portraits and his innovations in colour photography. **2 William.** 1644–1718, English Quaker and founder of Pennsylvania.

Penn. *abbrev. for* Pennsylvania.

penna ('pɛnə) *n, pl* **-nae** (-niː). *Ornithol.* any large feather that has a vane and forms part of the main plumage of a bird. [Latin: feather] ▸ **pennaceous** (pɛ'neɪʃəs) *adj*

pen name *n* an author's pseudonym. Also called: **nom de plume.**

pennant ('pɛnənt) *n* **1** a type of pennon, esp. one flown from vessels as identification or for signalling. **2** *Chiefly U.S., Canadian, and Austral.* **2a** a flag serving as an emblem of championship in certain sports. **2b** (*as modifier*): *pennant cricket.* **3** *Nautical.* another word for **pendant** (sense 5). [C17: probably a blend of PENDANT and PENNON]

pennate ('pɛneɪt) *or* **pennated** *adj Biology.* **1** having feathers, wings, or winglike structures. **2** another word for **pinnate.** [C19: from Latin *pennātus*, from *penna* wing]

penne ('pɛnɪ) *n* pasta in the form of short tubes. [C20: Italian, literally: quills]

Penney ('pɛnɪ) *n* **William George,** Baron Penney of East Hendred. 1909–91, British mathematician. He worked on the first atomic bomb and became chairman of the UK Atomic Energy Authority (1964–67).

penni ('pɛnɪ) *n, pl* **-niä** (-nɪə) *or* **-nis.** a Finnish monetary unit worth one hundredth of a markka. [Finnish, from Low German *pennig* PENNY]

penniless ('pɛnɪlɪs) *adj* very poor; almost totally without money. ▸ **'pennilessly** *adv* ▸ **'pennilessness** *n*

pennillion (pɪ'nɪlɪən) *n* a variant spelling of **penillion.**

Pennine Alps ('pɛnaɪn) *pl n* a range of the Alps between Switzerland and Italy. Highest peak: Monte Rosa, 4634 m (15 204 ft.).

Pennines ('pɛnaɪnz) *pl n* a system of hills in England, extending from the Cheviot Hills in the north to the River Trent in the south: forms the watershed for the main rivers of N England. Highest peak: Cross Fell, 893 m (2930 ft.). Also called: (the) **Pennine Chain.**

Pennine Way *n* a long-distance footpath extending from Edale, Derbyshire, for 402 km (250 miles) to Kirk Yetholm, Scottish Borders.

penninite ('pɛnɪˌnaɪt) *n* a bluish-green variety of chlorite occurring in the form of thick crystals. [C20: from German *Pennin* Pennine (Alps) + -ITE[1]]

pennon ('pɛnən) *n* **1** a long flag, often tapering and rounded, divided, or pointed at the end, originally a knight's personal flag. **2** a small tapering or triangular flag borne on a ship or boat. **3** a poetic word for **wing.** [C14: via Old French ultimately from Latin *penna* feather]

Pennsylvania (ˌpɛnsɪl'veɪnɪə) *n* a state of the northeastern U.S.: almost wholly in the Appalachians, with the Allegheny Plateau to the west and a plain in the southeast; the second most important U.S. state for manufacturing. Capital: Harrisburg. Pop.: 12 019 661 (1997 est.). Area: 116 462 sq. km (44 956 sq. miles). Abbrevs.: **Pa., Penn., Penna.,** or (with zip code) **PA**

Pennsylvania Dutch *n* **1** Also called: **Pennsylvania German.** a dialect of German spoken in E Pennsylvania. **2 the Pennsylvania Dutch.** (*functioning as pl*) a group of German-speaking people in E Pennsylvania, descended from 18th-century settlers from SW Germany and Switzerland.

Pennsylvanian (ˌpɛnsɪl'veɪnɪən) *adj* **1** of the state of Pennsylvania. **2** (in North America) of, denoting, or formed in the upper of two divisions of the Carboniferous period (see also **Mississippian** (sense 2)), which lasted 30 million years, during which coal measures were formed. ♦ *n* **3** an inhabitant or native of the state of Pennsylvania. **4 the.** the Pennsylvanian period or rock system, equivalent to the Upper Carboniferous of Europe.

penny ('pɛnɪ) *n, pl* **pennies** *or* **pence** (pɛns). **1** Also called (formerly): **new penny.** (in Britain) a bronze coin having a value equal to one hundredth of a pound. Symbol: **p 2** (in Britain before 1971) a bronze or copper coin having a value equal to one twelfth of a shilling or one two-hundred-and-fortieth of a pound. Abbrev.: **2d 3** a monetary unit of the Republic of Ireland worth one hundredth of a pound. **4** (*pl* **pennies**). (in the U.S. and Canada) a cent. **5** a coin of similar value, as used in several other countries. **6** (*used with a negative*) *Informal, chiefly Brit.* the least amount of money: *I don't have a penny.* **7 a bad penny.** *Informal, chiefly Brit.* an objectionable person or thing (esp. in the phrase **turn up like a bad penny**). **8 a pretty penny.** *Informal.* a considerable sum of money. **9 spend a penny.** *Brit. informal.* to urinate. **10 the penny dropped.** *Informal, chiefly Brit.* the explanation of something was finally realized. **11 two a penny.** plentiful but of little value. [Old English *penig, pening;* related to Old Saxon *penni(n)g,* Old High German *pfeni(n)c,* German *Pfennig*]

penny-a-liner *n Now rare.* a hack writer or journalist.

penny arcade *n Chiefly U.S.* a public place with various coin-operated machines for entertainment; amusement arcade.

Penny Black *n* the first adhesive postage stamp, issued in Britain in 1840; an imperforate stamp bearing the profile of Queen Victoria on a dark background.

pennyboy ('pɛnɪˌbɔɪ) *n Irish slang.* an employee whose duties include menial tasks, such as running errands.

pennycress ('pɛnɪˌkrɛs) *n* any of several cruciferous plants of the genus *Thlaspi* of temperate Eurasia and North America, typically having small white or mauve flowers and rounded or heart-shaped leaves.

penny-dreadful *n, pl* **-fuls.** *Brit. informal.* a cheap, often lurid or sensational book or magazine.

penny-farthing *n Brit.* an early type of bicycle with a large front wheel and a small rear wheel, the pedals being attached to the front wheel. U.S. name: **ordinary.** [C20: so called because of the similarity between the relative sizes of the wheels and the relative sizes of the (old) penny and farthing coins]

penny-pinching *adj Informal.* excessively careful with money. ▸ **'penny-ˌpincher** *n*

pennyroyal (ˌpɛnɪ'rɔɪəl) *n* **1** a Eurasian plant, *Mentha pulegium,* with hairy leaves and small mauve flowers, that yields an aromatic oil used in medicine: family *Labiatae* (labiates). **2** Also called: **mock pennyroyal.** a similar and related plant, *Hedeoma pulegioides,* of E North America. [C16: variant of Anglo-Norman *puliol real,* from Old French *pouliol* (from Latin *pūleium* pennyroyal) + *real* ROYAL]

penny shares *pl n Stock Exchange.* securities with a low market price, esp. less than 20p, enabling small investors to purchase a large number for a relatively small outlay.

pennyweight ('pɛnɪˌweɪt) *n* a unit of weight equal to 24 grains or one twentieth of an ounce (Troy).

penny whistle *n* a type of flageolet with six finger holes, esp. a cheap one made of metal. Also called: **tin whistle.**

penny-wise *adj* **1** greatly concerned with saving small sums of money. **2 penny-wise and pound-foolish.** careful about trifles but wasteful in large ventures.

pennywort ('pɛnɪˌwɜːt) *n* **1** Also called: **navelwort.** a crassulaceous Eurasian rock plant, *Umbilicus rupestris* (or *Cotyledon umbilicus*), with whitish-green tubular flowers and rounded leaves. **2** a marsh plant, *Hydrocotyle vulgaris,* of Europe and North Africa, having circular leaves and greenish-pink flowers: family *Hydrocotylaceae.* **3** a gentianaceous plant, *Obolaria virginica,* of E North America, with fleshy scalelike leaves and small white or purplish flowers. **4** any of various other plants with rounded penny-like leaves.

pennyworth ('pɛnɪˌwɜːθ) *n* **1** the amount that can be bought for a penny. **2** a small amount: *he hasn't got a pennyworth of sense.*

penology (piː'nɒlədʒɪ) *n* **1** the branch of the social sciences concerned with the punishment of crime. **2** the science of prison management. ♦ Also: **poenology.** [C19: from Greek *poinē* punishment] ▸ **penological** (ˌpiːnə'lɒdʒɪkᵊl) *adj* ▸ **ˌpeno'logically** *adv* ▸ **pe'nologist** *n*

pen pal *n* a person with whom one regularly exchanges letters, often a person in another country whom one has not met. Also called: **pen friend.**

penpusher ('pɛnˌpʊʃə) *n* a person who writes a lot, esp. a clerk involved with boring paperwork. ▸ **'penˌpushing** *adj, n*

Penrith (pɛn'rɪθ) *n* a market town in NW England, in Cumbria. Pop.: 12 049 (1991).

Penrose ('pɛnrəʊz) *n* Sir **Roger.** born 1931, British mathematician and theoretical physicist, noted for his investigation of black holes.

pensel *or* **pensil** ('pɛnsᵊl) *n* variants of **pencel.**

Penshurst Place ('pɛnzhɜːst) *n* a 14th-century mansion near Tunbridge Wells in Kent: birthplace of Sir Philip Sidney; gardens laid out from 1560.

pensile ('pɛnsaɪl) *adj Ornithol.* designating or building a hanging nest: *pensile birds.* [C17: from Latin *pensilis* hanging down, from *pendēre* to hang] ▸ **pensility** (pɛn'sɪlɪtɪ) *or* **'pensileness** *n*

pension[1] ('pɛnʃən) *n* **1** a regular payment made by the state to people over a certain age to enable them to subsist without having to work. **2** a regular payment made by an employer to former employees after they retire. **3** any regular payment made on charitable grounds, by way of patronage, or in recognition of merit, service, etc.: *a pension paid to a disabled soldier.* ♦ *vb* **4** (*tr*) to grant a pension to. [C14: via Old French from Latin *pēnsiō* a payment, from *pendere* to pay] ▸ **'pensionable** *adj* ▸ **'pensionless** *adj*

pension[2] *French.* (pɑ̃sjɔ̃) *n* (in France and some other countries) **1** a relatively cheap boarding house. **2** another name for **full board.** [C17: French; extended meaning of *pension* grant; see PENSION[1]]

pensionary ('pɛnʃənərɪ) *adj* **1** constituting a pension. **2** maintained by or receiving a pension. ♦ *n, pl* **-aries. 4** a person whose service can be bought; hireling.

pensioneer trustee (ˌpɛnʃə'nɪə) *n* (in Britain) a person authorized by the Inland Revenue to oversee the management of a pension fund.

pensioner ('pɛnʃənə) *n* **1** a person who is receiving a pension, esp. an old-age pension from the state. **2** a person dependent on the pay or bounty of another. **3** *Obsolete, Brit.* another name for **gentleman-at-arms.**

pension mortgage *n* an arrangement whereby a person takes out a mortgage and pays the capital repayment instalments into a pension fund and the interest to the mortgagee. The loan is repaid out of the tax-free lump sum proceeds of the pension plan on the borrower's retirement.

pension off *vb* (*tr, adv*) **1** to cause to retire from a post and pay a pension to. **2** to discard, because old and worn: *to pension off submarines.*

pensive ('pɛnsɪv) *adj* **1** deeply or seriously thoughtful, often with a tinge of sadness. **2** expressing or suggesting pensiveness. [C14: from Old French *pensif,* from *penser* to think, from Latin *pensāre* to consider; compare PENSION[1]] ▸ **'pensively** *adv* ▸ **'pensiveness** *n*

penstemon (pɛn'stiːmən) *n* a variant (esp. U.S.) of **pentstemon.**

penstock ('pɛnˌstɒk) *n* **1** a conduit that supplies water to a hydroelectric power plant. **2** a channel bringing water from the head gates to a water wheel. **3** a sluice for controlling water flow. [C17: from PEN[2] + STOCK]

pent (pɛnt) *vb* a past tense and past participle of **pen**[2].

penta- *combining form.* five: *pentagon; pentameter; pentaprism.* [from Greek *pente* five]

pentachlorophenol (ˌpɛntəˌklɔːrə'fiːnɒl) *n* a white crystalline water-insoluble compound used as a fungicide, herbicide, and preservative for wood. Formula: C_6Cl_5OH.

pentacle ('pɛntək^{ə}l) *n* another name for **pentagram.** [C16: from Italian *pentacolo* something having five corners; see PENTA-]

pentad ('pɛntæd) *n* **1** a group or series of five. **2** the number or sum of five. **3** a period of five years. **4** *Chem.* a pentavalent element, atom, . r radical. **5** *Meteorol.* a period of five days. [C17: from Greek *pentas* group of five]

pentadactyl (ˌpɛntəˈdæktɪl) *adj* (of the limbs of amphibians, reptiles, birds, and mammals) consisting of an upper arm or thigh, a forearm or shank, and a hand or foot bearing five digits.

pentagon ('pɛntəˌgɒn) *n* a polygon having five sides. ▸ **pentagonal** (pɛnˈtægən^{ə}l) *adj*

Pentagon ('pɛntəˌgɒn) *n* **1** the five-sided building in Arlington, Virginia, that houses the headquarters of the U.S. Department of Defense. **2** the military leadership of the U.S.

pentagram ('pɛntəˌgræm) *n* **1** a star-shaped figure formed by extending the sides of a regular pentagon to meet at five points. **2** such a figure used as a magical or symbolic figure by the Pythagoreans, black magicians, etc. ◆ Also called: **pentacle, pentangle.**

pentahedron (ˌpɛntəˈhiːdrən) *n, pl* **-drons** *or* **-dra** (-drə). a solid figure having five plane faces. See also **polyhedron.** ▸ **ˌpentaˈhedral** *adj*

pentamerous (pɛnˈtæmərəs) *adj* consisting of five parts, esp. (of flowers) having the petals, sepals, and other parts arranged in groups of five. ▸ **penˈtamerˌism** *n*

pentameter (pɛnˈtæmɪtə) *n* **1** a verse line consisting of five metrical feet. **2** (in classical prosody) a verse line consisting of two dactyls, one stressed syllable, two dactyls, and a final stressed syllable. ◆ *adj* **3** designating a verse line consisting of five metrical feet.

pentamidine (pɛnˈtæmɪˌdiːn, -dɪn) *n* a drug used to treat protozoal infections, esp. pneumonia caused by *Pneumocystis carinii* in AIDS patients.

pentane ('pɛnteɪn) *n* an alkane hydrocarbon having three isomers, esp. the isomer with a straight chain of carbon atoms (*n*-pentane) which is a colourless flammable liquid used as a solvent. Formula: C_5H_{12}.

pentangle ('pɛnˌtæŋg^{ə}l) *n* another name for **pentagram.**

pentangular (pɛnˈtæŋgjʊlə) *adj* having five angles.

pentanoic acid (ˌpɛntəˈnəʊɪk) *n* a colourless liquid carboxylic acid with an unpleasant odour, used in making perfumes, flavourings, and pharmaceuticals. Formula: $CH_3(CH_2)_3COOH$. Also called: **valeric acid.** [from PENTANE]

pentaprism ('pɛntəˌprɪzəm) *n* a five-sided prism that deviates light from any direction through an angle of 90°, typically used in single-lens reflex cameras between lens and viewfinder to present the image the right way round.

pentaquine ('pɛntəˌkwiːn, -kwɪn) *n* a synthetic drug used to treat malaria. Formula: $C_{18}H_{27}N_3O$. [C20: from PENTA- + QUINOLINE]

pentarchy ('pɛntɑːkɪ) *n, pl* **-chies. 1** government by five rulers. **2** a ruling body of five. **3** a union or association of five kingdoms, provinces, etc., each under its own ruler. **4** a country ruled by a body of five. ▸ **penˈtarchical** *adj*

pentastich ('pɛntəˌstɪk) *n* a poem, stanza, or strophe that consists of five lines.

Pentateuch ('pɛntəˌtjuːk) *n* the first five books of the Old Testament regarded as a unity. [C16: from Church Latin *pentateuchus*, from Greek PENTA- + *teukhos* tool (in Late Greek: scroll)] ▸ **ˌPentaˈteuchal** *adj*

pentathlon (pɛnˈtæθlən) *n* an athletic contest consisting of five different events, based on a competition in the ancient Greek Olympics. Compare **decathlon.** [C18: from Greek *pentathlon*, from PENTA- + *athlon* contest] ▸ **penˈtathlete** *n*

pentatomic (ˌpɛntəˈtɒmɪk) *adj Chem.* having five atoms in the molecule.

pentatonic scale (ˌpɛntəˈtɒnɪk) *n Music.* any of several scales consisting of five notes, the most commonly encountered one being composed of the first, second, third, fifth, and sixth degrees of the major diatonic scale.

pentavalent (ˌpɛntəˈveɪlənt) *adj Chem.* having a valency of five. Also: **quinquevalent.**

pentazocine (pɛnˈtæzəʊˌsiːn) *n* a powerful synthetic opiate used in medical practice as an analgesic.

Pentecost ('pɛntɪˌkɒst) *n* **1** a Christian festival occurring on Whit Sunday commemorating the descent of the Holy Ghost on the apostles. **2** Also called: **Feast of Weeks, Shavuot.** *Judaism.* the harvest festival celebrated fifty days after the second day of Passover on the sixth and seventh days of Sivan, and commemorating the giving the Torah on Mount Sinai. [Old English, from Church Latin *pentēcostē*, from Greek *pentēkostē* fiftieth]

Pentecostal (ˌpɛntɪˈkɒst^{ə}l) *adj* **1** (*usually prenominal*) of or relating to any of various Christian groups that emphasize the charismatic aspects of Christianity and adopt a fundamental attitude to the Bible. **2** of or relating to Pentecost or the influence of the Holy Ghost. ◆ *n* **3** a member of a Pentecostal Church. ▸ **ˌPenteˈcostalˌism** *n* ▸ **ˌPenteˈcostalist** *n, adj*

Pentelikon (pɛnˈtɛlɪkɒn) *n* a mountain in SE Greece, near Athens: famous for its white marble, worked regularly from the 6th century B.C., from which the chief buildings and sculptures in Athens are made. Height: 1109 m (3638 ft.). Latin name: **Penˈtelicus.**

pentene ('pɛntiːn) *n* a colourless flammable liquid alkene having several straight-chained isomeric forms, used in the manufacture of organic compounds. Formula: C_5H_{10}. Also called: **amylene.**

Penthesileia *or* **Penthesilea** (ˌpɛnθəsɪˈleɪə) *n Greek myth.* the daughter of Ares and queen of the Amazons, whom she led to the aid of Troy. She was slain by Achilles.

Pentheus ('pɛnθɪəs) *n Greek myth.* the grandson of Cadmus and his successor as king of Thebes, who resisted the introduction of the cult of Dionysus. In revenge the god drove him mad and he was torn to pieces by a group of bacchantes, one of whom was his mother.

penthouse ('pɛntˌhaʊs) *n* **1** a flat or maisonette built onto the top floor or roof of a block of flats. **2** a construction on the roof of a building, esp. one used to house machinery. **3** a shed built against a building, esp. one that has a sloping roof. **4** *Real Tennis.* the roofed corridor that runs along three sides of the court. [C14 *pentis* (later *penthouse*, by folk etymology), from Old French *apentis*, from Late Latin *appendicium* appendage, from Latin *appendere* to hang from; see APPENDIX]

pentimento (ˌpɛntɪˈmɛntəʊ) *n, pl* **-ti** (-tiː). **1** the revealing of a painting or part of a painting that has been covered over by a later painting. **2** the part of a painting thus revealed. [C20: Italian, literally: correction]

Pentland Firth ('pɛntlənd) *n* a channel between the mainland of N Scotland and the Orkney Islands: notorious for rough seas. Length: 32 km (20 miles). Width: up to 13 km (8 miles).

pentlandite ('pɛntlənˌdaɪt) *n* a brownish-yellow mineral consisting of an iron and nickel sulphide in cubic crystalline form: the principal ore of nickel. Formula: (Fe,Ni)S. [C19: from French; named after J. B. *Pentland* (1797–1873), Irish scientist who discovered it]

pentobarbitone sodium (ˌpɛntəˈbɑːbɪˌtəʊn) *n* a barbiturate drug used in medicine as a sedative and hypnotic. U.S. equivalent: **ˈsodium ˌpentaˈbarbital.** Formula: $C_{11}H_{17}N_2O_3Na$.

pentode ('pɛntəʊd) *n* **1** an electronic valve having five electrodes: a cathode, anode, and three grids. **2** (*modifier*) (of a transistor) having three terminals at the base or gate. [C20: from PENTA- + Greek *hodos* way]

pentomic (pɛnˈtɒmɪk) *adj* denoting or relating to the subdivision of an army division into five battle groups, esp. for nuclear warfare. [C20: from PENTA- + ATOMIC]

pentosan ('pɛntəˌsæn) *n Biochem.* any of a group of polysaccharides, having the general formula $(C_5H_8O_4)_n$: occur in plants, humus, etc. [C20: from PENTOSE + -AN]

pentose ('pɛntəʊs) *n* any monosaccharide containing five atoms of carbon per molecule: occur mainly in plants and the nucleic acids. [C20: from PENTA- + -OSE[2]]

pentose phosphate pathway *n* a sequence of metabolic reactions by which NADPH is synthesized, together with ribose phosphate, part of the synthesis of nucleic acids.

Pentothal sodium ('pɛntəˌθæl) *n* a trademark for **thiopentone sodium.**

pentoxide (pɛntˈɒksaɪd) *n* an oxide of an element with five atoms of oxygen per molecule.

pentstemon (pɛntˈstiːmən) *or esp. U.S.* **penstemon** *n* any scrophulariaceous plant of the North American genus *Pentstemon* (or *Penstemon*), having white, pink, red, blue, or purple flowers with five stamens, one of which is bearded and sterile. [C18: New Latin, from PENTA- + Greek *stēmōn* thread (here: stamen)]

pent-up *adj* (**pent up** *when postpositive*) **1** not released; repressed: *pent-up emotions.* **2** kept unwillingly: *I've been pent up in this office for over a year.*

pentyl ('pɛntaɪl, -tɪl) *n* (*modifier*) of, consisting of, or containing the monovalent group $CH_3CH_2CH_2CH_2CH_2$-: *a pentyl group or radical.*

pentyl acetate *n* a colourless combustible liquid used as a solvent for paints, in the extraction of penicillin, in photographic film, and as a flavouring. Formula: $CH_3COOC_5H_{11}$. Also called: **amyl acetate.** Nontechnical name: **banana oil.**

pentylenetetrazol (ˌpɛntɪliːnˈtɛtrəˌzɒl) *n* a white crystalline water-soluble substance with a bitter taste, used in medicine to stimulate the central nervous system. Formula: $C_6H_{10}N_4$. [C20: from *penta-methylene-tetrazole*]

penuche (pəˈnuːtʃɪ) *n* a variant of **panocha.**

penuchle *or* **penuckle** ('piːnʌk^{ə}l) *n* less common spellings of **pinochle.**

penult ('pɛnʌlt, pɪˈnʌlt) *or* **penultima** (pɪˈnʌltɪmə) *n* the last syllable but one in a word. [C16: Latin *paenultima syllaba*, from *paene ultima* almost the last]

penultimate (pɪˈnʌltɪmɪt) *adj* **1** next to the last. ◆ *n* **2** anything that is next to the last, esp. a penult. [C17: from Latin *paene* almost + ULTIMATE, on the model of Latin *paenultimus*]

penumbra (pɪˈnʌmbrə) *n, pl* **-brae** (-briː) *or* **-bras. 1** a fringe region of half shadow resulting from the partial obstruction of light by an opaque object. **2** *Astronomy.* the lighter and outer region of a sunspot. **3** *Painting.* the point or area in which light and shade blend. ◆ Compare **umbra.** [C17: via New Latin from Latin *paene* almost + *umbra* shadow] ▸ **peˈnumbral** *or* **peˈnumbrous** *adj*

penurious (pɪˈnjʊərɪəs) *adj* **1** niggardly with money. **2** lacking money or means. **3** yielding little; scanty. ▸ **peˈnuriously** *adv* ▸ **peˈnuriousness** *n*

penury ('pɛnjʊrɪ) *n* **1** extreme poverty. **2** extreme scarcity. [C15: from Latin *pēnūria* dearth, of obscure origin]

Penutian (pɪˈnjuːtɪən, -ʃən) *n* **1** a family of North American Indian languages of the Pacific coast. **2** a phylum of languages of North and South America, including Araucanian, Chinook, Mayan, and Sahaptin.

Penza (*Russian* ˈpjɛnzə) *n* a city in W Russia: manufacturing centre. Pop.: 534 000 (1995 est.).

Penzance (pɛnˈzæns) *n* a town in SW England, in SW Cornwall: the westernmost town in England; resort and fishing port. Pop.: 19 709 (1991).

Penzias ('pɛntsɪəs, 'pɛnz-) *n* **Arno Allan.** born 1933, U.S. astrophysicist, who shared the Nobel prize for physics (1978) with Robert W. Wilson for their discovery of cosmic microwave background radiation.

peon[1] ('piːən, 'piːɒn) *n* **1** a Spanish-American farm labourer or unskilled worker. **2** (formerly in Spanish America) a debtor compelled to work off his debts. **3** any very poor person. [C19: from Spanish *peón* peasant, from Medieval Latin *pedō* man who goes on foot, from Latin *pēs* foot; compare Old French *paon* PAWN[2]]

peon[2] (pjuːn, 'piːən, 'piːɒn) *n* (in India, Sri Lanka, etc., esp. formerly) **1** a messenger or attendant, esp. in an office. **2** a native policeman. **3** a foot soldier. [C17: from Portuguese *peão* orderly; see PEON[1]]

peonage ('piːənɪdʒ) *or* **peonism** ('piːəˌnɪzəm) *n* **1** the state of being a peon. **2** a system in which a debtor must work for his creditor until the debt is paid off.

peony *or* **paeony** ('piːənɪ) *n, pl* **-nies. 1** any of various ranunculaceous shrubs and plants of the genus *Paeonia*, of Eurasia and North America, having large pink, red, white, or yellow flowers. **2** the flower of any of these plants. [Old English *peonie*, from Latin *paeōnia*, from Greek *paiōnia;* related to *paiōnios* healing, from *paiōn* physician]

people ('piːpᵊl) *n* (*usually functioning as pl*) **1** persons collectively or in general. **2** a group of persons considered together: *blind people*. **3** (*pl* **peoples**) the persons living in a country and sharing the same nationality: *the French people*. **4** one's family: *he took her home to meet his people*. **5** persons loyal to someone powerful: *the king's people accompanied him in exile*. **6 the people. 6a** the mass of persons without special distinction, privileges, etc. **6b** the body of persons in a country, esp. those entitled to vote. ◆ *vb* **7** (*tr*) to provide with or as if with people or inhabitants. [C13: from Old French *pople*, from Latin *populus;* see POPULACE]

USAGE See at **person**.

people carrier *n* another name for **multipurpose vehicle**.

people mover *n* **1** any of various automated forms of transport for large numbers of passengers over short distances, such as a moving pavement, driverless cars, etc. **2** another name for **multipurpose vehicle**.

people's democracy *n* (in Communist ideology) a country or form of government in transition from bourgeois democracy to socialism. In this stage there is more than one class, the largest being the proletariat, led by the Communist Party, which is therefore the dominant power.

people's front *n* a less common term for **popular front**.

People's Party *n U.S. history*. the political party of the Populists.

Peoria (piː'ɔːrɪə) *n* a port in N central Illinois, on the Illinois River. Pop.: 112 306 (1996 est.).

pep (pɛp) *n* **1** high spirits, energy, or vitality. ◆ *vb* **peps, pepping, pepped. 2** (*tr;* usually foll. by *up*) to liven by imbuing with new vigour. [C20: short for PEPPER]

PEP (pɛp) *n acronym for* **1** personal equity plan: a method of saving in the U.K. with certain tax advantages, in which investments up to a fixed annual value can be purchased. ◆ *abbrev. for* **2** political and economic planning.

peperomia (pɛpə'rəʊmɪə) *n* any plant of the large genus *Peperomia* from tropical and subtropical America with slightly fleshy ornamental leaves, some of which are grown as pot plants: family *Piperaceae*. [New Latin, from Greek *peperi* pepper + *homoios* similar + -IA]

Pepin the Short ('pɛpɪn) *n* died 768 A.D., king of the Franks (751–768); son of Charles Martel and father of Charlemagne. He deposed the Merovingian king (751) and founded the Carolingian dynasty.

peplos *or* **peplus** ('pɛpləs) *n, pl* **-loses** *or* **-luses**. (in ancient Greece) the top part of a woman's attire, caught at the shoulders and hanging in folds to the waist. Also called: **peplum**. [C18: from Greek, of obscure origin]

peplum ('pɛpləm) *n, pl* **-lums** *or* **-la** (-lə). **1** a flared ruffle attached to the waist of a jacket, bodice, etc. **2** a variant of **peplos**. [C17: from Latin: full upper garment, from Greek *peplos* shawl]

pepo ('piːpəʊ) *n, pl* **-pos**. the fruit of any of various cucurbitaceous plants, such as the melon, squash, cucumber, and pumpkin, having a firm rind, fleshy watery pulp, and numerous seeds. [C19: from Latin: pumpkin, from Greek *pepōn* edible gourd, from *peptein* to ripen]

pepper ('pɛpə) *n* **1** a woody climbing plant, *Piper nigrum*, of the East Indies, having small black berry-like fruits: family *Piperaceae*. **2** the dried fruit of this plant, which is ground to produce a sharp hot condiment. See also **black pepper, white pepper. 3** any of various other plants of the genus *Piper*. See **cubeb, betel, kava. 4** Also called: **capsicum**. any of various tropical plants of the solanaceous genus *Capsicum*, esp. *C. frutescens*, the fruits of which are used as a vegetable and a condiment. See also **bird pepper, sweet pepper, red pepper, cayenne pepper. 5** the fruit of any of these capsicums, which has a mild or pungent taste. **6** the condiment made from the fruits of any of these plants. **7** any of various similar but unrelated plants, such as water pepper. ◆ *vb* (*tr*) **8** to season with pepper. **9** to sprinkle liberally; dot: *his prose was peppered with alliteration*. **10** to pelt with small missiles. [Old English *piper*, from Latin, from Greek *peperi;* compare French *poivre*, Old Norse *piparr*]

pepper-and-salt *adj* **1** (of cloth) marked with a fine mixture of black and white. **2** (of hair) streaked with grey.

peppercorn ('pɛpəˌkɔːn) *n* **1** the small dried berry of the pepper plant (*Piper nigrum*). **2** something trifling.

peppercorn rent *n* a rent that is very low or nominal.

peppered moth *n* a European geometrid moth, *Biston betularia*, occurring in a pale grey speckled form in rural areas and a black form in industrial regions. See also **melanism** (sense 1).

peppergrass ('pɛpəˌgrɑːs) *n* the usual U.S. and Canadian name for **pepperwort** (sense 2).

pepper mill *n* a small hand mill used to grind peppercorns.

peppermint ('pɛpəˌmɪnt) *n* **1** a temperate mint plant, *Mentha piperita*, with purple or white flowers: cultivated for its downy leaves, which yield a pungent oil. **2** the oil from this plant, which is used as a flavouring. **3** a sweet flavoured with peppermint.

pepperoni (ˌpɛpə'rəʊnɪ) *n* a highly seasoned dry sausage of pork and beef spiced with pepper, used esp. on pizza. [C20: from Italian *peperoni*, plural of *peperone* cayenne pepper]

pepper pot *n* **1** a small container with perforations in the top for sprinkling pepper. **2** a Caribbean stew of meat, rice, vegetables, etc., highly seasoned with cassareep.

pepper tree *n* any of several evergreen anacardiaceous trees of the chiefly South American genus *Schinus*, esp. *S. molle* (also called: **mastic tree**), having yellowish-white flowers and bright red ornamental fruits.

peppertree ('pɛpəˌtriː) *n N.Z.* another name for **kawakawa**.

pepperwort ('pɛpəˌwɜːt) *n* **1** any of various temperate and tropical aquatic or marsh ferns of the genus *Marsilea*, having floating leaves consisting of four leaflets: family *Marsileaceae*. **2** any of several cruciferous plants of the genus *Lepidium*, esp. *L. campestre*, of dry regions of Eurasia, having small white flowers and pungent seeds. Usual U.S. and Canadian name: **peppergrass**.

peppery ('pɛpərɪ) *adj* **1** flavoured with or tasting of pepper. **2** quick-tempered; irritable. **3** full of bite and sharpness: *a peppery speech*. ▸ **'pepperiness** *n*

pep pill *n Informal*. a tablet containing a stimulant drug.

peppy ('pɛpɪ) *adj* **-pier, -piest**. *Informal*. full of vitality; bouncy or energetic. ▸ **'peppily** *adv* ▸ **'peppiness** *n*

pepsin *or* **pepsine** ('pɛpsɪn) *n* a proteolytic enzyme produced in the stomach in the inactive form pepsinogen, which, when activated by acid, splits proteins into peptones. [C19: via German from Greek *pepsis*, from *peptein* to digest]

pepsinate ('pɛpsɪˌneɪt) *vb* (*tr*) **1** to treat (a patient) with pepsin. **2** to mix or infuse (something) with pepsin.

pepsinogen (pɛp'sɪnədʒən) *n* the inactive precursor of pepsin produced by the stomach.

pep talk *n Informal*. an enthusiastic talk designed to increase confidence, production, cooperation, etc.

peptic ('pɛptɪk) *adj* **1** of, relating to, or promoting digestion. **2** of, relating to, or caused by pepsin or the action of the digestive juices. [C17: from Greek *peptikos* capable of digesting, from *pepsis* digestion, from *peptein* to digest]

peptic ulcer *n Pathol*. an ulcer of the mucous membrane lining those parts of the alimentary tract exposed to digestive juices. It can occur in the oesophagus, the stomach, the duodenum, the jejunum, or in parts of the ileum.

peptidase ('pɛptɪˌdeɪs, -ˌdeɪz) *n* any of a group of proteolytic enzymes that hydrolyse peptides to amino acids.

peptide ('pɛptaɪd) *n* any of a group of compounds consisting of two or more amino acids linked by chemical bonding between their respective carboxyl and amino groups. See also **peptide bond, polypeptide**.

peptide bond *n Biochem*. a chemical amide linkage, –NH–CO–, formed by the condensation of the amino group of one amino acid with the carboxyl group of another.

peptize *or* **peptise** ('pɛptaɪz) *vb* (*tr*) *Chem*. to disperse (a substance) into a colloidal state, usually to form a sol. ▸ **'peptizable** *or* **'peptisable** *adj* ▸ **ˌpepti'zation** *or* **ˌpepti'sation** *n* ▸ **'peptizer** *or* **'peptiser** *n*

peptone ('pɛptəʊn) *n Biochem*. any of a group of compounds that form an intermediary group in the digestion of proteins to amino acids. See also **proteose**. [C19: from German *Pepton*, from Greek *pepton* something digested, from *peptein* to digest] ▸ **peptonic** (pɛp'tɒnɪk) *adj*

peptonize *or* **peptonise** ('pɛptəˌnaɪz) *vb* (*tr*) to hydrolyse (a protein) to peptones by enzymic action, esp. by pepsin or pancreatic extract. ▸ **ˌpeptoni'zation** *or* **ˌpeptoni'sation** *n* ▸ **'peptoˌnizer** *or* **'peptoˌniser** *n*

Pepys (piːps) *n* **Samuel**. 1633–1703, English diarist and naval administrator. His diary, which covers the period 1660–69, is a vivid account of London life through such disasters as the Great Plague, the Fire of London, and the intrusion of the Dutch fleet up the Thames.

Péquiste (peɪ'kiːst) *n* (*sometimes not cap.*) (in Canada) a member or supporter of the Parti Québecois. [from the French pronunciation of PQ + *-iste*]

Pequot ('piːkwɒt) *n* **1** (*pl* **-quot** *or* **-quots**) a member of a North American Indian people formerly living in S New England. **2** the language of this people, belonging to the Algonquian family. [probably based on Narraganset *paquatanog* destroyers]

per (pɜː; *unstressed* pə) *determiner* **1** for every: *three pence per pound*. ◆ *prep* **2** (esp. in some Latin phrases) by; through. **3 as per**. according to: *as per specifications*. **4 as per usual**. *Informal*. as usual. [C15: from Latin: by, for each]

PER (in Britain) *abbrev. for* Professional Employment Register.

per. *abbrev. for:* **1** period. **2** person.

per- *prefix* **1** through: *pervade*. **2** throughout: *perennial*. **3** away, beyond: *perfidy*. **4** completely, throughly: *perplex*. **5** (intensifier): *perfervid*. **6** indicating that a chemical compound contains a high proportion of a specified element: *peroxide; perchloride*. **7** indicating that a chemical element is in a higher than usual state of oxidation: *permanganate; perchlorate*. **8** (*not in technical usage*) a variant of **peroxy-**: *persulphuric acid*. [from Latin *per* through]

Pera ('pɪərə) *n* the former name of **Beyoğlu**.

peracid (pɜː'ræsɪd) *n* **1** an acid, such as perchloric acid, in which the element forming the acid radical exhibits its highest valency. **2** (*not in technical usage*) an acid, such as persulphuric acid, that contains the -OOH group. Recommended names: **per'oxo acid, per'oxy acid**. ▸ **peracidity** (ˌpɜːrə'sɪdɪtɪ) *n*

peradventure (pərəd'vɛntʃə, ˌpɜːr-) *Archaic*. ◆ *adv* **1** by chance; perhaps. ◆ *n* **2** chance, uncertainty, or doubt. [C13: from Old French *par aventure* by chance]

Peraea *or* **Perea** (pə'riːə) *n* a region of ancient Palestine, east of the River Jordan and the Dead Sea.

Perak ('pɛərə, 'pɪərə, pɪ'ræk) *n* a state of NW Peninsular Malaysia, on the Strait of Malacca: tin mining. Capital: Ipoh. Pop.: 2 222 400 (1993 est.). Area: 20 680 sq. km (8030 sq. miles).

perambulate (pə'ræmbjʊˌleɪt) *vb* **1** to walk about (a place). **2** (*tr*) to walk round in order to inspect. [C16: from Latin *perambulāre* to traverse, from *per* through + *ambulāre* to walk] ▸ **perˌambu'lation** *n* ▸ **perambulatory** (pə'ræmbjʊlətərɪ, -trɪ) *adj*

perambulator (pə'ræmbjʊˌleɪtə) *n* **1** a formal word for **pram**[1]. **2** a wheel-like instrument used by surveyors to measure distances.

per annum (pər 'ænəm) *adv* every year or by the year.

per ardua ad astra *Latin.* (pɜːr ˈɑːdjuə æd ˈæstrə) through difficulties to the stars: the motto of the RAF.

P/E ratio *abbrev. for* **price-earnings ratio.**

perborate (pəˈbɔːreɪt) *n* any of certain salts derived, or apparently derived, from perboric acid. Perborates are used as bleaches in washing powders. See **sodium perborate.**

percale (pəˈkeɪl, -ˈkɑːl) *n* a close-textured woven cotton fabric, plain or printed, used esp. for sheets. [C17: via French from Persian *pargālah* piece of cloth]

percaline (ˈpɜːkəˌliːn, -lɪn) *n* a fine light cotton fabric, used esp. for linings. [C19: from French; see PERCALE]

per capita (pə ˈkæpɪtə) *adj, adv* of or for each person. [Latin, literally: according to heads]

perceive (pəˈsiːv) *vb* **1** to become aware of (something) through the senses, esp. the sight; recognize or observe. **2** (*tr; may take a clause as object*) to come to comprehend; grasp. [C13: from Old French *perçoivre,* from Latin *percipere* seize entirely, from PER- (thoroughly) + *capere* to grasp] ▸ **perˈceivable** *adj* ▸ **perˌceivaˈbility** *n* ▸ **perˈceivably** *adv* ▸ **perˈceiver** *n*

perceived noise decibel *n* a unit for measuring perceived levels of noise by comparison with the sound pressure level of a reference sound judged equally noisy by a normal listener. Abbrev.: **PNdB.**

per cent (pə ˈsɛnt) *adv* **1** Also: **per centum.** in or for every hundred. ◆ *n also* **perˈcent. 2** a percentage or proportion. **3** (*often pl*) securities yielding a rate of interest as specified: *he bought three percents.* [C16: from Medieval Latin *per centum* out of every hundred]

percentage (pəˈsɛntɪdʒ) *n* **1** proportion or rate per hundred parts. **2** *Commerce.* the interest, tax, commission, or allowance on a hundred items. **3** any proportion in relation to the whole. **4** *Informal.* profit or advantage.

percentile (pəˈsɛntaɪl) *n* one of 99 actual or notional values of a variable dividing its distribution into 100 groups with equal frequencies; the 90th percentile is the value of a variable such that 90% of the relevant population is below that value. Also called: **centile.**

percept (ˈpɜːsɛpt) *n* **1** a concept that depends on recognition by the senses, such as sight, of some external object or phenomenon. **2** an object or phenomenon that is perceived. [C19: from Latin *perceptum,* from *percipere* to PERCEIVE]

perceptible (pəˈsɛptəbᵊl) *adj* able to be perceived; noticeable or recognizable. ▸ **perˌceptiˈbility** *n* ▸ **perˈceptibly** *adv*

perception (pəˈsɛpʃən) *n* **1** the act or the effect of perceiving. **2** insight or intuition gained by perceiving. **3** the ability or capacity to perceive. **4** way of perceiving; awareness or consciousness; view: *advertising affects the customer's perception of a product.* **5** the process by which an organism detects and interprets information from the external world by means of the sensory receptors. **6** *Law.* the collection, receipt, or taking into possession of rents, crops, etc. [C15: from Latin *perceptiō* comprehension; see PERCEIVE] ▸ **perˈceptional** *adj*

perceptive (pəˈsɛptɪv) *adj* **1** quick at perceiving; observant. **2** perceptual. **3** able to perceive. ▸ **perˈceptively** *adv* ▸ **perˈceptiveness** *or* **ˌpercepˈtivity** *n*

perceptual (pəˈsɛptjuəl) *adj* of or relating to perception. ▸ **perˈceptually** *adv*

perceptual defence *n Psychol.* the process by which it is thought that certain stimuli are either not perceived or are distorted due to their offensive, unpleasant, or threatening nature.

perceptual mapping *n Marketing.* the use of a graph or map in the development of a new product, in which the proximity of consumers' images of the new product to those of an ideal product provide an indication of the new product's likely success.

Perceval (ˈpɜːsɪvᵊl) *n* **Spencer.** 1762–1812, British statesman; prime minister (1809–12); assassinated.

perch[1] (pɜːtʃ) *n* **1** a pole, branch, or other resting place above ground on which a bird roosts or alights. **2** a similar resting place for a person or thing. **3** another name for **rod** (sense 7). **4** a solid measure for stone, usually taken as 198 inches by 18 inches by 12 inches. **5** a pole joining the front and rear axles of a carriage. **6** a frame on which cloth is placed for inspection. **7** *Obsolete or dialect.* a pole. ◆ *vb* **8** (usually foll. by *on*) to alight, rest, or cause to rest on or as if on a perch: *the bird perched on the branch; the cap was perched on his head.* **9** (*tr*) to inspect (cloth) on a perch. [C13 *perche* stake, from Old French, from Latin *pertica* long staff] ▸ **ˈpercher** *n*

perch[2] (pɜːtʃ) *n, pl* **perch** *or* **perches. 1** any freshwater spiny-finned teleost fish of the family *Percidae,* esp. those of the genus *Perca,* such as *P. fluviatilis* of Europe and *P. flavescens* (**yellow perch**) of North America: valued as food and game fishes. **2** any of various similar or related fishes. Related adj: **percoid.** [C13: from Old French *perche,* from Latin *perca,* from Greek *perkē;* compare Greek *perkos* spotted]

perchance (pəˈtʃɑːns) *adv Archaic or poetic.* **1** perhaps; possibly. **2** by chance; accidentally. [C14: from Anglo-French *par chance;* see PER, CHANCE]

Percheron (ˈpɜːʃəˌrɒn) *n* a compact heavy breed of carthorse, grey or black in colour. [C19: from French, from *le Perche,* region of NW France where the breed originated]

perchery (ˈpɜːtʃərɪ) *n, pl* **-eries. a** a barn in which hens are allowed to move without restriction. **b** (*as modifier*): *perchery eggs.* [C20: from PERCH[1]]

perchlorate (pəˈklɔːreɪt) *n* any salt or ester of perchloric acid. Perchlorate salts contain the ion ClO_4^-.

perchloric acid (pəˈklɔːrɪk) *n* a colourless syrupy oxyacid of chlorine containing a greater proportion of oxygen than chloric acid. It is a powerful oxidizing agent and is used as a laboratory reagent. Formula: $HClO_4$. Systematic name: **chloric(VII) acid.**

perchloride (pəˈklɔːraɪd) *n* a chloride that contains more chlorine than other chlorides of the same element.

perchloroethylene (pəˌklɔːrəʊˈɛθɪliːn) *or* **perchloroethene** (pəˌklɔːrəʊˈɛθiːn) *n* a colourless liquid used as a dry-cleaning solvent. Formula: $CCl_2{:}CCl_2$.

percipient (pəˈsɪpɪənt) *adj* **1** able to perceive. **2** perceptive. ◆ *n* **3** a person or thing that perceives. [C17: from Latin *percipiens* observing, from *percipere* to grasp; see PERCEIVE] ▸ **perˈcipience** *n* ▸ **perˈcipiently** *adv*

Percival *or* **Perceval** (ˈpɜːsɪvᵊl) *n* (in Arthurian legend) a knight in King Arthur's court. German equivalent: **Parzival.**

percoid (ˈpɜːkɔɪd) *or* **percoidean** (pəˈkɔɪdɪən) *adj* **1** of, relating to, or belonging to the *Percoidea,* a suborder of spiny-finned teleost fishes including the perches, sea bass, red mullet, cichlids, etc. **2** of, relating to, or resembling a perch. ◆ *n* **3** any fish belonging to the suborder *Percoidea.* [C19: from Latin *perca* PERCH[2] + -OID]

percolate *vb* (ˈpɜːkəˌleɪt). **1** to cause (a liquid) to pass through a fine mesh, porous substance, etc., or (of a liquid) to pass through a fine mesh, porous substance, etc.; trickle: *rain percolated through the roof.* **2** to permeate; penetrate gradually: *water percolated the road.* **3** (*intr*) *U.S. informal.* to become active or lively: *she percolated with happiness.* **4** to make (coffee) or (of coffee) to be made in a percolator. ◆ *n* (ˈpɜːkəlɪt, -ˌleɪt). **5** a product of percolation. [C17: from Latin *percolāre,* from PER + *cōlāre* to strain, from *cōlum* a strainer; see COLANDER] ▸ **percolable** (ˈpɜːkələbᵊl) *adj* ▸ **ˌpercoˈlation** *n* ▸ **ˈpercolative** *adj*

percolator (ˈpɜːkəˌleɪtə) *n* a kind of coffeepot in which boiling water is forced up through a tube and filters down through the coffee grounds into a container.

per contra (ˈpɜː ˈkɒntrə) *adv* on the contrary. [from Latin]

percuss (pəˈkʌs) *vb* (*tr*) **1** to strike sharply, rapidly, or suddenly. **2** *Med.* to tap on (a body surface) with the fingertips or a special hammer to aid diagnosis or for therapeutic purposes. [C16: from Latin *percutere,* from *per-* through + *quatere* to shake] ▸ **perˈcussor** *n*

percussion (pəˈkʌʃən) *n* **1** the act, an instance, or an effect of percussing. **2** *Music.* the family of instruments in which sound arises from the striking of materials with sticks or hammers. **3** *Music.* **3a** instruments of this family constituting a section of an orchestra, band, etc. **3b** (*as modifier*): *a percussion ensemble.* **4** *Med.* the act of percussing a body surface. **5** the act of exploding a percussion cap. [C16: from Latin *percussiō,* from *percutere* to hit; see PERCUSS]

percussion cap *n* a detonator consisting of a paper or thin metal cap containing material that explodes when struck and formerly used in certain firearms.

percussion instrument *n* any of various musical instruments that produce a sound when their resonating surfaces are struck directly, as with a stick or mallet, or by leverage action. They may be of definite pitch (as a kettledrum or xylophone), indefinite pitch (as a gong or rattle), or a mixture of both (as various drums).

percussionist (pəˈkʌʃənɪst) *n Music.* a person who plays any of several percussion instruments, esp. in an orchestra.

percussion lock *n* a gunlock in which the hammer strikes a percussion cap.

percussion tool *n* a power driven tool which operates by striking rapid blows: the power may be electricity or compressed air.

percussive (pəˈkʌsɪv) *adj* of, caused by, or relating to percussion. ▸ **perˈcussively** *adv* ▸ **perˈcussiveness** *n*

percutaneous (ˌpɜːkjuˈteɪnɪəs) *adj Med.* effected through the skin, as in the absorption of an ointment.

Percy (ˈpɜːsɪ) *n* **1** Sir **Henry,** known as *Harry Hotspur.* 1364–1403, English rebel, who was killed leading an army against Henry IV. **2 Thomas.** 1729–1811, English bishop and antiquary. His *Reliques of Ancient English Poetry* (1765) stimulated the interest of Romantic writers in old English and Scottish ballads.

Perdido (*Spanish* perˈðiðo) *n* **Monte** (ˈmɔnte). a mountain in NE Spain, in the central Pyrenees. Height: 3352 m (10 997 ft.). French name: (Mont) **Perdu.**

per diem (ˈpɜː ˈdaɪɛm, ˈdiːɛm) *adv* **1** every day or by the day. ◆ *n* **2a** an allowance for daily expenses, usually those incurred while working. **2b** (*as modifier*): *a per-diem allowance.* [from Latin]

perdition (pəˈdɪʃən) *n* **1** *Christianity.* **1a** final and irrevocable spiritual ruin. **1b** this state as one that the wicked are said to be destined to endure for ever. **2** another word for **hell. 3** *Archaic.* utter disaster, ruin, or destruction. [C14: from Late Latin *perditiō* ruin, from Latin *perdere* to lose, from PER- (away) + *dāre* to give]

perdu *or* **perdue** (ˈpɜːdjuː) *adj* **1** *Obsolete.* (of a soldier) placed on hazardous sentry duty. **2** *Obsolete.* (of a soldier) placed in a hazardous ambush. **3** (of a person or thing) hidden or concealed. ◆ *n* **4** *Obsolete.* a soldier placed on hazardous sentry duty. **5** *Obsolete.* a soldier placed in a hazardous ambush. [C16: via French: lost, from *perdre* to lose, from Latin *perdere* to destroy]

Perdu (pɛrdy) *n* **Mont.** the French name for (Monte) **Perdido.**

perdurable (pəˈdjʊərəbᵊl) *adj Rare.* extremely durable. [C13: from Late Latin *perdūrābilis,* from Latin *per-* (intensive) + *dūrābilis* long-lasting, from *dūrus* hard] ▸ **ˌperduraˈbility** *n* ▸ **ˈperdurably** *adv*

père *French.* (pɛr; *English* pɛə) *n* an addition to a French surname to specify the father rather than the son of the same name: *Dumas père.* Compare **fils**[1].

Perea (pəˈriːə) *n* a variant spelling of **Peraea.**

Père David's deer *n* a large grey deer, *Elaphurus davidianus,* surviving only in captivity as descendants of a herd preserved in the Imperial hunting park near Beijing. [C20: named after Father A. *David* (died 1900), French missionary]

peregrinate (ˈpɛrɪɡrɪˌneɪt) *vb* **1** (*intr*) to travel or wander about from place to place; voyage. **2** (*tr*) to travel through (a place). ◆ *adj* **3** an obsolete word for **foreign.** [C16: from Latin, from *peregrīnārī* to travel; see PEREGRINE] ▸ **ˈperegriˌnator** *n*

peregrination (ˌpɛrɪɡrɪˈneɪʃən) *n* **1** a voyage, esp. an extensive one. **2** the act or process of travelling.

peregrine (ˈpɛrɪɡrɪn) *adj Archaic.* **1** coming from abroad. **2** travelling or migratory; wandering. [**C14**: from Latin *peregrīnus* foreign, from *pereger* being abroad, from *per* through + *ager* land (that is, beyond one's own land)]

peregrine falcon *n* a falcon, *Falco peregrinus,* occurring in most parts of the world, having a dark plumage on the back and wings and lighter underparts. See also **duck hawk.**

Pereira (*Spanish* peˈreira) *n* a town in W central Colombia: cattle trading and coffee processing. Pop.: 434 267 (1997 est.).

pereira bark (pəˈrɛərə) *n* the bark of a South American apocynaceous tree, *Geissospermum vellosii:* source of a substance formerly used for treating malaria. [named after Jonathan *Pereira* (1804–53), English pharmacologist]

Perelman (ˈpɛrəlmən, ˈpɜːl-) *n* **S(idney) J(oseph).** 1904–79, U.S. humorous writer. After scriptwriting for the Marx Brothers, he published many collections of articles, including *Crazy Like a Fox* (1944) and *Eastward, Hi!* (1977).

peremptory (pəˈrɛmptərɪ) *adj* **1** urgent or commanding: *a peremptory ring on the bell.* **2** not able to be remitted or debated; decisive. **3** positive or assured in speech, manner, etc.; dogmatic. **4** *Law.* **4a** admitting of no denial or contradiction; precluding debate. **4b** obligatory rather than permissive. [**C16**: from Anglo-Norman *peremptorie,* from Latin *peremptōrius* decisive, from *perimere* to take away completely, from PER- (intensive) + *emere* to take] ▸ **perˈemptorily** *adv* ▸ **perˈemptoriness** *n*

Perendale (ˈpɛrənˌdeɪl) *n N.Z.* a Romney-Cheviot crossbreed of sheep. [**C20**: named after Sir Geoffrey S. *Peren,* New Zealand agriculturist]

perennate (ˈpɛrɪˌneɪt, pəˈrɛneɪt) *vb (intr)* (of plants) to live from one growing season to another, usually with a period of reduced activity between seasons. [**C17**: from Latin *perennātus,* from *perennāre,* from PER- (through) + *annus* year]

perennial (pəˈrɛnɪəl) *adj* **1** lasting throughout the year or through many years. **2** everlasting; perpetual. ◆ *n* **3** a woody or herbaceous plant that continues its growth for at least three years. Compare **annual** (sense 3), **biennial** (sense 3). [**C17**: from Latin *perennis* continual, from *per* through + *annus* year] ▸ **perˈennially** *adv*

perentie *or* **perenty** (pəˈrɛntɪ) *n, pl* **-ties.** a large dark-coloured monitor lizard, *Varanus giganteus,* of central and west Australia which grows to 7 ft. [from a native Australian language]

Peres (ˈpɛrɛs) *n* **Shimon** (ʃiːˈməʊn). born 1923, Israeli statesman, born in Poland: prime minister (1984–86; 1995–96); Nobel peace prize 1994 jointly with Yasser Arafat and Yitzhak Rabin.

perestroika (ˌpɛrəˈstrɔɪkə) *n* the policy of reconstructing the economy, etc., of the former Soviet Union under the leadership of Mikhail Gorbachov. [**C20**: Russian, literally: reconstruction]

Pérez de Cuéllar (ˈpɛrɛs də ˈkwerjɑː) *n* **Javier** (ˈhævɪeɪ) born 1920, Peruvian diplomat and UN secretary-general (1982–91).

Pérez Galdós (ˈpɛrɛs ɡɑːlˈdəʊs) *n* **Benito.** 1843–1920, Spanish novelist. His works include the *Episodios nacionales* (1873–1912), a series of historical novels, and *Fortunata y Jacinta* (1886–87).

perf. *abbrev. for:* **1** perfect. **2** perforated. **3** perforation.

perfect *adj* (ˈpɜːfɪkt). **1** having all essential elements. **2** unblemished; faultless: *a perfect gemstone.* **3** correct or precise: *perfect timing.* **4** utter or absolute: *a perfect stranger.* **5** excellent in all respects: *a perfect day.* **6** *Maths.* exactly divisible into equal integral or polynomial roots: *36 is a perfect square.* **7** *Botany.* **7a** (of flowers) having functional stamens and pistils. **7b** (of plants) having all parts present. **8** *Grammar.* denoting a tense of verbs used in describing an action that has been completed by the subject. In English this is a compound tense, formed with *have* or *has* plus the past participle. **9** *Music.* **9a** of or relating to the intervals of the unison, fourth, fifth, and octave. **9b** (of a cadence) ending on the tonic chord, giving a feeling of conclusion. Also: **full, final.** Compare **imperfect** (sense 6). **10** *Archaic.* positive certain, or assured. ◆ *n* (ˈpɜːfɪkt). **11** *Grammar.* **11a** the perfect tense. **11b** a verb in this tense. ◆ *vb* (pəˈfɛkt). *(tr)* **12** to make perfect; improve to one's satisfaction: *he is in Paris to perfect his French.* **13** to make fully accomplished. **14** *Printing.* to print the reverse side of (a printed sheet of paper). [**C13**: from Latin *perfectus,* from *perficere* to perform, from *per* through + *facere* to do] ▸ **ˈperfectness** *n*

USAGE For most of its meanings, the adjective *perfect* describes an absolute state, i.e. one that cannot be qualified; thus something is either *perfect* or *not perfect,* and cannot be *more perfect* or *less perfect.* However when *perfect* means excellent in all respects, a comparative can be used with it without absurdity: *the next day the weather was even more perfect.*

perfect binding *n* See **adhesive binding.**

perfect competition *n Economics.* a market situation in which there exists a homogeneous product, freedom of entry, and a large number of buyers and sellers none of whom individually can affect price.

perfect gas *n* another name for **ideal gas.**

perfectible (pəˈfɛktəbᵊl) *adj* capable of becoming or being made perfect. ▸ **perˌfectiˈbility** *n*

perfection (pəˈfɛkʃən) *n* **1** the act of perfecting or the state or quality of being perfect. **2** the highest degree of a quality, etc.: *the perfection of faithfulness.* **3** an embodiment of perfection. [**C13**: from Latin *perfectiō* a completing, from *perficere* to finish]

perfectionism (pəˈfɛkʃəˌnɪzəm) *n* **1** *Philosophy.* the doctrine that man can attain perfection in this life. **2** the demand for the highest standard of excellence.

perfectionist (pəˈfɛkʃənɪst) *n* **1** a person who strives for or demands the highest standards of excellence in work, etc. **2** a person who believes the doctrine of perfectionism. ◆ *adj* **3** of or relating to perfectionism.

perfective (pəˈfɛktɪv) *adj* **1** tending to perfect. **2** *Grammar.* denoting an aspect of verbs in some languages, including English, used to express that the action or event described by the verb is or was completed: *I lived in London for ten years* is perfective; *I have lived in London for ten years* is imperfective, since the implication is that I still live in London.

perfectly (ˈpɜːfɪktlɪ) *adv* **1** completely, utterly, or absolutely. **2** in a perfect way; extremely well.

perfect number *n* an integer, such as 28, that is equal to the sum of all its possible factors, excluding itself.

perfecto (pəˈfɛktəʊ) *n, pl* **-tos.** a large cigar that is tapered from both ends. [Spanish, literally: perfect]

perfector *or* **perfecter** (ˈpɜːfɪktə) *n* **1** a person who completes or makes something perfect. **2** *Printing.* a machine or press capable of printing both sides of the paper in a single operation.

perfect participle *n* another name for **past participle.**

perfect pitch *n* another name (not in technical usage) for **absolute pitch** (sense 1).

perfect rhyme *n* **1** Also called: **full rhyme.** rhyme between words in which the stressed vowels and any succeeding consonants are identical although the consonants preceding the stressed vowels may be different, as between *part/hart* or *believe/conceive.* **2** a rhyme between two words that are pronounced the same although differing in meaning, as in *bough/bow.*

perfervid (pɜːˈfɜːvɪd) *adj Literary.* extremely ardent, enthusiastic, or zealous. [**C19**: from New Latin *perfervidus,* from Latin *per-* (intensive) + *fervidus* FERVID] ▸ **perˈfervidly** *adv* ▸ **perˈfervidness** *n*

perfidious (pəˈfɪdɪəs) *adj* guilty, treacherous, or faithless; deceitful. ▸ **perˈfidiously** *adv* ▸ **perˈfidiousness** *n*

perfidy (ˈpɜːfɪdɪ) *n, pl* **-dies.** a perfidious act. [**C16**: from Latin *perfidia,* from *perfidus* faithless, from *per* beyond + *fidēs* faith]

perfin (ˈpɜːfɪn) *n Philately.* the former name for **spif.** [from *perf(orated with) in(itials)*]

perfoliate (pəˈfəʊlɪɪt, -ˌeɪt) *adj* (of a leaf) having a base that completely encloses the stem, so that the stem appears to pass through it. [**C17**: from New Latin *perfoliātus,* from Latin *per-* through + *folium* leaf] ▸ **perˌfoliˈation** *n*

perforate *vb* (ˈpɜːfəˌreɪt). **1** to make a hole or holes in (something); penetrate. **2** *(tr)* to punch rows of holes between (stamps, coupons, etc.) for ease of separation. ◆ *adj* (ˈpɜːfərɪt). **3** *Biology.* **3a** pierced by small holes: *perforate shells.* **3b** marked with small transparent spots. **4** *Philately.* another word for **perforated** (sense 2). [**C16**: from Latin *perforāre,* from *per-* through + *forāre* to pierce] ▸ **perforable** (ˈpɜːfərəbᵊl) *adj* ▸ **ˈperforative** *or* **ˈperforatory** *adj* ▸ **ˈperfoˌrator** *n*

perforated (ˈpɜːfəˌreɪtɪd) *adj* **1** pierced with one or more holes. **2** (esp. of stamps) having perforations. Abbrev.: **perf.**

perforated tape *n* a U.S. name for paper tape.

perforation (ˌpɜːfəˈreɪʃən) *n* **1** the act of perforating or the state of being perforated. **2** a hole or holes made in something. **3a** a method of making individual stamps, coupons, etc., easily separable by punching holes along their margins. **3b** the holes punched in this way. Abbrev.: **perf.**

perforated tape *n* a U.S. name for **paper tape.**

perforation (ˌpɜːfəˈreɪʃən) *n* **1** the act of perforating or the state of being perforated. **2** a hole or holes made in something. **3a** a method of making individual stamps, coupons, etc., easily separable by punching holes along their margins. **3b** the holes punched in this way. Abbrev.: **perf.**

perforation gauge *n* a graduated scale for measuring perforations and roulettes of postage stamps.

perforce (pəˈfɔːs) *adv* by necessity; unavoidably. [**C14**: from Old French *par force;* see PER, FORCE[1]]

perform (pəˈfɔːm) *vb* **1** to carry out or do (an action). **2** *(tr)* to fulfil or comply with: *to perform someone's request.* **3** to present or enact (a play, concert, etc.) before or otherwise entertain an audience: *the group performed Hamlet.* **4** *(intr) Informal.* to accomplish sexual intercourse: *he performed well.* [**C14**: from Anglo-Norman *perfourmer* (influenced by *forme* FORM), from Old French *parfournir,* from *par-* PER- +*fournir* to provide; see FURNISH] ▸ **perˈformable** *adj* ▸ **perˈformer** *n*

performance (pəˈfɔːməns) *n* **1** the act, process, or art of performing. **2** an artistic or dramatic production: *last night's performance was terrible.* **3** manner or quality of functioning: *a machine's performance.* **4** *Informal.* mode of conduct or behaviour, esp. when distasteful or irregular: *what did you mean by that performance at the restaurant?* **5** *Informal.* any tiresome procedure: *what a performance dressing the children to play in the snow!* **6** any accomplishment. **7** *Linguistics.* (in transformational grammar) the form of the human language faculty, viewed as concretely embodied in speakers. Compare **competence** (sense 5), **langue, parole** (sense 5).

performance appraisal *n* the assessment, at regular intervals, of an employee's performance at work.

performance art *n* a theatrical presentation that incorporates various art forms, such as dance, sculpture, music, etc.

performance bond *n* a bond given by a bank to a third party guaranteeing that if a specified customer fails to fulfil all the terms of a specified contract, the bank will be responsible for any loss sustained by the third party.

performance test *n Psychol.* a test designed to assess a person's manual ability.

performative (pəˈfɔːmətɪv) *adj Linguistics, philosophy.* **1a** denoting an utterance that constitutes some act, esp. the act described by the verb. For example, *I confess that I was there* is itself a confession, and so is performative in the narrower sense, while *I'd like you to meet …* (effecting an introduction) is performative only in the looser sense. See also **locutionary act, illocution, perlocution.** **1b** *(as n): that sentence is a performative.* **2a** denoting a verb that may be used as the main verb in such an utterance. **2b** *(as n): "promise" is a performative.* ▸ **perˈformatively** *adv*

performing (pəˈfɔːmɪŋ) *adj* (of an animal) trained to perform tricks before an audience, as in a circus.

performing arts *pl n* the arts that are primarily performed before an audience, such as dance and drama.

perfume *n* (ˈpɜːfjuːm). **1** a mixture of alcohol and fragrant essential oils extracted from flowers, spices, etc., or made synthetically, used esp. to impart a pleasant long-lasting scent to the body, stationery, etc. See also **cologne, toilet water. 2** a scent or odour, esp. a fragrant one. ◆ *vb* (pəˈfjuːm). **3** (*tr*) to impart a perfume to. **[C16:** from French *parfum,* probably from Old Provençal *perfum,* from *perfumar* to make scented, from *per* through (from Latin) + *fumar* to smoke, from Latin *fumāre* to smoke**]**

perfumer (pəˈfjuːmə) *or* **perfumier** (pəˈfjuːmɪeɪ) *n* a person who makes or sells perfume.

perfumery (pəˈfjuːmərɪ) *n, pl* **-eries. 1** a place where perfumes are sold. **2** a factory where perfumes are made. **3** the process of making perfumes. **4** perfumes in general.

perfunctory (pəˈfʌŋktərɪ) *adj* **1** done superficially, only as a matter of routine; careless or cursory. **2** dull or indifferent. **[C16:** from Late Latin *perfunctōrius* negligent, from *perfunctus* dispatched, from *perfungī* to fulfil; see FUNCTION**]** ▸ **perˈfunctorily** *adv* ▸ **perˈfunctoriness** *n*

perfuse (pəˈfjuːz) *vb* (*tr*) **1** to suffuse or permeate (a liquid, colour, etc.) through or over (something). **2** *Surgery.* to pass (a fluid) through organ tissue to ensure adequate exchange of oxygen and carbon monoxide. **[C16:** from Latin *perfūsus* wetted, from *perfundere* to pour over, from PER- + *fundere* to pour**]** ▸ **perˈfusion** *n* ▸ **perˈfusionist** *n* ▸ **perˈfusive** *adj* ▸ **perˈfused** *adj*

Pergamum (ˈpɜːgəməm) *n* an ancient city in NW Asia Minor, in Mysia: capital of a major Hellenistic monarchy of the same name that later became a Roman province.

pergola (ˈpɜːgələ) *n* a horizontal trellis or framework, supported on posts, that carries climbing plants and may form a covered walk. **[C17:** via Italian from Latin *pergula* projection from a roof, from *pergere* to go forward**]**

Pergolesi (*Italian* pergoˈleːsi) *n* **Giovanni Battista** (dʒoˈvanni batˈtista). 1710–36, Italian composer: his works include the operetta *La Serva padrona* (1733) and the *Stabat Mater* (1736) for women's voices.

perhaps (pəˈhæps; *informal* præps) *adv* **1a** possibly; maybe. **1b** (*as sentence modifier*): *he'll arrive tomorrow, perhaps; perhaps you'll see him tomorrow.* ◆ *sentence substitute.* **2** it may happen, be so, etc.; maybe. **[C16** *perhappes,* from *per* by + *happes* chance, HAP[1]**]**

peri (ˈpɪərɪ) *n, pl* **-ris. 1** (in Persian folklore) one of a race of beautiful supernatural beings. **2** any beautiful fairy-like creature. **[C18:** from Persian: fairy, from Avestan *pairikā* witch**]**

peri- *prefix* **1** enclosing, encircling, or around: *pericardium; pericarp; perigon.* **2** near or adjacent: *perihelion.* **[**from Greek *peri* around, near, about**]**

perianth (ˈpɛrɪˌænθ) *n* the outer part of a flower, consisting of the calyx and corolla. **[C18:** from French *périanthe,* from New Latin, from PERI- + Greek *anthos* flower**]**

periapt (ˈpɛrɪˌæpt) *n Rare.* a charm or amulet. **[C16:** via French from Greek *periapton,* from PERI- + *haptos* clasped, from *haptein* to fasten**]**

periastron (ˌpɛrɪˈæstrɒn) *n Astronomy.* the point in the orbit of a body around a star when it is nearest to the star, esp. applied to double-star systems.

periblem (ˈpɛrɪˌblɛm) *n Botany.* a layer of meristematic tissue in stems and roots that gives rise to the cortex. **[C19:** via German from Greek *periblēma* protection, from *periballein* to throw around, from PERI- + *ballein* to throw**]**

pericarditis (ˌpɛrɪkɑːˈdaɪtɪs) *n* inflammation of the pericardium. ▸ **pericarditic** (ˌpɛrɪkɑːˈdɪtɪk) *adj*

pericardium (ˌpɛrɪˈkɑːdɪəm) *n, pl* **-dia** (-dɪə). the membranous sac enclosing the heart. **[C16:** via New Latin from Greek *perikardion,* from PERI- + *kardia* heart**]** ▸ **ˌperiˈcardial** *or* **ˌperiˈcardiˌac** *adj*

pericarp (ˈpɛrɪˌkɑːp) *n* **1** the part of a fruit enclosing the seeds that develops from the wall of the ovary. **2** a layer of tissue around the reproductive bodies of some algae and fungi. **[C18:** via French from New Latin *pericarpium***]** ▸ **ˌperiˈcarpial** *or* **ˌperiˈcarpic** *adj*

perichondrium (ˌpɛrɪˈkɒndrɪəm) *n, pl* **-dria** (-drɪə). the white fibrous membrane that covers the surface of cartilage. **[C18:** New Latin, from PERI- + Greek *chondros* cartilage**]** ▸ **ˌperiˈchondrial** *adj*

periclase (ˈpɛrɪˌkleɪs) *n* a mineral consisting of magnesium oxide in the form of isometric crystals or grains: occurs in limestone masses. **[C19:** from New Latin *periclasia,* from Greek *peri* very + *klasis* a breaking, referring to its perfect cleavage**]** ▸ **periclastic** (ˌpɛrɪˈklæstɪk) *adj*

Periclean (ˌpɛrɪˈkliːən) *adj* of or relating to Pericles or to the period when Athens was the intellectual and artistic leader of the Greek city-states.

Pericles (ˈpɛrɪˌkliːz) *n* ?495–429 B.C., Athenian statesman and leader of the popular party, who contributed greatly to Athens' political and cultural supremacy in Greece. In power from about 460 B.C., he was responsible for the construction of the Parthenon. He conducted the Peloponnesian War (431–404 B.C.) successfully until his death.

periclinal (ˌpɛrɪˈklaɪnᵊl) *adj* **1** of or relating to a pericline. **2** *Botany.* **2a** denoting or relating to cell walls that are parallel to the surface of a plant part, such as a meristem. **2b** (of chimeras) having one component completely enclosed by the other component.

pericline (ˈpɛrɪˌklaɪn) *n* **1** a white translucent variety of albite in the form of elongated crystals. **2** Also called: **dome.** a dome-shaped formation of stratified rock with its slopes following the direction of folding. **[C19:** from Greek *periklinēs* sloping on all sides, from PERI- + *klinein* to lean**]**

pericope (pəˈrɪkəpɪ) *n* a selection from a book, esp. a passage from the Bible read at religious services. **[C17:** via Late Latin from Greek *perikopē* piece cut out, from PERI- + *kopē* a cutting**]** ▸ **pericopic** (ˌpɛrɪˈkɒpɪk) *adj*

pericranium (ˌpɛrɪˈkreɪnɪəm) *n, pl* **-nia** (-nɪə). the fibrous membrane covering the external surface of the skull. **[C16:** New Latin, from Greek *perikranion***]** ▸ **ˌperiˈcranial** *adj*

pericycle (ˈpɛrɪˌsaɪkᵊl) *n* a layer of plant tissue beneath the endodermis: surrounds the conducting tissue in roots and certain stems. **[C19:** from Greek *perikuklos***]** ▸ **pericyclic** (ˌpɛrɪˈsaɪklɪk, -ˈsɪk-) *adj*

pericynthion (ˌpɛrɪˈsɪnθɪən) *n* the point at which a spacecraft launched from earth into a lunar orbit is nearest the moon. Compare **perilune, apocynthion. [C20:** from PERI- + *-cynthion,* from CYNTHIA**]**

periderm (ˈpɛrɪˌdɜːm) *n* the outer corky protective layer of woody stems and roots, consisting of cork cambium, phelloderm and cork. **[C19:** from New Latin *peridermis***]** ▸ **ˌperiˈdermal** *or* **ˌperiˈdermic** *adj*

peridium (pəˈrɪdɪəm) *n, pl* **-ridia** (-ˈrɪdɪə). the distinct outer layer of the spore-bearing organ in many fungi. **[C19:** from Greek *pēridion* a little wallet, from *pēra* leather bag, of obscure origin**]**

peridot (ˈpɛrɪˌdɒt) *n* a pale green transparent variety of the olivine chrysolite, used as a gemstone. **[C14:** from Old French *peritot,* of unknown origin**]**

peridotite (ˌpɛrɪˈdəʊtaɪt) *n* a dark coarse-grained ultrabasic plutonic igneous rock consisting principally of olivine. **[C19:** from French, from PERIDOT**]** ▸ **peridotitic** (ˌpɛrɪdəʊˈtɪtɪk) *adj*

perigee (ˈpɛrɪˌdʒiː) *n* the point in its orbit around the earth when the moon or an artificial satellite is nearest the earth. Compare **apogee** (sense 1). **[C16:** via French from Greek *perigeion,* from PERI- + *gea* earth**]** ▸ **ˌperiˈgean** *or* **ˌperiˈgeal** *adj*

periglacial (ˌpɛrɪˈgleɪʃəl) *adj* relating to a region bordering a glacier: *periglacial climate.*

perigon (ˈpɛrɪgən) *n* an angle of 360°. Also called: **round angle. [C19:** from PERI- + Greek *gonia* angle**]**

Perigordian (ˌpɛrɪˈgɔːdɪən) *adj* **1** of, relating to, or characteristic of an Upper Palaeolithic culture in Europe, esp. in France. ◆ *n* **2 the.** the Perigordian culture. **[C20:** after *Périgord,* district in France**]**

Périgueux (ˌpɛrɪˈgɜː; *French* perigø) *n* a town in SW France, capital of the Dordogne: noted for its Roman remains, medieval cathedral, and pâté de foie gras. Pop.: 32 850 (1990).

perigynous (pəˈrɪdʒɪnəs) *adj* **1** (of a flower) having a concave or flat receptacle with a distinct gynoecium surrounded by the other floral parts, as in the rose-hip. **2** of or relating to the parts of a flower arranged in this way. **[C19:** from New Latin *perigynus;* see PERI-, -GYNOUS**]** ▸ **peˈrigyny** *n*

perihelion (ˌpɛrɪˈhiːlɪən) *n, pl* **-lia** (-lɪə). the point in its orbit when a planet or comet is nearest the sun. Compare **aphelion. [C17:** from New Latin *perihēlium,* from PERI- + Greek *hēlios* sun**]**

peril (ˈpɛrɪl) *n* exposure to risk or harm; danger or jeopardy. **[C13:** via Old French from Latin *perīculum***]**

perilous (ˈpɛrɪləs) *adj* very hazardous or dangerous: *a perilous journey.* ▸ **ˈperilously** *adv* ▸ **ˈperilousness** *n*

perilune (ˈpɛrɪˌluːn) *n* the point in a lunar orbit when a spacecraft launched from the moon is nearest the moon. Compare **apolune, pericynthion. [C20:** from PERI- + *-lune,* from Latin *lūna* moon**]**

perilymph (ˈpɛrɪˌlɪmf) *n* the fluid filling the space between the membranous and bony labyrinths of the internal ear.

perimeter (pəˈrɪmɪtə) *n* **1** *Maths.* **1a** the curve or line enclosing a plane area. **1b** the length of this curve or line. **2a** any boundary around something, such as a field. **2b** (*as modifier*): *a perimeter fence; a perimeter patrol.* **3** a medical instrument for measuring the limits of the field of vision. **[C16:** from French *périmètre,* from Latin *perimetros;* see PERI-, -METER**]** ▸ **perimetric** (ˌpɛrɪˈmɛtrɪk) *or* **ˌperiˈmetrical** *adj* ▸ **ˌperiˈmetrically** *adv* ▸ **peˈrimetry** *n*

perimorph (ˈpɛrɪˌmɔːf) *n* a mineral that encloses another mineral of a different type. ▸ **ˌperiˈmorphic** *or* **ˌperiˈmorphous** *adj* ▸ **ˌperiˈmorˌphism** *n*

perimysium (ˌpɛrɪˈmɪzɪəm) *n, pl* **-ia** (-ɪə). *Anatomy.* the sheath of fibrous connective tissue surrounding the primary bundles of muscle fibres. **[C19:** from PERI- + *-mysium,* from Greek *mus* muscle**]**

perinatal (ˌpɛrɪˈneɪtᵊl) *adj* of, relating to, or occurring in the period from about three months before to one month after birth.

perineal gland *n Zoology.* one of a pair of glands that are situated near the anus in some mammals and secrete an odorous substance.

perinephrium (ˌpɛrɪˈnɛfrɪəm) *n, pl* **-ria** (-rɪə). *Anatomy.* the fatty and connective tissue surrounding the kidney. **[C19:** from PERI- + *-nephrium,* from Greek *nephros* kidney**]** ▸ **ˌperiˈnephric** *adj*

perineum (ˌpɛrɪˈniːəm) *n, pl* **-nea** (-ˈniːə). **1** the region of the body between the anus and the genital organs, including some of the underlying structures. **2** the nearly diamond-shaped surface of the human trunk between the thighs. **[C17:** from New Latin, from Greek *perinaion,* from PERI- + *inein* to empty out**]** ▸ **ˌperiˈneal** *adj*

perineuritis (ˌpɛrɪnjʊˈraɪtɪs) *n* inflammation of the perineurium. ▸ **perineuritic** (ˌpɛrɪnjʊˈrɪtɪk) *adj*

perineurium (ˌpɛrɪˈnjʊərɪəm) *n* the connective tissue forming a sheath around a single bundle of nerve fibres. **[C19:** from New Latin, from PERI- + Greek *neuron* nerve**]** ▸ **ˌperiˈneurial** *adj*

period (ˈpɪərɪəd) *n* **1** a portion of time of indefinable length: *he spent a period away from home.* **2a** a portion of time specified in some way: *the Arthurian period; Picasso's blue period.* **2b** (*as modifier*): *period costume.* **3** a nontechnical name for an occurrence of menstruation. **4** *Geology.* a unit of geological time during which a system of rocks is formed: *the Jurassic period.* **5** a division of time, esp. of the academic day. **6** *Physics, maths.* **6a** the time taken to complete one cycle of a regularly recurring phenomenon; the reciprocal of frequency. Symbol: T **6b** an interval in which the values of a periodic function follow a certain pattern that is duplicated over successive intervals: $\sin x = \sin (x + 2\pi)$, *where* 2π *is the period.* **7** *Astronomy.* **7a** the time required by a body to make one complete rotation on its axis. **7b** the time interval between two successive maxima or minima of light variation of a variable star. **8** *Chem.* one of the horizontal rows of elements in the periodic table. Each period starts with an alkali metal and ends with a rare gas. Compare **group** (sense 11). **9** another term (esp. U.S. and Canadian) for **full stop. 10** a complete sentence, esp. a complex one with several clauses. **11** *Music.* a passage or division of a piece of music, usually consisting of two or more contrasting or complementary musical phrases and ending on a cadence. Also called: **sentence. 12** (in classical prosody) a unit consisting of two or more cola. **13** *Rare.* a completion or end. [C14 *peryod,* from Latin *periodus,* from Greek *periodos* circuit, from PERI- + *hodos* way]

periodate (pɜːˈraɪəˌdeɪt) *n* any salt or ester of a periodic acid.

periodic (ˌpɪərɪˈɒdɪk) *adj* **1** happening or recurring at intervals; intermittent. **2** of, relating to, or resembling a period. **3** having or occurring in repeated periods or cycles. ▸ ˌ**periˈodically** *adv* ▸ **periodicity** (ˌpɪərɪəˈdɪsɪtɪ) *n*

periodic acid (ˌpɜːraɪˈɒdɪk) *n* any of various oxyacids of iodine containing a greater proportion of oxygen than iodic acid and differing from each other in water content, esp. either of the crystalline compounds HIO_4 (**metaperiodic acid**) and H_5IO_6 (**paraperiodic acid**). [C19: from PER- + IODIC]

periodical (ˌpɪərɪˈɒdɪkᵊl) *n* **1** a publication issued at regular intervals, usually monthly or weekly. ◆ *adj* **2** of or relating to such publications. **3** published at regular intervals. **4** periodic or occasional.

periodic function (ˌpɪərɪˈɒdɪk) *n Maths.* a function, such as sin *x*, whose value is repeated at constant intervals.

periodic law (ˌpɪərɪˈɒdɪk) *n* the principle that the chemical properties of the elements are periodic functions of their atomic weights (also called: **Mendeleev's law**) or, more accurately, of their atomic numbers.

periodic sentence (ˌpɪərɪˈɒdɪk) *n Rhetoric.* a sentence in which the completion of the main clause is left to the end, thus creating an effect of suspense.

periodic system (ˌpɪərɪˈɒdɪk) *n* the classification of the elements based on the periodic law.

periodic table (ˌpɪərɪˈɒdɪk) *n* a table of the elements, arranged in order of increasing atomic number, based on the periodic law. Elements having similar chemical properties and electronic structures appear in vertical columns (groups).

periodic tenancy *n Social welfare.* the letting of a dwelling for a repeated short term, as by the week, month, or quarter, with no end date.

periodization *or* **periodisation** (ˌpɪərɪədaɪˈzeɪʃən) *n* the act or process of dividing history into periods.

period of revolution *n Astronomy.* the mean time taken for one body, such as a planet, to complete a revolution about another, such as the sun.

periodontal (ˌperɪəˈdɒntᵊl) *adj* of, denoting, or affecting the gums and other tissues surrounding the teeth: *periodontal disease.*

periodontics (ˌperɪəˈdɒntɪks) *n* (*functioning as sing*) the branch of dentistry concerned with diseases affecting the tissues and structures that surround teeth. Also called: **periodontology**. [C19: from PERI- + *-odontics,* from Greek *odōn* tooth] ▸ ˌ**perioˈdontic** *adj* ▸ ˌ**perioˈdontically** *adv*

period piece *n* an object, a piece of music, a play, etc., valued for its quality of evoking a particular historical period: often one regarded as of little except historical interest.

perionychium (ˌperɪəʊˈnɪkɪəm) *n, pl* **-ia** (-ɪə). the skin that surrounds a fingernail or toenail. [C19: New Latin, from PERI- + Greek *onux* a nail]

periosteum (ˌperɪˈɒstɪəm) *n, pl* **-tea** (-tɪə). a thick fibrous two-layered membrane covering the surface of bones. [C16: New Latin, from Greek *periosteon,* from PERI- + *osteon* bone] ▸ ˌ**periˈosteal** *adj*

periostitis (ˌperɪɒˈstaɪtɪs) *n* inflammation of the periosteum. ▸ **periostitic** (ˌperɪɒˈstɪtɪk) *adj*

periotic (ˌperɪˈəʊtɪk, ˈɒtɪk) *adj* **1** of or relating to the structures situated around the internal ear. **2** situated around the ear. [C19: from PERI- + *-otic,* from Greek *ous* ear]

peripatetic (ˌperɪpəˈtetɪk) *adj* **1** itinerant. **2** *Brit.* employed in two or more educational establishments and travelling from one to another: *a peripatetic football coach.* ◆ *n* **3** a peripatetic person. [C16: from Latin *peripatēticus,* from Greek *peripatētikos,* from *peripatein* to pace to and fro] ▸ ˌ**peripaˈtetically** *adv*

Peripatetic (ˌperɪpəˈtetɪk) *adj* **1** of or relating to the teachings of Aristotle, who used to teach philosophy while walking about the Lyceum in ancient Athens. ◆ *n* **2** a student of Aristotelianism.

peripatus (pəˈrɪpətəs) *n* any of a genus of wormlike arthropods having a segmented body and short unjointed limbs: belonging to the phylum *Onychophora.* [from New Latin, from Greek *peripatos* a pacing about; see PERIPATETIC]

peripeteia, peripetia (ˌperɪpɪˈtaɪə, -ˈtɪə), *or* **peripety** (pəˈrɪpətɪ) *n* (esp. in drama) an abrupt turn of events or reversal of circumstances. [C16: from Greek, from PERI- + *piptein* to fall (to change suddenly, literally: to fall around)] ▸ ˌ**peripeˈteian** *or* ˌ**peripeˈtian** *adj*

peripheral (pəˈrɪfərəl) *adj* **1** not relating to the most important part of something; incidental, minor, or superficial. **2** of, relating to, or of the nature of a periphery. **3** *Anatomy.* of, relating to, or situated near the surface of the body: *a peripheral nerve.* ▸ **peˈripherally** *adv*

peripheral device *or* **unit** *n Computing.* any device, such as a disk, printer, modem, or screen, concerned with input/output, storage, etc. Often shortened to **peripheral.**

periphery (pəˈrɪfərɪ) *n, pl* **-eries. 1** the outermost boundary of an area. **2** the outside surface of something. **3** *Anatomy.* the surface or outermost part of the body or one of its organs or parts. [C16: from Late Latin *peripheria,* from Greek, from PERI- + *pherein* to bear]

periphrasis (pəˈrɪfrəsɪs) *n, pl* **-rases** (-rəˌsiːz) **1** a roundabout way of expressing something; circumlocution. **2** an expression of this kind. [C16: via Latin from Greek, from PERI- + *phrazein* to declare]

periphrastic (ˌperɪˈfræstɪk) *adj* **1** employing or involving periphrasis. **2** expressed in two or more words rather than by an inflected form of one: used esp. of a tense of a verb where the alternative element is an auxiliary verb. For example, *He does go* and *He will go* involve periphrastic tenses. ▸ ˌ**periˈphrastically** *adv*

periphyton (pəˈrɪfɪˌtɒn) *n* aquatic organisms, such as certain algae, that live attached to rocks or other surfaces. [C20: from Greek, from PERI- + *phutos,* from *phuein* to grow]

peripteral (pəˈrɪptərəl) *adj* having a row of columns on all sides. [C19: from PERI- + *-pteral,* from Greek *pteron* wing]

perique (pəˈriːk) *n* a strong highly-flavoured tobacco cured in its own juices and grown in Louisiana. [C19: apparently from *Périque,* nickname of Pierre Chenet, American tobacco planter who first grew it in Louisiana]

perisarc (ˈperɪˌsɑːk) *n* the outer chitinous layer secreted by colonial hydrozoan coelenterates, such as species of *Obelia.* [C19: from PERI- + *-sarc,* from Greek *sarx* flesh] ▸ ˌ**periˈsarcal** *or* ˌ**periˈsarcous** *adj*

periscope (ˈperɪˌskəʊp) *n* any of a number of optical instruments that enable the user to view objects that are not in the direct line of vision, such as one in a submarine for looking above the surface of the water. They have a system of mirrors or prisms to reflect the light and often contain focusing lenses. [C19: from Greek *periskopein* to look around; see PERI-, -SCOPE]

periscopic (ˌperɪˈskɒpɪk) *adj* (of a lens) having a wide field of view. ▸ ˌ**periˈscopically** *adv*

perish (ˈperɪʃ) *vb* (*intr*) **1** to be destroyed or die, esp. in an untimely way. **2** to rot: *leather perishes if exposed to bad weather.* **3 perish the thought!** may it never be or happen thus. ◆ *n* **4 do a perish.** *Austral. informal.* to die or come near to dying of thirst or starvation. [C13: from Old French *périr,* from Latin *perīre* to pass away entirely, from PER- (away) + *īre* to go]

perishable (ˈperɪʃəbᵊl) *adj* **1** liable to rot or wither. ◆ *n* **2** (*often pl*) a perishable article, esp. food. ▸ ˌ**perishaˈbility** *or* ˈ**perishableness** *n* ▸ ˈ**perishably** *adv*

perished (ˈperɪʃt) *adj Informal.* (of a person, part of the body, etc.) extremely cold.

perishing (ˈperɪʃɪŋ) *adj* **1** *Informal.* (of weather, etc.) extremely cold. **2** *Slang.* (intensifier qualifying something undesirable): *it's a perishing nuisance!* ▸ ˈ**perishingly** *adv*

perisperm (ˈperɪˌspɜːm) *n* the nutritive tissue surrounding the embryo in certain seeds, and developing from the nucellus of the ovule. ▸ ˌ**periˈspermal** *adj*

perispomenon (ˌperɪˈspəʊməˌnɒn) *adj* **1** (of a Greek word) bearing a circumflex accent on the last syllable. ◆ *n* **2** a word having such an accent. [from Greek, from PERI- (around) + *spaein* to pull, draw]

perissodactyl (pəˌrɪsəʊˈdæktɪl) *or* **perissodactyle** (pəˌrɪsəʊˈdæktaɪl) *n* **1** any placental mammal of the order *Perissodactyla,* having hooves with an odd number of toes: includes horses, tapirs, and rhinoceroses. ◆ *adj* **2** of, relating to, or belonging to the *Perissodactyla.* [C19: from New Latin *perissodactylus,* from Greek *perissos* uneven + *daktulos* digit] ▸ **peˌrissoˈdactylous** *adj*

peristalsis (ˌperɪˈstælsɪs) *n, pl* **-ses** (-siːz). *Physiol.* the succession of waves of involuntary muscular contraction of various bodily tubes, esp. of the alimentary tract, where it effects transport of food and waste products. [C19: from New Latin, from PERI- + Greek *stalsis* compression, from *stellein* to press together] ▸ ˌ**periˈstaltic** *adj* ▸ ˌ**periˈstaltically** *adv*

peristome (ˈperɪˌstəʊm) *n* **1** a fringe of pointed teeth surrounding the opening of a moss capsule. **2** any of various parts surrounding the mouth of invertebrates, such as echinoderms and earthworms, and of protozoans. [C18: from New Latin *peristoma,* from PERI- + Greek *stoma* mouth] ▸ ˌ**periˈstomal** *or* ˌ**periˈstomial** *adj*

peristyle (ˈperɪˌstaɪl) *n* **1** a colonnade that surrounds a court or building. **2** an area that is surrounded by a colonnade. [C17: via French from Latin *peristȳlum,* from Greek *peristulon,* from PERI- + *stulos* column] ▸ ˌ**periˈstylar** *adj*

perithecium (ˌperɪˈθiːsɪəm) *n, pl* **-cia** (-sɪə). *Botany.* a flask-shaped structure containing asci that are discharged from an apical pore; a type of ascocarp. [C19: from New Latin, from PERI- + Greek *thēkē* case]

peritoneum (ˌperɪtəˈniːəm) *n, pl* **-nea** (-ˈniːə) *or* **-neums.** a thin translucent serous sac that lines the walls of the abdominal cavity and covers most of the viscera. [C16: via Late Latin from Greek *peritonaion,* from *peritonos* stretched around, from PERI- + *tenein* to stretch] ▸ ˌ**peritoˈneal** *adj*

peritonitis (ˌperɪtəˈnaɪtɪs) *n* inflammation of the peritoneum. ▸ **peritonitic** (ˌperɪtəˈnɪtɪk) *adj*

peritrack (ˈperɪˌtræk) *n* another name for **taxiway.**

peritricha (pəˈrɪtrɪkə) *pl n, sing* **peritrich** (ˈperɪtrɪk). **1** ciliate protozoans, of the order *Peritrichida,* in which the cilia are restricted to a spiral around the mouth. **2** bacteria having the entire cell surface covered with cilia. [C19: from New Latin, from PERI- + Greek *thrix* hair] ▸ **peˈritrichous** *adj*

periwig (ˈperɪˌwɪg) *n* a wig, such as a peruke. [C16 *perwyke,* changed from French *perruque* wig, PERUKE]

periwinkle[1] (ˈperɪˌwɪŋkᵊl) *n* any of various edible marine gastropods of the genus *Littorina,* esp. *L. littorea,* having a spirally coiled shell. Often shortened to **winkle.** [C16: of unknown origin]

periwinkle[2] (ˈperɪˌwɪŋkᵊl) *n* **1** Also called (U.S.): **creeping myrtle, trailing myrtle.** any of several Eurasian apocynaceous evergreen plants of the genus *Vinca,* such as *V. minor* (**lesser periwinkle**) and *V. major* (**greater periwinkle**), having trailing stems and blue flowers. **2a** a light purplish-blue colour. **2b** (*as adj*): *a periwinkle coat.* [C14 *pervenke,* from Old English *perwince,* from Late Latin *pervinca*]

perjink (pərˈdʒɪŋk) *adj Scot.* prim or finicky. [C19: of unknown origin]

perjure (ˈpɜːdʒə) *vb* (*tr*) *Criminal law.* to render (oneself) guilty of perjury.

[C15: from Old French *parjurer,* from Latin *perjūrāre,* from PER- + *jūrāre* to make an oath, from *jūs* law] ▸ **'perjurer** *n*

perjured ('pɜːdʒəd) *adj Criminal law.* **1a** having sworn falsely. **1b** having committed perjury. **2** involving or characterized by perjury: *perjured evidence.*

perjury ('pɜːdʒərɪ) *n, pl* **-juries.** *Criminal law.* the offence committed by a witness in judicial proceedings who, having been lawfully sworn or having affirmed, wilfully gives false evidence. [C14: from Anglo-French *parjurie,* from Latin *perjūrium* a false oath; see PERJURE] ▸ **perjurious** (pɜː'dʒʊərɪəs) *adj* ▸ **per'juriously** *adv*

perk[1] (pɜːk) *adj* **1** pert; brisk; lively. ◆ *vb* **2** See **perk up.** [C16: see PERK UP]

perk[2] (pɜːk) *vb Informal.* **1** (*intr*) (of coffee) to percolate. **2** (*tr*) to percolate (coffee).

perk[3] (pɜːk) *n Brit. informal.* short for **perquisite.**

perkin ('pɜːkɪn) *n* a variant of **parkin.**

Perkin's mauve ('pɜːkɪnz) *n* another name for **mauve** (sense 2). [C19: named after Sir William Henry *Perkin* (1838–1907), who first synthesized it]

perk up *vb* (*adv*) **1** to make or become more cheerful, hopeful, or lively. **2** to rise or cause to rise briskly: *the dog's ears perked up.* **3** (*tr*) to make smarter in appearance: *she perked up her outfit with a bright scarf.* **4** (*intr*) *Austral. slang.* to vomit. [C14 *perk,* perhaps from Norman French *perquer;* see PERCH[1]]

perky ('pɜːkɪ) *adj* **perkier, perkiest. 1** jaunty; lively. **2** confident; spirited. ▸ **'perkily** *adv* ▸ **'perkiness** *n*

Perl (pɜːl) *n* a computer language that is used for text manipulation, esp. on the World Wide Web. [C20: from *p(ractical) e(xtraction and) r(eport) l(anguage)*]

perlemoen ('peələˌmʊn) *n S. African.* another name for **abalone.** [from Afrikaans, from Dutch *paarlemoer* mother of pearl]

Perlis ('peəlɪs, 'pɜː-) *n* a state of NW Peninsular Malaysia, on the Andaman Sea: a dependency of Thailand until 1909. Capital: Kangar. Pop.: 187 600 (1993 est.). Area: 803 sq. km (310 sq. miles).

perlite *or* **pearlite** ('pɜːlaɪt) *n* a variety of obsidian consisting of masses of small pearly globules: used as a filler, insulator, and soil conditioner. [C19: from French, from *perle* PEARL[1]] ▸ **perlitic** *or* **pearlitic** (pɜː'lɪtɪk) *adj*

Perlman ('pɜːlmən) *n* **Itzhak** ('ɪtzæk). born 1945, Israeli violinist; polio victim.

perlocution (ˌpɜːlɒ'kjuːʃən) *n Philosophy.* the effect that someone has by uttering certain words, such as frightening a person. Also called: **perlocutionary act.** Compare **illocution.** [C16 (in the obsolete sense: the action of speaking): from Medieval or New Latin *perlocūtiō;* see PER-, LOCUTION] ▸ **ˌperlo'cutionary** *adj*

perm[1] (pɜːm) *n* **1** a hairstyle produced by treatment with heat, chemicals, etc. which gives long-lasting waves, curls, or other shaping. Also called (esp. formerly) **permanent wave. 2** the act of giving or receiving such a hairstyle. ◆ *vb* **3** (*tr*) to give a perm to (hair).

perm[2] (pɜːm) *n* short for **permutation** (sense 4).

Perm (*Russian* pjermj) *n* a port in W Russia, on the Kama River: oil refinery; university (1916). Pop.: 1 032 000 (1995 est.). Former name (1940–62): **Molotov.**

permaculture ('pɜːməˌkʌltʃə) *n* the practice of producing food, energy, etc., using ways that do not deplete the earth's natural resources. [C20: coined by Bill Mollison (born 1928), Australian ecologist, from *perma(nent agri)culture*]

permafrost ('pɜːməˌfrɒst) *n* ground that is permanently frozen, often to great depths, the surface sometimes thawing in the summer. [C20: from PERMA(NENT) + FROST]

permalloy (pɜːm'ælɔɪ) *n* any of various alloys containing iron and nickel (45–80 per cent) and sometimes smaller amounts of chromium and molybdenum. [C20: from PERM(EABILITY) + ALLOY]

permanence ('pɜːmənəns) *n* the state or quality of being permanent.

permanency ('pɜːmənənsɪ) *n, pl* **-cies. 1** a person or thing that is permanent. **2** another word for **permanence.**

permanent ('pɜːmənənt) *adj* **1** existing or intended to exist for an indefinite period: *a permanent structure.* **2** not expected to change for an indefinite time; not temporary: *a permanent condition.* [C15: from Latin *permanens* continuing, from *permanēre* to stay to the end, from *per-* through + *manēre* to remain] ▸ **'permanently** *adv*

Permanent Court of Arbitration *n* the official name of the **Hague Tribunal.**

permanent hardness *n Chem.* hardness of water that cannot be removed by boiling as it results mainly from the presence of calcium and magnesium chlorides and sulphates.

permanent health insurance *n* a form of insurance that provides up to 75 per cent of a person's salary, until retirement, in case of prolonged illness or disability.

permanent magnet *n* a magnet, often of steel, that retains its magnetization after the magnetic field producing it has been removed. ▸ **permanent magnetism** *n*

permanent press *n* **a** a chemical treatment for clothing that makes the fabric crease-resistant and sometimes provides a garment with a permanent crease or pleats. **b** (*as modifier*): *permanent-press skirts.*

permanent set *n Engineering.* the change in shape of a material that results when the load to which it is subjected causes the elastic limit to be exceeded and is then removed.

permanent wave *n* another name (esp. formerly) for **perm**[1] (sense 1).

permanent way *n Chiefly Brit.* the track of a railway, including the ballast, sleepers, rails, etc.

permanganate (pə'mæŋgəˌneɪt, -nɪt) *n* a salt of permanganic acid.

permanganic acid (ˌpɜːmæn'gænɪk) *n* a monobasic acid known only in solution and in the form of permanganate salts. Formula: $HMnO_4$. Systematic name: **manganic(VII) acid.**

permeability (ˌpɜːmɪə'bɪlɪtɪ) *n* **1** the state or quality of being permeable. **2** a measure of the ability of a medium to modify a magnetic field, expressed as the ratio of the magnetic flux density in the medium to the field strength; measured in henries per metre. Symbol: μ See also **relative permeability, magnetic constant. 3** *Civil engineering.* the rate of diffusion of fluid under pressure through soil. **4** the rate at which gas diffuses through the surface of a balloon or airship, usually expressed in litres per square metre per day.

permeability coefficient *n* the volume of an incompressible fluid that will flow in unit time through a unit cube of a porous substance across which a unit pressure difference is maintained.

permeable ('pɜːmɪəbᵊl) *adj* capable of being permeated, esp. by liquids. [C15: from Late Latin *permeābilis,* from Latin *permeāre* to pervade; see PERMEATE] ▸ **'permeableness** *n* ▸ **'permeably** *adv*

permeance ('pɜːmɪəns) *n* **1** the act of permeating. **2** the reciprocal of the reluctance of a magnetic circuit. Symbol: Λ ▸ **'permeant** *adj, n*

permeate ('pɜːmɪˌeɪt) *vb* **1** to penetrate or pervade (a substance, area, etc.): *a lovely smell permeated the room.* **2** to pass through or cause to pass through by osmosis or diffusion: *to permeate a membrane.* [C17: from Latin *permeāre,* from *per-* through + *meāre* to pass] ▸ **ˌperme'ation** *n* ▸ **'permeative** *adj*

per mensem *Latin.* ('pɜː 'mɛnsəm) *adv* every month or by the month.

Permian ('pɜːmɪən) *adj* **1** of, denoting, or formed in the last period of the Palaeozoic era, between the Carboniferous and Triassic periods, which lasted for 45 000 000 years. ◆ *n* **2 the.** the Permian period or rock system. [C19: after PERM, Russia]

per mill *or* **mil** (pə 'mɪl) *adv* by the thousand or in each thousand. [C19: from PER + French or Latin *mille* thousand, on the model of PER CENT]

permissible (pə'mɪsəbᵊl) *adj* permitted; allowable. ▸ **perˌmissi'bility** *n* ▸ **per'missibly** *adv*

permission (pə'mɪʃən) *n* authorization to do something.

permissive (pə'mɪsɪv) *adj* **1** tolerant; lenient: *permissive parents.* **2** indulgent in matters of sex: *a permissive society.* **3** granting permission. **4** *Archaic.* not obligatory. ▸ **per'missively** *adv* ▸ **per'missiveness** *n*

permit *vb* (pə'mɪt), **-mits, -mitting, -mitted. 1** (*tr*) to grant permission to do something: *you are permitted to smoke.* **2** (*tr*) to consent to or tolerate: *she will not permit him to come.* **3** (when *intr,* often foll. by *of;* when *tr,* often foll. by an infinitive) to allow the possibility (of): *the passage permits of two interpretations; his work permits him to relax nowadays.* ◆ *n* ('pɜːmɪt). **4** an official certificate or document granting authorization; licence. **5** permission, esp. written permission. [C15: from Latin *permittere,* from *per-* through + *mittere* to send] ▸ **per'mitter** *n*

permittivity (ˌpɜːmɪ'tɪvɪtɪ) *n, pl* **-ties.** a measure of the ability of a substance to transmit an electric field, expressed as the ratio of its electric displacement to the applied field strength; measured in farads per metre. Symbol: ε See also **relative permittivity, electric constant.**

permutate ('pɜːmjʊˌteɪt) *vb* to alter the sequence or arrangement (of); treat by permutation: *endlessly permutating three basic designs.*

permutation (ˌpɜːmjʊ'teɪʃən) *n* **1** *Maths.* **1a** an ordered arrangement of the numbers, terms, etc., of a set into specified groups: *the permutations of a, b, and c, taken two at a time, are ab, ba, ac, ca, bc, cb.* **1b** a group formed in this way. The number of permutations of *n* objects taken *r* at a time is $n!/(n-r)!$. Symbol: $_nP_r$. ◆ Compare **combination** (sense 6). **2** a combination of items made by reordering. **3** an alteration; transformation. **4** a fixed combination for selections of results on football pools. Usually shortened to **perm.** [C14: from Latin *permūtātiō,* from *permūtāre* to change thoroughly; see MUTATION] ▸ **ˌpermu'tational** *adj*

permute (pə'mjuːt) *vb* (*tr*) **1** to change the sequence of. **2** *Maths.* to subject to permutation. [C14: from Latin *permūtāre,* from PER- + *mūtāre* to change, alter] ▸ **per'mutable** *adj* ▸ **perˌmuta'bility** *or* **per'mutableness** *n* ▸ **per'mutably** *adv*

Pernambuco (ˌpɜːnəm'bjuːkəʊ; *Portuguese* pernəm'buku) *n* **1** a state of NE Brazil, on the Atlantic: consists of a humid coastal plain rising to a high inland plateau. Capital: Recife. Pop.: 7 445 200 (1995 est.). Area: 98 280 sq. km (37 946 sq. miles). **2** the former name of **Recife.**

pernicious (pə'nɪʃəs) *adj* **1** wicked or malicious: *pernicious lies.* **2** causing grave harm; deadly. [C16: from Latin *perniciōsus,* from *perniciēs* ruin, from PER- (intensive) + *nex* death] ▸ **per'niciously** *adv* ▸ **per'niciousness** *n*

pernicious anaemia *n* a form of anaemia characterized by lesions of the spinal cord, weakness, sore tongue, numbness in the arms and legs, diarrhoea, etc.: associated with inadequate absorption of vitamin B_{12}.

pernickety (pə'nɪkɪtɪ) *or U.S.* **persnickety** *adj Informal.* **1** excessively precise and attentive to detail; fussy. **2** (of a task) requiring close attention; exacting. [C19: originally Scottish, of unknown origin] ▸ **per'nicketiness** *or U.S.* **per'snicketiness** *n*

Pernik (*Bulgarian* 'pɛrnik) *n* an industrial town in W Bulgaria, on the Struma River. Pop.: 99 643 (1990). Former name (1949–62): **Dimitrovo.**

Pernod ('peənəʊ; *French* pɛrno) *n Trademark.* an aniseed-flavoured apéritif from France.

Perón (*Spanish* pe'rɔn) *n* **1 Juan Domingo** (xwan do'mɪngo). 1895–1974, Argentine soldier and statesman; dictator (1946–55). He was deposed in 1955, remaining in exile until 1973, when he was elected president (1973–74). **2** his third wife, **María Estella** (ma'ria es'teʎa), known as *Isabel.* born 1931, president of Argentina (1974–76); deposed. **3** (**María**) **Eva** (**Duarte**) **de Perón** ('eβa), known as *Evita.* Second wife of Juan Domingo Perón. 1919–52, Argentine film actress: active in politics and social welfare (1946–52). ▸ **Pe'ronist** *n, adj*

peroneal (ˌperə'niːəl) *adj Anatomy.* of or relating to the fibula or the outer side of the leg. [C19: from New Latin *peronē* fibula, from Greek: fibula]

perorate ('perəˌreɪt) *vb* (*intr*) **1** to speak at length, esp. in a formal manner. **2** to conclude a speech or sum up, esp. with a formal recapitulation.

peroration (ˌpɛrəˈreɪʃən) *n Rhetoric.* the conclusion of a speech or discourse, in which points made previously are summed up or recapitulated, esp. with greater emphasis. [C15: from Latin *perōrātiō,* from *perōrāre,* from PER- (thoroughly) + *ōrāre* to speak]

perovskite (pəˈrɒvskaɪt) *n* a yellow, brown, or greyish-black mineral form of calcium titanate with some rare-earth elements, which is used in certain high-temperature ceramic superconductors. [C19: named after Count Lev Alekseevich *Perovski* (1792–1856), Russian statesman]

peroxidase (pəˈrɒksɪˌdeɪs, -ˌdeɪz) *n* any of a group of enzymes that catalyse the oxidation of a compound by the decomposition of hydrogen peroxide or an organic peroxide. They generally consist of a protein combined with haem.

peroxidation (pəˌrɒksɪˈdeɪʃən) *n* a type of reaction in which oxygen atoms are formed leading to the production of peroxides. It is stimulated in the body by certain toxins and infections.

peroxide (pəˈrɒksaɪd) *n* **1** short for **hydrogen peroxide,** esp. when used for bleaching hair. **2** any of a class of metallic oxides, such as sodium peroxide, Na_2O_2, that contain the divalent ion $^-O\text{-}O^-$. **3** (*not in technical usage*) any of certain dioxides, such as manganese peroxide, MnO_2, that resemble peroxides in their formula but do not contain the $^-O\text{-}O^-$ ion. **4** any of a class of organic compounds whose molecules contain two oxygen atoms bound together. They tend to be explosive. **5** (*modifier*) of, relating to, bleached with, or resembling peroxide. ◆ *vb* **6** (*tr*) to bleach (the hair) with peroxide.

peroxide blonde *n Usually disparaging.* a woman having hair that is bleached rather than naturally blonde and that looks harsh or unnatural.

peroxisome (pəˈrɒksɪˌsəʊm) *n* a type of organelle present in most eukaryotic cells that carry out oxidative reactions, such as oxidation of alcohol in the liver.

peroxy- *or esp. for inorganic compounds* **peroxo-** *combining form.* indicating the presence of the peroxide group, -O-O-: *peroxysulphuric acid.* Also (not in technical usage): **per-.**

peroxysulphuric acid (pəˌrɒksɪsʌlˈfjʊərɪk) *n* a white hygroscopic crystalline unstable oxidizing acid. Formula: H_2SO_5. Also called (not in technical usage): **persulphuric acid, Caro's acid.**

perpend[1] (ˈpɜːpənd) *or* **perpent** *n* a large stone that passes through a wall from one side to the other. Also called: **parpend, perpend stone.** [C15: from Old French *parpain,* of uncertain origin]

perpend[2] (pəˈpɛnd) *vb* an archaic word for **ponder.** [C16: from Latin *perpendere* to examine, from PER- (thoroughly) + *pendere* to weigh]

perpendicular (ˌpɜːpənˈdɪkjʊlə) *adj* **1** Also: **normal.** at right angles to a horizontal plane. **2** denoting, relating to, or having the style of Gothic architecture used in England during the 14th and 15th centuries, characterized by tracery having vertical lines, a four-centred arch, and fan vaulting. **3** upright; vertical. ◆ *n* **4** *Geometry.* a line or plane perpendicular to another. **5** any instrument used for indicating the vertical line through a given point. **6** *Mountaineering.* a nearly vertical face. [C14: from Latin *perpendiculāris,* from *perpendiculum* a plumb line, from *per-* through + *pendēre* to hang] ▸ **perpendicularity** (ˌpɜːpənˌdɪkjʊˈlærɪtɪ) *n* ▸ **ˌperpenˈdicularly** *adv*

perpetrate (ˈpɜːpɪˌtreɪt) *vb* (*tr*) to perform or be responsible for (a deception, crime, etc.). [C16: from Latin *perpetrāre,* from *per-* (thoroughly) + *patrāre* to perform, perhaps from *pater* father, leader in the performance of sacred rites] ▸ **ˌperpeˈtration** *n* ▸ **ˈperpeˌtrator** *n*

USAGE *Perpetrate* and *perpetuate* are sometimes confused: *he must answer for the crimes he has perpetrated* (not *perpetuated*); *the book helped to perpetuate* (not *perpetrate*) *some of the myths surrounding his early life.*

perpetual (pəˈpɛtjʊəl) *adj* **1** (*usually prenominal*) eternal; permanent. **2** (*usually prenominal*) seemingly ceaseless because often repeated: *your perpetual complaints.* **3** *Horticulture.* blooming throughout the growing season or year. ◆ *n* **4** a plant that blooms throughout the growing season. [C14: via Old French from Latin *perpetuālis* universal, from *perpes* continuous, from *per-* (thoroughly) + *petere* to go towards] ▸ **perˈpetually** *adv*

perpetual check *n Chess.* a consecutive series of checks that the checked player cannot avoid, leading to a drawn game.

perpetual debenture *n* a bond or debenture that can either never be redeemed or cannot be redeemed on demand.

perpetual inventory *n* a form of stock control in which running records are kept of all acquisitions and disposals.

perpetual motion *n* **1** Also called: **perpetual motion of the first kind.** motion of a hypothetical mechanism that continues indefinitely without any external source of energy. It is impossible in practice because of friction. **2** Also called: **perpetual motion of the second kind.** motion of a hypothetical mechanism that derives its energy from a source at a lower temperature. It is impossible in practice because of the second law of thermodynamics.

perpetuate (pəˈpɛtjʊˌeɪt) *vb* (*tr*) to cause to continue or prevail: *to perpetuate misconceptions.* [C16: from Latin *perpetuāre* to continue without interruption, from *perpetuus* PERPETUAL] ▸ **perˌpetuˈation** *n*

USAGE See at **perpetrate.**

perpetuity (ˌpɜːpɪˈtjuːɪtɪ) *n, pl* **-ties. 1** eternity. **2** the state or quality of being perpetual. **3** *Property law.* a limitation preventing the absolute disposal of an estate for longer than the period allowed by law. **4** an annuity with no maturity date and payable indefinitely. **5 in perpetuity.** for ever. [C15: from Old French *perpetuite,* from Latin *perpetuitās* continuity; see PERPETUAL]

Perpignan (*French* pɛrpiɲɑ̃) *n* a town in S France: historic capital of Roussillon. Pop.: 108 049 (1990).

perplex (pəˈplɛks) *vb* (*tr*) **1** to puzzle; bewilder; confuse. **2** to complicate: *to perplex an issue.* [C15: from obsolete *perplex* (adj) intricate, from Latin *perplexus* entangled, from *per-* (thoroughly) + *plectere* to entwine]

perplexity (pəˈplɛksɪtɪ) *n, pl* **-ties. 1** the state of being perplexed. **2** the state of being intricate or complicated. **3** something that perplexes.

per pro (ˈpɜː ˈprəʊ) *prep* by delegation to; through the agency of: used when signing documents on behalf of someone else. [Latin: abbreviation of *per prōcūrātiōnem*]

USAGE See at **pp.**

perquisite (ˈpɜːkwɪzɪt) *n* **1** an incidental benefit gained from a certain type of employment, such as the use of a company car. **2** a customary benefit received in addition to a regular income. **3** a customary tip. **4** something expected or regarded as an exclusive right. ◆ Often shortened (informal) to **perk.** [C15: from Medieval Latin *perquīsītum* an acquired possession, from Latin *perquīrere* to seek earnestly for something, from *per-* (thoroughly) + *quaerere* to ask for, seek]

Perrault (*French* pero) *n* **Charles** (ʃarl). 1628–1703, French author, noted for his *Contes de ma mère l'oye* (1697), which contains the fairy tales *Little Red Riding Hood, Cinderella,* and *The Sleeping Beauty.*

Perrier water *or* **Perrier** (ˈpɛrɪeɪ) *n Trademark.* a sparkling mineral water from the south of France. [C20: named after a spring *Source Perrier,* at Vergèze, France]

Perrin (*French* pɛrɛ̃) *n* **Jean Baptiste** (ʒɑ̃ batist). 1870–1942, French physicist. His researches on the distribution and diffusion of particles in colloids (1911) gave evidence for the physical reality of molecules, confirmed the explanation of Brownian movement in terms of kinetic theory, and determined the magnitude of the Avogadro constant. He also studied cathode rays: Nobel prize for physics 1926.

perron (ˈpɛrən) *n* an external flight of steps, esp. one at the front entrance of a building. [C14: from Old French, from *pierre* stone, from Latin *petra*]

perry (ˈpɛrɪ) *n, pl* **-ries.** wine made of pears, similar in taste to cider. [C14 *pereye,* from Old French *peré,* ultimately from Latin *pirum* pear]

Perry (ˈpɛrɪ) *n* **1 Fred(erick John).** 1909–95, English tennis and table-tennis player; world singles table-tennis champion (1929); Wimbledon singles champion (1934–36). **2 Matthew Calbraith.** 1794–1858, U.S. naval officer, who led a naval expedition to Japan that obtained a treaty (1854) opening up Japan to western trade. **3** his brother, **Oliver Hazard.** 1785–1819, U.S. naval officer. His defeat of a British squadron on Lake Erie (1813) was the turning point in the War of 1812, leading to the recapture of Detroit.

pers. *abbrev. for:* **1** person. **2** personal.

Pers. *abbrev. for* Persia(n).

persalt (ˈpɜːˌsɔːlt) *n* any salt of a peracid.

perse (pɜːs) *n* **a** a dark greyish-blue colour. **b** (*as adj*): *perse cloth.* [C14: from Old French, from Medieval Latin *persus,* perhaps changed from Latin *Persicus* Persian]

per se (ˈpɜː ˈseɪ) *adv* by or in itself; intrinsically. [Latin]

Perse (pɜːs; *French* pɛrs) *n* **Saint-John** (ˈsɪndʒən), real name *Alexis Saint-Léger.* 1887–1975, French poet, born in Guadeloupe. His works include *Anabase* (1922) and *Chronique* (1960). Nobel prize for literature 1960.

persecute (ˈpɜːsɪˌkjuːt) *vb* (*tr*) **1** to oppress, harass, or maltreat, esp. because of race, religion, etc. **2** to bother persistently. [C15: from Old French *persecuter,* back formation from *persecuteur,* from Late Latin *persecūtor* pursuer, from *persequī* to take vengeance upon] ▸ **ˈperseˌcutive** *or* **ˈperseˌcutory** *adj* ▸ **ˈperseˌcutor** *n*

persecution (ˌpɜːsɪˈkjuːʃən) *n* the act of persecuting or the state of being persecuted.

persecution complex *n Psychol.* an acute irrational fear that other people are plotting one's downfall and that they are responsible for one's failures.

Perseid (ˈpɜːsɪɪd) *n* any member of a meteor shower occurring annually during early August and appearing to radiate from a point in the constellation Perseus. [C19: from Greek *Perseïdes* daughters of PERSEUS[1]]

Persephone (pəˈsɛfənɪ) *n Greek myth.* a daughter of Zeus and Demeter, abducted by Hades and made his wife and queen of the underworld, but allowed part of each year to leave it. Roman counterpart: **Proserpina.**

Persepolis (pəˈsɛpəlɪs) *n* the capital of ancient Persia in the Persian Empire and under the Seleucids: founded by Darius; sacked by Alexander the Great in 330 B.C.

Perseus[1] (ˈpɜːsɪəs) *n Greek myth.* a son of Zeus and Danaë, who with Athena's help slew the Gorgon Medusa and rescued Andromeda from a sea monster.

Perseus[2] (ˈpɜːsɪəs) *n, Latin genitive* **Persei** (ˈpɜːsɪˌaɪ). a conspicuous constellation in the N hemisphere lying between Auriga and Cassiopeia and crossed by the Milky Way. It contains the eclipsing binary, Algol.

perseverance (ˌpɜːsɪˈvɪərəns) *n* **1** continued steady belief or efforts, withstanding discouragement or difficulty; persistence. **2** *Christianity.* persistence in remaining in a state of grace until death. ▸ **ˌperseˈverant** *adj*

perseveration (pɜːˌsɛvəˈreɪʃən) *n Psychol.* **1** the tendency for an impression, idea, or feeling to dissipate only slowly and to recur during subsequent experiences. **2** an inability to change one's method of working when transferred from one task to another.

persevere (ˌpɜːsɪˈvɪə) *vb* (*intr;* often foll. by *in*) to show perseverance. [C14: from Old French *perseverer,* from Latin *persevērāre,* from *perseverus* very strict; see SEVERE] ▸ **ˌperseˈvering** *adj* ▸ **ˌperseˈveringly** *adv*

Pershing[1] (ˈpɜːʃɪŋ) *n* **John Joseph,** nickname *Black Jack.* 1860–1948, U.S. general. He was commander in chief of the American Expeditionary Force in Europe (1917–19).

Pershing[2] (ˈpɜːʃɪŋ) *n* a U.S. ballistic missile capable of carrying a nuclear or conventional warhead.

Persia (ˈpɜːʃə) *n* **1** the former name (until 1935) of **Iran. 2** another name for **Persian Empire.**

Persian (ˈpɜːʃən) *adj* **1** of or relating to ancient Persia or modern Iran, their inhabitants, or their languages. ◆ *n* **2** a native, citizen, or inhabitant of modern Iran; an Iranian. **3** a member of an Indo-European people of West Iranian speech who established a great empire in SW Asia in the 6th century B.C. **4** (loosely) the language of Iran or Persia in any of its ancient or modern forms, belonging to the West Iranian branch of the Indo-European family. See also **Avestan, Old Persian, Pahlavi**[2], **Farsi.**

Persian blinds *pl n* another term for **persiennes.**

Persian carpet *or* **rug** *n* a carpet or rug made in Persia or other countries of the Near East by knotting silk or wool yarn by hand onto a woven backing, characterized by rich colours and flowing or geometric designs.

Persian cat *n* a long-haired variety of domestic cat with a stocky body, round face, and short thick legs.

Persian Empire *n* the S Asian empire established by Cyrus the Great in the 6th century B.C. and overthrown by Alexander the Great in the 4th century B.C. At its height it extended from India to Europe.

Persian greyhound *n* another name for the **Saluki.**

Persian Gulf *n* a shallow arm of the Arabian Sea between SW Iran and Arabia: linked with the Arabian Sea by the Strait of Hormuz and the Gulf of Oman; important for the oilfields on its shores. Area: 233 000 sq. km (90 000 sq. miles).

Persian lamb *n* **1** a black loosely curled fur obtained from the skin of the karakul lamb. **2** a karakul lamb.

Persian melon *n* another name for **winter melon.**

persicaria (ˌpɜːsɪˈkɛərɪə) *n* another name for **red shank.**

persiennes (ˌpɜːsɪˈɛnz) *pl n* outside window shutters having louvres to keep out the sun while maintaining ventilation. Also called: **Persian blinds. [C19:** from French, from *persien* Persian**]**

persiflage (ˈpɜːsɪˌflɑːʒ) *n* light frivolous conversation, style, or treatment; friendly teasing. **[C18:** via French, from *persifler* to tease, from *per-* (intensive) + *siffler* to whistle, from Latin *sībilāre* to whistle**]**

persimmon (pɜːˈsɪmən) *n* **1** any of several tropical trees of the genus *Diospyros,* typically having hard wood and large orange-red fruit: family *Ebenaceae.* **2** the sweet fruit of any of these trees, which is edible when completely ripe. ◆ See also **ebony** (sense 1). **[C17:** of Algonquian origin; related to Delaware *pasĭmĕnan* dried fruit**]**

Persis (ˈpɜːsɪs) *n* an ancient region of SW Iran: homeland of the Achaemenid dynasty.

persist (pəˈsɪst) *vb (intr)* **1** (often foll. by *in*) to continue steadfastly or obstinately despite opposition or difficulty. **2** to continue to exist or occur without interruption: *the rain persisted throughout the night.* **[C16:** from Latin *persistere,* from *per-* (intensive) + *sistere* to stand steadfast, from *stāre* to stand**]** ▸ **perˈsister** *n*

persistence (pəˈsɪstəns) *or* **persistency** *n* **1** the quality of persisting; tenacity. **2** the act of persisting; continued effort or existence. **3** the continuance of an effect after the cause of it has stopped: *persistence of vision.*

persistent (pəˈsɪstənt) *adj* **1** showing persistence. **2** incessantly repeated; unrelenting: *your persistent questioning.* **3** (of plant parts) remaining attached to the plant after the normal time of withering: *a fruit surrounded by a persistent perianth.* **4** *Zoology.* **4a** (of parts normally present only in young stages) present in the adult: *persistent gills in axolotls.* **4b** continuing to grow or develop after the normal period of growth: *persistent teeth.* **5** (of a chemical, esp. when used as an insecticide) slow to break down; not easily degradable. ▸ **perˈsistently** *adv*

persistent cruelty *n Brit. law.* conduct causing fear of danger to the life or health of a spouse (used in matrimonial proceedings before magistrates).

persistent vegetative state *n Medicine.* an irreversible condition, resulting from brain damage, characterized by lack of consciousness, thought, and feeling, although reflex activities (such as breathing) continue. Abbrev: **PVS.**

persnickety (pəˈsnɪkɪtɪ) *adj* the U.S. word for **pernickety.**

person (ˈpɜːsᵊn) *n, pl* **persons. 1** an individual human being. **2** the body of a human being, sometimes including his or her clothing: *guns hidden on his person.* **3** a grammatical category into which pronouns and forms of verbs are subdivided depending on whether they refer to the speaker, the person addressed, or some other individual, thing, etc. **4** a human being or a corporation recognized in law as having certain rights and obligations. **5** *Philosophy.* a being characterized by consciousness, rationality, and a moral sense, and traditionally thought of as consisting of both a body and a mind or soul. **6** *Archaic.* a character or role; guise. **7 in person. 7a** actually present: *the author will be there in person.* **7b** without the help or intervention of others. **[C13:** from Old French *persone,* from Latin *persōna* mask, perhaps from Etruscan *phersu* mask**]**

USAGE *People* is the word usually used to refer to more than one individual: *there were a hundred people at the reception. Persons* is rarely used, except in official English: *several persons were interviewed.*

Person (ˈpɜːsᵊn) *n Christianity.* any of the three hypostases existing as distinct in the one God and constituting the Trinity. They are the **First Person,** the Father, the **Second Person,** the Son, and the **Third Person,** the Holy Ghost.

-person *suffix forming nouns.* sometimes used instead of *-man* and *-woman* or *-lady: chairperson; salesperson.*

USAGE See at **-man.**

persona (pɜːˈsəʊnə) *n, pl* **-nae** (-niː). **1** (*often pl*) a character in a play, novel, etc. **2** an assumed identity or character. **3** (in Jungian psychology) the mechanism that conceals a person's true thoughts and feelings, esp. in his adaptation to the outside world. **[**Latin: mask**]**

personable (ˈpɜːsənəbᵊl) *adj* pleasant in appearance and personality. ▸ **ˈpersonableness** *n* ▸ **ˈpersonably** *adv*

personage (ˈpɜːsənɪdʒ) *n* **1** an important or distinguished person. **2** another word for **person** (sense 1): *a strange personage.* **3** *Rare.* a figure in literature, history, etc.

persona grata *Latin.* (pɜːˈsəʊnə ˈgrɑːtə) *n, pl* ***personae gratae*** (pɜːˈsəʊniː ˈgrɑːtiː). an acceptable person, esp. a diplomat acceptable to the government of the country to which he or she is sent.

personal (ˈpɜːsənᵊl) *adj* **1** of or relating to the private aspects of a person's life: *personal letters; a personal question.* **2** (*prenominal*) of or relating to a person's body, its care, or its appearance: *personal hygiene; great personal beauty.* **3** belonging to or intended for a particular person and no-one else: *as a personal favour; for your personal use.* **4** (*prenominal*) undertaken by an individual himself: *a personal appearance by a celebrity.* **5** referring to, concerning, or involving a person's individual personality, intimate affairs, etc., esp. in an offensive way: *personal remarks; don't be so personal.* **6** having the attributes of an individual conscious being: *a personal God.* **7** of or arising from the personality: *personal magnetism.* **8** of, relating to, or denoting grammatical person. **9** *Law.* of or relating to movable property, such as money. Compare **real**[1] (sense 8). ◆ *n* **10** *Law.* an item of movable property.

personal column *n* a newspaper column containing personal messages, advertisements by charities, requests for friendship, holiday companions, etc.

personal computer *n* a small inexpensive computer used in word processing, playing computer games, etc.

personal equation *n* **1** the variation or error in observation or judgment caused by individual characteristics. **2** the allowance made for such variation.

personal equity plan *n* the full name for **PEP.**

personalism (ˈpɜːsənəˌlɪzəm) *n* **1** a philosophical movement that stresses the value of persons. **2** an idiosyncratic mode of behaviour or expression. ▸ **ˌpersonalˈistic** *adj* ▸ **ˈpersonalist** *n, adj*

personality (ˌpɜːsəˈnælɪtɪ) *n, pl* **-ties. 1** *Psychol.* the sum total of all the behavioural and mental characteristics by means of which an individual is recognized as being unique. **2** the distinctive character of a person that makes him socially attractive: *a salesman needs a lot of personality.* **3** a well-known person in a certain field, such as sport or entertainment. **4** a remarkable person: *the old fellow is a real personality.* **5** the quality of being a unique person. **6** the distinctive atmosphere of a place or situation. **7** (*often pl*) a personal remark.

personality cult *n* deliberately cultivated adulation of a person, esp. a political leader.

personality disorder *n Psychiatry.* any of a group of mental disorders characterized by a permanent disposition to behave in ways causing suffering to oneself or others.

personality inventory *n Psychol.* a form of personality test in which the subject answers questions about himself. The results are used to determine dimensions of personality, such as extroversion.

personality type *n Psychol.* a cluster of personality traits commonly occurring together.

personalize *or* **personalise** (ˈpɜːsənəˌlaɪz) *vb (tr)* **1** to endow with personal or individual qualities or characteristics. **2** to mark (stationery, clothing, etc.) with a person's initials, name, etc. **3** to take (a remark, etc.) personally. **4** another word for **personify.** ▸ **ˌpersonaliˈzation** *or* **ˌpersonaliˈsation** *n*

personally (ˈpɜːsənəlɪ) *adv* **1** without the help or intervention of others: *I'll attend to it personally.* **2** (*sentence modifier*) in one's own opinion or as regards oneself: *personally, I hate onions.* **3** as if referring to oneself: *to take the insults personally.* **4** as a person: *we like him personally, but professionally he's incompetent.*

personal organizer *n* **1** a diary that stores personal records, appointments, notes, etc. **2** a pocket-sized electronic device that performs the same functions.

personal pronoun *n* a pronoun having a definite person or thing as an antecedent and functioning grammatically in the same way as the noun that it replaces. In English, the personal pronouns include *I, you, he, she, it, we,* and *they,* and are inflected for case.

personal property *n Law.* movable property, such as furniture or money. Compare **real property.** Also called: **personalty.**

personal stereo *n* a very small audio cassette player designed to be worn attached to a belt and used with lightweight headphones.

personalty (ˈpɜːsənəltɪ) *n, pl* **-ties.** *Law.* another word for **personal property. [C16:** from Anglo-French, from Late Latin *persōnālitās* personality**]**

persona non grata *Latin.* (pɜːˈsəʊnə nɒn ˈgrɑːtə) *n, pl* ***personae non gratae*** (pɜːˈsəʊniː nɒn ˈgrɑːtiː). **1** an unacceptable or unwelcome person. **2** a diplomatic or consular officer who is not acceptable to the government or sovereign to whom he or she is accredited.

personate[1] (ˈpɜːsəˌneɪt) *vb (tr)* **1** to act the part of (a character in a play); portray. **2** a less common word for **personify. 3** *Criminal law.* to assume the identity of (another person) with intent to deceive. ▸ **ˌpersonˈation** *n* ▸ **ˈpersonative** *adj* ▸ **ˈpersonˌator** *n*

personate[2] (ˈpɜːsənɪt, -ˌneɪt) *adj* (of the corollas of certain flowers) having two lips in the form of a face. **[C18:** from New Latin *persōnātus* masked, from Latin *persōna;* see PERSON**]**

personification (pɜːˌsɒnɪfɪˈkeɪʃən) *n* **1** the attribution of human characteristics to things, abstract ideas, etc., as for literary or artistic effect. **2** the representation of an abstract quality or idea in the form of a person, creature, etc., as in art and literature. **3** a person or thing that personifies. **4** a person or thing regarded as an embodiment of a quality: *he is the personification of optimism.*

personify (pɜːˈsɒnɪˌfaɪ) *vb* **-fies, -fying, -fied.** *(tr)* **1** to attribute human characteristics to (a thing or abstraction). **2** to represent (an abstract quality) in human or animal form. **3** (of a person or thing) to represent (an abstract quality), as in art or literature. **4** to be the embodiment of. ▸ **perˈsoniˌfiable** *adj* ▸ **perˈsoniˌfier** *n*

personnel (ˌpɜːsəˈnɛl) *n* **1** the people employed in an organization or for a service or undertaking. Compare **materiel. 2a** the office or department that interviews, appoints, or keeps records of employees. **2b** (*as modifier*): *a personnel officer.* **[C19:** from French, ultimately from Late Latin *persōnālis* personal (adj); see PERSON**]**

perspective (pəˈspɛktɪv) *n* **1** a way of regarding situations, facts, etc., and judging their relative importance. **2** the proper or accurate point of view or the ability to see it; objectivity: *try to get some perspective on your troubles.* **3** the theory or art of suggesting three dimensions on a two-dimensional surface, in order to recreate the appearance and spatial relationships that objects or a scene in recession present to the eye. **4** the appearance of objects, buildings, etc., relative to each other, as determined by their distance from the viewer, or the effects of this distance on their appearance. **5** a view over some distance in space or time; vista; prospect. **6** a picture showing perspective. [C14: from Medieval Latin *perspectīva ars* the science of optics, from Latin *perspicere* to inspect carefully, from *per-* (intensive) + *specere* to behold] ▸ **per'spectively** *adv*

Perspex ('pɜːspɛks) *n Trademark.* any of various clear acrylic resins, used chiefly as a substitute for glass.

perspicacious (ˌpɜːspɪ'keɪʃəs) *adj* **1** acutely perceptive or discerning. **2** *Archaic.* having keen eyesight. [C17: from Latin *perspicax,* from *perspicere* to look at closely; see PERSPECTIVE] ▸ **ˌperspi'caciously** *adv* ▸ **perspicacity** (ˌpɜːspɪ'kæsɪtɪ) *or* **ˌperspi'caciousness** *n*

perspicuity (ˌpɜːspɪ'kjuːɪtɪ) *n* **1** the quality of being perspicuous. **2** another word for **perspicacity.**

perspicuous (pə'spɪkjuəs) *adj* (of speech or writing) easily understood; lucid. [C15: from Latin *perspicuus* transparent, from *perspicere* to explore thoroughly; see PERSPECTIVE] ▸ **per'spicuously** *adv* ▸ **per'spicuousness** *n*

perspiration (ˌpɜːspə'reɪʃən) *n* **1** the salty fluid secreted by the sweat glands of the skin. **2** the act or process of secreting this fluid.

perspiratory (pə'spaɪərətərɪ, -trɪ) *adj* of, relating to, or stimulating perspiration.

perspire (pə'spaɪə) *vb* to secrete or exude (perspiration) through the pores of the skin. [C17: from Latin *perspīrāre* to blow, from *per-* (through) + *spīrāre* to breathe; compare INSPIRE] ▸ **per'spiringly** *adv*

persuade (pə'sweɪd) *vb (tr; may take a clause as object or an infinitive)* **1** to induce, urge, or prevail upon successfully: *he finally persuaded them to buy it.* **2** to cause to believe; convince: *even with the evidence, the police were not persuaded.* [C16: from Latin *persuādēre,* from *per-* (intensive) + *suādēre* to urge, advise] ▸ **per'suadable** *or* **per'suasible** *adj* ▸ **perˌsuada'bility** *or* **perˌsuasi'bility** *n* ▸ **per'suader** *n*

persuasion (pə'sweɪʒən) *n* **1** the act of persuading or of trying to persuade. **2** the power to persuade. **3** the state of being persuaded; strong belief. **4** an established creed or belief, esp. a religious one. **5** a sect, party, or faction. [C14: from Latin *persuāsiō;* see PERSUADE]

persuasive (pə'sweɪsɪv) *adj* having the power or ability to persuade; tending to persuade: *a persuasive salesman.* ▸ **per'suasively** *adv* ▸ **per'suasiveness** *n*

persulphuric acid *or U.S.* **persulfuric acid** (ˌpɜːsʌl'fjuərɪk) *n* other names (not in technical usage) for **peroxysulphuric acid.**

pert (pɜːt) *adj* **1** saucy, impudent, or forward. **2** jaunty: *a pert little hat.* **3** *Obsolete.* clever or brisk. [C13: variant of earlier *apert,* from Latin *apertus* open, from *aperīre* to open; influenced by Old French *aspert,* from Latin *expertus* EXPERT] ▸ **'pertly** *adv* ▸ **'pertness** *n*

PERT (pɜːt) *n acronym for* programme evaluation and review technique.

pert. *abbrev. for* pertaining.

pertain (pə'teɪn) *vb (intr;* often foll. by *to)* **1** to have reference, relation, or relevance: *issues pertaining to women.* **2** to be appropriate: *the product pertains to real user needs.* **3** to belong (to) or be a part (of); be an adjunct, attribute, or accessory (of). [C14: from Latin *pertinēre,* from *per-* (intensive) + *tenēre* to hold]

Perth (pɜːθ) *n* **1** a city in central Scotland, in Perth and Kinross on the River Tay: capital of Scotland from the 12th century until the assassination of James I there in 1437. Pop.: 41 453 (1991). **2** a city in SW Australia, capital of Western Australia, on the Swan River: major industrial centre; University of Western Australia (1911). Pop.: 1 262 600 (1995 est.).

Perth and Kinross (kɪn'rɒs) *n* a council area of N central Scotland, corresponding mainly to the historical counties of Perthshire and Kinross-shire: part of Tayside Region from 1975 until 1996: chiefly mountainous, with agriculture, tourism, and forestry. Administrative centre: Perth. Pop.: 132 570 (1996 est.). Area: 5321 sq. km (2019 sq. miles).

Perthshire ('pɜːθˌʃɪə, -ʃə) *n* (until 1975) a county of central Scotland, now part of Perth and Kinross council area.

pertinacious (ˌpɜːtɪ'neɪʃəs) *adj* **1** doggedly resolute in purpose or belief; unyielding. **2** stubbornly persistent. [C17: from Latin *pertinax,* from *per-* (intensive) + *tenāx* clinging, from *tenēre* to hold] ▸ **ˌperti'naciously** *adv* ▸ **pertinacity** (ˌpɜːtɪ'næsɪtɪ) *or* **ˌperti'naciousness** *n*

pertinent ('pɜːtɪnənt) *adj* relating to the matter at hand; relevant. [C14: from Latin *pertinēns,* from *pertinēre* to PERTAIN] ▸ **'pertinence** *n* ▸ **'pertinently** *adv*

perturb (pə'tɜːb) *vb (tr; often passive)* **1** to disturb the composure of; trouble. **2** to throw into disorder. **3** *Physics, astronomy.* to cause (a planet, electron, etc.) to undergo a perturbation. [C14: from Old French *pertourber,* from Latin *perturbāre* to confuse, from *per-* (intensive) + *turbāre* to agitate, from *turba* confusion] ▸ **per'turbable** *adj* ▸ **per'turbably** *adv* ▸ **per'turbing** *adj* ▸ **per'turbingly** *adv*

perturbation (ˌpɜːtə'beɪʃən) *n* **1** the act of perturbing or the state of being perturbed. **2** a cause of disturbance or upset. **3** *Physics.* a secondary influence on a system that modifies simple behaviour, such as the effect of the other electrons on one electron in an atom. **4** *Astronomy.* a small continuous deviation in the inclination and eccentricity of the orbit of a planet or comet, due to the attraction of neighbouring planets.

pertussis (pə'tʌsɪs) *n* the technical name for **whooping cough.** [C18: New Latin, from Latin *per-* (intensive) + *tussis* cough] ▸ **per'tussal** *adj*

Peru (pə'ruː) *n* a republic in W South America, on the Pacific: the centre of the great Inca Empire when conquered by the Spanish in 1532; gained independence in 1824 by defeating Spanish forces with armies led by San Martín and Bolívar; consists of a coastal desert, rising to the Andes; an important exporter of minerals and a major fishing nation. Official languages: Spanish, Quechua, and Aymara. Official religion: Roman Catholic. Currency: nuevo sol. Capital: Lima. Pop.: 24 801 000 (1998 est.). Area: 1 285 215 sq. km (496 222 sq. miles). ▸ **Peruvian** (pə'ruːvɪən) *adj, n*

Peru Current *n* another name for the **Humboldt Current.**

Perugia (pə'ruːdʒə; *Italian* pe'ruːdʒa) *n* **1** a city in central Italy, in Umbria: centre of the Umbrian school of painting (15th century); university (1308); Etruscan and Roman remains. Pop.: 151 118 (1996 est.). Ancient name: **Pe'rusia. 2 Lake.** another name for (Lake) **Trasimene.**

Perugino (*Italian* peru'dʒino) *n* **Il** (il), real name *Pietro Vannucci.* 1446–1523, Italian painter; master of Raphael. His works include the fresco *Christ giving the Keys to Peter* in the Sistine Chapel, Rome.

peruke (pə'ruːk) *n* a type of wig for men, fashionable in the 17th and 18th centuries. Also called: **periwig.** [C16: from French *perruque,* from Italian *perrucca* wig, of obscure origin]

peruse (pə'ruːz) *vb (tr)* **1** to read or examine with care; study. **2** to browse or read through in a leisurely way. [C15 (meaning: to use up): from PER- (intensive) + USE] ▸ **pe'rusal** *n* ▸ **pe'ruser** *n*

Perutz (pə'rʊts) *n* **Max Ferdinand.** born 1914, British biochemist, born in Austria. With J. C. Kendrew, he worked on the structure of haemoglobin and shared the Nobel prize for chemistry 1962.

Peruvian bark *n* another name for **cinchona** (sense 2).

Peruzzi (*Italian* pe'ruttsi) *n* **Baldassare Tommaso** (baldas'saːre tom'maːzo). 1481–1536, Italian architect and painter of the High Renaissance. The design of the Palazzo Massimo, Rome, is attributed to him.

perv (pɜːv) *Slang.* ◆ *n* **1** a pervert. **2** *Austral.* an erotic glance or look. ◆ *vb also* **perve.** *(intr)* **3** *Austral.* to give a person an erotic look.

pervade (pɜː'veɪd) *vb (tr)* to spread through or throughout, esp. subtly or gradually; permeate. [C17: from Latin *pervādere,* from *per-* through + *vādere* to go] ▸ **per'vader** *n* ▸ **pervasion** (pɜː'veɪʒən) *n*

pervasive (pɜː'veɪsɪv) *adj* pervading or tending to pervade. [C18: from Latin *pervāsus,* past participle of *pervādere* to PERVADE] ▸ **per'vasively** *adv* ▸ **per'vasiveness** *n*

perverse (pə'vɜːs) *adj* **1** deliberately deviating from what is regarded as normal, good, or proper. **2** persistently holding to what is wrong. **3** wayward or contrary; obstinate; cantankerous. **4** *Archaic.* perverted. [C14: from Old French *pervers,* from Latin *perversus* turned the wrong way] ▸ **per'versely** *adv* ▸ **per'verseness** *n*

perversion (pə'vɜːʃən) *n* **1** any abnormal means of obtaining sexual satisfaction. **2** the act of perverting or the state of being perverted. **3** a perverted form or usage.

perversity (pə'vɜːsɪtɪ) *n, pl* **-ties. 1** the quality or state of being perverse. **2** a perverse action, comment, etc.

perversive (pə'vɜːsɪv) *adj* perverting or tending to pervert.

pervert *vb* (pə'vɜːt). *(tr)* **1** to use wrongly or badly. **2** to interpret wrongly or badly; distort. **3** to lead into deviant or perverted beliefs or behaviour; corrupt. **4** to debase. ◆ *n* ('pɜːvɜːt). **5** a person who practises sexual perversion. [C14: from Old French *pervertir,* from Latin *pervertere* to turn the wrong way, from *per-* (indicating deviation) + *vertere* to turn] ▸ **per'verter** *n* ▸ **per'vertible** *adj*

perverted (pə'vɜːtɪd) *adj* **1** deviating greatly from what is regarded as normal or right; distorted. **2** of or practising sexual perversion. **3** incorrectly interpreted. ▸ **per'vertedly** *adv* ▸ **per'vertedness** *n*

pervious ('pɜːvɪəs) *adj* **1** able to be penetrated; permeable. **2** receptive to new ideas; open-minded. [C17: from Latin *pervius,* from *per-* (through) + *via* a way] ▸ **'perviously** *adv* ▸ **'perviousness** *n*

pes (peɪz, piːz) *n, pl* **pedes** ('pɛdiːz). **1** the technical name for the human **foot. 2** the corresponding part in higher vertebrates. **3** any footlike part. [C19: New Latin: foot]

Pesach *or* **Pesah** ('peɪsɑːk; *Hebrew* 'pesax) *n* other words for **Passover** (sense 1). [from Hebrew *pesaḥ;* see PASSOVER]

pesade (pe'sɑːd) *n Dressage.* a position in which the horse stands on the hind legs with the forelegs in the air. [C18: from French, from *posade,* from Italian *posata* a halt, from *posare* to stop, from Latin *pausa* end]

Pesaro (*Italian* 'peːzaro) *n* a port and resort in E central Italy, in the Marches on the Adriatic. Pop.: 90 340 (1990). Ancient name: **Pisaurum** (pɪ'saurəm).

Pescadores (ˌpɛskə'dɔːrɪz) *pl n* a group of 64 islands in Formosa Strait, separated from Taiwan (to which it belongs) by the **Pescadores Channel.** Pop.: 91 263 (1995). Area: 127 sq. km (49 sq. miles). Chinese names: **Penghu, P'eng-hu.**

Pescara (*Italian* pes'kaːra) *n* a city and resort in E central Italy, on the Adriatic. Pop.: 118 764 (1996 est.).

peseta (pə'seɪtə; *Spanish* pe'seta) *n* the standard monetary unit of Spain and its dependencies, divided into 100 céntimos. [C19: from Spanish, diminutive of PESO]

pesewa (pɪ'seɪwɑː) *n* a Ghanaian monetary unit worth one hundredth of a cedi.

Peshawar (pə'ʃɔːə) *n* a city in N Pakistan, at the E end of the Khyber Pass: one of the oldest cities in Pakistan and capital of the ancient kingdom of Gandhara; university (1950). Pop.: 1 676 000 (1995 est.).

Peshitta (pə'ʃiːtə) *or* **Peshito** (pə'ʃiːtəʊ) *n* the principal Syriac version of the Bible. [C18 *Peshito,* from Syriac]

pesky ('pɛskɪ) *adj* **peskier, peskiest.** *Informal, chiefly U.S. and Canadian.* troublesome: *pesky flies.* [C19: probably changed from *pesty;* see PEST] ▸ **'peskily** *adv* ▸ **'peskiness** *n*

peso ('peɪsəʊ; *Spanish* 'peso) *n, pl* **-sos** (-səʊz; *Spanish* -sos). **1** the standard monetary unit, comprising 100 centavos, of Argentina, Chile, Colombia, Cuba, the Dominican Republic, Guinea-Bissau, Mexico, and the Philippines. **2** the standard monetary unit of Uruguay, divided into 100 centesimos. **3** a coin or currency note worth a peso. **4** another name for **piece of eight.** [C16: from Spanish: weight, from Latin *pēnsum* something weighed out, from *pendere* to weigh]

pessary ('pɛsərɪ) *n, pl* **-ries.** *Med.* **1** a device for inserting into the vagina, either as a support for the uterus or (**diaphragm pessary**) as a contraceptive. **2** a medicated vaginal suppository. [C14: from Late Latin *pessārium,* from Latin *pessum,* from Greek *pessos* plug]

pessimism ('pɛsɪˌmɪzəm) *n* **1** the tendency to expect the worst and see the worst in all things. **2** the doctrine of the ultimate triumph of evil over good. **3** the doctrine that this world is corrupt and that man's sojourn in it is a preparation for some other existence. [C18: from Latin *pessimus* worst, from *malus* bad] ▸ **'pessimist** *n* ▸ **ˌpessi'mistic** *or (less commonly)* **ˌpessi'mistical** *adj* ▸ **ˌpessi'mistically** *adv*

Pessoa (pɛ'səuə) *n* **Fernando.** 1888–1935, Portuguese poet, who ascribed much of his work to three imaginary poets, Alvaro de Campos, Alberto Caeiro, and Ricardo Reis.

pest (pɛst) *n* **1** a person or thing that annoys, esp. by imposing itself when it is not wanted; nuisance. **2a** any organism that damages crops, injures or irritates livestock or man, or reduces the fertility of land. **2b** *(as modifier): pest control.* **3** *Rare.* an epidemic disease or pestilence. [C16: from Latin *pestis* plague, of obscure origin]

Pestalozzi (ˌpɛstə'lɒtsɪ) *n* **Johann Heinrich** (jo'han 'hainrɪç). 1746–1827, Swiss educational reformer. His emphasis on learning by observation exerted a wide influence on elementary education.

pester ('pɛstə) *vb (tr)* to annoy or nag continually. [C16: from Old French *empestrer* to hobble (a horse), from Vulgar Latin *impāstōriāre* (unattested) to use a hobble, from *pāstōria* (unattested) a hobble, from Latin *pāstōrius* relating to a herdsman, from *pastor* herdsman] ▸ **'pesterer** *n* ▸ **'pesteringly** *adv*

pesthouse ('pɛstˌhaus) *n Obsolete.* a hospital for treating persons with infectious diseases. Also called: **lazaretto.**

pesticide ('pɛstɪˌsaɪd) *n* a chemical used for killing pests, esp. insects and rodents. ▸ **ˌpesti'cidal** *adj*

pestiferous (pɛ'stɪfərəs) *adj* **1** *Informal.* troublesome; irritating. **2** breeding, carrying, or spreading infectious disease. **3** corrupting; pernicious. [C16: from Latin *pestifer,* from *pestis* contagious disease, PEST + *ferre* to bring] ▸ **pes'tiferously** *adv* ▸ **pes'tiferousness** *n*

pestilence ('pɛstɪləns) *n* **1a** any epidemic outbreak of a deadly and highly infectious disease, such as the plague. **1b** such a disease. **2** an evil influence or idea.

pestilent ('pɛstɪlənt) *adj* **1** annoying; irritating. **2** highly destructive morally or physically; pernicious. **3** infected with or likely to cause epidemic or infectious disease. [C15: from Latin *pestilens* unwholesome, from *pestis* plague] ▸ **'pestilently** *adv*

pestilential (ˌpɛstɪ'lɛnʃəl) *adj* **1** dangerous or troublesome; harmful or annoying. **2** of, causing, or resembling pestilence. ▸ **ˌpesti'lentially** *adv*

pestle ('pɛsᵊl) *n* **1** a club-shaped instrument for mixing or grinding substances in a mortar. **2** a tool for pounding or stamping. ◆ *vb* **3** to pound (a substance or object) with or as if with a pestle. [C14: from Old French *pestel,* from Latin *pistillum;* related to *pinsāre* to crush]

pesto ('pɛstəu) *n* a sauce for pasta, consisting of basil leaves, nuts, garlic, oil, and Parmesan cheese, all crushed together. [Italian, shortened form of *pestato,* past participle of *pestare* to pound, crush]

pet[1] (pɛt) *n* **1** a tame animal kept in a household for companionship, amusement, etc. **2** a person who is fondly indulged; favourite: *teacher's pet.* ◆ *adj* **3** kept as a pet: *a pet dog.* **4** of or for pet animals: *pet food.* **5** particularly cherished; favourite: *a pet theory; a pet hatred.* **6** familiar or affectionate: *a pet name.* **7 pet day.** *Scot. and Irish.* a single fine day during a period of bad weather. ◆ *vb* **pets, petting, petted. 8** *(tr)* to treat (a person, animal, etc.) as a pet; pamper. **9** *(tr)* to pat or fondle (an animal, child, etc.). **10** *(intr) Informal.* (of two people) to caress each other in an erotic manner, as during lovemaking (often in the phrase **heavy petting**). [C16: origin unknown] ▸ **'petter** *n*

pet[2] (pɛt) *n* **1** a fit of sulkiness, esp. at what is felt to be a slight; pique. ◆ *vb* **pets, petting, petted. 2** *(intr)* to take offence; sulk. [C16: of uncertain origin]

PET *abbrev. for* positron emission tomography.

Pet. *Bible. abbrev. for* Peter.

peta- *prefix* denoting 10^{15}: *petametres.* Symbol: P [C20: so named because it is the SI prefix after TERA-; on the model of PENTA-, the prefix after TETRA-]

Pétain *(French* petɛ̃) *n* **Henri Philippe Omer** (ɑ̃ri filip ɔmɛr). 1856–1951, French marshal, noted for his victory at Verdun (1916) in World War I and his leadership of the pro-Nazi government of unoccupied France at Vichy (1940–44); imprisoned for treason (1945).

petal ('pɛtᵊl) *n* any of the separate parts of the corolla of a flower: often brightly coloured. [C18: from New Latin *petalum,* from Greek *petalon* leaf; related to *petannunai* to lie open] ▸ **'petaline** *adj* ▸ **'petal-ˌlike** *adj* ▸ **'petalled** *adj*

-petal *adj combining form.* seeking: *centripetal.* [from New Latin *-petus,* from Latin *petere* to seek]

petaliferous (ˌpɛtə'lɪfərəs) *or* **petalous** *adj* bearing or having petals.

petalody ('pɛtəˌləudɪ) *n* a condition in certain plants in which stamens or other parts of the flower assume the form and function of petals. [C19: from Greek *petalōdēs* like a leaf, from *petalon* leaf] ▸ **petalodic** (ˌpɛtə'lɒdɪk) *adj*

petaloid ('pɛtəˌlɔɪd) *adj Biology.* resembling a petal, esp. in shape: *the petaloid pattern on a sea urchin.*

pétanque (ˌpeɪ'tɑ̃k; *French* petɑ̃k) *n* another name, esp. in the South of France, for ***boules.*** [French, from Provençal *pèd tanco* foot fixed (to the ground)]

petard (pɪ'tɑːd) *n* **1** (formerly) a device containing explosives used to breach a wall, doors, etc. **2 hoist with one's own petard.** being the victim of one's own schemes. **3** a type of explosive firework. [C16: from French: firework, from *péter* to break wind, from Latin *pēdere*]

petasus ('pɛtəsəs) *or* **petasos** ('pɛtəsəs, -ˌsɒs) *n* a broad-brimmed hat worn by the ancient Greeks, such as one with wings on either side as traditionally worn by Mercury. [C16: via Latin from Greek *petasos*]

petaurist (pə'tɔːrɪst) *n* another name for **flying phalanger.** [C20: from Latin *petaurista* tightrope walker]

petcock ('pɛtˌkɒk) *n* a small valve for checking the water content of a steam boiler or draining waste from the cylinder of a steam engine. [C19: from PET[1] or perhaps French *pet,* from *péter* to break wind + COCK[1]]

petechia (pɪ'tiːkɪə) *n, pl* **-chiae** (-kɪˌiː). a minute discoloured spot on the surface of the skin or mucous membrane, caused by an underlying ruptured blood vessel. [C18: via New Latin from Italian *petecchia* freckle, of obscure origin] ▸ **pe'techial** *adj*

peter[1] ('piːtə) *vb (intr;* foll. by *out* or *away)* to fall (off) in volume, intensity, etc., and finally cease: *the cash petered out in three months.* [C19: of unknown origin]

peter[2] ('piːtə) *Bridge, whist. vb (intr)* **1** to play a high card before a low one in a suit, usually a conventional signal of a doubleton holding or of strength in that suit. ◆ *n* **2** the act of petering. [C20: perhaps a special use of PETER[1] (to fall off in power)]

peter[3] ('piːtə) *n Slang.* **1** a safe, till, or cash box. **2** a prison cell. **3** the witness box in a courtroom. **4** *Chiefly U.S.* a taboo slang word for **penis.** [C17 (meaning a case): from the name *Peter*]

Peter ('piːtə) *n New Testament.* **1 Saint.** Also called: **Simon Peter.** died ?67 A.D., a fisherman of Bethsaida, who became leader of the apostles and is regarded by Roman Catholics as the first pope; probably martyred at Rome. Feast day: June 29 or Jan. 18. **2** either of two epistles traditionally ascribed to Peter (in full **The First Epistle** and **The Second Epistle of Peter**).

Peter I *n* known as *Peter the Great.* 1672–1725, tsar of Russia (1682–1725), who assumed sole power in 1689. He introduced many reforms in government, technology, and the western European ideas. He also acquired new territories for Russia in the Baltic and founded the new capital of St Petersburg (1703).

Peter III *n* 1728–62, grandson of Peter I and tsar of Russia (1762): deposed in a coup d'état led by his wife (later Catherine II); assassinated.

Peterborough ('piːtəbərə, -brə) *n* **1** a city and from 1998 a unitary authority in central England, in N Cambridgeshire on the River Nene: industrial centre; under development as a new town since 1968. Pop.: 158 700 (1995 est.). Area: 402 sq. km (155 sq. miles). **2 Soke of.** a former administrative unit of E central England, generally considered part of Northamptonshire or Huntingdonshire: absorbed into Cambridgeshire in 1974. **3** a city in SE Canada, in SE Ontario: manufacturing centre. Pop.: 68 371 (1991). **4** a traditional type of wooden canoe formerly made in Peterborough, SE Ontario.

Peterlee ('piːtəˌliː) *n* a new town in Co. Durham, founded in 1948. Pop.: 23 500 (1990).

Peterloo Massacre (ˌpiːtə'luː) *n* an incident at St Peter's Fields, Manchester, in 1819 in which a radical meeting was broken up by a cavalry charge, resulting in about 500 injuries and 11 deaths. [C19: from *St Peter's Fields* + WATERLOO]

peterman ('piːtəmən) *n, pl* **-men.** *Slang.* a burglar skilled in safe-breaking. [C19: from PETER[3]]

Petermann Peak ('piːtəmən) *n* a mountain in E Greenland. Height: 2932 m (9645 ft.).

Peter Pan *n* a youthful, boyish, or immature man. [C20: after the main character in *Peter Pan* (1904), a play by J. M. BARRIE]

Peter Pan collar *n* a collar on a round neck, having two rounded ends at the front.

Peter Principle *n* **the.** the theory, usually taken facetiously, that all members in a hierarchy rise to their own level of incompetence. [C20: from the book *The Peter Principle* (1969) by Dr. Lawrence J. *Peter* and Raymond Hull, in which the theory was originally propounded]

Petersburg ('piːtəzˌbɜːg) *n* a city in SE Virginia, on the Appomattox River: scene of prolonged fighting (1864–65) during the final months of the American Civil War. Pop.: 38 386 (1990).

petersham ('piːtəʃəm) *n* **1** a thick corded ribbon used to stiffen belts, button bands, etc. **2** a heavy woollen fabric used esp. for coats. **3** a kind of overcoat made of such fabric. [C19: named after Viscount *Petersham* (died 1851), English army officer]

Peterson ('piːtəsᵊn) *n* **Oscar (Emmanuel).** born 1925, Canadian jazz pianist and singer, who led his own trio from the early 1950s.

Peter's pence *or* **Peter pence** *n* **1** an annual tax, originally of one penny, formerly levied for the maintenance of the Papal See: abolished by Henry VIII in 1534. **2** a voluntary contribution made by Roman Catholics in many countries for the same purpose. [C13: referring to St PETER, considered as the first pope]

Peters' projection *n* a form of modified Mercator's map projection that gives prominence to Third World countries. [C20: named after Arno *Peters,* German historian]

Peter the Hermit *n* ?1050–1115, French monk and preacher of the First Crusade.

pethidine ('pɛθɪˌdiːn) *n* another name for **meperidine.** [C20: perhaps a blend of PIPERIDINE + ETHYL]

pétillant *French* (petijɑ̃) *adj* (of wine) slightly effervescent. [French, from *pétiller* to effervesce]

petiolate ('pɛtɪəˌleɪt) *or* **petiolated** *adj* (of a plant or leaf) having a leafstalk. Compare **sessile** (sense 1).

petiole ('pɛtɪˌəul) *n* **1** the stalk by which a leaf is attached to the rest of the plant. **2** *Zoology.* a slender stalk or stem, such as the connection between the thorax and abdomen of ants. [C18: via French from Latin *petiolus* little foot, from *pēs* foot]

petiolule ('piːtɪəʊl,juːl) *n* the stalk of any of the leaflets making up a compound leaf. [C19: from New Latin *petiolūlus,* diminutive of Latin *petiolus;* see PETIOLE]

Petipa (*French* pətipa) *n* **Marius.** 1819–1910, French ballet dancer and choreographer of the Russian imperial ballet: collaborated with Tchaikovsky on *The Sleeping Beauty* (1890).

petit ('pɛtɪ) *adj* (*prenominal*) *Chiefly law.* of little or lesser importance; small: *petit jury.* [C14: from Old French: little, of obscure origin]

Petit (*French* pəti) *n* **Roland** (rɔlɑ̃). born 1924, French ballet dancer and choreographer. His innovative ballets include *Carmen* (1949), *Kraanerg* (1969), and *The Blue Angel* (1985); he also choreographed films, such as *Anything Goes* (1956) and *Black Tights* (1960).

petit bourgeois ('pɛtɪ 'bʊəʒwɑː; *French* pəti burʒwa) *n, pl* **petits bourgeois** ('pɛtɪ 'bʊəʒwɑːz; *French* pəti burʒwa). **1** Also called: **petite bourgeoisie, petty bourgeoisie.** the section of the middle class with the lowest social status, generally composed of shopkeepers, lower clerical staff, etc. **2** a member of this stratum. ◆ *adj* **3** of, relating to, or characteristic of the petit bourgeois, esp. indicating a sense of self-righteousness and a high degree of conformity to established standards of behaviour.

petite (pəˈtiːt) *adj* (of a woman) small, delicate, and dainty. [C18: from French, feminine of *petit* small]

petit four ('pɛtɪ 'fɔː; *French* pəti fur) *n, pl* **petits fours** ('pɛtɪ 'fɔːz; *French* pəti fur). any of various very small rich sweet cakes and biscuits, usually decorated with fancy icing, marzipan, etc. [French, literally: little oven]

petition (pɪˈtɪʃən) *n* **1** a written document signed by a large number of people demanding some form of action from a government or other authority. **2** any formal request to a higher authority or deity; entreaty. **3** *Law.* a formal application in writing made to a court asking for some specific judicial action: *a petition for divorce.* **4** the action of petitioning. ◆ *vb* **5** (*tr*) to address or present a petition to (a person in authority, government, etc.): *to petition Parliament.* **6** (*intr;* foll. by *for*) to seek by petition: *to petition for a change in the law.* [C14: from Latin *petītiō,* from *petere* to seek] ▸ **peˈtitionary** *adj*

petitioner (pɪˈtɪʃənə) *n* **1** a person who presents a petition. **2** *Chiefly Brit.* the plaintiff in a divorce suit.

petitio principii (pɪˈtɪʃɪ,əʊ prɪnˈkɪpɪ,aɪ) *n Logic.* a form of fallacious reasoning in which the conclusion has been assumed in the premises; begging the question. Sometimes shortened to **petitio.** [C16: Latin, translation of Greek *to en arkhei aiteisthai* an assumption at the beginning]

petit jury *n* a jury of 12 persons empanelled to determine the facts of a case and decide the issue pursuant to the direction of the court on points of law. Also called: **petty jury.** Compare **grand jury.** ▸ **petit juror** *n*

petit larceny *n* **1** (formerly in England) the stealing of property valued at 12 pence or under. Abolished 1827. **2** (in some states of the U.S.) the theft of property having a value below a certain figure. ◆ Also called: **petty larceny.** Compare **grand larceny.** ▸ **petit larcenist** *n*

petit mal ('pɛtɪ 'mæl; *French* pəti mal) *n* a mild form of epilepsy characterized by periods of impairment or loss of consciousness for up to 30 seconds. Compare **grand mal.** [C19: French: little illness]

petit point ('pɛtɪ 'pɔɪnt; *French* pəti pwɛ̃) *n* **1** Also called: **tent stitch.** a small diagonal needlepoint stitch used for fine detail. **2** work done with such stitches, esp. fine tapestry. ◆ Compare **gros point.** [French: small point]

petits pois (*French* pəti pwa) *pl n* small sweet fresh green peas. [French: small peas]

Petöfi (*Hungarian* ˈpɛtøːfi) *n* **Sándor** (ˈʃaːndor). 1823–49, Hungarian lyric poet and patriot.

Petra ('pɛtrə, 'piːtrə) *n* an ancient city in the south of present-day Jordan; capital of the Nabataean kingdom.

Petrarch ('pɛtrɑːk) *n* Italian name *Francesco Petrarca.* 1304–74, Italian lyric poet and scholar, who greatly influenced the values of the Renaissance. His collection of poems *Canzoniere,* inspired by his ideal love for Laura, was written in the Tuscan dialect. He also wrote much in Latin, esp. the epic poem *Africa* (1341) and the *Secretum* (1342), a spiritual self-analysis. ▸ **Peˈtrarchan** *adj*

Petrarchan sonnet *n* a sonnet form associated with the poet Petrarch, having an octave rhyming a b b a a b b a and a sestet rhyming either c d e c d e or c d c d c d. Also called: **Italian sonnet.**

petrel ('pɛtrəl) *n* any oceanic bird of the order *Procellariiformes,* having a hooked bill and tubular nostrils: includes albatrosses, storm petrels, and shearwaters. See also **storm petrel.** [C17: variant of earlier *pitteral,* associated by folk etymology with St *Peter,* because the bird appears to walk on water]

Petri dish ('pɛtrɪ) *n* a shallow circular flat-bottomed dish, often with a fitting cover, used in laboratories, esp. for producing cultures of microorganisms. [C19: named after J. R. *Petri* (1852–1921), German bacteriologist]

Petrie ('piːtrɪ) *n* Sir (**William Matthew**) **Flinders.** 1853–1942, British Egyptologist and archaeologist.

petrifaction (,pɛtrɪˈfækʃən) *or* **petrification** (,pɛtrɪfɪˈkeɪʃən) *n* **1** the act or process of forming petrified organic material. **2** the state of being petrified.

Petrified Forest *n* a national park in E Arizona, containing petrified coniferous trees about 170 000 000 years old.

petrify ('pɛtrɪ,faɪ) *vb* **-fies, -fying, -fied. 1** (*tr; often passive*) to convert (organic material, esp. plant material) into a fossilized form by impregnation with dissolved minerals so that the original appearance is preserved. **2** to make or become dull, unresponsive, insensitive, etc.; deaden. **3** (*tr; often passive*) to stun or daze with horror, fear, etc. [C16: from French *pétrifier,* ultimately from Greek *petra* stone, rock] ▸ **ˈpetri,fier** *n*

Petrine ('piːtraɪn) *adj* **1** *New Testament.* of or relating to St Peter, his position of leadership, or the epistles, etc., attributed to him. **2** *R.C. Church.* of or relating to the supremacy in the Church that the pope is regarded as having inherited from St Peter: *the Petrine claims.*

petro- *or before a vowel* **petr-** *combining form.* **1** indicating stone or rock: *petrology.* **2** indicating petroleum, its products, etc.: *petrochemical.* **3** of or relating to a petroleum-producing country: *petrostate.* [from Greek *petra* rock or *petros* stone]

petrochemical (,pɛtrəʊˈkɛmɪkᵊl) *n* **1** any substance, such as acetone or ethanol, obtained from petroleum or natural gas. ◆ *adj* **2** of, concerned with, or obtained from petrochemicals or related to petrochemistry. ▸ **,petroˈchemically** *adv*

petrochemistry (,pɛtrəʊˈkɛmɪstrɪ) *n* **1** the chemistry of petroleum and its derivatives. **2** the branch of chemistry concerned with the chemical composition of rocks.

petrodollar ('pɛtrəʊ,dɒlə) *n* money, paid in dollars, earned by a country for the exporting of petroleum.

petrog. *abbrev. for* petrography.

petroglyph ('pɛtrə,glɪf) *n* a drawing or carving on rock, esp. a prehistoric one. [C19: via French from Greek *petra* stone + *gluphē* carving]

Petrograd ('pɛtrəʊ,græd; *Russian* pɪtraˈgrat) *n* a former name (1914–24) of **Saint Petersburg.**

petrography (pɛˈtrɒgrəfɪ) *n* the branch of petrology concerned with the description and classification of rocks. Abbrev.: **petrog.** ▸ **peˈtrographer** *n* ▸ **petrographic** (,pɛtrəˈgræfɪk) *or* **,petroˈgraphical** *adj* ▸ **,petroˈgraphically** *adv*

petrol ('pɛtrəl) *n* any one of various volatile flammable liquid mixtures of hydrocarbons, mainly hexane, heptane, and octane, obtained from petroleum and used as a solvent and a fuel for internal-combustion engines. Usually petrol also contains additives such as antiknock compounds and corrosion inhibitors. U.S. and Canadian name: **gasoline.** [C16: via French from Medieval Latin PETROLEUM]

petrol. *abbrev. for* petrology.

petrolatum (,pɛtrəˈleɪtəm) *n* a translucent gelatinous substance obtained from petroleum; used as a lubricant and in medicine as an ointment base and protective dressing. Also called: **mineral jelly, petroleum jelly.** [C19: from PETROL + Latin *-atum* -ATE[1]]

petrol bomb *n* **1** a home-made incendiary device, consisting of a bottle filled with petrol and stoppered with a wick, that is thrown by hand; Molotov cocktail. ◆ *vb* **petrol-bomb.** (*tr*) **2** to attack with petrol bombs. ▸ **petrol bomber** *n*

petrol engine *n* an internal-combustion engine that uses petrol as fuel.

petroleum (pəˈtrəʊlɪəm) *n* a dark-coloured thick flammable crude oil occurring in sedimentary rocks around the Persian Gulf, in parts of North and South America, and below the North Sea, consisting mainly of hydrocarbons. Fractional distillation separates the crude oil into petrol, paraffin, diesel oil, lubricating oil, etc. Fuel oil, paraffin wax, asphalt, and carbon black are extracted from the residue. [C16: from Medieval Latin, from Latin *petra* stone + *oleum* oil]

petroleum ether *n* a volatile mixture of the higher alkane hydrocarbons, obtained as a fraction of petroleum and used as a solvent.

petroleum jelly *n* another name for **petrolatum.**

petrolic (pɛˈtrɒlɪk) *adj* of, relating to, containing, or obtained from petroleum.

petrology (pɛˈtrɒlədʒɪ) *n, pl* **-gies.** the study of the composition, origin, structure, and formation of rocks. Abbrev.: **petrol.** ▸ **petrological** (,pɛtrəˈlɒdʒɪkᵊl) *adj* ▸ **,petroˈlogically** *adv* ▸ **peˈtrologist** *n*

petrol pump *n* a device at a filling station that is used to deliver petrol to the tank of a car and which displays the quantity, quality, and usually the cost of the petrol delivered.

petrol station *n Brit.* another term for **filling station.**

petronel ('pɛtrə,nɛl) *n* a firearm of large calibre used in the 16th and early 17th centuries, esp. by cavalry soldiers. [C16: from French, literally: of the breast, from *poitrine* breast, from Latin *pectus*]

Petronius (pɪˈtrəʊnɪəs) *n* **Gaius** ('gaɪəs), known as *Petronius Arbiter.* died 66 A.D., Roman satirist, supposed author of the *Satyricon,* a picaresque account of the licentiousness of contemporary society.

Petropavlovsk (*Russian* pɪtraˈpavləfsk) *n* a city in N Kazakhstan on the Ishim River. Pop.: 239 000 (1995 est.).

Petrópolis (*Portuguese* peˈtrɔpulis) *n* a city in SE Brazil, north of Rio de Janeiro: resort. Pop.: 164 849 (1991).

petrosal (pɛˈtrəʊsᵊl) *adj Anatomy.* of, relating to, or situated near the dense part of the temporal bone that surrounds the inner ear. [C18: from Latin *petrōsus* full of rocks, from *petra* a rock, from Greek]

Petrosian (pɪˈtrəʊʒən) *n* **Tigran** (tigˈran). 1929–84, Soviet chess player; world champion (1963–69).

petrous ('pɛtrəs, 'piː-) *adj* **1** *Anatomy.* denoting the dense part of the temporal bone that surrounds the inner ear. **2** *Rare.* like rock or stone. [C16: from Latin *petrōsus* full of rocks]

Petrovsk (*Russian* pɪˈtrɔfsk) *n* the former name (until 1921) of **Makhachkala.**

Petrozavodsk (*Russian* pɪtrəzaˈvɔtsk) *n* a city in NW Russia, capital of the Karelian Autonomous Republic, on Lake Onega: developed around ironworks established by Peter the Great in 1703; university (1940). Pop.: 280 000 (1995 est.).

pe-tsai cabbage ('peɪˈtsaɪ) *n* another name for **Chinese cabbage** (sense 1). [from Chinese (Beijing) *pe ts'ai,* literally: white vegetable]

Petsamo (*Finnish* ˈpɛtsɑmɔ) *n* a former territory of N Finland ceded by the Soviet Union to Finland in 1920 and taken back in 1940; now in NW Russia.

petticoat ('pɛtɪ,kəʊt) *n* **1** a woman's light undergarment in the form of an underskirt or including a bodice supported by shoulder straps. **2** *Informal.* **2a** a humorous or mildly disparaging name for a woman. **2b** (*as modifier*): *petticoat politics.* [C15: see PETTY, COAT]

pettifog ('pɛtɪˌfɒg) *vb* **-fogs, -fogging, -fogged.** (*intr*) to be a pettifogger.

pettifogger ('pɛtɪˌfɒgə) *n* **1** a lawyer of inferior status who conducts unimportant cases, esp. one who is unscrupulous or resorts to trickery. **2** any person who quibbles or fusses over details. [C16: from PETTY + *fogger,* of uncertain origin, perhaps from *Fugger,* name of a family (C15–16) of German financiers] ▸ **'pettiˌfoggery** *n*

pettifogging ('pɛtɪˌfɒgɪŋ) *adj* **1** petty: *pettifogging details.* **2** mean; quibbling: *pettifogging lawyers.*

pettish ('pɛtɪʃ) *adj* peevish; petulant: *a pettish child.* [C16: from PET[2]] ▸ **'pettishly** *adv* ▸ **'pettishness** *n*

pettitoes ('pɛtɪˌtəʊz) *pl n* pig's trotters, esp. when used as food. [C16: from Old French *petite oie,* literally: little goose (giblets of a goose)]

petty ('pɛtɪ) *adj* **-tier, -tiest. 1** trivial; trifling; inessential: *petty details.* **2** of a narrow-minded, mean, or small-natured disposition or character: *petty spite.* **3** minor or subordinate in rank: *petty officialdom.* **4** *Law.* of lesser importance. [C14: from Old French PETIT] ▸ **'pettily** *adv* ▸ **'pettiness** *n*

petty cash *n* a small cash fund kept on a firm's premises for the payment of minor incidental expenses.

petty jury *n* a variant spelling of **petit jury.** ▸ **petty juror** *n*

petty larceny *n* a variant spelling of **petit larceny.**

petty officer *n* a noncommissioned officer in a naval service, comparable in rank to a sergeant in an army or marine corps.

petty sessions *n* (*functioning as sing or pl*) another term for **magistrates' court.**

petulant ('pɛtjʊlənt) *adj* irritable, impatient, or sullen in a peevish or capricious way. [C16: via Old French from Latin *petulāns* bold, from *petulāre* (unattested) to attack playfully, from *petere* to assail] ▸ **'petulance** *or* **'petulancy** *n* ▸ **'petulantly** *adv*

petunia (pɪ'tjuːnɪə) *n* any solanaceous plant of the tropical American genus *Petunia:* cultivated for their white, pink, blue, or purple funnel-shaped flowers. [C19: via New Latin from obsolete French *petun* variety of tobacco, from Tupi *petyn*]

petuntse *or* **petuntze** (pɪ'tʌntsɪ, -'tʊn-) *n* a fusible feldspathic mineral used in hard-paste porcelain; china stone. [C18: from Chinese (Beijing) *pe tun tzu,* from *pe* white + *tun* heap + *tzu* offspring]

Petworth House ('pɛtwɜːθ) *n* a mansion in Petworth in Sussex: rebuilt (1688–96) for Charles Seymour, 6th Duke of Somerset; gardens laid out by Capability Brown; subject of paintings by Turner.

Pevsner ('pɛvznə) *n* **1 Antoine** (ɑ̃twan). 1886–1962, French constructivist sculptor and painter, born in Russia; brother of Naum Gabo. **2** Sir **Nikolaus** ('nɪkəlaus). 1902–83, British architectural historian, born in Germany: his series *Buildings of England* (1951–74) describes every structure of account in the country.

pew (pjuː) *n* **1** (in a church) **1a** one of several long benchlike seats with backs, used by the congregation. **1b** an enclosed compartment reserved for the use of a family or other small group. **2** *Brit. informal.* a seat (esp. in the phrase **take a pew**). [C14 *pywe,* from Old French *puye,* from Latin *podium* a balcony, from Greek *podion* supporting structure, from *pous* foot]

pewee *or* **peewee** ('piːwiː) *n* any of several small North American flycatchers of the genus *Contopus,* having a greenish-brown plumage. [C19: imitative of its cry]

pewit ('piːwɪt) *n* another name for **lapwing.** [C13: imitative of the bird's cry]

pewter ('pjuːtə) *n* **1a** any of various alloys containing tin (80–90 per cent), lead (10–20 per cent), and sometimes small amounts of other metals, such as copper and antimony. **1b** (*as modifier*): *pewter ware; a pewter tankard.* **2a** a bluish-grey colour. **2b** (*as adj*): *pewter tights.* **3** plate or kitchen utensils made from pewter. [C14: from Old French *peaultre,* of obscure origin; related to Old Provençal *peltre* pewter] ▸ **'pewterer** *n*

peyote (peɪ'əʊtɪ, pɪ-) *n* another name for **mescal** (sense 1). [Mexican Spanish, from Nahuatl *peyotl*]

pF *symbol for* picofarad.

pf. *abbrev for:* **1** perfect. **2** Also: **pfg.** pfennig. **3** preferred.

Pfalz (pfalts) *n* the German name for the **Palatinate.**

pfennig ('fɛnɪg; *German* 'pfɛnɪç) *n, pl* **-nigs** *or* **-nige** (*German* -nɪgə). **1** a German monetary unit worth one hundredth of a Deutschmark. **2** (formerly) a monetary unit worth one hundredth of an East German ostmark. [German: PENNY]

PFI (in Britain) *abbrev. for* Private Finance Initiative.

Pforzheim (*German* 'pfɔrtshaim) *n* a city in SW Germany, in W Baden-Württemberg: centre of the German watch and jewellery industry. Pop.: 118 763 (1996 est.).

PFP *abbrev. for* partnerships for peace: a NATO initiative forging links with the former communist countries of eastern Europe.

PG[1] *symbol for* a film certified for viewing by anyone, but which contains scenes that may be unsuitable for children, for whom parental guidance is necessary. [C20: from abbreviation of *parental guidance*]

PG[2] *abbrev. for:* **1** paying guest. **2** postgraduate.

pg. *abbrev. for* page.

Pg. *abbrev. for:* **1** Portugal. **2** Portuguese.

PGA *abbrev. for* Professional Golfers' Association.

PGR *abbrev. for* psychogalvanic response.

pH *n* potential of hydrogen; a measure of the acidity or alkalinity of a solution equal to the common logarithm of the reciprocal of the concentration of hydrogen ions in moles per cubic decimetre of solution. Pure water has a pH of 7, acid solutions have a pH less than 7, and alkaline solutions a pH greater than 7.

Ph *chemical symbol for* phenyl group or radical.

ph. *abbrev. for* phase.

phacelia (fə'siːlɪə) *n* any plant of the mostly annual American genus *Phacelia,* esp. *P. campanularia,* grown for its large, deep blue bell flowers: family *Hydrophyllaceae.* [New Latin, from Greek *phakelos* cluster (from the habit of the flowers) + -IA]

Phaeacian (fiː'eɪʃən) *n Greek myth.* one of a race of people inhabiting the island of Scheria visited by Odysseus on his way home from the Trojan War.

Phaedra ('fiːdrə) *n Greek myth.* the wife of Theseus, who falsely accused her stepson Hippolytus of raping her because he spurned her amorous advances.

Phaedrus ('fiːdrəs) *n* ?15 B.C.–?50 A.D., Roman author of five books of Latin verse fables, based chiefly on Aesop.

phaeic ('fiːɪk) *adj* (of animals) having dusky coloration; less dark than melanic. [C19: from Greek *phaiós* dusky] ▸ **'phaeism** *n*

Phaethon ('feɪəθən) *n* a small asteroid that has an orbit approaching close to the sun and releases fragments of dust that enter the earth's atmosphere as meteors.

Phaëthon ('feɪəθən) *n Greek myth.* the son of Helios (the sun god) who borrowed his father's chariot and nearly set the earth on fire by approaching too close to it. Zeus averted the catastrophe by striking him down with a thunderbolt.

phaeton ('feɪtᵊn) *n* a light four-wheeled horse-drawn carriage with or without a top, usually having two seats. [C18: from PHAËTHON]

phage (feɪdʒ) *n* short for **bacteriophage.**

-phage *n combining form.* indicating something that eats or consumes something specified: *bacteriophage.* [from Greek *-phagos;* see PHAGO-] ▸ **-phagous** *adj combining form.*

phagedaena *or* **phagedena** (ˌfædʒɪ'diːnə) *n Pathol.* a rapidly spreading ulcer that destroys tissues as it increases in size. [C17: via Latin from Greek, from *phagein* to eat]

phago- *or before a vowel* **phag-** *combining form.* eating, consuming, or destroying: *phagocyte.* [from Greek *phagein* to consume]

phagocyte ('fægəˌsaɪt) *n* an amoeboid cell or protozoan that engulfs particles, such as food substances or invading microorganisms. ▸ **phagocytic** (ˌfægə'sɪtɪk) *adj*

phagocytosis (ˌfægəsaɪ'təʊsɪs) *n* the process by which a cell, such as a white blood cell, ingests microorganisms, other cells, and foreign particles.

phagomania (ˌfægəʊ'meɪnɪə) *n* a compulsive desire to eat. ▸ **ˌphago'maniˌac** *n*

-phagy *or* **-phagia** *n combining form.* indicating an eating or devouring: *anthropophagy.* [from Greek *-phagia;* see PHAGO-]

phalange ('fælændʒ) *n, pl* **phalanges** (fæ'lændʒiːz). *Anatomy.* another name for **phalanx** (sense 5). [C16: via French, ultimately from Greek PHALANX]

phalangeal (fə'lændʒɪəl) *adj Anatomy.* of or relating to a phalanx or phalanges.

phalanger (fə'lændʒə) *n* any of various Australasian arboreal marsupials, such as *Trichosurus vulpecula* (**brush-tailed phalanger**), having dense fur and a long tail: family *Phalangeridae.* Also called (Australian and N.Z.): **possum.** See also **flying phalanger.** [C18: via New Latin from Greek *phalaggion* spider's web, referring to its webbed hind toes]

Phalangist (fə'lændʒɪst) *n* **a** a member of a Lebanese Christian paramilitary organization founded in 1936 and originally based on similar ideas to the fascist Falange in Spain. **b** (*as modifier*): *Phalangist leaders.*

phalanstery ('fælənstərɪ, -strɪ) *n, pl* **-steries. 1** (in Fourierism) **1a** buildings occupied by a phalanx. **1b** a community represented by a phalanx. **2** any similar association or the buildings occupied by such an association. [C19: from French *phalanstère,* from *phalange* PHALANX, on the model of *monastère* MONASTERY]

phalanx ('fælæŋks) *n, pl* **phalanxes** *or* **phalanges** (fæ'lændʒiːz). **1** an ancient Greek and Macedonian battle formation of hoplites presenting long spears from behind a wall of overlapping shields. **2** any closely ranked unit or mass of people: *the police formed a phalanx to protect the embassy.* **3** a number of people united for a common purpose. **4** (in Fourierism) a group of approximately 1800 persons forming a commune in which all property is collectively owned. **5** *Anatomy.* any of the bones of the fingers or toes. Related adj: **phalangeal. 6** *Botany.* a bundle of stamens, joined together by their stalks (filaments). [C16: via Latin from Greek: infantry formation in close ranks, bone of finger or toe]

phalarope ('fæləˌrəʊp) *n* any aquatic shore bird of the family *Phalaropidae,* such as *Phalaropus fulicarius* (**grey phalarope**), of northern oceans and lakes, having a long slender bill and lobed toes: order *Charadriiformes.* [C18: via French from New Latin *Phalaropus,* from Greek *phalaris* coot + *pous* foot]

phallic ('fælɪk) *adj* **1** of, relating to, or resembling a phallus: *a phallic symbol.* **2** *Psychoanal.* **2a** relating to a stage of psychosexual development during which a male child's interest is concentrated on the genital organs. **2b** designating personality traits, such as conceit and self-assurance, due to fixation at the phallic stage of development. Compare **anal** (sense 2), **oral** (sense 7), **genital** (sense 2). **2c** (in Freudian theory) denoting a phase of early childhood in which there is a belief that both sexes possess a phallus. **3** of or relating to phallicism.

phallicism ('fælɪˌsɪzəm) *or* **phallism** *n* the worship or veneration of the phallus. ▸ **'phallicist** *or* **'phallist** *n*

phallocentric (ˌfæləʊ'sɛntrɪk) *adj* dominated by male attitudes. [C20: from PHALLUS + -CENTRIC] ▸ **ˌphallocen'tricity** *or* **ˌphallo'centrism** *n*

phalloidin (fə'lɔɪdɪn) *n* a peptide toxin, responsible for the toxicity of the death cap mushroom, *Amanita phalloides.* [C20: New Latin, from PHALLUS + -OID + -IN]

phallus ('fæləs) *n, pl* **-luses** *or* **-li** (-laɪ). **1** another word for **penis. 2** an image of the penis, esp. as a religious symbol of reproductive power. [C17: via Late Latin from Greek *phallos*]

-phane *n combining form.* indicating something resembling a specified substance: *cellophane.* [from Greek *phainein* to shine, (in passive) appear]

phanerocrystalline (ˌfænərəʊˈkrɪstəlɪn, -ˌlaɪn) *adj* (of igneous and metamorphic rocks) having a crystalline structure in which the crystals are large enough to be seen with the naked eye. [C19: from Greek *phaneros* visible + CRYSTALLINE]

phanerogam (ˈfænərəʊˌgæm) *n* any plant of the former major division *Phanerogamae,* which included all seed-bearing plants; a former name for **spermatophyte.** Compare **cryptogam.** [C19: from New Latin *phanerogamus,* from Greek *phaneros* visible + *gamos* marriage] ▸ ˌ**phaneroˈgamic** *or* **phanerogamous** (ˌfænəˈrɒgəməs) *adj*

phanerophyte (ˈfænərəˌfaɪt, fəˈnɛrə-) *n* a tree or shrub that bears its perennating buds more than 25 cm above the level of the soil. [C20: from Greek *phanero-* visible + -PHYTE]

Phanerozoic (ˌfænərəˈzəʊɪk) *adj* **1** of or relating to that part of geological time represented by rocks in which the evidence of life is abundant, comprising the Palaeozoic, Mesozoic, and Cenozoic eras. ◆ *n* **2 the.** the Phanerozoic era. ◆ Compare **Cryptozoic.**

phantasm (ˈfæntæzəm) *n* **1** a phantom. **2** an illusory perception of an object, person, etc. **3** (in the philosophy of Plato) objective reality as distorted by perception. [C13: from Old French *fantasme,* from Latin *phantasma,* from Greek; related to Greek *phantazein* to cause to be seen, from *phainein* to show] ▸ **phanˈtasmal** *or* **phanˈtasmic** *adj* ▸ **phanˈtasmally** *or* **phanˈtasmically** *adv*

phantasmagoria (ˌfæntæzməˈgɔːrɪə) *or* **phantasmagory** (fænˈtæzməgərɪ) *n* **1** *Psychol.* a shifting medley of real or imagined figures, as in a dream. **2** *Films.* a sequence of pictures made to vary in size rapidly while remaining in focus. **3** *Rare.* a shifting scene composed of different elements. [C19: probably from French *fantasmagorie* production of phantasms, from PHANTASM + *-agorie,* perhaps from Greek *ageirein* to gather together] ▸ **phantasmagoric** (ˌfæntæzməˈgɒrɪk) *or* ˌ**phantasmaˈgorical** *adj* ▸ ˌ**phantasmaˈgorically** *adv*

phantasy (ˈfæntəsɪ) *n, pl* **-sies.** an archaic spelling of **fantasy.**

phantom (ˈfæntəm) *n* **1a** an apparition or spectre. **1b** (*as modifier*): *a phantom army marching through the sky.* **2** the visible representation of something abstract, esp. as appearing in a dream or hallucination: *phantoms of evil haunted his sleep.* **3** something apparently unpleasant or horrific that has no material form. **4** *Med.* another name for **manikin** (sense 2b). [C13: from Old French *fantosme,* from Latin *phantasma,* PHANTASM]

phantom limb *n* the illusion that a limb still exists following its amputation, sometimes with pain (**phantom limb pain**).

phantom pregnancy *n* the occurrence of signs of pregnancy, such as enlarged abdomen and absence of menstruation, when no embryo is present, due to hormonal imbalance. Also called: **false pregnancy.** Technical name: **pseudocyesis.**

phantom withdrawal *n* the unauthorized removal of funds from a bank account using an automated teller machine.

-phany *n combining form.* indicating a manifestation: *theophany.* [from Greek *-phania,* from *phainein* to show; see -PHANE] ▸ **-phanous** *adj combining form.*

phar., Phar., pharm., *or* **Pharm.** *abbrev. for:* **1** pharmaceutical. **2** pharmacist. **3** pharmacopoeia. **4** pharmacy.

Pharaoh (ˈfɛərəʊ) *n* the title of the ancient Egyptian kings. [Old English *Pharaon,* via Latin, Greek, and Hebrew ultimately from Egyptian *pr-ʻo* great house] ▸ **Pharaonic** (fɛəˈrɒnɪk) *adj*

Pharaoh ant *or* **Pharaoh's ant** *n* a small yellowish-red ant, *Monomorium pharaonis,* of warm regions: accidentally introduced into many countries, infesting heated buildings.

Pharisaic (ˌfærɪˈseɪɪk) *or* **Pharisaical** *adj* **1** *Judaism.* of, relating to, or characteristic of the Pharisees or Pharisaism. **2** (*often not cap.*) righteously hypocritical. ▸ ˌ**Phariˈsaically** *adv* ▸ ˌ**Phariˈsaicalness** *n*

Pharisaism (ˈfærɪseɪˌɪzəm) *or* **Phariseeism** (ˈfærɪsiːˌɪzəm) *n* **1** *Judaism.* the tenets and customs of the Pharisees. **2** (*often not cap.*) observance of the external forms of religion without genuine belief; hypocrisy.

Pharisee (ˈfærɪˌsiː) *n* **1** *Judaism.* a member of an ancient Jewish sect that was opposed to the Sadducees, teaching strict observance of Jewish tradition as interpreted rabbinically and believing in life after death and in the coming of the Messiah. **2** (*often not cap.*) a self-righteous or hypocritical person. [Old English *Farisēus,* ultimately from Aramaic *perīshāiyā,* pl. of *perīsh* separated]

pharmaceutical (ˌfɑːməˈsjuːtɪkᵊl) *or* (*less commonly*) **pharmaceutic** *adj* of or relating to drugs or pharmacy. [C17: from Late Latin *pharmaceuticus,* from Greek *pharmakeus* purveyor of drugs; see PHARMACY] ▸ ˌ**pharmaˈceutically** *adv*

pharmaceutics (ˌfɑːməˈsjuːtɪks) *n* **1** (*functioning as sing*) another term for **pharmacy** (sense 1). **2** pharmaceutical remedies.

pharmacist (ˈfɑːməsɪst) *or* (*less commonly*) **pharmaceutist** (ˌfɑːməˈsjuːtɪst) *n* a person qualified to prepare and dispense drugs.

pharmaco- *combining form.* indicating drugs: *pharmacology; pharmacopoeia.* [from Greek *pharmakon* drug, potion]

pharmacodynamics (ˌfɑːməkəʊdaɪˈnæmɪks) *n* (*functioning as sing*) the branch of pharmacology concerned with the action of drugs on the physiology of the body. ▸ ˌ**pharmacodyˈnamic** *adj*

pharmacognosy (ˌfɑːməˈkɒgnəsɪ) *n* the branch of pharmacology concerned with crude drugs of plant and animal origin. [C19: from PHARMACO- + *gnosy,* from Greek *gnosis* knowledge] ▸ ˌ**pharmaˈcognosist** *n* ▸ **pharmacognostic** (ˌfɑːməkɒgˈnɒstɪk) *adj*

pharmacokinetics (ˌfɑːməkəʊkɪˈnɛtɪks, -kaɪ-) *n* the branch of pharmacology concerned with the way drugs are taken into, move through, and are eliminated from, the body. ▸ ˌ**pharmacokiˈnetic** *adj* ▸ ˌ**pharmacokiˈnetically** *adv* ▸ **pharmacokineticist** (ˌfɑːməkəʊkɪˈnɛtɪsɪst) *n*

pharmacol. *abbrev. for* pharmacology.

pharmacology (ˌfɑːməˈkɒlədʒɪ) *n* the science of drugs, including their characteristics and uses. ▸ **pharmacological** (ˌfɑːməkəˈlɒdʒɪkᵊl) *adj* ▸ ˌ**pharmacoˈlogically** *adv* ▸ ˌ**pharmaˈcologist** *n*

pharmacopoeia *or U.S.* (*sometimes*) **pharmacopeia** (ˌfɑːməkəˈpiːə) *n* an authoritative book containing a list of medicinal drugs with their uses, preparation, dosages, formulas, etc. [C17: via New Latin from Greek *pharmakopoiia* art of preparing drugs, from PHARMACO- + *-poiia,* from *poiein* to make] ▸ ˌ**pharmacoˈpoeial** *or* ˌ**pharmacoˈpoeic** *adj* ▸ ˌ**pharmacoˈpoeist** *n*

pharmacy (ˈfɑːməsɪ) *n, pl* **-cies. 1** Also called: **pharmaceutics.** the practice or art of preparing and dispensing drugs. **2** a dispensary. [C14: from Medieval Latin *pharmacia,* from Greek *pharmakeia* making of drugs, from *pharmakon* drug]

Pharos (ˈfɛərɒs) *n* a large Hellenistic lighthouse built on an island off Alexandria in Egypt in about 280 B.C. and destroyed by an earthquake in the 14th century: usually included among the Seven Wonders of the World.

Pharsalus (fɑːˈseɪləs) *n* an ancient town in Thessaly in N Greece. Several major battles were fought nearby, including Caesar's victory over Pompey (48 B.C.).

pharyngeal (ˌfærɪnˈdʒiːəl) *or* **pharyngal** (fəˈrɪŋgᵊl) *adj* **1** of, relating to, or situated in or near the pharynx. **2** *Phonetics.* pronounced or supplemented in pronunciation with an articulation in or constriction of the pharynx. ◆ *n* **3** *Phonetics.* a pharyngeal speech sound. [C19: from New Latin *pharyngeus;* see PHARYNX]

pharyngeal tonsil *n* the technical name for **adenoids.**

pharyngitis (ˌfærɪnˈdʒaɪtɪs) *n* inflammation of the pharynx.

pharyngo- *or before a vowel* **pharyng-** *combining form.* pharynx: *pharyngoscope.*

pharyngology (ˌfærɪŋˈgɒlədʒɪ) *n* the branch of medical science concerned with the pharynx and its diseases. ▸ **pharyngological** (ˌfærɪŋgəˈlɒdʒɪkᵊl) *adj* ▸ ˌ**pharynˈgologist** *n*

pharyngoscope (fəˈrɪŋgəˌskəʊp) *n* a medical instrument for examining the pharynx. ▸ **pharyngoscopic** (fəˌrɪŋgəˈskɒpɪk) *adj* ▸ **pharyngoscopy** (ˌfærɪŋˈgɒskəpɪ) *n*

pharyngotomy (ˌfærɪŋˈgɒtəmɪ) *n, pl* **-mies.** surgical incision into the pharynx.

pharynx (ˈfærɪŋks) *n, pl* **pharynges** (fæˈrɪndʒiːz) *or* **pharynxes.** the part of the alimentary canal between the mouth and the oesophagus. Compare **nasopharynx.** Related adj: **pharyngeal.** [C17: via New Latin from Greek *pharunx* throat; related to Greek *pharanx* chasm]

phase (feɪz) *n* **1** any distinct or characteristic period or stage in a sequence of events or chain of development: *there were two phases to the resolution; his immaturity was a passing phase.* **2** *Astronomy.* one of the recurring shapes of the portion of the moon or an inferior planet illuminated by the sun: *the new moon, first quarter, full moon, and last quarter are the four principal phases of the moon.* **3** *Physics.* **3a** the fraction of a cycle of a periodic quantity that has been completed at a specific reference time, expressed as an angle. **3b** (*as modifier*): *a phase shift.* **4** *Physics.* a particular stage in a periodic process or phenomenon. **5 in phase.** (of two waveforms) reaching corresponding phases at the same time. **6 out of phase.** (of two waveforms) not in phase. **7** *Chem.* a distinct state of matter characterized by homogeneous composition and properties and the possession of a clearly defined boundary. **8** *Zoology.* a variation in the normal form of an animal, esp. a colour variation, brought about by seasonal or geographical change. **9** *Biology.* (*usually in combination*) a stage in mitosis or meiosis: *prophase; metaphase.* **10** *Electrical engineering.* one of the circuits in a system in which there are two or more alternating voltages displaced by equal amounts in phase (sense 5). See also **polyphase** (sense 1). **11** (in systemic grammar) the type of correspondence that exists between the predicators in a clause that has two or more predicators; for example connection by *to,* as in *I managed to do it,* or *-ing,* as in *we heard him singing.* ◆ *vb* (*tr*) **12** (*often passive*) to execute, arrange, or introduce gradually or in stages: *a phased withdrawal.* **13** (sometimes foll. by *with*) to cause (a part, process, etc.) to function or coincide with (another part, process, etc.): *he tried to phase the intake and output of the machine; he phased the intake with the output.* **14** *Chiefly U.S.* to arrange (processes, goods, etc.) to be supplied or executed when required. [C19: from New Latin *phases,* pl. of *phasis,* from Greek: aspect; related to Greek *phainein* to show] ▸ ˈ**phaseless** *adj* ▸ ˈ**phasic** *or* ˈ**phaseal** *adj*

phase-contrast microscope *n* a microscope that makes visible details of colourless transparent objects. It employs a method of illumination such that small differences of refractive index of the materials in the object cause differences of luminous intensity by interference.

phase in *vb* (*tr, adv*) to introduce in a gradual or cautious manner: *the legislation was phased in over two years.*

phase modulation *n* a type of modulation, used in communication systems, in which the phase of a radio carrier wave is varied by an amount proportional to the instantaneous amplitude of the modulating signal.

phase out *vb* **1** (*tr, adv*) to discontinue or withdraw gradually. ◆ *n* **phase-out. 2** the action or an instance of phasing out: *a phase-out of conventional forces.*

phase rule *n* the principle that in any system in equilibrium the number of degrees of freedom is equal to the number of components less the number of phases plus two. See also **degree of freedom, component** (sense 4).

phase speed *or* **velocity** *n Physics.* the speed at which the phase of a wave is propagated, the product of the frequency times the wavelength. This is the quantity that is determined by methods using interference. In a dispersive medium it differs from the group speed. Also called: **wave speed, wave velocity.**

-phasia *n combining form.* indicating speech disorder of a specified kind: *aphasia.* [from Greek, from *phanai* to speak] ▸ **-phasic** *adj and n combining form.*

phasing ('feɪzɪŋ) *n Electrical engineering.* a tonal sweep achieved by varying the phase relationship of two similar audio signals by mechanical or electronic means.

phasmid ('fæzmɪd) *n* **1** any plant-eating insect of the mainly tropical order *Phasmida:* includes the leaf insects and stick insects. ◆ *adj* **2** of, relating to, or belonging to the order *Phasmida.* [C19: from New Latin *Phasmida,* from Greek *phasma* spectre]

phasor ('feɪzɔː) *n Electrical engineering.* a rotating vector representing a quantity, such as an alternating current or voltage, that varies sinusoidally.

phatic ('fætɪk) *adj* (of speech, esp. of conversational phrases) used to establish social contact and to express sociability rather than specific meaning. [C20: from Greek *phat(os)* spoken + -IC]

PHC *abbrev. for* Pharmaceutical Chemist.

PhD *abbrev. for* Doctor of Philosophy. Also: **DPhil.**

pheasant ('fez^ənt) *n* **1** any of various long-tailed gallinaceous birds of the family *Phasianidae,* esp. *Phasianus colchicus* (**ring-necked pheasant**), having a brightly-coloured plumage in the male: native to Asia but introduced elsewhere. **2** any of various other gallinaceous birds of the family *Phasianidae,* including the quails and partridges. **3** *U.S. and Canadian.* any of several other gallinaceous birds, esp. the ruffed grouse. [C13: from Old French *fesan,* from Latin *phāsiānus,* from Greek *phasianos ornis* Phasian bird, named after the River *Phasis,* in Colchis]

pheasant's eye *n* **1** an annual ranunculaceous plant, *Adonis annua* (or *autumnalis*), with scarlet flowers and finely divided leaves: native to S Europe but naturalized elsewhere. **2** a type of narcissus, *Narcissus poeticus,* that has white petals and a small red-ringed cup.

Phebe ('fiːbɪ) *n* a variant spelling of **Phoebe**[1].

Pheidippides *or* **Phidippides** (faɪ'dɪpɪˌdiːz) *n* Athenian athlete, who ran to Sparta to seek help against the Persians before the Battle of Marathon (490 B.C.).

phellem ('feləm) *n Botany.* the technical name for **cork** (sense 4). [C20: from Greek *phellos* cork + PHLOEM]

phelloderm ('feləʊˌdɜːm) *n* a layer of thin-walled cells produced by the inner surface of the cork cambium. [C19: from Greek *phellos* cork + -DERM] ▸ ˌ**phello'dermal** *adj*

phellogen ('felədʒən) *n Botany.* the technical name for **cork cambium.** [C19: from Greek *phellos* cork + -GEN] ▸ **phellogenetic** (ˌfeləʊdʒɪ'netɪk) *or* **phellogenic** (ˌfeləʊ'dʒenɪk) *adj*

phenacaine ('fiːnəˌkeɪn, 'fen-) *n* a crystalline basic compound that is the hydrochloride of holocaine: used as a local anaesthetic in ophthalmic medicine. Formula: $C_{18}H_{22}N_2O_2HCl$. [C20: from PHENO- + ACETO- + COCAINE]

phenacetin (fɪ'næsɪtɪn) *n* a white crystalline solid used in medicine to relieve pain and fever. Formula: $CH_3CONHC_6H_4OC_2H_5$. Also called: **acetophenetidin.** [C19: from PHENETIDINE + ACETYL + -IN]

phenacite ('fenəˌsaɪt) *or* **phenakite** ('fenəˌkaɪt) *n* a colourless or white glassy mineral consisting of beryllium silicate in hexagonal crystalline form: occurs in veins in granite. Formula: Be_2SiO_4. [C19: from Greek *phenax* a cheat, because of its deceptive resemblance to quartz]

phenanthrene (fɪ'nænθriːn) *n* a colourless crystalline aromatic compound isomeric with anthracene: used in the manufacture of dyes, drugs, and explosives. Formula: $C_{14}H_{10}$. [C19: from PHENO- + ANTHRACENE]

phenazine ('fenəˌziːn) *n* a yellow crystalline compound that is the parent compound of many azine dyes and some antibiotics. Formula: $C_6H_4N_2C_6H_4$. [C19: from PHENO- + AZINE]

phencyclidine (fen'sɪklɪˌdiːn) *n* See **PCP.**

phenetics (fɪ'netɪks) *n* (*functioning as sing*) *Biology.* a system of classification based on similarities between organisms without regard to their evolutionary relationships. [C20: from PHEN(OTYPE) + (GEN)ETICS] ▸ **phe'netic** *adj*

phenetidine (fɪ'netɪˌdiːn, -dɪn) *n* a liquid amine that is a derivative of phenetole, existing in three isomeric forms: used in the manufacture of dyestuffs. Formula: $H_2NC_6H_4OC_2H_5$. [C19: from PHENETOLE + -ID[3] + -INE[2]]

phenetole ('fenɪˌtəʊl, -ˌtɒl) *n* a colourless oily compound; phenyl ethyl ether. Formula: $C_6H_5OC_2H_5$. [C19: from PHENO- + ETHYL + -OLE[1]]

phenformin (fen'fɔːmɪn) *n* a biguanide administered orally in the treatment of diabetes to lower blood levels of glucose. Formula: $C_{10}H_{15}N_5$. [C20: from PHEN(YL) + FORM(ALDEHYDE) + -IN]

phenix ('fiːnɪks) *n* a U.S. spelling of **phoenix.**

pheno- *or before a vowel* **phen-** *combining form.* **1** showing or manifesting: *phenotype.* **2** indicating that a molecule contains benzene rings: *phenobarbitone.* [from Greek *phaino-* shining, from *phainein* to show; its use in a chemical sense is exemplified in *phenol,* so called because originally prepared from illuminating gas]

phenobarbitone (ˌfiːnəʊ'bɑːbɪˌtəʊn) *or* **phenobarbital** (ˌfiːnəʊ'bɑːbɪt^əl) *n* a white crystalline derivative of barbituric acid used as a sedative for treating insomnia and epilepsy. Formula: $C_{12}H_{12}N_2O_3$.

phenocopy ('fiːnəʊˌkɒpɪ) *n, pl* **-copies.** a noninheritable change in an organism that is caused by environmental influence during development but resembles the effects of a genetic mutation.

phenocryst ('fiːnəˌkrɪst, 'fen-) *n* any of several large crystals that are embedded in a mass of smaller crystals in igneous rocks such as porphyry. [C19: from PHENO- (shining) + CRYSTAL]

phenol ('fiːnɒl) *n* **1** Also called: **carbolic acid.** a white crystalline soluble poisonous acidic derivative of benzene, used as an antiseptic and disinfectant and in the manufacture of resins, nylon, dyes, explosives, and pharmaceuticals; hydroxybenzene. Formula: C_6H_5OH. **2** *Chem.* any of a class of weakly acidic organic compounds whose molecules contain one or more hydroxyl groups bound directly to a carbon atom in an aromatic ring.

phenolate ('fiːnəˌleɪt) *vb* **1** (*tr*) Also: **carbolize.** to treat or disinfect with phenol. ◆ *n* **2** another name (not in technical usage) for **phenoxide.**

phenolic (fɪ'nɒlɪk) *adj* of, containing, or derived from phenol.

phenolic resin *n* any one of a class of resins derived from phenol, used in paints, adhesives, and as thermosetting plastics. See also **Bakelite.**

phenology (fɪ'nɒlədʒɪ) *n* the study of recurring phenomena, such as animal migration, esp. as influenced by climatic conditions. [C19: from PHENO(MENON) + -LOGY] ▸ **phenological** (ˌfiːnə'lɒdʒɪk^əl) *adj* ▸ **phe'nologist** *n*

phenolphthalein (ˌfiːnɒl'θeɪliːn, -lɪɪn, -'θæl-) *n* a colourless crystalline compound used in medicine as a laxative and in chemistry as an indicator. Formula: $C_{20}H_{14}O_4$.

phenomena (fɪ'nɒmɪnə) *n* a plural of **phenomenon.**

phenomenal (fɪ'nɒmɪn^əl) *adj* **1** of or relating to a phenomenon. **2** extraordinary; outstanding; remarkable: *a phenomenal achievement.* **3** *Philosophy.* known or perceived by the senses rather than the mind. ▸ **phe'nomenally** *adv*

phenomenalism (fɪ'nɒmɪnəˌlɪzəm) *n Philosophy.* the doctrine that statements about physical objects and the external world can be analysed in terms of possible or actual experiences, and that entities, such as physical objects, are only mental constructions out of phenomenal appearances. Compare **idealism** (sense 3), **realism** (sense 6). ▸ **phe'nomenalist** *n, adj* ▸ **pheˌnomenal'istically** *adv*

phenomenology (fɪˌnɒmɪ'nɒlədʒɪ) *n Philosophy.* **1** the movement founded by Husserl that concentrates on the detailed description of conscious experience, without recourse to explanation, metaphysical assumptions, and traditional philosophical questions. **2** the science of phenomena as opposed to the science of being. ▸ **phenomenological** (fɪˌnɒmɪnə'lɒdʒɪk^əl) *adj* ▸ **pheˌnomeno'logically** *adv* ▸ **pheˌnome'nologist** *n*

phenomenon (fɪ'nɒmɪnən) *n, pl* **-ena** (-ɪnə) *or* **-enons. 1** anything that can be perceived as an occurrence or fact by the senses. **2** any remarkable occurrence or person. **3** *Philosophy.* **3a** the object of perception, experience, etc. **3b** (in the writings of Kant) a thing as it appears and is interpreted in perception and reflection, as distinguished from its real nature as a thing-in-itself. Compare **noumenon.** [C16: via Late Latin from Greek *phainomenon,* from *phainesthai* to appear, from *phainein* to show]

USAGE Although *phenomena* is often treated as if it were singular, correct usage is to employ *phenomenon* with a singular construction and *phenomena* with a plural: *that is an interesting phenomenon* (not *phenomena*); *several new phenomena were recorded in his notes.*

phenothiazine (ˌfiːnəʊ'θaɪəziːn) *n* **1** a colourless to light yellow insoluble crystalline compound used as an anthelmintic for livestock and in insecticides. Formula: $C_{12}H_9NS$. **2** any of several drugs derived from phenothiazine and used as strong tranquillizers and in the treatment of schizophrenia.

phenotype ('fiːnəʊˌtaɪp) *n* the physical constitution of an organism as determined by the interaction of its genetic constitution and the environment. Compare **genotype.** ▸ **phenotypic** (ˌfiːnəʊ'tɪpɪk) *or* ˌ**pheno'typical** *adj* ▸ ˌ**pheno'typically** *adv*

phenoxide (fɪ'nɒksaɪd) *n* any of a class of salts of phenol. They contain the ion $C_6H_5O^-$. Also called: **phenolate.**

phenoxy resin (fɪ'nɒksɪ) *n Chem.* any of a class of resins derived from polyhydroxy ethers.

phenyl ('fiːnaɪl, 'fenɪl) *n* (*modifier*) of, containing, or consisting of the monovalent group C_6H_5, derived from benzene: *a phenyl group or radical.*

phenylalanine (ˌfiːnaɪl'æləˌniːn, ˌfenɪl-) *n* an aromatic essential amino acid; a component of proteins.

phenylamine (ˌfiːnaɪlə'miːn, ˌfenɪl-) *n* another name for **aniline.**

phenylbutazone (ˌfiːnaɪl'bjuːtəˌzəʊn) *n* an anti-inflammatory drug used in the treatment of rheumatic diseases. [C20: from *(dioxodi)phenylbut(ylpyr)azo(lidi)ne*]

phenylketonuria (ˌfiːnaɪlˌkiːtə'njʊərɪə) *n* a congenital metabolic disorder characterized by the abnormal accumulation of phenylalanine in the body fluids, resulting in various degrees of mental deficiency. [C20: New Latin; see PHENYL, KETONE, -URIA]

phenytoin (ˌfenɪ'təʊɪn) *n* an anticonvulsant drug used in the treatment of epilepsy. [C20: from *(di)pheny(lhydan)toin*]

pheromone ('ferəˌməʊn) *n* a chemical substance, secreted externally by certain animals, such as insects, affecting the behaviour or physiology of other animals of the same species. [C20: *phero-,* from Greek *pherein* to bear + (HOR)MONE]

phew (fjuː) *interj* an exclamation of relief, surprise, disbelief, weariness, etc.

phi (faɪ) *n, pl* **phis.** the 21st letter in the Greek alphabet, Φ, φ, a consonant, transliterated as *ph* or *f.*

phial ('faɪəl) *n* a small bottle for liquids; vial. [C14: from Old French *fiole,* from Latin *phiola* saucer, from Greek *phialē* wide shallow vessel]

Phi Beta Kappa ('faɪ 'beɪtə 'kæpə, 'biːtə) *n* (in the U.S.) **1** a national honorary society, founded in 1776, membership of which is based on high academic ability. **2** a member of this society. [from the initials of the Greek motto *philosophia biou kubernētēs* philosophy the guide of life]

Phidias ('fɪdɪˌæs) *n* 5th century B.C., Greek sculptor, regarded as one of the greatest of sculptors. He executed the sculptures of the Parthenon and the colossal statue of Zeus at Olympia, one of the Seven Wonders of the World: neither survives in the original. ▸ **'Phidian** *adj*

Phidippides (faɪ'dɪpɪˌdiːz) *n* a variant spelling of **Pheidippides.**

phil. *abbrev. for:* **1** philosophy. **2** philharmonic.

Phil. *abbrev. for:* **1** Philippians. **2** Philippines. **3** Philadelphia. **4** Philharmonic.

Philadelphia (ˌfɪlə'dɛlfɪə) *n* a city and port in SE Pennsylvania, at the confluence of the Delaware and Schuylkill Rivers: the fourth largest city in the U.S.; founded by Quakers in 1682; cultural and financial centre of the American colonies and the federal capital (1790–1800); scene of the Continental Congresses (1774–83) and the signing of the Declaration of Independence (1776). Pop.: 1 478 002 (1996 est.).

philadelphus (ˌfɪlə'delfəs) *n* any shrub of the N temperate genus *Philadelphus,* cultivated for their strongly scented showy flowers: family *Philadelphaceae.* See also **mock orange** (sense 1). **[C19:** New Latin, from Greek *philadelphon* mock orange, literally: loving one's brother**]**

Philae ('faɪli:) *n* an island in Upper Egypt, in the Nile north of the Aswan Dam: of religious importance in ancient times; almost submerged since the raising of the level of the dam.

philander (fɪ'lændə) *vb* (*intr;* often foll. by *with*) (of a man) to flirt with women. **[C17:** from Greek *philandros* fond of men, from *philos* loving + *anēr* man; used as a name for a lover in literary works**]** ▸ **phi'landerer** *n* ▸ **phi'landering** *n, adj*

philanthropic (ˌfɪlən'θrɒpɪk) *or* **philanthropical** *adj* showing concern for humanity, esp. by performing charitable actions, donating money, etc. ▸ **ˌphilan'thropically** *adv*

philanthropy (fɪ'lænθrəpɪ) *n, pl* **-pies. 1** the practice of performing charitable or benevolent actions. **2** love of mankind in general. **[C17:** from Late Latin *philanthrōpia,* from Greek: love of mankind, from *philos* loving + *anthrōpos* man**]** ▸ **phi'lanthropist** *or* **philanthrope** ('fɪlənˌθrəʊp) *n*

philately (fɪ'lætəlɪ) *n* the collection and study of postage stamps and all related material concerned with postal history. **[C19:** from French *philatélie,* from PHILO- + Greek *ateleia* exemption from charges (here referring to stamps), from A-[1] + *telos* tax, payment**]** ▸ **philatelic** (ˌfɪlə'telɪk) *adj* ▸ **ˌphila'telically** *adv* ▸ **phi'latelist** *n*

Philby ('fɪlbɪ) *n* **1 Harold Adrian Russell,** known as *Kim.* 1912–88, English double agent; defected to the Soviet Union (1963). **2** his father, **H(arry) Saint John (Bridger).** 1885–1960, British explorer, civil servant, and Arabist.

-phile *or* **-phil** *n combining form.* indicating a person or thing having a fondness or preference for something specified: *bibliophile; Francophile.* **[**from Greek *philos* loving**]**

Philem. *Bible. abbrev. for* Philemon.

Philemon[1] (faɪ'li:mɒn) *n New Testament.* **1** a Christian of Colossae whose escaped slave came to meet Paul. **2** the book (in full **The Epistle of Paul the Apostle to Philemon**), asking Philemon to forgive the slave for escaping.

Philemon[2] (faɪ'li:mɒn) *n Greek myth.* a poor Phrygian, who with his wife Baucis offered hospitality to the disguised Zeus and Hermes.

philharmonic (ˌfɪlhɑ:'mɒnɪk, ˌfɪlə-) *adj* **1** fond of music. **2** (*cap. when part of a name*) denoting an orchestra, choir, society, etc., devoted to the performance, appreciation, and study of music. ◆ *n* **3** (*cap. when part of a name*) a specific philharmonic choir, orchestra, or society. **[C18:** from French *philharmonique,* from Italian *filarmonico* music-loving; see PHILO-, HARMONY**]**

philhellene (fɪl'heli:n) *or* **philhellenist** (fɪl'helɪnɪst) *n* **1** a lover of Greece and Greek culture. **2** *European history.* a supporter of the cause of Greek national independence. ▸ **philhellenic** (ˌfɪlhe'li:nɪk) *adj* ▸ **philhellenism** (fɪl'helɪˌnɪzəm) *n*

-philia *n combining form.* **1** indicating a tendency towards: *haemophilia.* **2** indicating an abnormal liking for: *necrophilia.* **[**from Greek *philos* loving**]** ▸ **-philiac** *n combining form.* ▸ **-philous** *or* **-philic** *adj combining form.*

philibeg ('fɪlɪˌbeg) *n* a variant spelling of **filibeg.**

Philip ('fɪlɪp) *n* **1** *New Testament.* **1a** an apostle from Bethsaida (John 1:43–51; 6:5–7; 12:21; 14:8). **1b** Also called: **Philip the Evangelist.** one of the seven deacons appointed by the early Church. **1c** Also called: **Philip the Tetrarch.** one of the sons of Herod the Great, who was ruler of part of former Judaea (4 B.C.–34 A.D.) (Luke 3:1). **2 King,** American Indian name *Metacomet.* died 1676, American Indian chief, the son of Massasoit. He waged King Philip's War against the colonists of New England (1675–76) and was killed in battle. **3 Prince.** another name for the (Duke of) **Edinburgh.**

Philip I *n* **1** known as *Philip the Handsome.* 1478–1506, king of Castile (1506); father of Emperor Charles V and founder of the Hapsburg dynasty in Spain. **2** title of Philip II of Spain as king of Portugal.

Philip II *n* **1** 382–336 B.C., king of Macedonia (359–336); the father of Alexander the Great. **2** known as *Philip Augustus.* 1165–1223, Capetian king of France (1180–1223); set out on the Third Crusade with Richard I of England (1190). **3** 1527–98, king of Spain (1556–98) and, as Philip I, king of Portugal (1580–98); the husband of Mary I of England (1554–58). He championed the Counter-Reformation, sending the Armada against England (1588).

Philip IV *n* known as *Philip the Fair.* 1268–1314, king of France (1285–1314): he challenged the power of the papacy, obtaining the elevation of Clement V as pope residing at Avignon (the beginning of the Babylonian captivity of the papacy).

Philip V *n* 1683–1746, king of Spain (1700–46) and founder of the Bourbon dynasty in Spain. His accession began the War of Spanish Succession (1701–13).

Philip VI *n* 1293–1350, first Valois king of France (1328–50). Edward III of England claimed his throne, which with other disputes led to the beginning of the Hundred Years' War (1337).

Philippeville ('fɪlɪpˌvɪl) *n* the former name of **Skikda.**

Philippi (fɪ'lɪpaɪ, 'fɪlɪ-) *n* an ancient city in NE Macedonia: scene of the victory of Antony and Octavian over Brutus and Cassius (42 B.C.). ▸ **Phi'lippian** *adj*

Philippians (fɪ'lɪpɪəns) *n* (*functioning as sing*) a book of the New Testament (in full **The Epistle of Paul the Apostle to the Philippians**).

philippic (fɪ'lɪpɪk) *n* a bitter or impassioned speech of denunciation; invective.

Philippics (fɪ'lɪpɪks) *pl n* **1** Demosthenes' orations against Philip of Macedon. **2** Cicero's orations against Antony.

Philippine ('fɪlɪˌpi:n) *adj* another word for **Filipino** (sense 3).

Philippine mahogany ('fɪlɪˌpi:n) *n* any of various Philippine hardwood trees of the genus *Shorea* and related genera: family *Dipterocarpaceae.*

Philippines ('fɪlɪˌpi:nz, ˌfɪlɪ'pi:nz) *n* (*functioning as sing*) **Republic of the.** a republic in SE Asia, occupying an archipelago of about 7100 islands (including Luzon, Mindanao, Samar, and Negros): became a Spanish colony in 1571 but ceded to the U.S. in 1898 after the Spanish-American War; gained independence in 1946. The islands are generally mountainous and volcanic. Official languages: Filipino, based on Tagalog, and English. Religion: Roman Catholic majority. Currency: peso. Capital: Manila. Pop.: 73 131 000 (1998 est.). Area: 300 076 sq. km (115 860 sq. miles). Related word: **Filipino.**

Philippine Sea *n* part of the NW Pacific Ocean, east and north of the Philippines.

Philippopolis (ˌfɪlɪ'pɒpəlɪs) *n* transliteration of the Greek name for **Plovdiv.**

Philip the Bold *n* 1342–1404, duke of Burgundy (1363–1404), noted for his courage at Poitiers (1356) in the Hundred Years' War: regent of France for his nephew Charles VI (1368–88, 1392–1404).

Philip the Good *n* 1396–1467, duke of Burgundy (1419–67), under whose rule Burgundy was one of the most powerful states in Europe.

Philip the Magnanimous *n* 1504–67, German prince; landgrave of Hesse (1509–67). He helped to crush (1525) the Peasants' Revolt and formed (1531) the League of Schmalkaden, an alliance of German Protestant rulers.

Philistia (fɪ'lɪstɪə) *n* an ancient country on the coast of SW Palestine. ▸ **Phi'listian** *adj*

Philistine ('fɪlɪˌstaɪn) *n* **1** a person who is unreceptive to or hostile towards culture, the arts, etc.; a smug boorish person. **2** a member of the non-Semitic people who inhabited ancient Philistia. ◆ *adj* **3** (*sometimes not cap.*) boorishly uncultured. **4** of or relating to the ancient Philistines. ▸ **Philistinism** ('fɪlɪstɪˌnɪzəm) *n*

Phillip ('fɪlɪp) *n* **Arthur.** 1738–1814, English naval commander; captain general of the First Fleet, which carried convicts from Portsmouth to Sydney Cove, Australia, where he founded New South Wales.

Phillips ('fɪlɪps) *n* Captain **Mark.** born 1948, English three-day-event horseman; married to Anne, the Princess Royal, divorced 1992.

Phillips curve *n Economics.* a curve that purports to plot the relationship between unemployment and inflation on the theory that as inflation falls unemployment rises and vice versa. **[C20:** named after A. W. H. *Phillips* (1914–75), English economist who formulated the theory**]**

Phillips screw *n Trademark.* a screw having a cruciform slot into which a screwdriver with a cruciform point (**Phillips screwdriver** (*Trademark*)) fits.

phillumenist (fɪ'lju:mənɪst, -'lu:-) *n* a person who collects matchbox labels. **[C20:** from PHILO- + Latin *lumen* light + -IST**]** ▸ **phil'lumeny** *n*

philo- *or before a vowel* **phil-** *combining form.* indicating a love of: *philology; philanthropic.* **[**from Greek *philos* loving**]**

Philoctetes (ˌfɪlɒk'ti:ti:z, fɪ'lɒktɪˌti:z) *n Greek myth.* a hero of the Trojan War, in which he killed Paris with the bow and poisoned arrows given to him by Hercules.

philodendron (ˌfɪlə'dendrən) *n, pl* **-drons** *or* **-dra** (-drə). any aroid evergreen climbing plant of the tropical American genus *Philodendron:* cultivated as house plants. **[C19:** New Latin from Greek: lover of trees**]**

philogyny (fɪ'lɒdʒɪnɪ) *n Rare.* fondness for women. Compare **misogyny. [C17:** from Greek *philogunia,* from PHILO- + *gunē* woman**]** ▸ **phi'logynist** *n* ▸ **phi'logynous** *adj*

Philo Judaeus ('faɪləʊ dʒu:'di:əs) *n* ?20 B.C.–?50 A.D., Jewish philosopher, born in Alexandria. He sought to reconcile Judaism with Greek philosophy.

philol. *abbrev. for:* **1** philological. **2** philology.

philology (fɪ'lɒlədʒɪ) *n* **1** comparative and historical linguistics. **2** the scientific analysis of written records and literary texts. **3** (no longer in scholarly use) the study of literature in general. **[C17:** from Latin *philologia,* from Greek: love of language**]** ▸ **philological** (ˌfɪlə'lɒdʒɪk°l) *adj* ▸ **ˌphilo'logically** *adv* ▸ **phi'lologist** *or* (*less commonly*) **phi'lologer** *n*

philomel ('fɪləˌmel) *or* **philomela** (ˌfɪləʊ'mi:lə) *n* poetic names for a **nightingale. [C14** *philomene,* via Medieval Latin from Latin *philomēla,* from Greek**]**

Philomela (ˌfɪləʊ'mi:lə) *n Greek myth.* an Athenian princess, who was raped and had her tongue cut out by her brother-in-law Tereus, and subsequently was transformed into a nightingale. See **Procne.**

philoprogenitive (ˌfɪləʊprəʊ'dʒenɪtɪv) *adj Rare.* **1** fond of children. **2** producing many offspring.

philos. *abbrev. for:* **1** philosopher. **2** philosophical.

philosopher (fɪ'lɒsəfə) *n* **1** a student, teacher, or devotee of philosophy. **2** a person of philosophical temperament, esp. one who is patient, wise, and stoical. **3** (formerly) an alchemist or devotee of occult science. **4** a person who establishes the ideology of a cult or movement: *the philosopher of the revolution.*

philosopher kings *pl n* **1** (in the political theory of Plato) the elite whose education has given them true knowledge of the Forms and esp. of the Form of the Good, thus enabling them alone to rule justly. **2** *Informal.* any ideologically motivated elite.

philosopher's stone *n* a stone or substance thought by alchemists to be capable of transmuting base metals into gold.

philosophical (ˌfɪlə'sɒfɪk°l) *or* **philosophic** *adj* **1** of or relating to philosophy or philosophers. **2** reasonable, wise, or learned. **3** calm and stoical, esp. in the face of difficulties or disappointments. **4** (formerly) of or relating to science or natural philosophy. ▸ **ˌphilo'sophically** *adv* ▸ **ˌphilo'sophicalness** *n*

philosophical logic *n* the branch of philosophy that studies the relationship between formal logic and ordinary language, esp. the extent to which the former can be held accurately to represent the latter.

philosophize *or* **philosophise** (fɪˈlɒsəˌfaɪz) *vb* **1** (*intr*) to make philosophical pronouncements and speculations. **2** (*tr*) to explain philosophically. ► **phiˌlosophiˈzation** *or* **phiˌlosophiˈsation** *n* ► **phiˈlosoˌphizer** *or* **phiˈlosoˌphiser** *n*

philosophy (fɪˈlɒsəfɪ) *n, pl* **-phies. 1** the academic discipline concerned with making explicit the nature and significance of ordinary and scientific beliefs and investigating the intelligibility of concepts by means of rational argument concerning their presuppositions, implications, and interrelationships; in particular, the rational investigation of the nature and structure of reality (metaphysics), the resources and limits of knowledge (epistemology), the principles and import of moral judgment (ethics), and the relationship between language and reality (semantics). **2** the particular doctrines relating to these issues of some specific individual or school: *the philosophy of Descartes.* **3** the critical study of the basic principles and concepts of a discipline: *the philosophy of law.* **4** *Archaic or literary.* the investigation of natural phenomena, esp. alchemy, astrology, and astronomy. **5** any system of belief, values, or tenets. **6** a personal outlook or viewpoint. **7** serenity of temper. **[C13:** from Old French *filosofie,* from Latin *philosophia,* from Greek, from *philosophos* lover of wisdom**]**

-philous *or* **-philic** *adj combining form.* indicating love of or fondness for: *heliophilous.* **[**from Latin *-philus,* from Greek *-philos;* see -PHILE**]**

philtre *or U.S.* **philter** (ˈfɪltə) *n* a drink supposed to arouse love, desire, etc. **[C16:** from Latin *philtrum,* from Greek *philtron* love potion, from *philos* loving**]**

philtrum (ˈfɪltrəm) *n, pl* **philtra.** the indentation above the upper lip. **[C17:** from Latin, see PHILTRE**]**

phimosis (faɪˈməʊsɪs) *n* abnormal tightness of the foreskin, preventing its being retracted over the tip of the penis. **[C17:** via New Latin from Greek: a muzzling, from *phimos* a muzzle**]**

phi-phenomenon (ˈfaɪfɪˌnɒmɪnən) *n, pl* **-na** (-nə). *Psychol.* **1** the illusion that when two lights are rapidly turned on and off in succession something appears to move backwards and forwards between them while the lights stay stationary. **2** a similar illusion in which one light appears to move smoothly backwards and forwards. **[C20:** arbitrary use of Greek *phi***]**

phiz (fɪz) *n Slang, chiefly Brit.* the face or a facial expression: *an ugly phiz.* Also called: **phizog** (ˈfɪzɒg, fɪˈzɒg). **[C17:** colloquial shortening of PHYSIOGNOMY**]**

Phiz (fɪz) *n* real name *Hablot Knight Browne.* 1815–82, English painter, noted for his illustrations for Dickens' novels.

phlebectomy (flɪˈbɛktəmɪ) *n* the surgical excision of a vein or part of a vein.

phlebitis (flɪˈbaɪtɪs) *n* inflammation of a vein. **[C19:** via New Latin from Greek; see PHLEBO-, -ITIS**]** ► **phlebitic** (flɪˈbɪtɪk) *adj*

phlebo- *or before a vowel* **phleb-** *combining form.* indicating a vein: *phlebotomy.* **[**from Greek *phleps, phleb-* vein**]**

phlebography (flɪˈbɒgrəfɪ) *n* another name for **venography.**

phlebosclerosis (ˌflɛbəʊsklɪˈrəʊsɪs) *n Pathol.* hardening and loss of elasticity of the veins. Also called: **venosclerosis.**

phlebotomize *or* **phlebotomise** (flɪˈbɒtəˌmaɪz) *vb* (*tr*) *Surgery.* to perform phlebotomy on (a patient).

phlebotomy (flɪˈbɒtəmɪ) *n, pl* **-mies.** surgical incision into a vein. Also called: **venesection. [C14:** from Old French *flebothomie,* from Late Latin *phlebotomia,* from Greek**]** ► **phlebotomic** (ˌflɛbəˈtɒmɪk) *or* **ˌphleboˈtomical** *adj* ► **phleˈbotomist** *n*

Phlegethon (ˈflɛgɪˌθɒn) *n Greek myth.* a river of fire in Hades. **[C14:** from Greek, literally: blazing, from *phlegethein* to flame, blaze**]**

phlegm (flɛm) *n* **1** the viscid mucus secreted by the walls of the respiratory tract. **2** *Archaic.* one of the four bodily humours. **3** apathy; stolidity; indifference. **4** self-possession; imperturbability; coolness. **[C14:** from Old French *fleume,* from Late Latin *phlegma,* from Greek: inflammation, from *phlegein* to burn**]** ► **ˈphlegmy** *adj*

phlegmatic (flɛgˈmætɪk) *or* **phlegmatical** *adj* **1** having a stolid or unemotional disposition. **2** not easily excited. ► **phlegˈmatically** *adv* ► **phlegˈmaticalness** *or* **phlegˈmaticness** *n*

phloem (ˈfləʊɛm) *n* tissue in higher plants that conducts synthesized food substances to all parts of the plant. **[C19:** via German from Greek *phloos* bark**]**

phlogistic (flɒˈdʒɪstɪk) *adj* **1** *Pathol.* of inflammation; inflammatory. **2** *Chem.* of, concerned with, or containing phlogiston.

phlogiston (flɒˈdʒɪstɒn, -tən) *n Chem.* a hypothetical substance formerly thought to be present in all combustible materials and to be released during burning. **[C18:** via New Latin from Greek, from *phlogizein* to set alight; related to *phlegein* to burn**]**

phlogopite (ˈflɒgəˌpaɪt) *n* a brownish mica consisting of a hydrous silicate of potassium, magnesium, and aluminium, occurring principally in marble and dolomite. Formula: $KMg_3AlSi_3O_{10}(OH)_2$. See also **mica. [C19:** from Greek *phlogōpos* of fiery appearance, from *phlox* flame + *ōps* eye**]**

phlox (flɒks) *n, pl* **phlox** *or* **phloxes.** any polemoniaceous plant of the chiefly North American genus *Phlox:* cultivated for their clusters of white, red, or purple flowers. **[C18:** via Latin from Greek: a plant of glowing colour, literally: flame**]**

phlyctena *or* **phlyctaena** (flɪkˈtiːnə) *n, pl* **-nae** (-niː). *Pathol.* a small blister, vesicle, or pustule. **[C17:** via New Latin from Greek *phluktaina,* from *phluzein* to swell**]**

Phnom Penh *or* **Pnom Penh** (ˌnɒm ˈpɛn) *n* the capital of Cambodia, a port in the south at the confluence of the Mekong and Tonle Sap Rivers: capital of the country since 1865; university (1960). Pop.: 920 000 (1994 est.).

-phobe *n combining form.* indicating a person or thing that fears or hates: *Germanophobe; xenophobe.* **[**from Greek *-phobos* fearing**]** ► **-phobic** *adj combining form.*

phobia (ˈfəʊbɪə) *n Psychiatry.* an abnormal intense and irrational fear of a given situation, organism, or object. **[C19:** from Greek *phobos* fear**]**

-phobia *n combining form.* indicating an extreme abnormal fear of or aversion to: *acrophobia; claustrophobia.* **[**via Latin from Greek, from *phobos* fear**]** ► **-phobic** *adj combining form.*

phobic (ˈfəʊbɪk) *adj* **1** of, relating to, or arising from a phobia. ◆ *n* **2** a person suffering from a phobia.

Phobos (ˈfəʊbɒs) *n* the larger of the two satellites of Mars and the closer to the planet. Approximate diameter: 23 km. Compare **Deimos.**

Phocaea (fəʊˈsiːə) *n* an ancient port in Asia Minor, the northernmost of Ionian cities on the W coast of Asia Minor: an important maritime state (about 1000–600 B.C.).

phocine (ˈfəʊsaɪn) *adj* **1** of, relating to, or resembling a seal. **2** of, relating to, or belonging to the *Phocinae,* a subfamily that includes the harbour seal and grey seal. **[C19:** ultimately from Greek *phōkē* a seal**]**

Phocis (ˈfəʊsɪs) *n* an ancient district of central Greece, on the Gulf of Corinth: site of the Delphic oracle.

phocomelia (ˌfəʊkəʊˈmiːlɪə) *or* **phocomely** (fəʊˈkɒməlɪ) *n* a congenital deformity resulting from prenatal interference with the development of the fetal limbs, characterized esp. by short stubby hands or feet attached close to the body. **[C19:** via New Latin from Greek *phōkē* a seal + *melos* a limb**]** ► **ˌphocoˈmelic** *adj*

phoebe (ˈfiːbɪ) *n* any of several greyish-brown North American flycatchers of the genus *Sayornis,* such as *S. phoebe* (**eastern phoebe**). **[C19:** imitative of the bird's call**]**

Phoebe[1] *or* **Phebe** (ˈfiːbɪ) *n* **1** *Classical myth.* a Titaness, who later became identified with Artemis (Diana) as goddess of the moon. **2** *Poetic.* a personification of the moon.

Phoebe[2] (ˈfiːbɪ) *n* the outermost satellite of the planet Saturn. It has retrograde motion.

Phoebus (ˈfiːbəs) *n* **1** Also called: **Phoebus Apollo.** *Greek myth.* Apollo as the sun god. **2** *Poetic.* a personification of the sun. **[C14:** via Latin from Greek *Phoibos* bright; related to *phaos* light**]**

Phoenicia (fəˈnɪʃɪə, -ˈniː-) *n* an ancient maritime country extending from the Mediterranean Sea to the Lebanon Mountains, now occupied by the coastal regions of Lebanon and parts of Syria and Israel: consisted of a group of city-states, at their height between about 1200 and 1000 B.C., that were leading traders of the ancient world.

Phoenician (fəˈniːʃən, -ˈnɪʃɪən) *n* **1** a member of an ancient Semitic people of NW Syria who dominated the trade of the ancient world in the first millennium B.C. and founded colonies throughout the Mediterranean. **2** the extinct language of this people, belonging to the Canaanitic branch of the Semitic subfamily of the Afro-Asiatic family. ◆ *adj* **3** of or relating to Phoenicia, the Phoenicians, or their language.

phoenix *or U.S.* **phenix** (ˈfiːnɪks) *n* **1** a legendary Arabian bird said to set fire to itself and rise anew from the ashes every 500 years. **2** a person or thing of surpassing beauty or quality. **[**Old English *fenix,* via Latin from Greek *phoinix;* identical in form with Greek *Phoinix* Phoenician, purple**]**

Phoenix[1] (ˈfiːnɪks) *n, Latin genitive* **Phoenices** (ˈfiːnɪˌsiːz). a constellation in the S hemisphere lying between Grus and Eridanus.

Phoenix[2] (ˈfiːnɪks) *n* a city in central Arizona, capital city of the state, on the Salt River. Pop.: 1 159 014 (1996 est.).

Phoenix Islands *pl n* a group of eight coral islands in the central Pacific: administratively part of Kiribati. Area: 28 sq. km (11 sq. miles).

Phomvihane (ˈpɒmvɪhaːn) *n* **Kaysone** (ˈkaɪsɒn). 1920–92, Laotian Communist statesman; prime minister of Laos (1975–91); president (1991–92).

phon (fɒn) *n* a unit of loudness that measures the intensity of a sound by the number of decibels it is above a reference tone having a frequency of 1000 hertz and a root-mean-square sound pressure of 20×10^{-6} pascal. **[C20:** via German from Greek *phōnē* sound, voice**]**

phon. *abbrev. for:* **1** Also: **phonet.** phonetics. **2** phonology.

phonate (fəʊˈneɪt) *vb* (*intr*) to articulate speech sounds, esp. to cause the vocal cords to vibrate in the execution of a voiced speech sound. **[C19:** from Greek *phōnē* voice**]** ► **phoˈnation** *n* ► **phonatory** (ˈfəʊnətərɪ, -trɪ) *adj*

phone[1] (fəʊn) *n, vb* short for **telephone.**

phone[2] (fəʊn) *n Phonetics.* a single uncomplicated speech sound. **[C19:** from Greek *phōnē* sound, voice**]**

-phone *combining form.* **1** (*forming nouns*) indicating voice, sound, or a device giving off sound: *microphone; telephone.* **2** (*forming nouns and adjectives*) (a person) speaking a particular language: *Francophone.* **[**from Greek *phōnē* voice, sound**]** ► **-phonic** *adj combining form.*

phonecard (ˈfəʊnˌkaːd) *n* a card for use in a cardphone that operates for the number or duration of calls paid for in the purchase price of the card.

phone-in *n* **a** a radio or television programme in which listeners' or viewers' questions, comments, etc., are telephoned to the studio and broadcast live. **b** (*as modifier*): *a phone-in discussion.*

phoneme (ˈfəʊniːm) *n Linguistics.* one of the set of speech sounds in any given language that serve to distinguish one word from another. A phoneme may consist of several phonetically distinct articulations, which are regarded as identical by native speakers, since one articulation may be substituted for another without any change of meaning. Thus /p/ and /b/ are separate phonemes in English because they distinguish such words as *pet* and *bet,* whereas the light and dark /l/ sounds in *little* are not separate phonemes since they may be transposed without changing meaning. **[C20:** via French from Greek *phōnēma* sound, speech**]**

phonemic (fəˈniːmɪk) *adj Linguistics.* **1** of or relating to the phoneme. **2** relating to or denoting speech sounds that belong to different phonemes rather than being allophonic variants of the same phoneme. Compare **phonetic** (sense 2). **3** of or relating to phonemics. ► **phoˈnemically** *adv*

phonemics (fəˈniːmɪks) *n* (*functioning as sing*) that aspect of linguistics concerned with the classification, analysis, interrelation, and environmental changes of the phonemes of a language. ▸ **pho'nemicist** *n*

phonendoscope (fə'nɛndə,skəʊp) *n* an instrument that amplifies small sounds, esp. within the human body. [C20: from PHONO- + ENDO- + -SCOPE]

phoner ('fəʊnə) *n Informal.* a person making a telephone call.

phonetic (fə'nɛtɪk) *adj* **1** of or relating to phonetics. **2** denoting any perceptible distinction between one speech sound and another, irrespective of whether the sounds are phonemes or allophones. Compare **phonemic** (sense 2). **3** conforming to pronunciation: *phonetic spelling.* [C19: from New Latin *phōnēticus,* from Greek *phōnētikos,* from *phōnein* to make sounds, speak] ▸ **pho'netically** *adv*

phonetic alphabet *n* a list of the words used in communications to represent the letters of the alphabet, as in E for Echo, T for Tango.

phonetician (,fəʊnɪ'tɪʃən) *n* a person skilled in phonetics or one who employs phonetics in his work.

phonetics (fə'nɛtɪks) *n* (*functioning as sing*) the science concerned with the study of speech processes, including the production, perception, and analysis of speech sounds from both an acoustic and a physiological point of view. This science, though capable of being applied to language studies, technically excludes linguistic considerations. Compare **phonology.**

phonetist ('fəʊnɪtɪst) *n* **1** another name for **phonetician. 2** a person who advocates or uses a system of phonetic spelling.

phoney *or esp. U.S.* **phony** ('fəʊnɪ) *Informal.* ◆ *adj* **-nier, -niest. 1** not genuine; fake. **2** (of a person) insincere or pretentious. ◆ *n, pl* **-neys** *or* **-nies. 3** an insincere or pretentious person. **4** something that is not genuine; a fake. [C20: origin uncertain] ▸ **'phoneyness** *or esp. U.S.* **'phoniness** *n*

phonics ('fɒnɪks) *n* (*functioning as sing*) **1** an obsolete name for **acoustics** (sense 1). **2** a method of teaching people to read by training them to associate letters with their phonetic values. ▸ **'phonic** *adj* ▸ **'phonically** *adv*

phono- *or before a vowel* **phon-** *combining form.* indicating a sound or voice: *phonograph; phonology.* [from Greek *phōnē* sound, voice]

phonochemistry (,fəʊnəʊ'kɛmɪstrɪ) *n* the branch of chemistry concerned with the chemical effects of sound and ultrasonic waves.

phonogram ('fəʊnə,græm) *n* **1** any written symbol standing for a sound, syllable, morpheme, or word. **2** a sequence of written symbols having the same sound in a variety of different words, for example, *ough* in *bought, ought,* and *brought.* ▸ **,phono'gramic** *or* **,phono'grammic** *adj*

phonograph ('fəʊnə,grɑːf, -,græf) *n* **1** an early form of gramophone capable of recording and reproducing sound on wax cylinders. **2** another U.S. and Canadian word for **gramophone** or **record player.**

phonography (fəʊ'nɒgrəfɪ) *n* **1** a writing system that represents sounds by individual symbols. Compare **logography. 2** the employment of such a writing system. ▸ **pho'nographer** *or* **pho'nographist** *n* ▸ **phonographic** (,fəʊnə'græfɪk) *adj*

phonol. *abbrev. for* phonology.

phonolite ('fəʊnə,laɪt) *n* a fine-grained volcanic igneous rock consisting of alkaline feldspars and nepheline. [C19: via French from German *Phonolith;* see PHONO-, -LITE] ▸ **phonolitic** (,fəʊnə'lɪtɪk) *adj*

phonology (fə'nɒlədʒɪ) *n, pl* **-gies. 1** the study of the sound system of a language or of languages in general. Compare **syntax** (senses 1, 2), **semantics. 2** such a sound system. ▸ **phonological** (,fəʊnə'lɒdʒɪkᵊl, ,fɒn-) *adj* ▸ **,phono'logically** *adv* ▸ **pho'nologist** *n*

phonometer (fə'nɒmɪtə) *n* an apparatus that measures the intensity of sound, esp. one calibrated in phons. ▸ **phonometric** (,fəʊnə'mɛtrɪk) *or* **,phono'metrical** *adj*

phonon ('fəʊnɒn) *n Physics.* a quantum of vibrational energy in the acoustic vibrations of a crystal lattice. [C20: from PHONO- + -ON]

phono plug ('fəʊnəʊ) *n Electrical engineering.* a type of coaxial connector, used esp. in audio equipment.

phonoscope ('fəʊnə,skəʊp) *n* a device that renders visible the vibrations of sound waves.

phonotactics ('fəʊnəʊ,tæktɪks) *n* (*functioning as sing*) *Linguistics.* the study of the possible arrangement of the sounds of a language in the words of that language. [C20: from PHONO- + *-tactics,* on the model of *syntactic;* see SYNTAX]

phonotype ('fəʊnə,taɪp) *n Printing.* **1** a letter or symbol representing a sound. **2** text printed in phonetic symbols. ▸ **phonotypic** (,fəʊnə'tɪpɪk) *or* **,phono'typical** *adj*

phonotypy ('fəʊnə,taɪpɪ) *n* the transcription of speech into phonetic symbols. ▸ **'phono,typist** *or* **'phono,typer** *n*

phony ('fəʊnɪ) *adj* **-nier, -niest,** *n, pl* **-nies.** a variant spelling (esp. U.S.) of **phoney.** ▸ **'phoniness** *n*

-phony *n combining form.* indicating a specified type of sound: *cacophony; euphony.* [from Greek *-phōnia,* from *phōnē* sound] ▸ **-phonic** *adj combining form.*

phony war *n* **1** (in wartime) a period of apparent calm and inactivity, esp. the period at the beginning of World War II. **2** (in peacetime) a contrived embattled atmosphere; mock war.

phooey ('fuːɪ) *interj Informal.* an exclamation of scorn, contempt, disbelief, etc. [C20: probably variant of PHEW]

-phore *n combining form.* indicating a person or thing that bears or produces: *gonophore; semaphore.* [from New Latin *-phorus,* from Greek *-phoros* bearing, from *pherein* to bear] ▸ **-phorous** *adj combining form.*

-phoresis *n combining form.* indicating a transmission: *electrophoresis.* [from Greek *phorēsīs* being carried, from *pherein* to bear]

phoresy ('fɒrəsɪ) *n* an association in which one animal clings to another to ensure movement from place to place, as some mites use some insects. [C20: from New Latin *phoresia,* from Greek *phorēsis,* from *pherein* to carry]

phormium ('fɔːmɪəm) *n* any plant of the New Zealand bulbous genus *Phormium,* with leathery evergreen leaves and red or yellow flowers in panicles. [New Latin, from Greek *phormos* a basket (from a use for the fibres)]

phosgene ('fɒzdʒiːn) *n* a colourless easily liquefied poisonous gas, carbonyl chloride, with an odour resembling that of new-mown hay: used in chemical warfare as a lethal choking agent and in the manufacture of pesticides, dyes, and polyurethane resins. Formula: $COCl_2$. [C19: from Greek *phōs* light + *-gene,* variant of -GEN]

phosgenite ('fɒzdʒɪ,naɪt) *n* a rare fluorescent secondary mineral consisting of lead chloro-carbonate in the form of greyish tetragonal crystals. Formula: $Pb_2(Cl_2CO_3)$.

phosphatase ('fɒsfə,teɪs, -,teɪz) *n* any of a group of enzymes that catalyse the hydrolysis of organic phosphates.

phosphate ('fɒsfeɪt) *n* **1** any salt or ester of any phosphoric acid, esp. a salt of orthophosphoric acid. **2** (*often pl*) any of several chemical fertilizers containing phosphorous compounds. [C18: from French *phosphat;* see PHOSPHORUS, -ATE[1]] ▸ **phosphatic** (fɒs'fætɪk) *adj*

phosphatide ('fɒsfə,taɪd) *n* another name for **phospholipid.**

phosphatidylcholine (,fɒsfətɪdaɪl'kəʊliːn) *n* the systematic name for **lecithin.**

phosphatidylethanolamine (,fɒsfətɪdaɪl,ɛθə'nɒləmiːn) *n* the systematic name for **cephalin.**

phosphatidylserine (,fɒsfətɪdaɪl'sɪəriːn) *n* any of a class of phospholipids occurring in biological membranes and fats.

phosphatize *or* **phosphatise** ('fɒsfə,taɪz) *vb* **1** (*tr*) to treat with a phosphate or phosphates, as by applying a fertilizer. **2** to change or be changed into a phosphate. ▸ **,phosphati'zation** *or* **,phosphati'sation** *n*

phosphaturia (,fɒsfə'tjʊərɪə) *n Pathol.* an abnormally large amount of phosphates in the urine. [C19: New Latin, from PHOSPHATE + -URIA] ▸ **,phospha'turic** *adj*

phosphene ('fɒsfiːn) *n* the sensation of light caused by pressure on the eyelid of a closed eye or by other mechanical or electrical interference with the visual system. [C19: from Greek *phōs* light + *phainein* to show]

phosphide ('fɒsfaɪd) *n* any compound of phosphorus with another element, esp. a more electropositive element.

phosphine ('fɒsfiːn) *n* a colourless flammable gas that is slightly soluble in water and has a strong fishy odour: used as a pesticide. Formula: PH_3.

phosphite ('fɒsfaɪt) *n* any salt or ester of phosphorous acid.

phospho- *or before a vowel* **phosph-** *combining form.* containing phosphorus: *phosphocreatine.* [from French, from *phosphore* PHOSPHORUS]

phosphocreatine (,fɒsfə'kriːə,tiːn) *or* **phosphocreatin** *n* a compound of phosphoric acid and creatine found in vertebrate muscle.

phospholipid (,fɒsfə'lɪpɪd) *n* any of a group of compounds composed of fatty acids, phosphoric acid, and a nitrogenous base: important constituents of all membranes. Also called: **phosphatide.**

phosphonic acid (fɒs'fɒnɪk) *n* the systematic name for **phosphorous acid.**

phosphoprotein (,fɒsfə'prəʊtiːn) *n* any of a group of conjugated proteins, esp. casein, in which the protein molecule is bound to phosphoric acid.

phosphor ('fɒsfə) *n* a substance, such as the coating on a cathode-ray tube, capable of emitting light when irradiated with particles of electromagnetic radiation. [C17: from French, ultimately from Greek *phōsphoros* PHOSPHORUS]

phosphorate ('fɒsfə,reɪt) *vb* **1** to treat or combine with phosphorus. **2** (*tr*) *Rare.* to cause (a substance) to exhibit phosphorescence.

phosphor bronze *n* any of various hard corrosion-resistant alloys containing copper, tin (2–8 per cent), and phosphorus (0.1–0.4 per cent): used in gears, bearings, cylinder casings, etc.

phosphoresce (,fɒsfə'rɛs) *vb* (*intr*) to exhibit phosphorescence.

phosphorescence (,fɒsfə'rɛsəns) *n* **1** *Physics.* **1a** a fluorescence that persists after the bombarding radiation producing it has stopped. **1b** a fluorescence for which the average lifetime of the excited atoms is greater than 10^{-8} seconds. **2** the light emitted in phosphorescence. **3** the emission of light during a chemical reaction, such as bioluminescence, in which insufficient heat is evolved to cause fluorescence. Compare **fluorescence.**

phosphorescent (,fɒsfə'rɛsᵊnt) *adj* exhibiting or having the property of phosphorescence. ▸ **,phospho'rescently** *adv*

phosphoric (fɒs'fɒrɪk) *adj* of or containing phosphorus in the pentavalent state.

phosphoric acid *n* **1** a colourless solid tribasic acid used in the manufacture of fertilizers and soap. Formula: H_3PO_4. Systematic name: **phosphoric(V) acid.** Also called: **orthophosphoric acid. 2** any oxyacid of phosphorus produced by reaction between phosphorus pentoxide and water. See also **metaphosphoric acid, pyrophosphoric acid, hypophosphoric acid.**

phosphorism ('fɒsfə,rɪzəm) *n* poisoning caused by prolonged exposure to phosphorus.

phosphorite ('fɒsfə,raɪt) *n* **1** a fibrous variety of the mineral apatite. **2** any of various mineral deposits that consist mainly of calcium phosphate. ▸ **phosphoritic** (,fɒsfə'rɪtɪk) *adj*

phosphoroscope (fɒs'fɒrə,skəʊp) *n* an instrument for measuring the duration of phosphorescence after the source of radiation causing it has been removed.

phosphorous ('fɒsfərəs) *adj* of or containing phosphorus in the trivalent state.

phosphorous acid *n* **1** a white or yellowish hygroscopic crystalline dibasic acid. Formula: H_3PO_3. Systematic name: **phosphoric acid.** Also called: **orthophosphorous acid. 2** any oxyacid of phosphorus containing less oxygen than the corresponding phosphoric acid.

phosphorus ('fɒsfərəs) *n* **1** an allotropic nonmetallic element occurring in phosphates and living matter. Ordinary phosphorus is a toxic flammable phosphorescent white solid; the red form is less reactive and nontoxic: used in matches, pesticides, and alloys. The radioisotope **phosphorus-32 (radio-**

phosphorus), with a half-life of 14.3 days, is used in radiotherapy and as a tracer. Symbol: P; atomic no.: 15; atomic wt.: 30.973762; valency: 3 or 5; relative density: 1.82 (white), 2.20 (red); melting pt.: 44.1°C (white); boiling pt.: 280°C (white). **2** a less common name for a **phosphor.** [C17: via Latin from Greek *phōsphoros* light-bringing, from *phōs* light + *pherein* to bring]

Phosphorus ('fɒsfərəs) *n* a morning star, esp. Venus.

phosphorus pentoxide *n* a white odourless solid produced when phosphorus burns: has a strong affinity for water with which it forms phosphoric acids. Formula: P_2O_5 (commonly existing as the dimer P_4O_{10}). Also called: **phosphoric anhydride.**

phosphorylase (fɒs'fɒrɪˌleɪs, -ˌleɪz) *n* any of a group of enzymes that catalyse the hydrolysis of glycogen to glucose-1-phosphate. [C20: from PHOSPHORUS + -YL + -ASE]

phosphorylation (ˌfɒsfɒrɪ'leɪʃən) *n* the chemical or enzymic introduction into a compound of a phosphoryl group (a trivalent radical of phosphorus and oxygen).

phossy jaw ('fɒsɪ) *n* a gangrenous condition of the lower jawbone caused by prolonged exposure to phosphorus fumes. [C19: *phossy,* colloquial shortening of PHOSPHORUS]

phot (fɒt, fəʊt) *n* a unit of illumination equal to one lumen per square centimetre. 1 phot is equal to 10 000 lux. [C20: from Greek *phōs* light]

phot. *abbrev. for:* **1** photograph. **2** photographic. **3** photography.

photic ('fəʊtɪk) *adj* **1** of or concerned with light. **2** *Biology.* of or relating to the production of light by organisms. **3** Also: **photobathic.** designating the zone of the sea where photosynthesis takes place. [C19: from PHOTO- + -IC]

photo ('fəʊtəʊ) *n, pl* **-tos.** short for **photograph** (sense 1).

photo- *combining form.* **1** of, relating to, or produced by light: *photosynthesis.* **2** indicating a photographic process: *photolithography.* [from Greek *phōs, phōt-* light]

photoactinic (ˌfəʊtəʊæk'tɪnɪk) *adj* emitting actinic radiation.

photoactive (ˌfəʊtəʊ'æktɪv) *adj* (of a substance) capable of responding to light or other electromagnetic radiation.

photo-ageing *n* premature wrinkling of the skin caused by overexposure to sunlight. ► ˌ**photo-'aged** *adj*

photoautotrophic (ˌfəʊtəʊˌɔːtəʊ'trɒfɪk) *adj* (of plants) capable of using light as the energy source in the synthesis of food from inorganic matter. See also **photosynthesis.**

photobathic (ˌfəʊtəʊ'bæθɪk) *adj* another word for **photic** (sense 3). [from PHOTO- + Greek *bathus* deep + -IC]

photobiology (ˌfəʊtəʊbaɪ'ɒlədʒɪ) *n* the branch of biology concerned with the effect of light on living organisms. ► **photobiological** (ˌfəʊtəʊˌbaɪə'lɒdʒɪkᵊl) *adj* ► ˌ**photobi'ologist** *n*

photo call *n* a time arranged for photographers, esp. press photographers, to take pictures of a celebrity, the cast of a play, etc., usually for publicity purposes.

photocatalysis (ˌfəʊtəʊkə'tælɪsɪs) *n, pl* **-ses** (-siːz). the alteration of the rate of a chemical reaction by light or other electromagnetic radiation.

photocathode (ˌfəʊtəʊ'kæθəʊd) *n* a cathode that undergoes or is used for photoemission.

photocell ('fəʊtəʊˌsel) *n* a device in which the photoelectric or photovoltaic effect or photoconductivity is used to produce a current or voltage when exposed to light or other electromagnetic radiation. They are used in exposure meters, burglar alarms, etc. Also called: **photoelectric cell, electric eye.**

photochemistry (ˌfəʊtəʊ'kemɪstrɪ) *n* the branch of chemistry concerned with the chemical effects of light and other electromagnetic radiations. Also called: **actinochemistry.** ► **photochemical** (ˌfəʊtəʊ'kemɪkᵊl) *adj* ► ˌ**photo'chemically** *adv* ► ˌ**photo'chemist** *n*

photochromic (ˌfəʊtəʊ'krəʊmɪk) *adj* (of glass) changing colour with the intensity of incident light, used, for example, in sunglasses that darken as the sunlight becomes brighter.

photochronograph (ˌfəʊtəʊ'krɒnəˌgrɑːf, -ˌgræf) *n Physics.* an instrument for measuring very small time intervals by the trace made by a beam of light on a moving photographic film. ► **photochronography** (ˌfəʊtəʊkrə'nɒgrəfɪ) *n*

photocompose (ˌfəʊtəʊkəm'pəʊz) *vb (tr)* to set (type matter) by photocomposition. ► ˌ**photocom'poser** *n*

photocomposition (ˌfəʊtəʊˌkɒmpə'zɪʃən) *n Printing.* typesetting by exposing type characters onto photographic film or photosensitive paper in order to make printing plates. Also called: **photosetting, phototypesetting.**

photoconduction (ˌfəʊtəʊkən'dʌkʃən) *n* conduction of electricity resulting from the absorption of light. See **photoconductivity.**

photoconductivity (ˌfəʊtəʊˌkɒndʌk'tɪvɪtɪ) *n* the change in the electrical conductivity of certain substances, such as selenium, as a result of the absorption of electromagnetic radiation. ► **photoconductive** (ˌfəʊtəʊkən'dʌktɪv) *adj* ► ˌ**photocon'ductor** *n*

photocopier ('fəʊtəʊˌkɒpɪə) *n* an instrument using light-sensitive photographic materials to reproduce written, printed, or graphic work.

photocopy ('fəʊtəʊˌkɒpɪ) *n, pl* **-copies. 1** a photographic reproduction of written, printed, or graphic work. See also **microcopy.** ◆ *vb* **-copies, -copying, -copied. 2** to reproduce (written, printed, or graphic work) on photographic material.

photocurrent ('fəʊtəʊˌkʌrənt) *n* an electric current produced by electromagnetic radiation in the photoelectric effect, photovoltaic effect, or photoconductivity.

photodegradable (ˌfəʊtəʊdɪ'greɪdəbᵊl) *adj* (of plastic) capable of being decomposed by prolonged exposure to light.

photodiode (ˌfəʊtəʊ'daɪəʊd) *n* a semiconductor diode, the conductivity of which is controlled by incident illumination.

photodisintegration (ˌfəʊtəʊdɪˌsɪntɪ'greɪʃən) *n* disintegration of an atomic nucleus as a result of its absorption of a photon, usually a gamma ray.

photodynamic (ˌfəʊtəʊdaɪ'næmɪk) *adj* **1** of or concerned with photodynamics. **2** involving or producing an adverse or toxic reaction to light, esp. ultraviolet light. **3** *Med.* denoting a therapy for cancer in which a cytotoxic drug is activated by a laser beam.

photodynamics (ˌfəʊtəʊdaɪ'næmɪks) *n (functioning as sing)* the branch of biology concerned with the effects of light on the actions of plants and animals.

photoelasticity (ˌfəʊtəʊɪlæ'stɪsɪtɪ) *n* the effects of stress, such as double refraction, on the optical properties of transparent materials.

photoelectric (ˌfəʊtəʊɪ'lektrɪk) *or* **photoelectrical** *adj* of or concerned with electric or electronic effects caused by light or other electromagnetic radiation. ► ˌ**photoe'lectrically** *adv* ► **photoelectricity** (ˌfəʊtəʊɪlek'trɪsɪtɪ) *n*

photoelectric cell *n* another name for **photocell.**

photoelectric effect *n* **1** the ejection of electrons from a solid by an incident beam of sufficiently energetic electromagnetic radiation. **2** any phenomenon involving electricity and electromagnetic radiation, such as photoemission.

photoelectric magnitude *n Astronomy.* the magnitude of a star, determined with great accuracy using a photometer plus a filter to select light or other radiation of the desired wavelength.

photoelectron (ˌfəʊtəʊɪ'lektrɒn) *n* an electron ejected from an atom, molecule, or solid by an incident photon.

photoelectrotype (ˌfəʊtəʊɪ'lektrəʊˌtaɪp) *n* an electrotype mode using photography.

photoemission (ˌfəʊtəʊɪ'mɪʃən) *n* the emission of electrons due to the impact of electromagnetic radiation, esp. as a result of the photoelectric effect. ► ˌ**photoe'missive** *adj*

photoengrave (ˌfəʊtəʊɪn'greɪv) *vb (tr)* to reproduce (an illustration) by photoengraving. ► ˌ**photoen'graver** *n*

photoengraving (ˌfəʊtəʊɪn'greɪvɪŋ) *n* **1** a photomechanical process for producing letterpress printing plates. **2** a plate made by this process. **3** a print made from such a plate.

photo finish *n* **1** a finish of a race in which contestants are so close that a photograph is needed to decide the result. **2** any race or competition in which the winners or placed contestants are separated by a very small margin.

Photofit ('fəʊtəʊˌfɪt) *n Trademark.* **a** a method of combining photographs of facial features, hair, etc., into a composite picture of a face: used by the police to trace suspects from witnesses' descriptions. **b** *(as modifier): a Photofit picture.*

photoflash ('fəʊtəʊˌflæʃ) *n* another name for **flashbulb.**

photoflood ('fəʊtəʊˌflʌd) *n* a highly incandescent tungsten lamp used as an artificial light source for indoor photography, television, etc. The brightness is obtained by operating with higher than normal current.

photofluorography (ˌfəʊtəʊfluə'rɒgrəfɪ) *n Med.* the process of taking a photograph (**photofluorogram**) of a fluoroscopic image: used in diagnostic screening.

photog. *abbrev. for:* **1** photograph. **2** photographer. **3** photographic. **4** photography.

photogelatine process (ˌfəʊtəʊ'dʒelətiːn) *n* another name for **collotype** (sense 1).

photogene ('fəʊtəʊˌdʒiːn) *n* another name for **afterimage.** [C19: from Greek *phōtogenēs* light-produced. See PHOTO-, -GENE]

photogenic (ˌfəʊtə'dʒenɪk) *adj* **1** (esp. of a person) having features, colouring, and a general facial appearance that look attractive in photographs. **2** *Biology.* producing or emitting light: *photogenic bacteria.* ► ˌ**photo'genically** *adv*

photogeology (ˌfəʊtəʊdʒɪ'ɒlədʒɪ) *n* the study and identification of geological phenomena using aerial photographs.

photogram ('fəʊtəˌgræm) *n* **1** a picture, usually abstract, produced on a photographic material without the use of a camera, as by placing an object on the material and exposing to light. **2** *Obsolete.* a photograph, often of the more artistic kind rather than a mechanical record.

photogrammetry (ˌfəʊtəʊ'græmɪtrɪ) *n* the process of making measurements from photographs, used esp. in the construction of maps from aerial photographs and also in military intelligence, medical and industrial research, etc. ► **photogrammetric** (ˌfəʊtəʊgrə'metrɪk) *adj* ► ˌ**photo'grammetrist** *n*

photograph ('fəʊtəˌgrɑːf, -ˌgræf) *n* **1** an image of an object, person, scene, etc., in the form of a print or slide recorded by a camera on photosensitive material. Often shortened to **photo.** ◆ *vb* **2** to take a photograph of (an object, person, scene, etc.).

photographer (fə'tɒgrəfə) *n* a person who takes photographs, either as a hobby or a profession.

photographic (ˌfəʊtə'græfɪk) *adj* **1** of or relating to photography: *a photographic society; photographic materials.* **2** like a photograph in accuracy or detail. **3** (of a person's memory) able to retain facts, appearances, etc., in precise detail, often after only a very short view of or exposure to them. ► ˌ**photo'graphically** *adv*

photography (fə'tɒgrəfɪ) *n* **1** the process of recording images on sensitized material by the action of light, X-rays, etc., and the chemical processing of this material to produce a print, slide, or cine film. **2** the art, practice, or occupation of taking and printing photographs, making cine films, etc.

photogravure (ˌfəʊtəʊgrə'vjʊə) *n* **1** any of various methods in which an intaglio plate for printing is produced by the use of photography. **2** matter printed from such a plate. ◆ Former name: **heliogravure.** [C19: from PHOTO- + French *gravure* engraving]

photojournalism (ˌfəʊtəʊ'dʒɜːnᵊˌlɪzəm) *n* journalism in which photographs are the predominant feature. ► ˌ**photo'journalist** *n* ► ˌ**photoˌjournal'istic** *adj*

photokinesis (ˌfəʊtəʊkɪ'niːsɪs, -kaɪ-) *n Biology.* the movement of an organism in response to the stimulus of light. ▸ **photokinetic** (ˌfəʊtəʊkɪˈnɛtɪk, -kaɪ-) *adj* ▸ **ˌphotokiˈnetically** *adv*

photolithograph (ˌfəʊtəʊˈlɪθəˌgrɑːf, -ˌgræf) *n* **1** a picture printed by photolithography. ◆ *vb* **2** (*tr*) to reproduce (pictures, text, etc.) by photolithography.

photolithography (ˌfəʊtəʊlɪˈθɒgrəfɪ) *n* **1** a lithographic printing process using photographically made plates. Often shortened to **photolitho** (ˌfəʊtəʊˈlaɪθəʊ). **2** *Electronics.* a process used in the manufacture of semiconductor devices, thin-film circuits, and printed circuits in which a particular pattern is transferred from a photograph onto a substrate, producing a pattern that acts as a mask during an etching or diffusion process. See also **planar process.** ▸ **ˌphotoliˈthographer** *n* ▸ **photolithographic** (ˌfəʊtəʊˌlɪθəˈgræfɪk) *adj* ▸ **ˌphotoˌlithoˈgraphically** *adv*

photoluminescence (ˌfəʊtəʊˌluːmɪˈnɛsəns) *n* luminescence resulting from the absorption of light or infrared or ultraviolet radiation. ▸ **ˌphotoˌlumiˈnescent** *adj*

photolysis (fəʊˈtɒlɪsɪs) *n* chemical decomposition caused by light or other electromagnetic radiation. Compare **radiolysis.** ▸ **photolytic** (ˌfəʊtəʊˈlɪtɪk) *adj*

photom. *abbrev. for* photometry.

photomap (ˈfəʊtəʊˌmæp) *n* **1** a map constructed by adding grid lines, place names, etc., to one or more aerial photographs. ◆ *vb* **-maps, -mapping, -mapped. 2** (*tr*) to map (an area) using aerial photography.

photomechanical (ˌfəʊtəʊmɪˈkænɪk^əl) *adj* **1** of or relating to any of various methods by which printing plates are made using photography. ◆ *n* **2** a final paste-up of artwork or typeset matter or both for photographing and processing into a printing plate. Often shortened to **mechanical.** ▸ **ˌphotomeˈchanically** *adv*

photomechanical transfer *n* a method of producing photographic prints or offset printing plates from paper negatives by a chemical transfer process rather than by exposure to light.

photometer (fəʊˈtɒmɪtə) *n* an instrument used in photometry, usually one that compares the illumination produced by a particular light source with that produced by a standard source. See also **spectrophotometer.**

photometry (fəʊˈtɒmɪtrɪ) *n* **1** the measurement of the intensity of light. **2** the branch of physics concerned with such measurements. ▸ **photometric** (ˌfəʊtəˈmɛtrɪk) *adj* ▸ **ˌphotoˈmetrically** *adv* ▸ **phoˈtometrist** *n*

photomicrograph (ˌfəʊtəʊˈmaɪkrəˌgrɑːf, -ˌgræf) *n* **1** a photograph of a microscope image. Sometimes called **microphotograph. 2** a less common name for **microphotograph** (sense 1). ▸ **photomicrographer** (ˌfəʊtəʊmaɪˈkrɒgrəfə) *n* ▸ **photomicrographic** (ˌfəʊtəʊˌmaɪkrəˈgræfɪk) *adj* ▸ **ˌphotoˌmicroˈgraphically** *adv* ▸ **ˌphotomiˈcrography** *n*

photomontage (ˌfəʊtəʊmɒnˈtɑːʒ) *n* **1** the technique of producing a composite picture by combining several photographs: used esp. in advertising. **2** the composite picture so produced.

photomosaic (ˌfəʊtəʊməˈzeɪɪk) *n* a large-scale detailed picture made up of many photographs. See also **mosaic** (sense 5).

photomultiplier (ˌfəʊtəʊˈmʌltɪˌplaɪə) *n* a device sensitive to electromagnetic radiation, consisting of a photocathode, from which electrons are released by incident photons, and an electron multiplier, which amplifies and produces a detectable pulse of current.

photomural (ˌfəʊtəʊˈmjʊərəl) *n* a decoration covering all or part of a wall consisting of a single enlarged photograph or a montage.

photon (ˈfəʊtɒn) *n* a quantum of electromagnetic radiation, regarded as a particle with zero rest mass and charge, unit spin, and energy equal to the product of the frequency of the radiation and the Planck constant.

photonasty (ˈfəʊtəʊˌnæstɪ) *n, pl* **-ties.** *Botany.* a nastic movement in response to a change in light intensity. ▸ **ˌphotoˈnastic** *adj*

photonegative (ˌfəʊtəʊˈnɛgətɪv) *adj Physics.* (of a material) having an electrical conductivity that decreases with increasing illumination.

photoneutron (ˌfəʊtəʊˈnjuːtrɒn) *n* a neutron emitted from a nucleus as a result of photodisintegration.

photonics (fəʊˈtɒnɪks) *n (functioning as sing)* the study and design of devices and systems, such as optical fibres, that depend on the transmission, modulation, or amplification of streams of photons.

photonuclear (ˌfəʊtəʊˈnjuːklɪə) *adj Physics.* of or concerned with a nuclear reaction caused by a photon.

photo-offset *n Printing.* an offset process in which the plates are produced photomechanically.

photo opportunity *n* an opportunity, either preplanned or accidental, for the press to photograph a politician, celebrity, or event.

photoperiod (ˌfəʊtəʊˈpɪərɪəd) *n* the period of daylight in every 24 hours, esp. in relation to its effects on plants and animals. See also **photoperiodism.** ▸ **ˌphotoˌperiˈodic** *adj* ▸ **ˌphotoˌperiˈodically** *adv*

photoperiodism (ˌfəʊtəʊˈpɪərɪəˌdɪzəm) *n* the response of plants and animals by behaviour, growth, etc., to photoperiods.

photophilous (fəʊˈtɒfələs) *adj* (esp. of plants) growing best in strong light. ▸ **phoˈtophily** *n*

photophobia (ˌfəʊtəʊˈfəʊbɪə) *n* **1** *Pathol.* abnormal sensitivity of the eyes to light, esp. as the result of inflammation. **2** *Psychiatry.* abnormal fear of or aversion to sunlight or well-lit places. ▸ **ˌphotoˈphobic** *adj*

photophore (ˈfəʊtəˌfɔː) *n Zoology.* any light-producing organ in animals, esp. in certain fishes.

photopia (fəʊˈtəʊpɪə) *n* the normal adaptation of the eye to light; day vision. [C20: New Latin, from PHOTO- + -OPIA] ▸ **photopic** (fəʊˈtɒpɪk, -ˈtəʊ-) *adj*

photopolymer (ˌfəʊtəʊˈpɒlɪmə) *n* a polymeric material that is sensitive to light: used in printing plates, microfilms, etc.

photopositive (ˌfəʊtəʊˈpɒzɪtɪv) *adj Physics.* (of a material) having an electrical conductivity that increases with increasing illumination.

photorealism (ˌfəʊtəʊˈrɪəˌlɪzəm) *n* a style of painting and sculpture that depicts esp. commonplace urban images with meticulously accurate detail. ▸ **ˌphotoˈrealist** *n, adj*

photoreceptor (ˌfəʊtəʊrɪˈsɛptə) *n Zoology, physiol.* a light-sensitive cell or organ that conveys impulses through the sensory neuron connected to it.

photoreconnaissance (ˌfəʊtəʊrɪˈkɒnɪsəns) *n Chiefly military.* reconnaissance from the air by camera.

photo relief *n* a method of showing the configuration of the relief of an area by photographing a model of it that is illuminated by a lamp in the northwest corner.

photosensitive (ˌfəʊtəʊˈsɛnsɪtɪv) *adj* sensitive to electromagnetic radiation, esp. light: *a photosensitive photographic film.* ▸ **ˌphotoˌsensiˈtivity** *n*

photosensitize *or* **photosensitise** (ˌfəʊtəʊˈsɛnsɪˌtaɪz) *vb* (*tr*) to make (an organism or substance) photosensitive. ▸ **ˌphotoˌsensitiˈzation** *or* **ˌphotoˌsensitiˈsation** *n*

photoset (ˈfəʊtəʊˌsɛt) *vb* **-sets, -setting, -set.** (*tr*) to set (type matter) by photosetting. ▸ **ˈphotoˌsetter** *n*

photosetting (ˈfəʊtəʊˌsɛtɪŋ) *n Printing.* another word for **photocomposition.**

photosphere (ˈfəʊtəʊˌsfɪə) *n* the visible surface of the sun. ▸ **photospheric** (ˌfəʊtəʊˈsfɛrɪk) *adj*

photostat (ˈfəʊtəʊˌstæt) *n* **1** a machine or process used to make quick positive or negative photographic copies of written, printed, or graphic matter. **2** any copy made by such a machine. ◆ *vb* **-stats, -statting** *or* **-stating, -statted** *or* **-stated. 3** to make a photostat copy (of). ▸ **ˌphotoˈstatic** *adj*

photosynthate (ˌfəʊtəʊˈsɪnˌθeɪt) *n* any substance synthesized in photosynthesis, esp. a sugar.

photosynthesis (ˌfəʊtəʊˈsɪnθɪsɪs) *n* **1** (in plants) the synthesis of organic compounds from carbon dioxide and water (with the release of oxygen) using light energy absorbed by chlorophyll. **2** the corresponding process in certain bacteria. ▸ **photosynthetic** (ˌfəʊtəʊsɪnˈθɛtɪk) *adj* ▸ **ˌphotosynˈthetically** *adv*

photosynthesize *or* **photosynthesise** (ˌfəʊtəʊˈsɪnθɪˌsaɪz) *vb* (of plants and some bacteria) to carry out photosynthesis.

photosystem (ˈfəʊtəʊˌsɪstəm) *n Botany.* either of two pigment-containing systems, photosystem I or II, in which the light-dependent chemical reactions of photosynthesis occur in the chloroplasts of plants.

phototaxis (ˌfəʊtəʊˈtæksɪs) *or* **phototaxy** *n* the movement of an entire organism in response to light. ▸ **phototactic** (ˌfəʊtəʊˈtæktɪk) *adj*

phototherapy (ˌfəʊtəʊˈθɛrəpɪ) *or* **phototherapeutics** (ˌfəʊtəʊˌθɛrəˈpjuːtɪks) *n (functioning as sing)* the use of light in the treatment of disease. ▸ **ˌphotoˌtheraˈpeutic** *adj* ▸ **ˌphotoˌtheraˈpeutically** *adv*

photothermic (ˌfəʊtəʊˈθɜːmɪk) *or* **photothermal** *adj* of or concerned with light and heat, esp. the production of heat by light. ▸ **ˌphotoˈthermically** *or* **ˌphotoˈthermally** *adv*

phototonus (fəʊˈtɒtənəs) *n* the condition of plants that enables them to respond to the stimulus of light. [C19: from PHOTO- + Greek *tonos* TONE] ▸ **phototonic** (ˌfəʊtəʊˈtɒnɪk) *adj*

phototopography (ˌfəʊtəʊtəˈpɒgrəfɪ) *n* the preparation of topographic maps from photographs.

phototransistor (ˌfəʊtəʊtrænˈzɪstə) *n* a junction transistor, whose base signal is generated by illumination of the base. The emitter current, and hence collector current, increases with the intensity of the light.

phototroph (ˈfəʊtəʊˌtrɒf) *n* an organism that obtains energy from sunlight for the synthesis of organic compounds. ▸ **phototrophic** (ˌfəʊtəʊˈtrɒfɪk) *adj*

phototropism (ˌfəʊtəʊˈtrəʊpɪzəm) *n* **1** the growth response of plant parts to the stimulus of light, producing a bending towards the light source. **2** the response of animals to light: sometimes used as another word for **phototaxis.** ▸ **ˌphotoˈtropic** *adj*

phototropy (ˌfəʊtəʊˈtrəʊpɪ) *n Chem.* **1** an alteration in the colour of certain substances as a result of being exposed to light of different wavelengths. **2** the reversible loss of colour of certain dyestuffs when illuminated at a particular wavelength.

phototube (ˈfəʊtəʊˌtjuːb) *n* a type of photocell in which radiation falling on a photocathode causes electrons to flow to an anode and thus produce an electric current.

phototype (ˈfəʊtəʊˌtaɪp) *Printing.* ◆ *n* **1a** a printing plate produced by photography. **1b** a print produced from such a plate. ◆ *vb* **2** (*tr*) to reproduce (an illustration) using a phototype. ▸ **phototypic** (ˌfəʊtəʊˈtɪpɪk) *adj* ▸ **ˌphotoˈtypically** *adv*

phototypeset (ˌfəʊtəʊˈtaɪpˌsɛt) *vb* **-sets, -setting, -set.** (*tr*) to set (type matter) by phototypesetting.

phototypesetting (ˌfəʊtəʊˈtaɪpˌsɛtɪŋ) *n Printing.* another word for **photocomposition.**

phototypography (ˌfəʊtəʊtaɪˈpɒgrəfɪ) *n* any printing process involving the use of photography. ▸ **phototypographical** (ˌfəʊtəʊˌtaɪpəˈgræfɪk^əl) *adj* ▸ **ˌphotoˌtypoˈgraphically** *adv*

photovoltaic (ˌfəʊtəʊvɒlˈteɪɪk) *adj* of, concerned with, or producing electric current or voltage caused by electromagnetic radiation.

photovoltaic effect *n* the effect observed when electromagnetic radiation falls on a thin film of one solid deposited on the surface of a dissimilar solid producing a difference in potential between the two materials.

photozincography (ˌfəʊtəʊzɪŋˈkɒgrəfɪ) *n* a photoengraving process using a printing plate made of zinc. ▸ **photozincograph** (ˌfəʊtəʊˈzɪŋkəˌgrɑːf, -ˌgræf) *n*

phr. *abbrev. for* phrase.

phrasal (ˈfreɪz^əl) *adj* of, relating to, or composed of phrases. ▸ **ˈphrasally** *adv*

phrasal verb *n* (in English grammar) a phrase that consists of a verb plus an adverbial or prepositional particle, esp. one the meaning of which cannot be deduced by analysis of the meaning of the constituents: *"take in" meaning "deceive" is a phrasal verb.*

phrase (freɪz) *n* **1** a group of words forming an immediate syntactic constituent of a clause. Compare **clause** (sense 1), **noun phrase, verb phrase. 2** a particular expression, esp. an original one. **3** *Music.* a small group of notes forming a coherent unit of melody. **4** (in choreography) a short sequence of dance movements. ◆ *vb (tr)* **5** *Music.* to divide (a melodic line, part, etc.) into musical phrases, esp. in performance. **6** to express orally or in a phrase. **[C16:** from Latin *phrasis,* from Greek: speech, from *phrazein* to declare, tell**]**

phrase book *n* a book containing frequently used expressions and their equivalents in a foreign language, esp. for the use of tourists.

phrase marker *n Linguistics.* a representation, esp. one in the form of a tree diagram, of the constituent structure of a sentence.

phraseogram ('freɪzɪəˌgræm) *n* a symbol representing a phrase, as in shorthand.

phraseograph ('freɪzɪəˌgrɑːf) *n* a phrase for which there exists a phraseogram. ▸ **phraseographic** (ˌfreɪzɪə'græfɪk) *adj* ▸ **phraseography** (ˌfreɪzɪ'ɒgrəfɪ) *n*

phraseologist (ˌfreɪzɪ'ɒlədʒɪst) *n* a person who is interested in or collects phrases or who affects a particular phraseology.

phraseology (ˌfreɪzɪ'ɒlədʒɪ) *n, pl* **-gies. 1** the manner in which words or phrases are used. **2** a set of phrases used by a particular group of people. ▸ **phraseological** (ˌfreɪzɪə'lɒdʒɪkᵊl) *adj* ▸ **ˌphraseo'logically** *adv*

phrase-structure grammar *n* a grammar in which relations among the words and morphemes of a sentence are described, but not deeper or semantic relations. Abbrev.: **PSG.** Compare **transformational grammar.**

phrase-structure rule *n Generative grammar.* a rule of the form A → X where A is a syntactic category label, such as *noun phrase* or *sentence,* and X is a sequence of such labels and/or morphemes, expressing the fact that A can be replaced by X in generating the constituent structure of a sentence. Also called: **rewrite rule.** Compare **transformational rule.**

phrasing ('freɪzɪŋ) *n* **1** the way in which something is expressed, esp. in writing; wording. **2** *Music.* the division of a melodic line, part, etc., into musical phrases.

phratry ('freɪtrɪ) *n, pl* **-tries.** *Anthropol.* a group of people within a tribe who have a common ancestor. **[C19:** from Greek *phratria* clan, from *phratēr* fellow clansman; compare Latin *frāter* brother**]** ▸ **'phratric** *adj*

phreatic (frɪ'ætɪk) *adj Geography.* of or relating to ground water occurring below the water table. Compare **vadose. [C19:** from Greek *phrear* a well**]**

phreatophyte (frɪ'ætəfaɪt) *n* a plant having very long roots that reach down to the water table or the layer above it. **[C20:** from Greek *phrear* a well + -PHYTE**]**

phren. *or* **phrenol.** *abbrev. for* phrenology.

phrenetic (frɪ'netɪk) *adj* an obsolete spelling of **frenetic.** ▸ **phre'netically** *adv* ▸ **phre'neticness** *n*

phrenic ('frenɪk) *adj* **1a** of or relating to the diaphragm. **1b** *(as n): the phrenic.* **2** *Obsolete.* of or relating to the mind. **[C18:** from New Latin *phrenicus,* from Greek *phrēn* mind, diaphragm**]**

phrenitis (frɪ'naɪtɪs) *n Rare.* **1** another name for **encephalitis. 2** a state of frenzy; delirium. **[C17:** via Late Latin from Greek: delirium, from *phrēn* mind, diaphragm + -ITIS**]** ▸ **phrenitic** (frɪ'nɪtɪk) *adj*

phreno- *or before a vowel* **phren-** *combining form.* **1** mind or brain: *phrenology.* **2** of or relating to the diaphragm: *phrenic.* **[**from Greek *phrēn* mind, diaphragm**]**

phrenology (frɪ'nɒlədʒɪ) *n* (formerly) the branch of science concerned with localization of function in the human brain, esp. determination of the strength of the faculties by the shape and size of the skull overlying the parts of the brain thought to be responsible for them. ▸ **phrenological** (ˌfrenə'lɒdʒɪkᵊl) *adj* ▸ **phre'nologist** *n*

phrensy ('frenzɪ) *n, pl* **-sies,** *vb* an obsolete spelling of **frenzy.**

Phrixus ('frɪksəs) *n Greek myth.* the son of Athamas and Nephele who escaped the wrath of his father's mistress, Ino, by flying to Colchis on a winged ram with a golden fleece. See also **Helle, Golden Fleece.**

Phrygia ('frɪdʒɪə) *n* an ancient country of W central Asia Minor.

Phrygian ('frɪdʒɪən) *adj* **1** of or relating to ancient Phrygia, its inhabitants, or their extinct language. **2** *Music.* of or relating to an authentic mode represented by the natural diatonic scale from E to E. See **Hypo-. 3** *Music.* (of a cadence) denoting a progression that leads a piece of music out of the major key and ends on the dominant chord of the relative minor key. ◆ *n* **4** a native or inhabitant of ancient Phrygia. **5** an ancient language of Phrygia, belonging to the Thraco-Phrygian branch of the Indo-European family: recorded in a few inscriptions.

Phrygian cap *n* a conical cap of soft material worn during ancient times that became a symbol of liberty during the French Revolution.

Phryne ('fraɪnɪ) *n,* real name *Muesarete.* 4th century B.C., Greek courtesan; lover of Praxiteles and model for Apelles' painting *Aphrodite Rising from the Waves.*

PHS (in the U.S.) *abbrev. for* Public Health Service.

phthalein ('θeɪliːn, -lɪɪn, 'θæl-, 'fθæl-) *n* any of a class of organic compounds obtained by the reaction of phthalic anhydride with a phenol and used in dyes. **[C19:** from *phthal-,* shortened form of NAPHTHALENE + -IN**]**

phthalic acid ('θælɪk, 'fθæl-) *n* a soluble colourless crystalline acid used in the synthesis of dyes and perfumes; 1,2-benzenedicarboxylic acid. Formula: $C_6H_4(COOH)_2$. **[C19** *phthalic,* from *phthal-* (see PHTHALEIN) + -IC**]**

phthalic anhydride *n* a white crystalline substance used mainly in producing dyestuffs. Formula: $C_6H_4(CO)_2O$.

phthalocyanine (ˌθæləʊ'saɪəˌniːn, ˌθeɪ-, ˌfθæl-) *n* **1** a cyclic blue-green organic pigment. Formula: $(C_6H_4C_2N)_4N_4$. **2** any of a class of compounds derived by coordination of this compound with a metal atom. They are blue or green pigments used in printing inks, plastics, and enamels. **[C20:** from *phthal-* (see PHTHALEIN) + CYANINE**]**

phthiriasis (θɪ'raɪəsɪs) *n Pathol.* the state or condition of being infested with lice; pediculosis. **[C16:** via Latin from Greek, from *phtheir* louse**]**

phthisic ('θaɪsɪk, 'fθaɪsɪk, 'taɪsɪk) *Obsolete.* ◆ *adj* **1** relating to or affected with phthisis. ◆ *n* **2** another name for **asthma. [C14:** from Old French *tisike,* from Latin *phthisicus,* from Greek *phthisikos;* see PHTHISIS**]** ▸ **'phthisical** *adj*

phthisis ('θaɪsɪs, 'fθaɪ-, 'taɪ-) *n* any disease that causes wasting of the body, esp. pulmonary tuberculosis. **[C16:** via Latin from Greek: a wasting away, from *phthinein* to waste away**]**

Phuket (ˌpuː'ket) *n* **1** an island and province of S Thailand, in the Andaman Sea: mainly flat. Area: 534 sq. km (206 sq. miles). **2** the chief town of the island of Phuket; a popular tourist resort.

phut (fʌt) *Informal.* ◆ *n* **1** a representation of a muffled explosive sound. ◆ *adv* **2 go phut.** to break down or collapse. **[C19:** of imitative origin**]**

phyco- *combining form.* seaweed: *phycology.* **[**from Greek *phukos***]**

phycobilin (ˌfaɪkəʊ'baɪlɪn) *n Biology.* any of a class of red or blue-green pigments found in the red algae and cyanobacteria.

phycobiont (ˌfaɪkəʊ'baɪɒnt) *n Botany.* the algal constituent of a lichen. Compare **mycobiont.**

phycology (faɪ'kɒlədʒɪ) *n* the study of algae. ▸ **phycological** (ˌfaɪkə'lɒdʒɪkᵊl) *adj* ▸ **phy'cologist** *n*

phycomycete (ˌfaɪkəʊ'maɪsiːt) *n* any of a primitive group of fungi, formerly included in the class *Phycomycetes* but now classified in different phyla: includes certain mildews and moulds. ▸ **ˌphycomy'cetous** *adj*

Phyfe *or* **Fife** (faɪf) *n* **Duncan.** ?1768–1854, U.S. cabinet-maker, born in Scotland.

phyla ('faɪlə) *n* the plural of **phylum.**

phylactery (fɪ'læktərɪ) *n, pl* **-teries. 1** *Judaism.* (*usually pl*) Also called: **Tefillah.** either of the pair of blackened square cases containing parchments inscribed with biblical passages, bound by leather thongs to the head and left arm, and worn by Jewish men during weekday morning prayers. **2** a reminder or aid to remembering. **3** *Archaic.* an amulet or charm. **[C14:** from Late Latin *phylactērium,* from Greek *phulaktērion* outpost, from *phulax* a guard**]**

phyle ('faɪlɪ) *n, pl* **-lae** (-liː). a tribe or clan of an ancient Greek people such as the Ionians. **[C19:** from Greek *phulē* tribe, clan**]** ▸ **'phylic** *adj*

phyletic (faɪ'letɪk) *or* **phylogenetic** (ˌfaɪləʊdʒɪ'netɪk) *adj* of or relating to the evolutionary development of organisms. **[C19:** from Greek *phuletikos* tribal**]** ▸ **phy'letically** *or* **ˌphyloge'netically** *adv*

-phyll *or* **-phyl** *n combining form.* leaf: *chlorophyll.* **[**from Greek *phullon***]**

phyllid ('fɪlɪd) *n Botany.* the leaf of a liverwort or moss.

phyllite ('fɪlaɪt) *n* a compact lustrous metamorphic rock, rich in mica, derived from a clay rock. **[C19:** from PHYLL(O)- + -ITE[1]**]** ▸ **phyllitic** (fɪ'lɪtɪk) *adj*

phyllo ('fɪləʊ) *n* a variant of **filo. [C20:** from Greek: leaf**]**

phyllo- *or before a vowel* **phyll-** *combining form.* leaf: *phyllopod.* **[**from Greek *phullon* leaf**]**

phylloclade ('fɪləʊˌkleɪd) *or* **phylloclad** ('fɪləʊˌklæd) *n* other names for **cladode. [C19:** from New Latin *phyllocladium,* from PHYLLO- + Greek *klados* branch**]**

phyllode ('fɪləʊd) *n* a flattened leafstalk that resembles and functions as a leaf. **[C19:** from New Latin *phyllodium,* from Greek *phullōdēs* leaflike**]** ▸ **phyl'lodial** *adj*

phylloid ('fɪlɔɪd) *adj* resembling a leaf.

phyllome ('fɪləʊm) *n* a leaf or a leaflike organ. ▸ **phyllomic** (fɪ'lɒmɪk, -'ləʊ-) *adj*

phylloplane ('fɪləʊˌpleɪn) *n Ecology.* the surface of a leaf considered as a habitat, esp. for microorganisms. Also called: **phyllosphere.**

phylloquinone (ˌfɪləʊkwɪ'nəʊn) *n* a viscous fat-soluble liquid occurring in plants: essential for the production of prothrombin, required in blood clotting. Formula: $C_{31}H_{46}O_2$. Also called: **vitamin K_1.**

phyllosilicate (ˌfɪləʊ'sɪlɪkeɪt) *n* any of a class of silicate minerals, including talc, consisting of thin sheets.

phyllosphere ('fɪləʊˌsfɪə) *n* another name for **phylloplane.**

phyllotaxis (ˌfɪlə'tæksɪs) *or* **phyllotaxy** *n, pl* **-taxes** (-'tæksiːz) *or* **-taxies. 1** the arrangement of the leaves on a stem. **2** the study of this arrangement in different plants. ▸ **ˌphyllo'tactic** *adj*

-phyllous *adj combining form.* having leaves of a specified number or type: *monophyllous.* **[**from Greek *-phullos* of a leaf**]**

phylloxera (ˌfɪlɒk'sɪərə, fɪ'lɒksərə) *n, pl* **-rae** (-riː) *or* **-ras.** any homopterous insect of the genus *Phylloxera,* such as *P. vitifolia* (or *Viteus vitifolii*) (**vine phylloxera**), typically feeding on plant juices, esp. of vines: family *Phylloxeridae.* **[C19:** New Latin, from PHYLLO- + *xēros* dry**]**

phylo- *or before a vowel* **phyl-** *combining form.* tribe; race; phylum: *phylogeny.* **[**from Greek *phulon* race**]**

phylogeny (faɪ'lɒdʒɪnɪ) *or* **phylogenesis** (ˌfaɪləʊ'dʒenɪsɪs) *n, pl* **-nies** *or* **-geneses** (-'dʒenɪˌsiːz). *Biology.* the sequence of events involved in the evolution of a species, genus, etc. Compare **ontogeny. [C19:** from PHYLO- + -GENY**]** ▸ **phylogenic** (ˌfaɪləʊ'dʒenɪk) *or* **phylogenetic** (ˌfaɪləʊdʒɪ'netɪk) *adj*

phylum ('faɪləm) *n, pl* **-la** (-lə). **1** a major taxonomic division of living organisms that contain one or more classes. An example is the phylum *Arthropoda* (insects, crustaceans, arachnids, etc., and myriapods). **2** any analogous group, such as a group of related language families or linguistic stocks. **[C19:** New Latin, from Greek *phulon* race**]**

phys. *abbrev. for:* **1** physical. **2** physician. **3** physics. **4** physiological. **5** physiology.

physalis (faɪ'seɪlɪs) *n* See **Chinese lantern, strawberry tomato. [**New Latin, from Greek *physallis* a bladder (from the form of the calyx)**]**

physiatrics (ˌfɪzɪ'ætrɪks) *n* (*functioning as sing*) *Med., U.S.* another name for **physiotherapy. [C19:** from PHYSIO- + -IATRICS**]** ▸ **ˌphysi'atric** *or* **ˌphysi'atrical** *adj*

physic ('fɪzɪk) *n* **1** *Rare.* a medicine or drug, esp. a cathartic or purge. **2** *Archaic.* the art or skill of healing. **3** an archaic term for **physics** (sense 1). ◆ *vb* **-ics, -icking, -icked.** **4** (*tr*) *Archaic.* to treat (a patient) with medicine. [C13: from Old French *fisique,* via Latin, from Greek *phusikē,* from *phusis* nature] ▸ **'physicky** *adj*

physical ('fɪzɪkᵊl) *adj* **1** of or relating to the body, as distinguished from the mind or spirit. **2** of, relating to, or resembling material things or nature: *the physical universe.* **3** involving or requiring bodily contact: *rugby is a physical sport.* **4** of or concerned with matter and energy. **5** of or relating to physics. **6** perceptible to the senses; apparent: *a physical manifestation.* ◆ *n* **7** short for **physical examination.** ◆ See also **physicals.** ▸ **'physically** *adv* ▸ **'physicalness** *n*

physical anthropology *n* the branch of anthropology dealing with the genetic aspect of human development and its physical variations.

physical chemistry *n* the branch of chemistry concerned with the way in which the physical properties of substances depend on and influence their chemical structure, properties, and reactions.

physical education *n* training and practice in sports, gymnastics, etc., as in schools and colleges. Abbrev.: **PE.**

physical examination *n Med.* the process of examining the body by means of sight, touch, percussion, or auscultation to diagnose disease or verify fitness.

physical geography *n* the branch of geography that deals with the natural features of the earth's surface.

physical handicap *n* loss of or failure to develop a specific bodily function or functions, whether of movement, sensation, coordination, or speech, but excluding mental impairments or disabilities. ▸ **physically handicapped** *adj*

physicalism ('fɪzɪkᵊ,lɪzəm) *n Philosophy.* the doctrine that all phenomena can be described in terms of space and time and that all meaningful statements are either analytic, as in logic and mathematics, or can be reduced to empirically verifiable assertions. See also **logical positivism, identity theory.** ▸ **'physicalist** *n, adj* ▸ **,physical'istic** *adj*

physicality (,fɪzɪ'kælɪtɪ) *n* **1** the state or quality of being physical. **2** the physical characteristics of a person, object, etc.

physical jerks *pl n Brit. informal.* See **jerk**[1] (sense 6).

physical medicine *n* the branch of medicine devoted to the management of physical disabilities, as resulting from rheumatic disease, asthma, poliomyelitis, etc. See also **rehabilitation** (sense 2).

physicals ('fɪzɪkᵊlz) *pl n Commerce.* commodities that can be purchased and used, as opposed to those bought and sold in a futures market. Also called: **actuals.**

physical science *n* any of the sciences concerned with nonliving matter, energy, and the physical properties of the universe, such as physics, chemistry, astronomy, and geology. Compare **life science.**

physical therapy *n* another term for **physiotherapy.**

physician (fɪ'zɪʃən) *n* **1** a person legally qualified to practise medicine, esp. one specializing in areas of treatment other than surgery; doctor of medicine. **2** *Archaic.* any person who treats diseases; healer. [C13: from Old French *fisicien,* from *fisique* PHYSIC]

physicist ('fɪzɪsɪst) *n* a person versed in or studying physics.

physicochemical (,fɪzɪkəʊ'kemɪkᵊl) *adj* of, concerned with, or relating to physical chemistry or both physics and chemistry. ▸ **,physico'chemically** *adv*

physics ('fɪzɪks) *n* (*functioning as sing*) **1** the branch of science concerned with the properties of matter and energy and the relationships between them. It is based on mathematics and traditionally includes mechanics, optics, electricity and magnetism, acoustics, and heat. Modern physics, based on quantum theory, includes atomic, nuclear, particle, and solid-state studies. It can also embrace applied fields such as geophysics and meteorology. **2** physical properties of behaviour: *the physics of the electron.* **3** *Archaic.* natural science or natural philosophy. [C16: from Latin *physica,* translation of Greek *ta phusika* natural things, from *phusis* nature]

physio ('fɪzɪəʊ) *n Informal.* short for **physiotherapy.**

physio- *or before a vowel* **phys-** *combining form.* **1** of or relating to nature or natural functions: *physiology.* **2** physical: *physiotherapy.* [from Greek *phusio,* from *phusis* nature, from *phuein* to make grow]

physiocrat ('fɪzɪəʊ,kræt) *n* a follower of Quesnay's doctrines of government, believing that the inherent natural order governing society was based on land and its natural products as the only true form of wealth. [C18: from French *physiocrate;* see PHYSIO-, -CRAT] ▸ **physiocracy** (,fɪzɪ'ɒkrəsɪ) *n* ▸ **,physio'cratic** *adj*

physiognomy (,fɪzɪ'ɒnəmɪ) *n* **1** a person's features or characteristic expression considered as an indication of personality. **2** the art or practice of judging character from facial features. **3** the outward appearance of something, esp. the physical characteristics of a geographical region. [C14: from Old French *phisonomie,* via Medieval Latin, from Late Greek *phusiognōmia,* erroneous for Greek *phusiognōmonia,* from *phusis* nature + *gnōmōn* judge] ▸ **physiognomic** (,fɪzɪə'nɒmɪk) *or* **,physiog'nomical** *adj* ▸ **,physiog'nomically** *adv* ▸ **,physi'ognomist** *n*

physiography (,fɪzɪ'ɒgrəfɪ) *n* another name for **geomorphology** or **physical geography.** ▸ **,physi'ographer** *n* ▸ **physiographic** (,fɪzɪə'græfɪk) *or* **,physio'graphical** *adj* ▸ **,physio'graphically** *adv*

physiol. *abbrev. for:* **1** physiological. **2** physiology.

physiological (,fɪzɪə'lɒdʒɪkᵊl) *adj* **1** of or relating to physiology. **2** of or relating to normal healthful functioning; not pathological. ▸ **,physio'logically** *adv*

physiological psychology *n* the branch of psychology concerned with the study and correlation of physiological and psychological events.

physiology (,fɪzɪ'ɒlədʒɪ) *n* **1** the branch of science concerned with the functioning of organisms. **2** the processes and functions of all or part of an organism. [C16: from Latin *physiologia,* from Greek] ▸ **,physi'ologist** *n*

physiotherapy (,fɪzɪəʊ'θɛrəpɪ) *n* the therapeutic use of physical agents or means, such as massage, exercises, etc. Also called: **physical therapy,** (Informal) **physio,** (U.S.) **physiatrics.** ▸ **,physio'therapist** *n*

physique (fɪ'ziːk) *n* the general appearance of the body with regard to size, shape, muscular development, etc. [C19: via French, from *physique* (adj) natural, from Latin *physicus* physical]

physoclistous (,faɪsəʊ'klɪstəs) *adj* (of fishes) having an air bladder that is not connected to the alimentary canal. Compare **physostomous.** [C19: from Greek *phusa* bladder + *-clistous,* from *kleistos* closed]

physostigmine (,faɪsəʊ'stɪgmiːn) *or* **physostigmin** (,faɪsəʊ'stɪgmɪn) *n* an alkaloid found in the Calabar bean used esp. in eye drops to reduce pressure inside the eyeball. Formula: $C_{15}H_{21}N_3O_2$. Also called: **eserine.** [C19: from New Latin *Physostigma* genus name, from Greek *phusa* bladder + *stigma* mark]

physostomous (faɪ'sɒstəməs) *adj* (of fishes) having a duct connecting the air bladder to part of the alimentary canal. Compare **physoclistous.** [C19: from Greek *phusa* bladder + *-stomous,* from *stoma* mouth]

-phyte *n combining form.* indicating a plant of a specified type or habitat: *lithophyte; thallophyte.* [from Greek *phuton* plant] ▸ **-phytic** *adj combining form.*

phyto- *or before a vowel* **phyt-** *combining form.* indicating a plant or vegetation: *phytogenesis.* [from Greek *phuton* plant, from *phuein* to make grow]

phytoalexin (,faɪtəʊə'lɛksɪn) *n Botany.* any of a group of substances produced by plants that inhibit the growth of pathogenic fungi that infect them. [C20: from PHYTO- + Greek *alexein* to ward off]

phytochemistry (,faɪtəʊ'kɛmɪstrɪ) *n* the branch of chemistry concerned with plants, their chemical composition and processes. ▸ **,phyto'chemist** *n*

phytochrome ('faɪtəʊ,krəʊm) *n Botany.* a blue-green pigment, present in most plants, that mediates many light-dependent processes, including photoperiodism and the greening of leaves.

phytogenesis (,faɪtəʊ'dʒɛnɪsɪs) *or* **phytogeny** (faɪ'tɒdʒənɪ) *n* the branch of botany concerned with the origin and evolution of plants. ▸ **phytogenetic** (,faɪtəʊdʒɪ'nɛtɪk) *adj* ▸ **,phytoge'netically** *adv*

phytogenic (,faɪtəʊ'dʒɛnɪk) *adj* derived from plants: *coal is a phytogenic substance.*

phytogeography (,faɪtəʊdʒɪ'ɒgrəfɪ) *n* the branch of botany that is concerned with the geographical distribution of plants. ▸ **,phytoge'ographer** *n* ▸ **,phyto,geo'graphic** *or* **,phyto,geo'graphical** *adj*

phytography (faɪ'tɒgrəfɪ) *n* the branch of botany that is concerned with the detailed description of plants. ▸ **phytographic** (,faɪtə'græfɪk) *adj*

phytohormone (,faɪtəʊ'hɔːməʊn) *n* a hormone-like substance produced by a plant.

phytology (faɪ'tɒlədʒɪ) *n* a rare name for **botany** (sense 1). ▸ **phytological** (,faɪtə'lɒdʒɪkᵊl) *adj* ▸ **,phyto'logically** *adv* ▸ **phy'tologist** *n*

phyton ('faɪtɒn) *n* a unit of plant structure, usually considered as the smallest part of the plant that is capable of growth when detached from the parent plant. [C20: from Greek. See -PHYTE]

phytopathology (,faɪtəʊpə'θɒlədʒɪ) *n* the branch of botany concerned with diseases of plants. ▸ **phytopathological** (,faɪtəʊ,pæθə'lɒdʒɪkᵊl) *adj* ▸ **,phytopa'thologist** *n*

phytophagous (faɪ'tɒfəgəs) *adj* (esp. of insects) feeding on plants. ▸ **phytophagy** (faɪ'tɒfədʒɪ) *n*

phytoplankton (,faɪtə'plæŋktən) *n* the photosynthesizing constituent of plankton, mainly unicellular algae. Compare **zooplankton.** ▸ **phytoplanktonic** (,faɪtəplæŋk'tɒnɪk) *adj*

phytosociology (,faɪtəʊ,səʊsɪ'ɒlədʒɪ, -,səʊʃɪ-) *n* the branch of ecology that is concerned with the origin, development, etc., of plant communities. ▸ **phytosociological** (,faɪtəʊ,səʊsɪə'lɒdʒɪkᵊl, -,səʊʃɪə-) *adj* ▸ **,phyto,socio'logically** *adv* ▸ **,phyto,soci'ologist** *n*

phytotoxin (,faɪtə'tɒksɪn) *n* a toxin, such as strychnine, that is produced by a plant. Compare **zootoxin.** ▸ **,phyto'toxic** *adj*

phytotron ('faɪtəʊ,trɒn) *n* a building in which plants can be grown on a large scale, under controlled conditions. [C20: from PHYTO- + -TRON, on the model of CYCLOTRON]

pi[1] (paɪ) *n, pl* **pis.** **1** the 16th letter in the Greek alphabet (Π, π), a consonant, transliterated as *p.* **2** *Maths.* a transcendental number, fundamental to mathematics, that is the ratio of the circumference of a circle to its diameter. Approximate value: 3.141 592...; symbol: π [C18 (mathematical use): representing the first letter of Greek *periphereia* PERIPHERY]

pi[2] *or* **pie** (paɪ) *n, pl* **pies.** **1** a jumbled pile of printer's type. **2** a jumbled mixture. ◆ *vb* **pies, piing, pied** *or* **pies, pieing, pied.** (*tr*) **3** to spill and mix (set type) indiscriminately. **4** to mix up. [C17: of uncertain origin]

pi[3] (paɪ) *adj Brit. slang.* short for **pious** (senses 2, 3).

PI *abbrev. for:* **1** Philippine Islands. **2** private investigator.

Piacenza (*Italian* pja'tʃentsa) *n* a town in N Italy, in Emilia-Romagna on the River Po. Pop.: 101 692 (1994 est.). Latin name: **Placentia** (plə'sɛntʃɪə).

piacular (paɪ'ækjʊlə) *adj* **1** making expiation for a sacrilege. **2** requiring expiation. [C17: from Latin *piāculum* propitiatory sacrifice, from *piāre* to appease]

Piaf (*French* pjaf) *n* **Edith** (edit), real name *Edith Giovanna Gassion,* known as *the Little Sparrow,* 1915–63, French singer.

piaffe (pɪ'æf) *n Dressage.* a passage done on the spot. [C18: from French, from *piaffer* to strut]

Piaget (*French* pjaʒɛ) *n* **Jean** (ʒɑ̃). 1896–1980, Swiss psychologist, noted for his work on the development of the cognitive functions in children.

pia mater ('paɪə 'meɪtə) *n* the innermost of the three membranes (see **meninges**) that cover the brain and spinal cord. [C16: from Medieval Latin, literally: pious mother, intended to translate Arabic *umm raqīqah* tender mother]

pianism ('piːəˌnɪzəm) *n* technique, skill, or artistry in playing the piano. ▸ ˌ**pia'nistic** *adj*

pianissimo (pɪə'nɪsɪˌməʊ) *adj, adv Music.* (to be performed) very quietly. Symbol: *pp* [C18: from Italian, superlative of *piano* soft]

pianist ('pɪənɪst) *n* a person who plays the piano.

piano[1] (pɪ'ænəʊ) *n, pl* **-anos.** a musical stringed instrument resembling a harp set in a vertical or horizontal frame, played by depressing keys that cause hammers to strike the strings and produce audible vibrations. See also **grand piano, upright piano.** [C19: short for PIANOFORTE]

piano[2] ('pjɑːnəʊ) *adj, adv Music.* (to be performed) softly. Symbol: *p* [C17: from Italian, from Latin *plānus* flat; see PLAIN[1]]

piano accordion *n* an accordion in which the right hand plays a piano-like keyboard. See **accordion.** ▸ **piano accordionist** *n*

pianoforte (pɪ'ænəʊ'fɔːtɪ) *n* the full name for **piano**[1]. [C18: from Italian, originally (*gravecembalo col*) *piano e forte* (harpsichord with) soft and loud; see PIANO[2], FORTE[2]]

Pianola (pɪə'nəʊlə) *n Trademark.* a type of mechanical piano in which the keys are depressed by air pressure from bellows, this air flow being regulated by perforations in a paper roll. Also called: **player piano.**

piano nobile ('pjɑːnəʊ 'nəʊbɪlɪ) *n Architect.* the main floor of a large house, containing the reception rooms: usually of lofty proportions. [Italian: great floor]

piano player *n* **1** another name for **pianist. 2** any of various devices for playing a piano automatically.

piano roll *n* a perforated roll of paper actuating the playing mechanism of a Pianola. Also called: **music roll.**

piano stool *n* a stool on which a pianist sits when playing a piano, esp. one whose height is adjustable.

piano trio *n* **1** an instrumental ensemble consisting of a piano, a violin, and a cello. **2** a piece of music written for such an ensemble, usually having the form and commonest features of a sonata.

piassava (ˌpiːə'sɑːvə) *or* **piassaba** (ˌpiːə'sɑːbə) *n* **1** either of two South American palm trees, *Attalea funifera* or *Leopoldinia piassaba.* **2** the coarse fibre obtained from either of these trees, used to make brushes and rope. [C19: via Portuguese from Tupi *piaçaba*]

piastre *or* **piaster** (pɪ'æstə) *n* **1** (formerly) the standard monetary unit of South Vietnam, divided into 100 cents. **2** a fractional monetary unit of Egypt, Lebanon, and Syria worth one hundredth of a pound. Its use in the Sudan is being phased out. **3** another name for **kuruş. 4** a rare word for **piece of eight.** [C17: from French *piastre,* from Italian *piastra d'argento* silver plate; related to Italian *piastro* PLASTER]

Piauí (*Portuguese* pja'ui) *n* a state of NE Brazil, on the Atlantic: rises to a semiarid plateau, with the more humid Parnaíba valley in the west. Capital: Teresina. Pop.: 2 725 900 (1995 est.). Area: 250 934 sq. km (96 886 sq. miles).

Piave (*Italian* 'pjaːve) *n* a river in NE Italy, rising near the border with Austria and flowing south and southeast to the Adriatic: the main line of Italian defence during World War I. Length: 220 km (137 miles).

piazza (pɪ'ætsə, -'ædzə; *Italian* 'pjattsa) *n* **1** a large open square in an Italian town. **2** *Chiefly Brit.* a covered passageway or gallery. [C16: from Italian: marketplace, from Latin *platēa* courtyard, from Greek *plateia;* see PLACE]

pibroch ('piːbrɒk; *Gaelic* 'piːbrɒx) *n* **1** a form of music for Scottish bagpipes, consisting of a theme and variations. **2** a piece of such music. [C18: from Gaelic *piobaireachd,* from *piobair* piper]

pic (pɪk) *n, pl* **pics** *or* **pix.** *Informal.* a photograph, picture, or illustration. [C20: shortened from PICTURE]

pica[1] ('paɪkə) *n* **1** Also called: **em, pica em.** a printer's unit of measurement, equal to 12 points or 0.166 ins. **2** (formerly) a size of printer's type equal to 12 point. **3** a typewriter type size having 10 characters to the inch. [C15: from Anglo-Latin *pīca* list of ecclesiastical regulations, apparently from Latin *pīca* magpie, with reference to its habit of making collections of miscellaneous items; the connection between the original sense (ecclesiastical list) and the typography meanings is obscure]

pica[2] ('paɪkə) *n Pathol.* an abnormal craving to ingest substances such as clay, dirt, or hair, sometimes occurring during pregnancy, in persons with chlorosis, etc. [C16: from medical Latin, from Latin: magpie, being an allusion to its omnivorous feeding habits]

Picabia (pɪ'kɑːbɪə; *French* pikabja) *n* **Francis.** 1879–1953, French painter, designer, and writer, associated with the cubist, Dadaist, and surrealist movements.

picador ('pɪkəˌdɔː) *n Bullfighting.* a horseman who pricks the bull with a lance in the early stages of a fight to goad and weaken it. [C18: from Spanish, literally: pricker, from *picar* to prick; see PIQUE[1]]

Picard (*French* pikar) *n* **Jean** (ʒɑ̃). 1620–82, French astronomer. He was the first to make a precise measurement of a longitude line, enabling him to estimate the earth's radius.

Picardy ('pɪkədɪ) *n* a region of N France: mostly low-lying; scene of heavy fighting in World War I. French name: **Picardie** (pikardi).

Picardy third *n Music.* a major chord used in the final chord of a piece of music in the minor mode. Also called: **tierce de Picardie.** [translation of French *tierce de Picardie,* from its use in the church music of Picardy]

picaresque (ˌpɪkə'rɛsk) *adj* **1** of or relating to a type of fiction in which the hero, a rogue, goes through a series of episodic adventures. It originated in Spain in the 16th century. **2** of or involving rogues or picaroons. [C19: via French from Spanish *picaresco,* from *pícaro* a rogue]

picaroon *or* **pickaroon** (ˌpɪkə'ruːn) *n Archaic.* an adventurer or rogue. [C17: from Spanish *picarón,* from *pícaro*]

Picasso (pɪ'kæsəʊ) *n* **Pablo** ('pæbləʊ). 1881–1973, Spanish painter and sculptor, resident in France: a highly influential figure in 20th-century art and a founder, with Braque, of cubism. A prolific artist, his works include *The Dwarf Dancer* (1901), belonging to his blue period; the first cubist painting *Les Demoiselles d'Avignon* (1907); *Three Dancers* (1925), which appeared in the first surrealist exhibition; and *Guernica* (1937), inspired by an event in the Spanish Civil War.

picayune (ˌpɪkə'juːn) *adj also* **picayunish.** *U.S. and Canadian informal.* **1** of small value or importance. **2** mean; petty. ◆ *n* **3** the half real, an old Spanish-American coin. **4** *U.S.* any coin of little value, esp. a five-cent piece. [C19: from French *picaillon* coin from Piedmont, from Provençal *picaioun,* of unknown origin] ▸ ˌ**pica'yunishly** *adv* ▸ ˌ**pica'yunishness** *n*

Piccadilly (ˌpɪkə'dɪlɪ) *n* one of the main streets of London, running from Piccadilly Circus to Hyde Park Corner.

piccalilli ('pɪkəˌlɪlɪ) *n* a pickle of mixed vegetables, esp. onions, cauliflower, and cucumber, in a mustard sauce. [C18 *piccalillo,* perhaps a coinage based on PICKLE]

piccanin ('pɪkəˌnɪn, ˌpɪkə'nɪn) *n S. African offensive.* a Black African child. [variant of PICCANINNY]

piccaninny *or esp. U.S.* **pickaninny** (ˌpɪkə'nɪnɪ) *n, pl* **-nies. 1** *Offensive.* a small Black or Aboriginal child. **2** (*modifier*) tiny: *a piccaninny fire won't last long.* [C17: perhaps from Portuguese *pequenino* tiny one, from *pequeno* small]

Piccard (*French* pikar) *n* **1 Auguste** (ogyst). 1884–1962, Swiss physicist, whose study of cosmic rays led to his pioneer balloon ascents in the stratosphere (1931–32). **2** his twin brother, **Jean Félix** (ʒɑ̃ feliks). 1884–1963, U.S. chemist and aeronautical engineer, born in Switzerland, noted for his balloon ascent into the stratosphere (1934).

piccolo ('pɪkəˌləʊ) *n, pl* **-los.** a woodwind instrument, the smallest member of the flute family, lying an octave above that of the flute. See **flute** (sense 1). [C19: from Italian: small; compare English PETTY, French *petit*]

pice (paɪs) *n, pl* **pice.** a former Indian coin worth one sixty-fourth of a rupee. [C17: from Mahratti *paisā*]

piceous ('pɪsɪəs, 'paɪsɪəs) *adj* of, relating to, or resembling pitch. [C17: from Latin *piceus,* from *pix* PITCH[2]]

pi character *n Printing.* any special character, such as an accent or mathematical symbol, which is not normally obtained in a standard type fount.

pichiciego (ˌpɪtʃɪsɪ'eɪgəʊ) *n, pl* **-gos. 1** a very small Argentine armadillo, *Chlamyphorus truncatus,* with white silky hair and pale pink plates on the head and back. **2 greater pichiciego.** a similar but larger armadillo, *Burmeisteria retusa.* [C19: from Spanish, probably from Guarani *pichey* small armadillo + Spanish *ciego* blind]

pick[1] (pɪk) *vb* **1** to choose (something) deliberately or carefully, from or as if from a group or number; select. **2** to pluck or gather (fruit, berries, or crops) from (a tree, bush, field, etc.): *to pick hops; to pick a whole bush.* **3** (*tr*) to clean or prepare (fruit, poultry, etc.) by removing the indigestible parts. **4** (*tr*) to remove loose particles from (the teeth, the nose, etc.). **5** (esp. of birds) to nibble or gather (corn, etc.). **6** (*tr*) to pierce, dig, or break up (a hard surface) with a pick. **7** (*tr*) to form (a hole) in this way. **8** (when *intr,* foll. by *at*) to nibble (at) fussily or without appetite. **9** to separate (strands, fibres, etc.), as in weaving. **10** (*tr*) to provoke (an argument, fight, etc.) deliberately. **11** (*tr*) to steal (money or valuables) from (a person's pocket). **12** (*tr*) to open (a lock) with an instrument other than a key. **13** to pluck the strings of (a guitar, banjo, etc.). **14** (*tr*) to make (one's way) carefully on foot: *they picked their way through the rubble.* **15 pick and choose.** to select fastidiously, fussily, etc. **16 pick someone's brains.** to obtain information or ideas from someone. ◆ *n* **17** freedom or right of selection (esp. in the phrase **take one's pick**). **18** a person, thing, etc., that is chosen first or preferred: *the pick of the bunch.* **19** the act of picking. **20** the amount of a crop picked at one period or from one area. **21** *Printing.* a speck of dirt or paper fibre or a blob of ink on the surface of set type or a printing plate. ◆ See also **pick at, pick off, pick on, pick out, pick-up.** [C15: from earlier *piken* to pick, influenced by French *piquer* to pierce; compare Middle Low German *picken,* Dutch *pikken*] ▸ '**pickable** *adj*

pick[2] (pɪk) *n* **1** a tool with a handle carrying a long steel head curved and tapering to a point at one or both ends, used for loosening soil, breaking rocks, etc. **2** any of various tools used for picking, such as an ice pick or toothpick. **3** a plectrum. [C14: perhaps variant of PIKE[2]]

pick[3] (pɪk) (in weaving) ◆ *vb* **1** (*tr*) to cast (a shuttle). ◆ *n* **2** one casting of a shuttle. **3** a weft or filling thread. [C14: variant of PITCH[1]]

pickaback ('pɪkəˌbæk) *n, adv, adj, vb* another word for **piggyback.**

pickaninny (ˌpɪkə'nɪnɪ) *n, pl* **-nies.** a variant spelling (esp. U.S.) of **piccaninny.**

pickaroon (ˌpɪkə'ruːn) *n* a variant spelling of **picaroon.**

pick at *vb* (*intr, prep*) to make criticisms of in a niggling or petty manner.

pickaxe *or U.S.* **pickax** ('pɪkˌæks) *n* **1** a large pick or mattock. ◆ *vb* **2** to use a pickaxe on (earth, rocks, etc.). [C15: from earlier *pikois* (but influenced also by AXE), from Old French *picois,* from *pic* PICK[2]; compare also PIQUE[1]]

picker ('pɪkə) *n* **1** a person or thing that picks, esp. that gathers fruit, crops, etc. **2** (in weaving) a person or the part of the loom that casts the shuttle.

pickerel ('pɪkərəl, 'pɪkrəl) *n, pl* **-el** *or* **-els.** any of several North American freshwater game fishes, such as *Esox americanus* and *E. niger:* family *Esocidae* (pikes, walleye, etc.). [C14: a small pike; diminutive of PIKE[1]]

pickerelweed ('pɪkərəlˌwiːd, 'pɪkrəl-) *n* any of several North American freshwater plants of the genus *Pontederia,* esp. *P. cordata,* having arrow-shaped leaves and purple flowers: family *Pontederiaceae.*

Pickering ('pɪkərɪŋ) *n* **1 Edward Charles.** 1846–1919, U.S. astronomer, who invented the meridian photometer. **2** his brother, **William Henry.** 1858–1938, U.S. astronomer, who discovered Phoebe, the ninth satellite of Saturn, and predicted (1919) the existence and position of Pluto.

picket ('pɪkɪt) *n* **1** a pointed stake, post, or peg that is driven into the ground to support a fence, provide a marker for surveying, etc. **2** an individual or group that stands outside an establishment to make a protest, to dissuade or prevent employees or clients from entering, etc. **3** Also: **picquet.** a small detachment of troops or warships positioned towards the enemy to give early warning of attack. ◆ *vb* **4** to post or serve as pickets at (a factory, embassy, etc.): *let's go and picket the shop.* **5** to guard (a main body or place) by using or acting as a picket. **6** (*tr*) to fasten (a horse or other animal) to a picket. **7** (*tr*) to fence (an area, boundary, etc.) with pickets. [C18: from French *piquet,* from Old French *piquer* to prick; see PIKE²] ▸ **'picketer** *n*

picket fence *n* a fence consisting of pickets supported at close regular intervals by being driven into the ground, by interlacing with strong wire, or by nailing to horizontal timbers fixed to posts in the ground.

picket line *n* a line of people acting as pickets.

Pickford ('pɪkfəd) *n* **Mary,** real name *Gladys Mary Smith.* 1893–1979, U.S. actress in silent films, born in Canada.

pickin ('pɪkɪn) *n W African.* a small child. [from Portuguese *pequeno;* see PICCANINNY]

pickings ('pɪkɪŋz) *pl n* (*sometimes sing*) money, profits, etc., acquired easily or by more or less dishonest means; spoils.

pickle ('pɪkᵊl) *n* **1** (*often pl*) vegetables, such as cauliflowers, onions, etc., preserved in vinegar, brine, etc.. **2** any food preserved in this way. **3** a liquid or marinade, such as spiced vinegar, for preserving vegetables, meat, fish, etc. **4** *Chiefly U.S. and Canadian.* a cucumber that has been preserved and flavoured in a pickling solution, such as brine or vinegar. **5** *Informal.* an awkward or difficult situation: *to be in a pickle.* **6** *Brit. informal.* a mischievous child. ◆ *vb* (*tr*) **7** to preserve in a pickling liquid. **8** to immerse (a metallic object) in a liquid, such as an acid, to remove surface scale. [C14: perhaps from Middle Dutch *pekel;* related to German *Pökel* brine] ▸ **'pickler** *n*

pickled ('pɪkᵊld) *adj* **1** preserved in a pickling liquid. **2** *Informal.* intoxicated; drunk.

picklock ('pɪkˌlɒk) *n* **1** a person who picks locks, esp. one who gains unlawful access to premises by this means. **2** an instrument for picking locks.

pick-me-up *n Informal.* a tonic or restorative, esp. a special drink taken as a stimulant.

pick 'n' mix *n* **1** a selection made by the customer from a variety of loose sweets displayed on a self-service counter. **2a** a selection extracted from a variety of sources to best serve one's needs. **2b** (*as modifier*): *a pick 'n' mix holiday.*

pick off *vb* (*tr, adv*) to aim at and shoot one by one.

pick on *vb* (*intr, prep*) to select for something unpleasant, esp. in order to bully, blame, or cause to perform a distasteful task.

pick out *vb* (*tr, adv*) **1** to select for use or special consideration, illustration, etc., as from a group. **2** to distinguish (an object from its surroundings), as in painting: *she picked out the woodwork in white.* **3** to perceive or recognize (a person or thing previously obscured): *we picked out his face among the crowd.* **4** to distinguish (sense or meaning) from or as if from a mass of detail or complication. **5** to play (a tune) tentatively, by or as if by ear.

pickpocket ('pɪkˌpɒkɪt) *n* a person who steals from the pockets or handbags of others in public places.

pick-up *n* **1** Also called: **pick-up arm, tone arm.** the light balanced arm of a record player that carries the wires from the cartridge to the preamplifier. **2** an electromagnetic transducer that converts the vibrations of the steel strings of an electric guitar or other amplified instrument into electric signals. **3** another name for **cartridge** (sense 3). **4** Also called: **pick-up truck.** a small truck with an open body and low sides, used for light deliveries. **5** *Informal, chiefly U.S.* an ability to accelerate rapidly: *this car has good pick-up.* **6** *Informal.* a casual acquaintance, usually one made with sexual intentions. **7** *Informal.* **7a** a stop to collect passengers, goods, etc. **7b** the people or things collected. **8** *Slang.* a free ride in a motor vehicle. **9** *Informal.* an improvement. **10** *Slang.* a pick-me-up. ◆ *adj* **11** *U.S. and Canadian.* organized, arranged, or assembled hastily and without planning: *a pick-up band; pick-up games.* ◆ *vb* **pick up.** (*adv*) **12** (*tr*) to gather up in the hand or hands. **13** (*tr*) to acquire, obtain, or purchase casually, incidentally, etc. **14** (*tr*) to catch (a disease): *she picked up a bad cold during the weekend.* **15** (*intr*) to improve in health, condition, activity, etc.: *the market began to pick up.* **16** (*reflexive*) to raise (oneself) after a fall or setback. **17** (*tr*) to notice or sense: *she picked up a change in his attitude.* **18** to resume where one left off; return to: *we'll pick up after lunch; they picked up the discussion.* **19** (*tr*) to learn gradually or as one goes along. **20** (*tr*) to take responsibility for paying (a bill): *he picked up the bill for dinner.* **21** (*tr*) *Informal.* to reprimand: *he picked her up on her table manners.* **22** (*tr*) to collect or give a lift to (passengers, hitchhikers, goods, etc.). **23** (*tr*) *Informal.* to become acquainted with, esp. with a view to having sexual relations. **24** (*tr*) *Informal.* to arrest. **25** to increase (speed): *the cars picked up down the straight.* **26** (*tr*) to receive (electrical signals, a radio signal, sounds, etc.), as for transmission or amplification. **27 pick up the pieces.** to restore a situation to normality after a crisis or collapse.

Pickwickian (pɪk'wɪkɪən) *adj* **1** of, relating to, or resembling Mr Pickwick in Charles Dickens' *The Pickwick Papers,* esp. in being naive or benevolent. **2** (of the use or meaning of a word, etc.) odd or unusual.

picky ('pɪkɪ) *adj* **pickier, pickiest.** *Informal.* fussy; finicky; choosy. ▸ **'pickily** *adv* ▸ **'pickiness** *n*

picnic ('pɪknɪk) *n* **1** a trip or excursion to the country, seaside, etc., on which people bring food to be eaten in the open air. **2a** any informal meal eaten outside. **2b** (*as modifier*): *a picnic lunch.* **3** *Informal, chiefly Austral.* a troublesome situation or experience. **4 no picnic.** *Informal.* a hard or disagreeable task. ◆ *vb* **-nics, -nicking, -nicked. 5** (*intr*) to eat a picnic. [C18: from French *piquenique,* of unknown origin] ▸ **'picnicker** *n*

picnic races *pl n Austral.* horse races for amateur riders held in rural areas.

pico- *prefix* denoting 10^{-12}: *picofarad.* Symbol: p [from Spanish *pico* small quantity, odd number, peak]

Pico de Aneto (*Spanish* 'piko de a'neto) *n* See **Aneto.**

Pico della Mirandola (*Italian* 'pi:ko ˌdɛlla mi'randola) *n* Count **Giovanni** (dʒo'vanni). 1463–94, Italian Platonist philosopher. His attempt to reconcile the ideas of classical, Christian, and Arabic writers in a collection of 900 theses, prefaced by his *Oration on the Dignity of Man* (1486), was condemned by the pope.

Pico de Teide (*Spanish* 'piko de 'teiðe) *n* See **Teide.**

picofarad ('pi:kəʊˌfærəd, -æd) *n* a million millionth of a farad; 10^{-12} farad. Symbol: pF

picoline ('pɪkəˌli:n, -lɪn) *n* a liquid derivative of pyridine found in bone oil and coal tar; methylpyridene. Formula: $C_5H_4N(CH_3)$. [C19: from Latin *pic-, pix* PITCH² + -OL² + -INE²] ▸ **picolinic** (ˌpɪkə'lɪnɪk) *adj*

picong ('pɪkɒŋ) *n Caribbean.* any teasing or satirical banter, originally a verbal duel in song. [from Spanish *picón* mocking, from *picar* to pierce; compare PICADOR]

picosecond ('pi:kəʊˌsɛkənd, 'paɪkəʊ-) *n* a million millionth of a second; 10^{-12} second.

picot ('pi:kəʊ) *n* any of a pattern of small loops, as on lace. [C19: from French: small point, from *pic* point]

picotee (ˌpɪkə'ti:) *n* a type of carnation having pale petals edged with a darker colour, usually red. [C18: from French *picoté* marked with points, from PICOT]

picquet ('pɪkɪt) *n* a variant spelling of **picket** (sense 3).

picrate ('pɪkreɪt) *n* **1** any salt or ester of picric acid, such as sodium picrate. **2** a charge-transfer complex formed by picric acid.

picric acid ('pɪkrɪk) *n* a toxic sparingly soluble crystalline yellow acid used as a dye, antiseptic, and explosive. Formula: $C_6H_2OH(NO_2)_3$. Systematic name: **2,4,6-trinitrophenol.** See also **lyddite.**

picrite ('pɪkraɪt) *n* a coarse-grained ultrabasic igneous rock consisting of olivine and augite with small amounts of plagioclase feldspar.

picro- *or before a vowel* **picr-** *combining form.* bitter: *picrotoxin.* [from Greek *pikros*]

picrotoxin (ˌpɪkrə'tɒksɪn) *n* a bitter poisonous crystalline compound used as an antidote for barbiturate poisoning. Formula: $C_{30}H_{34}O_{13}$.

Pict (pɪkt) *n* a member of any of the peoples who lived in Britain north of the Forth and Clyde in the first to the fourth centuries A.D.: later applied chiefly to the inhabitants of NE Scotland. Throughout Roman times the Picts carried out border raids. [Old English *Peohtas;* later forms from Late Latin *Pictī* painted men, from *pingere* to paint]

Pictish ('pɪktɪʃ) *n* **1** the language of the Picts, of which few records survive. Its origins are much disputed and it was extinct by about 900 A.D. ◆ *adj* **2** of or relating to the Picts.

pictogram ('pɪktəˌgræm) *n* another word for **pictograph.**

pictograph ('pɪktəˌgrɑ:f, -ˌgræf) *n* **1** a picture or symbol standing for a word or group of words, as in written Chinese. **2** a chart on which symbols are used to represent values, such as population levels or consumption. [C19: from Latin *pictus,* from *pingere* to paint] ▸ **pictographic** (ˌpɪktə'græfɪk) *adj* ▸ **pictography** (pɪk'tɒgrəfɪ) *n*

Pictor ('pɪktə) *n, Latin genitive* **Pictoris** (pɪk'tɔ:rɪs). a faint constellation in the S hemisphere lying between Dorado and Carina. [Latin: painter]

pictorial (pɪk'tɔ:rɪəl) *adj* **1** relating to, consisting of, or expressed by pictures. **2** (of books, newspapers, etc.) containing pictures. **3** of or relating to painting or drawing. **4** (of language, style, etc.) suggesting a picture; vivid; graphic. ◆ *n* **5a** a magazine, newspaper, etc., containing many pictures. **5b** (*cap. when part of a name*): *the Sunday Pictorial.* [C17: from Late Latin *pictōrius,* from Latin *pictor* painter, from *pingere* to paint] ▸ **pic'torially** *adv*

picture ('pɪktʃə) *n* **1a** a visual representation of something, such as a person or scene, produced on a surface, as in a photograph, painting, etc. **1b** (*as modifier*): *picture gallery; picture postcard.* Related adj: **pictorial. 2** a mental image or impression: *a clear picture of events.* **3** a verbal description, esp. one that is vivid. **4** a situation considered as an observable scene: *the political picture.* **5** a person or thing that bears a close resemblance to another: *he was the picture of his father.* **6** a person, scene, etc., considered as typifying a particular state or quality: *the picture of despair.* **7** a beautiful person or scene: *you'll look a picture.* **8** a complete image on a television screen, comprising two interlaced fields. **9a** a motion picture; film. **9b** (*as modifier*): *picture theatre.* **10 the pictures.** *Chiefly Brit. and Austral.* a cinema or film show. **11** another name for **tableau vivant. 12 get the picture.** *Informal.* to understand a situation. **13 in the picture.** informed about a given situation. ◆ *vb* (*tr*) **14** to visualize or imagine. **15** to describe or depict, esp. vividly. **16** (*often passive*) to put in a picture or make a picture of: *they were pictured sitting on the rocks.* [C15: from Latin *pictūra* painting, from *pingere* to paint]

picture card *n* another name for **court card.**

picturegoer ('pɪktʃəˌgəʊə) *n Brit., old-fashioned.* a person that goes to the cinema, esp. frequently.

picture hat *n* a decorated hat with a very wide brim, esp. as worn by women in paintings by Gainsborough and Reynolds.

picture house *n Chiefly Brit.* an old-fashioned name for **cinema** (sense 1a).

picture moulding *n* **1** the edge around a framed picture. **2** Also called: **picture rail.** the moulding or rail near the top of a wall from which pictures can be hung.

picture palace *n Brit.* an old-fashioned name for **cinema** (sense 1a).

picturesque (ˌpɪktʃə'rɛsk) *adj* **1** visually pleasing, esp. in being striking or vivid: *a picturesque view.* **2** having a striking or colourful character, nature, etc. **3** (of language) graphic; vivid. [C18: from French *pittoresque* (but also influenced by PICTURE), from Italian *pittoresco,* from *pittore* painter, from Latin *pictor*] ▸ ˌ**pictur'esquely** *adv* ▸ ˌ**pictur'esqueness** *n*

picture tube *n* another name for **television tube.**
picture window *n* a large window having a single pane of glass, usually placed so that it overlooks a view.
picture writing *n* **1** any writing system that uses pictographs. **2** a system of artistic expression and communication using pictures or symbolic figures.
picul ('pɪkᵊl) *n* a unit of weight, used in China, Japan, and SE Asia, equal to approximately 60 kilograms or 133 pounds. [C16: from Malay *pīkul* a grown man's load]
PID *abbrev. for* pelvic inflammatory disease.
piddle ('pɪdᵊl) *vb* **1** (*intr*) *Informal.* to urinate. **2** (when *tr,* often foll. by *away*) to spend (one's time) aimlessly; fritter. [C16: origin unknown] ▸ **'piddler** *n*
piddling ('pɪdlɪŋ) *adj Informal.* petty; trifling; trivial. ▸ **'piddlingly** *adv*
piddock ('pɪdək) *n* any marine bivalve of the family *Pholadidae,* boring into rock, clay, or wood by means of sawlike shell valves. See also **shipworm.** [C19: origin uncertain]
pidgin ('pɪdʒɪn) *n* a language made up of elements of two or more other languages and used for contacts, esp. trading contacts, between the speakers of other languages. Unlike creoles, pidgins do not constitute the mother tongue of any speech community. [C19: perhaps from Chinese pronunciation of English *business*]
pidgin English *n* a pidgin in which one of the languages involved is English.
pi-dog *n* a variant spelling of **pye-dog.**
pie[1] (paɪ) *n* **1** a baked food consisting of a sweet or savoury filling in a pastry-lined dish, often covered with a pastry crust. **2 have a** (*or* **one's**) **finger in the pie. 2a** to have an interest in or take part in some activity. **2b** to meddle or interfere. **3 pie in the sky.** illusory hope or promise of some future good; false optimism. [C14: of obscure origin]
pie[2] (paɪ) *n* an archaic or dialect name for **magpie.** [C13: via Old French from Latin *pīca* magpie; related to Latin *pīcus* woodpecker]
pie[3] (paɪ) *n, vb Printing.* a variant spelling of **pi**[2].
pie[4] (paɪ) *n* a very small former Indian coin worth one third of a pice. [C19: from Hindi *pā'ī,* from Sanskrit *pādikā* a fourth]
pie[5] *or* **pye** (paɪ) *n History.* a book for finding the Church service for any particular day. [C15: from Medieval Latin *pica* almanac; see PICA[1]]
pie[6] (paɪ) *adj* **be pie on.** *N.Z. informal.* to be keen on. [from Maori *pai ana*]
piebald ('paɪˌbɔːld) *adj* **1** marked or spotted in two different colours, esp. black and white: *a piebald horse.* ♦ *n* **2** a black-and-white pied horse. [C16: PIE[2] + BALD; see also PIED]
pie cart *n N.Z.* a mobile van selling warmed-up food and drinks.
piece (piːs) *n* **1** an amount or portion forming a separate mass or structure; bit: *a piece of wood.* **2** a small part, item, or amount forming part of a whole, esp. when broken off or separated: *a piece of bread.* **3** a length by which a commodity is sold, esp. cloth, wallpaper, etc. **4** an instance or occurrence: *a piece of luck.* **5** *Slang.* a girl or woman regarded as an object of sexual attraction: *a nice piece.* **6** an example or specimen of a style or type, such as an article of furniture: *a beautiful piece of Dresden china.* **7** *Informal.* an opinion or point of view: *to state one's piece.* **8** a literary, musical, or artistic composition. **9** a coin having a value as specified: *fifty-pence piece.* **10** a small object, often individually shaped and designed, used in playing certain games, esp. board games: *chess pieces.* **11a** a firearm or cannon. **11b** (*in combination*): *fowling-piece.* **12** any chessman other than a pawn. **13** *U.S. and Canadian.* a short time or distance: *down the road a piece.* **14** *Scot. and English dialect.* **14a** a slice of bread or a sandwich. **14b** a packed lunch taken to work, school, etc. **15** (*usually pl*) *Austral. and N.Z.* fragments of fleece wool. See also **oddment** (sense 2). **16 give someone a piece of one's mind.** *Informal.* to criticize or censure someone frankly or vehemently. **17 go to pieces. 17a** (of a person) to lose control of oneself; have a breakdown. **17b** (of a building, organization, etc.) to disintegrate. **18 nasty piece of work.** *Brit. informal.* a cruel or mean person. **19 of a piece.** of the same kind; alike. **20 piece of cake.** *Informal.* something easily obtained or achieved. ♦ *vb* (*tr*) **21** (often foll. by *together*) to fit or assemble piece by piece. **22** (often foll. by *up*) to patch or make up (a garment) by adding pieces. **23** *Textiles.* to join (broken threads) during spinning. ♦ See also **piece out.** [C13 *pece,* from Old French, of Gaulish origin; compare Breton *pez* piece, Welsh *peth* portion]
pièce de résistance *French.* (pjɛs də rezistɑ̃s) *n* **1** the principal or most outstanding item in a series or creative artist's work. **2** the main dish of a meal. [lit: piece of resistance]
piece-dyed *adj* (of fabric) dyed after weaving. Compare **yarn-dyed.**
piece goods *pl n* goods, esp. fabrics, made in standard widths and lengths. Also called: **yard goods.**
piecemeal ('piːsˌmiːl) *adv* **1** by degrees; bit by bit; gradually. **2** in or into pieces or piece from piece: *to tear something piecemeal.* ♦ *adj* **3** fragmentary or unsystematic: *a piecemeal approach.* [C13 *pecemele,* from PIECE + *-mele,* from Old English *mælum* quantity taken at one time]
piece of eight *n, pl* **pieces of eight.** a former Spanish coin worth eight reals; peso.
piece out *vb* (*tr, adv*) **1** to extend by adding pieces. **2** to cause to last longer by using only a small amount at a time: *to piece out rations.*
piecer ('piːsə) *n Textiles.* a person who mends, repairs, or joins something, esp. broken threads on a loom.
piece rate *n* a fixed rate paid according to the quantity produced.
piecework ('piːsˌwɜːk) *n* work paid for according to the quantity produced. Compare **timework.**
pie chart *n* a circular graph divided into sectors proportional to the magnitudes of the quantities represented.
piecrust table ('paɪˌkrʌst) *n* a round table, ornamented with carved moulding suggestive of a pie crust.
pied (paɪd) *adj* having markings of two or more colours. [C14: from PIE[2]; an allusion to the magpie's black-and-white colouring]
pied-à-terre (ˌpjeɪtɑːˈtɛə) *n, pl* **pieds-à-terre** (ˌpjeɪtɑːˈtɛə). a flat, house, or other lodging for secondary or occasional use. [French, literally: foot on (the) ground]
piedmont ('piːdmɒnt) *adj* (*prenominal*) (of glaciers, plains, etc.) formed or situated at the foot of a mountain or mountain range. [via French from Italian *piémonte,* from *pié,* variant of *piede* foot + *mont* mountain]
Piedmont ('piːdmɒnt) *n* **1** a region of NW Italy: consists of the upper Po Valley; mainly agricultural. Chief town: Turin. Pop.: 4 288 866 (1996 est.). Area: 25 399 sq. km (9807 sq. miles). Italian name: **Piemonte. 2** a low plateau of the eastern U.S., between the coastal plain and the Appalachian Mountains.
piedmontite ('piːdmɒnˌtaɪt, -mən-) *n* a dark red mineral occurring in metamorphic rocks: a complex hydrated silicate containing calcium, aluminium, iron, and manganese. Formula: $Ca_2(Al,Fe,Mn)_3(SiO_4)_3OH$. [C19: from PIEDMONT in Italy]
pie-dog *n* a variant spelling of **pye-dog.**
Pied Piper *n* **1** Also called: **the Pied Piper of Hamelin.** (in German legend) a piper who rid the town of Hamelin of rats by luring them away with his music and then, when he was not paid for his services, lured away its children. **2** (*sometimes not caps.*) a person who entices others to follow him.
pied-piping *n Transformational grammar.* the principle that a noun phrase may take with it the rest of a prepositional phrase or a larger noun phrase in which it is contained, when moved in a transformation. For example, when the interrogative pronoun is moved to initial position, other words are moved too, as in *to whom did you speak?*
pied wagtail *n* a British songbird, *Motacilla alba yarrellii,* with a black throat and back, long black tail, and white underparts and face: family *Motacillidae* (wagtails and pipits).
pie-eyed *adj* a slang term for **drunk** (sense 1).
pieman ('paɪmən) *n, pl* **-men.** *Brit., obsolete.* a seller of pies.
Piemonte (*Italian* pjeˈmonte) *n* the Italian name for **Piedmont** (sense 1).
pier (pɪə) *n* **1** a structure with a deck that is built out over water, and used as a landing place, promenade, etc. **2** a pillar that bears heavy loads, esp. one of rectangular cross section. **3** the part of a wall between two adjacent openings. **4** another name for **buttress** (sense 1). [C12 *per,* from Anglo-Latin *pera* pier supporting a bridge]
pierce (pɪəs) *vb* (*mainly tr*) **1** to form or cut (a hole) in (something) with or as if with a sharp instrument. **2** to thrust into or penetrate sharply or violently: *the thorn pierced his heel.* **3** to force (a way, route, etc.) through (something). **4** (of light) to shine through or penetrate (darkness). **5** (*also intr*) to discover or realize (something) suddenly or (of an idea) to become suddenly apparent. **6** (of sounds or cries) to sound sharply through (the silence). **7** to move or affect (a person's emotions, bodily feelings, etc.) deeply or sharply: *the cold pierced their bones.* **8** (*intr*) to penetrate or be capable of penetrating: *piercing cold.* [C13 *percen,* from Old French *percer,* ultimately from Latin *pertundere,* from *per* through + *tundere* to strike] ▸ **'pierceable** *adj* ▸ **'piercer** *n* ▸ **'piercing** *adj* ▸ **'piercingly** *adv*
Pierce (pɪəs) *n* **Franklin.** 1804–69, U.S. statesman; 14th president of the U.S. (1853–57).
pier glass *n* a tall narrow mirror, usually one of a pair or set, designed to hang on the wall between windows, usually above a pier table.
Pieria (paɪˈɪərɪə) *n* a region of ancient Macedonia, west of the Gulf of Salonika: site of the Pierian Spring.
Pierian (paɪˈɪərɪən) *adj* **1** of or relating to the Muses or artistic or poetic inspiration. **2** of or relating to Pieria.
Pierian Spring *n* a sacred fountain in Pieria, in Greece, fabled to inspire those who drank from it.
Pierides (paɪˈɪərɪˌdiːz) *pl n Greek myth.* **1** another name for the Muses (see **Muse**). **2** nine maidens of Thessaly, who were defeated in a singing contest by the Muses and turned into magpies for their effrontery.
pieridine (paɪˈɛərɪˌdaɪn) *adj* of, relating to, or belonging to the *Pieridae,* a family of butterflies including the whites and brimstones.
pieris ('paɪərɪs) *n* any plant of a genus, *Pieris,* of American and Asiatic shrubs, esp. *P. formosa forestii,* grown for the bright red colour of its young foliage: family *Ericaceae.* [New Latin, from Greek *Pierides,* a name for the Muses]
Piero della Francesca (*Italian* ˈpjeːro ˌdella franˈtʃeska) *n* ?1420–92, Italian painter, noted particularly for his frescoes of the *Legend of the True Cross* in San Francesco, Arezzo.
Piero di Cosimo (*Italian* ˈpjeːro di ˈkɔːzimo) *n* 1462–1521, Italian painter, noted for his mythological works.
Pierre (pɪə) *n* a city in central South Dakota, capital of the state, on the Missouri River. Pop.: 12 906 (1990).
Pierrot ('pɪərəʊ; *French* pjɛro) *n* **1** a male character from French pantomime with a whitened face, white costume, and pointed hat. **2** (*usually not cap.*) a clown or masquerader so made up.
pier table *n* a side table designed to stand against a wall between windows.
Piesporter ('piːzˌpɔːtə) *n* any of various white wines from the area around the village of Piesport in the Moselle valley in Germany.
pietà (pɪɛˈtɑː) *n* a sculpture, painting, or drawing of the dead Christ, supported by the Virgin Mary. [Italian: pity, from Latin *pietās* PIETY]
Pietermaritzburg (ˌpiːtəˈmærɪtsˌbɜːg) *n* a city in E South Africa, in KwaZulu/Natal: founded in 1839 by the Boers: gateway to Natal's mountain resorts; capital of the former province of Natal. Pop.: 156 473 (1991).
pietism ('paɪɪˌtɪzəm) *n* **1** a less common word for **piety. 2** excessive, exaggerated, or affected piety or saintliness. ▸ **'pietist** *n* ▸ **ˌpie'tistic** *or* **ˌpie'tistical** *adj*
Pietism ('paɪɪˌtɪzəm) *n History.* a reform movement in the German Lutheran

Churches during the 17th and 18th centuries that strove to renew the devotional ideal. ▸ **'Pietist** *n*

piet-my-vrou ('pi:t,meɪ'frəʊ) *n S. African.* a cuckoo, *Notococcyx solitarius,* having a red breast. [from Afrikaans *piet* Peter + *my* my + *vrou* wife: onomatopoeic, based on the bird's three clear notes]

Pietro da Cortona (*Italian* 'pjɛ:tro da kor'to:na) *n* real name *Pietro Berrettini.* 1596–1669, Italian baroque painter and architect.

piety ('paɪɪtɪ) *n, pl* **-ties. 1** dutiful devotion to God and observance of religious principles. **2** the quality or characteristic of being pious. **3** a pious action, saying, etc. **4** *Now rare.* devotion and obedience to parents or superiors. [C13 *piete,* from Old French, from Latin *pietās* piety, dutifulness, from *pius* PIOUS]

piezo- (paɪ'i:zəʊ-, pi:'eɪzəʊ-, 'pi:tsəʊ-) *combining form.* pressure: *piezometer.* [from Greek *piezein* to press]

piezochemistry (paɪ,i:zəʊ'kɛmɪstrɪ) *n* the study of chemical reactions at high pressures.

piezoelectric crystal (paɪ,i:zəʊɪ'lɛktrɪk) *n* a crystal, such as quartz, that produces a potential difference across its opposite faces when under mechanical stress. See also **piezoelectric effect.**

piezoelectric effect *or* **piezoelectricity** (paɪ,i:zəʊɪlɛk'trɪsɪtɪ) *n Physics.* **a** the production of electricity or electric polarity by applying a mechanical stress to certain crystals. **b** the converse effect in which stress is produced in a crystal as a result of an applied potential difference. ▸ **pi,ezoe'lectrically** *adv*

piezomagnetic effect (paɪ,i:zəʊmæg'nɛtɪk) *or* **piezomagnetism** (paɪ,i:zəʊ'mægnɪtɪzəm) *n Physics.* **a** the production of a magnetic field by applying a mechanical stress to certain crystals. **b** the converse effect in which stress is produced in a crystal as a result of an applied magnetic field. ▸ **pi,ezomag'netically** *adj*

piezometer (,paɪɪ'zɒmɪtə) *n* any instrument for the measurement of pressure (**piezometry**), esp. very high pressure, or for measuring the compressibility of materials under pressure. ▸ **piezometric** (paɪ,i:zəʊ'mɛtrɪk) *adj* ▸ **pi-,ezo'metrically** *adv*

piffle ('pɪf^əl) *Informal.* ◆ *n* **1** nonsense: *to talk piffle.* ◆ *vb* **2** (*intr*) to talk or behave feebly. [C19: origin uncertain]

piffling ('pɪflɪŋ) *adj* worthless, trivial.

pig (pɪg) *n* **1** any artiodactyl mammal of the African and Eurasian family *Suidae,* esp. *Sus scrofa* (**domestic pig**), typically having a long head with a movable snout, a thick bristle-covered skin, and, in wild species, long curved tusks. **2** a domesticated pig weighing more than 120 pounds (54 kg). **3** *Informal.* a dirty, greedy, or bad-mannered person. **4** the meat of swine; pork. **5** *Derogatory.* a slang word for **policeman. 6a** a mass of metal, such as iron, copper, or lead, cast into a simple shape for ease of storing or transportation. **6b** a mould in which such a mass of metal is formed. **7** *Brit. informal.* something that is difficult or unpleasant. **8** an automated device propelled through a duct or pipeline to clear impediments or check for faults, leaks, etc. **9 a pig in a poke.** something bought or received without prior sight or knowledge. **10 make a pig of oneself.** *Informal.* to overindulge oneself. **11 on the pig's back.** *Irish and N.Z.* successful; established: *he's on the pig's back now.* ◆ Related adj (for senses 1, 2): **porcine.** ◆ *vb* **pigs, pigging, pigged. 12** (*intr*) (of a sow) to give birth. **13** (*intr*) Also: **pig it.** *Informal.* to live in squalor. **14** (*tr*) *Informal.* to devour (food) greedily. ◆ See also **pig out.** [C13 *pigge,* of obscure origin]

pig bed *n* a bed of sand in which pig iron is cast.

pig dog *n N.Z.* a dog bred for hunting wild pigs in the bush.

pigeon[1] ('pɪdʒɪn) *n* **1** any of numerous birds of the family *Columbidae,* having a heavy body, small head, short legs, and long pointed wings: order *Columbiformes.* See **rock dove. 2** *Slang.* a victim or dupe. [C14: from Old French *pijon* young dove, from Late Latin *pīpiō* young bird, from *pīpīre* to chirp]

pigeon[2] ('pɪdʒɪn) *n Brit. informal.* concern or responsibility (often in the phrase **it's his, her,** etc., **pigeon**). [C19: altered from PIDGIN]

pigeon breast *n* a deformity of the chest characterized by an abnormal protrusion of the breastbone, caused by rickets or by obstructed breathing during infancy. Also called: **chicken breast.**

pigeon hawk *n* the North American variety of the merlin.

pigeon-hearted *or* **pigeon-livered** *adj* of a timid or fearful disposition.

pigeonhole ('pɪdʒɪn,həʊl) *n* **1** a small compartment for papers, letters, etc., as in a bureau. **2** a hole or recess in a dovecote for pigeons to nest in. **3** *Informal.* a category or classification. ◆ *vb* (*tr*) **4** to put aside or defer. **5** to classify or categorize, esp. in a rigid manner.

pigeon pea *n* another name for **dhal.**

pigeon-toed *adj* having the toes turned inwards.

pigeonwing ('pɪdʒɪn,wɪŋ) *n Chiefly U.S.* a fancy step in dancing in which the feet are clapped together.

pigface ('pɪg,feɪs) *n Austral.* a creeping succulent plant of the genus *Carpobrotus,* having bright-coloured flowers and red fruits and often grown for ornament: family *Aizoaceae.*

pig fern *n N.Z.* giant bracken.

pigfish ('pɪg,fɪʃ) *n, pl* **-fish** *or* **-fishes. 1** Also called: **hogfish.** any of several grunts, esp. *Orthopristis chrysopterus,* of the North American Atlantic coast. **2** any of several wrasses, such as *Achoerodus gouldii* (**giant pigfish**), that occur around the Great Barrier Reef.

piggery ('pɪgərɪ) *n, pl* **-geries. 1** a place where pigs are kept and reared. **2** great greediness; piggishness.

piggin ('pɪgɪn) *n* a small wooden bucket or tub. Also called: **pipkin.** [C16: origin unknown]

piggish ('pɪgɪʃ) *adj* **1** like a pig, esp. in appetite or manners. **2** *Informal, chiefly Brit.* obstinate or mean. ▸ **'piggishly** *adv* ▸ **'piggishness** *n*

Piggott ('pɪgət) *n* **Lester (Keith).** born 1935, English flat-racing jockey: he won the Derby nine times.

piggy ('pɪgɪ) *n, pl* **-gies. 1** a child's word for a pig, esp. a piglet. **2 piggy in the middle. 2a** a children's game in which one player attempts to retrieve a ball thrown over him or her by at least two other players. **2b** a situation in which a person or group is caught up in a disagreement between other people or groups. **3** a child's word for toe or, sometimes, finger. ◆ *adj* **-gier, -giest. 4** another word for **piggish.**

piggyback ('pɪgɪ,bæk) *or* **pickaback** *n* **1** a ride on the back and shoulders of another person. **2** a system whereby a vehicle, aircraft, etc., is transported for part of its journey on another vehicle, such as a flat railway wagon, another aircraft, etc. ◆ *adv* **3** on the back and shoulders of another person. **4** on or as an addition to something else. ◆ *adj* **5** of or for a piggyback: *a piggyback ride; piggyback lorry trains.* **6** of or relating to a type of heart transplant in which the transplanted heart functions in conjunction with the patient's own heart. ◆ *vb* (*tr*) **7** to give (a person) a piggyback on one's back and shoulders. **8** to transport (one vehicle) on another.

piggy bank *n* a child's coin bank shaped like a pig with a slot for coins.

pig-headed *adj* stupidly stubborn. ▸ **,pig-'headedly** *adv* ▸ **,pig-'headedness** *n*

pig iron *n* crude iron produced in a blast furnace and poured into moulds in preparation for making wrought iron, steels, alloys, etc.

Pig Island *n N.Z. informal.* New Zealand. ▸ **Pig Islander** *n*

pig-jump *vb* (*intr*) (of a horse) to jump from all four legs.

Pig Latin *n* a secret language used by children in which any consonants at the beginning of a word are placed at the end, followed by *-ay;* for example *cathedral* becomes *athedralcay.*

piglet ('pɪglɪt) *n* a young pig.

pigmeat ('pɪg,mi:t) *n* a less common name for **pork, ham**[1] (sense 2), or **bacon** (sense 1).

pigment ('pɪgmənt) *n* **1** a substance occurring in plant or animal tissue and producing a characteristic colour, such as chlorophyll in green plants and haemoglobin in red blood. **2** any substance used to impart colour. **3** a powder that is mixed with a liquid to give a paint, ink, etc. [C14: from Latin *pigmentum,* from *pingere* to paint] ▸ **'pigmentary** *adj*

pigmentation (,pɪgmən'teɪʃən) *n* **1** coloration in plants, animals, or man caused by the presence of pigments. **2** the deposition of pigment in animals, plants, or man.

Pigmy ('pɪgmɪ) *n, pl* **-mies.** a variant spelling of **Pygmy.**

pignut ('pɪg,nʌt) *n* **1** Also called: **hognut. 1a** the bitter nut of any of several North American hickory trees, esp. *Carya glabra* (**brown hickory**). **1b** any of the trees bearing such a nut. **2** another name for **earthnut.**

pig out *vb* (*intr, adv*) *Slang.* to gorge oneself.

pigpen ('pɪg,pɛn) *n* a U.S. and Canadian word for **pigsty.**

pig-root *vb* (*intr*) *N.Z.* another term for **pig-jump.**

pigs (pɪgz) *interj Austral. slang.* an expression of derision or disagreement. Also: **pig's arse, pig's bum.**

Pigs (pɪgz) *n* **Bay of.** See **Bay of Pigs.**

pig's ear *n* something that has been badly or clumsily done; a botched job (esp. in the phrase **make a pig's ear of (something)**).

pig's fry *n* the heart, liver, lights, and sweetbreads of a pig cooked, esp. fried, together.

pigskin ('pɪg,skɪn) *n* **1** the skin of the domestic pig. **2** leather made of this skin. **3** *U.S. and Canadian informal.* a football. ◆ *adj* **4** made of pigskin.

pigstick ('pɪg,stɪk) *vb* (*intr*) (esp. in India) to hunt and spear wild boar, esp. from horseback.

pigsticker ('pɪg,stɪkə) *n* **1** a person that hunts wild boar. **2** *Slang.* a large sharp hunting knife.

pigsticking ('pɪg,stɪkɪŋ) *n* the sport of hunting wild boar.

pigsty ('pɪg,staɪ) *or U.S. and Canadian* **pigpen** *n, pl* **-sties. 1** a pen for pigs; sty. **2** *Brit.* a dirty or untidy place.

pigswill ('pɪg,swɪl) *n* waste food or other edible matter fed to pigs. Also called: **pig's wash.**

pigtail ('pɪg,teɪl) *n* **1** a bunch of hair or one of two bunches on either side of the face, worn loose or plaited. **2** a twisted roll of tobacco. ▸ **'pig,tailed** *adj*

pigweed ('pɪg,wi:d) *n* **1** Also called: **redroot.** any of several coarse North American amaranthaceous weeds of the genus *Amaranthus,* esp. *A. retroflexus,* having hairy leaves and green flowers. **2** a U.S. name for **fat hen.**

pika ('paɪkə) *n* any burrowing lagomorph mammal of the family *Ochotonidae* of mountainous regions of North America and Asia, having short rounded ears, a rounded body, and rudimentary tail. Also called: **cony.** [C19: from Tungusic *piika*]

pikau ('pi:kaʊ) *n N.Z.* a pack, knapsack, or rucksack. [Maori]

pike[1] (paɪk) *n, pl* **pike** *or* **pikes. 1** any of several large predatory freshwater teleost fishes of the genus *Esox,* esp. *E. lucius* (**northern pike**), having a broad flat snout, strong teeth, and an elongated body covered with small scales: family *Esocidae.* **2** any of various similar fishes. [C14: short for *pikefish,* from Old English *pīc* point, with reference to the shape of its jaw]

pike[2] (paɪk) *n* **1** a medieval weapon consisting of an iron or steel spearhead joined to a long pole, the pikestaff. **2** a point or spike. ◆ *vb* **3** (*tr*) to stab or pierce using a pike. [Old English *pīc* point, of obscure origin]

pike[3] (paɪk) *n* short for **turnpike** (sense 1).

pike[4] (paɪk) *n Northern English dialect.* a pointed or conical hill. [Old English *pīc,* of obscure origin]

pike[5] (paɪk) *or* **piked** (paɪkt) *adj* (of the body position of a diver) bent at the hips but with the legs straight. [C20: of obscure origin]

pikelet ('paɪklɪt) *n* a dialect word for a **crumpet** (sense 1). [C18: from Welsh *bara pyglyd* pitchy bread]

pikeman ('paɪkmən) *n, pl* **-men.** (formerly) a soldier armed with a pike.

pikeperch ('paɪk,pɜ:tʃ) *n, pl* **-perch** *or* **-perches.** any of various pikelike freshwater teleost fishes of the genera *Stizostedion* (or *Lucioperca*), such as *S. lucioperca* of Europe: family *Percidae* (perches).

piker ('paɪkə) *n Slang.* **1** *Austral.* a wild bullock. **2** *Austral. and N.Z.* a useless person; failure. **3** *U.S., Austral., and N.Z.* a lazy person; shirker. **4** a mean person. [C19: perhaps related to PIKE[3]]

Pikes Peak *n* a mountain in central Colorado, in the Rockies. Height: 4300 m (14 109 ft.).

pikestaff ('paɪkˌstɑːf) *n* the wooden handle of a pike.

pilaster (pɪ'læstə) *n* a shallow rectangular column attached to the face of a wall. [C16: from French *pilastre*, from Latin *pīla* pillar] ▸ **pi'lastered** *adj*

Pilate ('paɪlət) *n* **Pontius** ('pɒnʃəs, 'pɒntɪəs). Roman procurator of Judaea (?26–?36 A.D.), who ordered the crucifixion of Jesus, allegedly reluctantly against his better judgment.

Pilates (pɪ'lɑːtiːz) *n* a system of gentle exercise performed lying down that stretches and lengthens the muscles, designed to improve posture, flexibility, etc. [C20: named after Joseph *Pilates* (1880–1967), its German inventor]

Pilatus (*German* pi'laːtʊs) *n* a mountain in central Switzerland, in Unterwalden canton: derives its name from the legend that the body of Pontius Pilate lay in a former lake on the mountain. Height: 2122 m (6962 ft.).

pilau (pɪ'laʊ), **pilaf, pilaff** ('pɪlæf), **pilao** (pɪ'laʊ), *or* **pilaw** (pɪ'lɔː) *n* a dish originating from the East, consisting of rice flavoured with spices and cooked in stock, to which meat, poultry, or fish may be added. [C17: from Turkish *pilāw*, from Persian]

pilch (pɪltʃ) *n Brit., archaic.* **1** an outer garment, originally one made of skin. **2** an infant's outer wrapping, worn over the napkin. [C17: from Old English *pylce* a garment made of skin and fur, from Late Latin *pellicia*, from Latin *pellis* fur]

pilchard ('pɪltʃəd) *n* a European food fish, *Sardina* (or *Clupea*) *pilchardus*, with a rounded body covered with large scales: family *Clupeidae* (herrings). [C16 *pylcher*, of obscure origin]

Pilcomayo (*Spanish* pilko'majo) *n* a river in S central South America, rising in W central Bolivia and flowing southeast, forming the border between Argentina and Paraguay, to the Paraguay River at Asunción. Length: about 1600 km (1000 miles).

pile[1] (paɪl) *n* **1** a collection of objects laid on top of one another or of other material stacked vertically; heap; mound. **2** *Informal.* a large amount of money (esp. in the phrase **make a pile**). **3** (*often pl*) *Informal.* a large amount: *a pile of work.* **4** a less common word for **pyre. 5** a large building or group of buildings. **6** short for **voltaic pile. 7** *Physics.* a structure of uranium and a moderator used for producing atomic energy; nuclear reactor. **8** *Metallurgy.* an arrangement of wrought-iron bars that are to be heated and worked into a single bar. **9** the point of an arrow. ◆ *vb* **10** (often foll. by *up*) to collect or be collected into or as if into a pile: *snow piled up in the drive.* **11** (*intr;* foll. by *in, into, off, out,* etc.) to move in a group, esp. in a hurried or disorganized manner: *to pile off the bus.* **12 pile arms.** to prop a number of rifles together, muzzles together and upwards, butts forming the base. **13 pile it on.** *Informal.* to exaggerate. ◆ See also **pile up.** [C15: via Old French from Latin *pīla* stone pier]

pile[2] (paɪl) *n* **1** a long column of timber, concrete, or steel that is driven into the ground to provide a foundation for a structure. **2** *Heraldry.* an ordinary shaped like a wedge, usually displayed point-downwards. ◆ *vb* (*tr*) **3** to drive (piles) into the ground. **4** to provide or support (a structure) with piles. [Old English *pīl*, from Latin *pīlum*]

pile[3] (paɪl) *n* **1** *Textiles.* **1a** the yarns in a fabric that stand up or out from the weave, as in carpeting, velvet, etc. **1b** one of these yarns. **2** soft fine hair, fur, wool, etc. [C15: from Anglo-Norman *pyle*, from Latin *pilus* hair]

pilea ('pɪlɪə) *n* any plant of the tropical annual or perennial genus *Pilea*, esp. *P. muscosa*, the artillery or gunpowder plant, which releases a cloud of pollen when shaken; some others are grown for their ornamental foliage: family *Urticaceae.* [New Latin, from Greek *pilos* cap (from the shape of the segments of the perianth)]

pileate ('paɪlɪɪt, -ˌeɪt, 'pɪl-) *or* **pileated** ('paɪlɪˌeɪtɪd, 'pɪl-) *adj* **1** (of birds) having a crest. **2** *Botany.* having a pileus. [C18: from Latin *pīleātus* wearing a felt cap, from PILEUS]

pile-driver *n* **1** a machine that drives piles into the ground either by repeatedly allowing a heavy weight to fall on the head of the pile or by using a steam hammer. **2** *Informal.* a forceful punch or kick.

pileous ('paɪlɪəs, 'pɪl-) *adj Biology.* **1** hairy. **2** of or relating to hair. [C19: ultimately from Latin *pilus* a hair]

piles (paɪlz) *pl n* a nontechnical name for **haemorrhoids.** [C15: from Latin *pilae* balls (referring to the appearance of external piles)]

pile shoe *n* an iron casting shaped to a point and fitted to a lower end of a wooden or concrete pile. Also called: **shoe.**

pileum ('paɪlɪəm, 'pɪl-) *n, pl* **-lea** (-lɪə). the top of a bird's head from the base of the bill to the occiput. [C19: New Latin, from Latin PILEUS]

pile up *vb* (*adv*) **1** to gather or be gathered in a pile; accumulate. **2** *Informal.* to crash or cause to crash. ◆ *n* **pile-up. 3** *Informal.* a multiple collision of vehicles.

pileus ('paɪlɪəs, 'pɪl-) *n, pl* **-lei** (-lɪˌaɪ). the upper cap-shaped part of a mushroom or similar spore-producing body. [C18 (botanical use): New Latin, from Latin: felt cap]

pilewort ('paɪlˌwɜːt) *n* any of several plants, such as lesser celandine, thought to be effective in treating piles.

pilfer ('pɪlfə) *vb* to steal (minor items), esp. in small quantities. [C14 *pylfre* (n) from Old French *pelfre* booty; see PELF] ▸ **'pilferer** *n* ▸ **'pilfering** *n*

pilferage ('pɪlfərɪdʒ) *n* **1** the act or practice of stealing small quantities or articles. **2** the amount so stolen.

pilgarlic (pɪl'gɑːlɪk) *n* **1** *Obsolete.* a bald head or a man with a bald head. **2** *Dialect.* a pitiable person. [C16: literally: peeled garlic]

pilgrim ('pɪlgrɪm) *n* **1** a person who undertakes a journey to a sacred place as an act of religious devotion. **2** any wayfarer. [C12: from Provençal *pelegrin*, from Latin *peregrīnus* foreign, from *per* through + *ager* field, land; see PEREGRINE]

Pilgrim ('pɪlgrɪm) *n* See **Canterbury Pilgrims** (sense 2).

pilgrimage ('pɪlgrɪmɪdʒ) *n* **1** a journey to a shrine or other sacred place. **2** a journey or long search made for exalted or sentimental reasons. ◆ *vb* **3** (*intr*) to make a pilgrimage.

Pilgrimage of Grace *n* a rebellion in 1536 in N England against the Reformation and Henry VIII's government.

Pilgrim Fathers *or* **Pilgrims** *pl n* **the.** the English Puritans who sailed on the Mayflower to New England, where they founded Plymouth Colony in SE Massachusetts (1620).

pili[1] (pɪ'liː) *n, pl* **-lis. 1** a burseraceous Philippine tree, *Canarium ovatum*, with edible seeds resembling almonds. **2** Also called: **pili nut.** the seed of this tree. [from Tagalog]

pili[2] ('paɪlɪ) *pl n, sing* **pilus** ('paɪləs). *Bacteriol.* short curled hairlike processes on the surface of certain bacteria that are involved in conjugation and the attachment of the bacteria to other cells. [C20: from Latin: hairs]

piliferous (paɪ'lɪfərəs) *adj* **1** (esp. of plants or their parts) bearing or ending in a hair or hairs. **2** designating the outer layer of root epidermis, which bears the root hairs. [C19: from Latin *pilus* hair + -FEROUS. Compare PILE[3]]

piliform ('pɪlɪˌfɔːm) *adj Botany.* resembling a long hair.

piling ('paɪlɪŋ) *n* **1** the act of driving piles. **2** a number of piles. **3** a structure formed of piles.

Pílion ('piljɔn) *n* transliteration of the Modern Greek name for **Pelion.**

pill[1] (pɪl) *n* **1** a small spherical or ovoid mass of a medicinal substance, intended to be swallowed whole. **2 the.** (*sometimes cap.*) *Informal.* an oral contraceptive. **3** something unpleasant that must be endured (esp. in the phrase **bitter pill to swallow**). **4** *Slang.* a ball or disc. **5** *Slang.* an unpleasant or boring person. ◆ *vb* **6** (*tr*) to give pills to. **7** (*tr*) to make pills of. **8** (*intr*) to form into small balls. **9** (*tr*) *Slang.* to blackball. ◆ See also **pills.** [C15: from Middle Flemish *pille*, from Latin *pilula* a little ball, from *pila* ball]

pill[2] (pɪl) *vb* **1** *Archaic or dialect.* to peel or skin (something). **2** *Archaic.* to pillage or plunder (a place). **3** *Obsolete.* to make or become bald. [Old English *pilian*, from Latin *pilāre* to strip]

pillage ('pɪlɪdʒ) *vb* **1** to rob (a town, village, etc.) of (booty or spoils), esp. during a war. ◆ *n* **2** the act of pillaging. **3** something obtained by pillaging; booty. [C14: via Old French from *piller* to despoil, probably from *peille* rag, from Latin *pīleus* felt cap] ▸ **'pillager** *n*

pillar ('pɪlə) *n* **1** an upright structure of stone, brick, metal, etc., that supports a superstructure or is used for ornamentation. **2** something resembling this in shape or function: *a pillar of stones; a pillar of smoke.* **3** a tall, slender, usually sheer rock column, forming a separate top. **4** a prominent supporter: *a pillar of the Church.* **5 from pillar to post.** from one place to another. ◆ *vb* **6** (*tr*) to support with or as if with pillars. [C13: from Old French *pilier*, from Latin *pīla;* see PILE[1]]

pillar box *n* **1** (in Britain) a red pillar-shaped public letter box situated on a pavement. ◆ *adj* **pillar-box. 2** characteristic of a pillar box (in the phrase **pillar-box red**).

Pillars of Hercules *pl n* the two promontories at the E end of the Strait of Gibraltar: the Rock of Gibraltar on the European side and the Jebel Musa on the African side; according to legend, formed by Hercules.

pill beetle *n* a very common beetle, *Byrrhus pilula*, typical of the family *Byrrhidae*, that can feign death by withdrawing legs and antennae into grooves underneath the oval body.

pillbox ('pɪlˌbɒks) *n* **1** a box for pills. **2** a small enclosed fortified emplacement, usually made of reinforced concrete. **3** a small round hat, now worn esp. by women.

pill bug *n* any of various woodlice of the genera *Armadillidium* and *Oniscus*, capable of rolling up into a ball when disturbed.

pillion ('pɪljən) *n* **1** a seat or place behind the rider of a motorcycle, scooter, horse, etc. ◆ *adv* **2** on a pillion: *to ride pillion.* [C16: from Gaelic; compare Scottish *pillean*, Irish *pillīn* couch; related to Latin *pellis* skin]

pilliwinks ('pɪlɪˌwɪŋks) *pl n* a medieval instrument of torture for the fingers and thumbs. [C14: of uncertain origin]

pillock ('pɪlək) *n Brit. slang.* a stupid or annoying person. [C14: from Scandinavian dialect *pillicock* penis]

pillory ('pɪlərɪ) *n, pl* **-ries. 1** a wooden framework into which offenders were formerly locked by the neck and wrists and exposed to public abuse and ridicule. **2** exposure to public scorn or abuse. ◆ *vb* **-ries, -rying, -ried.** (*tr*) **3** to expose to public scorn or ridicule. **4** to punish by putting in a pillory. [C13: from Anglo-Latin *pillorium*, from Old French *pilori*, of uncertain origin; related to Provençal *espillori*]

pillow ('pɪləʊ) *n* **1** a cloth case stuffed with feathers, foam rubber, etc., used to support the head, esp. during sleep. **2** Also called: **cushion.** a padded cushion or board on which pillow lace is made. **3** anything like a pillow in shape or function. ◆ *vb* (*tr*) **4** to rest (one's head) on or as if on a pillow. **5** to serve as a pillow for. [Old English *pylwe*, from Latin *pulvīnus* cushion; compare German *Pfühl*]

pillow block *n Machinery.* a block, such as a simple journal, that supports a shaft.

pillowcase ('pɪləʊˌkeɪs) *or* **pillowslip** ('pɪləʊˌslɪp) *n* a removable washable cover of cotton, linen, nylon, etc., for a pillow.

pillow fight *n* a mock fight in which participants thump each other with pillows.

pillow lace *n* lace made by winding thread around bobbins on a padded cushion or board. Compare **point lace.**

pillow lava *n* lava that has solidified under water, having a characteristic structure comprising a series of close-fitting pillow-shaped masses.
pillow sham *n Chiefly U.S.* a decorative cover for a bed pillow.
pillow talk *n* intimate conversation in bed.
pills (pɪlz) *pl n* a taboo slang word for **testicles.**
pillwort ('pɪl,wɜːt) *n* a small Eurasian water fern, *Pilularia globulifera,* with globular spore-producing bodies. [C19: from PILL[1] + WORT]
pilocarpine (,paɪləʊ'kɑːpaɪn, -pɪn) *or* **pilocarpin** (,paɪləʊ'kɑːpɪn) *n* an alkaloid extracted from the leaves of the jaborandi tree, formerly used to induce sweating. Formula: $C_{11}H_{16}N_2O_2$. [C19: from New Latin *Pilocarpus* genus name, from Greek *pilos* hair + *karpos* fruit]
pilomotor (,paɪləʊ'məʊtə) *adj Physiol.* causing movement of hairs: *pilomotor nerves.*
Pílos ('pilɔs) *n* transliteration of the Modern Greek name for **Pylos.**
pilose ('paɪləʊz) *or* **pilous** *adj Biology.* covered with fine soft hairs: *pilose leaves.* [C18: from Latin *pilōsus,* from *pilus* hair] ► **pilosity** (paɪ'lɒsɪtɪ) *n*
pilot ('paɪlət) *n* **1a** a person who is qualified to operate an aircraft or spacecraft in flight. **1b** (*as modifier*): *pilot error.* **2a** a person who is qualified to steer or guide a ship into or out of a port, river mouth, etc. **2b** (*as modifier*): *a pilot ship.* **3** a person who steers a ship. **4** a person who acts as a leader or guide. **5** *Machinery.* a guide, often consisting of a tongue or dowel, used to assist in joining two mating parts together. **6** *Machinery.* a plug gauge for measuring an internal diameter. **7** *Films.* a colour test strip accompanying black-and-white rushes from colour originals. **8** an experimental programme on radio or television. **9** See **pilot film. 10** (*modifier*) used in or serving as a test or trial: *a pilot project.* **11** (*modifier*) serving as a guide: *a pilot beacon.* ◆ *vb* (*tr*) **12** to act as pilot of. **13** to control the course of. **14** to guide or lead (a project, people, etc.). [C16: from French *pilote,* from Medieval Latin *pilotus,* ultimately from Greek *pēdon* oar; related to Greek *pous* foot]
pilotage ('paɪlətɪdʒ) *n* **1** the act of piloting an aircraft or ship. **2** a pilot's fee. **3** the navigation of an aircraft by the observation of ground features and use of charts.
pilot balloon *n* a meteorological balloon used to observe air currents.
pilot bird *n* a warbler of forest floors in SE Australia, *Pycnoptilus floccosus,* named from its alleged habit of accompanying the superb lyrebird.
pilot biscuit *n* another term for **hardtack.**
pilot cloth *n* a type of thick blue cloth used esp. to make sailor's coats.
pilot engine *n* a locomotive that leads one or more other locomotives at the head of a train of coaches or wagons.
pilot film *n* a film of short duration serving as a guide to a projected series.
pilot fish *n* **1** a small carangid fish, *Naucrates ductor,* of tropical and subtropical seas, marked with dark vertical bands: often accompanies sharks and other large fishes. **2** any of various similar or related fishes.
pilot house *n Nautical.* an enclosed structure on the bridge of a vessel from which it can be navigated; wheelhouse.
piloting ('paɪlətɪŋ) *n* **1** the navigational handling of a ship near land using buoys, soundings, landmarks, etc., or the finding of a ship's position by such means. **2** the occupation of a pilot.
pilot lamp *n* a small light in an electric circuit or device that lights up when the circuit is closed or when certain conditions prevail.
pilot light *n* **1** a small auxiliary flame that ignites the main burner of a gas appliance when the control valve opens. **2** a small electric light used as an indicator.
pilot officer *n* the most junior commissioned rank in the British Royal Air Force and in certain other air forces.
pilot plant *n* a small-scale industrial plant in which problems can be identified and solved before the full-scale plant is built.
pilot study *n* a small-scale experiment or set of observations undertaken to decide how and whether to launch a full-scale project.
pilot whale *n* any of several black toothed whales of the genus *Globicephala,* such as *G. melaena,* that occur in all seas except polar seas: family *Delphinidae.* Also called: **black whale, blackfish.**
pilous ('paɪləs) *adj* a variant of **pilose.**
Pils (pɪlz, pɪls) *n* a type of lager-like beer. [C20: abbrev. of PILSNER]
Pilsen ('pɪlzən) *n* the German name for **Plzeň.**
Pilsner ('pɪlznə) *or* **Pilsener** *n* a type of pale beer with a strong flavour of hops. [named after PILSEN, where it was originally brewed]
Piłsudski (*Polish* piw'sutski) *n* **Józef** ('juzef). 1867–1935, Polish nationalist leader and statesman; president (1918–21) and premier (1926–28; 1930).
Piltdown man ('pɪlt,daʊn) *n* an advanced hominid postulated from fossil bones found in Sussex in 1912, but shown by modern dating methods in 1953 to be a hoax, which was perpetrated by a student museum assistant who was refused a wage.
pilule ('pɪljuːl) *n* a small pill. [C16: via French from Latin *pilula* little ball, from *pila* ball] ► **'pilular** *adj*
pimento (pɪ'mɛntəʊ) *n, pl* **-tos.** another name for **allspice** or **pimiento.** [C17: from Spanish *pimiento* pepper plant, from Medieval Latin *pigmenta* spiced drink, from Latin *pigmentum* PIGMENT]
pi meson *n* another name for **pion.**
pimiento (pɪ'mjɛntəʊ, -'mɛn-) *n, pl* **-tos.** a Spanish pepper, *Capsicum annuum,* with a red fruit used raw in salads, cooked as a vegetable, and as a stuffing for green olives. Also called: **pimento.** [variant of PIMENTO]
pimp[1] (pɪmp) *n* **1** a man who solicits for a prostitute or brothel and lives off the earnings. **2** a man who procures sexual gratification for another; procurer; pander. ◆ *vb* **3** (*intr*) to act as a pimp. [C17: of unknown origin]
pimp[2] (pɪmp) *Slang, chiefly Austral. and N.Z.* ◆ *n* **1** a spy or informer. ◆ *vb* **2** (*intr;* often foll. by *on*) to inform (on). [of unknown origin]
pimpernel ('pɪmpə,nɛl, -pᵊl) *n* **1** any of several plants of the primulaceous genus *Anagallis,* such as the scarlet pimpernel, typically having small star-shaped flowers. **2** any of several similar and related plants, such as *Lysimachia nemorum* (**yellow pimpernel**). [C15: from Old French *pimpernelle,* ultimately from Latin *piper* PEPPER; compare Old English *pipeneale*]
pimple ('pɪmpᵊl) *n* a small round usually inflamed swelling of the skin. [C14: related to Old English *pipilian* to break out in spots; compare Latin *papula* pimple] ► **'pimpled** *adj* ► **'pimply** *adj* ► **'pimpliness** *n*
pin (pɪn) *n* **1a** a short stiff straight piece of wire pointed at one end and either rounded or having a flattened head at the other: used mainly for fastening pieces of cloth, paper, etc., esp. temporarily. **1b** (*in combination*): *pinhole.* **2** short for **cotter pin, hairpin, panel pin, rolling pin,** or **safety pin. 3** an ornamental brooch, esp. a narrow one. **4** a badge worn fastened to the clothing by a pin. **5** something of little or no importance (esp. in the phrases **not care** *or* **give a pin (for)**). **6** a peg or dowel. **7** anything resembling a pin in shape, function, etc. **8** (in various bowling games) a usually club-shaped wooden object set up in groups as a target. **9** Also called: **safety pin.** a clip on a hand grenade that prevents its detonation until removed or released. **10** *Nautical.* **10a** See **belaying pin. 10b** the axle of a sheave. **10c** the sliding closure for a shackle. **11** *Music.* a metal tuning peg on a piano, the end of which is inserted into a detachable key by means of which it is turned. **12** *Surgery.* a metal rod, esp. of stainless steel, for holding together adjacent ends of fractured bones during healing. **13** *Chess.* a position in which a piece is pinned against a more valuable piece or the king. **14** *Golf.* the flagpole marking the hole on a green. **15a** the cylindrical part of a key that enters a lock. **15b** the cylindrical part of a lock where this part of the key fits. **16** *Wrestling.* a position in which a person is held tight or immobile, esp. with both shoulders touching the ground. **17** a dovetail tenon used to make a dovetail joint. **18** (in Britain) a miniature beer cask containing 4½ gallons. **19** (*usually pl*) *Informal.* a leg. **20 be put to the pin on one's collar.** *Irish.* to be forced to make an extreme effort. ◆ *vb* **pins, pinning, pinned.** (*tr*) **21** to attach, hold, or fasten with or as if with a pin or pins. **22** to transfix with a pin, spear, etc. **23** (foll. by *on*) *Informal.* to place (the blame for something): *he pinned the charge on his accomplice.* **24** *Chess.* to cause (an enemy piece) to be effectively immobilized by attacking it with a queen, rook, or bishop so that moving it would reveal a check or expose a more valuable piece to capture. **25** Also: **underpin.** to support (masonry), as by driving in wedges over a beam. ◆ See also **pin down.** [Old English *pinn;* related to Old High German *pfinn,* Old Norse *pinni* nail]
PIN (pɪn) *n acronym for* personal identification number: a number used by a holder of a cash card or credit card used in EFTPOS.
p-i-n *abbrev. for* p-type, intrinsic, n-type: a form of construction of semiconductor devices.
pinaceous (paɪ'neɪʃəs) *adj* of, relating to, or belonging to the *Pinaceae,* a family of conifers with needle-like leaves: includes pine, spruce, fir, larch, and cedar. [C19: via New Latin from Latin *pīnus* a pine]
piña cloth ('piːnjə) *n* a fine fabric made from the fibres of the pineapple leaf. [C19: from Spanish *piña* pineapple]
piña colada ('piːnjə kə'lɑːdə) *n* a drink consisting of pineapple juice, coconut, and rum. [C20: from Spanish, literally: strained pineapple]
pinafore ('pɪnə,fɔː) *n* **1** *Chiefly Brit.* an apron, esp. one with a bib. **2** *Chiefly Brit.* short for **pinafore dress. 3** *Chiefly U.S.* an overdress buttoning at the back. [C18: from PIN + AFORE]
pinafore dress *n Brit.* a sleeveless dress worn over a blouse or sweater. Often shortened to **pinafore.** U.S. and Canadian name: **jumper.**
Pinar del Río (*Spanish* pi'nar ðel 'rrio) *n* a city in W Cuba: tobacco industry. Pop.: 128 570 (1994 est.).
pinaster (paɪ'næstə, pɪ-) *n* a Mediterranean pine tree, *Pinus pinaster,* with paired needles and prickly cones. Also called: **maritime** (*or* **cluster**) **pinaster.** [C16: from Latin: wild pine, from *pinus* pine]
pinball ('pɪn,bɔːl) *n* **a** a game in which the player shoots a small ball through several hazards on a table, electrically operated machine, etc. **b** (*as modifier*): *a pinball machine.*
pince-nez ('pæns,neɪ, 'pɪns-; *French* pɛ̃sne) *n, pl* **pince-nez.** eyeglasses that are held in place only by means of a clip over the bridge of the nose. [C19: French, literally: pinch-nose]
pincer movement ('pɪnsə) *n* a military tactical movement in which two columns of an army follow a curved route towards each other with the aim of isolating and surrounding an enemy. Also called: **envelopment.**
pincers ('pɪnsəz) *pl n* **1** Also called: **pair of pincers.** a gripping tool consisting of two hinged arms with handles at one end and, at the other, curved bevelled jaws that close on the workpiece: used esp. for extracting nails. **2** the pair or pairs of jointed grasping appendages in lobsters and certain other arthropods. [C14: from Old French *pinceour,* from Old French *pincier* to PINCH]
pinch (pɪntʃ) *vb* **1** to press (something, esp. flesh) tightly between two surfaces, esp. between a finger and the thumb (see **nip**[1]). **2** to confine, squeeze, or painfully press (toes, fingers, etc.) because of lack of space: *these shoes pinch.* **3** (*tr*) to cause stinging pain to: *the cold pinched his face.* **4** (*tr*) to make thin or drawn-looking, as from grief, lack of food, etc. **5** (usually foll. by *on*) to provide (oneself or another person) with meagre allowances, amounts, etc. **6 pinch pennies.** to live frugally because of meanness or to economize. **7** (*tr*) *Nautical.* to sail (a sailing vessel) so close to the wind that her sails begin to luff and she loses way. **8** (*intr;* sometimes foll. by *out*) (of a vein of ore) to narrow or peter out. **9** (usually foll. by *off, out,* or *back*) to remove the tips of (buds, shoots, etc.) to correct or encourage growth. **10** (*tr*) *Informal.* to steal or take without asking. **11** (*tr*) *Informal.* to arrest. ◆ *n* **12** a squeeze or sustained nip. **13** the quantity of a substance, such as salt, that can be taken between a thumb and finger. **14** a very small quantity. **15** a critical situation; predicament; emergency: *if it comes to the pinch we'll have to manage.* **16** (usually preceded by *the*) sharp, painful, or extreme stress, need, etc.: *feeling the pinch of poverty.* **17** See **pinch bar. 18** *Slang.* a robbery. **19** *Slang.* a police raid or arrest. **20 at a**

pinch. if absolutely necessary. **21 with a pinch** *or* **grain of salt.** without wholly believing; sceptically. [C16: probably from Old Norman French *pinchier* (unattested); related to Old French *pincier* to pinch; compare Late Latin *punctiāre* to prick]

pinch bar *n* a crowbar with a lug formed on it to provide a fulcrum.

pinchbeck ('pɪntʃ,bɛk) *n* **1** an alloy of copper and zinc, used as imitation gold. **2** a spurious or cheap imitation; sham. ◆ *adj* **3** made of pinchbeck. **4** sham, spurious, or cheap. [C18 (the alloy), C19 (something spurious): after Christopher *Pinchbeck* (?1670–1732), English watchmaker who invented it]

pinchcock ('pɪntʃ,kɒk) *n* a clamp used to compress a flexible tube to control the flow of fluid through it.

pinch effect *n* the constriction of a beam of charged particles, caused by a force on each particle due to its motion in the magnetic field generated by the movement of the other particles.

pinch-hit *vb* **-hits, -hitting, -hit.** (*intr*) **1** *Baseball.* to bat as a substitute for the scheduled batter. **2** *U.S. and Canadian informal.* to act as a substitute. ▸ **pinch hitter** *n*

pinchpenny ('pɪntʃ,pɛnɪ) *adj* **1** niggardly; miserly. ◆ *n, pl* **-nies. 2** a miserly person; niggard.

Pinckney ('pɪŋknɪ) *n* **1 Charles.** 1757–1824, U.S. statesman, who was a leading member of the convention that framed the U.S. Constitution (1787). **2** his cousin, **Charles Cotesworth.** 1746–1825, U.S. soldier, statesman, and diplomat, who also served at the Constitutional Convention. **3** his brother, **Thomas.** 1750–1828, U.S. soldier and politician. He was U.S. minister to Britain (1792–96) and special envoy to Spain (1795–96).

pin curl *n* a small section of hair wound in a circle and secured with a hairpin to set it in a curl.

Pincus ('pɪŋkəs) *n* **Gregory Goodwin.** 1903–67, U.S. physiologist, whose work on steroid hormones led to the development of the first contraceptive pill.

pincushion ('pɪn,kʊʃən) *n* a small well-padded cushion in which pins are stuck ready for use.

pindan ('pɪn,dæn) *n* **1** a desert region of Western Australia. **2** the vegetation growing in this region. [from a native Australian language]

Pindar ('pɪndə) *n* ?518–?438 B.C., Greek lyric poet, noted for his *Epinikia,* odes commemorating victories in the Greek games.

Pindaric (pɪn'dærɪk) *adj* **1** of, relating to, or resembling the style of Pindar. **2** *Prosody.* having a complex metrical structure, either regular or irregular. ◆ *n* **3** See **Pindaric ode.**

Pindaric ode *n* a form of ode associated with Pindar consisting of a triple unit or groups of triple units, with a strophe and an antistrophe of identical structure followed by an epode of a different structure. Often shortened to **Pindaric.**

pindling ('pɪndlɪŋ) *adj Dialect.* **1** *Western Brit.* peevish or fractious. **2** *U.S.* sickly or puny. [C19: perhaps changed from *spindling*]

pin down *vb* (*tr, adv*) **1** to force (someone) to make a decision or carry out a promise. **2** to define clearly: *he had a vague suspicion that he couldn't quite pin down.* **3** to confine to a place: *the fallen tree pinned him down.*

Pindus ('pɪndəs) *n* a mountain range in central Greece between Epirus and Thessaly. Highest peak: Mount Smólikas, 2633 m (8639 ft.). Modern Greek name: **Píndhos** ('pinðɔs).

pine[1] (paɪn) *n* **1** any evergreen resinous coniferous tree of the genus *Pinus,* of the N hemisphere, with long needle-shaped leaves and brown cones: family *Pinaceae.* See also **longleaf pine, nut pine, pitch pine, Scots pine. 2** any other tree or shrub of the family *Pinaceae.* **3** the wood of any of these trees. **4** any of various similar but unrelated plants, such as ground pine and screw pine. [Old English *pīn,* from Latin *pīnus* pine]

pine[2] (paɪn) *vb* **1** (*intr;* often foll. by *for* or an infinitive) to feel great longing or desire; yearn. **2** (*intr;* often foll. by *away*) to become ill, feeble, or thin through worry, longing, etc. **3** (*tr*) *Archaic.* to mourn or grieve for. [Old English *pīnian* to torture, from *pīn* pain, from Medieval Latin *pēna,* from Latin *poena* PAIN]

pineal ('pɪnɪəl, paɪ'niːəl) *adj* **1** resembling a pine cone. **2** of or relating to the pineal gland. [C17: via French from Latin *pīnea* pine cone]

pineal eye *n* an outgrowth of the pineal gland that forms an eyelike structure on the top of the head in certain cold-blooded vertebrates.

pineal gland *or* **body** *n* a pea-sized organ in the brain, situated beneath the posterior part of the corpus callosum, that secretes melatonin into the bloodstream. Technical names: **epiphysis, epiphysis cerebri.**

pineapple ('paɪn,æpᵊl) *n* **1** a tropical American bromeliaceous plant, *Ananas comosus,* cultivated in the tropics for its large fleshy edible fruit. **2** the fruit of this plant, consisting of an inflorescence clustered around a fleshy axis and surmounted by a tuft of leaves. **3** *Military slang.* a hand grenade. [C14 *pinappel* pine cone; C17: applied to the fruit because of its appearance]

pineapple weed *n* an Asian plant, *Matricaria matricarioides,* naturalized in Europe and North America, having greenish-yellow flower heads, and smelling of pineapple when crushed: family *Compositae* (composites).

pine cone *n* the seed-producing structure of a pine tree. See **cone** (sense 3a).

pine end *n Dialect.* the gable or gable end of a building.

pine marten *n* a marten, *Martes martes,* of N European and Asian coniferous woods, having dark brown fur with a creamy-yellow patch on the throat. See also **sweet marten.**

pinene ('paɪniːn) *n* either of two isomeric terpenes, found in many essential oils and constituting the main part of oil of turpentine. The commonest structural isomer (α-**pinene**) is used in the manufacture of camphor, solvents, plastics, and insecticides. Formula: $C_{10}H_{16}$. [C20: from PINE[1] + -ENE]

pine needle *n* any of the fine pointed leaves of a pine.

pine nut *or* **kernel** *n* the edible seed of certain pine trees.

Pinero (pɪ'nɪərəʊ) *n* Sir **Arthur Wing.** 1855–1934, English dramatist. His works include the farce *Dandy Dick* (1887) and the problem play *The Second Mrs Tanqueray* (1893).

pinery ('paɪnərɪ) *n, pl* **-neries. 1** a place, esp. a hothouse, where pineapples are grown. **2** a forest of pine trees, esp. one cultivated for timber.

Pines (paɪnz) *n* **Isle of.** the former name of the (Isle of) **Youth.**

pine tar *n* a brown or black semisolid or viscous substance, produced by the destructive distillation of pine wood, used in roofing compositions, paints, medicines, etc.

pinetum (paɪ'niːtəm) *n, pl* **-ta** (-tə). an area of land where pine trees and other conifers are grown. [C19: from Latin, from *pīnus* PINE[1]]

pin-eyed *adj* (of flowers, esp. primulas) having the stigma in the mouth of the corolla, on the end of a long style with the stamens lower in the tube. Compare **thrum-eyed.**

pinfall ('pɪn,fɔːl) *n Wrestling.* another name for **fall** (sense 48).

pinfeather ('pɪn,fɛðə) *n Ornithol.* a feather emerging from the skin and still enclosed in its horny sheath.

pinfish ('pɪn,fɪʃ) *n, pl* **-fish** *or* **-fishes.** a small porgy, *Lagodon rhomboides,* occurring off the SE North American coast of the Atlantic. Also called: **sailor's choice.** [so named because it has spines]

pinfold ('pɪn,fəʊld) *n* **1a** a pound for stray cattle. **1b** a fold or pen for sheep or cattle. ◆ *vb* **2** (*tr*) to gather or confine in or as if in a pinfold. [Old English *pundfald,* from POUND[3] + FOLD[2]]

ping (pɪŋ) *n* **1** a short high-pitched resonant sound, as of a bullet striking metal or a sonar echo. ◆ *vb* **2** (*intr*) to make such a noise. [C19: of imitative origin] ▸ **'pinging** *adj*

pinger ('pɪŋə) *n* a device that makes a pinging sound, esp. one that can be preset to ring at a particular time.

pingo ('pɪŋgəʊ) *n, pl* **-gos.** a mound of earth or gravel formed through pressure from a layer of water trapped between newly frozen ice and underlying permafrost in Arctic regions. [C20: from Eskimo]

Ping-Pong ('pɪŋ,pɒŋ) *n Trademark.* another name for **table tennis.** Also called: **ping pong.**

pinguid ('pɪŋgwɪd) *adj* fatty, oily, or greasy; soapy. [C17: from Latin *pinguis* fat, rich] ▸ **pin'guidity** *n*

pinhead ('pɪn,hɛd) *n* **1** the head of a pin. **2** something very small. **3** *Informal.* a stupid or contemptible person.

pinheaded ('pɪn,hɛdɪd) *adj Informal.* stupid or silly. ▸ **'pin,headedness** *n*

pinhole ('pɪn,həʊl) *n* **1** a small hole made with or as if with a pin. **2** *Archery.* the exact centre of an archery target, in the middle of the gold zone.

pinhole camera *n* a camera with a pinhole as an aperture instead of a lens.

pinion[1] ('pɪnjən) *n* **1** *Chiefly poetic.* a bird's wing. **2** the part of a bird's wing including the flight feathers. ◆ *vb* (*tr*) **3** to hold or bind (the arms) of (a person) so as to restrain or immobilize him. **4** to confine or shackle. **5** to make (a bird) incapable of flight by removing that part of (the wing) from which the flight feathers grow. [C15: from Old French *pignon* wing, from Latin *pinna* wing]

pinion[2] ('pɪnjən) *n* a cogwheel that engages with a larger wheel or rack, which it drives or by which it is driven. [C17: from French *pignon* cogwheel, from Old French *peigne* comb, from Latin *pecten* comb; see PECTEN]

Piniós (pi'njɔs) *n* transliteration of the Modern Greek name for the **Salambria.**

pinite ('pɪnaɪt, 'paɪ-) *n* a greyish-green or brown mineral containing amorphous aluminium and potassium sulphates. [C19: from German *Pinit,* named after the *Pini* mine, Schneeberg, Saxony]

pin joint *n* a mechanical joint that will transmit axial load but will not transmit torque.

pink[1] (pɪŋk) *n* **1** any of a group of colours with a reddish hue that are of low to moderate saturation and can usually reflect or transmit a large amount of light; a pale reddish tint. **2** pink cloth or clothing: *dressed in pink.* **3** any of various Old World plants of the caryophyllaceous genus *Dianthus,* such as *D. plumarius* (**garden pink**), cultivated for their fragrant flowers. See also **carnation** (sense 1). **4** any of various plants of other genera, such as the moss pink. **5** the flower of any of these plants. **6** the highest or best degree, condition, etc. (esp. in the phrases **in the pink of health, in the pink**). **7a** a huntsman's scarlet coat. **7b** a huntsman who wears a scarlet coat. ◆ *adj* **8** of the colour pink. **9** *Brit. informal.* left-wing. **10** *U.S. derogatory.* **10a** sympathetic to or influenced by Communism. **10b** leftist or radical, esp. half-heartedly. **11** *Informal.* of or relating to homosexuals or homosexuality: *the pink vote.* **12** (of a huntsman's coat) scarlet or red. ◆ *vb* **13** (*intr*) another word for **knock** (sense 7). [C16 (the flower), C18 (the colour): perhaps a shortening of PINKEYE] ▸ **'pinkish** *adj* ▸ **'pinkness** *n* ▸ **'pinky** *adj*

pink[2] (pɪŋk) *vb* (*tr*) **1** to prick lightly with a sword or rapier. **2** to decorate (leather, cloth, etc.) with a perforated or punched pattern. **3** to cut with pinking shears. [C14: perhaps of Low German origin; compare Low German *pinken* to peck]

pink[3] (pɪŋk) *n* a sailing vessel with a narrow overhanging transom. [C15: from Middle Dutch *pinke,* of obscure origin]

pink-collar *adj* of, relating to, or designating low-paid occupations traditionally associated with female workers. Compare **blue-collar, white-collar.**

pink elephants *pl n* a facetious name applied to hallucinations caused by drunkenness.

Pinkerton ('pɪŋkətən) *n* **Allan.** 1819–84, U.S. private detective, born in Scotland. He founded the first detective agency in the U.S. (1850) and organized an intelligence system for the Federal States of America (1861).

pinkeye ('pɪŋk,aɪ) *n* **1** Also called: **acute conjunctivitis.** an acute contagious inflammation of the conjunctiva of the eye, characterized by redness, discharge, etc.: usually caused by bacterial infection. **2** Also called: **infectious keratitis.** a similar condition affecting the cornea of horses and cattle. [C16: partial translation of obsolete Dutch *pinck oogen* small eyes]

pink-footed goose *n* a Eurasian goose, *Anser brachyrhynchus,* having a reddish-brown head, pink legs, and a pink band on its black beak.

pink gin *n* a mixture of gin and bitters.

pinkie *or* **pinky** ('pɪŋkɪ) *n, pl* **-ies.** *Scot., U.S., and Canadian.* the little finger. [C19: from Dutch *pinkje,* diminutive of PINK[1]; compare PINKEYE]

pinking shears *pl n* scissors with a serrated edge on one or both blades, producing a wavy edge to material cut, thus preventing fraying.

pink noise *n* noise containing a mixture of frequencies, but excluding higher frequencies.

pinko ('pɪŋkəʊ) *n, pl* **-os** *or* **-oes.** *U.S. derogatory.* a person regarded as mildly left-wing.

pinkroot ('pɪŋk,ruːt) *n* **1** any of several loganiaceous plants of the genus *Spigelia,* esp. *S. marilandica,* of the southeastern U.S., having red-and-yellow flowers and pink roots. **2** the powdered root of this plant, used as a vermifuge. **3** a fungal disease of onions and related plants resulting in stunted growth and shrivelled pink roots.

pink salmon *n* **1** any salmon having pale pink flesh, esp. *Oncorhynchus gorbuscha,* of the Pacific Ocean. **2** the flesh of such a fish.

pink slip *n U.S. informal.* a notice of redundancy issued to an employee.

pin money *n* **1** an allowance by a husband to his wife for personal expenditure. **2** money saved or earned to be used for incidental expenses.

pinna ('pɪnə) *n, pl* **-nae** (-niː) *or* **-nas. 1** any leaflet of a pinnate compound leaf. **2** *Zoology.* a feather, wing, fin, or similarly shaped part. **3** another name for **auricle** (sense 2). [C18: via New Latin from Latin: wing, feather, fin]

pinnace ('pɪnɪs) *n* any of various kinds of ship's tender. [C16: from French *pinace,* apparently from Old Spanish *pinaza,* literally: something made of pine, ultimately from Latin *pīnus* pine]

pinnacle ('pɪnək^əl) *n* **1** the highest point or level, esp. of fame, success, etc. **2** a towering peak, as of a mountain. **3** a slender upright structure in the form of a cone, pyramid, or spire on the top of a buttress, gable, or tower. ♦ *vb (tr)* **4** to set on or as if on a pinnacle. **5** to furnish with a pinnacle or pinnacles. **6** to crown with a pinnacle. [C14: via Old French from Late Latin *pinnāculum* a peak, from Latin *pinna* wing]

pinnate ('pɪneɪt, 'pɪnɪt) *or* **pinnated** *adj* **1** like a feather in appearance. **2** (of compound leaves) having the leaflets growing opposite each other in pairs on either side of the stem. [C18: from Latin *pinnātus,* from *pinna* feather] ▸ **'pinnately** *adv* ▸ **pin'nation** *n*

pinnati- *combining form.* pinnate or pinnately: *pinnatifid.*

pinnatifid (pɪ'nætɪfɪd) *adj* (of leaves) pinnately divided into lobes reaching more than halfway to the midrib. ▸ **pin'natifidly** *adv*

pinnatipartite (pɪ,nætɪ'pɑːtaɪt) *adj* (of leaves) pinnately divided into lobes reaching just over halfway to the midrib.

pinnatiped (pɪ'nætɪ,pɛd) *adj* (of birds) having lobate feet.

pinnatisect (pɪ'nætɪ,sɛkt) *adj* (of leaves) pinnately divided almost to the midrib but not into separate leaflets.

pinner ('pɪnə) *n* **1** a person or thing that pins. **2** a small dainty apron. **3** a cap with two long flaps pinned on.

pinniped ('pɪnɪ,pɛd) *or* **pinnipedian** (,pɪnɪ'piːdɪən) *adj* **1** of, relating to, or belonging to the *Pinnipedia,* an order of aquatic placental mammals having a streamlined body and limbs specialized as flippers: includes seals, sea lions, and the walrus. ♦ *n* **2** any pinniped animal. ♦ Compare **fissiped.** [C19: from New Latin *pinnipēs,* from Latin *pinna* feather, fin + *pēs* foot]

pinnule ('pɪnjuːl) *or* **pinnula** ('pɪnjʊlə) *n, pl* **pinnules** *or* **pinnulae** ('pɪnjʊ,liː). **1** any of the lobes of a leaflet of a pinnate compound leaf, which is itself pinnately divided. **2** *Zoology.* any feather-like part, such as any of the arms of a sea lily. [C16: from Latin *pinnula,* diminutive of *pinna* feather] ▸ **'pinnular** *adj*

pinny ('pɪnɪ) *n, pl* **-nies.** a child's or informal name for **pinafore** (sense 1).

Pinochet (Ugarte) ('piːnə,ʃeɪ) *n* **Augusto** (au'ɣusto). born 1915, Chilean general and statesman; president of Chile (1974–90) following his overthrow of Allende (1973).

pinochle, penuchle, penuckle, *or* **pinocle** ('piːnʌk^əl) *n* **1** a card game for two to four players similar to bezique. **2** the combination of queen of spades and jack of diamonds in this game. [C19: of unknown origin]

pinole (pɪ'nəʊlɪ) *n* (in the southwestern United States) flour made of parched ground corn, mesquite beans, sugar, etc. [from American Spanish, from Nahuatl]

pinotage ('pɪnətɑːʒ) *n* **1** a red grape variety of South Africa, a cross between the Pinot Noir and the Hermitage. **2** any of the red wines made from this grape.

Pinot Noir (piː'nəʊ nwɑː) *n* **1** a variety of black grape, grown esp. for winemaking. **2** any of the red wines made from this grape. [French]

pinpoint ('pɪn,pɔɪnt) *vb (tr)* **1** to locate or identify exactly: *to pinpoint a problem; to pinpoint a place on a map.* ♦ *n* **2** an insignificant or trifling thing. **3** the point of a pin. **4** *(modifier)* exact: *a pinpoint aim.*

pinprick ('pɪn,prɪk) *n* **1** a slight puncture made by or as if by a pin. **2** a small irritation. ♦ *vb* **3** *(tr)* to puncture with or as if with a pin.

pin rail *n Nautical.* a strong wooden rail or bar containing holes for belaying pins to which lines are fastened on sailing vessels. Compare **fife rail.**

pins and needles *n (functioning as sing) Informal.* **1** a tingling sensation in the fingers, toes, legs, etc., caused by the return of normal blood circulation after its temporary impairment. **2 on pins and needles.** in a state of anxious suspense or nervous anticipation.

Pinsk (*Russian* pinsk) *n* a city in SW Belarus: capital of a principality (13th–14th centuries). Pop.: 130 000 (1996 est.).

pinstripe ('pɪn,straɪp) *n* (in textiles) **a** a very narrow stripe in fabric or the fabric itself, used esp. for men's suits. **b** *(as modifier): a pinstripe suit.*

pint (paɪnt) *n* **1** a unit of liquid measure of capacity equal to one eighth of a gallon. 1 Brit. pint is equal to 0.568 litre, 1 U.S. pint to 0.473 litre. **2** a unit of dry measure of capacity equal to one half of a quart. 1 U.S. dry pint is equal to one sixty-fourth of a U.S. bushel or 0.5506 litre. **3** a measure having such a capacity. **4** *Brit. informal.* **4a** a pint of beer. **4b** a drink of beer: *he's gone out for a pint.* [C14: from Old French *pinte,* of uncertain origin; perhaps from Medieval Latin *pincta* marks used in measuring liquids, ultimately from Latin *pingere* to paint; compare Middle Low German, Middle Dutch *pinte*]

pinta[1] ('pɪntə) *n* a tropical infectious skin disease caused by the bacterium *Treponema carateum* and characterized by the formation of papules and loss of pigmentation in circumscribed areas. Also called: **mal de pinto.** [C19: from American Spanish, from Spanish: spot, ultimately from Latin *pictus* painted, from *pingere* to paint]

pinta[2] ('paɪntə) *n Informal.* a pint of milk. [C20: phonetic rendering of *pint of*]

Pinta ('pɪntə) *n* **the.** one of the three ships commanded by Columbus on his first voyage to America (1492).

pintadera (,pɪntə'dɛərə) *n* a decorative stamp, usually made of clay, found in the Neolithic of the E Mediterranean and in many American cultures. [from Spanish, literally: an instrument for making decorations on bread, from *pintado* mottled, from *pintar* to PAINT]

pintado petrel (pɪn'tɑːdəʊ) *n* another name for **Cape pigeon.** [C19: Portuguese: past participle of *pintar* to paint, referring to the mottled coloration]

pintail ('pɪn,teɪl) *n, pl* **-tails** *or* **-tail.** a greyish-brown duck, *Anas acuta,* with slender pointed wings and a pointed tail.

Pinter ('pɪntə) *n* **Harold.** born 1930, English dramatist. His plays, such as *The Caretaker* (1960), *The Homecoming* (1965), *Landscape* (1968), and *Ashes to Ashes* (1996), are noted for their equivocal and halting dialogue. ▸ **,Pinter'esque** *adj*

pintle ('pɪnt^əl) *n* **1** a pin or bolt forming the pivot of a hinge. **2** the link bolt, hook, or pin on a vehicle's towing bracket. **3** the needle or plunger of the injection valve of an oil engine. [Old English *pintel* penis]

pinto ('pɪntəʊ) *U.S. and Canadian.* ♦ *adj* **1** marked with patches of white; piebald. ♦ *n, pl* **-tos. 2** a pinto horse. [C19: from American Spanish (originally: painted, spotted), ultimately from Latin *pingere* to paint]

pinto bean *n* a variety of kidney bean that has mottled seeds and is grown for food and fodder in the southwestern U.S.

pint-size *or* **pint-sized** *adj Informal.* very small; tiny.

Pintubi ('pɪntəbɪ) *n* **1** *(pl* **-bi** *or* **-bis)** an Aboriginal people of the southern border area of Western Australia and the Northern Territory. **2** the language of this people.

pin tuck *n* a narrow ornamental fold used esp. on shirt fronts and dress bodices.

Pinturicchio (*Italian* pintu'rikkjo) *or* **Pintoricchio** (*Italian* pinto'rikkjo) *n* real name *Bernardino di Betto.* ?1454–1513, Italian painter of the Umbrian school.

pin-up *n* **1** *Informal.* **1a** a picture of a sexually attractive person, esp. when partially or totally undressed. **1b** *(as modifier): a pin-up magazine.* **2** *Slang.* a person who has appeared in such a picture. **3** a photograph of a famous personality. **4** *(modifier) U.S.* designed to be hung from a wall: *a pin-up lamp.*

pinwheel ('pɪn,wiːl) *n* **1** another name for **Catherine wheel** (sense 1). **2** a cogwheel whose teeth are formed by small pins projecting either axially or radially from the rim of the wheel. **3** the U.S. and Canadian name for **windmill** (sense 3).

pinwork ('pɪn,wɜːk) *n* (in needlepoint lace) the fine raised stitches.

pinworm ('pɪn,wɜːm) *n* a parasitic nematode worm, *Enterobius vermicularis,* infecting the colon, rectum, and anus of humans: family *Oxyuridae.* Also called: **threadworm.**

pin wrench *n* a wrench fitted with a cylindrical pin that registers in a hole in the part to be rotated, used to improve the application of the turning moment.

pinxit *Latin.* ('pɪŋksɪt) he (or she) painted it: an inscription sometimes found on paintings following the artist's name.

piny ('paɪnɪ) *adj* **pinier, piniest.** of, resembling, or covered with pine trees.

Pinyin ('pɪn'jɪn) *n* a system of romanized spelling developed in China in 1958: used to transliterate Chinese characters into the Roman alphabet.

Pinzón (*Spanish* pin'θon) *n* **1 Martín Alonzo** (mar'tin a'lɔnθo). ?1440–93, Spanish navigator, who commanded the *Pinta* on Columbus' first expedition (1492–93), which he abandoned in a vain attempt to be the first to arrive back in Spain. **2** his brother, **Vicente Yáñez** (bi'θente 'jaɲeθ). ?1460–?1524, Spanish navigator, who commanded the *Niña* on Columbus' first expedition (1492–93).

piolet (pjəʊ'leɪ) *n* a type of ice axe. [C19: from French (Savoy) dialect *piola* axe]

pion ('paɪɒn) *or* **pi meson** *n Physics.* a meson having a positive or negative charge and a rest mass 273 times that of the electron, or no charge and a rest mass 264 times that of the electron. [C20: from Greek letter PI[1] + ON]

pioneer (,paɪə'nɪə) *n* **1a** a colonist, explorer, or settler of a new land, region, etc. **1b** *(as modifier): a pioneer wagon.* **2** an innovator or developer of something new. **3** *Military.* a member of an infantry group that digs entrenchments, makes roads, etc. **4** *Ecology.* the first species of plant or animal to colonize an area of bare ground. ♦ *vb* **5** to be a pioneer (in or of). **6** *(tr)* to initiate, prepare, or open up: *to pioneer a medical programme.* [C16: from Old French *paonier* infantryman, from *paon* PAWN[2]; see also PEON[1]]

Pioneer[1] (,paɪə'nɪə) *n* a total abstainer from alcoholic drink, esp. a member of the **Pioneer Total Abstinence Association,** a society devoted to abstention.

Pioneer[2] (,paɪə'nɪə) *n* any of a series of U.S. spacecraft that studied the solar system, esp. **Pioneer 10,** which made the first flyby of Jupiter (1973), and **Pioneer 11,** which made the first flyby of Saturn (1979).

pious ('paɪəs) *adj* **1** having or expressing reverence for a god or gods; religious; devout. **2** marked by reverence. **3** marked by false reverence; sanctimonious. **4** sacred; not secular. **5** *Archaic.* having or expressing devotion for one's parents or others. [C17: from Latin *pius,* related to *piāre* to expiate] ▸ 'piously *adv* ▸ 'piousness *n*

Piozzi ('pjɔːtsɪ) *n* **Hester Lynch.** See (Hester Lynch) **Thrale.**

pip[1] (pɪp) *n* **1** the seed of a fleshy fruit, such as an apple or pear. **2** any of the segments marking the surface of a pineapple. **3** a rootstock or flower of the lily of the valley or certain other plants. [C18: short for PIPPIN]

pip[2] (pɪp) *n* **1** a short high-pitched sound, a sequence of which can act as a time signal, esp. on radio. **2** a radar blip. **3a** a spot or single device, such as a spade, diamond, heart, or club on a playing card. **3b** any of the spots on dice or dominoes. **4** *Informal.* the emblem worn on the shoulder by junior officers in the British Army, indicating their rank. ◆ *vb* **pips, pipping, pipped. 5** (of a young bird) **5a** (*intr*) to chirp; peep. **5b** to pierce (the shell of its egg) while hatching. **6** (*intr*) to make a short high-pitched sound. [C16 (in the sense: spot or speck); C17 (vb); C20 (in the sense: short high-pitched sound): of obscure, probably imitative origin; senses 1 and 5 are probably related to PEEP[2]]

pip[3] (pɪp) *n* **1** a contagious disease of poultry characterized by the secretion of thick mucus in the mouth and throat. **2** *Facetious slang.* a minor human ailment. **3** *Brit. slang.* a bad temper or depression (esp. in the phrase **give (someone) the pip**). ◆ *vb* **pips, pipping, pipped. 4** *Brit. slang.* to cause to be annoyed or depressed. [C15: from Middle Dutch *pippe,* ultimately from Latin *pituita* phlegm; see PITUITARY]

pip[4] (pɪp) *vb* **pips, pipping, pipped.** (*tr*) *Brit. slang.* **1** to wound or kill, esp. with a gun. **2** to defeat (a person), esp. when his success seems certain (often in the phrase **pip at the post**). **3** to blackball or ostracize. [C19 (originally in the sense: to blackball): probably from PIP[2]]

pipa ('piːpə) *n* a tongueless South American toad, *Pipa pipa,* that carries its young in pits in the skin of its back. [C18: from Surinam dialect, probably of African origin]

pipage ('paɪpɪdʒ) *n* **1** pipes collectively. **2** conveyance by pipes. **3** the money charged for such conveyance.

pipal ('paɪpᵊl) *n* a variant of **peepul.**

pipe[1] (paɪp) *n* **1** a long tube of metal, plastic, etc., used to convey water, oil, gas, etc. **2** a long tube or case. **3a** an object made in any of various shapes and sizes, consisting of a small bowl with an attached tubular stem, in which tobacco or other substances are smoked. **3b** (*as modifier*): *a pipe bowl.* **4** Also called: **'pipeful.** the amount of tobacco that fills the bowl of a pipe. **5** *Zoology, botany.* any of various hollow organs, such as the respiratory passage of certain animals. **6a** any musical instrument whose sound production results from the vibration of an air column in a simple tube. **6b** any of the tubular devices on an organ, in which air is made to vibrate either directly, as in a flue pipe, or by means of a reed. **7** an obsolete three-holed wind instrument, held in the left hand while played and accompanied by the tabor. See **tabor. 8 the pipes.** See **bagpipes. 9** a shrill voice or sound, as of a bird. **10a** a boatswain's pipe. **10b** the sound it makes. **11** (*pl*) *Informal.* the respiratory tract or vocal cords. **12** *Metallurgy.* a conical hole in the head of an ingot, made by escaping gas as the metal cools. **13** a cylindrical vein of rich ore, such as one of the vertical diamond-bearing veins at Kimberley, South Africa. **14** Also called: **volcanic pipe.** a vertical cylindrical passage in a volcano through which molten lava is forced during eruption. **15** *U.S. slang.* something easy to do, esp. a simple course in college. **16 put that in your pipe and smoke it.** *Informal.* accept that fact if you can. ◆ *vb* **17** to play (music) on a pipe. **18** (*tr*) to summon or lead by a pipe: *to pipe the dancers.* **19** to utter (something) shrilly. **20a** to signal orders to (the crew) by a boatswain's pipe. **20b** (*tr*) to signal the arrival or departure of: *to pipe the admiral aboard.* **21** (*tr*) to convey (water, gas, etc.) by a pipe or pipes. **22** (*tr*) to provide with pipes. **23** (*tr*) to trim (an article, esp. of clothing) with piping. **24** (*tr*) to force (cream, icing, etc.) through a shaped nozzle to decorate food. ◆ See also **pipe down, pipe up.** [Old English *pīpe* (n), *pīpian* (vb), ultimately from Latin *pīpāre* to chirp] ▸ **'pipeless** *adj* ▸ **'pipy** *adj*

pipe[2] (paɪp) *n* **1** a large cask for wine, oil, etc. **2** a measure of capacity for wine equal to four barrels. 1 pipe is equal to 126 U.S. gallons or 105 Brit. gallons. **3** a cask holding this quantity with its contents. [C14: via Old French (in the sense: tube, tubular vessel), ultimately from Latin *pīpāre* to chirp; compare PIPE[1]]

pipeclay ('paɪp,kleɪ) *n* **1** a fine white pure clay, used in the manufacture of tobacco pipes and pottery and for whitening leather and similar materials. ◆ *vb* **2** (*tr*) to whiten with pipeclay.

pipe cleaner *n* a short length of thin wires twisted so as to hold tiny tufts of yarn: used to clean the stem of a tobacco pipe.

piped music *n* light popular music prerecorded and played through amplifiers in a shop, restaurant, factory, etc., as background music. See also **Muzak.**

pipe down *vb* (*intr, adv*) *Informal.* to stop talking, making noise, etc.

pipe dream *n* a fanciful or impossible plan or hope. [alluding to dreams produced by smoking an opium pipe]

pipefish ('paɪp,fɪʃ) *n, pl* **-fish** *or* **-fishes.** any of various teleost fishes of the genera *Nerophis, Syngnathus,* etc., having a long tubelike snout and an elongated body covered with bony plates: family *Syngnathidae.* Also called: **needlefish.**

pipefitting ('paɪp,fɪtɪŋ) *n* **1a** the act or process of bending, cutting to length, and joining pipes. **1b** the branch of plumbing involving this. **2** the threaded gland nuts, unions, adaptors, etc., used for joining pipes. ▸ **'pipe,fitter** *n*

pipe jacking *n* a method of laying underground pipelines by assembling the pipes at the foot of an access shaft and pushing them through the ground.

pipeline ('paɪp,laɪn) *n* **1** a long pipe, esp. underground, used to transport oil, natural gas, etc., over long distances. **2** a medium of communication, esp. a private one. **3 in the pipeline.** in the process of being completed, delivered, or produced. ◆ *vb* (*tr*) **4** to convey by pipeline. **5** to supply with a pipeline.

pipe major *n* the noncommissioned officer, generally of warrant officer's rank, who is responsible for the training, duty, and discipline of a military or civilian pipe band.

pip-emma ('pɪp'ɛmə) *adv Old-fashioned.* in the afternoon; p.m. Compare **ack-emma.** [World War I phonetic alphabet for P, M]

pipe organ *n* another name for **organ** (the musical instrument). Compare **reed organ.**

piper ('paɪpə) *n* **1** a person who plays a pipe or bagpipes. **2 pay the piper and call the tune.** to bear the cost of an undertaking and control it.

Piper ('paɪpə) *n* **John.** 1903–92, British artist. An official war artist in World War II, he is known esp. for his watercolours of bombed churches and his stained glass in Coventry Cathedral.

piperaceous (,pɪpə'reɪʃəs) *adj* of, relating to, or belonging to the *Piperaceae,* a family of pungent tropical shrubs and climbing flowering plants: includes pepper, betel, and cubeb. [C17: via New Latin from Latin *piper* PEPPER]

piperazine (pɪ'pɛrə,ziːn, -zɪn) *n* a white crystalline deliquescent heterocyclic nitrogen compound used as an insecticide, corrosion inhibitor, and veterinary anthelmintic. Formula: $C_4H_{10}N_2$.

piperidine (pɪ'pɛrɪ,diːn, -dɪn) *n* a colourless liquid heterocyclic compound with a peppery ammoniacal odour: used in making rubbers and curing epoxy resins. Formula: $C_5H_{11}N$.

piperine ('pɪpə,raɪn, -rɪn) *n* a crystalline insoluble alkaloid that is the active ingredient of pepper, used as a flavouring and as an insecticide. Formula: $C_{17}H_{19}NO_3$. [C19: from Latin *piper* PEPPER]

pipe roll *n History.* an annual record of the accounts of a sheriff or other minister of the crown kept at the British Exchequer from the 12th to the 19th centuries. Also called: **the Great Roll of the Exchequer.** [C17: from PIPE[1] and ROLL; perhaps from documents being rolled into a pipe shape]

piperonal ('pɪpərəʊ,næl) *n* a white fragrant aldehyde used in flavourings, perfumery, and suntan lotions. Formula: $C_6H_3O_2CH_2CHO$. Also called: **heliotropin.**

pipes of Pan *pl n* another term for **panpipes.**

pipestone ('paɪp,stəʊn) *n* a variety of consolidated red clay used by American Indians to make tobacco pipes.

pipette (pɪ'pɛt) *n* **1** a calibrated glass tube drawn to a fine bore at one end, filled by sucking liquid into the bulb, and used to transfer or measure known volumes of liquid. ◆ *vb* **2** (*tr*) to transfer or measure out (a liquid) using a pipette. [C19: via French: little pipe, from *pipe* PIPE[1]]

pipe up *vb* (*intr, adv*) **1** to commence singing or playing a musical instrument: *the band piped up.* **2** to speak up, esp. in a shrill voice.

pipewort ('paɪp,wɜːt) *n* a perennial plant, *Eriocaulon septangulare,* of wet places in W Republic of Ireland, the Scottish Hebrides, and the eastern U.S., having a twisted flower stalk and a greenish-grey scaly flower head: family *Eriocaulaceae.*

pipi ('pɪpiː) *n, pl* **pipi** *or* **pipis.** any of various shellfishes, esp. *Plebidonax deltoides* of Australia or *Mesodesma novae-zelandiae* of New Zealand. [Maori]

piping ('paɪpɪŋ) *n* **1** pipes collectively, esp. pipes formed into a connected system, as in the plumbing of a house. **2** a cord of icing, whipped cream, etc., often used to decorate desserts and cakes. **3** a thin strip of covered cord or material, used to edge hems, etc. **4** the sound of a pipe or a set of bagpipes. **5** the art or technique of playing a pipe or bagpipes. **6** a shrill voice or sound, esp. a whistling sound. ◆ *adj* **7** making a shrill sound. **8** *Archaic.* relating to the pipe (associated with peace), as opposed to martial instruments, such as the fife or trumpet. ◆ *adv* **9 piping hot.** extremely hot.

pipistrelle (,pɪpɪ'strɛl) *n* any of numerous small brownish insectivorous bats of the genus *Pipistrellus,* occurring in most parts of the world: family *Vespertilionidae.* [C18: via French from Italian *pipistrello,* from Latin *vespertīliō* a bat, from *vesper* evening, because of its nocturnal habits]

pipit ('pɪpɪt) *n* any of various songbirds of the genus *Anthus* and related genera, having brownish speckled plumage and a long tail: family *Motacillidae.* Also called: **titlark.** [C18: probably of imitative origin]

pipiwharauroa ('piːpiː,færæuː,rɔːə) *n N.Z.* a Pacific migratory bird with a metallic green-gold plumage.

pipkin ('pɪpkɪn) *n* **1** a small metal or earthenware vessel. **2** another name for **piggin.** [C16: perhaps a diminutive of PIPE[2]; see -KIN]

pippin ('pɪpɪn) *n* **1** any of several varieties of eating apple with a rounded oblate shape. **2** the seed of any of these fruits. [C13: from Old French *pepin,* of uncertain origin]

pipsissewa (pɪp'sɪsəwə) *n* any of several ericaceous plants of the Asian and American genus *Chimaphila,* having jagged evergreen leaves and white or pinkish flowers. Also called: **wintergreen.** [C19: from Cree *pipisisikweu,* literally: it breaks it into pieces, so called because it was believed to be efficacious in treating bladder stones]

pipsqueak ('pɪp,skwiːk) *n Informal.* a person or thing that is insignificant or contemptible. [C20: from PIP[2] + SQUEAK]

piquant ('piːkənt, -kɑːnt) *adj* **1** having an agreeably pungent or tart taste. **2** lively or stimulating to the mind. [C16: from French (literally: prickling), from *piquer* to prick, goad; see PIQUE[1]] ▸ **'piquancy** *or* (*less commonly*) **'piquantness** *n* ▸ **'piquantly** *adv*

pique[1] (piːk) *n* **1** a feeling of resentment or irritation, as from having one's pride wounded. ◆ *vb* **piques, piquing, piqued.** (*tr*) **2** to cause to feel resentment or irritation. **3** to excite or arouse. **4** (foll. by *on* or *upon*) to pride or congratulate (oneself). [C16: from French, from *piquer* to prick, sting; see PICK[1]]

pique[2] (piːk) *Piquet.* ◆ *n* **1** a score of 30 points made by a player from a combination of cards held before play begins and from play while his opponent's score is nil. ◆ *vb* **2** to score a pique (against). [C17: from French *pic,* of uncertain origin]

piqué ('piːkeɪ) *n* a close-textured fabric of cotton, silk, or spun rayon woven with lengthwise ribs. [C19: from French *piqué* pricked, from *piquer* to prick]

piquet (pɪ'kɛt, -'keɪ) *n* a card game for two people playing with a reduced pack and scoring points for card combinations and tricks won. **[C17:** from French, of unknown origin; compare PIQUE[2]**]**

Pir (pir) *n* a title given to Sufi masters. [Persian]

piracy ('paɪrəsɪ) *n, pl* **-cies. 1** *Brit.* robbery on the seas within admiralty jurisdiction. **2** a felony, such as robbery or hijacking, committed aboard a ship or aircraft. **3** the unauthorized use or appropriation of patented or copyrighted material, ideas, etc. **[C16:** from Anglo-Latin *pirātia,* from Late Greek *peirāteia;* see PIRATE**]**

Piraeus *or* **Peiraeus** (paɪ'riːəs, pɪ'reɪ-) *n* a port in SE Greece, adjoining Athens: the country's chief port; founded in the 5th century B.C. as the port of Athens. Pop.: 169 622 (1991). Modern Greek name: **Piraiévs** (ˌpirɛ'ɛfs).

piragua (pɪ'rɑːgwə, -'ræg-) *n* another word for **pirogue. [C17:** via Spanish from Carib: dugout canoe**]**

Pirandello (*Italian* piran'dɛllo) *n* **Luigi** (lu'iːdʒi). 1867–1936, Italian short-story writer, novelist, and dramatist. His plays include *Right you are* (*If you think so*) (1917), *Six Characters in Search of an Author* (1921), and *Henry IV* (1922): Nobel prize for literature 1934.

Piranesi (*Italian* pira'neːsi) *n* **Giambattista** (dʒambat'tista). 1720–78, Italian etcher and architect: etchings include *Imaginary Prisons* and *Views of Rome.*

piranha *or* **piraña** (pɪ'rɑːnjə) *n* any of various small freshwater voracious fishes of the genus *Serrasalmus* and related genera, of tropical America, having strong jaws and sharp teeth: family *Characidae* (characins). **[C19:** via Portuguese from Tupi: fish with teeth, from *pirá* fish + *sainha* tooth**]**

pirate ('paɪrɪt) *n* **1** a person who commits piracy. **2a** a vessel used by pirates. **2b** (*as modifier*): *a pirate ship.* **3** a person who illicitly uses or appropriates someone else's literary, artistic, or other work. **4a** a person or group of people who broadcast illegally. **4b** (*as modifier*): *a pirate radio station.* ◆ *vb* **5** (*tr*) to use, appropriate, or reproduce (artistic work, ideas, etc.) illicitly. **[C15:** from Latin *pīrāta,* from Greek *peiratēs* one who attacks, from *peira* an attempt, attack**]** ▸ **piratical** (paɪ'rætɪkᵊl) *or* **pi'ratic** *adj* ▸ **pi'ratically** *adv*

Pirithoüs (paɪ'rɪθəʊəs) *n Greek myth.* a prince of the Lapiths, who accomplished many great deeds with his friend Theseus.

pirn (pɜːn; *Scot.* pɪrn) *n Scot.* **1** a reel or bobbin. **2** (in weaving) the spool of a shuttle. **3** a fishing reel. **[C15:** of uncertain origin**]**

pirog (pɪ'rəʊg) *n, pl* **-rogi** (-'rəʊgɪ). a large pie filled with meat, vegetables, etc. [from Russian: pie]

pirogue (pɪ'rəʊg) *or* **piragua** *n* any of various kinds of dugout canoes. **[C17:** via French from Spanish PIRAGUA**]**

pirouette (ˌpɪrʊ'ɛt) *n* **1** a body spin, esp. in dancing, on the toes or the ball of the foot. ◆ *vb* **2** (*intr*) to perform a pirouette. **[C18:** from French, from Old French *pirouet* spinning top; related to Italian *pirolo* little peg**]**

pirozhki *or* **piroshki** (pɪ'rɒʃkɪ) *pl n, sing* **pirozhok** (ˌpɪrə'ʒɒk). small triangular pastries filled with meat, vegetables, etc. **[C20:** from Russian, from *pirozhók,* diminutive of PIROG**]**

Pisa ('piːzə; *Italian* 'piːsa) *n* a city in Tuscany, NW Italy, near the mouth of the River Arno: flourishing maritime republic (11th–12th centuries), contains a university (1343), a cathedral (1063), and the Leaning Tower (begun in 1174 and about 5 m (17 ft.) from perpendicular); tourism. Pop.: 102 150 (1990).

pis aller *French.* (piz ale) *n* a last resort; stopgap. [literally: (at) the worst going]

Pisanello (*Italian* pisa'nɛllo) *n* **Antonio** (an'tɔːnjo). ?1395–?1455, Italian painter and medallist; a major exponent of the International Gothic style. He is best known for his portrait medals and drawings of animals.

Pisano (*Italian* pi'saːno) *n* **1 Andrea** (an'drɛa), real name *Andrea de Pontedera.* ?1290–1348, Italian sculptor and architect, noted for his bronze reliefs on the door of the baptistry in Florence. **2 Giovanni** (dʒo'vanni). ?1250–?1320, Italian sculptor, who successfully integrated classical and Gothic elements in his sculptures, esp. in his pulpit in St Andrea, Pistoia. **3** his father, **Nicola** (ni'kɔːla) ?1220–?84, Italian sculptor, who pioneered the classical style and is often regarded as a precursor of the Italian Renaissance: noted esp. for his pulpit in the baptistry of Pisa Cathedral.

piscary ('pɪskərɪ) *n, pl* **-ries. 1** a place where fishing takes place. **2** the right to fish in certain waters. **[C15:** from Latin *piscārius* fishing, from *piscis* a fish**]**

piscatorial (ˌpɪskə'tɔːrɪəl) *or* **piscatory** ('pɪskətərɪ, -trɪ) *adj* **1** of or relating to fish, fishing, or fishermen. **2** devoted to fishing. **[C19:** from Latin *piscātōrius,* from *piscātor* fisherman**]** ▸ **ˌpisca'torially** *adv*

Pisces ('paɪsiːz, 'pɪ-) *n, Latin genitive* **Piscium** ('paɪsɪəm). **1** *Astronomy.* a faint extensive zodiacal constellation lying between Aquarius and Aries on the ecliptic. **2** *Astrology.* **2a** Also called: the **Fishes.** the twelfth sign of the zodiac, symbol ♓, having a mutable water classification and ruled by the planets Jupiter and Neptune. The sun is in this sign between about Feb. 19 and March 20. **2b** a person born when the sun is in this sign. **3a** a taxonomic group that comprises all fishes. See **fish** (sense 1). **3b** a taxonomic group that comprises the bony fishes only. See **teleost.** ◆ *adj* **4** *Astrology.* born under or characteristic of Pisces. ◆ Also (for senses 2b, 4): **Piscean** ('paɪsɪən). **[C14:** Latin: the fishes**]**

pisci- *combining form.* fish: *pisciculture.* **[**from Latin *piscis***]**

pisciculture ('pɪsɪˌkʌltʃə) *n* the rearing and breeding of fish under controlled conditions. ▸ **ˌpisci'cultural** *adj* ▸ **ˌpisci'culturally** *adv* ▸ **ˌpisci'culturist** *n, adj*

piscina (pɪ'siːnə) *n, pl* **-nae** (-niː) *or* **-nas.** *R.C. Church.* a stone basin, with a drain, in a church or sacristy where water used at Mass is poured away. **[C16:** from Latin: fish pond, from *piscis* a fish**]** ▸ **piscinal** ('pɪsɪnᵊl) *adj*

piscine ('pɪsaɪn) *adj* of, relating to, or resembling a fish.

Piscis Austrinus ('pɪsɪs ɒ'straɪnəs, 'paɪ-) *n, Latin genitive* **Piscis Austrini** (ɒ'straɪnaɪ). a small constellation in the S hemisphere lying between Aquarius and Grus and containing the first-magnitude star Fomalhaut. **[**Latin: the Southern Fish**]**

piscivorous (pɪ'sɪvərəs) *adj* feeding on fish: *piscivorous birds.*

pisé ('piːzeɪ) *n* rammed earth or clay used to make floors or walls. Also called: **pisé de terre. [C18:** French, from past participle of *piser,* from Latin *pisare* to beat, pound**]**

Pisgah ('pɪzgə) *n* **Mount.** *Old Testament.* the mountain slopes to the northeast of the Dead Sea, from one of which, Mount Nebo, Moses viewed Canaan.

pish (pʃ, pɪʃ) *interj* **1** an exclamation of impatience or contempt. ◆ *vb* **2** to make this exclamation at (someone or something).

pishogue (pɪ'ʃəʊg) *n Irish.* sorcery; witchcraft. **[**from Irish *piseog, pisreog***]**

Pishpek (pɪʃ'pɛk) *n* a variant transliteration of the Kyrgyz name for **Bishkek.**

pisiform ('pɪsɪˌfɔːm) *adj* **1** *Zoology, botany.* resembling a pea. ◆ *n* **2** a small pealike bone on the ulnar side of the carpus. **[C18:** via New Latin from Latin *pīsum* pea + *forma* shape**]**

Pisistratus (paɪ'sɪstrətəs) *n* ?600–527 B.C., tyrant of Athens: he established himself in firm control of the city following his defeat of his aristocratic rivals at Pallene (546).

pismire ('pɪsˌmaɪə) *n* an archaic or dialect word for an **ant. [C14** (literally: urinating ant, from the odour of formic acid characteristic of an ant hill): from PISS + obsolete *mire* ant, of Scandinavian origin; compare Old Norse *maurr,* Middle Low German *mīre* ant**]**

pisolite ('paɪsəʊˌlaɪt) *n* any sedimentary rock consisting of pea-sized concentric formations (**pisoliths**) within a fine matrix. **[C18:** from New Latin *pisolithus* pea stone, from Greek *pisos* pea + *lithos* -LITE**]** ▸ **pisolitic** (ˌpaɪsəʊ'lɪtɪk) *adj*

piss (pɪs) *Slang.* ◆ *vb* **1** (*intr*) *Taboo.* to urinate. **2** (*tr*) *Taboo.* to discharge as or in one's urine: *to piss blood.* ◆ *n* **3** *Taboo.* an act of urinating. **4** *Taboo.* urine. **5** *Austral.* beer. **6 on the piss.** drinking alcohol, esp. in large quantities. **7 take the piss.** to tease or make fun of someone or something. **[C13:** from Old French *pisser,* probably of imitative origin**]** ▸ **'pisser** *n*

piss about *or* **around** *vb* (*adv*) *Taboo slang.* **1** (*intr*) to behave in a casual or silly way. **2** (*tr*) to waste the time of.

Pissarro (pɪ'sɑːrəʊ; *French* pisaro) *n* **Camille** (kamij). 1830–1903, French impressionist painter, esp. of landscapes.

piss artist *n Slang.* **1** a boastful or incompetent person. **2** a person who drinks heavily and gets drunk frequently.

pissed (pɪst) *adj Brit., Austral., and N.Z. slang.* intoxicated; drunk.

pisshead ('pɪsˌhɛd) *n Slang.* a drunkard.

piss off *vb* (*adv*) *Taboo slang.* **1** (*tr; often passive*) to annoy, irritate, or disappoint. **2** (*intr*) *Chiefly Brit.* to go away; depart, often used to dismiss a person.

pissoir ('piːswɑː; *French* piswar) *n* a public urinal, usu. enclosed by a wall or screen. [French, from *pisser* to urinate]

piss-up *n Slang, chiefly Brit.* a drinking session.

pistachio (pɪ'stɑːʃɪˌəʊ) *n, pl* **-os. 1** an anacardiaceous tree, *Pistacia vera,* of the Mediterranean region and W Asia, with small hard-shelled nuts. **2** Also called: **pistachio nut.** the nut of this tree, having an edible green kernel. **3** the sweet flavour of the pistachio nut, used esp. in ice creams. ◆ *adj* **4** of a yellowish-green colour. **[C16:** via Italian and Latin from Greek *pistakion* pistachio nut, from *pistakē* pistachio tree, from Persian *pistah***]**

pistareen (ˌpɪstə'riːn) *n* a Spanish coin, used in the U.S. and the West Indies until the 18th century. **[C18:** perhaps changed from PESETA**]**

piste (piːst) *n* **1** a trail, slope, or course for skiing. **2** a rectangular area for fencing bouts. **[C18:** via Old French from Old Italian *pista,* from *pistare* to tread down**]**

pistil ('pɪstɪl) *n* the female reproductive part of a flower, consisting of one or more separate or fused carpels; gynoecium. **[C18:** from Latin *pistillum* PESTLE**]**

pistillate ('pɪstɪlɪt, -ˌleɪt) *adj* (of plants) **1** having pistils but no anthers. **2** having or producing pistils.

Pistoia (*Italian* pis'toːja) *n* a city in N Italy, in N Tuscany: scene of the defeat and death of Catiline in 62 B.C. Pop.: 89 972 (1990).

pistol ('pɪstᵊl) *n* **1** a short-barrelled handgun. **2 hold a pistol to a person's head.** to threaten a person in order to force him to do what one wants. ◆ *vb* **-tols, -tolling, -tolled** *or U.S.* **-tols, -toling, -toled. 3** (*tr*) to shoot with a pistol. **[C16:** from French *pistole,* from German, from Czech *pišt'ala* pistol, pipe; related to Russian *pischal* shepherd's pipes**]**

pistole (pɪs'təʊl) *n* any of various gold coins of varying value, formerly used in Europe. **[C16:** from Old French, shortened from *pistolet,* literally: little PISTOL**]**

pistoleer (ˌpɪstə'lɪə) *n Obsolete.* a person, esp. a soldier, who is armed with or fires a pistol.

pistol grip *n* **a** a handle shaped like the butt of a pistol. **b** (*as modifier*): *a pistol-grip camera.*

pistol-whip *vb* **-whips, -whipping, -whipped.** (*tr*) *U.S.* to beat or strike with a pistol barrel.

piston ('pɪstən) *n* a disc or cylindrical part that slides to and fro in a hollow cylinder. In an internal-combustion engine it is forced to move by the expanding gases in the cylinder head and is attached by a pivoted connecting rod to a crankshaft or flywheel, thus converting reciprocating motion into rotation. **[C18:** via French from Old Italian *pistone,* from *pistare* to pound, grind, from Latin *pinsere* to crush, beat**]**

piston ring *n* a split ring, usually made of cast iron, that fits into a groove on the rim of a piston to provide a spring-loaded seal against the cylinder wall.

piston rod *n* **1** the rod that connects the piston of a reciprocating steam engine to the crosshead. **2** a less common name for a **connecting rod.**

piston slap *n* the characteristic sound of a seriously worn piston in a cylinder (usually of the engine of a motor car).

pit[1] (pɪt) *n* **1** a large, usually deep opening in the ground. **2a** a mine or excavation with a shaft, esp. for coal. **2b** the shaft in a mine. **2c** (*as modifier*): *pit pony; pit prop.* **3** a concealed danger or difficulty. **4 the pit.** hell. **5** Also called: **orchestra pit.** the area that is occupied by the orchestra in a theatre, located in front of the stage. **6** an enclosure for fighting animals or birds, esp. gamecocks. **7** *Anatomy.* **7a** a small natural depression on the surface of a body, organ, structure, or part; fossa. **7b** the floor of any natural bodily cavity: *the pit of the* *stomach.* **8** *Pathol.* a small indented scar at the site of a former pustule; pockmark. **9** any of various small areas in a plant cell wall that remain unthickened when the rest of the cell becomes lignified. **10** a working area at the side of a motor-racing track for servicing or refuelling vehicles. **11** a section on the floor of a commodity exchange devoted to a special line of trading. **12** a rowdy card game in which players bid for commodities. **13** an area of sand or other soft material at the end of a long-jump approach, behind the bar of a pole vault, etc., on which an athlete may land safely. **14** the ground floor of the auditorium of a theatre. **15** *Brit.* a slang word for **bed** (sense 1) or **bedroom** (sense 1). **16** another word for **pitfall** (sense 2). ◆ *vb* **pits, pitting, pitted. 17** (*tr;* often foll. by *against*) to match in opposition, esp. as antagonists. **18** to mark or become marked with pits. **19** (*tr*) to place or bury in a pit. ◆ See also **pits.** [Old English *pytt,* from Latin *puteus;* compare Old French *pet,* Old High German *pfuzzi*]

pit[2] (pɪt) *Chiefly U.S. and Canadian.* ◆ *n* **1** the stone of a cherry, plum, etc. ◆ *vb* **pits, pitting, pitted. 2** (*tr*) to extract the stone from (a fruit). [C19: from Dutch: kernel; compare PITH]

pit[3] (pɪt) *vb* a Scot. word for **put.**

pita ('pi:tə) *n* **1** any of several agave plants yielding a strong fibre. See also **istle. 2** a species of pineapple, *Ananas magdalenae,* the leaves of which yield a white fibre. **3** Also called: **pita fibre.** the fibre obtained from any of these plants, used in making cordage and paper. [C17: via Spanish from Quechua]

pitapat (ˌpɪtə'pæt) *adv* **1** with quick light taps or beats. ◆ *vb* **-pats, -patting, -patted. 2** (*intr*) to make quick light taps or beats. ◆ *n* **3** such taps or beats.

pit bull terrier *n* a dog resembling the Staffordshire bull terrier but somewhat larger: developed for dog-fighting; it is not recognized by kennel clubs. Also called: **American pit bull terrier.**

Pitcairn Island (pɪt'kɛən, 'pɪtkɛən) *n* an island in the S Pacific: forms with other islands a UK Overseas Territory; uninhabited until the landing in 1790 of the mutineers of H.M.S. *Bounty* and their Tahitian companions. Pop.: 54 (1995). Area: 4.6 sq. km (1.75 sq. miles).

pitch[1] (pɪtʃ) *vb* **1** to hurl or throw (something); cast; fling. **2** (*usually tr*) to set up (a camp, tent, etc.). **3** (*tr*) to place or thrust (a stake, spear, etc.) into the ground. **4** (*intr*) to move vigorously or irregularly to and fro or up and down. **5** (*tr*) to aim or fix (something) at a particular level, position, style, etc.: *if you advertise privately you may pitch the price too low.* **6** (*tr*) to aim to sell (a product) to a specified market or on a specified basis. **7** (*intr*) to slope downwards. **8** (*intr*) to fall forwards or downwards. **9** (*intr*) (of a vessel) to dip and raise its bow and stern alternately. **10** *Cricket.* to bowl (a ball) so that it bounces on a certain part of the wicket, or (of a ball) to bounce on a certain part of the wicket. **11** (*intr*) (of a missile, aircraft, etc.) to deviate from a stable flight attitude by movement of the longitudinal axis about the lateral axis. Compare **yaw** (sense 1), **roll** (sense 14). **12** (*tr*) (in golf) to hit (a ball) steeply into the air, esp. with backspin to minimize roll. **13** (*tr*) *Music.* **13a** to sing or play accurately (a note, interval, etc.). **13b** (*usually passive*) (of a wind instrument) to specify or indicate its basic key or harmonic series by its size, manufacture, etc. **14** (*tr*) *Cards.* to lead (a suit) and so determine trumps for that trick. **15** *Baseball.* **15a** (*tr*) to throw (a baseball) to a batter. **15b** (*intr*) to act as pitcher in a baseball game. **16** *Southwest English dialect.* (used with *it* as subject) to snow without the settled snow melting. **17 in there pitching.** *U.S. and Canadian informal.* taking part with enthusiasm. **18 pitch a tale** (*or* **yarn**). to tell a story, usually of a fantastic nature. ◆ *n* **19** the degree of elevation or depression. **20a** the angle of descent of a downward slope. **20b** such a slope. **21** the extreme height or depth. **22** *Mountaineering.* a section of a route between two belay points, sometimes equal to the full length of the rope but often shorter. **23** the degree of slope of a roof, esp. when expressed as a ratio of height to span. **24** the distance between corresponding points on adjacent members of a body of regular form, esp. the distance between teeth on a gearwheel or between threads on a screw thread. **25** the distance between regularly spaced objects such as rivets, bolts, etc. **26** the pitching motion of a ship, missile, etc. **27a** the distance a propeller advances in one revolution, assuming no slip. **27b** the blade angle of a propeller or rotor. **28** *Music.* **28a** the auditory property of a note that is conditioned by its frequency relative to other notes: *high pitch; low pitch.* **28b** an absolute frequency assigned to a specific note, fixing the relative frequencies of all other notes. The fundamental frequencies of the notes A–G, in accordance with the frequency A = 440 hertz, were internationally standardized and accepted in 1939. See also **concert pitch** (sense 1), **international pitch. 29** *Cricket.* the rectangular area between the stumps, 22 yards long and 10 feet wide; the wicket. **30** *Geology.* the inclination of the axis of an anticline or syncline or of a stratum or vein from the horizontal. **31** another name for **seven-up. 32** the act or manner of pitching a ball, as in cricket. **33** *Chiefly Brit.* a vendor's station, esp. on a pavement. **34** *Slang.* a persuasive sales talk, esp. one routinely repeated. **35** *Chiefly Brit.* (in many sports) the field of play. **36** Also called: **pitch shot.** *Golf.* an approach shot in which the ball is struck in a high arc. **37 make a pitch for.** *U.S. and Canadian slang.* **37a** to give verbal support to. **37b** to attempt to attract (someone) sexually or romantically. **38 queer someone's pitch.** *Brit. informal.* to upset someone's plans. ◆ See also **pitch in, pitch into, pitch on.** [C13 *picchen;* possibly related to PICK[1]]

pitch[2] (pɪtʃ) *n* **1** any of various heavy dark viscid substances obtained as a residue from the distillation of tars. See also **coal-tar pitch. 2** any of various similar substances, such as asphalt, occurring as natural deposits. **3** any of various similar substances obtained by distilling certain organic substances so that they are incompletely carbonized. **4** crude turpentine obtained as sap from pine trees. ◆ Related adj: **piceous.** ◆ *vb* **5** (*tr*) to apply pitch to (something). [Old English *pic,* from Latin *pix*]

pitch accent *n* (in languages such as Ancient Greek or modern Swedish) an accent in which emphatic syllables are pronounced on a higher musical pitch relative to other syllables. Also called: **tonic accent.**

pitch and putt *n* a type of miniature golf in which the holes are usually between 50 to 100 metres in length.

pitch-and-toss *n* a game of skill and chance in which the player who pitches a coin nearest to a mark has the first chance to toss all the coins, winning those that land heads up.

pitchbend ('pɪtʃˌbɛnd) *n* an electronic device that enables a player to bend the pitch of a note being sounded on a synthesizer, usually with a pitch wheel, strip, or lever.

pitch-black *adj* **1** extremely dark; unlit: *the room was pitch-black.* **2** of a deep black colour.

pitchblende ('pɪtʃˌblɛnd) *n* a blackish mineral that is a type of uraninite and occurs in veins, frequently associated with silver: the principal source of uranium and radium. Formula: UO_2. [C18: partial translation of German *Pechblende,* from *Pech* PITCH[2] (from its black colour) + BLENDE]

pitch circle *n* an imaginary circle passing through the teeth of a gearwheel, concentric with the gearwheel, and having a radius that would enable it to be in contact with a similar circle around a mating gearwheel.

pitch-cone angle *n* (in a bevel gear) the apex angle of the truncated cone (pitch cone) which forms the reference surface on which the teeth of a bevel gear are cut.

pitch-dark *adj* extremely or completely dark.

pitched battle *n* **1** a battle ensuing from the deliberate choice of time and place, engaging all the planned resources. **2** any fierce encounter, esp. one with large numbers.

pitcher[1] ('pɪtʃə) *n* **1** a large jug, usually rounded with a narrow neck and often of earthenware, used mainly for holding water. **2** *Botany.* any of the urn-shaped leaves of the pitcher plant. [C13: from Old French *pichier,* from Medieval Latin *picārium,* variant of *bicārium* BEAKER]

pitcher[2] ('pɪtʃə) *n* **1** *Baseball.* the player on the fielding team who pitches the ball to the batter. **2** a granite stone used in paving.

pitcher plant *n* any of various insectivorous plants of the genera *Sarracenia, Nepenthes,* and *Darlingtonia,* having leaves modified to form pitcher-like organs that attract and trap insects, which are then digested. See also **huntsman's-cup.**

pitchfork ('pɪtʃˌfɔ:k) *n* **1** a long-handled fork with two or three long curved tines for lifting, turning, or tossing hay. ◆ *vb* (*tr*) **2** to use a pitchfork on (something). **3** to thrust (someone) unwillingly into a position.

pitch in *vb* (*intr, adv*) **1** to cooperate or contribute. **2** to begin energetically.

pitching tool *n* a masonry chisel for rough work.

pitching wedge *n Golf.* a club with a face angle of more than 50°, used for short, lofted pitch shots.

pitch into *vb* (*intr, prep*) *Informal.* **1** to assail physically or verbally. **2** to get on with doing (something).

Pitch Lake *n* a deposit of natural asphalt in the Caribbean, in SW Trinidad. Area: 46 hectares (114 acres).

pitchman ('pɪtʃmən) *n, pl* **-men.** *U.S. and Canadian.* **1** an itinerant pedlar of small merchandise who operates from a stand at a fair, etc. **2** any high-pressure salesman or advertiser.

pitchometer (pɪtʃ'ɒmɪtə) *n* an instrument embodying a clinometer, for measuring the pitch of a ship's propeller.

pitch on *or* **upon** *vb* (*intr, prep*) to determine or decide.

pitch pine *n* **1** any of various coniferous trees of the genus *Pinus,* esp. *P. rigida,* of North America, having red-brown bark and long lustrous light brown cones: valued as a source of turpentine and pitch. **2** the wood of any of these trees.

pitch pipe *n* a small pipe, esp. one having a reed like a harmonica, that sounds a note or notes of standard frequency. It is used for establishing the correct starting note for unaccompanied singing.

pitchstone ('pɪtʃˌstəʊn) *n* a dark glassy acid volcanic rock similar in composition to granite, usually intruded as dykes, sills, etc. [C18: translation of German *Pechstein*]

pitchy ('pɪtʃɪ) *adj* **pitchier, pitchiest. 1** full of or covered with pitch. **2** resembling pitch. ▸ **'pitchiness** *n*

piteous ('pɪtɪəs) *adj* **1** exciting or deserving pity. **2** *Archaic.* having or expressing pity. ▸ **'piteously** *adv* ▸ **'piteousness** *n*

pitfall ('pɪtˌfɔ:l) *n* **1** an unsuspected difficulty or danger. **2** a trap in the form of a concealed pit, designed to catch men or wild animals. [Old English *pytt* PIT[1] + *fealle* trap]

pith (pɪθ) *n* **1** the soft fibrous tissue lining the inside of the rind in fruits such as the orange and grapefruit. **2** the essential or important part, point, etc. **3** weight; substance. **4** Also called: **medulla.** *Botany.* the central core of unspecialized cells surrounded by conducting tissue in stems. **5** the soft central part of a bone, feather, etc. ◆ *vb* (*tr*) **6** to destroy the brain and spinal cord of (a laboratory animal) by piercing or severing. **7** to kill (animals) by severing the spinal cord. **8** to remove the pith from (a plant). [Old English *pitha;* compare Middle Low German *pedik,* Middle Dutch *pitt(e)*]

pithead ('pɪtˌhɛd) *n* the top of a mine shaft and the buildings, hoisting gear, etc., situated around it.

pithecanthropus (ˌpɪθɪkæn'θrəʊpəs, -'kænθrə-) *n, pl* **-pi** (-ˌpaɪ). any primitive apelike man of the former genus *Pithecanthropus,* now included in the genus *Homo.* See **Java man, Peking man.** [C19: New Latin, from Greek *pithēkos* ape + *anthrōpos* man] ▸ **ˌpitheˈcanthroˌpine** *or* **ˌpitheˈcanthroˌpoid** *adj*

pith helmet *n* a lightweight hat made of pith that protects the wearer from the sun. Also called: **topee, topi.**

pithos ('pɪθɒs, 'paɪ-) *n, pl* **-thoi** (-θɔɪ). a large ceramic container for oil or grain. [from Greek]

pithy ('pɪθɪ) *adj* **pithier, pithiest. 1** terse and full of meaning or substance. **2** of, resembling, or full of pith. ▸ **'pithily** *adv* ▸ **'pithiness** *n*

pitiable ('pɪtɪəbᵊl) *adj* exciting or deserving pity or contempt. ▸ **'pitiableness** *n* ▸ **'pitiably** *adv*

pitiful ('pɪtɪfʊl) *adj* **1** arousing or deserving pity. **2** arousing or deserving contempt. **3** *Archaic.* full of pity or compassion. ▸ **'pitifully** *adv* ▸ **'pitifulness** *n*

pitiless ('pɪtɪlɪs) *adj* having or showing little or no pity or mercy. ▸ **'pitilessly** *adv* ▸ **'pitilessness** *n*

Pitjantjatjara (,pɪtjəntjə'tjærə) *or* **Pitjantjara** (,pɪtjən'dʒærə) *n* **1** (*pl* **-ra** *or* **-ras**) an Aboriginal people of the desert area of South Australia. **2** the language of this people.

pitman ('pɪtmən) *n, pl* **-men.** *Chiefly Scot. and northern English.* a person who works down a mine, esp. a coal miner.

Pitman ('pɪtmən) *n* Sir **Isaac.** 1813–97, English inventor of a system of phonetic shorthand (1837).

piton ('pi:tɒn; *French* pitɔ̃) *n Mountaineering.* a metal spike that may be driven into a crevice of rock or into ice and used to secure a rope. [**C20**: from French: ringbolt]

Pitot-static tube ('pi:təʊ'stætɪk) *n* combined Pitot and static pressure tubes placed in a fluid flow to measure the total and static pressures. The difference in pressures, as recorded on a manometer or airspeed indicator, indicates the fluid velocity. Also called: **Pitot tube.**

Pitot tube ('pi:təʊ) *n* **1** a small tube placed in a fluid with its open end upstream and the other end connected to a manometer. It measures the total pressure of the fluid. **2** short for **Pitot-static tube,** esp. one fitted to an aircraft. [**C18**: named after its inventor, Henri *Pitot* (1695–1771), French physicist]

pits (pɪts) *pl n Slang.* **the.** the worst possible person, place, or thing. [**C20**: perhaps shortened from *armpits*]

pitsaw ('pɪt,sɔ:) *n* a large saw formerly used for cutting logs into planks, operated by two men, one standing on top of the log and the other in a pit underneath it.

pit-sawn *adj* (of timber, esp. formerly) sawn into planks by hand in a saw-pit.

pit stop *n* **1** *Motor racing.* a brief stop made at a pit by a racing car for repairs, refuelling, etc. **2** *Informal.* any stop made during a car journey for refreshment, rest, or refuelling.

Pitt (pɪt) *n* **1 William,** known as *Pitt the Elder,* 1st Earl of Chatham. 1708–78, British statesman. He was first minister (1756–57; 1757–61; 1766–68) and achieved British victory in the Seven Years' War (1756–63). **2** his son **William,** known as *Pitt the Younger.* 1759–1806, British statesman. As prime minister (1783–1801; 1804–06), he carried through important fiscal and tariff reforms. From 1793, his attention was focused on the wars with revolutionary and Napoleonic France.

pitta bread *or* **pitta** ('pɪtə) *n* a flat rounded slightly leavened bread, originally from the Middle East, with a hollow inside like a pocket, which can be filled with food. Also called: **Arab bread, Greek bread.** [from Modern Greek: a cake]

pittance ('pɪtᵊns) *n* a small amount or portion, esp. a meagre allowance of money. [**C16**: from Old French *pietance* ration, ultimately from Latin *pietās* duty]

pitter-patter ('pɪtə,pætə) *n* **1** the sound of light rapid taps or pats, as of raindrops. ◆ *vb* **2** (*intr*) to make such a sound. ◆ *adv* **3** with such a sound: *the rain fell pitter-patter on the window.*

Pitt-Rivers ('pɪt'rɪvəz) *n* **Augustus Henry Lane Fox.** 1827–1900, British archaeologist; first inspector of ancient monuments (1882): assembled a major anthropological collection of tools and weapons (now in the **Pitt-Rivers Museum,** Oxford).

Pittsburgh ('pɪtsbɜ:g) *n* a port in SW Pennsylvania, at the confluence of the Allegheny and Monongahela Rivers, which form the Ohio River: settled around Fort Pitt in 1758; developed rapidly with the discovery of iron deposits and one of the world's richest coalfields; the largest river port in the U.S. and an important industrial centre, formerly with large steel mills. Pop.: 350 363 (1996 est.).

Pitt Street Farmer *n Austral. slang.* another name for **Collins Street Farmer.** [**C20**: after a principal business street in Sydney, Australia]

pituitary (pɪ'tju:ɪtərɪ, -trɪ) *n, pl* **-taries. 1** See **pituitary gland, pituitary extract.** ◆ *adj* **2** of or relating to the pituitary gland. **3** *Archaic.* of or relating to phlegm or mucus. [**C17**: from Late Latin *pītuītārius* slimy, from *pītuīta* phlegm]

pituitary extract *n* a preparation of the pituitary gland, used in medicine for the therapeutic effects of its hormones.

pituitary gland *or* **body** *n* the master endocrine gland, attached by a stalk to the base of the brain. Its two lobes (see **adenohypophysis** and **neurohypophysis**) secrete hormones affecting skeletal growth, development of the sex glands, and the functioning of the other endocrine glands. Also called: **hypophysis, hypophysis cerebri.**

pituri ('pɪtʃərɪ) *n, pl* **-ris.** an Australian solanaceous shrub, *Duboisia hopwoodii,* the leaves of which are the source of a narcotic used by the native Australians. [**C19**: from a native Australian name]

pit viper *n* any venomous snake of the New World family *Crotalidae,* having a heat-sensitive organ in a pit on each side of the head: includes the rattlesnakes.

pity ('pɪtɪ) *n, pl* **pities. 1** sympathy or sorrow felt for the sufferings of another. **2 have** (*or* **take**) **pity on.** to have sympathy or show mercy for. **3** something that causes regret or pity. **4** an unfortunate chance: *what a pity you can't come.* **5 more's the pity.** it is highly regrettable (that). ◆ *vb* **pities, pitying, pitied. 6** (*tr*) to feel pity for. [**C13**: from Old French *pité,* from Latin *pietās* duty] ▸ **'pitying** *adj* ▸ **'pityingly** *adv*

pityriasis (,pɪtɪ'raɪəsɪs) *n* **1** any of a group of skin diseases characterized by the shedding of dry flakes of skin. **2** a similar skin disease of certain domestic animals. [**C17**: via New Latin from Greek *pituriasis* scurfiness, from *pituron* bran]

più (pju:) *adv Music.* (*in combination*) more (quickly, softly, etc.): *più allegro, più mosso, più lento.* [Italian, from Latin *plus* more]

piupiu ('pi:u:,pi:u:) *n* a skirt made from the leaves of the New Zealand flax, worn by Maoris on ceremonial occasions. [Maori]

Piura (*Spanish* 'pjura) *n* a city in NW Peru: the oldest colonial city in Peru, founded by Pizarro in 1532; commercial centre of an agricultural district. Pop.: 277 964 (1993).

Pius II ('paɪəs) *n* pen name *Aeneas Silvius,* original name *Enea Silvio de' Piccolomini.* 1405–64, Italian ecclesiastic, humanist, poet, and historian; pope (1458–64).

Pius IV *n* original name *Giovanni Angelo de' Medici.* 1499–1565, pope (1559–65). He reconvened the Council of Trent (1562), confirming its final decrees.

Pius V *n* **Saint.** original name *Michele Ghislieri.* 1504–72, Italian ecclesiastic; pope (1566–72). He attempted to enforce the reforms decreed by the Council of Trent, excommunicated Elizabeth I of England (1570), and organized the alliance that defeated the Turks at Lepanto (1571). Feast day: 30 April.

Pius VI *n* original name *Giovanni Angelico Braschi.* 1717–99, Italian ecclesiastic; pope (1775–99). He opposed French attempts to limit papal authority and denounced (1791) the French Revolution: he died a prisoner of the French in the Revolutionary Wars.

Pius VII *n* original name *Luigi Barnaba Chiaramonti.* 1740–1823, Italian ecclesiastic; pope (1800–23). He concluded a concordat with Napoleon (1801) and consecrated him as emperor of France (1804), but resisted his annexation of the Papal States (1809).

Pius IX *n* original name *Giovanni Maria Mastai-Ferretti.* 1792–1878, Italian ecclesiastic; pope (1846–78). He refused to recognize the incorporation of Rome and the Papal States in the kingdom of Italy, confining himself to the Vatican after 1870. He decreed the dogma of the Immaculate Conception (1854) and convened the Vatican Council, which laid down the doctrine of papal infallibility (1870).

Pius X *n* **Saint.** original name *Giuseppe Sarto.* 1835–1914, Italian ecclesiastic; pope (1903–14). He condemned Modernism (1907) and initiated a new codification of canon law. Feast day: Aug. 21.

Pius XI *n* original name *Achille Ratti.* 1857–1939, Italian ecclesiastic; pope (1922–39). He signed the Lateran Treaty (1929), by which the Vatican City was recognized as an independent state. His encyclicals condemned Nazism and Communism.

Pius XII *n* original name *Eugenio Pacelli.* 1876–1958, Italian ecclesiastic; pope (1939–58): his attitude towards Nazi German anti-Semitism has been a matter of controversy.

Piute ('paɪ,u:t, paɪ'ju:t) *n* a variant spelling of **Paiute.**

pivot ('pɪvət) *n* **1** a short shaft or pin supporting something that turns; fulcrum. **2** the end of a shaft or arbor that terminates in a bearing. **3** a person or thing upon which progress, success, etc., depends. **4** the person or position from which a military formation takes its reference, as when altering position. ◆ *vb* **5** (*tr*) to mount on or provide with a pivot or pivots. **6** (*intr*) to turn on or as if on a pivot. [**C17**: from Old French; perhaps related to Old Provençal *pua* tooth of a comb]

pivotal ('pɪvətᵊl) *adj* **1** of, involving, or acting as a pivot. **2** of crucial importance. ▸ **'pivotally** *adv*

pivot bridge *n* another name for **swing bridge.**

pivot grammar *n Psychol.* a loose grammar said to govern two-word utterances by children.

pix[1] (pɪks) *pl n Informal.* photographs; prints.

pix[2] (pɪks) *n* a less common spelling of **pyx.**

pixel ('pɪksᵊl) *n* any of a number of very small picture elements that make up a picture, as on a visual display unit. [**C20**: from *pix* pictures + *el(ement)*]

pixelation (,pɪksɪ'leɪʃən) *n* a video technique in which an image is blurred by being overlaid with a grid of squares, usually to disguise the identity of a person.

pixie *or* **pixy** ('pɪksɪ) *n, pl* **pixies.** (in folklore) a fairy or elf. [**C17**: of obscure origin]

pixilated *or* **pixillated** ('pɪksɪ,leɪtɪd) *adj Chiefly U.S.* **1** eccentric or whimsical. **2** *Slang.* drunk. [**C20**: from PIXIE + *-lated,* as in *stimulated, titillated,* etc.] ▸ **,pixi'lation** *or* **,pixil'lation** *n*

Pizarro (pɪ'zɑ:rəʊ; *Spanish* pi'θarrɔ) *n* **Francisco** (fran'θisko). ?1475–1541, Spanish conqueror of Peru. He landed in Peru (1532), murdered the Inca King Atahualpa (1533), and founded Lima as the new capital of Peru (1535). He was murdered by his own followers.

pize (paɪz) *vb* (*tr*) *Yorkshire dialect.* to strike (someone a blow). [of obscure origin]

pizz. *Music. abbrev. for* pizzicato.

pizza ('pi:tsə) *n* a dish of Italian origin consisting of a baked disc of dough covered with cheese and tomatoes, usually with the addition of mushrooms, anchovies, sausage, or ham. [**C20**: from Italian, perhaps from Vulgar Latin *picea* (unattested), from Latin *piceus* relating to PITCH[2]; perhaps related to Modern Greek *pitta* cake]

pizzazz *or* **pizazz** (pə'zæz) *n Informal.* an attractive combination of energy and style; sparkle, vitality, glamour. Also called: **pazzazz, pazazz, pzazz.** [**C20**: origin obscure]

pizzeria (,pi:tsə'ri:ə) *n* a place where pizzas are made, sold, or eaten. [**C20**: from Italian, from PIZZA + *-eria* -ERY]

pizzicato (,pɪtsɪ'kɑ:təʊ) *Music.* ◆ *adj, adv* **1** (in music for the violin family) to be plucked with the finger. ◆ *n* **2** the style or technique of playing a normally bowed stringed instrument in this manner. [**C19**: from Italian: pinched, from *pizzicare* to twist, twang]

pizzle ('pɪzᵊl) *n Archaic or dialect.* the penis of an animal, esp. a bull. [**C16**: of

Germanic origin; compare Low German *pēsel,* Flemish *pēzel,* Middle Dutch *pēze* sinew]

pk *pl* **pks** *abbrev. for:* **1** pack. **2** park. **3** peak.

PK 1 *abbrev. for* psychokinesis. **2** *international car registration for* Pakistan.

pkg. *pl* **pkgs.** *abbrev. for* package.

pkt *abbrev. for* packet.

pl *abbrev. for:* **1** place. **2** plate. **3** plural.

PL 1 (in transformational grammar) *abbrev. for* plural. **2** *international car registration for* Poland.

Pl. (in street names) *abbrev. for* Place.

PL/1 *n* programming language 1: a high-level computer programming language designed for mathematical and scientific purposes. [C20: *p(rogramming) l(anguage) 1*]

PLA *abbrev. for* Port of London Authority.

plaas (plɑːs) *n S. African.* a farm. [Afrikaans]

placable ('plækəbəl) *adj* easily placated or appeased. [C15: via Old French from Latin *plācābilis,* from *plācāre* to appease; related to *placēre* to please] ▸ ˌ**placa'bility** *or* '**placableness** *n* ▸ '**placably** *adv*

placard ('plækɑːd) *n* **1** a printed or written notice for public display; poster. **2** a small plaque or card. ◆ *vb (tr)* **3** to post placards on or in. **4** to publicize or advertise by placards. **5** to display as a placard. [C15: from Old French *plaquart,* from *plaquier* to plate, lay flat; see PLAQUE]

placate (plə'keɪt) *vb (tr)* to pacify or appease. [C17: from Latin *plācāre;* see PLACABLE] ▸ **pla'cation** *n*

placatory (plə'keɪtərɪ; 'plækətərɪ, -trɪ) *or (less commonly)* **placative** (plə'keɪtɪv, 'plækətɪv) *adj* placating or intended to placate.

place (pleɪs) *n* **1** a particular point or part of space or of a surface, esp. that occupied by a person or thing. **2** a geographical point, such as a town, city, etc. **3** a position or rank in a sequence or order. **4a** an open square lined with houses of a similar type in a city or town. **4b** *(cap. when part of a street name): Grosvenor Place.* **5** space or room. **6** a house or living quarters. **7** a country house with grounds. **8** any building or area set aside for a specific purpose. **9** a passage in a book, play, film, etc.: *to lose one's place.* **10** proper or appropriate position or time: *he still thinks a woman's place is in the home.* **11** right or original position: *put it back in its place.* **12** suitable, appropriate, or customary surroundings (esp. in the phrases **out of place, in place**). **13** right, prerogative, or duty: *it is your place to give a speech.* **14** appointment, position, or job: *a place at college.* **15** position, condition, or state: *if I were in your place.* **16a** a space or seat, as at a dining table. **16b** *(as modifier): place mat.* **17** *Maths.* the relative position of a digit in a number. See also **decimal place. 18** any of the best times in a race. **19** *Horse racing.* **19a** *Brit.* the first, second, or third position at the finish. **19b** *U.S. and Canadian.* the first or usually the second position at the finish. **19c** *(as modifier): a place bet.* **20** *Theatre.* one of the three unities. See **unity** (sense 8). **21** *Archaic.* an important position, rank, or role. **22 all over the place.** in disorder or disarray. **23 another place.** *Brit., Parliamentary procedure.* **23a** (in the House of Commons) the House of Lords. **23b** (in the House of Lords) the House of Commons. **24 give place (to).** to make room (for) or be superseded (by). **25 go places.** *Informal.* **25a** to travel. **25b** to become successful. **26 in place of. 26a** instead of; in lieu of: *go in place of my sister.* **26b** in exchange for: *he gave her it in place of her ring.* **27 know one's place.** to be aware of one's inferior position. **28 pride of place.** the highest or foremost position. **29 put someone in his** (*or* **her**) **place.** to humble someone who is arrogant, conceited, forward, etc. **30 take one's place.** to take up one's usual or specified position. **31 take the place of.** to be a substitute for. **32 take place.** to happen or occur. **33 the other place.** *Facetious.* **33a** (at Oxford University) Cambridge University. **33b** (at Cambridge University) Oxford University. ◆ *vb (mainly tr)* **34** to put or set in a particular or appropriate place. **35** to find or indicate the place of. **36** to identify or classify by linking with an appropriate context: *to place a face.* **37** to regard or view as being: *to place prosperity above sincerity.* **38** to make (an order, a bet, etc.). **39** to find a home or job for (someone). **40** to appoint to an office or position. **41** (often foll. by *with*) to put under the care (of). **42** to direct or aim carefully. **43** *(passive) Brit.* to cause (a racehorse, greyhound, athlete, etc.) to arrive in first, second, third, or sometimes fourth place. **44** *(intr) U.S. and Canadian.* (of a racehorse, greyhound, etc.) to finish among the first three in a contest, esp. in second position. **45** to invest (funds). **46** to sing (a note) with accuracy of pitch. **47** to insert (an advertisement) in a newspaper, journal, etc. [C13: via Old French from Latin *platēa* courtyard, from Greek *plateia,* from *platus* broad; compare French *plat* flat]

Place (pleɪs) *n* **Francis.** 1771–1854, British radical, who campaigned for the repeal (1824) of the Combination Acts, which forbade the forming of trade unions, and for parliamentary reform.

placebo (plə'siːbəʊ) *n, pl* **-bos** *or* **-boes. 1** *Med.* an inactive substance or other sham form of therapy administered to a patient usually to compare its effects with those of a real drug or treatment, but sometimes for the psychological benefit to the patient through his believing he is receiving treatment. See also **control group, placebo effect. 2** something said or done to please or humour another. **3** *R.C. Church.* a traditional name for the vespers of the office for the dead. [C13 (in the ecclesiastical sense): from Latin *Placebo Domino* I shall please the Lord (from the opening of the office for the dead); C19 (in the medical sense)]

placebo effect *n Med.* a positive therapeutic effect claimed by a patient after receiving a placebo believed by him to be an active drug. See **control group.**

place card *n* a card placed on a dinner table before a seat, as at a formal dinner, indicating who is to sit there.

place kick *Football.* ◆ *n* **1** a kick in which the ball is placed in position before it is kicked. ◆ *vb* **place-kick. 2** to kick (a ball) using a place kick. ◆ Compare **drop kick, punt**[2].

placeman ('pleɪsmən) *n, pl* **-men.** *Brit., derogatory.* a person who holds a public office, esp. for private profit and as a reward for political support.

placement ('pleɪsmənt) *n* **1** the act of placing or the state of being placed. **2** arrangement or position. **3** the process or business of finding employment.

place name *n* the name of a geographical location, such as a town or area.

placenta (plə'sɛntə) *n, pl* **-tas** *or* **-tae** (-tiː). **1** the vascular organ formed in the uterus during pregnancy, consisting of both maternal and embryonic tissues and providing oxygen and nutrients for the fetus and transfer of waste products from the fetal to the maternal blood circulation. See also **afterbirth. 2** the corresponding organ or part in certain mammals. **3** *Botany.* **3a** the part of the ovary of flowering plants to which the ovules are attached. **3b** the mass of tissue in nonflowering plants that bears the sporangia or spores. [C17: via Latin from Greek *plakoeis* flat cake, from *plax* flat]

placental (plə'sɛntəl) *or* **placentate** *adj* (esp. of animals) having a placenta: *placental mammals.* See also **eutherian.**

placentation (ˌplæsɛn'teɪʃən) *n* **1** *Botany.* the way in which ovules are attached in the ovary. **2** *Zoology.* **2a** the way in which the placenta is attached in the uterus. **2b** the process of formation of the placenta.

place of safety order *n Social welfare, law.* (in Britain) under the Children and Young Persons Act 1969, an order granted by a justice to a person or agency granting authority to detain a child or young person and take him or her to a place of safety for not more than 28 days, because of the child's actual or likely ill-treatment or neglect, etc.

placer ('plæsə) *n* **a** surface sediment containing particles of gold or some other valuable mineral. **b** *(in combination): placer-mining.* [C19: from American Spanish: deposit, from Spanish *plaza* PLACE]

place setting *n* the set of items of cutlery, crockery, and glassware laid for one person at a dining table.

placet ('pleɪsɛt) *n* a vote or expression of assent by saying the word *placet.* [C16: from Latin, literally: it pleases]

place-value *adj* denoting a series in which successive digits represent successive powers of the base.

placid ('plæsɪd) *adj* having a calm appearance or nature. [C17: from Latin *placidus* peaceful; related to *placēre* to please] ▸ **placidity** (plə'sɪdɪtɪ) *or* '**placidness** *n* ▸ '**placidly** *adv*

placing ('pleɪsɪŋ) *n Stock Exchange.* a method of issuing securities to the public using an intermediary, such as a stockbroking firm.

placket ('plækɪt) *n Dressmaking.* **1** a piece of cloth sewn in under a closure with buttons, hooks and eyes, zips, etc. **2** the closure itself. [C16: perhaps from Middle Dutch *plackaet* breastplate, from Medieval Latin *placca* metal plate]

placoderm ('plækəˌdɜːm) *n* any extinct bony-plated fishlike vertebrate of the class *Placodermi,* of Silurian to Permian times: thought to have been the earliest vertebrates with jaws. [C19: from Greek *plac-, plax* a flat plate + -DERM]

placoid ('plækɔɪd) *adj* **1** platelike or flattened. **2** (of the scales of sharks and other elasmobranchs) toothlike; composed of dentine with an enamel tip and basal pulp cavity. [C19: from Greek *plac-, plax* flat]

plafond (plə'fɒn; *French* plafɔ̃) *n* **1** a ceiling, esp. one having ornamentation. **2** a card game, a precursor of contract bridge. [C17: from French, literally: ceiling, maximum, from *plat* flat + *fond* bottom, from Latin *fundus* bottom]

plagal ('pleɪgəl) *adj* **1** (of a cadence) progressing from the subdominant to the tonic chord, as in the *Amen* of a hymn. **2** (of a mode) commencing upon the dominant of an authentic mode, but sharing the same final as the authentic mode. Plagal modes are designated by the prefix *Hypo-* before the name of their authentic counterparts: *the Hypodorian mode.* ◆ Compare **authentic** (sense 5). [C16: from Medieval Latin *plagālis,* from *plaga,* perhaps from Greek *plagos* side]

plage (plɑːʒ) *n Astronomy.* a bright patch in the sun's chromosphere. [French, literally: beach, strand]

plagiarism ('pleɪdʒəˌrɪzəm) *n* **1** the act of plagiarizing. **2** something plagiarized. ▸ '**plagiarist** *n* ▸ ˌ**plagia'ristic** *adj*

plagiarize *or* **plagiarise** ('pleɪdʒəˌraɪz) *vb* to appropriate (ideas, passages, etc.) from (another work or author). ▸ '**plagiaˌrizer** *or* '**plagiaˌriser** *n*

plagiary ('pleɪdʒərɪ) *n, pl* **-ries.** *Archaic.* a person who plagiarizes or a piece of plagiarism. [C16: from Latin *plagiārus* plunderer, from *plagium* kidnapping; related to *plaga* snare]

plagio- *combining form.* slanting, inclining, or oblique: *plagiotropism.* [from Greek *plagios,* from *plagos* side]

plagioclase ('pleɪdʒɪəʊˌkleɪz) *n* a series of feldspar minerals consisting of a mixture of sodium and calcium aluminium silicates in triclinic crystalline form: includes albite, oligoclase, and labradorite. ▸ **plagioclastic** (ˌpleɪdʒɪəʊ'klæstɪk) *adj*

plagioclimax (ˌpleɪdʒɪəʊ'klaɪmæks) *n Ecology.* the climax stage of a community, influenced by man or some other outside factor.

plagiotropism (ˌpleɪdʒɪəʊ'trəʊˌpɪzəm) *n* the growth of a plant at an angle to the vertical in response to a stimulus. ▸ ˌ**plagio'tropic** *adj*

plague (pleɪg) *n* **1** any widespread and usually highly contagious disease with a high fatality rate. **2** an infectious disease of rodents, esp. rats, transmitted to man by the bite of the rat flea (*Xenopsylla cheopis*). **3** See **bubonic plague. 4** something that afflicts or harasses. **5** *Informal.* an annoyance or nuisance. **6** a pestilence, affliction, or calamity on a large scale, esp. when regarded as sent by God. **7** *Archaic.* used to express annoyance, disgust, etc.: *a plague on you.* ◆ *vb* **plagues, plaguing, plagued.** *(tr)* **8** to afflict or harass. **9** to bring down a plague upon. **10** *Informal.* to annoy. [C14: from Late Latin *plāga* pestilence, from Latin: a blow; related to Greek *plēgē* a stroke, Latin *plangere* to strike] ▸ '**plaguer** *n*

plaguy *or* **plaguey** ('pleɪgɪ) *Archaic, informal.* ◆ *adj* **1** disagreeable or vexing. ◆ *adv* **2** disagreeably or annoyingly. ▸ '**plaguily** *adv*

plaice (pleɪs) *n, pl* **plaice** *or* **plaices. 1** a European flatfish, *Pleuronectes* *platessa*, having an oval brown body marked with red or orange spots and valued as a food fish: family *Pleuronectidae*. **2** *U.S. and Canadian*. any of various other fishes of the family *Pleuronectidae*, esp. *Hippoglossoides platessoides*. [C13: from Old French *plaïz*, from Late Latin *platessa* flatfish, from Greek *platus* flat]

plaid (plæd, pleɪd) *n* **1** a long piece of cloth of a tartan pattern, worn over the shoulder as part of Highland costume. **2a** a crisscross weave or cloth. **2b** (*as modifier*): *a plaid scarf*. [C16: from Scottish Gaelic *plaide*, of obscure origin]

Plaid Cymru (ˌplaɪd ˈkʌmrɪ) *n* the Welsh nationalist party. [C20: Welsh, literally: party of Wales]

plain[1] (pleɪn) *adj* **1** flat or smooth; level. **2** not complicated; clear: *the plain truth*. **3** not difficult; simple or easy: *a plain task*. **4** honest or straightforward. **5** lowly, esp. in social rank or education. **6** without adornment or show: *a plain coat*. **7** (of fabric) without pattern or of simple untwilled weave. **8** not attractive. **9** not mixed; simple: *plain vodka*. **10** *Knitting*. of or done in plain. ♦ *n* **11** a level or almost level tract of country, esp. an extensive treeless region. **12** a simple stitch in knitting made by putting the right needle into a loop on the left needle, passing the wool round the right needle, and pulling it through the loop, thus forming a new loop. **13** (in billiards) **13a** the unmarked white ball, as distinguished from the spot balls. **13b** the player using this ball. **14** (in Ireland) short for **plain porter**, a light porter: *two pints of plain, please*. ♦ *adv* **15** (intensifier): *just plain tired*. ♦ See also **plains**. [C13: from Old French: simple, from Latin *plānus* level, distinct, clear] ▸ **ˈplainly** *adv* ▸ **ˈplainness** *n*

plain[2] (pleɪn) *vb* a dialect or poetic word for **complain**. [C14 *pleignen*, from Old French *plaindre* to lament, from Latin *plangere* to beat]

plainchant (ˈpleɪnˌtʃɑːnt) *n* another name for **plainsong**. [C18: from French, rendering Medieval Latin *cantus plānus*; see PLAIN[1]]

plain chocolate *n* chocolate with a slightly bitter flavour and dark colour. Compare **milk chocolate**.

plain clothes *pl n* **a** ordinary clothes, as distinguished from uniform, as worn by a police detective on duty. **b** (*as modifier*): *a plain-clothes policeman*.

plain flour *n* flour to which no raising agent has been added.

plain-laid *adj* (of a cable or rope) made of three strands twisted together from left to right.

plains (pleɪnz) *pl n Chiefly U.S.* extensive tracts of level or almost level treeless countryside; prairies.

plain sailing *n* **1** *Informal*. smooth or easy progress. **2** *Nautical*. sailing in a body of water that is unobstructed; clear sailing. Compare **plane sailing**.

Plains Indian *n* a member of any of the North American Indian peoples formerly living in the Great Plains of the U.S. and Canada.

plainsman (ˈpleɪnzmən) *n, pl* **-men**. a person who lives in a plains region, esp. in the Great Plains of North America.

Plains of Abraham *n* (*functioning as sing*) a field in E Canada between Quebec City and the St Lawrence River: site of an important British victory (1759) in the Seven Years' War, which cost the French their possession of Canada.

plainsong (ˈpleɪnˌsɒŋ) *n* the style of unison unaccompanied vocal music used in the medieval Church, esp. in Gregorian chant. Also called: **plainchant**. [C16: translation of Medieval Latin *cantus plānus*]

plain-spoken *adj* candid; frank; blunt.

plaint (pleɪnt) *n* **1** *Archaic*. a complaint or lamentation. **2** *Law*. a statement in writing of grounds of complaint made to a court of law and asking for redress of the grievance. [C13: from Old French *plainte*, from Latin *planctus* lamentation, from *plangere* to beat]

plain text *n Telecomm*. a message set in a directly readable form rather than in coded groups.

plaintiff (ˈpleɪntɪf) *n* a person who brings a civil action in a court of law. Compare **defendant** (sense 1). [C14: from legal French *plaintif*, from Old French *plaintif* (adj) complaining, from *plainte* PLAINT]

plaintive (ˈpleɪntɪv) *adj* expressing melancholy; mournful. [C14: from Old French *plaintif* grieving, from *plainte* PLAINT] ▸ **ˈplaintively** *adv* ▸ **ˈplaintiveness** *n*

plaister (ˈpleɪstə) *n Obsolete or Scot*. plaster.

plait (plæt) *n* **1** a length of hair, ribbon, etc., that has been plaited. **2** (in Britain) a loaf of bread of several twisting or intertwining parts. **3** a rare spelling of **pleat**. ♦ *vb* **4** (*tr*) to intertwine (strands or strips) in a pattern. [C15 *pleyt*, from Old French *pleit*, from Latin *plicāre* to fold; see PLY[2]]

plan (plæn) *n* **1** a detailed scheme, method, etc., for attaining an objective. **2** (*sometimes pl*) a proposed, usually tentative idea for doing something. **3** a drawing to scale of a horizontal section through a building taken at a given level. Compare **ground plan** (sense 1), **elevation** (sense 5). **4** an outline, sketch, etc. **5** (in perspective drawing) any of several imaginary planes perpendicular to the line of vision and between the eye and object depicted. ♦ *vb* **plans, planning, planned. 6** to form a plan (for) or make plans (for). **7** (*tr*) to make a plan of (a building). **8** (*tr; takes a clause as object or an infinitive*) to have in mind as a purpose; intend. [C18: via French from Latin *plānus* flat; compare PLANE[1], PLAIN[1]]

planar (ˈpleɪnə) *adj* **1** of or relating to a plane. **2** lying in one plane; flat. [C19: from Late Latin *plānāris* on level ground, from Latin *plānus* flat] ▸ **planarity** (pleɪˈnærɪtɪ) *n*

planarian (pləˈnɛərɪən) *n* any free-living turbellarian flatworm of the mostly aquatic suborder *Tricladida*, having a three-branched intestine. [C19: from New Latin *Plānāria* type genus, from Late Latin *plānārius* level, flat; see PLANE[1]]

planar process *n* a method of producing diffused junctions in semiconductor devices. A pattern of holes is etched into an oxide layer formed on a silicon substrate, into which impurities are diffused through the holes.

planation (pleɪˈneɪʃən) *n* the erosion of a land surface until it is basically flat.

planchet (ˈplɑːntʃɪt) *n* a piece of metal ready to be stamped as a coin, medal, etc.; flan. [C17: from French: little board, from *planche* PLANK[1]]

planchette (plɑːnˈʃɛt) *n* a heart-shaped board on wheels, on which messages are written under supposed spirit guidance. [C19: from French: little board, from *planche* PLANK[1]]

Planck (plæŋk; *German* plaŋk) *n* **Max** (**Karl Ernst Ludwig**) (maks). 1858–1947, German physicist who first formulated the quantum theory (1900): Nobel prize for physics 1918.

Planck constant *or* **Planck's constant** *n* a fundamental constant equal to the energy of any quantum of radiation divided by its frequency. It has a value of 6.6262×10^{-34} joule seconds. Symbol: *h* See also **Dirac constant.**

Planck's law *n Physics*. a law that is the basis of quantum theory, which states that the energy of electromagnetic radiation is confined to indivisible packets (quanta), each of which has an energy equal to the product of the Planck constant and the frequency of the radiation.

plane[1] (pleɪn) *n* **1** *Maths*. a flat surface in which a straight line joining any two of its points lies entirely on that surface. **2** a flat or level surface. **3** a level of existence, performance, attainment, etc. **4a** short for **aeroplane**. **4b** a wing or supporting surface of an aircraft or hydroplane. ♦ *adj* **5** level or flat. **6** *Maths*. (of a curve, figure, etc.) lying entirely in one plane. ♦ *vb* (*intr*) **7** to fly without moving wings or using engines; glide. **8** (of a boat) to rise partly and skim over the water when moving at a certain speed. **9** to travel by aeroplane. [C17: from Latin *plānum* level surface] ▸ **ˈplaneness** *n*

plane[2] (pleɪn) *n* **1** a tool with an adjustable sharpened steel blade set obliquely in a wooden or iron body, for levelling or smoothing timber surfaces, cutting mouldings or grooves, etc. **2** a flat tool, usually metal, for smoothing the surface of clay or plaster in a mould. ♦ *vb* (*tr*) **3** to level, smooth, or cut (timber, wooden articles, etc.) using a plane or similar tool. **4** (often foll. by *off*) to remove using a plane. [C14: via Old French from Late Latin *plāna* plane, from *plānāre* to level]

plane[3] (pleɪn) *n* See **plane tree**.

plane angle *n* an angle between two intersecting lines.

plane chart *n* a chart used in plane sailing, in which the lines of latitude and longitude are straight and parallel.

plane geometry *n* the study of the properties of and relationships between plane curves, figures, etc.

plane polarization *n* a type of polarization in which waves of light or other electromagnetic radiation are restricted to vibration in a single plane.

planer (ˈpleɪnə) *n* **1** a machine with a cutting tool that makes repeated horizontal strokes across the surface of a workpiece: used to cut flat surfaces into metal. **2** a machine for planing wood, esp. one in which the cutting blades are mounted on a rotating drum. **3** *Printing*. a flat piece of wood used to level type in a chase. **4** any person or thing that planes.

plane sailing *n Nautical*. navigation without reference to the earth's curvature. Compare **plain sailing**.

plane surveying *n* the surveying of areas of limited size, making no corrections for the earth's curvature.

planet (ˈplænɪt) *n* **1** Also called: **major planet**. any of the nine celestial bodies, Mercury, Venus, Earth, Mars, Jupiter, Saturn, Uranus, Neptune, or Pluto, that revolve around the sun in elliptical orbits and are illuminated by light from the sun. **2** any celestial body revolving around a star, illuminated by light from that star. **3** *Astrology*. any of the planets of the solar system, excluding the earth but including the sun and moon, each thought to rule one or sometimes two signs of the zodiac. See also **house** (sense 9). [C12: via Old French from Late Latin *planēta*, from Greek *planētēs* wanderer, from *planaein* to wander]

plane table *n* **1** a surveying instrument consisting of a drawing board mounted on adjustable legs, and used in the field for plotting measurements directly. ♦ *vb* **plane-table. 2** to survey (a plot of land) using a plane table.

planetarium (ˌplænɪˈtɛərɪəm) *n, pl* **-iums** *or* **-ia** (-ɪə). **1** an instrument for simulating the apparent motions of the sun, moon, and planets against a background of constellations by projecting images of these bodies onto the inside of a domed ceiling. **2** a building in which such an instrument is housed. **3** a model of the solar system, sometimes mechanized to show the relative motions of the planets.

planetary (ˈplænɪtərɪ, -trɪ) *adj* **1** of or relating to a planet. **2** mundane; terrestrial. **3** wandering or erratic. **4** *Astrology*. under the influence of one of the planets. **5** (of a gear, esp. an epicyclic gear) having an axis that rotates around that of another gear. **6** (of an electron) having an orbit around the nucleus of an atom. ♦ *n, pl* **-taries. 7** a train of planetary gears.

planetary nebula *n* an expanding shell of gas surrounding a dying star, formed from matter ejected from the star's outer layers; the gas is ionized by the remaining hot stellar core, emitting light in the process. [C18: named from its (occasional) resemblance to a planetary disc]

planetesimal hypothesis (ˌplænɪˈtɛsɪməl) *n* the discredited theory that the close passage of a star to the sun caused many small bodies (**planetesimals**) to be drawn from the sun, eventually coalescing to form the planets. [C20: *planetesimal*, from PLANET + INFINITESIMAL]

planetoid (ˈplænɪˌtɔɪd) *n* another name for **asteroid** (sense 1). ▸ **ˌplaneˈtoidal** *adj*

planetology (ˌplænɪˈtɒlədʒɪ) *n Astronomy*. the study of the origin, composition, and distribution of matter in the planets.

plane tree *or* **plane** *n* any tree of the genus *Platanus*, having ball-shaped heads of fruits and leaves with pointed lobes: family *Platanaceae*. The hybrid *P. × hispanica* (**London plane**) is frequently planted in towns. Also called: **platan**. [C14 *plane*, from Old French, from Latin *platanus*, from Greek *platanos*, from *platos* wide, referring to the leaves]

planet-struck *or* **planet-stricken** *adj Astrology*. affected by the influence of a planet, esp. malignly.

planet wheel *or* **gear** *n* any one of the wheels of an epicyclic gear train that orbits the central axis of the train.

planform ('plæn,fɔːm) *n* the outline or silhouette of an object, esp. an aircraft, as seen from above.

plangent ('plændʒənt) *adj* **1** having a loud deep sound. **2** resonant and mournful in sound. [C19: from Latin *plangere* to beat (esp. the breast, in grief); see PLAIN[2]] ▸ **'plangency** *n* ▸ **'plangently** *adv*

planimeter (plæ'nɪmɪtə) *n* a mechanical integrating instrument for measuring the area of an irregular plane figure, such as the area under a curve, by moving a point attached to an arm around the perimeter of the figure.

planimetry (plæ'nɪmɪtrɪ) *n* the measurement of plane areas. ▸ **planimetric** (,plænɪ'metrɪk) *or* **,plani'metrical** *adj*

planish ('plænɪʃ) *vb (tr)* to give a final finish to (metal) by hammering or rolling to produce a smooth surface. [C16: from Old French *planir* to smooth out, from Latin *plānus* flat, PLAIN[1]] ▸ **'planisher** *n*

planisphere ('plænɪ,sfɪə) *n* a projection or representation of all or part of a sphere on a plane surface, such as a polar projection of the celestial sphere onto a chart. [C14: from Medieval Latin *plānisphaerium,* from Latin *plānus* flat + Greek *sphaira* globe] ▸ **planispheric** (,plænɪ'sferɪk) *adj*

plank[1] (plæŋk) *n* **1** a stout length of sawn timber. **2** something that supports or sustains. **3** one of the policies in a political party's programme. **4 walk the plank.** to be forced by pirates to walk to one's death off the end of a plank jutting out over the water from the side of a ship. ◆ *vb (tr)* **5** to cover or provide (an area) with planks. **6** to beat (meat) to make it tender. **7** *Chiefly U.S. and Canadian.* to cook or serve (meat or fish) on a special wooden board. [C13: from Old Norman French *planke,* from Late Latin *planca* board, from *plancus* flat-footed; probably related to Greek *plax* flat surface]

plank[2] (plæŋk) *vb (tr) Scot.* to hide; cache. [C19: a variant of *plant*]

planking ('plæŋkɪŋ) *n* **1** a number of planks. **2** the act of covering or furnishing with planks.

plank-sheer *n Nautical.* a plank or timber covering the upper ends of the frames of a wooden vessel. [C14 *plancher,* from Old French *planchier,* from *planche* plank, from Latin *planca;* spelling influenced by PLANK[1], SHEER[1]]

plankton ('plæŋktən) *n* the organisms inhabiting the surface layer of a sea or lake, consisting of small drifting plants and animals, such as diatoms. Compare **nekton.** [C19: via German from Greek *planktos* wandering, from *plazesthai* to roam] ▸ **planktonic** (plæŋk'tɒnɪk) *adj*

planned economy *n* another name for **command economy.**

planned obsolescence *n* the policy of deliberately limiting the life of a product in order to encourage the purchaser to replace it. Also called: **built-in obsolescence.**

planner ('plænə) *n* **1** a person who makes plans, esp. for the development of a town, building, etc. **2** a chart for recording future appointments, tasks, goals, etc.

planning blight *n* the harmful effects of uncertainty about likely restrictions on the types and extent of future development in a particular area on the quality of life of its inhabitants and the normal growth of its business and community enterprises.

planning permission *n* (in Britain) formal permission that must be obtained from a local authority before development or a change of use of land or buildings.

plano- *or sometimes before a vowel* **plan-** *combining form.* indicating flatness or planeness: *plano-concave.* [from Latin *plānus* flat, level]

plano-concave (,pleɪnəʊ'kɒnkeɪv) *adj* (of a lens) having one side concave and the other side plane.

plano-convex (,pleɪnəʊ'kɒnvɛks) *adj* (of a lens) having one side convex and the other side plane.

planogamete ('plænəgə,miːt) *n* a motile gamete, such as a spermatozoon. [C19: from Greek *planos* wandering (see PLANET) + GAMETE]

planography (plə'nɒgrəfɪ) *n Printing.* any process, such as lithography, for printing from a flat surface. ▸ **planographic** (,pleɪnə'græfɪk) *adj* ▸ **,plano'graphically** *adv*

planometer (plæ'nɒmɪtə) *n* a flat metal plate used for directly testing the flatness of metal surfaces in accurate metalwork. ▸ **planometric** (,pleɪnə'metrɪk) *adj* ▸ **,plano'metrically** *adv* ▸ **pla'nometry** *n*

planosol ('pleɪnə,sɒl) *n* a type of intrazonal soil of humid or subhumid uplands having a strongly leached upper layer overlying a clay hardpan. [C20: from Latin PLANO- + *solum* soil]

plant[1] (plɑːnt) *n* **1** any living organism that typically synthesizes its food from inorganic substances, possesses cellulose cell walls, responds slowly and often permanently to a stimulus, lacks specialized sense organs and nervous system, and has no powers of locomotion. **2** such an organism that is green, terrestrial, and smaller than a shrub or tree; a herb. **3** a cutting, seedling, or similar structure, esp. when ready for transplantation. **4** *Informal.* a thing positioned secretly for discovery by another, esp. in order to incriminate an innocent person. **5** *Snooker, etc.* a position in which the cue ball can be made to strike an intermediate which then pockets another ball. ◆ *vb (tr)* **6** (often foll. by *out*) to set (seeds, crops, etc.) into (ground) to grow. **7** to place firmly in position. **8** to establish; found. **9** to implant in the mind. **10** *Slang.* to deliver (a blow). **11** *Informal.* to position or hide, esp. in order to deceive or observe. **12** to place (young fish, oysters, spawn, etc.) in (a lake, river, etc.) in order to stock the water. ◆ See also **plant out.** [Old English, from Latin *planta* a shoot, cutting] ▸ **'plantable** *adj* ▸ **'plant,like** *adj*

plant[2] (plɑːnt) *n* **1a** the land, buildings, and equipment used in carrying on an industrial, business, or other undertaking or service. **1b** (*as modifier*): *plant costs.* **2** a factory or workshop. **3** mobile mechanical equipment for construction, road-making, etc. [C20: special use of PLANT[1]]

Plantagenet (plæn'tædʒɪnɪt) *n* a line of English kings, ruling from the ascent of Henry II (1154) to the death of Richard III (1485). [C12: from Old French, literally: sprig of broom, with reference to the crest of the Angevin kings, from Latin *planta* sprig + *genista* broom]

plant agreement *n* a collective agreement at plant level within industry.

plantain[1] ('plæntɪn) *n* any of various N temperate plants of the genus *Plantago,* esp. *P. major* (**great plantain**), which has a rosette of broad leaves and a slender spike of small greenish flowers: family *Plantaginaceae.* See also **ribwort.** [C14 *plauntein,* from Old French *plantein,* from Latin *plantāgō,* from *planta* sole of the foot]

plantain[2] ('plæntɪn) *n* **1** a large tropical musaceous plant, *Musa paradisiaca.* **2** the green-skinned banana-like fruit of this plant, eaten as a staple food in many tropical regions. [C16: from Spanish *platano* plantain, PLANE TREE]

plantain-eater *n* another name for **touraco.**

plantain lily *n* any of several Asian plants of the liliaceous genus *Hosta,* having broad ribbed leaves and clusters of white, blue, or lilac flowers. Also called: **day lily.**

plantar ('plæntə) *adj* of, relating to, or occurring on the sole of the foot or a corresponding part: *plantar warts.* [C18: from Latin *plantāris,* from *planta* sole of the foot]

plantation (plæn'teɪʃən) *n* **1** an estate, esp. in tropical countries, where cash crops such as rubber, oil palm, etc., are grown on a large scale. **2** a group of cultivated trees or plants. **3** (formerly) a colony or group of settlers. **4** *Rare.* the planting of seeds, shoots, etc.

planter ('plɑːntə) *n* **1** the owner or manager of a plantation. **2** a machine designed for rapid, uniform, and efficient planting of seeds in the ground. **3** a colonizer or settler. **4** a decorative pot or stand for house plants.

planter's punch *n* a cocktail consisting of rum with lime or lemon juice and sugar.

plantigrade ('plæntɪ,greɪd) *adj* **1** walking with the entire sole of the foot touching the ground, as, for example, man and bears. ◆ *n* **2** a plantigrade animal. [C19: via French from New Latin *plantigradus,* from Latin *planta* sole of the foot + *gradus* a step]

plant kingdom *n* a category of living organisms comprising all plants. Compare **animal kingdom, mineral kingdom.**

plant louse *n* **1** another name for an **aphid. 2 jumping plant louse.** any small active cicada-like insect of the homopterous family *Psyllidae* (or *Chermidae*), having hind legs adapted for leaping, and feeding on plant juices.

plantocracy (plɑːn'tɒkrəsɪ) *n, pl* **-cies.** a ruling social class composed of planters.

plant out *vb (tr, adv)* to set (a seedling that has been raised in a greenhouse, frame, or other sheltered place) to grow out in open ground.

plantsman ('plɑːntsmən) *or (fem)* **plantswoman** *n, pl* **-men** *or* **-women.** an experienced gardener who specializes in collecting rare or interesting plants.

planula ('plænjʊlə) *n, pl* **-lae** (-,liː). the ciliated free-swimming larva of hydrozoan coelenterates such as the hydra. [C19: from New Latin: a little plane, from Latin *plānum* level ground] ▸ **'planular** *adj*

plaque (plæk, plɑːk) *n* **1** an ornamental or commemorative inscribed tablet or plate of porcelain, wood, etc. **2** a small flat brooch or badge, as of a club, etc. **3** *Pathol.* any small abnormal patch on or within the body, such as the typical lesion of psoriasis. **4** short for **dental plaque. 5** *Bacteriol.* a clear area within a bacterial or tissue culture caused by localized destruction of the cells by a bacteriophage or other virus. [C19: from French, from *plaquier* to plate, from Middle Dutch *placken* to beat (metal) into a thin plate]

plash[1] (plæʃ) *vb, n* a less common word for **splash.** [Old English *plæsc,* probably imitative; compare Dutch *plas*]

plash[2] (plæʃ) *vb* another word for **pleach.** [C15: from Old French *plassier,* from *plais* hedge, woven fence, from Latin *plectere* to plait; compare PLEACH]

plashy ('plæʃɪ) *adj* **plashier, plashiest. 1** wet or marshy. **2** splashing or splashy.

-plasia *or* **-plasy** *n combining form.* indicating growth, development, or change: *hypoplasia.* [from New Latin, from Greek *plasis* a moulding, from *plassein* to mould]

plasm ('plæzəm) *n* **1** protoplasm of a specified type: *germ plasm.* **2** a variant of **plasma.**

-plasm *n combining form.* (in biology) indicating the material forming cells: *protoplasm; cytoplasm.* [from Greek *plasma* something moulded; see PLASMA] ▸ **-plasmic** *adj combining form.*

plasma ('plæzmə) *or* **plasm** *n* **1** the clear yellowish fluid portion of blood or lymph in which the corpuscles and cells are suspended. **2** short for **blood plasma. 3** a former name for **protoplasm** or **cytoplasm. 4** *Physics.* **4a** a hot ionized material consisting of nuclei and electrons. It is sometimes regarded as a fourth state of matter and is the material present in the sun, most stars, and fusion reactors. **4b** the ionized gas in an electric discharge or spark, containing positive ions and electrons and a small number of negative ions together with un-ionized material. **5** a green slightly translucent variety of chalcedony, used as a gemstone. **6** a less common term for **whey.** [C18: from Late Latin: something moulded, from Greek, from *plassein* to mould] ▸ **plasmatic** (plæz'mætɪk) *or* **'plasmic** *adj*

plasma engine *n* an engine that generates thrust by reaction to the emission of a jet of plasma.

plasmagel ('plæzmə,dʒɛl) *n* another name for **ectoplasm** (sense 1).

plasmagene ('plæzmə,dʒiːn) *n Biology.* a self-replicating particle occurring in the cytoplasm of a cell and functioning in a way similar to but independent of chromosomal genes. ▸ **plasmagenic** (,plæzmə'dʒenɪk) *adj*

plasmalemma (,plæzmə'lɛmə) *or* **plasma membrane** *n* other names for **cell membrane.**

plasmapheresis (,plæzmə'fɛrəsəs) *n* (in blood transfusion) a technique for removing healthy or infected plasma by separating it from the red blood cells by settling or using a centrifuge and retransfusing the red blood cells in a harmless fluid into the donor or patient. [C20: from PLASM + Greek *aphairesis* taking away]

plasmasol ('plæzmə,sɒl) *n* another name for **endoplasm.**

plasma torch *n* an electrical device for converting a gas into a plasma, used for melting metal.

plasmid ('plæzmɪd) *n* a small circle of bacterial DNA that is independent of the main bacterial chromosome. Plasmids often contain genes for drug resistances and can be transmitted between bacteria of the same and different species: used in genetic engineering. [C20: from PLASM + -ID[1]]

plasmin ('plæzmɪn) *n* a proteolytic enzyme that causes fibrinolysis in blood clots.

plasminogen (plæz'mɪnədʒən) *n Biochem.* a zymogen found in blood that gives rise to plasmin on activation.

plasmo- *or before a vowel* **plasm-** *combining form.* of, relating to, or resembling plasma: *plasmolysis.* [from Greek *plasma;* see PLASMA]

plasmodesma (,plæzmə'dɛzmə) *or* **plasmodesm** ('plæzmə,dɛzəm) *n, pl* **-desmata** (-'dɛzmətə) *or* **-desms.** *Botany.* any of various very fine cytoplasmic threads connecting the cytoplasm of adjacent cells via minute holes in the cell walls. [C20: from PLASMO- + Greek *desma* bond]

plasmodium (plæz'məʊdɪəm) *n, pl* **-dia** (-dɪə). **1** an amoeboid mass of protoplasm, containing many nuclei: a stage in the life cycle of certain organisms, esp. the nonreproductive stage of the slime moulds. **2** any parasitic sporozoan protozoan of the genus *Plasmodium,* such as *P. falciparum* and *P. vivax,* which cause malaria. [C19: New Latin; see PLASMA, -ODE[1]] ▸ **plas'modial** *adj*

plasmoid ('plæz,mɔɪd) *n Physics.* a section of a plasma having a characteristic shape.

plasmolyse *or U.S.* **plasmolyze** ('plæzmə,laɪz) *vb* to subject (a cell) to plasmolysis or (of a cell) to undergo plasmolysis.

plasmolysis (plæz'mɒlɪsɪs) *n* the shrinkage of protoplasm away from the cell walls that occurs as a result of excessive water loss, esp. in plant cells (see **exosmosis**). ▸ **plasmolytic** (,plæzmə'lɪtɪk) *adj* ▸ **,plasmo'lytically** *adv*

plasmon ('plæzmɒn) *n Genetics.* the sum total of plasmagenes in a cell. [C20: from German, from Greek *plasma.* See PLASMA]

plasmosome ('plæzmə,səʊm) *n* another name for **nucleolus.**

Plassey ('plæsɪ) *n* a village in NE India, in W Bengal: scene of Clive's victory (1757) over Siraj-ud-daula, which established British supremacy over India.

-plast *n combining form.* indicating an organized living cell or particle of living matter: *protoplast.* [from Greek *plastos* formed, from *plassein* to form]

plaster ('plɑːstə) *n* **1** a mixture of lime, sand, and water, sometimes stiffened with hair or other fibres, that is applied to the surface of a wall or ceiling as a soft paste that hardens when dry. **2** *Brit., Austral., and N.Z.* an adhesive strip of material, usually medicated, for dressing a cut, wound, etc. **3** short for **mustard plaster** or **plaster of Paris.** ◆ *vb* **4** to coat (a wall, ceiling, etc.) with plaster. **5** (*tr*) to apply like plaster: *she plastered make-up on her face.* **6** (*tr*) to cause to lie flat or to adhere. **7** (*tr*) to apply a plaster cast to. **8** (*tr*) *Slang.* to strike or defeat with great force. [Old English, from Medieval Latin *plastrum* medicinal salve, building plaster, via Latin from Greek *emplastron* curative dressing, from EM- + *plassein* to form] ▸ **'plasterer** *n* ▸ **'plastery** *adj*

plasterboard ('plɑːstə,bɔːd) *n* a thin rigid board, in the form of a layer of plaster compressed between two layers of fibreboard, used to form or cover walls.

plaster cast *n* **1** *Surgery.* a cast made of plaster of Paris. See **cast** (sense 40). **2** a copy or mould of a sculpture or other object cast in plaster of Paris.

plastered ('plɑːstəd) *adj Slang.* intoxicated; drunk.

plastering ('plɑːstərɪŋ) *n* a coating or layer of plaster.

plaster of Paris *n* **1** a white powder that sets to a hard solid when mixed with water, used for making sculptures and casts, as an additive for lime plasters, and for making casts for setting broken limbs. It is usually the hemihydrate of calcium sulphate, $2CaSO_4.H_2O$. **2** the hard plaster produced when this powder is mixed with water: a fully hydrated form of calcium sulphate. ◆ Sometimes shortened to **plaster.** [C15: from Medieval Latin *plastrum parisiense,* originally made from the gypsum of *Paris*]

plastic ('plæstɪk, 'plɑːs-) *n* **1** any one of a large number of synthetic usually organic materials that have a polymeric structure and can be moulded when soft and then set, esp. such a material in a finished state containing plasticizer, stabilizer, filler, pigments, etc. Plastics are classified as thermosetting (such as Bakelite) or thermoplastic (such as PVC) and are used in the manufacture of many articles and in coatings, artificial fibres, etc. Compare **resin** (sense 2). **2** short for **plastic money.** ◆ *adj* **3** made of plastic. **4** easily influenced; impressionable: *the plastic minds of children.* **5** capable of being moulded or formed. **6** *Fine arts.* **6a** of or relating to moulding or modelling: *the plastic arts.* **6b** produced or apparently produced by moulding: *the plastic draperies of Giotto's figures.* **7** having the power to form or influence: *the plastic forces of the imagination.* **8** *Biology.* of or relating to any formative process; able to change, develop, or grow: *plastic tissues.* **9** of or relating to plastic surgery. **10** *Slang.* superficially attractive yet unoriginal or artificial: *plastic food.* [C17: from Latin *plasticus* relating to moulding, from Greek *plastikos,* from *plassein* to form] ▸ **'plastically** *adv*

-plastic *adj combining form.* growing or forming: *neoplastic.* [from Greek *plastikos;* see PLASTIC]

plastic bomb *n* a bomb consisting of an adhesive jelly-like explosive fitted around a detonator.

plastic bullet *n* a solid PVC cylinder, 10 cm long and 38 mm in diameter, fired by police in riots to regain control. Formal name: **baton round.**

Plasticine ('plæstɪ,siːn) *n Trademark.* a soft coloured material used, esp. by children, for modelling.

plasticity (plæ'stɪsɪtɪ) *n* **1** the quality of being plastic or able to be moulded. **2** (in pictorial art) the quality of depicting space and form so that they appear three-dimensional.

plasticize *or* **plasticise** ('plæstɪ,saɪz) *vb* to make or become plastic, as by the addition of a plasticizer. ▸ **,plastici'zation** *or* **,plastici'sation** *n*

plasticizer *or* **plasticiser** ('plæstɪ,saɪzə) *n* any of a number of substances added to materials in order to modify their physical properties. Their uses include softening and improving the flexibility of plastics and preventing dried paint coatings from becoming too brittle.

plastic money *n* credit cards, used instead of cash. [C20: from the cards being made of plastic]

plastic surgery *n* the branch of surgery concerned with therapeutic or cosmetic repair or re-formation of missing, injured, or malformed tissues or parts. Also called: **anaplasty.** ▸ **plastic surgeon** *n*

plastid ('plæstɪd) *n* any of various small particles in the cytoplasm of the cells of plants and some animals that contain pigments (see **chromoplast**), starch, oil, protein, etc. [C19: via German from Greek *plastēs* sculptor, from *plassein* to form]

plastometer (plæ'stɒmɪtə) *n* an instrument for measuring plasticity. ▸ **plastometric** (,plæstəʊ'mɛtrɪk) *adj* ▸ **plas'tometry** *n*

plastron ('plæstrən) *n* the bony plate forming the ventral part of the shell of a tortoise or turtle. [C16: via French from Italian *piastrone,* from *piastra* breastplate, from Latin *emplastrum* PLASTER] ▸ **'plastral** *adj*

-plasty *n combining form.* indicating plastic surgery involving a bodily part, tissue, or a specified process: *rhinoplasty; neoplasty.* [from Greek *-plastia;* see -PLAST]

plat[1] (plæt) *n* a small area of ground; plot. [C16 (also occurring in Middle English in place names): originally variant of PLOT[2]]

plat[2] (plæt) *n, vb* **plats, platting, platted.** *Dialect.* a variant spelling of **plait.** [C16: variant of PLAIT]

plat. *abbrev. for:* **1** plateau. **2** platoon.

Plata (*Spanish* 'plata) *n* **Río de la** ('rio de la). an estuary on the SE coast of South America, between Argentina and Uruguay, formed by the Uruguay and Paraná Rivers. Length: 275 km (171 miles). Width: (at its mouth) 225 km (140 miles). Also called: **La Plata.** English name: (River) **Plate.**

Plataea (plə'tiːə) *n* an ancient city in S Boeotia, traditionally an ally of Athens: scene of the defeat of a great Persian army by the Greeks in 479 B.C.

platan ('plætᵊn) *n* another name for **plane tree.** [C14: from Latin *platanus,* from Greek *platanos;* see PLANE TREE]

plat du jour ('plɑː də 'ʒʊə; *French* pla dy ʒur) *n, pl* **plats du jour** ('plɑːz də 'ʒʊə; *French* pla dy ʒur). the specially prepared or recommended dish of the day on a restaurant's menu. [French, literally: dish of the day]

plate (pleɪt) *n* **1a** a shallow usually circular dish made of porcelain, earthenware, glass, etc., on which food is served or from which food is eaten. **1b** (*as modifier*): *a plate rack.* **2a** Also called: **'plateful.** the contents of a plate or the amount a plate will hold. **2b** *Austral. and N.Z.* a plate of cakes, sandwiches, etc., brought by a guest to a party: *everyone was asked to bring a plate.* **3** an entire course of a meal: *a cold plate.* **4** any shallow or flat receptacle, esp. for receiving a collection in church. **5** flat metal of uniform thickness obtained by rolling, usually having a thickness greater than about three millimetres. **6** a thin coating of metal usually on another metal, as produced by electrodeposition, chemical action, etc. **7** metal or metalware that has been coated in this way, esp. with gold or silver: *Sheffield plate.* **8** dishes, cutlery, etc., made of gold or silver. **9** a sheet of metal, plastic, rubber, etc., having a printing surface produced by a process such as stereotyping, moulding, or photographic deposition. **10** a print taken from such a sheet or from a woodcut, esp. when appearing in a book. **11** a thin flat sheet of a substance, such as metal or glass. **12** armour made of overlapping or articulated pieces of thin metal. **13** *Photog.* **13a** a sheet of glass, or sometimes metal, coated with photographic emulsion on which an image can be formed by exposure to light. **13b** (*as modifier*): *a plate camera.* **14** an orthodontic device, esp. one used for straightening children's teeth. **15** an informal word for **denture** (sense 1). **16** *Anatomy.* any flat platelike structure or part. **17a** a cup or trophy awarded to the winner of a sporting contest, esp. a horse race. **17b** a race or contest for such a prize. **18** any of the rigid layers of the earth's lithosphere of which there are believed to be at least 15. See also **plate tectonics. 19** *Electronics.* **19a** *Chiefly U.S.* the anode in an electronic valve. **19b** an electrode in an accumulator or capacitor. **20** a horizontal timber joist that supports rafters or studs. **21** a light horseshoe for flat racing. **22** a thin cut of beef from the brisket. **23** See **plate rail. 24** Also called: **Communion plate.** *R.C. Church.* a flat plate held under the chin of a communicant in order to catch any fragments of the consecrated Host. **25** *Archaic.* a coin, esp. one made of silver. **26 on a plate.** in such a way as to be acquired without further trouble: *he was handed the job on a plate.* **27 on one's plate.** waiting to be done or dealt with: *he has a lot on his plate at the moment.* ◆ *vb* (*tr*) **28** to coat (a surface, usually metal) with a thin layer of other metal by electrolysis, chemical reaction, etc. **29** to cover with metal plates, as for protection. **30** *Printing.* to make a stereotype or electrotype from (type or another plate). **31** to form (metal) into plate, esp. by rolling. **32** to give a glossy finish to (paper) by calendering. **33** to grow (microorganisms) in a culture medium. [C13: from Old French: thin metal sheet, something flat, from Vulgar Latin *plattus* (unattested); related to Greek *platus* flat]

Plate (pleɪt) *n* **River.** the English name for the (Río de la) **Plata.**

plate armour *n* armour made of thin metal plates, which superseded mail during the 14th century.

plateau ('plætəʊ) *n, pl* **-eaus** *or* **-eaux** (-əʊz). **1** a wide mainly level area of elevated land. **2** a relatively long period of stability; levelling off: *the rising prices reached a plateau.* ◆ *vb* (*intr*) **3** to remain at a stable level for a relatively long period. [C18: from French, from Old French *platel* something flat, from *plat* flat; see PLATE]

Plateau ('plætəʊ) *n* a state of central Nigeria, formed in 1976 from part of Benue-Plateau State: tin mining. Capital: Jos. Pop. (including Nassarawa state): 3 671 498 (1995 est.). Area (including Nassarawa state): 58 030 sq. km (22 405 sq. miles).

plated ('pleɪtɪd) *adj* **1a** coated with a layer of metal. **1b** (*in combination*): *gold-plated.* **2** (of a fabric) knitted in two different yarns so that one appears on the face and the other on the back.

plate glass *n* glass formed into a thin sheet by rolling, used for windows.

platelayer ('pleɪt,leɪə) *n Brit.* a workman who lays and maintains railway track. U.S. equivalent: **trackman.**

platelet ('pleɪtlɪt) *n* a minute particle occurring in the blood of vertebrates and involved in clotting of the blood. Formerly called: **thrombocyte.** [C19: a small PLATE]

platemark ('pleɪt,mɑːk) *n, vb* another name for **hallmark** (senses 1, 4).

platen ('plætᵊn) *n* **1** a flat plate in a printing press that presses the paper against the type. **2** the roller on a typewriter, against which the keys strike. **3** the worktable of a machine tool, esp. one that is slotted to enable clamping belts to be used. [C15: from Old French *platine,* from *plat* flat; see PLATE]

plater ('pleɪtə) *n* **1** a person or thing that plates. **2** *Horse racing.* **2a** a mediocre horse entered chiefly for minor races. **2b** a blacksmith who shoes racehorses with the special type of light shoe used for racing.

plate rail *n Railways.* an early flat rail with an extended flange on its outer edge to retain wheels on the track. Sometimes shortened to **plate.**

plate tectonics *n* (*functioning as sing*) *Geology.* the study of the structure of the earth's crust with reference to the theory that the earth's lithosphere is divided into large rigid blocks (**plates**) that are floating on semimolten rock and are thus able to interact with each other at their boundaries, and to the associated theories of continental drift and seafloor spreading.

platform ('plætfɔːm) *n* **1** a raised floor or other horizontal surface, such as a stage for speakers. **2** a raised area at a railway station, from which passengers have access to the trains. **3** See **drilling platform, production platform. 4** the declared principles, aims, etc., of a political party, an organization, or an individual. **5** a level raised area of ground. **6a** the thick raised sole of some high-heeled shoes. **6b** (*as modifier*): *platform shoes.* **7** a vehicle or level place on which weapons are mounted and fired. **8** a specific type of computer hardware or computer operating system. [C16: from French *plateforme,* from *plat* flat + *forme* form, layout]

platform game *n* a type of computer game that is played by moving a figure on the screen through a series of obstacles and problems.

platform rocker *n U.S. and Canadian.* a rocking chair supported on a stationary base.

platform ticket *n* a ticket for admission to railway platforms but not for travel.

Plath (plæθ) *n* **Sylvia.** 1932–63, U.S. poet living in England. She wrote two volumes of verse, *The Colossus* (1960) and *Ariel* (1965), and a novel, *The Bell Jar* (1963).

platina ('plætɪnə, plə'tiːnə) *n* an alloy of platinum and several other metals, including palladium, osmium, and iridium. [C18: from Spanish: silvery element, from *plata* silver, from Provençal: silver plate]

plating ('pleɪtɪŋ) *n* **1** a coating or layer of material, esp. metal. **2** a layer or covering of metal plates.

platinic (plə'tɪnɪk) *adj* of or containing platinum, esp. in the tetravalent state.

platiniferous (,plætɪ'nɪfərəs) *adj* platinum-bearing.

platiniridium (,plætɪnɪ'rɪdɪəm) *n* any alloy of platinum and iridium: used in jewellery, electrical contacts, and hypodermic needles.

platinize *or* **platinise** ('plætɪ,naɪz) *vb* (*tr*) to coat with platinum. ► **,platini'zation** *or* **,platini'sation** *n*

platino-, platini-, *or before a vowel* **platin-** *combining form.* of, relating to, containing, or resembling platinum: *platinotype.*

platinocyanic acid (,plætɪnəʊsaɪ'ænɪk) *n* a hypothetical tetrabasic acid known only in the form of platinocyanide salts. Formula: $H_2Pt(CN)_4$.

platinocyanide (,plætɪnəʊ'saɪə,naɪd, -nɪd) *n* any salt containing the divalent complex cation $[Pt(CN)_4]^{2-}$.

platinoid ('plætɪ,nɔɪd) *adj* containing or resembling platinum: *a platinoid metal.*

platinotype ('plætɪnəʊ,taɪp) *n* an obsolete process for producing photographic prints using paper coated with an emulsion containing platinum salts, the resulting image in platinum black being more permanent and of a richer tone than the usual silver image.

platinous ('plætɪnəs) *adj* of or containing platinum, esp. in the divalent state.

platinum ('plætɪnəm) *n* **1** a ductile malleable silvery-white metallic element, very resistant to heat and chemicals. It occurs free and in association with other platinum metals, esp. in osmiridium: used in jewellery, laboratory apparatus, electrical contacts, dentistry, electroplating, and as a catalyst. Symbol: Pt; atomic no.: 78; atomic wt.: 195.08; valency: 1–4; relative density: 21.45; melting pt.: 1769°C; boiling pt.: 3827±100°C. **2a** a medium to light grey colour. **2b** (*as adj*): *a platinum carpet.* [C19: New Latin, from PLATINA, on the model of other metals with the suffix *-um*]

platinum black *n Chem.* a black powder consisting of very finely divided platinum metal. It is used as a catalyst, esp. in hydrogenation reactions.

platinum-blond *or* (*fem*) **platinum-blonde** *adj* **1** (of hair) of a pale silver-blond colour. **2a** having hair of this colour. **2b** (*as n*): *she was a platinum blonde.*

platinum disc *n* **a** (in Britain) an album certified to have sold 300 000 copies or a single certified to have sold 600 000 copies. **b** (in the U.S.) an album or single certified to have sold one million copies. Compare **gold disc, silver disc.**

platinum metal *n* any of the group of precious metallic elements consisting of ruthenium, rhodium, palladium, osmium, iridium, and platinum.

platitude ('plætɪ,tjuːd) *n* **1** a trite, dull, or obvious remark or statement; a commonplace. **2** staleness or insipidity of thought or language; triteness. [C19: from French, literally: flatness, from *plat* flat] ► **,plati'tudinous** *adj*

platitudinize *or* **platitudinise** (,plætɪ'tjuːdɪ,naɪz) *vb* (*intr*) to speak or write in platitudes. ► **,plati'tudi,nizer** *or* **,plati'tudi,niser** *n*

Plato[1] ('pleɪtəʊ) *n* ?427–?347 B.C., Greek philosopher: with his teacher Socrates and his pupil Aristotle, he is regarded as the initiator of western philosophy. His influential theory of ideas, which makes a distinction between objects of sense perception and the universal ideas or forms of which they are an expression, is formulated in such dialogues as *Phaedo, Symposium,* and *The Republic.* Other works include *The Apology* and *Laws.*

Plato[2] ('pleɪtəʊ) *n* a crater in the NW quadrant of the moon, about 100 km in diameter, that has a conspicuous dark floor.

Platonic (plə'tɒnɪk) *adj* **1** of or relating to Plato or his teachings. **2** (*often not cap.*) free from physical desire: *Platonic love.* ► **Pla'tonically** *adv*

Platonic solid *n* any of the five possible regular polyhedra: cube, tetrahedron, octahedron, icosahedron, and dodecahedron. Also called (esp. formerly): **Platonic body.** [C17: named after PLATO[1], who was the first to list them]

Platonism ('pleɪtə,nɪzəm) *n* **1** the teachings of Plato and his followers, esp. the philosophical theory that the meanings of general words are real existing abstract entities (Forms) and that particular objects have properties in common by virtue of their relationship with these Forms. Compare **nominalism, conceptualism, intuitionism. 2** the realist doctrine that mathematical entities have real existence and that mathematical truth is independent of human thought. **3** See **Neo-Platonism.** ► **'Platonist** *n*

platoon (plə'tuːn) *n* **1** *Military.* a subunit of a company usually comprising three sections of ten to twelve men: commanded by a lieutenant. **2** a group or unit of people, esp. one sharing a common activity, characteristic, etc. [C17: from French *peloton* little ball, group of men, from *pelote* ball; see PELLET]

Plattdeutsch (*German* 'platdɔytʃ) *n* another name for **Low German.** [literally: flat (that is, low) German]

Platte (plæt) *n* a river system of the central U.S., formed by the confluence of the **North Platte** and **South Platte** at North Platte, Nebraska: flows generally east to the Missouri River. Length: 499 km (310 miles).

platteland ('platə,lant) *n* **the.** (in South Africa) the country districts or rural areas. [C20: from Afrikaans, from Dutch *plat* flat + *land* country]

platter ('plætə) *n* **1** a large shallow usually oval dish or plate, used for serving food. **2** a course of a meal, usually consisting of several different foods served on the same plate: *a seafood platter.* [C14: from Anglo-Norman *plater,* from *plat* dish, from Old French *plat* flat; see PLATE]

platy[1] ('pleɪtɪ) *adj* **platier, platiest.** of, relating to, or designating rocks the constituents of which occur in flaky layers: *platy fracture.* [C19: from PLATE + -Y[1]]

platy[2] ('plætɪ) *n, pl* **platy, platys,** *or* **platies.** any of various small brightly coloured freshwater cyprinodont fishes of the Central American genus *Xiphophorus,* esp. *X. maculatus.* [C20: shortened from New Latin *Platypoecilus* former genus name, from PLATY- + *-poecilus,* from Greek *poikilos* spotted]

platy- *combining form.* indicating something flat: *platyhelminth.* [from Greek *platus* flat]

platyhelminth (,plætɪ'helmɪnθ) *n* any invertebrate of the phylum *Platyhelminthes* (the flatworms). [C19: from New Latin *Platyhelmintha* flatworm, from PLATY- + Greek *helmins* worm] ► **,platyhel'minthic** *adj*

platykurtic (,plætɪ'kɜːtɪk) *adj Statistics.* (of a distribution) having kurtosis B_2 less than 3, less heavily concentrated about the mean than a normal distribution. Compare **leptokurtic, mesokurtic.** [C20: from PLATY- + Greek *kurtos* arched, bulging + -IC]

platypus ('plætɪpəs) *n, pl* **-puses.** See **duck-billed platypus.** [C18: New Latin, from PLATY- + *-pus,* from Greek *pous* foot]

platyrrhine ('plætɪ,raɪn) *or* **platyrrhinian** (,plætɪ'rɪnɪən) *adj* **1** (esp. of New World monkeys) having widely separated nostrils opening to the side of the face. **2** (of humans) having an unusually short wide nose. ◆ *n* **3** an animal or person with this characteristic. ◆ Compare **catarrhine.** [C19: from New Latin *platyrrhinus,* from PLATY- + *-rrhinus,* from Greek *rhis* nose]

plaudit ('plɔːdɪt) *n* (*usually pl*) **1** an expression of enthusiastic approval or approbation. **2** a round of applause. [C17: shortened from earlier *plauditē,* from Latin: applaud!, from *plaudere* to APPLAUD]

Plauen (*German* 'plauən) *n* a city in E central Germany, in Saxony: textile centre. Pop.: 70 860 (1991).

plausible ('plɔːzəbᵊl) *adj* **1** apparently reasonable, valid, truthful, etc.: *a plausible excuse.* **2** apparently trustworthy or believable: *a plausible speaker.* [C16: from Latin *plausibilis* worthy of applause, from *plaudere* to APPLAUD] ► **,plausi'bility** *or* **'plausibleness** *n* ► **'plausibly** *adv*

plausive ('plɔːsɪv) *adj* **1** expressing praise or approval; applauding. **2** *Obsolete.* plausible.

Plautus ('plɔːtəs) *n* **Titus Maccius** ('taɪtəs 'mæksɪəs). ?254–?184 B.C., Roman comic dramatist. His 21 extant works, adapted from Greek plays, esp. those by Menander, include *Menaechmi* (the basis of Shakespeare's *The Comedy of Errors*), *Miles Gloriosus, Rudens,* and *Captivi.*

play (pleɪ) *vb* **1** to occupy oneself in (a sport or diversion); amuse oneself in (a game). **2** (*tr*) to contend against (an opponent) in a sport or game: *Ed played Tony at chess and lost.* **3** to fulfil or cause to fulfil (a particular role) in a team game: *he plays defence; he plays in the defence.* **4** (*tr*) to address oneself to (a ball) in a game: *play the ball not the man.* **5** (*intr*; often foll. by *about* or *around*) to behave carelessly, esp. in a way that is unconsciously cruel or hurtful; trifle or dally (with): *to play about with a young girl's affections.* **6** (when *intr,* often foll. by *at*) to perform or act the part (of) in or as in a dramatic production; assume or simulate the role (of): *to play the villain; just what are you playing at?* **7** to act out or perform (a dramatic production). **8** to give a performance in (a place) or (of a performance) to be given in a place. **9** to have the ability to perform on (a musical instrument): *David plays the harp.* **10** to perform (on a musical instrument) as specified: *he plays out of tune.* **11** (*tr*) **11a** to reproduce (a tune, melody, piece of music, note, etc.) on an instrument. **11b** to perform works by (a specific composer): *to play Brahms.* **12** to discharge or cause to discharge: *he played the water from the hose onto the garden.* **13** to operate, esp. to cause (a record player, radio, etc.) to emit sound or (of a record player, radio, etc.) to emit (sound): *he played a record; the radio was playing loudly.* **14** to move or cause to move freely, quickly, or irregularly: *lights played on the scenery.* **15** (*tr*) *Stock Exchange.* to speculate or operate aggressively for gain in (a market). **16** (*tr*) *Angling.* to attempt to tire (a hooked fish) by alternately letting out and reeling in line and by using the rod's flexibility. **17** to put (a card, counter, piece, etc.) into play. **18** to gamble (money) on a game. **19 play ball.** *Informal.* to cooperate. **20 play fair** (*or* **false**). (often foll. by *with*) to prove oneself fair (or unfair) in one's dealings. **21 play by ear.** See **ear**[1] (sense 19). **22 play for time.** to delay the outcome of some activity so as to gain time to one's own advantage. **23 play into the hands of.** to act directly to the advantage of (an opponent). **24 play the fool.** See **fool**[1] (sense 7). **25 play the game.** See **game**[1] (sense 22). ◆ *n* **26** a dramatic composition written for performance by actors on a stage, on television, etc.; drama. **27a** the performance of a dramatic composition. **27b** (*in combination*): *playreader.* **28a** games, exercise, or other activity undertaken for pleasure, diversion, etc., esp. by children. **28b** (*in combination*): *playroom.* **28c** (*as modifier*): *play dough.* **29** manner of action, conduct, or playing: *fair play.* **30** the playing or conduct of a game or the period during which a game is in progress: *rain stopped play.* **31** *U.S. and Canadian.* a move or manoeuvre in a game: *a brilliant play.* **32** the situation of a ball that is within the defined area and being played according to the rules (in the phrases **in play, out of play**). **33** a turn to play: *it's my play.* **34** the act of playing for stakes; gambling. **35** action, activity, or operation: *the play of the imagination.* **36** freedom of or scope or space for movement: *too much play in the rope.* **37** light, free, or rapidly shifting motion: *the play of light on the water.* **38** fun, jest, or joking: *I only did it in play.* **39 make a play for.** *Informal.* **39a** to make an obvious attempt to gain. **39b** to attempt to attract or seduce. ◆ See also **play along, playback, play down, play off, play on, play out, play up, play with.** [Old English *plega* (n), *plegan* (vb); related to Middle Dutch *pleyen*] ▸ **'playable** *adj*

playa ('plɑːjə; *Spanish* 'plaja) *n* (in the U.S.) a temporary lake, or its dry often salty bed, in a desert basin. [Spanish: shore, from Late Latin *plagia,* from Greek *plagios* slanting, from *plagos* side; compare French *plage* beach]

play-act *vb* **1** (*intr*) to pretend or make believe. **2** (*intr*) to behave in an overdramatic or affected manner. **3** to act in or as in (a play). ▸ **'play-ˌacting** *n* ▸ **'play-ˌactor** *n*

play along *vb* (*adv*) **1** (*intr;* usually foll. by *with*) to cooperate (with), esp. as a temporary measure. **2** (*tr*) to manipulate as if in a game, esp. for one's own advantage: *he played the widow along until she gave him her money.*

playback ('pleɪˌbæk) *n* **1** the act or process of reproducing a recording, esp. on magnetic tape. **2** the part of a tape recorder serving to reproduce or used for reproducing recorded material. **3** (*modifier*) of or relating to the reproduction of signals from a recording: *the playback head of a tape recorder.* ◆ *vb* **play back.** (*adv*) **4** to reproduce (recorded material) on (a magnetic tape) by means of a tape recorder.

playbill ('pleɪˌbɪl) *n* **1** a poster or bill advertising a play. **2** the programme of a play.

playboy ('pleɪˌbɔɪ) *n* a man, esp. one of private means, who devotes himself to the pleasures of nightclubs, expensive holiday resorts, female company, etc.

play-centre *n* the N.Z. name for **playgroup.**

play down *vb* (*tr, adv*) to make little or light of; minimize the importance of.

player ('pleɪə) *n* **1** a person who participates in or is skilled at some game or sport. **2** a person who plays a game or sport professionally. **3** a person who plays a musical instrument. **4** an actor. **5** *Informal.* a participant, esp. a powerful one, in a particular field of activity: *a leading city player.* **6** See **record player. 7** the playing mechanism in a Pianola.

Player ('pleɪə) *n* **Gary** ('gærɪ). born 1935, South African professional golfer: won the British Open Championship (1959; 1968; 1974) and the U.S. Open Championship (1965).

player piano *n* a mechanical piano; Pianola.

playful ('pleɪfʊl) *adj* **1** full of high spirits and fun: *a playful kitten.* **2** good-natured and humorous: *a playful remark.* ▸ **'playfully** *adv* ▸ **'playfulness** *n*

playgoer ('pleɪˌgəʊə) *n* a person who goes to theatre performances, esp. frequently.

playground ('pleɪˌgraʊnd) *n* **1** an outdoor area for children's play, esp. one having swings, slides, etc., or adjoining a school. **2** a place or region particularly popular as a sports or holiday resort. **3** a sphere of activity: *reading was his private playground.*

playgroup ('pleɪˌgruːp) *n* a regular meeting of small children arranged by their parents or a welfare agency to give them an opportunity of supervised creative play. See also **preschool, playschool.**

playhouse ('pleɪˌhaʊs) *n* **1** a theatre where live dramatic performances are given. **2** a toy house, small room, etc., for children to play in.

playing card *n* one of a pack of 52 rectangular stiff cards, used for playing a variety of games, each card having one or more symbols of the same kind (diamonds, hearts, clubs, or spades) on the face, but an identical design on the reverse. See also **suit** (sense 4).

playing field *n Chiefly Brit.* a field or open space used for sport.

playlet ('pleɪlɪt) *n* a short play.

play-lunch *n N.Z.* a schoolchild's mid-morning snack.

playmaker ('pleɪˌmeɪkə) *n Sport.* a player whose role is to create scoring opportunities for his or her team-mates.

playmate ('pleɪˌmeɪt) *or* **playfellow** *n* a friend or partner in play or recreation: *childhood playmates.*

play off *vb* (*adv*) **1** (*tr;* usually foll. by *against*) to deal with or manipulate as if in playing a game: *to play one person off against another.* **2** (*intr*) to take part in a play-off. ◆ *n* **play-off. 3** *Sport.* an extra contest to decide the winner when two or more competitors are tied. **4** *Chiefly U.S. and Canadian.* a contest or series of games to determine a championship, as between the winners of two competitions.

play on *vb* (*intr*) **1** (*adv*) to continue to play. **2** (*prep*) Also: **play upon.** to exploit or impose upon (the feelings or weakness of another) to one's own advantage. **3** (*adv*) *Cricket.* to hit the ball into one's own wicket.

play on words *n* another term for **pun**[1] (sense 1).

play out *vb* (*tr, adv*) **1** to finish: *let's play the game out if we aren't too late.* **2** (*often passive*) *Informal.* to use up or exhaust. **3** to release gradually: *he played the rope out.*

playpen ('pleɪˌpɛn) *n* a small enclosure, usually portable, in which a young child can be left to play in safety.

playroom ('pleɪˌruːm, -ˌrʊm) *n* a recreation room, esp. for children.

playschool ('pleɪˌskuːl) *n* an informal nursery group taking preschool children in half-day sessions. Also called: **playgroup.**

playsuit ('pleɪˌsuːt, -ˌsjuːt) *n* a woman's or child's outfit, usually comprising shorts and a top.

plaything ('pleɪˌθɪŋ) *n* **1** a toy. **2** a person regarded or treated as a toy: *he thinks she is just his plaything.*

playtime ('pleɪˌtaɪm) *n* a time for play or recreation, esp. the school break.

play up *vb* (*adv*) **1** (*tr*) to emphasize or highlight: *to play up one's best features.* **2** *Brit. informal.* to behave irritatingly (towards). **3** (*intr*) *Brit. informal.* (of a machine, car, etc.) to function erratically: *the car is playing up again.* **4** *Brit. informal.* to hurt; give (one) pain or trouble: *my back's playing me up again.* **5 play up to. 5a** to support (another actor) in a performance. **5b** to try to gain favour with by flattery.

play with *vb* (*intr, prep*) **1** to consider without giving deep thought to or coming to a conclusion concerning: *we're playing with the idea of emigrating.* **2** to behave carelessly with: *to play with a girl's affections.* **3** to fiddle or mess about with: *he's just playing with his food.*

playwright ('pleɪˌraɪt) *n* a person who writes plays.

plaza ('plɑːzə; *Spanish* 'plaθa) *n* **1** an open space or square, esp. in Spain or a Spanish-speaking country. **2** *Chiefly U.S. and Canadian.* **2a** a modern complex of shops, buildings, and parking areas. **2b** (*cap. when part of a name*): *Rockefeller Plaza.* [C17: from Spanish, from Latin *platēa* courtyard, from Greek *plateia;* see PLACE]

plc *or* **PLC** *abbrev. for* public limited company. See also **limited** (sense 5).

plea (pliː) *n* **1** an earnest entreaty or request: *a plea for help.* **2a** *Law.* something alleged or pleaded by or on behalf of a party to legal proceedings in support of his claim or defence. **2b** *Criminal law.* the answer made by an accused to the charge: *a plea of guilty.* **2c** (in Scotland and formerly in England) a suit or action at law. **3** an excuse, justification, or pretext: *he gave the plea of a previous engagement.* [C13: from Anglo-Norman *plai,* from Old French *plaid* lawsuit, from Medieval Latin *placitum* court order (literally: what is pleasing), from Latin *placēre* to please]

plea bargaining *n* an agreement between the prosecution and defence, sometimes including the judge, in which the accused agrees to plead guilty to a lesser charge in return for more serious charges being dropped.

pleach (pliːtʃ) *vb Chiefly Brit.* to interlace the stems or boughs of (a tree or hedge). Also: **plash.** [C14 *plechen,* from Old North French *plechier,* from Latin *plectere* to weave, plait; compare PLASH[2]]

plead (pliːd) *vb* **pleads, pleading; pleaded, plead** (plɛd), *or esp. Scot. and U.S.* **pled** (plɛd). **1** (when *intr,* often foll. by *with*) to appeal earnestly or humbly (to). **2** (*tr; may take a clause as object*) to give as an excuse; offer in justification or extenuation: *to plead ignorance; he pleaded that he was insane.* **3** (*intr;* often foll. by *for*) to provide an argument or appeal (for): *her beauty pleads for her.* **4** *Law.* to declare oneself to be (guilty or not guilty) in answer to the charge. **5** *Law.* to advocate (a case) in a court of law. **6** (*intr*) *Law.* **6a** to file pleadings. **6b** to address a court as an advocate. [C13: from Old French *plaidier,* from Medieval Latin *placitāre* to have a lawsuit, from Latin *placēre* to please; see PLEA] ▸ **'pleadable** *adj* ▸ **'pleader** *n*

pleading ('pliːdɪŋ) *n Law.* **1** the act of presenting a case in court, as by a lawyer on behalf of his client. **2** the art or science of preparing the formal written statements of the parties to a legal action. See also **pleadings.**

pleadings ('pliːdɪŋz) *pl n Law.* the formal written statements presented alternately by the plaintiff and defendant in a lawsuit setting out the respective matters relied upon.

pleasance ('plɛzəns) *n* **1** a secluded part of a garden laid out with trees, walks, etc. **2** *Archaic.* enjoyment or pleasure. [C14 *plesaunce,* from Old French *plaisance,* from *plaisant* pleasant, from *plaisir* to PLEASE]

pleasant ('plɛzᵊnt) *adj* **1** giving or affording pleasure; enjoyable. **2** having pleasing or agreeable manners, appearance, habits, etc. **3** *Obsolete.* merry and lively. [C14: from Old French *plaisant,* from *plaisir* to PLEASE] ▸ **'pleasantly** *adv* ▸ **'pleasantness** *n*

Pleasant Island *n* the former name of **Nauru.**

pleasantry ('plɛzᵊntrɪ) *n, pl* **-ries. 1** (*often pl*) an agreeable or amusing remark, often one made in order to be polite: *they exchanged pleasantries.* **2** an agreeably humorous manner or style. **3** *Rare.* enjoyment; pleasantness: *a pleasantry of life.* [C17: from French *plaisanterie,* from *plaisant* PLEASANT]

please (pliːz) *vb* **1** to give satisfaction, pleasure, or contentment to (a person); make or cause (a person) to be glad. **2** to be the will of or have the wish (to): *if it pleases you; the court pleases.* **3 if you please.** if you will or wish, sometimes used in ironic exclamation. **4 pleased with.** happy because of. **5 please one-**

self. to do as one likes. ◆ *adv* **6** (*sentence modifier*) used in making polite requests and in pleading, asking for a favour, etc.: *please don't tell the police where I am.* **7 yes please.** a polite formula for accepting an offer, invitation, etc. [C14 *plese,* from Old French *plaisir,* from Latin *placēre* to please, satisfy] ► **'pleasable** *adj* ► **pleased** *adj* ► **pleasedly** ('pli:zɪdlɪ) *adv* ► **'pleaser** *n*

Pleasence ('plɛzəns) *n* **Donald.** 1919–95, British actor. His films include *Dr Crippen* (1962) and *Cul de Sac* (1966).

pleasing ('pli:zɪŋ) *adj* giving pleasure; likable or gratifying. ► **'pleasingly** *adv* ► **'pleasingness** *n*

pleasurable ('plɛʒərəbᵊl) *adj* enjoyable, agreeable, or gratifying. ► **'pleasurableness** *n* ► **'pleasurably** *adv*

pleasure ('plɛʒə) *n* **1** an agreeable or enjoyable sensation or emotion: *the pleasure of hearing good music.* **2** something that gives or affords enjoyment or delight: *his garden was his only pleasure.* **3a** amusement, recreation, or enjoyment. **3b** (*as modifier*): *a pleasure boat; pleasure ground.* **4** *Euphemistic.* sexual gratification or enjoyment: *he took his pleasure of her.* **5** a person's preference or choice. ◆ *vb* **6** (when *intr,* often foll. by *in*) to give pleasure to or take pleasure (in). [C14 *plesir,* from Old French; related to Old French *plaisir* to PLEASE] ► **'pleasureful** *adj* ► **'pleasureless** *adj*

pleasure principle *n Psychoanal.* the idea that psychological processes and actions are governed by the gratification of needs. It is seen as the governing process of the id, whereas the reality principle is the governing process of the ego. See also **hedonism.**

pleat (pli:t) *n* **1** any of various types of fold formed by doubling back fabric and pressing, stitching, or steaming into place. See also **box pleat, inverted pleat, kick pleat, knife pleat, sunburst pleats.** ◆ *vb* **2** (*tr*) to arrange (material, part of a garment, etc.) in pleats. [C16: variant of PLAIT]

pleater ('pli:tə) *n* an attachment on a sewing machine that makes pleats.

pleb (plɛb) *n* **1** short for **plebeian. 2** *Brit. informal, often derogatory.* a common vulgar person. ◆ See also **plebs.**

plebby ('plɛbɪ) *adj* **-bier, -biest.** *Brit. informal, often derogatory.* common or vulgar: *a plebby party.* [C20: shortened from PLEBEIAN]

plebe (pli:b) *n Informal.* a member of the lowest class at the U.S. Naval Academy or Military Academy; freshman. [C19: shortened from PLEBEIAN]

plebeian (plə'bi:ən) *adj* **1** of, relating to, or characteristic of the common people, esp. those of Rome. **2** lacking refinement; vulgar: *plebeian tastes.* ◆ *n* **3** one of the common people, esp. one of the Roman plebs. **4** a person who is coarse or lacking in discernment. [C16: from Latin *plēbēius* belonging to the people, from *plēbs* the common people of ancient Rome] ► **ple'beian,ism** *n*

plebiscite ('plɛbɪˌsaɪt, -sɪt) *n* **1** a direct vote by the electorate of a state, region, etc., on some question of usually national importance, such as union with another state or acceptance of a government programme. **2** any expression or determination of public opinion on some matter. ◆ See also **referendum.** [C16: from Old French *plébiscite,* from Latin *plēbiscītum* decree of the people, from *plēbs* the populace + *scītum,* from *scīscere* to decree, approve, from *scīre* to know] ► **plebiscitary** (plə'bɪsɪtərɪ) *adj*

plebs (plɛbz) *n* **1** (*functioning as pl*) the common people; the masses. **2** (*functioning as sing or pl*) common people of ancient Rome. Compare **patrician.** [C17: from Latin: the common people of ancient Rome]

plectognath ('plɛktɒgˌnæθ) *n* **1** any spiny-finned marine fish of the mainly tropical order *Plectognathi* (or *Tetraodontiformes*), having a small mouth, strong teeth, and small gill openings: includes puffers, triggerfish, trunkfish, sunfish, etc. ◆ *adj* **2** of, relating to, or belonging to the order *Plectognathi.* [C19: via New Latin from Greek *plektos* twisted + *gnathos* jaw]

plectrum ('plɛktrəm) *n, pl* **-trums** *or* **-tra** (-trə). any implement for plucking a string, such as a small piece of plastic, wood, etc., used to strum a guitar, or the quill that plucks the string of a harpsichord. [C17: from Latin *plēctrum* quill, plectrum, from Greek *plektron,* from *plessein* to strike]

pled (plɛd) *vb U.S. or* (*esp. in legal usage*) *Scot.* a past tense and past participle of **plead.**

pledge (plɛdʒ) *n* **1** a formal or solemn promise or agreement, esp. to do or refrain from doing something. **2a** collateral for the payment of a debt or the performance of an obligation. **2b** the condition of being collateral (esp. in the phrase **in pledge**). **3** a sign, token, or indication: *the gift is a pledge of their sincerity.* **4** an assurance of support or goodwill, conveyed by drinking to a person, cause, etc.; toast: *we drank a pledge to their success.* **5** a person who binds himself, as by becoming bail or surety for another. **6 take** *or* **sign the pledge.** to make a vow to abstain from alcoholic drink. ◆ *vb* **7** to promise formally or solemnly: *he pledged allegiance.* **8** (*tr*) to bind or secure by or as if by a pledge: *they were pledged to secrecy.* **9** to give, deposit, or offer (one's word, freedom, property, etc.) as a guarantee, as for the repayment of a loan. **10** to drink a toast to (a person, cause, etc.). [C14: from Old French *plege,* from Late Latin *plebium* gage, security, from *plebīre* to pledge, of Germanic origin; compare Old High German *pflegan* to look after, care for] ► **'pledgable** *adj*

pledgee (plɛdʒ'i:) *n* **1** a person to whom a pledge is given. **2** a person to whom property is delivered as a pledge.

pledget ('plɛdʒɪt) *n* a small flattened pad of wool, cotton, etc., esp. for use as a pressure bandage to be applied to wounds or sores. [C16: of unknown origin]

pledgor, pledgeor (plɛdʒ'ɔ:), *or* **pledger** ('plɛdʒə) *n* a person who gives or makes a pledge.

-plegia *n combining form.* indicating a specified type of paralysis: *paraplegia.* [from Greek, from *plēgē* stroke, from *plēssein* to strike] ► **-plegic** *adj and n combining form.*

pleiad ('plaɪəd) *n* a brilliant or talented group, esp. one with seven members. [C16: originally French *Pléiade,* name given by Ronsard to himself and six other poets after a group of Alexandrian Greek poets who were called this after the PLEIADES[1]]

Pleiad ('plaɪəd) *n* one of the Pleiades (stars or daughters of Atlas).

Pleiades[1] ('plaɪəˌdi:z) *pl n Greek myth.* the seven daughters of Atlas, placed as stars in the sky either to save them from the pursuit of Orion or, in another account, after they had killed themselves for grief over the death of their half-sisters the Hyades.

Pleiades[2] ('plaɪəˌdi:z) *pl n* a conspicuous open star cluster in the constellation Taurus, containing several hundred stars only six or seven of which are visible to the naked eye. Compare **Hyades**[1].

plein-air (ˌpleɪn'ɛə; *French* plɛnɛr) *adj* of or in the manner of various French 19th-century schools of painting, esp. impressionism, concerned with the observation of light and atmosphere effects outdoors. [C19: from French phrase *en plein air* in the open (literally: full) air] ► **plein-airist** (ˌpleɪn'ɛərɪst) *n*

pleio- *combining form.* a variant of **plio-.**

Pleiocene ('plaɪəʊˌsi:n) *adj, n* a variant spelling of **Pliocene.**

pleiotropism (plaɪ'ɒtrəˌpɪzəm) *n Genetics.* the condition of a gene of affecting more than one characteristic of the phenotype.

Pleistocene ('plaɪstəˌsi:n) *adj* **1** of, denoting, or formed in the first epoch of the Quaternary period, which lasted for about 1 600 000 years. It was characterized by extensive glaciations of the N hemisphere and the evolutionary development of man. ◆ *n* **2 the.** the Pleistocene epoch or rock series. [C19: from Greek *pleistos* most + *kainos* recent]

Plekhanov (*Russian* pljɪ'xanof) *n* **Georgi Valentinovich** ('gjɪorgji valɪn'tjinəvjɪtʃ). 1857–1918, Russian revolutionary; founder of Russian Marxism and leader of the Russian Social Democratic Workers' Party.

plenary ('pli:nərɪ, 'plɛn-) *adj* **1** full, unqualified, or complete: *plenary powers; plenary indulgence.* **2** (of assemblies, councils, etc.) attended by all the members. ◆ *n, pl* **-ries. 3** a book of the gospels or epistles and homilies read at the Eucharist. [C15: from Late Latin *plēnārius,* from Latin *plēnus* full; related to Middle English *plener;* see PLENUM] ► **'plenarily** *adv*

plenipotent (plə'nɪpətənt) *adj* a less common word for **plenipotentiary.**

plenipotentiary (ˌplɛnɪpə'tɛnʃərɪ) *adj* **1** (esp. of a diplomatic envoy) invested with or possessing full power or authority. **2** conferring full power or authority. **3** (of power or authority) full; absolute. ◆ *n, pl* **-aries. 4** a person invested with full authority to transact business, esp. a diplomat authorized to represent a country. See also **envoy**[1] (sense 1). [C17: from Medieval Latin *plēnipotentiārius,* from Latin *plēnus* full + *potentia* POWER]

plenish ('plɛnɪʃ) *vb* (*tr*) *Archaic or Scot.* to fill, stock, or resupply. [C15: from Old French *pleniss-,* from *plenir,* from Latin *plēnus* full] ► **'plenisher** *n* ► **'plenishment** *n*

plenitude ('plɛnɪˌtju:d) *n* **1** abundance; copiousness. **2** the condition of being full or complete. [C15: via Old French from Latin *plēnitūdō,* from *plēnus* full]

plenteous ('plɛntɪəs) *adj* **1** ample; abundant: *a plenteous supply of food.* **2** producing or yielding abundantly: *a plenteous grape harvest.* [C13 *plenteus,* from Old French *plentivous,* from *plentif* abundant, from *plenté* PLENTY] ► **'plenteously** *adv* ► **'plenteousness** *n*

plentiful ('plɛntɪfʊl) *adj* **1** ample; abundant. **2** having or yielding an abundance: *a plentiful year.* ► **'plentifully** *adv* ► **'plentifulness** *n*

plenty ('plɛntɪ) *n, pl* **-ties. 1** (often foll. by *of*) a great number, amount, or quantity; lots: *plenty of time; there are plenty of cars on display here.* **2** generous or ample supplies of wealth, produce, or resources: *the age of plenty.* **3 in plenty.** existing in abundance: *food in plenty.* ◆ *determiner* **4a** very many; ample: *plenty of people believe in ghosts.* **4b** (*as pronoun*): *there's plenty more; that's plenty, thanks.* ◆ *adv* **5** *Not standard, chiefly U.S.* (intensifier): *he was plenty mad.* **6** *Informal.* more than adequately; abundantly: *the water's plenty hot enough.* [C13: from Old French *plenté,* from Late Latin *plēnitās* fullness, from Latin *plēnus* full]

Plenty ('plɛntɪ) *n* **Bay of.** a large bay of the Pacific on the NE coast of the North Island, New Zealand.

plenum ('pli:nəm) *n, pl* **-nums** *or* **-na** (-nə). **1** an enclosure containing gas at a higher pressure than the surrounding environment. **2** a fully attended meeting or assembly, esp. of a legislative body. **3** (esp. in the philosophy of the Stoics) space regarded as filled with matter. Compare **vacuum** (sense 1). **4** the condition or quality of being full. [C17: from Latin: space filled by matter, from *plēnus* full]

plenum system *n* a type of air-conditioning system in which air is passed into a room at a pressure greater than atmospheric pressure.

pleo- *combining form.* a variant of **plio-**: *pleochroism; pleomorphism.*

pleochroism (plɪ'ɒkrəʊˌɪzəm) *n* a property of certain crystals of absorbing light to an extent that depends on the orientation of the electric vector of the light with respect to the optic axes of the crystal. The effect occurs in uniaxial crystals (**dichroism**) and esp. in biaxial crystals (**trichroism**). [C19: PLEO- + *-chroism* from Greek *khrōs* skin colour] ► **pleochroic** (ˌpli:ə'krəʊɪk) *adj*

pleomorphism (ˌpli:ə'mɔ:ˌfɪzəm) *or* **pleomorphy** ('pli:əˌmɔ:fɪ) *n* **1** the occurrence of more than one different form in the life cycle of a plant or animal. **2** the occurrence of more than one different form of crystal of one chemical compound; polymorphism. ► **ˌpleo'morphic** *adj*

pleonasm ('pli:əˌnæzəm) *n Rhetoric.* **1** the use of more words than necessary or an instance of this, such as *a tiny little child.* **2** a word or phrase that is superfluous. [C16: from Latin *pleonasmus,* from Greek *pleonasmos* excess, from *pleonazein* to be redundant] ► **ˌpleo'nastic** *adj* ► **ˌpleo'nastically** *adv*

pleopod ('pli:əˌpɒd) *n* another name for **swimmeret.** [C19: from Greek *plein* to swim + *pous* foot]

plesiosaur ('pli:sɪəˌsɔ:) *n* any of various extinct marine reptiles of the order *Sauropterygia,* esp. any of the suborder *Plesiosauria,* of Jurassic and Cretaceous times, having a long neck, short tail, and paddle-like limbs. See also **ichthyosaur.** Compare **dinosaur, pterosaur.** [C19: from New Latin *plēsiosaurus,* from Greek *plēsios* near + *sauros* a lizard]

plessor ('plɛsə) *n* another name for **plexor**.

plethora ('plɛθərə) *n* **1** superfluity or excess; overabundance. **2** *Pathol., obsolete.* a condition caused by dilation of superficial blood vessels, characterized esp. by a reddish face. [C16: via Medieval Latin from Greek *plēthōrē* fullness, from *plēthein* to grow full] ▸ **plethoric** (plɛ'θɒrɪk) *adj* ▸ **ple'thorically** *adv*

plethysmograph (plə'θɪzməˌgrɑːf, -ˌgræf, -'θɪs-) *n* a device for measuring the fluctuations in volume of a bodily organ or part, such as those caused by variations in the amount of blood it contains. [C19: from Greek *plēthusmos* enlargement + *graphein* to write]

pleugh *or* **pleuch** (pluː, pluːx) *n, vb* a Scot. word for **plough.**

pleura ('plʊərə) *n, pl* **pleurae** ('plʊəriː). **1** the thin transparent serous membrane enveloping the lungs and lining the walls of the thoracic cavity. **2** the plural of **pleuron.** [C17: via Medieval Latin from Greek: side, rib] ▸ **'pleural** *adj*

pleurisy ('plʊərɪsɪ) *n* inflammation of the pleura, characterized by pain that is aggravated by deep breathing or coughing. [C14: from Old French *pleurisie,* from Late Latin *pleurisis,* from Greek *pleuritis,* from *pleura* side] ▸ **pleuritic** (plʊ'rɪtɪk) *adj, n*

pleurisy root *n* **1** the root of the butterfly weed, formerly used as a cure for pleurisy. **2** another name for **butterfly weed.**

pleuro- *or before a vowel* **pleur-** *combining form.* **1** of or relating to the side: *pleurodont; pleurodynia.* **2** indicating the pleura: *pleurotomy.* [from Greek *pleura* side]

pleurocentesis (ˌplʊərəʊsɛn'tiːsɪs) *n* another name for **thoracentesis.**

pleurodont ('plʊərəʊˌdɒnt) *adj* **1** (of the teeth of some reptiles) having no roots and being fused by their lateral sides only to the inner surface of the jawbone. See also **acrodont** (sense 1). **2** having pleurodont teeth: *pleurodont lizards.* ◆ *n* **3** an animal having pleurodont teeth.

pleurodynia (ˌplʊərəʊ'dɪnɪə) *n* pain in the muscles between the ribs. [C19: from New Latin, from PLEURO- + Greek *-odynia,* from *odynē* pain]

pleuron ('plʊərɒn) *n, pl* **pleura** ('plʊərə). the part of the cuticle of arthropods that covers the lateral surface of a body segment. [C18: from Greek: side]

pleuropneumonia (ˌplʊərəʊnjuː'məʊnɪə) *n* the combined disorder of pleurisy and pneumonia.

pleurotomy (plʊ'rɒtəmɪ) *n, pl* **-mies.** surgical incision into the pleura, esp. to drain fluid, as in pleurisy.

pleuston ('pluːstən, -stɒn) *n* a mass of small organisms, esp. algae, floating at the surface of shallow pools. [C20: from Greek *pleusis* sailing, from *plein* to sail; for form, compare PLANKTON]

pleustonic (pluː'stɒnɪk) *adj* **1** of or relating to pleuston. **2** denoting a marine organism held at the surface of the water by a float, such as the Portuguese man-of-war.

Pleven (*Bulgarian* 'plɛvɛn) *or* **Plevna** (*Bulgarian* 'plɛvna) *n* a town in N Bulgaria: taken by Russia from the Turks in 1877 after a siege of 143 days. Pop.: 125 029 (1996 est.).

plew, plu, *or* **plue** (pluː) *n Canadian history.* a beaver skin used as a standard unit of value in the fur trade. [from Canadian French *pelu* (adj) hairy, from French *poilu,* from *poil* hair, from Latin *pilus*]

plexiform ('plɛksɪˌfɔːm) *adj* like or having the form of a network or plexus; intricate or complex.

Plexiglas ('plɛksɪˌglɑːs) *n U.S. trademark.* a transparent plastic, polymethyl-methacrylate, used for combs, plastic sheeting, etc.

plexor ('plɛksə) *or* **plessor** *n Med.* a small hammer with a rubber head for use in percussion of the chest and testing reflexes. [C19: from Greek *plēxis* a stroke, from *plēssein* to strike]

plexus ('plɛksəs) *n, pl* **-uses** *or* **-us. 1** any complex network of nerves, blood vessels, or lymphatic vessels. **2** an intricate network or arrangement. [C17: New Latin, from Latin *plectere* to braid, PLAIT]

pliable ('plaɪəbᵊl) *adj* easily moulded, bent, influenced, or altered. ▸ **ˌplia'bility** *or* **'pliableness** *n* ▸ **'pliably** *adv*

pliant ('plaɪənt) *adj* **1** easily bent; supple: *a pliant young tree.* **2** easily modified; adaptable; flexible: *a pliant system.* **3** yielding readily to influence; compliant. [C14: from Old French, from *plier* to fold, bend; see PLY[2]] ▸ **'pliancy** *or* **'pliantness** *n* ▸ **'pliantly** *adv*

plica ('plaɪkə) *n, pl* **plicae** ('plaɪsiː). **1** Also called: **fold.** *Anatomy.* a folding over of parts, such as a fold of skin, muscle, peritoneum, etc. **2** *Pathol.* a condition of the hair characterized by matting, filth, and the presence of parasites. [C17: from Medieval Latin: a fold, from Latin *plicāre* to fold; see PLY[2]] ▸ **'plical** *adj*

plicate ('plaɪkeɪt) *or* **plicated** *adj* having or arranged in parallel folds or ridges; pleated: *a plicate leaf; plicate rock strata.* [C18: from Latin *plicātus* folded, from *plicāre* to fold] ▸ **'plicately** *adv* ▸ **'plicateness** *n*

plication (plaɪ'keɪʃən) *or* **plicature** ('plɪkətʃə) *n* **1** the act of folding or the condition of being folded or plicate. **2** a folded part or structure, esp. a fold in a series of rock strata. **3** *Surgery.* the act or process of suturing together the walls of a hollow organ or part to reduce its size.

plié ('pliːeɪ) *n* a classic ballet practice posture with back erect and knees bent. [French: bent, from *plier* to bend]

plier ('plaɪə) *n* a person who plies a trade.

pliers ('plaɪəz) *pl n* a gripping tool consisting of two hinged arms with usually serrated jaws that close on the workpiece. [C16: from PLY[1]]

plight[1] (plaɪt) *n* a condition of extreme hardship, danger, etc. [C14 *plit,* from Old French *pleit* fold, PLAIT; probably influenced by Old English *pliht* peril, PLIGHT[2]]

plight[2] (plaɪt) *vb (tr)* **1** to give or pledge (one's word): *he plighted his word to attempt it.* **2** to promise formally or pledge (allegiance, support, etc.): *to plight aid.* **3 plight one's troth. 3a** to make a promise of marriage. **3b** to give one's solemn promise. ◆ *n* **4** *Archaic or dialect.* a solemn promise, esp. of engagement; pledge. [Old English *pliht* peril; related to Old High German, German *Pflicht* duty] ▸ **'plighter** *n*

plimsoll *or* **plimsole** ('plɪmsəl) *n Brit.* a light rubber-soled canvas shoe worn for various sports. Also called: **gym shoe, sandshoe.** [C20: so called because of the resemblance of the rubber sole to a Plimsoll line]

Plimsoll line ('plɪmsəl) *n* another name for **load line.** [C19: named after Samuel *Plimsoll* (1824–98), MP, who advocated its adoption]

Plinian ('plɪnɪən) *adj Geology.* (of a volcanic eruption) characterized by repeated explosions. [C20: named after PLINY the Younger, who described such eruptions]

plink (plɪŋk) *n* **1** a short sharp often metallic sound as of a string on a musical instrument being plucked or a bullet striking metal. ◆ *vb* **2** *(intr)* to make such a noise. **3** to hit (a target, such as a tin can) by shooting or to shoot at such a target. [C20: of imitative origin] ▸ **'plinking** *n, adj*

plinth (plɪnθ) *n* **1** Also called: **socle.** the rectangular slab or block that forms the lowest part of the base of a column, statue, pedestal, or pier. **2** Also called: **plinth course.** the lowest part of the wall of a building that appears above ground level, esp. one that is formed of a course of stone or brick. **3** a flat block on either side of a doorframe, where the architrave meets the skirting. **4** a flat base on which a structure or piece of equipment is placed. [C17: from Latin *plinthus,* from Greek *plinthos* brick, shaped stone]

Pliny ('plɪnɪ) *n* **1** known as *Pliny the Elder.* Latin name *Gaius Plinius Secundus.* 23–79 A.D., Roman writer, the author of the encyclopedic *Natural History* (77). **2** his nephew, known as *Pliny the Younger.* Latin name *Gaius Plinius Caecilius Secundus.* ?62–?113 A.D., Roman writer and administrator, noted for his letters.

plio-, pleo-, *or* **pleio-** *combining form.* greater in size, extent, degree, etc.; more: *Pliocene.* [from Greek *pleiōn* more, from *polus* much, many]

Pliocene *or* **Pleiocene** ('plaɪəʊˌsiːn) *adj* **1** of, denoting, or formed in the last epoch of the Tertiary period, which lasted for ten million years, during which many modern mammals appeared. ◆ *n* **2 the.** the Pliocene epoch or rock series. [C19: PLIO- + *-cene,* from Greek *kainos* recent]

plissé ('pliːseɪ, 'plɪs-) *n* **1** fabric with a wrinkled finish, achieved by treatment involving caustic soda: *cotton plissé.* **2** such a finish on a fabric. [French *plissé* pleated, from *plisser* to pleat; see PLY[2]]

PLO *abbrev. for* Palestine Liberation Organization.

ploat (pləʊt) *vb (tr) Northeastern English dialect.* **1** to thrash; beat soundly. **2** to pluck (a fowl). [from Dutch or Flemish *ploten* to pluck the feathers or fur from]

Płock (plɒk) *n* a town in central Poland, on the River Vistula: several Polish kings are buried in the cathedral: oil refining, petrochemical works. Pop.: 126 900 (1996 est.).

plod (plɒd) *vb* **plods, plodding, plodded. 1** to make (one's way) or walk along (a path, road, etc.) with heavy usually slow steps. **2** *(intr)* to work slowly and perseveringly. ◆ *n* **3** the act of plodding. **4** the sound of slow heavy steps. **5** *Brit. slang.* a policeman. [C16: of imitative origin] ▸ **'plodder** *n* ▸ **'plodding** *adj* ▸ **'ploddingly** *adv* ▸ **'ploddingness** *n*

plodge (plɒdʒ) *Northeastern English dialect.* ◆ *vb* **1** *(intr)* to wade in water, esp. the sea. ◆ *n* **2** the act of wading. [of imitative origin; related to PLOD]

Ploeşti (*Romanian* plo'jeʃtj) *n* a city in SE central Romania: centre of the Romanian petroleum industry. Pop.: 254 136 (1994 est.).

-ploid *adj and n combining form.* indicating a specific multiple of a single set of chromosomes: *diploid.* [from Greek *-pl(oos)* -fold + -OID] ▸ **-ploidy** *n combining form.*

Plomer ('pluːmə) *n* **William (Charles Franklyn).** 1903–73, British poet, novelist, and short-story writer, born in South Africa. His novels include *Turbott Wolfe* (1926) and *The Case is Altered* (1932).

plonk[1] (plɒŋk) *vb* **1** (often foll. by *down*) to drop or be dropped, esp. heavily or suddenly: *he plonked the money on the table.* ◆ *n* **2** the act or sound of plonking. ◆ *interj* **3** an exclamation imitative of this sound.

plonk[2] (plɒŋk) *n Brit., Austral., and N.Z. informal.* alcoholic drink, usually wine, esp. of inferior quality. [C20: perhaps from French *blanc* white, as in *vin blanc* white wine]

plonker ('plɒŋkə) *n Slang.* a stupid person. [C20: from PLONK[1]]

plonko ('plɒŋkəʊ) *n, pl* **plonkos.** *Austral. slang.* an alcoholic, esp. one who drinks wine. [C20: from PLONK[2]]

plook (plʊk) *n Scot.* a variant spelling of **plouk.**

plop (plɒp) *n* **1** the characteristic sound made by an object dropping into water without a splash. ◆ *vb* **plops, plopping, plopped. 2** to fall or cause to fall with the sound of a plop: *the stone plopped into the water.* ◆ *interj* **3** an exclamation imitative of this sound: *to go plop.* [C19: imitative of the sound]

plosion ('pləʊʒən) *n Phonetics.* the sound of an abrupt break or closure, esp. the audible release of a stop. Also called: **explosion.**

plosive ('pləʊsɪv) *Phonetics.* ◆ *adj* **1** articulated with or accompanied by plosion. ◆ *n* **2** a plosive consonant; stop. [C20: from French, from *explosif* EXPLOSIVE]

plot[1] (plɒt) *n* **1** a secret plan to achieve some purpose, esp. one that is illegal or underhand: *a plot to overthrow the government.* **2** the story or plan of a play, novel, etc. **3** *Military.* a graphic representation of an individual or tactical setting that pinpoints an artillery target. **4** *Chiefly U.S.* a diagram or plan, esp. a surveyor's map. **5 lose the plot.** *Informal.* to lose one's ability or judgment in a given situation. ◆ *vb* **plots, plotting, plotted. 6** to plan secretly (something illegal, revolutionary, etc.); conspire. **7** *(tr)* to mark (a course, as of a ship or aircraft) on a map. **8** *(tr)* to make a plan or map of. **9a** to locate and mark (one or more points) on a graph by means of coordinates. **9b** to draw (a curve) through these points. **10** *(tr)* to construct the plot of (a literary work). [C16: from PLOT[2], influenced in use by COMPLOT]

plot[2] (plɒt) *n* **1** a small piece of land: *a vegetable plot.* ◆ *vb* **plots, plotting,**

plotted. 2 (*tr*) to arrange or divide (land) into plots. [Old English: piece of land, plan of an area]

Plotinus (plɒ'taɪnəs) *n* ?205–?270 A.D., Roman Neo-Platonist philosopher, born in Egypt.

plotter ('plɒtə) *n* 1 an instrument for plotting lines or angles on a chart. 2 a person who plots; conspirator.

plough *or esp. U.S.* **plow** (plaʊ) *n* 1 an agricultural implement with sharp blades, attached to a horse, tractor, etc., for cutting or turning over the earth. 2 any of various similar implements, such as a device for clearing snow. 3 a plane with a narrow blade for cutting grooves in wood. 4 (in agriculture) ploughed land. 5 **put one's hand to the plough.** to begin or undertake a task. ◆ *vb* 6 to till (the soil) with a plough. 7 to make (furrows or grooves) in (something) with or as if with a plough. 8 (when *intr,* usually foll. by *through*) to move (through something) in the manner of a plough: *the ship ploughed the water.* 9 (*intr;* foll. by *through*) to work at slowly or perseveringly. 10 (*intr;* foll. by *into* or *through*) (of a vehicle) to run uncontrollably into something in its path: *the plane ploughed into the cottage roof.* 11 (*tr;* foll. by *in, up, under,* etc.) to turn over (a growing crop, manure, etc.) into the earth with a plough. 12 (*intr*) *Brit. slang.* to fail an examination. [Old English *plōg* plough land; related to Old Norse *plogr,* Old High German *pfluoc*] ▸ '**plougher** *or esp. U.S.* '**plower** *n*

Plough (plaʊ) *n* **the.** the group of the seven brightest stars in the constellation Ursa Major. Also called: **Charles's Wain.** Usual U.S. name: the **Big Dipper.**

plough back *vb* (*tr, adv*) to reinvest (the profits of a business) in the same business.

ploughboy *or esp. U.S.* **plowboy** ('plaʊ,bɔɪ) *n* 1 a boy who guides the animals drawing a plough. 2 any country boy.

ploughman *or esp. U.S.* **plowman** ('plaʊmən) *n, pl* **-men.** 1 a man who ploughs, esp. using horses. 2 any farm labourer. ▸ '**ploughmanship** *or esp. U.S.* '**plowmanship** *n*

ploughman's lunch *n* a snack lunch, served esp. in a pub, consisting of bread and cheese with pickle.

ploughman's spikenard *n* a European plant, *Inula conyza,* with tubular yellowish flower heads surrounded by purple bracts: family *Compositae* (composites). Also called: **fleawort.**

Plough Monday *n* the first Monday after Epiphany, which in N and E England used to be celebrated with a procession of ploughmen drawing a plough from house to house.

ploughshare *or esp. U.S.* **plowshare** ('plaʊ,ʃɛə) *n* the horizontal pointed cutting blade of a mouldboard plough.

ploughstaff *or esp. U.S.* **plowstaff** ('plaʊ,stɑːf) *n* 1 Also called: '**ploughtail.** one of the handles of a plough. 2 a spade-shaped tool used to clean the ploughshare and mouldboard.

plouk *or* **plook** (plʊk) *n Scot.* a pimple. [C15: of uncertain origin] ▸ '**plouky** *or* '**plooky** *adj*

Plovdiv (*Bulgarian* 'plɔvdif) *n* a city in S Bulgaria on the Maritsa River: the second largest town in Bulgaria; conquered by Philip II of Macedonia in 341 B.C.; capital of Roman Thracia; commercial centre of a rich agricultural region. Pop.: 344 326 (1996 est.). Greek name: **Philippopolis.**

plover ('plʌvə) *n* 1 any shore bird of the family *Charadriidae,* typically having a round head, straight bill, and large pointed wings: order *Charadriiformes.* 2 any of similar and related birds, such as the Egyptian plover (see **crocodile bird**) and the upland plover. 3 **green plover.** another name for **lapwing.** [C14: from Old French *plovier* rainbird, from Latin *pluvia* rain]

plow (plaʊ) *n, vb* the usual U.S. spelling of **plough.** ▸ '**plower** *n*

Plowright ('plaʊ,raɪt) *n* **Joan.** born 1929, British actress, married to Laurence Olivier (1961–89).

plowter *or* **plouter** ('plaʊtər) *Scot.* ◆ *vb* (*intr*) 1 to work or play in water or mud; dabble. 2 to potter. ◆ *n* 3 the act of plowtering. [C19: of uncertain origin]

ploy (plɔɪ) *n* 1 a manoeuvre or tactic in a game, conversation, etc.; stratagem; gambit. 2 any business, job, hobby, etc., with which one is occupied: *angling is his latest ploy.* 3 *Chiefly Brit.* a frolic, escapade, or practical joke. [C18: originally Scot. and northern English, perhaps from obsolete n sense of EMPLOY meaning an occupation]

PLP (in Britain) *abbrev. for* Parliamentary Labour Party.

PLR *abbrev. for* Public Lending Right.

plu *or* **plue** (pluː) *n* variant spellings of **plew.**

pluck (plʌk) *vb* 1 (*tr*) to pull off (feathers, fruit, etc.) from (a fowl, tree, etc.). 2 (when *intr,* usually foll. by *at*) to pull or tug. 3 (*tr;* foll. by *off, away,* etc.) *Archaic.* to pull (something) forcibly or violently (from something or someone). 4 (*tr*) to sound (the strings) of (a musical instrument) with the fingers, a plectrum, etc. 5 (*tr*) another word for **strip**[1] (sense 7). 6 (*tr*) *Slang.* to fleece or swindle. ◆ *n* 7 courage, usually in the face of difficulties or hardship. 8 a sudden pull or tug. 9 the heart, liver, and lungs, esp. of an animal used for food. [Old English *pluccian, plyccan;* related to German *pflücken*] ▸ '**plucker** *n*

pluck up *vb* (*tr, adv*) 1 to pull out; uproot. 2 to muster (courage, one's spirits, etc.).

plucky ('plʌkɪ) *adj* **pluckier, pluckiest.** having or showing courage in the face of difficulties, danger, etc. ▸ '**pluckily** *adv* ▸ '**pluckiness** *n*

plug (plʌg) *n* 1 a piece of wood, cork, or other material, often cylindrical in shape, used to stop up holes and gaps or as a wedge for taking a screw or nail. 2 such a stopper used esp. to close the waste pipe of a bath, basin, or sink while it is in use and removed to let the water drain away. 3 a device having one or more pins to which an electric cable is attached: used to make an electrical connection when inserted into a socket. 4 Also called: **volcanic plug.** a mass of solidified magma filling the neck of an extinct volcano. 5 See **sparking plug.** 6a a cake of pressed or twisted tobacco, esp. for chewing. 6b a small piece of such a cake. 7 *Angling.* a weighted artificial lure with one or more sets of hooks attached, used in spinning. 8 a seedling with its roots encased in potting compost, grown in a tray with compartments for each individual plant. 9 *Informal.* a recommendation or other favourable mention of a product, show, etc., as on television, on radio, or in newspapers. 10 *Slang.* a shot, blow, or punch (esp. in the phrase **take a plug at**). 11 *Informal.* the mechanism that releases water to flush a lavatory (esp. in the phrase **pull the plug**). 12 *Chiefly U.S.* an old horse. 13 **pull the plug on.** *Informal.* to put a stop to. ◆ *vb* **plugs, plugging, plugged.** 14 (*tr*) to stop up or secure (a hole, gap, etc.) with or as if with a plug. 15 (*tr*) to insert or use (something) as a plug: *to plug a finger into one's ear.* 16 (*tr*) *Informal.* to make favourable and often-repeated mentions of (a song, product, show, etc.), esp. on television, on radio, or in newspapers. 17 (*tr*) *Slang.* to shoot with a gun: *he plugged six rabbits.* 18 (*tr*) *Slang.* to punch or strike. 19 (*intr;* foll. by *along, away,* etc.) *Informal.* to work steadily or persistently. [C17: from Middle Dutch *plugge;* related to Middle Low German *plugge,* German *Pflock*] ▸ '**plugger** *n*

plug-and-play *adj Computing.* capable of detecting the addition of a new input or output device and automatically activating the appropriate control software.

plugboard ('plʌg,bɔːd) *n* another name for **patch board.**

plug compatible *adj Computing.* (of peripheral devices) designed to be plugged into computer systems produced by different manufacturers.

plug gauge *n Engineering.* an accurately machined plug used for checking the diameter of a hole. Compare **ring gauge.**

plughole ('plʌg,həʊl) *n* a hole, esp. in a bath, basin, or sink, through which waste water drains and which can be closed with a plug.

plug in *vb* (*tr, adv*) to connect (an electrical appliance) with a power source by means of an electrical plug.

plug-ugly *adj* 1 *Informal.* extremely ugly. ◆ *n, pl* **-lies.** 2 *U.S. slang.* a city tough; ruffian. [C19: origin obscure; originally applied to ruffians in New York who attempted to exert political pressure]

plum[1] (plʌm) *n* 1 a small rosaceous tree, *Prunus domestica,* with white flowers and an edible oval fruit that is purple, yellow, or green and contains an oval stone. See also **greengage, damson.** 2 the fruit of this tree. 3 a raisin, as used in a cake or pudding. 4a a dark reddish-purple colour. 4b (*as adj*): *a plum carpet.* 5 *Informal.* 5a something of a superior or desirable kind, such as a financial bonus. 5b (*as modifier*): *a plum job.* [Old English *plūme;* related to Latin *prunum,* German *Pflaume*] ▸ '**plum,like** *adj*

plum[2] (plʌm) *adj, adv* a variant spelling of **plumb** (senses 3–6).

plumage ('pluːmɪdʒ) *n* the layer of feathers covering the body of a bird. [C15: from Old French, from *plume* feather, from Latin *plūma* down]

plumate ('pluːmeɪt, -mɪt) *or* **plumose** *adj Zoology, botany.* 1 of, relating to, or possessing one or more feathers or plumes. 2 resembling a plume; covered with small hairs: *a plumate seed.* [C19: from Latin *plumātus* covered with feathers; see PLUME]

plumb (plʌm) *n* 1 a weight, usually of lead, suspended at the end of a line and used to determine water depth or verticality. 2 the perpendicular position of a freely suspended plumb line (esp. in the phrases **out of plumb, off plumb**). ◆ *adj also* **plum.** 3 (*prenominal*) *Informal, chiefly U.S.* (intensifier): *a plumb nuisance.* ◆ *adv also* **plum.** 4 in a vertical or perpendicular line. 5 *Informal, chiefly U.S.* (intensifier): *plumb stupid.* 6 *Informal.* exactly; precisely (also in the phrase **plumb on**). ◆ *vb* 7 (*tr;* often foll. by *up*) to test the alignment of or adjust to the vertical with a plumb line. 8 (*tr*) to undergo or experience (the worst extremes of misery, sadness, etc.): *to plumb the depths of despair.* 9 (*tr*) to understand or master (something obscure): *to plumb a mystery.* 10 to connect or join (a device such as a tap) to a water pipe or drainage system. [C13: from Old French *plomb* (unattested) lead line, from Old French *plon* lead, from Latin *plumbum* lead] ▸ '**plumbable** *adj*

plumbaginaceous (plʌm,bædʒɪ'neɪʃəs) *adj* of, relating to, or belonging to the *Plumbaginaceae,* a family of typically coastal plants having flowers with a brightly coloured calyx and five styles: includes leadwort, thrift, and sea lavender.

plumbago (plʌm'beɪgəʊ) *n, pl* **-gos.** 1 any plumbaginaceous plant of the genus *Plumbago,* of warm regions, having clusters of blue, white, or red flowers. See also **leadwort.** 2 another name for **graphite.** [C17: from Latin: lead ore, leadwort, translation of Greek *polubdaina* lead ore, from *polubdos* lead]

plumb bob *n* the weight, usually of lead, at the end of a plumb line; plummet.

plumbeous ('plʌmbɪəs) *adj* made of or relating to lead or resembling lead in colour. [C16: from Latin *plumbeus* leaden, from *plumbum* lead]

plumber ('plʌmə) *n* a person who installs and repairs pipes, fixtures, etc., for water, drainage, and gas. [C14: from Old French *plommier* worker in lead, from Late Latin *plumbārius,* from Latin *plumbum* lead]

plumbery ('plʌmərɪ) *n, pl* **-eries.** 1 the workshop of a plumber. 2 another word for **plumbing** (sense 1).

plumbic ('plʌmbɪk) *adj* of or containing lead in the tetravalent state.

Plumbicon ('plʌmbɪ,kɒn) *n Trademark.* a development of the vidicon television camera tube in which the photosensitive material is lead oxide.

plumbiferous (plʌm'bɪfərəs) *adj* (of ores, rocks, etc.) containing or yielding lead.

plumbing ('plʌmɪŋ) *n* 1 Also called: **plumbery.** the trade or work of a plumber. 2 the pipes, fixtures, etc., used in a water, drainage, or gas installation. 3 the act or procedure of using a plumb to gauge depth, a vertical, etc.

plumbism ('plʌm,bɪzəm) *n* chronic lead poisoning. [C19: from Latin *plumbum* lead]

plumb line *n* 1 a string with a metal weight at one end that, when suspended, points directly towards the earth's centre of gravity and so is used to determine verticality, the depth of water, etc. 2 another name for **plumb rule.**

plumbous ('plʌmbəs) *adj* of or containing lead in the divalent state. [C17: from Late Latin *plumbōsus* full of lead, from Latin *plumbum* lead]

plumb rule *n* a plumb line attached to a narrow board, used by builders, surveyors, etc.

plumbum ('plʌmbəm) *n* an obsolete name for **lead**[2] (the metal). [from Latin]

plume (plu:m) *n* **1** a feather, esp. one that is large or ornamental. **2** a feather or cluster of feathers worn esp. formerly as a badge or ornament in a headband, hat, etc. **3** *Biology.* any feathery part, such as the structure on certain fruits and seeds that aids dispersal by wind. **4** something that resembles a plume: *a plume of smoke.* **5** a token or decoration of honour; prize. **6** *Geology.* a rising column of magma within the earth's mantle, which spreads sideways and cools on reaching the top of the mantle. ◆ *vb (tr)* **7** to adorn or decorate with feathers or plumes. **8** (of a bird) to clean or preen (itself or its feathers). **9** (foll. by *on* or *upon*) to pride or congratulate (oneself). [C14: from Old French, from Latin *plūma* downy feather] ▸ **'plumeless** *adj* ▸ **'plume,like** *adj*

plume moth *n* **1** one of a family (*Pterophoridae*) of slender-bodied micro moths with narrow wings, each usually divided into two, three, or four "plumes". The type is the white *Pterophorus pentadactylus.* **2 many-plumed moth.** an unrelated species, *Alucita hexadactyla.*

plummet ('plʌmɪt) *vb* **-mets, -meting, -meted. 1** (*intr*) to drop down; plunge. ◆ *n* **2** another word for **plumb bob. 3** a lead plumb used by anglers to determine the depth of water. [C14: from Old French *plommet* ball of lead, from *plomb* lead, from Latin *plumbum*]

plummy ('plʌmɪ) *adj* **-mier, -miest. 1** of, full of, or resembling plums. **2** *Brit. informal.* (of speech) having a deep tone and a refined and somewhat drawling articulation. **3** *Brit. informal.* choice; desirable.

plumose ('plu:məʊs, -məʊz) *adj* another word for **plumate.** [C17: from Latin *plūmōsus* feathery] ▸ **'plumosely** *adv* ▸ **plumosity** (plu:'mɒsɪtɪ) *n*

plump[1] (plʌmp) *adj* **1** well filled out or rounded; fleshy or chubby: *a plump turkey.* **2** bulging, as with contents; full: *a plump wallet.* **3** (of amounts of money) generous; ample: *a plump cheque.* ◆ *vb* **4** (often foll. by *up* or *out*) to make or become plump: *to plump up a pillow.* [C15 (meaning: dull, rude), C16 (in current senses): perhaps from Middle Dutch *plomp* dull, blunt] ▸ **'plumply** *adv* ▸ **'plumpness** *n*

plump[2] (plʌmp) *vb* **1** (often foll. by *down, into,* etc.) to drop or fall suddenly and heavily: *to plump down on the sofa.* **2** (*intr;* foll. by *for*) to give support (to) or make a choice (of) one out of a group or number. ◆ *n* **3** a heavy abrupt fall or the sound of this. ◆ *adv* **4** suddenly or heavily: *he ran plump into the old lady.* **5** straight down; directly: *the helicopter landed plump in the middle of the field.* ◆ *adj, adv* **6** in a blunt, direct, or decisive manner. [C14: probably of imitative origin; compare Middle Low German *plumpen,* Middle Dutch *plompen*]

plump[3] (plʌmp) *n Archaic or dialect.* a group of people, animals, or things; troop; cluster. [C15: of uncertain origin]

plumper ('plʌmpə) *n* a pad carried in the mouth by actors to round out the cheeks.

plum pudding *n* (in Britain) a dark brown rich boiled or steamed pudding made with flour, suet, sugar, and dried fruit.

plumule ('plu:mju:l) *n* **1** the embryonic shoot of seed-bearing plants. **2** a down feather of young birds that persists in some adults. [C18: from Late Latin *plūmula* a little feather]

plumy ('plu:mɪ) *adj* **plumier, plumiest. 1** plumelike; feathery. **2** consisting of, covered with, or adorned with feathers.

plunder ('plʌndə) *vb* **1** to steal (valuables, goods, sacred items, etc.) from (a town, church, etc.) by force, esp. in time of war; loot. **2** (*tr*) to rob or steal (choice or desirable things) from (a place): *to plunder an orchard.* ◆ *n* **3** anything taken by plundering or theft; booty. **4** the act of plundering; pillage. [C17: probably from Dutch *plunderen* (originally: to plunder household goods); compare Middle High German *plunder* bedding, household goods] ▸ **'plunderable** *adj* ▸ **'plunderer** *n* ▸ **'plunderous** *adj*

plunderage ('plʌndərɪdʒ) *n* **1** *Maritime law.* **1a** the embezzlement of goods on board a ship. **1b** the goods embezzled. **2** the act of plundering.

plunge (plʌndʒ) *vb* **1** (usually foll. by *into*) to thrust or throw (something, oneself, etc.): *they plunged into the sea.* **2** to throw or be thrown into a certain state or condition: *the room was plunged into darkness.* **3** (usually foll. by *into*) to involve or become involved deeply (in): *he plunged himself into a course of Sanskrit.* **4** (*intr*) to move or dash violently or with great speed or impetuosity. **5** (*intr*) to descend very suddenly or steeply: *the ship plunged in heavy seas; a plunging neckline.* **6** (*intr*) *Informal.* to speculate or gamble recklessly, for high stakes, etc. ◆ *n* **7** a leap or dive as into water. **8** *Informal.* a swim; dip. **9** *Chiefly U.S.* a place where one can swim or dive, such as a swimming pool. **10** a headlong rush: *a plunge for the exit.* **11** a pitching or tossing motion. **12 take the plunge.** *Informal.* **12a** to resolve to do something dangerous or irrevocable. **12b** to get married. [C14: from Old French *plongier,* from Vulgar Latin *plumbicāre* (unattested) to sound with a plummet, from Latin *plumbum* lead]

plunge bath *n* a bath large enough to immerse the whole body or to dive into.

plunger ('plʌndʒə) *n* **1** a rubber suction cup fixed to the end of a rod, used to clear blocked drains. **2** a device or part of a machine that has a plunging or thrusting motion; piston. **3** *Informal.* a reckless gambler.

plunk (plʌŋk) *vb* **1** to pluck (the strings) of (a banjo, harp, etc.) or (of such an instrument) to give forth a sound when plucked. **2** (often foll. by *down*) to drop or be dropped, esp. heavily or suddenly. ◆ *n* **3** the act or sound of plunking. **4** *Informal.* a hard blow. ◆ *interj* **5** an exclamation imitative of the sound of something plunking. ◆ *adv* **6** *Informal.* exactly; squarely: *plunk into his lap.* [C20: imitative]

Plunket *or* **Plunkett** ('plʌŋkət) *n* **Saint Oliver.** 1629–81, Irish Roman Catholic churchman and martyr; wrongly executed as a supposed conspirator in the Popish Plot (1678). Feast day: July 11.

Plunket baby ('plʌŋkət) *n N.Z. informal.* a baby brought up in infancy under the dietary recommendations of the Plunket Society.

Plunket nurse *n N.Z.* a child-care nurse appointed by the Plunket Society.

Plunket Society *n* the Royal New Zealand Society for the Health of Women and Children. [named after Sir William Lee *Plunket* (1864–1920), Governor General of New Zealand at the time of its founding (1907)]

pluperfect (plu:'pɜ:fɪkt) *adj, n Grammar.* another term for **past perfect.** [C16: from the Latin phrase *plūs quam perfectum* more than perfect]

plur. *abbrev. for:* **1** plural. **2** plurality.

plural ('plʊərəl) *adj* **1** containing, involving, or composed of more than one person, thing, item, etc.: *a plural society.* **2** denoting a word indicating that more than one referent is being referred to or described. ◆ *n* **3** *Grammar.* **3a** the plural number. **3b** a plural form. [C14: from Old French *plurel,* from Late Latin *plūrālis* concerning many, from Latin *plūs* more] ▸ **'plurally** *adv*

pluralism ('plʊərə,lɪzəm) *n* **1** the holding by a single person of more than one ecclesiastical benefice or office. **2** *Sociol.* a theory of society as several autonomous but interdependent groups which either share power or continuously compete for power. **3** the existence in a society of groups having distinctive ethnic origin, cultural forms, religions, etc. **4** a theory that views the power of employers as being balanced by the power of trade unions in industrial relations such that the interests of both sides can be catered for. **5** *Philosophy.* **5a** the metaphysical doctrine that reality consists of more than two basic types of substance. Compare **monism** (sense 1), **dualism** (sense 2). **5b** the metaphysical doctrine that reality consists of independent entities rather than one unchanging whole. Compare **monism** (sense 1), **absolutism** (sense 2b). ▸ **'pluralist** *n, adj* ▸ **,plural'istic** *adj*

plurality (plʊə'rælɪtɪ) *n, pl* **-ties. 1** the state of being plural or numerous. **2** *Maths.* a number greater than one. **3** the U.S. and Canadian term for **relative majority. 4** a large number. **5** the greater number; majority. **6** another word for **pluralism** (sense 1).

pluralize *or* **pluralise** ('plʊərə,laɪz) *vb* **1** (*intr*) to hold more than one ecclesiastical benefice or office at the same time. **2** to make or become plural. ▸ **,plurali'zation** *or* **,plurali'sation** *n* ▸ **'plural,izer** *or* **'plural,iser** *n*

plural voting *n* **1** a system that enables an elector to vote more than once in an election. **2** (in Britain before 1948) a system enabling certain electors to vote in more than one constituency.

pluri- *combining form.* denoting several: *pluriliteral; pluripresence.* [from Latin *plur-, plus* more, *plures* several]

pluriliteral (,plʊrɪ'lɪtərəl) *adj* (in Hebrew grammar) containing more than three letters in the root.

pluripresence (,plʊrɪ'prezəns) *n Theol.* presence in more than one place at the same time.

plus (plʌs) *prep* **1** increased by the addition of: *four plus two* (written 4 + 2). **2** with or with the addition of: *a good job, plus a new car.* ◆ *adj* **3** (*prenominal*) Also: **positive.** indicating or involving addition: *a plus sign.* **4** another word for **positive** (senses 8, 9). **5** on the positive part of a scale or coordinate axis: *a value of +x.* **6** indicating the positive side of an electrical circuit. **7** involving positive advantage or good: *a plus factor.* **8** (*postpositive*) *Informal.* having a value above that which is stated or expected: *she had charm plus.* **9** (*postpositive*) slightly above a specified standard on a particular grade or percentage: *he received a B+ rating on his essay.* **10** *Botany.* designating the strain of fungus that can only undergo sexual reproduction with a minus strain. ◆ *n* **11** short for **plus sign. 12** a positive quantity. **13** *Informal.* something positive or to the good. **14** a gain, surplus, or advantage. ◆ Mathematical symbol: + [C17: from Latin: more; compare Greek *pleiōn,* Old Norse *fleiri* more, German *viel* much]

USAGE *Plus, together with,* and *along with* do not create compound subjects in the way that *and* does: the number of the verb depends on that of the subject to which *plus, together with,* or *along with* is added: *this task, plus all the others, was* (not *were*) *undertaken by the government; the doctor, together with the nurses, was* (not *were*) *waiting for the patient.*

plus fours *pl n* men's baggy knickerbockers reaching below the knee, now only worn for hunting, golf, etc. [C20: so called because the trousers are made with four inches of material to hang over at the knee]

plush (plʌʃ) *n* **1a** a fabric with a cut pile that is longer and softer than velvet. **1b** (*as modifier*): *a plush chair.* ◆ *adj* **2** Also: **'plushy.** *Informal.* lavishly appointed; rich; costly. [C16: from French *pluche,* from Old French *peluchier* to pluck, ultimately from Latin *pilus* a hair, PILE[3]] ▸ **'plushly** *adv* ▸ **'plushness** *n*

plus sign *n* the symbol +, indicating addition or positive quantity.

Plutarch ('plu:tɑ:k) *n* ?46–?120 A.D., Greek biographer and philosopher, noted for his *Parallel Lives* of distinguished Greeks and Romans.

Pluto[1] ('plu:təʊ) *n Greek myth.* the god of the underworld; Hades.

Pluto[2] ('plu:təʊ) *n* the smallest planet and the farthest known from the sun; it has one known satellite, Charon. Its existence was predicted before it was discovered in 1930. Mean distance from sun: 5907 million km; period of revolution around sun: 248.4 years; period of axial rotation: 6.4 days; diameter and mass: 18 and 0.3 per cent that of earth respectively. [Latin, from Greek *Ploutōn,* literally: the rich one]

PLUTO ('plu:təʊ) *n* the code name of pipelines laid under the English Channel to supply fuel to the Allied forces landing in Normandy in 1944. [C20: from *p(ipe)l(ine) u(nder) t(he) o(cean)*]

plutocracy (plu:'tɒkrəsɪ) *n, pl* **-cies. 1** the rule or control of society by the wealthy. **2** a state or government characterized by the rule of the wealthy. **3** a class that exercises power by virtue of its wealth. [C17: from Greek *ploutokratia* government by the rich, from *ploutos* wealth + *-kratia* rule, power] ▸ **plutocratic** (,plu:tə'krætɪk) *or* **,pluto'cratical** *adj* ▸ **,pluto'cratically** *adv*

plutocrat ('plu:tə,kræt) *n* a member of a plutocracy.

pluton ('plu:tɒn) *n* any mass of igneous rock that has solidified below the surface of the earth. [C20: back formation from PLUTONIC]

Plutonian (plu:ˈtəʊnɪən) *adj* of or relating to Pluto (the god) or the underworld; infernal.

plutonic (plu:ˈtɒnɪk) *adj* (of igneous rocks) derived from magma that has cooled and solidified below the surface of the earth. Also: **abyssal.** [C20: named after PLUTO[1]]

plutonium (plu:ˈtəʊnɪəm) *n* a highly toxic metallic transuranic element. It occurs in trace amounts in uranium ores and is produced in a nuclear reactor by neutron bombardment of uranium-238. The most stable and important isotope, **plutonium-239,** readily undergoes fission and is used as a reactor fuel in nuclear power stations and in nuclear weapons. Symbol: Pu; atomic no.: 94; half-life of ^{239}Pu: 24 360 years; valency: 3, 4, 5, or 6; relative density (alpha modification): 19.84; melting pt.: 640°C; boiling pt.: 3230°C. [C20: named after the planet *Pluto* because Pluto lies beyond Neptune and plutonium was discovered soon after NEPTUNIUM]

Plutus (ˈplu:tʊs) *n* the Greek god of wealth. [from Greek *ploutos* wealth]

pluvial (ˈplu:vɪəl) *adj* **1** of, characterized by, or due to the action of rain; rainy: *pluvial insurance.* ◆ *n* **2** *Geology.* a period of persistent heavy rainfall, esp. one occurring in unglaciated regions during the Pleistocene epoch. [C17: from Latin *pluviālis* rainy, from *pluvia* rain]

pluviometer (ˌplu:vɪˈɒmɪtə) *n* another word for **rain gauge.** ▸ pluviometric (ˌplu:vɪəˈmɛtrɪk) *adj* ▸ ˌ**pluvioˈmetrically** *adv* ▸ ˌ**pluviˈometry** *n*

Pluviôse *French.* (plyvjoz) *n* the rainy month: the fifth month of the French revolutionary calendar, extending from Jan. 21 to Feb. 19. [C19 *pluviose,* C15 *pluvious;* see PLUVIOUS]

pluvious (ˈplu:vɪəs) *or* **pluviose** *adj* of or relating to rain; rainy. [C15: from Late Latin *pluviōsus* full of rain, from *pluvia* rain, from *pluere* to rain]

ply[1] (plaɪ) *vb* **plies, plying, plied.** (*mainly tr*) **1** to carry on, pursue, or work at (a job, trade, etc.). **2** to manipulate or wield (a tool). **3** to sell (goods, wares, etc.), esp. at a regular place. **4** (usually foll. by *with*) to provide (with) or subject (to) repeatedly or persistently: *he plied us with drink the whole evening; to ply a horse with a whip; he plied the speaker with questions.* **5** (*intr*) to perform or work steadily or diligently: *to ply with a spade.* **6** (*also intr*) (esp. of a ship) to travel regularly along (a route) or in (an area): *to ply between Dover and Calais; to ply the trade routes.* [C14 *plye,* short for *aplye* to APPLY]

ply[2] (plaɪ) *n, pl* **plies. 1a** a layer, fold, or thickness, as of cloth, wood, yarn, etc. **1b** (*in combination*): *four-ply.* **2** a thin sheet of wood glued to other similar sheets to form plywood. **3** one of the strands twisted together to make rope, yarn, etc. ◆ *vb* (*tr*) **4** to twist together (two or more single strands) to make yarn. [C15: from Old French *pli* fold, from *plier* to fold, from Latin *plicāre*]

Plymouth (ˈplɪməθ) *n* **1** a port and from 1998 a unitary authority in SW England, in SW Devon on **Plymouth Sound** (an inlet of the English Channel): Britain's chief port in Elizabethan times; the last port visited by the Pilgrim Fathers in the *Mayflower* before sailing to America; naval base. Pop.: 257 500 (1995 est.). Area: 76 sq. km (30 sq. miles). **2** a city in SE Massachusetts, on **Plymouth Bay:** the first permanent European settlement in New England; founded by the Pilgrim Fathers. Pop.: 45 608 (1990).

Plymouth Brethren *pl n* a religious sect founded *c.* 1827, strongly Puritanical in outlook and prohibiting many secular occupations for its members. It combines elements of Calvinism, Pietism, and millenarianism, and has no organized ministry.

Plymouth Colony *n* the Puritan colony founded by the Pilgrim Fathers in SE Massachusetts (1620). See also **Mayflower.**

Plymouth Rock *n* **1** a heavy American breed of domestic fowl. **2** a boulder on the coast of Massachusetts: traditionally thought to be the landing place of the Pilgrim Fathers (1620). See also **Mayflower.**

plywood (ˈplaɪˌwʊd) *n* a structural board consisting of an odd number of thin layers of wood glued together under pressure, with the grain of one layer at right angles to the grain of the adjoining layer.

Plzeň (*Czech* ˈplzɛnj) *n* an industrial city in the Czech Republic. Pop.: 171 249 (1996 est.). German name: **Pilsen.**

pm *abbrev. for* premium.

Pm *the chemical symbol for* promethium.

PM *abbrev. for:* **1** Prime Minister. **2** Past Master (of a fraternity). **3** Paymaster. **4** Postmaster. **5** *Military.* Provost Marshal.

p.m., P.M., pm, *or* **PM** *abbrev. for:* **1** (indicating the time period from midday to midnight) post meridiem. Compare **a.m.** [Latin: after noon] **2** postmortem (examination).

PMG *abbrev. for:* **1** Paymaster General. **2** Postmaster General. **3** *Military.* Provost Marshal General.

PMS *abbrev. for* premenstrual syndrome.

PMT *abbrev. for:* **1** photomechanical transfer. **2** premenstrual tension.

PN, P/N, *or* **pn** *abbrev. for* promissory note.

PNdB *abbrev. for* perceived noise decibel.

pneuma (ˈnju:mə) *n Philosophy.* a person's vital spirit, soul, or creative energy. Compare **psyche.** [C19: from Greek: breath, spirit, wind; related to *pnein* to blow, breathe]

pneumatic (njʊˈmætɪk) *adj* **1** of or concerned with air, gases, or wind. Compare **hydraulic. 2** (of a machine or device) operated by compressed air or by a vacuum: *a pneumatic drill; pneumatic brakes.* **3** containing compressed air: *a pneumatic tyre.* **4** of or concerned with pneumatics. **5** *Theol.* **5a** of or relating to the soul or spirit. **5b** of or relating to the Holy Ghost or other spiritual beings. **6** (of the bones of birds) containing air spaces which reduce their weight as an adaptation to flying. **7** *Informal.* (of a woman) well rounded, esp. with a large bosom. ◆ *n* **8** short for **pneumatic tyre.** [C17: from Late Latin *pneumaticus* of air or wind, from Greek *pneumatikos* of air or breath, from PNEUMA] ▸ **pneuˈmatically** *adv*

pneumatic conveyor *n Engineering.* a tube through which powdered or granular material, such as cement, grain, etc. is transported by a flow of air.

pneumatics (njʊˈmætɪks) *n* (*functioning as sing*) the branch of physics concerned with the mechanical properties of gases, esp. air. Also called: **aerometry, pneumodynamics.**

pneumatic trough *n Chem.* a shallow dishlike vessel filled with a liquid, usually water, and used in collecting gases by displacement of liquid from a filled jar held with its open end under the surface of the liquid.

pneumatic tyre *n* a rubber tyre filled with air under pressure, used esp. on motor vehicles.

pneumato- *combining form.* air; breath or breathing; spirit: *pneumatophore; pneumatology.* [from Greek *pneuma, pneumat-,* breath; see PNEUMA]

pneumatology (ˌnju:məˈtɒlədʒɪ) *n* **1** the branch of theology concerned with the Holy Ghost and other spiritual beings. **2** an obsolete name for **psychology** (the science). **3** an obsolete term for **pneumatics.** ▸ **pneumatological** (ˌnju:mətəˈlɒdʒɪkᵊl) *adj* ▸ ˌ**pneumaˈtologist** *n*

pneumatolysis (ˌnju:məˈtɒlɪsɪs) *n* a type of metamorphism in which hot gases from solidifying magma react with surrounding rock.

pneumatometer (ˌnju:məˈtɒmɪtə) *n* an instrument for measuring the pressure exerted by air being inhaled or exhaled during a single breath. Compare **spirometer.** ▸ ˌ**pneumaˈtometry** *n*

pneumatophore (nju:ˈmætəʊˌfɔ:) *n* **1** a specialized root of certain swamp plants, such as the mangrove, that branches upwards and undergoes gaseous exchange with the atmosphere. **2** a polyp in coelenterates of the order *Siphonophora,* such as the Portuguese man-of-war, that is specialized as a float.

pneumectomy (nju:ˈmɛktəmɪ) *n, pl* **-mies.** *Surgery.* another word for **pneumonectomy.**

pneumo-, pneumono- *or before a vowel* **pneum-, pneumon-** *combining form.* of or related to a lung or the lungs; respiratory: *pneumoconiosis; pneumonitis.* [from Greek *pneumōn* lung or *pneuma* breath]

pneumobacillus (ˌnju:məʊbəˈsɪləs) *n, pl* **-li** (-laɪ). a rod-shaped bacterium that occurs in the respiratory tract, esp. the Gram-negative *Klebsiella pneumoniae,* which causes pneumonia.

pneumococcus (ˌnju:məʊˈkɒkəs) *n, pl* **-cocci** (-ˈkɒksaɪ). a spherical bacterium that occurs in the respiratory tract, esp. the Gram-positive *Diplococcus pneumoniae,* which causes pneumonia. ▸ ˌ**pneumoˈcoccal** *adj*

pneumoconiosis (ˌnju:məʊˌkəʊnɪˈəʊsɪs) *or* **pneumonoconiosis** (ˌnju:mənəʊˌkəʊnɪˈəʊsɪs) *n* any disease of the lungs or bronchi caused by the inhalation of metallic or mineral particles: characterized by inflammation, cough, and fibrosis. [C19: shortened from *pneumonoconiosis,* from PNEUMO- + *-coniosis,* from Greek *konis* dust]

pneumocystis (ˌnju:məʊˈsɪstɪs) *n* any protozoan of the genus *Pneumocystis,* esp. *P. carinii,* which is a cause of pneumonia in people whose immune defences have been lowered by drugs or a disease.

pneumodynamics (ˌnju:məʊdaɪˈnæmɪks) *n* (*functioning as sing*) another name for **pneumatics.**

pneumoencephalogram (ˌnju:məʊɛnˈsɛfələˌɡræm) *n* See **encephalogram.** ▸ **pneumoencephalography** (ˌnju:məʊɛnˌsɛfəˈlɒɡrəfɪ) *n*

pneumogastric (ˌnju:məʊˈɡæstrɪk) *adj Anatomy.* **1** of or relating to the lungs and stomach. **2** a former term for **vagus.**

pneumograph (ˈnju:məˌɡrɑ:f, -ˌɡræf) *n Med.* an instrument for making a record (**pneumogram**) of respiratory movements.

pneumonectomy (ˌnju:məʊˈnɛktəmɪ) *or* **pneumectomy** (nju:ˈmɛktəmɪ) *n, pl* **-mies.** the surgical removal of a lung or part of a lung. [C20: from Greek *pneumōn* lung + -ECTOMY]

pneumonia (nju:ˈməʊnɪə) *n* inflammation of one or both lungs, in which the air sacs (alveoli) become filled with liquid, which renders them useless for breathing. It is usually caused by bacterial (esp. pneumococcal) or viral infection. [C17: New Latin from Greek from *pneumōn* lung]

pneumonic (nju:ˈmɒnɪk) *adj* **1** of, relating to, or affecting the lungs; pulmonary. **2** of or relating to pneumonia. [C17: from New Latin *pneumonicus,* from Greek, from *pneumon* lung]

pneumonitis (ˌnju:mɒnˈaɪtɪs) *n* inflammation of the lungs.

pneumothorax (ˌnju:məʊˈθɔ:ræks) *n* **1** the abnormal presence of air between the lung and the wall of the chest (pleural cavity), resulting in collapse of the lung. **2** *Med.* the introduction of air into the pleural cavity to collapse the lung: a former treatment for tuberculosis.

PNG *international car registration for* Papua New Guinea.

PNI *abbrev. for* psychoneuroimmunology.

p-n junction *n Electronics.* a boundary between a p-type and n-type semiconductor that functions as a rectifier and is used in diodes and junction transistors.

Pnom Penh (ˈnɒm ˈpɛn) *n* a variant spelling of **Phnom Penh.**

po (pəʊ) *n, pl* **pos.** *Brit.* an informal word for **chamber pot.** [C19: from POT[1]]

Po[1] *the chemical symbol for* polonium.

Po[2] (pəʊ) *n* a river in N Italy, rising in the Cottian Alps and flowing northeast to Turin, then east to the Adriatic: the longest river in Italy. Length: 652 km (405 miles). Latin name: **Padus.**

PO *abbrev. for:* **1** Post Office. **2** Personnel Officer. **3** petty officer. **4** Pilot Officer. **5** Also: **p.o.** postal order.

poaceous (pəʊˈeɪʃəs) *adj* (in former botanic classification) of, relating to, or belonging to the plant family *Poaceae* (grasses). [C18: via New Latin from Greek *poa* grass]

poach[1] (pəʊtʃ) *vb* **1** to catch (game, fish, etc.) illegally by trespassing on private property. **2** to encroach on or usurp (another person's rights, duties, etc.) or steal (an idea, employee, etc.). **3** *Tennis, badminton, etc.* to take or play (shots that should belong to one's partner). **4** to break up (land) into wet muddy patches, as by riding over it, or (of land) to become broken up in this way. **5** (*intr*) (of the feet, shoes, etc.) to sink into heavy wet ground. [C17: from Old

French *pocher,* of Germanic origin; compare Middle Dutch *poken* to prod; see POKE[1]]

poach[2] (pəutʃ) *vb* to simmer (eggs, fish, etc.) very gently in water, milk, stock, etc. [C15: from Old French *pochier* to enclose in a bag (as the yolks are enclosed by the whites); compare POKE[2]]

poacher[1] ('pəutʃə) *n* a person who illegally hunts game, fish, etc., on someone else's property.

poacher[2] ('pəutʃə) *n* a metal pan with individual cups for poaching eggs.

POB *abbrev. for* Post Office Box.

Pocahontas (ˌpɒkə'hɒntəs) *n* original name *Matoaka;* married name *Rebecca Rolfe.* ?1595–1617, American Indian, who allegedly saved the colonist Captain John Smith from being killed.

pochard ('pəutʃəd) *n, pl* **-chards** *or* **-chard.** any of various diving ducks of the genera *Aythya* and *Netta,* esp. *A. ferina* of Europe, the male of which has a grey-and-black body and a reddish head. [C16: of unknown origin]

pochette (pɒ'ʃɛt) *n* an envelope-shaped handbag used by women and men. [C20: from French: little pocket]

pock (pɒk) *n* **1** any pustule resulting from an eruptive disease, esp. from smallpox. **2** another word for **pockmark** (sense 1). [Old English *pocc;* related to Middle Dutch *pocke,* perhaps to Latin *bucca* cheek] ▸ **'pocky** *adj*

pocket ('pɒkɪt) *n* **1** a small bag or pouch in a garment for carrying small articles, money, etc. **2** any bag or pouch or anything resembling this. **3a** a cavity or hollow in the earth, etc., such as one containing gold or other ore. **3b** the ore in such a place. **4** a small enclosed or isolated area: *a pocket of resistance.* **5** any of the six holes with pouches or nets let into the corners and sides of a billiard table. **6** a position in a race in which a competitor is hemmed in. **7** *Australian Rules football.* a player in one of two side positions at the ends of the ground: *back pocket; forward pocket.* **8** *S. African.* a bag or sack of vegetables or fruit. **9 in one's pocket.** under one's control. **10 in** *or* **out of pocket.** having made a profit or loss, as after a transaction. **11 line one's pockets.** to make money, esp. by dishonesty when in a position of trust. **12** (*modifier*) suitable for fitting in a pocket; small: *a pocket edition.* ◆ *vb* **-ets, -eting, -eted.** (*tr*) **13 to put into one's pocket. 14** to take surreptitiously or unlawfully; steal. **15** (*usually passive*) to enclose or confine in or as if in a pocket. **16** to receive (an insult, injury, etc.) without retaliating. **17** to conceal or keep back (feelings): *he pocketed his pride and accepted help.* **18** *Billiards, etc.* to drive (a ball) into a pocket. **19** *U.S.* (esp. of the President) to retain (a bill) without acting on it in order to prevent it from becoming law. See also **pocket veto. 20** to hem in (an opponent), as in racing. [C15: from Anglo-Norman *poket* a little bag, from *poque* bag, from Middle Dutch *poke* POKE[2], bag; related to French *poche* pocket] ▸ **'pocketable** *adj* ▸ **'pocketless** *adj*

pocket battleship *n* a small heavily armoured and armed battle cruiser specially built to conform with treaty limitations on tonnage and armament, esp. any of those built by Germany in the 1930s.

pocket billiards *n* (*functioning as sing*) *Billiards.* **1** another name for **pool**[2] (sense 5). **2** any game played on a table in which the object is to pocket the balls, esp. snooker and pool.

pocketbook ('pɒkɪtˌbuk) *n U.S. and Canadian.* a small bag or case for money, papers, etc., carried by a handle or in the pocket.

pocket borough *n* (before the Reform Act of 1832) an English borough constituency controlled by one person or family who owned the land. Compare **rotten borough.**

pocketful ('pɒkɪtful) *n, pl* **-fuls. 1** as much as a pocket will hold. **2** *Informal.* a large amount: *it cost him a pocketful of money.*

pocket gopher *n* the full name for **gopher** (sense 1).

pocketknife ('pɒkɪtˌnaɪf) *n, pl* **-knives.** a small knife with one or more blades that fold into the handle; penknife.

pocket money *n* **1** *Brit.* a small weekly sum of money given to children by parents as an allowance. **2** money for day-to-day spending, incidental expenses, etc.

pocket mouse *n* any small mouselike rodent with cheek pouches, of the genus *Perognathus,* of desert regions of W North America: family *Heteromyidae.*

pocket veto *n U.S.* **1** the action of the President in retaining unsigned a bill passed by Congress within the last ten days of a session and thus causing it to die. **2** any similar action by a state governor or other chief executive.

pockmark ('pɒkˌmɑːk) *n* **1** Also called: **pock.** a pitted scar left on the skin after the healing of a smallpox or similar pustule. **2** any pitting of a surface that resembles or suggests such scars. ◆ *vb* **3** (*tr*) to scar or pit (a surface) with pockmarks. ▸ **'pockˌmarked** *adj*

poco ('pəukəu; *Italian* 'pɔːko) *or* **un poco** *adj, adv Music.* (*in combination*) a little; to a small degree: *poco rit.; un poco meno mosso.* [from Italian: little, from Latin *paucus* few, scanty]

poco a poco *adv* (*in combination*) *Music.* little by little: *poco a poco rall.* [Italian]

pococurante (ˌpəukəukju'ræntɪ) *n* **1** a person who is careless or indifferent. ◆ *adj* **2** indifferent or apathetic. [C18: from Italian, from *poco* little + *curante* caring] ▸ **ˌpococu'ranteism** *or* **ˌpococu'rantism** *n*

pod[1] (pɒd) *n* **1a** the fruit of any leguminous plant, consisting of a long two-valved case that contains seeds and splits along both sides when ripe. **1b** the seedcase as distinct from the seeds. **2** any similar fruit. **3** a streamlined structure attached by a pylon to an aircraft and used to house a jet engine (**podded engine**), fuel tank, armament, etc. ◆ *vb* **pods, podding, podded. 4** (*tr*) to remove the pod or shell from (peas, beans, etc.). **5** (*intr*) (of a plant) to produce pods. [C17: perhaps back formation from earlier *podware* bagged vegetables, probably from *pod,* variant of COD[2] + WARE[1]]

pod[2] (pɒd) *n* a small group of animals, esp. seals, whales, or birds. [C19: of unknown origin]

pod[3] (pɒd) *n* **1** a straight groove along the length of certain augers and bits. **2** the socket that holds the bit in a boring tool. [C16: of unknown origin]

POD *abbrev. for* pay on delivery.

-pod *or* **-pode** *n combining form.* indicating a certain type or number of feet: *arthropod; tripod.* [from Greek *-podos* footed, from *pous* foot]

podagra (pə'dægrə) *n* gout of the foot or big toe. [C15: via Latin from Greek, from *pous* foot + *agra* a trap] ▸ **po'dagral, po'dagric, po'dagrical,** *or* **po'dagrous** *adj*

poddy ('pɒdɪ) *n, pl* **-dies.** *Austral.* **1** a handfed calf or lamb. **2** any creature at an early stage of growth: *poddy mullet.* [perhaps from *poddy* (adj) fat]

poddy-dodger ('pɒdɪˌdɒdʒə) *n Austral. informal.* a cattle thief who steals unbranded calves.

podesta (pɒ'dɛstə; *Italian* pode'sta) *n* **1** (in modern Italy) a subordinate magistrate in some towns. **2** (in Fascist Italy) the chief magistrate of a commune. **3** (in medieval Italy) **3a** any of the governors of the Lombard cities appointed by Frederick Barbarossa. **3b** a chief magistrate in any of various republics, such as Florence. [C16: from Italian: power, from Latin *potestās* ability, power, from *posse* to be able]

podge (pɒdʒ) *or* **pudge** (pʌdʒ) *n Informal.* a short chubby person.

Podgorica *or* **Podgoritsa** (*Russian* 'pɔdgɔˌriːtsa) *n* a city in Yugoslavia, the capital of Montenegro: under Turkish rule (1474–1878). Pop.: 117 875 (1991). Former name (1946–92): **Titograd.**

podgy ('pɒdʒɪ) *adj* **podgier, podgiest.** short and fat; chubby. ▸ **'podgily** *adv* ▸ **'podginess** *n*

podiatry (pɒ'diːətrɪ, -'daɪ-) *n* another word for **chiropody.** [C20: from Greek *pous* foot] ▸ **podiatric** (ˌpəudɪ'ætrɪk) *adj* ▸ **po'diatrist** *n*

podium ('pəudɪəm) *n, pl* **-diums** *or* **-dia** (-dɪə). **1** a small raised platform used by lecturers, orchestra conductors, etc.; dais. **2** a plinth that supports a colonnade or wall. **3** a low wall surrounding the arena of an ancient amphitheatre. **4** *Zoology.* **4a** the terminal part of a vertebrate limb. **4b** any footlike organ, such as the tube foot of a starfish. [C18: from Latin: platform, balcony, from Greek *podion* little foot, from *pous* foot]

-podium *n combining form.* a part resembling a foot: *pseudopodium.* [from New Latin: footlike; see PODIUM]

Podolsk (*Russian* pa'dɔljsk) *n* an industrial city in W Russia, near Moscow. Pop.: 202 000 (1995 est.).

podophyllin *or* **podophylin resin** (ˌpɒdəu'fɪlɪn) *n* a bitter yellow resin obtained from the dried underground stems of the May apple and mandrake: used as a cathartic and to treat warts. [C19: from New Latin *Podophyllum* genus of herbs including the May apple, from *podo-,* from Greek *pous* foot + *phullon* leaf]

-podous *adj combining form.* having feet of a certain kind or number: *cephalopodous.*

podzol ('pɒdzɒl) *or* **podsol** ('pɒdsɒl) *n* a type of soil characteristic of coniferous forest regions having a greyish-white colour in its upper leached layers. [C20: from Russian: ash ground, from *pod* ground + *zola* ashes] ▸ **pod'zolic** *or* **pod'solic** *adj*

podzolization (ˌpɒdzɒlaɪ'zeɪʃən), **podsolization** (ˌpɒdsɒlaɪ'zeɪʃən) *or* **podzolisation, podsolisation** *n* the process by which the upper layer of a soil becomes acidic through the leaching of bases which are deposited in the lower horizons.

podzolize ('pɒdzɒˌlaɪz), **podsolize** ('pɒdsɒˌlaɪz) *or* **podzolise, podsolise** *vb* (*usually passive*) to make into or form a podzol.

Poe (pəu) *n* **Edgar Allan.** 1809–49, U.S. short-story writer, poet, and critic. Most of his short stories, such as *The Fall of the House of Usher* (1839) and the *Tales of the Grotesque and Arabesque* (1840), are about death, decay, and madness. *The Murders in the Rue Morgue* (1841) is regarded as the first modern detective story.

POE *abbrev. for:* **1** *Military.* port of embarkation. **2** port of entry.

poem ('pəuɪm) *n* **1** a composition in verse, usually characterized by concentrated and heightened language in which words are chosen for their sound and suggestive power as well as for their sense, and using such techniques as metre, rhyme, and alliteration. **2** a literary composition that is not in verse but exhibits the intensity of imagination and language common to it: *a prose poem.* **3** anything resembling a poem in beauty, effect, etc. [C16: from Latin *poēma,* from Greek, variant of *poiēma* something composed, created, from *poiein* to make]

poenology (piː'nɒlədʒɪ) *n* a variant spelling of **penology.**

poep (pup) *n S. African taboo.* **1** an emission of intestinal gas from the anus. **2** a mean or despicable person.

poesy ('pəuɪzɪ) *n, pl* **-sies. 1** an archaic word for **poetry. 2** *Poetic.* the art of writing poetry. **3** *Archaic or poetic.* a poem or verse, esp. one used as a motto. [C14: via Old French from Latin *poēsis,* from Greek, from *poiēsis* poetic art, creativity, from *poiein* to make]

poet ('pəuɪt) *or* (*sometimes when fem*) **poetess** *n* **1** a person who writes poetry. **2** a person with great imagination and creativity. [C13: from Latin *poēta,* from Greek *poiētēs* maker, poet, from *poiein* to make]

poet. *abbrev. for:* **1** poetic(al). **2** poetry.

poetaster (ˌpəuɪ'tæstə, -'teɪ-) *n* a writer of inferior verse. [C16: from Medieval Latin; see POET, -ASTER]

poetic (pəu'ɛtɪk) *or* **poetical** *adj* **1** of or relating to poetry. **2** characteristic of poetry, as in being elevated, sublime, etc. **3** characteristic of a poet. **4** recounted in verse. ▸ **po'etically** *adv*

poeticize (pəu'ɛtɪˌsaɪz), **poetize** ('pəuɪˌtaɪz) *or* **poeticise, poetise** *vb* **1** (*tr*) to put into poetry or make poetic. **2** (*intr*) to speak or write poetically.

poetic justice *n* fitting retribution; just deserts.

poetic licence *n* justifiable departure from conventional rules of form, fact, logic, etc., as in poetry.

poetics (pəʊ'ɛtɪks) *n* (*usually functioning as sing*) **1** the principles and forms of poetry or the study of these, esp. as a form of literary criticism. **2** a treatise on poetry.

poet laureate *n, pl* **poets laureate.** *Brit.* the poet appointed as court poet of Britain who is given a lifetime post as an officer of the Royal Household. The first was Ben Jonson in 1616.

poetry ('pəʊɪtrɪ) *n* **1** literature in metrical form; verse. **2** the art or craft of writing verse. **3** poetic qualities, spirit, or feeling in anything. **4** anything resembling poetry in rhythm, beauty, etc. [C14: from Medieval Latin *poētria,* from Latin *poēta* POET]

POEU (in Britain) *abbrev. for* Post Office Engineers Union.

po-faced *adj* (of a person) wearing a disapproving stern expression. [C20: possibly from PO + POKER-FACED]

pogey *or* **pogy** ('pəʊgɪ) *n, pl* **pogeys** *or* **pogies.** *Canadian slang.* **1** financial or other relief given to the unemployed by the government; dole. **2** unemployment insurance. **3a** the office distributing relief to the unemployed. **3b** (*as modifier*): *pogey clothes.* [C20: from earlier *pogie* workhouse, of unknown origin]

pogge (pɒg) *n* **1** Also called: **armed bullhead.** a European marine scorpaenoid fish, *Agonus cataphractus,* of northern European waters, with a large head, long thin tail, and body completely covered with bony plates: family *Agonidae.* **2** any other fish of the family *Agonidae.* [C18: of unknown origin]

pogo ('pəʊgəʊ) *vb* **pogos, pogoing, pogoed.** (*intr*) to jump up and down in one spot, as in a punk dance of the 1970s. [C20: from POGO STICK; from the motion] ▸ **'pogoer** *n*

pogonia (pə'gəʊnɪə) *n* any orchid of the chiefly American genus *Pogonia,* esp. the snakesmouth, having pink or white fragrant flowers. [C19: New Latin, from Greek *pōgōnias* bearded, from *pōgōn* a beard]

pogo stick *n* a stout pole with a handle at the top, steps for the feet and a spring at the bottom, so that the user can spring up, down, and along on it. [C20: of uncertain origin]

pogrom ('pɒgrəm) *n* an organized persecution or extermination of an ethnic group, esp. of Jews. [C20: via Yiddish from Russian: destruction, from *po-* like + *grom* thunder]

pogy ('pəʊgɪ, 'pɒgɪ) *n* **1** (*pl* **pogies** *or* **pogy**) another name for the **porgy.** **2** (*pl* **pogies**) a variant spelling of **pogey.** [C19: perhaps from Algonquian *pohegan* menhaden]

Pohai (ˌpəʊ'haɪ) *n* a variant transliteration of the Chinese name for **Bohai.**

pohutukawa (pəˌhuːtə'kɑːwə) *n* a myrtaceous New Zealand tree, *Metrosideros excelsa,* with red flowers and hard red wood. [from Maori]

poi[1] (pɔɪ, 'pəʊɪ) *n* a Hawaiian dish made of the root of the taro baked, pounded to a paste, and fermented. [C19: from Hawaiian]

poi[2] (pɔɪ) *n N.Z.* a ball of woven flax swung rhythmically in poi dances. [Maori]

poi dance *n N.Z.* a women's formation dance that involves singing and manipulating a poi.

-poiesis *n combining form.* indicating the act of making or producing something specified: *haematopoiesis.* [from Greek, from *poiēsis* a making; see POESY] ▸ **-poietic** *adj combining form.*

poignant ('pɔɪnjənt, -nənt) *adj* **1** sharply distressing or painful to the feelings. **2** to the point; cutting or piercing: *poignant wit.* **3** keen or pertinent in mental appeal: *a poignant subject.* **4** pungent in smell. [C14: from Old French, from Latin *pungens* pricking, from *pungere* to sting, pierce, grieve] ▸ **'poignancy** *or* **'poignance** *n* ▸ **'poignantly** *adv*

poikilocyte ('pɔɪkɪləʊˌsaɪt) *n* an abnormally shaped red blood cell. [C19: from Greek *poikilos* various + -CYTE]

poikilothermic (ˌpɔɪkɪləʊ'θɜːmɪk) *or* **poikilothermal** (ˌpɔɪkɪləʊ'θɜːməl) *adj* (of all animals except birds and mammals) having a body temperature that varies with the temperature of the surroundings. Compare **homoiothermic.** [C19: from Greek *poikilos* various + THERMAL] ▸ **ˌpoikilo'thermism** *or* **ˌpoikilo'thermy** *n*

poilu ('pwɑːluː; *French* pwaly) *n* an infantryman in the French Army, esp. one in the front lines in World War I. [C20: from French, literally: hairy (that is, virile), from *poil* hair, from Latin *pilus* a hair]

Poincaré (*French* pwɛ̃kare) *n* **1 Jules Henri** (ʒyl ɑ̃ri). 1854–1912, French mathematician, physicist, and philosopher. He made important contributions to the theory of functions and to astronomy and electromagnetic theory. **2** his cousin, **Raymond** (rɛmɔ̃). 1860–1934, French statesman; premier of France (1912–13; 1922–24; 1926–29); president (1913–20).

poinciana (ˌpɔɪnsɪ'ɑːnə) *n* **1** any tree of the tropical caesalpiniaceous genus *Poinciana,* having large orange or red flowers. **2** See **royal poinciana.** [C17: New Latin, named after M. de *Poinci,* 17th-century governor of the French Antilles]

poind (pɪnd) *vb* (*tr*) *Scots Law.* **1** to take (property of a debtor) in execution or by way of distress; distrain. **2** to impound (stray cattle, etc.). [C15: from Scots, variant of Old English *pyndan* to impound]

poinsettia (pɔɪn'setɪə) *n* a euphorbiaceous shrub, *Euphorbia* (or *Poinsettia*) *pulcherrima,* of Mexico and Central America, widely cultivated for its showy scarlet bracts, which resemble petals. [C19: New Latin, from the name of J. P. *Poinsett* (1799–1851), U.S. Minister to Mexico, who introduced it to the U.S.]

point (pɔɪnt) *n* **1** a dot or tiny mark. **2** a location, spot, or position. **3** any dot or mark used in writing or printing, such as a decimal point or a full stop. **4** short for **vowel point.** **5** the sharp tapered end of a pin, knife, etc. **6** a pin, needle, or other object having such a point. **7** *Maths.* **7a** a geometric element having no dimensions and whose position in space is located by means of its coordinates. **7b** a location: *point of inflection.* **8** a promontory, usually smaller than a cape. **9** a specific condition or degree. **10** a moment: *at that point he left the room.* **11** an important or fundamental reason, aim, etc.: *the point of this exercise is to train new teachers.* **12** an essential element or thesis in an argument: *you've made your point; I take your point.* **13** a suggestion or tip. **14** a detail or item. **15** an important or outstanding characteristic, physical attribute, etc.: *he has his good points.* **16** a distinctive characteristic or quality of an animal, esp. one used as a standard in judging livestock. **17** (*often pl*) any of the extremities, such as the tail, ears, or feet, of a domestic animal. **18** *Ballet.* (*often pl*) the tip of the toes. **19** a single unit for measuring or counting, as in the scoring of a game. **20** *Australian Rules football.* an informal name for **behind** (sense 11). **21** *Printing.* a unit of measurement equal to one twelfth of a pica, or approximately 0.01384 inch. There are approximately 72 points to the inch. **22** *Finance.* **22a** a unit of value used to quote security and commodity prices and their fluctuations. **22b** a percentage unit sometimes payable by a borrower as a premium on a loan. **23** *Navigation.* **23a** one of the 32 marks on the circumference of a compass card indicating direction. **23b** the angle of 11°15′ between two adjacent marks. **23c** a point on the horizon indicated by such a mark. **24** *Cricket.* **24a** a fielding position at right angles to the batsman on the off side and relatively near the pitch. **24b** a fielder in this position. **25** any of the numbers cast in the first throw in craps with which one neither wins nor loses by throwing them: 4, 5, 6, 8, 9, or 10. **26** either of the two electrical contacts that make or break the current flow in the distributor of an internal-combustion engine. **27** *Brit.* (*often pl*) a junction of railway tracks in which a pair of rails can be moved so that a train can be directed onto either of two lines. U.S. and Canadian equivalent: **switch.** **28** (*often pl*) a piece of ribbon, cord, etc., with metal tags at the end: used during the 16th and 17th centuries to fasten clothing. **29** *Backgammon.* a place or position on the board. **30** *Brit.* **30a** short for **power point.** **30b** an informal name for **socket** (sense 2). **31** an aggressive position adopted in bayonet or sword drill. **32** the position of the body of a pointer or setter when it discovers game. **33** *Boxing.* a mark awarded for a scoring blow, knockdown, etc. **34** any diacritic used in a writing system, esp. in a phonetic transcription, to indicate modifications of vowels or consonants. **35** *Jewellery.* a unit of weight equal to 0.01 carat. **36** the act of pointing. **37** *Ice hockey.* the position just inside the opponents' blue line. **38 beside the point.** not pertinent; irrelevant. **39 case in point.** a specific, appropriate, or relevant instance or example. **40 in point of.** in the matter of; regarding. **41 make a point of.** **41a** to make (something) one's regular habit. **41b** to do (something) because one thinks it important. **42 not to put too fine a point on it.** to speak plainly and bluntly. **43 on** (*or* **at**) **the point of.** at the moment immediately before a specified condition, action, etc., is expected to begin: *on the point of leaving the room.* **44 score points off.** to gain an advantage at someone else's expense. **45 stretch a point.** **45a** to make a concession or exception not usually made. **45b** to exaggerate. **46 to the point.** pertinent; relevant. **47 up to a point.** not completely. ◆ *vb* **48** (usually foll. by *at* or *to*) to indicate the location or direction of by or as by extending (a finger or other pointed object) towards it: *he pointed to the front door; don't point that gun at me.* **49** (*intr;* usually foll. by *at* or *to*) to indicate or identify a specific person or thing among several: *he pointed at the bottle he wanted; all evidence pointed to Donald as the murderer.* **50** (*tr*) to direct or cause to go or face in a specific direction or towards a place or goal: *point me in the right direction.* **51** (*tr*) to sharpen or taper. **52** (*intr*) (of gun dogs) to indicate the place where game is lying by standing rigidly with the muzzle turned in its direction. **53** (*tr*) to finish or repair the joints of (brickwork, masonry, etc.) with mortar or cement. **54** (*tr*) *Music.* to mark (a psalm text) with vertical lines to indicate the points at which the music changes during chanting. **55** to steer (a sailing vessel) close to the wind or (of a sailing vessel) to sail close to the wind. **56** (*tr*) *Phonetics.* to provide (a letter or letters) with diacritics. **57** (*tr*) to provide (a Hebrew or similar text) with vowel points. ◆ See also **point off, point out, point up.** [C13: from Old French: spot, from Latin *punctum* a point, from *pungere* to pierce; also influenced by Old French *pointe* pointed end, from Latin *pungere*]

point after *n American football.* a score given for a successful kick between the goalposts and above the crossbar, following a touchdown.

point-blank *adj* **1a** aimed or fired at a target so close that it is unnecessary to make allowance for the drop in the course of the projectile. **1b** permitting such aim or fire without loss of accuracy: *at point-blank range.* **2** plain or blunt: *a point-blank question.* ◆ *adv* **3** directly or straight. **4** plainly or bluntly. [C16: from POINT + BLANK (in the sense: centre spot of an archery target]

point d'appui *French.* (pwɛ̃ dapɥi) *n, pl* ***points d'appui*** (pwɛ̃ dapɥi). **1** a support or prop. **2** (formerly) the base or rallying point for a military unit.

point defect *n* an imperfection in a crystal, characterized by one unoccupied lattice position or one interstitial atom, molecule, or ion.

Point de Galle (pɔɪnt də 'gɑːlə) *n* a former name of **Galle.**

point-device *Obsolete.* ◆ *adj* **1** very correct or perfect; precise. ◆ *adv* **2** to perfection; perfectly; precisely. [C14: perhaps from old French *à point devis* to the point arranged]

point duty *n* **1** the stationing of a policeman or traffic warden at a road junction to control and direct traffic. **2** the position at the head of a military patrol, regarded as being the most dangerous.

pointe (pɔɪnt) *n Ballet.* the tip of the toe (esp. in the phrase **on pointes**). [from French: point]

Pointe-à-Pitre (*French* pwɛ̃tapitrə) *n* the chief port of Guadeloupe, on SW Grande Terre Island in the Caribbean. Pop.: 26 029 (1990).

pointed ('pɔɪntɪd) *adj* **1** having a point. **2** cutting or incisive: *a pointed wit.* **3** obviously directed at or intended for a particular person or aspect: *pointed criticism.* **4** emphasized or made conspicuous: *pointed ignorance.* **5** (of an arch or style of architecture employing such an arch) Gothic. **6** *Music.* (of a psalm text) marked to show changes in chanting. **7** (of Hebrew text) with vowel points marked. ▸ **'pointedly** *adv* ▸ **'pointedness** *n*

pointed arch *n* another name for **lancet arch.**

Pointe-Noire (*French* pwɛ̃tnwar) *n* a port in the S Congo Republic, on the Atlantic: the country's chief port and former capital (1950–58). Pop.: 576 206 (1995 est.).

pointer ('pɔɪntə) *n* **1** a person or thing that points. **2** an indicator on a measuring instrument. **3** a long rod or cane used by a lecturer to point to parts of a map, blackboard, etc. **4** one of a breed of large swift smooth-coated dogs, usually white with black, liver, or lemon markings: when on shooting expeditions it points to the bird with its nose, body, and tail in a straight line. **5** a helpful piece of information or advice.

Pointers ('pɔɪntəz) *pl n* **the.** the two brightest stars in the Plough, which lie in the direction pointing towards the Pole Star and are therefore used to locate it.

point estimate *n Statistics.* a specific value assigned to a parameter of a population on the basis of sampling statistics. Compare **interval estimate.**

point group *n Crystallog.* another term for **crystal class.**

pointillism ('pwæntɪˌlɪzəm, -tiːˌɪzəm, 'pɔɪn-) *n* the technique of painting elaborated from impressionism, in which dots of unmixed colour are juxtaposed on a white ground so that from a distance they fuse in the viewer's eye into appropriate intermediate tones. Also called: **divisionism.** [C19: from French, from *pointiller* to mark with tiny dots, from *pointille* little point, from Italian *puntiglio,* from *punto* POINT] ▸ **'pointillist** *n, adj*

pointing ('pɔɪntɪŋ) *n* **1** the act or process of repairing or finishing joints in brickwork, masonry, etc., with mortar. **2a** the insertion of marks to indicate the chanting of a psalm or the vowels in a Hebrew text. **2b** the sequence of marks so inserted.

point lace *n* lace made by a needle with buttonhole stitch on a paper pattern. Also called: **needlepoint.** Compare **pillow lace.**

pointless ('pɔɪntlɪs) *adj* **1** without a point. **2** without meaning, relevance, or force. **3** *Sport.* without a point scored. ▸ **'pointlessly** *adv* ▸ **'pointlessness** *n*

point man *n Chiefly U.S.* **1** *Military.* a soldier who walks at the front of an infantry patrol in combat. **2** the leader or spokesperson of a campaign or organization.

point off *vb (tr, adv)* to mark off from the right-hand side (a number of decimal places) in a whole number to create a mixed decimal: *point off three decimal places in 12345 and you get 12.345.*

point of honour *n, pl* **points of honour.** a circumstance, event, etc., that involves the defence of one's principles, social honour, etc.

point of inflection *n, pl* **points of inflection.** *Maths.* a stationary point on a curve at which the tangent is horizontal or vertical and where tangents on either side have the same sign.

point of no return *n* **1** a point at which an irreversible commitment must be made to an action, progression, etc. **2** a point in a journey at which, if one continues, supplies will be insufficient for a return to the starting place.

point of order *n, pl* **points of order.** a question raised in a meeting or deliberative assembly by a member as to whether the rules governing procedures are being breached.

point of sale *n* (in retail distribution) the place at which a sale is made. Abbrev.: **POS.**

point-of-sale terminal *n* (in retail distribution) a device used to record and process information relating to sales. Abbrev.: **POST.**

point of view *n, pl* **points of view. 1** a position from which someone or something is observed. **2** a mental viewpoint or attitude. **3** the mental position from which a story is observed or narrated: *the omniscient point of view.*

point out *vb (tr, adv)* to indicate or specify.

pointsman ('pɔɪntsˌmæn, -mən) *n, pl* **-men. 1** a person who operates railway points. U.S. and Canadian equivalent: **switchman. 2** a policeman or traffic warden on point duty.

point source *n Optics.* a source of light or other radiation that can be considered to have negligible dimensions.

points system *n Brit.* a system used to assess applicants' eligibility for local authority housing, based on (points awarded for) such factors as the length of time the applicant has lived in the area, how many children are in the family, etc.

point system *n* **1** *Printing.* a system of measurement using the **point** (see sense 21) as its unit. **2** a system for evaluation of achievement, as in education or industry, based on awarding points. **3** any system of writing or printing, such as Braille, that uses protruding dots.

point-to-point *n* **1** *Brit.* **1a** a steeplechase organized by a recognized hunt or other body, usually restricted to amateurs riding horses that have been regularly used in hunting. **1b** *(as modifier): a point-to-point race.* ◆ *adj* **2** (of a route) from one place to the next. **3** (of a radiocommunication link) from one point to another, rather than broadcast.

point up *vb (tr, adv)* to emphasize, esp. by identifying: *he pointed up the difficulties we would encounter.*

pointy ('pɔɪntɪ) *adj* **pointier, pointiest.** having a sharp point or points; pointed.

poise[1] (pɔɪz) *n* **1** composure or dignity of manner. **2** physical balance or assurance in movement or bearing. **3** the state of being balanced or stable; equilibrium; stability. **4** the position of hovering. **5** suspense or indecision. ◆ *vb* **6** to be or cause to be balanced or suspended. **7** *(tr)* to hold, as in readiness: *to poise a lance.* **8** *(tr)* a rare word for **weigh**[1]. [C16: from Old French *pois* weight, from Latin *pēnsum,* from *pendere* to weigh]

poise[2] (pwɑːz, pɔɪz) *n* the cgs unit of viscosity; the viscosity of a fluid in which a tangential force of 1 dyne per square centimetre maintains a difference in velocity of 1 centimetre per second between two parallel planes 1 centimetre apart. It is equivalent to 0.1 newton second per square metre. Symbol: P [C20: named after Jean Louis Marie *Poiseuille* (1799–1869), French physician]

poised (pɔɪzd) *adj* **1** self-possessed; dignified; exhibiting composure. **2** balanced and prepared for action: *a skier poised at the top of the slope.*

poison ('pɔɪzᵊn) *n* **1** any substance that can impair function, cause structural damage, or otherwise injure the body. Related adj: **toxic. 2** something that destroys, corrupts, etc.: *the poison of fascism.* **3** a substance that retards a chemical reaction or destroys or inhibits the activity of a catalyst. **4** a substance that absorbs neutrons in a nuclear reactor and thus slows down the reaction. It may be added deliberately or formed during fission. **5 what's your poison?** *Informal.* what would you like to drink? ◆ *vb (tr)* **6** to give poison to (a person or animal) esp. with intent to kill. **7** to add poison to. **8** to taint or infect with or as if with poison. **9** (foll. by *against*) to turn (a person's mind) against: *he poisoned her mind against me.* **10** to retard or stop (a chemical or nuclear reaction) by the action of a poison. **11** to inhibit or destroy (the activity of a catalyst) by the action of a poison. [C13: from Old French *puison* potion, from Latin *pōtiō* a drink, esp. a poisonous one, from *pōtāre* to drink] ▸ **'poisoner** *n*

poison dogwood *or* **elder** *n* other names for **poison sumach.**

poison gas *n* a gaseous substance, such as chlorine, phosgene, or lewisite, used in warfare to kill or harm.

poison hemlock *n* the U.S. name for **hemlock** (sense 1).

poison ivy *n* any of several North American anacardiaceous shrubs or vines of the genus *Rhus* (or *Toxicodendron*), esp. *R. radicans,* which has small green flowers and whitish berries that cause an itching rash on contact. See also **sumach** (sense 1).

poison oak *n* **1** either of two North American anacardiaceous shrubs, *Rhus toxicodendron* or *R. diversiloba,* that are related to the poison ivy and cause a similar rash. See also **sumach** (sense 1). **2** *(not in technical use)* another name for **poison ivy.**

poisonous ('pɔɪzənəs) *adj* **1** having the effects or qualities of a poison. **2** capable of killing or inflicting injury; venomous. **3** corruptive or malicious. ▸ **'poisonously** *adv* ▸ **'poisonousness** *n*

poison-pen letter *n* a letter written in malice, usually anonymously, and intended to abuse, frighten, or insult the recipient.

poison pill *n Finance.* a tactic used by a company fearing an unwelcome takeover bid, in which the value of the company is automatically reduced, as by the sale of an issue of shares having an option unfavourable to the bidders, if the bid is successful.

poison sumach *n* an anacardiaceous swamp shrub, *Rhus* (or *Toxicodendron*) *vernix* of the southeastern U.S., that has greenish-white berries and causes an itching rash on contact with the skin. Also called: **poison dogwood, poison elder.** See also **sumach.**

Poisson (*French* pwasɔ̃) *n* **Siméon Denis** (simeɔ̃ dəni). 1781–1840, French mathematician, noted for his application of mathematical theory to physics, esp. electricity and magnetism.

Poisson distribution ('pwɑːsᵊn) *n Statistics.* a distribution that represents the number of events occurring randomly in a fixed time at an average rate λ; symbol: $P_0(\lambda)$. For large n and small p with $np = \lambda$ it approximates to the binomial distribution $Bi(n,p)$. [C19: named after S. D. POISSON]

Poisson's ratio *n* a measure of the elastic properties of a material expressed as the ratio of the fractional contraction in breadth to the fractional increase in length when the material is stretched. Symbol: μ or ν

Poitiers (*French* pwatje) *n* a city in S central France: capital of the former province of Poitou until 1790; scene of the battle (1356) in which the English under the Black Prince defeated the French; university (1432). Pop.: 78 894 (1990).

poitín ('pɒtiːn) *n* the Irish Gaelic spelling of **poteen.**

Poitou (*French* pwatu) *n* a former province of W central France, on the Atlantic. Chief town: Poitiers.

Poitou-Charentes (*French* pwatuʃarɑ̃t) *n* a region of W central France, on the Bay of Biscay: mainly low-lying.

poke[1] (pəʊk) *vb* **1** *(tr)* to jab or prod, as with the elbow, the finger, a stick, etc. **2** *(tr)* to make (a hole, opening, etc.) by or as by poking. **3** (when *intr,* often foll. by *at*) to thrust (at). **4** *(tr) Informal.* to hit with the fist; punch. **5** (usually foll. by *in, out, out of, through,* etc.) to protrude or cause to protrude: *don't poke your arm out of the window.* **6** *(tr)* to stir (a fire, pot, etc.) by poking. **7** *(intr)* to meddle or intrude. **8** *(intr;* often foll. by *about* or *around)* to search or pry. **9** *(intr;* often foll. by *along)* to loiter, potter, dawdle, etc. **10** *(tr) Taboo slang.* (of a man) to have sexual intercourse with. **11 poke fun at.** to mock or ridicule. **12 poke one's nose into.** See **nose** (sense 17). ◆ *n* **13** a jab or prod. **14** short for **slowpoke. 15** *Informal.* a blow with one's fist; punch. **16** *Taboo slang.* sexual intercourse. [C14: from Low German and Middle Dutch *poken* to thrust, prod, strike]

poke[2] (pəʊk) *n* **1** *Dialect.* a pocket or bag. **2 a pig in a poke.** See **pig** (sense 9). [C13: from Old Northern French *poque,* of Germanic origin; related to Old English *pocca* bag, Old Norse *poki* POUCH, Middle Dutch *poke* bag; compare POACH[2]]

poke[3] (pəʊk) *n* **1** Also called: **poke bonnet.** a woman's bonnet with a brim that projects at the front, popular in the 18th and 19th centuries. **2** the brim itself. [C18: from POKE[1] (in the sense: to thrust out, project)]

poke[4] (pəʊk) *n* short for **pokeweed.**

pokeberry ('pəʊkbərɪ) *n, pl* **-berries. 1** Also called: **inkberry.** the berry of the pokeweed. **2** another name for the **pokeweed.**

pokelogan ('pəʊkˌləʊgən) *n Canadian.* another name for **bogan.** [C19: from Ojibwa *pokenogun*]

poker[1] ('pəʊkə) *n* **1** a metal rod, usually with a handle, for stirring a fire. **2** a person or thing that pokes.

poker[2] ('pəʊkə) *n* a card game of bluff and skill in which bets are made on the hands dealt, the highest-ranking hand (containing the most valuable combinations of sequences and sets of cards) winning the pool. [C19: probably from French *poque* similar card game]

poker dice *n* **1** a dice marked on its six faces with the pictures of the playing cards from ace to nine. **2** a gambling game, based on poker hands, played with five such dice.

poker face *n Informal.* a face without expression, as that of a poker player attempting to conceal the value of his cards. ► **'poker-,faced** *adj*

poker machine *n Austral. and N.Z.* a fruit machine. Often shortened to **pokie.**

pokerwork ('pəukə,wɜːk) *n* **1** the art of decorating wood or leather by burning a design with a heated metal point; pyrography. **2** artefacts decorated in this way.

pokeweed ('pəuk,wiːd), **pokeberry,** *or* **pokeroot** *n* a tall North American plant, *Phytolacca americana,* that has small white flowers, juicy purple berries, and a poisonous purple root used medicinally: family *Phytolaccaceae.* Sometimes shortened to **poke.** Also called: **inkberry.** [C18 *poke,* shortened from Algonquian *puccoon* plant used in dyeing, from *pak* blood]

pokie *or* **pokey** ('pəukɪ) *n Austral. and N.Z. informal.* short for **poker machine.**

poky *or* **pokey** ('pəukɪ) *adj* **pokier, pokiest. 1** *Informal.* (esp. of rooms) small and cramped. **2** without speed or energy; slow. ◆ *n* **3 the.** *Chiefly U.S. and Canadian slang.* prison. [C19: from POKE[1] (in slang sense: to confine)] ► **'pokily** *adv* ► **'pokiness** *n*

POL *Military. abbrev. for* petroleum, oil, and lubricants.

pol. *abbrev. for:* **1** political. **2** politics.

Pol. *abbrev. for:* **1** Poland. **2** Polish.

Pola ('pɔːla) *n* the Italian name for **Pula.**

Polack ('pəulæk) *n Derogatory slang.* a Pole or a person of Polish descent. [C16: from Polish *Polak* Pole]

polacre (pəu'lɑːkə) *or* **polacca** (pəu'lækə) *n* a three-masted sailing vessel used in the Mediterranean. [C17: from either French *polacre* or Italian *polacca* Pole or Polish; origin unknown]

Poland ('pəulənd) *n* a republic in central Europe, on the Baltic: first united in the 10th century; dissolved after the third partition effected by Austria, Russia, and Prussia in 1795; re-established independence in 1918; invaded by Germany in 1939; ruled by a Communist government from 1947 to 1989, when a multi-party system was introduced. It consists chiefly of a low undulating plain in the north, rising to a low plateau in the south, with the Sudeten and Carpathian Mountains along the S border. Official language: Polish. Religion: Roman Catholic majority. Currency: zloty. Capital: Warsaw. Pop.: 38 665 000 (1998 est.). Area: 311 730 sq. km (120 359 sq. miles). Polish name: **Polska.**

Polanski (pə'lænskɪ) *n* **Roman.** born 1933, Polish film director with a taste for the macabre, as in *Repulsion* (1965) and *Rosemary's Baby* (1968): later films include *Tess* (1980) and *Death and the Maiden* (1995).

polar ('pəulə) *adj* **1** situated at or near, coming from, or relating to either of the earth's poles or the area inside the Arctic or Antarctic Circles: *polar regions.* **2** having or relating to a pole or poles. **3** pivotal or guiding in the manner of the Pole Star. **4** directly opposite, as in tendency or character. **5** *Chem.* **5a** (of a molecule or compound) being or having a molecule in which there is an uneven distribution of electrons and thus a permanent dipole moment: *water has polar molecules.* **5b** (of a crystal or substance) being or having a crystal that is bound by ionic bonds: *sodium chloride forms polar crystals.*

polar axis *n* the fixed line in a system of polar coordinates from which the polar angle, θ, is measured anticlockwise.

polar bear *n* a white carnivorous bear, *Thalarctos maritimus,* of coastal regions of the North Pole.

polar body *n Physiology.* a tiny cell containing little cytoplasm that is produced with the ovum during oogenesis when the oocyte undergoes meiosis.

polar circle *n* a term for either the **Arctic Circle** or **Antarctic Circle.**

polar coordinates *pl n* a pair of coordinates for locating a point in a plane by means of the length of a radius vector, *r,* which pivots about the origin to establish the angle, θ, that the position of the point makes with a fixed line. Usually written (*r,* θ). See also **Cartesian coordinates, spherical coordinates.**

polar distance *n* the angular distance of a star, planet, etc., from the celestial pole; the complement of the declination. Also called: **codeclination.**

polar equation *n* an equation in polar coordinates.

polar front *n Meteorol.* a front dividing cold polar air from warmer temperate or tropical air.

Polari (pə'lɑːrɪ) *or* **Parlyaree** (pɑː'ljɑːrɪ) *n* an English slang that is derived from the Lingua Franca of Mediterranean ports; brought to England by sailors from the 16th century onwards. A few words survive, esp. in male homosexual slang. [C19: from Italian *parlare* to speak]

polarimeter (,pəulə'rɪmɪtə) *n* **1** an instrument for measuring the amount of polarization of light. **2** an instrument for measuring the rotation of the plane of polarization of light as a result of its passage through a liquid or solution. See **optical activity.** ► **polarimetric** (,pəulərɪ'metrɪk) *adj* ► **,polar'imetry** *n*

Polaris (pə'lɑːrɪs) *n* **1** Also called: the **Pole Star,** the **North Star.** the brightest star in the constellation Ursa Minor, situated slightly less than 1° from the north celestial pole. It is a Cepheid variable, with a period of four days. Visual magnitude: 2.08–2.17; spectral type: F8. **2a** a type of U.S. two-stage intermediate-range ballistic missile, usually fired by a submerged submarine. **2b** (*as modifier*): *a Polaris submarine.* [shortened from Medieval Latin *stella polāris* polar star]

polariscope (pəu'lærɪ,skəup) *n* an instrument for detecting polarized light or for observing objects under polarized light, esp. for detecting strain in transparent materials. See **photoelasticity.**

polarity (pəu'lærɪtɪ) *n, pl* **-ties. 1** the condition of having poles. **2** the condition of a body or system in which it has opposing physical properties at different points, esp. magnetic poles or electric charge. **3** the particular state of a part of a body or system that has polarity: *an electrode with positive polarity.* **4** the state of having or expressing two directly opposite tendencies, opinions, etc.

polarization *or* **polarisation** (,pəulərai'zeɪʃən) *n* **1** the condition of having or giving polarity. **2** *Physics.* the process or phenomenon in which the waves of light or other electromagnetic radiation are restricted to certain directions of vibration.

polarize *or* **polarise** ('pəulə,raɪz) *vb* **1** to acquire or cause to acquire polarity. **2** to acquire or cause to acquire polarization: *to polarize light.* **3** to cause people to adopt extreme opposing positions: *to polarize opinion.* ► **'polar,izable** *or* **'polar,isable** *adj* ► **'polar,izer** *or* **'polar,iser** *n*

polar lights *pl n* the aurora borealis in the N hemisphere or the aurora australis in the S hemisphere.

polarography (,pəulə'rɒgrəfɪ) *n* a technique for analysing and studying ions in solution by using an electrolytic cell with a very small cathode and obtaining a graph (**polarogram**) of the current against the potential to determine the concentration and nature of the ions. Because the cathode is small, polarization occurs and each type of anion is discharged at a different potential. The apparatus (**polarograph**) usually employs a dropping-mercury cathode. ► **polarographic** (,pəulərə'græfɪk) *adj*

Polaroid ('pəulə,rɔɪd) *Trademark.* ◆ *n* **1** a type of plastic sheet that can polarize a transmitted beam of normal light because it is composed of long parallel molecules. It only transmits plane-polarized light if these molecules are parallel to the plane of polarization and, since reflected light is partly polarized, it is often used in sunglasses to eliminate glare. **2 Polaroid Land Camera.** any of several types of camera yielding a finished print by means of a special developing and processing technique that occurs inside the camera and takes only a few seconds to complete. **3** (*pl*) sunglasses with lenses made from Polaroid plastic. ◆ *adj* **4** of, relating to, using, or used in a Polaroid Land Camera: *Polaroid film.*

polar sequence *n Astronomy.* a series of stars in the vicinity of the N celestial pole whose accurately determined magnitudes serve as the standard for visual and photographic magnitudes of stars.

polar wandering *n Geology.* the movement of the earth's magnetic poles with respect to the geographic poles.

polder ('pəuldə, 'pɒl-) *n* a stretch of land reclaimed from the sea or a lake, esp. in the Netherlands. [C17: from Middle Dutch *polre*]

pole[1] (pəul) *n* **1** a long slender usually round piece of wood, metal, or other material. **2** the piece of timber on each side of which a pair of carriage horses are hitched. **3** another name for **rod** (sense 7). **4** *Horse racing, chiefly U.S. and Canadian.* **4a** the inside lane of a racecourse. **4b** (*as modifier*): *the pole position.* **4c** one of a number of markers placed at intervals of one sixteenth of a mile along the side of a racecourse. **5** *Nautical.* **5a** any light spar. **5b** the part of a mast between the head and the attachment of the uppermost shrouds. **6 under bare poles.** *Nautical.* (of a sailing vessel) with no sails set. **7 up the pole.** *Brit., Austral., and N.Z. informal.* **7a** slightly mad. **7b** mistaken; on the wrong track. ◆ *vb* **8** (*tr*) to strike or push with a pole. **9** (*tr*) **9a** to set out (an area of land or garden) with poles. **9b** to support (a crop, such as hops or beans) on poles. **10** (*tr*) to deoxidize (a molten metal, esp. copper) by stirring it with green wood. **11** to punt (a boat). [Old English *pāl,* from Latin *pālus* a stake, prop; see PALE[2]]

pole[2] (pəul) *n* **1** either of the two antipodal points where the earth's axis of rotation meets the earth's surface. See also **North Pole, South Pole. 2** *Astronomy.* short for **celestial pole. 3** *Physics.* **3a** either of the two regions at the extremities of a magnet to which the lines of force converge or from which they diverge. **3b** either of two points or regions in a piece of material, system, etc., at which there are opposite electric charges, as at the two terminals of a battery. **4** *Maths.* an isolated singularity of an analytical function. **5** *Biology.* **5a** either end of the axis of a cell, spore, ovum, or similar body. **5b** either end of the spindle formed during the metaphase of mitosis and meiosis. **6** *Physiol.* the point on a neuron from which the axon or dendrites project from the cell body. **7** either of two mutually exclusive or opposite actions, opinions, etc. **8** *Geom.* the origin in a system of polar or spherical coordinates. **9** any fixed point of reference. **10 poles apart** (*or* **asunder**). having widely divergent opinions, tastes, etc. **11 from pole to pole.** throughout the entire world. [C14: from Latin *polus* end of an axis, from Greek *polos* pivot, axis, pole; related to Greek *kuklos* circle]

Pole[1] (pəul) *n* a native, inhabitant, or citizen of Poland or a speaker of Polish.

Pole[2] (pəul) *n* **Reginald.** 1500–58, English cardinal; last Roman Catholic archbishop of Canterbury (1556–58).

poleaxe *or U.S.* **poleax** ('pəul,æks) *n* **1** another term for **battle-axe** (sense 1). **2** a former naval weapon with an axe blade on one side of the handle and a spike on the other. **3** an axe used by butchers to slaughter animals. ◆ *vb* **4** (*tr*) to hit or fell with or as if with a poleaxe. [C14 *pollax* battle-axe, from POLL + AXE]

polecat ('pəul,kæt) *n, pl* **-cats** *or* **-cat. 1** Also called (formerly): **foumart.** a dark brown musteline mammal, *Mustela putorius,* of woodlands of Europe, Asia, and N Africa, that is closely related to but larger than the weasel and gives off an unpleasant smell. See also **sweet marten. 2** any of various related animals, such as the **marbled polecat,** *Vormela peregusna.* **3** *U.S.* a nontechnical name for **skunk** (sense 1). [C14 *polcat,* perhaps from Old French *pol* cock, from Latin *pullus,* + CAT[1]; from its habit of preying on poultry]

pole horse *n* a horse harnessed alongside the shaft (pole) of a vehicle. Also called: **poler.**

pole house *n N.Z.* a timber house built on a steep section and supported by heavy debarked logs in long piles.

poleis ('pɒlaɪs) *n* the plural of **polis**[1].

polemarch ('pɒlɪ,mɑːk) *n* (in ancient Greece) a civilian official, originally a supreme general. [C16: from Greek *polemarchos,* from *polemos* war + *archos* ruler]

polemic (pə'lemɪk) *adj also* **po'lemical. 1** of or involving dispute or controversy. ◆ *n* **2** an argument or controversy, esp. over a doctrine, belief, etc. **3** a person engaged in such an argument or controversy. **[**C17: from Medieval Latin *polemicus,* from Greek *polemikos* relating to war, from *polemos* war**]** ► **po'lemically** *adv* ► **polemicist** (pə'lɛmɪsɪst) *or* **polemist** ('pɒlɪmɪst) *n*

polemics (pə'lɛmɪks) *n* (*functioning as sing*) the art or practice of dispute or argument, as in attacking or defending a doctrine or belief.

polemoniaceous (ˌpɒlɪˌməʊnɪ'eɪʃəs) *adj* of, relating to, or belonging to the *Polemoniaceae,* a chiefly North American family of plants that includes phlox and Jacob's ladder. **[**C19: from New Latin *Polemōnium* type genus, from Greek *polemōnion* a plant, perhaps valerian**]**

polenta (pəʊ'lɛntə) *n* a thick porridge made in Italy, usually from maize. **[**C16: via Italian from Latin: pearl barley, perhaps from Greek *palē* pollen**]**

pole piece *n Electrical engineering.* a piece of ferromagnetic material forming an extension of the magnetic circuit in an electric motor, etc., used to concentrate the magnetic field where it will be most effective.

pole position *n* **1** (in motor racing) the starting position on the inside of the front row, generally considered the best one. **2** an advantageous starting position.

poler ('pəʊlə) *n* **1** another name for **pole horse. 2** a person or thing that poles, esp. a punter.

pole star *n* a guiding principle, rule, standard, etc.

Pole Star *n* **the.** the star closest to the N celestial pole at any particular time. At present this is Polaris, but it will eventually be replaced by some other star owing to precession of the earth's axis.

pole vault *n* **1 the.** a field event in which competitors attempt to clear a high bar with the aid of an extremely flexible long pole. **2** a single attempt in the pole vault. ◆ *vb* **pole-vault. 3** (*intr*) to perform a pole vault or compete in the pole vault. ► **'pole-ˌvaulter** *n*

poley ('pəʊlɪ) *adj Austral.* (of cattle) hornless or polled.

poleyn ('pəʊleɪn) *n* a piece of armour for protecting the knee. Also called: **knee-cap.** **[**from Old French *polain***]**

police (pə'liːs) *n* **1a** (often preceded by *the*) the organized civil force of a state, concerned with maintenance of law and order, the detection and prevention of crime, etc. **1b** (*as modifier*): *a police inquiry.* **2** (*functioning as pl*) the members of such a force collectively. **3** any organized body with a similar function: *security police.* **4** *Archaic.* **4a** the regulation and control of a community, esp. in regard to the enforcement of law, the prevention of crime, etc. **4b** the department of government concerned with this. ◆ *vb* (*tr*) **5** to regulate, control, or keep in order by means of a police or similar force. **6** to observe or record the activity or enforcement of: *a committee was set up to police the new agreement on picketing.* **7** *U.S.* to make or keep (a military camp, etc.) clean and orderly. **[**C16: via French from Latin *polītīa* administration, government; see POLITY**]**

police court *n* **1** another name for **magistrates' court. 2** (in Scotland, formerly) a burgh court with limited jurisdiction, presided over by lay magistrates or a stipendiary magistrate: replaced in 1975 by the **district court.**

police dog *n* a dog, often an Alsatian, trained to help the police, as in tracking.

policeman (pə'liːsmən) *or* (*fem*) **policewoman** *n, pl* **-men** *or* **-women.** a member of a police force, esp. one holding the rank of constable.

policeman's helmet *n* a Himalayan balsaminaceous plant, *Impatiens glandulifera,* with large purplish-pink flowers, introduced into Britain.

Police Motu *n* a pidginized version of the Motu language, used as a lingua franca in Papua, originally chiefly by the police. Also called: **Hiri Motu.**

police officer *n* a member of a police force, esp. a constable; policeman. Often shortened to (esp. as form of address): **officer.**

police procedural *n* a novel, film, or television drama that deals realistically with police work.

police state *n* a state or country in which a repressive government maintains control through the police.

police station *n* the office or headquarters of the police force of a district.

police wagon *n U.S.* another term for **patrol wagon.**

policy[1] ('pɒlɪsɪ) *n, pl* **-cies. 1** a plan of action adopted or pursued by an individual, government, party, business, etc. **2** wisdom, prudence, shrewdness, or sagacity. **3** *Scot.* (*often pl*) the improved grounds surrounding a country house. **[**C14: from Old French *policie,* from Latin *polītīa* administration, POLITY**]**

policy[2] ('pɒlɪsɪ) *n, pl* **-cies.** a document containing a contract of insurance. **[**C16: from Old French *police* certificate, from Old Italian *polizza,* from Latin *apodixis* proof, from Greek *apodeixis* demonstration, proof**]**

policyholder ('pɒlɪsɪˌhəʊldə) *n* a person or organization in whose name an insurance policy is registered.

policy science *n* a branch of the social sciences concerned with the formulation and implementation of policy in bureaucracies, etc.

Polignac (*French* pɔliɲak) *n* **Prince de,** title of *Auguste Jules Armand Marie de Polignac.* 1780–1847, French statesman; prime minister (1829–30) to Charles X: his extreme royalist and ultramontane policies provoked the 1830 revolution.

polio ('pəʊlɪəʊ) *n* short for **poliomyelitis.**

poliomyelitis (ˌpəʊlɪəʊˌmaɪə'laɪtɪs) *n* an acute infectious viral disease, esp. affecting children. In its paralytic form (**acute anterior poliomyelitis**) the brain and spinal cord are involved, causing weakness, paralysis, and wasting of muscle. Often shortened to **polio.** Also called: **infantile paralysis.** **[**C19: New Latin, from Greek *polios* grey + *muelos* marrow**]**

polis[1] ('pɒlɪs) *n, pl* **poleis** ('pɒlaɪs). an ancient Greek city-state. **[**from Greek: city**]**

polis[2] ('pɒlɪs) *n Scot. and Irish.* the police or a police officer. **[**C19: a variant pronunciation of *police***]**

polish ('pɒlɪʃ) *vb* **1** to make or become smooth and shiny by rubbing, esp. with wax or an abrasive. **2** (*tr*) to make perfect or complete. **3** to make or become elegant or refined. ◆ *n* **4** a finish or gloss. **5** the act of polishing or the condition of having been polished. **6** a substance used to produce a smooth and shiny, often protective surface. **7** elegance or refinement, esp. in style, manner, etc. ◆ See also **polish off, polish up.** **[**C13 *polis,* from Old French *polir,* from Latin *polīre* to polish**]** ► **'polishable** *adj* ► **'polisher** *n*

Polish ('pəʊlɪʃ) *adj* **1** of, relating to, or characteristic of Poland, its people, or their language. ◆ *n* **2** the official language of Poland, belonging to the West Slavonic branch of the Indo-European family.

Polish Corridor *n* the strip of land through E Pomerania providing Poland with access to the sea (1919–39), given to her in 1919 in the Treaty of Versailles, and separating East Prussia from the rest of Germany. It is now part of Poland.

polished ('pɒlɪʃt) *adj* **1** accomplished: *a polished actor.* **2** impeccably or professionally done: *a polished performance.* **3** (of rice) having had the outer husk removed by milling.

Polish notation *n* a logical notation that dispenses with the need for brackets by writing the logical constants as operators preceding their arguments.

polish off *vb* (*tr, adv*) *Informal.* **1** to finish or process completely. **2** to dispose of or kill; eliminate.

polish up *vb* (*adv*) **1** to make or become smooth and shiny by polishing. **2** (when *intr,* foll. by *on*) to study or practise until adept at; improve: *polish up your spelling; he's polishing up on his German.*

polit. *abbrev. for:* **1** political. **2** politics.

Politburo ('pɒlɪtˌbjʊərəʊ) *n* **1** the executive and policy-making committee of a Communist Party. **2** the supreme policy-making authority in most Communist countries. **[**C20: from Russian: contraction of *Politicheskoe Buro* political bureau**]**

polite (pə'laɪt) *adj* **1** showing regard for others, in manners, speech, behaviour, etc.; courteous. **2** cultivated or refined: *polite society.* **3** elegant or polished: *polite letters.* **[**C15: from Latin *polītus* polished; see POLISH**]** ► **po'litely** *adv* ► **po'liteness** *n*

politesse (ˌpɒlɪ'tɛs) *n* formal or genteel politeness. **[**C18: via French from Italian *politezza,* ultimately from Latin *polīre* to POLISH**]**

Politian (pəʊ'lɪʃən, pɒ-) *n* Italian name *Angelo Polliziano;* original name *Angelo Ambrogini.* 1454–94, Florentine humanist and poet.

politic ('pɒlɪtɪk) *adj* **1** artful or shrewd; ingenious: *a politic manager.* **2** crafty or unscrupulous; cunning: *a politic old scoundrel.* **3** sagacious, wise, or prudent, esp. in statesmanship: *a politic choice.* **4** an archaic word for **political.** ◆ See also **body politic, politics.** **[**C15: from Old French *politique,* from Latin *polīticus* concerning civil administration, from Greek *politikos,* from *politēs* citizen, from *polis* city**]** ► **'politicly** *adv*

political (pə'lɪtɪkᵊl) *adj* **1** of or relating to the state, government, the body politic, public administration, policy-making, etc. **2a** of, involved in, or relating to government policy-making as distinguished from administration or law. **2b** of or relating to the civil aspects of government as distinguished from the military. **3** of, dealing with, or relating to politics: *a political person.* **4** of, characteristic of, or relating to the parties and the partisan aspects of politics. **5** organized or ordered with respect to government: *a political unit.* ► **po'litically** *adv*

political economy *n* the former name for **economics** (sense 1).

politically correct *adj* demonstrating progressive ideals, esp. by avoiding vocabulary that is considered offensive, discriminatory, or judgmental, esp. concerning race and gender. Abbrev.: **PC.** ► **political correctness** *n*

political prisoner *n* someone imprisoned for holding, expressing, or acting in accord with particular political beliefs.

political science *n* (esp. as an academic subject) the study of the state, government, and politics: one of the social sciences. ► **political scientist** *n*

politician (ˌpɒlɪ'tɪʃən) *n* **1** a person actively engaged in politics, esp. a full-time professional member of a deliberative assembly. **2** a person who is experienced or skilled in the art or science of politics, government, or administration; statesman. **3** *Disparaging, chiefly U.S.* a person who engages in politics out of a wish for personal gain, as realized by holding a public office.

politicize *or* **politicise** (pə'lɪtɪˌsaɪz) *vb* **1** (*tr*) to render political in tone, interest, or awareness. **2** (*intr*) to participate in political discussion or activity. ► **poˌliticiˈzation** *or* **poˌliticiˈsation** *n*

politicking ('pɒlɪˌtɪkɪŋ) *n* political activity, esp. seeking votes.

politico (pə'lɪtɪˌkəʊ) *n, pl* **-cos.** an informal word for a **politician** (senses 1, 3). **[**C17: from Italian or Spanish**]**

politico- *combining form.* denoting political or politics: *politicoeconomic.*

politics ('pɒlɪtɪks) *n* **1** (*functioning as sing*) the practice or study of the art and science of forming, directing, and administrating states and other political units; the art and science of government; political science. **2** (*functioning as sing*) the complex or aggregate of relationships of people in society, esp. those relationships involving authority or power. **3** (*functioning as pl*) political activities or affairs: *party politics.* **4** (*functioning as sing*) the business or profession of politics. **5** (*functioning as sing or pl*) any activity concerned with the acquisition of power, gaining one's own ends, etc.: *company politics are frequently vicious.* **6** (*functioning as pl*) opinions, principles, sympathies, etc., with respect to politics: *his conservative politics.* **7** (*functioning as pl*) **7a** the policy-formulating aspects of government as distinguished from the administrative, or legal. **7b** the civil functions of government as distinguished from the military.

polity ('pɒlɪtɪ) *n, pl* **-ties. 1** a form of government or organization of a state, church, society, etc.; constitution. **2** a politically organized society, state, city, etc. **3** the management of public or civil affairs. **4** political organization. **[**C16: from Latin *polītīa,* from Greek *politeia* citizenship, civil administration, from *politēs* citizen, from *polis* city**]**

polje ('pəʊljɛ) *n Geography.* a large elliptical depression in karst regions, sometimes containing a marsh or small lake. **[**Serbo-Croat, literally: field; related to FLOOR**]**

Polk (pəuk) *n* **James Knox.** 1795–1849, U.S. statesman; 11th president of the U.S. (1845–49). During his administration, Texas and territory now included in New Mexico, Colorado, Utah, Nevada, Arizona, Oregon, and California were added to the Union.

polka ('pɒlkə) *n, pl* **-kas. 1** a 19th-century Bohemian dance with three steps and a hop, in fast duple time. **2** a piece of music composed for or in the rhythm of this dance. ◆ *vb* **-kas, -kaing, -kaed. 3** (*intr*) to dance a polka. [C19: via French from Czech *pulka* half-step, from *pul* half]

polka dot *n* **1** one of a pattern of small circular regularly spaced spots on a fabric. **2a** a fabric or pattern with such spots. **2b** (*as modifier*): *a polka-dot dress.* [C19: of uncertain origin]

poll (pəul) *n* **1** the casting, recording, or counting of votes in an election; a voting. **2** the result or quantity of such a voting: *a heavy poll.* **3** Also called: **opinion poll. 3a** a canvassing of a representative sample of a large group of people on some question in order to determine the general opinion of the group. **3b** the results or record of such a canvassing. **4** any counting or enumeration: *a poll of the number of men with long hair.* **5** short for **poll tax. 6** a list or enumeration of people, esp. for taxation or voting purposes. **7** the striking face of a hammer. **8** the occipital or back part of the head of an animal. ◆ *vb* (*mainly tr*) **9** to receive (a vote or quantity of votes): *he polled 10 000 votes.* **10** to receive, take, or record the votes of: *he polled the whole town.* **11** to canvass (a person, group, area, etc.) as part of a survey of opinion. **12** *Chiefly U.S.* to take the vote, verdict, opinion, etc., individually of each member (of a jury, conference, etc.). **13** (*sometimes intr*) to cast (a vote) in an election. **14** *Computing.* (in data transmission when several terminals share communications channels) to check each channel rapidly to establish which are free, or to call for data from each terminal in turn. **15** to clip or shear. **16** to remove or cut short the horns of (cattle). [C13 (in the sense: a human head) and C17 (in the modern sense: a counting of heads, votes): from Middle Low German *polle* hair of the head, head, top of a tree; compare Swedish *pull* crown of the head]

pollack *or* **pollock** ('pɒlək) *n, pl* **-lacks, -lack** *or* **-locks, -lock.** a gadoid food fish, *Pollachius pollachius,* that has a dark green back and a projecting lower jaw and occurs in northern seas, esp. the North Atlantic Ocean. [C17: from earlier Scottish *podlok,* of obscure origin]

Pollack ('pɒlək) *n* **Sydney.** born 1934, U.S. film director. His films include *Tootsie* (1982), *Out of Africa* (1986), and *The Firm* (1993).

Pollaiuolo (*Italian* pollaj'wɔ:lo) *n* **1 Antonio** (an'tɔ:njo), ?1432–98, Florentine painter, sculptor, goldsmith, and engraver: his paintings include the *Martyrdom of St Sebastian.* **2** his brother **Piero** ('pjɛ:ro). ?1443–96, Florentine painter and sculptor.

pollan ('pɒlən) *n* any of several varieties of the whitefish *Coregonus pollan* that occur in lakes in Northern Ireland. [C18: probably from Irish *poll* lake]

pollard ('pɒləd) *n* **1** an animal, such as a sheep or deer, that has either shed its horns or antlers or has had them removed. **2** a tree that has had its top cut off to encourage the formation of a crown of branches. ◆ *vb* **3** (*tr*) to convert into a pollard; poll. [C16: hornless animal; see POLL]

polled (pəuld) *adj* **1** (of animals, esp. cattle) having the horns cut off or being naturally hornless. **2** *Archaic.* shorn of hair; bald.

pollen ('pɒlən) *n* a fine powdery substance produced by the anthers of seed-bearing plants, consisting of numerous fine grains containing the male gametes. [C16: from Latin: powder; compare Greek *palē* pollen] ▸ **pollinic** (pə'lɪnɪk) *adj*

Pollen ('pɒlən) *n* **Daniel.** 1813–96, New Zealand statesman, born in Ireland: prime minister of New Zealand (1876).

pollen analysis *n* another name for **palynology.**

pollen basket *n* the part of the hind leg of a bee that is specialized for carrying pollen, typically consisting of a trough bordered by long hairs. Technical name: **corbicula.**

pollen count *n* a measure of the pollen present in the air over a 24-hour period, often published to enable sufferers from hay fever to predict the severity of their attacks.

pollen tube *n* a hollow tubular outgrowth that develops from a pollen grain after pollination, grows down the style to the ovule, and conveys male gametes to the egg cell.

pollex ('pɒlɛks) *n, pl* **-lices** (-lɪ,si:z). the first digit of the forelimb of amphibians, reptiles, birds, and mammals, such as the thumb of man and other primates. [C19: from Latin: thumb, big toe] ▸ **pollical** ('pɒlɪkᵊl) *adj*

pollinate ('pɒlɪ,neɪt) *vb* (*tr*) to transfer pollen from the anthers to the stigma of (a flower). ▸ **,polli'nation** *n* ▸ **'polli,nator** *n*

polling ('pəulɪŋ) *n* **1a** the casting or registering of votes at an election. **1b** (*as modifier*): *polling day.* **2** the conducting of a public opinion poll. **3** *Computing.* the automatic interrogation of terminals by a central controlling machine to determine if they are ready to receive or transmit messages.

polling booth *n* a semienclosed space in which a voter stands to mark a ballot paper during an election.

polling station *n* a building, such as a school, designated as the place to which voters go during an election to cast their votes.

polliniferous *or* **polleniferous** (,pɒlɪ'nɪfərəs) *adj* **1** producing pollen: *polliniferous plants.* **2** specialized for carrying pollen: *the polliniferous legs of bees.*

pollinium (pə'lɪnɪəm) *n, pl* **-ia** (-ɪə). a mass of cohering pollen grains, produced by plants such as orchids and transported as a whole during pollination. [C19: New Latin; see POLLEN]

pollinosis *or* **pollenosis** (,pɒlɪ'nəusɪs) *n Pathol.* a technical name for **hay fever.**

polliwog *or* **pollywog** ('pɒlɪ,wɒg) *n* **1** *Brit. dialect, U.S., and Canadian.* another name for **tadpole. 2** *Informal.* a sailor who has not crossed the equator. Compare **shellback.** [C15 *polwygle;* see POLL, WIGGLE]

Pollock ('pɒlək) *n* **1** Sir **Frederick.** 1845–1937, English legal scholar: with Maitland, he wrote *History of English Law before the Time of Edward I* (1895). **2 Jackson.** 1912–56, U.S. abstract expressionist painter; chief exponent of action painting in the U.S.

pollster ('pəulstə) *n* a person who conducts opinion polls.

poll tax *n* **1** a tax levied per head of adult population. **2** an informal name for **community charge.**

pollucite ('pɒlju,saɪt, pə'lu:,saɪt) *n* a colourless rare mineral consisting of a hydrated caesium aluminium silicate, often containing some rubidium. It occurs in coarse granite, esp. in Manitoba, and is an important source of caesium. Formula: $CsAlSi_2O_6.\frac{1}{2}H_2O$. [C19: from Latin *polluc-,* stem of *Pollux* + -ITE[1]; originally called *pollux,* alluding to Castor and Pollux, since it was associated with another mineral called *castor* or *castorite*]

pollutant (pə'lu:tᵊnt) *n* a substance that pollutes, esp. a chemical or similar substance that is produced as a waste product of an industrial process.

pollute (pə'lu:t) *vb* (*tr*) **1** to contaminate, as with poisonous or harmful substances. **2** to make morally corrupt or impure; sully. **3** to desecrate or defile. [C14 *polute,* from Latin *polluere* to defile] ▸ **pol'luter** *n*

polluted (pə'lu:tɪd) *adj* **1** made unclean or impure; contaminated. **2** *U.S. slang.* intoxicated; drunk.

pollution (pə'lu:ʃən) *n* **1** the act of polluting or the state of being polluted. **2** harmful or poisonous substances introduced into an environment.

Pollux ('pɒləks) *n* **1** the brightest star in the constellation Gemini, lying close to the star **Castor.** Visual magnitude: 1.2; spectral type: K0; distance: 35 light years. **2** *Classical myth.* See **Castor and Pollux.**

Pollyanna (,pɒlɪ'ænə) *n* a person who is constantly or excessively optimistic. [C20: after the chief character in *Pollyanna* (1913), a novel by Eleanor Porter (1868–1920), U.S. writer]

polo ('pəuləu) *n* **1** a game similar to hockey played on horseback using long-handled mallets (**polo sticks**) and a wooden ball. **2** any of several similar games, such as one played on bicycles. **3** short for **water polo. 4** Also called: **polo neck. 4a** a collar on a garment, worn rolled over to fit closely round the neck. **4b** a garment, esp. a sweater, with such a collar. [C19: from Balti (dialect of Kashmir): ball, from Tibetan *pulu*]

Polo ('pəuləu) *n* **Marco** ('mɑ:kəu). 1254–1324, Venetian merchant, famous for his account of his travels in Asia. After travelling overland to China (1271–75), he spent 17 years serving Kublai Khan before returning to Venice by sea (1292–95).

polonaise (,pɒlə'neɪz) *n* **1** a ceremonial marchlike dance in three-four time from Poland. **2** a piece of music composed for or in the rhythm of this dance. **3** a woman's costume with a tight bodice and an overskirt drawn back to show a decorative underskirt. [C18: from French *danse polonaise* Polish dance]

polonium (pə'ləunɪəm) *n* a very rare radioactive element that occurs in trace amounts in uranium ores. The isotope **polonium-210** is produced artificially and is used as a lightweight power source in satellites and to eliminate static electricity in certain industries. Symbol: Po; atomic no.: 84; half-life of most stable isotope, ^{209}Po: 103 years; valency: –2, 0, 2, 4, or 6; relative density (alpha modification): 9.32; melting pt.: 254°C; boiling pt.: 962°C. [C19: New Latin, from Medieval Latin *Polōnia* Poland; named in honour of the Polish nationality of its discoverer, Marie Curie]

polony (pə'ləunɪ) *n, pl* **-nies.** *Brit.* another name for **bologna sausage.** [C16: perhaps from BOLOGNA[1]]

polo shirt *n* a knitted cotton short-sleeved shirt with a collar and three-button opening at the neck.

Pol Pot ('pɒl 'pɒt) *n* original name *Kompong Thom.* 1925–98, Cambodian Communist statesman; prime minister of Kampuchea (1976; 1977–79); his policies led to the deaths of thousands in labour camps before he was overthrown by Vietnamese forces; in 1997 his former supporters in the Khmer Rouge captured him and claimed to have tried and sentenced him to life imprisonment.

Polska ('pɔlska) *n* the Polish name for **Poland.**

Poltava (*Russian* pal'tavə) *n* a city in the E Ukraine: scene of the victory (1709) of the Russians under Peter the Great over the Swedes under Charles XII; centre of an agricultural region. Pop.: 321 000 (1996 est.).

poltergeist ('pɒltə,gaɪst) *n* a spirit believed to manifest its presence by rappings and other noises and also by acts of mischief, such as throwing furniture about. [C19: from German, from *poltern* to be noisy + *Geist* GHOST]

poltroon (pɒl'tru:n) *n* **1** an abject or contemptible coward. ◆ *adj* **2** a rare word for **cowardly.** [C16: from Old French *poultron,* from Old Italian *poltrone* lazy good-for-nothing, apparently from *poltrīre* to lie indolently in bed, from *poltro* bed]

poly ('pɒlɪ) *n, pl* **polys.** *Informal.* short for **polytechnic.**

poly- *combining form.* **1** more than one; many or much: *polyhedron.* **2** having an excessive or abnormal number or amount: *polycythaemia.* [from Greek *polus* much, many; related to Old English *fela* many]

polyadelphous (,pɒlɪə'dɛlfəs) *adj* **1** (of stamens) having united filaments so that they are arranged in three or more groups. **2** (of flowers) having polyadelphous stamens. [C19: from New Latin, from POLY- + *-adelphous* from Greek *adelphos* brother]

polyadic (,pɒlɪ'ædɪk) *adj Logic, maths.* (of a relation, operation, etc.) having several argument places, as ... *moves* ... *from* ... *to* ..., which might be represented as $Mpox_1y_1z_1t_1x_2y_2z_2t_2$ where *p* names a person, *o* an object, and each *t* a time, and each <*x,y,z*> the coordinates of a place. [C20: modelled on MONADIC]

polyamide (,pɒlɪ'æmaɪd, -mɪd) *n* any one of a class of synthetic polymeric materials containing recurring -CONH- groups. See also **nylon.**

polyandry ('pɒlɪ,ændrɪ) *n* **1** the practice or condition of being married to more than one husband at the same time. Compare **polygamy. 2** the practice in animals of a female mating with more than one male during one breeding season. **3** the condition in flowers of having a large indefinite number of stamens. ◆ Compare **polygyny.** [C18: from Greek *poluandria,* from POLY- + *-andria* from *anēr* man] ► ˌ**poly'androus** *adj*

polyanthus (ˌpɒlɪ'ænθəs) *n, pl* **-thuses. 1** any of several hybrid garden primroses, esp. *Primula polyantha,* which has brightly coloured flowers. **2 polyanthus narcissus.** a Eurasian amaryllidaceous plant, *Narcissus tazetta,* having clusters of small yellow or white fragrant flowers. [C18: New Latin, Greek: having many flowers]

polyarchy ('pɒlɪˌɑːkɪ) *n, pl* **-chies.** a political system in which power is dispersed. [C17: from POLY- + -ARCHY]

polyatomic (ˌpɒlɪə'tɒmɪk) *adj* (of a molecule) containing more than two atoms.

polybasic (ˌpɒlɪ'beɪsɪk) *adj* (of an acid) having two or more replaceable hydrogen atoms per molecule.

polybasite (ˌpɒlɪ'beɪsaɪt, pə'lɪbəˌsaɪt) *n* a grey to black mineral consisting of a sulphide of silver, antimony, and copper in the form of platelike monoclinic crystals. It occurs in veins of silver ore. Formula: $(Ag,Cu)_{16}Sb_2S_{11}$. [C19: from POLY- + BASE[1] + -ITE[1]]

Polybius (pəʊ'lɪbɪəs) *n* ?205–?123 B.C., Greek historian. Under the patronage of Scipio the Younger, he wrote in 40 books a history of Rome from 264 B.C. to 146 B.C.

polycarbonate (ˌpɒlɪ'kɑːbəˌneɪt, -nɪt) *n* any of a class of strong transparent thermoplastic resins used in moulding materials, laminates, etc.

polycarboxylate (ˌpɒlɪ'kɑːbɒkˌsɪleɪt) *n* a salt or ester of a polycarboxylic acid. Polycarboxylate esters are used in certain detergents.

polycarboxylic acid (ˌpɒlɪ'kɑːbɒkˌsɪlɪk) *n* a type of carboxylic acid containing two or more carboxyl groups.

Polycarp ('pɒlɪˌkɑːp) *n* **Saint.** ?69–?155 A.D., Christian martyr and bishop of Smyrna, noted for his letter to the church at Philippi. Feast day: Feb. 23.

polycarpellary (ˌpɒlɪkɑː'pelərɪ) *adj* (of a plant gynoecium) having or consisting of many carpels.

polycarpic (ˌpɒlɪ'kɑːpɪk) *or* **polycarpous** *adj* (of a plant) able to produce flowers and fruit several times in succession. ► **'polyˌcarpy** *n*

polycarpous (ˌpɒlɪ'kɑːpəs) *or* **polycarpic** *adj* (of a plant) having a gynoecium consisting of many distinct carpels.

polycentrism (ˌpɒlɪ'sentrɪzəm) *n* (formerly) the fact, principle, or advocacy of the existence of more than one guiding or predominant ideological or political centre in a political system, alliance, etc., in the Communist world.

polychaete ('pɒlɪˌkiːt) *n* **1** any marine annelid worm of the class *Polychaeta,* having a distinct head and paired fleshy appendages (parapodia) that bear bristles (chaetae or setae) and are used in swimming: includes the lugworms, ragworms, and sea mice. ◆ *adj also* **polychaetous. 2** of, relating to, or belonging to the class *Polychaeta.* [C19: from New Latin, from Greek *polukhaitēs:* having much hair; see CHAETA]

polychasium (ˌpɒlɪ'keɪzɪəm) *n, pl* **-sia** (-zɪə). *Botany.* a cymose inflorescence in which three or more branches arise from each node. [C20: from New Latin, from POLY- + *-chasium* as in DICHASIUM]

polychlorinated biphenyl (ˌpɒlɪ'klɔːrɪˌneɪtɪd) *n* any of a group of compounds in which chlorine atoms replace the hydrogen atoms in biphenyl: used in industry in electrical insulators and in the manufacture of plastics; a toxic pollutant that can become concentrated in animal tissue. Abbrev.: **PCB.**

polychromatic (ˌpɒlɪkrəʊ'mætɪk), **polychromic** (ˌpɒlɪ'krəʊmɪk), *or* **polychromous** *adj* **1** having various or changing colours. **2** (of light or other electromagnetic radiation) containing radiation with more than one wavelength. ► **polychromatism** (ˌpɒlɪ'krəʊməˌtɪzəm) *n*

polychrome ('pɒlɪˌkrəʊm) *adj* **1** having various or changing colours; polychromatic. **2** made with or decorated in various colours. ◆ *n* **3** a work of art or artefact in many colours.

polychromy ('pɒlɪˌkrəʊmɪ) *n* decoration in many colours, esp. in architecture or sculpture.

polyclinic (ˌpɒlɪ'klɪnɪk) *n* a hospital or clinic able to treat a wide variety of diseases: general hospital.

Polyclitus, Polycleitus (ˌpɒlɪ'klaɪtəs), *or* **Polycletus** (ˌpɒlɪ'kliːtəs) *n* 5th-century B.C. Greek sculptor, noted particularly for his idealized bronze sculptures of the male nude, such as the *Doryphoros.*

polyconic projection (ˌpɒlɪ'kɒnɪk) *n* a type of conic projection in which the parallels are not concentric and all meridians except the central one are curved lines. It is neither equal-area nor conformal, but is suitable for maps of areas or countries of great longitudinal extent.

polycotton ('pɒlɪkɒtᵊn) *n* a fabric made from a mixture of polyester and cotton.

polycotyledon (ˌpɒlɪˌkɒtɪ'liːdᵊn) *n* any of various plants, esp. gymnosperms, that have or appear to have more than two cotyledons. ► ˌ**polyˌcoty'ledonous** *adj*

Polycrates (pə'lɪkrəˌtiːz) *n* died ?522 B.C., Greek tyrant of Samos, who was crucified by a Persian satrap.

polycrystal ('pɒlɪˌkrɪstᵊl) *n* an object composed of randomly orient crystals, formed by rapid solidification.

polycyclic (ˌpɒlɪ'saɪklɪk) *adj* **1** (of a molecule or compound) containing or having molecules that contain two or more closed rings of atoms. **2** *Biology.* having two or more rings or whorls: *polycyclic shells; a polycyclic stele.* ◆ *n* **3** a polycyclic compound: *anthracene is a polycyclic.*

polycystic (ˌpɒlɪ'sɪstɪk) *adj Med.* containing many cysts: *a polycystic ovary.*

polycythaemia *or esp. U.S.* **polycythemia** (ˌpɒlɪsaɪ'θiːmɪə) *n* an abnormal condition of the blood characterized by an increase in the number of red blood cells. It can occur as a primary disease of unknown cause (**polycythaemia vera** or **erythraemia**) or in association with respiratory or circulatory diseases. [C19: from POLY- + CYTO- + -HAEMIA]

polydactyl (ˌpɒlɪ'dæktɪl) *adj also* **polydactylous. 1** (of man and other vertebrates) having more than the normal number of digits. ◆ *n* **2** a human or other vertebrate having more than the normal number of digits. [C19: via French from Greek *poludaktulos* many-toed; see DACTYL]

polydemic (ˌpɒlɪ'demɪk) *adj Ecology, rare.* growing in or inhabiting more than two regions. [C20: from POLY- + ENDEMIC]

Polydeuces (ˌpɒlɪ'djuːsiːz) *n* the Greek name of **Pollux.** See **Castor and Pollux.**

polydipsia (ˌpɒlɪ'dɪpsɪə) *n Pathol.* excessive thirst. [C18: New Latin, from POLY- + *-dipsia,* from Greek *dipsa* thirst] ► ˌ**poly'dipsic** *adj*

polyembryony (ˌpɒlɪ'embrɪənɪ) *n* the production of more than one embryo from a single fertilized egg cell: occurs in certain plants and parasitic hymenopterous insects. ► **polyembryonic** (ˌpɒlɪˌembrɪ'ɒnɪk) *adj*

polyene ('pɒlɪˌiːn) *n* a chemical compound containing a chain of alternating single and double carbon-carbon bonds.

polyester (ˌpɒlɪ'estə) *n* any of a large class of synthetic materials that are polymers containing recurring -COO- groups: used as plastics, textile fibres, and adhesives.

polyethene (ˌpɒlɪ'eθiːn) *n* the systematic name for **polythene.**

polyethylene (ˌpɒlɪ'eθɪˌliːn) *n* another name for **polythene.**

polygala (pə'lɪgələ) *n* any herbaceous plant or small shrub of the polygalaceous genus *Polygala.* See also **milkwort.** [C18: New Latin, from Greek *polugalon,* from POLY- + *gala* milk]

polygalaceous (ˌpɒlɪgə'leɪʃəs, pəˌlɪg-) *adj* of, relating to, or belonging to the *Polygalaceae,* a family of plants having flowers with two large outer petal-like sepals, three small sepals, and three to five petals: includes milkwort.

polygamy (pə'lɪgəmɪ) *n* **1** the practice of having more than one wife or husband at the same time. Compare **polyandry, polygyny. 2a** the condition of having male, female, and hermaphrodite flowers on the same plant. **2b** the condition of having these different types of flower on separate plants of the same species. **3** the practice in male animals of having more than one mate during one breeding season. [C16: via French from Greek *polugamia* from POLY- + -GAMY] ► **po'lygamist** *n* ► **po'lygamous** *adj* ► **po'lygamously** *adv*

polygene ('pɒlɪˌdʒiːn) *n* any of a group of genes that each produce a small quantitative effect on a particular characteristic of the phenotype, such as height.

polygenesis (ˌpɒlɪ'dʒenɪsɪs) *n* **1** *Biology.* evolution of a polyphyletic organism or group. **2** the hypothetical descent of the different races of man from different ultimate ancestors. ◆ Compare **monogenesis.** ► **polygenetic** (ˌpɒlɪdʒɪ'netɪk) *adj* ► ˌ**polyge'netically** *adv*

polyglot ('pɒlɪˌglɒt) *adj* **1** having a command of many languages. **2** written in, composed of, or containing many languages. ◆ *n* **3** a person with a command of many languages. **4** a book, esp. a Bible, containing several versions of the same text written in various languages. **5** a mixture or confusion of languages. [C17: from Greek *poluglōttos* literally: many-tongued, from POLY- + *glōtta* tongue] ► **'polyˌglotism** *or* **'polyˌglottism** *n*

Polygnotus (ˌpɒlɪg'nəʊtəs) *n* 5th century B.C., Greek painter: associated with Cimon in rebuilding Athens.

polygon ('pɒlɪˌgɒn) *n* a closed plane figure bounded by three or more straight sides that meet in pairs in the same number of vertices, and do not intersect other than at these vertices. The sum of the interior angles is $(n-2) \times 180°$ for n sides; the sum of the exterior angles is 360°. A **regular polygon** has all its sides and angles equal. Specific polygons are named according to the number of sides, such as triangle, pentagon, etc. [C16: via Latin from Greek *polugōnon* figure with many angles] ► **polygonal** (pə'lɪgənᵊl) *adj* ► **po'lygonally** *adv*

polygonaceous (ˌpɒlɪgə'neɪʃəs, pəˌlɪgə-) *adj* of, relating to, or belonging to the *Polygonaceae,* a chiefly N temperate family of plants having a sheathing stipule (ocrea) clasping the stem and small inconspicuous flowers: includes dock, sorrel, buckwheat, knotgrass, and rhubarb.

polygonum (pə'lɪgənəm) *n* any polygonaceous plant of the genus *Polygonum,* having stems with knotlike joints and spikes of small white, green, or pink flowers. See also **knotgrass, bistort, prince's-feather** (sense 2). [C18: New Latin, from Greek *polugonon* knotgrass, from *polu-* POLY- + *-gonon,* from *gonu* knee]

polygraph ('pɒlɪˌgrɑːf, -ˌgræf) *n* **1** an instrument for the simultaneous electrical or mechanical recording of several involuntary physiological activities, including blood pressure, skin resistivity, pulse rate, respiration, and perspiration, used esp. as a lie detector. **2** a device for producing copies of written, printed, or drawn matter. [C18: from Greek *polugraphos* writing copiously] ► **polygraphic** (ˌpɒlɪ'græfɪk) *adj* ► ˌ**poly'graphically** *adv*

polygyny (pə'lɪdʒɪnɪ) *n* **1** the practice or condition of being married to more than one wife at the same time. Compare **polygamy. 2** the practice in animals of a male mating with more than one female during one breeding season. **3** the condition in flowers of having many styles. ◆ Compare **polyandry.** [C18: from POLY- + *-gyny,* from Greek *gunē* a woman] ► **po'lygynist** *n* ► **po'lygynous** *adj*

polyhedral angle (ˌpɒlɪ'hiːdrəl) *n* a geometric configuration formed by the intersection of three or more planes, such as the faces of a polyhedron, that have a common vertex. See also **solid angle.**

polyhedron (ˌpɒlɪ'hiːdrən) *n, pl* **-drons** *or* **-dra** (-drə). a solid figure consisting of four or more plane faces (all polygons), pairs of which meet along an edge, three or more edges meeting at a vertex. In a **regular polyhedron** all the faces are identical regular polygons making equal angles with each other. Specific polyhedrons are named according to the number of faces, such as tetrahedron, icosahedron, etc. [C16: from Greek *poluedron,* from POLY- + *hedron* side, base] ► ˌ**poly'hedral** *adj*

polyhydric (ˌpɒlɪˈhaɪdrɪk) *adj* another word for **polyhydroxy,** esp. when applied to alcohols.

polyhydroxy (ˌpɒlɪhaɪˈdrɒksɪ) *adj* (of a chemical compound) containing two or more hydroxyl groups per molecule. Also: **polyhydric.**

Polyhymnia (ˌpɒlɪˈhɪmnɪə) *n Greek myth.* the Muse of singing, mime, and sacred dance. [Latin, from Greek *Polumnia* full of songs; see POLY-, HYMN]

polyisoprene (ˌpɒlɪˈaɪsəˌpriːn) *n* any of various polymeric forms of isoprene, occurring in rubbers.

polymath (ˈpɒlɪˌmæθ) *n* a person of great and varied learning. [C17: from Greek *polumathēs* having much knowledge] ▸ ˌ**polyˈmathic** *adj* ▸ **polymathy** (pəˈlɪməθɪ) *n*

polymer (ˈpɒlɪmə) *n* a naturally occurring or synthetic compound, such as starch or Perspex, that has large molecules made up of many relatively simple repeated units. Compare **copolymer, oligomer.** ▸ **polymerism** (pəˈlɪməˌrɪzəm, ˈpɒlɪmə-) *n*

polymerase (pəˈlɪməreɪz) *n* any enzyme that catalyses the synthesis of a polymer, esp. the synthesis of DNA or RNA.

polymeric (ˌpɒlɪˈmɛrɪk) *adj* of, concerned with, or being a polymer: *a polymeric compound.* [C19: from Greek *polumerēs* having many parts]

polymerization *or* **polymerisation** (pəˌlɪməraɪˈzeɪʃən, ˌpɒlɪməraɪ-) *n* the act or process of forming a polymer or copolymer, esp. a chemical reaction in which a polymer is formed.

polymerize *or* **polymerise** (ˈpɒlɪməˌraɪz, pəˈlɪmə-) *vb* to react or cause to react to form a polymer.

polymerous (pəˈlɪmərəs) *adj* **1** (of flowers) having the petals, sepals, and other parts arranged in whorls of many parts. **2** *Biology.* having or being composed of many parts.

polymorph (ˈpɒlɪˌmɔːf) *n* **1** a species of animal or plant that exhibits polymorphism. **2** any of the crystalline forms of a chemical compound that exhibits polymorphism. **3** Also called: **polymorphonuclear leucocyte.** a common type of white blood cell that has a lobed nucleus and granular cytoplasm and functions as a phagocyte. [C19: from Greek *polumorphos* having many forms]

polymorphic function *n Computing.* a function in a computer program that can deal with a number of different types of data.

polymorphism (ˌpɒlɪˈmɔːfɪzəm) *n* **1** *Biology.* **1a** the occurrence of more than one form of individual in a single species within an interbreeding population. **1b** the occurrence of more than one form in the individual polyps of a coelenterate colony. **2** the existence or formation of different types of crystal of the same chemical compound.

polymorphonuclear (ˌpɒlɪˌmɔːfəʊˈnjuːklɪə) *adj* (of a leucocyte) having a lobed or segmented nucleus. See also **polymorph** (sense 3).

polymorphous (ˌpɒlɪˈmɔːfəs) *or* **polymorphic** *adj* **1** having, taking, or passing through many different forms or stages. **2** (of a substance) exhibiting polymorphism. **3** (of an animal or plant) displaying or undergoing polymorphism.

polymyxin (ˌpɒlɪˈmɪksɪn) *n* any of several toxic polypeptide antibiotics active against Gram-negative bacteria, obtained from the soil bacterium *Bacillus polymyxa.* [C20: from New Latin *Bacillus polymyxa;* see POLY-, MYXO-, -IN]

Polynesia (ˌpɒlɪˈniːʒə, -ʒɪə) *n* one of the three divisions of islands in the Pacific, the others being Melanesia and Micronesia: includes Samoa, Society, Marquesas, Mangareva, Tuamotu, Cook, and Tubuai Islands, and Tonga. [C18: via French from POLY- + Greek *nēsos* island]

Polynesian (ˌpɒlɪˈniːʒən, -ʒɪən) *adj* **1** of or relating to Polynesia, its people, or any of their languages. ◆ *n* **2** a member of the people that inhabit Polynesia, generally of Caucasoid features with light skin and wavy hair. **3** a branch of the Malayo-Polynesian family of languages, including Maori and Hawaiian and a number of other closely related languages of the S and central Pacific.

polyneuritis (ˌpɒlɪnjʊˈraɪtɪs) *n* inflammation of many nerves at the same time.

Polynices (ˌpɒlɪˈnaɪsiːz) *n Greek myth.* a son of Oedipus and Jocasta, for whom the Seven Against Thebes sought to regain Thebes. He and his brother Eteocles killed each other in single combat before its walls.

polynomial (ˌpɒlɪˈnəʊmɪəl) *adj* **1** of, consisting of, or referring to two or more names or terms. ◆ *n* **2a** a mathematical expression consisting of a sum of terms each of which is the product of a constant and one or more variables raised to a positive or zero integral power. For one variable, *x*, the general form is given by: $a_0x^n + a_1x^{n-1} + \dots + a_{n-1}x + a_n$, where a_0, a_1, etc., are real numbers. **2b** Also called: **multinomial.** any mathematical expression consisting of the sum of a number of terms. **3** *Biology.* a taxonomic name consisting of more than two terms, such as *Parus major minor* in which *minor* designates the subspecies.

polynuclear (ˌpɒlɪˈnjuːklɪə) *or* **polynucleate** *adj* having many nuclei; multinuclear.

polynucleotide (ˌpɒlɪˈnjuːklɪəˌtaɪd) *n Biochem.* a molecular chain of nucleotides chemically bonded by a series of ester linkages between the phosphoryl group of one nucleotide and the hydroxyl group of the sugar in the adjacent nucleotide. Nucleic acids consist of long chains of polynucleotides.

polynya (ˈpɒlənˌjɑː) *n* a stretch of open water surrounded by ice, esp. near the mouths of large rivers, in arctic seas. [C19: from Russian, from *poly* open, hollowed-out]

polyonymous (ˌpɒlɪˈɒnɪməs) *adj* having or known by several different names.

polyp (ˈpɒlɪp) *n* **1** *Zoology.* one of the two forms of individual that occur in coelenterates. It usually has a hollow cylindrical body with a ring of tentacles around the mouth. Compare **medusa** (sense 2). **2** Also called: **polypus.** *Pathol.* a small vascularized growth arising from the surface of a mucous membrane, having a rounded base or a stalklike projection. [C16 *polip,* from French *polype* nasal polyp, from Latin *pōlypus* sea animal, nasal polyp, from Greek *polupous* having many feet] ▸ ˈ**polypous** *or* ˈ**polypoid** *adj*

polypary (ˈpɒlɪpərɪ) *or* **polyparium** (ˌpɒlɪˈpɛərɪəm) *n, pl* **-paries** *or* **-paria** (-ˈpɛərɪə). the common base and connecting tissue of a colony of coelenterate polyps, esp. coral. [C18: from New Latin *polypārium;* see POLYP]

polypeptide (ˌpɒlɪˈpɛptaɪd) *n* any of a group of natural or synthetic polymers made up of amino acids chemically linked together; this class includes the proteins. See also **peptide.**

polypetalous (ˌpɒlɪˈpɛtələs) *adj* (of flowers) having many distinct or separate petals. Compare **gamopetalous.**

polyphagia (ˌpɒlɪˈfeɪdʒə) *n* **1a** an abnormal desire to consume excessive amounts of food, esp. as the result of a neurological disorder. **1b** an insatiable appetite. **2** the habit of certain animals, esp. certain insects, of feeding on many different types of food. [C17: New Latin, from Greek, from *poluphagos* eating much; see POLY-, -PHAGY] ▸ **polyphagous** (pəˈlɪfəgəs) *adj*

polyphase (ˈpɒlɪˌfeɪz) *adj* **1** Also: **multiphase.** (of an electrical system, circuit, or device) having, generating, or using two or more alternating voltages of the same frequency, the phases of which are cyclically displaced by fractions of a period. See also **single-phase, two-phase, three-phase. 2** having more than one phase.

Polyphemus (ˌpɒlɪˈfiːməs) *n Greek myth.* a cyclops who imprisoned Odysseus and his companions in his cave. To effect his escape, Odysseus blinded him.

polyphone (ˈpɒlɪˌfəʊn) *n* a letter or character having more than one phonetic value, such as English *c,* pronounced (k) before *a, o,* or *u* or (s) before *e* or *i.*

polyphonic (ˌpɒlɪˈfɒnɪk) *adj* **1** *Music.* composed of relatively independent melodic lines or parts; contrapuntal. **2** many-voiced. **3** *Phonetics.* of, relating to, or denoting a polyphone. ▸ ˌ**polyˈphonically** *adv*

polyphonic prose *n* a rhythmically free prose employing poetic devices, such as assonance and alliteration.

polyphony (pəˈlɪfənɪ) *n, pl* **-nies. 1** polyphonic style of composition or a piece of music utilizing it. **2** the use of polyphones in a writing system. [C19: from Greek *poluphōnia* diversity of tones, from POLY- + *phōnē* speech, sound] ▸ **poˈlyphonous** *adj* ▸ **poˈlyphonously** *adv*

polyphosphoric acid (ˌpɒlɪfɒsˈfɒrɪk) *n* **1** any one of a series of oxyacids of phosphorus with the general formula $H_{n+2}P_nO_{3n+1}$. The first member is pyrophosphoric acid ($n = 2$) and the series includes the highly polymeric metaphosphoric acid. The higher acids exist in an equilibrium mixture. **2** a glassy or liquid mixture of orthophosphoric and polyphosphoric acids: used industrially as a dehydrating agent, catalyst, and oxidizing agent.

polyphyletic (ˌpɒlɪfaɪˈlɛtɪk) *adj Biology.* relating to or characterized by descent from more than one ancestral group of animals or plants. [C19: from POLY- + PHYLETIC] ▸ ˌ**polyphyˈletically** *adv*

polyphyodont (ˌpɒlɪˈfaɪəʊˌdɒnt) *adj* having many successive sets of teeth, as fishes and other lower vertebrates. Compare **diphyodont.** [C19: from Greek *poluphuēs* manifold (from *polu-* POLY- + *phuē* growth) + -ODONT]

polyploid (ˈpɒlɪˌplɔɪd) *adj* **1** (of cells, organisms, etc.) having more than twice the basic (haploid) number of chromosomes. ◆ *n* **2** an individual or cell of this type. ▸ ˌ**polyˈploidal** *or* ˌ**polyˈploidic** *adj* ▸ ˈ**polyˌploidy** *n*

polypod (ˈpɒlɪˌpɒd) *adj also* **polypodous** (pəˈlɪpədəs). **1** (esp. of insect larvae) having many legs or similar appendages. ◆ *n* **2** an animal of this type.

polypody (ˈpɒlɪˌpəʊdɪ) *n, pl* **-dies. 1** any of various ferns of the genus *Polypodium,* esp. *P. vulgare,* having deeply divided leaves and round naked sori: family *Polypodiaceae.* **2** any fern of the family *Polypodiaceae,* all having opaque leaves and all except the harts-tongue divided leaves. [C15: from Latin *polypodium,* from Greek, from POLY- + *pous* foot]

polypoid (ˈpɒlɪˌpɔɪd) *adj* **1** of, relating to, or resembling a polyp. **2** (of a coelenterate) having the body in the form of a polyp.

polypropylene (ˌpɒlɪˈprəʊpɪˌliːn) *n* any of various tough flexible synthetic thermoplastic materials made by polymerizing propylene and used for making moulded articles, laminates, bottles, pipes, and fibres for ropes, bristles, upholstery, and carpets. Systematic name: **polypropene.**

polyprotodont (ˌpɒlɪˈprəʊtəʊˌdɒnt) *n* any marsupial of the group *Polyprotodontia,* characterized by four or more upper incisor teeth on each side of the jaw: includes the opossums and bandicoots. Compare **diprotodont.** [C19: from POLY- + PROTO- + -ODONT]

polyptych (ˈpɒlɪptɪk) *n* an altarpiece consisting of more than three panels, set with paintings or carvings, and usually hinged for folding. Compare **diptych, triptych.** [C19: via Late Latin from Greek *poluptuchon* something folded many times, from POLY- + *ptuchē* a fold]

polypus (ˈpɒlɪpəs) *n, pl* **-pi** (-paɪ). *Pathol.* another word for **polyp** (sense 2). [C16: via Latin from Greek: POLYP]

polyrhythm (ˈpɒlɪˌrɪðəm) *n Music.* a style of composition in which each part exhibits different rhythms. ▸ ˌ**polyˈrhythmic** *adj*

polyribosome (ˌpɒlɪˈraɪbəˌsəʊm) *n Biochem.* an assemblage of ribosomes associated with a messenger RNA molecule, involved in peptide synthesis. Also called: **polysome.**

polysaccharide (ˌpɒlɪˈsækəˌraɪd, -rɪd) *or* **polysaccharose** (ˌpɒlɪˈsækəˌrəʊz, -ˌrəʊs) *n* any one of a class of carbohydrates whose molecules contain linked monosaccharide units: includes starch, inulin, and cellulose. General formula: $(C_6H_{10}O_5)_n$. See also **oligosaccharide.**

polysemy (ˌpɒlɪˈsiːmɪ, pəˈlɪsəmɪ) *n* the existence of several meanings in a single word. Compare **monosemy.** [C20: from New Latin *polysēmia,* from Greek *polusēmos* having many meanings, from POLY- + *sēma* a sign] ▸ ˌ**polyˈsemous** *adj*

polysepalous (ˌpɒlɪˈsɛpələs) *adj* (of flowers) having distinct separate sepals. Compare **gamosepalous.**

polysome (ˈpɒlɪˌsəʊm) *n* another name for **polyribosome.**

polysomic (ˌpɒlɪˈsəʊmɪk) *adj* of, relating to, or designating a basically diploid chromosome complement, in which some but not all the chromosomes are represented more than twice. [C20: from POLY- + -SOME[3] + -IC]

polystichous (ˌpɒlɪˈstaɪkəs) *adj* (of plant parts) arranged in a number of rows.

polystyrene (ˌpɒlɪˈstaɪriːn) *n* a synthetic thermoplastic material obtained by polymerizing styrene; used as a white rigid foam (**expanded polystyrene**) for insulating and packing and as a glasslike material in light fittings and water tanks.

polysulphide (ˌpɒlɪˈsʌlfaɪd) *n* any sulphide of a metal containing divalent anions in which there are chains of sulphur atoms, as in the polysulphides of sodium, Na_2S_2, Na_2S_3, Na_2S_4, etc.

polysyllable (ˈpɒlɪˌsɪləbᵊl) *n* a word consisting of more than two syllables. ► **polysyllabic** (ˌpɒlɪsɪˈlæbɪk) *or* ˌ**polysylˈlabical** *adj* ► ˌ**polysylˈlabically** *adv*

polysyllogism (ˌpɒlɪˈsɪləˌdʒɪzəm) *n* a chain of syllogisms in which the conclusion of one syllogism serves as a premise for the next.

polysyndeton (ˌpɒlɪˈsɪndɪtən) *n* **1** *Rhetoric.* the use of several conjunctions in close succession, esp. where some might be omitted, as in *he ran and jumped and laughed for joy.* **2** Also called: **syndesis.** *Grammar.* a sentence containing more than two coordinate clauses. [C16: POLY- + *-syndeton,* from Greek *sundetos* bound together]

polysynthetic (ˌpɒlɪsɪnˈθɛtɪk) *adj* denoting languages, such as Eskimo, in which single words may express the meaning of whole phrases or clauses by virtue of multiple affixes. Compare **synthetic** (sense 3), **analytic** (sense 3), **agglutinative** (sense 2). ► **polysynthesis** (ˌpɒlɪˈsɪnθɪsɪs) *n* ► ˌ**polyˈsynthesism** *n* ► ˌ**polysynˈthetically** *adv*

polytechnic (ˌpɒlɪˈtɛknɪk) *n* **1** *Brit.* a college offering advanced full- and part-time courses, esp. vocational courses, in many fields at and below degree standard. ◆ *adj* **2** of or relating to technical instruction and training. [C19: via French from Greek *polutekhnos* skilled in many arts. See TECHNIC]

polytene (ˈpɒlɪˌtiːn) *adj* denoting a type of giant-size chromosome consisting of many replicated genes in parallel, found esp. in *Drosophila* larvae. [C20: from POLY- + Greek *taenia* band]

polytetrafluoroethylene (ˌpɒlɪˌtɛtrəˌflʊərəʊˈɛθɪˌliːn) *n* a white thermoplastic material with a waxy texture, made by polymerizing tetrafluoroethylene. It is nonflammable, resists chemical action and radiation, and has a high electrical resistance and an extremely low coefficient of friction. It is used for making gaskets, hoses, insulators, bearings, and for coating metal surfaces in chemical plants and in nonstick cooking vessels. Abbrev.: **PTFE.** Also called (trademark): **Teflon.**

polytheism (ˈpɒlɪθiːˌɪzəm, ˌpɒlɪˈθiːɪzəm) *n* the worship of or belief in more than one god. ► ˈ**polyˌtheist** *n* ► ˌ**polytheˈistic** *adj* ► ˌ**polytheˈistically** *adv*

polythene (ˈpɒlɪˌθiːn) *n* any one of various light thermoplastic materials made from ethylene with properties depending on the molecular weight of the polymer. The common forms are a waxy flexible plastic (**low-density polythene**) and a tougher rigid more crystalline form (**high-density polythene**). Polythene is used for packaging, moulded articles, pipes and tubing, insulation, textiles, and coatings on metal. Systematic name: **polyethene.** Also called: **polyethylene.**

polytonality (ˌpɒlɪtəʊˈnælɪtɪ) *or* **polytonalism** *n Music.* the simultaneous use of more than two different keys or tonalities. ► ˌ**polyˈtonal** *adj* ► ˌ**polyˈtonally** *adv* ► ˌ**polyˈtonalist** *n*

polytrophic (ˌpɒlɪˈtrɒfɪk) *adj* (esp. of bacteria) obtaining food from several different organic sources.

polytypic (ˌpɒlɪˈtɪpɪk) *or* **polytypical** *adj* **1** existing in, consisting of, or incorporating several different types or forms. **2** *Biology.* (of a taxonomic group) having many subdivisions, esp. (of a species) having many subspecies and geographical races.

polyunsaturated (ˌpɒlɪʌnˈsætʃəˌreɪtɪd) *adj* of or relating to a class of animal and vegetable fats, the molecules of which consist of long carbon chains with many double bonds. Polyunsaturated compounds are less likely to be converted into cholesterol in the body. They are widely used in margarines and in the manufacture of paints and varnishes. See also **monounsaturated.**

polyurethane (ˌpɒlɪˈjʊərəˌθeɪn) *or* **polyurethan** (ˌpɒlɪˈjʊərəˌθæn) *n* a class of synthetic materials made by copolymerizing an isocyanate and a polyhydric alcohol and commonly used as a foam (**polyurethane foam**) for insulation and packing, as fibres and hard inert coatings, and in a flexible form (**polyurethane rubber**) for diaphragms and seals.

polyuria (ˌpɒlɪˈjʊərɪə) *n Pathol., physiol.* the state or condition of discharging abnormally large quantities of urine, often accompanied by a need to urinate frequently. ► ˌ**polyˈuric** *adj*

polyvalent (ˌpɒlɪˈveɪlənt, pəˈlɪvələnt) *adj* **1** *Chem.* having more than one valency. **2** (of a vaccine) **2a** effective against several strains of the same disease-producing microorganism, antigen, or toxin. **2b** produced from cultures containing several strains of the same microorganism. ► ˌ**polyˈvalency** *n*

polyvinyl (ˌpɒlɪˈvaɪnɪl, -ˈvaɪnᵊl) *n* (*modifier*) designating a plastic or resin formed by polymerization of a vinyl derivative.

polyvinyl acetate *n* a colourless odourless tasteless resin used in emulsion paints, adhesives, sealers, a substitute for chicle in chewing gum, and for sealing porous surfaces. Abbrev.: **PVA.**

polyvinyl chloride *n* the full name of **PVC.**

polyvinylidene chloride (ˌpɒlɪvaɪˈnɪlɪˌdiːn) *n* any one of a class of thermoplastic materials formed by the polymerization of vinylidene chloride: used in packaging and for making pipes and fittings for chemical equipment. Also called: **saran.**

polyvinyl resin *n* any of a class of thermoplastic resins that are made by polymerizing or copolymerizing a vinyl compound. The commonest type is PVC.

Polyxena (pɒˈlɪksɪnə) *n Greek myth.* a daughter of King Priam of Troy, who was sacrificed on the command of Achilles' ghost.

polyzoan (ˌpɒlɪˈzəʊən) *n, adj* another word for **bryozoan.** [C19: from New Latin, *Polyzoa* class name, from POLY- + *-zoan,* from Greek *zōion* an animal]

polyzoarium (ˌpɒlɪzəʊˈɛərɪəm) *n, pl* **-ia** (-ɪə). a colony of bryozoan animals or its supporting skeletal framework. ► ˌ**polyzoˈarial** *adj*

polyzoic (ˌpɒlɪˈzəʊɪk) *adj Zoology.* **1** (of certain colonial animals) having many zooids or similar polyps. **2** producing or containing many sporozoites.

pom (pɒm) *n Slang, Austral. and N.Z.* short for **pommy.**

POM *abbrev. for* prescription-only medicine (*or* medication).

pomace (ˈpʌmɪs) *n* **1** the pulpy residue of apples or similar fruit after crushing and pressing, as in cider-making. **2** any pulpy substance left after crushing, mashing, etc. [C16: from Medieval Latin *pōmācium* cider, from Latin *pōmum* apple]

pomaceous (pɒˈmeɪʃəs) *adj* of, relating to, or bearing pomes, such as the apple, pear, and quince trees. [C18: from New Latin *pōmāceus,* from Latin *pōmum* apple]

pomade (pəˈmɑːd, -ˈmeɪd) *n* **1** a perfumed oil or ointment put on the hair, as to make it smooth and shiny. ◆ *vb* **2** (*tr*) to put pomade on. ◆ Also: **pomatum** (pəˈmeɪtəm). [C16: from French *pommade,* from Italian *pomato* (originally made partly from apples), from Latin *pōmum* apple]

pomander (pəʊˈmændə) *n* **1** a mixture of aromatic substances in a sachet or an orange, formerly carried as scent or as a protection against disease. **2** a container for such a mixture. [C15: from Old French *pome d'ambre,* from Medieval Latin *pōmum ambrae* apple of amber]

Pombal (*Portuguese* pomˈbal) *n* **Marquês de** (mərkeʃ ˈdəː). title of *Sebastião José de Carvalho e Mello.* 1699–1782, Portuguese statesman, who dominated Portuguese government from 1750 to 1777 and instituted many administrative and economic reforms.

pombe (ˈpɔmbɛ) *n E African.* any alcoholic drink. [Swahili]

pome (pəʊm) *n* the fleshy fruit of the apple and related plants, consisting of an enlarged receptacle enclosing the ovary and seeds. [C15: from Old French, from Late Latin *pōma* apple, pl (assumed to be sing) of Latin *pōmum* apple]

pomegranate (ˈpɒmɪˌgrænɪt, ˈpɒmˌgrænɪt) *n* **1** an Asian shrub or small tree, *Punica granatum,* cultivated in semitropical regions for its edible fruit: family *Punicaceae.* **2** the many-chambered globular fruit of this tree, which has tough reddish rind, juicy red pulp, and many seeds. [C14: from Old French *pome grenate,* from Latin *pōmum* apple + *grenate,* from Latin *grānātum,* from *grānātus* full of seeds]

pomelo (ˈpɒmɪˌləʊ) *n, pl* **-los. 1** a tropical rutaceous tree, *Citrus maxima* (or *C. decumana*), grown widely in oriental regions for its large yellow grapefruit-like edible fruit. **2** the fruit of this tree. **3** *Chiefly U.S.* another name for **grapefruit.** ◆ Also called: **shaddock.** [C19: from Dutch *pompelmoes, perhaps from pompoen* big + Portuguese *limão* a lemon]

Pomerania (ˌpɒməˈreɪnɪə) *n* a region of N central Europe, extending along the S coast of the Baltic Sea from Stralsund to the Vistula River: now chiefly in Poland, with a small area in NE Germany. German name: **Pommern.** Polish name: **Pomorze.**

Pomeranian (ˌpɒməˈreɪnɪən) *adj* **1** of or relating to Pomerania or its inhabitants. ◆ *n* **2** a native or inhabitant of Pomerania, esp. a German. **3** a breed of toy dog of the spitz type with a long thick straight coat.

pomfret[1] (ˈpʌmfrɪt, ˈpɒm-) *or* **pomfret-cake** *n* a small black rounded confection of liquorice. Also called: **Pontefract cake.** [C19: from *Pomfret,* earlier form of PONTEFRACT, where the cake was originally made]

pomfret[2] (ˈpɒmfrɪt) *n* **1** any of various fishes of the genus *Stromateidae* of the Indian and Pacific oceans: valued as food fishes. **2** any of various scombroid fishes, esp. *Brama raii,* of northern oceans: valued as food fishes. [C18: perhaps from a diminutive form of Portuguese *pampo*]

pomiculture (ˈpɒmɪˌkʌltʃə) *n* the cultivation of fruit. [C19: from Latin *pōmum* apple, fruit + CULTURE]

pomiferous (pɒˈmɪfərəs) *adj* (of the apple, pear, etc.) producing pomes or pomelike fruits. [C17: from Latin *pomifer* fruit-bearing]

pommel (ˈpʌməl, ˈpɒm-) *n* **1** the raised part on the front of a saddle. **2** a knob at the top of a sword or similar weapon. ◆ *vb* **-mels, -melling, -melled** *or U.S.* **-mels, -meling, -meled. 3** a less common word for **pummel.** [C14: from Old French *pomel* knob, from Vulgar Latin *pōmellum* (unattested) little apple, from Latin *pōmum* apple]

Pommern (ˈpɔmərn) *n* the German name for **Pomerania.**

pommy (ˈpɒmɪ) *n, pl* **-mies.** (*sometimes cap.*) *Slang.* a mildly offensive word used by Australians and New Zealanders for an English person. Sometimes shortened to **pom.** [C20: of uncertain origin. Among a number of explanations are: (1) based on a blend of IMMIGRANT and POMEGRANATE (alluding to the red cheeks of English immigrants); (2) from the abbreviation *POME,* Prisoner of Mother England (referring to convicts)]

pomology (pɒˈmɒlədʒɪ) *n* the branch of horticulture that is concerned with the study and cultivation of fruit. [C19: from New Latin *pōmologia,* from Latin *pōmum* apple, fruit] ► **pomological** (ˌpɒməˈlɒdʒɪkᵊl) *adj* ► ˌ**pomoˈlogically** *adv* ► **pomˈologist** *n*

Pomona[1] (pəˈməʊnə) *n* another name for **Mainland** (in the Orkneys).

Pomona[2] (pəˈməʊnə) *n* the Roman goddess of fruit trees.

Pomorze (pɔˈmɔʒɛ) *n* the Polish name for **Pomerania.**

pomp (pɒmp) *n* **1** stately or magnificent display; ceremonial splendour. **2** vain display, esp. of dignity or importance. **3** *Obsolete.* a procession or pageant. [C14: from Old French *pompe,* from Latin *pompa* procession, from Greek *pompē;* related to Greek *pompein* to send]

pompadour (ˈpɒmpəˌdʊə) *n* an early 18th-century hairstyle for women, having the front hair arranged over a pad to give it greater height and bulk. [C18: named after the Marquise de POMPADOUR, who originated it]

Pompadour (*French* pɔ̃padur) *n* **Marquise de,** title of *Jeanne Antoinette Pois-*

son. 1721–64, mistress of Louis XV of France (1745–64), whom she greatly influenced.

pompano ('pɒmpə,nəʊ) *n, pl* **-no** *or* **-nos. 1** any of several deep-bodied carangid food fishes of the genus *Trachinotus,* esp. *T. carolinus,* of American coastal regions of the Atlantic. **2** a spiny-finned food fish, *Palometa simillima,* of North American coastal regions of the Pacific: family *Stromateidae* (butterfish, etc.). **[C19:** from Spanish *pámpano* type of fish, of uncertain origin**]**

Pompeii (pɒm'peiː) *n* an ancient city in Italy, southeast of Naples: buried by an eruption of Vesuvius (79 A.D.); excavation of the site, which is extremely well preserved, began in 1748. ▸ **Pompeiian** (pɒm'peɪən, -'piː-) *adj, n*

Pompey[1] ('pɒmpɪ) *n* an informal name for **Portsmouth.**

Pompey[2] ('pɒmpɪ) *n* called *Pompey the Great;* Latin name *Gnaeus Pompeius Magnus.* 106–48 B.C., Roman general and statesman; a member with Caesar and Crassus of the first triumvirate (60). He later quarrelled with Caesar, who defeated him at Pharsalus (48). He fled to Egypt and was murdered.

Pompidou (*French* pɔ̃pidu) *n* **Georges** (ʒɔrʒ). 1911–74, French statesman; president of France (1969–74).

pompilid ('pɒmpɪlɪd) *n* another name for the **spider-hunting wasp. [C20:** from New Latin *pompilus,* from Greek *pompilos* a fish that accompanies ships, from *pempein* to send, escort**]**

pompom ('pɒmpɒm) *or* **pompon** *n* **1** a ball of tufted silk, wool, feathers, etc., worn on a hat for decoration. **2a** the small globelike flower head of certain cultivated varieties of dahlia and chrysanthemum. **2b** (*as modifier*): *pompom dahlia.* **[C18:** from French, from Old French *pompe* knot of ribbons, of uncertain origin**]**

pom-pom ('pɒmpɒm) *n* an automatic rapid-firing, small-calibre cannon, esp. a type of antiaircraft cannon used in World War II. Also called: **pompom. [C19:** of imitative origin**]**

pomposity (pɒm'pɒsɪtɪ) *n, pl* **-ties. 1** vain or ostentatious display of dignity or importance. **2** the quality of being pompous. **3** ostentatiously lofty style, language, etc. **4** a pompous action, remark, etc.

pompous ('pɒmpəs) *adj* **1** exaggeratedly or ostentatiously dignified or self-important. **2** ostentatiously lofty in style: *a pompous speech.* **3** *Rare.* characterized by ceremonial pomp or splendour. ▸ **'pompously** *adv* ▸ **'pompousness** *n*

'pon (pɒn) *prep Poetic or archaic. contraction of* upon.

ponce (pɒns) *Derogatory slang, chiefly Brit.* ◆ *n* **1** a man given to ostentatious or effeminate display in manners, speech, dress, etc. **2** another word for **pimp**[1]. ◆ *vb* **3** (*intr;* often foll. by *around* or *about*) to act like a ponce. **[C19:** from Polari, from Spanish *pu(n)to* male prostitute or French *pront* prostitute**]** ▸ **'poncy** *or* **'poncey** *adj*

Ponce (*Spanish* 'pɔnθe) *n* a port in S Puerto Rico, on the Caribbean: the second largest town on the island; settled in the 16th century. Pop.: 189 988 (1996 est.).

Ponce de León ('pɒns də 'liːən; *Spanish* 'pɔnθe ðe le'ɔn) *n* **Juan** (xwan). ?1460–1521, Spanish explorer. He settled (1509) and governed (1510–12) Puerto Rico and discovered (1513) Florida.

poncho ('pɒntʃəʊ) *n, pl* **-chos.** a cloak of a kind originally worn in South America, made of a rectangular or circular piece of cloth, esp. wool, with a hole in the middle to put the head through. **[C18:** from American Spanish, from Araucanian *pantho* woollen material**]**

pond (pɒnd) *n* **a** a pool of still water, often artificially created. **b** (*in combination*): *a fishpond.* **[C13** *ponde* enclosure; related to POUND[3]**]**

ponder ('pɒndə) *vb* (when *intr,* sometimes foll. by *on* or *over*) to give thorough or deep consideration (to); meditate (upon). **[C14:** from Old French *ponderer,* from Latin *ponderāre* to weigh, consider, from *pondus* weight; related to *pendere* to weigh**]**

ponderable ('pɒndərəbᵊl) *adj* **1** able to be evaluated or estimated; appreciable. **2** capable of being weighed or measured. ◆ *n* **3** (*often pl*) something that can be evaluated or appreciated; a substantial thing. ▸ **,pondera'bility** *n* ▸ **'ponderably** *adv*

ponderous ('pɒndərəs) *adj* **1** of great weight; heavy; huge. **2** (esp. of movement) lacking ease or lightness; awkward, lumbering, or graceless. **3** dull or laborious: *a ponderous oration.* **[C14:** from Latin *ponderōsus* of great weight, from *pondus* weight**]** ▸ **'ponderously** *adv* ▸ **'ponderousness** *or* **ponderosity** (,pɒndə'rɒsɪtɪ) *n*

Pondicherry (,pɒndɪ'tʃerɪ) *n* **1** a Union Territory of SE India: transferred from French to Indian administration in 1954 and made a Union Territory in 1962. Capital: Pondicherry. Pop.: 894 000 (1994 est.). Area: 479 sq. km (185 sq. miles). **2** a port in SE India, capital of the Union Territory of Pondicherry, on the Coromandel Coast. Pop.: 203 065 (1991).

pond lily *n* another name for **water lily.**

Pondo ('pɒndəʊ) *n* **1** (*pl* **-do** *or* **-dos**) a member of a Negroid people of southern Africa, living chiefly in Pondoland. **2** the language of this people, belonging to the Bantu grouping of the Niger-Congo family, and closely related to Xhosa.

pondok ('pɒndɒk) *or* **pondokkie** (pɒn'dɒkɪ) *n* (in southern Africa) a crudely made house built of tin sheet, reeds, etc. **[C20:** from Malay *pondók* leaf house**]**

Pondoland ('pɒndəʊ,lænd) *n* an area in SE central South Africa: inhabited chiefly by the Pondo people.

pond scum *n* a greenish layer floating on the surface of stagnant waters, consisting of various freshwater algae.

pond-skater *n* any of various heteropterous insects of the family *Gerrididae,* esp. *Gerris lacustris* (**common pond-skater**), having a slender hairy body and long hairy legs with which they skim about on the surface of ponds. Also called: **water strider, water skater.**

pond snail *n* a general term for the freshwater snails: often specifically for the **great pond snail** (*Limnaea stagnalis*) and others of that genus. *L. truncatula* is a host of the liver fluke.

pondweed ('pɒnd,wiːd) *n* **1** any of various water plants of the genus *Potamogeton,* which grow in ponds and slow streams: family *Potamogetonaceae.* **2** Also called: **waterweed.** *Brit.* any of various unrelated water plants, such as Canadian pondweed, mare's-tail, and water milfoil, that have thin or much divided leaves.

pone[1] (pəʊn) *n Southern U.S.* **1** Also called: **pone bread, corn pone.** bread made of maize. **2** a loaf or cake of this. **[C17:** from Algonquian; compare Delaware *apán* baked**]**

pone[2] (pəʊn, 'pəʊnɪ) *n Cards.* the player to the right of the dealer, or the non-dealer in two-handed games. **[C19:** from Latin: put!, that is, play, from *ponere* to put**]**

pong (pɒŋ) *Brit. informal.* ◆ *n* **1** a disagreeable or offensive smell; stink. ◆ *vb* **2** (*intr*) to give off an unpleasant smell; stink. **[C20:** perhaps from Romany *pan* to stink**]** ▸ **'pongy** *adj*

ponga ('pɒŋə) *n* a tall tree fern, *Cyathea dealbata,* of New Zealand, with large feathery leaves. **[Maori]**

pongee (pɒn'dʒiː, 'pɒndʒiː) *n* **1** a thin plain-weave silk fabric from China or India, left in its natural colour. **2** a cotton or rayon fabric similar to or in imitation of this, but not necessarily in the natural colour. **[C18:** from Mandarin Chinese (Peking) *pen-chī* woven at home, on one's own loom, from *pen* own + *chi* loom**]**

pongid ('pɒŋgɪd, 'pɒndʒɪd) *n* **1** any primate of the family *Pongidae,* which includes the gibbons and the great apes. ◆ *adj* **2** of, relating to, or belonging to the family *Pongidae.* **[**from New Latin *Pongo* type genus, from Kongo *mpongi* ape**]**

pongo ('pɒŋgəʊ) *n, pl* **-gos. 1** an anthropoid ape, esp. an orang-utan or (formerly) a gorilla. **2** *Military slang.* a soldier or marine. **[C17:** from Kongo *mpongo***]**

poniard ('pɒnjəd) *n* **1** a small dagger with a slender blade. ◆ *vb* **2** (*tr*) to stab with a poniard. **[C16:** from Old French *poignard* dagger, from *poing* fist, from Latin *pugnus;* related to Latin *pugnāre* to fight**]**

pons (pɒnz) *n, pl* **pontes** ('pɒntiːz). **1** a bridge of connecting tissue. **2** short for **pons Varolii. [**Latin: bridge**]**

pons asinorum (,æsɪ'nɔːrəm) *n* the geometric proposition that the angles opposite the two equal sides of an isosceles triangle are equal. **[**Latin: bridge of asses, referring originally to the fifth proposition of the first book of Euclid, which was considered difficult for students to learn**]**

pons Varolii (və'rəʊlɪ,aɪ) *n, pl* **pontes Varolii** ('pɒntiːz). a broad white band of connecting nerve fibres that bridges the hemispheres of the cerebellum in mammals. Sometimes shortened to **pons. [C16:** New Latin, literally: bridge of Varoli, after Costanzo *Varoli* (?1543–75), Italian anatomist**]**

pont (pɒnt) *n* (in South Africa) a river ferry, esp. one that is guided by a cable from one bank to the other. **[C17:** from Dutch: ferryboat, PUNT[1]; reintroduced through Afrikaans in 19th or 20th century**]**

Ponta Delgada (*Portuguese* 'pontə ðel'gaðə) *n* a port in the E Azores, on S São Miguel Island: chief commercial centre of the archipelago. Pop.: 22 200 (latest est.).

Pontchartrain ('pɒntʃə,treɪn) *n* **Lake.** a shallow lagoon in SE Louisiana, linked with the Gulf of Mexico by a narrow channel, the **Rigolets:** resort and fishing centre. Area: 1620 sq. km (625 sq. miles).

Pontefract ('pɒntɪ,frækt) *n* an industrial town in N England, in Wakefield unitary authority, West Yorkshire: castle (1069), in which Richard II was imprisoned and murdered (1400). Pop.: 28 358 (1991).

Pontefract cake *n* another name for **pomfret**[1].

Pontevedra (*Spanish* pɔnte'βeðra) *n* a port in NW Spain: takes its name from a 12-arched Roman bridge, the Pons Vetus. Pop.: 74 850 (1991).

Pontiac ('pɒntɪ,æk) *n* died 1769, chief of the Ottawa Indians, who led a rebellion against the British (1763–66).

pontianak (,pɒntɪ'ɑːnæk) *n* (in Malay folklore) a female vampire; the ghost of a woman who has died in childbirth. **[**from Malay**]**

Pontianak (,pɒntɪ'ɑːnæk) *n* a port in Indonesia, on W coast of Borneo almost exactly on the equator. Pop.: 387 112 (1990).

Pontic ('pɒntɪk) *adj* denoting or relating to the Black Sea. **[C15:** from Latin *Ponticus,* from Greek, from *Pontos* PONTUS**]**

pontifex ('pɒntɪ,feks) *n, pl* **pontifices** (pɒn'tɪfɪ,siːz). (in ancient Rome) any of the senior members of the Pontifical College, presided over by the **Pontifex Maximus. [C16:** from Latin, perhaps from Etruscan but influenced by folk etymology as if meaning literally: bridge-maker, from *pons* bridge + *-fex* from *facere* to make**]**

pontiff ('pɒntɪf) *n* a former title of the pagan high priest at Rome, later used of popes and occasionally of other bishops, and now confined exclusively to the pope. **[C17:** from French *pontife,* from Latin PONTIFEX**]**

pontifical (pɒn'tɪfɪkᵊl) *adj* **1** of, relating to, or characteristic of a pontiff, the pope, or a bishop. **2** having an excessively authoritative manner; pompous. ◆ *n* **3** *R.C. Church, Church of England.* a book containing the prayers and ritual instructions for ceremonies restricted to a bishop. ◆ See also **pontificals.** ▸ **pon'tifically** *adv*

Pontifical College *n R.C. Church.* **1** a major theological college under the direct control of the Roman Curia. **2** the council of priests, being the chief hieratic body of the Church.

Pontifical Mass *n R.C. Church, Church of England.* a solemn celebration of Mass by a bishop.

pontificals (pɒn'tɪfɪkᵊlz) *pl n Chiefly R.C. Church.* the insignia and special vestments worn by a bishop, esp. when celebrating High Mass.

pontificate *vb* (pɒn'tɪfɪ,keɪt). (*intr*) **1** Also (*less commonly*): **pontify** ('pɒntɪ,faɪ). to speak or behave in a pompous or dogmatic manner. **2** to serve or officiate as a pontiff, esp. in celebrating a Pontifical Mass. ◆ *n* (pɒn'tɪfɪkɪt). **3** the office or term of office of a pontiff, now usually the pope.

pontil ('pɒntɪl) *n* a less common word for **punty**. [C19: from French, apparently from Italian *puntello;* see PUNTY]

pontine ('pɒntaɪn) *adj* **1** of or relating to bridges. **2** of or relating to the pons Varolii. [C19: from Latin *pons* bridge]

Pontine Marshes ('pɒntaɪn) *pl n* an area of W Italy, southeast of Rome: formerly malarial swamps, drained in 1932–34 after numerous attempts since 160 B.C. had failed. Italian name: **Agro Pontino** ('ɑ:gro pon'ti:no).

Pontius Pilate ('pɒnʃəs, 'pɒntɪəs 'paɪlət) *n* See **Pilate.**

pontonier (,pɒntə'nɪə) *n Military, obsolete.* a person in charge of or involved in building a pontoon bridge. [C19: from French *pontonnier,* from Latin *pontō* ferry boat, PONTOON[1]]

pontoon[1] (pɒn'tu:n) *n* **1a** a watertight float or vessel used where buoyancy is required in water, as in supporting a bridge, in salvage work, or where a temporary or mobile structure is required in military operations. **1b** (*as modifier*): *a pontoon bridge.* **2** *Nautical.* a float, often inflatable, for raising a vessel in the water. [C17: from French *ponton,* from Latin *pontō* punt, floating bridge, from *pōns* bridge]

pontoon[2] (pɒn'tu:n) *n* **1** Also called: **twenty-one** (esp. U.S.), **vingt-et-un.** a gambling game in which players try to obtain card combinations worth 21 points. **2** (in this game) the combination of an ace with a ten or court card when dealt to a player as his first two cards. [C20: probably an alteration of French *vingt-et-un,* literally: twenty-one]

Pontoppidan (*Danish* pont'topidan) *n* **Henrik.** 1857–1943, Danish novelist and short-story writer, author of the novel sequences *The Promised Land* (1891–95), *Lykke-Per* (1898–1904), and *The Empire of Death* (1912–16). Nobel prize for literature 1917.

Pontormo (*Italian* pon'tormo) *n* **Jacopo da** ('ja:kopo da). original name *Jacopo Carrucci.* 1494–1556, Italian mannerist painter.

Pontus ('pɒntəs) *n* an ancient region of NE Asia Minor, on the Black Sea: became a kingdom in the 4th century B.C.; at its height under Mithridates VI (about 115–63 B.C.), when it controlled all Asia Minor; defeated by the Romans in the mid-1st century B.C.

Pontus Euxinus (ju:k'saɪnəs) *n* the Latin name of the **Black Sea.**

Pontypool (,pɒntɪ'pu:l) *n* an industrial town in E Wales, in Torfaen county borough: famous for lacquered ironware in the 18th century. Pop.: 35 564 (1991).

Pontypridd (,pɒntɪ'pri:ð) *n* an industrial town in S Wales, in Rhondda Cynon Taff county borough. Pop.: 28 487 (1991).

pony ('pəʊnɪ) *n, pl* **ponies.** **1** any of various breeds of small horse, usually under 14.2 hands. **2a** a small drinking glass, esp. for liqueurs. **2b** the amount held by such a glass. **3** anything small of its kind. **4** *Brit. slang.* a sum of £25, esp. in bookmaking. **5** Also called: **trot.** *U.S. slang.* a literal translation used by students, often illicitly, in preparation for foreign language lessons or examinations; crib. [C17: from Scottish *powney,* perhaps from obsolete French *poulenet* a little colt, from *poulain* colt, from Latin *pullus* young animal, foal]

pony express *n* (in the American West) a system of mail transport that employed relays of riders and mounts, esp. that operating from Missouri to California in 1860–61.

ponytail ('pəʊnɪ,teɪl) *n* a hairstyle in which the hair is pulled tightly into a band or ribbon at the back of the head into a loose hanging fall.

pony trekking *n* the act of riding ponies cross-country, esp. as a pastime.

pooch (pu:tʃ) *n* a slang word for **dog** (sense 1). [of unknown origin]

pood (pu:d) *n* a unit of weight, used in Russia, equal to 36.1 pounds or 16.39 kilograms. [C16: from Russian *pud,* probably from Old Norse *pund* POUND[2]]

poodle ('pu:dᵊl) *n* **1** a breed of dog, with varieties of different sizes, having curly hair, which is generally clipped from ribs to tail: originally bred to hunt waterfowl. **2** a person who is servile; lackey. [C19: from German *Pudel,* short for *Pudelhund,* from *pudeln* to splash + *Hund* dog; the dogs were formerly trained as water dogs; see PUDDLE, HOUND[1]]

poodle-faker *n Slang, old-fashioned.* a young man or newly commissioned officer who makes a point of socializing with women; ladies' man.

poof (pʊf, pu:f) *or* **poove** *n Brit. derogatory slang.* a male homosexual. [C20: from French *pouffe* puff] ▸ **'poofy** *adj*

poofter ('pʊftə, 'pu:f-) *n Derogatory slang.* **1** a man who is considered effeminate or homosexual. **2** *N.Z.* a contemptible person. [C20: expanded form of POOF]

pooh (pu:) *interj* **1** an exclamation of disdain, contempt, or disgust. ◆ *n, vb* **2** a childish word for **faeces** *or* **defecate.**

Pooh-Bah ('pu:'bɑ:) *n* a pompous self-important official holding several offices at once and fulfilling none of them. [C19: after the character, the Lord-High-Everything-Else, in *The Mikado* (1885), a light opera by Gilbert and Sullivan]

pooh-pooh ('pu:'pu:) *vb* (*tr*) to express disdain or scorn for; dismiss or belittle.

pool[1] (pu:l) *n* **1** a small body of still water, usually fresh; small pond. **2** a small isolated collection of liquid spilt or poured on a surface; puddle: *a pool of blood.* **3** a deep part of a stream or river where the water runs very slowly. **4** an underground accumulation of oil or gas, usually forming a reservoir in porous sedimentary rock. **5** See **swimming pool.** [Old English *pōl;* related to Old Frisian *pōl,* German *Pfuhl*]

pool[2] (pu:l) *n* **1** any communal combination of resources, funds, etc.: *a typing pool.* **2** the combined stakes of the betters in many gambling sports or games; kitty. **3** *Commerce.* a group of producers who conspire to establish and maintain output levels and high prices, each member of the group being allocated a maximum quota; price ring. **4** *Finance, chiefly U.S.* **4a** a joint fund organized by security-holders for speculative or manipulative purposes on financial markets. **4b** the persons or parties involved in such a combination. **5** any of various billiard games in which the object is to pot all the balls with the cue ball, esp. that played with 15 coloured and numbered balls, popular in the U.S.; pocket billiards. ◆ *vb* (*tr*) **6** to combine (investments, money, interests, etc.) into a common fund, as for a joint enterprise. **7** *Commerce.* to organize a pool of (enterprises). **8** *Austral. informal.* to inform on or incriminate (someone). ◆ See also **pools.** [C17: from French *poule,* literally: hen used to signify stakes in a card game, from Medieval Latin *pulla* hen, from Latin *pullus* young animal]

Poole (pu:l) *n* **1** a port and resort in S England, in Poole unitary authority, Dorset, on **Poole Harbour.** Pop.: 138 479 (1991). **2** a unitary authority in S England, in Dorset. Pop.: 138 100 (1994 est.). Area: 37 sq. km (14 sq. miles).

Pool Malebo ('pu:l mə'li:bəʊ) *n* the Congolese name for **Stanley Pool.**

poolroom ('pu:l,ru:m, -,rʊm) *n U.S. and Canadian.* a hall or establishment where pool, billiards, etc., are played.

pools (pu:lz) *pl n Brit.* an organized nationwide principally postal gambling pool betting on the result of football matches. Also called: **football pools.** [C20: from POOL[2] (in the sense: a gambling kitty)]

pool table *n* a billiard table on which pool is played.

poon[1] (pu:n) *n* **1** any of several trees of the SE Asian genus *Calophyllum* having lightweight hard wood and shiny leathery leaves: family *Guttiferae.* **2** the wood of any of these trees, used to make masts and spars. [C17: from Singhalese *pūna*]

poon[2] (pu:n) *n Austral. slang.* a stupid or ineffectual person. [C20: from English dialect]

Poona *or* **Pune** ('pu:nə) *n* a city in W India, in W Maharashtra: under British rule served as the seasonal capital of the Bombay Presidency. Pop.: 1 566 651 (1991).

poonce (pu:ns) *n Austral. slang.* **1** a male homosexual. ◆ *vb* (*intr*) **2** to behave effeminately. [C20: perhaps a blend of POOF and PONCE]

poop[1] (pu:p) *Nautical.* ◆ *n* **1** a raised structure at the stern of a vessel, esp. a sailing ship. **2** See **poop deck.** ◆ *vb* **3** (*tr*) (of a wave or sea) to break over the stern of (a vessel). **4** (*intr*) (of a vessel) to ship a wave or sea over the stern, esp. repeatedly. [C15: from Old French *pupe,* from Latin *puppis* poop, ship's stern]

poop[2] (pu:p) *vb U.S. and Canadian slang.* **1** (*tr; usually passive*) to cause to become exhausted; tire: *he was pooped after the race.* **2** (*intr;* usually foll. by *out*) to give up or fail, esp. through tiredness: *he pooped out of the race.* [C14 *poupen* to blow, make a sudden sound, perhaps of imitative origin]

poop[3] (pu:p) *n U.S. and Canadian slang.* **a** information; the facts. **b** (*as modifier*): *a poop sheet.* [of unknown origin]

poop[4] (pu:p) *Informal.* ◆ *vb* (*intr*) **1** to defecate. ◆ *n* **2** faeces; excrement. [perhaps related to POOP[2]]

poop deck *n Nautical.* the deck on top of the poop.

pooper-scooper *n* a device used to remove dogs' excrement from public areas. [C20: POOP[4] + -ER[1] + SCOOP]

Poopó (*Spanish* poo'po) *n* **Lake.** a lake in SW Bolivia, at an altitude of 3688 m (12 100 ft.): fed by the Desaguadero River. Area: 2540 sq. km (980 sq. miles).

poor (pʊə, pɔ:) *adj* **1a** lacking financial or other means of subsistence; needy. **1b** (*as collective n; preceded by the*): *the poor.* **2** characterized by or indicating poverty: *the country had a poor economy.* **3** deficient in amount; scanty or inadequate: *a poor salary.* **4** (when *postpositive,* usually foll. by *in*) badly supplied (with resources, materials, etc.): *a region poor in wild flowers.* **5** lacking in quality; inferior. **6** giving no pleasure; disappointing or disagreeable: *a poor play.* **7** (*prenominal*) deserving of pity; unlucky: *poor John is ill again.* **8 poor man's (something).** a (cheaper) substitute for (something). [C13: from Old French *povre,* from Latin *pauper;* see PAUPER, POVERTY] ▸ **'poorness** *n*

poor box *n* a box, esp. one in a church, used for the collection of alms or money for the poor.

poorhouse ('pʊə,haʊs, 'pɔ:-) *n* (formerly) a publicly maintained institution offering accommodation to the poor.

poor law *n English history.* a law providing for the relief or support of the poor from public, esp. parish, funds.

poorly ('pʊəlɪ, 'pɔ:-) *adv* **1** in a poor way or manner; badly. ◆ *adj* **2** (*usually postpositive*) *Informal.* in poor health; rather ill: *she's poorly today.*

poor man's orange *n N.Z. informal, obsolete.* a grapefruit.

poor mouth *n* **1** *Irish.* unjustified complaining, esp. to excite sympathy: *she always has the poor mouth.* ◆ *vb* **poor-mouth.** (*tr*) **2** *Informal.* to speak of disparagingly; decry.

poor rate *n English history.* a rate or tax levied by parishes for the relief or support of the poor.

poor relation *n* a person or thing considered inferior to another or others: *plastic is a poor relation of real leather.*

poort (pʊət) *n* (in South Africa) a steep narrow mountain pass, usually following a river or stream. [C19: from Afrikaans, from Dutch: gateway; see PORT[4]]

poortith ('pu:r,tɪθ) *n Scot.* a variant of **puirtith.**

poor White *n Often offensive.* **a** a poverty-stricken and underprivileged White person, esp. in the southern U.S. and South Africa. **b** (*as modifier*): *poor White trash.*

Pooterish ('pu:tərɪʃ) *adj* characteristic of or resembling the fictional character Pooter, esp. in being bourgeois, genteel, or self-important. [C20: from Charles *Pooter,* the hero of *Diary of a Nobody* (1892), by George and Weedon Grossmith]

poove (pu:v) *n Brit. derogatory slang.* a variant of **poof.**

pop[1] (pɒp) *vb* **pops, popping, popped.** **1** to make or cause to make a light sharp explosive sound. **2** to burst open or cause to burst open with such a sound. **3** (*intr;* often foll. by *in, out,* etc.) *Informal.* to come (to) or go (from) rapidly or suddenly; to pay a brief or unexpected visit (to). **4** (*intr*) (esp. of the eyes) to protrude: *her eyes popped with amazement.* **5** to shoot or fire at (a target) with a firearm. **6** (*tr*) to place or put with a sudden movement: *she popped some tablets into her mouth.* **7** (*tr*) *Informal.* to pawn: *he popped his watch yesterday.* **8** (*tr*) *Slang.* to take (a drug) in pill form or as an injection: *pill popping.* **9 pop one's clogs.** See **clog** (sense 9). **10 pop the question.** *Informal.*

to propose marriage. ◆ *n* **11** a light sharp explosive sound; crack. **12** *Informal.* a flavoured nonalcoholic carbonated beverage. ◆ *adv* **13** with a popping sound. ◆ *interj* **14** an exclamation denoting a sharp explosive sound. ◆ See also **pop off, pop-up.** [C14: of imitative origin]

pop[2] (pɒp) *n* **1a** music of general appeal, esp. among young people, that originated as a distinctive genre in the 1950s. It is generally characterized by a heavy rhythmic element and the use of electrical amplification. **1b** (*as modifier*): *pop music; a pop record; a pop group.* **2** *Informal.* a piece of popular or light classical music. ◆ *adj* **3** *Informal.* short for **popular.**

pop[3] (pɒp) *n* **1** an informal word for **father. 2** *Informal.* a name used in addressing an old or middle-aged man.

POP *abbrev. for* Post Office Preferred (size of envelopes, etc.).

pop. *abbrev. for:* **1** popular. **2** popularly. **3** population.

pop art *n* a movement in modern art that imitates the methods, styles, and themes of popular culture and mass media, such as comic strips, advertising, and science fiction.

popcorn (ˈpɒpˌkɔːn) *n* **1** a variety of maize having hard pointed kernels that puff up when heated. **2** the puffed edible kernels of this plant. [C19: so called because of the noise the grains make when they swell up and burst on heating]

pope[1] (pəʊp) *n* **1** (*often cap.*) the bishop of Rome as head of the Roman Catholic Church. Related adj: **papal. 2** *Eastern Orthodox Churches.* **2a** a title sometimes given to a parish priest. **2b** a title sometimes given to the Greek Orthodox patriarch of Alexandria. **3** a person assuming or having a status or authority resembling that of a pope. [Old English *papa,* from Church Latin: bishop, esp. of Rome, from Late Greek *papas* father-in-God, from Greek *pappas* father]

pope[2] (pəʊp) *n* another name for **ruffe** (the fish).

Pope (pəʊp) *n* **Alexander.** 1688–1744, English poet, regarded as the most brilliant satirist of the Augustan period, esp. with his *Imitations of Horace* (1733–38). His technical virtuosity is most evident in *The Rape of the Lock* (1712–14). Other works include *The Dunciad* (1728; 1742), the *Moral Essays* (1731–35), and *An Essay on Man* (1733–34).

popedom (ˈpəʊpdəm) *n* **1** the office or dignity of a pope. **2** the tenure of office of a pope. **3** the dominion of a pope; papal government.

popery (ˈpəʊpərɪ) *n* a derogatory name for **Roman Catholicism.**

pope's eye *n* **1** (in sheep and cows) a gland in the middle of the thigh surrounded by fat. ◆ *adj* **popeseye. 2** (in Scotland) denoting a cut of steak.

pope's nose *n* another name for **parson's nose.**

popeyed (ˈpɒpˌaɪd) *adj* **1** having bulging prominent eyes. **2** staring in astonishment; amazed.

popgun (ˈpɒpˌɡʌn) *n* a toy gun that fires a pellet or cork by means of compressed air and makes a popping sound.

popinjay (ˈpɒpɪnˌdʒeɪ) *n* **1** a conceited, foppish, or excessively talkative person. **2** an archaic word for **parrot. 3** the figure of a parrot used as a target. [C13 *papeniai,* from Old French *papegay* a parrot, from Spanish *papagayo,* from Arabic *babaghā*]

popish (ˈpəʊpɪʃ) *adj Derogatory.* belonging to or characteristic of Roman Catholicism. ▸ **ˈpopishly** *adv*

Popish Plot *n* a supposed conspiracy (1678) to murder Charles II of England and replace him with his Catholic brother James: in reality a fabrication by the informer Titus Oates.

poplar (ˈpɒplə) *n* **1** any tree of the salicaceous genus *Populus,* of N temperate regions, having triangular leaves, flowers borne in catkins, and light soft wood. See also **aspen, balsam poplar, Lombardy poplar, white poplar. 2** any of various trees resembling the true poplars, such as the tulip tree. **3** the wood of any of these trees. [C14: from Old French *poplier,* from *pouple,* from Latin *pōpulus*]

poplin (ˈpɒplɪn) *n* **a** a strong fabric, usually of cotton, in plain weave with fine ribbing, used for dresses, children's wear, etc. **b** (*as modifier*): *a poplin shirt.* [C18: from French *papeline,* perhaps from *Poperinge,* a centre of textile manufacture in Flanders]

popliteal (pɒpˈlɪtɪəl, ˌpɒplɪˈtiːəl) *adj* of, relating to, or near the part of the leg behind the knee. [C18: from New Latin *popliteus* the muscle behind the knee joint, from Latin *poples* the ham of the knee]

popmobility (ˌpɒpməʊˈbɪlɪtɪ) *n* a form of exercise that combines aerobics in a continuous dance routine, performed to pop music. [C20: POP[2] + MOBILITY]

Popocatépetl (ˌpɒpəˈkætəpɛtᵊl, -ˌkætəˈpɛtᵊl; *Spanish* popokaˈtepetl) *n* a volcano in SE central Mexico, southeast of Mexico City. Height: 5452 m (17 887 ft.).

pop off *vb* (*intr, adv*) *Informal.* **1** to depart suddenly or unexpectedly. **2** to die, esp. suddenly or unexpectedly: *he popped off at the age of sixty.* **3** to speak out angrily or indiscreetly: *he popped off at his boss and got fired.*

Popov (*Russian* paˈpɔf) *n* **1 Alexander Stepanovich** (alɪkˈsandᵊr stɪˈpanəvitʃ). 1859–1906, Russian physicist, the first to use an aerial in experiments with radio waves. **2 Oleg** (**Konstantinovich**). born 1930, Russian clown, a member of the Moscow Circus.

popover (ˈpɒpˌəʊvə) *n* **1** *Brit.* an individual Yorkshire pudding, often served with roast beef. **2** *U.S. and Canadian.* a light puffy hollow muffin made from a batter mixture. **3** a simple garment for women or girls that is put on by being slipped over the head.

poppadom *or* **poppadum** (ˈpɒpədəm) *n* a thin round crisp Indian bread, fried or roasted and served with curry, etc. [from Hindi]

popper (ˈpɒpə) *n* **1** a person or thing that pops. **2** *Brit.* an informal name for **press stud. 3** *Chiefly U.S. and Canadian.* a container for cooking popcorn in. **4** *Slang.* an amyl nitrite capsule, which is crushed and its contents inhaled by drug users as a stimulant.

Popper (ˈpɒpə) *n* Sir **Karl.** 1902–94, British philosopher, born in Vienna. In *The Logic of Scientific Discovery* (1934), he proposes that knowledge cannot be absolutely confirmed, but rather that science progresses by the experimental refutation of the current theory and its consequent replacement by a new theory, equally provisional but covering more of the known data. *The Open Society and its Enemies* (1945) is a critique of dogmatic political philosophies, such as Marxism. Other works are *The Poverty of Historicism* (1957), *Conjectures and Refutations* (1963), and *Objective Knowledge* (1972). ▸ **Popperian** (pɒˈpɪərɪən) *n, adj*

poppet (ˈpɒpɪt) *n* **1** a term of affection for a small child or sweetheart. **2** Also called: **poppet valve.** a mushroom-shaped valve that is lifted from its seating by applying an axial force to its stem: commonly used as an exhaust or inlet valve in an internal-combustion engine. **3** *Nautical.* a temporary supporting brace for a vessel hauled on land or in a dry dock. [C14: early variant of PUPPET]

poppet head *n* the framework above a mining shaft that supports the winding mechanism.

poppied (ˈpɒpɪd) *adj* **1** covered with poppies. **2** of or relating to the effects of poppies, esp. in inducing drowsiness or sleep.

popping crease *n Cricket.* a line four feet in front of and parallel with the bowling crease, at or behind which the batsman stands. [C18: from POP[1] (in the obsolete or dialect sense: to hit) + CREASE[1]]

popple (ˈpɒpᵊl) *vb* (*intr*) **1** (of boiling water or a choppy sea) to heave or toss; bubble. **2** (often foll. by *along*) (of a stream or river) to move with an irregular tumbling motion: *the small rivulet poppled along over rocks and stones for half a mile.* [C14: of imitative origin; compare Middle Dutch *popelen* to bubble, throb]

poppy (ˈpɒpɪ) *n, pl* **-pies. 1** any of numerous papaveraceous plants of the temperate genus *Papaver,* having red, orange, or white flowers and a milky sap: see **corn poppy, Iceland poppy, opium poppy. 2** any of several similar or related plants, such as the California poppy, prickly poppy, horned poppy, and Welsh poppy. **3** any of the drugs, such as opium, that are obtained from these plants. **4a** a strong red to reddish-orange colour. **4b** (*as adj*): *a poppy dress.* **5** a less common name for **poppyhead** (sense 2). **6** an artificial red poppy flower worn to mark Remembrance Sunday. [Old English *popæg,* ultimately from Latin *papāver*]

poppycock (ˈpɒpɪˌkɒk) *n Informal.* senseless chatter; nonsense. [C19: from Dutch dialect *pappekak,* literally: soft excrement, from *pap* soft + *kak* dung; see PAP[1]]

Poppy Day *n* an informal name for **Remembrance Sunday.**

poppyhead (ˈpɒpɪˌhɛd) *n* **1** the hard dry seed-containing capsule of a poppy. See also **capsule** (sense 3a). **2** a carved ornament, esp. one used on the top of the end of a pew or bench in Gothic church architecture.

poppy seed *n* the small grey seeds of one type of poppy flower, used esp. on loaves and as a cake filling.

pop shop *n* a slang word for a **pawnshop.**

Popsicle (ˈpɒpsɪkᵊl) *n U.S. and Canadian trademark.* an ice lolly.

popsy (ˈpɒpsɪ) *n, pl* **-sies.** *Old-fashioned Brit. slang.* an attractive young woman. [C19: diminutive formed from *pop,* shortened from POPPET; originally a nursery term]

populace (ˈpɒpjʊləs) *n* (*sometimes functioning as pl*) **1** the inhabitants of an area. **2** the common people; masses. [C16: via French from Italian *popolaccio* the common herd, from *popolo* people, from Latin *populus*]

popular (ˈpɒpjʊlə) *adj* **1** appealing to the general public; widely favoured or admired. **2** favoured by an individual or limited group: *I'm not very popular with her.* **3** connected with, representing, or prevailing among the general public; common: *popular discontent.* **4** appealing to or comprehensible to the layman: *a popular lecture on physics.* ◆ *n* **5** (*usually pl*) cheap newspapers with mass circulation; the popular press. Also shortened to **pops.** [C15: from Latin *populāris* belonging to the people, democratic, from *populus* people] ▸ **popularity** (ˌpɒpjʊˈlærɪtɪ) *n*

popular etymology *n Linguistics.* another name for **folk etymology.**

popular front *n* (*often cap.*) any of the left-wing groups or parties that were organized from 1935 onwards to oppose the spread of fascism.

popularize *or* **popularise** (ˈpɒpjʊləˌraɪz) *vb* (*tr*) **1** to make popular; make attractive to the general public. **2** to make or cause to become easily understandable or acceptable. ▸ **ˌpopulariˈzation** *or* **ˌpopulariˈsation** *n* ▸ **ˈpopularˌizer** *or* **ˈpopularˌiser** *n*

popularly (ˈpɒpjʊləlɪ) *adv* **1** by the public as a whole; generally or widely. **2** usually; commonly: *his full name is Robert, but he is popularly known as Bob.* **3** in a popular manner.

popular music *n* music having wide appeal, esp. characterized by lightly romantic or sentimental melodies. See also **pop**[2].

popular sovereignty *n* (in the pre-Civil War U.S.) the doctrine that the inhabitants of a territory should be free from federal interference in determining their own domestic policy, esp. in deciding whether or not to allow slavery.

populate (ˈpɒpjʊˌleɪt) *vb* (*tr*) **1** (*often passive*) to live in; inhabit. **2** to provide a population for; colonize or people. [C16: from Medieval Latin *populāre* to provide with inhabitants, from Latin *populus* people]

population (ˌpɒpjʊˈleɪʃən) *n* **1** (*sometimes functioning as pl*) all the persons inhabiting a country, city, or other specified place. **2** the number of such inhabitants. **3** (*sometimes functioning as pl*) all the people of a particular race or class in a specific area: *the Chinese population of San Francisco.* **4** the act or process of providing a place with inhabitants; colonization. **5** *Ecology.* a group of individuals of the same species inhabiting a given area. **6** *Astronomy.* either of two main groups of stars classified according to age and location. **Population I** consists of hot white stars, many occurring in galactic clusters and forming the arms of spiral galaxies. Stars of **population II** are older, the brightest being red giants, and are found in the centre of spiral and elliptical galaxies in globular clusters. **7** Also called: **universe.** *Statistics.* the entire finite or infinite aggregate of individuals or items from which samples are drawn.

population control *n* a policy of attempting to limit the growth in numbers of a population, esp. in poor or densely populated parts of the world, by programmes of contraception or sterilization.

population explosion *n* a rapid increase in the size of a population caused by such factors as a sudden decline in infant mortality or an increase in life expectancy.

population pyramid *n* a pyramid-shaped diagram illustrating the age distribution of a population: the youngest are represented by a rectangle at the base, the oldest by one at the apex.

populism ('pɒpjʊˌlɪzəm) *n* a political strategy based on a calculated appeal to the interests or prejudices of ordinary people.

populist ('pɒpjʊlɪst) *adj* **1** appealing to the interests or prejudices of ordinary people. ◆ *n* **2** a person, esp. a politician, who appeals to the interests or prejudices of ordinary people.

Populist ('pɒpjʊlɪst) *n* **1** *U.S. history.* a member of the People's Party, formed largely by agrarian interests to contest the 1892 presidential election. The movement gradually dissolved after the 1904 election. ◆ *adj also* **Populistic. 2** of, characteristic of, or relating to the People's Party, the Populists, or any individual or movement with similar aims. ► **'Populism** *n*

populist shop steward *n* a shop steward who operates in a delegate role, putting the immediate interests of his members before union principles and policies.

populous ('pɒpjʊləs) *adj* containing many inhabitants; abundantly populated. **[C15:** from Late Latin *populōsus***]** ► **'populously** *adv* ► **'populousness** *n*

pop-up *adj* **1** (of an appliance) characterized by or having a mechanism that pops up: *a pop-up toaster.* **2** (of a book) having pages that rise when opened to simulate a three-dimensional form. ◆ *vb* **pop up. 3** (*intr, adv*) to appear suddenly from below.

porangi ('pɔːræŋɪ) *adj N.Z. informal.* crazy; mad. **[**Maori**]**

porbeagle ('pɔːˌbiːgᵊl) *n* any of several voracious sharks of the genus *Lamna,* esp. *L. nasus,* of northern seas: family *Isuridae.* Also called: **mackerel shark. [C18:** from Cornish *porgh-bugel,* of obscure origin**]**

porcelain ('pɔːslɪn, -leɪn, 'pɔːsə-) *n* **1** a more or less translucent ceramic material, the principal ingredients being kaolin and petuntse (hard paste) or other clays, ground glassy substances, soapstone, bone ash, etc. **2** an object made of this or such objects collectively. **3** (*modifier*) of, relating to, or made from this material: *a porcelain cup.* **[C16:** from French *porcelaine,* from Italian *porcellana* cowrie shell, porcelain (from its shell-like finish), literally: relating to a sow (from the resemblance between a cowrie shell and a sow's vulva), from *porcella* little sow, from *porca* sow, from Latin; see PORK**]** ► **porcellaneous** (ˌpɔːsəˈleɪnɪəs) *adj*

porcelain clay *n* another name for **kaolin.**

porch (pɔːtʃ) *n* **1** a low structure projecting from the doorway of a house and forming a covered entrance. **2** *U.S. and Canadian.* an exterior roofed gallery, often partly enclosed; veranda. **[C13:** from French *porche,* from Latin *porticus* portico**]**

porcine ('pɔːsaɪn) *adj* of, connected with, or characteristic of pigs. **[C17:** from Latin *porcīnus,* from *porcus* pig**]**

porcino (pɔːˈtʃiːnəʊ) *n, pl* **porcini** (pɔːˈtʃiːnɪ). an edible saprotrophic basidiomycetous woodland fungus, *Boletus edulis,* with a brown shining cap covering white spore-bearing tubes and having a rich nutty flavour: family *Boletineae.* Also called: **cep. [**Italian, from Latin *porcīnus,* from *porcus* pig**]**

porcupine ('pɔːkjʊˌpaɪn) *n* any of various large hystricomorph rodents of the families *Hystricidae,* of Africa, Indonesia, S Europe, and S Asia, and *Erethizontidae,* of the New World. All species have a body covering of protective spines or quills. **[C14** *porc despyne* pig with spines, from Old French *porc espin;* see PORK, SPINE**]** ► **'porcuˌpinish** *adj* ► **'porcuˌpiny** *adj*

porcupine fish *n* any of various plectognath fishes of the genus *Diodon* and related genera, of temperate and tropical seas, having a body that is covered with sharp spines and can be inflated into a globe: family *Diodontidae.* Also called: **globefish.**

porcupine grass *n Austral.* another name for **spinifex** (sense 2).

porcupine provisions *pl n Finance.* provisions, such as poison pills or staggered directorships, made in the bylaws of a company to deter takeover bids. Also called: **shark repellents.**

pore[1] (pɔː) *vb* (*intr*) **1** (foll. by *over*) to make a close intent examination or study (of a book, map, etc.): *he pored over the documents for several hours.* **2** (foll. by *over, on,* or *upon*) to think deeply (about): *he pored on the question of their future.* **3** (foll. by *over, on,* or *upon*) *Rare.* to look earnestly or intently (at); gaze fixedly (upon). **[C13** *pouren;* perhaps related to PEER[2]**]**

USAGE See at **pour.**

pore[2] (pɔː) *n* **1** *Anatomy, zoology.* any small opening in the skin or outer surface of an animal. **2** *Botany.* any small aperture, esp. that of a stoma through which water vapour and gases pass. **3** any other small hole, such as a space in a rock, soil, etc. **[C14:** from Late Latin *porus,* from Greek *poros* passage, pore**]**

porgy ('pɔːgɪ) *n, pl* **-gy** *or* **-gies. 1** Also called: **pogy.** any of various sparid fishes, many of which occur in American Atlantic waters. See also **scup, sheepshead. 2** any of various similar or related fishes. **[C18:** from Spanish *pargo,* from Latin *phager* type of fish, from Greek *phagros* sea bream**]**

Pori (*Finnish* 'pɔri) *n* a port in SW Finland, on the Gulf of Bothnia. Pop.: 76 561 (1994). Swedish name: **Björneborg.**

poriferan (pɔːˈrɪfərən) *n* **1** any invertebrate of the phylum *Porifera,* which comprises the sponges. ◆ *adj also* **poriferous. 2** of, relating to, or belonging to the phylum *Porifera.* **[C19:** from New Latin *porifer* bearing pores**]**

poriferous (pɔːˈrɪfərəs) *adj* **1** *Biology.* having many pores. **2** another word for **poriferan** (sense 2).

porina (pɒˈraɪnə) *n N.Z.* **a** the larva of a moth which causes damage to grassland. **b** (*as modifier*): *porina infestation.* **[**from New Latin**]**

Porirua (ˌpɔːrɪˈruːə) *n* a city in New Zealand, on the North Island just north of Wellington. Pop.: 46 601 (1991).

porism ('pɔːrɪzəm) *n* a type of mathematical proposition considered by Euclid, the meaning of which is now obscure. It is thought to be a proposition affirming the possibility of finding such conditions as will render a certain problem indeterminate or capable of innumerable solutions. **[C14:** from Late Latin *porisma,* from Greek: deduction, from *porizein* to deduce, carry; related to Greek *poros* passage**]** ► **porismatic** (ˌpɔːrɪzˈmætɪk) *adj*

pork (pɔːk) *n* the flesh of pigs used as food. **[C13:** from Old French *porc,* from Latin *porcus* pig**]**

pork barrel *n Slang, chiefly U.S.* a bill or project requiring considerable government spending in a locality to the benefit of the legislator's constituents who live there. **[C20:** term originally applied to the Federal treasury considered as a source of lucrative grants**]**

porker ('pɔːkə) *n* a pig, esp. a young one weighing between 40 and 67 kg, fattened to provide meat such as pork chops.

pork pie *n* **1** a pie filled with minced seasoned pork. **2** See **porky**[2].

porkpie hat ('pɔːkˌpaɪ) *n* a hat with a round flat crown and a brim that can be turned up or down.

pork pig *n* a pig, typically of a lean type, bred and used principally for pork.

pork scratchings *pl n* small pieces of crisply cooked pork crackling, eaten cold as an appetizer with drinks.

porky[1] ('pɔːkɪ) *adj* **porkier, porkiest. 1** belonging to or characteristic of pork: *a porky smell.* **2** *Informal.* fat; obese. ► **'porkiness** *n*

porky[2] ('pɔːkɪ) *n, pl* **porkies.** *Brit. slang.* a lie. Also called: **pork pie. [**from rhyming slang *pork pie* lie**]**

porn (pɔːn) *or* **porno** ('pɔːnəʊ) *n, adj Informal.* short for **pornography** or **pornographic.**

pornocracy (pɔːˈnɒkrəsɪ) *n* government or domination of government by whores. **[C19:** from Greek, from *pornē* a prostitute, harlot + -CRACY**]**

pornography (pɔːˈnɒgrəfɪ) *n* **1** writings, pictures, films, etc., designed to stimulate sexual excitement. **2** the production of such material. ◆ Sometimes (informal) shortened to **porn** *or* **porno. [C19:** from Greek *pornographos* writing of harlots, from *pornē* a harlot + *graphein* to write**]** ► **por'nographer** *n* ► **pornographic** (ˌpɔːnəˈgræfɪk) *adj* ► **ˌporno'graphically** *adv*

poromeric (ˌpɔːrəˈmɛrɪk) *adj* **1** (of a plastic) permeable to water vapour. ◆ *n* **2** a substance having this characteristic, esp. one based on polyurethane and used in place of leather in making shoe uppers. **[C20:** from PORO(SITY) + (POLY)MER + -IC**]**

porosity (pɔːˈrɒsɪtɪ) *n, pl* **-ties. 1** the state or condition of being porous. **2** *Geology.* the ratio of the volume of space to the total volume of a rock. **[C14:** from Medieval Latin *porōsitās,* from Late Latin *porus* PORE[2]**]**

porous ('pɔːrəs) *adj* **1** permeable to water, air, or other fluids. **2** *Biology, geology.* having pores; poriferous. **[C14:** from Medieval Latin *porōsus,* from Late Latin *porus* PORE[2]**]** ► **'porously** *adv* ► **'porousness** *n*

porphyria (pɔːˈfɪrɪə) *n* a hereditary disease of body metabolism, producing abdominal pain, mental confusion, etc. **[C19:** from New Latin, from *porphyrin* a purple substance excreted by patients suffering from this condition, from Greek *porphura* purple**]**

porphyrin ('pɔːfɪrɪn) *n* any of a group of pigments occurring widely in animal and plant tissues and having a heterocyclic structure formed from four pyrrole rings linked by four methylene groups. **[C20:** from Greek *porphura* purple, referring to its colour**]**

porphyritic (ˌpɔːfɪˈrɪtɪk) *adj* **1** (of rocks) having large crystals in a fine groundmass of minerals. **2** consisting of porphyry.

porphyrogenite (ˌpɔːfəˈrɒdʒɪˌnaɪt) *n* (*sometimes cap.*) a prince born after his father has succeeded to the throne. **[C17:** via Medieval Latin from Late Greek *porphurogenētos* born in the purple, from Greek *porphuros* purple**]**

porphyroid ('pɔːfɪˌrɔɪd) *adj* **1** (of metamorphic rocks) having a texture characterized by large crystals set in a finer groundmass. ◆ *n* **2** a metamorphic rock having this texture.

porphyropsin (ˌpɔːfɪˈrɒpsɪn) *n* a purple pigment occurring in the retina of the eye of certain freshwater fishes. **[C20:** from Greek *porphura* purple + -OPSIS + -IN, on the model of RHODOPSIN**]**

porphyry ('pɔːfɪrɪ) *n, pl* **-ries. 1** a reddish-purple rock consisting of large crystals of feldspar in a finer groundmass of feldspar, hornblende, etc. **2** any igneous rock with large crystals embedded in a finer groundmass of minerals. **[C14** *porfurie,* from Late Latin *porphyrītēs,* from Greek *porphuritēs* (*lithos*) purple (stone), from *porphuros* purple**]**

Porphyry ('pɔːfɪrɪ) *n* original name *Malchus.* 232–305 A.D., Greek Neo-Platonist philosopher, born in Syria; disciple and biographer of Plotinus.

porpoise ('pɔːpəs) *n, pl* **-poises** *or* **-poise. 1** any of various small cetacean mammals of the genus *Phocaena* and related genera, having a blunt snout and many teeth: family *Delphinidae* (or *Phocaenidae*). **2** (*not in technical use*) any of various related cetaceans, esp. the dolphin. **[C14:** from French *pourpois,* from Medieval Latin *porcopiscus* (from Latin *porcus* pig + *piscis* fish), replacing Latin *porcus marīnus* sea pig**]**

porrect (pəˈrɛkt) *adj Botany.* extended forwards. **[C20:** from Latin *porrectus,* from *porrigere* to stretch out**]**

porridge ('pɒrɪdʒ) *n* **1** a dish made from oatmeal or another cereal, cooked in water or milk to a thick consistency. **2** *Slang.* a term in prison (esp. in the phrase **do porridge**). **[C16:** variant (influenced by Middle English *porray* pottage) of POTTAGE**]**

porringer ('pɒrɪndʒə) *n* a small dish, often with a handle, for soup, porridge, etc. **[C16:** changed from Middle English *potinger, poteger,* from Old French *potager,* from *potage* soup, contents of a pot; see POTTAGE**]**

Porsena ('pɔːsɪnə) *or* **Porsenna** (pɔːˈsɛnə) *n* **Lars** (lɑːz). 6th century B.C., a legendary Etruscan king, alleged to have besieged Rome in a vain attempt to reinstate Tarquinius Superbus on the throne.

Porson ('pɔːsᵊn) *n* **Richard.** 1759–1808, English classical scholar, noted for his editions of Aeschylus and Euripides.

port[1] (pɔːt) *n* **1** a town or place alongside navigable water with facilities for the loading and unloading of ships. **2** See **port of entry.** [Old English, from Latin *portus* harbour, port]

port[2] (pɔːt) *n* **1** Also called (formerly): **larboard. 1a** the left side of an aircraft or vessel when facing the nose or bow. **1b** (*as modifier*): *the port bow.* Compare **starboard** (sense 1). ◆ *vb* **2** to turn or be turned towards the port. [C17: origin uncertain]

port[3] (pɔːt) *n* a sweet fortified dessert wine. [C17: after *Oporto,* Portugal, from where it came originally]

port[4] (pɔːt) *n* **1** *Nautical.* **1a** an opening in the side of a ship, fitted with a watertight door, for access to the holds. **1b** See **porthole** (sense 1). **2** a small opening in a wall, armoured vehicle, etc., for firing through. **3** an aperture, esp. one controlled by a valve, by which fluid enters or leaves the cylinder head of an engine, compressor, etc. **4** *Electronics.* a logical circuit for the input and ouput of data. **5** *Chiefly Scot.* a gate or portal in a town or fortress. [Old English, from Latin *porta* gate]

port[5] (pɔːt) *Military.* ◆ *vb* **1** (*tr*) to carry (a rifle, etc.) in a position diagonally across the body with the muzzle near the left shoulder. ◆ *n* **2** this position. [C14: from Old French, from *porter* to carry, from Latin *portāre*]

port[6] (pɔːt) *vb* (*tr*) *Computing technol.* to change (programs) from one system to another. [C20: probably from PORT[4]]

port[7] (pɔːt) *n Austral.* (esp. in Queensland) a suitcase or school case. [C20: shortened from PORTMANTEAU]

Port. *abbrev. for:* **1** Portugal. **2** Portuguese.

porta ('pɔːtə) *n Anatomy.* an aperture in an organ, such as the liver, esp. one providing an opening for blood vessels. [C14: from Latin: gate, entrance]

portable ('pɔːtəbᵊl) *adj* **1** able to be carried or moved easily, esp. by hand. **2** (of software, files, etc.) able to be transferred from one type of computer system to another. **3** *Archaic.* able to be endured; bearable. ◆ *n* **4** an article designed to be readily carried by hand, such as a television, typewriter, etc. [C14: from Late Latin *portābilis,* from Latin *portāre* to carry] ► **ˌporta'bility** *n* ► **'portably** *adv*

Port Adelaide *n* the chief port of South Australia, near Adelaide on St Vincent Gulf. Pop.: 39 000 (latest est.).

Portadown (ˌpɔːtə'daʊn) *n* a town in S Northern Ireland, in the district of Armagh. Pop.: 21 299 (1991).

portage ('pɔːtɪdʒ; *French* pɔrtaʒ) *n* **1** the act of carrying; transport. **2** the cost of carrying or transporting. **3** the act or process of transporting boats, supplies, etc., overland between navigable waterways. **4** the route overland used for such transport. ◆ *vb* **5** to transport (boats, supplies, etc.) overland between navigable waterways. [C15: from French, from Old French *porter* to carry]

Portakabin ('pɔːtəˌkæbɪn) *n Trademark.* a portable building quickly set up for use as a temporary office, etc.

portal ('pɔːtᵊl) *n* **1** an entrance, gateway, or doorway, esp. one that is large and impressive. **2** any entrance or access to a place.◆ *adj* **3** *Anatomy.* **3a** of or relating to a portal vein: *hepatic portal system.* **3b** of or relating to a porta. [C14: via Old French from Medieval Latin *portāle,* from Latin *porta* gate, entrance]

portal frame *n Civil engineering, building trades.* a frame, usually of steel, consisting of two uprights and a cross beam at the top: the simplest structural unit in a framed building or a doorway.

portal-to-portal *adj* of or relating to the period between the actual times workers enter and leave their mine, factory, etc.: *portal-to-portal pay.*

portal vein *n* any vein connecting two capillary networks, esp. in the liver (**hepatic portal vein**).

portamento (ˌpɔːtə'mɛntəʊ) *n, pl* **-ti** (-tɪ). *Music.* a smooth slide from one note to another in which intervening notes are not separately discernible. Compare **glissando.** [C18: from Italian: a carrying, from Latin *portāre* to carry]

Port Arthur *n* **1** a former penal settlement (1833–70) in Australia, on the S coast of the Tasman Peninsula, Tasmania. **2** the former name of **Lüshun.**

portative ('pɔːtətɪv) *adj* **1** a less common word for **portable. 2** concerned with the act of carrying. [C14: from French, from Latin *portāre* to carry]

portative organ *n Music.* a small portable organ with arm-operated bellows popular in medieval times.

Port-au-Prince ('pɔːtəʊ'prɪns; *French* pɔrtoprɛ̃s) *n* the capital and chief port of Haiti, in the south on the Gulf of Gonaïves: founded in 1749 by the French; university (1944). Pop.: 846 247 (1995 est.).

Port Blair (blɛə) *n* the capital of the Indian Union Territory of the Andaman and Nicobar Islands, a port on the SE coast of South Andaman Island: a former penal colony. Pop.: 74 955 (1991).

portcullis (pɔːt'kʌlɪs) *n* an iron or wooden grating suspended vertically in grooves in the gateway of a castle or fortified town and able to be lowered so as to bar the entrance. [C14 *port colice,* from Old French *porte coleïce* sliding gate, from *porte* door, entrance + *coleïce,* from *couler* to slide, flow, from Late Latin *cōlāre* to filter]

Porte (pɔːt) *n* short for **Sublime Porte;** the court or government of the Ottoman Empire. [C17: shortened from French *Sublime Porte* High Gate, rendering the Turkish title *Babi Ali,* the imperial gate, which was regarded as the seat of government]

porte-cochere (ˌpɔːtkɒ'ʃɛə) *n* **1** a large covered entrance for vehicles leading into a courtyard. **2** a large roof projecting over a drive to shelter travellers entering or leaving vehicles. [C17: from French: carriage entrance, from *porte* gateway + *coche* coach]

Port Elizabeth *n* a port in S South Africa, on Algoa Bay: motor-vehicle manufacture, fruit canning; resort. Pop.: 303 353 (1991).

portend (pɔː'tɛnd) *vb* (*tr*) **1** to give warning of; predict or foreshadow. **2** *Obsolete.* to indicate or signify; mean. [C15: from Latin *portendere* to indicate, foretell; related to *prōtendere* to stretch out]

portent ('pɔːtɛnt) *n* **1** a sign or indication of a future event, esp. a momentous or calamitous one; omen. **2** momentous or ominous significance: *a cry of dire portent.* **3** a miraculous occurrence; marvel. [C16: from Latin *portentum* sign, omen, from *portendere* to PORTEND]

portentous (pɔː'tɛntəs) *adj* **1** of momentous or ominous significance. **2** miraculous, amazing, or awe-inspiring; prodigious. **3** self-important or pompous. ► **por'tentously** *adv* ► **por'tentousness** *n*

porter[1] ('pɔːtə) *n* **1** a person employed to carry luggage, parcels, supplies, etc., esp. at a railway station or hotel. **2** (in hospitals) a person employed to move patients from place to place. **3** *U.S. and Canadian.* a railway employee who waits on passengers, esp. in a sleeper. **4** *E African.* a manual labourer. [C14: from Old French *portour,* from Late Latin *portātōr,* from Latin *portāre* to carry]

porter[2] ('pɔːtə) *n* **1** *Chiefly Brit.* a person in charge of a gate or door; doorman or gatekeeper. **2** a person employed by a university or college as a caretaker and doorkeeper who also answers enquiries. **3** a person in charge of the maintenance of a building, esp. a block of flats. **4** Also called: **ostiary.** *R.C. Church.* a person ordained to what was formerly the lowest in rank of the minor orders. [C13: from Old French *portier,* from Late Latin *portārius* doorkeeper, from Latin *porta* door]

porter[3] ('pɔːtə) *n Brit.* a dark sweet ale brewed from black malt. [C18: shortened from *porter's ale,* apparently because it was a favourite beverage of porters]

Porter ('pɔːtə) *n* **1 Cole.** 1893–1964, U.S. composer and lyricist of musical comedies. His most popular songs include *Night and Day* and *Let's do It.* **2 George,** Baron Porter of Luddenham. born 1920, British chemist, who shared a Nobel prize for chemistry in 1967 for his work on flash photolysis. **3 Katherine Anne.** 1890–1980, U.S. short-story writer and novelist. Her best-known collections of stories are *Flowering Judas* (1930) and *Pale Horse, Pale Rider* (1939). **4 Peter.** born 1929, Australian poet, living in Britain. **5 Rodney Robert.** 1917–85, British biochemist: shared the Nobel prize for physiology or medicine 1972 for determining the structure of an antibody. **6 William Sidney.** original name of **O. Henry.**

porterage ('pɔːtərɪdʒ) *n* **1** the work of carrying supplies, goods, etc., done by porters. **2** the charge made for this.

porterhouse ('pɔːtəˌhaʊs) *n* **1** Also called: **porterhouse steak.** a thick choice steak of beef cut from the middle ribs or sirloin. **2** (formerly) a place in which porter, beer, etc., and sometimes chops and steaks, were served. [C19 (sense 1): said to be named after a porterhouse or chophouse in New York]

portfire ('pɔːtˌfaɪə) *n* (formerly) a slow-burning fuse used for firing rockets and fireworks and, in mining, for igniting explosives. [C17: from French *porte-feu,* from *porter* to carry + *feu* fire]

portfolio (pɔːt'fəʊlɪəʊ) *n, pl* **-os. 1** a flat case, esp. of leather, used for carrying maps, drawings, etc. **2** the contents of such a case, such as drawings, paintings, or photographs, that demonstrate recent work: *an art student's portfolio.* **3** such a case used for carrying ministerial or state papers. **4** the responsibilities or role of the head of a government department: *the portfolio for foreign affairs.* **5 Minister without portfolio.** a cabinet minister who is not responsible for any government department. **6** the complete investments held by an individual investor or by a financial organization. [C18: from Italian *portafoglio,* from *portāre* to carry + *foglio* leaf, paper, from Latin *folium* leaf]

Port-Gentil (*French* pɔrʒɑ̃ti) *n* the chief port of Gabon, in the west near the mouth of the Ogooué River: oil refinery. Pop.: 80 841 (1993).

Port Harcourt ('hɑːkət, -kɔːt) *n* a port in S Nigeria, capital of Rivers state on the Niger delta: the nation's second largest port; industrial centre. Pop.: 410 000 (1996 est.).

porthole ('pɔːtˌhəʊl) *n* **1** a small aperture in the side of a vessel to admit light and air, usually fitted with a watertight glass or metal cover, or both. Sometimes shortened to **port. 2** an opening in a wall or parapet through which a gun can be fired; embrasure.

portico ('pɔːtɪkəʊ) *n, pl* **-coes** *or* **-cos. 1** a covered entrance to a building; porch. **2** a covered walkway in the form of a roof supported by columns or pillars, esp. one built on to the exterior of a building. [C17: via Italian from Latin *porticus* PORCH]

portière (ˌpɔːtɪ'ɛə; *French* pɔrtjɛr) *n* a curtain hung in a doorway. [C19: via French from Medieval Latin *portāria,* from Latin *porta* door] ► **ˌporti'èred** *adj*

Porţile de Fier (pɔr'tsiːlɛ dɛ 'fjɛr) *n* the Romanian name for the **Iron Gate.**

portion ('pɔːʃən) *n* **1** a part of a whole; fraction. **2** a part allotted or belonging to a person or group. **3** an amount of food served to one person; helping. **4** *Law.* **4a** a share of property, esp. one coming to a child from the estate of his parents. **4b** the property given by a woman to her husband at marriage; dowry. **5** a person's lot or destiny. ◆ *vb* (*tr*) **6** to divide up; share out. **7** to give a share to (a person); assign or allocate. **8** *Law.* to give a dowry or portion to (a person); endow. [C13: via Old French from Latin *portiō* portion, allocation; related to *pars* PART] ► **'portionless** *adj*

Port Jackson *n* an inlet of the Pacific on the coast of SE Australia, forming a fine natural harbour: site of the city of Sydney, spanned by Sydney Harbour Bridge.

Portland[1] ('pɔːtlənd) *n* **1 Isle of.** a rugged limestone peninsula in SW England, in Dorset, connected to the mainland by a narrow isthmus and by Chesil Bank: the lighthouse of **Portland Bill** lies at the S tip; famous for the quarrying of **Portland stone,** a fine building material. Pop. (town): 12 000 (latest est.). **2** an inland port in NW Oregon, on the Willamette River: the largest city in the state; shipbuilding and chemical industries. Pop.: 480 824 (1996 est.). **3** a port in SW Maine, on Casco Bay: the largest city in the state; settled by the English in 1632, destroyed successively by French, Indian, and British attacks, and rebuilt; capital of Maine (1820–32). Pop.: 64 358 (1990).

Portland[2] (ˈpɔːtlənd) *n* **3rd Duke of.** title of *William Henry Cavendish Bentinck.* 1738–1809, British statesman; prime minister (1783; 1807–09); father of Lord William Cavendish Bentinck.

Portland cement *n* a cement that hardens under water and is made by heating a slurry of clay and crushed chalk or limestone to clinker in a kiln. [C19: named after the Isle of PORTLAND, because its colour resembles that of the stone quarried there]

Portlaoise (ˌpɔːtˈliːʃə) *n* a town in central Republic of Ireland, county town of Laois: site of a top-security prison. Pop.: 9500 (1990 est.).

Port Louis (ˈluːɪs, ˈluːɪ) *n* the capital and chief port of Mauritius, on the NW coast on the Indian Ocean. Pop.: 145 584 (1995 est.).

portly (ˈpɔːtlɪ) *adj* **-lier, -liest. 1** stout or corpulent. **2** *Archaic.* stately; impressive. [C16: from PORT[5] (in the sense: deportment, bearing)] ▸ **ˈportliness** *n*

Port Lyautey (ljəʊˈteɪ) *n* the former name (1932–56) of **Mina Hassan Tani.**

portmanteau (pɔːtˈmæntəʊ) *n, pl* **-teaus** *or* **-teaux** (-təʊz). **1** (formerly) a large travelling case made of stiff leather, esp. one hinged at the back so as to open out into two compartments. **2** (*modifier*) embodying several uses or qualities: *the heroine is a portmanteau figure of all the virtues.* [C16: from French: cloak carrier, from *porter* to carry + *manteau* cloak MANTLE]

portmanteau word *n* another name for **blend** (sense 7). [C19: from the idea that two meanings are packed into one word]

Port Moresby (ˈmɔːzbɪ) *n* the capital and chief port of Papua New Guinea, on the SE coast on the Gulf of Papua: important Allied base in World War II. Pop.: 193 242 (1990).

Port Nicholson *n* **1** the first British settlement in New Zealand, established on Wellington Harbour in 1840: grew into Wellington. **2** the former name for Wellington Harbour. [C19: named after Capt. John *Nicholson*, Australian naval officer]

Pôrto (ˈportu) *n* the Portuguese name for **Oporto.**

Pôrto Alegre (*Portuguese* ˈportu aˈlɛgri) *n* a port in S Brazil, capital of the Rio Grande do Sul state: the country's chief inland port; the chief commercial centre of S Brazil, with two universities (1936 and 1948). Pop.: 1 237 223 (1991), with a conurbation of 3 349 000 (1995).

Portobello (ˌpɔːtəʊˈbɛləʊ) *n* a small port in Panama, on the Caribbean northeast of Colón: the most important port in South America in colonial times; declined with the opening of the Panama Canal. Pop.: 3026 (1990 est.).

port of call *n* **1** any port where a ship stops, excluding its home port. **2** any place visited on a traveller's itinerary.

port of entry *n Law.* an airport, harbour, etc., where customs officials are stationed to supervise the entry into and exit from a country of persons and merchandise.

Port of Spain *n* the capital and chief port of Trinidad and Tobago, on the W coast of Trinidad. Pop.: 52 000 (1995 est.).

Porto Novo (ˈpɔːtəʊ ˈnəʊvəʊ) *n* the capital of Benin, in the southwest on a coastal lagoon: formerly a centre of Portuguese settlement and the slave trade. Pop.: 200 000 (1994 est.).

Porto Rico (ˈpɔːtə ˈriːkəʊ) *n* the former name (until 1932) of **Puerto Rico.** ▸ **Porto Rican** *adj, n*

Pôrto Velho (*Portuguese* ˈportu ˈvɛʎu) *n* a city in W Brazil, capital of the federal territory of Rondônia on the Madeira River. Pop.: 226 198 (1991).

Port Phillip Bay *or* **Port Phillip** *n* a bay in SE Australia, which forms the harbour of Melbourne.

portrait (ˈpɔːtrɪt, -treɪt) *n* **1a** a painting, drawing, sculpture, photograph, or other likeness of an individual, esp. of the face. **1b** (*as modifier*): *a portrait gallery.* **2** a verbal description or picture, esp. of a person's character. ◆ *adj* **3** *Printing* (of a publication or an illustration in a publication) of greater height than width. Compare **landscape** (sense 5a).

portraitist (ˈpɔːtrɪtɪst, -treɪ-) *n* an artist, photographer, etc., who specializes in portraits.

portraiture (ˈpɔːtrɪtʃə) *n* **1** the practice or art of making portraits. **2a** another term for **portrait** (sense 1). **2b** portraits collectively. **3** a verbal description.

portray (pɔːˈtreɪ) *vb* (*tr*) **1** to represent in a painting, drawing, sculpture, etc.; make a portrait of. **2** to make a verbal picture of; depict in words. **3** to play the part of (a character) in a play or film. [C14: from Old French *portraire* to depict, from Latin *prōtrahere* to drag forth, bring to light, from PRO-[1] + *trahere* to drag] ▸ **porˈtrayable** *adj* ▸ **porˈtrayal** *n* ▸ **porˈtrayer** *n*

portress (ˈpɔːtrɪs) *n* a female porter, esp. a doorkeeper.

Port Royal *n* **1** a fortified town in SE Jamaica, at the entrance to Kingston harbour: capital of Jamaica in colonial times. **2** the former name (until 1710) of **Annapolis Royal. 3** (*French* pɔr rwajal) an educational institution about 27 km (17 miles) west of Paris that flourished from 1638 to 1704, when it was suppressed by papal bull as it had become a centre of Jansenism. Its teachers were noted esp. for their work on linguistics: their *Grammaire générale et raisonnée* exercised much influence.

Port Said (ˈsɑːiːd, saɪd) *n* a port in NE Egypt, at the N end of the Suez Canal: founded in 1859 when the Suez Canal was begun; became the largest coaling station in the world and later an oil-bunkering port; damaged in the Arab–Israeli wars of 1967 and 1973. Pop.: 460 000 (1994 est.).

Port-Salut (ˈpɔː səˈluː; *French* pɔrsaly) *n* a mild semihard whole-milk cheese of a round flat shape. Also called: **Port du Salut.** [C19: named after the Trappist monastery at *Port du Salut* in NW France where it was first made]

Portsmouth (ˈpɔːtsməθ) *n* **1** a port in S England, in Portsmouth unitary authority, Hampshire, on the English Channel: Britain's chief naval base. Pop.: 174 690 (1991). Informal name: **Pompey. 2** a unitary authority in S England, in Hampshire. Pop.: 189 300 (1994 est.). Area: 37 sq. km (14 sq. miles). **3** a port in SE Virginia, on the Elizabeth River: naval base; shipyards. Pop.: 101 308 (1996 est.).

Port Sudan *n* the chief port of the Sudan, in the NE on the Red Sea. Pop.: 305 385 (1993).

Port Talbot (ˈtɔːlbət, ˈtæl-) *n* a port in SE Wales, in Neath Port Talbot county borough on Swansea Bay: established as a coal port in the mid-19th century; large steelworks; ore terminal. Pop.: 37 647 (1991).

Portugal (ˈpɔːtjugᵊl) *n* a republic in SW Europe, on the Atlantic: became an independent monarchy in 1139 and expelled the Moors in 1249 after more than four centuries of Muslim rule; became a republic in 1910; under the dictatorship of Salazar from 1932 until 1968, when he was succeeded by Dr Caetano, who was overthrown by a junta in 1974. Mario Soares restored constitutional government in 1976 and served as president from 1986 until 1996. Portugal is a member of the European Union. Official language: Portuguese. Religion: Roman Catholic majority. Currency: euro and escudo. Capital: Lisbon. Pop.: 9 964 000 (1998 est.). Area: 91 831 sq. km (35 456 sq. miles).

Portuguese (ˌpɔːtjuˈgiːz) *n* **1** the official language of Portugal, its overseas territories, and Brazil: the native language of approximately 110 million people. It belongs to the Romance group of the Indo-European family and is derived from the Galician dialect of Vulgar Latin. **2** (*pl* **-guese**) a native, citizen, or inhabitant of Portugal. ◆ *adj* **3** relating to, denoting, or characteristic of Portugal, its inhabitants, or their language.

Portuguese East Africa *n* a former name (until 1975) of **Mozambique.**

Portuguese Guinea *n* the former name (until 1974) of **Guinea-Bissau.** ▸ **Portuguese Guinean** *adj, n*

Portuguese India *n* a former Portuguese overseas province on the W coast of India, consisting of Goa, Daman, and Diu: established between 1505 and 1510; annexed by India in 1961.

Portuguese man-of-war *n* any of several large complex colonial hydrozoans of the genus *Physalia,* esp. *P. physalis,* having an aerial float and long stinging tentacles: order *Siphonophora.* Sometimes shortened to **man-of-war.**

Portuguese Timor *n* a former Portuguese overseas province in the Malay Archipelago, consisting of the east of the island of Timor, an enclave on the NW coast, and the islands of Ataúro and Jaco: annexed illegally by Indonesia (1975); an independence movement has been violently suppressed by Indonesia. Also called: **East Timor.**

Portuguese West Africa *n* a former name (until 1975) of **Angola.**

portulaca (ˌpɔːtjuˈlækə, -ˈleɪkə) *n* any portulacaceous plant of the genus *Portulaca,* such as rose moss and purslane, of tropical and subtropical America, having yellow, pink, or purple showy flowers. [C16: from Latin: PURSLANE]

portulacaceous (ˌpɔːtjuləˈkeɪʃəs) *adj* of, relating to, or belonging to the *Portulacaceae,* a family of fleshy-leaved flowering plants common in the U.S.

port wine stain *n* a purplish birthmark, often large and on the face or neck.

POS *abbrev. for* point of sale.

pos. *abbrev. for:* **1** position. **2** positive.

posada *Spanish.* (poˈsaða) *n, pl* **-das** (-ðas). an inn in a Spanish-speaking country. [literally: place for stopping]

pose[1] (pəʊz) *vb* **1** to assume or cause to assume a physical attitude, as for a photograph or painting. **2** (*intr;* often foll. by *as*) to pretend to be or present oneself (as something one is not). **3** (*intr*) to affect an attitude or play a part in order to impress others. **4** (*tr*) to put forward, ask, or assert: *to pose a question.* ◆ *n* **5** a physical attitude, esp. one deliberately adopted for or represented by an artist or photographer. **6** a mode of behaviour that is adopted for effect. [C14: from Old French *poser* to set in place, from Late Latin *pausāre* to cease, put down (influenced by Latin *pōnere* to place)]

pose[2] (pəʊz) *vb* (*tr*) **1** *Rare.* to puzzle or baffle. **2** *Archaic.* to question closely. [C16: from obsolete *appose,* from Latin *appōnere* to put to, set against; see OPPOSE]

Poseidon (pɒˈsaɪdᵊn) *n* **1** *Greek myth.* the god of the sea and of earthquakes; brother of Zeus, Hades, and Hera. He is generally depicted in art wielding a trident. Roman counterpart: **Neptune. 2** a U.S. submarine-launched ballistic missile.

Posen (ˈpoːzən) *n* the German name for **Poznań.**

poser[1] (ˈpəʊzə) *n* **1** a person who poses. **2** *Informal.* a person who likes to be seen in trendsetting clothes in fashionable bars, discos, etc.

poser[2] (ˈpəʊzə) *n* a baffling or insoluble question.

poseur (pəʊˈzɜː) *n* a person who strikes an attitude or assumes a pose in order to impress others. [C19: from French, from *poser* to POSE[1]]

posey (ˈpəʊzɪ) *or* **poserish** (ˈpəʊzərɪʃ) *adj Informal.* (of a place) for, characteristic of, or full of posers; affectedly trendy.

posh (pɒʃ) *Informal, chiefly Brit.* ◆ *adj* **1** smart, elegant, or fashionable; exclusive: *posh clothes.* **2** upper-class or genteel. ◆ *adv* **3** in a manner associated with the upper class: *to talk posh.* [C19: often said to be an acronym of the phrase *port out, starboard home,* the most desirable location for a cabin in British ships sailing to and from the East, being the north-facing or shaded side; but more likely to be a development of obsolete slang *posh* a dandy]

posho (ˈpɔʃɔ) *n E African.* **1** corn meal. **2** payment of workers in foodstuffs rather than money. [from Swahili]

posit (ˈpɒzɪt) *vb* (*tr*) **1** to assume or put forward as fact or the factual basis for an argument; postulate. **2** to put in position. ◆ *n* **3** a fact, idea, etc., that is posited; assumption. [C17: from Latin *pōnere* to place, position]

positif (ˈpɒsɪtɪf) *n* (on older organs) a manual controlling soft stops. [from French: positive]

position (pəˈzɪʃən) *n* **1** the place, situation, or location of a person or thing: *he took up a position to the rear.* **2** the appropriate or customary location: *the telescope is in position for use.* **3** the arrangement or disposition of the body or a part of the body: *the corpse was found in a sitting position.* **4** the manner in which a person or thing is placed; arrangement. **5** *Military.* an area or point occupied for tactical reasons. **6** mental attitude; point of view; stand: *what's your position on this issue?* **7** social status or standing, esp. high social standing. **8** a post of employment; job. **9** the act of positing a fact or viewpoint. **10** something posited, such as an idea, proposition, etc. **11** *Sport.* the part of a field or playing area where a player is placed or where he generally operates. **12** *Music.* **12a** the vertical spacing or layout of the written notes in a chord. Chords arranged with the three upper voices close together are in **close position.** Chords whose notes are evenly or widely distributed are in **open position.** See also **root position. 12b** one of the points on the fingerboard of a stringed instrument, determining where a string is to be stopped. **13** (in classical prosody) **13a** the situation in which a short vowel may be regarded as long, that is, when it occurs before two or more consonants. **13b make position.** (of a consonant, either on its own or in combination with other consonants, such as x in Latin) to cause a short vowel to become metrically long when placed after it. **14** *Finance.* the market commitment of a dealer in securities, currencies, or commodities: *a long position; a short position.* **15 in a position.** (foll. by an infinitive) able (to): *I'm not in a position to reveal these figures.* ◆ *vb (tr)* **16** to put in the proper or appropriate place; locate. **17** *Sport.* to place (oneself or another player) in a particular part of the field or playing area. **18** *Rare.* to locate or ascertain the position of. **[C15:** from Late Latin *positiō* a positioning, affirmation, from *pōnere* to place, lay down**]** ▸ **po'sitional** *adj*

positional notation *n* the method of denoting numbers by the use of a finite number of digits, each digit having its value multiplied by its place value, as in 936 = (9 × 100) + (3 × 10) + 6.

position audit *n Commerce.* a systematic assessment of the current strengths and weaknesses of an organization as a prerequisite for future strategic planning.

position effect *n* the effect on the phenotype of interacting genes when their relative positions on the chromosome are altered, as by inversion.

positive ('pɒzɪtɪv) *adj* **1** characterized by or expressing certainty or affirmation: *a positive answer.* **2** composed of or possessing actual or specific qualities; real: *a positive benefit.* **3** tending to emphasize what is good or laudable; constructive: *he takes a very positive attitude when correcting pupils' mistakes.* **4** tending towards progress or improvement; moving in a beneficial direction. **5** *Philosophy.* **5a** constructive rather than sceptical. **5b** (of a concept) denoting the presence rather than the absence of some property. **6** independent of circumstances; absolute or unqualified. **7** (*prenominal*) *Informal.* (intensifier): *a positive delight.* **8** *Maths.* **8a** having a value greater than zero: *a positive number.* **8b** designating, consisting of, or graduated in one or more quantities greater than zero: *positive direction.* **9** *Maths.* **9a** measured in a direction opposite to that regarded as negative. **9b** having the same magnitude as but opposite sense to an equivalent negative quantity. **10** *Grammar.* denoting the usual form of an adjective as opposed to its comparative or superlative form. **11** *Biology.* indicating movement or growth towards a particular stimulus. **12** *Physics.* **12a** (of an electric charge) having an opposite polarity to the charge of an electron and the same polarity as the charge of a proton. **12b** (of a body, system, ion, etc.) having a positive electric charge; having a deficiency of electrons: *a positive ion.* **12c** (of a point in an electric circuit) having a higher electric potential than some other point with an assigned zero potential. **13** short for **electropositive. 14** (of a lens) capable of causing convergence of a parallel beam of light. **15** *Med.* (of the results of an examination or test) indicating the existence or presence of a suspected disorder or pathogenic organism. **16** *Med.* (of the effect of a drug or therapeutic regimen) beneficial or satisfactory. **17** short for **Rh positive. 18** (of a machine part) having precise motion with no hysteresis or backlash. **19** *Chiefly U.S.* (of a government) directly involved in activities beyond the minimum maintenance of law and order, such as social welfare or the organization of scientific research. **20** *Economics.* of or denoting an analysis that is free of ethical, political, or value judgments. **21** *Astrology.* of, relating to, or governed by the group of signs of the zodiac that belong to the air and fire classifications, which are associated with a self-expressive spontaneous nature. ◆ *n* **22** something that is positive. **23** *Maths.* a quantity greater than zero. **24** *Photog.* a print or slide showing a photographic image whose colours or tones correspond to those of the original subject. **25** *Grammar.* the positive degree of an adjective or adverb. **26** a positive object, such as a terminal or plate in a voltaic cell. **27** *Music.* **27a** Also called: **positive organ.** a medieval nonportable organ with one manual and no pedals. Compare **portative organ. 27b** a variant spelling of **positif.** ◆ Compare **negative. [C13:** from Late Latin *positīvus* positive, agreed on an arbitrary basis, from *pōnere* to place**]** ▸ **'positiveness** *or* **,posi'tivity** *n*

positive discrimination *or* **action** *n* the provision of special opportunities in employment, training, etc. for a disadvantaged group, such as women, ethnic minorities, etc. U.S. equivalent: **affirmative action.**

positive feedback *n* See **feedback** (sense 1).

positively ('pɒzɪtɪvlɪ) *adv* **1** in a positive manner. **2** (intensifier): *he disliked her; in fact, he positively hated her.* ◆ *sentence substitute.* **3** unquestionably; absolutely.

positive polarity *n Grammar.* the grammatical characteristic of a word or phrase, such as *delicious* or *rather,* that may normally only be used in a semantically or syntactically positive or affirmative context.

positive vetting *n* the checking of a person's background, political affiliation, etc., to assess his suitability for a position that may involve national security.

positivism ('pɒzɪtɪ,vɪzəm) *n* **1** a strong form of empiricism, esp. as established in the philosophical system of Auguste Comte, that rejects metaphysics and theology as seeking knowledge beyond the scope of experience, and holds that experimental investigation and observation are the only sources of substantial knowledge. See also **logical positivism. 2** Also called: **legal positivism.** the jurisprudential doctrine that the legitimacy of a law depends on its being enacted in proper form, rather than on its content. Compare **natural law** (sense 3). **3** the quality of being definite, certain, etc. ▸ **'positivist** *n, adj* ▸ **,positiv'istic** *adj* ▸ **,positiv'istically** *adv*

positron ('pɒzɪ,trɒn) *n Physics.* the antiparticle of the electron, having the same mass but an equal and opposite charge. It is produced in certain decay processes and in pair production, annihilation occurring when it collides with an electron. **[C20:** from *posi(tive + elec)tron***]**

positron emission tomography *n* a technique for assessing brain activity and function by recording the emission of positrons when radioactively labelled glucose, introduced into the brain, is metabolized.

positronium (,pɒzɪ'trəʊnɪəm) *n Physics.* a short-lived entity consisting of a positron and an electron bound together. It decays by annihilation to produce two or three photons. **[C20:** from POSITRON + -IUM**]**

posology (pə'sɒlədʒɪ) *n* the branch of medicine concerned with the determination of appropriate doses of drugs or agents. **[C19:** from French *posologie,* from Greek *posos* how much**]** ▸ **posological** (,pɒsə'lɒdʒɪkᵊl) *adj*

poss (pɒs) *vb (tr)* to wash (clothes) by agitating them with a long rod, pole, etc. **[**of uncertain origin**]**

poss. *abbrev. for:* **1** possession. **2** possessive. **3** possible. **4** possibly.

posse ('pɒsɪ) *n* **1** *U.S.* short for **posse comitatus,** the able-bodied men of a district assembled together and forming a group upon whom the sheriff may call for assistance in maintaining law and order. **2** *Law.* possibility (esp. in the phrase **in posse**). **3** *Slang.* a Jamaican street gang in the U.S. **4** *Informal.* a group of friends or associates. **[C16:** from Medieval Latin (n): power, strength, from Latin (vb): to be able, have power**]**

posse comitatus (,kɒmɪ'tɑːtəs) *n* the formal legal term for **posse** (sense 1). **[**Medieval Latin: strength (manpower) of the county**]**

possess (pə'zɛs) *vb (tr)* **1** to have as one's property; own. **2** to have as a quality, faculty, characteristic, etc.: *to possess good eyesight.* **3** to have knowledge or mastery of: *to possess a little French.* **4** to gain control over or dominate: *whatever possessed you to act so foolishly?* **5** (foll. by *of*) to cause to be the owner or possessor: *I am possessed of the necessary information.* **6** (often foll. by *with*) to cause to be influenced or dominated (by): *the news possessed him with anger.* **7** to have sexual intercourse with. **8** *Now rare.* to keep control over or maintain (oneself or one's feelings) in a certain state or condition: *possess yourself in patience until I tell you the news.* **9** *Archaic.* to gain or seize. **[C15:** from Old French *possesser,* from Latin *possidēre* to own, occupy; related to Latin *sedēre* to sit**]** ▸ **pos'sessor** *n*

possessed (pə'zɛst) *adj* **1** (foll. by *of*) owning or having. **2** (*usually postpositive*) under the influence of a powerful force, such as a spirit or strong emotion. **3** a less common word for **self-possessed.**

possession (pə'zɛʃən) *n* **1** the act of possessing or state of being possessed: *in possession of the crown.* **2** anything that is owned or possessed. **3** (*pl*) wealth or property. **4** the state of being controlled or dominated by or as if by evil spirits. **5** the physical control or occupancy of land, property, etc., whether or not accompanied by ownership: *to take possession of a house.* **6** a territory subject to a foreign state or to a sovereign prince: *colonial possessions.* **7** *Sport.* control of the ball, puck, etc., as exercised by a player or team: *he got possession in his own half.*

possession order *n* (in Britain) a court order that entitles a landlord legally to evict a tenant or squatter and regain possession of the property.

possessive (pə'zɛsɪv) *adj* **1** of or relating to possession or ownership. **2** having or showing an excessive desire to possess, control, or dominate: *a possessive mother.* **3** *Grammar.* **3a** another word for **genitive** (sense 1). **3b** denoting an inflected form of a noun or pronoun used to convey the idea of possession, association, etc., as *my* or *Harry's.* ◆ *n* **4** *Grammar.* **4a** the possessive case. **4b** a word or speech element in the possessive case. ▸ **pos'sessively** *adv* ▸ **pos'sessiveness** *n*

possessory (pə'zɛsərɪ) *adj* **1** of, relating to, or having possession. **2** *Law.* arising out of, depending upon, or concerned with possession: *a possessory title.*

posset ('pɒsɪt) *n* a drink of hot milk curdled with ale, beer, etc., flavoured with spices, formerly used as a remedy for colds. **[C15** *poshoote,* of unknown origin**]**

possibility (,pɒsɪ'bɪlɪtɪ) *n, pl* **-ties. 1** the state or condition of being possible. **2** anything that is possible. **3** a competitor, candidate, etc., who has a moderately good chance of winning, being chosen, etc. **4** (*often pl*) a future prospect or potential: *my new house has great possibilities.*

possible ('pɒsɪbᵊl) *adj* **1** capable of existing, taking place, or proving true without contravention of any natural law. **2** capable of being achieved: *it is not possible to finish in three weeks.* **3** having potential or capabilities for favourable use or development: *the idea is a possible money-spinner.* **4** that may or may not happen or have happened; feasible but less than probable: *it is possible that man will live on Mars.* **5** *Logic.* (of a statement, formula, etc.) capable of being true under some interpretation, or in some circumstances. Usual symbol: *Mp* or ◇*p*, where *p* is the given expression. ◆ *n* **6** another word for **possibility** (sense 3). **[C14:** from Latin *possibilis* that may be, from *posse* to be able, have power**]**

USAGE Although it is very common to talk about something being *very possible* or *more possible,* these uses are generally thought to be incorrect, since *possible* describes an absolute state, and therefore something can only be *possible* or *not possible: it is very likely* (not *very possible*) *that he will resign; it has now become easier* (not *more possible*) *to obtain an entry visa.*

possible world *n Logic.* (in modal logic) a semantic device formalizing the notion of what the world might have been like. A statement is necessarily true if and only if it is true in every possible world.

possibly ('pɒsɪblɪ) *sentence substitute, adv* **1a** perhaps or maybe. **1b** (*as sentence modifier*): *possibly he'll come.* ◆ *adv* **2** by any chance; at all: *he can't possibly come.*

possie *or* **pozzy** ('pɒzɪ) *n Austral. and N.Z. informal.* a place; position: *if we're early for the film we'll get a good possie at the back.*

possum ('pɒsəm) *n* **1** an informal name for **opossum** (sense 1). **2** an Austral. and N.Z. name for **phalanger. 3 play possum.** to pretend to be dead, ignorant, asleep, etc., in order to deceive an opponent.

post[1] (pəʊst) *n* **1** a length of wood, metal, etc., fixed upright in the ground to serve as a support, marker, point of attachment, etc. **2** *Horse racing.* **2a** either of two upright poles marking the beginning (**starting post**) and end (**winning post**) of a racecourse. **2b** the finish of a horse race. **3** any of the main upright supports of a piece of furniture, such as a four-poster bed. ◆ *vb (tr)* **4** (sometimes foll. by *up*) to fasten or put up (a notice) in a public place. **5** to announce by means of or as if by means of a poster: *to post banns.* **6** to publish (a name) on a list. [Old English, from Latin *postis;* related to Old High German *first* ridgepole, Greek *pastas* colonnade]

post[2] (pəʊst) *n* **1** a position to which a person is appointed or elected; appointment; job. **2** a position or station to which a person, such as a sentry, is assigned for duty. **3** a permanent military establishment. **4** *Brit.* either of two military bugle calls (**first post** and **last post**) ordering or giving notice of the time to retire for the night. **5** See **trading post** (senses 1, 2). ◆ *vb* **6** *(tr)* to assign to or station at a particular place or position. **7** *Chiefly Brit.* to transfer to a different unit or ship on taking up a new appointment, etc. [C16: from French *poste,* from Italian *posto,* ultimately from Latin *pōnere* to place]

post[3] (pəʊst) *n* **1** *Chiefly Brit.* letters, packages, etc., that are transported and delivered by the Post Office; mail. **2** *Chiefly Brit.* a single collection or delivery of mail. **3** *Brit.* an official system of mail delivery. **4** an item of electronic mail made publicly available. **5** (formerly) any of a series of stations furnishing relays of men and horses to deliver mail over a fixed route. **6** a rider who carried mail between such stations. **7** *Brit.* another word for **pillar box. 8** *Brit.* short for **post office. 9** a size of writing or printing paper, 15¼ by 19 inches or 16½ by 21 inches (**large post**). **10** any of various book sizes, esp. 5¼ by 8¼ inches (**post octavo**) and 8¼ by 10¼ inches (**post quarto**). **11 by return of post.** *Brit.* by the next mail in the opposite direction. ◆ *vb* **12** *(tr) Chiefly Brit.* to send by post. U.S. and Canadian word: **mail. 13** *(tr)* to make (electronic mail) publicly available. **14** *(tr) Book-keeping.* **14a** to enter (an item) in a ledger. **14b** (often foll. by *up*) to compile or enter all paper items in (a ledger). **15** *(tr)* to inform of the latest news (esp. in the phrase **keep someone posted**). **16** *(intr)* (of a rider) to rise from and reseat oneself in a saddle in time with the motions of a trotting horse; perform a rising trot. **17** *(intr)* (formerly) to travel with relays of post horses. **18** *Archaic.* to travel or dispatch with speed; hasten. ◆ *adv* **19** with speed; rapidly. **20** by means of post horses. [C16: via French from Italian *poste,* from Latin *posita* something placed, from *pōnere* to put, place]

POST *abbrev. for* point of sales terminal.

post- *prefix* **1** after in time or sequence; following; subsequent: *postgraduate.* **2** behind; posterior to: *postorbital.* [from Latin, from *post* after, behind]

postage ('pəʊstɪdʒ) *n* **a** the charge for delivering a piece of mail. **b** *(as modifier): postage charges.*

postage due stamp *n* a stamp affixed by a Post Office to a letter, parcel, etc., indicating that insufficient or no postage has been prepaid and showing the amount to be paid by the addressee on delivery.

postage meter *n Chiefly U.S. and Canadian.* a postal franking machine. Also called: **postal meter.**

postage stamp *n* **1** a printed paper label with a gummed back for attaching to mail as an official indication that the required postage has been paid. **2** a mark directly printed or embossed on an envelope, postcard, etc., serving the same function.

postal ('pəʊstᵊl) *adj* of or relating to a Post Office or to the mail-delivery service. ▸ **'postally** *adv*

postal card *n U.S.* another term for **postcard.**

postal note *n Austral. and N.Z.* the usual name for **postal order.**

postal order *n* a written order for the payment of a sum of money, to a named payee, obtainable and payable at a post office.

post-and-rail fence *n* a fence constructed of upright wooden posts with horizontal timber slotted through it.

post-and-rail tea *n Austral. informal.* (in the 19th century) a coarse tea in which floating particles resembled a post-and-rail fence.

postaxial (pəʊst'æksɪəl) *adj Anatomy.* **1** situated or occurring behind the axis of the body. **2** of or relating to the posterior part of a vertebrate limb.

postbag ('pəʊstˌbæg) *n* **1** *Chiefly Brit.* another name for **mailbag. 2** the mail received by a magazine, radio programme, public figure, etc.

post-bellum ('pəʊst'bɛləm) *adj (prenominal)* of or during the period after a war, esp. the American Civil War. [C19: Latin *post* after + *bellum* war]

postbox ('pəʊstˌbɒks) *n Chiefly Brit.* a box into which mail is put for collection by the postal service. Also called: **letter box.**

postboy ('pəʊstˌbɔɪ) *n* **1** a man or boy who brings the post round to offices. **2** another name for **postilion.**

postbus ('pəʊstˌbʌs) *n* (in Britain, esp. in rural districts) a vehicle carrying the mail that also carries passengers.

post captain *n History.* (formerly) a naval officer holding a commission as a captain, as distinct from an officer with the courtesy title of captain.

postcard ('pəʊstˌkɑːd) *n* a card, often bearing a photograph, picture, etc., on one side, (**picture postcard**), for sending a message by post without an envelope. Also called (U.S.): **postal card.**

postcava (pəʊst'kɑːvə, -'keɪvə) *n Anatomy.* the inferior vena cava. [C19: New Latin; see POST-, VENA CAVA] ▸ **post'caval** *adj*

post chaise *n* a closed four-wheeled horse-drawn coach used as a rapid means for transporting mail and passengers in the 18th and 19th centuries. [C18: from POST[3] + CHAISE]

postcode ('pəʊstˌkəʊd) *n Brit. and Austral.* a code of letters and digits used as part of a postal address to aid the sorting of mail. Also called: **postal code.** U.S. equivalent: **zip code.**

post-cyclic *adj Transformational grammar.* denoting rules that apply only after the transformations of a whole cycle. Compare **cyclic** (sense 6), **last-cyclic.**

postdate (pəʊst'deɪt) *vb (tr)* **1** to write a future date on (a document), as on a cheque to prevent it being paid until then. **2** to assign a date to (an event, period, etc.) that is later than its previously assigned date of occurrence. **3** to be or occur at a later date than.

postdiluvian (ˌpəʊstdɪ'luːvɪən, -daɪ-) *adj also* **postdiluvial. 1** existing or occurring after the biblical Flood. ◆ *n* **2** a person or thing existing after the biblical Flood. [C17: from POST- + *diluvian,* from Latin *diluvium* deluge, flood]

postdoctoral (pəʊst'dɒktərəl) *adj* of, relating to, or designating studies, research, or professional work above the level of a doctorate.

poster ('pəʊstə) *n* **1** a large printed picture, used for decoration. **2** a placard or bill posted in a public place as an advertisement.

poste restante ('pəʊst rɪ'stænt; *French* pɔst rɛstɑ̃t) *n* **1** (not in the U.S. and Canada) an address on mail indicating that it should be kept at a specified post office until collected by the addressee. **2** the mail-delivery service or post-office department that handles mail having this address. ◆ U.S. and Canadian equivalent: **general delivery.** [French, literally: mail remaining]

posterior (pɒ'stɪərɪə) *adj* **1** situated at the back of or behind something. **2** coming after or following another in a series. **3** coming after in time. **4** *Zoology.* (of lower animals) of or near the hind end. **5** *Botany.* (of a flower) situated nearest to the main stem. **6** *Anatomy.* dorsal or towards the spine. ◆ Compare **anterior.** ◆ *n* **7** the buttocks; rump. **8** *Statistics.* a posterior probability. [C16: from Latin: latter, from *posterus* coming next, from *post* after] ▸ **pos'teriorly** *adv*

posterior probability *n Statistics.* the probability assigned to some parameter or to an event on the basis of its observed frequency in a sample, and calculated from a prior probability by Bayes' theorem. Compare **prior probability.** See also **empirical** (sense 5).

posterity (pɒ'stɛrɪtɪ) *n* **1** future or succeeding generations. **2** all of one's descendants. [C14: from French *postérité,* from Latin *posteritās* future generations, from *posterus* coming after, from *post* after]

postern ('pɒstən) *n* **1** a back door or gate, esp. one that is for private use. ◆ *adj* **2** situated at the rear or the side. [C13: from Old French *posterne,* from Late Latin *posterula (jānua)* a back (entrance), from *posterus* coming behind; see POSTERIOR, POSTERITY]

poster paint *or* **colour** *n* a gum-based opaque watercolour paint used for writing posters, etc.

post exchange *n U.S.* a government-subsidized shop operated mainly for military personnel. Abbrev.: **PX.**

postexilian (ˌpəʊstɪg'zɪlɪən) *or* **postexilic** *adj Old Testament.* existing or occurring after the Babylonian exile of the Jews (587–539 B.C.).

postfeminist (pəʊst'fɛmɪnɪst) *adj* **1** resulting from or including the beliefs and ideas of feminism. **2** differing from or showing moderation of these beliefs and ideas.◆ *n* **3** a person who believes in or advocates any of the ideas that have developed from the feminist movement.

postfix *vb* (pəʊst'fɪks). **1** *(tr)* to add or append at the end of something; suffix. ◆ *n* ('pəʊstˌfɪks). **2** a less common word for **suffix.**

post-Fordism (ˌpəʊst'fɔːdɪzəm) *n* the idea that modern industrial production has moved away from mass production in huge factories, as pioneered by Henry Ford, towards specialized markets based on small flexible manufacturing units. ▸ **ˌpost-'Fordist** *adj*

post-free *adv, adj* **1** *Brit.* with the postage prepaid; post-paid. **2** free of postal charge.

postglacial (pəʊst'gleɪsɪəl) *adj* formed or occurring after a glacial period, esp. after the Pleistocene epoch.

postgraduate (pəʊst'grædjʊɪt) *n* **1** a student who has obtained a degree from a university, etc., and is pursuing studies for a more advanced qualification. **2** *(modifier)* of or relating to such a student or to his studies. ◆ Also (U.S. and Canadian): **graduate.**

posthaste ('pəʊst'heɪst) *adv* **1** with great haste; as fast as possible. ◆ *n* **2** *Archaic.* great haste.

post hoc ('pəʊst 'hɒk) *n Logic.* the fallacy of assuming that temporal succession is evidence of causal relation. [from Latin, short for *Post hoc ergo propter hoc* after this, therefore on account of this]

post horn *n* a simple valveless natural horn consisting of a long tube of brass or copper, either straight or coiled; formerly often used to announce the arrival of a mailcoach.

post horse *n* (formerly) a horse kept at an inn or post house for use by postriders or for hire to travellers.

post house *n* (formerly) a house or inn where horses were kept for postriders or for hire to travellers.

posthumous ('pɒstjʊməs) *adj* **1** happening or continuing after one's death. **2**

ˌpost-Car'tesian *adj*
post'classical *adj*
post'coital *adj*
ˌpostconso'nantal *adj*
ˌposte'lection *adj*

(of a book, etc.) published after the author's death. **3** (of a child) born after the father's death. [C17: from Latin *postumus* the last, but modified as though from Latin *post* after + *humus* earth, that is, after the burial] ▸ **'posthumously** *adv*

posthypnotic suggestion (ˌpəʊsthɪp'nɒtɪk) *n* a suggestion made to the subject while in a hypnotic trance, to be acted upon at some time after emerging from the trance.

postiche (pɒ'stiːʃ) *adj* **1** (of architectural ornament) inappropriately applied; sham. **2** false or artificial; spurious. ◆ *n* **3** another term for **hairpiece** (sense 2). **4** an imitation, counterfeit, or substitute. **5** anything that is false; sham or pretence. [C19: from French, from Italian *apposticcio* (n), from Late Latin *appositīcius* (adj); see APPOSITE]

posticous (pɒ'stiːkəs, -'staɪ-) *or* **postical** *adj* (of the position of plant parts) behind another part; posterior. [C19: from Latin *postīcus* that is behind, from *post* after]

postie ('pəʊstɪ) *n Scot., Austral., and N.Z. informal.* a postman.

postil ('pɒstɪl) *n* **1** a commentary or marginal note, as in a Bible. **2** a homily or collection of homilies. ◆ *vb* **-tils, -tiling, -tiled** *or* **-tils, -tilling, -tilled. 3** *Obsolete.* to annotate (a biblical passage). [C15 (*postille*): from Old French *postille* from Medieval Latin *postilla*, perhaps from *post illa* (*verba textus*), after these words in the text, often the opening phrase of such an annotation]

postilion *or* **postillion** (pɒ'stɪljən) *n* a person who rides the near horse of the leaders in order to guide a team of horses drawing a coach. [C16: from French *postillon*, from Italian *postiglione*, from *posta* POST[3]]

postimpressionism (ˌpəʊstɪm'preʃəˌnɪzəm) *n* a movement in painting in France at the end of the 19th century, begun by Cézanne and exemplified by Gauguin, Van Gogh, and Matisse, which rejected the naturalism and momentary effects of impressionism but adapted its use of pure colour to paint subjects with greater subjective emotion. ▸ **ˌpostim'pressionist** *n, adj* ▸ **ˌpostimˌpression'istic** *adj*

postindustrial (ˌpəʊstɪn'dʌstrɪəl) *adj* characteristic of, relating to, or denoting work or a society that is no longer based on heavy industry.

posting[1] ('pəʊstɪŋ) *n* a wrestling attack in which the opponent is hurled at the post in one of the corners of the ring.

posting[2] ('pəʊstɪŋ) *n* **1** an appointment to a position or post, usually in another town or country. **2** an electronic mail message that is publicly available.

postliminy (pəʊst'lɪmɪnɪ) *or* **postliminium** (ˌpəʊstlɪ'mɪnɪəm) *n, pl* **-inies** *or* **-ia** (-ɪə). *International law.* the right by which persons and property seized in war are restored to their former status on recovery. [C19: (in this sense): from Latin *postlīminium* a return behind one's threshold, from *līmen* threshold]

postlude ('pəʊstluːd) *n* **1** *Music.* a final or concluding piece or movement. **2** a voluntary played at the end of a Church service. [C19: from POST- + *-lude*, from Latin *lūdus* game; compare PRELUDE]

postman ('pəʊstmən) *or* (*fem*) **postwoman** *n, pl* **-men** *or* **-women.** a person who carries and delivers mail as a profession.

postman's knock *n* a children's party game in which a kiss is exchanged for a pretend letter.

postmark ('pəʊstˌmɑːk) *n* **1** any mark stamped on mail by postal officials, such as a simple obliteration, date mark, or indication of route. See also **cancellation.** ◆ *vb* **2** (*tr*) to put such a mark on mail.

postmaster ('pəʊstˌmɑːstə) *n* **1** Also (*fem*) **postmistress.** an official in charge of a local post office. **2** the person responsible for managing the electronic mail at a site.

postmaster general *n, pl* **postmasters general.** the executive head of the postal service in certain countries.

postmeridian (ˌpəʊstmə'rɪdɪən) *adj* after noon; in the afternoon or evening. [C17: from Latin *postmerīdiānus* in the afternoon; see POST-, MERIDIAN]

post meridiem ('pəʊst mə'rɪdɪəm) the full form of **p.m.** [C17: Latin: after noon]

post mill *n* a windmill built round a central post on which the whole mill can be turned so that the sails catch the wind.

postmillennial (ˌpəʊstmɪ'lenɪəl) *adj* existing or taking place after the millennium.

postmillennialism (ˌpəʊstmɪ'lenɪəˌlɪzəm) *n* the doctrine or belief that the Second Coming of Christ will be preceded by the millennium. ▸ **ˌpostmil'lennialist** *n*

postmodern (pəʊst'mɒdən) *adj* (in the arts, architecture, etc.) characteristic of a style and school of thought that rejects the dogma and practices of any form of modernism; in architecture, contrasting with international modernism and featuring elements from several periods, esp. the Classical, often with ironic use of decoration. ▸ **post'moderˌnism** *n* ▸ **post'modernist** *n, adj*

postmortem (pəʊst'mɔːtəm) *adj* **1** (*prenominal*) occurring after death. ◆ *n* **2** analysis or study of a recently completed event: *a postmortem on a game of chess.* **3** See **postmortem examination.** [C18: from Latin, literally: after death]

postmortem examination *n* dissection and examination of a dead body to determine the cause of death. Also called: **autopsy, necropsy.**

postnasal drip (pəʊst'neɪzᵊl) *n Med.* a mucus secretion from the rear part of the nasal cavity into the nasopharynx, usually as the result of a cold or an allergy.

post-obit (pəʊst'əʊbɪt, -'ɒbɪt) *Chiefly law.* ◆ *n* **1** Also called: **post-obit bond.** a bond given by a borrower, payable after the death of a specified person, esp. one given to a moneylender by an expectant heir promising to repay when his interest falls into possession. ◆ *adj* **2** taking effect after death. [C18: from Latin *post obitum* after death]

post office *n* a building or room where postage stamps are sold and other postal business is conducted.

Post Office *n* a government department or authority in many countries responsible for postal services and often telecommunications.

post office box *n* a private numbered place in a post office, in which letters received are kept until called for.

postoperative (pəʊst'ɒpərətɪv, -'ɒprətɪv) *adj* of, relating to, or occurring in the period following a surgical operation. ▸ **post'operatively** *adv*

postorbital (pəʊst'ɔːbɪtᵊl) *adj Anatomy.* situated behind the eye or the eye socket.

post-paid *adv, adj* with the postage prepaid.

postpartum (pəʊst'pɑːtəm) *adj Med.* following childbirth. [Latin: after the act of giving birth]

postpone (pəʊst'pəʊn, pə'spəʊn) *vb* (*tr*) **1** to put off or delay until a future time. **2** to put behind in order of importance; defer. [C16: from Latin *postpōnere* to put after, neglect, from POST- + *ponere* to place] ▸ **post'ponable** *adj* ▸ **post'ponement** *n* ▸ **post'poner** *n*

postposition (ˌpəʊstpə'zɪʃən) *n* **1** placement of a modifier or other speech element after the word that it modifies or to which it is syntactically related. **2** a word or speech element so placed. ▸ **ˌpostpo'sitional** *adj* ▸ **ˌpostpo'sitionally** *adv*

postpositive (pəʊst'pɒzɪtɪv) *adj* **1** (of an adjective or other modifier) placed after the word modified, either immediately after, as in *two men abreast,* or as part of a complement, as in *those men are bad.* ◆ *n* **2** a postpositive modifier. ▸ **post'positively** *adv*

postproduction (ˌpəʊstprə'dʌkʃən) *n* **a** the work on a film or a television programme, such as editing, dubbing, etc., that takes place after shooting or videotaping is completed. **b** (*as modifier*): *postproduction costs.*

postrider ('pəʊstˌraɪdə) *n* (formerly) a person who delivered post on horseback.

post road *n* a road or route over which post is carried and along which post houses were formerly sited.

postscript ('pəʊsˌskrɪpt, 'pəʊst-) *n* **1** a message added at the end of a letter, after the signature. **2** any supplement, as to a document or book. [C16: from Late Latin *postscribere* to write after, from POST- + *scribere* to write]

poststructuralism (pəʊst'strʌktʃərəˌlɪzəm) *n* an approach to literature that, proceeding from the tenets of structuralism, maintains that, as words have no absolute meaning, any text is open to an unlimited range of interpretations. ▸ **post'structuralist** *n, adj*

post town *n* a town having a main Post Office branch.

post-traumatic stress disorder *n* a psychological condition, characterized by anxiety, withdrawal, and a proneness to physical illness, that may follow a traumatic experience.

postulant ('pɒstjʊlənt) *n* a person who makes a request or application, esp. a candidate for admission to a religious order. [C18: from Latin *postulāns* asking, from *postulāre* to ask, demand] ▸ **'postulancy** *or* **'postulantˌship** *n*

postulate *vb* ('pɒstjʊˌleɪt). (*tr; may take a clause as object*) **1** to assume to be true or existent; take for granted. **2** to ask, demand, or claim. **3** to nominate (a person) to a post or office subject to approval by a higher authority. ◆ *n* ('pɒstjʊlɪt). **4** something taken as self-evident or assumed as the basis of an argument. **5** a necessary condition or prerequisite. **6** a fundamental principle. **7** *Logic, maths.* an unproved and indemonstrable statement that should be taken for granted: used as an initial premise or underlying hypothesis in a process of reasoning. [C16: from Latin *postulāre* to ask for, require; related to *pōscere* to request] ▸ **ˌpostu'lation** *n*

postulator ('pɒstjʊˌleɪtə) *n R.C. Church.* a person, usually a priest, deputed to prepare and present a plea for the beatification or canonization of some deceased person.

posture ('pɒstʃə) *n* **1** a position or attitude of the limbs or body. **2** a characteristic manner of bearing the body; carriage: *to have good posture.* **3** the disposition of the parts of a visible object. **4** a mental attitude or frame of mind. **5** a state, situation, or condition. **6** a false or affected attitude; pose. ◆ *vb* **7** to assume or cause to assume a bodily position or attitude. **8** (*intr*) to assume an affected or unnatural bodily or mental posture; pose. [C17: via French from Italian *postura*, from Latin *positūra*, from *pōnere* to place] ▸ **'postural** *adj* ▸ **'posturer** *n*

posturize *or* **posturise** ('pɒstʃəˌraɪz) *vb* a less common word for **posture** (senses 7, 8).

postviral syndrome (ˌpəʊst'vaɪrəl) *n* another name for **chronic fatigue syndrome.** Abbrev.: **PVS.**

postvocalic (ˌpəʊstvə'kælɪk) *adj Phonetics.* following a vowel.

posy ('pəʊzɪ) *n, pl* **-sies. 1** a small bunch of flowers or a single flower; nosegay. **2** *Archaic.* a brief motto or inscription, esp. one on a trinket or a ring. [C16: variant of POESY]

pot[1] (pɒt) *n* **1** a container made of earthenware, glass, or similar material; usually round and deep, often having a handle and lid, used for cooking and other domestic purposes. **2** short for **flowerpot, teapot. 3** the amount that a pot will hold; potful. **4** a chamber pot, esp. a small one designed for a baby or toddler. **5** a handmade piece of pottery. **6** a large mug or tankard, as for beer. **7** *Austral.* any of various measures used for serving beer. **8** *Informal.* a cup or trophy, esp.

ˌposthyp'notic *adj*	**post'nasal** *adj*	**post'prandial** *adj*	**post'season** *adj*
post-'Keynesian *adj*	**post'natal** *adj*	**ˌpost-Refor'mation** *adj*	**ˌpost-Tal'mudic** *adj*
ˌpostmeno'pausal *adj*	**post'nuptial** *adj*	**ˌpost-Revo'lutionary** *adj*	**ˌpost-'war** *adj*

of silver, awarded as a prize in a competition. **9** the money or stakes in the pool in gambling games, esp. poker. **10** (*often pl*) *Informal.* a large amount, esp. of money. **11** a wicker trap for catching fish, esp. crustaceans: *a lobster pot.* **12** *Billiards, etc.* a shot by which a ball is pocketed. **13** *Chiefly Brit.* short for **chimneypot. 14** *U.S. informal.* a joint fund created by a group of individuals or enterprises and drawn upon by them for specified purposes. **15** *Hunting.* See **pot shot. 16** See **potbelly. 17 go to pot.** to go to ruin; deteriorate. ◆ *vb* **pots, potting, potted.** (*mainly tr*) **18** to set (a plant) in a flowerpot to grow. **19** to put or preserve (goods, meat, etc.) in a pot. **20** to cook (food) in a pot. **21** to shoot (game) for food rather than for sport. **22** to shoot (game birds or animals) while they are on the ground or immobile rather than flying or running. **23** (*also intr*) to shoot casually or without careful aim at (an animal, etc.). **24** to sit (a baby or toddler) on a chamber pot. **25** (*also intr*) to shape clay as a potter. **26** *Billiards, etc.* to pocket (a ball). **27** *Informal.* to capture or win; secure. ◆ See also **pot on.** [Late Old English *pott,* from Medieval Latin *pottus* (unattested), perhaps from Latin *pōtus* a drink; compare Middle Low German *pot,* Old Norse *pottr*]

pot[2] (pɒt) *n* **a** *Scot. and northern English dialect.* a deep hole or pothole. **b** (*cap. when part of a name*): *Pen-y-Ghent Pot.* [C14: perhaps identical with POT[1] but possibly of Scandinavian origin; compare Swedish dialect *putt* water hole, pit]

pot[3] (pɒt) *n Slang.* cannabis used as a drug in any form, such as leaves (marijuana or hemp) or resin (hashish). [C20: perhaps shortened from Mexican Indian *potiguaya*]

pot[4] (pɒt) *n Informal.* short for **potentiometer.**

pot. *abbrev. for* potential.

potable (ˈpəʊtəbᵊl) *adj* **1** a less common word for **drinkable.** ◆ *n* **2** something fit to drink; a beverage. [C16: from Late Latin *pōtābilis* drinkable, from Latin *pōtāre* to drink] ▸ ˌ**potaˈbility** *n*

potae (ˈpɔtaɪ) *n N.Z.* a hat. [Maori]

potage *French.* (pɔtaʒ; *English* pəʊˈtɑːʒ) *n* any thick soup. [C16: from Old French; see POTTAGE]

potager (ˈpɒtɪdʒə) *n* a small kitchen garden. [C17: from French *potagère* vegetable garden]

potamic (pəˈtæmɪk) *adj* of or relating to rivers. [C19: from Greek *potamos* river]

potamology (ˌpɒtəˈmɒlədʒɪ) *n* the scientific study of rivers. [C19: from Greek *potamos* river + -LOGY]

potash (ˈpɒtˌæʃ) *n* **1** another name for **potassium carbonate,** esp. the form obtained by leaching wood ash. **2** another name for **potassium hydroxide. 3** potassium chemically combined in certain compounds: *chloride of potash.* [C17 *pot ashes,* translation of obsolete Dutch *potaschen;* so called because originally obtained by evaporating the lye of wood ashes in pots]

potash alum *n* the full name for **alum** (sense 1).

potassium (pəˈtæsɪəm) *n* a light silvery element of the alkali metal group that is highly reactive and rapidly oxidizes in air; occurs principally in carnallite and sylvite. It is used when alloyed with sodium as a cooling medium in nuclear reactors and its compounds are widely used, esp. in fertilizers. Symbol: K; atomic no.: 19; atomic wt.: 39.0983; valency: 1; relative density: 0.862; melting pt.: 63.71°C; boiling pt.: 759°C. [C19: New Latin *potassa* potash] ▸ **poˈtassic** *adj*

potassium-argon dating *n* a technique for determining the age of minerals based on the occurrence in natural potassium of a small fixed amount of radioisotope ^{40}K that decays to the stable argon isotope ^{40}Ar with a half-life of 1.28×10^9 years. Measurement of the ratio of these isotopes thus gives the age of the mineral. Compare **radiocarbon dating, rubidium-strontium dating.**

potassium bitartrate *n* another name (not in technical usage) for **potassium hydrogen tartrate.**

potassium bromide *n* a white crystalline soluble substance with a bitter saline taste used in making photographic papers and plates and in medicine as a sedative. Formula: KBr.

potassium carbonate *n* a white odourless substance used in making glass and soft soap and as an alkaline cleansing agent. Formula: K_2CO_3.

potassium chlorate *n* a white crystalline soluble substance used in fireworks, matches, and explosives, and as a disinfectant and bleaching agent. Formula: $KClO_3$.

potassium cyanide *n* a white poisonous granular soluble solid substance used in photography and in extracting gold from its ores. Formula: KCN.

potassium dichromate *n* an orange-red crystalline soluble solid substance that is a good oxidizing agent and is used in making chrome pigments and as a bleaching agent. Formula: $K_2Cr_2O_7$.

potassium ferricyanide *n* a bright red soluble crystalline substance used in making dyes, pigments, and light-sensitive paper. Formula: $K_3Fe(CN)_6$. Also called: **red prussiate of potash.**

potassium ferrocyanide *n* a yellow soluble crystalline compound used in case-hardening steel and making dyes and pigments. Formula: $K_4Fe(CN)_6$. Also called: **yellow prussiate of potash.**

potassium hydrogen tartrate *n* a colourless or white soluble crystalline salt used in baking powders, soldering fluxes, and laxatives. Formula: $KHC_4H_4O_6$. Also called (not in technical usage): **potassium bitartrate, cream of tartar.**

potassium hydroxide *n* a white deliquescent alkaline solid used in the manufacture of soap, liquid shampoos, and detergents. Formula: KOH. Also called: **caustic potash.** See also **lye.**

potassium nitrate *n* a colourless or white crystalline compound used in gunpowders, pyrotechnics, fertilizers, and as a preservative for foods, esp. as a curing salt for ham, sausages, etc. (**E252**). Formula: KNO_3. Also called: **saltpetre, nitre.**

potassium permanganate *n* a dark purple poisonous odourless soluble crystalline solid, used as a bleach, disinfectant, and antiseptic. Formula: $KMnO_4$. Systematic name: **potassium manganate(VII).**

potassium sulphate *n* a soluble substance usually obtained as colourless crystals of the decahydrate: used in making glass and as a fertilizer. Formula: K_2SO_4.

potation (pəʊˈteɪʃən) *n* **1** the act of drinking. **2** a drink or draught, esp. of alcoholic drink. [C15: from Latin *pōtātiō* a drinking, from *pōtāre* to drink]

potato (pəˈteɪtəʊ) *n, pl* **-toes. 1** Also called: **Irish potato, white potato. 1a** a solanaceous plant, *Solanum tuberosum,* of South America: widely cultivated for its edible tubers. **1b** the starchy oval tuber of this plant, which has a brown or red skin and is cooked and eaten as a vegetable. **2** any of various similar plants, esp. the sweet potato. **3 hot potato.** *Slang.* a delicate or awkward matter. [C16: from Spanish *patata* white potato, from Taino *batata* sweet potato]

potato beetle *n* another name for the **Colorado beetle.**

potato blight *n* a devastating disease of potatoes produced by the fungus *Phytophthora infestaris* and the cause of the Irish potato famine of the mid 19th century.

potato chip *n* **1** (*usually pl*) another name for **chip** (sense 4). **2** (*usually pl*) the U.S. and Canadian term for **crisp** (sense 10).

potato crisp *n* (*usually pl*) another name for **crisp** (sense 10).

potatory (ˈpəʊtətərɪ, -trɪ) *adj Rare.* of, relating to, or given to drinking. [C19: from Late Latin *pōtātōrius* concerning drinking, from Latin *pōtāre* to drink]

pot-au-feu (*French* pɔtofø) *n* **1** a traditional French stew of beef and vegetables. **2** the large earthenware casserole in which this is cooked. [literally: pot on the fire]

potbelly (ˈpɒtˌbelɪ) *n, pl* **-lies. 1** a protruding or distended belly. **2** a person having such a belly. **3** *U.S. and Canadian.* a small bulbous stove in which wood or coal is burned. ▸ ˈ**potˌbellied** *adj*

potboiler (ˈpɒtˌbɔɪlə) *n Informal.* a literary or artistic work of little merit produced quickly in order to make money.

pot-bound *adj* (of a pot plant) having grown to fill all the available root space and therefore lacking room for continued growth.

potboy (ˈpɒtˌbɔɪ) *or* **potman** (ˈpɒtmən) *n, pl* **-boys** *or* **-men.** *Chiefly Brit.* (esp. formerly) a youth or man employed at a public house to serve beer, etc.

potch (pɒtʃ) *n Chiefly Austral., slang.* inferior quality opal used in jewellery for mounting precious opals. [C20: of uncertain origin]

pot cheese *n U.S.* a type of coarse dry cottage cheese.

poteen *or* **poitín** (ˈpɒtiːn) *n* (in Ireland) illicit spirit, often distilled from potatoes. [C19: from Irish *poitín* little pot, from *pota* pot]

Potemkin *or* **Potyomkin** (pɒˈtemkɪn; *Russian* paˈtjɔmkin) *n* **Grigori Aleksandrovich** (griˈgɔrij alɪkˈsandrəvitʃ). 1739–91, Russian soldier and statesman; lover of Catherine II, whose favourite he remained until his death.

potency (ˈpəʊtᵊnsɪ) *or* **potence** *n, pl* **-tencies** *or* **-tences. 1** the state or quality of being potent. **2** latent or inherent capacity for growth or development. [C16: from Latin *potentia* power, from *posse* to be able]

potent[1] (ˈpəʊtᵊnt) *adj* **1** possessing great strength; powerful. **2** (of arguments, etc.) persuasive or forceful. **3** influential or authoritative. **4** tending to produce violent physical or chemical effects: *a potent poison.* **5** (of a male) capable of having sexual intercourse. [C15: from Latin *potēns* able, from *posse* to be able] ▸ ˈ**potently** *adv* ▸ ˈ**potentness** *n*

potent[2] (ˈpəʊtᵊnt) *adj Heraldry.* (of a cross) having flat bars across the ends of the arms. [C17: from obsolete *potent* a crutch, from Latin *potentia* power]

potentate (ˈpəʊtᵊnˌteɪt) *n* a person who possesses great power or authority, esp. a ruler or monarch. [C14: from Late Latin *potentātus* ruler, from Latin: rule, command, from *potens* powerful, from *posse* to be able]

potential (pəˈtenʃəl) *adj* **1a** possible but not yet actual. **1b** (*prenominal*) capable of being or becoming but not yet in existence; latent. **2** *Grammar.* (of a verb or form of a verb) expressing possibility, as English *may* and *might.* **3** an archaic word for **potent**[1]. ◆ *n* **4** latent but unrealized ability or capacity: *Jones has great potential as a sales manager.* **5** *Grammar.* a potential verb or verb form. **6** short for **electric potential.** [C14: from Old French *potencial,* from Late Latin *potentiālis,* from Latin *potentia* power] ▸ **poˈtentially** *adv*

potential difference *n* the difference in electric potential between two points in an electric field; the work that has to be done in transferring unit positive charge from one point to the other, measured in volts. Abbrev.: **pd.** Symbol: U, ΔV, or $\Delta\phi$ Compare **electromotive force.**

potential divider *n* a tapped or variable resistor or a chain of fixed resistors in series, connected across a source of voltage and used to obtain a desired fraction of the total voltage. Also called: **voltage divider.**

potential energy *n* the energy of a body or system as a result of its position in an electric, magnetic, or gravitational field. It is measured in joules (SI units), electronvolts, ergs, etc. Symbol: E_p, V, U, or ϕ Abbrev.: **PE.**

potentiality (pəˌtenʃɪˈælɪtɪ) *n, pl* **-ties. 1** latent or inherent capacity or ability for growth, fulfilment, etc. **2** a person or thing that possesses such a capacity.

potential well *n Physics.* a localized region in a field of force in which the potential suddenly decreases.

potentiate (pəˈtenʃɪˌeɪt) *vb* (*tr*) **1** to cause to be potent. **2** *Med.* to increase (the individual action or effectiveness) of two drugs by administering them in combination with each other.

potentilla (ˌpəʊtᵊnˈtɪlə) *n* any rosaceous plant or shrub of the N temperate genus *Potentilla,* having five-petalled flowers. See also **cinquefoil** (sense 1), **silverweed** (sense 1), **tormentil.** [C16: New Latin, from Medieval Latin: garden valerian, from Latin *potēns* powerful, POTENT[1]]

potentiometer (pəˌtenʃɪˈɒmɪtə) *n* **1** an instrument for determining a potential difference or electromotive force by measuring the fraction of it that balances a standard electromotive force. **2** a device with three terminals, two of which are connected to a resistance wire and the third to a brush moving along the wire, so that a variable potential can be tapped off: used in electronic circuits, esp. as a volume control. Sometimes shortened to **pot.** ▸ **po,tenti'ometry** *n*

potentiometric (pə,tɛnʃɪə'mɛtrɪk) *adj Chem.* (of a titration) having the end point determined by a change in potential of an electrode immersed in the solution.

potful ('pɒtfʊl) *n* the amount held by a pot.

pothead ('pɒt,hɛd) *n Slang.* a habitual user of cannabis.

pothecary ('pɒθɪkərɪ) *n, pl* **-caries.** an archaic or Brit. dialect variant of **apothecary.**

potheen ('pɒtiːn, 'pɒθiːn) *n* a rare variant of **poteen.**

pother ('pɒðə) *n* **1** a commotion, fuss, or disturbance. **2** a choking cloud of smoke, dust, etc. ◆ *vb* **3** to make or be troubled or upset. **[C16:** of unknown origin**]**

potherb ('pɒt,hɜːb) *n* any plant having leaves, flowers, stems, etc., that are used in cooking for seasoning and flavouring or are eaten as a vegetable.

pothole ('pɒt,həʊl) *n* **1** *Geography.* **1a** a deep hole in limestone areas resulting from action by running water. See also **sinkhole** (sense 1). **1b** a circular hole in the bed of a river produced by abrasion. **2** a deep hole, esp. one produced in a road surface by wear or weathering.

potholing ('pɒt,həʊlɪŋ) *n Brit.* a sport in which participants explore underground caves. ▸ **'pot,holer** *n*

pothook ('pɒt,hʊk) *n* **1** a curved or S-shaped hook used for suspending a pot over a fire. **2** a long hook used for lifting hot pots, lids, etc. **3** an S-shaped mark, often made by children when learning to write.

pothouse ('pɒt,haʊs) *n Brit.* (formerly) a small tavern or pub.

pothunter ('pɒt,hʌntə) *n* **1** a person who hunts for food or for profit without regard to the rules of sport. **2** *Informal.* a person who enters competitions for the sole purpose of winning prizes. ▸ **'pot,hunting** *n, adj*

potiche (pɒ'tiːʃ) *n, pl* **-tiches** (-'tiːʃɪz, -'tiːʃ). a tall vase or jar, as of porcelain, with a round or polygonal body that narrows towards the neck and a detached lid or cover. **[**French, from *pot* pot; compare POTTAGE**]**

potion ('pəʊʃən) *n* **1** a drink, esp. of medicine, poison, or some supposedly magic beverage. **2** a rare word for **beverage. [C13:** via Old French from Latin *pōtiō* a drink, especially a poisonous one, from *pōtāre* to drink**]**

Potiphar ('pɒtɪfə) *n Old Testament.* one of Pharaoh's officers, who bought Joseph as a slave (Genesis 37:36).

potlatch ('pɒt,lætʃ) *n* **1** *Anthropol.* a competitive ceremonial activity among certain North American Indians, esp. the Kwakiutl, involving a lavish distribution of gifts and the destruction of property to emphasize the wealth and status of the chief or clan. **2** *U.S. and Canadian informal.* a wild party or revel. **[C19:** from Chinook, from Nootka *patshatl* a giving, present**]**

pot liquor *n Chiefly U.S.* the broth in which meat, esp. pork or bacon, and vegetables have been cooked.

pot luck *n Informal.* **1a** whatever food happens to be available without special preparation. **1b** (*as modifier*): *a pot-luck dinner.* **2** whatever is available (esp. in the phrase **take pot luck**).

potman ('pɒtmən) *n, pl* **-men.** *Chiefly Brit.* another word for **potboy.**

pot marigold *n* a Central European and Mediterranean plant, *Calendula officinalis,* grown for its rayed orange-and-yellow showy flowers, the petals of which were formerly used to colour food: family *Compositae* (composites). See also **calendula.**

Potomac (pə'təʊmək) *n* a river in the E central U.S., rising in the Appalachian Mountains of West Virginia: flows northeast, then generally southeast to Chesapeake Bay. Length (from the confluence of headstreams): 462 km (287 miles).

potometer (pə,tɒmɪtə) *n* an apparatus that measures the rate of water uptake by a plant or plant part. **[**from Latin *pōtāre* to drink + -METER**]**

pot on *vb* (*tr, adv*) to transfer (a plant) to a larger flowerpot.

potoroo (,pɒtə'ruː) *n* another name for **kangaroo rat. [**from a native Australian language**]**

Potosí (*Spanish* poto'si) *n* a city in S Bolivia, at an altitude of 4066 m (13 340 ft.): one of the highest cities in the world; developed with the discovery of local silver in 1545; tin mining; university (1571). Pop.: 123 327 (1993 est.).

potpie ('pɒt,paɪ) *n* a meat and vegetable stew with a pie crust on top.

pot plant *n* a plant grown in a flowerpot, esp. indoors.

potpourri (,pəʊ'pʊərɪ) *n, pl* **-ris. 1** a collection of mixed flower petals dried and preserved in a pot to scent the air. **2** a collection of unrelated or disparate items; miscellany. **3** a medley of popular tunes. **4** a stew of meat and vegetables. **[C18:** from French, literally: rotten pot, translation of Spanish *olla podrida* miscellany**]**

pot roast *n* meat, esp. beef, that is browned and cooked slowly in a covered pot with very little water, often with vegetables added.

Potsdam ('pɒtsdæm; *German* 'pɔtsdam) *n* a city in Germany, the capital of Brandenburg on the Havel River: residence of Prussian kings and German emperors and scene of the **Potsdam Conference** of 1945. Pop.: 136 619 (1996 est.).

potsherd ('pɒt,ʃɜːd) *or* **potshard** ('pɒt,ʃɑːd) *n* a broken fragment of pottery. **[C14:** from POT[1] + *schoord* piece of broken crockery; see SHARD**]**

pot shot *n* **1** a chance shot taken casually, hastily, or without careful aim. **2** a shot fired to kill game in disregard of the rules of sport. **3** a shot fired at quarry within easy range, often from an ambush.

pot still *n* a type of still used in distilling whisky in which heat is applied directly to the pot in which the wash is contained.

potstone ('pɒt,stəʊn) *n* an impure massive variety of soapstone, formerly used for making cooking vessels.

pottage ('pɒtɪdʒ) *n* a thick meat or vegetable soup. **[C13:** from Old French *potage* contents of a pot, from *pot* POT[1]**]**

potted ('pɒtɪd) *adj* **1** placed or grown in a pot. **2** cooked or preserved in a pot: *potted shrimps.* **3** *Informal.* summarized or abridged: *a potted version of a novel.*

potter[1] ('pɒtə) *n* a person who makes pottery.

potter[2] ('pɒtə) *or esp. U.S. and Canadian* **putter** *Chiefly Brit.* ◆ *vb* **1** (*intr;* often foll. by *about* or *around*) to busy oneself in a desultory though agreeable manner. **2** (*intr;* often foll. by *along* or *about*) to move with little energy or direction: *to potter about town.* **3** (*tr;* usually foll. by *away*) to waste (time): *to potter the day away.* ◆ *n* **4** the act of pottering. **[C16** (in the sense: to poke repeatedly): from Old English *potian* to thrust; see PUT**]** ▸ **'potterer** *or esp. U.S. and Canadian* **'putterer** *n*

Potter ('pɒtə) *n* **1 (Helen) Beatrix.** 1866–1943, British author and illustrator of children's animal stories, such as *The Tale of Peter Rabbit* (1902). **2 Dennis (Christopher George).** 1935–94, British dramatist. His TV plays include *Pennies from Heaven* (1978), *The Singing Detective* (1986), and *Blackeyes* (1989). **3 Paulus.** 1625–54, Dutch painter, esp. of animals. **4 Stephen.** 1900–70, British humorist and critic. Among his best-known works are *Gamesmanship* (1947) and *One-Upmanship* (1952), on the art of achieving superiority over others.

Potteries ('pɒtərɪz) *pl n* (*sometimes functioning as sing*) **the.** a region of W central England, in Staffordshire, in which the china and earthenware industries are concentrated.

potter's field *n* **1** *U.S.* a cemetery where the poor or unidentified are buried at the public expense. **2** *New Testament.* the land bought by the Sanhedrin with the money paid for the betrayal of Jesus (which Judas had returned to them) to be used as a burial place for strangers and the friendless poor (Acts 1:19; Matthew 27:7).

potter's wheel *n* a device with a horizontal rotating disc, on which clay is shaped into pots, bowls, etc., by hand.

potter wasp *n* any of various solitary wasps of the genus *Eumenes,* which construct vaselike cells of mud or clay, in which they lay their eggs: family *Vespidae.*

pottery ('pɒtərɪ) *n, pl* **-teries. 1** articles, vessels, etc., made from earthenware and dried and baked in a kiln. **2** a place where such articles are made. **3** the craft or business of making such articles. ◆ Related adj: **fictile. [C15:** from Old French *poterie,* from *potier* potter, from *pot* POT[1]**]**

potting shed ('pɒtɪŋ) *n* a building in which plants are set in flowerpots and in which empty pots, potting compost, etc., are stored.

pottle ('pɒt°l) *n Archaic.* a liquid measure equal to half a gallon. **[C14:** *potel,* from Old French: a small POT[1]**]**

potto ('pɒtəʊ) *n, pl* **-tos. 1** Also called: **kinkajou.** a short-tailed prosimian primate, *Perodicticus potto,* having vertebral spines protruding through the skin in the neck region: family *Lorisidae.* **2 golden potto.** another name for **angwantibo. 3** another name for **kinkajou** (sense 1). **[C18:** of West African origin; compare Wolof *pata* type of tail-less monkey**]**

Pott's disease (pɒts) *n* a disease of the spine, usually caused by tubercular infection and characterized by weakening and gradual disintegration of the vertebrae and the intervertebral discs. **[C18:** named after Percivall *Pott* (1714–88), English surgeon**]**

Pott's fracture *n* a fracture of the lower part of the fibula, usually with dislocation of the ankle. **[C18:** see POTT'S DISEASE**]**

potty[1] ('pɒtɪ) *adj* **-tier, -tiest.** *Brit. informal.* **1** foolish or slightly crazy. **2** trivial or insignificant. **3** (foll. by *about* or *on*) very keen (about). **[C19:** perhaps from POT[1]**]** ▸ **'pottiness** *n*

potty[2] ('pɒtɪ) *n, pl* **-ties.** a child's word for **chamber pot.**

pot-walloper *or* **potwaller** ('pɒt,wɒlə) *n* (in some English boroughs) a man entitled to the franchise before 1832 by virtue of possession of his own fireplace. **[C18:** from POT[1] + *wallop* to boil furiously, from Old English *weallan* to boil**]**

Potyomkin (*Russian* pa'tjɔmkin) *n* a variant spelling of **Potemkin.**

pouch (paʊtʃ) *n* **1** a small flexible baglike container: *a tobacco pouch.* **2** a saclike structure in any of various animals, such as the abdominal receptacle marsupium in marsupials or the cheek fold in rodents. **3** *Anatomy.* any sac, pocket, or pouchlike cavity or space in an organ or part. **4** another word for **mailbag. 5** a Scot. word for **pocket.** ◆ *vb* **6** (*tr*) to place in or as if in a pouch. **7** to arrange or become arranged in a pouchlike form. **8** (*tr*) (of certain birds and fishes) to swallow. **[C14:** from Old Norman French *pouche,* from Old French *poche* bag; see POKE[2]**]** ▸ **'pouchy** *adj*

pouched (paʊtʃt) *adj* having a pouch or pouches.

pouf *or* **pouffe** (puːf) *n* **1** a large solid cushion, usually cylindrical or cubic in shape, used as a seat. **2a** a woman's hair style, fashionable esp. in the 18th century, in which the hair is piled up in rolled puffs. **2b** a pad set in the hair to make such puffs. **3** a stuffed pad worn under panniers. **4** (pʊf, puːf). *Brit. derogatory slang.* less common spellings of **poof. [C19:** from French; see PUFF**]**

Poujadism ('puːʒɑːdɪzəm) *n* a conservative reactionary movement to protect the business interests of small traders. **[C20:** named after Pierre *Poujade* (born 1920), French publisher and bookseller who founded such a movement in 1954**]** ▸ **'Poujadist** *n, adj*

poulard *or* **poularde** ('puːlɑːd) *n* a hen that has been spayed for fattening. Compare **capon. [C18:** from Old French *pollarde,* from *polle* hen; see PULLET**]**

Poulenc (*French* pulɛ̃ːk) *n* **Francis** (frɑ̃sis). 1899–1963, French composer; a member of Les Six. His works include the operas *Les Mamelles de Tirésias* (1947) and *Dialogues des Carmélites* (1957), and the ballet *Les Biches* (1924).

poult[1] (pəʊlt) *n* the young of a gallinaceous bird, esp. of domestic fowl. **[C15:** syncopated variant of *poulet* PULLET**]**

poult[2] (pʊlt) *n* a fine plain-weave fabric of silk, rayon, nylon, etc., with slight ribs across it. Also called: **poult-de-soie. [C20:** from French; of unknown origin; compare PADUASOY**]**

poulterer ('pəʊltərə) *n Brit.* another word for a **poultryman.** [C17: from obsolete *poulter,* from Old French *pouletier,* from *poulet* PULLET]

poultice ('pəʊltɪs) *n* **1** Also called: **cataplasm.** *Med.* a local moist and often heated application for the skin consisting of substances such as kaolin, linseed, or mustard, used to improve the circulation, treat inflamed areas, etc. **2** *Austral. slang.* a large sum of money, esp. a debt. [C16: from earlier *pultes,* from Latin *puls* a thick porridge]

poultry ('pəʊltrɪ) *n* domestic fowls collectively. [C14: from Old French *pouletrie,* from *pouletier* poultry-dealer]

poultryman ('pəʊltrɪmən) *or* **poulterer** *n, pl* **-trymen** *or* **-terers. 1** Also called: **chicken farmer.** a person who rears domestic fowls, esp. chickens, for their eggs or meat. **2** a dealer in poultry, esp. one who sells the dressed carcasses.

pounce[1] (paʊns) *vb* **1** (*intr;* often foll. by *on* or *upon*) to spring or swoop, as in capturing prey. ◆ *n* **2** the act of pouncing; a spring or swoop. **3** the claw of a bird of prey. [C17: apparently from Middle English *punson* pointed tool; see PUNCHEON[2]] ▸ **'pouncer** *n*

pounce[2] (paʊns) *vb* (*tr*) to emboss (metal) by hammering from the reverse side. [C15 *pounsen,* from Old French *poinçonner* to stamp; perhaps the same as POUNCE[1]]

pounce[3] (paʊns) *n* **1** a very fine resinous powder, esp. of cuttlefish bone, formerly used to dry ink or sprinkled over parchment or unsized writing paper to stop the ink from running. **2** a fine powder, esp. of charcoal, that is tapped through perforations in paper corresponding to the main lines of a design in order to transfer the design to another surface. **3** (*as modifier*): *a pounce box.* ◆ *vb* (*tr*) **4** to dust (paper) with pounce. **5** to transfer (a design) by means of pounce. [C18: from Old French *ponce,* from Latin *pūmex* PUMICE] ▸ **'pouncer** *n*

pouncet box ('paʊnsɪt) *n* a box with a perforated top used for containing perfume. [C16 *pouncet,* perhaps alteration of *pounced* punched, perforated; see POUNCE[1]]

pound[1] (paʊnd) *vb* **1** (when *intr,* often foll. by *on* or *at*) to strike heavily and often. **2** (*tr*) to beat to a pulp; pulverize. **3** (*tr*) to instil by constant drilling: *to pound Latin into him.* **4** (*tr;* foll. by *out*) to produce, as by typing heavily. **5** to walk (the pavement, street, etc.) repeatedly: *he pounded the pavement looking for a job.* **6** (*intr*) to throb heavily. ◆ *n* **7** a heavy blow; thump. **8** the act of pounding. [Old English *pūnian;* related to Dutch *puin* rubble] ▸ **'pounder** *n*

pound[2] (paʊnd) *n* **1** an avoirdupois unit of weight that is divided into 16 ounces and is equal to 0.453 592 kilograms. Abbrev.: **lb. 2** a troy unit of weight divided into 12 ounces equal to 0.373 242 kilograms. Abbrev.: **lb tr** *or* **lb t. 3** an apothecaries' unit of weight, used in the U.S., that is divided into 5760 grains and is equal to one pound troy. **4** (*not in technical usage*) a unit of force equal to the mass of 1 pound avoirdupois where the acceleration of free fall is 32.174 feet per second per second. Abbrev.: **lbf. 5a** the standard monetary unit of the United Kingdom and its dependencies, divided into 100 pence. Official name: **pound sterling. 5b** (*as modifier*): *a pound coin.* **6** the standard monetary unit of the following countries: **6a** Cyprus: divided into 100 cents. **6b** Egypt: divided into 100 piastres. **6c** Ireland: divided into 100 pence. **6d** Lebanon: divided into 100 piastres. **6e** Syria: divided into 100 piastres. **7** another name for **lira** (sense 2). **8** Also called: **pound Scots.** a former Scottish monetary unit originally worth an English pound but later declining in value to 1 shilling 8 pence. **9** a monetary unit of the Sudan, replaced by the dinar in 1992 and being phased out gradually. [Old English *pund,* from Latin *pondō* pound; related to German *Pfund* pound, Latin *pondus* weight]

pound[3] (paʊnd) *n* **1** an enclosure, esp. one maintained by a public authority, for keeping officially removed vehicles or distrained goods or animals, esp. stray dogs. **2** a place where people are confined. **3a** a trap for animals. **3b** a trap or keepnet for fish. See **pound net.** ◆ *vb* **4** (*tr*) to confine in or as if in a pound; impound, imprison, or restrain. [C14: from Late Old English *pund-* as in *pundfeald* PINFOLD]

Pound (paʊnd) *n* **Ezra (Loomis).** 1885–1972, U.S. poet, translator, and critic, living in Europe. Indicted for treason by the U.S. government (1945) for pro-Fascist broadcasts during World War II, he was committed to a mental hospital until 1958. He was a founder of imagism and championed the early work of such writers as T. S. Eliot, Joyce, and Hemingway. His life work, the *Cantos* (1925–70), is an unfinished sequence of poems, which incorporates mythological and historical materials in several languages as well as political, economic, and autobiographical elements.

poundage[1] ('paʊndɪdʒ) *n* **1** a tax, charge, or other payment of so much per pound of weight. **2** a tax, charge, or other payment of so much per pound sterling. **3** a weight expressed in pounds.

poundage[2] ('paʊndɪdʒ) *n Agriculture.* **a** confinement of livestock within a pound. **b** the fee required for freeing a head of livestock from a pound.

poundal ('paʊndᵊl) *n* the fps unit of force; the force that imparts an acceleration of 1 foot per second per second to a mass of 1 pound. 1 poundal is equivalent to 0.1382 newton or 1.382×10^{4} dynes. Abbrev.: **pdl.** [C19: from POUND[2] + QUINTAL]

pound cake *n* a rich fruit cake originally made with a pound each of butter, sugar, and flour.

pound cost averaging *n Stock Exchange.* a method of accumulating capital by investing a fixed sum in a particular security at regular intervals, in order to achieve an average purchase price below the arithmetic average of the market prices on the purchase dates.

-pounder ('paʊndə) *n* (*in combination*) **1** something weighing a specified number of pounds: *a 200-pounder.* **2** something worth a specified number of pounds: *a ten-pounder.* **3** a gun that discharges a shell weighing a specified number of pounds: *a two-pounder.*

pound net *n* a fishing trap having an arrangement of standing nets directing the fish into an enclosed net.

pound of flesh *n* something that is one's legal right but is an unreasonable demand (esp. in the phrase **to have one's pound of flesh**). [from Shakespeare's *The Merchant of Venice* (1596), Act IV, scene i]

pound sterling *n* the official name for the standard monetary unit of the United Kingdom. See **pound**[2] (sense 5).

pour (pɔː) *vb* **1** to flow or cause to flow in a stream. **2** (*tr*) to issue, emit, etc., in a profuse way. **3** (*intr;* often foll. by *down*) Also: **pour with rain.** to rain heavily: *it's pouring down outside.* **4** (*intr*) to move together in large numbers; swarm. **5** (*intr*) to serve tea, coffee, etc.: *shall I pour?* **6 it never rains but it pours.** events, esp. unfortunate ones, come together or occur in rapid succession. **7 pour cold water on.** *Informal.* to be unenthusiastic about or discourage. **8 pour oil on troubled waters.** to try to calm a quarrel, etc. ◆ *n* **9** a pouring, downpour, etc. [C13: of unknown origin] ▸ **'pourer** *n*

USAGE The verbs *pour* and *pore* are sometimes confused: *she poured cream over her strudel; she pored* (not *poured*) *over the manuscript.*

pourboire *French.* (purbwar) *n* a tip; gratuity. [literally: for drinking]

pour encourager les autres *French.* (pur ɑ̃kuraʒe lez otrə) in order to encourage the others: often used ironically.

pourparler *French.* (purparle; *English* pʊə'pɑːleɪ) *n* an informal or preliminary conference. [literally: for speaking]

pourpoint ('pʊəˌpɔɪnt) *n* a man's stuffed quilted doublet of a kind worn between the Middle Ages and the 17th century. [C15: from Old French, from *pourpoindre* to stick, from *pour-* variant of *par-,* from Latin *per* through + *poindre* to pierce, from Latin *pungere* to puncture]

pour point *n Chem.* the lowest temperature at which a mineral oil will flow under specified conditions.

pousse-café *French.* (puskafe) *n* **1** a drink of liqueurs of different colours in unmixed layers. **2** any liqueur taken with coffee at the end of a meal. [literally: coffee-pusher]

poussette (puː'sɛt) *n* **1** a figure in country dancing in which couples hold hands and move up or down the set to change positions. ◆ *vb* **2** (*intr*) to perform such a figure. [C19: from French, from *pousser* to push]

poussin (*French* pusɛ̃) *n* a young chicken reared for eating. [from French]

Poussin (*French* pusɛ̃) *n* **Nicolas** (nikɔlɑ). 1594–1665, French painter, regarded as a leader of French classical painting. He is best known for the austere historical and biblical paintings and landscapes of his later years.

pou sto ('puː 'stəʊ) *n, pl* **pou stos.** *Literary.* **1** a place upon which to stand. **2** a basis of operation. [Greek: where I may stand, from Archimedes' saying that he could move the earth if given a place to stand]

pout[1] (paʊt) *vb* **1** to thrust out (the lips), as when sullen, or (of the lips) to be thrust out. **2** (*intr*) to swell out; protrude. **3** (*tr*) to utter with a pout. ◆ *n* **4** (*sometimes* **the pouts**) a fit of sullenness. **5** the act or state of pouting. [C14: of uncertain origin; compare Swedish dialect *puta* inflated, Danish *pude* PILLOW] ▸ **'poutingly** *adv* ▸ **'pouty** *adj*

pout[2] (paʊt) *n, pl* **pout** *or* **pouts. 1** short for **horned pout** or **eelpout. 2** any of various gadoid food fishes, esp. the bib (also called **whiting pout**). **3** any of certain other stout-bodied fishes. [Old English *-pūte* as in *ǣlepūte* eelpout; related to Dutch *puit* frog]

pouter ('paʊtə) *n* **1** a person or thing that pouts. **2** a breed of domestic pigeon with a large crop capable of being greatly puffed out.

poverty ('pɒvətɪ) *n* **1** the condition of being without adequate food, money, etc. **2** scarcity or dearth: *a poverty of wit.* **3** a lack of elements conducive to fertility in land or soil. [C12: from Old French *poverté,* from Latin *paupertās* restricted means, from *pauper* POOR]

poverty-stricken *adj* suffering from extreme poverty.

poverty trap *n* the situation of being unable to escape poverty because of being dependent on state benefits, which are reduced by the same amount as any extra income gained.

pow[1] (paʊ) *interj* an exclamation imitative of a collision, explosion, etc.

pow[2] (paʊ) *n Scot.* the head or a head of hair. [a Scot. variant of POLL]

pow[3] (paʊ) *n Scot.* a creek or slow stream. [C15: from earlier Scots *poll*]

POW *abbrev. for* prisoner of war.

powan ('paʊən) *n* **1** a freshwater whitefish, *Coregonus clupeoides,* occurring in some Scottish lakes. **2** any of certain similar related fishes, such as the vendace. ◆ Also called: **lake herring.** [C17: Scottish variant of POLLAN]

powder ('paʊdə) *n* **1** a solid substance in the form of tiny loose particles. **2** any of various preparations in this form, such as gunpowder, face powder, or soap powder. **3** fresh loose snow, esp. when considered as skiing terrain. **4 take a powder.** *U.S. and Canadian slang.* to run away or disappear. ◆ *vb* **5** to turn into powder; pulverize. **6** (*tr*) to cover or sprinkle with or as if with powder. [C13: from Old French *poldre,* from Latin *pulvis* dust] ▸ **'powderer** *n* ▸ **'powdery** *adj*

powder blue *n* **a** a dusty pale blue colour. **b** (*as adj*) *a powder-blue coat.*

powder burn *n* a superficial burn of the skin caused by a momentary intense explosion, esp. of gunpowder.

powder compact *n* See **compact** (sense 11).

powder flask *n* a small flask or case formerly used to carry gunpowder.

powder horn *n* a powder flask consisting of the hollow horn of an animal.

powder keg *n* **1** a small barrel used to hold gunpowder. **2** *Informal.* a potential source or scene of violence, disaster, etc.

powder metallurgy *n* the science and technology of producing solid metal components from metal powder by compaction and sintering.

powder monkey *n* (formerly) a boy who carried powder from the magazine to the guns on warships.

powder puff *n* a soft pad or ball of fluffy material used for applying cosmetic powder to the skin.

powder room *n Euphemistic.* a lavatory for women in a restaurant, department store, etc.

powdery mildew *n* **1** a plant disease characterized by a superficial white powdery growth on stems and leaves, caused by parasitic ascomycetous fungi of the family *Erysiphaceae:* affects the rose, aster, apple, vine, oak, etc. **2** any of the fungi causing this disease. ◆ Compare **downy mildew.**

Powell ('paʊəl) *n* **1** ('pəʊəl). **Anthony (Dymoke)** ('dɪmək). born 1905, British novelist, best known for his sequence of novels under the general title *A Dance to the Music of Time* (1951–75). **2 Cecil Frank.** 1903–69, British physicist, who was awarded the Nobel prize for physics in 1950 for his discovery of the pi-meson. **3 Earl,** known as *Bud Powell.* 1924–1966, U.S. modern-jazz pianist. **4 (John) Enoch.** 1912–98, British politician. An outspoken opponent of Commonwealth immigration into Britain and of British membership of the Common Market (now the European Union), in 1974 he resigned from the Conservative Party, returning to Parliament as a United Ulster Unionist Council member (1974–87). **5 Michael.** 1905–90, British film writer, producer, and director, best known for his collaboration (1942–57) with Emeric Pressburger. Films include *The Life and Death of Colonel Blimp* (1943), *A Matter of Life and Death* (1946), *The Red Shoes* (1948), and *Peeping Tom* (1960).

power ('paʊə) *n* **1** ability or capacity to do something. **2** (*often pl*) a specific ability, capacity, or faculty. **3** political, financial, social, etc., force or influence. **4** control or dominion or a position of control, dominion, or authority. **5** a state or other political entity with political, industrial, or military strength. **6** a person who exercises control, influence, or authority: *he's a power in the state.* **7** a prerogative, privilege, or liberty. **8a** legal authority to act, esp. in a specified capacity, for another. **8b** the document conferring such authority. **9a** a military force. **9b** military potential. **10** *Maths.* **10a** the value of a number or quantity raised to some exponent. **10b** another name for **exponent** (sense 4). **11** *Statistics.* the probability of rejecting the null hypothesis in a test when it is false. The power of a test of a given null depends on the particular alternative hypothesis against which it is tested. **12** *Physics, engineering.* a measure of the rate of doing work expressed as the work done per unit time. It is measured in watts, horsepower, etc. Symbol: *P* **13a** the rate at which electrical energy is fed into or taken from a device or system. It is expressed, in a direct-current circuit, as the product of current and voltage and, in an alternating-current circuit, as the product of the effective values of the current and voltage and the cosine of the phase angle between them. It is measured in watts. **13b** (*as modifier*): *a power amplifier.* **14** the ability to perform work. **15a** mechanical energy as opposed to manual labour. **15b** (*as modifier*): *a power mower.* **16** a particular form of energy: *nuclear power.* **17a** a measure of the ability of a lens or optical system to magnify an object, equal to the reciprocal of the focal length. It is measured in dioptres. **17b** another word for **magnification. 18** *Informal.* a large amount or quantity: *a power of good.* **19 in one's power.** (*often foll. by an infinitive*) able or allowed (to). **20 in (someone's) power.** under the control or sway of (someone). **21 the powers that be.** the established authority or administration. ◆ *vb* (*tr*) **22** to give or provide power to. **23** to fit (a machine) with a motor or engine. **24** (*intr*) *Slang.* to travel with great speed or force. ◆ See also **power down, power up.** [C13: from Anglo-Norman *poer,* from Vulgar Latin *potēre* (unattested), from Latin *posse* to be able]

power amplifier *n Electronics.* an amplifier that is usually the final amplification stage in a device and is designed to give the required power output.

powerboat ('paʊə,bəʊt) *n* a boat propelled by an inboard or outboard motor.

powerboating ('paʊə,bəʊtɪŋ) *n* the sport of driving powerboats in racing competitions.

power cut *n* a temporary interruption or reduction in the supply of electrical power to a particular area. Sometimes shortened to **cut.**

power dive *n* **1** a steep dive by an aircraft with its engines at high power. ◆ *vb* **power-dive. 2** to cause (an aircraft) to perform a power dive or (of an aircraft) to perform a power dive.

power down *vb* (*tr, adv*) to shut down (a computer system) in a methodical way, concluding by switching the power off.

power dressing *n* a style of dressing in severely tailored suits, adopted by some women executives to project an image of efficiency.

power drill *n* a hand tool with a rotating chuck driven by an electric motor and designed to take an assortment of tools for drilling, grinding, polishing, etc.

power factor *n* (in an electrical circuit) the ratio of the power dissipated to the product of the input volts times amps.

powerful ('paʊəfʊl) *adj* **1** having great power, force, potency, or effect. **2** extremely effective or efficient in action: *a powerful drug; a powerful lens.* **3** *Dialect.* large or great: *a powerful amount of trouble.* ◆ *adv* **4** *Dialect.* extremely; very: *he ran powerful fast.* ▸ **'powerfully** *adv* ▸ **'powerfulness** *n*

powerhouse ('paʊə,haʊs) *n* **1** an electrical generating station or plant. **2** *Informal.* a forceful or powerful person or thing.

powerless ('paʊəlɪs) *adj* without power or authority. ▸ **'powerlessly** *adv* ▸ **'powerlessness** *n*

power line *n* a set of conductors used to transmit and distribute electrical energy. Sometimes shortened to **line.**

power lunch *n* a high-powered business meeting conducted over lunch.

power of appointment *n Property law.* authority to appoint persons either from a particular class (**special power**) or selected by the donee of the power (**general power**) to take an estate or interest in property.

power of attorney *n* **1** legal authority to act for another person in certain specified matters. **2** the document conferring such authority. ◆ Also called: **letter of attorney.**

power pack *n* a device for converting the current from a supply into direct or alternating current at the voltage required by a particular electrical or electronic device.

power plant *n* **1** the complex, including machinery, associated equipment, and the structure housing it, that is used in the generation of power, esp. electrical power. **2** the equipment supplying power to a particular machine or for a particular operation or process.

power point *n* **1** an electrical socket mounted on or recessed into a wall. **2** such a socket, esp. one installed before the introduction of 13 ampere ring mains, that is designed to provide a current of up to 15 amperes for supplying heaters, etc., rather than lights.

power politics *n* (*functioning as sing*) (in international affairs) the threat or use of force as an instrument of national policy.

power series *n* a mathematical series whose terms contain ascending positive integral powers of a variable, such as $a_0 + a_1x + a_2x^2 + \ldots$

power set *n Maths, logic.* a set the elements of which are all the subsets of a given set.

power-sharing *n* a political arrangement in which opposing groups in a society participate in government.

power station *n* an electrical generating station.

power steering *n* a form of steering used on vehicles, where the torque applied to the steering wheel is augmented by engine power. Also called: **power-assisted steering.**

power structure *n* **1** the structure or distribution of power and authority in a community. **2** the people and groups who are part of such a structure.

power tool *n* a tool powered by electricity.

power up *vb* (*tr, adv*) to switch on the power to (a computer system).

Powhatan (,paʊhə'tæn, paʊ'hætᵊn) *n* American Indian name *Wahunsonacock.* died 1618, American Indian chief of a confederacy of tribes; father of Pocahontas.

powwow ('paʊ,waʊ) *n* **1** a talk, conference, or meeting. **2** a magical ceremony of certain North American Indians, usually accompanied by feasting and dancing. **3** (among certain North American Indians) a medicine man. **4** a meeting of or negotiation with North American Indians. ◆ *vb* **5** (*intr*) to hold a powwow. [C17: from Algonquian; related to Natick *pauwau* one who practises magic, Narraganset *powwaw*]

Powys[1] ('paʊɪs) *n* a county in E Wales, formed in 1974 from most of Breconshire, Montgomeryshire, and Radnorshire. Administrative centre: Llandrindod Wells. Pop.: 122 000 (1995 est.). Area: 5077 sq. km (1960 sq. miles).

Powys[2] ('pəʊɪs) *n* **1 John Cowper** ('kuːpə). 1872–1963, British novelist, essayist, and poet, who spent much of his life in the U.S. His novels include *Wolf Solent* (1929), *A Glastonbury Romance* (1932), and *Owen Glendower* (1940). **2** his brother, **Llewelyn.** 1884–1939, British essayist and journalist. **3** his brother, **T(heodore) F(rancis).** 1875–1953, British novelist and short-story writer, noted for such religious fables as *Mr Weston's Good Wine* (1927) and *Unclay* (1931).

pox (pɒks) *n* **1** any disease characterized by the formation of pustules on the skin that often leave pockmarks when healed. **2** (usually preceded by *the*) an informal name for **syphilis. 3 a pox on (someone** *or* **something**). (*interj*) *Archaic.* an expression of intense disgust or aversion for (someone or something). [C15: changed from *pocks,* plural of POCK]

poxy ('pɒksɪ) *adj* **poxier, poxiest.** *Slang.* **1** having or having had syphilis. **2** rotten; lousy; unpleasant.

Poyang *or* **P'o-yang** ('pɔː'jæŋ) *n* a lake in E China, in N Jiangxi province, connected by canal with the Yangtze River: the second largest lake in China. Area (at its greatest): 2780 sq. km (1073 sq. miles).

Poynting theorem ('pɔɪntɪŋ) *n* the theorem that the rate of flow of electromagnetic energy through unit area is equal to the **Poynting vector,** i.e. the cross product of the electric and magnetic field intensities. [C19: named after John Henry *Poynting* (1852–1914), English physicist]

Poznań (*Polish* 'pɔznajn) *n* a city in W Poland, on the Warta River: the centre of Polish resistance to German rule (1815–1918, 1939–45). Pop.: 581 800 (1996 est.). German name: **Posen.**

Pozsony ('poʒonj) *n* the Hungarian name for **Bratislava.**

pozzuolana (,pɒtswə'lɑːnə) *or* **pozzolana** (,pɒtsə'lɑːnə) *n* **1** a type of porous volcanic ash used in making hydraulic cements. **2** any of various artificial substitutes for this ash used in cements. ◆ Also called: **puzzolana.** [C18: from Italian: of POZZUOLI]

Pozzuoli (*Italian* pot'twɔːli) *n* a port in SW Italy, in Campania on the **Gulf of Pozzuoli** (an inlet of the Bay of Naples): in a region of great volcanic activity; founded in the 6th century B.C. by the Greeks. Pop.: 65 025 (1987 est.).

pozzy ('pɒzɪ) *n, pl* **pozzies.** a variant spelling of **possie.**

pp *abbrev. for:* **1** past participle. **2** (in formal correspondence) per pro. [Latin *per procurationem*: by delegation to] **3** privately printed. ◆ **4** *Music. symbol for* pianissimo: an instruction to play very quietly.

USAGE In formal correspondence, when Brenda Smith is signing on behalf of Peter Jones, she should write *Peter Jones pp* (or *per pro*) *Brenda Smith,* not the other way about.

pp *or* **PP** *abbrev. for:* **1** parcel post. **2** prepaid. **3** post-paid. **4** (in prescriptions) post prandium. [Latin: after a meal]

PP *abbrev. for:* **1** Parish Priest. **2** past President.

pp. *abbrev. for* pages.

ppd *abbrev. for:* **1** post-paid. **2** prepaid.

PPE *abbrev. for* philosophy, politics, and economics: a university course.

ppm *abbrev. for:* **1** *Chem.* parts per million. **2** Also: **PPM.** peak programme meter.

PPP *abbrev. for* purchasing power parity: a rate of exchange between two currencies that gives them equal purchasing powers in their own economies.

ppr *or* **p.pr.** *abbrev. for* present participle.

PPS *abbrev. for:* **1** parliamentary private secretary. **2** Also: **pps** post postscriptum. [Latin: after postscript; additional postscript]

PPTA (in New Zealand) *abbrev. for* Post-primary Teachers Association.
pq *abbrev. for* previous question.
PQ (in Canada) *abbrev. for:* **1** Province of Quebec. **2** Parti Québecois.
pr *abbrev. for:* **1** (*pl* **prs**) pair. **2** paper. **3** (in prescriptions) per rectum. **[**Latin: through the rectum; to be inserted into the anus**]** **4** power.
Pr *the chemical symbol for* praseodymium.
PR *abbrev. for:* **1** proportional representation. **2** public relations. **3** Puerto Rico.
pr. *abbrev. for:* **1** Also: **Pr.** preferred stock. **2** price. **3** pronoun.
Pr. *abbrev. for:* **1** Priest. **2** Prince.
pracharak (prəˈtʃɑːrək) *n* (in India) a person appointed to propagate a cause through personal contact, meetings, public lectures, etc. **[**Hindi**]**
practicable (ˈpræktɪkəbᵊl) *adj* **1** capable of being done; feasible. **2** usable. **[C17:** from French *praticable,* from *pratiquer* to practise; see PRACTICAL**]** ▸ **ˌpracticaˈbility** *or* **ˈpracticableness** *n* ▸ **ˈpracticably** *adv*
USAGE See at **practical.**
practical (ˈpræktɪkᵊl) *adj* **1** of, involving, or concerned with experience or actual use; not theoretical. **2** of or concerned with ordinary affairs, work, etc. **3** adapted or adaptable for use. **4** of, involving, or trained by practice. **5** being such for all useful or general purposes; virtual. ♦ *n* **6** an examination in the practical skills of a subject: *a science practical.* **[C17:** from earlier *practic,* from French *pratique,* via Late Latin from Greek *praktikos,* from *prassein* to experience, negotiate, perform**]** ▸ **ˌpractiˈcality** *or* **ˈpracticalness** *n*
USAGE A distinction is usually made between *practical* and *practicable. Practical* refers to a person, idea, project, etc., as being more concerned with or relevant to practice than theory: *he is a very practical person; the idea had no practical application. Practicable* refers to a project or idea as being capable of being done or put into effect: *the plan was expensive, yet practicable.*
practical joke *n* a prank or trick usually intended to make the victim appear foolish. ▸ **practical joker** *n*
practically (ˈpræktɪkəlɪ, -klɪ) *adv* **1** virtually; almost: *it has rained practically every day.* **2** in actuality rather than in theory: *what can we do practically to help?*
practical reason *or* **reasoning** *n Philosophy, logic.* **1** the faculty by which human beings determine how to act. **2** reasoning concerning the relative merits of actions. **3** the principles governing arguments which issue in actions or intentions to act.
practice (ˈpræktɪs) *n* **1** a usual or customary action or proceeding: *it was his practice to rise at six; he made a practice of stealing stamps.* **2** repetition or exercise of an activity in order to achieve mastery and fluency. **3** the condition of having mastery of a skill or activity through repetition (esp. in the phrases **in practice, out of practice**). **4** the exercise of a profession: *he set up practice as a lawyer.* **5** the act of doing something: *he put his plans into practice.* **6** the established method of conducting proceedings in a court of law. ♦ *vb* **7** the U.S. spelling of **practise. [C16:** from Medieval Latin *practicāre* to practise, from Greek *praktikē* practical science, practical work, from *prattein* to do, act**]**
practise *or U.S.* **practice** (ˈpræktɪs) *vb* **1** to do or cause to do repeatedly in order to gain skill. **2** (*tr*) to do (something) habitually or frequently: *they practise ritual murder.* **3** to observe or pursue (something, such as a religion): *to practise Christianity.* **4** to work at (a profession, job, etc.): *he practises medicine.* **5** (foll. by *on* or *upon*) to take advantage of (someone, someone's credulity, etc.). **[C15:** see PRACTICE**]**
practised *or U.S.* **practiced** (ˈpræktɪst) *adj* **1** expert; skilled; proficient. **2** acquired or perfected by practice.
practitioner (prækˈtɪʃənə) *n* **1** a person who practises a profession or art. **2** *Christian Science.* a person authorized to practise spiritual healing. **[C16:** from *practician,* from Old French *praticien,* from *pratiquer* to PRACTISE**]**
Pradesh (prəˈdeɪʃ) *n Indian.* a state, esp. a state in the Union of India. **[**Hindi**]**
Prado (ˈprɑːdəʊ) *n* an art gallery in Madrid housing an important collection of Spanish paintings.
prae- *prefix* an archaic variant of **pre-.**
praedial *or* **predial** (ˈpriːdɪəl) *adj* **1** of or relating to land, farming, etc. **2** attached to or occupying land. **[C16:** from Medieval Latin *praediālis,* from Latin *praedium* farm, estate**]** ▸ **ˌpraediˈality** *or* **ˌprediˈality** *n*
praefect (ˈpriːfekt) *n* a variant spelling of **prefect** (senses 4–7). ▸ **praefectorial** (ˌpriːfekˈtɔːrɪəl) *adj*
praemunire (ˌpriːmjʊˈnaɪərɪ) *n English history.* **1** a writ charging with the offence of resorting to a foreign jurisdiction, esp. to that of the Pope, in a matter determinable in a royal court. **2** the statute of Richard II defining this offence. **[C14:** from the Medieval Latin phrase (in the text of the writ) *praemūnīre faciās,* literally: that you cause (someone) to be warned in advance, from Latin *praemūnīre* to fortify or protect in front, from *prae* in front + *mūnīre* to fortify; in Medieval Latin the verb was confused with Latin *praemonēre* to forewarn**]**
praenomen (priːˈnəʊmɛn) *n, pl* **-nomina** (-ˈnɒmɪnə) *or* **-nomens.** an ancient Roman's first or given name. See also **agnomen, cognomen, nomen. [C18:** from Latin, from *prae-* before + *nōmen* NAME**]** ▸ **praenominal** (priːˈnɒmɪnᵊl) *adj* ▸ **praeˈnominally** *adv*
Praesepe (praɪˈsiːpɪ) *n* an open cluster of several hundred stars in the constellation Cancer, visible to the naked eye as a hazy patch of light.
praesidium (prɪˈsɪdɪəm) *n* a variant spelling of **presidium.**
praetor *or* **pretor** (ˈpriːtə, -tɔː) *n* (in ancient Rome) any of several senior magistrates ranking just below the consuls. **[C15:** from Latin: one who leads the way, probably from *praeīre,* from *prae-* before + *īre* to go**]** ▸ **praeˈtorial** *or* **preˈtorial** *adj* ▸ **ˈpraetorship** *or* **ˈpretorship** *n*
praetorian *or* **pretorian** (priːˈtɔːrɪən) *adj* **1** of or relating to a praetor. ♦ *n* **2** a person holding praetorian rank; a praetor or ex-praetor.
Praetorian *or* **Pretorian** (priːˈtɔːrɪən) *adj* **1** of or relating to the Praetorian Guard. **2** (*sometimes not cap.*) resembling the Praetorian Guard, esp. with regard to corruption. ♦ *n* **3** a member of the Praetorian Guard.
Praetorian Guard *n* **1** the bodyguard of the Roman emperors, noted for its political corruption, which existed from 27 B.C. to 312 A.D. **2** a member of this bodyguard.
Praetorius (*German* prɛˈtoːrius) *n* **Michael** (ˈmɪçaeːl). 1571–1621, German composer and musicologist, noted esp. for his description of contemporary musical practices and instruments, *Syntagma musicum* (1615–19).
pragmatic (prægˈmætɪk) *adj* **1** advocating behaviour that is dictated more by practical consequences than by theory or dogma. **2** *Philosophy.* of or relating to pragmatism. **3** involving everyday or practical business. **4** of or concerned with the affairs of a state or community. **5** *Rare.* interfering or meddlesome; officious. Also (for senses 3, 5): **pragmatical. [C17:** from Late Latin *prāgmaticus,* from Greek *prāgmatikos* from *pragma* act, from *prattein* to do**]** ▸ **pragˌmatiˈcality** *n* ▸ **pragˈmatically** *adv*
pragmatics (prægˈmætɪks) *n* (*functioning as sing*) **1** the study of those aspects of language that cannot be considered in isolation from its use. **2** the study of the relation between symbols and those who use them.
pragmatic sanction *n* an edict, decree, or ordinance issued with the force of fundamental law by a sovereign.
pragmatism (ˈprægməˌtɪzəm) *n* **1** action or policy dictated by consideration of the immediate practical consequences rather than by theory or dogma. **2** *Philosophy.* **2a** the doctrine that the content of a concept consists only in its practical applicability. **2b** the doctrine that truth consists not in correspondence with the facts but in successful coherence with experience. See also **instrumentalism.** ▸ **ˈpragmatist** *n, adj* ▸ **ˌpragmaˈtistic** *adj*
Prague (prɑːg) *n* the capital and largest city of the Czech Republic, on the Vltava River: a rich commercial centre during the Middle Ages; site of Charles University (1348) and a technical university (1707); scene of defenestrations (1419 and 1618) that contributed to the outbreak of the Hussite Wars and the Thirty Years' War respectively. Pop.: 1 209 855 (1996 est.). Czech name: **Praha.**
Praha (ˈpraha) *n* the Czech name for **Prague.**
Praia (praɪə) *n* the capital of Cape Verde; a port and submarine cable station. Pop.: 68 000 (1995 est.).
Prairial *French.* (prɛrial) *n* the month of meadows: the ninth month of the French Revolutionary calendar, extending from May 21 to June 19. **[C18:** from French *prairie* meadow**]**
prairie (ˈprɛərɪ) *n* (*often pl*) a treeless grassy plain of the central U.S. and S Canada. Compare **pampas, steppe, savanna. [C18:** from French, from Old French *praierie,* from Latin *prātum* meadow**]**
prairie chicken, fowl, grouse, *or* **hen** *n* either of two mottled brown-and-white grouse, *Tympanuchus cupido* or *T. pallidicinctus,* of North America.
prairie dog *n* any of several gregarious sciurine rodents of the genus *Cynomys,* such as *C. ludovicianus,* that live in large complex burrows in the prairies of North America. Also called: **prairie marmot.**
prairie oyster *n* **1** a drink consisting of raw unbeaten egg, vinegar or Worcester sauce (**Worcester oyster**), salt, and pepper: a supposed cure for a hangover. **2** the testicles of a bull calf cooked and eaten.
Prairie Provinces *pl n* the Canadian provinces of Manitoba, Saskatchewan, and Alberta, which lie in the N Great Plains region of North America: the chief wheat and petroleum producing area of Canada.
prairie schooner *n Chiefly U.S.* a horse-drawn covered wagon similar to but smaller than a Conestoga wagon, used in the 19th century to cross the prairies of North America.
prairie soil *n* a soil type occurring in temperate areas formerly under prairie grasses and characterized by a black A horizon, rich in plant foods.
prairie turnip *n* another name for **breadroot.**
prairie wolf *n* another name for **coyote** (sense 1).
praise (preɪz) *n* **1** the act of expressing commendation, admiration, etc. **2** the extolling of a deity or the rendering of homage and gratitude to a deity. **3** the condition of being commended, admired, etc. **4** *Archaic.* the reason for praise. **5 sing someone's praises.** to commend someone highly. ♦ *vb* (*tr*) **6** to express commendation, admiration, etc., for. **7** to proclaim or describe the glorious attributes of (a deity) with homage and thanksgiving. **[C13:** from Old French *preisier,* from Late Latin *pretiāre* to esteem highly, from Latin *pretium* prize; compare PRIZE[2], PRECIOUS**]** ▸ **ˈpraiser** *n*
praiseworthy (ˈpreɪzˌwɜːðɪ) *adj* deserving of praise; commendable. ▸ **ˈpraiseˌworthily** *adv* ▸ **ˈpraiseˌworthiness** *n*
prajna (ˈprʊdʒnə, -njɑː) *n* wisdom or understanding considered as the goal of Buddhist contemplation. **[**from Sanskrit *prajñā,* from *prajānāti* he knows**]**
Prakrit (ˈprɑːkrɪt) *n* any of the vernacular Indic languages as distinguished from Sanskrit: spoken from about 300 B.C. to the Middle Ages. See also **Pali. [C18:** from Sanskrit *prākrta* original, from *pra-* before + *kr* to do, make + *-ta* indicating a participle**]** ▸ **Praˈkritic** *adj*
praline (ˈprɑːliːn) *n* **1** a confection of nuts with caramelized sugar, used in desserts and as a filling for chocolates. **2** Also called: **sugared almond.** a sweet consisting of an almond encased in sugar. **[C18:** from French, named after César de Choiseul, comte de Plessis-*Praslin* (1598-1675), French field marshal whose chef first concocted it**]**
pralltriller (ˈprɑːlˌtrɪlə) *n* **1** an ornament used in 18th-century music consisting of an inverted mordent with an added initial upper note. **2** another word for **inverted mordent. [**German: bouncing trill**]**
pram[1] (præm) *n Brit.* a cotlike four-wheeled carriage for a baby. U.S. and Canadian term: **baby carriage. [C19:** shortened and altered from PERAMBULATOR**]**
pram[2] (prɑːm) *n Nautical.* a light tender with a flat bottom and a bow formed from the ends of the side and bottom planks meeting in a small raised transom. **[C16:** from Middle Dutch *prame;* related to Old Frisian *prām***]**
prance (prɑːns) *vb* **1** (*intr*) to swagger or strut. **2** (*intr*) to caper, gambol, or

dance about. **3** (*intr*) **3a** (of a horse) to move with high lively springing steps. **3b** to ride a horse that moves in this way. **4** (*tr*) to cause to prance. ◆ *n* **5** the act or an instance of prancing. [C14 *prauncen;* perhaps related to German *prangen* to be in full splendour; compare Danish (dialect) *pransk* lively, spirited, used of a horse] ▸ **'prancer** *n* ▸ **'prancingly** *adv*

prandial ('prændɪəl) *adj Facetious.* of or relating to a meal. [C19: from Latin *prandium* meal, luncheon] ▸ **'prandially** *adv*

Prandtl (*German* 'prantᵊl) *n* **Ludwig** ('lu:tvɪç). 1875–1953, German physicist, who made important contributions to aerodynamics and aeronautics.

prang (præŋ) *Chiefly Brit. slang.* ◆ *n* **1** an accident or crash in an aircraft, car, etc. **2** an aircraft bombing raid. **3** an achievement. ◆ *vb* **4** to crash or damage (an aircraft, car, etc.). **5** to damage (a town, etc.) by bombing. [C20: possibly imitative of an explosion; perhaps related to Malay *perang* war, fighting]

prank[1] (præŋk) *n* a mischievous trick or joke, esp. one in which something is done rather than said. [C16: of unknown origin] ▸ **'prankish** *adj*

prank[2] (præŋk) *vb* **1** (*tr*) to dress or decorate showily or gaudily. **2** (*intr*) to make an ostentatious display. [C16: from Middle Dutch *pronken;* related to German *Prunk* splendour, *prangen* to be in full splendour]

prankster ('præŋkstə) *n* a practical joker.

Prasad (prə'sa:d) *n* **Rajendra** (ra:'dʒendrə). 1884–1963, Indian statesman and journalist; first president of India (1950–62).

prase (preɪz) *n* a light green translucent variety of chalcedony. [C14: from French, from Latin *prasius* a leek-green stone, from Greek *prasios,* from *prason* a leek]

praseodymium (ˌpreɪzɪəʊ'dɪmɪəm) *n* a malleable ductile silvery-white element of the lanthanide series of metals. It occurs principally in monazite and bastnaesite and is used with other rare earths in carbon-arc lights and as a pigment in glass. Symbol: Pr; atomic no.: 59; atomic wt.: 140.90765; valency: 3; relative density: 6.773; melting pt.: 931°C; boiling pt.: 3520°C. [C20: New Latin, from Greek *prasios* of a leek-green colour + DIDYMIUM]

prat (præt) *n Slang.* an incompetent or ineffectual person: often used as a term of abuse. [C20: probably special use of C16 *prat* buttocks, of unknown origin]

prate (preɪt) *vb* **1** (*intr*) to talk idly and at length; chatter. **2** (*tr*) to utter in an idle or empty way. ◆ *n* **3** idle or trivial talk; prattle; chatter. [C15: of Germanic origin; compare Middle Dutch *prāten,* Icelandic and Norwegian *prata,* Danish *prate*] ▸ **'prater** *n* ▸ **'pratingly** *adv*

pratfall ('præt,fɔ:l) *n U.S. and Canadian slang.* a fall upon one's buttocks. [C20: from C16 *prat* buttocks (of unknown origin) + FALL]

pratincole ('prætɪŋ,kəʊl, 'preɪ-) *n* any of various swallow-like shore birds of the southern Old World genus *Glareola* and related genera, esp. *G. pratincola,* having long pointed wings, short legs, and a short bill: family *Glareolidae,* order *Charadriiformes.* [C18: from New Latin *pratincola* field-dwelling, from Latin *prātum* meadow + *incola* inhabitant]

pratique ('præti:k, præ'ti:k) *n* formal permission given to a vessel to use a foreign port upon satisfying the requirements of local health authorities. [C17: from French, from Medieval Latin *practica* PRACTICE]

Prato (*Italian* 'pra:to) *n* a walled city in central Italy, in Tuscany: woollen industry. Pop.: 167 991 (1996 est.). Official name: **Prato in Toscana** (in tos'ka:na).

prattle ('prætᵊl) *vb* **1** (*intr*) to talk in a foolish or childish way; babble. **2** (*tr*) to utter in a foolish or childish way. ◆ *n* **3** foolish or childish talk. [C16: from Middle Low German *pratelen* to chatter; see PRATE] ▸ **'prattler** *n* ▸ **'prattlingly** *adv*

prau (praʊ) *n* another word for **proa.**

prawn (prɔ:n) *n* **1** any of various small edible marine decapod crustaceans of the genera *Palaemon, Penaeus,* etc., having a slender flattened body with a long tail and two pairs of pincers. **2 come the raw prawn.** *Austral. informal.* to attempt deception. [C15: of obscure origin] ▸ **'prawner** *n*

prawn cracker *n* a puffy savoury crisp made from rice flour and prawn flavouring, served with Chinese food.

praxis ('præksɪs) *n, pl* **praxises** *or* **praxes** ('præksi:z). **1** the practice and practical side of a profession or field of study, as opposed to the theory. **2** a practical exercise. **3** accepted practice or custom. [C16: via Medieval Latin from Greek: deed, action, from *prassein* to do]

Praxiteles (præk'sɪtɪ,li:z) *n* 4th-century B.C. Greek sculptor: his works include statues of Hermes at Olympia, which survives, and of Aphrodite at Cnidus.

pray (preɪ) *vb* **1** (when *intr,* often foll. by *for;* when *tr, usually takes a clause as object*) to utter prayers (to God or other object of worship): *we prayed to God for the sick child.* **2** (when *tr, usually takes a clause as object or an infinitive*) to make an earnest entreaty (to or for); beg or implore: *she prayed to be allowed to go; leave, I pray you.* **3** (*tr*) *Rare.* to accomplish or bring by praying: *to pray a soul into the kingdom.* ◆ *interj* **4** *Archaic.* I beg you; please: *pray, leave us alone.* [C13: from Old French *preier,* from Latin *precārī* to implore, from *prex* an entreaty; related to Old English *fricgan,* Old High German *frāgēn* to ask, Old Norse *fregna* to enquire]

prayer[1] (prɛə) *n* **1a** a personal communication or petition addressed to a deity, esp. in the form of supplication, adoration, praise, contrition, or thanksgiving. **1b** any other form of spiritual communion with a deity. **2** a similar personal communication that does not involve adoration, addressed to beings venerated as being closely associated with a deity, such as angels or saints. **3** the practice of praying: *prayer is our solution to human problems.* **4** (*often pl*) a form of devotion, either public or private, spent mainly or wholly praying: *morning prayers.* **5** (*cap. when part of a recognized name*) a form of words used in praying: *the Lord's Prayer.* **6** an object or benefit prayed for. **7** an earnest request, petition, or entreaty. **8** *Law.* a request contained in a petition to a court for the relief sought by the petitioner. **9** *Slang.* a chance or hope: *she doesn't have a prayer of getting married.* [C13 *preiere,* from Old French, from Medieval Latin *precāria,* from Latin *precārius* obtained by begging, from *prex* prayer] ▸ **'prayerless** *adj*

prayer[2] ('preɪə) *n* a person who prays.

prayer beads (prɛə) *pl n R.C. Church.* the beads of the rosary.

prayer book (prɛə) *n* **1** *Ecclesiast.* a book containing the prayers used at church services or recommended for private devotions. **2** *Church of England.* (*often caps.*) another name for **Book of Common Prayer.**

prayerful ('prɛəfʊl) *adj* inclined to or characterized by prayer. ▸ **'prayerfully** *adv* ▸ **'prayerfulness** *n*

prayer meeting (prɛə) *n Chiefly Protestantism.* a religious meeting at which the participants offer up prayers to God.

prayer rug (prɛə) *n* the small carpet on which a Muslim kneels and prostrates himself while saying his prayers. Also called: **prayer mat.**

prayer shawl (prɛə) *n Judaism.* another word for **tallit.**

prayer wheel (prɛə) *n Buddhism.* (esp. in Tibet) a wheel or cylinder inscribed with or containing prayers, each revolution of which is counted as an uttered prayer, so that such prayers can be repeated by turning it.

praying mantis *or* **mantid** *n* another name for **mantis.**

PRB *abbrev. for* (after the signatures of Pre-Raphaelite painters) Pre-Raphaelite Brotherhood.

pre- *prefix* before in time, rank, order, position, etc.: *predate; pre-eminent; premeditation; prefrontal; preschool.* [from Latin *prae-,* from *prae* before, beforehand, in front]

preach (pri:tʃ) *vb* **1** to make known (religious truth) or give religious or moral instruction or exhortation in (sermons). **2** to advocate (a virtue, action, etc.), esp. in a moralizing way. [C13: from Old French *prechier,* from Church Latin *praedicāre,* from Latin: to proclaim in public; see PREDICATE] ▸ **'preachable** *adj*

preacher ('pri:tʃə) *n* **1** a person who has the calling and function of preaching the Christian Gospel, esp. a Protestant clergyman. **2** a person who preaches.

Preacher ('pri:tʃə) *n* **the.** *Bible.* the author of Ecclesiastes or the book of Ecclesiastes.

preachify ('pri:tʃɪ,faɪ) *vb* **-fies, -fying, -fied.** (*intr*) *Informal.* to preach or moralize in a tedious manner. ▸ **'preachi,fying** *n*

preachment ('pri:tʃmənt) *n* **1** the act of preaching. **2** a tedious or pompous sermon or discourse.

preachy ('pri:tʃɪ) *adj* **preachier, preachiest.** *Informal.* inclined to or marked by preaching.

preacquisition profit (ˌpri:ækwɪ'zɪʃən) *n* the retained profit of a company earned before a takeover and therefore not eligible for distribution as a dividend to the shareholders of the acquiring company.

preadamite (pri:'ædə,maɪt) *n* **1** a person who believes that there were people on earth before Adam. **2** a person assumed to have lived before Adam. ◆ *adj also* **preadamic** (ˌpri:ə'dæmɪk). **3** of or relating to a preadamite.

preadaptation (ˌpri:ædæp'teɪʃən) *n Biology.* the possession by a species or other group of characteristics that may favour survival in a changed environment, such as the limblike fins of crossopterygian fishes, which are preadaptation to terrestrial life.

preamble (pri:'æmbᵊl) *n* **1** a preliminary or introductory statement, esp. attached to a statute or constitution setting forth its purpose. **2** a preliminary or introductory conference, event, fact, etc. [C14: from Old French *préambule,* from Late Latin *praeambulum* walking before, from Latin *prae-* before + *ambulāre* to walk]

preamplifier (pri:'æmplɪ,faɪə) *n* an electronic amplifier used to improve the signal-to-noise ratio of an electronic device. It boosts a low-level signal to an intermediate level before it is transmitted to the main amplifier. Sometimes shortened to **preamp.**

preaxial (pri:'æksɪəl) *adj Anatomy.* **1** situated or occurring in front of the axis of the body. **2** of or relating to the anterior part of a vertebrate limb. ▸ **pre'axially** *adv*

prebend ('prɛbənd) *n* **1** the stipend assigned by a cathedral or collegiate church to a canon or member of the chapter. **2** the land, tithe, or other source of such a stipend. **3** a less common word for **prebendary.** **4** *Church of England.* the office, formerly with an endowment, of a prebendary. [C15: from Old French *prébende,* from Medieval Latin *praebenda* pension, stipend, from Latin *praebēre* to offer, supply, from *prae* forth + *habēre* to have, offer] ▸ **prebendal** (prɪ'bɛndᵊl) *adj*

prebendary ('prɛbəndərɪ, -drɪ) *n, pl* **-daries.** **1** a canon or member of the chapter of a cathedral or collegiate church who holds a prebend. **2** *Church of England.* an honorary canon with the title of prebendary.

prec. *abbrev. for* preceding.

Precambrian *or* **Pre-Cambrian** (pri:'kæmbrɪən) *adj* **1** of, denoting, or formed in the earliest geological era, which lasted for about 4 000 000 000 years before the Cambrian period. ◆ *n* **2 the.** the Precambrian era. See **Archaeozoic, Proterozoic.**

precancel (pri:'kænsᵊl) *vb* **-cels, -celling, -celled** *or U.S.* **-cels, -celing, -celed.** **1** (*tr*) to cancel (postage stamps) before placing them on mail. ◆ *n* **2** a precancelled stamp. ▸ **pre,cancel'lation** *n*

precancerous *adj* (esp. of cells) displaying characteristics that may develop into cancer.

ˌprea'dapt *vb*	**ˌprear'range** *vb*	**ˌprear'rangement** *n*	**pre-'Buddhist** *adj*
ˌpreado'lescent *n, adj*	**ˌprear'ranged** *adj*	**ˌpreas'semble** *vb*	

precarious (prɪˈkɛərɪəs) *adj* **1** liable to failure or catastrophe; insecure; perilous. **2** *Archaic.* dependent on another's will. [C17: from Latin *precārius* obtained by begging (hence, dependent on another's will), from *prex* PRAYER[1]] ▸ **preˈcariously** *adv* ▸ **preˈcariousness** *n*

precast *adj* (ˈpriːˌkɑːst). **1** (esp. of concrete when employed as a structural element in building) cast in a particular form before being used. ◆ *vb* (priːˈkɑːst), **-casts, -casting, -cast. 2** *(tr)* to cast (concrete) in a particular form before use.

precatory (ˈprɛkətərɪ, -trɪ) *adj Rare.* of, involving, or expressing entreaty; supplicatory. Also: **precative** (ˈprɛkətɪv). [C17: from Late Latin *precātōrius* relating to petitions, from Latin *precārī* to beg, PRAY]

precaution (prɪˈkɔːʃən) *n* **1** an action taken to avoid a dangerous or undesirable event. **2** caution practised beforehand; circumspection. [C17: from French, from Late Latin *praecautiō*, from Latin *praecavēre* to guard against, from *prae* before + *cavēre* to beware] ▸ **preˈcautionary** *or* **preˈcautional** *adj* ▸ **preˈcautious** *adj*

precede (prɪˈsiːd) *vb* **1** to go or be before (someone or something) in time, place, rank, etc. **2** *(tr)* to preface or introduce. [C14: via Old French from Latin *praecēdere* to go before, from *prae* before + *cēdere* to move]

precedence (ˈprɛsɪdəns) *or* **precedency** *n* **1** the act of preceding or the condition of being precedent. **2** the ceremonial order or priority to be observed by persons of different stations on formal occasions: *the officers are seated according to precedence.* **3** a right to preferential treatment: *I take precedence over you.*

precedent *n* (ˈprɛsɪdənt). **1** *Law.* a judicial decision that serves as an authority for deciding a later case. **2** an example or instance used to justify later similar occurrences. ◆ *adj* (prɪˈsiːdᵊnt, ˈprɛsɪdənt). **3** preceding.

precedented (ˈprɛsɪˌdɛntɪd) *adj* (of a decision, etc.) supported by having a precedent.

precedential (ˌprɛsɪˈdɛnʃəl) *adj* **1** of, involving, or serving as a precedent. **2** having precedence. ▸ **ˌpreceˈdentially** *adv*

preceding (prɪˈsiːdɪŋ) *adj (prenominal)* going or coming before; former.

precentor (prɪˈsɛntə) *n* **1** a cleric who directs the choral services in a cathedral. **2** a person who leads a congregation or choir in the sung parts of church services. [C17: from Late Latin *praecentor* leader of the music, from *prae* before + *canere* to sing] ▸ **precentorial** (ˌpriːsɛnˈtɔːrɪəl) *adj* ▸ **preˈcentorˌship** *n*

precept (ˈpriːsɛpt) *n* **1** a rule or principle for action. **2** a guide or rule for morals; maxim. **3** a direction, esp. for a technical operation. **4** *Law.* **4a** a writ or warrant. **4b** a written order to a sheriff to arrange an election, the empanelling of a jury, etc. **4c** (in England) an order to collect money under a rate. [C14: from Latin *praeceptum* maxim, injunction, from *praecipere* to admonish, from *prae* before + *capere* to take]

preceptive (prɪˈsɛptɪv) *adj* **1** of, resembling, or expressing a precept or precepts. **2** didactic. ▸ **preˈceptively** *adv*

preceptor (prɪˈsɛptə) *n* **1** *U.S.* a practising physician giving practical training to a medical student. **2** the head of a preceptory. **3** *Rare.* a tutor or instructor. ▸ **preˈceptorate** *n* ▸ **preceptorial** (ˌpriːsɛpˈtɔːrɪəl) *or* **preˈceptoral** *adj* ▸ **preˈceptorˌship** *n* ▸ **preˈceptress** *fem n*

preceptory (prɪˈsɛptərɪ) *n, pl* **-ries.** (formerly) a subordinate house or community of the Knights Templars.

precess (prɪˈsɛs) *vb* to undergo or cause to undergo precession.

precession (prɪˈsɛʃən) *n* **1** the act of preceding. **2** See **precession of the equinoxes. 3** the motion of a spinning body, such as a top, gyroscope, or planet, in which it wobbles so that the axis of rotation sweeps out a cone. [C16: from Late Latin *praecessiō* a going in advance, from Latin *praecēdere* to PRECEDE] ▸ **preˈcessional** *adj* ▸ **preˈcessionally** *adv*

precession of the equinoxes *n* the slightly earlier occurrence of the equinoxes each year due to the slow continuous westward shift of the equinoctial points along the ecliptic by 50 seconds of arc per year. It is caused by the precession of the earth's axis.

precinct (ˈpriːsɪŋkt) *n* **1a** an enclosed area or building marked by a fixed boundary such as a wall. **1b** such a boundary. **2** an area in a town, often closed to traffic, that is designed or reserved for a particular purpose: *a shopping precinct; pedestrian precinct.* **3** *U.S.* **3a** a district of a city for administrative or police purposes. **3b** the police responsible for such a district. **4** *U.S.* a polling or electoral district. [C15: from Medieval Latin *praecinctum* (something) surrounded, from Latin *praecingere* to gird around, from *prae* before, around + *cingere* to gird]

precincts (ˈpriːsɪŋkts) *pl n* the surrounding region or area.

preciosity (ˌprɛʃɪˈɒsɪtɪ) *n, pl* **-ties.** fastidiousness or affectation, esp. in speech or manners.

precious (ˈprɛʃəs) *adj* **1** beloved; dear; cherished. **2** very costly or valuable. **3** held in high esteem, esp. in moral or spiritual matters. **4** very fastidious or affected, as in speech, manners, etc. **5** *Informal.* worthless: *you and your precious ideas!* ◆ *adv* **6** *Informal.* (intensifier): *there's precious little left.* [C13: from Old French *precios,* from Latin *pretiōsus* valuable, from *pretium* price, value] ▸ **ˈpreciously** *adv* ▸ **ˈpreciousness** *n*

precious coral *n* another name for **red coral.**

precious metal *n* any of the metals gold, silver, or platinum.

precious stone *n* any of certain rare minerals, such as diamond, ruby, sapphire, emerald, or opal, that are highly valued as gemstones.

precipice (ˈprɛsɪpɪs) *n* **1a** the steep sheer face of a cliff or crag. **1b** the cliff or crag itself. **2** a precarious situation. [C16: from Latin *praecipitium* steep place, from *praeceps* headlong] ▸ **ˈprecipiced** *adj*

precipitant (prɪˈsɪpɪtənt) *adj* **1** hasty or impulsive; rash. **2** rushing or falling rapidly or without heed. **3** abrupt or sudden. ◆ *n* **4** *Chem.* a substance or agent that causes a precipitate to form. ▸ **preˈcipitance** *or* **preˈcipitancy** *n* ▸ **preˈcipitantly** *adv*

precipitate *vb* (prɪˈsɪpɪˌteɪt). **1** *(tr)* to cause to happen too soon or sooner than expected; bring on. **2** to throw or fall from or as from a height. **3** to cause (moisture) to condense and fall as snow, rain, etc., or (of moisture, rain, etc.) to condense and fall thus. **4** *Chem.* to undergo or cause to undergo a process in which a dissolved substance separates from solution as a fine suspension of solid particles. ◆ *adj* (prɪˈsɪpɪtɪt). **5** rushing ahead. **6** done rashly or with undue haste. **7** sudden and brief. ◆ *n* (prɪˈsɪpɪtɪt). **8** *Chem.* a precipitated solid in its suspended form or after settling or filtering. [C16: from Latin *praecipitāre* to throw down headlong, from *praeceps* headlong, steep, from *prae* before, in front + *caput* head] ▸ **preˈcipitable** *adj* ▸ **preˌcipitaˈbility** *n* ▸ **preˈcipitately** *adv* ▸ **preˈcipitateness** *n* ▸ **preˈcipitative** *adj* ▸ **preˈcipiˌtator** *n*

precipitation (prɪˌsɪpɪˈteɪʃən) *n* **1** *Meteorol.* **1a** rain, snow, sleet, dew, etc., formed by condensation of water vapour in the atmosphere. **1b** the deposition of these on the earth's surface. **1c** the amount precipitated. **2** the production or formation of a chemical precipitate. **3** the act of precipitating or the state of being precipitated. **4** rash or undue haste. **5** *Spiritualism.* the appearance of a spirit in bodily form; materialization.

precipitation hardening *n Metallurgy.* a process in which alloys are strengthened by the formation, in their lattice, of a fine dispersion of one component when the metal is quenched from a high temperature and aged at an intermediate temperature.

precipitin (prɪˈsɪpɪtɪn) *n Immunol.* an antibody that causes precipitation when mixed with its specific antigen.

precipitous (prɪˈsɪpɪtəs) *adj* **1** resembling a precipice or characterized by precipices. **2** very steep. **3** hasty or precipitate. ▸ **preˈcipitously** *adv* ▸ **preˈcipitousness** *n*

USAGE The use of *precipitous* to mean *hasty* is thought by some people to be incorrect.

precis *or* **précis** (ˈpreɪsiː) *n, pl* **precis** *or* **précis** (ˈpreɪsiːz). **1** a summary of the essentials of a text; abstract. ◆ *vb* **2** *(tr)* to make a precis of. [C18: from French: PRECISE]

precise (prɪˈsaɪs) *adj* **1** strictly correct in amount or value: *a precise sum.* **2** designating a certain thing and no other; particular: *this precise location.* **3** using or operating with total accuracy: *precise instruments.* **4** strict in observance of rules, standards, etc.: *a precise mind.* [C16: from French *précis,* from Latin *praecīdere* to curtail, from *prae* before + *caedere* to cut] ▸ **preˈcisely** *adv* ▸ **preˈciseness** *n*

precisian (prɪˈsɪʒən) *n* a punctilious observer of rules or forms, esp. in the field of religion. ▸ **preˈcisianism** *n*

precision (prɪˈsɪʒən) *n* **1** the quality of being precise; accuracy. **2** *(modifier)* characterized by or having a high degree of exactness: *precision grinding; a precision instrument.* [C17: from Latin *praecīsiō* a cutting off; see PRECISE] ▸ **preˈcisionism** *n* ▸ **preˈcisionist** *n*

preclinical (priːˈklɪnɪkᵊl) *adj Med.* **1** of, relating to, or occurring during the early phases of a disease before accurate diagnosis is possible. **2** of, relating to, or designating an early period of scientific study by a medical student before practical experience with patients. ▸ **preˈclinically** *adv*

preclude (prɪˈkluːd) *vb (tr)* **1** to exclude or debar. **2** to make impossible, esp. beforehand. [C17: from Latin *praeclūdere* to shut up, from *prae* in front, before + *claudere* to close] ▸ **preˈcludable** *adj* ▸ **preclusion** (prɪˈkluːʒən) *n* ▸ **preclusive** (prɪˈkluːsɪv) *adj* ▸ **preˈclusively** *adv*

precocial (prɪˈkəʊʃəl) *adj* **1** (of the young of some species of birds after hatching) covered with down, having open eyes, and capable of leaving the nest within a few days of hatching. ◆ *n* **2** a precocial bird. ◆ Compare **altricial.** [C19: see PRECOCIOUS]

precocious (prɪˈkəʊʃəs) *adj* **1** ahead in development, such as the mental development of a child. **2** *Botany.* (of plants, fruit, etc.) flowering or ripening early. [C17: from Latin *praecox* early maturing, from *prae* early + *coquere* to ripen] ▸ **preˈcociously** *adv* ▸ **preˈcociousness** *or* **precocity** (prɪˈkɒsɪtɪ) *n*

precognition (ˌpriːkɒgˈnɪʃən) *n Psychol.* the alleged ability to foresee future events. See also **clairvoyance, clairaudience.** [C17: from Late Latin *praecognitiō* foreknowledge, from *praecognoscere* to foresee, from *prae* before + *cognoscere* to know, ascertain] ▸ **precognitive** (priːˈkɒgnɪtɪv) *adj*

pre-Columbian *adj* of or relating to the Americas before they were discovered by Columbus.

preconceive (ˌpriːkənˈsiːv) *vb (tr)* to form an idea of beforehand; conceive of ahead in time.

preconception (ˌpriːkənˈsɛpʃən) *n* **1** an idea or opinion formed beforehand. **2** a bias; prejudice.

precondition (ˌpriːkənˈdɪʃən) *n* **1** a necessary or required condition; prerequisite. ◆ *vb* **2** *(tr) Psychol.* to present successively two stimuli to (an organism) without reinforcement so that they become associated; if a response is then conditioned to the second stimulus on its own, the same response will be evoked by the first stimulus.

preconize *or* **preconise** (ˈpriːkəˌnaɪz) *vb (tr)* **1** to announce or commend publicly. **2** to summon publicly. **3** (of the pope) to approve the appointment of (a nominee) to one of the higher dignities in the Roman Catholic Church. [C15: from Medieval Latin *praecōnīzāre* to make an announcement, from Latin *praecō* herald] ▸ **ˌpreconiˈzation** *or* **ˌpreconiˈsation** *n*

pre-ˈCeltic *adj*
pre-ˈChristian *adj*
pre-ˈChristmas *adj*
preˈclassical *adj*
ˌpreconˈcert *vb*
preˈcook *vb*

preconscious (priːˈkɒnʃəs) *adj* **1** *Psychol.* prior to the development of consciousness. ◆ *n* **2** *Psychoanal.* mental contents or activity not immediately in consciousness but readily brought there. ◆ Compare **subconscious, unconscious.** ▸ preˈ**consciously** *adv* ▸ **preˈconsciousness** *n*

precontract *n* (priːˈkɒntrækt). **1** a contract or arrangement made beforehand, esp. a betrothal. ◆ *vb* (ˌpriːkənˈtrækt). **2** to betroth or enter into a betrothal by previous agreement. **3** to make (an agreement, etc.) by prior arrangement.

precritical (priːˈkrɪtɪkᵊl) *adj* of, relating to, or occurring during the period preceding a crisis or a critical state or condition: *a precritical phase of a disease.*

precursor (prɪˈkɜːsə) *n* **1** a person or thing that precedes and shows or announces someone or something to come; harbinger. **2** a predecessor or forerunner. **3** a chemical substance that gives rise to another more important substance. [C16: from Latin *praecursor* one who runs in front, from *praecurrere,* from prae in front + *currere* to run]

precursory (prɪˈkɜːsərɪ) *or* **precursive** *adj* **1** serving as a precursor. **2** preliminary or introductory.

pred. *abbrev. for* predicate.

predacious *or* **predaceous** (prɪˈdeɪʃəs) *adj* **1** (of animals) habitually hunting and killing other animals for food. **2** preying on others. [C18: from Latin *praeda* plunder; compare PREDATORY] ▸ **preˈdaciousness, preˈdaceousness,** *or* **predacity** (prɪˈdæsɪtɪ) *n*

predate (priːˈdeɪt) *vb* (*tr*) **1** to affix a date to (a document, paper, etc.) that is earlier than the actual date. **2** to assign a date to (an event, period, etc.) that is earlier than the actual or previously assigned date of occurrence. **3** to be or occur at an earlier date than; precede in time.

predation (prɪˈdeɪʃən) *n* a relationship between two species of animal in a community, in which one (the predator) hunts, kills, and eats the other (the prey).

predator (ˈprɛdətə) *n* **1** any carnivorous animal. **2** a predatory person or thing.

predatory (ˈprɛdətərɪ, -trɪ) *adj* **1** *Zoology.* another word for **predacious** (sense 1). **2** of, involving, or characterized by plundering, robbing, etc. [C16: from Latin *praedātōrius* rapacious, from *praedārī* to pillage, from *praeda* booty] ▸ **ˈpredatorily** *adv* ▸ **ˈpredatoriness** *n*

predatory pricing *n Commerce.* offering goods or services at such a low price that competitors are forced out of the market.

predecease (ˌpriːdɪˈsiːs) *vb* **1** to die before (some other person). ◆ *n* **2** *Rare.* earlier death.

predecessor (ˈpriːdɪˌsɛsə) *n* **1** a person who precedes another, as in an office. **2** something that precedes something else. **3** an ancestor; forefather. [C14: via Old French from Late Latin *praedēcessor,* from *prae* before + *dēcēdere* to go away, from *dē* away + *cēdere* to go]

predella (prɪˈdɛlə; *Italian* preˈdɛlla) *n, pl* **-le** (-liː; *Italian* -le). **1** a painting or sculpture or a series of small paintings or sculptures in a long narrow strip forming the lower edge of an altarpiece or the face of an altar step or platform. **2** a platform in a church upon which the altar stands. [C19: from Italian: stool, step, probably from Old High German *bret* board]

predestinarian (ˌpriːdɛstɪˈnɛərɪən) *Theol.* ◆ *n* **1** a person who believes in divine predestination. ◆ *adj* **2** of or relating to predestination or characterizing those who believe in it. ▸ **ˌpredestiˈnarianism** *n*

predestinate *vb* (priːˈdɛstɪˌneɪt). **1** (*tr*) another word for **predestine.** ◆ *adj* (priːˈdɛstɪnɪt, -ˌneɪt). **2** predestined or foreordained. **3** *Theol.* subject to predestination; decided by God from all eternity.

predestination (priːˌdɛstɪˈneɪʃən) *n* **1** *Theol.* **1a** the act of God foreordaining every event from eternity. **1b** the doctrine or belief, esp. associated with Calvin, that the final salvation of some of mankind is foreordained from eternity by God. **2** the act of predestining or the state of being predestined.

predestine (priːˈdɛstɪn) *or* **predestinate** *vb* (*tr*) **1** to foreordain; determine beforehand. **2** *Theol.* (of God) to decree from eternity (any event, esp. the final salvation of individuals). [C14: from Latin *praedestināre* to resolve beforehand, from *destināre* to determine, DESTINE] ▸ **preˈdestinable** *adj*

predeterminate (ˌpriːdɪˈtɜːmɪnɪt, -ˌneɪt) *adj* determined beforehand; predetermined. ▸ **ˌpredeˈterminately** *adv*

predetermine (ˌpriːdɪˈtɜːmɪn) *vb* (*tr*) **1** to determine beforehand. **2** to influence or incline towards an opinion beforehand; bias. ▸ **ˌpredeˌtermiˈnation** *n* ▸ **ˌpredeˈterminative** *adj* ▸ **ˌpredeˈterminer** *n*

predial (ˈpriːdɪəl) *adj* a variant spelling of **praedial.**

predicable (ˈprɛdɪkəbᵊl) *adj* **1** capable of being predicated or asserted. ◆ *n* **2** a quality, attribute, etc., that can be predicated. **3** *Logic, obsolete.* one of the five Aristotelian classes of predicates (**the five heads of predicables**), namely genus, species, difference, property, and relation. [C16: from Latin *praedicābilis,* from *praedicāre* to assert publicly; see PREDICATE, PREACH] ▸ **ˌpredicaˈbility** *or* **ˈpredicableness** *n*

predicament (prɪˈdɪkəmənt) *n* **1** a perplexing, embarrassing, or difficult situation. **2** (ˈprɛdɪkəmənt). *Logic, obsolete.* one of Aristotle's ten categories of being. **3** *Archaic.* a specific condition, circumstance, state, position, etc. [C14: from Late Latin *praedicāmentum* what is predicated, from *praedicāre* to announce, assert; see PREDICATE]

predicant (ˈprɛdɪkənt) *adj* **1** of or relating to preaching. ◆ *n* **2** a member of a religious order founded for preaching, esp. a Dominican. **3** (ˌprɛdɪˈkænt). a variant spelling of **predikant.** [C17: from Latin *praedicāns* preaching, from *praedicāre* to say publicly; see PREDICATE]

predicate *vb* (ˈprɛdɪˌkeɪt). (*mainly tr*) **1** (*also intr; when tr, may take a clause as object*) to proclaim, declare, or affirm. **2** to imply or connote. **3** (foll. by *on* or *upon*) to base or found (a proposition, argument, etc.). **4** *Logic.* **4a** to assert or affirm (a property, characteristic, or condition) of the subject of a proposition. **4b** to make (a term, expression, etc.) the predicate of a proposition. ◆ *n* (ˈprɛdɪkɪt). **5** *Grammar.* **5a** the part of a sentence in which something is asserted or denied of the subject of a sentence; one of the two major components of a sentence, the other being the subject. **5b** (*as modifier*): *a predicate adjective.* **6** *Logic.* **6a** an expression that is derived from a sentence by the deletion of a name. **6b** a property, characteristic, or attribute that may be affirmed or denied of something. The categorial statement *all men are mortal* relates two predicates, *is a man* and *is mortal.* **6c** the term of a categorial proposition that is affirmed or denied of its subject. In this example *all men* is the subject, and *mortal* is the predicate. **6d** a function from individuals to truth values, the truth set of the function being the extension of the predicate. ◆ *adj* (ˈprɛdɪkɪt). **7** of or relating to something that has been predicated. [C16: from Latin *praedicāre* to assert publicly, from *prae* in front, in public + *dīcere* to say] ▸ **ˌprediˈcation** *n*

predicate calculus *n* the system of symbolic logic concerned not only with relations between propositions as wholes but also with the representation by symbols of individuals and predicates in propositions and with quantification over individuals. Also called: **functional calculus.** See also **propositional calculus.**

predicative (prɪˈdɪkətɪv) *adj* **1** *Grammar.* relating to or occurring within the predicate of a sentence: *a predicative adjective.* Compare **attributive. 2** *Logic.* (of a definition) given in terms that do not require quantification over entities of the same type as that which is thereby defined. Compare **impredicative.** ▸ **preˈdicatively** *adv*

predicator (ˈprɛdɪˌkeɪtə) *n* (in systemic grammar) the part of a sentence or clause containing the verbal group; one of the four or five major components into which clauses can be divided, the others being subject, object, adjunct, and (in some versions of the grammar) complement.

predicatory (ˈprɛdɪˌkeɪtərɪ, ˌprɛdɪˈkeɪtərɪ) *adj* of, relating to, or characteristic of preaching or a preacher. [C17: from Late Latin *praedicātōrius,* from *praedicāre* to proclaim]

predict (prɪˈdɪkt) *vb* (*tr; may take a clause as object*) to state or make a declaration about in advance, esp. on a reasoned basis; foretell. [C17: from Latin *praedīcere* to mention beforehand, from *prae* before + *dīcere* to say] ▸ **preˈdictable** *adj* ▸ **preˌdictaˈbility** *or* **preˈdictableness** *n* ▸ **preˈdictably** *adv*

prediction (prɪˈdɪkʃən) *n* **1** the act of predicting. **2** something predicted; a forecast, prophecy, etc. ▸ **preˈdictive** *adj* ▸ **preˈdictively** *adv*

predictor (prɪˈdɪktə) *n* **1** a person or thing that predicts. **2** an instrument, used in conjunction with an anti-aircraft gun, that determines the speed, distance, height, and direction of hostile aircraft. **3** *Statistics.* a more modern term for **independent variable.**

predigest (ˌpriːdaɪˈdʒɛst, -dɪ-) *vb* (*tr*) to treat (food) artificially to aid subsequent digestion in the body. ▸ **ˌprediˈgestion** *n*

predikant *or* **predicant** (ˌprɛdɪˈkænt) *n* a minister in the Dutch Reformed Church, esp. in South Africa. [from Dutch, from Old French *predicant,* from Late Latin *praedicans* preaching, from *praedicāre* to PREACH]

predilection (ˌpriːdɪˈlɛkʃən) *n* a predisposition, preference, or bias. [C18: from French *prédilection,* from Medieval Latin *praedīligere* to prefer, from Latin *prae* before + *dīligere* to love]

predispose (ˌpriːdɪˈspəʊz) *vb* (*tr*) **1** (often foll. by *to* or *towards*) to incline or make (someone) susceptible to something beforehand. **2** *Chiefly law.* to dispose of (property, etc.) beforehand; bequeath. ▸ **ˌpredisˈposal** *n*

predisposition (ˌpriːdɪspəˈzɪʃən) *n* **1** the condition of being predisposed. **2** *Med.* susceptibility to a specific disease. Compare **diathesis.**

prednisolone (prɛdˈnɪsəˌləʊn) *n* a steroid drug derived from prednisone and having the same uses as cortisone. [C20: altered from PREDNISONE]

prednisone (ˈprɛdnɪˌsəʊn) *n* a steroid drug derived from cortisone and having the same uses. [C20: perhaps from PRE(GNANT) + -D(IE)N(E) + (CORT)ISONE]

predominant (prɪˈdɒmɪnənt) *adj* **1** having superiority in power, influence, etc., over others. **2** prevailing; prominent. ▸ **preˈdominance** *or* **preˈdominancy** *n* ▸ **preˈdominantly** *adv*

predominate (prɪˈdɒmɪˌneɪt) *vb* **1** (*intr;* often foll. by *over*) to have power, influence, or control. **2** (*intr*) to prevail or preponderate. **3** (*tr*) *Rare.* to dominate or have control over. ◆ *adj* (prɪˈdɒmɪnɪt). **4** another word for **predominant.** [C16: from Medieval Latin *praedominārī,* from Latin *prae* before + *dominārī* to bear rule, domineer] ▸ **preˈdominately** *adv* ▸ **preˌdomiˈnation** *n* ▸ **preˈdomiˌnator** *n*

pre-echo (priːˈɛkəʊ) *n* **1** something that has preceded and anticipated something else; precursor. **2** a fault in an audio recording in which a sound that is to come is heard too early: on tape sometimes caused by print-through.

pre-eclampsia (ˌpriːɪˈklæmpsɪə) *n Pathol.* a toxic condition of pregnancy characterized by high blood pressure, protein in the urine, abnormal weight gain, and oedema. Compare **eclampsia.**

pre-embryo (priːˈɛmbrɪəʊ) *n* the structure formed after fertilization of an ovum but before differentiation of embryonic tissue.

preemie *or* **premie** (ˈpriːmɪ) *n Slang, chiefly U.S. and Canadian.* a premature infant. [C20: altered from PREMATURE]

pre-eminent (prɪˈɛmɪnənt) *adj* extremely eminent or distinguished; outstanding. ▸ **pre-ˈeminence** *n* ▸ **pre-ˈeminently** *adv*

pre-empt (prɪˈɛmpt) *vb* **1** (*tr*) to acquire in advance of or to the exclusion of others; appropriate. **2** (*tr*) *Chiefly U.S.* to occupy (public land) in order to acquire a prior right to purchase. **3** (*intr*) *Bridge.* to make a high opening bid,

ˌpre-eˈlection *n* **ˌpre-exˈist** *vb*

often on a weak hand, to shut out opposition bidding. ▸ **pre-'emptor** *n* ▸ **pre-'emptory** *adj*

pre-emption (prɪ'ɛmpʃən) *n* **1** *Law.* the purchase of or right to purchase property in advance of or in preference to others. **2** *International law.* the right of a government to intercept and seize for its own purposes goods or property of the subjects of another state while in transit, esp. in time of war. [C16: from Medieval Latin *praeemptiō,* from *praeemere* to buy beforehand, from *emere* to buy]

pre-emptive (prɪ'ɛmptɪv) *adj* **1** of, involving, or capable of pre-emption. **2** *Bridge.* (of a high bid) made to shut out opposition bidding. **3** *Military.* designed to reduce or destroy an enemy's attacking strength before it can use it: *a pre-emptive strike.* ▸ **pre-'emptively** *adv*

preen[1] (pri:n) *vb* **1** (of birds) to maintain (feathers) in a healthy condition by arrangement, cleaning, and other contact with the bill. **2** to dress or array (oneself) carefully; primp. **3** (usually foll. by *on*) to pride or congratulate (oneself). [C14 *preinen,* probably from *prunen* to PRUNE[3], influenced by *prenen* to prick, pin (see PREEN[2]); suggestive of the pricking movement of the bird's beak] ▸ **'preener** *n*

preen[2] (pri:n) *n Scot.* a pin, esp. a decorative one. [Old English *prēon* a pin; related to Middle High German *pfrieme* awl, Dutch *priem* bodkin]

pre-exilian (ˌpri:ɪg'zɪlɪən) *or* **pre-exilic** *adj Old Testament.* prior to the Babylonian exile of the Jews (586–538 B.C.).

pref. *abbrev. for:* **1** preface. **2** prefatory. **3** preference. **4** preferred. **5** prefix.

prefab ('pri:ˌfæb) *n* **a** a building that is prefabricated, esp. a small house. **b** (*as modifier*): *a prefab house.*

prefabricate (pri:'fæbrɪˌkeɪt) *vb* (*tr*) to manufacture sections of (a building), esp. in a factory, so that they can be easily transported to and rapidly assembled on a building site. ▸ **pre'fabriˌcated** *adj* ▸ **preˌfabri'cation** *n*

preface ('prɛfɪs) *n* **1** a statement written as an introduction to a literary or other work, typically explaining its scope, intention, method, etc.; foreword. **2** anything introductory. **3** *R.C. Church.* a prayer of thanksgiving and exhortation serving as an introduction to the canon of the Mass. ◆ *vb* (*tr*) **4** to furnish with a preface. **5** to serve as a preface to. [C14: from Medieval Latin *praefātia,* from Latin *praefātiō* a saying beforehand, from *praefārī* to utter in advance, from *prae* before + *fārī* to say] ▸ **'prefacer** *n*

prefatory ('prɛfətərɪ, -trɪ) *or* **prefatorial** (ˌprɛfə'tɔ:rɪəl) *adj* of, involving, or serving as a preface; introductory. [C17: from Latin *praefārī* to say in advance; see PREFACE] ▸ **'prefatorily** *or* **ˌprefa'torially** *adv*

prefect ('pri:fɛkt) *n* **1** (in France, Italy, etc.) the chief administrative officer in a department. **2** (in France, etc.) the head of a police force. **3** *Brit.* a schoolchild appointed to a position of limited power over his fellows. **4** (in ancient Rome) any of several magistrates or military commanders. **5** Also called: **prefect apostolic.** *R.C. Church.* an official having jurisdiction over a missionary district that has no ordinary. **6** *R.C. Church.* one of two senior masters in a Jesuit school or college (the **prefect of studies** and the **prefect of discipline** or **first prefect**). **7** *R.C. Church.* a cardinal in charge of a congregation of the Curia. ◆ Also (for senses 4–7): **praefect.** [C14: from Latin *praefectus* one put in charge, from *praeficere* to place in authority over, from *prae* before + *facere* to do, make] ▸ **prefectorial** (ˌpri:fɛk'tɔ:rɪəl) *adj*

prefecture ('pri:fɛkˌtjʊə) *n* **1** the office, position, or area of authority of a prefect. **2** the official residence of a prefect in France, Italy, etc. ▸ **pre'fectural** *adj*

prefer (prɪ'fɜ:) *vb* **-fers, -ferring, -ferred.** **1** (when *tr, may take a clause as object or an infinitive*) to like better or value more highly: *I prefer to stand.* **2** *Law.* to give preference, esp. to one creditor over others. **3** (esp. of the police) to put (charges) before a court, judge, magistrate, etc., for consideration and judgment. **4** (*tr; often passive*) to advance in rank over another or others; promote. [C14: from Latin *praeferre* to carry in front, prefer, from *prae* in front + *ferre* to bear] ▸ **pre'ferrer** *n*

USAGE Normally, *to* is used after *prefer* and *preferable,* not *than: I prefer Brahms to Tchaikovsky; a small income is preferable to no income at all.* However, *than* or *rather than* should be used to link infinitives: *I prefer to walk than/rather than to catch the train.*

preferable ('prɛfərəb°l, 'prɛfrəb°l) *adj* preferred or more desirable. ▸ **ˌprefera'bility** *or* **'preferableness** *n* ▸ **'preferably** *adv*

USAGE Since *preferable* already means *more desirable,* one should not say something is *more preferable* or *most preferable.* See also at **prefer.**

preference ('prɛfərəns, 'prɛfrəns) *n* **1** the act of preferring. **2** something or someone preferred. **3** *Law.* **3a** the settling of the claims of one or more creditors before or to the exclusion of those of the others. **3b** a prior right to payment, as of a dividend or share in the assets of a company in the event of liquidation. **4** *International trade.* the granting of favour or precedence to particular foreign countries, as by levying differential tariffs.

preference shares *pl n Brit. and Austral.* shares representing part of the capital issued by a company and entitling their holders to priority with respect to both net profit and net assets. Preference shares usually carry a definite rate of dividend that is generally lower than that declared on ordinary shares. U.S. and Canadian name: **preferred stock.** Compare **ordinary shares, preferred ordinary shares.**

preferential (ˌprɛfə'rɛnʃəl) *adj* **1** showing or resulting from preference. **2** giving, receiving, or originating from preference in international trade. ▸ **preferentiality** (ˌprɛfəˌrɛnʃɪ'ælɪtɪ) *n* ▸ **ˌprefer'entially** *adv*

preferential voting *n* a system of voting in which the electors signify their choices, as of candidates, in order of preference.

preferment (prɪ'fɜ:mənt) *n* **1** the act of promoting or advancing to a higher position, office, etc. **2** the state of being preferred for promotion or social advancement. **3** the act of preferring.

preferred ordinary shares *pl n Brit.* shares issued by a company that rank between preference shares and ordinary shares in the payment of dividends. Compare **preference shares.**

preferred stock *n* the U.S. and Canadian name for **preference shares.**

prefiguration (ˌpri:fɪgə'reɪʃən) *n* **1** the act of prefiguring. **2** something that prefigures, such as a prototype. ▸ **pre'figurative** *adj* ▸ **pre'figuratively** *adv* ▸ **pre'figurativeness** *n*

prefigure (pri:'fɪgə) *vb* (*tr*) **1** to represent or suggest in advance. **2** to imagine or consider beforehand. ▸ **pre'figurement** *n*

prefix *n* ('pri:fɪks). **1** *Grammar.* an affix that precedes the stem to which it is attached, as for example *un-* in *unhappy.* Compare **suffix** (sense 1). **2** something coming or placed before. ◆ *vb* (pri:'fɪks, 'pri:fɪks). (*tr*) **3** to put or place before. **4** *Grammar.* to add (a morpheme) as a prefix to the beginning of a word. ▸ **prefixal** ('pri:fɪksəl, pri:'fɪks-) *adj* ▸ **'prefixally** *adv* ▸ **prefixion** (pri:'fɪkʃən) *n*

preformation (ˌpri:fɔ:'meɪʃən) *n* **1** the act of forming in advance; previous formation. **2** *Biology.* the theory, now discredited, that an individual develops by simple enlargement of a fully differentiated egg cell. Compare **epigenesis** (sense 1).

prefrontal (pri:'frʌnt°l) *adj* situated in, involving, or relating to the foremost part of the frontal lobe of the brain.

preggers ('prɛgəz) *adj Chiefly Brit.* an informal word for **pregnant** (sense 1).

preggy ('prɛgɪ) *adj N.Z.* an informal word for **pregnant** (sense 1).

preglacial (pri:'gleɪsɪəl) *adj* formed or occurring before a glacial period, esp. before the Pleistocene epoch.

pregnable ('prɛgnəb°l) *adj* capable of being assailed or captured. [C15 *prenable,* from Old French *prendre* to take, from Latin *prehendere* to lay hold of, catch] ▸ **ˌpregna'bility** *n*

pregnancy ('prɛgnənsɪ) *n, pl* **-cies.** **1** the state or condition of being pregnant. **2** the period from conception to childbirth.

pregnant ('prɛgnənt) *adj* **1** carrying a fetus or fetuses within the womb. **2** full of meaning or significance. **3** inventive or imaginative. **4** prolific or fruitful. [C16: from Latin *praegnāns* with child, from *prae* before + *(g)nascī* to be born] ▸ **'pregnantly** *adv*

prehensile (prɪ'hɛnsaɪl) *adj* adapted for grasping, esp. by wrapping around a support: *a prehensile tail.* [C18: from French *préhensile,* from Latin *prehendere* to grasp] ▸ **prehensility** (ˌpri:hɛn'sɪlɪtɪ) *n*

prehension (prɪ'hɛnʃən) *n* **1** the act of grasping. **2** apprehension by the senses or the mind.

prehistoric (ˌpri:hɪ'stɒrɪk) *or* **prehistorical** *adj* of or relating to man's development before the appearance of the written word. ▸ **ˌprehis'torically** *adv*

prehistory (pri:'hɪstərɪ) *n, pl* **-ries.** **1** the prehistoric period. **2** the study of this period, relying entirely on archaeological evidence. ▸ **prehistorian** (ˌpri:hɪ'stɔ:rɪən) *n*

prehominid (pri:'hɒmɪnɪd) *n* any of various extinct manlike primates. See **australopithecine.**

pre-ignition (ˌpri:ɪg'nɪʃən) *n* ignition of all or part of the explosive charge in an internal-combustion engine before the exact instant necessary for correct operation.

prejudge (pri:'dʒʌdʒ) *vb* (*tr*) to judge beforehand, esp. without sufficient evidence. ▸ **pre'judger** *n* ▸ **pre'judgment** *or* **pre'judgement** *n*

prejudice ('prɛdʒʊdɪs) *n* **1** an opinion formed beforehand, esp. an unfavourable one based on inadequate facts. **2** the act or condition of holding such opinions. **3** intolerance of or dislike for people of a specific race, religion, etc. **4** disadvantage or injury resulting from prejudice. **5** **in** (*or* **to**) **the prejudice of.** to the detriment of. **6** **without prejudice.** *Law.* without dismissing or detracting from an existing right or claim. ◆ *vb* (*tr*) **7** to cause to be prejudiced. **8** to disadvantage or injure by prejudice. [C13: from Old French *préjudice,* from Latin *praejūdicium* a preceding judgment, disadvantage, from *prae* before + *jūdicium* trial, sentence, from *jūdex* a judge]

prejudicial (ˌprɛdʒʊ'dɪʃəl) *adj* causing prejudice; detrimental or damaging. ▸ **ˌpreju'dicially** *adv*

prelacy ('prɛləsɪ) *n, pl* **-cies.** **1** Also called: **prelature** ('prɛlɪtʃə). **1a** the office or status of a prelate. **1b** prelates collectively. **2** Also called: **prelatism** ('prɛləˌtɪzəm). *Often derogatory.* government of the Church by prelates.

prelapsarian (ˌpri:læp'sɛərɪən) *adj* characteristic of or relating to the human state or time before the Fall: *prelapsarian innocence.*

prelate ('prɛlɪt) *n* a Church dignitary of high rank, such as a cardinal, bishop, or abbot. [C13: from Old French *prélat,* from Church Latin *praelātus,* from Latin *praeferre* to hold in special esteem, PREFER] ▸ **prelatic** (prɪ'lætɪk) *or* **pre'latical** *adj*

prelatism ('prɛləˌtɪzəm) *n* government of the Church by prelates; episcopacy. ▸ **'prelatist** *n*

prelect (prɪ'lɛkt) *vb* (*intr*) *Rare.* to lecture or discourse in public. [C17: from Late Latin *praelegere* to instruct by reading, lecture, from *prae* in front of, in public + *legere* to read, choose] ▸ **pre'lection** *n* ▸ **pre'lector** *n*

prelexical (pri:'lɛksɪk°l) *adj Transformational grammar.* denoting or applica-

ˌpre-ex'istence *n*
'pre'flight *adj*
pre'form *vb*
pre'heat *vb*
ˌprein'dustrial *adj*

ble at a stage in the formation of a sentence at which words and phrases have not yet replaced all of the underlying grammatical and semantic material of that sentence in the speaker's mind.

prelibation (ˌpriːlaɪˈbeɪʃən) *n Rare.* an advance taste or sample; foretaste. [C16: from Late Latin *praelībātiō* a tasting beforehand, offering of the first fruits, from Latin *prae* before + *lībāre* to taste]

prelim. *abbrev. for* preliminary.

preliminaries (prɪˈlɪmɪnərɪz) *pl n* the full word for **prelims**.

preliminary (prɪˈlɪmɪnərɪ) *adj* **1** (*usually prenominal*) occurring before or in preparation; introductory. ◆ *n, pl* **-naries. 2** a preliminary event or occurrence. **3** an eliminating contest held before the main competition. [C17: from New Latin *praelīmināris,* from Latin *prae* before + *līmen* threshold] ► **preˈliminarily** *adv*

prelims (ˈpriːlɪmz, prəˈlɪmz) *pl n* **1** Also called: **front matter.** the pages of a book, such as the title page and contents, before the main text. **2** the first public examinations taken for the bachelor's degree in some universities. **3** (in Scotland) the school examinations taken as practice before public examinations. [C19: a contraction of PRELIMINARIES]

prelingually deaf (priːˈlɪŋgwəlɪ) *adj* **a** deaf from birth or having acquired deafness before learning to speak. **b** (*as collective n; preceded by the*): *the prelingually deaf.*

preliterate (priːˈlɪtərɪt) *adj* relating to a society that has not developed a written language. ► **preliteracy** (priːˈlɪtərəsɪ) *n*

prelude (ˈprɛljuːd) *n* **1a** a piece of music that precedes a fugue, or forms the first movement of a suite, or an introduction to an act in an opera, etc. **1b** (esp. for piano) a self-contained piece of music. **2** something serving as an introduction or preceding event, occurrence, etc. ◆ *vb* **3** to serve as a prelude to (something). **4** (*tr*) to introduce by a prelude. [C16: (n) from Medieval Latin *praelūdium,* from *prae* before + *-lūdium* entertainment, from Latin *lūdus* play; (vb) from Late Latin *praelūdere* to play beforehand, rehearse, from *lūdere* to play] ► **preluder** (prɪˈljuːdə, ˈprɛljudə) *n* ► **preˈludial** *adj* ► **prelusion** (prɪˈljuːʒən) *n* ► **prelusive** (prɪˈljuːsɪv) *or* **prelusory** (prɪˈljuːsərɪ) *adj* ► **preˈlusively** *or* **preˈlusorily** *adv*

prem (prɛm) *n Informal.* a premature infant.

prem. *abbrev. for* premium.

premarital (priːˈmærɪtᵊl) *adj* (esp. of sexual relations) occurring before marriage. Compare **extramarital.**

premature (ˌprɛməˈtjʊə, ˈprɛməˌtjʊə) *adj* **1** occurring or existing before the normal or expected time. **2** impulsive or hasty: *a premature judgment.* **3** (of an infant) weighing less than 2500 g (5½ lbs) and usually born before the end of the full period of gestation. [C16: from Latin *praemātūrus,* very early from *prae* in advance + *mātūrus* ripe] ► ˌ**premaˈturely** *adv* ► ˌ**premaˈtureness** *or* ˌ**premaˈturity** *n*

premaxilla (ˌpriːmækˈsɪlə) *n, pl* **-lae** (-liː). either of two bones situated in the upper jaw between the maxillary bones. ► ˌ**premaxˈillary** *adj*

premed (priːˈmɛd) *Informal.* ◆ *adj* **1** short for **premedical.** ◆ *n also* **premedic. 2** short for **premedication. 3** a premedical student.

premedical (priːˈmɛdɪkᵊl) *adj* **1** of or relating to a course of study prerequisite for entering medical school. **2** of or relating to a person engaged in such a course of study: *a premedical student.* ► **preˈmedically** *adv*

premedication (ˌpriːmɛdɪˈkeɪʃən) *n Surgery.* any drugs administered to sedate and otherwise prepare a patient for general anaesthesia.

premeditate (prɪˈmɛdɪˌteɪt) *vb* to plan or consider (something, such as a violent crime) beforehand. ► **preˈmediˌtatedly** *adv* ► **preˈmediˌtative** *adj* ► **preˈmediˌtator** *n*

premeditation (prɪˌmɛdɪˈteɪʃən) *n* **1** *Law.* prior resolve to do some act or to commit a crime. **2** the act of premeditating.

premenstrual (priːˈmɛnstrʊəl) *adj* of or occurring before a menstrual period.

premenstrual syndrome

premenstrual syndrome *or* **tension** *n* any of various symptoms, including esp. nervous tension, that may be experienced as a result of hormonal changes in the days before a menstrual period starts. Abbrevs.: **PMS, PMT.**

premie (ˈpriːmɪ) *n* a variant spelling of **preemie.**

premier (ˈprɛmjə) *n* **1** another name for **prime minister. 2** any of the heads of governments of the Canadian provinces and the Australian states. **3** (*pl*) *Austral.* the winners of a premiership. ◆ *adj* (*prenominal*) **4** first in importance, rank, etc. **5** first in occurrence; earliest. [C15: from Old French: first, from Latin *prīmārius* principal, from *prīmus* first]

premier danseur *French.* (prəmje dɑ̃sœr) *or* (*fem*) ***première danseuse*** (prəmjɛr dɑ̃søz) *n, pl* ***premiers danseurs*** *or* (*fem*) ***premières danseuses.*** the principal dancer in a ballet company. [C19: literally: first dancer]

premiere (ˈprɛmɪˌɛə, ˈprɛmɪə) *n* **1** the first public performance of a film, play, opera, etc. **2** the leading lady in a theatre company. ◆ *vb* **3** to give or be the first public performance of. [C19: from French, feminine of *premier* first]

premiership (ˈprɛmjəʃɪp) *n* **1** the office of premier. **2a** a championship competition held among a number of sporting clubs. **2b** a victory in such a championship.

premillenarian (ˌpriːmɪlɪˈnɛərɪən) *n* **1** a believer in or upholder of the doctrines of premillennialism. ◆ *adj* **2** of or relating to premillennialism. ► ˌ**premilleˈnarianism** *n*

premillennial (ˌpriːmɪˈlɛnɪəl) *adj* of or relating to the period preceding the millennium.

premillennialism (ˌpriːmɪˈlɛnɪəˌlɪzəm) *n* the doctrine or belief that the millennium will be preceded by the Second Coming of Christ. ► ˌ**premilˈlennialist** *n*

Preminger (ˈprɛmɪndʒə) *n* **Otto (Ludwig).** 1906–86, U.S. film director, born in Austria. His films include *Carmen Jones* (1954) and *Anatomy of a Murder* (1959).

premise *n* (ˈprɛmɪs). **1** Also: ˈ**premiss.** *Logic.* a statement that is assumed to be true for the purpose of an argument from which a conclusion is drawn. ◆ *vb* (prɪˈmaɪz, ˈprɛmɪs). **2** (when *tr, may take a clause as object*) to state or assume (a proposition) as a premise in an argument, theory, etc. [C14: from Old French *prémisse,* from Medieval Latin *praemissa* sent on before, from Latin *praemittere* to dispatch in advance, from *prae* before + *mittere* to send]

premises (ˈprɛmɪsɪz) *pl n* **1** a piece of land together with its buildings, esp. considered as a place of business. **2** *Law.* **2a** (in a deed, etc.) the matters referred to previously; the aforesaid; the foregoing. **2b** the introductory part of a grant, conveyance, etc. **3** *Law.* (in the U.S.) the part of a bill in equity that states the names of the parties, details of the plaintiff's claims, etc.

premium (ˈpriːmɪəm) *n* **1** an amount paid in addition to a standard rate, price, wage, etc.; bonus. **2** the amount paid or payable, usually in regular instalments, for an insurance policy. **3** the amount above nominal or par value at which something sells. **4a** an offer of something free or at a specially reduced price as an inducement to buy a commodity or service. **4b** (*as modifier*): *a premium offer.* **5** a prize given to the winner of a competition; award. **6** *U.S.* an amount sometimes charged for a loan of money in addition to the interest. **7** great value or regard: *to put a premium on someone's services.* **8** a fee, now rarely required, for instruction or apprenticeship in a profession or trade. **9 at a premium. 9a** in great demand or of high value, usually because of scarcity. **9b** above par. [C17: from Latin *praemium* prize, booty, reward]

Premium Savings Bonds *pl n* (in Britain) bonds issued by the Treasury since 1956 for purchase by the public. No interest is paid but there is a monthly draw for cash prizes of various sums. Also called: **premium bonds.**

premolar (priːˈməʊlə) *adj* **1** situated before a molar tooth. ◆ *n* **2** any one of eight bicuspid teeth in the human adult, two situated on each side of both jaws between the first molar and the canine.

premonish (prɪˈmɒnɪʃ) *vb* (*tr*) *Rare.* to admonish beforehand; forewarn.

premonition (ˌprɛməˈnɪʃən) *n* **1** an intuition of a future, usually unwelcome, occurrence; foreboding. **2** an early warning of a future event; forewarning. [C16: from Late Latin *praemonitiō,* from Latin *praemonēre* to admonish beforehand, from *prae* before + *monēre* to warn, advise] ► **premonitory** (prɪˈmɒnɪtərɪ, -trɪ) *adj*

Premonstratensian (ˌpriːˌmɒnstrəˈtɛnsɪən) *n* **a** a member of a religious order founded at Prémontré in N France in 1120 by St Norbert (about 1080–1134). **b** (*as modifier*): *a Premonstratensian canon.* [C17: from Medieval Latin (*locus*) *praemonstrātus* the place foreshown, because it was said to have been prophetically pointed out by St Norbert]

premorse (prɪˈmɔːs) *adj Biology.* appearing as though the end had been bitten off: *a premorse leaf.* [C18: from Latin *praemorsus* bitten off in front, from *praemordēre,* from *prae* in front + *mordēre* to bite]

premunition (ˌpriːmjʊˈnɪʃən) *n Med.* a state of immunity acquired as the result of a persistent latent infection. [C15 (in the sense: to protect beforehand): from Latin *praemūnītiō,* from *praemūnīre,* from *prae* before + *mūnīre* to fortify]

prenatal (priːˈneɪtᵊl) *adj* **1** occurring or present before birth; during pregnancy. ◆ *n* **2** *Informal.* a prenatal examination. ◆ Also: **antenatal.** ► **preˈnatally** *adv*

prenomen (priːˈnəʊmɛn) *n, pl* **-nomina** (-ˈnɒmɪnə) *or* **-nomens.** *U.S.* a less common spelling of **praenomen.**

prenominal (priːˈnɒmɪnᵊl) *adj* **1** placed before a noun, esp. (of an adjective or sense of an adjective) used only before a noun. **2** of or relating to a praenomen.

prenotion (priːˈnəʊʃən) *n* a rare word for **preconception.**

prentice (ˈprɛntɪs) *n* an archaic word for **apprentice.**

prenuptial agreement *n* a contract made between a man and woman before they marry, agreeing on the distribution of their assets in the event of divorce.

preoccupation (priːˌɒkjʊˈpeɪʃən) *or* **preoccupancy** (priːˈɒkjʊpənsɪ) *n* **1** the state of being preoccupied, esp. mentally. **2** something that holds the attention or preoccupies the mind.

preoccupied (priːˈɒkjʊˌpaɪd) *adj* **1** engrossed or absorbed in something, esp. one's own thoughts. **2** already or previously occupied. **3** *Biology.* (of a taxonomic name) already used to designate a genus, species, etc.

preoccupy (priːˈɒkjʊˌpaɪ) *vb* **-pies, -pying, -pied.** (*tr*) **1** to engross the thoughts or mind of. **2** to occupy before or in advance of another. [C16: from Latin *praeoccupāre* to capture in advance, from *prae* before + *occupāre* to seize, take possession of]

preordain (ˌpriːɔːˈdeɪn) *vb* (*tr*) to ordain, decree, or appoint beforehand. ► **preordination** (ˌpriːɔːdɪˈneɪʃən) *n*

prep (prɛp) *n* **1** *Informal.* short for **preparation** (sense 5) or (chiefly U.S.) **preparatory school.** ◆ *vb* **preps, prepping, prepped. 2** (*tr*) to prepare (a patient) for a medical operation or procedure.

prep. *abbrev. for:* **1** preparation. **2** preparatory. **3** preposition.

preparation (ˌprɛpəˈreɪʃən) *n* **1** the act or process of preparing. **2** the state of being prepared; readiness. **3** (*often pl*) a measure done in order to prepare for something; provision: *to make preparations for something.* **4** something that is prepared, esp. a medicine. **5** (esp. in a boarding school) **5a** homework. **5b** the period reserved for this. Usually shortened to **prep. 6** *Music.* **6a** the anticipa-

preˈnuptial *adj*	preˈpack *vb*	preˈpackage *vb*	preˈpacked *adj*

tion of a dissonance so that the note producing it in one chord is first heard in the preceding chord as a consonance. **6b** a note so employed. **7** (*often cap.*) the preliminary prayers at Mass or divine service.

preparative (prɪˈpærətɪv) *adj* **1** serving to prepare; preparatory. ◆ *n* **2** something that prepares. ▸ **preˈparatively** *adv*

preparatory (prɪˈpærətərɪ, -trɪ) *adj* **1** serving to prepare. **2** introductory or preliminary. **3** occupied in preparation. **4 preparatory to.** as a preparation to; before: *a drink preparatory to eating.* ▸ **preˈparatorily** *adv*

preparatory school *n* **1** (in Britain) a private school, usually single-sex and for children between the ages of 6 and 13, generally preparing pupils for public school. **2** (in the U.S.) a private secondary school preparing pupils for college. ◆ Often shortened to **prep school.**

prepare (prɪˈpɛə) *vb* **1** to make ready or suitable in advance for a particular purpose or for some use, event, etc.: *to prepare a meal; to prepare to go.* **2** to put together using parts or ingredients; compose or construct. **3** (*tr*) to equip or outfit, as for an expedition. **4** (*tr*) *Music.* to soften the impact of (a dissonant note) by the use of preparation. **5 be prepared.** (*foll. by an infinitive*) to be willing and able (to do something): *I'm not prepared to reveal these figures.* [C15: from Latin *praeparāre,* from *prae* before + *parāre* to make ready] ▸ **preˈparer** *n*

preparedness (prɪˈpɛərɪdnɪs) *n* the state of being prepared or ready, esp. militarily ready for war. ▸ **preˈparedly** *adv*

prepared piano *n* a piano in which some strings have been damped by having objects placed between them or tuned differently from the rest for specific tonal effect. This process was pioneered by John Cage.

prepay (priːˈpeɪ) *vb* **-pays, -paying, -paid.** (*tr*) to pay for in advance. ▸ **preˈpayable** *adj* ▸ **preˈpayment** *n*

prepense (prɪˈpɛns) *adj* (*postpositive*) (usually in legal contexts) arranged in advance; premeditated (esp. in the phrase **malice prepense**). [C18: from Anglo-Norman *purpensé,* from Old French *purpenser* to consider in advance, from *penser* to think, from Latin *pēnsāre* to weigh, consider]

preponderant (prɪˈpɒndərənt) *adj* greater in weight, force, influence, etc. ▸ **preˈponderance** *or* **preˈponderancy** *n* ▸ **preˈponderantly** *adv*

preponderate (prɪˈpɒndəˌreɪt) *vb* (*intr*) **1** (often foll. by *over*) to be more powerful, important, numerous, etc. (than). **2** to be of greater weight than something else. [C17: from Late Latin *praeponderāre* to be of greater weight, from *pondus* weight] ▸ **preˈponderately** *adv* ▸ **preˈponderˌating** *adj* ▸ **preˌponderˈation** *n*

preposition (ˌprɛpəˈzɪʃən) *n* a word or group of words used before a noun or pronoun to relate it grammatically or semantically to some other constituent of a sentence. Abbrev.: **prep.** [C14: from Latin *praepositiō* a putting before, from *pōnere* to place] ▸ **ˌprepoˈsitional** *adj* ▸ **ˌprepoˈsitionally** *adv*

USAGE The practice of ending a sentence with a preposition (*Venice is a place I should like to go to*) was formerly regarded as incorrect, but is now acceptable and is the preferred form in many contexts.

prepositive (priːˈpɒzɪtɪv) *adj* **1** (of a word or speech element) placed before the word governed or modified. ◆ *n* **2** a prepositive element. ▸ **preˈpositively** *adv*

prepositor (priːˈpɒzɪtə) *or* **prepostor** (priːˈpɒstə) *n Brit., rare.* a prefect in any of certain public schools. [C16: from Latin *praepositus* placed before]

prepossess (ˌpriːpəˈzɛs) *vb* (*tr*) **1** to preoccupy or engross mentally. **2** to influence in advance for or against a person or thing; prejudice; bias. **3** to make a favourable impression on beforehand.

prepossessing (ˌpriːpəˈzɛsɪŋ) *adj* creating a favourable impression; attractive. ▸ **ˌpreposˈsessingly** *adv* ▸ **ˌpreposˈsessingness** *n*

prepossession (ˌpriːpəˈzɛʃən) *n* **1** the state or condition of being prepossessed. **2** a prejudice or bias, esp. a favourable one.

preposterous (prɪˈpɒstərəs) *adj* contrary to nature, reason, or sense; absurd; ridiculous. [C16: from Latin *praeposterus* reversed, from *prae* in front, before + *posterus* following] ▸ **preˈposterously** *adv* ▸ **preˈposterousness** *n*

prepotency (prɪˈpəʊtᵊnsɪ) *n* **1** the state or condition of being prepotent. **2** *Genetics.* the ability of one parent to transmit more characteristics to its offspring than the other parent. **3** *Botany.* the ability of pollen from one source to bring about fertilization more readily than that from other sources.

prepotent (prɪˈpəʊtᵊnt) *adj* **1** greater in power, force, or influence. **2** *Biology.* showing prepotency. [C15: from Latin *praepotens* very powerful, from *posse* to be able] ▸ **preˈpotently** *adv*

preppy (ˈprɛpɪ) *Informal.* ◆ *adj* **1** characteristic of or denoting a fashion style of neat, understated, and often expensive clothes; young but classic: suggesting that the wearer is well off, upper class, and conservative. ◆ *n, pl* **-pies. 2** a person exhibiting such style. [C20: originally U.S., from *preppy* a person who attends or has attended a preparatory school before college]

preproduction (ˌpriːprəˈdʌkʃən) *n* **1** preliminary work on or trial production of a play, industrial prototype, etc. ◆ *adj* **2** (of a period, model, etc.) preliminary; trial.

prep school *n Informal.* See **preparatory school.**

prepuce (ˈpriːpjuːs) *n* **1** the retractable fold of skin covering the tip of the penis. Nontechnical name: **foreskin. 2** a similar fold of skin covering the tip of the clitoris. [C14: from Latin *praepūtium*] ▸ **preputial** (priːˈpjuːʃəl) *adj*

prequel (ˈpriːkwəl) *n* a film that is made about an earlier stage of a story or character's life because the later part of it has already made a successful film. [C20: from PRE- + (*se*)*quel*]

Pre-Raphaelite (ˌpriːˈræfəlaɪt) *n* **1** a member of the **Pre-Raphaelite Brotherhood,** an association of painters and writers including Rossetti, Holman Hunt, and Millais, founded in 1848 to combat the shallow conventionalism of academic painting and revive the fidelity to nature and the vivid realistic colour that they considered typical of Italian painting before Raphael. ◆ *adj* **2** of, in the manner of, or relating to Pre-Raphaelite painting and painters. ▸ **ˌPre-ˈRaphaelˌitism** *n*

prerequisite (priːˈrɛkwɪzɪt) *adj* **1** required as a prior condition. ◆ *n* **2** something required as a prior condition.

prerogative (prɪˈrɒgətɪv) *n* **1** an exclusive privilege or right exercised by a person or group of people holding a particular office or hereditary rank. **2** any privilege or right. **3** a power, privilege, or immunity restricted to a sovereign or sovereign government. ◆ *adj* **4** having or able to exercise a prerogative. [C14: from Latin *praerogātīva* privilege, earlier: group with the right to vote first, from *prae* before + *rogāre* to ask, beg for]

pres. *abbrev. for:* **1** present (time). **2** presidential.

Pres. *abbrev. for* President.

presa (ˈpresɑː) *n, pl* **-se** (-seɪ). *Music.* a sign or symbol used in a canon, round, etc., to indicate the entry of each part. Usual signs: +, :S:, or ※ [Italian, literally: a taking up, from *prendere* to take, from Latin *prehendere* to grasp]

presage *n* (ˈprɛsɪdʒ). **1** an intimation or warning of something about to happen; portent; omen. **2** a sense of what is about to happen; foreboding. **3** *Archaic.* a forecast or prediction. ◆ *vb* (ˈprɛsɪdʒ, prɪˈseɪdʒ). **4** (*tr*) to have a presentiment of. **5** (*tr*) to give a forewarning of; portend. **6** (*intr*) to make a prediction. [C14: from Latin *praesāgium* presentiment, from *praesāgīre* to perceive beforehand, from *sāgīre* to perceive acutely] ▸ **preˈsageful** *adj* ▸ **preˈsagefully** *adv* ▸ **preˈsager** *n*

presale (ˈpriːseɪl) *n* the practice of arranging the sale of a product before it is available.

Presb. *abbrev. for* Presbyterian.

presbyopia (ˌprɛzbɪˈəʊpɪə) *n* a progressively diminishing ability of the eye to focus, noticeable from middle to old age, caused by loss of elasticity of the crystalline lens. [C18: New Latin, from Greek *presbus* old man + *ōps* eye] ▸ **presbyopic** (ˌprɛzbɪˈɒpɪk) *adj*

presbyter (ˈprɛzbɪtə) *n* **1a** an elder of a congregation in the early Christian Church. **1b** (in some Churches having episcopal politics) an official who is subordinate to a bishop and has administrative, teaching, and sacerdotal functions. **2** (in some hierarchical Churches) another name for **priest. 3** (in the Presbyterian Church) **3a** a teaching elder. **3b** a ruling elder. [C16: from Late Latin, from Greek *presbuteros* an older man, from *presbus* old man]

presbyterate (prɛzˈbɪtərɪt, -ˌreɪt) *n* **1** the status or office of a presbyter. **2** a group of presbyters.

presbyterial (ˌprɛzbɪˈtɪərɪəl) *adj* of or relating to a presbyter or presbytery. Also: **presbyteral** (prɛzˈbɪtərəl). ▸ **ˌpresbyˈterially** *adv*

presbyterian (ˌprɛzbɪˈtɪərɪən) *adj* **1** of, relating to, or designating Church government by presbyters or lay elders. ◆ *n* **2** an upholder of this type of Church government. ▸ **ˌpresbyˈterianism** *n* ▸ **ˌpresbyˌterianˈistic** *adj*

Presbyterian (ˌprɛzbɪˈtɪərɪən) *adj* **1** of or relating to any of various Protestant Churches governed by presbyters or lay elders and adhering to various modified forms of Calvinism. ◆ *n* **2** a member of a Presbyterian Church. ▸ **ˌPresbyˈterianism** *n*

presbytery (ˈprɛzbɪtərɪ, -trɪ) *n, pl* **-teries. 1** *Presbyterian Church.* **1a** a local Church court composed of ministers and elders. **1b** the congregations or churches within the jurisdiction of any such court. **2** the part of a cathedral or church east of the choir, in which the main altar is situated; sanctuary. **3** presbyters or elders collectively. **4** government of a church by presbyters or elders. **5** *R.C. Church.* the residence of a parish priest. [C15: from Old French *presbiterie,* from Church Latin *presbyterium,* from Greek *presbyterion;* see PRESBYTER]

preschool *or* **pre-school** (priːˈskuːl) *adj* **a** (of a child) under the age at which compulsory education begins. **b** (of services) for or relating to preschool children.

prescience (ˈprɛsɪəns) *n* knowledge of events before they take place; foreknowledge. [C14: from Latin *praescīre* to foreknow, from *prae* before + *scīre* to know] ▸ **ˈprescient** *adj* ▸ **ˈpresciently** *adv*

prescind (prɪˈsɪnd) *vb Rare.* **1** (*intr;* usually foll. by *from*) to withdraw attention (from something). **2** (*tr*) to isolate, remove, or separate, as for special consideration. [C17: from Late Latin *praescindere* to cut off in front, from Latin *prae* before + *scindere* to split]

Prescott (ˈprɛskət) *n* **1 John Leslie.** born 1938, British politician: deputy leader of the Labour Party from 1994; deputy prime minister from 1997. **2 William Hickling** (ˈhɪklɪŋ). 1796–1859, U.S. historian, noted for his work on the history of Spain and her colonies.

prescribe (prɪˈskraɪb) *vb* **1** to lay down as a rule or directive. **2** *Law.* to claim or acquire (a right, title, etc.) by prescription. **3** *Law.* to make or become invalid or unenforceable by lapse of time. **4** *Med.* to recommend or order the use of (a drug or other remedy). [C16: from Latin *praescrībere* to write previously, from *prae* before + *scrībere* to write] ▸ **preˈscriber** *n*

prescript *n* (ˈpriːskrɪpt). **1** something laid down or prescribed. ◆ *adj* (prɪˈskrɪpt, ˈpriːskrɪpt). **2** prescribed as a rule. [C16: from Latin *praescriptum* something written down beforehand, from *praescrībere* to PRESCRIBE]

preˈplan *vb,* **-ˈplans, -ˈplanning, -ˈplanned.**
preˈprandial *adj*
ˌprepuˈbescent *n, adj*
ˌprepubliˈcation *adj*
preˈreading *n, adj*
ˌprereˈcord *vb*
ˌprereˈcorded *adj*
ˌpre-Reforˈmation *adj*
ˌpre-Reˈnaissance *adj*
ˌpreretirement *adj*
pre-ˈRoman *adj*
ˌprescienˈtific *adj*

prescriptible (prɪ'skrɪptəb^{ə}l) *adj* **1** subject to prescription. **2** depending on or derived from prescription. ► **pre,scripti'bility** *n*

prescription (prɪ'skrɪpʃən) *n* **1a** written instructions from a physician, dentist, etc., to a pharmacist stating the form, dosage strength, etc., of a drug to be issued to a specific patient. **1b** the drug or remedy prescribed. **2** (*modifier*) (of drugs) available legally only with a doctor's prescription. **3a** written instructions from an optician specifying the lenses needed to correct defects of vision. **3b** (*as modifier*): *prescription glasses.* **4** the act of prescribing. **5** something that is prescribed. **6** a long established custom or a claim based on one. **7** *Law.* **7a** the uninterrupted possession of property over a stated period of time, after which a right or title is acquired (**positive prescription**). **7b** the barring of adverse claims to property, etc., after a specified period of time has elapsed, allowing the possessor to acquire title (**negative prescription**). **7c** the right or title acquired in either of these ways. **[C14:** from legal Latin *praescriptiō* an order, prescription; see PRESCRIBE**]**

prescriptive (prɪ'skrɪptɪv) *adj* **1** making or giving directions, rules, or injunctions. **2** sanctioned by long-standing usage or custom. **3** derived from or based upon legal prescription: *a prescriptive title.* ► **pre'scriptively** *adv* ► **pre'scriptiveness** *n*

prescriptivism (prɪ'skrɪptɪ,vɪzəm) *n Ethics.* the theory that moral utterances have no truth value but prescribe attitudes to others and express the conviction of the speaker. Compare **descriptivism, emotivism.**

presell (priː'sɛl) *vb* (*tr*) **-sells, -selling, -sold. 1** to promote (a product, entertainment, etc.) with publicity in advance of its appearance. **2** to prepare (the public) for a product, entertainment, etc., with advance publicity. **3** to agree a sale of (a product) before it is available. **4** to sell (a book) before its publication date.

presence ('prɛzəns) *n* **1** the state or fact of being present. **2** the immediate proximity of a person or thing. **3** personal appearance or bearing, esp. of a dignified nature. **4** an imposing or dignified personality. **5** an invisible spirit felt to be nearby. **6** *Electronics.* a recording control that boosts mid-range frequencies. **7** (of a recording) a quality that gives the impression that the listener is in the presence of the original source of the sound. **8** *Obsolete.* assembly or company. **9** *Obsolete.* short for **presence chamber. [C14:** via Old French from Latin *praesentia* a being before, from *praeesse* to be before, from *prae* before + *esse* to be**]**

presence chamber *n* the room in which a great person, such as a monarch, receives guests, assemblies, etc.

presence of mind *n* the ability to remain calm and act constructively during times of crisis.

presenile dementia (priː'siːnaɪl) *n* a form of dementia, of unknown cause, starting before a person is old.

present[1] ('prɛz^{ə}nt) *adj* **1** (*prenominal*) in existence at the moment in time at which an utterance is spoken or written. **2** (*postpositive*) being in a specified place, thing, etc.: *the murderer is present in this room.* **3** (*prenominal*) now in consideration or under discussion: *the present topic; the present author.* **4** *Grammar.* denoting a tense of verbs used when the action or event described is occurring at the time of utterance or when the speaker does not wish to make any explicit temporal reference. **5** *Archaic.* readily available; instant: *present help is at hand.* **6** *Archaic.* mentally alert; attentive. ◆ *n* **7 the present.** the time being; now. **8** *Grammar.* **8a** the present tense. **8b** a verb in this tense. **9 at present.** at the moment; now. **10 for the present.** for the time being; temporarily. ◆ See also **presents. [C13:** from Latin *praesens,* from *praeesse* to be in front of, from *prae-* before, in front + *esse* to be**]**

present[2] *vb* (prɪ'zɛnt). (*mainly tr*) **1** to introduce (a person) to another, esp. to someone of higher rank. **2** to introduce to the public: *to present a play.* **3** to introduce and compere (a radio or television show). **4** to show; exhibit: *he presented a brave face to the world.* **5** to put forward; submit: *she presented a proposal for a new book.* **6** to bring or suggest to the mind: *to present a problem.* **7** to give or award: *to present a prize.* **8** to endow with or as if with a gift or award: *to present a university with a foundation scholarship.* **9** to offer formally: *to present one's compliments.* **10** to offer or hand over for action or settlement: *to present a bill.* **11** to represent or depict in a particular manner: *the actor presented Hamlet as a very young man.* **12** to salute someone with (one's weapon) (usually in the phrase **present arms**). **13** to aim or point (a weapon). **14** to nominate (a clergyman) to a bishop for institution to a benefice in his diocese. **15** to lay (a charge, etc.) before a court, magistrate, etc., for consideration or trial. **16** to bring a formal charge or accusation against (a person); indict. **17** *Chiefly U.S.* (of a grand jury) to take notice of (an offence) from personal knowledge or observation, before any bill of indictment has been drawn up. **18** (*intr*) *Med., psychol., etc.* to seek treatment for a particular symptom or problem: *she presented with postnatal depression.* **19** (*intr*) *Informal.* to produce a favourable, etc. impression: *she presents well in public; he presents as harmless but has poisoned his family.* **20 present oneself.** to appear, esp. at a specific time and place. ◆ *n* ('prɛz^{ə}nt). **21** anything that is presented; a gift. **22 make someone a present of something.** to give someone something: *I'll make you a present of a new car.* **[C13:** from Old French *presenter,* from Latin *praesentāre* to exhibit, offer, from *praesens* PRESENT[1]**]**

presentable (prɪ'zɛntəb^{ə}l) *adj* **1** fit to be presented or introduced to other people. **2** fit to be displayed or offered. ► **pre'sentableness** *or* **pre,senta'bility** *n* ► **pre'sentably** *adv*

presentation (,prɛzən'teɪʃən) *n* **1** the act of presenting or state of being presented. **2** the manner of presenting, esp. the organization of visual details to create an overall impression: *the presentation of the project is excellent but the content poor.* **3** the method of presenting: *his presentation of the facts was muddled.* **4** a verbal report presented with illustrative material, such as slides, graphs, etc.: *a presentation on the company results.* **5a** an offering or bestowal, as of a gift. **5b** (*as modifier*): *a presentation copy of a book.* **6** a performance or representation, as of a play. **7** the formal introduction of a person, as into society or at court; debut. **8** the act or right of nominating a clergyman to a benefice. **9** *Med.* the position of a baby relative to the birth canal at the time of birth. **10** *Commerce.* another word for **presentment** (sense 4). **11** *Television.* linking material between programmes, such as announcements, trailers, or weather reports. **12** an archaic word for **gift. 13** *Philosophy.* a sense datum. **14** (*often cap.*) another name for (feast of) **Candlemas.** ► **,presen'tational** *adj*

presentationism (,prɛzən'teɪʃə,nɪzəm) *n Philosophy.* the theory that objects are identical with our perceptions of them. Compare **representationalism.** ► **,presen'tationist** *n, adj*

presentative (prɪ'zɛntətɪv) *adj* **1** *Philosophy.* **1a** able to be known or perceived immediately. **1b** capable of knowing or perceiving in this way. **2** subject to or conferring the right of ecclesiastical presentation. ► **pre'sentativeness** *n*

present-day *n* (*modifier*) of the modern day; current: *I don't like present-day fashions.*

presentee (,prɛzən'tiː) *n* **1** a person who is presented, as at court. **2** a person to whom something is presented.

presenter (prɪ'zɛntə) *n* **1** a person who presents something or someone. **2** *Radio, television.* a person who introduces a show, links items, interviews guests, etc.; compere.

presentient (prɪ'sɛnʃənt, -'zɛn-, priː-) *adj* characterized by or experiencing a presentiment. **[C19:** from Latin *praesentiens* present participle of *praesentire,* from *prae-* PRE- + *sentire* to feel**]**

presentiment (prɪ'zɛntɪmənt) *n* a sense of something about to happen; premonition. **[C18:** from obsolete French, from *pressentir* to sense beforehand; see PRE-, SENTIMENT**]**

presently ('prɛzəntlɪ) *adv* **1** in a short while; soon. **2** at the moment. **3** an archaic word for **immediately.**

presentment (prɪ'zɛntmənt) *n* **1** the act of presenting or state of being presented; presentation. **2** something presented, such as a picture, play, etc. **3** *Law, chiefly U.S.* a statement on oath by a grand jury of something within their own knowledge or observation, esp. the commission of an offence when the indictment has been laid before them. **4** *Commerce.* the presenting of a bill of exchange, promissory note, etc.

present participle *n* a participial form of verbs used adjectivally when the action it describes is contemporaneous with that of the main verb of a sentence and also used in the formation of certain compound tenses. In English this form ends in *-ing.* Compare **gerund.**

present perfect *adj, n Grammar.* another term for **perfect** (senses 8, 11).

presents ('prɛzənts) *pl n Law.* used in a deed or document to refer to itself: *know all men by these presents.*

present value *n* the current capital value of a future income or outlay or of a series of such incomes or outlays. It is computed by the process of discounting at a predetermined rate of interest.

preservative (prɪ'zɜːvətɪv) *n* **1** something that preserves or tends to preserve, esp. a chemical added to foods to inhibit decomposition. ◆ *adj* **2** tending or intended to preserve.

preserve (prɪ'zɜːv) *vb* (*mainly tr*) **1** to keep safe from danger or harm; protect. **2** to protect from decay or dissolution; maintain: *to preserve old buildings.* **3** to maintain possession of; keep up: *to preserve a façade of indifference.* **4** to prevent from decomposition or chemical change. **5** to prepare (food), as by freezing, drying, or salting, so that it will resist decomposition. **6** to make preserves of (fruit, etc.). **7** to rear and protect (game) in restricted places for hunting or fishing. **8** (*intr*) to maintain protection and favourable conditions for game in preserves. ◆ *n* **9** something that preserves or is preserved. **10** a special area or domain: *archaeology is the preserve of specialists.* **11** (*usually pl*) fruit, etc., prepared by cooking with sugar. **12** areas where game is reared for private hunting or fishing. **[C14:** via Old French, from Late Latin *praeservāre* literally: to keep safe in advance, from Latin *prae-* before + *servāre* to keep safe**]** ► **pre'servable** *adj* ► **pre,serva'bility** *n* ► **pre'servably** *adv* ► **preservation** (,prɛzə'veɪʃən) *n* ► **pre'server** *n*

preset (prɪ'sɛt) *vb* **-sets, -setting, -set.** (*tr*) **1** to set (a timing device) so that something begins to operate at the time specified. ◆ *n* **2** *Electronics.* a control, such as a variable resistor, that is not as accessible as the main controls and is used to set initial conditions.

preshrunk (priː'ʃrʌŋk) *adj* (of fabrics, garments, etc.) having undergone a shrinking process during manufacture so that further shrinkage will not occur.

preside (prɪ'zaɪd) *vb* (*intr*) **1** to sit in or hold a position of authority, as over a meeting. **2** to exercise authority; control. **3** to occupy a position as an instrumentalist: *he presided at the organ.* **[C17:** via French from Latin *praesidēre* to superintend, from *prae* before + *sedēre* to sit**]** ► **pre'sider** *n*

presidency ('prɛzɪdənsɪ) *n, pl* **-cies. 1a** the office, dignity, or term of a president. **1b** (*often cap.*) the office of president of a republic, esp. the office of the President of the U.S. **2** *Mormon Church.* **2a** a local administrative council consisting of a president and two executive members. **2b** (*often cap.*) the supreme administrative body composed of the Prophet and two councillors.

president ('prɛzɪdənt) *n* **1** (*often cap.*) the chief executive or head of state of a republic, esp. of the U.S. **2** (in the U.S.) the chief executive officer of a company, corporation, etc. **3** a person who presides over an assembly, meeting, etc. **4** the chief executive officer of certain establishments of higher education.

,prese'lect *vb* **pre'shrink** *vb*

[C14: via Old French from Late Latin *praesidens* ruler; see PRESIDE] ▸ **presidential** (ˌprezɪˈdenʃəl) *adj* ▸ **ˌpresiˈdentially** *adv* ▸ **ˈpresidentˌship** *n*

president-elect *n* a person who has been elected president but has not yet entered office.

presidio (prɪˈsɪdɪˌəʊ; *Spanish* preˈsiðjo) *n, pl* **-sidios** (-ˈsɪdɪˌəʊz; *Spanish* -ˈsiðjos). a military post or establishment, esp. in countries under Spanish control. [C19: from Spanish: garrison, from Latin *praesidium* a guard, protection; see PRESIDE]

presidium *or* **praesidium** (prɪˈsɪdɪəm) *n, pl* **-iums** *or* **-ia** (-ɪə). **1** (*often cap.*) (in Communist countries) a permanent committee of a larger body, such as a legislature, that acts for it when it is in recess. **2** a collective presidency, esp. of a nongovernmental organization. [C20: from Russian *prezidium,* from Latin *praesidium,* from *praesidēre* to superintend; see PRESIDE]

presignify (priːˈsɪgnɪˌfaɪ) *vb* **-fies, -fying, -fied.** (*tr*) to signify beforehand; foreshadow; foretell.

Presley (ˈprezlɪ) *n* **Elvis** (**Aaron** *or* **Aron**). 1935–77, U.S. rock and roll singer. His recordings include "That's all Right (Mama)" (1954), "Heartbreak Hotel" (1956), "Hound Dog" (1956), numbers from the films *Loving You* and *Jailhouse Rock* (both 1957), and *Elvis is back* (1960).

press[1] (pres) *vb* **1** to apply or exert weight, force, or steady pressure on: *he pressed the button on the camera.* **2** (*tr*) to squeeze or compress so as to alter in shape or form. **3** to apply heat or pressure to (clothing) so as to smooth out or mark with creases; iron. **4** to make (objects) from soft material by pressing with a mould, form, etc., esp. to make gramophone records from plastic. **5** (*tr*) to hold tightly or clasp, as in an embrace. **6** (*tr*) to extract or force out (juice) by pressure (from). **7** (*tr*) *Weightlifting.* to lift (a weight) successfully with a press: *he managed to press 280 pounds.* **8** (*tr*) to force, constrain, or compel. **9** to importune or entreat (a person) insistently; urge: *they pressed for an answer.* **10** to harass or cause harassment. **11** (*tr*) to plead or put forward strongly or importunately: *to press a claim.* **12** (*intr*) to be urgent. **13** (*tr;* usually passive) to have little of: *we're hard pressed for time.* **14** (when *intr*, often foll. by *on* or *forward*) to hasten or advance or cause to hasten or advance in a forceful manner. **15** (*intr*) to crowd; throng; push. **16** (*tr*) (formerly) to put to death or subject to torture by placing heavy weights upon. **17** (*tr*) *Archaic.* to trouble or oppress. **18** **press charges.** to bring charges against a person. ◆ *n* **19** any machine that exerts pressure to form, shape, or cut materials or to extract liquids, compress solids, or hold components together while an adhesive joint is formed. **20** See **printing press. 21** the art or process of printing. **22 at** *or* **in (the) press.** being printed. **23 to (the) press.** to be printed: *when is this book going to press?* **24 the press. 24a** news media and agencies collectively, esp. newspapers. **24b** (*as modifier*): *a press matter; press relations.* **25 the press.** those who work in the news media, esp. newspaper reporters and photographers. **26** the opinions and reviews in the newspapers, etc.: *the play received a poor press.* **27** the act of pressing or state of being pressed. **28** the act of crowding, thronging, or pushing together. **29** a closely packed throng of people; crowd; multitude. **30** urgency or hurry in business affairs. **31** a cupboard, esp. a large one used for storing clothes or linen. **32** a wood or metal clamp or vice to prevent tennis rackets, etc., from warping when not in use. **33** *Weightlifting.* a lift in which the weight is raised to shoulder level and then above the head. [C14 *pressen,* from Old French *presser,* from Latin *pressāre,* from *premere* to press]

press[2] (pres) *vb* (*tr*) **1** to recruit (men) by forcible measures for military service. **2** to use for a purpose other than intended, (esp. in the phrase **press into service**). ◆ *n* **3** recruitment into military service by forcible measures, as by a press gang. [C16: back formation from *prest* to recruit soldiers; see PREST[2]; also influenced by PRESS[1]]

press agency *n* another name for **news agency.**

press agent *n* a person employed to obtain favourable publicity, such as notices in newspapers, for an organization, actor, etc. Abbrev.: **PA.**

press box *n* an area reserved for reporters, as in a sports stadium.

Pressburg (ˈpresbʊrk) *n* the German name for **Bratislava.**

Pressburger (ˈpresˌbɜːgə) *n* **Emeric** (ˈemərɪk). 1902–88, Hungarian film writer and producer, living in Britain: best known for his collaboration (1942–57) with Michael Powell. Films include *The Life and Death of Colonel Blimp* (1943), *I Know Where I'm Going* (1945), and *A Matter of Life and Death* (1946).

press conference *n* an interview for press and television reporters given by a politician, film star, etc.

press fit *n Engineering.* a type of fit for mating parts, usually tighter than a sliding fit, used when the parts do not have to move relative to each other.

press gallery *n* an area set apart for newspaper reporters, esp. in a legislative assembly.

press gang *n* **1** (formerly) a detachment of men used to press civilians for service in the navy or army. ◆ *vb* **press-gang.** (*tr*) **2** to force (a person) to join the navy or army by a press gang. **3** to induce (a person) to perform a duty by forceful persuasion: *his friends press-ganged him into joining the committee.*

pressie *or* **prezzie** (ˈprezɪ) *n* an informal word for **present**[2] (sense 21).

pressing (ˈpresɪŋ) *adj* **1** demanding immediate attention. **2** persistent or importunate. ◆ *n* **3** a large specified number of gramophone records produced at one time from a master record. **4** a component formed in a press. **5** *Football.* the tactic of trying to stay very close to the opposition when they are in possession of the ball. ▸ **ˈpressingly** *adv* ▸ **ˈpressingness** *n*

pressman (ˈpresmən, -ˌmæn) *n, pl* **-men. 1** a person who works for the press. **2** a person who operates a printing press.

pressmark (ˈpresˌmɑːk) *n Library science.* a location mark on a book indicating a specific bookcase. [C19: from PRESS[1] (in the sense: cupboard) + MARK[1]]

press of sail *n Nautical.* the most sail a vessel can carry under given conditions. Also called: **press of canvas.**

pressor (ˈpresə, -sɔː) *adj Physiol.* relating to or producing an increase in blood pressure. [C19: from Latin *premere* to press]

press release *n* an official announcement or account of a news item circulated to the press.

pressroom (ˈpresˌruːm, -ˌrʊm) *n* the room in a printing establishment that houses the printing presses.

press stud *n* a fastening device consisting of one part with a projecting knob that snaps into a hole on another like part, used esp. in closures in clothing. Also called: **popper, snap fastener.**

press-up *n* an exercise in which the body is alternately raised from and lowered to the floor by the arms only, the trunk being kept straight with the toes and hands resting on the floor. Also called (U.S. and Canadian): **push-up.**

pressure (ˈpreʃə) *n* **1** the state of pressing or being pressed. **2** the exertion of force by one body on the surface of another. **3** a moral force that compels: *to bring pressure to bear.* **4** an urgent claim or demand or series of urgent claims or demands: *to work under pressure.* **5** a burdensome condition that is hard to bear: *the pressure of grief.* **6** the force applied to a unit area of a surface, usually measured in pascals (newtons per square metre), millibars, torr, or atmospheres. Symbol: *p* or *P* **7** short for **atmospheric pressure** or **blood pressure.** ◆ *vb* **8** (*tr*) to constrain or compel, as by the application of moral force. **9** another word for **pressurize.** [C14: from Late Latin *pressūra* a pressing, from Latin *premere* to press] ▸ **ˈpressureless** *adj*

pressure cabin *n* the pressurized cabin of an aircraft or spacecraft.

pressure-cook *vb* to cook (food) in a pressure cooker.

pressure cooker *n* **1** a strong hermetically sealed pot in which food may be cooked quickly under pressure at a temperature above the normal boiling point of water. **2** *N.Z. informal.* a trainee student attending a shortened qualifying course.

pressure drag *n* the part of the total drag of a body moving through a gas or liquid caused by the components of the pressures at right angles to the surface of the body.

pressure gauge *n* any instrument for measuring fluid pressure. See also **Bourdon gauge, manometer.**

pressure gradient *n* **1** the change of pressure per unit distance. See **adverse pressure gradient, favourable pressure gradient. 2** *Meteorol.* the decrease in atmospheric pressure per unit of horizontal distance, shown on a synoptic chart by the spacing of the isobars.

pressure group *n* a group of people who seek to exert pressure on legislators, public opinion, etc., in order to promote their own ideas or welfare.

pressure head *n Physics.* a more formal name for **head** (sense 24a).

pressure point *n* any of several points on the body above an artery that, when firmly pressed, will control bleeding from the artery at a point farther away from the heart.

pressure suit *n* an inflatable suit worn by a person flying at high altitudes or in space, to provide protection from low pressure.

pressure vessel *n Engineering.* a vessel designed for containing substances, reactions, etc., at pressures above atmospheric pressure.

pressurize *or* **pressurise** (ˈpreʃəˌraɪz) *vb* (*tr*) **1** to increase the pressure in (an enclosure, such as an aircraft cabin) in order to maintain approximately atmospheric pressure when the external pressure is low. **2** to increase pressure on (a fluid). **3** to make insistent demands of (someone); coerce. ▸ **ˌpressuriˈzation** *or* **ˌpressuriˈsation** *n* ▸ **ˈpressurˌizer** *or* **ˈpressurˌiser** *n*

pressurized-water reactor *n* a nuclear reactor using water as coolant and moderator at a pressure that is too high to allow boiling to take place inside the reactor. The fuel is enriched uranium oxide cased in zirconium. Abbrev.: **PWR.**

presswork (ˈpresˌwɜːk) *n* **1** the operation of a printing press. **2** the matter printed by a printing press.

prest[1] (prest) *adj Obsolete.* prepared for action or use; ready. [C13: via Old French from Late Latin *praestus* ready to hand; see PRESTO]

prest[2] (prest) *n Obsolete.* a loan of money. [C16: originally, loan money offered as an inducement to recruits, from Old French: advance pay in the army, from *prester* to lend, from Latin *praestāre* to provide, from *prae* before + *stāre* to stand]

Prestel (ˈpresˌtel) *n Trademark.* the Viewdata service operated by British Telecom. See **Viewdata.**

Prester John (ˈprestə) *n* a legendary Christian priest and king, believed in the Middle Ages to have ruled in the Far East, but identified in the 14th century with the king of Ethiopia. [C14 *Prestre Johan,* from Medieval Latin *presbyter Iohannes* Priest John]

prestidigitation (ˌprestɪˌdɪdʒɪˈteɪʃən) *n* another name for **sleight of hand.** [C19: from French: quick-fingeredness, from Latin *praestigiae* feats of juggling, tricks, probably influenced by French *preste* nimble, and Latin *digitus* finger; see PRESTIGE] ▸ **ˌprestiˈdigiˌtator** *n*

prestige (preˈstiːʒ) *n* **1** high status or reputation achieved through success, influence, wealth, etc.; renown. **2a** the power to influence or impress; glamour. **2b** (*modifier*): *a prestige car.* [C17: via French from Latin *praestigiae* feats of juggling, tricks; apparently related to Latin *praestringere* to bind tightly, blindfold, from *prae* before + *stringere* to draw tight, bind]

prestigious (preˈstɪdʒəs) *adj* **1** having status or glamour; impressive or influen-

ˈpresoak *n* **preˈsoak** *vb* **ˌpre-Soˈcratic** *adj*

tial. **2** *Rare.* characterized by or using deceit, cunning, or illusion; fraudulent. ▸ **pres'tigiously** *adv* ▸ **pres'tigiousness** *n*

prestissimo (prɛ'stɪsɪˌməʊ) *Music.* ◆ *adj, adv* **1** to be played as fast as possible. ◆ *n, pl* **-mos. 2** a piece or passage directed to be played in this way. [C18: from Italian: very quickly, from *presto* fast]

presto ('prɛstəʊ) *adj, adv* **1** *Music.* to be played very fast. ◆ *adv* **2** immediately, suddenly, or at once (esp. in the phrase **hey presto**). ◆ *n, pl* **-tos. 3** *Music.* a movement or passage directed to be played very quickly. [C16: from Italian: fast, from Late Latin *praestus* (adj) ready to hand, Latin *praestō* (adv) present]

Preston ('prɛstən) *n* a town in NW England, administrative centre of Lancashire, on the River Ribble: developed as a weaving centre (17th–18th centuries). Pop.: 177 660 (1991).

Prestonpans (ˌprɛstən'pænz) *n* a small town and resort in SE Scotland, in East Lothian on the Firth of Forth: scene of the battle (1745) in which the Jacobite army of Prince Charles Edward defeated government forces under Sir John Cope. Pop.: 7014 (1991).

prestress (ˌpri:'strɛs) *vb* (*tr*) to apply tensile stress to (the steel cables, wires, etc., of a precast concrete part) before the load is applied.

prestressed concrete *n* concrete that contains steel wires, cables, etc., that are prestressed within their elastic limit to counteract the stresses that will occur under load.

Prestwich ('prɛstwɪtʃ) *n* a town in NW England, in Bury unitary authority, Greater Manchester. Pop.: 31 801 (1991).

Prestwick ('prɛstwɪk) *n* a town in SW Scotland, in South Ayrshire on the Firth of Clyde; international airport, golf course: tourism. Pop.: 13 705 (1991).

presumable (prɪ'zju:məbᵊl) *adj* able to be presumed or taken for granted.

presumably (prɪ'zju:məblɪ) *adv* (*sentence modifier*) one presumes or supposes that: *presumably he won't see you, if you're leaving tomorrow.*

presume (prɪ'zju:m) *vb* **1** (when *tr, often takes a clause as object*) to take (something) for granted; assume. **2** (when *tr, often foll. by an infinitive*) to take upon oneself (to do something) without warrant or permission; dare: *do you presume to copy my work?* **3** (*intr;* foll. by *on* or *upon*) to rely or depend: *don't presume on his agreement.* **4** *Law.* to take as proved until contrary evidence is produced. [C14: via Old French from Latin *praesūmere* to take in advance, from *prae* before + *sūmere* to ASSUME] ▸ **presumedly** (prɪ'zju:mɪdlɪ) *adv* ▸ **pre'sumer** *n* ▸ **pre'suming** *adj* ▸ **pre'sumingly** *adv*

presumption (prɪ'zʌmpʃən) *n* **1** the act of presuming. **2** bold or insolent behaviour or manners. **3** a belief or assumption based on reasonable evidence. **4** a ground or basis on which to presume. **5** *Law.* an inference of the truth of a fact from other facts proved, admitted, or judicially noticed. [C13: via Old French from Latin *praesumptiō* a using in advance, anticipation, from *praesūmere* to take beforehand; see PRESUME]

presumptive (prɪ'zʌmptɪv) *adj* **1** based on presumption or probability. **2** affording reasonable ground for belief. **3** of or relating to embryonic tissues that become differentiated into a particular tissue or organ: *presumptive epidermis.* ▸ **pre'sumptively** *adv* ▸ **pre'sumptiveness** *n*

presumptuous (prɪ'zʌmptjʊəs) *adj* **1** characterized by presumption or tending to presume; bold; forward. **2** an obsolete word for **presumptive.** ▸ **pre'sumptuously** *adv* ▸ **pre'sumptuousness** *n*

presuppose (ˌpri:sə'pəʊz) *vb* (*tr*) **1** to take for granted; assume. **2** to require or imply as a necessary prior condition. **3** *Philosophy, logic, linguistics.* to require (a condition) to be satisfied as a precondition for a statement to be either true or false or for a speech act to be felicitous. *Have you stopped beating your wife?* presupposes that the person addressed has a wife and has beaten her. ▸ **presupposition** (ˌpri:sʌpə'zɪʃən) *n*

pret. *abbrev. for* preterite.

preteen (pri:'ti:n) *n* a boy or girl approaching his or her teens.

pretence *or U.S.* **pretense** (prɪ'tɛns) *n* **1** the act of pretending. **2** a false display; affectation. **3** a claim, esp. a false one, to a right, title, or distinction. **4** make-believe or feigning. **5** a false claim or allegation; pretext. **6** a less common word for **pretension** (sense 3).

pretend (prɪ'tɛnd) *vb* **1** (when *tr, usually takes a clause as object or an infinitive*) to claim or allege (something untrue). **2** (*tr; may take a clause as object or an infinitive*) to make believe, as in a play: *you pretend to be Ophelia.* **3** (*intr;* foll. by *to*) to present a claim, esp. a dubious one: *to pretend to the throne.* **4** (*intr;* foll. by *to*) *Obsolete.* to aspire as a candidate or suitor (for). ◆ *adj* **5** fanciful; make-believe; simulated: *a pretend gun.* [C14: from Latin *praetendere* to stretch forth, feign, from *prae* in front + *tendere* to stretch]

pretender (prɪ'tɛndə) *n* **1** a person who pretends or makes false allegations. **2** a person who mounts a claim, as to a throne or title.

pretension (prɪ'tɛnʃən) *n* **1** (*often pl*) a false or unsupportable claim, esp. to merit, worth, or importance. **2** a specious or unfounded allegation; pretext. **3** the state or quality of being pretentious.

pretensive (prɪ'tɛnsɪv) *adj Caribbean.* pretentious.

pretentious (prɪ'tɛnʃəs) *adj* **1** making claim to distinction or importance, esp. undeservedly. **2** having or creating a deceptive outer appearance of great worth; ostentatious. ▸ **pre'tentiously** *adv* ▸ **pre'tentiousness** *n*

preter- *prefix* beyond, more than, or exceeding: *preternatural.* [from Latin *praeter-*, from *praeter*]

preterhuman (ˌpri:tə'hju:mən) *adj Rare.* beyond what is human.

preterite *or U.S.* **preterit** ('prɛtərɪt) *Grammar.* ◆ *n* **1** a tense of verbs used to relate past action, formed in English by inflection of the verb, as *jumped, swam.* **2** a verb in this tense. ◆ *adj* **3** denoting this tense. [C14: from Late Latin *praeteritum* (*tempus*) past (time, tense), from Latin *praeterīre* to go by, from PRETER- + *īre* to go]

preterition (ˌprɛtə'rɪʃən) *n* **1** the act of passing over or omitting. **2** *Roman law.* the failure of a testator to name one of his children in his will, thus invalidating it. **3** (in Calvinist theology) the doctrine that God passed over or left unpredestined those not elected to final salvation. [C17: from Late Latin *praeteritiō* a passing over]

preteritive (prɪ'tɛrɪtɪv) *adj* (of a verb) having only past tense forms.

preterm (ˌpri:'tɜ:m) *adj* **1** (of a baby) born prematurely. ◆ *adv* **2** prematurely.

pretermit (ˌpri:tə'mɪt) *vb* **-mits, -mitting, -mitted.** (*tr*) *Rare.* **1** to overlook intentionally; disregard. **2** to fail to do; neglect; omit. [C16: from Latin *praetermittere* to let pass, from PRETER- + *mittere* to send, release] ▸ **pretermission** (ˌpri:tə'mɪʃən) *n* ▸ **ˌpreter'mitter** *n*

preternatural (ˌpri:tə'nætʃrəl) *adj* **1** beyond what is ordinarily found in nature; abnormal. **2** another word for **supernatural.** [C16: from Medieval Latin *praeternātūrālis,* from Latin *praeter natūram* beyond the scope of nature] ▸ **ˌpreter'naturally** *adv* ▸ **ˌpreter'naturalism** *n* ▸ **ˌpreter'naturalness** *or* **ˌpreterˌnatu'rality** *n*

pretext ('pri:tɛkst) *n* **1** a fictitious reason given in order to conceal the real one. **2** a specious excuse; pretence. [C16: from Latin *praetextum* disguise, from *praetexere* to weave in front, disguise; see TEXTURE]

pretonic (pri:'tɒnɪk) *adj* denoting or relating to the syllable before the one bearing the primary stress in a word.

pretor ('pri:tə) *n* a variant spelling of **praetor.**

Pretoria (prɪ'tɔ:rɪə) *n* a city in N South Africa, the administrative capital of South Africa; formerly capital of Transvaal province: two universities (1873, 1930); large steelworks. Pop.: 525 583 (1991).

Pretorius (prɪ'tɔ:rɪəs) *n* **1 Andries Wilhelmus Jacobus** ('ɑndri:s wɪl'hɛlmys ja:'ko:bys). 1799–1853, a Boer leader in the Great Trek (1838) to escape British sovereignty; he also led an expedition to the Transvaal (1848). The town Pretoria was named after him. **2** his son, **Marthinus Wessels** (mar'ti:nys'wɛsəls). 1819–1901, first president of the South African Republic (1857–71) and of the Orange Free State (1859–63).

prettify ('prɪtɪˌfaɪ) *vb* **-fies, -fying, -fied.** (*tr*) to make pretty, esp. in a trivial fashion; embellish. ▸ **ˌprettifi'cation** *n* ▸ **'prettiˌfier** *n*

pretty ('prɪtɪ) *adj* **-tier, -tiest. 1** pleasing or appealing in a delicate or graceful way. **2** dainty, neat, or charming. **3** *Informal, often ironical.* excellent, grand, or fine: *here's a pretty mess!* **4** *Informal.* lacking in masculinity; effeminate; foppish. **5** *Archaic or Scot.* vigorous or brave. **6** an archaic word for **elegant. 7 a pretty penny.** *Informal.* a large sum of money. **8 sitting pretty.** *Informal.* well placed or established financially, socially, etc. ◆ *n, pl* **-ties. 9** a pretty person or thing. ◆ *adv* **10** *Informal.* fairly or moderately; somewhat. **11** *Informal.* quite or very. ◆ *vb* **-ties, -tying, -tied. 12** (*tr;* often foll. by *up*) to make pretty; adorn. [Old English *prættig* clever; related to Middle Low German *prattich* obstinate, Dutch *prettig* glad, Old Norse *prettugr* cunning] ▸ **'prettily** *adv* ▸ **'prettiness** *n*

pretty-pretty *adj Informal.* excessively or ostentatiously pretty.

pretzel ('prɛtsəl) *n* a brittle savoury biscuit, in the form of a knot or stick, glazed and salted on the outside, eaten esp. in Germany and the U.S. [C19: from German, from Old High German *brezitella;* perhaps related to Medieval Latin *bracellus* bracelet, from Latin *bracchium* arm]

Preussen ('prɔysən) *n* the German name for **Prussia.**

prevail (prɪ'veɪl) *vb* (*intr*) **1** (often foll. by *over* or *against*) to prove superior; gain mastery: *skill will prevail.* **2** to be or appear as the most important feature; be prevalent. **3** to exist widely; be in force. **4** (often foll. by *on* or *upon*) to succeed in persuading or inducing. [C14: from Latin *praevalēre* to be superior in strength, from *prae* beyond + *valēre* to be strong] ▸ **pre'vailer** *n*

prevailing (prɪ'veɪlɪŋ) *adj* **1** generally accepted; widespread: *the prevailing opinion.* **2** most frequent or conspicuous; predominant: *the prevailing wind is from the north.* ▸ **pre'vailingly** *adv*

prevalent ('prɛvələnt) *adj* **1** widespread or current. **2** superior in force or power; predominant. [C16 (in the sense: powerful): from Latin *praevalens* very strong, from *praevalēre:*see PREVAIL] ▸ **'prevalence** *or* **'prevalentness** *n* ▸ **'prevalently** *adv*

prevaricate (prɪ'værɪˌkeɪt) *vb* (*intr*) to speak or act falsely or evasively with intent to deceive. [C16: from Latin *praevāricārī* to walk crookedly, from *prae* beyond + *vāricare* to straddle the legs; compare Latin *vārus* bent] ▸ **preˌvari'cation** *n* ▸ **pre'variˌcator** *n*

prevenient (prɪ'vi:nɪənt) *adj* coming before; anticipating or preceding. [C17: from Latin *praevenīre* to precede, PREVENT] ▸ **pre'veniently** *adv*

prevent (prɪ'vɛnt) *vb* **1** (*tr*) to keep from happening, esp. by taking precautionary action. **2** (*tr;* often foll. by *from*) to keep (someone from doing something); hinder; impede. **3** (*intr*) to interpose or act as a hindrance. **4** (*tr*) *Archaic.* to anticipate or precede. [C15: from Latin *praevenīre,* from *prae* before + *venīre* to come] ▸ **pre'ventable** *or* **pre'ventible** *adj* ▸ **preˌventa'bility** *or* **preˌventi'bility** *n* ▸ **pre'ventably** *or* **pre'ventibly** *adv*

preventer (prɪ'vɛntə) *n* **1** a person or thing that prevents. **2** *Nautical.* a rope or other piece of gear rigged to prevent a sail from gybing.

prevention (prɪ'vɛnʃən) *n* **1** the act of preventing. **2** a hindrance, obstacle, or impediment.

preventive (prɪ'vɛntɪv) *adj* **1** tending or intended to prevent or hinder. **2** *Med.* **2a** tending to prevent disease; prophylactic. **2b** of or relating to the branch of medicine concerned with prolonging life and preventing disease. **3** (in Britain)

'pretest *n* **pre'test** *vb*

of, relating to, or belonging to the customs and excise service or the coastguard. ◆ *n* **4** something that serves to prevent or hinder. **5** *Med.* any drug or agent that tends to prevent or protect against disease. **6** another name for **contraceptive.** ◆ Also (except for sense 3): **preventative** (prɪˈventətɪv). ▸ **preˈventively** *adv* ▸ **preˈventiveness** *n*

preverbal (ˌpriːˈvɜːbᵊl) *adj* **1** being before the development of speech: *preverbal infants.* **2** *Grammar.* coming before the verb.

Prévert (*French* prevɛr) *n* **Jacques** (ʒak). 1900–77, Parisian poet, satirist, and writer of film scripts, noted esp. for his song poems. He was a member of the surrealist group from 1925 to 1929.

preview *or U.S.* **prevue** (ˈpriːvjuː) *n* **1** an advance or preliminary view or sight. **2** an advance showing before public presentation of a film, art exhibition, etc., usually before an invited audience of celebrities and journalists. **3** a public performance of a play before the official first night. ◆ *vb* **4** (*tr*) to view in advance.

preview monitor *n* (in a television studio control room) a picture monitor used for inspecting a picture source before it is switched to transmission.

Previn (ˈprevɪn) *n* **André** (ˈɒndreɪ). born 1929, U.S. orchestral conductor, born in Germany; living in Britain.

previous (ˈpriːvɪəs) *adj* **1** (*prenominal*) existing or coming before something else in time or position; prior. **2** (*postpositive*) *Informal.* taking place or done too soon; premature. **3** **previous to.** before; prior to. [C17: from Latin *praevius* leading the way, from *prae* before + *via* way] ▸ **ˈpreviously** *adv* ▸ **ˈpreviousness** *n*

previous question *n* **1** (in the House of Commons) a motion to drop the present topic under debate, put in order to prevent a vote. **2** (in the House of Lords and U.S. legislative bodies) a motion to vote on a bill or other question without delay. ◆ See also **closure** (sense 4).

previse (prɪˈvaɪz) *vb* (*tr*) *Rare.* **1** to predict or foresee. **2** to notify in advance. [C16: from Latin *praevidēre* to foresee, from *prae* before + *vidēre* to see]

prevision (prɪˈvɪʒən) *n Rare.* **1** the act or power of foreseeing; prescience. **2** a prophetic vision or prophecy.

prevocalic (ˌpriːvəʊˈkælɪk) *adj* (of a consonant) coming immediately before a vowel. ▸ **ˌprevoˈcalically** *adv*

Prévost d'Exiles (*French* prevo dɛgzil) *n* **Antoine François** (ɑ̃twan frɑ̃swa), known as *Abbé Prévost.* 1697–1763, French novelist, noted for his romance *Manon Lescaut* (1731), which served as the basis for operas by Puccini and Massenet.

prewar (ˌpriːˈwɔː, ˈpriːˌwɔː) *adj* of or occurring in the period before a war, esp. before World War I or II.

prey (preɪ) *n* **1** an animal hunted or captured by another for food. **2** a person or thing that becomes the victim of a hostile person, influence, etc. **3** **bird** *or* **beast of prey.** a bird or animal that preys on others for food. **4** an archaic word for **booty.** ◆ *vb* (*intr;* often foll. by *on* or *upon*) **5** to hunt or seize food by killing other animals. **6** to make a victim (of others), as by profiting at their expense. **7** to exert a depressing or obsessive effect (on the mind, spirits, etc.); weigh heavily (upon). [C13: from Old French *preie,* from Latin *praeda* booty; see PREDATORY] ▸ **ˈpreyer** *n*

prezzie (ˈprezɪ) *n* a variant of **pressie**, an informal word for **present**² (sense 21).

Priam (ˈpraɪəm) *n Greek myth.* the last king of Troy, killed at its fall. He was father by Hecuba of Hector, Paris, and Cassandra.

priapic (praɪˈæpɪk, -ˈeɪ-) *or* **priapean** (ˌpraɪəˈpiːən) *adj* **1** (*sometimes cap.*) of or relating to Priapus. **2** a less common word for **phallic.**

priapism (ˈpraɪəˌpɪzəm) *n Pathol.* prolonged painful erection of the penis, caused by neurological disorders, obstruction of the penile blood vessels, etc. [C17: from Late Latin *priāpismus,* ultimately from Greek PRIAPUS]

Priapus (praɪˈeɪpəs) *n* **1** (in classical antiquity) the god of the male procreative power and of gardens and vineyards. **2** (*often not cap.*) a representation of the penis.

Pribilof Islands (ˈprɪbɪləf) *pl n* a group of islands in the Bering Sea, off SW Alaska, belonging to the U.S.: the breeding ground of the northern fur seal. Area: about 168 sq. km (65 sq. miles). Also called: **Fur Seal Islands.**

price (praɪs) *n* **1** the sum in money or goods for which anything is or may be bought or sold. **2** the cost at which anything is obtained. **3** the cost of bribing a person. **4** a sum of money offered or given as a reward for a capture or killing. **5** value or worth, esp. high worth. **6** *Gambling.* another word for **odds. 7 at any price.** whatever the price or cost. **8 at a price.** at a high price. **9 beyond** (*or* **without**) **price.** invaluable or priceless. **10 the price of** (**one**). *Irish.* what (one) deserves, esp. a fitting punishment: *it's just the price of him.* **11 what price** (**something**)? what are the chances of (something) happening now? ◆ *vb* (*tr*) **12** to fix or establish the price of. **13** to ascertain or discover the price of. **14 price out of the market.** to charge so highly for as to prevent the sale, hire, etc., of. [C13 *pris,* from Old French, from Latin *pretium* price, value, wage] ▸ **ˈpricer** *n*

Price Commission *n* (in Britain) a commission established by the government in 1973 with authority to control prices as a measure against inflation. It was abolished in 1980.

price control *n* the establishment and maintenance of maximum price levels for basic goods and services by a government, esp. during periods of war or inflation.

price discrimination *n Economics.* the setting of different prices to be charged to different consumers or in different markets for the same goods or services.

price-dividend ratio *n* the ratio of the price of a share on a stock exchange to the dividends per share paid in the previous year, used as a measure of a company's potential as an investment. Abbrevs.: **P-D ratio, PDR.**

price-earnings ratio *n* the ratio of the price of a share on a stock exchange to the earnings per share, used as a measure of a company's future profitability. Abbrev.: **P/E ratio.**

price-fixing *n* **1** the setting of prices by agreement among producers and distributors. **2** another name for **price control** or **resale price maintenance.**

price leadership *n Marketing.* the setting of the price of a product or service by a dominant firm at a level that competitors can match, in order to avoid a price war.

priceless (ˈpraɪslɪs) *adj* **1** of inestimable worth; beyond valuation; invaluable. **2** *Informal.* extremely amusing or ridiculous. ▸ **ˈpricelessly** *adv* ▸ **ˈpricelessness** *n*

price ring *n* a group of traders formed to maintain the prices of their goods.

prices and incomes policy *n* voluntary or statutory regulation of the level of increases in prices and incomes.

price-sensitive *adj* likely to affect the price of property, esp. shares and securities: *price-sensitive information.*

price support *n* government maintenance of specified price levels at a minimum above market equilibrium by subsidy or by purchase of the market surplus at the guaranteed levels.

price tag *n* **1** a ticket or label on an article for sale showing its price. **2** the cost, esp. of something not usually priced: *the price tag on a top footballer.*

price war *n* a period of intense competition among enterprises, esp. retail enterprises, in the same market, characterized by repeated price reductions rather than advertising, brand promotion, etc.

pricey *or* **pricy** (ˈpraɪsɪ) *adj* **pricier, priciest.** an informal word for **expensive.**

prick (prɪk) *vb* (*mainly tr*) **1a** to make (a small hole) in (something) by piercing lightly with a sharp point. **1b** to wound in this manner. **2** (*intr*) to cause or have a piercing or stinging sensation. **3** to cause to feel a sharp emotional pain: *knowledge of such poverty pricked his conscience.* **4** to puncture or pierce. **5** to mark, delineate, or outline by dots or punctures. **6** (*also intr;* usually foll. by *up*) to rise or raise erect; point: *the dog pricked his ears up at his master's call.* **7** (usually foll. by *out* or *off*) to transplant (seedlings) into a larger container. **8** (often foll. by *off*) *Navigation.* to measure or trace (a course, distance, etc.) on a chart with dividers. **9** *Archaic.* to rouse or impel; urge on. **10** (*intr*) *Archaic.* to ride fast on horseback; spur a horse on. **11 prick up one's ears.** to start to listen attentively; become interested. ◆ *n* **12** the act of pricking or the condition or sensation of being pricked. **13** a mark made by a sharp point; puncture. **14** a sharp emotional pain resembling the physical pain caused by being pricked: *a prick of conscience.* **15** a taboo slang word for **penis. 16** *Slang, derogatory.* an obnoxious or despicable man. **17** an instrument or weapon with a sharp point, such as a thorn, goad, bee sting, etc. **18** the footprint or track of an animal, esp. a hare. **19** *Obsolete.* a small mark caused by pricking a surface; dot; point. **20 kick against the pricks.** to hurt oneself by struggling against something in vain. [Old English *prica* point, puncture; related to Dutch *prik,* Icelandic *prik* short stick, Swedish *prick* point, stick]

pricker (ˈprɪkə) *n* **1** a person or thing that pricks. **2** *U.S.* a thorn; prickle.

pricket (ˈprɪkɪt) *n* **1** a male deer in the second year of life having unbranched antlers. **2** a sharp metal spike on which to stick a candle. **3** a candlestick having such a spike. [C14 *priket,* from *prik* PRICK]

prickle (ˈprɪkᵊl) *n* **1** *Botany.* a pointed process arising from the outer layer of a stem, leaf, etc., and containing no woody or conducting tissue. Compare **thorn** (sense 1). **2** a pricking or stinging sensation. ◆ *vb* **3** to feel or cause to feel a stinging sensation. **4** (*tr*) to prick, as with a thorn. [Old English *pricel;* related to Middle Low German *prekel,* German *Prickel*]

prickly (ˈprɪklɪ) *adj* **-lier, -liest. 1** having or covered with prickles. **2** stinging or tingling. **3** bad-tempered or irritable. **4** full of difficulties; knotty: *a prickly problem.* ▸ **ˈprickliness** *n*

prickly ash *n* a North American rutaceous shrub or small tree, *Zanthoxylum americanum,* having prickly branches, feathery aromatic leaves, and bark used as a remedy for toothache. Also called: **toothache tree.**

prickly heat *n* a nontechnical name for **miliaria.**

prickly pear *n* **1** any of various tropical cacti of the genus *Opuntia,* having flattened or cylindrical spiny joints and oval fruit that is edible in some species. See also **cholla, nopal** (sense 2). **2** the fruit of any of these plants.

prickly poppy *n* an annual papaveraceous plant, *Argemone mexicana,* of tropical America, having prickly stems and leaves and large yellow or white flowers.

prick song *n Obsolete.* **a** a piece of written vocal music. **b** vocal music sung from a copy. [C16: from *pricked song, prickt song,* from PRICK (in the sense: to mark out, notate)]

pride (praɪd) *n* **1** a feeling of honour and self-respect; a sense of personal worth. **2** excessive self-esteem; conceit. **3** a source of pride. **4** satisfaction or pleasure taken in one's own or another's success, achievements, etc. (esp. in the phrase **take** (**a**) **pride in**). **5** the better or most superior part of something; flower. **6** the most flourishing time. **7** a group (of lions). **8** the mettle of a horse; courage; spirit. **9** *Archaic.* sexual desire, esp. in a female animal. **10** *Archaic.* display, pomp, or splendour. **11 pride of place.** the most important position. ◆ *vb* **12** (*tr;* foll. by *on* or *upon*) to take pride in (oneself) for. **13** (*intr*) to glory or revel (in). [Old English *prȳda;* related to Latin *prodesse* to be useful, Old Norse *prūthr* stately; see PROUD] ▸ **ˈprideful** *adj* ▸ **ˈpridefully** *adv*

ˈprewash *n*	**preˈwash** *vb*

Pride (praɪd) *n* **Thomas.** died 1658, English soldier on the Parliamentary side during the Civil War. He expelled members of the Long Parliament hostile to the army (**Pride's Purge,** 1648) and signed Charles I's death warrant.

prie-dieu (priː'djɜː) *n* a piece of furniture consisting of a low surface for kneeling upon and a narrow front surmounted by a rest for the elbows or for books, for use when praying. **[C18:** from French, from *prier* to pray + *Dieu* God**]**

prier *or* **pryer** ('praɪə) *n* a person who pries.

priest (priːst) *or (fem)* **priestess** *n* **1** *Christianity.* a person ordained to act as a mediator between God and man in administering the sacraments, preaching, blessing, guiding, etc. **2** (in episcopal Churches) a minister in the second grade of the hierarchy of holy orders, ranking below a bishop but above a deacon. **3** a minister of any religion. **4** *Judaism.* a descendant of the family of Aaron who has certain privileges in the synagogue service. **5** (in some non-Christian religions) an official who offers sacrifice on behalf of the people and performs other religious ceremonies. **6** (*sometimes cap.*) a variety of fancy pigeon having a bald pate with a crest or peak at the back of the head. **7** *Angling.* a small club used to kill fish caught. ♦ *vb* (*tr*) **8** to make a priest; ordain. ♦ Related adj: **hieratic.** **[**Old English *prēost,* apparently from PRESBYTER; related to Old High German *prēster,* Old French *prestre***]** ▸ **'priest,like** *adj*

priestcraft ('priːst,krɑːft) *n* **1** the art and skills involved in the work of a priest. **2** *Derogatory.* the influence of priests upon politics or the use by them of secular power.

priest-hole *or* **priest's hole** *n* a secret chamber in certain houses in England, built as a hiding place for Roman Catholic priests when they were proscribed in the 16th and 17th centuries.

priesthood ('priːst,hʊd) *n* **1** the state, order, or office of a priest. **2** priests collectively.

Priestley ('priːstlɪ) *n* **1 J(ohn) B(oynton).** 1894–1984, English author. His works include the novels *The Good Companions* (1929) and *Angel Pavement* (1930) and the comedy *Laburnum Grove* (1933). **2 Joseph.** 1733–1804, English chemist, political theorist, and clergyman, in the U.S. from 1794. He discovered oxygen (1774) independently of Scheele and isolated and described many other gases.

priestly ('priːstlɪ) *adj* **-lier, -liest.** of, relating to, characteristic of, or befitting a priest. ▸ **'priestliness** *n*

priest-ridden *adj* dominated or governed by or excessively under the influence of priests.

prig[1] (prɪg) *n* a person who is smugly self-righteous and narrow-minded. **[C18:** of unknown origin**]** ▸ **'priggery** *or* **'priggishness** *n* ▸ **'priggish** *adj* ▸ **'priggishly** *adv* ▸ **'priggism** *n*

prig[2] (prɪg) *Brit. slang, archaic.* ♦ *vb* **prigs, prigging, prigged. 1** another word for **steal.** ♦ *n* **2** another word for **thief.** **[C16:** of unknown origin**]**

Prigogine (*French* prigoʒin) *n* Viscount **Ilya** (ilja). born 1917, Belgian chemist, born in Russia: Nobel prize for chemistry 1977 for his work on nonequilibrium thermodynamics.

prill (prɪl) *vb* **1** (*tr*) to convert (a material) into a granular free-flowing form. ♦ *n* **2** prilled material. **[C18:** originally a Cornish copper-mining term, of obscure origin**]**

prim (prɪm) *adj* **primmer, primmest. 1** affectedly proper, precise, or formal. ♦ *vb* **prims, primming, primmed. 2** (*tr*) to make prim. **3** to purse (the mouth) primly or (of the mouth) to be so pursed. **[C18:** of unknown origin**]** ▸ **'primly** *adv* ▸ **'primness** *n*

prim. *abbrev. for:* **1** primary. **2** primitive.

prima ballerina ('priːmə) *n* a leading female ballet dancer. **[**from Italian, literally: first ballerina**]**

primacy ('praɪməsɪ) *n, pl* **-cies. 1** the state of being first in rank, grade, etc. **2** *Christianity.* the office, rank, or jurisdiction of a primate or senior bishop or (in the Roman Catholic Church) the pope.

prima donna ('priːmə 'dɒnə) *n, pl* **prima donnas. 1** a female operatic star; diva. **2** *Informal.* a temperamental person. **[C19:** from Italian: first lady**]**

primaeval (praɪ'miːvᵊl) *adj* a variant spelling of **primeval.**

prima facie ('praɪmə 'feɪʃɪ) at first sight; as it seems at first. **[C15:** from Latin, from *prīmus* first + *faciēs* FACE**]**

prima-facie evidence *n Law.* evidence that is sufficient to establish a fact or to raise a presumption of the truth of a fact unless controverted.

primage ('praɪmɪdʒ) *n N.Z.* tax added to customs duty.

primal ('praɪməl) *adj* **1** first or original. **2** chief or most important. **[C17:** from Medieval Latin *prīmālis,* from Latin *prīmus* first**]**

primal therapy *n Psychol.* a form of psychotherapy in which patients are encouraged to scream abusively about their parents and agonizingly about their own suffering in infancy. Also called: **primal scream therapy, scream therapy.** **[C20:** from the book *The Primal Scream* (1970) by Arthur Janov, U.S. psychologist, who originated the treatment**]**

primaquine ('praɪmə,kwiːn) *n* a synthetic drug used in the treatment of malaria. Formula: $C_{15}H_{21}N_3O$. **[C20:** from *prima-,* from Latin *prīmus* first + QUIN(OLIN)E**]**

primarily ('praɪmərəlɪ) *adv* **1** principally; chiefly; mainly. **2** at first; originally.

primary ('praɪmərɪ) *adj* **1** first in importance, degree, rank, etc. **2** first in position or time, as in a series. **3** fundamental; basic. **4** being the first stage; elementary. **5** (*prenominal*) of or relating to the education of children up to the age of 11. **6** (of the flight feathers of a bird's wing) growing from the manus. **7a** being the part of an electric circuit, such as a transformer or induction coil, in which a changing current induces a current in a neighbouring circuit: *a primary coil.* **7b** (of a current) flowing in such a circuit. Compare **secondary. 8a** (of a product) consisting of a natural raw material; unmanufactured. **8b** (of production or industry) involving the extraction or winning of such products. Agriculture, fishing, forestry, hunting, and mining are primary industries. Compare **secondary** (sense 7), **tertiary** (sense 2). **9** *Chem.* **9a** (of an organic compound) having a functional group attached to a carbon atom that is attached to at least two hydrogen atoms. **9b** (of an amine) having only one organic group attached to the nitrogen atom; containing the group NH_2. **9c** (of a salt) derived from a tribasic acid by replacement of one acidic hydrogen atom with a metal atom or electropositive group. **10** *Linguistics.* **10a** derived from a word that is not a derivation but the ultimate form itself. *Lovable* is a primary derivative of *love.* **10b** (of Latin, Greek, or Sanskrit tenses) referring to present or future time. Compare **historic** (sense 3). **11** *Geology, obsolete.* relating to the Palaeozoic or earlier eras. ♦ *n, pl* **-ries. 12** a person or thing that is first in rank, occurrence, etc. **13** (in the U.S.) **13a** a preliminary election in which the voters of a state or region choose a party's convention delegates, nominees for office, etc. See also **closed primary, direct primary, open primary. 13b** a local meeting of voters registered with one party to nominate candidates, select convention delegates, etc. Full name: **primary election. 14** See **primary colour. 15** any of the flight feathers growing from the manus of a bird's wing. **16** a primary coil, winding, inductance, or current in an electric circuit. **17** *Astronomy.* a celestial body around which one or more specified secondary bodies orbit: *the sun is the primary of the earth.* **[C15:** from Latin *prīmārius* of the first rank, principal, from *prīmus* first**]**

primary accent *or* **stress** *n Linguistics.* the strongest accent in a word or breath group, as that on the first syllable of *agriculture.* Compare **secondary accent.**

primary cell *n* an electric cell that generates an electromotive force by the direct and usually irreversible conversion of chemical energy into electrical energy. It cannot be recharged efficiently by an electric current. Also called: **voltaic cell.** Compare **secondary cell.**

primary colour *n* **1** Also called: **additive primary.** any of three spectral colours (usually red, green, and blue) that can be mixed to match any other colour, including white light but excluding black. **2** Also called: **subtractive primary.** any one of the spectral colours cyan, magenta, or yellow that can be subtracted from white light to match any other colour. An equal mixture of the three produces a black pigment. **3** Also called: **psychological primary.** any one of the colours red, yellow, green, or blue. All other colours look like a mixture of two or more of these colours and they play a unique role in the processing of colour by the visual system. ♦ See also **secondary colour, complementary colour.**

primary effect *n Psychol.* the process whereby the first few items on a list are learnt more rapidly than the middle items.

primary election *n* See **primary** (sense 13).

primary processes *pl n Psychoanal.* unconscious, irrational thought processes, such as condensation or displacement, governed by the pleasure principle. Compare **secondary processes.**

primary qualities *pl n* (in empiricist philosophy) those properties of objects that are directly known by experience, such as size, shape, and number.

primary school *n* **1** (in Britain) a school for children below the age of 11. It is usually divided into an infant and a junior section. **2** (in the U.S. and Canada) a school equivalent to the first three or four grades of elementary school, sometimes including a kindergarten.

primary stress *n Linguistics.* another term for **primary accent.**

primate[1] ('praɪmeɪt) *n* **1** any placental mammal of the order *Primates,* typically having flexible hands and feet with opposable first digits, good eyesight, and, in the higher apes, a highly developed brain: includes lemurs, lorises, monkeys, apes, and man. ♦ *adj* **2** of, relating to, or belonging to the order *Primates.* **[C18:** from New Latin *primates,* plural of *prīmās* principal, from *prīmus* first**]** ▸ **primatial** (praɪ'meɪʃəl) *adj*

primate[2] ('praɪmeɪt) *n* **1** another name for **archbishop. 2 Primate of all England.** the Archbishop of Canterbury. **3 Primate of England.** the Archbishop of York. **[C13:** from Old French, from Latin *prīmās* principal, from *prīmus* first**]**

primatology (,praɪmə'tɒlədʒɪ) *n* the branch of zoology that is concerned with the study of primates. ▸ **,prima'tologist** *n*

prime (praɪm) *adj* **1** (*prenominal*) first in quality or value; first-rate. **2** (*prenominal*) fundamental; original. **3** (*prenominal*) first in importance, authority, etc.; chief. **4** *Maths.* **4a** having no factors except itself or one: $x^2 + x + 3$ *is a prime polynomial.* **4b** (foll. by *to*) having no common factors (with): *20 is prime to 21.* **5** *Finance.* having the best credit rating: *prime investments.* ♦ *n* **6** the time when a thing is at its best. **7** a period of power, vigour, etc., usually following youth (esp. in the phrase **the prime of life**). **8** the beginning of something, such as the spring. **9** *Maths.* short for **prime number. 10** *Linguistics.* a semantically indivisible element; minimal component of the sense of a word. **11** *Music.* **11a** unison. **11b** the tonic of a scale. **12** *Chiefly R.C. Church.* the second of the seven canonical hours of the divine office, originally fixed for the first hour of the day, at sunrise. **13** the first of eight basic positions from which a parry or attack can be made in fencing. ♦ *vb* **14** to prepare (something); make ready. **15** (*tr*) to apply a primer, such as paint or size, to (a surface). **16** (*tr*) to fill (a pump) with its working fluid before starting, in order to improve the sealing of the pump elements and to expel air from it before starting. **17** (*tr*) to increase the quantity of fuel in the float chamber of (a carburettor) in order to facilitate the starting of an engine. **18** (*tr*) to insert a primer into (a gun, mine, charge, etc.) preparatory to detonation or firing. **19** (*intr*) (of a steam engine or boiler) to operate with or produce steam mixed with large amounts of water. **20** (*tr*) to provide with facts, information, etc., beforehand; brief. **[**(adj) **C14:** from Latin *prīmus* first; (n) **C13:** from Latin *prīma* (*hora*) the first (hour); (vb) **C16:** of uncertain origin, probably connected with n**]** ▸ **'primely** *adv* ▸ **'primeness** *n*

prime cost *n* the portion of the cost of a commodity that varies directly with the amount of it produced, principally comprising materials and labour. Also called: **variable cost.** Compare **overheads.**

prime meridian *n* the 0° meridian from which the other meridians or lines of longitude are calculated, usually taken to pass through Greenwich.

prime minister *n* **1** the head of a parliamentary government. **2** the chief minister of a sovereign or a state. ▸ **prime ministership** *or* **prime ministry** *n*

prime mover *n* **1** the original or primary force behind an idea, enterprise, etc. **2a** the source of power, such as fuel, wind, electricity, etc., for a machine. **2b** the means of extracting power from such a source, such as a steam engine, electric motor, etc. **3** (in the philosophy of Aristotle) that which is the cause of all movement.

Prime Mover *n* (usually preceded by *the*) *Philosophy*. God, esp. when considered as a first cause.

prime number *n* an integer that cannot be factorized into other integers but is only divisible by itself or 1, such as 2, 3, 7, and 11. Sometimes shortened to **prime.** Compare **composite number.**

primer[1] ('praɪmə) *n* **1** an introductory text, such as a school textbook. **2** *Printing*. See **long primer, great primer.** [C14: via Anglo-Norman from Medieval Latin *primārius* (*liber*) a first (book), from Latin *prīmārius* PRIMARY]

primer[2] ('praɪmə) *n* **1** a person or thing that primes. **2** a device, such as a tube containing explosive, for detonating the main charge in a gun, mine, etc. **3** a substance, such as paint, applied to a surface as a base, sealer, etc. Also called (for senses 2, 3): **priming.** [C15: see PRIME (vb)]

prime rate *n* the lowest commercial interest rate charged by a bank at a particular time.

primero (prɪ'mɛərəʊ) *n Chiefly Brit.* a 16th- and 17th-century card game. [C16: from Spanish *primera* card game, from *primero* first, from Latin *prīmārius* chief]

primers ('prɪməz) *pl n N.Z. informal*. the youngest class in a primary school.

prime time *n* **1** the peak viewing time on television, for which advertising rates are the highest. ◆ *adj* **primetime. 2** occurring or designed for prime time: *a primetime drama.*

primeval *or* **primaeval** (praɪ'miːvᵊl) *adj* of or belonging to the first age or ages, esp. of the world. [C17: from Latin *prīmaevus* youthful, from *prīmus* first + *aevum* age] ▸ **pri'mevally** *or* **pri'maevally** *adv*

prime vertical *n Astronomy*. the great circle passing through the observer's zenith and meeting the horizon due east and west.

primigravida (ˌpraɪmɪ'grævɪdə) *n, pl* **-das** *or* **-dae** (-ˌdiː). *Obstetrics*. a woman who is pregnant for the first time. [C19: New Latin, from Latin *prima* first + *gravida* GRAVID (woman)]

primine ('praɪmɪn) *n Botany*. the integument surrounding an ovule or the outer of two such integuments. Compare **secundine.** [C19: via French from Latin *prīmus* first]

priming ('praɪmɪŋ) *n* **1** something used to prime. **2** a substance, used to ignite an explosive charge.

primipara (praɪ'mɪpərə) *n, pl* **-ras** *or* **-rae** (-ˌriː). *Obstetrics*. a woman who has borne only one child. Also written: **Para I.** [C19: from Latin, from *prīmus* first + *parere* to bring forth] ▸ **primiparity** (ˌprɪmɪ'pærɪtɪ) *n* ▸ **pri'miparous** *adj*

primitive ('prɪmɪtɪv) *adj* **1** of or belonging to the first or beginning; original. **2** characteristic of an early state, esp. in being crude or uncivilized: *a primitive dwelling.* **3** *Anthropol.* denoting or relating to a preliterate and nonindustrial social system. **4** *Biology*. **4a** of, relating to, or resembling an early stage in the evolutionary development of a particular group of organisms: *primitive amphibians.* **4b** another word for **primordial** (sense 3). **5** showing the characteristics of primitive painters; untrained, childlike, or naive. **6** *Geology*. of, relating to, or denoting rocks formed in or before the Palaeozoic era. **7** denoting a word from which another word is derived, as for example *hope,* from which *hopeless* is derived. **8** *Protestant theol.* of, relating to, or associated with a minority group that breaks away from a sect, denomination, or Church in order to return to what is regarded as the original simplicity of the Gospels. ◆ *n* **9** a primitive person or thing. **10a** an artist whose work does not conform to traditional, academic, or avant-garde standards of Western painting, such as a painter from an African or Oceanic civilization. **10b** a painter of the pre-Renaissance era in European painting. **10c** a painter of any era whose work appears childlike or untrained. Also called (for a, c): **naive. 11** a work by such an artist. **12** a word or concept from which another word or concept is derived. **13** *Maths*. a curve, function, or other form from which another is derived. [C14: from Latin *prīmitīvus* earliest of its kind, primitive, from *prīmus* first] ▸ **'primitively** *adv* ▸ **'primitiveness** *n*

primitivism ('prɪmɪtɪˌvɪzəm) *n* **1** the condition of being primitive. **2** the notion that the value of primitive cultures is superior to that of the modern world. **3** the principles, characteristics, etc., of primitive art and artists. ▸ **'primitivist** *n, adj* ▸ **ˌprimitiv'istic** *adj*

primo ('priːməʊ) *n, pl* **-mos** *or* **-mi** (-mɪ). *Music*. the upper or right-hand part in a piano duet. Compare **secondo.** [Italian: first, from Latin *prīmus*]

Primo de Rivera (*Spanish* 'primo de ri'βera) *n* **1 José Antonio** (xo'se an'tonjo). 1903–36, Spanish politician; founded Falangism. **2** his father, **Miguel** (mi'ɣɛl). 1870–1930, Spanish general; dictator of Spain (1923–30).

primogenitor (ˌpraɪməʊ'dʒɛnɪtə) *n* **1** a forefather; ancestor. **2** an earliest parent or ancestor, as of a race. [C17: alteration of PROGENITOR after PRIMOGENITURE]

primogeniture (ˌpraɪməʊ'dʒɛnɪtʃə) *n* **1** the state of being a first-born. **2** *Law*. the right of an eldest son to succeed to the estate of his ancestor to the exclusion of all others. Compare **ultimogeniture.** [C17: from Medieval Latin *prīmōgenitūra* birth of a first child, from Latin *prīmō* at first + Late Latin *genitūra* a birth] ▸ **primogenitary** (ˌpraɪməʊ'dʒɛnɪtərɪ, -trɪ) *adj*

primordial (praɪ'mɔːdɪəl) *adj* **1** existing at or from the beginning; earliest; primeval. **2** constituting an origin; fundamental. **3** *Biology*. of or relating to an early stage of development: *primordial germ cells.* ◆ *n* **4** an elementary or basic principle. [C14: from Late Latin *prīmōrdiālis* original, from Latin *prīmus* first + *ōrdīrī* to begin] ▸ **priˌmordi'ality** *n* ▸ **pri'mordially** *adv*

primordium (praɪ'mɔːdɪəm) *n, pl* **-dia** (-dɪə). *Biology*. an organ or part in the earliest stage of development.

primp (prɪmp) *vb* to dress (oneself), esp. in fine clothes; prink. [C19: probably from PRIM]

primrose ('prɪmˌrəʊz) *n* **1** any of various temperate primulaceous plants of the genus *Primula,* esp. *P. vulgaris* of Europe, which has pale yellow flowers. **2** short for **evening primrose. 3** Also called: **primrose yellow.** a light to moderate yellow, sometimes with a greenish tinge. ◆ *adj* **4** of, relating to, or abounding in primroses. **5** of the colour primrose. **6** pleasant or gay. [C15: from Old French *primerose,* from Medieval Latin *prīma rosa* first rose]

primrose path *n* (often preceded by *the*) a pleasurable way of life.

primula ('prɪmjʊlə) *n* any primulaceous plant of the N temperate genus *Primula,* having white, yellow, pink, or purple funnel-shaped flowers with five spreading petals: includes the primrose, oxlip, cowslip, and polyanthus. [C18: New Latin, from Medieval Latin *prīmula* (*vēris*) little first one (of the spring)]

primulaceous (ˌprɪmjʊ'leɪʃəs) *adj* of, relating to, or belonging to the *Primulaceae,* a family of plants having funnel-shaped or bell-shaped flowers: includes primrose, moneywort, pimpernel, and loosestrife.

primum mobile *Latin*. ('praɪmʊm 'məʊbɪlɪ) *n* **1** a prime mover. **2** *Astronomy*. the outermost empty sphere in the Ptolemaic system that was thought to revolve around the earth from east to west in 24 hours carrying with it the inner spheres of the planets, sun, moon, and fixed stars. [C15: from Medieval Latin: first moving (thing)]

primus ('praɪməs) *n Scottish Episcopal Church*. the presiding bishop in the Synod. [from Latin: first]

Primus ('praɪməs) *n Trademark*. a portable paraffin cooking stove, used esp. by campers. Also called: **Primus stove.**

primus inter pares *Latin*. ('praɪməs ɪntə 'pɑːriːz) first among equals.

prin. *abbrev. for:* **1** principal. **2** principle.

prince (prɪns) *n* **1** (in Britain) a son of the sovereign or of one of the sovereign's sons. **2** a nonreigning male member of a sovereign family. **3** the monarch of a small territory, such as Monaco, usually called a principality, that was at some time subordinate to an emperor or king. **4** any sovereign; monarch. **5** a nobleman in various countries, such as Italy and Germany. **6** an outstanding member of a specified group: *a merchant prince.* **7** *U.S. and Canadian informal*. a generous and charming man. [C13: via Old French from Latin *princeps* first man, ruler, chief] ▸ **'princeˌlike** *adj*

Prince (prɪns) *n* full name *Prince Rogers Nelson*. born 1958, U.S. rock singer, songwriter, record producer, and multi-instrumentalist. His albums include *Dirty Mind* (1981), *Purple Rain* (1984), *Parade* (1986), and *Emancipation* (1996). He changed his stage name to a symbol and is often referred to as 'The Artist formerly known as Prince'.

Prince Albert *n* a man's double-breasted frock coat worn esp. in the early 20th century.

prince consort *n* the husband of a female sovereign, who is himself a prince.

princedom ('prɪnsdəm) *n* **1** the dignity, rank, or position of a prince. **2** a land ruled by a prince; principality.

Prince Edward Island *n* an island in the Gulf of St Lawrence that constitutes the smallest Canadian province. Capital: Charlottetown. Pop.: 137 200 (1997 est.). Area: 5656 sq. km (2184 sq. miles). Abbrev.: **PE.** ▸ **Prince Edward Islander** *n*

princeling ('prɪnslɪŋ) *n* **1** Also called: **princekin.** a young prince. **2** Also called: **princelet.** the ruler of an insignificant territory; petty or minor prince.

princely ('prɪnslɪ) *adj* **-lier, -liest. 1** generous or lavish. **2** of, belonging to, or characteristic of a prince. ◆ *adv* **3** in a princely manner. ▸ **'princeliness** *n*

Prince of Darkness *n* another name for **Satan.**

Prince of Peace *n Bible*. the future Messiah (Isaiah 9:6): held by Christians to be Christ.

Prince of Wales[1] *n* the eldest son and heir apparent of the British sovereign.

Prince of Wales[2] *n* **Cape.** a cape in W Alaska, on the Bering Strait opposite the coast of the extreme northeast of Russia: the westernmost point of North America.

Prince of Wales Island *n* **1** an island in N Canada, in the Northwest Territories. Area: about 36 000 sq. km (14 000 sq. miles). **2** an island in SE Alaska, the largest island in the Alexander Archipelago. Area: about 4000 sq. km (1500 sq. miles). **3** an island in NE Australia, in N Queensland in the Torres Strait. **4** the former name (until about 1867) of the island of **Penang.**

prince regent *n* a prince who acts as regent during the minority, disability, or absence of the legal sovereign.

Prince Regent *n* George IV as regent of Great Britain and Ireland during the insanity of his father (1811–20).

prince royal *n* the eldest son of a monarch.

Prince Rupert *n* a port in W Canada, on the coast of British Columbia: one of the W termini of the Canadian National transcontinental railway. Pop.: 16 620 (1991).

prince's-feather *n* **1** an amaranthaceous garden plant, *Amaranthus hybridus hypochondriacus,* with spikes of bristly brownish-red flowers. **2** a tall tropical polygonaceous plant, *Polygonum orientale,* with hanging spikes of pink flowers.

princess (prɪn'sɛs) *n* **1** (in Britain) a daughter of the sovereign or of one of the sovereign's sons. **2** a nonreigning female member of a sovereign family. **3** the wife and consort of a prince. **4** any very attractive or outstanding woman. **5** Also called: **princess dress, princess line.** a style of dress with a fitted bodice and an A-line skirt that is shaped by seams from shoulder to hem without a seam at the waistline.

princess royal *n* **1** the eldest daughter of a British or (formerly) a Prussian sovereign: a title not always conferred. **2** (*caps.*) the title of Princess Anne.

Princeton ('prɪnstən) *n* a town in central New Jersey: settled by Quakers in 1696; an important educational centre, seat of Princeton University (founded at Elizabeth in 1747 and moved here in 1756); scene of the battle (1777) during the War of American Independence in which Washington's troops defeated the British on the university campus. Pop.: 12 016 (1990).

principal ('prɪnsɪp^{ə}l) *adj* (*prenominal*) **1** first in importance, rank, value, etc.; chief. **2** denoting or relating to capital or property as opposed to interest, etc. ♦ *n* **3** a person who is first in importance or directs some event, action, organization, etc. **4** (in Britain) a civil servant of an executive grade who is in charge of a section. **5** *Law.* **5a** a person who engages another to act as his agent. **5b** an active participant in a crime. **5c** the person primarily liable to fulfil an obligation. **6** the head of a school or other educational institution. **7** (in Scottish schools) a head of department. **8** *Finance.* **8a** capital or property, as contrasted with the income derived from it. **8b** the original amount of a debt on which interest is calculated. **9** a main roof truss or rafter. **10** *Music.* **10a** the chief instrumentalist in a section of the orchestra. **10b** one of the singers in an opera company. **10c** either of two types of open diapason organ stops, one of four-foot length and pitch and the other of eight-foot length and pitch. **11** the leading performer in a play. **[C13**: via Old French from Latin *principālis* chief, from *princeps* chief man, PRINCE**]** ► **'principally** *adv* ► **'principalship** *n*

USAGE See at **principle.**

principal axis *n* **1** the line passing through the centres of curvature of the faces of a lens or a curved mirror. **2** any of three mutually perpendicular axes about which the moment of inertia of a body is maximum.

principal boy *n* the leading male role in a pantomime, played by a woman.

principal focus *n* another name for **focal point.**

principalities (ˌprɪnsɪ'pælɪtɪz) *pl n* (*often cap.*) the seventh of the nine orders into which the angels are divided in medieval angelology.

principality (ˌprɪnsɪ'pælɪtɪ) *n, pl* **-ties. 1a** a territory ruled by a prince. **1b** a territory from which a prince draws his title. **2** the dignity or authority of a prince. **[C14** (in the sense: pre-eminence): via Old French from Latin *principālis* PRINCIPAL**]**

principal nursing officer *n* a grade of nurse concerned with administration in the British National Health Service.

principal parts *pl n* **1** *Grammar.* the main inflected forms of a verb, from which all other inflections may be deduced. In English they are generally considered to consist of the third person present singular, present participle, past tense, and past participle. **2** the sides and interior angles of a triangle.

principate ('prɪnsɪˌpeɪt) *n* **1** a state ruled by a prince. **2** a form of rule in the early Roman Empire in which some republican forms survived.

Principe ('prɪnsɪpiː; *Portuguese* 'prĩsipə) *n* an island in the Gulf of Guinea, off the W coast of Africa: part of São Tomé e Principe. Area: 150 sq. km (58 sq. miles).

principium (prɪn'sɪpɪəm) *n, pl* **-ia** (-ɪə). (*usually pl*) a principle, esp. a fundamental one. **[C17**: Latin: an origin, beginning**]**

principle ('prɪnsɪp^{ə}l) *n* **1** a standard or rule of personal conduct: *a man of principle.* **2** (*often pl*) a set of such moral rules: *he'd stoop to anything; he has no principles.* **3** adherence to such a moral code; morality: *it's not the money but the principle of the thing; torn between principle and expediency.* **4** a fundamental or general truth or law: *first principles.* **5** the essence of something: *the male principle.* **6** a source or fundamental cause; origin: *principle of life.* **7** a rule or law concerning a natural phenomenon or the behaviour of a system: *the principle of the conservation of mass.* **8** an underlying or guiding theory or belief: *the hereditary principle; socialist principles.* **9** *Chem.* a constituent of a substance that gives the substance its characteristics and behaviour: *bitter principle.* **10 in principle.** in theory or essence. **11 on principle.** because of or in demonstration of a principle. **[C14**: from Latin *principium* beginning, basic tenet**]**

USAGE *Principle* and *principal* are often confused: *the principal* (not *principle*) *reason for his departure; the plan was approved in principle* (not *in principal*).

Principle ('prɪnsɪp^{ə}l) *n Christian Science.* another word for **God.**

principled ('prɪnsɪp^{ə}ld) *adj* **a** having high moral principles. **b** (*in combination*): *high-principled.*

principle of economy *n* **the.** another name for **Ockham's razor.**

principle of indifference *n* the principle that, in the absence of any reason to expect one event rather than another, all the possible events should be assigned the same probability. See **mathematical probability.**

principle of least action *n* the principle that motion between any two points in a conservative dynamical system is such that the action has a minimum value with respect to all paths between the points that correspond to the same energy. Also called: **Maupertuis principle.**

prink (prɪŋk) *vb* **1** to dress (oneself, etc.) finely; deck out. **2** (*intr*) to preen oneself. **[C16**: probably changed from PRANK[2] (to adorn, decorate)**]** ► **'prinker** *n*

print (prɪnt) *vb* **1** to reproduce (text, pictures, etc.), esp. in large numbers, by applying ink to paper or other material by one of various processes. **2** to produce or reproduce (a manuscript, a book, data, etc.) in print, as for publication. **3** to write (letters, etc.) in the style of printed matter. **4** to mark or indent (a surface) by pressing (something) onto it. **5** to produce a photographic print from (a negative). **6** (*tr*) to implant or fix in the mind or memory. **7** (*tr*) to make (a mark or indentation) by applying pressure. ♦ *n* **8** printed matter such as newsprint. **9** a printed publication such as a newspaper or book. **10 in print. 10a** in printed or published form. **10b** (of a book, etc.) offered for sale by the publisher. **11 out of print.** no longer available from a publisher. **12** a design or picture printed from an engraved plate, wood block, or other medium. **13** printed text, esp. with regard to the typeface used: *small print.* **14** a positive photographic image in colour or black and white produced, usually on paper, from a negative image on film. Compare **slide** (sense 13). **15a** a fabric with a printed design. **15b** (*as modifier*): *a print dress.* **16a** a mark or indentation made by pressing something onto a surface. **16b** a stamp, die, etc., that makes such an impression. **16c** the surface subjected to such an impression. **17** See **fingerprint.** ♦ See also **print out. [C13** *priente,* from Old French: something printed, from *preindre* to make an impression, from Latin *premere* to press**]**

printable ('prɪntəb^{ə}l) *adj* **1** capable of being printed or of producing a print. **2** suitable for publication. ► **ˌprinta'bility** *or* **'printableness** *n*

printed circuit *n* an electronic circuit in which certain components and the connections between them are formed by etching a metallic coating or by electrodeposition on one or both sides of a thin insulating board. Also called: **printed circuit board** *or* **card.**

printer ('prɪntə) *n* **1** a person or business engaged in printing. **2** a machine or device that prints. **3** *Computing.* an output device for printing results on paper.

printer's devil *n* an apprentice or errand boy in a printing establishment.

printery ('prɪntərɪ) *n, pl* **-eries. 1** *Chiefly U.S.* an establishment in which printing is carried out. **2** an establishment in which fabrics are printed.

printhead ('prɪntˌhɛd) *n Computing.* a component in a printer that forms a printed character.

printing ('prɪntɪŋ) *n* **1a** the process, business, or art of producing printed matter. **1b** (*as modifier*): *printing ink.* **2** printed text. **3** Also called: **impression.** all the copies of a book or other publication printed at one time. **4** a form of writing in which letters resemble printed letters.

printing press *n* any of various machines used for printing.

printmaker ('prɪntˌmeɪkə) *n* a person who makes print, esp. a craftsman or artist in this field.

print out *vb* (*tr, adv*) **1** (of a computer output device, such as a line printer) to produce (printed information). ♦ *n* **print-out. 2** such printed information.

print shop *n* a place in which printing is carried out.

print-through *n* the unwanted transfer of a recorded magnetic field pattern from one turn of magnetic tape to the preceding or succeeding turn on a reel, causing distortion.

print unions *pl n* the trade unions within the printing industry.

printwheel ('prɪntˌwiːl) *n* another name for **daisywheel.**

prion[1] ('praɪən) *n* any of various dovelike petrels of the genus *Pachyptila* of the southern oceans that have a serrated bill. **[C19**: New Latin, from Greek *priōn* a saw**]**

prion[2] ('priːɒn) *n* a protein in the brain, an abnormal transmissible form of which is thought to be the agent responsible for certain spongiform encephalopathies, such as BSE, scrapie, Creutzfeldt-Jakob disease, and kuru. **[C20**: altered from *pro(teinaceous) in(fectious particle)***]**

prior[1] ('praɪə) *adj* **1** (*prenominal*) previous; preceding. **2 prior to.** before; until. ♦ *n* **3** *Statistics.* a prior probability. **[C18**: from Latin: previous**]**

prior[2] ('praɪə) *n* **1** the superior of a house and community in certain religious orders. **2** the deputy head of a monastery or abbey, ranking immediately below the abbot. **3** (formerly) a chief magistrate in medieval Florence and other Italian republics. **[C11**: from Late Latin: head, from Latin (adj): previous, from Old Latin *pri* before**]**

Prior ('praɪə) *n* **Matthew.** 1664–1721, English poet and diplomat, noted for his epigrammatic occasional verse.

priorate ('praɪərɪt) *n* the office, status, or term of office of a prior.

prioress ('praɪərɪs) *n* a nun holding an office in her convent corresponding to that of a prior in a male religious order.

prioritize *or* **prioritise** (praɪ'ɒrɪˌtaɪz) *vb* (*tr*) **1** to arrange (items to be attended to) in order of their relative importance. **2** to give priority to or establish as a priority. ► **ˌprioriti'zation** *or* **ˌprioriti'sation** *n*

priority (praɪ'ɒrɪtɪ) *n, pl* **-ties. 1** the condition of being prior; antecedence; precedence. **2** the right of precedence over others. **3** something given specified attention: *my first priority.*

prior probability *n Statistics.* the probability assigned to a parameter or to an event in advance of any empirical evidence, often subjectively or on the assumption of the principle of indifference. Compare **posterior probability.**

priory ('praɪərɪ) *n, pl* **-ories.** a religious house governed by a prior, sometimes being subordinate to an abbey. **[C13**: from Medieval Latin *priōria;* see PRIOR[2]**]**

Pripet ('priːpɪt) *n* a river in E Europe, rising in the NW Ukraine and flowing northeast into Belarus across the **Pripet Marshes** (the largest swamp in Europe), then east into the Dnieper River. Length: about 800 km (500 miles). Russian name: **Pripyat** ('prɪpjətj).

prisage ('praɪzɪdʒ) *n* a customs duty levied until 1809 upon wine imported into England. **[C16**: from Anglo-French, from Old French *prise* a taking or requisitioning, duty, from *prendre* to take; see PRISE**]**

Priscian ('prɪʃɪən) *n* Latin name *Priscianus Caesariensis.* 6th century A.D., Latin grammarian.

prise *or* **prize** (praɪz) *vb* (*tr*) **1** to force open by levering. **2** to extract or obtain with difficulty: *they had to prise the news out of him.* ♦ *n* **3** *Rare or dialect.* a tool involving leverage in its use or the leverage so employed. ♦ U.S. and Canadian equivalent: **pry. [C17**: from Old French *prise* a taking, from *prendre* to take, from Latin *prehendere;* see PRIZE[1]**]**

prisere ('praɪˌsɪə) *n Ecology.* a primary sere or succession from bare ground to the community climax. **[C20**: PRI(MARY) + SERE[2]**]**

prism ('prɪzəm) *n* **1** a transparent polygonal solid, often having triangular ends and rectangular sides, for dispersing light into a spectrum or for reflecting and deviating light. They are used in spectroscopes, binoculars, periscopes, etc. **2** a form of crystal with faces parallel to the vertical axis. **3** *Maths.* a polyhedron having parallel, polygonal, and congruent bases and sides that are parallelograms. **[C16**: from Medieval Latin *prisma,* from Greek: something shaped by sawing, from *prizein* to saw**]**

prismatic (prɪz'mætɪk) *adj* **1** concerned with, containing, or produced by a prism. **2** exhibiting bright spectral colours: *prismatic light.* **3** *Crystallog.* another word for **orthorhombic.** ► **pris'matically** *adv*

prismatoid ('prɪzmə,tɔɪd) *n* a polyhedron whose vertices lie in either one of two parallel planes. Compare **prism** (sense 3), **prismoid.** [C19: from Greek *prismatoeidēs* shaped like a prism; see PRISM, -OID] ► **,prisma'toidal** *adj*

prismoid ('prɪzmɔɪd) *n* a prismatoid having an equal number of vertices in each of the two parallel planes and whose sides are trapeziums or parallelograms. [C18: from French *prismoïde;* see PRISM, -OID] ► **pris'moidal** *adj*

prison ('prɪz°n) *n* **1** a public building used to house convicted criminals and accused persons remanded in custody and awaiting trial. See also **jail, penitentiary, reformatory. 2** any place of confinement or seeming confinement. [C12: from Old French *prisun,* from Latin *prēnsiō* a capturing, from *prehendere* to lay hold of]

prisoner ('prɪzənə) *n* **1** a person deprived of liberty and kept in prison or some other form of custody as a punishment for a crime, while awaiting trial, or for some other reason. **2** a person confined by any of various restraints: *we are all prisoners of time.* **3 take no prisoners.** *Informal.* to be uncompromising and determined in one's actions. **4 take (someone) prisoner.** to capture and hold (someone) as a prisoner, esp. as a prisoner of war.

prisoner of war *n* a person, esp. a serviceman, captured by an enemy in time of war. Abbrev.: **POW.**

prisoner's base *n* a children's game involving two teams, members of which chase and capture each other to increase the number of children in their own base.

prissy ('prɪsɪ) *adj* **-sier, -siest.** fussy and prim, esp. in a prudish way. [C20: probably from PRIM + SISSY] ► **'prissily** *adv* ► **'prissiness** *n*

Priština (*Serbo-Croat* 'priːʃtina) *n* a city in Yugoslavia in S Serbia, capital of Kosovo: under Turkish control until 1912; nearby is the 14th-century Gračanica monastery. Pop.: 155 499 (1991).

pristine ('prɪstaɪn, -tiːn) *adj* **1** of or involving the earliest period, state, etc.; original. **2** pure; uncorrupted. **3** fresh, clean, and unspoiled: *his pristine new car.* [C15: from Latin *pristinus* primitive; related to *prīmus* first, PRIME]

USAGE The use of *pristine* to mean *fresh, clean, and unspoiled* is considered by some people to be incorrect.

Pritchett ('prɪtʃɪt) *n* Sir **V(ictor) S(awdon).** 1900–97, British short-story writer, novelist, essayist, and autobiographer; his works include *Balzac* (1973) and *A Careless Widow* (1989).

prithee ('prɪðɪ) *interj Archaic.* pray thee; please. [C16: shortened from *I pray thee*]

prittle-prattle ('prɪt°l,præt°l) *n* foolish or idle talk; babble. [C16: reduplication of PRATTLE]

priv. *abbrev. for:* **1** private. **2** privative.

privacy ('praɪvəsɪ, 'prɪvəsɪ) *n* **1** the condition of being private or withdrawn; seclusion. **2** the condition of being secret; secrecy. **3** *Philosophy.* the condition of being necessarily restricted to a single person.

Privatdocent (*German* pri'vaːtdo'tsent) *n* (esp. in German-speaking countries) a university lecturer who formerly received fees from his students rather than a university salary. [German, from *privat* PRIVATE + *docent* (for *Dozent* lecturer) from Latin *docēre* to teach]

private ('praɪvɪt) *adj* **1** not widely or publicly known: *they had private reasons for the decision.* **2** confidential; secret: *a private conversation.* **3** not for general or public use: *a private bathroom.* **4** (*prenominal*) individual; special: *my own private recipe.* **5** (*prenominal*) having no public office, rank, etc.: *a private man.* **6** (*prenominal*) denoting a soldier of the lowest military rank: *a private soldier.* **7** of, relating to, or provided by a private individual or organization, rather than by the state or a public body: *the private sector; private housing.* **8** (of a place) retired; sequestered; not overlooked. **9** (of a person) reserved; uncommunicative. **10 in private.** in secret; confidentially. ♦ *n* **11** a soldier of the lowest rank, sometimes separated into qualification grades, in many armies and marine corps: *private first class.* [C14: from Latin *prīvātus* belonging to one individual, withdrawn from public life, from *prīvāre* to deprive, bereave] ► **'privately** *adv*

private bar *n Brit.* the saloon or lounge bar of a public house. Also called: **the private.** Compare **public bar.**

private bill *n* a bill presented to Parliament or Congress on behalf of a private individual, corporation, etc.

private company *n* a limited company that does not issue shares for public subscription and whose owners do not enjoy an unrestricted right to transfer their shareholdings. Compare **public company.**

private detective *n* an individual privately employed to investigate a crime, keep watch on a suspected person, or make other inquiries. Also called: **private investigator.**

private enterprise *n* **1** economic activity undertaken by private individuals or organizations under private ownership. Compare **public enterprise. 2** another name for **capitalism.**

privateer (,praɪvə'tɪə) *n* **1** an armed, privately owned vessel commissioned for war service by a government. **2** Also called: **privateersman.** a commander or member of the crew of a privateer. ♦ *vb* **3** (*intr*) to serve as a privateer.

private eye *n Informal.* a private detective.

Private Finance Initiative *n* (in Britain) a government scheme to encourage private investment in public projects. Abbrev.: **PFI.**

private health insurance *n* insurance against the need for medical treatment as a private patient.

private hotel *n* **1** a residential hotel or boarding house in which the proprietor has the right to refuse to accept a person as a guest, esp. a person arriving by chance. **2** *Austral. and N.Z.* a hotel not having a licence to sell alcoholic liquor.

private income *n* an income from sources other than employment, such as investment. Also called: **private means.**

private language *n Philosophy.* a language that is not merely secret or accidentally limited to one user, but that cannot in principle be communicated to another.

private law *n* the branch of law that deals with the rights and duties of private individuals and the relations between them. Compare **public law.**

private life *n* the social or family life or personal relationships of an individual, esp. of a person in the public eye, such as a politician or celebrity.

private member *n* a member of a legislative assembly, such as the House of Commons, not having an appointment in the government.

private member's bill *n* a public bill introduced in the House of Commons by a private member.

private parts *or* **privates** ('praɪvɪts) *pl n* euphemistic terms for **genitals.**

private patient *n Brit.* a patient receiving medical treatment not paid for by the National Health Service.

private pay bed *n* (in Britain) a bed in a National Health Service hospital, reserved for private patients who pay a consultant acting privately for treatment and who are charged by the health service for use of hospital facilities. Often shortened to **pay bed.** Compare **amenity bed.**

private practice *n Brit.* medical practice that is not part of the National Health Service.

private press *n* a printing establishment primarily run as a pastime.

private property *n* land or belongings owned by a person or group and kept for their exclusive use.

private school *n* a school under the financial and managerial control of a private body or charitable trust, accepting mostly fee-paying pupils.

private secretary *n* **1** a secretary entrusted with the personal and confidential matters of a business executive. **2** a civil servant who acts as aide to a minister or senior government official. Compare **parliamentary private secretary.**

private sector *n* the part of a country's economy that consists of privately owned enterprises. Compare **public sector.**

private treaty *n* a sale of property for a price agreed directly between seller and buyer.

private view *n* a preview, esp. of an art exhibition, for specially invited guests.

private viewdata *n* an interactive video text system with restricted access.

privation (praɪ'veɪʃən) *n* **1** loss or lack of the necessities of life, such as food and shelter. **2** hardship resulting from this. **3** the state of being deprived. **4** *Logic, obsolete.* the absence from an object of what ordinarily or naturally belongs to such objects. [C14: from Latin *prīvātiō* deprivation]

privative ('prɪvətɪv) *adj* **1** causing privation. **2** expressing lack or negation, as for example the English suffix *-less* and prefix *un-*. **3** *Logic, obsolete.* (of a proposition) that predicates a logical privation. [C16: from Latin *prīvātīvus* indicating loss, negative] ► **'privatively** *adv*

privatization issue *n* an issue of shares available for purchase by members of the public when a publicly owned organization is transferred to the private sector.

privatize *or* **privatise** ('praɪvɪ,taɪz) *vb* (*tr*) to transfer (the production of goods or services) from the public sector of an economy into private ownership and operation. ► **,privati'zation** *or* **,privati'sation** *n*

privet ('prɪvɪt) *n* **a** any oleaceous shrub of the genus *Ligustrum,* esp. *L. vulgare,* having oval dark green leaves, white flowers, and purplish-black berries. **b** (*as modifier*): *a privet hedge.* [C16: of unknown origin]

privet hawk *n* a hawk moth, *Sphinx ligustri,* with a mauve-and-brown striped body: frequents privets.

privilege ('prɪvɪlɪdʒ) *n* **1** a benefit, immunity, etc., granted under certain conditions. **2** the advantages and immunities enjoyed by a small usually powerful group or class, esp. to the disadvantage of others: *one of the obstacles to social harmony is privilege.* **3** any of the fundamental rights guaranteed to the citizens of a country by its constitution. **4a** the right of a lawyer to refuse to divulge information obtained in confidence from a client. **4b** the right claimed by any of certain other functionaries to refuse to divulge information: *executive privilege.* **5** the rights and immunities enjoyed by members of most legislative bodies, such as freedom of speech, freedom from arrest in civil cases during a session, etc. **6** *U.S. stock exchange.* a speculative contract permitting its purchaser to make optional purchases or sales of securities at a specified time over a limited period of time. See also **call** (sense 58), **put** (sense 20), **spread** (sense 24c), **straddle** (sense 9). ♦ *vb* (*tr*) **7** to bestow a privilege or privileges upon. **8** (foll. by *from*) to free or exempt. [C12: from Old French *privilēge,* from Latin *prīvilēgium* law relevant to rights of an individual, from *prīvus* an individual + *lēx* law]

privileged ('prɪvɪlɪdʒd) *adj* **1** enjoying or granted as a privilege or privileges. **2** *Law.* **2a** not actionable as a libel or slander. **2b** (of a communication, document, etc.) that a witness cannot be compelled to divulge. **3** *Nautical.* (of a vessel) having the right of way.

privily ('prɪvɪlɪ) *adv Archaic or literary.* in a secret way.

privity ('prɪvɪtɪ) *n, pl* **-ties. 1** a legally recognized relationship existing between two parties, such as that between lessor and lessee and between the parties to a contract: *privity of estate; privity of contract.* **2** secret knowledge that is shared. [C13: from Old French *priveté*]

privy ('prɪvɪ) *adj* **privier, priviest. 1** (*postpositive;* foll. by *to*) participating in the knowledge of something secret. **2** *Archaic.* secret, hidden, etc. **3** *Archaic.* of or relating to one person only. ♦ *n, pl* **privies. 4** a lavatory, esp. an outside one. **5** *Law.* a person in privity with another. See **privity** (sense 1). [C13: from Old French *privé* something private, from Latin *prīvātus* PRIVATE]

privy chamber *n* **1** a private apartment inside a royal residence. **2** *Archaic.* a private room reserved for the use of a specific person or group.

privy council *n* **1** the council of state of a monarch or noble, esp. formerly. **2** *Archaic.* a private or secret council.

Privy Council *n* the private council of the British sovereign, consisting of all current and former ministers of the Crown and other distinguished subjects, all of whom are appointed for life. See also **Judicial Committee of the Privy Council.** ► **Privy Counsellor** *n*

privy purse *n* (*often caps.*) **1a** (in Britain) an allowance voted by Parliament for the private expenses of the monarch: part of the civil list. **1b** (in other countries) a similar sum of money for the monarch. **2** an official of the royal household responsible for dealing with the monarch's private expenses. Full name: **Keeper of the Privy Purse.**

privy seal *n* (*often caps.*) (in Britain) a seal affixed to certain documents issued by royal authority: of less rank and importance than the great seal.

prix fixe (*French* pri fiks) *n, pl* **prix fixes** (fiks). a fixed price charged for one of a set number of meals offered on a menu. Compare **à la carte, table d'hôte.**

Prix Goncourt *n* an annual prize for a work of French fiction. [C20: after the Académie GONCOURT]

prize[1] (praɪz) *n* **1a** a reward or honour for victory or for having won a contest, competition, etc. **1b** (*as modifier*): *prize jockey; prize essay.* **2** something given to the winner of any game of chance, lottery, etc. **3** something striven for. **4** any valuable property captured in time of war, esp. a vessel. [C14: from Old French *prise* a capture, from Latin *prehendere* to seize; influenced also by Middle English *prise* reward; see PRICE]

prize[2] (praɪz) *vb* (*tr*) to esteem greatly; value highly. [C15 *prise,* from Old French *preisier* to PRAISE]

prize[3] (praɪz) *vb, n* a variant spelling of **prise.**

prize court *n Law.* a court having jurisdiction to determine how property captured at sea in wartime is to be distributed.

prizefight ('praɪz,faɪt) *n* a boxing match for a prize or purse, esp. one of the fights popular in the 18th and 19th centuries. ► **'prize,fighter** *n* ► **'prize,fighting** *n*

prize money *n* **1** any money offered, paid, or received as a prize. **2** (formerly) a part of the money realized from the sale of a captured vessel.

prize ring *n* **1** the enclosed area or ring used by prizefighters. **2 the prize ring.** the sport of prizefighting.

prizewinner ('praɪz,wɪnə) *n* a person, animal, or thing that wins a prize. ► **'prize,winning** *adj*

prn (in prescriptions) *abbrev. for* pro re nata. [Latin: as the situation demands; as needed]

pro[1] (prəʊ) *adv* **1** in favour of a motion, issue, course of action, etc. Compare **anti.** ◆ *prep* **2** in favour of. ◆ *n, pl* **pros. 3** (*usually pl*) an argument or vote in favour of a proposal or motion. See also **pros and cons. 4** (*usually pl*) a person who votes in favour of a proposal, motion, etc. ◆ Compare **con**[2]. [from Latin *prō* (prep) in favour of]

pro[2] (prəʊ) *n, pl* **pros,** *adj* **1** *Informal.* short for **professional. 2** *Slang.* a prostitute. [C19: by shortening]

PRO *abbrev. for:* **1** Public Records Office. **2** public relations officer.

pro-[1] *prefix* **1** in favour of; supporting: *pro-Chinese.* **2** acting as a substitute for: *proconsul; pronoun.* [from Latin *prō* (adv and prep). In compound words borrowed from Latin, *prō-* indicates: forward, out (*project*); forward and down (*prostrate*); away from a place (*prodigal*); onward in time or space (*proceed*); extension outwards (*propagate*); before in time or place (*provide, protect*); on behalf of (*procure*); acting as a substitute for (*pronominal*); and sometimes intensive force (*promiscuous*)]

pro-[2] *prefix* before in time or position; anterior; forward: *prophase; procephalic; prognathous.* [from Greek *pro* (prep) before (in time, position, rank, etc.)]

proa ('prəʊə) *or* **prau** *n* any of several kinds of canoe-like boats used in the South Pacific, esp. one equipped with an outrigger and sails. [C16: from Malay *parāhū* a boat]

proactive (prəʊ'æktɪv) *adj* **1** tending to initiate change rather than reacting to events. **2** *Psychol.* of or denoting a mental process that affects a subsequent process. [C20: from PRO-[2] + (RE)ACTIVE]

proactive inhibition *or* **interference** *n Psychol.* the tendency for earlier memories to interfere with the retrieval of material learned later. Compare **retroactive inhibition.**

pro-am ('prəʊ'æm) *adj* (of a golf tournament, snooker tournament, etc.) involving both professional and amateur players.

prob. *abbrev. for:* **1** probable. **2** probably. **3** problem.

probabilism ('prɒbəbɪ,lɪzəm) *n* **1** *Philosophy.* the doctrine that although certainty is impossible, probability is a sufficient basis for belief and action. **2** the principle of Roman Catholic moral theology that in a situation in which authorities differ as to what is the right course of action it is permissible to follow any course which has the support of some authority. ► **'probabilist** *n, adj* ► **,probabil'istic** *adj* ► **,probabil'istically** *adv*

probability (,prɒbə'bɪlɪtɪ) *n, pl* **-ties. 1** the condition of being probable. **2** an event or other thing that is probable. **3** *Statistics.* a measure or estimate of the degree of confidence one may have in the occurrence of an event, measured on a scale from zero (impossibility) to one (certainty). It may be defined as the proportion of favourable outcomes to the total number of possibilities if these are indifferent (**mathematical probability**), or the proportion observed in a sample (**empirical probability**), or the limit of this as the sample size tends to infinity (**relative frequency**), or by more subjective criteria (**subjective probability**).

probability density function *n Statistics.* a function representing the relative distribution of frequency of a continuous random variable from which parameters such as its mean and variance can be derived and having the property that its integral from *a* to *b* is the probability that the variable lies in this interval. Its graph is the limiting case of a histogram as the amount of data increases and the class intervals decrease in size. Also called: **density function.** Compare **cumulative distribution function, frequency distribution.**

probability function *n Statistics.* the function the values of which are probabilities of the distinct outcomes of a discrete random variable.

probable ('prɒbəbᵊl) *adj* **1** likely to be or to happen but not necessarily so. **2** most likely: *the probable cause of the accident.* ◆ *n* **3** a person who is probably to be chosen for a team, event, etc. [C14: via Old French from Latin *probābilis* that may be proved, from *probāre* to prove]

probable cause *n Law.* reasonable grounds for holding a belief, esp. such as will justify bringing legal proceedings against a person or will constitute a defence to a charge of malicious prosecution.

probably ('prɒbəblɪ) *adv* **1** (*sentence modifier; not used with a negative or in a question*) in all likelihood or probability: *I'll probably see you tomorrow.* ◆ *sentence substitute.* **2** I believe such a thing or situation may be the case.

proband ('prəʊbænd) *n* another name (esp. U.S.) for **propositus** (sense 2). [C20: from Latin *probandus,* gerundive of *probāre* to test]

probang ('prəʊbæŋ) *n Surgery.* a long flexible rod, often with a small sponge at one end, for inserting into the oesophagus, as to apply medication. [C17: variant, apparently by association with PROBE, of *provang,* name coined by W. Rumsey (1584–1660), Welsh judge, its inventor; of unknown origin]

probate ('prəʊbɪt, -beɪt) *n* **1** the act or process of officially proving the authenticity and validity of a will. **2a** the official certificate stating a will to be genuine and conferring on the executors power to administer the estate. **2b** the probate copy of a will. **3** (in the U.S.) all matters within the jurisdiction of a probate court. **4** (*modifier*) of, relating to, or concerned with probate: *probate value; a probate court.* ◆ *vb* **5** (*tr*) *Chiefly U.S. and Canadian.* to establish officially the authenticity and validity of (a will). [C15: from Latin *probāre* to inspect]

probation (prə'beɪʃən) *n* **1** a system of dealing with offenders by placing them under the supervision of a probation officer. **2 on probation. 2a** under the supervision of a probation officer. **2b** undergoing a test period. **3** a trial period, as for a teacher, religious novitiate, etc. **4** the act of proving or testing. **5** a period during which a new employee may have his employment terminated on the grounds of unsuitability. ► **pro'bational** *or* **pro'bationary** *adj* ► **pro'bationally** *adv*

probationary assistant *n N.Z.* a teacher in the first probationary years. Abbrev.: **PA.**

probationer (prə'beɪʃənə) *n* a person on probation.

probation officer *n* an officer of a court who supervises offenders placed on probation and assists and befriends them.

probative ('prəʊbətɪv) *or* **probatory** ('prəʊbətərɪ, -trɪ) *adj* **1** serving to test or designed for testing. **2** providing proof or evidence. [C15: from Late Latin *probātīvus* concerning proof] ► **'probatively** *adv*

probe (prəʊb) *vb* **1** (*tr*) to search into or question closely. **2** to examine (something) with or as if with a probe. ◆ *n* **3** something that probes, examines, or tests. **4** *Surgery.* a slender and usually flexible instrument for exploring a wound, sinus, etc. **5** a thorough inquiry, such as one by a newspaper into corrupt practices. **6** *Electronics.* a lead connecting to or containing a measuring or monitoring circuit used for testing. **7** *Electronics.* a conductor inserted into a waveguide or cavity resonator to provide coupling to an external circuit. **8** any of various devices that provide a coupling link, esp. a flexible tube extended from an aircraft to link it with another so that it can refuel. **9** See **space probe.** [C16: from Medieval Latin *proba* investigation, from Latin *probāre* to test] ► **'probeable** *adj* ► **'prober** *n*

probity ('prəʊbɪtɪ) *n* confirmed integrity; uprightness. [C16: from Latin *probitās* honesty, from *probus* virtuous]

problem ('prɒbləm) *n* **1a** any thing, matter, person, etc., that is difficult to deal with, solve, or overcome. **1b** (*as modifier*): *a problem child.* **2** a puzzle, question, etc., set for solution. **3** *Maths.* a statement requiring a solution usually by means of one or more operations or geometric constructions. **4** (*modifier*) designating a literary work that deals with difficult moral questions: *a problem play.* [C14: from Late Latin *problēma,* from Greek: something put forward; related to *proballein* to throw forwards, from PRO-[2] + *ballein* to throw]

problematic (,prɒblə'mætɪk) *or* **problematical** *adj* **1** having the nature or appearance of a problem; questionable. **2** *Logic, obsolete.* (of a proposition) asserting that a property may or may not hold. Compare **apodeictic** (sense 2), **assertoric.** ► **,problem'atically** *adv*

pro bono publico *Latin.* ('prəʊ 'bəʊnəʊ 'publɪkəʊ) for the public good.

proboscidean *or* **proboscidian** (,prəʊbɒ'sɪdɪən) *adj* **1** of, relating to, or belonging to the *Proboscidea,* an order of massive herbivorous placental mammals having tusks and a long trunk: contains the elephants. ◆ *n* **2** any proboscidean animal.

proboscis (prəʊ'bɒsɪs) *n, pl* **-cises** *or* **-cides** (-sɪ,di:z). **1** a long flexible prehensile trunk or snout, as of an elephant. **2** the elongated mouthparts of certain insects, adapted for piercing or sucking food. **3** any similar part or organ. **4** *Informal, facetious.* a person's nose, esp. if large. [C17: via Latin from Greek *proboskis* trunk of an elephant, from *boskein* to feed]

proboscis monkey *n* an Old World monkey, *Nasalis larvatus,* of Borneo, with an elongated bulbous nose.

proc. *abbrev. for:* **1** procedure. **2** proceedings. **3** process.

procaine ('prəʊkeɪn, prəʊ'keɪn) *n* a colourless or white crystalline water-soluble

,proa'bortion *adj*	**,pro-A'merican** *adj, n*	**pro-'British** *adj*	**pro'business** *adj*

substance used, as the hydrochloride, as a local anaesthetic; 2-diethylaminoethyl-4-amino benzoate. Formula: $NH_2C_6H_4COOC_2H_4N(C_2H_5)_2$. See also **Novocaine.** [C20: from PRO-[1] + (CO)CAINE]

procambium (prəʊ'kæmbɪəm) *n* undifferentiated plant tissue, just behind the growing tip in stems and roots, that develops into conducting tissues. [C19: from PRO-[2] + CAMBIUM] ▶ **pro'cambial** *adj*

procarp ('prəʊkɑːp) *n* a female reproductive organ in red algae. [C19: from New Latin *procarpium,* from PRO-[2] + *-carpium,* from Greek *karpos* fruit]

procaryote (prəʊ'kærɪɒt) *n* a variant spelling of **prokaryote.**

procathedral (ˌprəʊkə'θiːdrəl) *n* a church serving as a cathedral.

procedural agreement *n* regulations agreed between the parties to collective bargaining, defining the bargaining units, bargaining scope, procedures for collective bargaining, and the facilities to be provided to trade union representatives.

procedure (prə'siːdʒə) *n* **1** a way of acting or progressing in a course of action, esp. an established method. **2** the established mode or form of conducting the business of a legislature, the enforcement of a legal right, etc. **3** *Computing.* another name for **subroutine.** ▶ **pro'cedural** *adj* ▶ **pro'cedurally** *adv*

proceed (prə'siːd) *vb* (*intr*) **1** (often foll. by *to*) to advance or carry on, esp. after stopping. **2** (often foll. by *with*) to undertake and continue (something or to do something): *he proceeded with his reading.* **3** (often foll. by *against*) to institute or carry on a legal action. **4** to emerge or originate; arise: *evil proceeds from the heart.* ◆ See also **proceeds.** [C14: from Latin *prōcēdere* to advance, from PRO-[1] + *cēdere* to go] ▶ **pro'ceeder** *n*

proceeding (prə'siːdɪŋ) *n* **1** an act or course of action. **2a** the institution of a legal action. **2b** any step taken in a legal action. **3** (*pl*) the minutes of the meetings of a club, society, etc. **4** (*pl*) legal action; litigation. **5** (*pl*) the events of an occasion, meeting, etc.

proceeds ('prəʊsiːdz) *pl n* **1** the profit or return derived from a commercial transaction, investment, etc. **2** the result, esp. the revenue or total sum, accruing from some undertaking or course of action, as in commerce.

proceleusmatic (ˌprɒsɪluːs'mætɪk) *Prosody.* ◆ *adj* **1** denoting or consisting of a metrical foot of four short syllables. ◆ *n* **2** a proceleusmatic metrical foot. [C18: from Late Latin *proceleusmaticus,* from Greek *prokeleusmatikos,* from *prokeleuein* to drive on, from PRO-[2] + *keleuein* to give orders]

procephalic (ˌprəʊsɪ'fælɪk) *adj Anatomy.* of or relating to the anterior part of the head.

process[1] ('prəʊsɛs) *n* **1** a series of actions that produce a change or development: *the process of digestion.* **2** a method of doing or producing something. **3** a forward movement. **4** the course of time. **5a** a summons, writ, etc., commanding a person to appear in court. **5b** the whole proceedings in an action at law. **6** a natural outgrowth or projection of a part, organ, or organism. **7** a distinct subtask of a computer system which can be regarded as proceeding in parallel with other subtasks of the system. **8** (*modifier*) relating to the general preparation of a printing forme or plate by the use, at some stage, of photography. **9** (*modifier*) denoting a film, film scene, shot, etc., made by techniques that produce unusual optical effects. ◆ *vb* (*tr*) **10** to subject to a routine procedure; handle. **11** to treat or prepare by a special method, esp. to treat (food) in order to preserve it: *to process cheese.* **12a** to institute legal proceedings against. **12b** to serve a process on. **13** *Photog.* **13a** to develop, rinse, fix, wash, and dry (exposed film, etc.). **13b** to produce final prints or slides from (undeveloped film). **14** *Computing.* to perform mathematical and logical operations on (data) according to programmed instructions in order to obtain the required information. **15** to prepare (food) using a food processor. [C14: from Old French *procès,* from Latin *prōcessus* an advancing, from *prōcēdere* to PROCEED]

process[2] (prə'sɛs) *vb* (*intr*) to proceed in or as if in a procession. [C19: back formation from PROCESSION]

process camera *n Printing.* a large camera used in the photographic processes involved in the printing industry.

process colour *n Printing.* any of the four colours (cyan, magenta, yellow, and black) used in process printing.

process engineering *n* the branch of engineering concerned with industrial processes, esp. continuous ones, such as the production of petrochemicals. ▶ **process engineer** *n*

procession (prə'sɛʃən) *n* **1** the act of proceeding in a regular formation. **2** a group of people or things moving forwards in an orderly, regular, or ceremonial manner. **3** a hymn, litany, etc., sung in a procession. **4** *Christianity.* the emanation of the Holy Spirit. ◆ *vb* **5** (*intr*) *Rare.* to go in procession. [C12: via Old French from Latin *prōcessiō* a marching forwards] ▶ **pro'cessionary** *adj*

processional (prə'sɛʃənəl) *adj* **1** of, relating to, or suitable for a procession. ◆ *n* **2** *Christianity.* **2a** a book containing the prayers, hymns, litanies, and liturgy prescribed for processions. **2b** a hymn, litany, etc., used in a procession. ▶ **pro'cessionally** *adv*

processionary moth *n* a moth of the family *Thaumetopoeidae,* esp. the **oak processionary moth** (*Thaumetopoea processionea*), the larvae of which leave the communal shelter nightly for food in a V-shaped procession.

processor ('prəʊsɛsə) *n* **1** *Computing.* another name for **central processing unit. 2** a person or thing that carries out a process.

process printing *n* a method of making reproductions of a coloured picture, usually by using four halftone plates for different coloured inks.

process-server *n* a sheriff's officer who serves legal documents such as writs for appearance in court.

procès-verbal *French.* (prɔsɛvɛrbal) *n, pl* ***-baux*** (-bo). a written record of an official proceeding; minutes. [C17: from French: see PROCESS[1], VERBAL]

pro-choice *adj* (of an organization, pressure group, etc.) supporting the right of a woman to have an abortion. Compare **pro-life.**

prochronism ('prəʊkrəˌnɪzəm) *n* an error in dating that places an event earlier than it actually occurred. Compare **parachronism.** [C17: from PRO-[2] + Greek *khronos* time + -ISM, by analogy with ANACHRONISM]

proclaim (prə'kleɪm) *vb* (*tr*) **1** (*may take a clause as object*) to announce publicly; declare. **2** (*may take a clause as object*) to show or indicate plainly. **3** to praise or extol. [C14: from Latin *prōclāmāre* to shout aloud] ▶ **pro'claimer** *n* ▶ **proclamation** (ˌprɒklə'meɪʃən) *n* ▶ **proclamatory** (prə'klæmətərɪ, -trɪ) *adj*

proclitic (prəʊ'klɪtɪk) *adj* **1a** relating to or denoting a monosyllabic word or form having no stress or accent and pronounced as a prefix of the following word, as in English *'t* for *it* in *'twas.* **1b** (in classical Greek) relating to or denoting a word that throws its accent onto the following word. ◆ *n* **2** a proclitic word or form. ◆ Compare **enclitic.** [C19: from New Latin *proclīticus,* from Greek *proklinein* to lean forwards; formed on the model of ENCLITIC]

proclivity (prə'klɪvɪtɪ) *n, pl* **-ties.** a tendency or inclination. [C16: from Latin *prōclīvitās,* from *prōclīvis* steep, from PRO-[1] + *clīvus* a slope]

Proclus ('prəʊkləs, 'prɒk-) *n* ?410–485 A.D., Greek Neo-Platonist philosopher.

Procne ('prɒknɪ) *n Greek myth.* a princess of Athens, who punished her husband for raping her sister Philomela by feeding him the flesh of their son. She was changed at her death into a swallow. See **Philomela.**

proconsul (prəʊ'kɒnsᵊl) *n* **1** an administrator or governor of a colony, occupied territory, or other dependency. **2** (in ancient Rome) the governor of a senatorial province. [C14: from Latin, from *prō consule* (someone acting) for the consul. See PRO-[2], CONSUL] ▶ **proconsular** (prəʊ'kɒnsjʊlə) *adj* ▶ **pro'consulate** *or* **pro'consulship** *n*

Procopius (prəʊ'kəʊpɪəs) *n* ?490–?562 A.D., Byzantine historian, noted for his account of the wars of Justinian I against the Persians, Vandals, and Ostrogoths.

procrastinate (prəʊ'kræstɪˌneɪt, prə-) *vb* (*usually intr*) to put off or defer (an action) until a later time; delay. [C16: from Latin *prōcrāstināre* to postpone until tomorrow, from PRO-[1] + *crās* tomorrow] ▶ **proˌcrasti'nation** *n* ▶ **pro'crastiˌnator** *n*

procreate ('prəʊkrɪˌeɪt) *vb* **1** to beget or engender (offspring). **2** (*tr*) to bring into being. [C16: from Latin *prōcreāre,* from PRO-[1] + *creāre* to create] ▶ **'procreant** *or* **'procreˌative** *adj* ▶ **ˌprocre'ation** *n* ▶ **'procreˌator** *n*

Procrustean (prəʊ'krʌstɪən) *adj* tending or designed to produce conformity by violent or ruthless methods.

Procrustes (prəʊ'krʌstiːz) *n Greek myth.* a robber, who put travellers in his bed, stretching or lopping off their limbs so that they fitted it. [C16: from Greek *Prokroustēs* the stretcher, from *prokrouein* to extend by hammering out]

procryptic (prəʊ'krɪptɪk) *adj* (of animals) having protective coloration. [C19: from PRO-[2] + Greek *kruptein* to conceal] ▶ **pro'cryptically** *adv*

procto- *or before a vowel* **proct-** *combining form.* indicating the anus or rectum: *proctology.* [from Greek *prōktos*]

proctology (prɒk'tɒlədʒɪ) *n* the branch of medical science concerned with the rectum. ▶ **proctological** (ˌprɒktə'lɒdʒɪkᵊl) *adj* ▶ **proc'tologist** *n*

proctor ('prɒktə) *n* **1** a member of the teaching staff of any of certain universities having the duties of enforcing discipline. **2** *U.S.* (in a college or university) a supervisor or monitor who invigilates examinations, enforces discipline, etc. **3** (formerly) an agent, esp. one engaged to conduct another's case in a court. **4** (formerly) an agent employed to collect tithes. **5** *Church of England.* one of the elected representatives of the clergy in Convocation and the General Synod. ◆ *vb* **6** (*tr*) *U.S.* to invigilate (an examination). [C14: syncopated variant of PROCURATOR] ▶ **proctorial** (prɒk'tɔːrɪəl) *adj* ▶ **proc'torially** *adv*

proctoscope ('prɒktəˌskəʊp) *n* a medical instrument for examining the rectum. ▶ **proctoscopic** (ˌprɒktə'skɒpɪk) *adj* ▶ **proctoscopy** (prɒk'tɒskəpɪ) *n*

procumbent (prəʊ'kʌmbənt) *adj* **1** Also: **prostrate.** (of stems) growing along the ground. **2** leaning forwards or lying on the face. [C17: from Latin *prōcumbere* to fall forwards; compare INCUMBENT]

procuration (ˌprɒkjʊ'reɪʃən) *n* **1** the act of procuring. **2** *Law.* **2a** the appointment of an agent, procurator, or attorney. **2b** the office, function, or authority of such an official. **2c** the formal written authority given to such an official. See also **power of attorney. 3** *Criminal law.* the offence of procuring women for immoral purposes. **4** *Archaic.* the management of another person's affairs.

procurator ('prɒkjʊˌreɪtə) *n* **1** (in ancient Rome) a civil official of the emperor's administration, often employed as the governor of a minor province or as a financial agent. **2** *Rare.* a person engaged and authorized by another to manage his affairs. [C13: from Latin: a manager, from *prōcūrāre* to attend to] ▶ **procuracy** ('prɒkjʊrəsɪ) *or* **'procuˌratorship** *n* ▶ **procuratorial** (ˌprɒkjʊrə'tɔːrɪəl) *or* **procuratory** ('prɒkjʊrətərɪ, -trɪ) *adj*

procurator fiscal *n* (in Scotland) a legal officer who performs the functions of public prosecutor and coroner.

procuratory ('prɒkjʊrətərɪ) *n Law.* authorization to act on behalf of someone else.

procure (prə'kjʊə) *vb* **1** (*tr*) to obtain or acquire; secure. **2** to obtain (women or girls) to act as prostitutes. [C13: from Latin *prōcūrāre* to look after, from PRO-[1] + *cūrāre* to care for] ▶ **pro'curable** *adj* ▶ **pro'curance** *or* **pro'cural** *n*

procurement (prə'kjʊəmənt) *n* **1** the act or an instance of procuring. **2** *Commerce.* **2a** the act of buying. **2b** (*as modifier*): *procurement cost; procurement budget.*

procurer (prə'kjʊərə) *or* (*fem*) **procuress** (prə'kjʊərɪs) *n* a person who procures, esp. one who procures women or girls as prostitutes.

Procyon ('prəʊsɪən) *n* the brightest star in the constellation Canis Minor, a bi-

pro'capitalist *adj*	**pro-'Catholic** *n, adj*	**ˌpro-Chi'nese** *adj*	**pro-'Communist** *adj, n*

nary with a very faint companion. Visual magnitude: 0.4; spectral type: F3; distance: 11 light years. [C17: via Latin from Greek *Prokuōn* literally: before the Dog, from PRO-[2] + *kuōn* dog; so named because it rises just before Sirius, the Dog Star]

prod (prɒd) *vb* **prods, prodding, prodded.** **1** to poke or jab with or as if with a pointed object. **2** (*tr*) to rouse or urge to action. ◆ *n* **3** the act or an instance of prodding. **4** a sharp or pointed object. **5** a stimulus or reminder. [C16: of uncertain origin] ▸ **'prodder** *n*

prod. *abbrev. for:* **1** produce. **2** produced. **3** product.

Prodi ('prəʊdɪ) *n* **Romano** (rə'mɑːnəʊ). born 1939, Italian politician; prime minister (1996–98); president of the European Commission from 1999.

prodigal ('prɒdɪgᵊl) *adj* **1** recklessly wasteful or extravagant, as in disposing of goods or money. **2** lavish in giving or yielding: *prodigal of compliments.* ◆ *n* **3** a person who spends lavishly or squanders money. [C16: from Medieval Latin *prōdigālis* wasteful, from Latin *prōdigus* lavish, from *prōdigere* to squander, from PRO-[1] + *agere* to drive] ▸ **,prodi'gality** *n* ▸ **'prodigally** *adv*

prodigious (prə'dɪdʒəs) *adj* **1** vast in size, extent, power, etc. **2** wonderful or amazing. **3** *Obsolete.* threatening. [C16: from Latin *prōdigiōsus* marvellous, from *prōdigium* see PRODIGY] ▸ **pro'digiously** *adv* ▸ **pro'digiousness** *n*

prodigy ('prɒdɪdʒɪ) *n, pl* **-gies.** **1** a person, esp. a child, of unusual or marvellous talents. **2** anything that is a cause of wonder and amazement. **3** something monstrous or abnormal. **4** an archaic word for **omen.** [C16: from Latin *prōdigium* an unnatural happening, from PRO-[1] + *-igium*, probably from *āio* I say]

prodrome ('prəʊdrəʊm) *n Med.* any symptom that signals the impending onset of a disease. [C19: via French from New Latin *prodromus,* from Greek *prodromos* forerunner, from PRO-[2] + *dramein* to run] ▸ **pro'dromal** *or* **prodromic** (prəʊ'drɒmɪk) *adj*

produce *vb* (prə'djuːs). **1** to bring (something) into existence; yield. **2** to bring forth (a product) by mental or physical effort; make: *she produced a delicious dinner for us.* **3** (*tr*) to give birth to. **4** (*tr*) to manufacture (a commodity): *this firm produces cartons.* **5** (*tr*) to give rise to: *her joke produced laughter.* **6** (*tr*) to present to view: *to produce evidence.* **7** to bring before the public: *he produced two plays and a film last year.* **8** to conceive and create the overall sound of (a record) and supervise its arrangement, recording, and mixing. **9** (*tr*) *Geometry.* to extend (a line). ◆ *n* ('prɒdjuːs). **10** anything that is produced; product. **11** agricultural products regarded collectively: *farm produce.* [C15: from Latin *prōdūcere* to bring forward, from PRO-[1] + *dūcere* to lead] ▸ **pro'ducible** *adj* ▸ **pro,duci'bility** *n*

producer (prə'djuːsə) *n* **1** a person or thing that produces. **2** *Brit.* a person responsible for the artistic direction of a play, including interpretation of the script, preparation of the actors, and overall design. **3** *U.S. and Canadian.* a person who organizes the stage production of a play, including the finance, management, etc. **4** the person who takes overall administrative responsibility for a film or television programme. Compare **director** (sense 4). **5** the person who supervises the arrangement, recording, and mixing of a record. **6** *Economics.* a person or business enterprise that generates goods or services for sale. Compare **consumer** (sense 1). **7** *Chem.* an apparatus or plant for making producer gas. **8** (*often pl*) *Ecology.* an organism, esp. a green plant, that builds up its own tissues from simple inorganic compounds. See also **consumer** (sense 3), **decomposer.**

producer gas *n* a mixture of carbon monoxide and nitrogen produced by passing air over hot coke, used mainly as a fuel. Also called: **air gas.** See also **water gas.**

producer goods *or* **producer's goods** *pl n* other terms for **capital goods.**

product ('prɒdʌkt) *n* **1** something produced by effort, or some mechanical or industrial process. **2** the result of some natural process. **3** a result or consequence. **4** a substance formed in a chemical reaction. **5** *Maths.* **5a** the result of the multiplication of two or more numbers, quantities, etc. **5b** Also called: **set product.** another name for **intersection** (sense 3). **6** See **Cartesian product.** [C15: from Latin *prōductum* (something) produced, from *prōdūcere* to bring forth]

product differentiation *n Commerce.* the real or illusory distinction between competing products in a market.

production (prə'dʌkʃən) *n* **1** the act of producing. **2** anything that is produced; product. **3** the amount produced or the rate at which it is produced. **4** *Economics.* the creation or manufacture for sale of goods and services with exchange value. **5** any work created as a result of literary or artistic effort. **6** the organization and presentation of a film, play, opera, etc. **7** *Brit.* the artistic direction of a play. **8a** the supervision of the arrangement, recording, and mixing of a record. **8b** the overall sound quality or character of a recording: *the material is very strong but the production is poor.* **9** (*modifier*) manufactured by a mass-production process: *a production model of a car.* **10 make a production (out) of.** *Informal.* to make an unnecessary fuss about. ▸ **pro'ductional** *adj*

production line *n* a factory system in which parts or components of the end product are transported by a conveyor through a number of different sites at each of which a manual or machine operation is performed on them without interrupting the flow of production.

production platform *n* (in the oil industry) a platform from which development wells are drilled that also houses a processing plant and other equipment necessary to keep an oilfield in production.

productive (prə'dʌktɪv) *adj* **1** producing or having the power to produce; fertile. **2** yielding favourable or effective results. **3** *Economics.* **3a** producing or capable of producing goods and services that have monetary or exchange value: *productive assets.* **3b** of or relating to such production: *the productive processes of an industry.* **4** (*postpositive;* foll. by *of*) resulting in: *productive of good results.* **5** denoting an affix or combining form used to produce new words. ▸ **pro'ductively** *adv* ▸ **pro'ductiveness** *n*

productivity (,prɒdʌk'tɪvɪtɪ) *n* **1** the output of an industrial concern in relation to the materials, labour, etc., it employs. **2** the state of being productive.

productivity bargaining *n* the process of reaching an agreement (**productivity agreement**) through collective bargaining whereby the employees of an organization agree to changes which are intended to improve productivity in return for an increase in pay or other benefits.

product liability *n* the liability to the public of a manufacturer or trader for selling a faulty product.

product life cycle *n Marketing.* the four stages (introduction, growth, maturity, and decline) into one of which the sales of a product fall during its market life.

product line *n Marketing.* a group of related products marketed by the same company.

product placement *n* the practice of a company paying for its product to be placed in a prominent position in a film or television programme as a form of advertising.

proem ('prəʊɛm) *n* an introduction or preface, such as to a work of literature. [C14: from Latin *prooemium* introduction, from Greek *prooimion,* from PRO-[2] + *hoimē* song] ▸ **proemial** (prəʊ'iːmɪəl) *adj*

proenzyme (prəʊ'ɛnzaɪm) *n* the inactive form of an enzyme; zymogen.

proestrus (prəʊ'ɛstrəs, -'iːstrəs) *n* the usual U.S. spelling of **pro-oestrus.**

prof (prɒf) *n Informal.* short for **professor.**

Prof. *abbrev. for* Professor.

profane (prə'feɪn) *adj* **1** having or indicating contempt, irreverence, or disrespect for a divinity or something sacred. **2** not designed or used for religious purposes; secular. **3** not initiated into the inner mysteries or sacred rites. **4** vulgar, coarse, or blasphemous: *profane language.* ◆ *vb* (*tr*) **5** to treat or use (something sacred) with irreverence. **6** to put to an unworthy or improper use. [C15: from Latin *profānus* outside the temple, from PRO-[1] + *fānum* temple] ▸ **profanation** (,prɒfə'neɪʃən) *n* ▸ **profanatory** (prə'fænətərɪ, -trɪ) *adj* ▸ **pro'fanely** *adv* ▸ **pro'faneness** *n* ▸ **pro'faner** *n*

profanity (prə'fænɪtɪ) *n, pl* **-ties.** **1** the state or quality of being profane. **2** vulgar or irreverent action, speech, etc.

profess (prə'fɛs) *vb* **1** to affirm or announce (something, such as faith); acknowledge: *to profess ignorance; to profess a belief in God.* **2** (*tr*) to claim (something, such as a feeling or skill, or to be or do something), often insincerely or falsely: *to profess to be a skilled driver.* **3** to receive or be received into a religious order, as by taking vows. [C14: from Latin *prōfitērī* to confess openly, from PRO-[1] + *fatērī* to confess]

professed (prə'fɛst) *adj* (*prenominal*) **1** avowed or acknowledged. **2** alleged or pretended. **3** professing to be qualified as: *a professed philosopher.* **4** having taken vows of a religious order. ▸ **professedly** (prə'fɛsɪdlɪ) *adv*

profession (prə'fɛʃən) *n* **1** an occupation requiring special training in the liberal arts or sciences, esp. one of the three learned professions, law, theology, or medicine. **2** the body of people in such an occupation. **3** the act of professing; avowal; declaration. **4a** Also called: **profession of faith.** a declaration of faith in a religion, esp. as made on entering the Church of that religion or an order belonging to it. **4b** the faith or the religion that is the subject of such a declaration. [C13: from Medieval Latin *professiō* the taking of vows upon entering a religious order, from Latin: public acknowledgment; see PROFESS]

professional (prə'fɛʃənᵊl) *adj* **1** of, relating to, suitable for, or engaged in as a profession. **2** engaging in an activity for gain or as a means of livelihood. **3** extremely competent in a job, etc. **4** undertaken or performed for gain or by people who are paid. ◆ *n* **5** a person who belongs to or engages in one of the professions. **6** a person who engages for his livelihood in some activity also pursued by amateurs. **7** a person who engages in an activity with great competence. **8** an expert player of a game who gives instruction, esp. to members of a club by whom he is hired. ▸ **pro'fessionally** *adv*

professional association *n* a body of persons engaged in the same profession, formed usually to control entry into the profession, maintain standards, and represent the profession in discussions with other bodies.

professional foul *n Football.* a deliberate foul committed as a last-ditch tactic to prevent an opponent from scoring.

professionalism (prə'fɛʃənə,lɪzəm) *n* **1** the methods, character, status, etc., of a professional. **2** the pursuit of an activity for gain or livelihood. ▸ **pro'fessionalist** *n, adj*

professor (prə'fɛsə) *n* **1** the principal lecturer or teacher in a field of learning at a university or college; a holder of a university chair. **2** *Chiefly U.S. and Canadian.* any teacher in a university or college. See also **associate professor, assistant professor, full professor.** **3** a person who claims skill and instructs others in some sport, occupation, etc. **4** a person who professes his opinions, beliefs, etc. [C14: from Medieval Latin: one who has made his profession in a religious order, from Latin: a public teacher; see PROFESS] ▸ **professorial** (,prɒfɪ'sɔːrɪəl) *adj* ▸ **,profes'sorially** *adv*

professoriate (,prɒfɪ'sɔːrɪɪt) *or* **professorate** (prə'fɛsərɪt) *n* **1** a group of professors. **2** Also called (esp. Brit.): **professorship** (prə'fɛsəʃɪp). the rank or position of university professor.

proffer ('prɒfə) *vb* **1** (*tr*) to offer for acceptance; tender. ◆ *n* **2** the act of proffering. [C13: from Old French *proffrir,* from PRO-[1] + *offrir* to offer] ▸ **'profferer** *n*

proficient (prə'fɪʃənt) *adj* **1** having great facility (in an art, occupation, etc.);

,pro-Euro'pean *adj, n*	**pro'fascist** *adj, n*	**pro'feminist** *adj, n*

skilled. ◆ *n* 2 an archaic word for an **expert.** [C16: from Latin *prōficere* to make progress, from PRO-[1] + *facere* to make] ► **pro'ficiency** *n* ► **pro'ficiently** *adv*

profile ('prəʊfaɪl) *n* 1 a side view, outline, or representation of an object, esp. of a human face or head. 2 a view or representation of an object, esp. a building, in contour or outline. 3 a short biographical sketch of a subject. 4 a graph, table, or list of scores representing the extent to which a person, field, or object exhibits various tested characteristics or tendencies: *a population profile.* 5 a vertical section of soil from the ground surface to the parent rock showing the different horizons. 6a a vertical section of part of the earth's crust showing the layers of rock. 6b a representation of such a section. 7 the outline of the shape of a river valley either from source to mouth (**long profile**) or at right angles to the flow of the river (**cross profile**). ◆ *vb* (*tr*) 8 to draw, write, or make a profile of. 9 to cut out a shape from a blank (as of steel) with a cutter. [C17: from Italian *profilo,* from *profilare* to sketch lightly, from PRO-[1] + Latin *fīlum* thread] ► **'profiler** *or* **profilist** ('prəʊfɪlɪst) *n*

profile component *n Brit. Education.* attainment targets in different subjects brought together for the general assessment of a pupil.

profile drag *n* the sum of the surface friction drag and the form drag for a body moving subsonically through a fluid.

profit ('prɒfɪt) *n* 1 (*often pl*) excess of revenues over outlays and expenses in a business enterprise over a given period of time, usually a year. 2 the monetary gain derived from a transaction. 3a income derived from property or an investment, as contrasted with capital gains. 3b the ratio of this income to the investment or principal. 4 *Economics.* 4a the income or reward accruing to a successful entrepreneur and held to be the motivating factor of all economic activity in a capitalist economy. 4b (*as modifier*): *the profit motive.* 5 a gain, benefit, or advantage. ◆ *vb* 6 to gain or cause to gain profit. [C14: from Latin *prōfectus* advance, from *prōficere* to make progress; see PROFICIENT] ► **'profiter** *n* ► **'profitless** *adj*

profitable ('prɒfɪtəbᵊl) *adj* affording gain, benefit, or profit. ► **'profitably** *adv* ► **'profitableness** *or* **,profita'bility** *n*

profit and loss *n Book-keeping.* an account compiled at the end of a financial year showing that year's revenue and expense items and indicating gross and net profit or loss.

profit centre *n* a unit or department of a company that is responsible for its costs and its profits.

profiteer (,prɒfɪ'tɪə) *n* 1 a person who makes excessive profits, esp. by charging exorbitant prices for goods in short supply. ◆ *vb* 2 (*intr*) to make excessive profits. ► **,profi'teering** *n*

profiterole (,prɒfɪtə'rəʊl, 'prɒfɪtə,rəʊl, prə'fɪtə,rəʊl) *n* a small case of choux pastry with a sweet or savoury filling. [C16: from French, literally: a small profit, (related to the gifts, etc., given to a servant), from *profiter* to PROFIT]

profit-sharing *n* a system in which a portion of the net profit of a business is distributed to its employees, usually in proportion to their wages or their length of service.

profit taking *n* selling commodities, securities, etc., at a profit after a rise in market values or before an expected fall in values.

profligate ('prɒflɪgɪt) *adj* 1 shamelessly immoral or debauched. 2 wildly extravagant or wasteful. ◆ *n* 3 a profligate person. [C16: from Latin *prōflīgātus* corrupt, from *prōflīgāre* to overthrow, from PRO-[1] + *flīgere* to beat] ► **profligacy** ('prɒflɪgəsɪ) *n* ► **'profligately** *adv*

profluent ('prɒflʊənt) *adj* flowing smoothly or abundantly. [C15: from Latin *prōfluere* to flow along]

pro-form *n* a word having grammatical function but assuming the meaning of an antecedent word or phrase for which it substitutes: *the word "does" is a pro-form for "understands Greek" in "I can't understand Greek but he does."*

pro forma ('prəʊ 'fɔːmə) *adj* 1 prescribing a set form or procedure. ◆ *adv* 2 performed in a set manner. [Latin: for form's sake]

pro forma invoice *n* an invoice issued before an order is placed or before the goods are delivered giving all the details and the cost of the goods.

profound (prə'faʊnd) *adj* 1 penetrating deeply into subjects or ideas: *a profound mind.* 2 showing or requiring great knowledge or understanding: *a profound treatise.* 3 situated at or extending to a great depth. 4 reaching to or stemming from the depths of one's nature: *profound regret.* 5 intense or absolute: *profound silence.* 6 thoroughgoing; extensive: *profound changes.* ◆ *n* 7 *Archaic or literary.* a great depth; abyss. [C14: from Old French *profund,* from Latin *profundus* deep, from PRO-[1] + *fundus* bottom] ► **pro'foundly** *adv* ► **pro'foundness** *or* **profundity** (prə'fʌndɪtɪ) *n*

Profumo (prə'fjuːməʊ) *n* **John** (**Dennis**). born 1915, British Conservative politician; secretary of state for war (1960–63). He resigned after a scandal that threatened the government of Harold Macmillan.

profuse (prə'fjuːs) *adj* 1 plentiful, copious, or abundant: *profuse compliments.* 2 (often foll. by *in*) free or generous in the giving (of): *profuse in thanks.* [C15: from Latin *profundere* to pour lavishly] ► **pro'fusely** *adv* ► **pro'fuseness** *or* **pro'fusion** *n*

prog[1] (prɒg) *vb* **progs, progging, progged.** 1 (*intr*) *Brit. slang or dialect.* to prowl about for or as if for food or plunder. ◆ *n* 2 *Brit. slang or dialect.* food obtained by begging. 3 *Canadian dialect.* a Newfoundland word for **food.** [C17: of unknown origin]

prog[2] (prɒg) *Brit. slang, archaic.* 1 *n* short for **proctor** (sense 1). ◆ *vb* **progs, progging, progged.** 2 (*tr*) (of a proctor) to discipline (a student).

prog[3] (prɒg) *n Informal.* short for **programme,** esp. a television programme.

prog. *abbrev. for:* 1 programme. 2 progress. 3 progressive.

Prog. *abbrev. for* Progressive (Party, movement, etc.).

progenitive (prəʊ'dʒɛnɪtɪv) *adj* capable of bearing offspring. ► **pro'genitiveness** *n*

progenitor (prəʊ'dʒɛnɪtə) *n* 1 a direct ancestor. 2 an originator or founder of a future development; precursor. [C14: from Latin: ancestor, from PRO-[1] + *genitor* parent, from *gignere* to beget]

progeny ('prɒdʒɪnɪ) *n, pl* **-nies.** 1 the immediate descendant or descendants of a person, animal, etc. 2 a result or outcome. [C13: from Latin *prōgeniēs* lineage; see PROGENITOR]

progeria (prəʊ'dʒɪərɪə) *n Med.* premature old age, a rare condition occurring in children and characterized by small stature, absent or greying hair, wrinkled skin, and other signs of old age. [C20: from PRO-[2] + Greek *gēras* old age]

progestational (,prəʊdʒɛ'steɪʃənᵊl) *adj Physiol.* 1 of or relating to the phase of the menstrual cycle, lasting approximately 14 days, during which the uterus is prepared for pregnancy by the secretion of progesterone from the corpus luteum. 2 preceding gestation; before pregnancy.

progesterone (prəʊ'dʒɛstə,rəʊn) *n* a steroid hormone, secreted mainly by the corpus luteum in the ovary, that prepares and maintains the uterus for pregnancy. Formula: $C_{21}H_{30}O_2$. Also called: **corpus luteum hormone.** [C20: from PRO-[1] + GE(STATION) + STER(OL) + -ONE]

progestogen (prəʊ'dʒɛstədʒən) *or* **progestin** (prə'dʒɛstɪn) *n* any of a group of steroid hormones that have progesterone-like activity, used in oral contraceptives and in treating gynaecological disorders. [C20: from PROGEST(ERONE) + -IN]

proglottis (prəʊ'glɒtɪs) *or* **proglottid** *n, pl* **-glottides** (-'glɒtɪ,diːz). any of the segments that make up the body of a tapeworm. Each contains reproductive organs and separates from the worm when filled with fertilized eggs. [C19: from Greek *proglōssis, proglōttis* point of the tongue, from PRO-[2] + *glōssa, glōtta* (so called because of its shape)] ► **pro'glottic** *or* **,proglot'tidean** *adj*

prognathous (prɒg'neɪθəs) *or* **prognathic** (prɒg'næθɪk) *adj* having a projecting lower jaw. [C19: from PRO-[2] + Greek *gnathos* jaw] ► **prognathism** ('prɒgnə,θɪzəm) *n*

prognosis (prɒg'nəʊsɪs) *n, pl* **-noses** (-'nəʊsiːz). 1 *Med.* 1a a prediction of the course or outcome of a disease or disorder. 1b the chances of recovery from a disease. 2 any forecast or prediction. [C17: via Latin from Greek: knowledge beforehand]

prognostic (prɒg'nɒstɪk) *adj* 1 of, relating to, or serving as a prognosis. 2 foretelling or predicting. ◆ *n* 3 *Med.* any symptom or sign used in making a prognosis. 4 a sign or forecast of some future occurrence. [C15: from Old French *pronostique,* from Latin *prognōsticum,* from Greek *prognōstikon,* from *progignōskein* to know in advance]

prognosticate (prɒg'nɒstɪ,keɪt) *vb* 1 to foretell (future events) according to present signs or indications; prophesy. 2 (*tr*) to foreshadow or portend. [C16: from Medieval Latin *prognōsticāre* to predict] ► **prog,nosti'cation** *n* ► **prog'nosticative** *adj* ► **prog'nosti,cator** *n*

program *or* (*sometimes*) **programme** ('prəʊgræm) *n* 1 a sequence of coded instructions fed into a computer, enabling it to perform specified logical and arithmetical operations on data. ◆ *vb* **-grams, -gramming, -grammed** *or* **-grammes, -gramming, -grammed.** 2 (*tr*) to feed a program into (a computer). 3 (*tr*) to arrange (data) into a suitable form so that it can be processed by a computer. 4 (*intr*) to write a program.

program generator *n* a computer program that can be used to help to create other computer programs.

programmable *or* **programable** (prəʊ'græməbᵊl) *adj* (esp. of a device or operation) capable of being programmed for automatic operation or computer processing. ► **pro,gramma'bility** *n*

programmatic (,prəʊgrə'mætɪk) *adj* 1 of or relating to programme music. 2 of or relating to a programme.

programme *or U.S.* **program** ('prəʊgræm) *n* 1 a written or printed list of the events, performers, etc., in a public performance. 2 a performance or series of performances, often presented at a scheduled time, esp. on radio or television. 3 a specially arranged selection of things to be done: *what's the programme for this afternoon?* 4 a plan, schedule, or procedure. 5 a syllabus or curriculum. ◆ *vb* **-grammes, -gramming, -grammed** *or U.S.* **-grams, -graming, -gramed.** 6 to design or schedule (something) as a programme. ◆ *n, vb* 7 *Computing.* a variant spelling of **program.** [C17: from Late Latin *programma,* from Greek: written public notice, from PRO-[2] + *graphein* to write]

programmed camera *n Photog.* a camera with electronic facilities for setting both aperture and shutter speed automatically on the basis of a through-the-lens light value and a given film speed.

programmed learning *n* a teaching method in which the material to be learnt is broken down into easily understandable parts on which the pupil is able to test himself .

programme evaluation and review technique *n* a method of planning, controlling, and checking the times taken to finish important parts of complex operations, such as making aircraft, ships, or bridges. Acronym: **PERT.** Compare **critical path analysis.**

programme music *n* music that is intended to depict or evoke a scene or idea. Compare **absolute music.**

programme of study *n Brit. Education.* the prescribed syllabus that pupils must be taught at each key stage in the National Curriculum.

programmer ('prəʊgræmə) *n* a person who writes a program so that data may be processed by a computer.

pro-'German *adj*

programming language *n* a simple language system designed to facilitate the writing of computer programs. See **high-level language, low-level language, machine code.**

program statement *n* a single instruction in a computer program.

program trading *n* trading on international stock exchanges using a computer program to exploit differences between stock index futures and actual share prices on world equity markets.

progress *n* ('prəʊgres). **1** movement forwards, esp. towards a place or objective. **2** satisfactory development, growth, or advance: *she is making progress in maths.* **3** advance towards completion, maturity, or perfection: *the steady onward march of progress.* **4** (*modifier*) of or relating to progress: *a progress report.* **5** *Biology.* increasing complexity, adaptation, etc., during the development of an individual or evolution of a group. **6** *Brit.* a stately royal journey. **7 in progress.** taking place; under way. ◆ *vb* (prə'gres). **8** (*intr*) to move forwards or onwards, as towards a place or objective. **9** to move towards or bring nearer to completion, maturity, or perfection. **[C15:** from Latin *prōgressus* a going forwards, from *prōgredī* to advance, from PRO-[1] + *gradī* to step**]**

progress chaser *n* a person employed to make sure at each stage, esp. of a manufacturing process, that a piece of work is on schedule and is delivered to the customer on time. ► **progress chasing** *n*

progression (prə'greʃən) *n* **1** the act of progressing; advancement. **2** the act or an instance of moving from one thing or unit in a sequence to the next. **3** *Maths.* a sequence of numbers in which each term differs from the succeeding term by a constant relation. See also **arithmetic progression, geometric progression, harmonic progression.** **4** *Music.* movement, esp. of a logical kind, from one note to the next (**melodic progression**) or from one chord to the next (**harmonic progression**). **5** *Astrology.* one of several calculations, based on the movement of the planets, from which it is supposed that one can find the expected developments in a person's birth chart and the probable trends of circumstances for a year in his life. ► **pro'gressional** *adj* ► **pro'gressionally** *adv*

progressionist (prə'greʃənɪst) *or* **progressist** (prə'gresɪst) *n Rare.* an advocate of social, political, or economic progress; a member of a progressive political party. ► **pro'gressionism** *n*

progressive (prə'gresɪv) *adj* **1** of or relating to progress. **2** proceeding or progressing by steps or degrees. **3** (*often cap.*) favouring or promoting political or social reform through government action, or even revolution, to improve the lot of the majority: *a progressive policy.* **4** denoting or relating to an educational system that allows flexibility in learning procedures, based on activities determined by the needs and capacities of the individual child, the aim of which is to integrate academic with social development. **5** (of a tax or tax system) graduated so that the rate increases relative to the amount taxed. Compare **regressive** (sense 2). **6** (esp. of a disease) advancing in severity, complexity, or extent. **7** (of a dance, card game, etc.) involving a regular change of partners after one figure, one game, etc. **8** denoting an aspect of verbs in some languages, including English, used to express prolonged or continuous activity as opposed to momentary or habitual activity: *a progressive aspect of the verb "to walk" is "is walking."* ◆ *n* **9** a person who advocates progress, as in education, politics, etc. **10a** the progressive aspect of a verb. **10b** a verb in this aspect. ► **pro'gressively** *adv* ► **pro'gressiveness** *n* ► **pro'gressivism** *n* ► **pro'gressivist** *n*

Progressive (prə'gresɪv) *n* **1** *U.S. history.* a member or supporter of a Progressive Party. **2** *Canadian history.* a member or supporter of a chiefly agrarian reform movement advocating the nationalization of railways, low tariffs, an end to party politics, and similar measures: important in the early 1920s. ◆ *adj* **3** of, relating to, or characteristic of a Progressive Party, Progressive movement, or Progressives.

Progressive Conservative *n* (in Canada) a member or supporter of the Progressive Conservative Party.

Progressive Conservative Party *n* (in Canada) a major political party with conservative policies.

progressive dinner *n Austral. and N.Z.* a meal in which each course is served at the home of a different person.

Progressive Federal Party *n S. African.* a political party, formed in 1977 by a merger between the Progressive Party and members of the United Party, supporting qualified franchise for all South Africans irrespective of race, colour, or creed. See also **National Party, United Party.**

Progressive Party *n* **1** a U.S. political party, made up chiefly of dissident Republicans, that nominated Theodore Roosevelt as its presidential candidate in 1912 and supported primaries, progressive labour legislation, and other reforms. **2** a U.S. political party, composed mostly of farmers, socialists, and unionists, that nominated Robert La Follette for president in 1924 and supported public ownership of railways and of public utilities and other reforms. **3** a U.S. political party, composed chiefly of dissident Democrats, that nominated Henry Wallace for president in 1948 and supported the nationalization of key industries, advocated social reforms, and opposed the Cold War. **4** (in South Africa) the former name for the **Progressive Federal Party.**

progress payment *n* an instalment of a larger payment made to a contractor for work carried out up to a specified stage of the job.

prohibit (prə'hɪbɪt) *vb* (*tr*) **1** to forbid by law or other authority. **2** to hinder or prevent. **[C15:** from Latin *prohibēre* to prevent, from PRO-[1] + *habēre* to hold**]** ► **pro'hibiter** *or* **pro'hibitor** *n*

prohibition (ˌprəʊɪ'bɪʃən) *n* **1** the act of prohibiting or state of being prohibited. **2** an order or decree that prohibits. **3** (*sometimes cap.*) (esp. in the U.S.) a policy of legally forbidding the manufacture, transportation, sale, or consumption of alcoholic beverages except for medicinal or scientific purposes. **4** *Law.* an order of a superior court (in Britain the High Court) forbidding an inferior court to determine a matter outside its jurisdiction. ► **ˌprohi'bitionary** *adj*

Prohibition (ˌprəʊɪ'bɪʃən) *n* the period (1920–33) when the manufacture, sale, and transportation of intoxicating liquors was banned by constitutional amendment in the U.S. ► **ˌProhi'bitionist** *n*

prohibitionist (ˌprəʊɪ'bɪʃənɪst) *n* (*sometimes cap.*) a person who favours prohibition, esp. of alcoholic beverages. ► **ˌprohi'bitionism** *n*

prohibitive (prə'hɪbɪtɪv) *or* (*less commonly*) **prohibitory** (prə'hɪbɪtərɪ, -trɪ) *adj* **1** prohibiting or tending to prohibit. **2** (esp. of prices) tending or designed to discourage sale or purchase. ► **pro'hibitively** *adv* ► **pro'hibitiveness** *n*

project *n* ('prɒdʒekt). **1** a proposal, scheme, or design. **2a** a task requiring considerable or concerted effort, such as one by students. **2b** the subject of such a task. **3** *U.S.* short for **housing project.** ◆ *vb* (prə'dʒekt). **4** (*tr*) to propose or plan. **5** (*tr*) to predict; estimate; extrapolate: *we can project future needs on the basis of the current birth rate.* **6** (*tr*) to throw or cast forwards. **7** to jut or cause to jut out. **8** (*tr*) to send forth or transport in the imagination: *to project oneself into the future.* **9** (*tr*) to cause (an image) to appear on a surface. **10** to cause (one's voice) to be heard clearly at a distance. **11** *Psychol.* **11a** (*intr*) (esp. of a child) to believe that others share one's subjective mental life. **11b** to impute to others (one's hidden desires and impulses), esp. as a means of defending oneself. Compare **introject.** **12** (*tr*) *Geometry.* to draw a projection of. **13** (*intr*) to communicate effectively, esp. to a large gathering. **[C14:** from Latin *prōicere* to throw down, from PRO-[1] + *iacere* to throw**]**

projectile (prə'dʒektaɪl) *n* **1** an object or body thrown forwards. **2** any self-propelling missile, esp. one powered by a rocket or the rocket itself. **3** any object that can be fired from a gun, such as a bullet or shell. ◆ *adj* **4** capable of being or designed to be hurled forwards. **5** projecting or thrusting forwards. **6** *Zoology.* another word for **protrusile.** **[C17:** from New Latin *prōjectilis* jutting forwards**]**

projection (prə'dʒekʃən) *n* **1** the act of projecting or the state of being projected. **2** an object or part that juts out. **3** see **map projection.** **4** the representation of a line, figure, or solid on a given plane as it would be seen from a particular direction or in accordance with an accepted set of rules. **5** a scheme or plan. **6** a prediction based on known evidence and observations. **7a** the process of showing film on a screen. **7b** the image or images shown. **8** *Psychol.* **8a** the belief, esp. in children, that others share one's subjective mental life. **8b** the process of projecting one's own hidden desires and impulses. See also **defence mechanism.** **9** the mixing by alchemists of powdered philosopher's stone with molten base metals in order to transmute them into gold. ► **pro'jectional** *adj*

projectionist (prə'dʒekʃənɪst) *n* a person responsible for the operation of film projection machines.

projection room *n* a small room in a cinema in which the film projectors are operated.

projection television *n* a television receiver in which a very bright picture on a small cathode-ray tube screen is optically projected onto a large screen.

projective (prə'dʒektɪv) *adj* relating to or concerned with projection: *projective geometry.* ► **pro'jectively** *adv*

projective geometry *n* the branch of geometry concerned with the properties of solids that are invariant under projection and section.

projective test *n* any psychological test, such as the Rorschach test, in which the subject is asked to respond to vague material. It is thought that unconscious ideas are thus projected, which, when the responses are interpreted, reveal hidden aspects of the subject's personality.

projector (prə'dʒektə) *n* **1** an optical instrument that projects an enlarged image of individual slides onto a screen or wall. Full name: **slide projector.** **2** an optical instrument in which a strip of film is wound past a lens at a fixed speed so that the frames can be viewed as a continuously moving sequence on a screen or wall. Full name: **film** *or* **cine projector.** **3** a device for projecting a light beam. **4** a person who devises projects.

projet ('prɒʒeɪ) *n Diplomacy.* a draft of a proposed treaty; plan or proposition. **[C19:** via French from Latin *prōjectum* something projecting**]**

prokaryon (prəʊ'kærɪɒn) *n* the nucleus of a prokaryote.

prokaryote *or* **procaryote** (prəʊ'kærɪɒt) *n* any organism of the kingdom *Prokaryotae* having cells in each of which the genetic material is in a single filament of DNA, not enclosed in a nucleus. Bacteria are prokaryotes. Compare **eukaryote.** **[**from PRO-[2] + KARYO- + *-ote* as in *zygote***]** ► **prokaryotic** *or* **procaryotic** (prəʊˌkærɪ'ɒtɪk) *adj*

Prokofiev (prə'kɒfɪˌef; *Russian* pra'kɔfjɪf) *n* **Sergei Sergeyevich** (sɪr'gjej sɪr'gjejɪvitʃ). 1891–1953, Soviet composer. His compositions include the orchestral fairy tale *Peter and the Wolf* (1936), the opera *The Love for Three Oranges* (1921), and seven symphonies.

Prokopyevsk (*Russian* pra'kɔpjɪfsk) *n* a city in S Russia: the chief coal-mining centre of the Kuznetsk Basin. Pop.: 253 000 (1995 est.).

prolactin (prəʊ'læktɪn) *n* a gonadotrophic hormone secreted by the anterior lobe of the pituitary gland. In mammals it stimulates the secretion of progesterone by the corpus luteum and initiates and maintains lactation. Also called: **luteotrophin, luteotrophic hormone.** See also **follicle-stimulating hormone, luteinizing hormone.**

prolamine ('prəʊləˌmiːn, -mɪn; prəʊ'læmiːn) *n* any of a group of simple plant proteins, including gliadin, hordein, and zein. **[C20:** from PROL(INE) + AM(MONIA) + -INE[2]**]**

prolapse ('prəʊlæps, prəʊ'læps) *Pathol.* ◆ *n* **1** Also called: **prolapsus**

pro'labour *adj*

(prəʊ'læpsəs). the sinking or falling down of an organ or part, esp. the womb. Compare **proptosis.** ◆ *vb (intr)* **2** (of an organ, etc.) to sink from its normal position. [C17: from Latin *prōlābi* to slide along, from PRO-[1] + *lābī* to slip]

prolate ('prəʊleɪt) *adj* having a polar diameter of greater length than the equatorial diameter. Compare **oblate**[1]. [C17: from Latin *prōferre* to enlarge] ► **'prolately** *adv* ► **'prolateness** *n*

prole (prəʊl) *n, adj Derogatory slang, chiefly Brit.* short for **proletarian.**

proleg ('prəʊ,lɛg) *n* any of the short paired unjointed appendages on each abdominal segment of a caterpillar and any of certain other insect larvae. [C19: from PRO-[1] + LEG]

prolegomenon (,prəʊlɛ'gɒmɪnən) *n, pl* **-na** (-nə). *(often pl)* a preliminary discussion, esp. a formal critical introduction to a lengthy text. [C17: from Greek, from *prolegein*, from PRO-[2] + *legein* to say] ► **,prole'gomenal** *adj*

prolepsis (prəʊ'lɛpsɪs) *n, pl* **-ses** (-si:z). **1** a rhetorical device by which objections and counterarguments are anticipated and answered in advance. **2** use of a word after a verb in anticipation of its becoming applicable through the action of the verb, as *flat* in *hammer it flat.* [C16: via Late Latin from Greek: anticipation, from *prolambanein* to anticipate, from PRO-[2] + *lambanein* to take] ► **pro'leptic** *adj*

proletarian (,prəʊlɪ'tɛərɪən) *or (less commonly)* **proletary** ('prəʊlɪtərɪ, -trɪ) *adj* **1** of, relating, or belonging to the proletariat. ◆ *n, pl* **-tarians** *or* **-taries. 2** a member of the proletariat. [C17: from Latin *prōlētārius* one whose only contribution to the state was his offspring, from *prōlēs* offspring] ► **,prole'tarianism** *n* ► **,prole'tarianness** *n*

proletariat (,prəʊlɪ'tɛərɪət) *n* **1** all wage-earners collectively. **2** the lower or working class. **3** (in Marxist theory) the class of wage-earners, esp. industrial workers, in a capitalist society, whose only possession of significant material value is their labour. **4** (in ancient Rome) the lowest class of citizens, who had no property. [C19: via French from Latin *prōlētārius* PROLETARIAN]

pro-life *adj* (of an organization, pressure group, etc.) supporting the right to life of the unborn; against abortion, experiments on embryos, etc. ► **,pro-'lifer** *n*

proliferate (prə'lɪfə,reɪt) *vb* **1** to grow or reproduce (new parts, cells, etc.) rapidly. **2** to grow or increase or cause to grow or increase rapidly. [C19: from Medieval Latin *prōlifer* having offspring, from Latin *prōlēs* offspring + *ferre* to bear] ► **pro,lifer'ation** *n* ► **pro'liferative** *adj*

proliferous (prə'lɪfərəs) *adj* **1** (of plants) producing many side branches or offshoots. **2** (of plants and certain animals) reproducing by means of buds, offshoots, etc. [C17: from Medieval Latin *prōlifer* having offspring]

prolific (prə'lɪfɪk) *adj* **1** producing fruit, offspring, etc., in abundance. **2** producing constant or successful results. **3** (often foll. by *in* or *of*) rich or fruitful. [C17: from Medieval Latin *prōlificus*, from Latin *prōlēs* offspring] ► **pro'lifically** *adv* ► **pro'lificness** *or* **pro'lificacy** *n*

proline ('prəʊli:n, -lɪn) *n* a nonessential amino acid that occurs in protein. [C20: from PYRROLIDINE]

prolix ('prəʊlɪks, prəʊ'lɪks) *adj* **1** (of a speech, book, etc.) so long as to be boring; verbose. **2** indulging in prolix speech or writing; long-winded. [C15: from Latin *prōlixus* stretched out widely, from PRO-[1] + *līquī* to flow] ► **pro'lixity** *or (less commonly)* **pro'lixness** *n* ► **pro'lixly** *adv*

prolocutor (prəʊ'lɒkjʊtə) *n* a chairman, esp. of the lower house of clergy in a convocation of the Anglican Church. [C15: from Latin: advocate, from PRO-[1] + *loquī* to speak] ► **pro'locutor,ship** *n*

PROLOG *or* **Prolog** ('prəʊlɒg) *n* a computer programming language based on mathematical logic. [C20: from *pro(gramming in) log(ic)*]

prologue *or U.S. (often)* **prolog** ('prəʊlɒg) *n* **1a** the prefatory lines introducing a play or speech. **1b** the actor speaking these lines. **2** a preliminary act or event. **3** (in early opera) **3a** an introductory scene in which a narrator summarizes the main action of the work. **3b** a brief independent play preceding the opera, esp. one in honour of a patron. ◆ *vb* **-logues, -loguing, -logued** *or U.S.* **-logs, -loging, -loged. 4** *(tr)* to introduce or preface with or as if with a prologue. [C13: from Latin *prologus*, from Greek *prologos*, from PRO-[2] + *logos* discourse]

prolong (prə'lɒŋ) *vb (tr)* to lengthen in duration or space; extend. [C15: from Late Latin *prōlongāre* to extend, from Latin PRO-[1] + *longus* long] ► **prolongation** (,prəʊlɒŋ'geɪʃən) *n* ► **pro'longer** *n* ► **pro'longment** *n*

prolonge (prə'lɒndʒ) *n* (formerly) a specially fitted rope used as part of the towing equipment of a gun carriage. [C19: from French, from *prolonger* to PROLONG]

prolusion (prə'lu:ʒən) *n* **1** a preliminary written exercise. **2** an introductory essay, sometimes of a slight or tentative nature. [C17: from Latin *prōlūsiō* preliminary exercise, from *prōlūdere* to practise beforehand, from PRO-[1] + *lūdere* to play] ► **prolusory** (prə'lu:zərɪ) *adj*

prom (prɒm) *n* **1** *Brit.* short for **promenade** (sense 1) or **promenade concert. 2** *U.S. and Canadian informal.* short for **promenade** (sense 3).

PROM (prɒm) *n Computing. acronym for* programmable read only memory.

prom. *abbrev. for* promontory.

promenade (,prɒmə'nɑ:d) *n* **1** *Chiefly Brit.* a public walk, esp. at a seaside resort. **2** a leisurely walk, esp. one in a public place for pleasure or display. **3** *U.S. and Canadian.* a ball or formal dance at a high school or college. **4** a marchlike step in dancing. **5** a marching sequence in a square or country dance. ◆ *vb* **6** to take a promenade in or through (a place). **7** *(intr) Dancing.* to perform a promenade. **8** *(tr)* to display or exhibit (someone or oneself) on or as if on a promenade. [C16: from French, from *promener* to lead out for a walk, from Late Latin *prōmināre* to drive (cattle) along, from PRO-[1] + *mināre* to drive, probably from *minārī* to threaten] ► **,prome'nader** *n*

promenade concert *n* a concert at which some of the audience stand rather than sit. Often shortened to **prom.**

promenade deck *n* an upper covered deck of a passenger ship for the use of the passengers.

promethazine (prəʊ'mɛθə,zi:n) *n* an antihistamine drug used to treat allergies and to prevent vomiting, esp. in motion sickness. [C20: from PRO(PYL) + *(di)meth(ylamine)* + (PHENOTHI)AZINE]

Promethean (prə'mi:θɪən) *adj* **1** of or relating to Prometheus. **2** creative, original, or life-enhancing. ◆ *n* **3** a person who resembles Prometheus.

Prometheus (prə'mi:θɪəs) *n Greek myth.* a Titan, who stole fire from Olympus to give to mankind and in punishment was chained to a rock, where an eagle tore at his liver until Hercules freed him.

promethium (prə'mi:θɪəm) *n* a radioactive element of the lanthanide series artificially produced by the fission of uranium. Symbol: Pm; atomic no.: 61; half-life of most stable isotope, ^{145}Pm: 17.7 years; valency: 3; melting pt.: 1042°C; boiling pt.: 2460°C (approx.). [C20: New Latin from PROMETHEUS]

prominence ('prɒmɪnəns) *n* **1** the state or quality of being prominent. **2** something that is prominent, such as a protuberance. **3** relative importance or consequence. **4** *Astronomy.* an eruption of incandescent gas from the sun's surface that can reach an altitude of several hundred thousand kilometres. It is visible during a total eclipse.

prominent ('prɒmɪnənt) *adj* **1** jutting or projecting outwards. **2** standing out from its surroundings; noticeable. **3** widely known; eminent. [C16: from Latin *prōminēre* to jut out, from PRO-[1] + *ēminēre* to project] ► **'prominently** *adv* ► **'prominentness** *n*

prominent moth *n* any moth of the family *Notodontidae* characterized by tufts of scales on the back edge of the forewing that stand up prominently at rest and give the group its name. It includes the puss moth and buff-tip as well as those with *prominent* in the name.

promiscuity (,prɒmɪ'skju:ɪtɪ) *n* **1** promiscuous sexual behaviour. **2** indiscriminate mingling, mixture, or confusion, as of parts or elements.

promiscuous (prə'mɪskjʊəs) *adj* **1** indulging in casual and indiscriminate sexual relationships. **2** consisting of a number of dissimilar parts or elements mingled in a confused or indiscriminate manner. **3** indiscriminate in selection. **4** casual or heedless. [C17: from Latin *prōmiscuus* indiscriminate, from PRO-[1] + *miscēre* to mix] ► **pro'miscuously** *adv* ► **pro'miscuousness** *n*

promise ('prɒmɪs) *vb* **1** (often foll. by *to;* when *tr, may take a clause as object or an infinitive*) to give an assurance of (something to someone); undertake (to do something) in the future: *I promise that I will come.* **2** *(tr)* to undertake to give (something to someone): *he promised me a car for my birthday.* **3** (when *tr, takes an infinitive*) to cause one to expect that in the future one is likely (to be or do something): *she promises to be a fine soprano.* **4** *(usually passive)* to engage to be married; betroth: *I'm promised to Bill.* **5** *(tr)* to assure (someone) of the authenticity or inevitability of something (often in the parenthetic phrase **I promise you,** used to emphasize a statement): *there'll be trouble, I promise you.* ◆ *n* **6** an undertaking or assurance given by one person to another agreeing or guaranteeing to do or give something, or not to do or give something, in the future. **7** indication of forthcoming excellence or goodness: *a writer showing considerable promise.* **8** the thing of which an assurance is given. [C14: from Latin *prōmissum* a promise, from *prōmittere* to send forth] ► **'promiser** *n*

Promised Land *n* **1** *Old Testament.* the land of Canaan, promised by God to Abraham and his descendants as their heritage (Genesis 12:7). **2** heaven, esp. when considered as the goal towards which Christians journey in their earthly lives. **3** any longed-for place where one expects to find greater happiness or fulfilment.

promisee (,prɒmɪ'si:) *n Contract law.* a person to whom a promise is made. Compare **promisor.**

promising ('prɒmɪsɪŋ) *adj* showing promise of favourable development or future success. ► **'promisingly** *adv*

promisor (,prɒmɪ'sɔ:, 'prɒmɪ,sɔ:) *n Contract law.* a person who makes a promise. Compare **promisee.**

promissory ('prɒmɪsərɪ) *adj* **1** containing, relating to, or having the nature of a promise. **2** *Insurance.* stipulating how the provisions of an insurance contract will be fulfilled after it has been signed.

promissory note *n Chiefly U.S. commerce.* a document, usually negotiable, containing a signed promise to pay a stated sum of money to a specified person at a designated date or on demand. Also called: **note, note of hand.**

promo ('prəʊməʊ) *n, pl* **-mos.** *Informal.* something that is used to promote a product, esp. a videotape film used to promote a pop record. [C20: shortened from *promotion*]

promontory ('prɒməntərɪ, -trɪ) *n, pl* **-ries. 1** a high point of land, esp. of rocky coast, that juts out into the sea. **2** *Anatomy.* any of various projecting structures. [C16: from Latin *prōmunturium* headland; related to *prōminēre;* see PROMINENT]

promote (prə'məʊt) *vb (tr)* **1** to further or encourage the progress or existence of. **2** to raise to a higher rank, status, degree, etc. **3** to advance (a pupil or student) to a higher course, class, etc. **4** to urge the adoption of; work for: *to promote reform.* **5** to encourage the sale of (a product) by advertising or securing financial support. **6** *Chess.* to exchange (a pawn) for any piece other than a king when the pawn reaches the 8th rank. [C14: from Latin *prōmovēre* to push onwards, from PRO-[1] + *movēre* to move] ► **pro'motable** *adj* ► **pro'motion** *n* ► **pro'motional** *adj*

promoter (prə'məʊtə) *n* **1** a person or thing that promotes. **2** a person who

pro'military *adj*	**pro'monarchist** *adj, n*

helps to organize, develop, or finance an undertaking. **3** a person who organizes and finances a sporting event, esp. a boxing match. **4** *Chem.* a substance added in small amounts to a catalyst to increase its activity. **5** *Genetics.* the site on an operon that must bind with messenger RNA polymerase before transcription of the operon occurs.

promotive (prəˈməʊtɪv) *adj* tending to promote. ► **proˈmotiveness** *n*

prompt (prɒmpt) *adj* **1** performed or executed without delay. **2** quick or ready to act or respond. ◆ *adv* **3** *Informal.* punctually. ◆ *vb* **4** (*tr*) to urge (someone to do something). **5** to remind (an actor, singer, etc.) of lines forgotten during a performance. **6** (*tr*) to refresh the memory of. **7** (*tr*) to give rise to by suggestion: *his affairs will prompt discussion.* ◆ *n* **8** *Commerce.* **8a** the time limit allowed for payment of the debt incurred by purchasing goods or services on credit. **8b** the contract specifying this time limit. **8c** Also called: **prompt note.** a memorandum sent to a purchaser to remind him of the time limit and the sum due. **9** the act of prompting. **10** anything that serves to remind. **11** an aid to the operator of a computer in the form of a question or statement that appears on the screen showing that the equipment is ready to proceed and indicating the options available. [C15: from Latin *promptus* evident, from *prōmere* to produce, from PRO-[1] + *emere* to buy] ► **ˈpromptly** *adv* ► **ˈpromptness** *n*

promptbook (ˈprɒmptˌbʊk) *n* the production script of a play containing notes, cues, etc.

prompter (ˈprɒmptə) *n* **1** a person offstage who reminds the actors of forgotten lines or cues. **2** a person, thing, etc., that prompts.

promptitude (ˈprɒmptɪˌtjuːd) *n* the quality of being prompt; punctuality.

prompt side *n Theatre.* the side of the stage where the prompter is, usually to the actor's left in Britain and to his right in the United States.

promulgate (ˈprɒməlˌgeɪt) *vb* (*tr*) **1** to put into effect (a law, decree, etc.), esp. by formal proclamation. **2** to announce or declare officially. **3** to make widespread. ◆ Also (archaic): **promulge** (prəʊˈmʌldʒ). [C16: from Latin *prōmulgāre* to bring to public knowledge; probably related to *provulgāre* to publicize, from PRO-[1] + *vulgāre* to make common, from *vulgus* the common people] ► **ˌpromulˈgation** *n* ► **ˈpromulˌgator** *n*

promycelium (ˌprəʊmaɪˈsiːlɪəm) *n, pl* **-lia** (-lɪə). *Botany.* a short tubular outgrowth from certain germinating fungal spores that produces spores itself and then dies. [C19: New Latin from PRO-[1] + MYCELIUM] ► **ˌpromyˈcelial** *adj*

pron. *abbrev. for:* **1** pronominal. **2** pronoun. **3** pronounced. **4** pronunciation.

pronate (prəʊˈneɪt) *vb* (*tr*) to turn (the forearm or hand) so that the palmar surface is directed downwards. [C19: from Late Latin *prōnāre* to bend forwards, bow] ► **proˈnation** *n*

pronator (prəʊˈneɪtə) *n* any muscle that effects pronation.

prone (prəʊn) *adj* **1** lying flat or face downwards; prostrate. **2** sloping or tending downwards. **3** having an inclination to do something. [C14: from Latin *prōnus* bent forward, from PRO-[1]] ► **ˈpronely** *adv* ► **ˈproneness** *n*

-prone *adj combining form.* liable or disposed to suffer: *accident-prone.*

pronephros (prəʊˈnefrɒs) *n, pl* **-roi** (-rɔɪ) *or* **-ra** (-rə). the first-formed anterior part of the embryonic kidney in vertebrates, which remains functional in the larvae of the lower vertebrates. See also **mesonephros, metanephros.** [C19: New Latin, from PRO-[2] + Greek *nephros* kidney] ► **proˈnephric** *adj*

prong (prɒŋ) *n* **1** a sharply pointed end of an instrument, such as on a fork. **2** any pointed projecting part. ◆ *vb* **3** (*tr*) to prick or spear with or as if with a prong. [C15: related to Middle Low German *prange* a stake, Gothic *anaprangan* to afflict] ► **pronged** *adj*

pronghorn (ˈprɒŋˌhɔːn) *n* a ruminant mammal, *Antilocapra americana,* inhabiting rocky deserts of North America and having small branched horns: family *Antilocapridae.* Also called: **American antelope.**

prong key *n* a key or spanner with two prongs or projections which engage corresponding holes in the face of a nut or component to be turned for tightening, adjustment, etc.

pronominal (prəʊˈnɒmɪnᵊl) *adj* relating to or playing the part of a pronoun. [C17: from Late Latin *prōnōminālis,* from *prōnōmen* a PRONOUN] ► **proˈnominally** *adv*

pronominalize *or* **pronominalise** (prəʊˈnɒmɪnəˌlaɪz) *vb* (*tr*) to make (a word) into or treat as a pronoun. ► **proˌnominaliˈzation** *or* **proˌnominaliˈsation** *n*

pronotum (prəʊˈnəʊtəm) *n* the notum of the prothorax of an insect. [C19: PRO-[2] + NOTUM]

pronoun (ˈprəʊˌnaʊn) *n* one of a class of words that serves to replace a noun phrase that has already been or is about to be mentioned in the sentence or context. Abbrev.: **pron.** [C16: from Latin *prōnōmen,* from PRO-[1] + *nōmen* noun]

pronounce (prəˈnaʊns) *vb* **1** to utter or articulate (a sound or sequence of sounds). **2** (*tr*) to utter or articulate (sounds or words) in the correct way. **3** (*tr; may take a clause as object*) to proclaim officially and solemnly: *I now pronounce you man and wife.* **4** (when *tr, may take a clause as object*) to declare as one's judgment: *to pronounce the death sentence upon someone.* **5** (*tr*) to make a phonetic transcription of (sounds or words). [C14: from Latin *prōnuntiāre* to announce, from PRO-[1] + *nuntiāre* to announce] ► **proˈnounceable** *adj* ► **proˈnouncer** *n*

pronounced (prəˈnaʊnst) *adj* **1** strongly marked or indicated. **2** (of a sound) articulated with vibration of the vocal cords; voiced. ► **pronouncedly** (prəˈnaʊnsɪdlɪ) *adv*

pronouncement (prəˈnaʊnsmənt) *n* **1** an official or authoritative statement or announcement. **2** the act of pronouncing, declaring, or uttering formally.

pronto (ˈprɒntəʊ) *adv Informal.* at once; promptly. [C20: from Spanish: quick, from Latin *promptus* PROMPT]

pronuclear[1] (ˌprəʊˈnjuːklɪə) *adj* in favour of or supporting the use of nuclear power. ► **ˌproˈnuclearist** *n, adj*

pronuclear[2] (ˌprəʊˈnjuːklɪə) *adj* of or relating to a pronucleus.

pronucleus (ˌprəʊˈnjuːklɪəs) *n, pl* **-clei** (-klɪˌaɪ). the nucleus of a mature ovum or spermatozoan before fertilization.

pronunciamento (prəˌnʌnsɪəˈmentəʊ) *n, pl* **-tos.** **1** an edict, proclamation, or manifesto, esp. one issued by rebels in a Spanish-speaking country. **2** an authoritarian announcement. [C19: from Spanish: pronouncement]

pronunciation (prəˌnʌnsɪˈeɪʃən) *n* **1** the act, instance, or manner of pronouncing sounds. **2** the supposedly correct manner of pronouncing sounds in a given language. **3** a phonetic transcription of a word.

pro-oestrus (prəʊˈiːstrəs, -ˈestrəs) *or U.S.* **proestrus** *n* the period in the oestrous cycle that immediately precedes oestrus.

proof (pruːf) *n* **1** any evidence that establishes or helps to establish the truth, validity, quality, etc., of something. **2** *Law.* the whole body of evidence upon which the verdict of a court is based. **3** *Maths, logic.* a sequence of steps or statements that establishes the truth of a proposition. See also **direct** (sense 17), **induction** (senses 4, 8). **4** the act of testing the truth of something (esp. in the phrase **put to the proof**). **5** *Scots Law.* trial before a judge without a jury. **6** *Printing.* a trial impression made from composed type, or a print-out (from a laser printer, etc.) for the correction of errors. **7** (in engraving, etc.) a print made by an artist or under his supervision for his own satisfaction before he hands the plate over to a professional printer. **8** *Photog.* a trial print from a negative. **9a** the alcoholic strength of proof spirit. **9b** the strength of a beverage or other alcoholic liquor as measured on a scale in which the strength of proof spirit is 100 degrees. ◆ *adj* **10** (*usually postpositive;* foll. by *against*) able to resist; impervious (to): *the roof is proof against rain.* **11** having the alcoholic strength of proof spirit. **12** of proved strength or impenetrability: *proof armour.* ◆ *vb* **13** (*tr*) to take a proof from (type matter, a plate, etc.). **14** to proofread (text) or inspect (a print, etc.), as for approval. **15** to render (something) proof, esp. to waterproof. [C13: from Old French *preuve* a test, from Late Latin *proba,* from Latin *probāre* to test]

-proof *adj, vb combining form.* secure against (damage by); (make) impervious to: *waterproof; mothproof; childproof.* [from PROOF (adj)]

proofread (ˈpruːfˌriːd) *vb* **-reads, -reading, -read** (-ˌred). to read (copy or printer's proofs) to detect and mark errors to be corrected. ► **ˈproofˌreader** *n*

proof spirit *n* **1** (in Britain and Canada) a mixture of alcohol and water or an alcoholic beverage that contains 49.28 per cent of alcohol by weight, 57.1 per cent by volume at 51°F: up until 1980 used as a standard of alcoholic liquids. **2** (in the U.S.) a similar standard mixture containing 50 per cent of alcohol by volume at 60°F.

proof stress *n Engineering.* the equivalent of yield stress in materials which have no clearly defined yield point.

proof theory *n* the branch of logic that studies the syntactic properties of formal theories, esp. the syntactic characterization of deductive validity.

prop[1] (prɒp) *vb* **props, propping, propped.** (when *tr,* often foll. by *up*) **1** (*tr*) to support with a rigid object, such as a stick. **2** (*tr;* usually also foll. by *against*) to place or lean. **3** (*tr*) to sustain or support. **4** (*intr*) *Austral. and N.Z.* to stop suddenly or unexpectedly. ◆ *n* **5** something that gives rigid support, such as a stick. **6** a person or thing giving support, as of a moral or spiritual nature. **7** *Rugby.* either of the forwards at either end of the front row of a scrum. [C15: related to Middle Dutch *proppe* vine prop; compare Old High German *pfropfo* shoot, German *Pfropfen* stopper]

prop[2] (prɒp) *n* short for **property** (sense 8).

prop[3] (prɒp) *n* an informal word for **propeller.**

prop. *abbrev. for:* **1** proper(ly). **2** property. **3** proposition. **4** proprietor.

propaedeutic (ˌprəʊpɪˈdjuːtɪk) *n* **1** (*often pl*) preparatory instruction basic to further study of an art or science. ◆ *adj also* **propaedeutical.** **2** of, relating to, or providing such instruction. [C19: from Greek *propaideuein* to teach in advance, from PRO-[2] + *paideuein* to rear]

propagable (ˈprɒpəgəbᵊl) *adj* capable of being propagated. ► **ˌpropagaˈbility** *or* **ˈpropagableness** *n*

propaganda (ˌprɒpəˈgændə) *n* **1** the organized dissemination of information, allegations, etc., to assist or damage the cause of a government, movement, etc. **2** such information, allegations, etc. [C18: from Italian, use of *propāgandā* in the New Latin title *Sacra Congregatio de Propaganda Fide* Sacred Congregation for Propagating the Faith] ► **ˌpropaˈgandism** *n* ► **ˌpropaˈgandist** *n, adj*

Propaganda (ˌprɒpəˈgændə) *n R.C. Church.* a congregation responsible for directing the work of the foreign missions and the training of priests for these.

propagandize *or* **propagandise** (ˌprɒpəˈgændaɪz) *vb* **1** (*tr*) to spread by propaganda. **2** (*tr*) to subject to propaganda. **3** (*intr*) to spread or organize propaganda.

propagate (ˈprɒpəˌgeɪt) *vb* **1** *Biology.* to reproduce or cause to reproduce; breed. **2** (*tr*) *Horticulture.* to produce (plants) by layering, grafting, cuttings, etc. **3** (*tr*) to promulgate; disseminate. **4** *Physics.* to move through, cause to move through, or transmit, esp. in the form of a wave: *to propagate sound.* **5** (*tr*) to transmit (characteristics) from one generation to the next. [C16: from Latin *propāgāre* to increase (plants) by cuttings, from *propāgēs* a cutting, from *pangere* to fasten] ► **ˌpropaˈgation** *n* ► **ˌpropaˈgational** *adj* ► **ˈpropagative** *adj*

propagator (ˈprɒpəˌgeɪtə) *n* **1** a person or thing that propagates. **2** a shallow box with a heating element and cover used for germinating seeds or rooting cuttings.

propagule (ˈprɒpəˌgjuːl) *or* **propagulum** (prəʊˈpægjʊləm) *n* a plant part, such as a bud, that becomes detached from the rest of the plant and grows into a new plant. [C20: from PROPAG(ATE) + -ULE]

propane (ˈprəʊpeɪn) *n* a colourless flammable gaseous alkane found in petroleum and used as a fuel. Formula: $CH_3CH_2CH_3$. [C19: from PROPIONIC ACID + -ANE]

propanedioic acid (ˌprəʊpeɪndaɪˈəʊɪk) *n* a colourless crystalline compound occurring in sugar beet. Formula: $C_3H_4O_4,CH_2(COOH)_2$. Also called: **malonic acid.** [C20: from PROPANE + DI-[1] + -O- + -IC]

propanoic acid (ˌprəʊpəˈnəʊɪk) *n* a colourless liquid carboxylic acid used in inhibiting the growth of moulds in bread. Formula: CH_3CH_2COOH. Former name: **propionic acid.** [C20: from PROPANE + -O- + -IC]

proparoxytone (ˌprəʊpəˈrɒksɪˌtəʊn) *adj* **1** (in Ancient Greek) of, relating to, or denoting words having an acute accent on the third syllable from the end. ◆ *n* **2** a proparoxytone word. ◆ Compare **paroxytone.** [C18: from Greek *proparoxutonos;* see PRO-[2], PAROXYTONE]

pro patria *Latin.* (ˈprəʊ ˈpætrɪˌɑː) for one's country.

propel (prəˈpɛl) *vb* **-pels, -pelling, -pelled.** (*tr*) to impel, drive, or cause to move forwards. [C15: from Latin *prōpellere* to drive onwards, from PRO-[1] + *pellere* to drive]

propellant *or* **propellent** (prəˈpɛlənt) *n* **1** something that provides or causes propulsion, such as the explosive charge in a gun or the fuel in a rocket. **2** the gas used to carry the liquid droplets in an aerosol spray.

propellent (prəˈpɛlənt) *adj* able or tending to propel.

propeller (prəˈpɛlə) *n* **1** a device having blades radiating from a central hub that is rotated to produce thrust to propel a ship, aircraft, etc. **2** a person or thing that propels.

propeller shaft *n* the shaft that transmits power from the gearbox to the differential gear in a motor vehicle or from the engine to the propeller in a ship or aircraft.

propelling pencil *n* a pencil consisting of a metal or plastic case containing a replaceable lead. As the point is worn away the lead can be extended, usually by turning part of the case.

propend (prəʊˈpɛnd) *vb* (*intr*) *Obsolete.* to be inclined or disposed. [C16: from Latin *prōpendēre* to hang forwards]

propene (ˈprəʊpiːn) *n* a colourless gaseous alkene obtained by cracking petroleum: used in synthesizing many organic compounds. Formula: $CH_3CH{:}CH_2$. Also called: **propylene.**

propensity (prəˈpɛnsɪtɪ) *n, pl* **-ties. 1** a natural tendency or disposition. **2** *Obsolete.* partiality. [C16: from Latin *prōpensus* inclined to, from *prōpendēre* to PROPEND]

proper (ˈprɒpə) *adj* **1** (*usually prenominal*) appropriate or suited for some purpose: *in its proper place.* **2** correct in behaviour or conduct. **3** excessively correct in conduct; vigorously moral. **4** up to a required or regular standard. **5** (*immediately postpositive*) (of an object, quality, etc.) referred to or named specifically so as to exclude anything not directly connected with it: *his claim is connected with the deed proper.* **6** (*postpositive;* foll. by *to*) belonging to or characteristic of a person or thing. **7** (*prenominal*) *Brit. informal.* (intensifier): *I felt a proper fool.* **8** (*usually postpositive*) (of heraldic colours) considered correct for the natural colour of the object or emblem depicted: *three martlets proper.* **9** *Maths, logic.* (of a relation) distinguished from a weaker relation by excluding the case where the relata are identical. For example, every set is a subset of itself, but a **proper subset** must exclude at least one member of the containing set. See also **strict** (sense 6). **10** *Archaic.* pleasant or good. ◆ *adv* **11** *Brit. dialect.* (intensifier): *he's proper stupid.* **12 good and proper.** *Informal.* thoroughly: *to get drunk good and proper.* ◆ *n* **13** the parts of the Mass that vary according to the particular day or feast on which the Mass is celebrated. Compare **ordinary** (sense 10). [C13: via Old French from Latin *prōprius* special] ▸ **ˈproperly** *adv* ▸ **ˈproperness** *n*

properdin (ˈprəʊpədɪn) *n Immunol.* a protein present in blood serum that, acting with complement, is involved in the destruction of alien cells, such as bacteria.

proper fraction *n* a fraction in which the numerator has a lower absolute value than the denominator, as ½ or $x/(3 + x^2)$.

proper motion *n* the very small continuous change in the direction of motion of a star relative to the sun. It is determined from its radial and tangential motion.

proper noun *or* **name** *n* the name of a person, place, or object, as for example *Iceland, Patrick,* or *Uranus.* Compare **common noun.** Related adj: **onomastic.**

propertied (ˈprɒpətɪd) *adj* owning land or property.

Propertius (prəˈpɜːʃɪəs, -ʃəs) *n* **Sextus** (ˈsɛkstəs). ?50–?15 B.C., Roman elegiac poet.

property (ˈprɒpətɪ) *n, pl* **-ties. 1** something of value, either tangible, such as land, or intangible, such as patents, copyrights, etc. **2** *Law.* the right to possess, use, and dispose of anything. **3** possessions collectively or the fact of owning possessions of value. **4a** a piece of land or real estate, esp. used for agricultural purposes. **4b** (*as modifier*): *property rights.* **5** *Chiefly Austral.* a ranch or station, esp. a small one. **6** a quality, attribute, or distinctive feature of anything, esp. a characteristic attribute such as the density or strength of a material. **7** *Logic, obsolete.* another name for **proprium. 8** any movable object used on the set of a stage play or film. Usually shortened to **prop.** [C13: from Old French *propriété,* from Latin *proprietās* something personal, from *proprius* one's own]

property bond *n* a bond issued by a life-assurance company, the premiums for which are invested in a property-owning fund.

property centre *n* a service for buying and selling property, including conveyancing, provided by a group of local solicitors. In full: **solicitors' property centre.**

property man *n* a member of the stage crew in charge of the stage properties. Usually shortened to **propman.**

prophage (ˈprəʊfeɪdʒ) *n* a virus that exists in a bacterial cell and undergoes division with its host without destroying it. Compare **bacteriophage.** [C20: by contraction from French *probactériophage; see* PRO-[2], BACTERIOPHAGE]

prophase (ˈprəʊˌfeɪz) *n* **1** the first stage of mitosis, during which the nuclear membrane disappears and the nuclear material resolves itself into chromosomes. See also **metaphase, anaphase, telophase. 2** the first stage of meiosis, divided into leptotene, zygotene, pachytene, diplotene, and diakinesis phases.

prophecy (ˈprɒfɪsɪ) *n, pl* **-cies. 1. a** a message of divine truth revealing God's will. **b** the act of uttering such a message. **2** a prediction or guess. **3** the function, activity, or charismatic endowment of a prophet or prophets. [C13: ultimately from Greek *prophētēs* PROPHET]

prophesy (ˈprɒfɪˌsaɪ) *vb* **-sies, -sying, -sied. 1** to reveal or foretell (something, esp. a future event) by or as if by divine inspiration. **2** (*intr*) *Archaic.* to give instruction in religious subjects. [C14 *prophecien,* from PROPHECY] ▸ **ˈprophe̦siable** *adj* ▸ **ˈprophe̦sier** *n*

prophet (ˈprɒfɪt) *n* **1** a person who supposedly speaks by divine inspiration, esp. one through whom a divinity expresses his will. Related adj: **vatic. 2** a person who predicts the future: *a prophet of doom.* **3** a spokesman for a movement, doctrine, etc. **4** *Christian Science.* **4a** a seer in spiritual matters. **4b** the vanishing of material sense to give way to the conscious facts of spiritual truth. [C13: from Old French *prophète,* from Latin *prophēta,* from Greek *prophētēs* one who declares the divine will, from PRO-[2] + *phanai* to speak] ▸ **ˈprophetess** *fem n* ▸ **ˈprophet-ˌlike** *adj*

Prophet (ˈprɒfɪt) *pl n* **the. 1** the principal designation of Mohammed as the founder of Islam. **2** a name for Joseph Smith as founder of the Mormon Church.

prophetic (prəˈfɛtɪk) *adj* **1** of or relating to a prophet or prophecy. **2** containing or of the nature of a prophecy; predictive. ▸ **proˈphetically** *adv*

Prophets (ˈprɒfɪts) *pl n* the books constituting the second main part of the Hebrew Bible, which in Jewish tradition is subdivided into the **Former Prophets,** Joshua, Judges, I-II Samuel, and I-II Kings, and the **Latter Prophets,** comprising those books which in Christian tradition are alone called the **Prophets** and which are divided into **Major Prophets** and **Minor Prophets.** Compare **Law of Moses, Hagiographa.**

prophylactic (ˌprɒfɪˈlæktɪk) *adj* **1** protecting from or preventing disease. **2** protective or preventive. ◆ *n* **3** a prophylactic drug or device. **4** *Chiefly U.S.* another name for **condom.** [C16: via French from Greek *prophulaktikos,* from *prophulassein* to guard by taking advance measures, from PRO-[2] + *phulax* a guard]

prophylaxis (ˌprɒfɪˈlæksɪs) *n* the prevention of disease or control of its possible spread.

propinquity (prəˈpɪŋkwɪtɪ) *n* **1** nearness in place or time. **2** nearness in relationship. [C14: from Latin *propinquitās* closeness, from *propinquus* near, from *prope* near by]

propionate (ˈprəʊpɪəˌneɪt) *n* any ester or salt of propionic acid.

propionic acid (ˌprəʊpɪˈɒnɪk) *n* the former name for **propanoic acid.** [C19: from Greek *pro-* first + *pionic* from *piōn* fat, because it is first in order of the fatty acids]

propitiate (prəˈpɪʃɪˌeɪt) *vb* (*tr*) to appease or make well disposed; conciliate. [C17: from Latin *propitiāre* to appease, from *propitius* gracious] ▸ **proˈpitiable** *adj* ▸ **proˌpitiˈation** *n* ▸ **proˌpitiˈatious** *adj* ▸ **proˈpitiative** *adj* ▸ **proˈpitiˌator** *n*

propitiatory (prəˈpɪʃɪətərɪ) *adj* **1** designed or intended to propitiate; conciliatory; expiatory. ◆ *n* **2** the mercy seat. ▸ **proˈpitiatorily** *adv*

propitious (prəˈpɪʃəs) *adj* **1** favourable; auguring well. **2** gracious or favourably inclined. [C15: from Latin *propitius* well disposed, from *prope* close to] ▸ **proˈpitiously** *adv* ▸ **proˈpitiousness** *n*

propjet (ˈprɒpˌdʒɛt) *n* another name for **turboprop.**

propman (ˈprɒpˌmæn) *n, pl* **-men.** short for **property man.**

propolis (ˈprɒpəlɪs) *n* a greenish-brown resinous aromatic substance collected by bees from the buds of trees for use in the construction of hives. Also called: **bee glue, hive dross.** [C17: via Latin from Greek: suburb, bee glue, from *pro-* before + *polis* city]

propone (prəˈpon, -ˈpəʊn) *vb Scot.* to propose or put forward, esp. before a court. [C14: from Latin *prōpōnere* to PROPOSE]

proponent (prəˈpəʊnənt) *n* **1** a person who argues in favour of something. **2** *Law.* a person who seeks probate of a will. [C16: from Latin *prōpōnere* to PROPOSE]

Propontis (prəˈpɒntɪs) *n* the ancient name for (the Sea of) **Marmara.**

proportion (prəˈpɔːʃən) *n* **1** the relationship between different things or parts with respect to comparative size, number, or degree; relative magnitude or extent; ratio. **2** the correct or desirable relationship between parts of a whole; balance or symmetry. **3** a part considered with respect to the whole. **4** (*pl*) dimensions or size: *a building of vast proportions.* **5** a share, part, or quota. **6** *Maths.* a relationship that maintains a constant ratio between two variable quantities: *x increases in direct proportion to y.* **7** *Maths.* a relationship between four numbers or quantities in which the ratio of the first pair equals the ratio of the second pair. ◆ *vb* (*tr*) **8** to adjust in relative amount, size, etc. **9** to cause to be harmonious in relationship of parts. [C14: from Latin *prōportiō* (a translation of Greek *analogia*), from phrase *prō portione,* literally: for (its, his, one's) PORTION] ▸ **proˈportionable** *adj* ▸ **proˌportionaˈbility** *n* ▸ **proˈportionably** *adv* ▸ **proˈportionment** *n*

proportional (prəˈpɔːʃənᵊl) *adj* **1** of, involving, or being in proportion. **2** *Maths.* having or related by a constant ratio. ◆ *n* **3** *Maths.* an unknown term in a proportion: *in a/b = c/x, x is the fourth proportional.* ▸ **proˌportionˈality** *n* ▸ **proˈportionally** *adv*

proportional counter *n* an instrument for detecting and measuring the intensity of ionizing radiation. It is similar to a Geiger counter but operates at a lower potential difference such that the magnitude of the discharge is directly proportional to the number of gas molecules ionized by the detected particle. This may permit the identification of the particle or the determination of its energy.

proportional representation *n* representation of parties in an elective body in proportion to the votes they win. Abbrev.: **PR.** Compare **first-past-the-post.** See also **Additional Member System, Alternative Vote, party list, Single Transferable Vote.**

proportional spacing *n* a feature of some typewriters and other output devices whereby the space allotted to each character is determined by the width of the character.

proportionate *adj* (prəˈpɔːʃənɪt). **1** being in proper proportion. ◆ *vb* (prəˈpɔːʃəˌneɪt). **2** (*tr*) to make proportionate. ▸ **proˈportionately** *adv* ▸ **proˈportionateness** *n*

proposal (prəˈpəʊzᵊl) *n* **1** the act of proposing. **2** something proposed, as a plan. **3** an offer, esp. of marriage.

propose (prəˈpəʊz) *vb* **1** (when *tr, may take a clause as object*) to put forward (a plan, motion, etc.) for consideration or action. **2** (*tr*) to nominate, as for a position. **3** (*tr*) to plan or intend (to do something): *I propose to leave town now.* **4** (*tr*) to announce the drinking of (a toast) to (the health of someone, etc.). **5** (*intr; often foll. by to*) to make an offer of marriage (to someone). [C14: from Old French *proposer,* from Latin *prōpōnere* to display, from PRO-[1] + *pōnere* to place] ▸ **proˈposable** *adj* ▸ **proˈposer** *n*

proposition (ˌprɒpəˈzɪʃən) *n* **1** a proposal or topic presented for consideration. **2** *Philosophy.* **2a** the content of a sentence that affirms or denies something and is capable of being true or false. **2b** the meaning of such a sentence: *I am warm* always expresses the same proposition whoever the speaker is. Compare **statement** (sense 8). **3** *Maths.* a statement or theorem, usually containing its proof. **4** *Informal.* a person or matter to be dealt with: *he's a difficult proposition.* **5** an invitation to engage in sexual intercourse. ◆ *vb* **6** (*tr*) to propose a plan, deal, etc., to, esp. to engage in sexual intercourse. [C14 *proposicioun,* from Latin *prōpositiō* a setting forth; see PROPOSE] ▸ ˌ**propoˈsitional** *adj* ▸ ˌ**propoˈsitionally** *adv*

propositional attitude *n Logic, philosophy.* a relation between a person and a proposition, such as belief, desire, intention, etc.

propositional calculus *n* the system of symbolic logic concerned only with the relations between propositions as wholes, taking no account of their internal structure. Compare **predicate calculus.**

propositional function *n* another name for **open sentence.**

propositus (prəˈpɒzɪtəs) *or* (*fem*) **proposita** (prəˈpɒzɪtə) *n, pl* **-ti** (-ˌtaɪ) *or* (*fem*) **-tae** (-tiː). **1** *Law.* the person from whom a line of descent is traced. **2** *Med.* Also called (esp. U.S.): **proband.** the first patient to be investigated in a family study, to whom all relationships are referred. [from New Latin, from Latin *prōpōnere* to set forth; see PROPOUND]

propound (prəˈpaʊnd) *vb* (*tr*) **1** to suggest or put forward for consideration. **2** *English law.* **2a** to produce (a will or similar instrument) to the proper court or authority in order for its validity to be established. **2b** (of an executor) to bring (an action to obtain probate) in solemn form. [C16 *propone,* from Latin *prōpōnere* to set forth from PRO-[1] + *pōnere* to place] ▸ **proˈpounder** *n*

propr *abbrev. for* proprietor.

propraetor *or* **propretor** (prəʊˈpriːtə) *n* (in ancient Rome) a citizen, esp. an ex-praetor, granted a praetor's imperium to be exercised outside Rome, esp. in the provinces. [Latin, from *prō praetōre* one who acts for a praetor]

propranolol (prəʊˈprænəˌlɒl) *n* a drug used in the treatment of angina pectoris, arrhythmia, hypertension, and other forms of heart disease. Formula: $C_{16}H_{21}NO_2$. [C20: from PRO(PYL) + *pr(op)anol* (from PROPANE + -OL) + -OL]

proprietary (prəˈpraɪətərɪ, -trɪ) *adj* **1** of, relating to, or belonging to property or proprietors. **2** privately owned and controlled. **3** *Med.* of or denoting a drug or agent manufactured and distributed under a trade name. Compare **ethical** (sense 3). ◆ *n, pl* **-taries. 4** *Med.* a proprietary drug or agent. **5** a proprietor or proprietors collectively. **6a** right to property. **6b** property owned. **7** Also called: **lord proprietary.** (in Colonial America) an owner, governor, or grantee of a proprietary colony. [C15: from Late Latin *proprietārius* an owner, from *proprius* one's own] ▸ **proˈprietarily** *adv*

proprietary colony *n U.S. history.* any of various colonies, granted by the Crown in the 17th century to a person or group of people with full governing rights.

proprietary name *n* a name that is a trademark.

proprietor (prəˈpraɪətə) *n* **1** an owner of an unincorporated business enterprise. **2** a person enjoying exclusive right of ownership to some property. **3** *U.S. history.* a governor or body of governors of a proprietary colony. ▸ **proˈprietorship** *n* ▸ **proprietorial** (prəˌpraɪəˈtɔːrɪəl) *adj* ▸ **proˈprietress** *or* **proˈprietrix** *fem n*

propriety (prəˈpraɪətɪ) *n, pl* **-ties. 1** the quality or state of being appropriate or fitting. **2** conformity to the prevailing standard of behaviour, speech, etc. **3** (*pl*) **the proprieties.** the standards of behaviour considered correct by polite society. [C15: from Old French *propriété,* from Latin *proprietās* a peculiarity, from *proprius* one's own]

proprioceptor (ˌprəʊprɪəˈsɛptə) *n Physiol.* any receptor (as in the gut, blood vessels, muscles, etc.) that supplies information about the state of the body. Compare **exteroceptor, interoceptor.** [C20: from *proprio-,* from Latin *proprius* one's own + RECEPTOR] ▸ ˌ**proprioˈceptive** *adj*

proprium (ˈprəʊprɪəm) *n Logic, obsolete.* Also called: **property.** an attribute that is not essential to a species but is common and peculiar to it. [C16: Latin, neuter sing of *proprius* proper, own]

prop root *n* a root that grows from and supports the stem above the ground in plants such as mangroves.

proptosis (prɒpˈtəʊsɪs) *n, pl* **-ses** (-siːz). *Pathol.* the forward displacement of an organ or part, such as the eyeball. See also **exophthalmos.** Compare **prolapse.** [C17: via Late Latin from Greek, from *propiptein* to fall forwards]

propulsion (prəˈpʌlʃən) *n* **1** the act of propelling or the state of being propelled. **2** a propelling force. [C15: from Latin *prōpellere* to PROPEL] ▸ **propulsive** (prəˈpʌlsɪv) *or* **proˈpulsory** *adj*

propyl (ˈprəʊpɪl) *n* (*modifier*) of, consisting of, or containing the monovalent group of atoms C_3H_7-: *a propyl group or radical.* [C19: from PROP(IONIC ACID) + -YL]

propylaeum (ˌprɒpɪˈliːəm) *or* **propylon** (ˈprɒpɪˌlɒn) *n, pl* **-laea** (-ˈliːə) *or* **-lons, -la.** a portico, esp. one that forms the entrance to a temple. [C18: via Latin from Greek *propulaion* before the gate, from PRO-[2] + *pulē* gate]

propylene (ˈprəʊpɪˌliːn) *n* another name for **propene.** [C19: from PROPYL + -ENE]

propylene glycol *n* a colourless viscous hydroscopic sweet-tasting compound used as an antifreeze and brake fluid. Formula: $CH_3CHOHCH_2OH$. Systematic name: **1,2-dihydroxypropane.**

propylite (ˈprɒpɪˌlaɪt) *n Geology.* an altered andesite or similar rock containing calcite, chlorite, etc., produced by the action of hot water. [C20: from *propylon* (see PROPYLAEUM) + -ITE[1]; so named because it is associated with the start of the Tertiary volcanic era]

pro rata (ˈprəʊ ˈrɑːtə) in proportion. [Medieval Latin]

prorate (prəʊˈreɪt, ˈprəʊreɪt) *vb Chiefly U.S. and Canadian.* to divide, assess, or distribute (something) proportionately. [C19: from PRO RATA] ▸ **proˈratable** *adj* ▸ **proˈration** *n*

prorogue (prəˈrəʊg) *vb* to discontinue the meetings of (a legislative body) without dissolving it. [C15: from Latin *prorogāre* literally: to ask publicly, from *prō-* in public + *rogāre* to ask] ▸ **prorogation** (ˌprəʊrəˈgeɪʃən) *n*

pros. *abbrev. for* prosody.

prosaic (prəʊˈzeɪɪk) *adj* **1** lacking imagination. **2** having the characteristics of prose. [C16: from Late Latin *prōsaicus,* from Latin *prōsa* PROSE] ▸ **proˈsaically** *adv* ▸ **proˈsaicness** *n*

prosaism (prəʊˈzeɪɪzəm) *or* **prosaicism** (prəʊˈzeɪɪˌsɪzəm) *n* **1** prosaic quality or style. **2** a prosaic expression, thought, etc. ▸ **proˈsaist** *n*

pros and cons *pl n* the various arguments in favour of and against a motion, course of action, etc. [C16: from Latin *prō* for + *con,* from *contrā* against]

proscenium (prəˈsiːnɪəm) *n, pl* **-nia** (-nɪə) *or* **-niums. 1** the arch or opening separating the stage from the auditorium together with the area immediately in front of the arch. **2** (in ancient theatres) the stage itself. [C17: via Latin from Greek *proskēnion,* from *pro-* before + *skēnē* scene]

prosciutto (prəʊˈʃuːtəʊ; *Italian* proˈʃutto) *n* cured ham from Italy: usually served as an hors d'oeuvre. [Italian, literally: dried beforehand, from *pro-* PRE- + *asciutto* dried]

proscribe (prəʊˈskraɪb) *vb* (*tr*) **1** to condemn or prohibit. **2** to outlaw; banish; exile. **3** (in ancient Rome) to outlaw (a citizen) by posting his name in public. [C16: from Latin *prōscrībere* to put up a written public notice, from *prō-* in public + *scrībere* to write] ▸ **proˈscriber** *n*

proscription (prəʊˈskrɪpʃən) *n* **1** the act of proscribing or the state of being proscribed. **2** denunciation, prohibition, or exclusion. **3** outlawry or ostracism. [C14: from Latin *prōscriptiō;* see PROSCRIBE] ▸ **proˈscriptive** *adj* ▸ **proˈscriptively** *adv* ▸ **proˈscriptiveness** *n*

prose (prəʊz) *n* **1** spoken or written language as in ordinary usage, distinguished from poetry by its lack of a marked metrical structure. **2** a passage set for translation into a foreign language. **3** commonplace or dull discourse, expression, etc. **4** *R.C. Church.* a hymn recited or sung after the gradual at Mass. **5** (*modifier*) written in prose. **6** (*modifier*) matter-of-fact. ◆ *vb* **7** to write or say (something) in prose. **8** (*intr*) to speak or write in a tedious style. [C14: via Old French from Latin phrase *prōsa ōrātiō* straightforward speech, from *prorsus* prosaic, from *prōvertere* to turn forwards, from PRO-[1] + *vertere* to turn] ▸ **ˈproseˌlike** *adj*

prosector (prəʊˈsɛktə) *n* a person who prepares or dissects anatomical subjects for demonstration. [C19: from Latin, from *prōsecare* to cut up; probably on the model of French *prosecteur*]

prosecute (ˈprɒsɪˌkjuːt) *vb* **1** (*tr*) to bring a criminal action against (a person) for some offence. **2** (*intr*) **2a** to seek redress by legal proceedings. **2b** to institute or conduct a prosecution. **3** (*tr*) to engage in or practise (a profession or trade). **4** (*tr*) to continue to do (a task, etc.). [C15: from Latin *prōsequī* to follow, from *prō-* forward + *sequī* to follow] ▸ **ˈproseˌcutable** *adj*

prosecuting attorney *n U.S. Law.* (in some states) an officer in a judicial district appointed to conduct criminal prosecutions on behalf of the state and people.

prosecution (ˌprɒsɪˈkjuːʃən) *n* **1** the act of prosecuting or the state of being prosecuted. **2a** the institution and conduct of legal proceedings against a person. **2b** the proceedings brought in the name of the Crown to put an accused on trial. **3** the lawyers acting for the Crown to put the case against a person. Compare **defence** (sense 6). **4** the following up or carrying on of something begun, esp. with a view to its accomplishment or completion.

prosecutor (ˈprɒsɪˌkjuːtə) *n* a person who institutes or conducts legal proceedings, esp. in a criminal court.

proselyte (ˈprɒsɪˌlaɪt) *n* **1** a person newly converted to a religious faith or sect; a convert, esp. a gentile converted to Judaism. ◆ *vb* **2** a less common word for **proselytize.** [C14: from Church Latin *prosēlytus,* from Greek *prosēlutos* recent arrival, convert, from *proserchesthai* to draw near] ▸ **proselytism** (ˈprɒsɪlɪˌtɪzəm) *n* ▸ **proselytic** (ˌprɒsɪˈlɪtɪk) *adj*

proselytize *or* **proselytise** (ˈprɒsɪlɪˌtaɪz) *vb* to convert (someone) from one

ˌ**proreˈform** *adj*

religious faith to another. ▸ ˌproselytiˈzation *or* ˌproselytiˈsation *n* ▸ ˈproselytˌizer *or* ˈproselytˌiser *n*

prosencephalon (ˌprɒsɛnˈsɛfəlɒn) *n, pl* **-la** (-lə). the part of the brain that develops from the anterior portion of the neural tube. Compare **mesencephalon, rhombencephalon.** Nontechnical name: **forebrain.** [C19: from New Latin, from Greek *prosō* forward + *enkephalos* brain] ▸ **prosencephalic** (ˌprɒsɛnsɪˈfælɪk) *adj*

prosenchyma (prɒsˈɛŋkɪmə) *n* a plant tissue consisting of long narrow cells with pointed ends: occurs in conducting tissue. [C19: from New Latin, from Greek *pros-* towards + *enkhuma* infusion; compare PARENCHYMA] ▸ **prosenchymatous** (ˌprɒsɛnˈkaɪmətəs) *adj*

prose poem *n* a prose composition characterized by a poetic style.

Proserpina (prəʊˈsɜːpɪnə) *n* the Roman goddess of the underworld. Greek counterpart: **Persephone.**

prosimian (prəʊˈsɪmɪən) *n* **1** any primate of the primitive suborder *Prosimii,* including lemurs, lorises, and tarsiers. ◆ *adj* **2** of, relating to, or belonging to the *Prosimii.* ◆ Compare **anthropoid** (sense 4). [C19: via New Latin from PRO-[2] + Latin *sīmia* ape]

prosit *German.* (ˈproːzɪt) *interj* good health! cheers! [German, from Latin, literally: may it prove beneficial]

prosody (ˈprɒsədɪ) *n* **1** the study of poetic metre and of the art of versification, including rhyme, stanzaic forms, and the quantity and stress of syllables. **2** a system of versification. **3** the patterns of stress and intonation in a language. [C15: from Latin *prosōdia* accent of a syllable, from Greek *prosōidia* song set to music, from *pros* towards + *ōidē,* from *aoidē* song; see ODE] ▸ **prosodic** (prəˈsɒdɪk) *adj* ▸ ˈ**prosodist** *n*

prosoma (prəʊˈsəʊmə) *n, pl* **-mas** *or* **-mata** (-mətə). *Zoology.* the head and thorax of an arachnid.

prosopagnosia (ˌprɒsəpægˈnəʊsɪə) *n* an inability to recognize faces. [C20: from Greek *prosōpon* face + AGNOSIA]

prosopography (ˌprɒsəˈpɒgrəfɪ) *n* **1** a description of a person's life and career. **2** the study of such descriptions as part of history, esp. Roman history. [C16: from New Latin *prosopographia,* from Greek *prosōpon* face, person + -GRAPHY] ▸ ˌ**prosoˈpographer** *n* ▸ **prosopographical** (ˌprɒsəpəˈgræfɪkᵊl) *adj* ▸ ˌ**prosopoˈgraphically** *adv*

prosopopoeia *or* **prosopopeia** (ˌprɒsəpəˈpiːə) *n* **1** *Rhetoric.* another word for **personification. 2** a figure of speech that represents an imaginary, absent, or dead person speaking or acting. [C16: via Latin from Greek *prosōpopoiia* dramatization, from *prosōpon* face + *poiein* to make] ▸ ˌ**prosopoˈpoeial** *or* ˌ**prosopoˈpeial** *adj*

prospect *n* (ˈprɒspɛkt). **1** (*sometimes pl*) a probability or chance for future success, esp. as based on present work or aptitude: *a good job with prospects.* **2** a vision of the future; what is foreseen; expectation: *she was excited at the prospect of living in London; unemployment presents a grim prospect.* **3** a view or scene, esp. one offering an extended outlook. **4** a prospective buyer, project, etc. **5** a survey or observation. **6** *Mining.* **6a** a known or likely deposit of ore. **6b** the location of a deposit of ore. **6c** a sample of ore for testing. **6d** the yield of mineral obtained from a sample of ore. ◆ *vb* (prəˈspɛkt). **7** (when *intr,* often foll. by *for*) to explore (a region) for gold or other valuable minerals. **8** (*tr*) to work (a mine) to discover its profitability. **9** (*intr;* often foll. by *for*) to search (for). [C15: from Latin *prōspectus* distant view, from *prōspicere* to look into the distance, from *prō-* forward + *specere* to look] ▸ ˈ**prospectless** *adj*

prospective (prəˈspɛktɪv) *adj* **1** looking towards the future. **2** (*prenominal*) anticipated or likely. ▸ **proˈspectively** *adv*

prospector (prəˈspɛktə) *n* a person who searches for the natural occurrence of gold, petroleum, etc.

prospectus (prəˈspɛktəs) *n, pl* **-tuses. 1** a formal statement giving details of a forthcoming event, such as the publication of a book or an issue of shares. **2** a pamphlet or brochure giving details of courses, as at a college or school. [C18: Latin, literally: distant view; see PROSPECT]

prosper (ˈprɒspə) *vb* (*usually intr*) to thrive, succeed, etc., or cause to thrive, succeed, etc. in a healthy way. [C15: from Latin *prosperāre* to succeed, from *prosperus* fortunate, from PRO-[1] + *spēs* hope]

prosperity (prɒˈspɛrɪtɪ) *n* the condition of prospering; success or wealth.

prosperous (ˈprɒspərəs) *adj* **1** flourishing; prospering. **2** rich; affluent; wealthy. **3** favourable or promising. ▸ ˈ**prosperously** *adv* ▸ ˈ**prosperousness** *n*

Prost (*French* prɔst) *n* **Alain** (alɛ̃). born 1955, French motor-racing driver: world champion 1985, 1986, 1989, and 1993.

prostaglandin (ˌprɒstəˈglændɪn) *n* any of a group of potent hormone-like compounds composed of essential fatty acids and found in all mammalian tissues, esp. human semen. Prostaglandins stimulate the muscles of the uterus and affect the blood vessels; they are used to induce abortion or birth. [C20: from *prosta(te) gland* + -IN; it was originally believed to be secreted by the prostate gland]

prostate (ˈprɒsteɪt) *n* **1** Also called: **prostate gland.** a gland in male mammals that surrounds the neck of the bladder and urethra and secretes a liquid constituent of the semen. ◆ *adj* **2** Also: **prostatic** (prɒˈstætɪk). of or relating to the prostate gland. See also **PSA.** [C17: via Medieval Latin from Greek *prostatēs* something standing in front (of the bladder), from *pro-* in front + *histanai* to cause to stand]

prostatectomy (ˌprɒstəˈtɛktəmɪ) *n, pl* **-mies.** surgical removal of all or a part of the prostate gland.

prostatitis (ˌprɒstəˈtaɪtɪs) *n* inflammation of the prostate gland.

prosternum (prəʊˈstɜːnəm) *n, pl* **-na** (-nə) *or* **-nums.** the sternum of the prothorax of an insect.

prosthesis (ˈprɒsθɪsɪs, prɒsˈθiːsɪs) *n, pl* **-ses** (-ˌsiːz). **1** *Surgery.* **1a** the replacement of a missing bodily part with an artificial substitute. **1b** an artificial part such as a limb, eye, or tooth. **2** *Linguistics.* another word for **prothesis.** [C16: via Late Latin from Greek: an addition, from *prostithenai* to add, from *pros-* towards + *tithenai* to place] ▸ **prosthetic** (prɒsˈθɛtɪk) *adj* ▸ **prosˈthetically** *adv*

prosthetic group *n* the nonprotein component of a conjugated protein, such as the lipid group in a lipoprotein.

prosthetics (prɒsˈθɛtɪks) *n* (*functioning as sing*) the branch of surgery concerned with prosthesis.

prosthodontics (ˌprɒsθəˈdɒntɪks) *n* (*functioning as sing*) the branch of dentistry concerned with the artificial replacement of missing teeth. [C20: from PROSTH(ESIS) + -ODONT + -ICS] ▸ ˌ**prosthoˈdontist** *n*

prostitute (ˈprɒstɪˌtjuːt) *n* **1** a woman who engages in sexual intercourse for money. **2** a man who engages in such activity, esp. in homosexual practices. **3** a person who offers his talent or work for unworthy purposes. ◆ *vb* (*tr*) **4** to offer (oneself or another) in sexual intercourse for money. **5** to offer (a person, esp. oneself, or a person's talent) for unworthy purposes. [C16: from Latin *prōstituere* to expose to prostitution, from *prō-* in public + *statuere* to cause to stand] ▸ ˌ**prostiˈtution** *n* ▸ ˈ**prostiˌtutor** *n*

prostomium (prəʊˈstəʊmɪəm) *n, pl* **-mia** (-mɪə). the lobe at the head end of earthworms and other annelids: bears tentacles, palps, etc., or forms part of a sucker or proboscis. [via New Latin from Greek *prostomion* mouth] ▸ **proˈstomial** *adj*

prostrate *adj* (ˈprɒstreɪt). **1** lying with the face downwards, as in submission. **2** exhausted physically or emotionally. **3** helpless or defenceless. **4** (of a plant) growing closely along the ground. ◆ *vb* (prɒˈstreɪt). (*tr*) **5** to bow or cast (oneself) down, as in submission. **6** to lay or throw down flat, as on the ground. **7** to make helpless or defenceless. **8** to make exhausted. [C14: from Latin *prōsternere* to throw to the ground, from *prō-* before + *sternere* to lay low] ▸ **prosˈtration** *n*

prostyle (ˈprəʊstaɪl) *adj* **1** (of a building) having a row of columns in front, esp. as in the portico of a Greek temple. ◆ *n* **2** a prostyle building, portico, etc. [C17: from Latin *prostȳlos,* from Greek: with pillars in front, from PRO-[2] + *stulos* pillar]

prosy (ˈprəʊzɪ) *adj* **prosier, prosiest. 1** of the nature of or similar to prose. **2** dull, tedious, or long-winded. ▸ ˈ**prosily** *adv* ▸ ˈ**prosiness** *n*

Prot. *abbrev. for:* **1** Protestant. **2** Protectorate.

prot- *combining form.* a variant of **proto-** before a vowel.

protactinium (ˌprəʊtækˈtɪnɪəm) *n* a toxic radioactive metallic element that occurs in uranium ores and is produced by neutron irradiation of thorium. Symbol: Pa; atomic no.: 91; half-life of the most stable isotope, ^{231}Pa: 32 500 years; valency: 4 or 5; relative density: 15.37 (calc.); melting pt.: 1572°C. Former name: **protoactinium.**

protagonist (prəʊˈtægənɪst) *n* **1** the principal character in a play, story, etc. **2** a supporter, esp. when important or respected, of a cause, political party, etc. [C17: from Greek *prōtagōnistēs,* from *prōtos* first + *agōnistēs* actor] ▸ **proˈtagonism** *n*

Protagoras (prəʊˈtægəˌræs) *n* ?485–?411 B.C., Greek philosopher and sophist, famous for his dictum "Man is the measure of all things."

protamine (ˈprəʊtəˌmiːn) *n* any of a group of basic simple proteins that occur, in association with nucleic acids, in the sperm of some fish. [C19: from German: see PROTO-, AMINE]

protandrous (prəʊˈtændrəs) *adj* (of plants and hermaphrodite animals) producing male gametes before female gametes. Compare **protogynous.** ▸ **proˈtandry** *n*

protanopia (ˌprəʊtəˈnəʊpɪə) *n* a form of colour blindness characterized by a tendency to confuse reds and greens and by a loss of sensitivity to red light. [C20: New Latin, from PROTO- + AN- + -OPIA] ▸ **protanopic** (ˌprəʊtəˈnɒpɪk) *adj*

protasis (ˈprɒtəsɪs) *n, pl* **-ses** (-siːz). **1** *Logic, grammar.* the antecedent of a conditional statement, such as *it rains* in *if it rains the game will be cancelled.* Compare **apodosis. 2** (in classical drama) the introductory part of a play. [C17: via Latin from Greek: a proposal, from *pro-* before + *teinein* to extend] ▸ **protatic** (prɒˈtætɪk) *adj*

protea (ˈprəʊtɪə) *n* any shrub or small tree of the genus *Protea,* of tropical and southern Africa, having flowers with coloured bracts arranged in showy heads: family *Proteaceae.* [C20: from New Latin, from PROTEUS, referring to the large number of different forms of the plant] ▸ **proteaceous** (ˌprəʊtɪˈeɪʃəs) *adj*

protean (prəʊˈtiːən, ˈprəʊtɪən) *adj* readily taking on various shapes or forms; variable. [C16: from PROTEUS]

protease (ˈprəʊtɪˌeɪs) *n* any enzyme involved in proteolysis. [C20: from PROTEIN + -ASE]

protease inhibitor *n* any one of a class of antiviral drugs that impair the growth and replication of HIV by inhibiting the action of protease produced by the virus: used in the treatment of AIDS.

protect (prəˈtɛkt) *vb* (*tr*) **1** to defend from trouble, harm, attack, etc. **2** *Economics.* to assist (domestic industries) by the imposition of protective tariffs on imports. **3** *Commerce.* to provide funds in advance to guarantee payment of (a note, draft, etc.). [C16: from Latin *prōtegere* to cover before, from PRO-[1] + *tegere* to cover]

protectant (prəˈtɛktənt) *n* a chemical substance that affords protection, as against frost, rust, insects, etc.

proˈslavery *adj* **pro-ˈSoviet** *adj*

protection (prəˈtɛkʃən) *n* **1** the act of protecting or the condition of being protected. **2** something that protects. **3a** the imposition of duties or quotas on imports, designed for the protection of domestic industries against overseas competition, expansion of domestic employment, etc. **3b** Also called: **protectionism**. the system, policy, or theory of such restrictions. Compare **free trade**. **4** a document that grants protection or immunity from arrest or harassment to a person, esp. a traveller. **5** *Mountaineering*. security on a climb provided by running belays, etc. **6** *Informal*. **6a** Also called: **protection money**. money demanded by gangsters for freedom from molestation. **6b** freedom from molestation purchased in this way. ▸ **proˈtectionˌism** *n* ▸ **proˈtectionist** *n, adj*

protection ratio *n* the minimum acceptable ratio between the amplitudes of a wanted radio or television broadcast signal and any interfering signal.

protective (prəˈtɛktɪv) *adj* **1** giving or capable of giving protection. **2** *Economics*. of, relating to, or intended for protection of domestic industries. ◆ *n* **3** something that protects. **4** a condom. ▸ **proˈtectively** *adv* ▸ **proˈtectiveness** *n*

protective coloration *n* the coloration of an animal that enables it to blend with its surroundings and therefore escape the attention of predators.

protective tariff *n* a tariff levied on imports to protect the domestic economy rather than to raise revenue.

protector (prəˈtɛktə) *n* **1** a person or thing that protects. **2** *History*. a person who exercised royal authority during the minority, absence, or incapacity of the monarch. ▸ **proˈtectoral** *adj* ▸ **proˈtectress** *fem n*

Protector (prəˈtɛktə) *n* short for **Lord Protector**, the title borne by Oliver Cromwell (1653–58) and by Richard Cromwell (1658–59) as heads of state during the period known as the **Protectorate**.

protectorate (prəˈtɛktərɪt) *n* **1a** a territory largely controlled by but not annexed to a stronger state. **1b** the relation of a protecting state to its protected territory. **2** the office or period of office of a protector.

protectory (prəˈtɛktərɪ) *n, pl* **-ries**. an institution for the care of homeless, delinquent, or destitute children.

protégé *or* (*fem*) **protégée** (ˈprəʊtɪˌʒeɪ) *n* a person who is protected and aided by the patronage of another person. [C18: from French *protéger* to PROTECT]

protein (ˈprəʊtiːn) *n* any of a large group of nitrogenous compounds of high molecular weight that are essential constituents of all living organisms. They consist of one or more chains of amino acids linked by peptide bonds and are folded into a specific three-dimensional shape maintained by further chemical bonding. [C19: via German from Greek *prōteios* primary, from *protos* first + -IN] ▸ **ˌproteinˈaceous, proˈteinic,** *or* **proˈteinous** *adj*

proteinase (ˈprəʊtɪˌneɪs, -ˌneɪz) *n* another name for **endopeptidase**.

proteinuria (ˌprəʊtɪˈnjʊərɪə) *n Med*. another name for **albuminuria**.

pro tempore *Latin*. (ˈprəʊ ˈtɛmpərɪ) *adv, adj* for the time being. Often shortened to **pro tem** (ˈprəʊ ˈtɛm).

proteolysis (ˌprəʊtɪˈɒlɪsɪs) *n* the hydrolysis of proteins into simpler compounds by the action of enzymes: occurs esp. during digestion. [C19: from New Latin, from *proteo-* (from PROTEIN) + -LYSIS] ▸ **proteolytic** (ˌprəʊtɪəˈlɪtɪk) *adj*

proteose (ˈprəʊtɪˌəʊs, -ˌəʊz) *n Now rare*. any of a group of compounds formed during proteolysis that are less complex than metaproteins but more so than peptones. Also called (esp. U.S.): **albumose**. [C20: from PROTEIN + -OSE[2]]

protero- *combining form*. anterior or former in time, place, order, etc.: *proterozoic*. [from Greek *proteros* fore]

Proterozoic (ˌprəʊtərəʊˈzəʊɪk) *n* **1** the later of two divisions of the Precambrian era, during which the earliest plants and animals are assumed to have lived. Compare **Archaeozoic**. ◆ *adj* **2** of or formed in the late Precambrian era.

protest *n* (ˈprəʊtest). **1a** public, often organized, dissent or manifestation of such dissent. **1b** (*as modifier*): *a protest march*. **2** a declaration or objection that is formal or solemn. **3** an expression of disagreement or complaint: *without a squeak of protest*. **4a** a formal notarial statement drawn up on behalf of a creditor and declaring that the debtor has dishonoured a bill of exchange or promissory note. **4b** the action of drawing up such a statement. **4c** a formal declaration by a taxpayer disputing the legality or accuracy of his assessment. **5** a statement made by the master of a vessel attesting to the circumstances in which his vessel was damaged or imperilled. **6** the act of protesting. **7 under protest**. having voiced objections; unwillingly. ◆ *vb* (prəˈtest). **8** (when *intr*, foll. by *against, at, about*, etc.; when *tr, may take a clause as object*) to make a strong objection (to something, esp. a supposed injustice or offence). **9** (when *tr, may take a clause as object*) to assert or affirm in a formal or solemn manner. **10** (when *tr, may take a clause as object*) to put up arguments against; disagree; complain; object: *"I'm okay," she protested; he protested that it was not his turn to wash up*. **11** (*tr*) *Chiefly U.S.* to object forcefully to: *leaflets protesting Dr King's murder*. **12** (*tr*) to declare formally that (a bill of exchange or promissory note) has been dishonoured. [C14: from Latin *prōtestārī* to make a formal declaration, from *prō-* before + *testārī* to assert] ▸ **proˈtestant** *adj, n* ▸ **proˈtester** *or* **proˈtestor** *n* ▸ **proˈtestingly** *adv*

Protestant (ˈprɒtɪstənt) *n* **a** an adherent of Protestantism. **b** (*as modifier*): *the Protestant Church*.

Protestant Episcopal Church *n* the full title of the **Episcopal Church**.

Protestantism (ˈprɒtɪstənˌtɪzəm) *n* **1** the religion or religious system of any of the Churches of Western Christendom that are separated from the Roman Catholic Church and adhere substantially to principles established by Luther, Calvin, etc., in the Reformation. **2** the Protestant Churches collectively. **3** adherence to the principles of the Reformation.

protestation (ˌprəʊtesˈteɪʃən) *n* **1** the act of protesting. **2** something protested about. **3** a strong declaration.

Proteus (ˈprəʊtɪəs) *n Greek myth*. a prophetic sea god capable of changing his shape at will.

prothalamion (ˌprəʊθəˈleɪmɪən) *or* **prothalamium** *n, pl* **-mia** (-mɪə). a song or poem in celebration of a marriage. [C16: from Greek *pro-* before + *thalamos* marriage; coined by Edmund Spenser, on the model of EPITHALAMION]

prothallus (prəʊˈθæləs) *or* **prothallium** (prəʊˈθælɪəm) *n, pl* **-li** (-laɪ) *or* **-lia** (-lɪə). *Botany*. the small flat free-living green disc of tissue that bears the reproductive organs of ferns, horsetails, and club mosses. [C19: from New Latin, from *pro-* before + Greek *thallus* a young shoot] ▸ **proˈthallic** *or* **proˈthallial** *adj*

prothesis (ˈprɒθɪsɪs) *n* **1** a process in the development of a language by which a phoneme or syllable is prefixed to a word to facilitate pronunciation: *Latin "scala" gives Spanish "escala" by prothesis*. **2** *Eastern Orthodox Church*. the solemn preparation of the Eucharistic elements before consecration. [C16: via Late Latin from Greek: a setting out in public, from *pro-* forth + *thesis* a placing] ▸ **prothetic** (prəˈθɛtɪk) *adj* ▸ **proˈthetically** *adv*

prothonotary (ˌprəʊθəˈnəʊtərɪ, -trɪ, prəʊˈθɒnə-) *or* **protonotary** *n, pl* **-taries**. (formerly) a chief clerk in certain law courts. [C15: from Medieval Latin *prōthonotārius*, from *prōtho-* PROTO- + Late Latin *notārius* NOTARY] ▸ **prothonotarial** (prəʊˌθɒnəˈtɛərɪəl) *or* **proˌtonoˈtarial** *adj*

prothorax (prəʊˈθɔːræks) *n, pl* **-thoraxes** *or* **-thoraces** (-ˈθɔːrəˌsiːz). the first segment of the thorax of an insect, which bears the first pair of walking legs. See also **mesothorax, metathorax**.

prothrombin (prəʊˈθrɒmbɪn) *n Biochem*. a zymogen found in blood that gives rise to thrombin on activation. See also **phylloquinone**.

protist (ˈprəʊtɪst) *n* (in some classification systems) any organism belonging to the kingdom *Protista*, originally including bacteria, protozoans, algae, and fungi, regarded as distinct from plants and animals. It was later restricted to protozoans, unicellular algae, and simple fungi. See also **protoctist**. [C19: from New Latin *Protista* most primitive organisms, from Greek *prōtistos* the very first, from *prōtos* first]

protium (ˈprəʊtɪəm) *n* the most common isotope of hydrogen, having a mass number of 1. [C20: New Latin, from PROTO- + -IUM]

proto- *or sometimes before a vowel* **prot-** *combining form*. **1** indicating the first in time, order, or rank: *protomartyr*. **2** primitive, ancestral, or original: *prototype*. **3** indicating the reconstructed earliest stage of a language: *Proto-Germanic*. **4** indicating the first in a series of chemical compounds: *protoxide*. **5** indicating the parent of a chemical compound or an element: *protactinium*. [from Greek *prōtos* first, from *pro* before; see PRO-[2]]

protoactinium (ˌprəʊtəʊækˈtɪnɪəm) *n* the former name of **protactinium**.

protochordate (ˌprəʊtəʊˈkɔːdeɪt) *n* **1** any chordate animal of the subphyla *Hemichordata* (acorn worms), *Urochordata* (tunicates), and *Cephalochordata* (lancelets). ◆ *adj* **2** of or relating to protochordates.

protocol (ˈprəʊtəˌkɒl) *n* **1** the formal etiquette and code of behaviour, precedence, and procedure for state and diplomatic ceremonies. **2** a memorandum or record of an agreement, esp. one reached in international negotiations, a meeting, etc. **3a** an amendment to a treaty or convention. **3b** an annexe appended to a treaty to deal with subsidiary matters or to render the treaty more lucid. **3c** a formal international agreement or understanding on some matter. **4** *Philosophy*. In full: **protocol statement**. a statement that is immediately verifiable by experience. See **logical positivism**. **5** *Computing*. the set form in which data must be presented for handling by a particular computer configuration, esp. in the transmission of information between different computer systems. [C16: from Medieval Latin *prōtocollum*, from Late Greek *prōtokollon* sheet glued to the front of a manuscript, from PROTO- + *kolla* glue]

protoctist (prəʊˈtɒktɪst) *n* (in modern biological classifications) any unicellular or simple multicellular organism belonging to the kingdom *Protoctista*, which includes protozoans, algae, and slime moulds. [C19: from New Latin *protoctista*, perhaps from Greek *prototokos* first born]

protogenic (ˌprəʊtəˈdʒɛnɪk) *adj Chem*. (of a compound) able to donate a hydrogen ion (proton) in a chemical reaction.

Proto-Germanic *n* the prehistoric unrecorded language that was the ancestor of all Germanic languages.

protogynous (prəʊˈtɒdʒɪnəs) *adj* (of plants and hermaphrodite animals) producing female gametes before male ones. Compare **protandrous**. ▸ **proˈtogyny** *n*

protohistory (ˌprəʊtəʊˈhɪstərɪ, -ˈhɪstrɪ) *n* the period or stage of human development or of a particular culture immediately prior to the emergence of writing. ▸ **protohistoric** (ˌprəʊtəʊhɪˈstɒrɪk) *adj*

protohuman (ˌprəʊtəʊˈhjuːmən) *n* **1** any of various prehistoric primates that resembled modern man. ◆ *adj* **2** of or relating to any of these primates.

Proto-Indo-European *n* the prehistoric unrecorded language that was the ancestor of all Indo-European languages.

protolanguage (ˌprəʊtəʊˈlæŋgwɪdʒ) *n* an extinct and unrecorded language reconstructed by comparison of its recorded or living descendants. Also called: **Ursprache**.

protolithic (ˌprəʊtəʊˈlɪθɪk) *adj* of or referring to the earliest Stone Age.

protomartyr (ˌprəʊtəʊˈmɑːtə) *n* **1** St Stephen as the first Christian martyr. **2** the first martyr to lay down his life in any cause.

protomorphic (ˌprəʊtəʊˈmɔːfɪk) *adj Biology*. primitive in structure; primordial.

proton (ˈprəʊtɒn) *n* a stable, positively charged elementary particle, found in atomic nuclei in numbers equal to the atomic number of the element. It is a baryon with a charge of 1.6022×10^{-19} coulomb, a rest mass of $1.672\,52 \times 10^{-27}$ kilogram, and spin ½. [C20: from Greek *prōtos* first]

protonema (ˌprəʊtəˈniːmə) *n, pl* **-nemata** (-ˈniːmətə). a branched threadlike structure that grows from a moss spore and eventually develops into the moss plant. [C19: from New Latin, from PROTO- + Greek *nema* thread] ▸ ˌ**proto'nemal** *or* **protonematal** (ˌprəʊtə'ni:mət^əl, -'nɛmət^əl) *adj*

protonic (prəʊ'tɒnɪk) *adj Chem.* (of a solvent, such as water) able to donate hydrogen ions to solute molecules.

proton microscope *n* a powerful type of microscope that uses a beam of protons, giving high resolution and sharp contrast.

proton number *n* another name for **atomic number.** Symbol: *Z*

Proto-Norse *n* the North Germanic language of Scandinavia up to about 700 A.D. See also **Old Norse.**

protopathic (ˌprəʊtə'pæθɪk) *adj Physiol.* **1** of or relating to a sensory nerve that perceives only coarse stimuli, such as pain. **2** of or relating to such perception. [C20: from PROTO- + Greek *pathos* suffering, disease + -IC] ▸ **protopathy** (prəʊ'tɒpəθɪ) *n*

protophilic (ˌprəʊtə'fɪlɪk) *adj Chem.* having or involving an affinity for hydrogen ions (protons).

protoplasm ('prəʊtəˌplæzəm) *n Biology.* the living contents of a cell: a complex translucent colourless colloidal substance differentiated into cytoplasm and nucleoplasm. [C19: from New Latin, from PROTO- + Greek *plasma* form] ▸ ˌ**proto'plasmic** *adj*

protoplast ('prəʊtəˌplæst) *n* a unit consisting of the living parts of a cell, including the protoplasm and cell membrane but not the vacuoles or (in plants) the cell wall. [C16: from Late Latin *prōtoplastus* the first-formed, from Greek *prōtoplastos,* from PROTO- + *plassein* to shape] ▸ ˌ**proto'plastic** *adj*

protoporphyrin (ˌprəʊtəʊ'pɔ:fɪrɪn) *n* a type of porphyrin that, when combined with an iron atom, forms haem, the oxygen-bearing prosthetic group of the red blood pigment haemoglobin.

Protosemitic (ˌprəʊtəʊsɪ'mɪtɪk) *n* the hypothetical parent language of the Semitic group of languages.

protostar ('prəʊtəʊˌstɑ:) *n* a cloud of interstellar gas and dust that gradually collapses, forming a hot dense core, and evolves into a star once nuclear fusion can occur in the core.

protostele ('prəʊtəˌsti:l, -ˌsti:lɪ) *n* a simple type of stele with a central core of xylem surrounded by a cylinder of phloem: occurs in most roots and the stems of ferns, etc. ▸ ˌ**proto'stelic** *adj*

prototherian (ˌprəʊtəʊ'θɪərɪən) *adj* **1** of, relating to, or belonging to the *Prototheria,* a subclass of mammals that includes the monotremes. ◆ *n* **2** any prototherian mammal; a monotreme. ◆ Compare **eutherian, metatherian.** [C19: New Latin, from PROTO- + Greek *theria* wild animals]

prototrophic (ˌprəʊtə'trɒfɪk) *adj* **1** (esp. of bacteria) feeding solely on inorganic matter. **2** (of cultured bacteria, fungi, etc.) having no specific food requirements.

prototype ('prəʊtəˌtaɪp) *n* **1** one of the first units manufactured of a product, which is tested so that the design can be changed if necessary before the product is manufactured commercially. **2** a person or thing that serves as an example of a type. **3** *Biology.* the ancestral or primitive form of a species or other group; an archetype. ▸ ˌ**proto'typal, prototypic** (ˌprəʊtə'tɪpɪk), *or* ˌ**proto'typical** *adj*

protoxide (prəʊ'tɒksaɪd) *n* the oxide of an element that contains the smallest amount of oxygen of any of its oxides.

protoxylem (ˌprəʊtə'zaɪləm) *n* the first-formed xylem tissue, consisting of extensible thin-walled cells thickened with rings or spirals of lignin. Compare **metaxylem.**

protozoan (ˌprəʊtə'zəʊən) *n, pl* **-zoa** (-'zəʊə) *or* **-zoans. 1** Also called: **protozoon** (ˌprəʊtə'zəʊɒn), *pl* **-zoa.** any of various minute unicellular organisms formerly regarded as invertebrates of the phylum *Protozoa* but now usually classified in certain phyla of protoctists. Protozoans include flagellates, ciliates, sporozoans, amoebas, and foraminifers. ◆ *adj also* ˌ**proto'zoic. 2** of or relating to protozoans. [C19: via New Latin from Greek PROTO- + *zōion* animal]

protozoology (ˌprəʊtəʊzəʊ'ɒlədʒɪ) *n* the branch of biology concerned with the study of protozoans. ▸ **protozoological** (ˌprəʊtəʊˌzəʊə'lɒdʒɪk^əl) *adj* ▸ ˌ**protozo'ologist** *n*

protract (prə'trækt) *vb (tr)* **1** to lengthen or extend (a speech, etc.); prolong in time. **2** (of a muscle) to draw, thrust, or extend (a part, etc.) forwards. **3** to plot or draw using a protractor and scale. [C16: from Latin *prōtrahere* to prolong, from PRO-[1] + *trahere* to drag] ▸ **pro'tractedly** *adv* ▸ **pro'tractedness** *n* ▸ **pro'tractive** *adj*

protractile (prə'træktaɪl) *or* (*less commonly*) **protractible** *adj* able to be extended or protruded: *protractile muscle.*

protraction (prə'trækʃən) *n* **1** the act or process of protracting. **2** the state or condition of being protracted. **3** a prolongation or protrusion. **4** an extension of something in time or space. **5** something that is extended in time or space. **6** the irregular lengthening of a syllable that is usually short.

protractor (prə'træktə) *n* **1** an instrument for measuring or drawing angles on paper, usually a flat semicircular transparent plastic sheet graduated in degrees. **2** a person or thing that protracts. **3** a surgical instrument for removing a bullet from the body. **4** *Anatomy.* a former term for **extensor.**

protrude (prə'tru:d) *vb* **1** to thrust or cause to thrust forwards or outwards. **2** to project or cause to project from or as if from a surface. [C17: from Latin, from PRO-[2] + *trudere* to thrust] ▸ **pro'trudable** *adj* ▸ **pro'trudent** *adj*

protrusile (prə'tru:saɪl) *adj Zoology.* capable of being thrust forwards: *protrusile jaws.* Also: **projectile.**

protrusion (prə'tru:ʒən) *n* **1** something that protrudes. **2** the state or condition of being protruded. **3** the act or process of protruding.

protrusive (prə'tru:sɪv) *adj* **1** tending to project or jut outwards. **2** a less common word for **obtrusive. 3** *Archaic.* causing propulsion. ▸ **pro'trusively** *adv* ▸ **pro'trusiveness** *n*

protuberant (prə'tju:bərənt) *adj* swelling out from the surrounding surface; bulging. [C17: from Late Latin *prōtūberāre* to swell, from PRO-[1] + *tūber* swelling] ▸ **pro'tuberance** *or* **pro'tuberancy** *n* ▸ **pro'tuberantly** *adv*

protuberate (prə'tju:bəˌreɪt) *vb (intr) Rare.* to swell out or project from the surrounding surface; bulge out.

protyle ('prəʊtaɪl) *or* **protyl** ('prəʊtɪl) *n* a hypothetical primitive substance from which the chemical elements were supposed to have been formed. [C19: from Greek *prōt-* PROTO- + *hylē* substance]

proud (praʊd) *adj* **1** (foll. by *of,* an infinitive, or a clause) pleased or satisfied, as with oneself, one's possessions, achievements, etc, or with another person, his or her achievements, qualities, etc. **2** feeling honoured or gratified by or as if by some distinction. **3** having an inordinately high opinion of oneself; arrogant or haughty. **4** characterized by or proceeding from a sense of pride: *a proud moment.* **5** having a proper sense of self-respect. **6** stately or distinguished. **7** bold or fearless. **8** (of a surface, edge, etc.) projecting or protruding from the surrounding area. **9** (of animals) restive or excited, esp. sexually; on heat. ◆ *adv* **10 do (someone) proud. 10a** to entertain (someone) on a grand scale: *they did us proud at the hotel.* **10b** to honour or distinguish (a person): *his honesty did him proud.* [Late Old English *prūd,* from Old French *prud, prod* brave, from Late Latin *prōde* useful, from Latin *prōdesse* to be of value, from *prōd-,* variant of *prō-* for + *esse* to be] ▸ **'proudly** *adv* ▸ **'proudness** *n*

proud flesh *n* a nontechnical name for **granulation tissue.** [C14: from PROUD (in the sense: swollen, protruding)]

Proudhon (*French* prudɔ̃) *n* **Pierre Joseph** (pjɛr ʒozɛf). 1809–65, French socialist, whose pamphlet *What is Property?* (1840) declared that property is theft.

Proust (*French* prust) *n* **1 Joseph Louis** (ʒozɛf lwi). 1754–1826, French chemist, who formulated the law of constant proportions. **2 Marcel** (marsɛl). 1871–1922, French novelist whose long novel *À la recherche du temps perdu* (1913–27) deals with the relationship of the narrator to themes such as art, time, memory, and society.

Proustian ('pru:stɪən) *adj* **1** of or relating to Marcel Proust, his works, or his style. ◆ *n* **2** an admirer of Marcel Proust's works.

proustite ('pru:staɪt) *n* a red mineral consisting of silver arsenic sulphide in hexagonal crystalline form. Formula: Ag_3AsS_3. [C19: from French, named after J. L. PROUST]

Prout (praʊt) *n* **1 Ebenezer.** 1835–1909, English musicologist and composer, noted for his editions of works by Handel and J. S. Bach. **2 William.** 1785–1850, English chemist, noted for his modification of the atomic theory.

prov. *abbrev. for:* **1** province. **2** provincial. **3** provisional.

Prov. *abbrev. for:* **1** Provençal. **2** *Bible.* Proverbs. **3** Province. **4** Provost.

prove (pru:v) *vb* **proves, proving, proved; proved** *or* **proven.** (*mainly tr*) **1** (*may take a clause as object or an infinitive*) to establish or demonstrate the truth or validity of; verify, esp. by using an established sequence of procedures or statements. **2** to establish the quality of, esp. by experiment or scientific analysis. **3** *Law.* to establish the validity and genuineness of (a will). **4** to show (oneself) able or courageous. **5** (*copula*) to be found or shown (to be): *this has proved useless; he proved to be invaluable.* **6** *Printing.* to take a trial impression of (type, etc.). **7** (*intr*) (of dough) to rise in a warm place before baking. **8** *Archaic.* to undergo. [C12: from Old French *prover,* from Latin *probāre* to test, from *probus* honest] ▸ **'provable** *adj* ▸ ˌ**prova'bility** *n* ▸ **'provably** *adv*

proven ('pru:v^ən) *vb* **1** a past participle of **prove. 2** See **not proven.** ◆ *adj* **3** tried; tested: *a proven method.* ▸ **'provenly** *adv*

provenance ('prɒvɪnəns) *or* (*chiefly U.S.*) **provenience** (prəʊ'vi:nɪəns) *n* a place of origin, esp. that of a work of art or archaeological specimen. [C19: from French, from *provenir,* from Latin *prōvenīre* to originate, from *venīre* to come]

Provençal (ˌprɒvɒn'sɑ:l; *French* prɔvɑ̃sal) *adj* **1** relating to, denoting, or characteristic of Provence, its inhabitants, their dialect of French, or their Romance language. ◆ *n* **2** a language of Provence, closely related to Catalan, French, and Italian, belonging to the Romance group of the Indo-European family. It was important in the Middle Ages as a literary language, and attempts have been made since the 19th century to revive its literary status. See also **langue d'oc. 3** a native or inhabitant of Provence.

Provençale (ˌprɒvɒn'sɑ:l; *French* prɔvɑ̃sal) *adj* (of dishes) prepared with garlic, oil, and often tomatoes.

Provence (*French* prɔvɑ̃s) *n* a former province of SE France, on the Mediterranean, and the River Rhône: forms part of the administrative region of Provence-Alpes-Côte d'Azur.

provender ('prɒvɪndə) *n* **1** any dry feed or fodder for domestic livestock. **2** food in general. [C14: from Old French *provendre,* from Late Latin *praebenda* grant, from Latin *praebēre* to proffer; influenced also by Latin *prōvidēre* to look after]

proventriculus (ˌprəʊvɛn'trɪkjʊləs) *n, pl* **-triculi** (-'trɪkjʊˌlaɪ). **1** the first part of the stomach of birds, the gizzard. **2** the thick muscular stomach of crustaceans and insects; gizzard. [C19: from New Latin, from Latin PRO-[1] + *ventriculus* little belly, from *venter* belly] ▸ ˌ**proven'tricular** *adj*

proverb ('prɒvɜ:b) *n* **1** a short, memorable, and often highly condensed saying embodying, esp. with bold imagery, some commonplace fact or experience. **2** a person or thing exemplary in respect of a characteristic: *Antarctica is a proverb for extreme cold.* **3** *Ecclesiast.* a wise saying or admonition providing guidance. ◆ *vb (tr)* **4** to utter or describe (something) in the form of a proverb. **5** to make

pro'union *adj*

(something) a proverb. [C14: via Old French from Latin *prōverbium*, from *verbum* word]

proverbial (prə'vɜːbɪəl) *adj* **1** (*prenominal*) commonly or traditionally referred to, esp. as being an example of some peculiarity, characteristic, etc. **2** of, connected with, embodied in, or resembling a proverb. ▸ **pro'verbially** *adv*

Proverbs ('prɒvɜːbz) *n* (*functioning as sing*) a book of the Old Testament consisting of the proverbs of various Israelite sages including Solomon.

provide (prə'vaɪd) *vb* (*mainly tr*) **1** to put at the disposal of; furnish or supply. **2** to afford; yield: *this meeting provides an opportunity to talk*. **3** (*intr;* often foll. by *for* or *against*) to take careful precautions (over): *he provided against financial ruin by wise investment*. **4** (*intr;* foll. by *for*) to supply means of support (to), esp. financially: *he provides for his family*. **5** (in statutes, documents, etc.) to determine (what is to happen in certain contingencies), esp. by including a proviso condition. **6** to confer and induct into ecclesiastical offices. **7** *Now rare.* to have or get in store: *in summer many animals provide their winter food*. [C15: from Latin *prōvidēre* to provide for, from *prō-* beforehand + *vidēre* to see] ▸ **pro'vider** *n*

providence ('prɒvɪdəns) *n* **1a** *Christianity.* God's foreseeing protection and care of his creatures. **1b** such protection and care as manifest by some other force. **2** a supposed manifestation of such care and guidance. **3** the foresight or care exercised by a person in the management of his affairs or resources.

Providence[1] ('prɒvɪdəns) *n Christianity.* God, esp. as showing foreseeing care and protection of his creatures. [C14: via French from Latin *prōvidentia*, from *prōvidēre* to provide; see PROVIDE, -ENCE]

Providence[2] ('prɒvɪdəns) *n* a port in NE Rhode Island, capital of the state, at the head of Narragansett Bay: founded by Roger Williams in 1636. Pop.: 152 558 (1996 est.).

provident ('prɒvɪdənt) *adj* **1** providing for future needs. **2** exercising foresight in the management of one's affairs or resources. **3** characterized by or proceeding from foresight. [C15: from Latin *prōvidens* foreseeing, from *prōvidēre* to PROVIDE] ▸ **'providently** *adv*

provident club *n Brit.* a hire-purchase system offered by some large retail organizations.

providential (ˌprɒvɪ'denʃəl) *adj* relating to, characteristic of, or presumed to proceed from or as if from divine providence. ▸ **ˌprovi'dentially** *adv*

provident society *n* another name for **friendly society.**

providing (prə'vaɪdɪŋ) *or* **provided** *conj* (*subordinating;* sometimes foll. by *that*) on the condition or understanding (that): *I'll play, providing you pay me*.

province ('prɒvɪns) *n* **1** a territory governed as a unit of a country or empire. **2** a district, territory, or region. **3** (*pl;* usually preceded by *the*) those parts of a country lying outside the capital and other large cities and regarded as outside the mainstream of sophisticated culture. **4** *Ecology.* a subdivision of a region, characterized by a particular fauna and flora. **5** an area or branch of learning, activity, etc. **6** the field or extent of a person's activities or office. **7** *R.C. Church, Church of England.* an ecclesiastical territory, usually consisting of several dioceses, and having an archbishop or metropolitan at its head. **8** a major administrative and territorial subdivision of a religious order. **9** *History.* a region of the Roman Empire outside Italy ruled by a governor from Rome. [C14: from Old French, from Latin *prōvincia* conquered territory]

Provincetown ('prɒvɪnsˌtaʊn) *n* a village in SE Massachusetts, at the tip of Cape Cod: scene of the first landing place of the Pilgrims (1620) and of the signing of the Mayflower Compact (1620). Pop.: 3374 (1990).

provincewide ('prɒvɪnsˌwaɪd) *Canadian.* ◆ *adj* **1** covering or available to the whole of a province: *a provincewide referendum*. ◆ *adv* **2** throughout a province: *an advertising campaign to go provincewide*.

provincial (prə'vɪnʃəl) *adj* **1** of or connected with a province. **2** characteristic of or connected with the provinces; local. **3** having attitudes and opinions supposedly common to people living in the provinces; rustic or unsophisticated; limited. **4** *N.Z.* denoting a football team representing a province, one of the historical administrative areas of New Zealand. ◆ *n* **5** a person lacking the sophistications of city life; rustic or narrow-minded individual. **6** a person coming from or resident in a province or the provinces. **7** the head of an ecclesiastical province. **8** the head of a major territorial subdivision of a religious order. ▸ **provinciality** (prəˌvɪnʃɪ'ælɪtɪ) *n* ▸ **pro'vincially** *adv*

Provincial Council *n* (formerly) a council administering any of the New Zealand provinces.

provincialism (prə'vɪnʃəˌlɪzəm) *n* **1** narrowness of mind or outlook; lack of sophistication. **2** a word or attitude characteristic of a provincial. **3** attention to the affairs of one's province rather than the whole nation. **4** the state or quality of being provincial. ◆ Also called: **localism.**

proving ground *n* a place or situation in which something new, such as equipment or a theory, can be tested.

provirus ('prəʊˌvaɪrəs) *n* the inactive form of a virus in a host cell.

provision (prə'vɪʒən) *n* **1** the act of supplying or providing food, etc. **2** something that is supplied or provided. **3** preparations made beforehand (esp. in the phrase **make provision for**). **4** (*pl*) food and other necessities, esp. for an expedition. **5** (*pl*) food obtained for a household. **6** a demand, condition, or stipulation formally incorporated in a document; proviso. **7** the conferring of and induction into ecclesiastical offices. ◆ *vb* **8** (*tr*) to supply with provisions. [C14: from Latin *prōvīsiō* a providing; see PROVIDE] ▸ **pro'visioner** *n*

provisional (prə'vɪʒənᵊl) *or* (*less commonly*) **provisionary** (prə'vɪʒənərɪ) *adj* **1** subject to later alteration; temporary or conditional: *a provisional decision*. ◆ *n* **2** a postage stamp surcharged during an emergency to alter the stamp's denomination or significance until a new or regular issue is printed. ▸ **pro'visionally** *adv*

Provisional (prə'vɪʒənᵊl) *adj* **1** of, designating, or relating to the unofficial factions of the IRA and Sinn Féin that have existed since a split in late 1969. The Provisional movement follows a policy of terrorism to achieve Irish unity. ◆ *n* **2** Also called: **Provo.** a member of the Provisional IRA or Sinn Féin. ◆ Compare **Official.**

proviso (prə'vaɪzəʊ) *n, pl* **-sos** *or* **-soes. 1** a clause in a document or contract that embodies a condition or stipulation. **2** a condition or stipulation. [C15: from Medieval Latin phrase *prōvīsō quod* it being provided that, from Latin *prōvīsus* provided]

provisory (prə'vaɪzərɪ) *adj* **1** containing a proviso; conditional. **2** another word for **provisional.** ▸ **pro'visorily** *adv*

provitamin (prəʊ'vɪtəmɪn) *n* a substance, such as carotene, that is converted into a vitamin in animal tissues.

Provo ('prəʊvəʊ) *n, pl* **-vos.** another name for a **Provisional** (sense 2).

provocation (ˌprɒvə'keɪʃən) *n* **1** the act of provoking or inciting. **2** something that causes indignation, anger, etc. **3** *English criminal law.* words or conduct that incite a person to attack another with fatal results.

provocative (prə'vɒkətɪv) *adj* acting as a stimulus or incitement, esp. to anger or sexual desire; provoking: *a provocative look; a provocative remark*. ▸ **pro'vocatively** *adv* ▸ **pro'vocativeness** *n*

provoke (prə'vəʊk) *vb* (*tr*) **1** to anger or infuriate. **2** to cause to act or behave in a certain manner; incite or stimulate. **3** to promote (certain feelings, esp. anger, indignation, etc.) in a person. **4** *Obsolete.* to summon. [C15: from Latin *prōvocāre* to call forth, from *vocāre* to call] ▸ **pro'voking** *adj* ▸ **pro'vokingly** *adv*

provolone (ˌprəʊvə'ləʊnɪ) *n* a mellow, pale yellow, soft, and sometimes smoked cheese, made of cow's milk: usually moulded in the shape of a pear. [Italian, from *provola*, apparently from Medieval Latin *probula* cheese made from buffalo milk]

provost ('prɒvəst) *n* **1** an appointed person who superintends or presides. **2** the head of certain university colleges or schools. **3** (in Scotland) the chairman and civic head of certain district councils or (formerly) of a burgh council. Compare **convener** (sense 2). **4** *Church of England.* the senior dignitary of one of the more recent cathedral foundations. **5** *R.C. Church.* **5a** the head of a cathedral chapter in England and some other countries. **5b** (formerly) the member of a monastic community second in authority under the abbot. **6** (in medieval times) an overseer, steward, or bailiff in a manor. **7** *Obsolete.* a prison warder. **8** (prə'vəʊ). *Brit. and Canadian military.* a military policeman. [Old English *profost*, from Medieval Latin *prōpositus* placed at the head (of), from Latin *praepōnere* to place first, from *prae-* before + *pōnere* to put]

provost court (prə'vəʊ) *n* a military court for trying people charged with minor offences in an occupied area.

provost guard (prə'vəʊ) *n* (esp. in the U.S.) a detachment under command of the provost marshal.

provost marshal (prə'vəʊ) *n* the officer in charge of military police and thus responsible for military discipline in a large camp, area, or city.

prow (praʊ) *n* the bow of a vessel. [C16: from Old French *proue*, from Latin *prora*, from Greek *prōra;* related to Latin *pro* in front]

prowess ('praʊɪs) *n* **1** outstanding or superior skill or ability. **2** bravery or fearlessness, esp. in battle. [C13: from Old French *proesce*, from *prou* good; see PROUD]

prowl (praʊl) *vb* **1** (when *intr*, often foll. by *around* or *about*) to move stealthily around (a place) as if in search of prey or plunder. ◆ *n* **2** the act of prowling. **3 on the prowl. 3a** moving around stealthily. **3b** zealously pursuing members of the opposite sex. [C14 *prollen*, of unknown origin] ▸ **'prowler** *n*

prox. *abbrev. for* proximo (next month).

proxemics (prɒk'siːmɪks) *n* (*functioning as sing*) the study of spatial interrelationships in humans or in populations of animals of the same species.

Proxima ('prɒksɪmə) *n* a flare star in the constellation Centaurus that is the nearest star to the sun. It is a red dwarf of very low magnitude. Distance: 4.3 light years. Also called: **Proxima Centauri.** See also **Rigil Kent.**

proximal ('prɒksɪməl) *adj* **1** *Anatomy.* situated close to the centre, median line, or point of attachment or origin. Compare **distal. 2** another word for **proximate.** ▸ **'proximally** *adv*

proximate ('prɒksɪmɪt) *or* **proximal** *adj* **1** next or nearest in space or time. **2** very near; close. **3** immediately preceding or following in a series. **4** a less common word for **approximate.** [C16: from Late Latin *proximāre* to draw near, from Latin *proximus* next, from *prope* near] ▸ **'proximately** *adv* ▸ **'proximateness** *n* ▸ **ˌproxi'mation** *n*

proxime accessit ('prɒksɪmɪ æk'sesɪt) *n* the person coming next after the winner in a competitive examination or an academic prize giving; runner-up. [Latin: he came next]

proximity (prɒk'sɪmɪtɪ) *n* **1** nearness in space or time. **2** nearness or closeness in a series. [C15: from Latin *proximitās* closeness; see PROXIMATE]

proximity fuse *n* an electronically triggered device designed to detonate an explosive charge in a missile, etc., at a predetermined distance from the target.

proximo ('prɒksɪməʊ) *adv Now rare except when abbreviated in formal correspondence.* in or during the next or coming month: *a letter of the seventh proximo*. Abbrev.: **prox.** Compare **instant, ultimo.** [C19: from Latin: in or on the next, from *proximus* next]

proxy ('prɒksɪ) *n, pl* **proxies. 1** a person authorized to act on behalf of someone else; agent: *to vote by proxy*. **2** the authority, esp. in the form of a document,

'pro'war *adj*

given to a person to act on behalf of someone else. [C15: *prokesye,* contraction of *procuracy,* from Latin *prōcūrātiō* procuration; see PROCURE]

Prozac ('prəuzæk) *n Trademark.* a drug that prolongs the action of serotonin in the brain; used as an antidepressant.

PRP *abbrev. for:* **1** performance-related pay. **2** profit-related pay.

prs *abbrev. for* pairs.

PRT *abbrev. for* petroleum revenue tax.

prude (pru:d) *n* a person who affects or shows an excessively modest, prim, or proper attitude, esp. regarding sex. [C18: from French, from *prudefemme,* from Old French *prode femme* respectable woman; see PROUD] ▸ **'prudish** *adj* ▸ **'prudishly** *adv* ▸ **'prudishness** *or* **'prudery** *n*

prudence ('pru:dəns) *n* **1** caution in practical affairs; discretion or circumspection. **2** care taken in the management of one's resources. **3** consideration for one's own interests. **4** the condition or quality of being prudent.

prudent ('pru:dᵊnt) *adj* **1** discreet or cautious in managing one's activities; circumspect. **2** practical and careful in providing for the future. **3** exercising good judgment or common sense. [C14: from Latin *prūdēns* far-sighted, contraction of *prōvidens* acting with foresight; see PROVIDENT] ▸ **'prudently** *adv*

prudential (pru:'dɛnʃəl) *adj* **1** characterized by or resulting from prudence. **2** exercising prudence or sound judgment. ▸ **pru'dentially** *adv*

Prudentius (pru:'dɛnʃəs) *n* **Aurelius Clemens** (ɔ:'ri:lɪəs 'klɛmɛnz). 348–410 A.D., Latin Christian poet, born in Spain. His works include the allegory *Psychomachia.*

Prud'hon (*French* prydɔ̃) *n* **Pierre Paul** (pjɛr pɔl). 1758–1823, French painter, noted for the romantic and mysterious aura of his portraits.

pruinose ('pru:ɪ,nəus, -,nəuz) *adj Botany.* coated with a powdery or waxy bloom. [C19: from Latin *pruīnōsus* frost-covered, from *pruīna* hoarfrost]

prune[1] (pru:n) *n* **1** a purplish-black partially dried fruit of any of several varieties of plum tree. **2** *Slang, chiefly Brit.* a dull, uninteresting, or foolish person. [C14: from Old French *prune,* from Latin *prūnum* plum, from Greek *prounon*]

prune[2] (pru:n) *vb* **1** to remove (dead or superfluous twigs, branches, etc.) from (a tree, shrub, etc.), esp. by cutting off. **2** to remove (anything undesirable or superfluous) from (a book, etc.). [C15: from Old French *proignier* to clip, probably from *provigner* to prune vines, from *provain* layer (of a plant,) from Latin *propāgo* a cutting] ▸ **'prunable** *adj* ▸ **'pruner** *n*

prune[3] (pru:n) *vb* an archaic word for **preen**[1].

prunella[1] (pru:'nɛlə), **prunelle** (pru:'nɛl), *or* **prunello** (pru:'nɛləu) *n* a strong fabric, esp. a twill-weave worsted, used for gowns and the uppers of some shoes. [C17: perhaps from PRUNELLE, with reference to the colour of the cloth]

prunella[2] (pru:'nɛlə) *n* See **selfheal.** [New Latin, altered from *brunella,* from German *Braüne* quinsy, which it was thought to cure]

prunelle (pru:'nɛl) *n* a green French liqueur made from sloes. [C18: from French: a little plum, from *prune* PRUNE[1]]

pruning hook *n* a tool with a curved steel blade terminating in a hook, used for pruning.

prurient ('pruərɪənt) *adj* **1** unusually or morbidly interested in sexual thoughts or practices. **2** exciting or encouraging lustfulness; erotic. [C17: from Latin *prūrīre* to itch, to lust after] ▸ **'prurience** *n* ▸ **'pruriently** *adv*

prurigo (pruə'raɪgəu) *n* a chronic inflammatory disease of the skin characterized by the formation of papules and intense itching. [C19: from Latin: an itch] ▸ **pruriginous** (pruə'rɪdʒɪnəs) *adj*

pruritus (pruə'raɪtəs) *n Pathol.* **1** any intense sensation of itching. **2** any of various conditions characterized by intense itching. [C17: from Latin: an itching; see PRURIENT] ▸ **pruritic** (pruə'rɪtɪk) *adj*

Prus. *abbrev. for* Prussia(n).

prusik ('prʌsɪk) *n Mountaineering.* **1** Also: **prusik knot.** a sliding knot that locks under pressure and can be used to form a loop (**prusik loop**) in which a climber can place his foot in order to stand or ascend a rope. ◆ *vb* **-siks, -siking, -siked.** (*intr*) **2** to climb (up a standing rope) using prusik loops. [C20: named after Dr *Prusik,* Austrian climber who devised the knot]

Prussia ('prʌʃə) *n* a former German state in N and central Germany, extending from France and the Low Countries to the Baltic Sea and Poland: developed as the chief military power of the Continent, leading the North German Confederation from 1867–71, when the German Empire was established; dissolved in 1947 and divided between East and West Germany, Poland, and the former Soviet Union. Area: (in 1939) 294 081 sq. km (113 545 sq. miles). German name: **Preussen.**

Prussian ('prʌʃən) *adj* **1** of, relating to, or characteristic of Prussia or its people, esp. of the Junkers and their formal military tradition. ◆ *n* **2** a German native or inhabitant of Prussia. **3** a member of a Baltic people formerly inhabiting the coastal area of the SE Baltic. **4** See **Old Prussian.**

Prussian blue *n* **1** any of a number of blue pigments containing ferrocyanide or ferricyanide ions. **2a** the blue or deep greenish-blue colour of this pigment. **2b** (*as adj*): *a Prussian-blue carpet.*

Prussianism ('prʌʃə,nɪzəm) *n* the ethos of the Prussian state and aristocracy, esp. militarism and stern discipline.

Prussianize *or* **Prussianise** ('prʌʃə,naɪz) *vb* (*tr*) to make Prussian in character, esp. with respect to military matters. ▸ **,Prussiani'zation** *or* **,Prussiani'sation** *n*

prussiate ('prʌʃɪɪt) *n* any cyanide, ferrocyanide, or ferricyanide.

prussic acid ('prʌsɪk) *n* the weakly acidic extremely poisonous aqueous solution of hydrogen cyanide. [C18: from French *acide prussique* Prussian acid, so called because obtained from Prussian blue]

Prut (*Russian* prut) *n* a river in E Europe, rising in the SW Ukraine and flowing generally southeast, forming part of the border between Romania and Moldova, to join the River Danube. Length: 853 km (530 miles).

pry[1] (praɪ) *vb* **pries, prying, pried. 1** (*intr;* often foll. by *into*) to make an impertinent or uninvited inquiry (about a private matter, topic, etc.). ◆ *n, pl* **pries. 2** the act of prying. **3** a person who pries. [C14: of unknown origin]

pry[2] (praɪ) *vb* **pries, prying, pried.** the U.S. and Canadian word for **prise.** [C14: of unknown origin]

pryer ('praɪə) *n* a variant spelling of **prier.**

Prynne (prɪn) *n* **William.** 1600–69, English Puritan leader and pamphleteer, whose ears were cut off in punishment for his attacks on Laud.

prytaneum (,prɪtə'ni:əm) *n, pl* **-nea** (-'ni:ə). the public hall of a city in ancient Greece. [Latin, from Greek *prutaneion,* from *prutanis, prutaneus*]

Przemyśl (*Polish* 'pʃɛmiʃl) *n* a city in SE Poland, near the border with the Ukraine on the San River: a fortress in the early Middle Ages; belonged to Austria (1722–1918). Pop.: 67 000 (1989 est.).

Przewalski's horse (,pɜ:ʒə'vælskɪz) *n* a wild horse, *Equus przewalskii,* of W Mongolia, having an erect mane and no forelock: extinct in the wild, only a few survive in captivity. [C19: named after the Russian explorer Nikolai Mikhailovich *Przewalski* (1839–88), who discovered it]

PS *abbrev. for:* **1** Passenger Steamer. **2** phrase structure. **3** Police Sergeant. **4** Also: **ps.** postscript. **5** private secretary. **6** prompt side.

ps. *abbrev. for* pieces.

Ps. *or* **Psa.** *Bible. abbrev. for* Psalm.

PSA *abbrev. for:* **1** (in Britain) Property Services Agency: the section of the Department of the Environment responsible for providing buildings for government departments and the armed forces. **2** prostatic specific antigen: an enzyme secreted by the prostate gland, increased levels of which are found in the blood of patients with cancer of the prostate. **3** (in New Zealand) Public Service Association.

psalm (sɑ:m) *n* **1** (*often cap.*) any of the 150 sacred songs, lyric poems, and prayers that together constitute a book (Psalms) of the Old Testament. **2** a musical setting of one of these poems. **3** any sacred song or hymn. [Old English, from Late Latin *psalmus,* from Greek *psalmos* song accompanied on the harp, from *psallein* to play (the harp)] ▸ **'psalmic** *adj*

psalmist ('sɑ:mɪst) *n* the composer of a psalm or psalms, esp. (when *cap.* and preceded by *the*) David, traditionally regarded as the author of The Book of Psalms.

psalmody ('sɑ:mədɪ, 'sæl-) *n, pl* **-dies. 1** the act of singing psalms or hymns. **2** the art or practice of the setting to music or singing of psalms. [C14: via Late Latin from Greek *psalmōidia* singing accompanied by a harp, from *psalmos* (see PSALM) + *ōidē* ODE] ▸ **'psalmodist** *n* ▸ **psalmodic** (sɑ:'mɒdɪk, sæl-) *adj*

Psalms (sɑ:mz) *n* (*functioning as sing*) the collection of 150 psalms in the Old Testament, the full title of which is **The Book of Psalms.**

Psalter ('sɔ:ltə) *n* **1** another name for **Psalms,** esp. in the version in the Book of Common Prayer. **2** a translation, musical, or metrical version of the Psalms. **3** a devotional or liturgical book containing a version of Psalms, often with a musical setting. [Old English *psaltere,* from Late Latin *psaltērium,* from Greek *psaltērion* stringed instrument, from *psallein* to play a stringed instrument]

psalterium (sɔ:l'tɪərɪəm) *n, pl* **-teria** (-'tɪərɪə). the third compartment of the stomach of ruminants, between the reticulum and abomasum. Also called: **omasum.** [C19: from Latin *psaltērium* PSALTER; from the similarity of its folds to the pages of a book]

psaltery ('sɔ:ltərɪ) *n, pl* **-teries.** *Music.* an ancient stringed instrument similar to the lyre, but having a trapezoidal sounding board over which the strings are stretched. [Old English: see PSALTER]

psammite ('sæmaɪt) *n* a rare name for **sandstone.** [C19: from Greek *psammos* sand] ▸ **psammitic** (sæ'mɪtɪk) *adj*

p's and q's *pl n* behaviour within social conventions; manners (esp. in the phrase **to mind one's p's and q's**). [altered from *p(lea)se and (than)k-you's*]

PSBR (in Britain) *abbrev. for* public sector borrowing requirement: the excess of government expenditure over receipts (mainly from taxation) that has to be financed by borrowing from the banks or the public.

psephite ('si:faɪt) *n* any rock, such as a breccia, that consists of large fragments embedded in a finer matrix. [C19: via French from Greek *psēphos* a pebble] ▸ **psephitic** (si:'fɪtɪk) *adj*

psephology (sɛ'fɒlədʒɪ) *n* the statistical and sociological study of elections. [C20: from Greek *psephos* pebble, vote + -LOGY, from the ancient Greeks' custom of voting with pebbles] ▸ **psephological** (,sɛfə'lɒdʒɪkᵊl) *adj* ▸ **,psepho'logically** *adv* ▸ **pse'phologist** *n*

pseud (sju:d) *n* **1** *Informal.* a false, artificial, or pretentious person. ◆ *adj* **2** another word for **pseudo.**

pseud. *abbrev. for* pseudonym.

pseudaxis (sju:'dæksɪs) *n Botany.* another name for **sympodium.**

Pseudepigrapha (,sju:dɪ'pɪgrəfə) *pl n* various Jewish writings from the first century B.C. to the first century A.D. that claim to have been divinely revealed but which have been excluded from the Greek canon of the Old Testament. Also called (R.C. Church): **Apocrypha.** [C17: from Greek *pseudepigraphos* falsely entitled, from PSEUDO- + *epigraphein* to inscribe] ▸ **Pseudepigraphic** (,sju:depɪ'græfɪk), **,Pseudepi'graphical,** *or* **,Pseude'pigraphous** *adj*

pseudo ('sju:dəu) *adj Informal.* not genuine; pretended.

pseudo- *or sometimes before a vowel* **pseud-** *combining form.* **1** false, pretending, or unauthentic: *pseudo-intellectual.* **2** having a close resemblance to: *pseudopodium.* [from Greek *pseudēs* false, from *pseudein* to lie]

pseudoarthrosis (,sju:dəuɑ:'θrəusɪs) *or* **pseudarthrosis** (,sju:dɑ:'θrəusɪs) *n, pl* **-ses** (-si:z). a joint formed by fibrous tissue bridging the gap between the two fragments of bone of an old fracture that have not united. Nontechnical names: **false joint, false ankylosis.** Also called: **nearthrosis.**

pseudocarp ('sju:dəu,kɑ:p) *n* a fruit, such as the strawberry or apple, that includes parts other than the ripened ovary. Also called: **false fruit, accessory fruit.** ▸ **,pseudo'carpous** *adj*

pseudocopulation (,sju:dəu,kɒpju'leɪʃən) *n Botany.* pollination of plants, esp. orchids, by male insects while attempting to mate with flowers that resemble the female insect.

pseudocyesis (ˌsjuːdəʊsaɪˈiːsɪs) *n, pl* **-ces** (-siːz). the technical name for **phantom pregnancy.**

Pseudo-Dionysius (ˌsjuːdəʊˌdaɪəˈnɪsɪəs) *n* the name given to the unidentified author (c. 500 A.D.) of important theological works formerly attributed to **Dionysius the Areopagite.**

pseudohermaphroditism (ˌsjuːdəʊhɜːˈmæfrədaɪˌtɪzəm) *n* the congenital condition of having the organs of reproduction of one sex and the external genitalia, usually malformed, of the opposite sex. Compare **hermaphroditism.**

pseudo-intransitive *adj* denoting an occurrence of a normally transitive verb in which a direct object is not explicitly stated or forms the subject of the sentence, as in *Margaret is cooking* or *these apples cook well.*

pseudomonas (sjuːˈdɒmənəs) *n, pl* **pseudomonades** (ˌsjuːdəʊˈmɒnədiːz). any of a genus of rodlike Gram-negative bacteria that live in soil and decomposing organic matter: many species are pathogenic to plants and a few are pathogenic to man. [C20: from New Latin, from PSEUDO- + Greek *monas* unit]

pseudomorph (ˈsjuːdəʊˌmɔːf) *n* a mineral that has an uncharacteristic crystalline form as a result of assuming the shape of another mineral that it has replaced. ► **ˌpseudoˈmorphic** *or* **ˌpseudoˈmorphous** *adj* ► **ˌpseudoˈmorphism** *n*

pseudomutuality (ˌsjuːdəʊˌmjuːtjʊˈælɪtɪ) *n, pl* **-ties.** *Psychol.* a relationship between two persons in which conflict of views or opinions is solved by simply ignoring it.

pseudonym (ˈsjuːdəˌnɪm) *n* a fictitious name adopted, esp. by an author. [C19: via French from Greek *pseudōnumon*] ► **ˌpseudoˈnymity** *n*

pseudonymous (sjuːˈdɒnɪməs) *adj* **1** having or using a false or assumed name. **2** writing or having been written under a pseudonym. ► **pseuˈdonymously** *adv*

pseudopodium (ˌsjuːdəʊˈpəʊdɪəm) *n, pl* **-dia** (-dɪə). a temporary projection from the cell of a protozoan, leucocyte, etc., used for feeding and locomotion.

pseudoscalar (ˌsjuːdəʊˈskeɪlə) *n Maths.* a variable quantity that has magnitude but not direction and is an odd function of the coordinates. Compare **pseudovector, scalar** (sense 1), **tensor** (sense 2), **vector** (sense 1).

pseudovector (ˌsjuːdəʊˈvɛktə) *n Maths.* a variable quantity, such as angular momentum, that has magnitude and orientation with respect to an axis. The components are even functions of the coordinates. Also called: **axial vector.** Compare **pseudoscalar, scalar** (sense 1), **tensor** (sense 2), **vector** (sense 1).

psf *abbrev. for* pounds per square foot.

PSG *abbrev. for* phrase structure grammar.

pshaw (pʃɔː) *interj Becoming rare.* an exclamation of disgust, impatience, disbelief, etc.

psi[1] *abbrev. for* pounds per square inch.

psi[2] (psaɪ) *n* **1** the 23rd letter of the Greek alphabet (Ψ, ψ), a composite consonant, transliterated as *ps.* **2a** paranormal or psychic phenomena collectively. **2b** (*as modifier*): *psi powers.*

psia *abbrev. for* pounds per square inch, absolute.

psid *abbrev. for* pounds per square inch, differential.

psig *abbrev. for* pounds per square inch, gauge.

psilocybin (ˌsɪləˈsaɪbɪn, ˌsaɪlə-) *n* a crystalline phosphate ester that is the active principle of the hallucinogenic fungus *Psilocybe mexicana.* Formula: $C_{12}H_{17}N_2O_4P$. [C20: from New Latin *Psilocybe* (from Greek *psilos* bare + *kubē* head) + -IN]

psilomelane (sɪˈlɒmɪˌleɪn) *n* a common black to grey secondary mineral consisting of hydrated basic oxide of manganese and barium: a source of manganese. Formula: $BaMn_9O_{16}(OH)_4$. [C19: from Greek *psilos* bare + *melas* black]

psi particle *n* See **J/psi particle.**

psittacine (ˈsɪtəˌsaɪn, -sɪn) *adj* of, relating to, or resembling a parrot. [C19: from Late Latin *psittacīnus,* from Latin *psittacus* a parrot]

psittacosis (ˌsɪtəˈkəʊsɪs) *n* a disease of parrots, caused by the bacterium *Chlamydia psittaci,* that can be transmitted to man, in whom it produces inflammation of the lungs and pneumonia. Also called: **parrot fever.** [C19: from New Latin, from Latin *psittacus* a parrot, from Greek *psittakos;* see -OSIS]

PSK *abbrev. for* phase shift keying: a digital data modulation system in which binary data signals switch the phase of a radio frequency carrier.

Pskov (*Russian* pskɔf) *n* **1** a city in NW Russia, on the Velikaya River: one of the oldest Russian cities, at its height in the 13th and 14th centuries. Pop.: 207 000 (1995 est.). **2 Lake.** the S part of Lake Peipus in NW Russia, linked to the main part by a channel 24 km (15 miles) long. Area: about 1000 sq. km (400 sq. miles).

PSL *abbrev. for* private sector liquidity: a measure of the money supply. See **M4; M5.**

psoas (ˈsəʊəs) *n* either of two muscles of the loins that aid in flexing and rotating the thigh. [C17: from New Latin, from Greek *psoai* (pl)]

psoralea (səˈreɪlɪə) *n* any plant of the tropical and subtropical leguminous genus *Psoralea,* having curly leaves, white or purple flowers, and short one-seeded pods. See **breadroot.** [C19: via New Latin from Greek *psōraleos* mangy, from *psōra* mange, an allusion to the glandular dots of the plant]

psoriasis (səˈraɪəsɪs) *n* a skin disease characterized by the formation of reddish spots and patches covered with silvery scales: tends to run in families. [C17: via New Latin from Greek: itching disease, from *psōra* itch] ► **psoriatic** (ˌsɔːrɪˈætɪk) *adj*

PSS *or* **pss.** *abbrev. for* postscripts.

psst (pst) *interj* an exclamation of beckoning, esp. one made surreptitiously.

PST (in the U.S. and Canada) *abbrev. for* Pacific Standard Time.

PSTN *abbrev. for* public switched telephone network: the conventional message switched telephone network.

PSV (in Britain) *abbrev. for* public service vehicle (now called passenger carrying vehicle).

psych *or* **psyche** (saɪk) *vb (tr) Informal.* to psychoanalyse. See also **psych out, psych up.** [C20: shortened from PSYCHOANALYSE]

psych. *abbrev. for:* **1** psychological. **2** psychology.

psyche (ˈsaɪkɪ) *n* the human mind or soul. [C17: from Latin, from Greek *psukhē* breath, soul; related to Greek *psukhein* to breathe]

Psyche (ˈsaɪkɪ) *n Greek myth.* a beautiful girl loved by Eros (Cupid), who became the personification of the soul.

psychedelia (ˌsaɪkəˈdeɪlɪə, -ˈdiːlɪə) *n (functioning as sing or pl)* psychedelic objects, dress, music, etc.

psychedelic *or* **psychodelic** (ˌsaɪkɪˈdɛlɪk) *adj* **1** relating to or denoting new or altered perceptions or sensory experiences, as through the use of hallucinogenic drugs. **2** denoting any of the drugs, esp. LSD, that produce these effects. **3** *Informal.* (of painting, fabric design, etc.) having the vivid colours and complex patterns popularly associated with the visual effects of psychedelic states. [C20: from PSYCHE + Greek *delos* visible] ► **ˌpsycheˈdelically** *or* **ˌpsychoˈdelically** *adv*

psychiatric social worker *n Social welfare.* (in Britain) a qualified person who works with mentally disordered people and their families, based in a psychiatric hospital, child guidance clinic, or social services department area team, and who may also be an approved social worker.

psychiatry (saɪˈkaɪətrɪ) *n* the branch of medicine concerned with the diagnosis and treatment of mental disorders. ► **psychiatric** (ˌsaɪkɪˈætrɪk) *or* **ˌpsychiˈatrical** *adj* ► **ˌpsychiˈatrically** *adv* ► **psyˈchiatrist** *n*

psychic (ˈsaɪkɪk) *adj* **1a** outside the possibilities defined by natural laws, as mental telepathy. **1b** (of a person) sensitive to forces not recognized by natural laws. **2** mental as opposed to physical; psychogenic. **3** *Bridge.* (of a bid) based on less strength than would normally be required to make the bid. ◆ *n* **4** a person who is sensitive to parapsychological forces or influences. [C19: from Greek *psukhikos* of the soul or life] ► **ˈpsychical** *adj* ► **ˈpsychically** *adv*

psychic determinism *n Psychol.* the assumption, made esp. by Freud, that mental processes do not occur by chance but that a cause can always be found for them.

psycho (ˈsaɪkəʊ) *n, pl* **-chos,** *adj* an informal word for **psychopath** or **psychopathic.**

psycho- *or sometimes before a vowel* **psych-** *combining form.* indicating the mind or psychological or mental processes: *psychology; psychogenesis; psychosomatic.* [from Greek *psukhē* spirit, breath]

psychoacoustics (ˌsaɪkəʊəˈkuːstɪks) *n (functioning as sing) Psychol.* the study of the relationship between sounds and their physiological and psychological effects.

psychoactive (ˌsaɪkəʊˈæktɪv) *adj* capable of affecting mental activity: *a psychoactive drug.*

psychoanal. *abbrev. for* psychoanalysis.

psychoanalyse *or U.S.* **psychoanalyze** (ˌsaɪkəʊˈænəˌlaɪz) *vb (tr)* to examine or treat (a person) by psychoanalysis. ► **ˌpsychoˈanaˌlyser** *or U.S.* **ˌpsychoˈanaˌlyzer** *n*

psychoanalysis (ˌsaɪkəʊəˈnælɪsɪs) *n* a method of studying the mind and treating mental and emotional disorders based on revealing and investigating the role of the unconscious mind. ► **psychoanalyst** (ˌsaɪkəʊˈænəlɪst) *n* ► **psychoanalytic** (ˌsaɪkəʊˌænəˈlɪtɪk) *or* **ˌpsychoˌanaˈlytical** *adj* ► **ˌpsychoˌanaˈlytically** *adv*

psychobabble (ˈsaɪkəʊˌbæbᵊl) *n Informal.* the jargon of psychology, esp. as used and popularized in various types of psychotherapy.

psychobiography (ˌsaɪkəʊbaɪˈɒgrəfɪ) *n* a biography that pays particular attention to a person's psychological development. ► **psychobiographical** (ˌsaɪkəʊbaɪəʊˈgræfɪkᵊl) *adj*

psychobiology (ˌsaɪkəʊbaɪˈɒlədʒɪ) *n Psychol.* the attempt to understand the psychology of organisms in terms of their biological functions and structures. ► **psychobiological** (ˌsaɪkəʊˌbaɪəˈlɒdʒɪkᵊl) *adj* ► **ˌpsychobioˈlogically** *adv* ► **ˌpsychobiˈologist** *n*

psychochemical (ˌsaɪkəʊˈkɛmɪkᵊl) *n* **1** any of various chemical compounds whose primary effect is the alteration of the normal state of consciousness. ◆ *adj* **2** of or relating to such chemical compounds.

psychodrama (ˈsaɪkəʊˌdrɑːmə) *n Psychiatry.* a form of group therapy in which individuals act out, before an audience, situations from their past. ► **psychodramatic** (ˌsaɪkəʊdrəˈmætɪk) *adj*

psychodynamics (ˌsaɪkəʊdaɪˈnæmɪks) *n (functioning as sing) Psychol.* the study of interacting motives and emotions. ► **ˌpsychodyˈnamic** *adj* ► **ˌpsychodyˈnamically** *adv*

psychogalvanic response (ˌsaɪkəʊgælˈvænɪk) *n* another name for **galvanic skin response.** Abbrev.: **PGR.**

psychogenesis (ˌsaɪkəʊˈdʒɛnɪsɪs) *n Psychol.* the study of the origin and development of personality, human behaviour, and mental processes. ► **psychogenetic** (ˌsaɪkəʊdʒɪˈnɛtɪk) *adj* ► **ˌpsychogeˈnetically** *adv*

psychogenic (ˌsaɪkəʊˈdʒɛnɪk) *adj Psychol.* (esp. of disorders or symptoms) of mental, rather than organic, origin. ► **ˌpsychoˈgenically** *adv*

psychogeriatric (ˌsaɪkəʊdʒɛrɪˈætrɪk) *adj* **1** *Med.* (of an old person) no longer in touch with everyday realities; exhibiting delusions; mentally incompetent.

ˌpseudo-ˈGothic *adj* | **ˌpseudoˈmedical** *adj* | **ˌpseudoˈscience** *n* | **ˌpseudoˌscienˈtific** *adj*

◆ *n* **2a** *Derogatory.* a confused old person. **2b** an impersonal label for a patient, as a unit, requiring institutional services appropriate for a mentally disordered old person. ◆ See also **confused elderly, geriatric, senile.**

psychogeriatrics (ˌsaɪkəʊdʒerɪˈætrɪks) *n* (*functioning as sing*) *Med.* the branch of health care concerned with the study, diagnosis, and sometimes treatment of mentally disordered old people. Compare **geriatrics.**

psychognosis (saɪˈkɒgnəsɪs) *n Psychol.* **1** the use of hypnosis to study mental phenomena. **2** the study of personality by observation of outward bodily signs. ▸ **psychognostic** (ˌsaɪkɒgˈnɒstɪk) *adj*

psychographics (ˌsaɪkəʊˈgræfɪks) *pl n* (*functioning as sing*) the study and grouping of people according to their attitudes and tastes, esp. for market research.

psychohistory (ˌsaɪkəʊˈhɪstərɪ, -ˈhɪstrɪ) *n, pl* **-ries.** biography based on psychological theories of personality development.

psychokinesis (ˌsaɪkəʊkɪˈniːsɪs, -kaɪ-) *n* **1** (in parapsychology) alteration of the state of an object by mental influence alone, without any physical intervention. **2** *Psychiatry.* a state of violent uncontrolled motor activity. **[**C20: from PSYCHO- + Greek *kinēsis* motion**]** ▸ **psychokinetic** (ˌsaɪkəʊkɪˈnetɪk) *adj*

psychol. *abbrev. for:* **1** psychological. **2** psychology.

psycholinguistics (ˌsaɪkəʊlɪŋˈgwɪstɪks) *n* (*functioning as sing*) the psychology of language, including language acquisition by children, the mental processes underlying adult comprehension and production of speech, language disorders, etc. ▸ ˌ**psychoˈlinguist** *n* ▸ ˌ**psycholinˈguistic** *adj*

psychological (ˌsaɪkəˈlɒdʒɪkᵊl) *adj* **1** of or relating to psychology. **2** of or relating to the mind or mental activity. **3** having no real or objective basis; arising in the mind: *his backaches are all psychological.* **4** affecting the mind. ▸ ˌ**psychoˈlogically** *adv*

psychological block *n* See **block** (sense 21).

psychological moment *n* the most appropriate time for producing a desired effect: *he proposed to her at the psychological moment.*

psychological primary *n* one of a set of perceived colours (red, yellow, blue, green, black, and white) that can be used to characterize all other perceived colours.

psychological warfare *n* the military application of psychology, esp. to propaganda and attempts to influence the morale of enemy and friendly groups in time of war.

psychologism (saɪˈkɒləˌdʒɪzəm) *n* **1** the belief in the importance and relevance of psychology for other sciences. **2** the belief that psychology is the basis for all other natural and social sciences. ▸ **psyˌcholoˈgistic** *adj*

psychologize *or* **psychologise** (saɪˈkɒləˌdʒaɪz) *vb* (*intr*) **1** to make interpretations of behaviour and mental processes. **2** to carry out investigation in the field of psychology.

psychology (saɪˈkɒlədʒɪ) *n, pl* **-gies. 1** the scientific study of all forms of human and animal behaviour, sometimes concerned with the methods through which behaviour can be modified. See also **analytical psychology, clinical psychology, comparative psychology, educational psychology, experimental psychology. 2** *Informal.* the mental make-up or structure of an individual that causes him to think or act in the way he does. ▸ **psyˈchologist** *n*

psychomachia (ˌsaɪkəʊˈmækɪə) *or* **psychomachy** (ˈsaɪkəʊməkɪ) *n* conflict of the soul. **[**C17: from Late Latin *psȳchomachia,* title of a poem by Prudentius (about 400), from Greek *psukhē* spirit + *makhē* battle**]**

psychometrics (ˌsaɪkəʊˈmetrɪks) *n* (*functioning as sing*) **1** the branch of psychology concerned with the design and use of psychological tests. **2** the application of statistical and mathematical techniques to psychological testing.

psychometry (saɪˈkɒmɪtrɪ) *n Psychol.* **1** measurement and testing of mental states and processes. See also **psychometrics. 2** (in parapsychology) the supposed ability to deduce facts about events by touching objects related to them. ▸ **psychometric** (ˌsaɪkəʊˈmetrɪk) *or* ˌ**psychoˈmetrical** *adj* ▸ ˌ**psychoˈmetrically** *adv* ▸ **psychometrician** (ˌsaɪkəʊməˈtrɪʃən) *or* **psyˈchometrist** *n*

psychomotor (ˌsaɪkəʊˈməʊtə) *adj* of, relating to, or characterizing movements of the body associated with mental activity.

psychoneuroimmunology (ˌsaɪkəʊˌnjʊərəʊˌɪmjʊˈnɒlədʒɪ) *n* the study of the effects of psychological factors on the immune system. Abbrev.: **PNI.**

psychoneurosis (ˌsaɪkəʊnjʊˈrəʊsɪs) *n, pl* **-roses** (-ˈrəʊsiːz). another word for **neurosis.** ▸ **psychoneurotic** (ˌsaɪkəʊnjʊˈrɒtɪk) *adj*

psychopath (ˈsaɪkəʊˌpæθ) *n* a person afflicted with a personality disorder characterized by a tendency to commit antisocial and sometimes violent acts and a failure to feel guilt for such acts. Also called: **sociopath.** ▸ ˌ**psychoˈpathic** *adj* ▸ ˌ**psychoˈpathically** *adv*

psychopathic disorder *n Law.* (in England, according to the Mental Health Act 1983) a persistent disorder or disability of mind which results in abnormally aggressive or seriously irresponsible conduct on the part of the person concerned. See also **mental disorder.**

psychopathic personality *n Psychiatry.* an antisocial personality characterized by the failure to develop any sense of moral responsibility and the capability of performing violent or antisocial acts.

psychopathology (ˌsaɪkəʊpəˈθɒlədʒɪ) *n* the scientific study of mental disorders. ▸ **psychopathological** (ˌsaɪkəʊˌpæθəˈlɒdʒɪkᵊl) *adj* ▸ ˌ**psychopaˈthologist** *n*

psychopathy (saɪˈkɒpəθɪ) *n Psychiatry.* **1** another name for **psychopathic personality. 2** any mental disorder or disease.

psychopharmacology (ˌsaɪkəʊˌfɑːməˈkɒlədʒɪ) *n* the study of drugs that affect the mind. ▸ **psychopharmacological** (ˌsaɪkəʊˌfɑːməkəˈlɒdʒɪkᵊl) *adj* ▸ ˌ**psychoˌpharmaˈcologist** *n*

psychophysics (ˌsaɪkəʊˈfɪzɪks) *n* (*functioning as sing*) the branch of psychology concerned with the relationship between physical stimuli and the effects they produce in the mind. ▸ ˌ**psychoˈphysical** *adj*

psychophysiology (ˌsaɪkəʊˌfɪzɪˈɒlədʒɪ) *n* the branch of psychology concerned with the physiological basis of mental processes. ▸ **psychophysiological** (ˌsaɪkəʊˌfɪzɪəˈlɒdʒɪkᵊl) *adj* ▸ ˌ**psychoˌphysiˈologist** *n*

psychoprophylaxis (ˌsaɪkəʊˌprəʊfɪˈlæksɪs) *n* a method of preparing women for natural childbirth by means of special breathing and relaxation.

psychosexual (ˌsaɪkəʊˈseksjʊəl) *adj* of or relating to the mental aspects of sex, such as sexual fantasies. ▸ ˌ**psychoˌsexuˈality** *n* ▸ ˌ**psychoˈsexually** *adv*

psychosis (saɪˈkəʊsɪs) *n, pl* **-choses** (-ˈkəʊsiːz). any form of severe mental disorder in which the individual's contact with reality becomes highly distorted. Compare **neurosis. [**C19: New Latin, from PSYCHO- + -OSIS**]**

psychosocial (ˌsaɪkəʊˈsəʊʃəl) *adj* of or relating to processes or factors that are both social and psychological in origin.

psychosomatic (ˌsaɪkəʊsəˈmætɪk) *adj* of or relating to disorders, such as stomach ulcers, thought to be caused or aggravated by psychological factors such as stress.

psychosurgery (ˌsaɪkəʊˈsɜːdʒərɪ) *n* any surgical procedure on the brain, such as a frontal lobotomy, to relieve serious mental disorders. ▸ **psychosurgical** (ˌsaɪkəʊˈsɜːdʒɪkᵊl) *adj*

psychotherapy (ˌsaɪkəʊˈθerəpɪ) *or* (*less commonly*) **psychotherapeutics** (ˌsaɪkəʊˌθerəˈpjuːtɪks) *n* the treatment of nervous disorders by psychological methods. ▸ ˌ**psychoˌtheraˈpeutic** *adj* ▸ ˌ**psychoˌtheraˈpeutically** *adv* ▸ ˌ**psychoˈtherapist** *n*

psychotic (saɪˈkɒtɪk) *Psychiatry.* ◆ *adj* **1** of, relating to, or characterized by psychosis. ◆ *n* **2** a person suffering from psychosis. ▸ **psyˈchotically** *adv*

psychotomimetic (saɪˌkɒtəʊmɪˈmetɪk) *adj* (of drugs such as LSD and mescaline) capable of inducing psychotic symptoms.

psychotropic (ˌsaɪkəʊˈtrɒpɪk) *adj* another word for **psychoactive.**

psych out *vb* (*mainly tr, adv*) *Informal.* **1** to guess correctly the intentions of (another); outguess. **2** to analyse or solve (a problem, etc.) psychologically. **3** to intimidate or frighten. **4** (*intr, adv*) to lose control psychologically; break down.

psychro- *combining form.* cold: *psychrometer.* **[**from Greek *psukhros***]**

psychrometer (saɪˈkrɒmɪtə) *n* a type of hygrometer consisting of two thermometers, one of which has a dry bulb and the other a bulb that is kept moist and ventilated. The difference between the readings of the thermometers gives an indication of atmospheric humidity. Also called: **wet-and-dry-bulb thermometer.**

psychrophilic (ˌsaɪkrəʊˈfɪlɪk) *adj* (esp. of bacteria) showing optimum growth at low temperatures.

psych up *vb* (*tr, adv*) *Informal.* to get (oneself or another) into a state of psychological readiness for an action, performance, etc.

psyllid (ˈsɪlɪd) *or* **psylla** (ˈsɪlə) *n* any homopterous insect of the family *Psyllidae,* which comprises the jumping plant lice. See **plant louse** (sense 2). **[**C19: from Greek *psulla* flea**]**

pt *abbrev. for:* **1** part. **2** past tense. **3** patient. **4** payment. **5** point. **6** port. **7** pro tempore.

Pt *abbrev. for* (in place names): **1** Point. **2** Port. ◆ **3** *the chemical symbol for* platinum.

PT *abbrev. for:* **1** physical therapy. **2** physical training. **3** postal telegraph. **4** pupil teacher. **5** (in Britain, formerly) purchase tax.

pt. *abbrev. for:* **1** pint. **2** preterite.

pta *symbol for* peseta.

PTA *abbrev. for:* **1** Parent-Teacher Association. **2** (in Britain) Passenger Transport Authority.

Ptah (ptɑː, tɑː) *n* (in ancient Egypt) a major god worshipped as the creative power, esp. at Memphis.

ptarmigan (ˈtɑːmɪgən) *n, pl* **-gans** *or* **-gan. 1** any of several arctic and subarctic grouse of the genus *Lagopus,* esp. *L. mutus,* which has a white winter plumage. **2** (*sometimes cap.*) a created domestic fancy pigeon with ruffled or curled feathers on the wings and back. **[**C16: changed (perhaps influenced by Greek *pteron* wing) from Scottish Gaelic *tarmachan,* diminutive of *tarmach,* of obscure origin**]**

PT boat *n* patrol torpedo boat, the former U.S. term for an **MTB.**

Pte *Military. abbrev. for* private.

PTE (in Britain) *abbrev. for* Passenger Transport Executive.

pteridology (ˌterɪˈdɒlədʒɪ) *n* the branch of botany concerned with the study of ferns and related plants. **[**C19: from *pterido-,* from Greek *pteris* fern + -LOGY**]** ▸ **pteridological** (ˌterɪdəˈlɒdʒɪkᵊl) *adj* ▸ ˌ**pteriˈdologist** *n*

pteridophyte (ˈterɪdəʊˌfaɪt) *n* (in traditional classification) any plant of the division *Pteridophyta,* reproducing by spores and having vascular tissue, roots, stems, and leaves: includes the ferns, horsetails, and club mosses. In modern classifications these plants are placed in separate phyla. **[**C19: from *pterido-,* from Greek *pteris* fern + -PHYTE**]** ▸ **pteridophytic** (ˌterɪdəʊˈfɪtɪk) *or* **pteridophytous** (ˌterɪˈdɒfɪtəs) *adj*

pteridosperm (ˈterɪdəˌspɜːm) *n* any extinct seed-producing fernlike plant of the group *Pteridospermae.* Also called: **seed fern. [**C19: from Greek *pteris* a fern + -SPERM**]**

ptero- *combining form.* wing, feather, or a part resembling a wing: *pterodactyl.* **[**from Greek *pteron* wing, feather**]**

pterodactyl (ˌterəˈdæktɪl) *n* any extinct flying reptile of the genus *Pterodactylus* and related genera, having membranous wings supported on an elongated fourth digit. See also **pterosaur. [**C19: from PTERO- + Greek *daktulos* finger**]**

pteropod (ˈterəˌpɒd) *n* any small marine gastropod mollusc of the group or order *Pteropoda,* in which the foot is expanded into two winglike lobes for swimming and the shell is absent or thin-walled. Also called: **sea butterfly.**

pterosaur (ˈterəˌsɔː) *n* any extinct flying reptile of the order *Pterosauria,* of Jurassic and Cretaceous times: included the pterodactyls. Compare **dinosaur, plesiosaur.**

-pterous *or* **-pteran** *adj combining form.* indicating a specified number or type of wings: *dipterous.* [from Greek *-pteros,* from *pteron* wing]

pterygial (tə'rɪdʒɪəl) *adj Zoology.* of or relating to a fin or wing. [from Greek *pterux* wing]

pterygoid process ('tɛrɪ,gɔɪd) *n Anatomy.* either of two long bony plates extending downwards from each side of the sphenoid bone within the skull. [C18 *pterygoid,* from Greek *pterugoeidēs,* from *pterux* wing; see -OID]

pteryla ('tɛrɪlə) *n, pl* **-lae** (-,liː). *Ornithol.* any of the tracts of skin that bear contour feathers, arranged in lines along the body of a bird. [C19: from New Latin, from Greek *pteron* feather + *hulē* wood, forest]

PTFE *abbrev. for* polytetrafluoroethylene.

ptg *abbrev. for* printing.

ptisan (tɪ'zæn) *n* **1** grape juice drained off without pressure. **2** a variant spelling of **tisane.** [C14: from Old French *tisane,* from Latin *ptisana,* from Greek *ptisanē* barley groats]

PTN *abbrev. for* public telephone network: the telephone network provided in Britain by British Telecom.

PTO *or* **pto** *abbrev. for* please turn over.

ptochocracy (təʊ'kɒkrəsɪ) *n, pl* **-cies.** government by the poor. [C18: from Greek, from *ptochos* poor + -CRACY]

Ptolemaeus (,tɒlɪ'miːəs) *n* a crater in the SE quadrant of the moon, about 140 kilometres (90 miles) in diameter.

Ptolemaic (,tɒlɪ'meɪɪk) *adj* **1** of or relating to the ancient astronomer Ptolemy or to his conception of the universe. **2** of or relating to the Macedonian dynasty that ruled Egypt from the death of Alexander the Great (323 B.C.) to the death of Cleopatra (30 B.C.).

Ptolemaic system *n* the theory of planetary motion developed by Ptolemy from the hypotheses of earlier philosophers, stating that the earth lay at the centre of the universe with the sun, the moon, and the known planets revolving around it in complicated orbits. Beyond the largest of these orbits lay a sphere of fixed stars. See also **epicycle** (sense 1). Compare **Copernican system.**

Ptolemaist (,tɒlɪ'meɪɪst) *n* a believer in or adherent of the Ptolemaic system of the universe.

Ptolemy ('tɒlɪmɪ) *n* Latin name *Claudius Ptolemaeus.* 2nd century A.D., Greek astronomer, mathematician, and geographer. His *Geography* was the standard geographical textbook until the discoveries of the 15th century. His system of astronomy (see **Ptolemaic system**), as expounded in the *Almagest,* remained undisputed until the Copernican system was evolved.

Ptolemy I *n* called *Ptolemy Soter.* ?367–283 B.C., king of Egypt (323–285 B.C.), a general of Alexander the Great, who obtained Egypt on Alexander's death and founded the Ptolemaic dynasty: his capital Alexandria became the centre of Greek culture.

Ptolemy II *n* called *Philadelphus.* 309–246 B.C., the son of Ptolemy I; king of Egypt (285–246). Under his rule the power, prosperity, and culture of Egypt was at its height.

ptomaine *or* **ptomain** ('təʊmeɪn) *n* any of a group of amines, such as cadaverine or putrescine, formed by decaying organic matter. [C19: from Italian *ptomaina,* from Greek *ptoma* corpse, from *piptein* to fall]

ptomaine poisoning *n* a popular term for **food poisoning.** Ptomaines were once erroneously thought to be a cause of food poisoning.

ptosis ('təʊsɪs) *n, pl* **ptoses** ('təʊsiːz). prolapse or drooping of a part, esp. the eyelid. [C18: from Greek: a falling] ▸ **ptotic** ('tɒtɪk) *adj*

pts *abbrev. for:* **1** parts. **2** payments. **3** points. **4** ports.

pts. *abbrev. for* pints.

PTT *abbrev. for* Post Telephone and Telegraph Administration; the usually national monopolies used to provide postal, telephonic, and telegraphic communication services.

Pty *Austral., N.Z., and S. African. abbrev. for* proprietary: used to denote a private limited company.

ptyalin ('taɪəlɪn) *n Biochem.* an amylase secreted in the saliva of man and other animals. [C19: from Greek *ptualon* saliva, from *ptuein* to spit]

ptyalism ('taɪə,lɪzəm) *n* excessive secretion of saliva. [C17: from Greek *ptualismos,* from *ptualizein* to produce saliva, from *ptualon* saliva]

p-type *adj* **1** (of a semiconductor) having a density of mobile holes in excess of that of conduction electrons. **2** associated with or resulting from the movement of holes in a semiconductor: *p-type conductivity.* Compare **n-type.**

Pu *the chemical symbol for* plutonium.

pub (pʌb) *n* **1** *Chiefly Brit.* a building with a bar and one or more public rooms licensed for the sale and consumption of alcoholic drink, often also providing light meals. Formal name: **public house. 2** *Austral. and N.Z.* a hotel. ◆ *vb* **pubs, pubbing, pubbed. 3** (*intr*) *Informal* to visit a pub or pubs (esp. in the phrase **go pubbing**).

pub. *abbrev. for:* **1** public. **2** publication. **3** published. **4** publisher. **5** publishing.

pub-crawl *Informal, chiefly Brit.* ◆ *n* **1** a drinking tour of a number of pubs or bars. ◆ *vb* **2** (*intr*) to make such a tour.

puberty ('pjuːbətɪ) *n* the period at the beginning of adolescence when the sex glands become functional and the secondary sexual characteristics emerge. Also called: **pubescence.** Related adj: **hebetic.** [C14: from Latin *pūbertās* maturity, from *pūber* adult] ▸ **'pubertal** *adj*

puberulent (pju'bɛrjʊlənt) *adj Biology.* covered with very fine down; finely pubescent. [C19: from Latin *pūber*]

pubes ('pjuːbiːz) *n, pl* **pubes** ('pjuːbiːz). **1** the region above the external genital organs, covered with hair from the time of puberty. **2** pubic hair. **3** the pubic bones. **4** the plural of **pubis.** [from Latin]

pubescent (pjuː'bɛsᵊnt) *adj* **1** arriving or having arrived at puberty. **2** (of certain plants and animals or their parts) covered with a layer of fine short hairs or down. [C17: from Latin *pūbēscere* to reach manhood, from *pūber* adult] ▸ **pu'bescence** *n*

pub grub *n Informal.* food served in a pub.

pubic ('pjuːbɪk) *adj* of or relating to the pubes or pubis: *pubic hair.*

pubis ('pjuːbɪs) *n, pl* **-bes** (-biːz). one of the three sections of the hipbone that forms part of the pelvis. [C16: shortened from New Latin *os pūbis* bone of the PUBES]

publ. *abbrev. for:* **1** publication. **2** published. **3** publisher.

public ('pʌblɪk) *adj* **1** of, relating to, or concerning the people as a whole. **2** open or accessible to all: *public gardens.* **3** performed or made openly or in the view of all: *public proclamation.* **4** (*prenominal*) well-known or familiar to people in general: *a public figure.* **5** (*usually prenominal*) maintained at the expense of, serving, or for the use of a community: *a public library.* **6** open, acknowledged, or notorious: *a public scandal.* **7 go public. 7a** (of a private company) to issue shares for subscription by the public. **7b** to reveal publicly hitherto confidential information. ◆ *n* **8** the community or people in general. **9** a part or section of the community grouped because of a common interest, activity, etc.: *the racing public.* [C15: from Latin *pūblicus,* changed from *pōplicus* of the people, from *populus* people]

public-address system *n* a system of one or more microphones, amplifiers, and loudspeakers for increasing the sound level of speech or music, used in auditoriums, public gatherings, etc. Sometimes shortened to **PA system.**

publican ('pʌblɪkən) *n* **1** (in Britain) a person who keeps a public house. **2** (in ancient Rome) a public contractor, esp. one who farmed the taxes of a province. [C12: from Old French *publicain,* from Latin *pūblicānus* tax gatherer, from *pūblicum* state revenues]

public assistance *n U.S.* payment given to individuals by government agencies on the basis of need.

publication (,pʌblɪ'keɪʃən) *n* **1** the act or process of publishing a printed work. **2** any printed work offered for sale or distribution. **3** the act or an instance of making information public. **4** the act of disseminating defamatory matter, esp. by communicating it to a third person. See **libel, slander.** Archaic word: **publishment.** [C14: via Old French from Latin *pūblicātiō* confiscation of an individual's property, from *pūblicāre* to seize and assign to public use]

public bar *n Brit.* a bar in a public house usually serving drinks at a cheaper price than in the saloon bar. Also called: **the public.** Compare **private bar.**

public bill *n* (in Parliament) a bill dealing with public policy that usually applies to the whole country. Compare **private bill, hybrid bill.**

public company *n* a limited company whose shares may be purchased by the public and traded freely on the open market and whose share capital is not less than a statutory minimum; public limited company. Compare **private company.**

public convenience *n* a public lavatory, esp. one in a public place.

public corporation *n* (in Britain) an organization established to run a nationalized industry or state-owned enterprise. The chairman and board members are appointed by a government minister, and the government has overall control.

public debt *n Chiefly U.S.* **1** the total financial obligations incurred by all governmental bodies of a nation. **2** another name for **national debt.**

public defender *n* (in the U.S.) a lawyer engaged at public expense to represent indigent defendants.

public domain *n* **1** *U.S.* lands owned by a state or by the federal government. **2** the status of a published work or invention upon which the copyright or patent has expired or which has not been patented or subject to copyright. It may thus be freely used by the public. **3 in the public domain.** able to be discussed and examined freely by the general public.

public enemy *n* a notorious person, such as a criminal, who is regarded as a menace to the public.

public enterprise *n* economic activity by governmental organizations. Compare **private enterprise** (sense 1).

public expenditure *n* spending by central government, local authorities, and public corporations.

public footpath *n* a footpath along which the public has right of way.

public gallery *n* the gallery in a chamber of Parliament reserved for members of the public who wish to listen to the proceedings. Also called: **strangers' gallery.**

public health inspector *n* (in Britain) a former name for **Environmental Health Officer.**

public holiday *n* a holiday observed over the whole country.

public house *n* **1** *Brit.* the formal name for **pub. 2** *U.S. and Canadian.* an inn, tavern, or small hotel.

publicist ('pʌblɪsɪst) *n* **1** a person who publicizes something, esp. a press or publicity agent. **2** a journalist. **3** *Rare.* a person learned in public or international law.

publicity (pʌ'blɪsɪtɪ) *n* **1a** the technique or process of attracting public attention to people, products, etc., as by the use of the mass media. **1b** (*as modifier*): *a publicity agent.* **2** public interest resulting from information supplied by such a technique or process. **3** information used to draw public attention to people, products, etc. **4** the state of being public. [C18: via French from Medieval Latin *pūblicitās;* see PUBLIC]

publicize *or* **publicise** ('pʌblɪ,saɪz) *vb* (*tr*) to bring to public notice; advertise.

public law *n* **1** a law that applies to the public of a state or nation. **2** the branch of law that deals with relations between a state and its individual members. Compare **private law.**

Public Lending Right *n* the right of authors to receive payment when their books are borrowed from public libraries. Abbrev.: **PLR.**

public-liability insurance *n* (in Britain) a form of insurance, compulsory for any business in contact with the public, which pays compensation to a member of the public suffering injury or damage as a result of the policyholder or his employees failing to take reasonable care.

public limited company *n* another name for **public company**. Abbrev.: **plc** *or* **PLC.**

publicly ('pʌblɪklɪ) *adv* **1** in a public manner; without concealment; openly. **2** in the name or with the consent of the public.

public nuisance *n* **1** *Law.* an illegal act causing harm to members of a particular community rather than to any individual. **2** *Informal.* a person who is generally considered objectionable.

public opinion *n* the attitude of the public, esp. as a factor in determining the actions of government.

public ownership *n* ownership by the state; nationalization.

public prosecutor *n Law.* an official in charge of prosecuting important cases.

Public Record Office *n* an institution in which official records are stored and kept available for inspection by the public.

public relations *n* (*functioning as sing or pl*) **1a** the practice of creating, promoting, or maintaining goodwill and a favourable image among the public towards an institution, public body, etc. **1b** the methods and techniques employed. **1c** (*as modifier*): *the public relations industry.* **2** the condition of the relationship between an organization and the public. **3** the professional staff employed to create, promote, or maintain a favourable relationship between an organization and the public. Abbrev.: **PR.**

public school *n* **1** (in England and Wales) a private independent fee-paying secondary school. **2** (in the U.S.) any school that is part of a free local educational system.

public sector *n* the part of an economy that consists of state-owned institutions, including nationalized industries and services provided by local authorities. Compare **private sector.**

public servant *n* **1** an elected or appointed holder of a public office. **2** the Austral. and N.Z. name for **civil servant.**

public service *n* **1a** government employment. **1b** the management and administration of the affairs of a political unit, esp. the civil service. **2a** a service provided for the community: *buses provide a public service.* **2b** (*as modifier*): *a public-service announcement.* **3** the Austral. and N.Z. name for the **civil service.**

public-service corporation *n U.S.* a private corporation that provides services to the community, such as telephone service, public transport.

public speaking *n* the art or practice of making speeches to large audiences. ▸ **public speaker** *n*

public spending *n* expenditure by central government, local authorities, and public enterprises.

public-spirited *adj* having or showing active interest in public welfare or the good of the community.

public transport *n* a system of buses, trains, etc., running on fixed routes, on which the public may travel.

public utility *n* an enterprise concerned with the provision to the public of essentials, such as electricity or water. Also called (U.S.): **public-service corporation.**

public works *pl n* engineering projects and other constructions, financed and undertaken by a government for the community.

publish ('pʌblɪʃ) *vb* **1** to produce and issue (printed matter) for distribution and sale. **2** (*intr*) to have one's written work issued for publication. **3** (*tr*) to announce formally or in public. **4** (*tr*) to communicate (defamatory matter) to someone other than the person defamed: *to publish a libel.* [C14: from Old French *puplier,* from Latin *pūblicāre* to make PUBLIC] ▸ **'publishable** *adj* ▸ **'publishing** *n*

publisher ('pʌblɪʃə) *n* **1** a company or person engaged in publishing periodicals, books, music, etc. **2** *U.S. and Canadian.* the proprietor of a newspaper or his representative.

púcán ('pu:kɑ:n) *n Irish.* a traditional Connemara open sailing boat. [Irish Gaelic]

Puccini (pu'tʃi:nɪ) *n* **Giacomo** ('dʒa:komo). 1858–1924, Italian operatic composer, noted for the dramatic realism of his operas, which include *Manon Lescaut* (1893), *La Bohème* (1896), *Tosca* (1900), and *Madame Butterfly* (1904).

puccoon (pə'ku:n) *n* **1** Also called: **alkanet.** any of several North American boraginaceous plants of the genus *Lithospermum,* esp. *L. canescens,* that yield a red dye. See also **gromwell. 2** any of several other plants that yield a reddish dye, esp. the bloodroot (**red puccoon**). **3** the dye from any of these plants. [C17: of Algonquian origin; see POKEWEED]

puce (pju:s) *n* **a** a colour varying from deep red to dark purplish-brown. **b** (*as adj*): *a puce carpet.* [C18: shortened from French *couleur puce* flea colour, from Latin *pūlex* flea]

puck[1] (pʌk) *n* **1** a small disc of hard rubber used in ice hockey. **2** a stroke at the ball in hurling. **3** *Irish slang.* a sharp blow. ◆ *vb* (*tr*) **4** to strike (the ball) in hurling. **5** *Irish slang.* to strike hard; punch. [C19: of unknown origin]

puck[2] (pʌk) *n* (*often cap.*) a mischievous or evil spirit. Also called: **Robin Goodfellow.** [Old English *pūca,* of obscure origin] ▸ **'puckish** *adj*

pucka ('pʌkə) *adj* a less common spelling of **pukka.**

pucker ('pʌkə) *vb* **1** to gather or contract (a soft surface such as the skin of the face) into wrinkles or folds, or (of such a surface) to be so gathered or contracted. ◆ *n* **2** a wrinkle, crease, or irregular fold. [C16: perhaps related to POKE[2], from the creasing into baglike wrinkles]

puckerood (ˌpʌkə'ru:d) *adj N.Z. informal.* ruined; exhausted. [from Maori *pakaru* to shatter]

pud (pʊd) *n Brit. informal.* short for **pudding.**

pudding ('pʊdɪŋ) *n* **1** a sweetened usually cooked dessert made in many forms and of various ingredients, such as flour, milk, and eggs, with fruit, etc. **2** a savoury dish, usually soft and consisting partially of pastry or batter: *steak-and-kidney pudding.* **3** the dessert course in a meal. **4** a sausage-like mass of seasoned minced meat, oatmeal, etc., stuffed into a prepared skin or bag and boiled. [C13 *poding;* compare Old English *puduc* a wart, Low German *puddek* sausage] ▸ **'puddingy** *adj*

pudding club *n Slang.* the state of being pregnant (esp. in the phrase **in the pudding club**).

pudding stone *n* a conglomerate rock in which there is a difference in colour and composition between the pebbles and the matrix.

puddle ('pʌdᵊl) *n* **1** a small pool of water, esp. of rain. **2** a small pool of any liquid. **3** a worked mixture of wet clay and sand that is impervious to water and is used to line a pond or canal. **4** *Rowing.* the patch of eddying water left by the blade of an oar after completion of a stroke. ◆ *vb* **5** (*tr*) to make (clay, etc.) into puddle. **6** (*tr*) to subject (iron) to puddling. **7** (*intr*) to dabble or wade in puddles, mud, or shallow water. **8** (*intr*) to mess about. [C14 *podel,* diminutive of Old English *pudd* ditch, of obscure origin] ▸ **'puddler** *n* ▸ **'puddly** *adj*

puddling ('pʌdlɪŋ) *n* **1** a process for converting pig iron into wrought iron by heating it with ferric oxide in a furnace to oxidize the carbon. **2** *Building.* the process of making a puddle.

puddock ('pʌdək) *n* a Scot. variant of **paddock**[2].

pudency ('pju:dᵊnsɪ) *n* modesty, shame, or prudishness. [C17: from Late Latin *pudentia,* from Latin *pudēre* to feel shame]

pudendum (pju:'dɛndəm) *n, pl* **-da** (-də). (*often pl*) the human external genital organs collectively, esp. of a female. [C17: from Late Latin, from Latin *pudenda* the shameful (parts), from *pudēre* to be ashamed] ▸ **pu'dendal** *or* **pudic** ('pju:dɪk) *adj*

pudge (pʌdʒ) *n Informal.* a variant of **podge.** [C19: of uncertain origin; see PUDGY]

pudgy ('pʌdʒɪ) *adj* **pudgier, pudgiest.** a variant spelling (esp. U.S.) of **podgy.** [C19: of uncertain origin; compare earlier *pudsy* plump, perhaps from Scottish *pud* stomach, plump child] ▸ **'pudgily** *adv* ▸ **'pudginess** *n*

Pudovkin (*Russian* pu'dɔfkjɪn) *n* **Vsevolod** ('fsjevələt). 1893–1953, Russian film director; noted for his silent films, such as *Mother* (1926) and *Storm over Asia* (1928).

Pudsey ('pʌdzɪ) *n* a town in N England, in Leeds unitary authority, West Yorkshire. Pop.: 31 636 (1991).

pudu ('pu:ˌdu:) *n* a diminutive Andean antelope, *Pudu pudu,* some 35 cm (13 to 14 in.) tall at the shoulder, with short straight horns and reddish-brown spotted coat. [C19: its native name]

Puebla (*Spanish* 'pweβla) *n* **1** an inland state of S central Mexico, situated on the Anáhuac Plateau. Capital: Puebla. Pop.: 4 624 239 (1995 est.). Area: 33 919 sq. km (13 096 sq. miles). **2** a city in S Mexico, capital of Puebla state: founded in 1532; university (1537). Pop.: 1 007 170 (1990). Full name: **Puebla de Zaragoza** (de θara'ɣoθa).

pueblo ('pwɛbləʊ; *Spanish* 'pweβlo) *n, pl* **-los** (-ləʊz; *Spanish* -los). **1** a communal village, built by certain Indians of the southwestern U.S. and parts of Latin America, consisting of one or more flat-roofed stone or adobe houses. **2** (in Spanish America) a village or town. **3** (in the Philippines) a town or township. [C19: from Spanish: people, from Latin *populus*]

Pueblo[1] ('pwɛbləʊ) *n, pl* **-lo** *or* **-los.** a member of any of the North American Indian peoples who live in pueblos, including the Tanoans, Zuñi, and Hopi.

Pueblo[2] ('pwɛbləʊ) *n* a city in the U.S.A., in Colorado: a centre of the steel industry. Pop.: 99 406 (1996 est.).

puerile ('pjʊəraɪl) *adj* **1** exhibiting silliness; immature; trivial. **2** of or characteristic of a child. [C17: from Latin *puerīlis* childish, from *puer* a boy] ▸ **'puerilely** *adv* ▸ **puerility** (pjʊə'rɪlɪtɪ) *n*

puerilism ('pjʊərɪˌlɪzəm) *n Psychiatry.* immature or childish behaviour by an adult.

puerperal (pju:'ɜ:pərəl) *adj* of, relating to, or occurring during the puerperium. [C18: from New Latin *puerperālis* relating to childbirth; see PUERPERIUM]

puerperal fever *n* a serious, formerly widespread, form of blood poisoning caused by infection contracted during childbirth.

puerperal psychosis *n* a mental disorder sometimes occurring in women after childbirth, characterized by deep depression, delusions of the child's death, and homicidal feelings towards the child.

puerperium (pjuə'pɪərɪəm) *n* the period following childbirth, lasting approximately six weeks, during which the uterus returns to its normal size and shape. [C17: from Latin: childbirth, from *puerperus* relating to a woman in labour, from *puer* boy + *parere* to bear]

Puerto Rico ('pwɜ:təʊ 'ri:kəʊ, 'pwɛə-) *n* an autonomous commonwealth (in association with the U.S.) occupying the smallest and easternmost of the Greater Antilles in the Caribbean: one of the most densely populated areas in the world; ceded by Spain to the U.S. in 1899. Currency: U.S. dollar. Capital: San Juan. Pop.: 3 786 000 (1998 est.). Area: 9104 sq. km (3515 sq. miles). Former name (until 1932): **Porto Rico.** Abbrev.: **PR.** ▸ **Puerto Rican** *adj, n*

Pufendorf (*German* 'pu:fəndɔrf) *n* **Samuel von** ('zamuəl fon). 1632–94, German jurist and philosopher, who lived in Sweden and Denmark. His *De Jure naturae et gentium* (1672) was an important contribution to the philosophy of natural and international law.

puff (pʌf) *n* **1** a short quick draught, gust, or emission, as of wind, smoke, air, etc., esp. a forceful one. **2** the amount of wind, smoke, etc., released in a puff. **3** the sound made by or associated with a puff. **4** an instance of inhaling and expelling the breath as in smoking. **5** a swelling. **6** a light aerated pastry usually filled with cream, jam, etc. **7** a powder puff. **8** exaggerated praise, as of a book, product, etc., esp. through an advertisement. **9** a piece of clothing fabric gathered up so as to bulge in the centre while being held together at the edges. **10** a loose piece of hair wound into a cylindrical roll, usually over a pad, and pinned in place in a coiffure. **11** a less common word for **quilt** (sense 1). **12** one's breath (esp. in the phrase **out of puff**). **13** *Derogatory slang.* a male homosexual. **14** a dialect word for **puffball.** ◆ *vb* **15** to blow or breathe or cause to blow or breathe in short quick draughts or blasts. **16** (*tr;* often foll. by *out;* usually passive) to cause to be out of breath. **17** to take puffs or draws at (a cigarette, cigar, or pipe). **18** to move with or by the emission of puffs: *the steam train puffed up the incline.* **19** (often foll. by *up, out,* etc.) to swell, as with air, pride, etc. **20** (*tr*) to praise with exaggerated empty words, often in advertising. **21** (*tr*) to apply (cosmetic powder) from a powder puff to (the face). **22** *Auctioneering.* to increase the price of (a lot) artificially by having an accomplice make false bids. [Old English *pyffan;* related to Dutch German *puffen,* Swiss *pfuffen,* Norwegian *puffa,* all of imitative origin]

puff adder *n* **1** a large venomous African viper, *Bitis arietans,* that is yellowish-grey with brown markings and inflates its body when alarmed. **2** another name for **hognose snake.**

puffball (ˈpʌfˌbɔːl) *n* any of various basidiomycetous saprotrophic fungi of the genera *Calvatia* and *Lycoperdon,* having a round fruiting body that discharges a cloud of brown spores when mature.

puffbird (ˈpʌfˌbɜːd) *n* any of various brownish tropical American birds of the family *Bucconidae,* having a large head: order *Piciformes* (woodpeckers, etc.). [C19: so called because of its habit of puffing out its feathers]

puffer (ˈpʌfə) *n* **1** a person or thing that puffs. **2** Also called: **globefish.** any marine plectognath fish of the family *Tetraodontidae,* having an elongated spiny body that can be inflated to form a globe.

puffery (ˈpʌfərɪ) *n, pl* **-eries.** *Informal.* exaggerated praise, esp. in publicity or advertising.

puffin (ˈpʌfɪn) *n* any of various northern diving birds of the family Alcidae (auks, etc.), esp. *Fratercula arctica* (**common** or **Atlantic puffin**), having a black-and-white plumage and a brightly coloured vertically flattened bill: order *Charadriiformes.* [C14: perhaps of Cornish origin]

puff pastry *or U.S.* **puff paste** *n* a dough rolled in thin layers incorporating fat to make a rich flaky pastry for pies, rich pastries, etc.

puff-puff *n Brit.* a children's name for a steam locomotive or railway train.

puffy (ˈpʌfɪ) *adj* **puffier, puffiest. 1** short of breath. **2** swollen or bloated: *a puffy face.* **3** pompous or conceited. **4** blowing in gusts. ▸ **ˈpuffily** *adv* ▸ **ˈpuffiness** *n*

pug[1] (pʌg) *n* **1** Also called: **carlin.** a small compact breed of dog with a smooth coat, lightly curled tail, and a short wrinkled nose. **2** any of several small geometrid moths, mostly of the genus *Eupithecia,* with slim forewings held outstretched at rest. [C16: of uncertain origin] ▸ **ˈpuggish** *adj*

pug[2] (pʌg) *vb* **pugs, pugging, pugged.** (*tr*) **1** to mix or knead (clay) with water to form a malleable mass or paste, often in a **pug mill. 2** to fill or stop with clay or a similar substance. **3** (of cattle) to trample (the ground) into consolidated mud. [C19: of uncertain origin]

pug[3] (pʌg) *n* a slang name for **boxer** (sense 1). [C20: shortened from PUGILIST]

Pugachov (ˈpugətʃɒf) *n* **Yemelyan Ivanovich.** 1726–75, Russian Cossack rebel, leader of a major revolt against the government of Catherine II: executed.

Puget (*French* pyʒɛ) *n* **Pierre** (pjɛr). 1620–94, French Baroque sculptor, best known for his *Milo of Crotona* (c. 1680).

Puget Sound (ˈpjuːdʒɪt) *n* an inlet of the Pacific in NW Washington. Length: about 130 km (80 miles).

pugging (ˈpʌgɪŋ) *n* material such as clay, mortar, sawdust, sand, etc., inserted between wooden flooring and ceiling to reduce the transmission of sound. Also called: **pug.**

puggree, pugree (ˈpʌgrɪ) *or* **puggaree, pugaree** (ˈpʌgərɪ) *n* **1** the usual Indian word for **turban. 2** a scarf, usually pleated, around the crown of some hats, esp. sun helmets. [C17: from Hindi *pagrī,* from Sanskrit *parikara*]

puggy (ˈpʌgɪ) *adj* **-gier, -giest.** *Dialect and N.Z.* sticky, claylike. [probably from PUG[2]]

pugilism (ˈpjuːdʒɪˌlɪzəm) *n* the art, practice, or profession of fighting with the fists; boxing. [C18: from Latin *pugil* a boxer; related to *pugnus* fist, *pugna* a fight] ▸ **ˈpugilist** *n* ▸ **ˌpugiˈlistic** *adj* ▸ **ˌpugiˈlistically** *adv*

Pugin (ˈpjuːdʒɪn) *n* **Augustus** (**Welby Northmore**). 1812–52, British architect; a leader of the Gothic Revival. He collaborated with Sir Charles Barry on the Palace of Westminster (begun 1836).

Puglia (ˈpuʎʎa) *n* the Italian name for **Apulia.**

pugnacious (pʌgˈneɪʃəs) *adj* readily disposed to fight; belligerent. [C17: from Latin *pugnāx*] ▸ **pugˈnaciously** *adv* ▸ **pugnacity** (pʌgˈnæsɪtɪ) *or* **pugˈnaciousness** *n*

pug nose *n* a short stubby upturned nose. [C18: from PUG[1]] ▸ **ˈpug-ˌnosed** *adj*

Pugwash conferences (ˈpʌgˌwɒʃ) *pl n* international peace conferences of scientists held regularly to discuss world problems: Nobel peace prize 1995 awarded to Joseph Rotblat, one of the founders of the conferences, secretary-general (1957–73), and president from 1988. [C20: from *Pugwash,* Nova Scotia, where the first conference was held]

puha (ˈpuːhɑː) *n N.Z.* another name for **sow thistle.** [Maori]

puir (puːr, pyr) *adj* a Scot. word for **poor.**

puirtith *or* **poortith** (ˈpuːrˌtɪθ, ˈpyr-) *n Scot.* poverty. [C16: from Old French *pouerteit, poverteit;* compare POVERTY]

puisne (ˈpjuːnɪ) *adj* (esp. of a subordinate judge) of lower rank. [C16: from Anglo-French, from Old French *puisné* born later, from *puis* at a later date, from Latin *posteā* afterwards + *né* born, from *naistre* to be born, from Latin *nascī*]

puissance (ˈpjuːɪsᵊns, ˈpwiːsɑːns) *n* **1** a competition in showjumping that tests a horse's ability to jump a limited number of large obstacles. **2** *Archaic or poetic.* power. [C15: from Old French; see PUISSANT]

puissant (ˈpjuːɪsᵊnt) *adj Archaic or poetic.* powerful. [C15: from Old French, ultimately from Latin *potēns* mighty, from *posse* to have power] ▸ **ˈpuissantly** *adv*

puja (ˈpuːdʒɑː) *n Hinduism.* a ritual in honour of the gods, performed either at home or in the mandir (temple). [from Sanskrit: worship]

puke (pjuːk) *Slang.* ◆ *vb* **1** to vomit. ◆ *n* **2** the act of vomiting. **3** the matter vomited. [C16: probably of imitative origin; compare German *spucken* to spit]

pukeko (ˈpʊkəkəʊ) *n, pl* **-kos.** a wading bird, *Porphyrio melanotus,* of New Zealand, with a brightly coloured plumage. [Maori]

pukka *or* **pucka** (ˈpʌkə) *adj* (esp. in India) **1** properly or perfectly done, constructed, etc.: *a pukka road.* **2** genuine: *pukka sahib.* [C17: from Hindi *pakkā* firm, from Sanskrit *pakva*]

pul (puːl) *n, pl* **puls** *or* **puli** (ˈpuːlɪ). an Afghan monetary unit worth one hundredth of an afghani. [via Persian from Turkish: small coin, from Late Greek *phollis* bag for money, from Latin *follis* bag]

pula (ˈpʊlə) *n* the standard monetary unit of Botswana, divided into 100 thebe.

Pula (*Serbo-Croat* ˈpuːla) *n* a port in NW Croatia at the S tip of the Istrian Peninsula: made a Roman military base in 178 B.C.; became the main Austro-Hungarian naval station and passed to Italy in 1919, to Yugoslavia in 1947, and is now in independent Croatia. Pop.: 62 300 (1991). Latin name: **Pietas Julia** (paɪˈɛɪtæsˈjuːlɪə). Italian name: **Pola.**

Pulau Pinang (ˈpʊlaʊ pɪˈnæŋ) *n* another name for **Penang.**

pulchritude (ˈpʌlkrɪˌtjuːd) *n Formal or literary.* physical beauty. [C15: from Latin *pulchritūdō,* from *pulcher* beautiful] ▸ **ˌpulchriˈtudinous** *adj*

Pulci (*Italian* ˈpultʃi) *n* **Luigi** (ˈlwiːdʒi). 1432–84, Italian poet. His masterpiece is the comic epic poem *Morgante* (1483).

pule (pjuːl) *vb* (*intr*) to cry plaintively; whimper. [C16: perhaps of imitative origin] ▸ **ˈpuler** *n*

puli (ˈpjuːlɪ, ˈpʊlɪ) *n* a breed of Hungarian sheepdog having a very long dense coat, usually black, that hangs in strands with a ropey or corded appearance. [Hungarian, literally: leader]

Pulitzer (ˈpʊlɪtsə) *n* **Joseph.** 1847–1911, U.S. newspaper publisher, born in Hungary. He established the Pulitzer prizes.

Pulitzer prize *n* one of a group of prizes established by Joseph Pulitzer and awarded yearly since 1917 for excellence in American journalism, literature, and music.

pull (pʊl) *vb* (*mainly tr*) **1** (*also intr*) to exert force on (an object) so as to draw it towards the source of the force. **2** to exert force on so as to remove; extract: *to pull a tooth.* **3** to strip of feathers, hair, etc.; pluck. **4** to draw the entrails from (a fowl). **5** to rend or tear. **6** to strain (a muscle, ligament, or tendon) injuriously. **7** (usually foll. by *off*) *Informal.* to perform or bring about: *to pull off a million-pound deal.* **8** (often foll. by *on*) *Informal.* to draw out (a weapon) for use: *he pulled a knife on his attacker.* **9** *Informal.* to attract: *the pop group pulled a crowd.* **10** (*also intr*) *Slang.* to attract (a sexual partner). **11** (*intr;* usually foll. by *on* or *at*) to drink or inhale deeply: *to pull at one's pipe; pull on a bottle of beer.* **12** to put on or make (a grimace): *to pull a face.* **13** (*also intr;* foll by *away, out, over,* etc.) to move (a vehicle) or (of a vehicle) be moved in a specified manner: *he pulled his car away from the roadside.* **14** *Printing.* to take (a proof) from type. **15** to withdraw or remove: *the board decided to pull their support.* **16** *Golf, baseball, etc.* to hit (a ball) so that it veers away from the direction in which the player intended to hit it (to the left for a right-handed player). **17** *Cricket.* to hit (a ball pitched straight or on the off side) to the leg side. **18** *Hurling.* to strike (a fast-moving ball) in the same direction as it is already moving. **19** (*also intr*) to row (a boat) or take a stroke of (an oar) in rowing. **20** to be rowed by: *a racing shell pulls one, two, four, or eight oars.* **21** (of a rider) to restrain (a horse), esp. to prevent it from winning a race. **22** (*intr*) (of a horse) to resist strongly the attempts of a rider to rein in or check it. **23 pull a fast one.** *Slang.* to play a sly trick. **24 pull apart** *or* **to pieces.** to criticize harshly. **25 pull your head in.** *Austral. informal.* be quiet! **26 pull (one's) punches. 26a** *Informal.* to restrain the force of one's criticisms or actions. **26b** *Boxing.* to restrain the force of one's blows, esp. when deliberately losing after being bribed, etc. **27 pull one's weight.** *Informal.* to do one's fair or proper share of a task. **28 pull strings.** *Informal.* to exercise personal influence, esp. secretly or unofficially. **29 pull (someone's) leg.** *Informal.* to make fun of, fool, or tease (someone). ◆ *n* **30** an act or an instance of pulling or being pulled. **31** the force or effort used in pulling: *the pull of the moon affects the tides on earth.* **32** the act or an instance of taking in drink or smoke. **33** something used for pulling, such as a knob or handle. **34** *Informal.* special advantage or influence: *his uncle is chairman of the company, so he has quite a lot of pull.* **35** *Informal.* the power to attract attention or support. **36** a period of rowing. **37** a single stroke of an oar in rowing. **38** the act of pulling the ball in golf, cricket, etc. **39** the act of checking or reining in a horse. **40** the amount of resistance in a bowstring, trigger, etc. ◆ See also **pull about, pull back, pull down, pull in, pull off, pull on, pull out, pull through, pull together, pull up.** [Old English *pullian;* related to Icelandic *pūla* to beat] ▸ **ˈpuller** *n*

pull about *vb* (*tr, adv*) to handle roughly: *the thugs pulled the old lady about.*

pull back *vb* (*adv*) **1** to return or be returned to a rearward position by pulling: *the army pulled back.* ◆ *n* **pullback. 2** the act of pulling back. **3** a device for restraining the motion of a mechanism, etc., or for returning it to its original position.

pull down *vb* (*tr, adv*) to destroy or demolish: *the old houses were pulled down.*

pullet (ˈpʊlɪt) *n* a young hen of the domestic fowl, less than one year old. [C14: from Old French *poulet* chicken, from Latin *pullus* a young animal or bird]

pulley (ˈpʊlɪ) *n* **1** a wheel with a grooved rim in which a rope, chain, or belt can run in order to change the direction or point of application of a force applied to the rope, etc. **2** a number of such wheels pivoted in parallel in a block, used to raise heavy loads. **3** a wheel with a flat, convex, or grooved rim mounted on a shaft and driven by or driving a belt passing around it. [C14 *poley,* from Old French *polie,* from Vulgar Latin *polidium* (unattested), apparently from Late Greek *polidion* (unattested) a little pole, from Greek *polos* axis]

pull in *vb* (*adv*) **1** (*intr;* often foll. by *to*) to reach a destination: *the train pulled in at the station.* **2** (*intr*) Also: **pull over.** (of a motor vehicle, driver, etc.) **2a** to draw in to the side of the road in order to stop or to allow another vehicle to pass. **2b** to stop (at a café, lay-by, etc.). **3** (*tr*) to draw or attract: *his appearance will pull in the crowds.* **4** (*tr*) *Slang.* to arrest. **5** (*tr*) to earn or gain (money). ◆ *n* **pull-in. 6** *Brit.* a roadside café, esp. for lorry drivers.

Pullman (ˈpʊlmən) *n, pl* **-mans.** a luxurious railway coach, esp. a sleeping car. Also called: **Pullman car.** [C19: named after George M. *Pullman* (1831–97), the U.S. inventor who first manufactured such coaches]

pull off *vb* (*tr*) **1** to remove (clothing) forcefully. **2** (*adv*) to succeed in performing (a difficult feat).

pull on *vb* (*tr, adv*) to don (clothing).

pullorum disease (pʊˈlɔːrəm) *n* an acute serious bacterial disease of very young birds, esp. chickens, characterized by a whitish diarrhoea: caused by *Salmonella pullorum,* transmitted during egg production. Also called: **bacillary white diarrhoea.** [Latin *pullōrum* of chickens, from *pullus* chicken]

pull out *vb* (*adv*) **1** (*tr*) to extract. **2** (*intr*) to depart: *the train pulled out of the station.* **3** *Military.* to withdraw or escape or be withdrawn or rescued, as from a difficult situation: *the troops were pulled out of the ruined city.* **4** (*intr*) (of a motor vehicle, driver, etc.) **4a** to draw away from the side of the road. **4b** to draw out from behind another vehicle to overtake. **5** (*intr*) to abandon a position or situation, esp. a dangerous or embarrassing one. **6** (foll. by *of*) to level out or cause to level out (from a dive). ◆ *n* **pull-out. 7** an extra leaf of a book that folds out. **8** a removable section of a magazine, etc. **9** a flight manoeuvre during which an aircraft levels out after a dive. **10** a withdrawal from a position or situation, esp. a dangerous or embarrassing one.

pullover (ˈpʊlˌəʊvə) *n* a garment, esp. a sweater, that is pulled on over the head.

pull through *vb* **1** Also: **pull round.** to survive or recover or cause to survive or recover, esp. after a serious illness or crisis. ◆ *n* **pull-through. 2** a weighted cord with a piece of cloth at the end used to clean the bore of a firearm.

pull together *vb* **1** (*intr, adv*) to cooperate or work harmoniously. **2 pull oneself together.** *Informal.* to regain one's self-control or composure.

pullulate (ˈpʌljʊˌleɪt) *vb* (*intr*) **1** (of animals, etc.) to breed rapidly or abundantly; teem; swarm. **2** (of plants or plant parts) to sprout, bud, or germinate. [C17: from Latin *pullulāre* to sprout, from *pullulus* a baby animal, from *pullus* young animal] ▸ **ˌpulluˈlation** *n*

pull up *vb* (*adv*) **1** (*tr*) to remove by the roots. **2** (often foll. by *with* or *on*) to move level (with) or ahead (of) or cause to move level (with) or ahead (of), esp. in a race. **3** to stop: *the car pulled up suddenly.* **4** (*tr*) to rebuke. ◆ *n* **pull-up. 5** *Brit.* a roadside café; pull-in.

pullus (ˈpʊləs) *n* a technical term for a chick or young bird. [C18: from Latin, from *pullulāre* to sprout]

pulmonary (ˈpʌlmənərɪ, -mənrɪ, ˈpʊl-) *adj* **1** of, or relating to or affecting the lungs. **2** having lungs or lunglike organs. [C18: from Latin *pulmōnārius,* from *pulmō* a lung; related to Greek *pleumōn* a lung]

pulmonary artery *n* either of the two arteries that convey oxygen-depleted blood from the heart to the lungs.

pulmonary vein *n* any one of the four veins that convey oxygen-rich blood from the lungs to the heart.

pulmonate (ˈpʌlmənɪt, ˈpʊl-) *adj* **1** having lungs or lunglike organs. **2** of, relating to, or belonging to the *Pulmonata,* a mostly terrestrial subclass or order of gastropod molluscs, including snails and slugs, in which the mantle is adapted as a lung. ◆ *n* **3** any pulmonate mollusc. [C19: from New Latin *pulmōnātus*]

pulmonic (pʌlˈmɒnɪk, pʊl-) *adj* **1** of or relating to the lungs; pulmonary. ◆ *n* **2** *Rare.* **2a** a person with lung disease. **2b** a drug or remedy for lung disease. [C17: from French *pulmonique,* from Latin *pulmō* a lung; see PULMONARY]

Pulmotor (ˈpʌlˌməʊtə, ˈpʊl-) *n Trademark.* an apparatus for pumping oxygen into the lungs during artificial respiration.

pulp (pʌlp) *n* **1** soft or fleshy plant tissue, such as the succulent part of a fleshy fruit. **2** a moist mixture of cellulose fibres, as obtained from wood, from which paper is made. **3a** a magazine or book containing trite or sensational material, and usually printed on cheap rough paper. **3b** (*as modifier*): *a pulp novel.* **4** *Dentistry.* the soft innermost part of a tooth, containing nerves and blood vessels. **5** any soft soggy mass or substance. **6** *Mining.* pulverized ore, esp. when mixed with water. ◆ *vb* **7** to reduce (a material or solid substance) to pulp or (of a material or solid substance) to be reduced to pulp. **8** (*tr*) to remove the pulp from (fruit). [C16: from Latin *pulpa*] ▸ **ˈpulper** *n*

pulpit (ˈpʊlpɪt) *n* **1** a raised platform, usually surrounded by a barrier, set up in churches as the appointed place for preaching, leading in prayer, etc. **2** any similar raised structure, such as a lectern. **3** a medium for expressing an opinion, such as a column in a newspaper. **4** (usually preceded by *the*) **4a** the preaching of the Christian message. **4b** the clergy or their message and influence. [C14: from Latin *pulpitum* a platform]

pulpwood (ˈpʌlpˌwʊd) *n* pine, spruce, or any other soft wood used to make paper.

pulpy (ˈpʌlpɪ) *adj* **pulpier, pulpiest.** having a soft or soggy consistency. ▸ **ˈpulpily** *adv* ▸ **ˈpulpiness** *n*

pulque (ˈpʊlkɪ; *Spanish* ˈpulke) *n* a light alcoholic drink from Mexico made from the juice of various agave plants, esp. the maguey. [C17: from Mexican Spanish, apparently from Nahuatl, from *puliuhqui* decomposed, since it will only keep for a day]

pulsar (ˈpʌlˌsɑː) *n* any of a number of very small extremely dense stars first discovered in 1967, which rotate very fast emitting regular pulses of polarized radiation, esp. radio waves. They are thought to be neutron stars formed during supernova explosions. [C20: from *puls(ating st)ar,* on the model of QUASAR]

pulsate (pʌlˈseɪt) *vb* (*intr*) **1** to expand and contract with a rhythmic beat; throb. **2** *Physics.* to vary in intensity, magnitude, size, etc.: *the current was pulsating.* **3** to quiver or vibrate. [C18: from Latin *pulsāre* to push] ▸ **pulsative** (ˈpʌlsətɪv) *adj* ▸ **ˈpulsatively** *adv*

pulsatile (ˈpʌlsəˌtaɪl) *adj* beating rhythmically; pulsating or throbbing. ▸ **pulsatility** (ˌpʌlsəˈtɪlɪtɪ) *n*

pulsatilla (ˌpʌlsəˈtɪlə) *n* another name for **pasqueflower.** [C16: from Medieval Latin, from *pulsāta* beaten (by the wind)]

pulsating star *n* a type of variable star, the variation in brightness resulting from expansion and subsequent contraction of the star.

pulsation (pʌlˈseɪʃən) *n* **1** the act of pulsating. **2** *Physiol.* a rhythmic beating or pulsing esp. of the heart or an artery.

pulsator (pʌlˈseɪtə) *n* **1** a device that stimulates rhythmic motion of a body; a vibrator. **2** any pulsating machine, device, or part.

pulsatory (ˈpʌlsətərɪ, -trɪ) *adj* **1** of or relating to pulsation. **2** throbbing or pulsating.

pulse[1] (pʌls) *n* **1** *Physiol.* **1a** the rhythmic contraction and expansion of an artery at each beat of the heart, often discernible to the touch at points such as the wrists. **1b** a single pulsation of the heart or arteries. **2** *Physics, electronics.* **2a** a transient sharp change in voltage, current, or some other quantity normally constant in a system. **2b** one of a series of such transient disturbances, usually recurring at regular intervals and having a characteristic geometric shape. **2c** (*as modifier*): *a pulse generator.* Less common name: **impulse. 3a** a recurrent rhythmic series of beats, waves, vibrations, etc. **3b** any single beat, wave, etc., in such a series. **4** bustle, vitality, or excitement: *the pulse of a city.* **5** the feelings or thoughts of a group or society as they can be measured: *the pulse of the voters.* **6 keep one's finger on the pulse.** to be well-informed about current events. ◆ *vb* **7** (*intr*) to beat, throb, or vibrate. [C14 *pous,* from Latin *pulsus* a beating, from *pellere* to beat] ▸ **ˈpulseless** *adj*

pulse[2] (pʌls) *n* **1** the edible seeds of any of several papilionaceous plants, such as peas, beans, and lentils. **2** the plant producing any of these seeds. [C13 *pols,* from Old French, from Latin *puls* pottage of pulse]

pulse code modulation *n Electronics.* a form of pulse modulation in which the information is carried by coded groups of pulses. Abbrev.: **pcm.**

pulse height analyser *n Electronics.* a multichannel analyser that sorts pulses into selected amplitude ranges.

pulsejet (ˈpʌlsˌdʒɛt) *n* a type of ramjet engine in which air is admitted through movable vanes that are closed by the pressure resulting from each intermittent explosion of the fuel in the combustion chamber, thus causing a pulsating thrust. Also called: **pulsejet engine, pulsojet** (ˈpʌlsəʊˌdʒɛt).

pulse modulation *n Electronics.* **1** a type of modulation in which a train of pulses is used as the carrier wave, one or more of its parameters, such as amplitude, being modulated or modified in order to carry information. **2** the modulation of a continuous carrier wave by means of pulses.

pulsimeter (pʌlˈsɪmɪtə) *n Med.* an instrument for measuring the strength and rate of the pulse. Also called: **pulsometer.**

pulsometer (pʌlˈsɒmɪtə) *n* **1** another name for **pulsimeter. 2** a vacuum pump that operates by steam being condensed and water admitted alternately in two chambers.

pulverable (ˈpʌlvərəbᵊl) *adj* able to be pulverized.

pulverize *or* **pulverise** (ˈpʌlvəˌraɪz) *vb* **1** to reduce (a substance) to fine particles, as by crushing or grinding, or (of a substance) to be so reduced. **2** (*tr*) to destroy completely; defeat or injure seriously. [C16: from Late Latin *pulverizare* or French *pulvériser,* from Latin *pulverum,* from *pulvis* dust] ▸ **ˈpulverˌizable** *or* **ˈpulverˌisable** *adj* ▸ **ˌpulveriˈzation** *or* **ˌpulveriˈsation** *n* ▸ **ˈpulverˌizer** *or* **ˈpulverˌiser** *n*

pulverulent (pʌlˈvɛrʊlənt) *adj* consisting of, covered with, or crumbling to dust or fine particles. [C17: from Latin *pulverulentus,* from *pulvis* dust] ▸ **pulˈverulence** *n*

pulvillus (pʌlˈvɪləs) *n, pl* **-li** (-laɪ). a small pad between the claws at the end of an insect's leg. [C18: from Latin, from *pulvīnulus,* diminutive of *pulvīnus* cushion]

pulvinate (ˈpʌlvɪˌneɪt) *or* **pulvinated** *adj* **1** *Architect.* (of a frieze) curved convexly; having a swelling. **2** *Botany.* **2a** shaped like a cushion. **2b** (of a leafstalk) having a pulvinus. [C19: from Latin *pulvīnātus* cushion-shaped]

pulvinus (pʌlˈvaɪnəs) *n, pl* **-ni** (-naɪ). a swelling at the base of a leafstalk: changes in its turgor pressure cause changes in the position of the leaf. [C19: from Latin: cushion]

puma (ˈpjuːmə) *n* a large American feline mammal, *Felis concolor,* that resembles a lion, having a plain greyish-brown coat and long tail. Also called: **cougar, mountain lion.** [C18: via Spanish from Quechuan]

pumice (ˈpʌmɪs) *n* **1** Also called: **pumice stone.** a light porous acid volcanic rock having the composition of rhyolite, used for scouring and, in powdered form, as an abrasive and for polishing. ◆ *vb* **2** (*tr*) to rub or polish with pumice. [C15 *pomys,* from Old French *pomis,* from Latin *pūmex*] ▸ **pumiceous** (pjuːˈmɪʃəs) *adj*

pumice country *n N.Z.* volcanic farmland in the North Island.

pummel (ˈpʌməl) *vb* **-mels, -melling, -melled** *or U.S.* **-mels, -meling, -meled.** (*tr*) to strike repeatedly with or as if with the fists. Also (less commonly): **pommel.** [C16: see POMMEL]

pump[1] (pʌmp) *n* **1** any device for compressing, driving, raising, or reducing the pressure of a fluid, esp. by means of a piston or set of rotating impellers. **2** *Biology.* a mechanism for the active transport of ions, such as protons, calcium ions, and sodium ions, across cell membranes: *a sodium pump.* ◆ *vb* **3** (when *tr,* usually foll. by *from, out, into, away,* etc.) to raise or drive (air, liquid, etc., esp. into or from something) with a pump or similar device. **4** (*tr;* usually foll. by *in* or *into*) to supply in large amounts: *to pump capital into a project.* **5** (*tr*) to deliver (shots, bullets, etc.) repeatedly with great force. **6** to operate (something, esp. a handle or lever) in the manner of a pump or (of something) to work in this way: *to pump the pedals of a bicycle.* **7** (*tr*) to obtain (information) from (a person) by persistent questioning. **8** (*intr;* usually foll. by *from* or *out of*) (of liquids) to flow freely in large spurts: *oil pumped from the fissure.* [C15: from Middle Dutch *pumpe* pipe, probably from Spanish *bomba,* of imitative origin]

pump[2] (pʌmp) *n* **1** a low-cut low-heeled shoe without fastenings, worn esp. for dancing. **2** a type of shoe with a rubber sole, used in games such as tennis; plimsoll. [C16: of unknown origin]

pumped storage *n* (in hydroelectric systems) a method of using power at a period of low demand to pump water back up to a high storage reservoir so that it can be released to generate electricity at a period of peak demand.

pumpernickel ('pʌmpəˌnɪkᵊl) *n* a slightly sour black bread, originating in Germany, made of coarse rye flour. [C18: from German, of uncertain origin]

pump gun *n* a repeating gun operated by a slide-action mechanism feeding ammunition from a magazine under the barrel into the breech.

pump iron *vb* (*intr*) *Slang.* to exercise with weights; do body-building exercises.

pumpkin ('pʌmpkɪn) *n* **1** any of several creeping cucurbitaceous plants of the genus *Cucurbita,* esp. *C. pepo* of North America and *C. maxima* of Europe. **2a** the large round fruit of any of these plants, which has a thick orange rind, pulpy flesh, and numerous seeds. **2b** (*as modifier*): *pumpkin pie.* [C17: from earlier *pumpion,* from Old French *pompon,* from Latin *pepo,* from Greek *pepōn,* from *pepōn* ripe, from *peptein* to ripen]

pumpkinseed ('pʌmpkɪnˌsiːd) *n* **1** the seed of the pumpkin. **2** a common North American freshwater sunfish, *Lepomis gibbosus,* with brightly coloured markings: family *Centrarchidae.*

pump priming *n* **1** the act or process of introducing fluid into a pump to improve the sealing of the pump parts on starting and to expel air from it. **2** *U.S.* government expenditure designed to stimulate economic activity in stagnant or depressed areas. **3** another term for **deficit financing.**

pump room *n* a building or room at a spa in which the water from a mineral spring may be drunk.

pun[1] (pʌn) *n* **1** the use of words or phrases to exploit ambiguities and innuendoes in their meaning, usually for humorous effect; a play on words. An example is: *"Ben Battle was a soldier bold, And used to war's alarms: But a cannonball took off his legs, So he laid down his arms."* (Thomas Hood). ◆ *vb* **puns, punning, punned. 2** (*intr*) to make puns. [C17: possibly from Italian *puntiglio* point of detail, wordplay; see PUNCTILIO]

pun[2] (pʌn) *vb* **puns, punning, punned.** (*tr*) *Brit.* to pack (earth, rubble, etc.) by pounding. [C16: dialectal variant of POUND[1]] ▸ **'punner** *n*

puna *Spanish.* ('puna) *n* **1** a high cold dry plateau, esp. in the Andes. **2** another name for **mountain sickness.** [C17: from American Spanish, from Quechuan]

Punakha *or* **Punaka** ('puːnəkə) *n* a town in W central Bhutan: a former capital of the country.

punch[1] (pʌntʃ) *vb* **1** to strike blows (at), esp. with a clenched fist. **2** (*tr*) *Western U.S.* to herd or drive (cattle), esp. for a living. **3** (*tr*) to poke or prod with a stick or similar object. ◆ *n* **4** a blow with the fist. **5** *Informal.* telling force, point, or vigour: *his arguments lacked punch.* **6 pull (one's) punches.** See at **pull** (sense 26). [C15: perhaps a variant of POUNCE[2]] ▸ **'puncher** *n*

punch[2] (pʌntʃ) *n* **1** a tool or machine for piercing holes in a material. **2** any of various tools used for knocking a bolt, rivet, etc., out of a hole. **3** a tool or machine used for stamping a design on something or shaping it by impact. **4** the solid die of a punching machine for cutting, stamping, or shaping material. **5** *Computing.* a device, such as a card punch or tape punch, used for making holes in a card or paper tape. **6** see **centre punch.** ◆ *vb* **7** (*tr*) to pierce, cut, stamp, shape, or drive with a punch. [C14: shortened from *puncheon,* from Old French *ponçon;* see PUNCHEON[2]]

punch[3] (pʌntʃ) *n* any mixed drink containing fruit juice and, usually, alcoholic liquor, generally hot and spiced. [C17: perhaps from Hindi *pānch,* from Sanskrit *pañca* five; the beverage originally included five ingredients]

Punch (pʌntʃ) *n* the main character in the traditional children's puppet show **Punch and Judy.**

punchbag ('pʌntʃˌbæg) *n* Also called (U.S. and Canadian): **punching bag.** a suspended stuffed bag that is punched for exercise, esp. boxing training.

punchball ('pʌntʃˌbɔːl) *n* **1** a stuffed or inflated ball, supported by a flexible rod, that is punched for exercise, esp. boxing training. **2** *U.S.* a game resembling baseball in which a light ball is struck with the fist.

punchboard ('pʌntʃˌbɔːd) *n* a board full of holes containing slips of paper, used in a gambling game in which a player attempts to push out a slip marked with a winning number.

punchbowl ('pʌntʃˌbəʊl) *n* **1** a large bowl for serving punch, lemonade, etc., usually with a ladle and often having small drinking glasses hooked around the rim. **2** *Brit.* a bowl-shaped depression in the land.

punch-drunk *adj* **1** demonstrating or characteristic of the behaviour of a person who has suffered repeated blows to the head, esp. a professional boxer. **2** dazed; stupefied.

punched card *or esp. U.S.* **punch card** *n* (formerly) a card on which data can be coded in the form of punched holes. In computing, there were usually 80 columns and 12 rows, each column containing a pattern of holes representing one character. Sometimes shortened to **card.**

punched tape *or U.S.* (*sometimes*) **perforated tape** *n* other terms for **paper tape.**

puncheon[1] ('pʌntʃən) *n* **1** a large cask of variable capacity, usually between 70 and 120 gallons. **2** the volume of such a cask used as a liquid measure. [C15 *poncion,* from Old French *ponchon,* of uncertain origin]

puncheon[2] ('pʌntʃən) *n* **1** a short wooden post that is used as a vertical strut. **2** a less common name for **punch**[2] (sense 1). [C14 *ponson,* from Old French *ponçon,* from Latin *punctiō* a puncture, from *pungere* to prick]

Punchinello (ˌpʌntʃɪ'nɛləʊ) *n, pl* **-los** *or* **-loes. 1** a type of clown from Italian burlesque or puppet shows, the prototype of Punch. **2** (*sometimes not cap.*) any grotesque or absurd character. [C17: from earlier *Polichinello,* from Italian (Neapolitan dialect) *Polecenella,* from Italian *pulcino* chicken, ultimately from Latin *pullus* young animal]

punch line *n* the culminating part of a joke, funny story, etc., that gives it its humorous or dramatic point.

punch-up *n Brit. informal.* a fight, brawl, or violent argument.

punchy ('pʌntʃɪ) *adj* **punchier, punchiest. 1** an informal word for **punch-drunk. 2** *Informal.* incisive or forceful: *a punchy article.* ▸ **'punchily** *adv* ▸ **'punchiness** *n*

punctate ('pʌŋkteɪt) *or* **punctated** *adj* having or marked with minute spots, holes, or depressions. [C18: from New Latin *punctātus,* from Latin *punctum* a point] ▸ **punc'tation** *n*

punctilio (pʌŋk'tɪlɪˌəʊ) *n, pl* **-os. 1** strict attention to minute points of etiquette. **2** a petty formality or fine point of etiquette. [C16: from Italian *puntiglio* small point, from *punto* point, from Latin *punctum* point]

punctilious (pʌŋk'tɪlɪəs) *adj* **1** paying scrupulous attention to correctness in etiquette. **2** attentive to detail. ▸ **punc'tiliously** *adv* ▸ **punc'tiliousness** *n*

punctual ('pʌŋktjʊəl) *adj* **1** arriving or taking place at an arranged time; prompt. **2** (of a person) having the characteristic of always keeping to arranged times, as for appointments, meetings, etc. **3** *Obsolete.* precise; exact; apposite. **4** *Maths.* consisting of or confined to a point in space. [C14: from Medieval Latin *punctuālis* concerning detail, from Latin *punctum* point] ▸ **ˌpunctu'ality** *n* ▸ **'punctually** *adv*

punctuate ('pʌŋktjʊˌeɪt) *vb* (*mainly tr*) **1** (*also intr*) to insert punctuation marks into (a written text). **2** to interrupt or insert at frequent intervals: *a meeting punctuated by heckling.* **3** to give emphasis to. [C17: from Medieval Latin *punctuāre* to prick, from Latin *punctum* a prick, from *pungere* to puncture] ▸ **'punctuˌator** *n*

punctuation (ˌpʌŋktjʊ'eɪʃən) *n* **1** the use of symbols not belonging to the alphabet of a writing system to indicate aspects of the intonation and meaning not otherwise conveyed in the written language. **2** the symbols used for this purpose. **3** the act or an instance of punctuating.

punctuation mark *n* any of the signs used in punctuation, such as a comma or question mark.

puncture ('pʌŋktʃə) *n* **1** a small hole made by a sharp object. **2** a perforation and loss of pressure in a pneumatic tyre, made by sharp stones, glass, etc. **3** the act of puncturing or perforating. ◆ *vb* **4** (*tr*) to pierce (a hole) in (something) with a sharp object. **5** to cause (something pressurized, esp. a tyre) to lose pressure by piercing, or (of a tyre, etc.) to be pierced and collapse in this way. **6** (*tr*) to depreciate (a person's self-esteem, pomposity, etc.). [C14: from Latin *punctūra,* from *pungere* to prick] ▸ **'puncturable** *adj* ▸ **'puncturer** *n*

pundit ('pʌndɪt) *n* **1** an expert. **2** (formerly) a learned person. **3** Also called: **pandit.** a Brahman learned in Sanskrit and, esp. in Hindu religion, philosophy or law. [C17: from Hindi *pandit,* from Sanskrit *pandita* learned man, from *pandita* learned]

Pune ('puːnə) *n* another name for **Poona.**

pung (pʌŋ) *n Eastern U.S. and Canadian.* a horse-drawn sleigh with a boxlike body on runners. [C19: shortened from Algonquian *tom-pung;* compare TOBOGGAN]

punga ('pʌŋə) *n* a variant spelling of **ponga.**

pungent ('pʌndʒənt) *adj* **1** having an acrid smell or sharp bitter flavour. **2** (of wit, satire, etc.) biting; caustic. **3** *Biology.* ending in a sharp point: *a pungent leaf.* [C16: from Latin *pungens* piercing, from *pungere* to prick] ▸ **'pungency** *n* ▸ **'pungently** *adv*

Punic ('pjuːnɪk) *adj* **1** of or relating to ancient Carthage or the Carthaginians. **2** characteristic of the treachery of the Carthaginians. ◆ *n* **3** the language of the ancient Carthaginians; a late form of Phoenician. [C15: from Latin *Pūnicus,* variant of *Poenicus* Carthaginian, from Greek *Phoinix*]

Punic Wars *pl n* three wars (264–241 B.C., 218–201 B.C., and 149–146 B.C.), in which Rome crushed Carthaginian power, destroying Carthage itself.

punish ('pʌnɪʃ) *vb* **1** to force (someone) to undergo a penalty or sanction, such as imprisonment, fines, death, etc., for some crime or misdemeanour. **2** (*tr*) to inflict punishment for (some crime, etc.). **3** (*tr*) to use or treat harshly or roughly, esp. as by overexertion: *to punish a horse.* **4** (*tr*) *Informal.* to consume (some commodity) in large quantities: *to punish the bottle.* [C14 *punisse,* from Old French *punir,* from Latin *pūnīre* to punish, from *poena* penalty] ▸ **'punisher** *n* ▸ **'punishing** *adj* ▸ **'punishingly** *adv*

punishable ('pʌnɪʃəbᵊl) *adj* liable to be punished or deserving of punishment. ▸ **ˌpunisha'bility** *n*

punishment ('pʌnɪʃmənt) *n* **1** a penalty or sanction given for any crime or offence. **2** the act of punishing or state of being punished. **3** *Informal.* rough treatment. **4** *Psychol.* any aversive stimulus administered to an organism as part of training.

punitive ('pjuːnɪtɪv) *or* (*less commonly*) **punitory** ('pjuːnɪtərɪ, -trɪ) *adj* relating to, involving, or with the intention of inflicting punishment: *a punitive expedition.* [C17: from Medieval Latin *pūnītīvus* concerning punishment, from Latin *pūnīre* to punish] ▸ **'punitively** *adv* ▸ **'punitiveness** *n*

Punjab (pʌn'dʒɑːb, 'pʌndʒɑːb) *n* **1** (formerly) a province in NW British India: divided between India and Pakistan in 1947. **2** a state of NW India: reorganized in 1966 as a Punjabi-speaking state, a large part forming the new state of Haryana; mainly agricultural. Capital: Chandigarh. Pop.: 21 695 000 (1994 est.). Area: 50 255 sq. km (19 403 sq. miles). **3** a province of W Pakistan: created in 1947. Capital: Lahore. Pop.: 53 840 000 (1985 est.). Area: 205 344 sq. km (127 595 sq. miles).

Punjabi *or* **Panjabi** (pʌnˈdʒɑːbɪ) *n* **1** a member of the chief people of the Punjab. **2** the state language of the Punjab, belonging to the Indic branch of the Indo-European family. ♦ *adj* **3** of or relating to the Punjab, its people, or their language.

Punjab States *pl n* (formerly) a group of states in NW India, amalgamated in 1956 with Punjab state.

punk[1] (pʌŋk) *n* **1a** a youth movement of the late 1970s, characterized by anti-Establishment slogans and outrageous clothes and hairstyles. **1b** an adherent of punk. **1c** short for **punk rock. 1d** (*as modifier*): *a punk record.* **2** an inferior, rotten, or worthless person or thing. **3** worthless articles collectively. **4** a petty criminal or hoodlum. **5** *Obsolete.* a young male homosexual; catamite. **6** *Obsolete.* a prostitute. ♦ *adj* **7** inferior, rotten, or worthless. [C16: via Polari from Spanish *pu(n)ta* prostitute, *pu(n)to* male prostitute] ► **ˈpunkish** *adj*

punk[2] (pʌŋk) *n* **1** dried decayed wood that smoulders when ignited: used as tinder. **2** any of various other substances that smoulder when ignited, esp. one used to light fireworks. [C18: of uncertain origin]

punka *or* **punkah** (ˈpʌŋkə) *n* a fan made of a palm leaf or leaves. [C17: from Hindi *pankhā*, from Sanskrit *paksaka* fan, from *paksa* wing]

punk rock *n* a fast abrasive style of rock music of the late 1970s, characterized by aggressive or offensive lyrics and performance. Sometimes shortened to **punk.** ► **punk rocker** *n*

punnet (ˈpʌnɪt) *n Chiefly Brit.* a small basket for fruit, such as strawberries. [C19: perhaps diminutive of dialect *pun* POUND[2]]

punster (ˈpʌnstə) *n* a person who is fond of making puns, esp. one who makes a tedious habit of this.

punt[1] (pʌnt) *n* **1** an open flat-bottomed boat with square ends, propelled by a pole. See **quant**[1]. ♦ *vb* **2** to propel (a boat, esp. a punt) by pushing with a pole on the bottom of a river, etc. [Old English *punt* shallow boat, from Latin *pontō* punt, PONTOON[1]]

punt[2] (pʌnt) *n* **1** a kick in certain sports, such as rugby, in which the ball is released and kicked before it hits the ground. **2** any long high kick. ♦ *vb* **3** to kick (a ball, etc.) using a punt. [C19: perhaps a variant of English dialect *bunt* to push, perhaps a nasalized variant of BUTT[3]]

punt[3] (pʌnt) *Chiefly Brit.* ♦ *vb* **1** (*intr*) to gamble; bet. ♦ *n* **2** a gamble or bet, esp. against the bank, as in roulette, or on horses. **3** Also called: **punter.** a person who bets. **4 take a punt at.** *Austral. and N.Z. informal.* to have an attempt or try at (something). [C18: from French *ponter* to punt, from *ponte* bet laid against the banker, from Spanish *punto* point, from Latin *punctum*]

punt[4] (pʊnt) *n* the Irish pound. [Irish Gaelic: pound]

Punta Arenas (*Spanish* ˈpunta aˈrenas) *n* a port in S Chile, on the Strait of Magellan: the southernmost city in the world. Pop.: 117 206 (1995 est.). Former name: **Magallanes.**

punter[1] (ˈpʌntə) *n* a person who punts a boat.

punter[2] (ˈpʌntə) *n* a person who kicks a ball.

punter[3] (ˈpʌntə) *n* **1** a person who places a bet. **2** *Informal.* any member of the public, esp. when a customer: *the punters flock into the sales.* **3** *Slang.* a prostitute's client. **4** *Slang.* a victim of a con man.

punty (ˈpʌntɪ) *n, pl* **-ties.** a long iron rod used in the finishing process of glass-blowing. Also called: **pontil.** [C17: see PONTIL]

puny (ˈpjuːnɪ) *adj* **-nier, -niest. 1** having a small physique or weakly constitution. **2** paltry; insignificant. [C16: from Old French *puisne* PUISNE] ► **ˈpunily** *adv* ► **ˈpuniness** *n*

pup (pʌp) *n* **1a** a young dog, esp. when under one year of age; puppy. **1b** the young of various other animals, such as the seal. **2 in pup.** (of a bitch) pregnant. **3** *Informal, chiefly Brit., contemptuous.* a conceited young man (esp. in the phrase **young pup**). **4 sell (someone) a pup.** to swindle (someone) by selling him something worthless. **5 the night's a pup.** *Austral. slang.* it's early yet. ♦ *vb* **pups, pupping, pupped. 6** (of dogs, seals, etc.) to give birth to (young). [C18: back formation from PUPPY]

pupa (ˈpjuːpə) *n, pl* **-pae** (-piː) *or* **-pas.** an insect at the immobile nonfeeding stage of development between larva and adult, when many internal changes occur. See **coarctate, exarate, obtect.** [C19: via New Latin, from Latin: a doll, puppet] ► **ˈpupal** *adj*

puparium (pjuːˈpeərɪəm) *n, pl* **-ia** (-ɪə). a hard barrel-shaped case enclosing the pupae of the housefly and other dipterous insects. ► **puˈparial** *adj*

pupate (pjuːˈpeɪt) *vb* (*intr*) (of an insect larva) to develop into a pupa. ► **puˈpation** *n*

pupil[1] (ˈpjuːpᵊl) *n* **1** a student who is taught by a teacher, esp. a young student. **2** *Civil and Scots Law.* a boy under 14 or a girl under 12 who is in the care of a guardian. [C14: from Latin *pupillus* an orphan, from *pūpus* a child]

pupil[2] (ˈpjuːpᵊl) *n* the dark circular aperture at the centre of the iris of the eye, through which light enters. [C16: from Latin *pūpilla*, diminutive of *pūpa* girl, puppet; from the tiny reflections in the eye]

pupillage *or U.S.* **pupilage** (ˈpjuːpɪlɪdʒ) *n* **1** the condition of being a pupil or duration for which one is a pupil. **2** (in England) the period spent by a newly called barrister in the chambers of a member of the bar.

pupillary[1] *or* **pupilary** (ˈpjuːpɪlərɪ) *adj* of or relating to a pupil or legal ward. [C17: from PUPIL[1] + -ARY] ► **ˌpupilˈlarity** *or* **ˌpupiˈlarity** *n*

pupillary[2] *or* **pupilary** (ˈpjuːpɪlərɪ) *adj* of or relating to the pupil of the eye. [C18: from Latin *pūpilla* PUPIL[2]]

pupiparous (pjuːˈpɪpərəs) *adj* (of certain dipterous flies) producing young that have already reached the pupa stage at the time of hatching. [C19: from New Latin *pupiparus*, from PUPA + *parere* to bring forth]

puppet (ˈpʌpɪt) *n* **1a** a small doll or figure of a person or animal moved by strings attached to its limbs or by the hand inserted in its cloth body. **1b** (*as modifier*): *a puppet theatre.* **2a** a person, group, state, etc., that appears independent but is in fact controlled by another. **2b** (*as modifier*): *a puppet government.* [C16 *popet*, perhaps from Old French *poupette* little doll, ultimately from Latin *pūpa* girl, doll]

puppeteer (ˌpʌpɪˈtɪə) *n* a person who manipulates puppets.

puppetry (ˈpʌpɪtrɪ) *n* **1** the art of making and manipulating puppets and presenting puppet shows. **2** unconvincing or specious presentation.

Puppis (ˈpʌpɪs) *n, Latin genitive* **Puppis.** a constellation in the S hemisphere lying between Vela and Canis Major, a section of which is crossed by the Milky Way. [Latin: the ship, the POOP of a ship]

puppy (ˈpʌpɪ) *n, pl* **-pies. 1** a young dog; pup. **2** *Informal, contemptuous.* a brash or conceited young man; pup. [C15 *popi*, from Old French *popée* doll; compare PUPPET] ► **ˈpuppyˌhood** *n* ► **ˈpuppyish** *adj*

puppy fat *n* fatty tissue that develops in childhood or adolescence and usually disappears by maturity.

puppy love *n* another term for **calf love.**

pup tent *n* another name for **shelter tent.**

Purana (puˈrɑːnə) *n* any of a class of Sanskrit writings not included in the Vedas, characteristically recounting the birth and deeds of Hindu gods and the creation, destruction, or recreation of the universe. [C17: from Sanskrit: ancient, from *purā* formerly] ► **Puˈranic** *adj*

Purbeck marble *or* **stone** (ˈpɜːbɛk) *n* a fossil-rich limestone that takes a high polish: used for building, etc. [C15: named after *Purbeck*, Dorset, where it is quarried]

purblind (ˈpɜːˌblaɪnd) *adj* **1** partly or nearly blind. **2** lacking in insight or understanding; obtuse. [C13: see PURE, BLIND; compare PARBOIL]

Purcell (ˈpɜːsᵊl) *n* **1 Edward Mills.** 1912–97, U.S. physicist, noted for his work on the magnetic moments of atomic nuclei: shared the Nobel prize for physics (1952). **2 Henry.** ?1659–95, English composer, noted chiefly for his rhythmic and harmonic subtlety in setting words. His works include the opera *Dido and Aeneas* (1689), music for the theatrical pieces *King Arthur* (1691) and *The Fairy Queen* (1692), several choral odes, fantasias, sonatas, and church music.

purchasable (ˈpɜːtʃɪsəbᵊl) *adj* **1** able to be bribed or corrupted. **2** able to be bought. ► **ˌpurchasaˈbility** *n*

purchase (ˈpɜːtʃɪs) *vb* (*tr*) **1** to obtain (goods, etc.) by payment. **2** to obtain by effort, sacrifice, etc.: *to purchase one's freedom.* **3** to draw, haul, or lift (a load) with the aid of mechanical apparatus. **4** to acquire (an estate) other than by inheritance. ♦ *n* **5** something that is purchased, esp. an article bought with money. **6** the act of buying. **7** acquisition of an estate by any lawful means other than inheritance. **8** a rough measure of the mechanical advantage achieved by a lever. **9** a firm foothold, grasp, etc., as for climbing or levering something. **10** a means of achieving some influence, advantage, etc. [C13: from Old French *porchacier* to strive to obtain, from *por-* for + *chacier* to CHASE[1]] ► **ˈpurchaser** *n*

purchase ledger *n Commerce.* a record of a company's purchases of goods and services showing the amounts paid and due.

purchase tax *n Brit.* a tax levied on nonessential consumer goods and added to selling prices by retailers.

purdah *or* **purda** (ˈpɜːdə) *n* **1** the custom in some Muslim and Hindu communities of keeping women in seclusion, with clothing that conceals them completely when they go out. **2** a screen in a Hindu house used to keep the women out of view. **3** a veil worn by Hindu women of high caste. [C19: from Hindi *parda* veil, from Persian *pardah*]

purdonium (pɜːˈdəʊnɪəm) *n* a type of coal scuttle having a slanted cover that is raised to open it, and an inner removable metal container for the coal. [C19: named after its inventor, a Mr *Purdon*]

pure (pjʊə) *adj* **1** not mixed with any extraneous or dissimilar materials, elements, etc.: *pure nitrogen.* **2** free from tainting or polluting matter; clean; wholesome: *pure water.* **3** free from moral taint or defilement: *pure love.* **4** (*prenominal*) (intensifier): *pure stupidity; a pure coincidence.* **5** (of a subject, etc.) studied in its theoretical aspects rather than for its practical applications: *pure mathematics; pure science.* Compare **applied. 6** (of a vowel) pronounced with more or less unvarying quality without any glide; monophthongal. **7** (of a consonant) not accompanied by another consonant. **8** of supposedly unmixed racial descent. **9** *Genetics, biology.* breeding true for one or more characteristics; homozygous. **10** *Music.* **10a** (of a sound) composed of a single frequency without overtones. **10b** (of intervals in the system of just intonation) mathematically accurate in respect to the ratio of one frequency to another. [C13: from Old French *pur*, from Latin *pūrus* unstained] ► **ˈpureness** *n*

purebred *adj* (ˈpjʊəˈbrɛd). **1** denoting a pure strain obtained through many generations of controlled breeding. ♦ *n* (ˈpjʊəˌbrɛd). **2** a purebred animal. Compare **grade** (sense 9), **crossbred** (sense 2).

pure culture *n Bacteriol.* a culture containing a single species of microorganism.

puree *or* **puri** (ˈpuːrɪ) *n* an unleavened flaky Indian bread, that is deep-fried in ghee and served hot. [Hindi]

purée (ˈpjʊəreɪ) *n* **1** a smooth thick pulp of cooked and sieved fruit, vegetables, meat, or fish. ♦ *vb* **-rées, -réeing, -réed. 2** (*tr*) to make (cooked foods) into a purée. [C19: from French *purer* to PURIFY]

Pure Land sects *pl n* Mahayana Buddhist sects venerating the Buddha as the compassionate saviour.

pure line *n* a breed or strain of animals or plants in which certain characters appear in successive generations as a result of inbreeding or self-fertilization.

purely (ˈpjʊəlɪ) *adv* **1** in a pure manner. **2** entirely: *purely by chance.* **3** in a chaste or innocent manner.

purfle (ˈpɜːfᵊl) *n also* **purfling. 1** a ruffled or curved ornamental band, as on clothing, furniture, etc. ♦ *vb* **2** (*tr*) to decorate with such a band or bands. [C14: from Old French *purfiler* to decorate with a border, from *filer* to spin, from *fil* thread, from Latin *filum*]

purgation (pɜːˈɡeɪʃən) *n* the act of purging or state of being purged; purification.

purgative (ˈpɜːɡətɪv) *Med.* ◆ *n* **1** a drug or agent for purging the bowels. ◆ *adj* **2** causing evacuation of the bowels; cathartic. ▸ **ˈpurgatively** *adv*

purgatorial (ˌpɜːɡəˈtɔːrɪəl) *adj* **1** serving to purify from sin. **2** of, relating to, or like purgatory. ▸ **ˌpurgaˈtorially** *adv*

purgatory (ˈpɜːɡətərɪ, -trɪ) *n* **1** *Chiefly R.C. Church.* a state or place in which the souls of those who have died in a state of grace are believed to undergo a limited amount of suffering to expiate their venial sins and become purified of the remaining effects of mortal sin. **2** a place or condition of suffering or torment, esp. one that is temporary. **[C13:** from Old French *purgatoire,* from Medieval Latin *pūrgātōrium,* literally: place of cleansing, from Latin *pūrgāre* to PURGE**]**

purge (pɜːdʒ) *vb* **1** (*tr*) to rid (something) of (impure or undesirable elements). **2** (*tr*) to rid (a state, political party, etc.) of (dissident or troublesome people). **3** (*tr*) **3a** to empty (the bowels) by evacuation of faeces. **3b** to cause (a person) to evacuate his bowels. **4a** to clear (a person) of a charge. **4b** to free (oneself) of guilt, as by atonement: *to purge contempt.* **5** (*intr*) to be cleansed or purified. ◆ *n* **6** the act or process of purging. **7** the elimination of opponents or dissidents from a state, political party, etc. **8** a purgative drug or agent; cathartic. **[C14:** from Old French *purger,* from Latin *pūrgāre* to purify**]** ▸ **ˈpurger** *n*

Puri (ˈpʊəriː, pʊəˈriː) *n* a port in E India, in Orissa on the Bay of Bengal: 12th-century temple of Jagannath. Pop.: 125 199 (1991).

Purification of the Virgin Mary *n* **the.** *Christianity.* **1** the presentation of Jesus in the Temple after the completion of Mary's purification (Luke 2:22). **2** Also called: **Candlemas.** the feast commemorating this (Feb. 2).

purificator (ˈpjʊərɪfɪˌkeɪtə) *n Christianity.* a small white linen cloth used to wipe the chalice and paten and also the lips and fingers of the celebrant at the Eucharist.

purify (ˈpjʊərɪˌfaɪ) *vb* **-fies, -fying, -fied. 1** to free (something) of extraneous, contaminating, or debasing matter. **2** (*tr*) to free (a person, etc.) from sin or guilt. **3** (*tr*) to make clean, as in a ritual, esp. the churching of women after childbirth. **[C14:** from Old French *purifier,* from Late Latin *pūrificāre* to cleanse, from *pūrus* pure + *facere* to make**]** ▸ **ˌpurifiˈcation** *n* ▸ **purificatory** (ˈpjʊərɪfɪˌkeɪtərɪ) *adj* ▸ **ˈpuriˌfier** *n*

Purim (ˈpʊərɪm; *Hebrew* puːˈriːm) *n* a Jewish holiday celebrated on Adar 14, in February or March, and in Adar Sheni in leap years, to commemorate the deliverance of the Jews from the massacre planned for them by Haman (Esther 9). [Hebrew *pūrīm,* plural of *pūr* lot; from the casting of lots by Haman]

purine (ˈpjʊəriːn) *or* **purin** (ˈpjʊərɪn) *n* **1** a colourless crystalline solid that can be prepared from uric acid. Formula: $C_5H_5N_4$. **2** Also called: **purine base.** any of a number of nitrogenous bases, such as guanine and adenine, that are derivatives of purine and constituents of nucleic acids and certain coenzymes. **[C19:** from German *Purin;* see PURE, URIC, -INE[2]**]**

puriri (puːˈriːriː) *n, pl* **-ris.** a forest tree, *Vitex lucens,* of New Zealand, having red berries and glossy green leaves and yielding a durable dark brown timber.

purism (ˈpjʊəˌrɪzəm) *n* insistence on traditional canons of correctness of form or purity of style or content, esp. in language, art, or music. ▸ **ˈpurist** *adj, n* ▸ **puˈristic** *adj* ▸ **puˈristically** *adv*

puritan (ˈpjʊərɪtᵊn) *n* **1** a person who adheres to strict moral or religious principles, esp. one opposed to luxury and sensual enjoyment. ◆ *adj* **2** characteristic of a puritan. **[C16:** from Late Latin *pūritās* PURITY**]** ▸ **ˈpuritanˌism** *n*

Puritan (ˈpjʊərɪtᵊn) (in the late 16th and 17th centuries) ◆ *n* **1** any of the more extreme English Protestants, most of whom were Calvinists, who wished to purify the Church of England of most of its ceremony and other aspects that they deemed to be Catholic. ◆ *adj* **2** of, characteristic of, or relating to the Puritans. ▸ **ˈPuritanˌism** *n*

puritanical (ˌpjʊərɪˈtænɪkᵊl) *or* (*less commonly*) **puritanic** *adj* **1** *Usually disparaging.* strict in moral or religious outlook, esp. in shunning sensual pleasures. **2** (*sometimes cap.*) of or relating to a puritan or the Puritans. ▸ **ˌpuriˈtanically** *adv* ▸ **ˌpuriˈtanicalness** *n*

purity (ˈpjʊərɪtɪ) *n* **1** the state or quality of being pure. **2** *Physics.* a measure of the amount of a single-frequency colour in a mixture of spectral and achromatic colours.

purl[1] (pɜːl) *n* **1** Also called: **purl stitch.** a knitting stitch made by doing a plain stitch backwards. **2** a decorative border, as of lace. **3** gold or silver wire thread. ◆ *vb* **4** to knit (a row or garment) in purl stitch. **5** to edge (something) with a purl. ◆ Also (for senses 2, 3, 5): **pearl. [C16:** from dialect *pirl* to twist into a cord**]**

purl[2] (pɜːl) *vb* **1** (*intr*) (of a stream, etc.) to flow with a gentle curling or rippling movement and a murmuring sound. ◆ *n* **2** a curling movement of water; eddy. **3** a murmuring sound, as of a shallow stream. **[C16:** related to Norwegian *purla* to bubble**]**

purler[1] (ˈpɜːlə) *n Informal.* a headlong or spectacular fall (esp. in the phrase **come a purler**).

purler[2] (ˈpɜːlə) *n Austral. slang.* something outstanding in its class. [of unknown origin]

purlieu (ˈpɜːljuː) *n* **1** *English history.* land on the edge of a forest that was once included within the bounds of the royal forest but was later separated although still subject to some of the forest laws, esp. regarding hunting. **2** (*usually pl*) a neighbouring area; outskirts. **3** (*often pl*) a place one frequents; haunt. **4** *Rare.* a district or suburb, esp. one that is poor or squalid. **[C15** *purlewe,* from Anglo-French *puralé* a going through (influenced also by Old French *lieu* place), from Old French *puraler* to traverse, from *pur* through + *aler* to go**]**

purlin *or* **purline** (ˈpɜːlɪn) *n* a horizontal beam that provides intermediate support for the common rafters of a roof construction. **[C15:** of uncertain origin**]**

purloin (pɜːˈlɔɪn) *vb* to take (something) dishonestly; steal. **[C15:** from Old French *porloigner* to put at a distance, from *por-* for + *loin* distant, from Latin *longus* long**]** ▸ **purˈloiner** *n*

purple (ˈpɜːpᵊl) *n* **1** any of various colours with a hue lying between red and blue and often highly saturated; a nonspectral colour. **2** a dye or pigment producing such a colour. **3** cloth of this colour, often used to symbolize royalty or nobility. **4** (usually preceded by *the*) high rank; nobility. **5a** the official robe of a cardinal. **5b** the rank, office, or authority of a cardinal as signified by this. **6 the purple.** bishops collectively. ◆ *adj* **7** of the colour purple. **8** (of writing) excessively elaborate or full of imagery: *purple prose.* **9** noble or royal. **[**Old English, from Latin *purpura* purple dye, from Greek *porphura* the purple fish (*Murex*)**]** ▸ **ˈpurpleness** *n* ▸ **ˈpurplish** *adj* ▸ **ˈpurply** *adj*

purple emperor *n* any of several Old World nymphalid butterflies of the genus *Apatura,* esp. *A. iris,* having mottled purple-and-brown wings.

purple-fringed orchid *or* **orchis** *n* either of two North American orchids, *Habenaria psychodes* or *H. fimbriata,* having purple fringed flowers.

purple gallinule *n* a long-toed purple aquatic bird, *Porphyrio porphyrio* (or *Porphyrula martinica*), of the southern U.S. and Europe, with red legs and red bill: family *Rallidae* (rails, etc.).

purple heart *n* **1** any of several tropical American leguminous trees of the genus *Peltogyne.* **2** the decorative purple heartwood of any of these trees. **3** *Informal, chiefly Brit.* a heart-shaped purple tablet consisting mainly of amphetamine.

Purple Heart *n* a decoration awarded to members of the U.S. Armed Forces for a wound incurred in action.

purple medic *n* another name for **alfalfa.**

purple patch *n* **1** Also called: **purple passage.** a section in a piece of writing characterized by rich, fanciful, or ornate language. **2** *Slang.* a period of success, good fortune, etc.

purport *vb* (pɜːˈpɔːt). (*tr*) **1** to claim (to be a certain thing, etc.) by manner or appearance, esp. falsely. **2** (esp. of speech or writing) to signify or imply. ◆ *n* (ˈpɜːpɔːt). **3** meaning; significance; import. **4** purpose; object; intention. **[C15:** from Anglo-French: contents, from Old French *porporter* to convey, from *por-* forth + *porter* to carry, from Latin *portāre***]**

purported (pɜːˈpɔːtɪd) *adj* alleged; supposed; rumoured: *a purported two million deal.* ▸ **purˈportedly** *adv*

purpose (ˈpɜːpəs) *n* **1** the reason for which anything is done, created, or exists. **2** a fixed design, outcome, or idea that is the object of an action or other effort. **3** fixed intention in doing something; determination: *a man of purpose.* **4** practical advantage or use: *to work to good purpose.* **5** that which is relevant or under consideration (esp. in the phrase **to** or **from the purpose**). **6** *Archaic.* purport. **7 on purpose.** intentionally. ◆ *vb* (*tr*) **8** to intend or determine to do (something). **[C13:** from Old French *porpos,* from *porposer* to plan, from Latin *prōpōnere* to PROPOSE**]**

purpose-built *adj* made to serve a specific purpose.

purposeful (ˈpɜːpəsfʊl) *adj* **1** having a definite purpose in view. **2** fixed in one's purpose; determined. ▸ **ˈpurposefully** *adv* ▸ **ˈpurposefulness** *n*

USAGE *Purposefully* is sometimes wrongly used where *purposely* is meant: *he had purposely* (not *purposefully*) *left the door unlocked.*

purposeless (ˈpɜːpəslɪs) *adj* having no fixed plan or intention. ▸ **ˈpurposelessly** *adv* ▸ **ˈpurposelessness** *n*

purposely (ˈpɜːpəslɪ) *adv* for a definite reason; on purpose.

USAGE See at **purposeful.**

purposive (ˈpɜːpəsɪv) *adj* **1** relating to, having, or indicating conscious intention. **2** serving a purpose; useful. ▸ **ˈpurposively** *adv* ▸ **ˈpurposiveness** *n*

purpura (ˈpɜːpjʊrə) *n Pathol.* any of several blood diseases causing purplish spots or patches on the skin due to subcutaneous bleeding. **[C18:** via Latin from Greek *porphura* a shellfish yielding purple dye**]** ▸ **ˈpurpuric** *adj*

purpure (ˈpɜːpjʊə) *n, adj* (*usually postpositive*) *Heraldry.* purple. **[**Old English from Latin *purpura* PURPLE**]**

purpurin (ˈpɜːpjʊrɪn) *n* a red crystalline compound used as a stain for biological specimens; 1,2,4-trihydroxyanthraquinone. Formula: $C_{14}H_5O_2(OH)_3$. **[C19:** from Latin *purpura* PURPLE + -IN**]**

purr (pɜː) *vb* **1** (*intr*) (esp. of cats) to make a low vibrant sound, usually considered as expressing pleasure, etc. **2** (*tr*) to express (pleasure, etc.) by this sound. ◆ *n* **3** a purring sound. **[C17:** of imitative origin; compare French *ronronner* to purr, German *schnurren,* Dutch *snorren***]**

purse (pɜːs) *n* **1** a small bag or pouch, often made of soft leather, for carrying money, esp. coins. **2** *U.S. and Canadian.* a woman's handbag. **3** anything resembling a small bag or pouch in form or function. **4** wealth; funds; resources. **5** a sum of money that is offered, esp. as a prize. ◆ *vb* **6** (*tr*) to contract (the mouth, lips, etc.) into a small rounded shape. **[**Old English *purs,* probably from Late Latin *bursa* bag, ultimately from Greek: leather**]**

purser (ˈpɜːsə) *n* an officer aboard a passenger ship, merchant ship, or aircraft who keeps the accounts and attends to the welfare of the passengers.

purse seine *n* a large net towed, usually by two boats, that encloses a school of fish and is then closed at the bottom by means of a line resembling the string formerly used to draw shut the neck of a money pouch or purse.

purse strings *pl n* control of finance or expenditure (esp. in such phrases as **hold** or **control the purse strings**).

purslane (ˈpɜːslɪn, -leɪn) *n* **1** a weedy portulacaceous plant, *Portulaca oleracea,* with small yellow flowers and fleshy leaves, which are used in salads and as a potherb. **2** any of various similar or related plants, such as sea purslane and water purslane. **[C14** *purcelane,* from Old French *porcelaine,* from Late Latin *porcillāgō,* from Latin *porcilāca,* variant of *portulāca***]**

pursuance (pəˈsjuːəns) *n* the carrying out or pursuing of an action, plan, etc.

pursuant (pəˈsjuːənt) *adj* **1** (*usually postpositive;* often foll. by *to*) *Chiefly law.* in agreement or conformity. **2** *Archaic.* pursuing. **[C17:** related to Middle

English *poursuivant* following after, from Old French; see PURSUE] ▸ **pur'suantly** *adv*

pursue (pə'sjuː) *vb* **-sues, -suing, -sued.** (*mainly tr*) **1** (*also intr*) to follow (a fugitive, etc.) in order to capture or overtake. **2** (esp. of something bad or unlucky) to follow closely or accompany: *ill health pursued her.* **3** to seek or strive to attain (some object, desire, etc.). **4** to follow the precepts of (a plan, policy, etc.). **5** to apply oneself to (one's studies, hobbies, interests, etc.). **6** to follow persistently or seek to become acquainted with. **7** to continue to discuss or argue (a point, subject, etc.). [C13: from Anglo-Norman *pursiwer,* from Old French *poursivre,* from Latin *prōsequī* to follow after] ▸ **pur'suer** *n*

pursuit (pə'sjuːt) *n* **1a** the act of pursuing, chasing, or striving after. **1b** (*as modifier*): *a pursuit plane.* **2** an occupation, hobby, or pastime. **3** (in cycling) a race in which the riders set off at intervals along the track and attempt to overtake each other. [C14: from Old French *poursieute,* from *poursivre* to prosecute, PURSUE]

pursuivant ('pɜːsɪvənt) *n* **1** the lowest rank of heraldic officer. **2** *History.* a state or royal messenger. **3** *History.* a follower or attendant. [C14: from Old French, from *poursivre* to PURSUE]

pursy ('pɜːsɪ) *adj* **1** short-winded. **2** *Archaic.* fat; over-weight. [C15: alteration of earlier *pursive,* from Anglo-French *porsif,* ultimately from Latin *pulsāre* to PULSATE]

purtenance ('pɜːtɪnəns) *n Archaic.* the inner organs, viscera. [C14: from Old French *pertinance* something that belongs; see APPURTENANCE]

purulent ('pjʊərʊlənt) *adj* of, relating to, or containing pus. [C16: from Latin *pūrulentus,* from PUS] ▸ **'purulence** *or* **'purulency** *n* ▸ **'purulently** *adv*

Purús (*Spanish, Portuguese* pu'rus) *n* a river in NW central South America, rising in SE Peru and flowing northeast to the Amazon. Length: about 3200 km (2000 miles).

purvey (pə'veɪ) *vb* (*tr*) **1** to sell or provide (commodities, esp. foodstuffs) on a large scale. **2** to publish or make available (lies, scandal, etc.). ◆ *n* ('pɜːvɪ). **3** *Scot.* the food and drink laid on at a wedding reception, etc. [C13: from Old French *porveeir,* from Latin *prōvidēre* to PROVIDE]

purveyance (pə'veɪəns) *n* **1** *History.* the collection or requisition of provisions for a sovereign. **2** *Rare.* the act of purveying. **3** *Rare.* that which is purveyed.

purveyor (pə'veɪə) *n* **1** (*often pl*) a person, organization, etc., that supplies food and provisions. **2** a person who spreads, repeats, or sells (information, lies, etc.). **3** a person or thing that habitually provides or supplies a particular thing or quality: *a purveyor of humour.* **4** *History.* an officer providing or exacting provisions, lodging, etc., for a sovereign.

purview ('pɜːvjuː) *n* **1** the scope of operation or concern of something. **2** the breadth or range of outlook or understanding. **3** *Law.* the body of a statute, containing the enacting clauses. [C15: from Anglo-Norman *purveu,* from *porveeir* to furnish; see PURVEY]

pus (pʌs) *n* the yellow or greenish fluid product of inflammation, composed largely of dead leucocytes, exuded plasma, and liquefied tissue cells. [C16: from Latin *pūs;* related to Greek *puon* pus]

Pusan ('puː'sæn) *n* a port in SE South Korea, on the Korea Strait: the second largest city and chief port of the country; industrial centre; two universities. Pop.: 3 813 814 (1995).

Pusey ('pjuːzɪ) *n* **Edward Bouverie** ('buːvərɪ). 1800–82, British ecclesiastic; a leader with Keble and Newman of the Oxford Movement.

Puseyism ('pjuːzɪˌɪzəm) *n* a derogatory term for the **Oxford Movement,** used by its contemporary opponents. [C19: after E. B. PUSEY] ▸ **'Puseyite** *n, adj*

push (pʊʃ) *vb* **1** (when *tr,* often foll. by *off, away,* etc.) to apply steady force to (something) in order to move it. **2** to thrust (one's way) through something, such as a crowd, by force. **3** (when *intr,* often foll. by *for*) to apply oneself vigorously (to achieving a task, plan, etc.). **4** (*tr*) to encourage or urge (a person) to some action, decision, etc. **5** (when *intr,* often foll. by *for*) to be an advocate or promoter (of): *to push for acceptance of one's theories.* **6** (*tr*) to use one's influence to help (a person): *to push one's own candidate.* **7** to bear upon (oneself or another person) in order to achieve more effort, better results, etc.: *she was a woman who liked to push her husband.* **8** (*tr*) **8a** to take undue risks, esp. through overconfidence, thus risking failure: *to push one's luck.* **8b** (*intr*) to act overconfidently. **9** *Tennis, cricket, etc.* to hit (a ball) with a stiff pushing stroke. **10** (*tr*) *Informal.* to sell (narcotic drugs) illegally. **11** (*intr;* foll. by *out, into,* etc.) (esp. of geographical features) to reach or extend: *the cliffs pushed out to the sea.* **12** (*tr*) to overdevelop (a photographic film), usually by the equivalent of up to two stops, to compensate for underexposure or increase contrast. **13** **push up (the) daisies.** *Slang.* to be dead and buried. ◆ *n* **14** the act of pushing; thrust. **15** a part or device that is pressed to operate some mechanism. **16** *Informal.* ambitious or enterprising drive, energy, etc. **17** *Informal.* a special effort or attempt to advance, as of an army in a war: *to make a push.* **18** *Informal.* a number of people gathered in one place, such as at a party. **19** *Austral. slang.* a group or gang, esp. one considered to be a clique. **20** *Tennis, cricket, etc.* a stiff pushing stroke. **21** **at a push.** *Informal.* with difficulty; only just. **22** **the push.** *Informal, chiefly Brit.* dismissal, esp. from employment. **23** **when push comes to shove.** *Informal.* when matters become critical; when a decision needs to be made. ◆ See also **push about, push along, push in, push off, push on, push through.** [C13: from Old French *pousser,* from Latin *pulsāre,* from *pellere* to drive]

push about *or* **around** *vb* (*tr, adv*) *Slang.* to bully; keep telling (a person) what to do in a bossy manner.

push along *vb* (*intr, adv*) *Informal.* to go away; leave.

pushball ('pʊʃˌbɔːl) *n Chiefly U.S. and Canadian.* a game in which two teams try to push a heavy ball towards opposite goals.

push-bike *n Brit.* an informal name for **bicycle.**

push button *n* **1** an electrical switch operated by pressing a button, which closes or opens a circuit. **2** (*modifier*) **push-button. 2a** operated by a push button: *a push-button radio.* **2b** initiated as simply as by pressing a button: *push-button warfare.*

pushcart ('pʊʃˌkɑːt) *n* another name (esp. U.S. and Canadian) for **barrow**[1] (sense 3).

pushchair ('pʊʃˌtʃɛə) *n* a usually collapsible chair-shaped carriage in which a small child may be wheeled. Also called: **baby buggy, buggy.** U.S. and Canadian word: **stroller.** Austral. words: **pusher, stroller.**

pushed (pʊʃt) *adj* (often foll. by *for*) *Informal.* short (of) or in need (of time, money, etc.).

pusher ('pʊʃə) *n* **1** *Informal.* a person who sells illegal drugs, esp. narcotics such as heroin and morphine. **2** *Informal.* an actively or aggressively ambitious person. **3a** a type of aircraft propeller placed behind the engine. **3b** a type of aircraft using such a propeller. **4** a person or thing that pushes. **5** *Brit.* a rakelike implement used by small children to push food onto a spoon. **6** *Austral.* the usual name for **pushchair.**

push fit *n Engineering.* another name for **sliding fit.**

push in *vb* (*intr, adv*) to force one's way into a group of people, queue, etc.

pushing ('pʊʃɪŋ) *adj* **1** enterprising, resourceful, or aggressively ambitious. **2** impertinently self-assertive. ◆ *adv* **3** almost or nearly (a certain age, speed, etc.): *pushing fifty.* ▸ **'pushingly** *adv* ▸ **'pushingness** *n*

Pushkin[1] ('pʊʃkɪn) *n* a town in NW Russia: site of the imperial summer residence and Catherine the Great's palace. Pop.: 97 000 (1989). Former name: **Tsarskoye Selo** (1708–1937).

Pushkin[2] ('pʊʃkɪn) *n* **Aleksander Sergeyevich** (alɪk'sandr sɪr'gjejɪvɪtʃ). 1799–1837, Russian poet, novelist, and dramatist. His works include the romantic verse tale *The Prisoner of the Caucasus* (1822), the verse novel *Eugene Onegin* (1833), the tragedy *Boris Godunov* (1825), and the novel *The Captain's Daughter* (1836).

push money *n* a cash inducement provided by a manufacturer or distributor for a retailer or his staff, to reward successful selling.

push off *vb* (*adv*) **1** Also: **push out.** to move into open water, as by being cast off from a mooring. **2** (*intr*) *Informal.* to go away; leave.

push on *vb* (*intr, adv*) to resume one's course; carry on one's way steadily; press on.

pushover ('pʊʃˌəʊvə) *n Informal.* **1** something that is easily achieved or accomplished. **2** a person, team, etc., that is easily taken advantage of or defeated.

pushpin ('pʊʃˌpɪn) *n U.S. and Canadian.* a pin with a small ball-shaped head.

push-pull *n* (*modifier*) using two similar electronic devices, such as matched valves, made to operate 180° out of phase with each other. The outputs are combined to produce a signal that replicates the input waveform: *a push-pull amplifier.*

pushrod ('pʊʃˌrɒd) *n* a metal rod transmitting the reciprocating motion that operates the valves of an internal-combustion engine having the camshaft in the crankcase.

push-start *vb* (*tr*) **1** to start (a motor vehicle) by pushing it while it is in gear, thus turning the engine. ◆ *n* **2** the act or process of starting a vehicle in this way.

push through *vb* (*tr*) to compel to accept: *the bill was pushed through Parliament.*

Pushto ('pʌʃtəʊ) *or* **Pushtu** ('pʌʃtuː) *n, adj* variant spellings of **Pashto.**

push-up *n* the U.S. and Canadian term for **press-up.**

pushy ('pʊʃɪ) *adj* **pushier, pushiest.** *Informal.* **1** offensively assertive or forceful. **2** aggressively or ruthlessly ambitious. ▸ **'pushily** *adv* ▸ **'pushiness** *n*

pusillanimous (ˌpjuːsɪ'lænɪməs) *adj* characterized by a lack of courage or determination. [C16: from Late Latin *pusillanimis* from Latin *pusillus* weak + *animus* courage] ▸ **pusillanimity** (ˌpjuːsɪlə'nɪmɪtɪ) *n* ▸ **ˌpusil'lanimously** *adv*

puss[1] (pʊs) *n* **1** an informal name for a **cat.** See also **pussy**[1] (sense 1). **2** *Slang.* a girl or woman. **3** an informal name for a **hare.** [C16: related to Middle Low German *pūs,* Dutch *poes,* Lithuanian *puz*]

puss[2] (pʊs) *n Slang.* **1** the face. **2** *Irish.* a gloomy or sullen expression. [C17: from Irish *pus*]

puss moth *n* a large pale prominent moth, *Cerura vinula,* whose larvae feed on willow and poplar, and are bright green with a masklike red head and claspers modified as "tails" that are protruded and raised in a state of alarm: family *Notodontidae.*

pussy[1] ('pʊsɪ) *n, pl* **pussies. 1** Also called: **puss, pussycat** ('pʊsɪˌkæt). an informal name for a **cat. 2** a furry catkin, esp. that of the pussy willow. **3** a rare word for **tipcat. 4** *Taboo slang.* the female pudenda. **5** *Taboo slang.* a woman considered as a sexual object. [C18: from PUSS[1]]

pussy[2] ('pʌsɪ) *adj* **-sier, -siest.** containing or full of pus.

pussyfoot ('pʊsɪˌfʊt) *Informal.* ◆ *vb* (*intr*) **1** to move about stealthily or warily like a cat. **2** to avoid committing oneself. ◆ *n, pl* **-foots. 3** a person who pussyfoots.

pussy willow ('pʊsɪ) *n* **1** an American willow tree, *Salix discolor,* with silvery silky catkins: widely planted for ornament. **2** any of various similar willows.

pustulant ('pʌstjʊlənt) *adj* **1** causing the formation of pustules. ◆ *n* **2** an agent causing such formation.

pustulate *vb* ('pʌstjʊˌleɪt). **1** to form or cause to form into pustules. ◆ *adj* ('pʌstjʊlɪt, -ˌleɪt). **2** covered with pustules. ▸ **ˌpustu'lation** *n*

pustule ('pʌstjuːl) *n* **1** a small inflamed elevated area of skin containing pus. **2** any small distinct spot resembling a pimple or blister. [C14: from Latin *pustula* a blister, variant of *pūsula;* compare Greek *phusallis* bladder, *phusa* bellows] ▸ **pustular** ('pʌstjʊlə) *adj*

put (pʊt) *vb* **puts, putting, put.** (*mainly tr*) **1** to cause to be (in a position or place): *to put a book on the table.* **2** to cause to be (in a state, relation, etc.): *to put one's things in order.* **3** (foll. by *to*) to cause (a person) to experience the endurance or suffering (of): *to put to death; to put to the sword.* **4** to set or commit (to an action, task, or duty), esp. by force: *he put him to work.* **5** to render, transform, or translate: *to put into English.* **6** to set (words) in a musical form (esp. in the phrase **put to music**). **7** (foll. by *at*) to estimate: *he put the distance at fifty miles.* **8** (foll. by *to*) to utilize (for the purpose of): *he put his knowledge to good use.* **9** (foll. by *to*) to couple a female animal (with a male) for the purpose of breeding: *the farmer put his heifer to the bull.* **10** to state; express: *to put it bluntly.* **11** to set or make (an end or limit): *he put an end to the proceedings.* **12** to present for consideration in anticipation of an answer or vote; propose: *he put the question to the committee; I put it to you that one day you will all die.* **13** to invest (money) in; give (support) to: *he put five thousand pounds into the project.* **14** to impart: *to put zest into a party.* **15** to throw or cast. **16 not know where to put oneself.** to feel awkward or embarrassed. **17 put paid to.** to destroy irrevocably and utterly: *the manager's disfavour put paid to their hopes for promotion.* **18 stay put.** to refuse to leave; keep one's position. ◆ *n* **19** a throw or cast, esp. in putting the shot. **20** Also called: **put option.** *Stock Exchange.* an option to sell a stated amount of securities at a specified price during a specified limited period. Compare **call** (sense 58). ◆ See also **put about, put across, put aside, put away, put back, put by, put down, put forth, put forward, put in, put off, put on, put on to, put out, put over, put through, put up, put upon.** [C12 *puten* to push; related to Old English *potian* to push, Norwegian, Icelandic *pota* to poke]

put about *vb* (*adv*) **1** *Nautical.* to change course or cause to change course: *we put about and headed for home.* **2** (*tr*) to make widely known: *he put about the news of the air disaster.* **3** (*tr; usually passive*) to disconcert or disturb: *she was quite put about by his appearance.*

put across *vb* (*tr*) **1** (*adv*) to communicate in a comprehensible way: *he couldn't put things across very well.* **2 put one across.** *Informal.* to get (someone) to accept or believe a claim, excuse, etc., by deception: *they put one across their teacher.*

putamen (pjuː'teɪmɛn) *n, pl* **-tamina** (-'tæmɪnə). the hard endocarp or stone of fruits such as the peach, plum, and cherry. [C19: from Latin: clippings, from *putāre* to prune]

put aside *vb* (*tr, adv*) **1** to move (an object, etc.) to one side, esp. in rejection. **2** to store up; save: *to put money aside for a rainy day.* **3** to ignore or disregard: *let us put aside our differences.*

putative ('pjuːtətɪv) *adj* **1** (*prenominal*) commonly regarded as being: *the putative father.* **2** (*prenominal*) considered to exist or have existed; inferred. **3** *Grammar.* denoting a mood of the verb in some languages used when the speaker does not have direct evidence of what he is asserting, but has inferred it on the basis of something else. [C15: from Late Latin *putātīvus* supposed, from Latin *putāre* to consider] ► **'putatively** *adv*

put away *vb* (*tr, adv*) **1** to return (something) to the correct or proper place: *he put away his books.* **2** to save: *to put away money for the future.* **3** to lock up in a prison, mental institution, etc.: *they put him away for twenty years.* **4** to eat or drink, esp. in large amounts. **5** to put to death, because of old age or illness: *the dog had to be put away.*

put back *vb* (*tr, adv*) **1** to return to its former place. **2** to move to a later time or date: *the wedding was put back a fortnight.* **3** to delay or impede the progress of: *the strike put back production severely.*

put by *vb* (*tr, adv*) to set aside (money, goods, etc.) to be kept for the future; store; save.

put down *vb* (*tr, adv*) **1** to make a written record of. **2** to repress: *to put down a rebellion.* **3** to consider; account: *they put him down for an ignoramus.* **4** to attribute: *I put the mistake down to his inexperience.* **5** to put to death, because of old age or illness: *the vet put the cat down.* **6** to table on the agenda: *the MPs put down a motion on the increase in crime.* **7** to put (a baby) to bed. **8** to dismiss, reject, or humiliate. ◆ *n* **put-down. 9** a cruelly crushing remark.

put forth *vb* (*tr, adv*) *Formal.* **1** to present; propose. **2** (of a plant) to produce or bear (leaves, branches, shoots, etc.).

put forward *vb* (*tr, adv*) **1** to propose; suggest. **2** to offer the name of; nominate.

put in *vb* (*adv*) **1** (*intr*) *Nautical.* to bring a vessel into port, esp. for a brief stay: *we put in for fresh provisions.* **2** (often foll. by *for*) to apply or cause to apply (for a job, in a competition, etc.). **3** (*tr*) to submit: *he put in his claims form.* **4** to intervene with (a remark) during a conversation. **5** (*tr*) to devote (time, effort, etc.) to a task: *he put in three hours overtime last night.* **6** (*tr*) to establish or appoint: *he put in a manager.* **7** (*tr*) *Cricket.* to cause (a team, esp. the opposing one) to bat: *England won the toss and put the visitors in to bat.* ◆ *n* **put-in. 8** *Rugby.* the act of throwing the ball into a scrum.

putlog ('pʌtˌlɒg) *or* **putlock** *n* a short horizontal beam that with others supports the floor planks of a scaffold. [C17: changed (through influence of LOG[1]) from earlier *putlock*, probably from PUT (past participle) + LOCK[1]]

Putnam ('pʌtnəm) *n* **1 Israel.** 1718–90, American general in the War of Independence. **2** his cousin **Rufus.** 1738–1824, American soldier in the War of Independence; surveyor general of the U.S. (1796–1803).

put off *vb* **1** (*tr, adv*) to postpone or delay: *they have put off the dance until tomorrow.* **2** (*tr, adv*) to evade (a person) by postponement or delay: *they tried to put him off, but he came anyway.* **3** (*tr, adv*) to confuse; disconcert: *he was put off by her appearance.* **4** (*tr, prep*) to cause to lose interest in or enjoyment of: *the accident put him off driving.* **5** (*intr, adv*) *Nautical.* to be launched off from shore or from a ship: *we put off in the lifeboat towards the ship.* **6** (*tr, adv*) *Archaic.* to remove (clothes). ◆ *n* **putoff. 7** *Chiefly U.S.* a pretext or delay.

put on *vb* (*tr, mainly adv*) **1** to clothe oneself in: *to put on a coat.* **2** (*usually passive*) to adopt (an attitude or feeling) insincerely: *his misery was just put on.* **3** to present or stage (a play, show, etc.). **4** to increase or add: *she put on weight; the batsman put on fifty runs before lunch.* **5** to cause (an electrical device) to function. **6** (*also prep*) to wager (money) on a horse race, game, etc.: *he put ten pounds on the favourite.* **7** (*also prep*) to impose as a burden or levy: *to put a tax on cars.* **8** *Cricket.* to cause (a bowler) to bowl. **9 put (someone) on. 9a** to connect (a person) by telephone. **9b** *Slang.* to mock or tease. ◆ *n* **put-on.** *Slang, chiefly U.S. and Canadian.* **10** a hoax or piece of mockery. **11** an affected manner or mode of behaviour.

put on to *vb* (*tr, prep*) **1** to connect by telephone. **2** to inform (someone) of (a person's location or activities): *I'll put the police on to you if you don't stop.* **3** to tell (a person) about (someone or something beneficial): *can you put me on to a cheap supermarket?*

put out *vb* (*tr, adv*) **1** (*often passive*) **1a** to annoy; anger. **1b** to confound or disturb; confuse. **2** to extinguish or douse (a fire, light, etc.): *he put out the fire.* **3** to poke forward: *to put out one's tongue.* **4** to be or present a source of inconvenience or annoyance to (a person): *I hope I'm not putting you out.* **5** to issue or publish; broadcast: *the authorities put out a leaflet.* **6** to render unconscious. **7** to dislocate: *he put out his shoulder in the accident.* **8** to show or exert: *the workers put out all their energy in the campaign.* **9** to pass, give out (work to be done) at different premises. **10** to lend (money) at interest. **11** *Cricket.* to dismiss (a player or team). **12** *Baseball.* to cause (a batter or runner) to be out by a fielding play. ◆ *n* **putout. 13** *Baseball.* a play in which the batter or runner is put out.

put over *vb* (*tr, adv*) **1** *Informal.* to communicate (facts, information, etc.) comprehensibly: *he puts his thoughts over badly.* **2** *Chiefly U.S.* to postpone; defer: *the match was put over a week.* Brit. equivalent: **put off. 3 put (a fast) one over on.** *Informal.* to get (someone) to accept or believe a claim, excuse, etc., by deception: *he put one over on his boss.*

put-put ('pʌtˌpʌt) *Informal.* ◆ *n* **1** a light chugging or popping sound, as made by a petrol engine. **2** a vehicle powered by an engine making such a sound. ◆ *vb* **-puts, -putting, -putted. 3** (*intr*) to make or travel along with such a sound.

putrefy ('pjuːtrɪˌfaɪ) *vb* **-fies, -fying, -fied.** (of organic matter) to decompose or rot with an offensive smell. [C15: from Old French *putrefier* + Latin *putrefacere*, from *puter* rotten + *facere* to make] ► **putrefaction** (ˌpjuːtrɪ'fækʃən) *n* ► **ˌputre'factive** *or* **putrefacient** (ˌpjuːtrɪ'feɪʃənt) *adj* ► **'putreˌfiable** *adj* ► **'putreˌfier** *n*

putrescent (pjuː'trɛsᵊnt) *adj* **1** becoming putrid; rotting. **2** characterized by or undergoing putrefaction. [C18: from Latin *putrescere* to become rotten] ► **pu'trescence** *n*

putrescible (pjuː'trɛsɪbᵊl) *adj* **1** liable to become putrid. ◆ *n* **2** a putrescible substance. [C18: from Latin *putrescere* to decay] ► **puˌtresci'bility** *n*

putrescine (pjuː'trɛsiːn, -ɪn) *n* a colourless crystalline amine produced by decaying animal matter; 1,4-diaminobutane. Formula: $H_2N(CH_2)_4NH_2$. [C20: from Latin *putrescere* + -INE[2]]

putrid ('pjuːtrɪd) *adj* **1** (of organic matter) in a state of decomposition, usually giving off a foul smell: *putrid meat.* **2** morally corrupt or worthless. **3** sickening; foul: *a putrid smell.* **4** *Informal.* deficient in quality or value: *a putrid film.* [C16: from Latin *putridus* rotten, from *putrēre* to be rotten] ► **pu'tridity** *or* **'putridness** *n* ► **'putridly** *adv*

putsch (pʊtʃ) *n* a violent and sudden uprising; political revolt, esp. a coup d'état. [C20: from German: from Swiss German: a push, of imitative origin]

putt (pʌt) *Golf.* ◆ *n* **1** a stroke on the green with a putter to roll the ball into or near the hole. ◆ *vb* **2** to strike (the ball) in this way. [C16: of Scottish origin; related to PUT]

puttee *or* **putty** ('pʌtɪ) *n, pl* **-tees** *or* **-ties.** (*usually pl*) a strip of cloth worn wound around the legs from the ankle to the knee, esp. as part of a military uniform in World War I. [C19: from Hindi *paṭṭī*, from Sanskrit *paṭṭikā*, from *paṭṭa* cloth]

putter[1] ('pʌtə) *n Golf.* **1** a club for putting, usually having a solid metal head. **2** a golfer who putts: *he is a good putter.*

putter[2] ('pʌtə) *vb* the usual U.S. and Canadian word for **potter**[2]. ► **'putterer** *n*

putter[3] ('pʊtə) *n* **1** a person who puts: *the putter of a question.* **2** a person who puts the shot.

put through *vb* (*tr, mainly adv*) **1** to carry out to a conclusion: *he put through his plan.* **2** (*also prep*) to organize the processing of: *she put through his application to join the organization.* **3** to connect by telephone. **4** to make (a telephone call).

putting green ('pʌtɪŋ) *n* **1** (on a golf course) the area of closely mown grass at the end of a fairway where the hole is. **2** an area of smooth grass with several holes for putting games.

Puttnam ('pʌtnəm) *n* Baron **David.** British film producer. Films include *Chariots of Fire* (1981), *The Killing Fields* (1984), and *Memphis Belle* (1990).

putto ('pʊtəʊ) *n, pl* **-ti** (-tɪ). a representation of a small boy, a cherub or cupid, esp. in baroque painting or sculpture. See also **amoretto.** [from Italian, from Latin *putus* boy]

putty ('pʌtɪ) *n, pl* **-ties. 1** a stiff paste made of whiting and linseed oil that is used to fix glass panes into frames and to fill cracks or holes in woodwork, etc. **2** any substance with a similar consistency, function, or appearance. **3** a mixture of lime and water with sand or plaster of Paris used on plaster as a finishing coat. **4** (*as modifier*): *a putty knife.* **5** See **putty powder. 6** a person who is easily influenced or persuaded: *he's putty in her hands.* **7a** a colour varying from a greyish-yellow to a greyish-brown or brownish-grey. **7b** (*as adj*): *putty-coloured.* **8 up to putty.** *Austral. informal.* worthless or useless. ◆ *vb* **-ties, -tying, -tied. 9** (*tr*) to fix, fill, or coat with putty. [C17: from French *potée* a potful]

putty powder *n* a powder, either tin oxide or tin and lead oxide, used for polishing glassware, metal, etc.

Putumayo (*Spanish* putu'majo) *n* a river in NW South America, rising in S Colombia and flowing southeast as most of the border between Colombia and Peru, entering the Amazon in Brazil: scene of the Putumayo rubber scandal

(1910–11) during the rubber boom, in which many Indians were enslaved and killed by rubber exploiters. Length: 1578 km (980 miles). Brazilian name: **Içá**.

put up *vb* (*adv, mainly tr*) **1** to build; erect: *to put up a statue*. **2** to accommodate or be accommodated at: *can you put me up for tonight?* **3** to increase (prices). **4** to submit or present (a plan, case, etc.). **5** to offer: *to put a house up for sale*. **6** to provide or supply; give: *to put up a good fight*. **7** to provide (money) for; invest in: *they put up five thousand for the new project*. **8** to preserve or can (jam, etc.). **9** to pile up (long hair) on the head in any of several styles. **10** (*also intr*) to nominate or be nominated as a candidate, esp. for a political or society post: *he put his wife up as secretary; he put up for president*. **11** *Archaic*. to return (a weapon) to its holder, as a sword to its sheath: *put up your pistol!* **12 put up to. 12a** to inform or instruct (a person) about (tasks, duties, etc.). **12b** to urge or goad (a person) on to; incite to. **13 put up with.** *Informal*. to endure; tolerate. ◆ *adj* **put-up. 14** dishonestly or craftily prearranged or conceived (esp. in the phrase **put-up job**).

put upon *vb* (*intr, prep, usually passive*) **1** to presume on (a person's generosity, good nature, etc.); take advantage of: *he's always being put upon*. **2** to impose hardship on; maltreat: *he was sorely put upon*.

putz (pʌts) *n U.S. slang*. a despicable or stupid person. [from Yiddish *puts* ornament]

Puvis de Chavannes (*French* pyvis də ʃavan) *n* **Pierre Cécile** (pjer sesil). 1824–98, French mural painter.

Puy de Dôme (pwi də dom) *n* **1** a department of central France in Auvergne region. Capital: Clermont-Ferrand. Pop.: 601 100 (1995). Area: 8016 sq. km (3094 sq. miles). **2** a mountain in central France, in the Auvergne Mountains: a volcanic plug. Height: 1485 m (4872 ft.).

Puy de Sancy (*French* pwi də sɑ̃si) *n* a mountain in S central France: highest peak of the Monts Dore. Height: 1886 m (6188 ft.).

Pu-yi ('puː'jiː) *n* **Henry**. 1906–67, last emperor of China as Xuan-Tong (1908–12); emperor of the Japanese puppet state of Manchukuo as Kang-de (1934–45).

puzzle ('pʌzᵊl) *vb* **1** to perplex or be perplexed. **2** (*intr*; foll. by *over*) to attempt the solution (of); ponder (about): *he puzzled over her absence*. **3** (*tr*; usually foll. by *out*) to solve by mental effort: *he puzzled out the meaning of the inscription*. ◆ *n* **4** a person or thing that puzzles. **5** a problem that cannot be easily or readily solved. **6** the state or condition of being puzzled. **7** a toy, game, or question presenting a problem that requires skill or ingenuity for its solution. See **jigsaw puzzle, Chinese puzzle.** [C16: of unknown origin] ▸ **'puzzling** *adj*

puzzlement ('pʌzᵊlmənt) *n* the state or condition of being puzzled; perplexity.

puzzler ('pʌzlə) *n* a person or thing that puzzles.

puzzolana (ˌputsə'lɑːnə) *n* a variant of **pozzuolana**.

PVA *abbrev. for* polyvinyl acetate.

PVC *abbrev. for* polyvinyl chloride; a synthetic thermoplastic material made by polymerizing vinyl chloride. The properties depend on the added plasticizer. The flexible forms are used in hosepipes, insulation, shoes, garments, etc. Rigid PVC is used for moulded articles.

PVS *abbrev. for:* **1** persistent vegetative state. **2** postviral syndrome.

Pvt. *Military. abbrev. for* private.

PW *abbrev. for* policewoman.

PWD *abbrev. for* Public Works Department.

PWR *abbrev. for* pressurized-water reactor.

pwt *abbrev. for* pennyweight.

PX *U. S. military. abbrev. for* Post Exchange.

PY *international car registration for* Paraguay.

py- *combining form*. variant of **pyo-** before a vowel.

pya (pjɑː, pɪ'ɑː) *n* a monetary unit of Myanmar worth one hundredth of a kyat. [from Burmese]

pyaemia *or* **pyemia** (paɪ'iːmɪə) *n* blood poisoning characterized by pus-forming microorganisms in the blood. [C19: from New Latin, from Greek *puon* pus + *haima* blood] ▸ **py'aemic** *or* **py'emic** *adj*

pyat, pyot, *or* **pyet** ('paɪət) *Scot*. ◆ *n* **1** the magpie. ◆ *adj* **2** pied. [Middle English *piot*, from PIE[2]]

pycnidium (pɪk'nɪdɪəm) *n, pl* **-ia** (-ɪə). a small flask-shaped structure containing spores that occurs in ascomycetes and certain other fungi. [C19: from New Latin, from Greek *puknos* thick]

pycno- *or before a vowel* **pycn-** *combining form*. indicating thickness or density: *pycnometer*. [via New Latin from Greek *puknos* thick]

pycnometer (pɪk'nɒmɪtə) *n* a small glass bottle of known volume for determining the relative density of liquids and solids by weighing. ▸ **pycnometric** (ˌpɪknə'metrɪk) *adj*

Pydna ('pɪdnə) *n* a town in ancient Macedonia: site of a major Roman victory over the Macedonians, resulting in the downfall of their kingdom (168 B.C.).

pye (paɪ) *n* a variant spelling of **pie**[5].

pye-dog, pie-dog *or* **pi-dog** *n* an ownerless half-wild Asian dog. [C19: Anglo-Indian *pye, paë*, from Hindi *pāhī* outsider]

pyelitis (ˌpaɪə'laɪtɪs) *n* inflammation of the pelvis of the kidney. Compare **pyelonephritis.** ▸ **pyelitic** (ˌpaɪə'lɪtɪk) *adj*

pyelo- *or before a vowel* **pyel-** *combining form*. denoting the renal pelvis: *pyelonephritis*. [from Greek *puelos* trough, pan; in the sense: pelvis]

pyelography (ˌpaɪə'lɒgrəfɪ) *n Med*. the branch of radiology concerned with examination of the kidney and associated structures by means of an X-ray picture called a **pyelogram** ('paɪələʊˌgræm). Also called: **urography.** ▸ **pyelographic** (ˌpaɪələʊ'græfɪk) *adj*

pyelonephritis (ˌpaɪələʊnɪ'fraɪtɪs) *n* inflammation of the kidney and renal pelvis. Compare **pyelitis.**

pygidium (paɪ'dʒɪdɪəm, -'gɪd-) *n, pl* **-ia** (-ɪə). the terminal segment, division, or other structure in certain annelids, arthropods, and other invertebrates. [C19: from New Latin, from Greek *pugē* rump] ▸ **py'gidial** *adj*

Pygmalion (pɪg'meɪlɪən) *n Greek myth*. a king of Cyprus, who fell in love with the statue of a woman he had sculpted and which his prayers brought to life as Galatea.

pygmy *or* **pigmy** ('pɪgmɪ) *n, pl* **-mies. 1** an abnormally undersized person. **2** something that is a very small example of its type. **3** a person of little importance or significance. **4** (*modifier*) of very small stature or size. [C14 *pigmeis* the Pygmies, from Latin *Pygmaeus* a Pygmy, from Greek *pugmaios* undersized, from *pugmē* fist] ▸ **pygmaean** *or* **pygmean** (pɪg'miːən) *adj*

Pygmy *or* **Pigmy** ('pɪgmɪ) *n, pl* **-mies.** a member of one of the dwarf peoples of Equatorial Africa, noted for their hunting and forest culture.

pyinkado (pjɪŋ'kɑːdəʊ) *n* **1** a leguminous tree, *Xylia xylocarpa* (or *dolabriformis*), native to India and Myanmar. **2** the heavy durable timber of this tree, used for construction. [C19: from Burmese]

pyjama *or U.S.* **pajama** (pə'dʒɑːmə) *n* (*modifier*) **1** of or forming part of pyjamas: *pyjama top*. **2** requiring pyjamas to be worn: *a pyjama party*. ◆ See also **pyjamas.** [C19: via Persian or Urdu from Persian *pāē, pāy* foot, leg + *jāmah* clothing, garment]

pyjamas *or U.S.* **pajamas** (pə'dʒɑːməz) *pl n* **1** loose-fitting nightclothes comprising a jacket or top and trousers. **2** full loose-fitting ankle-length trousers worn by either sex in various Eastern countries. **3** women's flared trousers or trouser suit used esp. for leisure wear.

pyknic ('pɪknɪk) *adj* (of a physical type) characterized by a broad squat fleshy physique with a large chest and abdomen. [C20: from Greek *puknos* thick]

pylon ('paɪlən) *n* **1** a large vertical steel tower-like structure supporting high-tension electrical cables. **2** a post or tower for guiding pilots or marking a turning point in a race. **3** a streamlined aircraft structure for attaching an engine pod, external fuel tank, etc., to the main body of the aircraft. **4** a monumental gateway, such as one at the entrance to an ancient Egyptian temple. **5** a temporary artificial leg. [C19: from Greek *pulōn* a gateway]

pylorectomy (ˌpaɪlɔː'rektəmɪ) *n, pl* **-mies.** the surgical removal of all or part of the pylorus, often including the adjacent portion of the stomach (**partial gastrectomy**).

pylorus (paɪ'lɔːrəs) *n, pl* **-ri** (-raɪ). the small circular opening at the base of the stomach through which partially digested food (chyme) passes to the duodenum. [C17: via Late Latin from Greek *pulōrus* gatekeeper, from *pulē* gate + *ouros* guardian] ▸ **py'loric** *adj*

Pylos ('paɪlɒs) *n* a port in SW Greece, in the SW Peloponnese; scene of a defeat of the Spartans by the Athenians (425 B.C.) during the Peloponnesian War and of the Battle of Navarino (see **Navarino**). Italian name: **Navarino.** Modern Greek name: **Pílos.**

Pym (pɪm) *n* **1 Barbara** (**Mary Crampton**). 1913–80, British novelist, noted for such comedies of middle-class English life as *Excellent Women* (1952), *A Glass of Blessings* (1958), and *The Sweet Dove Died* (1978). **2 John.** ?1584–1643, leading English parliamentarian during the events leading to the Civil War. He took a prominent part in the impeachment of Buckingham (1626) and of Strafford and Laud (1640).

Pynchon ('pɪntʃən) *n* **Thomas.** born 1937, U.S. novelist, author of *V* (1963), *The Crying of Lot 49* (1967), *Gravity's Rainbow* (1973), and *Mason and Dixon* (1997).

pyo- *or before a vowel* **py-** *combining form*. denoting pus: *pyosis*. [from Greek *puon*]

pyoderma (ˌpaɪəʊ'dɜːmə) *n Pathol*. any skin eruption characterized by pustules or the formation of pus.

pyogenesis (ˌpaɪəʊ'dʒenɪsɪs) *n Pathol*. the formation of pus. ▸ **ˌpyo'genic** *adj*

pyoid ('paɪɔɪd) *adj* resembling pus.

Pyongyang *or* **P'yŏng-yang** ('pjɒŋ'jæŋ) *n* the capital of North Korea, in the southwest on the Taedong River: industrial centre; university (1946). Pop.: 2 355 000 (1987 est.).

pyorrhoea *or esp. U.S.* **pyorrhea** (ˌpaɪə'rɪə) *n* inflammation of the gums characterized by the discharge of pus and loosening of the teeth; periodontal disease. ▸ **ˌpyor'rhoeal, ˌpyor'rhoeic** *or esp. U.S.* **ˌpyor'rheal, ˌpyor'rheic** *adj*

pyosis (paɪ'əʊsɪs) *n Pathol*. the formation of pus.

pyr- *combining form*. a variant of **pyro-** before a vowel.

pyracantha (ˌpaɪrə'kænθə) *n* any rosaceous shrub of the genus *Pyracantha*, esp. the firethorn, widely cultivated for ornament. [C17: from Greek *purakantha* name of a shrub, from PYRO- + *akantha* thorn]

pyralid ('pɪrəlɪd) *n* **1** any moth of the mostly tropical family *Pyralidae*, typically having narrow forewings and broad fringed hind wings: includes the bee moths and the corn borer. ◆ *adj* **2** of, relating to, or belonging to the family *Pyralidae*. [C19: via New Latin from Greek *puralis:* a mythical winged insect believed to live in fire, from *pur* fire]

pyramid ('pɪrəmɪd) *n* **1** a huge masonry construction that has a square base and, as in the case of the ancient Egyptian royal tombs, four sloping triangular sides. **2** an object, formation, or structure resembling such a construction. **3** *Maths*. a solid having a polygonal base and triangular sides that meet in a common vertex. **4** *Crystallog*. a crystal form in which three planes intersect all three axes of the crystal. **5** *Anatomy*. any pointed or cone-shaped bodily structure or part. **6** *Finance*. a group of enterprises containing a series of holding companies structured so that the top holding company controls the entire group with a relatively small proportion of the total capital invested. **7** *Chiefly U.S.* the series of transactions involved in pyramiding securities. **8** (*pl*) a game similar to billiards with fifteen coloured balls. ◆ *vb* **9** to build up or be arranged in the form of a pyramid. **10** *Chiefly U.S.* to speculate in (securities or property) by increasing purchases on additional margin or collateral derived from paper profits associated with high prices of securities and property in a boom. **11** *Finance.* to form (companies) into a pyramid. **[C16** (earlier *pyramis*): from Latin *pyramis,* from Greek *puramis,* probably from Egyptian**]** ▸ **pyramidal** (pɪˈræmɪdᵊl), ˌ**pyraˈmidical,** *or* ˌ**pyraˈmidic** *adj* ▸ **pyˈramidally** *or* ˌ**pyraˈmidically** *adv*

pyramidal orchid *n* a chalk-loving orchid, *Anacamptis pyramidalis,* bearing a dense cone-shaped spike of purplish-pink flowers with a long curved spur.

pyramidal peak *n Geology.* a sharp peak formed where the ridges separating three or more cirques intersect; horn.

pyramid selling *n* a practice adopted by some manufacturers of advertising for distributors and selling them batches of goods. The first distributors then advertise for more distributors who are sold subdivisions of the original batches at an increased price. This process continues until the final distributors are left with a stock that is unsaleable except at a loss.

Pyramus and Thisbe (ˈpɪrəməs; ˈθɪzbɪ) *n* (in Greek legend) two lovers of Babylon: Pyramus, wrongly supposing Thisbe to be dead, killed himself and she, encountering him in his death throes, did the same.

pyran (ˈpaɪræn, paɪˈræn) *n* an unsaturated heterocyclic compound having a ring containing five carbon atoms and one oxygen atom and two double bonds. It has two isomers depending on the position of the saturated carbon atom relative to the oxygen. **[C20:** from PYRO- + -AN**]**

pyranometer (ˌpaɪrəˈnɒmɪtə) *n Physics.* another name for **solarimeter.**

pyrargyrite (paɪˈrɑːdʒɪˌraɪt) *n* a dark red to black mineral consisting of silver antimony sulphide in hexagonal crystalline form: occurs in silver veins and is an important ore of silver. Formula: Ag_3SbS_3. **[C19:** from German *Pyrargyrit,* from PYRO- + Greek *arguros* silver**]**

pyrazole (ˈpaɪrəˌzəʊl) *n* a crystalline soluble basic heterocyclic compound; 1,2-diazole. Formula: $C_3H_4N_2$. **[C19:** from German, from PYRROLE + inserted *-az-* (see AZO-)**]**

pyre (paɪə) *n* a heap or pile of wood or other combustible material, esp. one used for cremating a corpse. **[C17:** from Latin *pyra,* from Greek *pura* hearth, from *pur* fire**]**

pyrene[1] (ˈpaɪriːn) *n* a solid polynuclear aromatic hydrocarbon extracted from coal tar. Formula: $C_{16}H_{10}$. **[C19:** from PYRO- + -ENE**]**

pyrene[2] (ˈpaɪriːn) *n Botany.* any of several small hard stones that occur in a single fruit and contain a single seed each. **[C19:** from New Latin *pyrena,* from Greek *purēn***]**

Pyrenean mountain dog *n* a large heavily built dog of an ancient breed originally used to protect sheep from wild animals: it has a long thick white coat with a dense ruff.

Pyrenees (ˌpɪrəˈniːz) *pl n* a mountain range between France and Spain, extending from the Bay of Biscay to the Mediterranean. Highest peak: Pico de Aneto, 3404 m (11 168 ft.). ▸ ˌ**Pyreˈnean** *adj*

Pyrénées *or* **Pyrénées-Atlantiques** (*French* pirenez-atlɑ̃tik) *n* a department of SW France in Aquitaine region. Capital: Pau. Pop.: 592 200 (1995). Area: 7712 sq. km (3008 sq. miles). Former name: **Basses-Pyrénées.**

Pyrénées-Orientales (*French* pirenezɔrjɑ̃tal) *n* a department of S France, in Languedoc-Roussillon region. Capital: Perpignan. Pop.: 376 200 (1995). Area: 4144 sq. km (1616 sq. miles).

pyrenoid (ˈpaɪrəˌnɔɪd) *n* any of various small protein granules that occur in certain algae, mosses, and protozoans and are involved in the synthesis of starch. **[C19:** from PYRENE[2] + -OID**]**

pyrethrin (paɪˈriːθrɪn) *n* **1** Also called: **pyrethrin I.** an oily water-insoluble compound used as an insecticide. Formula: $C_{21}H_{28}O_3$. **2** Also called: **pyrethrin II.** a compound of similar chemical structure and action, also found in pyrethrum. Formula: $C_{22}H_{28}O_5$. **[C19:** from PYRETHRUM + -IN**]**

pyrethroid (paɪˈriːθrɔɪd) *n* **1** any of various chemical compounds having similar insecticidal properties to pyrethrin. ♦ *adj* **2** of or relating to such compounds.

pyrethrum (paɪˈriːθrəm) *n* **1** any of several cultivated Eurasian chrysanthemums, such as *Chrysanthemum coccineum* and *C. roseum,* with white, pink, red, or purple flowers. **2** any insecticide prepared from the dried flowers of any of these plants, esp. *C. roseum.* **[C16:** via Latin from Greek *purethron* feverfew, probably from *puretos* fever; see PYRETIC**]**

pyretic (paɪˈrɛtɪk) *adj Pathol.* of, relating to, or characterized by fever. Compare **antipyretic. [C18:** from New Latin *pyreticus,* from Greek *puretos* fever, from *pur* fire**]**

Pyrex (ˈpaɪrɛks) *n Trademark.* **a** any of a variety of borosilicate glasses that have low coefficients of expansion, making them suitable for heat-resistant glassware used in cookery and chemical apparatus. **b** (*as modifier*): *a Pyrex dish.*

pyrexia (paɪˈrɛksɪə) *n* a technical name for **fever. [C18:** from New Latin, from Greek *purexis,* from *puressein* to be feverish, from *pur* fire**]** ▸ **pyˈrexial** *or* **pyˈrexic** *adj*

pyrgeometer (ˌpɜːdʒɪˈɒmɪtə) *n Physics.* an instrument for measuring the loss of heat by radiation from the earth's surface.

pyrheliometer (pəˌhiːlɪˈɒmɪtə) *n* an instrument for measuring the intensity of the sun's radiant energy. ▸ **pyrheliometric** (pəˌhiːlɪəʊˈmɛtrɪk) *adj*

pyridine (ˈpɪrɪˌdiːn) *n* a colourless hygroscopic liquid with a characteristic odour. It is a basic heterocyclic compound containing one nitrogen atom and five carbon atoms in its molecules and is used as a solvent and in preparing other organic chemicals. Formula: C_5H_5N. **[C19:** from PYRO- + -ID[3] + -INE[2]**]**

pyridoxal (ˌpɪrɪˈdɒksəl) *n Biochem.* a naturally occurring derivative of pyridoxine that is a precursor of a coenzyme (**pyridoxal phosphate**) involved in several enzymic reactions. Formula: $(CH_2OH)(CHO)C_5HN(OH)(CH_3)$.

pyridoxamine (ˌpɪrɪˈdɒksəmiːn) *n Biochem.* a metabolic form of pyridoxine.

pyridoxine (ˌpɪrɪˈdɒksiːn) *n Biochem.* a derivative of pyridine that is a precursor of the compounds pyridoxal and pyridoxamine. Also called: **vitamin B_6. [C20:** from PYRID(INE) + OX(YGEN) + -INE[2]**]**

pyriform (ˈpɪrɪˌfɔːm) *adj* (esp. of organs of the body) pear-shaped. **[C18:** from New Latin *pyriformis,* from *pyri-,* erroneously from Latin *pirum* pear + *-formis* -FORM**]**

pyrimidine (paɪˈrɪmɪˌdiːn) *n* **1** a liquid or crystalline organic compound with a penetrating odour; 1,3-diazine. It is a weakly basic soluble heterocyclic compound and can be prepared from barbituric acid. Formula: $C_4H_4N_2$. **2** Also called: **pyrimidine base.** any of a number of similar compounds having a basic structure that is derived from pyrimidine, including cytosine, thymine, and uracil, which are constituents of nucleic acids. **[C20:** variant of PYRIDINE**]**

pyrite (ˈpaɪraɪt) *n* a yellow mineral, found in igneous and metamorphic rocks and in veins. It is a source of sulphur and is used in the manufacture of sulphuric acid. Composition: iron sulphide. Formula: FeS_2. Crystal structure: cubic. Also called: **iron pyrites, pyrites.** Nontechnical name: **fool's gold. [C16:** from Latin *pyrites* flint, from Greek *puritēs* (*lithos*) fire (stone), that is, capable of withstanding or striking fire, from *pur* fire**]** ▸ **pyritic** (paɪˈrɪtɪk) *or* **pyˈritous** *adj*

pyrites (paɪˈraɪtiːz, *in combination* ˈpaɪraɪts) *n, pl* **-tes. 1** another name for **pyrite. 2** any of a number of other disulphides of metals, esp. of copper and tin.

pyro- *or before a vowel* **pyr-** *combining form.* **1** denoting fire, heat, or high temperature: *pyromania; pyrometer.* **2** caused or obtained by fire or heat: *pyroelectricity.* **3** *Chem.* **3a** denoting a new substance obtained by heating another: *pyroboric acid is obtained by heating boric acid.* **3b** denoting an acid or salt with a water content intermediate between that of the ortho- and meta-compounds: *pyro-phosphoric acid.* **4** *Mineralogy.* **4a** having a property that changes upon the application of heat: *pyromorphite.* **4b** having a flame-coloured appearance: *pyroxylin.*

pyrocatechol (ˌpaɪrəʊˈkætɪˌtʃɒl, -kɒl) *or* **pyrocatechin** (ˌpaɪrəʊˈkætɪkɪn) *n* another name for **catechol.**

pyrochemical (ˌpaɪrəʊˈkɛmɪkᵊl) *adj* of, concerned with, being, producing, or resulting from chemical changes at high temperatures. ▸ ˌ**pyroˈchemically** *adv*

pyroclastic (ˌpaɪrəʊˈklæstɪk) *adj* (of rocks) formed from the solid fragments ejected during a volcanic eruption.

pyroconductivity (ˌpaɪrəʊˌkɒndʌkˈtɪvɪtɪ) *n* conductivity that can be induced in certain solids by heating them.

pyroelectric (ˌpaɪrəʊɪˈlɛktrɪk) *adj* **1** of, concerned with, or exhibiting pyroelectricity. ♦ *n* **2** a pyroelectric substance.

pyroelectricity (ˌpaɪrəʊɪlɛkˈtrɪsɪtɪ, -ˌiːlɛk-) *n* the development of opposite charges at the ends of the axis of certain hemihedral crystals, such as tourmaline, as a result of a change in temperature.

pyrogallate (ˌpaɪrəʊˈgæleɪt) *n* any salt or ester of pyrogallol.

pyrogallol (ˌpaɪrəʊˈgælɒl) *n* a white lustrous crystalline soluble phenol with weakly acidic properties; 1,2,3-trihydroxybenzene: used as a photographic developer and for absorbing oxygen in gas analysis. Formula: $C_6H_3(OH)_3$. **[C20:** from PYRO- + GALL(IC)[2] + -OL[1]**]** ▸ ˌ**pyroˈgallic** *adj*

pyrogen (ˈpaɪrəʊˌdʒɛn) *n* any of a group of substances that cause a rise in temperature in an animal body.

pyrogenic (ˌpaɪrəʊˈdʒɛnɪk) *or* **pyrogenous** (paɪˈrɒdʒɪnəs) *adj* **1** produced by or producing heat. **2** *Pathol.* causing or resulting from fever. **3** *Geology.* less common words for **igneous.**

pyrognostics (ˌpaɪrɒgˈnɒstɪks) *pl n* the characteristics of a mineral, such as fusibility and flame coloration, that are revealed by the application of heat. **[C19:** from PYRO- + *-gnostics,* from Greek *gnōsis* knowledge**]**

pyrography (paɪˈrɒgrəfɪ) *n, pl* **-phies. 1** the art or process of burning designs on wood or leather with heated tools or a flame. **2** a design made by this process. ▸ **pyˈrographer** *n* ▸ **pyrographic** (ˌpaɪrəʊˈgræfɪk) *adj*

pyroligneous (ˌpaɪrəʊˈlɪgnɪəs) *or* **pyrolignic** *adj* (of a substance) produced by the action of heat on wood, esp. by destructive distillation. **[C18:** from French *pyroligneux,* from PYRO- + *ligneus* LIGNEOUS**]**

pyroligneous acid *n* the crude reddish-brown acidic liquid obtained by the distillation of wood and containing acetic acid, methanol, and acetone. Also called: **wood vinegar.**

pyrolusite (ˌpaɪrəʊˈluːsaɪt) *n* a blackish fibrous or soft powdery mineral consisting of manganese dioxide in tetragonal crystalline form. It occurs in association with other manganese ores and is an important source of manganese. Formula: MnO_2. **[C19:** from PYRO- + Greek *lousis* a washing + -ITE[1], from its use in purifying glass**]**

pyrolyse *or U.S.* **pyrolyze** (ˈpaɪrəʊˌlaɪz) *vb* (*tr*) to subject to pyrolysis. ▸ ˈ**pyroˌlyser** *or* ˈ**pyroˌlyzer** *n*

pyrolysis (paɪˈrɒlɪsɪs) *n* **1** the application of heat to chemical compounds in order to cause decomposition. **2** chemical decomposition of compounds caused by high temperatures. ▸ **pyrolytic** (ˌpaɪrəʊˈlɪtɪk) *adj*

pyromagnetic (ˌpaɪrəʊmægˈnɛtɪk) *adj* a former term for **thermomagnetic.**

pyromancy (ˈpaɪrəʊˌmænsɪ) *n* divination by fire or flames. ▸ ˈ**pyroˌmancer** *n* ▸ ˌ**pyroˈmantic** *adj*

pyromania (ˌpaɪrəʊˈmeɪnɪə) *n Psychiatry.* the uncontrollable impulse and practice of setting things on fire. ▸ ˌ**pyroˈmaniˌac** *n* ▸ **pyromaniacal** (ˌpaɪrəʊməˈnaɪəkᵊl) *adj*

pyrometallurgy (ˌpaɪrəʊmɛˈtælədʒɪ, -ˈmɛtəˌlɜːdʒɪ) *n* the branch of metallurgy involving processes performed at high temperatures, including sintering, roasting, smelting, casting, refining, alloying, and heat treatment.

pyrometer (paɪˈrɒmɪtə) *n* an instrument for measuring high temperatures, esp. by measuring the brightness (**optical pyrometer**) or total quantity (**radiation pyrometer**) of the radiation produced by the source. Other types include the resistance thermometer and the thermocouple. ▸ **pyrometric** (ˌpaɪrəʊˈmɛtrɪk) *or* ˌ**pyroˈmetrical** *adj* ▸ ˌ**pyroˈmetrically** *adv* ▸ **pyˈrometry** *n*

pyromorphite (ˌpaɪrəʊˈmɔːfaɪt) *n* a green, yellow, brown, or grey secondary mineral that consists of lead chloro-phosphate in the form of hexagonal crystals. Formula: $Pb_5Cl(PO_4)_3$. [C19: from German *Pyromorphit,* from PYRO- + Greek *morphē* form + -ITE[1], an allusion to the fact that it assumes a crystalline form when heated]

pyrone ('paɪrəun, paɪ'rəun) *n* **1** either of two heterocyclic compounds that have a ring containing five carbon atoms and one oxygen atom with two double bonds and a second oxygen atom attached to a carbon atom in either the *ortho*-position (**alpha pyrone**) or the *para*-position (**gamma pyrone**). **2** any one of a class of compounds that are substituted derivatives of a pyrone.

pyrope ('paɪrəup) *n* a deep yellowish-red garnet that consists of magnesium aluminium silicate and is used as a gemstone. Formula: $Mg_3Al_2(SiO_4)_3$. [C14 (used loosely of a red gem; modern sense C19): from Old French *pirope,* from Latin *pyrōpus* bronze, from Greek *purōpus* fiery-eyed, from *pur* fire +*ōps* eye]

pyrophoric (ˌpaɪrəu'fɒrɪk) *adj* **1** (of a chemical) igniting spontaneously on contact with air. **2** (of an alloy) producing sparks when struck or scraped: *lighter flints are made of pyrophoric alloy.* [C19: from New Latin *pyrophorus,* from Greek *purophoros* fire-bearing, from *pur* fire + *pherein* to bear]

pyrophosphate (ˌpaɪrəu'fɒsfeɪt) *n* any salt or ester of pyrophosphoric acid.

pyrophosphoric acid (ˌpaɪrəufɒs'fɒrɪk) *n* a crystalline soluble solid acid formed by the reaction between one molecule of phosphorus pentoxide and two water molecules. Formula: $H_4P_2O_7$. See also **polyphosphoric acid.**

pyrophotometer (ˌpaɪrəufəu'tɒmɪtə) *n* a type of pyrometer in which the temperature of an incandescent body is determined by photometric measurement of the light it emits. ► ˌ**pyropho'tometry** *n*

pyrophyllite (ˌpaɪrəu'fɪlaɪt) *n* a white, silvery, or green micaceous mineral that consists of hydrated aluminium silicate in monoclinic crystalline form and occurs in metamorphic rocks. Formula: $Al_2Si_4O_{10}(OH)_2$.

pyrosis (paɪ'rəusɪs) *n Pathol.* a technical name for **heartburn.** [C18: from New Latin, from Greek: a burning, from *puroun* to burn, from *pur* fire]

pyrostat ('paɪrəuˌstæt) *n* **1** a device that activates an alarm or extinguisher in the event of a fire. **2** a thermostat for use at high temperatures. ► ˌ**pyro'static** *adj*

pyrosulphate (ˌpaɪrəu'sʌlfeɪt) *n* any salt of pyrosulphuric acid. Also called: **disulphate.**

pyrosulphuric acid (ˌpaɪrəusʌl'fjuərɪk) *n* a fuming liquid acid made by adding sulphur trioxide to concentrated sulphuric acid. Formula: $H_2S_2O_7$. Also called: **disulphuric acid.** See also **fuming sulphuric acid.**

pyrotechnics (ˌpaɪrəu'teknɪks) *n* **1** (*functioning as sing*) the art or craft of making fireworks. **2** (*functioning as sing or pl*) a firework display. **3** (*functioning as sing or pl*) brilliance of display, as in the performance of music. ◆ Also called: **'pyroˌtechny.** ► ˌ**pyro'technic** *or* ˌ**pyro'technical** *adj*

pyroxene (paɪ'rɒksiːn) *n* any of a group of silicate minerals having the general formula $ABSi_2O_6$, where A is usually calcium, sodium, magnesium, or iron, and B is usually magnesium, iron, chromium, manganese, or aluminium. Pyroxenes occur in basic igneous rocks and some metamorphic rocks, and have colours ranging from white to dark green or black. They may be monoclinic (clinopyroxenes) or orthorhombic (orthopyroxenes) in crystal structure. Examples are augite (the most important pyroxene), diopside, enstatite, hypersthene, and jadeite. [C19: PYRO- + *-xene* from Greek *xenos* foreign, because it was mistakenly thought to have originated elsewhere when found in igneous rocks] ► **pyroxenic** (ˌpaɪrɒk'senɪk) *adj*

pyroxenite (paɪ'rɒksɪˌnaɪt) *n* a very dark coarse-grained ultrabasic rock consisting entirely of pyroxene minerals.

pyroxylin (paɪ'rɒksɪlɪn) *n* a yellow substance obtained by nitrating cellulose with a mixture of nitric and sulphuric acids; guncotton: used to make collodion, plastics, lacquers, and adhesives. [C19: from PYRO- + XYL(O)- + -IN]

Pyrrha ('pɪrə) *n Greek myth.* the wife of Deucalion, saved with him from the flood loosed upon mankind by Zeus.

pyrrhic[1] ('pɪrɪk) *Prosody.* ◆ *n* **1** a metrical foot of two short or unstressed syllables. ◆ *adj* **2** of or relating to such a metrical foot. **3** (of poetry) composed in pyrrhics. [C16: via Latin, from Greek *purrhikhē,* traditionally said to be named after its inventor *Purrhikhos*]

pyrrhic[2] ('pɪrɪk) *n* **1** a war dance of ancient Greece. ◆ *adj* **2** of or relating to this dance. [C17: Latin from Greek *purrhikhios* belonging to the *purrhikhē* war dance performed in armour; see PYRRHIC[1]]

Pyrrhic victory *n* a victory in which the victor's losses are as great as those of the defeated. Also called: **Cadmean victory.** [named after PYRRHUS, who defeated the Romans at Asculum in 279 B.C. but suffered heavy losses]

Pyrrho ('pɪrəu) *n* ?365–?275 B.C., Greek philosopher; founder of scepticism. He maintained that true wisdom and happiness lie in suspension of judgment, since certain knowledge is impossible to attain. ► **'Pyrrhonism** *n* ► **'Pyrrhonist** *n, adj*

pyrrhotite ('pɪrəˌtaɪt) *or* **pyrrhotine** ('pɪrəˌtiːn, -ˌtaɪn, -tɪn) *n* a common bronze-coloured magnetic mineral consisting of ferrous sulphide in hexagonal crystalline form. Formula: FeS. [C19: from Greek *purrhotēs* redness, from *purrhos* fiery, from *pur* fire]

pyrrhuloxia (ˌpɪrə'lɒksɪə) *n* a grey-and-pink crested bunting, *Pyrrhuloxia sinuata,* of Central and SW North America, with a short parrot-like bill. [from New Latin *Pyrrhula* genus of the finches (from Greek *purrhoulas* a flame-coloured bird, from *purrhos* red, from *pur* fire) + *Loxia* genus of the crossbills, from Greek *loxos* oblique]

Pyrrhus ('pɪrəs) *n* **1** 319–272 B.C., king of Epirus (306–272). He invaded Italy but was ultimately defeated by the Romans (275 B.C.). **2** another name for **Neoptolemus.** ► **'Pyrrhic** *adj*

pyrrole ('pɪrəul, pɪ'rəul) *n* a colourless insoluble toxic liquid having a five-membered ring containing one nitrogen atom, found in many naturally occurring compounds, such as chlorophyll. Formula: C_4H_5N. Also called: **azole.** [C19: from Greek *purrhos* red, from *pur* fire + -OLE[1]] ► **pyrrolic** (pɪ'rɒlɪk) *adj*

pyrrolidine (pɪ'rɒlɪˌdiːn) *n* an almost colourless liquid occurring in tobacco leaves and made commercially by hydrogenating pyrrole. It is a strongly alkaline heterocyclic base with molecules that contain a ring of four carbon atoms and one nitrogen atom. Formula: C_4H_9N.

pyruvic acid (paɪ'ruːvɪk) *n* a colourless pleasant-smelling liquid formed as an intermediate in the metabolism of proteins and carbohydrates, helping to release energy to the body; 2-oxopropanoic acid. Formula: $CH_3COCOOH$. [C19: *pyruvic* from PYRO- + Latin *ūva* grape]

Pythagoras[1] (paɪ'θægərəs) *n* ?580–?500 B.C., Greek philosopher and mathematician. He founded a religious brotherhood, which followed a life of strict asceticism and greatly influenced the development of mathematics and its application to music and astronomy.

Pythagoras[2] (paɪ'θægərəs) *n* a deep crater in the NE quadrant of the moon, 136 kilometres in diameter.

Pythagoras' theorem *n* the theorem that in a right-angled triangle the square of the length of the hypotenuse equals the sum of the squares of the other two sides.

Pythagorean (paɪˌθægə'riːən) *adj* **1** of or relating to Pythagoras. **2** *Music.* denoting the diatonic scale of eight notes arrived at by Pythagoras and based on a succession of fifths. ◆ *n* **3** a follower of Pythagoras.

Pythagoreanism (paɪˌθægə'riːəˌnɪzəm) *n* the teachings of Pythagoras and his followers, esp. that the universe is essentially a manifestation of mathematical relationships.

Pytheas ('pɪθɪəs) *n* 4th century B.C., Greek navigator. He was the first Greek to visit and describe the coasts of Spain, France, and the British Isles and may have reached Iceland.

Pythia ('pɪθɪə) *n Greek myth.* the priestess of Apollo at Delphi, who transmitted the oracles.

Pythian ('pɪθɪən) *adj also* **Pythic. 1** of or relating to Delphi or its oracle. ◆ *n* **2** the priestess of Apollo at the oracle of Delphi. **3** an inhabitant of ancient Delphi. [C16: via Latin *Pȳthius* from Greek *Puthios* of Delphi]

Pythian Games *pl n* (in ancient Greece) the second most important Panhellenic festival, celebrated in the third year of each Olympiad near Delphi. The four-year period between celebrations was known as a **Pythiad** ('pɪθɪˌæd).

Pythias ('pɪθɪˌæs) *n* See **Damon and Pythias.**

python ('paɪθən) *n* any large nonvenomous snake of the family *Pythonidae* of Africa, S Asia, and Australia, such as *Python reticulatus* (**reticulated python**). They can reach a length of more than 20 feet and kill their prey by constriction. [C16: New Latin, after PYTHON] ► **pythonic** (paɪ'θɒnɪk) *adj*

Python ('paɪθən) *n Greek myth.* a dragon, killed by Apollo at Delphi.

Pythonesque (ˌpaɪθə'nesk) *adj* denoting a kind of humour that is absurd and unpredictable; zany; surreal. [C20: named after the British television show *Monty Python's Flying Circus,* first broadcast in 1969]

pythoness ('paɪθəˌnes) *n* **1** a woman, such as Apollo's priestess at Delphi, believed to be possessed by an oracular spirit. **2** a female soothsayer. [C14 *phitonesse,* ultimately from Greek *Puthōn* PYTHON]

pyuria (paɪ'juərɪə) *n Pathol.* any condition characterized by the presence of pus in the urine. [C19: from New Latin, from Greek *puon* pus + *ouron* urine]

pyx *or* (*less commonly*) **pix** (pɪks) *n* **1** Also called: **pyx chest.** the chest in which coins from the British mint are placed to be tested for weight, etc. **2** *Christianity.* any receptacle in which the Eucharistic Host is kept. [C14: from Latin *pyxis* small box, from Greek, from *puxos* box tree]

pyxidium (pɪk'sɪdɪəm) *or* **pyxis** ('pɪksɪs) *n, pl* **-ia** (-ɪə) *or* **pyxides** ('pɪksɪˌdiːz). the dry fruit of such plants as the plantain: a capsule whose upper part falls off when mature so that the seeds are released. [C19: via New Latin from Greek *puxidion* a little box, from *puxis* box, PYX]

pyxie ('pɪksɪ) *n* a creeping evergreen shrub, *Pyxidanthera barbulata,* of the eastern U.S. with small white or pink star-shaped flowers: family *Diapensiaceae.* [C19: shortened from New Latin *Pyxidanthera,* from PYXIS + ANTHER]

pyxis ('pɪksɪs) *n, pl* **pyxides** ('pɪksɪˌdiːz). **1** a small box used by the ancient Greeks and Romans to hold medicines, etc. **2** a rare word for **pyx. 3** another name for **pyxidium.** [C14: via Latin from Greek: box]

Pyxis ('pɪksɪs) *n, Latin genitive* **Pyxidis** ('pɪksɪdɪs). an inconspicuous constellation close to Puppis that was originally considered part of the more extensive constellation Argo.

pzazz (pə'zæz) *n Informal.* a variant of **pizzazz.**

Qq

q *or* **Q** (kjuː) *n, pl* **q's, Q's,** *or* **Qs. 1** the 17th letter and 13th consonant of the modern English alphabet. **2** a speech sound represented by this letter, in English usually a voiceless velar stop, as in *unique* and *quick*.
q *symbol for* quintal.
Q *symbol for:* **1** *Chess.* queen. **2** question. **3** *Physics.* heat.
q. *abbrev. for:* **1** quart. **2** quarter. **3** quarterly. **4** query. **5** question. **6** quire.
Q. *abbrev. for:* **1** quartermaster. **2** (*pl* **Qq., qq.**) Also: **q.** quarto. **3** Quebec. **4** Queen. **5** question. **6** *Electronics.* Q factor.
Qabis (ˈkɑːbɪs) *n* the Arabic name for **Gabès.**
Qaboos bin Said (kəˈbuːs bɪn ˈsaɪd) *n* born 1940, sultan of Oman from 1970.
Qaddafi (gəˈdɑːfɪ) *n* **Moamar al** (ˈməʊə,mɑː ,æl). See (Moamar al) **Gaddafi.**
Qaddish (ˈkædɪʃ) *n, pl* **Qaddishim.** a variant spelling of **Kaddish.**
qadi (ˈkɑːdɪ, ˈkeɪdɪ) *n, pl* **-dis.** a variant spelling of **cadi.**
Qairwan (kaɪəˈwɑːn) *n* a variant of **Kairouan.**
QANTAS (ˈkwɒntəs) *n* the Australian national airline. [acronym of Queensland *a*nd Northern *T*erritory *A*erial *S*ervices, its original name: founded 1920]
Qaraghandy (*Kazakh* karaɣanˈdɪ) *n* a variant transliteration of the Kazakh name for **Karaganda.**
QARANC *abbrev. for* Queen Alexandra's Royal Army Nursing Corps.
qat (kæt, kɑːt) *n* a variant spelling of **khat.**
Qatar *or* **Katar** (kæˈtɑː) *n* a state in E Arabia, occupying a peninsula in the Persian Gulf: under Persian rule until the 19th century; became a British protectorate in 1916; declared independence in 1971; exports petroleum and natural gas. Official language: Arabic. Official religion: (Sunni) Muslim. Currency: riyal. Capital: Doha. Pop.: 579 000 (1998 est.). Area: about 11 000 sq. km (4250 sq. miles). ▸ **Qaˈtari** *or* **Kaˈtari** *adj, n*
Qattara Depression (kəˈtɑːrə) *n* an arid basin in the Sahara, in NW Egypt, impassable to vehicles. Area: about 18 000 sq. km (7000 sq. miles). Lowest point: 133 m (435 ft.) below sea level.
qawwali (kəˈvɑːlɪ) *n* an Islamic religious song, esp. in Asia.
QB 1 *abbrev. for* Queen's Bench. **2** *Chess. symbol for* queen's bishop.
QBP *Chess. symbol for* queen's bishop's pawn.
QC *abbrev. for* Queen's Counsel.
QCA (in Britain) *abbrev. for* Qualifications and Curriculum Authority.
QCD *abbrev. for* quantum chromodynamics.
q.e. *abbrev. for* quod est. [Latin: which is]
QED *abbrev. for:* **1** quod erat demonstrandum. [Latin: which was to be shown or proved] **2** quantum electrodynamics.
QEF *abbrev. for* quod erat faciendum. [Latin: which was to be done]
Qeshm (ˈkɛʃəm) *or* **Qishm** *n* **1** the largest island in the Persian Gulf: part of Iran. Area: 1336 sq. km (516 sq. miles). **2** the chief town of this island.
QF *abbrev. for* quick-firing.
Q factor *n* **1** a measure of the relationship between stored energy and rate of energy dissipation in certain electrical components, devices, etc., thus indicating their efficiency. **2** Also called: **Q value.** the heat released in a nuclear reaction, usually expressed in millions of electronvolts for each individual reaction. Symbol: Q [C20: short for *quality factor*]
QFD *abbrev. for* quantum flavourdynamics.
Q fever *n* an acute disease characterized by fever and pneumonia, transmitted to man by the rickettsia *Coxiella burnetii.* [C20: from *q(uery) fever* (the cause being unknown when it was named)]
qi (tʃiː) *n* a variant of **chi**[2].
Qian Long (ˈtʃɪˈæn ˈlɒŋ) *or* **Ch'ien-lung,** *n* , original name *Hong-li.* 1711–99, Chinese emperor of the Qing dynasty. He expanded the Chinese empire and was a patron of the arts.
qibla (ˈkɪblə) *n* a variant of **kiblah.**
qi gong (ˈtʃiː ˈgɒŋ) *n* a system of breathing and exercise designed to benefit both physical and mental health. [C20: from Chinese *qi* energy + *gong* exercise]
Qingdao (ˈtʃɪŋˈdaʊ), **Tsingtao,** *or* **Chingtao** *n* a port in E China, in E Shandong province on Jiazhou Bay, developed as a naval base and fort in 1891. Shandong university (1926). Pop.: 2 060 000 (1991 est.).
Qinghai, Tsinghai, *or* **Chinghai** (ˈtʃɪŋˈhaɪ) *n* **1** a province of NW China: consists largely of mountains and high plateaus. Capital: Xining. Pop.: 4 810 000 (1996 est.). Area: 721 000 sq. km (278 400 sq. miles). **2** the Pinyin transliteration of the Chinese name for **Koko Nor.**
qintar (kɪnˈtɑː, ˈkɪntɑː) *or* **qindar** (kɪnˈdɑː) *n* an Albanian monetary unit worth one hundredth of a lek.
Qiqihar, Chichihaerh, Ch'i-ch'i-haerh, *or* **Tsitsihar** (ˈtʃiː,tʃiːˈhɑː) *n* a city in NE China, in Heilongjiang province on the Nonni River. Pop.: 1 380 000 (1991 est.).
Qishm (ˈkɪʃəm) *n* a variant of **Qeshm.**
QKt *Chess. symbol for* queen's knight.
QKtP *Chess. symbol for* queen's knight's pawn.
ql *abbrev. for* quintal.
q.l. (in prescriptions) *abbrev. for* quantum libet. [Latin: as much as you please]
Qld *or* **QLD** *abbrev. for* Queensland.
qm (in prescriptions) *abbrev. for* quaque mane. [Latin: every morning]
QM *abbrev. for* Quartermaster.
QMC *abbrev. for* Quartermaster Corps.
Q-methodology *n* a statistical methodology used by psychologists to identify alternative world-views, opinions, interpretations, etc. in terms of statistically independent patterns of response recognized by clustering together individuals whose orderings of items, typically attitude statements, are similar. Compare **R-methodology.**
QMG *abbrev. for* Quartermaster General.
QMS *abbrev. for* Quartermaster Sergeant.
QMV *abbrev. for* Qualified Majority Voting.
qn (in prescriptions) *abbrev. for* quaque nocte. [Latin: every night]
QN *Chess. symbol for* queen's knight.
QNP *Chess. symbol for* queen's knight's pawn.
Qom (kɒm), **Qum,** *or* **Kum** *n* a city in NW central Iran: a place of pilgrimage for Shiite Muslims. Pop.: 780 453 (1994 est.).
qoph (kuf, kɒf; *Hebrew* kɔf) *n* a variant of **koph.**
qorma (ˈkɔːmə) *n* a variant spelling of **korma.**
QP *Chess. symbol for* queen's pawn.
Qq. *or* **qq.** *abbrev. for:* **1** quartos. **2** questions.
qqv *abbrev. for* quae vide (denoting a cross reference to more than one item). Compare **qv.** [New Latin: which (words, items, etc.) see]
QR *Chess. symbol for* queen's rook.
qr. *pl* **qrs.** *abbrev. for:* **1** quarter. **2** quarterly. **3** quire.
QRP *Chess. symbol for* queen's rook's pawn.
qs *abbrev. for:* **1** (in prescriptions) quantum sufficit. [Latin: as much as will suffice] **2** quarter section (of land).
QS *abbrev. for* quarter sessions.
Q-ship *n* a merchant ship with concealed guns, used to decoy enemy ships into the range of its weapons. [named from *q(uery)*]
QSM (in New Zealand) *abbrev. for* Queen's Service Medal.
QSO *abbrev. for:* **1** *Astronomy.* quasi-stellar object. **2** (in New Zealand) Queen's Service Order.
Q-sort *n* a psychological test requiring subjects to sort items relative to one another along a dimension such as "agree"/"disagree" for analysis by Q-methodological statistics.
qt *pl* **qt** *or* **qts** *abbrev. for* quart.
q.t. *Informal.* **1** *abbrev. for* quiet. **2 on the q.t.** secretly.
qto *abbrev. for* quarto.
qty *abbrev. for* quantity.
qu. *abbrev. for:* **1** queen. **2** query. **3** question.
qua (kweɪ, kwɑː) *prep* in the capacity of; by virtue of being. [C17: from Latin, ablative singular (feminine) of *qui* who]
quack[1] (kwæk) *vb (intr)* **1** (of a duck) to utter a harsh guttural sound. **2** to make a noise like a duck. ◆ *n* **3** the harsh guttural sound made by a duck. [C17: of imitative origin; related to Dutch *kwakken,* German *quacken*]
quack[2] (kwæk) *n* **1a** an unqualified person who claims medical knowledge or other skills. **1b** (*as modifier*): *a quack doctor.* **2** *Brit., Austral., and N.Z. informal.* a doctor; physician or surgeon. ◆ *vb* **3** *(intr)* to act in the manner of a quack. [C17: short for QUACKSALVER] ▸ **ˈquackish** *adj*
quackery (ˈkwækərɪ) *n, pl* **-eries.** the activities or methods of a quack.
quack grass *n* another name for **couch grass.** [C19: a variant of QUICK GRASS]
quacksalver (ˈkwæk,sælvə) *n* an archaic word for **quack**[2]. [C16: from Dutch, from *quack,* apparently: to hawk + *salf* SALVE[1]]
quad[1] (kwɒd) *n* short for **quadrangle** (sense 2).
quad[2] (kwɒd) *n Printing.* a block of type metal used for spacing.
quad[3] (kwɒd) *n* a variant spelling of **quod** (prison).
quad[4] (kwɒd) *n* short for **quadruplet** (sense 1).
quad[5] (kwɒd) *adj, n* short for **quadraphonic** *or* **quadraphonics.**
quad. *abbrev. for:* **1** quadrangle. **2** quadrant. **3** quadrilateral.
quadr- *combining form.* a variant of **quadri-** before a vowel.
quadragenarian (,kwɒdrədʒɪˈnɛərɪən) *n* **1** a person who is between 40 and 49 years old. ◆ *adj* **2** being from 40 to 49 years old. [C19: from Latin *quadrāgēnārius* consisting of forty, from *quādrāgintā* forty]
Quadragesima (,kwɒdrəˈdʒɛsɪmə) *n* **1** Also called: **Quadragesima Sunday.** the first Sunday in Lent. **2** *Obsolete.* the forty days of Lent. [C16: from Medieval Latin *quadrāgēsima dies* the fortieth day]
Quadragesimal (,kwɒdrəˈdʒɛsɪməl) *adj* of, relating to, or characteristic of Lent or the season of Lent.
quadrangle (ˈkwɒd,ræŋgᵊl) *n* **1** *Geometry.* a plane figure consisting of four points connected by four lines. In a **complete quadrangle,** six lines connect all pairs of points. **2** a rectangular courtyard, esp. one having buildings on all four sides. Often shortened to **quad. 3** the building surrounding such a courtyard. [C15: from Late Latin *quadrangulum* figure having four corners] ▸ **quadrangular** (kwɒˈdræŋgjʊlə) *adj*
quadrant (ˈkwɒdrənt) *n* **1** *Geometry.* **1a** a quarter of the circumference of a circle. **1b** the area enclosed by two perpendicular radii of a circle and its circumference. **1c** any of the four sections into which a plane is divided by two coordinate axes. **2** a piece of a mechanism in the form of a quarter circle, esp.

one used as a cam or a gear sector. **3** an instrument formerly used in astronomy and navigation for measuring the altitudes of stars, consisting of a graduated arc of 90° and a sighting mechanism attached to a movable arm. [C14: from Latin *quadrāns* a quarter] ▸ **quadrantal** (kwɒˈdrænt^{ə}l) *adj*

Quadrantid (ˈkwɒˌdræntɪd) *n* any member of a meteor shower occurring annually in early January and appearing to radiate from a point in the constellation Boötes.

quadraphonics *or* **quadrophonics** (ˌkwɒdrəˈfɒnɪks) *n* (*functioning as sing*) a system of sound recording and reproduction that uses four independent loudspeakers to give directional sources of sound. The speakers are fed by four separate amplified signals. ▸ ˌ**quadraˈphonic** *or* ˌ**quadroˈphonic** *adj* ▸ **quadraphony** *or* **quadrophony** (kwɒdˈrɒfənɪ) *n*

quadrat (ˈkwɒdrət) *n Ecology.* an area of vegetation, usually one square metre, selected at random for study of the plants in the surrounding area. [C14 (meaning"a square"): variant of QUADRATE]

quadrate *n* (ˈkwɒdrɪt, -reɪt). **1** a cube, square, or a square or cubelike object. **2** one of a pair of bones of the upper jaw of fishes, amphibians, reptiles, and birds that articulates with the lower jaw. In mammals it forms the incus. ◆ *adj* (ˈkwɒdrɪt, -reɪt). **3** of or relating to this bone. **4** square or rectangular. ◆ *vb* (kwɒˈdreɪt). **5** (*tr*) to make square or rectangular. **6** (often foll. by *with*) to conform or cause to conform. [C14: from Latin *quadrāre* to make square]

quadratic (kwɒˈdrætɪk) *Maths.* ◆ *n* **1** Also called: **quadratic equation.** an equation containing one or more terms in which the variable is raised to the power of two, but no terms in which it is raised to a higher power. ◆ *adj* **2** of or relating to the second power.

quadratics (kwɒˈdrætɪks) *n* (*functioning as sing*) the branch of algebra concerned with quadratic equations.

quadrature (ˈkwɒdrətʃə) *n* **1** *Maths.* the process of determining a square having an area equal to that of a given figure or surface. **2** the process of making square or dividing into squares. **3** *Astronomy.* a configuration in which two celestial bodies, usually the sun and the moon or a planet, form an angle of 90° with a third body, usually the earth. **4** *Electronics.* the relationship between two waves that are 90° out of phase.

quadrella (kwɒˈdrɛlə) *n Austral.* four nominated horseraces in which the punter bets on selecting the four winners.

quadrennial (kwɒˈdrɛnɪəl) *adj* **1** occurring every four years. **2** relating to or lasting four years. ◆ *n* **3** a period of four years. ▸ **quadˈrennially** *adv*

quadrennium (kwɒˈdrɛnɪəm) *n, pl* **-niums** *or* **-nia** (-nɪə). a period of four years. [C17: from Latin *quadriennium,* from QUADRI- + *annus* year]

quadri- *or before a vowel* **quadr-** *combining form.* four: *quadrilateral; quadrilingual; quadrisyllabic.* [from Latin; compare *quattuor* four]

quadric (ˈkwɒdrɪk) *Maths.* ◆ *adj* **1** having or characterized by an equation of the second degree, usually in two or three variables. **2** of the second degree. ◆ *n* **3** a quadric curve, surface, or function.

quadricentennial (ˌkwɒdrɪsɛnˈtɛnɪəl) *n* **1** a 400th anniversary. ◆ *adj* **2** of, relating to, or celebrating a 400th anniversary.

quadriceps (ˈkwɒdrɪˌsɛps) *n, pl* **-cepses** (-ˌsɛpsɪz) *or* **-ceps.** *Anatomy.* a large four-part muscle of the front of the thigh, which extends the leg. [C19: New Latin, from QUADRI- + *-ceps* as in BICEPS] ▸ **quadricipital** (ˌkwɒdrɪˈsɪpɪt^{ə}l) *adj*

quadrifid (ˈkwɒdrɪfɪd) *adj Botany.* divided into four lobes or other parts: *quadrifid leaves.*

quadriga (kwɒˈdriːgə) *n, pl* **-gas** *or* **-gae** (-dʒiː). (in the classical world) a two-wheeled chariot drawn by four horses abreast. [C18: from Latin, from earlier *quadrijugae* a team of four, from QUADRI- + *jugum* yoke]

quadrilateral (ˌkwɒdrɪˈlætərəl) *adj* **1** having or formed by four sides. ◆ *n* **2** Also called: **tetragon.** a polygon having four sides. A **complete quadrilateral** consists of four lines and their six points of intersection.

quadrille[1] (kwɒˈdrɪl, kwə-) *n* **1** a square dance of five or more figures for four or more couples. **2** a piece of music for such a dance, alternating between simple duple and compound duple time. [C18: via French from Spanish *cuadrilla,* diminutive of *cuadro* square, from Latin *quadra*]

quadrille[2] (kwɒˈdrɪl, kwə-) *n* an old card game for four players. [C18: from French, from Spanish *cuartillo,* from *cuarto* fourth, from Latin *quartus,* influenced by QUADRILLE[1]]

quadrillion (kwɒˈdrɪljən) *n* **1** (in Britain, France, and Germany) the number represented as one followed by 24 zeros (10^{24}). U.S. and Canadian word: **septillion.** **2** (in the U.S. and Canada) the number represented as one followed by 15 zeros (10^{15}). ◆ *determiner* **3** (preceded by *a* or a numeral) **3a** amounting to this number: *a quadrillion atoms.* **3b** (*as pronoun*): *a quadrillion.* [C17: from French *quadrillon,* from QUADRI- + *-illion,* on the model of *million*] ▸ **quadˈrillionth** *adj*

quadrinomial (ˌkwɒdrɪˈnəʊmɪəl) *n* an algebraic expression containing four terms.

quadripartite (ˌkwɒdrɪˈpɑːtaɪt) *adj* **1** divided into or composed of four parts. **2** maintained by or involving four participants or groups of participants.

quadriplegia (ˌkwɒdrɪˈpliːdʒɪə, -dʒə) *n Pathol.* paralysis of all four limbs, usually as the result of injury to the spine. Also called: **tetraplegia.** Compare **hemiplegia, paraplegia.** [C20: from QUADRI- + Greek *plēgē* a blow, from *plēssein* to strike] ▸ **quadriplegic** (ˌkwɒdrɪˈpliːdʒɪk) *adj, n*

quadripole (ˈkwɒdrɪˌpəʊl) *n Physics.* an electric circuit with two input and two output terminals.

quadrisect (ˈkwɒdrɪˌsɛkt) *vb* to divide into four parts, esp. into four equal parts. ▸ ˌ**quadriˈsection** *n*

quadrivalent (ˌkwɒdrɪˈveɪlənt) *adj Chem.* another word for **tetravalent.** ▸ ˌ**quadriˈvalency** *or* ˌ**quadriˈvalence** *n*

quadrivial (kwɒˈdrɪvɪəl) *adj* **1** having or consisting of four roads meeting at a point. **2** (of roads or ways) going in four directions. **3** of or relating to the quadrivium.

quadrivium (kwɒˈdrɪvɪəm) *n, pl* **-ia** (-ɪə) (in medieval learning) the higher division of the seven liberal arts, consisting of arithmetic, geometry, astronomy, and music. Compare **trivium.** [from Medieval Latin, from Latin: crossroads, meeting of four ways, from QUADRI- + *via* way]

quadroon (kwɒˈdruːn) *n* the offspring of a Mulatto and a White; a person who is one-quarter Black. [C18: from Spanish *cuarterón,* from *cuarto* quarter, from Latin *quartus*]

quadrophonics (ˌkwɒdrəˈfɒnɪks) *n* a variant spelling of **quadraphonics.**

quadrumanous (kwɒˈdruːmənəs) *adj* (of monkeys and apes) having all four feet specialized for use as hands. [C18: from New Latin *quadrumanus,* from QUADRI- + Latin *manus* hand]

quadruped (ˈkwɒdrʊˌpɛd) *n* **1** an animal, esp. a mammal, that has all four limbs specialized for walking. ◆ *adj* **2** having four feet. [C17: from Latin *quadrupēs,* from *quadru-* (see QUADRI-) + *pēs* foot] ▸ **quadrupedal** (kwɒˈdruːpɪd^{ə}l, ˌkwɒdrʊˈpɛd^{ə}l) *adj*

quadruple (ˈkwɒdrʊp^{ə}l, kwɒˈdruːp^{ə}l) *vb* **1** to multiply by four or increase fourfold. ◆ *adj* **2** four times as much or as many; fourfold. **3** consisting of four parts. ◆ *n* **4** a quantity or number four times as great as another. [C16: via Old French from Latin *quadruplus,* from *quadru-* (see QUADRI-) + *-plus* -fold] ▸ ˈ**quadruply** *adv*

quadruplet (ˈkwɒdrʊplɪt, kwɒˈdruːplɪt) *n* **1** one of four offspring born at one birth. Often shortened to **quad.** **2** a group or set of four similar things. **3** *Music.* a group of four notes to be played in a time value of three.

quadruple time *n* musical time in which there are four beats in each bar.

quadruplex (ˈkwɒdrʊˌplɛks, kwɒˈdruːplɛks) *adj* **1** consisting of four parts; fourfold. **2** denoting a type of television video tape recorder having four transversely rotating heads. [C19: from Latin, from *quadru-* (see QUADRI-) + *-plex* -fold] ▸ **quadruplicity** (ˌkwɒdrʊˈplɪsɪtɪ) *n*

quadruplicate *adj* (kwɒˈdruːplɪkɪt, -ˌkeɪt). **1** fourfold or quadruple. ◆ *vb* (kwɒˈdruːplɪˌkeɪt). **2** to multiply or be multiplied by four. ◆ *n* (kwɒˈdruːplɪkɪt, -ˌkeɪt). **3** a group or set of four things. [C17: from Latin *quadruplicāre* to increase fourfold] ▸ **quadˌrupliˈcation** *n*

quadrupole (ˈkwɒdrʊˌpəʊl) *n Physics.* a set of four associated electric charges or two associated magnetic dipoles.

quaere (ˈkwɪərɪ) *Rare.* ◆ *n* **1** a query or question. ◆ *interj* **2** ask or inquire: used esp. to introduce a question. [C16: Latin, imperative of *quaerere* to inquire]

quaestor (ˈkwiːstə, -tɔː) *or U.S.* (*sometimes*) **questor** (ˈkwɛstə) *n* any of several magistrates of ancient Rome, usually a financial administrator. [C14: from Latin, from *quaerere* to inquire] ▸ **quaestorial** (kwɛˈstɔːrɪəl) *adj* ▸ ˈ**quaestorˌship** *n*

quaff (kwɒf, kwɑːf) *vb* to drink heartily or in one draught. [C16: perhaps of imitative origin; compare Middle Low German *quassen* to eat or drink excessively] ▸ ˈ**quaffable** *adj* ▸ ˈ**quaffer** *n*

quag (kwæg, kwɒg) *n* another word for **quagmire.** [C16: perhaps related to QUAKE; compare Middle Low German *quabbe*]

quagga (ˈkwægə) *n, pl* **-gas** *or* **-ga.** a recently extinct member of the horse family (*Equidae*), *Equus quagga,* of southern Africa: it had a sandy brown colouring with zebra-like stripes on the head and shoulders. [C18: from obsolete Afrikaans, from Khoikhoi *qŭagga;* compare Xhosa *i-qwara* something striped]

quaggy (ˈkwægɪ, ˈkwɒgɪ) *adj* **-gier, -giest.** **1** resembling a marsh or quagmire; boggy. **2** yielding, soft, or flabby. ▸ ˈ**quagginess** *n*

quagmire (ˈkwægˌmaɪə, ˈkwɒg-) *n* **1** a soft wet area of land that gives way under the feet; bog. **2** an awkward, complex, or embarrassing situation. [C16: from QUAG + MIRE]

quahog (ˈkwɑːˌhɒg) *n* an edible clam, *Venus* (or *Mercenaria*) *mercenaria,* native to the Atlantic coast of North America, having a large heavy rounded shell. Also called: **hard-shell clam, hard-shell, round clam.** Compare **soft-shell clam.** [C18: from Narraganset, short for *poquauhock,* from *pohkeni* dark + *hogki* shell]

quaich *or* **quaigh** (kwex, kweɪx) *n, plu.* **quaichs** *or* **quaighs.** *Scot.* a small shallow drinking cup, usually with two handles. [from Scottish Gaelic *cuach* cup]

Quai d'Orsay (*French* ke dɔrsɛ) *n* the quay along the S bank of the Seine, Paris, where the French foreign office is situated.

quail[1] (kweɪl) *n, pl* **quails** *or* **quail.** **1** any small Old World gallinaceous game bird of the genus *Coturnix* and related genera, having a rounded body and small tail: family *Phasianidae* (pheasants). **2** any of various similar and related American birds, such as the bobwhite. [C14: from Old French *quaille,* from Medieval Latin *quaccula,* probably of imitative origin]

quail[2] (kweɪl) *vb* (*intr*) to shrink back with fear; cower. [C15: perhaps from Old French *quailler,* from Latin *coāgulāre* to curdle]

quaint (kweɪnt) *adj* **1** attractively unusual, esp. in an old-fashioned style: *a quaint village.* **2** odd, peculiar, or inappropriate: *a quaint sense of duty.* [C13 (in the sense: clever): from Old French *cointe,* from Latin *cognitus* known, from *cognoscere* to ascertain] ▸ ˈ**quaintly** *adv* ▸ ˈ**quaintness** *n*

quair (kwer, kweə) *n Scot.* a book. [a variant of QUIRE[1]]

quake (kweɪk) *vb* (*intr*) **1** to shake or tremble with or as with fear. **2** to convulse or quiver, as from instability. ◆ *n* **3** the act or an instance of quaking. **4** *Informal.* short for **earthquake.** [Old English *cwacian;* related to Old English *cweccan* to shake, Old Irish *bocaim,* German *wackeln*]

Quaker (ˈkweɪkə) *n* **1** a member of the Society of Friends, a Christian sect founded by George Fox about 1650, whose central belief is the doctrine of the Inner Light. Quakers reject sacraments, ritual, and formal ministry, hold meetings at which any member may speak, and have promoted many causes for social reform. ◆ *adj* **2** of, relating to, or designating the Religious Society of Friends or its religious beliefs or practices. [C17: originally a derogatory nickname, alluding either to their alleged ecstatic fits, or to George Fox's injunction to "*quake* at the word of the Lord"] ▸ '**Quakeress** *fem n* ▸ '**Quakerish** *adj* ▸ '**Quakerism** *n*

Quaker gun *n* a dummy gun, as of wood. [alluding to the Quakers' traditional pacifism]

Quaker meeting *n* a gathering of the Quakers for worship, characterized by periods of silence and by members speaking as moved by the Spirit.

quaking ('kweɪkɪŋ) *adj* unstable or unsafe to walk on, as a bog or quicksand: *a quaking bog; quaking sands.*

quaking grass *n* any grass of the genus *Briza,* of N temperate regions and South America, having delicate flower branches that shake in the wind.

quaky ('kweɪkɪ) *adj* **quakier, quakiest.** inclined to quake; shaky; tremulous. ▸ '**quakily** *adv* ▸ '**quakiness** *n*

quale ('kwɑːlɪ, 'kweɪ-) *n, pl* **-lia** (-lɪə). *Philosophy.* an essential property or quality. [C17: Latin, neuter singular of *qualis* of what kind]

qualification (ˌkwɒlɪfɪ'keɪʃən) *n* **1** an ability, quality, or attribute, esp. one that fits a person to perform a particular job or task: *he has no qualifications to be a teacher.* **2** a condition that modifies or limits; restriction. **3** the act of qualifying or state of being qualified.

qualified ('kwɒlɪˌfaɪd) *adj* **1** having the abilities, qualities, attributes, etc., necessary to perform a particular job or task. **2** limited, modified, or restricted; not absolute.

Qualified Majority Voting *n* a voting system, used by the EU Council of Ministers, enabling certain resolutions to be passed without unanimity. Abbrev.: **QMV.**

qualifier ('kwɒlɪˌfaɪə) *n* **1** a person or thing that qualifies, esp. a contestant in a competition who wins a preliminary heat or contest and so earns the right to take part in the next round. **2** a preliminary heat or contest. **3** *Grammar.* another word for **modifier** (sense 1).

qualify ('kwɒlɪˌfaɪ) *vb* **-fies, -fying, -fied. 1** to provide or be provided with the abilities or attributes necessary for a task, office, duty, etc.: *his degree qualifies him for the job; he qualifies for the job, but would he do it well?* **2** (*tr*) to make less strong, harsh, or violent; moderate or restrict. **3** (*tr*) to modify or change the strength or flavour of. **4** (*tr*) *Grammar.* another word for **modify** (sense 3). **5** (*tr*) to attribute a quality to; characterize. **6** (*intr*) to progress to the final stages of a competition, as by winning preliminary contests. [C16: from Old French *qualifier,* from Medieval Latin *quālificāre* to characterize, from Latin *quālis* of what kind + *facere* to make] ▸ '**qualiˌfiable** *adj* ▸ **qualificatory** ('kwɒlɪfɪkətərɪ, -ˌkeɪ-) *adj*

qualitative ('kwɒlɪtətɪv, -ˌteɪ-) *adj* involving or relating to distinctions based on quality or qualities. Compare **quantitative.** ▸ '**qualitatively** *adv*

qualitative analysis *n* See **analysis** (sense 4).

qualitative identity *n Logic.* the relation that holds between two relata that have properties in common. This term is used to distinguish many uses of the words *identical* or *same* in ordinary language from strict identity or numerical identity.

quality ('kwɒlɪtɪ) *n, pl* **-ties. 1** a distinguishing characteristic, property, or attribute. **2** the basic character or nature of something. **3** a trait or feature of personality. **4** degree or standard of excellence, esp. a high standard. **5** (formerly) high social status or the distinction associated with it. **6** musical tone colour; timbre. **7** *Logic.* the characteristic of a proposition that is dependent on whether it is affirmative or negative. **8** *Phonetics.* the distinctive character of a vowel, determined by the configuration of the mouth, tongue, etc., when it is articulated and distinguished from the pitch and stress with which it is uttered. **9** (*modifier*) having or showing excellence or superiority: *a quality product.* [C13: from Old French *qualité,* from Latin *quālitās* state, nature, from *quālis* of what sort]

quality control *n* control of the relative quality of a manufactured product, usually by statistical sampling techniques.

quality factor *n* a property of ionizing radiations that affects their ability to cause biological effects. For weakly ionizing radiations such as gamma rays it has value 1 whilst for alpha rays it is about 20. Former name: **relative biological effectiveness.**

qualm (kwɑːm) *n* **1** a sudden feeling of sickness or nausea. **2** a pang or sudden feeling of doubt, esp. concerning moral conduct; scruple. **3** a sudden sensation of misgiving or unease. [Old English *cwealm* death or plague; related to Old High German *qualm* despair, Dutch *kwalm* smoke, stench] ▸ '**qualmish** *adj* ▸ '**qualmishly** *adv* ▸ '**qualmishness** *n*

quamash ('kwɒmæʃ, kwə'mæʃ) *n* another name for **camass** (sense 1).

quandary ('kwɒndrɪ, -dərɪ) *n, pl* **-ries.** a situation or circumstance that presents problems difficult to solve; predicament; dilemma. [C16: of uncertain origin; perhaps related to Latin *quandō* when]

quandong, quandang ('kwɒnˌdɒŋ), *or* **quantong** ('kwɒnˌtɒŋ) *n* **1** Also called: **native peach. 1a** a small Australian santalaceous tree, *Eucarya acuminata* (or *Fusanus acuminatus*). **1b** the edible fruit or nut of this tree, used in preserves. **2 silver quandong. 2a** an Australian tree, *Elaeocarpus grandis:* family *Elaeocarpaceae.* **2b** the pale easily worked timber of this tree. [from a native Australian language]

quango ('kwæŋgəʊ) *n, pl* **-gos.** a semipublic government-financed administrative body whose members are appointed by the government. [C20: *qu(asi-)a(utonomous) n(on)g(overnmental) o(rganization)*]

quangocracy (kwæŋ'gɒkrəsɪ) *n, pl* **-cies. 1** the control or influence ascribed to quangos. **2** quangos collectively.

quant[1] (kwɒnt) *n* **1** a long pole for propelling a boat, esp. a punt, by pushing on the bottom of a river or lake. ◆ *vb* **2** to propel (a boat) with a quant. [C15: probably from Latin *contus* a pole, from Greek *kontos*]

quant[2] (kwɒnt) *n Informal.* a highly paid computer specialist with a degree in a quantitative science, employed by a financial house, to predict the future price movements of securities, commodities, currencies, etc. [C20: from QUANTITATIVE]

Quant (kwɒnt) *n* **Mary.** born 1934, British fashion designer, whose Chelsea Look of miniskirts and geometrically patterned fabrics dominated London fashion in the 1960s.

quanta ('kwɒntə) *n* the plural of **quantum.**

quantal ('kwɒntəl) *adj* **1** of or relating to a quantum or an entity that is quantized. **2** denoting something that is capable of existing in only one of two states.

quantic ('kwɒntɪk) *n* a homogeneous function of two or more variables in a rational and integral form, as in $x^2 + 3xy + y^2$. [C19: from Latin *quantus* how great]

quantifier ('kwɒntɪˌfaɪə) *n* **1** *Logic.* **1a** a symbol including a variable that indicates the degree of generality of the expression in which that variable occurs, as (∃*x*) in (∃*x*)*Fx*, rendered "something is an F", (*x*) in (*x*)(*Fx*→*Gx*), rendered "all Fs are Gs". **1b** any other symbol with an analogous interpretation: *the existential quantifier,* (∃*x*), *corresponds to the words "there is something, x, such that..."* **2** *Grammar.* a word or phrase in a natural language having this role, such as *some, all,* or *many* in English.

quantify ('kwɒntɪˌfaɪ) *vb* **-fies, -fying, -fied.** (*tr*) **1** to discover or express the quantity of. **2** *Logic.* to specify the quantity of (a term) by using a quantifier, such as *all, some,* or *no.* [C19: from Medieval Latin *quantificāre,* from Latin *quantus* how much + *facere* to make] ▸ '**quantifiable** *adj* ▸ ˌ**quantifi'cation** *n*

quantitative ('kwɒntɪtətɪv, -ˌteɪ-) *or* **quantitive** *adj* **1** involving or relating to considerations of amount or size. Compare **qualitative. 2** capable of being measured. **3** *Prosody.* denoting or relating to a metrical system, such as that in Latin and Greek verse, that is based on the relative length rather than stress of syllables. ▸ '**quantitatively** *or* '**quantitively** *adv*

quantitative analysis *n* See **analysis** (sense 4).

quantity ('kwɒntɪtɪ) *n, pl* **-ties. 1a** a specified or definite amount, weight, number, etc. **1b** (*as modifier*): *a quantity estimate.* **2** the aspect or property of anything that can be measured, weighed, counted, etc. **3** a large or considerable amount. **4** *Maths.* an entity having a magnitude that may be denoted by a numerical expression. **5** *Physics.* a specified magnitude or amount; the product of a number and a unit. **6** *Logic.* the characteristic of a proposition dependent on whether it is a universal or particular statement, considering all or only part of a class. **7** *Prosody.* the relative duration of a syllable or the vowel in it. [C14: from Old French *quantité,* from Latin *quantitās* extent, amount, from *quantus* how much]

USAGE The use of a plural noun after *quantity of* as in *a large quantity of bananas* was formerly considered incorrect, but is now acceptable.

quantity surveyor *n* a person who estimates the cost of the materials and labour necessary for a construction job.

quantity theory *n Economics.* a theory stating that the general price level varies directly with the quantity of money in circulation and the velocity with which it is circulated, and inversely with the volume of production expressed by the total number of money transactions.

quantize *or* **quantise** ('kwɒntaɪz) *vb* (*tr*) **1** *Physics.* to restrict (a physical quantity) to one of a set of values characterized by quantum numbers. **2** *Maths.* to limit (a variable) to values that are integral multiples of a basic unit. ▸ ˌ**quanti'zation** *or* ˌ**quanti'sation** *n*

quantometer (kwɒn'tɒmɪtə) *n Engineering.* a spectroscopic instrument for measuring the percentage of different metals present in a sample.

quantum ('kwɒntəm) *n, pl* **-ta** (-tə). **1** *Physics.* **1a** the smallest quantity of some physical property, such as energy, that a system can possess according to the quantum theory. **1b** a particle with such a unit of energy. **2** amount or quantity, esp. a specific amount. **3** (*often used with a negative*) the least possible amount that can suffice: *there is not a quantum of evidence for your accusation.* **4** something that can be quantified or measured. **5** (*modifier*) loosely, sudden, spectacular, or vitally important: *a quantum improvement.* [C17: from Latin *quantus* (adj) how much]

quantum chromodynamics *n Physics.* a theory describing the strong interaction in terms of quarks and gluons, with the colour of quarks used as an analogue of charge and the gluon as an analogue of the photon. Abbrev.: **QCD.** [C20: *chromodynamics* from CHROMO- (referring to quark colour) + DYNAMICS, modelled on QUANTUM ELECTRODYNAMICS]

quantum efficiency *n* **1** *Physics.* the number of electrons released by a photocell per photon of incident radiation of a given energy. **2** *Chem.* the number of chemical species that undergo reaction per photon of absorbed radiation of a given energy.

quantum electrodynamics *n Physics.* a relativistic quantum mechanical theory concerned with electromagnetic interactions. Abbrev.: **QED.**

quantum electronics *n* the application of quantum mechanics to the study of the generation and amplification of power at microwave frequencies in solid crystals.

quantum field theory *n Physics.* quantum mechanical theory concerned with elementary particles, which are represented by fields whose normal modes of oscillation are quantized.

quantum flavourdynamics *n* a gauge theory of the electromagnetic and weak interactions. Also called: **electroweak theory.** Abbrev.: **QFD.** [C20: *flavourdynamics* from FLAVOUR (referring to quark flavour) + DYNAMICS, modelled on QUANTUM ELECTRODYNAMICS]

quantum gravity *n Physics.* a theory of the gravitational interaction that involves quantum mechanics to explain the force.

quantum leap *or* **jump** *n* a sudden highly significant advance; breakthrough. [C20: from its use in physics meaning the sudden jump of an electron, atom, etc. from one energy level to another]

quantum mechanics *n (functioning as sing)* the branch of mechanics, based on the quantum theory used for interpreting the behaviour of elementary particles and atoms, which do not obey Newtonian mechanics.

quantum meruit *Latin.* ('mɛruːɪt) as much as he has earned: denoting a payment for goods or services in partial fulfilment of a contract or for those supplied when no price has been agreed.

quantum number *n Physics.* one of a set of integers or half-integers characterizing the energy states of a particle or system of particles. A function of the number multiplied by a fixed quantity gives the amount of some specified physical quantity possessed by the system.

quantum state *n Physics.* a state of a system characterized by a set of quantum numbers and represented by an eigenfunction. Each state has energy which has a value that is precise within the limits imposed by the uncertainty principle but which may be changed by applying a field of force. States that have the same energy are called **degenerate.** See also **energy level.**

quantum statistics *n (functioning as sing) Physics.* statistics concerned with the distribution of a number of identical elementary particles, atoms, ions, or molecules among possible quantum states.

quantum theory *n* a theory concerning the behaviour of physical systems based on Planck's idea that they can only possess certain properties, such as energy and angular momentum, in discrete amounts (quanta). The theory later developed in several equivalent mathematical forms based on De Broglie's theory (see **wave mechanics**) and on the Heisenberg uncertainty principle.

quaquaversal (ˌkwɑːkwəˈvɜːsəl) *adj Geology.* directed outwards in all directions from a common centre: *the quaquaversal dip of a pericline.* [C18: from Latin *quāquā* in every direction + *versus* towards]

quar. *abbrev. for:* **1** quarter. **2** quarterly.

quarantine ('kwɒrən,tiːn) *n* **1** a period of isolation or detention, esp. of persons or animals arriving from abroad, to prevent the spread of disease, usually consisting of the maximum known incubation period of the suspected disease. **2** the place or area where such detention is enforced. **3** any period or state of enforced isolation. ◆ *vb* **4** *(tr)* to isolate in or as if in quarantine. [C17: from Italian *quarantina* period of forty days, from *quaranta* forty, from Latin *quadrāgintā*]

quarantine flag *n Nautical.* the yellow signal flag for the letter Q, flown alone from a vessel to indicate that there is no disease aboard and to request pratique or, with a second signal flag, to indicate that there is disease aboard. Also called: **yellow flag, yellow jack.**

quare (kwɛə) *adj Irish dialect.* **1** remarkable or strange: *a quare fellow.* **2** great or good: *you're in a quare mess.* [probably variant of QUEER]

quark[1] (kwɑːk) *n Physics.* any of a set of six hypothetical elementary particles together with their antiparticles thought to be fundamental units of all baryons and mesons but unable to exist in isolation. The magnitude of their charge is either two thirds or one third of that of the electron. [C20: coined by James JOYCE in the novel *Finnegans Wake,* and given special application in physics]

quark[2] (kwɑːk) *n* a type of low-fat soft cheese. [from German]

Quarles (kwɔːlz, kwɑːlz) *n* **Francis.** 1592–1644, English poet.

quarrel[1] ('kwɒrəl) *n* **1** an angry disagreement; argument. **2** a cause of disagreement or dispute; grievance. ◆ *vb* **-rels, -relling, -relled** *or U.S.* **-rels, -reling, -reled.** *(intr; often foll. by with)* **3** to engage in a disagreement or dispute; argue. **4** to find fault; complain. [C14: from Old French *querele,* from Latin *querēlla* complaint, from *querī* to complain] ▸ **'quarreller** *or U.S.* **'quarreler** *n*

quarrel[2] ('kwɒrəl) *n* **1** an arrow having a four-edged head, fired from a crossbow. **2** a small square or diamond-shaped pane of glass, usually one of many in a fixed or casement window and framed with lead. [C13: from Old French *quarrel* pane, from Medieval Latin *quadrellus,* diminutive of Latin *quadrus* square]

quarrelsome ('kwɒrəlsəm) *adj* inclined to quarrel or disagree; belligerent. ▸ **'quarrelsomely** *adv* ▸ **'quarrelsomeness** *n*

quarrian *or* **quarrion** ('kwɒrɪən) *n* a cockatiel, *Leptolophus hollandicus,* of scrub and woodland regions of inland Australia, that feeds on seeds and grasses. [C20: probably from a native Australian language]

quarrier ('kwɒrɪə) *n* another word for **quarryman.**

quarry[1] ('kwɒrɪ) *n, pl* **-ries. 1** an open surface excavation for the extraction of building stone, slate, marble, etc., by drilling, blasting, or cutting. **2** a copious source of something, esp. information. ◆ *vb* **-ries, -rying, -ried. 3** to extract (stone, slate, etc.) from or as if from a quarry. **4** *(tr)* to excavate a quarry in. **5** to obtain (something, esp. information) diligently and laboriously: *he was quarrying away in the reference library.* [C15: from Old French *quarriere,* from *quarre* (unattested) square-shaped stone, from Latin *quadrāre* to make square]

quarry[2] ('kwɒrɪ) *n, pl* **-ries. 1** an animal, bird, or fish that is hunted, esp. by other animals; prey. **2** anything pursued or hunted. [C14 *quirre* entrails offered to the hounds, from Old French *cuirée* what is placed on the hide, from *cuir* hide, from Latin *corium* leather; probably also influenced by Old French *coree* entrails, from Latin *cor* heart]

quarry[3] ('kwɒrɪ) *n, pl* **-ries. 1** a square or diamond shape. **2** something having this shape. **3** another word for **quarrel**[2]. [C16: from Old French *quarré;* see QUARREL[2]]

quarryman ('kwɒrɪmən) *n, pl* **-men.** a man who works in or manages a quarry.

quarry tile *n* a square or diamond-shaped unglazed floor tile. [C20: from QUARRY[3]]

quart[1] (kwɔːt) *n* **1** a unit of liquid measure equal to a quarter of a gallon or two pints. 1 U.S. quart (0.946 litre) is equal to 0.8326 U.K. quart. 1 U.K. quart (1.136 litres) is equal to 1.2009 U.S. quarts. **2** a unit of dry measure equal to 2 pints or one eighth of a peck. [C14: from Old French *quarte,* from Latin *quartus* fourth]

quart[2] *n* **1** (kɑːt) *Piquet.* a sequence of four cards in the same suit. **2** (kart). *Fencing.* a variant spelling of **quarte.** [C17: from French *quarte* fourth]

quart. *abbrev. for:* **1** quarter. **2** quarterly.

quartan ('kwɔːtᵊn) *adj* (esp. of a malarial fever) occurring every third day. [C13: from Latin *febris quartāna* fever occurring every fourth day, reckoned inclusively]

quarte *French.* (kart) *n* the fourth of eight basic positions from which a parry or attack can be made in fencing. [C18: from French, fem of *quart* a quarter]

quarter ('kwɔːtə) *n* **1** one of four equal or nearly equal parts of an object, quantity, amount, etc. **2** Also called: **fourth.** the fraction equal to one divided by four (1/4). **3** *U.S., Canada, etc.* a quarter of a dollar; 25-cent piece. **4** a unit of weight equal to a quarter of a hundredweight. 1 U.S. quarter is equal to 25 pounds; 1 Brit. quarter is equal to 28 pounds. **5** short for **quarter-hour. 6** a fourth part of a year; three months. **7** *Astronomy.* **7a** one fourth of the moon's period of revolution around the earth. **7b** either of two phases of the moon, **first quarter** or **last quarter,** when half of the lighted surface is visible from the earth. **8** *Informal.* a unit of weight equal to a quarter of a pound or 4 ounces. **9** *Brit.* a unit of capacity for grain, etc., usually equal to 8 U.K. bushels. **10** *Sport.* one of the four periods into which certain games are divided. **11** *Nautical.* the part of a vessel's side towards the stern, usually aft of the aftermost mast: *the port quarter.* **12** *Nautical.* the general direction along the water in the quadrant between the beam of a vessel and its stern: *the wind was from the port quarter.* **13** a region or district of a town or city: *the Spanish quarter.* **14** a region, direction, or point of the compass. **15** *(sometimes pl)* an unspecified person or group of people: *to get word from the highest quarter.* **16** mercy or pity, as shown to a defeated opponent (esp. in the phrases **ask for** or **give quarter**). **17** any of the four limbs, including the adjacent parts, of the carcass of a quadruped or bird: *a hind quarter of beef.* **18** *Vet. science.* the side part of the wall of a horse's hoof. **19** the part of a shoe or boot covering the heel and joining the vamp. **20** *Heraldry.* one of four more or less equal quadrants into which a shield may be divided. **21** *Military slang.* short for **quartermaster.** ◆ *vb* **22** *(tr)* to divide into four equal or nearly equal parts. **23** *(tr)* to divide into any number of parts. **24** *(tr)* (esp. formerly) to dismember (a human body): *to be drawn and quartered.* **25** to billet or be billeted in lodgings, esp. (of military personnel) in civilian lodgings. **26** *(intr)* (of gun dogs or hounds) to range over an area of ground in search of game or the scent of quarry. **27** *(intr) Nautical.* (of the wind) to blow onto a vessel's quarter: *the wind began to quarter.* **28** *(tr) Heraldry.* **28a** to divide (a shield) into four separate bearings with a cross. **28b** to place (one set of arms) in diagonally opposite quarters to another. ◆ *adj* **29** being or consisting of one of four equal parts: *a quarter pound of butter.* ◆ See also **quarters.** [C13: from Old French *quartier,* from Latin *quartārius* a fourth part, from *quartus* fourth]

quarterage ('kwɔːtərɪdʒ) *n* **1** an allowance or payment made quarterly. **2** *Rare.* shelter or lodging.

quarterback ('kwɔːtə,bæk) *n U.S. and Canadian.* **1** a player in American or Canadian football, positioned usually behind the centre, who directs attacking play. **2 Monday-morning quarterbacking.** wisdom after the event, esp. by spectators.

quarter-bound *adj* (of a book) having a binding consisting of two types of material, the better type being used on the spine.

quarter crack *n Vet. science.* a sand crack on the inside of the forefoot of a horse.

quarter day *n* any of four days in the year when certain payments become due. In England, Wales, and Northern Ireland these are Lady Day, Midsummer's Day, Michaelmas, and Christmas. In Scotland they are Candlemas, Whit Sunday, Lammas, and Martinmas.

quarterdeck ('kwɔːtə,dɛk) *n Nautical.* the after part of the weather deck of a ship, traditionally the deck on a naval vessel for official or ceremonial use.

quartered ('kwɔːtəd) *adj* **1** *Heraldry.* (of a shield) divided into four sections, each having contrasting arms or having two sets of arms, each repeated in diagonally opposite corners. **2** (of a log) sawn into four equal parts along two diameters at right angles to each other; quartersawn.

quarterfinal ('kwɔːtə,faɪnᵊl) *n* the round before the semifinal in a competition.

quarter grain *n* the grain of quartersawn timber.

quarter horse *n* a small powerful breed of horse, originally bred for sprinting in quarter-mile races in Virginia in the late 18th century.

quarter-hour *n* **1** a period of 15 minutes. **2** any of the points on the face of a timepiece that mark 15 minutes before or after the hour, and sometimes 30 minutes after. ▸ **,quarter-'hourly** *adv, adj*

quartering ('kwɔːtərɪŋ) *n* **1** *Military.* the allocation of accommodation to service personnel. **2** *Heraldry.* **2a** the marshalling of several coats of arms on one shield, usually representing intermarriages. **2b** any coat of arms marshalled in this way.

quarterlight ('kwɔːtə,laɪt) *n Brit.* a small pivoted window in the door of a car for ventilation.

quarterly ('kwɔːtəlɪ) *adj* **1** occurring, done, paid, etc., at intervals of three months. **2** of, relating to, or consisting of a quarter. ◆ *n, pl* **-lies. 3** a periodical issued every three months. ◆ *adv* **4** once every three months. **5** *Heraldry.* into or in quarters: *a shield divided quarterly.*

quartermaster ('kwɔːtə,mɑːstə) *n* **1** an officer responsible for accommodation, food, and equipment in a military unit. **2** a rating in the navy, usually a petty officer, with particular responsibility for steering a ship and other navigational duties.

quarter-miler *n* an athlete who specializes in running the quarter mile.

quartern ('kwɔːtən) *n* **1** a fourth part of certain weights or measures, such as a peck or a pound. **2** Also called: **quartern loaf.** *Brit.* **2a** a type of loaf 4 inches square, used esp. for making sandwiches. **2b** any loaf weighing 1600 g when baked. [C13: from Old French *quarteron,* from *quart* a quarter]

quarter note *n* the usual U.S. and Canadian name for **crotchet** (sense 1).
quarter-phase *adj* another term for **two-phase.**
quarter plate *n* a photographic plate measuring 3¼ × 4¼ inches (8.3 × 10.8 cm).
quarter round *n Architect.* another name for **ovolo.**
quarters ('kwɔːtəz) *pl n* **1** housing or accommodation, esp. as provided for military personnel and their families. **2** the stations assigned to military personnel, esp. to each crew member of a warship: *general quarters.* **3** (in India) housing provided by an employer or by the government. **4** (*functioning as sing*) *Military slang.* short for **quartermaster.**
quartersaw ('kwɔːtəˌsɔː) *vb* **-saws, -sawing, -sawed, -sawed** *or* **-sawn.** (*tr*) to saw (timber) into quarters along two diameters of a log at right angles to each other.
quarter section *n U.S. and Canadian.* a land measure, used in surveying, with sides half a mile long; 160 acres.
quarter sessions *n* (*functioning as sing or pl*) **1** (in England and Wales, formerly) a criminal court held four times a year before justices of the peace or a recorder, empowered to try all but the most serious offences and to hear appeals from petty sessions. Replaced in 1972 by **crown courts.** Compare **assizes. 2** (in Scotland, formerly) a court held by justices of the peace four times a year, empowered to hear appeals from justice of the peace courts and to deal with some licensing matters: abolished in 1975.
quarterstaff ('kwɔːtəˌstɑːf) *n, pl* **-staves** (-ˌsteɪvz, -ˌstɑːvz). **1** a stout iron-tipped wooden staff about 6ft. long, formerly used in England as a weapon. **2** the use of such a staff in fighting, sport, or exercise. [C16: of uncertain origin]
quarter tone *n Music.* a quarter of a whole tone; a pitch interval corresponding to 50 cents measured on the well-tempered scale.
quartet *or* **quartette** (kwɔː'tet) *n* **1** a group of four singers or instrumentalists or a piece of music composed for such a group. See **string quartet. 2** any group of four. [C18: from Italian *quartetto,* diminutive of *quarto* fourth]
quartic ('kwɔːtɪk) *adj, n* another word for **biquadratic.** [C19: from Latin *quartus* fourth]
quartile ('kwɔːtaɪl) *n* **1** *Statistics.* one of three actual or notional values of a variable dividing its distribution into four groups with equal frequencies. ◆ *adj* **2** *Statistics.* denoting or relating to a quartile. **3** *Astrology.* denoting an aspect of two heavenly bodies when their longitudes differ by 90°. **4** a quarter part of a distribution. [C16: from Medieval Latin *quartīlis,* from Latin *quartus* fourth]
quarto ('kwɔːtəʊ) *n, pl* **-tos. 1** a book size resulting from folding a sheet of paper, usually crown or demy, into four leaves or eight pages, each one quarter the size of the sheet. Often written: **4to, 4°. 2** (formerly) a size of cut paper 10 in. by 8 in. (25.4 cm by 20.3 cm). [C16: from New Latin phrase *in quartō* in quarter]
quartz (kwɔːts) *n* **1** a colourless mineral often tinted by impurities, found in igneous, sedimentary, and metamorphic rocks. It is used in the manufacture of glass, abrasives, and cement, and also as a gemstone; the violet-purple variety is amethyst, the brown variety is cairngorm, the yellow variety is citrine, and the pink variety is rose quartz. Composition: silicon dioxide. Formula: SiO_2. Crystal structure: hexagonal. **2** short for **quartz glass.** [C18: from German *Quarz,* of Slavic origin]
quartz clock *or* **watch** *n* a clock or watch that is operated by the vibrations of a quartz crystal controlled by a microcircuit.
quartz crystal *n* a thin plate or rod cut in certain directions from a piece of piezoelectric quartz and accurately ground so that it vibrates at a particular frequency.
quartz glass *n* a colourless glass composed of almost pure silica, resistant to very high temperatures and transparent to near-ultraviolet radiation. Sometimes shortened to **quartz.**
quartziferous (kwɔːt'sɪfərəs) *adj* containing or composed of quartz.
quartz-iodine lamp *or* **quartz lamp** *n* a type of tungsten-halogen lamp containing small amounts of iodine and having a quartz envelope, operating at high temperature and producing an intense light for use in car headlamps, etc.
quartzite ('kwɔːtsaɪt) *n* **1** a white or grey sandstone composed of quartz. **2** a very hard metamorphic rock consisting of a mosaic of intergrown quartz crystals.
quasar ('kweɪzɑː, -sɑː) *n* any of a class of celestial objects that emit an immense amount of energy in the form of light, infrared radiation, etc., from a compact source. They are extremely distant and hence the youngest objects observed in the universe, and their energy generation is thought to involve a black hole located in a galaxy. [C20: *quas(i-stell)ar (object)*]
quash (kwɒʃ) *vb* (*tr*) **1** to subdue forcefully and completely; put down; suppress. **2** to annul or make void (a law, decision, etc.). **3** to reject (an indictment, writ, etc.) as invalid. [C14: from Old French *quasser,* from Latin *quassāre* to shake]
Quashi *or* **Quashie** ('kwɑːʃɪ) *n Caribbean.* an unsophisticated or gullible male Black peasant: *I'm not a Quashi that anyone can fool.* [from Twi]
quasi ('kweɪzaɪ, -saɪ; 'kwɑːzɪ) *adv* as if; as it were. [from Latin, literally: as if]
quasi- *combining form.* **1** almost but not really; seemingly: *a quasi-religious cult.* **2** resembling but not actually being; so-called: *a quasi-scholar.*
quasi-contract *n* an implied contract which arises without the express agreement of the parties.
quasi-judicial *adj* denoting or relating to powers and functions similar to those of a judge, such as those exercised by an arbitrator, administrative tribunal, etc.
Quasimodo (ˌkwɔːzɪ'məʊdəʊ) *n* **1** another name for **Low Sunday.** [from the opening words of the Latin introit for that day, *quasimodo geniti infantes* as new-born babies] **2** a character in Victor Hugo's novel *Notre-Dame de Paris* (1831), a grotesque hunch-backed bellringer of the cathedral of Notre Dame. **3** (*Italian* kwa'ziːmodo) **Salvatore** (salva'toːre). 1901–68, Italian poet, whose early work expresses symbolist ideas and techniques. His later work is more concerned with political and social issues: Nobel prize for literature 1959.
quasi-quotation *n Logic.* a metalinguistic device for referring to the form of an expression containing variables without referring to the symbols for those variables. Thus while *"not p"* refers to the expression consisting of the word *not* followed by the letter *p,* the quasi-quotation ⌜ *not p* ⌝ refers to the form of any expression consisting of the word *not* followed by any value of the variable *p.* Usual symbol: ⌜ ⌝ (**corners**).
quasi-stellar object *n* a member of any of several classes of astronomical bodies, including **quasars** (strong radio sources) and **quasi-stellar galaxies** (no traceable radio emission), both of which have exceptionally large red shifts. Abbrev.: **QSO.**
quass (kvɑːs, kwɑːs) *n* a variant of **kvass.**
quassia ('kwɒʃə) *n* **1** any tree of the tropical American simaroubaceous genus *Quassia,* having bitter bark and wood. **2** the bark and wood of *Quassia amara* and of a related tree, *Picrasma excelsa,* used in furniture making. **3** a bitter compound extracted from this bark and wood, formerly used as a tonic and anthelmintic, now used in insecticides. [C18: from New Latin, named after Graman *Quassi,* a slave who discovered (1730) the medicinal value of the root]
quatercentenary (ˌkwætəsɛn'tiːnərɪ) *n, pl* **-naries.** a 400th anniversary or the year or celebration marking it. [C19: from Latin *quater* four times + CENTENARY] ▸ ˌ**quatercen'tennial** *adj, n*
quaternary (kwə'tɜːnərɪ) *adj* **1** consisting of fours or by fours. **2** fourth in a series. **3** *Chem.* containing or being an atom bound to four other atoms or groups: *a quaternary ammonium compound.* **4** *Maths.* having four variables. ◆ *n, pl* **-naries. 5** the number four or a set of four. [C15: from Latin *quaternārius* each containing four, from *quaternī* by fours, distributive of *quattuor* four]
Quaternary (kwə'tɜːnərɪ) *adj* **1** of, denoting, or formed in the most recent period of geological time, which succeeded the Tertiary period one million years ago. ◆ *n* **2 the.** the Quaternary period or rock system, divided into Pleistocene and Holocene (Recent) epochs or series.
quaternary ammonium compound *n* a type of ionic compound that can be regarded as derived from ammonium compounds by replacing the hydrogen atoms with organic groups.
quaternion (kwə'tɜːnɪən) *n* **1** *Maths.* a generalized complex number consisting of four components, $x = x_0 + x_1i + x_2j + x_3k$, where $x, x_0...x_3$ are real numbers and $i^2 = j^2 = k^2 = -1$, $ij = -ji = k$, etc. **2** another word for **quaternary** (sense 5). [C14: from Late Latin *quaterniōn,* from Latin *quaternī* four at a time]
quaternity (kwə'tɜːnɪtɪ) *n, pl* **-ties.** a group of four, esp. a concept of God as consisting of four persons. [C16: from Late Latin *quaternitās,* from Latin *quaternī* by fours; see QUATERNARY]
Quathlamba (kwɑːt'lɑːmbɑː) *n* the Sotho name for the **Drakensberg.**
quatrain ('kwɒtreɪn) *n* a stanza or poem of four lines, esp. one having alternate rhymes. [C16: from French, from *quatre* four, from Latin *quattuor*]
quatre ('kætrə; *French* katrə) *n* a playing card with four pips. [French: four]
Quatre Bras (*French* katrə bra) *n* a village in Belgium near Brussels; site of a battle in June 1815 where Wellington defeated the French under Marshal Ney, immediately preceding the battle of Waterloo.
quatrefoil ('kætrəˌfɔɪl) *n* **1** a leaf, such as that of certain clovers, composed of four leaflets. **2** *Architect.* a carved ornament having four foils arranged about a common centre, esp. one used in tracery. [C15: from Old French, from *quatre* four + *-foil* leaflet; compare TREFOIL]
quattrocento (ˌkwætrəʊ'tʃɛntəʊ; *Italian* kwattro'tʃento) *n* the 15th century, esp. in reference to Renaissance Italian art and literature. [Italian, shortened from *milquattrocento* 1400]
quaver ('kweɪvə) *vb* **1** to say or sing (something) with a trembling voice. **2** (*intr*) (esp. of the voice) to quiver, tremble, or shake. **3** (*intr*) *Rare.* to sing or play quavers or ornamental trills. ◆ *n* **4** *Music.* a note having the time value of an eighth of a semibreve. Usual U.S. and Canadian name: **eighth note. 5** a tremulous sound or note. [C15 (in the sense: to vibrate, QUIVER[1]): from *quaven* to tremble, of Germanic origin; compare Low German *quabbeln* to tremble] ▸ **'quaverer** *n* ▸ **'quavering** *adj* ▸ **'quaveringly** *adv* ▸ **'quavery** *adj*
quay (kiː) *n* a wharf, typically one built parallel to the shoreline. Compare **pier** (sense 1). [C14 *keye,* from Old French *kai,* of Celtic origin; compare Cornish *kē* hedge, fence, Old Breton *cai* fence]
quayage ('kiːɪdʒ) *n* **1** a system of quays. **2** a charge for the use of a quay.
Quayle (kweɪl) *n* Sir (**John**) **Anthony.** 1913–89, British actor and theatrical producer: director (1948–56) of the Shakespeare Memorial Theatre.
quayside ('kiːˌsaɪd) *n* the edge of a quay along the water.
Que. *abbrev. for* Quebec.
quean (kwiːn) *n* **1** *Archaic.* **1a** a boisterous, impudent, or disreputable woman. **1b** a prostitute; whore. **2** *Scot.* a young unmarried woman or girl. [Old English *cwene;* related to Old Saxon, Old High German *quena,* Gothic *qino,* Old Norse *kona,* Greek *gunē* woman. Compare QUEEN]
queasy ('kwiːzɪ) *adj* **-sier, -siest. 1** having the feeling that one is about to vomit; nauseous. **2** feeling or causing uneasiness: *a queasy conscience.* [C15: of uncertain origin] ▸ **'queasily** *adv* ▸ **'queasiness** *n*
Quebec (kwɪ'bɛk, kə-, kɛ-) *n* **1** a province of E Canada: the largest Canadian province; a French colony from 1608 to 1763, when it passed to Britain; lying mostly on the Canadian Shield, it has vast areas of forest and extensive tundra and is populated mostly in the plain around the St Lawrence River. Capital: Quebec. Pop.: 7 419 900 (1997 est.). Area: 1 540 680 sq. km (594 860 sq. miles). Abbrev.: **PQ. 2** a port in E Canada, capital of the province of Quebec, situated on the St Lawrence River: founded in 1608 by Champlain; scene of the battle of the Plains of Abraham (1759), by which the British won Canada from the French. Pop.: 167 517 (1991). **3** *Communications.* a code word for the letter *q.* ▸ **Que'becker** *or* **Que'becer** *n*
Québecois (*French* kebɛkwa) *n, pl* **-cois** (-kwa). a native or inhabitant of the province of Quebec, esp. a French-speaking one.

quebracho (keɪ'brɑːtʃəʊ; *Spanish* ke'βratʃo) *n, pl* **-chos** (-tʃəʊz; *Spanish* -tʃos). **1** either of two anacardiaceous South American trees, *Schinopsis lorentzii* or *S. balansae,* having a tannin-rich hard wood used in tanning and dyeing. **2** an apocynaceous South American tree, *Aspidosperma quebrachoblanco,* whose bark yields alkaloids used in medicine and tanning. **3** the wood or bark of any of these trees. **4** any of various other South American trees having hard wood. [C19: from American Spanish, from *quiebracha,* from *quebrar* to break (from Latin *crepāre* to rattle) + *hacha* axe (from French *hache*)]

Quechua, Kechua ('kɛtʃwə), *or* **Quichua** *n* **1** (*pl* **-uas** *or* **-ua**) a member of any of a group of South American Indian peoples of the Andes, including the Incas. **2** the language or family of languages spoken by these peoples, possibly distantly related to the Tupi-Guarani family. ▸ **'Quechuan, 'Kechuan,** *or* **'Quichuan** *adj, n*

queen (kwiːn) *n* **1** a female sovereign who is the official ruler or head of state. **2** the wife or widow of a king. **3** a woman or a thing personified as a woman considered the best or most important of her kind: *a beauty queen; the queen of ocean liners.* **4** *Slang.* an effeminate male homosexual. **5a** the only fertile female in a colony of social insects, such as bees, ants, and termites, from the eggs of which the entire colony develops. **5b** (*as modifier*): *a queen bee.* **6** an adult female cat. **7** one of four playing cards in a pack, one for each suit, bearing the picture of a queen. **8** a chess piece, theoretically the most powerful piece, able to move in a straight line in any direction or diagonally, over any number of squares. ◆ *vb* **9** *Chess.* to promote (a pawn) to a queen when it reaches the eighth rank. **10** (*tr*) to crown as queen. **11** (*intr*) to reign as queen. **12 queen it.** (often foll. by *over*) *Informal.* to behave in an overbearing manner. [Old English *cwēn;* related to Old Saxon *quān* wife, Old Norse *kvæn,* Gothic *qēns* wife]

Queen (kwiːn) *n* **Ellery** ('ɛlərɪ). pseudonym of *Frederic Dannay* (1905–82) and *Manfred B. Lee* (1905–71), U.S. coauthors of detective novels featuring a sleuth also called Ellery Queen.

Queen-Anne *n* **1** a style of furniture popular in England about 1700–20 and in America about 1720–70, characterized by the use of unencumbered curves, walnut veneer, and the cabriole leg. ◆ *adj* **2** in or of this style. **3** denoting or relating to a style of architecture popular in England during the early 18th century, characterized by red-brick construction with classical ornamentation.

Queen Anne's Bounty *n Church of England.* **1** a fund formed by Queen Anne in 1704 for the augmentation of the livings of the poorer Anglican clergy. In 1948 the administrators of the fund were replaced by the Church Commissioners for England. **2** the office or board administering this fund.

Queen Anne's lace *n* another name for the **wild carrot.**

Queen Anne's War *n* those conflicts (1702–13) of the War of the Spanish Succession that were fought in North America.

queen bee *n* **1** the fertile female bee in a hive. **2** *Informal.* a woman in a position of dominance or ascendancy over her peers or associates.

Queenborough in Sheppey ('kwiːnbərə; 'ʃɛpɪ) *n* a town in SE England, in Kent: formed in 1968 by the amalgamation of Queenborough, Sheerness, and Sheppey. Pop.: 30 790 (1991).

queencake ('kwiːn,keɪk) *n* a small light cake containing currants.

Queen Charlotte Islands *pl n* a group of about 150 islands off the W coast of Canada: part of British Columbia. Pop.: 5316 (1991). Area: 9596 sq. km (3705 sq. miles).

queen consort *n* the wife of a reigning king.

queen dowager *n* the widow of a king.

Queen Elizabeth Islands *pl n* a group of islands off the N coast of Canada: the northernmost islands of the Canadian Arctic archipelago, lying N of latitude 74°N; part of the Northwest Territories. Area: about 390 000 sq. km (150 000 sq. miles).

queenly ('kwiːnlɪ) *adj* **-lier, -liest. 1** resembling or appropriate to a queen. **2** having the rank of queen. ◆ *adv* **3** in a manner appropriate to a queen. ▸ **'queenliness** *n*

Queen Mab (mæb) *n* (in British folklore) a bewitching fairy who rules over men's dreams.

Queen Maud Land (mɔːd) *n* the large section of Antarctica between Coats Land and Enderby Land: claimed by Norway in 1939.

Queen Maud Range *n* a mountain range in Antarctica, in S Ross Dependency, extending for about 800 km (500 miles).

queen mother *n* the widow of a former king who is also the mother of the reigning sovereign.

queen of puddings *n* a pudding made of moist but firm breadcrumb and custard mixture topped with jam and meringue.

queen olive *n* a variety of olive having large fleshy fruit suitable for pickling, esp. one from around Seville in Spain.

queen post *n* one of a pair of vertical posts that connect the tie beam of a truss to the principal rafters. Compare **king post.**

queen regent *n* a queen who acts as regent.

queen regnant *n* a queen who reigns on her own behalf.

Queens (kwiːnz) *n* a borough of E New York City, on Long Island. Pop.: 1 951 598 (1990).

Queen's Award *n* either of two awards instituted by royal warrant (1976) for a sustained increase in export earnings by a British firm (**Queen's Award for Export Achievement**) or for an advance in technology (**Queen's Award for Technological Achievement**).

Queen's Bench Division *n* (in England when the sovereign is female) one of the divisions of the High Court of Justice. Also called (when the sovereign is male): **King's Bench.**

Queensberry rules ('kwiːnzbərɪ, -brɪ) *pl n* **1** the code of rules followed in modern boxing, requiring the use of padded gloves, rounds of three minutes, and restrictions on the types of blows allowed. **2** *Informal.* gentlemanly or polite conduct, esp. in a dispute. [C19: named after the ninth Marquess of *Queensberry,* who originated the rules in 1869]

Queen's Counsel *n* (in England when the sovereign is female) a barrister or advocate appointed Counsel to the Crown on the recommendation of the Lord Chancellor, entitled to sit within the bar of the court and to wear a silk gown. Also called (when the sovereign is male): **King's Counsel.**

Queen's County *n* the former name of **Laois.**

queen's English *n* (when the British sovereign is female) standard Southern British English.

queen's evidence *n English law.* (when the sovereign is female) evidence given for the Crown against his former associates in crime by an accomplice (esp. in the phrase **turn queen's evidence**). Also called (when the sovereign is male): **king's evidence.** U.S. equivalent: **state's evidence.**

Queen's Guide *n* (in Britain and the Commonwealth when the sovereign is female) a Guide who has passed the highest tests of proficiency.

queen's highway *n* (in Britain when the sovereign is female) any public road or right of way.

Queen's House *n* **the.** a Palladian mansion in Greenwich, London: designed (1616–35) by Inigo Jones; now part of the National Maritime Museum; restored 1984–90.

Queensland ('kwiːnz,lænd, -lənd) *n* a state of NE Australia: fringed on the Pacific side by the Great Barrier Reef; the Great Dividing Range lies in the east, separating the coastal lowlands from the dry Great Artesian Basin in the south. Capital: Brisbane. Pop.: 3 339 000 (1996 est.). Area: 1 727 500 sq. km (667 000 sq. miles). ▸ **'Queens,lander** *n*

Queensland blue *n Austral.* a pumpkin with a bluish skin.

Queensland cane toad *n Austral.* a toad, *Bufo marinus,* introduced into Queensland from Hawaii to control insect pests, becoming a pest itself.

Queensland lungfish *n* a lungfish, *Neoceratodus forsteri,* reaching a length of six feet: occurs in Queensland rivers but introduced elsewhere.

Queensland nut *n* another name for **macadamia.**

Queen's proctor *n* (in England when the sovereign is female) an official empowered to intervene in divorce and certain other cases when it is alleged that material facts are being suppressed.

Queen's Regulations *pl n* (in Britain and certain other Commonwealth countries when the sovereign is female) the code of conduct for members of the armed forces.

Queen's Scout *n* (in Britain and the Commonwealth when the sovereign is female) a Scout who has passed the highest tests of endurance, proficiency, and skill. U.S. equivalent: **Eagle Scout.**

queen's shilling *n* See **king's shilling.**

Queen's speech *n* (in Britain and the dominions of the Commonwealth when the sovereign is female) another name for the **speech from the throne.**

Queenstown ('kwiːnz,taʊn) *n* the former name (1849–1922) of **Cóbh.**

Queen Street Farmer *n N.Z.* a businessman who runs a farm, often for a tax loss. [from *Queen Street,* the main business street in Auckland]

queen substance *n* a pheromone secreted by queen honeybees and consumed by the workers, in whom it causes suppression of egg-laying.

Queensware ('kwiːnz,wɛə) *or* **Queen's ware** *n* a type of light white earthenware with a brilliant glaze developed from creamware by Josiah Wedgwood and named in honour of his patroness, Queen Charlotte.

queer (kwɪə) *adj* **1** differing from the normal or usual in a way regarded as odd or strange. **2** suspicious, dubious, or shady. **3** faint, giddy, or queasy. **4** *Informal, derogatory.* homosexual. **5** *Informal.* odd or unbalanced mentally; eccentric or slightly mad. **6** *Slang.* worthless or counterfeit. ◆ *n* **7** *Informal, derogatory.* a homosexual, usually a male. ◆ *vb* (*tr*) *Informal.* **8** to spoil or thwart (esp. in the phrase **queer someone's pitch**). **9** to put in a difficult or dangerous position. [C16: perhaps from German *quer* oblique, ultimately from Old High German *twërh*] ▸ **'queerish** *adj* ▸ **'queerly** *adv* ▸ **'queerness** *n*

USAGE Although the term *queer* meaning homosexual is still considered derogatory when used by non-homosexuals, it is now being used by homosexuals of themselves as a positive term, as in *queer politics, queer cinema.*

queer-bashing *n Brit. slang.* the activity of making vicious and unprovoked verbal or physical assaults upon homosexuals or supposed homosexuals. ▸ **'queer-,basher** *n*

queer fish *n Brit. informal.* an eccentric or odd person.

queer street *n* (*sometimes caps.*) *Informal.* a difficult situation, such as debt or bankruptcy (in the phrase **in queer street**).

quell (kwɛl) *vb* (*tr*) **1** to suppress or beat down (rebellion, disorder, etc.); subdue. **2** to overcome or allay: *to quell pain; to quell grief.* [Old English *cwellan* to kill; related to Old Saxon *quellian,* Old High German *quellen,* Old Norse *kvelja* to torment] ▸ **'queller** *n*

Quelpart ('kwɛl,pɑːt) *n* another name for **Cheju.**

quelquechose ('kɛlkə'ʃəʊz) *n* an insignificant thing; mere trifle. [French, literally: something]

Quemoy (kɛ'mɔɪ) *n* an island in Formosa Strait, off the SE coast of China: administratively part of Taiwan. Pop. (with associated islets): 53 237 (1996 est.). Area: 130 sq. km (50 sq. miles).

quench (kwɛntʃ) *vb* (*tr*) **1** to satisfy (one's thirst, desires, etc.); slake. **2** to put out (a fire, flame, etc.); extinguish. **3** to put down or quell; suppress: *to quench a rebellion.* **4** to cool (hot metal) by plunging it into cold water. **5** *Physics.* to reduce the degree of (luminescence or phosphorescence) in (excited molecules or a material) by adding a suitable substance. **6** *Electronics.* **6a** to suppress (sparking) when the current is cut off in an inductive circuit. **6b** to suppress (an oscillation or discharge) in a component or device. [Old English *ācwencan* to extinguish; related to Old Frisian *quinka* to vanish] ▸ **'quenchable** *adj* ▸ **'quencher** *n* ▸ **'quenchless** *adj*

Queneau (*French* kɑno) *n* **Raymond** (rɛmɔ̃). 1903–76. French writer, influenced in the 1920s by surrealism. His novels include *Zazie dans le métro* (1959).

quenelle (kəˈnɛl) *n* a finely sieved mixture of cooked meat or fish, shaped into various forms and cooked in stock or fried as croquettes. [C19: from French, from German *Knödel* dumpling, from Old High German *knodo* knot]

quercetin *or* **quercitin** (ˈkwɜːsɪtɪn) *n* a yellow crystalline pigment found naturally as its glycosides in the rind and bark of many plants. It is used in medicine to treat fragile capillaries. Formula: $C_{15}H_{10}O_7$; melting pt: 316–7°C. Also called: **flavin.** [C19: from Latin *quercētum* an oak forest (from *quercus* an oak) + -IN] ▸ **quercetic** (kwɜːˈsɛtɪk, -ˈsiː-) *adj*

Quercia (*Italian* ˈkwertʃa) *n* **Jacopo della.** See **Jacopo della Quercia.**

Querétaro (*Spanish* keˈretaro) *n* **1** an inland state of central Mexico: economy based on agriculture and mining. Capital: Querétaro. Pop.: 1 248 844 (1995 est.). Area: 11 769 sq. km (4544 sq. miles). **2** a city in central Mexico, capital of Querétaro state: scene of the signing (1848) of the treaty ending the U.S.-Mexican War and of the execution of Emperor Maximilian (1867). Pop.: 385 503 (1990).

querist (ˈkwɪərɪst) *n* a person who makes inquiries or queries; questioner.

quern (kwɜːn) *n* a stone hand mill for grinding corn. [Old English *cweorn;* related to Old Frisian *quern,* Old High German *kurn,* Old Norse *kverna,* Gothic *quairnus* millstone]

quernstone (ˈkwɜːnˌstəʊn) *n* **1** another name for **millstone** (sense 1). **2** one of the two small circular stones used in a quern.

querulous (ˈkwɛrʊləs, ˈkwɛrjʊ-) *adj* **1** inclined to make whining or peevish complaints. **2** characterized by or proceeding from a complaining fretful attitude or disposition: *a querulous tone.* [C15: from Latin *querulus* from *querī* to complain] ▸ **ˈquerulously** *adv* ▸ **ˈquerulousness** *n*

query (ˈkwɪərɪ) *n, pl* **-ries. 1** a question, esp. one expressing doubt, uncertainty, or an objection. **2** a less common name for **question mark.** ◆ *vb* **-ries, -rying, -ried.** (*tr*) **3** to express uncertainty, doubt, or an objection concerning (something). **4** to express as a query: *"What's up now?"* she queried. **5** *U.S.* to put a question to (a person); ask. [C17: from earlier *quere,* from Latin *quaere* ask!, from *quaerere* to seek, inquire]

query language *n Computing.* the instructions and procedures used to retrieve information from a database.

ques. *abbrev. for* question.

Quesnay (*French* kɛnɛ) *n* **François** (frɑ̃swa). 1694–1774, French political economist, encyclopedist, and physician. He propounded the theory championed by the physiocrats in his *Tableau économique* (1758).

quest (kwɛst) *n* **1** the act or an instance of looking for or seeking; search: *a quest for diamonds.* **2** (in medieval romance) an expedition by a knight or company of knights to accomplish some prescribed task, such as finding the Holy Grail. **3** the object of a search; goal or target: *my quest is the treasure of the king.* **4** *Rare.* a collection of alms. ◆ *vb* (*mainly intr*) **5** (foll. by *for* or *after*) to go in search (of). **6** to go on a quest. **7** (of gun dogs or hounds) **7a** to search for game. **7b** to bay when in pursuit of game. **8** *Rare.* to collect alms. **9** (*also tr*) *Archaic.* to go in search of (a thing); seek or pursue. [C14: from Old French *queste,* from Latin *quaesita* sought, from *quaerere* to seek] ▸ **ˈquester** *n* ▸ **ˈquesting** *adj* ▸ **ˈquestingly** *adv*

question (ˈkwɛstʃən) *n* **1** a form of words addressed to a person in order to elicit information or evoke a response; interrogative sentence. **2** a point at issue: *it's only a question of time until she dies; the question is how long they can keep up the pressure.* **3** a difficulty or uncertainty; doubtful point: *a question of money; there's no question about it.* **4a** an act of asking. **4b** an investigation into some problem or difficulty. **5** a motion presented for debate by a deliberative body. **6 put the question.** to require members of a deliberative assembly to vote on a motion presented. **7** *Law.* a matter submitted to a court or other tribunal for judicial or quasi-judicial decision. **8 question of fact.** (in English law) that part of the issue before a court that is decided by the jury. **9 question of law.** (in English law) that part of the issue before a court that is decided by the judge. **10 beg the question. 10a** to avoid giving a direct answer by posing another question. **10b** to assume the truth of that which is intended to be proved. See **petitio principii. 11 beyond (all) question.** beyond (any) dispute or doubt. **12 call in** *or* **into question. 12a** to make (something) the subject of disagreement. **12b** to cast doubt upon the validity, truth, etc., of (something). **13 in question.** under discussion: *this is the man in question.* **14 out of the question.** beyond consideration; unthinkable or impossible: *the marriage is out of the question.* **15 pop the question.** *Informal.* to propose marriage. ◆ *vb* (*mainly tr*) **16** to put a question or questions to (a person); interrogate. **17** to make (something) the subject of dispute or disagreement. **18** to express uncertainty about the validity, truth, etc., of (something); doubt. [C13: via Old French from Latin *quaestiō,* from *quaerere* to seek] ▸ **ˈquestioner** *n*

USAGE *The question whether* should be used rather than *the question of whether* or *the question as to whether: this leaves open the question whether he acted correctly.*

questionable (ˈkwɛstʃənəbᵊl) *adj* **1** (esp. of a person's morality or honesty) admitting of some doubt; dubious. **2** of disputable value or authority: *a questionable text.* ▸ **ˈquestionableness** *or* **ˌquestionaˈbility** *n* ▸ **ˈquestionably** *adv*

questioning (ˈkwɛstʃənɪŋ) *adj* **1** proceeding from or characterized by a feeling of doubt or uncertainty. **2** enthusiastic or eager for philosophical or other investigations; intellectually stimulated: *an alert and questioning mind.* ▸ **ˈquestioningly** *adv*

questionless (ˈkwɛstʃənlɪs) *adj* **1** blindly adhering, as to a principle or course of action; unquestioning. **2** a less common word for **unquestionable.** ▸ **ˈquestionlessly** *adv*

question mark *n* **1** the punctuation mark **?**, used at the end of questions and in other contexts where doubt or ignorance is implied. **2** this mark used for any other purpose, as to draw attention to a possible mistake, as in a chess commentary. **3** an element of doubt or uncertainty.

question master *n Brit.* the chairman of a quiz or panel game.

questionnaire (ˌkwɛstʃəˈnɛə, ˌkɛs-) *n* a set of questions on a form, submitted to a number of people in order to collect statistical information. [C20: from French, from *questionner* to ask questions]

question time *n* (in parliamentary bodies of the British type) a period of time set aside each day for members to question government ministers.

questor (ˈkwɛstə) *n U.S.* a variant of **quaestor.** ▸ **questorial** (kwɛˈstɔːrɪəl) *adj* ▸ **ˈquestorˌship** *n*

Quetta (ˈkwɛtə) *n* a city in W central Pakistan, at an altitude of 1650 m (5500 ft.): a summer resort, military station, and trading centre. Pop.: 285 000 (1981).

quetzal (ˈkɛtsəl) *or* **quezal** (kɛˈsɑːl) *n, pl* **-zals** *or* **-zales** (-ˈsɑːlɛs). **1** Also called: **resplendent trogon.** a crested bird, *Pharomachrus mocinno,* of Central and N South America, which has a brilliant green, red, and white plumage and, in the male, long tail feathers: family *Trogonidae,* order *Trogoniformes* (trogons). **2** the standard monetary unit of Guatemala, divided into 100 centavos. [via American Spanish from Nahuatl *quetzalli* brightly coloured tail feather]

Quetzalcoatl (ˌkɛtsəlkəʊˈætᵊl) *n* a god of the Aztecs and Toltecs, represented as a feathered serpent.

queue (kjuː) *Chiefly Brit.* ◆ *n* **1** a line of people, vehicles, etc., waiting for something: *a queue at the theatre.* **2** *Computing.* a list in which entries are deleted from one end and inserted at the other. **3** a pigtail. **4 jump the queue.** See **queue-jump.** ◆ *vb* **queues, queuing** *or* **queueing, queued. 5** (*intr;* often foll. by *up*) to form or remain in a line while waiting. **6** *Computing.* to arrange (a number of programs) in a predetermined order for accessing by a computer. ◆ U.S. and Canadian word: **line.** [C16 (in the sense: tail); C18 (in the sense: pigtail): via French from Latin *cauda*tail]

queue-jump *vb* (*intr*) **1** to take a place in a queue ahead of those already queuing; push in. **2** to obtain prior consideration or some other advantage out of turn or unfairly. Also: **jump the queue.** ▸ **queue-jumper** *n*

queuing theory *n* a mathematical approach to the rate at which components queue to be processed by a machine, instructions are accessed by a computer, orders need to be serviced, etc., to achieve the optimum flow.

Quevedo y Villegas (kɛˈveɪðəʊiː vɪlˈjeɪgæs) *n* **Francisco Gómez de.** 1580–1645, Spanish poet and writer, noted for his satires and the picaresque novel *La historia de la vida del Buscón* (1626).

Quezon City (ˈkeɪzɒn) *n* a city in the Philippines, on central Luzon adjoining Manila: capital of the Philippines from 1948 to 1976; seat of the University of the Philippines (1908). Pop.: 1 676 644 (1994 est.).

Quezon y Molina (ˈkeɪzɒn iː mɒˈliːnə; *Spanish* keˈθon i moˈlina) *n* **Manuel Luis** (maˈnwɛl lwis). 1878–1944, Philippine statesman: first president of the Philippines (from 1935) and head of the government in exile after the Japanese conquest of the islands in World War II.

quibble (ˈkwɪbᵊl) *vb* (*intr*) **1** to make trivial objections; prevaricate. **2** *Archaic.* to play on words; pun. ◆ *n* **3** a trivial objection or equivocation, esp. one used to avoid an issue. **4** *Archaic.* a pun. [C17: probably from obsolete *quib,* perhaps from Latin *quibus* (from *quī* who, which), as used in legal documents, with reference to their obscure phraseology] ▸ **ˈquibbler** *n* ▸ **ˈquibbling** *adj, n* ▸ **ˈquibblingly** *adv*

Quiberon (*French* kibrɔ̃) *n* a peninsula of NW France, on the S coast of Brittany: a naval battle was fought off its coast in 1759 during the Seven Years' War, in which the British defeated the French.

quiche (kiːʃ) *n* an open savoury tart with a rich custard filling to which bacon, onion, cheese, etc., are added: *quiche Lorraine.* [French, from German *Kuchen* cake]

Quichua (ˈkɪtʃwə) *n, pl* **-uas** *or* **-ua.** a variant of **Quechua.**

quick (kwɪk) *adj* **1** (of an action, movement, etc.) performed or occurring during a comparatively short time: *a quick move.* **2** lasting a comparatively short time; brief: *a quick flight.* **3** accomplishing something in a time that is shorter than normal: *a quick worker.* **4** characterized by rapidity of movement; swift or fast: *a quick walker.* **5** immediate or prompt: *a quick reply.* **6** (*postpositive*) eager or ready to perform (an action): *quick to criticize.* **7** responsive to stimulation; perceptive or alert; lively: *a quick eye.* **8** eager or enthusiastic for learning: *a quick intelligence.* **9** easily excited or aroused: *a quick temper.* **10** skilfully swift or nimble in one's movements or actions; deft: *quick fingers.* **11** *Archaic.* **11a** alive; living. **11b** (*as n*) living people (esp. in the phrase **the quick and the dead**). **12** *Archaic or dialect.* lively or eager: *a quick dog.* **13** (of a fire) burning briskly. **14** composed of living plants: *a quick hedge.* **15** *Dialect.* (of sand) lacking firmness through being wet. **16 quick with child.** *Archaic.* pregnant, esp. being in an advanced state of pregnancy, when the movements of the fetus can be felt. ◆ *n* **17** any area of living flesh that is highly sensitive to pain or touch, esp. that under a toenail or fingernail or around a healing wound. **18** the vital or most important part (of a thing). **19** short for **quickset** (sense 1). **20 cut (someone) to the quick.** to hurt (someone's) feelings deeply; offend gravely. ◆ *adv Informal.* **21** in a rapid or speedy manner; swiftly. **22** soon: *I hope he comes quick.* ◆ *interj* **23** a command requiring the hearer to perform an action immediately or in as short a time as possible. [Old English *cwicu* living; related to Old Saxon *quik,* Old High German *queck,* Old Norse *kvikr* alive, Latin *vīvus* alive, Greek *bios* life] ▸ **ˈquickly** *adv* ▸ **ˈquickness** *n*

quick assets *pl n Accounting.* assets readily convertible into cash; liquid current assets.

quick-change artist *n* an actor or entertainer who undertakes several rapid changes of costume during his performance.

quicken (ˈkwɪkən) *vb* **1** to make or become faster; accelerate: *he quickened his walk; her heartbeat quickened with excitement.* **2** to impart to or receive vigour, enthusiasm, etc.; stimulate or be stimulated: *science quickens man's* *imagination.* **3** to make or become alive; revive. **4a** (of an unborn fetus) to begin to show signs of life. **4b** (of a pregnant woman) to reach the stage of pregnancy at which movements of the fetus can be felt.

quick fire *n* **1** rapid continuous gunfire, esp. at a moving target. ◆ *adj* **quick-fire. 2** Also: **quick-firing.** capable of or designed for quick fire. **3** *Informal.* rapid or following one another in rapid succession: *quick-fire questions.*

quick-freeze *vb* **-freezes, -freezing, -froze, -frozen.** (*tr*) to preserve (food) by subjecting it to rapid refrigeration at temperatures of 0°C or lower.

quick grass *n* another name for **couch grass.** [C17: Scot. and northern English variant of *couch grass,* from the earlier *quick* living; compare QUITCH GRASS]

quickie ('kwɪkɪ) *n Informal.* **1** Also called (esp. Brit.): **quick one.** a speedily consumed alcoholic drink. **2a** anything made, done, produced, or consumed rapidly or in haste. **2b** (*as modifier*): *a quickie divorce.*

quicklime ('kwɪk,laɪm) *n* another name for **calcium oxide.** [C15: from QUICK (in the archaic sense: living) + LIME[1]]

quick march *n* **1** a march at quick time or the order to proceed at such a pace. ◆ *interj* **2** a command to commence such a march.

quick response *n Marketing.* the rapid replenishment of a customer's stock by a supplier with direct access to data from the customer's point of sale.

quicksand ('kwɪk,sænd) *n* a deep mass of loose wet sand that submerges anything on top of it.

quickset ('kwɪk,sɛt) *Chiefly Brit.* ◆ *n* **1a** a plant or cutting, esp. of hawthorn, set so as to form a hedge. **1b** such plants or cuttings collectively. **2** a hedge composed of such plants. ◆ *adj* **3** composed of such plants. [C15: from *quick* in the archaic sense live, growing + *set* to plant, set in the ground]

quicksilver ('kwɪk,sɪlvə) *n* **1** another name for **mercury** (sense 1). ◆ *adj* **2** rapid or unpredictable in movement or change: *a quicksilver temper.* [Old English, from *cwicu* alive (see QUICK) + *seolfer* silver]

quickstep ('kwɪk,stɛp) *n* **1** a modern ballroom dance in rapid quadruple time. **2** a piece of music composed for or in the rhythm of this dance. ◆ *vb* **-steps, -stepping, -stepped. 3** (*intr*) to perform this dance.

quick-tempered *adj* readily roused to anger; irascible.

quickthorn ('kwɪk,θɔːn) *n* hawthorn, esp. when planted as a hedge. [C17: probably from *quick* in the sense "fast-growing": compare QUICKSET]

quick time *n Military.* the normal marching rate of 120 paces to the minute. Compare **double time** (senses 3, 4).

quick trick *n Bridge.* a high card almost certain to win a trick, usually an ace or a king: the unit in one of the systems of hand valuation.

quick-witted *adj* having a keenly alert mind, esp. as used to avert danger, make effective reply, etc. ▸ **,quick-'wittedly** *adv* ▸ **,quick-'wittedness** *n*

quid[1] (kwɪd) *n* a piece of tobacco, suitable for chewing. [Old English *cwidu* chewing resin; related to Old High German *quiti* glue, Old Norse *kvātha* resin; see CUD]

quid[2] (kwɪd) *n, pl* **quid. 1** *Brit.* a slang word for **pound** (sterling). **2** (**be**) **quids in.** *Brit. slang.* to be in a very favourable or advantageous position. **3 not the full quid.** *Austral. and N.Z. slang.* mentally subnormal. [C17: of obscure origin]

quiddity ('kwɪdɪtɪ) *n, pl* **-ties. 1** *Philosophy.* the essential nature of something. Compare **haecceity. 2** a petty or trifling distinction; quibble. [C16: from Medieval Latin *quidditās,* from Latin *quid* what]

quidnunc ('kwɪd,nʌŋk) *n* a person eager to learn news and scandal; gossipmonger. [C18: from Latin, literally: what now]

quid pro quo ('kwɪd prəʊ 'kwəʊ) *n, pl* **quid pro quos. 1** a reciprocal exchange. **2** something given in compensation, esp. an advantage or object given in exchange for another. [C16: from Latin: something for something]

quiescent (kwɪ'ɛsᵊnt) *adj* quiet, inactive, or dormant. [C17: from Latin *quiescere* to rest] ▸ **qui'escence** *or* **qui'escency** *n* ▸ **qui'escently** *adv*

quiescent tank *n* a tank, usually for sewage sludge, in which the sludge is allowed to remain for a time so that sedimentation can occur.

quiet ('kwaɪət) *adj* **1** characterized by an absence or near absence of noise: *a quiet street.* **2** characterized by an absence of turbulent motion or disturbance; peaceful, calm, or tranquil: *a quiet glade; the sea is quiet tonight.* **3** free from activities, distractions, worries, etc.; untroubled: *a quiet life; a quiet day at work.* **4** marked by an absence of work, orders, etc.; not busy: *the factory is very quiet at the moment.* **5** private; not public; secret: *a quiet word with someone.* **6** free from anger, impatience, or other extreme emotion: *a quiet disposition.* **7** free from pretentiousness or vain display; modest or reserved: *quiet humour.* **8** *Astronomy.* (of the sun) exhibiting a very low number of sunspots, solar flares, and other surface phenomena; inactive. Compare **active** (sense 8). ◆ *n* **9** the state of being silent, peaceful, or untroubled. **10 on the quiet.** without other people knowing; secretly. ◆ *vb* **11** a less common word for **quieten.** [C14: from Latin *quiētus,* past participle of *quiēscere* to rest, from *quiēs* repose, rest] ▸ **'quietness** *n*

quieten ('kwaɪətᵊn) *vb Chiefly Brit.* **1** (often foll. by *down*) to make or become calm, silent, etc.; pacify or become peaceful. **2** (*tr*) to allay (fear, doubts, etc.).

quietism ('kwaɪə,tɪzəm) *n* **1** a form of religious mysticism originating in Spain in the late 17th century, requiring withdrawal of the spirit from all human effort and complete passivity to God's will. **2** a state of passivity and calmness of mind towards external events. ▸ **'quietist** *n, adj*

quietly ('kwaɪətlɪ) *adv* **1** in a quiet manner. **2 just quietly.** *Austral.* between you and me; confidentially.

quietude ('kwaɪə,tjuːd) *n* the state or condition of being quiet, peaceful, calm, or tranquil.

quietus (kwaɪ'iːtəs, -'eɪtəs) *n, pl* **-tuses. 1** anything that serves to quash, eliminate, or kill; *to give the quietus to a rumour.* **2** a release from life; death. **3** the discharge or settlement of debts, duties, etc. [C16: from Latin *quiētus est,* literally: he is at rest, QUIET]

quiff (kwɪf) *n Brit.* a prominent tuft of hair, esp. one brushed up above the forehead. [C19: of unknown origin]

quill (kwɪl) *n* **1a** any of the large stiff feathers of the wing or tail of a bird. **1b** the long hollow central part of a bird's feather; calamus. **2** a bird's feather made into a pen for writing. **3** any of the stiff hollow spines of a porcupine or hedgehog. **4** a device, formerly usually made from a crow quill, for plucking a harpsichord string. **5** *Angling.* a length of feather barb stripped of barbules and used for the body of some artificial flies. **6** a small roll of bark, esp. one of dried cinnamon. **7** (in weaving) a bobbin or spindle. **8** a fluted fold, as in a ruff. **9** a hollow shaft that rotates upon an inner spindle or concentrically about an internal shaft. ◆ *vb* (*tr*) **10** to wind (thread, yarn, etc.) onto a spool or bobbin. **11** to make or press fluted folds in (a ruff). [C15 (in the sense: hollow reed or pipe): of uncertain origin; compare Middle Low German *quiele* quill]

quillai (kɪ'laɪ) *n* another name for **soapbark** (sense 1). [C19: via American Spanish from Araucanian]

Quiller-Couch (,kwɪlə'kuːtʃ) *n* Sir **Arthur** (**Thomas**), known as Q. 1863–1944, British critic and novelist, who edited the *Oxford Book of English Verse* (1900).

quillet ('kwɪlɪt) *n Archaic.* a quibble or subtlety. [C16: from earlier *quillity,* perhaps an alteration of QUIDDITY]

quilling ('kwɪlɪŋ) *n* decorative craftwork in which a material such as glass, fabric, or paper is formed into small bands or rolls that form the basis of a design.

quillon (*French* kijɔ̃) *n* (*often pl*) either half of the extended crosspiece of a sword or dagger. [C19: from French, diminutive of *quille* bowling pin, ultimately from Old High German *kegil* club, stake]

quill pen *n* another name for **quill** (sense 2).

quillwort ('kwɪl,wɜːt) *n* any aquatic tracheophyte plant of the genus *Isoetes,* with quill-like leaves at the bases of which are spore-producing structures: family *Isoetaceae,* phylum *Lycopodophyta* (club mosses, etc.).

Quilmes (*Spanish* 'kilmes) *n* a city in E Argentina: a resort and suburb of Buenos Aires. Pop.: 509 445 (1991).

quilt (kwɪlt) *n* **1** a thick warm cover for a bed, consisting of a soft filling sewn between two layers of material, usually with crisscross seams. **2** a bedspread or counterpane. **3** anything quilted or resembling a quilt. ◆ *vb* (*tr*) **4** to stitch together (two pieces of fabric) with (a thick padding or lining) between them: *to quilt cotton and wool.* **5** to create (a garment, covering, etc.) in this way. **6** to pad with material. **7** *Austral. informal.* to strike; clout. [C13: from Old French *coilte* mattress, from Latin *culcita* stuffed item of bedding] ▸ **'quilter** *n*

quilting ('kwɪltɪŋ) *n* **1** material used for making a quilt. **2** the act or process of making a quilt. **3** quilted work.

quim (kwɪm) *n Brit. taboo.* the female genitals. [C19: of uncertain origin]

Quimper (*French* kɛ̃pɛr) *n* a city in NW France: capital of Finistère department. Pop.: 62 540 (1990).

quin (kwɪn) *n Brit.* short for **quintuplet** (sense 2). U.S. and Canadian word: **quint.**

quinacrine ('kwɪnə,kriːn) *n* **1** another name for **mepacrine. 2 quinacrine mustard.** a nitrogen mustard derived from mepacrine and used as a stain for chromosomes. [C20: from QUIN(INE) + ACR(ID) + -INE[2]]

quinary ('kwaɪnərɪ) *adj* **1** consisting of fives or by fives. **2** fifth in a series. **3** (of a number system) having a base of five. ◆ *n, pl* **-ries. 4** a set of five. [C17: from Latin *quīnārius* containing five, from *quīnī* five each]

quinate ('kwaɪneɪt) *adj Botany.* arranged in or composed of five parts: *quinate leaflets.* [C19: from Latin *quīnī* five each]

quince (kwɪns) *n* **1** a small widely cultivated Asian rosaceous tree, *Cydonia oblonga,* with pinkish-white flowers and edible pear-shaped fruits. **2** the acid-tasting fruit of this tree, much used in preserves. [C14 *qwince* plural of *quyn* quince, from Old French *coin,* from Latin *cotōneum,* from Greek *kudōnion* quince, Cydonian (apple)]

quincentenary (,kwɪnsɛn'tiːnərɪ) *n, pl* **-naries.** a 500th anniversary or the year or celebration marking it. [C19: irregularly from Latin *quinque* five + CENTENARY] ▸ **quincentennial** (,kwɪnsɛn'tɛnɪəl) *adj, n*

quincuncial (kwɪn'kʌnʃəl) *adj* **1** consisting of or having the appearance of a quincunx. **2** (of the petals or sepals of a five-membered corolla or calyx in the bud) arranged so that two members overlap another two completely and the fifth overlaps on one margin and is itself overlapped on the other. ▸ **quin'cuncially** *adv*

quincunx ('kwɪnkʌŋks) *n* **1** a group of five objects arranged in the shape of a rectangle with one at each of the four corners and the fifth in the centre. **2** *Botany.* a quincuncial arrangement of sepals or petals in the bud. **3** *Astrology.* an aspect of 150° between two planets. [C17: from Latin: five twelfths, from *quinque* five + *uncia* twelfth; in ancient Rome, this was a coin worth five twelfths of an AS[2] and marked with five spots]

quindecagon (kwɪn'dɛkəgən) *n* a geometric figure having 15 sides and 15 angles. [C16: from Latin *quindecim* fifteen + *-agon,* as in *decagon*]

quindecaplet (kwɪn'dɛkə,plɛt) *n* **1** a group of 15. **2** one of a group of 15. [C20: irregularly formed on the models of *quadruplet, quintuplet,* etc.]

quindecennial (,kwɪndɪ'sɛnɪəl) *adj* **1** occurring once every 15 years or over a period of 15 years. ◆ *n* **2** a 15th anniversary. [C20: from Latin *quindecim* fifteen + *annus* year, on the model of *biennial*]

quine (kwəɪn) *n Scot.* a variant of **quean** (sense 2).

Quine (kwaɪn) *n* **Willard van Orman.** born 1908, U.S. philosopher. His works include *Word and Object* (1960), *Philosophy of Logic* (1970), *The Roots of Reference* (1973), and *The Logic of Sequences* (1990).

quinella (kwɪ'nɛlə) *n Austral. and N.Z.* a form of betting on a horse race in which the punter bets on selecting the first and second place-winners in any order. [from American Spanish *quiniela* a game of chance]

Qui Nhong ('kwiː 'njɒŋ) *n* a port in SE Vietnam, on the South China Sea. Pop.: 163 385 (1992 est.).

quinic acid ('kwɪnɪk) *n* a white crystalline soluble optically active carboxylic acid, found in cinchona bark, bilberries, coffee beans, and the leaves of certain other plants; 1,3,4,5-tetrahydroxycyclohexanecarboxylic acid. Formula: $C_6H_7(OH)_4COOH$.

quinidine ('kwɪnɪˌdiːn) *n* a crystalline alkaloid drug that is an optically active isomer of quinine: used to treat heart arrhythmias. Formula: $C_{20}H_{24}N_2O_2$.

quinine (kwɪ'niːn; *U.S.* 'kwaɪnaɪn) *n* a bitter crystalline alkaloid extracted from cinchona bark, the salts of which are used as a tonic, antipyretic, analgesic, etc., and (usually in combination with chloroquine and similar drugs) in malaria therapy. Formula: $C_{20}H_{24}N_2O_2$. [C19: from Spanish *quina* cinchona bark, from Quechua *kina* bark]

Quinn (kwɪn) *n* **Anthony.** born 1915, U.S. film actor, born in Mexico: noted esp. for his performances in *La Strada* (1954) and *Zorba the Greek* (1964).

quinnat salmon ('kwɪnæt) *n* another name for **Chinook salmon.** [C19: from Salish *t'kwinnat*]

quino- *or before a vowel* **quin-** *combining form.* indicating cinchona, cinchona bark, or quinic acid: *quinidine; quinol; quinoline.* [see QUININE]

quinol ('kwɪnɒl) *n* another name for **hydroquinone.**

quinoline ('kwɪnəˌliːn, -lɪn) *n* **1** an oily colourless insoluble basic heterocyclic compound synthesized by heating aniline, nitrobenzene, glycerol, and sulphuric acid: used as a food preservative and in the manufacture of dyes and antiseptics. Formula: C_9H_7N. **2** any substituted derivative of quinoline.

quinone (kwɪ'nəʊn, 'kwɪnəʊn) *n* another name for **benzoquinone.**

quinonoid ('kwɪnəˌnɔɪd, kwɪ'nəʊnɔɪd) *or* **quinoid** *adj* of, resembling, or derived from quinone.

quinquagenarian (ˌkwɪŋkwədʒɪ'nɛərɪən) *n* **1** a person between 50 and 59 years old. ◆ *adj* **2** being between 50 and 59 years old. **3** of or relating to a quinquagenarian. [C16: from Latin *quinquāgēnārius* containing fifty, from *quinquāgēnī* fifty each]

Quinquagesima (ˌkwɪŋkwə'dʒɛsɪmə) *n* the Sunday preceding Ash Wednesday, the beginning of Lent. Also called: **Quinquagesima Sunday.** [C14: via Medieval Latin from Latin *quinquāgēsima diēs* fiftieth day]

quinque- *combining form.* five: *quinquevalent.* [from Latin *quinque*]

quinquecentenary (ˌkwɪŋkwɪsen'tiːnərɪ) *n, pl* **-naries.** another name for **quincentenary.**

quinquefoliate (ˌkwɪŋkwɪ'fəʊlɪɪt, -ˌeɪt) *adj* (of leaves) having or consisting of five leaflets.

quinquennial (kwɪn'kwenɪəl) *adj* **1** occurring once every five years or over a period of five years. ◆ *n* **2** another word for **quinquennium. 3** a fifth anniversary. ▸ **quin'quennially** *adv*

quinquennium (kwɪn'kwenɪəm) *n, pl* **-nia** (-nɪə). a period or cycle of five years. [C17: from Latin *quinque* five + *annus* year]

quinquepartite (ˌkwɪŋkwɪ'pɑːtaɪt) *adj* **1** divided into or composed of five parts. **2** maintained by or involving five participants or groups of participants.

quinquereme (ˌkwɪŋkwɪ'riːm) *n* an ancient Roman galley with five banks of oars on each side. [C16: from Latin *quinquerēmis,* from QUINQUE- + *rēmus* oar]

quinquevalent (ˌkwɪŋkwɪ'veɪlənt, kwɪn'kwevələnt) *adj Chem.* another word for **pentavalent.** ▸ ˌ**quinque'valency** *or* **quinquevalence** (ˌkwɪŋkwɪ'veɪləns, kwɪn'kwevələns) *n*

quinsy ('kwɪnzɪ) *n* inflammation of the tonsils and surrounding tissues with the formation of abscesses. [C14: via Old French and Medieval Latin from Greek *kunankhē,* from *kuōn* dog + *ankhein* to strangle]

quint[1] *n* **1** (kwɪnt). an organ stop sounding a note a fifth higher than that normally produced by the key depressed. **2** (kɪnt). *Piquet.* a sequence of five cards in the same suit. [C17: from French *quinte,* from Latin *quintus* fifth]

quint[2] (kwɪnt) *n* the U.S. and Canadian word for **quin.**

quinta ('kɪntə) *n Winemaking.* a Portuguese vineyard where grapes for wine or port are grown. [C20: from Portuguese, literally: a country estate, farm]

quintain ('kwɪntɪn) *n* (esp. in medieval Europe) **1** a post or target set up for tilting exercises for mounted knights or foot soldiers. **2** the exercise of tilting at such a target. [C14: from Old French *quintaine,* from Latin: street in a Roman camp between the fifth and sixth maniples, from *quintus* fifth]

quintal ('kwɪntᵊl) *n* **1** a unit of weight equal to 100 pounds. **2** a unit of weight equal to 100 kilograms. [C15: via Old French from Arabic *qintār,* possibly from Latin *centēnārius* consisting of a hundred]

quintan ('kwɪntən) *adj* (of a fever) occurring every fourth day. [C17: from Latin *febris quintāna* fever occurring every fifth day, reckoned inclusively]

Quintana Roo (*Spanish* kin'tana 'rɔo) *n* a state of SE Mexico, on the E Yucatán Peninsula: hot, humid, forested, and inhabited chiefly by Maya Indians. Capital: Chetumal. Pop.: 703 442 (1995 est.). Area: 50 350 sq. km (19 463 sq. miles).

quinte *French.* (kɛ̃t) *n* the fifth of eight basic positions from which a parry or attack can be made in fencing. [C18: French, from Latin *quinta,* fem. of *quintus* fifth, from *quinque* five]

quintessence (kwɪn'tɛsəns) *n* **1** the most typical representation of a quality, state, etc. **2** an extract of a substance containing its principle in its most concentrated form. **3** (in ancient and medieval philosophy) ether, the fifth and highest essence or element after earth, water, air, and fire, which was thought to be the constituent matter of the heavenly bodies and latent in all things. [C15: via French from Medieval Latin *quinta essentia* the fifth essence, translation of Greek *pemptē ousia*] ▸ **quintessential** (ˌkwɪntɪ'sɛnʃəl) *adj* ▸ ˌ**quintes'sentially** *adv*

quintet *or* **quintette** (kwɪn'tɛt) *n* **1** a group of five singers or instrumentalists or a piece of music composed for such a group. **2** any group of five. [C19: from Italian *quintetto,* from *quinto* fifth]

quintic ('kwɪntɪk) *adj Maths.* of or relating to the fifth degree: *a quintic equation.*

quintile ('kwɪntaɪl) *n Astrology.* **1** an aspect of 72° between two heavenly bodies. **2** a fifth part of a distribution. [C17: from Latin *quintus* fifth]

Quintilian (kwɪn'tɪljən) *n* Latin name *Marcus Fabius Quintilianus.* ?35–?96 A.D., Roman rhetorician and teacher.

quintillion (kwɪn'tɪljən) *n, pl* **-lions** *or* **-lion. 1** (in Britain, France, and Germany) the number represented as one followed by 30 zeros (10^{30}). U.S. and Canadian word: **nonillion. 2** (in the U.S. and Canada) the number represented as one followed by 18 zeros (10^{18}). Brit. word: **trillion.** [C17: from Latin *quintus* fifth + *-illion,* as in MILLION] ▸ **quin'tillionth** *adj*

quintuple ('kwɪntjʊpᵊl, kwɪn'tjuːpᵊl) *vb* **1** to multiply by five. ◆ *adj* **2** five times as much or as many; fivefold. **3** consisting of five parts. ◆ *n* **4** a quantity or number five times as great as another. [C16: from French, from Latin *quintus,* on the model of QUADRUPLE]

quintuplet ('kwɪntjʊplɪt, kwɪn'tjuːplɪt) *n* **1** a group or set of five similar things. **2** one of five offspring born at one birth. Often shortened to **quin. 3** *Music.* a group of five notes to be played in a time value of three, four, or some other value.

quintuplicate *adj* (kwɪn'tjuːplɪkɪt). **1** fivefold or quintuple. ◆ *vb* (kwɪn'tjuːplɪˌkeɪt). **2** to multiply or be multiplied by five. ◆ *n* (kwɪn'tjuːplɪkɪt). **3** a group or set of five things. ▸ **quinˌtupli'cation** *n*

quinze (*French* kɛ̃z) *n* a card game with rules similar to those of vingt-et-un, except that the score aimed at is 15 rather than 21. [French: fifteen]

quip (kwɪp) *n* **1** a sarcastic or cutting remark; gibe. **2** a witty or clever saying: *a merry quip.* **3** *Archaic.* another word for **quibble.** ◆ *vb* **quips, quipping, quipped. 4** (*intr*) to make a quip. [C16: from earlier *quippy,* probably from Latin *quippe* indeed, to be sure]

quipster ('kwɪpstə) *n* a person inclined to make sarcastic or witty remarks.

quipu *or* **quippu** ('kiːpuː, 'kwɪpuː) *n* a device of the Incas of Peru used to record information, consisting of an arrangement of variously coloured and knotted cords attached to a base cord. [C17: from Spanish *quipo,* from Quechua *quipu,* literally: knot]

quire[1] (kwaɪə) *n* **1** a set of 24 or 25 sheets of paper; a twentieth of a ream. **2a** four sheets of paper folded once to form a section of 16 pages. **2b** a section or gathering. **3** a set of all the sheets in a book. [C15 *quayer,* from Old French *quaier,* from Latin *quaternī* four at a time, from *quater* four times]

quire[2] (kwaɪə) *n* an obsolete spelling of **choir.**

Quirinal ('kwɪrɪnᵊl) *n* one of the seven hills on which ancient Rome was built.

Quirinus (kwɪ'raɪnəs) *n Roman myth.* a god of war, who came to be identified with the deified Romulus.

Quirites (kwɪ'raɪtiːz) *pl n* the citizens of ancient Rome. [from Latin: inhabitants of *Cures,* later applied generally to Roman citizens]

quirk (kwɜːk) *n* **1** an individual peculiarity of character; mannerism or foible. **2** an unexpected twist or turn: *a quirk of fate.* **3** a continuous groove in an architectural moulding. **4** a flourish, as in handwriting. [C16: of unknown origin] ▸ **'quirky** *adj* ▸ **'quirkily** *adv* ▸ **'quirkiness** *n*

quirt (kwɜːt) *U.S. and S. African* ◆ *n* **1** a whip with a leather thong at one end. ◆ *vb* (*tr*) **2** to strike with a quirt. [C19: from Spanish *cuerda* CORD]

quis custodiet ipsos custodes? *Latin.* (kwɪs kus'təʊdɪˌɛt 'ɪpsɒs kus'təʊdiːz) who will guard the guards?

quisling ('kwɪzlɪŋ) *n* a traitor who aids an occupying enemy force; collaborator. [C20: after Major Vidkun *Quisling* (1887–1945), Norwegian collaborator with the Nazis]

quist (kwɪst) *n, pl* **quists** *or* **quist.** *West Midland and southwestern English dialect.* a wood pigeon. [of obscure origin]

quit (kwɪt) *vb* **quits, quitting, quitted** *or* (*chiefly U.S.*) **quit. 1** (*tr*) to depart from; leave: *he quitted the place hastily.* **2** to resign; give up (a job): *he quitted his job today.* **3** (*intr*) (of a tenant) to give up occupancy of premises and leave them: *they received notice to quit.* **4** to desist or cease from (something or doing something); break off: *quit laughing.* **5** (*tr*) to pay off (a debt); discharge or settle. **6** (*tr*) *Archaic.* to conduct or acquit (oneself); comport (oneself): *he quits himself with great dignity.* ◆ *adj* **7** (*usually predicative;* foll. by *of*) free (from); released (from): *he was quit of all responsibility for their safety.* [C13: from Old French *quitter,* from Latin *quiētus* QUIET; see QUIETUS]

quitch grass (kwɪtʃ) *n* another name for **couch grass.** Sometimes shortened to **quitch.** [Old English *cwice;* perhaps related to *cwicu* living, QUICK (with the implication that the grass cannot be killed); compare Dutch *kweek,* Norwegian *kvike,* German *Queckengras*]

quitclaim ('kwɪtˌkleɪm) *Law.* ◆ *n* **1** a formal renunciation of any claim against a person or of a right to land. ◆ *vb* **2** (*tr*) **2a** to renounce (a claim) formally. **2b** to declare (a person) free from liability. [C14: from Anglo-French *quiteclame,* from *quite* QUIT + *clamer* to declare (from Latin *clamāre* to shout)]

quite (kwaɪt) *adv* **1** to the greatest extent; completely or absolutely: *you're quite right; quite the opposite.* **2** (*not used with a negative*) to a noticeable or partial extent; somewhat: *she's quite pretty.* **3** in actuality; truly: *he thought the bag was heavy, but it was quite light; it's quite the thing to do.* **4 quite a** *or* **an.** (*not used with a negative*) of an exceptional, considerable, or noticeable kind: *quite a girl; quite a long walk.* **5 quite something.** a remarkable or noteworthy thing or person. ◆ *sentence substitute.* **6** Also: **quite so.** an expression used to indicate agreement or assent. [C14: adverbial use of *quite* (adj) QUIT]

USAGE See at **very.**

Quito ('kiːtəʊ; *Spanish* 'kito) *n* the capital of Ecuador, in the north at an altitude of 2850 m (9350 ft.), just south of the equator: the oldest capital in South America, existing many centuries before the Incan conquest in 1487; a cultural centre since the beginning of Spanish rule (1534); two universities. Pop.: 1 487 513 (1997 est.).

quitrent ('kwɪtˌrent) *n* (formerly) a rent payable by a freeholder or copyholder to his lord that released him from liability to perform services.

quits (kwɪts) *Informal.* ◆ *adj* (*postpositive*) **1** on an equal footing; even: *now we* *are quits.* **2 call it quits.** to agree to end a dispute, contest, etc., agreeing that honours are even. ◆ *interj* **3** an exclamation indicating willingness to give up.

quittance ('kwɪtᵊns) *n* **1** release from debt or other obligation. **2** a receipt or other document certifying this. [C13: from Old French, from *quitter* to release from obligation; see QUIT]

quitter ('kwɪtə) *n* a person who gives up easily; defeatist, deserter, or shirker.

quittor ('kwɪtə) *n Vet. science.* infection of the cartilages on the side of a horse's foot, characterized by inflammation and the formation of pus. [C13: perhaps from Old French *cuiture* a boiling, from Latin *coctūra* a cooking, from *coquere* to cook]

quiver[1] ('kwɪvə) *vb* **1** (*intr*) to shake with a rapid tremulous movement; tremble. ◆ *n* **2** the state, process, or noise of shaking or trembling. [C15: from obsolete *cwiver* quick, nimble; compare QUAVER] ▸ **'quiverer** *n* ▸ **'quivering** *adj* ▸ **'quiveringly** *adv* ▸ **'quivery** *adj*

quiver[2] ('kwɪvə) *n* a case for arrows. [C13: from Old French *cuivre;* related to Old English *cocer,* Old Saxon *kokari,* Old High German *kohhari,* Medieval Latin *cucurum*]

quiverful ('kwɪvəfʊl) *n* **1** the amount that a quiver can hold. **2** *Literary.* a fair number or full complement: *a quiverful of children.*

qui vive (ˌkiː 'viːv) *n* **on the qui vive.** on the alert; attentive. [C18: from French, literally: long live who?, sentry's challenge (equivalent to "To whose party do you belong?" or "Whose side do you support?")]

Quixote ('kwɪksət; *Spanish* ki'xote) *n* See **Don Quixote.**

quixotic (kwɪk'sɒtɪk) *adj* preoccupied with an unrealistically optimistic or chivalrous approach to life; impractically idealistic. [C18: after DON QUIXOTE] ▸ **quix'otically** *adv* ▸ **quixotism** ('kwɪksəˌtɪzəm) *n*

quiz (kwɪz) *n, pl* **quizzes. 1a** an entertainment in which the general or specific knowledge of the players is tested by a series of questions, esp. as a radio or television programme. **1b** (*as modifier*): *a quiz programme.* **2** any set of quick questions designed to test knowledge. **3** an investigation by close questioning; interrogation. **4** *Obsolete.* a practical joke; hoax. **5** *Obsolete.* a puzzling or eccentric individual. **6** *Obsolete.* a person who habitually looks quizzically at others, esp. through a small monocle. ◆ *vb* **quizzes, quizzing, quizzed.** (*tr*) **7** to investigate by close questioning; interrogate. **8** *U.S. and Canadian informal.* to test or examine the knowledge of (a student or class). **9** (*tr*) *Obsolete.* to look quizzically at, esp. through a small monocle. [C18: of unknown origin] ▸ **'quizzer** *n*

quizmaster ('kwɪzˌmɑːstə) *n* a person who puts questions to contestants on a quiz programme.

quizzical ('kwɪzɪkᵊl) *adj* questioning and mocking or supercilious: *a quizzical look.* ▸ **ˌquizzi'cality** *n* ▸ **'quizzically** *adv*

Qum (kʊm) *n* a variant of **Qom.**

Qumran ('kʊmrɑːn) *n* See **Khirbet Qumran.**

Qungur ('kʊŋgʊə) *n* a variant transliteration of the Chinese name for **Kongur Shan.**

quod (kwɒd) *n Chiefly Brit.* a slang word for **jail.** [C18: of uncertain origin; perhaps changed from *quad,* short for *quadrangle*]

quod erat demonstrandum *Latin.* ('kwɒd 'ɛræt ˌdɛmən'strændʊm) (at the conclusion of a proof, esp. of a theorem in Euclidean geometry) which was to be proved. Abbrev.: **QED.**

quodlibet ('kwɒdlɪˌbɛt) *n* **1** a light piece of music based on two or more popular tunes. **2** a subtle argument, esp. one prepared as an exercise on a theological topic. [C14: from Latin, from *quod* what + *libet* pleases, that is, whatever you like] ▸ **ˌquodli'betical** *adj* ▸ **ˌquodli'betically** *adv*

quoin, coign, *or* **coigne** (kwɔɪn, kɔɪn) *n* **1** an external corner of a wall. **2** Also called: **cornerstone.** a stone forming the external corner of a wall. **3** another name for **keystone** (sense 1). **4** *Printing.* a metal or wooden wedge or an expanding mechanical device used to lock type up in a chase. **5** a wedge used for any of various other purposes, such as (formerly) to adjust elevation in muzzle-loading cannon. [C16: variant of COIN (corner)]

quoin post *n* the vertical post at the side of a lock gate, about which the gate swings.

quoit (kɔɪt) *n* **1** a ring of iron, plastic, rope, etc., used in the game of quoits. **2** *Austral. slang.* a variant spelling of **coit.** [C15: of unknown origin]

quoits (kɔɪts) *pl n* (*usually functioning as sing*) a game in which quoits are tossed at a stake in the ground in attempts to encircle it.

quokka ('kwɒkə) *n* a small wallaby, *Setonix brachyurus,* formerly abundant in swampy coastal regions of Western Australia but now rare, occurring mostly on offshore islands. [from a native Australian language]

quondam ('kwɒndæm) *adj* (*prenominal*) of an earlier time; former: *her quondam lover.* [C16: from Latin adv: formerly]

Quonset hut ('kwɒnsɪt) *n Trademark, U.S.* a military shelter made of corrugated steel sheet, having a semicircular cross section. Brit. equivalent: **Nissen hut.**

quorate ('kwɔːˌreɪt) *adj Brit.* constituting or having a quorum.

Quorn (kwɔːn) *n Trademark.* a vegetable protein developed from a type of fungus and used in cooking as a meat substitute.

quorum ('kwɔːrəm) *n* a minimum number of members in an assembly, society, board of directors, etc., required to be present before any valid business can be transacted: *the quorum is forty.* [C15: from Latin, literally: of whom, occurring in Latin commissions in the formula *quorum vos…duos* (etc.) *volumus* of whom we wish that you be…two]

quot. *abbrev. for* quotation.

quota ('kwəʊtə) *n* **1** the proportional share or part of a whole that is due from, due to, or allocated to a person or group. **2** a prescribed number or quantity, as of items to be manufactured, imported, or exported, immigrants admitted to a country, or students admitted to a college. [C17: from Latin *quota pars* how big a share?, from *quotus* of what number]

quotable ('kwəʊtəbᵊl) *adj* apt or suitable for quotation: *his remarks are not quotable in mixed company.* ▸ **ˌquota'bility** *n*

quotation (kwəʊ'teɪʃən) *n* **1** a phrase or passage from a book, poem, play, etc., remembered and spoken, esp. to illustrate succinctly or support a point or an argument. **2** the act or habit of quoting from books, plays, poems, etc. **3** *Commerce.* a statement of the current market price of a security or commodity. **4** an estimate of costs submitted by a contractor to a prospective client; tender. **5** *Stock Exchange.* registration granted to a company or governmental body, enabling the shares and other securities of the company or body to be officially listed and traded. **6** *Printing.* a large block of type metal that is less than type-high and is used to fill up spaces in type pages.

quotation mark *n* either of the punctuation marks used to begin or end a quotation, respectively " and " or ' and ' in English printing and writing. When double marks are used, single marks indicate a quotation within a quotation, and vice versa. Also called: **inverted comma.**

quote (kwəʊt) *vb* **1** to recite a quotation (from a book, play, poem, etc.), esp. as a means of illustrating or supporting a statement. **2** (*tr*) to put quotation marks round (a word, phrase, etc.). **3** *Stock Exchange.* to state (a current market price) of (a security or commodity). ◆ *n* **4** an informal word for **quotation** (senses 1–4). **5** (*often pl*) an informal word for **quotation mark:** *put it in quotes.* ◆ *interj* **6** an expression used parenthetically to indicate that the words that follow it form a quotation: *the president said, quote, I shall not run for office in November, unquote.* [C14: from Medieval Latin *quotāre* to assign reference numbers to passages, from Latin *quot* how many]

quote-driven *adj* denoting an electronic market system, esp. for stock exchanges, in which prices are determined by quotations made by market makers or dealers. Compare **order-driven.**

quoth (kwəʊθ) *vb Archaic.* (used with all pronouns except *thou* and *you,* and with nouns) another word for **said**[1] (sense 2). [Old English *cwæth,* third person singular of *cwethan* to say; related to Old Frisian *quetha* to say, Old Saxon, Old High German *quethan;* see BEQUEATH]

quotha ('kwəʊθə) *interj Archaic.* an expression of mild sarcasm, used in picking up a word or phrase used by someone else: *Art thou mad? Mad, quotha! I am more sane than thou.* [C16: from *quoth a* quoth he]

quotidian (kwəʊ'tɪdɪən) *adj* **1** (esp. of attacks of malarial fever) recurring daily. **2** everyday; commonplace. ◆ *n* **3** a malarial fever characterized by attacks that recur daily. [C14: from Latin *quotīdiānus,* variant of *cottīdiānus* daily]

quotient ('kwəʊʃənt) *n* **1a** the result of the division of one number or quantity by another. **1b** the integral part of the result of division. **2** a ratio of two numbers or quantities to be divided. [C15: from Latin *quotiens* how often]

quo vadis ('kwəʊ 'vɑːdɪs) whither goest thou? [Latin: from the Vulgate version of John 16:5]

quo warranto ('kwəʊ wɒ'ræntəʊ) *n Law.* a proceeding initiated to determine or (formerly) a writ demanding by what authority a person claims an office, franchise, or privilege. [from Medieval Latin: by what warrant]

Qu Qiu Bai ('tʃuː 'tʃjuː 'beɪ) *or* **Ch'ü Ch'iu-pai** *n* 1889–1935, Chinese communist leader who was also an important literary figure: executed by the Nationalist forces in Shanghai.

Qur'an (kʊ'rɑːn, -'ræn) *n* a variant of **Koran.**

qv (denoting a cross reference) *abbrev. for* quod vide. [New Latin: which (word, item, etc.) see]

Qwaqwa ('kwɑːkwə) *n* (formerly, in South Africa) a Bantu homeland in N South Africa; the only Bantu homeland without exclaves: abolished in 1994. Also called: **Basotho-Qwaqwa.** Former name (until 1972): **Basotho-Ba-Borwa.**

qwerty *or* **QWERTY keyboard** ('kwɜːtɪ) *n* the standard English language typewriter keyboard layout with the characters q, w, e, r, t, and y positioned on the top row of alphabetic characters at the left side of the keyboard.

qy *abbrev. for* query.

Rr

r *or* **R** (ɑː) *n, pl* **r's, R's,** *or* **Rs. 1** the 18th letter and 14th consonant of the modern English alphabet. **2** a speech sound represented by this letter, in English usually an alveolar semivowel, as in *red.* **3** See **three Rs.**

R *symbol for:* **1** *Chem.* radical. **2** *Currency.* **2a** rand. **2b** rupee. **3** Réaumur (scale). **4** *Physics, electronics.* resistance. **5** roentgen *or* röntgen. **6** *Chess.* rook. **7** Royal. **8** *Chem.* gas constant. **9** (in the U.S. and Australia) **9a** restricted exhibition (used to describe a category of film certified as unsuitable for viewing by anyone under the age of 18). **9b** (*as modifier*): *an R film.*

r. *abbrev. for:* **1** rare. **2** recipe. **3** recto. **4** Also: **r** rod (unit of length). **5** ruled. **6** *Cricket, baseball, etc.* run(s).

R. *abbrev. for:* **1** rabbi. **2** rector. **3** Regiment. **4** Regina. **[**Latin: Queen**] 5** Republican. **6** response (in Christian liturgy). **7** Rex. **[**Latin: King**] 8** River. **9** Royal.

R. *or* **r.** *abbrev. for:* **1** radius. **2** railway. **3** registered (trademark). **4** right. **5** river. **6** road. **7** rouble.

Ra[1] *the chemical symbol for* radium.

Ra[2] (rɑː) *or* **Re** *n* the ancient Egyptian sun god, depicted as a man with a hawk's head surmounted by a solar disc and serpent.

RA *abbrev. for:* **1** rear admiral. **2** *Astronomy.* right ascension. **3** (in Britain) Royal Academician *or* Academy. **4** (in Britain) Royal Artillery. ◆ **5** *international car registration for* Argentina (officially Argentine Republic).

RAAF *abbrev. for* Royal Australian Air Force.

Rabat (rəˈbɑːt) *n* the capital of Morocco, in the northwest on the Atlantic coast, served by the port of Salé: became a military centre in the 12th century and a Corsair republic in the 17th century. Pop. (with Salé): 1 386 000 (1994 est.).

rabato *or* **rebato** (rəˈbɑːtəʊ) *n, pl* **-tos.** a wired or starched collar, often of intricate lace, that stood up at the back and sides: worn in the 17th century. **[**C16: from French *rabat* collar, with the ending *-o* added as if the word were from Italian**]**

Rabaul (rɑːˈbaʊl) *n* a port in Papua New Guinea, on NE New Britain Island, in the Bismarck Archipelago: capital of the Territory of New Guinea until 1941; almost surrounded by volcanoes. Pop.: 17 022 (1990).

Rabbath Ammon (ˈræbəθ ˈæmən) *n Old Testament.* the ancient royal city of the Ammonites, on the site of modern Amman.

rabbet (ˈræbɪt) *or* **rebate** *n* **1** a recess, groove, or step, usually of rectangular section, cut into a surface or along the edge of a piece of timber to receive a mating piece. **2** a joint made between two pieces of timber using a rabbet. ◆ *vb* (*tr*) **3** to cut or form a rabbet in (timber). **4** to join (pieces of timber) using a rabbet. **[**C15: from Old French *rabattre* to beat down**]**

rabbi (ˈræbaɪ) *n, pl* **-bis.** *Judaism.* **1** (in Orthodox Judaism) a man qualified in accordance with traditional religious law to expound, teach, and rule in accordance with this law. **2** the religious leader of a congregation; the minister of a synagogue. **3 the Rabbis.** the early Jewish scholars whose teachings are recorded in the Talmud. ◆ See also **Rav.** **[**Hebrew, from *rabh* master + *-ī* my**]**

rabbinate (ˈræbɪnɪt) *n* **1** the position, function, or tenure of office of a rabbi. **2** rabbis collectively.

rabbinic (rəˈbɪnɪk) *or* **rabbinical** *adj* of or relating to the rabbis, their teachings, writings, views, language, etc. ▸ **rab'binically** *adv*

Rabbinic (rəˈbɪnɪk) *or* **Rabbinical Hebrew** *n* the form of the Hebrew language used by the rabbis of the Middle Ages.

rabbinics (rəˈbɪnɪks) *n* (*functioning as sing*) the study of rabbinic literature of the post-Talmudic period.

rabbinism (ˈræbɪˌnɪzəm) *n* the teachings and traditions of the rabbis of the Talmudic period. ▸ **'rabbinist** *n, adj* ▸ **ˌrabbi'nistic** *adj*

rabbit (ˈræbɪt) *n, pl* **-bits** *or* **-bit. 1** any of various common gregarious burrowing leporid mammals, esp. *Oryctolagus cuniculus* of Europe and North Africa and the cottontail of America. They are closely related and similar to hares but are smaller and have shorter ears. **2** the fur of such an animal. **3** *Brit. informal.* a novice or poor performer at a game or sport. ◆ *vb* **4** (*intr;* often foll. by *on* or *away*) *Brit. informal.* to talk inconsequentially; chatter. **[**C14: perhaps from Walloon *robett,* diminutive of Flemish *robbe* rabbit, of obscure origin: C20 in sense 4, from rhyming slang *rabbit and pork* talk**]**

rabbiter (ˈræbɪtə) *n Chiefly Austral.* a person who traps and sells rabbits.

rabbit fever *n Pathol.* another name for **tularaemia.**

rabbitfish (ˈræbɪtˌfɪʃ) *n, pl* **-fish** *or* **-fishes. 1** a large chimaera, *Chimaera monstrosa,* common in European seas, with separate caudal and anal fins and a long whiplike tail. **2** any of the spiny-finned tropical marine fishes of the family *Siganidae* of Indo-Pacific waters. They have a rabbit-like snout and spines on the pelvic or ventral fins.

rabbiting (ˈræbɪtɪŋ) *n* the activity of hunting rabbits.

rabbitoh *or* **rabbito** (ˈræbɪtˌəʊ) *n Austral. informal.* (formerly) an itinerant seller of rabbits for eating. **[**C20: from such a seller's cry**]**

rabbit-proof fence *n* **a** a fence through which rabbits are unable to pass. **b** *Austral. informal.* a boundary between certain Australian states, marked by such a fence.

rabbit punch *n* a sharp blow to the back of the neck that can cause loss of consciousness or even death. Austral. name: **rabbit killer.**

rabbitry (ˈræbɪtrɪ) *n, pl* **-ries. 1** a place where tame rabbits are kept and bred. **2** the rabbits kept in such a place.

rabble[1] (ˈræbᵊl) *n* **1** a disorderly crowd; mob. **2 the.** *Contemptuous.* the common people. **[**C14 (in the sense: a pack of animals): of uncertain origin; perhaps related to Middle Dutch *rabbelen* to chatter, rattle**]**

rabble[2] (ˈræbᵊl) *n* **1** Also called: **'rabbler.** an iron tool or mechanical device for stirring, mixing, or skimming a molten charge in a roasting furnace. ◆ *vb* **2** (*tr*) to stir, mix, or skim (the molten charge) in a roasting furnace. **[**C17: from French *râble,* from Latin *rutābulum* rake for a furnace, from *ruere* to rake, dig up**]**

rabble-rouser *n* a person who manipulates the passions of the mob; demagogue. ▸ **'rabble-ˌrousing** *adj, n*

Rabelais (ˈræbəˌleɪ; *French* rablɛ) *n* **François** (frɑ̃swa). ?1494–1553, French writer. His written works, esp. *Gargantua and Pantagruel* (1534), contain a lively mixture of earthy wit, common sense, and satire.

Rabelaisian (ˌræbəˈleɪzɪən, -ʒən) *adj* **1** of, relating to, or resembling the work of Rabelais, esp. by broad, often bawdy humour and sharp satire. ◆ *n* **2** a student or admirer of Rabelais. ▸ **ˌRabe'laisianism** *n*

rabi (ˈrʌbɪ) *n* (in Pakistan, India, etc.) a crop that is harvested at the end of winter. Compare **kharif.** **[**Urdu: spring crop, from Arabic *rabī'* spring**]**

Rabi (ˈrɑːbɪ) *n* **Isidor Isaac.** 1898–1988, U.S. physicist, born in Austria, who devised the atomic and molecular beam resonance method of observing atomic spectra. Nobel prize for physics 1944.

Rabia[1] (rəˈbɪə) *n* either the third or the fourth month of the Muslim year, known as **Rabia I** and **Rabia II** respectively; the Muslim spring.

Rabia[2] *or* **Rabiah** (ˈrɑːbɪə) *n* full name *Rabia al-Adawiyyah.* c. 713–801 A.D., Islamic saint, mystic, and religious leader; her teachings inspired the Sufi movement.

rabid (ˈræbɪd, ˈreɪ-) *adj* **1** relating to or having rabies. **2** zealous; fanatical; violent; raging. **[**C17: from Latin *rabidus* frenzied, mad, from *rabere* to be mad**]** ▸ **rabidity** (rəˈbɪdɪtɪ) *or* **'rabidness** *n* ▸ **'rabidly** *adv*

rabies (ˈreɪbiːz) *n Pathol.* an acute infectious viral disease of the nervous system transmitted by the saliva of infected animals, esp. dogs. It is characterized by excessive salivation, aversion to water, convulsions, and paralysis. Also called: **hydrophobia, lyssa.** **[**C17: from Latin: madness, from *rabere* to rave**]** ▸ **rabic** (r!1bɪk) *or* **rabietic** (ˌreɪbɪˈetɪk) *adj*

Rabin (rəˈbiːn) *n* **Yitzhak.** 1922–95, Israeli statesman; prime minister of Israel (1974–77; 1992–95); assassinated.

RAC *abbrev. for:* **1** Royal Automobile Club. **2** Royal Armoured Corps.

raccoon *or* **racoon** (rəˈkuːn) *n, pl* **-coons** *or* **-coon. 1** any omnivorous mammal of the genus *Procyon,* esp. *P. lotor* (**North American raccoon**), inhabiting forests of North and Central America and the Caribbean: family *Procyonidae,* order *Carnivora* (carnivores). Raccoons have a pointed muzzle, long tail, and greyish-black fur with black bands around the tail and across the face. **2** the fur of the North American raccoon. **[**C17: from Algonquian *ärähkun,* from *ärähkuněm* he scratches with his hands**]**

raccoon dog *n* **1** a canine mammal, *Nyctereutes procyonoides,* inhabiting woods and forests near rivers in E Asia. It has long yellowish-brown black-tipped hair and facial markings resembling those of a raccoon. **2** Also called: **coonhound.** an American breed of dog having a short smooth black coat with tan markings, bred to hunt raccoons.

race[1] (reɪs) *n* **1** a contest of speed, as in running, swimming, driving, riding, etc. **2** any competition or rivalry: *the race for the White House.* **3** rapid or constant onward movement: *the race of time.* **4** a rapid current of water, esp. one through a narrow channel that has a tidal range greater at one end than the other. **5** a channel of a stream, esp. one for conducting water to or from a water wheel or other device for utilizing its energy: *a mill race.* **6a** a channel or groove that contains ball bearings or roller bearings or that restrains a sliding component. **6b** the inner or outer cylindrical ring in a ball bearing or roller bearing. **7** *Austral. and N.Z.* a narrow passage or enclosure in a sheep yard through which sheep pass individually, as to a sheep dip. **8** *Austral.* a wire tunnel through which footballers pass from the changing room onto a football field. **9** *N.Z.* a line of containers coupled together, used in mining to transport coal. **10** another name for **slipstream** (sense 1). **11** *Archaic.* the span or course of life. **12 not in the race.** *Austral. informal.* given or having no chance. ◆ *vb* **13** to engage in a contest of speed with (another). **14** to engage (oneself or one's representative) in a race, esp. as a profession or pastime: *to race pigeons.* **15** to move or go as fast as possible. **16** to run (an engine, shaft, propeller, etc.) or (of an engine, shaft, propeller, etc.) to run at high speed, esp. after reduction of the load or resistance. ◆ See also **race off, races.** **[**C13: from Old Norse *rās* running; related to Old English *rǣs* attack**]**

race[2] (reɪs) *n* **1** a group of people of common ancestry, distinguished from others by physical characteristics, such as hair type, colour of eyes and skin, stature, etc. Principal races are Caucasoid, Mongoloid, and Negroid. **2 the human race.** human beings collectively. **3** a group of animals or plants having common characteristics that distinguish them from other members of the same species, usually forming a geographically isolated group; subspecies. **4** a group of people sharing the same interests, characteristics, etc.: *the race of authors.* **[**C16: from French, from Italian *razza,* of uncertain origin**]**

race[3] (reɪs) *n* a ginger root. **[**C15: from Old French *rais,* from Latin *rādīx* a root**]**

Race (reɪs) *n* **Cape.** a cape at the SE extremity of Newfoundland, Canada.

racecard ('reɪs,kɑːd) *n* a card or booklet at a race meeting with the times of the races, names of the runners, etc., printed on it.

racecourse ('reɪs,kɔːs) *n* a long broad track, usually of grass, enclosed between rails, and with starting and finishing points marked upon it, over which horses are raced. Also called (esp. U.S. and Canada): **racetrack.**

racegoer ('reɪs,gəʊə) *n* one who attends a race meeting, esp. a habitual frequenter of race meetings.

racehorse ('reɪs,hɔːs) *n* a horse specially bred for racing.

raceme (rə'siːm) *n* an inflorescence in which the flowers are borne along the main stem, with the oldest flowers at the base. It can be simple, as in the foxglove, or compound (see **panicle**). **[C18:** from Latin *racēmus* bunch of grapes**]**

race meeting *n* a prearranged fixture for racing horses (or sometimes greyhounds) over a set course at set times.

racemic (rə'siːmɪk, -'sem-) *adj Chem.* of, concerned with, or being a mixture of dextrorotatory and laevorotatory isomers in such proportions that the mixture has no optical activity. **[C19:** from RACEME (as in *racemic acid*) + -IC**]** ▸ **racemism** ('ræsɪ,mɪzəm, rə'siːmɪzəm) *n*

racemic acid *n* the optically inactive form of tartaric acid that is sometimes found in grape juice.

racemize *or* **racemise** ('ræsɪ,maɪz) *vb* to change or cause to change into a racemic mixture. ▸ **,racemi'zation** *or* **,racemi'sation** *n*

racemose ('ræsɪ,məʊs, -,məʊz) *or* **racemous** *adj* being or resembling a raceme. **[C17:** from Latin *racēmōsus* clustering**]** ▸ **'race,mosely** *or* **'racemously** *adv*

race off *vb (tr, adv) Austral. informal.* to entice (a person) away with a view to seduction.

racer ('reɪsə) *n* **1** a person, animal, or machine that races. **2** a turntable used to traverse a heavy gun. **3** any of several long slender nonvenomous North American snakes of the colubrid genus *Coluber* and related genera, such as *C. lateralis* (**striped racer**).

race relations *n* **1** (*functioning as pl*) the relations between members of two or more human races, esp. within a single community. **2** (*functioning as sing*) the branch of sociology concerned with such relations.

race riot *n* a riot among members of different races in the same community.

races ('reɪsɪz) *pl n* **the.** a series of contests of speed between horses (or sometimes greyhounds) over a set course at prearranged times; a race meeting.

racetrack ('reɪs,træk) *n* **1** a circuit or course, esp. an oval one, used for motor racing, speedway, etc. **2** the usual U.S. and Canadian word for a **racecourse.**

raceway ('reɪs,weɪ) *n* **1** another word for **race**[1] (sense 5). **2** a racetrack, esp. one for banger racing. **3** another word (esp. U.S.) for **race**[1] (sense 6).

Rachel *n* **1** ('reɪtʃəl). *Old Testament.* the second and best-loved wife of Jacob; mother of Joseph and Benjamin (Genesis 29–35). **2** (*French* raʃel). original name *Elisa Félix.* 1820–58, French tragic actress, famous for her roles in the plays of Racine and Corneille.

rachiotomy (,reɪkɪ'ɒtəmɪ) *n* another name for **laminectomy.**

rachis *or* **rhachis** ('reɪkɪs) *n, pl* **rachises, rhachises** *or* **rachides, rhachides** ('rækɪ,diːz,'reɪ-). **1** *Botany.* the main axis or stem of an inflorescence or compound leaf. **2** *Ornithol.* the shaft of a feather, esp. the part that carries the barbs. **3** another name for **vertebral column. [C17:** via New Latin from Greek *rhakhis* ridge**]** ▸ **rachial, rhachial** ('reɪkɪəl) *or* **rachidial, rhachidial** (rə'kɪdɪəl) *adj*

rachitis (rə'kaɪtɪs) *n Pathol.* another name for **rickets. [C18:** New Latin, from Greek *rhakitis;* see RACHIS**]** ▸ **rachitic** (rə'kɪtɪk) *adj*

Rachmaninoff *or* **Rachmaninov** (ræk'mænɪ,nɒf; *Russian* rax'maninəf) *n* **Sergei Vassilievich** (sɪr'gjej va'siljɪvitʃ). 1873–1943, Russian piano virtuoso and composer.

Rachmanism ('rækmə,nɪzəm) *n* extortion or exploitation by a landlord of tenants of dilapidated or slum property, esp. when involving intimidation or use of racial fears to drive out sitting tenants whose rent is fixed at a low rate. **[C20:** after Perec *Rachman* (1920–62), British property-owner born in Poland**]**

racial ('reɪʃəl) *adj* **1** denoting or relating to the division of the human species into races on grounds of physical characteristics. **2** characteristic of any such group. **3** relating to or arising from differences between the races: *racial harmony.* **4** of or relating to a subspecies. ▸ **'racially** *adv*

racial unconscious *n Psychol.* another term for **collective unconscious.**

Racine (*French* rasin) *n* **Jean Baptiste** (ʒɑ̃ batist). 1639–99, French tragic poet and dramatist. His plays include *Andromaque* (1667), *Bérénice* (1670), and *Phèdre* (1677).

racing ('reɪsɪŋ) *adj* **1** denoting or associated with horse races: *the racing fraternity; a racing man.* ◆ *n* **2** the practice of engaging horses (or sometimes greyhounds) in contests of speed.

racism ('reɪsɪzəm) *or* **racialism** ('reɪʃə,lɪzəm) *n* **1** the belief that races have distinctive cultural characteristics determined by hereditary factors and that this endows some races with an intrinsic superiority over others. **2** abusive or aggressive behaviour towards members of another race on the basis of such a belief. ▸ **'racist** *or* **'racialist** *n, adj*

rack[1] (ræk) *n* **1** a framework for holding, carrying, or displaying a specific load or object: *a plate rack; a hat rack; a hay rack; a luggage rack.* **2** a toothed bar designed to engage a pinion to form a mechanism that will interconvert rotary and rectilinear motions. **3** a framework fixed to an aircraft for carrying bombs, rockets, etc. **4** (usually preceded by *the*) an instrument of torture that stretched the body of the victim. **5** a cause or state of mental or bodily stress, suffering, etc.; anguish; torment (esp. in the phrase **on the rack**). **6** *U.S. and Canadian.* (in pool, snooker, etc.) **6a** the triangular frame used to arrange the balls for the opening shot. **6b** the balls so grouped. Brit. equivalent: **frame.** ◆ *vb (tr)* **7** to torture on the rack. **8** Also: **wrack.** to cause great stress or suffering to: *guilt racked his conscience.* **9** Also: **wrack.** to strain or shake (something) violently, as by great physical force: *the storm racked the town.* **10** to place or arrange in or on a rack: *to rack bottles of wine.* **11** to move (parts of machinery or a mechanism) using a toothed rack. **12** to raise (rents) exorbitantly; rack-rent. **13** **rack one's brains.** to strain in mental effort, esp. to remember something or to find the solution to a problem. ◆ See also **rack up. [C14** *rekke,* probably from Middle Dutch *rec* framework; related to Old High German *recchen* to stretch, Old Norse *rekja* to spread out**]** ▸ **'racker** *n*

USAGE See at **wrack**[1].

rack[2] (ræk) *n* destruction; wreck (obsolete except in the phrase **go to rack and ruin**). **[C16:** variant of WRACK[1]**]**

rack[3] (ræk) *n* another word for **single-foot,** a gait of the horse. **[C16:** perhaps based on ROCK[2]**]**

rack[4] (ræk) *n* **1** a group of broken clouds moving in the wind. ◆ *vb* **2** *(intr)* (of clouds) to be blown along by the wind. **[**Old English *wrǣc* what is driven; related to Gothic *wraks* persecutor, Swedish *vrak* wreckage**]**

rack[5] (ræk) *vb (tr)* **1** to clear (wine, beer, etc.) as by siphoning it off from the dregs. **2** to fill a container with (beer, wine, etc.). **[C15:** from Old Provençal *arraca,* from *raca* dregs of grapes after pressing**]**

rack[6] (ræk) *n* the neck or rib section of mutton, pork, or veal. **[**Old English *hrace;* related to Old High German *rahho,* Danish *harke,* Swedish *harkla* to clear one's throat**]**

rack-and-pinion *n* **1** a device for converting rotary into linear motion and vice versa, in which a gearwheel (the pinion) engages with a flat toothed bar (the rack). ◆ *adj* **2** (of a type of steering gear in motor vehicles) having a track rod with a rack along part of its length that engages with a pinion attached to the steering column.

racket[1] ('rækɪt) *n* **1** a noisy disturbance or loud commotion; clamour; din. **2** gay or excited revelry, dissipation, etc. **3** an illegal enterprise carried on for profit, such as extortion, fraud, prostitution, drug peddling, etc. **4** *Slang.* a business or occupation: *what's your racket?* **5** *Music.* **5a** a medieval woodwind instrument of deep bass pitch. **5b** a reed stop on an organ of deep bass pitch. ◆ *vb* **6** *(intr; often foll. by about) Now rare.* to go about gaily or noisily, in search of pleasure, excitement, etc. **[C16:** probably of imitative origin; compare RATTLE[1]**]**

racket[2] *or* **racquet** ('rækɪt) *n* **1** a bat consisting of an open network of nylon or other strings stretched in an oval frame with a handle, used to strike the ball in tennis, badminton, etc. **2** a snowshoe shaped like a tennis racket. ◆ *vb* **3** *(tr)* to strike (a ball, shuttlecock, etc.) with a racket. ◆ See also **rackets. [C16:** from French *raquette,* from Arabic *rāhat* palm of the hand**]**

racketeer (,rækɪ'tɪə) *n* **1** a person engaged in illegal enterprises for profit. ◆ *vb* **2** *(intr)* to operate a racket. ▸ **,racket'eering** *n*

racket press *n* a device consisting of a frame closed by a spring mechanism, for keeping taut the strings of a tennis racket, squash racket, etc.

rackets ('rækɪts) *n (functioning as sing)* **a** a game similar to squash played in a large four-walled court by two or four players using rackets and a small hard ball. **b** (*as modifier*): *a rackets court; a rackets championship.*

racket-tail *n* any of several birds with a racket-shaped tail, such as certain hummingbirds and kingfishers.

rackety ('rækɪtɪ) *adj* **1** noisy, rowdy, or boisterous. **2** socially lively and, sometimes, mildly dissolute: *a rackety life.*

Rackham ('rækəm) *n* **Arthur.** 1867–1939, English artist, noted for his book illustrations, esp. of fairy tales.

rack off *vb (intr, adv; usually imperative) Austral. slang.* to go away; depart.

rack railway *n* a steep mountain railway having a middle rail fitted with a rack that engages a pinion on the locomotive to provide traction. Also called: **cog railway.**

rack-rent *n* **1** a high rent that annually equals or nearly equals the value of the property upon which it is charged. **2** any extortionate rent. ◆ *vb* **3** to charge an extortionate rent for (property, land, etc.). **[C17:** from RACK[1] (sense 12) + RENT[1]**]** ▸ **'rack-,renter** *n*

rack saw *n Building trades.* a wide-toothed saw.

rack up *vb (tr, adv)* **1** to accumulate (points). **2** Also: **rack down.** to adjust the vertical alignment of (the picture from a film projector or telecine machine) so that the upper or lower edges of the frame do not show.

racon ('reɪkɒn) *n* another name for **radar beacon. [C20:** from *ra(dar)* + *(bea)con***]**

raconteur (,rækɒn'tɜː) *n* a person skilled in telling stories. **[C19:** French, from *raconter* to tell**]**

racoon (rə'kuːn) *n, pl* **-coons** *or* **-coon.** a variant spelling of **raccoon.**

racquet ('rækɪt) *n* a variant spelling of **racket**[2].

racy ('reɪsɪ) *adj* **racier, raciest. 1** (of a person's manner, literary style, etc.) having a distinctively lively and spirited quality; fresh. **2** having a characteristic or distinctive flavour: *a racy wine.* **3** suggestive; slightly indecent; risqué: *a racy comedy.* ▸ **'racily** *adv* ▸ **'raciness** *n*

rad[1] (ræd) *n* a former unit of absorbed ionizing radiation dose equivalent to an energy absorption per unit mass of 0.01 joule per kilogram of irradiated material. 1 rad is equivalent to 0.01 gray. **[C20:** shortened from RADIATION**]**

rad[2] *symbol for* radian.

rad. *abbrev. for:* **1** radical. **2** radius. **3** radix. **4** radiator.

RADA ('rɑːdə) *n* (in Britain) *acronym for* Royal Academy of Dramatic Art.

radar ('reɪdɑː) *n* **1** a method for detecting the position and velocity of a distant object, such as an aircraft. A narrow beam of extremely high-frequency radio pulses is transmitted and reflected by the object back to the transmitter, the signal being displayed on a radarscope. The direction of the reflected beam and the time between transmission and reception of a pulse determine the position of the object. Former name: **radiolocation. 2** the equipment used in such detection. **[C20** *ra(dio) d(etecting) a(nd) r(anging)***]**

radar astronomy *n* the use of radar to map the surfaces of the planets, their satellites, and other bodies.

radar beacon *n* a device for transmitting a coded radar signal in response to a signal from an aircraft or ship. The coded signal is then used by the navigator to determine his position. Also called: **racon.**

radarscope ('reɪdɑːˌskəʊp) *n* a cathode-ray oscilloscope on which radar signals can be viewed. In a **plan position indicator,** the target is represented by a blip on a radial line that rotates around a point, representing the antenna.

radar trap *n* See **speed trap.**

Radcliffe ('rædklɪf) *n* **Ann.** 1764–1823, British novelist, noted for her Gothic romances *The Mysteries of Udolpho* (1794) and *The Italian* (1797).

raddle[1] ('rædᵊl) *vb* (*tr*) another word for **interweave.** [C17: from obsolete n sense of *raddle* meaning a rod, wattle, or lath, from Old French *redalle* a stick, pole; of obscure origin]

raddle[2] ('rædᵊl) *vb* **1** (*tr*) *Chiefly Brit.* to paint (the face) with rouge. ◆ *n, vb* **2** another word for **ruddle.** [C16: variant of RUDDLE]

raddled ('rædᵊld) *adj* (esp. of a person) unkempt or run-down in appearance. [C17: from RADDLE[2]]

Radek (*Russian* radjɪk) *n* **Karl** (**Bernhardovich**), original name *Karl Sobelsohn.* 1885–?1939, Soviet politician and journalist who was secretary of Comintern (1920–24). He was accused of treason (1937) and probably died in a labour camp.

Radetzky (*German* ra'dɛtski) *n* Count **Joseph** ('joːzɛf). 1766–1858, Austrian field marshal: served in the war against Sardinia (1848–9), winning brilliant victories at Custozza (1848) and Novara (1849): governor of Lombardy-Venetia in N Italy (1849-57).

radial ('reɪdɪəl) *adj* **1** (of lines, bars, beams of light, etc.) emanating from a common central point; arranged like the radii of a circle. **2** of, like, or relating to a radius or ray. **3** spreading out or developing uniformly on all sides. **4** of or relating to the arms of a starfish or similar radiating structures. **5** *Anatomy.* of or relating to the radius or forearm. **6** *Astronomy.* (of velocity) in a direction along the line of sight of a celestial object and measured by means of the red shift (or blue shift) of the spectral lines of the object. Compare **tangential** (sense 2). ◆ *n* **7** a radial part or section. **8** *Zoology.* **8a** any of the basal fin rays of most bony fishes. **8b** a radial or radiating structure, such as any of the ossicles supporting the oral disc of a sea star. **9** short for **radial tyre** or **radial drilling machine.** [C16: from Medieval Latin *radiālis,* from RADIUS] ▸ **'radially** *adv*

radial drilling machine *n* a machine in which the drilling head is mounted to slide along a radial arm which can be rotated, raised, or lowered on a vertical mast to adjust the position of the drill above the workpiece. Often shortened to **radial.**

radial engine *n* an internal-combustion engine having a number of cylinders arranged about a central crankcase.

radial keratotomy (ˌkɛrə'tɒtəmɪ) *n* an operation designed to improve shortsightedness in which a number of cuts are made around the cornea to change the shape of it. [C20: from KERATO- + -TOMY]

radial-ply *adj* (of a motor tyre) having the fabric cords in the outer casing running radially to enable the sidewalls to be flexible. Compare **cross-ply.**

radial symmetry *n* a type of structure of an organism or part of an organism in which a vertical cut through the axis in any of two or more planes produces two halves that are mirror images of each other. Compare **bilateral symmetry.**

radial tyre *n* a motor-vehicle tyre having a radial-ply casing. Often shortened to **radial.**

radial velocity *n* the component of the velocity of an object, esp. a celestial body, directed along a line from the observer to the object.

radian ('reɪdɪən) *n* an SI unit of plane angle; the angle between two radii of a circle that cut off on the circumference an arc equal in length to the radius. 1 radian is equivalent to 57.296 degrees and $\pi/2$ radians equals a right angle. Symbol: **rad** [C19: from RADIUS]

radiance ('reɪdɪəns) *or* **radiancy** *n, pl* **-ances** *or* **-ancies. 1** the quality or state of being radiant. **2** a measure of the amount of electromagnetic radiation leaving or arriving at a point on a surface. It is the radiant intensity in a given direction of a small element of surface area divided by the orthogonal projection of this area onto a plane at right angles to the direction. Symbol: L_e

radiant ('reɪdɪənt) *adj* **1** sending out rays of light; bright; shining. **2** characterized by health, intense joy, happiness, etc.: *a radiant countenance.* **3** emitted or propagated by or as radiation; radiated: *radiant heat.* **4** sending out heat by radiation: *a radiant heater.* **5** *Physics.* (of a physical quantity in photometry) evaluated by absolute energy measurements: *radiant flux; radiant efficiency.* Compare **luminous.** ◆ *n* **6** a point or object that emits radiation, esp. the part of a heater that gives out heat. **7** *Astronomy.* the point in space from which a meteor shower appears to emanate. [C15: from Latin *radiāre* to shine, from *radius* ray of light, RADIUS] ▸ **'radiantly** *adv*

radiant efficiency *n* the ratio of the power emitted by a source of radiation to the power consumed by it. Symbol: η_e

radiant energy *n* energy that is emitted or propagated in the form of particles or electromagnetic radiation. It is measured in joules. Symbol: Q_e

radiant exitance *n* the ability of a surface to emit radiation expressed as the radiant flux emitted per unit area at a specified point on the surface. Symbol: M_e

radiant flux *n* the rate of flow of energy as radiation. It is measured in watts. Symbol: Φ_e

radiant heat *n* heat transferred in the form of electromagnetic radiation rather than by conduction or convection; infrared radiation.

radiant heating *n* a system of heating a building by radiant heat emitted from panels containing electrical conductors, hot water, etc.

radiant intensity *n* a measure of the amount of radiation emitted from a point expressed as the radiant flux per unit solid angle leaving this source. Symbol: I_e

radiata pine (ˌreɪdɪ'ɑːtə) *n N.Z.* a pine tree, *Pinus radiata,* grown in Australia and New Zealand to produce building timber. Often shortened to **radiata.** [from New Latin]

radiate *vb* ('reɪdɪˌeɪt). **1** Also: **eradiate.** to emit (heat, light, or some other form of radiation) or (of heat, light, etc.) to be emitted as radiation. **2** (*intr*) (of lines, beams, etc.) to spread out from a centre or be arranged in a radial pattern. **3** (*tr*) (of a person) to show (happiness, health, etc.) to a great degree. ◆ *adj* ('reɪdɪɪt, -ˌeɪt). **4** having rays; radiating. **5** (of a capitulum) consisting of ray flowers. **6** (of animals or their parts) showing radial symmetry. **7** adorned or decorated with rays: *a radiate head on a coin.* [C17: from Latin *radiāre* to emit rays]

radiation (ˌreɪdɪ'eɪʃən) *n* **1** *Physics.* **1a** the emission or transfer of radiant energy as particles, electromagnetic waves, sound, etc. **1b** the particles, etc., emitted, esp. the particles and gamma rays emitted in nuclear decay. **2** Also called: **radiation therapy.** *Med.* treatment using a radioactive substance. **3** *Anatomy.* a group of nerve fibres that diverge from their common source. **4** See **adaptive radiation. 5** the act, state, or process of radiating or being radiated. **6** *Surveying.* the fixing of points around a central plane table by using an alidade and measuring tape. ▸ ˌ**radi'ational** *adj*

radiation belt *n* a region in the magnetosphere of a planet in which charged particles are trapped by the planet's magnetic field, an example being the earth's Van Allen belts.

radiation pattern *n* the graphic representation of the strength and direction of electromagnetic radiation in the vicinity of a transmitting aerial. Also called: **antenna pattern.**

radiation pyrometer *n* See **pyrometer.**

radiation resistance *n* the resistive component of the impedance of a radio transmitting aerial that arises from the radiation of power.

radiation sickness *n Pathol.* illness caused by overexposure of the body or a part of the body to ionizing radiations from radioactive material or X-rays. It is characterized by vomiting, diarrhoea, and in severe cases by sterility and cancer.

radiative ('reɪdɪətɪv) *or* **radiatory** ('reɪdɪətərɪ, -trɪ) *adj Physics.* emitting or causing the emission of radiation: *a radiative collision.*

radiator ('reɪdɪˌeɪtə) *n* **1** a device for heating a room, building, etc., consisting of a series of pipes through which hot water or steam passes. **2** a device for cooling an internal-combustion engine, consisting of thin-walled tubes through which water passes. Heat is transferred from the water through the walls of the tubes to the airstream, which is created either by the motion of the vehicle or by a fan. **3** *Austral. and N.Z.* an electric fire. **4** *Electronics.* the part of an aerial or transmission line that radiates electromagnetic waves. **5** an electric space heater.

radical ('rædɪkᵊl) *adj* **1** of, relating to, or characteristic of the basic or inherent constitution of a person or thing; fundamental: *a radical fault.* **2** concerned with or tending to concentrate on fundamental aspects of a matter; searching or thoroughgoing: *radical thought; a radical re-examination.* **3** favouring or tending to produce extreme or fundamental changes in political, economic, or social conditions, institutions, habits of mind, etc.: *a radical party.* **4** *Med.* (of treatment) aimed at removing the source of a disease: *radical surgery.* **5** *Slang, chiefly U.S.* very good; excellent. **6** of, relating to, or arising from the root or the base of the stem of a plant: *radical leaves.* **7** *Maths.* of, relating to, or containing roots of numbers or quantities. **8** *Linguistics.* of or relating to the root of a word. ◆ *n* **9** a person who favours extreme or fundamental change in existing institutions or in political, social, or economic conditions. **10** *Maths.* a root of a number or quantity, such as $\sqrt[3]{5}$, $\sqrt{x}$. **11** *Chem.* **11a** short for **free radical. 11b** another name for **group** (sense 10). **12** *Linguistics.* another word for **root**[1] (sense 9). **13** (in logographic writing systems such as that used for Chinese) a character conveying lexical meaning. [C14: from Late Latin *rādīcālis* having roots, from Latin *rādix* a root] ▸ **'radicalness** *n*

radical axis *n* a line from any point of which tangents to two given circles are of equal length. It is the line joining the points of intersection of two circles.

radicalism ('rædɪkəˌlɪzəm) *n* **1** the principles, desires, or practices of political radicals. **2** a radical movement, esp. in politics. **3** the state or nature of being radical, esp. in politics. ▸ ˌ**radical'istic** *adj* ▸ ˌ**radical'istically** *adv*

radically ('rædɪkəlɪ) *adv* thoroughly; completely; fundamentally: *to alter radically.*

radical sign *n* the symbol √ placed before a number or quantity to indicate the extraction of a root, esp. a square root. The value of a higher root is indicated by a raised digit in front of the symbol, as in $\sqrt[3]{}$.

radicand ('rædɪˌkænd, ˌrædɪ'kænd) *n* a number or quantity from which a root is to be extracted, usually preceded by a radical sign: 3 *is the radicand of* $\sqrt{3}$. [C20: from Latin *rādīcandum,* literally: that which is to be rooted, from *rādīcāre* to take root, from *rādīx* root]

radicchio (ræ'diːkɪəʊ) *n, pl* **chios.** an Italian variety of chicory, having purple leaves streaked with white that are eaten raw in salads.

radicel ('rædɪˌsɛl) *n* a very small root; radicle. [C19: from New Latin *radicella* a little root, from Latin *rādix* root]

radices ('reɪdɪˌsiːz) *n* a plural of **radix.**

radicle ('rædɪkᵊl) *n* **1** *Botany.* **1a** part of the embryo of seed-bearing plants that develops into the main root. **1b** a very small root or rootlike part. **2** *Anatomy.* any bodily structure resembling a rootlet, esp. one of the smallest branches of a vein or nerve. **3** *Chem.* a variant spelling of **radical** (sense 11). [C18: from Latin *rādīcula* a little root, from *rādīx* root]

Radiguet (*French* radigɛ) *n* **Raymond** (rɛmɔ̃). 1903–23, French novelist; the author of *The Devil in the Flesh* (1923) and *Count d'Orgel* (1924).

radii ('reɪdɪˌaɪ) *n* a plural of **radius.**

radio ('reɪdɪəʊ) *n, pl* **-os. 1** the use of electromagnetic waves, lying in the radio-frequency range, for broadcasting, two-way communications, etc. **2** an electronic device designed to receive, demodulate, and amplify radio signals from sound broadcasting stations, etc. **3** a similar device permitting both transmission and reception of radio signals for two-way communications. **4** the broadcasting, content, etc., of sound radio programmes: *he thinks radio is poor these days.* **5a** the occupation or profession concerned with any aspect of the broadcasting of sound radio programmes: *he's in radio.* **5b** (*modifier*) relating to, produced for, or transmitted by sound radio: *radio drama.* **6** short for **radiotelegraph, radiotelegraphy,** or **radiotelephone. 7** (*modifier*) **7a** of, relating to, employed in, or sent by radio signals: *a radio station.* **7b** of, concerned with, using, or operated by radio frequencies: *radio spectrum.* **8** (*modifier*) (of a motor vehicle) equipped with a radio for communication: *radio car.* ◆ *vb* **-os, -oing, -oed. 9** to transmit (a message) to (a person, radio station, etc.) by means of radio waves. ◆ Also called (esp. Brit.): **wireless.** [C20: short for *radiotelegraphy*]

radio- *combining form.* **1** denoting radio, broadcasting, or radio frequency: *radiogram.* **2** indicating radioactivity or radiation: *radiochemistry; radiolucent.* **3** indicating a radioactive isotope or substance: *radioactinium; radiothorium; radioelement.* [from French, from Latin *radius* ray; see RADIUS]

radioactivate (ˌreɪdɪəʊˈæktɪˌveɪt) *vb* (*tr*) to make radioactive. ► **ˌradioˌactiˈvation** *n*

radioactive (ˌreɪdɪəʊˈæktɪv) *adj* exhibiting, using, or concerned with radioactivity. ► **ˌradioˈactively** *adv*

radioactive dating *n* another term for **radiometric dating.**

radioactive decay *n* disintegration of a nucleus that occurs spontaneously or as a result of electron capture. One or more different nuclei are formed and usually particles and gamma rays are emitted. Sometimes shortened to **decay.** Also called: **disintegration.**

radioactive series *n Physics.* a series of nuclides each of which undergoes radioactive decay into the next member of the series, ending with a stable element, usually lead. See **uranium series, neptunium series, thorium series, actinium series.**

radioactive tracer *n Med.* See **tracer** (sense 3).

radioactive waste *n* any waste material containing radionuclides. Also called: **nuclear waste.**

radioactivity (ˌreɪdɪəʊækˈtɪvɪtɪ) *n* the spontaneous emission of radiation from atomic nuclei. The radiation can consist of alpha, beta, and gamma radiation.

radio astronomy *n* a branch of astronomy in which a radio telescope is used to detect and analyse radio signals received on earth from radio sources in space.

radioautograph (ˌreɪdɪəʊˈɔːtəˌgrɑːf, -ˌgræf) *n* another name for **autoradiograph.**

radio beacon *n* a fixed radio transmitting station that broadcasts a characteristic signal by means of which a vessel or aircraft can determine its bearing or position. Sometimes shortened to **beacon.**

radio beam *n* a narrow beam of radio signals transmitted by a radio or radar beacon, radio telescope, or some other directional aerial, used for communications, navigation, etc. Sometimes shortened to **beam.**

radiobiology (ˌreɪdɪəʊbaɪˈɒlədʒɪ) *n* the branch of biology concerned with the effects of radiation on living organisms and the study of biological processes using radioactive substances as tracers. ► **radiobiological** (ˌreɪdɪəʊˌbaɪəˈlɒdʒɪk^{ə}l) *adj* ► **ˌradioˌbioˈlogically** *adv* ► **ˌradiobiˈologist** *n*

radiocarbon (ˌreɪdɪəʊˈkɑːb^{ə}n) *n* a radioactive isotope of carbon, esp. carbon-14. See **carbon** (sense 1).

radiocarbon dating *n* a technique for determining the age of organic materials, such as wood, based on their content of the radioisotope ^{14}C acquired from the atmosphere when they formed part of a living plant. The ^{14}C decays to the nitrogen isotope ^{14}N with a half-life of 5730 years. Measurement of the amount of radioactive carbon remaining in the material thus gives an estimate of its age. Also called: **carbon-14 dating.**

radiochemistry (ˌreɪdɪəʊˈkɛmɪstrɪ) *n* the chemistry of radioactive elements and their compounds. ► **ˌradioˈchemical** *adj* ► **ˌradioˈchemist** *n*

radiocommunication (ˌreɪdɪəʊkəˌmjuːnɪˈkeɪʃən) *n* communication by means of radio waves.

radio compass *n* any navigational device that gives a bearing by determining the direction of incoming radio waves transmitted from a particular radio station or beacon. See also **goniometer** (sense 2).

radio control *n* remote control by means of radio signals from a transmitter. ► **ˈradio-conˈtrolled** *adj*

radioelement (ˌreɪdɪəʊˈɛlɪmənt) *n* an element that is naturally radioactive.

radio frequency *n* **1a** a frequency or band of frequencies that lie in the range 10 kilohertz to 300 000 megahertz and can be used for radio communications and broadcasting. Abbrevs.: **rf, RF.** See also **frequency band. 1b** (*as modifier*): *a radio-frequency amplifier.* **2** the frequency transmitted by a particular radio station.

radio galaxy *n* a galaxy that is a strong emitter of radio waves.

radiogenic (ˌreɪdɪəʊˈdʒɛnɪk) *adj* produced or caused by radioactive decay: *a radiogenic element; radiogenic heat.*

radiogoniometer (ˌreɪdɪəʊˌgəʊnɪˈɒmɪtə) *n* a device used to detect the direction of radio waves, consisting of a coil that is free to rotate within two fixed coils at right angles to each other.

radiogram (ˈreɪdɪəʊˌgræm) *n* **1** *Brit.* a unit comprising a radio and record player. **2** a message transmitted by radiotelegraphy. **3** another name for **radiograph.**

radiograph (ˈreɪdɪəʊˌgrɑːf, -ˌgræf) *n* an image produced on a specially sensitized photographic film or plate by radiation, usually by X-rays or gamma rays. Also called: **radiogram, shadowgraph.**

radiography (ˌreɪdɪˈɒgrəfɪ) *n* the production of radiographs of opaque objects for use in medicine, surgery, industry, etc. ► **ˌradiˈographer** *n* ► **radiographic** (ˌreɪdɪəʊˈgræfɪk) *adj* ► **ˌradioˈgraphically** *adv*

radio-immuno-assay (ˈreɪdɪəʊˌɪmjunəʊˈæseɪ) *n* a sensitive immunological assay, making use of radioactive labelling, for the detection and quantification of biologically important substances, such as hormone levels in the blood.

radio interferometer *n* a type of radio telescope in which two or more aerials connected to the same receiver produce interference patterns that can be analysed to provide information about the source of the radio waves.

radioisotope (ˌreɪdɪəʊˈaɪsətəʊp) *n* an isotope that is radioactive. ► **radioisotopic** (ˌreɪdɪəʊˌaɪsəˈtɒpɪk) *adj*

radiolarian (ˌreɪdɪəʊˈlɛərɪən) *n* any of various marine protozoans constituting the order *Radiolaria,* typically having a siliceous shell and stiff radiating cytoplasmic projections: phylum *Actinopoda* (actinopods). [C19: from New Latin *Radiolaria,* from Late Latin *radiolus* little sunbeam, from Latin *radius* ray, RADIUS]

radiolocation (ˌreɪdɪəʊləˈkeɪʃən) *n* a former name for **radar.** ► **ˌradioloˈcational** *adj*

radiological (ˌreɪdɪəˈlɒdʒɪk^{ə}l) *adj* **1** of, relating to, or concerning radiology or the equipment used in radiology. **2** of, relating to, or involving radioactive materials: *radiological warfare.* ► **ˌradioˈlogically** *adv*

radiology (ˌreɪdɪˈɒlədʒɪ) *n* the use of X-rays and radioactive substances in the diagnosis and treatment of disease. ► **ˌradiˈologist** *n*

radiolucent (ˌreɪdɪəʊˈluːs^{ə}nt) *adj* almost transparent to electromagnetic radiation, esp. X-rays.

radioluminescence (ˌreɪdɪəʊˌluːmɪˈnɛsəns) *n Physics.* luminescence that is induced by radiation from a radioactive material. ► **ˌradioˌlumiˈnescent** *adj*

radiolysis (ˌreɪdɪˈɒlɪsɪs) *n* chemical decomposition caused by radiation, such as a beam of electrons or X-rays. ► **radiolytic** (ˌreɪdɪəʊˈlɪtɪk) *adj*

radiometeorograph (ˌreɪdɪəʊˈmiːtɪərəˌgrɑːf, -ˌgræf) *n* another name for **radiosonde.**

radiometer (ˌreɪdɪˈɒmɪtə) *n* any instrument for the detection or measurement of radiant energy. ► **radiometric** (ˌreɪdɪəʊˈmɛtrɪk) *adj* ► **ˌradiˈometry** *n*

radiometric dating *n* any method of dating material based on the decay of its constituent radioactive atoms, such as potassium-argon dating or rubidium-strontium dating. Also called: **radioactive dating.**

radiomicrometer (ˌreɪdɪəʊmaɪˈkrɒmɪtə) *n* an instrument for detecting and measuring small amounts of radiation, usually by a sensitive thermocouple.

radio microphone *n* a microphone incorporating a radio transmitter so that the user can move around freely.

radiomimetic (ˌreɪdɪəʊmɪˈmɛtɪk) *adj* (of drugs) producing effects similar to those produced by X-rays.

radionuclide (ˌreɪdɪəʊˈnjuːklaɪd) *n* a nuclide that is radioactive.

radiopager (ˈreɪdɪəʊˌpeɪdʒə) *n* a small radio receiver fitted with a buzzer to alert a person to telephone their home, office, etc., to receive a message. ► **ˈradioˌpaging** *n*

radiopaque (ˌreɪdɪəʊˈpeɪk) *or* **radio-opaque** *adj* not permitting X-rays or other radiation to pass through. ► **radiopacity** (ˌreɪdɪəʊˈpæsɪtɪ) *or* **ˌradio-oˈpacity** *n*

radiophone (ˈreɪdɪəʊˌfəʊn) *n* another name for **radiotelephone** (sense 1).

radiophonic (ˌreɪdɪəʊˈfɒnɪk) *adj* denoting or relating to music produced by electronic means. ► **ˌradioˈphonically** *adv* ► **radiophony** (ˌreɪdɪˈɒfənɪ) *n*

radio receiver *n* an apparatus that receives incoming modulated radio waves and converts them into sound.

radioresistant (ˌreɪdɪəʊrɪˈsɪstənt) *adj Med.* resistant to the effects of radiation.

radioscope (ˈreɪdɪəʊˌskəʊp) *n* an instrument, such as a fluoroscope, capable of detecting radiant energy.

radioscopy (ˌreɪdɪˈɒskəpɪ) *n* another word for **fluoroscopy.** ► **radioscopic** (ˌreɪdɪəʊˈskɒpɪk) *adj* ► **ˌradioˈscopically** *adv*

radiosensitive (ˌreɪdɪəʊˈsɛnsɪtɪv) *adj* affected by or sensitive to radiation. ► **ˌradioˈsensitively** *adv* ► **ˌradioˌsensiˈtivity** *n*

radiosonde (ˈreɪdɪəʊˌsɒnd) *n* an airborne instrument to send meteorological information back to earth by radio. Also called: **radiometeorograph.** [C20: RADIO- + French *sonde* sounding line]

radio source *n* a celestial object, such as a supernova remnant or quasar, that is a source of radio waves.

radio spectrum *n* the range of electromagnetic frequencies used in radio transmission, lying between 10 kilohertz and 300 000 megahertz.

radio star *n* a former name for **radio source.**

radio station *n* **1** an installation consisting of one or more transmitters or receivers, etc., used for radiocommunications. **2** a broadcasting organization.

radiotelegram (ˌreɪdɪəʊˈtɛlɪˌgræm) *n* a message transmitted by radiotelegraphy. Also called: **radiogram.**

radiotelegraph (ˌreɪdɪəʊˈtɛlɪˌgrɑːf) *vb* **1** to send (a message) by radiotelegraphy. ◆ *n* **2** a message sent by radiotelegraphy.

radiotelegraphy (ˌreɪdɪəʊtɪˈlɛgrəfɪ) *n* a type of telegraphy in which messages (usually in Morse code) are transmitted by radio waves; its use is no longer widespread as it has been superseded by satellite technology. Also called: **wireless telegraphy.** ► **radiotelegraphic** (ˌreɪdɪəʊˌtɛlɪˈgræfɪk) *adj* ► **ˌradioˌteleˈgraphically** *adv*

radiotelemetry (ˌreɪdɪəʊtɪˈlɛmɪtrɪ) *n* the use of radio waves for transmitting information from a distant instrument to a device that indicates or records the measurements. Sometimes shortened to **telemetry.**

radiotelephone (ˌreɪdɪəʊˈtɛlɪˌfəʊn) *n* **1** Also called: **radiophone, wireless telephone.** a device for communications by means of radio waves rather than by transmitting along wires or cables. ◆ *vb* **2** to telephone (a person) by radiotelephone. ◆ Sometimes shortened to **radio.** ► **radiotelephonic** (ˌreɪdɪəʊˌtɛlɪˈfɒnɪk) *adj* ► **radiotelephony** (ˌreɪdɪəʊtɪˈlɛfənɪ) *n*

radio telescope *n* an instrument consisting of an antenna or system of antennas connected to one or more radio receivers, used in radio astronomy to detect and analyse radio waves from space.

radioteletype (ˌreɪdɪəʊˈtɛlɪˌtaɪp) *n* **1** a teleprinter that transmits or receives information by means of radio waves rather than by cable or wire. **2** a network of such devices widely used for communicating news, messages, information, etc. Abbrevs.: **RTT, RTTY.**

radiotherapy (ˌreɪdɪəʊˈθɛrəpɪ) *n* the treatment of disease, esp. cancer, by means of alpha or beta particles emitted from an implanted or ingested radioisotope, or by means of a beam of high-energy radiation. Compare **chemotherapy.** ► **radiotherapeutic** (ˌreɪdɪəʊˌθɛrəˈpjuːtɪk) *adj* ► **ˌradioˌtheraˈpeutically** *adv* ► **ˌradioˈtherapist** *n*

radiothermy (ˈreɪdɪəʊˌθɜːmɪ) *n Med.* the treatment of disease by means of heat generated by electromagnetic radiation.

radiotoxic (ˌreɪdɪəʊˈtɒksɪk) *adj* of or denoting the toxic effects of radiation or radioactive substances.

radio valve *n* another name for **valve** (sense 3).

radio wave *n* an electromagnetic wave of radio frequency.

radio window *n* a gap in ionospheric reflection that allows radio waves, with frequencies in the range 10 000 to 40 000 megahertz, to pass from or into space.

radish (ˈrædɪʃ) *n* **1** any of various cruciferous plants of the genus *Raphanus,* esp. *R. sativus* of Europe and Asia, cultivated for its edible root. **2** the root of this plant, which has a pungent taste and is eaten raw in salads. **3 wild radish.** another name for **white charlock.** See **charlock** (sense 2). [Old English *rǣdīc,* from Latin *rādīx* root]

radium (ˈreɪdɪəm) *n* **a** a highly radioactive luminescent white element of the alkaline earth group of metals. It occurs in pitchblende, carnotite, and other uranium ores, and is used in radiotherapy and in luminous paints. Symbol: Ra; atomic no.: 88; half-life of most stable isotope, ^{226}Ra: 1620 years; valency: 2; relative density: 5; melting pt.: 700°C; boiling pt.: 1140°C. **b** *(as modifier): radium needle.* [C20: from Latin *radius* ray]

radium therapy *n* treatment of disease, esp. cancer, by exposing affected tissues to radiation from radium.

radius (ˈreɪdɪəs) *n, pl* **-dii** (-dɪˌaɪ) *or* **-diuses. 1** a straight line joining the centre of a circle or sphere to any point on the circumference or surface. **2** the length of this line, usually denoted by the symbol *r.* **3** the distance from the centre of a regular polygon to a vertex (**long radius**) or the perpendicular distance to a side (**short radius**). **4** *Anatomy.* the outer and slightly shorter of the two bones of the human forearm, extending from the elbow to the wrist. **5** a corresponding bone in other vertebrates. **6** any of the veins of an insect's wing. **7** a group of ray flowers, occurring in such plants as the daisy. **8a** any radial or radiating part, such as a spoke. **8b** *(as modifier): a radius arm.* **9** the lateral displacement of a cam or eccentric wheel. **10** a circular area of a size indicated by the length of its radius: *the police stopped every lorry within a radius of four miles.* **11** the operational limit of a ship, aircraft, etc. [C16: from Latin: rod, ray, spoke]

radius of action *n Military.* the maximum distance that a ship, aircraft, or land vehicle can travel from its base and return without refuelling.

radius of curvature *n* the absolute value of the reciprocal of the curvature of a curve at a given point; the radius of a circle the curvature of which is equal to that of the given curve at that point. See also **centre of curvature.**

radius vector *n* **1** *Maths.* a line joining a point in space to the origin of polar or spherical coordinates. **2** *Astronomy.* an imaginary line joining a satellite to the planet or star around which it is orbiting.

radix (ˈreɪdɪks) *n, pl* **-dices** (-dɪˌsiːz) *or* **-dixes. 1** *Maths.* any number that is the base of a number system or of a system of logarithms: *10 is the radix of the decimal system.* **2** *Biology.* the root or point of origin of a part or organ. **3** *Linguistics.* a less common word for **root**[1] (sense 9). [C16: from Latin *rādīx* root; compare Greek *rhadix* small branch, *rhiza* root]

radix point *n* a point, such as the decimal point in the decimal system, separating the integral part of a number from the fractional part.

Radnorshire (ˈrædnəˌʃɪə, -ʃə) *or* **Radnor** *n* (until 1974) a county of E Wales, now part of Powys.

Radom *(Polish* ˈradɔm) *n* a city in E Poland: under Austria from 1795 to 1815 and Russia from 1815 to 1918. Pop.: 232 300 (1996 est.).

radome (ˈreɪdəʊm) *n* a protective housing for a radar antenna made from a material that is transparent to radio waves. [C20: RA(DAR) + DOME]

radon (ˈreɪdɒn) *n* a colourless radioactive element of the rare gas group, the most stable isotope of which, radon-222, is a decay product of radium. It is used as an alpha particle source in radiotherapy. Symbol: Rn; atomic no.: 86; half-life of ^{222}Rn: 3.82 days; valency: 0; density: 9.73 kg/m^3; melting pt.: −71°C; boiling pt.: −61.7°C. [C20: from RADIUM + -ON]

radula (ˈrædjʊlə) *n, pl* **-lae** (-ˌliː). a horny tooth-bearing strip on the tongue of molluscs that is used for rasping food. [C19: from Late Latin: a scraping iron, from Latin *rādere* to scrape] ► **ˈradular** *adj*

RAE (in Britain) *abbrev. for* Royal Aircraft Establishment.

Raeburn (ˈreɪˌbɜːn) *n* Sir **Henry.** 1756–1823, Scottish portrait painter.

RAEC *abbrev. for* Royal Army Educational Corps.

RAF *(Not standard* ræf) *abbrev. for* Royal Air Force.

raff (ræf) *n Archaic or dialect.* **1** rubbish; refuse. **2** rabble or riffraff. [C14: perhaps from Old French *rafle* a snatching up; compare RAFFLE, RIFFRAFF]

Rafferty (ˈræfətɪ) *or* **Rafferty's rules** *pl n Austral. and N.Z. slang.* no rules at all. [C20: of uncertain origin]

raffia *or* **raphia** (ˈræfɪə) *n* **1** Also called: **raffia palm.** a palm tree, *Raphia ruffia,* native to Madagascar, that has large plumelike leaves, the stalks of which yield a useful fibre. **2** the fibre obtained from this plant, used for tying, weaving, etc. **3** any of several related palms or the fibre obtained from them. [C19: from Malagasy]

raffinate (ˈræfɪˌneɪt) *n* the liquid left after a solute has been extracted by solvent extraction. [C20: from French *raffiner* to refine + -ATE[1]]

raffinose (ˈræfɪˌnəʊz, -ˌnəʊs) *n Biochem.* a trisaccharide of fructose, glucose, and galactose that occurs in sugar beet, cotton seed, certain cereals, etc. Formula: $C_{18}H_{32}O_{16}$. [C19: from French *raffiner* to refine + -OSE[2]]

raffish (ˈræfɪʃ) *adj* **1** careless or unconventional in dress, manners, etc.; rakish. **2** tawdry; flashy; vulgar. [C19: see RAFF] ► **ˈraffishly** *adv* ► **ˈraffishness** *n*

raffle (ˈræfᵊl) *n* **1a** a lottery in which the prizes are goods rather than money. **1b** *(as modifier): a raffle ticket.* ◆ *vb* **2** *(tr;* often foll. by *off)* to dispose of (goods) in a raffle. [C14 (a dice game): from Old French, of obscure origin] ► **ˈraffler** *n*

Raffles (ˈræfᵊlz) *n* Sir **Thomas Stamford.** 1781–1826, British colonial administrator: founded Singapore (1819) as a station for the British East India Company.

rafflesia (ræˈfliːzɪə) *n* any of various tropical Asian parasitic leafless plants constituting the genus *Rafflesia,* esp. *R. arnoldi,* the flowers of which grow up to 45 cm (18 inches) across, smell of putrid meat, and are pollinated by carrion flies: family *Rafflesiaceae.* [C19: New Latin, named after Sir Stamford RAFFLES, who discovered it]

Rafsanjani (ˌræfsænˈdʒɑːnɪ) *n* **Hojatoleslam Hashemi Ali Akbar.** born 1934, Iranian politician: president of Iran (1989–97).

raft[1] (rɑːft) *n* **1** a buoyant platform of logs, planks, etc., used as a vessel or moored platform. **2** a thick slab of reinforced concrete laid over soft ground to provide a foundation for a building. ◆ *vb* **3** to convey on or travel by raft, or make a raft from. [C15: from Old Norse *raptr* RAFTER] ► **ˈrafting** *n*

raft[2] (rɑːft) *n Informal.* a large collection or amount: *a raft of old notebooks discovered in a cupboard.* [C19: from RAFF]

rafter (ˈrɑːftə) *n* any one of a set of sloping beams that form the framework of a roof. [Old English *ræfter;* related to Old Saxon *rehter,* Old Norse *raptr,* Old High German *rāvo;* see RAFT[1]]

RAFVR *abbrev. for* Royal Air Force Volunteer Reserve.

rag[1] (ræg) *n* **1a** a small piece of cloth, such as one torn from a discarded garment, or such pieces of cloth collectively. **1b** *(as modifier): a rag doll; a rag book; rag paper.* **2** a fragmentary piece of any material; scrap; shred. **3** *Informal.* a newspaper or other journal, esp. one considered as worthless, sensational, etc. **4** *Informal.* an item of clothing. **5** *Informal.* a handkerchief. **6** *Brit. slang, esp. naval.* a flag or ensign. **7 lose one's rag.** to lose one's temper suddenly. ◆ See also **rags.** [C14: probably back formation from RAGGED, from Old English *raggig;* related to Old Norse *rögg* tuft]

rag[2] (ræg) *vb* **rags, ragging, ragged.** *(tr)* **1** to draw attention facetiously and persistently to the shortcomings or alleged shortcomings of (a person). **2** *Brit.* to play rough practical jokes on. ◆ *n* **3** *Brit.* a boisterous practical joke, esp. one on a fellow student. **4** (in British universities) **4a** a period, usually a week, in which various events are organized to raise money for charity, including a procession of decorated floats and tableaux. **4b** *(as modifier): rag day.* [C18: of uncertain origin]

rag[3] (ræg) *Jazz.* ◆ *n* **1** a piece of ragtime music. ◆ *vb* **rags, ragging, ragged. 2** *(tr)* to compose or perform in ragtime. [C20: shortened from RAGTIME]

rag[4] (ræg) *n* a roofing slate that is rough on one side. [C13: of obscure origin]

raga (ˈrɑːgə) *n* (in Indian music) **1** any of several conventional patterns of melody and rhythm that form the basis for freely interpreted compositions. Each pattern is associated with different aspects of religious devotion. **2** a composition based on one of these patterns. [C18: from Sanskrit *rāga* tone, colour]

ragamuffin (ˈrægəˌmʌfɪn) *n* **1** a ragged unkempt person, esp. a child. **2** another name for **ragga.** [C14 *Ragamoffyn,* name of a demon in the poem *Piers Plowman* (1393); probably based on RAG[1]]

rag-and-bone man *n Brit.* a man who buys and sells discarded clothing, furniture, etc. Also called: **ˈragˌman, ˈragˌpicker.** U.S. equivalent: **junkman.**

ragbag (ˈrægˌbæg) *n* **1** a bag for storing odd rags. **2** a confused assortment; jumble: *a ragbag of ideas.* **3** *Informal.* a scruffy or slovenly person. [C19]

ragbolt (ˈrægˌbəʊlt) *n* a bolt that has angled projections on it to prevent it working loose once it has been driven home.

rage (reɪdʒ) *n* **1** intense anger; fury. **2** violent movement or action, esp. of the sea, wind, etc. **3** great intensity of hunger, sexual desire, or other feelings. **4** a fashion or craze (esp. in the phrase **all the rage**). **5** *Austral. and N.Z. informal.* a dance or party. ◆ *vb (intr)* **6** to feel or exhibit intense anger. **7** (esp. of storms, fires, etc.) to move or surge with great violence. **8** (esp. of a disease or epidemic) to spread rapidly and uncontrollably. **9** *Austral. and N.Z. informal.* to have a good time. [C13: via Old French from Latin *rabiēs* madness]

ragga (ˈrægə) *n* a dance-orientated style of reggae. Also called: **ragamuffin.** [C20: shortened from RAGAMUFFIN]

ragged (ˈrægɪd) *adj* **1** (of clothes) worn to rags; tattered. **2** (of a person) dressed in shabby tattered clothes. **3** having a neglected or unkempt appearance: *ragged weeds.* **4** having a loose, rough, or uneven surface or edge; jagged. **5** uneven or irregular: *a ragged beat; a ragged shout.* [C13: probably from *ragge* RAG[1]] ► **ˈraggedly** *adv* ► **ˈraggedness** *n*

ragged robin *n* a caryophyllaceous plant, *Lychnis floscuculi,* native to Europe and Asia, that has pink or white flowers with ragged petals. Also called: **cuckooflower.** See also **catchfly.**

ragged school *n* (in Britain, formerly) a free elementary school for poor children.

raggedy (ˈrægɪdɪ) *adj Informal.* somewhat ragged; tattered: *a raggedy doll.*

raggle (ˈrægᵊl) *n Chiefly Scot.* a thin groove cut in stone or brickwork, esp. to hold the edge of a roof. [C19: of obscure origin]

raggle-taggle (ˈrægᵊlˈtægᵊl) *adj* motley or unkempt: *a raggle-taggle Gypsy.* [augmented form of RAGTAG]

ragi, raggee, *or* **raggy** (ˈrægɪ) *n* a cereal grass, *Eleusine coracana,* cultivated in Africa and Asia for its edible grain. [C18: from Hindi]

raglan (ˈræglən) *n* **1** a coat with sleeves that continue to the collar instead of having armhole seams. ◆ *adj* **2** cut in this design: *a raglan sleeve.* [C19: named after Lord RAGLAN]

Raglan (ˈræglən) *n* **Fitzroy James Henry Somerset,** 1st Baron Raglan.

1788–1855, British field marshal, diplomatist, politician, and protégé of Wellington: commanded British troops (1854–55) in the Crimean War.

ragman ('ræg,mæn) *n, pl* **-men.** another name for **rag-and-bone man.**

Ragman rolls ('rægmən) *pl n History.* a set of parchment rolls of 1296 enumerating the Scottish nobles who owed allegiance to Edward I of England, important as the only full list of the nobility of Scotland in the later 13th century. [C18: from obsolete *ragman* in the sense: statute, roll, list]

Ragnarök *or* **Ragnarok** ('rɑːgnə,rɒk) *n Norse myth.* the ultimate destruction of the gods in a cataclysmic battle with evil, out of which a new order will arise. German equivalent: **Götterdämmerung.** [Old Norse *ragnarökkr,* from *regin* the gods + *rökkr* twilight]

ragout (ræ'guː) *n* **1** a richly seasoned stew of meat or poultry and vegetables. ◆ *vb* **-gouts** (-'guːz), **-gouting** (-'guːɪŋ), **-gouted** (-'guːd). **2** (*tr*) to make into a ragout. [C17: from French, from *ragoûter* to stimulate the appetite again, from *ra-* RE- + *goûter* from Latin *gustāre* to taste]

rag-rolling *n* a decorating technique in which paint is applied with a roughly folded cloth in order to create a marbled effect.

rags (rægz) *pl n* **1** torn, old, or shabby clothing. **2** cotton or linen cloth waste used in the manufacture of rag paper. **3 glad rags.** *Informal.* best clothes; finery. **4 from rags to riches.** *Informal.* **4a** from poverty to great wealth. **4b** (*as modifier*): *a rags-to-riches tale.*

ragstone ('ræg,stəʊn) *n* a hard sandstone or limestone, esp. when used for building. Also called: **rag** *or* **ragg.** [C14: from RAG[4] + STONE]

ragtag ('ræg,tæg) *n Disparaging.* the common people; rabble (esp. in the phrase **ragtag and bobtail**). [C19]

ragtime ('ræg,taɪm) *n* a style of jazz piano music, developed by Scott Joplin around 1900, having a two-four rhythm base and a syncopated melody. [C20: probably from RAGGED + TIME]

rag trade *n Informal.* the clothing business, esp. the aspects concerned with the manufacture and sale of dresses.

Ragusa (*Italian* ra'guːza) *n* **1** an industrial town in SE Sicily. Pop.: 68 850 (1990). **2** the Italian name (until 1918) for **Dubrovnik.**

ragweed ('ræg,wiːd) *n* any plant of the chiefly North American genus *Ambrosia,* such as *A. artemisiifolia* (**common ragweed**): family *Compositae* (composites). Their green tassel-like flowers produce large amounts of pollen, which causes hay fever. Also called: **ambrosia.**

ragworm ('ræg,wɜːm) *n* any polychaete worm of the genus *Nereis,* living chiefly in burrows in sand or mud and having a flattened body with a row of fleshy parapodia along each side. U.S. name: **clamworm.**

ragwort ('ræg,wɜːt) *n* any of several plants of the genus *Senecio,* esp. *S. jacobaea* of Europe, that have yellow daisy-like flowers: family *Compositae* (composites). See also **groundsel** (sense 1).

rah (rɑː) *interj Informal, chiefly U.S.* short for **hurrah.**

rah-rah ('rɑː,rɑː) *adj Informal, chiefly U.S.* like or marked by boisterous and uncritical enthusiasm and excitement. [C20: a reduplication of RAH]

rai (raɪ) *n* a type of Algerian popular music based on traditional Algerian music influenced by modern Western pop. [C20: Arabic, literally: opinion]

raia ('rɑːjə, 'raɪə) *n* a less common variant of **rayah.**

raid (reɪd) *n* **1** a sudden surprise attack: *an air raid.* **2** a surprise visit by police searching for criminals or illicit goods: *a fraud-squad raid.* See also **bear raid, dawn raid.** ◆ *vb* **3** to make a raid against (a person, thing, etc.). **4** to sneak into (a place) in order to take something, steal, etc.: *raiding the larder.* [C15: Scottish dialect, from Old English *rād* military expedition; see ROAD] ▸ **'raider** *n*

rail[1] (reɪl) *n* **1** a horizontal bar of wood, metal, etc., supported by vertical posts, functioning as a fence, barrier, handrail, etc. **2** a horizontal bar fixed to a wall on which to hang things: *a picture rail.* **3** a horizontal framing member in a door or piece of panelling. Compare **stile**[2]. **4** short for **railing. 5** one of a pair of parallel bars laid on a prepared track, roadway, etc., that serve as a guide and running surface for the wheels of a railway train, tramcar, etc. **6a** short for **railway. 6b** (*as modifier*): *rail transport.* **7** *Nautical.* a trim for finishing the top of a bulwark. **8 off the rails. 8a** into or in a state of dysfunction or disorder. **8b** eccentric or mad. ◆ *vb* (*tr*) **9** to provide with a rail or railings. **10** (usually foll. by *in* or *off*) to fence (an area) with rails. [C13: from Old French *raille* rod, from Latin *rēgula* ruler, straight piece of wood] ▸ **'railless** *adj*

rail[2] (reɪl) *vb* (*intr;* foll. by *at* or *against*) to complain bitterly or vehemently: *to rail against fate.* [C15: from Old French *railler* to mock, from Old Provençal *ralhar* to chatter, joke, from Late Latin *ragere* to yell, neigh] ▸ **'railer** *n*

rail[3] (reɪl) *n* any of various small wading birds of the genus *Rallus* and related genera: family *Rallidae,* order *Gruiformes* (cranes, etc.). They have short wings, long legs, and dark plumage. [C15: from Old French *raale,* perhaps from Latin *rādere* to scrape]

railcar ('reɪl,kɑː) *n* a passenger-carrying railway vehicle consisting of a single coach with its own power unit.

railcard ('reɪl,kɑːd) *n Brit.* an identity card that young people or pensioners in Britain can buy, which allows them to buy train tickets more cheaply.

rail gauge *n* See **gauge** (sense 11).

railhead ('reɪl,hɛd) *n* **1** a terminal of a railway. **2** the farthest point reached by completed track on an unfinished railway. **3** *Military.* the point at which material and personnel are transferred from rail to another conveyance. **4** the upper part of a railway rail, on which the traffic wheels run.

railing ('reɪlɪŋ) *n* **1** (*often pl*) a fence, balustrade, or barrier that consists of rails supported by posts. **2** rails collectively or material for making rails.

raillery ('reɪlərɪ) *n, pl* **-leries. 1** light-hearted satire or ridicule; banter. **2** an example of this, esp. a bantering remark. [C17: from French, from *railler* to tease, banter; see RAIL[2]]

railroad ('reɪl,rəʊd) *n* **1** the usual U.S. word for **railway.** ◆ *vb* **2** (*tr*) *Informal.* to force (a person) into (an action) with haste or by unfair means.

railway ('reɪl,weɪ) *or U.S.* **railroad** *n* **1** a permanent track composed of a line of parallel metal rails fixed to sleepers, for transport of passengers and goods in trains. **2** any track on which the wheels of a vehicle may run: *a cable railway.* **3** the entire equipment, rolling stock, buildings, property, and system of tracks used in such a transport system. **4** the organization responsible for operating a railway network. **5** (*modifier*) of, relating to, or used on a railway or railways: *a railway engine; a railway strike.*

railwayman ('reɪl,weɪmən) *n, pl* **-men.** *Brit.* a worker on a railway, esp. one other than a driver.

raiment ('reɪmənt) *n Archaic or poetic.* attire; clothing; garments. [C15: shortened from *arrayment,* from Old French *areement;* see ARRAY]

rain (reɪn) *n* **1a** precipitation from clouds in the form of drops of water, formed by the condensation of water vapour in the atmosphere. **1b** a fall of rain; shower. **1c** (*in combination*): *a raindrop.* Related adjs.: **hyetal, pluvious. 2** a large quantity of anything falling rapidly or in quick succession: *a rain of abuse.* **3** (**come**) **rain or shine. 3a** regardless of the weather. **3b** regardless of circumstances. **4 right as rain.** *Brit. informal.* perfectly all right; perfectly fit. ◆ *vb* **5** (*intr;* with *it* as subject) to be the case that rain is falling. **6** (often with *it* as subject) to fall or cause to fall like rain: *the lid flew off and popcorn rained on everyone.* **7** (*tr*) to bestow in large measure: *to rain abuse on someone.* **8 rain cats and dogs.** *Informal.* to rain heavily; pour. **9 rained off.** cancelled or postponed on account of rain. U.S. and Canadian term: **rained out.** ◆ See also **rains.** [Old English *regn;* related to Old Frisian *rein,* Old High German *regan,* Gothic *rign*] ▸ **'rainless** *adj*

rainband ('reɪn,bænd) *n* a dark band in the solar spectrum caused by water in the atmosphere.

rainbird ('reɪn,bɜːd) *n* any of various birds, such as (in Britain) the green woodpecker, whose cry is supposed to portend rain.

rainbow ('reɪn,bəʊ) *n* **1** a bow-shaped display in the sky of the colours of the spectrum, caused by the refraction and reflection of the sun's rays through rain or mist. **2a** any similar display of bright colours. **2b** (*as modifier*): *a rainbow pattern.* **3** an illusory hope: *to chase rainbows.* **4** (*modifier*) of or relating to a political grouping together by several minorities, esp. of different races: *the rainbow coalition.*

rainbow bird *n* an Australian bee-eater, *Merops ornatus,* with a brightly-coloured plumage. It feeds in flight and nests in sandy burrows.

Rainbow Bridge *n* a natural stone bridge over a creek in SE Utah. Height: 94 m (309 ft.). Span: 85 m (278 ft.).

rainbow nation *n S. African.* an epithet, alluding to its multiracial population, of **South Africa.** [C20: coined by Nelson MANDELA following the end of apartheid]

rainbow quartz *n Mineralogy.* another name for **iris** (sense 3).

rainbow trout *n* a freshwater trout of North American origin, *Salmo gairdneri,* having a body marked with many black spots and two longitudinal red stripes.

rain check *n* **1** *U.S. and Canadian.* a ticket stub for a baseball or other game that allows readmission on a future date if the event is cancelled because of rain. **2** the deferral of acceptance of an offer, esp., a voucher issued to a customer wishing to purchase a sale item that is temporarily out of stock, enabling him to buy it at the special price when next the item is available. **3 take a rain check.** *Informal.* to accept the postponement of an offer.

raincoat ('reɪn,kəʊt) *n* a coat made of a waterproof material.

rainfall ('reɪn,fɔːl) *n* **1** precipitation in the form of raindrops. **2** *Meteorol.* the amount of precipitation in a specified place and time.

rainforest ('reɪn,fɒrɪst) *n* dense forest found in tropical areas of heavy rainfall. The trees are broad-leaved and evergreen, and the vegetation tends to grow in three layers (undergrowth, intermediate trees and shrubs, and very tall trees, which form a canopy). Also called: **selva.**

rain gauge *n* an instrument for measuring rainfall or snowfall, consisting of a cylinder covered by a funnel-like lid. Also called: **pluviometer.**

Rainier ('reɪnɪə; reɪ'nɪə, rə-) *n* **Mount.** a mountain in W Washington State: the highest mountain in the state and in the Cascade Range. Height: 4392 m (14 410 ft.).

Rainier III ('reɪnɪ,eɪ; *French* rɛnje) *n* full name *Rainier Louis Henri Maxence Bertrand de Grimaldi.* born 1923, ruling prince of Monaco from 1949. He married (1956) the U.S. actress Grace Kelly (1929–82).

rainmaker ('reɪn,meɪkə) *n* (among American Indians) a professional practitioner of ritual incantations or other actions intended to cause rain to fall. ▸ **'rain,making** *n*

rainout ('reɪn,aʊt) *n* radioactive fallout or atmospheric pollution carried to the earth by rain.

rainproof ('reɪn,pruːf) *adj* **1** Also: **'rain,tight.** (of garments, materials, buildings, etc.) impermeable to rainwater. ◆ *vb* **2** (*tr*) to make rainproof.

rains (reɪnz) *pl n* **the.** the season of heavy rainfall, esp. in the tropics.

rain shadow *n* the relatively dry area on the leeward side of high ground in the path of rain-bearing winds.

rainstorm ('reɪn,stɔːm) *n* a storm with heavy rain.

rain tree *n* a leguminous tree, *Samanea saman,* native to Central America and widely planted in the tropics for ornament. It has red-and-yellow feathery flowers and pinnate leaves whose leaflets close at the approach of rain.

rainwater ('reɪn,wɔːtə) *n* water from rain (as distinguished from spring water, tap water, etc.).

rainwater pipe *n Brit.* another name for **downpipe.**

rainy ('reɪnɪ) *adj* **rainier, rainiest. 1** characterized by a large rainfall: *a rainy climate.* **2** wet or showery; bearing rain. ▸ **'rainily** *adv* ▸ **'raininess** *n*

rainy day *n* a future time of need, esp. financial.

Rais (*French* rɛs) *or* **Retz** *n* **Gilles de** (ʒil də). 1404–40, French nobleman who fought with Joan of Arc: marshal of France (1429–40). He was executed for the torture and murder of more than 140 children.

raise (reɪz) *vb* (*mainly tr*) **1** to move, cause to move, or elevate to a higher position or level; lift. **2** to set or place in an upright position. **3** to construct, build, or erect: *to raise a barn.* **4** to increase in amount, size, value, etc.: *to raise prices.* **5** to increase in degree, strength, intensity, etc.: *to raise one's voice.* **6** to advance in rank or status; promote. **7** to arouse or awaken from or as if from sleep or death. **8** to stir up or incite; activate: *to raise a mutiny.* **9 raise Cain** (*or* **the devil, hell, the roof,** etc.). **9a** to create a boisterous disturbance. **9b** to react or protest heatedly. **10** to give rise to; cause or provoke: *to raise a smile.* **11** to put forward for consideration: *to raise a question.* **12** to cause to assemble or gather together; collect: *to raise an army.* **13** to grow or cause to grow: *to raise a crop.* **14** to bring up; rear: *to raise a family.* **15** to cause to be heard or known; utter or express: *to raise a shout; to raise a protest.* **16** to bring to an end; remove: *to raise a siege; raise a ban.* **17** to cause (dough, bread, etc.) to rise, as by the addition of yeast. **18** *Poker.* to bet more than (the previous player). **19** *Bridge.* to bid (one's partner's suit) at a higher level. **20** *Nautical.* to cause (something) to seem to rise above the horizon by approaching: *we raised land after 20 days.* **21** to establish radio communications with: *we managed to raise Moscow last night.* **22** to obtain (money, funds, capital, etc.). **23** to bring (a surface, a design, etc.) into relief; cause to project. **24** to cause (a blister, welt, etc.) to form on the skin. **25** to expel (phlegm) by coughing. **26** *Phonetics.* to modify the articulation of (a vowel) by bringing the tongue closer to the roof of the mouth. **27** *Maths.* to multiply (a number) by itself a specified number of times: *8 is 2 raised to the power 3.* **28a** to institute (a suit or action at law). **28b** to draw up (a summons). **29** *Chiefly U.S. and Canadian.* to increase the amount payable on (a cheque, money order, etc.) fraudulently. **30** *Curling.* to push (a stone) towards the tee with another stone. **31 raise an eyebrow 31a** Also: **raise one's eyebrows.** to look quizzical or surprised. **31b** to give rise to doubt or disapproval. **32 raise one's glass** (**to**). to drink the health of (someone); drink a toast (to). **33 raise one's hat.** *Old-fashioned.* to take one's hat briefly off one's head as a greeting or mark of respect. ♦ *n* **34** the act or an instance of raising. **35** *Chiefly U.S. and Canadian.* an increase, esp. in salary, wages, etc.; rise. [C12: from Old Norse *reisa;* related to Old English *rǣran* to REAR[2]] ► **'raisable** *or* **'raiseable** *adj* ► **'raiser** *n*

raised beach *n* a wave-cut platform raised above the shoreline by a relative fall in the water level.

raised bog *n Ecology.* a bog of convex shape produced by growth of sphagnum and other bog plants in acid conditions and the subsequent build up of acid peat.

raisin ('reɪzᵊn) *n* a dried grape. [C13: from Old French: grape, ultimately from Latin *racēmus* cluster of grapes; compare Greek *rhax* berry, grape] ► **'raisiny** *adj*

raising ('reɪzɪŋ) *n Transformational grammar.* a rule that moves a constituent from an embedded clause into the main clause. See also **subject-raising, negative-raising.**

raison d'être *French.* (rɛzɔ̃ dɛtrə) *n, pl* ***raisons d'être*** (rɛzɔ̃ dɛtrə). reason or justification for existence.

raita ('reɪtə, raɪ'iːtə) *n* an Indian dish of finely chopped cucumber, peppers, mint, etc., in yogurt, served with curries. [C20: from Hindi]

raj (rɑːdʒ) *n* (in India) government; rule. [C19: from Hindi, from Sanskrit *rājya,* from *rājati* he rules]

Raj (rɑːdʒ) *n* **the.** the British government in India before 1947.

Rajab (rə'dʒæb) *n* the seventh month of the Muslim year.

rajah *or* **raja** ('rɑːdʒə) *n* **1** (in India, formerly) a ruler or landlord: sometimes used as a form of address or as a title preceding a name. **2** a Malayan or Javanese prince or chieftain. [C16: from Hindi *rājā,* from Sanskrit *rājan* king; see RAJ; compare Latin *rex* king]

RAJAR ('reɪdʒɑː) *n acronym for* Radio Joint Audience Research.

Rajasthan (ˌrɑːdʒə'stɑːn) *n* a state of NW India, bordering on Pakistan: formed in 1958; contains the Thar Desert in the west. Capital: Jaipur. Pop.: 48 040 000 (1994 est.). Area: 342 239 sq. km (132 111 sq. miles).

raja yoga ('rɑːdʒə) *n* (*sometimes caps.*) a form of yoga chiefly concerned with controlling and using the energy of the mind by meditation. Compare **hatha yoga.** [C19: from Sanskrit *rājan* king + YOGA]

Rajkot ('rɑːdʒkəʊt) *n* a city in W India, in S Gujarat. Pop.: 559 407 (1991).

Rajput *or* **Rajpoot** ('rɑːdʒpʊt) *n Hinduism.* one of a Hindu military caste claiming descent from the Kshatriya, the original warrior caste. [C16: from Hindi, from Sanskrit *rājan* king; see RAJ]

Rajputana (ˌrɑːdʒpʊ'tɑːnə) *n* a former group of princely states in NW India: now mostly part of Rajasthan.

Rajya Sabha ('rɑːdʒjə 'sʌbə) *n* the upper chamber of India's Parliament. Compare **Lok Sabha.** [C20: Hindi, *rajya* state + *sabha* assembly]

Rakata (rə'kɑːtə) *n* another name for **Krakatoa.**

rake[1] (reɪk) *n* **1** a hand implement consisting of a row of teeth set in a headpiece attached to a long shaft and used for gathering hay, straw, leaves, etc., or for smoothing loose earth. **2** any of several mechanical farm implements equipped with rows of teeth or rotating wheels mounted with tines and used to gather hay, straw, etc. **3** any of various implements similar in shape or function, such as a tool for drawing out ashes from a furnace. **4** the act of raking. **5** *N.Z.* a line of wagons coupled together as one unit, used on railways. ♦ *vb* **6** to scrape, gather, or remove (leaves, refuse, etc.) with or as if with a rake. **7** to level or prepare (a surface, such as a flower bed) with a rake or similar implement. **8** (*tr;* sometimes foll. by *out*) to clear (ashes, clinker, etc.) from (a fire or furnace). **9** (*tr;* foll. by *up* or *together*) to gather (items or people) with difficulty, as from a scattered area or limited supply. **10** (*tr;* often foll. by *through, over,* etc.) to search or examine carefully. **11** (when *intr,* foll. by *against, along,* etc.) to scrape or graze: *the ship raked the side of the quay.* **12** (*tr*) to direct (gunfire) along the length of (a target): *machine-guns raked the column.* **13** (*tr*) to sweep (one's eyes) along the length of (something); scan. ♦ See also **rake in, rake-off, rake up.** [Old English *raca;* related to Old Norse *raka,* Old High German *rehho* a rake, Gothic *rikan* to heap up, Latin *rogus* funeral pile] ► **'raker** *n*

rake[2] (reɪk) *n* a dissolute man, esp. one in fashionable society; roué. [C17: short for RAKEHELL]

rake[3] (reɪk) *vb* (*mainly intr*) **1** to incline from the vertical by a perceptible degree, esp. (of a ship's mast or funnel) towards the stern. **2** (*tr*) to construct with a backward slope. ♦ *n* **3** the degree to which an object, such as a ship's mast, inclines from the perpendicular, esp. towards the stern. **4** *Theatre.* the slope of a stage from the back towards the footlights. **5** *Aeronautics.* **5a** the angle between the wings of an aircraft and the line of symmetry of the aircraft. **5b** the angle between the line joining the centroids of the section of a propeller blade and a line perpendicular to the axis. **6** the angle between the working face of a cutting tool and a plane perpendicular to the surface of the workpiece. **7** a slanting ledge running across a crag in the Lake District. [C17: of uncertain origin; perhaps related to German *ragen* to project, Swedish *raka*]

rake[4] (reɪk) *vb* (*intr*) **1** (of gun dogs or hounds) to hunt with the nose to the ground. **2** (of hawks) **2a** to pursue quarry in full flight. **2b** (often foll. by *away*) to fly wide of the quarry, esp. beyond the control of the falconer. [Old English *racian* to go forward, of uncertain origin]

rakehell ('reɪkˌhɛl) *Archaic.* ♦ *n* **1** a dissolute man; rake. ♦ *adj also* **rakehelly. 2** profligate; dissolute. [C16: from RAKE[1] + HELL; but compare Middle English *rakel* rash]

rake in *vb* (*tr, adv*) *Informal.* to acquire (money) in large amounts.

rake-off *Slang.* ♦ *n* **1** a share of profits, esp. one that is illegal or given as a bribe. ♦ *vb* **rake off. 2** (*tr, adv*) to take or receive (such a share of profits).

rake up *vb* (*tr, adv*) to revive, discover, or bring to light (something forgotten): *to rake up an old quarrel.*

raki *or* **rakee** (rɑː'kiː, 'rækɪ) *n* a strong spirit distilled in Turkey, Yugoslavia, etc., from grain, usually flavoured with aniseed or other aromatics. [C17: from Turkish *rāqī*]

rakish[1] ('reɪkɪʃ) *adj* dissolute; profligate. [C18: from RAKE[2] + -ISH] ► **'rakishly** *adv* ► **'rakishness** *n*

rakish[2] ('reɪkɪʃ) *adj* **1** dashing; jaunty: *a hat set at a rakish angle.* **2** *Nautical.* (of a ship or boat) having lines suggestive of speed. [C19: probably from RAKE[3] (sense 1), with reference to the sloping masts of pirate ships]

rale *or* **râle** (rɑːl) *n Med.* an abnormal crackling sound heard on auscultation of the chest, usually caused by the accumulation of fluid in the lungs. [C19: from French *râle,* from *râler* to breathe with a rattling sound; compare RAIL[3]]

Raleigh[1] ('rɔːlɪ, 'rɑː-) *n* a city in E central North Carolina, capital of the state. Pop.: 243 835 (1996 est.).

Raleigh[2] *or* **Ralegh** ('rɔːlɪ, 'rɑː-) *n* Sir **Walter.** ?1552–1618, English courtier, explorer, and writer; favourite of Elizabeth I. After unsuccessful attempts to colonize Virginia (1584–89), he led two expeditions to the Orinoco to search for gold (1595; 1616). He introduced tobacco and potatoes into England, and was imprisoned (1603–16) for conspiracy under James I. He was beheaded in 1618.

rall. *Music. abbrev. for* rallentando.

rallentando (ˌrælən'tændəʊ) *adj, adv Music.* becoming slower. Abbrev.: **rall.** Also: **ritardando, ritenuto.** [C19: Italian, from *rallentare* to slow down]

ralline ('rælaɪn, -ɪn) *adj* of, relating to, or belonging to the *Rallidae,* a family of birds that includes the rails, crakes, and coots. [C19: from New Latin *Rallus* RAIL[3]]

rally[1] ('rælɪ) *vb* **-lies, -lying, -lied. 1** to bring (a group, unit, etc.) into order, as after dispersal, or (of such a group) to reform and come to order: *the troops rallied for a final assault.* **2** (when *intr,* foll. by *to*) to organize (supporters, etc.) for a common cause or (of such people) to come together for a purpose. **3** to summon up (one's strength, spirits, etc.) or (of a person's health, strength, or spirits) to revive or recover. **4** (*intr*) *Stock Exchange.* to increase sharply after a decline: *steels rallied after a bad day.* **5** (*intr*) *Tennis, squash, etc.* to engage in a rally. ♦ *n, pl* **-lies. 6** a large gathering of people for a common purpose, esp. for some political cause: *the Nuremberg Rallies.* **7** a marked recovery of strength or spirits, as during illness. **8** a return to order after dispersal or rout, as of troops, etc. **9** *Stock Exchange.* a sharp increase in price or trading activity after a decline. **10** *Tennis, squash, etc.* an exchange of several shots before one player wins the point. **11** a type of motoring competition over public and closed roads. [C16: from Old French *rallier,* from RE- + *alier* to unite; see ALLY] ► **'rallier** *n*

rally[2] ('rælɪ) *vb* **-lies, -lying, -lied.** to mock or ridicule (someone) in a good-natured way; chaff; tease. [C17: from Old French *railler* to tease; see RAIL[2]]

rallycross ('rælɪˌkrɒs) *n* a form of motor sport in which cars race over a one-mile circuit of rough grass with some hard-surfaced sections. See also **autocross, motocross.**

rally round *vb* (*intr*) to come to the aid of (someone); offer moral or practical support.

ram (ræm) *n* **1** an uncastrated adult sheep. **2** a piston or moving plate, esp. one driven hydraulically or pneumatically. **3** the falling weight of a pile driver or similar device. **4** short for **battering ram. 5** Also called: **rostrum, beak.** a pointed projection in the stem of an ancient warship for puncturing the hull of enemy ships. **6** a warship equipped with a ram. **7** *Slang.* a sexually active man. ♦ *vb* **rams, ramming, rammed. 8** (*tr;* usually foll. by *into*) to force or drive, as by heavy blows: *to ram a post into the ground.* **9** (of a moving object) to crash with force (against another object) or (of two moving objects) to collide in this way: *the ships rammed the enemy.* **10** (*tr;* often foll. by *in* or *down*) to stuff or cram (something into a hole, etc.). **11** (*tr;* foll. by *onto, against,* etc.) to thrust violently: *he rammed the books onto the desk.* **12** (*tr*) to present (an idea, argument, etc.) forcefully or aggressively (esp. in the phrase **ram (something) down someone's throat**). **13** (*tr*) to drive (a charge) into a firearm. [Old

English *ramm;* related to Old High German *ram* ram, Old Norse *ramr* fierce, *rimma* to fight] ▸ **'rammer** *n*

Ram (ræm) *n* **the.** the constellation Aries, the first sign of the zodiac.

RAM[1] (ræm) *n Computing. acronym for* random access memory: semiconductor memory in which all storage locations can be rapidly accessed in the same amount of time. It forms the main memory of a computer, used by applications to perform tasks while the device is operating.

RAM[2] *abbrev. for* Royal Academy of Music.

r.a.m. *abbrev. for* relative atomic mass.

Rama ('rɑːmə) *n* (in Hindu mythology) any of Vishnu's three incarnations (the heroes Balarama, Parashurama, or Ramachandra). [from Sanskrit *Rāma* black, dark]

Ramachandra (ˌrɑːmə'tʃʌndrə) *n* (in Hindu mythology) an incarnation of Vishnu; the hero of the *Ramayana* and a character in the *Mahabharata.* See also **Rama.**

Ramadan, Rhamadhan (ˌræmə'dɑːn), *or* **Ramazan** (ˌræmə'zɑːn) *n* **1** the ninth month of the Muslim year, lasting 30 days, during which strict fasting is observed from sunrise to sunset. **2** the fast itself. [**C16**: from Arabic, literally: the hot month, from *ramad* dryness]

ram-air turbine *n* a small air-driven turbine fitted to an aircraft to provide power in the event of a failure of the normal systems.

Ramakrishna (ˌrɑːmə'krɪʃnə) *n* **Sri** (sriː). 1834–86, Hindu yogi and religious reformer. He preached the equal value of all religions as different paths to God.

Raman effect ('rɑːmən) *n* the change in wavelength of light that is scattered by electrons within a material. The effect is used in **Raman spectroscopy** for studying molecules. [**C20**: named after Sir Chandasekhara *Raman* (1888–1970), Indian physicist]

Ramanuja (ˌræmæ'nuːdʒə) *n* 11th century A.D., Indian Hindu philosopher and theologian.

Ramat Gan (rɑː'mɑːt 'gɑːn) *n* a city in Israel, E of Tel Aviv. Pop.: 121 700 (1997 est.).

Ramayana (rɑː'maɪənə) *n* a Sanskrit epic poem, composed about 300 B.C., recounting the feats of Ramachandra.

Rambert ('rɒmbɛə) *n* Dame **Marie.** 1888–1982, British ballet dancer and teacher, born in Poland: founded the **Ballet Rambert** (1926).

ramble ('ræmb^{ə}l) *vb (intr)* **1** to stroll about freely, as for relaxation, with no particular direction. **2** (of paths, streams, etc.) to follow a winding course; meander. **3** (of plants) to grow in a random fashion. **4** (of speech, writing, etc.) to lack organization. ◆ *n* **5** a leisurely stroll, esp. in the countryside. [**C17**: probably related to Middle Dutch *rammelen* to ROAM (of animals); see RAM]

rambler ('ræmblə) *n* **1** a weak-stemmed plant, esp. any of various cultivated hybrid roses that straggle over other vegetation. **2** a person who rambles, esp. one who takes country walks. **3** a person who lacks organization in his speech or writing.

rambling ('ræmblɪŋ) *adj* **1** straggling or sprawling haphazardly; unplanned: *a rambling old house.* **2** (of speech or writing) lacking a coherent plan; diffuse and disconnected. **3** (of a plant, esp. a rose) profusely climbing and straggling. **4** nomadic; wandering.

Ramboesque (ˌræmbəʊ'ɛsk) *adj* looking or behaving like or characteristic of Rambo, a fictional film character noted for his mindless brutality. [**C20**: after *Rambo, First Blood II,* released in Britain 1985] ▸ **'Rambo,ism** *n*

Rambouillet[1] (*French* rɑ̃bujɛ) *n* a town in N France, in the Yvelines department: site of the summer residence of French presidents. Pop.: 25 300 (1990).

Rambouillet[2] ('rɒmbuˌjeɪ, 'ræmbuˌleɪ; *French* rɑ̃bujɛ) *n* a fine-woolled merino-like breed of sheep. [**C19**: from RAMBOUILLET[1]]

rambunctious (ræm'bʌŋkʃəs) *adj Informal.* boisterous; unruly. [**C19**: probably from Icelandic *ram-* (intensifying prefix) + *-bunctious,* from BUMPTIOUS] ▸ **ram'bunctiously** *adv* ▸ **ram'bunctiousness** *n*

rambutan (ræm'buːt^{ə}n) *n* **1** a sapindaceous tree, *Nephelium lappaceum,* native to SE Asia, that has bright red edible fruit. **2** the fruit of this tree. [**C18**: from Malay, from *rambut* hair]

RAMC *abbrev. for* Royal Army Medical Corps.

Rameau (*French* ramo) *n* **Jean Philippe** (ʒɑ̃ filip). 1683–1764, French composer. His works include the opera *Castor et Pollux* (1737), chamber music, harpsichord pieces, church music, and cantatas. His *Traité de l'harmonie* (1722) was of fundamental importance in the development of modern harmony.

ramekin *or* **ramequin** ('ræmɪkɪn) *n* **1** a savoury dish made from a cheese mixture baked in a fireproof container. **2** the container itself. [**C18**: French *ramequin,* of Germanic origin]

ramentum (rə'mɛntəm) *n, pl* **-ta** (-tə). any of the thin brown scales that cover the stems and leaves of young ferns. [**C17**: from Latin *rādere* to scrape] ▸ **ramentaceous** (ˌræmɛn'teɪʃəs) *adj*

Rameses ('ræmɪˌsiːz) *n* a variant of **Ramses.**

rami ('reɪmaɪ) *n* the plural of **ramus.**

ramie *or* **ramee** ('ræmɪ) *n* **1** a woody urticaceous shrub of Asia, *Boehmeria nivea,* having broad leaves and a stem that yields a flaxlike fibre. **2** the fibre from this plant, used in making fabrics, cord, etc. [**C19**: from Malay *rami*]

ramification (ˌræmɪfɪ'keɪʃən) *n* **1** the act or process of ramifying or branching out. **2** an offshoot or subdivision. **3** (*often pl*) a subsidiary consequence, esp. one that complicates. **4** a structure of branching parts.

ramiform ('ræmɪˌfɔːm) *adj* having a branchlike shape. [**C19**: from Latin *rāmus* branch + -FORM]

ramify ('ræmɪˌfaɪ) *vb* **-fies, -fying, -fied. 1** to divide into branches or branchlike parts. **2** (*intr*) to develop complicating consequences; become complex. [**C16**: from French *ramifier,* from Latin *rāmus* branch + *facere* to make]

Ramillies ('ræmɪliːz; *French* ramiji) *n* a village in central Belgium where the Duke of Marlborough defeated the French in 1706.

ramjet *or* **ramjet engine** ('ræmˌdʒɛt) *n* **a** a type of jet engine in which fuel is burned in a duct using air compressed by the forward speed of the aircraft. **b** an aircraft powered by such an engine. Also called: **athodyd.**

rammish ('ræmɪʃ) *adj* like a ram, esp. in being lustful or foul-smelling. ▸ **'rammishly** *adv* ▸ **'rammishness** *n*

rammy ('ræmɪ) *n, pl* **-mies.** *Central Scot. urban dialect.* a noisy disturbance or free-for-all. [**C20**: perhaps from earlier Scot. *rammle* row, uproar]

ramose ('reɪməʊs, ræ'məʊs) *or* **ramous** ('reɪməs) *adj* having branches. [**C17**: from Latin *rāmōsus,* from *rāmus* branch] ▸ **'ramosely** *or* **'ramously** *adv* ▸ **ramosity** (ræ'mɒsɪtɪ) *n*

ramp (ræmp) *n* **1** a sloping floor, path, etc., that joins two surfaces at different levels. **2** a movable stairway by which passengers enter and leave an aircraft. **3** the act of ramping. **4** *Brit. slang.* a swindle, esp. one involving exorbitant prices. **5** an N.Z. name for **sleeping policeman.** ◆ *vb* **6** (*intr;* often foll. by *about* or *around*) (esp. of animals) to rush around in a wild excited manner. **7** to act in a violent or threatening manner, as when angry (esp. in the phrase **ramp and rage**). **8** (*tr*) *Finance.* to buy (a security) in the market with the object of raising its price and enhancing the image of the company behind it for financial gain. [**C18** (n): from **C13** *rampe,* from Old French *ramper* to crawl or rear, probably of Germanic origin; compare Middle Low German *ramp* cramp]

rampage *vb* (ræm'peɪdʒ). **1** (*intr*) to rush about in an angry, violent, or agitated fashion. ◆ *n* ('ræmpeɪdʒ, ræm'peɪdʒ). **2** angry or destructive behaviour. **3 on the rampage.** behaving violently or destructively. [**C18**: from Scottish, of uncertain origin; perhaps based on RAMP] ▸ **ram'pageous** *adj* ▸ **ram'pageously** *adv* ▸ **ram'pageousness** *n* ▸ **'rampager** *n*

rampant ('ræmpənt) *adj* **1** unrestrained or violent in behaviour, desire, opinions, etc. **2** growing or developing unchecked. **3** (*postpositive*) *Heraldry.* (of a beast) standing on the hind legs, the right foreleg raised above the left. **4** (of an arch) having one abutment higher than the other. [**C14**: from Old French *ramper* to crawl, rear; see RAMP] ▸ **'rampancy** *n* ▸ **'rampantly** *adv*

rampart ('ræmpɑːt) *n* **1** the surrounding embankment of a fort, often including any walls, parapets, walks, etc., that are built on the bank. **2** anything resembling a rampart in form or function, esp. in being a defence or bulwark. ◆ *vb* **3** (*tr*) to provide with a rampart; fortify. [**C16**: from Old French, from *remparer,* from RE- + *emparer* to take possession of, from Old Provençal *antparar,* from Latin *ante* before + *parāre* to prepare]

Ramphal (ˌræm'fɑːl) *n* Sir **Shridath Surendranath,** known as *Sunni.* born 1928, Guyanese diplomat and Commonwealth Secretary-General (1975–90).

rampion ('ræmpɪən) *n* **1** a campanulaceous plant, *Campanula rapunculus,* native to Europe and Asia, that has clusters of bluish flowers and an edible white tuberous root used in salads. **2** any of several plants of the related genus *Phyteuma* that are native to Europe and Asia and have heads of blue flowers. [**C16**: probably from Old French *raiponce,* from Old Italian *raponzo,* from *rapa* turnip, from Latin *rāpum* turnip; see RAPE[2]]

Rampur ('ræmpʊə) *n* a city in N India, in N Uttar Pradesh. Pop.: 243 742 (1991).

ram raid *n Informal.* a raid in which a stolen car is driven through a shop window in order to steal goods from the shop. ▸ **ram raiding** *n* ▸ **ram raider** *n*

ramrod ('ræmˌrɒd) *n* **1** a rod for cleaning the barrel of a rifle or other small firearms. **2** a rod for ramming in the charge of a muzzle-loading firearm.

Ramsay ('ræmzɪ) *n* **1 Allan.** ?1686–1758, Scottish poet, editor, and bookseller, noted particularly for his pastoral comedy *The Gentle Shepherd* (1725): first person to introduce the circulating library in Scotland. **2** his son, **Allan.** 1713–84, Scottish portrait painter. **3 James Andrew Broun.** See (1st Marquis and 10th Earl of) **Dalhousie. 4** Sir **William.** 1852–1916, Scottish chemist. He discovered argon (1894) with Rayleigh, isolated helium (1895), and identified neon, krypton, and xenon: Nobel prize for chemistry 1904.

Ramses ('ræmsiːz) *or* **Rameses** *n* any of 12 kings of ancient Egypt, who ruled from ?1315 to ?1090 B.C.

Ramses II *or* **Rameses II** *n* died ?1225 B.C., king of ancient Egypt (?1292–?25). His reign was marked by war with the Hittites and the construction of many colossal monuments, esp. the rock temple at Abu Simbel.

Ramses III *or* **Rameses III** *n* died ?1167 B.C., king of ancient Egypt (?1198–?67). His reign was marked by wars in Libya and Syria.

Ramsey ('ræmzɪ) *n* Sir **Alf(red) (Ernest).** 1922–99, English footballer and football manager, who played for England 32 times and managed England when they won the World Cup (1966).

Ramsgate ('ræmzˌgeɪt) *n* a port and resort in SE England, in E Kent on the North Sea coast. Pop.: 37 895 (1991).

ramshackle ('ræmˌʃæk^{ə}l) *adj* (esp. of buildings) badly constructed or maintained; rickety, shaky, or derelict. [**C17** *ramshackled,* from obsolete *ransackle* to RANSACK]

ramshorn snail ('ræmzˌhɔːn) *n* any of various freshwater snails of the genus *Planorbis* that are widely used in aquariums.

Ram Singh ('ræm 'sɪŋ) *n* 1816–85, Indian leader of a puritanical Sikh sect, the Kukas, who tried to remove the British from India through a policy of noncooperation.

ramsons ('ræmzənz, -sənz) *pl n* (*usually functioning as sing*) **1** a broad-leaved garlic, *Allium ursinum,* native to Europe and Asia. **2** the bulbous root of this plant, eaten as a relish. [Old English *hramesa;* related to Middle Low German *ramese,* Norwegian *rams*]

ramstam ('ræm'stæm) *Scot.* ◆ *adv* **1** headlong; hastily. ◆ *adj* **2** headlong; precipitate. [**C18**: perhaps from RAM + dialect *stam* to stamp]

ramtil ('ræmtɪl) *n* **1** an African plant, *Guizotia abyssinica,* grown in India: family *Compositae* (composites). **2** Also called: **Niger seed.** the seed of this plant, used as a source of oil and a bird food. [**C19**: from Hindi, from Sanskrit *rāma* black + *tila* sesame]

ramulose ('ræmjʊ,ləʊs) *or* **ramulous** ('ræmjʊləs) *adj* (of the parts or organs of animals and plants) having many small branches. **[C18:** from Latin *rāmulōsus* full of branching veins, from *rāmulus* twig, from *rāmus* branch**]**

ramus ('reɪməs) *n, pl* **-mi** (-maɪ). **1** the barb of a bird's feather. **2** either of the two parts of the lower jaw of a vertebrate. **3** any part or organ that branches from another part. **[C19:** from Latin: branch**]**

ran (ræn) *vb* the past tense of **run.**

RAN *abbrev. for* Royal Australian Navy.

Rancagua (*Spanish* raŋ'kagwa) *n* a city in central Chile. Pop.: 193 755 (1995 est.).

rance (rɑːns) *n* a type of red marble, often with white or blue graining, that comes from Belgium. **[C19:** apparently from French *ranche* rod, pole**]**

ranch (rɑːntʃ) *n* **1** a large tract of land, esp. one in North America, together with the necessary personnel, buildings, and equipment, for rearing livestock, esp. cattle. **2a** any large farm for the rearing of a particular kind of livestock or crop: *a mink ranch.* **2b** the buildings, land, etc., connected with it. ♦ *vb* **3** (*intr*) to manage or run a ranch. **4** (*tr*) to raise (animals) on or as if on a ranch. **[C19:** from Mexican Spanish *rancho* small farm; see RANCHO**]**

rancher ('rɑːntʃə) *n* a person who owns, manages, or works on a ranch.

rancherie ('rɑːntʃərɪ) *n* (in British Columbia, Canada) a settlement of North American Indians, esp. on a reserve. **[**from Spanish *rancheria***]**

ranchero (rɑːn'tʃeərəʊ) *n, pl* **-ros.** *Southwestern U.S.* another word for **rancher. [C19:** from American Spanish**]**

Ranchi ('ræntʃɪ) *n* an industrial city in E India, in S Bihar between the coal and iron belts of the Chota Nagpur Plateau. Pop.: 599 306 (1991).

rancho ('rɑːntʃəʊ) *n, pl* **-chos.** *Southwestern U.S.* **1** a hut or group of huts for housing ranch workers. **2** another word for **ranch. [C17:** from Mexican Spanish: camp, from Old Spanish *ranchar* to be billeted, from Old French *ranger* to place**]**

rancid ('rænsɪd) *adj* **1** (of butter, bacon, etc.) having an unpleasant stale taste or smell as the result of decomposition. **2** (of a taste or smell) rank or sour; stale. **[C17:** from Latin *rancidus* rank, from *rancēre* to stink**]** ▸ **rancidity** (ræn'sɪdɪtɪ) *or* **'rancidness** *n*

rancour *or U.S.* **rancor** ('ræŋkə) *n* malicious resentfulness or hostility; spite. **[C14:** from Old French, from Late Latin *rancor* rankness**]** ▸ **'rancorous** *adj* ▸ **'rancorously** *adv* ▸ **'rancorousness** *n*

rand[1] (rænd, rɒnt) *n* the standard monetary unit of the Republic of South Africa, divided into 100 cents. **[C20:** from Afrikaans, shortened from WITWATERSRAND, referring to the gold-mining there; related to RAND[2]**]**

rand[2] (rænd) *n* **1** *Shoemaking.* a leather strip put in the heel of a shoe before the lifts are put on. **2** *Dialect.* **2a** a strip or margin; border. **2b** a strip of cloth; selvage. **[**Old English; related to Old High German *rant* border, rim of a shield, Old Norse *rönd* shield, rim**]**

Rand (rænd) *n* **the.** short for **Witwatersrand.**

R & A *abbrev. for* Royal and Ancient (Golf Club, St Andrews).

randan[1] (ræn'dæn, 'rændæn) *n* a boat rowed by three people, in which the person in the middle uses two oars and the people fore and aft use one oar each. **[C19:** of uncertain origin**]**

randan[2] (,ræn'dæn, 'ræn,dæn) *n* rowdy behaviour; a spree. **[C18:** perhaps changed from RANDOM**]**

R & B *abbrev. for* rhythm and blues.

R & D *abbrev. for* research and development.

randem ('rændɛm) *adv* **1** with three horses harnessed together as a team. ♦ *n* **2** a carriage or team of horses so driven. **[C19:** probably from RANDOM + TANDEM**]**

Randers (*Danish* 'randərs) *n* a port and industrial centre in Denmark, in E Jutland on **Randers Fjord** (an inlet of the Kattegat). Pop.: 61 435 (1995).

Randolph ('rændɒlf, -dəlf) *n* **1 Edmund Jennings,** 1753–1813, U.S. politician. He was a member of the convention that framed the U.S. constitution (1787), attorney general (1789–94), and secretary of state (1794–95). **2 John,** called *Randolph of Roanoke.* 1773–1833, U.S. politician, noted for his eloquence: in 1820 he opposed the Missouri Compromise that outlawed slavery. **3** Sir **Thomas;** 1st Earl of Moray. Died 1332, Scottish soldier: regent after the death of Robert the Bruce (1329).

random ('rændəm) *adj* **1** lacking any definite plan or prearranged order; haphazard: *a random selection.* **2** *Statistics.* **2a** having a value which cannot be determined but only described probabilistically: a *random variable.* **2b** chosen without regard to any characteristics of the individual members of the population so that each has an equal chance of being selected: *random sampling.* ♦ *n* **3 at random.** in a purposeless fashion; not following any prearranged order. **[C14:** from Old French *randon,* from *randir* to gallop, of Germanic origin; compare Old High German *rinnan* to run**]** ▸ **'randomly** *adv* ▸ **'randomness** *n*

random access *n* another name for **direct access.**

randomize *or* **randomise** ('rændə,maɪz) *vb* (*tr*) to set up (a selection process, sample, etc.) in a deliberately random way in order to enhance the statistical validity of any results obtained. ▸ **,randomi'zation** *or* **,randomi'sation** *n* ▸ **'random,izer** *or* **'random,iser** *n*

random numbers *pl n* a sequence of numbers that do not form any progression, used to facilitate unbiased sampling of a population. A **random-number generator** is part of the software of most computers and many calculators.

random rubble *n* masonry in which untooled stones are set without coursing.

random variable *n Statistics.* a quantity that may take any of a range of values, either continuous or discrete, which cannot be predicted with certainty but only described probabilistically. Abbrev.: **rv.**

random walk *n* **1** a mathematical model used to describe physical processes, such as diffusion, in which a particle moves in straight-line steps of constant length but random direction. **2** *Statistics.* a route consisting of successive and connected steps in which each step is chosen by a random mechanism uninfluenced by any previous step.

random walk theory *n Stock Exchange.* the theory that the future movement of share prices does not reflect past movements and therefore will not follow a discernible pattern.

R and R *U.S. military. abbrev. for* rest and recreation.

randy ('rændɪ) *adj* **randier, randiest. 1** *Informal, chiefly Brit.* **1a** sexually excited or aroused. **1b** sexually eager or lustful. **2** *Chiefly Scot.* lacking any sense of propriety or restraint; reckless. ♦ *n, pl* **randies. 3** *Chiefly Scot.* **3a** a rude or reckless person. **3b** a coarse rowdy woman. **[C17:** probably from obsolete *rand* to RANT**]** ▸ **'randily** *adv* ▸ **'randiness** *n*

ranee ('rɑːnɪ) *n* a variant spelling of **rani.**

Ranelagh Gardens ('rænɪlə) *pl n* a public garden in Chelsea opened in 1742: a centre for members of fashionable society to meet and promenade. The gardens were closed in 1804. Also called: **Ranelagh. [**named after the Earl of *Ranelagh,* in whose grounds they were sited**]**

Ranfurly Shield (ræn'fɜːlɪ) *n* (in New Zealand) the premier rugby trophy, competed for annually by provincial teams. **[C20:** named after the Earl of *Ranfurly* (1856–1933), 15th Governor of New Zealand (1897–1904), who presented it to the New Zealand Rugby Football Union in 1902**]**

rang (ræŋ) *vb* the past tense of **ring**[2].

USAGE See at **ring**[2].

rangatira (,rʌŋgə'tɪərə) *n N.Z.* a Maori chief of either sex. **[**Maori**]**

range (reɪndʒ) *n* **1** the limits within which a person or thing can function effectively: *the range of vision.* **2** the limits within which any fluctuation takes place: *a range of values.* **3** the total products of a manufacturer, designer, or stockist: *the new autumn range.* **4a** the maximum effective distance of a projectile fired from a weapon. **4b** the distance between a target and a weapon. **5** an area set aside for shooting practice or rocket testing. **6** the total distance which a ship, aircraft, or land vehicle is capable of covering without taking on fresh fuel: *the range of this car is about 160 miles.* **7** *Physics.* the distance that a particle of ionizing radiation, such as an electron or proton, can travel through a given medium, esp. air, before ceasing to cause ionization. **8** *Maths, logic.* **8a** (of a function) the set of values that the function takes for all possible arguments. Compare **domain** (sense 7a). **8b** (of a variable) the set of values that a variable can take. **8c** (of a quantifier) the set of values that the variable bound by the quantifier can take. **9** *Statistics.* a measure of dispersion obtained by subtracting the smallest from the largest sample values. **10** the extent of pitch difference between the highest and lowest notes of a voice, instrument, etc. **11** *U.S. and Canadian.* **11a** an extensive tract of open land on which livestock can graze. **11b** (*as modifier*): *range cattle.* **12** the geographical region in which a species of plant or animal normally grows or lives. **13** a rank, row, or series of items. **14** a series or chain of mountains. **15** a large stove with burners and one or more ovens, usually heated by solid fuel. **16** the act or process of ranging. **17** *Nautical.* a line of sight taken from the sea along two or more navigational aids that mark a navigable channel. **18** the extension or direction of a survey line, established by marking two or more points. **19** a double-faced bookcase, as in a library. **20 range of significance.** *Philosophy, logic.* the set of subjects for which a given predicate is intelligible. ♦ *vb* **21** to establish or be situated in a line, row, or series. **22** (*tr; often reflexive,* foll. by *with*) to put into a specific category; classify: *she ranges herself with the angels.* **23** (foll. by *on*) to aim or point (a telescope, gun, etc.) or (of a gun, telescope, etc.) to be pointed or aimed. **24** to establish the distance of (a target) from (a weapon). **25** (*intr*) (of a gun or missile) to have a specified range. **26** (when *intr;* foll. by *over*) to wander about (in) an area; roam (over). **27** (*intr;* foll. by *over*) (of an animal or plant) to live or grow in its normal habitat. **28** (*tr*) to put (cattle) to graze on a range. **29** (*intr*) to fluctuate within specific limits: *their ages range from 18 to 21.* **30** (*intr*) to extend or run in a specific direction. **31** (*tr*) *Nautical.* to coil (an anchor rope or chain) so that it will pay out smoothly. **32** (*intr*) *Nautical.* (of a vessel) to swing back and forth while at anchor. **33** (*tr*) to make (lines of printers' type) level or even at the margin. **[C13:** from Old French: row, from *ranger* to position, from *renc* line**]**

rangefinder ('reɪndʒ,faɪndə) *n* **1** an instrument for determining the distance of an object from the observer, esp. in order to sight a gun or focus a camera. **2** another word for **tacheometer.**

rangeland ('reɪndʒ,lænd) *n* (*often pl*) land that naturally produces forage plants suitable for grazing but where rainfall is too low or erratic for growing crops.

range light *n Nautical.* **1** one of a pattern of navigation lights, usually fixed ashore, used by vessels for manoeuvring in narrow channels at night. **2** one of a distinctive pattern of lights shown at night on the masts of a powered vessel, such as a tugboat, to aid in identifying its size, number of barges in tow, etc.

ranger ('reɪndʒə) *n* **1** (*sometimes cap.*) an official in charge of a forest, park, estate, nature reserve, etc. **2** *Chiefly U.S.* a person employed to patrol a State or national park or forest. Brit. equivalent: **warden. 3** *U.S.* one of a body of armed troops employed to police a State or district: *a Texas ranger.* **4** (in the U.S. and certain other armies) a commando specially trained in making raids. **5** a person who wanders about large areas of country; a rover.

Ranger[1] *or* **Ranger Guide** ('reɪndʒə) *n Brit.* a member of the senior branch of the Guides.

Ranger[2] ('reɪndʒə) *n* any of a series of nine American lunar probes launched between 1961 and 1965, three of which transmitted to earth photographs of the moon.

ranging pole *or* **rod** *n* a pole for marking positions in surveying. Also called: **range pole, rod.**

rangiora (,ræŋgɪ'ɔːrə, ,ræŋɪ-) *n* an evergreen shrub or small tree, *Brachyglottis repanda,* of New Zealand, having large ovate leaves and small greenish-white flowers: family *Compositae* (composites). **[**Maori**]**

Rangoon (ræŋ'gu:n) *n* the former name (until 1989) of **Yangon**.

rangy ('reɪndʒɪ) *adj* **rangier, rangiest. 1** (of animals or people) having long slender limbs. **2** adapted to wandering or roaming. **3** allowing considerable freedom of movement; spacious; roomy. [C19: from RANGE + -Y[1]] ▸ **'rangily** *adv* ▸ **'ranginess** *n*

rani *or* **ranee** ('rɑ:nɪ) *n* (in oriental countries, esp. India) a queen or princess; the wife of a rajah. [C17: from Hindi: queen, from Sanskrit *rājñī*, feminine of *rājan* RAJAH]

Ranjit Singh ('rʌndʒɪt 'sɪŋ) *n* called *the Lion of the Punjab*. 1780–1839; founder of the Sikh kingdom in the Punjab.

rank[1] (ræŋk) *n* **1** a position, esp. an official one, within a social organization, esp. the armed forces: *the rank of captain*. **2** high social or other standing; status. **3** a line or row of people or things. **4** the position of an item in any ordering or sequence. **5** *Brit.* a place where taxis wait to be hired. **6** a line of soldiers drawn up abreast of each other. Compare **file**[1] (sense 5). **7** any of the eight horizontal rows of squares on a chessboard. **8** (in systemic grammar) one of the units of description of which a grammar is composed. Ranks of English grammar are sentence, clause, group, word, and morpheme. **9** *Music.* a set of organ pipes controlled by the same stop. **10** *Maths.* (of a matrix) the largest number of linearly independent rows or columns; the number of rows (or columns) of the nonzero determinant of greatest order that can be extracted from the matrix. **11 break ranks.** *Military.* to fall out of line, esp. when under attack. **12 close ranks.** to maintain discipline or solidarity, esp. in anticipation of attack. **13 pull rank.** to get one's own way by virtue of one's superior position or rank. ◆ *vb* **14** (*tr*) to arrange (people or things) in rows or lines; range. **15** to accord or be accorded a specific position in an organization, society, or group. **16** (*tr*) to array (a set of objects) as a sequence, esp. in terms of the natural arithmetic ordering of some measure of the elements: *to rank students by their test scores*. **17** (*intr*) to be important; rate: *money ranks low in her order of priorities*. **18** *Chiefly U.S.* to take precedence or surpass in rank: *the colonel ranks at this camp*. [C16: from Old French *ranc* row, rank, of Germanic origin; compare Old High German *hring* circle]

rank[2] (ræŋk) *adj* **1** showing vigorous and profuse growth: *rank weeds*. **2** highly offensive or disagreeable, esp. in smell or taste. **3** (*prenominal*) complete or absolute; utter: *a rank outsider*. **4** coarse or vulgar; gross: *his language was rank*. [Old English *ranc* straight, noble; related to Old Norse *rakkr* upright, Dutch, Swedish *rank* tall and thin, weak] ▸ **'rankly** *adv* ▸ **'rankness** *n*

Rank *n* **1** (ræŋk). **J(oseph) Arthur,** 1st Baron. 1888–1972, British industrialist and film executive, whose companies dominated the British film industry in the 1940s and 1950s. **2** (*German* raŋk). **Otto** ('ɔto). 1884–1939, Austrian psychoanalyst, noted for his theory that the trauma of birth may be reflected in certain forms of mental illness.

rank and file *n* **1** the ordinary soldiers of an army, excluding the officers. **2** the great mass or majority of any group or organization, as opposed to the leadership. **3** (*modifier*) of, relating to, or characteristic of the rank and file: *rank-and-file opinion; rank-and-file support*. ▸ **rank and filer** *n*

ranker ('ræŋkə) *n* **1** a soldier in the ranks. **2** a commissioned officer who entered service as a recruit, esp. in the army.

Rankine cycle ('ræŋkɪn) *n* the thermodynamic cycle in steam engines by which water is pumped into a boiler at one end and the steam is condensed at the other. [C19: named after W. J. M. *Rankine* (1820–72), Scottish physicist]

Rankine scale *n* an absolute scale of temperature in which the unit of temperature is equal to that on the Fahrenheit scale and the zero value of temperature is equal to −459.67°F. Compare **Kelvin scale.**

ranking ('ræŋkɪŋ) *adj* **1** *Chiefly U.S. and Canadian.* prominent; high ranking. **2** *Caribbean slang.* possessed of style; fashionable; exciting. ◆ *n* **3** a position on a scale; rating: *a ranking in a tennis tournament*.

rankle ('ræŋk^əl) *vb* (*intr*) to cause severe and continuous irritation, anger, or bitterness; fester: *his failure to win still rankles*. [C14 *ranclen*, from Old French *draoncler* to fester, from *draoncle* ulcer, from Latin *dracunculus* small serpent, from *dracō* serpent; see DRAGON]

rankshift ('ræŋk,ʃɪft) (in systemic grammar) ◆ *n* **1** a phenomenon in which a unit at one rank in the grammar has the function of a unit at a lower rank, as for example in the phrase *the house on the corner*, where the words *on the corner* shift down from the rank of group to the rank of word. ◆ *vb* **2** to shift or be shifted from one linguistic rank to another.

ransack ('rænsæk) *vb* (*tr*) **1** to search through every part of (a house, box, etc.); examine thoroughly. **2** to plunder; pillage. [C13: from Old Norse *rann* house + *saka* to search, SEEK] ▸ **'ransacker** *n*

ransom ('rænsəm) *n* **1** the release of captured prisoners, property, etc., on payment of a stipulated price. **2** the price demanded or stipulated for such a release. **3** rescue or redemption of any kind. **4 hold to ransom. 4a** to keep (prisoners, property, etc.) in confinement until payment for their release is made or received. **4b** to attempt to force (a person or persons) to comply with one's demands. **5 a king's ransom.** a very large amount of money or valuables. ◆ *vb* (*tr*) **6** to pay a stipulated price and so obtain the release of (prisoners, property, etc.). **7** to set free (prisoners, property, etc.) upon receiving the payment demanded. **8** to redeem; rescue: *Christ ransomed men from sin*. [C14: from Old French *ransoun*, from Latin *redemptiō* a buying back, REDEMPTION] ▸ **'ransomer** *n*

Ransom ('rænsəm) *n* **John Crowe.** 1888–1974, U.S. poet and critic.

Ransome ('rænsəm) *n* **Arthur.** 1884–1967, English writer, best known for his books for children, including *Swallows and Amazons* (1930) and *Great Northern?* (1947).

rant (rænt) *vb* **1** to utter (something) in loud, violent, or bombastic tones. **2** (*intr*) *Chiefly Scot.* to make merry; frolic. ◆ *n* **3** loud, declamatory, or extravagant speech; bombast. **4** *Chiefly Scot.* a wild revel. **5** *Scot.* an energetic dance or its tune. [C16: from Dutch *ranten* to rave; related to German *ranzen* to gambol] ▸ **'ranter** *n* ▸ **'ranting** *adj, n* ▸ **'rantingly** *adv*

ranunculaceous (rə,nʌŋkju'leɪʃəs) *adj* of, relating to, or belonging to the *Ranunculaceae*, a N temperate family of flowering plants typically having flowers with five petals and numerous anthers and styles. The family includes the buttercup, clematis, hellebore, and columbine.

ranunculus (rə'nʌŋkjʊləs) *n, pl* **-luses** *or* **-li** (-,laɪ). any ranunculaceous plant of the genus *Ranunculus*, having finely divided leaves and typically yellow five-petalled flowers. The genus includes buttercup, crowfoot, spearwort, and lesser celandine. [C16: from Latin: tadpole, from *rāna* a frog]

RAOC *abbrev. for* Royal Army Ordnance Corps.

rap[1] (ræp) *vb* **raps, rapping, rapped. 1** to strike (a fist, stick, etc.) against (something) with a sharp quick blow; knock: *he rapped at the door*. **2** (*intr*) to make a sharp loud sound, esp. by knocking. **3** (*tr*) to rebuke or criticize sharply. **4** (*tr*; foll. by *out*) to put (forth) in sharp rapid speech; utter in an abrupt fashion: *to rap out orders*. **5** (*intr*) *Slang.* to talk, esp. volubly. **6** (*intr*) to perform a rhythmic monologue with a musical backing. **7 rap over the knuckles.** to reprimand. ◆ *n* **8** a sharp quick blow or the sound produced by such a blow. **9** a sharp rebuke or criticism. **10** *Slang.* voluble talk; chatter: *stop your rap*. **11a** a fast, rhythmic monologue over a prerecorded instrumental track. **11b** (*as modifier*): *rap music*. **12** *Slang.* a legal charge or case. **13 beat the rap.** *U.S. and Canadian slang.* to escape punishment or be acquitted of a crime. **14 take the rap.** *Slang.* to suffer the consequences of a mistake, misdeed, or crime, whether guilty or not. [C14: probably of Scandinavian origin; compare Swedish *rappa* to beat] ▸ **'rapping** *n*

rap[2] (ræp) *n* (*used with a negative*) the least amount (esp. in the phrase **not to care a rap**). [C18: probably from *ropaire* counterfeit coin formerly current in Ireland]

rap[3] (ræp) *vb, n Austral. informal.* a variant spelling of **wrap** (senses 8, 12).

rapacious (rə'peɪʃəs) *adj* **1** practising pillage or rapine. **2** greedy or grasping. **3** (of animals, esp. birds) subsisting by catching living prey. [C17: from Latin *rapāx* grasping, from *rapere* to seize] ▸ **ra'paciously** *adv* ▸ **rapacity** (rə'pæsɪtɪ) *or* **ra'paciousness** *n*

Rapacki (*Polish* ra'patski) *n* **Adam** ('adam). 1909–70, Polish politician: foreign minister (1956–68): proposed (1957) the denuclearization of Poland, Czechoslovakia, East Germany, and West Germany (the **Rapacki Plan**): rejected by the West because of Soviet predominance in conventional weapons.

Rapallo (*Italian* ra'pallo) *n* a port and resort in NW Italy, in Liguria on the **Gulf of Rapallo** (an inlet of the Ligurian Sea): scene of the signing of two treaties after World War I. Pop.: 30 000 (1990 est.).

Rapa Nui ('rɑ:pɑ: 'nu:ɪ) *n* another name for **Easter Island.**

rape[1] (reɪp) *n* **1** the offence of forcing a person, esp. a woman, to submit to sexual intercourse against that person's will. See also **statutory rape. 2** the act of despoiling a country in warfare; rapine. **3** any violation or abuse: *the rape of justice*. **4** *Archaic.* abduction: *the rape of the Sabine women*. ◆ *vb* (*mainly tr*) **5** to commit rape upon (a person). **6** (*also intr*) to plunder or despoil (a place) in war. **7** *Archaic.* to carry off by force; abduct. [C14: from Latin *rapere* to seize]

rape[2] (reɪp) *n* a Eurasian cruciferous plant, *Brassica napus*, that has bright yellow flowers and is cultivated for its seeds, which yield a useful oil, and as a fodder plant. Also called: **colza, cole.** [C14: from Latin *rāpum* turnip]

rape[3] (reɪp) *n* (*often pl*) the skins and stalks of grapes left after wine-making: used in making vinegar. [C17: from French *râpe*, of Germanic origin; compare Old High German *raspōn* to scrape together]

rapeseed ('reɪp,si:d) *n* the seed of the rape plant.

rapeseed oil *n* oil extracted from rapeseed, used as a lubricant, as a constituent of soaps, etc. Also called: **rape oil, colza oil.**

Raphael ('ræfeɪəl) *n* **1** *Bible.* one of the archangels; the angel of healing and the guardian of Tobias (Tobit 3:17; 5-12). Feast day: Sept. 29. **2** original name *Raffaello Santi* or *Sanzio*. 1483–1520, Italian painter and architect, regarded as one of the greatest artists of the High Renaissance. His many paintings include the *Sistine Madonna* (?1513) and the *Transfiguration* (unfinished, 1520). ▸ **,Raphael'esque** *adj*

raphe ('reɪfɪ) *n, pl* **-phae** (-fi:). **1** an elongated ridge of conducting tissue along the side of certain seeds. **2** a longitudinal groove on the valve of a diatom. **3** *Anatomy.* a connecting ridge, as that between the two halves of the medulla oblongata. [C18: via New Latin from Greek *rhaphē* a seam, from *rhaptein* to sew together]

raphia ('ræfɪə) *n* a variant spelling of **raffia.**

raphide ('reɪfaɪd) *or* **raphis** ('reɪfɪs) *n, pl* **raphides** ('ræfɪ,di:z). any of numerous needle-shaped crystals, usually of calcium oxalate, that occur in many plant cells as a metabolic product. [C18: from French, from Greek *rhaphis* needle]

rapid ('ræpɪd) *adj* **1** (of an action or movement) performed or occurring during a short interval of time; quick: *a rapid transformation*. **2** characterized by high speed: *rapid movement*. **3** acting or moving quickly; fast: *a rapid worker*. ◆ See also **rapids.** [C17: from Latin *rapidus* tearing away, from *rapere* to seize; see RAPE[1]] ▸ **'rapidly** *adv* ▸ **rapidity** (rə'pɪdɪtɪ) *or* **'rapidness** *n*

rapid eye movement *n* movement of the eyeballs under closed eyelids during paradoxical sleep, which occurs while the sleeper is dreaming. Abbrev.: **REM.**

rapid fire *n* **1** a fast rate of gunfire. ◆ *adj* **rapid-fire. 2a** firing shots rapidly. **2b** denoting medium-calibre mounted guns designed for rapid fire. **3** done, delivered, or occurring in rapid succession.

rapids ('ræpɪdz) *pl n* part of a river where the current is very fast and turbulent.

rapid transit chess *n* the U.S. name for **lightning chess.** [from the name of the New York City underground railway system]

rapier ('reɪpɪə) *n* **1** a long narrow two-edged sword with a guarded hilt, used as a thrusting weapon, popular in the 16th and 17th centuries. **2** a smaller single-edged 18th-century sword, used principally in France. [C16: from Old French *espee rapiere,* literally: rasping sword; see RASP[1]] ▸ **'rapier-,like** *adj*

rapine ('ræpaɪn) *n* the seizure of property by force; pillage. [C15: from Latin *rapīna* plundering, from *rapere* to snatch]

rapist ('reɪpɪst) *n* a person who commits rape.

rapparee (,ræpə'riː) *n* **1** an Irish irregular soldier of the late 17th century. **2** *Obsolete.* any plunderer or robber. [C17: from Irish *rapairidhe* pike, probably from English RAPIER]

rappee (ræ'piː) *n* a moist English snuff of the 18th and 19th centuries. [C18: from French *tabac râpé,* literally: scraped tobacco, from *râper* to scrape; see RAPE[3], RASP[1]]

rappel (ræ'pɛl) *vb* **-pels, -pelling, -pelled,** *n* **1** another word for **abseil.** ◆ *n* **2** (formerly) a drumbeat to call soldiers to arms. [C19: from French, from *rappeler* to call back, from Latin *appellāre* to summon]

rapper ('ræpə) *n* **1** something used for rapping, such as a knocker on a door. **2** a performer of rap music.

rapport (ræ'pɔː) *n* (often foll. by *with*) a sympathetic relationship or understanding. See also **en rapport.** [C15: from French, from *rapporter* to bring back, from RE- + *aporter,* from Latin *apportāre,* from *ad* to + *portāre* to carry]

rapporteur (,ræpɔː'tɜː) *n* a person appointed by a committee to prepare reports of meetings or carry out an investigation. [C18: from French, literally: recorder, reporter]

rapprochement *French.* (raprɔʃmɑ̃) *n* a resumption of friendly relations, esp. between two countries. [C19: literally: bringing closer]

rapscallion (ræp'skæljən) *n* a disreputable person; rascal or rogue. [C17: from earlier *rascallion;* see RASCAL]

rapt[1] (ræpt) *adj* **1** totally absorbed; engrossed; spellbound, esp. through or as if through emotion: *rapt with wonder.* **2** characterized by or proceeding from rapture: *a rapt smile.* [C14: from Latin *raptus* carried away, from *rapere* to seize; see RAPE[1]] ▸ **'raptly** *adv*

rapt[2] (ræpt) *adj* Also: **wrapped.** *Austral. and N.Z. informal.* very pleased: delighted.

raptor ('ræptə) *n* another name for **bird of prey.** [C17: from Latin: plunderer, from *rapere* to take by force]

raptorial (ræp'tɔːrɪəl) *adj Zoology.* **1** (of the feet of birds) adapted for seizing prey. **2** (esp. of birds) feeding on prey; predatory. **3** of or relating to birds of prey. [C19: from Latin *raptor* a robber, from *rapere* to snatch]

rapture ('ræptʃə) *n* **1** the state of mind resulting from feelings of high emotion; joyous ecstasy. **2** (*often pl*) an expression of ecstatic joy. **3** the act of transporting a person from one sphere of existence to another, esp. from earth to heaven. ◆ *vb* **4** (*tr*) *Archaic or literary.* to entrance; enrapture. [C17: from Medieval Latin *raptūra,* from Latin *raptus* RAPT[1]]

rapturous ('ræptʃərəs) *adj* experiencing or manifesting ecstatic joy or delight. ▸ **'rapturously** *adv* ▸ **'rapturousness** *n*

RAR *abbrev. for* Royal Australian Regiment.

rara avis ('rɛərə 'eɪvɪs) *n, pl* **rarae aves** ('rɛəriː 'eɪviːz). an unusual, uncommon, or exceptional person or thing. [Latin: rare bird]

rare[1] (rɛə) *adj* **1** not widely known; not frequently used or experienced; uncommon or unusual: *a rare word.* **2** occurring seldom: *a rare appearance.* **3** not widely distributed; not generally occurring: *a rare herb.* **4** (of a gas, esp. the atmosphere at high altitudes) having a low density; thin; rarefied. **5** uncommonly great; extreme: *kind to a rare degree.* **6** exhibiting uncommon excellence; superlatively good or fine: *rare skill.* **7** highly valued because of its uncommonness: *a rare prize.* [C14: from Latin *rārus* sparse] ▸ **'rareness** *n*

rare[2] (rɛə) *adj* (of meat, esp. beef) very lightly cooked. [Old English *hrēr;* perhaps related to *hreaw* RAW]

rarebit ('rɛəbɪt) *n* another term for **Welsh rabbit.** [C18: by folk etymology from (WELSH) RABBIT; see RARE[2], BIT[1]]

rare earth *n* **1** any oxide of a lanthanide. **2** Also called: **rare-earth element.** another name for **lanthanide.**

raree show ('rɛəriː) *n* **1** a street show or carnival. **2** another name for **peepshow.** [C17: *raree* from RARE[1]]

rarefaction (,rɛərɪ'fækʃən) *or* **rarefication** (,rɛərɪfɪ'keɪʃən) *n* the act or process of making less dense or the state of being less dense. ▸ **,rare'factional, ,rarefi'cational,** *or* **,rare'factive** *adj*

rarefied ('rɛərɪ,faɪd) *adj* **1** exalted in nature or character; lofty: *a rarefied spiritual existence.* **2** current within only a small group; esoteric or exclusive. **3** (of a gas, esp. the atmosphere at high altitudes) having a low density; thin.

rarefy ('rɛərɪ,faɪ) *vb* **-fies, -fying, -fied.** to make or become rarer or less dense; thin out. [C14: from Old French *raréfier,* from Latin *rārēfacere,* from *rārus* RARE[1] + *facere* to make] ▸ **'rare,fiable** *adj* ▸ **'rare,fier** *n*

rare gas *n* another name for **inert gas** (sense 1).

rarely ('rɛəlɪ) *adv* **1** hardly ever; seldom: *I'm rarely in town these days.* **2** to an unusual degree; exceptionally. **3** *Dialect.* uncommonly well; excellently: *he did rarely at market yesterday.*

USAGE Since *rarely* means *hardly ever,* one should not say something *rarely ever* happens.

rareripe ('rɛə,raɪp) *U.S.* ◆ *adj* **1** ripening early. ◆ *n* **2** a fruit or vegetable that ripens early. [C18 *rare,* variant of RATHE + RIPE]

raring ('rɛərɪŋ) *adj* ready; willing; enthusiastic (esp. in the phrase **raring to go**). [C20: from *rare,* variant of REAR[2]]

rarity ('rɛərɪtɪ) *n, pl* **-ties. 1** a rare person or thing, esp. something interesting or valued because it is uncommon. **2** the state or quality of being rare.

Rarotonga (,rɛərə'tɒŋgə) *n* an island in the S Pacific, in the SW Cook Islands: the chief island of the group. Chief settlement: Avarua. Pop.: 9281 (1986). Area: 67 sq. km (26 sq. miles).

RAS *abbrev. for:* **1** Royal Agricultural Society. **2** Royal Astronomical Society.

rasbora (ræz'bɔːrə) *n* any of the small cyprinid fishes constituting the genus *Rasbora* of tropical Asia and East Africa. Many species are brightly coloured and are popular aquarium fishes. [from New Latin, from an East Indian language]

RASC *abbrev. for* (the former) Royal Army Service Corps, now called Royal Corps of Transport.

rascal ('rɑːskᵊl) *n* **1** a disreputable person; villain. **2** a mischievous or impish rogue. **3** an affectionate or mildly reproving term for a child or old man: *you little rascal; the wicked old rascal kissed her.* **4** *Obsolete.* a person of lowly birth. ◆ *adj* **5** (*prenominal*) *Obsolete.* **5a** belonging to the mob or rabble. **5b** dishonest; knavish. [C14: from Old French *rascaille* rabble, perhaps from Old Norman French *rasque* mud, filth]

rascality (rɑː'skælɪtɪ) *n, pl* **-ties.** mischievous, disreputable, or dishonest character, behaviour, or action.

rascally ('rɑːskəlɪ) *adj* **1** dishonest or mean; base. **2** *Archaic.* (esp. of places) wretchedly unpleasant; miserable. ◆ *adv* **3** in a dishonest or mean fashion.

rase (reɪz) *vb* a variant spelling of **raze.**

rash[1] (ræʃ) *adj* **1** acting without due consideration or thought; impetuous. **2** characterized by or resulting from excessive haste or impetuosity: *a rash word.* [C14: from Old High German *rasc* hurried, clever; related to Old Norse *roskr* brave] ▸ **'rashly** *adv* ▸ **'rashness** *n*

rash[2] (ræʃ) *n* **1** *Pathol.* any skin eruption. **2** a series of unpleasant and unexpected occurrences: *a rash of forest fires.* [C18: from Old French *rasche,* from *raschier* to scratch, from Latin *rādere* to scrape] ▸ **'rash,like** *adj*

rasher ('ræʃə) *n* a thin slice of bacon or ham. [C16: of unknown origin]

Rashid (ræ'ʃiːd) *n* a town in N Egypt, on the Nile delta. Pop.: 52 014 (1986). Former name: **Rosetta.**

Rasht (ræʃt) *or* **Resht** *n* a city in NW Iran, near the Caspian Sea: agricultural and commercial centre in a rice-growing area. Pop.: 374 475 (1994 est.).

Rask (*Danish* rasg) *n* **Rasmus Christian** ('rasmus'kresdjan). 1787–1832, Danish philologist. He pioneered comparative philology with his work on Old Norse (1818).

Rasmussen (*Danish* 'rasmusən) *n* **Knud Johan Victor** (knuð jo'han 'viktɔr). 1879–1933, Danish arctic explorer and ethnologist. He led several expeditions through the Arctic in support of his theory that the North American Indians were originally migrants from Asia.

rasorial (rə'sɔːrɪəl) *adj* (of birds such as domestic poultry) adapted for scratching the ground for food. [C19: from New Latin *Rasores* such birds, from Latin *rādere* to scrape]

rasp[1] (rɑːsp) *n* **1** a harsh grating noise. **2** a coarse file with rows of raised teeth. ◆ *vb* **3** (*tr*) to scrape or rub (something) roughly, esp. with a rasp; abrade. **4** to utter with or make a harsh grating noise. **5** to irritate (one's nerves or senses); grate (upon). [C16: from Old French *raspe,* of Germanic origin; compare Old High German *raspōn* to scrape] ▸ **'rasper** *n* ▸ **'raspish** *adj*

rasp[2] (rɑːsp) *n* another name, now Scot. or informal, for **raspberry.**

raspatory ('rɑːspətərɪ, -trɪ) *n, pl* **-ies.** a surgical instrument for abrading; surgeon's rasp. [C16: from Medieval Latin *raspatorium*]

raspberry ('rɑːzbərɪ, -brɪ) *n, pl* **-ries. 1** any of the prickly shrubs of the rosaceous genus *Rubus,* such as *R. strigosus* of E North America and *R. idaeus* of Europe, that have pinkish-white flowers and typically red berry-like fruits (drupelets). See also **bramble. 2a** the fruit of any such plant. **2b** (*as modifier*): *raspberry jelly.* **3 black raspberry.** Popular name: **blackcap. 3a** a related plant, *Rubus occidentalis,* of E North America, that has black berry-like fruits. **3b** the fruit of this plant. **4a** a dark purplish-red colour. **4b** (*as adj*): *a raspberry dress.* **5** a spluttering noise made with the tongue and lips to express contempt (esp. in the phrase **blow a raspberry**). [C17: from earlier *raspis* raspberry, of unknown origin + BERRY: C19 in sense 5, from rhyming slang *raspberry tart* fart]

rasping ('rɑːspɪŋ) *or* **raspy** *adj* (esp. of a noise) harsh or grating; rough.

raspings ('rɑːspɪŋz) *pl n* browned breadcrumbs for coating fish and other foods before frying, baking, etc.

Rasputin (ræ'spjuːtɪn; *Russian* ras'putin) *n* **Grigori Efimovich** (gri'gɔrij jɪ'fimɘvitʃ). ?1871–1916, Siberian peasant monk, notorious for his debauchery, who wielded great influence over Tsarina Alexandra. He was assassinated by a group of Russian noblemen.

rasse ('ræsɪ, ræs) *n* a small civet, *Viverricula indica,* of S and SE Asia. [C19: from Javanese *rase*]

Rasta ('ræstə) *n, adj* short for **Rastafarian.**

Ras Tafari (ræs tə'fɑːrɪ) *n* See **Haile Selassie.**

Rastafarian (,ræstə'fɛərɪən) *n* **1** a member of an originally Jamaican religion that regards **Ras Tafari** (the former emperor of Ethiopia, Haile Selassie) as God. ◆ *adj* **2** of, characteristic of, or relating to the Rastafarians.

raster ('ræstə) *n* a pattern of horizontal scanning lines traced by an electron beam, esp. on a television screen. [C20: via German from Latin: rake, from *rādere* to scrape]

rat (ræt) *n* **1** any of numerous long-tailed murine rodents, esp. of the genus *Rattus,* that are similar to but larger than mice and are now distributed all over the world. See also **brown rat, black rat. 2** *Informal.* a person who deserts his friends or associates, esp. in time of trouble. **3** *Informal.* a worker who works during a strike; blackleg; scab. **4** *Slang, chiefly U.S.* an informer; stool pigeon. **5** *Informal.* a despicable person. **6 smell a rat.** to detect something suspicious. ◆ *vb* **rats, ratting, ratted. 7** (*intr;* usually foll. by *on*) *Informal.* **7a** to divulge secret information (about); betray the trust (of). **7b** to default (on); abandon: *he ratted on the project at the last minute.* **8** to hunt and kill rats. ◆ See also **rats.** [Old English *rætt;* related to Old Saxon *ratta,* Old High German *rato*] ▸ **'rat,like** *adj*

rata ('rɑːtə) *n* either of two New Zealand myrtaceous forest trees, *Metrosideros robusta* or *M. lucida,* having crimson flowers and hard wood. [C19: from Maori]

ratable *or* **rateable** ('reɪtəbᵊl) *adj* **1** able to be rated or evaluated. **2** *Brit.* (of property) liable to payment of rates. ► ˌrataˈbility, ˌrateaˈbility *or* ˈratableness, ˈrateableness *n* ► ˈratably *or* ˈrateably *adv*

ratable value *or* **rateable value** *n Brit.* (formerly) a fixed value assigned to a property by a local authority, on the basis of which variable annual rates are charged.

ratafia (ˌrætəˈfɪə) *or* **ratafee** (ˌrætəˈfiː) *n* **1** any liqueur made from fruit or from brandy with added fruit. **2** a flavouring essence made from almonds. **3** *Chiefly Brit.* Also called: **ratafia biscuit.** a small macaroon flavoured with almonds. [C17: from West Indian Creole French]

ratal (ˈreɪtᵊl) *Brit.* ◆ *n* **1** the amount on which rates are assessed; ratable value. ◆ *adj* **2** of or relating to rates (local taxation). [C19: see RATE[1]]

ratan (ræˈtæn) *n* a variant spelling of **rattan.**

rat-a-tat-tat (ˈrætəˌtætˈtæt) *or* **rat-a-tat** (ˈrætəˈtæt) *n* the sound of knocking on a door.

ratatouille (ˌrætəˈtwiː) *n* a vegetable casserole made of tomatoes, aubergines, peppers, etc., fried in oil and stewed slowly. [C19: from French, from *touiller* to stir, from Latin *tudiculāre,* from *tudes* hammer]

ratbag (ˈrætˌbæg) *n Slang.* a despicable person. [C20: from RAT + BAG]

ratbaggery (ˈrætˌbægərɪ) *n Austral. slang.* nonsense, eccentricity.

ratbite fever *or* **disease** (ˈrætˌbaɪt) *n Pathol.* an acute infectious febrile disease caused by the bite of a rat infected with either of two pathogenic bacteria (*Streptobacillus moniliformis* or *Spirillum minus*).

rat-catcher *n* a person whose job is to destroy or drive away vermin, esp. rats.

ratchet (ˈrætʃɪt) *n* **1** a device in which a toothed rack or wheel is engaged by a pawl to permit motion in one direction only. **2** the toothed rack or wheel forming part of such a device. [C17: from French *rochet,* from Old French *rocquet* blunt head of a lance, of Germanic origin: compare Old High German *rocko* distaff]

ratchet effect *n Economics.* an effect that occurs when a price or wage increases as a result of temporary pressure but fails to fall back when the pressure is removed.

rate[1] (reɪt) *n* **1** a quantity or amount considered in relation to or measured against another quantity or amount: *a rate of 70 miles an hour.* **2a** a price or charge with reference to a standard or scale: *rate of interest; rate of discount.* **2b** *(as modifier)*: *a rate card.* **3** a charge made per unit for a commodity, service, etc. **4** See **rates. 5** the relative speed of progress or change of something variable; pace: *he works at a great rate; the rate of production has doubled.* **6a** relative quality; class or grade. **6b** *(in combination)*: *first-rate ideas.* **7** *Statistics.* a measure of the frequency of occurrence of a given event, such as births and deaths, usually expressed as the number of times the event occurs for every thousand of the total population considered. **8** a wage calculated against a unit of time. **9** the amount of gain or loss of a timepiece. **10 at any rate.** in any case; at all events; anyway. ◆ *vb (mainly tr)* **11** *(also intr)* to assign or receive a position on a scale of relative values; rank: *he is rated fifth in the world.* **12** to estimate the value of; evaluate: *we rate your services highly.* **13** to be worthy of; deserve: *this hotel does not rate four stars.* **14** to consider; regard: *I rate him among my friends.* **15** *Brit.* to assess the value of (property) for the purpose of local taxation. **16** *Slang.* to think highly of: *the clients do not rate the new system.* [C15: from Old French, from Medieval Latin *rata,* from Latin *prō ratā parte* according to a fixed proportion, from *ratus* fixed, from *rērī* to think, decide]

rate[2] (reɪt) *vb (tr)* to scold or criticize severely; rebuke harshly. [C14: perhaps related to Swedish *rata* to chide]

rateable (ˈreɪtəbᵊl) *adj* a variant spelling of **ratable.**

rate-cap (ˈreɪtˌkæp) *vb (tr)* **-caps, -capping, -capped.** (formerly in Britain) to impose on (a local authority) an upper limit on the level of the rate it may levy. ► ˈrate-ˌcapping *n*

rateen (ræˈtiːn) *n* a variant spelling of **ratine.**

ratel (ˈreɪtᵊl) *n* **1** a musteline mammal, *Mellivora capensis,* inhabiting wooded regions of Africa and S Asia. It has a massive body, strong claws, and a thick coat that is paler on the back and it feeds on honey and small animals. Also called: **honey badger. 2** *S. African.* a six-wheeled armoured vehicle. [C18: from Afrikaans]

rate of exchange *n* See **exchange rate.**

rate of return *n Finance.* the ratio of the annual income from an investment to the original investment, often expressed as a percentage.

ratepayer (ˈreɪtˌpeɪə) *n Brit.* (formerly) a person who paid local rates, esp. a householder.

rates (reɪts) *pl n Brit.* a tax formerly levied on property by a local authority.

ratfink (ˈrætˌfɪŋk) *n Slang, chiefly U.S. and Canadian.* a contemptible or undesirable person. [C20: from RAT + FINK]

ratfish (ˈrætˌfɪʃ) *n, pl* **-fish** *or* **-fishes. 1** another name for **rabbitfish** (sense 1). **2** a chimaera, *Hydrolagus colliei,* of the North Pacific Ocean, which has a long narrow tail.

rath (raθ) *n Irish history.* a circular enclosure surrounded by an earthen wall: used as a dwelling and stronghold in former times. [C16: from Irish Gaelic]

ratha (rʌt) *n* (in India) a four-wheeled carriage drawn by horses or bullocks; chariot. [Hindi]

rathe (reɪð) *or* **rath** (rɑːθ) *adj Archaic or literary.* **1** blossoming or ripening early in the season. **2** eager or prompt. [Old English *hrathe;* related to Old High German *hrado,* Old Norse *hrathr*]

Rathenau (*German* ˈraːtənau) *n* **Walther** (ˈvaltər). 1867–1922, German industrialist and statesman: he organized the German war industries during World War I, became minister of reconstruction (1921) and of foreign affairs (1922), and was largely responsible for the treaty of Rapallo with Russia. His assassination by right-wing extremists caused a furore.

rather (ˈrɑːðə) *adv (in senses 1-4, not used with a negative)* **1** relatively or fairly; somewhat: *it's rather dull.* **2** to a significant or noticeable extent; quite: *she's rather pretty.* **3** to a limited extent or degree: *I rather thought that was the case.* **4** with better or more just cause: *this text is rather to be deleted than rewritten.* **5** more readily or willingly; sooner: *I would rather not see you tomorrow.* ◆ *sentence connector.* **6** on the contrary: *it's not cold. Rather, it's very hot indeed.* ◆ *sentence substitute.* (ˈrɑːˈðɜː). **7** an expression of strong affirmation, often in answer to a question: *Is it worth seeing? Rather!* [Old English *hrathor* comparative of *hræth* READY, quick; related to Old Norse *hrathr*]

USAGE Both *would* and *had* are used with *rather* in sentences such as *I would rather* (or *had rather*) *go to the film than to the play. Had rather* is less common and now widely regarded as slightly old-fashioned.

rathouse (ˈræthaʊs) *n Austral. slang.* a psychiatric hospital or asylum.

ratify (ˈrætɪˌfaɪ) *vb* **-fies, -fying, -fied.** *(tr)* to give formal approval or consent to. [C14: via Old French from Latin *ratus* fixed (see RATE[1]) + *facere* to make] ► ˈratiˌfiable *adj* ► ˌratifiˈcation *n* ► ˈratiˌfier *n*

ratine, rateen, ratteen (ræˈtiːn), *or* **ratiné** (ˈrætɪˌneɪ) *n* a coarse loosely woven cloth. [C17: from French, from *ratine,* of obscure origin]

rating[1] (ˈreɪtɪŋ) *n* **1** a classification according to order or grade; ranking. **2** (in certain navies) a sailor who holds neither commissioned nor warrant rank; an ordinary seaman. **3** *Sailing.* a handicap assigned to a racing boat based on its dimensions, sail area, weight, draught, etc. **4** the estimated financial or credit standing of a business enterprise or individual. **5** *Radio, television, etc.* a figure based on statistical sampling indicating what proportion of the total listening and viewing audience tune in to a specific programme or network.

rating[2] (ˈreɪtɪŋ) *n* a sharp scolding or rebuke.

ratio (ˈreɪʃɪˌəʊ) *n, pl* **-tios. 1** a measure of the relative size of two classes expressible as a proportion: *the ratio of boys to girls is 2 to 1.* **2** *Maths.* a quotient of two numbers or quantities. See also **proportion** (sense 6). [C17: from Latin: a reckoning, from *rērī* to think; see REASON]

ratiocinate (ˌrætɪˈɒsɪˌneɪt) *vb (intr)* to think or argue logically and methodically; reason. [C17: from Latin *ratiōcinārī* to calculate, from *ratiō* REASON] ► ˌratiˌociˈnation *n* ► ˌratiˈocinative *adj* ► ˌratiˈociˌnator *n*

ration (ˈræʃən) *n* **1a** a fixed allowance of food, provisions, etc., esp. a statutory one for civilians in time of scarcity or soldiers in time of war: *a tea ration.* **1b** *(as modifier)*: *a ration book.* **2** a sufficient or adequate amount: *you've had your ration of television for today.* ◆ *vb (tr)* **3** (often foll. by *out*) to distribute (provisions), esp. to an army. **4** to restrict the distribution or consumption of (a commodity) by (people): *the government has rationed sugar; sugar is short, so I'll have to ration you.* ◆ See also **rations.** [C18: via French from Latin *ratiō* calculation; see REASON]

rational (ˈræʃənᵊl) *adj* **1** using reason or logic in thinking out a problem. **2** in accordance with the principles of logic or reason; reasonable. **3** of sound mind; sane: *the patient seemed quite rational.* **4** endowed with the capacity to reason; capable of logical thought: *man is a rational being.* **5** *Maths.* **5a** expressible as a ratio of two integers: *a rational number.* **5b** (of an expression, equation, etc.) containing no variable either in irreducible radical form or raised to a fractional power. ◆ *n* **6** *Maths.* a rational number. [C14: from Latin *ratiōnālis,* from *ratiō* REASON] ► ˈrationally *adv* ► ˈrationalness *n*

rationale (ˌræʃəˈnɑːl) *n* a reasoned exposition, esp. one defining the fundamental reasons for a course of action, belief, etc. [C17: from New Latin, from Latin *ratiōnālis*]

rationalism (ˈræʃənəˌlɪzəm) *n* **1** reliance on reason rather than intuition to justify one's beliefs or actions. **2** *Philosophy.* **2a** the doctrine that knowledge about reality can be obtained by reason alone without recourse to experience. **2b** the doctrine that human knowledge can all be encompassed within a single, usually deductive, system. **2c** the school of philosophy initiated by Descartes which held both the above doctrines. **3** the belief that knowledge and truth are ascertained by rational thought and not by divine or supernatural revelation. ► ˈrationalist *n* ► ˌrationalˈistic *adj* ► ˌrationalˈistically *adv*

rationality (ˌræʃəˈnælɪtɪ) *n, pl* **-ties. 1** the state or quality of being rational or logical. **2** the possession or utilization of reason or logic. **3** a reasonable or logical opinion. **4** *Economics.* the assumption that an individual will compare all possible combinations of goods and their prices when making purchases.

rationalize *or* **rationalise** (ˈræʃənəˌlaɪz) *vb* **1** to justify (one's actions, esp. discreditable actions, or beliefs) with plausible reasons, esp. after the event. **2** *Psychol.* to indulge, often unchallenged, in excuses for or explanations of (behaviour about which one feels uncomfortable or guilty). **3** to apply logic or reason to (something). **4** *(tr)* to eliminate unnecessary equipment, personnel, or processes from (a group of businesses, factory, etc.), in order to make it more efficient. **5** *(tr) Maths.* to eliminate one or more radicals without changing the value of (an expression) or the roots of (an equation). ► ˌrationaliˈzation *or* ˌrationaliˈsation *n* ► ˈrationalˌizer *or* ˈrationalˌiser *n*

rational number *n* any real number of the form *a*/*b*, where *a* and *b* are integers and *b* is not zero, as 7 or 7/3.

rations (ˈræʃənz) *pl n (sometimes sing)* a fixed daily allowance of food, esp. to military personnel or when supplies are limited. See also **iron rations.**

ratio scale *n Statistics.* a scale of measurement of data which permits the comparison of differences of values; a scale having a fixed zero value. The distances travelled by a projectile, for instance, are measured on a ratio scale since it makes sense to talk of one projectile travelling twice as far as another. Compare **ordinal scale, interval scale, nominal scale.**

Ratisbon (ˈrætɪzˌbɒn) *n* the former English name for **Regensburg.**

ratite (ˈrætaɪt) *adj* **1** (of flightless birds) having a breastbone that lacks a keel for the attachment of flight muscles. **2** of or denoting the flightless birds, formerly classified as a group (the *Ratitae*), that have a flat breastbone, feathers lacking vanes, and reduced wings. ◆ *n* **3** a bird, such as an ostrich, kiwi, or rhea, that belongs to this group; a flightless bird. [C19: from Latin *ratis* raft]

rat kangaroo *n* any of several ratlike kangaroos of the genera *Bettongia, Potorous, Aepyprymnus,* etc., found on the Australian mainland and in Tasmania.

ratline *or* **ratlin** ('rætlɪn) *n Nautical.* any of a series of light lines tied across the shrouds of a sailing vessel for climbing aloft. [C15: of unknown origin]

RATO ('reɪtəʊ) *n acronym for* rocket-assisted takeoff.

ratoon *or* **rattoon** (ræ'tu:n) *n* **1** a new shoot that grows from near the root or crown of crop plants, esp. the sugar cane, after the old growth has been cut back. ♦ *vb* **2** to propagate or cause to propagate by such a growth. [C18: from Spanish *retoño* young shoot, from RE- + *otoñar* to sprout in autumn, from *otoño* AUTUMN]

ratpack ('ræt,pæk) *n Derogatory slang.* those members of the press who give wide, often intrusive, coverage of the private lives of celebrities: *the royal ratpack.*

rat race *n* a continual routine of hectic competitive activity: *working in the City is a real rat race.*

rats (ræts) *interj* **1** an exclamation of rejection or disdain. ♦ *adj* **2** *Austral. slang.* deranged; insane.

ratsbane ('ræts,beɪn) *n* rat poison, esp. arsenic oxide.

Ratskeller *German.* ('ra:tskɛlər) *n* **1** the cellar of a town hall, esp. one used as a beer hall or restaurant. **2** any similar establishment, esp. in the U.S. [German: from *Rat(haus)* town hall + *Keller* cellar]

rat snake *n* any of various nonvenomous rodent-eating colubrid snakes, such as *Elaphe obsoleta* of North America and *Ptyas mucosus* of Asia.

rat-tail *n* **1** another name for **grenadier** (the fish). **2a** a horse's tail that has no hairs. **2b** a horse having such a tail. **3** a style of spoon in which the line of the handle is prolonged in a tapering moulding along the back of the bowl. **4** a kind of woodworking or metalworking file.

rattan *or* **ratan** (ræ'tæn) *n* **1** any of the climbing palms of the genus *Calamus* and related genera, having tough stems used for wickerwork and canes. **2** the stems of such plants collectively. **3** a stick made from one of these stems. [C17: from Malay *rōtan*]

rat-tat ('ræt,tæt) *n* a variant of **rat-a-tat-tat.**

ratteen (ræ'ti:n) *n* a variant spelling of **ratine.**

ratter ('rætə) *n* **1** a dog or cat that catches and kills rats. **2** another word for **rat** (senses 3, 4).

Rattigan ('rætɪgən) *n* Sir **Terence Mervyn.** 1911–77, English playwright. His plays include *The Winslow Boy* (1946), *Separate Tables* (1954), and *Ross* (1960).

rattish ('rætɪʃ) *adj* of, resembling, or infested with rats.

rattle[1] ('ræt^əl) *vb* **1** to make or cause to make a rapid succession of short sharp sounds, as of loose pellets colliding when shaken in a container. **2** to shake or cause to shake with such a sound: *the explosion rattled the windows.* **3** to send, move, drive, etc., with such a sound: *the car rattled along the country road.* **4** (*intr;* foll. by *on*) to chatter idly; talk, esp. at length: *he rattled on about his work.* **5** (*tr,* foll. by *off, out,* etc.) to recite perfunctorily or rapidly. **6** (*tr*) *Informal.* to disconcert; make frightened or anxious. ♦ *n* **7** a rapid succession of short sharp sounds. **8** a baby's toy filled with small pellets that rattle when shaken. **9** a series of loosely connected horny segments on the tail of a rattlesnake, vibrated to produce a rattling sound. **10** any of various European scrophulariaceous plants having a capsule in which the seeds rattle, such as *Pedicularis palustris* (**red rattle**) and *Rhinanthus minor* (**yellow rattle**). **11** idle chatter. **12** an idle chatterer. **13** *Med.* another name for **rale.** [C14: from Middle Dutch *ratelen;* related to Middle High German *razzen,* of imitative origin]

rattle[2] ('ræt^əl) *vb* (*tr;* often foll. by *down*) to fit (a vessel or its rigging) with ratlines. [C18: back formation from *rattling,* variant of RATLINE]

Rattle ('ræt^əl) *n* Sir **Simon.** born 1955, British conductor. Principal conductor (1980–91) and music director of the City of Birmingham Symphony Orchestra (1991–98); appointed chief conductor of the Berlin Philharmonic Orchestra, to commence in 2002.

rattlebox ('ræt^əl,bɒks) *n* any of various tropical and subtropical leguminous plants that have inflated pods within which the seeds rattle.

rattler ('rætlə) *n* **1** something that rattles. **2** *Chiefly U.S. and Canadian.* an informal name for **rattlesnake.**

rattlesnake ('ræt^əl,sneɪk) *n* any of the venomous New World snakes constituting the genera *Crotalus* and *Sistrurus,* such as *C. horridus* (**black** or **timber rattlesnake**): family *Crotalidae* (pit vipers). They have a series of loose horny segments on the tail that are vibrated to produce a buzzing or whirring sound.

rattlesnake plantain *n* any of various small temperate and tropical orchids of the genus *Goodyera,* having mottled or striped leaves and spikes of yellowish-white flowers.

rattletrap ('ræt^əl,træp) *n Informal.* a broken-down old vehicle, esp. an old car.

rattling ('rætlɪŋ) *adv Informal.* (intensifier qualifying something good, fine, pleasant, etc.): *a rattling good lunch.*

rattly ('rætlɪ) *adj* **-tlier, -tliest.** having a rattle; rattling.

rattoon (ræ'tu:n) *n, vb* a variant spelling of **ratoon.**

rat-trap *n* **1** a device for catching rats. **2** *Informal.* a type of bicycle pedal having serrated steel foot pads and a toe clip.

ratty ('rætɪ) *adj* **-tier, -tiest. 1** *Brit. and N.Z. informal.* irritable; annoyed. **2** *Informal.* (of the hair) unkempt or greasy. **3** *U.S. and Canadian slang.* shabby; dilapidated. **4** *Austral. slang.* **4a** angry. **4b** mad. **5** of, like, or full of rats. ▸ **'rattily** *adv* ▸ **'rattiness** *n*

Ratushinskaya (,rætu:'ʃɪnskaɪjɑ:) *n* **Irina** (ɪ'ri:nə). born 1954, Russian poet and writer, living in Britain: imprisoned (1983–86) in a Soviet labour camp on charges of subversion. Her publications include *Poems* (1984), *Grey is the Colour of Hope* (1988), and *The Odessans* (1992).

raucous ('rɔ:kəs) *adj* (of voices, cries, etc.) harshly or hoarsely loud. [C18: from Latin *raucus* hoarse] ▸ **'raucously** *adv* ▸ **'raucousness** *or* (*less commonly*) **raucity** ('rɔ:sɪtɪ) *n*

raunch (rɔ:ntʃ) *n Slang.* **1** lack of polish or refinement; crudeness. **2** *Chiefly U.S.* slovenliness or untidiness.

raunchy ('rɔ:ntʃɪ) *adj* **-chier, -chiest.** *Slang.* **1** openly sexual; lusty; earthy. **2** *Chiefly U.S.* slovenly or untidy. [C20: of unknown origin] ▸ **'raunchily** *adv* ▸ **'raunchiness** *n*

rauriki ('raurəki:) *n, pl* **-kis.** *N.Z.* another name for **sow thistle.** [Maori]

Rauschenberg ('rauʃənbɜ:g) *n* **Robert.** born 1925, U.S. artist; one of the foremost exponents of pop art.

rauwolfia (rɔ:'wʊlfɪə, raʊ-) *n* **1** any tropical tree or shrub of the apocynaceous genus *Rauwolfia,* esp. *R. serpentina* of SE Asia. **2** the powdered root of *R. serpentina:* a source of various drugs, esp. reserpine. [C19: New Latin, named after Leonhard *Rauwolf* (died 1596), German botanist]

Rav (ræv; *Hebrew* rav) *n Judaism.* **1** a rabbi who is a person's religious mentor, or one to whom questions are addressed for authoritative decision. **2** the title preferred by many orthodox rabbis to distinguish them from the clergy of other brands of Judaism.

ravage ('rævɪdʒ) *vb* **1** to cause extensive damage to. ♦ *n* **2** (*often pl*) destructive action: *the ravages of time.* [C17: from French, from Old French *ravir* to snatch away, RAVISH] ▸ **'ravagement** *n*

RAVC *abbrev. for* Royal Army Veterinary Corps.

rave[1] (reɪv) *vb* **1** to utter (something) in a wild or incoherent manner, as when mad or delirious. **2** (*intr*) to speak in an angry uncontrolled manner. **3** (*intr*) (of the sea, wind, etc.) to rage or roar. **4** (*intr;* foll. by *over* or *about*) *Informal.* to write or speak (about) with great enthusiasm. **5** (*intr*) *Brit. slang.* to enjoy oneself wildly or uninhibitedly. ♦ *n* **6** *Informal.* **6a** enthusiastic or extravagant praise. **6b** (*as modifier*): *a rave review.* **7** *Brit. slang.* **7a** Also called: **rave-up.** a party. **7b** a professionally organized party for young people, with electronic dance music, sometimes held in a field or disused building. **8** *Brit. slang.* a fad or fashion: *the latest rave.* **9** a name given to various types of dance music, such as techno, that feature fast electronic rhythm. [C14 *raven,* apparently from Old French *resver* to wander]

rave[2] (reɪv) *n* a vertical sidepiece on a wagon. [C16: modification of dialect *rathe,* of uncertain origin]

ravel ('ræv^əl) *vb* **-els, -elling, -elled** *or U.S.* **-els, -eling, -eled. 1** to tangle (threads, fibres, etc.) or (of threads, fibres, etc.) to become entangled. **2** (often foll. by *out*) to tease or draw out (the fibres of a fabric or garment) or (of a garment or fabric) to fray out in loose ends; unravel. **3** (*tr;* usually foll. by *out*) to disentangle or resolve: *to ravel out a complicated story.* **4** to break up (a road surface) in patches or (of a road surface) to begin to break up; fret; scab. **5** *Archaic.* to make or become confused or complicated. ♦ *n* **6** a tangle or complication. [C16: from Middle Dutch *ravelen*] ▸ **'raveller** *n* ▸ **'ravelly** *adj*

Ravel (*French* ravɛl) *n* **Maurice (Joseph)** (mɔris). 1875–1937, French composer, noted for his use of unresolved dissonances and mastery of tone colour. His works include *Gaspard de la Nuit* (1908) and *Le Tombeau de Couperin* (1917) for piano, *Boléro* (1928) for orchestra, and the ballet *Daphnis et Chloé* (1912).

ravelin ('rævlɪn) *n Fortifications.* an outwork having two embankments at a salient angle. [C16: from Italian *ravellino* a little bank, from *riva* bank, from Latin *rīpa*]

ravelment ('rævəlmənt) *n Rare.* a ravel or tangle.

raven[1] ('reɪv^ən) *n* **1** a large passerine bird, *Corvus corax,* having a large straight bill, long wedge-shaped tail, and black plumage: family *Corvidae* (crows). It has a hoarse croaking cry. **2a** a shiny black colour. **2b** (*as adj*): *raven hair.* [Old English *hræfn;* related to Old High German *hraban,* Old Norse *hrafn*]

raven[2] ('ræv^ən) *vb* **1** to seize or seek (plunder, prey, etc.). **2** to eat (something) voraciously or greedily; be ravenous in eating. [C15: from Old French *raviner* to attack impetuously; see RAVENOUS] ▸ **'ravener** *n*

ravening ('rævənɪŋ) *adj* (esp. of animals such as wolves) voracious; predatory. ▸ **'raveningly** *adv*

Ravenna (rə'venə; *Italian* ra'venna) *n* a city and port in NE Italy, in Emilia-Romagna: capital of the Western Roman Empire from 402 to 476, of the Ostrogoths from 493 to 526, and of the Byzantine exarchate from 584 to 751; famous for its ancient mosaics. Pop.: 137 216 (1996 est.).

ravenous ('rævənəs) *adj* **1** famished; starving. **2** rapacious; voracious. [C16: from Old French *ravineux,* from Latin *rapīna* plunder, from *rapere* to seize] ▸ **'ravenously** *adv* ▸ **'ravenousness** *n*

raver ('reɪvə) *n* **1** *Brit. slang.* a person who leads a wild or uninhibited social life. **2** *Slang.* a person who enjoys rave music, esp. one who frequents raves.

ravin ('rævɪn) *vb* an archaic spelling of **raven**[2].

ravine (rə'vi:n) *n* a deep narrow steep-sided valley, esp. one formed by the action of running water. [C15: from Old French: torrent, from Latin *rapīna* robbery, influenced by Latin *rapidus* RAPID, both from *rapere* to snatch]

raving ('reɪvɪŋ) *adj* **1a** delirious; frenzied. **1b** (*as adv*): *raving mad.* **2** *Informal.* (intensifier): *a raving beauty.* ♦ *n* **3** (*usually pl*) frenzied, irrational, or wildly extravagant talk or utterances. ▸ **'ravingly** *adv*

ravioli (,rævɪ'əʊlɪ) *n* small squares of pasta containing a savoury mixture of meat, cheese, etc. [C19: from Italian dialect, literally: little turnips, from Italian *rava* turnip, from Latin *rāpa*]

ravish ('rævɪʃ) *vb* (*tr*) **1** (*often passive*) to give great delight to; enrapture. **2** to rape. **3** *Archaic.* to carry off by force. [C13: from Old French *ravir,* from Latin *rapere* to seize] ▸ **'ravisher** *n* ▸ **'ravishment** *n*

ravishing ('rævɪʃɪŋ) *adj* delightful; lovely; entrancing. ▸ **'ravishingly** *adv*

raw (rɔ:) *adj* **1** (of food) not cooked: *raw onion.* **2** (*prenominal*) in an unfinished, natural, or unrefined state; not treated by manufacturing or other processes: *raw materials for making steel; raw brick.* **3** (of the skin, a wound, etc.) having the surface exposed or abraded, esp. painfully. **4** ignorant, inexperienced, or immature: *a raw recruit.* **5** (*prenominal*) not selected or modified: *raw statistics.* **6** frank or realistic: *a raw picture of the breakdown of a marriage.* **7** (of spirits) undiluted. **8** *Chiefly U.S.* coarse, vulgar, or obscene. **9** *Chiefly U.S.* recently done; fresh: *raw paintwork.* **10** (of the weather) harshly cold and damp. **11** *Informal.* unfair; unjust (esp. in the phrase **a raw deal**). ◆ *n* **12 the raw.** *Brit. informal.* a sensitive point: *his criticism touched me on the raw.* **13 in the raw. 13a** *Informal.* without clothes; naked. **13b** in a natural or unmodified state: *life in the raw.* [Old English *hreaw;* related to Old High German *hrao,* Old Norse *hrār* raw, Latin *cruor* thick blood, Greek *kreas* meat] ▸ **'rawish** *adj* ▸ **'rawly** *adv* ▸ **'rawness** *n*

Rawalpindi (rɔːl'pɪndɪ) *n* an ancient city in N Pakistan: interim capital of Pakistan (1959–67) during the building of Islamabad. Pop.: 1 290 000 (1995 est.).

rawboned ('rɔː'bəʊnd) *adj* having a lean bony physique.

rawhide ('rɔːˌhaɪd) *n* **1** untanned hide. **2** a whip or rope made of strips cut from such a hide.

rawhide hammer *n* a hammer, used to avoid damaging a surface, having a head consisting of a metal tube from each end of which a tight roll of hide protrudes.

rawinsonde ('reɪwɪnˌsɒnd) *n* a hydrogen balloon carrying meteorological instruments and a radar target, enabling the velocity of winds in the atmosphere to be measured. [C20: blend of *radar* + *wind* + *radiosonde*]

Rawlplug ('rɔːlplʌg) *n Trademark.* a short fibre or plastic tube used to provide a fixing in a wall for a screw.

raw material *n* **1** material on which a particular manufacturing process is carried out. **2** a person or thing regarded as suitable for some particular purpose: *raw material for the army.*

raw milk *n* unpasteurized milk.

raw silk *n* **1** untreated silk fibres reeled from the cocoon. **2** fabric woven from such fibres.

Rawsthorne ('rɔːsˌθɔːn) *n* **Alan.** 1905–71, English composer, whose works include three symphonies, several concertos, and a set of *Symphonic Studies* (1939).

rax (ræks) *Scot.* ◆ *vb* **1** (*tr*) to stretch or extend. **2** (*intr*) to reach out. **3** (*tr*) to pass or give (something to a person) with the outstretched hand; reach: *rax me the salt.* **4** (*tr*) to strain or sprain. ◆ *n* **5** the act of stretching or straining. [Old English *raxan*]

ray[1] (reɪ) *n* **1** a narrow beam of light; gleam. **2** a slight indication, esp. of something anticipated or hoped for: *a ray of solace.* **3** *Maths.* a straight line extending from a point. **4** a thin beam of electromagnetic radiation or particles. **5** any of the bony or cartilaginous spines of the fin of a fish that form the support for the soft part of the fin. **6** any of the arms or branches of a starfish or other radiate animal. **7** *Astronomy.* any of a number of bright streaks that radiate from the youngest lunar craters, such as Tycho; they are composed of crater ejecta not yet darkened, and extend considerable distances. **8** *Botany.* any strand of tissue that runs radially through the vascular tissue of some higher plants. See **medullary ray.** ◆ *vb* **9** (of an object) to emit (light) in rays or (of light) to issue in the form of rays. **10** (*intr*) (of lines, etc.) to extend in rays or on radiating paths. **11** (*tr*) to adorn (an ornament, etc.) with rays or radiating lines. [C14: from Old French *rai,* from Latin *radius* spoke, RADIUS]

ray[2] (reɪ) *n* any of various marine selachian fishes typically having a flattened body, greatly enlarged winglike pectoral fins, gills on the undersurface of the fins, and a long whiplike tail. They constitute the orders *Torpediniformes* (**electric rays**) and *Rajiformes.* [C14: from Old French *raie,* from Latin *raia*]

ray[3] (reɪ) *n Music.* (in tonic sol-fa) the second degree of any major scale; supertonic. [C14: see GAMUT]

Ray[1] (reɪ) *n* **Cape.** a promontory in SW Newfoundland, Canada.

Ray[2] (reɪ) *n* **1 John.** 1627–1705, English naturalist. He originated natural botanical classification and the division of flowering plants into monocotyledons and dicotyledons. **2 Man,** real name *Emmanuel Rudnitsky.* 1890–1976, U.S. surrealist photographer. **3 Satyajit** ('sætjədʒɪt). 1921–92, Indian film director.

rayah ('rɑːjə, 'raɪə) *n* (formerly) a non-Muslim subject of the Ottoman Empire. Also (less common) **raia.** [C19: from Turkish *raiyye,* from Arabic *ra'iyah* herd, flock]

Raybans ('reɪˌbænz) *pl n Trademark.* a brand of sunglasses.

ray flower *or* **floret** *n* any of the small strap-shaped flowers in the flower head of certain composite plants, such as the daisy. Compare **disc flower.**

ray gun *n* (in science fiction) a gun that emits rays to paralyse, stun, or destroy.

Rayleigh ('reɪlɪ) *n* **Lord,** title of *John William Strutt,* 1842–1919, British physicist. He discovered argon (1894) with Ramsay and made important contributions to the theory of sound, the theory of scattering of radiation, etc. Nobel prize for physics 1904.

Rayleigh disc *n* a small light disc suspended in the path of a sound wave, used to measure the intensity of the sound by analysing the resulting deflection of the disc.

Rayleigh scattering *n* a process in which electromagnetic radiation is elastically deflected by particles of matter, without a change of frequency but with a phase change.

rayless ('reɪlɪs) *adj* **1** dark; gloomy. **2** lacking rays: *a rayless flower.* ▸ **'raylessly** *adv* ▸ **'raylessness** *n*

raylet ('reɪlɪt) *n* a small ray.

Raynaud's disease ('reɪnəʊz) *n* a disease, mainly affecting women, in which spasms in the blood vessels of the fingers or toes restrict blood flow to the affected part, which becomes pale, numb, and sometimes painful. Often shortened to **Raynaud's.** [named after Maurice *Raynaud* (1834–81), French physician who first described it]

rayon ('reɪɒn) *n* **1** any of a number of textile fibres made from wood pulp or other forms of cellulose. **2** any fabric made from such a fibre. **3** (*modifier*) consisting of or involving rayon: *a rayon shirt.* [C20: from French, from Old French *rai* RAY[1]]

raze *or* **rase** (reɪz) *vb* (*tr*) **1** to demolish (a town, buildings, etc.) completely; level (esp. in the phrase **raze to the ground**). **2** to delete; erase. **3** *Archaic.* to graze. [C16: from Old French *raser* from Latin *rādere* to scrape] ▸ **'razer** *or* **'raser** *n*

razee (ræ'ziː) *History.* ◆ *n, pl* **razees. 1** a sailing ship that has had its upper deck or decks removed. ◆ *vb* **razees, razeeing, razeed.** (*tr*) **2** to remove the upper deck or decks of (a sailing ship). [C19: from French *rasée* shaved close, from *raser* to RAZE]

razoo (rɑ'zuː) *n Austral. and N.Z. informal.* an imaginary coin: *not a brass razoo; they took every last razoo.* [C20: of uncertain origin]

razor ('reɪzə) *n* **1** a sharp implement used esp. by men for shaving the face. **2 on a razor's edge** *or* **razor-edge.** in an acute dilemma. ◆ *vb* **3** (*tr*) to cut or shave with a razor. [C13: from Old French *raseor,* from *raser* to shave; see RAZE]

razorback ('reɪzəˌbæk) *n* **1** Also called: **finback.** another name for the **common rorqual** (see **rorqual**). **2** a semiwild or wild pig of the southeastern U.S., having a narrow body, long legs, and a ridged back.

razorbill ('reɪzəˌbɪl) *or* **razor-billed auk** *n* a common auk, *Alca torda,* of the North Atlantic, having a thick laterally compressed bill with white markings.

razor blade *n* a small rectangular piece of metal sharpened on one or both long edges for use in a razor for shaving.

razor-cut *vb* **-cuts, -cutting, -cut. 1** (*tr*) to trim or shape (the hair) with a razor. ◆ *n* **razor cut. 2** a fluffy hairstyle, usually tapering at the neck, trimmed by a razor.

razor-shell *n* any of various sand-burrowing bivalve molluscs of the genera *Ensis* and *Solen,* which have a long tubular shell. U.S. name: **razor clam.**

razor wire *n* strong wire with pieces of sharp metal set across it at close intervals, used to make fences or barriers.

razz (ræz) *U.S. and Canadian slang.* ◆ *vb* **1** (*tr*) to make fun of; deride. ◆ *n* **2** short for **raspberry** (sense 5).

razzia ('ræzɪə) *n, pl* **-zias.** *History.* a raid for plunder or slaves, esp. one carried out by Moors in North Africa. [C19: from French, from Arabic *ghaziah* war]

razzle-dazzle ('ræzᵊl'dæzᵊl) *or* **razzmatazz** ('ræzmə'tæz) *n Slang.* noisy or showy fuss or activity. [C19: rhyming compound based on DAZZLE]

Rb *the chemical symbol for* rubidium.

RB *international car registration for* (Republic of) Botswana.

RB- *abbrev. for* reconnaissance bomber: *RB-57.*

RBE *abbrev. for* relative biological effectiveness.

rc *abbrev. for* reinforced concrete.

RC *abbrev. for:* **1** Red Cross. **2** Reserve Corps. **3** Also: **R.C.** Roman Catholic. ◆ **4** *international car registration for* Taiwan (Nationalist Republic of China).

RCA *abbrev. for:* **1** (formerly) Radio Corporation of America. **2** Royal Canadian Academy. **3** Royal College of Art. ◆ **4** *international car registration for* Central African Republic.

RCAF *abbrev. for* Royal Canadian Air Force.

RCB(CG) *international car registration for* (Republic of the) Congo.

rcd *abbrev. for* received.

RCD *abbrev. for* residual current device.

RCH *international car registration for* (Republic of) Chile.

RCM *abbrev. for* Royal College of Music.

RCMP *abbrev. for* Royal Canadian Mounted Police.

RCN *abbrev. for:* **1** Royal Canadian Navy. **2** Royal College of Nursing.

RCO *abbrev. for* Royal College of Organists.

r-colour *or* **r-colouring** *n Phonetics.* an (r) quality imparted to certain vowels, usually by retroflexion. ▸ **'r-ˌcoloured** *adj*

RCP *abbrev. for* Royal College of Physicians.

rcpt *abbrev. for* receipt.

RCS *abbrev. for:* **1** Royal College of Science. **2** Royal College of Surgeons.

rct *Military. abbrev. for* recruit.

RCT *abbrev. for* Royal Corps of Transport.

RCVS *abbrev. for* Royal College of Veterinary Surgeons.

rd *abbrev. for:* **1** rendered. **2** rod (unit of length). **3** road. **4** round. **5** *Physics.* rutherford.

rd *or* **RD** (on a cheque) *abbrev. for* refer to drawer.

Rd *abbrev. for* Road.

RD (in New Zealand) *abbrev. for* Rural Delivery.

RDC (in Britain, formerly) *abbrev. for* Rural District Council.

RDS *abbrev. for* radio data system: a system in which digital signals are transmitted with normal radio programme to effect automatic tuning of receivers and other functions.

RDX *abbrev. for* Research Department Explosive; another name for **cyclonite.**

re[1] (reɪ, riː) *n Music.* a variant spelling of **ray**[3].

re[2] (riː) *prep* with reference to. [C18: from Latin *rē,* ablative case of *rēs* thing]

USAGE *Re,* in contexts such as *re your letter, your remarks have been noted* or *he spoke to me re your complaint,* is common in business or official correspondence. In general English *with reference to* is preferable in the former case and *about* or *concerning* in the latter. Even in business correspondence, the use of *re* is often restricted to the letter heading.

Re[1] (reɪ) *n* another name for **Ra**[2].

Re[2] *the chemical symbol for* rhenium.

Re[3] *or* **re** *symbol for* rupee.

RE *abbrev. for:* **1** Reformed Episcopal. **2** Religious Education. **3** Right Excellent. **4** Royal Engineers.

re- *prefix* **1** indicating return to a previous condition, restoration, withdrawal, etc.: *rebuild; renew; retrace; reunite.* **2** indicating repetition of an action: *recopy; remarry.* [from Latin]

USAGE Verbs beginning with *re-* indicate repetition or restoration. It is unnecessary to add an adverb such as *back* or *again: This must not occur again* (not *recur again*); *we recounted the votes* (not *recounted the votes again,* which implies that the votes were counted three times, not twice).

're *contraction of* are: *we're, you're, they're.*

reach (riːtʃ) *vb* **1** (*tr*) to arrive at or get to (a place, person, etc.) in the course of movement or action: *to reach the office.* **2** to extend as far as (a point or place): *to reach the ceiling; can you reach?* **3** (*tr*) to come to (a certain condition, stage, or situation): *to reach the point of starvation.* **4** (*intr*) to extend in influence or operation: *the Roman conquest reached throughout England.* **5** (*tr*) *Informal.* to pass or give (something to a person) with the outstretched hand: *to reach someone a book.* **6** (*intr;* foll. by *out, for,* or *after*) to make a movement (towards), as if to grasp or touch: *to reach for something on a shelf.* **7** (*intr;* foll. by *for* or *after*) to strive or yearn: *to reach for the impossible.* **8** (*tr*) to make contact or communication with (someone): *we tried to reach him all day.* **9** (*tr*) to strike, esp. in fencing or boxing. **10** (*tr*) to amount to (a certain sum): *to reach the five million mark.* **11** (*intr*) *Nautical.* to sail on a tack with the wind on or near abeam. ◆ *n* **12** the act of reaching. **13** the extent or distance of reaching: *within reach of safety; beyond her reach.* **14** the range of influence, power, jurisdiction, etc. **15** an open stretch of water, esp. on a river. **16** *Nautical.* the direction or distance sailed by a vessel on one tack. **17** a bar on the rear axle of a vehicle connecting it with some part at the front end. **18** *Television, radio.* the percentage of the population selecting a broadcast programme or channel for more than a specified time during a day or week. **19** *Advertising.* the proportion of a market that an advertiser hopes to reach at least once in a campaign. [Old English *rǣcan;* related to Old Frisian *rēka,* Old High German *reihheu*] ▸ **'reachable** *adj* ▸ **'reacher** *n*

reach-me-down *n Informal.* **1a** (*often pl*) a garment that is cheaply ready-made or second-hand. **1b** (*as modifier*): *reach-me-down finery.* **2** (*pl*) trousers. **3** (*modifier*) not original; derivative; stale: *a stock of reach-me-down ideas.*

react (rɪ'ækt) *vb* **1** (*intr;* foll. by *to, upon,* etc.) (of a person or thing) to act in response to another person, a stimulus, etc. or (of two people or things) to act together in a certain way. **2** (*intr;* foll. by *against*) to act in an opposing or contrary manner. **3** (*intr*) *Physics.* to exert an equal force in the opposite direction to an acting force. **4** *Chem.* to undergo or cause to undergo a chemical reaction. [C17: from Late Latin *reagere,* from RE- + Latin *agere* to drive, do]

re-act (riː'ækt) *vb* (*tr*) to act or perform again.

reactance (rɪ'æktəns) *n* **1** the opposition to the flow of alternating current by the capacitance or inductance of an electrical circuit; the imaginary part of the impedance Z, $Z = R + iX$, where R is the resistance, $i = \sqrt{-1}$, and X is the reactance. It is expressed in ohms. Compare **resistance** (sense 3). **2** the opposition to the flow of an acoustic or mechanical vibration, usually due to inertia or stiffness. It is the magnitude of the imaginary part of the acoustic or mechanical impedance.

reactant (rɪ'æktənt) *n* a substance that participates in a chemical reaction, esp. a substance that is present at the start of the reaction. Compare **product** (sense 4).

reaction (rɪ'ækʃən) *n* **1** a response to some foregoing action or stimulus. **2** the reciprocal action of two things acting together. **3** opposition to change, esp. political change, or a desire to return to a former condition or system. **4** a response indicating a person's feelings or emotional attitude. **5** *Med.* **5a** any effect produced by the action of a drug, esp. an adverse effect. Compare **side effect.** **5b** any effect produced by a substance (allergen) to which a person is allergic. **6** the simultaneous equal and opposite force that acts on a body whenever it exerts a force on another body. **7** short for **chemical reaction** or **nuclear reaction.** **8** *Stock Exchange.* a sharp fall in price interrupting a general rise. ▸ **re'actional** *adj*

USAGE *Reaction* is used to refer both to an instant response (*her reaction was one of amazement*) and to a considered response in the form of a statement (*the Minister gave his reaction to the court's decision*). Some people think this second use is incorrect.

reactionary (rɪ'ækʃənərɪ, -ʃənrɪ) *or* **reactionist** *adj* **1** of, relating to, or characterized by reaction, esp. against radical political or social change. ◆ *n, pl* **-aries** *or* **-ists.** **2** a person opposed to radical change. ▸ **re'actionism** *n*

reaction chamber *n Engineering.* the chamber in a rocket engine in which the reaction or combustion of fuel occurs.

reaction engine *or* **motor** *n* an engine, such as a jet or rocket engine, that ejects gas at high velocity and develops its thrust from the ensuing reaction.

reaction formation *n Psychoanal.* a defence mechanism by which a person at a conscious level condemns a repressed wish: thus, a latent homosexual may denounce homosexuality.

reaction time *n Physiol.* another name for **latent time.**

reaction turbine *n* a turbine in which the working fluid is accelerated by expansion in both the static nozzles and the rotor blades. Torque is produced by the momentum changes in the rotor and by reaction from fluid accelerating out of the rotor. Compare **impulse turbine.**

reactivate (rɪ'æktɪˌveɪt) *vb* (*tr*) to make (something) active or functional again. ▸ **reˌacti'vation** *n*

reactive (rɪ'æktɪv) *adj* **1** readily partaking in chemical reactions: *sodium is a reactive metal; free radicals are very reactive.* **2** of, concerned with, or having a reactance. **3** responsive to stimulus. **4** (of mental illnesses) precipitated by an external cause: *reactive depression.* ▸ **re'actively** *adv* ▸ **reactivity** (ˌriːæk'tɪvɪtɪ) *or* **re'activeness** *n*

reactor (rɪ'æktə) *n* **1** *Chem.* a substance, such as a reagent, that undergoes a reaction. **2** short for **nuclear reactor.** **3** a vessel, esp. one in industrial use, in which a chemical reaction takes place. **4** a coil of low resistance and high inductance that introduces reactance into a circuit. **5** *Med.* a person sensitive to a particular drug or agent.

read[1] (riːd) *vb* **reads, reading, read** (rɛd). **1** to comprehend the meaning of (something written or printed) by looking at and interpreting the written or printed characters. **2** to be occupied in such an activity: *he was reading all day.* **3** (when *tr,* often foll. by *out*) to look at, interpret, and speak aloud (something written or printed): *he read to us from the Bible.* **4** (*tr*) to interpret the significance or meaning of through scrutiny and recognition: *he read the sky and predicted rain; to read a map.* **5** (*tr*) to interpret or understand the meaning of (signs, characters, etc.) other than by visual means: *to read Braille.* **6** (*tr*) to have sufficient knowledge of (a language) to understand the written or printed word: *do you read German?* **7** (*tr*) to discover or make out the true nature or mood of: *to read someone's mind.* **8** to interpret or understand (something read) in a specified way, or (of something read) to convey a particular meaning or impression: *I read this speech as satire; this book reads well.* **9** (*tr*) to adopt as a reading in a particular passage: *for "boon" read "bone".* **10** (*intr*) to have or contain a certain form or wording: *the sentence reads as follows.* **11** to undertake a course of study in (a subject): *to read history; read for the bar.* **12** to gain knowledge by reading: *he read about the war.* **13** (*tr*) to register, indicate, or show: *the meter reads 100.* **14** (*tr*) to bring or put into a specified condition by reading: *to read a child to sleep.* **15** (*tr*) to hear and understand, esp. when using a two-way radio: *we are reading you loud and clear.* **16** *Computing.* to obtain (data) from a storage device, such as magnetic tape. Compare **write** (sense 16). **17** (*tr*) to understand (written or printed music) by interpretation of the notes on the staff and to be able to reproduce the musical sounds represented by these notes. **18 read a lesson** (*or* **lecture**). *Informal.* to censure or reprimand, esp. in a long-winded manner. **19 read between the lines.** to perceive or deduce a meaning that is hidden or implied rather than being openly stated. **20 you wouldn't read about it.** *Austral. informal.* an expression of dismay, disgust, or disbelief. ◆ *n* **21** matter suitable for reading: *this new book is a very good read.* **22** the act of reading. ◆ See also **read in, read into, read out, read up.** [Old English *rǣdan* to advise, explain; related to Old Frisian *rēda,* Old High German *rātan,* Gothic *garēdan*]

read[2] (red) *vb* **1** the past tense and past participle of **read**[1]. ◆ *adj* **2** having knowledge gained from books (esp. in the phrases **widely read, well-read**). **3 take (something) as read.** to take (something) for granted as a fact; understand or presume.

readable ('riːdəbᵊl) *adj* **1** (of handwriting, etc.) able to be read or deciphered; legible. **2** (of style of writing) interesting, easy, or pleasant to read. ▸ **ˌreada'bility** *or* **'readableness** *n* ▸ **'readably** *adv*

Reade (riːd) *n* **Charles.** 1814–84, English novelist: author of *The Cloister and the Hearth* (1861), a historical romance.

reader ('riːdə) *n* **1** a person who reads. **2** a person who is fond of reading. **3a** *Chiefly Brit.* at a university, a member of staff having a position between that of a senior lecturer and a professor. **3b** *U.S.* a teaching assistant in a faculty who grades papers, examinations, etc., on behalf of a professor. **4a** a book that is part of a planned series for those learning to read. **4b** a standard textbook, esp. for foreign-language learning. **5** a person who reads aloud in public. **6** a person who reads and assesses the merit of manuscripts submitted to a publisher. **7** a person employed to read proofs and indicate errors by comparison with the original copy; proofreader. **8** short for **lay reader.** **9** *Judaism, chiefly Brit.* another word for **cantor** (sense 1).

readership ('riːdəʃɪp) *n* **1** all the readers collectively of a particular publication or author: *a readership of five million; Dickens's readership.* **2** *Chiefly Brit.* the office, position, or rank of university reader.

readies ('rɛdɪz) *pl n Informal.* a variant of **ready** (sense 8): see **ready money.**

readily ('rɛdɪlɪ) *adv* **1** promptly; eagerly; willingly. **2** without difficulty or delay; easily or quickly.

read in (riːd) *vb* (*adv*) **1** to read (data) into a computer memory or storage device. **2 read oneself in.** *Church of England.* to assume possession of a benefice by publicly reading the Thirty-nine Articles.

readiness ('rɛdɪnɪs) *n* **1** the state of being ready or prepared, as for use or action. **2 in readiness.** **2a** prepared and waiting: *all was in readiness for the guests' arrival.* **2b** in preparation for: *he tidied the house in readiness for the guests' arrival.* **3** willingness or eagerness to do something. **4** ease or promptness.

reading ('riːdɪŋ) *n* **1a** the act of a person who reads. **1b** (*as modifier*): *a reading room; a reading lamp.* **2a** ability to read. **2b** (*as modifier*): *the reading public; a child of reading age.* **3** any matter that can be read; written or printed text. **4** a public recital or rendering of a literary work. **5** the form of a particular word or passage in a given text, esp. where more than one version exists. **6** an interpretation, as of a piece of music, a situation, or something said or written. **7** knowledge gained from books: *a person of little reading.* **8** a measurement indicated by a gauge, dial, scientific instrument, etc. **9** *Parliamentary procedure.* **9a** the formal recital of the body or title of a bill in a legislative assembly in order to begin one of the stages of its passage. **9b** one of the three stages in the passage of a bill through a legislative assembly. See **first reading, second reading, third reading.** **10** the formal recital of something written, esp. a will.

Reading ('rɛdɪŋ) *n* **1** a town in S England, on the River Thames: university (1892). Pop.: 134 600 (1991). **2** a unitary authority in S England, in Berkshire. Pop.: 142 900 (1996 est.). Area: 37 sq. km (14 sq. miles).

read into (riːd) *vb* (*tr, prep*) to discern in or infer from a statement (meanings not intended by the speaker or writer).

readjust (ˌriːə'dʒʌst) *vb* to adjust or adapt (oneself or something) again, esp. after an initial failure. ▸ **ˌread'justable** *adj* ▸ **ˌread'juster** *n* ▸ **ˌread'justment** *n*

ˌreab'sorb *vb*	**ˌreac'custom** *vb*	**ˌreacqui'sition** *n*	**ˌreadap'tation** *n*
ˌreab'sorption *n*	**ˌreac'quire** *vb*	**ˌrea'dapt** *vb*	**ˌread'dress** *vb*

read out (riːd) *vb* (*adv*) **1** (*tr*) to read (something) aloud. **2** to retrieve information from a computer memory or storage device. **3** (*tr*) *U.S. and Canadian.* to expel (someone) from a political party or other society. ◆ *n* **read-out. 4a** the act of retrieving information from a computer memory or storage device. **4b** the information retrieved.

read up (riːd) *vb* (*adv;* when *intr,* often foll. by *on*) to acquire information about (a subject) by reading intensively.

read-write head (ˈriːdˈraɪt) *n Computing.* an electromagnet that can both read and write information on a magnetic medium such as magnetic tape or disk.

ready (ˈrɛdɪ) *adj* **readier, readiest. 1** in a state of completion or preparedness, as for use or action. **2** willing or eager: *ready helpers.* **3** prompt or rapid: *a ready response.* **4** (*prenominal*) quick in perceiving; intelligent: *a ready mind.* **5** (*postpositive*) (foll. by *to*) on the point (of) or liable (to): *ready to collapse.* **6** (*postpositive*) conveniently near (esp. in the phrase **ready to hand**). **7 make** *or* **get ready.** to prepare (oneself or something) for use or action. ◆ *n* **8** *Informal.* (often preceded by *the*) short for **ready money. 9 at** *or* **to the ready. 9a** poised for use or action: *with pen at the ready.* **9b** (of a rifle) in the position normally adopted immediately prior to aiming and firing. ◆ *vb* **10** (*tr*) to put in a state of readiness; prepare. [Old English *(ge)rǣde;* related to Old Frisian *rēde,* Old High German *reiti,* Old Norse *reithr* ready]

ready-made *adj* **1** made for purchase and immediate use by any customer: *a ready-made jacket.* **2** extremely convenient or ideally suited: *a ready-made solution.* **3** unoriginal or conventional: *ready-made phrases.* ◆ *n* **4** a ready-made article, esp. a garment.

ready-mix *n* **1** (*modifier*) consisting of ingredients blended in advance, esp. of food that is ready to cook or eat after addition of milk or water: *a ready-mix cake.* **2** concrete that is mixed before or during delivery to a building site.

ready money *or* **cash** *n* funds for immediate use; cash. Also called: **the ready, the readies.**

ready reckoner *n* a table of numbers used to facilitate simple calculations, esp. one for applying rates of discount, interest, charging, etc. to different sums.

ready-to-wear *adj* (**ready to wear** *when postpositive*). **1** (of clothes) not tailored for the wearer; of a standard size. ◆ *n* **2** an article or suit of such clothes.

ready-witted *adj* quick to learn or perceive.

reafforest (ˌriːəˈfɒrɪst) *or* **reforest** *vb* (*tr*) to replant (an area that was formerly forested). ▸ **ˌreafˌforestˈation** *or* **ˌreforestˈation** *n*

Reagan (ˈreɪgən) *n* **Ronald.** born 1911, U.S. film actor and Republican statesman: Governor of California (1966–74): 40th president of the U.S. (1981–89).

reagent (riːˈeɪdʒənt) *n* a substance for use in a chemical reaction, esp. for use in chemical synthesis and analysis.

reagin (ˈrɪədʒɪn) *n Immunol.* a type of antibody that is formed against an allergen and is attached to the cells of a tissue. The antigen–antibody reaction that occurs on subsequent contact with the allergen causes tissue damage, leading to the release of histamine and other substances responsible for an allergic reaction. [C20: from German *reagieren* to react + -IN]

real[1] (ˈrɪəl) *adj* **1** existing or occurring in the physical world; not imaginary, fictitious, or theoretical; actual. **2** (*prenominal*) true; actual; not false: *the real reason.* **3** (*prenominal*) deserving the name; rightly so called: *a real friend; a real woman.* **4** not artificial or simulated; genuine: *real sympathy; real fur.* **5** (of food, etc.) traditionally made and having a distinct flavour: *real ale; real cheese.* **6** *Philosophy.* existent or relating to actual existence (as opposed to nonexistent, potential, contingent, or apparent). **7** (*prenominal*) *Economics.* (of prices, incomes, wages, etc.) considered in terms of purchasing power rather than nominal currency value. **8** (*prenominal*) denoting or relating to immovable property such as land and tenements: *real property.* Compare **personal. 9** *Physics.* See **image** (sense 2). **10** *Maths.* involving or containing real numbers alone; having no imaginary part. **11** *Music.* **11a** (of the answer in a fugue) preserving the intervals as they appear in the subject. **11b** denoting a fugue as having such an answer. Compare **tonal** (sense 3). **12** *Informal.* (intensifier): *a real fool; a real genius.* **13 the real thing.** the genuine article, not an inferior or mistaken substitute. ◆ *n* **14** short for **real number. 15 the real.** that which exists in fact; reality. **16 for real.** *Slang.* not as a test or trial; in earnest. [C15: from Old French *réel,* from Late Latin *reālis,* from Latin *rēs* thing] ▸ **ˈrealness** *n*

real[2] (reɪˈɑːl; *Spanish* reˈal) *n, pl* **reals** *or* **reales** (*Spanish* reˈales). a former small Spanish or Spanish-American silver coin. [C17: from Spanish, literally: royal, from Latin *rēgālis;* see REGAL[1]]

real[3] (*Portuguese* reˈal) *n, pl* **reais** (rəjʃ). **1** the standard monetary unit of Brazil, divided into 100 centavos. **2** a former coin of Portugal. [ultimately from Latin *rēgālis* REGAL[1]]

real ale *or* **beer** *n* any beer which is allowed to ferment in the cask and which when served is pumped up without using carbon dioxide.

real estate *n* another term for **real property.**

realgar (rɪˈælgə) *n* a rare orange-red soft mineral consisting of arsenic sulphide in monoclinic crystalline form. It occurs in Utah and Romania and as a deposit from hot springs. It is an important ore of arsenic and is also used as a pigment. Formula: AsS. [C14: via Medieval Latin from Arabic *rahj al-ghar* powder of the mine]

realia (rɪˈeɪlɪə) *pl n* real-life facts and material used in teaching. [C20: from neuter pl of Late Latin *reālis;* see REAL[1]]

realism (ˈrɪəˌlɪzəm) *n* **1** awareness or acceptance of the physical universe, events, etc., as they are, as opposed to the abstract or ideal. **2** awareness or acceptance of the facts and necessities of life; a practical rather than a moral or dogmatic view of things. **3** a style of painting and sculpture that seeks to represent the familiar or typical in real life, rather than an idealized, formalized, or romantic interpretation of it. **4** any similar school or style in other arts, esp. literature. **5** *Philosophy.* the thesis that general terms such as common nouns refer to entities that have a real existence separate from the individuals which fall under them. See also **universal** (sense 11b). Compare **Platonism, nominalism, conceptualism, naive realism. 6** *Philosophy.* the theory that physical objects continue to exist whether they are perceived or not. Compare **idealism, phenomenalism. 7** *Logic, philosophy.* the theory that the sense of a statement is given by a specification of its truth conditions, or that there is a reality independent of the speaker's conception of it that determines the truth or falsehood of every statement.

realist (ˈrɪəlɪst) *n* **1** a person who is aware of and accepts the physical universe, events, etc., as they are; pragmatist. **2** an artist or writer who seeks to represent the familiar or typical in real life rather than an idealized, formalized, or romantic interpretation. **3** *Philosophy.* a person who accepts realism. **4** (*modifier*) of, relating to, or characteristic of realism or realists in the arts, philosophy, etc.: *a realist school.*

realistic (ˌrɪəˈlɪstɪk) *adj* **1** showing awareness and acceptance of reality. **2** practical or pragmatic rather than ideal or moral. **3** (of a book, film, etc.) depicting or emphasizing what is real and actual rather than abstract or ideal. **4** of or relating to philosophical realism. ▸ **ˌrealˈistically** *adv*

reality (rɪˈælɪtɪ) *n, pl* **-ties. 1** the state of things as they are or appear to be, rather than as one might wish them to be. **2** something that is real. **3** the state of being real. **4** *Philosophy.* **4a** that which exists, independent of human awareness. **4b** the totality of facts as they are independent of human awareness of them. See also **conceptualism.** Compare **appearance** (sense 6). **5 in reality.** actually; in fact.

reality principle *n Psychoanal.* control of behaviour by the ego to meet the conditions imposed by the external world.

realize *or* **realise** (ˈrɪəˌlaɪz) *vb* **1** (when *tr, may take a clause as object*) to become conscious or aware of (something). **2** (*tr, often passive*) to bring (a plan, ambition, etc.) to fruition; make actual or concrete. **3** (*tr*) to give (something, such as a drama or film) the appearance of reality. **4** (*tr*) (of goods, property, etc.) to sell for or make (a certain sum): *this table realized £800.* **5** (*tr*) to convert (property or goods) into cash. **6** (*tr*) (of a musicologist or performer) **6a** to expand or complete (a thorough-bass part in a piece of baroque music) by supplying the harmonies indicated in the figured bass. **6b** to reconstruct (a composition) from an incomplete set of parts. **7** to sound or utter (a phoneme or other speech sound) in actual speech; articulate. ▸ **ˈrealˌizable** *or* **ˈrealˌisable** *adj* ▸ **ˈrealˌizably** *or* **ˈrealˌisably** *adv* ▸ **ˌrealiˈzation** *or* **ˌrealiˈsation** *n* ▸ **ˈrealˌizer** *or* **ˈrealˌiser** *n*

real life *n* **a** actual human life, as lived by real people, esp. contrasted with the lives of fictional or fantasy characters: *miracles don't happen in real life.* **b** (*as modifier*): *a real-life mystery.*

really (ˈrɪəlɪ) *adv* **1** in reality; in actuality; assuredly: *it's really quite harmless.* **2** truly; genuinely: *really beautiful.* ◆ *interj* **3** an exclamation of dismay, disapproval, doubt, surprise, etc. **4 not really?** an exclamation of surprise or polite doubt.

USAGE See at **very.**

realm (rɛlm) *n* **1** a royal domain; kingdom (now chiefly in such phrases as **Peer of the Realm**). **2** a field of interest, study, etc.: *the realm of the occult.* [C13: from Old French *reialme,* from Latin *regimen* rule, influenced by Old French *reial* royal, from Latin *rēgālis* REGAL[1]]

real number *n* any rational or irrational number. See **number** (sense 1).

real part *n* the term *a* in a complex number $a + ib$, where $i = \sqrt{-1}$.

realpolitik (reɪˈɑːlpɒlɪˈtiːk) *n* a ruthlessly realistic and opportunist approach to statesmanship, rather than a moralistic one, esp. as exemplified by Bismarck. [C19: German: politics of realism]

real presence *n* the doctrine that the body of Christ is actually present in the Eucharist.

real property *n* immovable property, esp. land and buildings, including proprietary rights over land, such as mineral rights. Compare **personal property.** Also called: **real estate.**

real tennis *n* an ancient form of tennis played in a four-walled indoor court with various openings, a sloping-roofed corridor along three sides, and a buttress on the fourth side. Also called: **royal tennis.**

real-time *adj* denoting or relating to a data-processing system in which a computer receives constantly changing data, such as information relating to air-traffic control, travel booking systems, etc., and processes it sufficiently rapidly to be able to control the source of the data.

Realtor (ˈrɪəltə, -ˌtɔː) *n* a U.S. and Canadian word for an **estate agent,** esp. an accredited one. [C20: from a trademark]

realty (ˈrɪəltɪ) *n* another term for **real property.**

real wages *pl n Economics.* wages evaluated with reference to their purchasing power rather than to the money actually paid. Compare **money wages.**

ream[1] (riːm) *n* **1** a number of sheets of paper, formerly 480 sheets (**short ream**), now 500 sheets (**long ream**) or 516 sheets (**printer's ream** or **perfect ream**). One ream is equal to 20 quires. **2** (*often pl*) *Informal.* a large quantity, esp. of

ˌreadˈmission *n*
ˌreadˈmit *vb,* **-ˈmits, -ˈmitting, -ˈmitted.**
ˌreadˈmittance *n*
ˌreaˈdopt *vb*
ˌreafˈfirm *vb*
ˌreaffirˈmation *n*
ˌreaˈlign *vb*
ˌreaˈlignment *n*
reˈalloˌcate *vb*
ˌrealloˈcation *n*
reˈalter *vb*

written matter: *he wrote reams.* [C14: from Old French *raime,* from Spanish *rezma,* from Arabic *rizmah* bale]

ream[2] (ri:m) *vb (tr)* **1** to enlarge (a hole) by use of a reamer. **2** *U.S.* to extract (juice) from (a citrus fruit) using a reamer. [C19: perhaps from C14 *remen* to open up, from Old English *rȳman* to widen]

reamer ('ri:mə) *n* **1** a steel tool with a cylindrical or tapered shank around which longitudinal teeth are ground, used for smoothing the bores of holes accurately to size. **2** *U.S.* a utensil with a conical projection used for extracting juice from citrus fruits; lemon squeezer.

rean (ri:n) *n* a variant spelling of **reen.**

reap (ri:p) *vb* **1** to cut or harvest (a crop), esp. corn, from (a field or tract of land). **2** *(tr)* to gain or get (something) as a reward for or result of some action or enterprise. [Old English *riopan;* related to Norwegian *ripa* to scratch, Middle Low German *repen* to card, ripple (flax)] ► **'reapable** *adj*

reaper ('ri:pə) *n* **1** a person who reaps or a machine for reaping. **2 the grim reaper.** death.

rear[1] (rɪə) *n* **1** the back or hind part. **2** the area or position that lies at the back: *a garden at the rear of the house.* **3** the section of a military force or procession farthest from the front. **4** an informal word for **buttocks** (see **buttock**). **5 bring up the rear.** to be at the back in a procession, race, etc. **6 in the rear.** at the back. **7** *(modifier)* of or in the rear: *the rear legs; the rear side.* [C17: probably abstracted from REARWARD OF REARGUARD]

rear[2] (rɪə) *vb* **1** *(tr)* to care for and educate (children) until maturity; bring up; raise. **2** *(tr)* to breed (animals) or grow (plants). **3** *(tr)* to place or lift (a ladder, etc.) upright. **4** *(tr)* to erect (a monument, building, etc.); put up. **5** *(intr;* often foll. by *up)* (esp. of horses) to lift the front legs in the air and stand nearly upright. **6** *(intr;* often foll. by *up* or *over)* (esp. of tall buildings) to rise high; tower. **7** *(intr)* to start with anger, resentment, etc. [Old English *rǣran;* related to Old High German *rēren* to distribute, Old Norse *reisa* to RAISE] ► **'rearer** *n*

rear admiral *n* an officer holding flag rank in any of certain navies, junior to a vice admiral.

Reardon ('rɪədən) *n* **Ray.** born 1932, Welsh snooker player: world champion 1970, 1973–76, 1978.

rearguard ('rɪə,gɑ:d) *n* **1** a detachment detailed to protect the rear of a military formation, esp. in retreat. **2** an entrenched or conservative element, as in a political party. **3 rearguard action. 3a** an action fought by a rearguard. **3b** a defensive action undertaken to try to stop something happening or continuing. [C15: from Old French *rereguarde* (modern French *arrière-garde*), from *rer,* from Latin *retro* back + *guarde* GUARD; compare VANGUARD]

rear light *or* **lamp** *n* a red light, usually one of a pair, attached to the rear of a motor vehicle. Also called: **tail-light, tail lamp.**

rearm (ri:'ɑ:m) *vb* **1** to arm again. **2** *(tr)* to equip (an army, a nation, etc.) with better weapons. ► **re'armament** *n*

rearmost ('rɪə,məust) *adj* nearest the rear; coming last.

rearmouse ('rɪə,maus) *n, pl* **-mice.** an archaic or dialect word for **bat** (the animal). [See REREMOUSE]

rearrange (,ri:ə'reɪndʒ) *vb (tr)* **1** to put (something) into a new order: *to rearrange the lighting.* **2** to put (something) back in its original order after it has been displaced. **3** to fix a new date or time for (something postponed): *to rearrange a match.* ► **,rear'ranger** *n* ► **,rear'rangement** *n*

rear sight *n* the sight of a gun nearest to the breech.

rear-view mirror *n* a mirror on a motor vehicle enabling the driver to see traffic behind him.

rearward ('rɪəwəd) *adj, adv* **1** Also (for adv only): **rearwards.** towards or in the rear. ◆ *n* **2** a position in the rear, esp. the rear division of a military formation. [C14 (as a noun: the part of an army positioned behind the main body of troops): from Anglo-French *rerewarde,* variant of *reregarde;* see REARGUARD]

Rea Silvia ('rɪə 'sɪlvɪə) *n* a variant spelling of **Rhea Silvia.**

reason ('ri:zᵊn) *n* **1** the faculty of rational argument, deduction, judgment, etc. **2** sound mind; sanity. **3** a cause or motive, as for a belief, action, etc. **4** an argument in favour of or a justification for something. **5** *Philosophy.* the intellect regarded as a source of knowledge, as contrasted with experience. **6** *Logic.* grounds for a belief; a premise of an argument supporting that belief. **7 by reason of.** because of. **8 in** *or* **within reason.** within moderate or justifiable bounds. **9 it stands to reason.** it is logical or obvious: *it stands to reason that he will lose.* **10 listen to reason.** to be persuaded peaceably. **11 reasons of State.** political justifications for an immoral act. ◆ *vb* **12** (when *tr, takes a clause as object)* to think logically or draw (logical conclusions) from facts or premises. **13** *(intr;* usually foll. by *with)* to urge or seek to persuade by reasoning. **14** *(tr;* often foll. by *out)* to work out or resolve (a problem) by reasoning. [C13: from Old French *reisun,* from Latin *ratiō* reckoning, from *rērī* to think] ► **'reasoner** *n*

USAGE The expression *the reason is because...* should be avoided. Instead one should say either *this is because. . .* or *the reason is that. . .*

reasonable ('ri:zənəbᵊl) *adj* **1** showing reason or sound judgment. **2** having the ability to reason. **3** having modest or moderate expectations; not making unfair demands. **4** moderate in price; not expensive. **5** fair; average: *reasonable weather.* ► **'reasonably** *adv* ► **'reasonableness** *n*

reasoned ('ri:zᵊnd) *adj* well thought-out or well presented: *a reasoned explanation.* ► **'reasonedly** *adv*

reasoning ('ri:zənɪŋ) *n* **1** the act or process of drawing conclusions from facts, evidence, etc. **2** the arguments, proofs, etc., so adduced.

reassure (,ri:ə'ʃuə) *vb (tr)* **1** to relieve (someone) of anxieties; restore confidence to. **2** another term for **reinsure.** ► **,reas'surance** *n* ► **,reas'surer** *n* ► **,reas'suringly** *adv*

reast (ri:st) *vb* a variant spelling of **reest.**

Réaum. *abbrev. for* Réaumur (scale).

Réaumur ('reɪə,mjuə) *adj* indicating measurement on the Réaumur scale of temperature.

Réaumur scale *n* a scale of temperature in which the freezing point of water is taken as 0° and the boiling point is 80°. [C18: named after René Antoine Ferchault de *Réaumur* (1683–1757), French physicist, who introduced it]

reave[1] (ri:v) *vb* **reaves, reaving, reaved** *or* **reft** (rɛft). *Archaic.* **1** to carry off (property, prisoners, etc.) by force. **2** *(tr;* foll. by *of)* to deprive; strip. See also **reive.** [Old English *reāfian;* related to Old High German *roubōn* to rob, Old Norse *raufa* to break open]

reave[2] (ri:v) *vb* **reaves, reaving, reaved** *or* **reft** (rɛft). *Archaic.* to break or tear (something) apart; cleave. [C13 *reven,* probably from REAVE[1] and influenced in meaning by RIVE]

reb (rɛb) *n (sometimes cap.) U.S. informal.* a Confederate soldier in the American Civil War (1861–65). Also called: **Johnny Reb.** [short for REBEL]

Reb (rɛb) *n Judaism.* an honorific title, corresponding to *Mr,* for those who do not have rabbinic qualifications: usually followed by the person's forename: *Reb Dovid.* [Yiddish, from Hebrew *rabbī* rabbi, master]

rebarbative (rɪ'bɑ:bətɪv) *adj* fearsome; forbidding. [C19: from French *rébarbatif,* from Old French *rebarber* to repel (an enemy), to withstand (him) face to face, from RE- + *barbe* beard, from Latin *barba*]

rebate[1] *n* ('ri:beɪt). **1** a refund of a fraction of the amount payable or paid, as for goods purchased in quantity; discount. ◆ *vb* (rɪ'beɪt). *(tr)* **2** to deduct (a part) of a payment from (the total). **3** *Archaic.* to reduce or diminish (something or the effectiveness of something). [C15: from Old French *rabattre* to beat down, hence reduce, deduct, from RE- + *abatre* to put down; see ABATE] ► **re'batable** *or* **re'bateable** *adj* ► **'rebater** *n*

rebate[2] ('ri:beɪt, 'ræbɪt) *n, vb* another word for **rabbet.**

rebato (rə'bɑ:təu) *n, pl* **-tos.** a variant spelling of **rabato.**

Rebbe ('rɛbə) *n Judaism.* **1** the usually dynastic leader of a Chassidic sect. **2** an individual's chosen spiritual mentor. [Yiddish, from Hebrew *rabbī* rabbi]

rebbetzin ('rɛbətsən) *n Judaism.* the wife of a rabbi. [from Yiddish]

rebec *or* **rebeck** ('ri:bɛk) *n* a medieval stringed instrument resembling the violin but having a lute-shaped body. [C16: from Old French *rebebe,* from Arabic *rebāb;* perhaps also influenced by Old French *bec* beak]

Rebecca (rɪ'bɛkə) *n Old Testament.* the sister of Laban, who became the wife of Isaac and the mother of Esau and Jacob (Genesis 24–27). Douay spelling: **Rebekah.**

rebel *vb* (rɪ'bɛl), **-bels, -belling, -belled.** *(intr;* often foll. by *against)* **1** to resist or rise up against a government or other authority, esp. by force of arms. **2** to dissent from an accepted moral code or convention of behaviour, dress, etc. **3** to show repugnance (towards). ◆ *n* ('rɛbᵊl). **4a** a person who rebels. **4b** *(as modifier): a rebel soldier; a rebel leader.* **5** a person who dissents from some accepted moral code or convention of behaviour, dress, etc. [C13: from Old French *rebelle,* from Latin *rebellis* insurgent, from RE- + *bellum* war] ► **'rebeldom** *n*

rebellion (rɪ'bɛljən) *n* **1** organized resistance or opposition to a government or other authority. **2** dissent from an accepted moral code or convention of behaviour, dress, etc. [C14: via Old French from Latin *rebelliō* revolt (of those conquered); see REBEL]

rebellious (rɪ'bɛljəs) *adj* **1** showing a tendency towards rebellion. **2** (of a problem, etc.) difficult to overcome; refractory. ► **re'belliously** *adv* ► **re'belliousness** *n*

rebellow (rɪ'bɛləu) *vb Archaic or literary.* to re-echo loudly.

rebirth (ri:'bɜ:θ) *n* **1** a revival or renaissance: *the rebirth of learning.* **2** a second or new birth; reincarnation.

rebirthing (ri:'bɜ:θɪŋ) *n* a form of psychotherapy in which the subject supposedly "relives" the experience of being born, in order to confront and overcome traumas and anxieties stemming from birth.

reboot (ri:'bu:t) *vb* to shut down and restart (a computer system) or (of a computer system) to shut down and restart.

rebore *n* ('ri:,bɔ:). **1** the process of boring out the cylinders of a worn reciprocating engine and fitting oversize pistons. ◆ *vb* (ri:'bɔ:). **2** *(tr)* to carry out this process.

reborn (ri:'bɔ:n) *adj* born or as if born again, esp. in having undergone spiritual regeneration.

rebound *vb* (rɪ'baund). *(intr)* **1** to spring back, as from a sudden impact. **2** to

,rea'nalysis *n, pl* **-ses.**
re'ani,mate *vb*
,reani'mation *n*
,reap'pear *vb*
,reap'pearance *n*
,reappli'cation *n*
,reap'ply *vb,* **-'plies, -'plying, -'plied.**
,reap'point *vb*
,reap'pointment *n*
,reap'portion *vb*
,reap'praisal *n*
,reap'praise *vb*
,rear'rest *vb, n*
,reas'semble *vb*
,reas'sembly *n, pl* **-blies.**
,reas'sert *vb*
,reas'sertion *n*
,reas'sess *vb*
,reas'sessment *n*
,reas'sign *vb*
,reas'signment *n*
,reat'tach *vb*
,reat'tachment *n*
,rea'waken *vb*
,rebap'tize *or* **,rebap'tise** *vb*
re'bid *vb,* **-'bids, -'bidding, -'bid.**
re'bind *vb,* **-'binds, -'binding, -'bound.**
re'boil *vb*

misfire, esp. so as to hurt the perpetrator: *the plan rebounded.* ◆ *n* ('riːbaʊnd). **3** the act or an instance of rebounding. **4** **on the rebound. 4a** in the act of springing back. **4b** *Informal.* in a state of recovering from rejection, disappointment, etc.: *he married her on the rebound from an unhappy love affair.* [C14: from Old French *rebondir,* from RE- + *bondir* to BOUND[2]]
rebozo (rɪ'bəʊzəʊ; *Spanish* re'βoθo) *n, pl* **-zos** (-zəʊz; *Spanish* -θos). a long wool or linen scarf covering the shoulders and head, worn by Latin American women. [C19: from Spanish: shawl, from *rebozar* to muffle]
rebuff (rɪ'bʌf) *vb (tr)* **1** to snub, reject, or refuse (a person offering help or sympathy, an offer of help, etc.) abruptly or out of hand. **2** to beat back (an attack); repel. ◆ *n* **3** a blunt refusal or rejection; snub. **4** any sudden check to progress or action. [C16: from Old French *rebuffer,* from Italian *ribuffare,* from *ribuffo* a reprimand, from *ri-* RE- + *buffo* puff, gust, apparently of imitative origin]
rebuke (rɪ'bjuːk) *vb* **1** *(tr)* to scold or reprimand (someone). ◆ *n* **2** a reprimand or scolding. [C14: from Old Norman French *rebuker,* from RE- + Old French *buchier* to hack down, from *busche* log, of Germanic origin] ▸ **re'bukable** *adj* ▸ **re'buker** *n*
rebus ('riːbəs) *n, pl* **-buses. 1** a puzzle consisting of pictures representing syllables and words; in such a puzzle the word *hear* might be represented by H followed by a picture of an ear. **2** a heraldic emblem or device that is a pictorial representation of or pun on the name of the bearer. [C17: from French *rébus,* from the Latin *rēbus* by things, from RES]
rebut (rɪ'bʌt) *vb* **-buts, -butting, -butted.** *(tr)* to refute or disprove, esp. by offering a contrary contention or argument. [C13: from Old French *reboter,* from RE- + *boter* to thrust, BUTT[3]] ▸ **re'buttable** *adj* ▸ **re'buttal** *n*
rebutter (rɪ'bʌtə) *n* **1** *Law.* a defendant's pleading in reply to a plaintiff's surrejoinder. **2** a person who rebuts.
rec (rɛk) *n Informal.* short for **recreation** (ground).
rec. *abbrev. for:* **1** receipt. **2** recipe. **3** record. **4** recorder.
recalcitrant (rɪ'kælsɪtrənt) *adj* **1** not susceptible to control or authority; refractory. ◆ *n* **2** a recalcitrant person. [C19: via French from Latin *recalcitrāre,* from RE- + *calcitrāre* to kick, from *calx* heel] ▸ **re'calcitrance** *n*
recalesce (ˌriːkə'lɛs) *vb (intr)* to undergo recalescence.
recalescence (ˌriːkə'lɛsəns) *n* a sudden spontaneous increase in the temperature of cooling iron resulting from an exothermic change in crystal structure occurring at a particular temperature. [C19: from Latin *recalēscere* to grow warm again, from RE- + *calēscere,* from *calēre* to be hot] ▸ ˌ**reca'lescent** *adj*
recall (rɪ'kɔːl) *vb (tr)* **1** *(may take a clause as object)* to bring back to mind; recollect; remember. **2** to order to return; call back permanently or temporarily: *to recall an ambassador.* **3** to revoke or take back. **4** to cause (one's thoughts, attention, etc.) to return from a reverie or digression. **5** *Poetic.* to restore or revive. ◆ *n* **6** the act of recalling or state of being recalled. **7** revocation or cancellation. **8** the ability to remember things; recollection. **9** *Military.* (esp. formerly) a signal to call back troops, etc., usually a bugle call: *to sound the recall.* **10** *U.S.* the process by which elected officials may be deprived of office by popular vote. ▸ **re'callable** *adj*
recant (rɪ'kænt) *vb* to repudiate or withdraw (a former belief or statement), esp. formally in public. [C16: from Latin *recantāre* to sing again, from RE- + *cantāre* to sing; see CHANT] ▸ **recantation** (ˌriːkæn'teɪʃən) *n* ▸ **re'canter** *n*
recap *vb* ('riːˌkæp, riː'kæp), **-caps, -capping, -capped,** *n* ('riːˌkæp). **1** *Informal.* short for **recapitulate** *or* **recapitulation.** ◆ *n* ('riːˌkæp). **2** *Austral. and N.Z.* another name for **retread.** ▸ **re'cappable** *adj*
recapitulate (ˌriːkə'pɪtjʊˌleɪt) *vb* **1** to restate the main points of (an argument, speech, etc.); summarize. **2** *(tr)* (of an animal) to repeat (stages of its evolutionary development) during the embryonic stages of its life. **3** to repeat at some point during a piece of music (material used earlier in the same work). [C16: from Late Latin *recapitulāre,* literally: to put back under headings; see CAPITULATE] ▸ ˌ**reca'pitulative** *or* ˌ**reca'pitulatory** *adj*
recapitulation (ˌriːkəˌpɪtjʊ'leɪʃən) *n* **1** the act of recapitulating, esp. summing up, as at the end of a speech. **2** Also called: **palingenesis.** *Biology.* the apparent repetition in the embryonic development of an animal of the changes that occurred during its evolutionary history. Compare **caenogenesis. 3** *Music.* the repeating of earlier themes, esp. when forming the final section of a movement in sonata form.
recaption (riː'kæpʃən) *n Law.* the process of taking back one's own wife, child, property, etc., without causing a breach of the peace. [C17: from RE- + CAPTION (in the sense: seizure)]
recapture (riː'kæptʃə) *vb (tr)* **1** to capture or take again. **2** to recover, renew, or repeat (a lost or former ability, sensation, etc.): *she soon recaptured her high spirits.* **3** *U.S.* (of the government) to take lawfully (a proportion of the profits of a public-service undertaking). ◆ *n* **4** the act of recapturing or fact of being recaptured. **5** *U.S.* the seizure by the government of a proportion of the profits of a public-service undertaking.
recce ('rɛkɪ) *n, vb,* **-ces, -ceing, -ced** *or* **-ceed.** a slang word for **reconnaissance** or **reconnoitre.**
recd *or* **rec'd** *abbrev. for* received.
recede (rɪ'siːd) *vb (intr)* **1** to withdraw from a point or limit; go back: *the tide receded.* **2** to become more distant: *hopes of rescue receded.* **3** to slope backwards: *apes have receding foreheads.* **4a** (of a man's hair) to cease to grow at the temples and above the forehead. **4b** (of a man) to start to go bald in this way. **5** to decline in value or character. **6** (usually foll. by *from*) to draw back or retreat, as from a promise. [C15: from Latin *recēdere* to go back, from RE- + *cēdere* to yield, CEDE]
re-cede (riː'siːd) *vb (tr)* to restore to a former owner.
receipt (rɪ'siːt) *n* **1** a written acknowledgment by a receiver of money, goods, etc., that payment or delivery has been made. **2** the act of receiving or fact of being received. **3** *(usually pl)* an amount or article received. **4** *Obsolete or U.S. dialect.* another word for **recipe.** ◆ *vb* **5** *(tr)* to acknowledge payment of (a bill), as by marking it. **6** *Chiefly U.S.* to issue a receipt for (money, goods, etc.). [C14: from Old Norman French *receite,* from Medieval Latin *recepta,* from Latin *recipere* to RECEIVE]
receiptor (rɪ'siːtə) *n Chiefly U.S.* a person who receipts.
receivable (rɪ'siːvəb[ə]l) *adj* **1** suitable for or capable of being received, esp. as payment or legal tender. **2** (of a bill, etc.) awaiting payment: *accounts receivable.* ◆ *n* **3** *(usually pl)* the part of the assets of a business represented by accounts due for payment.
receive (rɪ'siːv) *vb (mainly tr)* **1** to take (something offered) into one's hand or possession. **2** to have (an honour, blessing, etc.) bestowed. **3** to accept delivery or transmission of (a letter, telephone call, etc.). **4** to be informed of (news or information). **5** to hear and consent to or acknowledge (an oath, confession, etc.). **6** (of a vessel or container) to take or hold (a substance, commodity, or certain amount). **7** to support or sustain (the weight of something); bear. **8** to apprehend or perceive (ideas, etc.). **9** to experience, undergo, or meet with: *to receive a crack on the skull.* **10** *(also intr)* to be at home to (visitors). **11** to greet or welcome (visitors or guests), esp. in formal style. **12** to admit (a person) to a place, society, condition, etc.: *he was received into the priesthood.* **13** to accept or acknowledge (a precept or principle) as true or valid. **14** to convert (incoming radio signals) into sounds, pictures, etc., by means of a receiver. **15** *(also intr) Tennis.* to play at the other end from the server; be required to return (service). **16** *(also intr)* to partake of (the Christian Eucharist). **17** *(intr) Chiefly Brit.* to buy and sell stolen goods. [C13: from Old French *receivre,* from Latin *recipere* to take back, from RE- + *capere* to take]
received (rɪ'siːvd) *adj* generally accepted or believed: *received wisdom.*
Received Pronunciation *n* the accent of standard Southern British English. Abbrev.: **RP.**
receiver (rɪ'siːvə) *n* **1** a person who receives something; recipient. **2** a person appointed by a court to manage property pending the outcome of litigation, during the infancy of the owner, or after the owner(s) has been declared bankrupt or of unsound mind. **3** *Chiefly Brit.* a person who receives stolen goods knowing that they have been stolen. **4** the equipment in a telephone, radio, or television that receives incoming electrical signals or modulated radio waves and converts them into the original audio or video signals. **5** the part of a telephone containing the earpiece and mouthpiece that is held by the telephone user. **6** the equipment in a radar system, radio telescope, etc., that converts incoming radio signals into a useful form, usually displayed on the screen of a cathode-ray oscilloscope. **7** an obsolete word for **receptacle. 8** *Chem.* a vessel in which the distillate is collected during distillation. **9** *U.S. sport.* a player whose function is to receive the ball, esp. a footballer who catches long passes. **10** the metallic frame situated behind the breech of a gun to guide the round into the chamber.
receivership (rɪ'siːvəʃɪp) *n Law.* **1** the office or function of a receiver. **2** the condition of being administered by a receiver.
receiving order *n Brit.* a court order appointing a receiver to manage the property of a debtor or bankrupt.
recency effect ('riːsənsɪ) *n Psychol.* the phenomenon that when people are asked to recall in any order the items on a list, those that come at the end of the list are more likely to be recalled than the others.
recension (rɪ'sɛnʃən) *n* **1** a critical revision of a literary work. **2** a text revised in this way. [C17: from Latin *recēnsiō,* from *recēnsēre* to survey, from RE- + *cēnsēre* to assess]
recent ('riːs[ə]nt) *adj* having appeared, happened, or been made not long ago; modern, fresh, or new. [C16: from Latin *recens* fresh; related to Greek *kainos* new] ▸ **'recently** *adv* ▸ **'recentness** *or* **'recency** *n*
Recent ('riːs[ə]nt) *adj, n Geology.* another word for **Holocene.**
recept ('riːsɛpt) *n Psychol.* an idea or image formed in the mind by repeated experience of a particular pattern of sensory stimulation. [C20: from RE- + (CON)CEPT]
receptacle (rɪ'sɛptək[ə]l) *n* **1** an object that holds something; container. **2** *Botany.* **2a** the enlarged or modified tip of the flower stalk that bears the parts of the flower. **2b** the shortened flattened stem bearing the florets of the capitulum of composite flowers such as the daisy. **2c** the part of lower plants that bears the reproductive organs or spores. [C15: from Latin *receptāculum* a store-place, from *receptāre* to receive again, from *recipere* to RECEIVE]
reception (rɪ'sɛpʃən) *n* **1** the act of receiving or state of being received. **2** the manner in which something, such as a guest or a new idea, is received: *a cold reception.* **3** a formal party for guests, such as one after a wedding. **4** an area in an office, hotel, etc., where visitors or guests are received and appointments or reservations dealt with. **5** short for **reception room. 6** the quality or fidelity of a received radio or television broadcast: *the reception was poor.* **7** *Brit.* **7a** the first class in an infant school. **7b** a class in a school designed to receive new immigrants, esp. those whose knowledge of English is poor. **7c** *(as modifier): a reception teacher.* [C14: from Latin *receptiō* a receiving, from *recipere* to RECEIVE]

re'broadcast *vb,* **-casts, -casting, -cast.**
re'build *vb,* **-'builds, -'building, -'built.**
re'burial *n*
re'calcuˌlate *vb*
re'cast *vb,* **-'casts, -'casting, -'cast.**
re'caution *vb*

reception centre *n Social welfare.* (in Britain) **1** a place to which distressed people, such as vagrants, addicts, victims of a disaster, refugees, etc., go pending more permanent arrangements. **2** a local-authority home where children are looked after in a family crisis or where long-term placement is arranged for a child whose family cannot provide a home.

receptionist (rɪ'sɛpʃənɪst) *n* a person employed in an office, hotel, doctor's surgery, etc., to receive clients, guests, or patients, answer the telephone, and arrange appointments, etc.

reception room *n* **1** a room in a private house suitable for entertaining guests, esp. a lounge or dining room. **2** a room in a hotel suitable for large parties, receptions, etc.

receptive (rɪ'sɛptɪv) *adj* **1** able to apprehend quickly. **2** tending to receive new ideas or suggestions favourably. **3** able to hold or receive. ▸ **re'ceptively** *adv* ▸ **receptivity** (ˌriːsɛp'tɪvɪtɪ) *or* **re'ceptiveness** *n*

receptor (rɪ'sɛptə) *n* **1** *Physiol.* a sensory nerve ending that changes specific stimuli into nerve impulses. **2** any of various devices that receive information, signals, etc.

recess *n* (rɪ'sɛs, 'riːsɛs). **1** a space, such as a niche or alcove, set back or indented. **2** (*often pl*) a secluded or secret place: *recesses of the mind.* **3** a cessation of business, such as the closure of Parliament during a vacation. **4** *Anatomy.* a small cavity or depression in a bodily organ, part, or structure. **5** *U.S. and Canadian.* a break between classes at a school. ◆ *vb* (rɪ'sɛs). **6** (*tr*) to place or set (something) in a recess. **7** (*tr*) to build a recess or recesses in (a wall, building, etc.). [C16: from Latin *recessus* a retreat, from *recēdere* to RECEDE]

recession[1] (rɪ'sɛʃən) *n* **1** a temporary depression in economic activity or prosperity. **2** the withdrawal of the clergy and choir in procession from the chancel at the conclusion of a church service. **3** the act of receding. **4** a part of a building, wall, etc., that recedes. [C17: from Latin *recessio;* see RECESS]

recession[2] (riː'sɛʃən) *n* the act of restoring possession to a former owner. [C19: from RE- + CESSION]

recessional (rɪ'sɛʃənᵊl) *adj* **1** of or relating to recession. ◆ *n* **2** a hymn sung as the clergy and choir withdraw from the chancel at the conclusion of a church service.

recessionary (rɪ'sɛʃənərɪ) *adj* of, caused by, or undergoing economic recession.

recessive (rɪ'sɛsɪv) *adj* **1** tending to recede or go back; receding. **2** *Genetics.* **2a** (of a gene) capable of producing its characteristic phenotype in the organism only when its allele is identical. **2b** (of a character) controlled by such a gene. Compare **dominant** (sense 4). **3** *Linguistics.* (of stress) tending to be placed on or near the initial syllable of a polysyllabic word. ◆ *n* **4** *Genetics.* **4a** a recessive gene or character. **4b** an organism having such a gene or character. ▸ **re'cessively** *adv* ▸ **re'cessiveness** *n*

Rechabite ('rɛkəˌbaɪt) *n* a total abstainer from alcoholic drink, esp. a member of the **Independent Order of Rechabites,** a society devoted to abstention. [C14: via Medieval Latin from Hebrew *Rēkābīm* descendants of *Rēkāb.* See Jeremiah 35:6]

RECHAR ('riːtʃɑː) *n* an EU funding programme providing grants for the reconversion or development of depressed mining areas. [C20: from French: *Re*conversion de Bassins *Char*bonniers, literally: reconversion of coal fields]

recharge (ˌriː'tʃɑːdʒ) *vb* (*tr*) **1** to cause (an accumulator, capacitor, etc.) to take up and store electricity again. **2** to revive or renew (one's energies) (esp. in **recharge one's batteries**). ▸ **re'chargeable** *adj*

réchauffé *French.* (reʃofe) *n* **1** warmed-up leftover food. **2** old, stale, or reworked material. [C19: from French *réchauffer* to reheat, from RE- + *chauffer* to warm; see CHAFE]

recherché (rə'ʃɛəʃeɪ; *French* rəʃɛrʃe) *adj* **1** known only to connoisseurs; choice or rare. **2** studiedly refined or elegant. [C18: from French: past participle of *rechercher* to make a thorough search for; see RESEARCH]

recidivism (rɪ'sɪdɪˌvɪzəm) *n* habitual relapse into crime. [C19: from Latin *recidīvus* falling back, from RE- + *cadere* to fall] ▸ **re'cidivist** *n, adj* ▸ **reˌcidi'vistic** *or* **re'cidivous** *adj*

Recife (rɛ'siːfə) *n* a port at the easternmost point of Brazil on the Atlantic: capital of Pernambuco state; built partly on an island, with many waterways and bridges. Pop. (city): 1 296 995 (1991), with a conurbation of 3 168 000 (1995). Former name: **Pernambuco.**

recipe ('rɛsɪpɪ) *n* **1** a list of ingredients and directions for making something, esp. a food preparation. **2** *Med.* (formerly) a medical prescription. **3** a method for achieving some desired objective: *a recipe for success.* [C14: from Latin, literally: take (it)! from *recipere* to take, RECEIVE]

recipience (rɪ'sɪpɪəns) *n* **1** the act of receiving. **2** the quality of being receptive; receptiveness.

recipient (rɪ'sɪpɪənt) *n* **1** a person who or thing that receives. ◆ *adj* **2** a less common word for **receptive.** [C16: via French from Latin *recipiēns,* from *recipere* to RECEIVE]

reciprocal (rɪ'sɪprəkᵊl) *adj* **1** of, relating to, or designating something given by each of two people, countries, etc., to the other; mutual: *reciprocal friendship; reciprocal trade.* **2** given or done in return: *a reciprocal favour.* **3** (of a pronoun) indicating that action is given and received by each subject; for example, *each other* in the sentence *they started to shout at each other.* **4** *Maths.* of or relating to a number or quantity divided into one. **5** *Navigation.* denoting a course or bearing that is 180° from the previous or assumed one. ◆ *n* **6** something that is reciprocal. **7** Also called: **inverse.** *Maths.* a number or quantity that when multiplied by a given number or quantity gives a product of one: *the reciprocal of 2 is 0.5.* [C16: from Latin *reciprocus* alternating] ▸ **reˌcipro'cality** *n* ▸ **re'ciprocally** *adv*

reciprocate (rɪ'sɪprəˌkeɪt) *vb* **1** to give or feel in return. **2** to move or cause to move backwards and forwards. **3** (*intr*) to be correspondent or equivalent. [C17: from Latin *reciprocāre,* from *reciprocus* RECIPROCAL] ▸ **reˌcipro'cation** *n* ▸ **re'ciprocative** *or* **re'reciproˌcatory** *adj* ▸ **re'ciproˌcator** *n*

reciprocating engine *n* an engine in which one or more pistons move backwards and forwards inside a cylinder or cylinders.

reciprocity (ˌrɛsɪ'prɒsɪtɪ) *n, pl* **-ities. 1** reciprocal action or relation. **2** a mutual exchange of commercial or other privileges. [C18: via French from Latin *reciprocus* RECIPROCAL]

reciprocity failure *n Photog.* a failure of the two exposure variables, light intensity and exposure time, to behave in a reciprocal fashion at very high or very low values.

recision (rɪ'sɪʒən) *n* the act of cancelling or rescinding; annulment: *the recision of a treaty.* [C17: from Latin *recīsiō,* from *recīdere* to cut back]

recit. *Music. abbrev. for* recitative.

recital (rɪ'saɪtᵊl) *n* **1** a musical performance by a soloist or soloists. Compare **concert** (sense 1). **2** the act of reciting or repeating something learned or prepared. **3** an account, narration, or description. **4** a detailed statement of facts, figures, etc. **5** (*often pl*) *Law.* the preliminary statement in a deed showing the reason for its existence and leading up to and explaining the operative part. ▸ **re'citalist** *n*

recitation (ˌrɛsɪ'teɪʃən) *n* **1** the act of reciting from memory, or a formal reading of verse before an audience. **2** something recited.

recitative[1] (ˌrɛsɪtə'tiːv) *n* a passage in a musical composition, esp. the narrative parts in an oratorio, set for one voice with either continuo accompaniment only or full accompaniment, reflecting the natural rhythms of speech. [C17: from Italian *recitativo;* see RECITE]

recitative[2] (rɪ'saɪtətɪv) *adj* of or relating to recital.

recite (rɪ'saɪt) *vb* **1** to repeat (a poem, passage, etc.) aloud from memory before an audience, teacher, etc. **2** (*tr*) to give a detailed account of. **3** (*tr*) to enumerate (examples, etc.). [C15: from Latin *recitāre* to cite again, from RE- + *citāre* to summon; see CITE] ▸ **re'citable** *adj* ▸ **re'citer** *n*

reck (rɛk) *vb Archaic.* (*used mainly with a negative*) **1** to mind or care about (something): *to reck nought.* **2** (*usually impersonal*) to concern or interest (someone). [Old English *reccan;* related to Old High German *ruohhen* to take care, Old Norse *rækja,* Gothic *rakjan*]

reckless ('rɛklɪs) *adj* having or showing no regard for danger or consequences; heedless; rash: *a reckless driver; a reckless attempt.* [Old English *recceleās* (see RECK, -LESS); related to Middle Dutch *roekeloos,* Old High German *ruahhalōs*] ▸ **'recklessly** *adv* ▸ **'recklessness** *n*

Recklinghausen (*German* rɛklɪŋ'hauzən) *n* an industrial city in NW Germany, in North Rhine-Westphalia on the N edge of the Ruhr. Pop.: 127 216 (1996 est.).

reckon ('rɛkən) *vb* **1** to calculate or ascertain by calculating; compute. **2** (*tr*) to include; count as part of a set or class: *I reckon her with the angels.* **3** (*usually passive*) to consider or regard: *he is reckoned clever.* **4** (when *tr, takes a clause as object*) to think or suppose; be of the opinion: *I reckon you don't know where to go next.* **5** (*intr;* foll. by *with*) to settle accounts (with). **6** (*intr;* foll. by *with* or *without*) to take into account or fail to take into account: *the bully reckoned without John's big brother.* **7** (*intr;* foll. by *on* or *upon*) to rely or depend: *I reckon on your support in this crisis.* **8** (*tr*) *Slang.* to regard as good: *I don't reckon your chances of success.* **9** (*tr*) *Informal.* to have a high opinion of: *she was sensitive to bad reviews, even from people she did not reckon.* **10 to be reckoned with.** of considerable importance or influence. [Old English (*ge*)*recenian* recount; related to Old Frisian *rekenia,* Old High German *rehhanôn* to count]

reckoner ('rɛkənə) *n* any of various devices or tables used to facilitate reckoning, esp. a ready reckoner.

reckoning ('rɛkənɪŋ) *n* **1** the act of counting or calculating. **2** settlement of an account or bill. **3** a bill or account. **4** retribution for one's actions (esp. in the phrase **day of reckoning**). **5** *Navigation.* short for **dead reckoning.**

reclaim (rɪ'kleɪm) *vb* (*tr*) **1** to claim back: *to reclaim baggage.* **2** to convert (desert, marsh, waste ground, etc.) into land suitable for growing crops. **3** to recover (useful substances) from waste products. **4** to convert (someone) from sin, folly, vice, etc. **5** *Falconry.* to render (a hawk or falcon) tame. ◆ *n* **6** the act of reclaiming or state of being reclaimed. [C13: from Old French *réclamer,* from Latin *reclāmāre* to cry out, protest, from RE- + *clāmāre* to shout] ▸ **re'claimable** *adj* ▸ **re'claimant** *or* **re'claimer** *n*

reclamation (ˌrɛklə'meɪʃən) *n* **1** the conversion of desert, marsh, or other waste land into land suitable for cultivation. **2** the recovery of useful substances from waste products. **3** the act of reclaiming or state of being reclaimed.

réclame *French.* (reklam) *n* **1** public acclaim or attention; publicity. **2** the capacity for attracting publicity.

reclinate ('rɛklɪˌneɪt) *adj* (esp. of a leaf or stem) naturally curved or bent backwards so that the upper part rests on the ground. [C18: from Latin *reclīnātus* bent back]

recline (rɪ'klaɪn) *vb* to rest or cause to rest in a leaning position. [C15: from Old French *recliner,* from Latin *reclīnāre* to lean back, from RE- + *clīnāre* to LEAN[1]] ▸ **re'clinable** *adj* ▸ **reclination** (ˌrɛklɪ'neɪʃən) *n*

re'check *vb, n*
re'circuˌlate *vb*
ˌreclassifi'cation *n*
re'classiˌfy *vb,* **-ˌfies, -ˌfying, -ˌfied.**

recliner (rɪˈklaɪnə) *n* a type of armchair having a back that can be adjusted to slope at various angles and, usually, a leg rest.

recluse (rɪˈkluːs) *n* **1** a person who lives in seclusion. **2** a person who lives in solitude to devote himself to prayer and religious meditation; a hermit, anchorite, or anchoress. ◆ *adj* **3** solitary; retiring. [C13: from Old French *reclus*, from Late Latin *reclūdere* to shut away, from Latin RE- + *claudere* to close] ▶ **reclusion** (rɪˈkluːʒən) *n* ▶ **reˈclusive** *adj*

recognition (ˌrɛkəgˈnɪʃən) *n* **1** the act of recognizing or fact of being recognized. **2** acceptance or acknowledgment of a claim, duty, fact, truth, etc. **3** a token of thanks or acknowledgment. **4** formal acknowledgment of a government or of the independence of a country. **5** *Chiefly U.S. and Canadian.* an instance of a chairman granting a person the right to speak in a deliberative body, debate, etc. [C15: from Latin *recognitiō*, from *recognoscere* to know again, from RE- + *cognoscere* to know, ascertain] ▶ **recognitive** (rɪˈkɒgnɪtɪv) *or* **reˈcognitory** *adj*

recognizance *or* **recognisance** (rɪˈkɒgnɪzəns) *n* **1** *Law.* **1a** a bond entered into before a court or magistrate by which a person binds himself to do a specified act, as to appear in court on a stated day, keep the peace, or pay a debt. **1b** a monetary sum pledged to the performance of such an act. **2** an obsolete word for **recognition.** [C14: from Old French *reconoissance*, from *reconoistre* to RECOGNIZE] ▶ **reˈcognizant** *or* **reˈcognisant** *adj*

recognize *or* **recognise** (ˈrɛkəgˌnaɪz) *vb* (*tr*) **1** to perceive (a person, creature, or thing) to be the same as or belong to the same class as something previously seen or known; know again. **2** to accept or be aware of (a fact, duty, problem, etc.): *to recognize necessity.* **3** to give formal acknowledgment of the status or legality of (a government, an accredited representative, etc.). **4** *Chiefly U.S. and Canadian.* to grant (a person) the right to speak in a deliberative body, debate, etc. **5** to give a token of thanks for (a service rendered, etc.). **6** to make formal acknowledgment of (a claim, etc.). **7** to show approval or appreciation of (something good or pleasing). **8** to acknowledge or greet (a person), as when meeting by chance. **9** (*intr*) *Chiefly U.S.* to enter into a recognizance. [C15: from Latin *recognoscere* to know again, from RE- + *cognoscere* to know, ascertain] ▶ **ˈrecogˌnizable** *or* **ˈrecogˌnisable** *adj* ▶ **ˌrecogˌnizaˈbility** *or* **ˌrecogˌnisaˈbility** *n* ▶ **ˈrecogˌnizably** *or* **ˈrecogˌnisably** *adv* ▶ **ˈrecogˌnizer** *or* **ˈrecogˌniser** *n*

recognizee *or* **recognisee** (rɪˌkɒgnɪˈziː) *n Law.* the person to whom one entering into a recognizance is bound.

recognizor *or* **recognisor** (rɪˌkɒgnɪˈzɔː) *n Law.* a person who enters into a recognizance.

recoil *vb* (rɪˈkɔɪl). (*intr*) **1** to jerk back, as from an impact or violent thrust. **2** (often foll. by *from*) to draw back in fear, horror, or disgust: *to recoil from the sight of blood.* **3** (foll. by *on* or *upon*) to go wrong, esp. so as to hurt the perpetrator. **4** (of a nucleus, atom, molecule, or elementary particle) to change momentum as a result of the emission of a photon or particle. ◆ *n* (rɪˈkɔɪl, ˈriːkɔɪl). **5a** the backward movement of a gun when fired. **5b** the distance moved. **6** the motion acquired by a particle as a result of its emission of a photon or other particle. **7** the act of recoiling. [C13: from Old French *reculer*, from RE- + *cul* rump, from Latin *cūlus*] ▶ **reˈcoiler** *n*

recoilless (rɪˈkɔɪllɪs) *adj* denoting a gun, esp. an antitank weapon, in which the blast is vented to the rear so as to eliminate or reduce recoil.

recollect (ˌrɛkəˈlɛkt) *vb* (when *tr, often takes a clause as object*) to recall from memory; remember. [C16: from Latin *recolligere* to gather again, from RE- + *colligere* to COLLECT[1]] ▶ **ˌrecolˈlection** *n* ▶ **ˌrecolˈlective** *adj* ▶ **ˌrecolˈlectively** *adv*

recombinant (riːˈkɒmbɪnənt) *Genetics.* ◆ *adj* **1** produced by the combining of genetic material from more than one origin. ◆ *n* **2** a chromosome, cell, organism, etc., the genetic makeup of which results from recombination.

recombinant DNA *n* DNA molecules that are extracted from different sources and chemically joined together; for example DNA comprising an animal gene may be recombined with DNA from a bacterium.

recombination (ˌriːkɒmbɪˈneɪʃən) *n* **1** *Genetics.* any of several processes by which genetic material of different origins becomes combined. It most commonly occurs between two sets of parental chromosomes during production of germ cells. **2** *Physics.* the union of free electrons and holes in a semiconductor.

recommend (ˌrɛkəˈmɛnd) *vb* (*tr*) **1** (*may take a clause as object or an infinitive*) to advise as the best course or choice; counsel: *to recommend prudence.* **2** to praise or commend: *to recommend a new book.* **3** to make attractive or advisable: *the trip has little to recommend it.* **4** *Archaic.* to entrust (a person or thing) to someone else's care; commend. [C14: via Medieval Latin from Latin RE- + *commendāre* to COMMEND] ▶ **ˌrecomˈmendable** *adj* ▶ **ˌrecomˈmender** *n*

recommendation (ˌrɛkəmɛnˈdeɪʃən) *n* **1** the act of recommending. **2** something that recommends, esp. a letter presenting someone as suitable for a job, etc. **3** something that is recommended, such as a course of action.

recommendatory (ˌrɛkəˈmɛndətərɪ, -trɪ) *adj* intended to or serving to recommend.

recommit (ˌriːkəˈmɪt) *vb* **-mits, -mitting, -mitted.** (*tr*) **1** to send (a bill) back to a committee for further consideration. **2** to commit again. ▶ **ˌrecomˈmitment** *or* **ˌrecomˈmittal** *n*

recompense (ˈrɛkəmˌpɛns) *vb* **1** (*tr*) to pay or reward for service, work, etc. **2** (*tr*) to compensate for loss, injury, etc. ◆ *n* **3** compensation for loss, injury, etc.: *to make recompense.* **4** reward, remuneration, or repayment. [C15: from Old French *recompenser*, from Latin RE- + *compensāre* to balance in weighing; see COMPENSATE] ▶ **ˈrecomˌpensable** *adj* ▶ **ˈrecomˌpenser** *n*

recompose (ˌriːkəmˈpəʊz) *vb* (*tr*) **1** to restore to composure or calmness. **2** to arrange or compose again; reform. ▶ **recomposition** (ˌriːkɒmpəˈzɪʃən) *n*

reconcilable (ˈrɛkənˌsaɪləbᵊl, ˌrɛkənˈsaɪ-) *adj* able or willing to be reconciled. ▶ **ˌreconˌcilaˈbility** *or* **ˈreconˌcilableness** *n* ▶ **ˈreconˌcilably** *adv*

reconcile (ˈrɛkənˌsaɪl) *vb* (*tr*) **1** (*often passive;* usually foll. by *to*) to make (oneself or another) no longer opposed; cause to acquiesce in something unpleasant: *she reconciled herself to poverty.* **2** to become friendly with (someone) after estrangement or to re-establish friendly relations between (two or more people). **3** to settle (a quarrel or difference). **4** to make (two apparently conflicting things) compatible or consistent with each other. **5** to reconsecrate (a desecrated church, etc.). [C14: from Latin *reconciliāre* to bring together again, from RE- + *conciliāre* to make friendly, CONCILIATE] ▶ **ˈreconˌcilement** *n* ▶ **ˈreconˌciler** *n* ▶ **reconciliation** (ˌrɛkənˌsɪlɪˈeɪʃən) *n* ▶ **reconciliatory** (ˌrɛkənˈsɪlɪətərɪ, -trɪ) *adj*

Reconciliation (ˌrɛkənˌsɪlɪˈeɪʃən) *n R.C. Church.* a sacrament in which repentant sinners are absolved and gain reconciliation with God and the Church, on condition of confession of their sins to a priest and of performing a penance.

recondite (rɪˈkɒndaɪt, ˈrɛkənˌdaɪt) *adj* **1** requiring special knowledge to be understood; abstruse. **2** dealing with abstruse or profound subjects. [C17: from Latin *reconditus* hidden away, from RE- + *condere* to conceal] ▶ **reˈconditely** *adv* ▶ **reˈconditeness** *n*

recondition (ˌriːkənˈdɪʃən) *vb* (*tr*) to restore to good condition or working order: *to recondition an engine.*

reconnaissance *or* **reconnoissance** (rɪˈkɒnɪsəns) *n* **1** the act of reconnoitring. **2** the process of obtaining information about the position, activities, resources, etc., of an enemy or potential enemy. **3** a preliminary inspection of an area of land before an engineering survey is made. [C18: from French, from Old French *reconoistre* to explore, RECOGNIZE]

reconnoitre *or U.S.* **reconnoiter** (ˌrɛkəˈnɔɪtə) *vb* **1** to survey or inspect (an enemy's position, region of land, etc.); make a reconnaissance (of). ◆ *n* **2** the act or process of reconnoitring; a reconnaissance. [C18: from obsolete French *reconnoître* to inspect, explore; see RECOGNIZE] ▶ **ˌreconˈnoitrer** *or U.S.* **ˌreconˈnoiterer** *n*

reconsider (ˌriːkənˈsɪdə) *vb* **1** to consider (something) again, with a view to changing one's policy or course of action. **2** (in a legislative assembly or similar body) to consider again (a bill or other matter) that has already been voted upon. ▶ **ˌreconˌsiderˈation** *n*

reconstitute (riːˈkɒnstɪˌtjuːt) *vb* (*tr*) **1** to restore (food, etc.) to its former or natural state or a semblance of it, as by the addition of water to a concentrate: *reconstituted lemon juice.* **2** to reconstruct; form again. ▶ **reconstituent** (ˌriːkənˈstɪtjʊənt) *adj, n* ▶ **ˌreconstiˈtution** *n*

reconstruct (ˌriːkənˈstrʌkt) *vb* (*tr*) **1** to construct or form again; rebuild: *to reconstruct a Greek vase from fragments.* **2** to form a picture of (a crime, past event, etc.) by piecing together evidence or acting out a version of what might have taken place. ▶ **ˌreconˈstructible** *adj* ▶ **ˌreconˈstruction** *n* ▶ **ˌreconˈstructive** *or* **ˌreconˈstructional** *adj* ▶ **ˌreconˈstructor** *n*

Reconstruction (ˌriːkənˈstrʌkʃən) *n U.S. history.* the period after the Civil War when the South was reorganized and reintegrated into the Union (1865–77).

reconvert (ˌriːkənˈvɜːt) *vb* (*tr*) **1** to change (something) back to a previous state or form. **2** to bring (someone) back to his former religion. **3** *Property law.* to convert back (property previously converted) into its original form, as land into money and vice versa. See also **conversion** (sense 5). ▶ **reconversion** (ˌriːkənˈvɜːʃən) *n*

record *n* (ˈrɛkɔːd). **1** an account in permanent form, esp. in writing, preserving knowledge or information about facts or events. **2** a written account of some transaction that serves as legal evidence of the transaction. **3** a written official report of the proceedings of a court of justice or legislative body, including the judgments given or enactments made. **4** anything serving as evidence or as a memorial: *the First World War is a record of human folly.* **5** (*often pl*) information or data on a specific subject collected methodically over a long period: *weather records.* **6a** the best or most outstanding amount, rate, height, etc., ever attained, as in some field of sport: *an Olympic record; a world record; to break the record for the long jump.* **6b** (*as modifier*): *a record time.* **7** the sum of one's recognized achievements, career, or performance: *the officer has an excellent record.* **8** a list of crimes of which an accused person has previously been convicted, which are known to the police but may only be disclosed to a court in certain circumstances. **9 have a record.** to be a known criminal; have a previous conviction or convictions. **10** Also called: **gramophone record, disc.** a thin disc of a plastic material upon which sound has been recorded. Each side has a spiral groove, which undulates in accordance with the frequency and amplitude of the sound. Records were formerly made from a shellac-based compound but are now usually made from vinyl plastics. **11** the markings made by a recording instrument such as a seismograph. **12** *Computing.* a group of data or piece of information preserved as a unit in machine-readable form. **13** (in some computer languages) a data structure designed to allow the handling of groups of related pieces of information as though the group was a single entity. **14 for the record.** for the sake of strict factual accuracy. **15 go on record.** to state one's views publicly. **16** See **off the record. 17 on record. 17a** stated in a public document. **17b** publicly known. **18 set** *or* **put the record straight.** to correct an error or misunderstanding. ◆ *vb* (rɪˈkɔːd). (*mainly tr*) **19** to set

ˌrecoloniˈzation *or* **ˌrecoloniˈsation** *n*
reˈcolour *vb*
ˌrecomˈbine *vb*
ˌrecomˈmence *vb*
ˌrecomˈmencement *n*
ˌreconˈfirm *vb*
ˌreconˈnect *vb*
ˌreconˈnection *n*
reˈconquer *vb*
reˈconquest *n*
reˈconseˌcrate *vb*
ˌreconˈvene *vb*
reˈcopy *vb*, **-ˈcopies, -ˈcopying, -ˈcopied.**

down in some permanent form so as to preserve the true facts of: *to record the minutes of a meeting.* **20** to contain or serve to relate (facts, information, etc.). **21** to indicate, show, or register: *his face recorded his disappointment.* **22** to remain as or afford evidence of: *these ruins record the life of the Romans in Britain.* **23** (*also intr*) to make a recording of (music, speech, etc.) for reproduction, esp. on a record player or tape recorder, or for later broadcasting. **24** (*also intr*) (of an instrument) to register or indicate (information) on a scale: *the barometer recorded a low pressure.* [C13: from Old French *recorder* to call to mind, from Latin *recordārī* to remember, from RE- + *cor* heart] ► **reˈcordable** *adj*

record-changer *n* a device in a record player for changing records automatically.

recorded delivery *n* a Post Office service by which an official record of posting and delivery is obtained for a letter or package. Compare **registered post.**

recorder (rɪˈkɔːdə) *n* **1** a person who records, such as an official or historian. **2** something that records, esp. an apparatus that provides a permanent record of experiments, etc. **3** short for **tape recorder. 4** *Music.* a wind instrument of the flute family, blown through a fipple in the mouth end, having a reedlike quality of tone. There are four usual sizes: bass, tenor, treble, and descant. **5** (in England) a barrister or solicitor of at least ten years' standing appointed to sit as a part-time judge in the crown court. [sense 4 probably from *record* (*vb*) in the archaic sense "to sing"] ► **reˈcorderˌship** *n*

recording (rɪˈkɔːdɪŋ) *n* **1a** the act or process of making a record, esp. of sound on a gramophone record or magnetic tape. **1b** (*as modifier*): *recording studio; recording head.* **2** the record or tape so produced. **3** something that has been recorded, esp. a radio or television programme.

Recording Angel *n* an angel who supposedly keeps a record of every person's good and bad acts.

record of achievement *n Brit.* a statement of the personal and educational development of each pupil.

record player *n* a device for reproducing the sounds stored on a record, consisting of a turntable, usually electrically driven, that rotates the record at a fixed speed of 33, 45, or (esp. formerly) 78 revolutions a minute. A stylus vibrates in accordance with undulations in the groove in the record: these vibrations are converted into electric currents, which, after amplification, are recreated in the form of sound by one or more loudspeakers. See also **monophonic, quadraphonics, stereophonic.**

reco-reco (ˈrɛkəʊˈrɛkəʊ) *n, pl* **reco-recos.** a percussion instrument consisting of a ridged gourd or bamboo cane that is scraped with a piece of wood or metal. [C20: from a native Brazilian language]

recount (rɪˈkaʊnt) *vb* (*tr*) to tell the story or details of; narrate. [C15: from Old French *reconter,* from RE- + *conter* to tell, relate; see COUNT[1]] ► **reˈcountal** *n*

re-count *vb* (riːˈkaʊnt). **1** to count (votes, etc.) again. ◆ *n* (ˈriːˌkaʊnt). **2** a second or further count, esp. of votes in a closely contested election.

recoup (rɪˈkuːp) *vb* **1** to regain or make good (a financial or other loss). **2** (*tr*) to reimburse or compensate (someone), as for a loss. **3** *Law.* to keep back (something due), having rightful claim to do so; withhold; deduct. [C15: from Old French *recouper* to cut back, from RE- + *couper* to cut, from *coper* to behead; see COUP[1]] ► **reˈcoupable** *adj* ► **reˈcoupment** *n*

recourse (rɪˈkɔːs) *n* **1** the act of resorting to a person, course of action, etc., in difficulty or danger (esp. in the phrase **have recourse to**). **2** a person, organization, or course of action that is turned to for help, protection, etc. **3** the right to demand payment, esp. from the drawer or endorser of a bill of exchange or other negotiable instrument when the person accepting it fails to pay. **4 without recourse.** a qualified endorsement on such a negotiable instrument, by which the endorser protects himself from liability to subsequent holders. [C14: from Old French *recours,* from Late Latin *recursus* a running back, from RE- + *currere* to run]

recover (rɪˈkʌvə) *vb* **1** (*tr*) to find again or obtain the return of (something lost). **2** to regain (loss of money, position, time, etc.); recoup. **3** (of a person) to regain (health, spirits, composure, etc.), as after illness, a setback, or a shock, etc. **4** to regain (a former and usually better condition): *industry recovered after the war.* **5** *Law.* **5a** (*tr*) to gain (something) by the judgment of a court of law: *to recover damages.* **5b** (*intr*) to succeed in a lawsuit. **6** (*tr*) to obtain (useful substances) from waste. **7** (*intr*) (in fencing, swimming, rowing, etc.) to make a recovery. [C14: from Old French *recoverer,* from Latin *recuperāre* RECUPERATE] ► **reˈcoverable** *adj* ► **reˌcoveraˈbility** *n* ► **reˈcoverer** *n*

re-cover (riːˈkʌvə) *vb* (*tr*) **1** to cover again. **2** to provide (a piece of furniture, book, etc.) with a new cover.

recovered memory *n* the alleged recollection of traumatic events from childhood by a person undergoing psychotherapy. See also **false memory syndrome.**

recovery (rɪˈkʌvərɪ) *n, pl* **-eries. 1** the act or process of recovering, esp. from sickness, a shock, or a setback; recuperation. **2** restoration to a former or better condition. **3** the regaining of something lost. **4** the extraction of useful substances from waste. **5** *Law.* **5a** the obtaining of a right, etc., by the judgment of a court. **5b** (in the U.S.) the final judgment or verdict in a case. **6** *Fencing.* a return to the position of guard after making an attack. **7** *Swimming, rowing, etc.* the action of bringing the arm, oar, etc., forward for another stroke. **8** *Golf.* a stroke played from the rough or a bunker to the fairway or green.

recovery stock *n Stock Exchange.* a security that has fallen in price but is believed to have the ability to recover.

recreant (ˈrɛkrɪənt) *Archaic.* ◆ *adj* **1** cowardly; faint-hearted. **2** disloyal. ◆ *n* **3** a disloyal or cowardly person. [C14: from Old French, from *recroire* to surrender, from RE- + Latin *crēdere* to believe; compare MISCREANT] ► **ˈrecreance** *or* **ˈrecreancy** *n* ► **ˈrecreantly** *adv*

recreate (ˈrɛkrɪˌeɪt) *vb Rare.* to amuse (oneself or someone else). [C15: from Latin *recreāre* to invigorate, renew, from RE- + *creāre* to CREATE] ► **ˈrecreative** *adj* ► **ˈrecreatively** *adv* ► **ˈrecreˌator** *n*

re-create (ˌriːkrɪˈeɪt) *vb* to create anew; reproduce. ► **ˌre-creˈation** *n* ► **ˌre-creˈator** *n*

recreation (ˌrɛkrɪˈeɪʃən) *n* **1** refreshment of health or spirits by relaxation and enjoyment. **2** an activity or pastime that promotes this. **3a** an interval of free time between school lessons. **3b** (*as modifier*): *recreation period.*

recreational (ˌrɛkrɪˈeɪʃənᵊl) *adj* **1** of, relating to, or used for recreation: *recreational facilities.* **2** (of a drug) taken for pleasure rather than for medical reasons or because of an addiction.

recreation ground *n* an open space for public recreation, esp. one in a town, with swings and slides, etc., for children. Often shortened (informal) to: **rec.**

recreation room *n U.S. and Canadian.* **1** the full name for **rec room. 2** a room in a hotel, hospital, etc., for entertainment and social gatherings.

recrement (ˈrɛkrɪmənt) *n* **1** *Physiol.* any substance, such as bile, that is secreted from a part of the body and later reabsorbed instead of being excreted. **2** waste matter; refuse; dross. [C16: via Old French from Latin *recrēmentum* slag, filth, from RE- + *cernere* to sift] ► **ˌrecreˈmental** *adj*

recriminate (rɪˈkrɪmɪˌneɪt) *vb* (*intr*) to return an accusation against someone or engage in mutual accusations. [C17: from Medieval Latin *recrīmināre,* from Latin *crīmināri* to accuse, from *crīmen* an accusation; see CRIME] ► **reˈcriminative** *or* **reˈcriminatory** *adj* ► **reˈcrimiˌnator** *n*

recrimination (rɪˌkrɪmɪˈneɪʃən) *n* **1** the act or an instance of recriminating. **2** *Law.* a charge made by an accused against his accuser; countercharge.

rec room *n U.S. and Canadian.* a room in a house used by the family for relaxation and entertainment. In full: **recreation room.**

recrudesce (ˌriːkruːˈdɛs) *vb* (*intr*) (of a disease, trouble, etc.) to break out or appear again after a period of dormancy; recur. [C19: from Latin *recrūdēscere* to become raw again, from RE- + *crūdēscere* to grow worse, from *crūdus* bloody, raw; see CRUDE] ► **ˌrecruˈdescence** *n* ► **ˌrecruˈdescent** *adj*

recruit (rɪˈkruːt) *vb* **1a** to enlist (men) for military service. **1b** to raise or strengthen (an army, navy, etc.) by enlistment. **2** (*tr*) to enrol or obtain (members, support, etc.). **3** to furnish or be furnished with a fresh supply; renew. **4** *Archaic.* to recover (health, strength, spirits, etc.). ◆ *n* **5** a newly joined member of a military service. **6** any new member or supporter. [C17: from French *recrute* literally: new growth, from *recroître* to grow again, from Latin *recrēscere,* from RE- + *crēscere* to grow] ► **reˈcruitable** *adj* ► **reˈcruiter** *n* ► **reˈcruitment** *n*

recrystallize *or* **recrystallise** (riːˈkrɪstəˌlaɪz) *vb* **1** *Chem.* to dissolve and subsequently crystallize (a substance) from the solution, as in purifying chemical compounds, or (of a substance) to crystallize in this way. **2** to undergo or cause to undergo the process in which a deformed metal forms a new set of undeformed crystal grains. ► **reˌcrystalliˈzation** *or* **reˌcrystalliˈsation** *n*

rect *or* **rec't** *abbrev. for* receipt.

Rect. *abbrev. for:* **1** Rector. **2** Rectory.

recta (ˈrɛktə) *n* a plural of **rectum.**

rectal (ˈrɛktəl) *adj* of or relating to the rectum. ► **ˈrectally** *adv*

rectangle (ˈrɛkˌtæŋgᵊl) *n* a parallelogram having four right angles. Compare **rhombus.** [C16: from Medieval Latin *rectangulum,* from Latin *rectus* straight + *angulus* angle]

rectangular (rɛkˈtæŋgjʊlə) *adj* **1** shaped like a rectangle. **2** having or relating to right angles. **3** mutually perpendicular: *rectangular coordinates.* **4** having a base or section shaped like a rectangle. ► **recˌtanguˈlarity** *n* ► **recˈtangularly** *adv*

rectangular coordinates *pl n* the Cartesian coordinates in a system of mutually perpendicular axes.

rectangular hyperbola *n* a hyperbola with perpendicular asymptotes.

recti (ˈrɛktaɪ) *n* the plural of **rectus.**

recti- *or before a vowel* **rect-** *combining form.* straight or right: *rectilinear; rectangle.* [from Latin *rectus*]

rectified spirit *n Chem.* a constant-boiling mixture of ethanol and water, containing 95.6 per cent ethanol.

rectifier (ˈrɛktɪˌfaɪə) *n* **1** an electronic device, such as a semiconductor diode or valve, that converts an alternating current to a direct current by suppression or inversion of alternate half cycles. **2** *Chem.* an apparatus for condensing a hot vapour to a liquid in distillation; condenser. **3** a thing or person that rectifies.

rectify (ˈrɛktɪˌfaɪ) *vb* **-fies, -fying, -fied.** (*tr*) **1** to put right; correct; remedy. **2** to separate (a substance) from a mixture or refine (a substance) by fractional distillation. **3** to convert (alternating current) into direct current. **4** *Maths.* to determine the length of (a curve). **5** to cause (an object) to assume a linear motion or characteristic. [C14: via Old French from Medieval Latin *rectificāre* to adjust, from Latin *rectus* straight + *facere* to make] ► **ˈrectiˌfiable** *adj* ► **ˌrectifiˈcation** *n*

rectilinear (ˌrɛktɪˈlɪnɪə) *or* **rectilineal** *adj* **1** in, moving in, or characterized by a straight line or lines: *the rectilinear propagation of light.* **2** consisting of, bounded by, or formed by a straight line or lines. ► **ˌrectiˈlinearly** *or* **ˌrectiˈlineally** *adv*

rectitude (ˈrɛktɪˌtjuːd) *n* **1** moral or religious correctness. **2** correctness of judgment. [C15: from Late Latin *rectitūdō,* from Latin *rectus* right, straight, from *regere* to rule]

ˌre-creˈation *n*   **reˈcross** *vb*

recto ('rɛktəʊ) *n, pl* **-tos. 1** the front of a sheet of printed paper. **2** the right-hand pages of a book, bearing the odd numbers. Compare **verso** (sense 1b). [C19: from Latin *rectus* right, in *rectō foliō* on the right-hand page]

rectocele ('rɛktəʊˌsiːl) *n Pathol.* a protrusion or herniation of the rectum into the vagina. [C19: New Latin, from RECTUM + -CELE]

rector ('rɛktə) *n* **1** *Church of England.* a clergyman in charge of a parish in which, as its incumbent, he would formerly have been entitled to the whole of the tithes. Compare **vicar. 2** *R.C. Church.* a cleric in charge of a college, religious house, or congregation. **3** *Protestant Episcopal Church.* a clergyman in charge of a parish. **4** *Chiefly Brit.* the head of certain schools or colleges. **5** (in Scotland) a high-ranking official in a university: now a public figure elected for three years by the students. [C14: from Latin: director, ruler, from *regere* to rule] ▸ **'rectorate** *n* ▸ **rectorial** (rɛk'tɔːrɪəl) *adj* ▸ **'rectorship** *n*

rectory ('rɛktərɪ) *n, pl* **-ries. 1** the official house of a rector. **2** *Church of England.* the office and benefice of a rector.

rectrix ('rɛktrɪks) *n, pl* **rectrices** ('rɛktrɪˌsiːz, rɛk'traɪsiːz). any of the large stiff feathers of a bird's tail, used in controlling the direction of flight. [C17: from Late Latin, feminine of *rector* governor, RECTOR] ▸ **rectricial** (rɛk'trɪʃəl) *adj*

rectum ('rɛktəm) *n, pl* **-tums** *or* **-ta** (-tə). the lower part of the alimentary canal, between the sigmoid flexure of the colon and the anus. [C16: shortened from New Latin *rectum intestinum* the straight intestine]

rectus ('rɛktəs) *n, pl* **-ti** (-taɪ). *Anatomy.* a straight muscle, esp. either of two muscles of the anterior abdominal wall (**rectus abdominis**). [C18: from New Latin *rectus musculus*]

recumbent (rɪ'kʌmbənt) *adj* **1** lying down; reclining. **2** (of a part or organ) leaning or resting against another organ or the ground: *a recumbent stem.* **3** (of a fold in a rock formation) having strata nearly parallel to those of the surrounding formation. [C17: from Latin *recumbere* to lie back, from RE- + *cumbere* to lie] ▸ **re'cumbence** *or* **re'cumbency** *n* ▸ **re'cumbently** *adv*

recuperate (rɪ'kuːpəˌreɪt, -'kjuː-) *vb* **1** (*intr*) to recover from illness or exhaustion. **2** to recover (losses of money, etc.). [C16: from Latin *recuperāre* to recover, from RE- + *capere* to gain, take] ▸ **reˌcuper'ation** *n* ▸ **re'cuperative** *adj*

recuperator (rɪ'kuːpəˌreɪtə, -'kjuː-) *n* **1** a person that recuperates. **2** a device employing springs or pneumatic power to return a gun to the firing position after the recoil. **3** *Chemical engineering.* a system of flues that transfers heat from the hot gases leaving a furnace to the incoming air.

recur (rɪ'kɜː) *vb* **-curs, -curring, -curred.** (*intr*) **1** to happen again, esp. at regular intervals. **2** (of a thought, idea, etc.) to come back to the mind. **3** (of a problem, etc.) to come up again. **4** *Maths.* (of a digit or group of digits) to be repeated an infinite number of times at the end of a decimal fraction. [C15: from Latin *recurrere,* from RE- + *currere* to run] ▸ **re'curring** *adj* ▸ **re'curringly** *adv*

recurrent (rɪ'kʌrənt) *adj* **1** happening or tending to happen again or repeatedly. **2** *Anatomy.* (of certain nerves, branches of vessels, etc.) turning back, so as to run in the opposite direction. ▸ **re'currently** *adv* ▸ **re'currence** *n*

recurrent fever *n* another name for **relapsing fever.**

recurring decimal *n* a rational number that contains a pattern of digits repeated indefinitely after the decimal point. Also called: **circulating decimal, repeating decimal.**

recursion (rɪ'kɜːʃən) *n* **1** the act or process of returning or running back. **2** *Logic, maths.* the application of a function to its own values to generate an infinite sequence of values. The **recursion formula** or **clause** of a definition specifies the progression from one term to the next, as given the base clause $f(0) = 0$, $f(n + 1) = f(n) + 3$ specifies the successive terms of the sequence $f(n) = 3n$. [C17: from Latin *recursio,* from *recurrere* RECUR] ▸ **re'cursive** *adj*

recursive function *n Logic, maths.* a function defined in terms of the repeated application of a number of simpler functions to their own values, by specifying a base clause and a recursion formula.

recursive subroutine *n Computing.* a subroutine that can call itself as part of its execution.

recurvate (rɪ'kɜːvɪt, -veɪt) *adj Rare.* bent back.

recurve (rɪ'kɜːv) *vb* to curve or bend (something) back or down or (of something) to be so curved or bent. [C16: from Latin *recurvāre* from RE- + *curvāre* to CURVE]

recusant ('rɛkjʊzənt) *n* **1** (in 16th to 18th century England) a Roman Catholic who did not attend the services of the Church of England, as was required by law. **2** any person who refuses to submit to authority. ◆ *adj* **3** (formerly, of Catholics) refusing to attend services of the Church of England. **4** refusing to submit to authority. [C16: from Latin *recūsāns* refusing, from *recūsāre* from RE- + *causārī* to dispute, from *causa* a CAUSE] ▸ **'recusance** *or* **'recusancy** *n*

recycle (riː'saɪkᵊl) *vb* (*tr*) **1** to pass (a substance) through a system again for further treatment or use. **2** to reclaim (packaging or products with a limited useful life) for further use. **3** to institute a different cycle of processes or events in (a machine, system, etc.). **4** to repeat (a series of operations). ◆ *n* **5** the repetition of a fixed sequence of events. ▸ **re'cyclable** *or* **re'cycleable** *adj*

red[1] (rɛd) *n* **1** any of a group of colours, such as that of a ripe tomato or fresh blood, that lie at one end of the visible spectrum, next to orange, and are perceived by the eye when light in the approximate wavelength range 740–620 nanometres falls on the retina. Red is the complementary colour of cyan and forms a set of primary colours with blue and green. Related adjs.: **rubicund, ruddy. 2** a pigment or dye of or producing these colours. **3** red cloth or clothing: *dressed in red.* **4** a red ball in snooker, billiards, etc. **5** (in roulette and other gambling games) one of two colours on which players may place even bets, the other being black. **6** Also called: **inner.** *Archery.* a red ring on a target, between the blue and the gold, scoring seven points. **7 in the red.** *Informal.* in debit; owing money. **8 see red.** *Informal.* to become very angry. ◆ *adj* **redder, reddest. 9** of the colour red. **10** reddish in colour or having parts or marks that are reddish: *red hair; red deer.* **11** having the face temporarily suffused with blood, being a sign of anger, shame, etc. **12** (of the complexion) rosy; florid. **13** (of the eyes) bloodshot. **14** (of the hands) stained with blood, as after committing murder. **15** bloody or violent: *red revolution.* **16** (of wine) made from black grapes and coloured by their skins. **17** denoting the highest degree of urgency in an emergency; used by the police and the army and informally (esp. in the phrase **red alert**). ◆ *vb* **reds, redding, redded. 18** another word for **redden.** [Old English *rēad;* compare Old High German *rōt,* Gothic *rauths,* Latin *ruber,* Greek *eruthros,* Sanskrit *rohita*] ▸ **'redly** *adv* ▸ **'redness** *n*

red[2] (rɛd) *vb* **reds, redding, red** *or* **redded.** (*tr*) a variant spelling of **redd**[1].

Red (rɛd) *Informal.* ◆ *adj* **1** Communist, Socialist, or Soviet. **2** radical, leftist, or revolutionary. ◆ *n* **3** a member or supporter of a Communist or Socialist Party or a national of a state having such a government, esp. the former Soviet Union. **4** a radical, leftist, or revolutionary. [C19: from the colour chosen to symbolize revolutionary socialism]

red. *abbrev. for* reduce(d).

redact (rɪ'dækt) *vb* (*tr*) **1** to compose or draft (an edict, proclamation, etc.). **2** to put (a literary work, etc.) into appropriate form for publication; edit. [C15: from Latin *redigere* to bring back, from *red-* RE- + *agere* to drive] ▸ **re'daction** *n* ▸ **re'dactional** *adj* ▸ **re'dactor** *n*

red admiral *n* a nymphalid butterfly, *Vanessa atalanta,* of temperate Europe and Asia, having black wings with red and white markings. See also **white admiral.**

red algae *pl n* the numerous algae that constitute the phylum *Rhodophyta,* which contain a red pigment in addition to chlorophyll. The group includes carrageen, dulse, and laver. Also called: **red seaweed.**

redan (rɪ'dæn) *n* a fortification of two parapets at a salient angle. [C17: from French, from earlier *redent* notching of a saw edge, from RE- + *dent* tooth, from Latin *dēns*]

Red Army Faction *n* another name for the **Baader-Meinhof Gang.**

red-backed shrike *n* a common Eurasian shrike, *Lanius collurio,* the male of which has a grey crown and rump, brown wings and back, and a black-and-white face.

redback spider *n* a small venomous Australian spider, *Latrodectus hasselti,* having long thin legs and, in the female, a red stripe on the back of its globular abdomen.

red bag *n* (in Britain) a fabric bag for a barrister's robes, presented by a Queen's Counsel to a junior in appreciation of good work in a case. See also **blue bag.**

red bark *n* a kind of cinchona containing a high proportion of alkaloids.

red beds *pl n* sequences of red sedimentary rocks, usually sandstones or shales, coloured by the oxidization of the iron in them.

red biddy *n Informal.* cheap red wine fortified with methylated spirits.

red blood cell *or* **corpuscle** *n* another name for **erythrocyte.**

red-blooded *adj Informal.* vigorous; virile. ▸ **ˌred-'bloodedness** *n*

redbreast ('rɛdˌbrɛst) *n* any of various birds having a red breast, esp. the Old World robin (see **robin** (sense 1)).

redbrick ('rɛdˌbrɪk) *n* (*modifier*) denoting, relating to, or characteristic of a provincial British university of relatively recent foundation, esp. as distinguished from Oxford and Cambridge.

Redbridge ('rɛdˌbrɪdʒ) *n* a borough of NE Greater London: includes part of Epping Forest. Pop.: 225 100 (1994 est.). Area: 56 sq. km (22 sq. miles).

Red Brigades *pl n* **the.** a group of urban guerrillas, based in Italy, who kidnapped and murdered Aldo Moro in 1978.

redbud ('rɛdˌbʌd) *n* an American leguminous tree, *Cercis canadensis,* that has heart-shaped leaves and small budlike pink flowers. Also called: **American Judas tree.**

redbug ('rɛdˌbʌg) *n U.S.* another name for **chigger** (sense 1).

redcap ('rɛdˌkæp) *n* **1** *Brit. informal.* a military policeman. **2** *U.S. and Canadian.* a porter at an airport or station.

Redcar and Cleveland ('rɛdkɑː) *n* a unitary authority in NE England, in North Yorkshire: formerly (1975–96) part of Cleveland county. Pop.: 144 000 (1996 est.). Area: 240 sq. km (93 sq. miles).

red card *Soccer, etc.* ◆ *n* **1** a card of a red colour displayed by a referee to indicate that a player has been sent off. ◆ *vb* **red-card. 2** (*tr*) to send off (a player).

red carpet *n* **1** a strip of red carpeting laid for important dignitaries to walk on when arriving or departing. **2a** deferential treatment accorded to a person of importance. **2b** (*as modifier*): *the returning hero had a red-carpet reception.*

red cedar *n* **1** any of several North American coniferous trees, esp. *Juniperus virginiana,* a juniper that has fragrant reddish wood used for making pencils, and *Thuja plicata,* an arbor vitae. **2** the wood of any of these trees.

red cent *n* (*used with a negative*) *Informal, chiefly U.S.* a cent considered as a trivial amount of money (esp. in the phrases **not have a red cent, not worth a red cent,** etc.).

Red China *n* an unofficial name for (the People's Republic of) **China.**

red clover *n* a papilionaceous plant, *Trifolium pratense,* native to Europe and Asia, frequently planted as a forage crop. It has fragrant red flowers and three-lobed compound leaves.

redcoat ('rɛdˌkəʊt) *n* (formerly) a British soldier.

red cod *n* a deep-sea fish, *Physiculus bachus,* of Australia and New Zealand, with a grey-and-pink body that turns red when it is removed from water.

red coral *n* any of several corals of the genus *Corallium,* the skeletons of which are pinkish red in colour and used to make ornaments, etc. Also called: **precious coral.**

red corpuscle *or* **blood cell** *n* another name for **erythrocyte.**

Red Crescent *n* a national branch of or the emblem of the Red Cross Society in a Muslim country.

Red Cross *n* **1** an international humanitarian organization (**Red Cross Society**) formally established by the Geneva Convention of 1864. It was originally limited to providing medical care for war casualties but its services now include liaison between prisoners of war and their families, relief to victims of natural disasters, etc. **2** any national branch of this organization. **3** the emblem of this organization, consisting of a red cross on a white background.

redcurrant (ˈrɛdˈkʌrənt) *n* **1** a N temperate shrub, *Ribes rubrum,* having greenish flowers and small edible rounded red berries: family *Grossulariaceae.* **2a** the fruit of this shrub. **2b** (*as modifier*): *redcurrant jelly.*

redd[1] *or* **red** (rɛd) *Scot. and northern English dialect.* ♦ *vb* **redds, redding, redd** *or* **redded. 1** (*tr;* often foll. by *up*) to bring order to; tidy (up). ♦ *n* **2** the act or an instance of redding. [C15 *redden* to clear, perhaps a variant of RID] ▸ ˈ**redder** *n*

redd[2] (rɛd) *n* a hollow in sand or gravel on a river bed, scooped out as a spawning place by salmon, trout, or other fish. [C17 (originally: spawn): of obscure origin]

red deer *n* a large deer, *Cervus elaphus,* formerly widely distributed in the woodlands of Europe and Asia. The coat is reddish brown in summer and the short tail is surrounded by a patch of light-coloured hair.

Red Deer *n* **1** a town in S Alberta on the Red Deer River: trade centre for mixed farming, dairying region, and natural gas processing. Pop: 58 134 (1991). **2** a river in W Canada, in SW Alberta, flowing southeast into the South Saskatchewan River. Length: about 620 km (385 miles). **3** a river in W Canada, flowing east through **Red Deer Lake** into Lake Winnipegosis. Length: about 225 km (140 miles).

redden (ˈrɛdᵊn) *vb* **1** to make or become red. **2** (*intr*) to flush with embarrassment, anger, etc.; blush.

Redding (ˈrɛdɪŋ) *n* **Otis.** 1941–67, U.S. soul singer and songwriter. His recordings include "Respect" (1965), *Dictionary of Soul* (1966), and "(Sittin' on) The Dock of the Bay" (1968).

reddish (ˈrɛdɪʃ) *adj* somewhat red. ▸ ˈ**reddishly** *adv* ▸ ˈ**reddishness** *n*

Redditch (ˈrɛdɪtʃ) *n* a town in W central England, in N Worcestershire: designated a new town in the mid-1960s; metal-working industries. Pop.: 73 372 (1991).

reddle (ˈrɛdᵊl) *n, vb* a variant spelling of **ruddle.**

red duster *n Brit.* an informal name for the **Red Ensign.**

red dwarf *n* one of a class of small cool main-sequence stars.

rede (riːd) *Archaic.* ♦ *n* **1** advice or counsel. **2** an explanation. ♦ *vb* (*tr*) **3** to advise; counsel. **4** to explain. [Old English *rǣdan* to rule; see READ[1]]

red earth *n* a clayey zonal soil of tropical savanna lands, formed by extensive chemical weathering, coloured by iron compounds, and less strongly leached than laterite.

redeem (rɪˈdiːm) *vb* (*tr*) **1** to recover possession or ownership of by payment of a price or service; regain. **2** to convert (bonds, shares, etc.) into cash. **3** to pay off (a promissory note, loan, etc.). **4** to recover (something pledged, mortgaged, or pawned). **5** to convert (paper money) into bullion or specie. **6** to fulfil (a promise, pledge, etc.). **7** to exchange (trading stamps, coupons, etc.) for goods. **8** to reinstate in someone's estimation or good opinion; restore to favour: *he redeemed himself by his altruistic action.* **9** to make amends for. **10** to recover from captivity, esp. by a money payment. **11** *Christianity.* (of Christ as Saviour) to free (men) from sin by his death on the Cross. [C15: from Old French *redimer,* from Latin *redimere* to buy back, from *red-* RE- + *emere* to buy] ▸ **reˈdeemer** *n*

redeemable (rɪˈdiːməbᵊl) *or* **redemptible** (rɪˈdɛmptəbᵊl) *adj* (of bonds, shares, etc.) **1** subject to cancellation by repayment at a specified date or under specified conditions. **2** payable in or convertible into cash. ▸ **reˌdeemaˈbility** *n* ▸ **reˈdeemably** *adv*

Redeemer (rɪˈdiːmə) *n* **The.** Jesus Christ as having brought redemption to mankind.

redeeming (rɪˈdiːmɪŋ) *adj* serving to compensate for faults or deficiencies in quality, etc.: *one redeeming feature.*

redemption (rɪˈdɛmpʃən) *n* **1** the act or process of redeeming. **2** the state of being redeemed. **3** *Christianity.* **3a** deliverance from sin through the incarnation, sufferings, and death of Christ. **3b** atonement for guilt. **4** conversion of paper money into bullion or specie. **5a** removal of a financial obligation by paying off a note, bond, etc. **5b** (*as modifier*): *redemption date.* [C14: via Old French from Latin *redemptiō* a buying back; see REDEEM] ▸ **reˈdemptional, reˈdemptive,** *or* **reˈdemptory** *adj* ▸ **reˈdemptively** *adv*

redemptioner (rɪˈdɛmpʃənə) *n History.* an emigrant to Colonial America who paid for his passage by becoming an indentured servant.

redemption yield *n Stock Exchange.* the yield produced by a redeemable gilt-edged security taking into account the annual interest it pays and an annualized amount to account for any profit or loss when it is redeemed.

Redemptorist (rɪˈdɛmptərɪst) *n R.C. Church.* a member of a religious congregation founded in 1732 to do missionary work among the poor. [C19: from French *rédemptoriste,* from Old French or Latin *redemptor,* from Latin *redimere,* see REDEEM]

Red Ensign *n* the ensign of the British Merchant Navy, having the Union Jack on a red background at the upper corner of the vertical edge alongside the hoist. Compare **White Ensign, Blue Ensign.**

redeploy (ˌriːdɪˈplɔɪ) *vb* to assign new positions or tasks to (labour, troops, etc.). ▸ ˌ**redeˈployment** *n*

redevelop (ˌriːdɪˈvɛləp) *vb* (*tr*) **1** to rebuild or replan (a building, area, etc.). **2** *Photog.* to develop (a negative or print) for a second time, in order to improve the contrast, colour, etc. **3** to develop (something) again. ▸ ˌ**redeˈveloper** *n* ▸ ˌ**redeˈvelopment** *n*

redevelopment area *n* an urban area in which all or most of the buildings are demolished and rebuilt.

redeye (ˈrɛdˌaɪ) *n* **1** *U.S. slang.* inferior whiskey. **2** *Canadian slang.* a drink incorporating beer and tomato juice. **3** another name for **rudd. 4** *Slang.* **4a** an aeroplane flight leaving late at night or arriving early in the morning. **4b** (*as modifier*): *a redeye flight.*

red eye *n Photog.* an undesirable effect that sometimes appears in flashlight portraits when light from the flash enters the eye and is reflected from the retina on to the film, producing a red colour.

red-faced *adj* **1** flushed with embarrassment or anger. **2** having a florid complexion. ▸ **red-facedly** (ˌrɛdˈfeɪsɪdlɪ, -ˈfeɪstlɪ) *adv*

redfin (ˈrɛdˌfɪn) *n* any of various small cyprinid fishes of the genus *Notropis,* esp. *N. cornutus.* They have reddish fins and are popular aquarium fishes.

red fir *n* **1** a North American coniferous tree, *Abies magnifica,* having reddish wood valued as timber: family *Pinaceae.* **2** any of various other pinaceous trees that have reddish wood. **3** the wood of any of these trees.

red fire *n* any combustible material that burns with a bright red flame: used in flares and fireworks. The colour is usually produced by strontium salts.

redfish (ˈrɛdˌfɪʃ) *n, pl* **-fish** *or* **-fishes. 1** a male salmon that has recently spawned. Compare **blackfish** (sense 2). **2** any of several red European scorpaenid fishes of the genus *Sebastes,* esp. *S. marinus,* valued as a food fish.

red flag *n* **1** a symbol of socialism, communism, or revolution. **2** a warning of danger or a signal to stop.

Red Flag *n* **the.** a socialist song, written by James Connell in 1889.

Redford (ˈrɛdfəd) *n* **Robert.** born 1937, U.S. film actor and director. His films include (as actor) *The Chase* (1966), *Butch Cassidy and the Sundance Kid* (1969), *The Sting* (1973), *All the President's Men* (1976), *Up Close and Personal* (1996) and (as director) *Ordinary People* (1980), *A River Runs Through It* (1992), *Quiz Show* (1994), and *The Horse Whisperer* (1998).

red fox *n* the common fox, *Vulpes vulpes,* which has a reddish-brown coat: family *Canidae,* order *Carnivora* (carnivores).

red giant *n* a giant star that emits red light (spectral type M).

Redgrave (ˈrɛdˌgreɪv) *n* **1 Lynn.** born 1944, British stage and film actress. Her films include *Georgy Girl* (1966), *The Virgin Soldiers* (1969), *The National Health* (1973), *The Happy Hooker* (1975), and *Gods and Monsters* (1999). **2** her father, Sir **Michael.** 1908–85, British stage and film actor. Among his films are *The Lady Vanishes* (1938), *The Dam Busters* (1955), *The Loneliness of the Long Distance Runner* (1963), and *The Go-Between* (1971). **3** his elder daughter, **Vanessa.** born 1937, British stage and film actress, whose roles include performances in the films *Blow Up* (1966), *Isadora* (1968), *Mary, Queen of Scots* (1972), *Howards End* (1992), and *Wilde* (1997): noted also for her active commitment to left-wing politics.

red grouse *n* a reddish-brown grouse, *Lagopus scoticus,* of upland moors of Great Britain: an important game bird.

Red Guard *n* a member of a Chinese youth movement that attempted to effect the Cultural Revolution (1965–71).

red gum *n* **1** any of several Australian myrtaceous trees of the genus *Eucalyptus,* esp. *E. camaldulensis,* which has reddish wood. See also **blue gum. 2** the hard red wood from this tree, used for making railway sleepers, posts, etc. **3** another name for **sweet gum.**

red-handed *adj* (*postpositive*) in the act of committing a crime or doing something wrong or shameful (esp. in the phrase **catch red-handed**). [C19 (earlier, C15 *red hand*)] ▸ ˌ**red-ˈhandedly** *adv* ▸ ˌ**red-ˈhandedness** *n*

red hat *n* **1** the broad-brimmed crimson hat given to cardinals as the symbol of their rank and office. **2** the rank and office of a cardinal.

redhead (ˈrɛdˌhɛd) *n* **1** a person with red hair. **2** a diving duck, *Aythya americana,* of North America, the male of which has a grey-and-black body and a reddish-brown head.

red-headed *adj* **1** (of a person) having red hair. **2** (of an animal) having a red head.

red heat *n* **1** the temperature at which a substance is red-hot. **2** the state or condition of being red-hot.

red herring *n* **1** anything that diverts attention from a topic or line of inquiry. **2** a herring cured by salting and smoking.

red-hot *adj* **1** (esp. of metal) heated to the temperature at which it glows red: *iron is red-hot at about 500°C.* **2** extremely hot: *the stove is red-hot, so don't touch it.* **3** keen, excited, or eager; enthusiastic. **4** furious; violent: *red-hot anger.* **5** very recent or topical: *red-hot information.* **6** *Austral. slang.* extreme, unreasonable, or unfair: *the charges are red-hot.*

red-hot poker *n* See **kniphofia.**

redia (ˈriːdɪə) *n, pl* **diae** (-dɪˌiː). a parasitic larva of flukes that has simple locomotory organs, pharynx, and intestine and gives rise either to other rediae or to a different larva (the cercaria). [C19: from New Latin, named after Francesco *Redi* (1629–97), Italian naturalist]

Rediffusion (ˌriːdɪˈfjuːʒən) *n Brit. trademark.* a system by which radio or television programmes are relayed to subscribers from a receiver via cables.

Red Indian *n, adj* another name, now considered offensive, for **American Indian.** [see REDSKIN]

redingote (ˈrɛdɪŋˌgəʊt) *n* **1** a woman's coat with a close-fitting top and a full skirt. **2** a man's or woman's full-skirted outer coat of the 18th and 19th centu-

reˈdecoˌrate *vb*
reˌdecoˈration *n*
reˈdediˌcate *vb*
reˌdediˈcation *n*
ˌ**redeˈfine** *vb*
ˌ**redeˈsign** *vb*
ˌ**redeˈtermine** *vb*
reˈdial *vb,* **-ˈdials, -ˈdialling, -ˈdialled.**
ˌ**rediˈgest** *vb*

ries. **3** a woman's light dress or coat of the 18th century, with an open-fronted skirt, revealing a decorative underskirt. **[C19**: from French, from English *riding coat*]

redintegrate (rɛ'dɪntɪ,greɪt) *vb* **1** (*tr*) to make whole or complete again; restore to a perfect state; renew. **2** (*intr*) *Psychol.* to engage in the process of redintegration. **[C15**: from Latin *redintegrāre* to renew, from *red-* RE- + *integer* complete] ▸ **red'inte,grative** *adj*

redintegration (rɛ,dɪntɪ'greɪʃən) *n* **1** the act or process of making whole again; renewal. **2** *Psychol.* the process of responding to a part of a situation in the same manner as one has responded to the whole situation, as in the case of a souvenir reminding one of a holiday.

redivivus (,rɛdɪ'vaɪvəs) *adj Rare.* returned to life; revived. **[C17**: from Late Latin, from Latin *red-* RE- + *vīvus* alive]

red kowhai *n* another name for **kaka beak**.

red lead (lɛd) *n* a bright-red poisonous insoluble oxide of lead usually obtained as a powder by heating litharge in air. It is used as a pigment in paints. Formula: Pb_3O_4. Also called: **minium**.

red-lead ore ('rɛd'lɛd) *n* another name for **crocoite**.

redleg ('rɛd,lɛg) *n Caribbean, derogatory.* a poor White.

red-legged partridge *n* a partridge, *Alectoris rufa*, having a reddish tail, red legs and bill, and flanks barred with chestnut, black, and white: common on farmlands and heaths in SW Europe, including Britain.

red-letter day *n* a memorably important or happy occasion. **[C18**: from the red letters used in ecclesiastical calendars to indicate saints' days and feasts]

red light *n* **1** a signal to stop, esp. a red traffic signal in a system of traffic lights. **2** a danger signal. **3** an instruction to stop or discontinue. **4a** a red lamp in a window of or outside a house indicating that it is a brothel. **4b** (*as modifier*): *a red-light district*.

redline ('rɛd,laɪn) *vb* (*tr*) (esp. of a bank or group of banks) to refuse a loan to (a person or country) because of the presumed risks involved.

red man *n Archaic.* a North American Indian. **[C18**: see REDSKIN]

red meat *n* any meat that is dark in colour, esp. beef and lamb. Compare **white meat**.

red mist *n Informal.* a feeling of extreme anger that clouds one's judgment temporarily.

Redmond ('rɛdmənd) *n* **John Edward.** 1856–1918, Irish politician. He led the Parnellites from 1891 and helped to procure the Home Rule bill of 1912, but was considered too moderate by extreme nationalists.

red mullet *n* any of the marine percoid fishes constituting the family *Mullidae*, esp. *Mullus surmuletus*, a food fish of European waters. They have a pair of long barbels beneath the chin and a reddish coloration. U.S. name: **goatfish**.

redneck ('rɛd,nɛk) *n Disparaging.* **1** (in the southwestern U.S.) a poor uneducated White farm worker. **2** a person or institution that is extremely reactionary. ◆ *adj* **3** reactionary and bigoted: *redneck laws*.

red ned (nɛd) *n Austral. slang.* any cheap red wine.

redo (ri:'du:) *vb* **-does, -doing, -did, -done.** (*tr*) **1** to do over again. **2** *Informal.* to redecorate, esp. thoroughly: *we redid the house last summer*.

red oak *n* **1** any of several deciduous oak trees, esp. *Quercus borealis*, native to North America, having bristly leaves with triangular lobes and acorns with small cups. **2** the hard cross-grained reddish wood of this tree.

red ochre *n* any of various natural red earths containing ferric oxide: used as pigments.

redolent ('rɛdəulənt) *adj* **1** having a pleasant smell; fragrant. **2** (*postpositive*; foll. by *of* or *with*) having the odour or smell (of); scented (with): *a room redolent of country flowers*. **3** (*postpositive*; foll. by *of* or *with*) reminiscent or suggestive (of): *a picture redolent of the 18th century*. **[C14**: from Latin *redolens* smelling (of), from *redolēre* to give off an odour, from *red-* RE- + *olēre* to smell] ▸ **'redolence** or (*less commonly*) **'redolency** *n* ▸ **'redolently** *adv*

Redon (*French* rədõ) *n* **Odilon** (ɔdilõ). 1840–1916, French symbolist painter and etcher. He foreshadowed the surrealists in his paintings of fantastic dream images.

red osier *n* any of several willow trees that have red twigs used for basketwork.

red-osier dogwood *n* a North American shrub, *Cornus stolonifera*, having bright or dark red wood, white flowers, and whitish fruit.

redouble (rɪ'dʌbᵊl) *vb* **1** to make or become much greater in intensity, number, etc.: *to redouble one's efforts*. **2** to send back (sounds) or (of sounds) to be sent back; echo or re-echo. **3** *Bridge.* to double (an opponent's double). ◆ *n* **4** the act of redoubling.

redoubt (rɪ'daut) *n* **1** an outwork or detached fieldwork defending a pass, hilltop, etc. **2** a temporary defence work built inside a fortification as a last defensive position. **[C17**: via French from obsolete Italian *ridotta*, from Medieval Latin *reductus* shelter, from Latin *redūcere* to withdraw, from RE- + *dūcere* to lead]

redoubtable (rɪ'dautəbᵊl) *adj* **1** to be feared; formidable. **2** worthy of respect. **[C14**: from Old French, from *redouter* to dread, from RE- + *douter* to be afraid, DOUBT] ▸ **re'doubtableness** *n* ▸ **re'doubtably** *adv*

redound (rɪ'daund) *vb* **1** (*intr*; foll. by *to*) to have an advantageous or disadvantageous effect (on): *brave deeds redound to your credit*. **2** (*intr*; foll. by *on* or *upon*) to recoil or rebound. **3** (*intr*) *Archaic.* to arise; accrue: *wealth redounding from wise investment*. **4** (*tr*) *Archaic.* to reflect; bring: *his actions redound dishonour upon him*. **[C14**: from Old French *redonder*, from Latin *redundāre* to stream over, from *red-* RE- + *undāre* to rise in waves, from *unda* a wave]

redowa ('rɛdəvə, -wə) *n* a Bohemian folk dance similar to the waltz. **[C19**: via French and German from Czech *rejdovák*, from *rejdovati* to guide around]

redox ('ri:dɒks) *n* (*modifier*) another term for **oxidation-reduction**. **[C20**: from RED(UCTION) + OX(IDATION)]

red packet *n* (in Hong Kong, Malaysia, etc.) **1** a sum of money folded inside red paper and given at the Chinese New Year to unmarried younger relatives. **2** such a gift given at Chinese weddings by the parents to the bride and groom and by the bride and groom to unmarried younger relatives.

red-pencil *vb* **-cils, -cilling, -cilled** or *U.S.* **-cils, -ciling, -ciled.** (*tr*) to revise or correct (a book, manuscript, etc.).

red pepper *n* **1** any of several varieties of the pepper plant *Capsicum frutescens*, cultivated for their hot pungent red podlike fruits. **2** the fruit of any of these plants. **3** the ripe red fruit of the sweet pepper. **4** another name for **cayenne pepper**.

red pine *n* a coniferous tree, *Dacrydium cupressinum*, of New Zealand, having narrow sharp pointed leaves: family *Taxaceae*. Also called: **rimu**.

Red Planet *n* **the.** an informal name for **Mars**^{2}.

redpoll ('rɛd,pɒl) *n* either of two widely distributed finches, *Acanthis flammea* or *A. hornemanni* (**arctic** or **hoary redpoll**), having a greyish-brown plumage with a red crown and pink breast.

Red Poll or **Polled** *n* a red hornless short-haired breed of beef and dairy cattle.

redraft *n* ('ri:,drɑ:ft). **1** a second draft. **2** a bill of exchange drawn on the drawer or endorser of a protested bill by the holder for the amount of the protested bill plus costs and charges. **3** a re-exported commodity. ◆ *vb* (ri:'drɑ:ft). (*tr*) **4** to make a second copy of; draft again: *to redraft proposals for a project*.

red rag *n* a provocation; something that infuriates. [so called because red objects supposedly infuriate bulls]

red rattle *n* See **rattle** (sense 10).

redress (rɪ'drɛs) *vb* (*tr*) **1** to put right (a wrong), esp. by compensation; make reparation for: *to redress a grievance*. **2** to correct or adjust (esp. in the phrase **redress the balance**). **3** to make compensation to (a person) for a wrong. ◆ *n* **4** the act or an instance of setting right a wrong; remedy or cure: *to seek redress of grievances*. **5** compensation, amends, or reparation for a wrong, injury, etc. **6** relief from poverty or want. **[C14**: from Old French *redrecier* to set up again, from RE- + *drecier* to straighten; see DRESS] ▸ **re'dressable** or **re'dressible** *adj* ▸ **re'dresser** or (*less commonly*) **re'dressor** *n*

re-dress (ri:'drɛs) *vb* (*tr*) to dress (something) again.

Red River *n* **1** Also called: **Red River of the South.** a river in the S central U.S., flowing east from N Texas through Arkansas into the Mississippi in Louisiana. Length: 1639 km (1018 miles). **2** a river in the northern U.S., flowing north as the border between North Dakota and Minnesota and into Lake Winnipeg, Canada. Length: 515 km (320 miles). **3** a river in SE Asia, rising in SW China in Yünnan province and flowing southeast across N Vietnam to the Gulf of Tongkin: the chief river of N Vietnam, with an extensive delta. Length: 500 km (310 miles). Vietnamese name: **Song Koi**.

redroot ('rɛd,ru:t) *n* **1** a bog plant, *Lachnanthes tinctoria*, of E North America, having woolly yellow flowers and roots that yield a red dye: family *Haemodoraceae*. **2** another name for **pigweed** (sense 1).

red rose *n English history.* the emblem of the House of Lancaster. See also **Wars of the Roses, white rose**.

red route *n* an urban through route where the penalties for illegal parking are severe and are immediately enforced.

red run *n Skiing.* a run of some difficulty, suitable for intermediate skiers.

red salmon *n* **1** any salmon having reddish flesh, esp. the sockeye salmon. **2** the flesh of such a fish, esp. canned.

Red Sea *n* a long narrow sea between Arabia and NE Africa, linked with the Mediterranean in the north by the Suez Canal and with the Indian Ocean in the south: occasionally reddish in appearance through algae. Area: 438 000 sq. km (169 000 sq. miles).

red seaweed *n* another term for **red algae**.

red setter *n* a popular name for **Irish setter**.

redshank ('rɛd,ʃæŋk) *n* either of two large common European sandpipers, *Tringa totanus* or *T. erythropus* (**spotted redshank**), having red legs.

red shank *n* an annual polygonaceous plant, *Polygonum persicaria*, of N temperate regions, having red stems, narrow leaves, and oblong spikes of pink flowers. Also called: **persicaria, lady's-thumb**.

red shift *n* a shift in the lines of the spectrum of an astronomical object towards a longer wavelength (the red end of an optical spectrum), relative to the wavelength of these lines in the terrestrial spectrum, usually as a result of the Doppler effect caused by the recession of the object.

redskin ('rɛd,skɪn) *n* an informal name, now considered offensive, for an **American Indian**. **[C17**: so called because one particular tribe, the now extinct Beothuks of Newfoundland, painted themselves with red ochre]

red snapper *n* any of various marine percoid food fishes of the genus *Lutjanus*, esp. *L. blackfordi*, having a reddish coloration, common in American coastal regions of the Atlantic: family *Lutjanidae* (snappers).

red spider *n* short for **red spider mite** (see **spider mite**).

Red Spot See **Great Red Spot**.

red squirrel *n* **1** a reddish-brown squirrel, *Sciurus vulgaris*, inhabiting woodlands of Europe and parts of Asia. **2 American red squirrel.** Also called: **chickaree.** either of two reddish-brown squirrels, *Tamiasciurus hudsonicus* or *T. douglasii*, inhabiting forests of North America.

,redi'rect *vb*
,redi'rection *n*
re'discount *vb, n*
,redis'cover *vb*
,redis'covery *n, pl* **-eries.**
,redis'tribute *vb*
,redistri'bution *n*
,redis'tributive *adj*
,redi'vision *n*
re'draw *vb*, **-'draws, -'drawing, -'drew, -'drawn.**

redstart ('rɛd,stɑːt) *n* **1** any European songbird of the genus *Phoenicurus,* esp. *P. phoenicurus,* in which the male has a black throat, orange-brown tail and breast, and grey back: family *Muscicapidae* (thrushes, etc.). **2** any North American warbler of the genus *Setophaga,* esp. *S. ruticilla.* [Old English *rēad* RED[1] + *steort* tail; compare German *Rotsterz*]

red tape *n* obstructive official routine or procedure; time-consuming bureaucracy. [C18: from the red tape used to bind official government documents]

red tide *n* a discoloration of sea water caused by an explosive growth in phytoplankton density: sometimes toxic to fish life and, through accumulation in shellfish, to humans.

reduce (rɪ'djuːs) *vb* (*mainly tr*) **1** (*also intr*) to make or become smaller in size, number, extent, degree, intensity, etc. **2** to bring into a certain state, condition, etc.: *to reduce a forest to ashes; to reduce someone to despair.* **3** (*also intr*) to make or become slimmer; lose or cause to lose excess weight. **4** to impoverish (esp. in the phrase **in reduced circumstances**). **5** to bring into a state of submission to one's authority; subjugate: *the whole country was reduced after three months.* **6** to bring down the price of (a commodity): *the shirt was reduced in the sale.* **7** to lower the rank or status of; demote: *he was reduced from corporal to private; reduced to the ranks.* **8** to set out systematically as an aid to understanding; simplify: *his theories have been reduced in a popular treatise.* **9** *Maths.* to modify or simplify the form of (an expression or equation), esp. by substitution of one term by another. **10** *Cookery.* to make (a sauce, stock, etc.) more concentrated by boiling away some of the water in it. **11** to thin out (paint) by adding oil, turpentine, etc.; dilute. **12** (*also intr*) *Chem.* **12a** to undergo or cause to undergo a chemical reaction with hydrogen or formation of a hydride. **12b** to lose or cause to lose oxygen atoms. **12c** to undergo or cause to undergo an increase in the number of electrons. Compare **oxidize. 13** *Photog.* to lessen the density of (a negative or print) by converting some of the blackened silver in the emulsion to soluble silver compounds by an oxidation process using a photographic reducer. **14** *Surgery.* to manipulate or reposition (a broken or displaced bone, organ, or part) back to its normal site. **15** (*also intr*) *Biology.* to undergo or cause to undergo meiosis. [C14: from Latin *redūcere* to bring back, from RE- + *dūcere* to lead] ▸ **re'ducible** *adj* ▸ **re,duci'bility** *n* ▸ **re'ducibly** *adv*

reduced level *n Surveying.* calculated elevation in relation to a particular datum.

reducer (rɪ'djuːsə) *n* **1** *Photog.* a chemical solution used to lessen the density of a negative or print by oxidizing some of the blackened silver to soluble silver compounds. Compare **intensifier** (sense 3). **2** a pipe fitting connecting two pipes of different diameters. **3** a person or thing that reduces.

reducing agent *n Chem.* a substance that reduces another substance in a chemical reaction, being itself oxidized in the process. Compare **oxidizing agent.**

reducing glass *n* a lens or curved mirror that produces an image smaller than the object observed.

reductase (rɪ'dʌkteɪz) *n* any enzyme that catalyses a biochemical reduction reaction. [C20: from REDUCTION + -ASE]

reductio ad absurdum (rɪ'dʌktɪəʊ æd æb'sɜːdəm) *n* **1** a method of disproving a proposition by showing that its inevitable consequences would be absurd. **2** a method of indirectly proving a proposition by assuming its negation to be true and showing that this leads to an absurdity. **3** application of a principle or proposed principle to an instance in which it is absurd. [Latin, literally: reduction to the absurd]

reduction (rɪ'dʌkʃən) *n* **1** the act or process or an instance of reducing. **2** the state or condition of being reduced. **3** the amount by which something is reduced. **4** a form of an original resulting from a reducing process, such as a copy on a smaller scale. **5** a simplified form, such as an orchestral score arranged for piano. **6** *Maths.* **6a** the process of converting a fraction into its decimal form. **6b** the process of dividing out the common factors in the numerator and denominator of a fraction; cancellation. ▸ **re'ductive** *adj*

reduction division *n* another name for **meiosis.**

reduction formula *n Maths.* a formula, such as $\sin (90° \pm A) = \cos A$, expressing the values of a trigonometric function of any angle greater than 90° in terms of a function of an acute angle.

reductionism (rɪ'dʌkʃə,nɪzəm) *n* **1** the analysis of complex things, data, etc., into less complex constituents. **2** *Often disparaging.* any theory or method that holds that a complex idea, system, etc., can be completely understood in terms of its simpler parts or components. ▸ **re'ductionist** *n, adj* ▸ **re,duc-tion'istic** *adj*

redundancy (rɪ'dʌndənsɪ) *n, pl* **-cies. 1a** the state or condition of being redundant or superfluous, esp. superfluous in one's job. **1b** (*as modifier*): *a redundancy payment.* **2** excessive proliferation or profusion, esp. of superfluity. **3** duplication of components in electronic or mechanical equipment so that operations can continue following failure of a part. **4** repetition of information or inclusion of additional information to reduce errors in telecommunication transmissions and computer processing.

redundancy payment *n* a sum of money given by an employer to an employee who has been made redundant: usually calculated on the basis of the employee's rate of pay and length of service.

redundant (rɪ'dʌndənt) *adj* **1** surplus to requirements; unnecessary or superfluous. **2** verbose or tautological. **3** deprived of one's job because it is no longer necessary for efficient operation: *he has been made redundant.* **4** (of components, information, etc.) duplicated or added as a precaution against failure, error, etc. [C17: from Latin *redundans* overflowing, from *redundāre* to run back, stream over; see REDOUND] ▸ **re'dundantly** *adv*

red underwing *n* a large noctuid moth, *Catocala nupta,* having dull forewings and hind wings coloured red and black.

redupl. *abbrev. for* reduplicate *or* reduplication.

reduplicate *vb* (rɪ'djuːplɪ,keɪt). **1** to make or become double; repeat. **2** to repeat (a sound or syllable) in a word or (of a sound or syllable) to be repeated, esp. in forming inflections in certain languages. ◆ *adj* (rɪ'djuːplɪkɪt). **3** doubled or repeated. **4** (of petals or sepals) having the margins curving outwards. ▸ **re'duplicative** *adj*

reduplication (rɪ,djuːplɪ'keɪʃən) *n* **1** the process or an instance of redoubling. **2** the state, condition, or quality of being redoubled. **3** a thing that has been redoubled. **4** repetition of a sound or syllable in a word, as in the formation of the Latin perfect *tetigi* from *tangere* "touch".

reduviid (rɪ'djuːvɪɪd) *n* **1** any hemipterous bug of the family *Reduviidae,* which includes the assassin bugs and the wheel bug. ◆ *adj* **2** of, relating to, or belonging to the family *Reduviidae.* [C19: from New Latin *Reduviidae,* from Latin *reduvia* a hangnail]

redware ('rɛd,wɛə) *n* another name for **kelp** (the seaweed).

red water *n* **1** a disease of cattle caused by the protozoan *Babesia* (or *Piroplasma*) *bovis,* which destroys the red blood cells, characterized by the passage of red or blackish urine. **2** any of various other animal diseases characterized by haematuria.

redwing ('rɛd,wɪŋ) *n* **1** a small European thrush, *Turdus iliacus,* having a speckled breast, reddish flanks, and brown back. **2** a North American oriole, *Agelaius phoeniceus,* the male of which has a black plumage with a red-and-yellow patch on each wing.

redwood ('rɛd,wʊd) *n* a giant coniferous tree, *Sequoia sempervirens,* of coastal regions of California, having reddish fibrous bark and durable timber: family *Taxodiaceae.* The largest specimen is over 120 metres (360 feet) tall. See also **sequoia.**

Redwood seconds *n* (*functioning as sing*) a scale of measurement of viscosity based on the time in seconds taken for fluid to flow through a standard orifice: accepted as standard in the U.K. in 1886. See also **Saybolt universal seconds, Engler degrees.** [named after Sir B. *Redwood* (1846–1919), English chemist who proposed it]

reebok ('riːbʌk, -bɒk) *n, pl* **-boks** *or* **-bok.** a variant spelling of **rhebok.**

re-echo (riː'ɛkəʊ) *vb* **-oes, -oing, -oed. 1** to echo (a sound that is already an echo); resound. **2** (*tr*) to repeat like an echo.

reed (riːd) *n* **1** any of various widely distributed tall grasses of the genus *Phragmites,* esp. *P. communis,* that grow in swamps and shallow water and have jointed hollow stalks. **2** the stalk, or stalks collectively, of any of these plants, esp. as used for thatching. **3** *Music.* **3a** a thin piece of cane or metal inserted into the tubes of certain wind instruments, which sets in vibration the air column inside the tube. **3b** a wind instrument or organ pipe that sounds by means of a reed. **4** one of the several vertical parallel wires on a loom that may be moved upwards to separate the warp threads. **5** a small semicircular architectural moulding. See also **reeding. 6** an ancient Hebrew unit of length equal to six cubits. **7** an archaic word for **arrow. 8 broken reed.** a weak, unreliable, or ineffectual person. ◆ *vb* (*tr*) **9** to fashion into or supply with reeds or reeding. **10** to thatch using reeds. [Old English *hreod;* related to Old Saxon *hriod,* Old High German *hriot*]

Reed (riːd) *n* **1** Sir **Carol.** 1906–76, English film director. His films include *The Third Man* (1949), *An Outcast of the Islands* (1951), and *Oliver!* (1968), for which he won an Oscar. **2 Lou.** born 1942, U.S. rock singer, songwriter, and guitarist: member of the Velvet Underground (1965–70). His albums include *Transformer* (1972), *Berlin* (1973), *Street Hassle* (1978), *New York* (1989), and *Magic and Loss* (1992). **3 Walter.** 1851–1902, U.S. physician, who proved that yellow fever is transmitted by mosquitoes (1900).

reedbird ('riːd,bɜːd) *n* any of several birds that frequent reed beds, esp. (in the U.S. and Canada) the bobolink.

reedbuck ('riːd,bʌk) *n, pl* **-bucks** *or* **-buck.** any antelope of the genus *Redunca,* of Africa south of the Sahara, having a buff-coloured coat and inward-curving horns.

reed bunting *n* a common European bunting, *Emberiza schoeniclus,* that occurs near reed beds and has a brown streaked plumage with, in the male, a black head.

reed grass *n* a tall perennial grass, *Glyceria maxima,* of rivers and ponds of Europe, Asia, and Canada.

reeding ('riːdɪŋ) *n* **1** a set of small semicircular architectural mouldings. **2** the milling on the edges of a coin.

reedling ('riːdlɪŋ) *n* a titlike Eurasian songbird, *Panurus biarmicus,* common in reed beds: family *Muscicapidae* (Old World flycatchers, etc.). It has a tawny back and tail and, in the male, a grey-and-black head. Also called: **bearded tit.**

reed mace *n* **1** Also called: (popularly) **bulrush, false bulrush, cat's-tail.** a tall reedlike marsh plant, *Typha latifolia,* with straplike leaves and flowers in long brown sausage-shaped spikes: family *Typhaceae.* See also **bulrush** (sense 2). **2** a related and similar plant, *Typha angustifolia.*

reed organ *n* **1** a wind instrument, such as the harmonium, accordion, or harmonica, in which the sound is produced by reeds, each reed producing one note only. **2** a type of pipe organ, such as the regal, in which all the pipes are fitted with reeds.

reed pipe *n* **1** a wind instrument, such as a clarinet or oboe, whose sound is produced by a vibrating reed. **2** an organ pipe sounded by a vibrating reed.

re-'edit *vb*

reed stop *n* an organ stop controlling a rank of reed pipes.
reed warbler *n* any of various common Old World warblers of the genus *Acrocephalus,* esp. *A. scirpaceus,* that inhabit marshy regions and have a brown plumage.
reedy ('ri:dɪ) *adj* **reedier, reediest. 1** (of a place, esp. a marsh) abounding in reeds. **2** of or like a reed. **3** having a tone like a reed instrument; shrill or piping: *a reedy voice.* ▸ **'reedily** *adv* ▸ **'reediness** *n*
reef[1] (ri:f) *n* **1** a ridge of rock, sand, coral, etc., the top of which lies close to the surface of the sea. **2** a vein of ore, esp. one of gold-bearing quartz. [C16: from Middle Dutch *ref,* from Old Norse *rif* RIB[1], REEF[2]]
reef[2] (ri:f) *Nautical.* ◆ *n* **1** the part gathered in when sail area is reduced, as in a high wind. ◆ *vb* **2** to reduce the area of (sail) by taking in a reef. **3** (*tr*) to shorten or bring inboard (a spar). [C14: from Middle Dutch *rif;* related to Old Norse *rif* reef, RIB[1], German *reffen* to reef; see REEF[1]]
Reef (ri:f) *n* **the. 1** another name for the **Great Barrier Reef. 2** another name for the **Witwatersrand.**
reefer[1] ('ri:fə) *n* **1** *Nautical.* a person who reefs, such as a midshipman. **2** another name for **reefing jacket. 3** *Slang.* a hand-rolled cigarette, esp. one containing cannabis. [C19: from REEF[2]; applied to the cigarette because of its resemblance to the rolled reef of a sail]
reefer[2] ('ri:fə) *n* a ship, lorry, or other form of transport designed to carry refrigerated cargo. [C20: shortened and adapted from *refrigerator*]
reefing jacket *n* a man's short double-breasted jacket of sturdy wool. Also called: **reefer.**
reef knot *n* a knot consisting of two overhand knots turned opposite ways. Also called: **square knot.**
reef point *n Nautical.* one of several short lengths of line stitched through a sail for tying a reef.
reek (ri:k) *vb* **1** (*intr*) to give off or emit a strong unpleasant odour; smell or stink. **2** (*intr;* often foll. by *of*) to be permeated (by); be redolent (of): *the letter reeks of subservience.* **3** (*tr*) to treat with smoke; fumigate. **4** (*tr*) *Chiefly dialect.* to give off or emit (smoke, fumes, vapour, etc.). ◆ *n* **5** a strong offensive smell; stink. **6** *Chiefly dialect.* smoke or steam; vapour. [Old English *rēocan;* related to Old Frisian *riāka* to smoke, Old High German *rouhhan,* Old Norse *rjūka* to smoke, steam] ▸ **'reeking** *adj* ▸ **'reekingly** *adv* ▸ **'reeky** *adj*
reel[1] (ri:l, rɪəl) *n* **1** any of various cylindrical objects or frames that turn on an axis and onto which film, magnetic tape, paper tape, wire, thread, etc., may be wound. U.S. equivalent: **spool. 2** *Angling.* a device for winding, casting, etc., consisting of a revolving spool with a handle, attached to a fishing rod. **3** a roll of celluloid exhibiting a sequence of photographs to be projected. ◆ *vb* (*tr*) **4** to wind (cotton, thread, etc.) onto a reel. **5** (foll. by *in, out,* etc.) to wind or draw with a reel: *to reel in a fish.* [Old English *hrēol;* related to Old Norse *hræll* weaver's rod, Greek *krekein* to weave] ▸ **'reelable** *adj* ▸ **'reeler** *n*
reel[2] (ri:l, rɪəl) *vb* (*mainly intr*) **1** to sway, esp. under the shock of a blow or through dizziness or drunkenness. **2** to whirl about or have the feeling of whirling about: *his brain reeled.* ◆ *n* **3** a staggering or swaying motion or sensation. [C14 *relen,* probably from REEL[1]]
reel[3] (ri:l, rɪəl) *n* **1** any of various lively Scottish dances, such as the **eightsome reel** and **foursome reel,** for a fixed number of couples who combine in square and circular formations. **2** a piece of music having eight quavers to the bar composed for or in the rhythm of this dance. [C18: from REEL[2]]
reel-fed *adj Printing.* involving or printing on a web of paper: *a reel-fed press.* Compare **sheet-fed.**
reel man *n Austral. and N.Z.* (formerly) the member of a beach life-saving team who controlled the reel on which the line was wound.
reel off *vb* (*tr, adv*) to recite or write fluently and without apparent effort: *to reel off items on a list.*
reel of three *n* (in Scottish country dancing) a figure-of-eight movement danced by three people.
reel-to-reel *adj* **1** (of magnetic tape) wound from one reel to another in use. **2** (of a tape recorder) using magnetic tape wound from one reel to another, as opposed to cassettes.
reen *or* **rean** (ri:n) *n Southwest English dialect.* a ditch, esp. a drainage channel. [from earlier *rhine,* from Old English *ryne*]
re-entering angle *n* an interior angle of a polygon that is greater than 180°. Also called: **re-entrant angle.**
re-entrant (ri:'entrənt) *adj* **1** (of an angle, esp. in fortifications) pointing inwards. Compare **salient** (sense 2). **2** *Maths.* (of an angle in a polygon) greater than 180° and thus pointing inwards. ◆ *n* **3** an angle or part that points inwards.
re-entry (ri:'entrɪ) *n, pl* **-tries. 1** the act of retaking possession of land, etc., under a right reserved in an earlier transfer of the property, such as a lease. **2** the return of a spacecraft into the earth's atmosphere.
re-entry vehicle *n* the portion of a ballistic missile that carries a nuclear warhead and re-enters the earth's atmosphere.
reest *or* **reast** (ri:st) *vb* (*intr*) *Northern English dialect.* (esp. of horses) to be noisily uncooperative. [probably from Scottish *arreest* ARREST; perhaps related to RESTIVE]
reeve[1] (ri:v) *n* **1** *English history.* the local representative of the king in a shire (under the ealdorman) until the early 11th century. Compare **sheriff. 2** (in medieval England) a manorial steward who supervised the daily affairs of the manor: often a villein elected by his fellows. **3** *Canadian government.* (in certain provinces) a president of a local council, esp. in a rural area. **4** (formerly) a minor local official in any of several parts of England and the U.S. [Old English *gerēva;* related to Old High German *ruova* number, array]
reeve[2] (ri:v) *vb* **reeves, reeving; reeved** *or* **rove** (rəʊv). (*tr*) *Nautical.* **1** to pass (a rope or cable) through an eye or other narrow opening. **2** to fasten by passing through or around something. [C17: perhaps from Dutch *rēven* REEF[2]]
reeve[3] (ri:v) *n* the female of the ruff (the bird). [C17: of uncertain origin]
re-examine (ˌri:ɪg'zæmɪn) *vb* (*tr*) **1** to examine again. **2** *Law.* to examine (one's own witness) again upon matters arising out of his cross-examination. ▸ **ˌre-ex'aminable** *adj* ▸ **ˌre-exˌami'nation** *n* ▸ **ˌre-ex'aminer** *n*
re-export *vb* (ˌri:ɪk'spɔ:t, ri:'ekspɔ:t). **1** to export (imported goods, esp. after processing). ◆ *n* (ri:'ekspɔ:t). **2** the act of re-exporting. **3** a re-exported commodity. ▸ **ˌre-expor'tation** *n* ▸ **ˌre-ex'porter** *n*
ref (ref) *n Informal.* short for **referee.**
ref. *abbrev. for:* **1** referee. **2** reference. **3** reformed.
reface (ri:'feɪs) *vb* (*tr*) **1** to repair or renew the facing of (a wall). **2** to put a new facing on (a garment).
Ref. Ch. *abbrev. for* Reformed Church.
refection (rɪ'fekʃən) *n* refreshment with food and drink. [C14: from Latin *refectiō* a restoring, from *reficere* to remake, from RE- + *facere* to make]
refectory (rɪ'fektərɪ, -trɪ) *n, pl* **-tories.** a communal dining hall in a religious, academic, or other institution. [C15: from Late Latin *refectōrium,* from Latin *refectus* refreshed]
refectory table *n* a long narrow dining table supported by two trestles joined by a stretcher or set into a base.
refer (rɪ'fɜ:) *vb* **-fers, -ferring, -ferred.** (often foll. by *to*). **1** (*intr*) to make mention (of). **2** (*tr*) to direct the attention of (someone) for information, facts, etc.: *the reader is referred to Chomsky, 1965.* **3** (*intr*) to seek information (from): *I referred to Directory Enquiries; he referred to his notes.* **4** (*intr*) to be relevant (to); pertain or relate (to): *this song refers to an incident in the Civil War.* **5** (*tr*) to assign or attribute: *Cromwell referred his victories to God.* **6** (*tr*) to hand over for consideration, reconsideration, or decision: *to refer a complaint to another department.* **7** (*tr*) to hand back to the originator as unacceptable or unusable. **8** (*tr*) *Brit.* to fail (a student) in an examination. **9** (*tr*) *Brit.* to send back (a thesis) to a student for improvement. **10 refer to drawer.** a request by a bank that the payee consult the drawer concerning a cheque payable by that bank (usually because the drawer has insufficient funds in his account), payment being suspended in the meantime. **11** (*tr*) to direct (a patient) for treatment to another doctor, usually a specialist. **12** (*tr*) *Social welfare.* to direct (a client) to another agency or professional for a service. [C14: from Latin *referre* to carry back, from RE- + *ferre* to BEAR[1]] ▸ **referable** ('refərəbᵊl) *or* **referrable** (rɪ'fɜ:rəbᵊl) *adj* ▸ **re'ferral** *n* ▸ **re'ferrer** *n*

USAGE The common practice of adding *back* to *refer* is tautologous, since this meaning is already contained in the *re-* of *refer: this refers to* (not *back to*) *what has already been said.* However, when *refer* is used in the sense of passing a document or question for further consideration to the person from whom it was received, it may be appropriate to say *he referred the matter back.*

referee (ˌrefə'ri:) *n* **1** a person to whom reference is made, esp. for an opinion, information, or a decision. **2** the umpire or judge in any of various sports, esp. football and boxing, responsible for ensuring fair play according to the rules. **3** a person who is willing to testify to the character or capabilities of someone. **4** *Law.* See **Official Referee.** ◆ *vb* **-ees, -eeing, -eed. 5** to act as a referee (in); preside (over).
reference ('refərəns, 'refrəns) *n* **1** the act or an instance of referring. **2** something referred, esp. proceedings submitted to a referee in law. **3** a direction of the attention to a passage elsewhere or to another book, document, etc. **4** a book or passage referred to. **5** a mention or allusion: *this book contains several references to the Civil War.* **6** *Philosophy.* **6a** the relation between a word, phrase, or symbol and the object or idea to which it refers. **6b** the object referred to by an expression. Compare **sense** (sense 13). **7a** a source of information or facts. **7b** (*as modifier*): *a reference book; a reference library.* **8** a written testimonial regarding one's character or capabilities. **9** a person referred to for such a testimonial. **10a** (foll. by *to*) relation or delimitation, esp. to or by membership of a specific class or group; respect or regard: *all people, without reference to sex or age.* **10b** (*as modifier*): *a reference group.* **11 terms of reference.** the specific limits of responsibility that determine the activities of an investigating body, etc. **12 point of reference.** a fact forming the basis of an evaluation or assessment; criterion. ◆ *vb* (*tr*) **13** to furnish or compile a list of references for (an academic thesis, publication, etc.). **14** to make a reference to; refer to: *he referenced Chomsky 1956.* ◆ *prep* **15** *Business jargon.* with reference to: *reference your letter of the 9th inst.* Abbrev.: **re.** ▸ **'referencer** *n* ▸ **referential** (ˌrefə'renʃəl) *adj*
reference book *n* **1** a book, such as an encyclopedia, dictionary, etc., from which information may be obtained. **2** *S. African.* another name for **passbook** (sense 4).
referendum (ˌrefə'rendəm) *n, pl* **-dums** *or* **-da** (-də). **1** submission of an issue

re-'eduˌcate *vb*	**ˌre-e'mergence** *n*	**ˌre-en'gage** *vb*	**ˌre-es'tablish** *vb*
re-ˌedu'cation *n*	**ˌre-em'ploy** *vb*	**re-'engineering** *n, adj*	**ˌre-es'tablishment** *n*
ˌre-e'lect *vb*	**ˌre-em'ployment** *n*	**re-'enter** *vb*	**ˌre-e'valuˌate** *vb*
ˌre-e'lection *n*	**ˌre-en'act** *vb*	**ˌre-e'quip** *vb*, **-'quips, -'quipping, -'quipped.**	**ˌre-eˌvalu'ation** *n*
re-'eligible *adj*	**ˌre-en'actment** *n*	**ˌre-e'rect** *vb*	**ˌre-ex'perience** *vb*
ˌre-e'merge *vb*	**ˌre-en'force** *vb*		**re'fashion** *vb*

of public importance to the direct vote of the electorate. **2** a vote on such a measure. **3** a poll of the members of a club, union, or other group to determine their views on some matter. **4** a diplomatic official's note to his government requesting instructions. ◆ See also (for senses 1, 2) **plebiscite**. [C19: from Latin: something to be carried back, from *referre* to REFER]

referent ('rɛfərənt) *n* the object or idea to which a word or phrase refers. Compare **sense** (sense 13). [C19: from Latin *referens*, from *referre* to REFER]

referred pain *n Psychol.* pain felt in the body at some place other than its actual place of origin.

reffo ('rɛfəʊ) *n, pl* **reffos**. *Austral. slang*. an offensive name for a European refugee after World War II.

refill *vb* (riː'fɪl). **1** to fill (something) again. ◆ *n* ('riːfɪl). **2** a replacement for a consumable substance in a permanent container. **3** a second or subsequent filling: *a refill at the petrol station*. **4** *Informal*. another drink to replace one already drunk. ► **re'fillable** *adj*

refinancing (ˌriːfɪ'nænsɪŋ) *n* a method of paying a debt by borrowing additional money thus creating a second debt in order to pay the first.

refine (rɪ'faɪn) *vb* **1** to make or become free from impurities, sediment, or other foreign matter; purify. **2** (*tr*) to separate (a mixture) into pure constituents, as in an oil refinery. **3** to make or become free from coarse characteristics; make or become elegant or polished. **4** (*tr*; often foll. by *out*) to remove (something impure or extraneous). **5** (*intr*; often foll. by *on* or *upon*) to enlarge or improve (upon) by making subtle or fine distinctions. **6** (*tr*) to make (language) more subtle or polished. [C16: from RE- + FINE[1]] ► **re'finable** *adj* ► **re'finer** *n*

refined (rɪ'faɪnd) *adj* **1** not coarse or vulgar; genteel, elegant, or polite. **2** subtle; discriminating. **3** freed from impurities; purified.

refinement (rɪ'faɪnmənt) *n* **1** the act of refining or the state of being refined. **2** a fine or delicate point, distinction, or expression; a subtlety. **3** fineness or precision of thought, expression, manners, etc.; polish or cultivation. **4** a device, change, adaptation, etc., designed to improve performance or increase efficiency.

refinery (rɪ'faɪnərɪ) *n, pl* **-eries**. a factory for the purification of some crude material, such as ore, sugar, oil, etc.

refit *vb* (riː'fɪt), **-fits, -fitting, -fitted**. **1** to make or be made ready for use again by repairing, re-equipping, or resupplying. ◆ *n* ('riːˌfɪt). **2** a repair or re-equipping, as of a ship, for further use. ► **re'fitment** *n*

refl. *abbrev. for:* **1** reflection. **2** reflective. **3** reflex(ive).

reflate (riː'fleɪt) *vb* to inflate or be inflated again. [C20: back formation from REFLATION]

reflation (riː'fleɪʃən) *n* **1** an increase in economic activity. **2** an increase in the supply of money and credit designed to cause such an increase. ◆ Compare **inflation** (sense 2). [C20: from RE- + *-flation*, as in INFLATION or DEFLATION]

reflect (rɪ'flɛkt) *vb* **1** to undergo or cause to undergo a process in which light, other electromagnetic radiation, sound, particles, etc., are thrown back after impinging on a surface. **2** (of a mirror, etc.) to form an image of (something) by reflection. **3** (*tr*) to show or express: *his tactics reflect his desire for power*. **4** (*tr*) to bring as a consequence: *the success of the project reflected great credit on all the staff*. **5** (*intr*; foll. by *on* or *upon*) to cause to be regarded in a specified way: *her behaviour reflects well on her*. **6** (*intr*; foll. by *on* or *upon*) to cast dishonour, discredit, etc. (on): *his conduct reflects on his parents*. **7** (*intr*; usually foll. by *on*) to think, meditate, or ponder. [C15: from Latin *reflectere* to bend back, from RE- + *flectere* to bend; see FLEX]

reflectance (rɪ'flɛktəns) *or* **reflection factor** *n* a measure of the ability of a surface to reflect light or other electromagnetic radiation, equal to the ratio of the reflected flux to the incident flux. Symbol: ρ Compare **transmittance, absorptance**.

reflecting telescope *n* a type of telescope in which the initial image is formed by a concave mirror. Also called: **reflector**. Compare **refracting telescope**.

reflection *or* (*less commonly*) **reflexion** (rɪ'flɛkʃən) *n* **1** the act of reflecting or the state of being reflected. **2** something reflected or the image so produced, as by a mirror. **3** careful or long consideration or thought. **4** implicit or explicit attribution of discredit or blame. **5** *Maths*. a transformation in which the direction of one axis is reversed or changes the polarity of one of the variables. **6** *Anatomy*. the bending back of a structure or part upon itself. ► **re'flectional** *or* **re'flexional** *adj*

reflection density *n Physics*. a measure of the extent to which a surface reflects light or other electromagnetic radiation, equal to the logarithm to base ten of the reciprocal of the reflectance. Symbol: *D* Former name: **optical density**.

reflective (rɪ'flɛktɪv) *adj* **1** characterized by quiet thought or contemplation. **2** capable of reflecting: *a reflective surface*. **3** produced by reflection. ► **re'flectively** *adv*

reflectivity (ˌriːflɛk'tɪvɪtɪ) *n* **1** *Physics*. a measure of the ability of a surface to reflect radiation, equal to the reflectance of a layer of material sufficiently thick for the reflectance not to depend on the thickness. **2** Also called: **reflectiveness**. the quality or capability of being reflective.

reflectometer (ˌriːflɛk'tɒmɪtə) *n Physics*. an instrument for measuring the ratio of the energy of a reflected wave to the incident wave in a system.

reflector (rɪ'flɛktə) *n* **1** a person or thing that reflects. **2** a surface or object that reflects light, sound, heat, etc. **3** a small translucent red disc, strip, etc., with a reflecting backing on the rear of a road vehicle, which reflects the light of the headlights of a following vehicle. **4** another name for **reflecting telescope**. **5** part of an aerial placed so as to increase the forward radiation of the radiator and decrease the backward radiation.

reflet (rə'fleɪ) *n* an iridescent glow or lustre, as on ceramic ware. [C19: from French: a reflection, from Italian *riflesso*, from Latin *reflexus*, from *reflectere* to REFLECT]

reflex *n* ('riːflɛks). **1a** an immediate involuntary response, esp. one that is innate, such as coughing or removal of the hand from a hot surface, evoked by a given stimulus. **1b** (*as modifier*): *a reflex action*. See also **reflex arc**. **2a** a mechanical response to a particular situation, involving no conscious decision. **2b** (*as modifier*): *a reflex response*. **3** a reflection; an image produced by or as if by reflection. **4** a speech element derived from a corresponding form in an earlier state of the language: *"sorrow" is a reflex of Middle English "sorwe."* ◆ *adj* ('riːflɛks). **5** *Maths*. (of an angle) between 180° and 360°. **6** (*prenominal*) turned, reflected, or bent backwards. ◆ *vb* (rɪ'flɛks). **7** (*tr*) to bend, turn, or reflect backwards. [C16: from Latin *reflexus* bent back, from *reflectere* to reflect] ► **re'flexible** *adj* ► **reˌflexi'bility** *n*

reflex arc *n Physiol*. the neural pathway over which impulses travel to produce a reflex action, consisting of at least one afferent (receptor) and one efferent (effector) neuron.

reflex camera *n* a camera in which the image is composed and focused on a large ground-glass viewfinder screen. In a **single-lens reflex** the light enters through the camera lens and falls on the film when the viewfinder mirror is retracted. In a **twin-lens reflex** the light enters through a separate lens and is deflected onto the viewfinder screen.

reflexion (rɪ'flɛkʃən) *n Brit*. a less common spelling of **reflection**. ► **re'flexional** *adj*

reflexive (rɪ'flɛksɪv) *adj* **1** denoting a class of pronouns that refer back to the subject of a sentence or clause. Thus, in the sentence *that man thinks a great deal of himself*, the pronoun *himself* is reflexive. **2** denoting a verb used transitively with the reflexive pronoun as its direct object, as the French *se lever* "to get up" (literally "to raise oneself") or English *to dress oneself*. **3** *Physiol*. of or relating to a reflex. **4** *Logic, maths*. (of a relation) holding between any member of its domain and itself: *"... is a member of the same family as ..." is reflexive*. Compare **irreflexive, nonreflexive**. ◆ *n* **5** a reflexive pronoun or verb. ► **re'flexively** *adv* ► **re'flexiveness** *or* **reflexivity** (ˌriːflɛk'sɪvɪtɪ) *n*

reflexology (ˌriːflɛk'sɒlədʒɪ) *n* **1** a form of therapy practised as a treatment in alternative medicine in which the soles of the feet are massaged: designed to stimulate the blood supply and nerves and thus relieve tension. **2** *Psychol*. the belief that behaviour can be understood in terms of combinations of reflexes. ► **ˌreflex'ologist** *n*

refluent ('rɛflʊənt) *adj Rare*. flowing back; ebbing. [C18: from Latin *refluere* to flow back] ► **'refluence** *n*

reflux ('riːflʌks) *vb* **1** *Chem*. to boil or be boiled in a vessel attached to a condenser, so that the vapour condenses and flows back into the vessel. ◆ *n* **2** *Chem*. **2a** an act of refluxing. **2b** (*as modifier*): *a reflux condenser*. **3** the act or an instance of flowing back; ebb. [C15: from Medieval Latin *refluxus*, from Latin *refluere* to flow back]

reflux oesophagitis (iːˌsɒfə'dʒaɪtɪs) *n* inflammation of the gullet caused by regurgitation of stomach acids, producing heartburn: may be associated with a hiatus hernia.

reforest (riː'fɒrɪst) *vb* (*tr*) another word for **reafforest**.

reform (rɪ'fɔːm) *vb* **1** (*tr*) to improve (an existing institution, law, practice, etc.) by alteration or correction of abuses. **2** to give up or cause to give up a reprehensible habit or immoral way of life. **3** *Chem*. to change the molecular structure of (a hydrocarbon) to make it suitable for use as petrol by heat, pressure, and the action of catalysts. ◆ *n* **4** an improvement or change for the better, esp. as a result of correction of legal or political abuses or malpractices. **5** a principle, campaign, or measure aimed at achieving such change. **6** improvement of morals or behaviour, esp. by giving up some vice. [C14: via Old French from Latin *reformāre* to form again] ► **re'formable** *adj* ► **re'formative** *adj* ► **re'former** *n*

re-form (riː'fɔːm) *vb* to form anew. ► **ˌre-for'mation** *n*

reformation (ˌrɛfə'meɪʃən) *n* the act or an instance of reforming or the state of being reformed. ► **ˌrefor'mational** *adj*

Reformation (ˌrɛfə'meɪʃən) *n* a religious and political movement of 16th-century Europe that began as an attempt to reform the Roman Catholic Church and resulted in the establishment of the Protestant Churches.

reformatory (rɪ'fɔːmətərɪ, -trɪ) *n, pl* **-ries**. **1** Also called: **reform school**. (formerly) a place of instruction where young offenders were sent for corrective training. Compare **approved school**. ◆ *adj* **2** having the purpose or function of reforming.

Reform Bill *or* **Act** *n British history*. any of several bills or acts extending the franchise or redistributing parliamentary seats, esp. the acts of 1832 and 1867.

Reformed (rɪ'fɔːmd) *adj* **1** of or designating a Protestant Church, esp. the Calvinist as distinct from the Lutheran. **2** of or designating Reform Judaism.

reformism (rɪ'fɔːmɪzəm) *n* a doctrine or movement advocating reform, esp. political or religious reform, rather than abolition. ► **re'formist** *n, adj*

Reform Judaism *n* a movement in Judaism originating in the 19th century, which does not require strict observance of the law, but adapts the historical forms of Judaism to the contemporary world. Compare **Orthodox Judaism, Conservative Judaism**.

re'file *vb*
re'fire *vb*
re'float *vb*
re'focus *vb*, **-cuses, -cusing, -cused** *or* **-cusses, -cussing, -cussed**.
re'fold *vb*

refract (rɪˈfrækt) *vb* (*tr*) **1** to cause to undergo refraction. **2** to measure the refractive capabilities of (the eye, a lens, etc.). [C17: from Latin *refractus* broken up, from *refringere*, from RE- + *frangere* to break] ▸ **reˈfractable** *adj*
refracting telescope *n* a type of telescope in which the image is formed by a set of lenses. Also called: **refractor**. Compare **reflecting telescope**.
refraction (rɪˈfrækʃən) *n* **1** *Physics*. the change in direction of a propagating wave, such as light or sound, in passing from one medium to another in which it has a different velocity. **2** the amount by which a wave is refracted. **3** the ability of the eye to refract light. **4** the determination of the refractive condition of the eye. **5** *Astronomy*. the apparent elevation in position of a celestial body resulting from the refraction of light by the earth's atmosphere.
refractive (rɪˈfræktɪv) *adj* **1** of or concerned with refraction. **2** (of a material or substance) capable of causing refraction. ▸ **reˈfractively** *adv* ▸ **reˈfractiveness** *or* **refractivity** (ˌriːfrækˈtɪvɪtɪ) *n*
refractive index *n Physics*. a measure of the extent to which radiation is refracted on passing through the interface between two media. It is the ratio of the sine of the angle of incidence to the sine of the angle of refraction, which can be shown to be equal to the ratio of the phase speed in the first medium to that in the second. In the case of electromagnetic radiation, esp. light, it is usual to give values of the **absolute refractive index** of a medium, that is for radiation entering the medium from free space. Symbol: ν, μ
refractometer (ˌriːfrækˈtɒmɪtə) *n* any instrument for determining the refractive index of a substance. ▸ **refractometric** (rɪˌfræktəˈmɛtrɪk) *adj* ▸ **ˌrefracˈtometry** *n*
refractor (rɪˈfræktə) *n* **1** an object or material that refracts. **2** another name for **refracting telescope**.
refractory (rɪˈfræktərɪ) *adj* **1** unmanageable or obstinate. **2** *Med*. not responding to treatment. **3** *Physiol*. (of a nerve or muscle) incapable of responding to stimulation, esp. during the period (**refractory period**) immediately following a previous stimulation. **4** (of a material) able to withstand high temperatures without fusion or decomposition. ♦ *n, pl* **-ries**. **5** a material, such as fireclay or alumina, that is able to withstand high temperatures: used to line furnaces, kilns, etc. [C17: variant of obsolete *refractary*; see REFRACT] ▸ **reˈfractorily** *adv* ▸ **reˈfractoriness** *n*
refrain[1] (rɪˈfreɪn) *vb* (*intr*; usually foll. by *from*) to abstain (from action); forbear. [C14: from Latin *refrēnāre* to check with a bridle, from RE- + *frēnum* a bridle] ▸ **reˈfrainer** *n* ▸ **reˈfrainment** *n*
refrain[2] (rɪˈfreɪn) *n* **1** a regularly recurring melody, such as the chorus of a song. **2** a much repeated saying or idea. [C14: via Old French, ultimately from Latin *refringere* to break into pieces]
refrangible (rɪˈfrændʒɪbᵊl) *adj* capable of being refracted. [C17: from Latin *refringere* to break up, from RE- + *frangere* to break] ▸ **reˌfrangiˈbility** *or* **reˈfrangibleness** *n*
refresh (rɪˈfrɛʃ) *vb* **1** (*usually tr or reflexive*) to make or become fresh or vigorous, as through rest, drink, or food; revive or reinvigorate. **2** (*tr*) to enliven (something worn or faded), as by adding new decorations. **3** (*tr*) to stimulate (the memory). **4** (*tr*) to replenish, as with new equipment or stores. [C14: from Old French *refreschir*; see RE-, FRESH] ▸ **reˈfreshful** *adj*
refresher (rɪˈfrɛʃə) *n* **1** something that refreshes, such as a cold drink. **2** *English law*. a fee, additional to that marked on the brief, paid to counsel in a case that lasts more than a day.
refresher course *n* a short educational course for people to review their subject and developments in it.
refreshing (rɪˈfrɛʃɪŋ) *adj* **1** able to or tending to refresh; invigorating. **2** pleasantly different or novel. ▸ **reˈfreshingly** *adv*
refreshment (rɪˈfrɛʃmənt) *n* **1** the act of refreshing or the state of being refreshed. **2** (*pl*) snacks and drinks served as a light meal.
refrigerant (rɪˈfrɪdʒərənt) *n* **1** a fluid capable of changes of phase at low temperatures: used as the working fluid of a refrigerator. **2** a cooling substance, such as ice or solid carbon dioxide. **3** *Med*. an agent that provides a sensation of coolness or reduces fever. ♦ *adj* **4** causing cooling or freezing.
refrigerate (rɪˈfrɪdʒəˌreɪt) *vb* to make or become frozen or cold, esp. for preservative purposes; chill or freeze. [C16: from Latin *refrīgerāre* to make cold, from RE- + *frīgus* cold] ▸ **reˌfrigerˈation** *n* ▸ **reˈfrigerative** *adj* ▸ **reˈfrigeratory** *adj, n*
refrigerator (rɪˈfrɪdʒəˌreɪtə) *n* a chamber in which food, drink, etc., are kept cool. Informal word: **fridge**.
refringent (rɪˈfrɪndʒənt) *adj Physics*. of, concerned with, or causing refraction; refractive. [C18: from Latin *refringere* to break up; see REFRACT] ▸ **reˈfringency** *or* **reˈfringence** *n*
reft (rɛft) *vb* a past tense and past participle of **reave**.
refuel (riːˈfjuːəl) *vb* **-els, -elling, -elled** *or U.S.* **-els, -eling, -eled**. to supply or be supplied with fresh fuel.
refuge (ˈrɛfjuːdʒ) *n* **1** shelter or protection, as from the weather or danger. **2** any place, person, action, or thing that offers or appears to offer protection, help, or relief: *accused of incompetence, he took refuge in lying*. **3** another name for a traffic island. See **island** (sense 2). ♦ *vb* **4** *Archaic*. to take refuge or give refuge to. [C14: via Old French from Latin *refugium*, from *refugere* to flee away, from RE- + *fugere* to escape]
refugee (ˌrɛfjuˈdʒiː) *n* **a** a person who has fled from some danger or problem, esp. political persecution: *refugees from Rwanda*. **b** (*as modifier*): *a refugee camp; a refugee problem*. ▸ **ˌrefuˈgeeism** *n*
refugee capital *n Finance*. money from abroad invested, esp. for a short term, in the country offering the highest interest rate.
refugium (rɪˈfjuːdʒɪəm) *n, pl* **-gia** (-dʒɪə). a geographical region that has remained unaltered by a climatic change affecting surrounding regions and that therefore forms a haven for relict fauna and flora. [C20: Latin: refuge]
refulgent (rɪˈfʌldʒənt) *adj Literary*. shining, brilliant, or radiant. [C16: from Latin *refulgēre* to shine brightly, from RE- + *fulgēre* to shine] ▸ **reˈfulgence** *or* (*less commonly*) **reˈfulgency** *n* ▸ **reˈfulgently** *adv*
refund *vb* (rɪˈfʌnd). (*tr*) **1** to give back (money), as when an article purchased is unsatisfactory. **2** to reimburse (a person). ♦ *n* (ˈriːˌfʌnd). **3** return of money to a purchaser or the amount so returned. [C14: from Latin *refundere* to pour back, from RE- + *fundere* to pour] ▸ **reˈfundable** *adj* ▸ **reˈfunder** *n*
re-fund (riːˈfʌnd) *vb* (*tr*) *Finance*. **1** to discharge (an old or matured debt) by new borrowing, as by a new bond issue. **2** to replace (an existing bond issue) with a new one. [C20: from RE- + FUND]
refurbish (riːˈfɜːbɪʃ) *vb* (*tr*) to make neat, clean, or complete, as by renovating, re-equipping, or restoring. ▸ **reˈfurbishing** *or* **reˈfurbishment** *n*
refusal (rɪˈfjuːzᵊl) *n* **1** the act or an instance of refusing. **2** the opportunity to reject or accept; option.
refuse[1] (rɪˈfjuːz) *vb* **1** (*tr*) to decline to accept (something offered): *to refuse a present; to refuse promotion*. **2** to decline to give or grant (something) to (a person, organization, etc.). **3** (when *tr*, *takes an infinitive*) to express determination not (to do something); decline: *he refuses to talk about it*. **4** (of a horse) to be unwilling to take (a jump), as by swerving or stopping. **5** (*tr*) (of a woman) to declare one's unwillingness to accept (a suitor) as a husband. [C14: from Old French *refuser*, from Latin *refundere* to pour back; see REFUND] ▸ **reˈfusable** *adj* ▸ **reˈfuser** *n*
refuse[2] (ˈrɛfjuːs) *n* **a** anything thrown away; waste; rubbish. **b** (*as modifier*): *a refuse collection*. [C15: from Old French *refuser* to REFUSE[1]]
refusenik *or* **refusnik** (rɪˈfjuːznɪk) *n* **1** (formerly) a Jew in the Soviet Union who had been refused permission to emigrate. **2** a person who refuses to cooperate with a system or comply with a law because of a moral conviction. [C20: from REFUSE[1] + -NIK]
refutation (ˌrɛfjuˈteɪʃən) *n* **1** the act or process of refuting. **2** something that refutes; disproof.
refute (rɪˈfjuːt) *vb* **1** (*tr*) to prove (a statement, theory, charge, etc.) of (a person) to be false or incorrect; disprove. **2** to deny (a claim, charge, allegation, etc.). [C16: from Latin *refūtāre* to rebut] ▸ **refutable** (ˈrɛfjutəbᵊl, rɪˈfjuː-) *adj* ▸ **refutability** (ˌrɛfjutəˈbɪlɪtɪ, rɪˌfjuː-) *n* ▸ **ˈrefutably** *adv* ▸ **reˈfuter** *n*
USAGE The use of *refute* to mean *deny* is thought by many people to be incorrect.
reg. *abbrev. for*: **1** regiment. **2** register(ed). **3** registrar. **4** registry. **5** regular(ly). **6** regulation. **7** regulator.
Reg. *abbrev. for*: **1** Regent. **2** Regina.
regain (rɪˈgeɪn) *vb* (*tr*) **1** to take or get back; recover. **2** to reach again. ▸ **reˈgainable** *adj* ▸ **reˈgainer** *n*
regal[1] (ˈriːgᵊl) *adj* of, relating to, or befitting a king or queen; royal. [C14: from Latin *rēgālis*, from *rēx* king] ▸ **ˈregally** *adv*
regal[2] (ˈriːgᵊl) *n* (*sometimes pl*) a portable organ equipped only with small reed pipes, popular from the 15th century and recently revived for modern performance. [C16: from French *régale*; of obscure origin]
regale (rɪˈgeɪl) *vb* (*tr*; usually foll. by *with*) **1** to give delight or amusement to: *he regaled them with stories of his youth*. **2** to provide with choice or abundant food or drink. ♦ *n* **3** *Archaic*. **3a** a feast. **3b** a delicacy of food or drink. [C17: from French *régaler*, from *gale* pleasure; related to Middle Dutch *wale* riches; see also GALA] ▸ **reˈgalement** *n*
regalia (rɪˈgeɪlɪə) *pl n* (*sometimes functioning as sing*) **1** the ceremonial emblems or robes of royalty, high office, an order, etc. **2** any splendid or special clothes; finery. [C16: from Medieval Latin: royal privileges, from Latin *rēgālis* REGAL[1]]
regality (riːˈgælɪtɪ) *n, pl* **-ties**. **1** the state or condition of being royal; kingship or queenship; royalty. **2** the rights or privileges of royalty. **3** *Scot. history*. **3a** jurisdiction conferred by the sovereign on a powerful subject. **3b** a territory under such jurisdiction.
regard (rɪˈgɑːd) *vb* **1** to look closely or attentively at (something or someone); observe steadily. **2** (*tr*) to hold (a person or thing) in respect, admiration, or affection: *we regard your work very highly*. **3** (*tr*) to look upon or consider in a specified way: *she regarded her brother as her responsibility*. **4** (*tr*) to relate to; concern; have a bearing on. **5** to take notice of or pay attention to (something); heed: *he has never regarded the conventions*. **6** **as regards**. (*prep*) in respect of; concerning. ♦ *n* **7** a gaze; look. **8** attention; heed: *he spends without regard to his bank balance*. **9** esteem, affection, or respect. **10** reference, relation, or connection (esp. in the phrases **with regard to** *or* **in regard to**). **11** (*pl*) good wishes or greetings (esp. in the phrase **with kind regards**, used at the close of a letter). **12** **in this regard**. on this point. [C14: from Old French *regarder* to look at, care about, from RE- + *garder* to GUARD] ▸ **reˈgardable** *adj*
regardant (rɪˈgɑːdᵊnt) *adj* (*usually postpositive*) *Heraldry*. (of a beast) shown looking backwards over its shoulder. [C15: from Old French; see REGARD]
regardful (rɪˈgɑːdfʊl) *adj* **1** (often foll. by *of*) showing regard (for); heedful (of). **2** showing regard, respect, or consideration. ▸ **reˈgardfully** *adv* ▸ **reˈgardfulness** *n*
regarding (rɪˈgɑːdɪŋ) *prep* in respect of; on the subject of.

reˈformuˌlate *vb* **ˌreformuˈlation** *n* **reˈframe** *vb* **reˈfreeze** *vb*, **-ˈfreezes, -ˈfreezing, -ˈfroze, -ˈfrozen**.

regardless (rɪˈgɑːdlɪs) *adj* **1** (usually foll. by *of*) taking no regard or heed; heedless. ◆ *adv* **2** in spite of everything; disregarding drawbacks: *to carry on regardless.* ▸ **reˈgardlessly** *adv* ▸ **reˈgardlessness** *n*

regatta (rɪˈgætə) *n* an organized series of races of yachts, rowing boats, etc. [C17: from obsolete Italian (Venetian dialect) *rigatta* contest, of obscure origin]

regd *abbrev. for* registered.

regelate (ˈriːdʒɪˌleɪt) *vb Physics.* to undergo or cause to undergo regelation. [C19: from RE- + stem of participle of Latin *gelāre* to freeze]

regelation (ˌriːdʒɪˈleɪʃən) *n* the rejoining together of two pieces of ice as a result of melting under pressure at the interface between them and subsequent refreezing.

regency (ˈriːdʒənsɪ) *n, pl* **-cies. 1** government by a regent or a body of regents. **2** the office of a regent or body of regents. **3** a territory under the jurisdiction of a regent or body of regents. [C15: from Medieval Latin *regentia,* from Latin *regere* to rule]

Regency (ˈriːdʒənsɪ) *n* (preceded by *the*) **1** (in England) the period (1811–20) during which the Prince of Wales (later George IV) acted as regent during his father's periods of insanity. **2** (in France) the period of the regency of Philip, Duke of Orleans, during the minority of Louis XV (1715–23). ◆ *adj* **3** characteristic of or relating to the Regency periods in France or England or to the styles of architecture, furniture, art, literature, etc., produced in them.

regenerate *vb* (rɪˈdʒɛnəˌreɪt). **1** to undergo or cause to undergo moral, spiritual, or physical renewal or invigoration. **2** to form or be formed again; come or bring into existence once again. **3** to replace (lost or damaged tissues or organs) by new growth, or to cause (such tissues) to be replaced. **4** *Chem.* to restore or be restored to an original physical or chemical state. **5** (*tr*) *Electronics.* (in a digital system) to reshape (distorted incoming pulses) for onward transmission. ◆ *adj* (rɪˈdʒɛnərɪt). **6** morally, spiritually, or physically renewed or reborn; restored or refreshed. ▸ **reˈgenerable** *adj* ▸ **reˈgeneracy** *n* ▸ **reˈgenerative** *adj* ▸ **reˈgeneratively** *adv* ▸ **reˈgenerˌator** *n*

regeneration (rɪˌdʒɛnəˈreɪʃən) *n* **1** the act or process of regenerating or the state of being regenerated; rebirth or renewal. **2** the regrowth by an animal or plant of an organ, tissue, or part that has been lost or destroyed. **3** *Electronics.* the use of positive feedback to increase the amplification of a radio frequency stage.

regenerative cooling *n* the process of cooling the walls of the combustion chamber of a rocket by circulating the propellant around the chamber before combustion.

Regensburg (*German* ˈreːgənsburk) *n* a city in SE Germany, in Bavaria on the River Danube: a free Imperial city from 1245 and the leading commercial city of S Germany in the 12th and 13th centuries; the Imperial Diet was held in the town hall from 1663 to 1806. Pop.: 125 836 (1996 est.). Former English name: **Ratisbon.**

regent (ˈriːdʒənt) *n* **1** the ruler or administrator of a country during the minority, absence, or incapacity of its monarch. **2** (formerly) a senior teacher or administrator in any of certain universities. **3** *U.S. and Canadian.* a member of the governing board of certain schools and colleges. **4** *Rare.* any person who governs or rules. ◆ *adj* **5** (*usually postpositive*) acting or functioning as a regent: *a queen regent.* **6** *Rare.* governing, ruling, or controlling. [C14: from Latin *regēns* ruling, from *regere* to rule] ▸ **ˈregental** *adj* ▸ **ˈregentship** *n*

regent-bird *n* an Australian bower bird, *Sericulus chrysocephalus,* the male of which has a showy yellow and velvety-black plumage. [after the PRINCE REGENT]

Regent's Park *n* a park in central London, laid out as Marylebone Park by John Nash; now known for the London Zoo, its open-air theatre, and Nash's curved terraces.

Reger (*German* ˈreːgər) *n* **Max** (maks). 1873–1916, German composer, noted esp. for his organ works.

reggae (ˈrɛgeɪ) *n* a type of West Indian popular music having four beats to the bar, the upbeat being strongly accented. [C20: of West Indian origin]

Reggio di Calabria (*Italian* ˈreddʒo di kaˈlaːbrja) *n* a port in S Italy, in Calabria on the Strait of Messina: founded about 720 B.C. by Greek colonists. Pop.: 179 623 (1996 est.).

Reggio nell'Emilia (*Italian* ˈreddʒo nɛlleˈmiːlja) *n* a city in N central Italy, in Emilia-Romagna: founded in the 2nd century B.C. by Marcus Aemilius Lepidus; ruled by the Este family in the 15th–18th centuries. Pop.: 135 406 (1996 est.).

regicide (ˈrɛdʒɪˌsaɪd) *n* **1** the killing of a king. **2** a person who kills a king. [C16: from Latin *rēx* king + -CIDE] ▸ **ˌregiˈcidal** *adj*

regime *or* **régime** (reɪˈʒiːm) *n* **1** a system of government or a particular administration: *a fascist regime; the regime of Fidel Castro.* **2** a social system or order. **3** *Med.* another word for **regimen** (sense 1). [C18: from French, from Latin *regimen* guidance, from *regere* to rule]

regimen (ˈrɛdʒɪˌmɛn) *n* **1** Also called: **regime.** a systematic way of life or course of therapy, often including exercise and a recommended diet. **2** administration or rule. [C14: from Latin: guidance]

regiment *n* (ˈrɛdʒɪmənt). **1** a military formation varying in size from a battalion to a number of battalions. **2** a large number in regular or organized groups: *regiments of beer bottles.* ◆ *vb* (ˈrɛdʒɪˌmɛnt). (*tr*) **3** to force discipline or order on, esp. in a domineering manner. **4** to organize into a regiment or regiments. **5** to form into organized groups. **6** to assign to a regiment. [C14: via Old French from Late Latin *regimentum* government, from Latin *regere* to rule] ▸ **ˌregiˈmental** *adj* ▸ **ˌregiˈmentally** *adv* ▸ **ˌregimenˈtation** *n*

regimentals (ˌrɛdʒɪˈmɛntᵊlz) *pl n* **1** the uniform and insignia of a regiment. **2** military dress.

regimental sergeant major *n Military.* the senior Warrant Officer I in a British or Commonwealth regiment or battalion, responsible under the adjutant for all aspects of duty and discipline of the warrant officers, NCOs, and men. Abbrev.: **RSM.** Compare **company sergeant major.** See also **warrant officer.**

Regin (ˈreɪgɪn) *n Norse myth.* a dwarf smith, tutor of Sigurd, whom he encouraged to kill Fafnir for the gold he guarded.

Regina[1] (rɪˈdʒaɪnə) *n* queen: now used chiefly in documents, inscriptions, etc. Compare **Rex.**

Regina[2] (rɪˈdʒaɪnə) *n* a city in W Canada, capital and largest city of Saskatchewan: founded in 1882 as Pile O'Bones. Pop.: 179 178 (1991).

Regiomontanus (ˌriːdʒɪəumɒnˈteɪnəs, -ˈtɑː-, -ˈtæn-) *n* original name *Johann Müller.* 1436–76, German mathematician and astronomer, who furthered the development of trigonometry.

region (ˈriːdʒən) *n* **1** any large, indefinite, and continuous part of a surface or space. **2** an area considered as a unit for geographical, functional, social, or cultural reasons. **3** an administrative division of a country: *Tuscany is one of the regions of the Italian Republic.* **4** a realm or sphere of activity or interest. **5** range, area, or scope: *in what region is the price likely to be?* **6** (in Scotland from 1975 until 1996) any of the nine territorial divisions into which the mainland of Scotland was divided for purposes of local government; replaced in 1996 by council areas. See also **islands council.** [C14: from Latin *regiō,* from *regere* to govern]

regional (ˈriːdʒənᵊl) *adj* of, characteristic of, or limited to a region: *the regional dialects of English.* ▸ **ˈregionally** *adv*

regional enteritis *n* another name for **Crohn's disease.**

regionalism (ˈriːdʒənəˌlɪzəm) *n* **1** division of a country into administrative regions having partial autonomy. **2** advocacy of such division. **3** loyalty to one's home region; regional patriotism. **4** the common interests of national groups, people, etc., living in the same part of the world. **5** a word, custom, accent, or other characteristic associated with a specific region. ▸ **ˈregionalist** *n, adj*

régisseur *French.* (reʒisœr) *n* an official in a dance company with varying duties, usually including directing productions. [from *régir* to manage]

register (ˈrɛdʒɪstə) *n* **1** an official or formal list recording names, events, or transactions. **2** the book in which such a list is written. **3** an entry in such a list. **4** a recording device that accumulates data, totals sums of money, etc.: *a cash register.* **5** a movable plate that controls the flow of air into a furnace, chimney, room, etc. **6** *Computing.* one of a set of word-sized locations in the central processing unit in which items of data are placed temporarily before they are operated on by program instructions. **7** *Music.* **7a** the timbre characteristic of a certain manner of voice production. See **head voice, chest voice. 7b** any of the stops on an organ as classified in respect of its tonal quality: *the flute register.* **8** *Printing.* **8a** the correct alignment of the separate plates in colour printing. **8b** the exact correspondence of lines of type, columns, etc., on the two sides of a printed sheet of paper. **9** a form of a language associated with a particular social situation or subject matter, such as obscene slang, legal language, or journalese. **10** the act or an instance of registering. ◆ *vb* **11** (*tr*) to enter or cause someone to enter (an event, person's name, ownership, etc.) on a register; formally record. **12** to show or be shown on a scale or other measuring instrument: *the current didn't register on the meter.* **13** to show or be shown in a person's face, bearing, etc.: *his face registered surprise.* **14** (*intr*) to have an effect; make an impression: *the news of her uncle's death just did not register.* **15** to send (a letter, package, etc.) by registered post. **16** (*tr*) *Printing.* to adjust (a printing press, forme, etc.) to ensure that the printed matter is in register. **17** (*intr;* often foll. by *with*) (of a mechanical part) to align (with another part). **18** *Military.* to bring (a gun) to bear on its target by adjustment according to the accuracy of observed single rounds. [C14: from Medieval Latin *registrum,* from Latin *regerere* to transcribe, from RE- + *gerere* to bear] ▸ **ˈregisterer** *n* ▸ **ˈregistrable** *adj*

registered disabled *adj Social welfare.* (in Britain) **1** (of a handicapped person) on a local authority register under the Chronically Sick and Disabled Persons Act 1970. **2** on a register kept by the Manpower Services Commission for employment purposes, and holding a green identity card, thus qualifying for special services. ◆ Also called: **registered handicapped.** See also **green card** (sense 3), **handicap register.**

Registered General Nurse *n* (in Britain) a nurse who has completed a three-year training course in all aspects of nursing care to enable the nurse to be registered with the United Kingdom Central Council for Nursing, Midwifery, and Health Visiting. Abbrev.: **RGN.**

registered post *n* **1** a Post Office service by which compensation is paid for loss or damage to mail for which a registration fee has been paid. Compare **recorded delivery. 2** mail sent by this service.

Registered Trademark *n* See **trademark** (sense 1).

register mark *n Printing.* any of several marks incorporated on to printing plates to assist in the accurate positioning of images during printing.

register office *n Brit.* a government office where civil marriages are performed and births, marriages, and deaths are recorded. Often called: **registry office.**

register ton *n* the full name for **ton**[1] (sense 7).

registrant (ˈrɛdʒɪstrənt) *n* a person who registers a trademark or patent.

registrar (ˌrɛdʒɪˈstrɑː, ˈrɛdʒɪˌstrɑː) *n* **1** a person who keeps official records. **2** an administrative official responsible for student records, enrolment procedure, etc., in a school, college, or university. **3** *Brit. and N.Z.* a hospital doctor senior to a houseman but junior to a consultant, specializing in either medicine (**medical registrar**) or surgery (**surgical registrar**). **4** *Chiefly U.S.* a person

reˈgather *vb*

employed by a company to maintain a register of its security issues. ▸ **ˈregistrarship** *n*

registration (ˌrɛdʒɪˈstreɪʃən) *n* **1a** the act of registering or state of being registered. **1b** (*as modifier*): *a registration number.* **2** an entry in a register. **3** a group of people, such as students, who register at a particular time. **4** a combination of organ or harpsichord stops used in the performance of a piece of music. ▸ **ˌregisˈtrational** *adj*

registration document *n Brit.* a document giving identification details of a motor vehicle, including its manufacturer, date of registration, engine and chassis numbers, and owner's name. Compare **logbook** (sense 2).

registration number *n* a sequence of letters and numbers assigned to a motor vehicle when it is registered, usually indicating the year and place of registration, displayed on numberplates at the front and rear of the vehicle, and by which the vehicle may be identified.

registration plate *n* the Australian and N.Z. name for **numberplate.**

registry (ˈrɛdʒɪstrɪ) *n, pl* **-tries. 1** a place where registers are kept, such as the part of a church where the bride and groom sign a register after a wedding. **2** the registration of a ship's country of origin: *a ship of Liberian registry.* **3** another word for **registration.**

registry office *n Brit.* a name often used for a **register office.**

Regius professor (ˈriːdʒɪəs) *n Brit.* a person appointed by the Crown to a university chair founded by a royal patron. [C17: *regius*, from Latin: royal, from *rex* king]

reglet (ˈrɛglɪt) *n* **1** a flat narrow architectural moulding. **2** *Printing.* a strip of oiled wood used for spacing between lines of hot metal type.. Compare **lead**[2] (sense 7). [C16: from Old French, literally: a little rule, from *regle* rule, from Latin *rēgula*]

regmaker (ˈrɛxˌmɑːkə) *n S. African.* a drink taken to relieve the symptoms of a hangover; a pick-me-up. [Afrikaans]

regnal (ˈrɛgnəl) *adj* **1** of a sovereign, reign, or kingdom. **2** designating a year of a sovereign's reign calculated from the date of his or her accession. [C17: from Medieval Latin *rēgnālis*, from Latin *rēgnum* sovereignty; see REIGN]

regnant (ˈrɛgnənt) *adj* **1** (*postpositive*) reigning. **2** prevalent; current. [C17: from Latin *regnāre* to REIGN] ▸ **ˈregnancy** *n*

rego (ˈrɛdʒəʊ) *n Austral. slang.* **a** the registration of a motor vehicle. **b** a fee paid for this.

regolith (ˈrɛgəlɪθ) *n* the layer of loose material covering the bedrock of the earth and moon, etc., comprising soil, sand, rock fragments, volcanic ash, glacial drift, etc. [C20: from Greek *rhēgos* covering, blanket + *lithos* stone]

regorge (rɪˈgɔːdʒ) *vb* **1** (*tr*) to vomit up; disgorge. **2** (*intr*) (esp. of water) to flow or run back. [C17: from French *regorger;* see GORGE]

regosol (ˈrɛgəˌsɒl) *n* a type of azonal soil consisting of unconsolidated material derived from freshly deposited alluvium or sands. [C20: from Greek *rhēgos* covering, blanket + Latin *solum* soil]

Reg. prof. *abbrev. for* Regius professor.

regrate (rɪˈgreɪt) *vb* (*tr*) **1** to buy up (commodities) in advance so as to raise their price for profitable resale. **2** to resell (commodities so purchased); retail. **3** *Building trades.* to redress the surface of (hewn stonework). [C15: from Old French *regrater* perhaps from RE- + *grater* to scratch] ▸ **reˈgrater** *n*

regress *vb* (rɪˈgrɛs). **1** (*intr*) to return or revert, as to a former place, condition, or mode of behaviour. **2** (*tr*) *Statistics.* to measure the extent to which (a dependent variable) is associated with one or more independent variables. ◆ *n* (ˈriːgrɛs). **3** the act of regressing. **4** movement in a backward direction; retrogression. **5** *Logic.* a supposed explanation each stage of which requires to be similarly explained, as saying that knowledge requires a justification in terms of propositions themselves known to be true. [C14: from Latin *regressus* a retreat, from *regredī* to go back, from RE- + *gradī* to go] ▸ **reˈgressor** *n*

regression (rɪˈgrɛʃən) *n* **1** *Psychol.* the adoption by an adult or adolescent of behaviour more appropriate to a child, esp. as a defence mechanism to avoid anxiety. **2** *Statistics.* **2a** the analysis or measure of the association between one variable (the dependent variable) and one or more other variables (the independent variables), usually formulated in an equation in which the independent variables have parametric coefficients, which may enable future values of the dependent variable to be predicted. **2b** (*as modifer*): *regression curve.* **3** *Astronomy.* the slow movement around the ecliptic of the two points at which the moon's orbit intersects the ecliptic. One complete revolution occurs about every 19 years. **4** *Geology.* the retreat of the sea from the land. **5** the act of regressing.

regressive (rɪˈgrɛsɪv) *adj* **1** regressing or tending to regress. **2** (of a tax or tax system) levied or graduated so that the rate decreases as the amount taxed increases. Compare **progressive** (sense 5). **3** of, relating to, or characteristic of regression. ▸ **reˈgressively** *adv* ▸ **reˈgressiveness** *n*

regret (rɪˈgrɛt) *vb* **-grets, -gretting, -gretted.** (*tr*) **1** (*may take a clause as object or an infinitive*) to feel sorry, repentant, or upset about. **2** to bemoan or grieve the death or loss of. ◆ *n* **3** a sense of repentance, guilt, or sorrow, as over some wrong done or an unfulfilled ambition. **4** a sense of loss or grief. **5** (*pl*) a polite expression of sadness, esp. in a formal refusal of an invitation. [C14: from Old French *regreter*, of Scandinavian origin; compare Old Norse *grāta* to weep] ▸ **reˈgretful** *adj* ▸ **reˈgretfully** *adv* ▸ **reˈgretfulness** *n* ▸ **reˈgrettable** *adj* ▸ **reˈgrettably** *adv* ▸ **reˈgretter** *n*

USAGE *Regretful* and *regretfully* are sometimes wrongly used where *regrettable* and *regrettably* are meant: *he gave a regretful smile; he smiled regretfully; this is a regrettable* (not *regretful*) *mistake; regrettably* (not *regretfully*), *I shall be unable to attend.*

regroup (riːˈgruːp) *vb* **1** to reorganize (military forces), esp. after an attack or a defeat. **2** (*tr*) to rearrange into a new grouping or groupings.

Regt *abbrev. for:* **1** Regent. **2** Regiment.

regulable (ˈrɛgjʊləbᵊl) *adj* able to be regulated.

regular (ˈrɛgjʊlə) *adj* **1** normal, customary, or usual. **2** according to a uniform principle, arrangement, or order: *trees planted at regular intervals.* **3** occurring at fixed or prearranged intervals: *to make a regular call on a customer.* **4** following a set rule or normal practice; methodical or orderly. **5** symmetrical in appearance or form; even: *regular features.* **6** (*prenominal*) organized, elected, conducted, etc., in a proper or officially prescribed manner. **7** (*prenominal*) officially qualified or recognized: *he's not a regular doctor.* **8** (*prenominal*) (intensifier): *a regular fool.* **9** *U.S. and Canadian informal.* likable, dependable, or nice (esp. in the phrase **a regular guy**). **10** denoting or relating to the personnel or units of the permanent military services: *a regular soldier; the regular army.* **11** (of flowers) having any of their parts, esp. petals, alike in size, shape, arrangement, etc.; symmetrical. **12** (of the formation, inflections, etc., of a word) following the usual pattern of formation in a language. **13** *Maths.* **13a** (of a polygon) equilateral and equiangular. **13b** (of a polyhedron) having identical regular polygons as faces that make identical angles with each other. **13c** (of a prism) having regular polygons as bases. **13d** (of a pyramid) having a regular polygon as a base and the altitude passing through the centre of the base. **13e** another name for **analytic** (sense 5). **14** *Botany.* another word for **actinomorphic. 15** (*postpositive*) subject to the rule of an established religious order or community: *canons regular.* **15** *U.S. politics.* of, selected by, or loyal to the leadership or platform of a political party: *a regular candidate; regular policies.* **16** *Crystallog.* another word for **cubic** (sense 4). ◆ *n* **17** a professional long-term serviceman in a military unit. **18** *Informal.* a person who does something regularly, such as attending a theatre or patronizing a shop. **19** a member of a religious order or congregation, as contrasted with a secular. **20** *U.S. politics.* a party member loyal to the leadership, organization, platform, etc., of his party. [C14: from Old French *reguler, from* Latin *rēgulāris* of a bar of wood or metal, from *rēgula* ruler, model] ▸ **ˌreguˈlarity** *n* ▸ **ˈregularly** *adv*

regularize *or* **regularise** (ˈrɛgjʊləˌraɪz) *vb* (*tr*) to make regular; cause to conform. ▸ **ˌregulariˈzation** *or* **ˌregulariˈsation** *n*

regulate (ˈrɛgjʊˌleɪt) *vb* (*tr*) **1** to adjust (the amount of heat, sound, etc., of something) as required; control. **2** to adjust (an instrument or appliance) so that it operates correctly. **3** to bring into conformity with a rule, principle, or usage. [C17: from Late Latin *rēgulāre* to control, from Latin *rēgula* a ruler] ▸ **ˈregulative** *or* **ˈregulatory** *adj* ▸ **ˈregulatively** *adv*

regulated tenancy *n Social welfare.* (in Britain) the letting of a dwelling by a nonresident private landlord, usually at a registered fair rent, from which the landlord cannot evict the tenant without a possession order from a court. Compare **assured tenancy.**

regulation (ˌrɛgjʊˈleɪʃən) *n* **1** the act or process of regulating. **2** a rule, principle, or condition that governs procedure or behaviour. **3** a governmental or ministerial order having the force of law. **4** *Embryol.* the ability of an animal embryo to develop normally after its structure has been altered or damaged in some way. **5** (*modifier*) as required by official rules or procedure: *regulation uniform.* **6** (*modifier*) normal; usual; conforming to accepted standards: *a regulation haircut.* **7** *Electrical engineering.* the change in voltage occurring when a load is connected across a power supply, caused by internal resistance (for direct current) or internal impedance (alternating current).

regulator (ˈrɛgjʊˌleɪtə) *n* **1** a person or thing that regulates. **2** the mechanism, including the hairspring and the balance wheel, by which the speed of a timepiece is regulated. **3** a timepiece, known to be accurate, by which others are timed and regulated. **4** any of various mechanisms or devices, such as a governor valve, for controlling fluid flow, pressure, temperature, voltage, etc. **5** Also called: **regulator gene.** a gene the product of which controls the synthesis of a product from another gene.

regulo (ˈrɛgjʊləʊ) *n* any of a number of temperatures to which a gas oven may be set: *cook at regulo 4 for 40 minutes.* [C20: from *Regulo*, trademark for a type of thermostatic control on gas ovens]

regulus (ˈrɛgjʊləs) *n, pl* **-luses** *or* **-li** (-ˌlaɪ). impure metal forming beneath the slag during the smelting of ores. [C16: from Latin: a petty king, from *rēx* king; formerly used for *antimony*, because it combines readily with gold, thought of as the king of metals] ▸ **ˈreguline** *adj*

Regulus[1] (ˈrɛgjʊləs) *n* **Marcus Atilius** (ˈmɑːkəs əˈtɪlɪəs). died ?250 B.C., Roman general; consul (267; 256). Captured by the Carthaginians in the First Punic War, he was sent to Rome on parole to deliver the enemy's peace terms, advised the Senate to refuse them, and was tortured to death on his return to Carthage.

Regulus[2] (ˈrɛgjʊləs) *n* the brightest star in the constellation Leo. Visual magnitude: 1.3; spectral type: B8; distance: 69 light years.

regurgitate (rɪˈgɜːdʒɪˌteɪt) *vb* **1** to vomit forth (partially digested food). **2** (of some birds and certain other animals) to bring back to the mouth (undigested or partly digested food with which to feed the young). **3** (*intr*) to be cast up or out, esp. from the mouth. **4** *(intr) Med.* (of blood) to flow backwards, in a direction opposite to the normal one, esp. through a defective heart valve. [C17: from Medieval Latin *regurgitāre,* from RE- + *gurgitāre* to flood, from Latin *gurges* gulf, whirlpool] ▸ **reˈgurgitant** *n, adj* ▸ **reˌgurgiˈtation** *n*

rehab (ˈriːhæb) *n* **1** short for **rehabilitation. 2** *N.Z. informal.* short for **Rehabilitation Department.**

rehabilitate (ˌriːəˈbɪlɪˌteɪt) *vb* (*tr*) **1** to help (a person who has acquired a disability or addiction or who has just been released from prison) to readapt to so-

reˈgrow *vb*, **-ˈgrows, -ˈgrowing, -ˈgrew, -ˈgrown.**

reˈgrowth *n*

ciety or a new job, as by vocational guidance, retraining, or therapy. **2** to restore to a former position or rank. **3** to restore the good reputation of. [C16: from Medieval Latin *rehabilitāre* to restore, from RE- + Latin *habilitās* skill, ABILITY] ► ˌ**rehaˈbilitative** *adj*

rehabilitation (ˌriːəˌbɪlɪˈteɪʃən) *n* **1** the act or process of rehabilitating. **2** *Med.* **2a** the treatment of physical disabilities by massage, electrotherapy, and exercises. **2b** (*as modifier*): *rehabilitation centre.*

Rehabilitation Department *n N.Z.* a government department set up after World War II to assist ex-servicemen. Often shortened to **rehab.**

rehash (riːˈhæʃ) *vb* **1** (*tr*) to rework, reuse, or make over (old or already used material). ◆ *n* **2** something consisting of old, reworked, or reused material. [C19: from RE- + HASH[1] (to chop into pieces)]

rehearsal (rɪˈhɜːsᵊl) *n* **1** a session of practising a play, concert, speech etc., in preparation for public performance. **2** the act of going through or recounting; recital: *rehearsal of his own virtues was his usual occupation.* **3 in rehearsal.** being prepared for public performance.

rehearse (rɪˈhɜːs) *vb* **1** to practise (a play, concert, etc.), in preparation for public performance. **2** (*tr*) to run through; recount; recite: *the official rehearsed the grievances of the committee.* **3** (*tr*) to train or drill (a person or animal) for the public performance of a part in a play, show, etc. [C16: from Anglo-Norman *rehearser,* from Old French *rehercier* to harrow a second time, from RE- + *herce* harrow] ► **reˈhearser** *n*

reheat *vb* (riːˈhiːt). **1** to heat or be heated again: *to reheat yesterday's soup.* **2** (*tr*) to add fuel to (the exhaust gases of an aircraft jet engine) to produce additional heat and thrust. ◆ *n* (ˈriːhiːt), *also* **reheating.** **3** *Aeronautics.* another name (esp. Brit.) for **afterburning** (sense 1). ► **reˈheater** *n*

rehoboam (ˌriːəˈbəʊəm) *n* a wine bottle holding the equivalent of six normal bottles (approximately 156 ounces). [C19: named after *Rehoboam,* a son of King Solomon, from Hebrew, literally: the nation is enlarged]

Reich[1] (raɪk; *German* raiç) *n* **1** the Holy Roman Empire (**First Reich**). **2** the Hohenzollern empire from 1871 to 1919 (**Second Reich**). **3** the Weimar Republic from 1919 to 1933. **4** the Nazi dictatorship from 1933 to 1945 (**Third Reich**). [German: kingdom]

Reich[2] (raɪk) *n* **1 Steve.** born 1936, U.S. composer, whose works are characterized by the repetition and modification of small rhythmic motifs. His works include *Drumming* (1971), *Music for Large Ensemble* (1978), and *The Desert Music* (1984). **2** (*German* raiç) *n* **Wilhelm** (ˈvɪlhɛlm). 1897–1957, Austrian psychologist, lived in the U.S. An ardent socialist and advocate of sexual freedom, he proclaimed a cosmic unity of all energy and built a machine (the orgone accumulator) to concentrate this energy on human beings. His books include *The Function of the Orgasm* (1927).

Reichenberg (ˈraiçənbɛrk) *n* the German name for **Liberec.**

Reichsmark (ˈraɪksˌmɑːk; *German* ˈraiçsmark) *n, pl* **-marks** *or* **-mark.** the standard monetary unit of Germany between 1924 and 1948, divided into 100 **Reichspfennigs.**

Reichsrat (*German* ˈraiçsrat) *n* **1** the bicameral parliament of the Austrian half of Austria-Hungary (1867–1918). **2** the council of representatives of state governments within Germany from 1919 to 1934.

Reichstag (ˈraiksˌtɑːg; *German* ˈraiçstak) *n* **1** Also called: **diet.** (in medieval Germany) the estates or a meeting of the estates. **2** the legislative assembly representing the people in the North German Confederation (1867–71) and in the German empire (1871–1919). **3** the sovereign assembly of the Weimar Republic (1919–33). **4** the building in Berlin in which this assembly met and from 1999 in which the German government meets: its destruction by fire on Feb. 27, 1933 (probably by agents of the Nazi government) marked the end of Weimar democracy. It was restored in the 1990s following German reunification.

Reid (riːd) *n* **1** Sir **George Houston.** 1845–1918, Australian statesman, born in Scotland: premier of New South Wales (1894–99); prime minister of Australia (1904–05). **2 Thomas.** 1710–96, Scottish philosopher and founder of what came to be known as the philosophy of common sense.

reify (ˈriːɪˌfaɪ) *vb* **-fies, -fying, -fied.** (*tr*) to consider or make (an abstract idea or concept) real or concrete. [C19: from Latin *rēs* thing; compare DEIFY] ► ˌ**reifiˈcation** *n* ► ˌ**reifiˈcatory** *adj* ► ˈ**reiˌfier** *n*

Reigate (ˈraɪgɪt, -geɪt) *n* a town in S England, in Surrey at the foot of the North Downs. Pop.: 47 602 (1991).

reign (reɪn) *n* **1** the period during which a monarch is the official ruler of a country. **2** a period during which a person or thing is dominant, influential, or powerful: *the reign of violence is over.* ◆ *vb* (*intr*) **3** to exercise the power and authority of a sovereign. **4** to be accorded the rank and title of a sovereign without having ruling authority, as in a constitutional monarchy. **5** to predominate; prevail: *a land where darkness reigns.* **6** (*usually present participle*) to be the most recent winner of a competition, contest, etc.: *the reigning heavyweight champion.* [C13: from Old French *reigne,* from Latin *rēgnum* kingdom, from *rēx* king]

USAGE *Reign* is sometimes wrongly written for *rein* in certain phrases: *he gave full rein* (not *reign*) *to his feelings; it will be necessary to rein in* (not *reign in*) *public spending.*

Reign of Terror *n* the period of Jacobin rule during the French Revolution, during which thousands of people were executed for treason (Oct. 1793–July 1794).

reimburse (ˌriːɪmˈbɜːs) *vb* (*tr*) to repay or compensate (someone) for (money already spent, losses, damages, etc.): *your fare will be reimbursed after your interview.* [C17: from RE- + *imburse,* from Medieval Latin *imbursāre* to put in a moneybag, from *bursa* PURSE] ► ˌ**reimˈbursable** *adj* ► ˌ**reimˈbursement** *n* ► ˌ**reimˈburser** *n*

reimport *vb* (ˌriːɪmˈpɔːt, riːˈɪmpɔːt). **1** (*tr*) to import (goods manufactured from exported raw materials). ◆ *n* (riːˈɪmpɔːt). **2** the act of reimporting. **3** a reimported commodity. ► ˌ**reimporˈtation** *n* ► ˌ**reimˈporter** *n*

reimpression (ˌriːɪmˈprɛʃən) *n* a reprinting of a book without editorial changes or additions.

Reims *or* **Rheims** (riːmz; *French* rɛ̃s) *n* a city in NE France: scene of the coronation of most French monarchs. Pop.: 185 164 (1990).

rein (reɪn) *n* **1** (*often pl*) one of a pair of long straps, usually connected together and made of leather, used to control a horse, running from the side of the bit or the headstall to the hand of the rider, driver, or trainer. **2** a similar device used to control a very young child. **3** any form or means of control: *to take up the reins of government.* **4** the direction in which a rider turns (in phrases such as **on a left** (*or* **right**) **rein, change the rein**). **5** something that restrains, controls, or guides. **6 give** (**a**) **free rein.** to allow considerable freedom; remove restraints. **7 keep a tight rein on.** to control carefully; limit: *we have to keep a tight rein on expenditure.* **8 on a long rein.** with the reins held loosely so that the horse is relatively unconstrained. **9 shorten the reins.** to take up the reins so that the distance between hand and bit is lessened, in order that the horse may be more collected. ◆ *vb* **10** (*tr*) to check, restrain, hold back, or halt with or as if with reins. **11** to control or guide (a horse) with a rein or reins: *they reined left.* ◆ See also **rein in.** [C13: from Old French *resne,* from Latin *retinēre* to hold back, from RE- + *tenēre* to hold; see RESTRAIN]

USAGE See at **reign.**

reincarnate *vb* (riːˈɪnkɑːneɪt) (*tr; often passive*). **1** to cause to undergo reincarnation; be born again. ◆ *adj* (ˌriːɪnˈkɑːnɪt). **2** born again in a new body.

reincarnation (ˌriːɪnkɑːˈneɪʃən) *n* **1** the belief that on the death of the body the soul transmigrates to or is born again in another body. **2** the incarnation or embodiment of a soul in a new body after it has left the old one at physical death. **3** embodiment again in a new form, as of a principle or idea. ► ˌ**reincarˈnationist** *n, adj*

reindeer (ˈreɪnˌdɪə) *n, pl* **-deer** *or* **-deers.** a large deer, *Rangifer tarandus,* having large branched antlers in the male and female and inhabiting the arctic regions of Greenland, Europe, and Asia. It also occurs in North America, where it is known as a caribou. [C14: from Old Norse *hreindȳri,* from *hreinn* reindeer + *dyr* animal; related to Dutch *rendier,* German *Rentier;* see DEER]

Reindeer Lake *n* a lake in W Canada, in Saskatchewan and Manitoba: drains into the Churchill River via the **Reindeer River.** Area: 6390 sq. km (2467 sq. miles).

reindeer moss *n* any of various lichens of the genus *Cladonia,* esp. *C. rangiferina,* which occur in arctic and subarctic regions, providing food for reindeer.

reinforce (ˌriːɪnˈfɔːs) *vb* (*tr*) **1** to give added strength or support to. **2** to give added emphasis to; stress, support, or increase: *his rudeness reinforced my determination.* **3** to give added support to (a military force) by providing more men, supplies, etc. **4** *Psychol.* to reward an action or response of (a human or animal) so that it becomes more likely to occur again. [C17: from obsolete *renforce,* from French *renforcer;* see RE- + *inforce* ENFORCE] ► ˌ**reinˈforcement** *n*

reinforced concrete *n* concrete with steel bars, mesh, etc., embedded in it to enable it to withstand tensile and shear stresses.

reinforced plastic *n* plastic with fibrous matter, such as carbon fibre, embedded in it to confer additional strength.

Reinhardt (ˈraɪnˌhɑːt) *n* **1 Django** (ˈdʒæŋgəʊ), real name *Jean Baptiste Reinhardt.* 1910–53, French jazz guitarist, whose work was greatly influenced by Gypsy music. With Stéphane Grappelli, he led the Quintet of the Hot Club of France between 1934 and 1939. **2 Max,** original name *Max Goldmann.* 1873–1943, Austrian theatre producer and director, in the U.S. after 1933.

rein in *vb* (*adv*) to stop (a horse) by pulling on the reins.

reins (reɪnz) *pl n Archaic.* the kidneys or loins. [C14: from Old French, from Latin *rēnēs* the kidneys]

reinsman (ˈreɪnzmən) *n, pl* **-men.** *Austral. and N.Z.* the driver in a trotting race.

reinstate (ˌriːɪnˈsteɪt) *vb* (*tr*) to restore to a former rank or condition. ► ˌ**reinˈstatement** *n* ► ˌ**reinˈstator** *n*

reinsure (ˌriːɪnˈʃʊə, -ʃɔː) *vb* (*tr*) **1** to insure again. **2** (of an insurer) to obtain partial or complete insurance coverage from another insurer for (a risk on which a policy has already been issued). ► ˌ**reinˈsurance** *n* ► ˌ**reinˈsurer** *n*

reinvent (ˌriːɪnˈvent) *vb* (*tr*) **1** to replace (a product, etc.) with an entirely new version. **2** to duplicate (something that already exists) in what is therefore a wasted effort (esp. in the phrase **reinvent the wheel**).

reˈhang *vb,* **-ˈhangs, -ˈhanging, -ˈhung.**
reˈharden *vb*
reˈhear *vb*
reˈhouse *vb*
ˌ**reigˈnite** *vb*
ˌ**reimˈpose** *vb*
ˌ**reimpoˈsition** *n*
ˌ**reinˈcorpoˌrate** *vb*
ˌ**reincorpoˈration** *n*
ˌ**reinˈfect** *vb*
ˌ**reinˈfection** *n*
ˌ**reinˈstall** *or* ˌ**reinˈstal** *vb*
ˌ**reinstalˈlation** *n*
reˈinteˌgrate *vb*
ˌ**reinteˈgration** *n*
ˌ**reinˈter** *vb,* **-ˈters, -ˈterring, -ˈterred.**
ˌ**reinˈterpret** *vb*
ˌ**reinˌterpreˈtation** *n*
ˌ**reintroˈduce** *vb*
ˌ**reintroˈduction** *n*
ˌ**reinˈvest** *vb.*
ˌ**reinˈvestiˌgate** *vb*
ˌ**reinˌvestiˈgation** *n*
ˌ**reinˈvigorˌate** *vb*
ˌ**reinˌvigorˈation** *n*

reissue (ˌriːˈɪʃjuː) *vb* (*tr*) **1** to issue (a recording, book, etc.) again. ◆ *n* **2** something, esp. a recording or book, which has been issued again.
reiterate (riːˈɪtəˌreɪt) *vb* (*tr; may take a clause as object*) to say or do again or repeatedly. [C16: from Latin *reiterāre* to repeat, from RE- + *iterāre* to do again, from *iterum* again] ▸ **reˈiterant** *adj* ▸ **reˌiterˈation** *n* ▸ **reˈiterative** *adj* ▸ **reˈiteratively** *adv*
Reith (riːθ) *n* **John** (**Charles Walsham**), 1st Baron. 1889–1971, British public servant: first general manager (1922–27) and first director general (1927–38) of the BBC. ▸ **ˈReithian** *or* **ˈReithean** *adj*
reive (riːv) *vb* (*intr*) *Scot. and northern English dialect.* to go on a plundering raid. [variant of REAVE[1]] ▸ **ˈreiver** *n*
reject *vb* (rɪˈdʒɛkt). (*tr*) **1** to refuse to accept, acknowledge, use, believe, etc. **2** to throw out as useless or worthless; discard. **3** to rebuff (a person). **4** (of an organism) to fail to accept (a foreign tissue graft or organ transplant) because of immunological incompatibility. ◆ *n* (ˈriːdʒɛkt). **5** something rejected as imperfect, unsatisfactory, or useless. [C15: from Latin *rēicere* to throw back, from RE- + *jacere* to hurl] ▸ **reˈjectable** *adj* ▸ **reˈjecter** *or* **reˈjector** *n* ▸ **reˈjection** *n* ▸ **reˈjective** *adj*
rejig (riːˈdʒɪg) *vb* **-jigs, -jigging, -jigged.** (*tr*) **1** to re-equip (a factory or plant). **2** to rearrange, alter, or manipulate, sometimes in a slightly unscrupulous way. ◆ *n* **3** the act or process of rejigging. ▸ **reˈjigger** *n*
rejoice (rɪˈdʒɔɪs) *vb* **1** (when *tr, takes a clause as object or an infinitive;* when *intr,* often foll. by *in*) to feel or express great joy or happiness. **2** (*tr*) *Archaic.* to cause to feel joy. [C14: from Old French *resjoir,* from RE- + *joir* to be glad, from Latin *gaudēre* to rejoice] ▸ **reˈjoicer** *n* ▸ **reˈjoicing** *n*
rejoin[1] (riːˈdʒɔɪn) *vb* **1** to come again into company with (someone or something). **2** (*tr*) to put or join together again; reunite.
rejoin[2] (rɪˈdʒɔɪn) *vb* (*tr*) **1** to say (something) in reply; answer, reply, or retort. **2** *Law.* to answer (a plaintiff's reply). [C15: from Old French *rejoign-,* stem of *rejoindre;* see RE-, JOIN]
rejoinder (rɪˈdʒɔɪndə) *n* **1** a reply or response to a question or remark, esp. a quick witty one; retort. **2** *Law.* (in pleading) the answer made by a defendant to the plaintiff's reply. [C15: from Old French *rejoindre* to REJOIN[2]]
rejuvenate (rɪˈdʒuːvɪˌneɪt) *vb* (*tr*) **1** to give new youth, restored vitality, or youthful appearance to. **2** (*usually passive*) *Geography.* **2a** to cause (a river) to begin eroding more vigorously to a new lower base level, usually because of uplift of the land. **2b** to cause (a land surface) to develop youthful features. [C19: from RE- + Latin *juvenis* young] ▸ **reˌjuveˈnation** *n* ▸ **reˈjuveˌnator** *n*
rejuvenesce (rɪˌdʒuːvəˈnɛs) *vb* **1** to make or become youthful or restored to vitality. **2** *Biology.* to convert (cells) or (of cells) to be converted into a more active form. ▸ **reˌjuveˈnescence** *n* ▸ **reˌjuveˈnescent** *adj*
rel. *abbrev. for:* **1** relating. **2** relative(ly). **3** released. **4** religion. **5** religious.
relapse (rɪˈlæps) *vb* (*intr*) **1** to lapse back into a former state or condition, esp. one involving bad habits. **2** to become ill again after apparent recovery. ◆ *n* **3** the act or an instance of relapsing. **4** the return of ill health after an apparent or partial recovery. [C16: from Latin *relabī* to slip back, from RE- + *labī* to slip, slide] ▸ **reˈlapser** *n*
relapsing fever *n* any of various infectious diseases characterized by recurring fever, caused by the bite of body lice or ticks infected with spirochaetes of the genus *Borrelia.* Also called: **recurrent fever.**
relata (rɪˈleɪtə) *n* the plural of **relatum.**
relate (rɪˈleɪt) *vb* **1** (*tr*) to tell or narrate (a story, information, etc.). **2** (often foll. by *to*) to establish association (between two or more things) or (of something) to have relation or reference (to something else). **3** (*intr;* often foll. by *to*) to form a sympathetic or significant relationship (with other people, things, etc.). [C16: from Latin *relātus* brought back, from *referre* to carry back, from RE- + *ferre* to bear; see REFER] ▸ **reˈlatable** *adj* ▸ **reˈlater** *n*
related (rɪˈleɪtɪd) *adj* **1** connected; associated. **2** connected by kinship or marriage. **3** (in diatonic music) denoting or relating to a key that has notes in common with another key or keys. ▸ **reˈlatedness** *n*
relation (rɪˈleɪʃən) *n* **1** the state or condition of being related or the manner in which things are related. **2** connection by blood or marriage; kinship. **3** a person who is connected by blood or marriage; relative; kinsman. **4** reference or regard (esp. in the phrase **in** *or* **with relation to**). **5** the position, association, connection, or status of one person or thing with regard to another or others. **6** the act of relating or narrating. **7** an account or narrative. **8** *Law.* the principle by which an act done at one time is regarded in law as having been done antecedently. **9** *Law.* the statement of grounds of complaint made by a relator. **10** *Logic, maths.* **10a** an association between ordered pairs of objects, numbers, etc., such as ... *is greater than* .... **10b** the set of ordered pairs whose members have such an association. **11** *Philosophy.* **11a internal relation.** a relation that necessarily holds between its relata, as *4 is greater than 2.* **11b external relation.** a relation that does not so hold. ◆ See also **relations.** [C14: from Latin *relātiō* a narration, a relation (between philosophical concepts)]
relational (rɪˈleɪʃənᵊl) *adj* **1** *Grammar.* indicating or expressing syntactic relation, as for example the case endings in Latin. **2** having relation or being related. **3** *Computing.* based on data stored in a tabular form: *a relational database.*
relations (rɪˈleɪʃənz) *pl n* **1** social, political, or personal connections or dealings between or among individuals, groups, nations, etc.: *to enjoy good relations.* **2** family or relatives. **3** *Euphemistic.* sexual intercourse.
relationship (rɪˈleɪʃənʃɪp) *n* **1** the state of being connected or related. **2** association by blood or marriage; kinship. **3** the mutual dealings, connections, or feelings that exist between two parties, countries, people, etc.: *a business relationship.* **4** an emotional or sexual affair or liaison. **5** *Logic, maths.* another name for **relation** (sense 10).
relationship marketing *n* a type of marketing aimed at encouraging long-term customer loyalty.
relative (ˈrɛlətɪv) *adj* **1** having meaning or significance only in relation to something else; not absolute: *a relative value.* **2** (*prenominal*) (of a scientific quantity) being measured or stated relative to some other substance or measurement: *relative humidity; relative density.* Compare **absolute** (sense 10). **3** (*prenominal*) comparative or respective: *the relative qualities of speed and accuracy.* **4** (*postpositive;* foll. by *to*) in proportion (to); corresponding (to): *earnings relative to production.* **5** having reference (to); pertinent (to): *matters not relative to the topic under discussion.* **6** *Grammar.* denoting or belonging to a class of words that function as subordinating conjunctions in introducing relative clauses. In English, relative pronouns and determiners include *who, which,* and *that.* Compare **demonstrative** (sense 5), **interrogative** (sense 3). **7** *Grammar.* denoting or relating to a clause (**relative clause**) that modifies a noun or pronoun occurring earlier in the sentence. **8** (of a musical key or scale) having the same key signature as another key or scale: *C major is the relative major of A minor.* ◆ *n* **9** a person who is related by blood or marriage; relation. **10** a relative pronoun, clause, or grammatical construction. [C16: from Late Latin *relātīvus* referring] ▸ **ˈrelatively** *adv* ▸ **ˈrelativeness** *n*
relative aperture *n Photog.* the ratio of the equivalent focal length of a lens to the effective aperture of the lens; written as *f/n, f:n,* or *fn,* where *n* is the numerical value of this ratio and is equivalent to the f-number.
relative atomic mass *n* the ratio of the average mass per atom of the naturally occurring form of an element to one-twelfth the mass of an atom of carbon-12. Symbol: A_r Abbrev.: **r.a.m.** Former name: **atomic weight.**
relative density *n* the ratio of the density of a substance to the density of a standard substance under specified conditions. For liquids and solids the standard is usually water at 4°C or some other specified temperature. For gases the standard is often air or hydrogen at the same temperature and pressure as the substance. Symbol: *d* See also **specific gravity, vapour density.**
relative frequency *n* **a** the ratio of the actual number of favourable events to the total possible number of events; often taken as an estimate of probability. **b** the proportion of the range of a random variable taking a given value or lying in a given interval.
relative humidity *n* the mass of water vapour present in the air expressed as a percentage of the mass that would be present in an equal volume of saturated air at the same temperature. Compare **absolute humidity.**
relative majority *n Brit.* the excess of votes or seats won by the winner of an election over the runner-up when no candidate or party has more than 50 per cent. Compare **absolute majority.**
relative molecular mass *n* the sum of all the relative atomic masses of the atoms in a molecule; the ratio of the average mass per molecule of a specified isotopic composition of a substance to one-twelfth the mass of an atom of carbon-12. Symbol: M_r Abbrev.: **r.m.m.** Former name: **molecular weight.**
relative permeability *n* the ratio of the permeability of a medium to that of free space. Symbol: μ_r
relative permittivity *n* the ratio of the permittivity of a substance to that of free space. Symbol: ε_r Also called: **dielectric constant.**
relativism (ˈrɛlətɪˌvɪzəm) *n* any theory holding that truth or moral or aesthetic value, etc., is not universal or absolute but may differ between individuals or cultures. See also **historicism.** ▸ **ˈrelativist** *n, adj*
relativistic (ˌrɛlətɪˈvɪstɪk) *adj* **1** *Physics.* having or involving a speed close to that of light so that the behaviour is described by the theory of relativity rather than by Newtonian mechanics: *a relativistic electron; a relativistic velocity.* **2** *Physics.* of, concerned with, or involving relativity. **3** of or relating to relativism. ▸ **ˌrelativˈistically** *adv*
relativity (ˌrɛləˈtɪvɪtɪ) *n* **1** either of two theories developed by Albert Einstein, the **special theory of relativity,** which requires that the laws of physics shall be the same as seen by any two different observers in uniform relative motion, and the **general theory of relativity,** which considers observers with relative acceleration and leads to a theory of gravitation. **2** *Philosophy.* dependence upon some variable factor such as the psychological, social, or environmental context. See **relativism. 3** the state or quality of being relative.
relativize *or* **relativise** (ˈrɛlətɪvaɪz) *vb* **1** to make or become relative. **2** (*tr*) to apply the theory of relativity to. ▸ **ˌrelativiˈzation** *or* **ˌrelativiˈsation** *n*
relator (rɪˈleɪtə) *n* **1** a person who relates a story; narrator. **2** *English law.* a person who gives information upon which the attorney general brings an action. **3** *U.S. law.* a person who institutes proceedings by criminal information or quo warranto.
relatum (rɪˈleɪtəm) *n, pl* **-ta** (-tə). *Logic.* one of the objects between which a relation is said to hold.
relax (rɪˈlæks) *vb* **1** to make (muscles, a grip, etc.) less tense or rigid or (of muscles, a grip, etc.) to become looser or less rigid. **2** (*intr*) to take rest or recreation, as from work or effort: *on Sundays, she just relaxes; she relaxes by playing golf.* **3** to lessen the force of (effort, concentration, etc.) or (of effort) to become diminished. **4** to make (rules or discipline) less rigid or strict or (of rules, etc.) to diminish in severity. **5** (*intr*) (of a person) to become less formal; unbend. [C15: from Latin *relaxāre* to loosen, from RE- + *laxāre* to loosen, from *laxus* loose, LAX] ▸ **reˈlaxable** *adj* ▸ **reˈlaxed** *adj* ▸ **relaxedly** (rɪˈlæksɪdlɪ) *adv* ▸ **reˈlaxer** *n*

reˈjudge *vb*
reˈkindle *vb*
reˈlabel *vb,* **-bels, -belling, -belled.**

relaxant (rɪˈlæksᵊnt) *n* **1** *Med.* a drug or agent that relaxes, esp. one that relaxes tense muscles. ◆ *adj* **2** of, relating to, or tending to produce relaxation.

relaxation (ˌriːlækˈseɪʃən) *n* **1** rest or refreshment, as after work or effort; recreation. **2** a form of rest or recreation: *his relaxation is cricket.* **3** a partial lessening of a punishment, duty, etc. **4** the act of relaxing or state of being relaxed. **5** *Physics.* the return of a system to equilibrium after a displacement from this state. **6** *Maths.* a method by which errors resulting from an approximation are reduced by using new approximations.

relaxation oscillator *n Electronics.* a nonsinusoidal oscillator, the timing of which is controlled by the charge and discharge time constants of resistance and capacitance components.

relaxin (rɪˈlæksɪn) *n* **1** a mammalian polypeptide hormone secreted by the corpus luteum during pregnancy, which relaxes the pelvic ligaments. **2** a preparation of this hormone, used to facilitate childbirth. [C20: from RELAX + -IN]

relay *n* (ˈriːleɪ). **1** a person or team of people relieving others, as on a shift. **2** a fresh team of horses, dogs, etc., posted at intervals along a route to relieve others. **3** the act of relaying or process of being relayed. **4a** short for **relay race. 4b** one of the sections of a relay race. **5** an automatic device that controls the setting of a valve, switch, etc., by means of an electric motor, solenoid, or pneumatic mechanism. **6** *Electronics.* an electrical device in which a small change in current or voltage controls the switching on or off of circuits or other devices. **7** *Radio.* **7a** a combination of a receiver and transmitter designed to receive radio signals and retransmit them, in order to extend their range. **7b** (*as modifier*): *a relay station.* ◆ *vb* (rɪˈleɪ). (*tr*) **8** to carry or spread (something, such as news or information) by relays. **9** to supply or replace with relays. **10** to retransmit (a signal) by means of a relay. **11** *Brit.* to broadcast (a performance) by sending out signals through a transmitting station: *this concert is being relayed from the Albert Hall.* [C15 *relaien,* from Old French *relaier* to leave behind, from RE- + *laier* to leave, ultimately from Latin *laxāre* to loosen; see RELAX]

relay fast *n* (esp. in India) a form of protest in which a number of persons go without food by turns. Also called: **relay hunger strike.**

relay race *n* a race between two or more teams of contestants in which each contestant covers a specified portion of the distance.

release (rɪˈliːs) *vb* (*tr*) **1** to free (a person, animal, etc.) from captivity or imprisonment. **2** to free (someone) from obligation or duty. **3** to free (something) from (one's grip); let go or fall. **4** to issue (a record, film, book, etc.) for sale or circulation. **5** to make (news or information) known or allow (news, information, etc.) to be made known: *to release details of an agreement.* **6** *Law.* to relinquish (a right, claim, title, etc.) in favour of someone else. **7** *Ethology.* to evoke (a response) through the presentation of a stimulus that produces the response innately. ◆ *n* **8** the act of freeing or state of being freed, as from captivity, imprisonment, duty, pain, life, etc. **9** the act of issuing for sale or publication. **10** something issued for sale or public showing, esp. a film or a record: *a new release from Bob Dylan.* **11** a news item, document, etc., made available for publication, broadcasting, etc. **12** *Law.* the surrender of a claim, right, title, etc., in favour of someone else. **13** a control mechanism for starting or stopping an engine. **14a** the opening of the exhaust valve of a steam engine near the end of the piston stroke. **14b** the moment at which this valve opens. **15** the electronic control regulating how long a note sounds after a synthesizer key has been released. **16** the control mechanism for the shutter in a camera. [C13: from Old French *relesser,* from Latin *relaxāre* to slacken; see RELAX] ▸ **reˈleaser** *n*

relegate (ˈrɛlɪˌgeɪt) *vb* (*tr*) **1** to move to a position of less authority, importance, etc.; demote. **2** (*usually passive*) *Chiefly Brit.* to demote (a football team, etc.) to a lower division. **3** to assign or refer (a matter) to another or others, as for action or decision. **4** (foll. by *to*) to banish or exile. **5** to assign (something) to a particular group or category. [C16: from Latin *relēgāre* to send away, from RE- + *lēgāre* to send] ▸ **ˈreleˌgatable** *adj* ▸ **ˌreleˈgation** *n*

relent (rɪˈlɛnt) *vb* (*intr*) **1** to change one's mind about some decided course, esp. a harsh one; become more mild or amenable. **2** (of the pace or intensity of something) to slacken. **3** (of the weather) to become more mild. [C14: from RE- + Latin *lentāre* to bend, from *lentus* flexible, tenacious]

relentless (rɪˈlɛntlɪs) *adj* **1** (of an enemy, hostile attitude, etc.) implacable; inflexible; inexorable. **2** (of pace or intensity) sustained; unremitting. ▸ **reˈlentlessly** *adv* ▸ **reˈlentlessness** *n*

relevant (ˈrɛlɪvənt) *adj* **1** having direct bearing on the matter in hand; pertinent. **2** *Linguistics.* another word for **distinctive** (sense 2). [C16: from Medieval Latin *relevans,* from Latin *relevāre* to lighten, from RE- + *levāre* to raise, RELIEVE] ▸ **ˈrelevance** *or* **ˈrelevancy** *n* ▸ **ˈrelevantly** *adv*

reliable (rɪˈlaɪəbᵊl) *adj* able to be trusted; predictable or dependable. ▸ **reˌliaˈbility** *or* (*less commonly*) **reˈliableness** *n* ▸ **reˈliably** *adv*

reliance (rɪˈlaɪəns) *n* **1** dependence, confidence, or trust. **2** something or someone upon which one relies. ▸ **reˈliant** *adj* ▸ **reˈliantly** *adv*

relic (ˈrɛlɪk) *n* **1** something that has survived from the past, such as an object or custom. **2** something kept as a remembrance or treasured for its past associations; keepsake. **3** (*usually pl*) a remaining part or fragment. **4** *R.C. Church, Eastern Church.* part of the body of a saint or something supposedly used by or associated with a saint, venerated as holy. **5** *Informal.* an old or old-fashioned person or thing. **6** (*pl*) *Archaic.* the remains of a dead person; corpse. **7** *Ecology.* a less common term for **relict** (sense 1). [C13: from Old French *relique,* from Latin *reliquiae* remains, from *relinquere* to leave behind, RELINQUISH]

relict (ˈrɛlɪkt) *n* **1** *Ecology.* **1a** a group of animals or plants that exists as a remnant of a formerly widely distributed group in an environment different from that in which it originated. **1b** (*as modifier*): *a relict fauna.* **2** *Geology.* **2a** a mountain, lake, glacier, etc., that is a remnant of a pre-existing formation after a destructive process has occurred. **2b** a mineral that remains unaltered after metamorphism of the rock in which it occurs. **3** an archaic word for **widow** (sense 1). **4** an archaic word for **relic** (sense 6). [C16: from Latin *relictus* left behind, from *relinquere* to RELINQUISH]

relief (rɪˈliːf) *n* **1** a feeling of cheerfulness or optimism that follows the removal of anxiety, pain, or distress. **2** deliverance from or alleviation of anxiety, pain, distress, etc. **3a** help or assistance, as to the poor, needy, or distressed. **3b** (*as modifier*): *relief work.* **4** something that affords a diversion from monotony. **5** a person who replaces or relieves another at some task or duty. **6** a bus, shuttle plane, etc., that carries additional passengers when a scheduled service is full. **7** a road (**relief road**) carrying traffic round an urban area; bypass. **8a** the act of freeing a beleaguered town, fortress, etc.: *the relief of Mafeking.* **8b** (*as modifier*): *a relief column.* **9** Also called: **relievo, rilievo.** *Sculpture, architecture, etc.* **9a** the projection of forms or figures from a flat ground, so that they are partly or wholly free of it. **9b** a piece of work of this kind. **10** a printing process, such as engraving, letterpress, etc., that employs raised surfaces from which ink is transferred to the paper. **11** any vivid effect resulting from contrast: *comic relief.* **12** variation in altitude in an area; difference between highest and lowest level: *a region of low relief.* **13** *Mechanical engineering.* the removal of the surface material of a bearing area to allow the access of lubricating fluid. **14** *Law.* redress of a grievance or hardship: *to seek relief through the courts.* **15** *European history.* a succession of payments made by an heir to a fief to his lord: the size of the relief was determined by the lord within bounds set by custom. **16 on relief.** *U.S. and Canadian.* (of people) in receipt of government aid because of personal need. [C14: from Old French, from *relever* to raise up; see RELIEVE]

relief map *n* a map that shows the configuration and height of the land surface, usually by means of contours.

relieve (rɪˈliːv) *vb* (*tr*) **1** to bring alleviation of (pain, distress, etc.) to (someone). **2** to bring aid or assistance to (someone in need, a disaster area, etc.). **3** to take over the duties or watch of (someone). **4** to bring aid or a relieving force to (a besieged town, city, etc.). **5** to free (someone) from an obligation. **6** to make (something) less unpleasant, arduous, or monotonous. **7** to bring into relief or prominence, as by contrast. **8** (foll. by *of*) *Informal.* to take from: *the thief relieved him of his watch.* **9 relieve oneself.** to urinate or defecate. [C14: from Old French *relever,* from Latin *relevāre* to lift up, relieve, from RE- + *levāre* to lighten] ▸ **reˈlievable** *adj* ▸ **reˈliever** *n*

relieved (rɪˈliːvd) *adj* **1** (*postpositive;* often foll. by *at, about,* etc.) experiencing relief, esp. from worry or anxiety. **2** *Mechanical engineering.* having part of the surface cut away to avoid friction or wear.

relievo (rɪlˈjeɪvəʊ, rɪˈliːvəʊ) *n, pl* **-vos.** another name for **relief** (sense 9). [from Italian, literally: raised work]

religieuse *French.* (rəliʒjøz) *n* a nun. [C18: feminine of RELIGIEUX]

religieux *French.* (rəliʒjø) *n, pl* ***-gieux*** (-ʒjø). a member of a monastic order or clerical body. [C17: from Latin *religiōsus* religious]

religion (rɪˈlɪdʒən) *n* **1** belief in, worship of, or obedience to a supernatural power or powers considered to be divine or to have control of human destiny. **2** any formal or institutionalized expression of such belief: *the Christian religion.* **3** the attitude and feeling of one who believes in a transcendent controlling power or powers. **4** *Chiefly R.C. Church.* the way of life determined by the vows of poverty, chastity, and obedience entered upon by monks, friars, and nuns: *to enter religion.* **5** something of overwhelming importance to a person: *football is his religion.* **6** *Archaic.* **6a** the practice of sacred ritual observances. **6b** sacred rites and ceremonies. [C12: via Old French from Latin *religiō* fear of the supernatural, piety, probably from *religāre* to tie up, from RE- + *ligāre* to bind]

religionism (rɪˈlɪdʒəˌnɪzəm) *n* extreme religious fervour. ▸ **reˈligionist** *n, adj*

religiose (rɪˈlɪdʒɪˌəʊs) *adj* affectedly or extremely pious; sanctimoniously religious. ▸ **reˈligiˌosely** *adv* ▸ **religiosity** (rɪˌlɪdʒɪˈɒsɪtɪ) *n*

religious (rɪˈlɪdʒəs) *adj* **1** of, relating to, or concerned with religion. **2a** pious; devout; godly. **2b** (*as collective n;* preceded by *the*): *the religious.* **3** appropriate to or in accordance with the principles of a religion. **4** scrupulous, exact, or conscientious. **5** *Christianity.* of or relating to a way of life dedicated to religion by the vows of poverty, chastity, and obedience, and defined by a monastic rule. ◆ *n* **6** *Christianity.* a member of an order or congregation living by such a rule; a monk, friar, or nun. ▸ **reˈligiously** *adv* ▸ **reˈligiousness** *n*

Religious Society of Friends *n* the official name for the **Quakers.**

relinquish (rɪˈlɪŋkwɪʃ) *vb* (*tr*) **1** to give up (a task, struggle, etc.); abandon. **2** to surrender or renounce (a claim, right, etc.). **3** to release; let go. [C15: from French *relinquir,* from Latin *relinquere* to leave behind, from RE- + *linquere* to leave] ▸ **reˈlinquisher** *n* ▸ **reˈlinquishment** *n*

reliquary (ˈrɛlɪkwərɪ) *n, pl* **-quaries.** a receptacle or repository for relics, esp. relics of saints. [C17: from Old French *reliquaire,* from *relique* RELIC]

relique (rəˈliːk, ˈrɛlɪk) *n* an archaic spelling of **relic.**

reliquiae (rɪˈlɪkwɪˌiː) *pl n* fossil remains of animals or plants. [C19: from Latin: remains]

relish (ˈrɛlɪʃ) *vb* (*tr*) **1** to savour or enjoy (an experience) to the full. **2** to anticipate eagerly; look forward to. **3** to enjoy the taste or flavour of (food, etc.); savour. **4** to give appetizing taste or flavour to (food), by or as if by the addition of pickles or spices. ◆ *n* **5** liking or enjoyment, as of something eaten or experi-

re-ˈlay *vb,* **-ˈlays, -ˈlaying, -ˈlaid.**
reˈlearn *vb*
reˈlet *vb,* **-ˈlets, -ˈletting, -ˈlet.**
reˈlight *vb,* **-ˈlights, -ˈlighting; -ˈlighted** *or* **-lit.**
reˈline *vb*

enced (esp. in the phrase **with relish**). **6** pleasurable anticipation: *he didn't have much relish for the idea.* **7** an appetizing or spicy food added to a main dish to enhance its flavour. **8** an appetizing taste or flavour. **9** a zestful trace or touch: *there was a certain relish in all his writing.* **10** *Music.* (in English lute, viol, and keyboard music of the 16th and 17th centuries) a trilling ornament, used esp. at cadences. [C16: from earlier *reles* aftertaste, from Old French: something remaining, from *relaisser* to leave behind; see RELEASE] ▸ **'relishable** *adj*

relive (riːˈlɪv) *vb* (*tr*) to experience (a sensation, event, etc.) again, esp. in the imagination. ▸ **re'livable** *adj*

relocate (ˌriːləʊˈkeɪt) *vb* **1** to move or be moved to a new place, esp. (of an employee, a business, etc.) to a new area or place of employment. **2** (*intr*) (of an employee, a business, etc.) to move for reasons of business to a new area or place of employment. ▸ **,relo'cation** *n*

relocation costs *or* **expenses** *pl n* payment made by an employer or a government agency to cover removal expenses and other costs incurred by an employee who is required to take up employment elsewhere.

relucent (rɪˈluːsᵊnt) *adj Archaic.* bright; shining. [C16: from Latin *relūcēre* to shine out, from RE- + *lūcēre* to shine, from *lūx* light]

reluct (rɪˈlʌkt) *vb* (*intr*) *Archaic.* **1** (often foll. by *against*) to struggle or rebel. **2** to object; show reluctance. [C16: from Latin *reluctārī* to resist, from RE- + *luctārī* to struggle]

reluctance (rɪˈlʌktəns) *or* (*less commonly*) **reluctancy** *n* **1** lack of eagerness or willingness; disinclination. **2** *Physics.* a measure of the resistance of a closed magnetic circuit to a magnetic flux, equal to the ratio of the magnetomotive force to the magnetic flux.

reluctant (rɪˈlʌktənt) *adj* **1** not eager; unwilling; disinclined. **2** *Archaic.* offering resistance or opposition. [C17: from Latin *reluctārī* to resist; see RELUCT] ▸ **re'luctantly** *adv*

reluctivity (ˌrɛlʌkˈtɪvɪtɪ) *n, pl* **-ties.** *Physics.* a specific or relative reluctance of a magnetic material. [C19: RELUCT + *-ivity* on the model of *conductivity*]

relume (rɪˈluːm) *or* **relumine** (rɪˈluːmɪn) *vb* (*tr*) *Archaic.* to light or brighten again; rekindle. [C17: from Late Latin *relūmināre*, from Latin RE- + *illūmināre* to ILLUMINE]

rely (rɪˈlaɪ) *vb* **-lies, -lying, -lied.** (*intr*; foll. by *on* or *upon*) **1** to be dependent (on): *he relies on his charm.* **2** to have trust or confidence (in): *you can rely on us.* [C14: from Old French *relier* to fasten together, repair, from Latin *religāre* to tie back, from RE- + *ligāre* to tie]

REM[1] *abbrev. for* rapid eye movement.

REM[2] *or* **rem** (rɛm) *n acronym for* roentgen equivalent man.

remain (rɪˈmeɪn) *vb* (*mainly intr*) **1** to stay behind or in the same place: *to remain at home; only Tom remained.* **2** (*copula*) to continue to be: *to remain cheerful.* **3** to be left, as after use, consumption, the passage of time, etc.: *a little wine still remained in the bottle.* **4** to be left to be done, said, etc.: *it remains to be pointed out.* ◆ See also **remains.** [C14: from Old French *remanoir*, from Latin *remanēre* to be left, from RE- + *manēre* to stay]

remainder (rɪˈmeɪndə) *n* **1** a part or portion that is left, as after use, subtraction, expenditure, the passage of time, etc.: *the remainder of the milk; the remainder of the day.* **2** *Maths.* **2a** the amount left over when one quantity cannot be exactly divided by another: *for 10 ÷ 3, the remainder is 1.* **2b** another name for **difference** (sense 7b). **3** *Property law.* a future interest in property; an interest in a particular estate that will pass to one at some future date, as on the death of the current possessor. **4** a number of copies of a book left unsold when demand slows or ceases, which are sold at a reduced price by the publisher. ◆ *vb* **5** (*tr*) to sell (copies of a book) as a remainder. [C15: from Anglo-French, from Old French *remaindre* (infinitive used as noun), variant of *remanoir*; see REMAIN]

remainderman (rɪˈmeɪndəˌmæn) *n, pl* **-men.** *Property law.* the person entitled to receive a particular estate on its determination. Compare **reversioner.**

remains (rɪˈmeɪnz) *pl n* **1** any pieces, scraps, fragments, etc., that are left unused or still extant, as after use, consumption, the passage of time, etc.: *the remains of a meal; archaeological remains.* **2** the body of a dead person; corpse. **3** Also called: **literary remains.** the unpublished writings of an author at the time of his death.

remake *n* (ˈriːˌmeɪk). **1** something that is made again, esp. a new version of an old film. **2** the act of making again or anew. ◆ *vb* (riːˈmeɪk), **-makes, -making, -made. 3** (*tr*) to make again or anew.

remand (rɪˈmɑːnd) *vb* (*tr*) **1** *Law.* (of a court or magistrate) to send (a prisoner or accused person) back into custody or admit him to bail, esp. on adjourning a case for further inquiries to be made. **2** to send back. ◆ *n* **3** the sending of a prisoner or accused person back into custody (or sometimes admitting him to bail) to await trial or continuation of his trial. **4** the act of remanding or state of being remanded. **5 on remand.** in custody or on bail awaiting trial or completion of one's trial. [C15: from Medieval Latin *remandāre* to send back word, from Latin RE- + *mandāre* to command, confine; see MANDATE] ▸ **re'mandment** *n*

remand centre *n* (in Britain) an institution to which accused persons are sent for detention while awaiting appearance before a court. Until 1967 remand centres were for young people between 14 and 21 years of age.

remand home *n* (no longer in technical use) an institution to which juvenile offenders between 8 and 14 years may be remanded or committed for detention. See also **community home.**

remanence (ˈrɛmənəns) *n Physics.* the ability of a material to retain magnetization, equal to the magnetic flux density of the material after the removal of the magnetizing field. Also called: **retentivity.** [C17: from Latin *remanēre* to stay behind, REMAIN]

remanent (ˈrɛmənənt) *adj Rare.* remaining or left over.

remark (rɪˈmɑːk) *vb* **1** (when *intr*, often foll. by *on* or *upon*; when *tr*, *may take a clause as object*) to pass a casual comment (about); reflect in informal speech or writing. **2** (*tr; may take a clause as object*) to perceive; observe; notice. ◆ *n* **3** a brief casually expressed thought or opinion; observation. **4** notice, comment, or observation: *the event passed without remark.* **5** *Engraving.* a variant spelling of **remarque.** [C17: from Old French *remarquer* to observe, from RE- + *marquer* to note, MARK[1]] ▸ **re'marker** *n*

remarkable (rɪˈmɑːkəbᵊl) *adj* **1** worthy of note or attention: *a remarkable achievement.* **2** unusual, striking, or extraordinary: *a remarkable sight.* ▸ **re'markableness** *or* **re,marka'bility** *n* ▸ **re'markably** *adv*

remarque *or* **remark** (rɪˈmɑːk) *n* **1** a mark in the margin of an engraved plate to indicate the stage of production of the plate. It is removed before the plate is finished. **2** a plate so marked. **3** a print or proof from a plate so marked. [C19: from French; see REMARK]

Remarque (rɪˈmɑːk) *n* **Erich Maria** (ˈeːrɪç maˈriːa). 1898–1970, U.S. novelist, born in Germany, noted for his novel of World War I, *All Quiet on the Western Front* (1929).

remaster (riːˈmɑːstə) *vb* (*tr*) to make a new master audio recording, now usually digital, from (an earlier recording), to produce compact discs or stereo records with improved sound reproduction.

rematch *n* (ˈriːˌmætʃ). **1** *Sport.* a second or return match between contestants. ◆ *vb* (riːˈmætʃ). **2** (*tr*) to match (two contestants) again.

remblai (*French* rɑ̃blɛ) *n* earth used for an embankment or rampart. [C18: from French, from *remblayer* to embank, from *emblayer* to pile up]

Rembrandt (ˈrɛmbrænt) *n* full name *Rembrandt Harmensz* (or *Harmenszoon*) *van Rijn* (or *van Ryn*). 1606–69, Dutch painter, noted for his handling of shade and light, esp. in his portraits. ▸ **,Rembrandt'esque** *adj*

REME (ˈriːmiː) *n acronym for* Royal Electrical and Mechanical Engineers.

remedial (rɪˈmiːdɪəl) *adj* **1** affording a remedy; curative. **2** denoting or relating to special teaching, teaching methods, or material for backward and slow learners: *remedial education.* ▸ **re'medially** *adv*

remedy (ˈrɛmɪdɪ) *n, pl* **-dies. 1** (usually foll. by *for* or *against*) any drug or agent that cures a disease or controls its symptoms. **2** (usually foll. by *for* or *against*) anything that serves to put a fault to rights, cure defects, improve conditions, etc.: *a remedy for industrial disputes.* **3** the legally permitted variation from the standard weight or quality of coins; tolerance. ◆ *vb* (*tr*) **4** to relieve or cure (a disease, illness, etc.) by or as if by a remedy. **5** to put to rights (a fault, error, etc.); correct. [C13: from Anglo-Norman *remedie*, from Latin *remedium* a cure, from *remedērī* to heal again, from RE- + *medērī* to heal; see MEDICAL] ▸ **remediable** (rɪˈmiːdɪəbᵊl) *adj* ▸ **re'mediably** *adv* ▸ **'remediless** *adj*

remember (rɪˈmɛmbə) *vb* **1** to become aware of (something forgotten) again; bring back to one's consciousness; recall. **2** to retain (an idea, intention, etc.) in one's conscious mind: *to remember Pythagoras' theorem; remember to do one's shopping.* **3** (*tr*) to give money, etc., to (someone), as in a will or in tipping. **4** (*tr;* foll. by *to*) to mention (a person's name) to another person, as by way of greeting or friendship: *remember me to your mother.* **5** (*tr*) to mention (a person) favourably, as in prayer. **6** (*tr*) to commemorate (a person, event, etc.): *to remember the dead of the wars.* **7 remember oneself.** to recover one's good manners after a lapse; stop behaving badly. [C14: from Old French *remembrer*, from Late Latin *rememorārī* to recall to mind, from Latin RE- + *memor* mindful; see MEMORY] ▸ **re'memberer** *n*

remembrance (rɪˈmɛmbrəns) *n* **1** the act of remembering or state of being remembered. **2** something that is remembered; reminiscence. **3** a memento or keepsake. **4** the extent in time of one's power of recollection. **5a** the act of honouring some past event, person, etc. **5b** (*as modifier*): *a remembrance service.*

remembrancer (rɪˈmɛmbrənsə) *n Archaic.* a reminder, memento, or keepsake.

Remembrancer (rɪˈmɛmbrənsə) *n* (in Britain) **1** any of several officials of the Exchequer esp. one (**Queen's** *or* **King's Remembrancer**) whose duties include collecting debts due to the Crown. **2** an official (**City Remembrancer**) appointed by the Corporation of the City of London to represent its interests to Parliament and elsewhere.

Remembrance Sunday *n Brit.* the second Sunday in November, which is the Sunday closest to November 11, the anniversary of the armistice of 1918 that ended World War I, on which the dead of both World Wars are commemorated. Also called: **Remembrance Day.**

remex (ˈriːmɛks) *n, pl* **remiges** (ˈrɛmɪˌdʒiːz). any of the large flight feathers of a bird's wing. [C18: from Latin: a rower, from *rēmus* oar] ▸ **remigial** (rɪˈmɪdʒɪəl) *adj*

remind (rɪˈmaɪnd) *vb* (*tr;* usually foll. by *of; may take a clause as object or an infinitive*) to cause (a person) to remember (something or to do something); make (someone) aware (of something he may have forgotten): *remind me to phone home; flowers remind me of holidays.*

reminder (rɪˈmaɪndə) *n* **1** something that recalls the past. **2** a note to remind a person of something not done.

remindful (rɪˈmaɪndfʊl) *adj* **1** serving to remind. **2** (*postpositive*) bearing in mind; mindful.

reminisce (ˌrɛmɪˈnɪs) *vb* (*intr*) to talk or write about old times, past experiences, etc.

re'load *vb*
re'mail *vb*
re'man *vb*, -'mans, -'manning, -'manned.
re'marriage *n*
re'marry *vb*, -ries, -rying, -ried.
re'melt *vb*
re'mend *vb*

reminiscence (ˌrɛmɪˈnɪsəns) *n* **1** the act of recalling or narrating past experiences. **2** (*often pl*) some past experience, event, etc., that is recalled or narrated; anecdote. **3** an event, phenomenon, or experience that reminds one of something else. **4** (in the philosophy of Plato) the doctrine that perception and recognition of particulars is possible because the mind has seen the universal forms of all things in a previous disembodied existence. **5** *Psychol.* the ability to perform a task better when tested some time after the task has been learnt than when tested immediately after learning it.

reminiscent (ˌrɛmɪˈnɪsᵊnt) *adj* **1** (*postpositive;* foll. by *of*) stimulating memories (of) or comparisons (with). **2** characterized by reminiscence. **3** (of a person) given to reminiscing. **[C18:** from Latin *reminiscī* to call to mind, from RE- + *mēns* mind**]** ▸ ˌ**remiˈniscently** *adv*

remise (rɪˈmaɪz) *vb* **1** (*tr*) *Law.* to give up or relinquish (a right, claim, etc.); surrender. **2** *Fencing.* to make a renewed thrust on the same lunge after the first has missed. ◆ *n* **3** *Fencing.* a second thrust made on the same lunge after the first has missed. **4** *Obsolete.* a hired carriage. **5** *Obsolete.* a coach house. **[C17:** from French *remettre* to put back, from Latin *remittere* to send back, from RE- + *mittere* to send**]**

remiss (rɪˈmɪs) *adj* (*postpositive*) **1** lacking in care or attention to duty; negligent. **2** lacking in energy; dilatory. **[C15:** from Latin *remissus, from remittere* to release, from RE- + *mittere* to send**]** ▸ **reˈmissly** *adv* ▸ **reˈmissness** *n*

remissible (rɪˈmɪsəbᵊl) *adj* able to be remitted. **[C16:** from Latin *remissibilis;* see REMIT**]** ▸ **reˌmissiˈbility** *or* **reˈmissibleness** *n*

remission (rɪˈmɪʃən) *or* (*less commonly*) **remittal** (rɪˈmɪtᵊl) *n* **1** the act of remitting or state of being remitted. **2** a reduction of the term of a sentence of imprisonment, as for good conduct: *he got three years' remission.* **3** forgiveness for sin. **4** discharge or release from penalty, obligation, etc. **5** lessening of intensity; abatement, as in the severity of symptoms of a disease. ▸ **reˈmissive** *adj* ▸ **reˈmissively** *adv*

remit *vb* (rɪˈmɪt). **-mits, -mitting, -mitted.** (*mainly tr*) **1** (*also intr*) to send (money, payment, etc.), as for goods or service, esp. by post. **2** *Law.* (esp. of an appeal court) to send back (a case or proceeding) to an inferior court for further consideration or action. **3** to cancel or refrain from exacting (a penalty or punishment). **4** (*also intr*) to relax (pace, intensity, etc.) or (of pace or the like) to slacken or abate. **5** to postpone; defer. **6** *Archaic.* to pardon or forgive (crime, sins, etc.). ◆ *n* (ˈriːmɪt, rɪˈmɪt). **7** the area of authority or responsibility of an individual or a group: *by taking that action, the committee has exceeded its remit.* **8** *Law.* the transfer of a case from one court or jurisdiction to another, esp. from an appeal court to an inferior tribunal. **9** the act of remitting. **10** something remitted. **11** *N.Z.* a proposal from a branch of an organization put forward for discussion at the annual general meeting. **[C14:** from Latin *remittere* to send back, release, RE- + *mittere* to send**]** ▸ **reˈmittable** *adj* ▸ **reˈmittal** *n*

remittance (rɪˈmɪtəns) *n* **1** payment for goods or services received or as an allowance, esp. when sent by post. **2** the act of remitting.

remittance man *n* a man living abroad on money sent from home, esp. in the days of the British Empire.

remittee (rɪˌmɪtˈiː) *n* the recipient of a remittance; one to whom payment is sent.

remittent (rɪˈmɪtᵊnt) *adj* (of a fever or the symptoms of a disease) characterized by periods of diminished severity. ▸ **reˈmittence** *or* **reˈmittency** *n* ▸ **reˈmittently** *adv*

remitter (rɪˈmɪtə) *n* **1** Also called: **remittor.** a person who remits. **2** *Property law.* the principle by which a person out of possession of land to which he had a good title is adjudged to regain this when he again enters into possession of the land.

remix *vb* (riːˈmɪks). **1** to change the balance and separation of (a recording), usually to emphasize the rhythm section. ◆ *n* (ˈriːmɪks). **2** a remixed version of a recording.

remnant (ˈrɛmnənt) *n* **1** (*often pl*) a part left over after use, processing, etc. **2** a surviving trace or vestige, as of a former era: *a remnant of imperialism.* **3** a piece of material from the end of a roll, sold at a lower price. ◆ *adj* **4** remaining; left over. **[C14:** from Old French *remenant* remaining, from *remanoir* to REMAIN**]**

remonetize *or* **remonetise** (riːˈmʌnɪˌtaɪz) *vb* (*tr*) to reinstate as legal tender: *to remonetize silver.* ▸ **reˌmonetiˈzation** *or* **reˌmonetiˈsation** *n*

remonstrance (rɪˈmɒnstrəns) *n* **1** the act of remonstrating; protestation. **2** a protest or reproof, esp. a petition presented in protest against something.

Remonstrance (rɪˈmɒnstrəns) *n History.* **1** See **Grand Remonstrance. 2** the statement of Arminian principles drawn up in 1610 in Gouda in the Netherlands.

remonstrant (rɪˈmɒnstrənt) *n* **1** a person who remonstrates, esp. one who signs a remonstrance. ◆ *adj* **2** *Rare.* remonstrating or protesting.

Remonstrant (rɪˈmɒnstrənt) *n* a Dutch supporter of the Arminian Remonstrance of 1610.

remonstrate (ˈrɛmənˌstreɪt) *vb* (*intr*) **1** (usually foll. by *with, against,* etc.) to argue in protest or objection: *to remonstrate with the government.* **2** *Archaic.* to show or point out. **[C16:** from Medieval Latin *remonstrāre* to point out (errors), from Latin RE- + *monstrāre* to show**]** ▸ ˌ**remonˈstration** *n* ▸ **remonstrative** (rɪˈmɒnstrətɪv) *adj* ▸ ˈ**remonˌstrator** *n*

remontant (rɪˈmɒntənt) *adj* **1** (esp. of cultivated roses) flowering more than once in a single season. ◆ *n* **2** a rose having such a growth. **[C19:** from French: coming up again, from *remonter;* see REMOUNT**]**

remontoir *or* **remontoire** (ˌrɛmənˈtwɑː) *n* any of various devices used in watches, clocks, etc., to compensate for errors arising from the changes in the force driving the escapement. **[C19:** from French: winding mechanism, from *remonter* to wind; see REMOUNT**]**

remora (ˈrɛmərə) *n* any of the marine spiny-finned fishes constituting the family *Echeneidae.* They have a flattened elongated body and attach themselves to larger fish, rocks, etc., by a sucking disc on the top of the head. **[C16:** from Latin, from RE- + *mora* delay; an allusion to its alleged habit of delaying ships**]**

remorse (rɪˈmɔːs) *n* **1** a sense of deep regret and guilt for some misdeed. **2** compunction; pity; compassion. **[C14:** from Medieval Latin *remorsus* a gnawing, from Latin *remordēre* to bite again, from RE- + *mordēre* to bite**]** ▸ **reˈmorseful** *adj* ▸ **reˈmorsefully** *adv* ▸ **reˈmorsefulness** *n*

remorseless (rɪˈmɔːslɪs) *adj* **1** without compunction, pity, or compassion. **2** not abating in intensity; relentless: *a remorseless wind.* ▸ **reˈmorselessly** *adv* ▸ **reˈmorselessness** *n*

remote (rɪˈməʊt) *adj* **1** located far away; distant. **2** far from any centre of population, society, or civilization; out-of-the-way. **3** distant in time. **4** distantly related or connected: *a remote cousin.* **5** removed, as from the source or point of action. **6** slight or faint (esp. in the phrases **not the remotest idea, a remote chance**). **7** (of a person's manner) aloof or abstracted. **8** operated from a distance; remote-controlled: *a remote monitor.* **[C15:** from Latin *remōtus* far removed, from *removēre,* from RE- + *movēre* to move**]** ▸ **reˈmotely** *adv* ▸ **reˈmoteness** *n*

remote access *n Computing.* access to a computer from a physically separate terminal.

remote control *n* control of a system or activity by a person at a different place, usually by means of radio or ultrasonic signals or by electrical signals transmitted by wire. ▸ **reˈmote-conˈtrolled** *adj*

remote sensor *n* any instrument, such as a radar device or camera, that scans the earth or another planet from space in order to collect data about some aspect of it. ▸ **remote-sensing** *adj, n*

rémoulade (ˌreməˈleɪd; *French* remulad) *n* a mayonnaise sauce flavoured with herbs, mustard, and capers, served with salads, cold meat, etc. **[C19:** from French, from Picard dialect *ramolas* horseradish, from Latin *armoracea***]**

remould *vb* (ˌriːˈməʊld). (*tr*) **1** to mould again. **2** to bond a new tread onto the casing of (a worn pneumatic tyre). ◆ *n* (ˈriːˌməʊld). **3** a tyre made by this process. ◆ Also (for senses 2, 3): **retread.**

remount *vb* (riːˈmaʊnt). **1** to get on (a horse, bicycle, etc.) again. **2** (*tr*) to mount (a picture, jewel, exhibit, etc.) again. ◆ *n* (ˈriːmaʊnt). **3** a fresh horse, esp. (formerly) to replace one killed or injured in battle.

removal (rɪˈmuːvᵊl) *n* **1** the act of removing or state of being removed. **2a** a change of residence. **2b** (*as modifier*): *a removal company.* **3** dismissal from office.

removalist (rɪˈmuːvəlɪst) *n Austral.* a person or company that transports household effects to a new home.

remove (rɪˈmuːv) *vb* (*mainly tr*) **1** to take away and place elsewhere. **2** to displace (someone) from office; dismiss. **3** to do away with (a grievance, cause of anxiety, etc.); abolish. **4** to cause (dirt, stains, or anything unwanted) to disappear; get rid of. **5** *Euphemistic.* to assassinate; kill. **6** (*intr*) *Formal.* to change the location of one's home or place of business: *the publishers have removed to Mayfair.* ◆ *n* **7** the act of removing, esp. (formal) a removal of one's residence or place of work. **8** the degree of difference separating one person, thing, or condition from another: *only one remove from madness.* **9** *Brit.* (in certain schools) a class or form, esp. one for children of about 14 years, designed to introduce them to the greater responsibilities of a more senior position in the school. **10** (at a formal dinner, formerly) a dish to be changed while the rest of the course remains on the table. **[C14:** from Old French *removoir,* from Latin *removēre;* see MOVE**]** ▸ **reˈmovable** *adj* ▸ **reˌmovaˈbility** *or* **reˈmovableness** *n* ▸ **reˈmovably** *adv* ▸ **reˈmover** *n*

removed (rɪˈmuːvd) *adj* **1** separated by distance or abstract distinction. **2** (*postpositive*) separated by a degree of descent or kinship: *the child of a person's first cousin is his first cousin once removed.* ▸ **removedness** (rɪˈmuːvɪdnɪs) *n*

Remscheid (*German* ˈrɛmʃaɪt) *n* an industrial city in W Germany, in North Rhine-Westphalia. Pop.: 122 260 (1996 est.).

remunerate (rɪˈmjuːnəˌreɪt) *vb* (*tr*) to reward or pay for work, service, etc. **[C16:** from Latin *remūnerārī* to reward, from RE- + *mūnerāre* to give, from *mūnus* a gift; see MUNIFICENT**]** ▸ **reˌmuneraˈbility** *n* ▸ **reˈmunerable** *adj* ▸ **reˈmunerative** *adj* ▸ **reˈmuneratively** *adv* ▸ **reˈmunerativeness** *n* ▸ **reˈmunerˌator** *n*

remuneration (rɪˌmjuːnəˈreɪʃən) *n* **1** the act of remunerating. **2** pay; recompense.

Remus (ˈriːməs) *n Roman myth.* the brother of Romulus.

renaissance (rəˈneɪsəns; *U.S. also* ˈrɛnəˌsɒns) *or* **renascence** *n* a revival or rebirth, esp. of culture and learning. **[C19:** from French, from Latin RE- + *nascī* to be born**]**

Renaissance (rəˈneɪsəns; *U.S. also* ˈrɛnəˌsɒns) *n* **1 the.** the period of European history marking the waning of the Middle Ages and the rise of the modern world: usually considered as beginning in Italy in the 14th century. **2a** the spirit, culture, art, science, and thought of this period. Characteristics of the Renaissance are usually considered to include intensified classical scholarship, scientific and geographical discovery, a sense of individual human potentialities, and the assertion of the active and secular over the religious and contemplative life. **2b** (*as modifier*): *Renaissance writers.* See also **Early Renaissance, High Renaissance.** ◆ *adj* **3** of, characteristic of, or relating to the Renaissance, its culture, etc.

reˈmodel *vb,* **-els, -elling, -elled.** **reˈmortgage** *vb*

Renaissance man *n* a man of any period who has a broad range of intellectual interests.

renal ('riːnᵊl) *adj* of, relating to, resembling, or situated near the kidney. [C17: from French, from Late Latin *rēnālis,* from Latin *rēnēs* kidneys, of obscure origin]

renal pelvis *n* a small funnel-shaped cavity of the kidney into which urine is discharged before passing into the ureter.

Renan (*French* ranɑ̃) *n* **(Joseph) Ernest** (ernest). 1823–92, French philosopher, theologian, and historian; best known for his *Life of Jesus* (1863), which discounted the supernatural aspects of the Gospels.

renascence (rɪ'næsəns, -'neɪ-) *n* a variant of **renaissance.**

renascent (rɪ'næsᵊnt, -'neɪ-) *adj* becoming active or vigorous again; reviving: *renascent nationalism.* [C18: from Latin *renascī* to be born again]

rencounter (rɛn'kaʊntə) *Archaic.* ♦ *n also* **rencontre** (rɛn'kɒntə). **1** an unexpected meeting. **2** a hostile clash, as of two armies, adversaries, etc.; skirmish. ♦ *vb* **3** to meet (someone) unexpectedly. [C16: from French *rencontre,* from *rencontrer;* see ENCOUNTER]

rend (rɛnd) *vb* **rends, rending, rent. 1** to tear with violent force or to be torn in this way; rip. **2** (*tr*) to tear or pull (one's clothes, etc.), esp. as a manifestation of rage or grief. **3** (*tr*) (of a noise or cry) to disturb (the air, silence, etc.) with a shrill or piercing tone. **4** (*tr*) to pain or distress (the heart, conscience, etc.). [Old English *rendan;* related to Old Frisian *renda*] ► **'rendible** *adj*

Rendell ('rɛndᵊl, rɛn'dɛl) *n* Baroness **Ruth (Barbara).** born 1930, British crime writer: author of detective novels, such as *Wolf to the Slaughter* (1967), and psychological thrillers, such as *The Lake of Darkness* (1980) and (under the name **Barbara Vine**) *A Fatal Inversion* (1987) and *No Night is Too Long* (1994).

render ('rɛndə) *vb* (*tr*) **1** to present or submit (accounts, etc.) for payment, approval, or action. **2** to give or provide (aid, charity, a service, etc.). **3** to show (obedience), as due or expected. **4** to give or exchange, as by way of return or requital: *to render blow for blow.* **5** to cause to become: *grief had rendered him simple-minded.* **6** to deliver (a verdict or opinion) formally. **7** to portray or depict (something), as in painting, music, or acting. **8** to translate (something) into another language or form. **9** (sometimes foll. by *up*) to yield or give: *the tomb rendered up its secret.* **10** (often foll. by *back*) to return (something); give back. **11** to cover the surface of (brickwork, stone, etc.) with a coat of plaster. **12** (often foll. by *down*) to extract (fat) from (meat) by melting. **13** *Nautical.* **13a** to reeve (a line). **13b** to slacken (a rope, etc.). **14** *History.* (of a feudal tenant) to make (payment) in money, goods, or services to one's overlord. ♦ *n* **15** a first thin coat of plaster applied to a surface. **16** *History.* a payment in money, goods, or services made by a feudal tenant to his lord. [C14: from Old French *rendre,* from Latin *reddere* to give back (influenced by Latin *prendere* to grasp), from RE- + *dare* to give] ► **'renderable** *adj* ► **'renderer** *n*

rendering ('rɛndərɪŋ) *n* **1** the act or an instance of performing a play, piece of music, etc. **2** a translation of a text from a foreign language. **3** Also called: **rendering coat, render.** a coat of plaster or cement mortar applied to a surface. **4** a perspective drawing showing an architect's idea of a finished building, interior, etc.

rendezvous ('rɒndɪˌvuː) *n, pl* **-vous** (-ˌvuːz). **1** a meeting or appointment to meet at a specified time and place. **2** a place where people meet. **3** an arranged meeting of two spacecraft. ♦ *vb* **4** to meet or cause to meet at a specified time or place. [C16: from French, from *rendez-vous!* present yourselves! from *se rendre* to present oneself; see RENDER]

rendition (rɛn'dɪʃən) *n* **1** a performance of a musical composition, dramatic role, etc. **2** a translation of a text. **3** the act of rendering. **4** *Archaic.* surrender. [C17: from obsolete French, from Late Latin *redditiō;* see RENDER]

rendzina (rɛn'dziːnə) *n* a dark interzonal type of soil found in grassy or formerly grassy areas of moderate rainfall, esp. on chalklands. [C20: from Polish]

renegade ('rɛnɪˌgeɪd) *n* **1a** a person who deserts his cause or faith for another; apostate; traitor. **1b** (*as modifier*): *a renegade priest.* **2** any outlaw or rebel. [C16: from Spanish *renegado,* from Medieval Latin *renegāre* to renounce, from Latin RE- + *negāre* to deny]

renegado (ˌrɛnɪ'gɑːdəʊ) *n, pl* **-dos.** an archaic word for **renegade.**

renege *or* **renegue** (rɪ'niːg, -'neɪg) *vb* **1** (*intr;* often foll. by *on*) to go back (on one's promise, etc.). ♦ *vb, n* **2** *Cards.* other words for **revoke.** [C16 (in the sense: to deny, renounce): from Medieval Latin *renegāre* to renounce; see RENEGADE] ► **re'neger** *or* **re'neguer** *n*

renew (rɪ'njuː) *vb* (*mainly tr*) **1** to take up again. **2** (*also intr*) to begin (an activity) again; recommence: *to renew an attempt.* **3** to restate or reaffirm (a promise, etc.). **4** (*also intr*) to make (a lease, licence, or contract) valid or effective for a further period. **5** to extend the period of loan of (a library book). **6** to regain or recover (vigour, strength, activity, etc.). **7** to restore to a new or fresh condition. **8** to replace (an old or worn-out part or piece). **9** to replenish (a supply, etc.). ► **re'newable** *adj* ► **reˌnewa'bility** *n* ► **re'newer** *n*

renewable energy *n* another name for **alternative energy.**

renewables *pl n* sources of alternative energy, such as wind and wave power.

renewal (rɪ'njuːəl) *n* **1** the act of renewing or state of being renewed. **2** something that is renewed.

Renfrew ('rɛnfruː) *n* an industrial town in W central Scotland, in Renfrewshire, W of Glasgow. Pop.: 20 764 (1991).

Renfrewshire ('rɛnfruːʃɪə, -ʃə) *n* **1** a council area of W central Scotland, on the River Clyde W of Glasgow: corresponds to part of the historical county of Renfrewshire; part of Strathclyde region from 1975 to 1996: agricultural and residential, with clothing and manufacturing industries in Paisley. Administrative centre: Paisley. Pop.: 178 550 (1996 est.). Area: 261 sq. km (101 sq. miles). **2** a former county of W central Scotland, on the Firth of Clyde: became part of Strathclyde region in 1975; now covered by the council areas of Renfrewshire, East Renfrewshire, and Inverclyde.

reni- *combining form.* kidney or kidneys: *reniform.* [from Latin *rēnēs*]

Reni (*Italian* 'rɛːni) *n* **Guido** ('gwiːdo). 1575–1642, Italian baroque painter and engraver.

reniform ('rɛnɪˌfɔːm) *adj* having the shape or profile of a kidney: *a reniform leaf; a reniform mass of haematite.*

renin ('riːnɪn) *n* a proteolytic enzyme secreted by the kidneys, which plays an important part in the maintenance of blood pressure. [C20: from RENI- + -IN]

renitent (rɪ'naɪtᵊnt, 'rɛnɪtənt) *adj Rare.* **1** reluctant; recalcitrant. **2** not flexible. [C18: from Latin *renītī* to strive afresh, from RE- + *nītī* to endeavour] ► **re'nitence** *or* **re'nitency** *n*

Rennes (*French* rɛn) *n* a city in NW France: the ancient capital of Brittany. Pop.: 203 533 (1990).

rennet ('rɛnɪt) *n* **1a** the membrane lining the fourth stomach (abomasum) of a young calf. **1b** the stomach of certain other young animals. **2** a substance, containing the enzyme rennin, prepared esp. from the stomachs of calves and used for curdling milk in making cheese and junket. [C15: related to Old English *gerinnan* to curdle, RUN]

Rennie ('rɛnɪ) *n* **John.** 1761–1821, British civil engineer who designed bridges, canals, docks, and harbours, including three London bridges and the London and East India docks.

rennin ('rɛnɪn) *n* an enzyme that occurs in gastric juice and is a constituent of rennet. It coagulates milk by converting caseinogen to casein. Also called: **chymosin.** [C20: from RENNET + -IN]

Reno ('riːnəʊ) *n* a city in W Nevada, at the foot of the Sierra Nevada: noted as a divorce, wedding, and gambling centre by reason of its liberal laws. Pop.: 155 499 (1996 est.).

Renoir ('rɛnwɑː; *French* rənwar) *n* **1 Jean** (ʒɑ̃). 1894–1979, French film director: his films include *La grande illusion* (1937), *La règle du jeu* (1939), and *Diary of a Chambermaid* (1945). **2** his father, **Pierre Auguste** (pjɛr ogyst). 1841–1919, French painter. One of the initiators of impressionism, he broke away from the movement with his later paintings, esp. his many nude studies, which are more formal compositions.

renounce (rɪ'naʊns) *vb* **1** (*tr*) to give up (a claim or right), esp. by formal announcement: *to renounce a title.* **2** (*tr*) to repudiate: *to renounce Christianity.* **3** (*tr*) to give up (some habit, pursuit, etc.) voluntarily: *to renounce smoking.* **4** (*intr*) *Cards.* to fail to follow suit because one has no cards of the suit led. ♦ *n* **5** *Rare.* a failure to follow suit in a card game. [C14: from Old French *renoncer,* from Latin *renuntiāre* to disclaim, from RE- + *nuntiāre* to announce, from *nuntius* messenger] ► **re'nouncement** *n* ► **re'nouncer** *n*

renovate ('rɛnəˌveɪt) *vb* (*tr*) **1** to restore (something) to good condition: *to renovate paintings.* **2** to revive or refresh (one's spirits, health, etc.). [C16: from Latin *renovāre,* from RE- + *novāre* to make new, from *novus* NEW] ► **ˌreno'vation** *n* ► **'renoˌvative** *adj* ► **'renoˌvator** *n*

renown (rɪ'naʊn) *n* widespread reputation, esp. of a good kind; fame. [C14: from Anglo-Norman *renoun,* from Old French *renom,* from *renomer* to celebrate, from RE- + *nomer* to name, from Latin *nōmināre*] ► **re'nowned** *adj*

rensselaerite ('rɛnsələˌraɪt, ˌrɛnsə'lɛəraɪt) *n* a white or yellow compact variety of talc, used for ornaments. [C19: named after Stephen Van *Rensselaer* (1764–1839), American army officer and politician]

rent[1] (rɛnt) *n* **1** a payment made periodically by a tenant to a landlord or owner for the occupation or use of land, buildings, or other property, such as a telephone. **2** *Economics.* **2a** that portion of the national income accruing to owners of land and real property. **2b** the return derived from the cultivation of land in excess of production costs. **2c** See **economic rent. 3 for rent.** *Chiefly U.S. and Canadian.* available for use and occupation subject to the payment of rent. ♦ *vb* **4** (*tr*) to grant (a person) the right to use one's property in return for periodic payments. **5** (*tr*) to occupy or use (property) in return for periodic payments. **6** (*intr;* often foll. by *at*) to be let or rented (for a specified rental). [C12: from Old French *rente* revenue, from Vulgar Latin *rendere* (unattested) to yield; see RENDER] ► **ˌrenta'bility** *n* ► **'rentable** *adj*

rent[2] (rɛnt) *n* **1** a slit or opening made by tearing or rending; tear. **2** a breach or division, as in relations. ♦ *vb* **3** the past tense and past participle of **rend.**

rent-a- *prefix* **1** denoting a rental service. **2** *Derogatory or facetious.* denoting a person or group that performs a function as if hired from a rental service: *rent-a-mob.*

rental ('rɛntᵊl) *n* **1a** the amount paid by a tenant as rent. **1b** an income derived from rents received. **2** property available for renting. **3** a less common name for **rent-roll.** ♦ *adj* **4** of or relating to rent.

rent boy *n* a young male prostitute.

rent control *n* regulation by law of the rent a landlord can charge for domestic accommodation and of his right to evict tenants.

rente *French.* (rɑ̃t) *n* **1** annual income from capital investment; annuity. **2** government securities of certain countries, esp. France. **3** the interest on such securities.

renter ('rɛntə) *n* **1** a person who lets his property in return for rent, esp. a landlord. **2** a person who rents property from another; tenant. **3** a distributor of films to cinemas for commercial showing.

rent-free *adj, adv* without payment of rent.

rentier *French.* (rɑ̃tje) *n* **a** a person whose income consists primarily of fixed un-

re'name *vb*	ˌrene'gotiˌate *vb*	ˌrenegoti'ation *n*	ˌrenomi'nation *n*

earned amounts, such as rent or bond interest. **b** (*as modifier*): *the rentier class.* [from *rente;* see RENT[1]]

rent-roll *n* **1** a register of lands and buildings owned by a person, company, etc., showing the rent due and total amount received from each tenant. **2** the total income arising from rented property.

renunciation (rɪˌnʌnsɪˈeɪʃən) *n* **1** the act or an instance of renouncing. **2** a formal declaration renouncing something. **3** *Stock Exchange.* the surrender to another of the rights to buy new shares in a rights issue. [C14: from Latin *renunciātiō* a declaration, from *renuntiāre* to report, RENOUNCE] ▸ **reˈnunciative** *or* **reˈnunciatory** *adj*

renvoi (rɛnˈvɔɪ) *n* the referring of a dispute or other legal question to a jurisdiction other than that in which it arose. [C17: from French: a sending back, from *renvoyer,* from RE- + *envoyer* to send; see ENVOY[1]]

rep[1] *or* **repp** (rɛp) *n* a silk, wool, rayon, or cotton fabric with a transversely corded surface. [C19: from French *reps,* perhaps from English *ribs;* see RIB[1]] ▸ **repped** *adj*

rep[2] (rɛp) *n Theatre.* short for **repertory (company)**.

rep[3] (rɛp) *n* short for **representative** (senses 2, 5).

rep[4] (rɛp) *n U.S. informal.* short for **reputation.**

rep. *abbrev. for:* **1** report. **2** reported. **3** reporter. **4** representative. **5** reprint.

Rep. *abbrev. for:* **1** *U.S.* Representative. **2** *U.S.* Republican. **3** Republic.

repair[1] (rɪˈpɛə) *vb* (*tr*) **1** to restore (something damaged or broken) to good condition or working order. **2** to heal (a breach or division) in (something): *to repair a broken marriage.* **3** to make good or make amends for (a mistake, injury, etc.). ◆ *n* **4** the act, task, or process of repairing. **5** a part that has been repaired. **6** state or condition: *in good repair.* [C14: from Old French *reparer,* from Latin *reparāre,* from RE- + *parāre* to make ready] ▸ **reˈpairable** *adj* ▸ **reˈpairer** *n*

repair[2] (rɪˈpɛə) *vb* (*intr*) **1** (usually foll. by *to*) to go (to a place): *to repair to the country.* **2** (usually foll. by *to*) to have recourse (to) for help, etc.: *to repair to one's lawyer.* **3** (usually foll. by *from*) *Archaic.* to come back; return. ◆ *n Archaic.* **4** the act of going or returning. **5** a haunt or resort. [C14: from Old French *repairier,* from Late Latin *repatriāre* to return to one's native land, from Latin RE- + *patria* fatherland; compare REPATRIATE]

repairman (rɪˈpɛəˌmæn) *n, pl* **-men.** a man whose job it is to repair machines, appliances, etc.

repand (rɪˈpænd) *adj Botany.* having a wavy margin: *a repand leaf.* [C18: from Latin *repandus* bent backwards, from RE- + *pandus* curved] ▸ **reˈpandly** *adv*

reparable (ˈrɛpərəbᵊl, ˈrɛprə-) *adj* able to be repaired, recovered, or remedied: *a reparable loss.* [C16: from Latin *reparābilis,* from *reparāre* to REPAIR[1]] ▸ **ˌreparaˈbility** *n* ▸ **ˈreparably** *adv*

reparation (ˌrɛpəˈreɪʃən) *n* **1** the act or process of making amends: *an injury admitting of no reparation.* **2** (*usually pl*) compensation exacted as an indemnity from a defeated nation by the victors: esp. the compensation demanded of Germany by the Treaty of Versailles after World War I. **3** the act or process of repairing or state of having been repaired. [C14 *reparacioun,* ultimately from Latin *reparāre* to REPAIR[1]] ▸ **reparative** (rɪˈpærətɪv) *or* **reˈparatory** *adj*

repartee (ˌrɛpɑːˈtiː) *n* **1** a sharp, witty, or aphoristic remark made as a reply. **2** terse rapid conversation consisting of such remarks. **3** skill in making sharp witty replies or conversation. [C17: from French *repartie,* from *repartir* to retort, from RE- + *partir* to go away]

repartition (ˌriːpɑːˈtɪʃən) *n* **1** distribution or allotment. **2** the act or process of distributing afresh. ◆ *vb* **3** (*tr*) to divide up again; reapportion or reallocate.

repast (rɪˈpɑːst) *n* **1** a meal or the food provided at a meal: *a light repast.* **2** *Archaic.* **2a** food in general; nourishment. **2b** the act of taking food or refreshment. ◆ *vb* **3** (*intr*) *Archaic.* to feed (on). [C14: from Old French, from *repaistre* to feed, from Late Latin *repāscere* to nourish again, from Latin RE- + *pāscere* to feed, pasture (of animals)]

repatriate *vb* (*tr*) (riːˈpætrɪˌeɪt). **1** to send back (a refugee, prisoner of war, etc.) to the country of his birth or citizenship. **2** to send back (a sum of money previously invested abroad) to its country of origin. ◆ *n* (riːˈpætrɪɪt). **3** a person who has been repatriated. [C17: from Late Latin *repatriāre,* from Latin RE- + *patria* fatherland; compare REPAIR[2]] ▸ **reˌpatriˈation** *n*

repay (rɪˈpeɪ) *vb* **-pays, -paying, -paid.** **1** to pay back (money) to (a person); refund or reimburse. **2** to make a return for (something) by way of compensation: *to repay kindness.* ▸ **reˈpayable** *adj* ▸ **reˈpayment** *n*

repeal (rɪˈpiːl) *vb* (*tr*) **1** to annul or rescind officially (something previously ordered); revoke: *these laws were repealed.* **2** *Obsolete.* to call back (a person) from exile. ◆ *n* **3** an instance or the process of repealing; annulment. [C14: from Old French *repeler,* from RE- + *apeler* to call, APPEAL] ▸ **reˈpealable** *adj* ▸ **reˈpealer** *n*

Repeal (rɪˈpiːl) *n* (esp. in the 19th century) the proposed dissolution of the Union between Great Britain and Ireland.

repeat (rɪˈpiːt) *vb* **1** (when *tr, may take a clause as object*) to say or write (something) again, either once or several times; restate or reiterate. **2** to do or experience (something) again once or several times. **3** (*intr*) to occur more than once: *the last figure repeats.* **4** (*tr; may take a clause as object*) to reproduce (the words, sounds, etc.) uttered by someone else; echo. **5** (*tr*) to utter (a poem, speech, etc.) from memory; recite. **6** (*intr*) **6a** (of food) to be tasted again after ingestion as the result of belching or slight regurgitation. **6b** to belch. **7** (*tr; may take a clause as object*) to tell to another person (the words, esp. secrets, imparted to one by someone else). **8** (*intr*) (of a clock) to strike the hour or quarter-hour just past, when a spring is pressed. **9** (*intr*) *U.S.* to vote (illegally) more than once in a single election. **10 repeat oneself.** to say or do the same thing more than once, esp. so as to be tedious. ◆ *n* **11a** the act or an instance of repeating. **11b** (*as modifier*): *a repeat performance.* **12** a word, action, etc., that is repeated. **13** an order made out for goods, provisions, etc., that duplicates a previous order. **14** a duplicate copy of something; reproduction. **15** *Radio, television.* a second broadcast of a programme, film, etc., which has already been broadcast before. **16** *Music.* a passage that is an exact restatement of the passage preceding it. [C14: from Old French *repeter,* from Latin *repetere* to seek again, from RE- + *petere* to seek] ▸ **reˌpeataˈbility** *n* ▸ **reˈpeatable** *adj*

USAGE Since *again* is part of the meaning of *repeat,* one should not say something is *repeated again.*

repeated (rɪˈpiːtɪd) *adj* done, made, or said again and again; continual or incessant. ▸ **reˈpeatedly** *adv*

repeater (rɪˈpiːtə) *n* **1** a person or thing that repeats. **2** Also called: **repeating firearm.** a firearm capable of discharging several shots without reloading. **3** a timepiece having a mechanism enabling it to strike the hour or quarter-hour just past, when a spring is pressed. **4** *Electrical engineering.* a device that amplifies or augments incoming electrical signals and retransmits them, thus compensating for transmission losses. **5** Also called: **substitute.** *Nautical.* one of three signal flags hoisted with others to indicate that one of the top three is to be repeated.

repeating decimal *n* another name for **recurring decimal.**

repechage (ˌrɛpɪˈʃɑːʒ) *n* a heat of a competition, esp. in rowing or fencing, in which eliminated contestants have another chance to qualify for the next round or the final. [C19: from French *repêchage* literally: fishing out again, from RE- + *pêcher* to fish + -AGE]

repel (rɪˈpɛl) *vb* **-pels, -pelling, -pelled.** (*mainly tr*) **1** to force or drive back (something or somebody, esp. an attacker). **2** (*also intr*) to produce a feeling of aversion or distaste in (someone or something); be disgusting (to). **3** to push aside; dismiss: *he repelled the suggestion as wrong and impossible.* **4** to be effective in keeping away, controlling, or resisting: *an aerosol spray that repels flies.* **5** to have no affinity for; fail to mix with or absorb: *water and oil repel each other.* **6** to disdain to accept (something); turn away from or spurn: *she repelled his advances.* **7** (*also intr*) to exert an opposing force on (something): *an electric charge repels another charge of the same sign.* [C15: from Latin *repellere,* from RE- + *pellere* to push, drive] ▸ **reˈpeller** *n*

USAGE See at **repulse.**

repellent (rɪˈpɛlənt) *adj* **1** giving rise to disgust or aversion; distasteful or repulsive. **2** driving or forcing away or back; repelling. ◆ *n also* **repellant.** **3** something, esp. a chemical substance, that repels: *insect repellent.* **4** a substance with which fabrics are treated to increase their resistance to water. ▸ **reˈpellence** *or* **reˈpellency** *n* ▸ **reˈpellently** *adv*

repent[1] (rɪˈpɛnt) *vb* to feel remorse (for); be contrite (about); show penitence (for): *he repents of his extravagance; he repented his words.* [C13: from Old French *repentir,* from RE- + *pentir* to be contrite, from Latin *paenitēre* to repent] ▸ **reˈpenter** *n*

repent[2] (ˈriːpᵊnt) *adj Botany.* lying or creeping along the ground; reptant: *repent stems.* [C17: from Latin *rēpere* to creep]

repentance (rɪˈpɛntəns) *n* **1** remorse or contrition for one's past actions or sins. **2** an act or the process of being repentant; penitence.

repentant (rɪˈpɛntənt) *adj* **1** reproaching oneself for one's past actions or sins; contrite. **2** characterized by or proceeding from a sense of contrition: *a repentant heart; his repentant words.* ▸ **reˈpentantly** *adv*

repercussion (ˌriːpəˈkʌʃən) *n* **1** (*often pl*) a result or consequence, esp. one that is somewhat removed from the action or event which precipitated it: *the repercussions of the war are still keenly felt.* **2** a recoil after impact; a rebound. **3** a reflection, esp. of sound; echo or reverberation. **4** *Music.* the reappearance of a fugal subject and answer after an episode. [C16: from Latin *repercussiō,* from *repercutere* to strike back; see PERCUSSION] ▸ **ˌreperˈcussive** *adj*

repertoire (ˈrɛpəˌtwɑː) *n* **1** all the plays, songs, operas, or other works collectively that a company, actor, singer, dancer, etc., has prepared and is competent to perform. **2** the entire stock of things available in a field or of a kind: *the comedian's repertoire of jokes was becoming stale.* **3 in repertoire.** denoting the performance of two or more plays, ballets, etc., by the same company in the same venue on different evenings over a period of time: *"Nutcracker" returns to Covent Garden over Christmas in repertoire with "Giselle".* [C19: from French, from Late Latin *repertōrium* inventory; see REPERTORY]

repertory (ˈrɛpətərɪ, -trɪ) *n, pl* **-ries.** **1** the entire stock of things available in a field or of a kind; repertoire. **2** a building or place where a stock of things is kept; repository. **3** short for **repertory company.** [C16: from Late Latin *repertōrium* storehouse, from Latin *reperīre* to obtain, from RE- + *parere* to bring forth] ▸ **ˌreperˈtorial** *adj*

repertory company *n* a theatrical company that performs plays from a repertoire, esp. at its own theatre. U.S. name: **stock company.**

repertory society *n N.Z.* a group that supports amateur performances of plays by its members.

reˈnumber *vb*
ˌreoccuˈpation *n*
reˈoccuˌpy *vb,* **-ˌpies, -ˌpying, -ˌpied.**
ˌreocˈcur *vb,* **-ˈcurs, -ˈcurring, -ˈcurred.**
ˌreocˈcurrence *n*
reˈopen *vb*
reˈorder *vb*
ˌreorganiˌzation *or* **ˌreorganiˈsation** *n*
reˈorganˌize *or* **reˈorganˌise** *vb*
reˈoriˌent *vb*
ˌreorienˈtation *n*
reˈpack *vb*
reˈpackage *vb*
reˈpaint *vb, n*
reˈpaper *vb*
reˈpeople *vb*

repetend ('rɛpɪˌtɛnd, ˌrɛpɪ'tɛnd) *n* **1** *Maths.* the digit or series of digits in a recurring decimal that repeats itself. **2** anything repeated. [C18: from Latin *repetendum* what is to be repeated, from *repetere* to REPEAT]

répétiteur *French.* (repetitœr) *n* a member of an opera company who accompanies rehearsals on the piano and coaches the singers. ▸ ***répétiteuse*** (repetitœz) *fem n*

repetition (ˌrɛpɪ'tɪʃən) *n* **1** the act or an instance of repeating; reiteration. **2** a thing, word, action, etc., that is repeated. **3** a replica or copy. **4** *Civil and Scots Law.* the recovery or repayment of money paid or received by mistake, as when the same bill has been paid twice.

repetitious (ˌrɛpɪ'tɪʃəs) *adj* characterized by unnecessary repetition. ▸ **ˌrepe'titiously** *adv* ▸ **ˌrepe'titiousness** *n*

repetitive (rɪ'pɛtɪtɪv) *adj* characterized by or given to unnecessary repetition; boring: *dull, repetitive work.* ▸ **re'petitively** *adv* ▸ **re'petitiveness** *n*

repetitive strain *or* **stress injury** *n* a condition, characterized by arm or wrist pains, that can affect musicians, computer operators, etc., who habitually perform awkward hand movements. Abbrev.: **RSI**.

rephrase (riː'freɪz) *vb* (*tr*) to phrase again, esp. so as to express more clearly.

repine (rɪ'paɪn) *vb* (*intr*) to be fretful or low-spirited through discontent. [C16: from RE- + PINE[2]]

repique (rɪ'piːk) *Piquet.* ◆ *n* **1** a score of 30 points made from the cards held by a player before play begins. ◆ *vb* **2** to score a repique against (someone). [from French *repiq*]

replace (rɪ'pleɪs) *vb* (*tr*) **1** to take the place of; supersede: *the manual worker is being replaced by the machine.* **2** to substitute a person or thing for (another which has ceased to fulfil its function); put in place of: *to replace an old pair of shoes.* **3** to put back or return; restore to its rightful place. ▸ **re'placeable** *adj* ▸ **reˌplacea'bility** *n* ▸ **re'placer** *n*

replacement (rɪ'pleɪsmənt) *n* **1** the act or process of replacing. **2** a person or thing that replaces another. **3** *Geology.* the growth of a mineral within another of different chemical composition by gradual simultaneous deposition and removal.

replant (riː'plɑːnt) *vb* (*tr*) **1** to plant again: *she replanted the bulbs that the dog had dug up.* **2** to reattach (a severed limb or part) by surgery.

replantation (ˌriːplæn'teɪʃən) *n* the reattachment of (severed limbs or parts) by surgery.

replay *n* ('riːˌpleɪ). **1** Also called: **action replay.** *Television.* a showing again of a sequence of action, esp. of part of a sporting contest immediately after it happens either in slow motion (a **slow-motion replay**) or at normal speed. **2** a rematch. ◆ *vb* (riː'pleɪ). **3** to play again (a record, television sequence, sporting contest, etc.).

replenish (rɪ'plɛnɪʃ) *vb* (*tr*) **1** to make full or complete again by supplying what has been used up or is lacking. **2** to put fresh fuel on (a fire). [C14: from Old French *replenir,* from RE- + *plenir* to fill, from Latin *plēnus* full] ▸ **re'plenisher** *n* ▸ **re'plenishment** *n*

replete (rɪ'pliːt) *adj* (*usually postpositive*) **1** (often foll. by *with*) copiously supplied (with); abounding (in). **2** having one's appetite completely or excessively satisfied by food and drink; stuffed; gorged; satiated. [C14: from Latin *replētus,* from *replēre* to refill, from RE- + *plēre* to fill] ▸ **re'pletely** *adv* ▸ **re'pleteness** *n*

repletion (rɪ'pliːʃən) *n* **1** the state or condition of being replete; fullness, esp. excessive fullness due to overeating. **2** the satisfaction of a need or desire.

replevin (rɪ'plɛvɪn) *Law.* ◆ *n* **1** the recovery of goods unlawfully taken, made subject to establishing the validity of the recovery in a legal action and returning the goods if the decision is adverse. **2** (formerly) a writ of replevin. ◆ *vb* **3** another word for **replevy.** [C15: from Anglo-French, from Old French *replevir* to give security for, from RE- + *plevir* to PLEDGE]

replevy (rɪ'plɛvɪ) *Law.* ◆ *vb* **-plevies, -plevying, -plevied.** (*tr*) **1** to recover possession of (goods) by replevin. ◆ *n, pl* **-plevies. 2** another word for **replevin.** [C15: from Old French *replevir; see* REPLEVIN] ▸ **re'pleviable** *or* **re'plevisable** *adj*

replica ('rɛplɪkə) *n* an exact copy or reproduction, esp. on a smaller scale. [C19: from Italian, literally: a reply, from *replicare* to repeat, from Latin: to bend back, repeat]

replicate *vb* ('rɛplɪˌkeɪt). (*mainly tr*) **1** (*also intr*) to make or be a copy of; reproduce. **2** to fold (something) over on itself; bend back. **3** to reply to. ◆ *adj* ('rɛplɪkɪt). **4** folded back on itself: *a replicate leaf.* [C19: from Latin *replicātus* bent back; see REPLICA] ▸ **'replicative** *adj*

replication (ˌrɛplɪ'keɪʃən) *n* **1** a reply or response. **2** *Law.* (formerly) the plaintiff's reply to a defendant's answer or plea. **3** *Biology.* the production of exact copies of complex molecules, such as DNA molecules, that occurs during growth of living tissue. **4** repetition of a procedure, such as a scientific experiment, in order to reduce errors. **5** a less common word for **replica.** [C14: via Old French from Latin *replicātiō* a folding back, from *replicāre* to unroll; see REPLY]

replicon ('rɛplɪˌkɒn) *n Genetics.* a region of a DNA molecule that is replicated from a single origin.

reply (rɪ'plaɪ) *vb* **-plies, -plying, -plied.** (*mainly intr*) **1** to make answer (to) in words or writing or by an action; respond: *he replied with an unexpected move.* **2** (*tr; takes a clause as object*) to say (something) in answer: *he replied that he didn't want to come.* **3** *Law.* to answer a defendant's plea. **4** to return (a sound); echo. ◆ *n, pl* **-plies. 5** an answer made in words or writing or through an action; response. **6** the answer made by a plaintiff or petitioner to a defendant's case. [C14: from Old French *replier* to fold again, reply, from Latin *replicāre* to fold back, from RE- + *plicāre* to fold] ▸ **re'plier** *n*

repo ('riːpəʊ) *n Informal* short for: **1** repurchase agreement. **2a** repossession of property. **2b** (*as modifier*): *a repo car.*

repoint (ˌriː'pɔɪnt) *vb* (*tr*) to repair the joints of (brickwork, masonry, etc.) with mortar or cement.

repone (rɪ'pəʊn) *vb* (*tr*) *Scots Law.* to restore (someone) to his former status, office, etc.; rehabilitate. [C16: from Latin *repōnere* to put back, replace]

report (rɪ'pɔːt) *n* **1** an account prepared for the benefit of others, esp. one that provides information obtained through investigation and published in a newspaper or broadcast. **2** a statement made widely known; rumour: *according to report, he is not dead.* **3** an account of the deliberations of a committee, body, etc.: *a report of parliamentary proceedings.* **4** *Brit.* a statement on the progress, academic achievement, etc., of each child in a school, written by teachers and sent to the parents or guardian annually or each term. **5** a written account of a case decided at law, giving the main points of the argument on each side, the court's findings, and the decision reached. **6** comment on a person's character or actions; reputation: *he is of good report here.* **7** a sharp loud noise, esp. one made by a gun. ◆ *vb* (when *tr, may take a clause as object;* when *intr,* often foll. by *on*) **8** to give an account (of); describe. **9** to give an account of the results of an investigation (into): *to report on housing conditions.* **10** (of a committee, legislative body, etc.) to make a formal report on (a bill). **11** (*tr*) to complain about (a person), esp. to a superior: *I'll report you to the teacher.* **12** (*tr*) to reveal information about (a fugitive, escaped prisoner, etc.) esp. concerning his whereabouts. **13** (*intr*) to present oneself or be present at an appointed place or for a specific purpose: *report to the manager's office.* **14** (*intr*) to say or show that one is (in a certain state): *to report fit.* **15** (*intr;* foll. by *to*) to be responsible to and under the authority of: *the plant manager reports to the production controller.* **16** (*intr*) to act as a reporter for a newspaper or for radio or television. **17** *Law.* to take down in writing details of (the proceedings of a court of law) as a record or for publication. [C14: from Old French, from *reporter* to carry back, from Latin *reportāre,* from RE- + *portāre* to carry] ▸ **re'portable** *adj*

reportage (rɪ'pɔːtɪdʒ, ˌrəpɔː'tɑːʒ) *n* **1** the act or process of reporting news or other events of general interest. **2** a journalist's style of reporting. **3** a technique of documentary film or photo journalism that tells a story entirely through pictures.

reported clause *n Grammar.* a bound clause that reports what someone has said or thought, bound to a main clause that contains a verb of saying or thinking.

reportedly (rɪ'pɔːtɪdlɪ) *adv* according to rumour or report: *he is reportedly living in Australia.*

reported speech *n* another term for **indirect speech.**

reporter (rɪ'pɔːtə) *n* **1** a person who reports, esp. one employed to gather news for a newspaper, news agency, or broadcasting organization. **2** a person, esp. a barrister, authorized to write official accounts of judicial proceedings. **3** a person authorized to report the proceedings of a legislature. **4** (in Scotland) *Social welfare.* an official who arranges and conducts children's panel hearings and who may investigate cases and decide on the action to be taken.

reportorial (ˌrɛpɔː'tɔːrɪəl) *adj Chiefly U.S.* of or relating to a newspaper reporter. [C20: from REPORTER, influenced by EDITORIAL] ▸ **repor'torially** *adv*

report stage *n* the stage preceding the third reading in the passage of a bill through Parliament, at which the bill, as amended in committee, is reported back to the chamber considering it.

repose[1] (rɪ'pəʊz) *n* **1** a state of quiet restfulness; peace or tranquillity. **2** dignified calmness of manner; composure. ◆ *vb* **3** to place (oneself or one's body) in a state of quiet relaxation; lie or lay down at rest. **4** (*intr*) to lie when dead, as in the grave. **5** (*intr;* foll. by *on, in,* etc.) *Formal.* to take support (from) or be based (on): *your plan reposes on a fallacy.* [C15: from Old French *reposer,* from Late Latin *repausāre,* from RE- + *pausāre* to stop; see PAUSE] ▸ **re'posal** *n* ▸ **re'poser** *n* ▸ **re'poseful** *adj* ▸ **re'posefully** *adv* ▸ **re'posefulness** *n*

repose[2] (rɪ'pəʊz) *vb* (*tr*) **1** to put (trust or confidence) in a person or thing. **2** to place or put (an object) somewhere. [C15: from Latin *repōnere* to store up, from RE- + *pōnere* to put] ▸ **re'posal** *n*

reposit (rɪ'pɒzɪt) *vb* (*tr*) to put away, deposit, or store up. [C17: from Latin *repositus* replaced, from *repōnere;* see REPOSE[2], POSIT]

reposition (ˌriːpə'zɪʃən) *n* **1** the act or process of depositing or storing. **2** *Surgery.* the return of a broken or displaced organ, or part to its normal site. **3** *Archaic.* the reinstatement of a person in a post or office. ◆ *vb* (*tr*) **4** to place in a new position. **5** to target (a product or brand) at a new market by changing its image.

repository (rɪ'pɒzɪtərɪ, -trɪ) *n, pl* **-ries. 1** a place or container in which things can be stored for safety. **2** a place where things are kept for exhibition; museum. **3** a place where commodities are kept before being sold; warehouse. **4** a place of burial; sepulchre. **5** a receptacle containing the relics of the dead. **6** a person to whom a secret is entrusted; confidant. [C15: from Latin *repositōrium,* from *repōnere* to place]

repossess (ˌriːpə'zɛs) *vb* (*tr*) **1** to take back possession of (property), esp. for nonpayment of money due under a hire-purchase agreement. **2** to restore ownership of (something) to someone. ▸ **repossession** (ˌriːpə'zɛʃən) *n* ▸ **ˌrepos'sessor** *n*

repot (riː'pɒt) *vb* **-pots, -potting, -potted.** (*tr*) to put (a house plant) into a new usually larger pot.

re'photoˌgraph *vb*	**re'pin** *vb,* **-'pins, -'pinning, -'pinned.**	**re'plan** *vb,* **-'plans, -'planning, -'planned.**	**re'popuˌlate** *vb*

repoussé (rəˈpu:seɪ) *adj* **1** raised in relief, as a design on a thin piece of metal hammered through from the underside. **2** decorated with such designs. ◆ *n* **3** a design or surface made in this way. **4** the technique of hammering designs in this way. [C19: from French, from *repousser* to push back, from RE- + *pousser* to PUSH]

repp (rɛp) *n* a variant spelling of **rep**[1].

repr. *abbrev. for:* **1** represented. **2** representing. **3** reprint(ed).

reprehend (ˌrɛprɪˈhɛnd) *vb (tr)* to find fault with; criticize. [C14: from Latin *reprehendere* to hold fast, rebuke, from RE- + *prendere* to grasp] ▸ **ˌrepreˈhendable** *adj* ▸ **ˌrepreˈhender** *n*

reprehensible (ˌrɛprɪˈhɛnsəbᵊl) *adj* open to criticism or rebuke; blameworthy. [C14: from Late Latin *reprehensibilis,* from Latin *reprehendere* to hold back, reprove; see REPREHEND] ▸ **ˌrepreˌhensiˈbility** *or* **ˌrepreˈhensibleness** *n* ▸ **ˌrepreˈhensibly** *adv*

reprehension (ˌrɛprɪˈhɛnʃən) *n* the act or an instance of reprehending; reproof or rebuke. ▸ **ˌrepreˈhensive** *or (rarely)* **ˌrepreˈhensory** *adj* ▸ **ˌrepreˈhensively** *adv*

represent (ˌrɛprɪˈzɛnt) *vb (tr)* **1** to stand as an equivalent of; correspond to: *our tent represents home to us when we go camping.* **2** to act as a substitute or proxy (for). **3** to act as or be the authorized delegate or agent for (a person, country, etc.): *an MP represents his constituency.* **4** to serve or use as a means of expressing: *letters represent the sounds of speech.* **5** to exhibit the characteristics of; exemplify; typify: *romanticism in music is represented by Beethoven.* **6** to present an image of through the medium of a picture or sculpture; portray. **7** to bring clearly before the mind. **8** to set forth in words; state or explain. **9** to describe as having a specified character or quality; make out to be: *he represented her as a saint.* **10** to act out the part of on stage; portray. **11** to perform or produce (a play); stage. [C14: from Latin *repraesentāre* to exhibit, from RE- + *praesentāre* to PRESENT[2]] ▸ **ˌrepreˈsentable** *adj* ▸ **ˌrepreˌsentaˈbility** *n*

re-present (ˌri:prɪˈzɛnt) *vb (tr)* to present again. ▸ **re-presentation** (ˌri:prɛzənˈteɪʃən) *n*

representation (ˌrɛprɪzɛnˈteɪʃən) *n* **1** the act or an instance of representing or the state of being represented. **2** anything that represents, such as a verbal or pictorial portrait. **3** anything that is represented, such as an image brought clearly to mind. **4** the principle by which delegates act for a constituency. **5** a body of representatives. **6** *Contract law.* an assertion of fact made by one party to induce another to enter into a contract. **7** an instance of acting for another, on his authority, in a particular capacity, such as executor or administrator. **8** a dramatic production or performance. **9** *(often pl)* a statement of facts, true or alleged, esp. one set forth by way of remonstrance or expostulation. **10** *Linguistics.* an analysis of a word, sentence, etc., into its constituents: *phonetic representation.*

representational (ˌrɛprɪzɛnˈteɪʃənᵊl) *adj* **1** *Fine art.* depicting or attempting to depict objects, scenes, figures, etc., directly as seen; naturalistic. **2** of or relating to representation.

representationalism (ˌrɛprɪzɛnˈteɪʃənəˌlɪzəm) *or* **representationism** *n* **1** *Philosophy.* the doctrine that in perceptions of objects what is before the mind is not the object but a representation of it. Compare **presentationism, naive realism.** See also **barrier of ideas. 2** *Fine art.* the practice or advocacy of attempting to depict objects, scenes, figures, etc., directly as seen. ▸ **ˌrepresenˌtationalˈistic** *adj* ▸ **ˌrepresenˈtationist** *n, adj*

representative (ˌrɛprɪˈzɛntətɪv) *n* **1** a person or thing that represents another or others. **2** a person who represents and tries to sell the products or services of a firm, esp. a travelling salesman. Often shortened to **rep. 3** a typical example. **4** a person representing a constituency in a deliberative, legislative, or executive body, esp. *(cap.)* a member of the **House of Representatives** (the lower house of Congress). **5** *N.Z.* a rugby player, football player, etc., chosen to represent a province in interprovincial sports. ◆ *adj* **6** serving to represent; symbolic. **7a** exemplifying a class or kind; typical: *a representative example of the species.* **7b** containing or including examples of all the interests, types, etc., in a group: *a representative collection.* **8** acting as deputy or proxy for another or others. **9** acting for or representing a constituency or the whole people in the process of government: *a representative council.* **10** of, characterized by, or relating to the political principle of representation of the people: *representative government.* **11** of or relating to a mental picture or representation. ▸ **ˌrepreˈsentatively** *adv* ▸ **ˌrepreˈsentativeness** *n*

repress (rɪˈprɛs) *vb (tr)* **1** to keep (feelings, etc.) under control; suppress or restrain: *to repress a desire.* **2** to put into a state of subjugation: *to repress a people.* **3** *Psychoanal.* to banish (thoughts and impulses that conflict with conventional standards of conduct) from one's conscious mind. [C14: from Latin *reprimere* to press back, from RE- + *premere* to PRESS[1]] ▸ **reˈpresser** *n* ▸ **reˈpressible** *adj* ▸ **reˈpressive** *adj* ▸ **reˈpressively** *adv* ▸ **reˈpressiveness** *n*

repressed (rɪˈprɛst) *adj* (of a person) repressing feelings, instincts, desires, etc.

repression *n* **1** the act or process of repressing or the condition of being repressed. **2** *Psychoanal.* the subconscious rejection of thoughts and impulses that conflict with conventional standards of conduct. Compare **suppression** (sense 2).

repressor (rɪˈprɛsə) *n Biochem.* a protein synthesized under the control of a repressor gene, which has the capacity to bind to the operator gene and thereby shut off the expression of the structural genes of the operon.

reprieve (rɪˈpri:v) *vb (tr)* **1** to postpone or remit the punishment of (a person, esp. one condemned to death). **2** to give temporary relief to (a person or thing), esp. from otherwise irrevocable harm: *the government has reprieved the company with a huge loan.* ◆ *n* **3** a postponement or remission of punishment, esp. of a person condemned to death. **4** a warrant granting a postponement. **5** a temporary relief from pain or harm; respite. **6** the act of reprieving or the state of being reprieved. [C16: from Old French *repris* (something) taken back, from *reprendre* to take back, from Latin *reprehendere;* perhaps also influenced by obsolete English *repreve* to reprove] ▸ **reˈprievable** *adj* ▸ **reˈpriever** *n*

reprimand (ˈrɛprɪˌmɑ:nd) *n* **1** a reproof or formal admonition; rebuke. ◆ *vb* **2** *(tr)* to admonish or rebuke, esp. formally; reprove. [C17: from French *réprimande,* from Latin *reprimenda* (things) to be repressed; see REPRESS]

reprint *n* (ˈri:ˌprɪnt). **1** a reproduction in print of any matter already published; offprint. **2** a reissue of a printed work using the same type, plates, etc., as the original. ◆ *vb* (ri:ˈprɪnt). **3** *(tr)* to print again. ▸ **reˈprinter** *n*

reprisal (rɪˈpraɪzᵊl) *n* **1** *(often pl)* retaliatory action against an enemy in wartime, such as the execution of prisoners of war, destruction of property, etc. **2** the act or an instance of retaliation in any form. **3** (formerly) the forcible seizure of the property or subjects of one nation by another. [C15: from Old French *reprisaille,* from Old Italian *ripresaglia,* from *riprendere* to recapture, from Latin *reprehendere* to hold fast; see REPREHEND]

reprise (rɪˈpri:z) *Music.* ◆ *n* **1** the repeating of an earlier theme. ◆ *vb* **2** to repeat (an earlier theme). [C14: from Old French, from *reprendre* to take back, from Latin *reprehendere;* see REPREHEND]

repro (ˈri:prəʊ) *n, pl* **-pros. 1** short for **reproduction** (sense 2): *repro furniture.* **2** short for **reproduction proof.**

reproach (rɪˈprəʊtʃ) *vb (tr)* **1** to impute blame to (a person) for an action or fault; rebuke. **2** *Archaic.* to bring disgrace or shame upon. ◆ *n* **3** the act of reproaching. **4** rebuke or censure; reproof: *words of reproach.* **5** disgrace or shame: *to bring reproach upon one's family.* **6** something that causes or merits blame, rebuke, or disgrace. **7 above** *or* **beyond reproach.** perfect; beyond criticism. [C15: from Old French *reprochier,* from Latin RE- + *prope* near] ▸ **reˈproachable** *adj* ▸ **reˈproachableness** *n* ▸ **reˈproachably** *adv* ▸ **reˈproacher** *n*

reproachful (rɪˈprəʊtʃfʊl) *adj* **1** full of or expressing reproach. **2** *Archaic.* deserving of reproach; disgraceful. ▸ **reˈproachfully** *adv* ▸ **reˈproachfulness** *n*

reprobate (ˈrɛprəʊˌbeɪt) *adj* **1** morally unprincipled; depraved. **2** *Christianity.* destined or condemned to eternal punishment in hell. ◆ *n* **3** an unprincipled, depraved, or damned person. **4** a disreputable or roguish person: *the old reprobate.* ◆ *vb (tr)* **5** to disapprove of; condemn. **6** (of God) to destine, consign, or condemn to eternal punishment in hell. [C16: from Late Latin *reprobātus* held in disfavour, from Latin RE- + *probāre* to APPROVE[1]] ▸ **reprobacy** (ˈrɛprəbəsɪ) *n* ▸ **ˈreproˌbater** *n*

reprobation (ˌrɛprəʊˈbeɪʃən) *n* **1** disapproval, blame, or censure. **2** *Christianity.* condemnation to eternal punishment in hell; rejection by God. ▸ **reprobative** (ˈrɛprəbətɪv) *or* **ˌreproˈbationary** *adj* ▸ **ˈreprobatively** *adv*

reproduce (ˌri:prəˈdju:s) *vb (mainly tr)* **1** to make a copy, representation, or imitation of; duplicate. **2** *(also intr) Biology.* to undergo or cause to undergo a process of reproduction. **3** to produce or exhibit again. **4** to bring back into existence again; re-create. **5** to bring before the mind again (a scene, event, etc.) through memory or imagination. **6** *(intr)* to come out (well, badly, etc.), when copied. **7** to replace (damaged parts or organs) by a process of natural growth; regenerate. **8** to cause (a sound or television recording) to be heard or seen. ▸ **ˌreproˈducible** *adj* ▸ **ˌreproˈducibly** *adv* ▸ **ˌreproˌduciˈbility** *n*

reproducer (ˌri:prəˈdju:sə) *n* **1** a person or thing that makes reproductions. **2** a complete sound reproduction system. **3** another name for **loudspeaker.**

reproduction (ˌri:prəˈdʌkʃən) *n* **1** *Biology.* any of various processes, either sexual or asexual, by which an animal or plant produces one or more individuals similar to itself. **2a** an imitation or facsimile of a work of art, esp. of a picture made by photoengraving. **2b** *(as modifier): a reproduction portrait.* Sometimes shortened to **repro. 3** the quality of sound from an audio system: *this amplifier gives excellent reproduction.* **4** the act or process of reproducing. **5** the state of being reproduced. **6** a revival of an earlier production, as of a play.

reproduction proof *n Printing.* a proof of very good quality used for photographic reproduction to make a printing plate. Sometimes shortened to **repro** or **repro proof.**

reproductive (ˌri:prəˈdʌktɪv) *adj* of, relating to, characteristic of, or taking part in reproduction. ▸ **ˌreproˈductively** *adv* ▸ **ˌreproˈductiveness** *n*

reprography (rɪˈprɒgrəfɪ) *n* the art or process of copying, reprinting, or reproducing printed material. ▸ **reprographic** (ˌrɛprəˈgræfɪk) *adj* ▸ **ˌreproˈgraphically** *adv*

reproof (rɪˈpru:f) *n* an act or expression of rebuke or censure. Also called: **reproval** (rɪˈpru:vᵊl). [C14 *reproffe,* from Old French *reprove,* from Late Latin *reprobāre* to disapprove of; see REPROBATE]

re-proof (ri:ˈpru:f) *vb (tr)* **1** to treat (a coat, jacket, etc.) so as to renew its texture, waterproof qualities, etc. **2** to provide a new proof of (a book, galley, etc.)

reprove (rɪˈpru:v) *vb (tr)* to speak disapprovingly to (a person); rebuke or scold. [C14: from Old French *reprover,* from Late Latin *reprobāre,* from Latin RE- + *probāre* to examine, APPROVE[1]] ▸ **reˈprovable** *adj* ▸ **reˈprover** *n* ▸ **reˈproving** *adj* ▸ **reˈprovingly** *adv*

rept *abbrev. for:* **1** receipt. **2** report.

reptant (ˈrɛptənt) *adj Biology.* creeping, crawling, or lying along the ground. Also: **repent.** [C17: from Latin *reptāre* to creep]

reptile (ˈrɛptaɪl) *n* **1** any of the cold-blooded vertebrates constituting the class *Reptilia,* characterized by lungs, an outer covering of horny scales or plates, and young produced in amniotic eggs. The class today includes the tortoises,

reˈprocess *vb* **reˈprocessing** *adj*

turtles, snakes, lizards, and crocodiles; in Mesozoic times it was the dominant group, containing the dinosaurs and related forms. **2** a grovelling insignificant person: *you miserable little reptile!* ◆ *adj* **3** creeping, crawling, or squirming. **4** grovelling or insignificant; mean; contemptible. [C14: from Late Latin *reptilis* creeping, from Latin *rēpere* to crawl]

reptilian (rɛp'tɪlɪən) *adj* **1** of, relating to, resembling, or characteristic of reptiles. **2** mean or treacherous; contemptible: *reptilian behaviour.* ◆ *n* **3** a less common name for **reptile.**

Repton ('rɛptᵊn) *n* **Humphry.** 1752–1818, English landscape gardener.

Repub. *abbrev. for:* **1** Republic. **2** Republican.

republic (rɪ'pʌblɪk) *n* **1** a form of government in which the people or their elected representatives possess the supreme power. **2** a political or national unit possessing such a form of government. **3** a constitutional form in which the head of state is an elected or nominated president. **4** any community or group that resembles a political republic in that its members or elements exhibit a general equality, shared interests, etc.: *the republic of letters.* [C17: from French *république,* from Latin *rēspublica* literally: the public thing, from *rēs* thing + *publica* PUBLIC]

republican (rɪ'pʌblɪkən) *adj* **1** of, resembling, or relating to a republic. **2** supporting or advocating a republic. ◆ *n* **3** a supporter or advocate of a republic.

Republican (rɪ'pʌblɪkən) *adj* **1** of, belonging to, or relating to a Republican Party. **2** of, belonging to, or relating to the Irish Republican Army. ◆ *n* **3** a member or supporter of a Republican Party. **4** a member or supporter of the Irish Republican Army.

republicanism (rɪ'pʌblɪkəˌnɪzəm) *n* **1** the principles or theory of republican government. **2** support for a republic. **3** (*often cap.*) support for a Republican Party or for the Irish Republican Army.

republicanize *or* **republicanise** (rɪ'pʌblɪkəˌnaɪz) *vb* (*tr*) to make republican. ▸ **reˌpublicani'zation** *or* **reˌpublicani'sation** *n*

Republican Party *n* **1** the more conservative of the two major political parties in the U.S.: established around 1854. Compare **Democratic Party. 2** any of a number of political parties in other countries, usually so named to indicate their opposition to monarchy. **3** *U.S. history.* another name for the **Democratic-Republican Party.**

Republic of Ireland *n* See **Ireland**[1] (sense 2).

repudiate (rɪ'pjuːdɪˌeɪt) *vb* (*tr*) **1** to reject the authority or validity of; refuse to accept or ratify: *Congress repudiated the treaty that the President had negotiated.* **2** to refuse to acknowledge or pay (a debt). **3** to cast off or disown (a son, lover, etc.). [C16: from Latin *repudiāre* to put away, from *repudium* a separation, divorce, from RE- + *pudēre* to be ashamed] ▸ **re'pudiable** *adj* ▸ **reˌpudi'ation** *n* ▸ **re'pudiative** *adj* ▸ **re'pudiˌator** *n*

repugn (rɪ'pjuːn) *vb Archaic.* to oppose or conflict (with). [C14: from Old French *repugner,* from Latin *repugnāre* to fight against, from RE- + *pugnāre* to fight]

repugnant (rɪ'pʌgnənt) *adj* **1** repellent to the senses; causing aversion. **2** distasteful; offensive; disgusting. **3** contradictory; inconsistent or incompatible. [C14: from Latin *repugnāns* resisting; see REPUGN] ▸ **re'pugnance** *or* (*now rare*) **re'pugnancy** *n* ▸ **re'pugnantly** *adv*

repulse (rɪ'pʌls) *vb* (*tr*) **1** to drive back or ward off (an attacking force); repel; rebuff. **2** to reject with coldness or discourtesy: *she repulsed his advances.* **3** to produce a feeling of aversion or distaste. ◆ *n* **4** the act or an instance of driving back or warding off; rebuff. **5** a cold discourteous rejection or refusal. [C16: from Latin *repellere* to drive back, REPEL] ▸ **re'pulser** *n*

USAGE Some people think that the use of *repulse* in sentences such as *he was repulsed by what he saw* is incorrect and that the correct word is *repel.*

repulsion (rɪ'pʌlʃən) *n* **1** a feeling of disgust or aversion. **2** *Physics.* a force tending to separate two objects, such as the force between two like electric charges or magnetic poles.

repulsive (rɪ'pʌlsɪv) *adj* **1** causing or occasioning repugnance; loathsome; disgusting or distasteful: *a repulsive sight.* **2** tending to repel, esp. by coldness and discourtesy. **3** *Physics.* concerned with, producing, or being a repulsion. ▸ **re'pulsively** *adv* ▸ **re'pulsiveness** *n*

repurchase (riː'pɜːtʃɪs) *vb* (*tr*) **1** to buy back or buy again goods, securities, assets, etc. ◆ *n* **2** an act or instance of repurchasing.

repurchase agreement *n* an agreement in which a security or asset is sold and later repurchased at an agreed price to raise ready money. Sometimes shortened to **repo.**

reputable ('rɛpjʊtəbᵊl) *adj* **1** having a good reputation; honoured, trustworthy, or respectable. **2** (of words) acceptable as good usage; standard. ▸ **ˌreputa'bility** *n* ▸ **'reputably** *adv*

reputation (ˌrɛpjʊ'teɪʃən) *n* **1** the estimation in which a person or thing is generally held; opinion. **2** a high opinion generally held about a person or thing; esteem. **3** notoriety or fame, esp. for some specified characteristic. **4 have a reputation.** to be known or notorious, esp. for promiscuity, excessive drinking, or the like. [C14: from Latin *reputātiō* a reckoning, from *reputāre* to calculate, meditate; see REPUTE] ▸ **ˌrepu'tationless** *adj*

repute (rɪ'pjuːt) *vb* **1** (*tr; usually passive*) to consider (a person or thing) to be as specified: *he is reputed to be intelligent.* ◆ *n* **2** public estimation; reputation: *a writer of little repute.* [C15: from Old French *reputer,* from Latin *reputāre* to think over, from RE- + *putāre* to think]

reputed (rɪ'pjuːtɪd) *adj* (*prenominal*) generally reckoned or considered; supposed or alleged: *he is the reputed writer of a number of romantic poems.* ▸ **re'putedly** *adv*

req. *abbrev. for:* **1** request. **2** required. **3** requisition.

request (rɪ'kwɛst) *vb* (*tr*) **1** to express a desire for, esp. politely; ask for or demand: *to request a bottle of wine.* ◆ *n* **2a** the act or an instance of requesting, esp. in the form of a written statement; petition or solicitation: *a request for a song.* **2b** (*as modifier*): *a request programme.* **3 at the request of.** in accordance with the specific demand or wish of (someone). **4 by request.** in accordance with someone's desire. **5 in request.** in demand; popular: *he is in request in concert halls all over the world.* **6 on request.** on the occasion of a demand or request: *application forms are available on request.* [C14: from Old French *requeste,* from Vulgar Latin *requaerere* (unattested) to seek after; see REQUIRE, QUEST] ▸ **re'quester** *n*

request stop *n* a point on a route at which a bus will stop only if signalled to do so. U.S. equivalent: **flag stop.**

Requiem ('rɛkwɪˌɛm) *n* **1** *R.C. Church.* a Mass celebrated for the dead. **2** a musical setting of this Mass. **3** any piece of music composed or performed as a memorial to a dead person or persons. [C14: from Latin *requiēs* rest, from the opening of the introit, *Requiem aeternam dona eis* Rest eternal grant unto them]

requiem shark *n* any shark of the family *Carcharhinidae,* occurring mostly in tropical seas and characterized by a nictitating membrane and a heterocercal tail. The family includes the tiger shark and the soupfin. [C17: French *requiem* probably assimilated from a native name]

requiescat (ˌrɛkwɪ'ɛskæt) *n* a prayer for the repose of the souls of the dead. [Latin, from *requiescat in pace* may he rest in peace]

require (rɪ'kwaɪə) *vb* (*mainly tr; may take a clause as object or an infinitive*) **1** to have need of; depend upon; want. **2** to impose as a necessity; make necessary: *this work requires precision.* **3** (*also intr*) to make formal request (for); insist upon or demand, esp. as an obligation. **4** to call upon or oblige (a person) authoritatively; order or command: *to require someone to account for his actions.* [C14: from Old French *requerre,* from Vulgar Latin *requaerere* (unattested) to seek after, from Latin *requīrere* to seek to know, but also influenced by *quaerere* to seek] ▸ **re'quirable** *adj* ▸ **re'quirer** *n*

USAGE The use of *require to* as in *I require to see the manager* or *you require to complete a special form* is thought by many people to be incorrect: *I need to see the manager; you are required to complete a special form.*

requirement (rɪ'kwaɪəmənt) *n* **1** something demanded or imposed as an obligation: *Latin is no longer a requirement for entry to university.* **2** a thing desired or needed. **3** the act or an instance of requiring.

requisite ('rɛkwɪzɪt) *adj* **1** absolutely essential; indispensable. ◆ *n* **2** something indispensable; necessity. [C15: from Latin *requisītus* sought after, from *requīrere* to seek for, REQUIRE] ▸ **'requisitely** *adv* ▸ **'requisiteness** *n*

requisition (ˌrɛkwɪ'zɪʃən) *n* **1** a request or demand, esp. an authoritative or formal one. **2** an official form on which such a demand is made. **3** the act of taking something over, esp. temporarily for military or public use in time of emergency. **4** a necessary or essential condition; requisite. **5** a formal request by one government to another for the surrender of a fugitive from justice. ◆ *vb* (*tr*) **6** to demand and take for use or service, esp. by military or public authority. **7** (*may take an infinitive*) to require (someone) formally to do (something): *to requisition a soldier to drive a staff officer's car.* ▸ **ˌrequi'sitionary** *adj*

requital (rɪ'kwaɪtᵊl) *n* **1** the act or an instance of requiting. **2** a return or compensation for a good or bad action.

requite (rɪ'kwaɪt) *vb* (*tr*) to make return to (a person for a kindness or injury); repay with a similar action. [C16: RE- + obsolete *quite* to discharge, repay; see QUIT] ▸ **re'quitable** *adj* ▸ **re'quitement** *n* ▸ **re'quiter** *n*

reradiation (ˌriːreɪdɪ'eɪʃən) *n* radiation resulting from the previous absorption of primary radiation.

reredorter ('rɪəˌdɔːtə) *n History.* a privy at the back of a monastic dormitory.

reredos ('rɪədɒs) *n* **1** a screen or wall decoration at the back of an altar, in the form of a hanging, tapestry, painting, or piece of metalwork or sculpture. **2** another word for **fireback** (sense 1). [C14: from Old French *areredos,* from *arere* behind + *dos* back, from Latin *dorsum*]

reremouse *or* **rearmouse** ('rɪəˌmaʊs) *n, pl* **-mice.** an archaic or dialect word for **bat** (the animal). [Old English *hrēremūs,* probably from *hrēran* to move + *mūs* MOUSE]

rerun *vb* (riː'rʌn), **-runs, -running, -ran.** (*tr*) **1** to broadcast or put on (a film, play, series, etc.) again. **2** to run (a race, etc.) again. ◆ *n* ('riːˌrʌn). **3** a film, play, series, etc., that is broadcast or put on again; repeat. **4** a race that is run again. **5** *Computing.* the repeat of a part of a computer program.

res (reɪs) *n, pl* **res.** *Latin.* a thing, matter, or object.

res. *abbrev. for:* **1** research. **2** reserve. **3** residence. **4** resides. **5** resigned. **6** resolution.

res adjudicata ('reɪs əˌdʒuːdɪ'kɑːtə) *n* another term for **res judicata.**

resale ('riːˌseɪl, riː'seɪl) *n* the selling again of something purchased. ▸ **re'salable** *or* **re'saleable** *adj*

resale price maintenance *n* the practice by which a manufacturer establishes a fixed or minimum price for the resale of a brand product by retailers or other distributors. U.S. equivalent: **fair trade.** Abbrev.: **rpm.**

reschedule (riː'ʃɛdjuːl; *also, esp. U.S.* -skɛdʒʊəl) *vb* (*tr*) **1** to change the time, date, or schedule of. **2** to arrange a revised schedule for repayment of (a debt).

rescind (rɪ'sɪnd) *vb* (*tr*) to annul or repeal. [C17: from Latin *rēscindere* to cut off, from *re-* (intensive) + *scindere* to cut] ▸ **re'scindable** *adj* ▸ **re'scinder** *n* ▸ **re'scindment** *n*

rescissible (rɪ'sɪsəbᵊl) *adj* able to be rescinded.

ˌrepubli'cation *n*
re'read *vb,* **-'reads, -'reading, -'read.**
ˌrere'cord *vb*
ˌrere'cording *n*
re'route *vb*

rescission (rɪˈsɪʒən) *n* **1** the act of rescinding. **2** *Law.* the right to have a contract set aside if it has been entered into mistakenly, as a result of misrepresentation, undue influence, etc.
rescissory (rɪˈsɪsərɪ) *adj* having the power to rescind.
rescript (ˈriːˌskrɪpt) *n* **1** (in ancient Rome) an ordinance taking the form of a reply by the emperor to a question on a point of law. **2** any official announcement or edict; a decree. **3** something rewritten. **4** the act or process of rewriting. [C16: from Latin *rēscriptum* a reply, from *rēscribere* to write back]
rescue (ˈrɛskjuː) *vb* **-cues, -cuing, -cued.** (*tr*) **1** to bring (someone or something) out of danger, attack, harm, etc.; deliver or save. **2** to free (a person) from legal custody by force. **3** *Law.* to seize (goods or property) by force. ◆ *n* **4a** the act or an instance of rescuing. **4b** (*as modifier*): *a rescue party.* **5** the forcible removal of a person from legal custody. **6** *Law.* the forcible seizure of goods or property. [C14: *rescowen,* from Old French *rescourre,* from RE- + *escourre* to pull away, from Latin *excutere* to shake off, from *quatere* to shake] ▸ **ˈrescuable** *adj* ▸ **ˈrescuer** *n*
research (rɪˈsɜːtʃ, ˈriːsɜːtʃ) *n* **1** systematic investigation to establish facts or principles or to collect information on a subject. ◆ *vb* **2** to carry out investigations into (a subject, problem, etc.). [C16: from Old French *recercher* to seek, search again, from RE- + *cercher* to SEARCH] ▸ **reˈsearchable** *adj* ▸ **reˈsearcher** *n*
research and development *n* the part of a commercial company's activity concerned with applying the results of scientific research to develop new products and improve existing ones. Abbrev.: **R & D.**
reseat (riːˈsiːt) *vb* (*tr*) **1** to show (a person) to a new seat. **2** to put a new seat on (a chair, etc.). **3** to provide new seats for (a hall, theatre, etc.). **4** to re-form the seating of (a valve).
reseau (ˈrɛzəʊ) *n, pl* **-seaux** (-zəʊ, -zəʊz) *or* **-seaus. 1** a mesh background to a lace or other pattern. **2** *Astronomy.* a network of fine lines cut into a glass plate used as a reference grid on star photographs. **3** *Photog.* a screen covered in a regular pattern of minute coloured dots or lines, formerly used in colour photography. [C19: from French, from Old French *resel* a little net, from *rais* net, from Latin *rēte*]
resect (rɪˈsɛkt) *vb* (*tr*) *Surgery.* to cut out part of (a bone, an organ, or other structure or part). [C17: from Latin *resecāre* to cut away, from RE- + *secāre* to cut]
resection (rɪˈsɛkʃən) *n* **1** *Surgery.* excision of part of a bone, organ, or other part. **2** *Surveying.* a method of fixing the position of a point by making angular observations to three fixed points. ▸ **reˈsectional** *adj*
reseda (ˈrɛsɪdə) *n* **1** any plant of the genus *Reseda,* of the Mediterranean region, including mignonette and dyer's rocket, which has small spikes of grey-green flowers. ◆ *adj* **2** of a greyish-green colour; mignonette. [C18: from New Latin, from Latin: heal! from *resēdāre* to assuage, from RE- + *sēdāre* to soothe; see SEDATE[2]]
reselect (ˌriːsɪˈlɛkt) *vb* (*tr*) to choose (someone or something) again, esp. to choose an existing office-holder as candidate for re-election. ▸ **ˌreseˈlection** *n*
resemblance (rɪˈzɛmbləns) *n* **1** the state or quality of resembling; likeness or similarity in nature, appearance, etc. **2** the degree or extent to which or the respect in which a likeness exists. **3** something resembling something else; semblance; likeness. ▸ **reˈsemblant** *adj*
resemble (rɪˈzɛmbᵊl) *vb* (*tr*) to possess some similarity to; be like. [C14: from Old French *resembler,* from RE- + *sembler* to look like, from Latin *similis* like] ▸ **reˈsembler** *n*
resent (rɪˈzɛnt) *vb* (*tr*) to feel bitter, indignant, or aggrieved at. [C17: from French *ressentir,* from RE- + *sentir* to feel, from Latin *sentīre* to perceive; see SENSE]
resentful (rɪˈzɛntfʊl) *adj* feeling or characterized by resentment. ▸ **reˈsentfully** *adv* ▸ **reˈsentfulness** *n*
resentment (rɪˈzɛntmənt) *n* anger, bitterness, or ill will.
reserpine (ˈrɛsəpɪn) *n* an insoluble alkaloid, extracted from the roots of the plant *Rauwolfia serpentina,* used medicinally to lower blood pressure and as a sedative and tranquillizer. Formula: $C_{33}H_{40}N_2O_9$; melting pt.: 264–5°C. [C20: from German *Reserpin,* probably from the New Latin name of the plant]
reservation (ˌrɛzəˈveɪʃən) *n* **1** the act or an instance of reserving. **2** something reserved, esp. hotel accommodation, a seat on an aeroplane, in a theatre, etc. **3** (*often pl*) a stated or unstated qualification of opinion that prevents one's wholehearted acceptance of a proposal, claim, statement, etc. **4** an area of land set aside, esp. (in the U.S.) for American Indian peoples. **5** *Brit.* the strip of land between the two carriageways of a dual carriageway. **6** the act or process of keeping back, esp. for oneself; withholding. **7** *Law.* a right or interest retained by the grantor in property granted, conveyed, leased, etc., to another: *a reservation of rent.*
reserve (rɪˈzɜːv) *vb* (*tr*) **1** to keep back or set aside, esp. for future use or contingency; withhold. **2** to keep for oneself; retain: *I reserve the right to question these men later.* **3** to obtain or secure by advance arrangement: *I have reserved two tickets for tonight's show.* **4** to delay delivery of (a judgment), esp. in order to allow time for full consideration of the issues involved. ◆ *n* **5a** something kept back or set aside, esp. for future use or contingency. **5b** (*as modifier*): *a reserve stock.* **6** the state or condition of being reserved: *I have plenty in reserve.* **7** a tract of land set aside for the protection and conservation of wild animals, flowers, etc.: *a nature reserve.* **8** the usual Canadian name for **reservation** (sense 4). **9** *Austral. and N.Z.* an area of publicly owned land set aside for sport, recreation, etc. **10** the act of reserving; reservation. **11** a member of a team who only plays if a playing member drops out; a substitute. **12** (*often pl*) **12a** a part of an army or formation not committed to immediate action in a military engagement. **12b** that part of a nation's armed services not in active service. **13** coolness or formality of manner; restraint, silence, or reticence. **14** *Finance.* **14a** a portion of capital not invested (a **capital reserve**) or a portion of profits not distributed (a **revenue** or **general reserve**) by a bank or business enterprise and held to meet legal requirements, future liabilities, or contingencies. **14b** (*often pl*) liquid assets held by an organization, government, etc., to meet expenses and liabilities. **15 without reserve.** without reservations; fully; wholeheartedly. [C14: from Old French *reserver,* from Latin *reservāre* to save up, from RE- + *servāre* to keep] ▸ **reˈservable** *adj* ▸ **reˈserver** *n*
re-serve (riːˈsɜːv) *vb* (*tr*) to serve again.
reserve bank *n* one of the twelve banks forming part of the U.S. Federal Reserve System.
reserve currency *n* foreign currency that is acceptable as a medium of international payments and that is therefore held in reserve by many countries.
reserved (rɪˈzɜːvd) *adj* **1** set aside for use by a particular person or people: *this table is reserved.* **2** cool or formal in manner; restrained, silent, or reticent. **3** destined; fated: *a man reserved for great things.* ▸ **reservedly** (rɪˈzɜːvɪdlɪ) *adv* ▸ **reˈservedness** *n*
reserved list *n Brit.* a list of retired naval, army, or air-force officers available for recall to active service in an emergency.
reserved occupation *n Brit.* in time of war, an occupation from which one will not be called up for military service.
reserved word *n* a word in a programming language or computer system that has a fixed meaning and therefore cannot be redefined by a programmer.
reserve-grade *adj Austral.* denoting a sporting team of the second rank in a club.
reserve price *n Brit.* the minimum price acceptable to the owner of property being auctioned or sold. Also called (esp. Scot. and U.S.): **upset price.**
reserve tranche *n* the quota of 25 per cent to which a member of the IMF has unconditional access. Prior to 1978 it was paid in gold and known as the **gold tranche.**
reservist (rɪˈzɜːvɪst) *n* one who serves in the reserve formations of a nation's armed forces.
reservoir (ˈrɛzəˌvwɑː) *n* **1** a natural or artificial lake or large tank used for collecting and storing water, esp. for community water supplies or irrigation. **2** a receptacle for storing gas, esp. one attached to a stove. **3** *Biology.* a vacuole or cavity in an organism, containing a secretion or some other fluid. **4** *Anatomy.* another name for **cisterna. 5** a place where a great stock of anything is accumulated. **6** a large supply of something; reserve: *a reservoir of talent.* [C17: from French *réservoir,* from *réserver* to RESERVE]
reset[1] *vb* (riːˈsɛt), **-sets, -setting, -set.** (*tr*) **1** to set again (a broken bone, matter in type, a gemstone, etc.). **2** to restore (a gauge, dial, etc.) to zero. **3** Also: **clear.** to restore (the contents of a register or similar device) in a computer system to zero. ◆ *n* (ˈriːˌsɛt). **4** the act or an instance of setting again. **5** a thing that is set again. **6** a plant that has been recently transplanted. **7** a device for resetting instruments, controls, etc. ▸ **reˈsetter** *n*
reset[2] *Scot.* ◆ *vb* (riːˈsɛt). **-sets, -setting, -set. 1** to receive or handle goods knowing they have been stolen. ◆ *n* (ˈriːsɛt). **2** the receiving of stolen goods. [C14: from Old French *receter,* from Latin *receptāre,* from *recipere* to receive] ▸ **reˈsetter** *n*
res gestae (ˈreɪs ˈdʒɛstiː) *pl n* **1** things done or accomplished; achievements. **2** *Law.* incidental facts and circumstances that are admissible in evidence because they introduce or explain the matter in issue. [Latin]
resh (reɪʃ; *Hebrew* reʃ) *n* the 20th letter in the Hebrew alphabet (ר), transliterated as *r.* [from Hebrew, from *rōsh* head]
Resht (rɛʃt) *n* a variant of **Rasht.**
reshuffle (riːˈʃʌfᵊl) *n* **1** an act of shuffling again. **2** a reorganization, esp. of jobs within a government or cabinet. ◆ *vb* **3** to carry out a reshuffle (on).
reside (rɪˈzaɪd) *vb* (*intr*) *Formal.* **1** to live permanently or for a considerable time (in a place); have one's home (in): *he now resides in London.* **2** (of things, qualities, etc.) to be inherently present (in); be vested (in): *political power resides in military strength.* [C15: from Latin *residēre* to sit back, from RE- + *sedēre* to sit] ▸ **reˈsider** *n*
residence (ˈrɛzɪdəns) *n* **1** the place in which one resides; abode or home. **2** a large imposing house; mansion. **3** the fact of residing in a place or a period of residing. **4** the official house of the governor of any of various countries. **5** the state of being officially present. **6 in residence. 6a** actually resident: *the royal standard indicates that the Queen is in residence.* **6b** designating a creative artist resident for a set period at a university, college, etc., whose role is to stimulate an active interest in the subject: *composer in residence.* **7** the seat of some inherent quality, characteristic, etc.
residency (ˈrɛzɪdənsɪ) *n, pl* **-cies. 1** a variant of **residence. 2** a regular series of concerts by a band or singer at one venue. **3** *U.S. and Canadian.* the period, following internship, during which a physician undergoes further clinical training, usually in one medical speciality. **4** (in India, formerly) the official house of the governor general at the court of a native prince.
resident (ˈrɛzɪdənt) *n* **1** a person who resides in a place. **2** *Social welfare.* an occupant of a welfare agency home. Former name: **inmate. 3** (esp. formerly) a representative of the British government in a British protectorate. **4** (esp. in the

reˈseal *vb*
reˈsealable *adj*
re-ˈsearch *vb*
reˈsell *vb,* **-ˈsells, -ˈselling, -ˈsold.**
reˈsettle *vb*
reˈsettlement *n*
reˈshape *vb*
reˈship *vb,* **-ˈships, -ˈshipping, -ˈshipped.**

17th century) a diplomatic representative ranking below an ambassador. **5** (in India, formerly) a representative of the British governor general at the court of a native prince. **6** a bird or other animal that does not migrate. **7** *U.S. and Canadian.* a physician who lives in the hospital where he works while undergoing specialist training after completing his internship. Compare **house physician. 8** *Brit. and N.Z.* a junior doctor who lives in the hospital where he works. ◆ *adj* **9** living in a place; residing. **10** living or staying at a place in order to discharge a duty, etc. **11** (of qualities, characteristics, etc.) existing or inherent (in). **12** (of birds and other animals) not in the habit of migrating. ► **'resident,ship** *n*

resident commissioner *n* the representative of Puerto Rico in the U.S. House of Representatives. He may speak but has no vote.

residential (ˌrezɪ'denʃəl) *adj* **1** suitable for or allocated for residence: *a residential area.* **2** relating to or having residence. ► **ˌresi'dentially** *adv*

residential care *n Social welfare.* the provision by a welfare agency of a home with social-work supervision for people who need more than just housing accommodation, such as children in care or mentally handicapped adults.

residential school *n* (in Canada) a boarding school maintained by the Canadian government for Indian and Inuit children from sparsely populated settlements.

residentiary (ˌrezɪ'denʃərɪ) *adj* **1** residing in a place, esp. officially; resident. **2** subject to an obligation to reside in an official residence: *a residentiary benefice.* ◆ *n, pl* **-tiaries. 3** a clergyman obliged to reside in the place of his official appointment.

residents association *n* an organization composed of voluntary members living in a particular neighbourhood, which aims to improve the social and communal facilities of the neighbourhood and to conserve or improve its environmental advantages. See also **community association, tenants association.**

residual (rɪ'zɪdjʊəl) *adj* **1** of, relating to, or designating a residue or remainder; remaining; left over. **2** (of deposits, soils, etc.) formed by the weathering of pre-existing rocks and the removal of disintegrated material. **3** of or relating to the payment of residuals. ◆ *n* **4** something left over as a residue; remainder. **5** *Statistics.* **5a** the difference between the mean of a set of observations and one particular observation. **5b** the difference between the numerical value of one particular observation and the theoretical result. **6** (*often pl*) payment made to an actor, actress, musician, etc., for subsequent use of film in which the person appears. ► **re'sidually** *adv*

residual current device *n* a circuit-breaking device installed in electrical equipment to protect the operator from electrocution. Abbrev.: **RCD.**

residual unemployment *n* the unemployment that remains in periods of full employment, as a result of those mentally, physically, or emotionally unfit to work.

residuary (rɪ'zɪdjʊərɪ) *adj* **1** of, relating to, or constituting a residue; residual. **2** *Law.* entitled to the residue of an estate after payment of debts and distribution of specific gifts.

residue ('rezɪˌdjuː) *n* **1** matter remaining after something has been removed. **2** *Law.* what is left of an estate after the discharge of debts and distribution of specific gifts. **[C14:** from Old French *residu,* from Latin *residuus* remaining over, from *residēre* to stay behind, RESIDE**]**

residuum (rɪ'zɪdjʊəm) *n, pl* **-ua** (-jʊə). a more formal word for **residue.**

resign (rɪ'zaɪn) *vb* **1** (when *intr,* often foll. by *from*) to give up tenure of (a job, office, etc.). **2** (*tr*) to reconcile (oneself) to; yield: *to resign oneself to death.* **3** (*tr*) to give up (a right, claim, etc.); relinquish: *he resigned his claim to the throne.* **[C14:** from Old French *resigner,* from Latin *resignāre* to unseal, invalidate, destroy, from RE- + *signāre* to seal; see SIGN**]** ► **re'signer** *n*

re-sign (riː'saɪn) *vb* to sign (a document, etc.) again.

resignation (ˌrezɪg'neɪʃən) *n* **1** the act of resigning. **2** a formal document stating one's intention to resign. **3** a submissive unresisting attitude; passive acquiescence.

resigned (rɪ'zaɪnd) *adj* characteristic of or proceeding from an attitude of resignation; acquiescent or submissive. ► **resignedly** (rɪ'zaɪnɪdlɪ) *adv* ► **re'signedness** *n*

resile (rɪ'zaɪl) *vb* (*intr*) to spring or shrink back; recoil or resume original shape. **[C16:** from Old French *resilir,* from Latin *resilīre* to jump back, from RE- + *salīre* to jump**]** ► **re'silement** *n*

resilience (rɪ'zɪlɪəns) *n* **1** Also called: **resiliency.** the state or quality of being resilient. **2** *Ecology.* the ability of an ecosystem to return to its original state after being disturbed. **3** *Physics.* the amount of potential energy stored in an elastic material when deformed.

resilient (rɪ'zɪlɪənt) *adj* **1** (of an object or material) capable of regaining its original shape or position after bending, stretching, compression, or other deformation; elastic. **2** (of a person) recovering easily and quickly from shock, illness, hardship, etc.; irrepressible. ► **re'siliently** *adv*

resin ('rezɪn) *n* **1** any of a group of solid or semisolid amorphous compounds that are obtained directly from certain plants as exudations. They are used in medicine and in varnishes. **2** any of a large number of synthetic, usually organic, materials that have a polymeric structure, esp. such a substance in a raw state before it is moulded or treated with plasticizer, stabilizer, filler, etc. Compare **plastic** (sense 1). ◆ *vb* **3** (*tr*) to treat or coat with resin. **[C14:** from Old French *resine,* from Latin *rēsīna,* from Greek *rhētinē* resin from a pine**]** ► **'resinous** *adj* ► **'resinously** *adv* ► **'resinousness** *n*

resinate ('rezɪˌneɪt) *vb* (*tr*) to impregnate with resin.

resiniferous (ˌrezɪ'nɪfərəs) *adj* yielding or producing resin.

resinoid ('rezɪˌnɔɪd) *adj* **1** resembling, characteristic of, or containing resin. ◆ *n* **2** any resinoid substance, esp. a synthetic compound.

resipiscence (ˌresɪ'pɪsəns) *n Literary.* acknowledgment that one has been mistaken. **[C16:** from Late Latin *resipiscentia,* from *resipiscere* to recover one's senses, from Latin *sapere* to know**]** ► **ˌresi'piscent** *adj*

res ipsa loquitur (reɪs ˌɪpsɑː 'lɒkwɪtə) *Law.* the thing or matter speaks for itself. **[**Latin**]**

resist (rɪ'zɪst) *vb* **1** to stand firm (against); not yield (to); fight (against). **2** (*tr*) to withstand the deleterious action of; be proof against: *to resist corrosion.* **3** (*tr*) to oppose; refuse to accept or comply with: *to resist arrest; resist the introduction of new technology.* **4** (*tr*) to refrain from, esp. in spite of temptation (esp. in the phrases **cannot** *or* **could not resist** (**something**)). ◆ *n* **5** a substance used to protect something, esp. a coating that prevents corrosion. **[C14:** from Latin *resistere* to stand still, oppose, from RE- + *sistere* to stand firm**]** ► **re'sister** *n* ► **re'sistible** *adj* ► **reˌsisti'bility** *n* ► **re'sistibly** *adv*

resistance (rɪ'zɪstəns) *n* **1** the act or an instance of resisting. **2** the capacity to withstand something, esp. the body's natural capacity to withstand disease. **3a** the opposition to a flow of electric current through a circuit component, medium, or substance. It is the magnitude of the real part of the impedance and is measured in ohms. Symbol: *R* Compare **reactance** (sense 1). **3b** (*as modifier*): *resistance coupling; a resistance thermometer.* **4** any force that tends to retard or oppose motion: *air resistance; wind resistance.* **5** (in psychoanalytical theory) the tendency of a person to prevent the translation of repressed thoughts and ideas from the unconscious to the conscious and esp. to resist the analyst's attempt to bring this about. **6** *Physics.* the magnitude of the real part of the acoustic or mechanical impedance. **7 line of least resistance.** the easiest, but not necessarily the best or most honourable, course of action. **8** See **passive resistance.**

Resistance (rɪ'zɪstəns) *n* **the.** an illegal organization fighting for national liberty in a country under enemy occupation, esp. in France during World War II.

resistance thermometer *n* an accurate type of thermometer in which temperature is calculated from the resistance of a coil of wire (usually of platinum) or of a semiconductor placed at the point at which the temperature is to be measured.

resistance welding *n* a welding technique in which the parts to be joined are held together under pressure and heat is produced by passing a current through the contact resistance formed between the two surfaces.

resistant (rɪ'zɪstənt) *adj* **1** characterized by or showing resistance; resisting. **2a** impervious to the action of corrosive substances, heat, etc.: *a highly resistant surface.* **2b** (*in combination*): *a heat-resistant surface.* ◆ *n* **3** a person or thing that resists.

Resistencia (*Spanish* resis'tenθja) *n* a city in NE Argentina, on the Paraná River. Pop.: 292 350 (1991).

resistive (rɪ'zɪstɪv) *adj* **1** another word for **resistant. 2** exhibiting electrical resistance.

resistivity (ˌriːzɪs'tɪvɪtɪ) *n* **1** the electrical property of a material that determines the resistance of a piece of given dimensions. It is equal to RA/l, where R is the resistance, A the cross-sectional area, and l the length, and is the reciprocal of conductivity. It is measured in ohms. Symbol: ρ Former name: **specific resistance. 2** the power or capacity to resist; resistance.

resistless (rɪ'zɪstlɪs) *adj Archaic.* **1** unresisting. **2** irresistible. ► **re'sistlessly** *adv*

resistor (rɪ'zɪstə) *n* an electrical component designed to introduce a known value of resistance into a circuit.

resit *vb* (riː'sɪt), **-sits, -sitting, -sat.** (*tr*) **1** to sit (an examination) again. ◆ *n* ('riːsɪt). **2** an examination taken again by a person who has not been successful in a previous attempt.

res judicata ('reɪs ˌdʒuːdɪ'kɑːtə) *or* **res adjudicata** *n Law.* a matter already adjudicated upon that cannot be raised again. **[**Latin**]**

reskill (riː'skɪl) *vb* (*tr*) to train (workers) to acquire new or improved skills. ► **re'skilling** *n*

Resnais (*French* rɛnɛ) *n* **Alain** (alɛ̃). born 1922, French film director, whose films include *Hiroshima mon amour* (1959), *L'Année dernière à Marienbad* (1961), *La Vie est un roman* (1983), and *On Connaît la Chanson* (1998).

resnatron ('reznəˌtrɒn) *n* a tetrode used to generate high power at high frequencies. **[C20:** from RESONATOR + -TRON**]**

resoluble (rɪ'zɒljub$^{\circ}$l, 'rezəl-) *adj* another word for **resolvable.**

re-soluble (riː'sɒljub$^{\circ}$l) *adj* capable of being dissolved again. ► **re-'solubleness** *or* **re-ˌsolu'bility** *n* ► **re-'solubly** *adv*

resolute ('rezəˌluːt) *adj* **1** firm in purpose or belief; steadfast. **2** characterized by resolution; determined: *a resolute answer.* **[C16:** from Latin *resolutus,* from *resolvere* to RESOLVE**]** ► **'resoˌlutely** *adv* ► **'resoˌluteness** *n*

resolution (ˌrezə'luːʃən) *n* **1** the act or an instance of resolving. **2** the condition or quality of being resolute; firmness or determination. **3** something resolved or determined; decision. **4** a formal expression of opinion by a meeting, esp. one agreed by a vote. **5** a judicial decision on some matter; verdict; judgment. **6** the act or process of separating something into its constituent parts or elements. **7** *Med.* **7a** return from a pathological to a normal condition. **7b** subsidence of the symptoms of a disease, esp. the disappearance of inflammation without the formation of pus. **8** *Music.* the process in harmony whereby a dissonant note or chord is followed by a consonant one. **9** the ability of a television or film image to reproduce fine detail. **10** *Physics.* another word for **resolving power.** ► **ˌreso'lutioner** *or* **ˌreso'lutionist** *n*

resolutive (rɪ'zɒljutɪv) *adj* **1** capable of dissolving; causing disintegration. **2** *Law.* denoting a condition the fulfilment of which terminates a contract or other legal obligation.

resolvable (rɪ'zɒlvəb$^{\circ}$l) *or* **resoluble** *adj* able to be resolved or analysed. ► **reˌsolva'bility, reˌsolu'bility** *or* **re'solvableness, re'solubleness** *n*

resolve (rɪ'zɒlv) *vb* (*mainly tr*) **1** (*takes a clause as object or an infinitive*) to decide or determine firmly. **2** to express (an opinion) formally, esp. (of a public meeting) one agreed by a vote. **3** (*also intr;* usually foll. by *into*) to separate or cause to separate (into) (constituent parts or elements). **4** (*usually reflexive*) to change, alter, or appear to change or alter: *the ghost resolved itself into a tree.* **5**

to make up the mind of; cause to decide: *the tempest resolved him to stay at home.* **6** to find the answer or solution to; solve: *to resolve a problem.* **7** to explain away or dispel: *to resolve a doubt.* **8** to bring to an end; conclude: *to resolve an argument.* **9** *Med.* to cause (a swelling or inflammation) to subside, esp. without the formation of pus. **10** (*also intr*) to follow (a dissonant note or chord) or (of a dissonant note or chord) to be followed by one producing a consonance. **11** *Chem.* to separate (a racemic mixture) into its optically active constituents. **12** *Physics.* **12a** to distinguish between (separate parts) of (an image) as in a microscope, telescope, or other optical instrument. **12b** to separate (two adjacent peaks) in a spectrum by means of a spectrometer. **13** *Maths.* to split (a vector) into its components in specified directions. **14** an obsolete word for **dissolve.** ◆ *n* **15** something determined or decided; resolution: *he had made a resolve to work all day.* **16** firmness of purpose; determination: *nothing can break his resolve.* [C14: from Latin *resolvere* to unfasten, reveal, from RE- + *solvere* to loosen; see SOLVE] ▸ **re'solver** *n*

resolved (rɪ'zɒlvd) *adj* fixed in purpose or intention; determined. ▸ **resolvedly** (rɪ'zɒlvɪdlɪ) *adv* ▸ **re'solvedness** *n*

resolvent (rɪ'zɒlvənt) *adj* **1** serving to dissolve or separate something into its elements; resolving. ◆ *n* **2** something that resolves; solvent. **3** a drug or agent able to reduce swelling or inflammation.

resolving power *n* **1** Also called: **resolution.** *Physics.* **1a** the ability of a microscope, telescope, or other optical instrument to produce separate images of closely placed objects. **1b** the ability of a spectrometer to separate two adjacent peaks in a spectrum. **2** *Photog.* the ability of an emulsion to show up fine detail in an image.

resonance ('rɛzənəns) *n* **1** the condition or quality of being resonant. **2** sound produced by a body vibrating in sympathy with a neighbouring source of sound. **3** the condition of a body or system when it is subjected to a periodic disturbance of the same frequency as the natural frequency of the body or system. At this frequency the system displays an enhanced oscillation or vibration. **4** amplification of speech sounds by sympathetic vibration in the bone structure of the head and chest, resounding in the cavities of the nose, mouth, and pharynx. **5** *Electronics.* the condition of an electrical circuit when the frequency is such that the capacitive and inductive reactances are equal in magnitude. In a series circuit there is then maximum alternating current whilst in a parallel circuit there is minimum alternating current. **6** *Med.* the sound heard when tapping a hollow bodily structure, esp. the chest or abdomen. Change in the quality of the sound often indicates an underlying disease or disorder. **7** *Chem.* the phenomenon in which the electronic structure of a molecule can be represented by two or more hypothetical structures involving single, double, and triple chemical bonds. The true structure is considered to be an average of these theoretical structures. **8** *Physics.* **8a** the condition of a system in which there is a sharp maximum probability for the absorption of electromagnetic radiation or capture of particles. **8b** a type of elementary particle of extremely short lifetime. Resonances are regarded as excited states of more stable particles. [C16: from Latin *resonāre* to RESOUND]

resonant ('rɛzənənt) *adj* **1** (of sound) resounding or re-echoing. **2** producing or enhancing resonance, as by sympathetic vibration. **3** characterized by resonance. ▸ **'resonantly** *adv*

resonant cavity *n* another name for **cavity resonator.**

resonate ('rɛzəˌneɪt) *vb* **1** to resound or cause to resound; reverberate. **2** (of a mechanical system, electrical circuit, chemical compound, etc.) to exhibit or cause to exhibit resonance. [C19: from Latin *resonāre*] ▸ **ˌreso'nation** *n*

resonator ('rɛzəˌneɪtə) *n* any body or system that displays resonance, esp. a tuned electrical circuit or a conducting cavity in which microwaves are generated by a resonant current.

resorb (rɪ'sɔːb) *vb* (*tr*) to absorb again. [C17: from Latin *resorbēre,* from RE- + *sorbēre* to suck in; see ABSORB] ▸ **re'sorbent** *adj* ▸ **re'sorptive** *adj*

resorcinol (rɪ'zɔːsɪˌnɒl) *n* a colourless crystalline phenol with a sweet taste, used in making dyes, drugs, resins, and adhesives. Formula: $C_6H_4(OH)_2$; relative density: 1.27; melting pt.: 111°C; boiling pt. at 1 atm.: 276 °C. [C19: New Latin, from RESIN + ORCINOL] ▸ **re'sorcinal** *adj*

resorption (rɪ'sɔːpʃən) *n* **1** the process of resorbing or the state of being resorbed. **2** *Geology.* the remelting of a mineral by magma, resulting in a new crystal form being produced.

resort (rɪ'zɔːt) *vb* (*intr*) **1** (usually foll. by *to*) to have recourse (to) for help, use, etc.: *to resort to violence.* **2** to go, esp. often or habitually; repair: *to resort to the beach.* ◆ *n* **3** a place to which many people go for recreation, rest, etc.: *a holiday resort.* **4** the use of something as a means, help, or recourse. **5** the act of going to a place, esp. for recreation, rest, etc. **6 last resort.** the last possible course of action open to one. [C14: from Old French *resortir* to come out again, from RE- + *sortir* to emerge] ▸ **re'sorter** *n*

re-sort (riː'sɔːt) *vb* (*tr*) to sort again.

resound (rɪ'zaʊnd) *vb* (*intr*) **1** to ring or echo with sound; reverberate: *the hall resounded with laughter.* **2** to make a prolonged echoing noise: *the trumpet resounded.* **3** (of sounds) to echo or ring. **4** to be widely famous: *his achievements resounded throughout India.* [C14: from Old French *resoner,* from Latin *resonāre* to sound again]

re-sound (riː'saʊnd) *vb* to sound or cause to sound again.

resounding (rɪ'zaʊndɪŋ) *adj* **1** clear and emphatic; unmistakable: *a resounding vote of confidence.* **2** full of or characterized by resonance; reverberating: *a resounding slap.* ▸ **re'soundingly** *adv*

resource (rɪ'zɔːs, -'sɔːs) *n* **1** capability, ingenuity, and initiative; quick-wittedness: *a man of resource.* **2** (*often pl*) a source of economic wealth, esp. of a country (mineral, land, labour, etc.) or business enterprise (capital, equipment, personnel, etc.). **3** a supply or source of aid or support; something resorted to in time of need. **4** a means of doing something; expedient. [C17: from Old French *ressourse* relief, from *resourdre* to rise again, from Latin *resurgere,* from RE- + *surgere* to rise] ▸ **re'sourceless** *adj* ▸ **re'sourcelessness** *n*

resourceful (rɪ'zɔːsfʊl, -'sɔːs-) *adj* ingenious, capable, and full of initiative, esp. in dealing with difficult situations. ▸ **re'sourcefully** *adv* ▸ **re'sourcefulness** *n*

resp. *abbrev. for:* **1** respective(ly). **2** respondent.

respect (rɪ'spɛkt) *n* **1** an attitude of deference, admiration, or esteem; regard. **2** the state of being honoured or esteemed. **3** a detail, point, or characteristic; particular: *he differs in some respects from his son.* **4** reference or relation (esp. in the phrases **in respect of, with respect to**). **5** polite or kind regard; consideration: *respect for people's feelings.* **6** (*often pl*) an expression of esteem or regard (esp. in the phrase **pay one's respects**). ◆ *vb* (*tr*) **7** to have an attitude of esteem towards; show or have respect for: *to respect one's elders.* **8** to pay proper attention to; not violate: *to respect Swiss neutrality.* **9** to show consideration for; treat courteously or kindly. **10** *Archaic.* to concern or refer to. [C14: from Latin *rēspicere* to look back, pay attention to, from RE- + *specere* to look]

respectable (rɪ'spɛktəbᵊl) *adj* **1** having or deserving the respect of other people; estimable; worthy. **2** having good social standing or reputation. **3** having socially or conventionally acceptable morals, standards, etc.: *a respectable woman.* **4** relatively or fairly good; considerable: *a respectable salary.* **5** fit to be seen by other people; presentable. ▸ **reˌspecta'bility** *or* (*less commonly*) **re'spectableness** *n* ▸ **re'spectably** *adv*

respecter (rɪ'spɛktə) *n* **1** a person who respects someone or something. **2 no respecter of persons.** a person whose attitude and behaviour is uninfluenced by consideration of another's rank, power, wealth, etc.

respectful (rɪ'spɛktfʊl) *adj* full of, showing, or giving respect. ▸ **re'spectfully** *adv* ▸ **re'spectfulness** *n*

respecting (rɪ'spɛktɪŋ) *prep* concerning; regarding.

respective (rɪ'spɛktɪv) *adj* **1** belonging or relating separately to each of several people or things; several: *we took our respective ways home.* **2** an archaic word for **respectful.** ▸ **re'spectiveness** *n*

respectively (rɪ'spɛktɪvlɪ) *adv* (in listing a number of items or attributes that refer to another list) separately in the order given: *he gave Janet and John a cake and a chocolate respectively.*

Respighi (*Italian* res'piːgi) *n* **Ottorino** (otto'riːno). 1879–1936, Italian composer, noted esp. for his suites *The Fountains of Rome* (1917) and *The Pines of Rome* (1924).

respirable ('rɛspɪrəbᵊl) *adj* **1** able to be breathed. **2** suitable or fit for breathing. ▸ **ˌrespira'bility** *n*

respiration (ˌrɛspə'reɪʃən) *n* **1** the process in living organisms of taking in oxygen from the surroundings and giving out carbon dioxide (**external respiration**). In terrestrial animals this is effected by breathing air. **2** the chemical breakdown of complex organic substances, such as carbohydrates and fats, that takes place in the cells and tissues of animals and plants, during which energy is released and carbon dioxide produced (**internal respiration**). ▸ **respiratory** ('rɛspərətərɪ, -trɪ) *or* (*rarely*) **ˌrespi'rational** *adj*

respirator ('rɛspəˌreɪtə) *n* **1** an apparatus for providing long-term artificial respiration. **2** Also called: **gas mask.** a device worn over the mouth and nose to prevent inhalation of noxious fumes or to warm cold air before it is breathed.

respiratory failure *n* a condition in which the respiratory system is unable to provide an adequate supply of oxygen or to remove carbon dioxide efficiently.

respiratory quotient *n Biology.* the ratio of the volume of carbon dioxide expired to the volume of oxygen consumed by an organism, tissue, or cell in a given time.

respiratory system *n* the specialized organs, collectively, concerned with external respiration: in humans and other mammals it includes the trachea, bronchi, bronchioles, lungs, and diaphragm.

respire (rɪ'spaɪə) *vb* **1** to inhale and exhale (air); breathe. **2** (*intr*) to undergo the process of respiration. **3** *Literary.* to breathe again in a relaxed or easy manner, as after stress or exertion. [C14: from Latin *rēspīrāre* to exhale, from RE- + *spīrāre* to breathe; see SPIRIT[1]]

respite ('rɛspɪt, -paɪt) *n* **1** a pause from exertion; interval of rest. **2** a temporary delay. **3** a temporary stay of execution; reprieve. ◆ *vb* **4** (*tr*) to grant a respite to; reprieve. [C13: from Old French *respit,* from Latin *respectus* a looking back; see RESPECT] ▸ **'respiteless** *adj*

respite care *n Social welfare.* occasional usually planned residential care for dependent old or handicapped people, to provide relief for their permanent carers.

resplendent (rɪ'splɛndənt) *adj* having a brilliant or splendid appearance. [C15: from *rēsplendēre* to shine brightly, from RE- + *splendēre* to shine; see SPLENDOUR] ▸ **re'splendence** *or* **re'splendency** *n* ▸ **re'splendently** *adv*

respond (rɪ'spɒnd) *vb* **1** to state or utter (something) in reply. **2** (*intr*) to act in reply; react: *to respond by issuing an invitation.* **3** (*intr;* foll. by *to*) to react favourably: *this patient will respond to treatment.* **4** an archaic word for **correspond.** ◆ *n* **5** *Architect.* a pilaster or an engaged column that supports an arch or a lintel. **6** *Christianity.* a choral anthem chanted in response to a lesson read at a church service. [C14: from Old French *respondre,* from Latin *rēspondēre* to return like for like, from RE- + *spondēre* to pledge; see SPOUSE, SPONSOR] ▸ **re'spondence** *or* **re'spondency** *n* ▸ **re'sponder** *n*

respondent (rɪ'spɒndənt) *n* **1** *Law.* a person against whom a petition, esp. in a divorce suit, or appeal is brought. ◆ *adj* **2** a less common word for **responsive.**

responsa (rɪ'spɒnsə) *n Judaism.* **1** the plural of **responsum. 2** that part of rabbinic literature concerned with written rulings in answer to questions.

response (rɪ'spɒns) *n* **1** the act of responding; reply or reaction. **2** *Bridge.* a bid replying to a partner's bid or double. **3** (*usually pl*) *Christianity.* a short sentence or phrase recited or sung by the choir or congregation in reply to the officiant at a church service. **4** *Electronics.* the ratio of the output to the input level, at a particular frequency, of a transmission line or electrical device. **5** any pattern of glandular, muscular, or electrical reactions that arises from stimulation of the nervous system. [C14: from Latin *rēsponsum* answer, from *rēspondēre* to RESPOND] ▸ **re'sponseless** *adj*

responser *or* **responsor** (rɪ'spɒnsə) *n* a radio or radar receiver used in conjunction with an interrogator to receive and display signals from a transponder.

response time *n Computing.* the length of time taken by a system to respond to an instruction.

response variable *n Statistics.* a more modern term for **dependent variable** (sense 2).

responsibility (rɪˌspɒnsə'bɪlɪtɪ) *n, pl* **-ties. 1** the state or position of being responsible. **2** a person or thing for which one is responsible. **3** the ability or authority to act or decide on one's own, without supervision.

responsible (rɪ'spɒnsəbᵊl) *adj* **1** (*postpositive;* usually foll. by *for*) having control or authority (over). **2** (*postpositive;* foll. by *to*) being accountable for one's actions and decisions (to): *to be responsible to one's commanding officer.* **3** (of a position, duty, etc.) involving decision and accountability. **4** (often foll. by *for*) being the agent or cause (of some action): *to be responsible for a mistake.* **5** able to take rational decisions without supervision; accountable for one's own actions: *a responsible adult.* **6** able to meet financial obligations; of sound credit. [C16: from Latin *rēsponsus,* from *rēspondēre* to RESPOND] ▸ **re'sponsibleness** *n* ▸ **re'sponsibly** *adv*

responsive (rɪ'spɒnsɪv) *adj* **1** reacting or replying quickly or favourably, as to a suggestion, initiative, etc. **2** (of an organism) reacting to a stimulus. ▸ **re'sponsively** *adv* ▸ **re'sponsiveness** *n*

responsory (rɪ'spɒnsərɪ) *n, pl* **-ries.** *Christianity.* an anthem or chant consisting of versicles and responses and recited or sung after a lesson in a church service. [C15: from Late Latin *rēsponsōrium,* from Latin *rēspondēre* to answer]

responsum (rɪ'spɒnsəm) *n, pl* **-sa** (-sə). *Judaism.* a written answer from a rabbinic authority to a question submitted. [Latin, literally: reply, RESPONSE]

res publica ('reɪs 'pʊblɪˌkɑː) *n* the state, republic, or commonwealth. [Latin, literally: the public thing]

rest[1] (rɛst) *n* **1a** relaxation from exertion or labour. **1b** (*as modifier*): *a rest period.* **2** repose; sleep. **3** any relief or refreshment, as from worry or something troublesome. **4** calm; tranquillity. **5** death regarded as repose: *eternal rest.* **6** cessation from motion. **7 at rest. 7a** not moving; still. **7b** calm; tranquil. **7c** dead. **7d** asleep. **8** a pause or interval. **9** a mark in a musical score indicating a pause of specific duration. **10** *Prosody.* a pause in or at the end of a line; caesura. **11** a shelter or lodging: *a seaman's rest.* **12** a thing or place on which to put something for support or to steady it; prop. **13** *Billiards, snooker.* any of various special poles used as supports for the cue in shots that cannot be made using the hand as a support. **14 come to rest.** to slow down and stop. **15 lay to rest.** to bury (a dead person). **16 set (someone's mind) at rest.** to reassure (someone) or settle (someone's mind). ◆ *vb* **17** to take or give rest, as by sleeping, lying down, etc. **18** to place or position (oneself, etc.) for rest or relaxation. **19** (*tr*) to place or position for support or steadying: *to rest one's elbows on the table.* **20** (*intr*) to be at ease; be calm. **21** to cease or cause to cease from motion or exertion; halt. **22** to lie dead and buried. **23** (*intr*) to remain without further attention or action: *let the matter rest.* **24** to direct (one's eyes) or (of one's eyes) to be directed: *her eyes rested on the sleeping child.* **25** to depend or cause to depend; base; rely: *the whole argument rests on one crucial fact.* **26** to place or be placed, as blame, censure, etc. **27** (*intr;* foll. by *with, on, upon,* etc.) to be a responsibility (of): *it rests with us to apportion blame.* **28** *Law.* to finish the introduction of evidence in (a case). **29 rest on one's laurels.** See **laurel** (sense 9). **30 rest on one's oars. 30a** to stop rowing for a time. **30b** to stop doing anything for a time. [Old English *ræst, reste,* of Germanic origin; related to Gothic *rasta* a mile, Old Norse *röst* mile] ▸ **'rester** *n*

rest[2] (rɛst) *n* (usually preceded by *the*) **1** something left or remaining; remainder. **2** the others: *the rest of the world.* ◆ *vb* **3** (*copula*) to continue to be (as specified); remain: *rest assured.* [C15: from Old French *rester* to remain, from Latin *rēstāre,* from RE- + *stāre* to STAND]

rest area *n Austral. and N.Z.* a motorists' stopping place, usually off a highway, equipped with tables, seats, etc.

restate (riː'steɪt) *vb* (*tr*) to state or affirm again or in a new way. ▸ **re'statement** *n*

restaurant ('rɛstəˌrɒŋ, 'rɛstrɒŋ, -rɒnt) *n* a commercial establishment where meals are prepared and served to customers. [C19: from French, from *restaurer* to RESTORE]

restaurant car *n Brit.* a railway coach in which meals are served. Also called: **dining car.**

restaurateur (ˌrɛstərə'tɜː) *n* a person who owns or runs a restaurant. [C18: via French from Late Latin *restaurātor* one who restores, from Latin *restaurāre* to RESTORE]

rest-cure *n* **1** a rest taken as part of a course of medical treatment, as for stress, anxiety, etc. **2** an easy undemanding time or assignment: usually used with a negative: *it's no rest-cure, I can assure you.*

restful ('rɛstfʊl) *adj* **1** giving or conducive to rest. **2** being at rest; tranquil; calm. ▸ **'restfully** *adv* ▸ **'restfulness** *n*

restharrow ('rɛstˌhærəʊ) *n* any of several Eurasian papilionaceous plants of the genus *Ononis,* such as *O. repens* and *O. spinosa,* with tough woody stems and roots. [C16: from *rest,* variant of ARREST (to hinder, stop) + HARROW[1]]

rest-home *n* an old people's home.

restiform ('rɛstɪˌfɔːm) *adj* (esp. of bundles of nerve fibres) shaped like a cord or rope; cordlike. [C19: from New Latin *restiformis,* from Latin *restis* a rope + *forma* shape]

resting ('rɛstɪŋ) *adj* **1** not moving or working; at rest. **2** *Euphemistic.* (of an actor) out of work. **3** (esp. of plant spores) undergoing a period of dormancy before germination. **4** (of cells) not undergoing mitosis.

resting place *n* a place where someone or something rests, esp. (**last resting place**) the grave.

restitution (ˌrɛstɪ'tjuːʃən) *n* **1** the act of giving back something that has been lost or stolen. **2** *Law.* the act of compensating for loss or injury by reverting as far as possible to the position before such injury occurred. **3** the return of an object or system to its original state, esp. a restoration of shape after elastic deformation. [C13: from Latin *rēstitūtiō,* from *rēstituere* to rebuild, from RE- + *statuere* to set up] ▸ **'restiˌtutive** *or* **ˌresti'tutory** *adj*

restive ('rɛstɪv) *adj* **1** restless, nervous, or uneasy. **2** impatient of control or authority. [C16: from Old French *restif* balky, from *rester* to remain] ▸ **'restively** *adv* ▸ **'restiveness** *n*

restless ('rɛstlɪs) *adj* **1** unable to stay still or quiet. **2** ceaselessly active or moving: *the restless wind.* **3** worried; anxious; uneasy. **4** not restful; without repose: *a restless night.* ▸ **'restlessly** *adv* ▸ **'restlessness** *n*

rest mass *n* the mass of an object that is at rest relative to an observer. It is the mass used in Newtonian mechanics.

restoration (ˌrɛstə'reɪʃən) *n* **1** the act of restoring or state of being restored, as to a former or original condition, place, etc. **2** the replacement or giving back of something lost, stolen, etc. **3** something restored, replaced, or reconstructed. **4** a model or representation of an extinct animal, landscape of a former geological age, etc.

Restoration (ˌrɛstə'reɪʃən) *n British history.* **a** the re-establishment of the monarchy in 1660 or the reign of Charles II (1660–85). **b** (*as modifier*): *Restoration drama.*

restorationism (ˌrɛstə'reɪʃəˌnɪzəm) *n* belief in a future life in which human beings will be restored to a state of perfection and happiness. ▸ **ˌresto'rationist** *n, adj*

restorative (rɪ'stɒrətɪv) *adj* **1** tending to revive or renew health, spirits, etc. ◆ *n* **2** anything that restores or revives, esp. a drug or agent that promotes health or strength.

restore (rɪ'stɔː) *vb* (*tr*) **1** to return (something, esp. a work of art or building) to an original or former condition. **2** to bring back to health, good spirits, etc. **3** to return (something lost, stolen, etc.) to its owner. **4** to reintroduce or re-enforce: *to restore discipline.* **5** to reconstruct (an extinct animal, former landscape, etc.). [C13: from Old French, from Latin *rēstaurāre* to rebuild, from RE- + *-staurāre,* as in *instaurāre* to renew] ▸ **re'storable** *adj* ▸ **re'storableness** *n* ▸ **re'storer** *n*

restrain (rɪ'streɪn) *vb* (*tr*) **1** to hold (someone) back from some action, esp. by force. **2** to deprive (someone) of liberty, as by imprisonment. **3** to limit or restrict. [C14 *restreyne,* from Old French *restreindre,* from Latin *rēstringere* to draw back tightly, from RE- + *stringere* to draw, bind; see STRAIN[1]] ▸ **re'strainable** *adj*

restrained (rɪ'streɪnd) *adj* **1** (of a person or person's manner) calm and unemotional. **2** (of clothes, décor, etc.) subtle and tasteful. ▸ **restrainedly** (rɪ'streɪnɪdlɪ) *adv*

restrainer (rɪ'streɪnə) *n* **1** a person who restrains. **2** a chemical, such as potassium bromide, added to a photographic developer in order to reduce the amount of fog on a film and to retard the development.

restraint (rɪ'streɪnt) *n* **1** the ability to control or moderate one's impulses, passions, etc.: *to show restraint.* **2** the act of restraining or the state of being restrained. **3** something that restrains; restriction. [C15: from Old French *restreinte,* from *restreindre* to RESTRAIN]

restraint of trade *n* action tending to interfere with the freedom to compete in business.

restrict (rɪ'strɪkt) *vb* (often foll. by *to*) to confine or keep within certain often specified limits or selected bounds: *to restrict one's drinking to the evening.* [C16: from Latin *rēstrictus* bound up, from *rēstringere;* see RESTRAIN]

restricted (rɪ'strɪktɪd) *adj* **1** limited or confined. **2** not accessible to the general public or (*esp. U.S.*) out of bounds to military personnel. **3** *Brit.* denoting or in a zone in which a speed limit or waiting restrictions for vehicles apply. ▸ **re'strictedly** *adv* ▸ **re'strictedness** *n*

restricted users group *n* a group of people who, with knowledge of a secret password, or by some other method, have access to restricted information stored in a computer. Abbrev.: **RUG.**

restriction (rɪ'strɪkʃən) *n* **1** something that restricts; a restrictive measure, law, etc. **2** the act of restricting or the state of being restricted. **3** *Logic, maths.* a condition that imposes a constraint on the possible values of a variable or on the domain of arguments of a function. ▸ **re'strictionist** *n, adj*

restriction enzyme *n* any of several enzymes produced by bacteria as a defence against viral infection and commonly used to cut DNA for genetic manipulation or diagnosis.

restriction fragment *n Genetics.* a fragment of a DNA molecule cleaved by a restriction enzyme. See also **RFLP.**

restrictive (rɪ'strɪktɪv) *adj* **1** restricting or tending to restrict. **2** *Grammar.* denoting a relative clause or phrase that restricts the number of possible referents of its antecedent. The relative clause in *Americans who live in New York* is restrictive; the relative clause in *Americans, who are generally extrovert,* is nonrestrictive. ▸ **re'strictively** *adv* ▸ **re'strictiveness** *n*

restrictive covenant *n Law.* a covenant imposing a restriction on the use of land for the purpose of preserving the enjoyment or value of adjoining land.

restrictive practice *n Brit.* **1** a trading agreement against the public interest.

re'spray *vb, n*	**re'stage** *vb*	**re'start** *vb,* **'restart** *n*	**re'stock** *vb*

2 a practice of a union or other group tending to limit the freedom of other workers or employers.

rest room *n* a room in a public building having lavatories, washing facilities, and sometimes couches.

restructure (riːˈstrʌktʃə) *vb* (*tr*) to organize (a system, business, society, etc.) in a different way: *radical attempts to restructure the economy.* ▸ **reˈstructuring** *n*

rest stop *n* the U.S. name for **lay-by** (sense 1).

result (rɪˈzʌlt) *n* **1** something that ensues from an action, policy, course of events, etc.; outcome; consequence. **2** a number, quantity, or value obtained by solving a mathematical problem. **3** *U.S.* a decision of a legislative body. **4** (*often pl*) the final score or outcome of a sporting contest. **5** a favourable result, esp. a victory or success. ◆ *vb* (*intr*) **6** (often foll. by *from*) to be the outcome or consequence (of). **7** (foll. by *in*) to issue or terminate (in a specified way, state, etc.); end: *to result in tragedy.* **8** *Property law.* (of an undisposed or partially disposed of interest in land) to revert to a former owner when the prior interests come to an end. [C15: from Latin *resultāre* to rebound, spring from, from RE- + *saltāre* to leap]

resultant (rɪˈzʌltənt) *adj* **1** that results; resulting. ◆ *n* **2** *Maths, physics.* a single vector that is the vector sum of two or more other vectors.

resultant tone *n* a musical sound sometimes heard when two loud notes are sounded together, either lower in pitch than either (**differential tone**) or higher (**summational tone**).

resume (rɪˈzjuːm) *vb* **1** to begin again or go on with (something adjourned or interrupted). **2** (*tr*) to occupy again, take back, or recover: *to resume one's seat; resume possession.* **3** (*tr*) to assume (a title, office, etc.) again: *to resume the presidency.* **4** *Archaic.* to summarize; make a résumé of. [C15: from Latin *resūmere* to take up again, from RE- + *sūmere* to take up] ▸ **reˈsumable** *adj* ▸ **reˈsumer** *n*

résumé (ˈrɛzjʊˌmeɪ) *n* **1** a short descriptive summary, as of events. **2** *U.S. and Canadian.* another name for **curriculum vitae.** [C19: from French, from *résumer* to RESUME]

resumption (rɪˈzʌmpʃən) *n* the act of resuming or beginning again. [C15: via Old French from Late Latin *resumptiō*, from Latin *resūmere* to RESUME] ▸ **reˈsumptive** *adj* ▸ **reˈsumptively** *adv*

resupinate (rɪˈsjuːpɪnɪt) *adj Botany.* (of plant parts) reversed or inverted in position, so as to appear to be upside down. [C18: from Latin *resupīnātus* bent back, from *resupīnāre*, from RE- + *supīnāre* to place on the back; see SUPINE] ▸ **reˌsupiˈnation** *n*

resupine (rɪˈsjuːpaɪn) *adj Rare.* lying on the back; supine. [C17: from Latin *resupīnus* lying on the back]

resurge (rɪˈsɜːdʒ) *vb* (*intr*) *Rare.* to rise again from or as if from the dead. [C16: from Latin *resurgere* to rise again, reappear, from RE- + *surgere* to lift, arise, SURGE]

resurgent (rɪˈsɜːdʒənt) *adj* rising again, as to new life, vigour, etc.: *resurgent nationalism.* ▸ **reˈsurgence** *n*

resurrect (ˌrɛzəˈrɛkt) *vb* **1** to rise or raise from the dead; bring or be brought back to life. **2** (*tr*) to bring back into use or activity; revive: *to resurrect an ancient law.* **3** (*tr*) to renew (one's hopes, etc.). **4** (*tr*) *Facetious.* (formerly) to exhume and steal (a body) from its grave, esp. in order to sell it.

resurrection (ˌrɛzəˈrɛkʃən) *n* **1** a supposed act or instance of a dead person coming back to life. **2** belief in the possibility of this as part of a religious or mystical system. **3** the condition of those who have risen from the dead: *we shall all live in the resurrection.* [C13: via Old French from Late Latin *resurrectiō*, from Latin *resurgere* to rise again; see RESURGE] ▸ **ˌresurˈrectional** *or* **ˌresurˈrectionary** *adj*

Resurrection (ˌrɛzəˈrɛkʃən) *n Christian theol.* **1** the rising again of Christ from the tomb three days after his death. **2** the rising again from the dead of all men at the Last Judgment.

resurrectionism (ˌrɛzəˈrɛkʃəˌnɪzəm) *n* **1** belief that men will rise again from the dead, esp. the Christian doctrine of the Resurrection of Christ and of all men at the Last Judgment. **2** *Facetious.* (formerly) body snatching.

resurrectionist (ˌrɛzəˈrɛkʃənɪst) *n* **1** *Facetious.* (formerly) a body snatcher. **2** a member of an Anglican religious community founded in 1892. **3** a person who believes in the Resurrection.

resurrection plant *n* any of several unrelated desert plants that form a tight ball when dry and unfold and bloom when moistened. The best-known examples are the cruciferous *Anastatica hierochuntica*, club mosses of the genus *Selaginella*, and the composite *Asteriscus pygmoeus*. Also called: **rose of Jericho.**

resuscitate (rɪˈsʌsɪˌteɪt) *vb* (*tr*) to restore to consciousness; revive. [C16: from Latin *resuscitāre*, from RE- + *suscitāre* to raise, from *sub-* up from below + *citāre* to rouse, from *citus* quick] ▸ **reˈsuscitable** *adj* ▸ **reˌsusciˈtation** *n* ▸ **reˈsuscitative** *adj*

resuscitator (rɪˈsʌsɪˌteɪtə) *n* **1** an apparatus for forcing oxygen or a mixture containing oxygen into the lungs. **2** a person who resuscitates.

ret (rɛt) *vb* **rets, retting, retted.** (*tr*) to moisten or soak (flax, hemp, jute, etc.) to promote bacterial action in order to facilitate separation of the fibres from the woody tissue by beating. [C15: of Germanic origin; related to Middle Dutch *reeten*, Swedish *röta*, German *rösten*; see ROT[1]]

ret. *abbrev. for:* **1** retain. **2** retired. **3** return(ed).

retable (rɪˈteɪbᵊl) *n* an ornamental screenlike structure above and behind an altar, esp. one used as a setting for a religious picture or carving. [C19: from French, from Spanish *retablo*, from Latin *retrō* behind + *tabula* board; see REAR[1], TABLE]

retail (ˈriːteɪl) *n* **1** the sale of goods individually or in small quantities to consumers. Compare **wholesale** (sense 1). ◆ *adj* **2** of, relating to, or engaged in such selling: *retail prices.* ◆ *adv* **3** in small amounts or at a retail price. ◆ *vb* **4** to sell or be sold in small quantities to consumers. **5** (rɪˈteɪl). (*tr*) to relate (gossip, scandal, etc.) in detail, esp. persistently. [C14: from Old French *retaillier* to cut off, from RE- + *taillier* to cut; see TAILOR] ▸ **ˈretailer** *n*

retail price index *n* (in Britain) a list, based on government figures and usually published monthly, that shows the extent of change in the prices of a range of goods selected as being essential items in the budget of a normal household. Abbrev.: **RPI.**

retain (rɪˈteɪn) *vb* (*tr*) **1** to keep in one's possession. **2** to be able to hold or contain: *soil that retains water.* **3** (of a person) to be able to remember (information, facts, etc.) without difficulty. **4** to hold in position. **5** to keep for one's future use, as by paying a retainer or nominal charge: *to retain one's rooms for the holidays.* **6** *Law.* to engage the services of (a barrister) by payment of a preliminary fee. **7** (in selling races) to buy back a winner that one owns when it is auctioned after the race. **8** (of racehorse trainers) to pay an advance fee to (a jockey) so as to have prior or exclusive claims upon his services throughout the season. [C14: from Old French *retenir*, from Latin *retinēre* to hold back, from RE- + *tenēre* to hold] ▸ **reˈtainable** *adj* ▸ **reˈtainment** *n*

retained object *n Grammar.* a direct or indirect object of a passive verb. The phrase *the drawings* in the sentence *Harry was given the drawings* is a retained object.

retainer (rɪˈteɪnə) *n* **1** *History.* a supporter or dependant of a person of rank, esp. a soldier. **2** a servant, esp. one who has been with a family for a long time. **3** a clip, frame, or similar device that prevents a part of a machine, engine, etc., from moving. **4** a dental appliance for holding a loose tooth or prosthetic device in position. **5** a fee paid in advance to secure first option on the services of a barrister, jockey, etc. **6** a reduced rent paid for a flat, room, etc., during absence to reserve it for future use.

retaining ring *n* another name for **circlip.**

retaining wall *n* a wall constructed to hold back earth, loose rock, etc. Also called: **revetment.**

retake *vb* (riːˈteɪk), **-takes, -taking, -took, -taken.** (*tr*) **1** to take back or capture again: *to retake a fortress.* **2** *Films.* to shoot again (a shot or scene). **3** to tape again (a recording). ◆ *n* (ˈriːˌteɪk). **4** *Films.* a rephotographed shot or scene. **5** a retaped recording. ▸ **reˈtaker** *n*

retaliate (rɪˈtælɪˌeɪt) *vb* **1** (*intr*) to take retributory action, esp. by returning some injury or wrong in kind. **2** (*tr*) *Rare.* to avenge (an injury, wrong, etc.). [C17: from Late Latin *retāliāre*, from Latin RE- + *tālis* of such kind] ▸ **reˌtaliˈation** *n* ▸ **reˈtaliative** *or* **reˈtaliatory** *adj* ▸ **reˈtaliˌator** *n*

retard (rɪˈtɑːd) *vb* (*tr*) to delay or slow down (the progress, speed, or development) of (something). [C15: from Old French *retarder*, from Latin *retardāre*, from RE- + *tardāre* to make slow, from *tardus* sluggish; see TARDY]

retardant (rɪˈtɑːdᵊnt) *n* **1** a substance that reduces the rate of a chemical reaction. ◆ *adj* **2** having a slowing effect.

retardate (rɪˈtɑːdeɪt) *n Psychol.* a person who is retarded.

retardation (ˌriːtɑːˈdeɪʃən) *or* (*less commonly*) **retardment** (rɪˈtɑːdmənt) *n* **1** the act of retarding or the state of being retarded. **2** something that retards; hindrance. **3** the rate of deceleration. **4** *Psychiatry.* the slowing down of mental functioning and bodily movement. ▸ **reˈtardative** *or* **reˈtardatory** *adj*

retarded (rɪˈtɑːdɪd) *adj* underdeveloped, esp. mentally and esp. having an IQ of 70 to 85. See also **ESN, mental handicap, subnormal** (sense 2).

retarder (rɪˈtɑːdə) *n* **1** a person or thing that retards. **2** a substance added to slow down the rate of a chemical change, such as one added to cement to delay its setting.

retch (rɛtʃ, riːtʃ) *vb* **1** (*intr*) to undergo an involuntary spasm of ineffectual vomiting; heave. **2** to vomit. ◆ *n* **3** an involuntary spasm of ineffectual vomiting. [Old English *hrǣcan*; related to Old Norse *hrǣkja* to spit]

retd *abbrev. for:* **1** retired. **2** retained. **3** returned.

rete (ˈriːtɪ) *n, pl* **retia** (ˈriːʃɪə, -tɪə). *Anatomy.* any network of nerves or blood vessels; plexus. [C14 (referring to a metal network used with an astrolabe): from Latin *rēte* net] ▸ **ˈretial** *adj*

retene (ˈriːtiːn, ˈrɛt-) *n* a yellow crystalline hydrocarbon found in tar oils from pine wood and in certain fossil resins. Formula: $C_{18}H_{18}$. [C19: from Greek *rhētinē* resin]

retention (rɪˈtɛnʃən) *n* **1** the act of retaining or state of being retained. **2** the capacity to hold or retain liquid. **3** the capacity to remember. **4** *Pathol.* the abnormal holding within the body of urine, faeces, etc., that are normally excreted. **5** *Commerce.* a sum of money owed to a contractor but not paid for an agreed period as a safeguard against any faults found in the work carried out. **6** (*pl*) *Account.* profits earned by a company but not distributed as dividends; retained earnings. [C14: from Latin *retentiō*, from *retinēre* to RETAIN]

retentionist (rɪˈtɛnʃənɪst) *n* a person who advocates the retention of something, esp. capital punishment.

retentive (rɪˈtɛntɪv) *adj* having the capacity to retain or remember. ▸ **reˈtentively** *adv* ▸ **reˈtentiveness** *n*

retentivity (ˌriːtɛnˈtɪvɪtɪ) *n* **1** the state or quality of being retentive. **2** *Physics.* another name for **remanence.**

rethink *vb* (riːˈθɪŋk), **-thinks, -thinking, -thought. 1** to think about (some-

reˈstyle *vb*
ˌresubˈmit *vb*, **-ˈmits, -ˈmitting, -ˈmitted.**
ˌresupˈply *vb*, **-ˈplies, -ˈplying, -ˈplied.**
reˈsurface *vb*
reˈtell *vb*, **-ˈtells, -ˈtelling, -ˈtold.**

thing) again, esp. with a view to changing one's tactics or opinions. ◆ *n* ('riːˌθɪŋk). **2** the act or an instance of thinking again.

Réti ('reɪtɪ) *n* **Richard.** 1889–1929, Hungarian chess player and theorist; influential in enunciating the theories of the hypermodern school.

retiarius (ˌriːtɪ'eərɪəs, ˌriːʃɪ-) *n, pl* **-arii** (-'eərɪˌaɪ). (in ancient Rome) a gladiator armed with a net and trident. [Latin, from *rēte* net]

retiary ('riːtɪərɪ, -ʃɪə-) *adj Rare.* of, relating to, or resembling a net or web. [C17: from Latin RETIARIUS]

reticent ('retɪsənt) *adj* not open or communicative; not saying all that one knows; taciturn; reserved. [C19: from Latin *reticēre* to keep silent, from RE- + *tacēre* to be silent] ▸ **'reticence** *n* ▸ **'reticently** *adv*

reticle ('retɪkᵊl) *or* (*less commonly*) **reticule** *n* a network of fine lines, wires, etc., placed in the focal plane of an optical instrument to assist measurement of the size or position of objects under observation. Also called: **graticule.** [C17: from Latin *rēticulum* a little net, from *rēte* net]

reticulate (rɪ'tɪkjʊlɪt) *adj also* **reticular** (rɪ'tɪkjʊlə). **1** in the form of a network or having a network of parts: *a reticulate leaf.* **2** resembling, covered with, or having the form of a net. ◆ *vb* (rɪ'tɪkjʊˌleɪt). **3** to form or be formed into a net. [C17: from Late Latin *rēticulātus* made like a net] ▸ **re'ticulately** *adv* ▸ **reˌticu'lation** *n*

reticule ('retɪˌkjuːl) *n* **1** (in the 18th and 19th centuries) a woman's small bag or purse, usually in the form of a pouch with a drawstring and made of net, beading, brocade, etc. **2** a variant of **reticle.** [C18: from French *réticule,* from Latin *rēticulum* RETICLE]

reticulocyte (rɪ'tɪkjʊləˌsaɪt) *n* an immature red blood cell containing a network of granules or filaments. [C20: from RETICULUM + -CYTE]

reticuloendothelial (rɪˌtɪkjʊləʊˌendəʊ'θiːlɪəl) *adj Physiol.* denoting or relating to a bodily system that consists of all the cells able to ingest bacteria, colloidal particles, etc., with the exception of the leucocytes. See also **macrophage.** [C20: from RETICULUM + ENDOTHELIAL]

reticulum (rɪ'tɪkjʊləm) *n, pl* **-la** (-lə). **1** any fine network, esp. one in the body composed of cells, fibres, etc. **2** the second compartment of the stomach of ruminants, situated between the rumen and psalterium. [C17: from Latin: little net, from *rēte* net]

Reticulum (rɪ'tɪkjʊləm) *n, Latin genitive* **Reticuli** (rɪ'tɪkjʊˌlaɪ). a small constellation in the S hemisphere lying between Dorado and Hydrus.

retiform ('riːtɪˌfɔːm, 'ret-) *adj Rare.* netlike; reticulate. [C17: from Latin *rēte* net + *forma* shape]

retina ('retɪnə) *n, pl* **-nas** *or* **-nae** (-ˌniː). the light-sensitive membrane forming the inner lining of the posterior wall of the eyeball, composed largely of a specialized terminal expansion of the optic nerve. Images focused here by the lens of the eye are transmitted to the brain as nerve impulses. [C14: from Medieval Latin, perhaps from Latin *rēte* net] ▸ **'retinal** *adj*

retinaculum (ˌretɪ'nækjʊləm) *n, pl* **-la** (-lə). **1** connection or retention or something that connects or retains. **2** *Zoology.* a small hook that joins the forewing and hind wing of a moth during flight. [C18 (a surgical instrument used in castration): Latin, from *rētinēre* to hold back] ▸ **ˌreti'nacular** *adj*

retinal rivalry *n Psychol.* another name for **binocular rivalry.**

retinene ('retɪˌniːn) *or* **retinal** ('retɪnəl) *n* the aldehyde form of the polyene, retinol (vitamin A), that associates with the protein, opsin, to form the visual purple pigment, rhodopsin. [C20: from RETINA + -ENE]

retinite ('retɪˌnaɪt) *n* any of various resins of fossil origin, esp. one derived from lignite. [C19: from French *rétinite,* from Greek *rhētinē* resin + -ITE[1]]

retinitis (ˌretɪ'naɪtɪs) *n* inflammation of the retina. [C20: from New Latin, from RETINA + -ITIS]

retinol ('retɪˌnɒl) *n* another name for **vitamin A** and **rosin oil.** [C19: from Greek *rhētinē* resin + -OL[1]]

retinoscopy (ˌretɪ'nɒskəpɪ) *n Ophthalmol.* a procedure for detecting errors of refraction in the eye by means of an instrument (**retinoscope**) that reflects a beam of light from a mirror into the eye. Diagnosis is made by observing the areas of shadow and the direction in which the light moves when the mirror is rotated. Also called: **skiascopy, shadow test.** ▸ **retinoscopic** (ˌretɪnə'skɒpɪk) *adj* ▸ **ˌretino'scopically** *adv* ▸ **ˌreti'noscopist** *n*

retinue ('retɪˌnjuː) *n* a body of aides and retainers attending an important person, royalty, etc. [C14: from Old French *retenue,* from *retenir* to RETAIN] ▸ **'retiˌnued** *adj*

retiral (rɪ'taɪərᵊl) *n Scot.* the act of retiring from office, one's work, etc.; retirement.

retire (rɪ'taɪə) *vb* (*mainly intr*) **1** (*also tr*) to give up or to cause (a person) to give up his work, a post, etc., esp. on reaching pensionable age (in Britain and Australia usually 65 for men, 60 for women). **2** to go away, as into seclusion, for recuperation, etc. **3** to go to bed. **4** to recede or disappear: *the sun retired behind the clouds.* **5** to withdraw from a sporting contest, esp. because of injury. **6** (*also tr*) to pull back (troops, etc.) from battle or an exposed position or (of troops, etc.) to fall back. **7** (*tr*) **7a** to remove (bills, bonds, shares, etc.) from circulation by taking them up and paying for them. **7b** to remove (money) from circulation. [C16: from French *retirer,* from Old French RE- + *tirer* to pull, draw] ▸ **re'tirer** *n*

retired (rɪ'taɪəd) *adj* **1a** having given up one's work, office, etc., esp. on completion of the normal period of service: *a retired headmistress.* **1b** (*as collective n;* preceded by *the*): *the retired.* **2** withdrawn; secluded: *a retired life; a retired cottage in the woods.*

retiree (rɪˌtaɪə'riː) *n Chiefly U.S.* a person who has retired from work.

retirement (rɪ'taɪəmənt) *n* **1a** the act of retiring from one's work, office, etc. **1b** (*as modifier*): *retirement age.* **2** the period of being retired from work: *she had many plans for her retirement.* **3** seclusion from the world; privacy. **4** the act of going away or retreating.

retirement pension *n* a pension given to a person who has retired from regular employment, either one paid by the state or one arising from the person's former employment.

retirement relief *n* (in Britain) relief from capital-gains tax given to persons over 60 when disposing of business assets.

retiring (rɪ'taɪərɪŋ) *adj* shunning contact with others; shy; reserved. ▸ **re'tiringly** *adv*

retool (riː'tuːl) *vb* **1** to replace, re-equip, or rearrange the tools in (a factory, etc.). **2** *Chiefly U.S. and Canadian.* to revise or reorganize.

retorsion (rɪ'tɔːʃən) *n Rare.* retaliatory action taken by a state whose citizens have been mistreated by a foreign power by treating the subjects of that power similarly; reprisal. [C17: from French; see RETORT[1]]

retort[1] (rɪ'tɔːt) *vb* **1** (when *tr, takes a clause as object*) to utter (something) quickly, sharply, wittily, or angrily, in response. **2** to use (an argument) against its originator; turn the tables by saying (something). ◆ *n* **3** a sharp, angry, or witty reply. **4** an argument used against its originator. [C16: from Latin *retorquēre* to twist back, from RE- + *torquēre* to twist, wrench] ▸ **re'torter** *n*

retort[2] (rɪ'tɔːt) *n* **1** a glass vessel with a round bulb and long tapering neck that is bent down, used esp. in a laboratory for distillation. **2** a vessel in which large quantities of material may be heated, esp. one used for heating ores in the production of metals or heating coal to produce gas. ◆ *vb* **3** (*tr*) to heat in a retort. [C17: from French *retorte,* from Medieval Latin *retorta,* from Latin *retorquēre* to twist back; see RETORT[1]]

retortion (rɪ'tɔːʃən) *n* **1** the act of retorting. **2** a variant spelling of **retorsion.**

retouch (riː'tʌtʃ) *vb* (*tr*) **1** to restore, correct, or improve (a painting, make-up, etc.) with new touches. **2** *Photog.* to alter (a negative or print) by painting over blemishes or adding details. **3** to make small finishing improvements to. **4** *Archaeol.* to detach small flakes from (a blank) in order to make a tool. ◆ *n* **5** the art or practice of retouching. **6** a detail that is the result of retouching. **7** a photograph, painting, etc., that has been retouched. **8** *Archaeol.* fine percussion to shape flakes of stone into usable tools. ▸ **re'touchable** *adj* ▸ **re'toucher** *n*

retrace (rɪ'treɪs) *vb* (*tr*) **1** to go back over (one's steps, a route, etc.) again: *we retraced the route we took last summer.* **2** to go over (a past event) in the mind; recall. **3** to go over (a story, account, etc.) from the beginning. ▸ **re'traceable** *adj* ▸ **re'tracement** *n*

re-trace (riː'treɪs) *vb* (*tr*) to trace (a map, drawing, etc.) again.

retract (rɪ'trækt) *vb* **1** (*tr*) to draw in (a part or appendage): *a snail can retract its horns; to retract the landing gear of an aircraft.* **2** to withdraw (a statement, opinion, charge, etc.) as invalid or unjustified. **3** to go back on (a promise or agreement). **4** (*intr*) to shrink back, as in fear. **5** *Phonetics.* to modify the articulation of (a vowel) by bringing the tongue back away from the lips. [C16: from Latin *retractāre* to withdraw, from *tractāre* to pull, from *trahere* to drag] ▸ **re'tractable** *or* **re'tractible** *adj* ▸ **reˌtracta'bility** *or* **reˌtracti'bility** *n* ▸ **retractation** (ˌriːtræk'teɪʃən) *n* ▸ **re'tractive** *adj*

retractile (rɪ'træktaɪl) *adj* capable of being drawn in: *the retractile claws of a cat.* ▸ **retractility** (ˌriːtræk'tɪlɪtɪ) *n*

retraction (rɪ'trækʃən) *n* **1** the act of retracting or state of being retracted. **2** the withdrawal of a statement, charge, etc.

retractor (rɪ'træktə) *n* **1** *Anatomy.* any of various muscles that retract an organ or part. **2** *Surgery.* an instrument for holding back the edges of a surgical incision or organ or part. **3** a person or thing that retracts.

retral ('riːtrəl, 'retrəl) *adj Rare.* at, near, or towards the back. [C19: from Latin *retrō* backwards] ▸ **'retrally** *adv*

retread *vb* (riː'tred), **-treads, -treading, -treaded.** **1** (*tr*) another word for **remould** (sense 2). ◆ *n* ('riːˌtred). **2** another word for **remould** (sense 3). **3** *N.Z. informal.* a pensioner who has resumed employment, esp. in a former profession.

re-tread (riː'tred) *vb* **-treads, -treading, -trod, -trodden** *or* **-trod.** (*tr*) to tread or walk over (one's steps) again.

retreat (rɪ'triːt) *vb* (*mainly intr*) **1** *Military.* to withdraw or retire in the face of or from action with an enemy, either due to defeat or in order to adopt a more favourable position. **2** to retire or withdraw, as to seclusion or shelter. **3** (of a person's features) to slope back; recede. **4** (*tr*) *Chess.* to move (a piece) back. ◆ *n* **5** the act of retreating or withdrawing. **6** *Military.* **6a** a withdrawal or retirement in the face of the enemy. **6b** a bugle call signifying withdrawal or retirement, esp. (formerly) to within a defended fortification. **7** retirement or seclusion. **8** a place, such as a sanatorium or monastery, to which one may retire for refuge, quiet, etc. **9** a period of seclusion, esp. for religious contemplation. **10** an institution, esp. a private one, for the care and treatment of the mentally ill, infirm, elderly, etc. [C14: from Old French *retret,* from *retraire* to withdraw, from Latin *retrahere* to pull back; see RETRACT]

retrench (rɪ'trentʃ) *vb* **1** to reduce or curtail (costs); economize. **2** (*tr*) to shorten, delete, or abridge. **3** (*tr*) to protect by a retrenchment. [C17: from Old French *retrenchier,* from RE- + *trenchier* to cut, from Latin *truncāre* to lop; see TRENCH] ▸ **re'trenchable** *adj*

retrenchment (rɪ'trentʃmənt) *n* **1** the act of reducing expenditure in order to improve financial stability. **2** an extra interior fortification to reinforce outer walls.

re'test *vb*
re'tie *vb,* **-'ties, -'tying, -'tied.**
re'train *vb*
ˌretrans'mission *n*
ˌretrans'mit *vb,* **-'mits, -'mitting, -'mitted.**

retrial (riːˈtraɪəl) *n* a second or new trial, esp. of a case that has already been adjudicated upon.

retribution (ˌrɛtrɪˈbjuːʃən) *n* **1** the act of punishing or taking vengeance for wrongdoing, sin, or injury. **2** punishment or vengeance. [C14: via Old French from Church Latin *retribūtiō*, from Latin *retribuere* to repay, from RE- + *tribuere* to pay; see TRIBUTE] ▸ **retributive** (rɪˈtrɪbjutɪv) *or (less commonly)* **reˈtributory** *adj* ▸ **reˈtributively** *adv*

retrieval (rɪˈtriːvᵊl) *n* **1** the act or process of retrieving. **2** the possibility of recovery, restoration, or rectification (esp. in the phrase **beyond retrieval**). **3** a computer filing operation that recalls records or other data from a file.

retrieve (rɪˈtriːv) *vb* (*mainly tr*) **1** to get or fetch back again; recover: *he retrieved his papers from various people's drawers.* **2** to bring back to a more satisfactory state; revive. **3** to extricate from trouble or danger; rescue or save. **4** to recover or make newly available (stored information) from a computer system. **5** (*also intr*) (of dogs) to find and fetch (shot game). **6** *Tennis, badminton, etc.* to return successfully (a shot difficult to reach). **7** to recall; remember. ◆ *n* **8** the act of retrieving. **9** the chance of being retrieved. [C15: from Old French *retrover*, from RE- + *trouver* to find, perhaps from Vulgar Latin *tropāre* (unattested) to compose; see TROVER, TROUBADOUR] ▸ **reˈtrievable** *adj* ▸ **reˌtrievaˈbility** *n* ▸ **reˈtrievably** *adv*

retriever (rɪˈtriːvə) *n* **1** one of a breed of large gun dogs that can be trained to retrieve game: see **golden retriever, labrador retriever. 2** any dog used to retrieve shot game. **3** a person or thing that retrieves.

retro (ˈrɛtrəʊ) *n, pl* **-ros. 1** short for **retrorocket.** ◆ *adj* **2** denoting something associated with or revived from the past: *retro dressing; retro fashion.*

retro- *prefix* **1** back or backwards: *retroactive.* **2** located behind: *retrolental.* [from Latin *retrō* behind, backwards]

retroact (ˈrɛtrəʊˌækt) *vb* (*intr*) **1** to act in opposition. **2** to influence or have reference to past events.

retroaction (ˌrɛtrəʊˈækʃən) *n* **1** an action contrary or reciprocal to a preceding action. **2** a retrospective action, esp. a law affecting events prior to its enactment.

retroactive (ˌrɛtrəʊˈæktɪv) *adj* **1** applying or referring to the past: *retroactive legislation.* **2** effective or operative from a date or for a period in the past. ▸ **ˌretroˈactively** *adv* ▸ **ˌretroˈactiveness** *or* **ˌretroacˈtivity** *n*

retroactive inhibition *or* **interference** *n Psychol.* the tendency for the retention of learned material or skills to be impaired by subsequent learning, esp. by learning of a similar kind. Compare **proactive inhibition.**

retrocede (ˌrɛtrəʊˈsiːd) *vb* **1** (*tr*) to give back; return. **2** (*intr*) to go back or retire; recede. ▸ **retrocession** (ˌrɛtrəʊˈsɛʃən) *or* **ˌretroˈcedence** *n* ▸ **ˌretroˈcessive** *or* **ˌretroˈcedent** *adj*

retrochoir (ˈrɛtrəʊˌkwaɪə) *n* the space in a large church or cathedral behind the high altar.

retrofire (ˈrɛtrəʊˌfaɪə) *n* **1** *Phonetics.* the act of firing a retrorocket. **2** the moment at which it is fired.

retrofit (ˈrɛtrəʊˌfɪt) *vb* **-fits, -fitting, -fitted.** (*tr*) to equip (a vehicle, piece of equipment, etc.) with new parts, safety devices, etc., after manufacture.

retroflex (ˈrɛtrəʊˌflɛks) *or* **retroflexed** *adj* **1** bent or curved backwards. **2** *Phonetics.* of, relating to, or involving retroflexion. [C18: from Latin *retrōflexus*, from *retrōflectere*, from RETRO- + *flectere* to bend]

retroflexion *or* **retroflection** (ˌrɛtrəʊˈflɛkʃən) *n* **1** the act or condition of bending or being bent backwards. **2** *Phonetics.* the act of turning the tip of the tongue upwards and backwards towards the hard palate in the articulation of a vowel or a consonant.

retrograde (ˈrɛtrəʊˌɡreɪd) *adj* **1** moving or bending backwards. **2** (esp. of order) reverse or inverse. **3** tending towards an earlier worse condition; declining or deteriorating. **4** *Astronomy.* **4a** occurring or orbiting in a direction opposite to that of the earth's motion around the sun. Compare **direct** (sense 18). **4b** occurring or orbiting in a direction around a planet opposite to the planet's rotational direction: *the retrograde motion of the satellite Phoebe around Saturn.* **4c** appearing to move in a clockwise direction due to the rotational period exceeding the period of revolution around the sun: *Venus has retrograde rotation.* **5** *Biology.* tending to retrogress; degenerate. **6** *Music.* of, concerning, or denoting a melody or part that is played backwards. **7** *Obsolete.* opposed, contrary, or repugnant to. ◆ *vb* (*intr*) **8** to move in a retrograde direction; retrogress. **9** *U.S. military.* another word for **retreat** (sense 1). [C14: from Latin *retrōgradī* to go backwards, from *gradi* to walk, go] ▸ **ˌretrograˈdation** *n* ▸ **ˈretroˌgradely** *adv*

retrograde amnesia *n* amnesia caused by a trauma such as concussion, in which the memory loss relates to material learnt before the trauma. Compare **anterograde amnesia.**

retrogress (ˌrɛtrəʊˈɡrɛs) *vb* (*intr*) **1** to go back to an earlier, esp. worse, condition; degenerate or deteriorate. **2** to move backwards; recede. **3** *Biology.* to develop characteristics or features of lower or simpler organisms; degenerate. [C19: from Latin *retrōgressus* having moved backwards, from *retrōgradī*; see RETROGRADE] ▸ **ˌretroˈgression** *n* ▸ **ˌretroˈgressive** *adj* ▸ **ˌretroˈgressively** *adv*

retroject (ˌrɛtrəʊˈdʒɛkt) *vb* (*tr*) to throw backwards (opposed to *project*). [C19: from RETRO- + *-ject* as in PROJECT] ▸ **ˌretroˈjection** *n*

retrolental (ˌrɛtrəʊˈlɛntᵊl) *adj* behind a lens, esp. of the eye. [C20: from RETRO- + *-lental*, from New Latin: LENS]

retro-operative *adj* affecting or operating on past events; retroactive.

retropack (ˈrɛtrəʊˌpæk) *n* a system of retrorockets on a spacecraft.

retropulsion (ˌrɛtrəʊˈpʌlʃən) *n Med.* an abnormal tendency to walk backwards: a symptom of Parkinson's disease.

retrorocket (ˈrɛtrəʊˌrɒkɪt) *n* a small auxiliary rocket engine on a larger rocket, missile, or spacecraft, that produces thrust in the opposite direction to the direction of flight in order to decelerate the vehicle or make it move backwards. Often shortened to **retro.**

retrorse (rɪˈtrɔːs) *adj* (esp. of plant parts) pointing backwards or in a direction opposite to normal. [C19: from Latin *retrōrsus*, shortened form of *retrōversus* turned back, from RETRO- + *vertere* to turn] ▸ **reˈtrorsely** *adv*

retrospect (ˈrɛtrəʊˌspɛkt) *n* **1** the act of surveying things past (often in the phrase **in retrospect**). ◆ *vb Archaic.* **2** to contemplate (anything past); look back on (something). **3** (*intr*; often foll. by *to*) to refer. [C17: from Latin *retrōspicere* to look back, from RETRO- + *specere* to look]

retrospection (ˌrɛtrəʊˈspɛkʃən) *n* the act of recalling things past, esp. in one's personal experience.

retrospective (ˌrɛtrəʊˈspɛktɪv) *adj* **1** looking or directed backwards, esp. in time; characterized by retrospection. **2** applying to the past; retroactive. ◆ *n* **3** an exhibition of an artist's life's work or a representative selection of it. ▸ **ˌretroˈspectively** *adv* ▸ **ˌretroˈspectiveness** *n*

retroussé (rəˈtruːseɪ; *French* rətruse) *adj* (of a nose) turned up. [C19: from French *retrousser* to tuck up; see TRUSS]

retroversion (ˌrɛtrəʊˈvɜːʃən) *n* **1** the act of turning or condition of being turned backwards. **2** the condition of a part or organ, esp. the uterus, that is turned or tilted backwards. ▸ **ˈretroˌverse** *adj* ▸ **ˈretroˌverted** *adj*

Retrovir (ˈrɛtrəʊˌvɪə) *n Trademark.* a preparation of the drug zidovudine.

retrovirus (ˈrɛtrəʊˌvaɪrəs) *n* any of several viruses whose genetic specification is encoded in RNA rather than DNA and that are able to reverse the normal flow of genetic information from DNA to RNA by transcribing RNA into DNA: many retroviruses are known to cause cancer in animals. ▸ **ˈretroˌviral** *adj*

retry (riːˈtraɪ) *vb* **-tries, -trying, -tried.** (*tr*) to try again (a case already determined); give a new trial to.

retsina (rɛtˈsiːnə, ˈrɛtsɪnə) *n* a Greek wine flavoured with resin. [Modern Greek, from Italian *resina* RESIN]

return (rɪˈtɜːn) *vb* **1** (*intr*) to come back to a former place or state. **2** (*tr*) to give, take, or carry back; replace or restore. **3** (*tr*) to repay or recompense, esp. with something of equivalent value: *return the compliment.* **4** (*tr*) to earn or yield (profit or interest) as an income from an investment or venture. **5** (*intr*) to come back or revert in thought or speech: *I'll return to that later.* **6** (*intr*) to recur or reappear: *the symptoms have returned.* **7** to answer or reply. **8** (*tr*) to vote into office; elect. **9** (*tr*) *Law.* (of a jury) to deliver or render (a verdict). **10** (*tr*) to send back or reflect (light or sound): *the canyon returned my shout.* **11** (*tr*) to submit (a report, etc.) about (someone or something) to someone in authority. **12** (*tr*) *Cards.* to lead back (the suit led by one's partner). **13** (*tr*) *Ball games.* to hit, throw, or play (a ball) back. **14** (*tr*) *Architect.* to turn (a part, decorative moulding, etc.) away from its original direction. **15 return thanks.** (of Christians) to say grace before a meal. ◆ *n* **16** the act or an instance of coming back. **17** something that is given or sent back, esp. unsatisfactory merchandise returned to the maker or supplier or a theatre ticket sent back by a purchaser for resale. **18** the act or an instance of putting, sending, or carrying back; replacement or restoration. **19** (*often pl*) the yield, revenue, or profit accruing from an investment, transaction, or venture. **20** the act or an instance of reciprocation or repayment (esp. in the phrase **in return for**). **21** a recurrence or reappearance. **22** an official report, esp. of the financial condition of a company. **23a** a form (a **tax return**) on which a statement concerning one's taxable income is made. **23b** the statement itself. **24** (*often pl*) a statement of the votes counted at an election or poll. **25** an answer or reply. **26** *Brit.* short for **return ticket. 27** *N.Z. informal.* a second helping of food served at a table. **28** *Architect.* **28a** a part of a building that forms an angle with the façade. **28b** any part of an architectural feature that forms an angle with the main part. **29** *Law.* a report by a bailiff or other officer on the outcome of a formal document such as a writ, summons, etc., issued by a court. **30** *Cards.* a lead of a card in the suit that one's partner has previously led. **31** *Ball games.* the act of playing or throwing a ball back. **32 by return (of post).** *Brit.* by the next post back to the sender. **33 many happy returns (of the day).** a conventional greeting to someone on his or her birthday. **34 the point of no return.** the point at which a person's commitment is irrevocable. ◆ *adj* **35** of, relating to, or characterized by a return: *a return visit; a return performance.* **36** denoting a second, reciprocated occasion: *a return match.* [C14: from Old French *retorner*; see RE-, TURN]

returnable (rɪˈtɜːnəbᵊl) *adj* **1** able to be taken, given, or sent back. **2** required to be returned by law, as a writ to the court from which it issued. ▸ **reˌturnaˈbility** *n*

return crease *n Cricket.* one of two lines marked at right-angles to each bowling crease, from inside which a bowler must deliver the ball.

returned soldier *n Austral. and N.Z.* a soldier who has served abroad. Also (Austral.): **returned man.**

returnee (rɪˈtɜːˌniː) *n Chiefly U.S. and Canadian.* a person who returns to his native country, esp. after war service.

returner (rɪˈtɜːnə) *n* **1** a person or thing that returns. **2** a person who goes back to work after a break, esp. a woman who has had children.

returning officer *n* (in Britain, Canada, Australia, etc.) an official in charge of conducting an election in a constituency or electoral district, who supervises the counting of votes and announces the results.

return ticket *n Brit.* a ticket entitling a passenger to travel to his destination and back again. U.S. and Canadian equivalent: **round-trip ticket.**

retuse (rɪˈtjuːs) *adj Botany.* having a rounded apex and a central depression: *retuse leaves.* [C18: from Latin *retundere* to make blunt, from RE- + *tundere* to pound]

Retz (*French* rɛts) *n* **Gilles de.** See (Gilles de) **Rais.**

Reuben (ˈruːbɪn) *n Old Testament.* **1** the eldest son of Jacob and Leah: one of the 12 patriarchs of Israel (Genesis 29:30). **2** the Israelite tribe descended from him. **3** the territory of this tribe, lying to the northeast of the Dead Sea. Douay spelling: **Ruben.**

Reuchlin (*German* 'rɔyçliːn) *n* **Johann** (jo'han). 1455–1522, German humanist, who promoted the study of Greek and Hebrew.

reunify (riː'juːnɪˌfaɪ) *vb* **-fies, -fying, -fied.** (*tr*) to bring together again (something, esp. a country previously divided). ▸ **ˌreunifi'cation** *n*

reunion (riː'juːnjən) *n* **1** the act or process of coming together again. **2** the state or condition of having been brought together again. **3** a gathering of relatives, friends, or former associates.

Réunion (riː'juːnjən; *French* reynjɔ̃) *n* an island in the Indian Ocean, in the Mascarene Islands: an overseas region of France, having been in French possession since 1642. Capital: Saint-Denis. Pop.: 692 000 (1998 est.). Area: 2510 sq. km (970 sq. miles).

reunionist (riː'juːnjənɪst) *n* a person who desires or works for reunion between the Roman Catholic Church and the Church of England. ▸ **re'unionism** *n* ▸ **reˌunion'istic** *adj*

reunite (ˌriːjuː'naɪt) *vb* to bring or come together again. ▸ **ˌreu'nitable** *adj* ▸ **ˌreu'niter** *n*

Reus (*Spanish* reus) *n* a city in NE Spain, northwest of Tarragona: became commercially important after the establishment of an English colony (about 1750). Pop.: 86 864 (1991).

reuse *vb* (riː'juːz). (*tr*) **1** to use again. ◆ *n* (riː'juːs) **2** the act or process of using again.

Reuter ('rɔɪtə) *n* Baron **Paul Julius von** (paul 'juːlius fɔn). original name *Israel Beer Josaphat.* 1816–99, German telegrapher, who founded a news agency in London (1851).

Reutlingen (*German* 'rɔytlɪŋən) *n* a city in SW Germany, in Baden-Württemberg: founded in the 11th century; an Imperial free city from 1240 until 1802; textile industry. Pop.: 108 565 (1996 est.).

rev (rɛv) *Informal.* ◆ *n* **1** revolution per minute: *the engine was doing 5000 revs.* ◆ *vb* **revs, revving, revved. 2** (often foll. by *up*) to increase the speed of revolution of (an engine).

rev. *abbrev. for:* **1** revenue. **2** reverse(d). **3** review. **4** revise(d). **5** revision. **6** revolution. **7** revolving.

Rev. *abbrev. for:* **1** *Bible.* Revelation. **2** Reverend.

Reval ('reːval) *n* the German name for **Tallinn.**

revalorize *or* **revalorise** (riː'vælərаɪz) *vb* (*tr*) **1** to change the valuation of (assets). **2** to replace (a currency unit) by another. ▸ **reˌvalori'zation** *or* **reˌvalori'sation** *n*

revalue (riː'væljuː) *or U.S.* **revaluate** *vb* **1** to adjust the exchange value of (a currency), esp. upwards. Compare **devalue. 2** (*tr*) to make a fresh valuation or appraisal of. ▸ **reˌvalu'ation** *n*

revamp (riː'væmp) *vb* (*tr*) **1** to patch up or renovate; repair or restore. ◆ *n* **2** something that has been renovated or revamped. **3** the act or process of revamping. [C19: from RE- + VAMP[2]] ▸ **re'vamper** *n* ▸ **re'vamping** *n*

revanchism (rɪ'væntʃɪzəm) *n* **1** a foreign policy aimed at revenge or the regaining of lost territories. **2** desire or support for such a policy. [C20: from French *revanche* REVENGE] ▸ **re'vanchist** *n, adj*

rev counter *n Brit.* an informal name for **tachometer.**

Revd *abbrev. for* Reverend.

reveal (rɪ'viːl) *vb* (*tr*) **1** (*may take a clause as object or an infinitive*) to disclose (a secret); divulge. **2** to expose to view or show (something concealed). **3** (of God) to disclose (divine truths) either directly or through the medium of prophets, etc. ◆ *n* **4** *Architect.* the vertical side of an opening in a wall, esp. the side of a window or door between the frame and the front of the wall. [C14: from Old French *reveler,* from Latin *revēlāre* to unveil, from RE- + *vēlum* a VEIL] ▸ **re'vealable** *adj* ▸ **reˌveala'bility** *n* ▸ **re'vealer** *n* ▸ **re'vealment** *n*

revealed religion *n* **1** religion based on the revelation by God to man of ideas that he would not have arrived at by his natural reason alone. **2** religion in which the existence of God depends on revelation.

revealing (rɪ'viːlɪŋ) *adj* **1** of significance or import: *a very revealing experience.* **2** showing or designed to show more of the body than is usual or conventional: *a revealing costume.* ▸ **re'vealingly** *adv* ▸ **re'vealingness** *n*

revegetate (riː'vɛdʒɪˌteɪt) *vb* (*intr*) (of plants) to grow again and produce new tissue. ▸ **reˌvege'tation** *n*

reveille (rɪ'vælɪ) *n* **1** a signal, given by a bugle, drum, etc., to awaken soldiers or sailors in the morning. **2** the hour at which this takes place. ◆ Also called (esp. U.S.): **rouse.** [C17: from French *réveillez!* awake! from RE- + Old French *esveillier* to be wakeful, ultimately from Latin *vigilāre* to keep watch; see VIGIL]

revel ('rɛvəl) *vb* **-els, -elling, -elled** *or U.S.* **-els, -eling, -eled.** (*intr*) **1** (foll. by *in*) to take pleasure or wallow: *to revel in success.* **2** to take part in noisy festivities; make merry. ◆ *n* **3** (*often pl*) an occasion of noisy merrymaking. **4** a less common word for **revelry.** [C14: from Old French *reveler* to be merry, noisy, from Latin *rebellāre* to revolt, REBEL] ▸ **'reveller** *n* ▸ **'revelment** *n*

revelation (ˌrɛvə'leɪʃən) *n* **1** the act or process of disclosing something previously secret or obscure, esp. something true. **2** a fact disclosed or revealed, esp. in a dramatic or surprising way. **3** *Christianity.* **3a** God's disclosure of his own nature and his purpose for mankind, esp. through the words of human intermediaries. **3b** something in which such a divine disclosure is contained, such as the Bible. [C14: from Church Latin *revēlātiō,* from Latin *revēlāre* to REVEAL] ▸ **ˌreve'lational** *adj*

Revelation (ˌrɛvə'leɪʃən) *n* (*popularly, often pl*) the last book of the New Testament, containing visionary descriptions of heaven, of conflicts between good and evil, and of the end of the world. Also called: the **Apocalypse,** the **Revelation of Saint John the Divine.**

revelationist (ˌrɛvə'leɪʃənɪst) *n* a person who believes that God has revealed certain truths to man.

revelry ('rɛvəlrɪ) *n, pl* **-ries.** noisy or unrestrained merrymaking.

revenant ('rɛvɪnənt) *n* something, esp. a ghost, that returns. [C19: from French: ghost, from *revenir* to come back, from Latin *revenīre,* from RE- + *venīre* to come]

revenge (rɪ'vɛndʒ) *n* **1** the act of retaliating for wrongs or injury received; vengeance. **2** something done as a means of vengeance. **3** the desire to take vengeance or retaliate. **4** a return match, regarded as a loser's opportunity to even the score. ◆ *vb* (*tr*) **5** to inflict equivalent injury or damage for (injury received); retaliate in return for. **6** to take vengeance for (oneself or another); avenge. [C14: from Old French *revenger,* from Late Latin *revindicāre,* from RE- + *vindicāre* to VINDICATE] ▸ **re'vengeless** *adj* ▸ **re'venger** *n* ▸ **re'venging** *adj* ▸ **re'vengingly** *adv*

revengeful (rɪ'vɛndʒfʊl) *adj* full of or characterized by desire for vengeance; vindictive. ▸ **re'vengefully** *adv* ▸ **re'vengefulness** *n*

revenue ('rɛvɪˌnjuː) *n* **1** the income accruing from taxation to a government during a specified period of time, usually a year. **2a** a government department responsible for the collection of government revenue. **2b** (*as modifier*): *revenue men.* **3** the gross income from a business enterprise, investment, property, etc. **4** a particular item of income. **5** something that yields a regular financial return; source of income. [C16: from Old French, from *revenir* to return, from Latin *revenīre;* see REVENANT] ▸ **'reveˌnued** *adj*

revenue cutter *n* a small lightly armed boat used to enforce customs regulations and catch smugglers.

revenuer ('rɛvɪˌnjuːə) *n U.S. slang.* a revenue officer or cutter.

revenue tariff *n* a tariff for the purpose of producing public revenue. Compare **protective tariff.**

reverb (rɪ'vɜːb) *n* an electronic device that creates artificial acoustics.

reverberate (rɪ'vɜːbəˌreɪt) *vb* **1** (*intr*) to resound or re-echo: *the explosion reverberated through the castle.* **2** to reflect or be reflected many times. **3** (*intr*) to rebound or recoil. **4** (*intr*) (of the flame or heat in a reverberatory furnace) to be deflected onto the metal or ore on the hearth. **5** (*tr*) to heat, melt, or refine (a metal or ore) in a reverberatory furnace. [C16: from Latin *reverberāre* to strike back, from RE- + *verberāre* to beat, from *verber* a lash] ▸ **re'verberant** *or* (*less commonly*) **re'verberative** *adj* ▸ **re'verberantly** *adv* ▸ **re'verber'ation** *n*

reverberation time *n* a measure of the acoustic properties of a room, equal to the time taken for a sound to fall in intensity by 60 decibels. It is usually measured in seconds.

reverberator (rɪ'vɜːbəˌreɪtə) *n* **1** anything that produces or undergoes reverberation. **2** another name for **reverberatory furnace.**

reverberatory (rɪ'vɜːbərətərɪ, -trɪ) *adj* **1** characterized by, utilizing, or produced by reverberation. ◆ *n, pl* **-ries. 2** short for **reverberatory furnace.**

reverberatory furnace *n* a metallurgical furnace having a curved roof that deflects heat onto the charge so that the fuel is not in direct contact with the ore.

revere (rɪ'vɪə) *vb* (*tr*) to be in awe of and respect deeply; venerate. [C17: from Latin *reverērī,* from RE- + *verērī* to fear, be in awe of] ▸ **re'verable** *adj* ▸ **re'verer** *n*

Revere (rɪ'vɪə) *n* **Paul.** 1735–1818, American patriot and silversmith, best known for his night ride on April 18, 1775, to warn the Massachusetts colonists of the coming of the British troops.

reverence ('rɛvərəns) *n* **1** a feeling or attitude of profound respect, usually reserved for the sacred or divine; devoted veneration. **2** an outward manifestation of this feeling, esp. a bow or act of obeisance. **3** the state of being revered or commanding profound respect. **4 saving your reverence.** *Archaic.* a form of apology for using an obscene or taboo expression. ◆ *vb* **5** (*tr*) to revere or venerate. ▸ **'reverencer** *n*

Reverence ('rɛvərəns) *n* (preceded by *Your* or *His*) a title sometimes used to address or refer to a Roman Catholic priest.

reverend ('rɛvərənd) *adj* **1** worthy of reverence. **2** relating to or designating a clergyman or the clergy. ◆ *n* **3** *Informal.* a clergyman. [C15: from Latin *reverendus* fit to be revered; see REVERE]

Reverend ('rɛvərənd) *adj* a title of respect for a clergyman. Abbrevs.: **Rev., Revd.** See also **Very Reverend, Right Reverend, Most Reverend.**

USAGE *Reverend* with a surname alone (*Reverend Smith*), as a term of address (*"Yes, Reverend"*), or in the salutation of a letter (*Dear Rev. Mr Smith*) are all generally considered to be wrong usage. Preferred are (*the*) *Reverend John Smith* or *Reverend Mr Smith* and *Dear Mr Smith.*

Reverend Mother *n* a title of respect or form of address for the Mother Superior of a convent.

reverent ('rɛvərənt, 'rɛvrənt) *adj* feeling, expressing, or characterized by reverence. [C14: from Latin *reverēns* respectful] ▸ **'reverently** *adv* ▸ **'reverentness** *n*

reverential (ˌrɛvə'rɛnʃəl) *adj* resulting from or showing reverence: *a pilgrimage is a reverential act, performed by reverent people.* ▸ **ˌrever'entially** *adv*

reverie *or* **revery** ('rɛvərɪ) *n, pl* **-eries. 1** an act or state of absent-minded daydreaming: *to fall into a reverie.* **2** a piece of instrumental music suggestive of a daydream. **3** *Archaic.* a fanciful or visionary notion; daydream. [C14: from Old French *resverie* wildness, from *resver* to behave wildly, of uncertain origin; see RAVE[1]]

revers (rɪ'vɪə) *n, pl* **-vers** (-'vɪəz). (*usually pl*) the turned-back lining of part of a garment, esp. of a lapel or cuff. [C19: from French, literally: REVERSE]

re'type *vb* **ˌreup'holster** *vb* **re'usable** *adj*

reversal (rɪˈvɜːsᵊl) *n* **1** the act or an instance of reversing. **2** a change for the worse; reverse: *a reversal of fortune.* **3** the state of being reversed. **4** the annulment of a judicial decision, esp. by an appeal court on grounds of error or irregularity.

reversal film *n* photographic film that can be processed to produce a positive transparent image for direct projection, rather than a negative for printing.

reverse (rɪˈvɜːs) *vb* (*mainly tr*) **1** to turn or set in an opposite direction, order, or position. **2** to change into something different or contrary; alter completely: *reverse one's policy.* **3** (*also intr*) to move or cause to move backwards or in an opposite direction: *to reverse a car.* **4** to run (machinery, etc.) in the opposite direction to normal. **5** to turn inside out. **6** *Law.* to revoke or set aside (a judgment, decree, etc.); annul. **7** (often foll. by *out*) to print from plates so made that white lettering or design of (a page, text, display, etc.) appears on a black or coloured background. **8 reverse arms.** *Military.* to turn one's arms upside down, esp. as a token of mourning. **9 reverse the charge(s).** to make a telephone call at the recipient's expense. ◆ *n* **10** the opposite or contrary of something. **11** the back or rear side of something. **12** a change to an opposite position, state, or direction. **13** a change for the worse; setback or defeat. **14a** the mechanism or gears by which machinery, a vehicle, etc., can be made to reverse its direction. **14b** (*as modifier*): *reverse gear.* **15** the side of a coin bearing a secondary design. Compare **obverse** (sense 5). **16a** printed matter in which normally black or coloured areas, esp. lettering, appear white, and vice versa. **16b** (*as modifier*): *reverse plates.* **17 in reverse.** in an opposite or backward direction. **18 the reverse of.** emphatically not; not at all: *he was the reverse of polite when I called.* ◆ *adj* **19** opposite or contrary in direction, position, order, nature, etc.; turned backwards. **20** back to front; inverted. **21** operating or moving in a manner contrary to that which is usual. **22** denoting or relating to a mirror image. [C14: from Old French, from Latin *reversus,* from *revertere* to turn back] ▸ **reˈversely** *adv* ▸ **reˈverser** *n*

reverse-charge *adj* (*prenominal*) (of a telephone call) made at the recipient's expense. U.S. equivalent: **collect.**

reverse takeover *n Finance.* the purchase of a larger company by a smaller company, esp. of a public company by a private company.

reverse transcriptase (trænˈskrɪpteɪz) *n* an enzyme present in retroviruses that copies RNA into DNA, thus reversing the usual flow of genetic information in which DNA is copied into RNA.

reverse video *n Computing.* a highlighting feature achieved by reversing the colours of normal characters and background on a visual display unit.

reversi (rɪˈvɜːsɪ) *n* a game played on a draughtboard with 64 pieces, black on one side and white on the other. When pieces are captured they are turned over to join the capturing player's forces; the winner is the player who fills the board with pieces of his colour. [C19: from French; see REVERSE]

reversible (rɪˈvɜːsəbᵊl) *adj* **1** capable of being reversed: *a reversible decision.* **2** capable of returning to an original condition. **3** *Chem., physics.* capable of assuming or producing either of two possible states and changing from one to the other: *a reversible reaction.* **4** *Thermodynamics.* (of a change, process, etc.) occurring through a number of intermediate states that are all in thermodynamic equilibrium. **5** (of a fabric or garment) woven, printed, or finished so that either side may be used as the outer side. ◆ *n* **6** a reversible garment, esp. a coat. ▸ **reˌversiˈbility** ▸ **reˈversibly** *adv*

reversing light *n* a light on the rear of a motor vehicle to warn others that the vehicle is being reversed.

reversion (rɪˈvɜːʃən) *n* **1** a return to or towards an earlier condition, practice, or belief; act of reverting. **2** the act of reversing or the state of being reversed; reversal. **3** *Biology.* **3a** the return of individuals, organs, etc., to a more primitive condition or type. **3b** the reappearance of primitive characteristics in an individual or group. **4** *Property law.* **4a** an interest in an estate that reverts to the grantor or his heirs at the end of a period, esp. at the end of the life of a grantee. **4b** an estate so reverting. **4c** the right to succeed to such an estate. **5** the benefit payable on the death of a life-insurance policyholder. ▸ **reˈversionally** *adv* ▸ **reˈversionary** *or* **reˈversional** *adj*

reversionary bonus *n Insurance.* a bonus added to the sum payable on death or at the maturity of a with-profits assurance policy.

reversioner (rɪˈvɜːʃənə) *n Property law.* a person entitled to an estate in reversion. Compare **remainderman.**

reverso (rɪˈvɜːsəʊ) *n, pl* **-sos.** another name for **verso.**

revert *vb* (rɪˈvɜːt). (*intr;* foll. by *to*). **1** to go back to a former practice, condition, belief, etc.: *she reverted to her old wicked ways.* **2** to take up again or come back to a former topic. **3** *Biology.* (of individuals, organs, etc.) to return to a more primitive, earlier, or simpler condition or type. **4** *Property law.* (of an estate or interest in land) to return to its former owner or his heirs when a grant, esp. a grant for the lifetime of the grantee, comes to an end. **5 revert to type.** to resume characteristics that were thought to have disappeared. ◆ *n* (ˈriːˌvɜːt). **6** a person who, having been converted, has returned to his former beliefs or Church. [C13: from Latin *revertere* to return, from RE- + *vertere* to turn] ▸ **reˈverter** *n* ▸ **reˈvertible** *adj*

USAGE Since *back* is part of the meaning of *revert,* one should not say that someone *reverts back* to a certain type of behaviour.

revest (riːˈvɛst) *vb* (often foll. by *in*) to restore (former power, authority, status, etc., to a person) or (of power, authority, etc.) to be restored. [C16: from Old French *revestir* to clothe again, from Latin RE- + *vestīre* to clothe; see VEST]

revet (rɪˈvɛt) *vb* **-vets, -vetting, -vetted.** to face (a wall or embankment) with stones. [C19: from French *revêt,* from Old French *revestir* to reclothe; see REVEST]

revetment (rɪˈvɛtmənt) *n* **1** a facing of stones, sandbags, etc., to protect a wall, embankment, or earthworks. **2** another name for **retaining wall.** [C18: from French *revêtement* literally, a reclothing, from *revêtir;* see REVEST]

review (rɪˈvjuː) *vb* (*mainly tr*) **1** to look at or examine again: *to review a situation.* **2** to look back upon (a period of time, sequence of events, etc.); remember: *he reviewed his achievements with pride.* **3** to inspect, esp. formally or officially: *the general reviewed his troops.* **4** to read through or go over in order to correct. **5** *Law.* to re-examine (a decision) judicially. **6** to write a critical assessment of (a book, film, play, concert, etc.), esp. as a profession. ◆ *n* **7** Also called: **reviewal.** the act or an instance of reviewing. **8** a general survey or report: *a review of the political situation.* **9** a critical assessment of a book, film, play, concert, etc., esp. one printed in a newspaper or periodical. **10a** a publication containing such articles. **10b** (*cap. when part of a name*): *the Saturday Review.* **11** a second consideration; re-examination. **12** a retrospective survey. **13** a formal or official inspection. **14** a U.S. and Canadian word for **revision** (sense 2). **15** *Law.* judicial re-examination of a case, esp. by a superior court. **16** a less common spelling of **revue.** [C16: from French, from *revoir* to see again, from Latin *re-* RE- + *vidēre* to see] ▸ **reˈviewable** *adj* ▸ **reˈviewer** *n*

review copy *n* a copy of a book sent by a publisher to a journal, newspaper, etc., to enable it to be reviewed.

revile (rɪˈvaɪl) *vb* to use abusive or scornful language against (someone or something). [C14: from Old French *reviler,* from RE- + *vil* VILE] ▸ **reˈvilement** *n* ▸ **reˈviler** *n*

revise (rɪˈvaɪz) *vb* **1** (*tr*) to change, alter, or amend: *to revise one's opinion.* **2** *Brit.* to reread (a subject or notes on it) so as to memorize it, esp. in preparation for an examination. **3** (*tr*) to prepare a new version or edition of (a previously printed work). ◆ *n* **4** the act, process, or result of revising; revision. [C16: from Latin *revīsere* to look back at, from RE- + *vīsere* to inspect, from *vidēre* to see; see REVIEW, VISIT] ▸ **reˈvisable** *adj* ▸ **reˈvisal** *n* ▸ **reˈviser** *n*

Revised Standard Version *n* a revision by American scholars of the American Standard Version of the Bible. The New Testament was published in 1946 and the entire Bible in 1953.

Revised Version *n* a revision of the Authorized Version of the Bible prepared by two committees of British scholars, the New Testament being published in 1881 and the Old in 1885.

revision (rɪˈvɪʒən) *n* **1** the act or process of revising. **2** *Brit.* the process of rereading a subject or notes on it, esp. in preparation for an examination. **3** a corrected or new version of a book, article, etc. ▸ **reˈvisionary** *adj*

revisionism (rɪˈvɪʒəˌnɪzəm) *n* **1** (*sometimes cap.*) **1a** a moderate, nonrevolutionary version of Marxism developed in Germany around 1900. **1b** (in Marxist-Leninist ideology) any dangerous departure from the true interpretation of Marx's teachings. **2** the advocacy of revision of some political theory, religious doctrine, historical or critical interpretation, etc. **3** (*usually cap.*) an ultra-nationalist form of Zionism that arose in Palestine in the 1940s. ▸ **reˈvisionist** *n, adj*

revisit (riːˈvɪzɪt) *vb* (*tr*) **1** to visit again. **2** (used in the past participle) to re-examine (a topic or theme) after an interval, with a view to making a fresh appraisal: *Hitchcock revisited.*

revisory (rɪˈvaɪzərɪ) *adj* of, relating to, or having the power to revise.

revitalize *or* **revitalise** (riːˈvaɪtᵊˌlaɪz) *vb* (*tr*) to restore vitality or animation to. ▸ **reˌvitaliˈzation** *or* **reˌvitaliˈsation** *n*

revival (rɪˈvaɪvᵊl) *n* **1** the act or an instance of reviving or the state of being revived. **2** an instance of returning to life or consciousness; restoration of vigour or vitality. **3** a renewed use, acceptance of, or interest in (past customs, styles, etc.): *a revival of learning; the Gothic revival.* **4** a new production of a play that has not been recently performed. **5** a reawakening of faith or renewal of commitment to religion. **6** an evangelistic meeting or service intended to effect such a reawakening in those present. **7** the re-establishment of legal validity, as of a judgment, contract, etc.

revivalism (rɪˈvaɪvəˌlɪzəm) *n* **1** a movement, esp. an evangelical Christian one, that seeks to reawaken faith. **2** the tendency or desire to revive former customs, styles, etc.

revivalist (rɪˈvaɪvəlɪst) *n* **1** a person who holds, promotes, or presides over religious revivals. **2** a person who revives customs, institutions, ideas, etc. ◆ *adj* **3** of, relating to, or characterizing revivalism or religious revivals: *a revivalist meeting.* ▸ **reˌvivalˈistic** *adj*

revive (rɪˈvaɪv) *vb* **1** to bring or be brought back to life, consciousness, or strength; resuscitate or be resuscitated: *revived by a drop of whisky.* **2** to give or assume new vitality; flourish again or cause to flourish again. **3** to make or become operative or active again: *the youth movement was revived.* **4** to bring or come into use or currency again: *to revive a language.* **5** (*tr*) to take up again: *he revived his old hobby.* **6** to bring or come back to mind. **7** (*tr*) *Theatre.* to mount a new production of (an old play). [C15: from Old French *revivre* to live again, from Latin *revīvere,* from RE- + *vīvere* to live; see VIVID] ▸ **reˈvivable** *adj* ▸ **reˌvivaˈbility** *n* ▸ **reˈvivably** *adv* ▸ **reˈviver** *n* ▸ **reˈviving** *adj* ▸ **reˈvivingly** *adv*

revivify (rɪˈvɪvɪˌfaɪ) *vb* **-fies, -fying, -fied.** (*tr*) to give new life or spirit to; revive. ▸ **reˌvivifiˈcation** *n*

reviviscence (ˌrɛvɪˈvɪsəns, rɪˈvɪvɪsəns) *n Rare.* restoration to life or animation; revival. [C17: from Latin, from *revīviscere* come back to life, related to *vīvere* to live; see REVIVE] ▸ **ˌreviˈviscent** *adj*

revocable (ˈrɛvəkəbᵊl) *or* **revokable** (rɪˈvəʊkəbᵊl) *adj* capable of being revoked; able to be cancelled. ▸ **ˌrevocaˈbility** *or* **reˌvokaˈbility** *n* ▸ **ˈrevocably** *or* **reˈvokably** *adv*

revocation (ˌrɛvəˈkeɪʃən) *n* **1** the act of revoking or state of being revoked; cancellation. **2a** the cancellation or annulment of a legal instrument, esp. a will. **2b** the withdrawal of an offer, power of attorney, etc. ▸ **revocatory** (ˈrɛvəkətərɪ, -trɪ) *adj*

revoice (riːˈvɔɪs) *vb* (*intr*) **1** to utter again; echo. **2** to adjust the design of (an organ pipe or wind instrument) as after disuse or to conform with modern pitch.

revoke (rɪˈvəʊk) *vb* **1** (*tr*) to take back or withdraw; cancel; rescind: *to revoke a* *law.* 2 (*intr*) *Cards.* to break a rule of play by failing to follow suit when able to do so; renege. ◆ *n* 3 *Cards.* the act of revoking; a renege. [C14: from Latin *revocāre* to call back, withdraw, from RE- + *vocāre* to call] ▸ **re'voker** *n*

revolt (rɪ'vəult) *n* 1 a rebellion or uprising against authority. 2 **in revolt.** in the process or state of rebelling. ◆ *vb* 3 (*intr*) to rise up in rebellion against authority. 4 (*usually passive*) to feel or cause to feel revulsion, disgust, or abhorrence. [C16: from French *révolter* to revolt, from Old Italian *rivoltare* to overturn, ultimately from Latin *revolvere* to roll back, REVOLVE] ▸ **re'volter** *n*

revolting (rɪ'vəultɪŋ) *adj* 1 causing revulsion; nauseating, disgusting, or repulsive. 2 *Informal.* unpleasant or nasty: *that dress is revolting.* ▸ **re'voltingly** *adv*

revolute ('rɛvə,lu:t) *adj* (esp. of the margins of a leaf) rolled backwards and downwards. [C18: from Latin *revolūtus* rolled back; see REVOLVE]

revolution (,rɛvə'lu:ʃən) *n* 1 the overthrow or repudiation of a regime or political system by the governed. 2 (in Marxist theory) the violent and historically necessary transition from one system of production in a society to the next, as from feudalism to capitalism. 3 a far-reaching and drastic change, esp. in ideas, methods, etc. 4a movement in or as if in a circle. 4b one complete turn in such a circle: *a turntable rotating at 33 revolutions per minute.* 5a the orbital motion of one body, such as a planet or satellite, around another. Compare **rotation** (sense 5a). 5b one complete turn in such motion. 6 a cycle of successive events or changes. 7 *Geology.* a profound change in conditions over a large part of the earth's surface, esp. one characterized by mountain building: *an orogenic revolution.* [C14: via Old French from Late Latin *revolūtiō*, from Latin *revolvere* to REVOLVE]

revolutionary (,rɛvə'lu:ʃənərɪ) *n, pl* **-aries.** 1 a person who advocates or engages in revolution. ◆ *adj* 2 relating to or characteristic of a revolution. 3 advocating or engaged in revolution. 4 radically new or different: *a revolutionary method of making plastics.* 5 rotating or revolving. ▸ **,revo'lutionarily** *adv*

Revolutionary (,rɛvə'lu:ʃənərɪ) *adj* 1 *Chiefly U.S.* of or relating to the conflict or period of the War of American Independence (1775–83). 2 of or relating to any of various other Revolutions, esp. the **Russian Revolution** (1917) or the **French Revolution** (1789).

Revolutionary calendar *n* the calendar adopted by the French First Republic in 1793 and abandoned in 1805. Dates were calculated from Sept. 22, 1792. The months were called Vendémiaire, Brumaire, Frimaire, Nivôse, Pluviôse, Ventôse, Germinal, Floréal, Prairial, Messidor, Thermidor, and Fructidor.

Revolutionary Wars *pl n* the series of wars (1792–1802) fought against Revolutionary France by a combination of other powers, esp. England, Austria, and Prussia.

revolutionist (,rɛvə'lu:ʃənɪst) *n* 1 a less common word for a **revolutionary.** ◆ *adj* 2 of, characteristic of, or relating to revolution or revolutionaries.

revolutionize *or* **revolutionise** (,rɛvə'lu:ʃə,naɪz) *vb* (*tr*) 1 to bring about a radical change in: *science has revolutionized civilization.* 2 to inspire or infect with revolutionary ideas: *they revolutionized the common soldiers.* 3 to cause a revolution in (a country, etc.). ▸ **,revo'lution,izer** *or* **,revo'lution,iser** *n*

revolve (rɪ'vɒlv) *vb* 1 to move or cause to move around a centre or axis; rotate. 2 (*intr*) to occur periodically or in cycles. 3 to consider or be considered. 4 (*intr*; foll. by *around* or *about*) to be centred or focused (upon): *Juliet's thoughts revolved around Romeo.* ◆ *n* 5 *Theatre.* a circular section of a stage that can be rotated by electric power to provide a scene change. [C14: from Latin *revolvere*, from RE- + *volvere* to roll, wind] ▸ **re'volvable** *adj* ▸ **re'volvably** *adv*

revolver (rɪ'vɒlvə) *n* a pistol having a revolving multichambered cylinder that allows several shots to be discharged without reloading.

revolving (rɪ'vɒlvɪŋ) *adj* denoting or relating to an engine, such as a radial aero engine, in which the cylinders revolve about a fixed shaft. ▸ **re'volvingly** *adv*

revolving credit *n* a letter of credit for a fixed sum, specifying that the beneficiary may make repeated use of the credit provided that the fixed sum is never exceeded.

revolving door *n* 1 a door that rotates about a central vertical axis, esp. one with four leaves arranged at right angles to each other, thereby excluding draughts. 2a *Informal.* a tendency to change personnel on a frequent basis. 2b (*as modifier*): *a revolving-door band.* 3a *Informal.* the hiring of former government employees by private companies with which they had dealings when they worked for the government. 3b (*as modifier*): *revolving-door consultancies.*

revolving fund *n* a fund set up for a specific purpose and constantly added to by income from its investments.

revue *or* (*less commonly*) **review** (rɪ'vju:) *n* a form of light entertainment consisting of a series of topical sketches, songs, dancing, comic turns, etc. [C20: from French; see REVIEW]

revulsion (rɪ'vʌlʃən) *n* 1 a sudden and unpleasant violent reaction in feeling, esp. one of extreme loathing. 2 the act or an instance of drawing back or recoiling from something. 3 the diversion of disease or congestion from one part of the body to another by cupping, counterirritants, etc. [C16: from Latin *revulsiō* a pulling away, from *revellere*, from RE- + *vellere* to pull, tear] ▸ **re'vulsionary** *adj*

revulsive (rɪ'vʌlsɪv) *adj* 1 of or causing revulsion. ◆ *n* 2 *Med.* a counterirritant. ▸ **re'vulsively** *adv*

Rev. Ver. *abbrev. for* Revised Version (of the Bible).

reward (rɪ'wɔ:d) *n* 1 something given or received in return for a deed or service rendered. 2 a sum of money offered, esp. for help in finding a criminal or for the return of lost or stolen property. 3 profit or return. 4 something received in return for good or evil; deserts. 5 *Psychol.* any pleasant event that follows a response and therefore increases the likelihood of the response recurring in the future. ◆ *vb* 6 (*tr*) to give (something) to (someone), esp. in gratitude for a service rendered; recompense. [C14: from Old Norman French *rewarder* to regard, from RE- + *warder* to care for, guard, of Germanic origin; see WARD] ▸ **re'wardable** *adj* ▸ **re'warder** *n* ▸ **re'wardless** *adj*

reward claim *n Austral. history.* a claim granted to a miner who discovered gold in a new area.

rewarding (rɪ'wɔ:dɪŋ) *adj* giving personal satisfaction; gratifying: *caring for the elderly is rewarding.*

rewa-rewa ('reɪwə'reɪwə) *n* a tall proteaceous tree of New Zealand, *Knightia excelsa,* yielding a beautiful reddish timber. [C19: from Maori]

rewind *vb* (ri:'waɪnd), **-winds, -winding, -wound.** 1 (*tr*) to wind back, esp. a film or tape onto the original reel. ◆ *n* ('ri:,waɪnd, ri:'waɪnd). 2 something rewound. 3 the act of rewinding. ▸ **re'winder** *n*

rewire (ri:'waɪə) *vb* (*tr*) to provide (a house, engine, etc.) with new wiring. ▸ **re'wirable** *adj*

reword (ri:'wɜ:d) *vb* (*tr*) to alter the wording of; express differently.

rework (ri:'wɜ:k) *vb* (*tr*) 1 to use again in altered form: *the theme has been reworked in countless well-known poems.* 2 to rewrite or revise. 3 to reprocess for use again.

rewrite *vb* (ri:'raɪt), **-writes, -writing, -wrote, -written.** (*tr*) 1 to write (written material) again, esp. changing the words or form. 2 *Computing.* to return (data) to a store when it has been erased during reading. ◆ *n* ('ri:,raɪt). 3 something rewritten.

rewrite rule *n Generative grammar.* another name for **phrase-structure rule.**

Rex (rɛks) *n* king: part of the official title of a king, now used chiefly in documents, legal proceedings, inscriptions on coins, etc. Compare **Regina**[1]. [Latin]

Rexine ('rɛksi:n) *n Trademark.* a form of artificial leather.

Reye's syndrome (raɪz, reɪz) *n* a rare metabolic disease in children that can be fatal, involving damage to the brain, liver, and kidneys. [C20: named after R. D. K. *Reye* (1912–78) Australian paediatrician]

Reykjavik ('reɪkjə,vi:k) *n* the capital and chief port of Iceland, situated in the southwest: its buildings are heated by natural hot water. Pop.: 105 487 (1996 est.).

Reynard ('rɛnəd, 'rɛnɑ:d, 'reɪnəd, 'reɪnɑ:d) *n* a name for a fox, used in medieval tales, fables, etc. [from earlier *Renard, Renart,* hero of the French bestiary *Roman de Renart:* ultimately from the Old High German name *Reginhart,* literally, strong in counsel]

Reynaud (*French* rɛno) *n* **Paul** (pɔl). 1878–1966, French statesman: premier during the defeat of France by Germany (1940); later imprisoned by the Germans.

Reynolds ('rɛnəldz) *n* 1 **Albert.** born 1935, Irish politician: leader of the Fianna Fáil party and prime minister of the Republic of Ireland (1994–96). 2 Sir **Joshua.** 1723–92, English portrait painter. He was the first president of the Royal Academy (1768): the annual lectures he gave there, published as *Discourses,* are important contributions to art theory and criticism.

Reynolds number *n* a number, $v\rho l/\eta$, where v is the fluid velocity, ρ the density, η the viscosity and l a dimension of the system. The value of the number indicates the type of fluid flow. [C19: named after Osborne *Reynolds* (1842–1912), British physicist]

Reynosa (*Spanish* re'nosa) *n* a city in E Mexico, in Tamaulipas state on the Rio Grande. Pop.: 265 663 (1990).

rf *Music. abbrev. for* rinforzando. Also: **rfz.**

Rf *the chemical symbol for* rutherfordium.

RF *abbrev. for* radio frequency.

RF- (in the U.S. Air Force) *abbrev. for* reconnaissance fighter: *RF-4E.*

RFC *abbrev. for:* 1 Rugby Football Club. 2 Royal Flying Corps.

RFLP *abbrev. for* restriction fragment length polymorphism: any variation in DNA between individuals revealed by restriction enzymes that cut DNA into fragments of different lengths in consequence of such variations. It is used forensically and in the diagnosis of hereditary disease.

RGB *abbrev. for* red, green, blue: *RGB components of a colour; RGB signal.*

RGN (in Britain) *abbrev. for* Registered General Nurse.

RGS *abbrev. for* Royal Geographical Society.

Rgt *abbrev. for* regiment.

rh *or* **RH** *abbrev. for* right hand.

Rh 1 *the chemical symbol for* rhodium. ◆ 2 *abbrev. for* rhesus (esp. in **Rh factor**).

RH 1 *abbrev. for* Royal Highness. ◆ 2 *international car registration for* (Republic of) Haiti.

RHA *abbrev. for* 1 Regional Health Authority. 2 Royal Horse Artillery.

rhabdomancy ('ræbdə,mænsɪ) *n* divination for water or mineral ore by means of a rod or wand; dowsing; divining. [C17: via Late Latin from Late Greek *rhabdomanteia,* from *rhabdos* a rod + *manteia* divination] ▸ **'rhabdo,mantist** *or* **'rhabdo,mancer** *n*

rhabdomyoma (,ræbdəumaɪ'əumə) *n, pl* **-mas** *or* **-mata** (-mətə). *Pathol.* a benign tumour of striated muscle. [C19: from New Latin, from Greek *rhabdos* a rod + MYOMA]

rhachis ('reɪkɪs) *n, pl* **rhachises** *or* **rhachides** ('rækɪ,di:z, 'reɪ-). a variant spelling of **rachis.**

Rhadamanthus *or* **Rhadamanthys** (,rædə'mænθəs) *n Greek myth.* one of the judges of the dead in the underworld. ▸ **,Rhada'manthine** *adj*

re'warm *vb*	**re'wash** *vb*

Rhaetia ('ri:ʃɪə) *n* an Alpine province of ancient Rome including parts of present-day Tyrol and E Switzerland.

Rhaetian ('ri:ʃən) *n* 1 Also called: **Rhaeto-Romanic** ('ri:təurəu'mænɪk). a group of Romance languages or dialects spoken in certain valleys of the Alps, including Romansch, Ladin, and Friulian. ♦ *adj* 2 denoting or relating to this group of languages. 3 of or relating to Rhaetia.

Rhaetian Alps *pl n* a section of the central Alps along E Switzerland's borders with Austria and Italy. Highest peak: Piz Bernina, 4049 m (13 284 ft.).

Rhaetic *or* **Rhetic** ('ri:tɪk) *adj* 1 of or relating to a series of rocks formed between the Triassic and Jurassic periods. ♦ *n* 2 **the.** the Rhaetic series.

Rhamadhan (ˌræmə'dɑ:n) *n* a variant spelling of **Ramadan.**

rhamnaceous (ræm'neɪʃəs) *adj* of, relating to, or belonging to the *Rhamnaceae,* a widely distributed family of trees and shrubs having small inconspicuous flowers. The family includes the buckthorns. [C19: from New Latin *Rhamnaceae,* from Greek *rhamnos* a thorn]

rhapsodic (ræp'sɒdɪk) *adj* 1 of or like a rhapsody. 2 lyrical or romantic. ▸ **rhap'sodically** *adv*

rhapsodist ('ræpsədɪst) *n* 1 a person who speaks or writes rhapsodies. 2 a person who speaks with extravagant enthusiasm. 3 Also called: **rhapsode** ('ræpsəud). (in ancient Greece) a professional reciter of poetry, esp. of Homer. ▸ **ˌrhapso'distic** *adj*

rhapsodize *or* **rhapsodise** ('ræpsəˌdaɪz) *vb* 1 to speak or write (something) with extravagant enthusiasm. 2 (*intr*) to recite or write rhapsodies.

rhapsody ('ræpsədɪ) *n, pl* **-dies.** 1 *Music.* a composition free in structure and highly emotional in character. 2 an expression of ecstatic enthusiasm. 3 (in ancient Greece) an epic poem or part of an epic recited by a rhapsodist. 4 a literary work composed in an intense or exalted style. 5 rapturous delight or ecstasy. 6 *Obsolete.* a medley. [C16: via Latin from Greek *rhapsōidia,* from *rhaptein* to sew together + *ōidē* song]

rhatany ('rætənɪ) *n, pl* **-nies.** 1 either of two South American leguminous shrubs, *Krameria triandra* or *K. argentea,* that have thick fleshy roots. 2 the dried roots of such shrubs for use as an astringent. ♦ Also called: **krameria.** [C19: from New Latin *rhatānia,* ultimately from Quechua *ratánya*]

rhd *abbrev. for* right-hand drive.

rhea ('rɪə) *n* either of two large fast-running flightless birds, *Rhea americana* or *Pterocnemia pennata,* inhabiting the open plains of S South America: order *Rheiformes* (see **ratite**). They are similar to but smaller than the ostrich, having three-toed feet and a completely feathered body. [C19: New Latin; arbitrarily named after RHEA[1]]

Rhea[1] ('rɪə) *n Greek myth.* a Titaness, wife of Cronus and mother of several of the gods, including Zeus: a fertility goddess. Roman counterpart: **Ops.**

Rhea[2] ('rɪə) *n* a large satellite of the planet Saturn.

Rhea Silvia *or* **Rea Silvia** ('sɪlvɪə) *n Roman myth.* the mother of Romulus and Remus by Mars. See also **Ilia.**

rhebok *or* **reebok** ('ri:bʌk, -bɒk) *n, pl* **-boks** *or* **-bok.** an antelope, *Pelea capreolus,* of southern Africa, having woolly brownish-grey hair. [C18: Afrikaans, from Dutch *reebok* ROEBUCK]

Rhee (ri:) *n* **Syngman** ('sɪŋmən). 1875–1965, Korean statesman, leader of the campaign for independence from Japan; first president of South Korea (1948–60). Popular unrest forced his resignation.

Rheims (ri:mz; *French* rɛ̃s) *n* a variant spelling of **Reims.**

Rhein (raɪn) *n* the German name for the **Rhine.**

Rheinland ('raɪnlant) *n* the German name for the **Rhineland.**

Rheinland-Pfalz ('raɪnlant'pfalts) *n* the German name for **Rhineland-Palatinate.**

rheme (ri:m) *n Linguistics.* the constituent of a sentence that adds most new information, in addition to what has already been said in the discourse. The rheme is usually, but not always, associated with the subject. Compare **theme** (sense 5). [C20: from Greek *rhēma* that which is said]

Rhemish ('ri:mɪʃ) *adj* of, relating to, or originating in Reims.

Rhenish ('rɛnɪʃ, 'ri:-) *adj* 1 of or relating to the River Rhine or the lands adjacent to it, esp. the Rhineland-Palatinate. ♦ *n* 2 another word for **hock** (the wine).

rhenium ('ri:nɪəm) *n* a dense silvery-white metallic element that has a high melting point. It occurs principally in gadolinite and molybdenite and is used, alloyed with tungsten or molybdenum, in high-temperature thermocouples. Symbol: Re; atomic no.: 75; atomic wt.: 186.207; valency: -1 or 1–7; relative density: 21.02; melting pt.: 3186°C; boiling pt.: 5596°C (est.). [C19: New Latin, from *Rhēnus* the Rhine]

rheo. *abbrev. for* rheostat.

rheo- *combining form.* indicating stream, flow, or current: *rheometer; rheoscope.* [from Greek *rheos* stream, anything flowing, from *rhein* to flow]

rheobase ('ri:əuˌbeɪs) *n Physiol.* the minimum nerve impulse required to elicit a response from a tissue.

rheology (rɪ'ɒlədʒɪ) *n* the branch of physics concerned with the flow and change of shape of matter, esp. the viscosity of liquids. ▸ **rheological** (ˌri:ə'lɒdʒɪkᵊl) *adj* ▸ **rhe'ologist** *n*

rheometer (rɪ'ɒmɪtə) *n* 1 *Med.* an instrument for measuring the velocity of the blood flow. 2 another word for **galvanometer.** ▸ **rheometric** (ˌri:ə'mɛtrɪk) *adj* ▸ **rhe'ometry** *n*

rheomorphism (ˌri:ə'mɔ:fɪzəm) *n Geology.* the liquefaction of rock, which results in its flowing and intruding into surrounding rocks. ▸ **ˌrheo'morphic** *adj*

rheoreceptor ('ri:ərɪˌsɛptə) *n Zoology.* a receptor in fish and some amphibians that responds to water currents.

rheostat ('ri:əˌstæt) *n* a variable resistance, usually consisting of a coil of wire with a terminal at one end and a sliding contact that moves along the coil to tap off the current. ▸ **ˌrheo'static** *adj*

rheotaxis (ˌri:ə'tæksɪs) *n* movement of an organism towards or away from a current of water. ▸ **rheotactic** (ˌri:ə'tæktɪk) *adj*

rheotropism (rɪ'ɒtrəˌpɪzəm) *n* growth of a plant or sessile animal in the direction of a current of water. ▸ **rheotropic** (ˌri:ə'trɒpɪk) *adj*

Rhesus ('ri:səs) *n Greek myth.* a king of Thrace, who arrived in the tenth year of the Trojan War to aid Troy. Odysseus and Diomedes stole his horses because an oracle had said that if these horses drank from the River Xanthus, Troy would not fall.

rhesus baby ('ri:səs) *n* a baby suffering from haemolytic disease at birth as its red blood cells (which are Rh positive) have been attacked in the womb by antibodies from its Rh negative mother. [C20: see RH FACTOR]

rhesus factor *n* See **Rh factor.**

rhesus monkey *n* a macaque monkey, *Macaca mulatta,* of S Asia: used extensively in medical research. [C19: New Latin, arbitrarily from Greek *Rhesos* RHESUS]

rhet. *abbrev. for* rhetoric(al).

Rhetic ('ri:tɪk) *adj, n* a variant spelling of **Rhaetic.**

rhetor ('ri:tə) *n* 1 a teacher of rhetoric. 2 (in ancient Greece) an orator. [C14: via Latin from Greek *rhētōr;* related to *rhēma* word]

rhetoric ('rɛtərɪk) *n* 1 the study of the technique of using language effectively. 2 the art of using speech to persuade, influence, or please; oratory. 3 excessive use of ornamentation and contrivance in spoken or written discourse; bombast. 4 speech or discourse that pretends to significance but lacks true meaning: *all the politician says is mere rhetoric.* [C14: via Latin from Greek *rhētorikē* (*tekhnē*) (the art of) rhetoric, from *rhētōr* RHETOR]

rhetorical (rɪ'tɒrɪkᵊl) *adj* 1 concerned with effect or style rather than content or meaning; bombastic. 2 of or relating to rhetoric or oratory. ▸ **rhe'torically** *adv*

rhetorical question *n* a question to which no answer is required: used esp. for dramatic effect. An example is *Who knows?* (with the implication *Nobody knows*).

rhetorician (ˌrɛtə'rɪʃən) *n* 1 a teacher of the art of rhetoric. 2 a stylish or eloquent writer or speaker. 3 a person whose speech is pompous or extravagant.

rheum (ru:m) *n* a watery discharge from the eyes or nose. [C14: from Old French *reume,* ultimately from Greek *rheuma* bodily humour, stream, from *rhein* to flow]

rheumatic (ru:'mætɪk) *adj* 1 of, relating to, or afflicted with rheumatism. ♦ *n* 2 a person afflicted with rheumatism. [C14: ultimately from Greek *rheumatikos,* from *rheuma* a flow; see RHEUM] ▸ **rheu'matically** *adv*

rheumatic fever *n* a disease characterized by sore throat, fever, inflammation, and pain in the joints.

rheumatics (ru:'mætɪks) *n* (*functioning as sing*) *Informal.* rheumatism.

rheumatism ('ru:məˌtɪzəm) *n* any painful disorder of joints, muscles, or connective tissue. Compare **arthritis, fibrositis.** [C17: from Latin *rheumatismus* catarrh, from Greek *rheumatismos;* see RHEUM]

rheumatoid ('ru:məˌtɔɪd) *adj* (of the symptoms of a disease) resembling rheumatism. ▸ **ˌrheuma'toidally** *adv*

rheumatoid arthritis *n* a chronic disease of the musculoskeletal system, characterized by inflammation and swelling of joints (esp. joints in the hands, wrists, knees, and feet), muscle weakness, and fatigue.

rheumatology (ˌru:mə'tɒlədʒɪ) *n* the branch of medicine concerned with the study of rheumatic diseases. ▸ **rheumatological** (ˌru:mətə'lɒdʒɪkᵊl) *adj* ▸ **ˌrheuma'tologist** *n*

rheumy ('ru:mɪ) *adj* 1 of the nature of rheum. 2 *Literary.* damp and unhealthy: *the rheumy air.*

rhexis ('rɛksɪs) *n Med.* the rupture of an organ or blood vessel. [C17: from Greek *rhēxis* a bursting]

Rh factor *n* an agglutinogen commonly found in human blood: it may cause a haemolytic reaction, esp. during pregnancy or following transfusion of blood that does not contain this agglutinogen. Full name: **rhesus factor.** See also **Rh positive, Rh negative.** [C20: named after the rhesus monkey, in which it was first discovered]

RHG *abbrev. for* Royal Horse Guards.

rhigolene ('rɪgəuˌli:n) *n* a volatile liquid obtained from petroleum and used as a local anaesthetic. [C19: from Greek *rhigos* cold; see -OLE, -ENE]

rhinal ('raɪnᵊl) *adj* of or relating to the nose; nasal. [C19: from Greek *rhis, rhin*]

Rhine (raɪn) *n* a river in central and W Europe, rising in SE Switzerland: flows through Lake Constance north through W Germany and west through the Netherlands to the North Sea. Length: about 1320 km (820 miles). Dutch name: **Rijn.** French name: **Rhin** (rɛ̃). German name: **Rhein.**

Rhineland ('raɪnˌlænd, -lənd) *n* the region of Germany surrounding the Rhine. German name: **Rheinland.**

Rhineland-Palatinate *n* a state of W Germany: formed in 1946 from the S part of the Prussian Rhine province, the Palatinate, and parts of Rhine-Hesse and Hesse-Nassau; part of West Germany until 1990: agriculture (with extensive vineyards) and tourism are important. Capital: Mainz. Pop.: 3 977 900 (1996 est.). Area: 19 832 sq. km (7657 sq. miles). German name: **Rheinland-Pfalz.**

rhinencephalon (ˌraɪnɛn'sɛfəˌlɒn) *n, pl* **-lons** *or* **-la** (-lə). *Anatomy.* the part of the brain that contains the olfactory bulb and tract and is concerned with the sense of smell. [C19: from RHINO- + ENCEPHALON] ▸ **rhinencephalic** (ˌraɪnɛnsɪ'fælɪk) *adj*

Rhine Palatinate *n* See **Palatinate.**

rhinestone ('raɪnˌstəun) *n* an imitation gem made of paste. [C19: translation of French *caillou du Rhin,* referring to Strasbourg, where such gems were made]

Rhine wine *n* any of several wines produced along the banks of the Rhine, characteristically a white table wine such as riesling.

rhinitis (raɪˈnaɪtɪs) *n* inflammation of the mucous membrane that lines the nose. ▸ **rhinitic** (raɪˈnɪtɪk) *adj*

rhino[1] (ˈraɪnəʊ) *n, pl* **-nos** *or* **-no.** short for **rhinoceros.**

rhino[2] (ˈraɪnəʊ) *n Brit.* a slang word for **money.** [C17: of unknown origin]

rhino- *or before a vowel* **rhin-** *combining form.* indicating the nose or nasal: *rhinology.* [from Greek *rhis, rhin*]

rhinoceros (raɪˈnɒsərəs, -ˈnɒsrəs) *n, pl* **-oses** *or* **-os.** any of several perissodactyl mammals constituting the family *Rhinocerotidae* of SE Asia and Africa and having either one horn on the nose, like the **Indian rhinoceros** (*Rhinoceros unicornis*), or two horns, like the African **white rhinoceros** (*Diceros simus*). They have a very thick skin, massive body, and three digits on each foot. [C13: via Latin from Greek *rhinokerōs,* from *rhis* nose + *keras* horn] ▸ **rhinocerotic** (ˌraɪnəʊsɪˈrɒtɪk) *adj*

rhinoceros beetle *n* any of various scarabaeid beetles having one or more horns on the head, esp. *Oryctes rhinoceros,* a serious pest on coconut plantations.

rhinoceros bird *n* another name for the **oxpecker.**

rhinology (raɪˈnɒlədʒɪ) *n* the branch of medical science concerned with the nose and its diseases. ▸ **rhinological** (ˌraɪnəˈlɒdʒɪkəl) *adj* ▸ **rhiˈnologist** *n*

rhinoplasty (ˈraɪnəʊˌplæstɪ) *n* plastic surgery of the nose. ▸ **ˌrhinoˈplastic** *adj*

rhinoscopy (raɪˈnɒskəpɪ) *n Med.* examination of the nasal passages, esp. with a special instrument called a **rhinoscope** (ˈraɪnəʊˌskəʊp). ▸ **rhinoscopic** (ˌraɪnəʊˈskɒpɪk) *adj*

rhizo- *or before a vowel* **rhiz-** *combining form.* root: *rhizomorphous.* [from Greek *rhiza*]

rhizobium (raɪˈzəʊbɪəm) *n, pl* **-bia** (-bɪə). any rod-shaped bacterium of the genus *Rhizobium,* typically occurring in the root nodules of leguminous plants and able to fix atmospheric nitrogen. See also **nitrogen fixation.** [C20: from RHIZO- + Greek *bios* life]

rhizocarpous (ˌraɪzəʊˈkɑːpəs) *adj* **1** (of plants) producing subterranean flowers and fruit. **2** (of perennial plants) having roots that persist throughout the year but stems and leaves that wither at the end of the growing season.

rhizocephalan (ˌraɪzəʊˈsɛfələn) *n* **1** any parasitic crustacean of the order *Rhizocephala,* esp. *Sacculina carcini,* which has a saclike body and sends out absorptive processes into the body of its host, the crab: subclass *Cirripedia* (barnacles). ◆ *adj also* **rhizocephalous. 2** of, relating to, or belonging to the order *Rhizocephala.* [C19: from New Latin *Rhizocephala* (literally: root-headed), from RHIZO- + *-cephala* from Greek *kephalē* head]

rhizogenic (ˌraɪzəʊˈdʒɛnɪk), **rhizogenetic** (ˌraɪzəʊdʒəˈnɛtɪk), *or* **rhizogenous** (raɪˈzɒdʒənəs) *adj* (of cells and tissues) giving rise to roots.

rhizoid (ˈraɪzɔɪd) *n* any of various slender hairlike structures that function as roots in mosses, ferns, and related plants and in fungi. ▸ **rhiˈzoidal** *adj*

rhizome (ˈraɪzəʊm) *n* a thick horizontal underground stem of plants such as the mint and iris whose buds develop into new plants. Also called: **rootstock, rootstalk.** [C19: from New Latin *rhizoma,* from Greek, from *rhiza* a root] ▸ **rhizomatous** (raɪˈzɒmətəs, -ˈzəʊ-) *adj*

rhizomorph (ˈraɪzəʊˌmɔːf) *n* a rootlike structure of certain fungi, such as the honey fungus *Armillaria mellea,* consisting of a dense mass of hyphae.

rhizomorphous (ˌraɪzəʊˈmɔːfəs) *adj Botany.* having the appearance of a root.

rhizopod (ˈraɪzəʊˌpɒd) *n* **1** any protozoan of the phylum *Rhizopoda,* characterized by naked protoplasmic processes (pseudopodia). The group includes the amoebas. ◆ *adj* **2** of, relating to, or belonging to the *Rhizopoda.* ▸ **rhizopodan** (raɪˈzɒpədən) *adj, n* ▸ **rhiˈzopodous** *adj*

rhizopus (ˈraɪzəʊpəs) *n* any zygomycetous fungus of the genus *Rhizopus,* esp. *R. nigricans,* a bread mould. [C19: New Latin, from RHIZO- + Greek *pous* foot]

rhizosphere (ˈraɪzəʊˌsfɪə) *n* the region of the soil in contact with the roots of a plant. It contains many microorganisms and its composition is affected by root activities.

rhizotomy (raɪˈzɒtəmɪ) *n, pl* **-mies.** surgical incision into the roots of spinal nerves, esp. for the relief of pain.

Rh negative *n* **1** blood that does not contain the Rh factor. **2** a person having such blood.

rho (rəʊ) *n, pl* **rhos.** the 17th letter in the Greek alphabet (Ρ, ρ), a consonant transliterated as *r* or *rh.*

rhodamine (ˈrəʊdəˌmiːn, -mɪn) *n* any one of a group of synthetic red or pink basic dyestuffs used for wool and silk. They are made from phthalic anhydride and aminophenols. [C20: from RHODO- + AMINE]

Rhode Island (rəʊd) *n* a state of the northeastern U.S., bordering on the Atlantic: the smallest state in the U.S.; mainly low-lying and undulating, with an indented coastline in the east and uplands in the northwest. Capital: Providence. Pop.: 987 429 (1997 est.). Area: 2717 sq. km (1049 sq. miles). Abbrevs.: **R.I.** or (with zip code) **RI**

Rhode Island Red *n* a breed of domestic fowl, originating in America, characterized by a dark reddish-brown plumage and the production of brown eggs.

Rhodes[1] (rəʊdz) *n* **1** a Greek island in the SE Aegean Sea, about 16 km (10 miles) off the Turkish coast: the largest of the Dodecanese and the most easterly island in the Aegean. Capital: Rhodes. Pop.: 40 392 (1981). Area: 1400 sq. km (540 sq. miles). **2** a port on this island, in the NE: founded in 408 B.C.; of great commercial and political importance in the 3rd century B.C.; suffered several earthquakes, notably in 225, when the Colossus was destroyed. Pop.: 41 000 (latest est.). ◆ Ancient Greek name: **Rhodos.** Modern Greek name: **Ródhos.**

Rhodes[2] (rəʊdz) *n* **Cecil John.** 1853–1902, British colonial financier and statesman in South Africa. He made a fortune in diamond and gold mining and, as prime minister of the Cape Colony (1890–96), he helped to extend British territory. He established the annual **Rhodes scholarships** to Oxford.

Rhodes grass *n* a perennial grass, *Chloris gayana,* native to Africa but widely cultivated in dry regions for forage. [C19: named after Cecil RHODES]

Rhodesia (rəʊˈdiːʃə, -zɪə) *n* a former name (1964–79) for **Zimbabwe.** ▸ **Rhoˈdesian** *adj, n*

Rhodesian Front *n* the governing party in Zimbabwe (then called Rhodesia) 1962–78.

Rhodesian man *n* a type of early man, *Homo rhodesiensis* (or *H. sapiens rhodesiensis*), occurring in Africa in late Pleistocene times and resembling Neanderthal man in many features.

Rhodesian ridgeback (ˈrɪdʒˌbæk) *n* a large short-haired breed of dog characterized by a ridge of hair growing along the back in the opposite direction to the rest of the coat.

Rhodesoid (rəʊˈdiːzɔɪd) *adj* relating to or resembling Rhodesian man.

Rhodes scholarship *n* one of 72 scholarships founded by Cecil Rhodes, awarded annually on merit to Commonwealth and U.S. students to study for two or sometimes three years at Oxford University. ▸ **Rhodes scholar** *n*

Rhodian (ˈrəʊdɪən) *adj* **1** of or relating to the island of Rhodes. ◆ *n* **2** a native or inhabitant of Rhodes.

rhodic (ˈrəʊdɪk) *adj* of or containing rhodium, esp. in the tetravalent state.

rhodinal (ˈrəʊdɪˌnæl) *n* another name for **citronellal.**

rhodium (ˈrəʊdɪəm) *n* a hard corrosion-resistant silvery-white element of the platinum metal group, occurring free with other platinum metals in alluvial deposits and in nickel ores. It is used as an alloying agent to harden platinum and palladium. Symbol: Rh; atomic no.: 45; atomic wt.: 102.90550; valency: 2–6; relative density: 12.41; melting pt.: 1963±3°C; boiling pt.: 3697±100°C. [C19: New Latin, from Greek *rhodon* rose, from the pink colour of its compounds]

rhodo- *or before a vowel* **rhod-** *combining form.* rose or rose-coloured: *rhododendron; rhodolite.* [from Greek *rhodon* rose]

rhodochrosite (ˌrəʊdəʊˈkrəʊsaɪt) *n* a pink, grey, or brown mineral that consists of manganese carbonate in hexagonal crystalline form and occurs in ore veins. Formula: $MnCO_3$. [C19: from Greek *rhodokhrōs* of a rosy colour, from *rhodon* rose + *khrōs* colour]

rhododendron (ˌrəʊdəˈdɛndrən) *n* any ericaceous shrub of the genus *Rhododendron,* native to S Asia but widely cultivated in N temperate regions. They are mostly evergreen and have clusters of showy red, purple, pink, or white flowers. Also called (U.S.): **rosebay.** See also **azalea.** [C17: from Latin: oleander, from Greek, from *rhodon* rose + *dendron* tree]

rhododendron bug *n* See **lace bug.**

rhodolite (ˈrɒdəˌlaɪt) *n* a pale violet or red variety of garnet, used as a gemstone.

rhodonite (ˈrɒdəˌnaɪt) *n* a brownish translucent mineral consisting of manganese silicate in triclinic crystalline form with calcium, iron, or magnesium sometimes replacing the manganese. It occurs in metamorphic rocks, esp. in New Jersey and Russia, and is used as an ornamental stone, glaze, and pigment. Formula: $MnSiO_3$. [C19: from German *Rhodonit,* from Greek *rhodon* rose + -ITE[1]]

Rhodope Mountains (ˈrɒdəpɪ, rɒˈdəʊ-) *pl n* a mountain range in SE Europe, in the Balkan Peninsula extending along the border between Bulgaria and Greece. Highest peak: Golyam Perelik (Bulgaria), 2191 m (7188 ft.).

rhodopsin (rəʊˈdɒpsɪn) *n* a red pigment in the rods of the retina in vertebrates. It is dissociated by light into retinene, the light energy being converted into nerve signals, and is re-formed in the dark. Also called: **visual purple.** See also **iodopsin.** [C20: from RHODO- + -OPSIS + -IN]

Rhodos (ˈrɔðɔs) *n* the Ancient Greek name for **Rhodes**[1].

rhoicissus (ˌrəʊɪˈsɪsəs) *n* any plant of the climbing genus *Rhoicissus,* related to and resembling cissus, esp. *R. rhomboidea* (grape ivy), grown for its shiny evergreen foliage: family *Vitaceae.* [New Latin, from Greek *rhoia* pomegranate + CISSUS]

rhomb (rɒm) *n* another name for **rhombus.**

rhombencephalon (ˌrɒmbɛnˈsɛfəˌlɒn) *n* the part of the brain that develops from the posterior portion of the embryonic neural tube. Compare **mesencephalon, prosencephalon.** Nontechnical name: **hindbrain.** [C20: from RHOMBUS + ENCEPHALON]

rhombic (ˈrɒmbɪk) *adj* **1** relating to or having the shape of a rhombus. **2** *Crystallog.* another word for **orthorhombic.**

rhombic aerial *n* a directional travelling-wave aerial, usually horizontal, consisting of two conductors each forming a pair of adjacent sides of a rhombus.

rhombohedral (ˌrɒmbəʊˈhiːdrəl) *adj* **1** of or relating to a rhombohedron. **2** *Crystallog.* another term for **trigonal** (sense 2).

rhombohedron (ˌrɒmbəʊˈhiːdrən) *n* a six-sided prism whose sides are parallelograms. [C19: from RHOMBUS + -HEDRON]

rhomboid (ˈrɒmbɔɪd) *n* **1** a parallelogram having adjacent sides of unequal length. ◆ *adj also* **rhomˈboidal. 2** having such a shape. [C16: from Late Latin *rhomboides,* from Greek *rhomboeidēs* shaped like a RHOMBUS]

rhomboideus (rɒmˈbɔɪdɪəs) *n, pl* **-dei** (-dɪˌaɪ). *Anatomy.* either of two muscles that connect the spinal vertebrae to the scapulae. [C19: New Latin, from Late Latin *rhomboides:* see RHOMBOID]

rhombus (ˈrɒmbəs) *n, pl* **-buses** *or* **-bi** (-baɪ). an oblique-angled parallelogram having four equal sides. Also called: **rhomb.** Compare **square** (sense 1). [C16: from Greek *rhombos* something that spins; related to *rhembein* to whirl]

rhonchus (ˈrɒŋkəs) *n, pl* **-chi** (-kaɪ). a rattling or whistling respiratory sound resembling snoring, caused by secretions in the trachea or bronchi. [C19: from Latin, from Greek *rhenkhos* snoring] ▸ **ˈrhonchal** *or* **ˈrhonchial** *adj*

Rhondda (ˈrɒndə) *n* an urban area in S Wales, in Rhondda Cynon Taff county borough on two branches of the **Rhondda Valley**: developed into a major coal-mining centre after 1807 and grew to a population of 167 900 in 1924: the last coal mine closed in 1990. Pop.: 59 947 (1991).

Rhondda Cynon Taff (ˈrɒndə ˈkʌnən ˈtæf) *n* a county borough in S Wales, created from part of Mid Glamorgan in 1996. Pop.: 232 581 (1996 est.). Area: 558 sq. km (215 sq. miles).

Rhône (rəʊn) *n* **1** a river in W Europe, rising in S Switzerland in the **Rhône glacier** and flowing to Lake Geneva, then into France through gorges between the Alps and Jura and south to its delta on the Gulf of Lions: important esp. for hydroelectricity and for wine production along its valley. Length: 812 km (505 miles). **2** a department of E central France, in the Rhône-Alpes region. Capital: Lyons. Pop.: 1 561 900 (1995). Area: 3233 sq. km (1261 sq. miles).

Rhône-Alpes (*French* ronalp) *n* a region of E France: mainly mountainous, rising to the edge of the Massif Central in the west and the French Alps in the east; drained by the Rivers Rhône, Saône, and Isère.

rhotacism (ˈrəʊtəˌsɪzəm) *n* excessive use or idiosyncratic pronunciation of *r*. [C19: from New Latin *rhōtacismus*, from Greek *rhōtakizein* (verb) from the letter *rho*] ▸ ˈ**rhotacist** *n* ▸ ˌ**rhotaˈcistic** *adj*

rhotic (ˈrəʊtɪk) *adj Phonetics.* denoting or speaking a dialect of English in which postvocalic *rs* are pronounced. [from Greek *rho*, the letter *r*] ▸ **rhoticity** (rəʊˈtɪsɪtɪ) *n*

Rh positive *n* **1** blood containing the Rh factor. **2** a person having such blood.

RHS *abbrev. for:* **1** Royal Historical Society. **2** Royal Horticultural Society. **3** Royal Humane Society.

rhubarb (ˈruːbɑːb) *n* **1** any of several temperate and subtropical plants of the polygonaceous genus *Rheum*, esp. *R. rhaponticum* (**common garden rhubarb**), which has long green and red acid-tasting edible leafstalks, usually eaten sweetened and cooked. **2** the leafstalks of this plant. **3** a related plant, *Rheum officinale*, of central Asia, having a bitter-tasting underground stem that can be dried and used medicinally as a laxative or astringent. **4** *U.S. and Canadian slang.* a heated discussion or quarrel. ◆ *interj, n, vb* **5** the noise made by actors to simulate conversation, esp. by repeating the word *rhubarb* at random. [C14: from Old French *reubarbe*, from Medieval Latin *reubarbum*, probably a variant of *rha barbarum* barbarian rhubarb, from *rha* rhubarb (from Greek, perhaps from *Rha* ancient name of the Volga) + Latin *barbarus* barbarian]

rhumb (rʌm) *n* short for **rhumb line**.

rhumba (ˈrʌmbə, ˈrum-) *n, pl* **-bas**. a variant spelling of **rumba**.

rhumbatron (ˈrʌmbəˌtrɒn) *n* another name for **cavity resonator**. [C20: from RHUMBA + -TRON, from the rhythmic variation of the waves]

rhumb line *n* **1** an imaginary line on the surface of a sphere, such as the earth, that intersects all meridians at the same angle. **2** the course navigated by a vessel or aircraft that maintains a uniform compass heading. ◆ Often shortened to **rhumb**. [C16: from Old Spanish *rumbo*, apparently from Middle Dutch *ruum* space, ship's hold, but also influenced by Latin RHOMBUS]

rhyme *or* (*Archaic*) **rime** (raɪm) *n* **1** identity of the terminal sounds in lines of verse or in words. **2** a word that is identical to another in its terminal sound: *"while" is a rhyme for "mile"*. **3** a verse or piece of poetry having corresponding sounds at the ends of the lines: *the boy made up a rhyme about his teacher.* **4** any verse or piece of poetry. **5** **rhyme or reason**. sense, logic, or meaning: *this proposal has no rhyme or reason.* ◆ *vb* **6** to use (a word) or (of a word) to be used so as to form a rhyme; be or make identical in sound. **7** to render (a subject) into rhyme. **8** to compose (verse) in a metrical structure. ◆ See also **masculine rhyme, feminine rhyme, eye rhyme**. [C12: from Old French *rime*, from *rimer* to rhyme, from Old High German *rīm* a number; spelling influenced by RHYTHM] ▸ ˈ**rhymeless** *or* ˈ**rimeless** *adj*

rhyme royal *n Prosody.* a stanzaic form introduced into English verse by Chaucer, consisting of seven lines of iambic pentameter rhyming a b a b b c c.

rhymester, rimester (ˈraɪmstə), **rhymer,** *or* **rimer** *n* a poet, esp. one considered to be mediocre or mechanical in diction; poetaster or versifier.

rhyming slang *n* slang in which a word is replaced by another word or phrase that rhymes with it; for example, *apples and pears* meaning *stairs.*

rhynchocephalian (ˌrɪŋkəʊsɪˈfælɪən) *adj* **1** of, relating to, or belonging to the *Rhyncocephalia*, an order of lizard-like reptiles common in the Mesozoic era but today represented only by the tuatara. ◆ *n* **2** any reptile belonging to the order *Rhyncocephalia.* [C19: from New Latin *Rhynchocephalia*, from Greek *rhunkhos* a snout + *kephalē* head]

rhynchophore (ˈrɪŋkəˌfɔː) *n* a member of the *Rhynchophora*, a former name for the superfamily of beetles (*Curculionoidea*) that comprises the weevils and bark beetles. [C19: New Latin *rhyncophora*, from Greek *rhunkhos* a snout + *-phoros* bearing]

rhyolite (ˈraɪəˌlaɪt) *n* a fine-grained igneous rock consisting of quartz, feldspars, and mica or amphibole. It is the volcanic equivalent of granite. [C19: *rhyo-* from Greek *rhuax* a stream of lava + -LITE] ▸ **rhyolitic** (ˌraɪəˈlɪtɪk) *adj*

Rhys (riːs) *n* **Jean** (**Ella Gwendolen Rees Williams**). ?1890–1979, Welsh novelist and short-story writer, born in Dominica. Her novels include *Voyage in the Dark* (1934), *Good Morning, Midnight* (1939), and *Wide Sargasso Sea* (1966).

rhythm (ˈrɪðəm) *n* **1a** the arrangement of the relative durations of and accents on the notes of a melody, usually laid out into regular groups (**bars**) of beats, the first beat of each bar carrying the stress. **1b** any specific arrangement of such groupings; time: *quadruple rhythm.* **2** (in poetry) **2a** the arrangement of words into a more or less regular sequence of stressed and unstressed or long and short syllables. **2b** any specific such arrangement; metre. **3** (in painting, sculpture, architecture, etc.) a harmonious sequence or pattern of masses alternating with voids, of light alternating with shade, of alternating colours, etc. **4** any sequence of regularly recurring functions or events, such as the regular recurrence of certain physiological functions of the body. [C16: from Latin *rhythmus*, from Greek *rhuthmos*; related to *rhein* to flow] ▸ ˈ**rhythmless** *adj*

rhythm and blues *n* (*functioning as sing*) any of various kinds of popular music derived from or influenced by the blues. Abbrev.: **R & B**.

rhythmic (ˈrɪðmɪk) *or* **rhythmical** (ˈrɪðmɪkᵊl) *adj* of, relating to, or characterized by rhythm, as in movement or sound; metrical, periodic, or regularly recurring. ▸ ˈ**rhythmically** *adv* ▸ **rhythmicity** (rɪðˈmɪsɪtɪ) *n*

rhythmic gymnastics *n* (*functioning as sing or pl*) a form of gymnastics involving movements using hand apparatus such as balls, hoops, and ribbons.

rhythmics (ˈrɪðmɪks) *n* (*functioning as sing*) the study of rhythmic movement.

rhythmist (ˈrɪðmɪst) *n Rare.* a person who has a good sense of rhythm.

rhythm method *n* a method of controlling conception without the aid of a contraceptive device, by restricting sexual intercourse to those days in a woman's menstrual cycle on which conception is considered least likely to occur. See also **safe period**.

rhythm section *n* those instruments in a band or group (usually piano, double bass, and drums) whose prime function is to supply the rhythm.

rhyton (ˈraɪtɒn) *n, pl* **-ta** (-tə). (in ancient Greece) a horn-shaped drinking vessel with a hole in the pointed end through which to drink. [C19: from Greek *rhuton*, from *rhutos* flowing; related to *rhein* to flow]

RI *abbrev. for:* **1** Regina et Imperatrix. [Latin: Queen and Empress] **2** Rex et Imperator. [Latin: King and Emperor] **3** Rhode Island. **4** Royal Institution. **5** religious instruction. ◆ **6** *international car registration for* (Republic of) Indonesia.

ria (ˈrɪə) *n* a long narrow inlet of the seacoast, being a former valley that was submerged by a rise in the level of the sea. Rias are found esp. on the coasts of SW Ireland and NW Spain. [C19: from Spanish, from *rio* river]

RIA *abbrev. for* Royal Irish Academy.

RIAA curve *n Electronics.* a graphical representation, adopted as a worldwide standard, of the amplitude in relation to frequency response required for correct reproduction of microgroove disc recordings, compensating for the characteristics of the recording process. [C20: *R*ecord *I*ndustry *A*ssociation of *A*merica]

rial (ˈraɪəl) *n* **1** the standard monetary and currency unit of Iran, divided into 100 dinars. **2** the standard monetary and currency unit of Oman, divided into 1000 baiza. **3** another name for **riyal**. [C14: from Persian, from Arabic *riyāl* RIYAL]

rialto (rɪˈæltəʊ) *n, pl* **-tos**. a market or exchange. [C19: after the RIALTO]

Rialto (rɪˈæltəʊ) *n* an island in Venice, Italy, linked with San Marco Island by the **Rialto Bridge** (1590) over the Grand Canal: the business centre of medieval and renaissance Venice.

riant (ˈraɪənt) *adj Rare.* laughing; smiling; cheerful. [C16: from French, from *rire* to laugh, from Latin *rīdēre*] ▸ ˈ**riantly** *adv*

rib[1] (rɪb) *n* **1** any of the 24 curved elastic arches of bone that together form the chest wall in man. All are attached behind to the thoracic part of the spinal column. Technical name: **costa**. Compare **true rib, false ribs, floating rib**. **2** the corresponding bone in other vertebrates. **3** a cut of meat including one or more ribs. **4** a part or element similar in function or appearance to a rib, esp. a structural or supporting member or a raised strip or ridge. **5** a structural member in a wing that extends from the leading edge to the trailing edge and maintains the shape of the wing surface. **6** a projecting moulding or band on the underside of a vault or ceiling, which may be structural or ornamental. **7** one of a series of raised rows in knitted fabric. See also **ribbing** (sense 3). **8** a raised ornamental line on the spine of a book where the stitching runs across it. **9** any of the transverse stiffening timbers or joists forming the frame of a ship's hull. **10** any of the larger veins of a leaf. **11** a metal strip running along the top of the barrel of a shotgun or handgun and guiding the alignment of the sights. **12** a vein of ore in rock. **13** a projecting ridge of a mountain; spur. ◆ *vb* **ribs, ribbing, ribbed.** (*tr*) **14** to furnish or support with a rib or ribs. **15** to mark with or form into ribs or ridges. **16** to knit plain and purl stitches alternately in order to make raised rows in (knitting). **17** *Archaic.* to enclose with or as if with ribs. [Old English *ribb*; related to Old High German *rippi*, Old Norse *rif* REEF[1]] ▸ ˈ**ribless** *adj* ▸ ˈ**ribˌlike** *adj*

rib[2] (rɪb) *Informal.* ◆ *vb* **ribs, ribbing, ribbed.** **1** (*tr*) to tease or ridicule. ◆ *n* **2** a joke or hoax. [C20: short for *rib-tickle* (vb)]

RIBA *abbrev. for* Royal Institute of British Architects.

ribald (ˈrɪbᵊld) *adj* **1** coarse, obscene, or licentious, usually in a humorous or mocking way. ◆ *n* **2** a ribald person. [C13: from Old French *ribauld*, from *riber* to live licentiously, of Germanic origin] ▸ ˈ**ribaldly** *adv*

ribaldry (ˈrɪbᵊldrɪ) *n* ribald language or behaviour.

riband *or* **ribband** (ˈrɪbənd) *n* **1** a ribbon, esp. one awarded for some achievement. See also **blue riband**. **2** a flat rail attached to posts in a palisade. [C14: variant of RIBBON]

ribbed and smoked sheet *n* another name for **smoked rubber**.

Ribbentrop (*German* ˈrɪbəntrɔp) *n* **Joachim von** (ˈjoːaxɪm fɔn). 1893–1946, German Nazi politician: foreign minister under Hitler (1938–45). He was hanged after conviction as a war criminal at Nuremberg.

ribbing (ˈrɪbɪŋ) *n* **1** a framework or structure of ribs. **2** ribs collectively. **3** a raised pattern in woven or knitted material, made in knitting by doing purl and plain stitches alternately.

Ribble (ˈrɪbᵊl) *n* a river in NW England, flowing south and west through Lancashire to the Irish Sea. Length: 121 km (75 miles).

ribbon (ˈrɪbᵊn) *n* **1** a narrow strip of fine material, esp. silk, used for trimming, tying, etc. **2** something resembling a ribbon; a long strip: *a ribbon of land.* **3** a long thin flexible band of metal used as a graduated measure, spring, etc. **4** a long narrow strip of ink-impregnated cloth for making the impression of type characters on paper in a typewriter or similar device. **5** (*pl*) ragged strips or shreds (esp. in the phrase **torn to ribbons**). **6** a small strip of coloured cloth signifying membership of an order or award of military decoration, prize, or other distinction. ◆ *vb* (*tr*) **7** to adorn with a ribbon or ribbons. **8** to mark with narrow ribbon-like marks. **9** to reduce to ribbons; tear into strips. [C14 *ryban*, from Old French *riban*, apparently of Germanic origin; probably related to RING[1], BAND[2]] ▸ ˈ**ribbon-ˌlike** *or* ˈ**ribbony** *adj*

ribbon development *n Brit.* the building of houses in a continuous row along a main road: common in England between the two World Wars.

ribbonfish (ˈrɪbᵊnˌfɪʃ) *n, pl* **-fish** *or* **-fishes**. any of various soft-finned deep-sea teleost fishes, esp. *Regalecus glesne* (see **oarfish**), that have an elongated compressed body. They are related to the opah and dealfishes.

ribbon microphone *n* a type of microphone in which the conductor is a thin ribbon of aluminium alloy moving perpendicularly in a magnetic field. It is strongly directional and can be used to reduce unwanted side noise.

ribbon strip *n* another name for **ledger board** (sense 2).

ribbonwood ('rɪbən,wʊd) *n* a small evergreen malvaceous tree, *Hoheria populnea*, of New Zealand. Its wood is used in furniture making and the tough bark for making cord. Also called: **lacebark.**

ribbon worm *n* another name for **nemertean** (sense 1).

ribcage ('rɪb,keɪdʒ) *n* the bony structure consisting of the ribs and their connective tissue that encloses and protects the lungs, heart, etc.

Ribeirão Prêto (*Portuguese* riβəi'rɐ̃u 'pretu) *n* a city in SE Brazil, in São Paulo state. Pop.: 416 186 (1991).

Ribera (*Spanish* ri'βera) *n* **José de** (xo'se de) also called *Jusepe de Ribera*, Italian nickname *Lo Spagnoletto* (The Little Spaniard). 1591–1652, Spanish artist, living in Italy. His religious pictures often dwell on horrible suffering, presented in realistic detail.

ribgrass ('rɪb,grɑːs) *n* another name for **ribwort.**

riboflavin *or* **riboflavine** (,raɪbəʊ'fleɪvɪn) *n* a yellow water-soluble vitamin of the B complex that occurs in green vegetables, germinating seeds, and in milk, fish, egg yolk, liver, and kidney. It is essential for the carbohydrate metabolism of cells. It is used as a permitted food colour, yellow or orange-yellow (**E101**). Formula: $C_{17}H_{20}N_4O_6$. Also called: **vitamin B$_2$, lactoflavin.** **[**C20: from RIBOSE + FLAVIN**]**

ribonuclease (,raɪbəʊ'njuːkliː,eɪs, -,eɪz) *n* any of a group of enzymes that catalyse the hydrolysis of RNA. **[**C20: from RIBONUCLE(IC ACID) + -ASE**]**

ribonucleic acid (,raɪbəʊnjuː'kliːɪk, -'kleɪ-) *n* the full name of **RNA.** **[**C20: from RIBO(SE) + NUCLEIC ACID**]**

ribose ('raɪbəʊz, -bəʊs) *n Biochem.* a pentose sugar that is an isomeric form of arabinose and that occurs in RNA and riboflavin. Formula: $CH_2OH(CHOH)_3CHO$. **[**C20: changed from ARABINOSE**]**

ribosomal RNA *n Biochem.* a type of RNA thought to be transcribed from DNA in the nucleoli of cell nuclei, subsequently forming the component of ribosomes on which the translation of messenger RNA into protein chains is accomplished. Sometimes shortened to **r-RNA.**

ribosome ('raɪbə,səʊm) *n* any of numerous minute particles in the cytoplasm of cells, either free or attached to the endoplasmic reticulum, that contain RNA and protein and are the site of protein synthesis. **[**C20: from RIBO(NUCLEIC ACID) + -SOME[3]**]** ▸ **,ribo'somal** *adj*

ribozyme ('raɪbəʊ,zaɪm) *n* an RNA molecule capable of catalysing a chemical reaction, usually the cleavage of another RNA molecule. **[**C20: from RIBO(NUCLEIC ACID) + (EN)ZYME**]**

rib-tickler *n* a very amusing joke or story. ▸ **'rib-,tickling** *adj*

ribwort ('rɪb,wɜːt) *n* a Eurasian plant, *Plantago lanceolata*, that has lancelike ribbed leaves, which form a rosette close to the ground, and a dense spike of small white flowers: family *Plantaginaceae*. Also called: **ribgrass.** See also **plantain**[1].

RIC *abbrev. for* Royal Institute of Chemistry.

Ricardo (rɪ'kɑːdəʊ) *n* **David.** 1772–1823, British economist. His main work is *Principles of Political Economy and Taxation* (1817). ▸ **Ri'cardian** *adj, n*

Ricci (*Italian* 'rittʃi) *n* **Matteo** (ma'teo). 1552–1610, Italian Jesuit missionary and scholar, who introduced Christianity to China. He was later censured by the Church for allowing his converts to retain some of their ancient religious customs.

Riccio ('rɪtsɪəʊ) *n* a variant of **Rizzio.**

rice (raɪs) *n* **1** an erect grass, *Oryza sativa*, that grows in East Asia on wet ground and has drooping flower spikes and yellow oblong edible grains that become white when polished. **2** the grain of this plant. ◆ *vb* **3** (*tr*) *U.S. and Canadian.* to sieve (potatoes or other vegetables) to a coarse mashed consistency, esp. with a ricer. ◆ See also **Indian rice.** **[**C13 *rys*, via French, Italian, and Latin from Greek *orūza*, of Oriental origin**]**

Rice (raɪs) *n* **Elmer,** original name *Elmer Reizenstein.* 1892–1967, U.S. dramatist. His plays include *The Adding Machine* (1923) and *Street Scene* (1929), which was made into a musical by Kurt Weill in 1947.

ricebird ('raɪs,bɜːd) *n* any of various birds frequenting rice fields, esp. the bobolink.

rice bowl *n* **1** a small bowl for eating rice out of, esp. a decorative one made of china or porcelain. **2** a fertile rice-producing region.

rice grass *n* another name for **cord grass.**

rice paper *n* **1** a thin semitransparent edible paper made from the straw of rice, on which macaroons and similar cakes are baked. **2** a thin delicate Chinese paper made from an araliaceous plant, *Tetrapanax papyriferum* (**rice-paper plant**) of Taiwan, the pith of which is pared and flattened into sheets.

ricer ('raɪsə) *n U.S. and Canadian.* a kitchen utensil with small holes through which cooked potatoes and similar soft foods are pressed to form a coarse mash.

ricercare (,riːtʃə'kɑːreɪ) *or* **ricercar** ('riːtʃə,kɑː) *n, pl* **-cari** (-'kɑːriː) *or* **-cars.** (in music of the 16th and 17th centuries) **1** an elaborate polyphonic composition making extensive use of contrapuntal imitation and usually very slow in tempo. **2** an instructive composition to illustrate instrumental technique; étude. **[**Italian, literally: to seek again**]**

rich (rɪtʃ) *adj* **1a** well supplied with wealth, property, etc.; owning much. **1b** (*as collective n;* preceded by *the*): *the rich.* **2** (when *postpositive,* usually foll. by *in*) having an abundance of natural resources, minerals, etc.: *a land rich in metals.* **3** producing abundantly; fertile: *rich soil.* **4** (when *postpositive,* foll. by *in* or *with*) well supplied (with desirable qualities); abundant (in): *a country rich with cultural interest.* **5** of great worth or quality; valuable: *a rich collection of antiques.* **6** luxuriant or prolific: *a rich growth of weeds.* **7** expensively elegant, elaborate, or fine; costly: *a rich display.* **8** (of food) having a large proportion of flavoursome or fatty ingredients, such as spices, butter, or cream. **9** having a full-bodied flavour: *a rich ruby port.* **10** (of a smell) pungent or fragrant. **11** (of colour) intense or vivid; deep: *a rich red.* **12** (of sound or a voice) full, mellow, or resonant. **13** (of a fuel-air mixture) containing a relatively high proportion of fuel. Compare **weak** (sense 12). **14** very amusing, laughable, or ridiculous: *a rich joke; a rich situation.* ◆ *n* **15** See **riches.** **[**Old English *rīce* (originally of persons: great, mighty), of Germanic origin, ultimately from Celtic (compare Old Irish *rī* king)**]**

Rich (rɪtʃ) *n* **Buddy,** real name *Bernard Rich.* 1917–87, U.S. jazz drummer and band leader.

Richard ('rɪtʃəd) *n* Sir **Cliff,** real name *Harry Rodger Webb.* born 1940, British pop singer. Film musicals include *The Young Ones* (1961) and *Summer Holiday* (1962).

Richard I ('rɪtʃəd) *n* nicknamed *Coeur de Lion* or *the Lion-Heart.* 1157–99, king of England (1189–99); a leader of the third crusade (joining it in 1191). On his way home, he was captured in Austria (1192) and held to ransom. After a brief return to England, where he was crowned again (1194), he spent the rest of his life in France.

Richard II *n* 1367–1400, king of England (1377–99), whose reign was troubled by popular discontent and baronial opposition. He was forced to abdicate in favour of Henry Bolingbroke, who became Henry IV.

Richard III *n* 1452–85, king of England (1483–85), notorious as the suspected murderer of his two young nephews in the Tower of London. He proved an able administrator until his brief reign was ended by his death at the hands of Henry Tudor (later Henry VII) at the battle of Bosworth Field.

Richards ('rɪtʃədz) *n* **1 I(vor) A(rmstrong).** 1893–1979, British literary critic and linguist, who, with C. K. Ogden, wrote *The Meaning of Meaning* (1923) and devised Basic English. **2** Sir **Gordon.** 1904–86, British jockey. **3 Viv,** full name *Isaac Vivian Alexander Richards.* born 1952, West Indian cricketer; captained the West Indies (1985–91).

Richardson ('rɪtʃədsən) *n* **1 Dorothy M(iller).** 1873–1957, British novelist, a pioneer of stream-of-consciousness writing: author of the novel sequence *Pilgrimage* (14 vols, 1915–67). **2 Henry Handel.** pen name of *Ethel Florence Lindesay Richardson,* 1870–1946, Australian novelist; author of the trilogy *The Fortunes of Richard Mahony* (1917–29). **3** Sir **Owen Willans.** 1879–1959, British physicist; a pioneer in the study of atomic physics: Nobel prize for physics 1928. **4** Sir **Ralph (David).** 1902–83, British stage and screen actor. **5 Samuel.** 1689–1761, British novelist whose psychological insight and use of the epistolary form exerted a great influence on the development of the novel. His chief novels are *Pamela* (1740) and *Clarissa* (1747).

Richelieu ('rɪʃə,ljɜː; *French* riʃəljø) *n* **Armand Jean du Plessis** (armɑ̃ ʒɑ̃ dy plesi). 1585–1642, French statesman and cardinal, principal minister to Louis XIII and virtual ruler of France (1624–42). He destroyed the power of the Huguenots and strengthened the crown in France and the role of France in Europe.

Richelieu River *n* a river in E Canada, in S Quebec, rising in Lake Champlain and flowing north to the St Lawrence River. Length: 338 km (210 miles).

riches ('rɪtʃɪz) *pl n* wealth; an abundance of money, valuable possessions, or property.

Richler ('rɪʃlə) *n* **Mordecai.** born 1931, Canadian novelist. His novels include *St Urbain's Horseman* (1971), *Solomon Gursky Was Here* (1990), and *Barney's Version* (1997).

richly ('rɪtʃlɪ) *adv* **1** in a rich or elaborate manner: *a richly decorated carving.* **2** fully and appropriately: *he was richly rewarded for his service.*

Richmond ('rɪtʃmənd) *n* **1** a borough of Greater London, on the River Thames: formed in 1965 by the amalgamation of Barnes, Richmond, and Twickenham; site of Hampton Court Palace and the Royal Botanic Gardens at Kew. Pop.: 172 000 (1994 est.). Area: 55 sq. km (21 sq. miles). Official name: **Richmond-upon-Thames. 2** a town in N England, in North Yorkshire: Norman castle. Pop.: 7862 (1991). **3** a port in E Virginia, the state capital, at the falls of the James River: developed after the establishment of a trading post (1637); scene of the Virginia Conventions of 1774 and 1775; Confederate capital in the American Civil War. Pop.: 198 267 (1996 est.). **4** a county of SW New York City: coextensive with Staten Island borough; consists of Staten Island and several smaller islands.

richness ('rɪtʃ,nɪs) *n* **1** the state or quality of being rich. **2** *Ecology.* the number of individuals of a species in a given area.

rich rhyme *n Prosody.* another term for **rime riche.**

richt (rɪxt) *adj, adv, n* a Scot. word for **right.**

Richter *n* **1** ('rɪktə) **Burton.** born 1931, U.S. physicist: shared the 1976 Nobel prize for physics with Samuel Tring for discovering the subatomic particle known as the J/psi particle. **2** (*German* 'rɪçtər). **Johann Friedrich** (jo'han 'friːdrɪç), wrote under the name *Jean Paul.* 1763–1825, German romantic novelist. His works include *Hesperus* (1795) and *Titan* (1800–03). **3** (*Russian* 'rixtɪr). **Sviatoslav** (svɪta'slaf). 1915–97, Ukrainian concert pianist.

Richter scale ('rɪxtə) *n* a scale for expressing the magnitude of an earthquake by the quantity of energy released, ranging from 0 to over 8. Compare **Mercalli scale.** See also **magnitude** (sense 5). **[**C20: named after Charles *Richter* (1900–85) U.S. seismologist**]**

Richthofen (*German* 'rɪçthoːfən) *n* Baron **Manfred von** ('manfreːt fɔn), nickname *the Red Baron.* 1892–1918, German aviator; commander during World War I of the 11th Chasing Squadron (**Richthofen's Flying Circus**). He was credited with 80 air victories before he was shot down.

ricin ('raɪsɪn, 'rɪs-) *n Biochem.* a highly toxic protein, a lectin, derived from castor-oil seeds: used in experimental cancer therapy. **[**C19: from New Latin *Ricinus* genus name, from Latin: castor-oil plant**]**

ricinoleic acid (,rɪsɪnəʊ'liːɪk, -'nəʊlɪɪk) *n* **1** an oily unsaturated carboxylic acid found, as the glyceride, in castor oil and used in the manufacture of soap and in finishing textiles; 12-hydroxy-9-octadecanoic acid. Formula: $C_{18}H_{34}O_3$. **2** the mixture of fatty acids obtained by hydrolysing castor oil. [C19: from RICIN + OLEIC ACID]

rick[1] (rɪk) *n* **1** a large stack of hay, corn, peas, etc., built in the open in a regular-shaped pile, esp. one with a thatched top. ◆ *vb* **2** (*tr*) to stack or pile into ricks. [Old English *hrēac;* related to Old Norse *hraukr*]

rick[2] (rɪk) *n* **1** a wrench or sprain, as of the back. ◆ *vb* **2** (*tr*) to wrench or sprain (a joint, a limb, the back, etc.). [C18: see WRICK]

ricker ('rɪkə) *n* a young kauri tree of New Zealand. [from earlier use of the trunks as ships' rigging]

rickets ('rɪkɪts) *n* (*functioning as sing or pl*) *Pathol.* a disease mainly of children, characterized by softening of developing bone, and hence bow legs, malnutrition, and enlargement of the liver and spleen, caused by a deficiency of vitamin D. [C17: of unknown origin]

rickettsia (rɪ'kɛtsɪə) *n, pl* **-siae** (-sɪˌiː) *or* **-sias.** any of a group of parasitic microorganisms, intermediate in structure between bacteria and viruses, that live in the tissues of ticks, mites, and other arthropods, and cause disease when transmitted to man. [C20: named after Howard T. *Ricketts* (1871–1910), U.S. pathologist] ▸ **rick'ettsial** *adj*

rickettsial disease *n* any of several acute infectious diseases caused by ticks, mites, or body lice infected with rickettsiae. The main types include typhus, spotted fever, Q fever, trench fever, and tsutsugamushi disease.

rickety ('rɪkɪtɪ) *adj* **1** (of a structure, piece of furniture, etc.) likely to collapse or break; shaky. **2** feeble with age or illness; infirm. **3** relating to, resembling, or afflicted with rickets. [C17: from RICKETS] ▸ **'ricketiness** *n*

rickey ('rɪkɪ) *n* a cocktail consisting of gin or vodka, lime juice, and soda water, served iced (esp. in the phrase **a gin rickey**). [C19: of uncertain origin]

rickle ('rɪkᵊl) *n Scot.* **1** an unsteady or shaky structure, esp. a dilapidated building. **2** a loose or disorganized heap. [C16: perhaps of Scandinavian origin]

rickrack *or* **ricrac** ('rɪkˌræk) *n* a zigzag braid used for trimming. [C20: dissimilated reduplication of RACK[1]]

rickshaw ('rɪkʃɔː) *or* **ricksha** ('rɪkʃə) *n* **1** Also called: **jinrikisha.** a small two-wheeled passenger vehicle drawn by one or two men, used in parts of Asia. **2** Also called: **trishaw.** a similar vehicle with three wheels, propelled by a man pedalling as on a tricycle. ◆ See also **autorickshaw.** [C19: shortened from JINRIKISHA]

ricochet ('rɪkəˌʃeɪ, 'rɪkəˌʃɛt) *vb* **-chets, -cheting** (-ˌʃeɪɪŋ), **-cheted** (-ˌʃeɪd) *or* **-chets, -chetting** (-ˌʃɛtɪŋ), **-chetted** (-ˌʃɛtɪd). **1** (*intr*) (esp. of a bullet) to rebound from a surface or surfaces, usually with a characteristic whining or zipping sound. ◆ *n* **2** the motion or sound of a rebounding object, esp. a bullet. **3** an object, esp. a bullet, that ricochets. [C18: from French, of unknown origin]

Ricoeur (*French* rikør) *n* **Paul** (pɔl) born 1913, French philosopher, noted for his work on theories of interpretation. His books include *Philosophy of the Will* (3 vols, 1950–60), *Freud and Philosophy* (1965), and *The Living Metaphor* (1975).

ricotta (rɪ'kɒtə) *n* a soft white unsalted cheese made from sheep's milk, used esp. in making ravioli and gnocchi. [C19: Italian, from Latin *recocta* recooked, from *recoquere,* from RE- + *coquere* to COOK]

RICS *abbrev. for* Royal Institution of Chartered Surveyors.

rictus ('rɪktəs) *n, pl* **-tus** *or* **-tuses. 1** the gap or cleft of an open mouth or beak. **2** a fixed or unnatural grin or grimace, as in horror or death. [C18: from Latin, from *ringī* to gape] ▸ **'rictal** *adj*

rid (rɪd) *vb* **rids, ridding, rid** *or* **ridded.** (*tr*) **1** (foll. by *of*) to relieve or deliver from something disagreeable or undesirable; make free (of): *to rid a house of mice.* **2 get rid of.** to relieve or free oneself of (something or someone unpleasant or undesirable). [C13 (meaning: to clear land): from Old Norse *rythja;* related to Old High German *riutan* to clear land] ▸ **'ridder** *n*

riddance ('rɪdᵊns) *n* the act of getting rid of something undesirable or unpleasant; deliverance or removal (esp. in the phrase **good riddance**).

ridden ('rɪdᵊn) *vb* **1** the past participle of **ride.** ◆ *adj* **2** (*in combination*) afflicted, affected, or dominated by something specified: *damp-ridden; disease-ridden.*

riddle[1] ('rɪdᵊl) *n* **1** a question, puzzle, or verse so phrased that ingenuity is required for elucidation of the answer or meaning; conundrum. **2** a person or thing that puzzles, perplexes, or confuses; enigma. ◆ *vb* **3** to solve, explain, or interpret (a riddle or riddles). **4** (*intr*) to speak in riddles. [Old English *rǣdelle, rǣdelse,* from *rǣd* counsel; related to Old Saxon *rādislo,* German *Rätsel*] ▸ **'riddler** *n*

riddle[2] ('rɪdᵊl) *vb* (*tr*) **1** (usually foll. by *with*) to pierce or perforate with numerous holes: *riddled with bullets.* **2** to damage or impair. **3** to put through a sieve; sift. ◆ *n* **4** a sieve, esp. a coarse one used for sand, grain, etc. [Old English *hriddel* a sieve, variant of *hridder;* related to Latin *crībrum* sieve] ▸ **'riddler** *n*

ride (raɪd) *vb* **rides, riding, rode, ridden. 1** to sit on and control the movements of (a horse or other animal). **2** (*tr*) to sit on and propel (a bicycle or similar vehicle). **3** (*intr;* often foll. by *on* or *in*) to be carried along or travel on or in a vehicle: *she rides to work on the bus.* **4** (*tr*) to travel over or traverse: *they rode the countryside in search of shelter.* **5** (*tr*) to take part in by riding: *to ride a race.* **6** to travel through or be carried across (sea, sky, etc.): *the small boat rode the waves; the moon was riding high.* **7** (*tr*) *U.S. and Canadian.* to cause to be carried: *to ride someone out of town.* **8** (*intr*) to be supported as if floating: *the candidate rode to victory on his new policies.* **9** (*intr*) (of a vessel) to lie at anchor. **10** (*tr*) (of a vessel) to be attached to (an anchor). **11** (esp. of a bone) to overlap or lie over (another structure or part). **12** *S. African informal.* **12a** (*intr*) to drive a car. **12b** (*tr*) to transport (goods, farm produce, etc.) by motor vehicle or cart. **13** (*tr*) (esp. of a male animal) to copulate with; mount. **14** (*tr; usually passive*) to tyrannize over or dominate: *ridden by fear.* **15** (*tr*) *Informal.* to persecute, esp. by constant or petty criticism: *don't ride me so hard over my failure.* **16** (*intr*) *Informal.* to continue undisturbed: *I wanted to change something, but let it ride.* **17** (*tr*) to endure successfully; ride out. **18** (*tr*) to yield slightly to (a blow or punch) in order to lessen its impact. **19** (*intr;* often foll. by *on*) (of a bet) to remain placed: *let your winnings ride on the same number.* **20** (*intr*) *Jazz.* to play well, esp. in freely improvising at perfect tempo. **21 ride roughshod over.** to domineer over or act with complete disregard for. **22 ride to hounds.** to take part in a fox hunt on horseback. **23 ride for a fall.** to act in such a way as to invite disaster. **24 ride again.** *Informal.* to return to a former activity or scene of activity. **25 riding high.** confident, popular, and successful. ◆ *n* **26** a journey or outing on horseback or in a vehicle. **27** a path specially made for riding on horseback. **28** transport in a vehicle, esp. when given freely to a pedestrian; lift: *can you give me a ride to the station?* **29** a device or structure, such as a roller coaster at a fairground, in which people ride for pleasure or entertainment. **30 take for a ride.** *Informal.* **30a** to cheat, swindle, or deceive. **30b** to take (someone) away in a car and murder him. ◆ See also **ride down, ride out, ride up.** [Old English *rīdan;* related to Old High German *rītan,* Old Norse *rītha*] ▸ **'ridable** *or* **'rideable** *adj*

ride down *vb* (*tr, adv*) **1** to trample under the hooves of a horse. **2** to catch up with or overtake by riding.

rident ('raɪdᵊnt) *adj Rare.* laughing, smiling, or gay. [C17: from Latin *rīdēre* to laugh; see RIANT]

ride out *vb* (*tr, adv*) to endure successfully; survive (esp. in the phrase **ride out the storm**).

rider ('raɪdə) *n* **1** a person or thing that rides, esp. a person who rides a horse, a bicycle, or a motorcycle. **2** an additional clause, amendment, or stipulation added to a legal or other document, esp. (in Britain) a legislative bill at its third reading. **3** *Brit.* a statement made by a jury in addition to its verdict, such as a recommendation for mercy. **4** any of various objects or devices resting on, surmounting, or strengthening something else. **5** a small weight that can be slid along one arm of a chemical balance to make fine adjustments during weighing. **6** *Geology.* a thin seam, esp. of coal or mineral ore, overlying a thicker seam. ▸ **'riderless** *adj*

ride up *vb* (*intr, adv*) to move or work away from the proper place or position: *her new skirt rode up uncomfortably.*

ridge (rɪdʒ) *n* **1** a long narrow raised land formation with sloping sides esp. one formed by the meeting of two faces of a mountain or of a mountain buttress or spur. **2** any long narrow raised strip or elevation, as on a fabric or in ploughed land. **3** *Anatomy.* any elongated raised margin or border on a bone, tooth, tissue membrane, etc. **4a** the top of a roof at the junction of two sloping sides. **4b** (*as modifier*): *a ridge tile.* **5** the back or backbone of an animal, esp. a whale. **6** *Meteorol.* an elongated area of high pressure, esp. an extension of an anticyclone. Compare **trough** (sense 4). ◆ *vb* **7** to form into a ridge or ridges. [Old English *hrycg;* related to Old High German *hrucki,* Old Norse *hryggr*] ▸ **'ridgeˌlike** *adj* ▸ **'ridgy** *adj*

ridgeling, ridgling ('rɪdʒlɪŋ), *or* **ridgel** ('rɪdʒəl) *n* **1** a domestic male animal with one or both testicles undescended, esp. a horse. **2** an imperfectly castrated male domestic animal. [C16: perhaps from RIDGE, from the belief that the undescended testicles were near the animal's ridge or back]

ridgepole ('rɪdʒˌpəʊl) *n* **1** a timber laid along the ridge of a roof, to which the upper ends of the rafters are attached. **2** the horizontal pole at the apex of a tent.

ridgetree ('rɪdʒˌtriː) *n* another name for **ridgepole** (sense 1).

ridgeway ('rɪdʒˌweɪ) *n Brit.* a road or track along a ridge, esp. one of great antiquity.

ridicule ('rɪdɪˌkjuːl) *n* **1** language or behaviour intended to humiliate or mock; derision. ◆ *vb* **2** (*tr*) to make fun of, mock, or deride. [C17: from French, from Latin *rīdiculus,* from *rīdēre* to laugh] ▸ **'ridiˌculer** *n*

ridiculous (rɪ'dɪkjʊləs) *adj* worthy of or exciting ridicule; absurd, preposterous, laughable, or contemptible. [C16: from Latin *rīdiculōsus,* from *rīdēre* to laugh] ▸ **ri'diculously** *adv* ▸ **ri'diculousness** *n*

riding[1] ('raɪdɪŋ) *n* **a** the art or practice of horsemanship. **b** (*as modifier*): *a riding school; riding techniques.*

riding[2] ('raɪdɪŋ) *n* **1** (*cap. when part of a name*) any of the three former administrative divisions of Yorkshire: **North Riding, East Riding,** and **West Riding. 2** (in Canada) a parliamentary constituency. **3** (in New Zealand) a rural electorate for local government. [from Old English *thriding,* from Old Norse *thrithjungr* a third. The *th-* was lost by assimilation to the *-t* or *-th* that preceded it, as in *west thriding,* etc.]

riding breeches *pl n* tough breeches with padding inside the knees, worn for riding horses.

riding crop *n* a short whip with a thong at one end and a handle for opening gates at the other.

riding habit *n* a woman's dress worn for riding, usually with a full or a divided skirt.

riding lamp *or* **light** *n* a light on a boat or ship showing that it is at anchor.

Ridley ('rɪdlɪ) *n* **Nicholas.** ?1500–55, English bishop, who helped to revise the liturgy under Edward VI. He was burnt at the stake for refusing to disavow his Protestant beliefs when Mary I assumed the throne.

ridotto (rɪ'dɒtəʊ) *n, pl* **-tos.** an entertainment with music and dancing, often in masquerade: popular in 18th-century England. [C18: from Italian: retreat, from Latin *reductus,* from *redūcere* to lead back]

Rie (riː) *n* Dame **Lucie,** original name *Lucie Gomperz.* 1902–95, British potter, born in Austria.

Riefenstahl (*German* 'riːfənʃtaːl) *n* **Leni.** ('leːni). born 1902, German photographer and film director, best known for her Nazi propaganda films, such as *Triumph of the Will* (1934).

riel ('riːəl) *n* the standard monetary and currency unit of Cambodia, divided into 100 sen.

Riemann (*German* 'riːman) *n* **Georg Friedrich Bernhard** ('geːɔrk 'friːdrɪç

ˈbɛrnhart). 1826–66, German mathematician whose non-Euclidean geometry was used by Einstein as a basis for his general theory of relativity. ► **Rieˈmannian** *adj*

Riemannian geometry *n* a branch of non-Euclidean geometry in which a line may have many parallels through a given point. It has a model on the surface of a sphere, with lines represented by great circles. Also called: **elliptic geometry.**

riempie (ˈrɪmpɪ) *n S. African.* a leather thong or lace used mainly to make chair seats. [C19 (earlier *riem*): from Afrikaans, diminutive of *riem*, from Dutch: RIM]

Rienzi (rɪˈɛnzɪ; *Italian* ˈrjɛntsi) *or* **Rienzo** (rɪˈɛnzəʊ; *Italian* ˈrjɛntso) *n* **Cola di** (ˈkɔːla di). 1313–54, Italian radical political reformer in Rome.

riesling (ˈriːzlɪŋ, ˈraɪz-) *n* **1** a white wine from the Rhine valley in Germany and from certain districts in other countries. **2** the grape used to make this wine. [C19: from German, from earlier *Rüssling*, of obscure origin]

Rievaulx Abbey (ˈriːvəʊ) *n* a ruined Cistercian abbey near Helmsley in Yorkshire: built in the 12th century and abandoned at the dissolution of the monasteries; landscaped in the 18th century.

Rif, Riff (rɪf), *or* **Rifi** (ˈrɪfɪ) *n* **1** (*pl* **Rifs, Riffs, Rifis** *or* **Rif, Riff, Rifi**) a member of a Berber people, inhabiting the Atlas Mountains in Morocco. **2** Also called: **Rifian, Riffian** (ˈrɪfɪən). the dialect of Berber spoken by this people. **3** See **Er Rif.**

rifampicin (rɪˈfæmpɪsɪn) *or U.S.* **rifampin** (rɪˈfæmpɪn) *n* a drug used in the treatment of tuberculosis, meningitis, and leprosy. [C20: from *rifam(y)cin*, from Italian *riformare* to reform + -MYCIN, + inserted PI(PERAZINE)]

rife (raɪf) *adj* (*postpositive*) **1** of widespread occurrence; prevalent or current: *rumour was rife in the village.* **2** very plentiful; abundant. **3** (foll. by *with*) abounding (in): *a land rife with poverty.* [Old English *rīfe*; related to Old Norse *rīfr* generous, Middle Dutch *rīve*] ► **ˈrifely** *adv* ► **ˈrifeness** *n*

riff (rɪf) *Jazz, rock.* ◆ *n* **1** a short series of chords. ◆ *vb* **2** (*intr*) to play or perform riffs. [C20: probably altered and shortened from REFRAIN[2]]

riffle (ˈrɪfᵊl) *vb* **1** (when *intr*, often foll. by *through*) to flick rapidly through (the pages of a book, magazine, etc.), esp. in a desultory manner. **2** to shuffle (playing cards) by halving the pack and flicking the adjacent corners together. **3** to make or become a riffle. ◆ *n* **4** *U.S. and Canadian.* **4a** a rapid in a stream. **4b** a rocky shoal causing a rapid. **4c** a ripple on water. **5** *Mining.* a contrivance on the bottom of a sluice, containing transverse grooves for trapping particles of gold. **6** the act or an instance of riffling. [C18: probably from RUFFLE[1], influenced by RIPPLE[1]]

riffler (ˈrɪflə) *n* a file with a curved face for filing concave surfaces. [C18: from French *rifloir*, from *rifler* to scratch]

riffraff (ˈrɪfˌræf) *n* (*sometimes functioning as pl*) **1** worthless people, esp. collectively; rabble. **2** *Dialect.* worthless rubbish. [C15 *rif and raf*, from Old French *rif et raf*; related to *rifler* to plunder, and *rafle* a sweeping up; see RIFLE[2], RAFFLE]

rifle[1] (ˈraɪfᵊl) *n* **1a** a firearm having a long barrel with a spirally grooved interior, which imparts to the bullet spinning motion and thus greater accuracy over a longer range. **1b** (*as modifier*): *rifle fire.* **2** (formerly) a large cannon with a rifled bore. **3** one of the grooves in a rifled bore. **4** (*pl*) **4a** a unit of soldiers equipped with rifles. **4b** (*cap. when part of a name*): *the King's Own Rifles.* ◆ *vb* (*tr*) **5** to cut or mould spiral grooves inside the barrel of (a gun). **6** to throw or hit (a ball) with great speed. [C18: from Old French *rifler* to scratch; related to Low German *rifeln* from *riefe* groove, furrow]

rifle[2] (ˈraɪfᵊl) *vb* (*tr*) **1** to search (a house, safe, etc.) and steal from it; ransack. **2** to steal and carry off: *to rifle goods from a shop.* [C14: from Old French *rifler* to plunder, scratch, of Germanic origin] ► **ˈrifler** *n*

riflebird (ˈraɪfᵊlˌbɜːd) *n* any of various birds of paradise of the genera *Ptiloris* and *Craspedophora*, such as *C. magnifica* (**magnificent riflebird**).

rifle green *n Brit.* **a** a dark olive green, as in the uniforms of certain rifle regiments. **b** (*as adj*): *rifle-green cloth.*

rifle grenade *n* a grenade fired from a rifle.

rifleman (ˈraɪfᵊlmən) *n, pl* **-men. 1** a person skilled in the use of a rifle, esp. a soldier. **2** a wren, *Acanthisitta chloris*, of New Zealand: family *Xenicidae.* See also **bush wren.**

rifle range *n* an area used for target practice with rifles.

riflery (ˈraɪfᵊlrɪ) *n U.S.* **1** rifle shots. **2** the practice or skill of rifle marksmanship.

rifling (ˈraɪflɪŋ) *n* **1** the cutting of spiral grooves on the inside of a firearm's barrel. **2** the series of grooves so cut.

rift[1] (rɪft) *n* **1** a gap or space made by cleaving or splitting; fissure. **2** *Geology.* a fault produced by tension on either side of the fault plane. **3** a gap between two cloud masses; break or chink: *he saw the sun through a rift in the clouds.* **4** a break in friendly relations between people, nations, etc. ◆ *vb* **5** to burst or cause to burst open; split. [C13: from Old Norse; related to Danish *rift* cleft, Icelandic *ript* breach of contract]

rift[2] (rɪft) *n U.S.* **1** a shallow or rocky part in a stream. **2** the backwash from a wave that has just broken. [C14: from Old Norse *rypta*; related to Icelandic *ropa* to belch]

rift valley *n* a long narrow valley resulting from the subsidence of land between two parallel faults.

rig[1] (rɪg) *vb* **rigs, rigging, rigged.** (*tr*) **1** *Nautical.* to equip (a vessel, mast, etc.) with (sails, rigging, etc.). **2** *Nautical.* to set up or prepare ready for use. **3** to put the components of (an aircraft, etc.) into their correct positions. **4** to manipulate in a fraudulent manner, esp. for profit: *to rig prices; to rig an election.* ◆ *n* **5** *Nautical.* the distinctive arrangement of the sails, masts, and other spars of a vessel. **6** in full: **drilling rig.** the installation used in drilling for and exploiting natural oil and gas deposits: *an oil rig.* **7** apparatus or equipment; gear. **8** an amateur radio operator's transmitting and receiving set. **9** *U.S. and Canadian.* a carriage together with one or more horses. **10** *U.S. and Canadian.* an articulated lorry. ◆ See also **rig down, rig out, rig up.** [C15: from Scandinavian; related to Norwegian *rigga* to wrap]

rig[2] (rɪg) *n Scot. and northern English dialect.* a ridge or raised strip of unploughed land in a ploughed field. [a variant of RIDGE]

Riga (ˈriːgə) *n* the capital of Latvia, on the **Gulf of Riga** at the mouth of the Western Dvina on the Baltic Sea: a port and major trading centre since Viking times. Pop.: 826 100 (1996 est.).

rigadoon (ˌrɪgəˈduːn) *or* **rigaudon** (*French* rigodɔ̃) *n* **1** an old Provençal couple dance, light and graceful, in lively duple time. **2** a piece of music for or in the rhythm of this dance. [C17: from French, allegedly from its inventor *Rigaud*, a dancing master at Marseille]

rigamarole (ˈrɪgəməˌrəʊl) *n* a variant of **rigmarole.**

rigatoni (ˌrɪgəˈtəʊnɪ) *n* macaroni in the form of short ridged often slightly curved pieces. [C20: Italian, plural of *rigato*, from *rigare* to draw lines, make stripes, from *riga* a line, of Germanic origin]

rig down *vb* (*adv*) *Nautical.* to disassemble and stow.

Rigel (ˈraɪdʒəl, ˈraɪgᵊl) *n* the brightest star, Beta Orionis, in the constellation Orion: a very luminous and extremely remote bluish-white supergiant, a double star. Visual magnitude: 0.1; spectral type: B8. [C16: from Arabic *rijl* foot; from its position in Orion's foot]

-rigged *adj* (*in combination*) (of a sailing vessel) having a rig of a certain kind: *ketch-rigged; schooner-rigged.*

rigger (ˈrɪgə) *n* **1** a workman who rigs vessels, etc. **2** *Rowing.* a bracket on a racing shell or other boat to support a projecting rowlock. **3** a person skilled in the use of pulleys, lifting gear, cranes, etc.

rigging (ˈrɪgɪŋ) *n* **1** the shrouds, stays, halyards, etc., of a vessel. **2** the bracing wires, struts, and lines of a biplane, balloon, etc. **3** any form of lifting gear, tackle, etc.

rigging loft *n* **1** a loft or gallery in a boatbuilder's yard from which rigging can be fitted. **2** a loft in a theatre from which scenery, etc., is raised and lowered.

right (raɪt) *adj* **1** in accordance with accepted standards of moral or legal behaviour, justice, etc.: *right conduct.* **2** in accordance with fact, reason, or truth; correct or true: *the right answer.* **3** appropriate, suitable, fitting, or proper: *the right man for the job.* **4** most favourable or convenient; preferred: *the right time to act.* **5** in a satisfactory condition; orderly: *things are right again now.* **6** indicating or designating the correct time: *the clock is right.* **7** correct in opinion or judgment. **8** sound in mind or body; healthy or sane. **9** (*usually prenominal*) of, designating, or located near the side of something or someone that faces east when the front is turned towards the north. Related adj: **dextral. 10** (*usually prenominal*) worn on a right hand, foot, etc. **11** (*sometimes cap.*) of, designating, supporting, belonging to, or relating to the political or intellectual right (see sense 39). **12** (*sometimes cap.*) conservative or reactionary: *the right wing of the party.* **13** *Geometry.* **13a** formed by or containing a line or plane perpendicular to another line or plane. **13b** having the axis perpendicular to the base: *a right circular cone.* **13c** straight: *a right line.* **14** relating to or designating the side of cloth worn or facing outwards. **15** *Informal.* (intensifier): *a right idiot.* **16 in one's right mind.** sane. **17 the right side of. 17a** in favour with: *you'd better stay on the right side of him.* **17b** younger than: *she's still on the right side of fifty.* ◆ *adv* **18** in accordance with correctness or truth; accurately: *to guess right.* **19** in the appropriate manner; properly: *do it right next time!* **20** in a straight line; directly: *right to the top.* **21** in the direction of the east from the point of view of a person or thing facing north. **22** absolutely or completely; utterly: *he went right through the floor.* **23** all the way: *the bus goes right to the city centre.* **24** without delay; immediately or promptly: *I'll be right over.* **25** exactly or precisely: *right here.* **26** in a manner consistent with a legal or moral code; justly or righteously: *do right by me.* **27** in accordance with propriety; fittingly or suitably: *it serves you right.* **28** to good or favourable advantage; well: *it all came out right in the end.* **29** (esp. in religious titles) most or very: *right reverend.* **30** *Informal or dialect.* (intensifier): *I'm right glad to see you.* **31 right, left, and centre.** on all sides; from every direction. **32 she'll be right.** *Austral. and N.Z. informal.* that's all right; not to worry. **33 right off the bat.** *Informal.* as the first in a series; to begin with. ◆ *n* **34** any claim, title, etc., that is morally just or legally granted as allowable or due to a person: *I know my rights.* **35** anything that accords with the principles of legal or moral justice. **36** the fact or state of being in accordance with reason, truth, or accepted standards (esp. in the phrase **in the right**). **37** *Irish.* an obligation or duty: *you had a right to lock the door.* **38** the right side, direction, position, area, or part: *the right of the army; look to the right.* **39** (*often cap.* and preceded by *the*) the supporters or advocates of social, political, or economic conservatism or reaction, based generally on a belief that things are better left unchanged (opposed to *radical* or *left*). **40** *Boxing.* **40a** a punch with the right hand. **40b** the right hand. **41** *Finance.* **41a** (*often pl*) the privilege of a company's shareholders to subscribe for new issues of the company's shares on advantageous terms. **41b** the negotiable certificate signifying this privilege. **42 by right** (*or* **rights**). properly; justly: *by rights you should be in bed.* **43 in one's own right.** having a claim or title oneself rather than through marriage or other connection: *a peeress in her own right.* **44 too right.** *Austral. and N.Z. informal.* an exclamation of agreement. **45 to rights.** consistent with justice, correctness, or orderly arrangement: *he put the matter to rights.* ◆ *vb* (*mainly tr*) **46** (*also intr*) to restore to or attain a normal, esp. an upright, position: *the raft righted in a few seconds.* **47** to make (something) accord with truth or facts; correct. **48** to restore to an orderly state or condition; put right. **49** to make reparation for; compensate for or redress (esp. in the phrase **right a wrong**). ◆ *sentence substitute.* **50a** indicating that a statement has been understood. **50b** asking whether a statement has been understood. **50c** indicating a subdividing point within a discourse. ◆ *interj* **51** an expression of agreement or compliance. [Old English *riht, reoht*; related to Old High German *reht*, Gothic *raihts*, Latin *rēctus*] ► **ˈrighter** *n*

rightable (ˈraɪtəbᵊl) *adj* capable of being righted. ► **ˈrightably** *adv* ► **ˈrightableness** *n*

right about *n* 1 a turn executed through 180°. ◆ *adj, adv* 2 in the opposite direction.
right angle *n* 1 the angle between two radii of a circle that cut off on the circumference an arc equal in length to one quarter of the circumference; an angle of 90° or π/2 radians. 2 **at right angles.** perpendicular or perpendicularly. Related adj: **orthogonal.** ► ˈ**right-ˌangled** *adj*
right-angled triangle *n* a triangle one angle of which is a right angle. U.S. and Canadian name: **right triangle.**
right ascension *n Astronomy.* the angular distance measured eastwards along the celestial equator from the vernal equinox to the point at which the celestial equator intersects a great circle passing through the celestial pole and the heavenly object in question. Symbol: α Compare **declination** (sense 1).
right away *adv* without delay; immediately or promptly.
right-down *adv, adj* a variant of **downright.**
righten (ˈraɪtᵊn) *vb* 1 (*tr*) to set right. 2 to restore to or attain a normal or upright position.
righteous (ˈraɪtʃəs) *adj* **1a** characterized by, proceeding from, or in accordance with accepted standards of morality, justice, or uprightness; virtuous: *a righteous man.* **1b** (*as collective n;* preceded by *the*): *the righteous.* 2 morally justifiable or right, esp. from one's own point of view: *righteous indignation.* [Old English *rihtwīs,* from RIGHT + WISE²] ► ˈ**righteously** *adv* ► ˈ**righteousness** *n*
right-footer *n* (esp. in Ireland) a Protestant.
rightful (ˈraɪtfʊl) *adj* 1 in accordance with what is right; proper or just. 2 (*prenominal*) having a legally or morally just claim: *the rightful owner.* 3 (*prenominal*) held by virtue of a legal or just claim: *my rightful property.* ► ˈ**rightfully** *adv* ► ˈ**rightfulness** *n*
right-hand *adj* (*prenominal*) 1 of, relating to, located on, or moving towards the right: *a right-hand bend; this car has right-hand drive.* 2 for use by the right hand; right-handed. 3 **right-hand man.** one's most valuable assistant or supporter.
right-handed *adj* 1 using the right hand with greater skill or ease than the left. 2 performed with the right hand: *right-handed writing.* 3 made for use by the right hand. 4 worn on the right hand. 5 turning from left to right; clockwise. ► ˌ**right-ˈhandedly** *adv* ► ˌ**right-ˈhandedness** *n*
right-hander *n* 1 a blow with the right hand. 2 a person who is right-handed.
Right Honourable *adj* 1 (in Britain and certain Commonwealth countries) a title of respect for a Privy Councillor or an appeal-court judge. 2 (in Britain) a title of respect for an earl, a viscount, a baron, or the Lord Mayor or Lord Provost of any of certain cities.
rightish (ˈraɪtɪʃ) *adj* somewhat right, esp. politically.
rightist (ˈraɪtɪst) *adj* 1 of, tending towards, or relating to the political right or its principles; conservative, traditionalist, or reactionary. ◆ *n* 2 a person who supports or belongs to the political right. ► ˈ**rightism** *n*
rightly (ˈraɪtlɪ) *adv* 1 in accordance with the facts; correctly. 2 in accordance with principles of justice or morality. 3 with good reason; justifiably: *he was rightly annoyed with her.* 4 properly or suitably; appropriately: *rightly dressed for a wedding.* 5 (*used with a negative*) *Informal.* with certainty; positively or precisely (usually in the phrases **I don't rightly know, I can't rightly say**).
right-minded *adj* holding opinions or principles that accord with what is right or with the opinions of the speaker. ► ˌ**right-ˈmindedly** *adv* ► ˌ**right-ˈmindedness** *n*
rightness (ˈraɪtnɪs) *n* the state or quality of being right.
righto *or* **right oh** (ˈraɪtˈəʊ) *sentence substitute. Brit. informal.* an expression of agreement or compliance.
right off *adv* immediately; right away.
right of search *n* the right of a belligerent to stop and search neutral merchant ships on the high seas in wartime.
right of way *n, pl* **rights of way.** 1 the right of one vehicle or vessel to take precedence over another, as laid down by law or custom. **2a** the legal right of someone to pass over another's land, acquired by grant or by long usage. **2b** the path or road used by this right. 3 *U.S.* the strip of land over which a power line, railway line, road, etc., extends.
right on *interj* 1 *Slang, chiefly U.S. and Canadian.* an exclamation of full agreement, concurrence, or compliance with the wishes, words, or actions of another. ◆ *adj* 2 *Informal.* modern, trendy, and socially aware or relevant: *right-on green politics.*
Right Reverend *adj* (in Britain) a title of respect for an Anglican or Roman Catholic bishop.
rights issue *n Stock Exchange.* an issue of new shares offered by a company to its existing shareholders on favourable terms. Also called: **capitalization issue.**
rightsize (ˈraɪtˌsaɪz) *vb* to restructure (an organization) to cut costs and improve effectiveness without ruthlessly downsizing.
right-thinking (ˈraɪtˌθɪŋkɪŋ) *adj* possessing reasonable and generally acceptable opinions.
right triangle *n* U.S. and Canadian name for **right-angled triangle.**
rightward (ˈraɪtwəd) *adj* 1 situated on or directed towards the right. ◆ *adv* 2 a variant of **rightwards.**
rightwards (ˈraɪtwədz) *or* **rightward** *adv* towards or on the right.
right whale *n* any large whalebone whale of the family *Balaenidae.* They are grey or black, have a large head, and, in most, no dorsal fin, and are hunted as a source of whalebone and oil. See also **bowhead.** [C19: perhaps so named because it was *right* for hunting]
right wing *n* 1 (*often caps.*) the conservative faction of an assembly, party, etc. 2 the part of an army or field of battle on the right from the point of view of one facing the enemy. **3a** the right-hand side of the field of play from the point of view of a team facing its opponent's goal. **3b** a player positioned in this area in any of various games. **3c** the position occupied by such a player. ◆ *adj* **right-wing.** 4 of, belonging to, or relating to the right wing. ► ˈ**right-ˈwinger** *n*
Rigi (ˈriːgɪ) *n* a mountain in the Alps of N central Switzerland, between Lakes Lucerne, Zug, and Lauerz.
rigid (ˈrɪdʒɪd) *adj* 1 not bending; physically inflexible or stiff: *a rigid piece of plastic.* 2 unbending; rigorously strict; severe: *rigid rules.* ◆ *adv* 3 completely or excessively: *the lecture bored him rigid.* [C16: from Latin *rigidus,* from *rigēre* to be stiff] ► ˈ**rigidly** *adv* ► **riˈgidity** *or* ˈ**rigidness** *n*
rigid designator *n Logic.* an expression that identifies the same individual in every possible world: for example, "Shakespeare" is a rigid designator since it is possible that Shakespeare might not have been a playwright but not that he might not have been Shakespeare.
rigidify (rɪˈdʒɪdɪˌfaɪ) *vb* **-fies, -fying, -fied.** to make or become rigid.
Rigil Kent (ˈraɪdʒɪl ˈkent) *n Astronomy.* the star Alpha Centauri. Often shortened to **Rigil.** [from *Rigil Kentaurus,* from Arabic *al Rigil al Kentaurus* the Centaur's foot]
rigmarole (ˈrɪgməˌrəʊl) *or* **rigamarole** *n* 1 any long complicated procedure. 2 a set of incoherent or pointless statements; garbled nonsense. [C18: from earlier *ragman roll* a list, probably a roll used in a medieval game, wherein various characters were described in verse, beginning with *Ragemon le bon* Ragman the good]
rigor (ˈraɪgɔː, ˈrɪgə) *n* 1 *Med.* a sudden feeling of chilliness, often accompanied by shivering: it sometimes precedes a fever. 2 (ˈrɪgə). *Pathol.* rigidity of a muscle; muscular cramp. 3 a state of rigidity assumed by some animals in reaction to sudden shock. 4 the inertia assumed by some plants in conditions unfavourable to growth. [see RIGOUR]
rigorism (ˈrɪgəˌrɪzəm) *n* 1 strictness in judgment or conduct. 2 the religious cult of extreme self-denial. 3 *R.C. Theol.* the doctrine that in cases of doubt in moral matters the stricter course must always be followed. ► ˈ**rigorist** *n* ► ˌ**rigorˈistic** *adj*
rigor mortis (ˈrɪgə ˈmɔːtɪs) *n Pathol.* the stiffness of joints and muscular rigidity of a dead body, caused by depletion of ATP in the tissues. It begins two to four hours after death and lasts up to about four days, after which the muscles and joints relax. [C19: Latin, literally: rigidity of death]
rigorous (ˈrɪgərəs) *adj* 1 characterized by or proceeding from rigour; harsh, strict, or severe: *rigorous discipline.* 2 severely accurate; scrupulous: *rigorous book-keeping.* 3 (esp. of weather) extreme or harsh. 4 *Maths, logic.* (of a proof) making the validity of the successive steps completely explicit. ► ˈ**rigorously** *adv* ► ˈ**rigorousness** *n*
rigour *or U.S.* **rigor** (ˈrɪgə) *n* 1 harsh but just treatment or action. 2 a severe or cruel circumstance; hardship: *the rigours of famine.* 3 strictness, harshness, or severity of character. 4 strictness in judgment or conduct; rigorism. 5 *Maths, logic.* logical validity or accuracy. 6 *Obsolete.* rigidity. [C14: from Latin *rigor*]
rig out *vb* 1 (*tr, adv;* often foll. by *with*) to equip or fit out (with): *his car is rigged out with gadgets.* 2 to dress or be dressed: *rigged out smartly.* ◆ *n* **rig-out.** 3 *Informal.* a person's clothing or costume, esp. a bizarre outfit.
rigsdaler (ˈrɪgzˌdɑːlə) *n* another word for **rix-dollar.**
rig up *vb* (*tr, adv*) to erect or construct, esp. as a temporary measure: *cameras were rigged up to televise the event.*
Rig-Veda (rɪgˈveɪdə, -ˈviːdə) *n* a compilation of 1028 Hindu poems dating from 2000 B.C. or earlier. [C18: from Sanskrit *rigveda,* from *ric* song of praise + VEDA]
Rijeka (rɪˈɛkə; *Serbo-Croat* riˈjɛka) *n* a port in Croatia: an ancient town, changing hands many times before passing to Yugoslavia in 1947 until Croatia became independent in 1991. Pop.: 167 964 (1991). Italian name: **Fiume.**
rijksdaaler (ˈraɪksˌdɑːlə) *n* a variant of **rix-dollar.**
Rijksmuseum (ˈraɪxsmjuːˌzɪəm) *n* a museum in Amsterdam housing the national art collection of the Netherlands.
Rijn (rɛjn) *n* the Dutch name for the **Rhine.**
rijsttafel (ˈraɪsˌtɑːfəl) *n* an Indonesian food consisting of a selection of rice dishes to which are added small pieces of a variety of other foods, such as meat, fish, fruit, pickles, and curry. [from Dutch *rijst* rice + *tafel* table]
Rijswijk (ˈraɪsvaɪk; *Dutch* ˈrɛjswɛjk) *n* a town in the SW Netherlands, in South Holland province on the SE outskirts of The Hague: scene of the signing (1697) of the **Treaty of Rijswijk,** ending the War of the Grand Alliance. Pop.: 48 000 (1991). English name: **Ryswick.**
rikishi (rɪˈkɪʃɪ) *n, pl* **rikishi.** a sumo wrestler. [Japanese, literally: strong man]
Riksdag (*Swedish* ˈriːksdag) *n* the Swedish parliament.
Riksmål *Norwegian.* (ˈriksmɔl) *n* a former name for **Bokmål.** [literally: language of the kingdom]
rile (raɪl) *vb* (*tr*) 1 to annoy or anger; irritate. 2 *U.S. and Canadian.* to stir up or agitate (water, etc.); roil or make turbid. [C19: variant of ROIL]
Riley[1] (ˈraɪlɪ) *n* **Bridget (Louise).** born 1931, British painter, best known for her black-and-white op art paintings of the 1960s.
Riley[2] (ˈraɪlɪ) *n* **the life of Riley.** a luxurious and carefree existence. [C20: origin unknown]
rilievo *Italian.* (riˈljevo; *English* ˌrɪlɪˈeɪvəʊ) *n, pl* **-vi** (-vi; *English* -viː). another name for **relief** (sense 9).
Rilke (ˈrɪlkə) *n* **Rainer Maria** (ˈrainər maˈriːa). 1875–1926, Austro-German poet, born in Prague. Author of intense visionary lyrics, notably in the *Duino Elegies* (1922) and *Sonnets to Orpheus* (1923).
rill (rɪl) *n* 1 a brook or stream; rivulet. 2 a small channel or gulley, such as one formed during soil erosion. 3 Also: **rille.** one of many winding cracks on the moon. [C15: from Low German *rille;* related to Dutch *ril*]
rillet (ˈrɪlɪt) *n* a little rill.
rim (rɪm) *n* 1 the raised edge of an object, esp. of something more or less circular such as a cup or crater. 2 the peripheral part of a wheel, to which the tyre is attached. 3 *Basketball.* the hoop from which the net is suspended. ◆ *vb* **rims,**

rimming, rimmed. (*tr*) **4** to put a rim on (a pot, cup, wheel, etc.). **5** *Slang.* to lick, kiss, or suck the anus of (one's sexual partner). **6** *Ball games.* (of a ball) to run around the edge of (a hole, basket, etc.). [Old English *rima;* related to Old Saxon *rimi,* Old Norse *rimi* ridge]

RIM *international car registration for* (Islamic Republic of) Mauritania.

rimaye (rɪ'meɪ) *n* another name for **bergschrund.** [C20: French, from Latin *rima* cleft]

Rimbaud (*French* rɛ̃bo) *n* **Arthur** (artyr). 1854–91, French poet, whose work, culminating in the prose poetry of *Illuminations* (published 1884), greatly influenced the symbolists. *A Season in Hell* (1873) draws on his tempestuous homosexual affair with Verlaine, after which he abandoned writing (aged about 20) and spent the rest of his life travelling.

rime[1] (raɪm) *n* **1** frost formed by the freezing of supercooled water droplets in fog onto solid objects. ◆ *vb* **2** (*tr*) to cover with rime or something resembling rime. [Old English *hrīm;* related to Dutch *rijm,* Middle High German *rīmeln* to coat with frost]

rime[2] (raɪm) *n, vb* an archaic spelling of **rhyme.**

rimer ('raɪmə) *n* another name for **rhymester.**

rime riche ('riːm 'riːʃ) *n, pl* **rimes riches** ('riːm'riːʃ). rhyme between words or syllables that are identical in sound, as in *command/demand, pair/pear.* [French, literally: rich rhyme]

rimester ('raɪmstə) *n* a variant spelling of **rhymester.**

rim-fire *adj* **1** (of a cartridge) having the primer in the rim of the base. **2** (of a firearm) adapted for such cartridges. ◆ Compare **centre-fire.**

Rimini ('rɪmɪnɪ) *n* a port and resort in NE Italy, in Emilia-Romagna on the N Adriatic coast. Pop.: 129 598 (1996 est.). Ancient name: **Ariminum.**

rimose (raɪ'məʊs, -'məʊz) *adj* (esp. of plant parts) having the surface marked by a network of intersecting cracks. [C18: from Latin *rīmōsus,* from *rīma* a split, crack] ▸ **'rimosely** *adv* ▸ **rimosity** (raɪ'mɒsɪtɪ) *n*

rimrock ('rɪm,rɒk) *n* rock forming the boundaries of a sandy or gravelly alluvial deposit.

Rimsky-Korsakov ('rɪmskɪ'kɔːsəkɒf; *Russian* 'rimskij'kɔrsəkəf) *n* **Nikolai Andreyevich** (nika'laj an'drjejɪvitʃ). 1844–1908, Russian composer; noted for such works as the orchestral suite *Scheherazade* (1888) and the opera *Le Coq d'or* (first performed in 1910).

rimu ('riːmuː) *n* another name for **red pine.** [from Maori]

rimy ('raɪmɪ) *adj* **rimier, rimiest.** coated with rime.

rind (raɪnd) *n* **1** a hard outer layer or skin on bacon, cheese, etc. **2** the outer layer of a fruit or of the spore-producing body of certain fungi. **3** the outer layer of the bark of a tree. [Old English *rinde;* Old High German *rinta,* German *Rinde*]

rinderpest ('rɪndə,pest) *n* an acute contagious viral disease of cattle, characterized by severe inflammation of the intestinal tract and diarrhoea. [C19: German: cattle pest]

rinforzando (,riːnfɔː'tsændəʊ) a less common term for **sforzando.** [Italian, literally: reinforcing]

ring[1] (rɪŋ) *n* **1** a circular band usually of a precious metal, esp. gold, often set with gems and worn upon the finger as an adornment or as a token of engagement or marriage. **2** any object or mark that is circular in shape. **3** a circular path or course: *to run around in a ring.* **4** a group of people or things standing or arranged so as to form a circle: *a ring of spectators.* **5** an enclosed space, usually circular in shape, where circus acts are performed. **6** a square apron or raised platform, marked off by ropes, in which contestants box or wrestle. **7 the ring.** the sport of boxing. **8** the field of competition or rivalry. **9 throw one's hat in the ring.** to announce one's intention to be a candidate or contestant. **10** a group of people usually operating illegally and covertly: *a drug ring; a paedophile ring; a ring of antique dealers.* **11** (esp. at country fairs) an enclosure, often circular, where horses, cattle, and other livestock are paraded and auctioned. **12** an area reserved for betting at a racecourse. **13** a circular strip of bark cut from a tree or branch, esp. in order to kill it. **14** a single turn in a spiral. **15** *Geometry.* the area of space lying between two concentric circles. **16** *Maths.* a set that is subject to two binary operations, addition and multiplication, such that the set is an Abelian group under addition and is closed under multiplication, this latter operation being associative. **17** *Botany.* short for **annual ring. 18** Also called: **closed chain.** *Chem.* a closed loop of atoms in a molecule. **19** *Astronomy.* any of the thin circular bands of small bodies orbiting a giant planet, esp. Saturn. See also **Saturn**[2] (sense 1). **20 run rings around.** *Informal.* to be greatly superior to; outclass completely. ◆ *vb* **rings, ringing, ringed.** (*tr*) **21** to surround with or as if with or form a ring; encircle. **22** to mark (a bird) with a ring or clip for subsequent identification. **23** to fit a ring in the nose of (a bull, pig, etc.) so that it can be led easily. **24** Also: **ringbark 24a** to cut away a circular strip of bark from (a tree or branch) in order to kill it. **24b** to cut a narrow or partial ring from (the trunk of a tree) in order to check or prevent vigorous growth. **25** *Austral. and N.Z.* to be the fastest shearer in a shearing shed (esp. in the phrase **ring the shed**). [Old English *hring;* related to Old Norse *hringr*]

ring[2] (rɪŋ) *vb* **rings, ringing, rang, rung. 1** to emit or cause to emit a sonorous or resonant sound, characteristic of certain metals when struck. **2** to cause (a bell) to emit a ringing sound by striking it once or repeatedly or (of a bell) to emit such a sound. **3a** (*tr*) to cause (a large bell, esp. a church bell) to emit a ringing sound by pulling on a rope that is attached to a wheel on which the bell swings back and forth, being sounded by a clapper inside it. Compare **chime**[1] (sense 6). **3b** (*intr*) (of a bell) to sound by being swung in this way. **4** (*intr*) (of a building, place, etc.) to be filled with sound; echo: *the church rang with singing.* **5** (*intr;* foll. by *for*) to call by means of a bell, buzzer, etc.: *to ring for the butler.* **6** Also: **ring up.** *Chiefly Brit.* to call (a person) by telephone. **7** (*tr*) to strike or tap (a coin) in order to assess its genuineness by the sound produced. **8** (*intr*) (of the ears) to have or give the sensation of humming or ringing. **9** (*intr*) *Electronics.* (of an electric circuit) to produce a damped oscillatory wave after the application of a sharp input transition. **10** *Slang.* to change the identity of (a stolen vehicle) by using the licence plate, serial number, etc., of another, usually disused, vehicle. **11 ring a bell.** to sound familiar; remind one of something, esp. indistinctly. **12 ring down the curtain. 12a** to lower the curtain at the end of a theatrical performance. **12b** (foll. by *on*) to put an end (to). **13 ring false.** to give the impression of being false. **14 ring the bell. 14a** to do, say, or be the right thing. **14b** to reach the pinnacle of success or happiness. **15 ring the changes.** to vary the manner or performance of an action that is often repeated. **16 ring true.** to give the impression of being true: *that story doesn't ring true.* ◆ *n* **17** the act of or a sound made by ringing. **18** a sound produced by or suggestive of a bell. **19** any resonant or metallic sound, esp. one sustained or re-echoed: *the ring of trumpets.* **20** *Informal, chiefly Brit.* a telephone call: *he gave her a ring last night.* **21** the complete set of bells in a tower or belfry: *a ring of eight bells.* See **peal**[1] (sense 3). **22** an inherent quality or characteristic: *his explanation has the ring of sincerity.* **23** *Electronics.* the damped oscillatory wave produced by a circuit that rings. ◆ See also **ring back, ring in, ring off, ring out, ring up.** [Old English *hringan;* related to Old High German *hringen,* Old Norse *hringja*]

USAGE *Rang* and *sang* are the correct forms of the past tenses of *ring* and *sing,* although *rung* and *sung* are still heard informally and dialectally: *he rung (rang) the bell.*

ring back *vb* (*adv*) to return a telephone call (to).

ringbark ('rɪŋ,bɑːk) *vb* another term for **ring**[1] (sense 24).

ring binder *n* a loose-leaf binder fitted with metal rings that can be opened to allow perforated paper to be inserted.

ringbolt ('rɪŋ,bəʊlt) *n* a bolt with a ring fitted through an eye attached to the bolt head.

ringbone ('rɪŋ,bəʊn) *n* an abnormal bony growth affecting the pastern of a horse, often causing lameness.

ring circuit *n* an electrical system in which distribution points are connected to the main supply in a continuous closed circuit.

ringdove ('rɪŋ,dʌv) *n* **1** another name for **wood pigeon. 2** an Old World turtledove, *Streptopelia risoria,* having a greyish plumage with a black band around the neck.

ring-dyke *n* a dyke having an approximately circular outcrop of rock.

ringed (rɪŋd) *adj* **1** displaying ringlike markings. **2** having or wearing a ring. **3** formed by rings; annular.

ringed plover *n* a European shorebird, *Charadrius hiaticula,* with a greyish-brown back, white underparts with a black throat band, and orange legs: family *Charadriidae* (plovers).

ringent ('rɪndʒənt) *adj* (of the corolla of plants such as the snapdragon) consisting of two distinct gaping lips. [C18: from Latin *ringī* to open the mouth wide]

ringer ('rɪŋə) *n* **1** a person or thing that rings a bell. **2** Also called: **dead ringer.** *Slang.* a person or thing that is almost identical to another. **3** *Slang.* a stolen vehicle the identity of which has been changed by the use of the licence plate, serial number, etc., of another, usually disused, vehicle. **4** *U.S.* a contestant, esp. a horse, entered in a competition under false representations of identity, record, or ability. **5** *Austral. and N.Z.* the fastest shearer in a shed. **6** *Austral. informal.* the fastest or best at anything. **7** a quoit thrown so as to encircle a peg. **8** such a throw.

Ringer's solution ('rɪŋəz) *n* a solution containing the chlorides of sodium, potassium, and calcium, used to correct dehydration and, in physiological experiments, as a medium for in vitro preparations.

ring-fence *vb* **1** to assign (money, a grant, fund, etc.) to one particular purpose, so as to restrict its use: *to ring-fence a financial allowance.* **2** to oblige (a person or organization) to use money for a particular purpose: *to ring-fence a local authority.* ◆ *n* **ring fence. 3** an agreement, contract, etc., in which the use of money is restricted to a particular purpose.

ring finger *n* the third finger, esp. of the left hand, on which a wedding ring is traditionally worn.

ring flash *n Photog.* a type of electronic flash in which the light source is arranged in a ring around the lens in order to produce a light without shadows.

ring gauge *n Engineering.* a ring having an internal diameter of a specified size used for checking the diameter of a cylindrical object or part. Compare **plug gauge.**

ringgit ('rɪŋgɪt) *n* the standard monetary unit of Malaysia, divided into 100 sens. [from Malay]

ring in *vb* (*adv*) **1** (*intr*) *Chiefly Brit.* to report to someone by telephone. **2** (*tr*) to accompany the arrival of with bells (esp. in the phrase **ring in the new year**). **3** (*tr*) *Austral.* to substitute (a horse) fraudulently for another horse in a race. **4** (*tr*) *Austral. and N.Z. informal.* to recruit or include (a person). ◆ *n* **ring-in. 5** *Austral. informal.* a horse that serves as a substitute. **6** *Austral. and N.Z. informal.* a person or thing that is not normally a member of a particular group; outsider.

ringing tone *n Brit.* a sequence of pairs of tones heard by the dialler on a telephone when the number dialled is ringing. Compare **engaged tone, dialling tone.**

ringleader ('rɪŋ,liːdə) *n* a person who leads others in any kind of unlawful or mischievous activity.

ringlet ('rɪŋlɪt) *n* **1** a lock of hair hanging down in a spiral curl. **2** any of numerous butterflies of the genus *Erebia,* most of which occur in S Europe and have dark brown wings marked with small black-and-white eyespots: family *Satyridae.* ▸ **'ringleted** *adj*

ring main *n* a domestic electrical supply in which outlet sockets are connected to the mains supply through a ring circuit.

ringmaster ('rɪŋ,mɑːstə) *n* the master of ceremonies in a circus.

ring-necked *adj* (of animals, esp. certain birds and snakes) having a band of distinctive colour around the neck.

ring-necked pheasant *n* a common pheasant, *Phasianus colchicus,* originating in Asia. The male has a bright plumage with a band of white around the neck and the female is mottled brown.

ring off *vb* (*intr, adv*) *Chiefly Brit.* to terminate a telephone conversation by replacing the receiver; hang up.

Ring of the Nibelung *n* **1** *Germanic myth.* a magic ring on which the dwarf Alberich placed a curse after it was stolen from him. **2** the four operas by Wagner, *Das Rheingold* (1869), *Die Walküre* (1870), *Siegfried* (1876), and *Götterdämmerung* (1876), based on this myth: often shortened to **The Ring**.

ring out *vb* (*adv*) **1** (*tr*) to accompany the departure of with bells (esp. in the phrase **ring out the old year**). **2** (*intr*) to send forth a loud resounding noise.

ring ouzel *n* a European thrush, *Turdus torquatus,* common in rocky areas. The male has a blackish plumage with a white band around the neck and the female is brown.

ring road *n* a main road that bypasses a town or town centre. U.S. names: **belt, beltway**.

ring-shout *n* a West African circle dance that has influenced jazz, surviving in the Black churches of the southern U.S.

ringside ('rɪŋˌsaɪd) *n* **1** the area immediately surrounding an arena, esp. the row of seats nearest a boxing or wrestling ring. **2a** any place affording a close uninterrupted view. **2b** (*as modifier*): *a ringside seat.*

ringster ('rɪŋstə) *n* a member of a ring controlling a market in antiques, art treasures, etc.

ringtail ('rɪŋˌteɪl) *n* **1** Also called: **ring-tailed cat.** another name for **cacomistle. 2** *Austral.* any of several possums having curling prehensile tails used to grasp branches while climbing.

ring-tailed *adj* (of an animal) having a tail marked with rings of a distinctive colour.

ring taw *n* a game of marbles in which players attempt to knock other players' marbles out of a ring.

ring up *vb* (*adv*) **1** *Chiefly Brit.* to make a telephone call (to). **2** (*tr*) to record on a cash register. **3** (*tr*) to chronicle; record: *to ring up another success.* **4 ring up the curtain. 4a** to begin a theatrical performance. **4b** (often foll. by *on*) to make a start (on).

ringworm ('rɪŋˌwɜːm) *n* any of various fungal infections of the skin (esp. the scalp) or nails, often appearing as itching circular patches. Also called: **tinea.**

rink (rɪŋk) *n* **1** an expanse of ice for skating on, esp. one that is artificially prepared and under cover. **2** an area for roller skating on. **3** a building or enclosure for ice skating or roller skating. **4** *Bowls.* a strip of the green, usually about 5–7 metres wide, on which a game is played. **5** *Curling.* the strip of ice on which the game is played, usually 41 by 4 metres. **6** (in bowls and curling) the players on one side in a game. [C14 (Scots): from Old French *renc* row, RANK[1]]

rinkhals ('rɪŋkˌhals) *n, pl* **-hals** *or* **-halses.** a venomous elapid snake, *Hemachatus hemachatus,* of southern Africa, which spits venom at its enemies from a distance. Also called: **spitting snake.** [Afrikaans, literally: ring neck]

rinse (rɪns) *vb* (*tr*) **1** to remove soap from (clothes, etc.) by applying clean water in the final stage in washing. **2** to wash lightly, esp. without using soap: *to rinse one's hands.* **3** to give a light tint to (hair). ◆ *n* **4** the act or an instance of rinsing. **5** *Hairdressing.* a liquid preparation put on the hair when wet to give a tint to it: *a blue rinse.* [C14: from Old French *rincer,* from Latin *recens* fresh, new] ▸ **'rinsable** *or* **'rinsible** *adj* ▸ **ˌrinsa'bility** *or* **ˌrinsi'bility** *n* ▸ **'rinser** *n*

Rinzai ('rɪnzaɪ) *n* a Zen Buddhist school of Japan, characterized by the use of koans to lead to moments of insight and enlightenment.

Rio Branco (*Portuguese* 'riu 'brɐ̃ŋku) *n* **1** a city in W Brazil, capital of Acre state. Pop.: 167 457 (1991). **2** a river in Brazil, flowing south to the Rio Negro. Length: 644 km (400 miles).

Río Bravo ('rio 'braβo) *n* the Mexican name for the **Rio Grande.**

Rio de Janeiro ('riːəʊ də dʒə'nɪərəʊ) *or* **Rio** *n* **1** a port in SE Brazil, on Guanabara Bay: the country's chief port and its capital from 1763 to 1960; backed by mountains, notably Sugar Loaf Mountain; founded by the French in 1555 and taken by the Portuguese in 1567. Pop.: 5 473 909 (1991), with a conurbation of 9 888 000 (1995). Related noun: **Cariocan. 2** a state of E Brazil. Capital: Rio de Janeiro. Pop.: 13 296 400 (1995 est.). Area: 42 911 sq. km (16 568 sq. miles).

Río de la Plata ('riːəʊ də lɑː 'plɑːtə) *n* See **Plata.**

Río de Oro (*Spanish* 'rio ðe 'oro) *n* a former region of W Africa: comprised the S part of the Spanish Sahara (now Western Sahara).

Rio Grande *n* **1** ('riːəʊ 'grænd, 'grændɪ). a river in North America, rising in SW Colorado and flowing southeast to the Gulf of Mexico, forming the border between the U.S. and Mexico. Length: about 3030 km (1885 miles). Mexican name: **Río Bravo. 2** (*Portuguese* 'riu 'grɐ̃ndi). a port in SE Brazil, in SE Rio Grande do Sul state: serves as the port for Pôrto Alegre. Pop.: 157 608 (1991).

Rio Grande do Norte (*Portuguese* 'riu 'grɐ̃ndi du 'nɔrti) *n* a state of NE Brazil, on the Atlantic: much of it is semiarid plateau. Capital: Natal. Pop.: 2 582 300 (1995 est.). Area: 53 014 sq. km (20 469 sq. miles).

Rio Grande do Sul (*Portuguese* 'riu 'grɐ̃ndi du 'sul) *n* a state of S Brazil, on the Atlantic. Capital: Pôrto Alegre. Pop.: 9 578 600 (1995 est.). Area: 282 183 sq. km (108 951 sq. miles).

rioja (riː'əʊxə) *n* a red or white wine, with a distinctive vanilla bouquet and flavour, produced around the Ebro river in central N Spain. [C20: from *La Rioja,* the area where it is produced]

Río Negro ('riːəʊ 'neɪgrəʊ, 'nɛg-; *Spanish* 'rio 'neγro) *n* See **Negro**[2].

riot ('raɪət) *n* **1a** a disturbance made by an unruly mob or (in law) three or more persons; tumult or uproar. **1b** (*as modifier*): *a riot gun; riot police; a riot shield.* **2** boisterous activity; unrestrained revelry. **3** an occasion of boisterous merriment. **4** *Slang.* a person who occasions boisterous merriment. **5** a dazzling or arresting display: *a riot of colour.* **6** *Hunting.* the indiscriminate following of any scent by hounds. **7** *Archaic.* wanton lasciviousness. **8 run riot. 8a** to behave wildly and without restraint. **8b** (of plants) to grow rankly or profusely. ◆ *vb* **9** (*intr*) to take part in a riot. **10** (*intr*) to indulge in unrestrained revelry or merriment. **11** (*tr;* foll. by *away*) to spend (time or money) in wanton or loose living: *he has rioted away his life.* [C13: from Old French *riote* dispute, from *ruihoter* to quarrel, probably from *ruir* to make a commotion, from Latin *rugīre* to roar] ▸ **'rioter** *n* ▸ **'rioting** *n*

Riot Act *n* **1** *Criminal law.* (formerly in England) a statute of 1715 by which persons committing a riot had to disperse within an hour of the reading of the act by a magistrate. **2 read the riot act (to).** to warn or reprimand severely.

riotous ('raɪətəs) *adj* **1** proceeding from or of the nature of riots or rioting. **2** inciting to riot. **3** characterized by wanton or lascivious revelry: *riotous living.* **4** characterized by boisterous or unrestrained merriment: *riotous laughter.* ▸ **'riotously** *adv* ▸ **'riotousness** *n*

riot shield *n* a large oblong curved transparent shield used by police controlling crowds.

rip[1] (rɪp) *vb* **rips, ripping, ripped. 1** to tear or be torn violently or roughly; split or be rent. **2** (*tr;* foll. by *off* or *out*) to remove hastily, carelessly, or roughly: *they ripped out all the old kitchen units.* **3** (*intr*) *Informal.* to move violently or precipitously; rush headlong. **4** (*intr;* foll. by *into*) *Informal.* to pour violent abuse (on); make a verbal attack (on). **5** (*tr*) to saw or split (wood) in the direction of the grain. **6 let rip.** to act or speak without restraint. ◆ *n* **7** the place where something is torn; a tear or split. **8** short for **ripsaw.** ◆ See also **rip off, rip up.** [C15: perhaps from Flemish *rippen;* compare Middle Dutch *rippen* to pull] ▸ **'rippable** *adj*

rip[2] (rɪp) *n* short for **riptide** (sense 1). [C18: perhaps from RIP[1]]

rip[3] (rɪp) *n Informal, archaic.* **1** something or someone of little or no value. **2** an old worn-out horse. **3** a dissolute character; reprobate. [C18: perhaps altered from *rep,* shortened from REPROBATE]

RIP *abbrev. for* requiescat *or* requiescant in pace. [Latin: may he, she, *or* they rest in peace]

riparian (raɪ'pɛərɪən) *adj* **1** of, inhabiting, or situated on the bank of a river. **2** denoting or relating to the legal rights of the owner of land on a river bank, such as fishing or irrigation. ◆ *n* **3** *Property law.* a person who owns land on a river bank. [C19: from Latin *rīpārius,* from *rīpa* a river bank]

ripcord ('rɪpˌkɔːd) *n* **1** a cord that when pulled opens a parachute from its pack. **2** a cord on the gas bag of a balloon that when pulled opens a panel, enabling gas to escape and the balloon to descend.

ripe (raɪp) *adj* **1** (of fruit, grain, etc.) mature and ready to be eaten or used; fully developed. **2** mature enough to be eaten or used: *ripe cheese.* **3** fully developed in mind or body. **4** resembling ripe fruit, esp. in redness or fullness: *a ripe complexion.* **5** (*postpositive;* foll. by *for*) ready or eager (to undertake or undergo an action). **6** (*postpositive;* foll. by *for*) suitable; right or opportune: *the time is not yet ripe.* **7** mature in judgment or knowledge. **8** advanced but healthy (esp. in the phrase **a ripe old age**). **9** *Slang.* **9a** complete; thorough. **9b** excessive; exorbitant. **10** *Slang.* slightly indecent; risqué. [Old English *rīpe;* related to Old Saxon *rīpi,* Old High German *rīfi,* German *reif*] ▸ **'ripely** *adv* ▸ **'ripeness** *n*

ripen ('raɪpᵊn) *vb* to make or become ripe. ▸ **'ripener** *n*

ripieno (rɪ'pjɛnəʊ; *Italian* ri'pjeːno) *n, pl* **-ni** (-niː) *or* **-nos.** (in baroque concertos and concerti grossi) the full orchestra, as opposed to the instrumental soloists. Also called: **concerto.** Compare **concertino** (sense 1). [C18: from Italian: from *ri-* RE- + *pieno,* from Latin *plēnus* full]

Ripley ('rɪplɪ) *n* **George.** 1802–80, U.S. social reformer and transcendentalist: founder of the Brook Farm experiment in communal living in Massachusetts (1841).

rip off *vb* **1** (*tr*) to tear violently or roughly (from). **2** (*adv*) *Slang.* to steal from or cheat (someone). ◆ *n* **rip-off. 3** *Slang.* an article or articles stolen. **4** *Slang.* a grossly overpriced article. **5** *Slang.* the act of stealing or cheating.

Ripon ('rɪpᵊn) *n* a city in N England, in North Yorkshire: cathedral (12th–16th centuries). Pop.: 13 806 (1991 est.).

riposte *or* **ripost** (rɪ'pɒst, rɪ'pəʊst) *n* **1** a swift sharp reply in speech or action. **2** *Fencing.* a counterattack made immediately after a successful parry. ◆ *vb* **3** (*intr*) to make a riposte. [C18: from French, from Italian *risposta,* from *rispondere* to reply, RESPOND]

ripper ('rɪpə) *n* **1** a person who rips. **2** a murderer who dissects or mutilates his victims' bodies. **3** *Informal, chiefly Austral. and N.Z.* a fine or excellent person or thing.

ripping ('rɪpɪŋ) *adj Archaic Brit. slang.* excellent; splendid. ▸ **'rippingly** *adv*

ripple[1] ('rɪpᵊl) *n* **1** a slight wave or undulation on the surface of water. **2** a small wave or undulation in fabric, hair, etc. **3** a sound reminiscent of water flowing quietly in ripples: *a ripple of laughter.* **4** *Electronics.* an oscillation of small amplitude superimposed on a steady value. **5** *U.S. and Canadian.* another word for **riffle** (sense 4). **6** another word for **ripple mark.** ◆ *vb* **7** (*intr*) to form ripples or flow with a rippling or undulating motion. **8** (*tr*) to stir up (water) so as to form ripples. **9** (*tr*) to make ripple marks. **10** (*intr*) (of sounds) to rise and fall gently: *her laughter rippled through the air.* [C17: perhaps from RIP[1]] ▸ **'rippler** *n* ▸ **'rippling** *adj* ▸ **'ripplingly** *adv* ▸ **'ripply** *adj*

ripple[2] ('rɪpᵊl) *n* **1** a special kind of comb designed to separate the seed from the stalks in flax, hemp, or broomcorn. ◆ *vb* **2** (*tr*) to comb with this tool. [C14: of Germanic origin; compare Middle Dutch *repelen,* Middle High German *reffen* to ripple] ▸ **'rippler** *n*

ripple control *n* the remote control of a switch by electrical impulses.

ripple effect *n* the repercussions of an event or situation experienced far beyond its immediate location.

ripple mark *n* one of a series of small wavy ridges of sand formed by waves on a beach, by a current in a sandy riverbed, or by wind on land: sometimes found fossilized on bedding planes of sedimentary rock.

ripplet ('rɪplɪt) *n* a tiny ripple.
rip-rap *n Civil engineering.* broken stones loosely deposited in water or on a soft bottom to provide a foundation and protect a riverbed or river banks from scour: used for revetments, embankments, breakwaters, etc. [C19: reduplication of RAP[1]]
rip-roaring *adj Informal.* characterized by excitement, intensity, or boisterous behaviour.
ripsaw ('rɪp,sɔː) *n* a handsaw for cutting along the grain of timber.
ripsnorter ('rɪp,snɔːtə) *n Slang.* a person or thing noted for intensity or excellence. [C19: from RIP[1] + SNORTER] ▸ **'rip,snorting** *adj*
riptide ('rɪp,taɪd) *n* **1** Also called: **rip, tide-rip.** a stretch of turbulent water in the sea, caused by the meeting of currents or abrupt changes in depth. **2** Also called: **rip current.** a strong current, esp. one flowing outwards from the shore, causing disturbance on the surface.
Ripuarian (,rɪpju'ɛərɪən) *adj* **1a** of or relating to the group of Franks who lived during the 4th century near Cologne along the Rhine. **1b** of or designating their code of laws. ◆ *n* **2** a Ripuarian Frank. [C18: from Medieval Latin *Ripuārius,* perhaps from Latin *rīpa* a river bank]
rip up *vb (tr, adv)* **1** to tear (paper) into small pieces. **2** to annul, cancel, or unilaterally disregard. **3** to dig up, dig into, or remove (a surface): *they are ripping up the street.*
Rip Van Winkle ('rɪp væn 'wɪŋkᵊl) *n Informal.* **1** a person who is oblivious to changes, esp. in social attitudes or thought. **2** a person who sleeps a lot. [C19: from a character who slept for 20 years, in a story (1819) by Washington Irving]
riroriro ('riːrəu,riːrəu) *n, pl* **-ros.** another name for the **grey warbler.** [Maori]
RISC (rɪsk) *n acronym for* reduced instruction set computer: a computer in which the set of instructions which it can perform has been reduced to the minimum, resulting in very fast data processing.
rise (raɪz) *vb* **rises, rising, rose** (rəuz), **risen** ('rɪzᵊn). *(mainly intr)* **1** to get up from a lying, sitting, kneeling, or prone position. **2** to get out of bed, esp. to begin one's day: *he always rises early.* **3** to move from a lower to a higher position or place; ascend. **4** to ascend or appear above the horizon: *the sun is rising.* **5** to increase in height or level: *the water rose above the normal level.* **6** to attain higher rank, status, or reputation: *he will rise in the world.* **7** to be built or erected: *those blocks of flats are rising fast.* **8** to become apparent; appear: *new troubles rose to afflict her.* **9** to increase in strength, degree, intensity, etc.: *her spirits rose; the wind is rising.* **10** to increase in amount or value: *house prices are always rising.* **11** to swell up: *dough rises.* **12** to become erect, stiff, or rigid: *the hairs on his neck rose in fear.* **13** (of one's stomach or gorge) to manifest or feel nausea; retch. **14** to become actively rebellious; revolt: *the people rose against their oppressors.* **15** to slope upwards: *the ground rises beyond the lake.* **16** to return from the dead; be resurrected. **17** to originate; come into existence: *that river rises in the mountains.* **18** (of a session of a court, legislative assembly, etc.) to come to an end; adjourn. **19** *Angling.* (of fish) to come to the surface of the water, as when taking flies. **20** *(tr) Nautical.* another term for **raise** (sense 20). **21** (often foll. by *to*) *Informal.* to respond (to teasing, etc.) or fall into a trap prepared for one. ◆ *n* **22** the act or an instance of rising; ascent. **23** an increase in height; elevation. **24** an increase in rank, status, or position. **25** an increase in amount, cost, or value. **26** an increase in degree or intensity. **27** *Brit.* an increase in salary or wages. U.S. and Canadian word: **raise. 28** a piece of rising ground. **29** an upward slope or incline. **30** the appearance of the sun, moon, or other celestial body above the horizon. **31** the vertical height of a step or of a flight of stairs. **32** the vertical height of a roof above the walls or columns. **33** the height of an arch above the impost level. **34** *Angling.* the act or instance of fish coming to the surface of the water to take flies, etc. **35** the beginning, origin, or source; derivation. **36** *Taboo slang.* an erection of the penis. **37 get** *or* **take a rise out of.** to provoke an angry or petulant reaction from. **38 give rise to.** to cause the development of; produce. [Old English *rīsan;* related to Old Saxon *rīsan,* Gothic *reisan*]
rise above *vb (intr, prep)* to overcome or be unaffected by (something mean or contemptible).
risen ('rɪzᵊn) *vb* **1** the past participle of **rise.** ◆ *adj* **2** restored from death; ascended into glory: *the risen Christ.*
riser ('raɪzə) *n* **1** a person who rises, esp. from bed: *an early riser.* **2** the vertical part of a stair or step. **3** a vertical pipe, esp. one within a building.
rise to *vb (intr, prep)* to respond adequately to (the demands of something, esp. a testing challenge).
risibility (,rɪzɪ'bɪlɪtɪ) *n, pl* **-ties. 1** a tendency to laugh. **2** hilarity; laughter.
risible ('rɪzɪbᵊl) *adj* **1** having a tendency to laugh. **2** causing laughter; ridiculous. [C16: from Late Latin *rīsibilis,* from Latin *rīdēre* to laugh] ▸ **'risibly** *adv*
rising ('raɪzɪŋ) *n* **1** an insurrection or rebellion; revolt. **2** the yeast or leaven used to make dough rise in baking. ◆ *adj (prenominal)* **3** increasing in rank, status, or reputation: *a rising young politician.* **4** increasing in maturity; growing up to adulthood: *the rising generation.* ◆ *adv* **5** *Informal.* approaching the age of; nearly: *she's rising 40.*
rising damp *n* capillary movement of moisture from the ground into the walls of buildings. It results in structural damage up to a level of three feet.
rising trot *n* a horse's trot in which the rider rises from the saddle every second beat. Compare **sitting trot.**
risk (rɪsk) *n* **1** the possibility of incurring misfortune or loss; hazard. **2** *Insurance.* **2a** chance of a loss or other event on which a claim may be filed. **2b** the type of such an event, such as fire or theft. **2c** the amount of the claim should such an event occur. **2d** a person or thing considered with respect to the characteristics that may cause an insured event to occur. **3 at risk. 3a** vulnerable; likely to be lost or damaged. **3b** *Social welfare.* vulnerable to personal damage, to the extent that a welfare agency might take protective responsibility. **4 no risk.** *Austral. informal.* an expression of assent. **5 take** *or* **run a risk.** to proceed in an action without regard to the possibility of danger involved in it. ◆ *vb (tr)* **6** to expose to danger or loss; hazard. **7** to act in spite of the possibility of (injury or loss): *to risk a fall in climbing.* [C17: from French *risque,* from Italian *risco,* from *rischiare* to be in peril, from Greek *rhiza* cliff (from the hazards of sailing along rocky coasts)] ▸ **'risker** *n*
risk capital *n Chiefly Brit.* capital invested in an issue of ordinary shares, esp. of a speculative enterprise. Also called: **venture capital.**
risk factor *n Med.* a factor, such as a habit or an environmental condition, that predisposes an individual to develop a particular disease.
risky ('rɪskɪ) *adj* **riskier, riskiest.** involving danger; perilous. ▸ **'riskily** *adv* ▸ **'riskiness** *n*
Risorgimento (rɪ,sɔːdʒɪ'mɛntəu) *n* the period of and the movement for the political unification of Italy in the 19th century. [Italian, from *risorgere* to rise again, from Latin *resurgere,* from RE- + *surgere* to rise]
risotto (rɪ'zɒtəu) *n, pl* **-tos.** a dish of rice cooked in stock and served variously with tomatoes, cheese, chicken, etc. [C19: from Italian, from *riso* RICE]
risqué ('rɪskeɪ) *adj* bordering on impropriety or indecency: *a risqué joke.* [C19: from French *risquer* to hazard, RISK]
Riss (rɪs) *n* the third major Pleistocene glaciation in Alpine Europe. See also **Günz, Mindel, Würm.** [C20: named after the river *Riss,* a tributary of the Danube in Germany]
rissole ('rɪsəul) *n* a mixture of minced cooked meat coated in egg and breadcrumbs and fried. Compare **croquette.** [C18: from French, probably ultimately from Latin *russus* red; see RUSSET]
risus sardonicus ('riːsəs sɑː'dɒnɪkəs) *n Pathol.* fixed contraction of the facial muscles resulting in a peculiar distorted grin, caused esp. by tetanus. Also called: **trismus cynicus** ('trɪzməs 'sɪnɪkəs). [C17: New Latin, literally: sardonic laugh]
rit. *Music. abbrev. for:* **1** ritardando. **2** ritenuto.
ritardando (,rɪtɑː'dændəu) *adj, adv* another term for **rallentando.** Abbrev.: **rit.** [C19: from Italian, from *ritardare* to slow down]
rite (raɪt) *n* **1** a formal act or procedure prescribed or customary in religious ceremonies: *fertility rites; the rite of baptism.* **2** a particular body of such acts or procedures, esp. of a particular Christian Church: *the Latin rite.* **3** a Christian Church: *the Greek rite.* [C14: from Latin *rītus* religious ceremony]
ritenuto (,rɪtə'nuːtəu) *adj, adv Music.* **1** held back momentarily. **2** another term for **rallentando.** Abbrev.: **rit.** [C19: from Italian, from past participle of *ritenere,* from Latin *retinēre* to hold back]
rite of passage *or* ***rite de passage*** (*French* rit də pɑsaʒ) *n* **1** a ceremony performed in some cultures at times when an individual changes his status, as at puberty and marriage. **2** a significant event in a transitional period of someone's life.
ritornello (,rɪtə'nɛləu) *n, pl* **-los** *or* **-li** (-liː). *Music.* **1** an orchestral passage between verses of an aria or song. **2** a ripieno passage in a concerto grosso. [C17: from Italian, literally: a little return, from *ritorno* a RETURN]
ritual ('rɪtjuəl) *n* **1** the prescribed or established form of a religious or other ceremony. **2** such prescribed forms in general or collectively. **3** stereotyped activity or behaviour. **4** *Psychol.* any repetitive behaviour, such as hand-washing, performed by a person with a compulsive personality disorder. **5** any formal act, institution, or procedure that is followed consistently: *the ritual of the law.* ◆ *adj* **6** of, relating to, or characteristic of religious, social, or other rituals. [C16: from Latin *rītuālis,* from *rītus* RITE] ▸ **'ritually** *adv*
ritualism ('rɪtjuə,lɪzəm) *n* **1** emphasis, esp. exaggerated emphasis, on the importance of rites and ceremonies. **2** the study of rites and ceremonies, esp. magical or religious ones. ▸ **'ritualist** *n* ▸ **,ritual'istic** *adj* ▸ **,ritual'istically** *adv*
ritualize *or* **ritualise** ('rɪtjuə,laɪz) *vb* **1** *(intr)* to engage in ritualism or devise rituals. **2** *(tr)* to make (something) into a ritual.
Ritz (rɪts) *n* **1** any very luxurious and expensive establishment: usually used with a negative: *this isn't the Ritz, you know.* **2 put on the Ritz.** *(sometimes not cap.)* to assume a superior air or make an ostentatious display. [from the luxury hotels created by the Swiss César *Ritz* (1850–1918)]
ritzy ('rɪtsɪ) *adj* **ritzier, ritziest.** *Slang.* luxurious or elegant. ▸ **'ritzily** *adv* ▸ **'ritziness** *n*
riv. *abbrev. for* river.
rivage ('rɪvɪdʒ) *n Archaic.* a bank, shore, or coast. [C14: from Old French, from *rive* river bank, from Latin *rīpa*]
rival ('raɪvᵊl) *n* **1a** a person, organization, team, etc., that competes with another for the same object or in the same field. **1b** *(as modifier): rival suitors; a rival company.* **2** a person or thing that is considered the equal of another or others: *she is without rival in the field of economics.* ◆ *vb* **-vals, -valling, -valled** *or U.S.* **-vals, -valing, -valed.** *(tr)* **3** to be the equal or near equal of: *an empire that rivalled Rome.* **4** to try to equal or surpass; compete with in rivalry. [C16: from Latin *rīvālis,* literally: one who shares the same brook, from *rīvus* a brook]
rivalry ('raɪvəlrɪ) *n, pl* **-ries. 1** the act of rivalling; competition. **2** the state of being a rival or rivals. ▸ **'rivalrous** *adj*
rive (raɪv) *vb* **rives, riving, rived, rived** *or* **riven** ('rɪvᵊn). *(usually passive)* **1** to split asunder: *a tree riven by lightning.* **2** to tear apart: *riven to shreds.* **3** *Archaic.* to break (the heart) or (of the heart) to be broken. [C13: from Old Norse *rīfa;* related to Old Frisian *rīva*]
river ('rɪvə) *n* **1a** a large natural stream of fresh water flowing along a definite course, usually into the sea, being fed by tributary streams. **1b** *(as modifier): river traffic; a river basin.* **1c** *(in combination): riverside; riverbed.* Related adjs: **fluvial, potamic. 2** any abundant stream or flow: *a river of blood.* **3 sell down the river.** *Informal.* to deceive or betray. [C13: from Old French *riviere,* from Latin *rīpārius* of a river bank, from *rīpa* bank] ▸ **'riverless** *adj*
Rivera (*Spanish* ri'βera) *n* **Diego** ('djeɣo). 1886–1957, Mexican painter, noted for his monumental murals in public buildings, which are influenced by Aztec art and depict revolutionary themes.

river blindness *n* another name for **onchocerciasis.**
river horse *n* an informal name for the **hippopotamus.**
riverine ('rɪvəˌraɪn) *adj* **1** of, like, relating to, or produced by a river. **2** located or dwelling near a river; riparian.
Rivers ('rɪvəz) *n* a state of S Nigeria, in the Niger River Delta on the Gulf of Guinea. Capital: Port Harcourt. Pop.: 4 103 372 (1995 est.). Area: 21 850 sq. km (8436 sq. miles).
Riverside ('rɪvəˌsaɪd) *n* a city in SW California. Pop.: 255 069 (1996 est.).
rivet ('rɪvɪt) *n* **1** a short metal pin for fastening two or more pieces together, having a head at one end, the other end being hammered flat after being passed through holes in the pieces. ♦ *vb* **-ets, -eting, -eted.** *(tr)* **2** to join by riveting. **3** to hammer in order to form into a head. **4** *(often passive)* to cause to be fixed or held firmly, as in fascinated attention, horror, etc.: *to be riveted to the spot.* **[**C14: from Old French, from *river* to fasten, fix, of unknown origin**]** ► **'riveter** *n*
riveting ('rɪvətɪŋ) *adj* absolutely fascinating; enthralling.
Riviera (ˌrɪvɪ'ɛərə) *n* the Mediterranean coastal region between Cannes, France, and La Spezia, Italy: contains some of Europe's most popular resorts. **[**C18: from Italian literally: shore, ultimately from Latin *rīpa* bank, shore**]**
rivière (ˌrɪvɪ'ɛə) *n* a necklace the diamonds or other precious stones of which gradually increase in size up to a large centre stone. **[**C19: from French: brook, RIVER**]**
rivulet ('rɪvjʊlɪt) *n* a small stream. **[**C16: from Italian *rivoletto,* from Latin *rīvulus,* from *rīvus* stream**]**
rix-dollar ('rɪksˌdɒlə) *n* any of various former Scandinavian or Dutch small silver coins. Also called: **rijksdaaler, rigsdaler.** **[**C16: partial translation of obsolete Dutch *rijksdaler; rijk* realm, kingdom**]**
Riyadh (rɪ'jɑːd) *n* the joint capital (with Mecca) of Saudi Arabia, situated in a central oasis: the largest city in the country. Pop.: 2 800 000 (1996 est.).
riyal (rɪ'jɑːl) *n* the standard monetary and currency unit of Qatar, Saudi Arabia, and Yemen. **[**from Arabic *riyāl,* from Spanish *real* REAL[2]**]**
Rizal[1] *(Spanish* ri'θal) *n* another name for **Pasay.**
Rizal[2] *(Spanish* ri'θal) *n* **Jose** (xo'se). 1861–96, Philippine nationalist, executed by the Spanish during the Philippine revolution of 1896.
Rizzio ('rɪtsɪəʊ) *or* **Riccio** *n* **David.** ?1533–66, Italian musician and courtier who became the secretary and favourite of Mary, Queen of Scots. He was murdered at the instigation of a group of nobles, including Mary's husband, Darnley.
RL 1 *abbrev. for* Rugby League. ♦ **2** *international car registration for* (Republic of) Lebanon.
rly *abbrev. for* railway.
rm *abbrev. for:* **1** ream. **2** room.
RM *abbrev. for:* **1** Royal Mail. **2** Royal Marines. ♦ **3** *international car registration for* Madagascar.
RMA *abbrev. for* Royal Military Academy (Sandhurst).
R-methodology *n* any statistical methodology in psychology that is contrasted with Q-methodology.
RMM *international car registration for* (Republic of) Mali.
r.m.m. *abbrev. for* relative molecular mass.
rms *abbrev. for* root mean square.
RMS *abbrev. for:* **1** Royal Mail Service. **2** Royal Mail Steamer.
RMT *abbrev. for* National Union of Rail, Maritime and Transport Workers.
Rn *the chemical symbol for* radon.
RN 1 *abbrev. for* Royal Navy. **2** *international car registration for* (Republic of) Niger.
RNA *n Biochem.* ribonucleic acid; any of a group of nucleic acids, present in all living cells, that play an essential role in the synthesis of proteins. On hydrolysis they yield the pentose sugar ribose, the purine bases adenine and guanine, the pyrimidine bases cytosine and uracil, and phosphoric acid. See also **messenger RNA, transfer RNA, ribosomal RNA, DNA.**
RNAS *abbrev. for:* **1** Royal Naval Air Service(s). **2** Royal Naval Air Station.
RNIB *Brit. abbrev. for* Royal National Institute for the Blind.
RNID *Brit. abbrev. for* Royal National Institute for Deaf People.
RNLI *abbrev. for* Royal National Lifeboat Institution.
RNR *abbrev. for* Royal Naval Reserve.
RNVR *abbrev. for* Royal Naval Volunteer Reserve.
RNWMP (in Canada) *abbrev. for* Royal Northwest Mounted Police: a former name for the Royal Canadian Mounted Police.
RNZAF *abbrev. for* Royal New Zealand Air Force.
RNZN *abbrev. for* Royal New Zealand Navy.
RO *international car registration for* Romania.
roach[1] (rəʊtʃ) *n, pl* **roaches** *or* **roach. 1** a European freshwater cyprinid food fish, *Rutilus rutilus,* having a deep compressed body and reddish ventral and tail fins. **2** any of various similar fishes. **[**C14: from Old French *roche,* of obscure origin**]**
roach[2] (rəʊtʃ) *n* **1** short for **cockroach. 2** *Slang.* the butt of a cannabis cigarette.
roach[3] (rəʊtʃ) *n Nautical.* **1** the amount by which the leech of a fore-and-aft sail projects beyond an imaginary straight line between the clew and the head. **2** the curve at the foot of a square sail. **[**C18: of unknown origin**]**
Roach (rəʊtʃ) *n* **Hal,** full name *Harald Eugene Roach.* 1892–1992, U.S. film producer, whose company produced numerous comedy films in the 1920s and 1930s, including those featuring Harold Lloyd and Laurel and Hardy.
roach clip *n Slang.* a small clip resembling tweezers, used to hold the butt of a cannabis cigarette, in order to prevent burning one's fingers.
roached (rəʊtʃt) *adj* arched convexly, as the back of certain breeds of dog, such as the whippet. **[**C19: from ROACH[3] or *roach* (vb) to cut (a sail) into a roach**]**
road (rəʊd) *n* **1a** an open way, usually surfaced with tarmac or concrete, providing passage from one place to another. **1b** *(as modifier): road traffic; a road map; a road sign.* **1c** *(in combination): the roadside.* **2a** a street. **2b** *(cap. when part of a name): London Road.* **3a** *U.S.* short for **railroad. 3b** *Brit.* one of the tracks of a railway. **4** a way, path, or course: *the road to fame.* **5** *(often pl)* Also called: **roadstead.** *Nautical.* a partly sheltered anchorage. **6** a drift or tunnel in a mine, esp. a level one. **7 hit the road.** *Slang.* to start or resume travelling. **8 on the road. 8a** travelling, esp. as a salesman. **8b** (of a theatre company, pop group, etc.) on tour. **8c** leading a wandering life. **9 take (to) the road.** to begin a journey or tour. **10 one for the road.** *Informal.* a last alcoholic drink before leaving. **[**Old English *rād;* related to *rīdan* to RIDE, and to Old Saxon *rēda,* Old Norse *reith***]** ► **'roadless** *adj*
road agent *n U.S.* (formerly) a bandit who robbed stagecoaches; highwayman.
road allowance *n Canadian.* land reserved by the government to be used for public roads.
roadbed ('rəʊdˌbɛd) *n* **1** the material used to make a road. **2** a layer of ballast that supports the sleepers of a railway track.
roadblock ('rəʊdˌblɒk) *n* a barrier set up across a road by the police or military, in order to stop a fugitive, inspect traffic, etc.
road book *n* a book of maps, sometimes including a gazetteer.
road-fund licence *n Brit.* a licence showing that the tax payable in respect of a motor vehicle has been paid. **[**C20: from the former *road fund* for the maintenance of public highways**]**
road hog *n Informal.* a selfish or aggressive driver.
roadholding ('rəʊdˌhəʊldɪŋ) *n* the extent to which a motor vehicle is stable and does not skid, esp. at high speeds, or on sharp bends or wet roads.
roadhouse ('rəʊdˌhaʊs) *n* a pub, restaurant, etc., that is situated at the side of a road, esp. a country road.
road hump *n* the official name for **sleeping policeman.**
roadie ('rəʊdɪ) *n Informal.* a person who transports and sets up equipment for a band or group.
roadkill ('rəʊdˌkɪl) *n Chiefly U.S.* the remains of an animal or animals killed on the road by motor vehicles.
road metal *n* crushed rock, broken stone, etc., used to construct a road.
road movie *n* a genre of film in which the chief character is on the run or travelling in search of, or to escape from, himself.
road rage *n* aggressive behaviour by a motorist in response to the actions of another road user.
roadroller ('rəʊdˌrəʊlə) *n* a motor vehicle with heavy rollers for compressing road surfaces during road-making.
roadrunner ('rəʊdˌrʌnə) *n* a terrestrial crested bird, *Geococcyx californianus,* of Central and S North America, having a streaked plumage and long tail: family *Cuculidae* (cuckoos). Also called: **chaparral cock.**
road show *n* **1a** a radio show broadcast live from one of a number of towns or venues being visited by a disc jockey who is touring an area. **1b** the touring disc jockey and the personnel and equipment needed to present such a show: *the Radio 1 road show will be in Brighton next week.* **2** a group of entertainers, esp. pop musicians, on tour. **3** any occasion when an organization attracts publicity while touring or visiting: *an antiques roadshow; a royal roadshow.*
roadstead ('rəʊdˌstɛd) *n Nautical.* another word for **road** (sense 5).
roadster ('rəʊdstə) *n* **1** an open car, esp. one seating only two. **2** a kind of bicycle.
road tax *n* a tax paid, usually annually, on motor vehicles in use on the roads.
road test *n* **1** a test to ensure that a vehicle is roadworthy, esp. after repair or servicing, by driving it on roads. **2** a test of something in actual use. ♦ *vb* **road-test.** *(tr)* **3** to test (a vehicle) in this way.
road train *n Austral.* a line of linked trailers pulled by a truck, used for transporting stock, etc.
roadway ('rəʊdˌweɪ) *n* **1** the surface of a road. **2** the part of a road that is used by vehicles.
roadwork ('rəʊdˌwɜːk) *n* sports training by running along roads.
roadworks ('rəʊdˌwɜːks) *pl n* repairs to a road or cable under a road, esp. when forming a hazard or obstruction to traffic.
roadworthy ('rəʊdˌwɜːðɪ) *adj* (of a motor vehicle) mechanically sound; fit for use on the roads. ► **'roadˌworthiness** *n*
roam (rəʊm) *vb* **1** to travel or walk about with no fixed purpose or direction; wander. ♦ *n* **2** the act of roaming. **[**C13: origin unknown**]** ► **'roamer** *n*
roan (rəʊn) *adj* **1** (of a horse) having a bay (**red roan**), chestnut (**strawberry roan**), or black (**blue roan**) coat sprinkled with white hairs. ♦ *n* **2** a horse having such a coat. **3** a soft unsplit sheepskin leather with a close tough grain, used in bookbinding, etc. **[**C16: from Old French, from Spanish *roano,* probably from Gothic *rauths* red**]**
Roanoke Island ('rəʊəˌnəʊk) *n* an island off the coast of North Carolina: site of the first attempted English settlement in America. Length: 19 km (12 miles). Average width: 5 km (3 miles).
roar (rɔː) *vb (mainly intr)* **1** (of lions and other animals) to utter characteristic loud growling cries. **2** *(also tr)* (of people) to utter (something) with a loud deep cry, as in anger or triumph. **3** to laugh in a loud hearty unrestrained manner. **4** (of horses) to breathe with laboured rasping sounds. See **roaring** (sense 6). **5** (of the wind, waves, etc.) to blow or break loudly and violently, as during a storm. **6** (of a fire) to burn fiercely with a roaring sound. **7** (of a machine, gun, etc.) to operate or move with a loud harsh noise. **8** *(tr)* to bring (oneself) into a certain condition by roaring: *to roar oneself hoarse.* ♦ *n* **9** a loud deep cry, uttered by a person or crowd, esp. in anger or triumph. **10** a prolonged loud cry of certain animals, esp. lions. **11** any similar noise made by a fire, the wind, waves, artillery, an engine, etc. **[**Old English *rārian;* related to Old High German *rērēn,* Middle Dutch *reren***]** ► **'roarer** *n*
roaring ('rɔːrɪŋ) *adj* **1** *Informal.* very brisk and profitable (esp. in the phrase **a roaring trade**). **2 the roaring days.** *Austral.* the period of the Australian goldrushes. **3** *Irish, derogatory informal.* (intensifier): *a roaring communist.*

◆ *adv* 4 noisily or boisterously (esp. in the phrase **roaring drunk**). ◆ *n* 5 a loud prolonged cry. 6 a debilitating breathing defect of horses characterized by rasping sounds with each breath: caused by inflammation of the respiratory tract or obstruction of the larynx. Compare **whistling.** ► **'roaringly** *adv*

Roaring Forties *pl n* **the.** *Nautical.* the areas of ocean between 40° and 50° latitude in the S Hemisphere, noted for gale-force winds.

roar up *vb (tr, adv) Austral. informal.* to rebuke or reprimand (a person).

roast (rəust) *vb (mainly tr)* **1** to cook (meat or other food) by dry heat, usually with added fat and esp. in an oven. **2** to brown or dry (coffee, etc.) by exposure to heat. **3** *Metallurgy.* to heat (an ore) in order to produce a concentrate that is easier to smelt. **4** to heat (oneself or something) to an extreme degree, as when sunbathing, sitting before the fire, etc. **5** *(intr)* to be excessively and uncomfortably hot. **6** *Informal.* to criticize severely. ◆ *n* **7** something that has been roasted, esp. meat. **[C13:** from Old French *rostir,* of Germanic origin; compare Middle Dutch *roosten* to roast**]** ► **'roaster** *n*

roasting ('rəustɪŋ) *Informal.* ◆ *adj* **1** extremely hot. ◆ *n* **2** severe criticism.

rob (rɒb) *vb* **robs, robbing, robbed. 1** to take something from (someone) illegally, as by force or threat of violence. **2** *(tr)* to plunder (a house, shop, etc.). **3** *(tr)* to deprive unjustly: *to be robbed of an opportunity.* **[C13:** from Old French *rober,* of Germanic origin; compare Old High German *roubōn* to rob**]** ► **'robber** *n*

robalo ('rɒbəˌləu, 'rəu-) *n, pl* **-los** *or* **-lo.** any percoid fish of the family *Centropomidae,* occurring in warm and tropical (mostly marine) waters. Some of the larger species, such as the snooks, are important food fishes and many of the smaller ones are aquarium fishes. **[**Spanish, probably changed from *lobaro* (unattested), from *lobo* wolf, from Latin *lupus***]**

roband ('rɒbənd, 'rəubənd) *or* **robbin** *n Nautical.* a piece of marline used for fastening a sail to a spar. **[C18:** probably related to Middle Dutch *rabant,* from *ra* sailyard + *bant* band**]**

Robbe-Grillet (*French* rɔbgrijɛ) *n* **Alain** (alɛ̃). born 1922, French novelist. Author of *The Voyeur* (1955) and *Jealousy* (1957), he is one of the leading practitioners of the antinovel.

Robben Island ('rɒbᵊn) *n* a small island in South Africa, 11 km (7 miles) off the Cape Peninsula: formerly used by the South African government to house political prisoners.

robber crab *n* a terrestrial crab, *Birgus latro,* of the Indo-Pacific region, known for its habit of climbing coconut palms to feed on the nuts.

robber fly *n* any of the predatory dipterous flies constituting the family *Asilidae,* which have a strong bristly body with piercing mouthparts and which prey on other insects. Also called: **bee killer, assassin fly.**

robber trench *n Archaeol.* a trench that originally contained the foundations of a wall, the stones of which have been taken away.

robbery ('rɒbərɪ) *n, pl* **-beries. 1** *Criminal law.* the stealing of property from a person by using or threatening to use force. **2** the act or an instance of robbing.

Robbia ('rəubɪə; *Italian* 'robbja) *n* **1 Andrea della** (an'drεːa 'dɛlla). 1435–1525, Florentine sculptor, best known for his polychrome reliefs and his statues of infants in swaddling clothes. **2** his uncle, **Luca della** ('luːka 'dɛlla). ?1400–82, Florentine sculptor, who perfected a technique of enamelling terra cotta for reliefs.

robbin ('rɒbɪn) *n Nautical.* another word for **roband.**

Robbins ('rɒbɪnz) *n* **Jerome.** 1918–98, U.S. ballet dancer and choreographer. He choreographed the musicals *The King and I* (1951) and *West Side Story* (1957).

robe (rəub) *n* **1** any loose flowing garment, esp. the official vestment of a peer, judge, or academic. **2** a dressing gown or bathrobe. **3** *Austral. informal.* a wardrobe. ◆ *vb* **4** to put a robe, etc., on (oneself or someone else); dress. **[C13:** from Old French: of Germanic origin; compare Old French *rober* to ROB, Old High German *roub* booty**]**

robe-de-chambre *French.* (rɔbdəʃɑ̃brə) *n, pl* ***robes-de-chambre*** (rɔbdəʃɑ̃brə). a dressing gown or bathrobe.

Robert I ('rɒbət) *n* known as *Robert the Bruce.* 1274–1329, king of Scotland (1306–29): he defeated the English army of Edward II at Bannockburn (1314) and gained recognition of Scotland's independence (1328).

Robert II *n* 1316–90, king of Scotland (1371–90).

Robert III *n* ?1337–1406, king of Scotland (1390–1406), son of Robert II.

Roberts ('rɒbəts) *n* **Frederick Sleigh,** 1st Earl. 1832–1914, British field marshal. He was awarded the Victoria Cross (1858) for his service during the Indian Mutiny and was commander in chief (1899–1900) in the second Boer War.

Robeson ('rəubsən) *n* **Paul.** 1898–1976, U.S. bass singer, actor, and leader in the Black civil rights movement.

Robespierre ('rəubzpjεə; *French* rɔbzpjɛr) *n* **Maximilien François Marie Isidore de** (maksimiljɛ̃ frɑ̃swa mari izidɔr də). 1758–94, French revolutionary and Jacobin leader: established the Reign of Terror as a member of the Committee of Public Safety (1793–94): executed in the coup d'état of Thermidor (1794).

Robey ('rəubɪ) *n* Sir **George,** original name *George Edward Wade,* known as *the prime minister of mirth.* 1869–1954, British music-hall comedian, who also appeared in films.

robin ('rɒbɪn) *n* **1** Also called: **robin redbreast.** a small Old World songbird, *Erithacus rubecula,* related to the thrushes: family *Muscicapidae.* The male has a brown back, orange-red breast and face, and grey underparts. **2** a North American thrush, *Turdus migratorius,* similar to but larger than the Old World robin. **3** any of various similar birds having a reddish breast. **[C16:** arbitrary use of given name**]**

Robin Goodfellow ('rɒbɪn 'gudˌfeləu) *n* another name for **puck**[2].

robing room *n* a room in a palace, court, legislature, etc., where official robes of office are put on.

Robin Hood *n* a legendary English outlaw of the reign of Richard I, who according to tradition lived in Sherwood Forest and robbed the rich to give to the poor.

robinia (rə'bɪnɪə) *n* any tree of the leguminous genus *Robinia,* esp. the locust tree (see **locust** (sense 2)).

robin's-egg blue *n Chiefly U.S.* **a** a light greenish-blue colour. **b** *(as adj): a robin's-egg-blue dress.*

Robinson ('rɒbɪnsən) *n* **1 Edward G.,** real name *Emanuel Goldenberg.* 1893–1973, U.S. film actor, born in Romania, famous esp. for gangster roles. His films include *Little Caesar* (1930), *Brother Orchid* (1940), *Double Indemnity* (1944), and *All My Sons* (1948). **2 Edwin Arlington.** 1869–1935, U.S. poet, author of narrative verse, often based on Arthurian legend. His works include *Collected Poems* (1922), *The Man Who Died Twice* (1924), and *Tristram* (1927). **3 (William) Heath.** 1872–1944, British cartoonist and book illustrator, best known for his comic drawings of fantastic machines. **4 John (Arthur Thomas).** 1919–83, British bishop and theologian, best known for his controversial *Honest to God* (1963), which popularized radical theological discussion. He was suffragan Bishop of Woolwich (1959–69). **5 Mary.** born 1944, Irish barrister and politician: president of Ireland 1990–97. **6 Smokey,** real name *William Robinson.* born 1940, U.S. Motown singer, songwriter, and producer. His hits include "The Tears of a Clown" (1970) (with the Miracles) and "Being with you" (1981). **7 "Sugar" Ray,** real name *Walker Smith.* 1921–89, U.S. boxer, winner of the world middleweight championship on five separate occasions.

Robinson Crusoe *n* the hero of Daniel Defoe's novel *Robinson Crusoe* (1719), who survived being shipwrecked on a desert island. See also **Selkirk.**

roble ('rəublɪ) *n* **1** Also called: **white oak.** an oak tree, *Quercus lobata,* of California, having leathery leaves and slender pointed acorns. **2** any of several similar or related trees. **[C19:** from Spanish: from Latin *rōbur* oak, strength**]**

roborant ('rəubərənt, 'rɒb-) *adj* **1** tending to fortify or increase strength. ◆ *n* **2** a drug or agent that increases strength. **[C17:** from Latin *roborāre* to strengthen, from *rōbur* an oak**]**

robot ('rəubɒt) *n* **1** any automated machine programmed to perform specific mechanical functions in the manner of a man. **2** *(modifier)* not controlled by man; automatic: *a robot pilot.* **3** a person who works or behaves like a machine; automaton. **4** *S. African.* a set of traffic lights. **[C20:** (used in *R.U.R.,* a play by Karel Čapek) from Czech *robota* work; related to Old Slavonic *rabota* servitude, German *Arbeit* work**]** ► **ro'botic** *adj* ► **'robotism** *or* **'robotry** *n* ► **'robot-ˌlike** *adj*

robot bomb *n* another name for the **V-1.**

robot dancing, robotics, *or* **robotic dancing** *n* a dance of the 1980s characterized by jerky mechanical movements.

robotics (rəu'bɒtɪks) *n (functioning as sing)* **1** the science or technology of designing, building, and using robots. **2** another name for **robot dancing.**

robotize *or* **robotise** ('rəubəˌtaɪz) *vb (tr)* **1** *Chiefly U.S.* to automate: *robotized assembly lines.* **2** to cause (a person) to be or become mechanical and lifeless, like a robot.

Rob Roy ('rɒb 'rɔɪ) *n* real name *Robert Macgregor.* 1671–1734, Scottish outlaw.

Robson[1] ('rɒbsən) *n* **Mount.** a mountain in SW Canada, in E British Columbia: the highest peak in the Canadian Rockies. Height: 3954 m (12 972 ft.).

Robson[2] ('rɒbsən) *n* **1 Bobby,** full name *Robert William.* born 1933, English footballer and manager of England (1982–90). **2 Bryan.** born 1957, English footballer and manager: captain of England (1982–90). **3** Dame **Flora.** 1902–84, English stage and film actress.

robust (rəu'bʌst, 'rəubʌst) *adj* **1** strong in constitution; hardy; vigorous. **2** sturdily built: *a robust shelter.* **3** requiring or suited to physical strength: *a robust sport.* **4** (esp. of wines) having a rich full-bodied flavour. **5** rough or boisterous. **6** (of thought, intellect, etc.) straightforward and imbued with common sense. **[C16:** from Latin *rōbustus,* from *rōbur* an oak, strength**]** ► **ro'bustly** *adv*

robustious (rəu'bʌstʃəs) *adj Archaic.* **1** rough; boisterous. **2** strong, robust, or stout. ► **ro'bustiously** *adv* ► **ro'bustiousness** *n*

robustness (rəu'bʌstnɪs) *n* **1** the quality of being robust. **2** *Computing.* the ability of a computer system to cope with errors during execution.

roc (rɒk) *n* (in Arabian legend) a bird of enormous size and power. **[C16:** from Arabic *rukhkh,* from Persian *rukh***]**

ROC *abbrev. for* Royal Observer Corps.

Roca ('rəukə) *n* **Cape.** a cape in SW central Portugal, near Lisbon: the westernmost point of continental Europe.

rocaille (rɒ'kaɪ) *n* decorative rock or shell work, esp. as ornamentation in a rococo fountain, grotto, or interior. **[**from French, from *roc* ROCK[1]**]**

rocambole ('rɒkəmˌbəul) *n* a variety of sand leek whose garlic-like bulb is used for seasoning. **[C17:** from French, from German *Rockenbolle,* literally: distaff bulb (with reference to its shape)**]**

Rocard (*French* rɔkaːr) *n* **Michel.** born 1930, French politician: prime minister of France (1988–91).

Rochdale ('rɒtʃˌdeɪl) *n* **1** a town in NW England, in Rochdale unitary authority, Greater Manchester: former centre of the textile industry. Pop.: 94 313 (1991). **2** a unitary authority in NW England, in Greater Manchester. Pop.: 207 600 (1995 est.). Area: 159 sq. km (61 sq. miles).

Roche limit (rɒʃ) *n Astronomy.* the distance from the centre of a body, such as a planet, at which the tidal forces are stronger than the mutual gravitational attraction between two adjacent orbiting objects. **[C19:** named after E. A. *Roche* (1820–83), French mathematician**]**

Rochelle powder (rɒ'ʃɛl) *n* another name for **Seidlitz powder. [C18:** named after *La Rochelle,* French port**]**

Rochelle salt *n* a white crystalline double salt used in Seidlitz powder. Formula: $KNaC_4H_4O_6.4H_2O$.

roche moutonnée ('rəuʃ ˌmuːtə'neɪ) *n, pl* **roches moutonnées** ('rəuʃ

ˌmuːtəˈneɪz). a rounded mass of rock smoothed and striated by ice that has flowed over it. **[**C19: French, literally: fleecy rock, from *mouton* sheep**]**

Rochester[1] (ˈrɒtʃɪstə) *n* **1** a city in SE England, in Kent on the River Medway: with Chatham and Gillingham forms the conurbation of the Medway towns. Pop.: 23 971 (1991). **2** a city in NW New York State, on Lake Ontario. Pop.: 221 594 (1996 est.). **3** a city in the U.S., in Minnesota: site of the Mayo Clinic. Pop.: 75 638 (1996 est.).

Rochester[2] (ˈrɒtʃɪstə) *n* **2nd Earl of**, title of *John Wilmot*. 1647–80, English poet, wit, and libertine. His poems include satires, notably *A Satire against Mankind* (1675), love lyrics, and bawdy verse.

rochet (ˈrɒtʃɪt) *n* a white surplice with tight sleeves, worn by bishops, abbots, and certain other Church dignitaries. **[**C14: from Old French, from *roc* coat, outer garment, of Germanic origin; compare Old High German *roc* coat**]**

rock[1] (rɒk) *n* **1** *Geology*. any aggregate of minerals that makes up part of the earth's crust. It may be unconsolidated, such as a sand, clay, or mud, or consolidated, such as granite, limestone, or coal. See also **igneous, sedimentary,** and **metamorphic. 2** any hard mass of consolidated mineral matter, such as a boulder. **3** *Chiefly U.S., Canadian and Austral.* a stone. **4** a person or thing suggesting a rock, esp. in being dependable, unchanging, or providing firm foundation. **5** *Brit.* a hard sweet, typically a long brightly-coloured peppermint-flavoured stick, sold esp. in holiday resorts. **6** *Slang*. a jewel, esp. a diamond. **7** short for **rock salmon. 8** (*pl*) *Taboo slang.* the testicles. **9** *Slang.* another name for **crack** (sense 29). **10 between a rock and a hard place.** having to choose between two equally unpleasant alternatives. **11 on the rocks. 11a** in a state of ruin or destitution. **11b** (of drinks, esp. whisky) served with ice. **[**C14: from Old French *roche,* of unknown origin**]**

rock[2] (rɒk) *vb* **1** to move or cause to move from side to side or backwards and forwards. **2** to reel or sway or cause (someone) to reel or sway, as with a violent shock or emotion. **3** (*tr*) to shake or move (something) violently. **4** (*intr*) to dance in the rock-and-roll style. **5** *Mining.* to wash (ore) or (of ore) to be washed in a cradle. **6** (*tr*) to roughen (a copper plate) with a rocker before engraving a mezzotint. **7 rock the boat.** *Informal.* to create a disturbance in the existing situation. ◆ *n* **8** a rocking motion. **9** short for **rock and roll. 10** Also called: **rock music.** any of various styles of pop music having a heavy beat, derived from rock and roll. **[**Old English *roccian;* related to Middle Dutch, Old High German *rocken,* German *rücken***]**

Rock (rɒk) *n* **the.** an informal name for **Gibraltar.**

rockabilly (ˈrɒkəˌbɪlɪ) *n* **a** a fast, spare style of White rock music which originated in the mid-1950s in the U.S. South. **b** (*as modifier*): *a rockabilly number.* **[**C20: from ROCK (AND ROLL) + (HILL)BILLY**]**

Rockall (ˈrɒkɔːl) *n* an uninhabited British island in the N Atlantic, 354 km (220 miles) W of the Outer Hebrides. Area: 0.07 ha (0.18 acres).

rock and roll *or* **rock'n'roll** *n* **1a** a type of pop music originating in the 1950s as a blend of rhythm and blues and country and western. It is generally based upon the twelve-bar blues, the first and third beats in each bar being heavily accented. **1b** (*as modifier*): *the rock-and-roll era.* **2** dancing performed to such music, with exaggerated body movements stressing the beat. ◆ *vb* **3** (*intr*) to perform this dance. ► **rock and roller** *or* **rock'n'roller** *n*

rockaway (ˈrɒkəˌweɪ) *n U.S.* a four-wheeled horse-drawn carriage, usually with two seats and a hard top.

rock bass (bæs) *n* **1** a North American freshwater percoid fish, *Ambloplites rupestris:* an important food fish; family *Centrarchidae* (sunfishes, etc.). **2** any similar or related fish.

rock boot *n* a tight-fitting rock-climbing boot with a canvas or suede upper and smooth rubber sole, designed to give good grip on small holds.

rock borer *n* any of various sea creatures that bore into rock, such as some sea urchins, sponges, annelid worms, barnacles, isopods, and molluscs.

rock bottom *n* **a** the lowest possible level. **b** (*as modifier*): *rock-bottom prices.*

rock-bound *adj* hemmed in or encircled by rocks. Also (poetic): **rock-girt.**

rock brake *n* any of various ferns of the genera *Pellaea* and *Cryptogramma,* which grow on rocky ground and have sori at the ends of the veins.

rock cake *n* a small cake containing dried fruit and spice, with a rough surface supposed to resemble a rock.

rock candy *n* the usual U.S. and Canadian name for **rock**[1] (sense 5).

rock chopper *n Austral. slang.* a Roman Catholic. **[**from the initials RC**]**

rock climb *n* **1** an instance of rock climbing or the route followed. ◆ *vb* **rock-climb** (*intr*) **2** to practise rock climbing.

rock climbing *n* the technique and sport of climbing on steep rock faces, usually with ropes and other equipment and as part of a team or pair.

rock cod *n N.Z.* another name for **blue cod.**

rock cress *n* another name for **arabis.**

rock crystal *n* a pure transparent colourless quartz, used in electronic and optical equipment. Formula: SiO_2.

rock dove *or* **pigeon** *n* a common dove, *Columba livia,* from which domestic and feral pigeons are descended. It has a pale grey plumage with black-striped wings.

Rockefeller (ˈrɒkəˌfɛlə) *n* **1 John D(avison).** 1839–1937, U.S. industrialist and philanthropist. **2** his son, **John D(avison).** 1874–1960, U.S. capitalist and philanthropist. **3** his son, **Nelson (Aldrich).** 1908–79, U.S. politician; governor of New York State (1958–74); vice president (1974–76).

rocker (ˈrɒkə) *n* **1** any of various devices that transmit or operate with a rocking motion. See also **rocker arm. 2** another word for **rocking chair. 3** either of two curved supports on the legs of a chair or other article of furniture on which it may rock. **4** a steel tool with a curved toothed cage, used to roughen the copper plate in engraving a mezzotint. **5** *Mining.* another word for **cradle** (sense 9). **6a** an ice skate with a curved blade. **6b** the curve itself. **7** *Skating.* **7a** a figure consisting of three interconnecting circles. **7b** a half turn in which the skater turns through 180°, so facing about while continuing to move in the same direction. **8** a rock-music performer, fan, or song. **9** *Brit.* an adherent of a youth movement rooted in the 1950s, characterized by motorcycle trappings. Compare **mod**[1]. **10 off one's rocker.** *Slang.* crazy; demented.

rocker arm *n* a lever that rocks about a pivot, esp. a lever in an internal-combustion engine that transmits the motion of a pushrod or cam to a valve.

rockery (ˈrɒkərɪ) *n, pl* **-eries.** a garden constructed with rocks, esp. one where alpine plants are grown. Also called: **rock garden.**

rocket[1] (ˈrɒkɪt) *n* **1** a self-propelling device, esp. a cylinder containing a mixture of solid explosives, used as a firework, distress signal, line carrier, etc. **2a** any vehicle propelled by a rocket engine, esp. one used to carry a warhead, spacecraft, etc. **2b** (*as modifier*): *rocket propulsion; rocket launcher.* **3** *Brit. and N.Z. informal.* a severe reprimand (esp. in the phrase **get a rocket**). **4 rocket scientist.** *Informal, chiefly U.S.* a person of considerable intelligence and ability (esp. in the phrase **not exactly a rocket scientist**). ◆ *vb* **-ets, -eting, -eted. 5** (*tr*) to propel (a missile, spacecraft, etc.) by means of a rocket. **6** (*intr;* foll. by *off, away,* etc.) to move off at high speed. **7** (*intr*) to rise rapidly: *he rocketed to the top.* **[**C17: from Old French *roquette,* from Italian *rochetto* a little distaff, from *rocca* distaff, of Germanic origin**]**

rocket[2] (ˈrɒkɪt) *n* **1** Also called: **arugula.** a Mediterranean cruciferous plant, *Eruca sativa,* having yellowish-white flowers and leaves used as a salad. **2** any of several plants of the related genus *Sisymbrium,* esp. *S. irio* (**London rocket**), which grow on waste ground and have pale yellow flowers. **3 yellow rocket.** any of several yellow-flowered plants of the related genus *Barbarea,* esp. *B. vulgaris.* **4 sea rocket.** any of several plants of the related genus *Cakile,* esp. *C. maritima,* which grow along the seashores of Europe and North America and have mauve, pink, or white flowers. **5 dame's rocket.** another name for **dame's violet.** ◆ See also **dyer's rocket, wall rocket. [**C16: from French *roquette,* from Italian *rochetta,* from Latin *ērūca* a caterpillar, hairy plant**]**

rocketeer (ˌrɒkɪˈtɪə) *n* an engineer or scientist concerned with the design, operation, or launching of rockets.

rocket engine *n* a reaction engine in which a fuel and oxidizer are burnt in a combustion chamber, the products of combustion expanding through a nozzle and producing thrust. Also called: **rocket motor.**

rocketry (ˈrɒkɪtrɪ) *n* the science and technology of the design, operation, maintenance, and launching of rockets.

rockfish (ˈrɒkˌfɪʃ) *n, pl* **-fish** *or* **-fishes. 1** any of various fishes that live among rocks, esp. scorpaenid fishes of the genus *Sebastodes* and related genera, such as *S. caurinus* (**copper rockfish**) of North American Pacific coastal waters. **2** *Brit.* any of several coarse fishes when used as food, esp. the dogfish or wolffish. Formerly called: **rock salmon.**

rock flour *n* very finely powdered rock, produced when rocks are ground together (as along the faces of a moving fault or during the motion of glaciers) and are thus chemically unweathered.

Rockford (ˈrɒkfəd) *n* a city in N Illinois, on the Rock River. Pop.: 143 531 (1996 est.).

rock garden *n* a garden featuring rocks or rockeries.

Rockhampton (rɒkˈhæmptən, -ˈhæmtən) *n* a port in Australia, in E Queensland on the Fitzroy River. Pop.: 65 868 (1993).

rockhopper (ˈrɒkˌhɒpə) *n* **1** a small penguin, *Eudyptes crestatus,* of Antarctica, the Falkland Islands, and New Zealand, with a yellow crest on each side of its head. **2** *Austral. informal.* a fisherman that fishes from the rocks on the sea coast.

Rockies (ˈrɒkɪz) *pl n* another name for the **Rocky Mountains.**

rocking chair *n* a chair set on curving supports so that the sitter may rock backwards and forwards.

Rockingham (ˈrɒkɪŋəm) *n* **Marquess of,** title of *Charles Watson-Wentworth.* 1730–82, British statesman and leader of the Whig opposition, whose members were known as the **Rockingham Whigs;** prime minister (1765–66; 1782). He opposed the war with the American colonists.

rocking horse *n* a toy horse mounted on a pair of rockers on which a child can rock to and fro in a seesaw movement.

rocking stone *n* a boulder so delicately poised that it can be rocked. Also called: **logan, logan-stone.**

rockling (ˈrɒklɪŋ) *n, pl* **-lings** *or* **-ling.** any small gadoid fish of the genera *Gaidropsarus, Ciliata,* etc. (formerly all included in *Motella*), which have an elongated body with barbels around the mouth and occur mainly in the North Atlantic Ocean. **[**C17: from ROCK[1] + -LING[1]**]**

rock lobster *n* another name for the **spiny lobster.**

rock mechanics *n* (*functioning as sing*) the study of the mechanical behaviour of rocks, esp. their strength, elasticity, permeability, porosity, density, and reaction to stress.

rock melon *n U.S., Austral., and N.Z.* another name for **cantaloupe.**

rock'n'roll *n* a variant spelling of **rock and roll.** ► **rock'n'roller** *n*

rock oil *n* another name for **petroleum.**

rockoon (rɒˈkuːn) *n* a rocket carrying scientific equipment for studying the upper atmosphere, fired from a balloon at high altitude. **[**C20: from ROCKET[1] + BALLOON**]**

rock pigeon *n* another name for **rock dove.**

rock plant *n* any plant that grows on rocks or in rocky ground.

rock rabbit *n S. African.* another name for the **dassie.**

rockrose (ˈrɒkˌrəuz) *n* any of various cistaceous shrubs or herbaceous plants of the Mediterranean genera *Helianthemum, Tuberaria,* and *Cistus,* cultivated for their yellow-white or reddish roselike flowers.

rock salmon *n Brit.* (formerly) any of several coarse fishes when used as food, esp. the dogfish or wolffish: now known as **catfish** or **rockfish.**

rock salt *n* another name for **halite.**

rockshaft (ˈrɒkˌʃɑːft) *n* a shaft that rotates backwards and forwards rather than continuously, esp. one used in the valve gear of a steam engine.

rock snake *or* **python** *n* any large Australasian python of the genus *Liasis*.

rock steady *n* a type of slow Jamaican dance music of the 1960s.

rock tripe *n Canadian.* any of various edible lichens, esp. of the genus *Umbilicaria,* that grow on rocks and are used in the North as a survival food.

rockweed ('rɒk,wiːd) *n* any of various seaweeds that grow on rocks exposed at low tide.

Rockwell ('rɒk,wɛl, -wəl) *n* **Norman.** 1894–1978, U.S. illustrator, noted esp. for magazine covers.

rock wool *n* another name for **mineral wool.**

rocky[1] ('rɒkɪ) *adj* **rockier, rockiest. 1** consisting of or abounding in rocks: *a rocky shore.* **2** hard or unyielding: *rocky determination.* **3** hard like rock: *rocky muscles.* ▸ **'rockily** *adv* ▸ **'rockiness** *n*

rocky[2] ('rɒkɪ) *adj* **rockier, rockiest. 1** weak, shaky, or unstable. **2** *Informal.* (of a person) dizzy; sickly; nauseated. ▸ **'rockily** *adv* ▸ **'rockiness** *n*

Rocky Mountain goat *n* a sure-footed goat antelope, *Oreamnos americanus,* inhabiting the Rocky Mountains. It has thick white hair and black backward-curving horns.

Rocky Mountains *or* **Rockies** *pl n* the chief mountain system of W North America, extending from British Columbia to New Mexico: forms the Continental Divide. Highest peak: Mount Elbert, 4399 m (14 431 ft.). Mount McKinley (6194 m (20 320 ft.)), in the Alaska Range, is not strictly part of the Rocky Mountains.

Rocky Mountain spotted fever *n* an acute rickettsial disease characterized by high fever, chills, pain in muscles and joints, skin rash, etc. It is caused by the bite of a tick infected with the microorganism *Rickettsia rickettsii.*

rococo (rə'kəʊkəʊ) *n* (*often cap.*) **1** a style of architecture and decoration that originated in France in the early 18th century, characterized by elaborate but graceful, light, ornamentation, often containing asymmetrical motifs. **2** an 18th-century style of music characterized by petite prettiness, a decline in the use of counterpoint, and extreme use of ornamentation. **3** any florid or excessively ornamental style. ♦ *adj* **4** denoting, being in, or relating to the rococo. **5** florid or excessively elaborate. **[C19**: from French, from ROCAILLE, from *roc* ROCK[1]**]**

rod (rɒd) *n* **1** a slim cylinder of metal, wood, etc.; stick or shaft. **2** a switch or bundle of switches used to administer corporal punishment. **3** any of various staffs of insignia or office. **4** power, esp. of a tyrannical kind: *a dictator's iron rod.* **5** a straight slender shoot, stem, or cane of a woody plant. **6** See **fishing rod. 7** Also called: **pole, perch. 7a** a unit of length equal to 5½ yards. **7b** a unit of square measure equal to 30¼ square yards. **8** a straight narrow board marked with the dimensions of a piece of joinery, as the spacing of steps on a staircase. **9** a metal shaft that transmits power in axial reciprocating motion: *piston rod.* Compare **shaft** (sense 5). **10** *Surveying.* another name (esp. U.S.) for **staff**[1] (sense 8). **11** Also called: **retinal rod.** any of the elongated cylindrical cells in the retina of the eye, containing the visual purple (rhodopsin), which are sensitive to dim light but not to colour. Compare **cone** (sense 5). **12** any rod-shaped bacterium. **13** a slang word for **penis. 14** *U.S.* a slang name for **pistol** (sense 1). **15** short for **hot rod. [**Old English *rodd;* related to Old Norse *rudda* club, Norwegian *rudda, rydda* twig**]** ▸ **'rod,like** *adj*

Rodchenko (rɒd'tʃɛŋkəʊ) *n* **Alexander (Mikhailovich).** 1891–1956, Soviet painter, sculptor, designer, and photographer, noted for his abstract geometrical style: a member of the constructivist movement.

Roddick ('rɒdɪk) *n* **Anita.** born 1942, British entrepreneur, founder (1976) of the Body Shop chain, selling natural beauty and health products.

rode[1] (rəʊd) *vb* the past tense of **ride.**

rode[2] (rəʊd) *n Nautical.* an anchor rope or chain. **[C17**: of unknown origin**]**

rode[3] (rəʊd) *vb* (*intr*) (of the male woodcock) to perform a display flight at dusk during the breeding season. **[C18**: in the sense "(of birds) to fly homeward in the evening"; of uncertain origin**]** ▸ **'roding** *n*

rodent ('rəʊdᵊnt) *n* **a** any of the relatively small placental mammals that constitute the order *Rodentia,* having constantly growing incisor teeth specialized for gnawing. The group includes porcupines, rats, mice, squirrels, marmots, etc. **b** (*as modifier*): *rodent characteristics.* **[C19**: from Latin *rōdere* to gnaw, corrode**]** ▸ **'rodent-,like** *adj*

rodenticide (rəʊ'dɛntɪ,saɪd) *n* a substance used for killing rats, mice, and other rodents.

rodent operative *n Brit.* a name sometimes used for an official (operative) employed by a local authority to destroy vermin.

rodeo ('rəʊdɪ,əʊ) *n, pl* **-os.** *Chiefly U.S. and Canadian.* **1** a display of the skills of cowboys, including bareback riding, steer wrangling, etc. **2** the rounding up of cattle for branding, counting, inspection, etc. **3** an enclosure for cattle that have been rounded up. **[C19**: from Spanish, from *rodear* to go around, from *rueda* a wheel, from Latin *rota***]**

Roderic ('rɒdərɪk) *n* See **Rory O'Connor.**

Rodgers ('rɒdʒəz) *n* **Richard.** 1902–79, U.S. composer of musical comedies. He collaborated with the librettist Lorenz Hart on such musicals as *A Connecticut Yankee* (1927), *On Your Toes* (1936), and *Pal Joey* (1940). After Hart's death his librettist was Oscar Hammerstein II. Two of their musicals, *Oklahoma!* (1943) and *South Pacific* (1949), received the Pulitzer Prize.

Ródhos ('rɔðɔs) *n* transliteration of the Modern Greek name for **Rhodes**[1].

Rodin (*French* rɔdɛ̃) *n* **Auguste** (ogyst). 1840–1917, French sculptor, noted for his portrayal of the human form. His works include *The Kiss* (1886), *The Burghers of Calais* (1896), and *The Thinker* (1905).

Rodney ('rɒdnɪ) *n* **George Brydges,** 1st Baron Rodney. 1719–92, English admiral: captured Martinique (1762): defeated the Spanish at Cape St Vincent (1780) and the French under Admiral de Grasse off Dominica (1782), restoring British superiority in the Caribbean.

rodomontade (,rɒdəmɒn'teɪd, -'tɑːd) *Literary.* ♦ *n* **1a** boastful words or behaviour; bragging. **1b** (*as modifier*): *rodomontade behaviour.* ♦ *vb* **2** (*intr*) to boast, bluster, or rant. **[C17**: from French, from Italian *rodomonte* a boaster, from *Rodomonte* the name of a braggart king of Algiers in epic poems by Boiardo and Ariosto**]**

Rodrigo (rɒ'driːgəʊ) *n* **Joaquín.** 1902–99, Spanish composer. His works include *Concierto de Aranjuez* (1940) for guitar and orchestra and *Concierto Pastorale* (1978).

roe[1] (rəʊ) *n* **1** Also called: **hard roe.** the ovary of a female fish filled with mature eggs. **2** Also called: **soft roe.** the testis of a male fish filled with mature sperm. **3** the ripe ovary of certain crustaceans, such as the lobster. **[C15**: from Middle Dutch *roge,* from Old High German *roga;* related to Old Norse *hrogn***]**

roe[2] (rəʊ) *n, pl* **roes** *or* **roe.** short for **roe deer. [**Old English *rā(ha),* related to Old High German *rēh(o),* Old Norse *rā***]**

Roe (rəʊ) *n* **Richard.** *Law.* (formerly) the defendant in a fictitious action, Doe versus Roe, to test a point of law. See also **Doe** (sense 1).

roebuck ('rəʊ,bʌk) *n, pl* **-bucks** *or* **-buck.** the male of the roe deer.

roe deer *n* a small graceful deer, *Capreolus capreolus,* of woodlands of Europe and Asia. The antlers are small and the summer coat is reddish-brown.

Roeg ('rəʊəg) *n* **Nic(olas).** born 1928, British film director and cinematographer. Films include *Walkabout* (1970), *Don't Look Now* (1972), *Insignificance* (1984), *The Witches* (1990), and *Heart of Darkness* (1994).

roentgen *or* **röntgen** ('rɒntgən, -tjən, 'rɛnt-) *n* a unit of dose of electromagnetic radiation equal to the dose that will produce in air a charge of 0.258×10^{-3} coulomb on all ions of one sign, when all the electrons of both signs liberated in a volume of air of mass one kilogram are stopped completely. Symbol: R or r

Roentgen *or* **Röntgen** ('rɒntgən, -tjən, 'rɛnt-; *German* 'rœntgən) *n* **Wilhelm Konrad** ('vɪlhɛlm 'kɔnraːt). 1845–1923, German physicist, who in 1895 discovered X-rays: Nobel prize for physics 1901.

roentgen equivalent man *n* the dose of ionizing radiation that produces the same effect in man as one roentgen of x- or gamma-radiation. Abbrev.: **REM** *or* **rem.**

roentgenize, roentgenise *or* **röntgenize, röntgenise** ('rɒntgə,naɪz, -tjə-, 'rɛnt-) *vb* (*tr*) to bombard with X-rays. ▸ **,roentgeni'zation, ,roentgeni'sation** *or* **,röntgeni'zation, ,röntgeni'sation** *n*

roentgeno- *or* **röntgeno-** *combining form.* indicating X-rays: *roentgenogram.* **[**from ROENTGEN**]**

roentgenogram, röntgenogram ('rɒntgənə,græm, -tjə-, 'rɛnt-) *or* **roentgenograph, röntgenograph** *n Chiefly U.S.* an X-ray.

roentgenology *or* **röntgenology** (,rɒntgə'nɒlədʒɪ, -tjə-, ,rɛnt-) *n* an obsolete name for **radiology.** ▸ **roentgenological** *or* **röntgenological** (,rɒntgənə'lɒdʒɪkᵊl, -tjə-, ,rɛnt-) *adj* ▸ **,roentgeno'logically** *or* **,röntgeno'logically** *adv* ▸ **,roentgen'ologist** *or* **,röntgen'ologist** *n*

roentgenopaque *or* **röntgenopaque** (,rɒntgənəʊ'peɪk, -tjən-, ,rɛnt-) *adj* (of a material) not allowing the transmission of X-rays.

roentgenoscope *or* **röntgenoscope** ('rɒntgənəʊ,skəʊp, -tjə-, 'rɛnt-) *n* a less common name for **fluoroscope.** ▸ **roentgenoscopic** *or* **röntgenoscopic** (,rɒntgənəʊ'skɒpɪk, -tjə-,,rɛnt-) *adj* ▸ **roentgenoscopy** *or* **röntgenoscopy** (,rɒntgə'nɒskəpɪ, -tjə-, ,rɛnt-) *n*

roentgenotherapy *or* **röntgenotherapy** (,rɒntgənə'θɛrəpɪ, -tjə-, ,rɛnt-) *n* the therapeutic use of X-rays.

roentgen ray *n* a former name for **X-ray.**

Roeselare ('ruːsəlaːrə) *n* the Flemish name for **Roulers.**

Roethke ('rɛtkə) *n* **Theodore.** 1908–63, U.S. poet, whose books include *Words for the Wind* (1957) and *The Far Field* (1964).

rogallo (rə'gæləʊ) *n, pl* **-los.** a flexible fabric delta wing, originally designed as a possible satellite retrieval vehicle but actually developed in the 1960s as the first successful hang-glider. **[C20**: after Francis M. *Rogallo,* the U.S. engineer who designed it**]**

rogation (rəʊ'geɪʃən) *n* (*usually pl*) *Christianity.* a solemn supplication, esp. in a form of ceremony prescribed by the Church. **[C14**: from Latin *rogātiō,* from *rogāre* to ask, make supplication**]**

Rogation Days *pl n* April 25 (the **Major Rogation**) and the Monday, Tuesday, and Wednesday before Ascension Day, observed by Christians as days of solemn supplication for the harvest and marked by processions, special prayers, and blessing of the crops.

rogatory ('rɒgətərɪ, -trɪ) *adj* (esp. in legal contexts) seeking or authorized to seek information. **[C19**: from Medieval Latin *rogātōrius,* from Latin *rogāre* to ask**]**

roger ('rɒdʒə) *interj* **1** (used in signalling, telecommunications, etc.) message received and understood. Compare **wilco. 2** an expression of agreement. ♦ *vb* **3** *Taboo slang.* (of a man) to copulate (with). **[C20**: from the name *Roger,* representing *R* for *received***]**

Roger II ('rɒdʒə) *n* 1095–1154, Norman king of Siciliy (1130–54). His court was an intellectual centre for Muslim and Christian scholars.

Rogers ('rɒdʒəz) *n* **1 Ginger,** real name *Virginia McMath.* 1911–95, U.S. dancer and film actress, who partnered Fred Astaire. **2 Richard,** Baron Rogers of Riverside. born 1933, British architect. His works include the Pompidou Centre in Paris (1971–77; with Renzo Piano), the Lloyd's building in London (1986), and the Millennium Dome in Greenwich, London. **3 William Penn Adair,** known as *Will.* 1879–1935, U.S. actor, newspaper columnist, and humorist in the homespun tradition.

Roget ('rɒʒeɪ) *n* **Peter Mark.** 1779–1869, English physician, who on retirement devised a *Thesaurus of English Words and Phrases* (1852), a classified list of synonyms.

rognon *French.* (rɔɲɔ̃) *n Mountaineering.* an isolated rock outcrop on a glacier. **[C20**: literally: kidney**]**

rogue (rəʊg) *n* **1** a dishonest or unprincipled person, esp. a man; rascal; scoundrel. **2** *Often jocular.* a mischievous or wayward person, often a child; scamp. **3** a crop plant which is inferior, diseased, or of a different, unwanted variety. **4a**

any inferior or defective specimen. **4b** (*as modifier*): *rogue heroin.* **5** *Archaic.* a vagrant. **6a** an animal of vicious character that has separated from the main herd and leads a solitary life. **6b** (*as modifier*): *a rogue elephant.* ◆ *vb* **7a** (*tr*) to rid (a field or crop) of plants that are inferior, diseased, or of an unwanted variety. **7b** to identify and remove such plants. [C16: of unknown origin; perhaps related to Latin *rogāre* to beg]

roguery ('rəugərɪ) *n, pl* **-gueries. 1** behaviour characteristic of a rogue. **2** a roguish or mischievous act.

rogues' gallery *n* **1** a collection of photographs of known criminals kept by the police for identification purposes. **2** a group of undesirable people.

roguish ('rəugɪʃ) *adj* **1** dishonest or unprincipled. **2** mischievous or arch. ▸ **'roguishly** *adv* ▸ **'roguishness** *n*

Röhm (*German* røm) *n* **Ernst** (ɛrnst). 1887–1934, German soldier, who organized (1921–34) Hitler's storm troops: murdered on Hitler's orders.

Rohypnol (ˌrəu'hɪpnɒl) *n Trademark.* a preparation of the drug flunitrazepam used as a hypnotic: its ability to render someone unconscious and disorientated on awakening has been exploited by rapists.

roil (rɔɪl) *vb* **1** (*tr*) to make (a liquid) cloudy or turbid by stirring up dregs or sediment. **2** (*intr*) (esp. of a liquid) to be agitated or disturbed. **3** (*intr*) *Dialect.* to be noisy or boisterous. **4** (*tr*) another word (now rare) for **rile** (sense 1). [C16: of unknown origin; compare RILE]

roily ('rɔɪlɪ) *adj* **roilier, roiliest.** *Rare.* cloudy or muddy.

roister ('rɔɪstə) *vb* (*intr*) **1** to engage in noisy merrymaking; revel. **2** to brag, bluster, or swagger. [C16: from Old French *rustre* lout, from *ruste* uncouth, from Latin *rusticus* rural; see RUSTIC] ▸ **'roisterer** *n* ▸ **'roisterous** *adj* ▸ **'roisterously** *adv*

rojak ('rodʒa) *n* (in Malaysia) a salad dish served in chilli sauce. [from Malay]

ROK *international car registration for* South Korea (Republic of Korea).

Roland ('rəulənd) *n* the greatest of the legendary 12 peers (paladins, of whom Oliver was another) in attendance on Charlemagne; he died in battle at Roncesvalles (778 A.D.).

role *or* **rôle** (rəul) *n* **1** a part or character in a play, film, etc., to be played by an actor or actress. **2** *Psychol.* the part played by a person in a particular social setting, influenced by his expectation of what is appropriate. **3** usual or customary function: *what is his role in the organization?* [C17: from French *rôle* ROLL, an actor's script]

role model *n* a person regarded by others, esp. younger people, as a good example to follow.

role-playing *n Psychol.* activity in which a person imitates, consciously or unconsciously, a role uncharacteristic of himself. See also **psychodrama.**

Rolf (rɒlf) *or* **Rolf the Ganger** *n* other names for **Rollo.**

Rolfe (rɒlf) *n* **Frederick William,** also known as *Baron Corvo.* 1860–1913, British novelist. His best-known work is *Hadrian the Seventh* (1904).

roll (rəul) *vb* **1** to move or cause to move along by turning over and over. **2** to move or cause to move along on wheels or rollers. **3** to flow or cause to flow onwards in an undulating movement: *billows of smoke rolled over the ground.* **4** (*intr*) to extend in undulations: *the hills roll down to the sea.* **5** (*intr;* usually foll. by *around*) to move or occur in cycles. **6** (*intr*) (of a planet, the moon, etc.) to revolve in an orbit. **7** (*intr;* foll. by *on, by,* etc.) to pass or elapse: *the years roll by.* **8** to rotate or cause to rotate wholly or partially: *to roll one's eyes.* **9** to curl, cause to curl, or admit of being curled, so as to form a ball, tube, or cylinder; coil. **10** to make or form by shaping into a ball, tube, or cylinder: *to roll a cigarette.* **11** (often foll. by *out*) to spread or cause to spread out flat or smooth under or as if under a roller: *to roll the lawn; to roll pastry.* **12** to emit, produce, or utter with a deep prolonged reverberating sound: *the thunder rolled continuously.* **13** to trill or cause to be trilled: *to roll one's r's.* **14** (*intr*) (of a vessel, aircraft, rocket, etc.) to turn from side to side around the longitudinal axis. Compare **pitch**[1] (sense 11), **yaw** (sense 1). **15** to cause (an aircraft) to execute a roll or (of an aircraft) to execute a roll (sense 40). **16** (*intr*) to walk with a swaying gait, as when drunk; sway. **17** (*intr;* often foll. by *over*) (of an animal, esp. a dog) to lie on its back and wriggle while kicking its legs in the air, without moving along. **18** (*intr*) to wallow or envelop oneself (in). **19** (*tr*) to apply ink to (type, etc.) with a roller or rollers. **20** to throw (dice). **21** (*intr*) to operate or begin to operate: *the presses rolled.* **22** (*intr*) *Informal.* to make progress; move or go ahead: *let the good times roll.* **23** (*tr*) *Informal, chiefly U.S. and N.Z.* to rob (a helpless person, such as someone drunk or asleep). **24** (*tr*) *Slang.* to have sexual intercourse or foreplay with (a person). **25 start** *or* **set the ball rolling.** to open or initiate (an action, discussion, movement, etc.). ◆ *n* **26** the act or an instance of rolling. **27** anything rolled up in a cylindrical form: *a roll of newspaper.* **28** an official list or register, esp. of names: *an electoral roll.* **29** a rounded mass: *rolls of flesh.* **30** a strip of material, esp. leather, fitted with pockets or pouches for holding tools, toilet articles, needles and thread, etc. **31** a cylinder used to flatten something; roller. **32** a small loaf of bread for one person: eaten plain, with butter, or as a light meal when filled with meat, cheese, etc. **33** a flat pastry or cake rolled up with a meat (**sausage roll**), jam (**jam roll**), or other filling. See also **swiss roll. 34** a swell, ripple, or undulation on a surface: *the roll of the hills.* **35** a swaying, rolling, or unsteady movement or gait. **36** a deep prolonged reverberating sound: *the roll of thunder.* **37** a rhythmic cadenced flow of words. **38** a trilling sound; trill. **39** a very rapid beating of the sticks on a drum. **40** a flight manoeuvre in which an aircraft makes one complete rotation about its longitudinal axis without loss of height or change in direction. **41** the angular displacement of a vessel, rocket, missile, etc., caused by rolling. **42** a throw of dice. **43** a bookbinder's tool having a brass wheel, used to impress a line or repeated pattern on the cover of a book. **44** *Slang.* an act of sexual intercourse or petting (esp. in the phrase **a roll in the hay**). **45** *U.S. slang.* an amount of money, esp. a wad of paper money. **46 on a roll.** *Slang.* experiencing continued good luck or success. **47 strike off the roll(s). 47a** to expel from membership. **47b** to debar (a solicitor) from practising, usually because of dishonesty. ◆ See also **roll in, roll off, roll on, roll over, roll up.** [C14 *rollen,* from Old French *roler,* from Latin *rotulus* a little wheel, from *rota* a wheel]

Rolland (*French* rɔlɑ̃) *n* **Romain** (rɔmɛ̃). 1866–1944, French novelist, dramatist, and essayist, known for his novels about a musical genius, *Jean-Christophe,* (1904–12): Nobel prize for literature 1915.

rollaway ('rəuləˌweɪ) *n* (*modifier*) mounted on rollers so as to be easily moved, esp. to be stored away after use.

rollbar ('rəulˌbɑː) *n* a bar that reinforces the frame of a car, esp. one used for racing, rallying, etc., to protect the driver if the car should turn over.

roll call *n* **1** the reading aloud of an official list of names, those present responding when their names are read out. **2** the time or signal for such a reading.

rolled gold *n* a metal, such as brass, coated with a thin layer of gold, usually of above 9 carat purity. It is used in inexpensive jewellery. Also called (U.S.): **filled gold.**

rolled paperwork *n* a form of decoration on small objects, such as boxes, in which a design is made up of tiny rolls of paper cut crossways and laid together: popular in the 18th and 19th centuries. Also called: **curled paperwork, paper filigree.**

rolled-steel joist *n* a steel beam, esp. one with a cross section in the form of a letter *H* or *I.* Abbrev.: **RSJ.**

roller ('rəulə) *n* **1** a cylinder having an absorbent surface and a handle, used for spreading paint. **2** Also called: **garden roller.** a heavy cast-iron cylinder or pair of cylinders on an axle to which a handle is attached; used for flattening lawns. **3** a long heavy wave of the sea, advancing towards the shore. Compare **breaker**[1] (sense 2). **4** a hardened cylinder of precision-ground steel that forms one of the rolling components of a roller bearing or of a linked driving chain. **5** a cylinder fitted on pivots, used to enable heavy objects to be easily moved; castor. **6** *Printing.* a cylinder, usually of hard rubber, used to ink a forme or plate before impression. **7** a cylindrical tube or barrel onto which material is rolled for transport or storage. **8** any of various other cylindrical devices that rotate about a cylinder, used for any of various purposes. **9** a small cylinder, esp. one that is heated, onto which a woman's hair may be rolled to make it curl. **10** *Med.* a bandage consisting of a long strip of muslin or cheesecloth rolled tightly into a cylindrical form before application. **11** a band fastened around a horse's belly to keep a blanket in position. **12** any of various Old World birds of the family *Coraciidae,* such as *Coracias garrulus* (**European roller**), that have a blue, green, and brown plumage, a slightly hooked bill, and an erratic flight: order *Coraciiformes* (kingfishers, etc.). **13** (*often cap.*) a variety of tumbler pigeon that performs characteristic backward somersaults in flight. **14** a breed of canary that has a soft trilling song in which the notes are run together. **15** a person or thing that rolls. **16** *Austral.* a man who rolls and trims fleeces after shearing. **17** short for **roadroller** or **steamroller. 18** short for **roller caption.**

rollerball ('rəuləˌbɔːl) *n* a pen having a small moving nylon, plastic, or metal ball as a writing point.

roller bearing *n* a bearing in which a shaft runs on a number of hardened-steel rollers held within a cage.

Rollerblade ('rəuləˌbleɪd) *n Trademark.* a type of roller skate in which the wheels are set in a single straight line under the boot.

roller caption *n Television.* caption lettering that moves progressively up or across the picture, as for showing the credits at the end of a programme. Often shortened to **roller.**

roller chain *n Engineering.* a chain for transmitting power in which each link consists of two free-moving rollers held in position by pins connected to sideplates.

roller coaster *n* another term for **big dipper.**

roller derby *n* a race on roller skates, esp. one involving aggressive tactics.

roller skate *n* **1** a device having clamps and straps for fastening to a boot or shoe and four small wheels that enable the wearer to glide swiftly over a floor or other surface. ◆ *vb* **roller-skate. 2** (*intr*) to move on roller skates. ▸ **roller skater** *n*

roller towel *n* **1** a towel with the two ends sewn together, hung on a roller. **2** a continuous towel wound inside a roller enabling a clean section to be pulled out when required.

roll film *n* a length of photographic film backed with opaque paper and rolled on a spool.

rollick ('rɒlɪk) *vb* **1** (*intr*) to behave in a carefree, frolicsome, or boisterous manner. ◆ *n* **2** a boisterous or carefree escapade or event. [C19: of Scottish dialect origin, probably from ROMP + FROLIC]

rollicking[1] ('rɒlɪkɪŋ) *adj* boisterously carefree and swaggering.

rollicking[2] ('rɒlɪkɪŋ) *n Brit. informal.* a very severe telling-off; dressing-down. [C20: from ROLLICK (vb) (in former sense: to be angry, make a fuss); perhaps influenced by BOLLOCKING]

roll in *vb* (*mainly intr*) **1** (*adv*) to arrive in abundance or in large numbers. **2** (*adv*) *Informal.* to arrive at one's destination. **3 be rolling in.** (*prep*) *Informal.* to abound or luxuriate in (wealth, money, etc.). **4** (*adv; also tr*) *Hockey.* to return (the ball) to play after it has crossed the touchline.

rolling ('rəulɪŋ) *adj* **1** having gentle rising and falling slopes; undulating: *rolling country.* **2** progressing or spreading by stages or by occurrences in different places in succession, with continued or increasing effectiveness: *three weeks of rolling strikes disrupted schools.* **3** subject to regular review and updating: *a rolling plan for overseas development.* **4** deeply resounding; reverberating: *rolling thunder.* **5** *Slang.* extremely rich. **6** that may be turned up or down: *a rolling hat brim.* ◆ *adv* **7** *Slang.* swaying or staggering (in the phrase **rolling drunk**).

rolling bearing *n* any bearing in which the antifriction action depends on the rolling action of balls or rollers.

rolling friction *n Engineering.* frictional resistance to rotation or energy losses in rolling bearings. Compare **sliding friction.**

rolling hitch *n* a knot used for fastening one rope to another or to a spar, being easily released but jamming when the rope is pulled.

rolling launch *n Marketing.* the process of introducing a new product into a market gradually. Compare **roll out** (sense 3).

rolling mill *n* **1** a mill or factory where ingots of heated metal are passed between rollers to produce sheets or bars of a required cross section and form. **2** a machine having rollers that may be shaped to reduce ingots, etc., to a required cross section and form.

rolling pin *n* a cylinder with handles at both ends, often of wood, used for rolling dough, pastry, etc., out flat.

rolling stock *n* the wheeled vehicles collectively used on a railway, including the locomotives, passenger coaches, freight wagons, guard's vans, etc.

rolling stone *n* a restless or wandering person.

Rolling Stones *pl n* **the.** British rock group (formed 1962): comprising Mick Jagger, Keith Richards (born 1943; guitar, vocals), Brian Jones (1942–69; guitar), Charlie Watts (born 1941; drums), Bill Wyman (born 1936; bass guitar), and subsequently Mick Taylor (born 1948; guitar; with the group 1969–74) and Ron Wood (born 1947; guitar; with the group from 1975). See also (Michael Philip) **Jagger.**

Rollins (ˈrɒlɪnz) *n* **Sonny,** original name *Theodore Walter Rollins.* born 1930, U.S. jazz tenor saxophonist, noted for his improvisation.

rollmop (ˈrəʊlˌmɒp) *n* a herring fillet rolled, usually around onion slices, and pickled in spiced vinegar. [C20: from German *Rollmops,* from *rollen* to ROLL + *Mops* pug dog]

rollneck (ˈrəʊlˌnɛk) *adj* **1** (of a garment) having a high neck that may be rolled over. ◆ *n* **2** a rollneck sweater or other garment.

Rollo (ˈrɒləʊ) *n* ?860–?930 A.D., Norse war leader who received from Charles the Simple a fief that formed the basis of the duchy of Normandy. Also called: **Rolf, Rolf the Ganger.**

roll off *vb* (*intr, adv*) *Electronics.* to exhibit gradually reduced response at the upper or lower ends of the working frequency range.

roll of honour *n* a list of those who have died in war for their country, esp. those from a particular locality or organization.

roll on *vb* **1** *Brit.* used to express the wish that an eagerly anticipated event or date will come quickly: *roll on Saturday.* ◆ *adj* **roll-on. 2** (of a deodorant, lip gloss, etc.) dispensed by means of a revolving ball fitted into the neck of the container. ◆ *n* **roll-on. 3** a woman's foundation garment, made of elasticized material and having no fastenings. **4** a liquid cosmetic, esp. a deodorant, packed in a container having an applicator consisting of a revolving ball.

roll-on/roll-off *adj* denoting a cargo ship or ferry designed so that vehicles can be driven straight on and straight off.

roll out *vb* (*tr, adv*) **1** to cause (pastry) to become flatter and thinner by pressure with a rolling pin. **2** to show (a new type of aircraft) to the public for the first time. **3** to launch (a new film, product, etc.) in a series of stages over an area, each stage involving an increased number of outlets. ◆ *n* **roll-out. 4** a presentation to the public of a new aircraft, product, etc.; a launch.

roll over *vb* (*adv*) **1** (*intr*) to overturn. **2** See **roll** (sense 17). **3** (*tr*) to allow (a loan, prize, etc.) to continue in force for a further period. ◆ *n* **rollover. 4a** an instance of such continuance of a loan, prize, etc. **4b** (*as modifier*): *a rollover jackpot.*

Rolls-Royce (ˌrəʊlzˈrɔɪs) *n Trademark.* **1** Also called (informal): **Rolls.** a make of very high-quality, luxurious, and prestigious British car. The Rolls-Royce company is no longer British-owned. **2** anything considered to be the very best of its kind. [named after its designers, Charles Stewart *Rolls* (1877–1910), English pioneer motorist and aviator, and Sir (Frederick) Henry *Royce* (1863–1933), English engineer, who founded the Rolls-Royce Company (1906)]

roll-top desk *n* a desk having a slatted wooden panel that can be pulled down over the writing surface when not in use. Also called: **roll-top.**

roll up *vb* (*adv*) **1** to form or cause to form a cylindrical shape. **2** (*tr*) to wrap (an object) round on itself or on an axis: *to roll up a map.* **3** (*intr*) *Informal.* to arrive, esp. in a vehicle. ◆ *n* **roll-up. 4** *Brit. informal.* a cigarette made by hand from loose tobacco and cigarette paper. **5** *Austral.* (in the 19th century) a mass meeting of workers on an issue of common concern. **6** *Austral. archaic.* the attendance at any fixture: *they had a good roll-up.*

rollway (ˈrəʊlˌweɪ) *n* **1** an incline down which logs are rolled for transportation. **2** a series of rollers laid parallel to each other, over which heavy loads may be moved.

roll-your-own *n Informal.* a hand-rolled cigarette.

Rolodex (ˈrəʊləˌdɛks) *n Trademark. Chiefly U.S.* a small file for holding names, addresses, and telephone numbers, consisting of cards attached horizontally to a rotatable central cylinder.

roly-poly (ˈrəʊlɪˈpəʊlɪ) *adj* **1** plump, buxom, or rotund. ◆ *n, pl* **-lies. 2** *Brit.* a strip of suet pastry spread with jam, fruit, or a savoury mixture, rolled up, and baked or steamed as a pudding. **3** a plump, buxom, or rotund person. **4** *Austral.* an informal name for **tumbleweed.** [C17: apparently by reduplication from *roly,* from ROLL]

Rom (rɒm) *n, pl* **Roma** (ˈrɒmə). a male Gypsy. [Romany]

ROM (rɒm) *n Computing. acronym for* read only memory: a storage device that holds data permanently and cannot in normal circumstances be altered by the programmer.

rom. *Printing. abbrev. for* roman (type).

Rom. *abbrev. for:* **1** Roman. **2** Romance (languages). **3** *Bible.* Romans. **4** Romania(n).

Roma (ˈroːma) *n* the Italian name for **Rome.**

Romagna (*Italian* roˈmaɲɲa) *n* an area of N Italy: part of the Papal States up to 1860.

Romaic (rəʊˈmeɪɪk) *Obsolete.* ◆ *n* **1** the modern Greek vernacular, esp. Demotic. ◆ *adj* **2** of or relating to Greek, esp. Demotic. [C19: from Greek *Rhōmaikos* Roman, with reference to the Eastern Roman Empire]

romaine (rəʊˈmeɪn) *n* the usual U.S. and Canadian name for **cos**[1] (lettuce). [C20: from French, from *romain* Roman]

Romains (*French* rɔmɛ̃) *n* **Jules** (ʒyl). pseudonym of *Louis Farigoule.* 1885–1972, French poet, dramatist, and novelist. His works include the novel *Men of Good Will* (1932–46).

romaji (ˈrəʊmɑːdʒɪ) *n* the Roman alphabet as used to write Japanese.

roman[1] (ˈrəʊmən) *adj* **1** of, relating to, or denoting a vertical style of printing type: the usual form of type for most printed matter. Compare **italic.** ◆ *n* **2** roman type or print. [C16: so called because the style of letters is that used in ancient Roman inscriptions]

roman[2] (*French* rɔmɑ̃) *n* a metrical narrative in medieval French literature derived from the *chansons de geste.*

Roman (ˈrəʊmən) *adj* **1** of or relating to Rome or its inhabitants in ancient or modern times. **2** of or relating to Roman Catholicism or the Roman Catholic Church. **3** denoting, relating to, or having the style of architecture used by the ancient Romans, characterized by large-scale masonry domes, barrel vaults, and semicircular arches. ◆ *n* **4** a citizen or inhabitant of ancient or modern Rome. **5** *Informal.* short for **Roman Catholic.**

roman à clef *French.* (rɔmɑ̃ a kle) *n, pl* ***romans à clef*** (rɔmɑ̃ a kle). a novel in which real people are depicted under fictitious names. [literally: novel with a key]

Roman alphabet *n* the alphabet evolved by the ancient Romans for the writing of Latin, based upon an Etruscan form derived from the Greeks and ultimately from the Phoenicians. The alphabet serves for writing most of the languages of W Europe and many other languages.

Roman arch *n* another name for **Norman arch.**

Roman blind *n* a window blind consisting of a length of material which, when drawn up, gathers into horizontal folds from the bottom.

Roman calendar *n* the lunar calendar of ancient Rome, replaced in 45 B.C. by the Julian calendar. It originally consisted of 10 months, with a special month intercalated between Feb. 23 and 24.

Roman candle *n* a firework that produces a continuous shower of sparks punctuated by coloured balls of fire. [C19: so called from its having been originated in Italy]

Roman Catholic *adj* **1** of or relating to the Roman Catholic Church. ◆ *n* **2** a member of this Church. ◆ Often shortened to **Catholic.**

Roman Catholic Church *n* the Christian Church over which the pope presides, with administrative headquarters in the Vatican. Also called: **Catholic Church, Church of Rome.**

Roman Catholicism *n* the beliefs, practices, and system of government of the Roman Catholic Church.

romance *n* (rəˈmæns, ˈrəʊmæns). **1** a love affair, esp. an intense and happy but short-lived affair involving young people. **2** love, esp. romantic love idealized for its purity or beauty. **3** a spirit of or inclination for adventure, excitement, or mystery. **4** a mysterious, exciting, sentimental, or nostalgic quality, esp. one associated with a place. **5** a narrative in verse or prose, written in a vernacular language in the Middle Ages, dealing with strange and exciting adventures of chivalrous heroes. **6** any similar narrative work dealing with events and characters remote from ordinary life. **7** the literary genre represented by works of these kinds. **8** (in Spanish literature) a short narrative poem, usually an epic or historical ballad. **9** a story, novel, film, etc., dealing with love, usually in an idealized or sentimental way. **10** an extravagant, absurd, or fantastic account or explanation. **11** a lyrical song or short instrumental composition having a simple melody. ◆ *vb* (rəˈmæns). **12** (*intr*) to tell, invent, or write extravagant or romantic fictions. **13** (*intr*) to tell extravagant or improbable lies. **14** (*intr*) to have romantic thoughts. **15** (*intr*) (of a couple) to indulge in romantic behaviour. **16** (*tr*) to be romantically involved with. [C13: *romauns,* from Old French *romans,* ultimately from Latin *Rōmānicus* Roman] ▸ **roˈmancer** *n*

Romance (rəˈmæns, ˈrəʊmæns) *adj* **1** denoting, relating to, or belonging to the languages derived from Latin, including Italian, Spanish, Portuguese, French, and Romanian. **2** denoting a word borrowed from a Romance language: *there are many Romance words in English.* ◆ *n* **3** this group of languages; the living languages that belong to the Italic branch of the Indo-European family.

Roman collar *n* another name for **clerical collar.**

Roman Empire *n* **1** the territories ruled by ancient Rome. At its height under Trajan, the Roman Empire included W and S Europe, Africa north of the Sahara, and SW Asia. In 395 A.D. it was divided by Theodosius into the **Eastern Roman Empire,** whose capital was Byzantium and which lasted until 1453, and the **Western Roman Empire,** which lasted until the sack of Rome in 476. **2** the government of Rome and its dominions by the emperors from 27 B.C. **3** the Byzantine Empire. **4** the Holy Roman Empire.

Romanes (ˈrɒmənɪs) *n* Romany; the language of the Gypsies. [from Romany]

Romanesque (ˌrəʊməˈnɛsk) *adj* **1** denoting, relating to, or having the style of architecture used in W and S Europe from the 9th to the 12th century, characterized by the rounded arch, the groin vault, massive-masonry wall construction, and a restrained use of mouldings. See also **Norman** (sense 6). **2** denoting or relating to a corresponding style in painting, sculpture, etc. [C18: see ROMAN, -ESQUE]

roman-fleuve *French.* (rɔmɑ̃flœv) *n, pl* ***romans-fleuves*** (rɔmɑ̃flœv). a novel or series of novels dealing with a family or other group over several generations. [literally: stream novel]

Roman holiday *n* entertainment or pleasure that depends on the suffering of others. [C19: from Byron's poem *Childe Harold* (IV, 141)]

Romani ('rɒmənɪ, 'rəʊ-) *n, pl* **-nis.** a variant spelling of **Romany.**

Romania (rəʊ'meɪnɪə), **Rumania,** *or* **Roumania** *n* a republic in SE Europe, bordering on the Black Sea: united in 1861; became independent in 1878; Communist government set up in 1945; became a socialist republic in 1965; a more democratic regime was installed after a revolution in 1989. It consists chiefly of a great central arc of the Carpathian Mountains and Transylvanian Alps, with the plains of Walachia, Moldavia, and Dobriya on the south and east and the Pannonian Plain in the west. Official language: Romanian. Religion: Romanian Orthodox (Christian) majority. Currency: leu. Capital: Bucharest. Pop.: 22 491 000 (1998 est.). Area: 237 500 sq. km (91 699 sq. miles).

Romanian (rəʊ'meɪnɪən), **Rumanian,** *or* **Roumanian** *n* **1** the official language of Romania, belonging to the Romance group of the Indo-European family. **2** a native, citizen, or inhabitant of Romania. ◆ *adj* **3** relating to, denoting, or characteristic of Romania, its people, or their language.

Romanic (rəʊ'mænɪk) *adj* another word for **Roman** or **Romance.**

Romanism ('rəʊməˌnɪzəm) *n* Roman Catholicism, esp. when regarded as excessively or superstitiously ritualistic.

Romanist ('rəʊmənɪst) *n* **1** a member of a Church, esp. the Church of England, who favours or is influenced by Roman Catholicism. **2** a Roman Catholic. **3** a student of classical Roman civilization or law. ▸ **ˌRoman'istic** *adj*

Romanize *or* **Romanise** ('rəʊməˌnaɪz) *vb* **1** (*tr*) to impart a Roman Catholic character to (a ceremony, practice, etc.). **2** (*intr*) to be converted to Roman Catholicism. **3** (*tr*) to transcribe or transliterate (a language) into the Roman alphabet. **4** to make Roman in character, allegiance, style, etc. ▸ **ˌRomani'zation** *or* **ˌRomani'sation** *n*

Roman law *n* **1** the system of jurisprudence of ancient Rome, codified under Justinian and forming the basis of many modern legal systems. **2** another term for **civil law.**

Roman mile *n* a unit of length used in ancient Rome, equivalent to about 1620 yards or 1481 metres.

Roman nose *n* a nose having a high prominent bridge.

Roman numerals *pl n* the letters used by the Romans for the representation of cardinal numbers, still used occasionally today. The integers are represented by the following letters: I (= 1), V (= 5), X (= 10), L (= 50), C (= 100), D (= 500), and M (= 1000). If a numeral is followed by another numeral of lower denomination, the two are added together; if it is preceded by one of lower denomination, the smaller numeral is subtracted from the greater. Thus VI = 6 (V + I), but IV = 4 (V – I). Other examples are XC (= 90), CL (= 150), XXV (= 25), XLIV (= 44). Multiples of a thousand are indicated by a superior bar: thus, $\bar{V}$ = 5000, $\bar{X}$ = 10 000, $\overline{XD}$ = 490 000, etc.

Romano[1] (rəʊ'mɑːnəʊ) *n* a hard light-coloured sharp-tasting cheese, similar to Parmesan.

Romano[2] (*Italian* ro'maːno) *n* See **Giulio Romano.**

Romanov ('rəʊmənɒf; *Russian* ra'manəf) *n* any of the Russian imperial dynasty that ruled from the crowning (1613) of Mikhail Fyodorovich to the abdication (1917) of Nicholas II during the February Revolution.

Roman pace *n* an ancient Roman measure of length, equal to 5 Roman feet or about 58 inches (147 centimetres). See also **geometric pace.**

Romans ('rəʊmənz) *n* (*functioning as sing*) a book of the New Testament (in full **The Epistle of Paul the Apostle to the Romans**), containing one of the fullest expositions of the doctrines of Saint Paul, written in 58 A.D.

Romansch *or* **Romansh** (rəʊ'mænʃ) *n* a group of Rhaetian dialects spoken in the Swiss canton of Graubünden; an official language of Switzerland since 1938. See also **Friulian, Ladin.** [C17: from Romansch, literally: Romance language, from Latin *Rōmānicus* ROMANIC]

Roman snail *n* a large edible European snail, *Helix pomatia,* the usual *escargot* of menus, erroneously thought to have been introduced to northern Europe by the Romans.

romantic (rəʊ'mæntɪk) *adj* **1** of, relating to, imbued with, or characterized by romance. **2** evoking or given to thoughts and feelings of love, esp. idealized or sentimental love: *a romantic woman; a romantic setting.* **3** impractical, visionary, or idealistic: *a romantic scheme.* **4** *Often euphemistic.* imaginary or fictitious: *a romantic account of one's war service.* **5** (*often cap.*) of or relating to a movement in European art, music, and literature in the late 18th and early 19th centuries, characterized by an emphasis on feeling and content rather than order and form, on the sublime, supernatural, and exotic, and the free expression of the passions and individuality. ◆ *n* **6** a person who is romantic, as in being idealistic, amorous, or soulful. **7** a person whose tastes in art, literature, etc., lie mainly in romanticism; romanticist. **8** (*often cap.*) a poet, composer, etc., of the romantic period or whose main inspiration or interest is romanticism. [C17: from French *romantique,* from obsolete *romant* story, romance, from Old French *romans* ROMANCE] ▸ **ro'mantically** *adv*

romanticism (rəʊ'mæntɪˌsɪzəm) *n* **1** (*often cap.*) the theory, practice, and style of the romantic art, music, and literature of the late 18th and early 19th centuries, usually opposed to classicism. **2** romantic attitudes, ideals, or qualities. ▸ **ro'manticist** *n*

romanticize *or* **romanticise** (rəʊ'mæntɪˌsaɪz) *vb* **1** (*intr*) to think or act in a romantic way. **2** (*tr*) to interpret according to romantic precepts. **3** to make or become romantic, as in style. ▸ **roˌmantici'zation** *or* **roˌmantici'sation** *n*

Romany *or* **Romani** ('rɒmənɪ, 'rəʊ-) *n* **1** (*pl* **-nies** *or* **-nis**) **1a** another name for a **Gypsy. 1b** (*as modifier*): *Romany customs.* **2** the language of the Gypsies, belonging to the Indic branch of the Indo-European family, but incorporating extensive borrowings from local European languages. Most of its 250 000 speakers are bilingual. It is extinct in Britain. [C19: from Romany *romani* (adj) Gypsy, ultimately from Sanskrit *domba* man of a low caste of musicians, of Dravidian origin]

romanza (rə'mænzə) *n Music.* a short instrumental piece of song-like character. [from Italian]

romaunt (rə'mɔːnt) *n Archaic.* a verse romance. [C16: from Old French; see ROMANTIC]

Romberg ('rɒmbɜːg) *n* **Sigmund.** 1887–1951, U.S. composer of operettas, born in Hungary. He wrote *The Student Prince* (1924) and *The Desert Song* (1926).

Rom. Cath. *abbrev. for* Roman Catholic.

Rome (rəʊm) *n* **1** the capital of Italy, on the River Tiber: includes the independent state of the Vatican City; traditionally founded by Romulus on the Palatine Hill in 753 B.C., later spreading to six other hills east of the Tiber; capital of the Roman Empire; a great cultural and artistic centre, esp. during the Renaissance. Pop.: 2 654 187 (1996 est.). Italian name: **Roma. 2** the Roman Empire. **3** the Roman Catholic Church or Roman Catholicism.

Romeo ('rəʊmɪəʊ) *n* **1** (*pl* **-os.**) an ardent male lover. **2** *Communications.* a code word for the letter *r.* [from the hero of Shakespeare's *Romeo and Juliet* (1594)]

Romish ('rəʊmɪʃ) *adj Usually derogatory.* of, relating to, or resembling Roman Catholic beliefs or practices.

Rommel (*German* 'rɔməl) *n* **Erwin** ('ɛrviːn), nicknamed *the Desert Fox.* 1891–1944, German field marshal, noted for his brilliant generalship in N Africa in World War II. Later a commander in N France, he committed suicide after the officers' plot against Hitler.

Romney ('rɒmnɪ, 'rʌm-) *n* **George.** 1734–1802, English painter, who painted more than 50 portraits of Lady Hamilton in various historical roles.

Romney Marsh ('rɒmnɪ, 'rʌm-) *n* **1** a marshy area of SE England, on the Kent coast between New Romney and Rye: includes Dungeness. **2** a type of hardy British sheep from this area, with long wool, bred for mutton.

romp (rɒmp) *vb* (*intr*) **1** to play or run about wildly, boisterously, or joyfully. **2 romp home** (*or* **in**). to win a race easily. ◆ *n* **3** a noisy or boisterous game or prank. **4** an instance of sexual activity between two or more people that is entered into light-heartedly and without emotional commitment: *naked sex romps.* **5** Also called: **romper.** *Archaic.* a playful or boisterous child, esp. a girl. **6** an easy victory. [C18: probably variant of RAMP, from Old French *ramper* to crawl, climb] ▸ **'rompish** *adj*

rompers ('rɒmpəz) *pl n* **1** a one-piece baby garment consisting of trousers and a bib with straps. **2** *N.Z.* a type of costume worn by schoolgirls for games and gymnastics.

romp through *vb* (*intr, prep*) *Informal.* to progress quickly and easily through something: *he romped through the work.*

Romulus ('rɒmjʊləs) *n Roman myth.* the founder of Rome, suckled with his twin brother Remus by a she-wolf after they were abandoned in infancy. Their parents were Rhea Silvia and Mars. Romulus later killed Remus in an argument over the new city.

Roncesvalles ('rɒnsəˌvælz; *Spanish* rɔnθez'βaʎes) *n* a village in N Spain, in the Pyrenees: a nearby pass was the scene of the defeat of Charlemagne and death of Roland in 778. French name: **Roncevaux** (rɔ̃svo).

rondavel ('rɒndɑːvəl) *n S. African.* a circular often thatched building with a conical roof. [of uncertain origin]

rondeau ('rɒndəʊ) *n, pl* **-deaux** (-dəʊ, -dəʊz). a poem consisting of 13 or 10 lines with two rhymes and having the opening words of the first line used as an unrhymed refrain. See also **roundel.** [C16: from Old French, from *rondel* a little round, from *rond* ROUND]

rondel ('rɒndᵊl) *n* **1** a rondeau consisting of three stanzas of 13 or 14 lines with a two-line refrain appearing twice or three times. **2** a figure in Scottish country dancing by means of which couples change position in the set. [C14: from Old French, literally: a little circle, from *rond* ROUND]

rondelet ('rɒndəˌlɛt) *n* a brief rondeau, having five or seven lines and a refrain taken from the first line. [C16: from Old French: a little RONDEL]

rondo ('rɒndəʊ) *n, pl* **-dos.** a piece of music in which a refrain is repeated between episodes: often constitutes the form of the last movement of a sonata or concerto. [C18: from Italian, from French RONDEAU]

Rondônia (*Portuguese* rõ'donja) *n* a state of W Brazil: consists chiefly of tropical rainforest; a centre of the Amazon rubber boom until about 1912. Capital: Pôrto Velho. Pop.: 1 339 500 (1995 est.). Area: 243 043 sq. km (93 839 sq. miles). Former name (until 1956): **Guaporé.**

rondure ('rɒndjʊə) *n Literary.* **1** a circle or curve. **2** roundness or curvature. [C17: from French *rondeur,* from *rond* ROUND]

rone (rəʊn; *Scot.* ron) *or* **ronepipe** ('rəʊnˌpaɪp; *Scot.* 'ronˌpəɪp) *n Scot.* a drainpipe or gutter for carrying rainwater from a roof. [C19: origin unknown]

Roneo ('rəʊnɪəʊ) *Trademark.* ◆ *vb* **-neos, -neoing, -neoed.** (*tr*) **1** to duplicate (a document) from a stencil. ◆ *n, pl* **-neos. 2** a document reproduced by this process.

ronggeng ('rɒŋgɛŋ) *n* a Malay traditional dance. [Malay]

ronin ('rəʊnɪn) *n Japanese history.* **1** a lordless samurai, esp. one whose feudal lord had been deprived of his territory. **2** such samurai collectively. [Japanese]

Ronsard (*French* rɔ̃sar) *n* **Pierre de** (pjɛr də). 1524–85, French poet, foremost of the *Pléiade.*

röntgen ('rɒntgən, -tjən, 'rɛnt-) *n* a variant spelling of **roentgen.**

Röntgen ('rɒntgən, -tjən, 'rɛnt-; *German* 'rœntgən) *n* a variant spelling of (Wilhelm Konrad) **Roentgen.**

roo (ruː) *n Austral. informal.* a kangaroo.

rood (ruːd) *n* **1a** a crucifix, esp. one set on a beam or screen at the entrance to the chancel of a church. **1b** (*as modifier*): *rood beam; rood arch; rood screen.* **2** the Cross on which Christ was crucified. **3** a unit of area equal to one quarter of an acre or 0.10117 hectares. **4** a unit of area equal to 40 square rods. [Old English *rōd;* related to Old Saxon *rōda,* Old Norse *rōtha*]

Roodepoort-Maraisburg ('ruːdəˌpʊət mə'reɪsbɜːg) *n* an industrial city in NE South Africa, on the Witwatersrand. Pop.: 162 632 (1991).

rood screen *n* a partition of stone or wood, often richly carved and decorated, that separates the chancel from the main part of a church: it is surmounted by a crucifix (rood), and was an important feature of medieval churches, though in England many rood screens were destroyed at the Reformation.

roof (ruːf) *n, pl* **roofs** (ruːfs, ruːvz). **1a** a structure that covers or forms the top of a building. **1b** (*in combination*): *the rooftop*. **1c** (*as modifier*): *a roof garden*. **2** the top covering of a vehicle, oven, or other structure: *the roof of a car*. **3** *Anatomy*. any structure that covers an organ or part: *the roof of the mouth*. **4** a highest or topmost point or part: *Mount Everest is the roof of the world*. **5** a house or other shelter: *a poor man's roof*. **6** *Mountaineering*. the underside of a projecting overhang. **7 hit** (*or* **go through**) **the roof**. *Informal*. **7a** to get extremely angry; become furious. **7b** to rise or increase steeply. **8 raise the roof**. **8a** to create a boisterous disturbance. **8b** to react or protest heatedly. ◆ *vb* **9** (*tr*) to provide or cover with a roof or rooflike part. [Old English *hrōf*; related to Middle Dutch, Old Norse *hrōf*] ► **'roofer** *n* ► **'roofless** *adj* ► **'roof,like** *adj*

roof garden *n* a garden on a flat roof of a building.

roofing ('ruːfɪŋ) *n* **1** material used to construct a roof. **2** the act of constructing a roof.

roof rack *n* a rack attached to the roof of a motor vehicle for carrying luggage, skis, etc.

rooftop ('ruːf,tɒp) *n* **1** the outside part of the roof of a building. **2 shout from the rooftops**. to proclaim (something) publicly.

rooftree ('ruːf,triː) *n* another name for **ridgepole**.

rooibos tea ('rɔɪbɒs) *n S. African*. tea prepared from any of several species of *Borbonia* or *Aspalanthus*, believed to have tonic properties. [from Afrikaans *rooi* red + *bos* bush]

rooikat ('rɔɪ,kæt) *n* a South African lynx, *Felis caracal*. [Afrikaans *rooi* red + *kat* cat]

rooinek ('rʊɪnɛk, 'rɔɪ-) *n S. African*. a contemptuous name for an Englishman. [C19: Afrikaans, literally: red neck]

rook[1] (rʊk) *n* **1** a large Eurasian passerine bird, *Corvus frugilegus*, with a black plumage and a whitish base to its bill: family *Corvidae* (crows). **2** *Slang*. a swindler or cheat, esp. one who cheats at cards. ◆ *vb* **3** (*tr*) *Slang*. to overcharge, swindle, or cheat. [Old English *hrōc*; related to Old High German *hruoh*, Old Norse *hrōkr*]

rook[2] (rʊk) *n* a chesspiece that may move any number of unoccupied squares in a straight line, horizontally or vertically. Also called: **castle**. [C14: from Old French *rok*, ultimately from Arabic *rukhkh*]

rookery ('rʊkərɪ) *n, pl* **-eries**. **1** a group of nesting rooks. **2** a clump of trees containing rooks' nests. **3a** a breeding ground or communal living area of certain other species of gregarious birds or mammals, esp. penguins or seals. **3b** a colony of any such creatures. **4** *Archaic*. an overcrowded slum tenement building or area of housing.

rookie ('rʊkɪ) *n Informal*. an inexperienced person or newcomer, esp. a raw recruit in the army. [C20: changed from RECRUIT]

rooky ('rʊkɪ) *adj* **rookier, rookiest**. *Literary*. abounding in rooks.

room (ruːm, rʊm) *n* **1** space or extent, esp. unoccupied or unobstructed space for a particular purpose: *is there room to pass?* **2** an area within a building enclosed by a floor, a ceiling, and walls or partitions. **3** (*functioning as sing or pl*) the people present in a room: *the whole room was laughing*. **4** (foll. by *for*) opportunity or scope: *room for manoeuvre*. **5** (*pl*) a part of a house, hotel, etc. that is rented out as separate accommodation; lodgings: *she got rooms quite easily in Dulwich Road*. **6** a euphemistic word for **lavatory** (sense 1). ◆ *vb* **7** (*intr*) *Chiefly U.S.* to occupy or share a room or lodging: *where does he room?* [Old English *rūm*; related to Gothic, Old High German *rūm*] ► **'roomer** *n*

roomette (ruː'mɛt, rʊ'mɛt) *n U.S. and Canadian*. a self-contained compartment in a railway sleeping car.

roomful ('ruːmfʊl, 'rʊm-) *n, pl* **-fuls**. a number or quantity sufficient to fill a room: *a roomful of furniture*.

rooming house *n U.S. and Canadian*. a house having self-contained furnished rooms or flats for renting.

roommate ('ruːm,meɪt, 'rʊm-) *n* a person with whom one shares a room or lodging.

room service *n* service in a hotel providing meals, drinks, etc., in guests' rooms.

room temperature *n* the normal temperature of a living room, usually taken as being around 20°C.

roomy ('ruːmɪ, 'rʊmɪ) *adj* **roomier, roomiest**. having ample room; spacious. ► **'roomily** *adv* ► **'roominess** *n*

roorback ('rʊə,bæk) *n U.S.* a false or distorted report or account, used to obtain political advantage. [C19: after Baron von *Roorback*, invented author of an imaginary *Tour through the Western and Southern States* (1844), which contained a passage defaming James K. Polk]

Roosevelt ('rəʊzə,vɛlt) *n* **1 (Anna) Eleanor**. 1884–1962, U.S. writer, diplomat, and advocate of liberal causes: delegate to the United Nations (1945–52). **2** her husband, **Franklin Delano** ('dɛlə,nəʊ), known as *FDR*. 1882–1945, 32nd president of the U.S. (1933–45); elected four times. He instituted major reforms (the **New Deal**) to counter the economic crisis of the 1930s and was a forceful leader during World War II. **3 Theodore**. 1858–1919, 26th president of the U.S. (1901–09). A proponent of extending military power, he won for the U.S. the right to build the Panama Canal (1903). He won the Nobel peace prize (1906), for mediating in the Russo-Japanese war.

roost (ruːst) *n* **1** a place, perch, branch, etc., where birds, esp. domestic fowl, rest or sleep. **2** a temporary place to rest or stay. **3 rule the roost**. See **rule** (sense 20). ◆ *vb* **4** (*intr*) to rest or sleep on a roost. **5** (*intr*) to settle down or stay. **6 come home to roost**. to have unfavourable repercussions. [Old English *hrōst*; related to Old Saxon *hrost* loft, German *Rost* grid]

Roost (ruːst) *n* **the**. a powerful current caused by conflicting tides around the Shetland and Orkney Islands. [C16: from Old Norse *röst*]

rooster ('ruːstə) *n Chiefly U.S. and Canadian*. the male of the domestic fowl; a cock.

root[1] (ruːt) *n* **1a** the organ of a higher plant that anchors the rest of the plant in the ground, absorbs water and mineral salts from the soil, and does not bear leaves or buds. **1b** (loosely) any of the branches of such an organ. **2** any plant part, such as a rhizome or tuber, that is similar to a root in structure, function, or appearance. **3a** the essential, fundamental, or primary part or nature of something: *your analysis strikes at the root of the problem*. **3b** (*as modifier*): *the root cause of the problem*. **4** *Anatomy*. the embedded portion of a tooth, nail, hair, etc. **5** origin or derivation, esp. as a source of growth, vitality, or existence. **6** (*pl*) a person's sense of belonging in a community, place, etc., esp. the one in which he was born or brought up. **7** an ancestor or antecedent. **8** *Bible*. a descendant. **9** the form of a word that remains after removal of all affixes; a morpheme with lexical meaning that is not further subdivisible into other morphemes with lexical meaning. Compare **stem**[1] (sense 9). **10** *Maths*. a number or quantity that when multiplied by itself a certain number of times equals a given number or quantity: *3 is a cube root of 27*. **11** Also called: **solution**. *Maths*. a number that when substituted for the variable satisfies a given equation: *2 is a root of* $x^3 - 2x - 4 = 0$. **12** *Music*. (in harmony) the note forming the foundation of a chord. **13** *Austral. and N.Z. slang*. sexual intercourse. **14 root and branch**. (*adv*) entirely; completely; utterly. ◆ Related adj: **radical**. ◆ *vb* **15** (*intr*) Also: **take root**. to put forth or establish a root and begin to grow. **16** (*intr*) Also: **take root**. to become established, embedded, or effective. **17** (*tr*) to fix or embed with or as if with a root or roots. **18** *Austral. and N.Z. slang*. to have sexual intercourse (with). ◆ See also **root out, root up**. [Old English *rōt*, from Old Norse; related to Old English *wyrt* WORT] ► **'rooter** *n* ► **'root,like** *adj* ► **'rooty** *adj* ► **'rootiness** *n*

root[2] (ruːt) *vb* (*intr*) **1** (of a pig) to burrow in or dig up the earth in search of food, using the snout. **2** (foll. by *about, around, in*, etc.) *Informal*. to search vigorously but unsystematically. [C16: changed (through influence of ROOT[1]) from earlier *wroot*, from Old English *wrōtan*; related to Old English *wrōt* snout, Middle Dutch *wrōte* mole] ► **'rooter** *n*

root[3] *vb* (*intr*; usually foll. by *for*) *Informal*. to give support to (a contestant, team, etc.), as by cheering. [C19: perhaps a variant of Scottish *rout* to make a loud noise, from Old Norse *rauta* to roar] ► **'rooter** *n*

root beer *n U.S. and Canadian*. an effervescent drink made from extracts of various roots and herbs.

root canal *n* the passage in the root of a tooth through which its nerves and blood vessels enter the pulp cavity.

root-canal therapy *n* another name for **root treatment**.

root cap *n* a hollow cone of loosely arranged cells that covers the growing tip of a root and protects it during its passage through the soil.

root climber *n* any of various climbing plants, such as the ivy, that adhere to a supporting structure by means of small roots growing from the side of the stem.

root crop *n* a crop, as of turnips or beets, cultivated for the food value of its roots.

rooted ('ruːtɪd) *adj* **1** having roots. **2** deeply felt: *rooted objections*. **3** *Austral. slang*. tired or defeated. **4 get rooted!** *Austral. taboo slang*. an exclamation of contemptuous anger or annoyance, esp. against another person.

root ginger *n* the raw underground stem of the ginger plant used finely chopped or grated, esp. in Chinese dishes.

root hair *n* any of the hollow hairlike outgrowths of the outer cells of a root, just behind the tip, that absorb water and salts from the soil.

rooting compound *n Horticulture*. a substance, usually a powder, containing auxins in which plant cuttings are dipped in order to promote root growth.

rootle ('ruːtᵊl) *vb* (*intr*) *Brit*. another word for **root**[2].

rootless ('ruːtlɪs) *adj* having no roots, esp. (of a person) having no ties with a particular place or community.

rootlet ('ruːtlɪt) *n* a small root or branch of a root.

root mean square *n* the square root of the average of the squares of a set of numbers or quantities: *the root mean square of* 1, 2, *and* 4 *is* $\sqrt{[(1^2 + 2^2 + 4^2)/3]} = \sqrt{7}$. Abbrev: **rms**.

root nodule *n* a swelling on the root of a leguminous plant, such as the pea or clover, that contains bacteria of the genus *Rhizobium*, capable of nitrogen fixation.

root out *vb* (*tr, adv*) to remove or eliminate completely: *we must root out inefficiency*.

root position *n Music*. the vertical distribution of the written notes of a chord in which the root of the chord is in the bass. See **position** (sense 12a), **inversion** (sense 5a).

roots music *n* **1** another name for **world music**. **2** reggae, esp. when regarded as authentic and uncommercialized.

rootstock ('ruːt,stɒk) *n* **1** another name for **rhizome**. **2** another name for **stock** (sense 7). **3** *Biology*. a basic structure from which offshoots have developed.

root treatment *n Dentistry*. a procedure, used for treating an abscess at the tip of the root of a tooth, in which the pulp is removed and a filling (**root filling**) inserted in the root canal. Also called: **root-canal therapy**.

root up *vb* (*tr, adv*) to tear or dig up by the roots.

ropable *or* **ropeable** ('rəʊpəbᵊl) *adj* **1** capable of being roped. **2** *Austral. and N.Z. informal*. **2a** angry. **2b** wild or intractable: *a ropable beast*.

rope (rəʊp) *n* **1a** a fairly thick cord made of twisted and intertwined hemp or other fibres or of wire or other strong material. **1b** (*as modifier*): *a rope bridge; a rope ladder*. **2** a row of objects fastened or united to form a line: *a rope of pearls; a rope of onions*. **3** a quantity of material twisted or wound in the form of a cord. **4** anything in the form of a filament or strand, esp. something viscous or glutinous: *a rope of slime*. **5 the rope**. **5a** a rope, noose, or halter used for hanging. **5b** death by hanging, strangling, etc. **6 give (someone) enough rope to hang himself**. to allow (someone) to accomplish his own downfall by his own foolish acts. **7 know the ropes. 7a** to have a thorough understanding of a particular sphere of activity. **7b** to be experienced in the ways of the world. **8 on the ropes. 8a** *Boxing.* driven against the ropes enclosing the ring by an opponent's attack. **8b** in a defenceless or hopeless position. ◆ *vb* **9** (*tr*) to bind or fasten with or as if with a rope. **10** (*tr; usually foll. by off*) to enclose or divide by means of a rope. **11** (*intr*) to become extended in a long filament or thread. **12** (when *intr,* foll. by *up*) *Mountaineering.* to tie (climbers) together with a rope. [Old English *rāp;* related to Old Saxon *rēp,* Old High German *reif*]

rope dancer *n* another name for a **tightrope walker.**

rope in *vb* (*tr, adv*) **1** *Brit.* to persuade to take part in some activity. **2** *U.S. and Canadian.* to trick or entice into some activity.

rope's end *n* a short piece of rope, esp. as formerly used for flogging sailors.

ropewalk ('rəʊp,wɔːk) *n* a long narrow usually covered path or shed where ropes are made.

rope yarn *n* the natural or synthetic fibres out of which rope is made.

ropey *or* **ropy** ('rəʊpɪ) *adj* **ropier, ropiest. 1** *Brit. informal.* **1a** inferior or inadequate. **1b** slightly unwell; below par. **2** (of a viscous or sticky substance) forming strands or filaments. **3** resembling a rope: *ropey muscles.* ▸ **'ropily** *adv* ▸ **'ropiness** *n*

roque (rəʊk) *n U.S.* a game developed from croquet, played on a hard surface with a resilient surrounding border from which the ball can rebound. [C19: variant of CROQUET]

Roquefort ('rɒkfɔː) *n* a blue-veined cheese with a strong flavour, made from ewe's and goat's milk: matured in caves. [C19: named after *Roquefort,* village in S France]

roquelaure ('rɒkə,lɔː) *n* a man's hooded knee-length cloak of the 18th and 19th centuries. [C18: from French, named after the Duc de *Roquelaure* (1656–1738), French marshal]

roquet ('rəʊkɪ) *Croquet.* ◆ *vb* **-quets** (-kɪz), **-queting** (-kɪɪŋ), **-queted** (-kɪd). **1** to drive one's ball against (another person's ball) in order to be allowed to croquet. ◆ *n* **2** the act of roqueting. [C19: variant of CROQUET]

Roraima (*Portuguese* rɔ'raima) *n* a state of N Brazil: chiefly rainforest. Capital: Boa Vista. Pop.: 262 200 (1995 est.). Area: 230 104 sq. km (89 740 sq. miles).

ro-ro ('rəʊrəʊ) *adj acronym for* **roll-on/roll-off.**

rorqual ('rɔːkwəl) *n* any of several whalebone whales of the genus *Balaenoptera,* esp. *B. physalus:* family *Balaenopteridae.* They have a dorsal fin and a series of grooves along the throat and chest. Also called: **finback.** [C19: from French, from Norwegian *rörhval,* from Old Norse *reytharhvalr,* from *reythr* (from *rauthr* red) + *hvalr* whale]

Rorschach test ('rɔːʃɑːk; *German* 'rɔrʃax) *n Psychol.* a personality test consisting of a number of unstructured ink blots presented for interpretation. [C20: named after Hermann *Rorschach* (1884–1922), Swiss psychiatrist]

rort (rɔːt) *Austral. informal.* ◆ *n* **1** a rowdy party or celebration. **2** a dishonest scheme. ◆ *vb* **3** to take unfair advantage of something. [C20: back formation from *rorty* (in the sense: good, splendid)] ▸ **'rorty** *adj*

Rory O'Connor (,rɔːrɪ əʊ'kɒnə) *n* Also called *Roderic.* ?1116–98, king of Connaught and last High King of Ireland.

Rosa[1] ('rəʊzə; *Italian* 'rɔːza) *n* **Monte** ('mɒntɪ; *Italian* 'monte). a mountain between Italy and Switzerland: the highest in the Pennine Alps. Height: 4634 m (15 204 ft.).

Rosa[2] (*Italian* 'rɔːza) *n* **Salvator** ('salvatɔr). 1615–73, Italian artist, noted esp. for his romantic landscapes.

rosace ('rəʊzeɪs) *n* **1** another name for **rose window. 2** another name for **rosette.** [C19: from French, from Latin *rosāceus* ROSACEOUS]

rosaceous (rəʊ'zeɪʃəs) *adj* **1** of, relating to, or belonging to the *Rosaceae,* a family of flowering plants typically having white, yellow, pink, or red five-petalled flowers. The family includes the rose, strawberry, blackberry, and many fruit trees such as apple, cherry, and plum. **2** of the colour rose; rose-coloured; rosy. [C18: from Latin *rosāceus* composed of roses, from *rosa* ROSE[1]]

rosaniline (rəʊ'zænɪ,liːn, -lɪn) *or* **rosanilin** *n* a reddish-brown crystalline insoluble derivative of aniline used, in the form of its soluble hydrochloride, as a red dye. See also **fuchsin.** [C19: from ROSE[1] + ANILINE]

rosarian (rəʊ'zɛərɪən) *n* a person who cultivates roses, esp. professionally.

Rosario (rəʊ'sɑːrɪəʊ; *Spanish* rɔ'sarjo) *n* an inland port in E Argentina, on the Paraná River: the second largest city in the country; industrial centre. Pop.: 1 157 372 (1992 est.).

rosarium (rəʊ'zɛərɪəm) *n, pl* **-sariums** *or* **-saria** (-'zɛərɪə). a rose garden. [C19: New Latin]

rosary ('rəʊzərɪ) *n, pl* **-saries. 1** *R.C. Church.* **1a** a series of prayers counted on a string of beads, usually consisting of five or 15 decades of Aves, each decade beginning with a Paternoster and ending with a Gloria. **1b** a string of 55 or 165 beads used to count these prayers as they are recited. **2** (in other religions) a similar string of beads used in praying. **3** a bed or garden of roses. **4** an archaic word for a **garland** (of flowers, leaves, etc.). [C14: from Latin *rosārium* rose garden, from *rosārius* of roses, from *rosa* ROSE[1]]

Roscius ('rɒskɪəs, -sɪəs) *n* **1** full name *Quintus Roscius Gallus.* died 62 B.C., Roman actor. **2** any actor. ▸ **'Roscian** *adj*

Roscommon (rɒs'kɒmən) *n* an inland county of N central Republic of Ireland, in Connacht: economy based on cattle and sheep farming. County town: Roscommon. Pop.: 52 000 (1996). Area: 2463 sq. km (951 sq. miles).

rose[1] (rəʊz) *n* **1a** any shrub or climbing plant of the rosaceous genus *Rosa,* typically having prickly stems, compound leaves, and fragrant flowers. **1b** (*in combination*): *rosebush; rosetree.* **2** the flower of any of these plants. **3** any of various similar plants, such as the rockrose and Christmas rose. **4a** a moderate purplish-red colour; purplish pink. **4b** (*as adj*): *rose paint.* **5** a rose, or a representation of one, as the national emblem of England. **6** *Jewellery.* **6a** a cut for a diamond or other gemstone, having a hemispherical faceted crown and a flat base. **6b** a gem so cut. **7** a perforated cap fitted to the spout of a watering can or the end of a hose, causing the water to issue in a spray. **8** a design or decoration shaped like a rose; rosette. **9** Also called: **ceiling rose.** *Electrical engineering.* a circular boss attached to a ceiling through which the flexible lead of an electric-light fitting passes. **10** *History.* See **red rose, white rose. 11 bed of roses.** a situation of comfort or ease. **12 under the rose.** in secret; privately; sub rosa. ◆ *vb* **13** (*tr*) to make rose-coloured; cause to blush or redden. [Old English, from Latin *rosa,* probably from Greek *rhodon* rose] ▸ **'rose,like** *adj*

rose[2] (rəʊz) *vb* the past tense of **rise.**

rosé ('rəʊzeɪ) *n* any pink wine, made either by removing the skins of red grapes after only a little colour has been extracted or by mixing red and white wines. [C19: from French, literally: pink, from Latin *rosa* ROSE[1]]

rose acacia *n* a leguminous shrub, *Robinia hispida,* of the southern U.S., having prickly branches bearing clusters of red scentless flowers. See also **locust** (sense 2).

rose apple *n* an ornamental myrtaceous tree, *Eugenia jambos,* of the East Indies, cultivated in the tropics for its edible fruit.

roseate ('rəʊzɪ,eɪt) *adj* **1** of the colour rose or pink. **2** excessively or idealistically optimistic. ▸ **'rose,ately** *adv*

Roseau (rəʊ'zəʊ) *n* the capital of Dominica, a port on the SW coast: botanical gardens. Pop.: 15 853 (1991).

rosebay ('rəʊz,beɪ) *n* **1** *U.S.* any of several rhododendrons, esp. *Rhododendron maximum* of E North America. **2 rosebay willowherb.** a perennial onagraceous plant, *Chamaenerion* (formerly *Epilobium*) *angustifolium,* that has spikes of deep pink flowers and is widespread in open places throughout N temperate regions. **3** another name for **oleander.**

Rosebery ('rəʊzbərɪ, -brɪ) *n* **Earl of,** title of *Archibald Philip Primrose.* 1847–1929, British Liberal statesman; prime minister (1894–95).

rosebud ('rəʊz,bʌd) *n* **1** the bud of a rose. **2** *Literary.* a pretty young woman.

rose campion *n* a European caryophyllaceous plant, *Lychnis coronaria,* widely cultivated for its pink flowers. Its stems and leaves are covered with white woolly down. Also called: **dusty miller.**

rose chafer *or* **beetle** *n* a British scarabaeid beetle, *Cetonia aurata,* that has a greenish-golden body with a metallic lustre and feeds on plants.

rose-coloured *adj* **1** of the colour rose; rosy. **2** See **rose-tinted. 3 see through rose-coloured** (*or* **rose-tinted**) **glasses** (*or* **spectacles**). to view in an excessively optimistic light.

rose-cut *adj* (of a gemstone) cut with a hemispherical faceted crown and a flat base.

rosefish ('rəʊz,fɪʃ) *n, pl* **-fish** *or* **-fishes. 1** a red scorpaenid food fish, *Sebastes marinus,* of North Atlantic coastal waters. **2** any of various other red fishes.

rose geranium *n* a small geraniaceous shrub, *Pelargonium graveolens,* grown in North America for its pink flowers and fragrant leaves, used for scenting perfumes and cosmetics.

rosehip ('rəʊz,hɪp) *n* the berry-like fruit of a rose plant. See **hip**[2].

rosella (rəʊ'zɛlə) *n* any of various Australian parrots of the genus *Platycercus,* such as *P. elegans* (**crimson rosella**), often kept as cage birds. [C19: probably alteration of *Rose-hiller,* after *Rose Hill,* Parramatta, near Sydney]

rosemaling ('rəʊzə,mɑːlɪŋ, -sə-) *n* a type of painted or carved decoration in Scandinavian peasant style consisting of floral motifs. [C20: from Norwegian, literally: rose painting]

rose mallow *n* **1** Also called (U.S. and Canadian): **marsh mallow.** any of several malvaceous marsh plants of the genus *Hibiscus,* such as *H. moscheutos,* of E North America, having pink or white flowers and downy leaves. **2** *U.S.* another name for the **hollyhock.**

rosemary ('rəʊzmərɪ) *n, pl* **-maries.** an aromatic European shrub, *Rosmarinus officinalis,* widely cultivated for its grey-green evergreen leaves, which are used in cookery for flavouring and yield a fragrant oil used in the manufacture of perfumes: family *Labiatae* (labiates). It is the traditional flower of remembrance. [C15: earlier *rosmarine,* from Latin *rōs* dew + *marīnus* marine; modern form influenced by folk etymology, as if ROSE[1] + MARY]

rose moss *n* a low-growing portulacaceous plant, *Portulaca grandiflora,* native to Brazil but widely cultivated as a garden plant for its brightly coloured flowers.

Rosenberg ('rəʊzənbɜːg) *n* **1 Alfred.** 1893–1946, German Nazi politician and writer, who devised much of the racial ideology of Nazism: hanged for war crimes. **2 Isaac.** 1890–1918, British poet and painter, best known for his poems about life in the trenches during World War I: died in action. **3 Julius.** 1918–53, U.S. spy, who, with his wife **Ethel** (1914–53), was executed for passing information about nuclear weapons to the Russians.

rose of Jericho *n* another name for the **resurrection plant.**

rose of Sharon *n* **1** Also called: **Aaron's beard.** a creeping shrub, *Hypericum calycinum,* native to SE Europe but widely cultivated, having large yellow flowers: family *Hypericaceae.* **2** Also called: **althaea.** a Syrian malvaceous shrub, *Hibiscus syriacus* (or *Althaea frutex*), cultivated for its red or purplish flowers.

roseola (rəʊ'ziːələ) *n Pathol.* **1** any red skin eruption or rash. **2** another name for **rubeola.** [C19: from New Latin, diminutive of Latin *roseus* rosy] ▸ **ro'seolar** *adj*

rose quartz *n* a rose-pink often translucent variety of quartz that is used for ornaments.

rose-root *n* a Eurasian crassulaceous mountain plant, *Sedum rosea,* with fleshy pink-tipped leaves, a thick fleshy pinkish underground stem, and a cluster of yellow flowers. Also called: **midsummer-men.**

rosery ('rəʊzərɪ) *n, pl* **-series.** a bed or garden of roses.

rose-tinted *adj* **1** Also **rose-coloured.** excessively optimistic. **2 see through rose-tinted** (*or* **rose-coloured**) **glasses** (*or* **spectacles**). to view in an excessively optimistic light.

rose topaz *n* a rose-pink form of topaz produced by heating yellow-brown topaz.

Rosetta (rəʊ'zɛtə) *n* the former name of **Rashid.**

Rosetta stone *n* a basalt slab discovered in 1799 at Rosetta, dating to the reign of Ptolemy V (196 B.C.) and carved with parallel inscriptions in Egyptian hieroglyphics, demotic characters, and Greek, which provided the key to the decipherment of ancient Egyptian texts.

rosette (rəʊ'zɛt) *n* **1** a decoration or pattern resembling a rose, esp. an arrangement of ribbons or strips formed into a rose-shaped design and worn as a badge or presented as a prize. **2** another name for **rose window. 3** a rose-shaped patch of colour, such as one of the clusters of spots marking a leopard's fur. **4** *Botany.* a circular cluster of leaves growing from the base of a stem. **5** any of various plant diseases characterized by abnormal leaf growth. **[C18:** from Old French: a little ROSE[1]**]**

Rosewall ('rəʊz,wɔːl) *n* **Ken(neth).** born 1934, Australian tennis player: Australian champion 1953, 1955, and 1971–72; U.S. champion 1956 and 1970.

rose-water *n* **1a** scented water used as a perfume and in cooking, made by the distillation of rose petals or by impregnation with oil of roses. **1b** (*as modifier*): *rose-water scent.* **2** (*modifier*) elegant or delicate, esp. excessively so.

rose window *n* a circular window, esp. one that has ornamental tracery radiating from the centre to form a symmetrical roselike pattern. Also called: **wheel window, rosette.**

rosewood ('rəʊz,wʊd) *n* **1** the hard dark wood of any of various tropical and subtropical leguminous trees, esp. of the genus *Dalbergia.* It has a roselike scent and is used in cabinetwork. **2** any of the trees yielding this wood.

Rosh Chodesh (rɒʃ 'xɔdəʃ) *n Judaism.* the first day of a new month, coinciding usually with the new moon, and also the preceding day if the previous month has 30 days, observed as a minor festival. See also **Jewish calendar.** [from Hebrew, literally: the beginning of the new moon]

Rosh Hashanah *or* **Rosh Hashana** ('rɒʃ hə'ʃɑːnə; *Hebrew* 'rɔʃ haʃa'na) *n* the festival marking the Jewish New Year, celebrated on the first and second days of Tishri, and marked by penitential prayers and by the blowing of the shofar. [from Hebrew *rōsh hasshānāh,* literally: beginning of the year, from *rōsh* head + *hash-shānāh* year]

Rosicrucian (,rəʊzɪ'kruːʃən) *n* **1** a member of a society professing esoteric religious doctrines, venerating the emblems of the rose and Cross as symbols of Christ's Resurrection and Redemption, and claiming various occult powers. ◆ *adj* **2** of, relating to, or designating the Rosicrucians or Rosicrucianism. **[C17:** from Latin *Rosae Crucis* Rose of the Cross, translation of the German name Christian *Rosenkreuz,* supposed founder of the society in the 15th century**]** ▸ **,Rosi'crucianism** *n*

Rosie Lee ('rəʊzɪ 'liː) *n Cockney rhyming slang.* tea.

rosin ('rɒzɪn) *n* **1** Also called: **colophony.** a translucent brittle amber substance produced in the distillation of crude turpentine oleoresin and used esp. in making varnishes, printing inks, and sealing waxes and for treating the bows of stringed instruments. **2** (not in technical usage) another name for **resin** (sense 1). ◆ *vb* **3** (*tr*) to treat or coat with rosin. **[C14:** variant of RESIN**]** ▸ **'rosiny** *adj*

Rosinante (,rɒzɪ'næntɪ) *n* a worn-out emaciated old horse. **[C18:** from Spanish, the name of Don Quixote's horse, from *rocin* old horse**]**

rosiner ('rɒzənə) *n Austral. slang.* a strong alcoholic drink. **[**from English dialect sense of *rosin* to supply with liquor**]**

rosin oil *n* a yellowish fluorescent oily liquid obtained from certain resins, used in the manufacture of carbon black, varnishes, and lacquers. Also called: **'rosinol, retinol.**

rosinweed ('rɒzɪn,wiːd) *n* any of several North American plants of the genus *Silphium* and related genera, esp. the compass plant, having resinous juice, sticky foliage, and a strong smell: family *Compositae* (composites).

Roskilde (*Danish* 'rɔskilə) *n* a city in Denmark, on NE Sjælland west of Copenhagen: capital of Denmark from the 10th century to 1443; scene of the signing (1658) of the **Peace of Roskilde** between Denmark and Sweden. Pop.: 49 080 (1990).

ROSPA ('rɒspə) *n* (in Britain) *acronym for* Royal Society for the Prevention of Accidents.

Ross (rɒs) *n* **1 Diana.** born 1944, U.S. singer: lead vocalist (1961–69) with Motown group the Supremes, whose hits include "Baby Love" (1964). Her subsequent recordings include *Lady Sings the Blues* (film soundtrack, 1972). **2** Sir **James Clark.** 1800–62, British naval officer; explorer of the Arctic and Antarctic. He located the north magnetic pole (1831) and discovered the Ross Sea during an Antarctic voyage (1839–43). **3** his uncle, Sir **John.** 1777–1856, Scottish naval officer and Arctic explorer. **4** Sir **Ronald.** 1857–1932, English bacteriologist, who discovered the transmission of malaria by mosquitoes: Nobel prize for physiology or medicine 1902.

Ross and Cromarty ('krɒmətɪ) *n* (until 1975) a county of N Scotland, including the island of Lewis and many islets: now split between the Highland and Western Isles council areas.

Ross Dependency *n* a section of Antarctica administered by New Zealand: includes the coastal regions of Victoria Land and King Edward VII Land, the Ross Sea and islands, and the Ross Ice Shelf. Area: about 414 400 sq. km (160 000 sq. miles).

Rossellini (rɒsə'liːnɪ) *n* **Roberto.** 1906–77, Italian film director. His films include *Rome, Open City* (1945), *Paisà* (1946), and *L'Amore* (1948).

Rossetti (rɒ'zɛtɪ) *n* **1 Christina Georgina.** 1830–94, British poet. **2** her brother, **Dante Gabriel.** 1828–82, British poet and painter: a leader of the Pre-Raphaelites.

Ross Ice Shelf *n* the ice shelf forming the S part of the Ross Sea, between Victoria Land and Byrd Land. Also called: **Ross Barrier, Ross Shelf Ice.**

Rossini (rɒ'siːnɪ) *n* **Gioacchino Antonio** (dʒoak'kiːno an'tɔːnjo). 1792–1868, Italian composer, esp. of operas, such as *The Barber of Seville* (1816) and *William Tell* (1829).

Ross Island *n* an island in the W Ross Sea: contains the active volcano Mount Erebus.

Rossiya (ra'siːjə) *n* transliteration of the Russian name for **Russia.**

Ross Sea *n* a large arm of the S Pacific in Antarctica, incorporating the Ross Ice Shelf and lying between Victoria Land and the Edward VII Peninsula.

Rostand (*French* rɔstɑ̃) *n* **Edmond** (ɛdmɔ̃). 1868–1918, French playwright and poet in the romantic tradition; best known for his verse drama *Cyrano de Bergerac* (1897).

rostellum (rɒ'stɛləm) *n, pl* **-la** (-lə). *Biology.* a small beaklike process, such as the hooked projection from the top of the head in tapeworms or the outgrowth from the stigma of an orchid. **[C18:** from Latin: a little beak, from *rōstrum* a beak**]** ▸ **ros'tellate** *or* **ros'tellar** *adj*

roster ('rɒstə) *n* **1** a list or register, esp. one showing the order of people enrolled for duty. ◆ *vb* **2** (*tr*) to place on a roster. **[C18:** from Dutch *rooster* grating or list (the lined paper looking like a grid)**]**

Rostock ('rɒstɒk) *n* a port in NE Germany, in Mecklenburg-West Pomerania on the Warnow estuary 13 km (8 miles) from the Baltic and its outport, Warnemünde: formerly the chief port of East Germany; university (1419). Pop.: 227 535 (1996 est.).

Rostov *or* **Rostov-on-Don** ('rɒstɒv) *n* a port in S Russia, on the River Don 48 km (30 miles) from the Sea of Azov: industrial centre. Pop.: 1 026 000 (1995 est.).

rostral ('rɒstrəl) *adj* **1** *Biology.* of or like a beak or snout. **2** adorned with the prows of ships: *a rostral column.*

rostrate ('rɒs,treɪt) *adj Biology.* having a beak or beaklike process.

Rostropovich (,rɒstrə'pəʊvɪtʃ; *Russian* rəstra'pɔvitʃ) *n* **Mstislav Leopoldovich** ('mɪstɪslɑːv; *Russian* msti'slaf lea'pɔldavitʃ). born 1927, Soviet cellist, composer, and conductor; became a U.S. citizen in 1978 after losing Soviet citizenship (restored in 1990).

rostrum ('rɒstrəm) *n, pl* **-trums** *or* **-tra** (-trə). **1** any platform, stage, or dais on which public speakers stand to address an audience. **2** a platform or dais in front of an orchestra on which the conductor stands. **3** another word for **ram** (sense 5). **4** the prow or beak of an ancient Roman ship. **5** *Biology, zoology.* a beak or beaklike part. **[C16:** from Latin *rōstrum* beak, ship's prow, from *rōdere* to nibble, gnaw; in plural, *rōstra,* orator's platform, because this platform in the Roman forum was adorned with the prows of captured ships**]**

rosy ('rəʊzɪ) *adj* **rosier, rosiest. 1** of the colour rose or pink. **2** having a healthy pink complexion: *rosy cheeks.* **3** optimistic, esp. excessively so: *a rosy view of social improvements.* **4** full of health, happiness, or joy: *rosy slumbers.* **5** resembling, consisting of, or abounding in roses. ▸ **'rosily** *adv* ▸ **'rosiness** *n*

rosy finch *n* any of several finches of the genus *Leucosticte,* occurring in mountainous regions of North America and Asia. They have brown or grey plumage with pink patches on the wings, rump, and tail.

rot[1] (rɒt) *vb* **rots, rotting, rotted. 1** to decay or cause to decay as a result of bacterial or fungal action. **2** (*intr;* usually foll. by *off* or *away*) to fall or crumble (off) or break (away), as from natural decay, corrosive action, or long use. **3** (*intr*) to become weak, debilitated, or depressed through inertia, confinement, etc.; languish: *rotting in prison.* **4** to become or cause to become morally corrupt or degenerate. **5** (*tr*) *Textiles.* another word for **ret.** ◆ *n* **6** the process of rotting or the state of being rotten. **7** something decomposed, disintegrated, or degenerate. Related adj: **putrid. 8** short for **dry rot. 9** *Pathol.* any putrefactive decomposition of tissues. **10** a condition in plants characterized by breakdown and decay of tissues, caused by parasitic bacteria, fungi, etc. **11** *Vet. science.* a contagious fungal disease of sheep characterized by inflammation, swelling, a foul-smelling discharge, and lameness. **12** (*also interj*) nonsense; rubbish. [Old English *rotian* (vb); related to Old Norse *rotna.* C13 (n), from Scandinavian]

rot[2] *abbrev. for* rotation (of a mathematical function).

rota ('rəʊtə) *n Chiefly Brit.* a register of names showing the order in which people take their turn to perform certain duties. **[C17:** from Latin: a wheel**]**

Rota ('rəʊtə) *n R.C. Church.* the supreme ecclesiastical tribunal for judging cases brought before the Holy See.

rota bed *n Social welfare.* a bed in an old people's home, reserved for the regular respite care of dependent old people.

rotachute ('rəʊtə,ʃuːt) *n* a device serving the same purpose as a parachute, in which the canopy is replaced by freely revolving rotor blades, used for the delivery of stores or recovery of missiles.

Rotameter ('rəʊtə,miːtə) *n Trademark.* a device used for measuring the flow of a fluid. It consists of a small float supported in a tapering glass by the flow of the fluid, the height of the float indicating the rate of flow.

rotaplane ('rəʊtə,pleɪn) *n* an aircraft that derives its lift from freely revolving rotor blades.

Rotarian (rəʊ'tɛərɪən) *n* **1** a member of a Rotary Club. ◆ *adj* **2** of or relating to Rotary Clubs or their members. ▸ **Ro'tarianism** *n*

rotary ('rəʊtərɪ) *adj* **1** of, relating to, or operating by rotation. **2** turning or able to turn; revolving. ◆ *n, pl* **-ries. 3** a part of a machine that rotates about an axis. **4** *U.S. and Canadian.* another term for **roundabout** (for traffic). **[C18:** from Medieval Latin *rotārius,* from Latin *rota* a wheel**]**

rotary clothesline *or* **clothes dryer** *n* an apparatus of radiating spokes that support lines on which clothes are hung to dry.

Rotary Club *n* any of the local clubs that form **Rotary International,** an international association of professional and businessmen founded in the U.S. in 1905 to promote community service.

rotary engine *n* **1** an internal-combustion engine having radial cylinders that rotate about a fixed crankshaft. **2** an engine, such as a turbine or wankel engine, in which power is transmitted directly to rotating components.

rotary plough *or* **tiller** *n* an implement with a series of blades mounted on a power-driven shaft, used to break up soil or weeds.

rotary press *n* a machine for printing from a revolving cylinder, or a plate attached to one, usually onto a continuous strip of paper.

rotary pump *n Engineering.* a pump in which a liquid is displaced through a shaped stator by a shaped rotor.

rotate *vb* (rəʊ'teɪt). **1** to turn or cause to turn around an axis, line, or point; revolve or spin. **2** to follow or cause to follow a set order or sequence. **3** to replace one group of personnel with another. ◆ *adj* ('rəʊteɪt). **4** *Botany.* designating a corolla the united petals of which radiate from a central point like the spokes of a wheel. ▸ **ro'tatable** *adj*

rotation (rəʊ'teɪʃən) *n* **1** the act of rotating; rotary motion. **2** a regular cycle of events in a set order or sequence. **3** a planned sequence of cropping according to which the crops grown in successive seasons on the same land are varied so as to make a balanced demand on its resources of fertility. **4** *Maths.* **4a** a circular motion of a configuration about a given point or line, without a change in shape. **4b** a transformation in which the coordinate axes are rotated by a fixed angle about the origin. **4c** another name for **curl** (sense 11). Abbrev. (for c.): **rot** **5a** the spinning motion of a body, such as a planet, about an internal axis. Compare **revolution** (sense 5a). **5b** one complete turn in such motion. ▸ **ro'tational** *adj*

rotator (rəʊ'teɪtə) *n* **1** a person, device, or part that rotates or causes rotation. **2** *Anatomy.* any of various muscles that revolve a part on its axis.

rotatory ('rəʊtətərɪ, -trɪ) *or (less commonly)* **rotative** ('rəʊtətɪv) *adj* of, relating to, possessing, or causing rotation. ▸ **'rotatively** *adv*

Rotavator *or* **Rotovator** ('rəʊtəˌveɪtə) *n Trademark.* a type of machine with rotating blades that will break up soil, as on rough or uncultivated ground, or work surface material into the soil. [C20: original form *Rotavator,* from *rota(ry) (culti)vator*]

Rotblat ('rɒtblæt) *n* **Joseph.** See **Pugwash conferences.**

rote[1] (rəʊt) *n* **1** a habitual or mechanical routine or procedure. **2 by rote.** by repetition; by heart (often in the phrase **learn by rote**). [C14: origin unknown]

rote[2] (rəʊt) *n* an ancient violin-like musical instrument; crwth. [C13: from Old French *rote,* of Germanic origin; related to Old High German *rotta,* Middle Dutch *rotte*]

rotenone ('rəʊtɪˌnəʊn) *n* a white odourless crystalline substance extracted from the roots of derris: a powerful insecticide. Formula: $C_{23}H_{22}O_6$; relative density: 1.27; melting pt.: 163°C. [C20: from Japanese *rōten* derris + -ONE]

rotgut ('rɒtˌgʌt) *n Facetious slang.* alcoholic drink, esp. spirits, of inferior quality.

Roth (rɒθ) *n* **Philip.** born 1933, U.S. novelist. His works include *Goodbye, Columbus* (1959), *Portnoy's Complaint* (1969), *My Life as a Man* (1974), *Sabbath's Theater* (1995), and *I Married a Communist* (1998).

Rotherham ('rɒðərəm) *n* **1** an industrial town in N England, in Rotherham unitary authority, South Yorkshire. Pop.: 121 380 (1991). **2** a unitary authority in N England, in South Yorkshire. Pop.: 256 300 (1996 est.). Area: 283 sq. km (109 sq. miles).

Rothermere ('rɒðəˌmɪə) *n* **Viscount.** title of *Harold Sidney Harmsworth.* 1868–1940, British newspaper magnate.

Rothesay ('rɒθsɪ) *n* a town in SW Scotland, in Argyll and Bute, on the E coast of Bute Island. Pop.: 5264 (1991).

Rothko ('rɒθkəʊ) *n* **Mark.** 1903–70, U.S. abstract expressionist painter, born in Russia.

Rothschild ('rɒθtʃaɪld, 'rɒθs-) *n* a powerful family of European Jewish bankers, prominent members of which were: **1 Lionel Nathan,** Baron de Rothschild. 1809–79, British banker and first Jewish member of Parliament. **2** his grandfather **Meyer Amschel** ('maɪər 'amʃəl). 1743–1812, German financier and founder of the Rothschild banking firm. **3** his son, **Nathan Meyer,** Baron de Rothschild. 1777–1836, British banker, born in Germany.

roti ('rəʊtɪ, 'ruːtɪ) *n* (in India and the Caribbean) a type of unleavened bread. [from Hindi: bread]

rotifer ('rəʊtɪfə) *n* any minute aquatic multicellular invertebrate of the phylum *Rotifera,* having a ciliated wheel-like organ used in feeding and locomotion: common constituents of freshwater plankton. Also called: **wheel animalcule.** [C18: from New Latin *Rotifera,* from Latin *rota* wheel + *ferre* to bear] ▸ **rotiferal** (rəʊ'tɪfərəl) *or* **ro'tiferous** *adj*

rotisserie (rəʊ'tɪsərɪ) *n* **1** a rotating spit on which meat, poultry, etc., can be cooked. **2** a shop or restaurant where meat is roasted to order. [C19: from French, from Old French *rostir* to ROAST]

rotl ('rɒtᵊl) *n, pl* **rotls** *or* **artal** ('ɑːtɑːl). a unit of weight used in Muslim countries, varying in value between about one and five pounds. [C17: from Arabic *ratl,* perhaps from Greek *litra* a pound]

rotogravure (ˌrəʊtəʊgrə'vjʊə) *n* **1** a printing process using a cylinder etched with many small recesses, from which ink is transferred to a moving web of paper, plastic, etc., in a rotary press. **2** printed material produced in this way, esp. magazines. ◆ Often shortened to **roto.** [C20: from Latin *rota* wheel + GRAVURE]

roton ('rəʊtɒn) *n Physics.* a quantum of rotational energy.

rotor ('rəʊtə) *n* **1** the rotating member of a machine or device, esp. the armature of a motor or generator or the rotating assembly of a turbine. Compare **stator.** **2** a device having blades radiating from a central hub that is rotated to produce thrust to lift and propel a helicopter. **3** the revolving arm of the distributor of an internal-combustion engine. **4** a violent rolling wave of air occurring in the lee of a mountain or hill, in which the air rotates about a horizontal axis. [C20: shortened form of ROTATOR]

Rotorua (ˌrəʊtə'ruːə) *n* a city in New Zealand, on N central North Island at the SW end of Lake Rotorua: centre of forestry; noted for volcanic activity. Pop.: 54 700 (1994).

rotovate *or* **rotavate** ('rəʊtəˌveɪt) *vb (tr)* to break up (the surface of the earth, or an area of ground) using a Rotovator.

rotten ('rɒtᵊn) *adj* **1** affected with rot; decomposing, decaying, or putrid. **2** breaking up, esp. through age or hard use; disintegrating: *rotten ironwork.* **3** morally despicable or corrupt. **4** untrustworthy, disloyal, or treacherous. **5** *Informal.* unpleasant, unfortunate, or nasty: *rotten luck; rotten weather.* **6** *Informal.* unsatisfactory or poor: *rotten workmanship.* **7** *Informal.* miserably unwell. **8** *Informal.* distressed, uncomfortable, and embarrassed: *I felt rotten when I told him to go.* **9** (of rocks, soils, etc.) soft and crumbling, esp. as a result of weathering. **10** *Slang, chiefly Austral. and N.Z.* intoxicated; drunk. ◆ *adv* *Informal.* **11** extremely; very much: *men fancy her rotten.* [C13: from Old Norse *rottin;* related to Old English *rotian* to ROT[1]] ▸ **'rottenly** *adv* ▸ **'rottenness** *n*

rotten borough *n* (before the Reform Act of 1832) any of certain English parliamentary constituencies with only a very few electors. Compare **pocket borough.**

rottenstone ('rɒtᵊnˌstəʊn) *n* a much-weathered limestone, rich in silica: used in powdered form for polishing metal.

rotter ('rɒtə) *n Slang, chiefly Brit.* a worthless, unpleasant, or despicable person.

Rotterdam ('rɒtəˌdæm) *n* a port in the SW Netherlands, in South Holland province: the second largest city of the Netherlands and one of the world's largest ports; oil refineries, shipbuilding yards, etc. Pop.: 592 745 (1996 est.).

Rottweiler ('rɒtˌvaɪlə) *n* a breed of large robustly built dog with a smooth coat of black with dark tan markings on the face, chest, and legs, and usually having a docked tail. [German, named after *Rottweil,* German city where the dog was originally bred]

rotund (rəʊ'tʌnd) *adj* **1** rounded or spherical in shape. **2** plump. **3** sonorous or grandiloquent; full in tone, style of speaking, etc. [C18: from Latin *rotundus* wheel-shaped, round, from *rota* wheel] ▸ **ro'tundity** *or* **ro'tundness** *n* ▸ **ro'tundly** *adv*

rotunda (rəʊ'tʌndə) *n* a building or room having a circular plan, esp. one that has a dome. [C17: from Italian *rotonda,* from Latin *rotundus* round, from *rota* a wheel]

ROU *international car registration for* (Republic of) Uruguay.

Rouault (ruː'əʊ; *French* rwo) *n* **Georges** (ʒɔrʒ). 1871–1958, French expressionist artist. His work is deeply religious; it includes much stained glass.

Roubaix (*French* rubɛ) *n* a city in N France near the Belgian border: forms, with Tourcoing, a large industrial conurbation. Pop.: 97 746 (1990).

Roubiliac *or* **Roubillac** (rubijak) *n* **Louis-François** (lwifrɑ̃swa). ?1695–1762, French sculptor: lived chiefly in England: his sculptures include the statue of Handel in Vauxhall Gardens (1737).

rouble *or* **ruble** ('ruːbᵊl) *n* **1** the standard monetary unit of Belarus and Russia, divided into 100 kopecks. **2** the standard monetary unit of Tajikistan, divided into 100 tanga. [C16: from Russian *rubl* silver bar, from Old Russian *rublĭ* bar, block of wood, from *rubiti* to cut up]

rouche (ruːʃ) *n* a variant spelling of **ruche.**

roucou ('ruːˌkuː) *n* another name for **annatto.** [C17: via French from Tupi *urucú*]

roué ('ruːeɪ) *n* a debauched or lecherous man; rake. [C19: from French, literally: one broken on the wheel, from *rouer,* from Latin *rotāre* to revolve, from *rota* a wheel; with reference to the fate deserved by a debauchee]

Rouen (*French* rwɑ̃) *n* a city in N France, on the River Seine: the chief river port of France; became capital of the duchy of Normandy in 912; scene of the burning of Joan of Arc (1431); university (1964). Pop.: 105 470 (1990).

rouge (ruːʒ) *n* **1** a red powder, used as a cosmetic for adding redness to the cheeks. **2** short for **jeweller's rouge.** ◆ *vb (tr)* **3** to apply rouge to. [C18: from French: red, from Latin *rubeus*]

Rouge Croix (ˌruːʒ 'krwɑː) *n* a pursuivant at the English college of arms.

Rouge Dragon (ˌruːʒ 'drægən) *n* a pursuivant at the English college of arms.

rouge et noir ('ruːʒ eɪ 'nwɑː; *French* ruʒ e nwar) *n* a card game in which the players put their stakes on any of two red and two black diamond-shaped spots marked on the table. Also called: **trente et quarante.** [French, literally: red and black]

Rouget de Lisle (*French* ruʒɛ də lil) *n* **Claude Joseph** (klod ʒozɛf). 1760–1836, French army officer: composer of the *Marseillaise* (1792), the French national anthem.

rough (rʌf) *adj* **1** (of a surface) not smooth; uneven or irregular. **2** (of ground) covered with scrub, boulders, etc. **3** denoting or taking place on uncultivated ground: *rough grazing; rough shooting.* **4** shaggy or hairy. **5** turbulent; agitated: *a rough sea.* **6** (of the performance or motion of something) uneven; irregular: *a rough engine.* **7** (of behaviour or character) rude, coarse, ill mannered, inconsiderate, or violent. **8** harsh or sharp: *rough words.* **9** *Informal.* severe or unpleasant: *a rough lesson.* **10** (of work, a task, etc.) requiring physical rather than mental effort. **11** *Informal.* ill or physically upset: *he felt rough after an evening of heavy drinking.* **12** unfair or unjust: *rough luck.* **13** harsh or grating to the ear. **14** harsh to the taste. **15** without refinement, luxury, etc. **16** not polished or perfected in any detail; rudimentary; not elaborate: *rough workmanship; rough justice.* **17** not prepared or dressed: *rough gemstones.* **18** (of a guess, estimate, etc.) approximate. **19** *Austral. informal.* (of a chance) not good. **20** having the sound of *h;* aspirated. **21 rough on.** *Informal, chiefly Brit.* **21a** severe towards. **21b** unfortunate for (a person). **22 the rough side of one's tongue.** harsh words; a reprimand, rebuke, or verbal attack. ◆ *n* **23** rough ground. **24** a sketch or preliminary piece of artwork. **25** an unfinished or crude state (esp. in the phrase **in the rough**). **26 the rough.** *Golf.* the part of the course bordering the fairways where the grass is untrimmed. **27** the side of a tennis or squash racket on which the binding strings form an uneven line. **28** *Informal.* a rough or violent person; thug. **29** the unpleasant side of something (esp. in the phrase **take the rough with the smooth**). ◆ *adv* **30** in a rough manner; roughly. **31 sleep rough.** to spend the night in the open; be without a home or without shelter. ◆ *vb* **32** (*tr*) to make rough; roughen. **33** (*tr*; foll. by *out, in*, etc.) to prepare (a sketch, report, piece of work, etc.) in preliminary form. **34 rough it.** *Informal.* to live without the usual comforts or conveniences of life. ◆ See also **rough out, rough up.** [Old English *rūh*; related to Old Norse *ruksa*, Middle Dutch *rūge, rūwe*, German *rauh*] ▸ **'roughness** *n*

roughage ('rʌfɪdʒ) *n* **1** the coarse indigestible constituents of food or fodder, which provide bulk to the diet and aid digestion. See also **dietary fibre. 2** any rough or coarse material.

rough-and-ready *adj* **1** crude, unpolished, or hastily prepared, but sufficient for the purpose. **2** (of a person) without formality or refinement; rudely vigorous. ▸ **'rough-and-'readiness** *n*

rough-and-tumble *n* **1** a fight or scuffle without rules. ◆ *adj* **2** characterized by roughness, disorderliness, and disregard for rules or conventions.

rough breathing *n* (in Greek) the sign (ʿ) placed over an initial letter, or a second letter if the word begins with a diphthong, indicating that (in ancient Greek) it was pronounced with an *h*. Compare **smooth breathing.**

roughcast ('rʌfˌkɑːst) *n* **1** a coarse plaster used to cover the surface of an external wall. **2** any rough or preliminary form, model, etc. ◆ *adj* **3** covered with or denoting roughcast. ◆ *vb* **-casts, -casting, -cast. 4** to apply roughcast to (a wall, etc.). **5** to prepare in rough. **6** (*tr*) another word for **rough-hew.** ▸ **'roughˌcaster** *n*

rough collie *n* a large long-haired collie having a distinctive ruff and a long narrow head without a pronounced stop.

rough-cut *n* a first edited version of a film with the scenes in sequence and the soundtrack synchronized.

rough diamond *n* **1** an unpolished diamond. **2** an intrinsically trustworthy or good person with uncouth manners or dress.

rough-dry *adj* **1** (of clothes or linen) dried ready for pressing. ◆ *vb* **-dries, -drying, -dried. 2** (*tr*) to dry (clothes or linen) without smoothing or pressing.

roughen ('rʌfᵊn) *vb* to make or become rough.

rough fish *n* a fish that is neither a sport fish nor useful as food or bait for sport fish.

rough-hew *vb* **-hews, -hewing, -hewed; -hewed** *or* **-hewn.** (*tr*) **1** to cut or hew (timber, stone, etc.) roughly without finishing the surface. **2** Also: **roughcast.** to shape roughly or crudely.

roughhouse ('rʌfˌhaʊs) *Slang.* ◆ *n* **1** rough, disorderly, or noisy behaviour. ◆ *vb* **2** to treat (someone) in a boisterous or rough way.

roughie[1] ('rʌfɪ) *n* a small food fish of the family *Arripididae*, found in southern and western Australian waters. Also called: **orange roughie.**

roughie[2] *n Austral. slang.* **1** something unfair, esp. a trick: *he put a roughie over.* **2** (in horse racing) an outsider that wins.

roughish ('rʌfɪʃ) *adj* somewhat rough.

rough-legged buzzard *n* a buzzard, *Buteo lagopus*, of Europe, Asia, and North America, having feathers covering its legs.

roughly ('rʌflɪ) *adv* **1** without being exact or fully authenticated; approximately: *roughly half the candidates were successful.* **2** in a clumsy, coarse, or violent manner: *his captors did not treat him roughly.* **3** in a crude or primitive manner: *a slab of roughly hewn stone.*

rough music *n* (formerly) a loud cacophony created with tin pans, drums, etc., esp. as a protest or demonstration of indignation outside someone's house.

roughneck ('rʌfˌnɛk) *n Slang.* **1** a rough or violent person; thug. **2** a worker in an oil-drilling operation.

rough out *vb* (*tr, adv*) **1** See **rough** (sense 33). **2** *Engineering.* to machine (a workpiece, such as a casting or forging) with heavy cuts leaving a rough surface to be finished.

rough passage *n* **1** a stormy sea journey. **2** a difficult or testing time.

rough puff pastry *n* a rich flaky pastry made with butter and used for piecrusts, flans, etc.

roughrider ('rʌfˌraɪdə) *n* a rider of wild or unbroken horses.

roughshod ('rʌfˌʃɒd) *adj* **1** (of a horse) shod with rough-bottomed shoes to prevent sliding. ◆ *adv* **2 ride roughshod over.** to domineer over or act with complete disregard for.

rough spin *n N.Z. informal.* hard or unfair treatment.

rough-spoken *adj* rude or uncouth in speech; blunt.

rough stuff *n Informal.* violence.

rough trade *n Slang.* (in homosexual use) a tough or violent sexual partner, esp. a lorry driver, construction worker, or docker, casually picked up.

rough up *vb* (*tr, adv*) **1** *Informal.* to treat violently; beat up. **2** to cause (feathers, hair, etc.) to stand up by rubbing against the grain.

roulade (ruːˈlɑːd) *n* **1** a slice of meat rolled, esp. around a stuffing, and cooked. **2** an elaborate run in vocal music. [C18: from French, literally: a rolling, from *rouler* to ROLL]

rouleau (ˈruːləʊ) *n, pl* **-leaux** (-ləʊ, -ləʊz) *or* **-leaus. 1** a roll of paper containing coins. **2** (*often pl*) a roll of ribbon. [C17: from French, from *role* ROLL]

Roulers (ruːˈlɛəz; *French* rulɛrs) *n* a city in NW Belgium, in West Flanders province: electronics. Pop.: 53 617 (1995 est.). Flemish name: **Roeselare.**

roulette (ruːˈlɛt) *n* **1** a gambling game in which a ball is dropped onto a spinning horizontal wheel divided into 37 or 38 coloured and numbered slots, with players betting on the slot into which the ball will fall. **2a** a toothed wheel for making a line of perforations. **2b** a tiny slit made by such a wheel on a sheet of stamps as an aid to tearing it apart. **3** a curve generated by a point on one curve rolling on another. ◆ *vb* (*tr*) **4** to use a roulette on (something), as in engraving, making stationery, etc. [C18: from French, from *rouelle* a little wheel, from *roue* a wheel, from Latin *rota*]

Roumania (ruːˈmeɪnɪə) *n* a variant of **Romania.** ▸ **Rouˈmanian** *adj, n*

Roumelia (ruːˈmiːlɪə) *n* a variant spelling of **Rumelia.**

round (raʊnd) *adj* **1** having a flat circular shape, as a disc or hoop. **2** having the shape of a sphere or ball. **3** curved; not angular. **4** involving or using circular motion. **5** (*prenominal*) complete; entire: *a round dozen.* **6** *Maths.* **6a** forming or expressed by an integer or whole number, with no fraction. **6b** expressed to the nearest ten, hundred, or thousand: *in round figures.* **7** (of a sum of money) considerable; ample. **8** fully depicted or developed, as a character in a book. **9** full and plump: *round cheeks.* **10** (of sound) full and sonorous. **11** (of pace) brisk; lively. **12** (*prenominal*) (of speech) candid; straightforward; unmodified: *a round assertion.* **13** (of a vowel) pronounced with rounded lips. ◆ *n* **14** a round shape or object. **15 in the round. 15a** in full detail. **15b** *Theatre.* with the audience all round the stage. **16** a session, as of a negotiation: *a round of talks.* **17** a series, cycle, or sequence: *a giddy round of parties.* **18 the daily round.** the usual activities of one's day. **19** a stage of a competition: *he was eliminated in the first round.* **20** (*often pl*) a series of calls, esp. in a set order: *a doctor's rounds; a milkman's round.* **21** a playing of all the holes on a golf course. **22** a single turn of play by each player, as in a card game. **23** one of a number of periods constituting a boxing, wrestling, or other match, each usually lasting three minutes. **24** *Archery.* a specified number of arrows shot from a specified distance. **25** a single discharge by a number of guns or a single gun. **26** a bullet, blank cartridge, or other charge of ammunition. **27** a number of drinks bought at one time for a group of people. **28** a single slice of bread or toast or two slices making a single serving of sandwiches. **29** a general outburst of applause, cheering, etc. **30** movement in a circle or around an axis. **31** *Music.* a part song in which the voices follow each other at equal intervals at the same pitch. **32** a sequence of bells rung in order of treble to tenor. Compare **change** (sense 29). **33** a dance in which the dancers move in a circle. **34** a cut of beef from the thigh between the rump and the shank. **35 go** *or* **make the rounds. 35a** to go from place to place, as in making deliveries or social calls. **35b** (of information, rumour, etc.) to be passed around, so as to be generally known. ◆ *prep* **36** surrounding, encircling, or enclosing: *a band round her head.* **37** on all or most sides of: *to look round one.* **38** on or outside the circumference or perimeter of: *the stands round the racecourse.* **39** situated at various points in: *a lot of shelves round the house.* **40** from place to place in: *driving round Ireland.* **41** somewhere in or near: *to stay round the house.* **42** making a circuit or partial circuit about: *the ring road round the town.* **43** reached by making a partial circuit about something: *the shop round the corner.* **44** revolving round a centre or axis: *the earth's motion round its axis.* **45** so as to have a basis in: *the story is built round a good plot.* ◆ *adv* **46** on all or most sides: *the garden is fenced all round; the crowd gathered round.* **47** on or outside the circumference or perimeter: *the racing track is two miles round.* **48** in all directions from a point of reference: *he owns the land for ten miles round.* **49** to all members of a group: *pass the food round.* **50** in rotation or revolution: *the wheels turn round.* **51** by a circuitous route: *the road to the farm goes round by the pond.* **52** to a specific place: *she came round to see me.* **53 all year round.** throughout the year; in every month. ◆ *vb* **54** to make or become round. **55** (*tr*) to encircle; surround. **56** to move or cause to move with circular motion: *to round a bend.* **57** (*tr*) **57a** to pronounce (a speech sound) with rounded lips. **57b** to purse (the lips). ◆ See also **round down, round off, round on, round out, round up.** [C13: from Old French *ront*, from Latin *rotundus* round, from *rota* a wheel] ▸ **'roundness** *n*

USAGE See at **around.**

roundabout ('raʊndəˌbaʊt) *n* **1** *Brit.* a revolving circular platform provided with wooden animals, seats, etc., on which people ride for amusement; merry-go-round. **2** a road junction in which traffic streams circulate around a central island. U.S. and Canadian name: **traffic circle. 3** an informal name for **boring mill.** ◆ *adj* **4** indirect or circuitous; devious. ◆ *adv, prep* **round about. 5** on all sides: *spectators standing round about.* **6** approximately: *at round about 5 o'clock.*

round and round *adv, prep* following a circuitous or circular course for a comparatively long time, esp. vainly.

round angle *n* another name for **perigon.**

round-arm *adj, adv Cricket.* denoting or using bowling with the arm held more or less horizontal.

round clam *n* another name for the **quahog.**

round dance *n* **1** a dance in which the dancers form a circle. **2** a ballroom dance, such as the waltz, in which couples revolve.

round down *vb* (*tr, adv*) to lower (a number) to the nearest whole number or ten, hundred, or thousand below it. Compare **round up** (sense 2).

rounded ('raʊndɪd) *adj* **1** round or curved. **2** having been made round or curved. **3** full, mature, or complete. **4** (of the lips) pursed, as in pronouncing the sound (uː). **5** (of a speech sound) articulated with rounded lips. ▸ **'roundedly** *adv* ▸ **'roundedness** *n*

roundel ('raʊndᵊl) *n* **1** a form of rondeau consisting of three stanzas each of three lines with a refrain after the first and the third. **2** a circular identifying mark in national colours on military aircraft. **3** a small ornamental circular window, panel, medallion, plate, disc, etc. **4** a round plate of armour used to protect the armpit. **5** *Heraldry.* a charge in the shape of a circle. **6** another word for **roundelay** (sense 1). [C13: from Old French *rondel* a little circle; see RONDEL]

roundelay ('raʊndɪˌleɪ) *n* **1** Also called: **roundel.** a slow medieval dance performed in a circle. **2** a song in which a line or phrase is repeated as a refrain. [C16: from Old French *rondelet* a little rondel, from *rondel*; also influenced by LAY[4]]

rounder ('raʊndə) *n* **1** a run round all four bases after one hit in rounders. **2** a tool or machine for rounding edges or surfaces.

rounders ('raʊndəz) *n* (*functioning as sing*) *Brit.* a ball game in which players run between posts after hitting the ball, scoring a **rounder** if they run round all four before the ball is retrieved.

round hand *n* a style of handwriting with large rounded curves. Compare **italic, copperplate** (sense 3).

Roundhead ('raʊnd,hɛd) *n English history.* a supporter of Parliament against Charles I during the Civil War. Compare **Cavalier.** [referring to their short-cut hair]

roundhouse ('raʊnd,haʊs) *n* **1** a circular building in which railway locomotives are serviced or housed, radial tracks being fed by a central turntable. **2** *Boxing slang.* **2a** a swinging punch or style of punching. **2b** (*as modifier*): *a roundhouse style.* **3** *Pinochle, U.S.* a meld of all four kings and queens. **4** an obsolete word for **jail.** **5** *Obsolete.* a cabin on the quarterdeck of a sailing ship.

rounding ('raʊndɪŋ) *n Computing.* a process in which a number is approximated as the closest number that can be expressed using the number of bits or digits available.

rounding error *n Computing.* an error introduced into a computation by the need to perform rounding.

roundish ('raʊndɪʃ) *adj* somewhat round.

roundlet ('raʊndlɪt) *n Literary.* a small circle. [C14: from Old French *rondelet,* from Old French RONDEL]

roundly ('raʊndlɪ) *adv* **1** frankly, bluntly, or thoroughly: *to be roundly criticized.* **2** in a round manner or so as to be round.

round off *vb* (*tr, adv*) **1** (often foll. by *with*) to bring to a satisfactory conclusion; complete, esp. agreeably: *we rounded off the evening with a brandy.* **2** to make round or less jagged.

round on *vb* (*intr, prep*) to attack or reply to (someone) with sudden irritation or anger.

round out *vb* (*tr, adv*) **1** to make or become bigger or plumper; fill out, esp. so as to be symmetrical. **2** to round up (a number).

round robin *n* **1** a letter, esp. a petition or protest, having the signatures in a circle in order to disguise the order of signing. **2** any letter or petition signed by a number of people. **3** *U.S. and Canadian.* a tournament, as in a competitive game or sport, in which each player plays against every other player.

round-shouldered *adj* denoting a faulty posture characterized by drooping shoulders and a slight forward bending of the back.

roundsman ('raʊndzmən) *n, pl* **-men. 1** *Brit.* a person who makes rounds, as for inspection or to deliver goods. **2** *Austral. and N.Z.* a reporter covering a particular district or topic.

round table *n* **a** a meeting of parties or people on equal terms for discussion. **b** (*as modifier*): *a round-table conference.*

Round Table *n* **the. 1** (in Arthurian legend) the table of King Arthur, shaped so that his knights could sit around it without any having precedence. **2** Arthur and his knights collectively. **3** one of an organization of clubs of young business and professional men who meet in order to further social and business activities and charitable work. **4** (in New Zealand) an organization of businessmen supporting policies of the New Right.

round-the-clock *adj* (*or as adv* **round the clock**) throughout the day and night.

round top *n* a platform round the masthead of a sailing ship.

round tower *n* a freestanding circular stone belfry built in Ireland from the 10th century beside a monastery and used as a place of refuge.

round trip *n* a trip to a place and back again, esp. returning by a different route.

roundtripping ('raʊnd,trɪpɪŋ) *n Finance.* a form of trading in which a company borrows a sum of money from one source and takes advantage of a short-term rise in interest rates to make a profit by lending it to another.

round-trip ticket *n* the usual U.S. and Canadian name for **return ticket.**

round up *vb* (*tr, adv*) **1** to gather (animals, suspects, etc.) together: *to round ponies up.* **2** to raise (a number) to the nearest whole number or ten, hundred, or thousand above it. Compare **round down.** ◆ *n* **roundup. 3** the act of gathering together livestock, esp. cattle, so that they may be branded, counted, or sold. **4** a collection of suspects or criminals by the police, esp. in a raid. **5** any similar act of collecting or bringing together: *a roundup of today's news.*

roundwood ('raʊnd,wʊd) *n Forestry.* small pieces of timber (about 5–15 cm, or 2–6 in.) in diameter; small logs.

roundworm ('raʊnd,wɜːm) *n* any nematode worm, esp. *Ascaris lumbricoides,* a common intestinal parasite of man and pigs.

roup[1] (ruːp) *n Vet. science.* any of various chronic respiratory diseases of birds, esp. poultry. [C16: of unknown origin] ▸ **'roupy** *adj*

roup[2] (raʊp) *Scot. and northern English dialect.* ◆ *vb* (*tr*) **1** to sell by auction. ◆ *n* **2** an auction. [C16 (originally: to shout): of Scandinavian origin; compare Icelandic *raupa* to boast]

rouse[1] (raʊz) *vb* **1** to bring (oneself or another person) out of sleep, unconsciousness, etc., or (of a person) to come to consciousness in this way. **2** (*tr*) to provoke, stir, or excite: *to rouse someone's anger.* **3 rouse oneself.** to become active or energetic. **4** *Hunting.* to start or cause to start from cover: *to rouse game birds.* **5** (*intr*) *Falconry.* (of hawks) to ruffle the feathers and cause them to stand briefly on end (a sign of contentment). **6** (raʊs). (*intr;* foll. by *on*) *Austral.* to speak scoldingly or rebukingly (to). ◆ *n* **7** *Chiefly U.S.* another term for **reveille.** [C15 (in sense 5): origin obscure] ▸ **rousedness** ('raʊzɪdnɪs) *n* ▸ **'rouser** *n*

rouse[2] (raʊz) *n Archaic.* **1** an alcoholic drink, esp. a full measure. **2** another word for **carousal.** [C17: probably a variant of CAROUSE (as in the phrase *drink a rouse,* erroneous for *drink carouse*);compare Danish *drikke en rus* to become drunk, German *Rausch* drunkenness]

rouseabout ('raʊsə,baʊt) *n Austral. and N.Z.* an unskilled labourer in a shearing shed. Also called: **roustabout.**

rousing ('raʊzɪŋ) *adj* tending to rouse or excite; lively, brisk, or vigorous: *a rousing chorus.* ▸ **'rousingly** *adv*

Rousseau (*French* ruso) *n* **1 Henri** (ɑ̃ri), known as *le Douanier.* 1844–1910, French painter, who created bold dreamlike pictures, often of exotic landscapes in a naive style. Among his works are *Sleeping Gypsy* (1897) and *Jungle with a Lion* (1904–06). He also worked as a customs official. **2 Jean Jacques** (ʒɑ̃ ʒak). 1712–78, French philosopher and writer, born in Switzerland, who strongly influenced the theories of the French Revolution and the romantics. Many of his ideas spring from his belief in the natural goodness of man, whom he felt was warped by society. His works include *Du contrat social* (1762), *Émile* (1762), and his *Confessions* (1782). **3 Théodore** (teɔdɔr). 1812–67, French landscape painter: leader of the Barbizon school.

Roussillon (*French* rusijɔ̃) *n* a former province of S France: united with Aragon in 1172; passed to the French crown in 1659; now forms part of the region of Languedoc-Roussillon.

roust (raʊst) *vb* (*tr;* often foll. by *out*) to rout or stir, as out of bed. [C17: perhaps an alteration of ROUSE[1]]

roustabout ('raʊstə,baʊt) *n* **1** *Chiefly U.S. and Canadian.* an unskilled labourer on an oil rig. **2** *Austral.* another word for **rouseabout.**

rout[1] (raʊt) *n* **1** an overwhelming defeat. **2** a disorderly retreat. **3** a noisy rabble. **4** *Law.* a group of three or more people proceeding to commit an illegal act. **5** *Archaic.* a large party or social gathering. ◆ *vb* **6** (*tr*) to defeat and cause to flee in confusion. [C13: from Anglo-Norman *rute,* from Old French: disorderly band, from Latin *ruptus* broken, from *rumpere* to burst; see ROUTE]

rout[2] (raʊt) *vb* **1** to dig over or turn up (something), esp. (of an animal) with the snout; root. **2** (*tr;* usually foll. by *out* or *up*) to get or find by searching. **3** (*tr;* usually foll. by *out*) to force or drive out: *they routed him out of bed at midnight.* **4** (*tr;* often foll. by *out*) to hollow or gouge out. **5** (*intr*) to search, poke, or rummage. [C16: variant of ROOT[2]]

route (ruːt) *n* **1** the choice of roads taken to get to a place. **2** a regular journey travelled. **3** (*cap.*) *U.S.* a main road between cities: *Route 66.* **4** *Mountaineering.* the direction or course taken by a climb. **5** *Med.* the means (mouth or injection) by which a drug or agent is administered or enters the body: *oral route.* ◆ *vb* **routes, routing** *or* **routeing, routed.** (*tr*) **6** to plan the route of; send by a particular route. [C13: from Old French *rute,* from Vulgar Latin *rupta via* (unattested), literally: a broken (established) way, from Latin *ruptus* broken, from *rumpere* to break, burst]

USAGE When forming the present participle or verbal noun from the verb *to route* it is preferable to retain the *e* in order to distinguish the word from *routing,* the present participle or verbal noun from *rout*[1], to defeat or *rout*[2], to dig, rummage: *the routeing of buses from the city centre to the suburbs.* The spelling *routing* in this sense is, however, sometimes encountered, esp. in American English.

routemarch ('ruːt,mɑːtʃ) *n* **1** *Military.* a long training march. **2** *Informal.* any long exhausting walk. ◆ *vb* **3** to go or send on a routemarch.

router[1] ('raʊtə) *n* any of various tools or machines for hollowing out, cutting grooves, etc.

router[2] ('ruːtə) *n Computing.* a device that allows packets of data to be moved efficiently between two points on a network.

routh *or* **rowth** (raʊθ) *Scot.* ◆ *n* **1** abundance. ◆ *adj* **2** abundant; plentiful. [C18: of uncertain origin]

routine (ruː'tiːn) *n* **1** a usual or regular method of procedure, esp. one that is unvarying. **2** *Computing.* a program or part of a program performing a specific function: *an input routine; an output routine.* **3** a set sequence of dance steps. **4** *Informal.* a hackneyed or insincere speech. ◆ *adj* **5** of, relating to, or characteristic of routine. [C17: from Old French, from *route* a customary way, ROUTE] ▸ **rou'tinely** *adv*

roux (ruː) *n* a mixture of equal amounts of fat and flour, heated, blended, and used as a basis for sauces. [C19: from French: brownish, from Latin *russus* RUSSET]

rove[1] (rəʊv) *vb* **1** to wander about (a place) with no fixed direction; roam. **2** (*intr*) (of the eyes) to look around; wander. **3 have a roving eye.** to show a widespread amorous interest in the opposite sex. **4** (*intr*) *Australian Rules football.* to play as a rover. ◆ *n* **5** the act of roving. [C15 *roven* (in archery) to shoot at a target chosen at random (C16: to wander, stray), from Scandinavian; compare Icelandic *rāfa* to wander]

rove[2] (rəʊv) *vb* **1** (*tr*) to pull out and twist (fibres of wool, cotton, etc.) lightly, as before spinning or in carding. ◆ *n* **2** wool, cotton, etc., thus prepared. [C18: of obscure origin]

rove[3] (rəʊv) *n* a metal plate through which a rivet is passed and then clenched over. [C15: from Scandinavian; compare Icelandic *ró*]

rove[4] (rəʊv) *vb* a past tense and past participle of **reeve**[2].

rove beetle *n* any beetle of the family *Staphylinidae,* characterized by very short elytra and an elongated body: typically they are of carnivorous or scavenging habits.

rove-over *adj Prosody.* (in sprung rhythm) denoting a metrical foot left incomplete at the end of one line and completed in the next.

rover[1] ('rəʊvə) *n* **1** a person who roves; wanderer. **2** *Archery.* a mark selected at random for use as a target. **3** *Croquet.* a ball that has been driven through all the hoops but has not yet hit the winning peg. **4** *Australian Rules football.* one of the three players in the ruck, usually smaller than the other two, selected for his agility in play. [C15: from ROVE[1]]

rover[2] ('rəʊvə) *n* a pirate or pirate ship. [C14: probably from Middle Dutch or Middle Low German, from *roven* to rob]

rover[3] ('rəʊvə) *n* a machine for roving wool, cotton, etc., or a person who operates such a machine. [C18: from ROVE[2]]

Rover *or* **Rover Scout** ('rəʊvə) *n Brit.* the former name for **Venture Scout.**

roving commission *n* authority or power given in a general area, without precisely defined terms of reference.

row[1] (rəʊ) *n* **1** an arrangement of persons or things in a line: *a row of chairs.* **2a** *Chiefly Brit.* a street, esp. a narrow one lined with identical houses. **2b** (*cap. when part of a street name*): *Church Row.* **3** a line of seats, as in a cinema, theatre, etc. **4** *Maths.* a horizontal linear arrangement of numbers, quantities, or terms, esp. in a determinant or matrix. **5** a horizontal rank of squares on a chessboard or draughtboard. **6 in a row.** in succession; one after the other: *he won two gold medals in a row.* **7 a hard row to hoe.** a difficult task or assignment. [Old English *rāw, rǣw;* related to Old High German *rīga* line, Lithuanian *raiwe* strip]

row[2] (rəʊ) *vb* **1** to propel (a boat) by using oars. **2** (*tr*) to carry (people, goods, etc.) in a rowing boat. **3** to be propelled by means of (oars or oarsmen). **4** (*intr*) to take part in the racing of rowing boats as a sport, esp. in eights, in which each member of the crew pulls one oar. Compare **scull** (sense 6). **5** (*tr*) to race against in a boat propelled by oars: *Oxford row Cambridge every year.* ◆ *n* **6** an act, instance, period, or distance of rowing. **7** an excursion in a rowing boat. ◆ See also **row over.** [Old English *rōwan;* related to Middle Dutch *roien,* Middle High German *rüejen,* Old Norse *rōa,* Latin *rēmus* oar] ► **'rower** *n* ► **'rowing** *n*

row[3] (raʊ) *n* **1** a noisy quarrel or dispute. **2** a noisy disturbance; commotion: *we couldn't hear the music for the row next door.* **3** a reprimand. **4 give (someone) a row.** *Informal.* to scold (someone); tell off. ◆ *vb* **5** (*intr;* often foll. by *with*) to quarrel noisily. **6** (*tr*) *Archaic.* to reprimand. [C18: origin unknown]

rowan ('rəʊən, 'raʊ-) *n* another name for the (European) **mountain ash.** [C16: from Scandinavian; compare Norwegian *rogn, raun,* Old Norse *reynir*]

rowboat ('rəʊˌbəʊt) *n* the usual U.S. and Canadian word for **rowing boat.**

rowdy ('raʊdɪ) *adj* **-dier, -diest. 1** tending to create noisy disturbances; rough, loud, or disorderly: *a rowdy gang of football supporters.* ◆ *n, pl* **-dies. 2** a person who behaves in a rough disorderly fashion. [C19: originally U.S. slang, perhaps related to ROW[3]] ► **'rowdily** *adv* ► **'rowdiness** *n*

rowdyism ('raʊdɪɪzəm) *n* rowdy behaviour or tendencies or a habitual pattern of rowdy behaviour: *the problem of rowdyism at football matches.*

Rowe (rəʊ) *n* **Nicholas.** 1674–1718, English dramatist, who produced the first critical edition of Shakespeare; poet laureate (1715–18). His plays include *Tamerlane* (1702) and *The Fair Penitent* (1703).

rowel ('raʊəl) *n* **1** a small spiked wheel attached to a spur. **2** *Vet. science.* a piece of leather or other material inserted under the skin of a horse to cause a discharge. ◆ *vb* **-els, -elling, -elled** *or U.S.* **-els, -eling, -eled.** (*tr*) **3** to goad (a horse) using a rowel. **4** *Vet. science.* to insert a rowel in (the skin of a horse) to cause a discharge. [C14: from Old French *roel* a little wheel, from *roe* a wheel, from Latin *rota*]

rowen ('raʊən) *n* another word for **aftermath** (sense 2). [C14 *reywayn,* corresponding to Old French *regaïn,* from RE- + *gaïn* rowen, from *gaignier* to till, earn; see GAIN[1]]

row house (rəʊ) *n* a U.S. and Canadian term for **terraced house.**

rowing boat ('rəʊɪŋ) *n Chiefly Brit.* a small boat propelled by one or more pairs of oars. Usual U.S. and Canadian word: **rowboat.**

rowing machine *n* a device with oars and a sliding seat resembling a sculling boat, used to provide exercise.

Rowlandson ('rəʊləndsən) *n* **Thomas.** 1756–1827, English caricaturist, noted for the vigour of his attack on sordid aspects of contemporary society and on statesmen such as Napoleon.

Rowley ('rəʊlɪ, 'raʊ-) *n* **Thomas.** ?1586–?1642, English dramatist, who collaborated with John Ford and Thomas Dekker on *The Witch of Edmonton* (1621) and with Thomas Middleton on *The Changeling* (1622).

rowlock ('rɒlək) *n* a swivelling device attached to the gunwale of a boat that holds an oar in place and acts as a fulcrum during rowing. Usual U.S. and Canadian word: **oarlock.**

row over (rəʊ) *vb* (*intr, adv*) **1** to win a rowing race unopposed, by rowing the course. ◆ *n* **rowover. 2** the act of doing this.

rowth (raʊθ) *n, adj Scot.* a variant spelling of **routh.**

Roxas y Acuña (*Spanish* 'roxas i a'kuɲa) *n* **Manuel** (ma'nwel). 1892–1948, Philippine statesman; first president of the Republic of the Philippines (1946–48).

Roxburghshire ('rɒksbərəʃɪə, -ʃə) *n* (until 1975) a county of SE Scotland, now part of Scottish Borders council area.

Roy (rɔɪ) *n Austral. slang.* a trendy Australian male.

royal ('rɔɪəl) *adj* **1** of, relating to, or befitting a king, queen, or other monarch; regal. **2** (*prenominal; often cap.*) established, chartered by, under the patronage or in the service of royalty: *the Royal Society of St George.* **3** being a member of a royal family. **4** above the usual or normal in standing, size, quality, etc. **5** *Informal.* unusually good or impressive; first-rate. **6** *Nautical.* just above the topgallant (in the phrase **royal mast**). ◆ *n* **7** (*sometimes cap.*) *Informal.* a member of a royal family. **8** Also called: **royal stag.** a stag with antlers having 12 or more branches. **9** *Nautical.* a sail set next above the topgallant, on a royal mast. **10** a size of printing paper, 20 by 25 inches. **11** Also called: **small royal.** *Chiefly Brit.* a size of writing paper, 19 by 24 inches. **12** any of various book sizes, esp. 6¼ by 10 inches (**royal octavo**), 6¾ by 10¼ inches (**super royal octavo**), and (chiefly Brit.) 10 by 12½ inches (**royal quarto**) and 10¼ by 13½ inches (**super royal quarto**). [C14: from Old French *roial,* from Latin *rēgālis,* fit for a king, from *rēx* king; compare REGAL[1]] ► **'royally** *adv*

Royal Academy *n* a society founded by George III in 1768 to foster a national school of painting, sculpture, and design in England. Full name: **Royal Academy of Arts.**

Royal Air Force *n* the air force of the United Kingdom. Abbrev.: **RAF.**

Royal Air Force List *n Brit.* an official list of all serving commissioned officers of the RAF and reserve officers liable for recall.

Royal and Ancient Club *n* **the.** a golf club, headquarters of the sport's ruling body, based in St Andrews, Scotland. Abbrev.: **R&A.**

royal assent *n* (in Britain) the formal signing of an act of Parliament by the sovereign, by which it becomes law.

royal blue *n* **a** a deep blue colour. **b** (*as adj*): *a royal-blue carpet.*

royal burgh *n* (in Scotland) a burgh that was established by a royal charter granted directly by the sovereign.

Royal Canadian Mounted Police *n* the federal police force of Canada. Abbrev.: **RCMP.**

Royal Commission *n* (in Britain) a body set up by the monarch on the recommendation of the prime minister to gather information about the operation of existing laws or to investigate any social, educational, or other matter. The commission has prescribed terms of reference and reports to the government on how any change might be achieved.

royal duke *n* a duke who is also a royal prince, being a member of the royal family.

Royal Engineers *pl n* a branch of the British army that undertakes the building of fortifications, mines, bridges, and other engineering works. Abbrev.: **RE.**

royal fern *n* a fern, *Osmunda regalis,* of damp regions, having large fronds up to 2 metres (7 feet) in height, some of which are modified for bearing spores: family *Osmundaceae.*

royal flush *n Poker.* a hand made up of the five top honours of a suit.

Royal Highness *n* a title of honour used in addressing or referring to a member of a royal family.

royal icing *n Brit.* a hard white icing made from egg whites and icing sugar, used for coating and decorating cakes, esp. fruit cakes.

Royal Institution *n* a British society founded in 1799 for the dissemination of scientific knowledge.

royalist ('rɔɪəlɪst) *n* **1** a supporter of a monarch or monarchy, esp. a supporter of the Stuarts during the English Civil War. **2** *Informal.* an extreme reactionary or conservative: *an economic royalist.* ◆ *adj also* (*less commonly*) **royalistic. 3** of, characteristic of, or relating to royalists. ► **'royalism** *n*

royal jelly *n* a substance secreted by the pharyngeal glands of worker bees and fed to all larvae when very young and to larvae destined to become queens throughout their development.

Royal Leamington Spa *n* the official name of **Leamington Spa.**

Royal Marines *pl n Brit.* a corps of soldiers specially trained in amphibious warfare. Abbrev.: **RM.**

Royal Mint *n* a British organization having the sole right to manufacture coins since the 16th century. In 1968 it moved from London to Llantrisant in Wales.

Royal National Theatre *n* a theatre complex in London, on the S bank of the Thames (opened 1976). The prefix Royal was added in 1988. It houses the Royal National Theatre Company.

Royal Navy *n* the navy of the United Kingdom. Abbrev.: **RN.**

royal palm *n* any of several palm trees of the genus *Roystonea,* esp. *R. regia,* of tropical America, having a tall trunk with a tuft of feathery pinnate leaves.

royal poinciana *n* a caesalpiniaceous tree, *Delonix regia,* that is native to Madagascar but widely cultivated elsewhere, having clusters of large scarlet flowers and long pods. Also called: **flamboyant.**

royal purple *n* **a** a deep reddish-purple colour, sometimes approaching a strong violet. **b** (*as adj*): *a royal-purple dress.*

royal road *n* an easy or direct way of achieving a desired end: *the royal road to success.*

Royal Scots Greys *pl n* **the.** a British cavalry regiment, the Second Dragoons. Also called: **Greys, Scots Greys.** [C17: from their grey uniforms]

Royal Society *n* an association founded in England by Charles II in 1660 to promote research in the sciences.

royal stag *n* See **royal** (sense 8).

Royal Standard *n* a flag bearing the arms of the British sovereign, flown only when she (or he) is present.

royal tennis *n* another name for **real tennis.**

royalty ('rɔɪəltɪ) *n, pl* **-ties. 1** the rank, power, or position of a king or queen. **2a** royal persons collectively. **2b** one who belongs to the royal family. **3** any quality characteristic of a monarch; kingliness or regal dignity. **4** a percentage of the revenue from the sale of a book, performance of a theatrical work, use of a patented invention or of land, etc., paid to the author, inventor, or proprietor.

Royal Victorian Order *n* (in Britain) an order of chivalry founded by Queen Victoria in 1896, membership of which is conferred for special services to the sovereign. Abbrev.: **VO.**

royal warrant *n* an authorization to a tradesman to supply goods to a royal household.

Royal Worcester *n* Worcester china made after 1862.

Royce (rɔɪs) *n* **Josiah.** 1855–1916, U.S. philosopher of monistic idealism. In his ethical studies he emphasized the need for individual loyalty to the world community.

rozzer ('rɒzə) *n Cockney slang.* a policeman. [C19: of unknown origin]

RP *abbrev. for:* **1** Received Pronunciation. **2** Reformed Presbyterian. **3** Regius Professor. **4** *international car registration for* (Republic of the) Philippines.

RPC *abbrev. for* Royal Pioneer Corps.

RPG *abbrev. for* report program generator: a business-oriented computer programming language.

RPI (in Britain) *abbrev. for* retail price index.

rpm *abbrev. for:* **1** revolutions per minute. **2** resale price maintenance.

rps *abbrev. for* revolutions per second.

RPS (in Britain) *abbrev. for* Royal Photographic Society.

rpt *abbrev. for* report.

RPV *abbrev. for* remotely piloted vehicle.

RQ *abbrev. for* respiratory quotient.

RR *abbrev. for* Right Reverend.

-rrhagia *n combining form.* (in pathology) an abnormal discharge or flow: *menorrhagia.* [from Greek *-rrhagia* a bursting forth, from *rhēgnunai* to burst, break]

-rrhoea *or esp. U.S.* **-rrhea** *n combining form.* (in pathology) a discharge or flow: *diarrhoea.* [from New Latin, from Greek *-rrhoia,* from *rhoia* a flowing, from *rhein* to flow]

r-RNA *abbrev. for* ribosomal RNA.

RRP *abbrev. for* recommended retail price.

Rs *symbol for* rupees.

RS (in Britain) *abbrev. for* Royal Society.

RSA *abbrev. for:* **1** Republic of South Africa. **2** Royal Scottish Academy. **3** Royal Scottish Academician. **4** Royal Society of Arts. **5** (in New Zealand) Returned Services Association.

RSC *abbrev. for:* **1** Royal Shakespeare Company. **2** Royal Society of Chemistry.

RSFSR *abbrev. for* (formerly) Russian Soviet Federative Socialist Republic.

RSG (in Britain) *abbrev. for:* **1** rate support grant. **2** *Civil Defence.* Regional Seat of Government.

RSGB *abbrev. for* Radio Society of Great Britain (amateur radio operators).

RSI *abbrev. for* repetitive strain *or* stress injury: a physical condition characterized by pain in the arm, affecting those who repeatedly perform awkward hand movements, such as computer-terminal operators and violinists.

RSJ *abbrev. for* rolled-steel joist.

RSL *abbrev. for:* **1** Royal Society of Literature. **2** (in Australia) Returned Services League.

RSM *abbrev. for:* **1** regimental sergeant major. **2** Royal School of Music. **3** Royal Society of Medicine. ◆ **4** *international car registration for* (Republic of) San Marino.

RSNO *abbrev. for* Royal Scottish National Orchestra.

RSNZ *abbrev. for* Royal Society of New Zealand.

RSPB (in Britain) *abbrev. for* Royal Society for the Protection of Birds.

RSPCA (in Britain and Australia) *abbrev. for* Royal Society for the Prevention of Cruelty to Animals.

RSV *abbrev. for* Revised Standard Version (of the Bible).

RSVP *abbrev. for* répondez s'il vous plaît. [French: please reply]

rt *abbrev. for* right.

RT *abbrev. for* radio telegraphy *or* radio telephony.

RTA *abbrev. for* road traffic accident.

RTC (in India) *abbrev. for:* **1** Road Transport Corporation. **2** Round Table Conference.

RTE *abbrev. for* Radio Telefis Éireann. [Irish Gaelic: Irish Radio and Television]

RTF *Computing. abbrev. for* rich text format: a standard file format allowing file transfer between different applications and operating systems.

Rt Hon. *abbrev. for* Right Honourable.

RTR *abbrev. for* Royal Tank Regiment.

Rt Rev. *abbrev. for* Right Reverend.

RTT *or* **RTTY** *abbrev. for* radioteletype.

Ru *the chemical symbol for* ruthenium.

RU 1 *abbrev. for* Rugby Union. ◆ **2** *international car registration for* Burundi.

RU486 *n Trademark.* a brand name for the **abortion pill.**

Ruanda-Urundi (rʊˈændəʊˈrʊndɪ) *n* a former territory of central Africa: part of German East Africa from 1890; a League of Nations mandate under Belgian administration from 1919; a United Nations trusteeship from 1946; divided into the independent states of Rwanda and Burundi in 1962.

rub (rʌb) *vb* **rubs, rubbing, rubbed. 1** to apply pressure and friction to (something) with a circular or backward and forward motion. **2** to move (something) with pressure along, over, or against (a surface). **3** to chafe or fray. **4** (*tr*) to bring into a certain condition by rubbing: *rub it clean.* **5** (*tr*) to spread with pressure, esp. in order to cause to be absorbed: *he rubbed ointment into his back.* **6** (foll. by *off, out, away,* etc.) to remove or be removed by rubbing. **7** *Bowls.* (of a bowl) to be slowed or deflected by an uneven patch on the green. **8** (*tr;* often foll. by *together*) to move against each other with pressure and friction (esp. in the phrases **rub one's hands,** often a sign of glee, anticipation, or satisfaction, and **rub noses,** a greeting among Eskimos). **9 rub (someone's) nose in it.** *Informal.* to remind (someone) unkindly of his failing or error. **10 rub (up) the wrong way.** to arouse anger (in); annoy. **11 rub shoulders** (*or* **elbows**) **with.** *Informal.* to mix with socially or associate with. ◆ *n* **12** the act of rubbing. **13** (preceded by *the*) an obstacle or difficulty (esp. in the phrase **there's the rub**). **14** something that hurts the feelings or annoys; rebuke. **15** *Bowls.* an uneven patch in the green. **16** any roughness or unevenness of surface. **17 rub of the green. 17a** *Golf.* an incident of accidental interference with the ball. **17b** *Informal.* a piece of good or bad luck. ◆ See also **rub along, rub down, rub in, rub off, rub out, rub up.** [C15: perhaps from Low German *rubben,* of obscure origin]

rubaboo (ˈrʌbəˌbuː) *n Canadian.* a soup or stew made by boiling pemmican with, if available, flour and vegetables. [C19: from Canadian French *rababou,* from Algonquian]

rubáiyát (ˈruːbaɪˌjæt) *n Prosody.* (in Persian poetry) a verse form consisting of four-line stanzas. See also **Omar Khayyám.** [C19: from Arabic *rubāʿīyah,* from *rubāʿīy* consisting of four elements]

Rub' al Khali (ˈrʊb æl ˈkɑːlɪ) *n* a desert in S Arabia, mainly in Saudi Arabia, extending southeast from Nejd to Hadramaut and northeast from Yemen to the United Arab Emirates. Area: about 777 000 sq. km (300 000 sq. miles). English names: **Great Sandy Desert, Empty Quarter.** Also called: **Ar Rimal, Dahna.**

rub along *vb* (*intr, adv*) *Brit.* **1** to continue in spite of difficulties. **2** to maintain an amicable relationship; not quarrel.

rubato (ruːˈbɑːtəʊ) *Music.* ◆ *n, pl* **-tos. 1** flexibility of tempo in performance. ◆ *adj, adv* **2** to be played with a flexible tempo. [C19: from the Italian phrase *tempo rubato,* literally: stolen time, from *rubare* to ROB]

rubber[1] (ˈrʌbə) *n* **1** Also called: **India rubber, gum elastic, caoutchouc.** a cream to dark brown elastic material obtained by coagulating and drying the latex from certain plants, esp. the tree *Hevea brasiliensis.* **2** any of a large variety of elastomers produced by improving the properties of natural rubber or by synthetic means. **3** *Chiefly Brit.* a piece of rubber or felt used for erasing something written, typed, etc.; eraser. **4** a coarse file. **5** a cloth, pad, etc., used for polishing or buffing. **6** a person who rubs something in order to smooth, polish, or massage. **7** (*often pl*) *Chiefly U.S. and Canadian.* a rubberized waterproof article, such as a mackintosh or overshoe. **8** *Slang.* a male contraceptive; condom. **9** (*modifier*) made of or producing rubber: *a rubber ball; a rubber factory.* [C17: from RUB + -ER[1]; the tree was so named because its product was used for rubbing out writing]

rubber[2] (ˈrʌbə) *n* **1** *Bridge, whist, etc.* **1a** a match of three games. **1b** the deal that wins such a match. **2** a series of matches or games in any of various sports. [C16: origin unknown]

rubber band *n* a continuous loop of thin rubber, used to hold papers, etc., together. Also called: **elastic band.**

rubber bridge *n* a form of bridge in which fresh hands are dealt for each round and the aim is to win a rubber. Compare **duplicate bridge.**

rubber cement *n* any of a number of adhesives made by dissolving rubber in a solvent such as benzene.

rubber cheque *n Facetious.* a cheque that bounces.

rubber goods *pl n Euphemistic.* contraceptives; condoms.

rubberize *or* **rubberise** (ˈrʌbəˌraɪz) *vb* (*tr*) to coat or impregnate with rubber.

rubberneck (ˈrʌbəˌnɛk) *Slang.* ◆ *n* **1** a person who stares or gapes inquisitively, esp. in a naive or foolish manner. **2** a sightseer or tourist. ◆ *vb* **3** (*intr*) to stare in a naive or foolish manner.

rubber plant *n* **1** a moraceous plant, *Ficus elastica,* with glossy leathery leaves: a tall tree in India and Malaya, it is cultivated as a house plant in Europe and America. **2** any of several tropical trees, the sap of which yields rubber. See also **rubber tree.**

rubber stamp *n* **1** a device used for imprinting dates or commonly used phrases on forms, invoices, etc. **2** automatic authorization of a payment, proposal, etc., without challenge. **3** a person who makes such automatic authorizations; a cipher or person of little account.◆ *vb* **rubber-stamp.** (*tr*) **4** to imprint (forms, invoices, etc.) with a rubber stamp. **5** *Informal.* to approve automatically.

rubber tree *n* a tropical American euphorbiaceous tree, *Hevea brasiliensis,* cultivated throughout the tropics, esp. in Malaya, for the latex of its stem, which is the major source of commercial rubber. See also **Pará rubber.**

rubbery (ˈrʌbərɪ) *adj* having the texture of or resembling rubber, esp. in flexibility or toughness.

rubbing (ˈrʌbɪŋ) *n* an impression taken of an incised or raised surface, such as a brass plate on a tomb, by laying paper over it and rubbing with wax, graphite, etc.

rubbing alcohol *n* a liquid usually consisting of 70 per cent denatured ethyl alcohol, used by external application as an antiseptic or rubefacient.

rubbish (ˈrʌbɪʃ) *n* **1** worthless, useless, or unwanted matter. **2** discarded or waste matter; refuse. **3** foolish words or speech; nonsense. ◆ *vb* **4** (*tr*) *Informal.* to criticize; attack verbally. [C14 *robys,* of uncertain origin] ► **ˈrubbishy** *adj*

rubbity (ˈrʌbətɪ) *or* **rubbidy** (ˈrʌbədɪ) *n, pl* **-ties** *or* **-dies.** *Austral. slang.* a pub. [from rhyming slang *rubbity dub*]

rubble (ˈrʌbᵊl) *n* **1** fragments of broken stones, bricks, etc. **2** any fragmented solid material. **3** *Quarrying.* the weathered surface layer of rock. **4** Also called: **ˈrubbleˌwork.** masonry constructed of broken pieces of rock, stone, etc. [C14 *robyl;* perhaps related to Middle English *rubben* to rub, or to RUBBISH] ► **ˈrubbly** *adj*

Rubbra (ˈrʌbrə) *n* (**Charles**) **Edmund.** 1901–86, English composer of works in a traditional idiom.

rubby (ˈrʌbɪ) *n, pl* **-bies.** *Canadian slang.* **1** rubbing alcohol, esp. when mixed with cheap wine for drinking. **2** a person who drinks such mixtures, esp. a derelict alcoholic.

rub down *vb* (*adv*) **1** to dry or clean (a horse, athlete, oneself, etc.) vigorously, esp. after exercise. **2** to make or become smooth by rubbing. **3** (*tr*) to prepare (a surface) for painting by rubbing it with sandpaper. ◆ *n* **rubdown. 4** the act of rubbing down. **5** the Hong Kong term for **dressing-down.**

rube (ruːb) *n U.S. and Canadian slang.* an unsophisticated countryman. [C20: probably from the name *Reuben*]

rubefy (ˈruːbɪˌfaɪ) *vb* **-fies, -fying, -fied.** (*tr*) to make red, esp. (of a counterirritant) to make the skin go red. [C19: from Latin *rubefacere,* from *rubeus* red + *facere* to make] ► **rubefacient** (ˌruːbɪˈfeɪʃənt) *adj, n* ► **rubefaction** (ˌruːbɪˈfækʃən) *n*

rubella (ruːˈbɛlə) *n* a mild contagious viral disease, somewhat similar to measles, characterized by cough, sore throat, skin rash, and occasionally vomiting. It can cause congenital defects if caught during the first three months of pregnancy. Also called: **German measles.** [C19: from New Latin, from Latin *rubellus* reddish, from *rubeus* red]

rubellite (ˈruːbɪˌlaɪt, ruːˈbɛl-) *n* a red transparent variety of tourmaline, used as a gemstone. [C18: from Latin *rubellus* reddish]

Rubenesque (ˌruːbəˌnɛsk) *adj* (of a woman) having the physique associated with Rubens' portraits of women; plump and attractive.

Rubens (ˈruːbɪnz) *n* Sir **Peter Paul.** 1577–1640, Flemish painter, regarded as the greatest exponent of the Baroque: appointed (1609) painter to Archduke Albert of Austria, who gave him many commissions, artistic and diplomatic. He was knighted by Charles I of England in 1629. His prolific output includes the triptych in Antwerp Cathedral, *Descent from the Cross* (1611–14), *The Rape of the Sabines* (1635), and his *Self-Portrait* (?1639).

rubeola (ruːˈbiːələ) *n* technical name for **measles.** Compare **rubella.** [C17: from New Latin, from Latin *rubeus* reddish, from *ruber* red] ► **ruˈbeolar** *adj*

rubescent (ruːˈbɛsᵊnt) *adj Literary.* reddening; blushing. [C18: from Latin *rubescere* to grow red, from *ruber* red] ► **ruˈbescence** *n*

rubiaceous (ˌruːbɪˈeɪʃəs) *adj* of, relating to, or belonging to the *Rubiaceae,* a widely distributed family of trees, shrubs, and herbaceous plants that includes the coffee and cinchona trees, gardenia, madder, and bedstraws. [C19: from New Latin *Rubiaceae,* from Latin *rubia* madder, from *rubeus* red]

Rubicon (ˈruːbɪkən) *n* **1** a stream in N Italy: in ancient times the boundary between Italy and Cisalpine Gaul. By leading his army across it and marching on Rome in 49 B.C., Julius Caesar broke the law that a general might not lead an army out of the province to which he was posted and so committed himself to civil war with the senatorial party. **2** (*sometimes not cap.*) a point of no return. **3** a penalty in piquet by which the score of a player who fails to reach 100 points in six hands is added to his opponent's. **4 cross** (*or* **pass**) **the Rubicon.** to commit oneself irrevocably to some course of action.

rubicund (ˈruːbɪkənd) *adj* of a reddish colour; ruddy; rosy. [C16: from Latin *rubicundus,* from *rubēre* to be ruddy, from *ruber* red] ▸ **rubicundity** (ˌruːbɪˈkʌndɪtɪ) *n*

rubidium (ruːˈbɪdɪəm) *n* a soft highly reactive radioactive element of the alkali metal group; the 16th most abundant element in the earth's crust (310 parts per million), occurring principally in pollucite, carnallite, and lepidolite. It is used in electronic valves, photocells, and special glass. Symbol: Rb; atomic no.: 37; atomic wt.: 85.4678; half-life of ^{87}Rb: 5×10^{11} years; valency: 1,2,3, or 4; relative density: 1.532 (solid), 1.475 (liquid); melting pt.: 39.48°C; boiling pt.: 688°C. [C19: from New Latin, from Latin *rubidus* dark red, with reference to the two red lines in its spectrum] ▸ **ruˈbidic** *adj*

rubidium-strontium dating *n* a technique for determining the age of minerals based on the occurrence in natural rubidium of a fixed amount of the radioisotope ^{87}Rb which decays to the stable strontium isotope ^{87}Sr with a half-life of 5×10^{10} years. Measurement of the ratio of these isotopes thus gives the age of a mineral, for ages of up to about 4×10^9 years.

rubiginous (ruːˈbɪdʒɪnəs) *adj* rust-coloured. [C17: from Latin *rūbīginōsus,* from *rūbīgō* rust, from *ruber* red]

Rubik cube (ˈruːbɪk) *or* **Rubik's cube** *n Trademark.* a puzzle consisting of a cube of six colours, each face of which is made up of nine squares, eight of which are individually rotatable. The aim is to swivel the squares until each face of the cube shows one colour only. [C20: named after Professor Erno *Rubik* (born 1944), its Hungarian inventor]

rub in *vb* (*tr, adv*) **1** to spread with pressure, esp. in order to cause to be absorbed. **2 rub it in.** *Informal.* to harp on (something distasteful to a person, of which he does not wish to be reminded).

Rubinstein (ˈruːbɪnˌstaɪn) *n* **1 Anton Grigorevich** (anˈtɔn griˈgɔrjɪvitʃ). 1829–94, Russian composer and pianist. **2 Artur** (ˈartur). 1886–1982, U.S. pianist, born in Poland.

rubious (ˈruːbɪəs) *adj Literary.* of the colour ruby; dark red. [C17: from RUBY + -OUS]

ruble (ˈruːbᵊl) *n* a variant spelling of **rouble.**

Rublyov (*Russian* ˈrubljɔv) *or* **Rublev,** *n* **Andrey** (ˈandre). ?1370–1430, Russian icon painter. His masterpiece is *The Old Testament Trinity.*

rub off *vb* **1** to remove or be removed by rubbing. **2** (*intr;* often foll. by *on* or *onto*) to have an effect through close association or contact, esp. so as to make similar: *her crude manners have rubbed off on you.*

rub out *vb* (*tr, adv*) **1** to remove or be removed with a rubber. **2** *U.S. slang.* to murder. **3** *Australian Rules football.* to suspend (a player).

rubric (ˈruːbrɪk) *n* **1** a title, heading, or initial letter in a book, manuscript, or section of a legal code, esp. one printed or painted in red ink or in some similarly distinguishing manner. **2** a set of rules of conduct or procedure. **3** a set of directions for the conduct of Christian church services, often printed in red in a prayer book or missal. **4** instructions to a candidate at the head of the examination paper. **5** an obsolete name for **red ochre.** ◆ *adj* **6** written, printed, or marked in red. [C15 *rubrike* red ochre, red lettering, from Latin *rubrīca* (*terra*) red (earth), ruddle, from *ruber* red] ▸ **ˈrubrical** *adj* ▸ **ˈrubrically** *adv*

rubricate (ˈruːbrɪˌkeɪt) *vb* (*tr*) **1** to print (a book or manuscript) with red titles, headings, etc. **2** to mark in red. **3** to supply with or regulate by rubrics. [C16: from Latin *rubricāre* to colour red, from *rubrīca* red earth; see RUBRIC] ▸ **ˌrubriˈcation** *n* ▸ **ˈrubriˌcator** *n*

rubrician (ruːˈbrɪʃən) *n* an authority on liturgical rubrics.

rubstone (ˈrʌbˌstəʊn) *n* a stone used for sharpening or smoothing, esp. a whetstone.

rub up *vb* (*adv*) *Chiefly Brit.* **1** (when *intr,* foll. by *on*) to refresh one's memory (of). **2** (*tr*) to smooth or polish.

ruby (ˈruːbɪ) *n, pl* **-bies. 1** a deep red transparent precious variety of corundum: occurs naturally in Myanmar and Sri Lanka but is also synthesized. It is used as a gemstone, in lasers, and for bearings and rollers in watchmaking. Formula: Al_2O_3. **2a** the deep-red colour of a ruby. **2b** (*as adj*): *ruby lips.* **3a** something resembling, made of, or containing a ruby. **3b** (*as modifier*): *ruby necklace.* **4** (*modifier*) denoting a fortieth anniversary: *our ruby wedding.* **5** (formerly) a size of printer's type approximately equal to 5½ point. [C14: from Old French *rubi,* from Latin *rubeus* reddish, from *ruber* red] ▸ **ˈruby-ˌlike** *adj*

ruby glass *n* glass that has a deep rich red colour produced from oxides of various minerals, such as lead, copper, and iron.

ruby silver *n* another name for **proustite** or **pyrargyrite.**

ruby spinel *n* a red transparent variety of spinel, used as a gemstone.

ruby-tail wasp *n* any of various brightly coloured wasps of the family *Chrysididae,* having a metallic sheen, which parasitize bees and other solitary wasps.

RUC *abbrev. for* Royal Ulster Constabulary.

ruche *or* **rouche** (ruːʃ) *n* a strip of pleated or frilled lawn, lace, etc., used to decorate blouses, dresses, etc., or worn around the neck like a small ruff as in the 16th century. [C19: from French, literally: beehive, from Medieval Latin *rūsca* bark of a tree, of Celtic origin]

ruching (ˈruːʃɪŋ) *n* **1** material used for a ruche. **2** a ruche or ruches collectively.

ruck[1] (rʌk) *n* **1** a large number or quantity; mass, esp. of ordinary or undistinguished people or things. **2** (in a race) a group of competitors who are well behind the leaders at the finish. **3** *Rugby.* a loose scrum that forms around the ball when it is on the ground. **4** *Australian Rules football.* the three players, two ruckmen and a rover, that do not have fixed positions but follow the ball closely. ◆ *vb* **5** (*intr*) *Rugby.* to try to win the ball by mauling and scrummaging. [C13 (meaning "heap of firewood"): perhaps from Scandinavian; compare Old Norse *hraukr* RICK[1]]

ruck[2] (rʌk) *n* **1** a wrinkle, crease, or fold. ◆ *vb* **2** (usually foll. by *up*) to become or make wrinkled, creased, or puckered. [C18: from Scandinavian; related to Old Norse *hrukka*]

ruck[3] (rʌk) *n Prison slang.* a fight. [C20: short for RUCKUS]

ruckle (ˈrʌkᵊl) *n, vb Brit.* another word for **ruck**[2].

rucksack (ˈrʌkˌsæk) *n* a large bag, usually having two straps and a supporting frame, carried on the back and often used by climbers, campers, etc. U.S. and Canadian name: **backpack.** [C19: from German, literally: back sack]

ruckus (ˈrʌkəs) *n, pl* **-uses.** *Informal.* an uproar; ruction. [C20: from RUCTION + RUMPUS]

ruction (ˈrʌkʃən) *n Informal.* **1** an uproar; noisy or quarrelsome disturbance. **2** (*pl*) a violent and unpleasant row; trouble: *there'll be ructions when she hears about it.* [C19: perhaps changed from INSURRECTION]

rudaceous (ruːˈdeɪʃəs) *adj* (of conglomerate, breccia, and similar rocks) composed of coarse-grained material. Compare **arenaceous** (sense 1), **argillaceous.** [C20: from Latin *rudis* coarse, rough + -ACEOUS]

Ruda Śląska (ˈruːdə ˈʃlɑnskə) *n* a town in SW Poland: coalmining. Pop.: 166 300 (1996 est.).

rudbeckia (rʌdˈbɛkɪə) *n* any plant of the North American genus *Rudbeckia,* cultivated for their showy flowers, which have golden-yellow rays and green or black conical centres: family *Compositae* (composites). See also **coneflower, black-eyed Susan.** [C18: New Latin, named after Olaus *Rudbeck* (1630–1702), Swedish botanist]

rudd (rʌd) *n* a European freshwater cyprinid fish, *Scardinius erythrophthalmus,* having a compressed dark greenish body and reddish ventral and tail fins. [C17: probably from dialect *rud* red colour, from Old English *rudu* redness]

Rudd (rʌd) *n* **Steele,** pen name of *Arthur Hoey Davis,* 1868–1935, Australian author. His works include *On Our Selection* (1899), *Our New Selection* (1902), and *Back at Our Selection* (1906), which featured the characters Dad and Dave.

rudder (ˈrʌdə) *n* **1** *Nautical.* a pivoted vertical vane that projects into the water at the stern of a vessel and can be controlled by a tiller, wheel, or other apparatus to steer the vessel. **2** a vertical control surface attached to the rear of the fin used to steer an aircraft, in conjunction with the ailerons. **3** anything that guides or directs. [Old English *rōther;* related to Old French *rōther,* Old High German *ruodar,* Old Norse *rōthr.* See ROW[2]] ▸ **ˈrudderless** *adj*

rudderhead (ˈrʌdəˌhɛd) *n Nautical.* the top of the rudderpost, to which the steering apparatus may be fixed.

rudderpost (ˈrʌdəˌpəʊst) *n Nautical.* **1** Also called: **rudderstock** (ˈrʌdəˌstɒk). a postlike member at the forward edge of a rudder. **2** the part of the stern frame of a vessel to which a rudder is fitted.

ruddle (ˈrʌdᵊl), **raddle,** *or* **reddle** *n* **1** a red ochre, used esp. to mark sheep. ◆ *vb* **2** (*tr*) to mark (sheep) with ruddle. [C16: diminutive formed from Old English *rudu* redness; see RUDD]

ruddock (ˈrʌdək) *n Brit.* a dialect name for the **robin** (sense 1). [Old English *rudduc;* related to *rudu* redness; see RUDD]

ruddy (ˈrʌdɪ) *adj* **-dier, -diest. 1** (of the complexion) having a healthy reddish colour, usually resulting from an outdoor life. **2** coloured red or pink: *a ruddy sky.* ◆ *adv, adj Informal, chiefly Brit.* **3** (intensifier) bloody; damned: *a ruddy fool.* [Old English *rudig,* from *rudu* redness (see RUDD); related to Old High German *rot* RED[1], Swedish *rod,* Old Norse *rythga* to make rusty] ▸ **ˈruddily** *adv* ▸ **ˈruddiness** *n*

ruddy duck *n* a small duck, *Oxyura jamaicensis,* that inhabits marshes, ponds, etc., in North America and N South America and has a stiff upright tail. The male has a reddish-brown body and blue bill in the breeding season.

rude (ruːd) *adj* **1** insulting or uncivil; discourteous; impolite: *he was rude about her hairstyle.* **2** lacking refinement; coarse or uncouth. **3** vulgar or obscene: *a rude joke.* **4** unexpected and unpleasant: *a rude awakening to the facts of economic life.* **5** roughly or crudely made: *we made a rude shelter on the island.* **6** rough or harsh in sound, appearance, or behaviour. **7** humble or lowly. **8** (*prenominal*) robust or sturdy: *in rude health.* **9** (*prenominal*) approximate or imprecise: *a rude estimate.* [C14: via Old French from Latin *rudis* coarse, unformed] ▸ **ˈrudely** *adv* ▸ **ˈrudeness** *or* (*informal*) **ˈrudery** *n*

rude awakening *n* an occurrence of being made to face an unpleasant fact.

ruderal (ˈruːdərəl) *n* **1** a plant that grows on waste ground. ◆ *adj* **2** growing in waste places. [C19: from New Latin *rūderālis,* from Latin *rūdus* rubble]

Rudesheimer (ˈruːdəsˌhaɪmə) *n* a white Rhine wine: named after the town of Rüdesheim on the Rhine.

rudiment (ˈruːdɪmənt) *n* **1** (*often pl*) the first principles or elementary stages of a subject. **2** (*often pl*) a partially developed version of something. **3** *Biology.* an organ or part in its earliest recognizable form, esp. one in an embryonic or vestigial state. [C16: from Latin *rudīmentum* a beginning, from *rudis* unformed; see RUDE]

rudimentary (ˌruːdɪˈmɛntərɪ) *or* (*less commonly*) **rudimental** *adj* **1** basic; fundamental; not elaborated or perfected. **2** incompletely developed; vestigial: *rudimentary leaves.* ▸ **ˌrudiˈmentarily** *or* (*less commonly*) **ˌrudiˈmentally** *adv*

rudish (ˈruːdɪʃ) *adj* somewhat rude.

Rudolf[1] (ˈruːdɒlf) *n* **Lake.** the former name (until 1979) of (Lake) **Turkana.**

Rudolf[2] *or* **Rudolph** (ˈruːdɒlf) *n* 1858–89, archduke of Austria, son of emperor

Franz Joseph: he and his mistress committed suicide at the royal hunting lodge in Mayerling.

Rudolf I *or* **Rudolph I** ('ru:dɒlf) *n* 1218–91, king of Germany (1273–91): founder of the Hapsburg dynasty based on the duchies of Styria and Austria.

rue[1] (ru:) *vb* **rues, ruing, rued. 1** to feel sorrow, remorse, or regret for (one's own wrongdoing, past events with unpleasant consequences, etc.). ◆ *n* **2** *Archaic.* sorrow, pity, or regret. [Old English *hrēowan;* related to Old Saxon *hreuwan,* Old High German *hriuwan*] ▸ **'ruer** *n*

rue[2] (ru:) *n* any rutaceous plant of the genus *Ruta,* esp. *R. graveolens,* an aromatic Eurasian shrub with small yellow flowers and evergreen leaves which yield an acrid volatile oil, formerly used medicinally as a narcotic and stimulant. Archaic name: **herb of grace.** Compare **goat's-rue, meadow rue, wall rue.** [C14: from Old French, from Latin *rūta,* from Greek *rhutē*]

rueful ('ru:fʊl) *adj* **1** feeling or expressing sorrow or repentance: *a rueful face.* **2** inspiring sorrow or pity. ▸ **'ruefully** *adv* ▸ **'ruefulness** *n*

rufescent (ru:'fɛsᵊnt) *adj Botany.* tinged with red or becoming red. [C19: from Latin *rūfescere* to grow reddish, from *rūfus* red, auburn] ▸ **ru'fescence** *n*

ruff[1] (rʌf) *n* **1** a circular pleated, gathered, or fluted collar of lawn, muslin, etc., often starched or wired, worn by both men and women in the 16th and 17th centuries. **2** a natural growth of long or coloured hair or feathers around the necks of certain animals or birds. **3a** an Old World shore bird, *Philomachus pugnax,* the male of which has a large erectile ruff of feathers in the breeding season: family *Scolopacidae* (sandpipers, etc.), order *Charadriiformes.* **3b** the male of this bird. Compare **reeve**[3]. [C16: back formation from RUFFLE[1]] ▸ **'ruff,like** *adj*

ruff[2] (rʌf) *n Cards.* **1** (*also vb*) another word for **trump**[1]. **2** an old card game similar to whist. [C16: from Old French *roffle;* perhaps changed from Italian *trionfa* TRUMP[1]]

ruffe *or* **ruff**[3] (rʌf) *n* a European freshwater teleost fish, *Acerina cernua,* having a single spiny dorsal fin: family *Percidae* (perches). Also called: **pope.** [C15: perhaps an alteration of ROUGH (referring to its scales)]

ruffed grouse *n* a large North American grouse, *Bonasa umbellus,* having brown plumage with darker markings around the neck and a black-tipped fan-shaped tail.

ruffian ('rʌfɪən) *n* a violent or lawless person; hoodlum or villain. [C16: from Old French *rufien,* from Italian *ruffiano,* perhaps related to Langobardic *hruf* scurf, scabbiness] ▸ **'ruffianism** *n* ▸ **'ruffianly** *adj*

ruffle[1] ('rʌfᵊl) *vb* **1** to make, be, or become irregular or rumpled: *to ruffle a child's hair; a breeze ruffling the water.* **2** to annoy, irritate, or be annoyed or irritated. **3** (*tr*) to make into a ruffle; pleat. **4** (of a bird) to erect (its feathers) in anger, display, etc. **5** (*tr*) to flick (cards, pages, etc.) rapidly with the fingers. ◆ *n* **6** an irregular or disturbed surface. **7** a strip of pleated material used for decoration or as a trim. **8** *Zoology.* another name for **ruff**[1] (sense 2). **9** annoyance or irritation. [C13: of Germanic origin; compare Middle Low German *ruffelen* to crumple, Old Norse *hrufla* to scratch]

ruffle[2] ('rʌfᵊl) *n* **1** a low continuous drumbeat. ◆ *vb* **2** (*tr*) to beat (a drum) with a low repetitive beat. [C18: from earlier *ruff,* of imitative origin]

ruffle[3] ('rʌfᵊl) *vb* (*intr*) *Archaic.* to behave riotously or arrogantly; swagger. [C15: of obscure origin]

ruffler ('rʌflə) *n* **1** a person or thing that ruffles. **2** an attachment on a sewing machine used for making frills.

rufiyaa (ru:'fi:jɑ:) *n* the standard monetary unit of the Maldives, divided into 100 laari.

rufous ('ru:fəs) *adj* reddish-brown. [C18: from Latin *rūfus*]

rug (rʌg) *n* **1** a floor covering, smaller than a carpet and made of thick wool or of other material, such as an animal skin. **2** *Chiefly Brit.* a blanket, esp. one used as a wrap or lap robe for travellers. **3** *Slang.* a wig. **4 pull the rug out from under.** to betray, expose, or leave defenceless. [C16: from Scandinavian; compare Norwegian *rugga,* Swedish *rugg* coarse hair. See RAG[1]] ▸ **'rug,like** *adj*

RUG *Computing. abbrev. for* restricted users group.

ruga ('ru:gə) *n, pl* **-gae** (-dʒi:). (*usually pl*) *Anatomy.* a fold, wrinkle, or crease. [C18: Latin]

rugby *or* **rugby football** ('rʌgbɪ) *n* **1** a form of football played with an oval ball in which the handling and carrying of the ball is permitted. Also called: **rugger. 2** *Canadian.* another name for **Canadian football.** See also **rugby league, rugby union.** [C19: named after the public school at Rugby, where it was first played]

Rugby ('rʌgbɪ) *n* a town in central England, in E Warwickshire: famous public school, founded in 1567. Pop.: 61 106 (1991). ▸ **'Rugbeian** *adj, n*

rugby league *n* a form of rugby football played between teams of 13 players.

rugby union *n* a form of rugby football played between teams of 15 players.

rugged ('rʌgɪd) *adj* **1** having an uneven or jagged surface. **2** rocky or steep: *rugged scenery.* **3** (of the face) strong-featured or furrowed. **4** rough, severe, or stern in character. **5** without refinement or culture; rude: *rugged manners.* **6** involving hardship; harsh: *he leads a rugged life in the mountains.* **7** difficult or hard: *a rugged test.* **8** (of equipment, machines, etc.) designed to withstand rough treatment or use in rough conditions: *a handheld rugged computer which can survive being submerged in water.* **9** *Chiefly U.S. and Canadian.* sturdy or strong; robust. [C14: from Scandinavian; compare Swedish *rugga* to make rough] ▸ **'ruggedly** *adv* ▸ **'ruggedness** *n*

ruggedize *or* **ruggedise** ('rʌgɪ,daɪz) *vb* (*tr*) to make durable, as for military use.

rugger ('rʌgə) *n Chiefly Brit.* an informal name for **rugby.**

rugose ('ru:gəʊs, -gəʊz), **rugous,** *or* **rugate** ('ru:geɪt, -gɪt) *adj* wrinkled: *rugose leaves.* [C18: from Latin *rūgōsus,* from *rūga* a wrinkle] ▸ **'rugosely** *adv* ▸ **rugosity** (ru:'gɒsɪtɪ) *n*

rug rat *n U.S. and Canadian informal.* a child not yet walking.

Ruhr (rʊə; *German* ru:r) *n* the chief coalmining and industrial region of Germany: in North Rhine-Westphalia around the valley of the **River Ruhr** (a tributary of the Rhine 235 km (146 miles) long). German name: **Ruhrgebiet** ('ru:rgə,bi:t).

ruin ('ru:ɪn) *n* **1** destroyed or decayed building or town. **2** the state or condition of being destroyed or decayed. **3** loss of wealth, position, etc., or something that causes such loss; downfall. **4** something that is severely damaged: *his life was a ruin.* **5** a person who has suffered a downfall, bankruptcy, etc. **6** loss of value or usefulness. **7** *Archaic.* loss of her virginity by a woman outside marriage. ◆ *vb* **8** (*tr*) to bring to ruin; destroy. **9** (*tr*) to injure or spoil: *the town has been ruined with tower blocks.* **10** (*intr*) *Archaic or poetic.* to fall into ruins; collapse. [C14: from Old French *ruine,* from Latin *ruīna* a falling down, from *ruere* to fall violently] ▸ **'ruinable** *adj* ▸ **'ruiner** *n*

ruination (,ru:ɪ'neɪʃən) *n* **1** the act of ruining or the state of being ruined. **2** something that causes ruin.

ruinous ('ru:ɪnəs) *adj* causing, tending to cause, or characterized by ruin or destruction: *a ruinous course of action.* ▸ **'ruinously** *adv* ▸ **'ruinousness** *n*

Ruisdael *or* **Ruysdael** ('ri:zdɑ:l, -deɪl, 'raɪz-; *Dutch* 'rœizda:l) *n* **Jacob van** ('ja:kɔp van). ?1628–82, Dutch landscape painter.

rule (ru:l) *n* **1** an authoritative regulation or direction concerning method or procedure, as for a court of law, legislative body, game, or other human institution or activity: *judges' rules; play according to the rules.* **2** the exercise of governmental authority or control: *the rule of Caesar.* **3** the period of time in which a monarch or government has power: *his rule lasted 100 days.* **4** a customary form or procedure; regular course of action: *he made a morning swim his rule.* **5** (usually preceded by *the*) the common order of things; normal condition: *violence was the rule rather than the exception.* **6** a prescribed method or procedure for solving a mathematical problem, or one constituting part of a computer program, usually expressed in an appropriate formalism. **7** a formal expression of a grammatical regularity in a linguistic description of a language. **8** any of various devices with a straight edge for guiding or measuring; ruler: *a carpenter's rule.* **9a** a printed or drawn character in the form of a long thin line. **9b** another name for **dash**[1] (sense 13): *en rule; em rule.* **9c** a strip of brass or other metal used to print such a line. **10** *Christianity.* a systematic body of prescriptions defining the way of life to be followed by members of a religious order. **11** *Law.* an order by a court or judge. **12 as a rule.** normally or ordinarily. ◆ *vb* **13** to exercise governing or controlling authority over (a people, political unit, individual, etc.): *he ruled for 20 years; his passion for her ruled his life.* **14** (when *tr, often takes a clause as object*) to decide authoritatively; decree: *the chairman ruled against the proposal.* **15** (*tr*) to mark with straight parallel lines or make one straight line, as with a ruler: *to rule a margin.* **16** (*tr*) to restrain or control: *to rule one's temper.* **17** (*intr*) to be customary or prevalent: *chaos rules in this school.* **18** (*intr*) to be pre-eminent or superior: *football rules in the field of sport.* **19** (*tr*) *Astrology.* (of a planet) to have a strong affinity with certain human attributes, activities, etc., associated with (one or sometimes two signs of the zodiac): *Mars rules Aries.* **20 rule the roost** (*or* **roast**). to be pre-eminent; be in charge. [C13: from Old French *riule,* from Latin *rēgula* a straight edge; see REGULATE] ▸ **'rulable** *adj*

rule of three *n* a mathematical rule asserting that the value of one unknown quantity in a proportion is found by multiplying the denominator of each ratio by the numerator of the other.

rule of thumb *n* **a** a rough and practical approach, based on experience, rather than a scientific or precise one based on theory. **b** (*as modifier*): *a rule-of-thumb decision.*

rule out *vb* (*tr, adv*) **1** to dismiss from consideration. **2** to make impossible; preclude or prevent: *the rain ruled out outdoor games.*

ruler ('ru:lə) *n* **1** a person who rules or commands. **2** Also called: **rule.** a strip of wood, metal, or other material, having straight edges graduated usually in millimetres or inches, used for measuring and drawing straight lines.

Rules (ru:lz) *pl n* **1** short for **Australian Rules** (football). **2 the Rules.** *English history.* the neighbourhood around certain prisons (esp. the Fleet and King's Bench prison) in which trusted prisoners were allowed to live under specified restrictions.

ruling ('ru:lɪŋ) *n* **1** a decision of someone in authority, such as a judge. **2** one or more parallel ruled lines. ◆ *adj* **3** controlling or exercising authority: *the ruling classes.* **4** prevalent or predominant.

rum[1] (rʌm) *n* spirit made from sugar cane, either coloured brownish-red by the addition of caramel or by maturation in oak containers, or left white. [C17: perhaps shortened from C16 *rumbullion,* of uncertain origin]

rum[2] (rʌm) *adj* **rummer, rummest.** *Brit. slang.* strange; peculiar; odd. [C19: perhaps from Romany *rom* man] ▸ **'rumly** *adv* ▸ **'rumness** *n*

rum[3] (rʌm) *n* short for **rummy**[1].

Rumania (ru:'meɪnɪə) *n* a variant of **Romania.** ▸ **Ru'manian** *adj, n*

rumba *or* **rhumba** ('rʌmbə, 'rʊm-) *n* **1** a rhythmic and syncopated Cuban dance in duple time. **2** a ballroom dance derived from this. **3** a piece of music composed for or in the rhythm of this dance. [C20: from Spanish: lavish display, of uncertain origin]

rumble ('rʌmbᵊl) *vb* **1** to make or cause to make a deep resonant sound: *thunder rumbled in the sky.* **2** to move with such a sound: *the train rumbled along.* **3** (*tr*) to utter with a rumbling sound: *he rumbled an order.* **4** (*tr*) to tumble (metal components, gemstones, etc.) in a barrel of smooth stone in order to polish them. **5** (*tr*) *Brit. informal.* to find out about (someone or something); discover (something): *the police rumbled their plans.* **6** (*intr*) *U.S. slang.* to be involved in a gang fight. ◆ *n* **7** a deep resonant sound. **8** a widespread murmur of discontent. **9** another name for **tumbler** (sense 4). **10** *U.S., Canadian, and N.Z. slang.* a gang fight. [C14: perhaps from Middle Dutch *rummelen;* related to German *rummeln, rumpeln*] ▸ **'rumbler** *n* ▸ **'rumbling** *adj* ▸ **'rumblingly** *adv*

rumble seat *n U.S. and Canadian.* a folding outside seat at the rear of some early cars; dicky.

rumble strip *n* one of a set of roughly surfaced strips set in a road on the approach to a junction or hazard, to alert drivers by means of a change in tyre noise.

rumbustious (rʌmˈbʌstjəs) *adj* boisterous or unruly. [C18: probably a variant of ROBUSTIOUS] ▸ **rumˈbustiously** *adv* ▸ **rumˈbustiousness** *n*

Rumelia (ruːˈmiːlɪə) *n History.* the possessions of the Ottoman Empire in the Balkan peninsula: including Macedonia, Albania, Thrace, and an autonomous province (**Eastern Rumelia**) ceded in 1885 to Bulgaria.

rumen (ˈruːmɛn) *n, pl* **-mens** *or* **-mina** (-mɪnə). the first compartment of the stomach of ruminants, behind the reticulum, in which food is partly digested before being regurgitated as cud. [C18: from Latin: throat, gullet]

Rumford (ˈrʌmfəd) *n* **Count.** See (Benjamin) **Thompson.**

ruminant (ˈruːmɪnənt) *n* **1** any artiodactyl mammal of the suborder *Ruminantia,* the members of which chew the cud and have a stomach of four compartments, one of which is the rumen. The group includes deer, antelopes, cattle, sheep, and goats. **2** any other animal that chews the cud, such as a camel. ◆ *adj* **3** of, relating to, or belonging to the suborder *Ruminantia.* **4** (of members of this suborder and related animals, such as camels) chewing the cud; ruminating. **5** meditating or contemplating in a slow quiet way.

ruminate (ˈruːmɪˌneɪt) *vb* **1** (of ruminants) to chew (the cud). **2** (when *intr,* often foll. by *upon, on,* etc.) to meditate or ponder (upon). [C16: from Latin *rūmināre* to chew the cud, from RUMEN] ▸ **ˌrumiˈnation** *n* ▸ **ˈruminative** *adj* ▸ **ˈruminatively** *adv* ▸ **ˈrumiˌnator** *n*

rummage (ˈrʌmɪdʒ) *vb* **1** (when *intr,* often foll. by *through*) to search (through) while looking for something, often causing disorder or confusion. ◆ *n* **2** an act of rummaging. **3** a jumble of articles. **4** *Obsolete.* confusion or bustle. [C14 (in the sense: to pack a cargo): from Old French *arrumage,* from *arrumer* to stow in a ship's hold, probably of Germanic origin] ▸ **ˈrummager** *n*

rummage out *or* **up** *vb* (*tr*) to find by searching vigorously; turn out.

rummage sale *n* **1** the U.S. and Canadian term for **jumble sale. 2** *U.S.* a sale of unclaimed property or unsold stock.

rummer (ˈrʌmə) *n* a drinking glass, typically having an ovoid bowl on a short stem. [C17: from Dutch *roemer* a glass for drinking toasts, from *roemen* to praise]

rummy[1] (ˈrʌmɪ) *or* **rum** *n* a card game based on collecting sets and sequences. [C20: perhaps from RUM[2]]

rummy[2] (ˈrʌmɪ) *adj* another word for **rum**[2].

rummy[3] (ˈrʌmɪ) *n, pl* **-mies. 1** *U.S. and Canadian.* a slang word for **drunkard.** ◆ *adj* **2** of or like rum in taste or smell.

rumour *or U.S.* **rumor** (ˈruːmə) *n* **1a** information, often a mixture of truth and untruth, passed around verbally. **1b** (*in combination*): *a rumour-monger.* **2** gossip or hearsay. **3** *Archaic.* din or clamour. **4** *Obsolete.* fame or reputation. ◆ *vb* **5** (*tr; usually passive*) to pass around or circulate in the form of a rumour: *it is rumoured that the Queen is coming.* **6** *Literary.* to make or cause to make a murmuring noise. [C14: via Old French from Latin *rūmor* common talk; related to Old Norse *rymja* to roar, Sanskrit *rāuti* he cries]

rump (rʌmp) *n* **1** the hindquarters of a mammal, not including the legs. **2** the rear part of a bird's back, nearest to the tail. **3** a person's buttocks. **4** Also called: **rump steak.** a cut of beef from behind the loin and above the round. **5** an inferior remnant. [C15: from Scandinavian; compare Danish *rumpe,* Icelandic *rumpr,* German *Rumpf* trunk of the body] ▸ **ˈrumpless** *adj*

Rumpelstiltskin (ˌrʌmpəlˈstɪltskɪn) *n* a dwarf in a German folktale who aids the king's bride on condition that she give him her first child or guess the dwarf's name. She guesses correctly and in his rage he destroys himself.

rumple (ˈrʌmpəl) *vb* **1** to make or become wrinkled, crumpled, ruffled, or dishevelled. ◆ *n* **2** a wrinkle, fold, or crease. [C17: from Middle Dutch *rompelen;* related to Old English *gerumpen* creased, wrinkled] ▸ **ˈrumply** *adj*

Rump Parliament *or* **the Rump** *n English history.* the remainder of the Long Parliament after Pride's Purge. It sat from 1648–53.

rumpus (ˈrʌmpəs) *n, pl* **-puses.** a noisy, confused, or disruptive commotion. [C18: of unknown origin]

rumpus room *n U.S., Canadian, and N.Z.* a room used for noisy activities, such as parties or children's games.

rumpy-pumpy (ˈrʌmpɪˈpʌmpɪ) *n Informal.* sexual intercourse.

Rum Rebellion *n Austral.* the deposition of Governor William Bligh in 1808 by officers of the New South Wales Corps, caused by his interference in their trading activities, esp. in the trafficking of rum.

run (rʌn) *vb* **runs, running, ran, run. 1** (*intr*) **1a** (of a two-legged creature) to move on foot at a rapid pace so that both feet are off the ground together for part of each stride. **1b** (of a four-legged creature) to move at a rapid gait; gallop or canter. **2** (*tr*) to pass over (a distance, route, etc.) in running: *to run a mile; run a race.* **3** (*intr*) to run in or finish a race as specified, esp. in a particular position: *John is running third.* **4** (*tr*) to perform or accomplish by or as if by running: *to run an errand.* **5** (*intr*) to flee; run away: *they took to their heels and ran.* **6** (*tr*) to bring into a specified state or condition by running: *to run oneself to a standstill.* **7** (*tr*) to track down or hunt (an animal): *to run a fox to earth.* **8** (*intr*) to move about freely and without restraint: *the children are running in the garden.* **9** (*intr;* usually foll. by *to*) to go or have recourse, as for aid, assistance, etc.: *he's always running to his mother when he's in trouble.* **10** (*tr*) to set (animals) loose on (a field or tract of land) so as to graze freely. **11** (*intr;* often foll. by *over, round,* or *up*) to make a short trip or brief informal visit: *I'll run over to your house this afternoon.* **12** to move quickly and easily on wheels by rolling, or in any of certain other ways: *a ball running along the ground; a sledge running over snow.* **13** to move or cause to move with a specified result or in a specified manner: *to run a ship aground; to run into a tree.* **14** (often foll. by *over*) to move or pass or cause to move or pass quickly: *to run a vacuum cleaner over the carpet; to run one's eyes over a page.* **15** (*tr;* foll. by *into, out of, through,* etc.) to force, thrust, or drive: *she ran a needle into her finger.* **16** (*tr*) to drive or maintain and operate (a vehicle). **17** (*tr*) to give a lift to (someone) in a vehicle; transport: *he ran her to the railway station.* **18** to ply or cause to ply between places on a route: *the bus runs from Piccadilly to Golders Green.* **19** to operate or be operated; function or cause to function: *the engine is running smoothly; to run a program on a computer.* **20** (*tr*) to be in charge of; manage: *to run a company.* **21** to extend or continue or cause to extend or continue in a particular direction, for a particular duration or distance, etc.: *the road runs north; the play ran for two years; the months ran into years.* **22** (*intr*) *Law.* **22a** to have legal force or effect: *the lease runs for two more years.* **22b** to accompany; be an integral part of or adjunct to: *an easement runs with the land.* **23** (*tr*) to be subjected to, be affected by, or incur: *to run a risk; run a temperature.* **24** (*intr;* often foll. by *to*) to be characterized (by); tend or incline: *her taste runs to extravagant hats; to run to fat.* **25** (*intr*) to recur persistently or be inherent: *red hair runs in my family.* **26** to cause or allow (liquids) to flow or (of liquids) to flow, esp. in a manner specified: *water ran from the broken pipe; the well has run dry.* **27** (*intr*) to melt and flow: *the wax grew hot and began to run.* **28** *Metallurgy.* **28a** to melt or fuse. **28b** (*tr*) to mould or cast (molten metal): *to run lead into ingots.* **29** (*intr*) (of waves, tides, rivers, etc.) to rise high, surge, or be at a specified height: *a high sea was running that night.* **30** (*intr*) to be diffused: *the colours in my dress ran when I washed it.* **31** (*intr*) (of stitches) to unravel or come undone or (of a garment) to have stitches unravel or come undone: *if you pull that thread the whole seam will run.* **32** to sew (an article) with continuous stitches. **33** (*intr*) (of growing vines, creepers, etc.) to trail, spread, or climb: *ivy running over a cottage wall.* **34** (*intr*) to spread or circulate quickly: *a rumour ran through the town.* **35** (*intr*) to be stated or reported: *his story runs as follows.* **36** to publish or print or be published or printed in a newspaper, magazine, etc.: *they ran his story in the next issue.* **37** (often foll. by *for*) *Chiefly U.S. and Canadian.* to be a candidate or present as a candidate for political or other office: *Anderson is running for president.* **38** (*tr*) to get past or through; evade: *to run a blockade.* **39** (*tr*) to deal in (arms, etc.), esp. by importing illegally: *he runs guns for the rebels.* **40** *Nautical.* to sail (a vessel, esp. a sailing vessel) or (of such a vessel) to be sailed with the wind coming from astern. **41** (*intr*) (of fish) **41a** to migrate upstream from the sea, esp. in order to spawn. **41b** to swim rapidly in any area of water, esp. during migration. **42** (*tr*) *Cricket.* to score (a run or number of runs) by hitting the ball and running between the wickets. **43** (*tr*) *Billiards, etc.* to make (a number of successful shots) in sequence. **44** (*tr*) *Golf.* to hit (the ball) so that it rolls along the ground. **45** (*tr*) *Bridge.* to cash (all one's winning cards in a long suit) successively. **46 run a bath.** to turn on the taps to fill a bath with water for bathing oneself. **47 run close.** to compete closely with; present a serious challenge to: *he got the job, but a younger man ran him close.* **48 run for it.** *Informal.* to attempt to escape from arrest, etc., by running. **49 be run off one's feet.** to be extremely busy. ◆ *n* **50** an act, instance, or period of running. **51** a gait, pace, or motion faster than a walk: *she went off at a run.* **52** a distance covered by running or a period of running: *a run of ten miles.* **53** an act, instance, or period of travelling in a vehicle, esp. for pleasure: *to go for a run in the car.* **54** free and unrestricted access: *we had the run of the house and garden for the whole summer.* **55a** a period of time during which a machine, computer, etc., operates. **55b** the amount of work performed in such a period. **56** a continuous or sustained period: *a run of good luck.* **57** a continuous sequence of performances: *the play had a good run.* **58** *Cards.* a sequence of winning cards in one suit, usually more than five: *a run of spades.* **59** tendency or trend: *the run of the market.* **60** type, class, or category: *the usual run of graduates.* **61** (usually foll. by *on*) a continuous and urgent demand: *a run on butter; a run on the dollar.* **62** a series of unravelled stitches, esp. in stockings or tights; ladder. **63** the characteristic pattern or direction of something: *the run of the grain on a piece of wood.* **64a** a continuous vein or seam of ore, coal, etc. **64b** the direction in which it lies. **65a** a period during which water or other liquid flows. **65b** the amount of such a flow. **66** a pipe, channel, etc., through which water or other liquid flows. **67** *U.S.* a small stream. **68** a steeply inclined pathway or course, esp. a snow-covered one used for skiing and bobsleigh racing. See also **green run, blue run, red run, black run. 69** an enclosure for domestic fowls or other animals, in which they have free movement: *a chicken run.* **70** (esp. in Australia and New Zealand) a tract of land for grazing livestock. **71** a track or area frequented by animals: *a deer run; a rabbit run.* **72** a group of animals of the same species moving together. **73** the migration of fish upstream in order to spawn. **74** *Nautical.* **74a** the tack of a sailing vessel in which the wind comes from astern. **74b** part of the hull of a vessel near the stern where it curves upwards and inwards. **75** *Military.* **75a** a mission in a warplane. **75b** short for **bombing run. 76** the movement of an aircraft along the ground during takeoff or landing. **77** *Music.* a rapid scalelike passage of notes. **78** *Cricket.* a score of one, normally achieved by both batsmen running from one end of the wicket to the other after one of them has hit the ball. Compare **extra** (sense 6), **boundary** (sense 2c). **79** *Baseball.* an instance of a batter touching all four bases safely, thereby scoring. **80** *Golf.* the distance that a ball rolls after hitting the ground. **81 a run for (one's) money.** *Informal.* **81a** a strong challenge or close competition. **81b** pleasure derived from an activity. **82 in the long run.** as the eventual outcome of a sequence of events, actions, etc.; ultimately. **83 in the short run.** as the immediate outcome of a series of events, etc. **84 on the run. 84a** escaping from arrest; fugitive. **84b** in rapid flight; retreating: *the enemy is on the run.* **84c** hurrying from place to place: *she's always on the run.* **85 the runs.** *Slang.* diarrhoea. ◆ See also **run about, run across, run after, run along, run around, run away, run down, run in, run into, run off, run on, run out, run over, run through, run to, run up.** [Old English *runnen,* past participle of *(ge)rinnan;* related to Old French, Old Norse *rinna,* Old Saxon, Gothic, Old High German *rinnan*]

runabout (ˈrʌnəˌbaʊt) *n* **1** a small car, esp. one for use in a town. **2** a light aircraft. **3** a light motorboat. **4** a person who moves about constantly or busily. ◆ *vb* **run about. 5** (*intr, adv*) to move busily from place to place.

run across *vb* (*intr, prep*) to meet unexpectedly; encounter by chance.

run after *vb* (*intr, prep*) *Informal.* **1** to pursue (a member of the opposite sex) with persistent attention. **2** to pursue (anything) persistently. **3** to care for in an excessively attentive or servile way: *she runs after her three grown sons as if they were babies.*

runagate ('rʌnəˌgeɪt) *n Archaic.* **a** a vagabond, fugitive, or renegade. **b** (*as modifier*): *a runagate priest.* [C16: variant (influenced by RUN) of RENEGADE]

run along *vb* (*intr, adv*) (often said patronizingly) to go away; leave.

run around *vb* (*intr, adv*) *Informal.* **1** (often foll. by *with*) to associate habitually (with). **2** to behave in a fickle or promiscuous manner. ◆ *n* **run-around. 3** *Informal.* deceitful or evasive treatment of a person (esp. in the phrase **give** *or* **get the run-around**). **4** *Printing.* an arrangement of printed matter in which the column width is narrowed to accommodate an illustration.

run away *vb* (*intr, adv*) **1** to take flight; escape. **2** to go away; depart. **3** (of a horse) to gallop away uncontrollably. **4 run away with. 4a** to abscond or elope with: *he ran away with his boss's daughter.* **4b** to make off with; steal. **4c** to escape from the control of: *his enthusiasm ran away with him.* **4d** to win easily or be assured of victory in (a competition): *he ran away with the race.* ◆ *n* **runaway. 5a** a person or animal that runs away. **5b** (*as modifier*): *a runaway horse.* **6** the act or an instance of running away. **7** (*modifier*) occurring as a result of the act of eloping: *a runaway wedding.* **8** (*modifier*) (of a race, victory, etc.) easily won.

runch (rʌntʃ) *n Scot. and northern English.* another name for **white charlock.** See **charlock** (sense 2). [C16: of obscure origin]

runcible spoon ('rʌnsɪbᵊl) *n* a forklike utensil with two broad prongs and one sharp curved prong. [*runcible* coined by Edward Lear in a nonsense poem (1871)]

Runcie ('rʌnsɪ) *n* **Robert** (**Alexander Kennedy**), Baron. born 1921, Archbishop of Canterbury (1980–91).

runcinate ('rʌnsɪnɪt, -ˌneɪt) *adj* (of a leaf) having a saw-toothed margin with the teeth or lobes pointing backwards. [C18: from New Latin *runcīnātus,* from Latin *runcīnāre* to plane off, from *runcīna* a carpenter's plane]

Runcorn ('rʌŋˌkɔːn) *n* a town in NW England, in N Cheshire on the Manchester Ship Canal: port and industrial centre; designated a new town in 1964. Pop.: 64 154 (1991).

rundale ('rʌnˌdeɪl) *n* (formerly) the name given, esp. in Ireland and earlier, in Scotland, to the system of land tenure in which each land-holder had several strips of land that were not contiguous. Also called (in Scotland): **'runrig.** [C16 *ryndale,* from RUN (vb) + *dale,* a northern variant of DOLE[1], in the sense "a portion"]

rundle ('rʌndᵊl) *n* **1** a rung of a ladder. **2** a wheel, esp. of a wheelbarrow. [C14: variant of ROUNDEL]

rundlet ('rʌndlɪt) *n Obsolete.* a liquid measure, generally about 15 gallons. [C14: see ROUNDLET]

run down *vb* (*mainly adv*) **1** to cause or allow (an engine, battery, etc.) to lose power gradually and cease to function or (of an engine, battery, etc.) to do this. **2** to decline or reduce in number or size: *the firm ran down its sales force.* **3** (*tr, usually passive*) to tire, sap the strength of, or exhaust: *he was thoroughly run down and needed a holiday.* **4** (*tr*) to criticize adversely; denigrate; decry. **5** (*tr*) to hit and knock to the ground with a moving vehicle. **6** *Nautical.* **6a** (*tr*) to collide with and cause to sink. **6b** (*intr, prep*) to navigate so as to move parallel to (a coast). **7** (*tr*) to pursue and find or capture: *to run down a fugitive.* **8** (*tr*) to read swiftly or perfunctorily: *he ran down their list of complaints.* ◆ *adj* **run-down. 9** tired; exhausted. **10** worn-out, shabby, or dilapidated: *a run-down old house.* ◆ *n* **rundown. 11** a brief review, résumé, or summary. **12** the process of a motor or mechanism coming gradually to a standstill after the source of power is removed. **13** a reduction in number or size.

Rundstedt ('rʊndstɛt; *German* 'rʊntʃtɛt) *n* **Karl Rudolf Gerd von** (karl 'ruːdɔlf gɛrt fɔn). 1875–1953, German field marshal; directed the conquest of Poland and France in World War II; commander of the Western Front (1942–44); led the Ardennes counteroffensive (Dec. 1944).

rune (ruːn) *n* **1** any of the characters of an ancient Germanic alphabet, derived from the Roman alphabet, in use, esp. in Scandinavia, from the 3rd century A.D. to the end of the Middle Ages. Each character was believed to have a magical significance. **2** any obscure piece of writing using mysterious symbols. **3** a kind of Finnish poem or a stanza in such a poem. [Old English *rūn,* from Old Norse *rūn* secret; related to Old Saxon, Old High German, Gothic *runa*] ▸ **'runic** *adj*

Runeberg ('ruːnəˌbɜːg, *Finnish* 'runəˌbærj) *n* **Johan Ludvig.** 1804–77, Finnish poet, who wrote in Swedish. His works include the epic *King Fialar* (1844) and patriotic poems including the Finnish national anthem.

rung[1] (rʌŋ) *n* **1** one of the bars or rods that form the steps of a ladder. **2** a crosspiece between the legs of a chair, etc. **3** *Nautical.* a spoke on a ship's wheel or a handle projecting from the periphery. **4** *Dialect.* a cudgel or staff. [Old English *hrung;* related to Old High German *runga,* Gothic *hrugga*] ▸ **'rungless** *adj*

rung[2] (rʌŋ) *vb* the past participle of **ring**[2].

run in *vb* (*adv*) **1** to run (an engine) gently, usually for a specified period when it is new, in order that the running surfaces may become polished. **2** (*tr*) to insert or include. **3** (*intr*) (of an aircraft) to approach a point or target. **4** (*tr*) *Informal.* to take into custody; arrest: *he was run in for assault.* ◆ *n* **run-in. 5** *Informal.* an argument or quarrel: *he had a run-in with the boss yesterday.* **6** an approach to the end of an event, etc.: *the run-in to the championship.* **7** *Printing.* matter inserted in an existing paragraph.

run into *vb* (*prep; mainly intr*) **1** (*also tr*) to collide with or cause to collide with: *her car ran into a tree.* **2** to encounter unexpectedly. **3** (*also tr*) to be beset by or cause to be beset by: *the project ran into financial difficulties.* **4** to extend to; be of the order of: *debts running into thousands.*

runlet ('rʌnlɪt) *n Archaic.* a cask for wine, beer, etc. [C14: from Old French *rondelet* ROUNDLET]

runnel ('rʌnᵊl) *n Literary.* a small stream. [C16: from Old English *rynele;* related to RUN]

runner ('rʌnə) *n* **1** a person who runs, esp. an athlete. **2** a messenger for a bank or brokerage firm. **3** an employee of an art or antique dealer who visits auctions to bid on desired lots. **4** a person engaged in the solicitation of business. **5** a person on the run; fugitive. **6a** a person or vessel engaged in smuggling; smuggler. **6b** (*in combination*): *a rum-runner.* **7** a person who operates, manages, or controls something. **8a** either of the strips of metal or wood on which a sledge runs. **8b** the blade of an ice skate. **9** a roller or guide for a sliding component. **10** the rotating element of a water turbine. **11** another name for **running belay. 12** any of various carangid fishes of temperate and tropical seas, such as *Caranx crysos* (**blue runner**) of American Atlantic waters. **13** *Botany.* **13a** Also called: **stolon.** a slender horizontal stem, as of the strawberry, that grows along the surface of the soil and propagates by producing roots and shoots at the nodes or tip. **13b** a plant that propagates in this way. **14** a strip of lace, linen, etc., placed across a table, dressing table, etc. for protection and decoration. **15** a narrow rug or carpet, as for a passage. **16** another word for **rocker** (on a rocking chair). **17 do a runner.** *Slang.* to run away in order to escape trouble or to avoid paying for something.

runner bean *n* another name for **scarlet runner.**

runner-up *n, pl* **runners-up.** a contestant finishing a race or competition in second place.

running ('rʌnɪŋ) *adj* **1** maintained continuously; incessant: *a running battle; running commentary.* **2** (*postpositive*) without interruption; consecutive: *he lectured for two hours running.* **3** denoting or relating to the scheduled operation of a public vehicle: *the running time of a train.* **4** accomplished at a run: *a running jump.* **5** (of a knot) sliding along the rope from which it is made, so as to form a noose which becomes smaller when the rope is pulled. **6** (of a wound, sore, etc.) discharging pus or a serous fluid. **7** denoting or relating to operations for maintenance: *running repairs.* **8** prevalent; current: *running prices.* **9** repeated or continuous: *a running design.* **10** (of certain plants, plant stems, etc.) creeping along the ground. **11** flowing: *running water.* **12** (of handwriting) having the letters run together. ◆ *n* **13** management or organization: *the running of a company.* **14** operation or maintenance: *the running of a machine.* **15** competition or a competitive situation (in the phrases **in the running, out of the running**). **16 make the running.** to set the pace in a competition or race. **17** *Rare.* the power or ability to run.

running belay *n Mountaineering.* the clipping of the rope through a karabiner attached to a sling, piton, nut, etc., secured to the mountain: used by a leading climber of a team to reduce the length of a possible fall. Also called: **runner.**

running board *n* a footboard along the side of a vehicle, esp. an early motorcar.

running commentary *n* a continuous spoken description of an event while it is happening.

running head *or* **title** *n Printing.* a heading printed at the top of every page or every other page of a book.

running light *n Nautical.* one of several white, red, or green lights displayed by vessels operating at night.

running mate *n* **1** *U.S.* a candidate for the subordinate of two linked positions, esp. a candidate for the vice-presidency. **2** a horse that pairs another in a team.

running repairs *pl n* repairs, as to a machine or vehicle, that are minor and can be made with little or no interruption in the use of the item.

running rigging *n Nautical.* the wires and ropes used to control the operations of a sailing vessel. Compare **standing rigging.**

running stitch *n* a simple form of hand stitching, consisting of small stitches that look the same on both sides of the fabric, usually used for gathering. Sometimes called: **gathering stitch.**

runny ('rʌnɪ) *adj* **-nier, -niest. 1** tending to flow; liquid. **2** (of the nose or nasal passages) exuding mucus.

Runnymede ('rʌnɪˌmiːd) *n* a meadow on the S bank of the Thames near Windsor, where King John met his rebellious barons in 1215 and acceded to Magna Carta.

run off *vb* (*adv*) **1** (*intr*) to depart in haste. **2** (*tr*) to produce quickly, as copies on a duplicating machine. **3** to drain (liquid) or (of liquid) to be drained. **4** (*tr*) to decide (a race) by a runoff. **5** (*tr*) to get rid of (weight, etc.) by running. **6** (*intr*) (of a flow of liquid) to begin to dry up; cease to run. **7 run off with. 7a** to steal; purloin. **7b** to elope with. ◆ *n* **runoff. 8a** an extra race to decide the winner after a tie. **8b** a contest or election held after a previous one has failed to produce a clear victory for any one person. **9** that portion of rainfall that runs into streams as surface water rather than being absorbed by the soil. **10** the overflow of a liquid from a container. **11** *N.Z.* grazing land for store cattle.

run-of-paper *adj* (of a story, advertisement, etc.) placed anywhere in a newspaper, at the discretion of the editor.

run-of-the-mill *adj* ordinary, average, or undistinguished in quality, character, or nature; not special or excellent.

run on *vb* (*adv*) **1** (*intr*) to continue without interruption. **2** to write with linked-up characters. **3** *Printing.* to compose text matter without indentation or paragraphing. ◆ *n* **run-on. 4** *Printing.* **4a** text matter composed without indenting. **4b** (*as modifier*): *run-on text matter.* **5a** a word added at the end of a dictionary entry whose meaning can be easily inferred from the definition of the headword. **5b** (*as modifier*): *a run-on entry.*

run out *vb* (*adv*) **1** (*intr;* often foll. by *of*) to exhaust (a supply of something) or (of a supply) to become exhausted. **2 run out on.** *Informal.* to desert or abandon. **3** (*tr*) *Cricket.* to dismiss (a running batsman) by breaking the wicket with the ball, or with the ball in the hand, while he is out of his ground. ◆ *n* **run-out.** 4 *Cricket.* dismissal of a batsman by running him out. 5 *Mechanical engineering.* an imperfection of a rotating component so that not all parts revolve in the same plane.

run over *vb* 1 (*tr, adv*) to knock down (a person) with a moving vehicle. 2 (*intr*) to overflow the capacity of (a container). 3 (*intr, prep*) to examine hastily or make a rapid survey of. 4 (*intr, prep*) to exceed (a limit): *we've run over our time.*

runt (rʌnt) *n* 1 the smallest and weakest young animal in a litter, esp. the smallest piglet in a litter. 2 *Derogatory.* an undersized or inferior person. 3 a large pigeon, originally bred for eating. [C16: origin unknown] ▸ **'runtish** *adj* ▸ **'runty** *adj* ▸ **'runtiness** *n*

run through *vb* 1 (*tr, adv*) to transfix with a sword or other weapon. 2 (*intr, prep*) to exhaust (money) by wasteful spending; squander. 3 (*intr, prep*) to practise or rehearse: *let's run through the plan.* 4 (*intr, prep*) to examine hastily. ◆ *n* **run-through.** 5 a practice or rehearsal. 6 a brief survey.

run time *n Computing.* the time during which a computer program is executed.

run to *vb* (*intr, prep*) to be sufficient for: *my income doesn't run to luxuries.*

run up *vb* (*tr, adv*) 1 to amass or accumulate; incur: *to run up debts.* 2 to make by sewing together quickly: *to run up a dress.* 3 to hoist: *to run up a flag.* ◆ *n* **run-up.** 4 an approach run by an athlete for a long jump, pole vault, etc. 5 a preliminary or preparatory period: *the run-up to the election.*

runway ('rʌn,weɪ) *n* 1 a hard level roadway or other surface from which aircraft take off and on which they land. 2 an enclosure for domestic animals; run. 3 *Forestry, North American.* a chute for sliding logs down. 4 *Chiefly U.S.* a narrow ramp extending from the stage into the audience in a theatre, nightclub, etc., esp. as used by models in a fashion show.

Runyon ('rʌnjən) *n* (**Alfred**) **Damon.** 1884–1946, U.S. short-story writer, best known for his humorous tales about racy Broadway characters. His story collections include *Guys and Dolls* (1932), which became the basis of a musical (1950).

rupee (ruː'piː) *n* the standard monetary unit of India, Nepal, and Pakistan (divided into 100 paisas), Sri Lanka, Mauritius, and the Seychelles (divided into 100 cents). [C17: from Hindi *rupaīyā,* from Sanskrit *rūpya* coined silver, from *rūpa* shape, beauty]

Rupert ('ruːpət) *n* **Prince.** 1619–82, German-born nephew of Charles I: Royalist general during the Civil War (until 1646) and commander of the Royalist fleet (1648–50). After the Restoration he was an admiral of the English fleet in wars against the Dutch.

Rupert's Land *n* (formerly, in Canada) the territories granted by Charles II to the Hudson's Bay Company in 1670 and ceded to the Canadian Government in 1870, comprising all the land watered by rivers flowing into Hudson Bay.

rupiah (ruː'piːə) *n, pl* **-ah** *or* **-ahs.** the standard monetary unit of Indonesia, divided into 100 sen. [from Hindi: RUPEE]

rupicolous (ruː'pɪkələs) *adj Biology.* living or growing on or among rocks. [C19: from Latin *rūp(ēs)* crag + -I- + -COLOUS]

rupture ('rʌptʃə) *n* 1 the act of breaking or bursting or the state of being broken or burst. 2 a breach of peaceful or friendly relations. 3 *Pathol.* 3a the breaking or tearing of a bodily structure or part. 3b another word for **hernia.** ◆ *vb* 4 to break or burst or cause to break or burst. 5 to affect or be affected with a rupture or hernia. 6 to undergo or cause to undergo a breach in relations or friendship. [C15: from Latin *ruptūra* a breaking, from *rumpere* to burst forth; see ERUPT] ▸ **'rupturable** *adj*

rural ('rʊərəl) *adj* 1 of, relating to, or characteristic of the country or country life. 2 living in or accustomed to the country. 3 of, relating to, or associated with farming. ◆ Compare **urban.** [C15: via Old French from Latin *rūrālis,* from *rūs* the country] ▸ **'ruralism** *n* ▸ **'ruralist** *n* ▸ **ru'rality** *n* ▸ **'rurally** *adv*

rural dean *n Chiefly Brit.* a clergyman having authority over a group of parishes.

rural delivery *n N.Z.* a mail service in a country area, often run by contractors for the Post Office.

rural district *n* (in England and Wales from 1888 to 1974 and Northern Ireland from 1898 to 1973) a rural division of a county.

ruralize *or* **ruralise** ('rʊərə,laɪz) *vb* 1 (*tr*) to make rural in character, appearance, etc. 2 (*intr*) to go into the country to live. ▸ **,rurali'zation** *or* **,rurali'sation** *n*

rural science *or* **studies** *n Brit.* the study and theory of agriculture, biology, ecology, and associated fields.

Rurik *or* **Ryurik** ('rʊərɪk) *n* died 879. Varangian (Scandinavian Viking) leader who founded the Russian monarchy. He gained control over Novgorod (?862) and his dynasty, the **Rurikids,** ruled until 1598.

Ruritania (,rʊərɪ'teɪnɪə, -njə) *n* 1 an imaginary kingdom of central Europe: setting of several novels by Anthony Hope, esp. *The Prisoner of Zenda* (1894). 2 any setting of adventure, romance, and intrigue. ▸ **,Ruri'tanian** *adj, n*

ruru ('ruːruː) *n N.Z.* another name for **mopoke.** [Maori]

Rus. *abbrev. for* Russia(n).

ruse (ruːz) *n* an action intended to mislead, deceive, or trick; stratagem. [C15: from Old French: trick, esp. to evade capture, from *ruser* to retreat, from Latin *recūsāre* to refuse]

Ruse ('ruːseɪ) *n* a city in NE Bulgaria, on the River Danube: the chief river port and one of the largest industrial centres in Bulgaria. Pop.: 168 051 (1996 est.).

rush[1] (rʌʃ) *vb* 1 to hurry or cause to hurry; hasten. 2 to make a sudden attack upon (a fortress, position, person, etc.). 3 (when *intr,* often foll. by *at, in,* or *into*) to proceed or approach in a reckless manner. 4 **rush one's fences.** to proceed with precipitate haste. 5 (*intr*) to come, flow, swell, etc., quickly or suddenly: *tears rushed to her eyes.* 6 *Slang.* to cheat, esp. by grossly overcharging. 7 (*tr*) *U.S. and Canadian.* to make a concerted effort to secure the agreement, participation, etc., of (a person). 8 (*intr*) *American football.* to gain ground by running forwards with the ball. ◆ *n* 9 the act or condition of rushing. 10 a sudden surge towards someone or something: *a gold rush.* 11 a sudden surge of sensation, esp. produced by a drug. 12 a sudden demand. ◆ *adj* (*prenominal*) 13 requiring speed or urgency: *a rush job.* 14 characterized by much movement, business, etc.: *a rush period.* [C14 *ruschen,* from Old French *ruser* to put to flight, from Latin *recūsāre* to refuse, reject] ▸ **'rusher** *n*

rush[2] (rʌʃ) *n* 1 any annual or perennial plant of the genus *Juncus,* growing in wet places and typically having grasslike cylindrical leaves and small green or brown flowers: family *Juncaceae.* Many species are used to make baskets. 2 any of various similar or related plants, such as the woodrush, scouring rush, and spike-rush. 3 something valueless; a trifle; straw: *not worth a rush.* 4 short for **rush light.** [Old English *risce, rysce;* related to Middle Dutch *risch,* Norwegian *rusk,* Old Slavonic *rozga* twig, rod] ▸ **'rush,like** *adj*

Rushdie ('rʊʃdɪ) *n* (**Ahmed**) **Salman** (sʌl'mɑːn). born 1947, British writer, born in India, whose novels include *Midnight's Children* (1981), which won the Booker prize, *Shame* (1983), and *The Ground Beneath Her Feet* (1998). His novel *The Satanic Verses* (1988) was regarded as blasphemous by many Muslims and he was forced into hiding (1989) when the Ayatollah Khomeini called for his death.

rushes (rʌʃɪz) *pl n* (*sometimes sing*) (in film-making) the initial prints of a scene or scenes before editing, usually prepared daily.

rush hour *n* a period at the beginning and end of the working day when large numbers of people are travelling to or from work.

rush light *or* **candle** *n* a narrow candle, formerly in use, made of the pith of various types of rush dipped in tallow.

Rushmore ('rʌʃmɔː) *n* **Mount.** a mountain in W South Dakota, in the Black Hills: a national memorial, with the faces of Washington, Lincoln, Jefferson, and Roosevelt carved into its side by Gutzon Borglum between 1927 and 1941. Height: 1841 m (6040 ft.).

rushy ('rʌʃɪ) *adj* **rushier, rushiest.** abounding in, covered with, or made of rushes. ▸ **'rushiness** *n*

rus in urbe *Latin.* (rʊs ɪn 'ɜːbɪ) the country in the town.

rusk (rʌsk) *n* a light bread dough, sweet or plain, baked twice until it is brown, hard, and crisp: often given to babies. [C16: from Spanish or Portuguese *rosca* screw, bread shaped in a twist, of unknown origin]

Rusk (rʌsk) *n* (**David**) **Dean.** 1909–94, U.S. statesman: secretary of state (1961–69). He defended U.S. military involvement in Vietnam and opposed recognition of communist China.

Ruskin ('rʌskɪn) *n* **John.** 1819–1900, English art critic and social reformer. He was a champion of the Gothic Revival and the Pre-Raphaelites and saw a close connection between art and morality. From about 1860 he argued vigorously for social and economic planning. His works include *Modern Painters* (1843–60), *The Stones of Venice* (1851–53), *Unto this Last* (1862), *Time and Tide* (1867), and *Fors Clavigera* (1871–84).

Russ (rʌs) *n, pl* **Russ** *or* **Russes,** *adj* an archaic word for **Russian** (person or language).

Russ. *abbrev. for* Russia(n).

RUSS *international car registration for* Russia.

Russborough House ('rʌsbərə) *n* a mansion near Blessington in Co. Wicklow, Republic of Ireland: built by Richard Castle and Francis Bindon for the 1st Earl of Miltown from 1740.

Russell ('rʌsᵊl) *n* 1 **Bertrand** (**Arthur William**), 3rd Earl. 1872–1970, British philosopher and mathematician. His books include *Principles of Mathematics* (1903), *Principia Mathematica* (1910–13) with A. N. Whitehead, *Introduction to Mathematical Philosophy* (1919), *The Problems of Philosophy* (1912), *The Analysis of Mind* (1921), and *An Enquiry into Meaning and Truth* (1940): Nobel prize for literature 1950. 2 **George William,** pen name æ. 1867–1935, Irish poet and journalist. 3 **Henry Norris.** 1877–1957, U.S. astronomer and astrophysicist, who originated one form of the Hertzsprung–Russell diagram. 4 **John,** 1st Earl. 1792–1878, British statesman; prime minister (1846–52; 1865–66). He led the campaign to carry the 1832 Reform Act. 5 **Ken.** born 1927, British film director. His films include *Women in Love* (1969), *The Music Lovers* (1970), *The Boy Friend* (1971), *Valentino* (1977), *Gothic* (1986), and *The Rainbow* (1989).

Russell diagram *n* See **Hertzsprung-Russell diagram.**

Russell's paradox *n Logic.* the paradox discovered by Bertrand Russell in the work of Gottlob Frege, that the class of all classes that are not members of themselves is a member of itself only if it is not, and is not only if it is. This undermines the notion of an all-inclusive universal class.

russet ('rʌsɪt) *n* 1 brown with a yellowish or reddish tinge. 2a a rough homespun fabric, reddish-brown in colour, formerly in use for clothing. 2b (*as modifier*): *a russet coat.* 3 any of various apples with rough brownish-red skins. 4 abnormal roughness on fruit, caused by parasites, pesticides, or frost. ◆ *adj* 5 (of tanned hide leather) dressed ready for staining. 6 *Archaic.* simple; homely; rustic: *a russet life.* 7 of the colour russet: *russet hair.* [C13: from Anglo-Norman, from Old French *rosset,* from *rous,* from Latin *russus;* related to Latin *ruber* red] ▸ **'russety** *adj*

Russia ('rʌʃə) *n* (full name **Russian Federation**) 1 the largest country in the world, covering N Eurasia and bordering on the Pacific and Arctic Oceans and the Baltic, Black, and Caspian Seas: originating from the principality of Muscovy in the 17th century, it expanded to become the Russian Empire; the Tsar was overthrown in 1917 and the Communist Russian Soviet Federative Socialist Republic was created; this merged with neighbouring Soviet Republics in 1922 to form the Soviet Union; on the disintegration of the Soviet Union in 1991 the Russian Federation was established as an independent state. Official language: Russian. Religion: nonreligious and Russian orthodox Christian. Currency: rouble. Capital: Moscow. Pop.: 146 861 000 (1998 est.). Area: 17 074 984 sq. km

(6 592 658 sq. miles). **2** another name for the **Russian Empire. 3** another name for the former **Soviet Union. 4** another name for the former **Russian Soviet Federative Socialist Republic.** ◆ Russian name: **Rossiya.**

Russia leather *n* a smooth dyed leather made from calfskin and scented with birch tar oil, originally produced in Russia.

Russian ('rʌʃən) *n* **1** the official language of Russia: an Indo-European language belonging to the East Slavonic branch. **2** the official language of the former Soviet Union. **3** a native or inhabitant of Russia. ◆ *adj* **4** of, relating to, or characteristic of Russia, its people, or their language.

Russian doll *n* any of a set of hollow wooden figures, each of which splits in half to contain the next smallest figure, down to the smallest.

Russian dressing *n* mayonnaise or vinaigrette with chilli sauce, chopped gherkins, etc.

Russian Empire *n* the tsarist empire in Asia and E Europe, overthrown by the Russian Revolution of 1917.

Russian Federation *n* See **Russia.**

Russianize *or* **Russianise** ('rʌʃəˌnaɪz) *vb* to make or become Russian in style, character, etc. ▸ **ˌRussianiˈzation** *or* **ˌRussianiˈsation** *n*

Russian Orthodox Church *n* the national Church of Russia, constituting a branch of the Eastern Church presided over by the Patriarch of Moscow.

Russian Revolution *n* **1** Also called (reckoned by the Julian calendar): **February Revolution.** the uprising in Russia in March 1917, during which the tsar abdicated and a provisional government was set up. **2** Also called (reckoned by the Julian calendar): **October Revolution.** the seizure of power by the Bolsheviks under Lenin in November 1917, transforming the uprising into a socialist revolution. This was followed by a period of civil war against counter-revolutionary armies (1918–22), which ended in eventual victory for the Bolsheviks.

Russian roulette *n* **1** a game of chance in which each player in turn spins the cylinder of a revolver loaded with only one cartridge and presses the trigger with the barrel against his own head. **2** any foolish or potentially suicidal undertaking.

Russian salad *n* a salad of cold diced cooked vegetables mixed with Russian dressing.

Russian Soviet Federative Socialist Republic *n* (formerly) the largest administrative division of the Soviet Union. Abbrev.: **RSFSR.**

Russian Turkestan *n* See **Turkestan.**

Russian wolfhound *n* a less common name for **borzoi.**

Russian Zone *n* another name for the **Soviet Zone.**

Russify ('rʌsɪˌfaɪ) *vb* **-fies, -fying, -fied.** *(tr)* to cause to become Russian in character. ▸ **ˌRussifiˈcation** *n*

Russky *or* **Russki** ('rʌskɪ) *n, pl* **-kies** *or* **-kis,** *adj Chiefly U.S.* a slang word for **Russian.** [C20]

Russo- ('rʌsəʊ-) *combining form.* Russia or Russian: *Russo-Japanese.*

Russo-Japanese War *n* a war (1904–05) between Russia and Japan, caused largely by rivalry over Korea and Manchuria. Russia suffered a series of major defeats.

Russophile ('rʌsəʊˌfaɪl) *or* **Russophil** *n* **1** an admirer of Russia or the former Soviet Union, its customs, political system, etc. ◆ *adj* **2** marked by or possessing admiration of Russia or the former Soviet Union.

Russophobe ('rʌsəʊˌfəʊb) *n* a person who feels intense and often irrational hatred (**Russophobia**) for Russia, or esp. the former Soviet Union, its political system, etc. ▸ **ˌRussoˈphobic** *adj*

russula ('rʌsjʊlə) *n, pl* **-lae** (-liː) *or* **-las.** any fungus of the large basidiomycetous genus *Russula,* of typical toadstool shape and often brightly coloured, such as the yellow *R. ochroleuca* and *R. lutea,* the green *R. aeruginea,* the violet-pink *R. fragilis,* and the purple *R. atropurpurea.*

rust (rʌst) *n* **1** a reddish-brown oxide coating formed on iron or steel by the action of oxygen and moisture. **2** Also called: **rust fungus.** *Plant pathol.* **2a** any basidiomycetous fungus of the order *Uredinales,* parasitic on cereal plants, conifers, etc. **2b** any of various plant diseases characterized by reddish-brown discoloration of the leaves and stem, esp. that caused by the rust fungi. **3a** a strong brown colour, sometimes with a reddish or yellowish tinge. **3b** *(as adj): a rust carpet.* **4** any corrosive or debilitating influence, esp. lack of use. ◆ *vb* **5** to become or cause to become coated with a layer of rust. **6** to deteriorate or cause to deteriorate through some debilitating influence or lack of use: *he allowed his talent to rust over the years.* [Old English *rūst;* related to Old Saxon, Old High German *rost*] ▸ **ˈrustless** *adj*

rust belt *n* an area where heavy industry is in decline, esp. in the Midwest of the U.S.

rust bucket *n* **1** *Slang.* something that is run-down or dilapidated, esp. a very badly rusted car. ◆ *adj* **rustbucket. 2** *Informal.* run-down or dilapidated: *rustbucket factories.*

rustic ('rʌstɪk) *adj* **1** of, characteristic of, or living in the country; rural. **2** having qualities ascribed to country life or people; simple; unsophisticated: *rustic pleasures.* **3** crude, awkward, or uncouth. **4** made of untrimmed branches: *a rustic seat.* **5** denoting or characteristic of a style of furniture popular in England in the 18th and 19th centuries, in which the legs and feet of chairs, tables, etc., were made to resemble roots, trunks, and branches of trees. **6** (of masonry) having a rusticated finish. ◆ *n* **7** a person who comes from or lives in the country. **8** an unsophisticated, simple, or clownish person from the country. **9** Also called: **ˈrusticˌwork.** brick or stone having a rough finish. [C16: from Old French *rustique,* from Latin *rūsticus,* from *rūs* the country] ▸ **ˈrustically** *adv* ▸ **rusticity** (rʌˈstɪsɪtɪ) *n*

rusticate ('rʌstɪˌkeɪt) *vb* **1** to banish or retire to the country. **2** to make or become rustic in style, behaviour, etc. **3** *(tr) Architect.* to finish (an exterior wall) with large blocks of masonry that are separated by deep joints and decorated with a bold, usually textured, design. **4** *(tr) Brit.* to send down from university for a specified time as a punishment. [C17: from Latin *rūsticārī,* from *rūs* the country] ▸ **ˌrustiˈcation** *n* ▸ **ˈrustiˌcator** *n*

rusticating ('rʌstɪˌkeɪtɪŋ) *n* (in New Zealand) a wide type of weatherboarding used in older houses. Also called: **rusticated.**

rustle[1] ('rʌsᵊl) *vb* **1** to make or cause to make a low crisp whispering or rubbing sound, as of dry leaves or paper. **2** to move with such a sound. ◆ *n* **3** such a sound or sounds. [Old English *hrūxlian;* related to Gothic *hrukjan* to CROW[2], Old Norse *hraukr* raven, CROW[1]] ▸ **ˈrustling** *adj, n* ▸ **ˈrustlingly** *adv*

rustle[2] ('rʌsᵊl) *vb* **1** *Chiefly U.S. and Canadian.* to steal (cattle, horses, etc.). **2** *U.S. and Canadian informal.* to move swiftly and energetically. [C19: probably special use of RUSTLE[1] (in the sense: to move with quiet sound)]

rustler ('rʌslə) *n* **1** *Chiefly U.S. and Canadian.* a cattle or horse thief. **2** *U.S. and Canadian informal.* an energetic or vigorous person.

rustle up *vb (tr, adv) Informal.* **1** to prepare (a meal, snack, etc.) rapidly, esp. at short notice. **2** to forage for and obtain.

rustproof ('rʌstˌpruːf) *adj* treated against rusting.

rusty ('rʌstɪ) *adj* **rustier, rustiest. 1** covered with, affected by, or consisting of rust: *a rusty machine; a rusty deposit.* **2** of the colour rust. **3** discoloured by age: *a rusty coat.* **4** (of the voice) tending to croak. **5** old-fashioned in appearance; seemingly antiquated: *a rusty old gentleman.* **6** out of practice; impaired in skill or knowledge by inaction or neglect. **7** (of plants) affected by the rust fungus. ▸ **ˈrustily** *adv* ▸ **ˈrustiness** *n*

rut[1] (rʌt) *n* **1** a groove or furrow in a soft road, caused by wheels. **2** any deep mark, hole, or groove. **3** a narrow or predictable way of life, set of attitudes, etc.; dreary or undeviating routine (esp. in the phrase **in a rut**). ◆ *vb* **ruts, rutting, rutted. 4** *(tr)* to make a rut or ruts in. [C16: probably from French *route* road]

rut[2] (rʌt) *n* **1** a recurrent period of sexual excitement and reproductive activity in certain male ruminants, such as the deer, that corresponds to the period of oestrus in females. **2** another name for **oestrus.** ◆ *vb* **ruts, rutting, rutted. 3** *(intr)* (of male ruminants) to be in a period of sexual excitement and activity. [C15: from Old French *rut* noise, roar, from Latin *rugītus,* from *rugīre* to roar]

rutabaga (ˌruːtəˈbeɪgə) *n* the U.S. and Canadian name for **swede.** [C18: from Swedish dialect *rotabagge,* literally: root bag]

rutaceous (ruːˈteɪʃəs) *adj* of, relating to, or belonging to the *Rutaceae,* a family of tropical and temperate flowering plants many of which have aromatic leaves. The family includes rue, citrus trees, and dittany. [C19: from New Latin *Rutaceae,* from Latin *rūta* RUE[2]]

ruth (ruːθ) *n Archaic.* **1** pity; compassion. **2** repentance; remorse. **3** grief or distress. [C12: from *rewen* to RUE[1]]

Ruth (ruːθ) *n* **1** *Old Testament.* **1a** a Moabite woman, who left her own people to remain with her mother-in-law Naomi, and became the wife of Boaz; an ancestress of David. **1b** the book in which these events are recounted. **2 George Herman,** nicknamed *Babe.* 1895–1948, U.S. professional baseball player from 1914 to 1935.

Ruthenia (ruːˈθiːnɪə) *n* a region of E Europe on the south side of the Carpathian Mountains: belonged to Hungary from the 14th century, to Czechoslovakia from 1918 to 1939, and was ceded to the former Soviet Union in 1945; in 1991 it became part of the newly independent Ukraine. Also called: **Carpatho-Ukraine.**

Ruthenian (ruːˈθiːnɪən) *adj* **1** of or relating to Ruthenia, its people, or their dialect of Ukrainian. ◆ *n* **2** a dialect of Ukrainian. **3** a native or inhabitant of Ruthenia.

ruthenic (ruːˈθenɪk) *adj* of or containing ruthenium, esp. in a high valency state.

ruthenious (ruːˈθiːnɪəs) *adj* of or containing ruthenium in a divalent state.

ruthenium (ruːˈθiːnɪəm) *n* a hard brittle white element of the platinum metal group. It occurs free with other platinum metals in pentlandite and other ores and is used to harden platinum and palladium. Symbol: Ru; atomic no.: 44; atomic wt.: 101.07; valency: 0–8; relative density: 12.41; melting pt.: 2334°C; boiling pt.: 4150°C. [C19: from Medieval Latin *Ruthenia* Russia, where it was first discovered]

rutherford ('rʌðəfəd) *n* a unit of activity equal to the quantity of a radioactive nuclide required to produce one million disintegrations per second. Abbrev.: **rd.** [C20: named after Ernest RUTHERFORD]

Rutherford ('rʌðəfəd) *n* **1 Ernest,** 1st Baron. 1871–1937, British physicist, born in New Zealand, who discovered the atomic nucleus (1909). Nobel prize for chemistry 1908. **2** Dame **Margaret.** 1892–1972, British stage and screen actress. Her films include *Passport to Pimlico* (1949), *Murder She Said* (1962), and *The VIPs* (1963). **3 Mark,** original name *William Hale White.* 1831–1913, British novelist and writer, whose work deals with his religious uncertainties: best known for *The Autobiography of Mark Rutherford* (1881) and the novel *The Revolution in Tanner's Lane* (1887).

rutherfordium (ˌrʌðəˈfɔːdɪəm) *n* a transactinide element produced by bombarding californium-249 nuclei with carbon-12 nuclei. Symbol: Rf; atomic no.: 104; atomic wt.: 261. Name in the former Soviet Union: **kurchatovium.** [C20: named after E. RUTHERFORD]

ruthful ('ruːθfʊl) *adj Archaic.* full of or causing sorrow or pity. ▸ **ˈruthfully** *adv* ▸ **ˈruthfulness** *n*

ruthless ('ruːθlɪs) *adj* feeling or showing no mercy; hardhearted. ▸ **ˈruthlessly** *adv* ▸ **ˈruthlessness** *n*

rutilant ('ruːtɪlənt) *adj Rare.* of a reddish colour or glow. [C15: from Latin *rutilāns* having a red glow, from *rutilāre,* from *rutilus* ruddy, red]

rutilated ('ruːtɪˌleɪtɪd) *adj* (of minerals, esp. quartz) containing needles of rutile.

rutile ('ruːtaɪl) *n* a black, yellowish, or reddish-brown mineral, found in igneous rocks, metamorphosed limestones, and quartz veins. It is a source of titanium.

Composition: titanium dioxide. Formula: TiO_2. Crystal structure: tetragonal. [C19: via French from German *Rutil,* from Latin *rutilus* red, glowing]

Rutland (ˈrʌtlənd) *n* an inland county of central England: the smallest of the historical English counties, it became part of Leicestershire in 1974 but was reinstated as an independent unitary authority in 1997: mainly agricultural. Administrative centre: Oakham. Pop.: 33 600 (1994 est.). Area: 394 sq. km (152 sq. miles).

ruttish (ˈrʌtɪʃ) *adj* **1** (of an animal) in a condition of rut. **2** lascivious or salacious. ▸ **ˈruttishly** *adv* ▸ **ˈruttishness** *n*

rutty (ˈrʌtɪ) *adj* **-tier, -tiest.** full of ruts or holes: *a rutty track.* ▸ **ˈruttily** *adv* ▸ **ˈruttiness** *n*

Ruwenzori (ˌruːwenˈzɔːrɪ) *n* a mountain range in central Africa, on the border between Uganda and the Democratic Republic of the Congo (formerly Zaïre) between Lakes Edward and Albert: generally thought to be Ptolemy's "Mountains of the Moon". Highest peak: Mount Stanley, 5109 m (16 763 ft.).

Ruysdael (ˈriːzdɑːl, -deɪl, ˈraɪz-; *Dutch* ˈrœizdaːl) *n* a variant spelling of **Ruisdael.**

Ruyter (ˈraɪtə; *Dutch* ˈrœitər) *n* **Michiel Adriaanszoon de** (miːˈxiːl ˌaːdriˈaːnsun də). 1607–76, Dutch admiral, noted for actions in the Anglo-Dutch wars in 1652–53, 1665–67, 1672, and 1673, when he prevented an Anglo-French invasion.

rv *Statistics. abbrev. for* random variable.

RV *abbrev. for* Revised Version (of the Bible).

RW *abbrev. for:* **1** Right Worshipful. **2** Right Worthy.

RWA *international car registration for* Rwanda.

Rwanda[1] (rʊˈændə) *n* a republic in central Africa: part of German East Africa from 1899 until 1917, when Belgium took over the administration; became a republic in 1961 after the successful Hutu revolt against the Tutsi (1959); fighting between the ethnic groups has broken out repeatedly since independence. Official languages: Rwanda, French, and English. Religion: Roman Catholic, African Protestant, Muslim, and animist. Currency: Rwanda franc. Capital: Kigali. Pop.: 7 965 000 (1998 est.). Area: 26 338 sq. km (10 169 sq. miles). Former name (until 1962): **Ruanda.** ▸ **Rˈwandan** *adj, n*

Rwanda[2] (rʊˈændə) *n* the official language of Rwanda, belonging to the Bantu group of the Niger-Congo family and closely related to Kirundi. Also called: **Kinyarwanda.**

rwd *abbrev. for* rear-wheel drive.

Rwy *or* **Ry** *abbrev. for* railway.

-ry *suffix forming nouns.* a variant of **-ery:** *dentistry.*

Ryazan (*Russian* rɪˈzanj) *n* a city in W central Russia: capital of a medieval principality; oil refineries and engineering industries. Pop.: 536 000 (1995 est.).

Rybinsk (*Russian* ˈribinsk) *n* a city in W central Russia, on the River Volga: an important river port, terminal of the Mariinsk Waterway (between Saint Petersburg and the Volga) at the SE end of the **Rybinsk Reservoir** (area: 4700 sq. km (1800 sq. miles)). Pop.: 248 000 (1995 est.). Former names: (from the Revolution until 1957) **Shcherbakov,** (1984–91) **Andropov.**

Rydal (ˈraɪdᵊl) *n* a village in NW England, in Cumbria on **Rydal Water** (a small lake). **Rydal Mount,** home of Wordsworth from 1813 to 1850, is situated here.

Ryder (ˈraɪdə) *n* **Susan,** Baroness Ryder of Warsaw. born 1923, British philanthropist; founder of the Sue Ryder Foundation for the Sick and Disabled, which is funded by a chain of charity shops: widow of Leonard Cheshire.

Ryder Cup (raɪdə) *n* **the.** the trophy awarded in a professional golfing competition between teams representing Europe and the U.S. [C20: named after Samuel *Ryder* (1859–1936), British businessman and golf patron]

rye[1] (raɪ) *n* **1** a tall hardy widely cultivated annual grass, *Secale cereale,* having soft bluish-green leaves, bristly flower spikes, and light brown grain. See also **wild rye. 2** the grain of this grass, used in making flour and whiskey, and as a livestock food. **3** Also called: **rye whiskey.** whiskey distilled from rye. U.S. whiskey must by law contain not less than 51 per cent rye. **4** *U.S.* short for **rye bread.** [Old English *ryge;* related to Old Norse *rugr,* Old French *rogga,* Old Saxon *roggo*]

rye[2] (raɪ) *n Gypsy dialect.* a gentleman. [from Romany *rai,* from Sanskrit *rājan* king; see RAJAH]

Rye (raɪ) *n* a resort in SE England, in East Sussex: one of the Cinque Ports. Pop.: 3708 (1991).

rye bread *n* any of various breads made entirely or partly from rye flour, often with caraway seeds.

rye-brome *n* a grass, *Bromus secalinus,* native to Europe and Asia, having rough leaves and wheatlike ears. U.S. names: **cheat, chess.**

rye-grass *n* any of various grasses of the genus *Lolium,* esp. *L. perenne,* native to Europe, N Africa, and Asia and widely cultivated as forage crops. They have a flattened flower spike and hairless leaves.

Ryle (raɪl) *n* **1 Gilbert.** 1900–76, British philosopher. His works include *The Concept of Mind* (1949). **2** Sir **Martin.** 1918–84, British astronomer, noted for his research on radio astronomy: Astronomer Royal 1972–82; shared the Nobel prize for physics in 1974.

Ryobu Shinto (riːˈəʊbuː) *n* a fusion of Shinto and Buddhism, which flourished in Japan in the 13th century. [from Japanese *ryō bu,* literally: two parts]

ryokan (rɪˈəʊkən) *n* a traditional Japanese inn. [Japanese]

ryot (ˈraɪət) *n* (in India) a peasant or tenant farmer. [C17: from Hindi *ra'īyat,* from Arabic *ra'īyah* flock, peasants, from *ra'ā* pasture]

Ryswick (ˈrɪzwɪk) *n* the English name for **Rijswijk.**

Ryukyu Islands (rɪˈuːkjuː) *pl n* a chain of 55 islands in the W Pacific, extending almost 650 km (400 miles) from S Japan to N Taiwan: an ancient kingdom, under Chinese rule from the late 14th century, invaded by Japan in the early 17th century, under full Japanese sovereignty from 1879 to 1945, and U.S. control from 1945 to 1972; now part of Japan again. They are subject to frequent typhoons. Chief town: Naha City (on Okinawa). Pop.: 1 273 508 (1995). Area: 2196 sq. km (849 sq. miles).

Ryurik (ˈrʊərɪk) *n* a variant spelling of **Rurik.**

Ss

s *or* **S** (ɛs) *n, pl* **s's, S's,** *or* **Ss. 1** the 19th letter and 15th consonant of the modern English alphabet. **2** a speech sound represented by this letter, usually an alveolar fricative, either voiceless, as in *sit,* or voiced, as in *dogs.* **3a** something shaped like an S. **3b** (*in combination*): *an S-bend in a road.*

s *symbol for* second (of time).

S *symbol for:* **1** satisfactory. **2** Society. **3** small (size). **4** South. **5** *Chem.* sulphur. **6** *Physics.* **6a** entropy. **6b** siemens. **6c** strangeness. **7** *Currency.* **7a** schilling. **7b** sol. **7c** sucre. ◆ **8** *international car registration for* Sweden.

s. *abbrev. for:* **1** section. **2** see. **3** semi-. **4** shilling. **5** sign(ed). **6** singular. **7** sire. **8** son. **9** substantive. **10** succeeded.

S. *abbrev. for:* **1** sabbath. **2** (*pl* **SS.**) Saint. **3** Saturday. **4** Saxon. **5** school. **6** Sea. **7** senate. **8** September. **9** Signor. **10** Socialist. **11** Society. **12** Sunday. **13** (in titles) Fellow. [Latin *socius*]

-s[1] *or* **-es** *suffix.* forming the plural of most nouns: *boys; boxes.* [from Old English *-as,* plural nominative and accusative ending of some masculine nouns]

-s[2] *or* **-es** *suffix.* forming the third person singular present indicative tense of verbs: *he runs; she washes.* [from Old English (northern dialect) *-es, -s,* originally the ending of the second person singular]

-s[3] *suffix of nouns.* forming nicknames and names expressing affection or familiarity: *Fats; Fingers; ducks.* [special use of -s[1]]

-'s *suffix.* **1** forming the possessive singular of nouns and some pronouns: *man's; one's.* **2** forming the possessive plural of nouns whose plurals do not end in *-s: children's.* **3** forming the plural of numbers, letters, or symbols: *20's; p's and q's.* **4** *Informal.* contraction of *is* or *has: he's here; John's coming; it's gone.* **5** *Informal.* contraction of *us* with *let: let's.* **6** *Informal.* contraction of *does* in some questions: *where's he live? what's he do?* [senses 1, 2: assimilated contraction from Middle English *-es,* from Old English, masculine and neuter genitive singular; sense 3, equivalent to -s[1]]

-s' *suffix.* forming the possessive of plural nouns ending in the sound *s* or *z* and of some singular nouns: *girls'; for goodness' sake.*

Sa *a former chemical symbol for* samarium.

SA *abbrev. for:* **1** Salvation Army. **2** Sociedad Anónima. [Spanish: limited company] **3** Société anonyme. [French: limited company] **4** South Africa. **5** South America. **6** South Australia. **7** *Sturmabteilung:* the Nazi terrorist militia, organized around 1924.

s.a. *abbrev. for:* **1** semiannual. **2** sex appeal. **3** sine anno. [Latin: without date]

Saadi (sɑː'diː) *n* a variant spelling of **Sadi.**

Saar (sɑː; *German* zaːr) *n* **1** a river in W Europe, rising in the Vosges Mountains and flowing north to the Moselle River in Germany. Length: 246 km (153 miles). French name: **Sarre. 2 the Saar.** another name for **Saarland.**

Saarbrücken (*German* zaːr'brykən) *n* an industrial city in W Germany, capital of Saarland state, on the Saar River. Pop.: 187 032 (1996 est.).

SAARC *abbrev. for* South Asian Association for Regional Cooperation.

Saarinen ('sɑːrɪnən) *n* **Eero** ('eɪrəʊ). 1910–61, U.S. architect, born in Finland. His works include the U.S. Embassy, London (1960).

Saarland (*German* 'zaːrlant) *n* a state of W Germany: formed in 1919; under League of Nations administration until 1935; occupied by France (1945–57); part of West Germany (1957–90): contains rich coal deposits and is a major industrial region. Capital: Saarbrücken. Pop.: 1 084 400 (1996 est.). Area: 2567 sq. km (991 sq. miles).

Sab. *abbrev. for* Sabbath.

Saba ('sɑːbə) *n* **1** an island in the NE Caribbean, in the Netherlands Antilles. Pop.: 1197 (1994 est.). Area: 13 sq. km (5 sq. miles). **2** another name for **Sheba**[1] (sense 1).

Sabadell (*Spanish* saβa'ðel) *n* a town in NE Spain, near Barcelona: textile manufacturing. Pop.: 188 386 (1995 est.).

sabadilla (ˌsæbə'dɪlə) *n* **1** a tropical American liliaceous plant, *Schoenocaulon officinale.* **2** the bitter brown seeds of this plant, which contain the alkaloids veratrine and veratridine and are used in insecticides. [C19: from Spanish *cebadilla,* diminutive of *cebada* barley, from Latin *cibāre* to feed, from *cibus* food]

Sabaean *or* **Sabean** (sə'biːən) *n* **1** an inhabitant or native of ancient Saba. **2** the ancient Semitic language of Saba. ◆ *adj* **3** of or relating to ancient Saba, its inhabitants, or their language. [C16: from Latin *Sabaeus, from Greek Sabaios* belonging to Saba (Sheba)]

Sabah ('sɑːbɑː) *n* a state of Malaysia, occupying N Borneo and offshore islands in the South China and Sulu Seas: became a British protectorate in 1888; gained independence and joined Malaysia in 1963. Capital: Kota Kinabalu. Pop.: 1 472 700 (1993 est.). Area: 76 522 sq. km (29 545 sq. miles). Former name (until 1963): **North Borneo.**

Sabaoth (sæ'beɪɒθ, 'sæbeɪɒθ) *n Bible.* hosts, armies (esp. in the phrase **the Lord of Sabaoth** in Romans 9:29). [C14: via Latin and Greek from Hebrew *ç'bāōth,* from *çābā*]

Sabatier (*French* sabatje) *n* **Paul** (pɔl). 1854–1941, French chemist, who discovered a process for the hydrogenation of organic compounds: shared the Nobel prize for chemistry (1912).

sabayon (ˌsæbaɪ'jɒn; *French* sabajɔ̃) *n* a dessert or sweet sauce made with egg yolks, sugar, and wine beaten together over heat till thick: served either hot or cold. [C20: from French, alteration of Italian *zabione* ZABAGLIONE]

sabbat ('sæbæt, -ət) *n* another word for **Sabbath** (sense 4).

Sabbatarian (ˌsæbə'tɛərɪən) *n* **1** a person advocating the strict religious observance of Sunday. **2** a person who observes Saturday as the Sabbath. ◆ *adj* **3** of or relating to the Sabbath or its observance. [C17: from Late Latin *sabbatārius* a Sabbath-keeper] ► **ˌSabba'tarianism** *n*

Sabbath ('sæbəθ) *n* **1** the seventh day of the week, Saturday, devoted to worship and rest from work in Judaism and in certain Christian Churches. **2** Sunday, observed by Christians as the day of worship and rest from work in commemoration of Christ's Resurrection. **3** (*not cap.*) a period of rest. **4** Also called: **sabbat, witches' Sabbath.** a midnight meeting or secret rendezvous for practitioners of witchcraft, sorcery, or devil worship. [Old English *sabbat,* from Latin *sabbatum,* from Greek *sabbaton,* from Hebrew *shabbāth,* from *shābath* to rest]

sabbath school *n* (*sometimes caps.*) *Chiefly U.S.* a school for religious instruction held on the Sabbath.

sabbatical (sə'bætɪkᵊl) *adj* **1** denoting a period of leave granted to university staff, teachers, etc., esp. approximately every seventh year: *a sabbatical year; sabbatical leave.* **2** denoting a post that renders the holder eligible for such leave. ◆ *n* **3** any sabbatical period. [C16: from Greek *sabbatikos;* see SABBATH]

Sabbatical (sə'bætɪkᵊl) *adj also* **Sabbatic. 1** of, relating to, or appropriate to the Sabbath as a day of rest and religious observance. ◆ *n* **2** short for **sabbatical year.**

sabbatical year *n* (*often caps.*) *Bible.* a year during which the land was to be left uncultivated, debts annulled, etc., supposed to be observed every seventh year by the ancient Israelites according to Leviticus 25.

SABC *abbrev. for* South African Broadcasting Corporation.

Sabellian (sə'belɪən) *n* **1** an extinct language or group of languages of ancient Italy, surviving only in a few inscriptions belonging to the Osco-Umbrian group. **2** a member of any of the ancient peoples speaking this language, including the Sabines. ◆ *adj* **3** of or relating to this language or its speakers. [C17: from Latin *Sabellī* group of Italian tribes]

saber ('seɪbə) *n, vb* the U.S. spelling of **sabre.**

sabin ('sæbɪn, 'seɪ-) *n Physics.* a unit of acoustic absorption equal to the absorption resulting from one square foot of a perfectly absorbing surface. [C20: introduced by Wallace C. *Sabine* (1868–1919), U.S. physicist]

Sabin ('seɪbɪn) *n* **Albert Bruce.** 1906–93, U.S. microbiologist, born in Poland. He developed the **Sabin vaccine** (1955), taken orally to immunize against poliomyelitis.

Sabine ('sæbaɪn) *n* **1** a member of an ancient Oscan-speaking people who lived in central Italy northeast of Rome. ◆ *adj* **2** of, characteristic of, or relating to this people or their language.

sabkha ('sæbxə, -kə) *n* a flat coastal plain with a salt crust, common in Arabia. [C19: from Arabic]

sable ('seɪbᵊl) *n, pl* **-bles** *or* **-ble. 1** a marten, *Martes zibellina,* of N Asian forests, with dark brown luxuriant fur. Related adj: **zibeline. 2a** the highly valued fur of this animal. **2b** (*as modifier*): *a sable coat.* **3 American sable.** the brown, slightly less valuable fur of the American marten, *Martes americana.* **4** the colour of sable fur: a dark brown to yellowish-brown colour. ◆ *adj* **5** of the colour of sable fur. **6** black; dark; gloomy. **7** (*usually postpositive*) *Heraldry.* of the colour black. [C15: from Old French, from Old High German *zobel,* of Slavic origin; related to Russian *sobol',* Polish *sobol*]

Sable ('seɪbᵊl) *n* **Cape. 1** a cape at the S tip of Florida: the southernmost point of continental U.S. **2** the southernmost point of Nova Scotia, Canada.

sable antelope *n* a large black E African antelope, *Hippotragus niger,* with long backward-curving horns.

sabot ('sæbəʊ; *French* sabo) *n* **1** a shoe made from a single block of wood. **2** a shoe with a wooden sole and a leather or cloth upper. **3** a lightweight sleeve in which a subcalibre round is enclosed in order to make it fit the rifling of a firearm. After firing the sabot drops away. **4** *Austral.* a small sailing boat with a shortened bow. [C17: from French, probably from Old French *savate* an old shoe, also influenced by *bot* BOOT[1]; related to Italian *ciabatta* old shoe, Old Provençal *sabata*]

sabotage ('sæbəˌtɑːʒ) *n* **1** the deliberate destruction, disruption, or damage of equipment, a public service, etc., as by enemy agents, dissatisfied employees, etc. **2** any similar action or behaviour. ◆ *vb* **3** (*tr*) to destroy, damage, or disrupt, esp. by secret means. [C20: from French, from *saboter* to spoil through clumsiness (literally: to clatter in sabots)]

saboteur (ˌsæbə'tɜː) *n* a person who commits sabotage. [C20: from French; see SABOTAGE]

sabra ('sɑːbrə) *n* a native-born Israeli Jew. [from Hebrew *Sabēr* prickly pear, common plant in the coastal areas of the country]

sabre *or U.S.* **saber** ('seɪbə) *n* **1** a stout single-edged cavalry sword, having a curved blade. **2** a sword used in fencing, having a narrow V-shaped blade, a semicircular guard, and a slightly curved hand. **3** a cavalry soldier. ◆ *vb* **4** (*tr*) to injure or kill with a sabre. [C17: via French from German (dialect) *Sabel,* from Middle High German *sebel,* perhaps from Magyar *szablya;* compare Russian *sablya* sabre]

sabre-rattling *n, adj Informal.* seeking to intimidate by an aggressive display of military power.

sabretache ('sæbəˌtæʃ) *n* a leather case suspended from a cavalryman's saddle. [C19: via French from German *Säbeltasche* sabre pocket]

sabre-toothed tiger *or* **cat** *n* any of various extinct Tertiary felines of the genus *Smilodon* and related genera, with long curved upper canine teeth.

sabulous ('sæbjʊləs) *or* **sabulose** ('sæbjʊləʊs) *adj* **1** like sand in texture; gritty. **2** Also: **sabuline** ('sæbjʊliːn). (of plants) growing in sand. [C17: from Latin *sabulōsus,* from *sabulum* SAND] ▸ **sabulosity** (ˌsæbjʊ'lɒsɪtɪ) *n*

sac (sæk) *n* a pouch, bag, or pouchlike part in an animal or plant. [C18: from French, from Latin *saccus;* see SACK[1]] ▸ **'sacˌlike** *adj*

SAC (in Britain) *abbrev. for* Special Area of Conservation.

sacaton (ˌsækə'təʊn) *n* a coarse grass, *Sporobolus wrightii,* of the southwestern U.S. and Mexico, grown for hay and pasture. [American Spanish *zacatón,* from *zacate* coarse grass, from Nahuatl *zacatl*]

saccade (sə'kɑːd, -'keɪd) *n* **1** the movement of the eye when it makes a sudden change of fixation, as in reading. **2** a sudden check given to a horse. [C18: from French: a jerk on the reins of a horse]

saccate ('sækeɪt) *adj Botany.* in the form of a sac; pouched. [C19: from New Latin *saccatus,* from *saccus:* see SACK[1]]

saccharase ('sækəˌreɪs) *n* another name for **invertase.**

saccharate ('sækəˌreɪt) *n* any salt or ester of saccharic acid.

saccharic acid (sæ'kærɪk) *n* a white soluble solid dicarboxylic acid obtained by the oxidation of cane sugar or starch; 2,3,4,5-tetrahydroxyhexanedioic acid. Formula: $COOH(CHOH)_4COOH$.

saccharide ('sækəˌraɪd, -rɪd) *n* any sugar or other carbohydrate, esp. a simple sugar.

saccharify (sæ'kærɪˌfaɪ), **saccharize,** *or* **saccharise** ('sækəˌraɪz) *vb* **-fies, -fying, -fied** *(tr)* to convert (starch) into sugar. ▸ **sacˌcharifi'cation, ˌsacchari'zation,** *or* **ˌsacchari'sation** *n*

saccharimeter (ˌsækə'rɪmɪtə) *n* any instrument for measuring the strength of sugar solutions, esp. a type of polarimeter for determining the concentration from the extent to which the solution rotates the plane of polarized light. ▸ **ˌsaccha'rimetry** *n*

saccharin ('sækərɪn) *n* a very sweet white crystalline slightly soluble powder used as a nonfattening sweetener. Formula: $C_7H_5NO_3S$. [C19: from SACCHARO- + -IN]

saccharine ('sækəˌraɪn, -ˌriːn) *adj* **1** excessively sweet; sugary: *a saccharine smile.* **2** of, relating to, of the nature of, or containing sugar or saccharin. ▸ **'saccharinely** *adv* ▸ **saccharinity** (ˌsækə'rɪnɪtɪ) *n*

saccharo- *or before a vowel* **sacchar-** *combining form.* sugar: *saccharomycete.* [via Latin from Greek *sakkharon,* ultimately from Sanskrit *śarkarā* sugar]

saccharoid ('sækəˌrɔɪd) *adj* **1** Also: **ˌsaccha'roidal.** *Geology.* having or designating a texture resembling that of loaf sugar: *saccharoid marble.* ◆ *n* **2** *Biochem.* any of a group of polysaccharides that remotely resemble sugars, but are not sweet and are often insoluble.

saccharometer (ˌsækə'rɒmɪtə) *n* a hydrometer used to measure the strengths of sugar solutions. It is usually calibrated directly to give a reading of concentration.

saccharose ('sækəˌrəʊz, -ˌrəʊs) *n* a technical name for **sugar** (sense 1).

Sacco ('sækəʊ) *n* **Nicola** (ni'kɔːla). 1891–1927, U.S. radical agitator, born in Italy. With Bartolomeo Vanzetti, he was executed for murder (1927) despite suspicions that their political opinions influenced the verdict: the case caused international protests.

saccular ('sækjʊlə) *adj* of or resembling a sac.

sacculate ('sækjʊlɪt, -ˌleɪt) *or* **sacculated** *adj* of, relating to, or possessing a saccule, saccules, or a sacculus. ▸ **ˌsaccu'lation** *n*

saccule ('sækjuːl) *or* **sacculus** ('sækjʊləs) *n, pl* **-cules** *or* **-li** (liː). **1** a small sac. **2** the smaller of the two parts of the membranous labyrinth of the internal ear. Compare **utricle** (sense 1). [C19: from Latin *sacculus* diminutive of *saccus* SACK[1]]

sacculiform (sæ'kjʊlɪˌfɔːm) *adj Biology.* (of plant parts, etc.) shaped like a small sac.

sacerdotal (ˌsæsə'dəʊt°l) *adj* of, relating to, or characteristic of priests. [C14: from Latin *sacerdōtālis,* from *sacerdōs* priest, from *sacer* sacred] ▸ **ˌsacer'dotally** *adv*

sacerdotalism (ˌsæsə'dəʊt°ˌlɪzəm) *n* **1** the principles, methods, etc., of the priesthood. **2** the belief that ordained priests are endowed with sacramental and sacrificial powers. **3** exaggerated respect for priests. **4** *Derogatory.* power over people's opinions and actions achieved by priests through sophistry or guile. ▸ **ˌsacer'dotalist** *n*

sachem ('seɪtʃəm) *n* **1** *U.S.* a leader of a political party or organization, esp. of Tammany Hall. **2** another name for **sagamore.** [C17: from Narraganset *săchim* chief] ▸ **sachemic** (seɪ'tʃɛmɪk, 'seɪtʃə-) *adj*

sachet ('sæʃeɪ) *n* **1** a small sealed envelope, usually made of plastic or paper, for containing sugar, salt, shampoo, etc. **2a** a small soft bag containing perfumed powder, placed in drawers to scent clothing. **2b** the powder contained in such a bag. [C19: from Old French: a little bag, from *sac* bag; see SACK[1]]

Sachs (*German* zaks) *n* **1 Hans** (hans). 1494–1576, German master shoemaker and Meistersinger, portrayed by Wagner in *Die Meistersinger von Nürnberg.* **2 Nelly** (**Leonie**). 1891–1970, German Jewish poet and dramatist, who escaped from Nazi Germany and settled in Sweden. Her works include *Eli: A Mystery Play of the Sufferings of Israel* (1951) and 'O the Chimneys', a poem about the Nazi extermination camps. Nobel prize for literature 1966 jointly with Shmuel Yosef Agnon.

Sachsen ('zaksən) *n* the German name for **Saxony.**

sack[1] (sæk) *n* **1** a large bag made of coarse cloth, thick paper, etc., used as a container. **2** Also called: **'sackˌful.** the amount contained in a sack, sometimes used as a unit of measurement. **3a** a woman's loose tube-shaped dress. **3b** Also called: **sacque.** a woman's full loose hip-length jacket, worn in the 18th and mid-20th centuries. **4** short for **rucksack. 5** *Cricket.* the Australian word for **bye**[1]. **6 the sack.** *Informal.* dismissal from employment. **7** a slang word for **bed. 8 hit the sack.** *Slang.* to go to bed. **9 rough as sacks.** *N.Z.* uncouth. ◆ *vb (tr)* **10** *Informal.* to dismiss from employment. **11** to put into a sack or sacks. [Old English *sacc,* from Latin *saccus* bag, from Greek *sakkos;* related to Hebrew *saq*] ▸ **'sackˌlike** *adj*

sack[2] (sæk) *n* **1** the plundering of a place by an army or mob, usually involving destruction, slaughter, etc. **2** *American football.* a tackle on a quarterback which brings him down before he has passed the ball. ◆ *vb* **3** *(tr)* to plunder and partially destroy (a place). **4** *American football.* to tackle and bring down a quarterback before he has passed the ball. [C16: from French phrase *mettre à sac,* literally: to put (loot) in a sack, from Latin *saccus* SACK[1]] ▸ **'sacker** *n*

sack[3] (sæk) *n Archaic except in trademarks.* any dry white wine formerly imported into Britain from SW Europe. [C16 *wyne seck,* from French *vin sec* dry wine, from Latin *siccus* dry]

sackbut ('sækˌbʌt) *n* a medieval form of trombone. [C16: from French *saqueboute,* from Old French *saquer* to pull + *bouter* to push; see BUTT[3]: used in the Bible (Daniel 3) as a mistranslation of Aramaic *sabb'ka* stringed instrument]

sackcloth ('sækˌklɒθ) *n* **1** coarse cloth such as sacking. **2** garments made of such cloth, worn formerly to indicate mourning or penitence. **3 sackcloth and ashes.** a public display of extreme grief, remorse, or repentance.

sacking ('sækɪŋ) *n* coarse cloth used for making sacks, woven from flax, hemp, jute, etc.

sack race *n* a race in which the competitors' legs and often bodies are enclosed in sacks. ▸ **sack racing** *n*

Sackville ('sækvɪl) *n* **Thomas,** 1st Earl of Dorset. 1536–1608, English poet, dramatist, and statesman. He collaborated with Thomas Norton on the early blank-verse tragedy *Gorboduc* (1561).

Sackville-West (ˌsækvɪl 'wɛst) *n* **Victoria** (**Mary**), known as *Vita.* 1892–1962, British writer and gardener, whose works include the novel *The Edwardians* (1930) and the poem *The Land* (1931). She is also noted for the gardens at Sissinghurst Castle, Kent. Married to Harold Nicolson.

sacral[1] ('seɪkrəl) *adj* of, relating to, or associated with sacred rites. [C19: from Latin *sacrum* sacred object]

sacral[2] ('seɪkrəl) *adj* of or relating to the sacrum. [C18: from New Latin *sacrālis* of the SACRUM]

sacrament ('sækrəmənt) *n* **1** an outward sign combined with a prescribed form of words and regarded as conferring some specific grace upon those who receive it. The Protestant sacraments are baptism and the Lord's Supper. In the Roman Catholic and Eastern Churches they are baptism, penance, confirmation, the Eucharist, holy orders, matrimony, and the anointing of the sick (formerly extreme unction). **2** *(often cap.)* the Eucharist. **3** the consecrated elements of the Eucharist, esp. the bread. **4** something regarded as possessing a sacred or mysterious significance. **5** a symbol; pledge. [C12: from Church Latin *sacrāmentum* vow, from Latin *sacrāre* to consecrate]

sacramental (ˌsækrə'mɛnt°l) *adj* **1** of, relating to, or having the nature of a sacrament. **2** bound by or as if by a sacrament. ◆ *n* **3** *R.C. Church.* a sacrament-like ritual action, such as the sign of the cross or the use of holy water. ▸ **ˌsacra'mentally** *adv* ▸ **sacramentality** (ˌsækrəmɛn'tælɪtɪ) *or* **ˌsacra'mentalness** *n*

sacramentalism (ˌsækrə'mɛnt°ˌlɪzəm) *n* belief in or special emphasis upon the efficacy of the sacraments for conferring grace. ▸ **ˌsacra'mentalist** *n*

Sacramentarian (ˌsækrəmɛn'tɛərɪən) *n* **1** any Protestant theologian, such as Zwingli, who maintained that the bread and wine of the Eucharist were the body and blood of Christ only in a figurative sense and denied his real presence in these elements. **2** one who believes in sacramentalism. ◆ *adj* **3** of or relating to Sacramentarians. **4** *(not cap.)* of or relating to sacraments. ▸ **ˌSacramen'tarianism** *n*

Sacramento (ˌsækrə'mɛntəʊ) *n* **1** an inland port in N central California, capital of the state at the confluence of the American and Sacramento Rivers: became a boom town in the gold rush of the 1850s. Pop.: 376 243 (1996 est.). **2** a river in N California, flowing generally south to San Francisco Bay. Length: 615 km (382 miles).

sacrarium (sæ'krɛərɪəm) *n, pl* **-craria** (-'krɛərɪə). **1** the sanctuary of a church. **2** *R.C. Church.* a place near the altar of a church, similar in function to the piscina, where materials used in the sacred rites are deposited or poured away. [C18: from Latin *sacrārium,* from *sacer* SACRED]

sacred ('seɪkrɪd) *adj* **1** exclusively devoted to a deity or to some religious ceremony or use; holy; consecrated. **2** worthy of or regarded with reverence, awe, or respect. **3** protected by superstition or piety from irreligious actions. **4** connected with or intended for religious use: *sacred music.* **5 sacred to.** dedicated to; in honour of. [C14: from Latin *sacrāre* to set apart as holy, from *sacer* holy] ▸ **'sacredly** *adv* ▸ **'sacredness** *n*

Sacred College *n* the collective body of the cardinals of the Roman Catholic Church.

sacred cow *n Informal.* a person, institution, custom, etc., unreasonably held to be beyond criticism. [alluding to the Hindu belief that cattle are sacred]

Sacred Heart *n R.C. Church.* **1** the heart of Jesus Christ, a symbol of His love and sacrifice. **2** a representation of this, usually bleeding, as an aid to devotion.

sacred mushroom *n* **1** any of various hallucinogenic mushrooms, esp. species of *Psilocybe* and *Amanita,* that have been eaten in rituals in various parts of the world. **2** a mescal button, used in a similar way.

sacrifice ('sækrɪˌfaɪs) *n* **1** a surrender of something of value as a means of gaining something more desirable or of preventing some evil. **2** a ritual killing of a person or animal with the intention of propitiating or pleasing a deity. **3** a symbolic offering of something to a deity. **4** the person, animal, or object surrendered, destroyed, killed, or offered. **5** a religious ceremony involving one or more sacrifices. **6** loss entailed by giving up or selling something at less than its value. **7** *Chess.* the act or an instance of sacrificing a piece. ◆ *vb* **8** to make a sacrifice (of); give up, surrender, or destroy (a person, thing, etc.). **9** *Chess.* to permit or force one's opponent to capture (a piece) freely, as in playing a combination or gambit: *he sacrificed his queen and checkmated his opponent on the next move.* [C13: via Old French from Latin *sacrificium,* from *sacer* holy + *facere* to make] ► **'sacri,ficeable** *adj* ► **'sacri,ficer** *n*

sacrifice paddock *n N.Z.* a grassed area allowed to be grazed completely, to be cultivated and resown later.

sacrificial (ˌsækrɪ'fɪʃəl) *adj* used in or connected with a sacrifice. ► **,sacri'ficially** *adv*

sacrificial anode *n Metallurgy.* an electropositive metal, such as zinc, that protects a more important electronegative part by corroding when attacked by electrolytic action.

sacrilege ('sækrɪlɪdʒ) *n* **1** the misuse or desecration of anything regarded as sacred or as worthy of extreme respect: *to play Mozart's music on a kazoo is sacrilege.* **2** the act or an instance of taking anything sacred for secular use. [C13: from Old French *sacrilège,* from Latin *sacrilegium,* from *sacrilegus* temple-robber, from *sacra* sacred things + *legere* to take] ► **sacrilegist** (ˌsækrɪ'liːdʒɪst) *n*

sacrilegious (ˌsækrɪ'lɪdʒəs) *adj* **1** of, relating to, or involving sacrilege; impious. **2** guilty of sacrilege. ► **,sacri'legiously** *adv* ► **,sacri'legiousness** *n*

sacring ('seɪkrɪŋ) *n Archaic.* the act or ritual of consecration, esp. of the Eucharist or of a bishop. [C13: from obsolete *sacren* to consecrate, from Latin *sacrāre;* see SACRED]

sacring bell *n Chiefly R.C. Church.* a small bell rung at the elevation of the Host and chalice during Mass.

sacristan ('sækrɪstən) *or* **sacrist** ('sækrɪst, 'seɪ-) *n* **1** a person who has charge of the contents of a church, esp. the sacred vessels, vestments, etc. **2** a less common word for **sexton** (sense 1). [C14: from Medieval Latin *sacristānus,* from *sacrista,* from Latin *sacer* holy]

sacristy ('sækrɪstɪ) *n, pl* **-ties.** a room attached to a church or chapel where the sacred vessels, vestments, etc., are kept and where priests attire themselves. [C17: from Medieval Latin *sacristia;* see SACRISTAN]

sacroiliac (ˌseɪkrəʊ'ɪlɪˌæk, ˌsæk-) *Anatomy.* ◆ *adj* **1** of or relating to the sacrum and ilium, their articulation, or their associated ligaments. ◆ *n* **2** the joint where these bones meet.

sacrosanct ('sækrəʊˌsæŋkt) *adj* very sacred or holy; inviolable. [C17: from Latin *sacrōsanctus* made holy by sacred rite, from *sacrō* by sacred rite, from *sacer* holy + *sanctus,* from *sancīre* to hallow] ► **,sacro'sanctity** *or* **'sacro,sanctness** *n*

sacrum ('seɪkrəm, 'sækrəm) *n, pl* **-cra** (-krə). **1** (in man) the large wedge-shaped bone, consisting of five fused vertebrae, in the lower part of the back. **2** the corresponding part in some other vertebrates. [C18: from Latin *os sacrum* holy bone, because it was used in sacrifices, from *sacer* holy]

sad (sæd) *adj* **sadder, saddest. 1** feeling sorrow; unhappy. **2** causing, suggestive, or expressive of such feelings: *a sad story.* **3** unfortunate; unsatisfactory; shabby; deplorable: *her clothes were in a sad state.* **4** *Brit. informal.* ludicrously contemptible; pathetic: *he's a sad, boring little wimp.* **5** (of pastry, cakes, etc.) not having risen fully; heavy. **6** (of a colour) lacking brightness; dull or dark. **7** *Archaic.* serious; grave. [Old English *sæd* weary; related to Old Norse *sathr,* Gothic *saths,* Latin *satur, satis* enough] ► **'sadly** *adv* ► **'sadness** *n*

SAD *abbrev. for* seasonal affective disorder.

Sadat (sə'dæt) *n* (**Mohammed**) **Anwar El** ('ænwɑː ɛl). 1918–81, Egyptian statesman: president of Egypt (1970–81); assassinated; Nobel peace prize jointly with Begin 1978.

Saddam Hussein (sæ'dæm) *n* See **Hussein** (sense 2).

sadden ('sædᵊn) *vb* to make or become sad.

saddle ('sædᵊl) *n* **1** a seat for a rider, usually made of leather, placed on a horse's back and secured with a girth under the belly. **2** a similar seat on a bicycle, tractor, etc., made of leather or steel. **3** a back pad forming part of the harness of a packhorse. **4** anything that resembles a saddle in shape, position, or function. **5** a cut of meat, esp. mutton, consisting of part of the backbone and both loins. **6** the part of a horse or similar animal on which a saddle is placed. **7** the part of the back of a domestic chicken that is nearest to the tail. **8** *Civil engineering.* a block on top of one of the towers of a suspension bridge over which the cables or chains pass. **9** *Engineering.* the carriage that slides on the bed of a lathe and supports the slide rest, tool post, or turret. **10** the nontechnical name for **clitellum. 11** another name for **col** (sense 1). **12** a raised piece of wood or metal for covering a doorsill. **13 in the saddle.** in a position of control. ◆ *vb* **14** (sometimes foll. by *up*) to put a saddle on (a horse). **15** (*intr*) to mount into the saddle. **16** (*tr*) to burden; charge: *I didn't ask to be saddled with this job.* [Old English *sadol, sædel;* related to Old Norse *sothull,* Old High German *satul*] ► **'saddleless** *adj* ► **'saddle-,like** *adj*

saddleback ('sædᵊlˌbæk) *n* **1** a marking resembling a saddle on the backs of various animals. **2** a rare bird of New Zealand, *Philesturnus carunculatus,* having a chestnut-coloured saddle-shaped marking across its back and wings. **3** another name for **saddle roof. 4** another name for **col** (sense 1).

saddle-backed *adj* **1** having the back curved in shape or concave like a saddle. **2** having a saddleback.

saddlebag ('sædᵊlˌbæg) *n* a pouch or small bag attached to the saddle of a horse, bicycle, etc.

saddlebill ('sædᵊlˌbɪl) *n* a large black-and-white stork, *Ephippiorhynchus senegalensis,* of tropical Africa, having a heavy red bill with a black band around the middle and a yellow patch at the base. Also called: **jabiru.** [C19 (as *saddlebill stork*): so called because of the appearance of its bill]

saddle block *n Surgery.* a type of spinal anaesthesia producing sensory loss in the buttocks, inner sides of the thighs, and perineum.

saddlebow ('sædᵊlˌbəʊ) *n* the pommel of a saddle.

saddlecloth ('sædᵊlˌklɒθ) *n* a light cloth put under a horse's saddle, so as to prevent rubbing.

saddle horse *n* a lightweight horse kept for riding only. Compare **carthorse.** Also called: **saddler.**

saddler ('sædlə) *n* a person who makes, deals in, or repairs saddles and other leather equipment for horses.

saddle roof *n* a roof that has a ridge and two gables. Also called: **saddleback.**

saddlery ('sædlərɪ) *n, pl* **-dleries. 1** saddles, harness, and other leather equipment for horses collectively. **2** the business, work, or place of work of a saddler.

saddle soap *n* a soft soap containing neat's-foot oil used to preserve and clean leather.

saddle-sore *adj* **1** sore after riding a horse. **2** (of a horse or rider) having sores caused by the chafing of the saddle. ◆ *n* **saddle sore. 3** such a sore.

saddle stitching *n* a method of binding in which the sections of a publication are inserted inside each other and secured through the middle fold with thread, or wire staples.

saddletree ('sædᵊlˌtriː) *n* the frame of a saddle.

Sadducee ('sædjʊˌsiː) *n Judaism.* a member of an ancient Jewish sect that was opposed to the Pharisees, denying the resurrection of the dead, the existence of angels, and the validity of oral tradition. [Old English *sadducēas,* via Latin and Greek from Late Hebrew *ṣāddūqī,* probably from *Ṣadoq* Zadok, high priest and supposed founder of the sect] ► **,Saddu'cean** *adj* ► **'Saddu,ceeism** *n*

Sade (sɑːd) *n* Comte **Donatien Alphonse François de** (dɔnasjɛ̃ alfɔ̃s frɑ̃swa də), known as the *Marquis de Sade.* 1740–1814, French soldier and writer, whose exposition of sexual perversion gave rise to the term sadism.

sadhana ('sɑːdʌnə) *n Hinduism.* one of a number of spiritual practices or disciplines which lead to perfection, these being contemplation, asceticism, worship of a god, and correct living. [from Sanskrit: effective]

sadhe, sade, *or* **tsade** ('sɑːdiː, 'tsɑːdiː; *Hebrew* 'tsadiː) *n* the 18th letter in the Hebrew alphabet (צ or, at the end of a word ץ), transliterated as *s* or *ts* and pronounced more or less like English *s* or *ts* with pharyngeal articulation.

sadhu *or* **saddhu** ('sɑːduː) *n* a Hindu wandering holy man. [Sanskrit, from *sādhu* good]

Sadi *or* **Saadi** (sɑː'diː) *n* original name *Sheikh Muslih Addin.* ?1184–1292, Persian poet. His best-known works are *Gulistān* (Flower Garden) and *Būstān* (Tree Garden), long moralistic poems in prose and verse.

sadiron ('sædˌaɪən) *n* a heavy iron pointed at both ends, for pressing clothes. [C19: from SAD (in the obsolete sense: heavy) + IRON]

sadism ('seɪdɪzəm, 'sæ-) *n* the gaining of pleasure or sexual gratification from the infliction of pain and mental suffering on another person. See also **algolagnia.** Compare **masochism.** [C19: from French, named after the Marquis de SADE] ► **'sadist** *n* ► **sadistic** (sə'dɪstɪk) *adj* ► **sa'distically** *adv*

Sadler's Wells ('sædləz wɛlz) *n* (*functioning as sing*) a theatre in London. It was renovated in 1931 by Lilian Bayliss and became the home of the Sadler's Wells Opera Company and the Sadler's Wells Ballet (now the Royal Ballet). [named after the medicinal *wells* on the site and its owner Thomas *Sadler,* who founded the original theatre on the site]

sadomasochism (ˌseɪdəʊ'mæsəˌkɪzəm, ˌsædəʊ-) *n* **1** the combination of sadistic and masochistic elements in one person, characterized by both aggressive and submissive periods in relationships with others. **2** sexual practice in which one partner adopts a sadistic role and the other a masochistic one. Abbrev.: **SM.** Compare **sadism, masochism.** ► **,sadomaso'chistic** *adj*

Sadowa ('sɑːdəʊvə) *n* a village in the Czech Republic, in NE Bohemia: scene of the decisive battle of the Austro-Prussian war (1866) in which the Austrians were defeated by the Prussians. Czech name: **Sadová** ('sadɔvaː).

sad sack *n U.S. slang.* an inept person who makes mistakes despite good intentions. [C20: from a cartoon character created by G. Baker, U.S. cartoonist]

sae (se) *adv* a Scot. word for **so**[1].

SAE (in the U.S.) *abbrev. for* Society of Automotive Engineers.

s.a.e. *abbrev. for* stamped addressed envelope.

Safar *or* **Saphar** (sə'fɑː) *n* the second month of the Muslim year. [from Arabic]

safari (sə'fɑːrɪ) *n, pl* **-ris. 1** an overland journey or hunting expedition, esp. in Africa. **2** the people, animals, etc., that go on the expedition. [C19: from Swahili: journey, from Arabic *safarīya,* from *safara* to travel]

safari jacket *n* another name for **bush jacket.**

safari park *n* an enclosed park in which lions and other wild animals are kept uncaged in the open and can be viewed by the public from cars, etc.

safari suit *n* an outfit made of tough cotton, denim, etc., consisting of a bush jacket with matching trousers, shorts, or skirt.

safe (seɪf) *adj* **1** affording security or protection from harm: *a safe place.* **2** (*postpositive*) free from danger: *you'll be safe here.* **3** secure from risk; certain; sound: *a safe investment; a safe bet.* **4** worthy of trust; prudent: *a safe companion.* **5** tending to avoid controversy or risk: *a safe player.* **6** unable to do harm; not dangerous: *a criminal safe behind bars; water safe to drink.* **7 on the safe side.** as a precaution. ◆ *adv* **8** in a safe condition: *the children are safe in bed now.* **9 play safe.** to act in a way least likely to cause danger, controversy, or defeat. ◆ *n* **10** a strong container, usually of metal and provided with a secure lock, for storing money or valuables. **11** a small ventilated cupboard-like container for storing food. **12** *U.S. and Canadian.* a slang word for **condom.** [C13: from Old French *salf,* from Latin *salvus;* related to Latin *salus* safety] ► **'safely** *adv* ► **'safeness** *n*

safe-blower *n* a person who uses explosives to open safes and rob them.

safe-breaker *n* a person who breaks open and robs safes. Also called: **safecracker.**

safe-conduct *n* **1** a document giving official permission to travel through a region, esp. in time of war. **2** the protection afforded by such a document. ◆ *vb* (*tr*) **3** to conduct (a person) in safety. **4** to give a safe-conduct to.

safe-deposit *or* **safety-deposit** *n* **a** a place or building with facilities for the safe storage of money or valuables. **b** (*as modifier*): *a safe-deposit box.*

safeguard ('seɪf,gɑːd) *n* **1** a person or thing that ensures protection against danger, damage, injury, etc. **2** a document authorizing safe-conduct. ◆ *vb* **3** (*tr*) to defend or protect.

safe house *n* a place used secretly by undercover agents, terrorists, etc., as a meeting place or refuge.

safekeeping ('seɪf'kiːpɪŋ) *n* the act of keeping or state of being kept in safety.

safelight ('seɪf,laɪt) *n Photog.* a light that can be used in a room in which photographic material is handled, transmitting only those colours to which a particular type of film, plate, or paper is relatively insensitive.

safe period *n Informal.* the period during the menstrual cycle when conception is considered least likely to occur. See also **rhythm method.**

safe seat *n* a Parliamentary seat that at an election is sure to be held by the same party as held it before.

safe sex *or* **safer sex** *n* sexual intercourse using physical protection, such as a condom, or nonpenetrative methods to prevent the spread of such diseases as AIDS.

safety ('seɪftɪ) *n, pl* **-ties. 1** the quality of being safe. **2** freedom from danger or risk of injury. **3** a contrivance or device designed to prevent injury. **4** *American football.* **4a** Also called: **'safety,man.** either of two players who defend the area furthest back in the field. **4b** a play in which the offensive team causes the ball to cross its own goal line and then grounds the ball behind that line, scoring two points for the opposing team. Compare **touchback.**

safety belt *n* **1** another name for **seat belt. 2** a belt or strap worn by a person working at a great height and attached to a fixed object to prevent him from falling.

safety catch *n* a device to prevent the accidental operation of a mechanism, e.g. in a firearm or lift.

safety chain *n* a chain on the fastening of a bracelet, watch, etc., to ensure that it cannot open enough to fall off accidentally. Also called: **guard.**

safety curtain *n* a curtain made of fireproof material that can be lowered to separate the auditorium and stage in a theatre to prevent the spread of a fire.

safety factor *n* another name for **factor of safety.**

safety film *n* photographic film consisting of a nonflammable cellulose acetate or polyester base.

safety fuse *n* **1** a slow-burning fuse for igniting detonators from a distance. **2** an electrical fuse that protects a circuit from overloading.

safety glass *n* glass made by sandwiching a layer of plastic or resin between two sheets of glass so that if broken the fragments will not shatter.

Safety Islands *pl n* a group of three small French islands in the Atlantic, off the coast of French Guiana. French name: **Îles du Salut.**

safety lamp *n* an oil-burning miner's lamp in which the flame is surrounded by a metal gauze to prevent it from igniting combustible gas. Also called: **Davy lamp.**

safety match *n* a match that will light only when struck against a specially prepared surface.

safety net *n* **1** a net used in a circus to catch high-wire and trapeze artistes if they fall. **2** any means of protection from hardship or loss, such as insurance.

safety pin *n* **1** a spring wire clasp with a covering catch, made so as to shield the point when closed and to prevent accidental unfastening. **2** another word for **pin** (sense 9).

safety razor *n* a razor with a guard or guards fitted close to the cutting edge or edges so that deep cuts are prevented and the risk of accidental cuts reduced.

safety valve *n* **1** a valve in a pressure vessel that allows fluid to escape when a predetermined level of pressure has been reached. **2** a harmless outlet for emotion, energy, etc.

saffian ('sæfɪən) *n* leather tanned with sumach and usually dyed a bright colour. [C16: via Russian and Turkish from Persian *sakhtiyān* goatskin, from *sakht* hard]

safflower ('sæflauə) *n* **1** a thistle-like Eurasian annual plant, *Carthamus tinctorius,* having large heads of orange-yellow flowers and yielding a dye and an oil used in paints, medicines, etc.: family *Compositae* (composites). **2** a red dye used for cotton and for colouring foods and cosmetics, or a drug obtained from the florets of this plant. ◆ Also called: **false saffron.** [C16: via Dutch *saffloer* or German *safflor* from Old French *saffleur,* from Early Italian *saffiore,* of uncertain origin. Influenced by SAFFRON, FLOWER]

saffron ('sæfrən) *n* **1** an Old World crocus, *Crocus sativus,* having purple or white flowers with orange stigmas. **2** the dried stigmas of this plant, used to flavour or colour food. **3 meadow saffron.** another name for **autumn crocus. 4 false saffron.** another name for **safflower. 5a** an orange to orange-yellow colour. **5b** (*as adj*): *a saffron dress.* [C13: from Old French *safran,* from Medieval Latin *safranum,* from Arabic *za'farān*]

Safi (*French* safi) *n* a port in W Morocco, 170 km (105 miles) northwest of Marrakech, to which it is the nearest port. Pop.: 364 648 (1994).

Safid Rud (sæ'fiːd 'ruːd) *n* a river in N Iran, flowing northeast to a delta on the Caspian Sea. Length: about 785 km (490 miles).

S.Afr. *abbrev. for* South Africa(n).

safranine *or* **safranin** ('sæfrənɪn, -,niːn) *n* any of a class of azine dyes, used for textiles and biological stains. [C19: from French *safran* SAFFRON + -INE[2]]

safrole ('sæfrəul) *n* a colourless or yellowish oily water-insoluble liquid present in sassafras and camphor oils and used in soaps and perfumes. Formula: $C_3H_5C_6H_3O_2CH_2$. [C19: from (SAS)SAFR(AS) + -OLE[1]]

saft (sæft) *adj* a Scot. word for **soft.**

sag (sæg) *vb* (*mainly intr*) **sags, sagging, sagged. 1** (*also tr*) to sink or cause to sink in parts, as under weight or pressure: *the bed sags in the middle.* **2** to fall in value: *prices sagged to a new low.* **3** to hang unevenly; droop. **4** (of courage, spirits, etc.) to weaken; flag. ◆ *n* **5** the act or an instance of sagging: *a sag in profits.* **6** *Nautical.* the extent to which a vessel's keel sags at the centre. Compare **hog** (sense 6), **hogged. 7a** a marshy depression in an area of glacial till, chiefly in the U.S. Middle West. **7b** (*as modifier*): *sag and swell topography.* [C15: from Scandinavian; compare Swedish *sacka,* Dutch *zakken,* Norwegian dialect *sakka* to subside, Danish *sakke* to lag behind]

saga ('sɑːgə) *n* **1** any of several medieval prose narratives written in Iceland and recounting the exploits of a hero or a family. **2** any similar heroic narrative. **3** Also called: **saga novel.** a series of novels about several generations or members of a family. **4** any other artistic production said to resemble a saga. **5** *Informal.* a series of events or a story stretching over a long period. [C18: from Old Norse: a narrative; related to Old English *secgan* to SAY[1]]

sagacious (sə'geɪʃəs) *adj* **1** having or showing sagacity; wise. **2** *Obsolete.* (of hounds) having an acute sense of smell. [C17: from Latin *sagāx,* from *sāgīre* to be astute] ▸ **sa'gaciously** *adv* ▸ **sa'gaciousness** *n*

sagacity (sə'gæsɪtɪ) *n* foresight, discernment, or keen perception; ability to make good judgments.

sagamore ('sægə,mɔː) *n* (among some North American Indians) a chief or eminent man. Also called: **sachem.** [C17: from Abnaki *sāgimau,* literally: he overcomes]

Sagan (*French* sagã) *n* **Françoise** (frãswɑːz), original name *Françoise Quoirez.* born 1935, French writer, best-known for the novels *Bonjour Tristesse* (1954) and *Aimez-vous Brahms?* (1959).

sag bag *n* another name for **bean bag** (sense 2).

sage[1] (seɪdʒ) *n* **1** a man revered for his profound wisdom. ◆ *adj* **2** profoundly wise or prudent. **3** *Obsolete.* solemn. [C13: from Old French, from Latin *sapere* to be sensible; see SAPIENT] ▸ **'sagely** *adv* ▸ **'sageness** *n*

sage[2] (seɪdʒ) *n* **1** a perennial Mediterranean plant, *Salvia officinalis,* having grey-green leaves and purple, blue, or white flowers: family *Labiatae* (labiates). **2** the leaves of this plant, used in cooking for flavouring. **3** short for **sagebrush.** [C14: from Old French *saulge,* from Latin *salvia,* from *salvus* safe, in good health (from the curative properties attributed to the plant)]

sagebrush ('seɪdʒ,brʌʃ) *n* any of several aromatic plants of the genus *Artemisia,* esp. *A. tridentata,* a shrub of W North America, having silver-green leaves and large clusters of small white flowers: family *Compositae* (composites).

sage Derby *n* See **Derby**[2] (sense 4).

sage grouse *n* a large North American grouse, *Centrocercus urophasianus,* the males of which perform elaborate courtship displays. [C19: so named because it lives among, and eats, SAGEBRUSH]

saggar *or* **sagger** ('sægə) *n* a clay box in which fragile ceramic wares are placed for protection during firing. [C17: perhaps alteration of SAFEGUARD]

Saghalien (sə'gɑːljən) *n* a variant of **Sakhalin.**

Sagitta (sə'gɪtə) *n, Latin genitive* **Sagittae** (sə'gɪtiː). a small constellation in the N hemisphere lying between Cygnus and Aquila and crossed by the Milky Way. [C16: from Latin, literally: an arrow]

sagittal ('sædʒɪtᵊl) *adj* **1** resembling an arrow; straight. **2** of or relating to the sagittal suture. **3** situated in a plane parallel to the sagittal suture. ▸ **'sagittally** *adv*

sagittal suture *n* a serrated line on the top of the skull that marks the junction of the two parietal bones.

Sagittarius (,sædʒɪ'teərɪəs) *n, Latin genitive* **Sagittarii** (,sædʒɪ'teərɪ,aɪ). **1** *Astronomy.* a large conspicuous zodiacal constellation in the S hemisphere lying between Scorpius and Capricornus on the ecliptic and crossed by the Milky Way. **2** Also called: the **Archer.** *Astrology.* **2a** the ninth sign of the zodiac, symbol ♐, having a mutable fire classification and ruled by the planet Jupiter. The sun is in this sign between Nov. 22 and Dec. 21. **2b** a person born when the sun is in this sign. ◆ *adj* **3** *Astrology.* born under or characteristic of Sagittarius. ◆ Also (for senses 2b, 3): **Sagittarian** (,sædʒɪ'teərɪən). [C14: from Latin: an archer, from *sagitta* an arrow]

sagittate ('sædʒɪ,teɪt) *or* **sagittiform** (sə'dʒɪtɪ,fɔːm,'sædʒ-) *adj* (esp. of leaves) shaped like the head of an arrow. [C18: from New Latin *sagittātus,* from Latin *sagitta* arrow]

sago ('seɪgəu) *n* a starchy cereal obtained from the powdered pith of a sago palm, used for puddings and as a thickening agent. [C16: from Malay *sāgū*]

sago grass *n Austral.* a tall tough grass, *Paspalidum globoideum,* grown as forage for cattle.

sago palm *n* **1** any of various tropical Asian palm trees, esp. any of the genera *Metroxylon, Arenga,* and *Caryota,* the trunks of which yield sago. **2** any of several palmlike cycads that yield sago, esp. *Cycas revoluta.*

saguaro (sə'gwɑːrəu, sə'wɑː-) *or* **sahuaro** (sə'wɑːrəu) *n, pl* **-ros.** a giant cactus, *Carnegiea gigantea,* of desert regions of Arizona, S California, and Mexico, having white nocturnal flowers and edible red pulpy fruits. [Mexican Spanish, variant of *sahuaro,* an Indian name]

Saguenay (,sægə'neɪ) *n* a river in SE Canada in S Quebec, rising as the Péribonca River on the central plateau and flowing south, then east to the St. Lawrence. Length: 764 km (475 miles).

Sagunto (*Spanish* sa'γunto) *n* an industrial town in E Spain, near Valencia: allied to Rome and made a heroic resistance to the Carthaginian attack led by Hannibal (219–218 B.C.). Pop.: 57 300 (1989). Ancient name: **Saguntum** (sə'guːntəm).

Sahaptin (sɑː'hæptɪn), **Sahaptan** (sɑː'hæptən), *or* **Sahaptian** (sɑː'hæptɪən) *n* **1** (*pl* **-tins, -tans, -tians** *or* **-tin, -tan, -tian**) a member of a North American Indian people of Oregon and Washington, including the Nez Percé. **2** the language of this people. ◆ Also: **Shahaptin** (ʃə'hæptɪn).

Sahara (sə'hɑːrə) *n* a desert in N Africa, extending from the Atlantic to the Red Sea and from the Mediterranean to central Mali, Niger, Chad, and the Sudan:

the largest desert in the world, occupying over a quarter of Africa; rises to over 3300 m (11 000 ft.) in the central mountain system of the Ahaggar and Tibesti massifs; large reserves of iron ore, oil, and natural gas. Area: 9 100 000 sq. km (3 500 000 sq. miles). Average annual rainfall: less than 254 mm (10 in.). Highest recorded temperature: 58°C (136.4°F).

Saharan (sə'hɑːrən) *n* **1** a group of languages spoken in parts of Chad and adjacent countries, now generally regarded as forming a branch of the Nilo-Saharan family. ♦ *adj* **2** relating to or belonging to this group of languages. **3** of or relating to the Sahara.

sahib ('sɑːhɪb) *or* **saheb** ('sɑːhɛb) *n* (in India) a form of address or title placed after a man's name or designation, used as a mark of respect. [C17: from Urdu, from Arabic *çāhib,* literally: friend]

Sahitya Akademi (sɑː'hɪtjə ə'kɑːdəmɪ) *n* a body set up by the Government of India for cultivating literature in Indian languages and in English.

saice (saɪs) *n* a variant spelling of **syce.**

said[1] (sɛd) *adj* **1** (*prenominal*) (in contracts, pleadings, etc.) named or mentioned previously; aforesaid. ♦ *vb* **2** the past tense and past participle of **say**[1].

said[2] ('sɑːɪd) *n* a variant of **sayyid.**

Saida ('sɑːɪdə) *n* a port in SW Lebanon, on the Mediterranean: on the site of ancient Sidon; terminal of the Trans-Arabian pipeline from Saudi Arabia. Pop.: 100 000 (1991 est.).

saiga ('saɪgə) *n* either of two antelopes, *Saiga tatarica* or *S. mongolica,* of the plains of central Asia, having an enlarged slightly elongated nose. [C19: from Russian]

Saigon (saɪ'gɒn) *n* the former name (until 1976) of **Ho Chi Minh City.**

Saigo Takamori (saɪ'iːgəʊ ˌtækə'mɔːrɪ) *n* 1828–77, Japanese samurai, who led (1868) the coup that restored imperial government. In 1877 he reluctantly led a samurai rebellion, committing suicide when it failed.

sail (seɪl) *n* **1** an area of fabric, usually Terylene or nylon (formerly canvas), with fittings for holding it in any suitable position to catch the wind, used for propelling certain kinds of vessels, esp. over water. **2** a voyage on such a vessel: *a sail down the river.* **3** a vessel with sails or such vessels collectively: *to travel by sail; we raised seven sail in the northeast.* **4** a ship's sails collectively. **5** something resembling a sail in shape, position, or function, such as the part of a windmill that is turned by the wind or the part of a Portuguese man-of-war that projects above the water. **6** the conning tower of a submarine. **7 in sail.** having the sail set. **8 make sail. 8a** to run up the sail or to run up more sail. **8b** to begin a voyage. **9 set sail. 9a** to embark on a voyage by ship. **9b** to hoist sail. **10 under sail. 10a** with sail hoisted. **10b** under way. ♦ *vb* (*mainly intr*) **11** to travel in a boat or ship: *we sailed to Le Havre.* **12** to begin a voyage; set sail: *we sail at 5 o'clock.* **13** (of a vessel) to move over the water: *the liner is sailing to the Caribbean.* **14** (*tr*) to manoeuvre or navigate a vessel: *he sailed the schooner up the channel.* **15** (*tr*) to sail over: *she sailed the Atlantic single-handed.* **16** (often foll. by *over, through,* etc.) to move fast or effortlessly: *we sailed through customs; the ball sailed over the fence.* **17** to move along smoothly; glide. **18** (often foll. by *in* or *into*) *Informal.* **18a** to begin (something) with vigour. **18b** to make an attack (on) violently with words or physical force. [Old English *segl;* related to Old Frisian *seil,* Old Norse *segl,* German *Segel*] ▸ **'sailable** *adj* ▸ **'sailless** *adj*

sailboard ('seɪlˌbɔːd) *n* the craft used for windsurfing, consisting of a moulded board like a surfboard, to which a mast bearing a single sail is attached by a swivel joint.

sailboarding ('seɪlˌbɔːdɪŋ) *n* another name for **windsurfing.**

sailcloth ('seɪlˌklɒθ) *n* **1** any of various fabrics from which sails are made. **2** a lighter cloth used for clothing, etc.

sailer ('seɪlə) *n* a vessel, esp. one equipped with sails, with specified sailing characteristics: *a good sailer.*

sailfish ('seɪlˌfɪʃ) *n, pl* **-fish** *or* **-fishes. 1** any of several large scombroid game fishes of the genus *Istiophorus,* such as *I. albicans* (**Atlantic sailfish**), of warm and tropical seas: family *Istiophoridae.* They have an elongated upper jaw and a long sail-like dorsal fin. **2** another name for **basking shark.**

sailing ('seɪlɪŋ) *n* **1** the practice, art, or technique of sailing a vessel. **2** a method of navigating a vessel: *rhumb-line sailing.* **3** an instance of a vessel's leaving a port: *scheduled for a midnight sailing.*

sailing boat *or esp. U.S. and Canadian* **sailboat** ('seɪlˌbəʊt) *n* a boat propelled chiefly by sail.

sailing ship *n* a large sailing vessel.

sailor ('seɪlə) *n* **1** any member of a ship's crew, esp. one below the rank of officer. **2** a person who sails, esp. with reference to the likelihood of his becoming seasick: *a good sailor.* **3** short for **sailor hat** or **sailor suit.** ▸ **'sailorly** *adj*

sailor hat *n* a hat with a flat round crown and fairly broad brim that is rolled upwards.

sailor's-choice *n* any of various small percoid fishes of American coastal regions of the Atlantic, esp. the grunt *Haemulon parra* and the pinfish.

sailor suit *n* a child's suit, usually navy and white, with a collar that is squared off at the back like a sailor's.

sailplane ('seɪlˌpleɪn) *n* a high-performance glider.

sain (seɪn) *vb* (*tr*) *Archaic.* to make the sign of the cross over so as to bless or protect from evil or sin. [Old English *segnian,* from Latin *signare* to SIGN (with the cross)]

sainfoin ('sænfɔɪn) *n* a Eurasian perennial papilionaceous plant, *Onobrychis viciifolia,* widely grown as a forage crop, having pale pink flowers and curved pods. [C17: from French, from Medieval Latin *sānum faenum* wholesome hay, referring to its former use as a medicine]

saint (seɪnt; *unstressed* sənt) *n* **1** a person who after death is formally recognized by a Christian Church, esp. the Roman Catholic Church, as having attained, through holy deeds or behaviour, a specially exalted place in heaven and the right to veneration. **2** a person of exceptional holiness or goodness. **3** (*pl*) *Bible.* the collective body of those who are righteous in God's sight. ♦ *vb* **4** (*tr*) to canonize; recognize formally as a saint. [C12: from Old French, from Latin *sanctus* holy, from *sancīre* to hallow] ▸ **'saintdom** *n* ▸ **'saintless** *adj* ▸ **'saintlike** *adj*

Saint Agnes's Eve *n, usually abbreviated to* **St Agnes's Eve.** the night of Jan. 20, when according to tradition a woman can discover the identity of her future husband by performing certain rites.

Saint Albans ('ɔːlbənz) *n, usually abbreviated to* **St Albans.** a city in SE England, in W Hertfordshire: founded in 948 A.D. around the Benedictine abbey first built in Saxon times on the site of the martyrdom (about 303 A.D.) of St Alban; present abbey built in 1077; Roman ruins. Pop.: 80 376 (1991). Latin name: **Verulamium.**

Saint Andrews *n, usually abbreviated to* **St Andrews.** a city in E Scotland, in Fife on the North Sea: the oldest university in Scotland (1411); famous golf links. Pop.: 11 136 (1991).

Saint Andrew's Cross *n, usually abbreviated to* **St Andrew's Cross. 1** a diagonal cross with equal arms. **2** a white diagonal cross on a blue ground. [C18: so called because Saint ANDREW is reputed to have been crucified on a cross of this shape]

Saint Anthony's Cross *n, usually abbreviated to* **St Anthony's Cross.** another name for **tau cross.**

Saint Anthony's fire *n, usually abbreviated to* **St Anthony's fire.** *Pathol.* another name for **ergotism** or **erysipelas.** [C16: so named because praying to *St Anthony* was believed to effect a cure]

Saint Augustine ('ɔːgəsˌtiːn) *n, usually abbreviated to* **St Augustine.** a resort in NE Florida, on the Intracoastal Waterway: the oldest town in North America (1565); the northernmost outpost of the Spanish colonial empire for over 200 years. Pop.: 11 692 (1990).

Saint Austell ('ɔːstəl) *n, usually abbreviated to* **St Austell.** a town in SW England, in S Cornwall on **St Austell Bay** (an inlet of the English Channel): china clay industry; administratively part of St Austell with Fowey since 1968. Pop. (with Fowey): 21 622 (1991).

Saint Bartholomew's Day Massacre *n, usually abbreviated to* **St Bartholomew's Day Massacre.** the murder of Huguenots in Paris that began on Aug. 24, 1572 on the orders of Charles IX, acting under the influence of his mother Catherine de' Medici.

Saint Bernard *n, usually abbreviated to* **St Bernard.** a large breed of dog with a dense red-and-white coat, formerly used as a rescue dog in mountainous areas. [C19: so called because they were kept by the monks of the hospice at the Great SAINT BERNARD PASS]

Saint Bernard Pass *n, usually abbreviated to* **St Bernard Pass.** either of two passes over the Alps: the **Great St Bernard Pass,** 2472 m (8110 ft.) high, east of Mont Blanc between Italy and Switzerland, or the **Little St Bernard Pass,** 2157 m (7077 ft.) high, south of Mont Blanc between Italy and France.

Saint-Brieuc (*French* sɛ̃briø) *n, usually abbreviated to* **St-Brieuc.** a market town in NW France, near the N coast of Brittany. Pop.: 47 370 (1990).

Saint Catharines *n, usually abbreviated to* **St Catharines.** an industrial city in S central Canada, in S Ontario on the Welland Canal. Pop.: 129 300 (1991).

Saint Christopher *n, usually abbreviated to* **St Christopher.** another name for **Saint Kitts.**

Saint Christopher-Nevis *n, usually abbreviated to* **St Christopher-Nevis.** the official name of **Saint Kitts-Nevis.**

Saint Clair (klɛə) *n, usually abbreviated to* **St Clair. Lake.** a lake between SE Michigan and Ontario: linked with Lake Huron by the **St Clair River** and with Lake Erie by the Detroit River. Area: 1191 sq. km (460 sq. miles).

Saint-Cloud (*French* sɛ̃klu) *n, usually abbreviated to* **St-Cloud.** a residential suburb of Paris: former royal palace; Sèvres porcelain factory. Pop.: 28 670 (1990).

Saint Croix (krɔɪ) *n, usually abbreviated to* **St Croix.** an island in the Caribbean, the largest of the Virgin Islands of the U.S.: purchased by the U.S. in 1917. Chief town: Christiansted. Pop.: 50 139 (1990). Area: 207 sq. km (80 sq. miles). Also called: **Santa Cruz** ('sæntə 'kruːz).

Saint Croix River *n, usually abbreviated to* **St Croix River.** a river on the border between the northeast U.S. and SE Canada, flowing from the Chiputneticook Lakes to Passamaquoddy Bay, forming the border between Maine, U.S., and New Brunswick, Canada. Length: 121 km (75 miles).

Saint David's *n, usually abbreviated to* **St David's.** a town in SW Wales, in Pembrokeshire: its cathedral was a place of pilgrimage in medieval times. Pop.: 1627 (1991).

Saint-Denis (*French* sɛ̃dni) *n, usually abbreviated to* **St-Denis. 1** a town in N France, on the Seine: 12th-century Gothic abbey church, containing the tombs of many French monarchs; an industrial suburb of Paris. Pop.: 89 988 (1990). **2** the capital of the French overseas region of Réunion, a port on the N coast. Pop.: 207 158 (1995).

Sainte-Beuve (*French* sɛ̃tbœv) *n* **Charles Augustin** (ʃarl ogystɛ̃). 1804–69, French critic, best known for his collections of essays *Port Royal* (1840–59) and *Les Causeries du Lundi* (1851–62).

sainted ('seɪntɪd) *adj* **1** canonized. **2** like a saint in character or nature. **3** hallowed or holy.

Sainte Foy (seɪnt 'fɔɪ, sənt) *n, usually abbreviated to* **Ste Foy.** a SW suburb of Quebec, on the St Lawrence River. Pop.: 71 133 (1991).

Saint Elias Mountains *pl n, usually abbreviated to* **St Elias Mountains.** a mountain range between SE Alaska and the SW Yukon, Canada. Highest peak: Mount Logan, 6050 m (19 850 ft.).

Saint Elmo's fire ('ɛlməʊz) *n, usually abbreviated to* **St Elmo's fire.** (not in technical usage) a luminous region that sometimes appears around church spires, the masts of ships, etc. It is a corona discharge in the air caused by atmospheric electricity. Also called: **corposant.** [C16: so called because it was associated with *Saint Elmo* (a corruption, via *Sant'Ermo*, of *Saint Erasmus*, died 303) the patron saint of Mediterranean sailors]

Saint-Émilion (*French* sɛ̃temiljɔ̃) *n* a full-bodied red wine, similar to a Burgundy, produced around the town of Saint-Émilion in Bordeaux.

Saint-Étienne (*French* sɛ̃tetjɛn) *n, usually abbreviated to* **St-Étienne.** a town in E central France: a major producer of textiles and armaments. Pop.: 201 569 (1990).

Saint-Exupéry (*French* sɛ̃tɛgzyperi) *n* **Antoine de** (ɑ̃twan də). 1900–44, French novelist and aviator. His novels of aviation include *Vol de nuit* (1931) and *Terre des hommes* (1939). He also wrote the fairy tale *Le petit prince* (1943).

Saint Gall (*French* sɛ̃ gal) *n, usually abbreviated to* **St Gall. 1** a canton of NE Switzerland. Capital: St Gall. Pop.: 440 744 (1995 est.). Area: 2012 sq. km (777 sq. miles). **2** a town in NE Switzerland, capital of St Gall canton: an important educational centre in the Middle Ages. Pop.: 75 541 (1994). ◆ German name: **Sankt Gallen** (zaŋkt 'galən).

Saint George's *n, usually abbreviated to* **St George's.** the capital of Grenada, a port in the southwest. Pop.: 4621 (1991).

Saint George's Channel *n, usually abbreviated to* **St George's Channel.** a strait between Wales and Ireland, linking the Irish Sea with the Atlantic. Length: about 160 km (100 miles). Width: up to 145 km (90 miles).

Saint George's Cross *n, usually abbreviated to* **St George's Cross.** a red Greek cross on a white background.

Saint George's mushroom *n* an edible whitish basidiomycetous fungus, *Tricholoma gambosum,* with a floury smell. [so named because it appears earlier than most fungi, around St George's day (23 April)]

Saint Gotthard ('gɒtəd) *n, usually abbreviated to* **St Gotthard. 1** a range of the Lepontine Alps in SE central Switzerland. **2** a pass over the St Gotthard mountains, in S Switzerland. Height: 2114 m (6935 ft.).

Saint Helena (ˌsentɪ'li:nə) *n, usually abbreviated to* **St Helena.** a volcanic island in the SE Atlantic, forming (with its dependencies Tristan da Cunha and Ascension) a UK Overseas Territory: discovered by the Portuguese in 1502 and annexed by England in 1651; scene of Napoleon's exile and death. Capital: Jamestown. Pop.: 5700 (1992). Area: 122 sq. km (47 sq. miles).

Saint Helens *n, usually abbreviated to* **St Helens. 1** a town in NW England, in St Helens unitary authority, Merseyside: glass industry. Pop.: 106 293 (1991). **2** a unitary authority in NW England, in Merseyside. Pop.: 181 000 (1994 est.). Area: 130 sq. km (50 sq. miles). **3 Mount.** a volcanic peak in S Washington state; it erupted in 1980 after lying dormant from 1857.

Saint Helier ('hɛlɪə) *n, usually abbreviated to* **St Helier.** a market town and resort in the Channel Islands, on the S coast of Jersey. Pop.: 27 523 (1996).

sainthood ('seɪnthʊd) *n* **1** the state or character of being a saint. **2** saints collectively.

Saint James's Palace *n, usually abbreviated to* **St James's Palace.** a palace in Pall Mall, London: residence of British monarchs from 1697 to 1837.

Saint John *n, usually abbreviated to* **St John. 1** a port in E Canada, at the mouth of the St John River: the largest city in New Brunswick. Pop.: 90 457 (1991). **2** an island in the Caribbean, in the Virgin Islands of the U.S. Pop.: 3504 (1990). Area: 49 sq. km (19 sq. miles). **3 Lake.** a lake in Canada, in S Quebec: drained by the Saguenay River. Area: 971 sq. km (375 sq. miles). **4** a river in E North America, rising in Maine, U.S., and flowing northeast to New Brunswick, Canada, then generally southeast to the Bay of Fundy. Length: 673 km (418 miles).

Saint-John Perse ('sɪndʒən 'pɜ:s) *n* See (Saint-John) **Perse.**

Saint John's *n, usually abbreviated to* **St John's. 1** a port in Canada, capital of Newfoundland, on the E coast of the Avalon Peninsula. Pop.: 95 770 (1991). **2** the capital of Antigua and Barbuda: a port on the NW coast of the island of Antigua. Pop.: 21 514 (1991).

Saint John's bread *n, usually abbreviated to* **St John's bread.** another name for **carob** (sense 2). [C16: so called because its beans were thought to be the "locusts" that JOHN THE BAPTIST ate in the desert]

Saint John's wort *n, usually abbreviated to* **St John's wort.** any of numerous shrubs or herbaceous plants of the temperate genus *Hypericum,* such as *H. perforatum,* having yellow flowers and glandular leaves: family *Hypericaceae.* See also **rose of Sharon** (sense 1), **tutsan.** [C15: so named because it was traditionally gathered on *Saint John's Eve* (June 23rd) as a protection against evil spirits]

Saint-Just (*French* sɛ̃ʒyst) *n* **Louis Antoine Léon de** (lwi ɑ̃twan leɔ̃ də). 1767–94, French Revolutionary leader and orator. A member of the Committee of Public Safety (1793–94), he was guillotined with Robespierre.

Saint Kilda ('kɪldə) *n, usually abbreviated to* **St Kilda. 1** a group of volcanic islands in the Atlantic, in the Outer Hebrides: uninhabited since 1930; bird sanctuary. **2** Also called: **Hirta.** the main island of this group.

Saint Kitts (kɪts) *n, usually abbreviated to* **St Kitts.** an island in the E Caribbean, in the Leeward Islands: part of the state of St Kitts-Nevis. Capital: Basseterre. Pop.: 40 618 (1991). Area: 168 sq. km (65 sq. miles). Also called: **Saint Christopher.**

Saint Kitts-Nevis *n, usually abbreviated to* **St Kitts-Nevis.** an independent state in the E Caribbean; comprises the two islands of St Kitts and Nevis: with the island of Anguilla formed a colony (1882–1967) and a British associated state (1967–83); Anguilla formally separated from the group in 1983; gained full independence in 1983 as a member of the Commonwealth. Official language: English. Religion: Protestant majority. Currency: E Caribbean dollar. Capital: Basseterre. Pop.: 42 300 (1998 est.). Area: 262 sq. km (101 sq. miles).

Saint Laurent (*French* sɛ̃ lɔrɑ̃) *n, usually abbreviated to* **St Laurent.** a W suburb of Montreal, Canada. Pop.: 72 402 (1991).

Saint-Laurent (*French* sɛ̃lɔrɑ̃) *n* **Yves** (iv), full name *Yves-Mathieu.* born 1936, French couturier: popularized trousers for women for all occasions.

Saint Lawrence *n, usually abbreviated to* **St Lawrence. 1** a river in SE Canada, flowing northeast from Lake Ontario, forming part of the border between Canada and the U.S., to the Gulf of St Lawrence: commercially one of the most important rivers in the world as the easternmost link of the St Lawrence Seaway. Length: 1207 km (750 miles). Width at mouth: 145 km (90 miles). **2 Gulf of.** a deep arm of the Atlantic off the E coast of Canada between Newfoundland and the mainland coasts of Quebec, New Brunswick, and Nova Scotia.

Saint Lawrence Seaway *n, usually abbreviated to* **St Lawrence Seaway.** an inland waterway of North America, passing through the Great Lakes, the St Lawrence River, and connecting canals and locks: one of the most important waterways in the world. Length: 3993 km (2480 miles).

Saint Leger ('lɛdʒə) *n, usually abbreviated to* **St Leger. the.** an annual horse race run at Doncaster since 1776: one of the classics of the flat-racing season.

Saint Leonard ('lɛnəd) *n, usually abbreviated to* **St Leonard.** a N suburb of Montreal, Canada. Pop.: 82 200 (latest est.).

Saint-Lô (*French* sɛ̃lo) *n, usually abbreviated to* **St-Lô.** a market town in NW France: a Calvinist stronghold in the 16th century. Pop.: 22 819 (1990).

Saint Louis ('lʊɪs) *n, usually abbreviated to* **St Louis.** a port in E Missouri, on the Mississippi River near its confluence with the Missouri: the largest city in the state; university; major industrial centre. Pop.: 351 565 (1996 est.).

Saint-Louis (*French* sɛ̃lwi) *n, usually abbreviated to* **St-Louis.** a port in NW Senegal, on an island at the mouth of the Senegal River: the first French settlement in W Africa (1689); capital of Senegal until 1958. Pop.: 179 000 (1995 est.).

Saint Lucia ('lu:ʃə) *n, usually abbreviated to* **St Lucia.** an island state in the Caribbean, in the Windward Islands group of the Lesser Antilles: a volcanic island; gained self-government in 1967 as a British Associated State; attained full independence within the Commonwealth in 1979. Official language: English. Religion: Roman Catholic majority. Currency: E Caribbean dollar. Capital: Castries. Pop.: 151 000 (1998 est.). Area: 616 sq. km (238 sq. miles).

Saint Luke's summer *n, usually abbreviated to* **St Luke's summer.** a period of unusually warm weather in the autumn. [referring to St Luke's feast-day, Oct. 7 in the pre-Gregorian calendar (now Oct. 18)]

saintly ('seɪntlɪ) *adj* **-lier, -liest.** like, relating to, or suitable for a saint. ► **'saintlily** *adv* ► **'saintliness** *n*

Saint Martin *n, usually abbreviated to* **St Martin.** an island in the E Caribbean, in the Leeward Islands: administratively divided since 1648, the north belonging to France (as a dependency of Guadeloupe) and the south belonging to the Netherlands (as part of the Netherlands Antilles); salt industry. Pop.: (French) 28 518 (1990); (Dutch) 37 256 (1994 est.). Areas: (French) 52 sq. km (20 sq. miles); (Dutch) 33 sq. km (13 sq. miles). Dutch name: **Sint Maarten.**

Saint Martin's summer *n, usually abbreviated to* **St Martin's summer.** a period of unusually warm weather in the late autumn, esp. early November. [referring to St Martin's feast-day, Oct. 31 in the pre-Gregorian calendar (now Nov. 11)]

Saint-Maur-des-Fossés (*French* sɛ̃mɔrdefose) *n, usually abbreviated to* **St-Maur-des-Fossés.** a town in N France, on the River Marne: a residential suburb of SE Paris. Pop.: 77 492 (1990).

Saint-Mihiel (*French* sɛ̃mjel) *n, usually abbreviated to* **St-Mihiel.** a village in NE France, on the River Meuse: site of a battle in World War I, in which the American army launched its first offensive in France.

Saint Moritz (mə'rɪts) *n, usually abbreviated to* **St Moritz.** a village in E Switzerland, in Graubünden canton in the Upper Engadine, at an altitude of 1856 m (6089 ft.): sports and tourist centre. Pop.: 5335 (1990 est.).

Saint-Nazaire (*French* sɛ̃nazɛr) *n, usually abbreviated to* **St-Nazaire.** a port in NW France, at the mouth of the River Loire: German submarine base in World War II; shipbuilding. Pop.: 64 812 (1990).

Saint-Ouen (*French* sɛ̃twɛ̃) *n, usually abbreviated to* **St-Ouen.** a town in N France, on the Seine: an industrial suburb of Paris; famous flea market. Pop.: 42 611 (1990).

Saint Paul *n, usually abbreviated to* **St Paul.** a port in SE Minnesota, capital of the state, at the head of navigation of the Mississippi: now contiguous with Minneapolis (the Twin Cities). Pop.: 259 606 (1996 est.).

saintpaulia (sənt'pɔ:lɪə) *n* another name for **African violet.** [C20: New Latin, named after Baron W. von *Saint Paul,* German soldier (died 1910), who discovered it]

Saint Paul's *n, usually abbreviated to* **St Paul's.** a cathedral in central London, built between 1675 and 1710 to replace an earlier cathedral destroyed during the Great Fire (1666): regarded as Wren's masterpiece.

Saint Peter's *n, usually abbreviated to* **St Peter's.** the basilica of the Vatican City, built between 1506 and 1615 to replace an earlier church: the largest church in the world, 188 m (615 ft.) long, and chief pilgrimage centre of Europe; designed by many architects, notably Bramante, Raphael, Sangallo, Michelangelo, and Bernini.

Saint Petersburg ('pi:təzˌbɜ:g) *n, usually abbreviated to* **St Petersburg. 1** a city and port in Russia, on the Gulf of Finland at the mouth of the Neva River: founded by Peter the Great in 1703 and built on low-lying marshes subject to frequent flooding; capital of Russia from 1712 to 1918; a cultural and educational centre, with a university (1819); a major industrial centre, with engineering, shipbuilding, chemical, textile, and printing industries. Pop.: 4 838 500 (1995 est.). Former names: **Petrograd** (1914–24), **Leningrad** (1924–91). **2** a city and resort in W Florida, on Tampa Bay. Pop.: 235 988 (1996 est.).

Saint Pierre (*French* sɛ̃ pjɛr) *n, usually abbreviated to* **St Pierre.** a former town on the coast of the French island of Martinique, destroyed by the eruption of Mont Pelée in 1902.

Saint-Pierre (*French* sɛ̃pjɛr) *n* **Jacques Henri Bernardin de** (ʒak ɑ̃ri bɛrnardɛ̃ də). 1737–1814, French author; his work, which was greatly influenced by the writings of Rousseau, includes *Voyage à l'Île de France* (1773), *Études de la nature* (1784, 1788), and *La chaumière indienne* (1791).

Saint Pierre and Miquelon (ˌmɪkəˈlɒn; *French* miklɔ̃) *n, usually abbreviated to* **St Pierre and Miquelon.** an archipelago in the Atlantic, off the S coast of Newfoundland: an overseas department of France, the only remaining French possession in North America; consists of the islands of St Pierre, with most of the population, and Miquelon, about ten times as large; fishing industries. Capital: St Pierre. Pop.: 6392 (1990). Area: 242 sq. km (94 sq. miles).

Saint Pölten (ˈpɜːltən) *n* See **Sankt Pölten.**

Saint-Quentin (*French* sɛ̃kɑ̃tɛ̃) *n, usually abbreviated to* **St-Quentin.** a town in N France, on the River Somme: textile industry. Pop.: 62 085 (1990).

Saint-Saëns (*French* sɛ̃sɑ̃s) *n* **(Charles) Camille** (kamij). 1835–1921, French composer, pianist, and organist. His works include the symphonic poem *Danse Macabre* (1874), the opera *Samson and Delilah* (1877), the humorous orchestral suite *Carnival of Animals* (1886), five symphonies, and five piano concertos.

Saintsbury (ˈseɪntsbərɪ, -brɪ) *n* **George Edward Bateman.** 1845–1933, British literary critic and historian; author of many works on English and French literature.

saint's day *n Christianity.* a day in the church calendar commemorating a saint.

Saint-Simon (*French* sɛ̃simɔ̃) *n* **1 Comte de** (kɔ̃t də), title of *Claude Henri de Rouvroy.* 1760–1825, French social philosopher, generally regarded as the founder of French socialism. He thought society should be reorganized along industrial lines and that scientists should be the new spiritual leaders. His most important work is *Nouveau Christianisme* (1825). **2 Duc de** (dyk də), title of *Louis de Rouvroy.* 1675–1755, French soldier, statesman, and writer: his *Mémoires* are an outstanding account of the period 1694–1723, during the reigns of Louis XIV and Louis XV.

Saint-Simonianism (səntsɪˈməunɪəˌnɪzəm) *or* **Saint-Simonism** (səntˈsaɪmənɪzəm) *n* the socialist system advocated by the Comte de Saint-Simon. ▸ **Saint-Siˈmonian** *n, adj*

Saint Swithin's Day *n, usually abbreviated to* **St Swithin's Day.** July 15, observed as a Church festival commemorating Saint Swithin. It is popularly supposed that if it rains on this day the rain will persist for the next 40 days.

Saint Thomas *n, usually abbreviated to* **St Thomas. 1** an island in the E Caribbean, in the Virgin Islands of the U.S. Capital: Charlotte Amalie. Pop.: 48 166 (1990). Area: 83 sq. km (28 sq. miles). **2** the former name (1921–37) of **Charlotte Amalie.**

Saint Valentine's Day *n, usually abbreviated to* **St Valentine's Day.** Feb. 14, the day on which valentines are exchanged, originally connected with the pagan festival of Lupercalia.

Saint Vincent *n, usually abbreviated to* **St Vincent. 1 Cape.** a headland at the SW extremity of Portugal: scene of several important naval battles, notably in 1797, when the British defeated the French and Spanish. **2 Gulf.** a shallow inlet of SE South Australia, to the east of the Yorke Peninsula: salt industry.

Saint Vincent and the Grenadines *n, usually abbreviated to* **St Vincent and the Grenadines.** an island state in the Caribbean, in the Windward Islands of the Lesser Antilles: comprises the island of St Vincent and the Northern Grenadines; formerly a British associated state (1969–79); gained full independence in 1979 as a member of the Commonwealth. Official language: English. Religion: Protestant majority. Currency: Caribbean dollar. Capital: Kingstown. Pop.: 113 000 (1998 est.). Area: 389 sq. km (150 sq. miles).

Saint Vitus's dance (ˈvaɪtəsɪz) *n, usually abbreviated to* **St Vitus's dance.** *Pathol.* a nontechnical name for **Sydenham's chorea.** **[C17:** so called because sufferers traditionally prayed to *Saint Vitus* (3rd-century child martyr) for relief**]**

Saipan (saɪˈpæn) *n* an island in the W Pacific, in the S central Mariana Islands: administrative centre of the U.S. Trust Territory of the Pacific Islands; captured by the Americans and used as an air base until the end of World War II; administered by the U.S. since 1946. Pop.: 38 896 (1990). Area: 180 sq. km (70 sq. miles).

sair (ser) *adj, adv* a Scot. word for **sore.**

Saïs (ˈseɪɪs) *n* (in ancient Egypt) a city in the W Nile delta; the royal capital of the 24th dynasty (about 730–715 B.C.) and the 26th dynasty (about 664–525 B.C.). ▸ **Saite** (ˈseraɪt) *n* ▸ **Saitic** (seɪˈɪtɪk) *adj*

saith (seθ) *vb* (used with *he, she,* or *it*) *Archaic.* a form of the present tense (indicative mood) of **say**[1].

saithe (seɪθ) *n Brit.* another name for **coalfish.** **[C19:** from Old Norse *seithr* coalfish; compare Gaelic *saigh, saighean* coalfish, Irish *saoidhean* young of fish**]**

Saiva (ˈsaɪvə, ˈʃaɪ-) *n* **1** a member of a branch of Hinduism devoted to the worship of Siva, but rejecting the notion of his incarnations. ◆ *adj* **2** of or relating to Saivism or Saivites. ▸ **ˈSaivism** *n* ▸ **ˈSaivite** *n*

sakai (ˈsakaɪ) *n* (in Malaysia) **1** a Malaysian aborigine. **2** a wild or uncouth person. **[**from Malay**]**

Sakai (sɑːˈkaɪ) *n* a port in S Japan, on S Honshu on Osaka Bay: an industrial satellite of Osaka. Pop.: 802 965 (1995).

sake[1] (seɪk) *n* **1** benefit or interest (esp. in the phrase **for (someone's** *or* **one's own) sake). 2** the purpose of obtaining or achieving (esp. in the phrase **for the sake of (something)). 3** used in various exclamations of impatience, urgency, etc.: *for heaven's sake; for pete's sake.* **[C13** (in the phrase *for the sake of,* probably from legal usage): from Old English *sacu* lawsuit (hence, a cause); related to Old Norse *sok,* German *Sache* matter**]**

sake[2], **saké,** *or* **saki** (ˈsækɪ) *n* a Japanese alcoholic drink made from fermented rice. **[C17:** from Japanese**]**

saker (ˈseɪkə) *n* a large falcon, *Falco cherrug,* of E Europe and central Asia: used in falconry. **[C14** *sagre,* from Old French *sacre,* from Arabic *saqr***]**

Sakhalin (*Russian* səxaˈlin) *or* **Saghalien** *n* an island in the Sea of Okhotsk, off the SE coast of Russia north of Japan: fishing, forestry, and mineral resources (coal and petroleum). Capital: Yuzhno-Sakhalinsk. Pop.: 673 000 (1995 est.). Area: 76 000 sq. km (29 300 sq. miles). Japanese name (1905–24): **Karafuto.**

Sakha Republic (*Russian* ˈsaxa) *n* an administrative division in E Russia, in NE Siberia on the Arctic Ocean: the coldest inhabited region of the world; it has rich mineral resources. Capital: Yakutsk. Pop.: 1 060 700 (1994). Area: 3 103 200 sq. km (1 197 760 sq. miles). Former names: **Yakut Republic, Yakutia.**

Sakharov (*Russian* zaˈxarəf) *n* **Andrei** (anˈdrjej). 1921–89, Soviet physicist and human-rights campaigner: Nobel peace prize 1975.

saki (ˈsɑːkɪ) *n* any of several small mostly arboreal New World monkeys of the genera *Pithecia* and *Chiropotes,* having long hair and a long bushy tail. **[C20:** French, from Tupi *saqi***]**

Saki (ˈsɑːkɪ) *n* pen name of (Hector Hugh) **Munro.**

Saktas (ˈsæktəs) *n* a Hindu sect worshipping female goddesses represented by the vulva. **[C19:** from Sanskrit. See SAKTI**]**

Sakti (ˈsæktɪ) *or* **Shakti** (ˈʃʌktɪ) *n Hinduism.* **1** the female principle or organ of reproduction and generative power in general. **2** this principle manifested in the consorts of the gods, esp. Kali. **[C19:** from Sanskrit *śákti* power**]**

Sakyamuni (ˌsɑːkjəˈmuːnɪ) *n* one of the titles of the Buddha, deriving from the name of Sakya where he was born. **[**Sanskrit, literally: hermit of the *Sākya* tribe**]**

sal (sæl) *n* a pharmacological term for **salt** (sense 3). **[**Latin**]**

salaam (səˈlɑːm) *n* **1** a Muslim form of salutation consisting of a deep bow with the right palm on the forehead. **2** a salutation signifying peace, used chiefly by Muslims. ◆ *vb* **3** to make a salaam or salute (someone) with a salaam. **[C17:** from Arabic *salām* peace, from the phrase *assalām ʻalaikum* peace be to you**]**

salable (ˈseɪləbᵊl) *adj* the U.S. spelling of **saleable.**

salacious (səˈleɪʃəs) *adj* **1** having an excessive interest in sex. **2** (of books, magazines, etc.) erotic, bawdy, or lewd. **[C17:** from Latin *salax* fond of leaping, from *salīre* to leap**]** ▸ **saˈlaciously** *adv* ▸ **saˈlaciousness** *or* **salacity** (səˈlæsɪtɪ) *n*

salad (ˈsæləd) *n* **1** a dish of raw vegetables, such as lettuce, tomatoes, etc., served as a separate course with cold meat, eggs, etc., or as part of a main course. **2** any dish of cold vegetables or fruit: *potato salad; fruit salad.* **3** any green vegetable used in such a dish, esp. lettuce. **[C15:** from Old French *salade,* from Old Provençal *salada,* from *salar* to season with salt, from Latin *sal* salt**]**

salad days *pl n* a period of youth and inexperience. **[**allusion to *Antony and Cleopatra* (1.v.73) by William Shakespeare: "my salad days When I was green in judgment, cold in blood"**]**

salad dressing *n* a sauce for salad, such as oil and vinegar or mayonnaise.

salade (səˈlɑːd) *n* another word for **sallet.**

salade niçoise (sæˈlɑːd niːˈswɑːz) *n* a cold dish consisting of hard-boiled eggs, anchovy fillets, olives, tomatoes, tuna fish, etc. **[C20:** from French, literally salad of or from *Nice,* S France**]**

Saladin (ˈsælədɪn) *n* Arabic name *Salah-ed-Din Yusuf ibn-Ayyub.* ?1137–93, sultan of Egypt and Syria and opponent of the Crusaders. He defeated the Christians near Tiberias (1187) and captured Acre, Jerusalem, and Ashkelon. He fought against Richard I of England and Philip II of France during the Third Crusade (1189–92).

Salado (*Spanish* saˈlaðo) *n* **1** a river in N Argentina, rising in the Andes as the Juramento and flowing southeast to the Paraná River. Length: 2012 km (1250 miles). **2** a river in W Argentina, rising near the Chilean border as the Desaguadero and flowing south to the Colorado River. Length: about 1365 km (850 miles).

Salamanca (*Spanish* salaˈmaŋka) *n* a city in W Spain: a leading cultural centre of Europe till the end of the 16th century; market town. Pop.: 167 316 (1995 est.).

salamander (ˈsæləˌmændə) *n* **1** any of various urodele amphibians, such as *Salamandra salamandra* **(European fire salamander)** of central and S Europe (family *Salamandridae*). They are typically terrestrial, have an elongated body, and only return to water to breed. **2** *Chiefly U.S. and Canadian.* any urodele amphibian. **3** a mythical reptile supposed to live in fire. **4** an elemental fire-inhabiting being. **5** any person or thing able to exist in fire or great heat. **6** *Metallurgy.* a residue of metal and slag deposited on the walls of a furnace. **7** a portable stove used to dry out a building under construction. **[C14:** from Old French *salamandre,* from Latin *salamandra,* from Greek**]** ▸ **salamandrine** (ˌsæləˈmændrɪn) *adj*

Salambria (səˈlæmbrɪə, ˌsɑːlɑːmˈbriə) *n* a river in N Greece, in Thessaly, rising in the Pindus Mountains and flowing southeast and east to the Gulf of Salonika. Length: about 200 km (125 miles). Ancient name: **Peneus.** Modern Greek name: **Piniós.**

salami (səˈlɑːmɪ) *n* a highly seasoned type of sausage, usually flavoured with garlic. **[C19:** from Italian, plural of *salame,* from Vulgar Latin *salāre* (unattested) to salt, from Latin *sal* salt**]**

Salamis (ˈsæləmɪs) *n* an island in the Saronic Gulf, Greece: scene of the naval battle in 480 B.C., in which the Greeks defeated the Persians. Pop.: 20 000 (latest est.). Area: 95 sq. km (37 sq. miles).

sal ammoniac *n* another name for **ammonium chloride.**

salaried (ˈsælərɪd) *adj* earning or yielding a salary: *a salaried worker; salaried employment.*

salary (ˈsælərɪ) *n, pl* **-ries. 1** a fixed regular payment made by an employer, often monthly, for professional or office work as opposed to manual work. Compare **wage** (sense 1). ◆ *vb* **-ries, -rying, -ried. 2** *(tr)* to pay a salary to. **[C14:** from Anglo-Norman *salarie,* from Latin *salārium* the sum given to Roman soldiers to buy salt, from *sal* salt**]**

salaryman (ˈsælərɪˌmæn) *n, pl* **-men.** (in Japan) an office worker.

Salazar (*Portuguese* salə'zar) *n* **Antonio de Oliveira** (ən'tɔnju 'də: oli'vaɪrə). 1889–1970, Portuguese statesman; dictator (1932–68).

salchow ('sɔ:lkəʊ) *n Figure skating.* a jump from the inner backward edge of one foot with one, two, or three full turns in the air, returning to the outer backward edge of the opposite foot. [C20: named after Ulrich *Salchow* (1877–1949), Swedish figure skater, who originated it]

Salduba (sæl'du:bə, 'sældəbə) *n* the pre-Roman (Celtiberian) name for **Zaragoza.**

sale (seɪl) *n* **1** the exchange of goods, property, or services for an agreed sum of money or credit. **2** the amount sold. **3** the opportunity to sell; market: *there was no sale for luxuries.* **4** the rate of selling or being sold: *a slow sale of synthetic fabrics.* **5a** an event at which goods are sold at reduced prices, usually to clear old stocks. **5b** (*as modifier*): *sale bargains.* **6** an auction. [Old English *sala,* from Old Norse *sala.* See also SELL]

Sale (seɪl) *n* **1** a town in NW England, in Trafford unitary authority, Greater Manchester: a residential suburb of Manchester. Pop.: 57 824 (1991). **2** a city in SE Australia, in SE Victoria: centre of an agricultural region. Pop.: 13 858 (1991).

Salé (*French* sale) *n* a port in NW Morocco, on the Atlantic adjoining Rabat. Pop.: 521 000 (1993 est.).

saleable *or U.S.* **salable** ('seɪləbᵊl) *adj* fit for selling or capable of being sold. ▸ **ˌsalea'bility, 'saleableness** *or U.S.* **ˌsala'bility, 'salableness** *n* ▸ **'saleably** *or U.S.* **'salably** *adv*

sale and lease back *n* a system of raising capital for a business by selling the business property and then renting it from the new owner for an agreed period.

Salem ('seɪləm) *n* **1** a city in S India, in Tamil Nadu: textile industries. Pop.: 366 712 (1991). **2** a city in NE Massachusetts, on the Atlantic: scene of the execution of 19 people after the witch hunts of 1692. Pop.: 38 091 (1990). **3** a city in the NW USA, the state capital of Oregon: food-processing. Pop.: 122 566 (1996 est.). **4** an Old Testament name for **Jerusalem.** (Genesis 14:18; Psalms 76:2).

sale of work *n Brit.* a sale of goods and handicrafts made by the members of a club, church congregation, etc., to raise money.

sale or return *or* **sale and return** *n* an arrangement by which a retailer pays only for goods sold, returning those that are unsold to the wholesaler or manufacturer.

salep ('sælɛp) *n* the dried ground starchy tubers of various orchids, used for food and formerly as drugs. [C18: via French and Turkish from Arabic *sahlab,* shortened from *khusy ath-tha'lab,* literally: fox's testicles, name of an orchid]

saleratus (ˌsælə'reɪtəs) *n* another name for **sodium bicarbonate,** esp. when used in baking powders. [C19: from New Latin *sal aerātus* aerated salt]

Salerno (*Italian* sa'lɛrno) *n* a port in SW Italy, in Campania on the **Gulf of Salerno:** first medical school of medieval Europe. Pop.: 143 863 (1996 est.).

saleroom ('seɪlˌru:m, -ˌrʊm) *n Chiefly Brit.* a room where objects are displayed for sale, esp. by auction.

salesclerk ('seɪlzˌklɜ:rk) *n U.S. and Canadian.* a shop assistant. Sometimes shortened to **clerk.**

sales forecast *n* a prediction of future sales of a product, either judgmental or based on previous sales patterns.

Salesian (sə'li:zjən, -ʒən) *adj* **1** of or relating to St Francis of Sales or to the religious orders founded by him or by St John Bosco in his name. See also **Visitation** (sense 2). ◆ *n* **2** a member of a Salesian order, esp. a member of the Society of St Francis of Sales founded in Turin by St John Bosco (1854), and dedicated to all types of educational work. [C19: from *Sales;* see FRANCIS OF SALES]

salesman ('seɪlzmən) *n, pl* **-men. 1** Also called: (*fem*) **'salesˌwoman, 'salesˌgirl, 'salesˌlady,** *or* **'salesˌperson.** a person who sells merchandise or services either in a shop or by canvassing in a designated area. **2** short for **travelling salesman.**

salesmanship ('seɪlzmənʃɪp) *n* **1** the technique, skill, or ability of selling. **2** the work of a salesman.

sales pitch *or* **talk** *n* an argument or other persuasion used in selling.

sales promotion *n* activities or techniques intended to create consumer demand for a product or service.

sales resistance *n* opposition of potential customers to selling, esp. aggressive selling.

salesroom ('seɪlzˌru:m, -ˌrʊm) *n* a room in which merchandise on sale is displayed.

sales tax *n* a tax levied on retail sales receipts and added to selling prices by retailers.

sales trader *n Stock Exchange.* a person employed by a market maker, or his firm, to find clients.

salet ('sælɪt) *n* a variant spelling of **sallet.**

saleyard ('seɪlˌjɑ:d) *n Austral. and N.Z.* an area with pens for holding animals before auction.

Salford ('sɔ:lfəd, 'sɒl-) *n* **1** a city in NW England in Salford unitary authority, Greater Manchester, on the Manchester Ship Canal: a major centre of the cotton industry in the 19th century; extensive docks. Pop.: 79 755 (1991). **2** a unitary authority in NW England, in Greater Manchester. Pop.: 230 500 (1995 est.). Area: 97 sq. km (37 sq. miles).

Salian ('seɪlɪən) *adj* **1** denoting or relating to a group of Franks (the **Salii**) who settled in the Netherlands in the 4th century A.D. and later conquered large areas of Gaul, esp. in the north. ◆ *n* **2** a member of this group.

salic ('sælɪk, 'seɪ-) *adj* (of rocks and minerals) having a high content of silica and alumina. [C20: from *s(ilica)* + *al(umina)* + -IC]

Salic *or* **Salique** ('sælɪk, 'seɪlɪk) *adj* of or relating to the Salian Franks or the Salic law.

salicaceous (ˌsælɪ'keɪʃəs) *adj* of, relating to, or belonging to the *Salicaceae,* a chiefly N temperate family of trees and shrubs having catkins: includes the willows and poplars. [C19: via New Latin from Latin *salix* a willow]

salicin *or* **salicine** ('sælɪsɪn) *n* a colourless or white crystalline water-soluble glucoside obtained from the bark of poplar trees and used as a medical analgesic. Formula: $C_{13}H_{18}O_7$. [C19: from French *salicine,* from Latin *salix* willow]

salicional (sə'lɪʃənəl) *or* **salicet** ('sælɪˌsɛt) *n* a soft-toned organ stop with a reedy quality. [C19: from German, from Latin *salix* willow]

Salic law *n History.* **1a** the code of laws of the Salic Franks and other Germanic tribes. **1b** a law within this code excluding females from inheritance. **2** a law excluding women from succession to the throne in certain countries, such as France and Spain.

salicornia (ˌsælɪ'kɔ:nɪə) *n* any chenopodiaceous plant of the genus *Salicornia,* of seashores and salt marshes: includes glasswort. [C19: from Late Latin, perhaps from Latin *sal* salt + *cornu* a horn]

salicylate (sə'lɪsɪˌleɪt) *n* any salt or ester of salicylic acid.

salicylic acid (ˌsælɪ'sɪlɪk) *n* a white crystalline slightly water-soluble substance with a sweet taste and bitter aftertaste, used in the manufacture of aspirin, dyes, and perfumes, and as a fungicide. Formula: $C_6H_4(OH)(COOH)$. [C19: from *salicyl* (via French from Latin *salix* a willow + -YL) + -IC]

salient ('seɪlɪənt) *adj* **1** prominent, conspicuous, or striking: *a salient feature.* **2** (esp. in fortifications) projecting outwards at an angle of less than 180°. Compare **re-entrant** (sense 1). **3** *Geometry.* (of an angle) pointing outwards from a polygon and hence less than 180°. Compare **re-entrant** (sense 2). **4** (esp. of animals) leaping. ◆ *n* **5** *Military.* a projection of the forward line into enemy-held territory. **6** a salient angle. [C16: from Latin *salīre* to leap] ▸ **'salience** *or* **'saliency** *n* ▸ **'saliently** *adv*

salientian (ˌseɪlɪ'ɛnʃɪən) *n, adj* another word for **anuran.** [C19: from New Latin *Salientia,* literally: leapers, from Latin *salīre* to leap]

Salieri (*Italian* ˌsal'jeri) *n* **Antonio** (an'tonjo). 1750–1825, Italian composer and conductor, who worked in Vienna (from 1766). The suggestion that he poisoned Mozart has no foundation.

saliferous (sæ'lɪfərəs) *adj* (esp. of rock strata) containing or producing salt. [C19: from Latin *sal* SALT + *ferre* to bear]

salify ('sælɪˌfaɪ) *vb* **-fies, -fying, -fied.** (*tr*) **1** to treat, mix with, or cause to combine with a salt. **2** to convert (a substance) into a salt: *to salify ammonia by treatment with hydrochloric acid.* [C18: from French *salifier,* from New Latin *salificāre,* from Latin *sal* salt + *facere* to make] ▸ **'saliˌfiable** *adj* ▸ **ˌsalifi'cation** *n*

salimeter (sæ'lɪmɪtə) *n* another word for **salinometer.** ▸ **salimetric** (ˌsælɪ'mɛtrɪk) *adj* ▸ **sal'imetry** *n*

salina (sə'laɪnə) *n* a salt marsh, lake, or spring. [C17: from Spanish, from Medieval Latin: salt pit, from Late Latin *salīnus* SALINE]

saline ('seɪlaɪn) *adj* **1** of, concerned with, consisting of, or containing common salt: *a saline taste.* **2** *Med.* of or relating to a saline. **3** of, concerned with, consisting of, or containing any chemical salt, esp. a metallic salt resembling sodium chloride. ◆ *n* **4** *Med.* an isotonic solution of sodium chloride and distilled water. [C15: from Late Latin *salīnus,* from Latin *sal* salt] ▸ **salinity** (sə'lɪnɪtɪ) *n*

Salinger ('sælɪndʒə) *n* **J(erome) D(avid).** born 1919, U.S. writer, noted particularly for his novel of adolescence *The Catcher in the Rye* (1951). His first novel for 34 years, *Hapworth 16, 1924* was published in 1997.

salinometer (ˌsælɪ'nɒmɪtə) *n* a hydrometer for determining the amount of salt in a solution, usually calibrated to measure concentration. Also called: **salimeter.** ▸ **salinometric** (ˌsælɪnə'mɛtrɪk) *adj* ▸ **ˌsali'nometry** *n*

Salique ('sælɪk, 'seɪlɪk) *adj* a variant spelling of **Salic.**

Salisbury[1] ('sɔ:lzbərɪ, -brɪ) *n* **1** the former name (until 1982) of **Harare. 2** a city in S Australia: an industrial suburb of N Adelaide. Pop.: 89 000 (latest est.). **3** a city in S England, in SE Wiltshire: nearby Old Sarum was the site of an Early Iron Age hill fort; its cathedral (1220–58) has the highest spire in England. Pop.: 39 268 (1991). Ancient name: **Sarum.** Official name: **New Sarum.**

Salisbury[2] ('sɔ:lzbərɪ, -brɪ) *n* **Robert Gascoyne Cecil** ('gæskɔɪn), 3rd Marquess of Salisbury. 1830–1903, British statesman; Conservative prime minister (1885–86; 1886–92; 1895–1902). His greatest interest was in foreign and imperial affairs.

Salisbury Plain *n* an open chalk plateau in S England, in Wiltshire: site of Stonehenge; military training area. Average height: 120 m (400 ft.).

Salish ('seɪlɪʃ) *or* **Salishan** ('seɪlɪʃən,'sæl-) *n* **1** a family of North American Indian languages spoken in the northwestern U.S. and W Canada. **2 the Salish.** (*functioning as pl*) the peoples collectively who speak these languages, divided in Canada into the **Coast Salish** and the **Interior Salish.**

saliva (sə'laɪvə) *n* the secretion of salivary glands, consisting of a clear usually slightly acid aqueous fluid of variable composition. It moistens the oral cavity and prepares food for swallowing. Related adj: **sialoid.** [C17: from Latin, of obscure origin] ▸ **salivary** (sə'laɪvərɪ,'sælɪvərɪ) *adj*

salivary gland *n* any of the glands in mammals that secrete saliva. In man the chief salivary glands are the **parotid, sublingual,** and **submaxillary glands.**

salivate ('sælɪˌveɪt) *vb* **1** (*intr*) to secrete saliva, esp. an excessive amount. **2** (*tr*) to cause (a laboratory animal, etc.) to produce saliva, as by the administration of mercury. ▸ **ˌsali'vation** *n*

Salk (sɔ:lk) *n* **Jonas Edward.** 1914–95, U.S. virologist: developed an injected vaccine against poliomyelitis (1954).

sallee *or* **sally** ('sælɪ) *n Austral.* **1** Also called: **snow gum.** a SE Australian eucalyptus tree, *Eucalyptus pauciflora,* with a pale grey bark. **2** any of various acacia trees. [probably of native origin]

sallet, salet ('sælɪt), *or* **salade** *n* a light round helmet extending over the back of the neck; replaced the basinet in the 15th century. [C15: from French *salade,* probably from Old Italian *celata,* from *celare* to conceal, from Latin]

sallow[1] ('sæləʊ) *adj* **1** (esp. of human skin) of an unhealthy pale or yellowish colour. ◆ *vb* **2** (*tr*) to make sallow. [Old English *salu;* related to Old Norse *sol* seaweed (Icelandic *sōlr* yellowish), Old High German *salo,* French *sale* dirty] ▸ **'sallowish** *adj* ▸ **'sallowly** *adv* ▸ **'sallowness** *n*

sallow[2] ('sæləʊ) *n* **1** any of several small willow trees, esp. the Eurasian *Salix cinerea* (**common sallow**), which has large catkins that appear before the leaves. **2** a twig or the wood of any of these trees. [Old English *sealh;* related to Old Norse *selja,* Old High German *salaha,* Middle Low German *salwīde,* Latin *salix*] ▸ **'sallowy** *adj*

Sallust ('sæləst) *n* full name *Gaius Sallustius Crispus.* 86–?34 B.C., Roman historian and statesman, noted for his histories of the Catiline conspiracy and the Roman war against Jugurtha.

sally[1] ('sælɪ) *n, pl* **-lies. 1** a sudden violent excursion, esp. by besieged forces to attack the besiegers; sortie. **2** a sudden outburst or emergence into action, expression, or emotion. **3** an excursion or jaunt. **4** a jocular retort. ◆ *vb* **-lies, -lying, -lied.** (*intr*) **5** to make a sudden violent excursion. **6** (often foll. by *forth*) to go out on an expedition, etc. **7** to come, go, or set out in an energetic manner. **8** to rush out suddenly. [C16: from Old French *saillie,* from *saillir* to dash forwards, from Latin *salīre* to leap] ▸ **'sallier** *n*

sally[2] ('sælɪ) *n, pl* **-lies.** *Bell-ringing.* the lower part of a bell rope, where it is caught at handstroke, into which coloured wool is woven to make a grip. [C19: perhaps from an obsolete or dialect sense of SALLY[1] leaping movement]

Sally ('sælɪ) *n, pl* **-lies.** *Austral. and N.Z. informal.* a member of the Salvation Army.

Sally Army *n Brit. informal.* short for **Salvation Army.**

Sally Lunn (lʌn) *n* a flat round cake made from a sweet yeast dough, usually served hot. [C19: said to be named after an 18th-century English baker who invented it]

sallyport ('sælɪˌpɔːt) *n* an opening in a fortified place from which troops may make a sally.

salmagundi *or* **salmagundy** (ˌsælmə'gʌndɪ) *n* **1** a mixed salad dish of cooked meats, eggs, beetroot, etc., popular in 18th-century England. **2** a miscellany; potpourri. [C17: from French *salmigondis,* perhaps from Italian *salami conditi* pickled salami]

Salmanazar (ˌsælmə'næzə) *n* a wine bottle holding the equivalent of twelve normal bottles (approximately 312 ounces). [C19: humorous allusion to an Assyrian king mentioned in the Bible (II Kings 17:3); compare JEROBOAM]

salmi *or* **salmis** ('sælmɪ) *n, pl* **-mis** (-mɪ). a ragout of game stewed in a rich brown sauce. [C18: from French, shortened form of *salmigondis* SALMAGUNDI]

salmon ('sæmən) *n, pl* **-ons** *or* **-on. 1** any soft-finned fish of the family *Salmonidae,* esp. *Salmo salar* of the Atlantic and *Oncorhynchus* species (sockeye, Chinook, etc.) of the Pacific, which are important food fishes. They occur in cold and temperate waters and many species migrate to fresh water to spawn. **2** *Austral.* any of several unrelated fish. **3** short for **salmon pink.** [C13: from Old French *saumon,* from Latin *salmō;* related to Late Latin *salar* trout]

salmonberry ('sæmənbərɪ, -brɪ) *n, pl* **-ries. 1** a spineless raspberry bush, *Rubus spectabilis,* of North America, having reddish-purple flowers and large red or yellow edible fruits. **2** the fruit of this plant. [C19: so called from the colour of the berries]

salmonella (ˌsælmə'nɛlə) *n, pl* **-lae** (-ˌliː). any Gram-negative rod-shaped aerobic bacterium of the genus *Salmonella,* including *S. typhosa,* which causes typhoid fever, and many species (notably *S. enteritidis*) that cause food poisoning (**salmonellosis**): family *Enterobacteriaceae.* [C19: New Latin, named after Daniel E. *Salmon* (1850–1914), U.S. veterinary surgeon]

salmonid ('sælmənɪd) *n* any fish of the family *Salmonidiae.*

salmon ladder *n* a series of steps in a river designed to enable salmon to bypass a dam and move upstream to their breeding grounds.

salmonoid ('sælməˌnɔɪd) *adj* **1** of, relating to, or belonging to the *Salmonoidea,* a suborder of soft-finned teleost fishes having a fatty fin between the dorsal and tail fins: includes the salmon, whitefish, grayling, smelt, and char. **2** of, relating to, or resembling a salmon. ◆ *n* **3** any fish belonging to the suborder *Salmonoidea,* esp. any of the family *Salmonidae* (salmon, trout, char).

salmon pink *n* **a** a yellowish-pink colour, sometimes with an orange tinge. **b** (*as adj*): *a salmon-pink hat.* ◆ Sometimes shortened to **salmon.**

salmon trout *n* any of various large trout, esp. the sea trout.

salol ('sælɒl) *n* a white sparingly soluble crystalline compound with a slight aromatic odour, used as a preservative and to absorb light in sun-tan lotions, plastics, etc.; phenyl salicylate. Formula: $C_6H_4(OH)COOC_6H_5$. [C19: from *salicyl* (see SALICYLIC ACID) + -OL]

Salome (sə'ləʊmɪ) *n New Testament.* the daughter of Herodias, at whose instigation she beguiled Herod by her seductive dancing into giving her the head of John the Baptist.

salon ('sælɒn) *n* **1** a room in a large house in which guests are received. **2** an assembly of guests in a fashionable household, esp. a gathering of major literary, artistic, and political figures from the 17th to the early 20th centuries. **3** a commercial establishment in which hairdressers, beauticians, etc., carry on their businesses: *beauty salon.* **4a** a hall for exhibiting works of art. **4b** such an exhibition, esp. one showing the work of living artists. [C18: from French, from Italian *salone,* augmented form of *sala* hall, of Germanic origin; compare Old English *sele* hall, Old High German *sal,* Old Norse *salr* hall]

Salonika *or* **Salonica** (sə'lɒnɪkə) *n* the English name for **Thessaloníki.**

salon music *n Sometimes derogatory.* light classical music intended esp. for domestic entertaining.

saloon (sə'luːn) *n* **1** Also called: **saloon bar.** *Brit.* another word for **lounge** (sense 5). **2** a large public room on a passenger ship. **3** any large public room used for a specific purpose: *a dancing saloon.* **4** *Chiefly U.S. and Canadian.* a place where alcoholic drink is sold and consumed. **5** a closed two-door or four-door car with four to six seats. U.S., Canadian, and N.Z. name: **sedan. 6** an obsolete word for **salon** (sense 1). [C18: from French SALON]

saloop (sə'luːp) *n* an infusion of aromatic herbs or other plant parts, esp. salep, formerly used as a tonic or cure. [C18: changed from SALEP]

Salop ('sæləp) *n* a former name (1974–80) of **Shropshire.** ▸ **Salopian** (sə'ləʊpjən) *n, adj*

salopettes (ˌsælə'pɛts) *pl n* a garment worn for skiing, consisting of quilted trousers reaching to the chest and held up by shoulder straps. [C20: from French]

salpa ('sælpə) *n, pl* **-pas** *or* **-pae** (-piː). any of various minute floating animals of the genus *Salpa,* of warm oceans, having a transparent barrel-shaped body with openings at either end: class *Thaliacea,* subphylum *Tunicata* (tunicates). [C19: from New Latin, from Latin: variety of stockfish, from Greek *salpē*] ▸ **salpiform** ('sælpɪˌfɔːm) *adj*

salpicon ('sælpɪkən) *n* a mixture of chopped fish, meat, or vegetables in a sauce, used as fillings for croquettes, pastries, etc. [C18: from French, from Spanish, from *salpicar* to sprinkle with salt]

salpiglossis (ˌsælpɪ'glɒsɪs) *n* any solanaceous plant of the Chilean genus *Salpiglossis,* some species of which are cultivated for their bright funnel-shaped flowers. [C19: New Latin, from Greek *salpinx* trumpet + *glōssa* tongue]

salpingectomy (ˌsælpɪn'dʒɛktəmɪ) *n, pl* **-mies.** surgical removal of a Fallopian tube. [C20: from SALPINX + -ECTOMY]

salpingitis (ˌsælpɪn'dʒaɪtɪs) *n* inflammation of a Fallopian tube. [C19: from SALPINX + -ITIS] ▸ **salpingitic** (ˌsælpɪn'dʒɪtɪk) *adj*

salpingo- *combining form.* indicating the Fallopian tubes: *salpingo-oophorectomy.* [C20: from SALPINX]

salpinx ('sælpɪŋks) *n, pl* **salpinges** (sæl'pɪndʒiːz). *Anatomy.* another name for the **Fallopian tube** or the **Eustachian tube.** [C19: from Greek: trumpet] ▸ **salpingian** (sæl'pɪndʒɪən) *adj*

salsa ('sælsə) *n* **1** a type of Latin American big-band dance music. **2** a dance performed to this kind of music. **3** *Mexican cookery.* a spicy tomato-based sauce. [C20: from Spanish: sauce]

salsify ('sælsɪfɪ) *n, pl* **-fies. 1** Also called: **oyster plant, vegetable oyster.** a Mediterranean plant, *Tragopogon porrifolius,* having grasslike leaves, purple flower heads, and a long white edible taproot: family *Compositae* (composites). **2** the root of this plant, which tastes of oysters and is eaten as a vegetable. [C17: from French *salsifis,* from Italian *sassefrica,* from Late Latin *saxifrica,* from Latin *saxum* rock + *fricāre* to rub]

sal soda *n* the crystalline decahydrate of sodium carbonate.

salt (sɔːlt) *n* **1** a white powder or colourless crystalline solid, consisting mainly of sodium chloride and used for seasoning and preserving food. **2** (*modifier*) preserved in, flooded with, containing, or growing in salt or salty water: *salt pork; salt marshes.* **3** *Chem.* any of a class of usually crystalline solid compounds that are formed from, or can be regarded as formed from, an acid and a base by replacement of one or more hydrogen atoms in the acid molecules by positive ions from the base. **4** liveliness or pungency: *his wit added salt to the discussion.* **5** dry or laconic wit. **6** a sailor, esp. one who is old and experienced. **7** short for **saltcellar. 8 rub salt into someone's wounds.** to make someone's pain, shame, etc., even worse. **9 salt of the earth.** a person or group of people regarded as the finest of their kind. **10 with a grain** (*or* **pinch**) **of salt.** with reservations; sceptically. **11 worth one's salt.** efficient; worthy of one's pay. ◆ *vb* (*tr*) **12** to season or preserve with salt. **13** to scatter salt over (an icy road, path, etc.) to melt the ice. **14** to add zest to. **15** (often foll. by *down* or *away*) to preserve or cure with salt or saline solution. **16** *Chem.* to treat with common salt or other chemical salt. **17** to provide (cattle, etc.) with salt. **18** to give a false appearance of value to, esp. to introduce valuable ore fraudulently into (a mine, sample, etc.). ◆ *adj* **19** not sour, sweet, or bitter; salty. **20** *Obsolete.* rank or lascivious (esp. in the phrase **a salt wit**). ◆ See also **salt away, salt out, salts.** [Old English *sealt;* related to Old Norse, Gothic *salt,* German *Salz,* Lettish *sāls,* Latin *sāl,* Greek *hals*] ▸ **'saltish** *adj* ▸ **'saltless** *adj* ▸ **'saltˌlike** *adj* ▸ **'saltness** *n*

SALT (sɔːlt) *n acronym for* Strategic Arms Limitation Talks *or* Treaty.

Salta (*Spanish* 'salta) *n* a city in NW Argentina: thermal springs. Pop.: 370 904 (1991).

saltant ('sæltənt) *adj* (of an organism) differing from others of its species because of a saltation. [C17: from Latin *saltāns* dancing, from *saltāre,* from *salīre* to spring]

saltarello (ˌsæltə'rɛləʊ) *n, pl* **-li** (-lɪ) *or* **-los. 1** a traditional Italian dance, usually in compound duple time. **2** a piece of music composed for or in the rhythm of this dance. [C18: from Italian, from *saltare* to dance energetically, from Latin; see SALTANT]

saltation (sæl'teɪʃən) *n* **1** *Biology.* an abrupt variation in the appearance of an organism, species, etc., usually caused by genetic mutation. **2** *Geology.* the leaping movement of sand or soil particles carried in water or by the wind. **3** a sudden abrupt movement or transition. [C17: from Latin *saltātiō* a dance, from *saltāre* to leap about]

saltatorial (ˌsæltə'tɔːrɪəl) *or* **saltatory** *adj* **1** *Biology.* specialized for or characterized by jumping: *the saltatorial legs of a grasshopper.* **2** of or relating to saltation. [C17 *saltatory,* from Latin *saltātōrius* concerning dancing, from *saltātor* a dancer; see SALTANT]

salt away *or* (*less commonly*) **down** *vb* (*tr, adv*) to hoard or save (money, valuables, etc.).

salt bath *n Metallurgy.* a bath of molten salts in which steel can be immersed to soak to a uniform and accurately maintained temperature as part of the process of heat treatment. Different salts are used for different temperatures.

saltbox ('sɔːltˌbɒks) *n* **1** a box for salt with a sloping lid. **2** *U.S.* a house that has two storeys in front and one storey at the back, with a gable roof that extends downwards over the rear.

saltbush ('sɔːltˌbʊʃ) *n* any of various chenopodiaceous shrubs of the genus *Atriplex* that grow in alkaline desert regions.

salt cake *n* an impure form of sodium sulphate obtained as a by-product in several industrial processes: used in the manufacture of detergents, glass, and ceramic glazes.

saltcellar ('sɔːltˌselə) *n* **1** a small container for salt used at the table. **2** *Brit. informal.* either of the two hollows formed above the collarbones of very slim people. [changed (through influence of cellar) from C15 *salt saler; saler* from Old French *saliere* container for salt, from Latin *salārius* belonging to salt, from *sal* salt]

saltchuck ('sɔːltˌtʃʌk) *n Canadian, chiefly W coast.* any body of salt water. [C20: from SALT + CHUCK[4]]

saltchucker ('sɔːltˌtʃʌkə) *n Canadian W coast informal.* a saltwater angler.

salt dome *or* **plug** *n* a domelike structure of stratified rocks containing a central core of salt: formed by the upward movement of a salt deposit.

salted ('sɔːltɪd) *adj* **1** seasoned, preserved, or treated with salt. **2** *Informal.* experienced in an occupation.

salter ('sɔːltə) *n* **1** a person who deals in or manufactures salt. **2** a person who treats meat, fish, etc., with salt.

saltern ('sɔːltən) *n* **1** another word for **saltworks. 2** a place where salt is obtained from pools of evaporated sea water. [Old English *saltærn,* from SALT + *ærn* house. Compare BARN[1], RANSACK]

saltfish ('sɔːltfɪʃ) *n Caribbean.* salted cod.

salt flat *n* a flat expanse of salt left by the total evaporation of a body of water.

saltigrade ('sæltɪˌgreɪd) *adj* (of animals) adapted for moving in a series of jumps. [C19: from New Latin *Saltigradae,* name formerly applied to jumping spiders, from Latin *saltus* a leap + *gradī* to move]

Saltillo (*Spanish* sal'tiʎo) *n* a city in N Mexico, capital of Coahuila state: resort and commercial centre of a mining region. Pop.: 420 947 (1990).

salting ('sɔːltɪŋ) *n* (*often pl*) an area of low ground regularly inundated with salt water; often taken to include its halophyte vegetation; a salt marsh.

saltire *or* (*less commonly*) **saltier** ('sɔːlˌtaɪə) *n Heraldry.* an ordinary consisting of a diagonal cross on a shield. [C14 *sawturoure,* from Old French *sauteour* cross-shaped barricade, from *saulter* to jump, from Latin *saltāre*]

salt lake *n* an inland lake of high salinity resulting from inland drainage in an arid area of high evaporation.

Salt Lake City *n* a city in N central Utah, near the Great Salt Lake at an altitude of 1330 m (4300 ft.): state capital; founded in 1847 by the Mormons as world capital of the Mormon Church; University of Utah (1850). Pop.: 172 575 (1996 est.).

salt lick *n* **1** a place where wild animals go to lick naturally occurring salt deposits. **2** a block of salt or a salt preparation given to domestic animals to lick.

salt marsh *n* an area of marshy ground that is intermittently inundated with salt water or that retains pools or rivulets of salt or brackish water, together with its characteristic halophytic vegetation.

Salto (*Spanish* 'salto) *n* a port in NW Uruguay, on the Uruguay River: Uruguay's second largest city. Pop.: 77 400 (1985).

salt out *vb* (*adv*) *Chem.* to cause (a dissolved substance) to come out of solution by adding an electrolyte.

saltpan ('sɔːltˌpæn) *n* a shallow basin, usually in a desert region, containing salt, gypsum, etc., that was deposited from an evaporated salt lake.

saltpetre *or U.S.* **saltpeter** (ˌsɔːlt'piːtə) *n* **1** another name for **potassium nitrate. 2** short for **Chile saltpetre.** [C16: from Old French *salpetre,* from Latin *sal petrae* salt of rock]

salt pork *n* pork, esp. the fat pork taken from the back, sides, and belly, that has been cured with salt.

salts (sɔːlts) *pl n* **1** *Med.* any of various mineral salts, such as magnesium sulphate or sodium sulphate, for use as a cathartic. **2** short for **smelling salts. 3 like a dose of salts.** *Informal.* very fast.

saltus ('sæltəs) *n, pl* **-tuses.** a break in the continuity of a sequence, esp. the omission of a necessary step in a logical argument. [Latin: a leap]

saltwater ('sɔːltˌwɔːtə) *adj* of, relating to, or inhabiting salt water, esp. the sea: *saltwater fishes.*

saltworks ('sɔːltˌwɜːks) *n* (*functioning as sing*) a place, building, or factory where salt is produced.

saltwort ('sɔːltˌwɜːt) *n* **1** Also called: **glasswort, kali.** any of several chenopodiaceous plants of the genus *Salsola,* esp. *S. kali,* of beaches and salt marshes, which has prickly leaves, striped stems, and small green flowers. See also **barilla. 2** another name for **sea milkwort.**

salty ('sɔːltɪ) *adj* **saltier, saltiest. 1** of, tasting of, or containing salt. **2** (esp. of humour) sharp; piquant. **3** relating to life at sea. ▸ **'saltily** *adv* ▸ **'saltiness** *n*

salubrious (sə'luːbrɪəs) *adj* conducive or favourable to health; wholesome. [C16: from Latin *salūbris,* from *salūs* health] ▸ **sa'lubriously** *adv* ▸ **sa'lubriousness** *or* **salubrity** (sə'luːbrɪtɪ) *n*

Saluki (sə'luːkɪ) *n* a tall breed of hound with a smooth coat and long fringes on the ears and tail. Also called: **Persian greyhound.** [C19: from Arabic *salūqīy* of Saluq, name of an ancient Arabian city]

salutary ('sæljʊtərɪ, -trɪ) *adj* **1** promoting or intended to promote an improvement or beneficial effect: *a salutary warning.* **2** promoting or intended to promote health. [C15: from Latin *salūtāris* wholesome, from *salūs* safety] ▸ **'salutarily** *adv* ▸ **'salutariness** *n*

salutation (ˌsælju'teɪʃən) *n* **1** an act, phrase, gesture, etc., that serves as a greeting. **2** a form of words used as an opening to a speech or letter, such as *Dear Sir* or *Ladies and Gentlemen.* **3** the act of saluting. [C14: from Latin *salūtātiō,* from *salūtāre* to greet; see SALUTE]

salutatory (sə'luːtətərɪ, -trɪ) *adj* of, relating to, or resembling a salutation. ▸ **sa'lutatorily** *adv*

salute (sə'luːt) *vb* **1** (*tr*) to address or welcome with friendly words or gestures of respect, such as bowing or lifting the hat; greet. **2** (*tr*) to acknowledge with praise or honour: *we salute your gallantry.* **3** *Military.* to pay or receive formal respect, as by presenting arms or raising the right arm. ◆ *n* **4** the act of saluting. **5** a formal military gesture of respect. [C14: from Latin *salūtāre* to greet, from *salūs* wellbeing] ▸ **sa'luter** *n*

salvable ('sælvəb[ə]l) *adj* capable of or suitable for being saved or salvaged. [C17: from Late Latin *salvāre* to save, from Latin *salvus* safe] ▸ ˌ**salva'bility** *or* **'salvableness** *n* ▸ **'salvably** *adv*

Salvador ('sælvəˌdɔː; *Portuguese* salva'dor) *n* a port in E Brazil, capital of Bahia state: founded in 1549 as capital of the Portuguese colony, which it remained until 1763; a major centre of the African slave trade in colonial times. Pop.: 2 070 296 (1991). Former name: **Bahia.** Official name: **São Salvador da Bahia de Todos os Santos** (sɐ̃u salva'dor 'dəː ba'ia 'dəː 'toːduʃ uʃ 'sɐ̃ntuʃ).

Salvadorian[1], **Salvadorean** (ˌsælvə'dɔːrɪən) *or* **Salvadoran** (ˌsælvə'dɔːrən) *n* **1** a native or inhabitant of El Salvador. ◆ *adj* **2** of or relating to El Salvador, or its people, culture, etc.

Salvadorian[2] (ˌsælvə'dɔːrɪən) *n* **1** a native or inhabitant of Salvador. ◆ *adj* **2** of or relating to Salvador or its inhabitants.

salvage ('sælvɪdʒ) *n* **1** the act, process, or business of rescuing vessels or their cargoes from loss at sea. **2a** the act of saving any goods or property in danger of damage or destruction. **2b** (*as modifier*): *a salvage operation.* **3** the goods or property so saved. **4** compensation paid for the salvage of a vessel or its cargo. **5** the proceeds from the sale of salvaged goods or property. ◆ *vb* (*tr*) **6** to save or rescue (goods or property) from fire, shipwreck, etc. **7** to gain (something beneficial) from a failure: *she salvaged little from the broken marriage.* [C17: from Old French, from Medieval Latin *salvāgium,* from *salvāre* to SAVE[1]] ▸ **'salvageable** *adj* ▸ **'salvager** *n*

salvation (sæl'veɪʃən) *n* **1** the act of preserving or the state of being preserved from harm. **2** a person or thing that is the means of preserving from harm. **3** *Christianity.* deliverance by redemption from the power of sin and from the penalties ensuing from it. **4** *Christian Science.* the realization that Life, Truth, and Love are supreme and that they can destroy such illusions as sin, death, etc. [C13: from Old French *sauvacion,* from Late Latin *salvātiō,* from Latin *salvātus* saved, from *salvāre* to SAVE[1]] ▸ **sal'vational** *adj*

Salvation Army *n* **a** a Christian body founded in 1865 by William Booth and organized on quasi-military lines for evangelism and social work among the poor. **b** (*as modifier*): *the Salvation Army Hymn Book.*

salvationist (sæl'veɪʃənɪst) *n* **1** a member of an evangelical sect emphasizing the doctrine of salvation. **2** (*often cap.*) a member of the Salvation Army. ◆ *adj* **3** stressing the doctrine of salvation. **4** (*often cap.*) of or relating to the Salvation Army. ▸ **sal'vationism** *n*

Salvation Jane (dʒeɪn) *n Austral.* another name, used in South Australia, for **viper's bugloss** (sense 2).

salva veritate *Latin.* ('sælvə ˌverɪ'tɑːteɪ) *adv Philosophy.* without affecting truth-value.

salve[1] (sælv, sɑːv) *n* **1** an ointment for wounds, sores, etc. **2** anything that heals or soothes. ◆ *vb* (*tr*) **3** to apply salve to (a wound, sore, etc.). **4** to soothe, comfort, or appease. [Old English *sealf;* related to Old High German *salba,* Greek *elpos* oil, Sanskrit *sarpis* lard]

salve[2] (sælv) *vb* **1** a less common word for **salvage. 2** an archaic word for **save**[1] (sense 3). [C18: from SALVAGE]

salver ('sælvə) *n* a tray, esp. one of silver, on which food, letters, visiting cards, etc., are presented. [C17: from French *salve,* from Spanish *salva* tray from which the king's taster sampled food, from Latin *salvāre* to SAVE[1]]

salverform ('sælvəˌfɔːm) *adj* (of the corolla of the phlox and certain other flowers) consisting of a narrow tube with flat spreading terminal petals.

salvia ('sælvɪə) *n* any herbaceous plant or small shrub of the genus *Salvia,* such as the sage, grown for their medicinal or culinary properties or for ornament: family *Labiatae* (labiates). [C19: from Latin: SAGE[2]]

salvo[1] ('sælvəʊ) *n, pl* **-vos** *or* **-voes. 1** a discharge of fire from weapons in unison, esp. on a ceremonial occasion. **2** concentrated fire from many weapons, as in a naval battle. **3** an outburst, as of applause. [C17: from Italian *salva,* from Old French *salve,* from Latin *salvē!* greetings! from *salvēre* to be in good health, from *salvus* safe]

salvo[2] ('sælvəʊ) *n, pl* **-vos.** *Rare.* **1** an excuse or evasion. **2** an expedient to save a reputation or soothe hurt feelings. **3** (in legal documents) a saving clause; reservation. [C17: from such Medieval Latin phrases as *salvō iure* the right of keeping safe, from Latin *salvus* safe]

Salvo ('sælvəʊ) *n, pl* **-vos.** *Austral. slang.* a member of the Salvation Army.

sal volatile (vɒ'lætɪlɪ) *n* **1** another name for **ammonium carbonate. 2** Also called: **spirits of ammonia** *or* (archaic) **hartshorn.** a solution of ammonium carbonate in alcohol and aqueous ammonia, often containing aromatic oils, used as smelling salts. [C17: from New Latin: volatile salt]

salvor *or* **salver** ('sælvə) *n* a person instrumental in salvaging a vessel or its cargo. [C17: from SALVAGE + -OR[1]]

Salween ('sælwiːn) *n* a river in SW Asia, rising in the Tibetan Plateau and flowing east and south through SW China and Myanmar to the Gulf of Martaban. Length: 2400 km (1500 miles).

Salyut (sæl'juːt) *n* any of a series of seven Soviet space stations. The first was launched into earth orbit in April 1971 and the last was launched in April 1982. The Salyut programme led to the Mir space station. [C20: Russian: salute]

Salzburg ('sæltsbɜːg; *German* 'zaltsbʊrk) *n* **1** a city in W Austria, capital of Salzburg province: 7th-century Benedictine abbey; a centre of music since the Middle Ages and birthplace of Mozart; tourist centre. Pop.: 143 978 (1991). **2** a state of W Austria. Pop.: 507 000 (1995 est.). Area: 7154 sq. km (2762 sq. miles).

Salzgitter (*German* zalts'gɪtər) *n* an industrial city in central Germany, in SE Lower Saxony. Pop.: 117 713 (1996 est.).

SAM (sæm) *n acronym for* surface-to-air missile.

Sam. *Bible. abbrev. for* Samuel.

S.Am. *abbrev. for* South America(n).

samadhi (sʌ'mɑ:di) *n Buddhism, Hinduism.* a state of deep meditative contemplation which leads to higher consciousness. [from Sanskrit: concentration, from *samā* together + *dhi* mind]

Samar ('sɑ:mə) *n* an island in the E central Philippines, separated from S Luzon by the San Bernardino Strait: the third largest island in the republic. Capital: Catbalogan. Pop.: 1 300 000 (latest est.). Area: 13 080 sq. km (5050 sq. miles).

samara (sə'mɑ:rə, 'sæmərə) *n* a dry indehiscent one-seeded fruit with a winglike extension to aid dispersal: occurs in the ash, maple, etc. Also called: **key fruit.** [C16: from New Latin, from Latin: seed of an elm]

Samara (*Russian* sa'marə) *n* a port in SW Russia, on the River Volga: centre of an important industrial complex; oil refining. Pop.: 1 184 000 (1995 est.). Former name (1935–91): **Kuibyshev** *or* **Kuybyshev.**

Samarang (sə'mɑ:rɑ:ŋ) *n* a variant spelling of **Semarang.**

Samaria (sə'mɛərɪə) *n* **1** the region of ancient Palestine that extended from Judaea to Galilee and from the Mediterranean to the River Jordan; the N kingdom of Israel. **2** the capital of this kingdom; constructed northwest of Shechem in the 9th century B.C.

samariform (sə'mɑ:rɪ,fɔ:m) *adj Botany.* shaped like a samara; winged.

Samaritan (sə'mærɪtᵊn) *n* **1** a native or inhabitant of Samaria. **2** short for **Good Samaritan. 3** a member of a voluntary organization (**the Samaritans**) which offers counselling to people in despair, esp. by telephone. **4** the dialect of Aramaic spoken in Samaria. ◆ *adj* **5** of or relating to Samaria. ► **Sa'maritanism** *n*

samarium (sə'mɛərɪəm) *n* a silvery metallic element of the lanthanide series occurring chiefly in monazite and bastnaesite and used in carbon-arc lighting, as a doping agent in laser crystals, and as a neutron-absorber. Symbol: Sm; atomic no.: 62; atomic wt.: 150.36; valency: 2 or 3; relative density: 7.520; melting pt.: 1074°C; boiling pt.: 1794°C. [C19: New Latin, from SAMARSKITE + -IUM]

Samarkand ('sæmə,kænd; *Russian* səmar'kant) *n* a city in E Uzbekistan: under Tamerlane it became the chief economic and cultural centre of central Asia, on trade routes from China and India (the "silk road"). Pop.: 368 000 (1996). Ancient name: **Maracanda.**

samarskite (sə'mɑ:skaɪt) *n* a velvety black mineral of complex composition occurring in pegmatites: used as a source of uranium and certain rare earth elements. [C19: named after Colonel von *Samarski,* 19th-century Russian inspector of mines]

Sama-Veda ('sɑ:mə'veɪdə) *n Hinduism.* the third Veda containing the rituals for sacrifices. [C18: from Sanskrit *sāman* a chant + VEDA]

samba ('sæmbə) *n, pl* **-bas. 1** a lively modern ballroom dance from Brazil in bouncy duple time. **2** a piece of music composed for or in the rhythm of this dance. ◆ *vb* **-bas, -baing, -baed. 3** (*intr*) to perform such a dance. [Portuguese, of African origin]

sambar *or* **sambur** ('sæmbə) *n, pl* **-bars, -bar** *or* **-burs, -bur.** a S Asian deer, *Cervus unicolor,* with three-tined antlers. [C17: from Hindi, from Sanskrit *śambarra,* of obscure origin]

sambo[1] ('sæmbəʊ) *n, pl* **-bos. 1** *Slang.* an offensive word for **Black**[1]: often used as a term of address. **2** the offspring of a Black and a member of another race or a mulatto. [C18: from American Spanish *zambo* a person of Black descent; perhaps related to Bantu *nzambu* monkey]

sambo[2] *or* **sambo wrestling** ('sæmbəʊ) *n* a type of wrestling based on judo that originated in Russia and now features in international competitions. [C20: from Russian *sam(ozashchita) b(ez) o(ruzhiya)* self-defence without weapons] ► **sambo wrestler** *n*

Sambre (*French* sɑ̃brə) *n* a river in W Europe, rising in N France and flowing east into Belgium to join the Meuse at Namur. Length: 190 km (118 miles).

Sam Browne belt *n* a military officer's wide belt supported by a strap passing from the left side of the belt over the right shoulder. [C20: named after Sir *Samuel J. Browne* (1824–1901), British general, who devised such a belt]

same (seɪm) *adj* (usually preceded by *the*) **1** being the very one: *she is wearing the same hat she wore yesterday.* **2a** being the one previously referred to; aforesaid. **2b** (*as n*): *a note received about same.* **3a** identical in kind, quantity, etc.: *two girls of the same age.* **3b** (*as n*): *we'd like the same, please.* **4** unchanged in character or nature: *his attitude is the same as ever.* **5 all the same. 5a** Also: **just the same.** nevertheless; yet. **5b** immaterial: *it's all the same to me.* ◆ *adv* **6** in an identical manner. [C12: from Old Norse *samr;* related to Old English adverbial phrase *swā same* likewise, Gothic *sama,* Latin *similis,* Greek *homos* same]

USAGE The use of *same* exemplified in *if you send us your order for the materials, we will deliver same tomorrow* is common in business and official English. In general English, however, this use of the word is avoided: *may I borrow your book? I'll return it* (not *same*) *tomorrow.*

samekh ('sɑ:mək; *Hebrew* 'samɛx) *n* the 15th letter in the Hebrew alphabet (ס) transliterated as *s.* [Hebrew, literally: a support]

sameness ('seɪmnɪs) *n* **1** the state or quality of being the same. **2** lack of change; monotony.

samey ('seɪmɪ) *adj Informal.* monotonous; repetitive; unvaried.

samfoo ('sæmfu:) *n* a style of casual dress worn by Chinese women, consisting of a waisted blouse and trousers. [from Chinese (Cantonese) *sam* dress + *foo* trousers]

Samian ('seɪmɪən) *adj* **1** of or relating to Samos or its inhabitants. ◆ *n* **2** a native or inhabitant of Samos.

Samian ware *n* **1** a fine earthenware pottery, reddish-brown or black in colour, found in large quantities on Roman sites. **2** Also called: **Arretine ware.** the earlier pottery from which this developed, an imitation of a type of Greek pottery, made during the first century B.C. at Arretium. [C19: named after the island of SAMOS, source of a reddish-coloured earth resembling terra sigillata, similar to the earth from which the pottery was made]

samiel ('sæmjɛl) *n* another word for **simoom.** [C17: from Turkish *samyeli,* from *sam* poisonous + *yel* wind]

samisen ('sæmɪ,sɛn) *n* a Japanese plucked stringed instrument with a long neck, an unfretted fingerboard, and a rectangular soundbox. [Japanese, from Chinese *san-hsien,* from *san* three + *hsien* string]

samite ('sæmaɪt, 'seɪ-) *n* a heavy fabric of silk, often woven with gold or silver threads, used in the Middle Ages for clothing. [C13: from Old French *samit,* from Medieval Latin *examitum,* from Greek *hexamiton,* from *hexamitos* having six threads, from *hex* six + *mitos* a thread]

samiti *or* **samithi** ('sʌmɪtɪ) *n* (in India) an association, esp. one formed to organize political activity. [Hindi]

samizdat (*Russian* səmiz'dat) *n* (in the former Soviet Union) **a** a system of clandestine printing and distribution of banned or dissident literature. **b** (*as modifier*): *a samizdat publication.* [C20: from Russian, literally: self-published]

sammy ('sæmɪ) *n, pl* **-mies.** *Informal.* (in South Africa) an Indian fruit and vegetable vendor who goes from house to house. [C20: from the forename *Sammy*]

Samnite ('sæmnaɪt) (in ancient Italy) ◆ *n* **1** a member of an Oscan-speaking people of the S Apennines, who clashed repeatedly with Rome between 350 B.C. and 200 B.C. ◆ *adj* **2** of or relating to this people.

Samnium ('sæmnɪəm) *n* an ancient country of central Italy inhabited by Oscan-speaking Samnites: corresponds to the present-day regions of Abruzzi, Molise, and part of Campania.

Samoa (sə'məʊə) *n* **1** an independent state occupying four inhabited islands and five uninhabited islands in the S Pacific archipelago of the Samoa Islands: established as a League of Nations mandate under New Zealand administration in 1920 and a UN trusteeship in 1946; gained independence as Western Samoa in 1962 as the first fully independent Polynesian state; officially changed its name to Samoa in 1997; a member of the Commonwealth. Languages: Samoan and English. Religion: Christian. Currency: tala. Capital: Apia. Pop.: 171 000 (1998 est.). Area 2841 sq. km (1097 sq. miles). **2** Also called: **Samoa Islands.** a group of islands in the S Pacific, northeast of Fiji: an independent kingdom until the mid 19th century, when it was divided administratively into **American Samoa** (in the east) and **German Samoa** (in the west); the latter was mandated to New Zealand in 1919 and gained full independence in 1962 as Western Samoa, now **Samoa** (sense 1). Area: 3038 sq. km (1173 sq. miles).

Samoan (sə'məʊən) *adj* **1** of or relating to Samoa, its people, or their language. ◆ *n* **2** a member of the people that inhabit Samoa. **3** the language of Samoa, belonging to the Polynesian family of languages.

Samos ('seɪmɒs) *n* an island in the E Aegean Sea, off the SW coast of Turkey: a leading commercial centre of ancient Greece. Pop.: 41 965 (1991). Area: 492 sq. km (190 sq. miles).

samosa (sə'məʊsə) *n, pl* **-sas** *or* **-sa.** (in Indian cookery) a small triangular pastry case containing spiced vegetables or meat and served fried. [C20: from Hindi]

Samothrace ('sæmə,θreɪs) *n* a Greek island in the NE Aegean Sea: mountainous. Pop.: 4000 (latest est.).

samovar ('sæmə,vɑ:, ,sæmə'vɑ:) *n* (esp. in Russia) a metal urn for making tea, in which the water is heated esp. formerly by charcoal held in an inner container or nowadays more usually by electricity. [C19: from Russian, from *samo-* self (related to SAME) + *varit'* to boil]

Samoyed (,sæmə'jɛd) *n* **1** (*pl* **-yed** *or* **-yeds**) a member of a group of peoples who migrated along the Russian Arctic coast and now live chiefly in the area of the N Urals: related to the Finns. **2** the languages of these peoples, related to Finno-Ugric within the Uralic family. **3** (sə'mɔɪɛd). a Siberian breed of dog of the spitz type, having a dense white or cream coat with a distinct ruff, and a tightly curled tail. [C17: from Russian *Samoed*] ► ,**Samo'yedic** *adj*

samp (sæmp) *n S. African.* crushed maize used for porridge. [C17: from Narraganset *nasaump* softened by water]

sampan ('sæmpæn) *n* any small skiff, widely used in the Orient, that is propelled by oars or a scull. [C17: from Chinese *san pan,* from *san* three + *pan* board]

samphire ('sæm,faɪə) *n* **1** Also called: **rock samphire.** an umbelliferous plant, *Crithmum maritimum,* of Eurasian coasts, having fleshy divided leaves and clusters of small white flowers. **2 golden samphire.** a Eurasian coastal plant, *Inula crithmoides,* with fleshy leaves and yellow flower heads: family *Compositae* (composites). **3 marsh samphire.** another name for **glasswort** (sense 1). **4** any of several other plants of coastal areas. [C16 *sampiere,* from French *herbe de Saint Pierre* Saint Peter's herb; perhaps influenced by *camphire* CAMPHOR]

sample ('sɑ:mpᵊl) *n* **1a** a small part of anything, intended as representative of the whole; specimen. **1b** (*as modifier*): *a sample bottle.* **2** Also called: **sampling.** *Statistics.* **2a** a set of individuals or items selected from a population for analysis to yield estimates of, or to test hypotheses about, parameters of the whole population. A **biased sample** is one in which the items selected share some property which influences their distribution, while a **random sample** is devised to avoid any such interference so that its distribution is affected only by, and so can be held to represent, that of the whole population. See also **matched sample. 2b** (*as modifier*): *sample distribution.* ◆ *vb* **3** (*tr*) to take a sample or samples of. **4** *Music.* **4a** to take a short extract from (one record) and mix it into a different backing track. **4b** to record (a sound) and feed it into a computerized synthesizer so that it can be reproduced at any pitch. [C13: from Old French *essample,* from Latin *exemplum* EXAMPLE]

sample point *n Statistics.* a single possible observed value of a variable; a member of the sample space of an experiment.

sampler ('sɑ:mplə) *n* **1** a person who takes samples. **2** a piece of embroidery executed as an example of the embroiderer's skill in using a variety of stitches: often incorporating numbers, letters, and the name and age of the embroiderer in a decorative panel. **3** *Music.* a piece of electronic equipment used for sampling. **4** a recording comprising a collection of tracks from other albums, intended to stimulate interest in the featured products.

sample space *n Statistics.* the set of possible outcomes of an experiment; the range of values of a random variable.

sampling ('sɑːmplɪŋ) *n* **1** the process of selecting a random sample. **2** a variant of **sample** (sense 2). **3** the process of taking a short extract from (a record) and mixing it into a different backing track. **4** a process in which a continuous electrical signal is approximately represented by a series of discrete values, usually regularly spaced.

sampling frame *n Statistics.* See **frame** (sense 13).

sampling statistic *n* any function of observed data, esp. one used to estimate the corresponding parameter of the underlying distribution, such as the sample mean, sample variance, etc. Compare **parameter** (sense 3).

Sampras ('sæmpˌræs) *n* **Pete.** born 1971, U.S. tennis player: U.S. singles champion (1990, 1993, 1995, 1996); Wimbledon singles champion (1993–95, 1997–99).

samsara (səm'sɑːrə) *n* **1** *Hinduism.* the endless cycle of birth, death, and rebirth. **2** *Buddhism.* the transmigration or rebirth of a person. [Sanskrit, literally: a passing through, from *sam* altogether + *sarati* it runs]

samshu ('sæmʃuː, -sjuː) *n* an alcoholic drink from China that is made from fermented rice and resembles sake. [C17: perhaps modification of Chinese *shao chiu* spirits that will burn, from *shao* to burn + *chiu* spirits]

Samson ('sæmsən) *n* **1** a judge of Israel, who performed herculean feats of strength against the Philistine oppressors until he was betrayed to them by his mistress Delilah (Judges 13–16). **2** any man of outstanding physical strength.

Samsun (*Turkish* 'sɑmsun) *n* a port in N Turkey, on the Black Sea. Pop.: 330 360 (1995 est.). Ancient name: **Amisus** (əmiːsəs).

Samuel ('sæmjuəl) *n Old Testament.* **1** a Hebrew prophet, seer, and judge, who anointed the first two kings of the Israelites (I Samuel 1–3; 8–15). **2** either of the two books named after him, **I** and **II Samuel.**

samurai ('sæmʊˌraɪ, 'sæmjʊ-) *n, pl* **-rai. 1** the Japanese warrior caste that provided the administrative and fighting aristocracy from the 11th to the 19th centuries. **2** a member of this aristocracy. [C19: from Japanese]

samurai bond *n* a bond issued in Japan and denominated in yen, available for purchase by nonresidents of Japan. Compare **shogun bond.**

san (sæn) *n Old-fashioned informal.* short for **sanatorium** (esp. sense 3).

San[1] (sɑːn) *n* a group of the Khoisan languages, spoken mostly by Bushmen.

San[2] (sɑːn) *n* a river in E central Europe, rising in the W Ukraine and flowing northwest across SE Poland to the Vistula River. Length: about 450 km (280 miles).

San'a *or* **Sanaa** (sɑː'nɑː) *n* the administrative capital of Yemen, on the central plateau at an altitude of 2350 m (7700 ft.): formerly the capital of North Yemen. Pop.: 972 000 (1995 est.).

San Antonio (sæn æn'təʊnɪˌəʊ) *n* a city in S Texas: site of the Alamo; the leading town in Texas until about 1930. Pop.: 1 067 816 (1996 est.). ► **San Antonian** *adj, n*

Sanatana Dharma (saˌnɑtana 'dɑrmaː) *n* the name used by Hindus for Hinduism. [from Sanskrit: the eternal way]

sanative ('sænətɪv) *adj* a less common word for **curative.** [C15: from Medieval Latin *sānātīvus,* from Latin *sānāre* to heal, from *sānus* healthy]

sanatorium (ˌsænə'tɔːrɪəm) *or U.S.* **sanitarium** *n, pl* **-riums** *or* **-ria** (-rɪə). **1** an institution for the medical care and recuperation of persons who are chronically ill. **2** a health resort. **3** *Brit.* a room in a boarding school where sick pupils may receive treatment in isolation. [C19: from New Latin, from Latin *sānāre* to heal]

sanbenito (ˌsænbə'niːtəʊ) *n, pl* **-tos. 1** a yellow garment bearing a red cross, worn by penitent heretics in the Inquisition. **2** a black garment bearing flames and devils, worn by impenitent heretics at an auto-da-fé. [C16: from Spanish *San Benito* Saint Benedict, an ironical allusion to its likeness to the Benedictine scapular]

San Bernardino (sæn ˌbɜːnə'diːnəʊ) *n* a city in SE California: founded in 1851 by Mormons from Salt Lake City. Pop.: 183 474 (1996 est.).

San Bernardino Pass *n* a pass over the Lepontine Alps in SE Switzerland. Highest point: 2062 m (6766 ft.).

San Blas ('sɑːn 'blɑːs) *n* **1 Isthmus of.** the narrowest part of the Isthmus of Panama. Width: about 50 km (30 miles). **2 Gulf of.** an inlet of the Caribbean on the N coast of Panama.

Sancerre (sɒn'sɛə; *French* sɑ̃sɛr) *n* a dry white wine produced in the Loire valley in France. [French]

San Cristóbal (*Spanish* saŋ kri'stoβal) *n* **1** Also called: **Chatham Island.** an island in the Pacific, in the Galápagos Islands. Area: 505 sq. km (195 sq. miles). **2** a city in SW Venezuela: founded in 1561 by Spanish conquistadores. Pop.: 220 675 (1990).

sanctified ('sæŋktɪˌfaɪd) *adj* **1** consecrated or made holy. **2** a less common word for **sanctimonious.**

sanctify ('sæŋktɪˌfaɪ) *vb* **-fies, -fying, -fied.** *(tr)* **1** to make holy. **2** to free from sin; purify. **3** to sanction (an action or practice) as religiously binding: *to sanctify a marriage.* **4** to declare or render (something) productive of or conductive to holiness, blessing, or grace. **5** *Obsolete.* to authorize to be revered. [C14: from Late Latin *sanctificāre,* from Latin *sanctus* holy + *facere* to make] ► **'sanctiˌfiable** *adj* ► **ˌsanctifi'cation** *n* ► **'sanctiˌfier** *n*

sanctimonious (ˌsæŋktɪ'məʊnɪəs) *adj* affecting piety or making a display of holiness. [C17: from Latin *sanctimonia* sanctity, from *sanctus* holy] ► **ˌsancti'moniously** *adv* ► **ˌsancti'moniousness** *n* ► **'sanctimony** *n*

sanction ('sæŋkʃən) *n* **1** final permission; authorization. **2** aid or encouragement. **3** something, such as an ethical principle, that imparts binding force to a rule, oath, etc. **4** the penalty laid down in a law for contravention of its provisions. **5** *(often pl)* a coercive measure, esp. one taken by one or more states against another guilty of violating international law. ◆ *vb (tr)* **6** to give authority to; permit. **7** to make authorized; confirm. [C16: from Latin *sanctiō* the establishment of an inviolable decree, from *sancīre* to decree] ► **'sanctionable** *adj* ► **'sanctioner** *n* ► **'sanctionless** *adj*

sanction mark *n* a mark on pieces of 19th-century French furniture signifying that the piece met the quality standards required by the Parisian guild of ebonists.

sanctitude ('sæŋktɪˌtjuːd) *n* saintliness; holiness.

sanctity ('sæŋktɪtɪ) *n, pl* **-ties. 1** the condition of being sanctified; holiness. **2** anything regarded as sanctified or holy. **3** the condition of being inviolable; sacredness: *the sanctity of marriage.* [C14: from Old French *saincteté,* from Latin *sanctitās,* from *sanctus* holy]

sanctuary ('sæŋktjʊərɪ) *n, pl* **-aries. 1** a holy place. **2** a consecrated building or shrine. **3** *Old Testament.* **3a** the Israelite temple at Jerusalem, esp. the holy of holies. **3b** the tabernacle in which the Ark was enshrined during the wanderings of the Israelites. **4** the chancel, or that part of a sacred building surrounding the main altar. **5a** a sacred building where fugitives were formerly entitled to immunity from arrest or execution. **5b** the immunity so afforded. **6** a place of refuge; asylum. **7** a place, protected by law, where animals, esp. birds, can live and breed without interference. [C14: from Old French *sainctuarie,* from Late Latin *sanctuārium* repository for holy things, from Latin *sanctus* holy]

sanctuary lamp *n Christianity.* a lamp, usually red, placed in a prominent position in the sanctuary of a church, that when lit indicates the presence of the Blessed Sacrament.

sanctum ('sæŋktəm) *n, pl* **-tums** *or* **-ta** (-tə). **1** a sacred or holy place. **2** a room or place of total privacy or inviolability. [C16: from Latin, from *sanctus* holy]

sanctum sanctorum (sæŋk'tɔːrəm) *n* **1** *Bible.* another term for the **holy of holies. 2** *Often facetious.* an especially private place. [C14: from Latin, literally: holy of holies, rendering Hebrew *qōdesh haqqodāshīm*]

Sanctus ('sæŋktəs) *n* **1** *Liturgy.* the hymn that occurs immediately after the preface in the celebration of the Eucharist. **2** a musical setting of this, usually incorporated into the Ordinary of the Roman Catholic Mass. [C14: from the first word of the hymn, *Sanctus sanctus sanctus* Holy, holy, holy, from Latin *sancīre* to consecrate]

Sanctus bell *n Chiefly R.C. Church.* a bell rung as the opening words of the Sanctus are pronounced and also at other important points during Mass.

sand (sænd) *n* **1** loose material consisting of rock or mineral grains, esp. rounded grains of quartz, between 0.2 and 2 mm in diameter. **2** *(often pl)* a sandy area, esp. on the seashore or in a desert. **3a** a greyish-yellow colour. **3b** *(as adj): sand upholstery.* **4** the grains of sandlike material in an hourglass. **5** *U.S. informal.* courage; grit. **6 the sands are running out.** there is not much time left before death or the end. ◆ *vb* **7** *(tr)* to smooth or polish the surface of with sandpaper or sand: *to sand a floor.* **8** *(tr)* to sprinkle or cover with or as if with sand; add sand to. **9** to fill or cause to fill with sand: *the channel sanded up.* [Old English; related to Old Norse *sandr,* Old High German *sant,* Greek *hamathos*] ► **'sandˌlike** *adj*

Sand (*French* sɑ̃d) *n* **George** (ʒɔrʒ), pen name of *Amandine Aurore Lucie Dupin.* 1804–76, French novelist, best known for such pastoral novels as *La Mare au diable* (1846) and *François le Champi* (1847–48) and for her works for women's rights to independence.

Sandage ('sændɪdʒ) *n* **Allan Rex.** born 1926, U.S. astronomer, who discovered the first quasar (1961).

Sandakan (sɑːn'dɑːkɑːn) *n* a port in Malaysia, on the NE coast of Sabah: capital (until 1947) of North Borneo. Pop.: 223 432 (1991).

sandal ('sænd^{ə}l) *n* **1** a light shoe consisting of a sole held on the foot by thongs, straps, etc. **2** a strap passing over the instep or around the ankle to keep a low shoe on the foot. [C14: from Latin *sandalium,* from Greek *sandalion* a small sandal, from *sandalon* sandal] ► **'sandalled** *adj*

sandalwood ('sænd^{ə}lˌwʊd) *or* **sandal** *n* **1** any of several evergreen trees of the genus *Santalum,* esp. *S. album* (**white sandalwood**), of S Asia and Australia, having hard light-coloured heartwood: family *Santalaceae.* **2** the wood of any of these trees, which is used for carving, is burned as incense, and yields an aromatic oil used in perfumery. **3** any of various similar trees or their wood, esp. *Pterocarpus santalinus* (**red sandalwood**), a leguminous tree of SE Asia having dark red wood used as a dye. [C14 *sandal,* from Medieval Latin *sandalum,* from Late Greek *sandanon,* from Sanskrit *candana* sandalwood]

Sandalwood Island *n* the former name for **Sumba.**

sandarac *or* **sandarach** ('sændəˌræk) *n* **1** Also called: **sandarac tree.** a pinaceous tree, *Tetraclinis articulata* (or *Callitris quadrivalvis*), of NW Africa, having hard fragrant dark wood. **2** a brittle pale yellow transparent resin obtained from the bark of this tree and used in making varnish and incense. **3** Also called: **citron wood.** the wood of this tree, used in building. [C16 *sandaracha,* from Latin *sandaraca* red pigment, from Greek *sandarakē*]

sandbag ('sændˌbæg) *n* **1** a sack filled with sand used for protection against gunfire, floodwater, etc., or as ballast in a balloon, ship, etc. **2** a bag filled with sand and used as a weapon. ◆ *vb* **-bags, -bagging, -bagged.** *(tr)* **3** to protect or strengthen with sandbags. **4** to hit with or as if with a sandbag. **5** *Finance.* to obstruct (an unwelcome takeover bid) by prolonging talks in the hope that an acceptable bidder will come forward. ► **'sandˌbagger** *n*

sandbank ('sændˌbæŋk) *n* a submerged bank of sand in a sea or river, that may be exposed at low tide.

sand bar *n* a ridge of sand in a river or sea, built up by the action of tides, currents, etc., and often exposed at low tide.

sandblast ('sændˌblɑːst) *n* **1** a jet of sand or grit blown from a nozzle under air pressure or steam pressure. ◆ *vb (tr)* **2** to clean, grind, or decorate (a surface) with a sandblast. ► **'sandˌblaster** *n*

sand-blind *adj* not completely blind; partially able to see. Compare **stone-blind.** [C15: changed (through influence of SAND) from Old English *sam-blind* (unattested), from *sam-* half, SEMI- + BLIND] ▸ **'sand-,blindness** *n*

sandbox ('sænd,bɒks) *n* **1** a container on a railway locomotive from which sand is released onto the rails to assist the traction. **2** a box with sand shaped for moulding metal. **3** a container of sand for small children to play in.

sandbox tree *n* a tropical American euphorbiaceous tree, *Hura crepitans,* having small woody seed capsules, which explode when ripe to scatter the seeds: formerly used to hold sand for blotting ink.

sandboy ('sænd,bɔɪ) *n* **happy** (*or* **jolly**) **as a sandboy.** very happy; high-spirited.

Sandburg ('sændbɜːg, 'sænbɜːg) *n* **Carl.** 1878–1967, U.S. writer, noted esp. for his poetry, often written in free verse.

sand-cast *vb* **-casts, -casting, -cast.** (*tr*) to produce (a casting) by pouring molten metal into a mould of sand. ▸ **'sand-,casting** *n*

sand castle *n* a mass of sand moulded into a castle-like shape, esp. as made by a child on the seashore.

sand crack *n Vet. science.* a deep crack or fissure in the wall of a horse's hoof, often causing lameness. See also **toe crack, quarter crack.**

sand dab *n* any of various small flatfishes of the genus *Citharichthys* that occur in American Pacific coastal waters and are important food fishes.

sand dollar *n* any of various flattened disclike echinoderms of the order *Clypeasteroida,* of shallow North American coastal waters: class *Echinoidea* (sea urchins).

sand eel *or* **lance** *n* any silvery eel-like marine spiny-finned fish of the family *Ammodytidae* found burrowing in sand or shingle. Popular name: **launce.**

sandek ('sɑn,dɛk) *n Judaism.* a man who holds a baby being circumcised. [Hebrew]

sander ('sændə) *n* **1** a power-driven tool for smoothing surfaces, esp. wood, plastic, etc., by rubbing with an abrasive disc. **2** a person who uses such a device.

sanderling ('sændəlɪŋ) *n* a small sandpiper, *Crocethia alba,* that frequents sandy shores. [C17: perhaps from SAND + Old English *erthling, eorthling* EARTHLING]

Sanderson ('sændəsən) *n* **Tessa.** born 1956, British javelin-thrower.

sand flea *n* another name for the **chigoe** (sense 1) and **sand hopper.**

sandfly ('sænd,flaɪ) *n, pl* **-flies. 1** any of various small mothlike dipterous flies of the genus *Phlebotomus* and related genera: the bloodsucking females transmit diseases including leishmaniasis: family *Psychodidae.* **2** any of various similar and related flies.

sandglass ('sænd,glɑːs) *n* a less common word for **hourglass.**

sandgrouse ('sænd,graʊs) *n* any bird of the family *Pteroclididae,* of dry regions of the Old World, having very short feet, a short bill, and long pointed wings and tail: order *Columbiformes.*

sandhi ('sændɪ) *n, pl* **-dhis.** *Linguistics.* modification of the form or sound of a word under the influence of an adjacent word. [from Sanskrit *samdhi* a placing together, from *sam* together + *dadhāti* he puts]

sandhog ('sænd,hɒg) *n Chiefly U.S. and Canadian.* a person who works in underground or underwater construction projects.

sand hopper *n* any of various small hopping amphipod crustaceans of the genus *Orchestia* and related genera, common in intertidal regions of seashores. Also called: **beach flea, sand flea.**

Sandhurst ('sænd,hɜːst) *n* a village in S England, in Berkshire: seat of the Royal Military Academy for the training of officer cadets in the British Army. Pop.: 19 153 (1991).

San Diego (,sæn dɪ'eɪgəʊ) *n* a port in S California, on the Pacific: naval base; two universities. Pop.: 1 171 121 (1996 est.).

Sandinista (,sændɪ'niːstə) *n* (in Nicaragua). **a** one of a left-wing group of revolutionaries who overthrew President Samoza in 1979 and formed a socialist coalition government. **b** (*as modifier*): *Nicaragua's Sandinista government.* [C20: from Spanish, named after Augusto César *Sandino* a Nicaraguan general and rebel leader, murdered in 1933]

sand lance *or* **launce** *n* another name for the **sand eel.**

sand leek *n* a Eurasian alliaceous plant, *Allium scorodoprasum,* having reddish-pink flowers, purple bulbils, and a garlic-like bulb. See also **rocambole.**

sand lizard *n* a small greyish-brown European lizard, *Lacerta agilis,* that has long clawed digits and, in the male, bright green underparts: family *Lacertidae.*

sandman ('sænd,mæn) *n, pl* **-men.** (in folklore) a magical person supposed to put children to sleep by sprinkling sand in their eyes.

sand martin *n* a small brown European songbird, *Riparia riparia,* with white underparts: it nests in tunnels bored in sand, river banks, etc.: family *Hirundinidae* (swallows and martins).

sand painting *n* a type of painting done by American Indians, esp. in the healing ceremonies of the Navaho, using fine coloured sand on a neutral ground.

sandpaper ('sænd,peɪpə) *n* **1** (formerly) a strong paper coated with sand for smoothing and polishing. **2** a common name for **glasspaper.** ◆ *vb* **3** (*tr*) to polish or grind (a surface) with or as if with sandpaper.

sandpiper ('sænd,paɪpə) *n* **1** any of numerous N hemisphere shore birds of the genera *Tringa, Calidris,* etc., typically having a long slender bill and legs and cryptic plumage: family *Scolopacidae,* order *Charadriiformes.* **2** any other bird of the family *Scolopacidae,* which includes snipes and woodcocks.

sandpit ('sænd,pɪt) *n* **1** a shallow pit or container holding sand for children to play in. **2** a pit from which sand is extracted.

Sandringham ('sændrɪŋəm) *n* a village in E England, in Norfolk near the E shore of the Wash: site of **Sandringham House,** a residence of the royal family.

Sandrocottus (,sændrəʊ'kɒtəs) *n* the Greek name of **Chandragupta.**

sandshoe ('sænd,ʃuː) *n Brit. and Austral.* a light canvas shoe with a rubber sole; plimsoll.

sand shrimp *n* See **shrimp** (sense 4).

sandsoap ('sænd,səʊp) *n* a gritty general-purpose soap.

sandstone ('sænd,stəʊn) *n* any of a group of common sedimentary rocks consisting of sand grains consolidated with such materials as quartz, haematite, and clay minerals: used widely in building.

sandstorm ('sænd,stɔːm) *n* a strong wind that whips up clouds of sand, esp. in a desert.

sand table *n Military* a surface on which sand can be modelled into a relief map on which to demonstrate tactics.

sand trap *n* another name (esp. U.S.) for **bunker** (sense 2).

sand viper *n* **1** a S European viper, *Vipera ammodytes,* having a yellowish-brown coloration with a zigzag pattern along the back. **2** another name for **horned viper.**

sand wasp *n* a solitary wasp of the subfamily *Sphecinae,* a subgroup of the digger wasps most of which nest in sandy ground.

sand wedge *n Golf.* a club with a flanged sole and a face angle of more than 50°, used in bunker shots to cut through sand, get under the ball, and lift it clear.

Sandwell ('sændwɛl) *n* a unitary authority in central England, in West Midlands. Pop.: 293 700 (1995 est.). Area: 86 sq. km (33 sq. miles).

sandwich ('sænwɪdʒ, -wɪtʃ) *n* **1** two or more slices of bread, usually buttered, with a filling of meat, cheese, etc. **2** anything that resembles a sandwich in arrangement. ◆ *vb* (*tr*) **3** to insert tightly between two other things. **4** to put into a sandwich. **5** to place between two dissimilar things. [C18: named after John Montagu, 4th Earl of *Sandwich* (1718–92), who ate sandwiches rather than leave the gambling table for meals]

sandwich board *n* one of two connected boards, usually bearing advertisements, that are hung over the shoulders in front of and behind a person.

sandwich cake *n* a cake that is made up of two or more layers with a jam or other filling. Also called: **layer cake.**

sandwich compound *n Chem.* any of a class of organometallic compounds whose molecules have a metal atom or ion bound between two plane parallel organic rings. See also **metallocene.**

sandwich course *n* any of several courses consisting of alternate periods of study and industrial work.

Sandwich Islands *pl n* the former name of **Hawaii.**

sandwich man *n* a man who carries sandwich boards.

sandwich tern *n* a European tern, *Sterna sandvicensis,* that has a yellow-tipped bill, whitish plumage, and white forked tail, and nests in colonies on beaches, etc. [C18: from the town of *Sandwich* in Kent]

sandworm ('sænd,wɜːm) *n* any of various polychaete worms that live in burrows on sandy shores, esp. the lugworm.

sandwort ('sænd,wɜːt) *n* **1** any of numerous caryophyllaceous plants of the genus *Arenaria,* which grow in dense tufts on sandy soil and have white or pink solitary flowers. **2** any of various related plants.

sandy ('sændɪ) *adj* **sandier, sandiest. 1** consisting of, containing, or covered with sand. **2** (esp. of hair) reddish-yellow. **3** resembling sand in texture. ▸ **'sandiness** *n*

sand yacht *n* a wheeled boat with sails, built to be propelled over sand, esp. beaches, by the wind.

sandy blight *n Austral.* a nontechnical name for any of various eye inflammations.

sane (seɪn) *adj* **1** sound in mind; free from mental disturbance. **2** having or showing reason, good judgment, or sound sense. **3** *Obsolete.* healthy. [C17: from Latin *sānus* healthy] ▸ **'sanely** *adv* ▸ **'saneness** *n*

San Fernando (*Spanish* san fer'nando) *n* **1** a port in Trinidad and Tobago, on Trinidad on the Gulf of Paria: the second-largest town in the country. Pop.: 30 100 (1990). **2** an inland port in W Venezuela, on the Apure River. Pop.: 84 179 (1989 est.). Official name: **San Fernando de Apure. 3** a port in SW Spain, on the Isla de León SE of Cádiz; site of an arsenal (founded 1790) and of the most southerly observatory in Europe. Pop.: 85 191 (1991).

Sanforized *or* **Sanforised** ('sænfə,raɪzd) *adj Trademark.* (of a fabric) preshrunk using a patented process.

San Francisco (,sæn fræn'sɪskəʊ) *n* a port in W California, situated around the Golden Gate: developed rapidly during the California gold rush; a major commercial centre and one of the world's finest harbours. Pop.: 735 315 (1996 est.). ▸ **San Franciscan** *n, adj*

San Francisco Bay *n* an inlet of the Pacific in W California, linked with the open sea by the Golden Gate strait. Length: about 80 km (50 miles). Greatest width: 19 km (12 miles).

sang[1] (sæŋ) *vb* the past tense of **sing.**

USAGE See at **ring**[2].

sang[2] (sæŋ) *n* a Scot. word for **song.**

sangar ('sʌŋgə) *n Military.* a breastwork of stone or sods. [C19: from Pashto]

sangaree (,sæŋgə'riː) *n* a spiced drink similar to sangria. [C18: from Spanish *sangría* a bleeding, from *sangre* blood, from Latin *sanguis;* see SANGUINE]

Sanger ('sæŋə) *n* **1 Frederick.** born 1918, English biochemist, who determined the molecular structure of insulin: awarded two Nobel prizes for chemistry (1958; 1980). **2 Margaret** (**Higgins**). 1883–1966, U.S. leader of the birth-control movement.

sang-froid (*French* sɑ̃frwa) *n* composure; self-possession; calmness. [C18: from French, literally: cold blood]

Sangh (sʌŋg) *n* (in India) an association or union, esp. a political or labour organization. [Hindi]

Sangha ('sɑn,gə) *n* **a** the Buddhist community. **b** (in Theravada Buddhism) the monastic order. [from Sanskrit: group, congregation]

sanghat (sʌŋgʌt) *n Sikhism.* a fellowship or assembly, esp. a local Sikh community or congregation. [Punjabi]

Sango ('sɑːŋgəʊ) *n* a language used in Chad, the Central African Republic, N Democratic Republic of the Congo (formerly Zaïre), and the Congo, belonging to the Adamawa branch of the Niger-Congo family.

sangoma (sæŋ'gəʊmə) *n S. African.* a witch doctor or herbalist. [from Zulu *isangoma*]

Sangrail, Sangraal (sæŋ'greɪl), *or* **Sangreal** ('sæŋgrɪəl) *n* another name for the **Holy Grail**. [C15: from Old French *Saint Graal.* See SAINT, HOLY GRAIL]

Sangre de Cristo Mountains ('sæŋgrɪ də 'krɪstəʊ) *pl n* a mountain range in S Colorado and N New Mexico: part of the Rocky Mountains. Highest peak: Blanca Peak, 4364 m (14 317 ft.).

sangria (sæŋ'griːə) *n* a Spanish drink of red wine, sugar, orange or lemon juice, and iced soda, sometimes laced with brandy. [Spanish: a bleeding; see SANGAREE]

sanguinaria (ˌsæŋgwɪ'nɛərɪə) *n* **1** the dried rhizome of the bloodroot, used as an emetic. **2** another name for **bloodroot** (sense 1). [C19: from New Latin *herba sanguināria,* literally: the bloody herb]

sanguinary ('sæŋgwɪnərɪ) *adj* **1** accompanied by much bloodshed. **2** bloodthirsty. **3** consisting of, flowing, or stained with blood. [C17: from Latin *sanguinārius*] ▸ **'sanguinarily** *adv* ▸ **'sanguinariness** *n*

sanguine ('sæŋgwɪn) *adj* **1** cheerful and confident; optimistic. **2** (esp. of the complexion) ruddy in appearance. **3** blood-red. **4** an obsolete word for **sanguinary** (sense 2). ◆ *n* **5** Also called: **red chalk**. a red pencil containing ferric oxide, used in drawing. [C14: from Latin *sanguineus* bloody, from *sanguis* blood] ▸ **'sanguinely** *adv* ▸ **'sanguineness** *or* **san'guinity** *n*

sanguineous (sæŋ'gwɪnɪəs) *adj* **1** of, containing, relating to, or associated with blood. **2** a less common word for **sanguine** (senses 1–3). ▸ **san'guineousness** *n*

sanguinolent (sæŋ'gwɪnələnt) *adj* containing, tinged with, or mixed with blood. [C15: from Latin *sanguinolentus,* from *sanguis* blood] ▸ **san'guinolency** *n*

Sanhedrin ('sænɪdrɪn) *n Judaism.* **1** the supreme judicial, ecclesiastical, and administrative council of the Jews in New Testament times, having 71 members. **2** a similar tribunal of 23 members having less important functions and authority. [C16: from Late Hebrew, from Greek *sunedrion* council, from *sun-* SYN- + *hedra* seat]

sanicle ('sænɪkᵊl) *n* any umbelliferous plant of the genus *Sanicula,* of most regions except Australia, having clusters of small white flowers and oval fruits with hooked bristles: formerly thought to have healing powers. [C15: via Old French from Medieval Latin *sānicula,* probably from Latin *sānus* healthy]

sanidine ('sænɪˌdiːn, -dɪn) *n* an alkali feldspar that is a high-temperature glassy form of orthoclase in flat, tabular crystals, found in lavas and dykes. Formula: $KAlSi_3O_8$. [C19: from German, from Greek *sanis, sanidos* a board]

sanies ('seɪnɪˌiːz) *n Pathol.* a thin greenish foul-smelling discharge from a wound, ulcer, etc., containing pus and blood. [C16: from Latin, of obscure origin]

San Ildefonso (*Spanish* san ilde'fonso) *n* a town in central Spain, near Segovia: site of the 18th-century summer palace of the kings of Spain. Also called: **La Granja**.

sanitarian (ˌsænɪ'tɛərɪən) *adj* **1** of or relating to sanitation. ◆ *n* **2** a sanitation expert.

sanitarium (ˌsænɪ'tɛərɪəm) *n, pl* **-riums** *or* **-ria** (-rɪə). the U.S. spelling of **sanatorium**. [C19: from Latin *sānitās* health]

sanitary ('sænɪtərɪ, -trɪ) *adj* **1** of or relating to health and measures for the protection of health. **2** conducive to or promoting health; free from dirt, germs, etc.; hygienic. [C19: from French *sanitaire,* from Latin *sānitās* health] ▸ **'sanitarily** *adv* ▸ **'sanitariness** *n*

sanitary belt *n* a belt for supporting a sanitary towel.

sanitary engineering *n* the branch of civil engineering associated with the supply of water, disposal of sewage, and other public health services. ▸ **sanitary engineer** *n*

sanitary inspector *n* (in Britain) a former name for **Environmental Health Officer**.

sanitary towel *or esp. U.S.* **napkin** *n* an absorbent pad worn externally by women during menstruation to absorb the menstrual flow.

sanitation (ˌsænɪ'teɪʃən) *n* the study and use of practical measures for the preservation of public health.

sanitize *or* **sanitise** ('sænɪˌtaɪz) *vb* (*tr*) **1** to make sanitary or hygienic, as by sterilizing. **2** to omit unpleasant details from (a news report, document, etc.) to make it more palatable to the recipients. ▸ **ˌsaniti'zation** *or* **ˌsaniti'sation** *n*

sanity ('sænɪtɪ) *n* **1** the state of being sane. **2** good sense or soundness of judgment. [C15: from Latin *sānitās* health, from *sānus* healthy]

sanjak ('sændʒæk) *n* (in the Turkish Empire) a subdivision of a vilayet. [C16: from Turkish *sancàk,* literally: a flag]

San Jose (ˌsæn həʊ'zeɪ) *n* a city in W central California: a leading world centre of the fruit drying and canning industry. Pop.: 838 744 (1996 est.).

San José (*Spanish* saŋ xo'se) *n* the capital of Costa Rica, on the central plateau: a major centre of coffee production in the mid-19th century; University of Costa Rica (1843). Pop.: 329 154 (1997 est.).

San Jose scale *n* a small E Asian homopterous insect, *Quadraspidiotus perniciosus,* introduced into the U.S. and other countries, where it has become a serious pest of fruit trees: family *Diaspididae.* [C20: from its first being seen in the United States at *San Jose,* California]

San Juan (*Spanish* saŋ 'xwan) *n* **1** the capital and chief port of Puerto Rico, on the NE coast; University of Puerto Rico; manufacturing centre. Pop.: 433 705 (1996 est.). **2** a city in W Argentina: almost completely destroyed by an earthquake in 1944. Pop.: 352 691 (1991).

San Juan Bautista (*Spanish* saŋ 'xwan bau'tista) *n* the former name of **Villahermosa**.

San Juan Islands (sæn 'wɑːn, 'hwɑːn) *pl n* a group of islands between NW Washington, U.S., and SE Vancouver Island, Canada: administratively part of Washington.

San Juan Mountains *pl n* a mountain range in SW Colorado and N New Mexico: part of the Rocky Mountains. Highest peak: Uncompahgre Peak, 4363 m (14 314 ft.).

sank (sæŋk) *vb* the past tense of **sink**.

Sankara ('sæŋkɑːrə) *n* 8th century A.D., Hindu philosopher, the leading exponent of the Vedantic school: noted for his commentaries on Hindu texts.

Sankey ('sæŋkɪ) *n* **Ira David**. 1840–1908, U.S. evangelist and hymnodist, noted for his revivalist campaigns in Britain and the U.S. with D. L. Moody.

Sankhya ('sæŋkjə) *n* one of the six orthodox schools of Hindu philosophy, teaching an eternal interaction of spirit and matter. [from Sanskrit *sāmkhya,* literally: based on calculation, from *samkhyāti* he reckons]

Sankt Pölten (*German* zaŋkt 'pœltən) *n, usually abbreviated to* **St. Pölten**. a city in NE Austria, the capital of Lower Austria state. Pop.: 50 026 (1991).

San Luis Potosí (*Spanish* san 'lwis poto'si) *n* **1** a state of central Mexico: mainly high plateau; economy based on mining (esp. silver) and agriculture. Capital: San Luis Potosí. Pop.: 2 191 712 (1995 est.). Area: 62 849 sq. km (24 266 sq. miles). **2** an industrial city in central Mexico, capital of San Luis Potosí state, at an altitude of 1850 m (6000 ft.). Pop.: 488 238 (1990).

San Marino (ˌsæn mə'riːnəʊ) *n* a republic in S central Europe in the Apennines, forming an enclave in Italy: the smallest republic in Europe, according to tradition founded by St Marinus in the 4th century. Official language: Italian. Religion: Roman Catholic majority. Currency: lira. Capital: San Marino. Pop.: 26 100 (1998 est.). Area: 62 sq. km (24 sq. miles). ▸ **San Marinese** (ˌsæn ˌmærɪ'niːz) *or* **Sammarinese** (səˌmærɪ'niːz) *adj, n*

San Martín (*Spanish* san mar'tin) *n* **José de** (xo'se de). 1778–1850, South American patriot, who played an important part in gaining independence for Argentina, Chile, and Peru. He was protector of Peru (1821–22).

Sanmicheli (*Italian* sanmi'kɛːli) *n* **Michele** (mi'kɛːle). ?1484–1559, Italian mannerist architect.

sannyasi (sʌn'jɑːsɪ) *or* **sannyasin** (sʌn'jɑːsɪn) *n* a Brahman who having attained the fourth and last stage of life as a beggar will not be reborn, but will instead be absorbed into the Universal Soul. [from Hindi: abandoning, from Sanskrit *samnyāsin*]

San Pedro Sula (*Spanish* san 'peðro 'sula) *n* a city in NW Honduras: the country's chief industrial centre. Pop.: 383 900 (1995 est.).

San Remo (*Italian* san 'rɛːmo) *n* a port and resort in NW Italy, in Liguria on the slopes of the Maritime Alps; flower market. Pop.: 60 800 (1987 est.).

sans (sænz) *prep* an archaic word for **without**. [C13: from Old French *sanz,* from Latin *sine* without, but probably also influenced by Latin *absentiā* in the absence of]

Sans. *or* **Sansk.** *abbrev. for* Sanskrit.

San Salvador (sæn 'sælvəˌdɔː; *Spanish* san salβa'ðor) *n* the capital of El Salvador, situated in the SW central part: became capital in 1841; ruined by earthquakes in 1854 and 1873; university (1841). Pop.: 422 570 (1992).

San Salvador Island *n* an island in the central Bahamas: the first land in the New World seen by Christopher Columbus (1492). Area: 156 sq. km (60 sq. miles). Also called: **Watling Island**.

sans-culotte (ˌsænzkju'lɒt; *French* sɑ̃kylɔt) *n* **1** (during the French Revolution) **1a** (originally) a revolutionary of the poorer class. **1b** (later) any revolutionary, esp. one having extreme republican sympathies. **2** any revolutionary extremist. [C18: from French, literally: without knee breeches, because the revolutionaries wore pantaloons or trousers rather than knee breeches] ▸ **ˌsans-cu'lottism** *n* ▸ **ˌsans-cu'lottist** *n*

San Sebastián (ˌsæn sə'bæstjən; *Spanish* san seβas'tjan) *n* a port and resort in N Spain on the Bay of Biscay: former summer residence of the Spanish court. Pop.: 169 933 (1991).

sansevieria (ˌsænsɪ'vɪərɪə) *n* any herbaceous perennial plant of the liliaceous genus *Sansevieria,* of Old World tropical regions. Some are cultivated as house plants for their erect bayonet-like fleshy leaves of variegated green (mother-in-law's tongue); others yield useful fibre (bowstring hemp). [New Latin, named after Raimondo di Sangro (1710–1771), Italian scholar and prince of *San Severo*]

Sanskrit ('sænskrɪt) *n* an ancient language of India, the language of the Vedas, of Hinduism, and of an extensive philosophical and scientific literature dating from the beginning of the first millennium B.C. It is the oldest recorded member of the Indic branch of the Indo-European family of languages; recognition of the existence of the Indo-European family arose in the 18th century from a comparison of Sanskrit with Greek and Latin. Although it is used only for religious purposes, it is one of the official languages of India. [C17: from Sanskrit *samskrta* perfected, literally: put together] ▸ **'Sanskritist** *n*

Sanskritic (sæn'skrɪtɪk) *adj* **1** of or relating to Sanskrit. **2** denoting or belonging to those Indic languages that developed directly from Sanskrit, such as Pali, Hindi, Punjabi, and Bengali. ◆ *n* **3** this group of languages.

Sanson-Flamsteed projection ('sænsən'flæmstiːd) *n* another name for **sinusoidal projection**. [devised by the cartographer *Sanson* in 1650, adapted by *Flamsteed* in 1729]

sans serif *or* **sanserif** (sæn'sɛrɪf) *n* a style of printer's typeface in which the characters have no serifs.

San Stefano (ˌsæn stɪ'fɑːnəʊ) *n* a village in NW Turkey, near Istanbul on the Sea of Marmara: scene of the signing (1878) of the treaty ending the Russo-Turkish War. Turkish name: **Yeşilköy**.

San Suu Kyi *n* See **Aung San Suu Kyi**.

Santa ('sæntə) *n Informal.* short for **Santa Claus**.

Santa Ana *n* **1** (*Spanish* 'santa 'ana). a city in NW El Salvador: the second largest city in the country; coffee-processing industry. Pop.: 202 337 (1992). **2** ('sæntə 'ænə). a city in SW California: commercial and processing centre of a rich agricultural region. Pop.: 302 419 (1996 est.).

Santa Anna *or* **Santa Ana** (*Spanish* 'santa 'ana) *n* **Antonio López de** (a'tonjo 'lopɛθ de). ?1795–1876, Mexican general, revolutionary, and president (1833–36, 1841–?45, 1847–48, 1853–55). In 1836, he captured the Alamo in an attempt to crush the Texan Revolution but was then defeated at San Jacinto.

Santa Catalina ('sæntə ˌkætəˈli:nə) *n* an island in the Pacific, off the coast of SW California: part of Los Angeles county: resort. Area: 181 sq. km (70 sq. miles). Also called: **Catalina Island.**

Santa Catarina (*Portuguese* 'santə kətə'rinə) *n* a state of S Brazil, on the Atlantic: consists chiefly of the Great Escarpment. Capital: Florianópolis. Pop.: 4 836 600 (1995 est.). Area: 95 985 sq. km (37 060 sq. miles).

Santa Clara (*Spanish* 'santa 'klara) *n* a city in W central Cuba: sugar and tobacco industries. Pop.: 205 400 (1994 est.).

Santa Claus ('sæntə ˌklɔ:z) *n* the legendary patron saint of children, commonly identified with Saint Nicholas, who brings presents to children on Christmas Eve or, in some European countries, on Saint Nicholas' Day. Often shortened to **Santa.** Also called: **Father Christmas.**

Santa Cruz[1] ('sæntə 'kru:z; *Spanish* 'santa 'kruθ) *n* **1** a province of S Argentina, on the Atlantic: consists of a large part of Patagonia, with the forested foothills of the Andes in the west. Capital: Río Gallegos. Pop.: 180 115 (1995 est.). Area: 243 940 sq. km (94 186 sq. miles). **2** a city in E Bolivia: the second largest town in Bolivia. Pop.: 767 260 (1993 est.). **3** another name for **Saint Croix.**

Santa Cruz[2] (*Spanish* 'santa 'kruθ) *n* **Alvaro de Bazán.** 1526–88, Spanish naval commander, who proposed, assembled, and prepared the Spanish Armada but died shortly before it sailed for England.

Santa Cruz de Tenerife ('sæntə 'kru:z də ˌtɛnə'ri:f; *Spanish* 'santa 'kruθ de tene'rife) *n* a port and resort in the W Canary Islands, on NE Tenerife: oil refinery. Pop.: 211 389 (1986).

Santa Fe *n* **1** ('sæntə 'feɪ). a city in N central New Mexico, capital of the state: one of the oldest European settlements in North America, founded in 1610 as the capital of the Kingdom of New Mexico; developed trade with the U.S. by the Santa Fe Trail in the early 19th century. Pop.: 62 514 (1994 est.). **2** (*Spanish* 'santa 'fe). an inland port in E Argentina, on the Salado River: University of the Littoral (1920). Pop.: 406 388 (1991). ▶ **'Santa 'Fean** *adj, n*

Santa Fe Trail ('sæntə 'feɪ) *n* an important trade route in the western U.S. from about 1821 to 1880, linking Independence, Missouri to Santa Fe, New Mexico.

Santa Gertrudis ('sæntə gə'tru:dɪs) *n* one of a breed of large red beef cattle developed in Texas.

Santa Isabel (*Spanish* 'santa isa'βel) *n* the former name (until 1973) of **Malabo.**

santalaceous (ˌsæntə'leɪʃəs) *adj* of, relating to, or belonging to the *Santalaceae,* a family of semiparasitic plants of Australia and Malaysia including sandalwood and quandong. [C19: via New Latin from Late Greek *santalon* sandalwood]

Santa Maria[1] ('sæntə mə'ri:ə) *n* **the.** the flagship of Columbus on his first voyage to America (1492).

Santa Maria[2] *n* **1** (*Portuguese* 'səntə ma'ria) a city in S Brazil, in Rio Grande do Sul state. Pop.: 193 294 (1991). **2** (*Spanish* 'santa ma'ria) an active volcano in SW Guatemala. Height: 3768 m (12 362 ft.).

Santa Marta (*Spanish* 'santa 'marta) *n* a port in NW Colombia, on the Caribbean: the oldest city in Colombia, founded in 1525; terminus of the Atlantic railway from Bogotá (opened 1961). Pop.: 343 038 (1997 est.).

Santa Maura ('santa 'maura) *n* the Italian name for **Levkás.**

Santander (*Spanish* santan'dɛr) *n* a port and resort in N Spain, on an inlet of the Bay of Biscay: noted for its prehistoric collection from nearby caves; shipyards and an oil refinery. Pop.: 194 837 (1995 est.).

Santarém (*Portuguese* sənta'rɐ̃j) *n* a port in N Brazil, in Pará state where the Tapajós River flows into the Amazon. Pop.: 168 153 (1991).

Santa Rosa de Copán (*Spanish* 'santa 'rɔsa de ko'pan) *n* a village in W Honduras: noted for the ruined Mayan city of Copán, which lies to the west.

Santayana (ˌsæntɪ'ænə) *n* **George.** 1863–1952, U.S. philosopher, poet, and critic, born in Spain. His works include *The Life of Reason* (1905–06) and *The Realms of Being* (1927–40).

Santee (sæn'ti:) *n* a river in SE central South Carolina, formed by the union of the Congaree and Wateree Rivers: flows southeast to the Atlantic; part of the **Santee-Wateree-Catawba River System,** an inland waterway 866 km (538 miles) long. Length: 230 km (143 miles).

Santer ('sæntə) *n* **Jacques.** born 1937, Luxembourg politician: prime minister of Luxembourg (1984–95); president of the European Commission (1994–99).

Santeria (ˌsæntə'rɪə) *n* a Caribbean religion composed of elements from both traditional African religion and Roman Catholicism. [American Spanish, literally: holiness]

Santiago (ˌsæntɪ'ɑ:gəʊ; *Spanish* san'tjaɣo) *n* **1** the capital of Chile, at the foot of the Andes: commercial and industrial centre; two universities. Pop.: 5 076 808 (1995 est.). Official name: **Santiago de Chile** (de 'tʃile). **2** a city in the N Dominican Republic. Pop.: 375 000 (1991 est.). Official name: **Santiago de los Caballeros** (de los kaβa'ʎeros).

Santiago de Compostela (*Spanish* de kɔmpɔs'tela) *n* a city in NW Spain: place of pilgrimage since the 9th century and the most visited (after Jerusalem and Rome) in the Middle Ages; cathedral built over the tomb of the apostle St. James. Pop.: 87 472 (1991). Latin name: **Campus Stellae** ('kæmpəs 'stɛli:).

Santiago de Cuba (*Spanish* de 'kuβa) *n* a port in SE Cuba, on **Santiago Bay** (a large inlet of the Caribbean): capital of Cuba until 1589; university (1947); industrial centre. Pop.: 440 084 (1994 est.).

Santiago del Estero (*Spanish* del es'tero) *n* a city in N Argentina: the oldest continuous settlement in Argentina, founded in 1553 by Spaniards from Peru. Pop.: 263 471 (1991).

Santo Domingo ('sæntəʊ də'mɪŋgəʊ; *Spanish* 'santo ðo'miŋgo) *n* **1** the capital and chief port of the Dominican Republic, on the S coast: the oldest continuous European settlement in the Americas, founded in 1496; university (1538). Pop. (capital district): 2 138 262 (1993). Former name (1936–61): **Ciudad Trujillo. 2** the former name (until 1844) of the **Dominican Republic. 3** another name (esp. in colonial times) for **Hispaniola.**

santolina (ˌsæntə'li:nə) *n* any plant of the evergreen Mediterranean genus *Santolina,* esp. *S. chamaecyparissus,* grown for its silvery-grey felted foliage: family *Compositae.* [New Latin, altered from SANTONICA]

santonica (sæn'tɒnɪkə) *n* **1** an oriental wormwood plant, *Artemisia cina* (or *maritima*). **2** the dried flower heads of this plant, formerly used as a vermifuge. ◆ Also called: **wormseed.** [C17: New Latin, from Late Latin *herba santonica* herb of the *Santones* (probably wormwood), from Latin *Santonī* a people of Aquitania]

santonin ('sæntənɪn) *n* a white crystalline soluble substance extracted from the dried flower heads of santonica and used in medicine as an anthelmintic. Formula: $C_{15}H_{18}O_3$. [C19: from SANTONICA + -IN]

Santos (*Portuguese* 'səntuʃ) *n* a port in S Brazil, in São Paulo state: the world's leading coffee port. Pop.: 415 554 (1991).

Santos-Dumont (*French* sɑ̃todymɔ̃) *n* **Alberto** (albɛrto). 1873–1932, Brazilian aeronaut, living in France. He constructed dirigibles and aircraft, including a monoplane (1909).

São Francisco (*Portuguese* sɐ̃u frɐ̃'sisku) *n* a river in E Brazil, rising in SW Minas Gerais state and flowing northeast, then southeast to the Atlantic northeast of Aracajú. Length: 3200 km (1990 miles).

São Luís (*Portuguese* sɐ̃u 'lwis) *or* **São Luíz** ('lwiʃ) *n* a port in NE Brazil, capital of Maranhão state, on the W coast of São Luís Island: founded in 1612 by the French and taken by the Portuguese in 1615. Pop.: 164 334 (1991).

São Miguel (*Portuguese* sɐ̃u mi'ɣɛl) *n* an island in the E Azores: the largest of the group. Pop.: 126 388 (1991 est.). Area: 854 sq. km (333 sq. miles).

Saône (*French* son) *n* a river in E France, rising in Lorraine and flowing generally south to join the Rhône at Lyon, as its chief tributary: canalized for 375 km (233 miles) above Lyon; linked by canals with the Rhine, Marne, Seine, and Loire Rivers. Length: 480 km (298 miles).

Saône-et-Loire (*French* sonelwar) *n* a department of central France, in Burgundy region. Capital: Mâcon. Pop.: 554 800 (1995). Area: 8627 sq. km (3365 sq. miles).

São Paulo (*Portuguese* sɐ̃um 'paulu) *n* **1** a state of SE Brazil: consists chiefly of tableland draining west into the Paraná River. Capital: São Paulo. Pop.: 33 699 600 (1995 est.). Area: 247 239 sq. km (95 459 sq. miles). **2** a city in S Brazil, capital of São Paulo state: the largest city and industrial centre in Brazil, with one of the busiest airports in the world; three universities; rapidly expanding population. Pop.: 25 000 (1874); 2 017 025 (1950); 9 393 753 (1991).

Saorstat Eireann ('sɛəstɑ:t 'ɛərən) *n* the Gaelic name for the **Irish Free State.**

São Salvador (*Portuguese* sɐ̃u salva'dor) *n* short for **São Salvador da Bahia de Todos os Santos,** the official name for **Salvador.**

São Tomé e Principe (*Portuguese* sɐ̃un tu'mɛ 'ɛ: 'prĩsipə) *n* a republic in the Gulf of Guinea, off the W coast of Africa, on the Equator: consists of the islands of Principe and São Tomé; colonized by the Portuguese in the late 15th century; became independent in 1975. Official language: Portuguese. Religion: Roman Catholic majority. Currency: dobra. Capital: São Tomé. Pop.: 136 000 (1998 est.). Area: 1001 sq. km (386 sq. miles).

sap[1] (sæp) *n* **1** a solution of mineral salts, sugars, etc., that circulates in a plant. **2** any vital body fluid. **3** energy; vigour. **4** *Slang.* a gullible or foolish person. **5** another name for **sapwood.** ◆ *vb* **saps, sapping, sapped.** (*tr*) **6** to drain of sap. [Old English *sæp;* related to Old High German *sapf,* German *Saft* juice, Middle Low German *sapp,* Sanskrit *sabar* milk juice] ▶ **'sapless** *adj*

sap[2] (sæp) *n* **1** a deep and narrow trench used to approach or undermine an enemy position, esp. in siege warfare. ◆ *vb* **saps, sapping, sapped. 2** to undermine (a fortification, etc.) by digging saps. **3** (*tr*) to weaken. [C16 *zappe,* from Italian *zappa* spade, of uncertain origin; perhaps from Old Italian (dialect) *zappo* a goat]

sapajou ('sæpəˌdʒu:) *n* another name for **capuchin** (monkey). [C17: from French, of Tupi origin]

sapanwood ('sæpənˌwʊd) *n* a variant spelling of **sappanwood.**

sapele (sə'pi:lɪ) *n* **1** any of several W African meliaceous trees of the genus *Entandrophragma,* esp. *E. cylindricum,* yielding a hard timber resembling mahogany. **2** the timber obtained from such a tree, used to make furniture. [C20: West African name]

Saphar (sə'fɑ:) *n* a variant spelling of **Safar.**

saphead[1] ('sæpˌhɛd) *n Slang.* a simpleton, idiot, or fool. ▶ **'sapˌheaded** *adj*

saphead[2] ('sæpˌhɛd) *n Military.* the end of a sap nearest to the enemy.

saphena (sə'fi:nə) *n, pl* **-nae** (-ni:). *Anatomy.* either of two large superficial veins of the legs. [C14: via Medieval Latin from Arabic *ṣāfin*] ▶ **sa'phenous** *adj*

sapid ('sæpɪd) *adj* **1** having a pleasant taste. **2** agreeable or engaging. [C17: from Latin *sapidus,* from *sapere* to taste] ▶ **sapidity** (sə'pɪdɪtɪ) *or* **'sapidness** *n*

sapient ('seɪpɪənt) *adj Often used ironically.* wise or sagacious. [C15: from Latin *sapere* to taste] ▶ **'sapience** *n* ▶ **'sapiently** *adv*

sapiential (ˌseɪpɪ'ɛnʃəl, ˌsæpɪ-) *adj* showing, having, or providing wisdom. ▶ **ˌsapi'entially** *adv*

sapindaceous (ˌsæpɪn'deɪʃəs) *adj* of, relating to, or belonging to the *Sapindaceae,* a tropical and subtropical family of trees, shrubs, and lianas including the soapberry, litchi, and supplejack. [C19: via New Latin from Latin *sāpō* soap + *Indus* Indian]

Sapir (səˈpɪə, ˈseɪ,pɪə) *n* **Edward.** 1884–1939, U.S. anthropologist and linguist, noted for his study of the ethnology and languages of North American Indians.

Sapir-Whorf hypothesis *n* the theory that human languages determine the structure of the real world as perceived by human beings, rather than vice versa, and that this structure is different and incommensurable from one language to another. [named after E. SAPIR and B. L. WHORF]

sapling (ˈsæplɪŋ) *n* **1** a young tree. **2** *Literary.* a youth.

sapodilla (,sæpəˈdɪlə) *n* **1** a large tropical American evergreen tree, *Achras zapota,* the latex of which yields chicle. **2** Also called: **sapodilla plum.** the edible brown rough-skinned fruit of this tree, which has a sweet yellowish pulp. ◆ Also called: **naseberry, sapota.** [C17: from Spanish *zapotillo,* diminutive of *zapote* sapodilla fruit, from Nahuatl *tsapotl*]

saponaceous (,sæpəʊˈneɪʃəs) *adj* resembling soap; soapy. [C18: from New Latin *sāpōnāceus,* from Latin *sāpō* SOAP] ▸ **,sapoˈnaceousness** *n*

saponaria (,sæpəʊˈnɛərɪə) *n* See **soapwort.** [New Latin, from Late Latin *saponarius* soapy]

saponify (səˈpɒnɪ,faɪ) *vb* **-fies, -fying, -fied.** *Chem.* **1** to undergo or cause to undergo a process in which a fat is converted into a soap by treatment with alkali. **2** to undergo or cause to undergo a reaction in which an ester is hydrolysed to an acid and an alcohol as a result of treatment with an alkali. [C19: from French *saponifier,* from Latin *sāpō* SOAP] ▸ **saˈponi,fiable** *adj* ▸ **saˈponi,fier** *n* ▸ **sa,ponifiˈcation** *n*

saponin (ˈsæpənɪn) *n* any of a group of plant glycosides with a steroid structure that foam when shaken and are used in detergents. [C19: from French *saponine,* from Latin *sāpō* SOAP]

saponite (ˈsæpə,naɪt) *n* a clay mineral consisting of hydrated magnesium aluminium silicate and occurring in metamorphic rocks such as serpentine. [C19: from Swedish *saponit* (a rendering of German *Seifenstein* soapstone), from Latin *sāpō* SOAP]

sapor (ˈseɪpɔː, -pə) *n Rare.* the quality in a substance that is perceived by the sense of taste; flavour. [C15: from Latin: SAVOUR] ▸ **,sapoˈrific** *or* **ˈsaporous** *adj*

sapota (səˈpəʊtə) *n* **1** (in tropical America) any of various different fruits. **2** another name for **sapodilla.** [C16: from Spanish *zapote,* from Nahuatl *tsapotl;* see SAPODILLA]

sapotaceous (,sæpəˈteɪʃəs) *adj* of, relating to, or belonging to the *Sapotaceae,* a family of leathery-leaved tropical plants: includes the gutta-percha and balata trees, sapodilla, and shea. [C19: from New Latin *sapota* SAPOTA]

sappanwood *or* **sapanwood** (ˈsæpən,wʊd) *n* **1** a small caesalpiniaceous tree, *Caesalpinia sappan,* of S Asia producing wood that yields a red dye. **2** the wood of this tree. [C16: *sapan,* via Dutch from Malay *sapang*]

sapper (ˈsæpə) *n* **1** a soldier who digs trenches. **2** (in the British Army) a private of the Royal Engineers.

Sapper (ˈsæpə) *n* real name *Herman Cyril McNeile.* 1888–1937, British novelist, author of the popular thriller *Bull-dog Drummond* (1920) and its sequels.

Sapphic (ˈsæfɪk) *adj* **1** *Prosody.* denoting a metre associated with Sappho, consisting generally of a trochaic pentameter line with a dactyl in the third foot. **2** of or relating to Sappho or her poetry. **3** lesbian. ◆ *n* **4** *Prosody.* a verse, line, or stanza written in the Sapphic form.

Sapphic ode *n* another term for **Horatian ode.**

Sapphira (sæˈfaɪrə) *n New Testament.* the wife of Ananias, who together with her husband was struck dead for fraudulently concealing their wealth from the Church (Acts 5).

sapphire (ˈsæfaɪə) *n* **1a** any precious corundum gemstone that is not red, esp. the highly valued transparent blue variety. A synthetic form is used in electronics and precision apparatus. Formula: Al_2O_3. **1b** (*as modifier*): *a sapphire ring.* **2a** the blue colour of sapphire. **2b** (*as adj*): *sapphire eyes.* [C13 *safir,* from Old French, from Latin *sapphīrus,* from Greek *sappheiros,* perhaps from Hebrew *sappīr,* ultimately perhaps from Sanskrit *śanipriya,* literally: beloved of the planet Saturn, from *śani* Saturn + *priya* beloved]

sapphirine (ˈsæfə,riːn, -rɪn) *n* **1** a rare blue or bluish-green mineral that consists of magnesium aluminium silicate in monoclinic crystalline form and occurs as small grains in some metamorphic rocks. **2** a blue variety of spinel. ◆ *adj* **3** relating to or resembling sapphire.

sapphism (ˈsæfɪzəm) *n* a less common word for **lesbianism.** [C19: after SAPPHO, who is believed to have been a lesbian]

Sappho (ˈsæfəʊ) *n* 6th century B.C., Greek lyric poetess of Lesbos.

Sapporo (ˈsɑːpəʊ,rəʊ) *n* a city in N Japan, on W Hokkaido: commercial centre; university (1918). Pop.: 1 756 968 (1995).

sappy (ˈsæpɪ) *adj* **-pier, -piest.** **1** (of plants) full of sap. **2** full of energy or vitality. **3** *Slang.* silly or fatuous. ▸ **ˈsappily** *adv* ▸ **ˈsappiness** *n*

sapraemia (sæˈpriːmɪə) *n Pathol.* blood poisoning caused by toxins of putrefactive bacteria. [C19: New Latin, from SAPRO- + -EMIA] ▸ **saˈpraemic** *adj*

sapro- *or before a vowel* **sapr-** *combining form.* indicating dead or decaying matter: *saprogenic; saprolite.* [from Greek *sapros* rotten]

saprobe (ˈsæprəʊb) *n* an organism, esp. a plant, that lives in stagnant or foul water. [C20: from Greek, from SAPRO- + *bios* life] ▸ **sapˈrobic** *adj*

saprobiont (,sæprəʊˈbaɪɒnt) *n* another name for **saprotroph.**

saprogenic (,sæprəʊˈdʒɛnɪk) *or* **saprogenous** (sæˈprɒdʒɪnəs) *adj* **1** producing or resulting from decay: *saprogenic bacteria.* **2** growing on decaying matter. ▸ **saprogenicity** (,sæprədʒəˈnɪsɪtɪ) *n*

saprolite (ˈsæprəʊlɪt) *n* a deposit of earth, clay, silt, etc., formed by decomposition of rocks that has remained in its original site. ▸ **,saproˈlitic** *adj*

sapropel (ˈsæprə,pɛl) *n* an unconsolidated sludge consisting of the decomposed remains of aquatic organisms, esp. algae, that accumulates at the bottoms of lakes and oceans. [C20: from SAPRO- + *-pel* from Greek *pēlos* mud] ▸ **,saproˈpelic** *adj*

saprophagous (sæˈprɒfəgəs) *adj* (of certain animals) feeding on dead or decaying organic matter.

saprophyte (ˈsæprəʊ,faɪt) *n* any plant that lives and feeds on dead organic matter; a saprotrophic plant. ▸ **saprophytic** (,sæprəʊˈfɪtɪk) *adj* ▸ **,saproˈphytically** *adv*

saprotroph (ˈsæprəʊ,trəʊf) *n* any organism, esp. a fungus or bacterium, that lives and feeds on dead organic matter. Also called: **saprobe, saprobiont.** ▸ **saprotrophic** (,sæprəʊˈtrəʊfɪk) *adj* ▸ **,saproˈtrophically** *adv*

saprozoic (,sæprəʊˈzəʊɪk) *adj* **1** (of animals or plants) feeding on dead organic matter. **2** of or relating to nutrition in which the nutrient substances are derived from dead organic matter.

sapsago (ˈsæpsə,gəʊ) *n* a hard greenish Swiss cheese made with sour skimmed milk and coloured and flavoured with clover. [C19: changed from German *Schabziger,* from *schaben* to grate + dialect *Ziger* a kind of cheese]

sapsucker (ˈsæp,sʌkə) *n* either of two North American woodpeckers, *Sphyrapicus varius* or *S. thyroideus,* that have white wing patches and feed on the sap from trees.

sapwood (ˈsæp,wʊd) *n* the soft wood, just beneath the bark in tree trunks, that consists of living tissue. Compare **heartwood.**

SAR *abbrev. for* Special Administrative Region (of China).

Sar. *abbrev. for* Sardinia(n).

sarabande *or* **saraband** (ˈsærə,bænd) *n* **1** a decorous 17th-century courtly dance. **2** *Music.* a piece of music composed for or in the rhythm of this dance, in slow triple time, often incorporated into the classical suite. [C17: from French, from Spanish *zarabanda,* of uncertain origin]

Saracen (ˈsærəsᵊn) *n* **1** *History.* a member of one of the nomadic Arabic tribes, esp. of the Syrian desert, that harassed the borders of the Roman Empire in that region. **2a** a Muslim, esp. one who opposed the crusades. **2b** (in later use) any Arab. ◆ *adj* **3** of or relating to Arabs of either of these periods, regions, or types. **4** designating, characterizing, or relating to Muslim art or architecture. [C13: from Old French *Sarrazin,* from Late Latin *Saracēnus,* from Late Greek *Sarakēnos,* perhaps from Arabic *sharq* sunrise, from *shāraqa* to rise] ▸ **Saracenic** (,særəˈsɛnɪk) *or* **,Saraˈcenical** *adj*

Saragossa (,særəˈgɒsə) *n* the English name for **Zaragoza.**

Sarah (ˈsɛərə) *n Old Testament.* the wife of Abraham and mother of Isaac (Genesis 17:15–22).

Sarajevo (*Serbo-Croat* ˈsarajɛvɔ) *or* **Serajevo** *n* the capital of Bosnia-Herzegovina: developed as a Turkish town in the 15th century; capital of the Turkish and Austro-Hungarian administrations in 1850 and 1878 respectively; scene of the assassination of Archduke Franz Ferdinand in 1914, precipitating World War I; besieged by Bosnian Serbs (1992–95). Pop.: 416 497 (1991).

saran (səˈræn) *n* any one of a class of thermoplastic resins based on vinylidene chloride, used in fibres, moulded articles, and coatings. [C20: after *Saran,* trademark coined by the Dow Chemical Co.]

Sarandon (ˈsærəndən) *n* **Susan Abigail.** born 1946, U.S. film actress: her films include *Thelma and Louise* (1991), *Lorenzo's Oil* (1992), *The Client* (1994), and *Dead Man Walking* (1996).

sarangi (sɑːˈrʌŋgɪ) *n Music.* a stringed instrument of India played with a bow. [Hindi]

Saransk (*Russian* saˈransk) *n* a city in W central Russia, capital of the Mordovian Republic: university (1957). Pop.: 320 000 (1995 est.).

Sarasvati (sʌˈrʌsvətɪ) *n Hinduism.* a goddess of learning and eloquence.

Saratov (*Russian* saˈratəf) *n* an industrial city in W Russia, on the River Volga: university (1919). Pop.: 895 000 (1995 est.).

Sarawak (səˈrɑːwək) *n* a state of Malaysia, on the NW coast of Borneo on the South China Sea: granted to Sir James Brooke by the Sultan of Brunei in 1841 as a reward for helping quell a revolt; mainly agricultural. Capital: Kuching. Pop.: 1 648 217 (1991). Area: about 121 400 sq. km (48 250 sq. miles).

sarcasm (ˈsɑːkæzəm) *n* **1** mocking, contemptuous, or ironic language intended to convey scorn or insult. **2** the use or tone of such language. [C16: from Late Latin *sarcasmus,* from Greek *sarkasmos,* from *sarkazein* to rend the flesh, from *sarx* flesh]

sarcastic (sɑːˈkæstɪk) *adj* **1** characterized by sarcasm. **2** given to the use of sarcasm. ▸ **sarˈcastically** *adv*

sarcenet *or* **sarsenet** (ˈsɑːsnɪt) *n* a fine soft silk fabric formerly from Italy and used for clothing, ribbons, etc. [C15: from Old French *sarzinet,* from *Sarrazin* SARACEN]

sarco- *or before a vowel* **sarc-** *combining form.* indicating flesh: *sarcoma.* [from Greek *sark-, sarx* flesh]

sarcocarp (ˈsɑːkəʊ,kɑːp) *n Botany.* **1** the fleshy mesocarp of such fruits as the peach or plum. **2** any fleshy fruit.

sarcoid (ˈsɑːkɔɪd) *adj* **1** of, relating to, or resembling flesh: *a sarcoid tumour.* ◆ *n* **2** a tumour resembling a sarcoma.

sarcolemma (,sɑːkəʊˈlɛmə) *n, pl* **-mas** *or* **-mata** (-mətə). the membrane covering a muscle fibre.

sarcoma (sɑːˈkəʊmə) *n, pl* **-mata** (-mətə) *or* **-mas.** *Pathol.* a usually malignant tumour arising from connective tissue. [C17: via New Latin from Greek *sarkōma* fleshy growth; see SARCO-, -OMA] ▸ **sarˈcoma,toid** *or* **sarˈcomatous** *adj*

sarcomatosis (sɑː,kəʊməˈtəʊsɪs) *n Pathol.* a condition characterized by the development of several sarcomas at various bodily sites. [C19: see SARCOMA, -OSIS]

sarcomere (ˈsɑːkəʊ,mɪə) *n* any of the units that together comprise striped muscle.

sarcophagus (sɑːˈkɒfəgəs) *n, pl* **-gi** (-,gaɪ) *or* **-guses.** a stone or marble coffin or tomb, esp. one bearing sculpture or inscriptions. [C17: via Latin from

Greek *sarkophagos* flesh-devouring; from the type of stone used, which was believed to destroy the flesh of corpses]

sarcoplasm ('sɑːkəʊˌplæzəm) *n* the cytoplasm of a muscle fibre. ▸ ˌ**sarcoˈplasmic** *adj*

sarcous ('sɑːkəs) *adj* (of tissue) muscular or fleshy. [C19: from Greek *sarx* flesh]

sard (sɑːd) *or* **sardius** ('sɑːdɪəs) *n* an orange, red, or brown variety of chalcedony, used as a gemstone. Formula: SiO_2. Also called: **sardine.** [C14: from Latin *sarda*, from Greek *sardios* stone from Sardis]

Sardanapalus (ˌsɑːdəˈnæpələs) *n* the Greek name of **Ashurbanipal.**

sardar *or* **sirdar** (səˈdɑː) *n* (in India) **1** a title used before the name of Sikh men. **2** a leader. [Hindi, from Persian]

Sardegna (sarˈdeɲɲa) *n* the Italian name for **Sardinia.**

sardine[1] (sɑːˈdiːn) *n, pl* **-dines** *or* **-dine. 1** any of various small marine food fishes of the herring family, esp. a young pilchard. See also **sild. 2 like sardines.** very closely crowded together. [C15: via Old French from Latin *sardīna*, diminutive of *sarda* a fish suitable for pickling]

sardine[2] ('sɑːdiːn, -dᵊn) *n* another name for **sard.** [C14: from Late Latin *sardinus*, from Greek *sardinos lithos* Sardian stone, from *Sardeis* Sardis]

Sardinia (sɑːˈdɪnɪə) *n* the second-largest island in the Mediterranean: forms, with offshore islands, an administrative region of Italy; ceded to Savoy by Austria in 1720 in exchange for Sicily and formed the Kingdom of Sardinia with Piedmont; became part of Italy in 1861. Capital: Cagliari. Pop.: 1 660 701 (1996 est.). Area: 24 089 sq. km (9301 sq. miles). Italian name: **Sardegna.**

Sardinian (sɑːˈdɪnɪən) *adj* **1** of or relating to Sardinia, its inhabitants, or their language. ♦ *n* **2** a native or inhabitant of Sardinia. **3** the spoken language of Sardinia, sometimes regarded as a dialect of Italian but containing many loan words from Spanish.

Sardis ('sɑːdɪs) *or* **Sardes** ('sɑːdiːz) *n* an ancient city of W Asia Minor: capital of Lydia.

sardius ('sɑːdɪəs) *n* **1** *Old Testament.* a precious stone, probably a ruby, set in the breastplate of the high priest. **2** another name for **sard.** [C14: via Late Latin from Greek *sardios*, from *Sardeis* Sardis]

sardonic (sɑːˈdɒnɪk) *adj* characterized by irony, mockery, or derision. [C17: from French *sardonique*, from Latin *sardonius*, from Greek *sardonios* derisive, literally: of Sardinia, alteration of Homeric *sardanios* scornful (laughter or smile)] ▸ **sarˈdonically** *adv* ▸ **sarˈdonicism** *n*

sardonyx ('sɑːdənɪks) *n* a variety of chalcedony with alternating reddish-brown and white parallel bands, used as a gemstone. Formula: SiO_2. [C14: via Latin from Greek *sardonux*, perhaps from *sardion* SARDINE[2] + *onux* nail]

Sardou (*French* sardu) *n* **Victorien** (viktɔrjɛ̃). 1831–1908, French dramatist. His plays include *Fédora* (1882) and *La Tosca* (1887), the source of Puccini's opera.

sargasso *or* **sargasso weed** (sɑːˈgæsəʊ) *n, pl* **-sos.** another name for **gulfweed.** [C16: from Portuguese *sargaço*, of unknown origin]

Sargasso Sea *n* a calm area of the N Atlantic, between the Caribbean and the Azores, where there is an abundance of floating seaweed of the genus *Sargassum.*

sargassum (sɑːˈgæsəm) *n* any floating brown seaweed of the genus *Sargassum*, such as gulfweed, of warm seas, having ribbon-like fronds containing air sacs. [C18: from New Latin; see SARGASSO]

sarge (sɑːdʒ) *n Informal.* sergeant: used esp. as a term of address.

Sargent ('sɑːdʒənt) *n* **1** Sir **(Harold) Malcolm (Watts).** 1895–1967, English conductor. **2 John Singer.** 1856–1925, U.S. painter, esp. of society portraits; in London from 1885.

Sargeson ('sɑːdʒəsᵊn) *n* **Frank.** 1903–82, New Zealand short-story writer and novelist. His work includes the short-story collection *That Summer and Other Stories* (1946) and the novel *I Saw in my Dream* (1949).

Sargodha (sɑːˈgəʊdə) *n* a city in NE Pakistan: grain market. Pop.: 294 000 (latest est.).

Sargon II ('sɑːgɒn) *n* died 705 B.C., king of Assyria (722–705). He developed a policy of transporting conquered peoples to distant parts of his empire.

Sargon of Akkad ('sɑːgɒn, 'ækæd) *n* 24th to 23rd century B.C., semilegendary Mesopotamian ruler whose empire extended from the Gulf to the Mediterranean.

sari *or* **saree** ('sɑːrɪ) *n, pl* **-ris** *or* **-rees.** the traditional dress of women of India, Pakistan, etc., consisting of a very long narrow piece of cloth elaborately swathed around the body. [C18: from Hindi *sārī*, from Sanskrit *śāṭī*]

sarin ('særɪn) *n* isopropyl methylphosphonofluoridate: used in chemical warfare as a lethal nerve gas producing asphyxia. Formula: $CH_3P(O)(F)OCH(CH_3)_2$. [C20: from German, of unknown origin]

sark (særk) *n Scot.* a shirt or (formerly) chemise. [Old English *serc*; related to Old Norse *serkr*]

Sark (sɑːk) *n* an island in the English Channel in the Channel Islands, consisting of **Great Sark** and **Little Sark**, connected by an isthmus: ruled by a hereditary seigneur or dame. Pop.: 550 (1986 est.). Area: 5 sq. km (2 sq. miles). French name: **Sercq.**

Sarka ('zɑːkə) *n* a variant spelling of **Zarqa.**

sarking ('sɑːkɪŋ, 'særkɪŋ) *n Scot., northern English, and N.Z.* a timber or felt cladding placed over the rafters of a roof before the tiles or slates are fixed in place. [C15: from verbal use of SARK]

sarky ('sɑːkɪ) *adj* **-kier, -kiest.** *Brit. informal.* sarcastic.

Sarmatia (sɑːˈmeɪʃɪə) *n* the ancient name of a region between the Volga and Vistula Rivers now covering parts of Poland, Belarus, and SW Russia. ▸ **Sarˈmatian** *n, adj* ▸ **Sarmatic** (sɑːˈmætɪk) *adj*

sarmentose (sɑːˈmɛntəʊs), **sarmentous** (sɑːˈmɛntəs), *or* **sarmentaceous** (ˌsɑːmənˈteɪʃəs) *adj* (of plants such as the strawberry) having stems in the form of runners. [C18: from Latin *sarmentōsus* full of twigs, from *sarmentum* brushwood, from *sarpere* to prune]

sarmie ('sɑːmɪ) *n S. African children's slang.* a sandwich. [C20: from Northern English SARNIE]

Sarnen (*German* 'zarnən) *n* a town in central Switzerland, capital of Obwalden demicanton: resort. Pop.: 7200 (1980).

Sarnia ('sɑːnɪə) *n* an inland port in S central Canada, in SW Ontario at the S end of Lake Huron: oil refineries. Pop.: 74 376 (1991).

sarnie ('sɑːnɪ) *n Brit. informal.* a sandwich. [C20: probably from Northern or dialect pronunciation of first syllable of *sandwich*]

sarod (sæˈrəʊd) *n* an Indian stringed musical instrument that may be played with a bow or plucked. [C19: from Hindi]

sarong (səˈrɒŋ) *n* **1** a draped skirtlike garment worn by men and women in the Malay Archipelago, Sri Lanka, the Pacific islands, etc. **2** a fashionable Western adaptation of this garment. [C19: from Malay, literally: sheath]

Saronic Gulf (səˈrɒnɪk) *n* an inlet of the Aegean on the SE coast of Greece. Length: about 80 km (50 miles). Width: about 48 km (30 miles). Also called: (Gulf of) **Aegina.**

saros ('seɪrɒs) *n* a cycle of about 18 years 11 days (6585.32 days) in which eclipses of the sun and moon occur in the same sequence and at the same intervals as in the previous such cycle. [C19: from Greek, from Babylonian *šāru* 3600 (years); modern astronomical use apparently based on mistaken interpretation of *šāru* as a period of 18½ years] ▸ **saronic** (səˈrɒnɪk) *adj*

Saros ('sɑːrɒs) *n* **Gulf of.** an inlet of the Aegean in NW Turkey, north of the Gallipoli Peninsula. Length: 59 km (37 miles). Width: 35 km (22 miles).

sarpanch (səˈpʌntʃ) *n* the head of a panchayat. [Urdu, from *sar* head + Sanskrit *panch* five; see PANCHAYAT]

Sarpedon (sɑːˈpiːdɒn) *n Greek myth.* a son of Zeus and Laodameia, or perhaps Europa, and king of Lycia. He was slain by Patroclus while fighting on behalf of the Trojans.

Sarpi (*Italian* 'sarpi) *n* **Paolo** ('paolo), real name *Pietro Soave Polano.* 1552–1623, Italian scholar, theologian, and patriot, who championed the Venetian republic in its dispute with Pope Paul V, arguing against papal absolutism and for the separation of church and state.

sarracenia (ˌsærəˈsiːnɪə) *n* any American pitcher plant of the genus *Sarracenia*, having single nodding flowers and leaves modified as pitchers that trap and digest insects: family *Sarraceniaceae.* [C18: New Latin, named after D. *Sarrazin*, 17th-century botanist of Quebec]

sarraceniaceous (ˌsærəˌsiːnɪˈeɪʃəs) *adj* of, relating to, or belonging to the *Sarraceniaceae*, an American family of pitcher plants.

Sarraute (*French* sarot) *n* **Nathalie** (natali). born 1900, French novelist, noted as an exponent of the anti-novel. Her novels include *Portrait of a Man Unknown* (1948), *Martereau* (1953), and *Ici* (1995).

Sarre (sar) *n* the French name for the **Saar.**

sarrusophone (səˈruːzəˌfəʊn) *n* a wind instrument resembling the oboe but made of brass. [C19: named after *Sarrus*, French bandmaster, who invented it (1856)]

sarsaparilla (ˌsɑːsəpəˈrɪlə, ˌsɑːspə-) *n* **1** any of various prickly climbing plants of the tropical American genus *Smilax* having large aromatic roots and heart-shaped leaves: family *Smilacaceae.* **2** the dried roots of any of these plants, formerly used as a medicine. **3** a nonalcoholic drink prepared from these roots. **4** any of various plants resembling true sarsaparilla, esp. the araliaceous plant *Aralia nudicaulis* (**wild sarsaparilla**), of North America. [C16: from Spanish *sarzaparrilla*, from *zarza* a bramble, (from Arabic *šaras*) + *-parrilla*, from Spanish *parra* a climbing plant]

sarsen ('sɑːsᵊn) *n* **1** *Geology.* a boulder of silicified sandstone, probably of Tertiary age, found in large numbers in S England. **2** such a stone used in a megalithic monument. Also called: **greywether.** [C17: probably a variant of SARACEN]

sarsenet ('sɑːsnɪt) *n* a variant spelling of **sarcenet.**

Sarthe (*French* sart) *n* a department of NW France, in Pays de la Loire region. Capital: Le Mans. Pop.: 521 600 (1995). Area: 6245 sq. km (2436 sq. miles).

Sarto (*Italian* 'sarto) *n* **Andrea del** (anˈdrεːa del). 1486–1531, Florentine painter. His works include *The Nativity of the Virgin* (1514) in the church of Sant' Annunziata, Florence.

sartor ('sɑːtə) *n* a humorous or literary word for **tailor.** [C17: from Latin: a patcher, from *sarcīre* to patch]

sartorial (sɑːˈtɔːrɪəl) *adj* **1** of or relating to a tailor or to tailoring. **2** *Anatomy.* of or relating to the sartorius. [C19: from Late Latin *sartōrius* from SARTOR] ▸ **sarˈtorially** *adv*

sartorius (sɑːˈtɔːrɪəs) *n, pl* **-torii** (-ˈtɔːrɪˌaɪ). *Anatomy.* a long ribbon-shaped muscle that aids in flexing the knee. [C18: New Latin, from *sartorius musculus*, literally: tailor's muscle, because it is used when one sits in the cross-legged position in which tailors traditionally sat while sewing]

Sartre (*French* sartrə) *n* **Jean-Paul** (ʒɑ̃pɔl). 1905–80, French philosopher, novelist, and dramatist; chief French exponent of atheistic existentialism. His works include the philosophical essay *Being and Nothingness* (1943), the novels *Nausea* (1938) and *Les Chemins de la liberté* (1945–49), a trilogy, and the plays *Les Mouches* (1943), *Huis clos* (1944), and *Les Mains sales* (1948).

Sarum ('sεərəm) *n* the ancient name of **Salisbury**[1] (sense 3).

Sarum use *n* the distinctive local rite or system of rites used at Salisbury cathedral in late medieval times.

Sarvodaya (səˈvəʊdəjə) *n* (in India) economic and social development and improvement of a community as a whole. [Hindi, from *sarva* all + *udaya* rise]

SAS *abbrev. for* Special Air Service.

Sasebo ('sɑːsəˌbəʊ) *n* a port in SW Japan, on NW Kyushu on Omura Bay: naval base. Pop.: 244 879 (1995).

sash[1] (sæʃ) *n* a long piece of ribbon, silk, etc., worn around the waist like a belt or over one shoulder, as a symbol of rank. [C16: from Arabic *shāsh* muslin]

sash[2] (sæʃ) *n* **1** a frame that contains the panes of a window or door. ◆ *vb* (*tr*) **2** to furnish with a sash, sashes, or sash windows. [C17: originally plural *sashes,* variant of *shashes,* from CHASSIS]

sashay (sæ'ʃeɪ) *vb* (*intr*) *Informal.* **1** to move, walk, or glide along casually. **2** to move or walk in a showy way; parade. [C19: from an alteration of *chassé,* a gliding dance step]

sash cord *n* a strong cord connecting a sash weight to a sliding sash.

sashimi ('sæʃɪmɪ) *n* a Japanese dish of thin fillets of raw fish. [C19: from Japanese *sashi* pierce + *mi* flesh]

sash saw *n* a small tenon saw used for cutting sashes.

sash weight *n* a weight used to counterbalance the weight of a sliding sash in a sash window and thus hold it in position at any height.

sash window *n* a window consisting of two sashes placed one above the other so that one or each can be slid over the other to open the window.

sasin ('sæsɪn) *n* another name for the **blackbuck.** [C19: of unknown origin]

sasine ('sesɪn, 'seɪ-) *n Scots Law.* the granting of legal possession of feudal property. [C17: Scots variant of SEISIN]

Sask. *abbrev. for* Saskatchewan.

Saskatchewan (sæs'kætʃɪwən) *n* **1** a province of W Canada: consists of Canadian Shield in the north and open prairie in the south; economy based chiefly on agriculture and mineral resources. Capital: Regina. Pop.: 1 023 500 (1997 est.). Area: 651 900 sq. km (251 700 sq. miles). Abbrevs.: **Sask., SK. 2** a river in W Canada, formed by the confluence of the North and South Saskatchewan Rivers: flows east to Lake Winnipeg. Length: 596 km (370 miles). ► **Saskatchewanian** (sæs,kætʃə'wɒnɪən) *n, adj*

saskatoon (,sæskə'tu:n) *n* a species of serviceberry, *Amelanchier alnifolia,* of W Canada: noted for its succulent purplish berries. [from Cree *misaskwatomin,* from *misaskwat* tree of many branches + *min* fruit]

Saskatoon (,sæskə'tu:n) *n* a city in W Canada, in S Saskatchewan on the South Saskatchewan River: oil refining; university (1907). Pop.: 186 058 (1991).

sasquatch ('sæs,kwætʃ) *n* (in Canadian folklore) in British Columbia, a hairy beast or manlike monster said to leave huge footprints. [from Salish]

sass (sæs) *U.S. and Canadian informal.* ◆ *n* **1** insolent or impudent talk or behaviour. ◆ *vb* (*intr*) **2** to talk or answer back in such a way. [C20: back formation from SASSY[1]]

sassaby ('sæsəbɪ) *n, pl* **-bies.** an African antelope, *Damaliscus lunatus,* of grasslands and semideserts, having angular curved horns and an elongated muzzle: thought to be the swiftest hoofed mammal. [C19: from Bantu *tshêsêbê*]

sassafras ('sæsə,fræs) *n* **1** an aromatic deciduous lauraceous tree, *Sassafras albidum,* of North America, having three-lobed leaves and dark blue fruits. **2** the aromatic dried root bark of this tree, used as a flavouring, and yielding sassafras oil. **3** *Austral.* any of several unrelated trees having a similar fragrant bark. [C16: from Spanish *sasafras,* of uncertain origin]

sassafras oil *n* a clear volatile oil that is extracted from the root of the sassafras tree and contains camphor, pinene, and safrole.

Sassanid ('sæsənɪd) *n, pl* **Sassanids** *or* **Sassanidae** (sæ'sænɪ,di:). any member of the native dynasty that built and ruled an empire in Persia from 224 to 636 A.D. ► **Sa'ssanian** *adj*

Sassari (*Italian* 'sassari) *n* a city in NW Sardinia, Italy: the second-largest city on the island; university (1565). Pop.: 121 639 (1996 est.).

Sassenach ('sæsə,næk; *Scot.* -næx) *n Scot. and occasionally Irish.* an English person or a Lowland Scot. [C18: from Scot. Gaelic *Sasunnach,* Irish *Sasanach,* from Late Latin *saxonēs* Saxons]

Sassoon (sæ'su:n) *n* **1 Siegfried** (**Lorraine**). 1886–1967, British poet and novelist, best known for his poems of the horrors of war collected in *Counterattack* (1918) and *Satirical Poems* (1926). He also wrote a semi-fictitious autobiographical trilogy *The Memoirs of George Sherston* (1928–36). **2 Vidal.** born 1928, British hair stylist: founder and chairman of Vidal Sassoon Inc.

sassy[1] ('sæsɪ) *adj* **-sier, -siest.** *U.S. informal.* insolent, impertinent. [C19: variant of SAUCY] ► **'sassily** *adv* ► **'sassiness** *n*

sassy[2] ('sæsɪ), **sasswood** ('sæs,wʊd), *or* **sassy wood** *n* **1** a W African leguminous tree, *Erythrophleum guineense,* with poisonous bark (**sassy bark**) and hard strong wood. **2** the bark or wood of this tree or the alkaloid derived from them, which is sometimes used in medicine. [C19: probably from a language of the Kwa family: compare Twi *sese* plane tree, Ewe *sesewu* a kind of timber tree]

sastra ('ʃɑ:strə) *n* a variant spelling of **shastra.**

sastruga (sə'stru:gə, sæ-) *or* **zastruga** *n* one of a series of ridges on snow-covered plains, caused by the action of wind laden with ice particles. [from Russian *zastruga* groove, from *za* by + *struga* deep place]

sat (sæt) *vb* the past tense and past participle of **sit.**

SAT *abbrev. for:* **1** (in the U.S.) Scholastic Aptitude Test. **2** South Australian Time.

Sat. *abbrev. for:* **1** Saturday. **2** Saturn.

Satan ('seɪtᵊn) *n* the devil, adversary of God, and tempter of mankind: sometimes identified with Lucifer (Luke 4:5–8). [Old English, from Late Latin, from Greek, from Hebrew: plotter, from *sātan* to plot against]

satang (sæ'tæŋ) *n, pl* **-tang.** a monetary unit of Thailand worth one hundredth of a baht. [from Thai *satān*]

satanic (sə'tænɪk) *or* (*now rare*) **satanical** *adj* **1** of or relating to Satan. **2** supremely evil or wicked; diabolic. ► **sa'tanically** *adv* ► **sa'tanicalness** *n*

Satanism ('seɪtᵊ,nɪzəm) *n* **1** the worship of Satan. **2** a form of such worship which includes blasphemous or obscene parodies of Christian prayers, etc. **3** a satanic disposition or satanic practices. ► **'Satanist** *n, adj*

satay, satai, *or* **saté** ('sæteɪ) *n* barbecued spiced meat cooked on skewers usually made from the stems of coconut leaves. [from Malay]

SATB *abbrev. for* soprano, alto, tenor, bass: a combination of voices in choral music.

satchel ('sætʃəl) *n* a rectangular bag, usually made of leather or cloth and provided with a shoulder strap, used for carrying books, esp. school books. [C14: from Old French *sachel* a little bag, from Late Latin *saccellus,* from Latin *saccus* SACK[1]] ► **'satchelled** *adj*

sate[1] (seɪt) *vb* (*tr*) **1** to satisfy (a desire or appetite) fully. **2** to supply beyond capacity or desire. [Old English *sadian;* related to Old High German *satōn;* see SAD, SATIATE]

sate[2] (sæt, seɪt) *vb Archaic.* a past tense and past participle of **sit.**

sateen (sæ'ti:n) *n* a glossy linen or cotton fabric, woven in such a way that it resembles satin. [C19: changed from SATIN, on the model of VELVETEEN]

satellite ('sætᵊ,laɪt) *n* **1** a celestial body orbiting around a planet or star: *the earth is a satellite of the sun.* **2** Also called: **artificial satellite.** a man-made device orbiting around the earth, moon, or another planet transmitting to earth scientific information or used for communication. See also **communications satellite. 3** a person, esp. one who is obsequious, who follows or serves another. **4** a country or political unit under the domination of a foreign power. **5** a subordinate area or community that is dependent upon a larger adjacent town or city. **6** (*modifier*) subordinate to or dependent upon another: *a satellite nation.* **7** (*modifier*) of, used in, or relating to the transmission of television signals from a satellite to the house: *a satellite dish aerial.* ◆ *vb* **8** (*tr*) to transmit by communications satellite. [C16: from Latin *satelles* an attendant, probably of Etruscan origin]

satellite broadcasting *n* the transmission of television or radio programmes from an artificial satellite at a power suitable for direct reception in the home.

satellite dish aerial *n* a parabolic aerial for reception from or transmission to an artificial satellite. Often shortened to **dish aerial** or **dish.**

satellitium (,sætᵊ'lɪtɪəm, -'lɪʃɪəm) *n Astrology.* a group of three or more planets lying in one sign of the zodiac. [C17: from Latin, literally: bodyguard, retinue, from *satelles* an attendant. See SATELLITE]

satem ('sɑ:təm, 'seɪ-) *adj* denoting or belonging to the group of Indo-European languages in which original velar stops became palatalized (k > s or ʃ). These languages belong to the Indic, Iranian, Armenian, Slavonic, Baltic, and Albanian branches and are traditionally regarded as the E group. Compare **centum.** [from Avestan *satəm* hundred; chosen to exemplify the variation of initial *s* with initial *k* (as in *centum*) in Indo-European languages]

satiable ('seɪʃɪəbᵊl, 'seɪʃə-) *adj* capable of being satiated. ► **,satia'bility** *n* ► **'satiably** *adv*

satiate ('seɪʃɪ,eɪt) *vb* (*tr*) **1** to fill or supply beyond capacity or desire, often arousing weariness. **2** to supply to satisfaction or capacity. [C16: from Latin *satiāre* to satisfy, from *satis* enough] ► **,sati'ation** *n*

Saticon ('sætɪ,kɒn) *n Trademark.* a high-resolution television camera tube used when high definition is required. [C20: from S(ELENIUM) + A(RSENIC) + T(ELLURIUM) (used in the tube screen) + ICON(OSCOPE)]

Satie (*French* sati) *n* **Erik** (**Alfred Leslie**) (erik). 1866–1925, French composer, noted for his eccentricity, experimentalism, and his direct and economical style. His music, including numerous piano pieces and several ballets, exercised a profound influence upon other composers, such as Debussy and Ravel.

satiety (sə'taɪɪtɪ) *n* the state of being satiated. [C16: from Latin *satietās,* from *satis* enough]

satin ('sætɪn) *n* **1** a fabric of silk, rayon, etc., closely woven to show much of the warp, giving a smooth glossy appearance. **2** (*modifier*) of or like satin in texture: *a satin finish.* [C14: via Old French from Arabic *zaitūnī* of *Zaytūn,* Arabic rendering of Chinese *Tseutung* (now *Tsinkiang*), port in southern China from which the cloth was probably first exported] ► **'satin-,like** *adj* ► **'satiny** *adj*

satinet *or* **satinette** (,sætɪ'net) *n* a thin or imitation satin. [C18: from French: small satin]

satinflower ('sætɪn,flaʊə) *n* another name for **greater stitchwort** (see **stitchwort**).

satinpod ('sætɪn,pɒd) *n* another name for **honesty** (the plant).

satin stitch *n* an embroidery stitch consisting of rows of flat stitches placed close together. [C17: so called from the satin-like appearance of embroidery using this stitch]

satin walnut *n* the brown heartwood of the sweet gum tree, used for furniture, fittings, and panelling.

satinwood ('sætɪn,wʊd) *n* **1** a tree, *Chloroxylon swietenia,* that occurs in the East Indies and has hard wood with a satiny texture: family *Flindersiaceae.* **2** the wood of this tree, used in veneering, cabinetwork, marquetry, etc. **3 West Indian satinwood.** another name for **yellowwood** (sense 2).

satire ('sætaɪə) *n* **1** a novel, play, entertainment, etc., in which topical issues, folly, or evil are held up to scorn by means of ridicule and irony. **2** the genre constituted by such works. **3** the use of ridicule, irony, etc., to create such an effect. [C16: from Latin *satira* a mixture, from *satur* sated, from *satis* enough]

satirical (sə'tɪrɪkᵊl) *or* **satiric** *adj* **1** of, relating to, or containing satire. **2** given to the use of satire. ► **sa'tirically** *adv* ► **sa'tiricalness** *n*

satirist ('sætərɪst) *n* **1** a person who writes satire. **2** a person given to the use of satire.

satirize *or* **satirise** ('sætə,raɪz) *vb* to deride (a person or thing) by means of satire. ► **,satiri'zation** *or* **,satiri'sation** *n* ► **'sati,rizer** *or* **'sati,riser** *n*

satisfaction (,sætɪs'fækʃən) *n* **1** the act of satisfying or state of being satisfied. **2** the fulfilment of a desire. **3** the pleasure obtained from such fulfilment. **4** a source of fulfilment. **5** reparation or compensation for a wrong done or received. **6** *R.C. Church, Church of England.* the performance by a repentant sinner of a penance. 7 *Christianity.* the atonement for sin by the death of Christ. [C15: via French from Latin *satisfactionem,* from *satisfacere* to SATISFY]

satisfactory (ˌsætɪsˈfæktərɪ, -trɪ) *adj* 1 adequate or suitable; acceptable: *a satisfactory answer.* 2 giving satisfaction. 3 constituting or involving atonement, recompense, or expiation for sin. ▸ **ˌsatisˈfactorily** *adv* ▸ **ˌsatisˈfactoriness** *n*

satisfice (ˈsætɪsˌfaɪs) *vb* 1 (*intr*) to act in such a way as to satisfy the minimum requirements for achieving a particular result. 2 (*tr*) *Obsolete.* to satisfy. [C16: altered from SATISFY] ▸ **ˈsatisˌficer** *n*

satisficing behaviour (ˈsætɪsˌfaɪsɪŋ) *n Economics.* the form of behaviour demonstrated by firms who seek satisfactory profits and satisfactory growth rather than maximum profits.

satisfy (ˈsætɪsˌfaɪ) *vb* **-fies, -fying, -fied.** (*mainly tr*) 1 (*also intr*) to fulfil the desires or needs of (a person). 2 to provide amply for (a need or desire). 3 to relieve of doubt; convince. 4 to dispel (a doubt). 5 to make reparation to or for. 6 to discharge or pay off (a debt) to (a creditor). 7 to fulfil the requirements of; comply with: *you must satisfy the terms of your lease.* 8 *Maths, logic.* to fulfil the conditions of (a theorem, assumption, etc.); to yield a truth by substitution of the given value: $x = 3$ *satisfies* $x^2 - 4x + 3 = 0$. [C15: from Old French *satisfier,* from Latin *satisfacere,* from *satis* enough + *facere* to make, do] ▸ **ˈsatisˌfiable** *adj* ▸ **ˈsatisˌfier** *n* ▸ **ˈsatisˌfying** *adj* ▸ **ˈsatisˌfyingly** *adv*

Sato Eisaku (ˈsɑːtəʊ eɪsaku) *n* 1901–75, Japanese statesman: prime minister (1964–72). During his term of office Japan became a major economic power. He shared the Nobel peace prize (1974) for opposing the proliferation of nuclear weapons.

satori (səˈtɔːrɪ) *n Zen Buddhism.* the state of sudden indescribable intuitive enlightenment. [from Japanese]

satrap (ˈsætrəp) *n* 1 (in ancient Persia) a provincial governor. 2 a subordinate ruler, esp. a despotic one. [C14: from Latin *satrapa,* from Greek *satrapēs,* from Old Persian *khshathrapāvan,* literally: protector of the land]

satrapy (ˈsætrəpɪ) *n, pl* **-trapies.** the province, office, or period of rule of a satrap.

SATs (sæts) *pl n Brit. education. acronym for* standard assessment tasks.

satsuma (sætˈsuːmə) *n* 1 a small citrus tree, *Citrus nobilis* var. *unshiu,* cultivated, esp. in Japan, for its edible fruit. 2 the fruit of this tree, which has a loose rind and easily separable segments. [C19: originally from the province of Satsuma, Japan]

Satsuma (ˈsætsʊˌmɑː) *n* a former province of SW Japan, on S Kyushu: famous for its porcelain.

Satsuma ware *n* 1 simple pottery made in Satsuma, Japan, from the late 16th century. 2 ornamental glazed porcelain ware made in Satsuma, Japan, from the late 18th century.

saturable (ˈsætʃərəbᵊl) *adj Chem.* capable of being saturated. ▸ **ˌsaturaˈbility** *n*

saturant (ˈsætʃərənt) *Chem.* ◆ *n* 1 the substance that causes a solution, etc., to be saturated. ◆ *adj* 2 (of a substance) causing saturation. [C18: from Latin *saturāns*]

saturate *vb* (ˈsætʃəˌreɪt). 1 to fill, soak, or imbue totally. 2 to make (a chemical compound, vapour, solution, magnetic material, etc.) saturated or (of a compound, vapour, etc.) to become saturated. 3 (*tr*) *Military.* to bomb or shell heavily. ◆ *adj* (ˈsætʃərɪt, -ˌreɪt). 4 a less common word for **saturated.** [C16: from Latin *saturāre,* from *satur* sated, from *satis* enough] ▸ **ˌsatuˈrater** *or* **ˌsatuˈrator** *n*

saturated (ˈsætʃəˌreɪtɪd) *adj* 1 (of a solution or solvent) containing the maximum amount of solute that can normally be dissolved at a given temperature and pressure. See also **supersaturated.** 2 (of a colour) having a large degree of saturation. 3 (of a chemical compound) 3a containing no multiple bonds and thus being incapable of undergoing additional reactions: *a saturated hydrocarbon.* 3b containing no unpaired valence electrons. 4 (of a fat, esp. an animal fat) containing a high proportion of fatty acids having single bonds. See also **polyunsaturated, unsaturated.** 5 (of a vapour) containing the equilibrium amount of gaseous material at a given temperature and pressure. See also **supersaturated.** 6 (of a magnetic material) fully magnetized. 7 extremely wet; soaked.

saturation (ˌsætʃəˈreɪʃən) *n* 1 the act of saturating or the state of being saturated. 2 *Chem.* the state of a chemical compound, solution, or vapour when it is saturated. 3 *Meteorol.* the state of the atmosphere when it can hold no more water vapour at its particular temperature and pressure, the relative humidity then being 100 per cent. 4 the attribute of a colour that enables an observer to judge its proportion of pure chromatic colour. See also **colour.** 5 *Physics.* the state of a ferromagnetic material in which it is fully magnetized. The magnetic domains are then all fully aligned. 6 *Electronics.* the state of a valve or semiconductor device that is carrying the maximum current of which it is capable and is therefore unresponsive to further increases of input signal. 7 the level beyond which demand for a product or service is not expected to increase. ◆ *modifier* 8 denoting the maximum possible intensity of coverage of an area: *saturation bombing; a saturation release of a film.*

saturation diving *n* a method of diving in which divers live in a complex of decompression chambers for up to 28 days, going to work via a diving bell, and only decompressing at the end of the period. Helium is substituted for nitrogen in the air supply to avoid the narcotic effects of nitrogen.

saturation point *n* 1 the point at which no more (people, things, ideas, etc.) can be absorbed, accommodated, used, etc. 2 *Chem.* the point at which no more solute can be dissolved in a solution or gaseous material absorbed in a vapour.

Saturday (ˈsætədɪ) *n* the seventh and last day of the week: the Jewish Sabbath. [Old English *sæternes dæg,* translation of Latin *Sāturnī diēs* day of Saturn; compare Middle Dutch *saterdach,* Dutch *zaterdag*]

Saturn[1] (ˈsætɜːn) *n* the Roman god of agriculture and vegetation. Greek counterpart: **Cronus.**

Saturn[2] (ˈsætɜːn) *n* 1 one of the **giant planets,** the sixth planet from the sun, around which revolve planar concentric rings (**Saturn's rings**) consisting of small frozen particles. The planet has at least 18 satellites. Mean distance from sun: 1425 million km; period of revolution around sun: 29.46 years; period of axial rotation: 10.23 hours; diameter and mass: 9.36 and 95.14 times that of the earth, respectively. See also **Titan**[2]. 2 a large U.S. rocket used for launching various objects, such as a spaceprobe or an Apollo spacecraft, into space. 3 the alchemical name for **lead**[2]. ▸ **Saturnian** (sæˈtɜːnɪən) *adj*

Saturnalia (ˌsætəˈneɪlɪə) *n, pl* **-lia** *or* **-lias.** 1 an ancient Roman festival celebrated in December: renowned for its general merrymaking. 2 (*sometimes not cap.*) a period or occasion of wild revelry. [C16: from Latin *Sāturnālis* relating to SATURN[1]] ▸ **ˌSaturˈnalian** *adj*

Saturnian (sæˈtɜːnɪən) *adj* 1 of or connected with the Roman god Saturn, whose reign was thought of as a golden age. 2 *Prosody.* denoting a very early verse form in Latin in which the accent was one of stress rather than quantity, there being an equal number of main stresses in each line, regardless of the number of unaccented syllables. ◆ *n* 3 a line in Saturnian metre.

saturniid (sæˈtɜːnɪɪd) *n* 1 any moth of the mainly tropical family *Saturniidae,* typically having large brightly coloured wings: includes the emperor, cecropia, and luna moths. ◆ *adj* 2 of, relating to, or belonging to the *Saturniidae.*

saturnine (ˈsætəˌnaɪn) *adj* 1 having a gloomy temperament; taciturn. 2 *Archaic.* 2a of or relating to lead. 2b having or symptomatic of lead poisoning. [C15: from French *saturnin,* from Medieval Latin *sāturnīnus* (unattested), from Latin *Sāturnus* Saturn, with reference to the gloomy influence attributed to the planet Saturn] ▸ **ˈsaturˌninely** *adv* ▸ **saturninity** (ˌsætəˈnɪnɪtɪ) *n*

saturnism (ˈsætəˌnɪzəm) *n Pathol.* another name for **lead poisoning.** [C19: from New Latin *sāturnismus;* properties similar to those of lead were attributed to the planet]

satyagraha (ˈsɔːtjɑːgrɔːhɑː) *n* 1 the policy of nonviolent resistance adopted by Mahatma Gandhi from about 1919 to oppose British rule in India. 2 any movement of nonviolent resistance. [via Hindi from Sanskrit, literally: insistence on truth, from *satya* truth + *agraha* fervour]

satyagrahi (ˈsʌtjəˌgrʌhiː) *n* an exponent of nonviolent resistance, esp. as a form of political protest.

satyr (ˈsætə) *n* 1 *Greek myth.* one of a class of sylvan deities, represented as goatlike men who drank and danced in the train of Dionysus and chased the nymphs. 2 a man who has strong sexual desires. 3 a man who has satyriasis. 4 any of various butterflies of the genus *Satyrus* and related genera, having dark wings often marked with eyespots: family *Satyridae.* [C14: from Latin *satyrus,* from Greek *saturos*] ▸ **satyric** (səˈtɪrɪk) *or* **saˈtyrical** *adj* ▸ **ˈsatyr-ˌlike** *adj*

satyriasis (ˌsætɪˈraɪəsɪs) *n* a neurotic condition in men in which the symptoms are a compulsion to have sexual intercourse with as many women as possible and an inability to have lasting relationships with them. Compare **nymphomania.** [C17: via New Latin from Greek *saturiasis;* see SATYR, -IASIS]

satyrid (səˈtaɪrɪd) *n* any butterfly of the family *Satyridae,* having typically brown or dark wings with paler markings: includes the graylings, satyrs, browns, ringlets, and gatekeepers.

satyr play *n* (in ancient Greek drama) a ribald play with a chorus of satyrs, presented at the Dionysian festival.

sauce (sɔːs) *n* 1 any liquid or semiliquid preparation eaten with food to enhance its flavour. 2 anything that adds piquancy. 3 *U.S. and Canadian.* stewed fruit. 4 *U.S. dialect.* vegetables eaten with meat. 5 *Informal.* impudent language or behaviour. ◆ *vb* (*tr*) 6 to prepare (food) with sauce. 7 to add zest to. 8 to make agreeable or less severe. 9 *Informal.* to be saucy to. [C14: via Old French from Latin *salsus* salted, from *salīre* to sprinkle with salt, from *sal* salt] ▸ **ˈsauceless** *adj*

sauce boat *n* another term for **gravy boat.**

saucebox (ˈsɔːsˌbɒks) *n Informal.* a saucy person.

saucepan (ˈsɔːspən) *n* a metal or enamel pan with a long handle and often a lid, used for cooking food.

saucer (ˈsɔːsə) *n* 1 a small round dish on which a cup is set. 2 any similar dish. [C14: from Old French *saussier* container for SAUCE] ▸ **ˈsaucerful** *n* ▸ **ˈsaucerless** *adj*

sauch *or* **saugh** (sɔːx) *n* a sallow or willow. [C15: from Old English *salh*]

saucy (ˈsɔːsɪ) *adj* **saucier, sauciest.** 1 impertinent. 2 pert; jaunty: *a saucy hat.* ▸ **ˈsaucily** *adv* ▸ **ˈsauciness** *n*

Saud (saʊd) *n* full name *Saud ibn Abdul-Aziz.* 1902–69, king of Saudi Arabia (1953–64); son of Ibn Saud. He was deposed by his brother Faisal.

Saudi Arabia (ˈsɔːdɪ, ˈsaʊ-) *n* a kingdom in SW Asia, occupying most of the Arabian peninsula between the Persian Gulf and the Red Sea: founded in 1932 by Ibn Saud, who united Hejaz and Nejd; consists mostly of desert plateau; large reserves of petroleum and natural gas. Official language: Arabic. Official religion: (Sunni) Muslim. Currency: riyal. Capital: Riyadh (royal), Jidda (administrative). Pop.: 20 786 000 (1998 est.). Area: 2 260 353 sq. km (872 722 sq. miles). ▸ **Saudi** *or* **Saudi Arabian** *adj, n*

sauerbraten (ˈsaʊəˌbrɑːtᵊn; *German* ˈzauərˌbraːtən) *n* beef marinated in vinegar, sugar, and seasonings, and then braised. [German, from *sauer* SOUR + *Braten* roast]

sauerkraut (ˈsaʊəˌkraʊt) *n* finely shredded and pickled cabbage. [German, from *sauer* SOUR + *Kraut* cabbage]

sauger (ˈsɔːgə) *n* a small North American pikeperch, *Stizostedion canadense,* with a spotted dorsal fin: valued as a food and game fish. [C19: of unknown origin]

Saul (sɔːl) *n* 1 *Old Testament.* the first king of Israel (?1020–1000 B.C.). He led Israel successfully against the Philistines, but was in continual conflict with the high priest Samuel. He became afflicted with madness and died by his own hand; succeeded by David. 2 *New Testament.* the name borne by Paul prior to his conversion (Acts 9: 1–30).

Sault Sainte Marie ('suː seɪnt mə'riː) *n, usually abbreviated to* **Sault Ste Marie.** 1 an inland port in central Canada, in Ontario on the St. Mary's River, which links Lake Superior and Lake Huron, opposite Sault Ste Marie, Michigan: canal bypassing the rapids completed in 1895. Pop.: 81 476 (1991). 2 an inland port in NE Michigan, opposite Sault Ste Marie, Ontario: canal around the rapids completed in 1855, enlarged and divided in 1896 and 1919 (popularly called **Soo Canals**). Pop.: 14 689 (1990).

sauna ('sɔːnə) *n* 1 an invigorating bath originating in Finland in which the bather is subjected to hot steam, usually followed by a cold plunge or by being lightly beaten with birch twigs. 2 the place in which such a bath is taken. [C20: from Finnish]

Saunders ('sɔːndəz) *n* Dame **Cicely.** born 1918, British philanthropist: founded St Christopher's Hospice in 1967 for the care of the terminally ill, upon which the modern hospice movement is modelled. Her books include *Living with Dying* (1983).

saunter ('sɔːntə) *vb* (*intr*) 1 to walk in a casual manner; stroll. ◆ *n* 2 a leisurely pace or stroll. 3 a leisurely old-time dance. [C17 (meaning: to wander aimlessly), C15 (to muse): of obscure origin] ▸ **'saunterer** *n*

-saur *or* **-saurus** *n combining form.* lizard: *dinosaur.* [from New Latin *saurus*]

saurel ('sɔːrəl) *n* a U.S. name for **horse mackerel** (sense 1). [C19: via French from Late Latin *saurus,* from Greek *sauros,* of obscure origin]

saurian ('sɔːrɪən) *adj* 1 of, relating to, or resembling a lizard. 2 of, relating to, or belonging to the *Sauria,* a former suborder of reptiles (now called *Lacertilia*), which included the lizards. ◆ *n* 3 a former name for **lizard.** [C15: from New Latin *Sauria,* from Greek *sauros*]

saurischian (sɔː'rɪskɪən) *adj* 1 of, relating to, or belonging to the *Saurischia,* an order of late Triassic dinosaurs including the theropods and sauropods. ◆ *n* 2 any dinosaur belonging to the order *Saurischia.* [C19: from New Latin *Saurischia,* from *saurus* + ISCHIUM]

sauropod ('sɔːrəˌpɒd) *n* any herbivorous quadrupedal saurischian dinosaur of the suborder *Sauropoda,* of Jurassic and Cretaceous times, including the brontosaurus, diplodocus, and titanosaurs. They had small heads and long necks and tails and were partly amphibious. [C19: from New Latin *sauropoda,* from Greek *sauros* lizard + *pous* foot] ▸ **sauropodous** (sɔː'rɒpədəs) *adj*

saury ('sɔːrɪ) *n, pl* **-ries.** any teleost fish, such as the Atlantic *Scomberesox saurus* of the family *Scomberesocidae* of tropical and temperate seas, having an elongated body and long toothed jaws. Also called: **skipper.** [C18: perhaps from Late Latin *saurus;* see SAUREL]

sausage ('sɒsɪdʒ) *n* 1 finely minced meat, esp. pork or beef, mixed with fat, cereal or bread, and seasonings (**sausage meat**), and packed into a tube-shaped animal intestine or synthetic casing. 2 an object shaped like a sausage. 3 *Aeronautics, informal.* a captive balloon shaped like a sausage. 4 **not a sausage.** nothing at all. [C15: from Old Norman French *saussiche,* from Late Latin *salsīcia,* from Latin *salsus* salted; see SAUCE] ▸ **'sausage-ˌlike** *adj*

sausage dog *n* an informal name for **dachshund.**

sausage roll *n Brit.* a roll of sausage meat in pastry.

Saussure (*French* sosyr) *n* **Ferdinand de** (fɛrdinɑ̃ də). 1857–1913, Swiss linguist. He pioneered structuralism in linguistics and the separation of scientific language description from historical philological studies. ▸ **Saus'surean** *adj, n*

saut (sɔːt) *n, vb, adj* a Scot. word for **salt.**

sauté ('səuteɪ) *vb* **-tés, -téing** *or* **-téeing, -téed.** 1 to fry (food) quickly in a little fat. ◆ *n* 2 a dish of sautéed food, esp. meat that is browned and then cooked in a sauce. ◆ *adj* 3 sautéed until lightly brown: *sauté potatoes.* [C19: from French: tossed, from *sauter* to jump, from Latin *saltāre* to dance, from *salīre* to spring]

Sauternes (səu'tɜːn) *n* (*sometimes not cap.*) a sweet white wine made in the southern Bordeaux district of France. [C18: from *Sauternes,* the district where it is produced]

sauve qui peut *French.* (sov ki pø) *n* a state of panic or disorder; rout. [literally: save (himself) who can]

Sauvignon Blanc ('səuvɪnjɒn 'blɒŋk) *n* 1 a white grape grown in the Bordeaux and Loire regions of France, New Zealand, and elsewhere, used for making wine. 2 any of various white wines made from this grape.

sav (sæv) *n Austral. and N.Z. informal.* short for **saveloy.**

Sava ('sɑːvə) *or* **Save** (sɑːv) *n* a river in SE Europe, rising in NW Slovenia and flowing east and south to the Danube at Belgrade. Length: 940 km (584 miles).

savage ('sævɪdʒ) *adj* 1 wild; untamed: *savage beasts of the jungle.* 2 ferocious in temper; vicious: *a savage dog.* 3 uncivilized; crude: *savage behaviour.* 4 (of peoples) nonliterate or primitive: *a savage tribe.* 5 (of terrain) rugged and uncultivated. 6 *Obsolete.* far from human habitation. ◆ *n* 7 a member of a nonliterate society, esp. one regarded as primitive. 8 a crude or uncivilized person. 9 a fierce or vicious person or animal. ◆ *vb* (*tr*) 10 to criticize violently. 11 to attack ferociously and wound: *the dog savaged the child.* [C13: from Old French *sauvage,* from Latin *silvāticus* belonging to a wood, from *silva* a wood] ▸ **'savagedom** *n* ▸ **'savagely** *adv* ▸ **'savageness** *n*

Savage ('sævɪdʒ) *n* **Michael Joseph.** 1872-1940, New Zealand statesman; prime minister of New Zealand (1935-40).

Savage Island *n* another name for **Niue.**

savagery ('sævɪdʒrɪ) *n, pl* **-ries.** 1 an uncivilized condition. 2 a savage act or nature. 3 savages collectively.

Savaii (sɑː'vaiː) *n* the largest island in Western Samoa: mountainous and volcanic. Pop.: 44 930 (1986). Area: 1174 sq. km (662 sq. miles).

savanna *or* **savannah** (sə'vænə) *n* open grasslands, usually with scattered bushes or trees, characteristic of much of tropical Africa. Whether this is the natural climax vegetation or the result of clearing or burning by man is disputed. [C16: from Spanish *zavana,* from Taino *zabana*]

Savannah (sə'vænə) *n* 1 a port in the U.S., in E Georgia, near the mouth of the Savannah River: port of departure of the *Savannah* for Liverpool (1819), the first steamship to cross the Atlantic. Pop.: 136 262 (1996 est.). 2 a river in the southeastern U.S., formed by the confluence of the Tugaloo and Seneca Rivers in NW South Carolina: flows southeast to the Atlantic. Length: 505 km (314 miles).

savant ('sævənt; *French* savɑ̃) *n* a man of great learning; sage. [C18: from French, from *savoir* to know, from Latin *sapere* to be wise; see SAPIENT] ▸ **'savante** *fem n*

savate (sə'væt) *n* a form of boxing in which blows may be delivered with the feet as well as the hands. [C19: from French, literally: old worn-out shoe; related to SABOT]

save[1] (seɪv) *vb* 1 (*tr*) to rescue, preserve, or guard (a person or thing) from danger or harm. 2 to avoid the spending, waste, or loss of (money, possessions, etc.). 3 (*tr*) to deliver from sin; redeem. 4 (often foll. by *up*) to set aside or reserve (money, goods, etc.) for future use. 5 (*tr*) to treat with care so as to avoid or lessen wear or degeneration: *use a good light to save your eyes.* 6 (*tr*) to prevent the necessity for; obviate the trouble of: *good work now will save future revision.* 7 (*tr*) *Soccer, hockey, etc.* to prevent (a goal) by stopping (a struck ball or puck). 8 (*intr*) *Chiefly U.S.* (of food) to admit of preservation; keep. ◆ *n* 9 *Soccer, hockey, etc.* the act of saving a goal. 10 *Computing.* an instruction to write information from the memory onto a tape or disk. [C13: from Old French *salver,* via Late Latin from Latin *salvus* safe] ▸ **'savable** *or* **'saveable** *adj* ▸ **'savableness** *or* **'saveableness** *n* ▸ **'saver** *n*

save[2] (seɪv) *Archaic or literary.* ◆ *prep* 1 (often foll. by *for*) Also: **saving.** with the exception of. ◆ *conj* 2 but; except. [C13 *sauf,* from Old French, from Latin *salvō,* from *salvus* safe]

save-all *n* 1 a device to prevent waste or loss. 2 *Nautical.* 2a a net used while loading a ship. 2b a light sail set to catch wind spilling from another sail. 3 *Dialect.* overalls or a pinafore. 4 *Brit.* a dialect word for **miser.**

save as you earn *n* (in Britain) a savings scheme operated by the government, in which monthly contributions earn tax-free interest. Abbrev.: **SAYE.**

saveloy ('sævɪˌlɔɪ) *n* a smoked sausage made from salted pork, well seasoned and coloured red with saltpetre. [C19: probably via French from Italian *cervellato,* from *cervello* brain, from Latin *cerebellum,* diminutive of *cerebrum* brain]

Savery ('seɪvərɪ) *n* **Thomas.** ?1650–1715, English engineer, who built (1698) the first practical steam engine, used to pump water from mines.

Savigny ('savɪɲɪ) *n* **Friedrich Karl von** ('friːdrɪç 'kal fɔn). 1779–1861, German legal scholar, who pioneered the historical approach to jurisprudence, emphasizing custom and precedent.

savin *or* **savine** ('sævɪn) *n* 1 a small spreading juniper bush, *Juniperus sabina,* of Europe, N Asia, and North America. 2 the oil derived from the shoots and leaves of this plant, formerly used in medicine to treat rheumatism, etc. 3 another name for **red cedar** (sense 1). [C14: from Old French *savine,* from Latin *herba Sabīna* the Sabine plant]

saving ('seɪvɪŋ) *adj* 1 tending to save or preserve. 2 redeeming or compensating (esp. in the phrase **saving grace**). 3 thrifty or economical. 4 *Law.* denoting or relating to an exception or reservation: *a saving clause in an agreement.* ◆ *n* 5 preservation or redemption, esp. from loss or danger. 6 economy or avoidance of waste. 7 reduction in cost or expenditure: *a saving of 20p.* 8 anything saved. 9 (*pl*) money saved for future use. 10 *Law.* an exception or reservation. ◆ *prep* 11 with the exception of. ◆ *conj* 12 except. ▸ **'savingly** *adv*

savings account *n* an account at a bank that accumulates interest.

savings and loan association *n* a U.S. name for a **building society.**

savings bank *n* 1 a bank that accepts the savings of depositors and pays interest on them. 2 a container, usually having a slot in the top, for saving coins.

savings ratio *n Economics.* the ratio of personal savings to disposable income, esp. using the difference between national figures for disposable income and consumer spending as a measure of savings.

saviour *or U.S.* **savior** ('seɪvjə) *n* a person who rescues another person or a thing from danger or harm. [C13 *saveour,* from Old French, from Church Latin *Salvātor* the Saviour; see SAVE[1]]

Saviour *or U.S.* **Savior** ('seɪvjə) *n Christianity.* Jesus Christ regarded as the saviour of men from sin.

Savitskaya (sæ'vɪtskaɪə) *n* **Svetlana** (svɛt'lɑːnə). born 1949, Soviet cosmonaut, the first woman to walk in space (1984). She was elected to the former Soviet parliament (1989).

Savoie (*French* savwa) *n* 1 a department of E France, in Rhône-Alpes region. Capital: Chambéry. Pop.: 366 800 (1995). Area: 6188 sq. km (2413 sq. miles). 2 the French name for **Savoy**[1].

savoir-faire ('sævwɑː'fɛə) *n* the ability to do the right thing in any situation. [French, literally: a knowing how to do]

savoir-vivre ('sævwɑː'viːvrə) *n* familiarity with the customs of good society; breeding. [French, literally: a knowing how to live]

Savona (*Italian* sa'voːna) *n* a port in NW Italy, in Liguria on the Mediterranean: an important centre of the Italian iron and steel industry. Pop.: 69 806 (1990).

Savonarola (*Italian* savona'rɔːla) *n* **Girolamo** (dʒi'rɔːlamo). 1452–98, Italian religious and political reformer. As a Dominican prior in Florence he preached against contemporary sinfulness and moral corruption. When the Medici were expelled from the city (1494) he instituted a severely puritanical republic but lost the citizens' support after being excommunicated (1497). He was hanged and burned as a heretic.

savory ('seɪvərɪ) *n, pl* **-vories.** 1 any of numerous aromatic plants of the genus

Satureja, esp. *S. montana* (**winter savory**) and *S. hortensis* (**summer savory**), of the Mediterranean region, having narrow leaves and white, pink, or purple flowers: family *Labiatae* (labiates). **2** the leaves of any of these plants, used as a potherb. [C14: probably from Old English *sætherie,* from Latin *saturēia,* of obscure origin]

savour *or U.S.* **savor** ('seɪvə) *n* **1** the quality in a substance that is perceived by the sense of taste or smell. **2** a specific taste or smell: *the savour of lime.* **3** a slight but distinctive quality or trace. **4** the power to excite interest: *the savour of wit has been lost.* **5** *Archaic.* reputation. ◆ *vb* **6** (*intr;* often foll. by *of*) to possess the taste or smell (of). **7** (*intr;* often foll. by *of*) to have a suggestion (of). **8** (*tr*) to give a taste to; season. **9** (*tr*) to taste or smell, esp. appreciatively. **10** (*tr*) to relish or enjoy. [C13: from Old French *savour,* from Latin *sapor* taste, from *sapere* to taste] ▸ **'savourless** *or U.S.* **'savorless** *adj* ▸ **'savorous** *adj*

savoury *or U.S.* **savory** ('seɪvərɪ) *adj* **1** attractive to the sense of taste or smell. **2** salty or spicy; not sweet: *a savoury dish.* **3** pleasant. **4** respectable. ◆ *n, pl* **-vouries. 5** *Chiefly Brit.* a savoury dish served as an hors d'oeuvre or dessert. [C13 *savure,* from Old French *savouré,* from *savourer* to SAVOUR] ▸ **'savourily** *or U.S.* **'savorily** *adv* ▸ **'savouriness** *or U.S.* **'savoriness** *n*

savoy (sə'vɔɪ) *n* a cultivated variety of cabbage, *Brassica oleracea capitata,* having a compact head and wrinkled leaves. [C16: named after the SAVOY region]

Savoy[1] (sə'vɔɪ) *n* an area of SE France, bordering on Italy, mainly in the Savoy Alps: a duchy in the late Middle Ages and part of the Kingdom of Sardinia from 1720 to 1860, when it became part of France. French name: **Savoie.**

Savoy[2] (sə'vɔɪ) *n* a noble family of Italy that ruled over the duchy of Savoy and became the royal house of Italy (1861–1946): the oldest reigning dynasty in Europe before the dissolution of the Italian monarchy.

Savoy Alps *pl n* a range of the Alps in SE France. Highest peak: Mont Blanc, 4807 m (15 772 ft.).

Savoyard[1] (sə'vɔɪɑːd; *French* savwajar) *n* **1** a native of Savoy. **2** the dialect of French spoken in Savoy. ◆ *adj* **3** of or relating to Savoy, its inhabitants, or their dialect.

Savoyard[2] (sə'vɔɪɑːd) *n* **1** a person keenly interested in the operettas of Gilbert and Sullivan. **2** a person who takes part in these operettas. [C20: from the *Savoy* Theatre, built in London in 1881 by Richard D'Oyly Carte for the presentation of operettas by Gilbert and Sullivan]

savvy ('sævɪ) *Slang.* ◆ *vb* **-vies, -vying, -vied. 1** to understand or get the sense of (an idea, etc.). **2 no savvy.** I don't (he doesn't, etc.) understand. ◆ *n* **3** comprehension. ◆ *adj* **-vier, -viest. 4** *Chiefly U.S.* shrewd; well-informed. [C18: corruption of Spanish *sabe (usted)* (you) know, from *saber* to know, from Latin *sapere* to be wise]

saw[1] (sɔː) *n* **1** any of various hand tools for cutting wood, metal, etc., having a blade with teeth along one edge. **2** any of various machines or devices for cutting by use of a toothed blade, such as a power-driven circular toothed wheel or toothed band of metal. ◆ *vb* **saws, sawing, sawed; sawed** *or* **sawn. 3** to cut with a saw. **4** to form by sawing. **5** to cut as if wielding a saw: *to saw the air.* **6** to move (an object) from side to side as if moving a saw. [Old English *sagu;* related to Old Norse *sog,* Old High German *saga,* Latin *secāre* to cut, *secūris* axe] ▸ **'sawer** *n* ▸ **'saw,like** *adj*

saw[2] (sɔː) *vb* the past tense of **see**[1].

saw[3] (sɔː) *n* a wise saying, maxim, or proverb. [Old English *sagu* a saying; related to SAGA]

SAW *abbrev. for* surface acoustic wave.

sawbill ('sɔː,bɪl) *n* **1** another name for **merganser** or **motmot. 2** any of various hummingbirds of the genus *Ramphodon.* [C19: so called because of their serrated bills]

sawbones ('sɔː,bəʊnz) *n, pl* **bones** *or* **boneses.** *Slang.* a surgeon or doctor.

sawbuck ('sɔː,bʌk) *n* **1** *U.S. and Canadian.* a sawhorse, esp. one having an X-shaped supporting structure. **2** *Chiefly U.S. and Canadian slang.* a ten-dollar bill. [C19: (in the sense: sawhorse) translated from Dutch *zaagbok;* (in the sense: ten-dollar bill) from the legs of a sawbuck forming the Roman numeral X]

sawder ('sɔːdə) *Informal.* ◆ *n* **1** flattery; compliments (esp. in the phrase **soft sawder**). ◆ *vb* (*tr*) **2** to flatter. [C19: metaphorical use of variant of SOLDER]

saw doctor *n N.Z.* a sawmill specialist who sharpens and services saw blades.

sawdust ('sɔː,dʌst) *n* particles of wood formed by sawing.

sawfish ('sɔː,fɪʃ) *n, pl* **-fish** *or* **-fishes.** any sharklike ray of the family *Pristidae* of subtropical coastal waters and estuaries, having a serrated bladelike mouth.

sawfly ('sɔː,flaɪ) *n, pl* **-flies.** any of various hymenopterous insects of the family *Tenthredinidae* and related families, the females of which have a sawlike ovipositor.

sawhorse ('sɔː,hɔːs) *n* a stand for timber during sawing.

sawmill ('sɔː,mɪl) *n* **1** an industrial establishment where timber is sawn into planks, etc. **2** a large sawing machine.

sawn (sɔːn) *vb* a past participle of **saw**[1].

Sawney ('sɔːnɪ) *n* **1** a derogatory word for **Scotsman. 2** (*also not cap.*) *Informal.* a fool. [C18: a Scots variant of *Sandy,* short for *Alexander*]

sawn-off *or esp. U.S.* **sawed-off** *adj* **1** (*prenominal*) (of a shotgun) having the barrel cut short, mainly to facilitate concealment of the weapon. **2** *Informal.* (of a person) small in stature.

saw palmetto *n* any of several dwarf prickly palms, esp. any of the genus *Sabal,* of the southeastern U.S.

saw-pit *n* (esp. formerly) a pit above which a log is sawn into planks with a large pitsaw.

saw set *n* a tool used for setting the teeth of a saw, consisting of a type of clamp used to bend each tooth in turn at a slight angle to the plane of the saw, alternate teeth being bent in the same direction.

sawtooth ('sɔː,tuːθ) *adj* **1** (of a waveform) having an amplitude that varies linearly with time between two values, the interval in one direction often being much greater than the other. **2** having or generating such a waveform.

saw-wort ('sɔː,wɜːt) *n* a perennial Old World plant, *Serratula tinctoria,* having serrated leaves that yield a yellow dye: family *Compositae* (composites).

sawyer ('sɔːjə) *n* a person who saws timber for a living. [C14 *sawier,* from SAW[1] + *-ier,* variant of -ER[1]]

sax[1] (sæks) *n* a tool resembling a small axe, used for cutting roofing slate. [Old English *seax* knife; related to Old Saxon *sahs,* Old Norse *sax*]

sax[2] (sæks) *n Informal.* short for **saxophone.**

Sax. *abbrev. for:* **1** Saxon. **2** Saxony.

saxatile ('sæksə,taɪl; *as specific name* sæk'sætɪlɪ) *adj* growing on or living among rocks. [C17: from Latin *saxitilis,* from *saxum* rock]

Saxe[1] (saks) *n* the French name for **Saxony.**

Saxe[2] (*French* saks) *n* **Hermann Maurice** (ɛrman mɔris) comte de Saxe. 1696–1750, French marshal born in Saxony: he distinguished himself in the War of the Austrian Succession (1740–48).

saxe blue (sæks) *n* **a** a light greyish-blue colour. **b** (*as adj*): *a saxe-blue dress.* [C19: from French *Saxe* Saxony, source of a dye of this colour]

Saxe-Coburg-Gotha (sæks'kəʊbɜːg'gəʊθə) *n* the ruling house of the former German duchy of Saxe-Coburg-Gotha (until 1918) and the name of the British royal family (1901–17) through Prince Albert.

saxhorn ('sæks,hɔːn) *n* a valved brass instrument used chiefly in brass and military bands, having a tube of conical bore and a brilliant tone colour. It resembles the tuba and constitutes a family of instruments related to the flugelhorn and cornet. [C19: named after Adolphe *Sax* (see SAXOPHONE), who invented it (1845)]

saxicolous (sæk'sɪkələs) *adj* living on or among rocks: *saxicolous plants.* Also: **saxicole, saxatile** ('sæksə,taɪl). [C19: from New Latin *saxicolus,* from Latin *saxum* rock + *colere* to dwell]

saxifragaceous (,sæksɪfrə'geɪʃəs) *adj* of, relating to, or belonging to the *Saxifragaceae,* a chiefly arctic and alpine family of plants having a basal rosette of leaves and small flowers: includes saxifrage.

saxifrage ('sæksɪ,freɪdʒ) *n* any saxifragaceous plant of the genus *Saxifraga,* having small white, yellow, purple, or pink flowers. [C15: from Late Latin *saxifraga,* literally: rock-breaker, from Latin *saxum* rock + *frangere* to break]

Saxo Grammaticus ('sæksəʊ grə'mætɪkəs) *n* ?1150–?1220, Danish chronicler, noted for his *Gesta Danorum,* a history of Denmark down to 1185, written in Latin, which is partly historical and partly mythological, and contains the Hamlet (Amleth) legend.

Saxon ('sæksən) *n* **1** a member of a West Germanic people who in Roman times spread from Schleswig across NW Germany to the Rhine. Saxons raided and settled parts of S Britain in the fifth and sixth centuries A.D. In Germany they established a duchy and other dominions, which changed and shifted through the centuries, usually retaining the name Saxony. **2** a native or inhabitant of Saxony. **3a** the Low German dialect of Saxony. **3b** any of the West Germanic dialects spoken by the ancient Saxons or their descendants. ◆ *adj* **4** of, relating to, or characteristic of the ancient Saxons, the Anglo-Saxons, or their descendants. **5** of, relating to, or characteristic of Saxony, its inhabitants, or their Low German dialect. ◆ See also **West Saxon, Anglo-Saxon.** [C13 (replacing Old English *Seaxe*): via Old French from Late Latin *Saxon-, Saxo,* from Greek; of Germanic origin and perhaps related to the name of a knife used by the Saxons; compare SAW[1]]

Saxon blue *n* a dye made by dissolving indigo in a solution of sulphuric acid. [C19: named after SAXONY, where it originated]

saxony ('sæksənɪ) *n* **1** a fine 3-ply yarn used for knitting and weaving. **2** a fine woollen fabric used for coats, etc. [C19: named after SAXONY, where it was produced]

Saxony ('sæksənɪ) *n* **1** a state in E Germany, formerly part of East Germany. Pop.: 4 566 600 (1996 est.). **2** a former duchy and electorate in SE and central Germany, whose territory changed greatly over the centuries. **3** (in the early Middle Ages) any territory inhabited or ruled by Saxons. ◆ Compare **Saxony-Anhalt, Lower Saxony.** German name: **Sachsen.** French name: **Saxe.**

Saxony-Anhalt ('sæksənɪ 'ɑːnhɑːlt) *n* a state of E Germany: created in 1947 from the state of Anhalt and those parts of Prussia formerly ruled by the duchy of Saxony: part of East Germany until 1990. Pop.: 2 738 900 (1996 est.).

saxophone ('sæksə,fəʊn) *n* a keyed wind instrument of mellow tone colour, used mainly in jazz and dance music. It is made in various sizes, has a conical bore, and a single reed. Often shortened to **sax.** [C19: named after Adolphe *Sax* (1814–94), Belgian musical-instrument maker, who invented it (1846)] ▸ **saxophonic** (,sæksə'fɒnɪk) *adj* ▸ **saxophonist** (sæk'sɒfənɪst) *n*

say[1] (seɪ) *vb* **says** (sɛz), **saying, said.** (*mainly tr*) **1** to speak, pronounce, or utter. **2** (*also intr*) to express (an idea) in words; tell: *we asked his opinion but he refused to say.* **3** (*also intr; may take a clause as object*) to state (an opinion, fact, etc.) positively; declare; affirm. **4** to recite: *to say grace.* **5** (*may take a clause as object*) to report or allege: *they say we shall have rain today.* **6** (*may take a clause as object*) to take as an assumption; suppose: *let us say that he is lying.* **7** (*may take a clause as object*) to convey by means of artistic expression: *the artist in this painting is saying that we should look for hope.* **8** to make a case for: *there is much to be said for either course of action.* **9** (*usually passive*) *Irish.* to persuade or coax (someone) to do something: *If I hadn't been said by her I wouldn't be in this fix.* **10 go without saying.** to be so obvious as to need no explanation. **11 I say!** *Chiefly Brit. informal.* an exclamation of surprise. **12 not to say.** even; and indeed. **13 that is to say.** in other words; more explicitly. **14 to say nothing of.** as well as; even disregarding: *he was warmly dressed in a shirt and heavy jumper, to say nothing of a thick overcoat.* **15 to say the least.** without the slightest exaggeration; at the very least. ◆ *adv* **16** approximately: *there were, say, 20 people present.* **17** for example: *choose a number, say, four.* ◆ *n* **18** the right or chance to speak: *let him have his say.* **19**

authority, esp. to influence a decision: *he has a lot of say in the company's policy.* **20** a statement of opinion: *you've had your say, now let me have mine.* ◆ *interj* **21** *U.S. and Canadian informal.* an exclamation to attract attention or express surprise, etc. [Old English *secgan;* related to Old Norse *segja,* Old Saxon *seggian,* Old High German *sagēn*] ► **'sayer** *n*

say[2] (seɪ) *n Archaic.* a type of fine woollen fabric. [C13: from Old French *saie,* from Latin *saga,* plural of *sagum* a type of woollen cloak]

Sayan Mountains (sɑː'jæn) *pl n* a mountain range in S central Russia, in S Siberia. Highest peak: Munku-Sardyk, 3437 m (11 457 ft.).

Saybolt universal seconds ('seɪˌbəult) *n* (*functioning as sing*) a U.S. measurement of viscosity similar in type to the British Redwood seconds. [named after G. M. *Saybolt* (died 1924), U.S. chemist, who proposed it]

SAYE *abbrev. for* save as you earn.

Sayers ('seɪəz) *n* **Dorothy L(eigh).** 1893–1957, English detective-story writer.

saying ('seɪɪŋ) *n* a maxim, adage, or proverb.

say-so *n Informal.* **1** an arbitrary assertion. **2** an authoritative decision. **3** the authority to make a final decision.

sayyid, sayid ('saɪɪd), *or* **said** *n* **1** a Muslim claiming descent from Mohammed's grandson Husain. **2** a Muslim honorary title. [C17: from Arabic: lord]

sazerac ('sæzəˌræk) *n U.S.* a mixed drink of whisky, Pernod, syrup, bitters, and lemon. [C20: of uncertain origin]

Sb *the chemical symbol for* antimony. [from New Latin *stibium*]

sb. *abbrev. for* substantive.

SBA *abbrev. for* standard beam approach: a radar navigation system that gives lateral guidance to aircraft when landing.

SBS *abbrev. for* Special Boat Service.

SBU *abbrev. for* strategic business unit: a division within an organization responsible for marketing its own range of products.

sc *Printing. abbrev. for* small capitals.

Sc *the chemical symbol for* scandium.

SC *abbrev. for:* **1** Signal Corps. **2** South Carolina. **3** (in New Zealand) School Certificate. **4** (in Canada) Star of Courage.

sc. *abbrev. for:* **1** scale. **2** scene. **3** science. **4** scilicet. **5** screw. **6** scruple (unit of weight).

SCAA (in Britain) *abbrev. for* School Curriculum and Assessment Authority: a statutory organization responsible for reviewing all aspects of the school curriculum.

scab (skæb) *n* **1** the dried crusty surface of a healing skin wound or sore. **2** a contagious disease of sheep resembling mange, caused by a mite (*Psoroptes communis*). **3** a fungal disease of plants characterized by crusty spots on the fruits, leaves, etc. **4** *Derogatory.* **4a** Also called: **blackleg.** a person who refuses to support a trade union's actions, esp. one who replaces a worker who is on strike. **4b** (*as modifier*): *scab labour.* **5** a despicable person. ◆ *vb* **scabs, scabbing, scabbed.** (*intr*) **6** to become covered with a scab. **7** (of a road surface) to become loose so that potholes develop. **8** to replace a striking worker. [Old English *sceabb;* related to Old Norse *skabb,* Latin *scabiēs,* Middle Low German *schabbe* scoundrel, German *schäbig* SHABBY] ► **'scabˌlike** *adj*

scabbard ('skæbəd) *n* a holder for a bladed weapon such as a sword or bayonet; sheath. [C13 *scauberc,* from Norman French *escaubers* (pl), of Germanic origin; related to Old High German *skār* blade and *bergan* to protect]

scabbard fish *n* any of various marine spiny-finned fishes of the family *Trichiuridae,* esp. of the genus *Lepidopus,* having a long whiplike scaleless body and long sharp teeth: most common in warm waters.

scabble ('skæbᵊl) *vb* (*tr*) to shape (stone) roughly. [C17: from earlier *scapple,* from French *escapler* to shape (timber)]

scabby ('skæbɪ) *adj* **-bier, -biest. 1** *Pathol.* having an area of the skin covered with scabs. **2** *Pathol.* having scabies. **3** *Informal.* despicable. ► **'scabbily** *adv* ► **'scabbiness** *n*

scabies ('skeɪbiːz, -bɪˌiːz) *n* a contagious skin infection caused by the mite *Sarcoptes scabiei,* characterized by intense itching, inflammation, and the formation of vesicles and pustules. [C15: from Latin: scurf, from *scabere* to scratch; see SHAVE] ► **scabietic** (ˌskeɪbɪ'ɛtɪk) *adj*

scabious[1] ('skeɪbɪəs) *adj* **1** having or covered with scabs. **2** of, relating to, or resembling scabies. [C17: from Latin *scabiōsus,* from SCABIES]

scabious[2] ('skeɪbɪəs) *n* **1** any plant of the genus *Scabiosa,* esp. *S. atropurpurea,* of the Mediterranean region, having blue, red, or whitish dome-shaped flower heads: family *Dipsacaceae.* **2** any of various similar plants of the related genus *Knautia.* **3** **devil's bit scabious.** a similar and related Eurasian marsh plant, *Succisa pratensis.* [C14: from Medieval Latin *scabiōsa herba* the scabies plant, referring to its use in treating scabies]

scablands ('skæbˌlændz) *pl n* a type of terrain, found for example in the NW U.S., consisting of bare rock surfaces, with little or no soil cover and scanty vegetation, that have been deeply channelled by glacial flood waters.

scabrid ('skæbrɪd) *adj* having a rough or scaly surface. [C19: see SCABROUS] ► **scabridity** (skə'brɪdɪtɪ) *n*

scabrous ('skeɪbrəs) *adj* **1** roughened because of small projections; scaly. **2** indelicate, indecent, or salacious: *scabrous humour.* **3** difficult to deal with; knotty. [C17: from Latin *scaber* rough; related to SCABIES] ► **'scabrously** *adv* ► **'scabrousness** *n*

scad (skæd) *n, pl* **scad** *or* **scads.** any of various carangid fishes of the genus *Trachurus,* esp. the horse mackerel. [C17: of uncertain origin; compare Swedish *skädde* flounder]

scads (skædz) *pl n Informal.* a large amount or number. [C19: of uncertain origin]

Scafell Pike (skɔː'fɛl) *n* a mountain in NW England, in Cumbria in the Lake District: the highest peak in England. Height: 978 m (3209 ft.).

scaffold ('skæfəld, -fəuld) *n* **1** a temporary metal or wooden framework that is used to support workmen and materials during the erection, repair, etc., of a building or other construction. **2** a raised wooden platform on which plays are performed, tobacco, etc., is dried, or (esp. formerly) criminals are executed. ◆ *vb* (*tr*) **3** to provide with a scaffold. **4** to support by means of a scaffold. [C14: from Old French *eschaffaut,* from Vulgar Latin *catafalicum* (unattested); see CATAFALQUE] ► **'scaffolder** *n*

scaffolding ('skæfəldɪŋ) *n* **1** a scaffold or system of scaffolds. **2** the building materials used to make scaffolds.

scag[1] *or* **skag** (skæg) *n* a slang name for **heroin.**

scag[2] (skæg) *South Wales and southwest English dialect.* ◆ *n* **1** a tear in a garment or piece of cloth. ◆ *vb* **scags, scagging, scagged. 2** (*tr*) to make a tear in (cloth). [apparently related to Old Norse *skaga* to project]

scagliola (skæl'jəulə) *n* imitation marble made of glued gypsum with a polished surface of coloured stone or marble dust. [C16: from Italian, diminutive of *scaglia* chip of marble, of Germanic origin; related to SHALE, SCALE[2]]

Scala ('skaːla) *n* **La.** See **La Scala.**

scalable ('skeɪləbᵊl) *adj* capable of being scaled or climbed. ► **'scalableness** *n* ► **'scalably** *adv*

scalade (skə'leɪd) *or* **scalado** (skə'leɪdəu) *n, pl* **-lades** *or* **-lados.** short for **escalade.** [C16: from Old Italian *scalada,* from *scala* a ladder; see SCALE[3]]

scalage ('skeɪlɪdʒ) *n* **1** *U.S.* a percentage deducted from the price of goods liable to shrink or leak. **2** *Forestry, U.S. and Canadian.* the estimated amount of usable timber in a log. [C19: from SCALE[3] + -AGE]

scalar ('skeɪlə) *n* **1** a quantity, such as time or temperature, that has magnitude but not direction and is an even function of the coordinates. Compare **vector** (sense 1), **tensor** (sense 2), **pseudoscalar, pseudovector. 2** *Maths.* an element of a field associated with a vector space. ◆ *adj* **3** having magnitude but not direction. [C17 (meaning: resembling a ladder): from Latin *scālāris,* from *scāla* ladder]

scalare (skə'lɛərɪ) *n* another name for **angelfish** (sense 2). [C19: from Latin *scālāris* of a ladder, SCALAR, referring to the runglike pattern on its body]

scalariform (skə'lærɪˌfɔːm) *adj Biology.* resembling a ladder: *a scalariform cell.* [C19: from New Latin *scālāriformis* from Latin *scālāris* of a ladder + -FORM]

scalar multiplication *n Maths.* an operation used in the definition of a vector space in which the product of a scalar and a vector is a vector, the operation is distributive over the addition of both scalars and vectors, and is associative with multiplication of scalars.

scalar product *n* the product of two vectors to form a scalar, whose value is the product of the magnitudes of the vectors and the cosine of the angle between them. Written: ***A•B*** or *AB* Compare **vector product.** Also called: **dot product.**

scalawag ('skæləˌwæg) *n* a variant of **scallywag.**

scald[1] (skɔːld) *vb* **1** to burn or be burnt with or as if with hot liquid or steam. **2** (*tr*) to subject to the action of boiling water, esp. so as to sterilize. **3** (*tr*) to heat (a liquid) almost to boiling point. **4** (*tr*) to plunge (tomatoes, peaches, etc.) into boiling water briefly in order to skin them more easily. ◆ *n* **5** the act or result of scalding. **6** an abnormal condition in plants, characterized by discoloration and wrinkling of the skin of the fruits, caused by exposure to excessive sunlight, gases, etc. [C13: via Old Norman French from Late Latin *excaldāre* to wash in warm water, from *calida* (*aqua*) warm (water), from *calēre* to be warm] ► **'scalder** *n*

scald[2] (skɔːld) *n* a variant spelling of **skald.**

scald[3] (skɔːld) *Obsolete.* ◆ *adj also* **scalled. 1** scabby. ◆ *n* **2** a scab or a skin disease producing scabs. [C16: from SCALL]

scald-crow *n Irish.* another name for **hooded crow.**

scaldfish ('skɔːldˌfɪʃ, 'skɑːld-) *n, pl* **-fish** *or* **-fishes.** a small European flatfish, *Arnoglossus laterna,* covered with large fragile scales: family *Bothidae.* [C19: from SCALD[3]]

scale[1] (skeɪl) *n* **1** any of the numerous plates, made of various substances resembling enamel or dentine, covering the bodies of fishes. **2a** any of the horny or chitinous plates covering a part or the entire body of certain reptiles and mammals. **2b** any of the numerous minute structures covering the wings of lepidoptera. Related adj: **squamous. 3** a thin flat piece or flake. **4** a thin flake of dead epidermis shed from the skin: excessive shedding may be the result of a skin disease. **5** a specialized leaf or bract, esp. the protective covering of a bud or the dry membranous bract of a catkin. **6** See **scale insect. 7** a flaky black oxide of iron formed on the surface of iron or steel at high temperatures. **8** any oxide formed on a metal during heat treatment. ◆ *vb* **9** (*tr*) to remove the scales or coating from. **10** to peel off or cause to peel off in flakes or scales. **11** (*intr*) to shed scales. **12** to cover or become covered with scales, incrustation, etc. **13** (*tr*) to throw (a disc or thin flat object) edgewise through the air or along the surface of water. **14** (*intr*) *Austral. informal.* to ride on public transport without paying a fare. [C14: from Old French *escale,* of Germanic origin; compare Old English *scealu* SHELL] ► **'scaleˌlike** *adj*

scale[2] (skeɪl) *n* **1** (*often pl*) a machine or device for weighing. **2** one of the pans of a balance. **3** **tip the scales. 3a** to exercise a decisive influence. **3b** (foll. by *at*) to amount in weight (to). ◆ *vb* (*tr*) **4** to weigh with or as if with scales. **5** to have a weight of. [C13: from Old Norse *skāl* bowl, related to Old High German *scāla* cup, Old English *scealu* SHELL, SCALE[1]]

scale[3] (skeɪl) *n* **1** a sequence of marks either at regular intervals or else representing equal steps used as a reference in making measurements. **2** a measuring instrument having such a scale. **3a** the ratio between the size of something real and that of a model or representation of it: *the scale of the map was so large that we could find our house on it.* **3b** (*as modifier*): *a scale model.* **4** a line, numerical ratio, etc., for showing this ratio. **5** a progressive or graduated table of things, wages, etc., in order of size, value, etc.: *a wage scale for carpenters.* **6** an established measure or standard. **7** a relative degree or extent: *he entertained on a grand scale.* **8** *Music.* a group of notes taken in ascending or descending order, esp. within the compass of one octave. **9** *Maths.* the notation of a given number system: *the decimal scale.* **10** a graded series of tests measuring mental development, etc. **11** *Obsolete.* a ladder or staircase. ◆ *vb* **12** to climb to the top of (a height) by or as if by a ladder. **13** (*tr*) to make or draw (a model, plan, etc.) according to a particular ratio of proportionate reduction. **14** (*tr; usually foll. by up or down*) to increase or reduce proportionately in size, etc. **15** *U.S. and Canadian.* (in forestry) to estimate the board footage of (standing timber or logs). [C15: via Italian from Latin *scāla* ladder; related to Old French *eschiele,* Spanish *escala*]

scaleboard ('skeɪlˌbɔːd, 'skæbəd) *n* a very thin piece of board, used for backing a picture, as a veneer, etc.

scale insect *n* any small homopterous insect of the family *Coccidae* and related families, which typically live and feed on plants and secrete a protective scale around themselves. Many species, such as the San Jose scale, are important pests.

scale leaf *n Botany.* a modified leaf, often small and membranous, protecting buds, etc.

scale moss *n* any of various leafy liverworts of the order *Jungermanniales,* which resemble mosses.

scalene ('skeɪliːn) *adj* **1** *Maths.* (of a triangle) having all sides of unequal length. **2** *Anatomy.* of or relating to any of the scalenus muscles. [C17: from Late Latin *scalēnus* with unequal sides, from Greek *skalēnos*]

scalenus (skə'liːnəs, skeɪ-) *n, pl* **-ni** (-naɪ). *Anatomy.* any one of the three muscles situated on each side of the neck extending from the cervical vertebrae to the first or second pair of ribs. [C18: from New Latin; see SCALENE]

scaler ('skeɪlə) *n* **1** a person or thing that scales. **2** Also called: **counter, scaling circuit.** an electronic device or circuit that aggregates electric pulses and gives a single output pulse for a predetermined number of input pulses.

Scales (skeɪlz) *n* **the.** the constellation Libra, the seventh sign of the zodiac.

Scaliger ('skælɪdʒə) *n* **1 Joseph Justus** ('dʒʌstəs). 1540–1609, French scholar, who revolutionized the study of ancient chronology by his work *De Emendatione temporum* (1583). **2** his father, **Julius Caesar.** 1484–1558, Italian classical scholar, and writer on biology and medicine.

scaling ladder *n* a ladder used to climb high walls, esp. one used formerly to enter a besieged town, fortress, etc.

scall (skɔːl) *n Pathol.* a former term for any of various diseases of the scalp characterized by itching and scab formation. [C14: from Old Norse *skalli* bald head. Compare SKULL] ▸ **scalled** *adj*

scallion ('skæljən) *n* any of various onions or similar plants, such as the spring onion, that have a small bulb and long leaves and are eaten in salads. Also called: **green onion.** [C14: from Anglo-French *scalun,* from Latin *Ascalōnia* (*caepa*) Ascalonian (onion), from *Ascalo* Ascalon, a Palestinian port]

scallop ('skɒləp, 'skæl-) *n* **1** any of various marine bivalves of the family *Pectinidae,* having a fluted fan-shaped shell: includes free-swimming species (genus *Pecten*) and species attached to a substratum (genus *Chlamys*). See also **pecten** (sense 3). **2** the edible adductor muscle of certain of these molluscs. **3** either of the shell valves of any of these molluscs. **4** a scallop shell or similarly shaped dish, in which fish, esp. shellfish, is cooked and served. **5** one of a series of curves along an edge, esp. an edge of cloth. **6** the shape of a scallop shell used as the badge of a pilgrim, esp. in the Middle Ages. **7** *Chiefly Austral.* a potato cake fried in batter. ◆ *vb* **8** (*tr*) to decorate (an edge) with scallops. **9** to bake (food) in a scallop shell or similar dish. **10** (*intr*) to collect scallops. [C14: from Old French *escalope* shell, of Germanic origin; see SCALP] ▸ **'scalloper** *n* ▸ **'scalloping** *n*

scally ('skælɪ) *n, pl* **-lies.** *Northwest English dialect.* a rascal; rogue. [C20: from SCALLYWAG]

scallywag ('skælɪˌwæg) *n* **1** *Informal.* a scamp; rascal. **2** (after the U.S. Civil War) a White Southerner who supported the Republican Party and its policy of Black emancipation. Scallywags were viewed as traitors by their fellow Southerners. ◆ Also: **scalawag, scallawag.** [C19: (originally undersized animal) of uncertain origin]

scaloppine *or* **scaloppini** (ˌskælə'piːnɪ) *pl n* escalopes of meat, esp. veal, cooked in a rich sauce, usually of wine with seasonings. [Italian: from *scaloppa* a fillet, probably from Old French *escalope* SCALLOP]

scalp (skælp) *n* **1** *Anatomy.* the skin and subcutaneous tissue covering the top of the head. **2** (among North American Indians) a part of this removed as a trophy from a slain enemy. **3** a trophy or token signifying conquest. **4** *Hunting, chiefly U.S.* a piece of hide cut from the head of a victim as a trophy or as proof of killing in order to collect a bounty. **5** *Informal, chiefly U.S.* a small speculative profit taken in quick transactions. **6** *Scottish dialect.* a projection of bare rock from vegetation. ◆ *vb* (*tr*) **7** to cut the scalp from. **8** *Informal, chiefly U.S.* to purchase and resell (securities) quickly so as to make several small profits. **9** *Informal.* to buy (tickets) cheaply and resell at an inflated price. [C13: probably from Scandinavian; compare Old Norse *skalpr* sheath, Middle Dutch *schelpe,* Danish *skalp* husk] ▸ **'scalper** *n*

scalpel ('skælpᵊl) *n* a surgical knife with a short thin blade. [C18: from Latin *scalpellum,* from *scalper* a knife, from *scalpere* to scrape] ▸ **scalpellic** (skæl'pelɪk) *adj*

scalping ('skælpɪŋ) *n* a process in which the top portion of a metal ingot is machined away before use, thus removing the layer containing defects and impurities.

scalp lock *n* a small tuft or plait of hair left on the shaven scalp by American Indian warriors as a challenge to enemies.

scaly ('skeɪlɪ) *adj* **scalier, scaliest. 1** resembling or covered in scales. **2** peeling off in scales. ▸ **'scaliness** *n*

scaly anteater *n* another name for **pangolin.**

scam (skæm) *n Slang.* a stratagem for gain; a swindle.

Scamander (skə'mændə) *n* the ancient name for the **Menderes** (sense 2).

scammony ('skæmənɪ) *n, pl* **-nies. 1** a twining Asian convolvulus plant, *Convolvulus scammonia,* having arrow-shaped leaves, white or purple flowers, and tuberous roots. **2** a resinous juice obtained from the roots of this plant and having purgative properties. **3** any of various similar medicinal resins or the plants that yield them. [Old English, via Latin from Greek *skammōnia,* of obscure origin] ▸ **scammoniate** (skæ'məʊnɪɪt) *adj*

scamp[1] (skæmp) *n* **1** an idle mischievous person; rascal. **2** a mischievous child. [C18: from *scamp* (vb) to be a highway robber, probably from Middle Dutch *schampen* to decamp, from Old French *escamper,* from *es-* EX-[1] + *-camper,* from Latin *campus* field] ▸ **'scampish** *adj*

scamp[2] (skæmp) *vb* a less common word for **skimp.** ▸ **'scamper** *n*

scamper ('skæmpə) *vb* (*intr*) **1** to run about playfully. **2** (often foll. by *through*) to hurry quickly through (a place, task, book, etc.) ◆ *n* **3** the act of scampering. [C17: probably from *scamp* (vb); see SCAMP[1]] ▸ **'scamperer** *n*

scampi ('skæmpɪ) *n* (*usually functioning as sing*) large prawns, usually eaten fried in breadcrumbs. [Italian: plural of *scampo* shrimp, of obscure origin]

scan (skæn) *vb* **scans, scanning, scanned. 1** (*tr*) to scrutinize minutely. **2** (*tr*) to glance over quickly. **3** (*tr*) *Prosody.* to read or analyse (verse) according to the rules of metre and versification. **4** (*intr*) *Prosody.* to conform to the rules of metre and versification. **5** (*tr*) *Electronics.* to move a beam of light, electrons, etc., in a predetermined pattern over (a surface or region) to obtain information, esp. either to sense and transmit or to reproduce a television image. **6** (*tr*) to examine data stored on (magnetic tape, etc.), usually in order to retrieve information. **7** to examine or search (a prescribed region) by systematically varying the direction of a radar or sonar beam. **8** *Physics.* to examine or produce or be examined or produced by a continuous charge of some variable: *to scan a spectrum.* **9** *Med.* to obtain an image of (a part of the body) by means of a scanner. ◆ *n* **10** the act or an instance of scanning. **11** *Med.* **11a** the examination of a part of the body by means of a scanner: *a brain scan; ultrasound scan.* **11b** the image produced by a scanner. [C14: from Late Latin *scandere* to scan (verse), from Latin: to climb] ▸ **'scannable** *adj*

Scand. *or* **Scan.** *abbrev. for* Scandinavia(n).

scandal ('skændᵊl) *n* **1** a disgraceful action or event: *his negligence was a scandal.* **2** censure or outrage arising from an action or event. **3** a person whose conduct causes reproach or disgrace. **4** malicious talk, esp. gossip about the private lives of other people. **5** *Law.* a libellous action or statement. ◆ *vb* (*tr*) *Obsolete.* **6** to disgrace. **7** to scandalize. [C16: from Late Latin *scandalum* stumbling block, from Greek *skandalon* a trap] ▸ **'scandalous** *adj* ▸ **'scandalously** *adv* ▸ **'scandalousness** *n*

scandalize *or* **scandalise** ('skændəˌlaɪz) *vb* (*tr*) to shock, as by improper behaviour. ▸ **ˌscandali'zation** *or* **ˌscandali'sation** *n* ▸ **'scandalˌizer** *or* **'scandalˌiser** *n*

scandalmonger ('skændᵊlˌmʌŋgə) *n* a person who spreads or enjoys scandal, gossip, etc.

Scandaroon (ˌskændə'ruːn) *n* a large variety of fancy pigeon having a long thin body and an elongated neck and head. [from *Scandaroon* the former name of *Ishenderon* a seaport in Turkey]

scandent ('skændənt) *adj* (of plants) having a climbing habit. [C17: from Latin *scandere* to climb]

Scanderbeg ('skændəˌbɛg) *n* original name *George Castriota;* Turkish name *Iskender Bey.* ?1403–68, Albanian patriot. He was an army commander for the sultan of Turkey until 1443, when he changed sides and drove the Turks from Albania.

Scandian ('skændɪən) *n* another name for a **Scandinavian.** [C17: from Latin *Scandia* Scandinavia]

scandic ('skændɪk) *adj* of or containing scandium.

Scandinavia (ˌskændɪ'neɪvɪə) *n* **1** Also called: **the Scandinavian Peninsula.** the peninsula of N Europe occupied by Norway and Sweden. **2** the countries of N Europe, esp. considered as a cultural unit and including Norway, Sweden, Denmark, and often Finland, Iceland, and the Faeroe Islands.

Scandinavian (ˌskændɪ'neɪvɪən) *adj* **1** of, relating to, or characteristic of Scandinavia, its inhabitants, or their languages. ◆ *n* **2** a native or inhabitant of Scandinavia. **3** Also called: **Norse.** the northern group of Germanic languages, consisting of Swedish, Danish, Norwegian, Icelandic, and Faeroese.

Scandinavian Shield *n* another name for **Baltic Shield.**

scandium ('skændɪəm) *n* a rare light silvery-white metallic element occurring in minute quantities in numerous minerals. Symbol: Sc; atomic no.: 21; atomic wt.: 44.955910; valency: 3; relative density: 2.989; melting pt.: 1541°C; boiling pt.: 2836°C. [C19: from New Latin, from Latin *Scandia* Scandinavia, where it was discovered]

scanner ('skænə) *n* **1** a person or thing that scans. **2** a device, usually electronic, used to measure or sample the distribution of some quantity or condition in a particular system, region, or area. **3** an aerial or similar device designed to transmit or receive signals, esp. radar signals, inside a given solid angle of space, thus allowing a particular region to be scanned. **4** any of various devices used in medical diagnosis to obtain an image of an internal organ or part. See **CAT scanner, nuclear magnetic resonance scanner, ultrasound scanner. 5** *Informal.* a television outside broadcast vehicle. **6** short for **optical scanner. 7** *Printing.* an electronic device which scans artwork and illustrations and converts the images to digital form for manipulation, and incorporation into printed publications

scanning electron microscope *n* a type of electron microscope that produces a three-dimensional image.

scansion ('skænʃən) *n* the analysis of the metrical structure of verse. See **quantity** (sense 7), **stress** (sense 4). [C17: from Latin: climbing up, from *scandere* to climb, SCAN]

scansorial (skæn'sɔːrɪəl) *adj Zoology.* specialized for, characterized by, or relating to climbing: *a scansorial bird.* [C19: from Latin *scānsōrius,* from *scandere* to climb]

scant (skænt) *adj* **1** scarcely sufficient; limited: *he paid her scant attention.* **2** (*prenominal*) slightly short of the amount indicated; bare: *a scant ten inches.* **3** (*postpositive;* foll. by *of*) having a short supply (of). ◆ *vb* (*tr*) **4** to limit in size or quantity. **5** to provide with a limited or inadequate supply of. **6** to treat in a slighting or inadequate manner. ◆ *adv* **7** scarcely; barely. [C14: from Old Norse *skamt,* from *skammr* short; related to Old High German *scam*] ▸ **'scantly** *adv* ▸ **'scantness** *n*

scantling ('skæntlɪŋ) *n* **1** a piece of sawn timber, such as a rafter, that has a small cross section. **2** the dimensions of a piece of building material or the structural parts of a ship, esp. those in cross section. **3** a building stone, esp. one that is more than 6 feet in length. **4** a small quantity or amount. [C16: changed (through influence of SCANT and -LING[1]) from earlier *scantillon,* a carpenter's gauge, from Old Norman French *escantillon,* ultimately from Latin *scandere* to climb; see SCAN]

scantlings ('skæntlɪŋz) *pl n* the structural casings of the internal gas paths in an aeroengine.

scanty ('skæntɪ) *adj* **scantier, scantiest. 1** limited; barely enough; meagre. **2** insufficient; inadequate. **3** lacking fullness; small. ▸ **'scantily** *adv* ▸ **'scantiness** *n*

Scapa Flow ('skæpə) *n* an extensive landlocked anchorage off the N coast of Scotland, in the Orkney Islands: major British naval base in both World Wars. Length: about 24 km (15 miles). Width: 13 km (8 miles).

scape[1] (skeɪp) *n* **1** a leafless stalk in plants that arises from a rosette of leaves and bears one or more flowers. **2** *Zoology.* a stalklike part, such as the first segment of an insect's antenna. [C17: from Latin *scāpus* stem, from (Doric) Greek *skapos;* see SHAFT] ▸ **'scapose** *adj*

scape[2] *or* **'scape** (skeɪp) *vb, n* an archaic word for **escape.**

-scape *suffix forming nouns.* indicating a scene or view of something, esp. a pictorial representation: *seascape.* [abstracted from LANDSCAPE]

scapegoat ('skeɪp,gəʊt) *n* **1** a person made to bear the blame for others. **2** *Old Testament.* a goat used in the ritual of Yom Kippur (Leviticus 16); it was symbolically laden with the sins of the Israelites and sent into the wilderness to be destroyed. ◆ *vb* **3** (*tr*) to make a scapegoat of. [C16: from ESCAPE + GOAT, coined by William Tyndale to translate Biblical Hebrew *azāzēl* (probably) goat for Azazel, mistakenly thought to mean "goat that escapes"]

scapegrace ('skeɪp,greɪs) *n* an idle mischievous person. [C19: from SCAPE[2] + GRACE, alluding to a person who lacks God's grace]

scapewheel ('skeɪp,wiːl) *n* a less common name for **escape wheel.**

scaphoid ('skæfɔɪd) *adj Anatomy.* an obsolete word for **navicular.** [C18: via New Latin from Greek *skaphoeidēs,* from *skaphē* boat]

scaphopod ('skæfə,pɒd) *n* any marine mollusc of the class *Scaphopoda,* which includes the tusk (or tooth) shells. [C20: from New Latin, from Greek *skaphē* boat + -POD]

scapolite ('skæpə,laɪt) *n* any of a group of colourless, white, grey, or violet fluorescent minerals consisting of sodium or calcium aluminium silicate, carbonate, and chloride in tetragonal crystalline form. They occur mainly in impure limestones and pegmatites. Also called: **wernerite.** [C19: from German *Skapolith,* from Greek *skapos* rod + -LITE]

scapula ('skæpjʊlə) *n, pl* **-lae** (-liː) *or* **-las. 1** either of two large flat triangular bones, one on each side of the back part of the shoulder in man. Nontechnical name: **shoulder blade. 2** the corresponding bone in most vertebrates. [C16: from Late Latin: shoulder]

scapular ('skæpjʊlə) *adj* **1** *Anatomy.* of or relating to the scapula. ◆ *n* **2** part of the monastic habit worn by members of many Christian, esp. Roman Catholic, religious orders, consisting of a piece of woollen cloth worn over the shoulders, and hanging down in front and behind to the ankles. **3** two small rectangular pieces of woollen cloth joined by tapes passing over the shoulders and worn under secular clothes in token of affiliation to a religious order. **4** any of the small feathers that are attached to the humerus of a bird and lie along the shoulder. ◆ Also called (for senses 2 and 3): **'scapulary.**

scar[1] (skɑː) *n* **1** any mark left on the skin or other tissue following the healing of a wound. **2** a permanent change in a person's character resulting from emotional distress: *his wife's death left its scars on him.* **3** the mark on a plant indicating the former point of attachment of a part, esp. the attachment of a leaf to a stem. **4** a mark of damage; blemish. ◆ *vb* **scars, scarring, scarred. 5** to mark or become marked with a scar. **6** (*intr*) to heal leaving a scar. [C14: via Late Latin from Greek *eskhara* scab]

scar[2] (skɑː) *n* **1** a bare craggy rock formation. **2** a similar formation in a river or sea. ◆ Also called (Scot): **scaur.** [C14: from Old Norse *sker* low reef, SKERRY]

scarab ('skærəb) *n* **1** any scarabaeid beetle, esp. *Scarabaeus sacer* (**sacred scarab**), regarded by the ancient Egyptians as divine. **2** the scarab as represented on amulets, etc., of ancient Egypt, or in hieroglyphics as a symbol of the solar deity. [C16: from Latin *scarabaeus;* probably related to Greek *karabos* horned beetle]

scarabaeid (,skærə'biːɪd) *or* **scarabaean** (,skærə'biːən) *n* **1** any beetle of the family *Scarabaeidae,* including the sacred scarab and other dung beetles, the chafers, goliath beetles, and rhinoceros beetles. ◆ *adj* **2** of, relating to, or belonging to the family *Scarabaeidae.* [C19: from New Latin]

scarabaeoid (,skærə'biːɔɪd) *adj* **1** Also: **scaraboid** ('skærə,bɔɪd). of, relating to, or resembling a scarabaeid. **2** a former word for **lamellicorn.**

scarabaeus (,skærə'biːəs) *n, pl* **-baeuses** *or* **-baei** (-'biːaɪ). a less common name for **scarab.**

Scaramouch *or* **Scaramouche** ('skærə,maʊtʃ, -,muːtʃ) *n* a stock character who appears as a boastful coward in commedia dell'arte and farce. [C17: via French from Italian *Scaramuccia,* from *scaramuccia* a SKIRMISH]

Scarborough ('skɑːbrə) *n* a fishing port and resort in NE England, in North Yorkshire on the North Sea: developed as a spa after 1660; ruined 12th-century castle. Pop.: 38 809 (1991).

scarce (skɛəs) *adj* **1** rarely encountered. **2** insufficient to meet the demand. **3 make oneself scarce.** *Informal.* to go away, esp. suddenly. ◆ *adv* **4** *Archaic or literary.* scarcely. [C13: from Old Norman French *scars,* from Vulgar Latin *excarpsus* (unattested) plucked out, from Latin *excerpere* to select; see EXCERPT] ▸ **'scarceness** *n*

scarcely ('skɛəslɪ) *adv* **1** hardly at all; only just. **2** *Often used ironically.* probably not or definitely not: *that is scarcely justification for your actions.*

USAGE See at **hardly.**

scarcement ('skɛəsmənt) *n* a ledge in a wall. [C16: probably from obsolete sense of SCARCE to reduce + -MENT]

scarcity ('skɛəsɪtɪ) *n, pl* **-ties. 1** inadequate supply; dearth; paucity. **2** rarity or infrequent occurrence.

scare (skɛə) *vb* **1** to fill or be filled with fear or alarm. **2** (*tr;* often foll. by *away* or *off*) to drive (away) by frightening. **3** (*tr*) *U.S. and Canadian informal.* (foll. by *up*) to produce (a meal) quickly from what is available. ◆ *n* **4** a sudden attack of fear or alarm. **5** a period of general fear or alarm. ◆ *adj* **6** causing (needless) fear or alarm: *a scare story.* [C12: from Old Norse *skirra;* related to Norwegian *skjerra,* Swedish dialect *skjarra*] ▸ **'scarer** *n*

scarecrow ('skɛə,krəʊ) *n* **1** an object, usually in the shape of a man, made out of sticks and old clothes to scare birds away from crops. **2** a person or thing that appears frightening but is not actually harmful. **3** *Informal.* **3a** an untidy-looking person. **3b** a very thin person.

scaredy-cat ('skɛədɪ,kæt) *n Informal.* someone who is easily frightened.

scaremonger ('skɛə,mʌŋgə) *n* a person who delights in spreading rumours of disaster. ▸ **'scare,mongering** *n*

scarf[1] (skɑːf) *n, pl* **scarves** (skɑːvz) *or* **scarfs. 1** a rectangular, triangular, or long narrow piece of cloth worn around the head, neck, or shoulders for warmth or decoration. ◆ *vb* (*tr*) *Rare.* **2** to wrap with or as if with a scarf. **3** to use as or in the manner of a scarf. [C16: of uncertain origin; compare Old Norman French *escarpe,* Medieval Latin *scrippum* pilgrim's pack; see SCRIP[2]]

scarf[2] (skɑːf) *n, pl* **scarfs. 1** Also called: **scarf joint, scarfed joint.** a lapped joint between two pieces of timber made by notching or grooving the ends and strapping, bolting, or gluing the two pieces together. **2** the end of a piece of timber shaped to form such a joint. **3** *N.Z.* a wedge-shaped cut made in a tree before felling, to determine the direction of the fall. **4** *Whaling.* an incision made along a whale's body before stripping off the blubber. ◆ *vb* (*tr*) **5** to join (two pieces of timber) by means of a scarf. **6** to make a scarf on (a piece of timber). **7** to cut a scarf in (a whale). [C14: probably from Scandinavian; compare Norwegian *skarv,* Swedish *skarf,* Low German, Dutch *scherf* SCARF[1]]

Scarfe (skɑːf) *n* **Gerald.** born 1936, British cartoonist, famous for his scathing caricatures of politicians and celebrities.

scarfskin ('skɑːf,skɪn) *n* the outermost layer of the skin; epidermis or cuticle. [C17: from SCARF[1] (in the sense: an outer covering)]

Scargill ('skɑːgɪl) *n* **Arthur.** born 1941, British trades union leader; president of the National Union of Mineworkers (from 1982). He led the miners in a long and bitter strike (1984–85), but failed to prevent pit closures.

scarificator ('skɛərɪfɪ,keɪtə, 'skærɪ-) *n* a surgical instrument for use in puncturing the skin or other tissue.

scarify[1] ('skɛərɪ,faɪ, 'skærɪ-) *vb* **-fies, -fying, -fied.** (*tr*) **1** *Surgery.* to make tiny punctures or superficial incisions in (the skin or other tissue), as for inoculating. **2** *Agriculture.* **2a** to break up and loosen (soil) to a shallow depth. **2b** to scratch or abrade the outer surface of (seeds) to increase water absorption or hasten germination. **3** to wound with harsh criticism. [C15: via Old French from Latin *scarīfāre* to scratch open, from Greek *skariphasthai* to draw, from *skariphos* a pencil] ▸ **,scarifi'cation** *n* ▸ **'scari,fier** *n*

scarify[2] ('skɛərɪ,faɪ) *vb* **-fies, -fying, -fied.** (*tr*) *Informal.* to make scared; frighten. [C18: from SCARE + -IFY] ▸ **'scari,fyingly** *adv*

USAGE *Scarify* is sometimes wrongly thought to mean the same as *scare: a frightening* (not *scarifying*) *film.*

scarious ('skɛərɪəs) *or* **scariose** ('skɛərɪ,əʊs) *adj* (of plant parts) membranous, dry, and brownish in colour: *scarious bracts.* [C19: from New Latin *scariōsus,* of uncertain origin]

scarlatina (,skɑːlə'tiːnə) *n* the technical name for **scarlet fever.** [C19: from New Latin, from Italian *scarlattina,* diminutive of *scarlatto* SCARLET] ▸ **,scarla'tinal** *adj*

Scarlatti (skɑː'lætɪ) *n* **1 Alessandro** (ales'sandro). ?1659–1725, Italian composer; regarded as the founder of modern opera. **2** his son, (**Giuseppe**) **Domenico** (do'meːniko). 1685–1757, Italian composer and harpsichordist, in Portugal and Spain from 1720. He wrote over 550 single-movement sonatas for harpsichord, many of them exercises in virtuoso technique.

scarlet ('skɑːlɪt) *n* **1** a vivid red colour, sometimes with an orange tinge. **2** cloth or clothing of this colour. ◆ *adj* **3** of the colour scarlet. **4** sinful or immoral, esp. unchaste. [C13: from Old French *escarlate* fine cloth, of unknown origin]

scarlet fever *n* an acute communicable disease characterized by fever, strawberry-coloured tongue, and a typical rash starting on the neck and chest and spreading to the abdomen and limbs, caused by the bacterium *Streptococcus pyogenes.* Technical name: **scarlatina.**

scarlet hat *n* another term for **red hat.**

scarlet letter *n* (esp. among U.S. Puritans) a scarlet letter *A* formerly worn by a person convicted of adultery.

scarlet pimpernel *n* a primulaceous plant, *Anagallis arvensis,* of temperate regions, having small red, purple, or white star-shaped flowers that close in bad weather. Also called: **shepherd's** (*or* **poor man's**) **weatherglass.**

scarlet runner *n* a climbing perennial bean plant, *Phaseolus multiflorus* (or *P. coccineus*), of tropical America, having scarlet flowers: widely cultivated for its long green edible pods containing edible seeds. Also called: **runner bean, string bean.**

scarlet tanager *n* an E North American tanager, *Piranga olivacea,* the male of which has a bright red head and body with black wings and tail.

scarlet woman *n* **1** *New Testament.* a sinful woman described in Revelation 17, interpreted as a figure either of pagan Rome or of the Roman Catholic Church regarded as typifying vice overlaid with gaudy pageantry. **2** any sexually promiscuous woman, esp. a prostitute.

scarp (skɑːp) *n* **1** a steep slope, esp. one formed by erosion or faulting; escarpment. See also **cuesta. 2** *Fortifications.* the side of a ditch cut nearest to and immediately below a rampart. ◆ *vb* **3** (*tr; often passive*) to wear or cut so as to form a steep slope. [C16: from Italian *scarpa*]

scarper (ˈskɑːpə) *Brit. slang.* ◆ *vb* (*intr*) **1** to depart in haste. ◆ *n* **2** a hasty departure. [C19: probably an adaptation of Italian *scappare* to escape; perhaps influenced by folk etymology *Scapa Flow* Cockney rhyming slang for *go*]

Scarron (*French* skarɔ̃) *n* **Paul** (pɔl). 1610–60, French comic dramatist and novelist, noted particularly for his picaresque novel *Le Roman comique* (1651–57).

scart (skært) *Scot.* ◆ *vb* **1** to scratch or scrape. ◆ *n* **2** a scratch or scrape. **3** a stroke of a pen. **4** a small amount; scraping. [C14: from earlier *scrat*]

Scart *or* **SCART** (skɑːt) *n Electronics.* **a** a 21-pin plug-and-socket system which carries picture, sound, and other signals, used especially in home entertainment systems. **b** (*as modifier*): *a Scart cable.* [C20: after Syndicat des Constructeurs des Appareils Radiorécepteurs et Téléviseurs, the company that designed it]

scarves (skɑːvz) *n* a plural of **scarf**[1].

scary (ˈskɛərɪ) *adj* **scarier, scariest.** *Informal.* **1** causing fear or alarm; frightening. **2** easily roused to fear; timid.

scat[1] (skæt) *vb* **scats, scatting, scatted.** (*intr; usually imperative*) *Informal.* to go away in haste. [C19: perhaps from a hiss + the word *cat,* used to frighten away cats]

scat[2] (skæt) *n* **1** a type of jazz singing characterized by improvised vocal sounds instead of words. ◆ *vb* **scats, scatting, scatted. 2** (*intr*) to sing jazz in this way. [C20: perhaps imitative]

scat[3] (skæt) *n* any marine and freshwater percoid fish of the Asian family *Scatophagidae,* esp. *Scatophagus argus,* which has a beautiful coloration. [C20: shortened from *Scatophagus;* see SCATO-]

scat[4] (skæt) *n* an animal dropping. [C20: see SCATO-]

scathe (skeɪð) *vb* (*tr*) **1** *Rare.* to attack with severe criticism. **2** *Archaic or dialect.* to injure. ◆ *n* **3** *Archaic or dialect.* harm. [Old English *sceatha;* related to Old Norse *skathi,* Old Saxon *scatho*] ▸ **ˈscatheless** *adj*

scathing (ˈskeɪðɪŋ) *adj* **1** harshly critical; scornful: *a scathing remark.* **2** damaging; painful. ▸ **ˈscathingly** *adv*

scato- *or before a vowel* **scat-** *combining form.* dung or excrement: *scatophagous.* [from Greek *skōr, skat-* dung]

scatology (skæˈtɒlədʒɪ) *n* **1** the scientific study of excrement, esp. in medicine for diagnostic purposes, and in palaeontology of fossilized excrement. **2** obscenity or preoccupation with obscenity, esp. in the form of references to excrement. ▸ **scatological** (ˌskætəˈlɒdʒɪkᵊl) *or* (*less commonly*) **ˌscatoˈlogic** *adj* ▸ **scaˈtologist** *n*

scatter (ˈskætə) *vb* **1** (*tr*) to throw about in various directions; strew. **2** to separate and move or cause to separate and move in various directions; disperse. **3** to deviate or cause to deviate in many directions, as in the diffuse reflection or refraction of light. ◆ *n* **4** the act of scattering. **5** a substance or a number of objects scattered about. [C13: probably a variant of SHATTER] ▸ **ˈscatterable** *adj* ▸ **ˈscatterer** *n*

scatterbrain (ˈskætəˌbreɪn) *n* a person who is incapable of serious thought or concentration. ▸ **ˈscatterˌbrained** *adj*

scatter diagram *n Statistics.* a graph that plots along two axes at right angles to each other the relationship between two variable quantities, such as height and weight.

scatter-gun *n* a shotgun.

scattering (ˈskætərɪŋ) *n* **1** a small amount. **2** *Physics.* the process in which particles, atoms, etc., are deflected as a result of collision.

scatter pin *n* a small decorative pin usually worn in groups of two or three.

scatter rug *n* a small rug used to cover a limited area.

scatty (ˈskætɪ) *adj* **-tier, -tiest.** *Brit. informal.* **1** empty-headed, frivolous, or thoughtless. **2** distracted (esp. in **drive someone scatty**). [C20: from SCATTERBRAINED] ▸ **ˈscattily** *adv* ▸ **ˈscattiness** *n*

scaud (skɔːd) *vb, n* a Scot. word for **scald**[1].

scaup *or* **scaup duck** (skɔːp) *n* either of two diving ducks, *Aythya marila* (**greater scaup**) or *A. affinis* (**lesser scaup**), of Europe and America, having a black-and-white plumage in the male. Also called (U.S.): **bluebill, broadbill.** [C16: Scottish variant of SCALP]

scauper (ˈskɔːpə) *n* a variant spelling of **scorper.**

scaur (skɔːr) *n* a Scot. variant of **scar**[2].

scavenge (ˈskævɪndʒ) *vb* **1** to search for (anything usable) among discarded material. **2** (*tr*) to purify (a molten metal) by bubbling a suitable gas through it. The gas may be inert or may react with the impurities. **3** to clean up filth from (streets, etc.). **4** *Chem.* to act as a scavenger for (atoms, molecules, ions, radicals, etc.).

scavenge pump *n Engineering.* an oil pump used in some internal-combustion engines to return oil from the crankcase to the oil tank.

scavenger (ˈskævɪndʒə) *n* **1** a person who collects things discarded by others. **2** any animal that feeds on decaying organic matter, esp. on refuse. **3** a substance added to a chemical reaction or mixture to counteract the effect of impurities. **4** a person employed to clean the streets. [C16: from Anglo-Norman *scawager,* from Old Norman French *escauwage* examination, from *escauwer* to scrutinize, of Germanic origin; related to Flemish *scauwen*] ▸ **ˈscavengery** *n*

scavenger beetle *n* any beetle of the mostly aquatic family *Hydrophilidae,* having clubbed antennae and long palps, and usually feeding on decaying vegetation.

scavenger hunt *n* a game in which players are required to collect an assortment of miscellaneous items: usually played outdoors.

scavenge stroke *or* **scavenging stroke** *n* (in a reciprocating engine) the stroke of a piston in a four-stroke cycle that pushes the burnt gases out as exhaust. Also called: **exhaust stroke.**

ScD *abbrev. for* Doctor of Science.

SCE (in Scotland) *abbrev. for* Scottish Certificate of Education: either of two public examinations in specific subjects taken as school-leaving qualifications or as qualifying examinations for entry into a university, college, etc. See also **higher** (sense 2), **O grade.**

scena (ˈʃeɪnə) *n, pl* **-ne** (-ˌneɪ). **1** a scene in an opera, usually longer than a single aria. **2** a dramatic vocal piece written in operatic style.

scenario (sɪˈnɑːrɪˌəʊ) *n, pl* **-narios. 1** a summary of the plot of a play, etc., including information about its characters, scenes, etc. **2** a predicted sequence of events: *let's try another scenario, involving the demise of democracy.* [C19: via Italian from Latin *scēnārium,* from *scēna;* see SCENE] ▸ **scenarist** (ˈsiːnərɪst, sɪˈnɑː-) *n*

scend *or* **send** (sɛnd) *Nautical.* ◆ *vb* **scends, scending, scended** *or* **sends, sending, sent. 1** (*intr*) (of a vessel) to surge upwards in a heavy sea. ◆ *n* **2** the upward heaving of a vessel pitching. **3** the forward lift given a vessel by the sea. [C17: perhaps from DESCEND or ASCEND]

scene (siːn) *n* **1** the place where an action or event, real or imaginary, occurs. **2** the setting for the action of a play, novel, etc. **3** an incident or situation, real or imaginary, esp. as described or represented. **4a** a subdivision of an act of a play, in which the time is continuous and the setting fixed. **4b** a single event, esp. a significant one, in a play. **5** *Films.* a shot or series of shots that constitutes a unit of the action. **6** the backcloths, stage setting, etc., for a play or film set; scenery. **7** the prospect of a place, landscape, etc. **8** a display of emotion, esp. an embarrassing one to the onlookers. **9** *Informal.* the environment for a specific activity: *the fashion scene.* **10** *Informal.* interest or chosen occupation: *classical music is not my scene.* **11** *Rare.* the stage, esp. of a theatre in ancient Greece or Rome. **12 behind the scenes.** out of public view; privately. [C16: from Latin *scēna* theatrical stage, from Greek *skēnē* tent, stage]

scene dock *or* **bay** *n* a place in a theatre where scenery is stored, usually near the stage.

scenery (ˈsiːnərɪ) *n, pl* **-eries. 1** the natural features of a landscape. **2** *Theatre.* the painted backcloths, stage structures, etc., used to represent a location in a theatre or studio. [C18: from Italian SCENARIO]

scenic (ˈsiːnɪk, ˈsɛn-) *adj* **1** of or relating to natural scenery. **2** having beautiful natural scenery: *a scenic drive.* **3** of or relating to the stage or stage scenery. **4** (in painting) representing a scene, such as a scene of action or a historical event. ▸ **ˈscenically** *adv*

scenic railway *n* **1** a miniature railway used for amusement in a park, zoo, etc. **2** a roller coaster.

scenic reserve *n N.Z.* an area of natural beauty, set aside for public recreation.

scenography (siːˈnɒgrəfɪ) *n* **1** the art of portraying objects or scenes in perspective. **2** scene painting, esp. in ancient Greece. [C17: via Latin from Greek *skēnographia* a drawing in perspective, from *skēnē* SCENE] ▸ **sceˈnographer** *n* ▸ **scenographic** (ˌsiːnəʊˈgræfɪk) *or* **ˌscenoˈgraphical** *adj* ▸ **ˌsceˈnoˈgraphically** *adv*

scent (sɛnt) *n* **1** a distinctive smell, esp. a pleasant one. **2** a smell left in passing, by which a person or animal may be traced. **3** a trail, clue, or guide. **4** an instinctive ability for finding out or detecting. **5** another word (esp. Brit.) for **perfume.** ◆ *vb* **6** (*tr*) to recognize or be aware of by or as if by the smell. **7** (*tr*) to have a suspicion of; detect: *I scent foul play.* **8** (*tr*) to fill with odour or fragrance. **9** (*intr*) (of hounds, etc.) to hunt by the sense of smell. **10** to smell (at): *the dog scented the air.* [C14: from Old French *sentir* to sense, from Latin *sentīre* to feel; see SENSE] ▸ **ˈscented** *adj* ▸ **ˈscentless** *adj*

scented orchid *n* a slender orchid, *Gymnadenia conopsea,* with fragrant pink flowers carried in a dense spike and having a three-lobed lip; found in calcareous turf. The less common **larger scented orchid** is *G. densiflora.* Also called **fragrant orchid.**

sceptic *or archaic and U.S.* **skeptic** (ˈskɛptɪk) *n* **1** a person who habitually doubts the authenticity of accepted beliefs. **2** a person who mistrusts people, ideas, etc., in general. **3** a person who doubts the truth of religion, esp. Christianity. ◆ *adj* **4** of or relating to sceptics; sceptical. [C16: from Latin *scepticus,* from Greek *skeptikos* one who reflects upon, from *skeptesthai* to consider] ▸ **ˈsceptical** *or archaic and U.S.* **ˈskeptical** *adj* ▸ **ˈsceptically** *or archaic and U.S.* **ˈskeptically** *adv* ▸ **ˈscepticism** *or archaic and U.S.* **ˈskepticism** *n*

Sceptic *or archaic and U.S.* **Skeptic** (ˈskɛptɪk) *n* **1** a member of one of the ancient Greek schools of philosophy, esp. that of Pyrrho, who believed that real knowledge of things is impossible. ◆ *adj* **2** of or relating to the Sceptics. ▸ **ˈScepticism** *or archaic and U.S.* **ˈSkepticism** *n*

sceptre *or U.S.* **scepter** (ˈsɛptə) *n* **1** a ceremonial staff held by a monarch as the symbol of authority. **2** imperial authority; sovereignty. ◆ *vb* **3** (*tr*) to invest with authority. [C13: from Old French *sceptre,* from Latin *scēptrum,* from Greek *skeptron* staff] ▸ **ˈsceptred** *or U.S.* **ˈsceptered** *adj*

SCG (in Australia) *abbrev. for* Sydney Cricket Ground.

sch. *abbrev. for* school.

Schadenfreude *German.* (ˈʃaːdənfrɔydə) *n* delight in another's misfortune. [German: from *Schaden* harm + *Freude* joy]

Schaerbeek (*Flemish* ˈsxaːrbeːk) *n* a city in central Belgium: an industrial suburb of Brussels. Pop.: 102 417 (1992 est.).

Schaffhausen (*German* ʃaːfˈhauzən) *n* **1** a small canton of N Switzerland. Pop.: 74 035 (1996 est.). Area: 298 sq. km (115 sq. miles). **2** a town in N Switzerland, capital of Schaffhausen canton, on the Rhine. Pop.: 35 000 (latest est.). French name: **Schaffhouse.**

schappe ('ʃæpə) *n* a yarn or fabric made from waste silk. [from German]

Schaumburg-Lippe (*German* 'ʃaumburk'lɪpə) *n* a former state of NW Germany, between Westphalia and Hanover: part of Lower Saxony since 1946.

schedule ('ʃedju:l; *also, esp. U.S.* 'skɛdʒuəl) *n* **1** a plan of procedure for a project, allotting the work to be done and the time for it. **2** a list of items: *a schedule of fixed prices.* **3** a list of times, esp. of arrivals and departures; timetable. **4** a list of tasks to be performed, esp. within a set period. **5** *Law.* a list or inventory, usually supplementary to a contract, will, etc. **6 on schedule.** at the expected or planned time. ♦ *vb* (*tr*) **7** to make a schedule of or place in a schedule. **8** to plan to occur at a certain time. [C14: earlier *cedule, sedule* via Old French from Late Latin *schedula* small piece of paper, from Latin *scheda* sheet of paper] ▸ **'schedular** *adj*

scheduled ('ʃedju:ld) *adj* **1** arranged or planned according to a programme, timetable, etc.: *a scheduled meeting; a change to the scheduled programmes on TV tonight.* **2** (of an aircraft or a flight) part of a regular service, not specially chartered. **3** *Brit.* (of a building, place of historic interest, etc.) entered on a list of places to be preserved. See also **listed building.**

scheduled castes *pl n* certain classes in Indian society officially granted special concessions. See **Harijan.**

scheduled territories *pl n* **the.** another name for **sterling area.**

Scheele (*Swedish* 'ʃe:lə) *n* **Karl Wilhelm** (kɑ:rl 'vilhɛlm). 1742–86, Swedish chemist. He discovered oxygen, independently of Priestley, and many other substances.

scheelite ('ʃi:laɪt) *n* a white, brownish, or greenish mineral, usually fluorescent, consisting of calcium tungstate in tetragonal crystalline form with some tungsten often replaced by molybdenum: occurs principally in contact metamorphic rocks and quartz veins, and is an important source of tungsten and purified calcium tungstate. Formula: $CaWO_4$. [C19: from German *Scheelit,* named after K. W. SCHEELE]

Scheldt (ʃɛlt, skɛlt) *n* a river in W Europe, rising in NE France and flowing north and northeast through W Belgium to Antwerp, then northwest to the North Sea in the SW Netherlands. Length: 435 km (270 miles). Flemish and Dutch name: **Schelde** ('sxɛldɛ). French name: **Escaut.**

Schelling (*German* 'ʃɛlɪŋ) *n* **Friedrich Wilhelm Joseph von** ('fri:drɪç 'vɪlhɛlm 'jo:zɛf fɔn). 1775–1854, German philosopher. He expanded Fichte's idea that there is one reality, the infinite and absolute Ego, by regarding nature as an absolute being working towards self-consciousness. His works include *Ideas towards a Philosophy of Nature* (1797) and *System of Transcendental Idealism* (1800). ▸ **Schellingian** (ʃɛ'lɪŋɪən) *adj*

schema ('ski:mə) *n, pl* **-mata** (-mətə). **1** a plan, diagram, or scheme. **2** (in the philosophy of Kant) a rule or principle that enables the understanding to apply its categories and unify experience: *universal succession is the schema of causality.* **3** *Psychol.* a mental model of aspects of the world or of the self that is structured in such a way as to facilitate the processes of cognition and perception. **4** *Logic.* an expression using metavariables that may be replaced by object language expressions to yield a well-formed formula. Thus $A = A$ is an axiom schema for identity, representing the infinite number of axioms, $x = x$, $y = y$, $z = z$, etc. [C19: from Greek: form]

schematic (skɪ'mætɪk, ski:-) *adj* **1** of or relating to the nature of a diagram, plan, or schema. ♦ *n* **2** a schematic diagram, esp. of an electrical circuit. ▸ **sche'matically** *adv*

schematism ('ski:mə,tɪzəm) *n* the general form, arrangement, or classification of something.

schematize *or* **schematise** ('ski:mə,taɪz) *vb* (*tr*) to form into or arrange in a scheme. ▸ **,schemati'zation** *or* **,schemati'sation** *n*

scheme (ski:m) *n* **1** a systematic plan for a course of action. **2** a systematic arrangement of correlated parts; system. **3** a secret plot. **4** a visionary or unrealizable project. **5** a chart, diagram, or outline. **6** an astrological diagram giving the aspects of celestial bodies at a particular time. **7** *Chiefly Brit.* a plan formally adopted by a commercial enterprise or governmental body, as for pensions, etc. **8** *Chiefly Scot.* an area of housing that is laid out esp. by a local authority; estate. ♦ *vb* **9** (*tr*) to devise a system for. **10** to form intrigues (for) in an underhand manner. [C16: from Latin *schema,* from Greek *skhēma* form] ▸ **'schemer** *n*

scheming ('ski:mɪŋ) *adj* **1** given to making plots; cunning. ♦ *n* **2** intrigues. ▸ **'schemingly** *adv*

Schengen Convention *or* **Agreement** ('ʃɛŋən) *n* an agreement, signed in 1985, but not implemented until 1995, to abolish border controls within Europe: ten countries had acceded by 1995; the UK is not a signatory.

scherzando (skɛə'tsændəu) *Music.* ♦ *adj, adv* **1** to be performed in a lighthearted manner. ♦ *n, pl* **-di** (-di:) *or* **-dos. 2** a movement, passage, etc., directed to be performed in this way. [Italian, literally: joking. See SCHERZO]

scherzo ('skɛətsəu) *n, pl* **-zos** *or* **-zi** (-tsi:). a brisk lively movement, developed from the minuet, with a contrastive middle section (a trio). See **minuet** (sense 2). [Italian: joke, of Germanic origin; compare Middle High German *scherzen* to jest]

Schiaparelli (*Italian* skjapa'rɛlli) *n* **1 Elsa** ('elsa). 1896–1973, Italian couturière, noted esp. for the dramatic colours of her designs. **2 Giovanni Virginio** (dʒo'vanni vir'dʒi:njo). 1835–1910, Italian astronomer, who discovered the asteroid Hesperia (1861) and the so-called canals of Mars (1877).

Schickard ('ʃɪkəd) *n* a large crater in the SW quadrant of the moon, about 227 kilometres (141 miles) in diameter.

Schick test (ʃɪk) *n Med.* a skin test to determine immunity to diphtheria: a dilute diphtheria toxin is injected into the skin; within two or three days a red inflamed area will develop if no antibodies are present. [C20: named after Bela *Schick* (1877–1967), U.S. paediatrician]

Schiedam (*Dutch* sxi:'dɑm) *n* a port in the SW Netherlands, in South Holland province west of Rotterdam: gin distilleries. Pop.: 72 515 (1994).

Schiele (*German* 'ʃi:lə) *n* **Egon** ('e:gɔn). 1890–1918, Austrian painter and draughtsman: a leading exponent of Austrian expressionism.

Schiff base (ʃɪf) *n* the product of the chemical association of an aldehyde with a primary amine. [C19: named after Hugo *Schiff* (1834–1915), German chemist]

schiller ('ʃɪlə) *n* an unusual metallic lustre in some minerals caused by internal reflection from certain inclusions such as gas cavities. [C19: from German *Schiller* iridescence, from Old High German *scilihen* to blink]

Schiller (*German* 'ʃɪlər) *n* **Johann Christoph Friedrich von** (jo'han 'krɪstɔf 'fri:drɪç fɔn). 1759–1805, German poet, dramatist, historian, and critic. His concern with the ideal freedom of the human spirit to rise above the constraints placed upon it is reflected in his great trilogy *Wallenstein* (1800) and in *Maria Stuart* (1800).

schilling ('ʃɪlɪŋ) *n* **1** the standard monetary unit of Austria, divided into 100 groschen. **2** an old German coin of low denomination. [C18: from German: SHILLING]

schipperke ('ʃɪpəkɪ, 'skɪp-) *n* a small Dutch breed of tailless dog with a foxy head, pricked ears, and usually a black coat. [C19: from Dutch, literally: little boatman (from its use as a guard dog on canal barges). See SKIPPER[1]]

schism ('sɪzəm, 'skɪz-) *n* **1** the division of a group into opposing factions. **2** the factions so formed. **3** division within or separation from an established Church, esp. the Roman Catholic Church, not necessarily involving differences in doctrine. [C14: from Church Latin *schisma,* from Greek *skhisma* a cleft, from *skhizein* to split]

schismatic (sɪz'mætɪk, skɪz-) *or* **schismatical** *adj* **1** of, relating to, or promoting schism. ♦ *n* **2** a person who causes schism or belongs to a schismatic faction. ▸ **schis'matically** *adv* ▸ **schis'maticalness** *n*

schist (ʃɪst) *n* any metamorphic rock that can be split into thin layers because its micaceous minerals have become aligned in thin parallel bands. [C18: from French *schiste,* from Latin *lapis schistos* stone that may be split, from Greek *skhizein* to split] ▸ **'schistose** *adj* ▸ **schistosity** (ʃɪ'stɒsɪtɪ) *n*

schistosome ('ʃɪstə,səum) *n* any of various blood flukes of the chiefly tropical genus *Schistosoma,* which cause disease in man and domestic animals. Also called: **bilharzia.** [C19: from New Latin *Schistosoma;* see SCHIST, -SOME[3]]

schistosomiasis (,ʃɪstəsəu'maɪəsɪs) *n* a disease caused by infestation of the body with blood flukes of the genus *Schistosoma.* Also called: **bilharziasis.**

schizanthus (skɪt'sænθəs) *n* any plant of the Chilean annual genus *Schizanthus,* some species of which are grown as pot or garden plants for their showy red, white, or yellow orchid-like flowers: family *Solanaceae.* Sometimes called: **poor man's orchid.** [New Latin, from Greek *schizein* to cut + *anthos* flower (from the deeply divided corolla)]

schizo ('skɪtsəu) *Offensive.* ♦ *adj* **1** schizophrenic. ♦ *n, pl* **-os. 2** a schizophrenic person.

schizo- *or before a vowel* **schiz-** *combining form.* indicating a cleavage, split, or division: *schizocarp; schizophrenia.* [from Greek *skhizein* to split]

schizocarp ('skɪzə,kɑ:p) *n Botany.* a dry fruit that splits into two or more one-seeded portions at maturity. ▸ **,schizo'carpous** *or* **,schizo'carpic** *adj*

schizogenesis (,skɪtsəu'dʒɛnɪsɪs) *n* asexual reproduction by fission of the parent organism or part. ▸ **schizogenetic** (,skɪtsəudʒɪ'nɛtɪk) *adj*

schizogony (skɪt'sɒgənɪ) *n* asexual reproduction in protozoans that is characterized by multiple fission.

schizoid ('skɪtsɔɪd) *adj* **1** *Psychol.* denoting a personality disorder characterized by extreme shyness and oversensitivity to others. **2** *Informal.* characterized by or showing conflicting or contradictory attitudes, ideas, etc. ♦ *n* **3** a person who has a schizoid personality.

schizomycete (,skɪtsəumaɪ'si:t) *n* any microscopic organism of the class *Schizomycetes,* which includes the bacteria. ▸ **schizomycetic** (,skɪtsəumaɪ'sɛtɪk) *or* **,schizomy'cetous** *adj*

schizont ('skɪtsɒnt) *n* a cell formed from a trophozoite during the asexual stage of the life cycle of sporozoan protozoans, such as the malaria parasite. [C19: from SCHIZO- + *-ont* a being, from Greek *einai* to be]

schizophrenia (,skɪtsəu'fri:nɪə) *n* **1** any of a group of psychotic disorders characterized by progressive deterioration of the personality, withdrawal from reality, hallucinations, delusions, social apathy, emotional instability, etc. See **catatonia, hebephrenia, paranoia. 2** *Informal.* behaviour that appears to be motivated by contradictory or conflicting principles. [C20: from SCHIZO- + Greek *phrēn* mind + -IA]

schizophrenic (,skɪtsəu'frɛnɪk) *adj* **1** exhibiting symptoms of schizophrenia. **2** *Informal.* experiencing or maintaining contradictory attitudes, emotions, etc. ♦ *n* **3** a person who is schizophrenic.

schizophrenogenic (,skɪtsəu,fri:nəu'dʒɛnɪk, -,frɛnəu-) *adj* tending to cause schizophrenia.

schizopod ('skɪtsəu,pɒd) *n* any of various shrimplike crustaceans of the former order *Schizopoda,* now separated into the orders *Mysidacea* (opossum shrimps) and *Euphausiacea.*

schizothymia (,skɪtsəu'θaɪmɪə) *n Psychiatry.* the condition of being schizoid or introverted. It encompasses elements of schizophrenia but does not involve the same depth of psychological disturbance. [C20: New Latin, from SCHIZO- + *-thymia,* from Greek *thumos* spirit] ▸ **,schizo'thymic** *adj*

Schlegel (*German* 'ʃle:gəl) *n* **1 August Wilhelm von** ('august 'vɪlhɛlm fɔn). 1767–1845, German romantic critic and scholar, noted particularly for his translations of Shakespeare. **2** his brother, **Friedrich von** ('fri:drɪç fɔn). 1772–1829, German philosopher and critic; a founder of the romantic movement in Germany.

Schleiermacher (*German* 'ʃlaiər,maxər) *n* **Friedrich Ernst Daniel** ('fri:drɪç ɛrnst 'da:njeːl). 1768–1834, German Protestant theologian and philosopher. His works include *The Christian Faith* (1821–22).

schlemiel, schlemihl, *or* **shlemiel** (ʃlə'mi:l) *n U.S. slang.* an awkward or unlucky person whose endeavours usually fail. [Yiddish, from German, after the hero of a novel by Chamisso (1781–1838)]

schlep (ʃlɛp) *U.S. slang.* ◆ *vb* **schleps, schlepping, schlepped. 1** to drag or lug (oneself or an object) with difficulty. ◆ *n* **2** a stupid or clumsy person. **3** an arduous journey or procedure. [Yiddish, from German *schleppen*]

Schlesien ('ʃle:ziən) *n* the German name for **Silesia.**

Schlesinger ('ʃlɛzɪŋə) *n* **John (Richard).** born 1926, British film and theatre director. Films include *Billy Liar* (1963), *Midnight Cowboy* (1969), *Sunday Bloody Sunday* (1971) and *Eye for an Eye* (1995).

Schleswig (*German* 'ʃle:svɪç) *n* **1** a fishing port in N Germany, in Schleswig-Holstein state: on an inlet of the Baltic. Pop.: 26 817 (1989 est.). **2** a former duchy, in the S Jutland Peninsula: annexed by Prussia in 1864; N part returned to Denmark after a plebiscite in 1920; S part forms part of the German state of Schleswig-Holstein. Danish name: **Slesvig.**

Schleswig-Holstein (*German* 'ʃle:svɪç'hɔlʃtain) *n* a state of N Germany, formerly in West Germany: drained chiefly by the River Elbe; mainly agricultural. Capital: Kiel. Pop.: 2 725 500 (1996 est.). Area: 15 658 sq. km (6045 sq. miles).

Schlick (ʃlɪk) *n* **Moritz.** 1882–1936, German philosopher, working in Austria, who founded (1924) the Vienna Circle to develop the doctrine of logical positivism. His works include the *General Theory of Knowledge* (1918) and *Problems of Ethics* (1930).

Schlieffen (*German* 'ʃli:fən) *n* **Alfred** ('alfre:t), Count von Schlieffen. 1833–1913, German field marshal, who devised the **Schlieffen Plan** (1905): it was intended to ensure German victory over a Franco-Russian alliance by holding off Russia with minimal strength and swiftly defeating France by a massive flanking movement through the Low Countries. In a modified form, it was unsuccessfully employed in World War I (1914).

Schliemann (*German* 'ʃli:man) *n* **Heinrich** ('hainrɪç). 1822–90, German archaeologist, who discovered nine superimposed city sites of Troy (1871–90). He also excavated the site of Mycenae (1876).

schlieren ('ʃlɪərən) *n* **1** *Physics.* visible streaks produced in a transparent fluid as a result of variations in the fluid's density leading to variations in refractive index. They can be recorded by flash photography (**schlieren photography**). **2** streaks or platelike masses of mineral in a rock mass, that differ in texture or composition from the main mass. [German, plural of *Schliere* streak] ▸ **'schlieric** *adj*

schlock (ʃlɒk) *Chiefly U.S. slang.* ◆ *n* **1** goods or produce of cheap or inferior quality; trash. ◆ *adj* **2** cheap, inferior, or trashy. [Yiddish: damaged merchandise, probably from German *Schlag* a blow; related to SLAY]

schlumbergera (ʃləm'bɜ:gərə) *n* See **Christmas cactus.**

schmaltz *or* **schmalz** (ʃmælts, ʃmɔ:lts) *n* **1** excessive sentimentality, esp. in music. **2** *U.S.* animal fat used in cooking. [C20: from German (*Schmalz*) and Yiddish: melted fat, from Old High German *smalz*] ▸ **'schmaltzy** *adj*

Schmidt (ʃmɪt) *n* **Helmut (Heinrich Waldemar)** ('hɛlmu:t). born 1918, German Social Democrat statesman; chancellor of West Germany (1974–82).

Schmidt telescope *or* **camera** *n* a catadioptric telescope designed to produce a very sharp image of a large area of sky in one photographic exposure. It incorporates a thin specially shaped glass plate at the centre of curvature of a short-focus spherical primary mirror so that the resulting image, which is focused on a photographic plate, is free from spherical aberration, coma, and astigmatism. [C20: named after B. V. *Schmidt* (1879–1935), Estonian-born German inventor]

Schmitt trigger *n Electronics.* a bistable circuit that gives a constant output when the input voltage is above a specified value. [C20: named after O. H. *Schmitt* (born 1913), U.S. scientist]

schmo *or* **shmo** (ʃməʊ) *n, pl* **schmoes** *or* **shmoes.** *U.S. slang.* a dull, stupid, or boring person. [from Yiddish *shmok*]

schmooze (ʃmu:z) *Slang.* ◆ *vb* **1** (*intr*) to chat or gossip. **2** (*tr*) to chat to (someone) for the purposes of self-promotion or to gain some advantage. ◆ *n* **3** a trivial conversation; chat. [Yiddish, from *schmues* a chat, from Hebrew *shemuoth* reports]

schmuck (ʃmʌk) *n U.S. slang.* a stupid or contemptible person; oaf. [from Yiddish *schmuck* penis, from German *Schmuck* decoration, from Middle High German *smucken* to press into]

schmutter ('ʃmʌtə) *n Slang.* cloth or clothing. [C20: from Yiddish *schmatte* rag, from Polish *szmata*]

Schnabel ('ʃnɑ:bᵊl) *n* **Artur** ('artʊr). 1882–1951, U.S. pianist and composer, born in Austria.

schnapper ('ʃnæpə) *n* a variant of **snapper** (senses 1, 2).

schnapps *or* **schnaps** (ʃnæps) *n* **1** a Dutch spirit distilled from potatoes. **2** (in Germany) any strong spirit. [C19: from German *Schnaps,* from *schnappen* to SNAP]

schnauzer ('ʃnaʊtsə) *n* a wire-haired breed of dog of the terrier type, originally from Germany, having a greyish coat and distinctive beard, moustache, and eyebrows. [C19: from German *Schnauze* SNOUT]

schnecken ('ʃnɛkən) *pl n, sing* **schnecke** ('ʃnɛkə). *Chiefly U.S.* a sweet spiral-shaped bread roll flavoured with cinnamon and nuts. [German, plural of *Schnecke* SNAIL]

Schneider Trophy ('ʃnaɪdə) *n* a trophy for air racing between seaplanes of any nation, first presented by Jacques Schneider in 1913; won outright by Britain in 1931.

Schnittke ('ʃnɪtkə) *n* **Alfred.** 1934–98, Russian composer: his works include four symphonies, four violin concertos, choral, chamber, and film music.

schnitzel ('ʃnɪtsəl) *n* a thin slice of meat, esp. veal. See also **Wiener schnitzel.** [German: cutlet, from *schnitzen* to carve, *schnitzeln* to whittle]

Schnitzler (*German* 'ʃnɪtslər) *n* **Arthur** ('artʊr). 1862–1931, Austrian dramatist and novelist. His best-known work is *Anatol* (1893), a series of one-act plays that reveal his psychological insight and preoccupation with sexuality.

schnook (ʃnʊk) *n U.S. slang.* a stupid or gullible person. [from Yiddish *shnok,* variant of *shmok* SCHMO]

schnorkel ('ʃnɔ:kᵊl) *n, vb* a less common variant of **snorkel.**

schnorrer ('ʃnɔ:rə) *n U.S. slang.* a person who lives off the charity of others; professional beggar. [Yiddish, from German *Schnurrer* beggar (who played an instrument), from Middle High German *snurren* to hum]

schnozzle ('ʃnɒzᵊl) *n Chiefly U.S.* a slang word for **nose** (sense 1). [alteration of Yiddish *shnoitsl,* diminutive of *shnoits,* from German *Schnauze* SNOUT]

Schoenberg *or* **Schönberg** ('ʃɜ:nbɜ:g; *German* 'ʃø:nbɛrk) *n* **Arnold** ('arnɔlt). 1874–1951, Austrian composer and musical theorist, in the U.S. after 1933. The harmonic idiom of such early works as the string sextet *Verklärte Nacht* (1899) gave way to his development of atonality, as in the song cycle *Pierrot Lunaire* (1912), and later of the twelve-tone technique. He wrote many choral, orchestral, and chamber works and the unfinished opera *Moses and Aaron.*

schola cantorum ('skəʊlə kæn'tɔ:rəm) *n, pl* **scholae cantorum** ('skəʊli:). a choir or choir school maintained by a church. [Medieval Latin: school of singers]

scholar ('skɒlə) *n* **1** a learned person, esp. in the humanities. **2** a person, esp. a child, who studies; pupil. **3** a student of merit at an educational establishment who receives financial aid, esp. from an endowment given for such a purpose. **4** *S. African.* a school pupil. [C14: from Old French *escoler,* via Late Latin from Latin *schola* SCHOOL¹] ▸ **'scholarly** *adj* ▸ **'scholarliness** *n*

scholarship ('skɒləʃɪp) *n* **1** academic achievement; erudition; learning. **2a** financial aid provided for a scholar because of academic merit. **2b** the position of a student who gains this financial aid. **2c** (*as modifier*): *a scholarship student.* **3** the qualities of a scholar.

scholar's mate *n Chess.* a simple mate by the queen on the f7 square, achievable by white's fourth move.

scholastic (skə'læstɪk) *adj* **1** of, relating to, or befitting schools, scholars, or education. **2** pedantic or precise. **3** (*often cap.*) characteristic of or relating to the medieval Schoolmen. ◆ *n* **4** a student or pupil. **5** a person who is given to quibbling or logical subtleties; pedant. **6** (*often cap.*) a disciple or adherent of scholasticism; Schoolman. **7a** a Jesuit student who is undergoing a period of probation prior to commencing his theological studies. **7b** the status and position of such a student. **8** a formalist in art. [C16: via Latin from Greek *skholastikos* devoted to learning, ultimately from *skholē* SCHOOL¹] ▸ **scho'lastically** *adv*

scholasticate (skə'læstɪˌkeɪt, -kɪt) *n R.C. Church.* the state of being a scholastic, the period during which a Jesuit student is a scholastic, or an institution where scholastics pass this period. [C19: from New Latin *scholasticātus,* from Latin *scholasticus* SCHOLASTIC]

scholasticism (skə'læstɪˌsɪzəm) *n* **1** (*sometimes cap.*) the system of philosophy, theology, and teaching that dominated medieval western Europe and was based on the writings of the Church Fathers and (from the 12th century) Aristotle. **2** strict adherence to traditional doctrines.

scholiast ('skəʊlɪˌæst) *n* a medieval annotator, esp. of classical texts. [C16: from Late Greek *skholiastēs,* from *skholiazein* to write a SCHOLIUM] ▸ **ˌscholi'astic** *adj*

scholium ('skəʊlɪəm) *n, pl* **-lia** (-lɪə). a commentary or annotation, esp. on a classical text. [C16: from New Latin, from Greek *skholion* exposition, from *skholē* SCHOOL¹]

Schönberg ('ʃɜ:nbɜ:g; *German* 'ʃø:nbɛrk) *n* See **Schoenberg.**

Schongauer (*German* 'ʃo:ngauər) *n* **Martin** ('marti:n). ?1445–91, German painter and engraver.

school¹ (sku:l) *n* **1a** an institution or building at which children and young people usually under 19 receive education. **1b** (*as modifier*): *school bus; school day.* **1c** (*in combination*): *schoolroom; schoolwork.* **2** any educational institution or building. **3** a faculty, institution, or department specializing in a particular subject: *a law school.* **4** the staff and pupils of a school. **5** the period of instruction in a school or one session of this: *he stayed after school to do extra work.* **6** meetings held occasionally for members of a profession, etc. **7** a place or sphere of activity that instructs: *the school of hard knocks.* **8** a body of people or pupils adhering to a certain set of principles, doctrines, or methods. **9** a group of artists, writers, etc., linked by the same style, teachers, or aims: *the Venetian school of painting.* **10** a style of life: *a gentleman of the old school.* **11** *Informal.* a group assembled for a common purpose, esp. gambling or drinking. ◆ *vb* (*tr*) **12** to train or educate in or as in a school. **13** to discipline or control. **14** an archaic word for **reprimand.** [Old English *scōl,* from Latin *schola* school, from Greek *skholē* leisure spent in the pursuit of knowledge]

school² (sku:l) *n* **1** a group of porpoises or similar aquatic animals that swim together. ◆ *vb* **2** (*intr*) to form such a group. [Old English *scolu* SHOAL²]

school attendance officer *n* a former name for **Educational Welfare Officer.**

school board *n* **1** (formerly in Britain) an elected board of ratepayers who provided local elementary schools between 1870 and 1902. **2** (in the U.S. and Canada) a local board of education.

schoolboy ('sku:lˌbɔɪ) *or* (*fem*) **schoolgirl** *n* a child attending school.

School Certificate *n* (in England and Wales between 1917 and 1951 and currently in New Zealand) a certificate awarded to school pupils who pass a public examination: the equivalent of O level. Abbrev.: **SC.**

School Committee *n* (in New Zealand) a parent group selected to support a primary school.

school crossing patrol *n* the official name for **lollipop man** *or* **lady.**

schoolhouse ('sku:lˌhaʊs) *n* **1** a building used as a school, esp. a rural school. **2** a house attached to a school.

schoolie ('sku:lɪ) *n Austral. slang.* a schoolteacher or a high school student.

schooling ('sku:lɪŋ) *n* **1** education, esp. when received at school. **2** the process of teaching or being taught in a school. **3** the training of an animal, esp. of a horse for dressage. **4** an archaic word for **reprimand.**

school-leaver *n* a pupil who is about to leave or has recently left school, esp. at the minimum school-leaving age. ► **'school-,leaving** *adj*

schoolman ('sku:lmən) *n, pl* **-men. 1** (*sometimes cap.*) a scholar versed in the learning of the Schoolmen. **2** *Rare, chiefly U.S.* a professional educator or teacher.

Schoolman ('sku:lmən) *n, pl* **-men.** (*sometimes not cap.*) a master in one of the schools or universities of the Middle Ages who was versed in scholasticism; scholastic.

schoolmarm ('sku:l,mɑ:m) *n Informal.* **1** a woman schoolteacher, esp. when considered to be prim, prudish, or old-fashioned. **2** *Brit.* any woman considered to be prim, prudish, or old-fashioned. **[C19:** from SCHOOL[1] + *marm,* variant of MA'AM. See MADAM**]** ► **'school,marmish** *adj*

schoolmaster ('sku:l,mɑ:stə) *n* **1** a man who teaches in or runs a school. **2** a person or thing that acts as an instructor. **3** a food fish, *Lutjanus apodus,* of the warm waters of the Caribbean and Atlantic: family *Lutjanidae* (snappers). ◆ *vb* (*intr*) **4** to be a schoolmaster. ► **'school,mastering** *n* ► **'school,masterish** *adj* ► **'school,masterly** *adj* ► **'school,mastership** *n*

schoolmate ('sku:l,meɪt) *or* **schoolfellow** *n* a companion at school; fellow pupil.

school milk *n Social welfare.* (formerly, in Britain) a third of a pint of milk, originally provided free by the local education authority to all young pupils, then later given only to children who passed a needs or means test.

schoolmistress ('sku:l,mɪstrɪs) *n* a woman who teaches in or runs a school. ► **'school,mistressy** *adj*

school of arts *n Austral.* a public building in a small town, originally one used for adult education.

Schools (sku:lz) *pl n* **1 the.** the medieval Schoolmen collectively. **2** (at Oxford University) **2a** the Examination Schools, the University building in which examinations are held. **2b** *Informal.* the Second Public Examination for the degree of Bachelor of Arts; finals.

school ship *n* a ship for training young men in seamanship, for a career in the regular or merchant navy.

schoolteacher ('sku:l,ti:tʃə) *n* a person who teaches in a school. ► **'school,teaching** *n*

school welfare officer *n* a former name for **Educational Welfare Officer.**

school year *n* **1** a twelve-month period, (in Britain) usually starting in late summer and continuing for three terms until the following summer, during which pupils remain in the same class. **2** the time during this period when the school is open.

schooner ('sku:nə) *n* **1** a sailing vessel with at least two masts, with all lower sails rigged fore-and-aft, and with the main mast stepped aft. **2** *Brit.* a large glass for sherry. **3** *U.S., Canadian, Austral., and N.Z.* a large glass for beer. **[C18:** origin uncertain**]**

schooner rig *n Nautical.* a rig in which the mainmast is taller than the foremast.

Schopenhauer (*German* 'ʃo:pənhauər) *n* **Arthur** ('artur). 1788–1860, German pessimist philosopher. In his chief work, *The World as Will and Idea* (1819), he expounded the view that will is the creative primary factor and idea the secondary receptive factor. ► **Schopenhauerian** (,ʃəupən'hauərɪən) *adj* ► **'Schopen,hauer,ism** *n*

schorl (ʃɔ:l) *n* a black tourmaline consisting of a borosilicate of sodium, iron, and aluminium. Formula: $NaFe_3B_3Al_3(Al_3Si_6O_{27})(OH)_4$. **[C18:** from German *Schörl,* origin unknown**]** ► **schor'laceous** *adj*

schottische (ʃɒ'ti:ʃ) *n* **1** a 19th-century German dance resembling a slow polka. **2** a piece of music composed for or in the manner of this dance. **[C19:** from German *der schottische Tanz* the Scottish dance**]**

Schottky defect ('ʃɒtkɪ) *n Physics.* a crystal defect in which vacancies exist in the lattice. **[C20:** named after Walter *Schottky* (1886–1976), German physicist**]**

Schottky effect *n Physics.* a reduction in the energy required to remove an electron from a solid surface in a vacuum when an electric field is applied to the surface.

Schottky noise *n* another name for **shot noise.**

Schouten Islands ('ʃaut°n) *pl n* a group of islands in the Pacific, off the N coast of Irian Jaya. Pop.: 25 487 (1966). Area: 3185 sq. km (1230 sq. miles).

Schreiner ('ʃraɪnə) *n* **Olive** (**Emilie Albertina**). 1855–1920, South African novelist and feminist writer, whose works include the autobiographical *The Story of an African Farm* (1883) and *Women and Labour* (1911).

Schrödinger (*German* 'ʃrø:dɪŋər) *n* **Erwin** ('ɛrvi:n). 1887–1961, Austrian physicist, who discovered the wave equation: shared the Nobel prize for physics 1933.

Schrödinger equation *n* an equation used in wave mechanics to describe a physical system. For a particle of mass *m* and potential energy *V* it is written $(ih/2\pi).(\partial\psi/\partial t) = (-h^2/8\pi^2 m)\nabla^2\psi + V\psi$, where $i = \sqrt{-1}$, *h* is the Planck constant, *t* the time, ∇^2 the Laplace operator, and ψ the wave function.

Schubert ('ʃu:bət) *n* **Franz** (**Peter**) (frants). 1797–1828, Austrian composer; the originator and supreme exponent of the modern German lied. His many songs include the cycles *Die Schöne Müllerin* (1823) and *Die Winterreise* (1827). His other works include symphonies and much piano and chamber music including string quartets and the *Trout* piano quintet (1819).

schul (ʃu:l) *n* a variant spelling of **shul.**

Schumacher (*German* 'ʃu:maxər) *n* **1 Ernst Friedrich** (ɛrnst 'fri:drɪç). 1911–77, British economist, born in Germany. He is best known for his book *Small is Beautiful* (1973). **2 Michael.** born 1969, German motor racing driver; Formula One world champion (1994, 1995).

Schuman *n* **1** (*French* ʃuman). **Robert** (rɔbɛr). 1886–1963, French statesman; prime minister (1947–48). He proposed (1950) pooling the coal and steel resources of W Europe. **2** ('ʃu:mən). **William** (**Howard**). 1910–91, U.S. composer.

Schumann ('ʃu:mən) *n* **1 Elisabeth** (e'li:zabɛt). 1885–1952, German soprano, noted esp. for her interpretations of lieder. **2 Robert Alexander** ('ro:bɛrt alɛ'ksandər). 1810–56, German romantic composer, noted esp. for his piano music, such as *Carneval* (1835) and *Kreisleriana* (1838), his songs, and four symphonies.

schuss (ʃus) *Skiing.* ◆ *n* **1** a straight high-speed downhill run. ◆ *vb* **2** (*intr*) to perform a schuss. **[**German: SHOT[1]**]**

Schütz (*German* ʃyts) *n* **Heinrich** ('hainrɪç). 1585–1672, German composer, esp. of church music and madrigals.

Schutzstaffel *German.* ('ʃutsʃtafəl) *n, pl* ***-feln*** (-fəln). See **SS.**

schwa *or* **shwa** (ʃwɑ:) *n* **1** a central vowel represented in the International Phonetic Alphabet by (ə). The sound occurs in unstressed syllables in English, as in *around, mother,* and *sofa.* **2** the symbol (ə) used to represent this sound. **[C19:** via German from Hebrew *shewā,* a diacritic indicating lack of a vowel sound**]**

Schwaben ('ʃva:bən) *n* the German name for **Swabia.**

Schwann (*German* ʃvan) *n* **Theodor** ('te:odo:r). 1810–82, German physiologist, who founded the theory that all animals consist of cells or cell products.

Schwarzkopf (*German* 'ʃvartskɔpf) *n* **1 Elisabeth** (e'li:zabɛt). born 1915, Austro-British operatic soprano, born in Germany. **2** ('ʃwɔ:ts,kɒpf). **Norman,** nicknamed *Stormin' Norman.* born 1934, U.S. general. As head of Central Command, the U.S. military district covering the Middle East, he became the victorious commander-in-chief of the U.S.-led UN forces in the Gulf War (1991).

Schwarzschild radius ('ʃwɔ:ts,ʃɪld; *German* 'ʃvartsʃɪlt) *n Astronomy.* the radius of a sphere (**Schwarzschild sphere**) surrounding an object, esp. a black hole, from within which no meaningful information can escape because of gravitational forces. **[C20:** named after Karl *Schwarzschild* (1873–1916), U.S. astrophysicist**]**

Schwarzwald ('ʃvartsvalt) *n* the German name for the **Black Forest.**

Schweinfurt (*German* 'ʃvainfurt) *n* a city in central Germany, in N Bavaria on the River Main. Pop.: 54 520 (1991).

Schweitzer ('ʃwaɪtsə, 'ʃvaɪt-) *n* **Albert.** 1875–1965, Franco-German medical missionary, philosopher, theologian, and organist, born in Alsace. He took up medicine in 1905 and devoted most of his life after 1913 to a medical mission at Lambaréné, Gabon: Nobel peace prize 1952.

Schweiz (ʃvaits) *n* the German name for **Switzerland.**

Schwerin (*German* ʃve'ri:n) *n* a city in N Germany, in Mecklenburg-West Pomerania on **Lake Schwerin.** Pop.: 114 688 (1996 est.).

Schwitters (*German* 'ʃvɪtərs) *n* **Kurt** (kurt). 1887–1948, German dadaist painter and poet, noted for his collages composed of discarded materials.

Schwyz (*German* ʃvi:ts) *n* **1** a canton of central Switzerland: played an important part in the formation of the Swiss confederation, to which it gave its name. Capital: Schwyz. Pop.: 122 409 (1996 est.). Area: 908 sq. km (351 sq. miles). **2** a town in E central Switzerland, capital of Schwyz canton: tourism. Pop.: 12 740 (1990).

sci. *abbrev. for:* **1** science. **2** scientific.

sciaenid (saɪ'i:nɪd) *or* **sciaenoid** *adj* **1** of, relating to, or belonging to the *Sciaenidae,* a family of mainly tropical and subtropical marine percoid fishes that includes the drums, grunts, and croakers. ◆ *n* **2** any sciaenid fish. **[C19:** from Latin *sciaena* a type of fish, from Greek *skiaina***]**

sciamachy (saɪ'æməkɪ), **sciomachy,** *or* **skiamachy** (skaɪ'æməkɪ) *n, pl* **-chies.** *Rare.* a fight with an imaginary enemy. **[C17:** from Greek *skiamakhia* a mock fight, from *skia* a shadow + *makhesthai* to fight**]**

sciatic (saɪ'ætɪk) *adj* **1** *Anatomy.* of or relating to the hip or the hipbone. **2** of, relating to, or afflicted with sciatica. **[C16:** from French *sciatique,* from Late Latin *sciaticus,* from Latin *ischiadicus* relating to pain in the hip, from Greek *iskhiadikos,* from *iskhia* hip joint**]**

sciatica (saɪ'ætɪkə) *n* a form of neuralgia characterized by intense pain and tenderness along the course of the body's longest nerve (**sciatic nerve**), extending from the back of the thigh down to the calf of the leg. **[C15:** from Late Latin *sciatica;* see SCIATIC**]**

SCID *abbrev. for* severe combined immune deficiency; a serious condition in which babies are born with reduced numbers of T- and B-lymphocytes, which impairs their immune systems and makes them susceptible to severe infections and cancer.

science ('saɪəns) *n* **1** the systematic study of the nature and behaviour of the material and physical universe, based on observation, experiment, and measurement, and the formulation of laws to describe these facts in general terms. **2** the knowledge so obtained or the practice of obtaining it. **3** any particular branch of this knowledge: *the pure and applied sciences.* **4** any body of knowledge organized in a systematic manner. **5** skill or technique. **6** *Archaic.* knowledge. **[C14:** via Old French from Latin *scientia* knowledge, from *scīre* to know**]**

science fiction *n* **a** a literary genre that makes imaginative use of scientific knowledge or conjecture. **b** (*as modifier*): *a science fiction writer.*

Science Museum *n* a museum in London, originating from 1852 and given its present name and site in 1899: contains collections relating to the history of science, technology, and industry.

science park *n* an area usually linked with a university where scientific research and commercial development are carried on in cooperation.

scienter (saɪ'ɛntə) *adv Law.* knowingly; wilfully. [from Latin]

sciential (saɪ'ɛnʃəl) *adj* **1** of or relating to science. **2** skilful or knowledgeable.

scientific (,saɪən'tɪfɪk) *adj* **1** (*prenominal*) of, relating to, derived from, or used in science: *scientific equipment.* **2** (*prenominal*) occupied in science: *scientific manpower.* **3** conforming with the principles or methods used in science: *a scientific approach.* ▸ ˌ**scien'tifically** *adv*

scientific method *n* a method of investigation in which a problem is first identified and observations, experiments, or other relevant data are then used to construct or test hypotheses that purport to solve it.

scientific socialism *n* Marxist socialism. Compare **utopian socialism.**

scientism ('saɪənˌtɪzəm) *n* **1** the application of, or belief in, the scientific method. **2** the uncritical application of scientific or quasi-scientific methods to inappropriate fields of study or investigation. ▸ ˌ**scien'tistic** *adj*

scientist ('saɪəntɪst) *n* a person who studies or practises any of the sciences or who uses scientific methods.

Scientist ('saɪəntɪst) *n* **1** *Christian Science.* Christ as supreme spiritual healer. **2** short for **Christian Scientist.**

Scientology (ˌsaɪən'tɒlədʒɪ) *n Trademark.* the philosophy of the Church of Scientology, a nondenominational movement founded in the U.S. in the 1950s, which emphasizes self-knowledge as a means of realizing full spiritual potential. [C20: from Latin *scient(ia)* SCIENCE + -LOGY] ▸ ˌ**Scien'tologist** *n*

sci-fi ('saɪˌfaɪ) *n* short for **science fiction.**

scilicet ('sɪlɪˌsɛt) *adv* namely; that is: used esp. in explaining an obscure text or supplying a missing word. [Latin: shortened from *scīre licet* it is permitted to know]

scilla ('sɪlə) *n* any liliaceous plant of the genus *Scilla,* of Old World temperate regions, having small bell-shaped flowers. See also **squill** (sense 3). [C19: via Latin from Greek *skilla;* compare SQUILL]

Scilly Isles, Scilly Islands ('sɪlɪ), *or* **Scillies** ('sɪlɪz) *pl n* a group of about 140 small islands (only five inhabited) off the extreme SW coast of England: tourist centre. Capital: Hugh Town. Pop.: 2900 (1991). Area: 16 sq. km (6 sq. miles). ▸ **Scillonian** (sɪ'ləʊnɪən) *adj, n*

scimitar *or* (*rarely*) **simitar** ('sɪmɪtə) *n* an oriental sword with a curved blade broadening towards the point. [C16: from Old Italian *scimitarra,* probably from Persian *shimshīr,* of obscure origin]

scincoid ('sɪŋkɔɪd) *or* **scincoidian** *adj* **1** of, relating to, or resembling a skink. ◆ *n* **2** any animal, esp. a lizard, resembling a skink. [C18: from New Latin *scincoidēs,* from Latin *scincus* a SKINK]

scindapsus (sɪn'dæpsəs) *n* any plant of the tropical Asiatic climbing genus *Scindapsus,* typically stem rooting, esp. *S. aureus* and *S. pictus,* grown as greenhouse or house plants for their leathery heart-shaped variegated leaves: family *Araceae.* [New Latin, from Greek *skindapsos* an ivy-like plant]

scintigraphy (ˌsɪn'tɪgrəfɪ) *n Med.* a diagnostic technique using a radioactive tracer and scintillation counter for producing pictures (**scintigrams**) of internal parts of the body. [C20: from SCINTI(LLATION) + -GRAPHY]

scintilla (sɪn'tɪlə) *n* a minute amount; hint, trace, or particle. [C17: from Latin: a spark]

scintillate ('sɪntɪˌleɪt) *vb* (*mainly intr*) **1** (*also tr*) to give off (sparks); sparkle; twinkle. **2** to be animated or brilliant. **3** *Physics.* to give off flashes of light as a result of the impact of particles or photons. [C17: from Latin *scintillāre,* from *scintilla* a spark] ▸ '**scintillant** *adj* ▸ '**scintillantly** *adv* ▸ '**scintilˌlating** *adj* ▸ '**scintilˌlatingly** *adv*

scintillation (ˌsɪntɪ'leɪʃən) *n* **1** the act of scintillating. **2** a spark or flash. **3** the twinkling of stars, caused by rapid changes in the density of the earth's atmosphere producing uneven refraction of starlight. **4** *Physics.* a flash of light produced when a material scintillates.

scintillation counter *n* an instrument for detecting and measuring the intensity of high-energy radiation. It consists of a phosphor with which particles collide producing flashes of light that are detected by a photomultiplier and converted into pulses of electric current that are counted by electronic equipment.

scintillator ('sɪntɪˌleɪtə) *n Physics.* a phosphor that produces scintillations.

scintillometer (ˌsɪntɪ'lɒmɪtə) *n Physics.* a device for observing ionizing radiation by the scintillations it produces in a suitable material.

scintillon (sɪn'tɪlən) *n* a luminescent body present in the cytoplasm of some dinoflagellates.

sciolism ('saɪəˌlɪzəm) *n Rare.* the practice of opinionating on subjects of which one has only superficial knowledge. [C19: from Late Latin *sciolus* someone with a smattering of knowledge, from Latin *scīre* to know] ▸ '**sciolist** *n* ▸ ˌ**scio'listic** *adj*

sciomachy (saɪ'ɒməkɪ) *n, pl* **-chies.** a variant of **sciamachy.**

sciomancy ('saɪəˌmænsɪ) *n* divination with the help of ghosts. [C17: via Latin from Greek *skia* ghost + -MANCY] ▸ '**sciomancer** *n* ▸ ˌ**scio'mantic** *adj*

scion ('saɪən) *n* **1** a descendant, heir, or young member of a family. **2** a shoot or twig of a plant used to form a graft. [C14: from Old French *cion,* of Germanic origin; compare Old High German *chīnan* to sprout]

sciophyte ('saɪəˌfaɪt) *n* any plant that grows best in the shade. [C20: via Latin from Greek *skia* shade + -PHYTE] ▸ **sciophytic** (ˌsaɪə'fɪtɪk) *adj*

Scipio ('skɪpɪˌəʊ, 'sɪpɪˌəʊ) *n* **1** full name *Publius Cornelius Scipio Africanus Major.* 237–183 B.C., Roman general. He commanded the Roman invasion of Carthage in the Second Punic War, defeating Hannibal at Zama (202). **2** full name *Publius Cornelius Scipio Aemilianus Africanus Minor.* ?185–129 B.C., Roman statesman and general; the grandson by adoption of Scipio Africanus Major. He commanded an army against Carthage in the last Punic War and razed the city to the ground (146). He became the leader (132) of the opposition in Rome to popular reforms.

scire facias ('saɪərɪ 'feɪʃɪˌæs) *n Law, rare.* **1** a judicial writ founded upon some record, such as a judgment, letters patent, etc., requiring the person against whom it is brought to show cause why the record should not be enforced or annulled. **2** a proceeding begun by the issue of such a writ. [C15: from legal Latin, literally: cause (him) to know]

scirrhous ('sɪrəs) *adj Pathol.* of or resembling a scirrhus; hard. ▸ **scirrhosity** (sɪ'rɒsɪtɪ) *n*

scirrhus ('sɪrəs) *n, pl* **-rhi** (-raɪ) *or* **-rhuses.** *Pathol.* a firm cancerous growth composed of fibrous tissues. [C17: from New Latin, from Latin *scirros,* from Greek *skirros,* from *skiros* hard] ▸ **scirrhoid** ('sɪrɔɪd) *adj*

scissel ('skɪsᵊl) *n* the waste metal left over from sheet metal after discs have been punched out of it. [C19: from French *cisaille,* from *cisailler* to clip]

scissile ('sɪsaɪl) *adj* capable of being cut or divided. [C17: from Latin *scissilis* that can be split, from *scindere* to cut]

scission ('sɪʃən) *n* the act or an instance of cutting, splitting, or dividing. [C15: from Late Latin *scissiō,* from *scindere* to split]

scissor ('sɪzə) *vb* to cut (an object) with scissors.

scissors ('sɪzəz) *pl n* **1** Also called: **pair of scissors.** a cutting instrument used for cloth, hair, etc., having two crossed pivoted blades that cut by a shearing action, with ring-shaped handles at one end. **2** a wrestling hold in which a wrestler wraps his legs round his opponent's body or head, locks his feet together, and squeezes. **3** any gymnastic or athletic feat in which the legs cross and uncross in a scissor-like movement. **4** *Athletics.* a technique in high-jumping, now little used, in which the legs perform a scissor-like movement in clearing the bar. [C14 *sisoures,* from Old French *cisoires,* from Vulgar Latin *cīsōria* (unattested), ultimately from Latin *caedere* to cut; see CHISEL] ▸ '**scissor-ˌlike** *adj*

scissors kick *n* **1** a type of swimming kick used esp. in the sidestroke, in which one leg is moved forward and the other bent back and they are then brought together again in a scissor-like action. **2** *Football.* a kick in which the player leaps into the air raising one leg and brings up his other leg to kick the ball.

scissure ('sɪʒə, 'sɪʃə) *n Rare.* a longitudinal cleft. [C15: from Latin *scissūra* a rending, from Latin *scindere* to split]

sciurine ('saɪjʊrɪn, -ˌraɪn) *adj* **1** of, relating to, or belonging to the *Sciuridae,* a family of rodents inhabiting most parts of the world except Australia and southern South America: includes squirrels, marmots, and chipmunks. ◆ *n* **2** any sciurine animal. [C19: from Latin *sciūrus,* from Greek *skiouros* squirrel, from *skia* a shadow + *oura* a tail]

sciuroid ('saɪjʊrɔɪd, saɪ'jʊərɔɪd) *adj* **1** (of an animal) resembling a squirrel. **2** (esp. of the spikes of barley) shaped like a squirrel's tail. [C19: from Latin *sciūrus* squirrel + -OID]

sclaff (sklæf) *Golf.* ◆ *vb* **1** to cause (the club) to hit (the ground behind the ball) when making a stroke. ◆ *n* **2** a sclaffing stroke or shot. ◆ Also: **duff.** [C19: from Scottish *sclaf* to shuffle] ▸ '**sclaffer** *n*

sclera ('sklɪərə) *n* the firm white fibrous membrane that forms the outer covering of the eyeball. Also called: **sclerotic.** [C19: from New Latin, from Greek *sklēros* hard]

sclere (sklɪə) *n Zoology.* a supporting anatomical structure, esp. a sponge spicule.

sclerenchyma (sklɪə'rɛŋkɪmə) *n* a supporting tissue in plants consisting of dead cells with very thick lignified walls. [C19: from SCLERO- + PARENCHYMA] ▸ **sclerenchymatous** (ˌsklɪərɛŋ'kɪmətəs) *adj*

sclerite ('sklɪəraɪt) *n Zoology.* **1** any of the hard chitinous plates that make up the exoskeleton of an arthropod. **2** any calcareous or chitinous part, such as a spicule or plate. [C19: from SCLERO- + -ITE[1]] ▸ **scleritic** (sklɪə'rɪtɪk) *adj*

scleritis (sklɪə'raɪtɪs) *or* **sclerotitis** (ˌsklɪərəʊ'taɪtɪs) *n Pathol.* inflammation of the sclera.

sclero- *or before a vowel* **scler-** *combining form.* **1** indicating hardness: *sclerosis.* **2** of or relating to the sclera: *sclerotomy.* [from Greek *sklēros* hard]

scleroderma (ˌsklɪərəʊ'dɜːmə), **sclerodermia** (ˌsklɪərəʊ'dɜːmɪə), *or* **scleriasis** (sklɪ'raɪəsɪs) *n* a chronic progressive disease most common among women, characterized by a local or diffuse thickening and hardening of the skin. [C19: from New Latin *sclerōdermus,* from Greek, from *sklēros* hard + *derma* skin]

sclerodermatous (ˌsklɪərəʊ'dɜːmətəs) *adj* **1** (of animals) possessing a hard external covering of scales or plates. **2** of or relating to scleroderma.

scleroid ('sklɪərɔɪd) *adj* (of organisms and their parts) hard or hardened.

scleroma (sklɪə'rəʊmə) *n, pl* **-mata** (-mətə) *or* **-mas.** *Pathol.* any small area of abnormally hard tissue, esp. in a mucous membrane. [C17: from New Latin, from Greek, from *sklēroun* to harden, from *sklēros* hard]

sclerometer (sklɪə'rɒmɪtə) *n* an instrument that determines the hardness of a mineral or metal by means of a diamond point. ▸ **sclerometric** (ˌsklɪərə'mɛtrɪk) *adj*

sclerophyll ('sklɛrəʊˌfɪl) *n* a woody plant with small leathery evergreen leaves that is the dominant plant form in certain hot dry areas, esp. the Mediterranean region. [C20: from Greek *sklēros* hard + *phullon* a leaf] ▸ **sclerophyllous** (sklɛ'rɒfɪləs) *adj*

scleroprotein (ˌsklɪərəʊ'prəʊtiːn) *n* any of a group of insoluble stable proteins such as keratin, elastin, and collagen that occur in skeletal and connective tissues. Also called: **albuminoid.**

sclerosed ('sklɪərəʊst) *adj Pathol.* hardened; sclerotic.

sclerosis (sklɪə'rəʊsɪs) *n, pl* **-ses** (-siːz). **1** *Pathol.* a hardening or thickening of organs, tissues, or vessels from chronic inflammation, abnormal growth of fibrous tissue, or degeneration of the myelin sheath of nerve fibres, or (esp. on the inner walls of arteries) deposition of fatty plaques. Compare **arteriosclerosis, atherosclerosis, multiple sclerosis. 2** the hardening of a plant cell wall or tissue by the deposition of lignin. [C14: via Medieval Latin from Greek *sklērōsis* a hardening] ▸ **scle'rosal** *adj*

sclerotic (sklɪə'rɒtɪk) *adj* **1** of or relating to the sclera. **2** of, relating to, or having sclerosis. **3** *Botany.* characterized by the hardening and strengthening of cell walls. ◆ *n* **4** another name for **sclera.** [C16: from Medieval Latin *sclērōticus,* from Greek; see SCLEROMA]

sclerotin ('sklɛrəutɪn) *n* a protein in the cuticle of insects that becomes hard and dark.

sclerotium (sklɪə'rəuʃɪəm) *n, pl* **-tia** (-ʃɪə). a compact mass of hyphae, that is formed by certain fungi and gives rise to new fungal growth or spore-producing structures. [C18: from New Latin, from Greek *sklēros* hard] ▸ **scle'rotioid** *or* **scle'rotial** *adj*

sclerotize *or* **sclerotise** ('sklɛrə,taɪz) *vb (tr; usually passive). Zoology.* to harden and darken (an insect's cuticle). ▸ **,scleroti'zation** *or* **,scleroti'sation** *n*

sclerotomy (sklɪə'rɒtəmɪ) *n, pl* **-mies.** surgical incision into the sclera.

sclerous ('sklɪərəs) *adj Anatomy, pathol.* hard; bony; indurated. [C19: from Greek *sklēros* hard]

SCM (in Britain) *abbrev. for:* **1** State Certified Midwife. **2** Student Christian Movement.

scoff[1] (skɒf) *vb* **1** (*intr;* often foll. by *at*) to speak contemptuously (about); express derision (for); mock. **2** (*tr*) *Obsolete.* to regard with derision. ◆ *n* **3** an expression of derision. **4** an object of derision. [C14: probably from Scandinavian; compare Old Frisian *skof* mockery, Danish *skof, skuf* jest] ▸ **'scoffer** *n* ▸ **'scoffing** *adj* ▸ **'scoffingly** *adv*

scoff[2] (skɒf) *Informal, chiefly Brit.* ◆ *vb* **1** to eat (food) fast and greedily; devour. ◆ *n* **2** food or rations. [C19: variant of *scaff* food; related to Afrikaans, Dutch *schoft* quarter of the day, one of the four daily meals]

scofflaw ('skɒflɔ:) *n U.S. informal.* a person who habitually flouts or violates the law, esp. one who fails to pay debts or answer summonses.

Scofield ('skəufi:ld) *n* (**David**) **Paul.** born 1922, English stage and film actor.

scold (skəuld) *vb* **1** to find fault with or reprimand (a person) harshly; chide. **2** (*intr*) to use harsh or abusive language. ◆ *n* **3** a person, esp. a woman, who constantly finds fault. [C13: from Old Norse SKALD] ▸ **'scoldable** *adj* ▸ **'scolder** *n* ▸ **'scolding** *n* ▸ **'scoldingly** *adv*

scolecite ('skɒlɪ,saɪt, 'skəul-) *n* a white zeolite mineral consisting of hydrated calcium aluminium silicate in groups of radiating monoclinic crystals. Formula: $CaAl_2Si_3O_{10}.3H_2O$. [C19: *scolec-* from Greek *skōlēx* SCOLEX + -ITE[1]]

scolex ('skəulɛks) *n, pl* **scoleces** (skəu'li:si:z) *or* **scolices** ('skɒlɪ,si:z, 'skəu-). the headlike part of a tapeworm, bearing hooks and suckers by which the animal is attached to the tissues of its host. [C19: from New Latin, from Greek *skōlēx* worm]

scoliosis (,skɒlɪ'əusɪs) *n Pathol.* an abnormal lateral curvature of the spine, of congenital origin or caused by trauma or disease of the vertebrae or hipbones. Compare **kyphosis, lordosis.** [C18: from New Latin, from Greek: a curving, from *skolios* bent] ▸ **scoliotic** (,skɒlɪ'ɒtɪk) *adj*

scollop[1] ('skɒləp) *n, vb* a variant of **scallop.**

scollop[2] ('skɒləp) *n* (in Ireland) a rod, pointed at both ends, used to pin down thatch. [C19: from Irish Gaelic *scolb*]

scolopendrid (,skɒlə'pɛndrɪd) *n* any centipede of the family *Scolopendridae,* including some large and poisonous species. [C19: from New Latin *Scolopendridae,* from Latin *scolopendra,* from Greek *skolopendra* legendary sea-fish] ▸ **scolopendrine** (,skɒlə'pɛndraɪn, -drɪn) *adj*

scolopendrium (skɒlə'pɛndrɪəm) *n* any of a genus of true ferns with undivided leaves, esp. hart's-tongue. [C17: from New Latin, from Greek *scolopendrion,* from a fancied resemblance of the fern and its sori to a centipede]

scombroid ('skɒmbrɔɪd) *adj* **1** of, relating to, or belonging to the *Scombroidea,* a suborder of marine spiny-finned fishes having a spindle-shaped body and a forked powerful tail: includes the mackerels, tunnies, bonitos, swordfish, and sailfish. ◆ *n* **2** any fish belonging to the suborder *Scombroidea.* [C19: from Greek *skombros* a mackerel; see -OID]

sconce[1] (skɒns) *n* **1** a bracket fixed to a wall for holding candles or lights. **2** a flat candlestick with a handle. [C14: from Old French *esconse* hiding place, lantern, or from Late Latin *sconsa,* from *absconsa* dark lantern]

sconce[2] (skɒns) *n* a small protective fortification, such as an earthwork. [C16: from Dutch *schans,* from Middle High German *schanze* bundle of brushwood]

sconce[3] (skɒns) (at Oxford and Cambridge Universities, esp. formerly) ◆ *vb* (*tr*) **1** to challenge (a fellow student) on the grounds of a social misdemeanour to drink a large quantity of beer without stopping. **2** *Obsolete.* to fine (a student) for some minor misdemeanour. ◆ *n* **3** the act of sconcing. **4** a mug or tankard used in sconcing. [C17: of obscure origin]

sconce[4] (skɒns) *n Archaic.* **1** the head or skull. **2** sense, brain, or wit. [C16: probably jocular use of SCONCE[1]]

scone *n* **1** (skɒn, skəun) a light plain doughy cake made from flour with very little fat, cooked in an oven or (esp. originally) on a griddle, usually split open and buttered. **2** (skɒn). *Austral.* a slang word for **head** (sense 1). **3 off one's scone.** *Austral. slang.* **3a** angry. **3b** insane. [C16: Scottish, perhaps from Middle Low German *schonbrot,* Middle Dutch *schoonbrot* fine bread]

Scone (sku:n) *n* a parish in Perth and Kinross, E Scotland, consisting of the two villages of New Scone and Old Scone, formerly the site of the Pictish capital and the stone upon which medieval Scottish kings were crowned. The stone was removed to Westminster Abbey by Edward I in 1296; it was returned to Scotland in 1996 and placed in Edinburgh Castle. Scone Palace was rebuilt in the Neo-Gothic style in the 19th century.

scoop (sku:p) *n* **1** a utensil used as a shovel or ladle, esp. a small shovel with deep sides and a short handle, used for taking up flour, corn, etc. **2** a utensil with a long handle and round bowl used for dispensing liquids. **3** a utensil with a round bowl and short handle, sometimes with a mechanical device to empty the bowl, for serving ice cream or mashed potato. **4** anything that resembles a scoop in action, such as the bucket on a dredge. **5** a spoonlike surgical instrument for scraping or extracting foreign matter, etc., from the body. **6** the quantity taken up by a scoop. **7** the act of scooping, dredging, etc. **8** a hollow cavity. **9** *Slang.* a large quick gain, as of money. **10** a news story reported in one newspaper before all the others; an exclusive. **11** any sensational piece of news. ◆ *vb* (*mainly tr*) **12** (often foll. by *up*) to take up and remove (an object or substance) with or as if with a scoop. **13** (often foll. by *out*) to hollow out with or as if with a scoop: *to scoop a hole in a hillside.* **14** to make (a large sudden profit). **15** to beat (rival newspapers) in uncovering a news item. **16** *Hockey, golf, etc.* to hit (the ball) on its underside so that it rises into the air. [C14: via Middle Dutch *schōpe* from Germanic; compare Old High German *scephan* to ladle, German *schöpfen, Schaufel* SHOVEL, Dutch *schoep* vessel for baling] ▸ **'scooper** *n* ▸ **'scoop,ful** *n*

scoop neck *n* a rounded low-cut neckline on a woman's garment.

scoosh (skuʃ) *Scot.* ◆ *vb* **1** to squirt. **2** (*intr*) (of liquid) to rush. ◆ *n* **3** a squirt or rush of liquid. **4** any fizzy drink. [C19: of imitative origin]

scoot (sku:t) *vb* **1** to go or cause to go quickly or hastily; dart or cause to dart off or away. **2** *Scot.* to squirt. ◆ *n* **3** the act of scooting. **4** *Scot.* a squirt. [C19 probably of Scandinavian origin; compare SHOOT]

scooter ('sku:tə) *n* **1** a child's vehicle consisting of a low footboard on wheels, steered by handlebars. It is propelled by pushing one foot against the ground. **2** See **motor scooter. 3** (in the U.S. and Canada) another term for **ice yacht.** ▸ **'scooterist** *n*

scop (skɒp) *n* (in Anglo-Saxon England) a bard or minstrel. [Old English: related to Old Norse *skop, skaup,* Old High German *scof, scopf* poem]

scopa ('skəupə) *n, pl* **-pae** (-,pi:). a tuft of hairs on the abdomen or hind legs of bees, used for collecting pollen. [C19: from Latin, used only in pl *scopae* twigs, brush]

Scopas ('skəupəs) *n* 4th century B.C., Greek sculptor and architect.

scope (skəup) *n* **1** opportunity for exercising the faculties or abilities; capacity for action. **2** range of view, perception, or grasp; outlook. **3** the area covered by an activity, topic, etc.; range: *the scope of his thesis was vast.* **4** *Nautical.* slack left in an anchor cable. **5** *Logic, linguistics.* that part of an expression that is governed by a given operator: the scope of the negation in $PV-(q\wedge r)$ is $-(q\wedge r)$. **6** *Informal.* short for **telescope, microscope, oscilloscope,** etc. **7** *Archaic.* purpose or aim. [C16: from Italian *scopo* goal, from Latin *scopus,* from Greek *skopos* target; related to Greek *skopein* to watch]

-scope *n combining form.* indicating an instrument for observing, viewing, or detecting: *microscope; stethoscope.* [from New Latin *-scopium,* from Greek *-skopion,* from *skopein* to look at] ▸ **-scopic** *adj combining form.*

scopolamine (skə'pɒlə,mi:n, -mɪn; ,skəupə'læmɪn) *n* a colourless viscous liquid alkaloid extracted from certain plants, such as henbane: used in preventing travel sickness and as an anticholinergic, sedative, and truth serum. Formula: $C_{17}H_{21}NO_4$. Also called: **hyoscine.** See also **atropine.** [C20: *scopol-* from New Latin *scopolia Japonica* Japanese belladonna (from which the alkaloid is extracted), named after G. A. *Scopoli* (1723–88), Italian naturalist, + AMINE]

scopoline ('skəupə,li:n, -lɪn) *n* a soluble crystalline alkaloid obtained from the decomposition of scopolamine and used as a sedative. Formula: $C_8H_{13}NO_2$. Also called: **oscine.** [C19: from *scopol-* (as in SCOPOLAMINE) + -INE[2]]

scopula ('skɒpjulə) *n, pl* **-las** *or* **-lae** (-,li:). a small tuft of dense hairs on the legs and chelicerae of some spiders. [C19: from Late Latin: a broom-twig, from *scōpa* thin twigs] ▸ **scopulate** ('skɒpju,leɪt, -lɪt) *adj*

Scopus ('skəupəs) *n* **Mount.** a mountain in central Israel, east of Jerusalem: a N extension of the Mount of Olives; site of the Hebrew University (1925). Height: 834 m (2736 ft.).

-scopy *n combining form.* indicating a viewing or observation: *microscopy.* [from Greek *-skopia,* from *skopein* to look at]

scorbutic (skɔ:'bju:tɪk) *adj* of, relating to, or having scurvy. [C17: from New Latin *scorbūticus,* from Medieval Latin *scorbūtus,* probably of Germanic origin; compare Old English *sceorf* scurf, Middle Low German *scorbuk* scurvy] ▸ **scor'butically** *adv*

scorch (skɔ:tʃ) *vb* **1** to burn or become burnt, so as to affect the colour, taste, etc., or to cause or feel pain. **2** to wither or parch or cause to wither from exposure to heat. **3** (*intr*) *Informal.* to be very hot: *it is scorching outside.* **4** (*tr*) *Informal.* to criticize harshly. **5** (*intr*) *Brit. slang.* to drive or ride very fast. ◆ *n* **6** a slight burn. **7** a mark caused by the application of too great heat. **8** *Horticulture.* a mark or series of marks on fruit, vegetables, etc., caused by pests or insecticides. [C15: probably from Old Norse *skorpna* to shrivel up] ▸ **'scorching** *adj*

scorched earth policy *n* **1** the policy in warfare of removing or destroying everything that might be useful to an invading enemy, esp. by fire. **2** *Business.* a manoeuvre by a company expecting an unwelcome takeover bid in which apparent profitability is greatly reduced by a reversible operation, such as borrowing at an exorbitant interest rate.

scorcher ('skɔ:tʃə) *n* **1** a person or thing that scorches. **2** something severe or caustic. **3** *Informal.* a very hot day. **4** *Brit. informal.* something remarkable.

score (skɔ:) *n* **1** an evaluative usually numerical record of a competitive game or match. **2** the total number of points made by a side or individual in a game or match. **3** the act of scoring, esp. a point or points. **4 the score.** *Informal.* the actual situation; the true facts: *to know the score.* **5** *U.S. and Canadian.* the result of a test or exam. **6** a group or set of twenty: *three score years and ten.* **7** (*usually pl;* foll. by *of*) a great number; lots: *I have scores of things to do.* **8** *Music.* **8a** the written or printed form of a composition in which the instrumental or vocal parts appear on separate staves vertically arranged on large pages (**full score**) or in a condensed version, usually for piano (**short score**) or voices and piano (**vocal score**). **8b** the incidental music for a film or play. **8c** the songs, music, etc., for a stage or film musical. **9** a mark or notch, esp. one made in keeping a tally. **10** an account of amounts due. **11** an amount recorded as due. **12** a reason or account: *the book was rejected on the score of length.* **13** a grievance. **14a** a line marking a division or boundary. **14b** (*as modifier*): *score line.* **15** *Informal.* the victim of a theft or swindle. **16** *Dancing.* notation indicating a dancer's moves. **17 over the score.** *Informal.* excessive; unfair. **18 settle** *or* **pay off a score. 18a** to avenge a wrong. **18b** to repay a debt. ◆ *vb*

19 to gain (a point or points) in a game or contest. 20 (*tr*) to make a total score of: *to score twelve.* 21 to keep a record of the score (of). 22 (*tr*) to be worth (a certain amount) in a game. 23 (*tr*) *U.S. and Canadian.* to evaluate (a test or exam) numerically; mark. 24 (*tr*) to record by making notches in. 25 to make (cuts, lines, etc.) in or on. 26 (*intr*) *Slang.* to obtain something desired, esp. to purchase an illegal drug. 27 (*intr*) *Slang.* (of a man) to be successful in seducing a person. 28 (*tr*) 28a to set or arrange (a piece of music) for specific instruments or voices. 28b to write the music for (a film, play, etc.). 29 to achieve (success or an advantage): *your idea really scored with the boss.* 30 (*tr*) *Chiefly U.S. and Canadian.* to criticize harshly; berate. 31 to accumulate or keep a record of (a debt). [Old English *scora;* related to Old Norse *skor* notch, tally, twenty] ► 'scorer *n*

scoreboard ('skɔː,bɔːd) *n Sport, etc.* a board for displaying the score of a game or match.

scorecard ('skɔː,kɑːd) *n* 1 a card on which scores are recorded in various games, esp. golf. 2 a card identifying the players in a sports match, esp. cricket or baseball.

score draw *n* (esp. in football) a result of a match in which both sides have scored an equal number of goals.

score off *vb* (*intr, prep*) to gain an advantage at someone else's expense.

score out *vb* (*tr, adv*) to delete or cancel by marking through with a line or lines; cross out.

scoria ('skɔːrɪə) *n, pl* **-riae** (-rɪ,iː). 1 a rough heavy mass of solidified lava containing many cavities. 2 refuse obtained from smelted ore; slag. [C17: from Latin: dross, from Greek *skōria,* from *skōr* excrement] ► **scoriaceous** (,skɔːrɪ'eɪʃəs) *adj*

scorify ('skɔːrɪ,faɪ) *vb* **-fies, -fying, -fied.** to remove (impurities) from metals by forming scoria. ► ,**scorifi'cation** *n* ► '**scori,fier** *n*

scoring ('skɔːrɪŋ) *n* 1 the act or practice of scoring. 2 another name for **orchestration** (see **orchestrate**).

scorn (skɔːn) *n* 1 open contempt or disdain for a person or thing; derision. 2 an object of contempt or derision. 3 *Archaic.* an act or expression signifying contempt. ◆ *vb* 4 to treat with contempt or derision. 5 (*tr*) to reject with contempt. [C12 *schornen,* from Old French *escharnir,* of Germanic origin; compare Old High German *scerōn* to behave rowdily, obsolete Dutch *schern* mockery] ► '**scorner** *n* ► '**scornful** *adj* ► '**scornfully** *adv* ► '**scornfulness** *n*

scorpaenid (skɔː'piːnɪd) *n* 1 any spiny-finned marine fish of the family *Scorpaenidae,* having sharp spines on the fins and a heavy armoured head: includes the scorpion fishes, rockfishes, and redfishes. ◆ *adj* 2 of, relating to, or belonging to the family *Scorpaenidae.* [via New Latin from Latin *scorpaena* a sea-scorpion; see SCORPION]

scorpaenoid (skɔː'piːnɔɪd) *adj* 1 of, relating to, or belonging to the *Scorpaenoidea,* a suborder of spiny-finned fishes having bony plates covering the head: includes the sculpins, scorpion fishes, gurnards, etc. ◆ *n* 2 any fish belonging to the suborder *Scorpaenoidea.*

scorper *or* **scauper** ('skɔːpə) *n* a kind of fine chisel with a square or curved tip used in wood engraving for clearing away large areas of the block or clearing away lines. [C19: erroneously for *scauper* scalper, from Latin *scalper* knife]

Scorpio ('skɔːpɪ,əʊ) *n* 1 Also called: the **Scorpion.** *Astrology.* 1a the eighth sign of the zodiac, symbol ♏, having a fixed water classification and ruled by the planets Mars and Pluto. The sun is in this sign between about Oct. 23 and Nov. 21. 1b a person born during a period when the sun is in this sign. 2 *Astronomy.* another name for **Scorpius.** ◆ *adj* 3 *Astrology.* born under or characteristic of Scorpio. ◆ Also (for senses 1b, 3): **Scorpionic** (,skɔːpɪ'ɒnɪk). [Latin: SCORPION]

scorpioid ('skɔːpɪ,ɔɪd) *adj* 1 of, relating to, or resembling scorpions or the order (*Scorpionida*) to which they belong. 2 *Botany.* (esp. of a cymose inflorescence) having the main stem coiled during development.

scorpion ('skɔːpɪən) *n* 1 any arachnid of the order *Scorpionida,* of warm dry regions, having a segmented body with a long tail terminating in a venomous sting. 2 **false scorpion.** any small nonvenomous arachnid of the order *Pseudoscorpionida* (or *Chelonethida*), which superficially resemble scorpions but lack the long tail. See **book scorpion.** 3 any of various other similar arachnids, such as the whip scorpion, or other arthropods, such as the water scorpion. 4 *Old Testament.* a barbed scourge (I Kings 12:11). 5 *History.* a war engine for hurling stones; ballista. [C13: via Old French from Latin *scorpiō,* from Greek *skorpios,* of obscure origin]

Scorpion ('skɔːpɪən) *n* **the.** the constellation Scorpio, the eighth sign of the zodiac.

scorpion fish *n* any of various scorpaenid fishes of the genus *Scorpaena* and related genera, of temperate and tropical seas, having venomous spines on the dorsal and anal fins.

scorpion fly *n* any of various insects of the family *Panorpidae,* of the N hemisphere, having a scorpion-like but nonvenomous tail in the males, long antennae, and a beaklike snout: order *Mecoptera.*

scorpion grass *n* another name for **forget-me-not.**

Scorpius ('skɔːpɪəs) *n, Latin genitive* **Scorpii** ('skɔːpɪ,aɪ). a large zodiacal constellation lying between Libra and Sagittarius and crossed by the Milky Way. It contains the first magnitude star Antares. Also called: **Scorpio.**

Scorsese (skɔː'seɪzɪ) *n* **Martin.** born 1942, U.S. film director, whose films include *Taxi Driver* (1976), *Raging Bull* (1980), *Casino* (1995), *Kundun* (1998), and the controversial *The Last Temptation of Christ* (1988).

Scot (skɒt) *n* 1 a native or inhabitant of Scotland. 2 a member of a tribe of Celtic raiders from the north of Ireland who carried out periodic attacks against the British mainland coast from the 3rd century A.D., eventually settling in N Britain during the 5th and 6th centuries.

Scot. *abbrev. for:* 1 Scotch (whisky). 2 Scotland. 3 Scottish.

scot and lot *n British history.* a municipal tax paid by burgesses and others that came to be regarded as a qualification for the borough franchise in parliamentary elections (until the Reform Act of 1832). [C13 *scot* tax, from Germanic; compare Old Norse *skot;* related to Old French *escot* (French *écot*) + LOT (in the obsolete sense: tax)]

scotch[1] (skɒtʃ) *vb* (*tr*) 1 to put an end to; crush: *bad weather scotched our plans.* 2 *Archaic.* to injure so as to render harmless. 3 *Obsolete.* to cut or score. ◆ *n* 4 *Archaic.* a gash; scratch. 5 a line marked down, as for hopscotch. [C15: of obscure origin]

scotch[2] (skɒtʃ) *vb* 1 (*tr*) to block, prop, or prevent from moving with or as if with a wedge. ◆ *n* 2 a block or wedge to prevent motion. [C17: of obscure origin]

Scotch[1] (skɒtʃ) *adj* 1 another word for **Scottish.** ◆ *n* 2 the Scots or their language.

USAGE In the north of England and in Scotland, *Scotch* is not used outside fixed expressions such as *Scotch whisky.* The use of *Scotch* for *Scots* or *Scottish* is otherwise felt to be incorrect, esp. when applied to persons.

Scotch[2] (skɒtʃ) *n* 1 Also called: **Scotch whisky.** whisky distilled esp. from fermented malted barley and made in Scotland. 2 *Northeast English.* a type of relatively mild beer.

Scotch broth *n Brit.* a thick soup made from mutton or beef stock, vegetables, and pearl barley.

Scotch egg *n Brit.* a hard-boiled egg enclosed in a layer of sausage meat, covered in egg and crumbs, and fried.

Scotchman ('skɒtʃmən) *n, pl* **-men.** (*regarded as bad usage by the Scots*) another word for **Scotsman.** ► '**Scotch,woman** *fem n*

Scotch mist *n* 1 a heavy wet mist. 2 drizzle. [C16: so called because it is common on Scottish hills]

Scotch pancake *n* another name for **drop scone.**

Scotch snap *n Music.* a rhythmic pattern consisting of a short note followed by a long one. Also called: **Scotch catch.** [C19: so named because it is characteristic of, though not exclusive to, Scottish dance music, esp. that for strathspeys]

Scotch tape *n Trademark, chiefly U.S.* a transparent or coloured adhesive tape made of cellulose or a similar substance.

Scotch terrier *n* another name for **Scottish terrier.**

Scotch woodcock *n* hot toast spread with anchovies or anchovy paste and topped with creamy scrambled eggs.

scoter ('skəʊtə) *n, pl* **-ters** *or* **-ter.** any sea duck of the genus *Melanitta,* such as *M. nigra* (**common scoter**), of northern regions. The male plumage is black with white patches around the head and eyes. [C17: origin unknown]

scot-free *adv, adj* (*predicative*) without harm, loss, or penalty. [C16: see SCOT AND LOT]

scotia ('skəʊʃə) *n* a deep concave moulding, esp. one used on the base of an Ionic column between the two torus mouldings. [C16: via Latin from Greek *skotia,* from *skotos* darkness (from the shadow in the cavity)]

Scotism ('skəʊtɪzəm) *n* the doctrines of Duns Scotus, esp. those holding that philosophy and theology are independent. See **haecceity.** ► '**Scotist** *n, adj* ► **Sco'tistic** *adj*

Scotland ('skɒtlənd) *n* a country that is part of the United Kingdom, occupying the north of Great Britain: the English and Scottish thrones were united under one monarch in 1603 and the parliaments in 1707: a separate Scottish parliament was established in 1999. Scotland consists of the Highlands in the north, the central Lowlands, and hilly uplands in the south; has a deeply indented coastline, about 800 offshore islands (mostly in the west), and many lochs. Capital: Edinburgh. Pop.: 4 998 567 (1991). Area: 78 768 sq. km (30 412 sq. miles). Related adjs: **Caledonian, Scottish.**

Scotland Yard *n* the headquarters of the police force of metropolitan London, controlled directly by the British Home Office and hence having certain national responsibilities. Official name: **New Scotland Yard.**

scotoma (skɒ'təʊmə) *n, pl* **-mas** *or* **-mata** (-mətə). 1 *Pathol.* a blind spot; a permanent or temporary area of depressed or absent vision caused by lesions of the visual system, viewing the sun directly (**eclipse scotoma**), squinting, etc. 2 *Psychol.* a mental blind spot; inability to understand or perceive certain matters. [C16: via Medieval Latin from Greek *skotōma* giddiness, from *skotoun* to make dark, from *skotos* darkness] ► **scotomatous** (skɒ'tɒmətəs) *adj*

scotopia (skə'təʊpɪə, skəʊ-) *n* the ability of the eye to adjust for night vision. [New Latin, from Greek *skotos* darkness + -OPIA] ► **scotopic** (skə'tɒpɪk, skəʊ-) *adj*

Scots (skɒts) *adj* 1 of, relating to, or characteristic of Scotland, its people, their English dialects, or their Gaelic language. ◆ *n* 2 any of the English dialects spoken or written in Scotland. See also **Lallans.**

Scots Greys *pl n* **the.** another name for (the) **Royal Scots Greys.**

Scotsman ('skɒtsmən) *n, pl* **-men.** a native or inhabitant of Scotland. ► '**Scots,woman** *fem n*

Scots pine *or* **Scotch pine** *n* 1 a coniferous tree, *Pinus sylvestris,* of Europe and W and N Asia, having blue-green needle-like leaves and brown cones with a small prickle on each scale: a valuable timber tree. 2 the wood of this tree. ◆ Also called: **Scots** (*or* **Scotch**) **fir.**

Scott (skɒt) *n* 1 Sir **George Gilbert.** 1811–78, British architect, prominent in the Gothic revival. He restored many churches and cathedrals and designed the Albert Memorial (1863) and St Pancras Station (1865). 2 his grandson, Sir **Giles Gilbert.** 1880–1960, British architect, whose designs include the Anglican cathedral in Liverpool (1904–78) and the new Waterloo Bridge (1939–45). 3 **Paul** (**Mark**). 1920–78, British novelist, who is best known for the series of novels known as the "Raj Quartet": *The Jewel in the Crown* (1966), *The Day of the Scorpion* (1968), *The Towers of Silence* (1972), and *A Division of the Spoils* (1975). *Staying On* (1977) won the Booker Prize. 4 Sir **Peter** (**Markham**). 1909–89, British naturalist, wildlife artist, and conservationist, noted esp. for his paintings of birds. He founded (1946) the Slimbridge refuge for waterfowl in Gloucestershire. 5 his father, **Robert Falcon.** 1868–1912, British naval officer and explorer of the Antarctic. He commanded two Antarctic expeditions (1901–04; 1910–12) and reached the South Pole on Jan. 18, 1912, shortly after Amundsen; he and the rest of his party died on the return journey. **6** Sir **Walter.** 1771–1832, Scottish romantic novelist and poet. He is remembered chiefly for the "Waverley" historical novels, including *Waverley* (1814), *Rob Roy* (1817), *The Heart of Midlothian* (1818), inspired by Scottish folklore and history, and *Ivanhoe* (1819), *Kenilworth* (1821), *Quentin Durward* (1823), and *Redgauntlet* (1824). His narrative poems include *The Lay of the Last Minstrel* (1805), *Marmion* (1808), and *The Lady of the Lake* (1810).

Scotticism (ˈskɒtɪˌsɪzəm) *n* a Scottish idiom, word, etc.

Scottie *or* **Scotty** (ˈskɒtɪ) *n, pl* **-ties. 1** See **Scottish terrier. 2** *Informal.* a Scotsman.

Scottish (ˈskɒtɪʃ) *adj* **1** of, relating to, or characteristic of Scotland, its people, their Gaelic language, or their English dialect. ♦ *n* **2 the.** (*functioning as pl*) the Scots collectively.

Scottish Blackface *n* a common breed of hardy mountain sheep having horns and a black face, kept chiefly on the mainland of Scotland.

Scottish Borders *n* a council area in SE Scotland, on the English border: created in 1996, it has the same boundaries as the former Borders Region: it is mainly hilly, with agriculture (esp. sheep farming) the chief economic activity. Administrative centre: Newtown St Boswells. Pop.: 106 100 (1996 est.). Area: 4734 sq. km (1827 sq. miles).

Scottish Certificate of Education *n* See **SCE.**

Scottish Gaelic *n* the Goidelic language of the Celts of Scotland, spoken in the Highlands and Western Isles.

Scottish National Party *n* a political party advocating the independence of Scotland, founded in 1934. Abbrev.: **SNP.** ▸ **Scottish Nationalist** *or* (*informal*) **Scot Nat** (næt) *n, adj*

Scottish terrier *n* a small but sturdy breed of terrier, having short legs and erect ears and tail and a longish, wiry, usually black coat. Often shortened to **Scottie.** Former name: **Aberdeen terrier.**

Scottish topaz *n* a form of yellow transparent quartz.

Scotus (ˈskəʊtəs) *n* See **Duns Scotus.**

scoundrel (ˈskaʊndrəl) *n* a worthless or villainous person. [C16: of unknown origin] ▸ ˈ**scoundrelly** *adj*

scour[1] (skaʊə) *vb* **1** to clean or polish (a surface) by washing and rubbing, as with an abrasive cloth. **2** to remove dirt from or have the dirt removed from. **3** (*tr*) to clear (a channel) by the force of water; flush. **4** (*tr*) to remove by or as if by rubbing. **5** (*intr*) (of livestock, esp. cattle) to have diarrhoea. **6** (*tr*) to cause (livestock) to purge their bowels. **7** (*tr*) to wash (wool) to remove wax, suint, and other impurities. ♦ *n* **8** the act of scouring. **9** the place scoured, esp. by running water. **10** something that scours, such as a cleansing agent. **11** (*often pl*) prolonged diarrhoea in livestock, esp. cattle. [C13: via Middle Low German *schūren,* from Old French *escurer,* from Late Latin *excūrāre* to cleanse, from *cūrāre;* see CURE] ▸ ˈ**scourer** *n*

scour[2] (skaʊə) *vb* **1** to range over (territory), as in making a search. **2** to move swiftly or energetically over (territory). [C14: from Old Norse *skūr*]

scourge (skɜːdʒ) *n* **1** a person who harasses, punishes, or causes destruction. **2** a means of inflicting punishment or suffering. **3** a whip used for inflicting punishment or torture. ♦ *vb* (*tr*) **4** to whip; flog. **5** to punish severely. [C13: from Anglo-French *escorge,* from Old French *escorgier* (unattested) to lash, from *es-* EX-[1] + Latin *corrigia* whip] ▸ ˈ**scourger** *n*

scouring rush *n* any of several horsetails, esp. *Equisetum hyemale,* that have rough-ridged stems and were formerly used for scouring and polishing.

scourings (ˈskaʊərɪŋz) *pl n* **1** the residue left after cleaning grain. **2** residue that remains after scouring.

scouse (skaʊs) *n Liverpool dialect.* a stew made from left-over meat. [C19: shortened from LOBSCOUSE]

Scouse (skaʊs) *Brit. informal.* ♦ *n* **1** Also called: **Scouser.** a person who lives in or comes from Liverpool. **2** the dialect spoken by such a person. ♦ *adj* **3** of or from Liverpool; Liverpudlian. [C20: from SCOUSE]

scout[1] (skaʊt) *n* **1** a person, ship, or aircraft sent out to gain information. **2** *Military.* a person or unit despatched to reconnoitre the position of the enemy. **3** *Sport.* a person employed by a club to seek new players. **4** the act or an instance of scouting. **5** (esp. at Oxford University) a college servant. Compare **gyp**[3]. **6** (in Britain) a patrolman of a motoring organization. **7** *Informal.* a fellow or companion. ♦ *vb* **8** to examine or observe (anything) in order to obtain information. **9** (*tr;* sometimes foll. by *out* or *up*) to seek. **10** (*intr*) to act as a scout for a sports club. **11** (*intr.;* foll. by *about* or *around*) to go in search (for). [C14: from Old French *ascouter* to listen to, from Latin *auscultāre* to AUSCULTATE] ▸ ˈ**scouter** *n*

scout[2] (skaʊt) *vb Archaic.* to reject (a person or thing) with contempt. [C17: from Old Norse *skūta* derision]

Scout (skaʊt) *n* (*sometimes not cap.*) a boy or (in some countries) a girl who is a member of a worldwide movement (the **Scout Association**) founded as the Boy Scouts in England in 1908 by Lord Baden-Powell with the aim of developing character and responsibility. See also **Air Scout, Girl Scout, Guide, Sea Scout, Venture Scout.**

scout car *n* a fast lightly armoured vehicle used for reconnaissance.

Scouting (ˈskaʊtɪŋ) *n* **a** the activities, programmes, principles, etc., of the Scout Association. **b** (*as modifier*): *the international Scouting movement.*

Scout Leader *n* the leader of a troop of Scouts.

scoutmaster (ˈskaʊtˌmɑːstə) *n* a former name for **Scout Leader.**

scow (skaʊ) *n* **1** an unpowered barge used for freight; lighter. **2** (esp. in the midwestern U.S.) a sailing yacht with a flat bottom, designed to plane. [C18: via Dutch *schouw* from Low German *schalde,* related to Old Saxon *skaldan* to push (a boat) into the sea]

scowl (skaʊl) *vb* **1** (*intr*) to contract the brows in a threatening or angry manner. ♦ *n* **2** a gloomy or threatening expression. [C14: probably from Scandinavian; compare Danish *skule* to look down, Old English *scūlēgede* squint-eyed] ▸ ˈ**scowler** *n*

SCP *abbrev. for* single-cell protein.

SCPS (in Britain) *abbrev. for* Society of Civil and Public Servants.

SCR *abbrev. for:* **1** (in British universities) senior common room. **2** silicon controlled rectifier.

scr. *abbrev. for* scruple (unit of weight).

scrabble (ˈskræbᵊl) *vb* **1** (*intr;* often foll. by *about* or *at*) to scrape (at) or grope (for), as with hands or claws. **2** to struggle (with). **3** (*intr;* often foll. by *for*) to struggle to gain possession, esp. in a disorderly manner. **4** to scribble. ♦ *n* **5** the act or an instance of scrabbling. **6** a scribble. **7** a disorderly struggle. [C16: from Middle Dutch *shrabbelen,* frequentative of *shrabben* to scrape] ▸ ˈ**scrabbler** *n*

Scrabble (ˈskræbᵊl) *n Trademark.* a board game in which words are formed by placing lettered tiles in a pattern similar to a crossword puzzle.

scrag (skræg) *n* **1** a thin or scrawny person or animal. **2** the lean end of a neck of veal or mutton. **3** *Informal.* the neck of a human being. ♦ *vb* **scrags, scragging, scragged.** (*tr*) **4** *Informal.* to wring the neck of; throttle. [C16: perhaps variant of CRAG; related to Norwegian *skragg,* German *Kragen* collar]

scraggly (ˈskræglɪ) *adj* **-glier, -gliest.** untidy or irregular.

scraggy (ˈskrægɪ) *adj* **-gier, -giest. 1** lean or scrawny. **2** rough; unkempt. ▸ ˈ**scraggily** *adv* ▸ ˈ**scragginess** *n*

scram[1] (skræm) *vb* **scrams, scramming, scrammed.** (*intr; often imperative*) *Informal.* to go away hastily; get out. [C20: shortened from SCRAMBLE]

scram[2] (skræm) *n* **1** an emergency shutdown of a nuclear reactor. ♦ *vb* **2** (of a nuclear reactor) to shut down or be shut down in an emergency. [C20: perhaps from SCRAM[1]]

scramb *or* **scram** (skræm) *vb* (*tr*) *Brit. dialect.* to scratch with nails or claws. [from Dutch *schrammen*]

scramble (ˈskræmbᵊl) *vb* **1** (*intr*) to climb or crawl, esp. by using the hands to aid movement. **2** (*intr*) to proceed hurriedly or in a disorderly fashion. **3** (*intr;* often foll. by *for*) to compete with others, esp. in a disordered manner: *to scramble for a prize.* **4** (*intr;* foll. by *through*) to deal with hurriedly and unsystematically. **5** (*tr*) to throw together in a haphazard manner; jumble. **6** (*tr*) to collect in a hurried or disorganized manner. **7** (*tr*) to cook (eggs that have been whisked up with milk and seasoning) in a pan containing a little melted butter. **8** *Military.* to order (a crew or aircraft) to take off immediately or (of a crew or aircraft) to take off immediately. **9** (*tr*) to render (speech) unintelligible during transmission by means of an electronic scrambler. ♦ *n* **10** the act of scrambling. **11** a climb over rocks that involves the use of the hands but not ropes, etc. **12** a disorderly struggle, esp. to gain possession. **13** *Military.* an immediate preparation for action, as of crew, aircraft, etc. **14** *Brit.* a motorcycle rally in which competitors race across rough open ground. [C16: blend of SCRABBLE and RAMP]

scrambled eggs *pl n Slang.* gold embroidery on the peak of a high-ranking military officer's cap.

scrambler (ˈskræmblə) *n* **1** a plant that produces long weak shoots by which it grows over other plants. **2** an electronic device that renders speech unintelligible during transmission, normal speech being restored at the receiving system.

scran (skræn) *n* **1** *Slang.* food; provisions. **2 bad scran to.** *Irish dialect.* bad luck to. [C18: of unknown origin]

scrannel (ˈskrænᵊl) *adj Archaic.* **1** thin. **2** harsh. [C17: probably from Norwegian *skran* lean. Compare SCRAWNY]

Scranton (ˈskræntən) *n* an industrial city in NE Pennsylvania: university (1888). Pop.: 77 189 (1996 est.).

scrap[1] (skræp) *n* **1** a small piece of something larger; fragment. **2** an extract from something written. **3a** waste material or used articles, esp. metal, often collected and reprocessed. **3b** (*as modifier*): *scrap iron.* **4** (*pl*) pieces of discarded food. ♦ *vb* **scraps, scrapping, scrapped.** (*tr*) **5** to make into scrap. **6** to discard as useless. [C14: from Old Norse *skrap;* see SCRAPE]

scrap[2] (skræp) *Informal.* ♦ *n* **1** a fight or argument. ♦ *vb* **scraps, scrapping, scrapped. 2** (*intr*) to quarrel or fight. [C17: perhaps from SCRAPE]

scrapbook (ˈskræpˌbʊk) *n* a book or album of blank pages in which to mount newspaper cuttings, pictures, etc.

scrape (skreɪp) *vb* **1** to move (a rough or sharp object) across (a surface), esp. to smooth or clean. **2** (*tr;* often foll. by *away* or *off*) to remove (a layer) by rubbing. **3** to produce a harsh or grating sound by rubbing against (an instrument, surface, etc.). **4** (*tr*) to injure or damage by rough contact: *to scrape one's knee.* **5** (*intr*) to be very economical or sparing in the use (of) (esp. in the phrase **scrimp and scrape**). **6** (*intr*) to draw the foot backwards in making a bow. **7** (*tr*) to finish (a surface) by use of a scraper. **8** (*tr*) to make (a bearing, etc.) fit by scraping. **9 bow and scrape.** to behave with excessive humility. ♦ *n* **10** the act of scraping. **11** a scraped place. **12** a harsh or grating sound. **13** *Informal.* an awkward or embarrassing predicament. **14** *Informal.* a conflict or struggle. [Old English *scrapian;* related to Old Norse *skrapa,* Middle Dutch *schrapen,* Middle High German *schraffen*] ▸ ˈ**scrapable** *adj* ▸ ˈ**scraper** *n*

scrape in *vb* (*intr, adv*) to succeed in entering with difficulty or by a narrow margin: *he only just scraped into university.* Also: **scrape into.**

scraperboard (ˈskreɪpəˌbɔːd) *n* **1** thin card covered with a layer of white china clay and a black top layer of Indian ink, which can be scraped away with a special tool to leave a white line. **2** a picture or design produced in this way.

scrape through *vb* (*adv*) **1** (*intr*) to manage or survive with difficulty. **2** to succeed in with difficulty or by a narrow margin: *he scraped through by one mark.*

scrape together *or* **up** *vb* (*tr, adv*) to collect with difficulty: *to scrape together money for a new car.*

scrapheap (ˈskræpˌhiːp) *n* **1** a pile of discarded material. **2 on the scrapheap.** (of people or things) having outlived their usefulness.

scrapie ('skreɪpɪ) *n* a usually fatal virus disease of sheep and goats affecting the central nervous system, characterized by intense itching. [C20: from SCRAPE + -IE]

scraping ('skreɪpɪŋ) *n* **1** the act of scraping. **2** a sound produced by scraping. **3** (*often pl*) something scraped off, together, or up; a small amount.

scrappy[1] ('skræpɪ) *adj* **-pier, -piest.** fragmentary; disjointed. ► **'scrappily** *adv* ► **'scrappiness** *n*

scrappy[2] ('skræpɪ) *adj* **-pier, -piest.** *Informal.* pugnacious.

scratch (skrætʃ) *vb* **1** to mark or cut (the surface of something) with a rough or sharp instrument. **2** (often foll. by *at, out, off,* etc.) to scrape (the surface of something), as with claws, nails, etc. **3** to scrape (the surface of the skin) with the nails, as to relieve itching. **4** to chafe or irritate (a surface, esp. the skin). **5** to make or cause to make a grating sound; scrape. **6** (*tr;* sometimes foll. by *out*) to erase by or as if by scraping. **7** (*tr*) to write or draw awkwardly. **8** (*intr;* sometimes foll. by *along*) to earn a living, manage, etc., with difficulty. **9** to withdraw (an entry) from a race, match, etc. **10** (*intr*) *Billiards, etc.* **10a** to make a shot resulting in a penalty. **10b** to make a lucky shot. **11** (*tr*) *U.S.* to cancel (the name of a candidate) from a party ticket in an election. **12** (*intr;* often foll. by *for*) *Austral. informal.* to be struggling or in difficulty, esp. in earning a living. **13 scratch the surface.** to treat (a subject) superficially. **14 you scratch my back and I'll scratch yours.** if you will help me, I will help you. ◆ *n* **15** the act of scratching. **16** a slight injury. **17** a mark made by scratching. **18** a slight grating sound. **19** (in a handicap sport) **19a** a competitor or the status of a competitor who has no allowance or receives a penalty. **19b** (*as modifier*): *a scratch player.* **20** the time, initial score, etc., of such a competitor. **21a** the line from which competitors start in a race. **21b** (formerly) a line drawn on the floor of a prize ring at which the contestants stood to begin or continue fighting. **22** a withdrawn competitor in a race, etc. **23** *Billiards, etc.* **23a** a shot that results in a penalty, as when the cue ball enters the pocket. **23b** a lucky shot. **24** poultry food. **25 from scratch.** *Informal.* from the very beginning. **26 up to scratch.** (*usually used with a negative*) *Informal.* up to standard. ◆ *adj* **27** *Sport.* (of a team) assembled hastily. **28** (in a handicap sport) with no allowance or penalty. **29** *Informal.* rough or haphazard. ◆ See also **scratches, scratch together.** [C15: via Old French *escrater* from Germanic; compare Old High German *krazzōn* (German *kratzen*); related to Old French *gratter* to GRATE[1]] ► **'scratcher** *n* ► **'scratchy** *adj* ► **'scratchily** *adv* ► **'scratchiness** *n*

scratchcard ('skrætʃˌkɑːd) *n* a ticket that reveals whether or not the holder is eligible for a prize when the surface is removed by scratching.

scratches ('skrætʃɪz) *n* (*functioning as sing*) a disease of horses characterized by eczematous weeping lesions in the region of the fetlock. [C16: so called because it makes the pastern appear to be scratched]

scratch file *n Computing.* a temporary store for use during the execution of a program.

scratchie ('skrætʃɪ) *n Austral. informal.* a scratchcard.

scratching ('skrætʃɪŋ) *n* a percussive effect obtained by rotating a gramophone record manually: a disc-jockey and dub technique.

scratch pad *n* **1** *Chiefly U.S. and Canadian.* a notebook, esp. one with detachable leaves. **2** *Computing.* a small semiconductor memory for temporary storage.

scratchplate ('skrætʃˌpleɪt) *n* a plastic or metal plate attached to the front of a guitar to protect it from pick scratches.

scratch sheet *n U.S. and Canadian informal.* another term for a **dope sheet.**

scratch test *n Med.* a skin test to determine allergic sensitivity to various substances by placing the allergen to be tested over an area of lightly scratched skin. A positive reaction is typically indicated by the formation of a weal.

scratch together *or* **up** *vb* (*tr, adv*) to assemble with difficulty: *he scratched up a team for the football match.*

scratch video *n* the technique or practice of recycling images from films or television to make collages.

scraw (skrɑː) *n Irish.* a sod from the surface of a peat bog or from a field. [from Irish Gaelic *scraith*]

scrawl (skrɔːl) *vb* **1** to write or draw (signs, words, etc.) carelessly or hastily; scribble. ◆ *n* **2** careless or scribbled writing, drawing, or marks. [C17: perhaps a blend of SPRAWL and CRAWL[1]] ► **'scrawler** *n* ► **'scrawly** *adj*

scrawny ('skrɔːnɪ) *adj* **scrawnier, scrawniest. 1** very thin and bony; scraggy. **2** meagre or stunted: *scrawny vegetation.* [C19: variant of dialect *scranny;* see SCRANNEL] ► **'scrawnily** *adv* ► **'scrawniness** *n*

screak (skriːk) *Dialect, chiefly U.S.* ◆ *vb* **1** (*intr*) to screech or creak. ◆ *n* **2** a screech or creak. [C16: from Old Norse *skrækja.* See SCREECH[1], SHRIEK] ► **'screaky** *adj*

scream (skriːm) *vb* **1** to utter or emit (a sharp piercing cry or similar sound or sounds), esp. as of fear, pain, etc. **2** (*intr*) to laugh wildly. **3** (*intr*) to speak, shout, or behave in a wild or impassioned manner. **4** (*tr*) to bring (oneself) into a specified state by screaming: *she screamed herself hoarse.* **5** (*intr*) to be extremely conspicuous: *these orange curtains scream, you need more restful colours in a bedroom.* ◆ *n* **6** a sharp piercing cry or sound, esp. one denoting fear or pain. **7** *Informal.* a person or thing that causes great amusement. [C13: from Germanic; compare Middle Dutch *schreem,* West Frisian *skrieme* to weep]

screamer ('skriːmə) *n* **1** a person or thing that screams. **2** any goose-like aquatic bird, such as *Chauna torquata* (**crested screamer**), of the family *Anhimidae* of tropical and subtropical South America: order *Anseriformes* (ducks, geese, etc.). **3** someone or something that raises screams of laughter or astonishment. **4** *U.S. and Canadian slang.* a sensational headline. **5** *Austral. slang.* **5a** a person or thing that is excellent of its kind. **5b** See **two-pot screamer.**

scream therapy *n* another name for **primal therapy.**

scree (skriː) *n* an accumulation of weathered rock fragments at the foot of a cliff or hillside, often forming a sloping heap. Also called: **talus.** [Old English *scrīthan* to slip; related to Old Norse *skrītha* to slide, German *schreiten* to walk]

screech[1] (skriːtʃ) *n* **1** a shrill, harsh, or high-pitched sound or cry. ◆ *vb* **2** to utter with or produce a screech. [C16: variant of earlier *scritch,* of imitative origin] ► **'screecher** *n* ► **'screechy** *adj*

screech[2] (skriːtʃ) *n Canadian.* (esp. in Newfoundland) a dark rum. [perhaps special use of SCREECH[1]]

screech owl *n* **1** a small North American owl, *Otus asio,* having ear tufts and a reddish-brown or grey plumage. **2** *Brit.* any owl that utters a screeching cry.

screed (skriːd) *n* **1** a long or prolonged speech or piece of writing. **2** a strip of wood, plaster, or metal placed on a surface to act as a guide to the thickness of the cement or plaster coat to be applied. **3** a mixture of cement, sand, and water applied to a concrete slab, etc., to give a smooth surface finish. **4** *Scot.* a rent or tear or the sound produced by this. [C14: probably variant of Old English *scrēade* SHRED]

screen (skriːn) *n* **1** a light movable frame, panel, or partition serving to shelter, divide, hide, etc. **2** anything that serves to shelter, protect, or conceal. **3** a frame containing a mesh that is placed over a window or opening to keep out insects. **4** a decorated partition, esp. in a church around the choir. See also **rood** (sense 1). **5** a sieve. **6** a system for selecting people, such as candidates for a job. **7** the wide end of a cathode-ray tube, esp. in a television set, on which a visible image is formed. **8** a white or silvered surface, usually fabric, placed in front of a projector to receive the enlarged image of a film or of slides. **9 the screen.** the film industry or films collectively. **10** *Photog.* a plate of ground glass in some types of camera on which the image of a subject is focused before being photographed. **11** *Printing.* a glass marked with fine intersecting lines, used in a camera for making half-tone reproductions. **12** men or ships deployed around and ahead of a larger military formation to warn of attack or protect from a specific threat. **13** *Sport, chiefly U.S. and Canadian.* a tactical ploy in which a player blocks an opponent's view. **14** *Psychoanal.* anything that prevents a person from realizing his true feelings about someone or something. **15** *Electronics.* See **screen grid.** ◆ *vb* (*tr*) **16** (sometimes foll. by *off*) to shelter, protect, or conceal. **17** to sieve or sort. **18** to test or check (an individual or group) so as to determine suitability for a task, etc. **19** to examine for the presence of a disease, weapons, etc.: *the authorities screened five hundred cholera suspects.* **20** to provide with a screen or screens. **21** to project (a film) onto a screen, esp. for public viewing. **22** *Printing.* to photograph (a picture) through a screen to render it suitable for half-tone reproduction. **23** *Sport, chiefly U.S. and Canadian.* to block the view of (an opposing player). [C15: from Old French *escren* (French *écran*); related to Old High German *skrank,* German *Schrank* cupboard] ► **'screenable** *adj* ► **'screener** *n* ► **'screenˌful** *n* ► **'screenˌlike** *adj*

screen grid *n Electronics.* an electrode placed between the control grid and anode of a valve and having a fixed positive potential relative to the grid. It acts as an electrostatic shield preventing capacitive coupling between grid and anode, thus increasing the stability of the device. Sometimes shortened to **screen.** See also **suppressor grid.**

screenings ('skriːnɪŋz) *pl n* refuse separated by sifting.

screening test *n* a simple test performed on a large number of people to identify those who have or are likely to develop a specified disease.

screen memory *n Psychoanal.* a memory that is tolerable but allied to a distressing event and which is unconsciously used to hide the distressing memory.

screenplay ('skriːnˌpleɪ) *n* the script for a film, including instructions for sets and camera work.

screen process *n* a method of printing using a fine mesh of silk, nylon, etc., treated with an impermeable coating except in the areas through which ink is subsequently forced onto the paper behind. Also called: **silk-screen printing.**

screensaver ('skriːnseɪvər) *n* a computer program that reduces screen damage resulting from an unchanging display when a computer is switched on but not in use by blanking the screen or generating moving patterns, etc.

screen test *n* **1** a filmed audition of a prospective actor or actress to test suitability. **2** the test film so made.

screen trading *n* a form of trading on a market or exchange in which the visual display unit of a computer replaces personal contact as in floor trading.

screenwriter ('skriːnˌraɪtə) *n* a person who writes screenplays.

screigh *or* **screich** (skriːx) *n, vb* a Scot. word for **screech**[1].

screw (skruː) *n* **1** a device used for fastening materials together, consisting of a threaded and usually tapered shank that has a slotted head by which it may be rotated so as to cut its own thread as it bores through the material. **2** Also called: **screw-bolt.** a threaded cylindrical rod that engages with a similarly threaded cylindrical hole; bolt. **3** a thread in a cylindrical hole corresponding with that on the bolt or screw with which it is designed to engage. **4** anything resembling a screw in shape or spiral form. **5** a twisting movement of or resembling that of a screw. **6** Also called: **screw-back.** *Billiards, snooker, etc.* **6a** a stroke in which the cue ball recoils or moves backward after striking the object ball, made by striking the cue ball below its centre. **6b** the motion resulting from this stroke. **7** another name for **propeller** (sense 1). **8** *Slang.* a prison guard. **9** *Brit. slang.* salary, wages, or earnings. **10** *Brit.* a small amount of salt, tobacco, etc., in a twist of paper. **11** *Slang.* a person who is mean with money. **12** *Slang.* an old, unsound, or worthless horse. **13** (*often pl*) *Slang.* force or compulsion (esp. in the phrase **put the screws on**). **14** *Taboo slang.* sexual intercourse. **15 have a screw loose.** *Informal.* to be insane. **16 turn** *or* **tighten the screw.** *Slang.* to increase the pressure. ◆ *vb* **17** (*tr*) to rotate (a screw or bolt) so as to drive it into or draw it out of a material. **18** (*tr*) to cut a screw thread in (a rod or hole) with a tap or die or on a lathe. **19** to turn or cause to turn in the manner of a screw. **20** (*tr*) to attach or fasten with a screw or screws. **21** (*tr*) *Informal.* to take advantage of; cheat. **22** (*tr;* often foll. by *up*) to distort or contort: *he screwed his face into a scowl.* **23** Also: **screw back.** to impart a screw to (a ball). **24** (*tr,* often foll. by *from* or *out of*) to coerce or force out of; extort. **25** *Taboo slang.* to have sexual intercourse (with). **26** (*tr*) *Slang.* to burgle. **27 have one's head**

screwed on (the right way). *Informal.* to be wise or sensible. ◆ See also **screw up.** [C15: from French *escroe,* from Medieval Latin *scrōfa* screw, from Latin: sow, presumably because the thread of the screw is like the spiral of the sow's tail] ▸ **ˈscrewer** *n* ▸ **ˈscrewˌlike** *adj*

screwball (ˈskruːˌbɔːl) *Slang, chiefly U.S. and Canadian.* ◆ *n* **1** an odd or eccentric person. ◆ *adj* **2** odd; zany; eccentric.

screw conveyor *n Engineering.* a duct along which material is conveyed by the rotational action of a spiral vane which lies along the length of the duct. Also called: **worm conveyor.**

screwdriver (ˈskruːˌdraɪvə) *n* **1** a tool used for turning screws, usually having a handle of wood, plastic, etc., and a steel shank with a flattened square-cut tip that fits into a slot in the head of the screw. **2** an alcoholic beverage consisting of orange juice and vodka.

screwed (skruːd) *adj* **1** fastened by a screw or screws. **2** having spiral grooves like a screw; threaded. **3** twisted or distorted. **4** *Brit.* a slang word for **drunk.**

screw eye *n* a wood screw with its shank bent into a ring.

screw jack *n* a lifting device utilizing the mechanical advantage of a screw thread, the effort being applied through a bevel drive. Also called: **jackscrew, jack.**

screw pile *n* a pile with a threaded tip that is screwed into the ground by a winch or capstan.

screw pine *n* any of various pandanaceous plants of the Old World tropical genus *Pandanus,* having a spiral mass of pineapple-like leaves and heavy cone-like fruits.

screw plate *n* a steel plate with threaded holes used for making male screws.

screw propeller *n* an early form of ship's propeller in which an Archimedes' screw is used to produce thrust by accelerating a flow of water. ▸ **ˈscrew-proˈpelled** *adj*

screw tap *n* another name for **tap**[2] (sense 6).

screw thread *n* the helical ridge on a screw formed by a die or lathe tool.

screw top *n* **1** a lid with a threaded rim that is turned on the corresponding thread on the neck of a bottle or container to close it securely. **2** a bottle or container having such a lid. ▸ **ˈscrew-ˌtop** *or* **ˈscrew-ˌtopped** *adj*

screw up *vb* (*tr, adv*) **1** to twist out of shape or distort. **2** to summon up or call upon: *to screw up one's courage.* **3** (*also intr*) *Informal.* to mishandle or make a mess (of). **4** (*often passive*) *Informal.* to cause to become very anxious, confused, or nervous: *he is really screwed up about his exams.*

screwworm (ˈskruːˌwɜːm) *n* **1** the larva of a dipterous fly, *Callitroga macellaria,* that develops beneath the skin of living mammals often causing illness or death. **2 screwworm fly.** the fly producing this larva: family *Calliphoridae.*

screwy (ˈskruːɪ) *adj* **screwier, screwiest.** *Informal.* odd, crazy, or eccentric.

Scriabin *or* **Skryabin** (ˈskrɪəbɪn; *Russian* ˈskrjabin) *n* **Aleksandr Nikolayevich** (alɪkˈsandr nikaˈlajɪvitʃ). 1872–1915, Russian composer, whose works came increasingly to express his theosophic beliefs. He wrote many piano works; his orchestral compositions include *Prometheus* (1911).

scribble[1] (ˈskrɪbᵊl) *vb* **1** to write or draw in a hasty or illegible manner. **2** to make meaningless or illegible marks (on). **3** *Derogatory or facetious.* to write poetry, novels, etc. ◆ *n* **4** hasty careless writing or drawing. **5** writing, esp. literary matter, of poor quality. **6** meaningless or illegible marks. [C15: from Medieval Latin *scrībillāre* to write hastily, from Latin *scrībere* to write] ▸ **ˈscribbler** *n* ▸ **ˈscribbly** *adj*

scribble[2] (ˈskrɪbᵊl) *vb* (*tr*) to card (wool, etc.). [C17: probably from Low German; compare *schrubben* SCRUB[1]]

scribbly gum (ˈskrɪbᵊlɪ) *n* any species of the genus *Eucalyptus* with smooth white bark marked with random patterns made by wood-boring insects.

scribe (skraɪb) *n* **1** a person who copies documents, esp. a person who made handwritten copies before the invention of printing. **2** a clerk or public copyist. **3** *Old Testament.* a recognized scholar and teacher of the Jewish Law. **4** *Judaism.* a man qualified to write certain documents in accordance with religious requirements. **5** an author or journalist: used humorously. **6** another name for **scriber.** ◆ *vb* **7** to score a line on (a surface) with a pointed instrument, as in metalworking. [(in the senses: writer, etc.) C14: from Latin *scrība* clerk, from *scrībere* to write; C17 (vb): perhaps from INSCRIBE] ▸ **ˈscribal** *adj*

Scribe (*French* skrib) *n* **Augustin Eugène** (ogystɛ̃ øʒɛn). 1791–1861, French author or coauthor of over 350 vaudevilles, comedies, and libretti for light opera.

scriber (ˈskraɪbə) *n* a pointed steel tool used to score materials as a guide to cutting, etc. Also called: **scribe.**

scrim (skrɪm) *n* an open-weave muslin or hessian fabric, used in upholstery, lining, building, and in the theatre to create the illusion of a solid wall or to suggest haziness, etc., according to the lighting. [C18: origin unknown]

scrimmage (ˈskrɪmɪdʒ) *n* **1** a rough or disorderly struggle. **2** *American football.* the clash of opposing linemen at every down. ◆ *vb* **3** (*intr*) to engage in a scrimmage. **4** (*tr*) to put (the ball) into a scrimmage. [C15: from earlier *scrimish,* variant of SKIRMISH] ▸ **ˈscrimmager** *n*

scrimp (skrɪmp) *vb* **1** (when *intr,* sometimes foll. by *on*) to be very economical or sparing in the use (of) (esp. in the phrase **scrimp and save**). **2** (*tr*) to treat meanly: *he is scrimping his children.* **3** (*tr*) to cut too small. ◆ *adj* **4** a less common word for **scant.** [C18: Scottish, origin unknown] ▸ **ˈscrimpy** *adj* ▸ **ˈscrimpily** *adv* ▸ **ˈscrimpiness** *n*

scrimshank (ˈskrɪmˌʃæŋk) *vb* (*intr*) *Brit. military slang.* to shirk work. [C19: of unknown origin]

scrimshaw (ˈskrɪmˌʃɔː) *n* **1** the art of decorating or carving shells, ivory, etc., done by sailors as a leisure activity. **2a** an article made in this manner. **2b** such articles collectively. ◆ *vb* **3** to produce scrimshaw (from). [C19: origin uncertain, perhaps after a surname]

scrip[1] (skrɪp) *n* **1** a written certificate, list, etc. **2** a small scrap, esp. of paper with writing on it. **3** *Finance.* **3a** a certificate representing a claim to part of a share of stock. **3b** the shares allocated in a bonus issue. [C18: in some senses, probably from SCRIPT; otherwise, short for *subscription receipt*]

scrip[2] (skrɪp) *n Archaic.* a small bag or wallet, as carried by pilgrims. [C14: from Old French *escreppe,* variant of *escarpe* SCARF[1]]

scrip[3] (skrɪp) *or* **script** *n Informal.* a medical prescription. [C20: short for PRESCRIPTION]

scrip issue *n* another name for **bonus issue.**

scripophily (skrɪˈpɒfɪlɪ) *n* the hobby of collecting bonds and share certificates, esp. those of historical interest. [C20: from SCRIP[1] + -O- + *-phily,* from Greek *philos* loving] ▸ **scripophile** (ˈskrɪpəʊˌfaɪl) *n*

script (skrɪpt) *n* **1** handwriting as distinguished from print, esp. cursive writing. **2** the letters, characters, or figures used in writing by hand. **3** any system or style of writing. **4** written copy for the use of performers in films and plays. **5** *Law.* **5a** an original or principal document. **5b** (esp. in England) a will or codicil or the draft for one. **6** any of various typefaces that imitate handwriting. **7** an answer paper in an examination. **8** another word for **scrip**[3]. ◆ *vb* **9** (*tr*) to write a script for. [C14: from Latin *scriptum* something written, from *scrībere* to write]

Script. *abbrev. for:* **1** scriptural. **2** Scripture(s).

scriptorium (skrɪpˈtɔːrɪəm) *n, pl* **-riums** *or* **-ria** (-rɪə). a room, esp. in a monastery, set apart for the writing or copying of manuscripts. [from Medieval Latin]

scriptural (ˈskrɪptʃərəl) *adj* **1** (*often cap.*) of, in accordance with, or based on Scripture. **2** of or relating to writing. ▸ **ˈscripturally** *adv*

scripture (ˈskrɪptʃə) *n* a sacred, solemn, or authoritative book or piece of writing. [C13: from Latin *scriptūra* written material, from *scrībere* to write]

Scripture (ˈskrɪptʃə) *n* **1** Also called: **Holy Scripture, Holy Writ, the Scriptures.** *Christianity.* the Old and New Testaments. **2** any book or body of writings, esp. when regarded as sacred by a particular religious group.

scriptwriter (ˈskrɪptˌraɪtə) *n* a person who prepares scripts, esp. for a film. ▸ **ˈscriptˌwriting** *n*

scrivener (ˈskrɪvnə) *n Archaic.* **1** a person who writes out deeds, letters, etc.; copyist. **2** a notary. [C14: from *scrivein* clerk, from Old French *escrivain,* ultimately from Latin *scrība* SCRIBE]

scrobiculate (skrəʊˈbɪkjʊlɪt, -ˌleɪt) *or* **scrobiculated** *adj Biology.* having a surface covered with small round pits or grooves. [C19: from Latin *scrobiculus* diminutive of *scrobis* a ditch]

scrod (skrɒd) *n U.S.* a young cod or haddock, esp. one split and prepared for cooking. [C19: perhaps from obsolete Dutch *schrood,* from Middle Dutch *schrode* SHRED (n); the name perhaps refers to the method of preparing the fish for cooking]

scrofula (ˈskrɒfjʊlə) *n Pathol.* (*no longer in technical use*) tuberculosis of the lymphatic glands. Also called (formerly): (the) **king's evil.** [C14: from Medieval Latin, from Late Latin *scrōfulae* swollen glands in the neck, literally: little sows (sows were thought to be particularly prone to the disease), from Latin *scrōfa* sow]

scrofulous (ˈskrɒfjʊləs) *adj* **1** of, relating to, resembling, or having scrofula. **2** morally degraded. ▸ **ˈscrofulously** *adv* ▸ **ˈscrofulousness** *n*

scroggin (ˈskrɒgɪn) *n N.Z. informal.* a tramper's home-made high-calorie sweetmeat.

scroll (skrəʊl) *n* **1** a roll of parchment, paper, etc., usually inscribed with writing. **2** an ancient book in the form of a roll of parchment, papyrus, etc. **3a** a decorative carving or moulding resembling a scroll. **3b** (*as modifier*): *a scroll saw.* **3c** (*in combination*): *scrollwork.* ◆ *vb* **4** (*tr*) to saw into scrolls. **5** to roll up like a scroll. **6** *Computing.* to move (text) from right to left or up and down on a screen in order to view text that cannot be contained within a single display image. [C15 *scrowle,* from *scrowe,* from Old French *escroe* scrap of parchment, but also influenced by ROLL]

scroll saw *n* a saw with a narrow blade for cutting intricate ornamental curves in wood.

scrollwork (ˈskrəʊlˌwɜːk) *n* ornamental work in scroll-like patterns, esp. when done with a scroll saw.

Scrooge (skruːdʒ) *n* a mean or miserly person. [C19: after a character in Dickens' story *A Christmas Carol* (1843)]

scroop (skruːp) *Dialect.* ◆ *vb* **1** (*intr*) to emit a grating or creaking sound. ◆ *n* **2** such a sound. [C18: of imitative origin]

scrophulariaceous (ˌskrɒfjʊˌlɛərɪˈeɪʃəs) *adj* of, relating to, or belonging to the *Scrophulariaceae,* a family of plants including figwort, snapdragon, foxglove, toadflax, speedwell, and mullein. [C19: from New Latin (*herba*) *scrophularia* scrofula (plant), from the use of such plants in treating scrofula]

scrotum (ˈskrəʊtəm) *n, pl* **-ta** (-tə) *or* **-tums.** the pouch of skin containing the testes in most mammals. [C16: from Latin] ▸ **ˈscrotal** *adj*

scrouge (skraʊdʒ, skruːdʒ) *vb* (*tr*) *Dialect.* to crowd or press. [C18: alteration of C16 *scruze* to squeeze, perhaps blend of SCREW + SQUEEZE]

scrounge (skraʊndʒ) *vb Informal.* **1** (when *intr,* sometimes foll. by *around*) to search in order to acquire (something) without cost. **2** to obtain or seek to obtain (something) by cadging or begging. [C20: variant of dialect *scrunge* to steal, of obscure origin] ▸ **ˈscrounger** *n*

scrub[1] (skrʌb) *vb* **scrubs, scrubbing, scrubbed. 1** to rub (a surface) hard, with or as if with a brush, soap, and water, in order to clean it. **2** to remove (dirt), esp. by rubbing with a brush and water. **3** (*intr;* foll. by *up*) (of a surgeon) to wash the hands and arms thoroughly before operating. **4** (*tr*) to purify (a vapour or gas) by removing impurities. **5** (*tr*) *Informal.* to delete or cancel. **6** (*intr*) *Horse-racing slang.* (of jockeys) to urge a horse forwards by moving the arms and whip rhythmically forwards and backwards alongside its neck. ◆ *n* **7** the act of or an instance of scrubbing. ◆ See also **scrub round.** [C14: from Middle Low German *schrubben,* or Middle Dutch *schrobben*]

scrub[2] (skrʌb) *n* **1a** vegetation consisting of stunted trees, bushes, and other plants growing in an arid area. **1b** (*as modifier*): *scrub vegetation.* **2** an area of arid land covered with such vegetation. **3a** an animal of inferior breeding or condition. **3b** (*as modifier*): *a scrub bull.* **4** a small or insignificant person. **5** anything stunted or inferior. **6** *Sport, U.S. and Canadian.* a player not in the first team. **7 the scrub.** *Austral. informal.* a remote place, esp. one where contact with people can be avoided. ◆ *adj* (*prenominal*) **8** small, stunted, or inferior. **9** *Sport, U.S. and Canadian.* **9a** (of a player) not in the first team. **9b** (of a team) composed of such players. **9c** (of a contest) between scratch or incomplete teams. [C16: variation of SHRUB[1]]

scrubber[1] ('skrʌbə) *n* **1** a person or thing that scrubs. **2** an apparatus for purifying a gas. **3** *Derogatory Brit. and Austral. slang.* a promiscuous woman.

scrubber[2] ('skrʌbə) *n Austral.* a domestic animal, esp. a bullock, that has run wild in the bush. [C19: from SCRUB[2]]

scrub bird *n* either of two fast-running wren-like passerine birds, *Atrichornis clamosus* or *A. rufescens,* that constitute the Australian family *Atrichornithidae.*

scrubby ('skrʌbɪ) *adj* **-bier, -biest.** **1** covered with or consisting of scrub. **2** (of trees or vegetation) stunted in growth. **3** *Brit. informal.* messy. ▸ **'scrubbiness** *n*

scrub fowl *or* **turkey** *n* another name for **megapode.**

scrubland ('skrʌb,lænd) *n* an area of scrub vegetation.

scrub round *vb* (*intr, prep*) *Informal.* to waive; avoid or ignore: *we can scrub round the rules.*

scrub typhus *n* an acute febrile disease characterized by severe headache, skin rash, chills, and swelling of the lymph nodes, caused by the bite of mites infected with the microorganism *Rickettsia tsutsugamushi:* occurs mainly in Asia, Australia, and the islands of the western Pacific.

scruff[1] (skrʌf) *n* the nape of the neck (esp. in the phrase **by the scruff of the neck**). [C18: variant of *scuft,* perhaps from Old Norse *skoft* hair; related to Old High German *scuft*]

scruff[2] (skrʌf) *n* **1** *Informal.* an untidy scruffy person. **2** *Informal.* a disreputable person, ruffian. **3** another name for **scum** (sense 3).

scruffy ('skrʌfɪ) *adj* **scruffier, scruffiest.** unkempt or shabby.

scrum (skrʌm) *n* **1** *Rugby.* the act or method of restarting play after an infringement when the two opposing packs of forwards group together with heads down and arms interlocked and push to gain ground while the scrum half throws the ball in and the hookers attempt to scoop it out to their own team. A scrum is usually called by the referee (**set scrum**) but may be formed spontaneously (**loose scrum**). **2** *Informal.* a disorderly struggle. ◆ *vb* **scrums, scrumming, scrummed.** **3** (*intr;* usually foll. by *down*) *Rugby.* to form a scrum. [C19: shortened from SCRUMMAGE]

scrum half *n Rugby.* **1** a player who puts in the ball at scrums and tries to get it away to his three-quarter backs. **2** this position in a team.

scrummage ('skrʌmɪdʒ) *n, vb* **1** *Rugby.* another word for **scrum. 2** a variant of **scrimmage.** [C19: variant of SCRIMMAGE] ▸ **'scrummager** *n*

scrump (skrʌmp) *vb Dialect.* to steal (apples) from an orchard or garden. [dialect variant of SCRIMP]

scrumple ('skrʌmpᵊl) *vb* (usually foll. by *up*) to crumple or crush (something, esp. a piece of paper) or (esp. of a piece of paper) to become crumpled or crushed. [C16: variant of CRUMPLE]

scrumptious ('skrʌmpʃəs) *adj Informal.* very pleasing; delicious. [C19: probably changed from SUMPTUOUS] ▸ **'scrumptiously** *adv* ▸ **'scrumptiousness** *n*

scrumpy ('skrʌmpɪ) *n* a rough dry cider, brewed esp. in the West Country. [from *scrump,* variant of SCRIMP (in obsolete sense: withered), referring to the apples used]

scrunch (skrʌntʃ) *vb* **1** to crumple, crush, or crunch or to be crumpled, crushed, or crunched. ◆ *n* **2** the act or sound of scrunching. [C19: variant of CRUNCH]

scrunchie ('skrʌntʃɪ) *n* a loop of elastic covered loosely with fabric, used to hold the hair in a ponytail, etc.

scruple ('skru:pᵊl) *n* **1** (*often pl*) a doubt or hesitation as to what is morally right in a certain situation. **2** *Archaic.* a very small amount. **3** a unit of weight equal to 20 grains (1.296 grams). **4** an ancient Roman unit of weight equivalent to approximately one twenty-fourth of an ounce. ◆ *vb* **5** (*obsolete when tr*) to have doubts (about), esp. for a moral reason. [C16: from Latin *scrūpulus* a small weight, from *scrūpus* rough stone] ▸ **'scrupleless** *adj*

scrupulous ('skru:pjʊləs) *adj* **1** characterized by careful observation of what is morally right. **2** very careful or precise. [C15: from Latin *scrūpulōsus* punctilious] ▸ **'scrupulously** *adv* ▸ **'scrupulousness** *n*

scrutable ('skru:təbᵊl) *adj Rare.* open to or able to be understood by scrutiny. [C17: from Latin *scrūtārī* to inspect closely; see SCRUTINY] ▸ **,scruta'bility** *n*

scrutator (skru:'teɪtə) *n* a person who examines or scrutinizes. [from Latin, from *scrūtārī* to search]

scrutineer (,skru:tɪ'nɪə) *n* a person who examines, esp. one who scrutinizes the conduct of an election poll.

scrutinize *or* **scrutinise** ('skru:tɪ,naɪz) *vb* (*tr*) to examine carefully or in minute detail. ▸ **'scruti,nizer** *or* **'scruti,niser** *n*

scrutiny ('skru:tɪnɪ) *n, pl* **-nies.** **1** close or minute examination. **2** a searching look. **3a** (in the early Christian Church) a formal testing that catechumens had to undergo before being baptized. **3b** a similar examination of candidates for holy orders. [C15: from Late Latin *scrūtinium* an investigation, from *scrūtārī* to search (originally referring to rag-and-bone men), from *scrūta* rubbish]

scry (skraɪ) *vb* **scries, scrying, scried.** (*intr*) to divine, esp. by crystal gazing. [C16: from DESCRY]

SCSI ('skʌzɪ) *acronym for* Small Computer Systems Interface: a system for connecting a computer to peripheral devices.

scuba ('skju:bə) *n* **a** an apparatus used in skindiving, consisting of a cylinder or cylinders containing compressed air attached to a breathing apparatus. **b** (*as modifier*): *scuba diving.* [C20: from the initials of *self-contained underwater breathing apparatus*]

scud (skʌd) *vb* **scuds, scudding, scudded.** **1** (*intr*) (esp. of clouds) to move along swiftly and smoothly. **2** (*intr*) *Nautical.* to run before a gale. **3** (*tr*) *Scot.* to hit; slap. ◆ *n* **4** the act of scudding. **5** *Meteorol.* **5a** a formation of low fractostratus clouds driven by a strong wind beneath rain-bearing clouds. **5b** a sudden shower or gust of wind. **6** *Scot.* a slap. [C16: probably of Scandinavian origin; related to Norwegian *skudda* to thrust, Swedish *skudda* to shake]

Scud (skʌd) *n Informal.* a Soviet-made surface-to-surface missile, originally designed to carry nuclear warheads and with a range of 300 km; later modified to achieve greater range: used in the Iran-Iraq War and in the Gulf War.

scudo ('sku:dəʊ) *n, pl* **-di** (-di:). any of several former Italian coins. [C17: from Italian: shield, from Latin *scūtum*]

scuff (skʌf) *vb* **1** to scrape or drag (the feet) while walking. **2** to rub or scratch (a surface) or (of a surface) to become rubbed or scratched. **3** (*tr*) *U.S.* to poke at (something) with the foot. ◆ *n* **4** the act or sound of scuffing. **5** a rubbed place caused by scuffing. **6** a backless slipper. [C19: probably of imitative origin]

scuffle[1] ('skʌfᵊl) *vb* (*intr*) **1** to fight in a disorderly manner. **2** to move by shuffling. **3** to move in a hurried or confused manner. ◆ *n* **4** a disorderly struggle. **5** the sound made by scuffling or shuffling. [C16: from Scandinavian; compare Swedish *skuff, skuffa* to push]

scuffle[2] ('skʌfᵊl) *n U.S.* a type of hoe operated by pushing rather than pulling. [C18: from Dutch *schoffel* SHOVEL]

scull (skʌl) *n* **1** a single oar moved from side to side over the stern of a boat to propel it. **2** one of a pair of short-handled oars, both of which are pulled by one oarsman, esp. in a racing shell. **3** a racing shell propelled by an oarsman or oarsmen pulling two oars. **4** (*pl*) a race between racing shells, each propelled by one, two, or four oarsmen pulling two oars. **5** an act, instance, period, or distance of sculling. ◆ *vb* **6** to propel (a boat) with a scull. [C14: of unknown origin] ▸ **'sculler** *n*

scullery ('skʌlərɪ) *n, pl* **-leries.** *Chiefly Brit.* a small room or part of a kitchen where washing up, vegetable preparation, etc. is done. [C15: from Anglo-Norman *squillerie,* from Old French *escuelerie,* from *escuele* a bowl, from Latin *scutella,* from *scutra* a flat tray]

Scullin ('skʌlɪn) *n* **James Henry.** 1876–1953, Australian statesman; prime minister of Australia (1929–31).

scullion ('skʌljən) *n* **1** a mean or despicable person. **2** *Archaic.* a servant employed to do rough household work in a kitchen. [C15: from Old French *escouillon* cleaning cloth, from *escouve* a broom, from Latin *scōpa* a broom]

sculp. *abbrev. for:* **1** Also: **sculpt.** sculpsit. **2** sculptor, sculptress, or sculpture.

sculpin ('skʌlpɪn) *n, pl* **-pin** *or* **-pins.** *U.S. and Canadian.* any of various fishes of the family *Cottidae* (bullheads and sea scorpions). [C17: of unknown origin]

sculpsit *Latin.* ('skʌlpsɪt) he (or she) sculptured it: an inscription following the artist's name on a sculpture.

sculpt (skʌlpt) *vb* **1** a variant of **sculpture** (senses 5–8). **2** (*intr*) to practise sculpture. ◆ Also: **sculp.** [C19: from French *sculpter,* from Latin *sculpere* to carve]

sculptor ('skʌlptə) *or* (*fem*) **sculptress** *n* a person who practises sculpture.

Sculptor ('skʌlptə) *n, Latin genitive* **Sculptoris** (skʌlp'tɔ:rɪs). a faint constellation in the S hemisphere between Phoenix and Cetus.

sculpture ('skʌlptʃə) *n* **1** the art of making figures or designs in relief or the round by carving wood, moulding plaster, etc., or casting metals, etc. **2** works or a work made in this way. **3** ridges or indentations as on a shell, formed by natural processes. **4** the gradual formation of the landscape by erosion. ◆ *vb* (*mainly tr*) **5** (*also intr*) to carve, cast, or fashion (stone, bronze, etc.) three dimensionally. **6** to portray (a person, etc.) by means of sculpture. **7** to form in the manner of sculpture, esp. to shape (landscape) by erosion. **8** to decorate with sculpture. ◆ Also (for senses 5–8): **sculpt.** [C14: from Latin *sculptūra* a carving; see SCULPT] ▸ **'sculptural** *adj* ▸ **'sculpturally** *adv*

sculpturesque (,skʌlptʃə'rɛsk) *adj* resembling sculpture. ▸ **,sculptur'esquely** *adv* ▸ **,sculptur'esqueness** *n*

scum (skʌm) *n* **1** a layer of impure matter that forms on the surface of a liquid, often as the result of boiling or fermentation. **2** the greenish film of algae and similar vegetation surface of a stagnant pond. **3** Also called: **dross, scruff.** the skin of oxides or impurities on the surface of a molten metal. **4** waste matter. **5** a worthless person or group of people. ◆ *vb* **scums, scumming, scummed.** **6** (*tr*) to remove scum from. **7** (*intr*) *Rare.* to form a layer of or become covered with scum. [C13: of Germanic origin; related to Old High German *scūm,* Middle Dutch *schūm,* Old French *escume;* see SKIM] ▸ **'scum,like** *adj* ▸ **'scummer** *n* ▸ **'scummy** *adj*

scumbag ('skʌm,bæg) *n Slang.* an offensive or despicable person. [C20: perhaps from earlier U.S. sense: condom, from U.S. slang *scum* semen + bag]

scumble ('skʌmbᵊl) *vb* **1** (in painting and drawing) to soften or blend (an outline or colour) with an upper coat of opaque colour, applied very thinly. ◆ *n* **2** the upper layer of colour applied in this way. **3** the technique or effects of scumbling. [C18: probably from SCUM]

scuncheon ('skʌntʃən) *n* the inner part of a door jamb or window frame. [C15: from Old French *escoinson,* from *coin* angle]

scunge (skʌndʒ) *Austral. and N.Z. slang.* ◆ *vb* **1** to borrow. ◆ *n* **2** a dirty or worthless person. **3** a person who borrows, esp. habitually. [C20: of unknown origin]

scungy ('skʌndʒɪ) *adj* **scungier, scungiest.** *Austral. and N.Z. informal.* miserable; sordid; dirty. [C20: of uncertain origin]

scunner ('skʌnə; *Scot.* 'skʌnər) *Dialect, chiefly Scot.* ◆ *vb* **1** (*intr*) to feel aversion. **2** (*tr*) to produce a feeling of aversion in. ◆ *n* **3** a strong aversion (often in the phrase **take a scunner to**). **4** an object of dislike; nuisance. [C14: from Scottish *skunner,* of unknown origin]

Scunthorpe ('skʌn,θɔːp) *n* a town in E England, in North Lincolnshire unitary authority, Lincolnshire: developed rapidly after the discovery of local iron ore in the late 19th century; iron and steel industries have declined. Pop.: 75 982 (1991).

scup (skʌp) *n* a common sparid fish, *Stenotomus chrysops,* of American coastal regions of the Atlantic. Also called: **northern porgy.** [C19: from Narraganset *mishcup,* from *mishe* big + *kuppe* close together; from the form of the scales]

scupper[1] ('skʌpə) *n* **1** *Nautical.* a drain or spout allowing water on the deck of a vessel to flow overboard. **2** an opening in the side of a building for draining off water. **3** a drain in a factory floor for running off the water from a sprinkler system. [C15 *skopper,* of uncertain origin; perhaps related to SCOOP]

scupper[2] ('skʌpə) *vb (tr) Brit.* **1** *Slang.* to overwhelm, ruin, or disable. **2** to sink (one's ship) deliberately. [C19: of unknown origin]

scuppernong ('skʌpə,nɒŋ) *n* **1** a sweet American wine, slightly golden, made from a variety of muscadine grape. **2** another name for **muscadine** (sense 2), esp. the variety from which this wine is made. [C19: named after *Scuppernong* River in North Carolina where the grape grows]

scurf (skɜːf) *n* **1** another name for **dandruff. 2** flaky or scaly matter adhering to or peeling off a surface. [Old English *scurf;* related to Old Norse *skurfóttr* scurfy, Old High German *scorf,* Danish *skurv*] ▸ **'scurfy** *adj*

scurrilous ('skʌrɪləs) *adj* **1** grossly or obscenely abusive or defamatory. **2** characterized by gross or obscene humour. [C16: from Latin *scurrīlis* derisive, from *scurra* buffoon] ▸ **scurrility** (skə'rɪlɪtɪ) *or* **'scurrilousness** *n* ▸ **'scurrilously** *adv*

scurry ('skʌrɪ) *vb* **-ries, -rying, -ried. 1** to move about or proceed hurriedly. **2** *(intr)* to whirl about. ◆ *n, pl* **-ries. 3** the act or sound of scurrying. **4** a brisk light whirling movement, as of snow. **5** *Horse racing.* a short race or sprint. [C19: probably shortened from *hurry-scurry*]

scurvy ('skɜːvɪ) *n* **1** a disease caused by a lack of vitamin C, characterized by anaemia, spongy gums, bleeding beneath the skin, and (in infants) malformation of bones and teeth. Related adj: **scorbutic.** ◆ *adj* **-vier, -viest. 2** mean or despicable. [C16: see SCURF] ▸ **'scurvily** *adv* ▸ **'scurviness** *n*

scurvy grass *n* any of various cruciferous plants of the genus *Cochlearia,* esp. *C. officinalis,* of Europe and North America, formerly used to treat scurvy.

scut (skʌt) *n* the short tail of animals such as the deer and rabbit. [C15: probably of Scandinavian origin; compare Old Norse *skutr* end of a vessel, Icelandic *skott* tail]

scuta ('skjuːtə) *n* the plural of **scutum.**

scutage ('skjuːtɪdʒ) *n* (in feudal society) a payment sometimes exacted by a lord from his vassal in lieu of military service. [C15: from Medieval Latin *scūtāgium,* literally: shield dues, from Latin *scūtum* a shield]

Scutari *n* **1** ('skuːtərɪ, skuː'tɑːrɪ). the former name of **Üsküdar. 2** (sku'tari). the Italian name for **Shkodër.**

scutate ('skjuːteɪt) *adj* **1** (of animals) having or covered with large bony or horny plates. **2** *Botany.* shaped like a round shield or buckler: *a scutate leaf.* [C19: from Latin *scūtātus* armed with a shield, from *scūtum* a shield] ▸ **scu'tation** *n*

scutch (skʌtʃ) *vb* **1** *(tr)* to separate the fibres from the woody part of (flax) by pounding. ◆ *n* **2** the tool used for this. Also called: **scutcher.** [C18: from obsolete French *escoucher,* from Vulgar Latin *excuticāre* (unattested) to beat out, from Latin EX-[1] + *quatere* to shake]

scutcheon ('skʌtʃən) *n* **1** a variant of **escutcheon. 2** any rounded or shield-shaped structure, esp. a scute. ▸ **'scutcheonless** *adj* ▸ **'scutcheon-,like** *adj*

scutch grass *n* another name for **Bermuda grass** and **couch grass.** Sometimes shortened to **scutch.** [variant of COUCH GRASS]

scute (skjuːt) *n Zoology.* a horny or chitinous plate that makes up part of the exoskeleton in armadillos, turtles, fishes, etc. [C14 (the name of a French coin; C19 in zoological sense): from Latin *scūtum* shield]

scutellation (,skjuːtɪ'leɪʃən) *n Zoology.* **1** the way in which scales or plates are arranged in an animal. **2** a covering of scales or scutella, as on a bird's leg. [C19: New Latin, from *scutella,* plural of SCUTELLUM + -ATION]

scutellum (skjuː'tɛləm) *n, pl* **-la** (-lə). *Biology.* **1** the last of three plates into which the notum of an insect's thorax is divided. **2** one of the scales on the tarsus of a bird's leg. **3** the cotyledon of a developing grass seed. **4** any other small shield-shaped part or structure. [C18: from New Latin: a little shield, from Latin *scūtum* a shield] ▸ **scu'tellar** *adj* ▸ **scutellate** ('skjuːtɪ,leɪt, -lɪt) *adj*

scutiform ('skjuːtɪ,fɔːm) *adj* (esp. of plant parts) shaped like a shield. [C17: from New Latin *scūtiformis,* from Latin *scūtum* a shield + *forma* shape]

scutter ('skʌtə) *vb, n Brit.* an informal word for **scurry.** [C18: probably from SCUTTLE[2], with -ER[1] as in SCATTER]

scuttle[1] ('skʌt[ə]l) *n* **1** See **coal scuttle. 2** *Dialect, chiefly Brit.* a shallow basket, esp. for carrying vegetables. **3** the part of a motor-car body lying immediately behind the bonnet. [Old English *scutel* trencher, from Latin *scutella* bowl, diminutive of *scutra* platter; related to Old Norse *skutill,* Old High German *scuzzila,* perhaps to Latin *scūtum* shield]

scuttle[2] ('skʌt[ə]l) *vb* **1** *(intr)* to run or move about with short hasty steps. ◆ *n* **2** a hurried pace or run. [C15: perhaps from SCUD, influenced by SHUTTLE]

scuttle[3] ('skʌt[ə]l) *vb* **1** *(tr) Nautical.* to cause (a vessel) to sink by opening the seacocks or making holes in the bottom. **2** *(tr)* to give up (hopes, plans, etc.). ◆ *n* **3** *Nautical.* a small hatch or its cover. [C15 (n): via Old French from Spanish *escotilla* a small opening, from *escote* opening in a piece of cloth, from *escotar* to cut out]

scuttlebutt ('skʌt[ə]l,bʌt) *n Nautical.* **1** a drinking fountain. **2** (formerly) a cask of drinking water aboard a ship. **3** *Chiefly U.S. slang.* rumour or gossip. [C19: from SCUTTLE[3] + BUTT[4]]

scutum ('skjuːtəm) *n, pl* **-ta** (-tə). **1** the middle of three plates into which the notum of an insect's thorax is divided. **2** another word for **scute. 3** a large Roman shield. [Latin: shield]

Scutum ('skjuːtəm) *n, Latin genitive* **Scuti** ('skjuːtaɪ). a small faint constellation in the S hemisphere lying between Sagittarius and Aquila and crossed by the Milky Way. Also called: **Scutum Sobieskii** (sɒ'bjeskɪ). [Latin, literally: the Shield]

scuzzy ('skʌzɪ) *adj* **-zier, -ziest.** *Slang, chiefly U.S.* unkempt, dirty, or squalid. [C20: perhaps from *disgusting* or perhaps from a blend of *scum and fuzz*]

Scylla ('sɪlə) *n* **1** *Greek myth.* a sea nymph transformed into a sea monster believed to drown sailors navigating the Strait of Messina. She was identified with a rock off the Italian coast. Compare **Charybdis. 2 between Scylla and Charybdis.** in a predicament in which avoidance of either of two dangers means exposure to the other.

scyphiform ('saɪfɪ,fɔːm) *adj* shaped like a cup or goblet: *a scyphiform cell.* [C19: from Greek *skuphos* cup + -FORM]

scyphistoma (saɪ'fɪstəmə) *n, pl* **-mae** (-,miː) *or* **-mas.** a sessile hydra-like individual representing the polyp stage of scyphozoans. It produces forms which become free-swimming jellyfish. [C19: from Greek *skuphos* cup + STOMA]

scyphozoan (,saɪfə'zəuən) *n* **1** any marine medusoid coelenterate of the class *Scyphozoa;* a jellyfish. ◆ *adj* **2** of, relating to, or belonging to the *Scyphozoa.* [C19: via New Latin from Greek *skuphos* bowl + *zōion* animal]

scyphus ('saɪfəs) *n, pl* **-phi** (-faɪ). **1** an ancient Greek two-handled drinking cup without a footed base. **2** *Botany.* a cuplike body formed at the end of the thallus in certain lichens. [C18: from Latin: goblet, from Greek *skuphos*]

Scyros ('skirɔs) *n* a variant spelling of **Skyros.**

scythe (saɪð) *n* **1** a manual implement for cutting grass, etc., having a long handle held with both hands and a curved sharpened blade that moves in a plane parallel to the ground. ◆ *vb* **2** *(tr)* to cut (grass, etc.) with a scythe. [Old English *sigthe;* related to Old Norse *sigthr,* Old High German *segansa*] ▸ **'scythe,like** *adj*

Scythia ('sɪðɪə) *n* an ancient region of SE Europe and Asia, north of the Black Sea: now part of the Ukraine.

Scythian ('sɪðɪən) *adj* **1** of or relating to ancient Scythia, its inhabitants, or their language. ◆ *n* **2** a member of an ancient nomadic people of Scythia. **3** the extinct language of this people, belonging to the East Iranian branch of the Indo-European family.

sd *abbrev. for:* **1** sine die. **2** sound. **3** *Philosophy.* sense datum.

SD *abbrev. for:* **1** South Dakota. **2** Also: **sd.** *Statistics.* standard deviation. ◆ **3** *international car registration for* Swaziland.

SDA (formerly) *abbrev. for* Scottish Development Agency.

S. Dak. *abbrev. for* South Dakota.

SDI *abbrev. for* Strategic Defense Initiative. See **Star Wars.**

SDLP (in Northern Ireland) *abbrev. for* Social Democratic and Labour Party.

SDP *abbrev. for* Social Democratic Party.

SDRs *abbrev. for* special drawing rights.

Se *the chemical symbol for* selenium.

SE *symbol for* southeast(ern).

sea (siː) *n* **1a** (usually preceded by *the*) the mass of salt water on the earth's surface as differentiated from the land. Related adjs: **marine, maritime, thalassic. 1b** *(as modifier): sea air.* **2** *(cap. when part of place name)* **2a** one of the smaller areas of ocean: *the Irish Sea.* **2b** a large inland area of water: *the Caspian Sea.* **3** turbulence or swell, esp. of considerable size: *heavy seas.* **4** *(cap. when part of a name) Astronomy.* any of many huge dry plains on the surface of the moon. See also **mare**[2]. **5** anything resembling the sea in size or apparent limitlessness. **6** the life or career of a sailor (esp. in the phrase **follow the sea**). **7 at sea. 7a** on the ocean. **7b** in a state of confusion. **8 go to sea.** to become a sailor. **9 put (out) to sea.** to embark on a sea voyage. [Old English *sǣ;* related to Old Norse *sǣr,* Old Frisian *sē,* Gothic *saiws,* Old High German *sēo*]

sea anchor *n Nautical.* any device, such as a bucket or canvas funnel, dragged in the water to keep a vessel heading into the wind or reduce drifting.

sea anemone *n* any of various anthozoan coelenterates, esp. of the order *Actiniaria,* having a polypoid body with oral rings of tentacles. See also **actinia.**

sea aster *n* a composite perennial plant of salt marshes, *Aster tripolium,* having yellow and purple flowers like those of the related Michaelmas daisy.

sea bag *n* a canvas bag, closed by a line threaded through grommets at the top, used by a seaman for his belongings.

sea bass (bæs) *n* any of various American coastal percoid fishes of the genus *Centropristes* and related genera, such as *C. striatus* (**black sea bass**), having an elongated body with a long spiny dorsal fin almost divided into two: family *Serranidae.*

Seabee ('siː,biː) *n* a member of the U.S. Navy's Construction Battalions established to build airstrips. [C20: from pronunciation of *CB,* for *Construction Battalion*]

sea beet *n* a name for the wild form of *Beta vulgaris.* See **beet.**

sea bird *n* a bird such as a gull, that lives on the sea.

sea biscuit *n* another term for **hardtack.**

seablite ('siː,blaɪt) *n* a prostrate annual plant of the goosefoot family, *Suaeda maritima,* of salt marshes, having fleshy alternate leaves and small green flowers. [C18: SEA + *blite,* via Latin from Greek *bliton* ORACHE]

seaboard ('siː,bɔːd) *n* **a** land bordering on the sea; the seashore. **b** *(as modifier): seaboard towns.*

Seaborg ('siːbɔːg) *n* **Glenn Theodore.** 1912–99, U.S. chemist and nuclear physicist. With E. M. McMillan, he discovered several transuranic elements, including plutonium (1940), curium, and americium (1944), and shared a Nobel prize for chemistry 1951.

seaborgium ('siːbɔːgɪəm) *n* a synthetic transuranic element, synthesized and identified in 1974. Symbol: Sg; atomic no.: 106. [C20: after Glenn SEABORG]

seaborne ('siː,bɔːn) *adj* **1** carried on or by the sea. **2** transported by ship.

sea bream *n* any sparid fish, esp. *Pagellus centrodontus,* of European seas, valued as a food fish.
sea breeze *n* a wind blowing from the sea to the land, esp. during the day when the land surface is warmer.
sea buckthorn *n* a thorny Eurasian shrub, *Hippophaë rhamnoides,* growing on sea coasts and having silvery leaves and orange fruits: family *Elaeagnaceae.*
sea butterfly *n* another name for **pteropod.**
SEAC ('si:æk) *n* (in Britain) *acronym for* School Examination and Assessment Council.
sea captain *n* the master of a ship, usually a merchant ship.
sea change *n* a seemingly magical change, as brought about by the action of the sea. **[**coined by Shakespeare, in Ariel's song "Full Fathom Five" in *The Tempest* (1611)**]**
sea chest *n* a usually large firm chest used by a sailor for storing personal property.
seacoast ('si:ˌkəʊst) *n* land bordering on the sea; a coast.
seacock ('si:ˌkɒk) *n Nautical.* a valve in the hull of a vessel below the water line for admitting sea water or for pumping out bilge water.
sea cow *n* **1** any sirenian mammal, such as a dugong or manatee. **2** an archaic name for **walrus.**
sea cucumber *n* any echinoderm of the class *Holothuroidea,* having an elongated body covered with a leathery skin and bearing a cluster of tentacles at the oral end. They usually creep on the sea bed or burrow in sand. **[**C17: so named because of its cucumber-like shape**]**
seadog ('si:ˌdɒg) *n* another word for **fogbow** or **fogdog.**
sea dog *n* an experienced or old sailor.
sea duck *n* any of various large diving ducks, such as the eider and the scoter, that occur along coasts.
sea eagle *n* any of various fish-eating eagles that live near the sea, esp. *Haliaetus albicilla* (**European sea eagle** or **white-tailed eagle**) having a brown plumage and white tail.
sea-ear *n* another name for the **ormer** (sense 1).
sea elephant *n* another name for **elephant seal.**
sea fan *n* any of various corals of the genus *Gorgonia* and related genera, having a treelike or fan-shaped horny skeleton: order *Gorgonacea* (gorgonians).
seafarer ('si:ˌfɛərə) *n* **1** a traveller who goes by sea. **2** a less common word for **sailor.**
seafaring ('si:ˌfɛərɪŋ) *adj* (*prenominal*) **1** travelling by sea. **2** working as a sailor. ◆ *n* **3** the act of travelling by sea. **4** the career or work of a sailor.
sea fir *n* another name for **hydroid** (sense 3).
seafloor spreading ('si:ˌflɔ:) *n* a series of processes in which new oceanic lithosphere is created at oceanic ridges, spreads away from the ridges, and returns to the earth's interior along Benioff zones. Also called: **ocean floor spreading.**
sea foam *n* **1** foam formed on the surface of the sea. **2** a former name for **meerschaum** (sense 1).
seafood ('si:ˌfu:d) *n* edible saltwater fish or shellfish.
sea fret *n* a wet mist or haze coming inland from the sea.
seafront ('si:ˌfrʌnt) *n* a built-up area facing the sea.
sea-girt *adj Literary.* surrounded by the sea.
seagoing ('si:ˌgəʊɪŋ) *adj* intended for or used at sea.
sea gooseberry *n* any of various ctenophores of the genus *Pleurobrachia* and related genera, having a rounded body with longitudinal rows of cilia and hairlike tentacles.
sea green *n* **a** a moderate green colour, sometimes with a bluish or yellowish tinge. **b** (*as adj*): *a sea-green carpet.*
seagull ('si:ˌgʌl) *n* **1** a popular name for the **gull** (the bird). **2** *N.Z.* a casual wharf labourer who is not a trade-union member.
sea hare *n* any of various marine gastropods of the order *Aplysiomorpha* (or *Anaspidea*), esp. *Aplysia punctata,* having a soft body with an internal shell and two pairs of earlike tentacles.
sea heath *n* a small tough perennial plant, *Frankenia laevis,* of Eurasian salt marshes, having minute leaves and pink flowers: family *Frankeniaceae.*
sea holly *n* a European umbelliferous plant, *Eryngium maritimum,* of sandy shores, having spiny bluish-green stems and blue flowers.
sea horse *n* **1** any marine teleost fish of the temperate and tropical genus *Hippocampus,* having a bony-plated body, a prehensile tail, and a horselike head and swimming in an upright position: family *Syngnathidae* (pipefishes). **2** an archaic name for the **walrus. 3** a fabled sea creature with the tail of a fish and the front parts of a horse.
sea-island cotton *n* **1** a cotton plant, *Gossypium barbadense,* of the Sea Islands, widely cultivated for its fine long fibres. **2** the fibre of this plant or the material woven from it.
Sea Islands *pl n* a chain of islands in the Atlantic off the coasts of South Carolina, Georgia, and Florida.
sea kale *n* a European coastal cruciferous plant, *Crambe maritima,* with broad fleshy leaves and white flowers: cultivated for its edible asparagus-like shoots. Compare **kale.**
seakale beet ('si:ˌkeɪl) *n* another name for **chard.**
sea king *n* any of the greater Viking pirate chiefs who led raids on the coasts of early medieval Europe.
seal[1] (si:l) *n* **1** a device impressed on a piece of wax, moist clay, etc., fixed to a letter, document, etc., as a mark of authentication. **2** a stamp, ring, etc., engraved with a device to form such an impression. **3** a substance, esp. wax, so placed over an envelope, document, etc., that it must be broken before the object can be opened or used. **4** any substance or device used to close or fasten tightly. **5** a material, such as putty or cement, that is used to close an opening to prevent the passage of air, water, etc. **6** a small amount of water contained in the trap of a drain to prevent the passage of foul smells. **7** an agent or device for keeping something hidden or secret. **8** anything that gives a pledge or confirmation. **9** a decorative stamp often sold in aid of charity. **10** *R.C. Church.* Also called: **seal of confession.** the obligation never to reveal anything said by a penitent in confession. **11 set one's seal on** (*or* **to**). **11a** to mark with one's sign or seal. **11b** to endorse. ◆ *vb* (*tr*) **12** to affix a seal to, as proof of authenticity. **13** to stamp with or as if with a seal. **14** to approve or authorize. **15** (sometimes foll. by *up*) to close or secure with or as if with a seal: *to seal one's lips; seal up a letter.* **16** (foll. by *off*) to enclose (a place) with a fence, wall, etc. **17** to decide irrevocably. **18** *Mormon Church.* to make (a marriage or adoption) perpetually binding. **19** to close tightly so as to render airtight or watertight. **20** to paint (a porous material) with a nonporous coating. **21** *Austral. and N.Z.* to consolidate (a road surface) with bitumen, tar, etc. **[**C13 *seel,* from Old French, from Latin *sigillum* little figure, from *signum* a sign**]** ► **'sealable** *adj*
seal[2] (si:l) *n* **1** any pinniped mammal of the families *Otariidae* (see **eared seal**) and *Phocidae* (see **earless seal**) that are aquatic but come on shore to breed. Related adjs: **otarid, phocine. 2** any earless seal (family *Phocidae*), esp. the common or harbour seal or the grey seal (*Halichoerus grypus*). **3** sealskin. ◆ *vb* **4** (*intr*) to hunt for seals. **[**Old English *seolh;* related to Old Norse *selr,* Old High German *selah,* Old Irish *selige* tortoise**]** ► **'seal-ˌlike** *adj*
sea lace *n* a brown seaweed, *Chorda filum,* that grows on stones under sandy bottoms and produces chordlike fronds up to 8.5 metres (28 ft.) long.
sea ladder *n* a rope ladder, set of steps, etc., by which a boat may be boarded at sea.
sea lamprey *n* a common anadromous lamprey, *Petromyzon marinus,* a form of which occurs in the Great Lakes of N America and causes great losses of fish.
sea lane *n* an established route for ships.
sealant ('si:lənt) *n* **1** any substance, such as wax, used for sealing documents, bottles, etc. **2** any of a number of substances used for stopping leaks, waterproofing wood, etc.
sea lavender *n* any of numerous perennial plants of the plumbaginaceous genus *Limonium,* of temperate salt marshes, having spikes of white, pink, or mauve flowers, several species of which are grown as garden plants. See also **statice.**
sea lawyer *n Nautical slang.* a contentious seaman.
seal brown *n* **a** a dark brown colour often with a yellowish or greyish tinge. **b** (*as adj*): *a seal-brown dress.*
sealed (si:ld) *vb* **1** the past participle of **seal**[1]. ◆ *adj* **2** *Austral. and N.Z.* (of a road) having a hard surface; made-up.
sealed-beam *adj* (esp. of a car headlight) having a lens and prefocused reflector sealed in the lamp vacuum.
sealed book *n* another term for **closed book.**
sealed move *n Chess.* the last move before an adjournment, which is written down by the player making it, sealed in an envelope, and kept secret from his opponent until play is resumed.
sealed orders *pl n* written instructions that are not to be read until a specified time.
sealed unit *n* a hard disk that is permanently sealed to prevent damage to the read/write head. See also **Winchester disk.**
sea legs *pl n Informal.* **1** the ability to maintain one's balance on board ship, esp. in rough weather. **2** the ability to resist seasickness, esp. in rough weather.
sealer[1] ('si:lə) *n* **1** a person or thing that seals. **2** (formerly in Britain and currently in the U.S.) an official who examines the accuracy of weights and measures. **3** a coating of paint, varnish, etc., applied to a surface to prevent the absorption of subsequent coats.
sealer[2] ('si:lə) *n* a person or ship occupied in hunting seals.
sealery ('si:lərɪ) *n, pl* **-eries. 1** the occupation of hunting seals. **2** any place where seals are regularly to be found, esp. a seal rookery.
sea letter *n* **1** Also called: **passport.** a document issued to a merchant vessel, esp. in wartime, authorizing it to leave a port or proceed freely. **2** (formerly) a document issued to a vessel in port, describing its cargo, crew, etc.
sea lettuce *n* any of various green seaweeds of the genus *Ulva,* which have edible wavy translucent fronds.
sea level *n* the level of the surface of the sea with respect to the land, taken to be the mean level between high and low tide, and used as a standard base for measuring heights and depths.
sea lily *n* any of various sessile echinoderms, esp. of the genus *Ptilocrinus,* in which the body consists of a long stalk attached to a hard surface and bearing a central disc with delicate radiating arms: class *Crinoidea* (crinoids).
sealing wax *n* a hard material made of shellac, turpentine, and pigment that softens when heated. It is used for sealing documents, parcels, letters, etc.
sea lion *n* any of various large eared seals, such as *Zalophus californianus* (**Californian sea lion**), of the N Pacific, often used as a performing animal.
sea loch *n* another name for **loch** (sense 2).
Sea Lord *n* (in Britain) either of the two serving naval officers (**First** and **Second Sea Lords**) who sit on the admiralty board of the Ministry of Defence.
seal-point *n* a popular variety of the Siamese cat, having a dark brown mask, paws, and tail, and a cream body.
seal ring *n* another term for **signet ring.**
sealskin ('si:lˌskɪn) *n* **1a** the skin or pelt of a fur seal, esp. when dressed with the outer hair removed and the underfur dyed dark brown. **1b** (*as modifier*): *a sealskin coat.* **2** a garment made of this skin.
Sealyham terrier ('si:lɪəm) *n* a short-legged wire-haired breed of terrier with a medium-length white coat. Often shortened to **Sealyham. [**named after *Sealyham,* village in S Wales, where it was bred in the 19th century**]**
seam (si:m) *n* **1** the line along which pieces of fabric are joined, esp. by stitching. **2** a ridge or line made by joining two edges. **3** a stratum of coal, ore, etc. **4 in a good seam.** *Northern English dialect.* doing well, esp. financially. **5** a linear

indentation, such as a wrinkle or scar. **6** *Surgery.* another name for **suture** (sense 1b). **7** *Anatomy.* another name for **raphe** (sense 3). **8** (*modifier*) *Cricket.* of or relating to a style of bowling in which the bowler utilizes the stitched seam round the ball in order to make it swing in flight and after touching the ground: *a seam bowler.* **9 bursting at the seams.** full to overflowing. ◆ *vb* **10** (*tr*) to join or sew together by or as if by a seam. **11** *U.S.* to make ridges in (knitting) using purl stitch. **12** to mark or become marked with or as if with a seam or wrinkle. [Old English; related to Old Norse *saumr,* Old High German *soum*]

seaman ('si:mən) *n, pl* **-men. 1** a rating trained in seamanship as opposed to electrical engineering, etc. **2** a man who serves as a sailor. **3** a person skilled in seamanship. ▸ **'seaman-,like** *adj* ▸ **'seamanly** *adj, adv*

seamanship ('si:mənʃɪp) *n* skill in and knowledge of the work of navigating, maintaining, and operating a vessel.

seamark ('si:,mɑ:k) *n Nautical.* an aid to navigation, such as a conspicuous object on a shore used as a guide.

sea mat *n* a popular name for a **bryozoan.**

seam bowler *or* **seamer** *n Cricket.* a fast bowler who makes the ball bounce on its seam so that it will change direction. ▸ **seam bowling** *n*

seamer ('si:mə) *n* **1** a person or thing that seams. **2** another name for **seam bowler.**

sea mew *n* another name for **mew**[2].

Seami (si:'ɑ:mɪ) *n* a variant spelling of **Zeami.**

sea mile *n* a unit of distance used in navigation, defined as the length of one minute of arc, measured along the meridian, in the latitude of the position. Its actual length varies slightly with latitude but is about 1853 metres (6080 feet). Symbol: M. See also **nautical mile.**

sea milkwort *n* a primulaceous plant, *Glaux maritima,* of estuary mud and seaside rocks of N temperate coasts, having trailing stems and small pink flowers. Also called: **saltwort, black saltwort.** Compare **milkwort.**

seamless ('si:mlɪs) *adj* **1** (of a garment) having no seams. **2** continuous or flowing: *seamless output; a seamless performance.*

seamount ('si:,maunt) *n* a submarine mountain rising more than 1000 metres above the surrounding ocean floor. Compare **guyot.**

sea mouse *n* any of several large polychaete worms of the genus *Aphrodite* and related genera, having a broad flattened body covered dorsally with a dense mat of iridescent hairlike chaetae. [C16: so called because of its appearance]

seamstress ('sɛmstrɪs) *or* (*rarely*) **sempstress** ('sɛmpstrɪs) *n* a woman who sews and makes clothes, esp. professionally.

seamy ('si:mɪ) *adj* **seamier, seamiest. 1** showing the least pleasant aspect; sordid. **2** (esp. of the inner side of a garment) showing many seams. ▸ **'seaminess** *n*

Seanad Éireann ('ʃænəð 'e:rən) *n* (in the Republic of Ireland) the upper chamber of parliament; the Senate. [from Irish, literally: senate of Ireland]

seance *or* **séance** ('seɪɑ̃ns, -ɑ:ns) *n* **1** a meeting at which spiritualists attempt to receive messages from the spirits of the dead. **2** a meeting of a society. [C19: from French, literally: a sitting, from Old French *seoir* to sit, from Latin *sedēre*]

sea onion *n* another name for **sea squill.**

sea otter *n* a large marine otter, *Enhydra lutris,* of N Pacific coasts, formerly hunted for its thick dark brown fur.

sea pen *n* any of various anthozoan coelenterates of the genus *Pennatula* and related genera, forming fleshy feather-like colonies in warm seas: order *Pennatulacea.*

sea perch *n* **1** any of various marine serranid fishes, such as the bass and stone bass, that have an elongated body with a very spiny dorsal fin and occur in all except polar seas. **2** another name for **surfperch.**

sea pink *n* another name for **thrift** (the plant).

seaplane ('si:,pleɪn) *n* any aircraft that lands on and takes off from water. Also called (esp. U.S.): **hydroplane.**

seaport ('si:,pɔ:t) *n* **1** a port or harbour accessible to seagoing vessels. **2** a town or city located at such a place.

sea power *n* **1** a nation that possesses great naval strength. **2** the naval strength of a country or nation.

sea purse *n* a tough horny envelope containing fertilized eggs, produced by the female of certain sharks and skates. Also called: **mermaid's purse.**

sea purslane *n* a small chenopodiaceous shrub, *Halimione portulacoides,* of salt marshes in Eurasia and parts of Africa, having oval leaves and inconspicuous flowers.

SEAQ ('si:,æk) *n acronym for* Stock Exchange Automated Quotation: a computerized system that collects and displays the prices and transactions in securities.

seaquake ('si:,kweɪk) *n* an agitation and disturbance of the sea caused by an earthquake at the sea bed.

sear[1] (sɪə) *vb* (*tr*) **1** to scorch or burn the surface of. **2** to brand with a hot iron. **3** to cause to wither or dry up. **4** *Rare.* to make callous or unfeeling. ◆ *n* **5** a mark caused by searing. ◆ *adj* **6** *Poetic.* dried up. [Old English *sēarian* to become withered, from *sēar* withered; related to Old High German *sōrēn,* Greek *hauos* dry, Sanskrit *sōsa* drought]

sear[2] (sɪə) *n* the catch in the lock of a small firearm that holds the hammer or firing pin cocked. [C16: probably from Old French *serre* a clasp, from *serrer* to hold firmly, from Late Latin *sērāre* to bolt, from Latin *sera* a bar]

sea ranger *n Brit.* a senior Guide training in seamanship. U.S. equivalent: **mariner.**

sea raven *n* a large fish, *Hemitripterus americanus,* of North American Atlantic coastal waters that inflates itself with air when caught: family *Cottidae* (bullheads and sea scorpions).

search (sɜ:tʃ) *vb* **1** to look through (a place, records, etc.) thoroughly in order to find someone or something. **2** (*tr*) to examine (a person) for concealed objects by running one's hands over the clothing. **3** to look at or examine (something) closely: *to search one's conscience.* **4** (*tr.*; foll. by *out*) to discover by investigation. **5** *Surgery.* **5a** to explore (a bodily cavity) during a surgical procedure. **5b** to probe (a wound). **6** (*tr.*) *Military.* to fire all over (an area). **7** *Computing.* to review (a file) to locate specific information. **8** *Archaic.* to penetrate. **9 search me.** *Informal.* I don't know. ◆ *n* **10** the act or an instance of searching. **11** the examination of a vessel by the right of search. **12** *Computing.* **12a** a review of a file to locate specific information. **12b** (*as modifier*): *a search routine.* **13 right of search.** *International law.* the right possessed by the warships of a belligerent state in time of war to board and search merchant vessels to ascertain whether ship or cargo is liable to seizure. [C14: from Old French *cerchier,* from Late Latin *circāre* to go around, from Latin *circus* CIRCLE] ▸ **'searchable** *adj* ▸ **'searcher** *n*

search engine *n Computing.* a service provided on the Internet enabling users to search for items of interest.

searching ('sɜ:tʃɪŋ) *adj* keenly penetrating: *a searching look.* ▸ **'searchingly** *adv* ▸ **'searchingness** *n*

searchlight ('sɜ:tʃ,laɪt) *n* **1** a device, consisting of a light source and a reflecting surface behind it, that projects a powerful beam of light in a particular direction. **2** the beam of light produced by such a device.

search party *n* a group of people taking part in an organized search, as for a lost, missing, or wanted person.

search warrant *n* a written order issued by a justice of the peace authorizing a constable or other officer to enter and search premises for stolen goods, drugs, etc.

Searle (sɜ:l) *n* **Ronald** (**William Fordham**). born 1920, British cartoonist, best known as the creator of the schoolgirls of St Trinian's.

sea robin *n* any of various American gurnards of the genus *Prionotus* and related genera, such as *P. carolinus* (**northern sea robin**).

sea room *n* sufficient space to manoeuvre a vessel.

sea salt *n* salt obtained by evaporation of sea water.

seascape ('si:,skeɪp) *n* a sketch, picture, etc., of the sea.

sea scorpion *n* any of various northern marine scorpaenoid fishes of the family *Cottidae,* esp. *Taurulus bubalis* (**long-spined sea scorpion**). They have a tapering body and a large head covered with bony plates and spines.

Sea Scout *n* a Scout belonging to any of a number of Scout troops whose main activities are canoeing, sailing, etc., and who wear sailors' caps as part of their uniform.

sea serpent *n* a huge legendary creature of the sea resembling a snake or dragon.

sea shanty *n* same as **shanty**[2].

seashell ('si:,ʃɛl) *n* the empty shell of a marine mollusc.

seashore ('si:,ʃɔ:) *n* **1** land bordering on the sea. **2** *Law.* the land between the marks of high and low water.

seasick ('si:,sɪk) *adj* suffering from nausea and dizziness caused by the motion of a ship at sea. ▸ **'sea,sickness** *n*

seaside ('si:,saɪd) *n* **a** any area bordering on the sea, esp. one regarded as a resort. **b** (*as modifier*): *a seaside hotel.*

sea slater *n* a large (2.5 cm or 1 in.) nocturnal isopod, *Ligea oceanica,* that lives in cracks in rocks or walls around the high-water mark.

sea slug *n* any of various shell-less marine gastropod molluscs, esp. those of the order *Nudibranchia.* See **nudibranch.**

sea snail *n* any small spiny-finned fish of the family *Liparidae,* esp. *Liparis liparis,* of cold seas, having a soft scaleless tadpole-shaped body with the pelvic fins fused into a sucker. Also called: **snailfish.**

sea snake *n* any venomous snake of the family *Hydrophiidae,* of tropical seas, that swims by means of a laterally compressed oarlike tail.

season ('si:zᵊn) *n* **1** one of the four equal periods into which the year is divided by the equinoxes and solstices, resulting from the apparent movement of the sun north and south of the equator during the course of the earth's orbit around it. These periods (spring, summer, autumn, and winter) have their characteristic weather conditions in different regions, and occur at opposite times of the year in the N and S hemispheres. **2** a period of the year characterized by particular conditions or activities: *the rainy season.* **3** the period during which any particular species of animal, bird, or fish is legally permitted to be caught or killed: *open season on red deer.* **4** a period during which a particular entertainment, sport, etc., takes place: *a season at the National Theatre; the football season; the tourist season.* **5** (esp. formerly) a period of fashionable social events in a particular place: *the London season.* **6** any definite or indefinite period. **7** any of the major periods into which the ecclesiastical calendar is divided, such as Lent, Advent, or Easter. **8** (*sometimes cap.*) Christmas (esp. in the phrases **compliments of the season, Season's greetings**). **9** a period or time that is considered proper, suitable, or natural for something. **10 in good season.** early enough. **11 in season. 11a** (of game) permitted to be caught or killed. **11b** (of fresh food) readily available. **11c** Also: **in** *or* **on heat.** (of some female mammals) sexually receptive. **11d** appropriate. ◆ *vb* **12** (*tr*) to add herbs, salt, pepper, or spice to (food). **13** (*tr*) to add zest to. **14** (in the preparation of timber) to undergo or cause to undergo drying. **15** (*tr; usually passive*) to make or become mature or experienced: *seasoned troops.* **16** (*tr*) to mitigate or temper: *to season one's admiration with reticence.* [C13: from Old French *seson,* from Latin *satiō* a sowing, from *serere* to sow] ▸ **'seasoned** *adj* ▸ **'seasoner** *n* ▸ **'seasonless** *adj*

seasonable ('si:zənəbᵊl) *adj* **1** suitable for the season. **2** taking place at the appropriate time. ▸ **'seasonableness** *n* ▸ **'seasonably** *adv*

seasonal ('si:zənᵊl) *adj* of, relating to, or occurring at a certain season or certain seasons of the year: *seasonal labour.* ▸ **'seasonally** *adv* ▸ **'seasonalness** *n*

seasonal affective disorder *n* a state of depression sometimes experienced by people in winter, thought to be related to lack of sunlight. Abbrev.: **SAD.**

seasoning ('si:zənɪŋ) *n* **1** something that enhances the flavour of food, such as salt or herbs. **2** another term (not now in technical usage) for **drying** (sense 2).

season ticket *n* a ticket for a series of events, number of journeys, etc., within a limited time, usually obtained at a reduced rate.

sea spider *n* a small marine arachnid, having four pairs of legs and somewhat resembling a spider, unusual in that the male carries the eggs once they are laid and cares for the offspring.

sea squill *or* **onion** *n* a Mediterranean liliaceous plant, *Urginea maritima,* having dense spikes of small white flowers, and yielding a bulb with medicinal properties.

sea squirt *n* any minute primitive marine animal of the class *Ascidiacea,* most of which are sedentary, having a saclike body with openings through which water enters and leaves. See also **ascidian.**

sea steps *pl n* projecting metal bars attached to a ship's side, used for boarding.

sea swallow *n* a popular name for **tern**[1].

seat (si:t) *n* **1** a piece of furniture designed for sitting on, such as a chair or sofa. **2** the part of a chair, bench, etc., on which one sits. **3** a place to sit, esp. one that requires a ticket: *I have two seats for the film tonight.* **4** another name for **buttocks** (see **buttock**). **5** the part of a garment covering the buttocks. **6** the part or area serving as the base of an object. **7** the part or surface on which the base of an object rests. **8** the place or centre in which something is located: *a seat of government.* **9** a place of abode, esp. a country mansion that is or was originally the chief residence of a family. **10** a membership or the right to membership in a legislative or similar body. **11** *Chiefly Brit.* a parliamentary constituency. **12** membership in a stock exchange. **13** the manner in which a rider sits on a horse. **14 by the seat of one's pants.** by instinct rather than knowledge or experience. **15 on seat.** *W African informal.* (of officials) in the office rather than on tour or on leave: *the agricultural advisor will be on seat tomorrow.* ◆ *vb* **16** (*tr*) to bring to or place on a seat; cause to sit down. **17** (*tr*) to provide with seats. **18** (*tr; often passive*) to place or centre: *the ministry is seated in the capital.* **19** (*tr*) to set firmly in place. **20** (*tr*) to fix or install in a position of power. **21** (*tr*) to put a seat on or in (an item of furniture, garment, etc.). **22** (*intr*) (of garments) to sag in the area covering the buttocks: *your thin skirt has seated badly.* [Old English *gesete;* related to Old Norse *sæti,* Old High German *gasāzi,* Middle Dutch *gesaete*] ▸ **'seatless** *adj*

sea tangle *n* any of various brown seaweeds, esp. any of the genus *Laminaria.*

seat belt *n* **1** Also called: **safety belt.** a belt or strap worn in a vehicle to restrain forward motion in the event of a collision. **2** a similar belt or strap worn in an aircraft at takeoff and landing and in rough weather.

-seater *n* a settee, vehicle, cinema, etc., having a number of seats as specified: *a forty-seater coach.*

seating ('si:tɪŋ) *n* **1** the act of providing with a seat or seats. **2a** the provision of seats, as in a theatre, cinema, etc. **2b** (*as modifier*): *seating arrangements.* **3** material used for covering or making seats.

Seaton Valley ('si:tᵊn) *n* a region in NE England, in SE Northumberland: consists of a group of former coal-mining villages. Pop.: 46 141 (latest est.).

sea trout *n* **1** a silvery marine variety of the brown trout that migrates to fresh water to spawn. Compare **brown trout. 2** any of several marine sciaenid fishes of the genus *Cynoscion,* such as *C. nebulosus* (**spotted sea trout**) and the weakfish, of North American coastal waters.

Seattle (sɪ'ætᵊl) *n* a port in W Washington, on the isthmus between Lake Washington and Puget Sound: the largest city in the state and chief commercial centre of the Northwest; two universities. Pop.: 524 704 (1996 est.).

sea urchin *n* any echinoderm of the class *Echinoidea,* such as *Echinus esculentus* (**edible sea urchin**), typically having a globular body enclosed in a rigid spiny test and occurring in shallow marine waters.

sea vegetable *n* an edible seaweed.

sea wall *n* a wall or embankment built to prevent encroachment or erosion by the sea or to serve as a breakwater. ▸ **'sea-,walled** *adj*

seawan *or* **sewan** ('si:wən) *n* shell beads, usually unstrung, used by certain North American Indians as money; wampum. [C18: from Narraganset *seawohn* loose]

seaward ('si:wəd) *adv* **1** a variant of **seawards.** ◆ *adj* **2** directed or moving towards the sea. **3** (esp. of a wind) coming from the sea.

seawards ('si:wədz) *or* **seaward** *adv* towards the sea.

seaware ('si:,wɛə) *n* any of numerous large coarse seaweeds, esp. when cast ashore and used as fertilizer. [Old English *sǣwār,* from *sǣ* SEA + *wār* seaweed]

sea wasp *n Austral.* another name for **box jellyfish.**

seaway ('si:,weɪ) *n* **1** a waterway giving access to an inland port, navigable by ocean-going ships. **2** a vessel's progress. **3** a rough or heavy sea. **4** a route across the sea.

seaweed ('si:,wi:d) *n* **1** any of numerous multicellular marine algae that grow on the seashore, in salt marshes, in brackish water, or submerged in the ocean. **2** any of certain other plants that grow in or close to the sea.

seaworthy ('si:,wɜ:ðɪ) *adj* in a fit condition or ready for a sea voyage. ▸ **'sea,worthiness** *n*

sea wrack *n* any of various seaweeds found on the shore, esp. any of the larger species.

sebaceous (sɪ'beɪʃəs) *adj* **1** of or resembling sebum, fat, or tallow; fatty. **2** secreting fat or a greasy lubricating substance. [C18: from Late Latin *sēbāceus,* from SEBUM]

sebaceous glands *pl n* the small glands in the skin that secrete sebum into hair follicles and onto most of the body surface except the soles of the feet and the palms of the hands.

sebacic acid (sɪ'bæsɪk, -'beɪ-) *n* another name for **decanedioic acid.**

Sebastian (sɪ'bæstjən) *n* **Saint.** died ?288 A.D., Christian martyr. According to tradition, he was first shot with arrows and then beaten to death. Feast day: Jan. 20.

Sebastopol (sɪ'bæstəpəl) *n* the English name for **Sevastopol.**

sebi- *or* **sebo-** *combining form.* fat or fatty matter: *sebiferous.* [from Latin *sēbum* tallow]

sebiferous (sɪ'bɪfərəs) *adj Biology.* producing or carrying a fatty, oily, or wax-like substance.

seborrhoea *or esp. U.S.* **seborrhea** (,sɛbə'rɪə) *n* a disease of the sebaceous glands characterized by excessive secretion of sebum and its accumulation on the skin surface. ▸ **,sebor'rhoeal, ,sebor'rhoeic** *or esp. U.S.* **,sebor'rheal, ,sebor'rheic** *adj*

sebum ('si:bəm) *n* the oily secretion of the sebaceous glands that acts as a lubricant for the hair and skin and provides some protection against bacteria. [C19: from New Latin, from Latin: tallow]

sec[1] (sɛk) *adj* **1** (of wines) dry. **2** (of champagne) of medium sweetness. [C19: from French, from Latin *siccus*]

sec[2] (sɛk) *n Informal.* short for **second**[2]: *wait a sec.*

sec[3] (sɛk) *abbrev. for* secant.

SEC *abbrev. for* Securities and Exchange Commission.

sec. *abbrev. for:* **1** second (of time). **2** secondary. **3** secretary. **4** section. **5** sector.

SECAM ('si:,kæm) *n acronym for* séquentiel couleur à mémoire: a colour-television broadcasting system used in France, the former Soviet Union, and some other countries.

secant ('si:kənt) *n* **1** (of an angle) a trigonometric function that in a right-angled triangle is the ratio of the length of the hypotenuse to that of the adjacent side; the reciprocal of cosine. Abbrev.: **sec. 2** a line that intersects a curve. [C16: from Latin *secāre* to cut] ▸ **'secantly** *adv*

secateurs ('sɛkətəz, ,sɛkə'tɜ:z) *pl n Chiefly Brit.* a small pair of shears for pruning, having a pair of pivoted handles, sprung so that they are normally open, and usually a single cutting blade that closes against a flat surface. [C19: plural of French *sécateur,* from Latin *secāre* to cut]

secco ('sɛkəʊ) *n, pl* **-cos. 1** wall painting done on dried plaster with tempera or pigments ground in limewater. Compare **fresco. 2** any wall painting other than true fresco. [C19: from Italian: dry, from Latin *siccus*]

secede (sɪ'si:d) *vb* (*intr;* often foll. by *from*) (of a person, section, etc.) to make a formal withdrawal of membership, as from a political alliance, church, organization, etc. [C18: from Latin *sēcēdere* to withdraw, from *sē-* apart + *cēdere* to go] ▸ **se'ceder** *n*

secern (sɪ'sɜ:n) *vb* (*tr*) *Rare.* **1** (of a gland or follicle) to secrete. **2** to distinguish or discriminate. [C17: from Latin *sēcernere* to separate, from *sē-* apart + *cernere* to distinguish] ▸ **se'cernment** *n*

secession (sɪ'sɛʃən) *n* **1** the act of seceding. **2** (*often cap.*) *Chiefly U.S.* the withdrawal in 1860–61 of 11 Southern states from the Union to form the Confederacy, precipitating the American Civil War. [C17: from Latin *sēcessiō* a withdrawing, from *sēcēdere* to SECEDE] ▸ **se'cessional** *adj* ▸ **se'cession,ism** *n* ▸ **se'cessionist** *n, adj*

sech (ʃɛk, sɛtʃ, 'sɛk'eɪtʃ) *n* hyperbolic secant; a hyperbolic function that is the reciprocal of cosh.

seclude (sɪ'klu:d) *vb* (*tr*) **1** to remove from contact with others. **2** to shut off or screen from view. [C15: from Latin *sēclūdere* to shut off, from *sē-* + *claudere* to imprison]

secluded (sɪ'klu:dɪd) *adj* **1** kept apart from the company of others: *a secluded life.* **2** sheltered; private. ▸ **se'cludedly** *adv* ▸ **se'cludedness** *n*

seclusion (sɪ'klu:ʒən) *n* **1** the act of secluding or the state of being secluded. **2** a secluded place. [C17: from Medieval Latin *sēclūsiō;* see SECLUDE]

seclusive (sɪ'klu:sɪv) *adj* **1** tending to seclude. **2** fond of seclusion. ▸ **se'clusively** *adv* ▸ **se'clusiveness** *n*

second[1] ('sɛkənd) *adj* (*usually prenominal*) **1a** coming directly after the first in numbering or counting order, position, time, etc.; being the ordinal number of *two:* often written 2nd. **1b** (*as n*): *the second in line.* **2** rated, graded, or ranked between the first and third levels. **3** alternate: *every second Thursday.* **4** additional; extra: *a second opportunity.* **5** resembling a person or event from an earlier period of history; unoriginal: *a second Wagner.* **6** of lower quality; inferior: *belonging to the second class.* **7** denoting the lowest but one forward ratio of a gearbox in a motor vehicle. **8** *Music.* **8a** relating to or denoting a musical part, voice, or instrument lower in pitch than another part, voice, or instrument (the first): *the second tenors.* **8b** of or relating to a part, instrument, or instrumentalist regarded as subordinate to another (the first): *the second flute.* **9 at second hand.** by hearsay. ◆ *n* **10** *Brit. education.* an honours degree of the second class, usually further divided into an upper and lower designation. Full term: **second-class honours degree. 11** the lowest but one forward ratio of a gearbox in a motor vehicle: *he changed into second on the bend.* **12** (in boxing, duelling, etc.) an attendant who looks after a competitor. **13** a speech seconding a motion or the person making it. **14** *Music.* **14a** the interval between one note and another lying next above or below it in the diatonic scale. **14b** one of two notes constituting such an interval in relation to the other. See also **minor** (sense 4), **major** (sense 13), **interval** (sense 5). **15** (*pl*) goods of inferior quality. **16** (*pl*) *Informal.* a second helping of food. **17** (*pl*) the second course of a meal. ◆ *vb* (*tr*) **18** to give aid or backing to. **19** (in boxing, etc.) to act as second to (a competitor). **20** to make a speech or otherwise express formal support for (a motion already proposed). ◆ *adv* **21** Also: **secondly.** in the second place. ◆ *sentence connector.* **22** Also: **secondly.** as the second point: linking what follows with the previous statement. [C13: via Old French from Latin *secundus* coming next in order, from *sequī* to follow] ▸ **'seconder** *n*

second[2] ('sɛkənd) *n* **1a** 1/60 of a minute of time. **1b** the basic SI unit of time: the duration of 9 192 631 770 periods of radiation corresponding to the transition between two hyperfine levels of the ground state of caesium-133. Symbol: s **2** 1/60 of a minute of angle. Symbol: ″ **3** a very short period of time; moment. [C14: from Old French, from Medieval Latin *pars minūta secunda* the second small part (a minute being the first small part of an hour); see SECOND[1]]

second[3] (sɪ'kɒnd) *vb (tr) Brit.* **1** to transfer (an employee) temporarily to another branch, etc. **2** *Military.* to transfer (an officer) to another post, often retiring him to a staff or nonregimental position. **[**C19: from French *en second* in second rank (or position)**]**

Second Advent *n* a less common term for the **Second Coming.**

secondary ('sɛkəndərɪ, -drɪ) *adj* **1** one grade or step after the first; not primary. **2** derived from or depending on what is primary, original, or first: *a secondary source.* **3** below the first in rank, importance, etc.; not of major importance. **4** (*prenominal*) of or relating to the education of young people between the ages of 11 and 18: *secondary education.* **5** (of the flight feathers of a bird's wing) growing from the ulna. **6a** being the part of an electric circuit, such as a transformer or induction coil, in which a current is induced by a changing current in a neighbouring coil: *a secondary coil.* **6b** (of a current) flowing in such a circuit. Compare **primary** (sense 7). **7** (of an industry) involving the manufacture of goods from raw materials. Compare **primary** (sense 8b), **tertiary** (sense 2). **8** *Geology.* (of minerals) formed by the alteration of pre-existing minerals. **9** *Chem.* **9a** (of an organic compound) having a functional group attached to a carbon atom that is attached to one hydrogen atom and two other groups. **9b** (of an amine) having only two organic groups attached to a nitrogen atom; containing the group NH. **9c** (of a salt) derived from a tribasic acid by replacement of two acidic hydrogen atoms with metal atoms or electropositive groups. **10** *Linguistics.* **10a** derived from a word that is itself a derivation from another word. Thus, *lovably* comes from *lovable* and is a secondary derivative from *love.* **10b** (of a tense in Latin, Greek, or Sanskrit) another word for **historic** (sense 3). ♦ *n, pl* **-aries. 11** a person or thing that is secondary. **12** a subordinate, deputy, or inferior. **13** a secondary coil, winding, inductance, or current in an electric circuit. **14** *Ornithol.* any of the flight feathers that grow from the ulna of a bird's wing. See **primary** (sense 6). **15** *Astronomy.* a celestial body that orbits around a specified primary body: *the moon is the secondary of the earth.* **16** *Med.* a cancerous growth in some part of the body away from the site of the original tumour. **17** *American football.* **17a** (usually preceded by *the*) cornerbacks and safeties collectively. **17b** their area in the field. **18** short for **secondary colour.** ▸ **'secondarily** *adv* ▸ **'secondariness** *n*

secondary accent *or* **stress** *n Phonetics.* (in a system of transcribing utterances recognizing three levels of stress) the accent on a syllable of a word or breath group that is weaker than the primary accent but stronger than the lack of stress: *in the word "agriculture" the secondary accent falls on the third syllable.* Compare **primary accent.**

secondary cell *n* an electric cell that can be recharged and can therefore be used to store electrical energy in the form of chemical energy. See also **accumulator** (sense 1). Compare **primary cell.**

secondary colour *n* a colour formed by mixing two primary colours. Sometimes shortened to **secondary.**

secondary emission *n Physics.* the emission of electrons (**secondary electrons**) from a solid as a result of bombardment with a beam of electrons, ions, or metastable atoms: used in electron multipliers.

secondary modern school *n Brit.* (formerly) a secondary school offering a more technical or practical and less academic education than a grammar school.

secondary picketing *n* the picketing by strikers of a place of work that supplies goods to or distributes goods from their employer. ▸ **secondary picket** *n*

secondary processes *pl n Psychoanal.* the logical conscious type of mental functioning, guided by external reality. Compare **primary processes.**

secondary qualities *pl n* (in empiricist philosophy) those properties of objects that are explained in terms of the primary properties of their parts, such as heat in terms of the motion of molecules.

secondary school *n* a school for young people, usually between the ages of 11 and 18.

secondary sexual characteristic *n* any of various features distinguishing individuals of different sex but not directly concerned in reproduction. Examples are the antlers of a stag and the beard of a man.

secondary stress *n* another term for **secondary accent.**

second ballot *n* an electoral procedure in which if no candidate emerges as a clear winner in a first ballot, candidates at the bottom of the poll are eliminated and another ballot is held among the remaining candidates.

second-best *adj* **1** next to the best. **2 come off second best.** *Informal.* to be defeated in competition. ♦ *n* **second best. 3** an inferior alternative.

second chamber *n* the upper house of a bicameral legislative assembly.

second childhood *n* dotage; senility (esp. in the phrases **in his, her,** etc., **second childhood**).

second class *n* **1** the class or grade next in value, quality, etc., to the first. ♦ *adj* (**second-class** *when prenominal*). **2** of the class or grade next to the best in quality, etc. **3** shoddy or inferior. **4** of or denoting the class of accommodation in a hotel or on a train, etc., lower in quality and price than first class. **5a** (in Britain) of or relating to mail that is processed more slowly than first-class mail. **5b** (in the U.S. and Canada) of or relating to mail that consists mainly of newspapers, etc. **6** *Education.* See **second**[1] (sense 10). ♦ *adv* **7** by second-class mail, transport, etc.

second-class citizen *n* a person whose rights and opportunities are treated as less important than those of other people in the same society.

Second Coming *or* (*less commonly*) **Second Advent** *n* the prophesied return of Christ to earth at the Last Judgment.

second cousin *n* the child of a first cousin of either of one's parents.

second-degree burn *n Pathol.* See **burn**[1] (sense 22).

seconde (sɪ'kɒnd; *French* səgɔ̃d) *n* the second of eight positions from which a parry or attack can be made in fencing. **[**C18: from French *seconde parade* the second parry**]**

Second Empire *n* **1a** the imperial government of France under Napoleon III. **1b** the period during which this government functioned (1852–70). **2** the style of furniture and decoration of the Second Empire, reviving the Empire style, but with fussier ornamentation.

second estate *n Rare.* the nobility collectively.

second fiddle *n Informal.* **1a** the second violin in a string quartet or one of the second violins in an orchestra. **1b** the musical part assigned to such an instrument. **2** a secondary status. **3** a person who has a secondary status.

second floor *n* **1** *Brit.* the storey of a building immediately above the first and two floors up from the ground. U.S. and Canadian term: **third floor. 2** the U.S. and Canadian term for **first floor.**

second generation *n* **1** offspring of parents born in a given country. ♦ (*modifier*) **2** of an improved or refined stage of development in manufacture: *a second-generation robot.*

second growth *n* natural regrowth of a forest after fire, cutting, or some other disturbance.

second-guess *vb Informal.* **1** to criticize or evaluate with hindsight. **2** to attempt to anticipate or predict (a person or thing). ▸ **'second-'guesser** *n*

second hand *n* a pointer on the face of a timepiece that indicates the seconds. Compare **hour hand, minute hand.**

second-hand *adj* **1** previously owned or used. **2** not from an original source or experience. **3** dealing in or selling goods that are not new: *a second-hand car dealer.* ♦ *adv* **4** from a source of previously owned or used goods: *he prefers to buy second-hand.* **5** not directly: *he got the news second-hand.*

Second International *n* **1 the.** an international association of socialist parties and trade unions that began in Paris in 1889 and collapsed during World War I. The right-wing elements reassembled at Berne in 1919. See also **Labour and Socialist International. 2** another name for the **Labour and Socialist International.**

second language *n* **1** a language other than the mother tongue that a person or community uses for public communication, esp. in trade, higher education, and administration. **2** a non-native language officially recognized and adopted in a multilingual country as a means of public communication.

second lieutenant *n* an officer holding the lowest commissioned rank in the armed forces of certain nations.

secondly ('sɛkəndlɪ) *adv* another word for **second**[1], usually used to precede the second item in a list of topics.

second man *n* a person who assists the driver in crewing a locomotive.

second mate *n* the next in command of a merchant vessel after the first mate. Also called: **second officer.**

secondment (sɪ'kɒndmənt) *n Brit.* a temporary transfer to another job or post within the same organization. **[**C19: from French *en second* in second rank (or position)**]**

second mortgage *n* a mortgage incurred after a first mortgage and having second claim against the security.

second name *n* another term for **surname** (sense 1).

second nature *n* a habit, characteristic, etc., not innate but so long practised or acquired as to seem so.

secondo (sɛ'kɒndəʊ) *n, pl* **-di** (-diː). the left-hand part in a piano duet. Compare **primo.** **[**Italian: SECOND[1]**]**

second person *n* a grammatical category of pronouns and verbs used when referring to or describing the individual or individuals being addressed.

second-rate *adj* **1** not of the highest quality; mediocre. **2** second in importance, etc. ▸ **'second-'rater** *n*

second reading *n* the second presentation of a bill in a legislative assembly, as to approve its general principles (in Britain), or to discuss a committee's report on it (in the U.S.).

Second Republic *n* **1** the republican government of France from the deposition of Louis Philippe (1848) until the Second Empire (1852). **2** the period during which this form of government existed (1848–52).

second sight *n* the alleged ability to foresee the future, see actions taking place elsewhere, etc.; clairvoyance. ▸ **'second-'sighted** *adj* ▸ **'second-'sightedness** *n*

second-strike *adj* **1** (of a nuclear weapon) intended to be used in a counterattack in response to a nuclear attack. **2** (of a strategy) based on the concept of surviving an initial nuclear attack with enough nuclear weaponry to retaliate.

second string *n* **1** *Chiefly Brit.* an alternative course of action, etc., intended to come into use should the first fail (esp. in the phrase **a second string to one's bow**). **2** a substitute or reserve player or team. ♦ *adj* **second-string.** *Chiefly U.S. and Canadian.* **3** *Sport.* **3a** being a substitute player. **3b** being the second-ranked player of a team in an individual sport. **4** second-rate or inferior.

second thought *n* (*usually pl*) a revised opinion or idea on a matter already considered.

second wind (wɪnd) *n* **1** the return of the ability to breathe at a comfortable rate, esp. following a period of exertion. **2** renewed ability to continue in an effort.

Second World War *n* another name for **World War II.**

secrecy ('siːkrɪsɪ) *n, pl* **-cies. 1** the state or quality of being secret. **2** the state of keeping something secret. **3** the ability or tendency to keep things secret.

secret ('siːkrɪt) *adj* **1** kept hidden or separate from the knowledge of others. Related adj: **cryptic. 2** known only to initiates: *a secret password.* **3** hidden from general view or use: *a secret garden.* **4** able or tending to keep things private or to oneself. **5** operating without the knowledge of outsiders: *a secret society.* **6** outside the normal range of knowledge. ♦ *n* **7** something kept or to be kept hidden. **8** something unrevealed; mystery. **9** an underlying explanation, reason, etc., that is not apparent: *the secret of success.* **10** a method, plan, etc., known only to initiates. **11** *Liturgy.* a variable prayer, part of the Mass, said by the celebrant after the offertory and before the preface. **12 in the secret.**

among the people who know a secret. [C14: via Old French from Latin *sēcrētus* concealed, from *sēcernere* to sift; see SECERN] ▸ **'secretly** *adv*

secret agent *n* a person employed in espionage.

secretagogue (sɪ'kri:təgɒg) *n Med.* a substance that stimulates secretion. ▸ **se,creta'gogic** *adj*

secretaire (,sɛkrɪ'tɛə) *n* an enclosed writing desk, usually having an upper cabinet section. [C19: from French *secrétaire;* see SECRETARY]

secretariat (,sɛkrɪ'tɛərɪət) *n* **1a** an office responsible for the secretarial, clerical, and administrative affairs of a legislative body, executive council, or international organization. **1b** the staff of such an office. **1c** the building or rooms in which such an office is housed. **2** a body of secretaries. **3** a secretary's place of work; office. **4** the position of a secretary. [C19: via French from Medieval Latin *sēcrētāriātus,* from *sēcrētārius* SECRETARY]

secretary ('sɛkrətrɪ) *n, pl* **-taries. 1** a person who handles correspondence, keeps records, and does general clerical work for an individual, organization, etc. **2** the official manager of the day-to-day business of a society or board. **3** (in Britain) a senior civil servant who assists a government minister. **4** (in the U.S. and New Zealand) the head of a government administrative department. **5** (in Britain) See **secretary of state. 6** (in Australia) the head of a public service department. **7** *Diplomacy.* the assistant to an ambassador or diplomatic minister of certain countries. **8** another name for **secretaire.** [C14: from Medieval Latin *sēcrētārius,* from Latin *sēcrētum* something hidden; see SECRET] ▸ **secretarial** (,sɛkrɪ'tɛərɪəl) *adj* ▸ **'secretaryship** *n*

secretary bird *n* a large African long-legged diurnal bird of prey, *Sagittarius serpentarius,* having a crest and tail of long feathers and feeding chiefly on snakes: family *Sagittariidae,* order *Falconiformes* (hawks, falcons, etc.). [C18: so called because its crest resembles a group of quill pens stuck behind the ear]

secretary-general *n, pl* **secretaries-general.** a chief administrative official, as of the United Nations.

secretary of state *n* **1** (in Britain) the head of any of several government departments. **2** (in the U.S.) the head of the government department in charge of foreign affairs (**State Department**). **3** (in certain U.S. states) an official with various duties, such as keeping records.

secrete[1] (sɪ'kri:t) *vb* (of a cell, organ, etc.) to synthesize and release (a secretion). [C18: back formation from SECRETION] ▸ **se'cretor** *n*

secrete[2] (sɪ'kri:t) *vb (tr)* to put in a hiding place. [C18: variant of obsolete *secret* to hide away; see SECRET (n)]

secretin (sɪ'kri:tɪn) *n* a peptic hormone secreted by the mucosae of the duodenum and jejunum when food passes from the stomach. [C20: from SECRETION + -IN]

secretion (sɪ'kri:ʃən) *n* **1** a substance that is released from a cell, esp. a glandular cell, and is synthesized in the cell from simple substances extracted from the blood or a similar fluid. **2** the process involved in producing and releasing such a substance from the cell. [C17: from Medieval Latin *sēcrētiō,* from Latin: a separation; see SECERN] ▸ **se'cretionary** *adj*

secretive ('si:krɪtɪv, sɪ'kri:tɪv) *adj* **1** inclined to secrecy; reticent. **2** another word for **secretory.** ▸ **'secretively** *adv* ▸ **'secretiveness** *n*

secretory (sɪ'kri:tərɪ) *adj* of, relating to, or producing a secretion: *a secretory cell; secretory function.*

secret police *n* a police force that operates relatively secretly to check subversion or political dissent.

secret service *n* **1** a government agency or department that conducts intelligence or counterintelligence operations. **2** such operations.

Secret Service *n* a U.S. government agency responsible for the protection of the president, the suppression of counterfeiting, and certain other police activities.

secret society *n* a society or organization that conceals its rites, activities, etc., from those who are not members.

sect (sɛkt) *n* **1** a subdivision of a larger religious group (esp. the Christian Church as a whole) the members of which have to some extent diverged from the rest by developing deviating beliefs, practices, etc. **2** *Often disparaging.* **2a** a schismatic religious body characterized by an attitude of exclusivity in contrast to the more inclusive religious groups called denominations or Churches. **2b** a religious group regarded as extreme or heretical. **3** a group of people with a common interest, doctrine, etc.; faction. [C14: from Latin *secta* faction, following, from the stem of *sequī* to follow]

sect. *abbrev. for* section.

-sect *vb combining form.* to cut or divide, esp. into a specified number of parts: *trisect.* [from Latin *sectus* cut, from *secāre* to cut; see SAW[1]]

sectarian (sɛk'tɛərɪən) *adj* **1** of, belonging or relating to, or characteristic of sects or sectaries. **2** adhering to a particular sect, faction, or doctrine. **3** narrow-minded, esp. as a result of rigid adherence to a particular sect. ◆ *n* **4** a member of a sect or faction, esp. one who is bigoted in his adherence to its doctrines or in his intolerance towards other sects, etc. ▸ **sec'tarian,ism** *n*

sectarianize *or* **sectarianise** (sɛk'tɛərɪə,naɪz) *vb (tr)* to render sectarian.

sectary ('sɛktərɪ) *n, pl* **-taries. 1** a member of a sect, esp. a person who belongs to a religious sect that is regarded as heretical or schismatic. **2** a person excessively devoted to a particular sect. **3** a member of a Nonconformist denomination, esp. one that is small. [C16: from Medieval Latin *sectārius,* from Latin *secta* SECT]

sectile ('sɛktaɪl) *adj* able to be cut smoothly. [C18: from Latin *sectilis,* from *secāre* to cut] ▸ **sectility** (sɛk'tɪlɪtɪ) *n*

section ('sɛkʃən) *n* **1** a part cut off or separated from the main body of something. **2** a part or subdivision of a piece of writing, book, etc.: *the sports section of the newspaper.* **3** one of several component parts. **4** a distinct part or subdivision of a country, community, etc. **5** *U.S. and Canadian.* an area one mile square (640 acres) in a public survey, esp. in the western parts of the U.S. and Canada. **6** *N.Z.* a plot of land for building on, esp. in a suburban area. **7** the section of a railway track that is maintained by a single crew or is controlled by a particular signal box. **8** the act or process of cutting or separating by cutting. **9** a representation of a portion of a building or object exposed when cut by an imaginary vertical plane so as to show its construction and interior. **10** *Geometry.* **10a** a plane surface formed by cutting through a solid. **10b** the shape or area of such a plane surface. ◆ Compare **cross section** (sense 1). **11** *Surgery.* any procedure involving the cutting or division of an organ, structure, or part. **12** a thin slice of biological tissue, mineral, etc., prepared for examination by microscope. **13** a segment of an orange or other citrus fruit. **14** a small military formation, typically comprising two or more squads or aircraft. **15** *Austral. and N.Z.* a fare stage on a bus, tram, etc. **16** *Music.* **16a** an extended division of a composition or movement that forms a coherent part of the structure: *the development section.* **16b** a division in an orchestra, band, etc., containing instruments belonging to the same class: *the brass section.* **17** Also called: **signature, gathering, gather, quire.** a folded printing sheet or sheets ready for gathering and binding. ◆ *vb (tr)* **18** to cut or divide into sections. **19** to cut through so as to reveal a section. **20** (in drawing, esp. mechanical drawing) to shade so as to indicate sections. **21** *Surgery.* to cut or divide (an organ, structure, or part). **22** *Brit., Social welfare.* to have (a mentally disturbed person) confined in a mental hospital under an appropriate section of the mental health legislation. [C16: from Latin *sectiō,* from *secāre* to cut]

sectional ('sɛkʃənəl) *adj* **1** composed of several sections. **2** of or relating to a section. ▸ **'sectionally** *adv*

sectionalism ('sɛkʃənə,lɪzəm) *n* excessive or narrow-minded concern for local or regional interests as opposed to the interests of the whole. ▸ **'sectionalist** *n, adj*

sectionalize *or* **sectionalise** ('sɛkʃənə,laɪz) *vb (tr)* **1** to render sectional. **2** to divide into sections, esp. geographically. ▸ **,sectionali'zation** *or* **,sectionali'sation** *n*

section mark *n Printing.* a mark (§) inserted into text matter to draw attention to a footnote or to indicate a section of a book, etc. Also called: **section.**

sector ('sɛktə) *n* **1** a part or subdivision, esp. of a society or an economy: *the private sector.* **2** *Geometry.* either portion of a circle included between two radii and an arc. Area: $\frac{1}{2}r^2\theta$, where *r* is the radius and θ is the central angle subtended by the arc (in radians). **3** a measuring instrument consisting of two graduated arms hinged at one end. **4** a part or subdivision of an area of military operations. **5** *Computing.* the smallest addressable portion of the track on a magnetic tape, disk, or drum store. [C16: from Late Latin: sector, from Latin: a cutter, from *secāre* to cut] ▸ **'sectoral** *adj*

sectorial (sɛk'tɔ:rɪəl) *adj* **1** of or relating to a sector. **2** *Zoology.* **2a** adapted for cutting: *the sectorial teeth of carnivores.* **2b** designating a vein in the wing of an insect that links certain branches of the radius vein.

secular ('sɛkjʊlə) *adj* **1** of or relating to worldly as opposed to sacred things; temporal. **2** not concerned with or related to religion. **3** not within the control of the Church. **4** (of an education, etc.) **4a** having no particular religious affinities. **4b** not including compulsory religious studies or services. **5** (of clerics) not bound by religious vows to a monastic or other order. **6** occurring or appearing once in an age or century. **7** lasting for a long time. **8** *Astronomy.* occurring slowly over a long period of time: *the secular perturbation of a planet's orbit.* ◆ *n* **9** a member of the secular clergy. **10** another word for **layman.** [C13: from Old French *seculer,* from Late Latin *saeculāris* temporal, from Latin: concerning an age, from *saeculum* an age] ▸ **'secularly** *adv*

secularism ('sɛkjʊlə,rɪzəm) *n* **1** *Philosophy.* a doctrine that rejects religion, esp. in ethics. **2** the attitude that religion should have no place in civil affairs. **3** the state of being secular. ▸ **'secularist** *n, adj* ▸ **,secular'istic** *adj*

secularity (,sɛkjʊ'lærɪtɪ) *n, pl* **-ties. 1** the state or condition of being secular. **2** interest in or adherence to secular things. **3** a secular concern or matter.

secularize *or* **secularise** ('sɛkjʊlə,raɪz) *vb (tr)* **1** to change from religious or sacred to secular functions, etc. **2** to dispense from allegiance to a religious order. **3** *Law.* to transfer (property) from ecclesiastical to civil possession or use. **4** *English legal history.* to transfer (an offender) from the jurisdiction of the ecclesiastical courts to that of the civil courts for the imposition of a more severe punishment. ▸ **,seculari'zation** *or* **,seculari'sation** *n* ▸ **'secular,izer** *or* **'secular,iser** *n*

secund (sɪ'kʌnd) *adj Botany.* having or designating parts arranged on or turned to one side of the axis. [C18: from Latin *secundus* following, from *sequī* to follow; see SECOND[1]] ▸ **se'cundly** *adv*

Secunderabad (sə'kʌndərə,bæd, -,bɑ:d) *n* a former town in S central India, in N Andra Pradesh: one of the largest British military stations in India: now part of Hyderabad city.

secundine ('sɛkən,daɪn, -dɪn) *n Botany.* the inner of two integuments surrounding the ovule of a plant. [C17: from Late Latin *secundīnae,* from Latin *secundus* following + -INE. See SECOND[1]]

secundines ('sɛkən,daɪnz, sɪ'kʌndɪnz) *pl n Physiol.* a technical word for **afterbirth.** [C14: from Late Latin *secundīnae,* from Latin *secundus* following; see SECOND[1]]

secure (sɪ'kjʊə) *adj* **1** free from danger, damage, etc. **2** free from fear, care, etc. **3** in safe custody. **4** not likely to fail, become loose, etc. **5** able to be relied on; certain: *a secure investment.* **6** *Nautical.* stowed away or made inoperative. **7** *Archaic.* careless or overconfident. ◆ *vb* **8** *(tr)* to obtain or get possession of: *I will secure some good seats.* **9** (when *intr,* often foll. by *against*) to make or become free from danger, fear, etc. **10** *(tr)* to make fast or firm; fasten. **11** (when *intr,* often foll. by *against*) to make or become certain; guarantee: *this plan will secure your happiness.* **12** *(tr)* to assure (a creditor) of payment, as by giving security. **13** *(tr)* to make (a military position) safe from attack. **14** *Nautical.* to make (a vessel or its contents) safe or ready by battening down hatches, stowing gear, etc. **15** *(tr) Nautical.* to stow or make inoperative: *to secure the radio.* [C16:

from Latin *sēcūrus* free from care, from *sē-* without + *cūra* care] ▸ **se'curable** *adj* ▸ **se'curely** *adv* ▸ **se'curement** *n* ▸ **se'cureness** *n* ▸ **se'curer** *n*

secure tenancy *n* (in Britain) *Social welfare.* the letting of a dwelling by a nonprivate landlord, usually a local council or housing association, under an agreement that allows security of tenure, subletting, improvements made to the property by the tenant without consequent rent increase, and the right to buy the dwelling at a discount after three years' occupancy.

Securities and Exchange Commission *n* a U.S. federal agency established in 1934 to supervise and regulate issues of and transactions in securities and to prosecute illegal stock manipulations. Abbrev.: **SEC.**

Securities and Investments Board *n* (from 1986 to 1997) a British regulatory body that oversaw London's financial markets, each of which has its own self-regulatory organization: replaced by the Financial Services Authority. Abbrev.: **SIB.**

securitization *or* **securitisation** (sɪˌkjuərɪtaɪ'zeɪʃən) *n Finance.* the use of such securities as eurobonds to enable investors to lend directly to borrowers with a minimum of risk but without using banks as intermediaries.

security (sɪ'kjuərɪtɪ) *n, pl* **-ties.** **1** the state of being secure. **2** assured freedom from poverty or want: *he needs the security of a permanent job.* **3** a person or thing that secures, guarantees, etc. **4** precautions taken to ensure against theft, espionage, etc.: *the security in the government offices was not very good.* **5** (*often pl*) **5a** a certificate of creditorship or property carrying the right to receive interest or dividend, such as shares or bonds. **5b** the financial asset represented by such a certificate. **6** the specific asset that a creditor can claim title to in the event of default on an obligation. **7** something given or pledged to secure the fulfilment of a promise or obligation. **8** a person who undertakes to fulfil another person's obligation. **9** the protection of data to ensure that only authorized personnel have access to computer files. **10** *Archaic.* carelessness or overconfidence.

security blanket *n* **1** a policy of temporary secrecy by police or those in charge of security, in order to protect a person, place, etc., threatened with danger, from further risk. **2** a baby's blanket, soft toy, etc., to which a baby or young child becomes very attached, using it as a comforter. **3** *Informal.* anything used or thought of as providing reassurance.

Security Council *n* a permanent organ of the United Nations established to maintain world peace. It consists of five permanent members (China, France, Russia, the UK, and the U.S.) and ten nonpermanent members.

security guard *n* a person employed to protect buildings, people, etc., and to collect and deliver large sums of money.

security of tenure *n* (in Britain) the right of a tenant to continue to occupy a dwelling or site unless the landlord obtains a court order for possession of the property or termination of the tenancy agreement.

security risk *n* a person deemed to be a threat to state security in that he could be open to pressure, have subversive political beliefs, etc.

secy *or* **sec'y** *abbrev. for* secretary.

SED *abbrev. for* Scottish Education Department.

sedan (sɪ'dæn) *n* **1** the U.S., Canadian, and N.Z. name for a **saloon** (sense 5). **2** short for **sedan chair.** [C17: of uncertain origin; compare Latin *sēdēs* seat]

Sedan (*French* sədɑ̃; *English* sɪ'dæn) *n* a town in NE France, on the River Meuse: passed to France in 1642; a Protestant stronghold (16th–17th centuries); scene of a French defeat (1870) during the Franco-Prussian War and of a battle (1940) in World War II, which began the German invasion of France. Pop.: 22 400 (1990).

sedan chair *n* a closed chair for one passenger, carried on poles by two bearers. It was commonly used in the 17th and 18th centuries. Sometimes shortened to **sedan.**

sedate[1] (sɪ'deɪt) *adj* **1** habitually calm and composed in manner; serene. **2** staid, sober, or decorous. [C17: from Latin *sēdāre* to soothe; related to *sedēre* to sit] ▸ **se'dately** *adv* ▸ **se'dateness** *n*

sedate[2] (sɪ'deɪt) *vb* (*tr*) to administer a sedative to. [C20: back formation from SEDATIVE]

sedation (sɪ'deɪʃən) *n* **1** a state of calm or reduced nervous activity. **2** the administration of a sedative.

sedative ('sɛdətɪv) *adj* **1** having a soothing or calming effect. **2** of or relating to sedation. ◆ *n* **3** *Med.* a sedative drug or agent. [C15: from Medieval Latin *sēdātīvus,* from Latin *sēdātus* assuaged; see SEDATE[1]]

Seddon ('sɛdᵊn) *n* **Richard John,** known as *King Dick.* 1845–1906, New Zealand statesman, born in England; prime minister of New Zealand (1893–1906).

sedentary ('sɛdᵊntərɪ, -trɪ) *adj* **1** characterized by or requiring a sitting position: *sedentary work.* **2** tending to sit about without taking much exercise. **3** (of animals) moving about very little, usually because of attachment to a rock or other surface. **4** (of birds) not migratory. [C16: from Latin *sedentārius,* from *sedēre* to sit] ▸ **'sedentarily** *adv* ▸ **'sedentariness** *n*

Seder ('seɪdə) *n Judaism.* a ceremonial meal with prescribed ritual reading of the Haggadah observed in Jewish homes on the first night or first two nights of Passover. [from Hebrew *sēdher* order]

sederunt (sɪ'derunt, sɪ'dɛərənt) *n* (in Scotland) **1** a sitting of an ecclesiastical assembly, court, etc. **2** the list of persons present. [C17: from Latin *sēdērunt* they were sitting, from *sedēre* to sit]

sedge (sɛdʒ) *n* **1** any grasslike cyperaceous plant of the genus *Carex,* typically growing on wet ground and having rhizomes, triangular stems, and minute flowers in spikelets. **2** any other plant of the family *Cyperaceae.* [Old English *secg;* related to Middle High German *segge* sedge, Old English *sagu* SAW[1]] ▸ **'sedgy** *adj*

sedge fly *n* an angler's name for various caddis flies, notably the grey sedge, the murragh, and the cinnamon sedge.

Sedgemoor ('sɛdʒˌmuə) *n* a plain in SW England, in central Somerset: scene of the defeat (1685) of the Duke of Monmouth.

sedge warbler *n* a European songbird, *Acrocephalus schoenobaenus,* of reed beds and swampy areas, having a streaked brownish plumage with white eye stripes: family *Muscicapidae* (Old World flycatchers, etc.).

Sedgwick ('sɛdʒwɪk) *n* **Adam.** 1785–1873, English geologist; played a major role in establishing parts of the geological time scale, esp. the Cambrian and Devonian periods.

sedilia (sɛ'daɪlɪə) *n* (*functioning as sing*) the group of three seats, each called a **sedile** (sɛ'daɪlɪ), often recessed, on the south side of a sanctuary where the celebrant and ministers sit at certain points during High Mass. [C18: from Latin, from *sedīle* a chair, from *sedēre* to sit]

sediment ('sɛdɪmənt) *n* **1** matter that settles to the bottom of a liquid. **2** material that has been deposited from water, ice, or wind. [C16: from Latin *sedimentum* a settling, from *sedēre* to sit] ▸ **sedimentous** (ˌsɛdɪ'mɛntəs) *adj*

sedimentary (ˌsɛdɪ'mentərɪ) *adj* **1** characteristic of, resembling, or containing sediment. **2** (of rocks) formed by the accumulation and consolidation of mineral and organic fragments that have been deposited by water, ice, or wind. Compare **igneous, metamorphic.** ▸ **ˌsedi'mentarily** *adv*

sedimentation (ˌsɛdɪmen'teɪʃən) *n* **1** the process of formation of sedimentary rocks. **2** the deposition or production of sediment. **3** *Chem., biochem.* the process by which large molecules or macroscopic particles are concentrated in a centrifugal field in a centrifuge or ultracentrifuge.

sedimentation tank *n* a tank into which sewage is passed to allow suspended solid matter to separate out.

sedimentology (ˌsɛdɪmɛn'tɒlədʒɪ) *n* the branch of geology concerned with sedimentary rocks and deposits. ▸ **ˌsedimen'tologist** *n*

sedition (sɪ'dɪʃən) *n* **1** speech or behaviour directed against the peace of a state. **2** an offence that tends to undermine the authority of a state. **3** an incitement to public disorder. **4** *Archaic.* revolt. [C14: from Latin *sēditiō* discord, from *sēd-* apart + *itiō* a going, from *īre* to go] ▸ **se'ditionary** *n, adj*

seditious (sɪ'dɪʃəs) *adj* **1** of, like, or causing sedition. **2** inclined to or taking part in sedition. ▸ **se'ditiously** *adv* ▸ **se'ditiousness** *n*

seduce (sɪ'djuːs) *vb* (*tr*) **1** to persuade to engage in sexual intercourse. **2** to lead astray, as from the right action. **3** to win over, attract, or lure. [C15: from Latin *sēdūcere* to lead apart, from *sē-* apart + *dūcere* to lead] ▸ **se'ducible** *or* **se'duceable** *adj*

seducer (sɪ'djuːsə) *or* (*fem*) **seductress** (sɪ'dʌktrɪs) *n* a person who entices, allures, or seduces, esp. one who entices another to engage in sexual intercourse.

seduction (sɪ'dʌkʃən) *n* **1** the act of seducing or the state of being seduced. **2** a means of seduction.

seductive (sɪ'dʌktɪv) *adj* tending to seduce or capable of seducing; enticing; alluring. ▸ **se'ductively** *adv* ▸ **se'ductiveness** *n*

sedulous ('sɛdjuləs) *adj* constant or persistent in use or attention; assiduous; diligent. [C16: from Latin *sēdulus,* of uncertain origin] ▸ **sedulity** (sɪ'djuːlɪtɪ) *or* **'sedulousness** *n* ▸ **'sedulously** *adv*

sedum ('siːdəm) *n* any crassulaceous rock plant of the genus *Sedum,* having thick fleshy leaves and clusters of white, yellow, or pink flowers. See also **stonecrop, rose-root, orpine.** [C15: from Latin: houseleek]

see[1] (siː) *vb* **sees, seeing, saw, seen.** **1** to perceive with the eyes. **2** (when *tr, may take a clause as object*) to perceive (an idea) mentally; understand: *I explained the problem but he could not see it.* **3** (*tr*) to perceive with any or all of the senses: *I hate to see you so unhappy.* **4** (*tr; may take a clause as object*) to be aware of in advance; foresee: *I can see what will happen if you don't help.* **5** (when *tr, may take a clause as object*) to ascertain or find out (a fact); learn: *see who is at the door.* **6** (when *tr, takes a clause as object;* when *intr,* foll. by *to*) to make sure (of something) or take care (of something): *see that he gets to bed early.* **7** (when *tr, may take a clause as object*) to consider, deliberate, or decide: *see if you can come next week.* **8** (*tr*) to have experience of; undergo: *he had seen much unhappiness in his life.* **9** (*tr*) to allow to be in a specified condition: *I cannot stand by and see a child in pain.* **10** (*tr*) to be characterized by: *this period of history has seen much unrest.* **11** (*tr*) to meet or pay a visit to: *to see one's solicitor.* **12** (*tr*) to receive, esp. as a guest or visitor: *the Prime Minister will see the deputation now.* **13** (*tr*) to frequent the company of: *she is seeing a married man.* **14** (*tr*) to accompany or escort: *I saw her to the door.* **15** (*tr*) to refer to or look up: *for further information see the appendix.* **16** (in gambling, esp. in poker) to match (another player's bet) or match the bet of (another player) by staking an equal sum. **17 as far as I can see.** to the best of my judgment or understanding. **18 see fit.** (*takes an infinitive*) to consider proper, desirable, etc.: *I don't see fit to allow her to come here.* **19 see (someone) hanged** *or* **damned first.** *Informal.* to refuse absolutely to do what one has been asked. **20 see (someone) right.** *Brit. informal.* to ensure fair treatment of (someone): *if he has cheated you, I'll see you right.* **21 see the light (of day).** See **light**[1] (sense 24). **22 see you, see you later,** *or* **be seeing you.** an expression of farewell. **23 you see.** *Informal.* a parenthetical filler phrase used to make a pause in speaking or add slight emphasis. ◆ See also **see about, see into, see of, see off, see out, see over, see through.** [Old English *sēon;* related to Old Norse *sjá,* Gothic *saihwan,* Old Saxon *sehan*] ▸ **'seeable** *adj*

see[2] (siː) *n* the diocese of a bishop, or the place within it where his cathedral or procathedral is situated. See also **Holy See.** [C13: from Old French *sed,* from Latin *sēdēs* a seat; related to *sedēre* to sit]

see about *vb* (*intr, prep*) **1** to take care of; look after: *he couldn't see about the matter because he was ill.* **2** to investigate; enquire into: *to see about a new car.*

Seebeck ('siːbɛk) *n Philately.* **1** any of a set of stamps issued (1890–99) in Nicaragua, Honduras, Ecuador, and El Salvador and named after Nicholas Frederick Seebeck, who provided them free to the respective governments. **2** any of the reprints issued later for personal gain by Seebeck.

Seebeck effect ('siːbɛk; *German* 'zeːbɛk) *n* the phenomenon in which a current is produced in a circuit containing two or more different metals when the junctions between the metals are maintained at different temperatures. Also called: **thermoelectric effect.** Compare **Peltier effect.** [C19: named after Thomas *Seebeck* (1770–1831), German physicist]

seed (si:d) *n* **1** *Botany.* a mature fertilized plant ovule, consisting of an embryo and its food store surrounded by a protective seed coat (testa). Related adj: **seminal. 2** the small hard seedlike fruit of plants such as wheat. **3** any propagative part of a plant, such as a tuber, spore, or bulb. **4** such parts collectively. **5** the source, beginning, or germ of anything: *the seeds of revolt.* **6** *Chiefly Bible.* offspring or descendants: *the seed of Abraham.* **7** an archaic or dialect term for **sperm** or **semen. 8** *Sport.* a seeded player. **9** the egg cell or cells of the lobster and certain other animals. **10** See **seed oyster. 11** *Chem.* a small crystal added to a supersaturated solution or supercooled liquid to induce crystallization. **12 go** *or* **run to seed. 12a** (of plants) to produce and shed seeds. **12b** to lose vigour, usefulness, etc. ◆ *vb* **13** to plant (seeds, grain, etc.) in (soil): *we seeded this field with oats.* **14** (*intr*) (of plants) to form or shed seeds. **15** (*tr*) to remove the seeds from (fruit, etc.). **16** (*tr*) *Chem.* to add a small crystal to (a supersaturated solution or supercooled liquid) in order to cause crystallization. **17** (*tr*) to scatter certain substances, such as silver iodide, in (clouds) in order to cause rain. **18** (*tr*) **18a** to arrange (the draw of a tournament) so that outstanding teams or players will not meet in the early rounds. **18b** to distribute (players or teams) in this manner. [Old English *sǣd;* related to Old Norse *sāth,* Gothic *sēths,* Old High German *sāt*] ▸ **'seed,like** *adj* ▸ **'seedless** *adj*

seedbed ('si:d,bɛd) *n* **1** a plot of land in which seeds or seedlings are grown before being transplanted. **2** the place where something develops: *the seedbed of discontent.*

seedcake ('si:d,keɪk) *n* a sweet cake flavoured with caraway seeds and lemon rind or essence.

seed capital *n Finance.* a small amount of capital required to finance the research necessary to produce a business plan for a new company.

seed capsule *or* **seedcase** ('si:d,keɪs) *n* the part of a fruit enclosing the seeds; pericarp.

seed coat *n* the nontechnical name for **testa.**

seed coral *n* small pieces of coral used in jewellery, etc.

seed corn *n* **1** the good quality ears or kernels of corn that are used as seed. **2** assets or investments that are expected to provide profits in the future.

seeder ('si:dəˈ) *n* **1** a person or thing that seeds. **2** a device used to remove seeds, as from fruit, etc. **3** any of various devices for sowing grass seed or grain on the surface of the ground.

seed fern *n* another name for **pteridosperm.**

seed leaf *n* the nontechnical name for **cotyledon.**

seedling ('si:dlɪŋ) *n* a plant produced from a seed, esp. a very young plant.

seed money *n* money used for the establishment of an enterprise.

seed oyster *n* a young oyster, esp. a cultivated oyster, ready for transplantation.

seed pearl *n* a tiny pearl weighing less than a quarter of a grain.

seed plant *n* any plant that reproduces by means of seeds: a gymnosperm or angiosperm.

seed pod *n* a carpel or pistil enclosing the seeds of a plant, esp. a flowering plant.

seed potato *n* a potato tuber used for planting.

seed vessel *n Botany.* a dry fruit, such as a capsule.

seedy ('si:dɪ) *adj* **seedier, seediest. 1** shabby or unseemly in appearance: *seedy clothes.* **2** (of a plant) at the stage of producing seeds. **3** *Informal.* not physically fit; sickly. ▸ **'seedily** *adv* ▸ **'seediness** *n*

Seeger ('si:gə) *n* **Pete.** born 1919. U.S. folk singer and songwriter, noted for his protest songs, which include "We shall Overcome" (1960), "Where have all the Flowers gone?" (1961), "If I had a Hammer" (1962), and "Little Boxes" (1962).

seeing ('si:ɪŋ) *n* **1** the sense or faculty of sight; vision. **2** *Astronomy.* the condition of the atmosphere with respect to observation of stars, planets, etc.: *the bad seeing was due to turbulent air.* ◆ *conj* **3** (*subordinating;* often foll. by *that*) in light of the fact (that); inasmuch as; since.

USAGE The use of *seeing as how* as in *seeing as (how) the bus is always late, I don't need to hurry* is generally thought to be incorrect or non-standard.

see into *vb* (*intr, prep*) **1** to examine or investigate. **2** to discover the true nature of: *I can't see into your thoughts.*

seek (si:k) *vb* **seeks, seeking, sought.** (*mainly tr*) **1** (when *intr,* often foll. by *for* or *after*) to try to find by searching; look for: *to seek a solution.* **2** (*also intr*) to try to obtain or acquire: *to seek happiness.* **3** to attempt (to do something); try: *I'm only seeking to help.* **4** (*also intr*) to enquire about or request (something): *to seek help.* **5** to go or resort to: *to seek the garden for peace.* **6** an archaic word for **explore.** [Old English *sēcan;* related to Old Norse *sōkja,* Gothic *sōkjan,* Old High German *suohhen,* Latin *sāgīre* to perceive by scent; see BESEECH] ▸ **'seeker** *n*

seek out *vb* (*tr, adv*) to search hard for a specific person or thing and find: *she sought out her friend from amongst the crowd.*

seel (si:l) *vb* (*tr*) **1** to sew up the eyelids of (a hawk or falcon) so as to render it quiet and tame. **2** *Obsolete.* to close up the eyes of, esp. by blinding. [C15 *silen,* from Old French *ciller,* from Medieval Latin *ciliāre,* from Latin *cilium* an eyelid]

Seeland ('ze:lant) *n* the German name for **Sjælland.**

seem (si:m) *vb* (may take an infinitive) **1** (*copula*) to appear to the mind or eye; look: *this seems nice; the car seems to be running well.* **2** to give the impression of existing; appear to be: *there seems no need for all this nonsense.* **3** used to diminish the force of a following infinitive to be polite, more noncommittal, etc.: *I can't seem to get through to you.* [C12: perhaps from Old Norse *soma* to beseem, from *sœmr* befitting; related to Old English *sēman* to reconcile; see SAME] ▸ **'seemer** *n*

USAGE See at **like.**

seeming ('si:mɪŋ) *adj* **1** (*prenominal*) apparent but not actual or genuine: *seeming honesty.* ◆ *n* **2** outward or false appearance. ▸ **'seemingly** *adv* ▸ **'seemingness** *n*

seemly ('si:mlɪ) *adj* **-lier, -liest. 1** proper or fitting. **2** *Obsolete.* pleasing or handsome in appearance. ◆ *adv* **3** *Archaic.* properly or decorously. [C13: from Old Norse *sœmiligr,* from *sœmr* befitting] ▸ **'seemliness** *n*

seen (si:n) *vb* the past participle of **see**[1].

see of *vb* (*tr, prep*) to meet; be in contact with: *we haven't seen much of him since he got married.*

see off *vb* (*tr, adv*) **1** to be present at the departure of (a person making a journey). **2** *Informal.* to cause to leave or depart, esp. by force.

see out *vb* (*tr, adv*) **1** to remain or endure until the end of: *we'll see the first half of the game out and then leave.* **2** to be present at the departure of (a person from a house, room, etc.).

see over *or* **round** *vb* (*intr, prep*) to inspect by making a tour of: *she said she'd like to see over the house.*

seep (si:p) *vb* **1** (*intr*) to pass gradually or leak through or as if through small openings; ooze. ◆ *n* **2** a small spring or place where water, oil, etc., has oozed through the ground. **3** another word for **seepage.** [Old English *sīpian;* related to Middle High German *sīfen,* Swedish dialect *sipa*]

seepage ('si:pɪdʒ) *n* **1** the act or process of seeping. **2** liquid or moisture that has seeped.

seer[1] (sɪə) *n* **1** a person who can supposedly see into the future; prophet. **2** a person who professes supernatural powers. **3** a person who sees. ▸ **'seeress** *fem n*

seer[2] (sɪə) *n* a variant spelling of **ser.**

seersucker ('sɪə,sʌkə) *n* a light cotton, linen, or other fabric with a crinkled surface and often striped. [C18: from Hindi *śīrśakar,* from Persian *shīr o shakkar,* literally: milk and sugar]

seesaw ('si:,sɔ:) *n* **1** a plank balanced in the middle so that two people seated on the ends can ride up and down by pushing on the ground with their feet. **2** the pastime of riding up and down on a seesaw. **3a** an up-and-down or back-and-forth movement. **3b** (*as modifier*): *a seesaw movement.* ◆ *vb* **4** (*intr*) to move up and down or back and forth in such a manner; oscillate. [C17: reduplication of SAW[1], alluding to the movement from side to side, as in sawing]

seethe (si:ð) *vb* **1** (*intr*) to boil or to foam as if boiling. **2** (*intr*) to be in a state of extreme agitation, esp. through anger. **3** (*tr*) to soak in liquid. **4** (*tr*) *Archaic.* to cook or extract the essence of (a food) by boiling. ◆ *n* **5** the act or state of seething. [Old English *sēothan;* related to Old Norse *sjōtha,* Old High German *siodan* to seethe] ▸ **'seething** *adj* ▸ **'seethingly** *adv*

see through *vb* **1** (*tr*) to help out in time of need or trouble: *I know you're short of money, but I'll see you through.* **2** (*tr, adv*) to remain with until the end or completion: *let's see the job through.* **3** (*intr, prep*) to perceive the true nature of: *I can see through your evasion.* ◆ *adj* **see-through. 4** partly or wholly transparent or translucent, esp. (of clothes) in a titillating way: *a see-through nightie.*

sefer ('sefɛr, 'seɪfɛr) *n Judaism.* **1** in full: **sefer torah.** the scrolls of the Law. **2** any book of Hebrew religious literature. [from Hebrew, literally: book]

Seferis (sə'fɛərɪs) *n* **George.** pen name of *Georgios Seferiades.* 1900–71, Greek poet and diplomat: Nobel prize for literature 1963.

Sefton ('sɛftᵊn) *n* a unitary authority in NW England, in Merseyside. Pop.: 291 000 (1995 est.). Area: 150 sq. km (58 sq. miles).

segment *n* ('sɛgmənt). **1** *Maths.* **1a** a part of a line or curve between two points. **1b** a part of a plane or solid figure cut off by an intersecting line, plane, or planes, esp. one between a chord and an arc of a circle. **2** one of several parts or sections into which an object is divided; portion. **3** *Zoology.* any of the parts into which the body or appendages of an annelid or arthropod are divided. **4** *Linguistics.* a speech sound considered in isolation. ◆ *vb* (sɛg'mɛnt). **5** to cut or divide (a whole object) into segments. [C16: from Latin *segmentum,* from *secāre* to cut] ▸ **segmentary** ('sɛgməntərɪ, -trɪ) *adj*

segmental (sɛg'mentᵊl) *adj* **1** of, like, or having the form of a segment. **2** divided into segments. **3** *Linguistics.* of, relating to, or constituting an isolable speech sound. ▸ **seg'mentally** *adv*

segmentation (,sɛgmɛn'teɪʃən) *n* **1** the act or an instance of dividing into segments. **2** *Embryol.* another name for **cleavage** (sense 4). **3** *Zoology.* another name for **metamerism** (sense 1).

segmentation cavity *n* another name for **blastocoel.**

segno ('sɛnjəu; *Italian* 'seɲɲo) *n, pl* **-gni** (-nji:; *Italian* -ɲɲi). *Music.* a sign at the beginning or end of a section directed to be repeated. Symbol: 𝄋 or :S: [Italian: a sign, from Latin *signum*]

Segovia[1] (sɪ'gəuvɪə; *Spanish* se'ɣoβja) *n* a town in central Spain: site of a Roman aqueduct, still in use, and the fortified palace of the kings of Castile (the Alcázar). Pop.: 58 060 (1991).

Segovia[2] (sɪ'gəuvɪə; *Spanish* se'ɣoβja) *n* **Andrés** (an'dres), Marquis of Salobreña. 1893–1987, Spanish classical guitarist.

Segrè (sə'greɪ) *n* **Emilio** (ɛm'i:lɪəu). 1905–89, U.S. physicist, born in Italy, who was the first to produce an artificial element. He shared the Nobel prize for physics (1959) with Owen Chamberlain for their discovery (1955) of the antiproton.

segregate ('sɛgrɪ,geɪt) *vb* **1** to set or be set apart from others or from the main group. **2** (*tr*) to impose segregation on (a racial or minority group). **3** *Genetics, metallurgy.* to undergo or cause to undergo segregation. [C16: from Latin *sēgregāre,* from *sē-* apart + *grex* a flock] ▸ **segregable** ('sɛgrɪgəbᵊl) *adj* ▸ **'segre,gative** *adj* ▸ **'segre,gator** *n*

segregation (,sɛgrɪ'geɪʃən) *n* **1** the act of segregating or state of being segregated. **2** *Sociol.* the practice or policy of creating separate facilities within the same society for the use of a minority group. **3** *Genetics.* the separation at meiosis of the two members of any pair of alleles into separate gametes. See also

Mendel's laws. **4** *Metallurgy.* the process in which a component of an alloy or solid solution separates in small regions within the solid or on the solid's surface. ▸ **ˌsegreˈgational** *adj*

segregationist (ˌsɛgrɪˈgeɪʃənɪst) *n* a person who favours, advocates, or practises racial segregation.

segue (ˈsɛgweɪ) *vb* **segues, segueing, segued.** (*intr*) **1** (often foll. by *into*) to proceed from one section or piece of music to another without a break. **2** (*imperative*) play on without pause: a musical direction. ◆ *n* **3** the practice or an instance of playing music in this way. [from Italian: follows, from *seguire* to follow, from Latin *sequī*]

seguidilla (ˌsɛgɪˈdiːljə) *n* **1** a Spanish dance in a fast triple rhythm. **2** a piece of music composed for or in the rhythm of this dance. **3** *Prosody.* a stanzaic form consisting of four to seven lines and marked by a characteristic rhythm. [Spanish: a little dance, from *seguida* a dance, from *seguir* to follow, from Latin *sequī*]

seicento (*Italian* seiˈtʃɛnto) *n* the 17th century with reference to Italian art and literature. [Italian, shortened from *mille seicento* one thousand six hundred]

seiche (seɪʃ) *n* a periodic oscillation of the surface of an enclosed or semi-enclosed body of water (lake, inland sea, bay, etc.) caused by such phenomena as atmospheric pressure changes, winds, tidal currents, and earthquakes. [C19: from Swiss French, first used to describe rise and fall of water in Lake Geneva; of obscure origin]

Seidlitz powder *or* **powders** (ˈsɛdlɪts) *n* a laxative consisting of two powders, tartaric acid and a mixture of sodium bicarbonate and Rochelle salt. Also called: **Rochelle powder.** [C19: named after *Seidlitz,* a village in Bohemia with mineral springs having similar laxative effects]

seif dune (seɪf) *n* (in deserts, esp. the Sahara) a long ridge of blown sand, often several miles long. [*seif,* from Arabic: sword, from the shape of the dune]

Seifert (ˈsiːˌfət) *n* **Jaroslav** (ˈjærəslæf). 1901–86, Czech poet and journalist, noted esp. for poems dealing with the German occupation of Prague during World War II. Nobel prize for literature 1984.

seigneur (seˈnjɜː; *French* sɛɲœr) *n* **1** a feudal lord, esp. in France. **2** (in French Canada, until 1854) the landlord of an estate that was subdivided among peasants who held their plots by a form of feudal tenure. [C16: from Old French, from Vulgar Latin *senior,* from Latin: an elderly man; see SENIOR] ▸ **seiˈgneurial** *adj*

seigneury (ˈseɪnjərɪ) *n, pl* **-gneuries.** the estate of a seigneur.

seignior (ˈseɪnjə) *n* **1** a less common name for a **seigneur. 2** (in England) the lord of a seigniory. [C14: from Anglo-French *segnour;* see SEIGNEUR] ▸ **seigniorial** (seɪˈnjɔːrɪəl) *adj*

seigniorage (ˈseɪnjərɪdʒ) *n* **1** something claimed by a sovereign or superior as a prerogative, right, or due. **2** a fee payable to a government for coining bullion. **3** the difference in value between the cost of bullion and the face value of the coin made from it.

seigniory (ˈseɪnjərɪ) *or* **signory** (ˈsiːnjərɪ) *n, pl* **-gniories** *or* **-gnories. 1** less common names for a **seigneury. 2** (in England) the fee or manor of a seignior; a feudal domain. **3** the authority of a seignior or the relationship between him and his tenants. **4** a body of lords.

seik (siːk) *adj* a Scot. word for **sick**[1].

seine (seɪn) *n* **1** a large fishing net that hangs vertically in the water by means of floats at the top and weights at the bottom. ◆ *vb* **2** to catch (fish) using this net. [Old English *segne,* from Latin *sagēna,* from Greek *sagēnē;* related to Old High German *segina,* Old French *saïne*]

Seine (seɪn; *French* sɛn) *n* a river in N France, rising on the Plateau de Langres and flowing northwest through Paris to the English Channel: the second longest river in France, linked by canal with the Rivers Somme, Scheldt, Meuse, Rhine, Saône, and Loire. Length: 776 km (482 miles).

Seine-et-Marne (*French* sɛnemarn) *n* a department of N central France, in Île-de-France region. Capital: Melun. Pop.: 1 179 300 (1995). Area: 5931 sq. km (2313 sq. miles).

Seine-Maritime (*French* sɛnmaritim) *n* a department of N France, in Haute-Normandie region. Capital: Rouen. Pop.: 1 241 500 (1995). Area: 6342 sq. km (2473 sq. miles).

Seine-Saint-Denis (*French* sɛnsɛ̃dni) *n* a department of N central France, in Île-de-France region. Capital: Bobigny. Pop.: 1 405 500 (1995). Area: 236 sq. km (92 sq. miles).

seise *or U.S.* **seize** (siːz) *vb* to put into legal possession of (property, etc.). [variant of SEIZE] ▸ **ˈseisable** *adj* ▸ **ˈseiser** *n*

seisin *or U.S.* **seizin** (ˈsiːzɪn) *n Property law.* feudal possession of an estate in land. [C13: from Old French *seisine,* from *seisir* to SEIZE]

seism (ˈsaɪzəm) *n* a less common name for **earthquake.** [C19: from Greek *seismos,* from *seiein* to shake]

seismic (ˈsaɪzmɪk) *adj* **1** Also (less commonly): **seismical** (ˈsaɪzmɪkᵊl). relating to or caused by earthquakes or artificially produced earth tremors. **2** of enormous proportions or having highly significant consequences: *seismic social change.* ▸ **ˈseismically** *adv*

seismic array *n* a system of linked seismographs arranged in a regular geometric pattern to increase sensitivity to earthquake detection.

seismicity (saɪzˈmɪsɪtɪ) *n* seismic activity; the phenomenon of earthquake activity or the occurrence of artificially produced earth tremors.

seismic wave *n* an earth vibration generated by an earthquake or explosion.

seismo- *or before a vowel* **seism-** *combining form.* earthquake: *seismology.* [from Greek *seismos*]

seismograph (ˈsaɪzməˌgrɑːf, -ˌgræf) *n* an instrument that registers and records the features of earthquakes. A **seismogram** (ˈsaɪzməˌgræm) is the record from such an instrument. Also called: **seisˈmometer.** ▸ **seismographic** (ˌsaɪzməˈgræfɪk) *adj* ▸ **seismographer** (saɪzˈmɒgrəfə) *n* ▸ **seisˈmography** *n*

seismology (saɪzˈmɒlədʒɪ) *n* the branch of geology concerned with the study of earthquakes. ▸ **seismologic** (ˌsaɪzməˈlɒdʒɪk) *or* **ˌseismoˈlogical** *adj* ▸ **ˌseismoˈlogically** *adv* ▸ **seisˈmologist** *n*

seismoscope (ˈsaɪzməˌskəʊp) *n* an instrument that indicates the occurrence of an earthquake. Compare **seismograph.** ▸ **seismoscopic** (ˌsaɪzməˈskɒpɪk) *adj*

sei whale (seɪ) *n* a rorqual, *Balaenoptera borealis.* [C20: from Norwegian *seihval,* from *sei* coalfish (see SAITHE) + *hval* whale: so called because it follows coalfish in search of food]

seize (siːz) *vb* (*mainly tr*) **1** (also *intr,* foll. by *on*) to take hold of quickly; grab: *she seized her hat and ran for the bus.* **2** (sometimes foll. by *on* or *upon*) to grasp mentally, esp. rapidly: *she immediately seized his idea.* **3** to take mental possession of: *alarm seized the crowd.* **4** to take possession of rapidly and forcibly: *the thief seized the woman's purse.* **5** to take legal possession of; take into custody. **6** to take by force or capture: *the army seized the undefended town.* **7** to take immediate advantage of: *to seize an opportunity.* **8** *Nautical.* to bind (two ropes together or a piece of gear to a rope). See also **serve** (sense 19). **9** (*intr;* often foll. by *up*) (of mechanical parts) to become jammed, esp. because of excessive heat. **10** (*passive;* usually foll. by *of*) to be apprised of; conversant with. **11** the usual U.S. spelling of **seise.** [C13 *saisen,* from Old French *saisir,* from Medieval Latin *sacīre* to position, of Germanic origin; related to Gothic *satjan* to SET[1]] ▸ **ˈseizable** *adj*

seizing (ˈsiːzɪŋ) *n Nautical.* a binding used for holding together two ropes, two spars, etc., esp. by lashing with a separate rope.

seizure (ˈsiːʒə) *n* **1** the act or an instance of seizing or the state of being seized. **2** *Pathol.* a sudden manifestation or recurrence of a disease, such as an epileptic convulsion.

sejant *or* **sejeant** (ˈsiːdʒənt) *adj* (*usually postpositive*) *Heraldry.* (of a beast) shown seated. [C16: variant of *seant,* from Old French, from *seoir* to sit, from Latin *sedēre*]

Sejm (seɪm) *n* the unicameral legislature of Poland. [Polish: assembly]

Sekondi (ˌsɛkənˈdiː) *n* a port in SW Ghana, 8 km (5 miles) northeast of Takoradi: linked administratively with Takoradi in 1946. Pop. (with Takoradi): 103 600 (1988 est.).

Sekt (zɛkt) *n* any of various German sparkling wines. [C20: from German, from Spanish *vino seco* dry wine]

sel (sɛl) *n* a Scot. word for **self.**

selachian (sɪˈleɪkɪən) *adj* **1** of, relating to, or belonging to the *Selachii* (or *Elasmobranchii*), a large subclass of cartilaginous fishes including the sharks, rays, dogfish, and skates. ◆ *n* **2** any fish belonging to the subclass *Selachii.* ◆ Also: **elasmobranch.** [C19: from New Latin *Selachiī,* from Greek *selakhē* a shark; related to Greek *selas* brightness]

selaginella (ˌsɛlədʒɪˈnɛlə) *n* any club moss of the genus *Selaginella,* having stems covered in small pointed leaves and small spore-bearing cones: family *Selaginellaceae.* See also **resurrection plant.** [C19: from New Latin, diminutive of Latin *selāgō* plant similar to the savin]

selah (ˈsiːlə) *n* a Hebrew word of unknown meaning occurring in the Old Testament psalms, and thought to be a musical direction. [C16: from Hebrew]

Selangor (səˈlæŋə) *n* a state of Peninsular Malaysia, on the Strait of Malacca: established as a British protectorate in 1874, became a Federated Malay State in 1896 and part of Malaysia in 1946; tin producer. Capital: Shah Alam. Pop.: 1 981 090 (1993 est.). Area: 8203 sq. km (3167 sq. miles).

Selby (ˈsɛlbɪ) *n* an inland port in N England, in N Yorkshire, on the River Ouse: centre for a major coalfield since 1983: agricultural products. Pop.: 15 292 (1991).

Selden (ˈsɛldən) *n* **John.** 1584–1654, English antiquary and politician. As a member of Parliament, he was twice imprisoned for opposing the king.

seldom (ˈsɛldəm) *adv* not often; rarely. [Old English *seldon;* related to Old Norse *sjāldan,* Old High German *seltan*]

select (sɪˈlɛkt) *vb* **1** to choose (someone or something) in preference to another or others. ◆ *adj also* **selected. 2** chosen in preference to another or others. **3** of particular quality or excellence. **4** limited as to membership or entry: *a select gathering.* **5** careful in making a choice. [C16: from Latin *sēligere* to sort, from *sē-* apart + *legere* to choose] ▸ **seˈlectly** *adv* ▸ **seˈlectness** *n*

select committee *n* (in Britain) a small committee composed of members of parliament, set up by either House of Parliament to investigate and report back on a specified matter of interest.

selectee (sɪˌlɛkˈtiː) *n U.S.* a person who is selected, esp. for military service.

selection (sɪˈlɛkʃən) *n* **1** the act or an instance of selecting or the state of being selected. **2** a thing or number of things that have been selected. **3** a range from which something may be selected: *this shop has a good selection of clothes.* **4** *Biology.* the natural or artificial process by which certain organisms or characters are reproduced and perpetuated in the species in preference to others. See also **natural selection. 5** a contestant in a race chosen as likely to win or come second or third. **6** *Austral.* **6a** the act of free-selecting. **6b** a tract of land acquired by free-selection.

selective (sɪˈlɛktɪv) *adj* **1** of or characterized by selection. **2** tending to choose carefully or characterized by careful choice. **3** *Electronics.* occurring at, operating at, or capable of separating out a particular frequency or band of frequencies. ▸ **seˈlectively** *adv* ▸ **seˈlectiveness** *n*

selective attention *n Psychol.* the process by which a person can selectively pick out one message from a mixture of messages occurring simultaneously.

selective service *n U.S.* (formerly) compulsory military service under which men were conscripted selectively.

selective synchronization *n* a sound-recording process that facilitates overdubs by feeding the recorded track to the performer straight from the recording head. Often shortened to **sel-sync.**

selectivity (sɪˌlɛkˈtɪvɪtɪ) *n* **1** the state or quality of being selective. **2** the degree to which a radio receiver or other circuit can respond to and separate the frequency of a desired signal from other frequencies by tuning. **3** the principle that welfare services should go only to those whose need is greatest, as revealed by needs tests, means tests, etc.

selectman (sɪ'lɛktmən) *n, pl* **-men.** any of the members of the local boards of most New England towns.

selector (sɪ'lɛktə) *n* **1** a person or thing that selects. **2** a device used in automatic telephone switching that connects one circuit with any one of a number of other circuits. **3** *Brit.* a person who chooses the members of a sports team. **4** *Austral.* the holder of a tract of land acquired by free-selection.

selenate ('sɛlɪˌneɪt) *n* any salt or ester formed by replacing one or both of the hydrogens of selenic acid with metal ions or organic groups. **[C19:** from SELENIUM + -ATE[1]**]**

Selene (sɪ'liːnɪ) *n* the Greek goddess of the moon. Roman counterpart: **Luna.**

selenic (sɪ'liːnɪk) *adj* of or containing selenium, esp. in the hexavalent state.

selenic acid *n* a colourless crystalline soluble strong dibasic acid analogous to sulphuric acid. Formula: H_2SeO_4.

selenious (sɪ'liːnɪəs) *or* **selenous** (sɪ'liːnəs) *adj* of or containing selenium in the divalent or tetravalent state.

selenious acid *n* a white soluble crystalline strong dibasic acid analogous to sulphurous acid. Formula: H_2SeO_3.

selenite ('sɛlɪˌnaɪt) *n* a colourless glassy variety of gypsum. **[C17:** via Latin from Greek *selēnitēs lithos* moonstone, from *selēnē* moon; so called because it was believed to wax and wane with the moon**]**

selenium (sɪ'liːnɪəm) *n* a nonmetallic element that exists in several allotropic forms. It occurs free in volcanic areas and in sulphide ores, esp. pyrite. The common form is a grey crystalline solid that is photoconductive, photovoltaic, and semiconducting: used in photocells, solar cells, and in xerography. Symbol: Se; atomic no.: 34; atomic wt.: 78.96; valency: –2, 4, or 6; relative density: 4.79 (grey); melting pt.: 221°C (grey); boiling pt.: 685°C (grey). **[C19:** from New Latin, from Greek *selēnē* moon; named by analogy to TELLURIUM (from Latin *tellus* earth)**]**

selenium cell *n* a photoelectric cell containing a strip of selenium between two metal electrodes.

seleno- *or before a vowel* **selen-** *combining form.* denoting the moon: *selenology.* **[**from Greek *selēnē* moon**]**

selenodont (sɪ'liːnəˌdɒnt) *adj* **1** (of the teeth of certain mammals) having crescent-shaped ridges on the crowns, as in deer. ◆ *n* **2** a mammal with selenodont teeth. **[C19:** from SELENO- (moon-shaped) + -ODONT**]**

selenography (ˌsiːlɪ'nɒgrəfɪ) *n* the branch of astronomy concerned with the description and mapping of the surface features of the moon. ► **selenograph** (sɪ'liːnəʊˌgrɑːf, -ˌgræf) *n* ► **ˌsele'nographer** *or* **ˌselle'nographist** *n* ► **selenographic** (sɪˌliːnəʊ'græfɪk) *or* **seˌleno'graphical** *adj* ► **seˌleno'graphically** *adv*

selenology (ˌsiːlɪ'nɒlədʒɪ) *n* the branch of astronomy concerned with the moon, its physical characteristics, nature, origin, etc. ► **selenological** (sɪˌliːnəʊ'lɒdʒɪk^{ə}l) *adj* ► **ˌsele'nologist** *n*

selenomorphology (sɪˌliːnəʊmɔː'fɒlədʒɪ) *n* the study of the lunar surface and landscape.

Seles ('sɛlɛz, -lɛʃ) *n* **Monica.** born 1973, U.S. tennis player, born in Yugoslavia: winner of the U.S. Open (1991, 1992); stabbed while on court in an unprovoked attack.

Seleucia (sɪ'luːʃɪə) *n* **1** an ancient city in Mesopotamia, on the River Tigris: founded by Seleucus Nicator in 312 B.C.; became the chief city of the Seleucid empire; sacked by the Romans around 162 A.D. **2** an ancient city in SE Asia Minor, on the River Calycadnus (modern Goksu Nehri): captured by the Turks in the 13th century; site of present-day Silifke (Turkey). Official name: **Seleucia Tracheotis** (ˌtrækɪ'əʊtɪs) or **Trachea** (trə'kɪə). **3** an ancient port in Syria, on the River Orontes: the port of Antioch, of military importance during the wars between the Ptolemies and Seleucids; largely destroyed by earthquake in 526; site of present-day Samandağ (Turkey). Official name: **Seleucia Pieria** (paɪ'iːrɪə).

Seleucid (sɪ'luːsɪd) *n, pl* **-cids** *or* **-cidae** (-sɪˌdiː). **1** a member of a royal dynasty (312–64 B.C.) that at the zenith of its power ruled over an area extending from Thrace to India. ◆ *adj* **2** of, relating to, or supporting the Seleucids or their dynasty. ► **Seleucidan** (sɪ'luːsɪd^{ə}n) *adj*

Seleucus I (sɪ'luːkəs) *n* surname *Nicator.* ?358–280 B.C., Macedonian general under Alexander the Great, who founded the Seleucid kingdom.

self (sɛlf) *n, pl* **selves** (sɛlvz). **1** the distinct individuality or identity of a person or thing. **2** a person's usual or typical bodily make-up or personal characteristics: *she looked her old self again.* **3 good self** (*or* **selves**). *Rare.* a polite way of referring to or addressing a person (or persons), used following *your, his, her,* or *their.* **4** one's own welfare or interests: *he only thinks of self.* **5** an individual's consciousness of his own identity or being. **6** *Philosophy.* (usually preceded by *the*) that which is essential to an individual, esp. the mind or soul in Cartesian metaphysics; the ego. **7** a bird, animal, etc., that is a single colour throughout, esp. a self-coloured pigeon. ◆ *pron* **8** *Not standard.* myself, yourself, etc.: *seats for self and wife.* ◆ *adj* **9** of the same colour or material: *a dress with a self belt.* See also **self-coloured. 10** *Obsolete.* the same. **[**Old English *seolf;* related to Old Norse *sjālfr,* Gothic *silba,* Old High German *selb***]**

self- *combining form.* **1** of oneself or itself: *self-defence; self-rule.* **2** by, to, in, due to, for, or from the self: *self-employed; self-inflicted; self-respect.* **3** automatic or automatically: *self-propelled.*

self-abnegation *n* the denial of one's own interests in favour of the interests of others. ► **ˌself-'abneˌgating** *adj*

self-absorption *n* **1** preoccupation with oneself to the exclusion of others or the outside world. **2** *Physics.* the process in which some of the radiation emitted by a material is absorbed by the material itself.

self-abuse *n* **1** disparagement or misuse of one's own abilities, etc. **2** a censorious term for **masturbation.**

self-acting *adj* not requiring an external influence or control to function; automatic. ► **ˌself-'action** *n*

self-actualization *n Psychol.* the process of establishing oneself as a whole person, able to develop one's abilities and to understand oneself.

self-addressed *adj* **1** addressed for return to the sender. **2** directed to oneself: *a self-addressed remark.*

self-advocacy *n Social welfare.* (esp. in the U.S.) **1a** the practice of having mentally handicapped people speak for themselves and control their own affairs, rather than having nonhandicapped people automatically assume responsibility for them. See also **normalization. 1b** (*as modifier*): *a self-advocacy group.* **2** the act or condition of representing oneself, either generally in society or in formal proceedings, such as a court.

self-aggrandizement *n* the act of increasing one's own power, importance, etc., esp. in an aggressive or ruthless manner. ► **ˌself-ag'granˌdizing** *adj*

self-annealing *adj Metallurgy.* denoting certain metals, such as lead, tin, and zinc, that recrystallize at air temperatures and so may be cold-worked without strain-hardening.

self-annihilation *n* the surrender of the self in mystical contemplation, union with God, etc.

self-appointed *adj* having assumed authority without the agreement of others: *a self-appointed critic.*

self-assertion *n* the act or an instance of putting forward one's own opinions, etc., esp. in an aggressive or conceited manner. ► **ˌself-as'serting** *adj* ► **ˌself-as'sertingly** *adv* ► **ˌself-as'sertive** *adj* ► **ˌself-as'sertively** *adv* ► **ˌself-as'sertiveness** *n*

self-assessment *n* **1** an evaluation of one's own abilities and failings. **2** *Finance.* a system to enable taxpayers to assess their own tax liabilities.

self-assurance *n* confidence in the validity, value, etc., of one's own ideas, opinions, etc.

self-assured *adj* confident of one's own worth. ► **ˌself-as'suredly** *adv* ► **ˌself-as'suredness** *n*

self-catering *adj* denoting accommodation in which the tenant or visitor provides and prepares his own food.

self-centred *adj* totally preoccupied with one's own concerns. ► **ˌself-'centredly** *adv* ► **ˌself-'centredness** *n*

self-certification *n* (in Britain) a formal assertion by a worker to his employer that absence from work for up to seven days was due to sickness. From 1982 this replaced a doctor's certificate for the purposes of paying sickness benefit. See also **sick note.**

self-coloured *adj* **1** having only a single and uniform colour: *self-coloured flowers; a self-coloured dress.* **2** (of cloth, material, etc.) **2a** having the natural or original colour. **2b** retaining the colour of the thread before weaving.

self-command *n* another term for **self-control.**

self-concept *n Psychol.* the whole set of attitudes, opinions, and cognitions that a person has of himself.

self-confessed *adj* according to one's own testimony or admission: *a self-confessed liar.*

self-confidence *n* confidence in one's own powers, judgment, etc. ► **ˌself-'confident** *adj* ► **ˌself-'confidently** *adv*

self-conscious *adj* **1** unduly aware of oneself as the object of the attention of others; embarrassed. **2** conscious of one's existence. ► **ˌself-'consciously** *adv* ► **ˌself-'consciousness** *n*

self-contained *adj* **1** containing within itself all parts necessary for completeness. **2** (of a flat) having its own kitchen, bathroom, and lavatory not shared by others and usually having its own entrance. **3** able or tending to keep one's feelings, thoughts, etc., to oneself; reserved. **4** able to control one's feelings or emotions in the presence of others. ► **ˌself-con'tainedly** *adv* ► **ˌself-con'tainedness** *n*

self-control *n* the ability to exercise restraint or control over one's feelings, emotions, reactions, etc. ► **ˌself-con'trolled** *adj* ► **ˌself-con'trolling** *adj*

self-deception *or* **self-deceit** *n* the act or an instance of deceiving oneself, esp. as to the true nature of one's feelings or motives. ► **ˌself-de'ceptive** *adj*

self-defence *n* **1** the act of defending oneself, one's actions, ideas, etc. **2** boxing as a means of defending the person (esp. in the phrase **noble art of self-defence**). **3** *Law.* the right to defend one's person, family, or property against

ˌself-a'basement *n*
ˌself-ab'sorbed *adj*
ˌself-ˌaccu'sation *n*
ˌself-ad'hesive *adj*
ˌself-ad'justing *adj*
ˌself-ad'ministered *adj*
ˌself-ˌadmi'ration *n*
ˌself-ad'vancement *n*
ˌself-ad'vertisement *n*
self-a'nalysis *n*
ˌself-ap'proval *n*
ˌself-a'ware *adj*
ˌself-be'trayal *n*
ˌself-'censorˌship *n*
ˌself-'cleaning *adj*
ˌself-con'cern *n*
ˌself-conˌgratu'lation *n*
ˌself-con'sistent *adj*
ˌself-con'tempt *n*
ˌself-ˌcontra'diction *n*
ˌself-ˌcontra'dictory *adj*
ˌself-cor'recting *adj*
ˌself-cre'ated *adj*
ˌself-'critical *adj*
ˌself-'critiˌcism *n*
ˌself-de'feating *adj*

attack or threat of attack by the use of no more force than is reasonable. ▸ **ˌself-deˈfensive** *adj*

self-denial *n* the denial or sacrifice of one's own desires. ▸ **ˌself-deˈnying** *adj* ▸ **ˌself-deˈnyingly** *adv*

self-deprecating *or* **self-depreciating** *adj* having a tendency to disparage oneself.

self-determination *n* **1** the power or ability to make a decision for oneself without influence from outside. **2** the right of a nation or people to determine its own form of government without influence from outside. ▸ **ˌself-deˈtermined** *adj* ▸ **ˌself-deˈtermining** *adj*

self-discipline *n* the act of disciplining or power to discipline one's own feelings, desires, etc., esp. with the intention of improving oneself. ▸ **ˌself-ˈdisciplined** *adj*

self-dissociation *n Chem.* the splitting of the molecules of certain highly polar liquids, such as water and liquid ammonia, into ions.

self-drive *adj* denoting or relating to a hired car that is driven by the hirer.

self-educated *adj* **1** educated through one's own efforts without formal instruction. **2** educated at one's own expense, without financial aid. ▸ **ˌself-ˌeduˈcation** *n*

self-effacement *n* the act of making oneself, one's actions, etc., inconspicuous, esp. because of humility or timidity. ▸ **ˌself-efˈfacing** *adj* ▸ **ˌself-efˈfacingly** *adv*

self-employed *adj* earning one's living in one's own business or through freelance work, rather than as the employee of another. ▸ **ˌself-emˈployment** *n*

self-esteem *n* **1** respect for or a favourable opinion of oneself. **2** an unduly high opinion of oneself; vanity.

self-evident *adj* containing its own evidence or proof without need of further demonstration. ▸ **ˌself-ˈevidence** *n* ▸ **ˌself-ˈevidently** *adv*

self-examination *n* scrutiny of one's own conduct, motives, desires, etc. ▸ **ˌself-exˈamining** *adj*

self-excited *adj* **1** (of an electrical machine) having the current for the magnetic field system generated by the machine itself or by an auxiliary machine coupled to it. **2** (of an oscillator) generating its own energy and depending on resonant circuits for frequency determination.

self-executing *adj* (of a law, treaty, or clause in a deed or contract, etc.) coming into effect automatically at a specified time, no legislation or other action being needed for enforcement.

self-existent *adj Philosophy.* existing independently of any other being or cause. ▸ **ˌself-exˈistence** *n*

self-explanatory *or (less commonly)* **self-explaining** *adj* understandable without explanation; self-evident.

self-expression *n* the expression of one's own personality, feelings, etc., as in painting, poetry, or other creative activity. ▸ **ˌself-exˈpressive** *adj*

self-feeder *n* any machine or device capable of automatically supplying materials when and where they are needed, esp. one for making measured quantities of food constantly available to farm livestock.

self-fertilization *n* fertilization in a plant or animal by the fusion of male and female gametes produced by the same individual. Compare **cross-fertilization** (sense 1). ▸ **ˌself-ˈfertiˌlized** *adj* ▸ **ˌself-ˈfertiˌlizing** *or* **ˌself-ˈfertile** *adj*

self-forgetful *adj* forgetful of one's own interests. ▸ **ˌself-forˈgetfully** *adv* ▸ **ˌself-forˈgetfulness** *n*

self-government *n* **1** the government of a country, nation, etc., by its own people. **2** the state of being self-controlled. **3** an archaic term for **self-control.** ▸ **ˌself-ˈgoverned** *adj* ▸ **ˌself-ˈgoverning** *adj*

selfheal (ˈselfˌhiːl) *n* **1** a low-growing European herbaceous plant, *Prunella vulgaris,* with tightly clustered violet-blue flowers and reputedly having healing powers: family *Labiatae* (labiates). **2** any of several other plants thought to have healing powers. ◆ Also called: **allheal, heal-all.**

self-help *n* **1** the act or state of providing the means to help oneself without relying on the assistance of others. **2a** the practice of solving one's problems by joining or forming a group designed to help those suffering from a particular problem. **2b** *(as modifier)*: *a self-help group.*

selfhood (ˈselfhʊd) *n* **1** *Philosophy.* **1a** the state of having a distinct identity. **1b** the individuality so possessed. **2** a person's character. **3** the quality of being egocentric.

self-identity *n* the conscious recognition of the self as having a unique identity.

self-image *n* one's own idea of oneself or sense of one's worth.

self-important *adj* having or showing an unduly high opinion of one's own abilities, importance, etc. ▸ **ˌself-imˈportantly** *adv* ▸ **ˌself-imˈportance** *n*

self-improvement *n* the improvement of one's status, position, education, etc., by one's own efforts.

self-induced *adj* **1** induced or brought on by oneself or itself. **2** *Electronics.* produced by self-induction.

self-inductance *n* the inherent inductance of a circuit, given by the ratio of the electromotive force produced in the circuit by self-induction to the rate of change of current producing it. It is usually expressed in henries. Symbol: *L* Also called: **coefficient of self-induction.**

self-induction *n* the production of an electromotive force in a circuit when the magnetic flux linked with the circuit changes as a result of a change in current in the same circuit. See also **self-inductance.** Compare **mutual induction.** ▸ **ˌself-inˈductive** *adj*

self-indulgent *adj* tending to indulge one's own desires, etc. ▸ **ˌself-inˈdulgence** *n* ▸ **ˌself-inˈdulgently** *adv*

self-insurance *n* the practice of insuring oneself or one's property by accumulating a reserve out of one's income or funds rather than by purchase of an insurance policy.

self-interest *n* **1** one's personal interest or advantage. **2** the act or an instance of pursuing one's own interest. ▸ **ˌself-ˈinterested** *adj* ▸ **ˌself-ˈinterestedness** *n*

selfish (ˈsɛlfɪʃ) *adj* **1** chiefly concerned with one's own interest, advantage, etc., esp. to the total exclusion of the interests of others. **2** relating to or characterized by self-interest. ▸ **ˈselfishly** *adv* ▸ **ˈselfishness** *n*

self-justification *n* the act or an instance of justifying or providing excuses for one's own behaviour, etc.

self-justifying *adj* offering excuses for one's behaviour, often when they are not called for.

self-knowledge *n* knowledge of one's own character, etc.

selfless (ˈsɛlflɪs) *adj* having little concern for one's own interests. ▸ **ˈselflessly** *adv* ▸ **ˈselflessness** *n*

self-liquidating *adj* **1** (of a loan, bill of exchange, etc.) used to finance transactions whose proceeds are expected to accrue before the date of redemption or repayment. **2** (of a business transaction, project, investment, etc.) yielding proceeds sufficient to cover the initial outlay or to finance any recurrent outlays.

self-loading *adj* (of a firearm) utilizing some of the force of the explosion to eject the empty shell and replace it with a new one. Also: **autoloading.** See also **automatic** (sense 5), **semiautomatic** (sense 2). ▸ **ˌself-ˈloader** *n*

self-love *n* the instinct or tendency to seek one's own well-being or to further one's own interest.

self-made *adj* **1** having achieved wealth, status, etc., by one's own efforts. **2** made by oneself.

self-opinionated *or (less commonly)* **self-opinioned** *adj* **1** having an unduly high regard for oneself or one's own opinions. **2** clinging stubbornly to one's own opinions.

self-pity *n* the act or state of pitying oneself, esp. in an exaggerated or self-indulgent manner. ▸ **ˌself-ˈpitying** *adj* ▸ **ˌself-ˈpityingly** *adv*

self-pollination *n* the transfer of pollen from the anthers to the stigma of the same flower. Compare **cross-pollination.** ▸ **ˌself-ˈpolliˌnated** *adj*

self-possessed *adj* having control of one's emotions, etc. ▸ **ˌself-posˈsessedly** *adv* ▸ **ˌself-posˈsession** *n*

self-preservation *n* the preservation of oneself from danger or injury, esp. as a basic instinct.

self-pronouncing *adj* (in a phonetic transcription) of, relating to, or denoting a word that, except for additional diacritic marks of stress, may keep the letters of its ordinary orthography to represent its pronunciation.

self-propelled *adj* (of a vehicle) provided with its own source of tractive power rather than requiring an external means of propulsion. ▸ **ˌself-proˈpelling** *adj*

self-raising *adj* (of flour) having a raising agent, such as baking powder, already added.

self-realization *n* the realization or fulfilment of one's own potential or abilities.

self-regard *n* **1** concern for one's own interest. **2** proper esteem for oneself.

self-regarding *adj* **1** self-centred; egotistical. **2** *Philosophy.* (of an action) affecting the interests of no-one other than the agent, and hence, according to John Stuart Mill, immune from moral criticism.

self-regulating organization *n* one of several British organizations set up in 1986 under the auspices of the Securities and Investment Board to regulate the activities of London investment markets. Abbrev.: **SRO.**

self-reliance *n* reliance on one's own abilities, decisions, etc. ▸ **ˌself-reˈliant** *adj* ▸ **ˌself-reˈliantly** *adv*

self-renunciation *n* the renunciation of one's own rights, claims, interest, etc., esp. in favour of those of others. ▸ **ˌself-reˈnunciatory** *adj*

self-reproach *n* the act of finding fault with or blaming oneself. ▸ **ˌself-reˈproachful** *adj* ▸ **ˌself-reˈproachfully** *adv*

self-respect *n* a proper sense of one's own dignity and integrity. ▸ **ˌself-reˈspectful** *or* **ˌself-reˈspecting** *adj*

ˌself-deˈlusion *n*
ˌself-deˈstruct *vb*
ˌself-deˈstruction *n*
ˌself-deˈvelopment *n*
ˌself-diˈrected *adj*
ˌself-ˈdoubt *n*
ˌself-eˈlected *adj*
ˌself-enˈclosed *adj*
ˌself-enˈrichment *n*
ˌself-fiˈnanced *adj*
ˌself-fiˈnancing *adj*
ˌself-fulˈfilling *adj*
ˌself-fulˈfilment *n*
ˌself-ˈgenerˌating *adj*
ˌself-ˈhate *n*
ˌself-ˈhatred *n*
ˌself-ˈhealing *n*
ˌself-hypˈnosis *n*
ˌself-ˌimmoˈlation *n*
ˌself-imˈposed *adj*
ˌself-inˈflicted *adj*
ˌself-inˈitiˌated *adj*
ˌself-ˈlocking *adj*
ˌself-ˈmastery *n*
ˌself-ˈmockery *n*
ˌself-ˈmotiˌvated *adj*
ˌself-ˈmoving *adj*
ˌself-ˌmutiˈlation *n*
ˌself-oˈpinion *n*
ˌself-ˈparody *n*
ˌself-perˈpetuˌating *adj*
ˌself-ˈportrait *n*
ˌself-ˈpowered *adj*
ˌself-ˈpraise *n*
ˌself-proˈclaimed *adj*
ˌself-proˈduced *adj*
ˌself-proˈfessed *adj*
ˌself-proˈmotion *n*
ˌself-ˈpropaˌgating *adj*
ˌself-proˈtection *n*
ˌself-proˈtective *adj*
ˌself-ˈpunishment *n*
ˌself-ˈquestioning *adj*
ˌself-reˈflection *n*
ˌself-ˈreguˌlating *adj*

self-restraint *n* restraint imposed by oneself on one's own feelings, desires, etc.
self-righteous *adj* having or showing an exaggerated awareness of one's own virtuousness or rights. ► ˌ**self-'righteously** *adv* ► ˌ**self-'righteousness** *n*
self-rule *n* another term for **self-government** (sense 1).
self-sacrifice *n* the sacrifice of one's own desires, interest, etc., for the sake of duty or for the well-being of others. ► ˌ**self-'sacriˌficing** *adj* ► ˌ**self-'sacriˌficingly** *adv*
selfsame ('sɛlfˌseɪm) *adj (prenominal)* the very same.
self-satisfied *adj* having or showing a complacent satisfaction with oneself, one's own actions, behaviour, etc. ► ˌ**self-ˌsatis'faction** *n*
self-sealing *adj* (esp. of an envelope) designed to become sealed with the application of pressure only.
self-seeking *n* **1** the act or an instance of seeking one's own profit or interest, esp. exclusively. ◆ *adj* **2** having or showing an exclusive preoccupation with one's own profit or interest: *a self-seeking attitude.* ► ˌ**self-'seeker** *n*
self-service *adj* **1** of or denoting a shop, restaurant, petrol station, etc., where the customer serves himself. ◆ *n* **2** the practice of serving oneself, as in a shop, etc.
self-serving *adj* habitually seeking one's own advantage, esp. at the expense of others.
self-sown *adj* (of plants) growing from seed dispersed by any means other than by the agency of man or animals. Also: **self-seeded.**
self-starter *n* **1** an electric motor used to start an internal-combustion engine. **2** the switch that operates this motor. **3** a person who is strongly motivated and shows initiative, esp. at work.
self-styled *adj (prenominal)* claiming to be of a specified nature, quality, profession, etc.: *a self-styled expert.*
self-sufficient *or* **self-sufficing** *adj* able to provide for or support oneself without the help of others. ► ˌ**self-suf'ficiency** *n* ► ˌ**self-suf'ficiently** *adv*
self-suggestion *n* another term for **autosuggestion.**
self-supporting *adj* **1** able to support or maintain oneself without the help of others. **2** able to stand up or hold firm without support, props, attachments, etc.
self-tapping *adj* (of a screw) cutting its own thread when screwed into a plain hole in a metal sheet.
self-tender *n* an offer by a company to buy back some or all of its shares from its shareholders, esp. as a protection against an unwelcome takeover bid.
self-violence *n Euphemistic.* suicide.
self-will *n* stubborn adherence to one's own will, desires, etc., esp. at the expense of others. ► ˌ**self-'willed** *adj*
self-winding *adj* (of a wrist watch) having a mechanism, activated by the movements of the wearer, in which a rotating or oscillating weight rewinds the mainspring.
Seljuk (sɛl'dʒuːk) *or* **Seljukian** (sɛl'dʒuːkɪən) *n* **1** a member of any of the pre-Ottoman Turkish dynasties ruling over large parts of Asia in the 11th, 12th, and 13th centuries A.D. ◆ *adj* **2** of or relating to these dynasties or to their subjects. **[C19:** from Turkish**]**
selkie ('sɛlkɪ) *n Scot.* a variant of **silkie.**
Selkirk ('sɛlˌkɜːk) *n* **Alexander.** original name *Alexander Selcraig.* 1676–1721, Scottish sailor, who was marooned on one of the islets of Juan Fernández and is regarded as the prototype of Defoe's *Robinson Crusoe.*
Selkirk Mountains *pl n* a mountain range in SW Canada, in SE British Columbia. Highest peak: Mount Sir Sandford, 3533 m (11 590 ft.).
Selkirkshire ('sɛlkɜːkˌʃɪə, -ʃə) *n* (until 1975) a county of SE Scotland, now part of Scottish Borders.
sell (sɛl) *vb* **sells, selling, sold. 1** to dispose of or transfer or be disposed of or transferred to a purchaser in exchange for money or other consideration; put or be on sale. **2** to deal in (objects, property, etc.): *he sells used cars for a living.* **3** *(tr)* to give up or surrender for a price or reward: *to sell one's honour.* **4** to promote or facilitate the sale of (objects, property, etc.): *publicity sells many products.* **5** to induce or gain acceptance of: *to sell an idea.* **6** *(intr)* to be in demand on the market: *these dresses sell well in the spring.* **7** *(tr) Informal.* to deceive or cheat. **8** *(tr;* foll. by *on)* to persuade to accept or approve (of): *to sell a buyer on a purchase.* **9 sell down the river.** *Informal.* to betray. **10 sell oneself. 10a** to convince someone else of one's potential or worth. **10b** to give up one's moral or spiritual standards, etc. **11 sell short. 11a** *Informal.* to disparage or belittle. **11b** *Finance.* to sell securities or goods without owning them in anticipation of buying them before delivery at a lower price. ◆ *n* **12** the act or an instance of selling. Compare **hard sell, soft sell. 13** *Informal.* **13a** a trick, hoax, or deception. **13b** *Irish.* a great disappointment: *the service in the hotel was a sell.* ◆ See also **sell off, sell out, sell up. [**Old English *sellan* to lend, deliver; related to Old Norse *selja* to sell, Gothic *saljan* to offer sacrifice, Old High German *sellen* to sell, Latin *cōnsilium* advice**]** ► **'sellable** *adj*
Sellafield ('sɛləˌfiːld) *n* the site of an atomic power station and nuclear reprocessing plant in NW England, in W Cumbria. Former name: **Windscale.**
sell-by date *n* **1** a date printed on the packaging of perishable goods, indicating the date after which the goods should not be offered for sale. **2 past one's sell-by date.** *Informal.* beyond one's prime.
seller ('sɛlə) *n* **1** a person who sells. **2** an article to be sold: *this item is always a good seller.* **3** short for **selling race.**
Sellers ('sɛləz) *n* **Peter.** 1925–80, English radio, stage, and film actor and comedian: noted for his gift of precise vocal mimicry, esp. in *The Goon Show* (with Spike Milligan and Harry Secombe; BBC Radio, 1952–60). His films include *The Lady Killers* (1955), *I'm All Right, Jack* (1959), *The Millionairess* (1961), *Only Two Can Play* (1962), *The Pink Panther* (1963), *Dr Strangelove* (1964), and *Being There* (1979).
sellers' market *n* a market in which demand exceeds supply and sellers can influence prices.
Sellers screw thread *n* a thread form in a system of standard sizes proposed by Sellers in 1884 and later accepted as standard in the U.S.A., having a 60° flank angle with a flat top and foot. **[**named after William *Sellers* (1824–1905), U.S. engineer**]**
selling-plater *n* **1** a horse that competes, or is only good enough to compete, in a selling race. **2** a person or thing of limited ability or value.
selling race *or* **plate** *n* a horse race in which the winner must be offered for sale at auction.
sell off *vb (tr, adv)* to sell (remaining or unprofitable items), esp. at low prices.
Sellotape ('sɛləˌteɪp) *n* **1** *Trademark.* a type of transparent adhesive tape made of cellulose or a similar substance. ◆ *vb* **2** *(tr)* to seal or stick using adhesive tape.
sell out *vb (adv)* **1** Also (chiefly Brit.): **sell up.** to dispose of (supplies of something) completely by selling. **2** *(tr) Informal.* to betray, esp. through a secret agreement. **3** *(intr) Informal.* to abandon one's principles, standards, etc.: *his best friends were accusing him of selling out.* ◆ *n* **sellout. 4** *Informal.* a performance for which all tickets are sold. **5** a commercial success. **6** *Informal.* a betrayal.
sell-through *adj* **1** (of prerecorded video cassettes) sold without first being available for hire only. ◆ *n* **2** the sale of prerecorded video cassettes in this way.
sell up *vb (adv) Chiefly Brit.* **1** *(tr)* to sell all (the possessions or assets) of (a bankrupt debtor) in order to discharge his debts as far as possible. **2** *(intr)* to sell a business.
selsyn ('sɛlsɪn) *n* another name for **synchro. [**from SEL(F-) + SYN(CHRONOUS)**]**
sel-sync ('sɛlˌsɪŋk) *n* short for **selective synchronization.**
Seltzer ('sɛltsə) *n* **1** a natural effervescent water with a high content of minerals. **2** a similar synthetic water, used as a beverage. ◆ Also called: **Seltzer water. [C18:** changed from German *Selterser Wasser* water from *(Nieder) Selters,* district where mineral springs are located, near Wiesbaden, Germany**]**
selva ('sɛlvə) *n* **1** dense equatorial forest, esp. in the Amazon basin, characterized by tall broad-leaved evergreen trees, epiphytes, lianas, etc. **2** a tract of such forest. **[C19:** from Spanish and Portuguese, from Latin *silva* forest**]**
selvage *or* **selvedge** ('sɛlvɪdʒ) *n* **1** the finished nonfraying edge of a length of woven fabric. **2** a similar strip of material allowed in fabricating a metal or plastic article, used esp. for handling components during manufacture. **[C15:** from SELF + EDGE; related to Dutch *selfegghe,* German *Selbende***]** ► **'selvaged** *adj*
selves (sɛlvz) *n* **a** the plural of **self. b** *(in combination): ourselves, yourselves, themselves.*
Selznick ('sɛlznɪk) *n* **David O(liver).** 1902–62, U.S. film producer, who produced such films as *A Star is Born* (1937), *Gone with the Wind* (1939), and *A Farewell to Arms* (1957).
sem. *abbrev. for:* **1** semester. **2** semicolon.
Sem. *abbrev. for:* **1** Seminary. **2** Semitic.
semanteme (sɪ'mæntiːm) *n* another word for **sememe** (sense 2).
semantic (sɪ'mæntɪk) *adj* **1** of or relating to meaning or arising from distinctions between the meanings of different words or symbols. **2** of or relating to semantics. **3** *Logic.* concerned with the interpretation of a formal theory, as when truth tables are given as an account of the sentential connectives. **[C19:** from Greek *sēmantikos* having significance, from *sēmainein* to signify, from *sēma* a sign**]** ► **se'mantically** *adv*
semantics (sɪ'mæntɪks) *n (functioning as sing)* **1** the branch of linguistics that deals with the study of meaning, changes in meaning, and the principles that govern the relationship between sentences or words and their meanings. **2** the study of the relationships between signs and symbols and what they represent. **3** *Logic.* **3a** the study of interpretations of a formal theory. **3b** the study of the relationship between the structure of a theory and its subject matter. **3c** (of a formal theory) the principles that determine the truth or falsehood of sentences within the theory, and the references of its terms. ► **se'manticist** *n*
semantic tableau *n Logic.* **1** a method of demonstrating the consistency or otherwise of a set of statements by constructing a diagrammatic representation of all the circumstances that satisfy the set of statements. **2** the diagram so constructed.
semaphore ('sɛməˌfɔː) *n* **1** an apparatus for conveying information by means of visual signals, as with movable arms or railway signals, flags, etc. **2** a system of signalling by holding a flag in each hand and moving the arms to designated positions to denote each letter of the alphabet. ◆ *vb* **3** to signal (information) by means of semaphore. **[C19:** via French, from Greek *sēma* a signal + -PHORE**]** ► **semaphoric** (ˌsɛmə'fɒrɪk) *or* ˌ**sema'phorical** *adj* ► ˌ**sema'phorically** *adv*
Semarang *or* **Samarang** (sə'mɑːrɑːŋ) *n* a port in S Indonesia, in N Java on the Java Sea. Pop.: 1 365 500 (1995 est.).
semasiology (sɪˌmeɪsɪ'ɒlədʒɪ) *n* another name for **semantics. [C19:** from Greek *sēmasia* meaning, from *sēmainein* to signify + -LOGY**]** ► **semasiological** (sɪˌmeɪsɪə'lɒdʒɪkᵊl) *adj* ► **seˌmasio'logically** *adv* ► **seˌmasi'ologist** *n*
sematic (sɪ'mætɪk) *adj* (of the conspicuous coloration of certain animals) acting as a warning, esp. to potential predators. **[C19:** from Greek *sēma* a sign**]**

ˌ**self-'righting** *adj*
ˌ**self-'taught** *adj*
ˌ**self-'torture** *n*
ˌ**self-ˌtransfor'mation** *n*
ˌ**self-'treatment** *n*
ˌ**self-ˌunder'standing** *n*
ˌ**self-'worth** *n*

sematology (ˌsɛmə'tɒlədʒɪ) *n* another name for **semantics**. [C19: from Greek *sēmat-*, *sēma* sign + -LOGY]

semblable ('sɛmbləbᵊl) *Archaic*. ◆ *adj* **1** resembling or similar. **2** apparent rather than real. ◆ *n* **3** something that resembles another thing. **4** a resemblance. [C14: from Old French, from *sembler* to seem; see SEMBLANCE] ▸ **'semblably** *adv*

semblance ('sɛmbləns) *n* **1** outward appearance, esp. without any inner substance or reality. **2** a resemblance or copy. [C13: from Old French, from *sembler* to seem, from Latin *simulāre* to imitate, from *similis* like]

semé *or* **semée** ('sɛmeɪ; *French* səme) *adj* (*postpositive*) (usually foll. by *of*) *Heraldry*. dotted (with): *semé of fleurs-de-lys gules*. [C16: from French, literally: sown, from *semer* to sow, from Latin *sēmināre*, from *sēmen* seed]

semei- for words beginning thus, see the more common spelling in **semi-**.

Semele ('sɛmɪlɪ) *n Greek myth*. mother of Dionysus by Zeus.

sememe ('siːmiːm) *n Linguistics*. **1** the meaning of a morpheme. **2** Also called: **semanteme**. a minimum unit of meaning in terms of which it is sometimes proposed that meaning in general might be analysed. [C20 (coined in 1933 by L. BLOOMFIELD): from Greek *sēma* a sign + -EME]

semen ('siːmɛn) *n* **1** the thick whitish fluid containing spermatozoa that is ejaculated from the male genital tract. **2** another name for **sperm**[1]. [C14: from Latin: seed]

Semeru *or* **Semeroe** (sə'mɛruː) *n* a volcano in Indonesia: the highest peak in Java. Height: 3676 m (12 060 ft.).

semester (sɪ'mɛstə) *n* **1** *Chiefly U.S. and Canadian*. either of two divisions of the academic year, ranging from 15 to 18 weeks. **2** (in German universities) a session of six months. [C19: via German from Latin *sēmestris* half-yearly, from *sex* six + *mensis* a month] ▸ **se'mestral** *adj*

semi ('sɛmɪ) *n, pl* **semis**. *Informal*. **1** *Brit*. short for **semidetached (house)**. **2** short for **semifinal**. **3** *U.S., Canadian, Austral., and N.Z.* short for **semi-trailer**.

semi- *prefix* **1** half: *semicircle*. Compare **demi-** (sense 1), **hemi-**. **2** partially, partly, not completely, or almost: *semiprofessional; semifinal*. **3** occurring twice in a specified period of time: *semiannual; semiweekly*. [from Latin; compare Old English *sōm-*, *sām-* half, Greek *hēmi-*]

semiannual (ˌsɛmɪ'ænjʊəl) *adj* **1** occurring every half-year. **2** lasting for half a year. ▸ **ˌsemi'annually** *adv*

semiaquatic (ˌsɛmɪə'kwætɪk) *adj* (of organisms, esp. plants) occurring close to the water and sometimes within it.

semiarid (ˌsɛmɪ'ærɪd) *adj* characterized by scanty rainfall and scrubby vegetation, often occurring in continental interiors. ▸ **ˌsemia'ridity** *n*

semiautomatic (ˌsɛmɪˌɔːtə'mætɪk) *adj* **1** partly automatic. **2** (of a firearm) self-loading but firing only one shot at each pull of the trigger. Compare **automatic** (sense 5). ◆ *n* **3** a semiautomatic firearm. ▸ **ˌsemiˌauto'matically** *adv*

Semi-Bantu *n* **1** a group of languages of W Africa, mainly SE Nigeria and Cameroon, that were not traditionally classed as Bantu but that show certain essential Bantu characteristics. They are now classed with Bantu in the Benue-Congo branch of the Niger-Congo family. ◆ *adj* **2** relating to or belonging to this group of languages.

semibold (ˌsɛmɪ'bəʊld) *Printing*. ◆ *adj* **1** denoting a weight of typeface between medium and bold face. **2** denoting matter printed in this. ◆ *n* **3** semibold type.

semibreve ('sɛmɪˌbriːv) *n Music*. a note, now the longest in common use, having a time value that may be divided by any power of 2 to give all other notes. Usual U.S. and Canadian name: **whole note**. See also **breve** (sense 2).

semicentennial (ˌsɛmɪsɛn'tɛnɪəl) *adj* **1** (*prenominal*) of or relating to the 50th anniversary of some event. **2** occurring once every 50 years. ◆ *n* **3** a 50th anniversary.

semicircle ('sɛmɪˌsɜːkᵊl) *n* **1a** one half of a circle. **1b** half the circumference of a circle. **2** anything having the shape or form of half a circle. ▸ **semicircular** (ˌsɛmɪ'sɜːkjʊlə) *adj* ▸ **ˌsemi'circularly** *adv*

semicircular canal *n Anatomy*. any of the three looped fluid-filled membranous tubes, at right angles to one another, that comprise the labyrinth of the ear: concerned with the sense of orientation and equilibrium.

semicolon (ˌsɛmɪ'kəʊlən) *n* the punctuation mark (;) used to indicate a pause intermediate in value or length between that of a comma and that of a full stop.

semiconductor (ˌsɛmɪkən'dʌktə) *n* **1** a substance, such as germanium or silicon, that has an electrical conductivity that increases with temperature and is intermediate between that of a metal and an insulator. The behaviour may be exhibited by the pure substance (**intrinsic semiconductor**) or as a result of impurities (**extrinsic semiconductor**). **2a** a device, such as a transistor or integrated circuit, that depends on the properties of such a substance. **2b** (*as modifier*): *a semiconductor diode*. ▸ **ˌsemicon'duction** *n*

semiconscious (ˌsɛmɪ'kɒnʃəs) *adj* not fully conscious. ▸ **ˌsemi'consciously** *adv* ▸ **ˌsemi'consciousness** *n*

semidetached (ˌsɛmɪdɪ'tætʃt) *adj* **a** (of a building) joined to another on one side by a common wall. **b** (*as n*): *they live in a suburban semidetached*.

semidiurnal (ˌsɛmɪdaɪ'ɜːnᵊl) *adj* **1** of or continuing during half a day. **2** occurring every 12 hours.

semidome ('sɛmɪˌdəʊm) *n* a half-dome, esp. one used to cover a semicircular apse.

semielliptical (ˌsɛmɪɪ'lɪptɪkᵊl) *adj* shaped like one half of an ellipse, esp. one divided along the major axis.

semifinal (ˌsɛmɪ'faɪnᵊl) *n* **a** the round before the final in a competition. **b** (*as modifier*): *the semifinal draw*.

semifinalist (ˌsɛmɪ'faɪnᵊlɪst) *n* a player or team taking part in a semifinal.

semifluid (ˌsɛmɪ'fluːɪd) *adj also* (*rarely*) **semifluidic** (ˌsɛmɪfluː'ɪdɪk). **1** having properties between those of a liquid and those of a solid. ◆ *n* **2** a substance that has such properties because of high viscosity: *tar is a semifluid*. ◆ Also: **semiliquid**. ▸ **ˌsemiflu'idity** *n*

semiliterate (ˌsɛmɪ'lɪtərɪt) *adj* **1** hardly able to read or write. **2** able to read but not to write.

Sémillon ('seɪmiːjɒn; *French* semijõ) *n* **1** a white grape grown in the Bordeaux area of France and in Australia, used for making wine. **2** any of various white wines made from this grape. [French]

semilunar (ˌsɛmɪ'luːnə) *adj* shaped like a crescent or half-moon.

semilunar valve *n Anatomy*. either of two crescent-shaped valves, one in the aorta and one in the pulmonary artery, that prevent regurgitation of blood into the heart.

seminal ('sɛmɪnəl) *adj* **1** potentially capable of development. **2** highly original, influential and important. **3** rudimentary or unformed. **4** of or relating to semen: *seminal fluid*. **5** *Biology*. of or relating to seed. [C14: from Late Latin *sēminālis* belonging to seed, from Latin *sēmen* seed] ▸ **ˌsemi'nality** *n* ▸ **'seminally** *adv*

seminar ('sɛmɪˌnɑː) *n* **1** a small group of students meeting regularly under the guidance of a tutor, professor, etc., to exchange information, discuss theories, etc. **2** one such meeting or the place in which it is held. **3** a higher course for postgraduates. **4** any group or meeting for holding discussions or exchanging information. [C19: via German from Latin *sēminārium* SEMINARY]

seminarian (ˌsɛmɪ'nɛərɪən) *n* a student at a seminary.

seminary ('sɛmɪnərɪ) *n, pl* **-naries**. **1** an academy for the training of priests, rabbis, etc. **2** *U.S.* another word for **seminar** (sense 1). **3** a place where something is grown. [C15: from Latin *sēminārium* a nursery garden, from *sēmen* seed] ▸ **ˌsemi'narial** *adj*

semination (ˌsɛmɪ'neɪʃən) *n Rare*. the production, dispersal, or sowing of seed. [C16: from Late Latin *sēminātiō*, from Latin *sēmināre* to sow, from *sēmen* seed]

seminiferous (ˌsɛmɪ'nɪfərəs) *adj* **1** containing, conveying, or producing semen: *the seminiferous tubules of the testes*. **2** (of plants) bearing or producing seeds. [C17: from Latin *sēmin-*, *sēmen* seed + connecting vowel + -FEROUS]

Seminole ('sɛmɪˌnəʊl) *n* **1** (*pl* **-noles** *or* **-nole**) a member of a North American Indian people consisting of Creeks who moved into Florida in the 18th century. **2** the language of this people, belonging to the Muskhogean family. [from Creek *simanó-li* fugitive, from American Spanish *cimarrón* runaway]

semiochemical (ˌsɛmɪəʊ'kɛmɪkᵊl) *n* a chemical substance produced by an animal and used in communications, such as a pheromone. [C20: *semio-* from Greek *sēmeion* a sign + CHEMICAL]

semiology *or* **semeiology** (ˌsɛmɪ'ɒlədʒɪ, ˌsiːmɪ-) *n* another word for **semiotics**. [C17 (in the sense "sign language"): from Greek *sēmeion* sign + -LOGY] ▸ **semiologic** (ˌsɛmɪə'lɒdʒɪk, ˌsiːmɪ-), **ˌsemio'logical** *or* **ˌsemeio'logic**, **ˌsemeio'logical** *adj* ▸ **ˌsemi'ologist** *or* **ˌsemei'ologist** *n*

semiotic *or* **semeiotic** (ˌsɛmɪ'ɒtɪk, ˌsiːmɪ-) *adj* **1** relating to signs and symbols, esp. spoken or written signs. **2** relating to semiotics. **3** of, relating to, or resembling the symptoms of disease; symptomatic. [C17: from Greek *sēmeiōtikos* taking note of signs, from *sēmeion* a sign]

semiotician (ˌsɛmɪə'tɪʃən) *n* a person who studies semiotics.

semiotics *or* **semeiotics** (ˌsɛmɪ'ɒtɪks, ˌsiːmɪ-) *n* (*functioning as sing*) **1** the study of signs and symbols, esp. the relations between written or spoken signs and their referents in the physical world or the world of ideas. See also **semantics, syntactics, pragmatics**. **2** the scientific study of the symptoms of disease; symptomatology. ◆ Also called: **semiology, semeiology**.

Semipalatinsk (*Russian* sɪmipa'latinsk) *n* a city in NE Kazakhstan on the Irtysh River; an important communications centre. Pop.: 320 200 (1995 est.).

semipalmate (ˌsɛmɪ'pælmɪt) *or* **semipalmated** *adj* (of the feet of some birds) having the front three toes partly webbed.

semiparasitic (ˌsɛmɪˌpærə'sɪtɪk) *adj* **1** (of plants) obtaining shelter and some food from a host but undergoing photosynthesis at the same time. **2** (of bacteria or fungi) usually parasitic but capable of living as a saprotroph. ▸ **semiparasite** (ˌsɛmɪ'pærəsaɪt) *n* ▸ **semiparasitism** (ˌsɛmɪ'pærəsɪˌtɪzəm) *n*

semipermeable (ˌsɛmɪ'pɜːmɪəbᵊl) *adj* (esp. of a cell membrane) selectively permeable. ▸ **ˌsemiˌpermea'bility** *n*

semipolar bond (ˌsɛmɪ'pəʊlə) *n Chem*. another name for **coordinate bond**.

semiporcelain (ˌsɛmɪ'pɔːslɪn) *n* a durable porcellaneous stoneware; stone china.

semipostal (ˌsɛmɪ'pəʊstᵊl) *adj Philately, chiefly U.S.* denoting stamps where all or part of the receipts from sale are given to some charitable cause.

semiprecious (ˌsɛmɪ'prɛʃəs) *adj* (of certain stones) having less value than a precious stone.

semipro ('sɛmɪˌprəʊ) *adj, n, pl* **-pros**. short for **semiprofessional**.

semiprofessional (ˌsɛmɪprə'fɛʃənᵊl) *adj* **1** (of a person) engaged in an activity or sport part-time but for pay. **2** (of an activity or sport) engaged in by semiprofessional people. **3** of or relating to a person whose activities are professional in some respects: *a semiprofessional pianist*. ◆ *n* **4** a semiprofessional person. ▸ **ˌsemipro'fessionally** *adv*

semiquaver ('sɛmɪˌkweɪvə) *n Music*. a note having the time value of one-sixteenth of a semibreve. Usual U.S. and Canadian name: **sixteenth note**.

Semiramis (sɛ'mɪrəmɪs) *n* the legendary founder of Babylon and wife of Ninus, king of Assyria, which she ruled with great skill after his death.

semirigid (ˌsɛmɪ'rɪdʒɪd) *adj* **1** partly but not wholly rigid. **2** (of an airship) maintaining shape by means of a main supporting keel and internal gas pressure.

semiskilled (ˌsɛmɪ'skɪld) *adj* partly skilled or trained but not sufficiently so to perform specialized work.

semisolid (ˌsɛmɪ'sɒlɪd) *adj* **1a** having a viscosity and rigidity intermediate between that of a solid and a liquid. **1b** partly solid. ◆ *n* **2** a substance in this state.

semisolus (ˌsɛmɪˈsəʊləs) *n* an advertisement that appears on the same page as another advertisement but not adjacent to it.

semisubmersible rig *n* (in the oil industry) a type of drilling platform that floats supported by underwater pontoons, with much of its structure below the water line for stability in high winds: usually used only for exploratory drilling for oil or gas. Sometimes shortened to **semisubmersible.**

Semite (ˈsiːmaɪt) *or (less commonly)* **Shemite** *n* **1** a member of the group of Caucasoid peoples who speak a Semitic language, including the Jews and Arabs as well as the ancient Babylonians, Assyrians, and Phoenicians. **2** another word for a **Jew.** [C19: from New Latin *sēmīta* descendant of Shem, via Greek *Sēm,* from Hebrew SHEM]

Semitic (sɪˈmɪtɪk) *or (less commonly)* **Shemitic** *n* **1** a branch or subfamily of the Afro-Asiatic family of languages that includes Arabic, Hebrew, Aramaic, Amharic, and such ancient languages as Akkadian and Phoenician. ◆ *adj* **2** denoting, relating to, or belonging to this group of languages. **3** denoting, belonging to, or characteristic of any of the peoples speaking a Semitic language, esp. the Jews or the Arabs. **4** another word for **Jewish.**

Semitics (sɪˈmɪtɪks) *n (functioning as sing)* the study of Semitic languages and culture. ► **Semitist** (ˈsɛmɪtɪst) *n*

Semito-Hamitic (ˈsɛmɪtəʊhæˈmɪtɪk) *n* **1** a former name for the **Afro-Asiatic** family of languages. ◆ *adj* **2** denoting or belonging to this family of languages.

semitone (ˈsɛmɪˌtəʊn) *n* an interval corresponding to a frequency difference of 100 cents as measured in the system of equal temperament, and denoting the pitch difference between certain adjacent degrees of the diatonic scale (**diatonic semitone**) or between one note and its sharpened or flattened equivalent (**chromatic semitone**); minor second. Also called (U.S. and Canadian): **half step.** Compare **whole tone.** ► **semitonic** (ˌsɛmɪˈtɒnɪk) *adj* ► ˌ**semiˈtonally** *adv*

semitrailer (ˌsɛmɪˈtreɪlə) *n* a type of trailer or articulated lorry that has wheels only at the rear, the front end being supported by the towing vehicle.

semitropical (ˌsɛmɪˈtrɒpɪkᵊl) *adj* **1** partly tropical. **2** another word for **subtropical.** ► ˌ**semiˈtropics** *pl n*

semivitreous (ˌsɛmɪˈvɪtrɪəs) *adj* **1** partially vitreous. **2** *Ceramics.* not wholly impervious to liquid.

semivocal (ˌsɛmɪˈvəʊkᵊl) *or* **semivocalic** (ˌsɛmɪvəʊˈkælɪk) *adj* of or relating to a semivowel.

semivowel (ˈsɛmɪˌvaʊəl) *n Phonetics.* **1** a vowel-like sound that acts like a consonant, in that it serves the same function in a syllable carrying the same amount of prominence as a consonant relative to a true vowel, the nucleus of the syllable. In English and many other languages the chief semivowels are (w) in *well* and (j), represented as *y,* in *yell.* **2** a frictionless continuant classified as one of the liquids; (l) or (r). ◆ Also called: **glide.**

semiyearly (ˌsɛmɪˈjɪəlɪ) *adj* another word for **semiannual.**

Semmelweis (ˈsɛməlˌvaɪs) *n* **Ignaz Philipp.** 1818–65, Hungarian obstetrician, who discovered the cause of puerperal infection and pioneered the use of antiseptics.

semmit (ˈsɪmɪt, ˈsɛm-) *n Scot.* a vest. [C15: of unknown origin]

semolina (ˌsɛməˈliːnə) *n* the large hard grains of wheat left after flour has been bolted, used for puddings, soups, etc. [C18: from Italian *semolino,* diminutive of *semola* bran, from Latin *simila* very fine wheat flour]

Sempach (*German* ˈzɛmpax) *n* a village in central Switzerland, in Lucerne canton on **Lake Sempach:** scene of the victory (1386) of the Swiss over the Hapsburgs.

semper fidelis *Latin.* (ˈsɛmpə fɪˈdeɪlɪs) always faithful.

semper paratus *Latin.* (ˈsɛmpə pəˈrɑːtəs) always prepared.

sempervivum (ˌsɛmpəˈvaɪvəm) *n* See **houseleek.** [New Latin, from Latin *sempervivus* ever-living, from *semper* always + *vivere* to live]

sempiternal (ˌsɛmpɪˈtɜːnᵊl) *adj Literary.* everlasting; eternal. [C15: from Old French *sempiternel,* from Late Latin *sempiternālis,* from Latin *sempiternus,* from *semper* always + *aeternus* ETERNAL] ► ˌ**sempiˈternally** *adv* ► **sempiternity** (ˌsɛmpɪˈtɜːnɪtɪ) *n*

semplice (ˈsɛmplɪtʃɪ) *adj, adv Music.* to be performed in a simple manner. [Italian: simple, from Latin *simplex*]

sempre (ˈsɛmprɪ) *adv Music.* (preceding a tempo or dynamic marking) always; consistently. It is used to indicate that a specified volume, tempo, etc., is to be sustained throughout a piece or passage. [Italian: always, from Latin *semper*]

sempstress (ˈsɛmpstrɪs) *n* a rare word for **seamstress.**

Semtex (ˈsɛmtɛks) *n* a pliable plastic explosive. [C20: originally a trade name]

sen (sɛn) *n, pl* **sen.** a monetary unit of Brunei, worth one hundredth of a dollar, Cambodia, worth one hundredth of a riel, Indonesia, worth one hundredth of a rupiah, Malaysia, worth one hundredth of a ringgit, and formerly of Japan (where it is still used as a unit of account). [C19: ultimately from Chinese *ch'ien* coin]

SEN (in Britain) *abbrev. for:* **1** (formerly) State Enrolled Nurse. **2** special educational needs: needs arising from any of a wide range of problems that affect a pupil's normal educational development and for which special provisions are made.

Sen. *or* **sen.** *abbrev. for:* **1** senate. **2** senator. **3** senior.

sena (ˈseɪnɑː) *n* (in India) the army: used in the names of certain paramilitary political organizations. [Hindi]

senarmontite (ˌsɛnɑːˈmɒntaɪt) *n* a white or grey mineral consisting of antimony trioxide in cubic crystalline form. Formula: Sb_2O_3. [C19: named after Henri de *Sénarmont* (died 1862), French mineralogist]

senary (ˈsiːnərɪ) *adj* of or relating to the number six; having six parts or units. [C17: from Latin *sēnārius,* from *sēnī* six each, from *sex* SIX]

senate (ˈsɛnɪt) *n* **1** any legislative or governing body considered to resemble a Senate. **2** the main governing body at some colleges and universities. [C13: from Latin *senātus* council of the elders, from *senex* an old man]

Senate (ˈsɛnɪt) *n (sometimes not cap.)* **1** the upper chamber of the legislatures of the U.S., Canada, Australia, and many other countries. **2** the legislative council of ancient Rome. Originally the council of the kings, the Senate became the highest legislative, judicial, and religious authority in republican Rome. **3** the ruling body of certain free cities in medieval and modern Europe.

senator (ˈsɛnətə) *n* **1** *(often cap.)* a member of a Senate or senate. **2** any legislator or statesman.

senatorial (ˌsɛnəˈtɔːrɪəl) *adj* **1** of, relating to, befitting, or characteristic of a senator. **2** composed of senators. **3** *Chiefly U.S.* electing or entitled to representation by a senator: *senatorial districts.* ► ˌ**senaˈtorially** *adv*

senatus consultum *Latin.* (səˈnɑːtəs kənˈsʊltəm) *n, pl* ***senatus consulta*** (kənˈsʊltə). a decree of the Senate of ancient Rome, taking the form of advice to a magistrate.

send[1] (sɛnd) *vb* **sends, sending, sent. 1** *(tr)* to cause or order (a person or thing) to be taken, directed, or transmitted to another place: *to send a letter; she sent the salesman away.* **2** (when *intr,* foll. by *for;* when *tr, takes an infinitive*) to dispatch a request or command (for something or to do something): *he sent for a bottle of wine; he sent to his son to come home.* **3** *(tr)* to direct or cause to go to a place or point: *his blow sent the champion to the floor.* **4** *(tr)* to bring to a state or condition: *this noise will send me mad.* **5** *(tr;* often foll. by *forth, out,* etc.) to cause to issue; emit: *his cooking sent forth a lovely smell from the kitchen.* **6** *(tr)* to cause to happen or come: *misery sent by fate.* **7** to transmit (a message) by radio, esp. in the form of pulses. **8** *(tr) Slang.* to move to excitement or rapture: *this music really sends me.* **9 send (someone) about his** *or* **her business.** to dismiss or get rid of (someone). **10 send (someone) packing.** to dismiss or get rid of (someone) peremptorily. ◆ *n* **11** another word for **swash** (sense 4). ◆ See also **send down, sendoff, send up.** [Old English *sendan;* related to Old Norse *senda,* Gothic *sandjan,* Old High German *senten*] ► ˈ**sendable** *adj* ► ˈ**sender** *n*

send[2] (sɛnd) *vb* **sends, sending, sent,** *n* a variant spelling of **scend.**

Sendai (sɛnˈdaɪ) *n* a city in central Japan, on NE Honshu: university (1907). Pop.: 971 263 (1995).

Sendak (ˈsɛndæk) *n* **Maurice (Bernard).** born 1928, U.S. artist and set designer, best known as an illustrator of children's books, including *Where the Wild Things Are* (1963), *In the Night Kitchen* (1971), and *Nutcracker* (1984).

sendal (ˈsɛndᵊl) *n* **1** a fine silk fabric used, esp. in the Middle Ages, for ceremonial clothing, etc. **2** a garment of such fabric. [C13: from Old French *cendal,* from Medieval Latin *cendalum;* probably related to Greek *sindon* fine linen]

send down *vb (tr, adv) Brit.* **1** to expel from a university, esp. permanently. **2** *Informal.* to send to prison.

sendoff (ˈsɛndˌɒf) *n Informal.* **1** a demonstration of good wishes to a person about to set off on a journey, new career, etc. **2** a start, esp. an auspicious one, to a venture. ◆ *vb* **send off.** *(tr, adv)* **3** to cause to depart; despatch. **4** *Soccer, rugby, etc.* (of the referee) to dismiss (a player) from the field of play for some offence. **5** *Informal.* to give a sendoff to.

send up *vb (tr, adv)* **1** *Slang.* to send to prison. **2** *Brit. informal.* to make fun of, esp. by doing an imitation or parody of: *he sent up the teacher marvellously.* ◆ *n* **send-up. 3** *Brit. informal.* a parody or imitation.

Seneca[1] (ˈsɛnɪkə) *n* **1** *(pl* **-cas** *or* **-ca)** a member of a North American Indian people formerly living south of Lake Ontario; one of the Iroquois peoples. **2** the language of this people, belonging to the Iroquoian family. [C19: from Dutch *Sennecaas* (plural), probably of Algonquian origin]

Seneca[2] (ˈsɛnɪkə) *n* **1 Lucius Annaeus** (əˈniːəs), called *the Younger.* ?4 B.C.–65 A.D., Roman philosopher, statesman, and dramatist; tutor and adviser to Nero. He was implicated in a plot to murder Nero and committed suicide. His works include Stoical essays on ethical subjects and tragedies that had a considerable influence on Elizabethan drama. **2** his father, **Marcus** (ˈmɑːkəs) *or* **Lucius Annaeus,** called *the Elder* or *the Rhetorician.* ?55 B.C.–?39 A.D., Roman writer on oratory and history.

senecio (sɪˈniːʃɪəʊ) *n, pl* **-cios.** See **cineraria.**

Senefelder (ˈzenəˌfɛldə) *n* **(Johan Nepomuk Franz) Aloys** (ˈaloɪs). 1771–1834, German dramatist and engraver, born in Czechoslovakia, who invented (1796) lithography.

senega (ˈsɛnɪgə) *n* **1** a milkwort plant, *Polygala senega,* of the eastern U.S., with small white flowers. **2** the root of this plant, used as an expectorant. ◆ Also called: **senega snakeroot, seneca snakeroot.** [C18: variant of *Seneca* (the Indian tribe)]

Senegal (ˌsɛnɪˈgɔːl) *n* a republic in West Africa, on the Atlantic: made part of French West Africa in 1895; became fully independent in 1960; mostly low-lying, with semidesert in the north and tropical forest in the southwest. Official language: French. Religion: Muslim majority. Currency: franc. Capital: Dakar. Pop.: 9 723 000 (1998 est.). Area: 197 160 sq. km (76 124 sq. miles). ► **Senegalese** (ˌsɛnɪgəˈliːz) *adj, n*

Senegambia (ˌsɛnəˈgæmbɪə) *n* a region of W Africa, between the Senegal and Gambia Rivers: now mostly in Senegal.

Senegambia Confederation *n* an economic and political union (1982–89) between Senegal and The Gambia.

senescent (sɪˈnɛsᵊnt) *adj* **1** growing old. **2** characteristic of old age. [C17: from Latin *senēscere* to grow old, from *senex* old] ► **seˈnescence** *n*

seneschal (ˈsɛnɪʃəl) *n* **1** a steward of the household of a medieval prince or nobleman who took charge of domestic arrangements, etc. **2** *Brit.* a cathedral official. [C14: from Old French, from Medieval Latin *siniscalcus,* of Germanic origin; related to Old High German *senescalh* oldest servant, from *sene-* old + *scalh* a servant]

Senghor (*French* sɑ̃gɔr) *n* **Léopold Sédar** (leɔpɔl sedar). born 1906, Senegalese statesman and writer; president of Senegal (1960–80).

senile (ˈsiːnaɪl) *adj* **1** of, relating to, or characteristic of old age. **2** mentally or physically weak or infirm on account of old age. **3** (of land forms or rivers) at an advanced stage in the cycle of erosion. See **old** (sense 18). **[C17:** from Latin *senīlis,* from *senex* an old man**]** ▸ **'senilely** *adv* ▸ **senility** (sɪ'nɪlɪtɪ) *n*

senile dementia *n* dementia starting in old age with no clear physical cause.

senior ('siːnjə) *adj* **1** higher in rank or length of service. **2** older in years: *senior citizens.* **3** of or relating to adulthood, maturity, or old age: *senior privileges.* **4** *Education.* **4a** of, relating to, or designating more advanced or older pupils. **4b** of or relating to a secondary school. **5** *U.S.* of, relating to, or designating students in the fourth and final year at college. ◆ *n* **6** a senior person. **7a** a senior pupil, student, etc. **7b** a fellow of senior rank in an English university. **[C14:** from Latin: older, from *senex* old**]**

Senior ('siːnjə) *adj Chiefly U.S.* being the older: used to distinguish the father from the son with the same first name or names: *Charles Parker, Senior.* Abbrevs.: **Sr, Sen.**

senior aircraftman *n* a rank in the Royal Air Force comparable to that of a private in the army, though not the lowest rank in the Royal Air Force.

senior citizen *n* an old age pensioner.

senior common room *n* (in British universities, colleges, etc.) a common room for the use of academic staff. Compare **junior common room.**

seniority (ˌsiːnɪ'ɒrɪtɪ) *n, pl* **-ties. 1** the state of being senior. **2** precedence in rank, etc., due to senior status.

senior management *n* another term for **top management.**

senior service *n Brit.* the Royal Navy.

Senlac ('sɛnlæk) *n* a hill in Sussex: site of the Battle of Hastings in 1066.

senna ('sɛnə) *n* **1** any of various tropical plants of the caesalpiniaceous genus *Cassia,* esp. *C. angustifolia* (**Arabian senna**) and *C. acutifolia* (**Alexandrian senna**), having typically yellow flowers and long pods. **2 senna leaf.** the dried leaflets of any of these plants, used as a cathartic and laxative. ◆ See also **bladder senna. [C16:** via New Latin from Arabic *sanā***]**

Senna ('sɛnə) *n* **Ayrton** ('ɛətən). 1960–94, Brazilian racing driver: world champion (1988, 1990, 1991).

Sennacherib (sɛ'nækərɪb) *n* died 681 B.C., king of Assyria (705–681); son of Sargon II. He invaded Judah twice, defeated Babylon, and rebuilt Nineveh.

Sennar ('sɛnɑː, sɛ'nɑː) *n* **1** a region of the E Sudan, between the White Nile and the Blue Nile: a kingdom from the 16th to 19th centuries. **2** a town in this region, on the Blue Nile: the nearby **Sennar Dam** (1925) supplies irrigation water to Gezira. Pop.: 8000 (latest est.).

sennet ('sɛnɪt) *n* a fanfare: used as a stage direction in Elizabethan drama. **[C16:** probably variant of SIGNET (meaning "a sign")**]**

Sennett ('sɛnət) *n* **Mack,** original name *Michael Sinott.* 1884–1960, U.S. film producer and director, born in Canada, who produced many silent comedy films featuring the Keystone Kops, Charlie Chaplin, and Harold Lloyd, for the Keystone Company.

sennight *or* **se'nnight** ('sɛnaɪt) *n* an archaic word for **week. [**Old English *seofan nihte;* see SEVEN, NIGHT**]**

sennit ('sɛnɪt) *n* **1** a flat braided cordage used on ships. **2** plaited straw, grass, palm leaves, etc., as for making hats. **[C17:** of unknown origin**]**

señor (sɛ'njɔː; *Spanish* se'ɲor) *n, pl* **-ñors** *or* **-ñores** (*Spanish* -'ɲores). a Spaniard or Spanish-speaking man: a title of address equivalent to *Mr* when placed before a name or *sir* when used alone. **[**Spanish, from Latin *senior* an older man, SENIOR**]**

señora (sɛ'njɔːrə; *Spanish* se'ɲora) *n, pl* **-ras** (-rəz; *Spanish* -ras). a married Spanish or Spanish-speaking woman: a title of address equivalent to *Mrs* when placed before a name or *madam* when used alone.

señorita (ˌsɛnjɔː'riːtə; *Spanish* seɲo'rita) *n, pl* **-tas** (-təz; *Spanish* -tas). an unmarried Spanish or Spanish-speaking woman: a title of address equivalent to *Miss* when placed before a name or *madam* or *miss* when used alone.

sensate ('sɛnseɪt) *adj* **1** perceived by the senses. **2** *Obsolete.* having the power of sensation. **[C16:** from Late Latin *sensātus* endowed with sense, from Latin *sensus* SENSE**]** ▸ **'sensately** *adv*

sensation (sɛn'seɪʃən) *n* **1** the power of perceiving through the senses. **2** a physical condition or experience resulting from the stimulation of one of the sense organs: *a sensation of warmth.* **3** a general feeling or awareness: *a sensation of fear.* **4** a state of widespread public excitement: *his announcement caused a sensation.* **5** anything that causes such a state: *your speech was a sensation.* **[C17:** from Medieval Latin *sensātiō,* from Late Latin *sensātus* SENSATE**]** ▸ **sen'sationless** *adj*

sensational (sɛn'seɪʃənᵊl) *adj* **1** causing or intended to cause intense feelings, esp. of curiosity, horror, etc.: *sensational disclosures in the press.* **2** *Informal.* extremely good: *a sensational skater.* **3** of or relating to the faculty of sensation. **4** *Philosophy.* of or relating to sensationalism. ▸ **sen'sationally** *adv*

sensationalism (sɛn'seɪʃənᵊˌlɪzəm) *n* **1** the use of sensational language, etc., to arouse an intense emotional response. **2** such sensational matter itself. **3** *Philosophy.* **3a** the doctrine that knowledge cannot go beyond the analysis of experience. **3b** *Ethics.* the doctrine that the ability to gratify the senses is the only criterion of goodness. **4** *Psychol.* the theory that all experience and mental life may be explained in terms of sensations and remembered images. **5** *Aesthetics.* the theory of the beauty of sensuality in the arts. ◆ Also called (for senses 3, 4): **sensationism.** ▸ **sen'sationalist** *n, adj* ▸ **senˌsational'istic** *adj*

sensationalize *or* **sensationalise** (sɛn'seɪʃənəˌlaɪz) *vb* (*tr*) to cause (events, esp. in newspaper reports) to seem more vivid, shocking, etc., than they really are.

sense (sɛns) *n* **1** any of the faculties by which the mind receives information about the external world or about the state of the body. In addition to the five traditional faculties of sight, hearing, touch, taste, and smell, the term includes the means by which bodily position, temperature, pain, balance, etc., are perceived. **2** such faculties collectively; the ability to perceive. **3** a feeling perceived through one of the senses: *a sense of warmth.* **4** a mental perception or awareness: *a sense of happiness.* **5** moral discernment; understanding: *a sense of right and wrong.* **6** (*sometimes pl*) sound practical judgment or intelligence: *he is a man without any sense.* **7** reason or purpose: *what is the sense of going out in the rain?* **8** substance or gist; meaning: *what is the sense of this proverb?* **9** specific meaning; definition: *in what sense are you using the word?* **10** an opinion or consensus. **11** *Maths.* one of two opposite directions measured on a directed line; the sign of the measure as contrasted with the magnitude of a vector. **12 make sense.** to be reasonable or understandable. **13** *Logic, linguistics.* **13a** the import of an expression as contrasted with its referent. Thus *the morning star* and *the evening star* have the same reference, Venus, but different senses. **13b** the property of an expression by virtue of which its referent is determined. **13c** that which one grasps in understanding an expression. **14 take leave of one's senses.** See **leave**[2] (sense 8). ◆ *vb* (*tr*) **15** to perceive through one or more of the senses. **16** to apprehend or detect without or in advance of the evidence of the senses. **17** to understand. **18** *Computing.* **18a** to test or locate the position of (a part of computer hardware). **18b** to read (data). **[C14:** from Latin *sēnsus,* from *sentīre* to feel**]**

sense datum *n Philosophy.* a sensation detached both from any information it may convey and from its putative source in the external world, such as the bare awareness of a red visual field. Sense data are held by some philosophers to be the immediate objects of experience providing certain knowledge from which knowledge of material objects is inferred. See also **representationalism** (sense 1), **apriorism.**

senseless ('sɛnslɪs) *adj* **1** lacking in sense; foolish: *a senseless plan.* **2** lacking in feeling; unconscious. **3** lacking in perception; stupid. ▸ **'senselessly** *adv* ▸ **'senselessness** *n*

sense organ *n* a structure in animals that is specialized for receiving external or internal stimuli and transmitting them in the form of nervous impulses to the brain.

sensi ('sɛnseɪ) *n* a teacher or instructor, esp. of karate or judo. **[**Japanese: teacher, leader**]**

sensibilia (ˌsɛnsɪ'bɪlɪə) *n* that which can be sensed. **[**Latin, neuter plural of *sensibilis* SENSIBLE**]**

sensibility (ˌsɛnsɪ'bɪlɪtɪ) *n, pl* **-ties. 1** the ability to perceive or feel. **2** (*often pl*) the capacity for responding to emotion, impression, etc. **3** (*often pl*) the capacity for responding to aesthetic stimuli. **4** mental responsiveness; discernment; awareness. **5** (*usually pl*) emotional or moral feelings: *cruelty offends most people's sensibilities.* **6** the condition of a plant of being susceptible to external influences, esp. attack by parasites.

sensible ('sɛnsɪbᵊl) *adj* **1** having or showing good sense or judgment: *a sensible decision.* **2** (of clothing) serviceable; practical: *sensible shoes.* **3** having the capacity for sensation; sensitive. **4** capable of being apprehended by the senses. **5** perceptible to the mind. **6** (sometimes foll. by *of*) having perception; aware: *sensible of your kindness.* **7** readily perceived; considerable: *a sensible difference.* ◆ *n* **8** Also called: **sensible note.** a less common term for **leading note. [C14:** from Old French, from Late Latin *sēnsibilis,* from Latin *sentīre* to sense**]** ▸ **'sensibleness** *n* ▸ **'sensibly** *adv*

sensible horizon *n* See under **horizon** (sense 2a).

sensillum (sɛn'sɪləm) *n, pl* **-la** (-lə). a sense organ in insects, typically consisting of a receptor organ in the integument connected to sensory neurons. **[**New Latin, diminutive of Latin *sensus* sense (Middle Latin: sense organ)**]**

sensitive ('sɛnsɪtɪv) *adj* **1** having the power of sensation. **2** responsive to or aware of feelings, moods, reactions, etc. **3** easily irritated; delicate: *sensitive skin.* **4** affected by external conditions or stimuli. **5** easily offended. **6** of or relating to the senses or the power of sensation. **7** capable of registering small differences or changes in amounts, quality, etc.: *a sensitive instrument.* **8** *Photog.* having a high sensitivity: *a sensitive emulsion.* **9** connected with matters affecting national security, esp. through access to classified information. **10** (of a stock market or prices) quickly responsive to external influences and thus fluctuating or tending to fluctuate. **[C14:** from Medieval Latin *sēnsitīvus,* from Latin *sentīre* to feel**]** ▸ **'sensitively** *adv* ▸ **'sensitiveness** *n*

sensitive plant *n* **1** a tropical American mimosa plant, *Mimosa pudica,* the leaflets and stems of which fold if touched. **2** any similar plant, such as the caesalpiniaceous plant *Cassia nictitans* of E North America. **3** *Informal.* a person who is easily upset.

sensitivity (ˌsɛnsɪ'tɪvɪtɪ) *n, pl* **-ties. 1** the state or quality of being sensitive. **2** *Physiol.* the state, condition, or quality of reacting or being sensitive to an external stimulus, drug, allergen, etc. **3** *Electronics.* the magnitude or time of response of an instrument, circuit, etc., to an input signal, such as a current. **4** *Photog.* the degree of response of an emulsion to light or other actinic radiation, esp. to light of a particular colour, expressed in terms of its speed.

sensitize *or* **sensitise** ('sɛnsɪˌtaɪz) *vb* **1** to make or become sensitive. **2** (*tr*) to render (an individual) sensitive to a drug, allergen, etc. **3** (*tr*) *Photog.* to make (a material) sensitive to light or to other actinic radiation, esp. to light of a particular colour, by coating it with a photographic emulsion often containing special chemicals, such as dyes. ▸ **ˌsensiti'zation** *or* **ˌsensiti'sation** *n* ▸ **'sensiˌtizer** *or* **'sensiˌtiser** *n*

sensitometer (ˌsɛnsɪ'tɒmɪtə) *n* an instrument for measuring the sensitivity to light of a photographic material over a range of exposures. ▸ **ˌsensi'tometry** *n*

sensor ('sɛnsə) *n* anything, such as a photoelectric cell, that receives a signal or stimulus and responds to it. **[C19:** from Latin *sēnsus* perceived, from *sentīre* to observe**]**

sensorimotor (ˌsɛnsərɪ'məʊtə) *or* **sensomotor** (ˌsɛnsə'məʊtə) *adj* of or relating to both the sensory and motor functions of an organism or to the nerves controlling them.

sensorium (sɛn'sɔːrɪəm) *n, pl* **-riums** *or* **-ria** (-rɪə). **1** the area of the brain considered responsible for receiving and integrating sensations from the outside world. **2** *Physiol.* the entire sensory and intellectual apparatus of the body. [C17: from Late Latin, from Latin *sēnsus* felt, from *sentīre* to perceive]

sensory ('sɛnsərɪ) *or* (*less commonly*) **sensorial** (sɛn'sɔːrɪəl) *adj* **1** of or relating to the senses or the power of sensation. **2** of or relating to those processes and structures within an organism that receive stimuli from the environment and convey them to the brain. [C18: from Latin *sensōrius*, from *sentīre* to feel]

sensory deprivation *n Psychol.* an experimental situation in which all stimulation is cut off from the sensory receptors.

sensual ('sɛnsjʊəl) *adj* **1** of or relating to any of the senses or sense organs; bodily. **2** strongly or unduly inclined to gratification of the senses. **3** tending to arouse the bodily appetites, esp. the sexual appetite. **4** of or relating to sensualism. [C15: from Late Latin *sensuālis*, from Latin *sēnsus* SENSE. Compare French *sensuel*, Italian *sensuale*] ▸ **'sensually** *adv* ▸ **'sensualness** *n*

sensualism ('sɛnsjʊəˌlɪzəm) *n* **1** the quality or state of being sensual. **2** another word for **sensationalism** (senses 3a, 3b).

sensuality (ˌsɛnsjʊ'ælɪtɪ) *n, pl* **-ties. 1** the quality or state of being sensual. **2** excessive indulgence in sensual pleasures. ▸ **sensualist** ('sɛnsjʊəlɪst) *n*

sensum ('sɛnsəm) *n, pl* **-sa** (-sə). another word for **sense datum.**

sensuous ('sɛnsjʊəs) *adj* **1** aesthetically pleasing to the senses. **2** appreciative of or moved by qualities perceived by the senses. **3** of, relating to, or derived from the senses. [C17: apparently coined by Milton to avoid the unwanted overtones of SENSUAL; not in common use until C19: from Latin *sēnsus* SENSE + -OUS] ▸ **'sensuously** *adv* ▸ **'sensuousness** *n*

sent (sɛnt) *vb* the past tense and past participle of **send**[1] and **send**[2].

sentence ('sɛntəns) *n* **1** a sequence of words capable of standing alone to make an assertion, ask a question, or give a command, usually consisting of a subject and a predicate containing a finite verb. **2** the judgment formally pronounced upon a person convicted in criminal proceedings, esp. the decision as to what punishment is to be imposed. **3** an opinion, judgment, or decision. **4** *Music.* another word for **period** (sense 11). **5** any short passage of scripture employed in liturgical use: *the funeral sentences.* **6** *Logic.* a well-formed expression, without variables. **7** *Archaic.* a proverb, maxim, or aphorism. ◆ *vb* **8** (*tr*) to pronounce sentence on (a convicted person) in a court of law: *the judge sentenced the murderer to life imprisonment.* [C13: via Old French from Latin *sententia* a way of thinking, from *sentīre* to feel] ▸ **sentential** (sɛn'tɛnʃəl) *adj* ▸ **sen'tentially** *adv*

sentence connector *n* a word or phrase that introduces a clause or sentence and serves as a transition between it and a previous clause or sentence, as for example *also* in *I'm buying eggs and also I'm looking for a dessert for tonight.* It may be preceded by a coordinating conjunction such as *and* in the above example.

sentence stress *n* the stress given to a word or words in a sentence, often conveying nuances of meaning or emphasis.

sentence substitute *n* a word or phrase, esp. one traditionally classified as an adverb, that is used in place of a finite sentence, such as *yes, no, certainly,* and *never.*

sentential calculus *n Logic.* the formal theory the intended interpretation of which concerns the logical relations between sentences treated only as a whole and without regard to their internal structure.

sentential function *n* another name for **open sentence.**

sententious (sɛn'tɛnʃəs) *adj* **1** characterized by or full of aphorisms, terse pithy sayings, or axioms. **2** constantly using aphorisms, etc. **3** tending to indulge in pompous moralizing. [C15: from Latin *sententiōsus* full of meaning, from *sententia;* see SENTENCE] ▸ **sen'tentiously** *adv* ▸ **sen'tentiousness** *n*

sentience ('sɛnʃəns) *or* **sentiency** *n* **1** the state or quality of being sentient; awareness. **2** sense perception not involving intelligence or mental perception; feeling.

sentient ('sɛntɪənt) *adj* **1** having the power of sense perception or sensation; conscious. ◆ *n* **2** *Rare.* a sentient person or thing. [C17: from Latin *sentiēns* feeling, from *sentīre* to perceive] ▸ **'sentiently** *adv*

sentiment ('sɛntɪmənt) *n* **1** susceptibility to tender, delicate, or romantic emotion: *she has too much sentiment to be successful.* **2** (*often pl*) a thought, opinion, or attitude. **3** exaggerated, overindulged, or mawkish feeling or emotion. **4** an expression of response to deep feeling, esp. in art or literature. **5** a feeling, emotion, or awareness: *a sentiment of pity.* **6** a mental attitude modified or determined by feeling: *there is a strong revolutionary sentiment in his country.* **7** a feeling conveyed, or intended to be conveyed, in words. [C17: from Medieval Latin *sentīmentum*, from Latin *sentīre* to feel]

sentimental (ˌsɛntɪ'mɛntᵊl) *adj* **1** tending to indulge the emotions excessively. **2** making a direct appeal to the emotions, esp. to romantic feelings. **3** relating to or characterized by sentiment. ▸ **ˌsenti'mentally** *adv*

sentimentalism (ˌsɛntɪ'mɛntᵊˌlɪzəm) *n* **1** the state or quality of being sentimental. **2** an act, statement, etc., that is sentimental. ▸ **ˌsenti'mentalist** *n*

sentimentality (ˌsɛntɪmɛn'tælɪtɪ) *n, pl* **-ties. 1** the state, quality, or an instance of being sentimental. **2** an act, statement, etc., that is sentimental.

sentimentalize *or* **sentimentalise** (ˌsɛntɪ'mɛntᵊˌlaɪz) *vb* to make sentimental or behave sentimentally. ▸ **ˌsentiˌmentali'zation** *or* **ˌsentiˌmentali'sation** *n*

sentimental value *n* the value of an article in terms of its sentimental associations for a particular person.

sentinel ('sɛntɪnᵊl) *n* **1** a person, such as a sentry, assigned to keep guard. **2** *Computing.* a character used to indicate the beginning or end of a particular block of information. ◆ *vb* **-nells, -nelling, -nelled.** (*tr*) **3** to guard as a sentinel. **4** to post as a sentinel. **5** to provide with a sentinel. [C16: from Old French *sentinelle*, from Old Italian *sentinella*, from *sentina* watchfulness, from *sentire* to notice, from Latin]

sentry ('sɛntrɪ) *n, pl* **-tries. 1** a soldier who guards or prevents unauthorized access to a place, keeps watch for danger, etc. **2** the watch kept by a sentry. [C17: perhaps shortened from obsolete *centrinel*, C16 variant of SENTINEL]

sentry box *n* a small shelter with an open front in which a sentry may stand to be sheltered from the weather.

Senussi *or* **Senusi** (sɛ'nuːsɪ) *n, pl* **-sis.** a member of a zealous and aggressive Muslim sect of North Africa and Arabia, founded in 1837 by **Sidi Mohammed ibn Ali al Senussi** (?1787–1859). ▸ **Se'nussian** *or* **Se'nusian** *adj*

senza ('sɛntsɑː) *prep Music.* without; omitting. [Italian]

Seoul (səʊl) *n* the capital of South Korea, in the west on the Han River: capital of Korea from 1392 to 1910, then seat of the Japanese administration until 1945; became capital of South Korea in 1948; cultural and educational centre. Pop.: 10 229 262 (1995).

sep. *abbrev. for:* **1** sepal. **2** separate.

Sep. *abbrev. for:* **1** September. **2** Septuagint.

SEPA *abbrev. for* Scottish Environment Protection Agency.

sepal ('sɛpᵊl) *n* any of the separate parts of the calyx of a flower. [C19: from New Latin *sepalum: sep-*, from Greek *skepē* a covering + *-alum*, from New Latin *petalum* PETAL] ▸ **'sepalled** *or* **sepalous** ('sɛpələs) *adj*

sepaloid ('siːpəˌlɔɪd) *or* **sepaline** *adj* (esp. of petals) resembling a sepal in structure and function.

-sepalous *adj combining form.* having sepals of a specified type or number: *polysepalous.* ▸ **-sepaly** *n combining form.*

separable ('sɛpərəbᵊl, 'sɛprəbᵊl) *adj* able to be separated, divided, or parted. ▸ **ˌsepara'bility** *or* **'separableness** *n* ▸ **'separably** *adv*

separate *vb* ('sɛpəˌreɪt). **1** (*tr*) to act as a barrier between: *a range of mountains separates the two countries.* **2** to put or force or be put or forced apart. **3** to part or be parted from a mass or group. **4** (*tr*) to discriminate between: *to separate the men from the boys.* **5** to divide or be divided into component parts; sort or be sorted. **6** to sever or be severed. **7** (*intr*) (of a married couple) to cease living together by mutual agreement or after obtaining a decree of judicial separation. ◆ *adj* ('sɛprɪt, 'sɛpərɪt). **8** existing or considered independently: *a separate problem.* **9** disunited or apart. **10** set apart from the main body or mass. **11** distinct, individual, or particular. **12** solitary or withdrawn. **13** (*sometimes cap.*) designating or relating to a Church or similar institution that has ceased to have associations with an original parent organization. [C15: from Latin *sēparāre*, from *sē-* apart + *parāre* to obtain] ▸ **'separately** *adv* ▸ **'separateness** *n*

separates ('sɛprɪts, 'sɛpərɪts) *pl n* women's outer garments that only cover part of the body and so are worn in combination with others, usually unmatching; skirts, blouses, jackets, trousers, etc. Compare **coordinates.**

separate school *n* (in Canada) a school for a large religious minority financed by its rates and administered by its own school board but under the authority of the provincial department of education.

separating funnel *n Chem.* a large funnel having a tap in its output tube, used to separate immiscible liquids.

separation (ˌsɛpə'reɪʃən) *n* **1** the act of separating or state of being separated. **2** the place or line where a separation is made. **3** a gap that separates. **4** *Family law.* the cessation of cohabitation between a man and wife, either by mutual agreement or under a decree of a court. See **judicial separation.** Compare **divorce. 5a** the act of jettisoning a burnt-out stage of a multistage rocket. **5b** the instant at which such a stage is jettisoned.

separatist ('sɛpərətɪst, 'sɛprə-) *or* **separationist** *n* **a** a person who advocates or practises secession from an organization or group. **b** (*as modifier*): *a separatist movement.* ▸ **'separaˌtism** *n* ▸ **ˌsepara'tistic** *adj*

Separatist ('sɛpərətɪst, 'sɛprə-) *n* (*sometimes not cap.*) a person who advocates the secession of a province, esp. Quebec, from Canada. ▸ **'Separaˌtism** *n*

separative ('sɛpərətɪv, 'sɛprə-) *adj* tending to separate or causing separation. ▸ **'separatively** *adv* ▸ **'separativeness** *n*

separator ('sɛpəˌreɪtə) *n* **1** a person or thing that separates. **2** a device for separating things into constituent parts, as milk into cream, etc. ▸ **'separatory** *adj*

separatrix ('sɛpəˌreɪtrɪks) *n, pl* **separatrices** (ˌsɛpə'reɪtrɪˌsiːz). another name for **solidus** (sense 1). [via New Latin from Late Latin, feminine of *sēparātor* one that separates]

Sephardi (sɪ'fɑːdiː) *n, pl* **-dim** (-dɪm). *Judaism.* **1a** a Jew of Spanish, Portuguese, or North African descent. **1b** (loosely) any Oriental Jew. **2** the pronunciation of Hebrew used by these Jews, and of Modern Hebrew as spoken in Israel. **3** (*modifier*) of or pertaining to the Sephardim, esp. to their liturgy and ritual. **4** (*modifier*) of or pertaining to the liturgy adopted by certain European, esp. Chassidic, communities who believe it to be more authentic but nonetheless differing from the genuine Oriental liturgy. ◆ Compare **Ashkenazi.** [C19: from Late Hebrew, from Hebrew *sepharad* a region mentioned in Obadiah 20, thought to have been Spain] ▸ **Se'phardic** *adj*

sepia ('siːpɪə) *n* **1** a dark reddish-brown pigment obtained from the inky secretion of the cuttlefish. **2** any cuttlefish of the genus *Sepia.* **3** a brownish tone imparted to a photograph, esp. an early one such as a calotype. It can be produced by first bleaching a print (after fixing) and then immersing it for a short time in a solution of sodium sulphide or of alkaline thiourea. **4** a brownish-grey to dark yellowish-brown colour. **5** a drawing or photograph in sepia. ◆ *adj* **6** of the colour sepia or done in sepia: *a sepia print.* [C16: from Latin: a cuttlefish, from Greek; related to Greek *sēpein* to make rotten]

sepiolite ('siːpɪəˌlaɪt) *n* another name for **meerschaum** (sense 1). [C19: from German *Sepiolith*, from Greek *sēpion* bone of a cuttlefish; see SEPIA, -LITE]

sepmag ('sɛpˌmæg) *adj* designating a film or television programme for which the sound is recorded on separate magnetic material and run in synchronism with the picture. [C20: from SEP(ARATE) + MAG(NETIC)]

sepoy ('siːpɔɪ) *n* (formerly) an Indian soldier in the service of the British. [C18:

from Portuguese *sipaio*, from Urdu *sipāhī*, from Persian: horseman, from *sipāh* army]

Sepoy Rebellion *or* **Mutiny** *n* the Indian Mutiny of 1857–58.

seppuku (sɛˈpuːkuː) *n* another word for **hara-kiri**. [from Japanese, from Chinese *ch'ieh* to cut + *fu* bowels]

sepsis (ˈsɛpsɪs) *n* the presence of pus-forming bacteria in the body. [C19: via New Latin from Greek *sēpsis* a rotting; related to Greek *sēpein* to cause to decay]

sept (sɛpt) *n* **1** *Anthropol.* a clan or group that believes itself to be descended from a common ancestor. **2** a branch of a tribe or nation, esp. in medieval Ireland or Scotland. [C16: perhaps variant of SECT]

Sept. *abbrev. for:* **1** September. **2** Septuagint.

septa (ˈsɛptə) *n* the plural of **septum**.

septal (ˈsɛptəl) *adj* of or relating to a septum.

septarium (sɛpˈtɛərɪəm) *n, pl* **-ia** (-ɪə). a mass of mineral substance having cracks filled with another mineral, esp. calcite. [C18: from New Latin, from Latin SEPTUM] ▸ **sepˈtarian** *adj*

septate (ˈsɛpteɪt) *adj* divided by septa: *a septate plant ovary*. [C19: from New Latin *septātus* having a SEPTUM]

septavalent (ˌsɛptəˈveɪlənt) *adj Chem.* another word for **heptavalent**. [C19: from SEPT(IVALENT) + (HEPT)AVALENT]

September (sɛpˈtɛmbə) *n* the ninth month of the year, consisting of 30 days. [Old English, from Latin: the seventh (month) according to the original calendar of ancient Rome, from *septem* seven]

September Massacre *n* (during the French Revolution) the massacre of royalist prisoners and others in Paris between Sept. 2 and 6, 1792.

Septembrist (sɛpˈtɛmbrɪst) *n French history.* a person who took part in the September Massacre.

septenary (ˈsɛptɪnərɪ) *adj* **1** of or relating to the number seven. **2** forming a group of seven. **3** another word for **septennial**. ◆ *n, pl* **-naries**. **4** the number seven. **5** a group of seven things. **6** a period of seven years. **7** *Prosody.* a line of seven metrical feet. [C16: from Latin *septēnārius*, from *septēnī* seven each, from *septem* seven]

septennial (sɛpˈtɛnɪəl) *adj* **1** occurring every seven years. **2** relating to or lasting seven years. [C17: from Latin *septennis*, from *septem* seven + *annus* a year] ▸ **sepˈtennially** *adv*

septennium (sɛpˈtɛnɪəm) *n, pl* **-niums** *or* **-nia** (-nɪə). a period or cycle of seven years. [C19: from Latin, from *septem* seven + *-ennium*, from *annus* year]

septentrion (sɛpˈtɛntrɪˌɒn) *n Archaic.* the northern regions or the north. [C14: from Latin *septentriōnēs*, literally: the seven ploughing oxen (the constellation of the Great Bear), from *septem* seven + *triōnēs* ploughing oxen] ▸ **sepˈtentrional** *adj*

septet *or* **septette** (sɛpˈtɛt) *n* **1** *Music.* a group of seven singers or instrumentalists or a piece of music composed for such a group. **2** a group of seven people or things. [C19: from German, from Latin *septem* seven]

septi-[1] *or before a vowel* **sept-** *combining form.* seven: *septivalent*. [from Latin *septem*]

septi-[2] *combining form.* septum: *septicidal*.

septic (ˈsɛptɪk) *adj* **1** of, relating to, or caused by sepsis. **2** of, relating to, or caused by putrefaction. ◆ *n* **3** *Austral. and N.Z. informal.* short for **septic tank**. [C17: from Latin *sēpticus*, from Greek *sēptikos*, from *sēptos* decayed, from *sēpein* to make rotten] ▸ **ˈseptically** *adv* ▸ **septicity** (sɛpˈtɪsɪtɪ) *n*

septicaemia *or U.S.* **septicemia** (ˌsɛptɪˈsiːmɪə) *n* any of various diseases caused by microorganisms in the blood. Nontechnical name: **blood poisoning**. See also **bacteraemia, pyaemia**. [C19: from New Latin, from Greek *sēptik(os)* SEPTIC + -AEMIA] ▸ **ˌseptiˈcaemic** *or U.S.* **ˌseptiˈcemic** *adj*

septicidal (ˌsɛptɪˈsaɪdᵊl) *adj Botany.* (of a dehiscence) characterized by splitting along the partitions of the seed capsule. [C19: from SEPTI-[2] + -CIDAL] ▸ **ˌseptiˈcidally** *adv*

septic tank *n* a tank, usually below ground, for containing sewage to be decomposed by anaerobic bacteria.

septifragal (sɛpˈtɪfrəgᵊl) *adj* (of a dehiscence) characterized by breaking apart from a natural line of division in the fruit. [C19: from SEPTI-[2] + *-fragal*, from Latin *frangere* to break]

septilateral (ˌsɛptɪˈlætərəl) *adj* having seven sides.

septillion (sɛpˈtɪljən) *n, pl* **-lions** *or* **-lion**. **1** (in Britain, France, and Germany) the number represented as one followed by 42 zeros (10^{42}). **2** (in the U.S. and Canada) the number represented as one followed by 24 zeros (10^{24}). Brit. word: **quadrillion**. [C17: from French, from *sept* seven + *-illion*, on the model of *million*] ▸ **sepˈtillionth** *adj, n*

septime (ˈsɛptiːm) *n* the seventh of eight basic positions from which a parry or attack can be made in fencing. [C19: from Latin *septimus* seventh, from *septem* seven]

septivalent (ˌsɛptɪˈveɪlənt) *or* **septavalent** (ˌsɛptəˈveɪlənt) *adj Chem.* another word for **heptavalent**.

septuagenarian (ˌsɛptjʊədʒɪˈnɛərɪən) *n* **1** a person who is from 70 to 79 years old. ◆ *adj* **2** being between 70 and 79 years old. **3** of or relating to a septuagenarian. [C18: from Latin *septuāgēnārius*, from *septuāgēnī* seventy each, from *septuāgintā* seventy]

Septuagesima (ˌsɛptjʊəˈdʒɛsɪmə) *n* the third Sunday before Lent. [C14: from Church Latin *septuāgēsima* (*diēs*) the seventieth (day); compare QUINQUAGESIMA]

Septuagint (ˈsɛptjʊəˌdʒɪnt) *n* the principal Greek version of the Old Testament, including the Apocrypha, believed to have been translated by 70 or 72 scholars. [C16: from Latin *septuāgintā* seventy]

septum (ˈsɛptəm) *n, pl* **-ta** (-tə). **1** *Biology, anatomy.* a dividing partition between two tissues or cavities. **2** a dividing partition or membrane between two cavities in a mechanical device. [C18: from Latin *saeptum* wall, from *saepīre* to enclose; related to Latin *saepēs* a fence]

septuple (ˈsɛptjʊpᵊl) *adj* **1** seven times as much or many; sevenfold. **2** consisting of seven parts or members. ◆ *vb* **3** (*tr*) to multiply by seven. [C17: from Late Latin *septuplus*, from *septem* seven; compare QUADRUPLE]

septuplet (sɛpˈtjuːplɪt, ˈsɛptjʊplɪt) *n* **1** *Music.* a group of seven notes played in a time value of six, eight, etc. **2** one of seven offspring produced at one birth. **3** a group of seven things.

septuplicate (sɛpˈtjuːplɪkət) *n* **1** a group or set of seven things. ◆ *adj* **2** having or being in seven parts; sevenfold.

sepulchral (sɪˈpʌlkrəl) *adj* **1** suggestive of a tomb; gloomy. **2** of or relating to a sepulchre. ▸ **seˈpulchrally** *adv*

sepulchre *or U.S.* **sepulcher** (ˈsɛpəlkə) *n* **1** a burial vault, tomb, or grave. **2** Also called: **Easter sepulchre**. a separate alcove in some medieval churches in which the Eucharistic elements were kept from Good Friday until the Easter ceremonies. ◆ *vb* **3** (*tr*) to bury in a sepulchre. [C12: from Old French *sépulcre*, from Latin *sepulcrum*, from *sepelīre* to bury]

sepulture (ˈsɛpəltʃə) *n* **1** the act of placing in a sepulchre. **2** an archaic word for **sepulchre**. [C13: via Old French from Latin *sepultūra*, from *sepultus* buried, from *sepelīre* to bury]

seq. *abbrev. for:* **1** sequel. **2** sequens. [Latin: the following (one)]

seqq. *abbrev. for* sequentia. [Latin: the following (ones)]

sequacious (sɪˈkweɪʃəs) *adj* **1** logically following in regular sequence. **2** ready to follow any leader; pliant. [C17: from Latin *sequāx* pursuing, from *sequī* to follow] ▸ **seˈquaciously** *adv* ▸ **sequacity** (sɪˈkwæsɪtɪ) *n*

sequel (ˈsiːkwəl) *n* **1** anything that follows from something else; development. **2** a consequence or result. **3** a novel, play, etc., that continues a previously related story. [C15: from Late Latin *sequēla*, from Latin *sequī* to follow]

sequela (sɪˈkwiːlə) *n, pl* **-lae** (-liː). (*often pl*) *Med.* **1** any abnormal bodily condition or disease related to or arising from a pre-existing disease. **2** any complication of a disease. [C18: from Latin: SEQUEL]

sequence (ˈsiːkwəns) *n* **1** an arrangement of two or more things in a successive order. **2** the successive order of two or more things: *chronological sequence*. **3** a sequentially ordered set of related things or ideas. **4** an action or event that follows another or others. **5a** *Cards.* a set of three or more consecutive cards, usually of the same suit. **5b** *Bridge.* a set of two or more consecutive cards. **6** *Music.* an arrangement of notes or chords repeated several times at different pitches. **7** *Maths.* **7a** an ordered set of numbers or other mathematical entities in one-to-one correspondence with the integers 1 to *n*. **7b** an ordered infinite set of mathematical entities in one-to-one correspondence with the natural numbers. **8** a section of a film constituting a single continuous uninterrupted episode. **9** *Biochem.* the unique order of amino acids in the polypeptide chain of a protein or of nucleotides in the polynucleotide chain of DNA or RNA. **10** *R.C. Church.* another word for **prose** (sense 4). ◆ *vb* (*tr*) **11** to arrange in a sequence. **12** *Biochem.* to determine the order of the units comprising (a protein, nucleic acid, genome, etc.). [C14: from Medieval Latin *sequentia* that which follows, from Latin *sequī* to follow]

sequence of tenses *n Grammar.* the sequence according to which the tense of a subordinate verb in a sentence is determined by the tense of the principal verb, as in *I believe he is lying, I believed he was lying*, etc.

sequencer (ˈsiːkwənsə) *n* **1** an electronic device that determines the order in which a number of operations occur. **2** an electronic device that sorts information into the required order for data processing. **3** a unit connected to a synthesizer, which is capable of memorizing sequences of notes.

sequencing (ˈsiːkwənsɪŋ) *n Biochem.* **1** the procedure of determining the order of amino acids in the polypeptide chain of a protein (**protein sequencing**) or of nucleotides in a DNA section comprising a gene (**gene sequencing**). **2** Also called: **priority sequencing**. *Commerce.* specifying the order in which jobs are to be processed, based on the allocation of priorities.

sequent (ˈsiːkwənt) *adj* **1** following in order or succession. **2** following as a result; consequent. ◆ *n* **3** something that follows; consequence. **4** *Logic.* a formal representation of an argument. The inference of *A* from *A & B* is written *A & B* ⊢ *A*. The sequent ⊢ *A* represents the derivation of *A* from no assumptions and thus indicates that *A* is a theorem. [C16: from Latin *sequēns*, from *sequī* to follow] ▸ **ˈsequently** *adv*

sequential (sɪˈkwɛnʃəl) *adj* **1** characterized by or having a regular sequence. **2** another word for **sequent**. ▸ sequentiality (sɪˌkwɛnʃɪˈælɪtɪ) *n* ▸ **seˈquentially** *adv*

sequential access *n* a method of reaching and reading data from a computer file by reading through the file from the beginning. Compare **direct access**.

sequential scanning *n* a system of scanning a television picture along the lines in numerical sequence. Compare **interlaced scanning**.

sequester (sɪˈkwɛstə) *vb* (*tr*) **1** to remove or separate. **2** (*usually passive*) to retire into seclusion. **3** *Law.* to take (property) temporarily out of the possession of its owner, esp. until the claims of creditors are satisfied or a court order is complied with. **4** *International law.* to requisition or appropriate (enemy property). [C14: from Late Latin *sequestrāre* to surrender for safekeeping, from Latin *sequester* a trustee] ▸ **seˈquestrable** *adj*

sequestrant (sɪˈkwɛstrənt) *n Chem.* any substance used to bring about sequestration, often by chelation. They are used in horticulture to counteract lime in the soil.

sequestrate (sɪˈkwɛstreɪt) *vb* (*tr*) **1** *Law.* a variant of **sequester** (sense 3). **2** *Chiefly Scots Law.* **2a** to place (the property of a bankrupt) in the hands of a trustee for the benefit of his creditors. **2b** to render (a person) bankrupt. **3** *Archaic.* to seclude or separate. [C16: from Late Latin *sequestrāre* to SEQUESTER] ▸ **sequestrator** (ˈsiːkwɛsˌtreɪtə, sɪˈkwɛsˌtreɪtə) *n*

sequestration (ˌsiːkwɛˈstreɪʃən) *n* **1** the act of sequestering or state of being sequestered. **2** *Law.* the sequestering of property. **3** *Chem.* the effective removal of ions from a solution by coordination with another type of ion or molecule to form complexes that do not have the same chemical behaviour as the original ions. See also **sequestrant.**

sequestrum (sɪˈkwɛstrəm) *n, pl* **-tra** (-trə). *Pathol.* a detached piece of necrotic bone that often migrates to a wound, abscess, etc. [C19: from New Latin, from Latin: something deposited; see SEQUESTER] ▸ **seˈquestral** *adj*

sequin (ˈsiːkwɪn) *n* **1** a small piece of shiny often coloured metal foil or plastic, usually round, used to decorate garments, etc. **2** Also called: **zecchino.** any of various gold coins formerly minted in Italy, Turkey, and Malta. [C17: via French from Italian *zecchino,* from *zecca* mint, from Arabic *sikkah* die for striking coins] ▸ **ˈsequined** *adj*

sequoia (sɪˈkwɔɪə) *n* either of two giant Californian coniferous trees, *Sequoia sempervirens* (**redwood**) or *Sequoiadendron giganteum* (formerly *Sequoia gigantea*) (**big tree** or **giant sequoia**): family *Taxodiaceae.* [C19: New Latin, named after *Sequoya,* known also as George Guess, (?1770–1843), American Indian scholar and leader]

Sequoia National Park *n* a national park in central California, in the Sierra Nevada Mountains: established in 1890 to protect groves of giant sequoias, some of which are about 4000 years old. Area: 1556 sq. km (601 sq. miles).

ser *or* **seer** (sɪə) *n* a unit of weight used in India, usually taken as one fortieth of a maund. [from Hindi]

ser. *abbrev. for:* **1** serial. **2** series. **3** sermon.

sera (ˈsɪərə) *n* a plural of **serum.**

sérac (ˈsɛræk) *n* a pinnacle of ice among crevasses on a glacier, usually on a steep slope. [C19: from Swiss French: a variety of white cheese (hence the ice that it resembles) from Medieval Latin *serācium,* from Latin *serum* whey]

seraglio (sɛˈrɑːlɪˌəʊ) *or* **serail** (səˈraɪ, -ˈraɪl, -ˈreɪl) *n, pl* **-raglios** *or* **-rails. 1** the harem of a Muslim house or palace. **2** a sultan's palace, esp. in the former Turkish empire. **3** the wives and concubines of a Muslim. [C16: from Italian *serraglio* animal cage, from Medieval Latin *serrāculum* bolt, from Latin *sera* a door bar; associated also with Turkish *seray* palace]

serai (sɛˈraɪ) *n* (in the East) a caravanserai or inn. [C17: from Turkish *saray* palace, from Persian *sarāī* palace; see CARAVANSERAI]

Serajevo (*Serbo-Croat* ˈsɛrajɛvɔ) *n* a variant of **Sarajevo.**

Seram *or* **Ceram** (sɪˈræm) *n* an island in Indonesia, in the Moluccas, separated from New Guinea by the **Ceram Sea:** mountainous and densely forested. Area: 17 150 sq. km (6622 sq. miles). Also called: **Serang** (səˈræŋ).

serape (səˈrɑːpɪ) *n* **1** a blanket-like shawl often of brightly-coloured wool worn by men in Latin America. **2** a large shawl worn around the shoulders by women as a fashion garment.

seraph (ˈsɛrəf) *n, pl* **-aphs** *or* **-aphim** (-əfɪm). **1** *Theol.* a member of the highest order of angels in the celestial hierarchies, often depicted as the winged head of a child. **2** *Old Testament.* one of the fiery six-winged beings attendant upon Jehovah in Isaiah's vision (Isaiah 6). [C17: back formation from plural *seraphim,* via Late Latin from Hebrew]

seraphic (sɪˈræfɪk) *or* **seraphical** *adj* **1** of or resembling a seraph. **2** blissfully serene; rapt. ▸ **seˈraphically** *adv*

Serapis (ˈsɛrəpɪs) *n* a Graeco-Egyptian god combining attributes of Apis and Osiris.

Serb (sɜːb) *n, adj* another word for **Serbian.** [C19: from Serbian *Srb*]

Serb. *abbrev. for* Serbia(n).

Serbia (ˈsɜːbɪə) *n* a constituent republic of Yugoslavia: declared a kingdom in 1882; precipitated World War I by the conflict with Austria; became part of the Kingdom of the Serbs, Croats, and Slovenes (later called Yugoslavia) in 1918; remained united with Montenegro to form the Federal Republic of Yugoslavia when the other constituent republics became independent in 1991–92. Capital: Belgrade. Pop.: 5 806 000 (1995 est.). Area: 88 361 sq. km (34 109 sq. miles). Former name: **Servia.** Serbian name: **Srbija.**

Serbian (ˈsɜːbɪən) *adj* **1** of, relating to, or characteristic of Serbia, its people, or their dialect of Serbo-Croat. ◆ *n* **2** the dialect of Serbo-Croat spoken in Serbia. **3a** a native or inhabitant of Serbia. **3b** a speaker of the Serbian dialect.

Serbo-Croat *or* **Serbo-Croatian** *n* **1** the language of the Serbs and the Croats, belonging to the South Slavonic branch of the Indo-European family. The Serbian dialect is usually written in the Cyrillic alphabet, the Croatian in Roman. Also called: **Croato-Serb.** ◆ *adj* **2** of or relating to this language.

SERC *Brit. abbrev. for* Science and Engineering Research Council.

Sercq (sɛrk) *n* the French name for **Sark.**

serdab (ˈsɜːdæb, səˈdæb) *n* a secret chamber in an ancient Egyptian tomb. [C19 (earlier, in the sense: cellar): from Arabic: cellar, from Persian *sardāb* ice cellar, from *sard* cold + *āb* water]

sere[1] *or* **sear** (sɪə) *adj* **1** *Archaic.* dried up or withered. ◆ *vb, n* **2** a rare spelling of **sear**[1]. [Old English *sēar;* see SEAR[1]]

sere[2] (sɪə) *n* the series of changes occurring in the ecological succession of a particular community. [C20: from SERIES]

serein (səˈreɪn) *n* fine rain falling from a clear sky after sunset, esp. in the tropics. [C19: via French, from Old French *serain* dusk, from Latin *sērus* late]

Seremban (səˈrɛmbən) *n* a town in Peninsular Malaysia, capital of Negri Sembilan state. Pop.: 182 584 (1991).

serenade (ˌsɛrɪˈneɪd) *n* **1** a piece of music appropriate to the evening, characteristically played outside the house of a woman. **2** a piece of music indicative or suggestive of this. **3** an extended composition in several movements similar to the modern suite or divertimento. ◆ *vb* **4** (*tr*) to play a serenade for (someone). **5** (*intr*) to play a serenade. ◆ Compare **aubade.** [C17: from French *sérénade,* from Italian *serenata,* from *sereno* peaceful, from Latin *serēnus* calm; also influenced in meaning by Italian *sera* evening, from Latin *sērus* late] ▸ **ˌsereˈnader** *n*

serenata (ˌsɛrɪˈnɑːtə) *n* **1** an 18th-century cantata, often dramatic in form. **2** another word for **serenade.** [C18: from Italian; see SERENADE]

serendipity (ˌsɛrənˈdɪpɪtɪ) *n* the faculty of making fortunate discoveries by accident. [C18: coined by Horace Walpole, from the Persian fairytale *The Three Princes of Serendip,* in which the heroes possess this gift] ▸ **ˌserenˈdipitous** *adj*

serene (sɪˈriːn) *adj* **1** peaceful or tranquil; calm. **2** clear or bright: *a serene sky.* **3** (*often cap.*) honoured: used as part of certain royal titles: *His Serene Highness.* [C16: from Latin *serēnus*] ▸ **seˈrenely** *adv* ▸ **seˈreneness** *n*

serenity (sɪˈrɛnɪtɪ) *n, pl* **-ties. 1** the state or quality of being serene. **2** (*often cap.*) a title of honour used of certain royal personages: preceded by *his, her,* etc.

serf (sɜːf) *n* (esp. in medieval Europe) an unfree person, esp. one bound to the land. If his lord sold the land, the serf was passed on to the new landlord. [C15: from Old French, from Latin *servus* a slave; see SERVE] ▸ **ˈserfdom** *or* **ˈserfhood** *n* ▸ **ˈserfˌlike** *adj*

serge (sɜːdʒ) *n* **1** a twill-weave woollen or worsted fabric used for clothing. **2** a similar twilled cotton, silk, or rayon fabric. [C14: from Old French *sarge,* from Vulgar Latin *sārica* (unattested), from Latin *sēricum,* from Greek *sērikon* silk, from *sērikos* silken, from *sēr* silkworm]

sergeant (ˈsɑːdʒənt) *n* **1** a noncommissioned officer in certain armed forces, usually ranking above a corporal. **2a** (in Britain) a police officer ranking between constable and inspector. **2b** (in the U.S.) a police officer ranking below a captain. **3** See **sergeant at arms. 4** a court or municipal officer who has ceremonial duties. **5** (formerly) a tenant by military service, not of knightly rank. **6** See **serjeant at law.** ◆ Also: **serjeant.** [C12: from Old French *sergent,* from Latin *serviēns,* literally: serving, from *servīre* to SERVE] ▸ **sergeancy** (ˈsɑːdʒənsɪ) *or* **ˈsergeantship** *n*

sergeant at arms *n* **1** an officer of a legislative or fraternal body responsible for maintaining internal order. **2** (formerly) an officer who served a monarch or noble, esp. as an armed attendant. ◆ Also called: **sergeant, serjeant at arms, serjeant.**

sergeant at law *n* a variant spelling of **serjeant at law.**

Sergeant Baker *n* a large brightly-coloured fish of the genus *Latropiscis,* found in temperate waters of Australia.

sergeant major *n* **1** a noncommissioned officer of the highest rank or having specific administrative tasks in branches of the armed forces of various countries. **2** a large damselfish, *Abudefduf saxatilis,* having a bluish-grey body marked with black stripes.

Sergipe (*Portuguese* serˈʒipi) *n* a state of NE Brazil: the smallest Brazilian state; a centre of resistance to Dutch conquest (17th century). Capital: Aracajú. Pop.: 1 605 300 (1995 est.). Area: 13 672 sq. km (8492 sq. miles).

Sergt *abbrev. for* Sergeant.

serial (ˈsɪərɪəl) *n* **1** a novel, play, etc., presented in separate instalments at regular intervals. **2** a publication, usually regularly issued and consecutively numbered. ◆ *adj* **3** of, relating to, or resembling a series. **4** published or presented as a serial. **5** of or relating to such publication or presentation. **6** *Computing.* of or operating on items of information, instructions, etc., in the order in which they occur. Compare **parallel** (sense 5). **7** of, relating to, or using the techniques of serialism. **8** *Logic, maths.* (of a relation) connected, transitive, and asymmetric, thereby imposing an order on all the members of the domain, as *less than* on the natural numbers. See also **ordering.** [C19: from New Latin *seriālis,* from Latin *seriēs* SERIES] ▸ **ˈserially** *adv*

serial correlation *n Statistics.* another name for **autocorrelation.**

serialism (ˈsɪərɪəˌlɪzəm) *n* (in 20th-century music) the use of a sequence of notes in a definite order as a thematic basis for a composition and a source from which the musical material is derived. See also **twelve-tone.**

serialize *or* **serialise** (ˈsɪərɪəˌlaɪz) *vb* (*tr*) to publish or present in the form of a serial. ▸ **ˌserialiˈzation** *or* **ˌserialiˈsation** *n*

serial killer *n* a person who carries out a series of murders.

serial monogamy *n* the practice of having a number of long-term romantic or sexual partners in succession.

serial number *n* any of the consecutive numbers assigned to machines, tools, books, etc.

seriate (ˈsɪərɪɪt) *adj* forming a series. ▸ **ˈseriately** *adv*

seriatim (ˌsɪərɪˈætɪm, ˌsɛr-) *adv* in a series; one after another in regular order. [C17: from Medieval Latin, from Latin *seriēs* SERIES]

sericeous (sɪˈrɪʃəs) *adj Botany.* **1** covered with a layer of small silky hairs: *a sericeous leaf.* **2** silky. [C18: from Late Latin *sēriceus* silken, from Latin *sēricus;* see SERGE]

sericin (ˈsɛrɪsɪn) *n* a gelatinous protein found on the fibres of raw silk. [C19: from Latin *sēricum* silk + -IN]

sericulture (ˈsɛrɪˌkʌltʃə) *n* the rearing of silkworms for the production of raw silk. [C19: via French; *seri-* from Latin *sēricum* silk, from Greek *sērikos* silken, from *sēr* a silkworm] ▸ **ˌseriˈcultural** *adj* ▸ **ˌseriˈculturist** *n*

seriema (ˌsɛrɪˈiːmə) *n* either of two cranelike South American birds, *Cariama cristata* or *Chunga burmeisteri,* having a crest just above the bill, rounded wings, and a long tail: family *Cariamidae,* order *Gruiformes* (cranes, rails, etc.). [C19: from New Latin, from Tupi *çariama* crested]

series (ˈsɪəriːz, -rɪz) *n, pl* **-ries. 1** a group or connected succession of similar or related things, usually arranged in order. **2** a set of radio or television programmes having the same characters and setting but different stories. **3** a set of books having the same format, related content, etc., published by one firm. **4** a set of stamps, coins, etc., issued at a particular time. **5** *Maths.* the sum of a finite or infinite sequence of numbers or quantities. See also **geometric series. 6** *Electronics.* **6a** a configuration of two or more components connected in a circuit so that the same current flows in turn through each of them (esp. in the phrase **in series**). **6b** (*as modifier*): *a series circuit.* Compare **parallel** (sense 10). **7** *Rhetoric.* a succession of coordinate elements in a sentence. **8** *Geology.* a stratigraphical unit that is a subdivision of a system and represents the rocks formed during an epoch. [C17: from Latin: a row, from *serere* to link]

series resonance *n* the resonance that results when circuit elements are connected with their inductance and capacitance in series, so that the impedance of the combination falls to a minimum at the resonant frequency. Compare **parallel resonance.**

series-wound ('sɪəri:z,waʊnd, -rɪz-) *adj* (of a motor or generator) having the field and armature circuits connected in series. Compare **shunt-wound.**

serif *or* (*rarely*) **seriph** ('serɪf) *n Printing.* a small line at the extremities of a main stroke in a type character. [C19: perhaps from Dutch *schreef* dash, probably of Germanic origin, compare Old High German *screvōn* to engrave]

serigraph ('serɪ,græf, -,grɑ:f) *n* a colour print made by an adaptation of the silk-screen process. [C19: from *seri-*, from Latin *sēricum* silk + -GRAPH] ► **serigraphy** (sə'rɪgrəfɪ) *n*

serin ('serɪn) *n* any of various small yellow-and-brown finches of the genus *Serinus,* esp. *S. serinus,* of parts of Europe. See also **canary.** [C16: from French, perhaps from Old Provençal *sirena* a bee-eater, from Latin *sīrēn,* a kind of bird, from SIREN]

serine ('seri:n, 'sɪəri:n, -rɪn) *n* a sweet-tasting amino acid that is synthesized in the body and is involved in the synthesis of cysteine; 2-amino-3-hydroxypropanoic acid. Formula: $CH_2(OH)CH(NH_2)COOH$. [C19: from SERICIN + -INE[2]]

seringa (sə'rɪŋgə) *n* **1** any of several euphorbiaceous trees of the Brazilian genus *Hevea,* that yield rubber. **2** a deciduous simaroubaceous tree, *Kirkia acuminata,* of southern Africa with a graceful shape. [C18: from Portuguese, variant of SYRINGA]

Seringapatam (sə,rɪŋgəpə'tæm) *n* a small town in S India, in Karnataka on **Seringapatam Island** in the Cauvery River: capital of Mysore from 1610 to 1799, when it was besieged and captured by the British. Pop.: 21 902 (1991 est.).

seriocomic (,sɪərɪəʊ'kɒmɪk) *or* (*less commonly*) **seriocomical** *adj* mixing serious and comic elements. ► **,serio'comically** *adv*

serious ('sɪərɪəs) *adj* **1** grave in nature or disposition; thoughtful: *a serious person.* **2** marked by deep feeling; in earnest; sincere: *is he serious or joking?* **3** concerned with important matters: *a serious conversation.* **4** requiring effort or concentration: *a serious book.* **5** giving rise to fear or anxiety; critical: *a serious illness.* **6** *Informal.* worthy of regard because of substantial quantity or quality: *serious money; serious wine.* **7** *Informal.* extreme or remarkable: *a serious haircut.* [C15: from Late Latin *sēriōsus,* from Latin *sērius;* probably related to Old English *swǣr* gloomy, Gothic *swers* esteemed] ► **'seriousness** *n*

seriously ('sɪərɪəslɪ) *adv* **1** in a serious manner or to a serious degree. **2** *Informal.* extremely or remarkably: *seriously tall.*

serjeant ('sɑ:dʒənt) *n* a variant spelling of **sergeant.**

serjeant at arms *n* a variant spelling of **sergeant at arms.**

serjeant at law *n* (formerly in England) a barrister of a special rank, to which he was raised by a writ under the Great Seal. Also called: **serjeant, sergeant at law, sergeant.**

Serlio (*Italian* 'serʎo) *n* **Sebastiano.** 1475–1554, Italian architect and painter, best known for his treatise *Complete Works on Architecture and Perspective* (1537–75), the first to set out the principles of classical architecture and to give rules for their application.

sermon ('sɜ:mən) *n* **1a** an address of religious instruction or exhortation, often based on a passage from the Bible, esp. one delivered during a church service. **1b** a written version of such an address. **2** a serious speech, esp. one administering reproof. [C12: via Old French from Latin *sermō* discourse, probably from *serere* to join together] ► **sermonic** (sɜ:'mɒnɪk) *or* **ser'monical** *adj*

sermonize *or* **sermonise** ('sɜ:mə,naɪz) *vb* to talk to or address (a person or audience) as if delivering a sermon. ► **'sermon,izer** *or* **'sermon,iser** *n*

Sermon on the Mount *n New Testament.* a major discourse delivered by Christ, including the Beatitudes and the Lord's Prayer (Matthew 5–7).

sero- *combining form.* indicating a serum: *serotherapy.*

seroconvert (,sɪərəʊkən'vɜ:t) *vb (intr)* (of an individual) to produce antibodies specific to, and in response to the presence in the blood of, a particular antigen, such as a virus or vaccine. ► **,serocon'version** *n*

serology (sɪ'rɒlədʒɪ) *n* the science concerned with serums. ► **serologic** (,sɪərə'lɒdʒɪk) *or* **,sero'logical** *adj* ► **se'rologist** *n*

seronegative (,sɪərəʊ'negətɪv) *adj* (of a person whose blood has been tested for a specific disease, such as AIDS) showing no serological reaction indicating the presence of the disease.

seropositive (,sɪərəʊ'pɒzɪtɪv) *adj* (of a person whose blood has been tested for a specific disease, such as AIDS) showing a serological reaction indicating the presence of the disease.

seropurulent (,sɪərəʊ'pjʊərələnt) *adj Pathol.* composed of or containing both serum and pus.

serosa (sɪ'rəʊsə) *n* **1** another name for **serous membrane. 2** one of the thin membranes surrounding the embryo in an insect's egg. [C19: from New Latin, from *serōsus* relating to SERUM]

serotherapy (,sɪərəʊ'θerəpɪ) *n* the treatment of disease by the injection of serum containing antibodies to the disease.

serotine ('serə,taɪn) *adj* **1** Also: **serotinal** (sɪ'rɒtɪn^əl), **serotinous.** *Biology.* produced, flowering, or developing late in the season. ◆ *n* **2** either of two insectivorous bats, *Eptesicus serotinus* or *Vespertilio serotinus:* family *Vespertilionidae.* [C16: from Latin *sērōtinus* late, from *sērus* late; applied to the bat because it flies late in the evening]

serotonin (,serə'təʊnɪn) *n* a compound that occurs in the brain, intestines, and blood platelets and acts as a neurotransmitter, as well as inducing vasoconstriction and contraction of smooth muscle; 5-hydroxytryptamine (5HT). [from SERO- + TON(IC) + -IN]

serous ('sɪərəs) *adj* of, resembling, producing, or containing serum. [C16: from Latin *serōsus,* from SERUM] ► **serosity** (sɪ'rɒsɪtɪ) *or* **'serousness** *n*

serous fluid *n* a thin watery fluid found in many body cavities, esp. those lined with serous membrane.

serous membrane *n* any of the smooth moist delicate membranes, such as the pleura or peritoneum, that line the closed cavities of the body.

serow ('serəʊ) *n* either of two antelopes, *Capricornis sumatraensis* and *C. crispus,* of mountainous regions of S and SE Asia, having a dark coat and conical backward-pointing horns. [C19: from Lepcha *să-ro* Tibetan goat]

Serpens ('sɜ:pənz) *n, Latin genitive* **Serpentis** (sə'pentɪs). a faint extensive constellation situated in the N and S equatorial regions and divided into two parts, **Serpens Caput** (the head) lying between Ophiuchus and Boötes and **Serpens Cauda** (the tail) between Ophiuchus and Aquila. [Latin: SERPENT]

serpent ('sɜ:pənt) *n* **1** a literary or dialect word for **snake. 2** *Old Testament.* a manifestation of Satan as a guileful tempter (Genesis 3:1–5). **3** a sly, deceitful, or unscrupulous person. **4** an obsolete wind instrument resembling a snake in shape, the bass form of the cornett. **5** a firework that moves about with a serpentine motion when ignited. [C14: via Old French from Latin *serpēns* a creeping thing, from *serpere* to creep; related to Greek *herpein* to crawl]

serpentine[1] ('sɜ:pən,taɪn) *adj* **1** of, relating to, or resembling a serpent. **2** twisting; winding. ◆ *n* **3** *Maths.* a curve that is symmetric about the origin of and asymptotic to the *x*-axis. [C14: from Late Latin *serpentīnus,* from *serpēns* SERPENT]

serpentine[2] ('sɜ:pən,taɪn) *n* **1** a dark green or brown mineral with a greasy or silky lustre, found in igneous and metamorphic rocks. It is used as an ornamental stone; and one variety (chrysotile) is known as asbestos. Composition: hydrated magnesium silicate. Formula: $Mg_3Si_2O_5.2H_2O$. Crystal structure: monoclinic. **2** any of a group of minerals having the general formula $(Mg,Fe)_3Si_2O_5(OH)_4$. [C15 *serpentyn,* from Medieval Latin *serpentīnum* SERPENTINE[1]; referring to the snakelike patterns of these minerals]

serpigo (sɜ:'paɪgəʊ) *n Pathol.* any progressive skin eruption, such as ringworm or herpes. [C14: from Medieval Latin, from Latin *serpere* to creep] ► **serpiginous** (sɜ:'pɪdʒɪnəs) *adj*

SERPS *or* **Serps** (sɜ:ps) *n* (in Britain) *acronym for* state earnings-related pension scheme.

serpulid ('sɜ:pjʊlɪd) *n* a marine polychaete worm of the family *Serpulidae,* which constructs and lives in a calcareous tube attached to stones or seaweed and has a crown of ciliated tentacles. [C19: Latin, from *serpula* a little serpent]

serra ('serə) *n, pl* **-rae** (-ri:). *Zoology.* a sawlike part or organ. [C19: from Latin: saw]

serranid (sə'rænɪd, 'serə-) *or* **serranoid** ('serə,nɔɪd) *n* **1** any of numerous mostly marine percoid fishes of the family *Serranidae:* includes the sea basses, sea perches, groupers, and jewfish. ◆ *adj* **2** of or belonging to the family *Serranidae.* [C19: from New Latin *Serranidae,* from *serrānus* genus name from Latin *serra* sawfish]

serrate *adj* ('serɪt, -eɪt). **1** (of leaves) having a margin of forward pointing teeth. **2** having a notched or sawlike edge. ◆ *vb* (se'reɪt). **3** *(tr)* to make serrate. [C17: from Latin *serrātus* saw-shaped, from *serra* a saw] ► **ser'rated** *adj*

serration (se'reɪʃən) *or* (*less commonly*) **serrature** ('serətʃə) *n* **1** the state or condition of being serrated. **2** a row of notches or toothlike projections on an edge. **3** a single notch.

serried ('serɪd) *adj* in close or compact formation: *serried ranks of troops.* [C17: from Old French *serré* close-packed, from *serrer* to shut up; see SEAR[2]]

serriform ('serɪ,fɔ:m) *adj Biology.* resembling a notched or sawlike edge. [*serri-,* from Latin *serra* saw]

serrulate ('serʊ,leɪt, -lɪt) *or* **serrulated** *adj* (esp. of leaves) minutely serrate. [C18: from New Latin *serrulātus,* from Latin *serrula* diminutive of *serra* a saw]

serrulation (,serʊ'leɪʃən) *n* **1** any of the notches in a serrulate object. **2** the condition of being serrulate.

Sertorius (sɜ:'tɔ:rɪəs) *n* **Quintus** ('kwɪntəs). ?123–72 B.C., Roman soldier who fought with Marius in Gaul (102) and led an insurrection in Spain against Sulla until he was assassinated.

sertularian (,sɜ:tjʊ'leərɪən) *n* any of various hydroid coelenterates of the genus *Sertularia,* forming feathery colonies of long branched stems bearing stalkless paired polyps. [C18: from New Latin *Sertulāria,* from Latin *sertula* diminutive of *serta* a garland]

serum ('sɪərəm) *n, pl* **-rums** *or* **-ra** (-rə). **1** See **blood serum. 2** antitoxin obtained from the blood serum of immunized animals. **3** *Physiol., zoology.* clear watery fluid, esp. that exuded by serous membranes. **4** a less common word for **whey.** [C17: from Latin: whey] ► **'serumal** *adj*

serum albumin *n* a form of albumin that is the most abundant protein constituent of blood plasma. See also **albumin.**

serum globulin *n* the blood serum component consisting of proteins with a larger molecular weight than serum albumin. See also **immunoglobulin.**

serum hepatitis *n* a former name for **hepatitis B.**

serum sickness *n* an allergic reaction, such as vomiting, skin rash, etc., that sometimes follows injection of a foreign serum.

serv. *abbrev. for:* **1** servant. **2** service.

serval ('sɜ:v^əl) *n, pl* **-vals** *or* **-val.** a slender feline mammal, *Felis serval,* of the African bush, having an orange-brown coat with black spots, large ears, and long legs. [C18: via French from Late Latin *cervālis* staglike, from Latin *cervus* a stag]

servant ('sɜ:v^ənt) *n* **1** a person employed to work for another, esp. one who performs household duties. **2** See **public servant.** [C13: via Old French, from *servant* serving, from *servir* to SERVE] ► **'servant-,like** *adj*

serve (sɜ:v) *vb* **1** to be in the service of (a person). **2** to render or be of service to (a person, cause, etc.); help. **3** (in a shop) to give (customers) information about articles for sale and to hand over articles purchased. **4** (*tr*) to provide (guests, customers, etc.) with food, drink, etc.: *she served her guests with cocktails.* **5** to distribute or provide (food, drink, etc.) for guests, customers, etc.: *do you serve coffee?* **6** (*tr; sometimes foll. by up*) to present (food, drink, etc.) in a specified manner: *cauliflower served with cheese sauce.* **7** (*tr*) to provide with a regular supply of. **8** (*tr*) to work actively for: *to serve the government.* **9** (*tr*) to pay homage to: *to serve God.* **10** to answer the requirements of; suit: *this will serve my purpose.* **11** (*intr; may take an infinitive*) to have a use; function: *this wood will serve to build a fire.* **12** to go through (a period of service, enlistment, imprisonment, etc.). **13** (*intr*) (of weather, conditions, etc.) to be favourable or suitable. **14** (*tr*) Also: **service.** (of a male animal) to copulate with (a female animal). **15** *Tennis, squash, etc.* to put (the ball) into play. **16** (*intr*) *R.C. Church.* to act as server at Mass or other services. **17** (*tr*) to deliver (a legal document, esp. a writ or summons) to (a person). **18** to provide (a machine, etc.) with an impulse or signal for control purposes or with a continuous supply of fuel, working material, etc. **19** (*tr*) *Nautical.* to bind (a rope, spar, etc.) with wire or fine cord to protect it from chafing, etc. See also **seize** (sense 8). **20 serve (a person) right.** *Informal.* to pay (a person) back, esp. for wrongful or foolish treatment or behaviour. ♦ *n* **21** *Tennis, squash, etc.* short for **service** (sense 17). **22** *Austral.* a portion or helping of food or drink. **[C13:** from Old French *servir,* from Latin *servīre,* from *servus* a slave**]** ▸ **'servable** *or* **'serveable** *adj*

server ('sɜːvə) *n* **1** a person who serves. **2** *Chiefly R.C. Church.* a person who acts as acolyte or assists the priest at Mass. **3** something that is used in serving food and drink. **4** the player who serves in racket games. **5** *Computing.* a computer or program that supplies data or resources to other machines on a network.

Servetus (sɜː'viːtəs) *n* **Michael,** Spanish name *Miguel Serveto.* 1511–53, Spanish theologian and physician. He was burnt at the stake by order of Calvin for denying the doctrine of the Trinity and the divinity of Christ.

Servia ('sɜːvɪə) *n* the former name of **Serbia.** ▸ **'Servian** *adj, n*

service[1] ('sɜːvɪs) *n* **1** an act of help or assistance. **2** an organized system of labour and material aids used to supply the needs of the public: *telephone service; bus service.* **3** the supply, installation, or maintenance of goods carried out by a dealer. **4** the state of availability for use by the public (esp. in the phrases **into** *or* **out of service**). **5** a periodic overhaul made on a car, machine, etc. **6** the act or manner of serving guests, customers, etc., in a shop, hotel, restaurant, etc. **7** a department of public employment and its employees: *civil service.* **8** employment in or performance of work for another: *he has been in the service of our firm for ten years.* **9** the work of a public servant. **10a** one of the branches of the armed forces. **10b** (*as modifier*): *service life.* **11** the state, position, or duties of a domestic servant (esp. in the phrase **in service**). **12** the act or manner of serving food. **13** a complete set of dishes, cups, etc., for use at table. **14** public worship carried out according to certain prescribed forms: *divine service.* **15** the prescribed form according to which a specific kind of religious ceremony is to be carried out: *the burial service.* **16** a unified collection of musical settings of the canticles and other liturgical items prescribed by the Book of Common Prayer as used in the Church of England. **17** *Tennis, squash, etc.* **17a** the act, manner, or right of serving a ball. **17b** the game in which a particular player serves: *he has lost his service.* Often shortened to **serve. 18** (in feudal law) the duty owed by a tenant to his lord. **19** the serving of a writ, summons, etc., upon a person. **20** *Nautical.* a length of tarred marline or small stuff used in serving. **21** (of male animals) the act of mating. **22** (*modifier*) of, relating to, or for the use of servants or employees. ♦ *vb* (*tr*) **23** to make fit for use. **24** to supply with assistance. **25** to overhaul (a car, machine, etc.). **26** (of a male animal) to mate with (a female). **27** *Brit.* to meet interest and capital payments on (debt). ♦ See also **services. [C12** *servise,* from Old French, from Latin *servitium* condition of a slave, from *servus* a slave**]**

service[2] ('sɜːvɪs) *n* See **service tree.**

serviceable ('sɜːvɪsəbᵊl) *adj* **1** capable of or ready for service; usable. **2** capable of giving good service; durable. **3** *Archaic.* diligent in service. ▸ **,servicea'bility** *or* **'serviceableness** *n* ▸ **'serviceably** *adv*

service area *n* **1** a place on a motorway providing garage services, restaurants, toilet facilities, etc. **2** the area within which a satisfactory signal can be received from a given radio transmitter.

serviceberry ('sɜːvɪs,berɪ) *n, pl* **-ries. 1** Also called: **shadbush.** any of various North American rosaceous trees or shrubs of the genus *Amelanchier,* esp. *A. canadensis,* which has white flowers and edible purplish berries. **2** the fruit of any of these plants. **3** the fruit of the service tree. ♦ Also called (for senses 1, 2): **shadberry, Juneberry.**

service ceiling *n* the height above sea level, measured under standard conditions, at which the rate of climb of an aircraft has fallen to a specified amount. Compare **absolute ceiling.**

service charge *n* a percentage of a bill, as at a restaurant or hotel, added to the total to pay for service.

service contract *n* a contract between an employer and a senior employee, esp. a director, executive, etc.

service flat *n Brit.* a flat in which domestic services are provided by the management. Also called (esp. Austral.): **serviced flat.**

service industry *n* an industry that provides services, such as transport or entertainment, rather than goods.

service line *n* (in certain racket games) **1** the line at the back of the court behind which the server must stand when serving. **2** a line indicating the boundary of a permissible service, as on the backwall of a squash court.

serviceman ('sɜːvɪs,mæn, -mən) *n, pl* **-men. 1** Also called (*fem*): **'service,woman.** a person who serves in the armed services of a country. **2** a man employed to service and maintain equipment.

service module *n* a section of an Apollo spacecraft housing the rocket engine, radar, fuel cells, etc., and jettisoned on re-entry into the earth's atmosphere. See also **lunar module, command module.**

service road *n Brit.* a relatively narrow road running parallel to a main road and providing access to houses, shops, offices, factories, etc., situated along its length.

services ('sɜːvɪsɪz) *pl n* **1** work performed for remuneration. **2** (usually preceded by *the*) the armed forces. **3** (*sometimes sing*) *Economics.* commodities, such as banking, that are mainly intangible and usually consumed concurrently with their production. Compare **goods** (sense 2). **4** a system of providing the public with gas, water, etc.

service station *n* **1** a place that supplies fuel, oil, etc., for motor vehicles and often carries out repairs, servicing, etc. **2** a place that repairs and sometimes supplies mechanical or electrical equipment.

service tree *n* **1** Also called: **sorb.** a Eurasian rosaceous tree, *Sorbus domestica,* cultivated for its white flowers and brown edible apple-like fruits. **2 wild service tree.** a similar and related Eurasian tree, *Sorbus torminalis.* **[***service,* from Old English *syrfe,* from Vulgar Latin *sorbea* (unattested), from Latin *sorbus* SORB**]**

servient tenement ('sɜːvɪənt) *n Property Law.* the land or tenement over which an easement or other servitude is exercised. Compare **dominant tenement.**

serviette (,sɜːvɪ'ɛt) *n Chiefly Brit.* a small square of cloth or paper used while eating to protect the clothes, wipe the mouth and hands, etc. **[C15:** from Old French, from *servir* to SERVE; formed on the model of OUBLIETTE**]**

servile ('sɜːvaɪl) *adj* **1** obsequious or fawning in attitude or behaviour; submissive. **2** of or suitable for a slave. **3** existing in or relating to a state of slavery. **4** (when *postpositive,* foll. by *to*) submitting or obedient. **[C14:** from Latin *servīlis,* from *servus* slave**]** ▸ **'servilely** *adv* ▸ **servility** (sɜː'vɪlɪtɪ) *or* **'servileness** *n*

servile work *n R.C. Church.* work of a physical nature that is forbidden on Sundays and on certain holidays.

serving ('sɜːvɪŋ) *n* a portion or helping of food or drink.

servitor ('sɜːvɪtə) *n Archaic.* a person who serves another. **[C14:** from Old French *servitour,* from Late Latin *servītor,* from Latin *servīre* to SERVE**]**

servitude ('sɜːvɪ,tjuːd) *n* **1** the state or condition of a slave; bondage. **2** the state or condition of being subjected to or dominated by a person or thing: *servitude to drink.* **3** *Law.* a burden attaching to an estate for the benefit of an adjoining estate or of some definite person. See also **easement. 4** short for **penal servitude. [C15:** via Old French from Latin *servitūdō,* from *servus* a slave**]**

servo ('sɜːvəʊ) *adj* **1** (*prenominal*) of, relating to, forming part of, or activated by a servomechanism: *servo brakes.* ♦ *n, pl* **-vos. 2** *Informal.* short for **servomechanism. [**see SERVOMOTOR**]**

servomechanism ('sɜːvəʊ,mɛkə,nɪzəm, ,sɜːvəʊ'mɛk-) *n* a mechanical or electromechanical system for control of the position or speed of an output transducer. Negative feedback is incorporated to minimize discrepancies between the output state and the input control setting. ▸ **servomechanical** (,sɜːvəʊmɪ'kænɪkᵊl) *adj*

servomotor ('sɜːvəʊ,məʊtə) *n* any motor that supplies power to a servomechanism. **[C19:** from French *servo-moteur,* from Latin *servus* slave + French *moteur* MOTOR**]**

servqual ('sɜːv,kwɒl) *n Marketing.* the provision of high-quality products by an organization backed by a high level of service for consumers. **[C20:** from SERV(ICE)[1] + QUAL(ITY)**]**

sesame ('sɛsəmɪ) *n* **1** a tropical herbaceous plant, *Sesamum indicum,* of the East Indies, cultivated, esp. in India, for its small oval seeds: family *Pedaliaceae.* **2** the seeds of this plant, used in flavouring bread and yielding an edible oil (**benne oil** or **gingili**). ♦ Also called: **benne, gingili, til. [C15:** from Latin *sēsamum,* from Greek *sēsamon, sēsamē,* of Semitic origin; related to Arabic *simsim***]**

sesamoid ('sɛsə,mɔɪd) *adj Anatomy.* **1** of or relating to various small bones formed in tendons, such as the patella. **2** of or relating to any of various small cartilages, esp. those of the nose. **[C17:** from Latin *sēsamoīdēs* like sesame (seed), from Greek**]**

Sesostris I (sɛ'sɒstrɪs) *n* 20th century B.C., king of Egypt of the 12th dynasty. He conquered Nubia and brought ancient Egypt to the height of its prosperity. The funerary complex at Lisht was built during his reign.

Sesotho (sɪ'suːtʊ) *n* the dialect of Sotho spoken by the Basotho: an official language of Lesotho. Also called: **Southern Sotho.** Former name: **Basuto.**

sesqui- *prefix* **1** indicating one and a half: *sesquicentennial.* **2** (in a chemical compound) indicating a ratio of two to three: *sesquioxide.* **[**from Latin, contraction of SEMI- + *as* AS[2] + *-que* and**]**

sesquialtera (,sɛskwɪ'æltərə) *n Music.* **1** a mixture stop on an organ. **2** another term for **hemiola. [C16:** from Latin *sesqui-* half + *alter* second, other**]**

sesquicarbonate (,sɛskwɪ'kɑːbə,neɪt, -nɪt) *n* a mixed salt consisting of a carbonate and a hydrogen carbonate, such as sodium sesquicarbonate, $Na_2CO_3.NaHCO_3.2H_2O$.

sesquicentennial (,sɛskwɪsɛn'tɛnɪəl) *adj* **1** of or relating to a period of 150 years. ♦ *n* **2** a period or cycle of 150 years. **3** a 150th anniversary or its celebration. ▸ **,sesquicen'tennially** *adv*

sesquioxide (,sɛskwɪ'ɒksaɪd) *n* any of certain oxides whose molecules contain three atoms of oxygen for every two atoms of the element: *chromium sesquioxide,* Cr_2O_3.

sesquipedalian (,sɛskwɪpɪ'deɪlɪən) *or* (*less commonly*) **sesquipedal** (sɛs'kwɪpədᵊl) *adj* **1** tending to use very long words. **2** (of words or expressions) long and ponderous; polysyllabic. ♦ *n* **3** a polysyllabic word. **[C17:** from Latin *sēsquipedālis* of a foot and a half (coined by Horace in *Ars Poetica*), from SESQUI- + *pedālis* of the foot, from *pēs* foot**]** ▸ **,sesquipe'dalianism** *n*

sesquiterpene (,sɛskwɪ'tɜːpiːn) *n* any of certain terpenes whose molecules contain one and a half times as many atoms as a normal terpene. Formula: $C_{15}H_{24}$.

Sesshu ('sɛʃuː) *n* original family name *Oda,* also called *Toyo.* 1420–1506, Japanese landscape painter, who introduced the Chinese technique of ink painting on long scrolls to Japan.

sessile ('sɛsaɪl) *adj* **1** (of flowers or leaves) having no stalk; growing directly from the stem. **2** (of animals such as the barnacle) permanently attached to a substratum. [C18: from Latin *sēssilis* concerning sitting, from *sedēre* to sit] ▸ **sessility** (sɛ'sɪlɪtɪ) *n*

sessile oak *n* another name for the **durmast** (sense 1).

session ('sɛʃən) *n* **1** the meeting of a court, legislature, judicial body, etc., for the execution of its function or the transaction of business. **2** a single continuous meeting of such a body. **3** a series or period of such meetings. **4** *Education.* **4a** the time during which classes are held. **4b** a school or university term or year. **5** *Presbyterian Church.* the judicial and administrative body presiding over a local congregation and consisting of the minister and elders. **6** a meeting of a group of musicians to record in a studio. **7** a meeting of a group of people to pursue an activity. **8** any period devoted to an activity. **9** See **Court of Session.** [C14: from Latin *sessiō* a sitting, from *sedēre* to sit] ▸ **'sessional** *adj* ▸ **'sessionally** *adv*

session musician *n* a studio musician, esp. one who works freelance.

sessions ('sɛʃənz) *pl n* the sittings or a sitting of justice in court. See **magistrates' court, quarter sessions.**

Sessions ('sɛʃənz) *n* **Roger** (**Huntington**). 1896–1985, U.S. composer.

sesterce ('sɛstɛːs) *or* **sestertius** (sɛ'stɜːtɪəs) *n* a silver or, later, bronze coin of ancient Rome worth a quarter of a denarius. [C16: from Latin *sēstertius* a coin worth two and a half asses, from *sēmis* half + *tertius* a third]

sestertium (sɛ'stɜːtɪəm) *n, pl* **-tia** (-tɪə). an ancient Roman money of account equal to 1000 sesterces. [C16: from Latin, from the phrase *mille sestertium* a thousand of sesterces; see SESTERCE]

sestet (sɛ'stɛt) *n* **1** *Prosody.* the last six lines of a Petrarchan sonnet. **2** *Prosody.* any six-line stanza. **3** another word for **sextet** (sense 1). [C19: from Italian *sestetto,* from *sesto* sixth, from Latin *sextus,* from *sex* six]

sestina (sɛ'stiːnə) *n* an elaborate verse form of Italian origin, normally unrhymed, consisting of six stanzas of six lines each and a concluding tercet. The six final words of the lines in the first stanza are repeated in a different order in each of the remaining five stanzas and also in the concluding tercet. Also called: **sextain.** [C19: from Italian, from *sesto* sixth, from Latin *sextus*]

Sestos ('sɛstɒs) *n* a ruined town in NW Turkey, at the narrowest point of the Dardanelles: N terminus of the bridge of boats built by Xerxes in 481 B.C. for the crossing of his armies of invasion.

set[1] (sɛt) *vb* **sets, setting, set.** (*mainly tr*) **1** to put or place in position or into a specified state or condition: *to set a book on the table; to set someone free.* **2** (*also intr;* foll. by *to* or *on*) to put or be put (to); apply or be applied: *he set fire to the house; they set the dogs on the scent.* **3** to put into order or readiness for use; prepare: *to set a trap; to set the table for dinner.* **4** (*also intr*) to put, form, or be formed into a jelled, firm, fixed, or rigid state: *the jelly set in three hours.* **5** (*also intr*) to put or be put into a position that will restore a normal state: *to set a broken bone.* **6** to adjust (a clock or other instrument) to a position. **7** to determine or establish: *we have set the date for our wedding.* **8** to prescribe or allot (an undertaking, course of study, etc.): *the examiners have set "Paradise Lost".* **9** to arrange in a particular fashion, esp. an attractive one: *she set her hair; the jeweller set the diamonds in silver.* **10** (of clothes) to hang or fit (well or badly) when worn. **11** Also: **set to music.** to provide music for (a poem or other text to be sung). **12** Also: **set up.** *Printing.* to arrange or produce (type, film, etc.) from (text or copy); compose. **13** to arrange (a stage, television studio, etc.) with scenery and props. **14** to describe or present (a scene or the background to a literary work, story, etc.) in words: *his novel is set in Russia.* **15** to present as a model of good or bad behaviour (esp. in the phrases **set an example, set a good example, set a bad example**). **16** (foll. by *on* or *by*) to value (something) at a specified price or estimation of worth: *he set a high price on his services.* **17** (foll. by *at*) to price (the value of something) at a specified sum: *he set his services at £300.* **18** (*also intr*) to give or be given a particular direction: *his course was set to the East.* **19** (*also intr*) to rig (a sail) or (of a sail) to be rigged so as to catch the wind. **20** (*intr*) (of the sun, moon, etc.) to disappear beneath the horizon. **21** to leave (dough, etc.) in one place so that it may prove. **22** to sharpen (a cutting blade) by grinding or honing the angle adjacent to the cutting edge. **23** to displace alternate teeth of (a saw) to opposite sides of the blade in order to increase the cutting efficiency. **24** to sink (the head of a nail) below the surface surrounding it by using a nail set. **25** *Computing.* to give (a binary circuit) the value 1. **26** (of plants) to produce (fruits, seeds, etc.) after pollination or (of fruits or seeds) to develop after pollination. **27** to plant (seeds, seedlings, etc.). **28** to place (a hen) on (eggs) for the purpose of incubation. **29** (*intr*) (of a gun dog) to turn in the direction of game, indicating its presence. **30** *Scot. and Irish.* to let or lease: *to set a house.* **31** *Bridge.* to defeat (one's opponents) in their attempt to make a contract. **32** a dialect word for **sit. 33 set eyes on.** to see. ◆ *n* **34** the act of setting or the state of being set. **35** a condition of firmness or hardness. **36** bearing, carriage, or posture: *the set of a gun dog when pointing.* **37** the fit or hang of a garment, esp. when worn. **38** the scenery and other props used in and identifying the location of a stage or television production, film, etc. **39** Also called: **set width.** *Printing.* **39a** the width of the body of a piece of type. **39b** the width of the lines of type in a page or column. **40** *Nautical.* **40a** the cut of the sails or the arrangement of the sails, spars, rigging, etc., of a vessel. **40b** the direction from which a wind is blowing or towards which a tide or current is moving. **41** *Psychol.* a temporary bias disposing an organism to react to a stimulus in one way rather than in others. **42** a seedling, cutting, or similar part that is ready for planting: *onion sets.* **43** a blacksmith's tool with a short head similar to a cold chisel set transversely onto a handle and used, when struck with a hammer, for cutting off lengths of iron bars. **44** See **nail set. 45** a mechanical distortion of shape or alignment. **46** a variant spelling of **sett.** ◆ *adj* **47** fixed or established by authority or agreement: *set hours of work.* **48** (*usually postpositive*) rigid or inflexible: *she is set in her ways.* **49** conventional, artificial, or stereotyped, rather than spontaneous: *she made her apology in set phrases.* **50** (*postpositive;* foll. by *on* or *upon*) resolute in intention: *he is set upon marrying.* **51** (of a book, etc.) prescribed for students' preparation for an examination. ◆ See also **set about, set against, set aside, set back, set down, set forth, set in, set off, set on, set out, set to, set up, set upon.** [Old English *settan,* causative of *sittan* to SIT; related to Old Frisian *setta,* Old High German *sezzan*]

set[2] (sɛt) *n* **1** a number of objects or people grouped or belonging together, often forming a unit or having certain features or characteristics in common: *a set of coins; John is in the top set for maths.* **2** a group of people who associate together, esp. a clique: *he's part of the jet set.* **3** *Maths, logic.* **3a** Also called: **class.** a collection of numbers, objects, etc., that is treated as an entity: {3, the moon} is the set the two members of which are the number 3 and the moon. **3b** (in some formulations) a class that can itself be a member of other classes. **4** any apparatus that receives or transmits television or radio signals. **5** *Tennis, squash, etc.* one of the units of a match, in tennis one in which one player or pair of players must win at least six games: *Graf lost the first set.* **6a** the number of couples required for a formation dance. **6b** a series of figures that make up a formation dance. **7a** a band's or performer's concert repertoire on a given occasion: *the set included no new numbers.* **7b** a continuous performance: *the Who played two sets.* ◆ *vb* **sets, setting, set. 8** (*intr*) (in square dancing and country dancing) to perform a sequence of steps while facing towards another dancer: *set to your partners.* **9** (*usually tr*) to divide into sets: *in this school we set our older pupils for English.* [C14 (in the obsolete sense: a religious sect): from Old French *sette,* from Latin *secta* SECT; later sense development influenced by the verb SET[1]]

SET (in Britain) *abbrev. for* selective employment tax: an employment payroll tax, first levied in 1966 and abolished when VAT was introduced in 1973.

seta ('siːtə) *n, pl* **-tae** (-tiː). (in invertebrates and some plants) any bristle or bristle-like appendage. [C18: from Latin] ▸ **setaceous** (sɪ'teɪʃəs) *adj* ▸ **se'taceously** *adv* ▸ **'setal** *adj*

set about *vb* (*intr, prep*) **1** to start or begin. **2** to attack physically or verbally.

set against *vb* (*tr, prep*) **1** to balance or compare: *to set a person's faults against his virtues.* **2** to cause to be hostile or unfriendly to.

set aside *vb* (*tr, adv*) **1** to reserve for a special purpose; put to one side. **2** to discard, dismiss, or quash.

set-aside *n* **a** (in the European Union) a scheme in which a proportion of farmland is taken out of production in order to reduce surpluses or maintain or increase prices of a specific crop. **b** (*as modifier*): *set-aside land.*

set back *vb* (*tr, adv*) **1** to hinder; impede. **2** *Informal.* to cost (a person) a specified amount. ◆ *n* **setback. 3** anything that serves to hinder or impede. **4** a recession in the upper part of a high building, esp. one that increases the daylight at lower levels. **5** Also called: **offset, setoff.** a steplike shelf where a wall is reduced in thickness.

set chisel *n* another name for **cold chisel.**

set down *vb* (*tr, adv*) **1** to write down or record. **2** to judge, consider, or regard: *he set him down as an idiot.* **3** (foll. by *to*) to ascribe; attribute: *his attitude was set down to his illness.* **4** to reprove; rebuke. **5** to snub; dismiss. **6** *Brit.* to allow (passengers) to alight from a bus, taxi, etc.

se tenant *French.* (sə tənɑ̃) *adj* **1** denoting two postage stamps of different face values and sometimes of different designs in an unseparated pair. ◆ *n* **2** such a pair of stamps. [literally: holding together]

set forth *vb* (*adv*) *Formal or archaic.* **1** (*tr*) to state, express, or utter: *he set forth his objections.* **2** (*intr*) to start out on a journey: *the expedition set forth on the first of July.*

Seth (sɛθ) *n Old Testament.* Adam's third son, given by God in place of the murdered Abel (Genesis 4:25).

SETI ('sɛtɪ) *n acronym for* Search for Extraterrestrial Intelligence; a scientific programme attempting, by radio transmissions, to make contact with beings from other planets.

setiferous (sɪ'tɪfərəs) *or* **setigerous** (sɪ'tɪdʒərəs) *adj Biology.* bearing bristles. [C19: see SETA, -FEROUS, -GEROUS]

setiform ('siːtɪˌfɔːm) *adj Biology.* shaped like a seta.

set in *vb* (*intr, adv*) **1** to become established: *the winter has set in.* **2** (of wind) to blow or (of current) to move towards shore. ◆ *adj* **set-in. 3** (of a part) made separately and then added to a larger whole: *a set-in sleeve.*

setline ('sɛtˌlaɪn) *n* any of various types of fishing line that consist of a long line suspended across a stream, between buoys, etc., and having shorter hooked and baited lines attached. See **trawl** (sense 2), **trotline.**

set off *vb* (*adv*) **1** (*intr*) to embark on a journey. **2** (*tr*) to cause (a person) to act or do something, such as laugh or tell stories. **3** (*tr*) to cause to explode. **4** (*tr*) to act as a foil or contrast to, esp. so as to improve: *that brooch sets your dress off well.* **5** (*tr*) *Accounting.* to cancel a credit on (one account) against a debit on another, both of which are in the name of the same person, enterprise, etc. **6** (*intr*) to bring a claim by way of setoff. ◆ *n* **setoff. 7** anything that serves as a counterbalance. **8** anything that serves to contrast with or enhance something else; foil. **9** another name for **setback** (sense 5). **10** a counterbalancing debt or claim offered by a debtor against a creditor. **11** a cross claim brought by a debtor that partly offsets the creditor's claim. See also **counterclaim.**

set-off *n Printing.* a fault in which ink is transferred from a heavily inked or undried printed sheet to the sheet next to it in a pile. Also called (esp. Brit.): **offset.**

Seton ('siːtᵊn) *n* **Ernest Thompson.** 1860–1946, U.S. author and illustrator of animal books, born in England.

set on *vb* (*tr*) **1** (*prep*) to cause to attack: *they set the dogs on him.* **2** (*adv*) to instigate or incite; urge: *he set the child on to demand food.*

Seto Naikai ('sɛtəʊ 'naɪkaɪ) *n* transliteration of the Japanese name for the **Inland Sea.**

setose ('siːtəʊs) *adj Biology.* covered with setae; bristly. [C17: from Latin *saetōsus,* from *saeta* a bristle]

set out *vb (adv, mainly tr)* **1** to present, arrange, or display: *he set the flowers out in the vase.* **2** to give a full account of; explain exactly: *he set out the matter in full.* **3** to plan or lay out (a garden, etc.). **4** *(intr)* to begin or embark on an undertaking, esp. a journey.

set piece *n* **1** a work of literature, music, etc., often having a conventional or prescribed theme, intended to create an impressive effect. **2** a piece of scenery built to stand independently as part of a stage set. **3** a display of fireworks. **4** *Sport.* a rehearsed team manoeuvre, usually attempted in continuous games at a restart of play, esp. when the other side has been penalized for improper play.

set point *n Tennis, etc.* a point that would enable one side to win a set.

setscrew ('sɛt,skruː) *n* a screw that fits into the boss or hub of a wheel, coupling, cam, etc., and prevents motion of the part relative to the shaft on which it is mounted.

set square *n* a thin flat piece of plastic, metal, etc., in the shape of a right-angled triangle, used in technical drawing.

sett *or* **set** (sɛt) *n* **1** a small rectangular paving block made of stone, such as granite, used to provide a durable road surface. Compare **cobblestone. 2** the burrow of a badger. **3a** a square in a pattern of tartan. **3b** the pattern itself. [C19: variant of SET[1] (n)]

settee (sɛ'tiː) *n* a seat, for two or more people, with a back and usually with arms. [C18: changed from SETTLE[2]]

setter ('sɛtə) *n* any of various breeds of large gun dog, having silky coats and plumed tails. See **English setter, Gordon setter, Irish setter.** [C16: so called because they can be used to indicate where game is: see SET[1]]

set theory *n* **1** *Maths.* the branch of mathematics concerned with the properties and interrelationships of sets. **2** *Logic.* a theory constructed within first-order logic that yields the mathematical theory of classes, esp. one that distinguishes sets from proper classes as a means of avoiding certain paradoxes.

setting ('sɛtɪŋ) *n* **1** the surroundings in which something is set; scene. **2** the scenery, properties, or background, used to create the location for a stage play, film, etc. **3** *Music.* a composition consisting of a certain text and music provided or arranged for it. **4** the metal mounting and surround of a gem: *diamonds in an antique gold setting.* **5** the tableware, cutlery, etc., for a single place at table. **6** any of a series of points on a scale or dial that can be selected to control the level as of temperature, speed, etc., at which a machine functions. **7** a clutch of eggs in a bird's nest, esp. a clutch of hen's eggs.

setting lotion *n* a perfumed solution of gum or a synthetic resin in a solvent, used in hairdressing to make a set last longer.

setting rule *n Printing.* a metal strip used in the hand-setting of type in a composing stick to separate the line being set from the previous one.

settle[1] ('sɛt[ə]l) *vb* **1** *(tr)* to put in order; arrange in a desired state or condition: *he settled his affairs before he died.* **2** to arrange or be arranged in a fixed or comfortable position: *he settled himself by the fire.* **3** *(intr)* to come to rest or a halt: *a bird settled on the hedge.* **4** to take up or cause to take up residence: *the family settled in the country.* **5** to establish or become established in a way of life, job, residence, etc. **6** *(tr)* to migrate to and form a community; colonize. **7** to make or become quiet, calm, or stable. **8** *(intr)* to be cast or spread; come down: *fog settled over a wide area.* **9** to make (a liquid) clear or (of a liquid) to become clear; clarify. **10** to cause (sediment) to sink to the bottom, as in a liquid, or (of sediment) to sink thus. **11** to subside or cause to subside and become firm or compact: *the dust settled.* **12** (sometimes foll. by *up*) to pay off or account for (a bill, debt, etc.). **13** *(tr)* to decide, conclude, or dispose of: *to settle an argument.* **14** *(intr;* often foll. by *on* or *upon)* to agree or fix: *to settle upon a plan.* **15** *(tr;* usually foll. by *on* or *upon)* to secure (title, property, etc.) to a person, as by making a deed of settlement, will, etc.: *he settled his property on his wife.* **16** to determine (a legal dispute, etc.) by agreement of the parties without resort to court action (esp. in the phrase **settle out of court**). ♦ See also **settle down, settle for, settle in, settle with.** [Old English *setlan;* related to Dutch *zetelen;* see SETTLE[2]] ▸ **'settleable** *adj*

settle[2] ('sɛt[ə]l) *n* a seat, for two or more people, usually made of wood with a high back and arms, and sometimes having a storage space in the boxlike seat. [Old English *setl;* related to Old Saxon, Old High German *sezzal*]

settle down *vb (adv, mainly intr)* **1** *(also tr)* to make or become quiet and orderly. **2** (often foll. by *to*) to apply oneself diligently: *please settle down to work.* **3** to adopt an orderly and routine way of life, take up a permanent post, etc., esp. after marriage.

settle for *vb (intr, prep)* to accept or agree to in spite of dispute or dissatisfaction.

settle in *vb (adv)* to become or help to become adapted to and at ease in a new home, environment, etc.

settlement ('sɛt[ə]lmənt) *n* **1** the act or state of settling or being settled. **2** the establishment of a new region; colonization. **3** a place newly settled; colony. **4** a collection of dwellings forming a community, esp. on a frontier. **5** a community formed by members of a group, esp. of a religious sect. **6** a public building used to provide educational and general welfare facilities for persons living in deprived areas. **7** a subsidence of all or part of a structure. **8a** the payment of an outstanding account, invoice, charge, etc. **8b** *(as modifier): settlement day.* **9** an adjustment or agreement reached in matters of finance, business, etc. **10** *Law.* **10a** a conveyance, usually to trustees, of property to be enjoyed by several persons in succession. **10b** the deed or other instrument conveying such property. **10c** the determination of a dispute, etc., by mutual agreement without resorting to legal proceedings.

settler ('sɛtlə) *n* a person who settles in a new country or a colony.

settler's clock *n Austral.* (formerly) an informal name for **kookaburra.** [C19: so called because its laugh was heard at dawn and sunset]

settle with *vb (prep)* **1** *(intr)* to pay a debt or bill to. **2** *(intr)* to make an agreement with. **3** to get one's revenge for (a wrong or injury) with (a person).

settlings ('sɛtlɪŋz) *pl n* any matter or substance that has settled at the bottom of a liquid; sediment; dregs.

settlor ('sɛtlə) *n Law.* a person who settles property on someone.

set to *vb (intr, adv)* **1** to begin working. **2** to start fighting. ♦ *n* **set-to. 3** *Informal.* a brief disagreement or fight.

Setúbal *(Portuguese* sə'tuβal) *n* a port in SW Portugal, on **Setúbal Bay** south of Lisbon: an earthquake in 1755 destroyed most of the old town. Pop.: 83 550 (1991).

set up *vb (adv, mainly tr)* **1** *(also intr)* to put into a position of power, etc. **2** *(also intr)* to begin or enable (someone) to begin (a new venture), as by acquiring or providing means, equipment, etc. **3** to build or construct: *to set up a shed.* **4** to raise, cause, or produce: *to set up a wail.* **5** to advance or propose: *to set up a theory.* **6** to restore the health of: *the sea air will set you up again.* **7** to establish (a record). **8** *Informal.* to cause (a person) to be blamed, accused, etc. **9** *Informal.* **9a** to provide (drinks, etc.) for: *set 'em up, Joe!* **9b** to pay for the drinks of: *I'll set up the next round.* **10** *Printing.* another term for **set**[1] (sense 12). ♦ *n* **setup. 11** *Informal.* the way in which anything is organized or arranged. **12** *Slang.* an event the result of which is prearranged: *it's a setup.* **13** a prepared arrangement of materials, machines, etc., for a job or undertaking. **14** a station at which a surveying instrument, esp. a theodolite, is set up. **15** *Films.* the position of the camera, microphones, and performers at the beginning of a scene. ♦ *adj* **set-up. 16** physically well-built.

set upon *vb (intr, prep)* to attack: *three thugs set upon him.*

set width *n* another name for **set**[1] (sense 39).

Seurat *(French* sœra) *n* **Georges** (ʒɔrʒ). 1859–91, French neoimpressionist painter. He developed the pointillist technique of painting, characterized by brilliant luminosity, as in *Dimanche à la Grande-Jatte* (1886).

Sevan (sɛ'vɑːn) *n* **Lake.** a lake in Armenia at an altitude of 1914 m (6279 ft.). Area: 1417 sq. km (547 sq. miles).

Sevastopol *(Russian* sɪvas'tɔpəlj) *n* a port, resort, and naval base in the S Ukraine, in the Crimea, on the Black Sea: captured and destroyed by British, French, and Turkish forces after a siege of 11 months (1854–55) during the Crimean War; taken by the Germans after a siege of 8 months (1942) during World War II. Pop.: 365 000 (1996 est.). English name: **Sebastopol.**

seven ('sɛv[ə]n) *n* **1** the cardinal number that is the sum of six and one and is a prime number. See also **number** (sense 1). **2** a numeral, 7, VII, etc., representing this number. **3** the amount or quantity that is one greater than six. **4** anything representing, represented by, or consisting of seven units, such as a playing card with seven symbols on it. **5** Also called: **seven o'clock.** seven hours after noon or midnight. ♦ *determiner* **6a** amounting to seven: *seven swans a-swimming.* **6b** *(as pronoun): you've eaten seven already.* ♦ Related prefixes: **hepta-, septi-.** ♦ See also **sevens.** [Old English *seofon;* related to Gothic *sibun,* German *sieben,* Old Norse *sjau,* Latin *septem,* Greek *hepta,* Sanskrit *saptá*]

Seven against Thebes *pl n Greek myth.* the seven members of an expedition undertaken to regain for Polynices, a son of Oedipus, his share in the throne of Thebes from his usurping brother Eteocles. The seven are usually listed as Polynices, Adrastus, Amphiaraus, Capaneus, Hippomedon, Tydeus, and Parthenopaeus. The campaign failed and the warring brothers killed each other in single combat before the Theban walls. See also **Adrastus.**

seven deadly sins *pl n* a fuller name for the **deadly sins.**

sevenfold ('sɛv[ə]n,fəʊld) *adj* **1** equal to or having seven times as many or as much. **2** composed of seven parts. ♦ *adv* **3** by or up to seven times as many or as much.

Seven Hills of Rome *pl n* the hills on which the ancient city of Rome was built: the Palatine, Capitoline, Quirinal, Caelian, Aventine, Esquiline, and Viminal.

sevens ('sɛv[ə]nz) *n (functioning as sing)* a Rugby Union match or series of matches played with seven players on each side.

seven seas *pl n* the oceans of the world considered as the N and S Pacific, the N and S Atlantic, and the Arctic, Antarctic, and Indian Oceans.

seven-segment display *n* an arrangement of seven bars forming a square figure of eight, used in electronic displays of alphanumeric characters: any letter or figure can be represented by illuminating selected bars.

Seven Sleepers *pl n* seven Christian youths from Ephesus who were walled up in a cave by the Emperor Decius in 250 A.D. and, according to legend, slept for 187 years.

seventeen ('sɛv[ə]n'tiːn) *n* **1** the cardinal number that is the sum of ten and seven and is a prime number. See also **number** (sense 1). **2** a numeral, 17, XVII, etc., representing this number. **3** the amount or quantity that is seven more than ten. **4** something represented by, representing, or consisting of 17 units. ♦ *determiner* **5a** amounting to seventeen: *seventeen attempts.* **5b** *(as pronoun): seventeen were sold.* [Old English *seofontīene*]

seventeenth ('sɛv[ə]n'tiːnθ) *adj* **1** *(usually prenominal)* **1a** coming after the sixteenth in numbering or counting order, position, time, etc.; being the ordinal number of *seventeen:* often written 17th. **1b** *(as n): the ship docks on the seventeenth.* ♦ *n* **2a** one of 17 approximately equal parts of something. **2b** *(as modifier): a seventeenth part.* **3** the fraction equal to one divided by 17 (1/17).

seventeen-year locust *n* an E North American cicada, *Magicicada septendecim,* appearing in great numbers at infrequent intervals because its nymphs take 13 or 17 years to mature. Also called: **periodical cicada.**

seventh ('sɛv[ə]nθ) *adj* **1** *(usually prenominal)* **1a** coming after the sixth and before the eighth in numbering or counting order, position, time, etc.; being the ordinal number of *seven:* often written 7th. **1b** *(as n): she left on the seventh;*

he was the seventh to arrive. ◆ *n* **2a** one of seven equal or nearly equal parts of an object, quantity, measurement, etc. **2b** (*as modifier*): *a seventh part.* **3** the fraction equal to one divided by seven (1/7). **4** *Music.* **4a** the interval between one note and another seven notes away from it counting inclusively along the diatonic scale. **4b** one of two notes constituting such an interval in relation to the other. See also **major** (sense 13), **minor** (sense 4), **interval** (sense 5). **4c** short for **seventh chord.** ◆ *adv* **5** Also: **seventhly.** after the sixth person, position, event, etc. ◆ *sentence connector.* **6** Also: **seventhly.** as the seventh point: linking what follows to the previous statements, as in a speech or argument.

seventh chord *n Music.* a chord consisting of a triad with a seventh added above the root. See **dominant seventh chord, diminished seventh chord, major seventh chord, minor seventh chord.**

Seventh-Day Adventist *n Protestant.* a member of that branch of the Adventists which constituted itself as a separate body after the expected Second Coming of Christ failed to be realized in 1844. They are strongly Protestant, believe that Christ's coming is imminent, and observe Saturday instead of Sunday as their Sabbath.

seventh heaven *n* **1** the final state of eternal bliss, esp. according to Talmudic and Muslim eschatology. **2** a state of supreme happiness. **[**C19: so named from the belief that there are seven levels of heaven, the seventh and most exalted being the abode of God and the angels**]**

seventieth (ˈsevᵊntɪɪθ) *adj* **1** (*usually prenominal*) **1a** being the ordinal number of *seventy* in numbering or counting order, position, time, etc.: often written 70th. **1b** (*as n*): *the seventieth in line.* ◆ *n* **2a** one of 70 approximately equal parts of something. **2b** (*as modifier*): *a seventieth part.* **3** the fraction equal to one divided by 70 (1/70).

seventy (ˈsevᵊntɪ) *n, pl* **-ties. 1** the cardinal number that is the product of ten and seven. See also **number** (sense 1). **2** a numeral, 70, LXX, etc., representing this number. **3** (*pl*) the numbers 70–79, esp. the 70th to the 79th year of a person's life or of a particular century. **4** the amount or quantity that is seven times as big as ten. **5** something represented by, representing, or consisting of 70 units. ◆ *determiner* **6a** amounting to seventy: *the seventy varieties of fabric.* **6b** (*as pronoun*): *to invite seventy to the wedding.* **[**Old English *seofontig***]**

seven-up *n* a card game in which the lead to each round determines the trump suit. Also called: **all fours, pitch.**

Seven Wonders of the World *pl n* the seven structures considered by ancient and medieval scholars to be the most wondrous of the ancient world. The list varies, but generally consists of the Pyramids of Egypt, the Hanging Gardens of Babylon, Phidias' statue of Zeus at Olympia, the temple of Artemis at Ephesus, the mausoleum of Halicarnassus, the Colossus of Rhodes, and the Pharos (or lighthouse) of Alexandria.

seven-year itch *n* **1** *Pathol.* an informal name for **scabies. 2** *Informal.* a tendency towards infidelity, traditionally said to begin after about seven years of marriage.

Seven Years' War *n* the war (1756–63) of Britain and Prussia, who emerged in the ascendant, against France and Austria, resulting from commercial and colonial rivalry between Britain and France and from the conflict in Germany between Prussia and Austria.

sever (ˈsevə) *vb* **1** to put or be put apart; separate. **2** to divide or be divided into parts. **3** (*tr*) to break off or dissolve (a tie, relationship, etc.). **[**C14 *severen,* from Old French *severer,* from Latin *sēparāre* to SEPARATE**]**

severable (ˈsevərəbᵊl) *adj* **1** able to be severed. **2** *Law.* capable of being separated, as a clause in an agreement: *a severable contract.*

several (ˈsevrəl) *determiner* **1a** more than a few; an indefinite small number: *several people objected.* **1b** (*as pronoun; functioning as pl*): *several of them know.* ◆ *adj* **2** (*prenominal*) various; separate: *the members with their several occupations.* **3** (*prenominal*) distinct; different: *three several times.* **4** *Law.* capable of being dealt with separately; not shared. Compare **joint** (sense 15). **[**C15: via Anglo-French from Medieval Latin *sēparālis,* from Latin *sēpār,* from *sēparāre* to SEPARATE**]**

severally (ˈsevrəlɪ) *adv* **1** separately, individually, or distinctly. **2** each in turn; respectively.

severalty (ˈsevrəltɪ) *n, pl* **-ties. 1** the state of being several or separate. **2** (usually preceded by *in*) *Property law.* the tenure of property, esp. land, in a person's own right and not jointly with another or others.

severance (ˈsevərəns) *n* **1** the act of severing or state of being severed. **2** a separation. **3** *Law.* the division into separate parts of a joint estate, contract, etc.

severance pay *n* compensation paid by an organization to an employee who leaves because, through no fault of his own, the job to which he was appointed ceases to exist, as during rationalization, and no comparable job is available to him.

severe (sɪˈvɪə) *adj* **1** rigorous or harsh in the treatment of others; strict: *a severe parent.* **2** serious in appearance or manner; stern. **3** critical or dangerous: *a severe illness.* **4** causing misery or discomfort by its harshness: *severe weather.* **5** strictly restrained in appearance; austere: *a severe way of dressing.* **6** hard to endure, perform, or accomplish: *a severe test.* **7** rigidly precise or exact. **[**C16: from Latin *sevērus***]** ▸ **seˈverely** *adv* ▸ **seˈvereness** *or* **severity** (sɪˈverɪtɪ) *n*

Severn (ˈsevᵊn) *n* **1** a river in E Wales and W England, rising in Powys and flowing northeast and east into England, then south to the Bristol Channel. Length: about 290 km (180 miles). **2** a river in SE central Canada, in Ontario, flowing northeast to Hudson Bay. Length: about 676 km (420 miles).

Severnaya Zemlya (*Russian* ˈsjevɪrnəjə zɪmˈlja) *n* an archipelago in the Arctic Ocean off the coast of N central Russia.

Severus (sɪˈvɪərəs) *n* **Lucius Septimius** (sɛpˈtɪmɪəs). 146–211 A.D., Roman soldier and emperor (193–211). He waged war successfully against the Parthians (197–202) and spent his last years in Britain (208–11).

Seveso (seˈveɪsəʊ) *n* a town in N Italy, near Milan: evacuated in 1976 after contamination by a poisonous cloud of dioxin gas released from a factory.

Sévigné (*French* seviɲe) *n* **Marquise de,** title of *Marie de Rabutin-Chantal.* 1626–96, French letter writer. Her correspondence with her daughter and others provides a vivid account of society during the reign of Louis XIV.

Seville (səˈvɪl) *n* a port in SW Spain, on the Guadalquivir River: chief town of S Spain under the Vandals and Visigoths (5th–8th centuries); centre of Spanish colonial trade (16th–17th centuries); tourist centre. Pop.: 719 588 (1995 est.). Ancient name: **Hispalis.** Spanish name: **Sevilla** (seˈβiʎa).

Seville orange *n* **1** an orange tree, *Citrus aurantium,* of tropical and semitropical regions: grown for its bitter fruit, which is used to make marmalade. **2** the fruit of this tree. ◆ Also called: **bitter orange.**

Sèvres (*French* sɛvrə) *n* porcelain ware manufactured at Sèvres, near Paris, from 1756, characterized by the use of clear colours and elaborate decorative detail.

sew (səʊ) *vb* **sews, sewing, sewed; sewn** *or* **sewed. 1** to join or decorate (pieces of fabric, etc.) by means of a thread repeatedly passed through with a needle or similar implement. **2** (*tr;* often foll. by *on* or *up*) to attach, fasten, or close by sewing. **3** (*tr*) to make (a garment, etc.) by sewing. ◆ See also **sew up.** **[**Old English *sēowan;* related to Old Norse *sȳja,* Gothic *siujan,* Old High German *siuwen,* Latin *suere* to sew, Sanskrit *sīvjati* he sews**]**

sewage (ˈsuːɪdʒ) *n* waste matter from domestic or industrial establishments that is carried away in sewers or drains for dumping or conversion into a form that is not toxic. **[**C19: back formation from SEWER[1]**]**

sewage farm *n* a place where sewage is treated, esp. for use as manure.

sewage gas *n* gas given off in the digestion of sewage consisting of approximately 66 per cent methane and 34 per cent carbon dioxide.

sewan (ˈsiːwən) *n* a variant spelling of **seawan.**

Seward (ˈsjuːəd) *n* **William Henry.** 1801–72, U.S. statesman; secretary of state (1861–69). He was a leading opponent of slavery and was responsible for the purchase of Alaska (1867).

Seward Peninsula *n* a peninsula of W Alaska, on the Bering Strait. Length: about 290 km (180 miles).

Sewell (ˈsuːəl) *n* **Henry.** 1807–79, New Zealand statesman, born in England: first prime minister of New Zealand (1856).

sewellel (sɪˈwɛləl) *n* another name for **mountain beaver** (see **beaver**[1] (sense 3)). **[**C19: probably from Chinook**]**

sewer[1] (ˈsuːə) *n* **1** a drain or pipe, esp. one that is underground, used to carry away surface water or sewage. ◆ *vb* **2** (*tr*) to provide with sewers. **[**C15: from Old French *esseveur,* from *essever* to drain, from Vulgar Latin *exaquāre* (unattested), from Latin EX-[1] + *aqua* water**]**

sewer[2] (ˈsəʊə) *n* a person or thing that sews.

sewer[3] (ˈsuːə) *n* (in medieval England) a servant of high rank in charge of the serving of meals and the seating of guests. **[**C14: shortened from Anglo-French *asseour,* from Old French *asseoir* to cause to sit, from Latin *assidēre,* from *sedēre* to sit**]**

sewerage (ˈsuːərɪdʒ) *n* **1** an arrangement of sewers. **2** the removal of surface water or sewage by means of sewers. **3** another word for **sewage.**

sewin *or* **sewen** (ˈsjuən) *n* (in Wales and Ireland) another name for the **sea trout.** **[**C16: origin unknown**]**

sewing (ˈsəʊɪŋ) *n* **a** a piece of cloth, etc., that is sewn or to be sewn. **b** (*as modifier*): *sewing basket.*

sewing machine *n* any machine designed to sew material. It is now usually driven by electric motor but is sometimes operated by a foot treadle or by hand.

sewn (səʊn) *vb* a past participle of **sew.**

sewn binding *n Bookbinding.* a style of binding where the backs of the gathered sections are sewn together before being inserted into a cover.

sew up *vb* (*tr, adv*) **1** to fasten or mend completely by sewing. **2** *U.S.* to acquire sole use or control of. **3** *Informal.* to complete or negotiate successfully: *to sew up a deal.*

sex (sɛks) *n* **1** the sum of the characteristics that distinguish organisms on the basis of their reproductive function. **2** either of the two categories, male or female, into which organisms are placed on this basis. **3** short for **sexual intercourse. 4** feelings or behaviour resulting from the urge to gratify the sexual instinct. **5** sexual matters in general. ◆ *modifier.* **6** of or concerning sexual matters: *sex education; sex hygiene.* **7** based on or arising from the difference between the sexes: *sex discrimination.* ◆ *vb* **8** (*tr*) to ascertain the sex of. **[**C14: from Latin *sexus;* compare *secāre* to divide**]**

sex- *combining form.* six: *sexcentennial.* **[**from Latin**]**

sexagenarian (ˌsɛksədʒɪˈnɛərɪən) *n* **1** a person from 60 to 69 years old. ◆ *adj* **2** being from 60 to 69 years old. **3** of or relating to a sexagenarian. **[**C18: from Latin *sexāgēnārius,* from *sexāgēnī* sixty each, from *sexāgintā* sixty**]** ▸ **sexagenary** (sɛkˈsædʒɪnərɪ) *adj, n*

Sexagesima (ˌsɛksəˈdʒɛsɪmə) *n* the second Sunday before Lent. **[**C16: from Latin: sixtieth, from *sexāgintā* sixty**]**

sexagesimal (ˌsɛksəˈdʒɛsɪməl) *adj* **1** relating to or based on the number 60: *sexagesimal measurement of angles.* ◆ *n* **2** a fraction in which the denominator is some power of 60; a sixtieth.

sex-and-shopping *adj* (*prenominal*) (of a novel) belonging to a genre of novel in which the central character, a woman, has a number of sexual encounters, and the author mentions the name of many up-market products: *a sex-and-shopping blockbuster.*

sexangular (sɛksˈæŋgjʊlə) *adj* another name for **hexagonal.** ▸ **sexˈangularly** *adv*

sex appeal *n* the quality or power of attracting the opposite sex.

sexcentenary (ˌsɛksɛnˈtiːnərɪ) *adj* **1** of or relating to 600 or a period of 600 years. **2** of, relating to, or celebrating a 600th anniversary. ◆ *n, pl* **-naries. 3** a 600th anniversary or its celebration. **[**C18: from Latin *sexcentēnī* six hundred each**]**

sex change *n* **a** a change in a person's physical sexual characteristics to those of the opposite sex, often achieved by surgery. **b** (*as modifier*): *a sex-change operation.*

sex chromosome *n* either of the chromosomes determining the sex of animals. See also **X-chromosome, Y-chromosome.**

sexed (sɛkst) *adj* **1** (*in combination*) having a specified degree of sexuality: *undersexed.* **2** of, relating to, or having sexual differentiation.

sexennial (sɛk'sɛnɪəl) *adj* **1** occurring once every six years or over a period of six years. ◆ *n* **2** a sixth anniversary. [C17: from Latin *sexennis* of six years, from *sex* six + *annus* a year] ▸ **sex'ennially** *adv*

sex hormone *n* an animal hormone affecting development and growth of reproductive organs and related parts.

sexism ('sɛksɪzəm) *n* discrimination on the basis of sex, esp. the oppression of women by men. [C20: from SEX + -ISM, on the model of RACISM] ▸ **'sexist** *n, adj*

sexivalent *or* **sexavalent** (ˌsɛksɪ'veɪlənt) *adj Chem.* another word for **hexavalent.**

sexless ('sɛkslɪs) *adj* **1** having or showing no sexual differentiation. **2** having no sexual desires. **3** sexually unattractive. ▸ **'sexlessly** *adv* ▸ **'sexlessness** *n*

sex-limited *adj Genetics.* of or designating a character or the gene producing it that appears in one sex only.

sex linkage *n Genetics.* the condition in which a particular gene is located on a sex chromosome, esp. on the X-chromosome, so that the character controlled by the gene is associated with either of the sexes. ▸ **'sex,linked** *adj*

sex object *n* a person viewed or treated as a means of obtaining sexual gratification.

sexology (sɛk'sɒlədʒɪ) *n* the study of sexual behaviour in human beings. ▸ **sex'ologist** *n* ▸ **sexological** (ˌsɛksə'lɒdʒɪkᵊl) *adj*

sexpartite (sɛks'pɑːtaɪt) *adj* **1** (esp. of vaults, arches, etc.) divided into or composed of six parts. **2** maintained by or involving six participants or groups of participants.

sexploitation (ˌsɛksplɔɪ'teɪʃən) *n* the commercial exploitation of sex in films and other media. [C20: blend of SEX + EXPLOITATION]

sexpot ('sɛksˌpɒt) *n Slang.* a person, esp. a young woman, considered as being sexually very attractive.

sex shop *n* **a** a shop selling aids purporting to increase the pleasurableness of sexual activity. **b** a shop selling erotica and pornographic material.

sex-starved *adj* deprived of sexual gratification.

sext (sɛkst) *n Chiefly R.C. Church.* the fourth of the seven canonical hours of the divine office or the prayers prescribed for it: originally the sixth hour of the day (noon). [C15: from Church Latin *sexta hōra* the sixth hour]

Sext (sɛkst) *n R.C. Church.* an official compilation of decretals issued by Boniface VIII in 1298 to supplement the five books of the Liber Extra. It forms part of the Corpus Juris Canonici. In full: **Liber Sextus.**

sextain ('sɛksteɪn) *n* another word for **sestina.** [C17: from obsolete French *sestine* SESTINA, but also influenced by obsolete *sixain* stanza of six lines]

sextan ('sɛkstən) *adj* (of a fever) marked by paroxysms that recur every fifth day. [C17: from Medieval Latin *sextana (febris)* (fever) of the sixth (day)]

Sextans ('sɛkstənz) *n, Latin genitive* **Sextantis** (sɛks'tæntɪs). a faint constellation lying on the celestial equator close to Leo and Hydra. [New Latin: SEXTANT]

sextant ('sɛkstənt) *n* **1** an optical instrument used in navigation and consisting of a telescope through which a sighting of a heavenly body is taken, with protractors for determining its angular distance above the horizon or from another heavenly body. **2** a sixth part of a circle having an arc which subtends an angle of 60°. [C17: from Latin *sextāns* one sixth of a unit]

sextet *or* **sextette** (sɛks'tɛt) *n* **1** *Music.* a group of six singers or instrumentalists or a piece of music composed for such a group. **2** a group of six people or things. [C19: variant of SESTET, with Latinization of *ses-*]

sex therapy *n* treatment by counselling, behaviour modification, etc., for psychosexual and physical problems in sexual intercourse. ▸ **sex therapist** *n*

sextile ('sɛkstaɪl) *n* **1** *Statistics.* one of five actual or notional values of a variable dividing its distribution into six groups with equal frequencies. **2** *Astrology, astronomy.* an aspect or position of 60° between two planets or other celestial bodies. [C16: from Latin *sextīlis* one sixth (of a circle), from *sextus* sixth]

sextillion (sɛks'tɪljən) *n, pl* **-lions** *or* **-lion. 1** (in Britain, France, and Germany) the number represented as one followed by 36 zeros (10^{36}). **2** (in the U.S. and Canada) the number represented as one followed by 21 zeros (10^{21}). [C17: from French, from SEX- + *-illion,* on the model of SEPTILLION] ▸ **sex'tillionth** *adj, n*

sexto ('sɛkstəʊ) *n, pl* **-tos.** *Bookbinding.* another word for **sixmo.** [C19: from Latin *sextus* sixth]

sextodecimo (ˌsɛkstəʊ'dɛsɪˌməʊ) *n, pl* **-mos.** *Bookbinding.* another word for **sixteenmo.** [C17: from Latin *sextusdecimus* sixteenth]

sexton ('sɛkstən) *n* **1** a person employed to act as caretaker of a church and its contents and graveyard, and often also as bell-ringer, gravedigger, etc. **2** another name for the **burying beetle.** [C14: from Old French *secrestein,* from Medieval Latin *sacristānus* SACRISTAN]

sex tourism *n* tourism with the intention of exploiting permissive or poorly enforced local laws concerning sex, esp. sex with children.

sextuple ('sɛkstjupᵊl) *n* **1** a quantity or number six times as great as another. ◆ *adj* **2** six times as much or many; sixfold. **3** consisting of six parts or members. **4** (of musical time or rhythm) having six beats per bar. [C17: Latin *sextus* sixth + *-uple,* as in QUADRUPLE]

sextuplet ('sɛkstjuplɪt) *n* **1** one of six offspring born at one birth. **2** a group of six things. **3** *Music.* a group of six notes played in a time value of four.

sextuplicate *n* (sɛks'tuːpləkɪt, -ˌkeɪt, -'tjuː-, -'tʌp-). **1** a group or set of six things, esp. identical copies. ◆ *adj* (sɛks'tuːpləkɪt, -ˌkeɪt, -'tjuː-, -'tʌp-). **2** six times as many, much, or often. **3** *Maths.* raised to the sixth power. ◆ *vb* (sɛks'tuːpləˌkeɪt, -'tjuː-, -'tʌp-). **4** to multiply or become multiplied by six. [C20: from SEXTU(PLE + DU)PLICATE]

sex-typed *adj* characterized as appropriate for or of one sex rather than the other. ▸ **'sex-ˌtyping** *n*

sexual ('sɛksjuəl) *adj* **1** of, relating to, or characterized by sex or sexuality. **2** (of reproduction) characterized by the union of male and female gametes. Compare **asexual** (sense 2). [C17: from Late Latin *sexuālis;* see SEX] ▸ **'sexually** *adv*

sexual dimorphism *n Biology.* differences in appearance between the males and females of a species.

sexual harassment *n* the persistent unwelcome directing of sexual remarks and looks, and unnecessary physical contact at a person, usually a woman, esp. in the workplace.

sexual intercourse *n* the act of sexual procreation in which the insertion of the male's erect penis into the female's vagina is followed by rhythmic thrusting usually culminating in orgasm; copulation; coitus. Related adj: **venereal.**

sexuality (ˌsɛksju'ælɪtɪ) *n* **1** the state or quality of being sexual. **2** preoccupation with or involvement in sexual matters. **3** the possession of sexual potency.

sexualize *or* **sexualise** ('sɛksjuəˌlaɪz) *vb* **1** to make or become sexual or sexually aware. **2** to give or acquire sexual associations. ▸ **ˌsexuali'zation** *or* **ˌsexuali'sation** *n*

sexual reproduction *n* reproduction involving the fusion of a male and female haploid gamete.

sexual selection *n* an evolutionary process in animals, in which selection by females of males with certain characters, such as large antlers or bright plumage, results in the preservation of these characters in the species.

sexy ('sɛksɪ) *adj* **sexier, sexiest.** *Informal.* **1** provoking or intended to provoke sexual interest: *a sexy dress; a sexy book.* **2** feeling sexual interest; aroused. **3** interesting, exciting, or trendy: *a sexy project; a sexy new car.* ▸ **'sexily** *adv* ▸ **'sexiness** *n*

Seychelles (seɪ'ʃɛl, -'ʃɛlz) *pl n* a group of volcanic islands in the W Indian Ocean: taken by the British from the French in 1744: became an independent republic within the Commonwealth in 1976, incorporating the British Indian Ocean Territory islands of Aldabra, Farquhar and Desroches. Languages: Creole, English, and French. Religion: Roman Catholic majority. Currency: rupee. Capital: Victoria. Pop.: 79 400 (1998 est.). Area: 455 sq. km (176 sq. miles).

Seyfert galaxy ('saɪfət) *n* any of a class of spiral galaxies having a very bright nucleus and inconspicuous arms. [C20: named after Carl K. *Seyfert* (died 1960), U.S. astronomer]

Seyhan (seɪ'hɑːn) *n* another name for **Adana.**

Seymour ('siːmɔː) *n* **Jane.** ?1509–37, third wife of Henry VIII of England; mother of Edward VI.

sf, sf., sfz, *or* **sfz.** *Music. abbrev. for* sforzando.

SF *or* **sf** *abbrev. for* science fiction.

SFA *abbrev. for:* **1** Scottish Football Association. **2** Sweet Fanny Adams. See **fanny adams.**

Sfax (sfæks) *n* a port in E Tunisia, on the Gulf of Gabès: the second largest town in Tunisia; commercial centre of a phosphate region. Pop.: 230 900 (1994).

sferics ('sfɛrɪks) *n* the usual U.S. spelling of **spherics**[2].

SFO *abbrev. for* Serious Fraud Office: the department of the British government which investigates cases of serious financial fraud.

Sforza (*Italian* 'sfɔrtsa) *n* **1** Count **Carlo** ('karlo). 1873–1952, Italian statesman; leader of the anti-Fascist opposition. **2 Francesco** (fran'tʃesko). 1401–66, duke of Milan (1450–66). **3** his father **Giacomuzzo** (dʒako'muttso) or **Muzio** ('muttsjo), original name *Attendolo.* 1369–1424, Italian condottiere and founder of the dynasty that ruled Milan (1450–1535). **4 Lodovico** (lodo'viːko), called *the Moor.* 1451–1508, duke of Milan (1494–1500), but effective ruler from 1480; patron of Leonardo da Vinci.

sforzando (sfɔː'tsɑːndəʊ) *or* **sforzato** (sfɔː'tsɑːtəʊ) *Music.* ◆ *adj, adv* **1** to be played with strong initial attack. Abbrev: **sf.** ◆ *n* **2** a symbol, mark, etc., such as >, written above a note, indicating this. [C19: from Italian, from *sforzare* to force, from EX-[1] + *forzare,* from Vulgar Latin *fortiāre* (unattested) to FORCE[1]]

sfumato (sfuː'mɑːtəʊ) *n* (in painting) a gradual transition between areas of different colour, avoiding sharp outlines. [from Italian, from *sfumato* shaded off, from *sfumare* to shade off, from Latin EX-[1] + *fūmāre* to smoke]

sg *abbrev. for* specific gravity.

SG *abbrev. for:* **1** (in transformational grammar) singular. **2** solicitor general.

sgd *abbrev. for* signed.

SGHWR *abbrev. for* steam-generating heavy-water reactor.

sgian-dhu ('skiːən'duː, 'skiːn-) *n Scot.* a dirk carried in the stocking by Highlanders. [Gaelic *sgian* knife + *dhu* black]

S. Glam *abbrev. for* South Glamorgan.

SGML *abbrev. for* standard generalized mark-up language: an international standard used in publishing for defining the structure and formatting of documents.

SGP *international car registration for* Singapore.

sgraffito (sgræ'fiːtəʊ) *n, pl* **-ti** (-tɪ). **1** a technique in mural or ceramic decoration in which the top layer of glaze, plaster, etc., is incised with a design to reveal parts of the ground. **2** such a decoration. **3** an object decorated in such a way. [C18: from Italian, from *sgraffire* to scratch; see GRAFFITI]

's Gravenhage (sxraːvən'haːxə) *n* the Dutch name for (The) **Hague.**

Sgt *abbrev. for* Sergeant.

Sgt Maj. *abbrev. for* Sergeant Major.

sh (*spelling pron* ʃʃʃ) *interj* an exclamation to request silence or quiet.

sh. *abbrev. for:* **1** *Stock Exchange.* share. **2** sheep. **3** shilling.

SHA *Navigation. abbrev. for* sidereal hour angle.

Shaanxi ('ʃæn'ʃiː) *or* **Shensi** *n* a province of NW China: one of the earliest centres of Chinese civilization; largely mountainous. Capital: Xi An. Pop.: 35 140 000 (1996 est.). Area: 195 800 sq. km (75 598 sq. miles).

Shaba ('ʃɑːbə) *n* a region of SE Democratic Republic of the Congo (formerly Zaïre): site of a secessionist movement during the 1960s and again declared itself independent in 1993; important for hydroelectric power and rich mineral resources (copper and tin ore). Area: 496 964 sq. km (191 878 sq. miles). Former name (until 1972): **Katanga.**

Shaban *or* **Shaaban** (ʃə'bɑːn, ʃɑː-) *n* the eighth month of the Muslim year. [from Arabic *sha'bān*]

Shabbat (ʃɑː'bɑːt), **Shabbos,** *or* **Shabbes** ('ʃɑːbəs) *n, pl* **Shabbatot** (ˌʃɑːbɑː'tot), **Shabbosos** (ʃɑː'bosəs), *or* **Shabbosim** (ʃɑːbosəm). *Judaism.* another word for the **Sabbath.** [from Hebrew *shabbāth;* see SABBATH]

shabby ('ʃæbɪ) *adj* **-bier, -biest. 1** threadbare or dilapidated in appearance. **2** wearing worn and dirty clothes; seedy. **3** mean, despicable, or unworthy: *shabby treatment.* **4** dirty or squalid. [C17: from Old English *sceabb* SCAB + -Y[1]] ▸ **'shabbily** *adv* ▸ **'shabbiness** *n*

shabby-genteel *adj* preserving or aspiring to the forms and manners of gentility despite appearing shabby.

Shabuoth (ʃə'vuːəs, -əus; *Hebrew* ʃavuː'ɔt) *n* a variant spelling of **Shavuot.**

Shacharis *Hebrew.* ('ʃɑxəˌras) *or* **Shaharith** (ˌʃɑxɑ'rit) *n Judaism.* the morning service.

Shache ('ʃæ'tʃeɪ), **Soche,** *or* **So-ch'e** *n* a town in W China, in the W Xinjiang Uygur AR: a centre of the caravan trade between China, India, and Transcaspian areas. Also called: **Yarkand.**

shack (ʃæk) *n* **1** a roughly built hut. ◆ *vb* **2** See **shack up.** [C19: perhaps from dialect *shackly* ramshackle, from dialect *shack* to shake]

shackle ('ʃækᵊl) *n* **1** (*often pl*) a metal ring or fastening, usually part of a pair used to secure a person's wrists or ankles; fetter. **2** (*often pl*) anything that confines or restricts freedom. **3** a rope, tether, or hobble for an animal. **4** a U-shaped bracket, the open end of which is closed by a bolt (**shackle pin**), used for securing ropes, chains, etc. ◆ *vb* (*tr*) **5** to confine with or as if with shackles. **6** to fasten or connect with a shackle. [Old English *sceacel;* related to Dutch *schakel,* Old Norse *skokull* wagon pole, Latin *cingere* to surround] ▸ **'shackler** *n*

Shackleton ('ʃækəltən) *n* Sir **Ernest Henry.** 1874–1922, British explorer. He commanded three expeditions to the Antarctic (1907–09; 1914–17; 1921–22), during which the south magnetic pole was located (1909).

shacko ('ʃækəu) *n, pl* **shackos** *or* **shackoes.** a variant spelling of **shako.**

shack up *vb* (*intr, adv;* usually foll. by *with*) *Slang.* to live or take up residence, esp. with a mistress or lover.

shad (ʃæd) *n, pl* **shad** *or* **shads. 1** any of various herring-like food fishes of the genus *Alosa* and related genera, such as *A. alosa* (**allis shad**) of Europe, that migrate from the sea to freshwater to spawn: family *Clupeidae* (herrings). **2** any of various similar but unrelated fishes. [Old English *sceadd;* related to Norwegian *skadd,* German *Schade* shad, Old Irish *scatān* herring, Latin *scatēre* to well up]

shadberry ('ʃædbərɪ, -brɪ) *n, pl* **-ries.** another name for **serviceberry** (senses 1, 2). [C19: perhaps so called because they appear when SHAD fish are in the rivers to spawn]

Shadbolt ('ʃædˌbəult) *n* **Maurice.** born 1932, New Zealand novelist.

shadbush ('ʃædˌbuʃ) *n* another name for **serviceberry** (sense 1).

shadchan *Yiddish.* (*Yiddish* 'ʃatxən; *Hebrew* ʃad'xan) *n, pl* ***shadchanim*** (ʃat'xɔnɪm) *or* ***shadchans.*** a Jewish marriage broker. [from Hebrew *shadhkhān,* from *shiddēkh* to arrange a marriage]

shaddock ('ʃædək) *n* another name for **pomelo.** [C17: named after Captain *Shaddock,* who brought its seed from the East Indies to Jamaica in 1696]

shade (ʃeɪd) *n* **1** relative darkness produced by the blocking out of light. **2** a place made relatively darker or cooler than other areas by the blocking of light, esp. sunlight. **3** a position of relative obscurity. **4** something used to provide a shield or protection from a direct source of light, such as a lampshade. **5** a darker area indicated in a painting, drawing, etc., by shading. **6** a colour that varies slightly from a standard colour due to a difference in hue, saturation, or luminosity: *a darker shade of green.* **7** a slight amount: *a shade of difference.* **8** *Literary.* a ghost. **9** an archaic word for **shadow. 10 put in the shade.** to appear better than (another); surpass. ◆ *vb* (*mainly tr*) **11** to screen or protect from heat, light, view, etc. **12** to make darker or dimmer. **13** to represent (a darker area) in (a painting, drawing, etc.), by means of hatching, using a darker colour, etc. **14** (*also intr*) to change or cause to change slightly. **15** to lower (a price) slightly. [Old English *sceadu;* related to Gothic *skadus,* Old High German *skato,* Old Irish *scāth* shadow, Greek *skotos* darkness, Swedish *skäddä* fog] ▸ **'shadeless** *adj*

shades (ʃeɪdz) *pl n* **1** gathering darkness at nightfall. **2** a slang word for **sunglasses. 3** (*often cap;* preceded by *the*) a literary term for **Hades. 4** (foll. by *of*) undertones or suggestions: *shades of my father!*

shading ('ʃeɪdɪŋ) *n* the graded areas of tone, lines, dots, etc., indicating light and dark in a painting or drawing.

shadoof *or* **shaduf** (ʃə'duːf) *n* a mechanism for raising water, consisting of a pivoted pole with a bucket at one end and a counterweight at the other, esp. as used in Egypt and the Near East. [C19: from Egyptian Arabic]

shadow ('ʃædəu) *n* **1** a dark image or shape cast on a surface by the interception of light rays by an opaque body. **2** an area of relative darkness. **3** the dark portions of a picture. **4** a hint, image, or faint semblance: *beyond a shadow of a doubt.* **5** a remnant or vestige: *a shadow of one's past self.* **6** a reflection. **7** a threatening influence; blight: *a shadow over one's happiness.* **8** a spectre. **9** an inseparable companion. **10** a person who trails another in secret, such as a detective. **11** *Med.* a dark area on an X-ray film representing an opaque structure or part. **12** (in Jungian psychology) the archetype that represents man's animal ancestors. **13** *Archaic or rare.* protection or shelter. **14** (*modifier*) *Brit.* designating a member or members of the main opposition party in Parliament who would hold ministerial office if their party were in power: *shadow Chancellor; shadow cabinet.* ◆ *vb* (*tr*) **15** to cast a shadow over. **16** to make dark or gloomy; blight. **17** to shade from light. **18** to follow or trail secretly. **19** (often foll. by *forth*) to represent vaguely. **20** *Painting, drawing, etc.* another word for **shade** (sense 13). [Old English *sceadwe,* oblique case of *sceadu* SHADE; related to Dutch *schaduw*] ▸ **'shadower** *n* ▸ **'shadowless** *adj*

shadow-box *vb* (*intr*) **1** *Boxing.* to practise blows and footwork against an imaginary opponent. **2** to act or speak unconvincingly, without saying what one means, etc.: *he's just shadow-boxing.* ▸ **'shadow-ˌboxing** *n*

shadowgraph ('ʃædəuˌgrɑːf, -ˌgræf) *n* **1** a silhouette made by casting a shadow, usually of the hands, on a lighted surface. **2** another name for **radiograph.**

shadow mask *n Television.* a perforated metal sheet mounted close to the phosphor-dotted screen in some colour television tubes. The holes are positioned so that each of the three electron beams strikes the correct phosphor dot producing the required colour mixture in the image.

shadow play *n* a theatrical entertainment using shadows thrown by puppets or actors onto a lighted screen.

shadow price *n Economics.* the calculated price of a good or service for which no market price exists.

shadow test *n Med.* another name for **retinoscopy.**

shadowy ('ʃædəuɪ) *adj* **1** full of shadows; dark; shady. **2** resembling a shadow in faintness; vague. **3** illusory or imaginary. **4** mysterious or secretive: *a shadowy underworld figure.* ▸ **'shadowiness** *n*

Shadrach ('ʃædræk, 'ʃeɪ-) *n Old Testament.* one of Daniel's three companions, who, together with Meshach and Abednego, was miraculously saved from destruction in Nebuchadnezzar's fiery furnace (Daniel 3:12–30).

shaduf (ʃə'duːf) *n* a variant spelling of **shadoof.**

Shadwell ('ʃædwəl) *n* **Thomas.** ?1642–92, English dramatist; poet laureate (1688–92). He was satirized by Dryden.

shady ('ʃeɪdɪ) *adj* **shadier, shadiest. 1** full of shade; shaded. **2** affording or casting a shade. **3** dim, quiet, or concealed. **4** *Informal.* dubious or questionable as to honesty or legality. ▸ **'shadily** *adv* ▸ **'shadiness** *n*

SHAEF (ʃeɪf) *n* (in World War II) *acronym for* Supreme Headquarters Allied Expeditionary Forces.

Shaffer ('ʃæfə) *n* **Peter.** born 1926, British dramatist. His plays include *The Royal Hunt of the Sun* (1964), *Equus* (1973), *Amadeus* (1979), and *The Gift of the Gorgon* (1992).

shaft (ʃɑːft) *n* **1** the long narrow pole that forms the body of a spear, arrow, etc. **2** something directed at a person in the manner of a missile: *shafts of sarcasm.* **3** a ray, beam, or streak, esp. of light. **4** a rod or pole forming the handle of a hammer, axe, golf club, etc. **5** a revolving rod that transmits motion or power: usually used of axial rotation. Compare **rod** (sense 9). **6** one of the two wooden poles by which an animal is harnessed to a vehicle. **7** *Anatomy.* **7a** the middle part (diaphysis) of a long bone. **7b** the main portion of any elongated structure or part. **8** the middle part of a column or pier, between the base and the capital. **9** a column, obelisk, etc., esp. one that forms a monument. **10** *Architect.* a column that supports a vaulting rib, sometimes one of a set. **11** a vertical passageway through a building, as for a lift. **12** a vertical passageway into a mine. **13** *Ornithol.* the central rib of a feather. **14** an archaic or literary word for **arrow. 15 get the shaft.** *U.S. and Canadian slang.* to be tricked or cheated. ◆ *vb* **16** *Slang.* to have sexual intercourse with (a woman). **17** *Slang.* to trick or cheat. [Old English *sceaft;* related to Old Norse *skapt,* German *Schaft,* Latin *scāpus* shaft, Greek *skeptron* SCEPTRE, Lettish *skeps* javelin]

Shaftesbury ('ʃɑːftsbərɪ, -brɪ) *n* **1 1st Earl of,** title of *Anthony Ashley Cooper.* 1621–83, English statesman, a major figure in the Whig opposition to Charles II. **2 7th Earl of,** title of *Anthony Ashley Cooper.* 1801–85, English evangelical churchman and social reformer. He promoted measures to improve conditions in mines (1842), factories (1833; 1847; 1850), and schools.

shaft feather *n Archery.* one of the two fletchings on an arrow. Compare **cock feather.**

shafting ('ʃɑːftɪŋ) *n* **1** an assembly of rotating shafts for transmitting power. **2** the stock from which shafts are made. **3** *Architect.* a set of shafts.

shag[1] (ʃæg) *n* **1** a matted tangle, esp. of hair, wool, etc. **2** a napped fabric, usually a rough wool. **3** shredded coarse tobacco. ◆ *vb* **shags, shagging, shagged. 4** (*tr*) to make shaggy. [Old English *sceacga;* related to *sceaga* SHAW[1], Old Norse *skegg* beard, *skagi* tip, *skōgr* forest]

shag[2] (ʃæg) *n* **1** another name for the **green cormorant** (*Phalacrocorax aristotelis*). **2 like a shag on a rock.** *Austral. slang.* abandoned and alone. [C16: special use of SHAG[1], with reference to its crest]

shag[3] (ʃæg) *Brit. slang.* ◆ *vb* **shags, shagging, shagged. 1** *Taboo.* to have sexual intercourse with (a person). **2** (*tr;* often foll. by *out; usually passive*) to exhaust; tire. ◆ *n* **3** *Taboo.* an act of sexual intercourse. [C20: of unknown origin]

shagbark ('ʃægˌbɑːk) *or* **shellbark** *n* **1** a North American hickory tree, *Carya ovata,* having loose rough bark and edible nuts. **2** the wood of this tree, used for tool handles, fuel, etc. **3** the light-coloured hard-shelled nut of this tree. [C18: so called because of the texture of its bark]

shaggy ('ʃægɪ) *adj* **-gier, -giest. 1** having or covered with rough unkempt fur, hair, wool, etc.: *a shaggy dog.* **2** rough or unkempt. **3** (in textiles) having a nap of long rough strands. ▸ **'shaggily** *adv* ▸ **'shagginess** *n*

shaggy cap *n* an edible saprotrophic agaricaceous fungus, *Coprinus comatus,* having a white cap covered with shaggy scales.

shaggy dog story *n Informal.* a long rambling joke ending in a deliberate anticlimax, such as a pointless punch line.

shagreen (ʃæ'griːn) *n* **1** the rough skin of certain sharks and rays, used as an abrasive. **2** a rough grainy leather made from certain animal hides. [C17:

from French *chagrin,* from Turkish *çagri* rump; also associated through folk etymology with SHAG[1], GREEN]

shagroon (ʃæ'gru:n) *n N.Z. history.* a nineteenth-century Australian settler in Canterbury. [perhaps from Irish *seachrān* wandering]

shah (ʃɑ:) *n* a ruler of certain Middle Eastern countries, esp. (formerly) Iran. [C16: from Persian: king] ▸ **'shahdom** *n*

shahada (ʃə'hɑ:də) *n* the Islamic declaration of faith, repeated daily by Muslims. [from Arabic, literally: witnessing]

Shahaptin (ʃə'hæptɪn), **Shahaptan** (ʃə'hæptən), *or* **Shahaptian** (ʃə'hæptɪən) *n* variants of **Sahaptin.**

Shah Jahan (dʒə'hɑ:n) *n* 1592–1666, Mogul emperor (1628–58). During his reign the finest monuments of Mogul architecture in India were built, including the Taj Mahal and the Pearl Mosque at Agra.

Shahjahanpur (ˌʃɑ:dʒəˌhɑ:n'pʊə) *n* a city in N India, in central Uttar Pradesh: founded in 1647 in the reign of Shah Jahan. Pop.: 237 713 (1991).

Shahn (ʃɑ:n) *n* **Ben.** 1898–1969, U.S. artist, born in Lithuania, best known as an exponent of social realism, especially in the series (1931–32) inspired by the executions of Sacco and Vanzetti.

Shah of Iran (ʃɑ:) *n* See (Mohammed Reza) **Pahlavi**[1].

Shaitan (ʃaɪ'tɑ:n) *n* (in Muslim countries) **a** Satan. **b** any evil spirit. **c** a vicious person or animal. [C17: from Arabic *shaytān,* from Hebrew *śāṭān;* see SATAN]

Shaka *or* **Chaka** ('ʃaka) *n* died 1828, Zulu military leader, who founded the Zulu Empire in southern Africa.

shake (ʃeɪk) *vb* **shakes, shaking, shook, shaken** ('ʃeɪkᵊn). **1** to move or cause to move up and down or back and forth with short quick movements; vibrate. **2** to sway or totter or cause to sway or totter. **3** to clasp or grasp (the hand) of (a person) in greeting, agreement, etc.: *he shook John by the hand; he shook John's hand; they shook and were friends.* **4 shake hands.** to clasp hands in greeting, agreement, etc. **5 shake on it.** *Informal.* to shake hands in agreement, reconciliation, etc. **6** to bring or come to a specified condition by or as if by shaking: *he shook free and ran.* **7** (*tr*) to wave or brandish: *he shook his sword.* **8** (*tr;* often foll. by *up*) to rouse, stir, or agitate. **9** (*tr*) to shock, disturb, or upset: *he was shaken by the news of her death.* **10** (*tr*) to undermine or weaken: *the crisis shook his faith.* **11** to mix (dice) by rattling in a cup or the hand before throwing. **12** (*tr*) *Austral. archaic slang.* to steal. **13** (*tr*) *U.S. and Canadian informal.* to escape from: *can you shake that detective?* **14** *Music.* to perform a trill on (a note). **15 shake a leg.** *Informal.* to hurry: usually used in the imperative. **16 shake in one's shoes.** to tremble with fear or apprehension. **17 shake one's head.** to indicate disagreement or disapproval by moving the head from side to side. **18 shake the dust from one's feet.** to depart gladly or with the intention not to return. ◆ *n* **19** the act or an instance of shaking. **20** a tremor or vibration. **21 the shakes.** *Informal.* a state of uncontrollable trembling or a condition that causes it, such as a fever. **22** *Informal.* a very short period of time; jiffy: *in half a shake.* **23** a shingle or clapboard made from a short log by splitting it radially. **24** a fissure or crack in timber or rock. **25** an instance of shaking dice before casting. **26** *Music.* another word for **trill**[1] (sense 1). **27** a dance, popular in the 1960s, in which the body is shaken convulsively in time to the beat. **28** an informal name for **earthquake. 29** short for **milk shake. 30 no great shakes.** *Informal.* of no great merit or value; ordinary. ◆ See also **shake down, shake off, shake up.** [Old English *sceacan;* related to Old Norse *skaka* to shake, Old High German *untscachōn* to be driven] ▸ **'shakable** *or* **'shakeable** *adj*

shake down *vb* (*adv*) **1** to fall or settle or cause to fall or settle by shaking. **2** (*tr*) *U.S. slang.* to extort money from, esp. by blackmail or threats of violence. **3** (*tr*) *U.S. slang.* to search thoroughly. **4** (*tr*) *Informal, chiefly U.S.* to submit (a vessel, etc.) to a shakedown test. **5** (*intr*) to go to bed, esp. to a makeshift bed. **6** (*intr*) (of a person, animal, etc.) to settle down. ◆ *n* **shakedown. 7** *U.S. slang.* a swindle or act of extortion. **8** *U.S. slang.* a thorough search. **9** a makeshift bed, esp. of straw, blankets, etc. **10** *Informal, chiefly U.S.* **10a** a voyage to test the performance of a ship or aircraft or to familiarize the crew with their duties. **10b** (*as modifier*): *a shakedown run.*

shake off *vb* (*adv*) **1** to remove or be removed with or as if with a quick movement: *she shook off her depression.* **2** (*tr*) to escape from; elude: *they shook off the police.*

shake-out *n* the process of reducing the number of people in a workforce in order to lower the costs of a company.

shaker ('ʃeɪkə) *n* **1** a person or thing that shakes. **2** a container, often having a perforated top, from which something, such as a condiment, is shaken. **3** a container in which the ingredients of alcoholic drinks are shaken together.

Shakers ('ʃeɪkəz) *pl n* **the.** an American millenarian sect, founded in 1747 as an offshoot of the Quakers, given to ecstatic shaking, advocating celibacy for its members, and practising common ownership of property.

Shakespeare ('ʃeɪkspɪə) *n* **William.** 1564–1616, English dramatist and poet. He was born and died at Stratford-upon-Avon but spent most of his life as an actor and playwright in London. His plays with approximate dates of composition are: *Henry VI, Parts I–III* (1590); *Richard III* (1592); *The Comedy of Errors* (1592); *Titus Andronicus* (1593); *The Taming of the Shrew* (1593); *The Two Gentlemen of Verona* (1594); *Love's Labour's Lost* (1594); *Romeo and Juliet* (1594); *Richard II* (1595); *A Midsummer Night's Dream* (1595); *King John* (1596); *The Merchant of Venice* (1596); *Henry IV, Parts I–II* (1597); *Much Ado about Nothing* (1598); *Henry V* (1598); *Julius Caesar* (1599); *As You Like It* (1599); *Twelfth Night* (1599); *Hamlet* (1600); *The Merry Wives of Windsor* (1600); *Troilus and Cressida* (1601); *All's Well that ends Well* (1602); *Measure for Measure* (1604); *Othello* (1604); *King Lear* (1605); *Macbeth* (1605); *Antony and Cleopatra* (1606); *Coriolanus* (1607); *Timon of Athens* (1607); *Pericles* (1608); *Cymbeline* (1609); *The Winter's Tale* (1610); *The Tempest* (1611); and, possibly in collaboration with John Fletcher, *Two Noble Kinsmen* (1612) and *Henry VIII* (1612). His *Sonnets,* variously addressed to a fair young man and a dark lady, were published in 1609.

Shakespearean *or* **Shakespearian** (ʃeɪk'spɪərɪən) *adj* **1** of, relating to, or characteristic of Shakespeare or his works. ◆ *n* **2** a student of or specialist in Shakespeare's works.

Shakespeareana ('ʃeɪkˌspɪərɪ'ɑ:nə, ʃeɪkˌspɪər-) *n* (*functioning as pl*) collected writings or items relating to Shakespeare.

Shakespearean sonnet *n* a sonnet form developed in 16th-century England and employed by Shakespeare, having the rhyme scheme a b a b c d c d e f e f g g. Also called: **Elizabethan sonnet, English sonnet.**

shake up *vb* (*tr, adv*) **1** to shake or agitate in order to mix. **2** to reorganize drastically. **3** to stir or rouse. **4** to restore the shape of (a pillow, cushion, etc.). **5** *Informal.* to disturb or shock mentally or physically. ◆ *n* **shake-up. 6** *Informal.* a radical or drastic reorganization.

Shakhty (*Russian* 'ʃaxtɪ) *n* an industrial city in W Russia: the chief town of the E Donets Basin; a major coal-mining centre. Pop.: 230 000 (1995 est.).

shaking palsy *n* another name for **Parkinson's disease.**

shako *or* **shacko** ('ʃækəʊ) *n, pl* **shakos, shakoes** *or* **shackos, shackoes.** a tall usually cylindrical military headdress, having a plume and often a peak, popular esp. in the 19th century. [C19: via French from Hungarian *csákó,* from Middle High German *zacke* a sharp point]

Shakta ('ʃʌktə) *n Hinduism.* a devotee of Sakti, the wife of Siva. [from Sanskrit *śākta* concerning Sakti] ▸ **'Shaktism** *n* ▸ **'Shaktist** *n*

Shakti ('ʃʌktɪ) *n* a variant of **Sakti.**

shaky ('ʃeɪkɪ) *adj* **shakier, shakiest. 1** tending to shake or tremble. **2** liable to prove defective; unreliable. **3** uncertain or questionable: *your arguments are very shaky.* ▸ **'shakily** *adv* ▸ **'shakiness** *n*

shale (ʃeɪl) *n* a dark fine-grained laminated sedimentary rock formed by compression of successive layers of clay. [Old English *scealu* SHELL; compare German *Schalstein* laminated limestone; see SCALE[1], SCALE[2]] ▸ **'shaly** *adj*

shale oil *n* an oil distilled from shales and used as fuel.

shall (ʃæl; *unstressed* ʃəl) *vb past* **should.** (takes an infinitive without *to* or an implied infinitive) used as an auxiliary: **1** (esp. with *I* or *we* as subject) to make the future tense: *we shall see you tomorrow.* Compare **will**[1] (sense 1). **2** (with *you, he, she, it, they,* or a noun as subject) **2a** to indicate determination on the part of the speaker, as in issuing a threat: *you shall pay for this!* **2b** to indicate compulsion, now esp. in official documents: *the Tenant shall return the keys to the Landlord.* **2c** to indicate certainty or inevitability: *our day shall come.* **3** (*with any noun or pronoun as subject, esp. in conditional clauses or clauses expressing doubt*) to indicate nonspecific futurity: *I don't think I shall ever see her again; he doubts whether he shall be in tomorrow.* [Old English *sceal;* related to Old Norse *skal,* Old High German *scal,* Dutch *zal*]

USAGE The usual rule given for the use of *shall* and *will* is that where the meaning is one of simple futurity, *shall* is used for the first person of the verb and *will* for the second and third: *I shall go tomorrow; they will be there now.* Where the meaning involves command, obligation, or determination, the positions are reversed: *it shall be done; I will definitely go.* However, *shall* has come to be largely neglected in favour of *will,* which has become the commonest form of the future in all three persons.

shalloon (ʃæ'lu:n) *n* a light twill-weave woollen fabric used chiefly for coat linings, etc. [C17: from Old French *chalon,* from the name of *Châlons-sur-Marne,* France, where it originated]

shallop ('ʃæləp) *n* **1** a light boat used for rowing in shallow water. **2** (formerly) a two-masted gaff-rigged vessel. [C16: from French *chaloupe,* from Dutch *sloep* SLOOP]

shallot (ʃə'lɒt) *n* **1** Also called: **scallion.** an alliaceous plant, *Allium ascalonicum,* cultivated for its edible bulb. **2** the bulb of this plant, which divides into small sections and is used in cooking for flavouring and as a vegetable. [C17: from Old French *eschalotte,* from Old French *eschaloigne,* from Latin *Ascalōnia caepa* Ascalonian onion, from *Ascalon,* a Palestinian town]

shallow ('ʃæləʊ) *adj* **1** having little depth. **2** lacking intellectual or mental depth or subtlety; superficial. ◆ *n* **3** (*often pl*) a shallow place in a body of water; shoal. ◆ *vb* **4** to make or become shallow. [C15: related to Old English *sceald* shallow; see SHOAL[1]] ▸ **'shallowly** *adv* ▸ **'shallowness** *n*

shalom aleichem *Hebrew.* (ʃa'lɔm a'lexem; *English* ʃə'lɒm ə'leɪxəm) *interj* peace be to you: used by Jews as a greeting or farewell. Often shortened to **shalom.**

shalt (ʃælt) *vb Archaic or dialect.* (used with the pronoun *thou* or its relative equivalent) a singular form of the present tense (indicative mood) of **shall.**

sham (ʃæm) *n* **1** anything that is not what it purports or appears to be. **2** something false, fake, or fictitious that purports to be genuine. **3** a person who pretends to be something other than he is. ◆ *adj* **4** counterfeit or false; simulated. ◆ *vb* **shams, shamming, shammed. 5** to falsely assume the appearance of (something); counterfeit: *to sham illness.* [C17: perhaps a Northern English dialect variant of SHAME] ▸ **'shammer** *n*

shaman ('ʃæmən) *n* **1** a priest of shamanism. **2** a medicine man of a similar religion, esp. among certain tribes of North American Indians. [C17: from Russian *shaman,* from Tungusian *šaman,* from Pali *samana* Buddhist monk, ultimately from Sanskrit *śrama* religious exercise] ▸ **shamanic** (ʃə'mænɪk) *adj*

shamanism ('ʃæməˌnɪzəm) *n* **1** the religion of certain peoples of northern Asia, based on the belief that the world is pervaded by good and evil spirits who can be influenced or controlled only by the shamans. **2** any similar religion involving forms of spiritualism. ▸ **'shamanist** *n, adj* ▸ **ˌshaman'istic** *adj*

Shamash ('ʃɑ:mæʃ) *n* the sun god of Assyria and Babylonia. [from Akkadian: sun]

shamateur ('ʃæməˌtɜ:, -ˌtjʊə, -tə, -tʃə) *n* a sportsperson who is officially an amateur but accepts payment. [C20: from a blend of SHAM + AMATEUR]

shamba ('ʃamba) *n* (in E Africa) any field used for growing crops. [Swahili]

shamble ('ʃæmbᵊl) *vb* **1** (*intr*) to walk or move along in an awkward or unsteady way. ◆ *n* **2** an awkward or unsteady walk. [C17: from *shamble* (adj) ungainly, perhaps from the phrase *shamble legs* legs resembling those of a meat vendor's table; see SHAMBLES] ▸ **'shambling** *adj, n*

shambles ('ʃæmbᵊlz) *n* (*functioning as sing or pl*) **1** a place of great disorder: *the room was a shambles after the party.* **2** a place where animals are brought to be slaughtered. **3** any place of slaughter or carnage. **4** *Brit. dialect.* a row of covered stalls or shops where goods, originally meat, are sold. [C14 *shamble* table used by meat vendors, from Old English *sceamel* stool, from Late Latin *scamellum* a small bench, from Latin *scamnum* stool]

shambolic (ʃæm'bɒlɪk) *adj Informal.* completely disorganized; chaotic. [C20: irregularly formed from SHAMBLES]

shame (ʃeɪm) *n* **1** a painful emotion resulting from an awareness of having done something dishonourable, unworthy, degrading, etc. **2** capacity to feel such an emotion. **3** ignominy or disgrace. **4** a person or thing that causes this. **5** an occasion for regret, disappointment, etc.: *it's a shame you can't come with us.* **6 put to shame. 6a** to disgrace. **6b** to surpass totally. ◆ *interj* **7** *S. African informal.* **7a** an expression of sympathy. **7b** an expression of pleasure or endearment. ◆ *vb* (*tr*) **8** to cause to feel shame. **9** to bring shame on; disgrace. **10** (often foll. by *into*) to compel through a sense of shame: *he shamed her into making an apology.* [Old English *scamu;* related to Old Norse *skömm,* Old High German *skama*] ▸ **'shamable** *or* **'shameable** *adj*

shamefaced ('ʃeɪm,feɪst) *adj* **1** bashful or modest. **2** showing a sense of shame. [C16: alteration of earlier *shamefast,* from Old English *sceamfæst;* see SHAME, FAST[1]] ▸ **shamefacedly** (ʃeɪm'feɪsɪdlɪ, 'ʃeɪm,feɪstlɪ) *adv* ▸ **shame'facedness** *n*

shameful ('ʃeɪmfʊl) *adj* causing or deserving shame; scandalous. ▸ **'shamefully** *adv* ▸ **'shamefulness** *n*

shameless ('ʃeɪmlɪs) *adj* **1** having no sense of shame; brazen. **2** done without shame; without decency or modesty. ▸ **'shamelessly** *adv* ▸ **'shamelessness** *n*

Shamir (ʃæ'mɪə) *n* **Yitzhak** ('jɪtʒæk). born 1915, Israeli statesman, born in Poland: prime minister (1983–84; 1986–92): foreign minister (1980–83; 1984–86).

shammes *or* **shammash** ('ʃɑːməs; *Hebrew* ʃa'maʃ) *n, pl* **shammosim** *or* **shammashim** (*Hebrew* ʃa'mɔsɪm). *Judaism.* **1** an official acting as the beadle, sexton, and caretaker of a synagogue. **2** the extra candle used on the Feast of Hanukkah to kindle the lamps or candles of the menorah. [from Hebrew *shāmmāsh,* from Aramaic *shĕmāsh* to serve]

shammy ('ʃæmɪ) *n, pl* **-mies.** *Informal.* another word for **chamois** (sense 3). Also called: **shammy leather.** [C18: variant, influenced by the pronunciation, of CHAMOIS]

Shamo ('ʃɑː'məʊ) *n* transliteration of the Chinese name for the **Gobi.**

shampoo (ʃæm'puː) *n* **1** a liquid or cream preparation of soap or detergent to wash the hair. **2** a similar preparation for washing carpets, etc. **3** the process of shampooing. ◆ *vb* **-poos, -pooing, -pooed. 4** (*tr*) to wash (the hair, etc.) with such a preparation. [C18: from Hindi *chāmpo,* from *chāmpnā* to knead] ▸ **sham'pooer** *n*

shamrock ('ʃæm,rɒk) *n* a plant having leaves divided into three leaflets, variously identified as the wood sorrel, red clover, white clover, and black medick: the national emblem of Ireland. [C16: from Irish Gaelic *seamrōg,* diminutive of *seamar* clover]

shamus ('ʃɑːməs, 'ʃeɪ-) *n, pl* **-muses.** *U.S. slang.* a police or private detective. [probably from SHAMMES, influenced by Irish *Séamas* James]

Shan (ʃɑːn) *n* **1** (*pl* **Shans** *or* **Shan**) a member of a Mongoloid people living in Myanmar, Thailand, and SW China. **2** the language or group of dialects spoken by the Shan, belonging to the Sino-Tibetan family and closely related to Thai.

Shandong ('ʃæn'dʌŋ) *or* **Shantung** *n* a province of NE China, on the Yellow Sea and the Gulf of Chihli: part of the earliest organized state of China (1520–1030 B.C.); consists chiefly of the fertile plain of the lower Yellow River, with mountains over 1500 m (5000 ft.) high in the centre. Capital: Jinan. Pop.: 87 050 000 (1996 est.). Area: 153 300 sq. km (59 189 sq. miles).

shandrydan ('ʃændrɪ,dæn) *n* **1** a two-wheeled cart or chaise, esp. one with a hood. **2** any decrepit old-fashioned conveyance. [C19: of unknown origin]

shandy ('ʃændɪ) *or U.S.* **shandygaff** ('ʃændɪ,gæf) *n, pl* **-dies** *or* **-gaffs.** an alcoholic drink made of beer and ginger beer or lemonade. [C19: of unknown origin]

Shang (ʃæŋ) *n* **1** the dynasty ruling in China from about the 18th to the 12th centuries B.C. ◆ *adj* **2** of or relating to the pottery produced during the Shang dynasty.

Shangaan ('ʃaŋgɑːn) *n* a member of any of the Tsonga-speaking Bantu peoples settled in Mozambique and NE Transvaal, esp. one who works in a gold mine.

shanghai ('ʃæŋhaɪ, ʃæŋ'haɪ) *Slang.* ◆ *vb* **-hais, -haiing, -haied.** (*tr*) **1** to kidnap (a man or seaman) for enforced service at sea, esp. on a merchant ship. **2** to force or trick (someone) into doing something, going somewhere, etc. **3** *Austral. and N.Z.* to shoot with a catapult. ◆ *n* **4** *Austral. and N.Z.* a catapult. [C19: from the city of SHANGHAI; from the forceful methods formerly used to collect crews for voyages to the Orient]

Shanghai ('ʃæŋ'haɪ) *n* a port in E China, in SE Jiangsu near the estuary of the Yangtze: the largest city in China and one of the largest ports in the world; a major cultural and industrial centre, with two universities. Pop.: 7 830 000 (1991 est.).

Shango ('ʃæŋgəʊ) *n* **a** a W African religious cult surviving in some parts of the Caribbean. **b** (*as modifier*): *Shango ritual.* [Yoruba]

Shangri-la (,ʃæŋgrɪ'lɑː) *n* a remote or imaginary utopia. [C20: from the name of an imaginary valley in the Himalayas, from *Lost Horizon* (1933), a novel by James Hilton]

shank (ʃæŋk) *n* **1** *Anatomy.* the shin. **2** the corresponding part of the leg in vertebrates other than man. **3** a cut of meat from the top part of an animal's shank. **4** the main part of a tool, between the working part and the handle. **5** the part of a bolt between the thread and the head. **6** the cylindrical part of a bit by which it is held in the drill. **7** the ring or stem on the back of some buttons. **8** the stem or long narrow part of a key, anchor, hook, spoon handle, nail, pin, etc. **9** the band of a ring as distinguished from the setting. **10a** the part of a shoe connecting the wide part of the sole with the heel. **10b** the metal or leather piece used for this. **11** *Printing.* the body of a piece of type, between the shoulder and the foot. **12** *Engineering.* a ladle used for molten metal. **13** *Music.* another word for **crook** (sense 6). ◆ *vb* **14** (*intr*) (of fruits, roots, etc.) to show disease symptoms, esp. discoloration. **15** (*tr*) *Golf.* to mishit (the ball) with the foot of the shaft rather than the face of the club. [Old English *scanca;* related to Old Frisian *schanke,* Middle Low German *schenke,* Danish, Swedish *skank* leg]

Shankar ('ʃæŋkɑː) *n* **Ravi** ('rɑːviː). born 1920, Indian sitarist.

Shankaracharya ('ʃʌŋkərɑː'tʃɑːrjə) *or* **Shankara** ('ʃʌŋkərə) *n* 9th century A.D., Hindu philosopher and teacher; chief exponent of Vedanta philosophy.

Shankly ('ʃæŋklɪ) *n* **Bill.** 1913–81, Scottish footballer and manager of Liverpool FC (1959–74).

shanks's pony *or U.S. and Canadian* **shanks's mare** ('ʃæŋksɪz) *n Informal.* one's own legs as a means of transportation. [C18: from SHANK (in the sense: lower leg); probably with a pun on the surname *Shanks*]

Shannon[1] ('ʃænən) *n* a river in the Republic of Ireland, rising in NW Co. Cavan and flowing south to the Atlantic by an estuary 113 km (70 miles) long: the longest river in the Republic of Ireland. Length: 260 km (161 miles).

Shannon[2] ('ʃænən) *n* **Claude** (**Elwood**). born 1916, U.S. mathematician, who first developed information theory.

shanny ('ʃænɪ) *n, pl* **-nies.** a European blenny, *Blennius pholis,* of rocky coastal waters. [C19: of obscure origin]

Shansi ('ʃæn'siː) *n* a variant transliteration of the Chinese name for **Shanxi.**

Shan State (ʃɑːn, ʃæn) *n* an administrative division of E Myanmar: formed in 1947 from the joining of the Federation of Shan States with the Wa States; consists of the **Shan plateau,** crossed by forested mountain ranges reaching over 2100 m (7000 ft.). Pop.: 4 416 000 (1994 est.). Area: 149 743 sq. km (57 816 sq. miles).

shan't (ʃɑːnt) *contraction of* shall not.

Shantou *or* **Shantow** ('ʃæn'taʊ) *n* a port in SE China, in E Guangdong near the mouth of the Han River: became a treaty port in 1869. Pop.: 578 630 (1990 est.). Also called: **Swatow.**

shantung (,ʃæn'tʌŋ) *n* **1** a heavy silk fabric with a knobbly surface. **2** a cotton or rayon imitation of this. [C19: so called because it was first imported to Britain from SHANTUNG in China]

Shantung ('ʃæn'tʌŋ) *n* a variant transliteration of the Chinese name for **Shandong.**

shanty[1] ('ʃæntɪ) *n, pl* **-ties. 1** a ramshackle hut; crude dwelling. **2** *Austral. and N.Z.* a public house, esp. an unlicensed one. **3** (formerly, in Canada) **3a** a log bunkhouse at a lumber camp. **3b** the camp itself. [C19: from Canadian French *chantier* cabin built in a lumber camp, from Old French *gantier* GANTRY]

shanty[2], **shantey** ('ʃæntɪ), **chanty,** *or U.S.* **chantey** ('ʃæntɪ, 'tʃæn-) *n, pl* **-ties** *or* **-teys.** a song originally sung by sailors, esp. a rhythmic one forming an accompaniment to work. [C19: from French *chanter* to sing; see CHANT]

shantytown ('ʃæntɪ,taʊn) *n* a town or section of a town or city inhabited by very poor people living in shanties.

Shanxi *or* **Shansi** ('ʃæn'ʃiː) *n* a province of N China: China's richest coal reserves and much heavy industry. Capital: Taiyuan. Pop.: 30 770 000 (1996 est.). Area: 157 099 sq. km (60 656 sq. miles).

shape (ʃeɪp) *n* **1** the outward form of an object defined by outline. **2** the figure or outline of the body of a person. **3** a phantom. **4** organized or definite form: *my plans are taking shape.* **5** the form that anything assumes; guise. **6** something used to provide or define form; pattern; mould. **7** condition or state of efficiency: *to be in good shape.* **8 out of shape. 8a** in bad physical condition. **8b** bent, twisted, or deformed. **9 take shape.** to assume a definite form. ◆ *vb* **10** (when *intr,* often foll. by *into* or *up*) to receive or cause to receive shape or form. **11** (*tr*) to mould into a particular pattern or form; modify. **12** (*tr*) to plan, devise, or prepare: *to shape a plan of action.* **13** an obsolete word for **appoint.** [Old English *gesceap,* literally: that which is created, from *scieppan* to create; related to *sceap* sexual organs, Old Norse *skap* destiny, Old High German *scaf* form] ▸ **'shapable** *or* **'shapeable** *adj* ▸ **'shaper** *n*

SHAPE (ʃeɪp) *n acronym for* Supreme Headquarters Allied Powers Europe.

-shaped (ʃeɪpt) *adj combining form.* having the shape of: *an L-shaped room; a pear-shaped figure.*

shapeless ('ʃeɪplɪs) *adj* **1** having no definite shape or form: *a shapeless mass; a shapeless argument.* **2** lacking a symmetrical or aesthetically pleasing shape: *a shapeless figure.* ▸ **'shapelessly** *adv* ▸ **'shapelessness** *n*

shapely ('ʃeɪplɪ) *adj* **-lier, -liest.** (esp. of a woman's body or legs) pleasing or attractive in shape. ▸ **'shapeliness** *n*

shape up *vb* (*intr, adv*) **1** *Informal.* to proceed or develop satisfactorily. **2** *Informal.* to develop a definite or proper form. ◆ *n* **shapeup. 3** *U.S. and Canadian.* (formerly) a method of hiring dockers for a day or shift by having a union hiring boss select them from a gathering of applicants.

Shapley ('ʃæplɪ) *n* **Harlow.** 1885–1972, U.S. astronomer, director of the Harvard College Observatory (1922–56): noted for his work on the size and structure of the galaxy.

shard (ʃɑːd) *or* **sherd** *n* **1** a broken piece or fragment of a brittle substance, esp. of pottery. **2** *Zoology.* a tough sheath, scale, or shell, esp. the elytra of a beetle. [Old English *sceard;* related to Old Norse *skarth* notch, Middle High German *scharte* notch]

share[1] (ʃεə) *n* **1** a part or portion of something owned, allotted to, or contributed by a person or group. **2** (*often pl*) any of the equal parts, usually of low par value, into which the capital stock of a company is divided: ownership of shares carries the right to receive a proportion of the company's profits. See also **ordinary shares, preference shares. 3 go shares.** *Informal.* to share (something) with another or others. ◆ *vb* **4** (*tr;* often foll. by *out*) to divide or apportion, esp. equally. **5** (when *intr,* often foll. by *in*) to receive or contribute a portion of: *we can share the cost of the petrol; six people shared in the inheritance.* **6** to join with another or others in the use of (something): *can I share your umbrella?* [Old English *scearu;* related to Old Norse *skor* amount, Old High German *scara* crowd; see SHEAR] ▸ **'sharable** *or* **'shareable** *adj* ▸ **'sharer** *n*

share[2] (ʃεə) *n* short for **ploughshare.** [Old English *scear;* related to Old Norse *skeri,* Old High German *scaro*]

share certificate *n* a document issued by a company certifying ownership of one or more of its shares. U.S. equivalent: **stock certificate.**

sharecrop ('ʃεə,krɒp) *vb* **-crops, -cropping, -cropped.** *Chiefly U.S.* to cultivate (farmland) as a sharecropper.

sharecropper ('ʃεə,krɒpə) *n Chiefly U.S.* a farmer, esp. a tenant farmer, who pays over a proportion of a crop or crops as rent.

shared care *n Social welfare.* an arrangement between a welfare agency and a family with a dependent handicapped member, whereby the agency takes the handicapped person into a home for respite care or in emergencies.

shared logic *n Computing.* the sharing of a central processing unit and associated software among several terminals.

shared ownership *n* (in Britain) a form of house purchase whereby the purchaser buys a proportion of the dwelling, usually from a local authority or housing association, and rents the rest.

shared resources *n* (*functioning as sing*) *Computing.* the sharing of peripherals among several terminals.

sharefarmer ('ʃεə,fɑːmə) *n Chiefly Austral.* a farmer who pays a fee to another in return for use of land to raise crops, etc.

shareholder ('ʃεə,həʊldə) *n* the owner of one or more shares in a company.

share index *n* an index showing the movement of share prices. See **Financial Times Industrial Ordinary Share Index, Financial Times Stock Exchange 100 Index.**

share-milker *n* (in New Zealand) a person who lives on a dairy farm milking the owner's herd for an agreed share of the profits and, usually, building his own herd simultaneously.

share option *n* a scheme giving employees an option to buy shares in the company for which they work at a favourable price or discount.

share premium *n Brit.* the excess of the amount actually subscribed for an issue of corporate capital over its par value. Also called (esp. U.S.): **capital surplus.**

share shop *n* a stockbroker, bank, or other financial intermediary that handles the buying and selling of shares for members of the public, esp. during a privatization issue.

shareware ('ʃεə,wεə) *n Computing.* software available to all users without the need for a licence and for which a token fee is requested.

Shari ('ʃɑːrɪ) *n* a variant spelling of **Chari** (the river).

sharia *or* **sheria** (ʃə'riːə) *n* the body of doctrines that regulate the lives of those who profess Islam. [Arabic]

sharif (ʃæ'riːf) *n* a variant transliteration of **sherif.**

shark[1] (ʃɑːk) *n* any of various usually ferocious selachian fishes, typically marine with a long body, two dorsal fins, rows of sharp teeth, and between five and seven gill slits on each side of the head. [C16: of uncertain origin] ▸ **'shark,like** *adj*

shark[2] (ʃɑːk) *n* **1** a person who preys on or victimizes others, esp. by swindling or extortion. ◆ *vb* **2** *Archaic.* to obtain (something) by cheating or deception. [C18: probably from German *Schurke* rogue; perhaps also influenced by SHARK[1]]

shark bell *n Chiefly Austral.* a bell sounded to warn swimmers of the presence of sharks. Also: **shark alarm.**

shark net *or* **mesh** *n Chiefly Austral.* **1** a net for catching sharks. **2** a long piece of netting strung across a bay, inlet, etc., to exclude sharks.

shark patrol *n Chiefly Austral.* a watch for sharks kept by an aircraft flying over beaches used by swimmers.

shark repellents *pl n Finance.* another name for **porcupine provisions.**

shark siren *n Chiefly Austral.* a siren sounded to warn swimmers of the presence of sharks.

sharkskin ('ʃɑːk,skɪn) *n* a smooth glossy fabric of acetate rayon, used for sportswear, etc.

sharksucker ('ʃɑːk,sʌkə) *n* an informal name for a **remora.**

shark watcher *n Informal.* a business consultant who assists companies in identifying and preventing unwelcome takeover bids.

Sharon ('ʃærən) *n* **Plain of.** a plain in W Israel, between the Mediterranean and the hills of Samaria, extending from Haifa to Tel Aviv.

sharon fruit ('ʃærən) *n* another name for **persimmon** (sense 2).

sharp (ʃɑːp) *adj* **1** having a keen edge suitable for cutting. **2** having an edge or point; not rounded or blunt. **3** involving a sudden change, esp. in direction: *a sharp bend.* **4** moving, acting, or reacting quickly, efficiently, etc.: *sharp reflexes.* **5** clearly defined. **6** mentally acute; clever; astute. **7** sly or artful; clever in an underhand way: *sharp practice.* **8** bitter or harsh: *sharp words.* **9** shrill or penetrating: *a sharp cry.* **10** having an acrid taste. **11** keen; biting: *a sharp wind; sharp pain.* **12** *Music.* **12a** (*immediately postpositive*) denoting a note that has been raised in pitch by one chromatic semitone: *B sharp.* **12b** (of an instrument, voice, etc.) out of tune by being or tending to be too high in pitch. Compare **flat**[1] (sense 23). **13** *Phonetics.* a less common word for **fortis. 14** *Informal.* **14a** stylish. **14b** too smart. **15 at the sharp end.** involved in the area of any activity where there is most difficulty, competition, danger, etc. ◆ *adv* **16** in a sharp manner. **17** exactly: *six o'clock sharp.* **18** *Music.* **18a** higher than a standard pitch. **18b** out of tune by being or tending to be too high in pitch: *she sings sharp.* Compare **flat**[1] (sense 29). ◆ *n* **19** *Music.* **19a** an accidental that raises the pitch of the following note by one chromatic semitone. Usual symbol: ♯ **19b** a note affected by this accidental. Compare **flat**[1] (sense 35). **20** a thin needle with a sharp point. **21** *Informal.* a sharper. ◆ *vb* **22** (*tr*) *Music.* the usual U.S. and Canadian word for **sharpen.** [Old English *scearp;* related to Old Norse *skarpr,* Old High German *scarpf,* Old Irish *cerb,* Lettish *skarbs*] ▸ **'sharply** *adv* ▸ **'sharpness** *n*

Sharp (ʃɑːp) *n* **Cecil (James).** 1859–1924, British musician, best known for collecting, editing, and publishing English folk songs.

sharpbender ('ʃɑːp,bεndə) *n Informal.* an organization that has been underperforming its competitors but suddenly becomes more successful, often as a result of new management or changes in its business strategy. [C20: from the sharp upward bend in its sales or profits]

sharpen ('ʃɑːpᵊn) *vb* **1** to make or become sharp or sharper. **2** *Music.* to raise the pitch of (a note), esp. by one chromatic semitone. Usual U.S. and Canadian word: **sharp.** ▸ **'sharpener** *n*

sharper ('ʃɑːpə) *n* a person who cheats or swindles; fraud.

Sharpeville ('ʃɑːpvɪl) *n* a town in E South Africa: scene of riots in 1960, when 69 demonstrators died, 1984, and 1985, when 19 died.

sharp-eyed *adj* **1** having very good eyesight. **2** observant or alert.

sharpie ('ʃɑːpɪ) *n Austral.* a member of a teenage group having short hair and distinctive clothes. Compare **skinhead.**

sharpish ('ʃɑːpɪʃ) *adj* **1** fairly sharp. ◆ *adv* **2** *Informal.* promptly; quickly.

sharp-set *adj* **1** set to give an acute cutting angle. **2** keenly hungry. **3** keen or eager.

sharpshooter ('ʃɑːp,ʃuːtə) *n* an expert marksman, esp. with a rifle. ▸ **'sharp,shooting** *n*

sharp-sighted *adj* having keen vision; sharp-eyed. ▸ **,sharp-'sightedly** *adv* ▸ **,sharp-'sightedness** *n*

sharp-tongued *adj* bitter or critical in speech; sarcastic.

sharp-witted *adj* having or showing a keen intelligence; perceptive. ▸ **,sharp-'wittedly** *adv* ▸ **,sharp-'wittedness** *n*

shashlik *or* **shashlick** (ʃɑː'ʃlɪk, 'ʃɑːʃlɪk) *n* a type of kebab. [from Russian, of Turkic origin; compare *shish kebab*]

Shasta daisy ('ʃæstə) *n* a Pyrenean plant, *Chrysanthemum maximum,* widely cultivated for its large white daisy-like flowers: family *Compositae* (composites). [named after Mount *Shasta* in California]

shastra ('ʃɑːstrə), **shaster** ('ʃɑːstə), *or* **sastra** *n* any of the sacred writings of Hinduism. [C17: from Sanskrit *śāstra,* from *śās* to teach]

shat (ʃæt) *vb Taboo.* a past tense and past participle of **shit.**

Shatt-al-Arab ('ʃætæl'ærəb) *n* a river in SE Iraq, formed by the confluence of the Tigris and Euphrates Rivers: flows southeast as part of the border between Iraq and Iran to the Persian Gulf. Length: 193 km (120 miles).

shatter ('ʃætə) *vb* **1** to break or be broken into many small pieces. **2** (*tr*) to impair or destroy: *his nerves were shattered by the torture.* **3** (*tr*) to dumbfound or thoroughly upset: *she was shattered by the news.* **4** (*tr*) *Informal.* to cause to be tired out or exhausted. **5** an obsolete word for **scatter.** ◆ *n* **6** (*usually pl*) *Obsolete or dialect.* a fragment. [C12: perhaps obscurely related to SCATTER] ▸ **'shattered** *adj* ▸ **'shatterer** *n* ▸ **'shattering** *adj* ▸ **'shatteringly** *adv*

shatterproof ('ʃætə,pruːf) *adj* designed to resist shattering.

shave (ʃeɪv) *vb* **shaves, shaving, shaved; shaved** *or* **shaven.** (*mainly tr*) **1** (*also intr*) to remove (the beard, hair, etc.) from (the face, head, or body) by scraping the skin with a razor. **2** to cut or trim very closely. **3** to reduce to shavings. **4** to remove thin slices from (wood, etc.) with a sharp cutting tool; plane or pare. **5** to touch or graze in passing. **6** *Informal.* to reduce (a price) by a slight amount. **7** *U.S. commerce.* to purchase (a commercial paper) at a greater rate of discount than is customary or legal. ◆ *n* **8** the act or an instance of shaving. **9** any tool for scraping. **10** a thin slice or shaving. **11** an instance of barely touching something. **12 close shave.** *Informal.* a narrow escape. [Old English *sceafan;* related to Old Norse *skafa,* Gothic *skaban* to shave, Latin *scabere* to scrape] ▸ **'shavable** *or* **'shaveable** *adj*

shaveling ('ʃeɪvlɪŋ) *n Archaic.* **1** *Derogatory.* a priest or clergyman with a shaven head. **2** a young fellow; youth.

shaven ('ʃeɪvᵊn) *adj* **a** closely shaved or tonsured. **b** (*in combination*): *clean-shaven.*

shaver ('ʃeɪvə) *n* **1** a person or thing that shaves. **2** Also called: **electric razor, electric shaver.** an electrically powered implement for shaving, having reciprocating or rotating blades behind a fine metal comb or pierced foil. **3** *Informal.* a youngster, esp. a young boy. **4** *Obsolete.* a person who makes hard or extortionate bargains.

Shavian ('ʃeɪvɪən) *adj* **1** of, relating to, or like George Bernard Shaw, his works, ideas, etc. ◆ *n* **2** an admirer of Shaw or his works. ▸ **'Shavianism** *n*

shaving ('ʃeɪvɪŋ) *n* **1** a thin paring or slice, esp. of wood, that has been shaved from something. ◆ *modifier.* **2** used when shaving the face, etc.: *shaving cream.*

Shavuot *or* **Shabuoth** (ʃə'vuːəs, -əʊs; *Hebrew* ʃavuː'ɔt) *n* the Hebrew name for **Pentecost** (sense 2). [from Hebrew *shābhūʿōth,* plural of *shābhūaʿ* week]

shaw[1] (ʃɔː) *n Archaic or dialect.* a small wood; thicket; copse. [Old English *sceaga;* related to Old Norse *skagi* tip, *skaga* to jut out, *skōgr* forest, *skegg* beard]

shaw[2] (ʃɔː) *Scot.* ◆ *vb* **1** to show. ◆ *n* **2** a show. **3** the part of a potato plant that is above ground.

Shaw (ʃɔː) *n* **1 Artie,** original name *Arthur Arshawsky.* born 1910, U.S. jazz clarinetist, band leader, and composer. **2 George Bernard,** often known as *GBS.* 1856–1950, Irish dramatist and critic, in England from 1876. He was an active socialist and became a member of the Fabian Society but his major works are effective as satiric attacks rather than political tracts. These include *Arms and the Man* (1894), *Candida* (1894), *Man and Superman* (1903), *Major Barbara* (1905), *Pygmalion* (1913), *Back to Methuselah* (1921), and *St. Joan* (1923): Nobel prize for literature 1925. **3 Richard Norman.** 1831–1912, English architect. **4 Thomas Edward.** the name assumed by (T. E.) **Lawrence** after 1927.

shawl (ʃɔːl) *n* a piece of fabric or knitted or crocheted material worn around the shoulders by women or wrapped around a baby. **[C17:** from Persian *shāl***]**

shawl collar *n* a collar rolled back in a continuous and tapering line along the surplice neckline of a garment.

shawlie (ˈʃɔːlɪ) *n Irish.* a disparaging term for a working-class woman who wears a shawl.

shawm (ʃɔːm) *n Music.* a medieval form of the oboe with a conical bore and flaring bell, blown through a double reed. **[C14** *shalmye,* from Old French *chalemie,* ultimately from Latin *calamus* a reed, from Greek *kalamos***]**

Shawnee (ʃɔːˈniː) *n* **1** (*pl* **-nees** *or* **-nee**) a member of a North American Indian people formerly living along the Tennessee River. **2** the language of this people, belonging to the Algonquian family. **[C20:** back formation from obsolete *Shawnese,* from Shawnee *Shaawanwaaki* people of the south, from *shaawanawa* south**]**

Shawwal (ʃəˈwɑːl) *n* the tenth month of the Muslim year. **[**from Arabic**]**

shay (ʃeɪ) *n* a dialect word for **chaise. [C18:** back formation from CHAISE, mistakenly thought to be plural**]**

Shays (ʃeɪz) *n* **Daniel.** ?1747–1825, American soldier and revolutionary leader of a rebellion of Massachusetts farmers against the U.S. government (1786–87).

Shcheglovsk (*Russian* ʃtʃɪɡˈlɔfsk) *n* the former name (until 1932) of **Kemerovo.**

Shcherbakov (*Russian* ʃtʃɪrbaˈkɔf) *n* a former name (from the Revolution until 1957) of **Rybinsk.**

she (ʃiː) *pron* (*subjective*) **1** refers to a female person or animal: *she is a doctor; she's a fine mare.* **2** refers to things personified as feminine, such as cars, ships, and nations. **3** *Austral. and N.Z.* an informal word for **it** (esp. in the phrases **she's apples, she'll be right,** etc.) ◆ *n* **4a** a female person or animal **4b** (*in combination*): *she-cat.* **[**Old English *sīe,* accusative of *sēo,* feminine demonstrative pronoun**]**

shea (ˈʃɪə) *n* **1** a tropical African sapotaceous tree, *Butyrospermum parkii,* with oily seeds. **2 shea butter.** the white butter-like fat obtained from the seeds of this plant and used as food, to make soaps, etc. **[C18:** from Bambara *si***]**

sheading (ˈʃiːdɪŋ) *n* any of the six subdivisions of the Isle of Man. **[**variant of *shedding;* see SHED[2]**]**

sheaf (ʃiːf) *n, pl* **sheaves** (ʃiːvz). **1** a bundle of reaped but unthreshed corn tied with one or two bonds. **2** a bundle of objects tied together. **3** the arrows contained in a quiver. ◆ *vb* **4** (*tr*) to bind or tie into a sheaf. **[**Old English *sceaf,* related to Old High German *skoub* sheaf, Old Norse *skauf* tail, Gothic *skuft* tuft of hair**]**

shear (ʃɪə) *vb* **shears, shearing, sheared** *or archaic, Austral. and N.Z. sometimes* **shore; sheared** *or* **shorn. 1** (*tr*) to remove (the fleece or hair) of (sheep, etc.) by cutting or clipping. **2** to cut or cut through (something) with shears or a sharp instrument. **3** *Engineering.* to cause (a part, member, shaft, etc.) to deform or fracture or (of a part, etc.) to deform or fracture as a result of excess torsion or transverse load. **4** (*tr;* often foll. by *of*) to strip or divest: *to shear someone of his power.* **5** (when *intr,* foll. by *through*) to move through (something) by or as if by cutting. **6** *Scot. or dialect.* to reap (corn, etc.) with a scythe or sickle. ◆ *n* **7** the act, process, or an instance of shearing. **8** a shearing of a sheep or flock of sheep, esp. when referred to as an indication of age: *a sheep of two shears.* **9** a form of deformation or fracture in which parallel planes in a body or assembly slide over one another. **10** *Physics.* the deformation of a body, part, etc., expressed as the lateral displacement between two points in parallel planes divided by the distance between the planes. **11** either one of the blades of a pair of shears, scissors, etc. **12** a machine that cuts sheet material by passing a knife blade through it. **13** a device for lifting heavy loads consisting of a tackle supported by a framework held steady by guy ropes. ◆ See also **shears, shore**[3]. **[**Old English *sceran;* related to Old Norse *skera* to cut, Old Saxon, Old High German *skeran* to shear; see SHARE[2]**]** ▸ **ˈshearer** *n*

shearing gang *n N.Z.* a group of itinerant workers who contract to shear, class, and bale a farmer's wool clip.

shearing shed *n N.Z.* a farm building equipped with power machinery for sheepshearing and equipment for baling wool. Also called: **woolshed.**

shearlegs (ˈʃɪəˌlɛɡz) *n* a variant spelling of **sheerlegs.**

shearling (ˈʃɪəlɪŋ) *n* **1** a young sheep after its first shearing. **2** the skin of such an animal.

shear pin *n* an easily replaceable pin inserted in a machine at a critical point and designed to break and stop the machine if the stress becomes too great.

shears (ʃɪəz) *pl n* **1a** large scissors, as for cutting cloth, jointing poultry, etc. **1b** a large scissor-like and usually hand-held cutting tool with flat blades, as for cutting hedges. **2** any of various analogous cutting or clipping implements or machines. **3** short for **sheerlegs. 4 off the shears.** *Austral. informal.* (of a sheep) newly shorn.

shear strength *n* the degree to which a material or bond is able to resist shear.

shearwater (ˈʃɪəˌwɔːtə) *n* any of several oceanic birds of the genera *Puffinus,* such as *P. puffinus* (**Manx shearwater**), *Procellaria,* etc., specialized for an aerial or aquatic existence: family *Procellariidae,* order *Procellariiformes* (petrels). **[C17:** so named because their wings seem to clip the waves when they are flying low**]**

sheatfish (ˈʃiːtˌfɪʃ) *n, pl* **-fish** *or* **-fishes.** another name for **European catfish** (see **silurid** (sense 1)). **[C16:** variant of *sheathfish;* perhaps influenced by German *Schaid* sheatfish; see SHEATH, FISH**]**

sheath (ʃiːθ) *n, pl* **sheaths** (ʃiːðz). **1** a case or covering for the blade of a knife, sword, etc. **2** any similar close-fitting case. **3** *Biology.* an enclosing or protective structure, such as a leaf base encasing the stem of a plant. **4** the protective covering on an electric cable. **5** a figure-hugging dress with a narrow tapering skirt. **6** another name for **condom.** ◆ *vb* **7** (*tr*) another word for **sheathe. [**Old English *scēath;* related to Old Norse *skeithir,* Old High German *sceida* a dividing; compare Old English *scādan* to divide**]**

sheathbill (ˈʃiːθˌbɪl) *n* either of two pigeon-like shore birds, *Chionis alba* or *C. minor,* of antarctic and subantarctic regions, constituting the family *Chionididae:* order *Charadriiformes.* They have a white plumage and a horny sheath at the base of the bill.

sheathe (ʃiːð) *vb* (*tr*) **1** to insert (a knife, sword, etc.) into a sheath. **2** (esp. of cats) to retract (the claws). **3** to surface with or encase in a sheath or sheathing.

sheathing (ˈʃiːðɪŋ) *n* **1** any material used as an outer layer, as on a ship's hull. **2** boarding, etc., used to cover the wall studding or roof joists of a timber frame.

sheath knife *n* a knife carried in or protected by a sheath.

sheave[1] (ʃiːv) *vb* (*tr*) to gather or bind into sheaves.

sheave[2] (ʃiːv) *n* a wheel with a grooved rim, esp. one used as a pulley. **[C14:** of Germanic origin; compare Old High German *scība* disc**]**

sheaves (ʃiːvz) *n* the plural of **sheaf.**

Sheba[1] (ˈʃiːbə) *n* **1** Also called: **Saba.** the ancient kingdom of the Sabeans: a rich trading nation dealing in gold, spices, and precious stones (I Kings 10). **2** the region inhabited by this nation, located in the SW corner of the Arabian peninsula: modern Yemen.

Sheba[2] (ˈʃiːbə) *n* **Queen of.** *Old Testament.* a queen of the Sabeans, who visited Solomon (I Kings 10:1–13).

shebang (ʃɪˈbæŋ) *n Slang.* **1** a situation, matter, or affair (esp. in the phrase **the whole shebang**). **2** a hut or shack. **[C19:** of uncertain origin**]**

Shebat (ʃeˈvat) *n* a variant spelling of **Shevat.**

shebeen *or* **shebean** (ʃɪˈbiːn) *n* **1** *Irish, Scot., S. African.* a place where alcoholic drink is sold illegally. **2** (in Ireland) alcohol, esp. home-distilled whiskey, sold without a licence. **3** (in South Africa) a place where Black African men engage in social drinking. **4** (in the U.S. and Ireland) weak beer. **[C18:** from Irish Gaelic *síbín* beer of poor quality**]**

Shechem (ˈʃɛkəm, -ɛm) *n* the ancient name of **Nablus.**

Shechina *or* **Shekinah** (ʃɛˈkaɪnə; *Hebrew* ʃəxiːˈna) *n Judaism.* **1** the radiance in which God's immanent presence in the midst of his people, esp. in the Temple, is visibly manifested. **2** the divine presence itself as contrasted with the divine transcendence. **[C17:** from Hebrew *shĕkhīnāh,* from *shākhan* to dwell**]**

shechita (ˈʃəxitɑ, ˈʃxitə) *n* the Jewish method of killing animals for food. **[**from Hebrew, literally: slaughter**]**

shed[1] (ʃɛd) *n* **1** a small building or lean-to of light construction, used for storage, shelter, etc. **2** a large roofed structure, esp. one with open sides, used for storage, repairing locomotives, sheepshearing, etc. **3** *N.Z.* another name for **freezing works. 4 in the shed.** *N.Z.* at work. ◆ *vb* **sheds, shedding, shedded. 5** (*tr*) *N.Z.* to store (hay or wool) in a shed. **[**Old English *sced;* probably variant of *scead* shelter, SHADE**]** ▸ **ˈshedˌlike** *adj*

shed[2] (ʃɛd) *vb* **sheds, shedding, shed.** (*mainly tr*) **1** to pour forth or cause to pour forth: *to shed tears; shed blood.* **2 shed** (*or* **throw**) **light on** *or* **upon.** to clarify or supply additional information about. **3** to cast off or lose: *the snake shed its skin; trees shed their leaves.* **4** (of a lorry) to drop (its load) on the road by accident. **5** to repel: *this coat sheds water.* **6** (*also intr*) (in weaving) to form an opening between (the warp threads) in order to permit the passage of the shuttle. **7** (*tr*) *Dialect.* to make a parting in (the hair). ◆ *n* **8** (in weaving) the space made by shedding. **9** short for **watershed. 10** *Chiefly Scot.* a parting in the hair. **[**Old English *sceadan;* related to Gothic *skaidan,* Old High German *skeidan* to separate; see SHEATH**]** ▸ **ˈshedable** *or* **ˈsheddable** *adj*

shed[3] (ʃɛd) *vb* **sheds, shedding, shed. 1** (*tr*) to separate or divide off (some farm animals) from the remainder of a group: *a good dog can shed his sheep in a matter of minutes.* ◆ *n* **2** (of a dog) the action of separating farm animals. **[**from SHED[2]**]** ▸ **ˈshedding** *n*

shed[4] (ʃɛd) *n Physics.* a unit of nuclear cross section equal to 10^{-52} square metre. **[C20:** from SHED[1]; so called by comparison to BARN[2] because of its smaller size**]**

she'd (ʃiːd) *contraction of* she had *or* she would.

shedder (ˈʃɛdə) *n* **1** a person or thing that sheds. **2** an animal, such as a llama, snake, or lobster, that moults. **3** *N.Z.* a person who milks cows in a milking shed.

shed hand *n Chiefly Austral. and N.Z.* a worker in a sheepshearing shed.

shed out *vb* (*tr, adv*) *N.Z.* to separate off (sheep that have lambed) and move them to better pasture.

shed up *vb* (*tr, adv*) *N.Z.* to store (hay) in a shed.

sheen (ʃiːn) *n* **1** a gleaming or glistening brightness; lustre. **2** *Poetic.* splendid clothing. ◆ *adj* **3** *Rare.* shining and beautiful; radiant. **[**Old English *sciene;* related to Old Norse *skjōni* white horse, Gothic *skauns* beautiful, Old High German *scōni* bright**]** ▸ **ˈsheeny** *adj*

Sheene (ʃiːn) *n* **Barry** (**Stephen Frank**). born 1950, British racing motorcyclist: 500 cc. world champion (1976, 1977).

sheeny (ˈʃiːnɪ) *n, pl* **sheenies.** *Slang.* a derogatory word for a **Jew. [C19:** of unknown origin**]**

sheep (ʃiːp) *n, pl* **sheep. 1** any of various bovid mammals of the genus *Ovis* and related genera, esp. *O. aries* (**domestic sheep**), having transversely ribbed horns and a narrow face. There are many breeds of domestic sheep, raised for their wool and for meat. Related adj: **ovine. 2 Barbary sheep.** another name for **aoudad. 3** a meek or timid person, esp. one without initiative. **4 separate the sheep from the goats.** to pick out the members of any group who are superior in some respects. **[**Old English *sceap;* related to Old Frisian *skēp,* Old Saxon *scāp,* Old High German *scāf***]** ▸ **ˈsheepˌlike** *adj*

sheepcote (ˈʃiːpˌkəʊt) *n Chiefly Brit.* another word for **sheepfold.**

sheep-dip *n* **1** any of several liquid disinfectants and insecticides in which sheep are immersed to kill vermin and germs in their fleece. **2** a deep trough containing such a liquid.

sheepdog ('ʃiːpˌdɒg) *n* **1** Also called: **shepherd dog.** a dog used for herding sheep. See **Border collie. 2** any of various breeds of dog reared originally for herding sheep. See **Old English sheepdog, Shetland sheepdog.**

sheepdog trial *n* (*often pl*) a competition in which sheepdogs are tested in their tasks.

sheepfold ('ʃiːpˌfəʊld) *n* a pen or enclosure for sheep.

sheepish ('ʃiːpɪʃ) *adj* **1** abashed or embarrassed, esp. through looking foolish or being in the wrong. **2** resembling a sheep in timidity or lack of initiative. ▸ **'sheepishly** *adv* ▸ **'sheepishness** *n*

sheep ked *or* **tick** *n* a wingless dipterous fly, *Melophagus ovinus,* that is an external parasite of sheep: family *Hippoboscidae.*

sheep measles *n* (*functioning as sing or pl*) a disease of sheep caused by infestation by the cysticerci of a dog tapeworm (*Taenia ovis*).

sheepo ('ʃiːpəʊ) *n, pl* **sheepos.** *N.Z.* a person employed to bring sheep to the catching pen in a shearing shed.

sheep race *n N.Z.* a single-file walkway for sheep at the entrance to a sheep-dip.

sheep's eyes *pl n Old-fashioned.* amorous or inviting glances.

sheep's fescue *n* a temperate perennial tufted grass, *Festuca ovina,* with narrow inwardly rolled leaves. **[C18:** so called because it is often used for sheep pastures**]**

sheepshank ('ʃiːpˌʃæŋk) *n* a knot consisting of two hitches at the ends of a bight made in a rope to shorten it temporarily.

sheepshead ('ʃiːpsˌhɛd) *n, pl* **-head** *or* **-heads.** any of several sparid fishes with strong crushing teeth, esp. *Archosargus rhomboidalis,* of the American Atlantic, which is marked with dark bands.

sheepshearing ('ʃiːpˌʃɪərɪŋ) *n* **1** the act or process of shearing sheep. **2** the season or an occasion of shearing sheep. **3** a feast held on such an occasion. ▸ **'sheepˌshearer** *n*

sheepskin ('ʃiːpˌskɪn) *n* **a** the skin of a sheep, esp. when used for clothing, etc., or with the fleece removed and used for parchment. **b** (*as modifier*): *a sheepskin coat.*

sheep sorrel *or* **sheep's sorrel** *n* a polygonaceous plant, *Rumex acetosella,* of the N hemisphere, having slightly bitter-tasting leaves and small reddish flowers.

sheep station *or* **run** *n Austral. and N.Z.* a large sheep farm. Also called: **run.**

sheep tick *n* **1** a tick, *Ixodes ricinus,* that is parasitic on sheep, cattle, and man and transmits the disease louping ill in sheep. **2** another name for **sheep ked.**

sheepwalk ('ʃiːpˌwɔːk) *n Chiefly Brit.* a tract of land for grazing sheep.

sheer[1] (ʃɪə) *adj* **1** perpendicular; very steep: *a sheer cliff.* **2** (of textiles) so fine as to be transparent. **3** (*prenominal*) absolute; unmitigated: *sheer folly.* **4** *Obsolete.* bright or shining. ◆ *adv* **5** steeply or perpendicularly. **6** completely or absolutely. ◆ *n* **7** any transparent fabric used for making garments. **[**Old English *scīr;* related to Old Norse *skīrr* bright, Gothic *skeirs* clear, Middle High German *schīr***]** ▸ **'sheerly** *adv* ▸ **'sheerness** *n*

sheer[2] (ʃɪə) *vb* (foll. by *off* or *away* (*from*)). **1** to deviate or cause to deviate from a course. **2** (*intr*) to avoid an unpleasant person, thing, topic, etc. ◆ *n* **3** the upward sweep of the deck or bulwarks of a vessel. **4** *Nautical.* the position of a vessel relative to its mooring. **[C17:** perhaps variant of SHEAR**]**

sheerlegs *or* **shearlegs** ('ʃɪəˌlɛgz) *n* (*functioning as sing*) a device for lifting heavy weights consisting of two or more spars lashed together at the upper ends from which a lifting tackle is suspended. Also called: **shears. [C19:** variant of *shear legs***]**

Sheerness (ˌʃɪə'nɛs) *n* a port and resort in SE England, in N Kent at the junction of the Medway estuary and the Thames: administratively part of Queenborough in Sheppey since 1968.

sheet[1] (ʃiːt) *n* **1** a large rectangular piece of cotton, linen, etc., generally one of a pair used as inner bedclothes. **2a** a thin piece of a substance such as paper, glass, or metal, usually rectangular in form. **2b** (*as modifier*): *sheet iron.* **3** a broad continuous surface; expanse or stretch: *a sheet of rain.* **4** a newspaper, esp. a tabloid. **5** a piece of printed paper to be folded into a section for a book. **6** a page of stamps, usually of one denomination and already perforated. **7** any thin tabular mass of rock covering a large area. ◆ *vb* **8** (*tr*) to provide with, cover, or wrap in a sheet. **9** (*intr*) (of rain, snow, etc.) to fall heavily. **[**Old English *sciete;* related to *sceat* corner, lap, Old Norse *skaut,* Old High German *scōz* lap**]**

sheet[2] (ʃiːt) *n Nautical.* a line or rope for controlling the position of a sail relative to the wind. **[**Old English *scēata* corner of a sail; related to Middle Low German *schōte* rope attached to a sail; see SHEET[1]**]**

sheet anchor *n* **1** *Nautical.* a large strong anchor for use in emergency. **2** a person or thing to be relied upon in an emergency. **[C17:** from earlier *shute anker,* from *shoot* (obsolete) the sheet of a sail**]**

sheet bend *n* a knot used esp. for joining ropes of different sizes. Also called: **becket bend, weaver's hitch.**

sheet down *vb* (*intr, adv*) (of rain) to fall heavily in sheets.

sheet-fed *adj Printing.* involving or printing on separate sheets of paper. Compare **reel-fed.**

sheeting ('ʃiːtɪŋ) *n* fabric from which sheets are made.

sheet lightning *n* lightning that appears as a broad sheet, caused by the reflection of more distant lightning.

sheet metal *n* metal in the form of a sheet, the thickness being intermediate between that of plate and that of foil.

sheet music *n* **1** the printed or written copy of a short composition or piece, esp. in the form of unbound leaves. **2** music in its written or printed form.

sheet pile *n Civil engineering.* one of a group of piles made of timber, steel, or prestressed concrete set close together to resist lateral pressure, as from earth or water. Compare **bearing pile.**

Sheffer's stroke *n Logic.* a function of two sentences, equivalent to the negation of their conjunction, and written *p*|*q* (*p* and *q* are both not true) where *p,q,* are the arguments: *p*|*q* is false only when *p,q* are both true. It is possible to construct all truth functions out of this one alone. **[**named after H. M. *Sheffer* (1883–1964), U.S. philosopher**]**

Sheffield ('ʃɛfiːld) *n* **1** a city in N England, in Sheffield unitary authority, South Yorkshire on the River Don: important centre of steel manufacture and of the cutlery industry; Sheffield University (1905) and Sheffield Hallam University. Pop.: 431 607 (1991). **2** a unitary authority in N England, in South Yorkshire. Pop.: 528 500 (1995 est.). Area: 368 sq. km (142 sq. miles).

Sheffield Shield *n* (in Australia) the prize of the annual interstate cricket competition. **[C19:** named after Lord *Sheffield,* sponsor of a visiting English side in 1891–92, who inaugurated the Sheffield Shield competition in 1892**]**

sheikh *or* **sheik** (ʃeɪk) *n* (in Muslim countries) **a** the head of an Arab tribe, village, etc. **b** a venerable old man. **c** a high priest or religious leader, esp. a Sufi master. **[C16:** from Arabic *shaykh* old man**]**

sheikhdom *or* **sheikdom** ('ʃeɪkdəm) *n* the territory ruled by a sheikh.

sheila ('ʃiːlə) *n Austral. and N.Z. old-fashioned.* an informal word for **girl** or **woman. [C19:** from the girl's name *Sheila***]**

shekel ('ʃɛk[ə]l) *n* **1** the standard monetary unit of modern Israel, divided into 100 agorot. **2** any of several former coins and units of weight of the Near East. **3** (*often pl*) *Informal.* any coin or money. **[C16:** from Hebrew *sheqel***]**

Shekinah (ʃɛ'kaɪnə; *Hebrew* ʃəxiː'na) *n Judaism.* a variant spelling of **Shechina.**

Shelburne ('ʃɛlbɜːn) *n* **2nd Earl of,** title of *William Petty Fitzmaurice,* also called (from 1784) *1st Marquess of Lansdowne.* 1737–1805, British statesman; prime minister (1782–83).

shelduck ('ʃɛlˌdʌk) *or* (*masc*) **sheldrake** ('ʃɛlˌdreɪk) *n, pl* **-ducks, -duck** *or* **-drakes, -drake.** any of various large usually brightly coloured gooselike ducks, such as *Tadorna tadorna* (**common shelduck**), of the Old World. **[C14:** *shel,* probably from dialect *sheld* pied; related to Middle Dutch *schillede* variegated**]**

shelf (ʃɛlf) *n, pl* **shelves** (ʃɛlvz). **1** a thin flat plank of wood, metal, etc., fixed horizontally against a wall, etc., for the purpose of supporting objects. **2** something resembling this in shape or function. **3** the objects placed on a shelf, regarded collectively: *a shelf of books.* **4** a projecting layer of ice, rock, etc., on land or in the sea. See also **continental shelf. 5** *Mining.* a layer of bedrock hit when sinking a shaft. **6** *Archery.* the part of the hand on which an arrow rests when the bow is grasped. **7** See **off the shelf. 8 on the shelf.** put aside or abandoned: used esp. of unmarried women considered to be past the age of marriage. ◆ *vb* **9** (*tr*) *Austral. slang.* to inform upon. **[**Old English *scylfe* ship's deck; related to Middle Low German *schelf* shelf, Old English *scylf* crag**]** ▸ **'shelfˌlike** *adj*

shelf ice *n* a less common term for **ice shelf.**

shelf life *n* the length of time a packaged food, chemical, etc., will last without deteriorating.

shell (ʃɛl) *n* **1** the protective calcareous or membranous outer layer of an egg, esp. a bird's egg. **2** the hard outer covering of many molluscs that is secreted by the mantle. **3** any other hard outer layer, such as the exoskeleton of many arthropods. **4** the hard outer layer of some fruits, esp. of nuts. **5** any hard outer case. **6** a hollow artillery projectile filled with explosive primed to explode either during flight, on impact, or after penetration. Compare **ball**[1] (sense 7a). **7** a small-arms cartridge comprising a hollow casing inside which is the primer, charge, and bullet. **8** a pyrotechnic cartridge designed to explode in the air. **9** *Rowing.* a very light narrow racing boat. **10** the external structure of a building, esp. one that is unfinished or one that has been gutted by fire. **11** the basic structural case of something, such as a machine, vehicle, etc. **12** *Physics.* **12a** a class of electron orbits in an atom in which the electrons have the same principal quantum number and differences in their energy are small compared with differences in energy between shells. **12b** an analogous energy state of nucleons in certain theories (**shell models**) of the structure of the atomic nucleus. **13** the pastry case of a pie, flan, etc. **14** a thin slab of concrete or a skeletal framework made of wood or metal that forms a shell-like roof. **15** *Brit.* (in some schools) a class or form. **16 come** (*or* **bring**) **out of one's shell.** to become (or help to become) less shy and reserved. ◆ *vb* **17** to divest or be divested of a shell, husk, pod, etc. **18** to separate or be separated from an ear, husk, cob, etc. **19** (*tr*) to bombard with artillery shells. ◆ See also **shell out. [**Old English *sciell;* related to Old Norse *skel* shell, Gothic *skalja* tile, Middle Low German *schelle* shell; see SCALE[1], SHALE**]** ▸ **'shell-less** *adj* ▸ **'shell-ˌlike** *adj* ▸ **'shelly** *adj*

she'll (ʃiːl; *unstressed* ʃɪl) *contraction of* she will *or* she shall.

shellac (ʃə'læk, 'ʃɛlæk) *n* **1** a yellowish resin secreted by the lac insect, esp. a commercial preparation of this used in varnishes, polishes, and leather dressings. **2** Also called: **shellac varnish.** a varnish made by dissolving shellac in ethanol or a similar solvent. **3** a gramophone record based on shellac. ◆ *vb* **-lacs, -lacking, -lacked.** (*tr*) **4** to coat or treat (an article) with a shellac varnish. **5** *U.S. slang.* to defeat completely. **[C18:** SHELL + LAC[1], translation of French *laque en écailles,* literally: lac in scales, that is, in thin plates**]** ▸ **shel'lacker** *n*

shellacking (ʃə'lækɪŋ, 'ʃɛlækɪŋ) *n Slang, chiefly U.S. and Canadian.* a complete defeat; a sound beating: *anyone who gives a shellacking to their bigger neighbours.*

shellback ('ʃɛlˌbæk) *n* **1** *Informal.* a sailor who has crossed the equator. Compare **polliwog** (sense 2). **2** an experienced or old sailor.

shellbark ('ʃɛlˌbɑːk) *n* another name for **shagbark. [C19:** so called from the texture of its bark**]**

shell bean *n U.S.* any of various bean plants that are cultivated for their edible seeds rather than for their pods.

shell company *n Business.* **1** a near-defunct company, esp. one with a stock-exchange listing, used as a vehicle for a thriving company. **2** a company that has ceased to trade but retains its registration and is sold for a small sum to enable its new owners to avoid the cost and trouble of registering a new company.

Shelley ('ʃɛlɪ) *n* **1 Mary (Wollstonecraft)** ('wʊlstən,krɑːft). 1797–1851, British writer; author of *Frankenstein* (1818); the daughter of William Godwin and Mary Wollstonecraft, she eloped with Percy Bysshe Shelley. **2 Percy Bysshe** (bɪʃ). 1792–1822, British romantic poet. His works include *Queen Mab* (1813), *Prometheus Unbound* (1820), and *The Triumph of Life* (1824). He wrote an elegy on the death of Keats, *Adonais* (1821), and shorter lyrics, including the odes 'To the West Wind' and 'To a Skylark' (both 1820). He was drowned in the Ligurian Sea while sailing from Leghorn to La Spezia.

shellfire ('ʃɛl,faɪə) *n* the firing of artillery shells.

shellfish ('ʃɛl,fɪʃ) *n, pl* **-fish** *or* **-fishes.** any aquatic invertebrate having a shell or shell-like carapace, esp. such an animal used as human food. Examples are crustaceans such as crabs and lobsters and molluscs such as oysters.

shell game *n* the U.S. name for **thimblerig.**

shell gland *n Zoology.* a gland in certain invertebrates that secretes the components required for forming the shell of an egg.

shell jacket *n* an army officer's waist-length mess jacket.

shell out *vb (adv) Informal.* to pay out or hand over (money). [C19: from SHELL (in the sense: to remove from a pod or (figuratively) a purse)]

shell program *n Computers.* a basic low-cost computer program that provides a framework within which the user can develop the program to suit his personal requirements.

shellproof ('ʃɛl,pruːf) *adj* designed, intended, or able to resist shellfire.

shell shock *n* loss of sight, memory, etc., resulting from psychological strain during prolonged engagement in warfare. Also called: **combat neurosis.** ▸ **'shell-,shocked** *adj*

shell star *n Astronomy.* a type of star, usually of spectral type B to F, surrounded by a gaseous shell.

shell suit *n* a lightweight tracksuit consisting of an inner cotton layer covered by a waterproof nylon layer.

Shelta ('ʃɛltə) *n* a secret language used by some itinerant tinkers in Ireland and parts of Britain, based on systematically altered Gaelic. [C19: from earlier *sheldrū,* perhaps an arbitrary alteration of Old Irish *bēlre* speech]

shelter ('ʃɛltə) *n* **1** something that provides cover or protection, as from weather or danger; place of refuge. **2** the protection afforded by such a cover; refuge. **3** the state of being sheltered. ◆ *vb* **4** *(tr)* to provide with or protect by a shelter. **5** *(intr)* to take cover, as from rain; find refuge. **6** *(tr)* to act as a shelter for; take under one's protection. [C16: of uncertain origin] ▸ **'shelterer** *n* ▸ **'shelterless** *adj*

shelter belt *n* a row of trees planted to protect an area from the wind.

sheltered ('ʃɛltəd) *adj* **1** protected from wind or weather: *a sheltered garden.* **2** protected from outside influences: *a sheltered upbringing.* **3** (of buildings) specially designed to provide a safe environment for the elderly, handicapped, or disabled: *sheltered workshops for the blind.* See also **sheltered housing.**

sheltered housing *n* accommodation designed esp. for the elderly or infirm consisting of a group of individual premises, often with some shared facilities and a caretaker. Also called: **sheltered accommodation, sheltered homes.**

shelter tent *n U.S.* a military tent for two men.

sheltie *or* **shelty** ('ʃɛltɪ) *n, pl* **-ties.** another name for **Shetland pony** or **Shetland sheepdog.** [C17: probably from Orkney dialect *sjalti,* from Old Norse *Hjalti* Shetlander, from *Hjaltland* Shetland]

shelve[1] (ʃɛlv) *vb (tr)* **1** to place on a shelf. **2** to provide with shelves. **3** to put aside or postpone from consideration. **4** to dismiss or cause to retire. [C16: from *shelves,* plural of SHELF] ▸ **'shelver** *n*

shelve[2] (ʃɛlv) *vb (intr)* to slope away gradually; incline. [C16: origin uncertain]

shelves (ʃɛlvz) *n* the plural of **shelf.**

shelving ('ʃɛlvɪŋ) *n* **1** material for making shelves. **2** a set of shelves; shelves collectively.

Shem (ʃɛm) *n Old Testament.* the eldest of Noah's three sons (Genesis 10:21). Douay spelling: **Sem** (sɛm).

Shema (ʃəˈmɑː) *n* **1** the central statement of Jewish belief, the sentence "Hear, O Israel: the Lord is your God; the Lord is One" (Deuteronomy 6:4). **2** the section of the liturgy consisting of this and related biblical passages, Deuteronomy 6:4–9 and 11:13–21 and Numbers 15:37–41, recited in the morning and evening prayers and on retiring at night. [Hebrew, literally: hear]

Shembe ('ʃɛmbe) *n* (in South Africa) an African sect that combines Christianity with aspects of Bantu religion.

Shemini Atseres ('ʃmini ɑ'tsɛrɛs) *or* **Shemini Atzereth** ('ʃəmini ɑ'tsɛrɛt) *n Judaism.* the festival which follows upon Sukkoth on Tishri 22 (and 23 outside Israel), and includes Simchat Torah.

Shemite ('ʃɛmaɪt) *n* another word for **Semite.**

Shemitic (ʃə'mɪtɪk) *n, adj* another word for **Semitic.**

Shemona Esrei *Hebrew.* (*Hebrew* ʃəmə'na ɛs'reɪ; *Yiddish* 'ʃmonə 'esreɪ) *n Judaism.* another name for **Amidah.** [literally: eighteen (blessings)]

shemozzle (ʃɪ'mɒzᵊl) *n Informal.* a noisy confusion or dispute; uproar. [C19: perhaps from Yiddish *shlimazl* misfortune]

Shenandoah National Park (,ʃɛnən'dəʊə) *n* a national park in N Virginia: established in 1935 to protect part of the Blue Ridge Mountains. Area: 782 sq. km (302 sq. miles).

shenanigan (ʃɪ'nænɪgən) *n Informal.* **1** *(usually pl)* roguishness; mischief. **2** an act of treachery; deception. [C19: of unknown origin]

shend (ʃɛnd) *vb* **shends, shending, shent** (ʃɛnt). *(tr) Archaic.* **1** to put to shame. **2** to chide or reproach. **3** to injure or destroy. [Old English *gescendan,* from *scand* SHAME]

Shensi ('ʃɛn'siː) *n* a variant transliteration of the Chinese name for **Shaanxi.**

Shenyang ('ʃɛn'jæŋ) *n* a walled city in NE China in S Manchuria, capital of Liaoning province: capital of the Manchu dynasty from 1644–1912; seized by the Japanese in 1931. Pop.: 4 540 000 (1991 est.). Former name: **Mukden.**

she-oak *n* any of various Australian trees of the genus *Casuarina.* See **casuarina.** [C18 *she* (in the sense: inferior) + OAK]

Sheol ('ʃiːəʊl, -ɒl) *n Old Testament.* **1** the abode of the dead. **2** *(often not cap.)* hell. [C16: from Hebrew *shĕ'ōl*]

Shepard ('ʃɛpəd) *n* **1 Alan Bartlett, Jr.** 1923–98, U.S. naval officer; first U.S. astronaut in space (1961). **2 Sam,** original name *Samuel Shepard Rogers.* born 1943, U.S. dramatist, film actor, and director. His plays include *Chicago* (1966), *The Tooth of Crime* (1972), and *Buried Child* (1978): films as actor include *Days of Heaven* (1978) and *The Right Stuff* (1983); films as director include *Far North* (1989) and *Silent Tongue* (1994).

shepherd ('ʃɛpəd) *n* **1** a person employed to tend sheep. Fem. equivalent: **shepherdess.** Related adjs: **bucolic, pastoral. 2** a person, such as a clergyman, who watches over or guides a group of people. ◆ *vb (tr)* **3** to guide or watch over in the manner of a shepherd. **4** *Australian Rules football.* to prevent opponents from tackling (a member of one's own team) by blocking their path. [from Old English *sceaphirde.* See SHEEP, HERD[2]]

Shepherd *n Astron.* a small moon of Saturn orbiting close to the rings and partly responsible for ring stability.

shepherd dog *n* another term for **sheepdog** (sense 1).

shepherd's needle *n* a European umbelliferous plant, *Scandix pectenveneris,* with long needle-like fruits.

shepherd's pie *n Chiefly Brit.* a baked dish of minced meat covered with mashed potato. Also called: **cottage pie.**

shepherd's-purse *n* a cruciferous plant, *Capsella bursa-pastoris,* having small white flowers and flattened triangular seed pods. [C15: compare Latin *bursa pastoris,* French *bourse-de-berger,* German *Hirtentasche,* Dutch *herdentasch*]

shepherd's weatherglass *n Brit.* another name for the **scarlet pimpernel.**

Sheppard ('ʃɛpəd) *n* **Jack.** 1702–24, English criminal, whose daring escapes from prison were celebrated in many contemporary ballads and plays.

Sheppey ('ʃɛpɪ) *n* **Isle of.** an island in SE England, off the N coast of Kent in the Thames estuary: separated from the mainland by **The Swale,** a narrow channel. Chief towns: Sheerness, Minster. Pop.: 31 854 (latest est.). Area: 80 sq. km (30 sq. miles).

sherardize *or* **sherardise** ('ʃɛrə,daɪz) *vb Metallurgy.* to coat (iron or steel) with zinc by heating in a container with zinc dust or (of iron or steel) to be coated in this way. [C20: process named after *Sherard* Cowper-Coles (died 1936), English inventor] ▸ **,sherardi'zation** *or* **,sherardi'sation** *n*

Sheraton[1] ('ʃɛrətən) *n* **Thomas.** 1751–1806, English furniture maker, author of the influential *Cabinet-Maker and Upholsterer's Drawing Book* (1791).

Sheraton[2] ('ʃɛrətən) *adj* denoting furniture made by or in the style of Thomas Sheraton, characterized by lightness, elegance, and the extensive use of inlay.

sherbet ('ʃɜːbət) *n* **1** a fruit-flavoured slightly effervescent powder, eaten as a sweet or used to make a drink: *lemon sherbet.* **2** another word (esp. U.S. and Canadian) for **sorbet** (sense 1). **3** *Austral. slang.* beer. **4** a cooling Oriental drink of sweetened fruit juice. [C17: from Turkish *şerbet,* from Persian *sharbat,* from Arabic *sharbah* drink, from *shariba* to drink]

Sherborne ('ʃɛːbɔːn) *n* a town in S England in Dorset: noted for its medieval abbey, ruined medieval castle, and **Sherborne Castle,** a mansion built by Sir Walter Raleigh in 1594. Pop.: 7606 (1991).

Sherbrooke ('ʃɜː,brʊk) *n* a city in E Canada, in S Quebec: industrial and commercial centre. Pop.: 76 429 (1991).

sherd (ʃɜːd) *n* a variant of **shard.**

sheria (ʃə'riːə) *n* a variant spelling of **sharia.**

Sheridan ('ʃɛrɪdən) *n* **1 Philip Henry.** 1831–88, American Union cavalry commander in the Civil War. He forced Lee's surrender to Grant (1865). **2 Richard Brinsley** ('brɪnzlɪ). 1751–1816, Irish dramatist, politician, and orator, noted for his comedies of manners *The Rivals* (1775), *School for Scandal* (1777), and *The Critic* (1779).

sherif *or* **shereef** (ʃɛ'riːf) *or* **sharif** *n, pl* **ashraf.** *Islam.* **1** a descendant of Mohammed through his daughter Fatima. **2** (formerly) the governor of Mecca. **3** an honorific title accorded to any Muslim ruler. [C16: from Arabic *sharīf* noble]

sheriff ('ʃɛrɪf) *n* **1** (in the U.S.) the chief law-enforcement officer in a county: popularly elected, except in Rhode Island. **2** (in England and Wales) the chief executive officer of the Crown in a county, having chiefly ceremonial duties. Related adj: **shrieval. 3** (in Scotland) a judge in any of the sheriff courts. **4** (in Australia) an administrative officer of the Supreme Court, who enforces judgments and the execution of writs, empanels juries, etc. **5** (in New Zealand) an officer of the High Court. [Old English *scīrgerēfa,* from *scīr* SHIRE[1] + *gerēfa* REEVE[1]] ▸ **'sheriffdom** *n*

sheriff court *n* (in Scotland) a court having jurisdiction to try summarily or on indictment all but the most serious crimes and to deal with most civil actions.

Sherman ('ʃɜːmən) *n* **William Tecumseh** (tɪ'kʌmsə). 1820–91, American Union commander during the Civil War. He led the victorious march through Georgia (1864), becoming commander of the army in 1869.

sherpa ('ʃɜːpə) *n* an official who makes preparations for or assists a government representative or important delegate at a summit meeting or conference. [C20: from SHERPA, a member of a people noted for providing assistance to mountaineers: from a pun on the different senses of SUMMIT]

Sherpa ('ʃɜːpə) *n, pl* **-pas** *or* **-pa.** a member of a people of Mongolian origin living on the southern slopes of the Himalayas in Nepal, noted as mountaineers.

Sherriff ('ʃɛrɪf) *n* **R(obert) C(edric).** 1896–1975, British dramatist and film writer, best known for his play of World War I *Journey's End* (1928). His film scripts include *Goodbye Mr. Chips* (1936) and *The Dam Busters* (1955).

Sherrington ('ʃɛrɪŋtən) *n* Sir **Charles Scott.** 1857–1952, English physiologist, noted for his work on reflex action, published in *The Integrative Action of the Nervous System* (1906): shared the Nobel prize for physiology or medicine with Adrian (1932).

sherry ('ʃɛrɪ) *n, pl* **-ries.** a fortified wine, originally from the Jerez region in S Spain, usually drunk as an apéritif. [C16: from earlier *sherris* (assumed to be plural), from Spanish *Xeres,* now *Jerez*]

's Hertogenbosch (*Dutch* shɛrto:xən'bɔs) *n* a city in the S Netherlands, capital of North Brabant province: birthplace of Hieronymus Bosch. Pop.: 125 044 (1996 est.). Also called: **Den Bosch.** French name: **Bois-le-Duc.**

sherwani (ʃɛə'wɑ:nɪ) *n, pl* **-nis.** a long coat closed up to the neck, worn by men in India. [Hindi]

Sherwood ('ʃɜ:,wʊd) *n* **Robert Emmet.** 1896–1955, U.S. dramatist. His plays include *The Petrified Forest* (1935), *Idiot's Delight* (1936), and *There shall be no Night* (1940).

Sherwood Forest *n* an ancient forest in central England, in Nottinghamshire: formerly a royal hunting ground and much more extensive; famous as the home of Robin Hood.

she's (ʃi:z) *contraction of* she is *or* she has.

Shetland *or* **Shetland Islands** ('ʃɛtlənd) *pl n* a group of about 100 islands (fewer than 20 inhabited), off the N coast of Scotland, which constitute an island authority of Scotland: a Norse dependency from the 8th century until 1472; noted for the breeding of Shetland ponies, knitwear manufacturing, and fishing; oil-related industries. Administrative centre: Lerwick. Pop.: 23 020 (1996 est.). Area: 1426 sq. km (550 sq. miles). Official name (until 1974): **Zetland.**

Shetland pony *n* a very small sturdy breed of pony with a long shaggy mane and tail. Also called: **sheltie.**

Shetland sheepdog *n* a small dog similar in appearance to a rough collie. Also called: **sheltie.**

Shetland wool *n* a fine loosely twisted wool yarn spun from the fleece of Shetland sheep and used esp. for sweaters.

sheuch *or* **sheugh** (ʃu:x, ʃʌx) *n Scot. dialect.* a ditch or trough. [dialect variant of SOUGH[2]]

Sheva Brachoth *or* **Sheva Brochos** *Hebrew.* (*Hebrew* 'ʃɛvɑ brɑ'xot; *Yiddish* 'ʃɛvə 'broxəs) *pl n Judaism.* **1** the seven blessings said during the marriage service and repeated at the celebration thereafter. **2** any of the celebratory meals held on the seven days after a wedding. [literally: seven blessings]

Shevardnadze (,ʃɛvəd'nɑ:dzə) *n* **Eduard (Amvrosiyevich).** born 1928, Georgian statesman; president of Georgia from 1995; Soviet minister of foreign affairs (1985–91), who played an important part in arms negotiations with the U.S.; president of the Georgian state council (1992–95).

Shevat *or* **Shebat** (ʃɛ'vat) *n* (in the Jewish calendar) the eleventh month of the year according to biblical reckoning and the fifth month of the civil year. [from Hebrew]

shew (ʃəʊ) *vb* **shews, shewing, shewed; shewn** (ʃəʊn) *or* **shewed.** an archaic spelling of **show.** ▸ **'shewer** *n*

shewbread *or* **showbread** ('ʃəʊ,brɛd) *n Old Testament.* the loaves of bread placed every Sabbath on the table beside the altar of incense in the tabernacle or temple of ancient Israel (Exodus 25:30; Leviticus 24:5–9). [on the model of German *Schaubrot,* a translation of the Greek *artoi enōpioi,* a translation of the Hebrew *lechem pānīm,* literally: bread of the presence]

SHF *or* **shf** *Radio. abbrev. for* superhigh frequency.

Shiah *or* **Shia** ('ʃi:ə) *n* **1** one of the two main branches of Islam (the other being the Sunni), now mainly in Iran, which regards Mohammed's cousin Ali and his successors as the true imams. **2** another name for **Shiite.** ◆ *adj* **3** designating or characteristic of this sect or its beliefs and practices. [C17: from Arabic *shī'ah* sect, from *shā'a* to follow]

shiai ('ʃi:aɪ) *n* a judo contest. [Japanese]

shiatsu (,ʃi:'ætsu:) *n* massage in which pressure is applied to the same points of the body as in acupuncture. Also called: **acupressure.** [Japanese, from Chinese *chǐ* finger + *yā* pressure]

shibboleth ('ʃɪbə,lɛθ) *n* **1** a belief, principle, or practice which is commonly adhered to but which is thought by some people to be inappropriate or out of date. **2** a custom, phrase, or use of language that acts as a test of belonging to, or as a stumbling block to becoming a member of, a particular social class, profession, etc. [C14: from Hebrew, literally: ear of grain; the word is used in the Old Testament by the Gileadites as a test word for the Ephraimites, who could not pronounce the sound *sh*]

shicker ('ʃɪkə) *n Austral. archaic slang.* alcoholic drink; liquor. [via Yiddish from Hebrew]

shickered ('ʃɪkəd) *adj Austral. and N.Z. slang.* drunk; intoxicated.

shidduch *Yiddish.* ('ʃɪdəx) *n, pl* **shidduchim** (ʃɪ'du:xɪm). *Judaism.* **1a** an arranged marriage. **1b** the arrangement of a marriage. **2** any negotiated agreement. [from Hebrew: see SHADCHAN]

shied (ʃaɪd) *vb* the past tense and past participle of **shy**[1] and **shy**[2].

shield (ʃi:ld) *n* **1** any protection used to intercept blows, missiles, etc., such as a tough piece of armour carried on the arm. **2** any similar protective device. **3** Also called: **scutcheon, escutcheon.** *Heraldry.* a pointed stylized shield used for displaying armorial bearings. **4** anything that resembles a shield in shape, such as a prize in a sports competition. **5** the protective outer covering of an animal, such as the shell of a turtle. **6** *Physics.* a structure of concrete, lead, etc., placed around a nuclear reactor or other source of radiation in order to prevent the escape of radiation. **7** a broad stable plateau of ancient Precambrian rocks forming the rigid nucleus of a particular continent. See **Baltic Shield, Canadian Shield. 8** short for **dress shield. 9** *Civil engineering.* a hollow steel cylinder that protects men driving a circular tunnel through loose, soft, or water-bearing ground. **10 the shield.** *Informal.* **10a** *Austral.* short for the **Sheffield Shield. 10b** *N.Z.* short for the **Ranfurly Shield.** ◆ *vb* **11** (*tr*) to protect, hide, or conceal (something) from danger or harm. [Old English *sceld;* related to Old Norse *skjöldr,* Gothic *skildus,* Old High German *scilt* shield, Old English *sciell* SHELL] ▸ **'shielder** *n* ▸ **'shield,like** *adj*

shield bug *n* any shield-shaped herbivorous heteropterous insect of the superfamily *Pentamoidea,* esp. any of the family *Pentatomidae.* Also called: **stink bug.**

shield cricket *n Austral.* the interstate cricket competition held for the Sheffield Shield.

shield fern *n* any temperate woodland fern of the genus *Polystichum* having shield-shaped flaps covering the spore-producing bodies.

shield match *n* **a** *Austral.* a cricket match for the Sheffield Shield. **b** *N.Z.* a rugby match for the Ranfurly Shield.

Shield of David *n* another term for the **Star of David.**

shield volcano *n* a broad volcano built up from the repeated nonexplosive eruption of basalt to form a low dome or shield, usually having a large caldera at the summit.

shieling ('ʃi:lɪŋ) *or* **shiel** (ʃi:l) *n Chiefly Scot.* **1** a rough, sometimes temporary, hut or shelter used by people tending cattle on high or remote ground. **2** pasture land for the grazing of cattle in summer. [C16: from Middle English *shale* hut, of unknown origin]

shier[1] ('ʃaɪə) *adj* a comparative of **shy**[1].

shier[2] *or* **shyer** ('ʃaɪə) *n* a horse that shies habitually.

shiest ('ʃaɪɪst) *adj* a superlative of **shy**[1].

shift (ʃɪft) *vb* **1** to move or cause to move from one place or position to another. **2** (*tr*) to change for another or others. **3** to change (gear) in a motor vehicle. **4** (*intr*) (of a sound or set of sounds) to alter in a systematic way. **5** (*intr*) to provide for one's needs (esp. in the phrase **shift for oneself**). **6** (*intr*) to proceed by indirect or evasive methods. **7** to remove or be removed, esp. with difficulty: *no detergent can shift these stains.* **8** (*intr*) *Slang.* to move quickly. **9** (*tr*) *Computing.* to move (bits held in a store location) to the left or right. ◆ *n* **10** the act or an instance of shifting. **11** a group of workers who work for a specific period. **12** the period of time worked by such a group. **13** an expedient, contrivance, or artifice. **14** the displacement of rocks, esp. layers or seams in mining, at a geological fault. **15** an underskirt or dress with little shaping. [Old English *sciftan;* related to Old Norse *skipta* to divide, Middle Low German *schiften,* to separate] ▸ **'shifter** *n*

shifting cultivation *n* a land-use system, esp. in tropical Africa, in which a tract of land is cultivated until its fertility diminishes, when it is abandoned until this is restored naturally.

shifting spanner *n Austral. and N.Z.* an adjustable spanner. Also called: **shifter.**

shift key *n* a key on a typewriter or computer keyboard used to type capital letters and certain numbers and symbols.

shiftless ('ʃɪftlɪs) *adj* lacking in ambition or initiative. ▸ **'shiftlessly** *adv* ▸ **'shiftlessness** *n*

shiftwork ('ʃɪft,wɜ:k) *n* a system of employment where an individual's normal hours of work are, in part, outside the period of normal day working and may follow a different pattern in consecutive periods of weeks.

shifty ('ʃɪftɪ) *adj* **shiftier, shiftiest. 1** given to evasions; artful. **2** furtive in character or appearance. **3** full of expedients; resourceful. ▸ **'shiftily** *adv* ▸ **'shiftiness** *n*

shigella (ʃɪ'gɛlə) *n* any rod-shaped Gram-negative bacterium of the genus *Shigella;* some species cause dysentery. [C20: named after K. *Shiga* (1870–1957), Japanese bacteriologist, who discovered it]

shih-tzu ('ʃi:'tsu:) *n* a small dog of a breed derived from crossing the Pekingese and the Tibetan apso. It has a long straight dense coat and carries its tail curled over its back. [from Chinese, literally: lion]

Shiism ('ʃi:ɪzəm) *n Islam.* the beliefs and practices of Shiah.

shiitake (,ʃɪɪ'tɑ:keɪ) *n, pl* **-take.** a kind of mushroom widely used in Oriental cookery. [C20: from Japanese *shii* tree + *take* mushroom]

Shiite ('ʃi:aɪt) *or* **Shiah** *Islam.* ◆ *n* **1** an adherent of Shiah. ◆ *adj* **2** of or relating to Shiah. ▸ **Shiitic** (ʃi:'ɪtɪk) *adj*

Shijiazhuang ('ʃi:dʒɑ:'dʒwæŋ), **Shihchiachuang,** *or* **Shihkiachwang** (,ʃi:tʃjɑ:'tʃwæŋ) *n* a city in NE China, capital of Hebei province: textile manufacturing. Pop.: 1 320 000 (1991 est.).

shikar (ʃɪ'kɑ:) (in India) ◆ *n* **1** hunting, esp. big-game hunting. ◆ *vb* **-kars, -karring, -karred. 2** to hunt (game, esp. big game). [C17: via Urdu from Persian]

shikari *or* **shikaree** (ʃɪ'kɑ:rɪ) *n, pl* **-ris** *or* **-rees.** (in India) a hunter.

Shikoku ('ʃi:kəʊ,ku:) *n* the smallest of the four main islands of Japan, separated from Honshu by the Inland Sea: forested and mountainous. Pop.: 4 183 000 (1995). Area: 17 759 sq. km (6857 sq. miles).

shiksa ('ʃɪksə) *n Often derogatory.* (used by Jews) **1** a non-Jewish girl. **2** a Jewish girl who fails to live up to traditional Jewish standards. [Yiddish *shikse,* feminine of *sheygets* non-Jewish youth, from Hebrew *sheqes* defect]

shill (ʃɪl) *n Slang.* a confidence trickster's assistant, esp. a person who poses as an ordinary customer, gambler, etc., in order to entice others to participate. [C20: perhaps shortened from *shillaber* a circus barker, of unknown origin]

shillelagh *or* **shillala** (ʃə'leɪlə, -lɪ; *Irish* ʃɪ'le:lə) *n* (in Ireland) a stout club or cudgel, esp. one made of oak or blackthorn. [C18: from Irish Gaelic *sail* cudgel + *éille* leash, thong]

shilling ('ʃɪlɪŋ) *n* **1** a former British and Australian silver or cupronickel coin worth one twentieth of a pound: not minted in Britain since 1970. Abbrevs.: **s., sh. 2** the standard monetary unit of Kenya, Somalia, Tanzania, and Uganda: divided into 100 cents. **3** an old monetary unit of the U.S. varying in value in different states. **4** (*in combination*) *Scot.* an indication of the strength and character of a beer, referring to the price after duty that was formerly paid per barrel: *sixty-shilling.* Usually abbreviated to: /-. [Old English *scilling;* related to Old Norse *skillingr,* Gothic *skilliggs,* Old High German *skilling*]

shilling mark *n* another name for **solidus** (sense 1). [so named because it was used to separate shillings from pence when writing amounts less than one pound before the introduction of decimal currency in Britain. For example, *three shillings and eleven pence* was written *3/11*]

Shillong (ʃɪˈlɒŋ) *n* a city in NE India, capital of Meghalaya: situated on the **Shillong Plateau** at an altitude of 1520 m (4987 ft.); destroyed by earthquake in 1897 and rebuilt. Pop.: 131 719 (1991).

shillyshally (ˈʃɪlɪˌʃælɪ) *Informal.* ◆ *vb* **-lies, -lying, -lied. 1** (*intr*) to be indecisive, esp. over unimportant matters; hesitate. ◆ *adv* **2** in an indecisive manner. ◆ *adj* **3** indecisive or hesitant. ◆ *n, pl* **-lies. 4** indecision or hesitation; vacillation. [C18: from *shill I shall I,* by reduplication of *shall I*] ▸ **ˈshilly,shallier** *n*

Shiloh (ˈʃaɪləʊ) *n* a town in central ancient Palestine, in Canaan on the E slope of Mount Ephraim: keeping place of the tabernacle and the ark; destroyed by the Philistines.

shilpit (ˈʃɪlpɪt) *adj Scot.* puny; thin; weak-looking. [C19: of unknown origin]

shily (ˈʃaɪlɪ) *adv* a less common spelling of **shyly.**

shim (ʃɪm) *n* **1** a thin packing strip or washer often used with a number of similar washers or strips to adjust a clearance for gears, etc. **2** *Physics.* a thin strip of magnetic material, such as soft iron, used to adjust a magnetic field. ◆ *vb* **shims, shimming, shimmed. 3** (*tr*) to modify a load, clearance, or magnetic field by the use of shims.

shimmer (ˈʃɪmə) *vb* **1** (*intr*) to shine with a glistening or tremulous light. ◆ *n* **2** a faint, glistening, or tremulous light. [Old English *scimerian;* related to Middle Low German *schēmeren* to grow dark, Old Norse *skimi* brightness] ▸ **ˈshimmering** *adj* ▸ **ˈshimmeringly** *adv* ▸ **ˈshimmery** *adj*

shimmy (ˈʃɪmɪ) *n, pl* **-mies. 1** an American ragtime dance with much shaking of the hips and shoulders. **2** abnormal wobbling motion in a motor vehicle, esp. in the front wheels or steering. **3** an informal word for **chemise.** ◆ *vb* **-mies, -mying, -mied.** (*intr*) **4** to dance the shimmy. **5** to vibrate or wobble. [C19: changed from CHEMISE, mistakenly assumed to be plural]

Shimonoseki (ˌʃɪmənəʊˈsɛkɪ) *n* a port in SW Japan, on SW Honshu: scene of the peace treaty (1895) ending the Sino-Japanese War; a heavy industrial centre. Pop.: 259 791 (1995).

shin[1] (ʃɪn) *n* **1** the front part of the lower leg. **2** the front edge of the tibia. **3** *Chiefly Brit.* a cut of beef, the lower foreleg. ◆ *vb* **shins, shinning, shinned. 4** (when *intr,* often foll. by *up*) to climb (a pole, tree, etc.) by gripping with the hands or arms and the legs and hauling oneself up. **5** (*tr*) to kick (a person) in the shins. [Old English *scinu;* related to Old High German *scina* needle, Norwegian dialect *skina* small disc]

shin[2] (ʃɪn) *n* the 22nd letter in the Hebrew alphabet (ש), transliterated as *sh.* [from Hebrew *shīn,* literally: tooth]

Shinar (ˈʃaɪnə) *n Old Testament.* the southern part of the valley of the Tigris and Euphrates, often identified with Sumer; Babylonia.

shinbone (ˈʃɪnˌbəʊn) *n* the nontechnical name for **tibia** (sense 1).

shindig (ˈʃɪnˌdɪg) *n Informal.* **1** a noisy party, dance, etc. **2** another word for **shindy.** [C19: variant of SHINDY]

shindy (ˈʃɪndɪ) *n, pl* **-dies.** *Informal.* **1** a quarrel or commotion (esp. in the phrase **kick up a shindy**). **2** another word for **shindig.** [C19: variant of SHINTY]

shine (ʃaɪn) *vb* **shines, shining, shone. 1** (*intr*) to emit light. **2** (*intr*) to glow or be bright with reflected light. **3** (*tr*) to direct the light of (a lamp, etc.): *he shone the torch in my eyes.* **4** (*tr; past tense and past participle* **shined**) to cause to gleam by polishing: *to shine shoes.* **5** (*intr*) to be conspicuously competent; excel: *she shines at tennis.* **6** (*intr*) to appear clearly; be conspicuous: *the truth shone out of his words.* ◆ *n* **7** the state or quality of shining; sheen; lustre. **8** (**come**) **rain or shine. 8a** whatever the weather. **8b** regardless of circumstances. **9** *Informal.* short for **moonshine** (whisky). **10** *Informal.* a liking or fancy (esp. in the phrase **take a shine to**). [Old English *scīnan;* related to Old Norse *skīna,* Gothic *skeinan,* Old High German *scīnan* to shine, Greek *skia* shadow]

shiner (ˈʃaɪnə) *n* **1** something that shines, such as a polishing device. **2** any of numerous small North American freshwater cyprinid fishes of the genus *Notropis* and related genera, such as *N. cornutus* (**common shiner**) and *Notemigonus crysoleucas* (**golden shiner**). **3** a popular name for the **mackerel. 4** *Informal.* a black eye. **5** *N.Z. old-fashioned, informal.* a vagrant or tramp.

shingle[1] (ˈʃɪŋgᵊl) *n* **1** a thin rectangular tile, esp. one made of wood, that is laid with others in overlapping rows to cover a roof or a wall. **2** a woman's short-cropped hairstyle. **3** *U.S. and Canadian.* a small signboard or nameplate fixed outside the office of a doctor, lawyer, etc. **4 a shingle short.** *Austral. informal.* unintelligent or mentally subnormal. ◆ *vb* (*tr*) **5** to cover (a roof or a wall) with shingles. **6** to cut (the hair) in a short-cropped style. [C12 *scingle,* from Late Latin *scindula* a split piece of wood, from Latin *scindere* to split] ▸ **ˈshingler** *n*

shingle[2] (ˈʃɪŋgᵊl) *n* **1** coarse gravel, esp. the pebbles found on beaches. **2** a place or area strewn with shingle. [C16: of Scandinavian origin; compare Norwegian *singl* pebbles, Frisian *singel* gravel] ▸ **ˈshingly** *adj*

shingle[3] (ˈʃɪŋgᵊl) *vb* (*tr*) *Metallurgy.* to hammer or squeeze the slag out of (iron) after puddling in the production of wrought iron. [C17: from Old French dialect *chingler* to whip, from *chingle* belt, from Latin *cingula* girdle; see CINGULUM]

shingles (ˈʃɪŋgᵊlz) *n* (*functioning as sing*) an acute viral disease affecting the ganglia of certain nerves, characterized by inflammation, pain, and skin eruptions along the course of the affected nerve. Technical names: **herpes zoster, zoster.** [C14: from Medieval Latin *cingulum* girdle, rendering Greek *zōnē* ZONE]

shinkin (ˈʃɪŋkɪn) *n South Wales dialect.* a worthless person. [Welsh, from the surname *Jenkin,* of Dutch origin]

shinleaf (ˈʃɪnˌliːf) *n, pl* **-leaves.** the usual U.S. name for **wintergreen** (sense 3).

shinplaster (ˈʃɪnˌplɑːstə) *n U.S., Canadian, and Austral.* a promissory note on brittle paper, issued by an individual. [C19: so called because of its resemblance to a sticking plaster]

shin splints *n* (*functioning as sing or pl*) a painful swelling of the front lower leg, associated with muscle or bone inflammation, and common among athletes and other sportspeople.

Shinto (ˈʃɪntəʊ) *n* the indigenous religion of Japan, polytheistic in character and incorporating the worship of a number of ethnic divinities, from the chief of which the emperor is believed to be descended. [C18: from Japanese: the way of the gods, from Chinese *shên* gods + *tao* way] ▸ **ˈShintoism** *n* ▸ **ˈShintoist** *n, adj*

shinty (ˈʃɪntɪ) *or U.S. and Canadian* **shinny** (ˈʃɪnɪ) *n, pl* **-ties** *or U.S. and Canadian* **-nies. 1** a simple form of hockey of Scottish origin played with a ball and sticks curved at the lower end. **2** the stick used in this game. ◆ *vb* **-ties, -tying, -tied** *or U.S. and Canadian* **-nies, -nying, -nied.** (*intr*) **3** to play shinty. [C17: possibly from Scottish Gaelic *sinteag* a pace, bound]

shiny (ˈʃaɪnɪ) *adj* **shinier, shiniest. 1** glossy or polished; bright. **2** (of clothes or material) worn to a smooth and glossy state, as by continual rubbing. ▸ **ˈshininess** *n*

ship (ʃɪp) *n* **1** a vessel propelled by engines or sails for navigating on the water, esp. a large vessel that cannot be carried aboard another, as distinguished from a boat. **2** *Nautical.* a large sailing vessel with three or more square-rigged masts. **3** the crew of a ship. **4** short for **airship** or **spaceship. 5** *Informal.* any vehicle or conveyance. **6 when one's ship comes in.** when one has become successful or wealthy. ◆ *vb* **ships, shipping, shipped. 7** to place, transport, or travel on any conveyance, esp. aboard a ship: *ship the microscopes by aeroplane; can we ship tomorrow?* **8** (*tr*) *Nautical.* to take (water) over the side. **9** to bring or go aboard a vessel: *to ship oars.* **10** (*tr;* often foll. by *off*) *Informal.* to send away, often in order to be rid of: *they shipped the children off to boarding school.* **11** (*intr*) to engage to serve aboard a ship: *I shipped aboard a Liverpool liner.* ◆ See also **ship out.** [Old English *scip;* related to Old Norse *skip,* Old High German *skif* ship, *scipfī* cup] ▸ **ˈshippable** *adj*

-ship *suffix forming nouns.* **1** indicating state or condition: *fellowship.* **2** indicating rank, office, or position: *lordship.* **3** indicating craft or skill: *horsemanship; workmanship; scholarship.* [Old English *-scipe;* compare SHAPE]

shipboard (ˈʃɪpˌbɔːd) *n* **1** (*modifier*) taking place, used, or intended for use aboard a ship: *a shipboard encounter.* **2 on shipboard.** on board a ship.

ship-broker *n* a person who acts for a shipowner by getting cargo and passengers for his ships and also handling insurance and other matters.

shipbuilder (ˈʃɪpˌbɪldə) *n* a person or business engaged in the building of ships. ▸ **ˈshipˌbuilding** *n*

ship chandler *n* a person or business dealing in supplies for ships. ▸ **ship chandlery** *n*

Shipka Pass (ˈʃɪpkə) *n* a pass over the Balkan Mountains in central Bulgaria: scene of a bloody Turkish defeat in the Russo-Turkish War (1877–78). Height: 1334 m (4376 ft.).

shipload (ˈʃɪpˌləʊd) *n* the quantity carried by a ship.

shipmaster (ˈʃɪpˌmɑːstə) *or* **shipman** (ˈʃɪpmən) *n, pl* **-masters** *or* **-men.** the master or captain of a ship.

shipmate (ˈʃɪpˌmeɪt) *n* a sailor who serves on the same ship as another.

shipment (ˈʃɪpmənt) *n* **1a** goods shipped together as part of the same lot: *a shipment of grain.* **1b** (*as modifier*): *a shipment schedule.* **2** the act of shipping cargo.

ship money *n English history.* a tax levied to finance the fitting out of warships: abolished 1640.

ship of the line *n Nautical.* (formerly) a warship large enough to fight in the first line of battle.

ship out *vb* (*adv*) to depart or cause to depart by ship: *we shipped out at dawn; they shipped out the new recruits.*

shipowner (ˈʃɪpˌəʊnə) *n* a person who owns or has shares in a ship or ships.

shipper (ˈʃɪpə) *n* a person or company in the business of shipping freight.

shipping (ˈʃɪpɪŋ) *n* **1a** the business of transporting freight, esp. by ship. **1b** (*as modifier*): *a shipping magnate; shipping line.* **2a** ships collectively: *there is a lot of shipping in the Channel.* **2b** the tonnage of a number of ships: *shipping for this year exceeded that of last.*

shipping agent *n* a person or company whose business is to prepare shipping documents, arrange shipping space and insurance, and deal with customs requirements.

shipping clerk *n* a person employed by a company to arrange, receive, record, and send shipments of goods.

shipping ton *n* the full name for **ton**[1] (sense 5).

ship-rigged *adj* rigged as a full-rigged ship.

ship's articles *or* **shipping articles** *pl n* a type of contract by which sailors agree to the conditions, payment, etc., for the ship in which they are going to work.

ship's biscuit *n* another name for **hardtack.**

ship's boy *n* a young man or boy employed to attend the needs of passengers or officers aboard ship.

shipshape (ˈʃɪpˌʃeɪp) *adj* **1** neat; orderly. ◆ *adv* **2** in a neat and orderly manner.

ship's papers *pl n* the documents that are required by law to be carried by a ship for the purpose of ascertaining details of her ownership, nationality, destination, and cargo or to prove her neutrality.

shipway (ˈʃɪpˌweɪ) *n* **1** the structure on which a vessel is built, then launched. **2** a canal used by ships.

shipworm (ˈʃɪpˌwɜːm) *n* any wormlike marine bivalve mollusc of the genus

Teredo and related genera and family *Teredinidae.* They bore into wooden piers, ships, etc., by means of drill-like shell valves. See also **piddock.**

shipwreck ('ʃɪp,rɛk) *n* **1** the partial or total destruction of a ship at sea. **2** a wrecked ship or part of such a ship. **3** ruin or destruction: *the shipwreck of all my hopes.* ◆ *vb (tr)* **4** to wreck or destroy (a ship). **5** to bring to ruin or destruction. [Old English *scipwræc,* from SHIP + *wræc* something driven by the sea; see WRACK[2]]

shipwright ('ʃɪp,raɪt) *n* an artisan skilled in one or more of the tasks required to build vessels.

shipyard ('ʃɪp,jɑːd) *n* a place or facility for the building, maintenance, and repair of ships.

shiralee (,ʃɪrə'liː) *n Austral. history, informal.* a swag; swagman's bundle. [C19: of unknown origin]

Shiraz[1] (ʃɪə'rɑːz) *n* a city in SW Iran, at an altitude of 1585 m (5200 ft.): an important Muslim cultural centre in the 14th century; university (1948); noted for fine carpets. Pop.: 1 042 801 (1995 est.).

Shiraz[2] (ʃɪə'rɑːz) *n* the name used in Australia for the Syrah grape and wines. [from SHIRAZ[1], where the wine supposedly originated]

shire[1] (ʃaɪə) *n* **1a** one of the British counties. **1b** *(in combination): Yorkshire.* **2** (in Australia) a rural district having its own local council. **3** See **shire horse. 4 the Shires.** the Midland counties of England, esp. Northamptonshire and Leicestershire, famous for hunting, etc. [Old English *scīr* office; related to Old High German *scīra* business]

shire[2] (ʃaɪə) *vb (tr) Ulster dialect.* to refresh or rest: *let me get my head shired.* [from Old English *scīr* clear]

Shiré ('ʃɪəreɪ) *n* a river in E central Africa, flowing from Lake Malawi through Malawi and Mozambique to the Zambezi. Length: 596 km (370 miles).

Shiré Highlands *pl n* an upland area of S Malawi. Average height: 900 m (3000 ft.).

shire horse *n* a large heavy breed of carthorse with long hair on the fetlocks. Often shortened to **shire.** [C19: so called because the breed was originally reared in *the Shires.* See SHIRE[1]]

shirk[1] (ʃɜːk) *vb* **1** to avoid discharging (work, a duty, etc.); evade. ◆ *n also* **shirker. 2** a person who shirks. [C17: probably from German *Schurke* rogue; see SHARK[2]]

shirk [2] (ʃɪːk) *n Islam.* **a** the fundamental sin of regarding anything as equal to Allah. **b** any belief that is considered to be in opposition to Allah and Islam. [from Arabic: association]

shirr (ʃɜː) *vb* **1** to gather (fabric) into two or more parallel rows to decorate a dress, blouse, etc., often using elastic thread. **2** *(tr)* to bake (eggs) out of their shells. ◆ *n also* **shirring. 3** a series of gathered rows decorating a dress, blouse, etc. [C19: of unknown origin]

shirt (ʃɜːt) *n* **1** a garment worn on the upper part of the body, esp. by men, usually of light material and typically having a collar and sleeves and buttoning up the front. **2** short for **nightshirt** or **undershirt. 3 keep your shirt on.** *Informal.* refrain from losing your temper (often used as an exhortation to another). **4 put** *or* **lose one's shirt on.** *Informal.* to bet or lose all one has on (a horse, etc.). [Old English *scyrte;* related to Old English *sceort* SHORT, Old Norse *skyrta* skirt, Middle High German *schurz* apron]

shirting ('ʃɜːtɪŋ) *n* fabric used in making men's shirts.

shirt-lifter *n Derogatory slang.* a homosexual.

shirtsleeve ('ʃɜːt,sliːv) *n* **1** the sleeve of a shirt. **2 in one's shirtsleeves.** not wearing a jacket.

shirt-tail *n* the part of a shirt that extends below the waist.

shirtwaister ('ʃɜːt,weɪstə) *or U.S. and Canadian* **shirtwaist** *n* a woman's dress with a tailored bodice resembling a shirt.

shirty ('ʃɜːtɪ) *adj* **shirtier, shirtiest.** *Slang, chiefly Brit.* bad-tempered or annoyed. [C19: perhaps based on such phrases as *to get someone's shirt out* to annoy someone] ▸ **'shirtily** *adv* ▸ **'shirtiness** *n*

shish kebab ('ʃiːʃ kə'bæb) *n* a dish consisting of small pieces of meat and vegetables threaded onto skewers and grilled. [from Turkish *şiş kebab,* from *şiş* skewer; see KEBAB]

shit (ʃɪt) *Taboo.* ◆ *vb* **shits, shitting; shitted, shit,** *or* **shat. 1** to defecate. **2** (usually foll. by *on*) *Slang.* to give the worst possible treatment (to). ◆ *n* **3** faeces; excrement. **4** rubbish; nonsense. **5** an obnoxious or worthless person. **6** cannabis resin or heroin. **7 in the shit.** in trouble. **8 the shit hits the fan.** the real trouble begins. ◆ *interj* **9** an exclamation expressing anger, disgust, etc. ◆ Also (esp. dialect): **shite** (ʃaɪt). [Old English *scite* (unattested) dung, *scītan* to defecate, of Germanic origin; related to Old English *scēadan* to separate, Old Norse *skīta* to defecate, Middle Dutch *schitte* excrement] ▸ **'shitty** *adj* ▸ **'shittily** *adv* ▸ **'shittiness** *n*

shithead ('ʃɪt,hɛd) *n Taboo slang.* a fool; idiot: used as a term of abuse.

shittah ('ʃɪtə) *n, pl* **shittim** ('ʃɪtɪm) *or* **shittahs.** a tree mentioned in the Old Testament, thought to be either of two Asian acacias, *Acacia seyal* or *A. tortilis,* having close-grained yellow-brown wood. [C17: from Hebrew *shiṭṭāh;* related to Egyptian *sout* acacia]

Shittim ('ʃɪtɪm) *n Old Testament.* the site to the east of the Jordan and northeast of the Dead Sea where the Israelites encamped before crossing the Jordan (Numbers 25:1–9).

shittim wood ('ʃɪtɪm) *n Old Testament.* a kind of wood, probably acacia, from which the Ark of the Covenant and parts of the tabernacle were made. [C14: from Hebrew *shiṭṭīm,* plural of SHITTAH]

shiur ('ʃiʊr, ʃi'uːr) *n, pl* **shiurim** (ʃiu'rim, ʃi'uːrim) *Judaism.* a lesson, esp. one in which a passage of the Talmud is studied together by a group of people. [from Hebrew, literally: measurement]

shiv (ʃɪv) *n* a variant spelling of **chiv.**

Shiva ('ʃiːvə, 'ʃɪvə) *n* a variant spelling of **Siva.** ▸ **'Shivaism** *n* ▸ **'Shivaist** *n, adj*

shivah ('ʃivɑ, 'ʃivə) *n Judaism.* **1** the period of formal mourning lasting seven days from the funeral during which the mourner stays indoors and sits on a low stool. **2 sit shivah.** to mourn. [from Hebrew, literally: seven (days)]

shivaree (,ʃɪvə'riː) *n* a variant (esp. U.S. and Canadian) of **charivari.**

shive (ʃaɪv) *n* **1** a flat cork or bung for wide-mouthed bottles. **2** an archaic word for **slice.** [C13: from Middle Dutch or Middle Low German *schīve;* see SHEAVE[1]]

shiver[1] ('ʃɪvə) *vb (intr)* **1** to shake or tremble, as from cold or fear. **2a** (of a sail) to luff; flap or shake. **2b** (of a sailing vessel) to sail close enough to the wind to make the sails luff. ◆ *n* **3** the act of shivering; a tremulous motion. **4 the shivers.** an attack of shivering, esp. through fear or illness. [C13 *chiveren,* perhaps variant of *chevelen* to chatter (used of teeth), from Old English *ceafl* JOWL[1]] ▸ **'shiverer** *n* ▸ **'shivering** *adj*

shiver[2] ('ʃɪvə) *vb* **1** to break or cause to break into fragments. ◆ *n* **2** a splintered piece. [C13: of Germanic origin; compare Old High German *scivaro,* Middle Dutch *scheveren* to shiver, Old Norse *skīfa* to split]

shivery ('ʃɪvərɪ) *adj* **1** inclined to shiver or tremble. **2** causing shivering, esp. through cold or fear.

Shizuoka (,ʃiːzuː'əʊkə) *n* a city in central Japan, on S Honshu: a centre for green tea; university (1949). Pop.: 474 089 (1995).

Shkodër (*Albanian* 'ʃkodər) *n* a market town in NW Albania, on **Lake Shkodër**: an Illyrian capital in the first millennium B.C. Pop.: 83 700 (1991 est.). Italian name: **Scutari.**

shloshim ('ʃləʃim, 'ʃləʊʃim) *n Judaism.* the period of thirty days' deep mourning following a death. [from Hebrew, literally: thirty (days)]

Shluh (ʃə'luː, ʃluː) *n* **1** *(pl* **Shluhs** *or* **Shluh)** a member of a Berber people inhabiting the Atlas Mountains in Morocco and Algeria. **2** the dialect of Berber spoken by this people.

SHM *abbrev. for* simple harmonic motion.

shmatte *Yiddish.* ('ʃmɑtə) *n* **1** a rag. **2** anything shabby. **3** *(modifier)* clothes: a jocular use: *the shmatte trade.*

shmo (ʃməʊ) *n, pl* **shmoes.** a variant form of **schmo.**

Shoah ('ʃɔɑː) *n* (in secular Judaism) a Hebrew word for **holocaust** (sense 2). See also **Churban** (sense 2). [literally: destruction]

shoal[1] (ʃəʊl) *n* **1** a stretch of shallow water. **2** a sandbank or rocky area in a stretch of water, esp. one that is visible at low water. ◆ *vb* **3** to make or become shallow. **4** *(intr) Nautical.* to sail into shallower water. ◆ *adj also* **shoaly. 5** a less common word for **shallow. 6** *Nautical.* (of the draught of a vessel) drawing little water. [Old English *sceald* SHALLOW] ▸ **'shoaliness** *n*

shoal[2] (ʃəʊl) *n* **1** a large group of fish. **2** a large group of people or things. ◆ *vb* **3** *(intr)* to collect together in such a group. [Old English *scolu;* related to Middle Low German, Middle Dutch *schōle* SCHOOL[2]]

shoat *or* **shote** (ʃəʊt) *n* a piglet that has recently been weaned. [C15: related to West Flemish *schote*]

shock[1] (ʃɒk) *vb* **1** to experience or cause to experience extreme horror, disgust, surprise, etc.: *the atrocities shocked us; she shocks easily.* **2** to cause a state of shock in (a person). **3** to come or cause to come into violent contact; jar. ◆ *n* **4** a sudden and violent jarring blow or impact. **5** something that causes a sudden and violent disturbance in the emotions: *the shock of her father's death made her ill.* **6** *Pathol.* a state of bodily collapse or near collapse caused by circulatory failure or sudden lowering of the blood pressure, as from severe bleeding, burns, fright, etc. [C16: from Old French *choc,* from *choquier* to make violent contact with, of Germanic origin; related to Middle High German *schoc*] ▸ **'shockable** *adj* ▸ **,shocka'bility** *n*

shock[2] (ʃɒk) *n* **1** a number of sheaves set on end in a field to dry. **2** a pile or stack of unthreshed corn. ◆ *vb* **3** *(tr)* to set up (sheaves) in shocks. [C14: probably of Germanic origin; compare Middle Low German, Middle Dutch *schok* shock of corn, group of sixty]

shock[3] (ʃɒk) *n* **1** a thick bushy mass, esp. of hair. ◆ *adj* **2** *Rare.* bushy; shaggy. [C19: perhaps from SHOCK[2]]

shock absorber *n* any device designed to absorb mechanical shock, esp. one fitted to a motor vehicle to damp the recoil of the road springs.

shocker ('ʃɒkə) *n Informal.* **1** a person or thing that shocks or horrifies. **2** a sensational novel, film, or play.

shockheaded ('ʃɒk,hɛdɪd) *adj* having a head of bushy or tousled hair.

shock-horror *adj Facetious.* (esp. of newspaper headlines) sensationalistic: *shock-horror stories about the British diet.* [C20: SHOCK[1] + HORROR]

shocking ('ʃɒkɪŋ) *adj* **1** causing shock, horror, or disgust. **2 shocking pink.** a vivid or garish shade of pink. **3** *Informal.* very bad or terrible: *shocking weather.* ▸ **'shockingly** *adv* ▸ **'shockingness** *n*

shock jock *n Informal.* a radio disc jockey who is deliberately controversial or provocative.

Shockley ('ʃɒklɪ) *n* **William Bradfield.** 1910–89, U.S. physicist, born in Britain, who shared the Nobel prize for physics (1956) with John Bardeen and Walter Brattain for developing the transistor. He also held controversial views on the connection between race and intelligence.

shockproof ('ʃɒk,pruːf) *adj* capable of absorbing shock without damage: *a shockproof watch.*

shockstall ('ʃɒk,stɔːl) *n* the loss of lift and increase of drag experienced by transonic aircraft when strong shock waves on the wings cause the airflow to separate from the wing surfaces.

shock therapy *or* **treatment** *n* the treatment of certain psychotic conditions by injecting drugs or by passing an electric current through the brain (**electroconvulsive therapy**) to produce convulsions or coma.

shock troops *pl n* soldiers specially trained and equipped to carry out an assault.

shock tube *n* an apparatus in which a gas is heated to very high temperatures by means of a shock wave, usually for spectroscopic investigation of the natures and reactions of the resulting radicals and excited molecules.

shock wave *n* a region across which there is a rapid pressure, temperature, and density rise caused by a body moving supersonically in a gas or by a detonation. Often shortened to **shock.** See also **sonic boom, shock tube.**

shod (ʃɒd) *vb* the past participle of **shoe.**

shoddy (ˈʃɒdɪ) *adj* **-dier, -diest. 1** imitating something of better quality. **2** of poor quality; trashy. **3** made of shoddy material. ◆ *n, pl* **-dies. 4** a yarn or fabric made from wool waste or clippings. **5** anything of inferior quality that is designed to simulate superior quality. [C19: of unknown origin] ▸ **ˈshoddily** *adv* ▸ **ˈshoddiness** *n*

shoe (ʃuː) *n* **1a** one of a matching pair of coverings shaped to fit the foot, esp. one ending below the ankle, having an upper of leather, plastic, etc., on a sole and heel of heavier leather, rubber, or synthetic material. **1b** (*as modifier*): *shoe cleaner.* **2** anything resembling a shoe in shape, function, position, etc., such as a horseshoe. **3** a band of metal or wood on the bottom of the runner of a sledge. **4** (in baccarat, etc.) a boxlike device for holding several packs of cards and allowing the cards to be dispensed singly. **5** a base for the supports of a superstructure of a bridge, roof, etc. **6** a metal collector attached to an electric train that slides along the third rail and picks up power for the motor. **7** *Engineering.* a lining to protect from and withstand wear: see **brake shoe, pile shoe. 8 be in (a person's) shoes.** *Informal.* to be in (another person's) situation. ◆ *vb* **shoes, shoeing, shod.** (*tr*) **9** to furnish with shoes. **10** to fit (a horse) with horseshoes. **11** to furnish with a hard cover, such as a metal plate, for protection against friction or bruising. [Old English *scōh;* related to Old Norse *skōr,* Gothic *skōhs,* Old High German *scuoh*]

shoebill (ˈʃuːˌbɪl) *n* a large wading bird, *Balaeniceps rex,* of tropical E African swamps, having a dark plumage, a large head, and a large broad bill: family *Balaenicipitidae,* order *Ciconiiformes.* [C19: so named because of the shape of its bill]

shoeblack (ˈʃuːˌblæk) *n* (esp. formerly) a person who shines boots and shoes.

shoehorn (ˈʃuːˌhɔːn) *n* **1** a smooth curved implement of horn, metal, plastic, etc., inserted at the heel of a shoe to ease the foot into it. ◆ *vb* **2** (*tr*) to cram (people or things) into a very small space.

shoelace (ˈʃuːˌleɪs) *n* a cord or lace for fastening shoes.

shoe leather *n* **1** leather used to make shoes. **2 save shoe leather.** to avoid wearing out shoes, as by taking a bus rather than walking.

shoemaker (ˈʃuːˌmeɪkə) *n* a person who makes or repairs shoes or boots. ▸ **ˈshoeˌmaking** *n*

Shoemaker-Levy 9 (ˈʃuːˌmeɪkə liːvaɪ) *n* a comet that was captured into an orbit around Jupiter and later broke up, the fragments colliding with Jupiter in July 1995. [C20: after *Carolyn Shoemaker* (born 1929), *Eugene Shoemaker* (born 1928), and *David Levy* (born 1948), U.S. astronomers, who discovered the orbiting fragments]

shoer (ˈʃuːə) *n Rare.* a person who shoes horses; farrier.

shoeshine (ˈʃuːˌʃaɪn) *n* **1** the act or an instance of polishing a pair of shoes. **2** the appearance or shiny surface of polished shoes.

shoestring (ˈʃuːˌstrɪŋ) *n* **1** another word for **shoelace. 2** *Informal.* **2a** a very small or petty amount of money (esp. in the phrase **on a shoestring**). **2b** (*as modifier*): *a shoestring budget.*

shoetree (ˈʃuːˌtriː) *n* a wooden or metal form inserted into a shoe or boot to stretch it or preserve its shape.

shofar *or* **shophar** (ˈʃəʊfɑː; *Hebrew* ʃoˈfar) *n, pl* **-fars, -phars** *or* **-froth, -phroth** (*Hebrew* -ˈfrɔt). *Judaism.* a ram's horn sounded in the synagogue daily during the month of Elul and repeatedly on Rosh Hashanah, and by the ancient Israelites as a warning, summons, etc. [from Hebrew *shōphār* ram's horn]

shogun (ˈʃəʊˌguːn) *n Japanese history.* **1** (from 794 A.D.) a chief military commander. **2** (from about 1192 to 1867) any of a line of hereditary military dictators who relegated the emperors to a position of purely theoretical supremacy. [C17: from Japanese, from Chinese *chiang chün* general, from *chiang* to lead + *chün* army] ▸ **ˈshoˌgunal** *adj*

shogunate (ˈʃəʊgʊnɪt, -ˌneɪt) *n Japanese history.* the office or rule of a shogun.

shogun bond *n* a bond sold on the Japanese market by a foreign institution and denominated in a foreign currency. Compare **samurai bond.**

shoji (ˈʃəʊʒiː, -dʒiː) *n, pl* **-ji** *or* **-jis. 1** a rice-paper screen in a sliding wooden frame, used in Japanese houses as a partition. **2** any similar screen. [C19: from Japanese, from *shō* to separate + *ji* a piece]

Sholapur (ˈʃəʊləˌpʊə) *n* a city in SW India, in S Maharashtra: major textile centre. Pop.: 604 215 (1991).

Sholem Aleichem *n* See (Sholem) **Aleichem.**

Sholes (ʃəʊlz) *n* **Christopher Latham.** 1819–90, U.S. inventor, who invented (1868) the typewriter and sold the patent to the Remington company (1873).

Sholokhov (*Russian* ˈʃɔləxəf) *n* **Mikhail Aleksandrovich** (mixaˈil alɪkˈsandrəvitʃ). 1905–84, Soviet author, noted particularly for *And Quiet flows the Don* (1934) and *The Don flows Home to the Sea* (1940), describing the effect of the Revolution and civil war on the life of the Cossacks: Nobel prize for literature 1965.

Shona (ˈʃɒnə) *n* **1** (*pl* **-na** *or* **-nas**) a member of a Sotho people of S central Africa, living chiefly in Zimbabwe and Mozambique. **2** the language of this people, belonging to the Bantu group of the Niger-Congo family.

shone (ʃɒn; *U.S.* ʃəʊn) *vb* the past tense and past participle of **shine.**

shoneen (ˈʃoːniːn) *n Irish.* an Irishman who imitates English ways. [C19: from Irish Gaelic *Seoinín,* diminutive of *Seon* John (taken as typical English name)]

shonky (ˈʃɒŋkɪ) *adj* **-kier, -kiest.** *Austral. and N.Z. informal.* **1** of dubious integrity or legality. **2** unreliable; unsound. [C19: perhaps from Yiddish *shonniker* or from SH(ODDY) + (W)ONKY]

shoo (ʃuː) *interj* **1** go away!: used to drive away unwanted or annoying people, animals, etc. ◆ *vb* **shoos, shooing, shooed. 2** (*tr*) to drive away by or as if by crying "shoo." **3** (*intr*) to cry "shoo." [C15: imitative; related to Middle High German *schū,* French *shou,* Italian *scio*]

shoofly pie (ˈʃuːˌflaɪ) *n U.S.* a dessert similar to treacle tart.

shoogle (ˈʃʊgᵊl) *Dialect, chiefly Scot.* ◆ *vb* **1** to shake, sway, or rock back and forth. ◆ *n* **2** a rocking motion; shake. [from dialectal *shog, shug;* apparently related to German *schaukeln* to shake] ▸ **ˈshoogly** *adj*

shoo-in *n U.S. and Canadian.* **1** a person or thing that is certain to win or succeed. **2** a match or contest that is easy to win.

shook[1] (ʃʊk) *n* **1** (in timber working) a set of parts ready for assembly, esp. of a barrel. **2** a group of sheaves piled together on end; shock. [C18: of unknown origin]

shook[2] (ʃʊk) *vb* **1** the past tense of **shake.** ◆ *adj* **2 shook on.** *Austral. and N.Z. informal.* keen on; enthusiastic about.

shool (ʃuːl) *n* a dialect word for **shovel.**

shoon (ʃuːn) *n Dialect, chiefly Scot.* a plural of **shoe.**

shoot (ʃuːt) *vb* **shoots, shooting, shot. 1** (*tr*) to hit, wound, damage, or kill with a missile discharged from a weapon. **2** to discharge (a missile or missiles) from a weapon. **3** to fire (a weapon) or (of a weapon) to be fired. **4** to send out or be sent out as if from a weapon: *he shot questions at her.* **5** (*intr*) to move very rapidly; dart. **6** (*tr*) to slide or push into or out of a fastening: *to shoot a bolt.* **7** to emit (a ray of light) or (of a ray of light) to be emitted. **8** (*tr*) to go or pass quickly over or through: *to shoot rapids.* **9** (*intr*) to hunt game with a gun for sport. **10** (*tr*) to pass over (an area) in hunting game. **11** to extend or cause to extend; project. **12** (*tr*) to discharge down or as if down a chute. **13** (*intr*) (of a plant) to produce (buds, branches, etc.). **14** (*intr*) (of a seed) to germinate. **15** to photograph or record (a sequence, subject, etc.). **16** (*tr; usually passive*) to variegate or streak, as with colour. **17** *Soccer, hockey, etc.* to hit or propel (the ball, etc.) towards the goal. **18** (*tr*) *Sport, chiefly U.S. and Canadian.* to score (points, strokes, etc.): *he shot 72 on the first round.* **19** (*tr*) to plane (a board) to produce a straight edge. **20** (*tr*) *Mining.* to detonate. **21** (*tr*) to measure the altitude of (a celestial body). **22** (often foll. by *up*) *Slang.* to inject (someone, esp. oneself) with (a drug, esp. heroin). **23 shoot a line.** See **line**[1] (sense 58). **24 shoot from the hip.** to speak bluntly or impulsively without concern for the consequences. **25 shoot one's bolt.** See **bolt**[1] (sense 13). **26 shoot oneself in the foot.** *Informal.* to damage one's own cause inadvertently. **27 shoot one's mouth off.** *Slang.* **27a** to talk indiscreetly. **27b** to boast or exaggerate. **28 shoot the breeze.** See **breeze**[1] (sense 5). ◆ *n* **29** the act of shooting. **30** the action or motion of something that is shot. **31** the first aerial part of a plant to develop from a germinating seed. **32** any new growth of a plant, such as a bud, young branch, etc. **33** *Chiefly Brit.* a meeting or party organized for hunting game with guns. **34** an area or series of coverts and woods where game can be hunted with guns. **35** a steep descent in a stream; rapid. **36** *Informal.* a photographic assignment. **37** *Geology, mining.* a narrow workable vein of ore. **38** *Obsolete.* the reach of a shot. **39 the whole shoot.** *Slang.* everything. ◆ *interj* **40** *U.S. and Canadian.* an exclamation expressing disbelief, scepticism, disgust, disappointment, etc. ◆ See also **shoot down, shoot out, shoot through, shoot up.** [Old English *sceōtan;* related to Old Norse *skjōta,* Old High German *skiozan* to shoot, Old Slavonic *iskydati* to throw out]

shoot down *vb* (*tr, adv*) **1** to shoot callously. **2** to cause to fall to earth by hitting with a missile. **3** to defeat or disprove: *he shot down her argument.*

shooter (ˈʃuːtə) *n* **1** a person or thing that shoots. **2** *Slang.* a gun. **3** *Cricket.* a ball that unexpectedly travels low on pitching.

shooting box *n* a small country house providing accommodation for a shooting party during the shooting season. Also called: **shooting lodge.**

shooting brake *n Brit.* a former name for **estate car.**

shooting gallery *n* **1** an area, often enclosed, designed for target practice, shooting, etc. **2** *Slang.* a house where heroin addicts inject themselves.

shooting iron *n U.S. slang.* a firearm, esp. a pistol.

shooting script *n Films.* written instructions indicating to the cameraman the order of shooting.

shooting star *n* an informal name for **meteor.**

shooting stick *n* a device that resembles a walking stick, having a spike at one end and a folding seat at the other.

shoot out *vb* (*tr, adv*) **1** to fight to the finish by shooting (esp. in the phrase **shoot it out**). ◆ *n* **shoot-out. 2** a conclusive gunfight.

shoot through *vb* (*intr, adv*) *Informal, chiefly Austral.* to leave; depart.

shoot up *vb* (*adv*) **1** (*intr*) to grow or become taller very fast. **2** (*tr*) to hit with a number of shots. **3** (*tr*) to spread terror throughout (a place) by lawless and wanton shooting. **4** (*tr*) *Slang.* to inject (someone, esp. oneself) with (a drug, esp. heroin).

shop (ʃɒp) *n* **1** a place, esp. a small building, for the retail sale of goods and services. **2** an act or instance of shopping, esp. household shopping: *the weekly shop.* **3** a place for the performance of a specified type of work; workshop. **4 all over the shop.** *Informal.* **4a** in disarray: *his papers were all over the shop.* **4b** in every direction: *I've searched for it all over the shop.* **5 shut up shop.** to close business at the end of the day or permanently. **6 talk shop.** to speak about one's work, esp. when meeting socially, sometimes with the effect of excluding those not similarly employed. ◆ *vb* **shops, shopping, shopped. 7** (*intr;* often foll. by *for*) to visit a shop or shops in search of (goods) with the intention of buying them. **8** (*tr*) *Slang, chiefly Brit.* to inform on or betray, esp. to the police. [Old English *sceoppa* stall, booth; related to Old High German *scopf* shed, Middle Dutch *schoppe* stall]

shopaholic (ˌʃɒpəˈhɒlɪk) *n Informal.* a compulsive shopper. [C20: from SHOP + -HOLIC]

shop around *vb* (*intr, adv*) *Informal.* **1** to visit a number of shops or stores to compare goods and prices. **2** to consider a number of possibilities before making a choice.

shop assistant *n* a person who serves in a shop.

shop floor *n* **1** the part of a factory housing the machines and men directly involved in production. **2a** workers, esp. factory workers organized in a union. **2b** (*as modifier*): *shop-floor protest.*

shophar ('ʃəʊfɑː; *Hebrew* ʃɔ'far) *n, pl* **-phars** *or* **-phroth** (*Hebrew* -'frɔt). a variant spelling of **shofar**.

shopkeeper ('ʃɒpˌkiːpə) *n* a person who owns or manages a shop or small store. ▸ **'shopˌkeeping** *n*

shoplifter ('ʃɒpˌlɪftə) *n* a person who steals goods from a shop during shopping hours. ▸ **'shopˌlifting** *n*

shopper ('ʃɒpə) *n* a person who buys goods in a shop.

shopping ('ʃɒpɪŋ) *n* **1** a number or collection of articles purchased. **2** the act or an instance of making purchases.

shopping bag lady *n* another name for **bag lady**.

shopping centre *n* **1** a purpose-built complex of shops, restaurants, etc., for the use of pedestrians. **2** the area of a town where most of the shops are situated.

shopping mall *n* a large enclosed shopping centre.

shopping precinct *n* a pedestrian area containing shops, restaurants, etc., forming a single architectural unit and usually providing car-parking facilities.

shopsoiled ('ʃɒpˌsɔɪld) *adj* **1** worn, faded, tarnished, etc., from being displayed in a shop or store. U.S. word: **shopworn**. **2** no longer new or fresh.

shop steward *n* a coworker elected by trade union members to represent them in discussions and negotiations with the management.

shoptalk ('ʃɒpˌtɔːk) *n* conversation concerning one's work, esp. when carried on outside business hours.

shopwalker ('ʃɒpˌwɔːkə) *n Brit.* a person employed by a departmental store to supervise sales personnel, assist customers, etc. U.S. equivalent: **floorwalker**.

shopworn ('ʃɒpˌwɔːn) *adj* the U.S. word for **shopsoiled**.

shoran ('ʃɔːræn) *n* a short-range radar system by which an aircraft, ship, etc., can accurately determine its position by the time taken for a signal to be sent to two radar beacons at known locations and be returned. **[C20:** *sho(rt) ra(nge) n(avigation)***]**

shore[1] (ʃɔː) *n* **1** the land along the edge of a sea, lake, or wide river. Related adj: **littoral**. **2a** land, as opposed to water (esp. in the phrase **on shore**). **2b** (*as modifier*): *shore duty.* **3** *Law.* the tract of coastland lying between the ordinary marks of high and low water. **4** (*often pl*) a country: *his native shores.* ◆ *vb* **5** (*tr*) to move or drag (a boat) onto a shore. **[C14:** probably from Middle Low German, Middle Dutch *schōre;* compare Old High German *scorra* cliff; see SHEAR**]**

shore[2] (ʃɔː) *n* **1** a prop, post, or beam used to support a wall, building, ship in dry dock, etc. ◆ *vb* **2** (*tr;* often foll. by *up*) to prop or make safe with or as if with a shore. **[C15:** from Middle Dutch *schōre;* related to Old Norse *skortha* prop**]** ▸ **'shoring** *n*

shore[3] (ʃɔː) *vb Archaic or Austral. and N.Z.* a past tense of **shear**.

shore bird *n* any of various birds that live close to water, esp. any bird of the families *Charadriidae* or *Scolopacidae* (plovers, sandpipers, etc.). Also called (Brit.): **wader**.

shore leave *n Naval.* **1** permission to go ashore. Compare **liberty** (sense 5). **2** time spent ashore during leave.

shoreless ('ʃɔːlɪs) *adj* **1** without a shore suitable for landing. **2** *Poetic.* boundless; vast: *the shoreless wastes.*

shoreline ('ʃɔːˌlaɪn) *n* the edge of a body of water.

shore patrol *n U.S.* a naval unit serving the same function as the military police.

shoreward ('ʃɔːwəd) *adj* **1** near or facing the shore. ◆ *adv also* **shorewards**. **2** towards the shore.

shoreweed ('ʃɔːˌwiːd) *n* a tufty aquatic perennial, *Littorella uniflora,* of the plantain family, that forms underwater mats but usually flowers only on muddy margins.

shorn (ʃɔːn) *vb* a past participle of **shear**.

short (ʃɔːt) *adj* **1** of little length; not long. **2** of little height; not tall. **3** of limited duration. **4** not meeting a requirement; deficient: *the number of places laid at the table was short by four.* **5** (*postpositive;* often foll. by *of* or *on*) lacking (in) or needful (of): *I'm always short of money.* **6** concise; succinct. **7** lacking in the power of retentiveness: *a short memory.* **8** abrupt to the point of rudeness: *the salesgirl was very short with him.* **9** *Finance.* **9a** not possessing the securities or commodities that have been sold under contract and therefore obliged to make a purchase before the delivery date. **9b** of or relating to such sales, which depend on falling prices for profit. **10** *Phonetics.* **10a** denoting a vowel of relatively brief temporal duration. **10b** classified as short, as distinguished from other vowels. Thus in English (ɪ) in *bin,* though of longer duration than (iː) in *beat,* is nevertheless regarded as a short vowel. **10c** (in popular usage) denoting the qualities of the five English vowels represented orthographically in the words *pat, pet, pit, pot, put,* and *putt.* **11** *Prosody.* **11a** denoting a vowel that is phonetically short or a syllable containing such a vowel. In classical verse short vowels are followed by one consonant only or sometimes one consonant plus a following *l* or *r.* **11b** (of a vowel or syllable in verse that is not quantitative) not carrying emphasis or accent; unstressed. **12** (of pastry) crumbly in texture. See also **shortcrust pastry**. **13** (of a drink of spirits) undiluted; neat. **14 have (someone) by the short and curlies.** *Informal.* to have (someone) completely in one's power. **15 in short supply.** scarce. **16 short and sweet.** unexpectedly brief. **17 short for.** an abbreviation for. ◆ *adv* **18** abruptly: *to stop short.* **19** briefly or concisely. **20** rudely or curtly. **21** *Finance.* without possessing the securities or commodities at the time of their contractual sale: *to sell short.* **22 caught** *or* **taken short.** having a sudden need to urinate or defecate. **23 fall short. 23a** to prove inadequate. **23b** (often foll. by *of*) to fail to reach or measure up to (a standard). **24 go short.** not to have a sufficient amount, etc. **25 short of.** except: *nothing short of a miracle can save him now.* ◆ *n* **26** anything that is short. **27** a drink of spirits as opposed to a long drink such as beer. **28** *Phonetics, prosody.* a short vowel or syllable. **29** *Finance.* **29a** a short contract or sale. **29b** a short seller. **30** a short film, usually of a factual nature. **31** See **short circuit** (sense 1). **32 for short.** *Informal.* as an abbreviation: *he is called Jim for short.* **33 in short. 33a** as a summary. **33b** in a few words. ◆ *vb* **34** See **short circuit** (sense 2). ◆ See also **shorts**. **[**Old English *scort;* related to Old Norse *skortr* a lack, *skera* to cut, Old High German *scurz* short**]** ▸ **'shortness** *n*

short account *n* **1** the aggregate of short sales on an open market, esp. a stock market. **2** the account of a stock-market speculator who sells short.

short-acting *adj* (of a drug) quickly effective, but requiring regularly repeated doses for long-term treatment, being rapidly absorbed, distributed in the bloodstream, and excreted. Compare **intermediate-acting, long-acting.**

shortage ('ʃɔːtɪdʒ) *n* a deficiency or lack in the amount needed, expected, or due; deficit.

short bill *n* a bill of exchange that is payable at sight, on demand, or within less than ten days.

shortbread ('ʃɔːtˌbrɛd) *n* a rich crumbly biscuit made from dough with a large proportion of butter. **[C19:** from SHORT (in the sense: crumbly)**]**

shortcake ('ʃɔːtˌkeɪk) *n* **1** a kind of shortbread made from a rich biscuit dough. **2** a dessert made of layers of shortcake filled with fruit and cream. **[C16:** from SHORT (in the sense: crumbly)**]**

short-change *vb* (*tr*) **1** to give less than correct change to. **2** *Slang.* to treat unfairly or dishonestly, esp. by giving less than is deserved or expected. ▸ **ˌshort-'changer** *n*

short circuit *n* **1** a faulty or accidental connection between two points of different potential in an electric circuit, bypassing the load and establishing a path of low resistance through which an excessive current can flow. It can cause damage to the components if the circuit is not protected by a fuse. ◆ *vb* **short-circuit. 2** to develop or cause to develop a short circuit. **3** (*tr*) to bypass (a procedure, regulation, etc.). **4** (*tr*) to hinder or frustrate (plans, etc.). ◆ Sometimes (for senses 1, 2) shortened to **short**.

shortcoming ('ʃɔːtˌkʌmɪŋ) *n* a failing, defect, or deficiency.

short corner *n Hockey.* another name for **penalty corner**.

short covering *n* **1** the purchase of securities or commodities by a short seller to meet delivery requirements. **2** the securities or commodities purchased.

shortcrust pastry ('ʃɔːtˌkrʌst) *n* a basic type of pastry that is made with half the quantity of fat to flour, and has a crisp but crumbly texture. Also called: **short pastry**.

short cut *n* **1** a route that is shorter than the usual one. **2** a means of saving time or effort. ◆ *vb* **short-cut, -cuts, -cutting, -cut. 3** (*intr*) to use a short cut. **[C16:** from CUT (in the sense: a direct route)**]**

short-dated *adj* (of a gilt-edged security) having less than five years to run before redemption. Compare **medium-dated, long-dated.**

short-day *adj* (of plants) able to flower only if exposed to short periods of daylight (less than 12 hours), each followed by a long dark period. Compare **long-day**.

short division *n* the division of numbers, usually integers, that can be worked out mentally rather than on paper.

shorten ('ʃɔːtᵊn) *vb* **1** to make or become short or shorter. **2** (*tr*) *Nautical.* to reduce the area of (sail). **3** (*tr*) to make (pastry, bread, etc.) short, by adding butter or another fat. **4** *Gambling.* to cause (the odds) to lessen or (of odds) to become less. ▸ **'shortener** *n*

shortening ('ʃɔːtᵊnɪŋ) *n* butter, lard, or other fat, used in a dough, cake mixture, etc., to make the mixture short.

Shorter Catechism *n Chiefly Presbyterian Church.* the more widely used and influential of two catechisms of religious instruction drawn up in 1647.

shortfall ('ʃɔːtˌfɔːl) *n* **1** failure to meet a goal or a requirement. **2** the amount of such a failure; deficiency.

short fuse *n Informal.* a quick temper.

shorthand ('ʃɔːtˌhænd) *n* **a** a system of rapid handwriting employing simple strokes and other symbols to represent words or phrases. **b** (*as modifier*): *a shorthand typist.*

short-handed *adj* **1** lacking the usual or necessary number of assistants, workers, etc. **2** *Sport. U.S. and Canadian.* with less than the full complement of players. ▸ **ˌshort-'handedness** *n*

shorthand typist *n Brit.* a person skilled in the use of shorthand and in typing. U.S. and Canadian name: **stenographer**.

short head *n Horse racing.* a distance shorter than the length of a horse's head.

shorthold tenancy ('ʃɔːtˌhəʊld) *n* (in Britain) the letting of a dwelling by a nonresident private landlord for a fixed term of between one and five years at a fair rent.

shorthorn ('ʃɔːtˌhɔːn) *n* a short-horned breed of cattle with several regional varieties. Also called: **Durham**.

short hundredweight *n* the full name for **hundredweight** (sense 2).

shortie *or* **shorty** ('ʃɔːtɪ) *n* **1** *Informal.* **1a** (*pl* **shorties**). a person or thing that is extremely short. **1b** (*as modifier*): *a shortie nightdress.* **2** a Scot. name for **shortbread**.

short jenny *n Billiards.* an in-off into a middle pocket. Compare **long jenny**. **[**from *Jenny,* pet form of *Janet***]**

short leg *n Cricket.* **a** a fielding position on the leg side near the batsman's wicket. **b** a fielder in this position.

short list *Chiefly Brit.* ◆ *n* **1** a list of suitable applicants for a job, post, etc., from which the successful candidate will be selected. ◆ *vb* (*tr*) **short-list. 2** to put (someone) on a short list.

short-lived *adj* living or lasting only for a short time.

shortly ('ʃɔːtlɪ) *adv* **1** in a short time; soon. **2** in a few words; briefly. **3** in a curt or rude manner.

short metre *n* a stanza form, used esp. for hymns, consisting of four lines, the third of which has eight syllables, while the rest have six.

short odds *pl n* (in betting) an almost even chance.

short order *n Chiefly U.S. and Canadian.* **a** food that is easily and quickly prepared. **b** (*as modifier*): *short-order counter.*

short-range *adj* of small or limited extent in time or distance: *a short-range forecast; a short-range gun.*

shorts (ʃɔːts) *pl n* **1** trousers reaching the top of the thigh or partway to the knee, worn by both sexes for sport, relaxing in summer, etc. **2** *Chiefly U.S. and Canadian.* men's underpants that usually reach mid-thigh. Usual Brit. word: **pants. 3** short-dated gilt-edged securities. **4** short-term bonds. **5** securities or commodities that have been sold short. **6** timber cut shorter than standard lengths. **7** a livestock feed containing a large proportion of bran and wheat germ. **8** items needed to make up a deficiency.

short shrift *n* **1** brief and unsympathetic treatment. **2** (formerly) a brief period allowed to a condemned prisoner to make confession. **3 make short shrift of.** to dispose of quickly and unsympathetically.

short-sighted *adj* **1** relating to or suffering from myopia. **2** lacking foresight: *a short-sighted plan.* ▶ **,short-'sightedly** *adv* ▶ **,short-'sightedness** *n*

short-spoken *adj* tending to be abrupt in speech.

short-staffed *adj* lacking an adequate number of staff, assistants, etc.

shortstop ('ʃɔːt,stɒp) *n Baseball.* **a** the fielding position to the left of second base viewed from home plate. **b** the player at this position.

short story *n* a prose narrative of shorter length than the novel, esp. one that concentrates on a single theme.

short straw *n* **draw the short straw.** be the person (as in drawing lots) to whom an unwelcome task or fate falls.

short subject *n Chiefly U.S.* a short film, esp. one presented between screenings of a feature film.

short-tempered *adj* easily moved to anger; irascible.

short-term *adj* **1** of, for, or extending over a limited period. **2** *Finance.* extending over, maturing within, or required within a short period of time, usually twelve months: *short-term credit; short-term capital.*

short-termism *n* the tendency to focus attention on short-term gains, often at the expense of long-term success or stability.

short-term memory *n Psychol.* that section of the memory storage system of limited capacity (approximately seven items) that is capable of storing material for a brief period of time. Compare **long-term memory.**

short time *or* **short-time working** *n* a system of working, usually for a temporary period, when employees are required to work and be paid for fewer than their normal hours per week due to a shortage of work.

short ton *n* the full name for **ton**[1] (sense 2).

short-waisted *adj* unusually short from the shoulders to the waist.

short wave *n* **a** a radio wave with a wavelength in the range 10–100 metres. **b** (*as modifier*): *a short-wave broadcast.*

short-winded *adj* **1** tending to run out of breath, esp. after exertion. **2** (of speech or writing) terse or abrupt.

Shoshone *or* **Shoshoni** (ʃəʊ'ʃəʊnɪ) *n* **1** (*pl* **-nes, -ne** *or* **-nis, -ni**) a member of a North American Indian people of the southwestern U.S., related to the Aztecs. **2** the language of this people, belonging to the Uto-Aztecan family.

Shoshonean *or* **Shoshonian** (ʃəʊ'ʃəʊnɪən,,ʃəʊʃə'niːən) *n* a subfamily of North American Indian languages belonging to the Uto-Aztecan family, spoken mainly in the southwestern U.S.

Shostakovich (,ʃɒstə'kəʊvɪtʃ; *Russian* ʃəsta'kɔvitʃ) *n* **Dmitri Dmitriyevich** ('dmitrij 'dmitrijɪvitʃ). 1906–75, Soviet composer, noted esp. for his 15 symphonies and his chamber music.

shot[1] (ʃɒt) *n* **1** the act or an instance of discharging a projectile. **2** (*pl* **shot**) a solid missile, such as an iron ball or a lead pellet, discharged from a firearm. **3a** small round pellets of lead collectively, as used in cartridges. **3b** metal in the form of coarse powder or small pellets. **4** the distance that a discharged projectile travels or is capable of travelling. **5** a person who shoots, esp. with regard to his ability: *he is a good shot.* **6** *Informal.* an attempt; effort. **7** *Informal.* a guess or conjecture. **8** any act of throwing or hitting something, as in certain sports. **9** the launching of a rocket, missile, etc., esp. to a specified destination: *a moon shot.* **10a** a single photograph: *I took 16 shots of the wedding.* **10b** a series of frames on cine film concerned with a single event. **10c** a length of film taken by a single camera without breaks, used with others to build up a full motion picture or television film. **11** *Informal.* an injection, as of a vaccine or narcotic drug. **12** *Informal.* a glass of alcoholic drink, esp. spirits. **13** *Sport.* a heavy metal ball used in the shot put. **14** an explosive charge used in blasting. **15** globules of metal occurring in the body of a casting that are harder than the rest of the casting. **16** a unit of chain length equal to 75 feet (Brit.) or 90 feet (U.S.). **17 call the shots.** *Slang.* to have control over an organization, course of action, etc. **18 have a shot at.** *Informal.* **18a** to attempt. **18b** *Austral.* to jibe at or vex. **19 like a shot.** very quickly, esp. willingly. **20 shot in the arm.** *Informal.* anything that regenerates, increases confidence or efficiency, etc.: *his arrival was a shot in the arm for the company.* **21 shot in the dark.** a wild guess. **22 that's the shot.** *Austral. informal.* that is the right thing to do. ◆ *vb* **shots, shotting, shotted. 23** (*tr*) to weight or load with shot. [Old English *scot;* related to Old Norse *skot,* Old High German *scoz* missile; see SHOOT]

shot[2] (ʃɒt) *vb* **1** the past tense and past participle of **shoot.** ◆ *adj* **2** (of textiles) woven to give a changing colour effect: *shot silk.* **3** streaked with colour. **4** *Slang.* exhausted. **5 get shot** *or* **shut of.** *Slang.* to get rid of.

shot-blasting *n* the cleaning of metal, etc., by a stream of shot.

shote (ʃəʊt) *n* a variant spelling of **shoat.**

shotgun ('ʃɒt,gʌn) *n* **1a** a shoulder firearm with unrifled bore designed for the discharge of small shot at short range and used mainly for hunting small game. **1b** (*as modifier*): *shotgun fire.* **2** *American football.* an offensive formation in which the quarterback lines up for a snap unusually far behind the line of scrimmage. ◆ *adj* **3** *Chiefly U.S.* involving coercion or duress: *a shotgun merger.* **4** *Chiefly U.S.* involving or relying on speculative suggestions, etc.: *a shotgun therapy.* ◆ *vb* **-guns, -gunning, -gunned. 5** (*tr*) *U.S.* to shoot or threaten with or as if with a shotgun.

shotgun wedding *n Informal.* a wedding into which one or both partners are coerced, usually because the woman is pregnant.

shot hole *n* a drilled hole into which explosive is put for blasting.

shot noise *or* **effect** *n* the inherent electronic noise arising in an electric current because of the discontinuous nature of conduction by electrons. Also called: **Schottky noise** ('ʃɒtkɪ).

shot put *n* **1** an athletic event in which contestants hurl or put a heavy metal ball or shot as far as possible. **2** a single put of the shot. ▶ **'shot-,putter** *n*

shott *or* **chott** (ʃɒt) *n* **1** a shallow temporary salt lake or marsh in the North African desert. **2** the hollow in which it lies. [C19: via French *chott* from Arabic *shatt*]

shotten ('ʃɒtᵊn) *adj* **1** (of fish, esp. herring) having recently spawned. **2** *Archaic.* worthless or undesirable. [C15: from obsolete past participle of SHOOT]

shot tower *n* a building formerly used in the production of shot, in which molten lead was graded and dropped from a great height into water, thus cooling it and forming the shot.

should (ʃʊd) *vb* the past tense of **shall:** used as an auxiliary verb to indicate that an action is considered by the speaker to be obligatory (*you should go*) or to form the subjunctive mood with *I* or *we* (*I should like to see you; if I should be late, go without me*). [Old English *sceold;* see SHALL]

USAGE *Should* has, as its most common meaning in modern English, the sense *ought* as in *I should go to the graduation, but I don't see how I can.* However, the older sense of the subjunctive of *shall* is often used with *I* or *we* to indicate a more polite form than *would: I should like to go, but I can't.* In much speech and writing, *should* has been replaced by *would* in contexts of this kind, but it remains in formal English when a conditional subjunctive is used: *should he choose to remain, he would be granted asylum.*

shoulder ('ʃəʊldə) *n* **1** the part of the vertebrate body where the arm or a corresponding forelimb joins the trunk: the pectoral girdle and associated structures. **2** the joint at the junction of the forelimb with the pectoral girdle. **3** a cut of meat including the upper part of the foreleg. **4** *Printing.* the flat surface of a piece of type from which the face rises. **5** *Tanning.* the portion of a hide covering the shoulders and neck of the animal, usually including the cheeks. **6** the part of a garment that covers the shoulder. **7** anything that resembles a shoulder in shape or position. **8** the strip of unpaved land that borders a road. **9** *Engineering.* a substantial projection or abrupt change in shape or diameter designed to withstand thrust. **10** *Photog.* the portion of the characteristic curve of a photographic material indicating the maximum density that can be produced on the material. **11** *Jewellery.* the part of a ring where the shank joins the setting. **12 a shoulder to cry on.** a person one turns to for sympathy with one's troubles. **13 give (someone) the cold shoulder.** *Informal.* **13a** to treat (someone) in a cold manner; snub. **13b** to ignore or shun (someone). **14 put one's shoulder to the wheel.** *Informal.* to work very hard. **15 rub shoulders with.** See **rub** (sense 11). **16 shoulder to shoulder. 16a** side by side or close together. **16b** in a corporate effort. ◆ *vb* **17** (*tr*) to bear or carry (a burden, responsibility, etc.) as if on one's shoulders. **18** to push (something) with or as if with the shoulder. **19** (*tr*) to lift or carry on the shoulders. **20 shoulder arms.** *Military.* to bring the rifle vertically close to the right side with the muzzle uppermost and held at the trigger guard. [Old English *sculdor;* related to Old High German *sculterra*]

shoulder blade *n* the nontechnical name for **scapula.**

shoulder pad *n* a small pad inserted to raise or give shape to the shoulder of a garment.

shoulder patch *n Military.* an emblem worn high on the arm as an insignia. Also called: **shoulder flash.**

shoulder strap *n* a strap over one or both of the shoulders, as to hold up a garment or to support a bag, etc.

shouldn't ('ʃʊdᵊnt) *vb contraction of* should not.

shouldst (ʃʊdst) *or* **shouldest** ('ʃʊdɪst) *vb Archaic or dialect.* (used with the pronoun *thou* or its relative equivalent) a form of the past tense of **shall.**

shouse (ʃaʊs) *Austral. slang.* ◆ *n* **1** a toilet; lavatory. ◆ *adj* **2** unwell or in poor spirits. [C20: shortening of *shithouse*]

shout (ʃaʊt) *n* **1** a loud cry, esp. to convey emotion or a command. **2** *Informal, Brit., Austral., and N.Z.* **2a** a round, esp. of drinks. **2b** one's turn to buy a round of drinks. ◆ *vb* **3** to utter (something) in a loud cry; yell. **4** (*intr*) to make a loud noise. **5** (*tr*) *Austral. and N.Z. informal.* to treat (someone) to (something), esp. a round of drinks. [C14: probably from Old Norse *skūta* taunt; related to Old Norse *skjōta* to SHOOT] ▶ **'shouter** *n*

shout down *vb* (*tr, adv*) to drown, overwhelm, or silence by shouting or talking loudly.

shove (ʃʌv) *vb* **1** to give a thrust or push to (a person or thing). **2** (*tr*) to give a violent push to; jostle. **3** (*intr*) to push one's way roughly. **4** (*tr*) *Informal.* to put (something) somewhere, esp. hurriedly or carelessly: *shove it in the bin.* ◆ *n* **5** the act or an instance of shoving. ◆ See also **shove off.** [Old English *scūfan;* related to Old Norse *skūfa* to push, Gothic *afskiuban* to push away, Old High German *skioban* to shove] ▶ **'shover** *n*

shove-halfpenny *n Brit.* a game in which players try to propel old halfpennies or polished discs with the hand into lined sections of a wooden or slate board.

shovel ('ʃʌvᵊl) *n* **1** an instrument for lifting or scooping loose material, such as earth, coal, etc., consisting of a curved blade or a scoop attached to a handle. **2**

any machine or part resembling a shovel in action. **3** Also called: **shovelful.** the amount that can be contained in a shovel. **4** short for **shovel hat.** ♦ *vb* **-els, -elling, -elled** *or U.S.* **-els, -eling, -eled. 5** to lift (earth, etc.) with a shovel. **6** (*tr*) to clear or dig (a path) with or as if with a shovel. **7** (*tr*) to gather, load, or unload in a hurried or careless way: *he shovelled the food into his mouth and rushed away.* [Old English *scofl;* related to Old High German *scūfla* shovel, Dutch *schoffel* hoe; see SHOVE] ▸ **'shoveller** *or U.S.* **'shoveler** *n*

shoveler ('ʃʌvələ) *n* a duck, *Anas* (or *Spatula*) *clypeata,* of ponds and marshes, having a spoon-shaped bill, a blue patch on each wing, and in the male a green head, white breast, and reddish-brown body.

shovel hat *n* a black felt hat worn by some clergymen, with a brim rolled up to resemble a shovel in shape.

shovelhead ('ʃʌvᵊl,hɛd) *n* a common shark, *Sphyrna tiburo,* of the Atlantic and Pacific Oceans, having a shovel-shaped head: family *Sphyrnidae* (hammerheads).

shovelnose ('ʃʌvᵊl,nəuz) *n* an American freshwater sturgeon, *Scaphirhynchus platorynchus,* having a broad shovel-like snout.

shove off *vb* (*intr, adv; often imperative*) **1** to move from the shore in a boat. **2** *Informal.* to go away; depart.

show (ʃəu) *vb* **shows, showing, showed; shown** *or* **showed. 1** to make, be, or become visible or noticeable: *to show one's dislike.* **2** (*tr*) to present to view; exhibit: *he showed me a picture.* **3** (*tr*) to indicate or explain; prove: *to show that the earth moves round the sun.* **4** (*tr*) to exhibit or present (oneself or itself) in a specific character: *to show oneself to be trustworthy.* **5** (*tr;* foll. by *how* and an infinitive) to instruct by demonstration: *show me how to swim.* **6** (*tr*) to indicate or register: *a barometer shows changes in the weather.* **7** (*tr*) to grant or bestow: *to show favour to someone.* **8** (*intr*) to appear: *to show to advantage.* **9** to exhibit, display, or offer (goods, etc.) for sale: *three artists were showing at the gallery.* **10** (*tr*) to allege, as in a legal document: *to show cause.* **11** to present (a play, film, etc.) or (of a play, etc.) to be presented, as at a theatre or cinema. **12** (*tr*) to guide or escort: *please show me to my room.* **13 show in** *or* **out.** to conduct a person into or out of a room or building by opening the door for him. **14** (*intr*) to win a place in a horse race, etc. **15** to give a performance of riding and handling (a horse) to display its best points. **16** (*intr*) *Informal.* to put in an appearance; arrive. ♦ *n* **17** a display or exhibition. **18** a public spectacle. **19** an ostentatious or pretentious display. **20** a theatrical or other entertainment. **21** a trace or indication. **22** *Obstetrics.* a discharge of blood at the onset of labour. **23** *U.S., Austral., and N.Z. informal.* a chance; opportunity (esp. in the phrases **give someone a show, he's got no show of winning,** etc.). **24** a sporting event consisting of contests in which riders perform different exercises to show their skill and their horses' ability and breeding. **25** *Slang, chiefly Brit.* a thing or affair (esp. in the phrases **good show, bad show,** etc.). **26** *Austral. and N.Z., mining.* a slight indication of the presence of gold. **27** a display of farm animals, with associated competitions. **28 for show.** in order to attract attention. **29 run the show.** *Informal.* to take charge of or manage an affair, business, etc. **30 steal the show.** to draw the most attention or admiration, esp. unexpectedly. **31 stop the show.** *Informal.* **31a** (of a stage act, etc.) to receive so much applause as to interrupt the performance. **31b** to be received with great enthusiasm. ♦ See also **show off, show up.** [Old English *scēawian;* related to Old High German *scouwōn* to look, Old Norse *örskār* careful, Greek *thuoskoos* seer]

show bill *n* a poster advertising a play or show. Also called: **show card.**

showboat ('ʃəu,bəut) *n* **1** a paddle-wheel river steamer with a theatre and a repertory company. ♦ *vb* **2** (*intr*) to perform or behave in a showy and flamboyant way.

showbread ('ʃəu,brɛd) *n* a variant spelling of **shewbread.**

show business *n* the entertainment industry, including theatre, films, television, and radio. Informal term: **show biz.**

show card *n* **1** *Commerce.* a tradesman's advertisement mounted on card as a poster. **2** another term for **show bill.**

showcase ('ʃəu,keɪs) *n* **1** a glass case used to display objects in a museum or shop. **2** a setting in which anything may be displayed to best advantage. ♦ *vb* **3** (*tr*) to exhibit or display. ♦ *adj* **4** displayed or meriting display as in a showcase.

show copy *n Films.* a positive print of a film for use at an important presentation such as a premiere.

showd (ʃaud) *Northeast Scot. dialect.* ♦ *vb* **1** (*intr*) to rock or sway to and fro. **2** (*tr*) to rock (a baby in one's arms or in a pram). ♦ *n* **3** a rocking motion. [from Old English *scūdan* to shake]

show day *n* (in Australia) a public holiday in a state on the date of its annual agricultural and industrial show.

showdown ('ʃəu,daun) *n* **1** *Informal.* an action that brings matters to a head or acts as a conclusion or point of decision. **2** *Poker.* the exposing of the cards in the players' hands on the table at the end of the game.

shower[1] ('ʃauə) *n* **1** a brief period of rain, hail, sleet, or snow. **2** a sudden abundant fall or downpour, as of tears, sparks, or light. **3** a rush; outpouring: *a shower of praise.* **4a** a kind of bath in which a person stands upright and is sprayed with water from a nozzle. **4b** the room, booth, etc., containing such a bath. Full name: **shower bath. 5** *Brit. slang.* a derogatory term applied to a person or group, esp. to a group considered as being slack, untidy, etc. **6** *U.S., Canadian, Austral., and N.Z.* a party held to honour and present gifts to a person, as to a prospective bride. **7** a large number of particles formed by the collision of a cosmic-ray particle with a particle in the atmosphere. **8** *N.Z.* a light fabric cover thrown over a tea table to protect the food from flies, dust, etc. ♦ *vb* **9** (*tr*) to sprinkle or spray with or as if with a shower: *shower the powder into the milk.* **10** (often with *it* as subject) to fall or cause to fall in the form of a shower. **11** (*tr*) to give (gifts, etc.) in abundance or present (a person) with (gifts, etc.): *they showered gifts on him.* **12** (*intr*) to take a shower. [Old English *scūr;* related to Old Norse *skūr,* Old High German *skūr* shower, Latin *caurus* northwest wind] ▸ **'showery** *adj*

shower[2] ('ʃəuə) *n* a person or thing that shows.

showerproof ('ʃauə,pru:f) *adj* (of a garment, etc.) resistant to or partly impervious to rain. ▸ **'shower,proofing** *n*

showgirl ('ʃəu,gɜ:l) *n* a girl who appears in variety shows, nightclub acts, etc., esp. as a singer or dancer.

showground ('ʃəu,graund) *n* an open-air setting for agricultural displays, competitions, etc. Also called (Austral. and N.Z.): **showgrounds.**

show house *n* a house on a new estate that is decorated and furnished for prospective buyers to view.

showing ('ʃəuɪŋ) *n* **1** a presentation, exhibition, or display. **2** manner of presentation; performance. **3** evidence.

showjumping ('ʃəu,dʒʌmpɪŋ) *n* the riding of horses in competitions to demonstrate skill in jumping over or between various obstacles. ▸ **'show-,jumper** *n*

showman ('ʃəumən) *n, pl* **-men. 1** a person who presents or produces a theatrical show, etc. **2** a person skilled at presenting anything in an effective manner. ▸ **'showmanship** *n*

shown (ʃəun) *vb* a past participle of **show.**

show off *vb* (*adv*) **1** (*tr*) to exhibit or display so as to invite admiration. **2** (*intr*) *Informal.* to behave in such a manner as to make an impression. ♦ *n* **show-off. 3** *Informal.* a person who makes a vain display of himself.

show of hands *n* the raising of hands to indicate voting for or against a proposition.

showpiece ('ʃəu,pi:s) *n* **1** anything displayed or exhibited. **2** anything prized as a very fine example of its type.

showplace ('ʃəu,pleɪs) *n* a place exhibited or visited for its beauty, historic interest, etc.

showroom ('ʃəu,ru:m, -,rum) *n* a room in which goods, such as cars, are on display.

show stopper *n Informal.* a stage act, etc., that receives so much applause as to interrupt the performance.

show trial *n* a trial conducted primarily to make a particular impression on the public or on other nations, esp. one that demonstrates the power of the state over the individual.

show up *vb* (*adv*) **1** to reveal or be revealed clearly. **2** (*tr*) to expose or reveal the faults or defects of by comparison. **3** (*tr*) *Informal.* to put to shame; embarrass: *he showed me up in front of my friends.* **4** (*intr*) *Informal.* to appear or arrive.

showy ('ʃəuɪ) *adj* **showier, showiest. 1** gaudy, flashy, or ostentatious. **2** making a brilliant or imposing display. ▸ **'showily** *adv* ▸ **'showiness** *n*

shpt *abbrev. for* shipment.

shr. *Stock Exchange. abbrev. for* share.

shrank (ʃræŋk) *vb* a past tense of **shrink.**

shrapnel ('ʃræpnᵊl) *n* **1a** a projectile containing a number of small pellets or bullets exploded before impact. **1b** such projectiles collectively. **2** fragments from this or any other type of shell. [C19: named after H. *Shrapnel* (1761–1842), English army officer, who invented it]

shred (ʃrɛd) *n* **1** a long narrow strip or fragment torn or cut off. **2** a very small piece or amount; scrap. ♦ *vb* **shreds, shredding, shredded** *or* **shred. 3** (*tr*) to tear or cut into shreds. [Old English *scread;* related to Old Norse *skrjōthr* torn-up book, Old High German *scrōt* cut-off piece; see SCROLL, SHROUD, SCREED] ▸ **'shredder** *n*

Shreveport ('ʃri:v,pɔ:t) *n* a city in NW Louisiana, on the Red River: centre of an oil and natural-gas region. Pop.: 191 558 (1995 est.).

shrew (ʃru:) *n* **1** Also called: **shrewmouse.** any small mouse-like long-snouted mammal, such as *Sorex araneus* (**common shrew**), of the family *Soricidae:* order *Insectivora* (insectivores). See also **water shrew.** Related adj: **soricine. 2** a bad-tempered or mean-spirited woman. [Old English *scrēawa;* related to Old High German *scrawaz* dwarf, Icelandic *skröggr* old man, Norwegian *skrugg* dwarf]

shrewd (ʃru:d) *adj* **1** astute and penetrating, often with regard to business. **2** artful and crafty: *a shrewd politician.* **3** *Obsolete.* **3a** piercing: *a shrewd wind.* **3b** spiteful. [C14: from *shrew* (obsolete vb) to curse, from SHREW] ▸ **'shrewdly** *adv* ▸ **'shrewdness** *n*

shrewdie ('ʃru:dɪ) *n Austral. and N.Z. informal.* a shrewd person. [C20: from SHREWD + -IE]

shrewish ('ʃru:ɪʃ) *adj* (esp. of a woman) bad-tempered and nagging. ▸ **'shrewishly** *adv* ▸ **'shrewishness** *n*

shrew mole *n* any of several moles, such as *Uropsilus soricipes* of E Asia or *Neurotrichus gibbsi* of E North America, having a long snout and long tail.

shrewmouse ('ʃru:,maus) *n, pl* **-mice.** another name for **shrew,** esp. the common shrew.

Shrewsbury ('ʃrəuzbərɪ, -brɪ, 'ʃru:z-) *n* a town in W central England, administrative centre of Shropshire, on the River Severn: strategically situated near the Welsh border; market town. Pop.: 90 900 (1991).

shriek (ʃri:k) *n* **1** a shrill and piercing cry. ♦ *vb* **2** to produce or utter (words, sounds, etc.) in a shrill piercing tone. [C16: probably from Old Norse *skrækja* to SCREECH[1]] ▸ **'shrieker** *n*

shrieval ('ʃri:vᵊl) *adj* of or relating to a sheriff.

shrievalty ('ʃri:vəltɪ) *n, pl* **-ties. 1** the office or term of office of a sheriff. **2** the jurisdiction of a sheriff. [C16: from SHRIEVE, on the model of *mayoralty*]

shrieve (ʃri:v) *n* an archaic word for **sheriff.**

shrift (ʃrɪft) *n Archaic.* the act or an instance of shriving or being shriven. See also **short shrift.** [Old English *scrift,* from Latin *scriptum* SCRIPT]

shrike (ʃraɪk) *n* **1** Also called: **butcherbird.** any songbird of the chiefly Old World family *Laniidae,* having a heavy hooked bill and feeding on smaller animals which they sometimes impale on thorns, barbed wire, etc. See also **bush**

shrike (sense 1). **2** any of various similar but unrelated birds, such as the cuckoo shrikes. **3 shrike thrush** *or* **tit.** another name for **thickhead** (the bird). [Old English *scrīc* thrush; related to Middle Dutch *schrīk* corncrake; see SCREECH[1], SHRIEK]

shrill (ʃrɪl) *adj* **1** sharp and high-pitched in quality. **2** emitting a sharp high-pitched sound. ♦ *vb* **3** to utter (words, sounds, etc.) in a shrill tone. **4** (*tr*) *Rare.* to cause to produce a shrill sound. [C14: probably from Old English *scralletan;* related to German *schrill* shrill, Dutch *schrallen* to shriek] ► **'shrillness** *n* ► **'shrilly** *adv*

shrimp (ʃrɪmp) *n* **1** any of various chiefly marine decapod crustaceans of the genus *Crangon* and related genera, having a slender flattened body with a long tail and a single pair of pincers. **2** any of various similar but unrelated crustaceans, such as the opossum shrimp and mantis shrimp. **3** Also called: **freshwater shrimp.** any of various freshwater shrimplike amphipod crustaceans of the genus *Gammarus,* esp. *G. pulex.* **4** Also called: **sand shrimp.** any of various shrimplike amphipod crustaceans of the genus *Gammarus,* esp. *G. locusta.* ♦ See also **opossum shrimp. 5** *Informal.* a diminutive person, esp. a child. ♦ *vb* **6** (*intr*) to fish for shrimps. [C14: probably of Germanic origin; compare Middle Low German *schrempen* to shrink; see SCRIMP, CRIMP] ► **'shrimper** *n*

shrine (ʃraɪn) *n* **1** a place of worship hallowed by association with a sacred person or object. **2** a container for sacred relics. **3** the tomb of a saint or other holy person. **4** a place or site venerated for its association with a famous person or event. **5** *R.C. Church.* a building, alcove, or shelf arranged as a setting for a statue, picture, or other representation of Christ, the Virgin Mary, or a saint. ♦ *vb* **6** short for **enshrine.** [Old English *scrīn,* from Latin *scrīnium* bookcase; related to Old Norse *skrín,* Old High German *skrīni*] ► **'shrine,like** *adj*

shrink (ʃrɪŋk) *vb* **shrinks, shrinking; shrank** *or* **shrunk; shrunk** *or* **shrunken. 1** to contract or cause to contract as from wetness, heat, cold, etc. **2** to become or cause to become smaller in size. **3** (*intr;* often foll. by *from*) **3a** to recoil or withdraw: *to shrink from the sight of blood.* **3b** to feel great reluctance (at): *to shrink from killing an animal.* ♦ *n* **4** the act or an instance of shrinking. **5** a slang word for **psychiatrist.** [Old English *scrincan;* related to Old Norse *skrokkr* torso, Old Swedish *skrunkin* wrinkled, Old Norse *hrukka* a crease, Icelandic *skrukka* wrinkled woman] ► **'shrinkable** *adj* ► **'shrinker** *n* ► **'shrinking** *adj* ► **'shrinkingly** *adv*

shrinkage ('ʃrɪŋkɪdʒ) *n* **1** the act or fact of shrinking. **2** the amount by which anything decreases in size, value, weight, etc. **3** the loss in body weight during shipment and preparation of livestock for marketing as meat. **4** *Retail.* the loss of merchandise through theft or damage.

shrink fit *n Engineering.* a tight fit of a collar or wheel boss on a shaft obtained by expanding the collar or boss by heating to enable it to be threaded onto the shaft and then allowing it to cool, or by freezing the shaft to reduce its diameter to enable it to be threaded into the collar or boss and then allowing the shaft temperature to rise.

shrinking violet *n Informal.* a shy person.

shrink-wrap *vb* **-wraps, -wrapping, -wrapped.** (*tr*) to package (a product) in a flexible plastic wrapping designed to shrink about its contours to protect and seal it.

shrive (ʃraɪv) *vb* **shrives, shriving; shrove** *or* **shrived; shriven** ('ʃrɪvᵊn) *or* **shrived.** *Chiefly R.C. Church.* **1** to hear the confession of (a penitent). **2** (*tr*) to impose a penance upon (a penitent) and grant him sacramental absolution. **3** (*intr*) to confess one's sins to a priest in order to obtain sacramental forgiveness. [Old English *scrīfan,* from Latin *scrībere* to write] ► **'shriver** *n*

shrivel ('ʃrɪvᵊl) *vb* **-els, -elling, -elled** *or U.S.* **-els, -eling, -eled. 1** to make or become shrunken and withered. **2** to lose or cause to lose vitality. [C16: probably of Scandinavian origin; compare Swedish dialect *skryvla* wrinkle]

shroff (ʃrɒf) *n* **1** (in China, Japan, etc., esp. formerly) an expert employed to separate counterfeit money or base coin from the genuine. **2** (in India) a moneychanger or banker. ♦ *vb* **3** (*tr*) to test (money) and separate out the counterfeit and base. [C17: from Portuguese *xarrafo,* from Hindi *sarrāf* moneychanger, from Arabic]

Shropshire ('ʃrɒpˌʃɪə, -ʃə) *n* a county of W central England: mainly agricultural. Administrative centre: Shrewsbury. Pop.: 416 500 (1994 est.). Area: 3490 sq. km (1347 sq. miles).

shroud (ʃraʊd) *n* **1** a garment or piece of cloth used to wrap a dead body. **2** anything that envelops like a garment: *a shroud of mist.* **3** a protective covering for a piece of equipment. **4** *Astronautics.* a streamlined protective covering used to protect the payload during a rocket-powered launch. **5** *Nautical.* one of a pattern of ropes or cables used to stay a mast. **6** any of a set of wire cables stretched between a smokestack or similar structure and the ground, to prevent side sway. **7** Also called: **shroud line.** any of a set of lines running from the canopy of a parachute to the harness. ♦ *vb* **8** (*tr*) to wrap in a shroud. **9** (*tr*) to cover, envelop, or hide. **10** *Archaic.* to seek or give shelter. [Old English *scrūd* garment; related to Old Norse *skrūth* gear] ► **'shroudless** *adj*

shroud-laid *adj* (of a rope) made with four strands twisted to the right, usually around a core.

shrove (ʃrəʊv) *vb* a past tense of **shrive.**

Shrovetide ('ʃrəʊvˌtaɪd) *n* the Sunday, Monday, and Tuesday before Ash Wednesday, formerly a time when confessions were made in preparation for Lent.

Shrove Tuesday *n* the last day of Shrovetide; Pancake Day.

shrub[1] (ʃrʌb) *n* a woody perennial plant, smaller than a tree, with several major branches arising from near the base of the main stem. [Old English *scrybb;* related to Middle Low German *schrubben* coarse, uneven, Old Swedish *skrubba* to SCRUB[1]] ► **'shrub,like** *adj*

shrub[2] (ʃrʌb) *n* **1** a mixed drink of rum, fruit juice, sugar, and spice. **2** mixed fruit juice, sugar, and spice made commercially to be mixed with rum or other spirits. [C18: from Arabic *sharāb,* variant of *shurb* drink; see SHERBET]

shrubbery ('ʃrʌbərɪ) *n, pl* **-beries. 1** a place where a number of shrubs are planted. **2** shrubs collectively.

shrubby ('ʃrʌbɪ) *adj* **-bier, -biest. 1** consisting of, planted with, or abounding in shrubs. **2** resembling a shrub. ► **'shrubbiness** *n*

shrub layer *n* See **layer** (sense 2).

shrug (ʃrʌg) *vb* **shrugs, shrugging, shrugged. 1** to draw up and drop (the shoulders) abruptly in a gesture expressing indifference, contempt, ignorance, etc. ♦ *n* **2** the gesture so made. **3** a woman's short jacket. [C14: of uncertain origin]

shrug off *vb* (*tr, adv*) **1** to minimize the importance of; dismiss. **2** to get rid of. **3** to wriggle out of or push off (clothing).

shrunk (ʃrʌŋk) *vb* a past participle and past tense of **shrink.**

shrunken ('ʃrʌŋkᵊn) *vb* **1** a past participle of **shrink.** ♦ *adj* **2** (*usually prenominal*) reduced in size.

shtg. *abbrev. for* shortage.

shtick (ʃtɪk) *n Slang.* a comedian's routine; act; piece. [C20: from Yiddish *shtik* piece, from Middle High German *stücke*]

shtoom (ʃtʊm) *adj Slang.* silent; dumb (esp. in **keep shtoom**). [from Yiddish, from German *stumm* silent]

shuck (ʃʌk) *n* **1** the outer covering of something, such as the husk of a grain of maize, a pea pod, or an oyster shell. ♦ *vb* (*tr*) **2** to remove the shucks from. **3** *Informal, chiefly U.S. and Canadian.* to throw off or remove (clothes, etc.). [C17: American dialect, of unknown origin] ► **'shucker** *n*

shucks (ʃʌks) *U.S. and Canadian informal.* ♦ *pl n* **1** something of little value (esp. in the phrase **not worth shucks**). ♦ *interj* **2** an exclamation of disappointment, annoyance, etc.

shudder ('ʃʌdə) *vb* **1** (*intr*) to shake or tremble suddenly and violently, as from horror, fear, aversion, etc. ♦ *n* **2** the act of shuddering; convulsive shiver. [C18: from Middle Low German *schōderen;* related to Old Frisian *skedda* to shake, Old High German *skutten* to shake] ► **'shuddering** *adj* ► **'shudderingly** *adv* ► **'shuddery** *adj*

shuffle ('ʃʌfᵊl) *vb* **1** to walk or move (the feet) with a slow dragging motion. **2** to change the position of (something), esp. quickly or in order to deceive others. **3** (*tr*) to mix together in a careless manner: *he shuffled the papers nervously.* **4** to mix up (cards in a pack) to change their order. **5** (*intr*) to behave in an awkward, evasive, or underhand manner; equivocate. **6** (when *intr,* often foll. by *into* or *out of*) to move or cause to move clumsily: *he shuffled out of the door.* **7** (*intr*) to dance the shuffle. ♦ *n* **8** the act or an instance of shuffling. **9** a dance or dance step with short dragging movements of the feet. [C16: probably from Low German *schüffeln;* see SHOVE] ► **'shuffler** *n*

shuffleboard ('ʃʌfᵊlˌbɔːd) *n* **1** a game in which players push wooden or plastic discs with a long cue towards numbered scoring sections marked on a floor, esp. a ship's deck. **2** the marked area on which this game is played.

shuffle off *vb* (*tr, adv*) to thrust off or put aside: *shuffle off responsibility.*

shuffle play *n* a facility on a compact disc player that randomly selects a track from one of a number of compact discs.

shufty *or* **shufti** ('ʃʊftɪ, 'ʃʌftɪ) *n, pl* **-ties.** *Brit. slang.* a look; peep. [C20: from Arabic]

Shufu *or* **Sufu** ('ʃuːˈfuː) *n* transliteration of the Chinese name for **Kashi.**

shuggy ('ʃʌgɪ) *n, pl* **-gies.** *Northeastern English dialect.* a swing, as at a fairground. [from *shog, shug* to shake; see SHOOGLE]

shul *or* **schul** (ʃuːl) *n* the Yiddish word for **synagogue.** [Yiddish: synagogue, from Old High German *scuola* SCHOOL[1]]

Shulamite ('ʃuːləˌmaɪt) *n Old Testament.* an epithet of uncertain meaning applied to the bride in the Song of Solomon 6:13.

Shulchan Aruch (ʃʊlˈxɑn ɑrˈʊx, 'ʃʊlxən 'ɑʊrəx) *n* the main codification of Jewish law derived from the Talmud, compiled by the 16th-century rabbi, Joseph Caro.

shun (ʃʌn) *vb* **shuns, shunning, shunned.** (*tr*) to avoid deliberately; keep away from. [Old English *scunian,* of obscure origin] ► **'shunnable** *adj* ► **'shunner** *n*

'shun (ʃʌn) *interj Military.* a clipped form of **attention** (sense 7).

shunt (ʃʌnt) *vb* **1** to turn or cause to turn to one side; move or be moved aside. **2** *Railways.* to transfer (rolling stock) from track to track. **3** *Electronics.* to divert or be diverted through a shunt. **4** (*tr*) to evade by putting off onto someone else. **5** (*tr*) *Motor racing slang.* to crash (a car). ♦ *n* **6** the act or an instance of shunting. **7** a railway point. **8** *Electronics.* a low-resistance conductor connected in parallel across a device, circuit, or part of a circuit to provide an alternative path for a known fraction of the current. **9** *Med.* a channel that bypasses the normal circulation of the blood: a congenital abnormality or surgically induced. **10** *Brit. informal.* a collision which occurs when a vehicle runs into the back of the vehicle in front. [C13: perhaps from *shunen* to SHUN]

shunter ('ʃʌntə) *n* a small railway locomotive used for manoeuvring coaches rather than for making journeys.

shunt-wound ('ʃʌntˌwaʊnd) *adj Electrical engineering.* (of a motor or generator) having the field and armature circuits connected in parallel. Compare **series-wound.**

shush (ʃʊʃ) *interj* **1** be quiet! hush! ♦ *vb* **2** to silence or calm (someone) by or as if by saying "shush". [C20: reduplication of SH, influenced by HUSH[1]]

Shushan ('ʃuːʃæn) *n* the Biblical name for **Susa.**

shut (ʃʌt) *vb* **shuts, shutting, shut. 1** to move (something) so as to cover an aperture; close: *to shut a door.* **2** to close (something) by bringing together the parts: *to shut a book.* **3** (*tr;* often foll. by *up*) to close or lock the doors of: *to shut up a house.* **4** (*tr;* foll. by *in, out,* etc.) to confine, enclose, or exclude: *to shut a child in a room.* **5** (*tr*) to prevent (a business, etc.) from operating. **6 shut one's eyes to.** to ignore deliberately. **7 shut the door on. 7a** to refuse to think about. **7b** to render impossible. ♦ *adj* **8** closed or fastened. ♦ *n* **9** the act or time of shutting. **10** the line along which pieces of metal are welded. **11 get**

shut *or* **shot of.** *Slang.* to get rid of. ◆ See also **shutdown, shut-off, shutout, shut up.** [Old English *scyttan;* related to Old Frisian *sketta* to shut in, Middle Dutch *schutten* to obstruct]

shutdown ('ʃʌtˌdaʊn) *n* **1a** the closing of a factory, shop, etc. **1b** *(as modifier): shutdown costs.* ◆ *vb* **shut down.** *(adv)* **2** to cease or cause to cease operation. **3** *(tr)* to close by lowering. **4** *(tr)* (of fog) to descend and envelop. **5** *(intr;* foll. by *on* or *upon) Informal.* to put a stop to; clamp down on. **6** *(tr)* to reduce the power level of (a nuclear reactor) to the lowest possible value.

Shute (ʃuːt) *n* **Nevil,** real name *Nevil Shute Norway.* 1899–1960, English novelist, in Australia after World War II: noted for his novels set in Australia, esp. *A Town like Alice* (1950) and *On the Beach* (1957).

shuteye ('ʃʌtˌaɪ) *n* an informal term for **sleep.**

shut-in *n* **1** *Chiefly U.S. and Canadian.* **1a** a person confined indoors by illness. **1b** *(as modifier): a shut-in patient.* **2** *Psychiatry.* a condition in which the person is highly withdrawn and unable to express his own feelings. See also **schizoid.**

shut-off *n* **1** a device that shuts something off, esp. a machine control. **2** a stoppage or cessation. ◆ *vb* **shut off.** *(tr, adv)* **3** to stem the flow of. **4** to block off the passage through. **5** to isolate or separate.

shutout ('ʃʌtˌaʊt) *n* **1** a less common word for a **lockout. 2** *Sport.* a game in which the opposing team does not score. ◆ *vb* **shut out.** *(tr, adv)* **3** to keep out or exclude. **4** to conceal from sight: *we planted trees to shut out the view of the road.* **5** to prevent (an opponent) from scoring.

shut-out bid *n Bridge.* a pre-emptive bid.

shutter ('ʃʌtə) *n* **1** a hinged doorlike cover, often louvred and usually one of a pair, for closing off a window. **2 put up the shutters.** to close business at the end of the day or permanently. **3** *Photog.* an opaque shield in a camera that, when tripped, admits light to expose the film or plate for a predetermined period, usually a fraction of a second. It is either built into the lens system or lies in the focal plane of the lens (**focal-plane shutter**). **4** *Photog.* a rotating device in a film projector that permits an image to be projected onto the screen only when the film is momentarily stationary. **5** *Music.* one of the louvred covers over the mouths of organ pipes, operated by the swell pedal. **6** a person or thing that shuts. ◆ *vb (tr)* **7** to close with or as if with a shutter or shutters. **8** to equip with a shutter or shutters.

shuttering ('ʃʌtərɪŋ) *n* another word (esp. Brit.) for **formwork.**

shutter priority *n Photog.* an automatic exposure system in which the photographer selects the shutter speed and the camera then automatically sets the correct aperture. Compare **aperture priority.**

shuttle ('ʃʌtᵊl) *n* **1** a bobbin-like device used in weaving for passing the weft thread between the warp threads. **2** a small bobbin-like device used to hold the thread in a sewing machine or in tatting, knitting, etc. **3a** a bus, train, aircraft, etc., that plies between two points, esp. one that offers a frequent service over a short route. **3b** short for **space shuttle. 4a** the movement between various countries of a diplomat in order to negotiate with rulers who refuse to meet each other. **4b** *(as modifier): shuttle diplomacy.* **5** *Badminton, etc.* short for **shuttlecock.** ◆ *vb* **6** to move or cause to move by or as if by a shuttle. [Old English *scytel* bolt; related to Middle High German *schüzzel,* Swedish *skyttel.* See SHOOT, SHOT]

shuttle armature *n* a simple H-shaped armature used in small direct-current motors.

shuttlecock ('ʃʌtᵊlˌkɒk) *n* **1** a light cone consisting of a cork stub with feathered flights, struck to and fro in badminton and battledore. Often shortened to **shuttle. 2** anything moved to and fro, as in an argument. ◆ *vb* **3** to move or cause to move to and fro, like a shuttlecock. [C16: from SHUTTLE + COCK[1]]

shut up *vb (adv)* **1** *(tr)* to prevent all access to. **2** *(tr)* to confine or imprison. **3** *Informal.* to cease to talk or make a noise or cause to cease to talk or make a noise: often used in commands. **4** *(intr)* (of horses in a race) to cease through exhaustion from maintaining a racing pace.

shwa (ʃwɑː) *n* a variant spelling of **schwa.**

shy[1] (ʃaɪ) *adj* **shyer, shyest** *or* **shier, shiest. 1** not at ease in the company of others. **2** easily frightened; timid. **3** (often foll. by *of)* watchful or wary. **4** *Poker.* (of a player) without enough money to back his bet. **5** (of plants and animals) not breeding or producing offspring freely. **6** (foll. by *of) Informal, chiefly U.S. and Canadian.* short (of). **7** *(in combination)* showing reluctance or disinclination: *workshy.* ◆ *vb* **shies, shying, shied.** *(intr)* **8** to move suddenly, as from fear: *the horse shied at the snake in the road.* **9** (usually foll. by *off* or *away)* to draw back; recoil. ◆ *n, pl* **shies. 10** a sudden movement, as from fear. [Old English *sceoh;* related to Old High German *sciuhen* to frighten away, Dutch *schuw* shy, Swedish *skygg*] ▸ **'shyer** *n* ▸ **'shyly** *adv* ▸ **'shyness** *n*

shy[2] (ʃaɪ) *vb* **shies, shying, shied. 1** to throw (something) with a sideways motion. ◆ *n, pl* **shies. 2** a quick throw. **3** *Informal.* a gibe. **4** *Informal.* an attempt; experiment. **5** short for **cockshy.** [C18: of Germanic origin; compare Old High German *sciuhen* to make timid, Middle Dutch *schüchteren* to chase away] ▸ **'shyer** *n*

Shylock ('ʃaɪˌlɒk) *n* a heartless or demanding creditor. [C19: after *Shylock,* the name of the heartless usurer in Shakespeare's *The Merchant of Venice* (1596)]

shypoo (ʃaɪ'puː) *n Austral. informal.* **a** a liquor of poor quality. **b** a place where this is sold. **c** *(as modifier): a shypoo shanty.* [C20: of uncertain origin]

shyster ('ʃaɪstə) *n Informal, chiefly U.S.* a person, esp. a lawyer or politician, who uses discreditable or unethical methods. [C19: probably based on *Scheuster,* name of a disreputable 19th-century New York lawyer]

si (siː) *n Music.* a variant of **te.**

Si[1] (ʃiː) *or* **Si Kiang** *n* a variant transliteration of the Chinese name for the **Xi.**

Si[2] *the chemical symbol for* silicon.

SI 1 *symbol for* Système International (d'Unités). See **SI unit. 2** *N.Z. abbrev. for* South Island.

sial ('saɪəl) *n* the silicon-rich and aluminium-rich rocks of the earth's continental upper crust, the most abundant individual rock being granite. [C20: *si(licon)* + *al(uminium)*] ▸ **sialic** (saɪ'ælɪk) *adj*

sialagogue *or* **sialogogue** ('saɪələˌɡɒɡ, saɪ'æləˌɡɒɡ) *n Med.* any drug or agent that can stimulate the flow of saliva. [C18: from New Latin *sialagōgus,* from Greek *sialon* saliva + -AGOGUE] ▸ **sialagogic** *or* **sialogogic** (ˌsaɪələ'ɡɒdʒɪk) *adj*

Sialkot (sɪ'ælkɒt) *n* a city in NE Pakistan: shrine of Guru Nanak. Pop.: 296 000 (1981).

sialoid ('saɪəˌlɔɪd) *adj* resembling saliva. [from Greek *sialon* saliva + -OID]

Siam (saɪ'æm, 'saɪæm) *n* **1** the former name (until 1939 and 1945–49) of **Thailand. 2 Gulf of.** an arm of the South China Sea between the Malay Peninsula and Indochina.

siamang ('saɪəˌmæŋ) *n* a large black gibbon, *Hylobates* (or *Symphalangus*) *syndactylus,* of Sumatra and the Malay Peninsula, having a large reddish-brown vocal sac beneath the chin and the second and third toes united. [C19: from Malay]

Siamese (ˌsaɪə'miːz) *n, pl* **-mese. 1** See **Siamese cat.** ◆ *adj* **2** characteristic of, relating to, or being a Siamese twin. ◆ *adj, n* **3** another word for **Thai.**

Siamese cat *n* a short-haired breed of cat with a tapering tail, blue eyes, and dark ears, mask, tail, and paws. [so called because the breed is believed to have originated in SIAM]

Siamese fighting fish *n* a brightly coloured labyrinth fish, *Betta splendens,* of Thailand and Malaysia, having large sail-like fins: the males are very pugnacious.

Siamese twins *pl n* twin babies born joined together at some point, such as at the hips. Some have lived for many years without being surgically separated. [C19: named after a famous pair of conjoined twins, Chang and Eng (1811–74), who were born in SIAM]

Sian (ʃjɑːn) *n* a variant transliteration of the Chinese name for **Xi An.**

Siang (ʃjɑːŋ) *n* a variant transliteration of the Chinese name for the **Xiang.**

Siangtan ('ʃjɑːŋ'tɑːn) *n* a variant transliteration of the Chinese name for **Xiangtan.**

sib (sɪb) *n* **1** a blood relative. **2** kinsmen collectively; kindred. **3** any social unit that is bonded by kinship through one line of descent only. [Old English *sibb;* related to Old Norse *sifjar* relatives, Old High German *sippa* kinship, Latin *suus* one's own; see GOSSIP]

SIB (in Britain) *abbrev. for* Securities and Investments Board: a body that regulates financial dealings in the City of London.

Sib. *abbrev. for* Siberia(n).

Sibelius (sɪ'beɪlɪəs) *n* **Jean** (ʒɑn). 1865–1957, Finnish composer, noted for his seven symphonies, his symphonic poems, such as *Finlandia* (1900) and *Tapiola* (1925), and his violin concerto (1905).

Siberia (saɪ'bɪərɪə) *n* a vast region of Russia and N Kazakhstan: extends from the Ural Mountains to the Pacific and from the Arctic Ocean to the borders with China and Mongolia; colonized after the building of the Trans-Siberian Railway. Area: 13 807 037 sq. km (5 330 896 sq. miles). ▸ **Si'berian** *n, adj*

sibilant ('sɪbɪlənt) *adj* **1** *Phonetics.* relating to or denoting the consonants (s, z, ʃ, ʒ), all pronounced with a characteristic hissing sound. **2** having a hissing sound: *the sibilant sound of wind among the leaves.* ◆ *n* **3** a sibilant consonant. [C17: from Latin *sībilāre* to hiss, of imitative origin; compare Greek *sizein* to hiss] ▸ **'sibilance** *or* **'sibilancy** *n* ▸ **'sibilantly** *adv*

sibilate ('sɪbɪˌleɪt) *vb* to pronounce or utter (words or speech) with a hissing sound. ▸ **ˌsibi'lation** *n*

Sibiu *(Romanian* si'biu) *n* an industrial town in W central Romania: originally a Roman city, refounded by German colonists in the 12th century. Pop.: 170 528 (1994 est.). German name: **Hermannstadt.** Hungarian name: **Nagyszeben.**

sibling ('sɪblɪŋ) *n* **1a** a person's brother or sister. **1b** *(as modifier): sibling rivalry.* **2** any fellow member of a sib. [C19: specialized modern use of Old English *sibling* relative, from SIB; see -LING[1]]

sibship ('sɪbʃɪp) *n* a group of children of the same parents.

sibyl ('sɪbɪl) *n* **1** (in ancient Greece and Rome) any of a number of women believed to be oracles or prophetesses, one of the most famous being the sibyl of Cumae, who guided Aeneas through the underworld. **2** a witch, fortune-teller, or sorceress. [C13: ultimately from Greek *Sibulla,* of obscure origin] ▸ **sibylline** ('sɪbɪˌlaɪn, sɪ'bɪlaɪn), **sibyllic,** *or* **sibylic** (sɪ'bɪlɪk) *adj*

Sibylline Books *pl n* (in ancient Rome) a collection of prophetic sayings, supposedly bought from the Cumaean sibyl, bearing upon Roman policy and religion.

sic[1] (sɪk) *adv* so or thus: inserted in brackets in a written or printed text to indicate that an odd or questionable reading is what was actually written or printed. [Latin]

sic[2] (sɪk) *vb* **sics, sicking, sicked.** *(tr)* **1** to turn on or attack: used only in commands, as to a dog. **2** to urge (a dog) to attack. [C19: dialect variant of SEEK]

sic[3] (sɪk) *determiner, adv* a Scot. word for **such.**

Sic. *abbrev. for:* **1** Sicilian. **2** Sicily.

Sica *(Italian* 'siːka) **Vittorio de.** See (Vittorio) **de Sica.**

Sicanian (sɪ'keɪnɪən) *adj* another word for **Sicilian.**

siccar ('sɪkər) *adj Scot.* sure; certain. Also: **sicker.** [Middle English, from Latin *sēcūrus* SECURE]

siccative ('sɪkətɪv) *n* a substance added to a liquid to promote drying: used in paints and some medicines. [C16: from Late Latin *siccātīvus,* from Latin *siccāre* to dry up, from *siccus* dry]

sice (saɪs) *n* a variant spelling of **syce.**

sicht (sɪxt) *n, vb* a Scot. word for **sight.**

Sichuan ('sɪ'tʃwɑːn) *or* **Szechwan** *n* a province of SW China: the most populous administrative division in the country, esp. in the central Red Basin, where it is crossed by three main tributaries of the Yangtze. Capital: Chengdu. Pop.: 98 650 000 (1996 est.). Area: about 569 800 sq. km (220 000 sq. miles).

Sicilia (si'tʃiːlja) *n* the Latin and Italian name for **Sicily**.

siciliano (sɪˌsɪlɪ'ɑːnəʊ, ˌsɪtʃɪ'ljɑːnəʊ) *n, pl* **-ianos**. **1** an old dance in six-beat or twelve-beat time. **2** music composed for or in the rhythm of this dance. [Italian: Sicilian]

Sicilian Vespers *n* (*functioning as sing*) a revolt in 1282 against French rule in Sicily, in which the ringing of the vesper bells on Easter Monday served as the signal to massacre and drive out the French.

Sicily ('sɪsɪlɪ) *n* the largest island in the Mediterranean, separated from the tip of SW Italy by the Strait of Messina: administratively an autonomous region of Italy; settled by Phoenicians, Greeks, and Carthaginians before the Roman conquest of 241 B.C.; under Normans (12th–13th centuries); formed the **Kingdom of the Two Sicilies** with Naples in 1815; mountainous and volcanic. Capital: Palermo. Pop.: 5 094 735 (1996 est.). Area: 25 460 sq. km (9830 sq. miles). Latin names: **Sicilia, Trinacria.** Italian name: **Sicilia.** ▸ **Sicilian** (sɪ'sɪlɪən) *adj, n*

sick[1] (sɪk) *adj* **1** inclined or likely to vomit. **2a** suffering from ill health. **2b** (*as collective n;* preceded by *the*)*: the sick.* **3a** of, relating to, or used by people who are unwell: *sick benefits.* **3b** (*in combination*)*: sickbed.* **4** deeply affected with a mental or spiritual feeling akin to physical sickness: *sick at heart.* **5** mentally, psychologically, or spiritually disturbed. **6** *Informal.* delighting in or catering for the macabre or sadistic; morbid: *sick humour.* **7** (often foll. by *of*) *Informal.* Also: **sick and tired.** disgusted or weary, esp. because satiated: *I am sick of his everlasting laughter.* **8** (often foll. by *for*) weary with longing; pining: *I am sick for my own country.* **9** pallid or sickly. **10** not in working order. **11** (of land) unfit for the adequate production of certain crops. **12 look sick.** *Slang.* to be outclassed. ◆ *n, vb* **13** an informal word for **vomit.** ◆ See also **sick-out.** [Old English *sēoc;* related to Old Norse *skjūkr,* Gothic *siuks,* Old High German *sioh*] ▸ **'sickish** *adj*

sick[2] (sɪk) *vb* a variant spelling of **sic**[2].

sickbay ('sɪkˌbeɪ) *n* a room or area for the treatment of the sick or injured, as on board a ship or at a boarding school.

sick building syndrome *n* a group of symptoms, such as headaches, eye irritation, and lethargy, that may be experienced by workers in air-conditioned offices.

sicken ('sɪkən) *vb* **1** to make or become sick, nauseated, or disgusted. **2** (*intr;* often foll. by *for*) to show symptoms (of an illness).

sickener ('sɪkᵊnə) *n* **1** something that induces sickness or nausea. **2** a bright red basidiomycetous fungus of either of two species of *Russula,* notably the poisonous *R. emetica.*

sickening ('sɪkənɪŋ) *adj* **1** causing sickness or revulsion. **2** *Informal.* extremely annoying. ▸ **'sickeningly** *adv*

Sickert ('sɪkət) *n* **Walter Richard.** 1860–1942, British impressionist painter, esp. of scenes of London music halls.

sick headache *n* **1** a headache accompanied by nausea. **2** a nontechnical name for **migraine.**

sickie ('sɪkɪ) *n Informal.* a day of sick leave from work, whether for genuine sickness or not. [C20: from SICK[1] + -IE]

sickle ('sɪkᵊl) *n* an implement for cutting grass, corn, etc., having a curved blade and a short handle. [Old English *sicol,* from Latin *sēcula;* related to *secāre* to cut]

sick leave *n* leave of absence from work through illness.

sicklebill ('sɪkᵊlˌbɪl) *n* any of various birds having a markedly curved bill, such as *Falculea palliata,* a Madagascan bird of the family *Vangidae, Hemignathus procerus,* a Hawaiian honey creeper, and certain hummingbirds and birds of paradise.

sickle-cell anaemia *n* a hereditary haemolytic anaemia, occurring in Black populations, and caused by mutant haemoglobin. The red blood cells become sickle-shaped. It is characterized by fever, abdominal pain, jaundice, leg ulcers, etc.

sickle feather *n* (*often pl*) any of the elongated tail feathers of certain birds, esp. the domestic cock. [C17: so called because of its shape]

sickle medick *n* a small Eurasian papilionaceous plant, *Medicago falcata,* having trifoliate leaves, yellow flowers, and sickle-shaped pods. Also called: **yellow medick.**

sick list *n* a list of the sick, esp. in the army or navy.

sickly ('sɪklɪ) *adj* **-lier, -liest. 1** disposed to frequent ailments; not healthy; weak. **2** of, relating to, or caused by sickness. **3** (of a smell, taste, etc.) causing revulsion or nausea. **4** (of light or colour) faint or feeble. **5** mawkish; insipid: *sickly affectation.* ◆ *adv* **6** in a sick or sickly manner. ▸ **'sickliness** *n*

sickness ('sɪknɪs) *n* **1** an illness or disease. **2** nausea or queasiness. **3** the state or an instance of being sick.

sickness benefit *n* **1** (in the British National Insurance scheme) a weekly payment to a person who has been off work through illness for more than three days and less than six months. **2** (in New Zealand) a payment made by the Department of Social Welfare to a person unable to work owing to a medical condition.

sick note *n Brit. informal.* a document given to an employer certifying that an employee's absence from work of more than four days was due to illness. If the absence is for more than seven days the note must be signed by a doctor. See also **self-certification.**

sicko ('sɪkəʊ) *Informal.* ◆ *n, pl* **sickos. 1** a person who is mentally disturbed or perverted. ◆ *adj* **2** perverted or in bad taste: *sicko prurience.* [C20: from SICK[1] (sense 5) + -O]

sick-out *U.S. and Caribbean.* ◆ *n* **1** a form of industrial action in which all workers in a factory, etc., report sick simultaneously. ◆ *vb* **sick out. 2** (*intr, adv*) to take part in such action.

sick pay *n* wages paid to an employee while he is on sick leave.

sickroom ('sɪkˌruːm, -ˌrʊm) *n* **1** a room to which a person who is ill is confined. **2** a room set aside, as in a school, for people who are taken ill.

sic passim *Latin.* ('sɪk 'pæsɪm) a phrase used in printed works to indicate that a word, spelling, etc., occurs in the same form throughout. [literally: thus everywhere]

sic transit gloria mundi *Latin.* ('sɪk 'trænsɪt 'glɔːrɪˌɑː 'mʊndiː) thus passes the glory of the world.

Sicyon ('sɪsɪˌɒn, 'sɪsɪən) *n* an ancient city in S Greece, in the NE Peloponnese near Corinth: declined after 146 B.C.

sidalcea (sɪ'dælsɪə) *n* any plant of the mostly perennial N American genus *Sidalcea,* related to and resembling mallow, esp. *S. malvaeflora,* grown for its spikes of lilac, pink, or red flowers: family *Malvaceae.* Also called **Greek mallow.** [New Latin, from Greek *sidē* a plant name + *alkea* a kind of mallow]

Siddhartha (sɪ'dɑːtə) *n* the personal name of the **Buddha.**

Siddons ('sɪdᵊnz) *n* **Sarah.** 1755–1831, English tragedienne.

siddur *Hebrew.* (siː'duːr; *English* 'sɪdʊə) *n, pl* **-durim** (-duː'riːm) *or* **-durs.** *Judaism.* the Jewish prayer book. [literally: order]

side (saɪd) *n* **1** a line or surface that borders anything. **2** *Geometry.* **2a** any line segment forming part of the perimeter of a plane geometric figure. **2b** another name for **face** (sense 13). **3** either of two parts into which an object, surface, area, etc., can be divided, esp. by a line, median, space, etc.: *the right side and the left side.* Related adj: **lateral. 4** either of the two surfaces of a flat object: *the right and wrong side of the cloth.* **5** a surface or part of an object that extends vertically: *the side of a cliff.* **6** either half of a human or animal body, esp. the area around the waist, as divided by the median plane: *I have a pain in my side.* **7** the area immediately next to a person or thing: *he stood at her side.* **8** a district, point, or direction within an area identified by reference to a central point: *the south side of the city.* **9** the area at the edge of a room, road, etc., as distinguished from the middle. **10** aspect or part: *look on the bright side; his cruel side.* **11** one of two or more contesting factions, teams, etc. **12** a page in an essay, book, etc. **13** a position, opinion, etc., held in opposition to another in a dispute. **14** line of descent: *he gets his brains from his mother's side.* **15** *Informal.* a television channel. **16** *Billiards, etc.* spin imparted to a ball by striking it off-centre with the cue. U.S. and Canadian equivalent: **English. 17** *Brit. slang.* insolence, arrogance, or pretentiousness: *to put on side.* **18 on one side.** set apart from the rest, as provision for emergencies, etc., or to avoid muddling. **19 on the side. 19a** apart from or in addition to the main object. **19b** as a sideline. **19c** *U.S.* as a side dish. **19d bit on the side.** See **bit** (sense 11). **20 side by side. 20a** close together. **20b** (foll. by *with*) beside or near to. **21 take sides.** to support one group, opinion, etc., as against another. **22 on the weak, heavy,** etc., **side.** tending to be too weak, heavy, etc. ◆ *adj* **23** being on one side; lateral. **24** from or viewed as if from one side. **25** directed towards one side. **26** not main; subordinate or incidental: *side door; side road.* ◆ *vb* **27** (*intr;* usually foll. by *with*) to support or associate oneself with a faction, interest, etc. **28** (*tr*) to provide with siding or sides. **29** (*tr;* often foll. by *away* or *up*) *Northern English dialect.* to tidy up or clear (dishes, a table, etc.). [Old English *sīde;* related to *sīd* wide, Old Norse *sītha* side, Old High German *sīta*]

side arms *pl n* weapons carried on the person, by sling, belt, or holster, such as a sword, pistol, etc.

sideband ('saɪdˌbænd) *n* the frequency band either above (**upper sideband**) or below (**lower sideband**) the carrier frequency, within which fall the spectral components produced by modulation of a carrier wave. See also **single sideband transmission.**

sideboard ('saɪdˌbɔːd) *n* a piece of furniture intended to stand at the side of a dining room, with drawers, cupboards, and shelves to hold silver, china, linen, etc.

sideboards ('saɪdˌbɔːdz) *pl n* another term for **sideburns.**

sideburns ('saɪdˌbɜːnz) *pl n* a man's whiskers grown down either side of the face in front of the ears. Also called: **sideboards, side whiskers,** (Austral.) **sidelevers.** [C19: variant of BURNSIDES]

sidecar ('saɪdˌkɑː) *n* **1** a small car attached on one side to a motorcycle, usually for one passenger, the other side being supported by a single wheel. **2** a cocktail containing brandy with equal parts of Cointreau and lemon juice.

side chain *n Chem.* a group of atoms bound to an atom, usually a carbon, that forms part of a larger chain or ring in a molecule.

-sided *adj* (*in combination*) having a side or sides as specified: *three-sided; many-sided.*

side deal *n* a transaction between two people for their private benefit, which is subsidiary to a contract negotiated by them on behalf of the organizations they represent.

side dish *n* a portion of food served in addition to the main dish.

side-dress *vb* (*tr*) to place fertilizers on or in the soil near the roots of (growing plants).

side drum *n* a small double-headed drum carried at the side with snares that produce a rattling effect.

side effect *n* **1** any unwanted nontherapeutic effect caused by a drug. Compare **aftereffect** (sense 2). **2** any secondary effect, esp. an undesirable one.

side-foot *Soccer.* ◆ *n* **1** a shot or pass played with the side of the foot. ◆ *vb* **2** (*tr*) to strike (a ball) with the side of the foot.

sidekick ('saɪdˌkɪk) *n Informal.* a close friend or follower who accompanies another on adventures, etc.

sidelight ('saɪdˌlaɪt) *n* **1** light coming from the side. **2** a side window. **3** either of the two navigational running lights used by vessels at night, a red light on the port and a green on the starboard. **4** *Brit.* either of two small lights on the front of a motor vehicle, used to indicate the presence of the vehicle at night rather than to assist the driver. **5** additional or incidental information.

sideline ('saɪdˌlaɪn) *n* **1** *Sport.* a line that marks the side boundary of a playing area. **2** a subsidiary interest or source of income. **3** an auxiliary business activity or line of merchandise. ◆ *vb* (*tr*) **4** to prevent (a player) from taking part in a game. **5** to prevent (a person) from pursuing a particular activity, operation, career, etc.

sidelines ('saɪd,laɪnz) *pl n* **1** *Sport.* the area immediately outside the playing area, where substitute players sit. **2** the peripheral areas of any region, organization, etc.

sidelong ('saɪd,lɒŋ) *adj* (*prenominal*) **1** directed or inclining to one side. **2** indirect or oblique. ♦ *adv* **3** from the side; obliquely.

sideman ('saɪdmən) *n, pl* **-men.** a member of a dance band or a jazz group other than the leader.

side meat *n U.S. informal.* salt pork or bacon. [C19: so called because it comes from the side of the pig]

sidereal (saɪ'dɪərɪəl) *adj* **1** of, relating to, or involving the stars. **2** determined with reference to one or more stars: *the sidereal day.* [C17: from Latin *sīdereus,* from *sīdus* a star, a constellation] ▸ **si'dereally** *adv*

sidereal day *n* See **day** (sense 5).

sidereal hour *n* a 24th part of a sidereal day.

sidereal month *n* See **month** (sense 5).

sidereal period *n Astronomy.* the period of revolution of a body about another with respect to one or more stars.

sidereal time *n* time based upon the rotation of the earth with respect to a particular star, the **sidereal day** being the unit of measurement.

sidereal year *n* See **year** (sense 5).

siderite ('saɪdə,raɪt) *n* **1** Also called: **chalybite.** a pale yellow to brownish-black mineral consisting chiefly of iron carbonate in hexagonal crystalline form. It occurs mainly in ore veins and sedimentary rocks and is an important source of iron. Formula: $FeCO_3$. **2** a meteorite consisting principally of metallic iron. ▸ **sideritic** (,saɪdə'rɪtɪk) *adj*

sidero- *or before a vowel* **sider-** *combining form.* indicating iron: *siderolite.* [from Greek *sidēros*]

sideroad ('saɪd,rəʊd) *n Canadian.* (esp. in Ontario) a road, usually north-south, going at right angles to concession roads.

siderolite ('saɪdərə,laɪt) *n* a meteorite consisting of a mixture of iron, nickel, and such ferromagnesian minerals as olivine and pyroxene.

siderophilin (,sɪdə'rɒfəlɪn) *n* another name for **transferrin.** [from SIDERO- + -PHIL(E) + -IN]

siderosis (,saɪdə'rəʊsɪs) *n* **1** a lung disease caused by breathing in fine particles of iron or other metallic dust. **2** an excessive amount of iron in the blood or tissues. ▸ **siderotic** (,sɪdə'rɒtɪk) *adj*

siderostat ('saɪdərəʊ,stæt) *n* an astronomical instrument consisting essentially of a plane mirror rotated by a clock mechanism about two axes so that light from a celestial body, esp. the sun, is reflected along a constant direction for a long period of time. See also **heliostat.** Compare **coelostat.** [C19: from *sidero-*, from Latin *sidus* a star + -STAT, on the model of HELIOSTAT] ▸ **,sidero'static** *adj*

side-saddle *n* **1** a riding saddle originally designed for women riders in skirts who sit with both legs on the near side of the horse. ♦ *adv* **2** on or as if on a side-saddle: *to be riding side-saddle.*

sideshow ('saɪd,ʃəʊ) *n* **1** a small show or entertainment offered in conjunction with a larger attraction, as at a circus or fair. **2** a subordinate event or incident.

sideslip ('saɪd,slɪp) *n* **1** a sideways skid, as of a motor vehicle. **2** a sideways and downward movement towards the inside of a turn by an aircraft in a sharp bank. ♦ *vb* **-slips, -slipping, -slipped. 3** another name for **slip**[1] (sense 12).

sidesman ('saɪdzmən) *n, pl* **-men.** *Church of England.* a man elected to help the parish church warden.

side-splitting *adj* **1** producing great mirth. **2** (of laughter) uproarious or very hearty.

sidestep ('saɪd,stɛp) *vb* **-steps, -stepping, -stepped. 1** to step aside from or out of the way of (something). **2** (*tr*) to dodge or circumvent. ♦ *n* **side step. 3** a movement to one side, as in dancing, boxing, etc. ▸ **'side,stepper** *n*

side street *n* a minor or unimportant street, esp. one leading off a main thoroughfare.

sidestroke ('saɪd,strəʊk) *n* a type of swimming stroke in which the swimmer lies sideways in the water paddling with his arms and making a scissors kick with his legs.

sideswipe ('saɪd,swaɪp) *n* **1** a glancing blow or hit along or from the side. ♦ *vb* **2** to strike (someone) with such a blow. ▸ **'side,swiper** *n*

side tone *n* sound diverted from a telephone microphone to the earpiece so that a speaker hears his own voice at the same level and position as that of the respondent.

sidetrack ('saɪd,træk) *vb* **1** to distract or be distracted from a main subject or topic. ♦ *n* **2** *U.S. and Canadian.* a railway siding. **3** the act or an instance of sidetracking; digression.

side-valve engine *n* a type of internal-combustion engine in which the inlet and exhaust valves are in the cylinder block at the side of the pistons. Compare **overhead-valve engine.**

sidewalk ('saɪd,wɔːk) *n* the U.S. and Canadian word for **pavement.**

sidewall ('saɪd,wɔːl) *n* either of the sides of a pneumatic tyre between the tread and the rim.

sideward ('saɪdwəd) *adj* **1** directed or moving towards one side. ♦ *adv also* **sidewards. 2** towards one side.

sideways ('saɪd,weɪz) *adv* **1** moving, facing, or inclining towards one side. **2** from one side; obliquely. **3** with one side forward. ♦ *adj* (*prenominal*) **4** moving or directed to or from one side. **5** towards or from one side.

sidewheel ('saɪd,wiːl) *n* one of the paddle wheels of a sidewheeler.

sidewheeler ('saɪd,wiːlə) *n* a vessel, esp. a river boat, propelled by two large paddle wheels, one on each side. Compare **stern-wheeler.**

side whiskers *pl n* another name for **sideburns.**

sidewinder ('saɪd,waɪndə) *n* **1** a North American rattlesnake, *Crotalus cerastes,* that moves forwards by a sideways looping motion. **2** *Boxing, U.S.* a heavy swinging blow from the side. **3** a U.S. air-to-air missile using infrared homing aids in seeking its target.

Sidi-bel-Abbès (*French* sidibelabɛs) *n* a city in NW Algeria: headquarters of the Foreign Legion until Algerian independence (1962). Pop.: 152 778 (1987).

siding ('saɪdɪŋ) *n* **1** a short stretch of railway track connected to a main line, used for storing rolling stock or to enable trains on the same line to pass. **2** a short railway line giving access to the main line for freight from a factory, mine, quarry, etc. **3** *U.S. and Canadian.* material attached to the outside of a building to make it weatherproof.

sidle ('saɪdᵊl) *vb* (*intr*) **1** to move in a furtive or stealthy manner; edge along. **2** to move along sideways. ♦ *n* **3** a sideways movement. [C17: back formation from obsolete *sideling* sideways] ▸ **'sidler** *n*

Sidmouth ('sɪdmuθ) *n* **1st Viscount.** See (Henry) **Addington.**

Sidney *or* **Sydney** ('sɪdnɪ) *n* **1 Algernon.** 1622–83, English Whig politician, beheaded for his supposed part in the Rye House Plot to assassinate Charles II and the future James II: author of *Discourses Concerning Government* (1689). **2** Sir **Philip.** 1554–86, English poet, courtier, and soldier. His works include the pastoral romance *Arcadia* (1590), the sonnet sequence *Astrophel and Stella* (1591), and *The Defence of Poesie* (1595), one of the earliest works of literary criticism in English.

Sidon ('saɪdᵊn) *n* the chief city of ancient Phoenicia: founded in the third millennium B.C.; wealthy through trade and the making of glass and purple dyes; now the Lebanese city of Saïda. ▸ **Sidonian** (saɪ'dəʊnɪən) *adj, n*

Sidra ('sɪdrə) *n* **Gulf of.** a wide inlet of the Mediterranean on the N coast of Libya.

SIDS *abbrev. for* sudden infant death syndrome. See **cot death.**

siècle *French.* (sjɛklə) *n* a century, period, or era.

Siegbahn ('siːgbɑːn) *n* **1 Kai** ('kaɪ). born 1918, Swedish physicist who worked on electron spectroscopy: Nobel prize for physics 1981. **2** his father, **Karl Manne Georg** (kaːrl 'manə 'jeːɔrj). 1886–1978, Swedish physicist, who discovered the M series in X-ray spectroscopy: Nobel prize for physics 1924.

siege (siːdʒ) *n* **1a** the offensive operations carried out to capture a fortified place by surrounding it, severing its communications and supply lines, and deploying weapons against it. **1b** (*as modifier*): *siege warfare.* **2** a persistent attempt to gain something. **3** a long tedious period, as of illness, etc. **4** *Obsolete.* a seat or throne. **5 lay siege to.** to besiege. ♦ *vb* **6** (*tr*) to besiege or assail. [C13: from Old French *sege* a seat, from Vulgar Latin *sēdicāre* (unattested) to sit down, from Latin *sedēre*]

siege mentality *n* a state of mind in which a person believes that he or she is being constantly oppressed or attacked.

Siegen ('siːgən) *n* a city in NW Germany, in North Rhine-Westphalia: manufacturing centre: birthplace of Rubens. Pop.: 111 398 (1996 est.).

Siege Perilous *n* (in Arthurian legend) the seat at the Round Table that could be filled only by the knight destined to find the Holy Grail and that was fatal to anyone else. [from SIEGE (in the archaic sense: a seat or throne)]

Siegfried ('siːgfriːd; *German* 'ziːkfriːt) *n German myth.* a German prince, the son of Sigmund and husband of Kriemhild, who, in the *Nibelungenlied,* assumes possession of the treasure of the Nibelungs by slaying the dragon that guards it, wins Brunhild for King Gunther, and is eventually killed by Hagen. Norse equivalent: **Sigurd.**

Siegfried line *n* the line of fortifications built by the Germans prior to and during World War II opposite the Maginot line in France.

Sieg Heil *German.* (ziːk hail) hail to victory: a Nazi salute, often accompanied by the raising of the right arm.

siemens ('siːmənz) *n, pl* **siemens.** the derived SI unit of electrical conductance equal to 1 reciprocal ohm. Symbol: S Formerly called: **mho.**

Siemens ('siːmənz) *n* **1 Ernst Werner von** (ɛrnst 'vɛrnər fɔn). 1816–92, German engineer, inventor, and pioneer in telegraphy. Among his inventions are the self-excited dynamo and an electrolytic refining process. **2** his brother, Sir **William,** original name *Karl Wilhelm Siemens.* 1823–83, British engineer, born in Germany, who invented the open-hearth process for making steel.

Siena (sɪ'ɛnə; *Italian* 'sjɛːna) *n* a walled city in central Italy, in Tuscany: founded by the Etruscans; important artistic centre (13th–14th centuries); university (13th century). Pop.: 58 278 (1990).

Sienkiewicz (*Polish* ʃɛŋ'kjɛvitʃ) *n* **Henryk** ('xɛnrik). 1846–1916, Polish novelist. His best-known works are *Quo Vadis?* (1896), set in Nero's Rome, and the war trilogy *With Fire and Sword* (1884), *The Deluge* (1886), and *Pan Michael* (1888), set in 17th-century Poland: Nobel prize for literature 1905.

sienna (sɪ'ɛnə) *n* **1** a natural earth containing ferric oxide used as a yellowish-brown pigment when untreated (**raw sienna**) or a reddish-brown pigment when roasted (**burnt sienna**). **2** the colour of this pigment. See also **burnt sienna.** [C18: from Italian *terra di Siena* earth of SIENA]

sierra (sɪ'ɛərə) *n* a range of mountains with jagged peaks, esp. in Spain or America. [C17: from Spanish, literally: saw, from Latin *serra;* see SERRATE] ▸ **si'erran** *adj*

Sierra (sɪ'ɛərə) *n Communications.* a code word for the letter *s.*

Sierra Leone (sɪ'ɛərə lɪ'əʊnɪ, lɪ'əʊn) *n* a republic in W Africa, on the Atlantic: became a British colony in 1808 and gained independence (within the Commonwealth) in 1961; declared a republic in 1971; became a one-party state in 1978; multiparty democracy restored in 1991 but military rule was imposed following a coup in 1992, which led to civil unrest; consists of coastal swamps rising to a plateau in the east. Official language: English. Religion: Muslim majority and animist. Currency: leone. Capital: Freetown. Pop.: 4 577 000 (1998 est.). Area: 71 740 sq. km (27 699 sq. miles). ▸ **Sierra Leonean** *adj, n*

Sierra Madre (*Spanish* 'sjerra 'maðre) *n* (*functioning as sing*) the main mountain system of Mexico, extending for 2500 km (1500 miles) southeast from the N border: consists of the **Sierra Madre Oriental** in the east, the **Sierra Madre**

Occidental in the west, and the **Sierra Madre del Sur** in the south. Highest peak: Citlaltépetl, 5699 m (18 698 ft.).

Sierra Morena (*Spanish* 'sjɛrra mo'rena) *n* (*functioning as sing*) a mountain range in SW Spain, between the Guadiana and Guadalquivir Rivers. Highest peak: Estrella, 1299 m (4262 ft.).

Sierra Nevada *n* (*functioning as sing*) **1** (sɪ'ɛərə nɪ'vɑːdə). a mountain range in E California, parallel to the Coast Ranges. Highest peak: Mount Whitney, 4418 m (14 495 ft.). **2** (*Spanish* 'sjɛrra ne'βaða). a mountain range in SE Spain, mostly in Granada and Almería provinces. Highest peak: Cerro de Mulhacén, 3478 m (11 411 ft.).

sies (sɪs, siːs) *interj S. African informal.* a variant of **sis**[2].

siesta (sɪ'ɛstə) *n* a rest or nap, usually taken in the early afternoon, as in hot countries. [C17: from Spanish, from Latin *sexta hōra* the sixth hour, that is, noon]

sieve (sɪv) *n* **1** a device for separating lumps from powdered material, straining liquids, grading particles, etc., consisting of a container with a mesh or perforated bottom through which the material is shaken or poured. **2** *Rare.* a person who gossips and spreads secrets. **3 a memory** *or* **head like a sieve.** a very poor memory. ♦ *vb* **4** to pass or cause to pass through a sieve. **5** (*tr;* often foll. by *out*) to separate or remove (lumps, materials, etc.) by use of a sieve. [Old English *sife;* related to Old Norse *sef* reed with hollow stalk, Old High German *sib* sieve, Dutch *zeef*] ► **'sieve,like** *adj*

sievert ('siːvət) *n* **1** the derived SI unit of dose equivalent, equal to 1 joule per kilogram. 1 sievert is equivalent to 100 rems. Symbol: Sv **2** (formerly) a unit of gamma radiation dose approximately equal to 8.4 × 10^{-2} gray. [C20: named after Rolf *Sievert* (1896–1966), Swedish physicist]

sieve tube *n Botany.* an element of phloem tissue consisting of a longitudinal row of thin-walled elongated cells with perforations in their connecting walls through which food materials pass.

Sieyès (*French* sjejɛs) *n* **Emmanuel Joseph** (ɛmanɥel ʒozɛf), called *Abbé Sieyès.* 1748–1836, French statesman, political theorist, and churchman, who became prominent during the Revolution following the publication of his pamphlet *Qu'est-ce que le tiers état?* (1789). He was instrumental in bringing Napoleon I to power (1799).

sifaka (sɪ'fɑːkə) *n* either of two large rare arboreal lemuroid primates, *Propithecus diadema* or *P. verreauxi*, of Madagascar, having long strikingly patterned or coloured fur: family *Indriidae.* [from Malagasy]

sift (sɪft) *vb* **1** (*tr*) to sieve (sand, flour, etc.) in order to remove the coarser particles. **2** to scatter (something) over a surface through a sieve. **3** (*tr*) to separate with or as if with a sieve; distinguish between. **4** (*tr*) to examine minutely: *to sift evidence.* **5** (*intr*) to move as if through a sieve. [Old English *siftan;* related to Middle Low German *siften* to sift, Dutch *ziften;* see SIEVE] ► **'sifter** *n*

siftings ('sɪftɪŋz) *pl n* material or particles separated out by or as if by a sieve.

sig. *abbrev. for:* **1** signature. **2** signor. **3** signore.

Sig. *abbrev. for:* **1** (in prescriptions) signā. [Latin: sign] **2** (in prescriptions) signature. **3** signor. **4** signore.

sigh (saɪ) *vb* **1** (*intr*) to draw in and exhale audibly a deep breath as an expression of weariness, despair, relief, etc. **2** (*intr*) to make a sound resembling this: *trees sighing in the wind.* **3** (*intr;* often foll. by *for*) to yearn, long, or pine. **4** (*tr*) to utter or express with sighing. ♦ *n* **5** the act or sound of sighing. [Old English *sīcan*, of obscure origin] ► **'sigher** *n*

sight (saɪt) *n* **1** the power or faculty of seeing; perception by the eyes; vision. Related adjs: **optical, visual. 2** the act or an instance of seeing. **3** the range of vision: *within sight of land.* **4** range of mental vision; point of view; judgment: *in his sight she could do nothing wrong.* **5** a glimpse or view (esp. in the phrases **catch sight of, lose sight of**). **6** anything that is seen. **7** (*often pl*) anything worth seeing; spectacle: *the sights of London.* **8** *Informal.* anything unpleasant or undesirable to see: *his room was a sight!* **9** any of various devices or instruments used to assist the eye in making alignments or directional observations, esp. such a device used in aiming a gun. **10** an observation or alignment made with such a device. **11** an opportunity for observation. **12** *Obsolete.* insight or skill. **13 a sight.** *Informal.* a great deal: *she's a sight too good for him.* **14 a sight for sore eyes.** a person or thing that one is pleased or relieved to see. **15 at** *or* **on sight. 15a** as soon as seen. **15b** on presentation: *a bill payable at sight.* **16 know by sight.** to be familiar with the appearance of without having personal acquaintance: *I know Mr Brown by sight but we have never spoken.* **17 not by a long sight.** *Informal.* on no account; not at all. **18 out of sight.** *Slang.* **18a** extreme or very unusual. **18b** (*as interj*) that's marvellous! **19 set one's sights on.** to have (a specified goal) in mind; aim for. **20 sight unseen.** without having seen the object at issue: *to buy a car sight unseen.* ♦ *vb* **21** (*tr*) to see, view, or glimpse. **22** (*tr*) **22a** to furnish with a sight or sights. **22b** to adjust the sight of. **23** to aim (a firearm) using the sight. [Old English *sihth;* related to Old High German *siht;* see SEE[1]] ► **'sightable** *adj*

sight bill *or* **draft** *n* variants of **demand bill.**

sighted ('saɪtɪd) *adj* **1** not blind. **2** (*in combination*) having sight of a specified kind: *short-sighted.*

sighter ('saɪtə) *n Shooting, archery.* any of six practice shots allowed to each competitor in a tournament.

sightless ('saɪtlɪs) *adj* **1** blind. **2** invisible. ► **'sightlessly** *adv* ► **'sightlessness** *n*

sightline ('saɪt,laɪn) *n* an uninterrupted line of vision, as in a theatre, etc., or from a vehicle joining a road.

sightly ('saɪtlɪ) *adj* **-lier, -liest. 1** pleasing or attractive to see. **2** *U.S.* providing a pleasant view. ► **'sightliness** *n*

sight-read ('saɪt,riːd) *vb* **-reads, -reading, -read** (-,rɛd). to sing or play (music in a printed or written form) without previous preparation. ► **'sight-,reader** *n* ► **'sight-,reading** *n*

sightscreen ('saɪt,skriːn) *n Cricket.* a large white screen placed near the boundary behind the bowler to help the batsman see the ball.

sightsee ('saɪt,siː) *vb* **-sees, -seeing, -saw, -seen.** *Informal.* to visit the famous or interesting sights of (a place). ► **'sight,seeing** *n* ► **'sight,seer** *n*

sigil ('sɪdʒɪl) *n Rare.* **1** a seal or signet. **2** a sign or image supposedly having magical power. [C17: from Latin *sigillum* a little sign, from *signum* a SIGN] ► **sigillary** ('sɪdʒɪlərɪ) *adj*

Sigismund ('sɪgɪsmənd) *n* 1368–1437, king of Hungary (1387–1437) and of Bohemia (1419–37); Holy Roman Emperor (1411–37). He helped to end the Great Schism in the Church; implicated in the death of Huss.

Sigismund II *n* called *Sigismund Augustus.* 1520–72, king of Poland (1548–72), who united Poland, Lithuania, and their dependencies by the Union of Lublin (1569).

sigla ('sɪglə) *n* the list of symbols used in a book, usually collected together as part of the preliminaries. [Latin: plural of *siglum,* diminutive of *signum* sign]

siglos ('sɪglɒs) *n, pl* **-loi** (-lɔɪ). a silver coin of ancient Persia worth one twentieth of a daric.

sigma ('sɪgmə) *n* **1** the 18th letter in the Greek alphabet (Σ, σ or, when final, ς), a consonant, transliterated as *S.* **2** *Maths.* the symbol Σ, indicating summation of the numbers or quantities indicated. [Greek, of Semitic origin; related to Hebrew SAMEKH]

sigmate ('sɪgmɪt, -meɪt) *adj* shaped like the Greek letter sigma or the Roman *S.* ► **sigmation** (sɪg'meɪʃən) *n*

sigmoid ('sɪgmɔɪd) *adj also* **sigmoidal. 1** shaped like the letter S. **2** of or relating to the sigmoid flexure of the large intestine. ♦ *n* **3** See **sigmoid flexure.** [C17: from Greek *sigmoeidēs* sigma-shaped]

sigmoid flexure *n* **1** the S-shaped bend in the final portion of the large intestine. **2** *Zoology.* an S-shaped curve, as in the necks of certain birds.

sigmoidoscope (sɪg'mɔɪdə,skəʊp) *n* an instrument incorporating a light for the direct observation of the colon, rectum, and sigmoid flexure. ► **sigmoidoscopic** (sɪg,mɔɪdə'skɒpɪk) *adj* ► **sigmoidoscopy** (,sɪgmɔɪd'ɒskəpɪ) *n*

Sigmund ('sɪgmənd, 'siːgmʊnd; *German* 'ziːkmʊnt) *n* **1** *Norse myth.* the father of the hero Sigurd. **2** Also called: **Siegmund** (*German* 'ziːkmʊnt). *German myth.* king of the Netherlands, father of Siegfried.

sign (saɪn) *n* **1** something that indicates or acts as a token of a fact, condition, etc., that is not immediately or outwardly observable. **2** an action or gesture intended to convey information, a command, etc. **3a** a board, placard, etc., displayed in public and inscribed with words or designs intended to inform, warn, etc. **3b** (*as modifier*)*: a sign painter.* **4** an arbitrary or conventional mark or device that stands for a word, phrase, etc. **5** *Maths, logic.* **5a** any symbol indicating an operation: *a plus sign; an implication sign.* **5b** the positivity or negativity of a number, quantity, or expression: *subtraction from zero changes the sign of an expression.* **6** an indication or vestige: *the house showed no signs of being occupied.* **7** a portentous or significant event. **8** an indication, such as a scent or spoor, of the presence of an animal. **9** *Med.* any objective evidence of the presence of a disease or disorder. Compare **symptom** (sense 1). **10** *Astrology.* See **sign of the zodiac.** ♦ *vb* **11** to write (one's name) as a signature to (a document, etc.) in attestation, confirmation, ratification, etc. **12** (*intr;* often foll. by *to*) to make a sign; signal. **13** to engage or be engaged by written agreement, as a player for a team, etc. **14** (*tr*) to outline in gestures a sign over, esp. the sign of the cross. **15** (*tr*) to indicate by or as if by a sign; betoken. **16** (*intr*) to use sign language. ♦ See also **sign away, sign in, sign off, sign on, sign out, sign up.** [C13: from Old French *signe,* from Latin *signum* a sign] ► **'signable** *adj* ► **'signer** *n*

Signac (*French* siɲak) *n* **Paul** (pɔl). 1863–1935, French neoimpressionist painter, influenced by Seurat.

signage ('saɪnɪdʒ) *n* signs collectively, esp. street signs or signs giving directions.

signal ('sɪgnᵊl) *n* **1** any sign, gesture, token, etc., that serves to communicate information. **2** anything that acts as an incitement to action: *the rise in prices was a signal for rebellion.* **3a** a variable parameter, such as a current or electromagnetic wave, by which information is conveyed through an electronic circuit, communications system, etc. **3b** the information so conveyed. **3c** (*as modifier*)*: signal strength; a signal generator.* ♦ *adj* **4** distinguished or conspicuous. **5** used to give or act as a signal. ♦ *vb* **-nals, -nalling, -nalled** *or U.S.* **-nals, -naling, -naled. 6** to communicate (a message, etc.) to (a person). [C16: from Old French *seignal,* from Medieval Latin *signāle,* from Latin *signum* SIGN] ► **'signaller** *or U.S.* **'signaler** *n*

signal box *n* **1** a building containing manually operated signal levers for all the railway lines in its section. **2** a control point for a large area of a railway system, operated electrically and semiautomatically.

signal generator *n Electrical engineering.* an apparatus used to generate a signal consisting of a known oscillating voltage, usually between 1 microvolt and 1 volt, over a range of frequencies, to test electronic equipment.

signalize *or* **signalise** ('sɪgnə,laɪz) *vb* (*tr*) **1** to make noteworthy or conspicuous. **2** to point out carefully.

signally ('sɪgnəlɪ) *adv* conspicuously or especially.

signalman ('sɪgnᵊlmən) *n, pl* **-men. 1** a railway employee in charge of the signals and points within a section. **2** a man who sends and receives signals, esp. in the navy.

signalment ('sɪgnᵊlmənt) *n U.S.* a detailed description of a person, for identification or use in police records. [from French *signalement,* from *signaler* to distinguish]

signal-to-noise ratio *n* the ratio of one parameter, such as power of a wanted signal to the same parameter of the noise at a specified point in an electronic circuit, etc.

signatory ('sɪgnətərɪ, -trɪ) *n, pl* **-ries. 1** a person who has signed a document such as a treaty or contract or an organization, state, etc., on whose behalf such a document has been signed. ◆ *adj* **2** having signed a document, treaty, etc. [C17: from Latin *signātōrius* concerning sealing, from *signāre* to seal, from *signum* a mark]

signature ('sɪgnɪtʃə) *n* **1** the name of a person or a mark or sign representing his name, marked by himself or by an authorized deputy. **2** the act of signing one's name. **3** a distinctive mark, characteristic, etc., that identifies a person or thing. **4** *Music.* See **key signature, time signature. 5** *U.S.* the part of a medical prescription that instructs a patient how frequently and in what amounts he should take a drug or agent. Abbrevs.: **Sig., S. 6** *Printing.* **6a** a sheet of paper printed with several pages that upon folding will become a section or sections of a book. **6b** such a sheet so folded. **6c** a mark, esp. a letter, printed on the first page of a signature. [C16: from Old French, from Medieval Latin *signātūra,* from Latin *signāre* to sign]

signature tune *n Brit.* a melody used to introduce or identify a television or radio programme, a dance band, a performer, etc. Also called (esp. U.S. and Canadian): **theme song.**

sign away *vb (tr, adv)* to dispose of or lose by or as if by signing a document: *he signed away all his rights.*

signboard ('saɪn,bɔːd) *n* a board carrying a sign or notice, esp. one used to advertise a product, event, etc.

signed minor *n Maths.* another name for **cofactor.**

signed-ranks test *n Statistics.* See **Wilcoxon test.**

signet ('sɪgnɪt) *n* **1** a small seal, esp. one as part of a finger ring. **2** a seal used to stamp or authenticate documents. **3** the impression made by such a seal. ◆ *vb* **4** *(tr)* to stamp or authenticate with a signet. [C14: from Medieval Latin *signētum* a little seal, from Latin *signum* a SIGN]

signet ring *n* a finger ring bearing a signet.

significance (sɪg'nɪfɪkəns) *n* **1** consequence or importance. **2** something signified, expressed, or intended. **3** the state or quality of being significant. **4** *Statistics.* **4a** a measure of the confidence that can be placed in a result, esp. a substantive causal hypothesis, as not being merely a matter of chance. **4b** *(as modifier): a significance level.* Compare **confidence level.** See also **hypothesis testing.**

significance test *n Statistics.* (in hypothesis testing) a test of whether the alternative hypothesis achieves the predetermined significance level in order to be accepted in preference to the null hypothesis.

significant (sɪg'nɪfɪkənt) *adj* **1** having or expressing a meaning; indicative. **2** having a covert or implied meaning; suggestive. **3** important, notable, or momentous. **4** *Statistics.* of or relating to a difference between a result derived from a hypothesis and its observed value that is too large to be attributed to chance and that therefore tends to refute the hypothesis. [C16: from Latin *significāre* to SIGNIFY] ► **sig'nificantly** *adv*

significant figures *or esp. U.S.* **significant digits** *pl n* **1** the figures of a number that express a magnitude to a specified degree of accuracy, rounding up or down the final figure: *3.141 59 to four significant figures is 3.142.* **2** the number of such figures: *3.142 has four significant figures.* Compare **decimal place** (sense 2).

significant other *n U.S. informal.* a spouse or lover.

signification (,sɪgnɪfɪ'keɪʃən) *n* **1** something that is signified; meaning or sense. **2** the act of signifying.

significative (sɪg'nɪfɪkətɪv) *adj* **1** (of a sign, mark, etc.) symbolic. **2** another word for **significant.** ► **sig'nificatively** *adv* ► **sig'nificativeness** *n*

signify ('sɪgnɪ,faɪ) *vb* **-fies, -fying, -fied.** (when *tr, may take a clause as object*) **1** *(tr)* to indicate, show, or suggest. **2** *(tr)* to imply or portend: *the clouds signified the coming storm.* **3** *(tr)* to stand as a symbol, sign, etc. (for). **4** *(intr) Informal.* to be significant or important. [C13: from Old French *signifier,* from Latin *significāre,* from *signum* a sign, mark + *facere* to make] ► **'signi,fiable** *adj* ► **'signi,fier** *n*

sign in *vb (adv)* **1** to sign or cause to sign a register, as at a hotel, club, etc. **2** to make or become a member, as of a club.

signing ('saɪnɪŋ) *n* a specific set of manual signs used to communicate with deaf people.

sign language *n* **1** another word for **signing. 2** any system of communication by manual signs or gestures.

sign manual *n Law.* a person's signature in his own hand, esp. that of a sovereign on an official document.

sign off *vb (adv)* **1** *(intr)* to announce the end of a radio or television programme, esp. at the end of a day. **2** *(intr) Bridge.* to make a conventional bid indicating to one's partner that one wishes the bidding to stop. **3** *(tr)* to withdraw or retire from (an activity). **4** *(tr)* (of a doctor) to declare (someone) unfit for work, because of illness. **5** *(intr) Brit.* to terminate one's claim to unemployment benefit.

sign of the cross *n Chiefly R.C. Church.* a gesture in which the right hand is moved from the forehead to the breast and from the left shoulder to the right to describe the form of a cross in order to invoke the grace of Christ.

sign of the zodiac *n* any of the 12 equal areas, 30° wide, into which the zodiac can be divided, named after the 12 zodiacal constellations. In astrology, it is thought that a person's psychological type and attitudes to life can be correlated with the sign in which the sun lay at the moment of his birth, with the ascendant sign, and to a lesser extent with the signs in which other planets lay at this time. Also called: **sign, star sign, sun sign.** See also **planet** (sense 3), **house** (sense 9).

sign on *vb (adv)* **1** *(tr)* to hire or employ. **2** *(intr)* to commit oneself to a job, activity, etc. **3** *(intr) Brit.* to register as unemployed with the Department of Social Security.

signor *or* **signior** ('siːnjɔː; *Italian* siɲ'ɲor) *n, pl* **-gnors** *or* **-gnori** (*Italian* -'ɲori). an Italian man: usually used before a name as a title equivalent to *Mr.*

signora (siːn'jɔːrə; *Italian* siɲ'ɲora) *n, pl* **-ras** *or* **-re** (*Italian* -re). a married Italian woman: a title of address equivalent to *Mrs* when placed before a name or *madam* when used alone. [Italian, feminine of SIGNORE]

signore (siːn'jɔːriː; *Italian* siɲ'ɲore) *n, pl* **-ri** (-rɪ; *Italian* -ri). an Italian man: a title of respect equivalent to *sir* when used alone. [Italian, ultimately from Latin *senior* an elder, from *senex* an old man]

Signorelli (*Italian* siɲɲo'rɛlli) *n* **Luca** ('luːka). ?1441–1523, Italian painter, noted for his frescoes.

Signoret (*French* siɲɔrɛ) *n* **Simone** (simɔ̃), original name *Simone Kaminker.* 1921–85, French stage and film actress, whose films include *La Ronde* (1950), *Casque d'Or* (1952), *Room at the Top* (1958), and *Ship of Fools* (1965): married the actor and singer Yves Montand (1921–91).

signorina (,siːnjɔː'riːnə; *Italian* siɲɲo'rina) *n, pl* **-nas** *or* **-ne** (*Italian* -ne). an unmarried Italian woman: a title of address equivalent to *Miss* when placed before a name or *madam* or *miss* when used alone. [Italian, diminutive of SIGNORA]

signory ('siːnjərɪ) *n, pl* **-gnories.** a variant spelling of **seigniory.**

sign out *vb (adv)* to sign (one's name) to indicate that one is leaving a place: *he signed out for the evening.*

signpost ('saɪn,pəʊst) *n* **1** a post bearing a sign that shows the way, as at a roadside. **2** something that serves as a clue or indication; sign. ◆ *vb (tr; usually passive)* **3** to mark with signposts. **4** to indicate direction towards: *the camp site is signposted from the road.*

sign test *n* a statistical test used to analyse the direction of differences of scores between the same or matched pairs of subjects under two experimental conditions.

sign up *vb (adv)* to enlist or cause to enlist, as for military service.

Sigurd ('sɪgʊəd; *German* 'ziːgʊrt) *n Norse myth.* a hero who killed the dragon Fafnir to gain the treasure of Andvari, won Brynhild for Gunnar by deception, and then was killed by her when she discovered the fraud. His wife was Gudrun. German counterpart: **Siegfried.**

Sihanouk ('sɪənʊk) *n* King **Norodom** (,nɒrə'dɒm). born 1922, Cambodian statesman; king of Cambodia (1941–55 and from 1993); prime minister (1955–60), after which he became head of state. He was deposed in 1970 but reinstated (1975–76) following the victory of the Khmer Rouge in the civil war. He was head of state in exile from 1982; returned in 1991 to join peace negotiations and became monarch in 1993 under a new constitution.

sika ('siːkə) *n* a Japanese forest-dwelling deer, *Cervus nippon,* having a brown coat, spotted with white in summer, and a large white patch on the rump. [from Japanese *shika*]

Sikang ('ʃiː'kæŋ) *n* a former province of W China: established in 1928 from part of W Sichuan and E Tibet; dissolved in 1955.

Sikh (siːk) *n* **1** a member of an Indian religion that separated from Hinduism and was founded in the 16th century, that teaches monotheism and that has the Granth as its chief religious document, rejecting the authority of the Vedas. ◆ *adj* **2** of or relating to the Sikhs or their religious beliefs and customs. [C18: from Hindi, literally: disciple, from Sanskrit *śikṣati* he studies] ► **'Sikh,ism** *n*

Si Kiang ('ʃiː 'kjæŋ, kaɪ'æŋ) *n* See **Xi.**

Siking ('siː'kɪŋ) *n* a former name for **Xi An.**

Sikkim ('sɪkɪm) *n* a state of NE India: under British control (1861–1947); became an Indian protectorate in 1950 and an Indian state in 1975; lies in the Himalayas, rising to 8600 m (28 216 ft.) at Kanchenjunga in the north. Capital: Gangtok. Pop.: 444 000 (1994 est.). Area: 7096 sq. km (2740 sq. miles). ► **,Sikki'mese** *adj, n*

Sikorski (sɪ'kɔːskiː) *n* **Władysław** ('vlædɪslæf). 1881–1943, Polish general and statesman: prime minister (1922–23) and prime minister of the Polish government in exile during World War II: died in an air crash.

Sikorsky (sɪ'kɔːskɪ) *n* **Igor.** 1889–1972, U.S. aeronautical engineer, born in Russia. He designed and flew the first four-engined aircraft (1913) and designed the first successful helicopter (1939).

silage ('saɪlɪdʒ) *n* any crop harvested while green for fodder and kept succulent by partial fermentation in a silo. Also called: **ensilage.** [C19: alteration (influenced by SILO) of ENSILAGE]

Silastic (sɪ'læstɪk) *n Trademark.* a flexible inert silicone rubber, used esp. in prosthetic medicine.

sild (sɪld) *n* any of various small young herrings, esp. when prepared and canned in Norway. [Norwegian]

sile (saɪl) *vb (intr) Northern English dialect.* to pour with rain. [probably from Old Norse; compare Swedish and Norwegian dialect *sila* to pass through a strainer]

silence ('saɪləns) *n* **1** the state or quality of being silent. **2** the absence of sound or noise; stillness. **3** refusal or failure to speak, communicate, etc., when expected: *his silence on the subject of their promotion was alarming.* **4** a period of time without noise. **5** oblivion or obscurity. ◆ *vb (tr)* **6** to bring to silence. **7** to put a stop to; extinguish: *to silence all complaint.* [C13: via Old French from Latin *silentium,* from *silēre* to be quiet. See SILENT]

silenced ('saɪlənst) *adj* (of a clergyman) forbidden to preach or perform his clerical functions: *a silenced priest.*

silencer ('saɪlənsə) *n* **1** any device designed to reduce noise, esp. the tubular device containing baffle plates in the exhaust system of a motor vehicle. U.S. and Canadian name: **muffler. 2** a tubular device fitted to the muzzle of a firearm to deaden the report. **3** a person or thing that silences.

silene (saɪ'liːnɪ) *n* any plant of the large perennial genus *Silene,* with mostly red or pink flowers; many, esp. *S.* or *Agrostemma coeli-rosa,* are grown as garden plants: family *Carophyllaceae.* See also **campion.** [New Latin from Latin *silenus* viscaria]

silent ('saɪlənt) *adj* **1** characterized by an absence or near absence of noise or sound: *a silent house.* **2** tending to speak very little or not at all. **3** unable to speak. **4** failing to speak, communicate, etc., when expected: *the witness* *chose to remain silent.* **5** not spoken or expressed: *silent assent.* **6** not active or in operation: *a silent volcano.* **7** (of a letter) used in the conventional orthography of a word but no longer pronounced in that word: *the "k" in "know" is silent.* **8** denoting a film that has no accompanying soundtrack, esp. one made before 1927, when such soundtracks were developed. ♦ *n* **9** a silent film. [C16: from Latin *silēns,* from *silēre* to be quiet] ► **'silently** *adv* ► **'silentness** *n*

silent cop *n Austral. informal.* a small hemispherical traffic marker at an intersection.

silent majority *n* a presumed moderate majority of the citizens who are too passive to make their views known.

silent partner *n* another name (esp. U.S. and Canadian) for **sleeping partner.**

Silenus (saɪ'liːnəs) *n Greek myth.* **1** chief of the satyrs and foster father to Dionysus: often depicted riding drunkenly on a donkey. **2** (*often not cap.*) one of a class of woodland deities, closely similar to the satyrs.

silesia (saɪ'liːʃɪə) *n* a twill-weave fabric of cotton or other fibre, used esp. for pockets, linings, etc. [C17: Latinized form of German *Schlesien* SILESIA]

Silesia (saɪ'liːʃɪə) *n* a region of central Europe around the upper and middle Oder valley: mostly annexed by Prussia in 1742 but became almost wholly Polish in 1945; rich coal and iron-ore deposits. Polish name: **Śląsk.** Czech name: **Slezsko.** German name: **Schlesien.** ► **Si'lesian** *adj, n*

silex ('saɪlɛks) *n* a type of heat-resistant glass made from fused quartz. [C16: from Latin: hard stone, flint]

silhouette (ˌsɪluː'ɛt) *n* **1** the outline of a solid figure as cast by its shadow. **2** an outline drawing filled in with black, often a profile portrait cut out of black paper and mounted on a light ground. ♦ *vb* **3** (*tr*) to cause to appear in silhouette. [C18: named after Étienne de *Silhouette* (1709–67), French politician, perhaps referring to silhouettes as partial portraits, with a satirical allusion to Silhouette's brief career as controller general (1759)]

silica ('sɪlɪkə) *n* **1** the dioxide of silicon, occurring naturally as quartz, cristobalite, and tridymite. It is a refractory insoluble material used in the manufacture of glass, ceramics, and abrasives. **2** short for **silica glass.** [C19: New Latin, from Latin: SILEX]

silica gel *n* an amorphous form of silica capable of absorbing large quantities of water: used in drying gases and oils, as a carrier for catalysts and an anticaking agent for cosmetics.

silica glass *n* another name for **quartz glass.**

silicate ('sɪlɪkɪt, -ˌkeɪt) *n* a salt or ester of silicic acid, esp. one of a large number of usually insoluble salts with polymeric negative ions having a structure formed of tetrahedrons of SiO_4 groups linked in rings, chains, sheets, or three dimensional frameworks. Silicates constitute a large proportion of the earth's minerals and are present in cement and glass.

siliceous *or* **silicious** (sɪ'lɪʃəs) *adj* **1** of, relating to, or containing silica: *siliceous deposits; a siliceous clay.* **2** (of plants) growing in or needing soil rich in silica.

silici- *or before a vowel* **silic-** *combining form.* indicating silica or silicon: *silicify.*

silicic (sɪ'lɪsɪk) *adj* of, concerned with, or containing silicon or an acid obtained from silicon.

silicic acid *n* a white gelatinous substance obtained by adding an acid to a solution of sodium silicate. It has an ill-defined composition and is best regarded as hydrated silica, $SiO_2.nH_2O$.

silicide ('sɪlɪˌsaɪd) *n* any one of a class of binary compounds formed between silicon and certain metals.

siliciferous (ˌsɪlɪ'sɪfərəs) *adj* containing or yielding silicon or silica.

silicify (sɪ'lɪsɪˌfaɪ) *vb* **-fies, -fying, -fied.** to convert or be converted into silica: *silicified wood.* ► **siˌlicifi'cation** *n*

silicium (sɪ'lɪsɪəm) *n* a rare name for **silicon.**

silicle ('sɪlɪkᵊl), **silicula** (sɪ'lɪkjʊlə), *or* **silicule** ('sɪlɪˌkjuːl) *n Botany.* a short broad siliqua, occurring in such cruciferous plants as honesty and shepherd's-purse. [C18: from Latin *silicula* a small pod; see SILIQUA]

silicon ('sɪlɪkən) *n* **a** a brittle metalloid element that exists in two allotropic forms; occurs principally in sand, quartz, granite, feldspar, and clay. It is usually a grey crystalline solid but is also found as a brown amorphous powder. It is used in transistors, rectifiers, solar cells, and alloys. Its compounds are widely used in glass manufacture, the building industry, and in the form of silicones. Symbol: Si; atomic no.: 14; atomic wt.: 28.0855; valency: 4; relative density: 2.33; melting pt.: 1414°C; boiling pt.: 3267°C. **b** (*modifier*) (*sometimes cap.*) denoting an area of a country that contains a density of high-technology industry. [C19: from SILICA, on the model of *boron, carbon*]

silicon carbide *n* an extremely hard bluish-black insoluble crystalline substance produced by heating carbon with sand at a high temperature and used as an abrasive and refractory material. Silicon carbide whiskers have a high tensile strength and are used in composites; very pure crystals are used as semiconductors. Formula: SiC.

silicon chip *n* another term for **chip** (sense 8).

silicon-controlled rectifier *n* a semiconductor rectifier whose forward current between two electrodes, the anode and cathode, is initiated by means of a signal applied to a third electrode, the gate. The current subsequently becomes independent of the signal. It is a type of thyristor. Abbrev.: **SCR.**

silicone ('sɪlɪˌkəʊn) *n Chem.* **a** any of a large class of polymeric synthetic materials that usually have resistance to temperature, water, and chemicals, and good insulating and lubricating properties, making them suitable for wide use as oils, water-repellents, resins, etc. Chemically they have alternate silicon and oxygen atoms with the silicon atoms bound to organic groups. **b** (*as modifier*): *silicone rubber.* ♦ See also **siloxane.**

silicon rectifier *n Electronics.* a rectifier consisting of a semiconductor diode using crystalline silicon.

Silicon Valley *n* **1** an industrial strip in W California, extending S of San Francisco, in which the U.S. information technology industry is concentrated. **2** any area in which industries associated with information technology are concentrated.

silicosis (ˌsɪlɪ'kəʊsɪs) *n Pathol.* a form of pneumoconiosis caused by breathing in tiny particles of silica, quartz, or slate, and characterized by shortness of breath and fibrotic changes in the tissues of the lungs.

siliculose (sɪ'lɪkjʊˌləʊs, -ˌləʊz) *adj* (of certain cruciferous plants such as honesty) producing silicles. [C18: from New Latin *siliculōsus,* from *silicula* a SILICLE]

siliqua (sɪ'liːkwə, 'sɪlɪkwə) *or* **silique** (sɪ'liːk, 'sɪlɪk) *n, pl* **-liquae** (-'liːkwiː), **-liquas,** *or* **-liques.** the long dry dehiscent fruit of cruciferous plants, such as the wallflower, consisting of two compartments separated by a central septum to which the seeds are attached. [C18: via French from Latin *siliqua* a pod] ► **siliquaceous** (ˌsɪlɪ'kweɪʃəs) *adj* ► **siliquose** ('sɪlɪˌkwəʊs) *or* **siliquous** ('sɪlɪkwəs) *adj*

silk (sɪlk) *n* **1** the very fine soft lustrous fibre produced by a silkworm to make its cocoon. **2a** thread or fabric made from this fibre. **2b** (*as modifier*): *a silk dress.* **3** a garment made of this. **4** a very fine fibre produced by a spider to build its web, nest, or cocoon. **5** the tuft of long fine styles on an ear of maize. **6** *Brit.* **6a** the gown worn by a Queen's (or King's) Counsel. **6b** *Informal.* a Queen's (or King's) Counsel. **6c take silk.** to become a Queen's (or King's) Counsel. ♦ *vb* **7** (*intr*) *U.S. and Canadian.* (of maize) to develop long hairlike styles. [Old English *sioluc;* compare Old Norse *silki,* Greek *sērikon,* Korean *sir;* all ultimately from Chinese *ssŭ* silk] ► **'silkˌlike** *adj*

silkaline *or* **silkalene** (ˌsɪlkə'liːn) *n* a fine smooth cotton fabric used for linings, etc. [C20: from SILK + *-aline,* from *-oline* as in CRINOLINE]

silk cotton *n* another name for **kapok.**

silk-cotton tree *n* any of several tropical bombacaceous trees of the genus *Ceiba,* esp. *Ceiba pentandra,* having seeds covered with silky hairs from which kapok is obtained. Also called: **kapok tree.**

silken ('sɪlkən) *adj* **1** made of silk. **2** resembling silk in smoothness or gloss. **3** dressed in silk. **4** soft and delicate. **5** *Rare.* luxurious or elegant.

silk hat *n* a man's top hat covered with silk.

silkie ('sɪlkɪ) *or* **selkie** *n* a Scot. word for a **seal** (the animal). [from earlier Scot. *selich,* Old English *seolh*]

silk-screen printing *n* another name for **screen process.**

silkweed ('sɪlkˌwiːd) *n* another name for **milkweed** (sense 1). [C19: so called because the pods contain a silklike down]

silkworm ('sɪlkˌwɜːm) *n* **1** the larva of the Chinese moth *Bombyx mori,* that feeds on the leaves of the mulberry tree: widely cultivated as a source of silk. **2** any of various similar or related larvae. **3 silkworm moth.** the moth of any of these larvae.

silky ('sɪlkɪ) *adj* **silkier, silkiest. 1** resembling silk in texture; glossy. **2** made of silk. **3** (of a voice, manner, etc.) suave; smooth. **4** *Botany.* covered with long fine soft hairs: *silky leaves.* ► **'silkily** *adv* ► **'silkiness** *n*

silky oak *n* any of several trees of the Australian genus *Grevillea,* esp. *G. robusta,* having divided leaves and showy clusters of orange, red, or white flowers: cultivated in the tropics as shade trees: family *Proteaceae.*

sill (sɪl) *n* **1** a shelf at the bottom of a window inside a room. **2** a horizontal piece along the outside lower member of a window, that throws water clear of the wall below. **3** the lower horizontal member of a window or door frame. **4** a continuous horizontal member placed on top of a foundation wall in order to carry a timber framework. **5** a flat usually horizontal mass of igneous rock, situated between two layers of older sedimentary rock, that was formed by an intrusion of magma. [Old English *syll;* related to Old Norse *svill* sill, Icelandic *svoli* tree trunk, Old High German *swella* sill, Latin *solum* ground]

sillabub ('sɪləˌbʌb) *n* a variant spelling of **syllabub.**

Sillanpää (*Finnish* 'sillɑmpæː) *n* **Frans Eemil** (frans 'eːmil). 1888–1964, Finnish writer, noted for his novels *Meek Heritage* (1919) and *The Maid Silja* (1931): Nobel prize for literature 1939.

siller ('sɪlər) *Scot.* ♦ *n* **1** silver. **2** money. ♦ *adj* **3** silver. [a Scot. variant of SILVER]

sillimanite ('sɪlɪməˌnaɪt) *n* a white, brown, or green fibrous mineral that consists of aluminium silicate in orthorhombic crystalline form and occurs in metamorphic rocks. Formula: Al_2SiO_5. [C19: named after Benjamin *Silliman* (1779–1864), U.S. chemist]

Sillitoe ('sɪlɪtəʊ) *n* **Alan.** born 1928, British novelist. His best-known works include *Saturday Night and Sunday Morning* (1958) and *The Loneliness of the Long Distance Runner* (1959).

Sills (sɪlz) *n* **Beverley,** original name *Belle Silverman.* born 1929, U.S. soprano: director of the New York City Opera (1979–89).

silly ('sɪlɪ) *adj* **-lier, -liest. 1** lacking in good sense; absurd. **2** frivolous, trivial, or superficial. **3** feeble-minded. **4** dazed, as from a blow. **5** *Obsolete.* homely or humble. ♦ *n* **6** (*modifier*) *Cricket.* (of a fielding position) near the batsman's wicket: *silly mid-on.* **7** (*pl* **-lies**) Also called: **silly-billy.** *Informal.* a foolish person. [C15 (in the sense: pitiable, hence the later senses: foolish): from Old English *sǣlig* (unattested) happy, from *sǣl* happiness; related to Gothic *sēls* good] ► **'silliness** *n*

silly season *n Brit.* a period, usually during the hot summer months, when journalists fill space reporting on frivolous events and activities.

silo ('saɪləʊ) *n, pl* **-los. 1** a pit, trench, horizontal container, or tower, often cylindrical in shape, in which silage is made and stored. **2** a strengthened underground position in which missile systems are sited for protection against attack. [C19: from Spanish, perhaps from Celtic]

Siloam (saɪ'ləʊəm, sɪ-) *n Bible.* a pool in Jerusalem where Jesus cured a man of his blindness (John 9).

Silone (*Italian* si'lo:ne) *n* **Ignazio** (iɲ'ɲattsjo). 1900–78, Italian writer, noted for his humanitarian socialistic novels, *Fontamara* (1933) and *Bread and Wine* (1937).

siloxane (sɪ'lɒkseɪn) *n* any of a class of compounds containing alternate silicon and oxygen atoms with the silicon atoms bound to hydrogen atoms or organic groups. Many are highly complex polymers. See also **silicone.** **[C20:** from SIL(ICON) + OX(YGEN) + (METH)ANE**]**

silt (sɪlt) *n* **1** a fine deposit of mud, clay, etc., esp. one in a river or lake. ◆ *vb* **2** (usually foll. by *up*) to fill or become filled with silt; choke. **[C15:** of Scandinavian origin; compare Norwegian, Danish *sylt* salt marsh; related to Old High German *sulza* salt marsh; see SALT**]** ▸ **sil'tation** *n* ▸ **'silty** *adj*

siltstone ('sɪlt,stəʊn) *n* a variety of fine sandstone formed from consolidated silt.

Silures (saɪ'lʊəri:z) *pl n* a powerful and warlike tribe of ancient Britain, living chiefly in SE Wales, who fiercely resisted Roman invaders in the 1st century A.D.

Silurian (saɪ'lʊərɪən) *adj* **1** of, denoting, or formed in the third period of the Palaeozoic era, between the Ordovician and Devonian periods, which lasted for 40 million years, during which fishes first appeared. **2** of or relating to the Silures. ◆ *n* **3 the.** the Silurian period or rock system.

silurid (saɪ'lʊərɪd) *n* **1** any freshwater teleost fish of the Eurasian family *Siluridae,* including catfish, such as *Silurus glanis* (**European catfish**), that have an elongated body, naked skin, and a long anal fin. ◆ *adj* **2** of, relating to, or belonging to the family *Siluridae.* **[C19:** from Latin *silūrus,* from Greek *silouros* a river fish**]**

silva ('sɪlvə) *n* a variant spelling of **sylva.**

silvan ('sɪlvən) *adj* a variant spelling of **sylvan.**

Silvanus *or* **Sylvanus** (sɪl'veɪnəs) *n Roman myth.* the Roman god of woodlands, fields, and flocks. Greek counterpart: **Pan.** **[**Latin: from *silva* woodland**]**

silver ('sɪlvə) *n* **1a** a very ductile malleable brilliant greyish-white element having the highest electrical and thermal conductivity of any metal. It occurs free and in argentite and other ores: used in jewellery, tableware, coinage, electrical contacts, and in electroplating. Its compounds are used in photography. Symbol: Ag; atomic no.: 47; atomic wt.: 107.8682; valency: 1 or 2; relative density: 10.50; melting pt.: 961.93°C; boiling pt.: 2163°C. **1b** (*as modifier*): *a silver coin.* Related adj: **argent. 2** coin made of, or having the appearance of, this metal. **3** cutlery, whether made of silver or not. **4** any household articles made of silver. **5** *Photog.* any of a number of silver compounds used either as photosensitive substances in emulsions or as sensitizers. **6a** a brilliant or light greyish-white colour. **6b** (*as adj*): *silver hair.* **7** short for **silver medal.** ◆ *adj* **8** well-articulated: *silver speech.* **9** (*prenominal*) denoting the 25th in a series, esp. an annual series: *a silver wedding anniversary.* ◆ *vb* **10** (*tr*) to coat with silver or a silvery substance: *to silver a spoon.* **11** to become or cause to become silvery in colour. **[**Old English *siolfor;* related to Old Norse *silfr,* Gothic *silubr,* Old High German *silabar,* Old Slavonic *sirebro***]** ▸ **'silverer** *n* ▸ **'silvering** *n*

silver age *n* **1** (in Greek and Roman mythology) the second of the world's major epochs, inferior to the preceding golden age and characterized by opulence and irreligion. **2** the postclassical period of Latin literature, occupying the early part of the Roman imperial era, characterized by an overindulgence in elegance for its own sake and empty scholarly rhetoric.

silverback ('sɪlvə,bæk) *n* an older male gorilla with grey hair on its back.

silver beet *n* a variety of beet, *Beta vulgaris cicla,* having large firm green leaves: staple cooked green vegetable in Australia and New Zealand.

silver bell *n* any of various deciduous trees of the styracaceous genus *Halesia,* esp. *H. carolina,* of North America and China, having white bell-shaped flowers. Also called: **snowdrop tree.**

silver belly *n N.Z.* a freshwater eel.

silver birch *n* a betulaceous tree, *Betula pendula,* of N temperate regions of the Old World, having silvery-white peeling bark. See also **birch** (sense 1).

silver bromide *n* a yellowish insoluble powder that darkens when exposed to light: used in making photographic emulsions. Formula: AgBr.

silver certificate *n* (formerly) a banknote issued by the U.S. Treasury to the public and redeemable in silver.

silver chloride *n* a white insoluble powder that darkens on exposure to light because of the production of metallic silver: used in making photographic emulsions and papers. Formula: AgCl.

silver disc *n* (in Britain) an album certified to have sold 60 000 copies or a single certified to have sold 200 000 copies. Compare **gold disc, platinum disc.**

silver-eye *n Austral. and N.Z.* another name for **white-eye.**

silver fern *n N.Z.* **1** another name for **ponga. 2** a formalized spray of fern leaf, silver on a black background: the symbol of New Zealand sporting teams, esp. the All Blacks.

silver fir *n* any of various fir trees the leaves of which have a silvery undersurface, esp. *Abies alba,* an important timber tree of central and S Europe.

silverfish ('sɪlvə,fɪʃ) *n, pl* **-fish** *or* **-fishes. 1** a silver variety of the goldfish *Carassius auratus.* **2** any of various other silvery fishes, such as the moonfish *Monodactylus argenteus.* **3** any of various small primitive wingless insects of the genus *Lepisma,* esp. *L. saccharina,* that have long antennae and tail appendages and occur in buildings, feeding on food scraps, bookbindings, etc.: order *Thysanura* (bristletails).

silver fox *n* **1** an American red fox in a colour phase in which the fur is black with long silver-tipped hairs. **2** the valuable fur or pelt of this animal.

silver frost *n* another name for **glaze ice.**

silver-gilt *n* silver covered with a thin film of gold.

silverhorn ('sɪlvə,hɔ:n) *n* any of various usually darkish caddis flies of the family *Leptoceridae,* characterized by very long pale antennae. The larvae are a favourite food of trout.

silver iodide *n* a yellow insoluble powder that darkens on exposure to light: used in photography and artificial rainmaking. Formula: AgI.

silver lining *n* a comforting or hopeful aspect of an otherwise desperate or unhappy situation (esp. in the phrase **every cloud has a silver lining**).

silver maple *n* a North American maple tree, *Acer saccharinum,* having five-lobed leaves that are green above and silvery-white beneath.

silver medal *n* a medal of silver awarded to a competitor who comes second in a contest or race. Compare **gold medal, bronze medal.**

silvern ('sɪlvən) *adj Archaic or poetic.* silver.

silver nitrate *n* a white crystalline soluble poisonous substance used in making photographic emulsions, other silver salts, and as a medical antiseptic and astringent. Formula: $AgNO_3$. See also **lunar caustic.**

silver plate *n* **1** a thin layer of silver deposited on a base metal. **2** articles, esp. tableware, made of silver plate. ◆ *vb* **silver-plate. 3** (*tr*) to coat (a metal, object, etc.) with silver, as by electroplating.

silverpoint ('sɪlvə,pɔɪnt) *n* a drawing technique popular esp. in the 15th and 16th centuries, using an instrument with a silver wire tip on specially prepared paper.

silver screen *n* **the.** *Informal.* **1** films collectively or the film industry. **2** the screen onto which films are projected.

silver service *n* (in restaurants) a style of serving food using a spoon and fork in one hand like a pair of tongs.

silverside ('sɪlvə,saɪd) *n* **1** *Brit. and N.Z.* a coarse cut of beef below the aitchbone and above the leg. **2** Also called: **silversides.** any small marine or freshwater teleost fish of the family *Atherinidae,* related to the grey mullets: includes the jacksmelt.

silversmith ('sɪlvə,smɪθ) *n* a craftsman who makes or repairs articles of silver. ▸ **'silver,smithing** *n*

silver standard *n* a monetary system in which the legal unit of currency is defined with reference to silver of a specified fineness and weight and sometimes (esp. formerly) freely redeemable for it.

silvertail ('sɪlvə,teɪl) *n Austral. informal.* a rich and influential person.

silver thaw *n Canadian.* **1** a freezing rainstorm. **2** another name for **glitter** (sense 7).

silver-tongued *adj* persuasive; eloquent.

silverware ('sɪlvə,wɛə) *n* articles, esp. tableware, made of or plated with silver.

silverweed ('sɪlvə,wi:d) *n* **1** a rosaceous perennial creeping plant, *Potentilla anserina,* with silvery pinnate leaves and yellow flowers. **2** any of various convolvulaceous shrubs of the genus *Argyreia,* of SE Asia and Australia, having silvery leaves and purple flowers.

silvery ('sɪlvərɪ) *adj* **1** of or having the appearance of silver: *the silvery moon.* **2** containing or covered with silver. **3** having a clear ringing sound. ▸ **'silveriness** *n*

silver-Y moth *n* a brownish noctuid moth, *Plusia gamma,* having a light Y-shaped marking on each forewing; it migrates in large flocks. Often shortened to **silver-Y.**

silviculture ('sɪlvɪ,kʌltʃə) *n* the branch of forestry that is concerned with the cultivation of trees. **[C20:** *silvi-,* from Latin *silva* woodland + CULTURE**]** ▸ **,silvi'cultural** *adj* ▸ **,silvi'culturist** *n*

s'il vous plaît *French.* (sil vu plɛ) if you please; please.

sima ('saɪmə) *n* **1** the silicon-rich and magnesium-rich rocks of the earth's oceanic crust, the most abundant individual rock being basalt. **2** the earth's continental lower crust, probably comprised of gabbro rather than basalt. **[C20:** from SI(LICA) + MA(GNESIA)**]** ▸ **simatic** (saɪ'mætɪk) *adj*

Si-ma Qian ('si:mɑ: 'tʃɪən) *or* **Ssu-ma Ch'ien** *n* ?145–?85 B.C., Chinese historian, author of the *Shih-chi,* a history of China from earliest times to the 2nd century B.C., usually considered the greatest historical work in Chinese.

simar (sɪ'mɑ:) *n* a variant spelling of **cymar.**

simarouba *or* **simaruba** (,sɪmə'ru:bə) *n* **1** any tropical American tree of the genus *Simarouba,* esp. *S. amara,* having divided leaves and fleshy fruits: family *Simaroubaceae.* **2** the medicinal bark of any of these trees. **[C18:** from New Latin, from Carib *simaruba***]**

simaroubaceous *or* **simarubaceous** (,sɪmərU:'beɪʃəs) *adj* of, relating to, or belonging to the *Simaroubaceae,* a mainly tropical family of trees and shrubs that includes ailanthus, seringa, and quassia.

simba ('sɪmbə) *n* an E African word for **lion.** **[**Swahili**]**

Simbirsk (*Russian* sim'birsk) *n* a city in W central Russia on the River Volga: birthplace of Lenin (V. I. Ulyanov). Pop.: 678 000 (1995 est.). Former name (1924–91): **Ulyanovsk.**

Simchath Torah, Simhath Torah, *or* **Simchas Torah** (sim'xɑt tɔr'ɑ:, 'simxɑs 'tɑʊrə) *n* a Jewish festival celebrated immediately after Sukkoth on Tishri 23 (in Israel, Tishri 22) to mark the completion of the annual cycle of Torah readings and its immediate recommencement. **[**from Hebrew *śimḥath tōrāh,* literally: celebration of the Torah**]**

Simenon ('sɪmənɒn; *French* simnɔ̃) *n* **Georges** (ʒɔrʒ). 1903–89, Belgian novelist. He wrote over two hundred novels, including the detective series featuring Maigret.

Simeon ('sɪmɪən) *n* **1a** *Old Testament.* the second son of Jacob and Leah. **1b** the tribe descended from him. **1c** the territory once occupied by this tribe in the extreme south of the land of Canaan. **2** *New Testament.* a devout Jew, who recognized the infant Jesus as the Messiah and uttered the canticle *Nunc Dimittis* over him in the Temple (Luke 2:25–35).

Simeon Stylites (staɪ'laɪti:z) *n* **Saint.** ?390–459 A.D., Syrian monk, first of the ascetics who lived on pillars. Feast day: Jan. 5 or Sept. 1.

Simferopol (*Russian* simfɪ'rɔpəlj) *n* a city in the S Ukraine on the S Crimean Peninsula: a Scythian town in the 1st century B.C.; seized by the Russians in 1736. Pop.: 348 000 (1996 est.).

simian ('sɪmɪən) *adj* **1** Also (rarely): **simious** ('sɪmɪəs). of, relating to, or resembling a monkey or ape. ◆ *n* **2** a monkey or ape. [C17: from Latin *sīmia* an ape, probably from *sīmus* flat-nosed, from Greek *sīmos*]

similar ('sɪmɪlə) *adj* **1** showing resemblance in qualities, characteristics, or appearance; alike but not identical. **2** *Geometry.* (of two or more figures) having corresponding angles equal and all corresponding sides in the same ratio. Compare **congruent** (sense 2). **3** *Maths.* (of two classes) equinumerous. [C17: from Old French *similaire,* from Latin *similis*] ▸ **similarity** (ˌsɪmɪ'lærɪtɪ) *n* ▸ **'similarly** *adv*

USAGE *As* should not be used after *similar: Wilson held a similar position to Jones* (not *a similar position as Jones*)*; the system is similar to the one in France* (not *similar as in France*).

simile ('sɪmɪlɪ) *n* a figure of speech that expresses the resemblance of one thing to another of a different category, usually introduced by *as* or *like.* Compare **metaphor.** [C14: from Latin *simile* something similar, from *similis* like]

similitude (sɪ'mɪlɪˌtjuːd) *n* **1** likeness; similarity. **2** a thing or sometimes a person that is like or the counterpart of another. **3** *Archaic.* a simile, allegory, or parable. [C14: from Latin *similitūdō,* from *similis* like]

simitar ('sɪmɪtə) *n* a rare spelling of **scimitar.**

Simla ('sɪmlə) *n* a city in N India, capital of Himachal Pradesh state: summer capital of India (1865–1939); hill resort and health centre. Pop.: 109 860 (1991).

simmer ('sɪmə) *vb* **1** to cook (food) gently at or just below the boiling point. **2** (*intr*) to be about to break out in rage or excitement. ◆ *n* **3** the act, sound, or state of simmering. [C17: perhaps of imitative origin; compare German *summen* to hum]

simmer dim ('sɪmər, -mə) *n Scot.* the night-long twilight found in the Northern Isles around midsummer. [Scottish form of SUMMER[1] + DIM]

simmer down *vb* (*adv*) **1** (*intr*) *Informal.* to grow calmer or quieter, as after intense rage or excitement. **2** (*tr*) to reduce the volume of (a liquid) by boiling slowly.

simnel cake ('sɪmnᵊl) *n Brit.* a fruit cake, often coloured with saffron and covered with a layer of marzipan, traditionally eaten in Lent or at Easter. [C13 *simenel,* from Old French, from Latin *simila* fine flour, probably of Semitic origin; related to Greek *semidalis* fine flour]

Simon ('saɪmən) *n* **1** the original name of (Saint) **Peter. 2** *New Testament.* **2a** See **Simon Zelotes. 2b** a relative of Jesus, who may have been identical with Simon Zelotes (Matthew 13:55). **2c** Also called: **Simon the Tanner.** a Christian of Joppa with whom Peter stayed (Acts of the Apostles 9:43). **3 John (Allsebrook),** 1st Viscount Simon. 1873–1954, British statesman and lawyer. He was Liberal home secretary (1915–16) and, as a leader of the National Liberals, foreign secretary (1931–35), home secretary (1935–37), Chancellor of the Exchequer (1937–40), Lord Chancellor (1940–45). **4 (Marvin) Neil.** born 1927, U.S. dramatist and librettist, whose plays include *Barefoot in the Park* (1963), *California Suite* (1976), *Biloxi Blues* (1985), *Lost in Yonkers* (1990), and *London Suite* (1995): many have been made into films. **5 Paul.** born 1942, U.S. pop singer and songwriter. His albums include: with Art Garfunkel (born 1941), *The Sounds of Silence* (1966), and *Bridge over Troubled Water* (1970); and, solo, *Graceland* (1986), and *The Rhythm of the Saints* (1990).

simoniac (sɪ'məʊnɪˌæk) *n* a person who is guilty of practising simony. ▸ **simoniacal** (ˌsaɪmə'naɪəkᵊl) *adj* ▸ **ˌsimo'niacally** *adv*

Simonides (saɪ'mɒnɪˌdiːz) *n* ?556–?468 B.C., Greek lyric poet and epigrammatist, noted for his odes to victory.

Simon Magus *n New Testament.* a Samaritan sorcerer, probably from Gitta, of the 1st century A.D. After being converted to Christianity, he tried to buy miraculous powers from the apostles (Acts of the Apostles 8:9–24). He is also identified as the founder of a Gnostic sect.

Simon Peter *n New Testament.* the full name of the apostle Peter, a combination of his original name and the name given him by Christ (Matthew 16:17–18).

simon-pure *adj* real; genuine; authentic. [C19: from the phrase *the real Simon Pure,* name of a character in the play *A Bold Stroke for a Wife* (1717) by Susannah Centlivre (1669–1723) who is impersonated by another character in some scenes]

simony ('saɪmənɪ) *n Christianity.* the practice, now usually regarded as a sin, of buying or selling spiritual or Church benefits such as pardons, relics, etc., or preferments. [C13: from Old French *simonie,* from Late Latin *sīmōnia,* from the name of SIMON MAGUS] ▸ **'simonist** *n*

Simon Zelotes (zɪ'ləʊtiːz) *n* **Saint.** one of the 12 apostles, who had probably belonged to the Zealot party before becoming a Christian (Luke 6:15). Owing to a misinterpretation of two similar Aramaic words he is also, but mistakenly, called *the Canaanite* (Matthew 10:4). Feast day: Oct. 28 or May 10.

simoom (sɪ'muːm) *or* **simoon** (sɪ'muːn) *n* a strong suffocating sand-laden wind of the deserts of Arabia and North Africa. Also called: **samiel.** [from Arabic *samūm* poisonous, from *sam* poison, from Aramaic *sammā* poison]

simp (sɪmp) *n U.S. slang.* short for **simpleton.**

simpatico (sɪm'pɑːtɪˌkəʊ, -'pæt-) *adj Informal.* **1** pleasant or congenial. **2** of similar mind or temperament; compatible. [Italian: from *simpatia* SYMPATHY]

simper ('sɪmpə) *vb* **1** (*intr*) to smile coyly, affectedly, or in a silly self-conscious way. **2** (*tr*) to utter (something) in a simpering manner. ◆ *n* **3** a simpering smile; smirk. [C16: probably from Dutch *simper* affected] ▸ **'simperer** *n* ▸ **'simpering** *adj, n* ▸ **'simperingly** *adv*

simple ('sɪmpᵊl) *adj* **1** not involved or complicated; easy to understand or do: *a simple problem.* **2** plain; unadorned: *a simple dress.* **3** consisting of one element or part only; not combined or complex: *a simple mechanism.* **4** unaffected or unpretentious: *although he became famous, he remained a simple and well-liked man.* **5** not guileful; sincere; frank: *her simple explanation was readily accepted.* **6** of humble condition or rank: *the peasant was of simple birth.* **7** weak in intelligence; feeble-minded. **8** (*prenominal*) without additions or modifications; mere: *the witness told the simple truth.* **9** (*prenominal*) ordinary or straightforward: *a simple case of mumps.* **10** *Chem.* (of a substance or material) consisting of only one chemical compound rather than a mixture of compounds. **11** *Maths.* **11a** (of a fraction) containing only integers. **11b** (of an equation) containing variables to the first power only; linear. **11c** (of a root of an equation) occurring only once; not multiple. **12** *Biology.* not divided into parts: *a simple leaf; a simple eye.* **13** *Music.* relating to or denoting a time where the number of beats per bar may be two, three, or four. ◆ *n Archaic.* **14** a simpleton; fool. **15** a plant, esp. a herbaceous plant, having medicinal properties. [C13: via Old French from Latin *simplex* plain] ▸ **'simpleness** *n*

simple fraction *n* a fraction in which the numerator and denominator are both integers expressed as a ratio rather than a decimal. Also called: **common fraction, vulgar fraction.**

simple fracture *n* a fracture in which the broken bone does not pierce the skin. Also called: **closed fracture.** Compare **compound fracture.**

simple fruit *n* a fruit, such as a grape or cherry, that is formed from only one ovary.

simple harmonic motion *n* a form of periodic motion of a particle, etc., in which the acceleration is always directed towards some equilibrium point and is proportional to the displacement from this point. Abbrev.: **SHM.**

simple-hearted *adj* free from deceit; open; frank; sincere.

simple interest *n* interest calculated or paid on the principal alone. Compare **compound interest.**

simple machine *n* a simple device for altering the magnitude or direction of a force. The six basic types are the lever, wheel and axle, pulley, screw, wedge, and inclined plane.

simple microscope *n* a microscope having a single lens; magnifying glass. Compare **compound microscope.**

simple-minded *adj* **1** stupid; foolish; feeble-minded. **2** unsophisticated; artless. ▸ **ˌsimple-'mindedly** *adv* ▸ **ˌsimple-'mindedness** *n*

simple sentence *n* a sentence consisting of a single main clause. Compare **compound sentence, complex sentence.**

Simple Simon *n* a foolish man or boy; simpleton. [C20: after the name of a character in a nursery rhyme]

simple tense *n Grammar.* a tense of verbs, in English and other languages, not involving the use of an auxiliary verb in addition to the main verb, as for example the past *He drowned* as opposed to the future *He will drown.*

simpleton ('sɪmpᵊltən) *n* a foolish or ignorant person.

simplex ('sɪmplɛks) *adj* **1** permitting the transmission of signals in only one direction in a radio circuit, etc. Compare **duplex.** ◆ *n* **2** *Linguistics.* a simple not a compound word. **3** *Geom.* the most elementary geometric figure in Euclidean space of a given dimension; a line in one-dimensional space or a triangle in two-dimensional space. [C16: from Latin: simple, literally: one-fold, from *sim-* one + *plex,* from *plicāre* to fold; compare DUPLEX]

simplicidentate (ˌsɪmplɪsɪ'dɛnteɪt) *adj* **1** of, relating to, or belonging to the *Simplicidentata,* a former suborder including all the mammals now classified as rodents: used when lagomorphs were included in the order *Rodentia.* ◆ *n* **2** any animal of this type.

simplicity (sɪm'plɪsɪtɪ) *n* the quality or condition of being simple.

simplify ('sɪmplɪˌfaɪ) *vb* **-fies, -fying, -fied.** (*tr*) **1** to make less complicated, clearer, or easier. **2** *Maths.* to reduce (an equation, fraction, etc.) to its simplest form by cancellation of common factors, regrouping of terms in the same variable, etc. [C17: via French from Medieval Latin *simplificāre,* from Latin *simplus* simple + *facere* to make] ▸ **ˌsimplifi'cation** *n* ▸ **'simplificative** *adj* ▸ **'simpliˌfier** *n*

simplistic (sɪm'plɪstɪk) *adj* **1** characterized by extreme simplicity; naive. **2** oversimplifying complex problems; making unrealistically simple judgments or analyses. ▸ **'simplism** *n* ▸ **sim'plistically** *adv*

USAGE Since *simplistic* already has *too* as part of its meaning, it is tautologous to talk about something being *too simplistic* or *over-simplistic.*

Simplon Pass ('sɪmplɒn) *n* a pass over the Lepontine Alps in S Switzerland, between Brig (Switzerland) and Iselle (Italy). Height: 2009 m (6590 ft.).

simply ('sɪmplɪ) *adv* **1** in a simple manner. **2** merely; only. **3** absolutely; altogether; really: *a simply wonderful holiday.* ◆ *sentence modifier.* **4** frankly; candidly.

Simpson ('sɪmpsᵊn, 'sɪmsᵊn) *n* **1** Sir **James Young.** 1811–70, Scottish obstetrician, who pioneered the use of chloroform as an anaesthetic. **2 Wallis (Warfield)** ('wɒlɪs). See **Edward VIII.**

Simpson Desert ('sɪmpsən) *n* an uninhabited arid region in central Australia, mainly in the Northern Territory. Area: about 145 000 sq. km (56 000 sq. miles).

simul ('sɪməl) *n* a shortened form of **simultaneous** (sense 2).

simulacrum (ˌsɪmjʊ'leɪkrəm) *n, pl* **-cra** (-krə). *Archaic.* **1** any image or representation of something. **2** a slight, unreal, or vague semblance of something; superficial likeness. [C16: from Latin: likeness, from *simulāre* to imitate, from *similis* like]

simulant ('sɪmjʊlənt) *adj* **1** simulating. **2** (esp. of plant parts) resembling another part in structure or function.

simular ('sɪmjʊlə) *Archaic.* ◆ *n* **1** a person or thing that simulates or imitates; sham. ◆ *adj* **2** fake; simulated.

simulate *vb* ('sɪmjʊˌleɪt). (*tr*) **1** to make a pretence of; feign: *to simulate anxiety.* **2** to reproduce the conditions of (a situation, etc.), as in carrying out an experiment: *to simulate weightlessness.* **3** to assume or have the appearance of; imitate. ◆ *adj* ('sɪmjʊlɪt, -ˌleɪt). **4** *Archaic.* assumed or simulated. [C17: from Latin *simulāre* to copy, from *similis* like] ▸ **'simulative** *adj* ▸ **'simulatively** *adv*

simulated ('sɪmjʊˌleɪtɪd) *adj* **1** (of fur, leather, pearls, etc.) being an imitation of the genuine article, usually made from cheaper material. **2** (of actions, qualities, emotions, etc.) imitated; feigned.

simulation (ˌsɪmjʊˈleɪʃən) *n* **1** the act or an instance of simulating. **2** the assumption of a false appearance or form. **3** a representation of a problem, situation, etc., in mathematical terms, esp. using a computer. **4** *Maths, statistics, computing.* the construction of a mathematical model for some process, situation, etc., in order to estimate its characteristics or solve problems about it probabilistically in terms of the model. **5** *Psychiatry.* the conscious process of feigning illness in order to gain some particular end; malingering.

simulator (ˈsɪmjʊˌleɪtə) *n* **1** any device or system that simulates specific conditions or the characteristics of a real process for the purposes of research or operator training: *space simulator.* **2** a person who simulates.

simulcast (ˈsɪməlˌkɑːst) *vb* **1** (*tr*) to broadcast (a programme, etc.) simultaneously on radio and television. ◆ *n* **2** a programme, etc., so broadcast. [C20: from SIMUL(TANEOUS) + (BROAD)CAST]

simultaneous (ˌsɪməlˈteɪnɪəs; *U.S.* ˌsaɪməlˈteɪnɪəs) *adj* **1** occurring, existing, or operating at the same time; concurrent. ◆ *n* **2** *Chess.* a display in which one player plays a number of opponents at once, walking from board to board. Sometimes shortened to **simul.** [C17: formed on the model of INSTANTANEOUS from Latin *simul* at the same time, together] ▸ ˌ**simulˈtaneously** *adv* ▸ ˌ**simulˈtaneousness** *or* **simultaneity** (ˌsɪməltəˈniːɪtɪ; *U.S.* ˌsaɪməltəˈniːɪtɪ) *n*

simultaneous equations *pl n* a set of equations that are all satisfied by the same values of the variables, the number of variables being equal to the number of equations.

sin[1] (sɪn) *n* **1** *Theol.* **1a** transgression of God's known will or any principle or law regarded as embodying this. **1b** the condition of estrangement from God arising from such transgression. See also **actual sin, mortal sin, original sin, venial sin. 2** any serious offence, as against a religious or moral principle. **3** any offence against a principle or standard. **4 live in sin.** *Informal.* (of an unmarried couple) to live together. ◆ *vb* (*intr*) **sins, sinning, sinned. 5** *Theol.* to commit a sin. **6** (usually foll. by *against*) to commit an offence (against a person, principle, etc.). [Old English *synn;* related to Old Norse *synth,* Old High German *suntea* sin, Latin *sons* guilty] ▸ ˈ**sinner** *n*

sin[2] (sɪn) *prep, conj, adv* a Scot. dialect word for **since.**

sin[3] (siːn) *n* the 21st letter in the Hebrew alphabet (ש), transliterated as *S.*

sin[4] (saɪn) *Maths. abbrev. for* sine.

Sinai (ˈsaɪnaɪ) *n* **1** a mountainous peninsula of NE Egypt at the N end of the Red Sea, between the Gulf of Suez and the Gulf of Aqaba: occupied by Israel in 1967; fully restored by 1982. **2 Mount.** the mountain where Moses received the Law from God (Exodus 19–20): often identified as Jebel Musa, sometimes as Jebel Serbal, both on the S Sinai Peninsula. ▸ **Sinaitic** (ˌsaɪnɪˈɪtɪk) *or* **Sinaic** (sɪˈneɪɪk) *adj*

Sinaloa (ˌsiːnəˈləʊə, ˌsɪn-; *Spanish* sinaˈloa) *n* a state of W Mexico. Capital: Culiacán. Pop.: 2 424 745 (1995 est.). Area: 58 092 sq. km (22 425 sq. miles).

sinanthropus (sɪnˈænθrəpəs) *n* a primitive apelike man of the genus *Sinanthropus,* now considered a subspecies of *Homo erectus.* See also **Java man, Peking man.** [C20: from New Latin, from Late Latin *Sīnae* the Chinese + *-anthropus,* from Greek *anthrōpos* man]

sinapism (ˈsɪnəˌpɪzəm) *n* a technical name for **mustard plaster.** [C17: from Late Latin *sināpismus,* from Greek *sinapismos* application of mustard plaster, from *sinapi* mustard, of Egyptian origin]

Sinarquist (ˈsɪnɑːkɪst, -kwɪst) *n* (in Mexico) a member of a fascist movement in the 1930s and 1940s having links with the Nazis and the Falangists: hostile towards the U.S., Communism, Jews, organized labour, etc. [C20: Mexican Spanish *sinarquista,* from Spanish *sin* without + *anarquista* anarchist] ▸ ˈ**Sinarquism** *n*

Sinatra (sɪˈnɑːtrə) *n* **Francis Albert,** known as *Frank.* 1915–98, U.S. popular singer and film actor. His recordings include "One for My Baby (and One More for the Road)" (1955) and "My Way" (1969).

sin bin *n* **1** *Slang.* (in ice hockey, etc.) an area off the field of play where a player who has committed a foul can be sent to sit for a specified period. **2** *Brit. informal.* a special unit on a separate site from a school that disruptive schoolchildren attend until they can be reintegrated into their normal classes.

since (sɪns) *prep* **1** during or throughout the period of time after: *since May it has only rained once.* ◆ *conj* (*subordinating*) **2** (sometimes preceded by *ever*) continuously from or starting from the time when: *since we last met, important things have happened.* **3** seeing that; because: *since you have no money, you can't come.* ◆ *adv* **4** since that time: *he left yesterday and I haven't seen him since.* [Old English *sīththan,* literally: after that; related to Old High German *sīd* since, Latin *sērus* late]

USAGE See at **ago.**

sincere (sɪnˈsɪə) *adj* **1** not hypocritical or deceitful; open; genuine: *a sincere person; sincere regret.* **2** *Archaic.* pure; unadulterated; unmixed. **3** *Obsolete.* sound; whole. [C16: from Latin *sincērus*] ▸ **sinˈcerely** *adv* ▸ **sincerity** (sɪnˈserɪtɪ) *or* **sinˈcereness** *n*

sinciput (ˈsɪnsɪˌpʌt) *n, pl* **sinciputs** *or* **sincipita** (sɪnˈsɪpɪtə). *Anatomy.* the forward upper part of the skull. [C16: from Latin: half a head, from SEMI- + *caput* head] ▸ **sinˈcipital** *adj*

Sinclair (sɪŋˈklɛə, ˈsɪŋklɛə) *n* **1** Sir **Clive (Marles).** born 1940, British electronics engineer, inventor, and entrepreneur, who produced such electronic goods as pocket calculators and some of the first home computers; however, the Sinclair C5, a small light electric vehicle for one person, proved a commercial failure. **2 Upton (Beall).** 1878–1968, U.S. novelist, whose *The Jungle* (1906) exposed the working and sanitary conditions of the Chicago meat-packing industry and prompted the passage of food inspection laws.

Sind (sɪnd) *n* a province of SE Pakistan, mainly in the lower Indus valley: formerly a province of British India; became a province of Pakistan in 1947; divided in 1955 between Hyderabad and Khairpur; reunited as a province in 1970. Capital: Karachi. Pop.: 21 682 000 (1985 est.). Area: 140 914 sq. km (54 407 sq. miles).

Sindhi (ˈsɪndɪ) *n* **1** (*pl* **-dhi** *or* **-dhis**) a former inhabitant of Sind. The Muslim majority now lives in Pakistan while the Hindu minority has mostly moved to India. **2** the language of this people, belonging to the Indic branch of the Indo-European family.

sine[1] (saɪn) *n* (of an angle) **a** a trigonometric function that in a right-angled triangle is the ratio of the length of the opposite side to that of the hypotenuse. **b** a function that in a circle centred at the origin of a Cartesian coordinate system is the ratio of the ordinate of a point on the circumference to the radius of the circle. Abbrev.: **sin.** [C16: from Latin *sinus* a bend; in New Latin, *sinus* was mistaken as a translation of Arabic *jiba* sine (from Sanskrit *jīva,* literally: bowstring) because of confusion with Arabic *jaib* curve]

sine[2] (ˈsaɪnɪ) *prep* (esp. in Latin phrases or legal terms) lacking; without.

sinecure (ˈsaɪnɪˌkjʊə) *n* **1** a paid office or post involving minimal duties. **2** a Church benefice to which no spiritual or pastoral charge is attached. [C17: from Medieval Latin phrase (*beneficium*) *sine cūrā* (benefice) without cure (of souls), from Latin *sine* without + *cūra* cure, care] ▸ ˈ**sineˌcurism** *n* ▸ ˈ**sineˌcurist** *n*

sine curve *n* a curve of the equation $y = \sin x$. Also called: **sinusoid.**

sine die *Latin.* (ˈsaɪnɪ ˈdaɪɪ) *adv, adj* without a day fixed: *an adjournment sine die.* [literally: without a day]

sine prole *Latin.* (ˈsaɪnɪ ˈprəʊlɪ) *adj, adv Law.* without issue (esp. in the phrase ***demisit sine prole*** (died without issue)).

sine qua non *Latin.* (ˈsaɪnɪ kweɪ ˈnɒn) *n* an essential condition or requirement. [literally: without which not]

sinew (ˈsɪnjuː) *n* **1** *Anatomy.* another name for **tendon. 2** (*often pl*) **2a** a source of strength or power. **2b** a literary word for **muscle.** [Old English *sionu;* related to Old Norse *sin,* Old Saxon *sinewa,* Old High German *senawa* sinew, Lettish *pasainis* string] ▸ ˈ**sinewless** *adj*

sine wave *n* any oscillation, such as a sound wave or alternating current, whose waveform is that of a sine curve.

sinewy (ˈsɪnjʊɪ) *adj* **1** consisting of or resembling a tendon or tendons. **2** muscular; brawny. **3** (esp. of language, style, etc.) vigorous; forceful. **4** (of meat, etc.) tough; stringy. ▸ ˈ**sinewiness** *n*

sinfonia (ˌsɪnfəˈnɪə) *n, pl* **-nie** (-ˈniːeɪ). **1** another word for **symphony** (senses 2, 3). **2** (*cap. when part of a name*) a symphony orchestra. [Italian]

sinfonietta (ˌsɪnfənˈjɛtə, -fəʊn-) *n* **1** a short or light symphony. **2** (*cap. when part of name*) a small symphony orchestra. [Italian: a little symphony, from SINFONIA]

sinful (ˈsɪnfʊl) *adj* **1** having committed or tending to commit sin: *a sinful person.* **2** characterized by or being a sin: *a sinful act.* ▸ ˈ**sinfully** *adv* ▸ ˈ**sinfulness** *n*

sing (sɪŋ) *vb* **sings, singing, sang, sung. 1** to produce or articulate (sounds, words, a song, etc.) with definite and usually specific musical intonation. **2** (when *intr,* often foll. by *to*) to perform (a song) to the accompaniment (of): *to sing to a guitar.* **3** (*intr;* foll. by *of*) to tell a story or tale in song (about): *I sing of a maiden.* **4** (*intr;* foll. by *to*) to address a song (to) or perform a song (for). **5** (*intr*) to perform songs for a living, as a professional singer. **6** (*intr*) (esp. of certain birds and insects) to utter calls or sounds reminiscent of music. **7** (when *intr,* usually foll. by *of*) to tell (something) or give praise (to someone), esp. in verse: *the poet who sings of the Trojan dead.* **8** (*intr*) to make a whining, ringing, or whistling sound: *the kettle is singing; the arrow sang past his ear.* **9** (*intr*) (of the ears) to experience a continuous ringing or humming sound. **10** (*tr*) (esp. in church services) to chant or intone (a prayer, psalm, etc.). **11** (*tr*) to bring to a given state by singing: *to sing a child to sleep.* **12** (*intr*) *Slang, chiefly U.S.* to confess or act as an informer. **13** (*intr*) *Austral.* (in Aboriginal witchcraft) to bring about a person's death by incantation. The same power can sometimes be used beneficently. ◆ *n* **14** *Informal.* an act or performance of singing. **15** a ringing or whizzing sound, as of bullets. ◆ See also **sing along, sing out.** [Old English *singan;* related to Old Norse *syngja* to sing, Gothic *siggwan,* Old High German *singan*] ▸ ˈ**singable** *adj* ▸ ˈ**singing** *adj, n*

USAGE See at **ring**[2].

sing. *abbrev. for* singular.

sing along *vb* (*intr, adv*) **1** to join in singing with a performer. ◆ *n* **sing-along. 2** such a singsong.

Singapore (ˌsɪŋəˈpɔː, ˌsɪŋgə-) *n* **1** a republic in SE Asia, occupying one main island and about 58 small islands at the S end of the Malay Peninsula: established as a British trading post in 1819 and became part of the Straits Settlements in 1826; occupied by the Japanese (1942–45); a British colony from 1946, becoming self-governing in 1959; part of the Federation of Malaysia from 1963 to 1965, when it became an independent republic (within the Commonwealth). Official languages: Chinese, Malay, English, and Tamil. Religion: Buddhist, Taoist, traditional beliefs, and Muslim. Currency: Singapore dollar. Capital: Singapore. Pop.: 3 164 000 (1998 est.). Area: 646 sq. km (250 sq. miles). **2** the capital of the republic of Singapore: a major international port; administratively not treated as a city. ▸ ˌ**Singaˈporean** *adj, n*

singe (sɪndʒ) *vb* **singes, singeing, singed. 1** to burn or be burnt superficially; scorch: *to singe one's clothes.* **2** (*tr*) to burn the ends of (hair, etc.). **3** (*tr*) to expose (a carcass) to flame to remove bristles or hair. ◆ *n* **4** a superficial burn. [Old English *sengan;* related to Middle High German *sengen* to singe, Dutch *sengel* spark, Norwegian *sengla* to smell of burning, Swedish *sjängla* to singe, Icelandic *sāngr*]

singer (ˈsɪŋə) *n* **1** a person who sings, esp. one who earns a living by singing. **2** a singing bird. **3** an obsolete word for **poet.**

Singer (ˈsɪŋə) *n* **1 Isaac Bashevis.** 1904–91, U.S. writer of Yiddish novels and short stories; born in Poland. His works include *Satan in Goray* (1935), *The Family Moscat* (1950), the autobiographical *In my Father's Court* (1966), and

The King of the Fields (1989): Nobel prize for literature 1978. **2 Isaac Merrit.** 1811–75, U.S. inventor, who originated and developed an improved chain-stitch sewing machine (1852).

singer-songwriter *n* a performer who writes his or her own songs.

Singh (sɪŋ) *n* a title assumed by a Sikh when he becomes a full member of the community. [from Hindi, from Sanskrit *sinhá* a lion]

Singhalese (ˌsɪŋəˈliːz) *n, pl* **-leses** *or* **-lese**, *adj* a variant spelling of **Sinalese.**

singing hinny *n* a type of currant cake popular in NE England which, when cooked on a griddle, makes a singing noise. [*hinny* Scottish and N English variant of HONEY]

singing telegram *n* a greetings service in which a person is employed to present greetings by singing to the person celebrating.

single (ˈsɪŋɡᵊl) *adj* (*usually prenominal*) **1** existing alone; solitary: *upon the hill stood a single tower.* **2** distinct from other things; unique or individual. **3** composed of one part. **4** designed for one user: *a single room; a single bed.* **5** (*also postpositive*) unmarried. **6** connected with the condition of being unmarried: *he led a single life.* **7** (esp. of combat) involving two individuals; one against one. **8** sufficient for one person or thing only: *a single portion of food.* **9** even one: *there wasn't a single person on the beach.* **10** (of a flower) having only one set or whorl of petals. **11** determined; single-minded: *a single devotion to duty.* **12** (of the eye) seeing correctly: *to consider something with a single eye.* **13** *Rare.* honest or sincere; genuine. **14** *Archaic.* (of ale, beer, etc.) mild in strength. ◆ *n* **15** something forming one individual unit. **16** an unmarried person. **17** a gramophone record, CD, or cassette with a short recording, usually of pop music, on it. **18** *Golf.* a game between two players. **19** *Cricket.* a hit from which one run is scored. **20a** *Brit.* a pound note. **20b** *U.S. and Canadian.* a dollar note. **21** See **single ticket.** ◆ *vb* **22** (*tr*; usually foll. by *out*) to select from a group of people or things; distinguish by separation: *he singled him out for special mention.* **23** (*tr*) to thin out (seedlings). **24** short for **single-foot.** ◆ See also **singles.** [C14: from Old French *sengle,* from Latin *singulus* individual] ▸ **ˈsingleness** *n*

single-acting *adj* (of a reciprocating engine or pump) having a piston or pistons that are pressurized on one side only. Compare **double-acting** (sense 1).

single-action *n* (*modifier*) (of a firearm) requiring the hammer to be cocked by hand before firing.

single-blind *adj* of or relating to an experiment, esp. one to discover people's reactions to certain commodities, drugs, etc., in which the experimenters but not the subjects know the particulars of the test items during the experiment. Compare **double-blind.**

single bond *n Chem.* a covalent bond formed between two atoms by the sharing of one pair of electrons.

single-breasted *adj* (of a garment) having the fronts overlapping only slightly and with one row of fastenings.

single-cell protein *n* protein that is produced by micro-organisms fermenting in liquid or gaseous petroleum fractions or other organic substances: used as a food supplement. Abbrev.: **SCP.**

single cream *n* cream having a low fat content that does not thicken with beating.

single-cross *n Genetics.* a hybrid of the first generation between two inbred lines.

single-cut file *n* a file with teeth in one direction only: used for filing soft material.

single-decker *n Brit. informal.* a bus with only one passenger deck.

single density *n Computing.* a disk with the normal capacity for storage.

single-end *n Scot. dialect.* accommodation consisting of a single room.

single-ended *adj Electronics.* (of an amplifier) having one side of the input and one side of the output connected to earth: used for an unbalanced signal.

single entry *n* **a** a simple book-keeping system in which transactions are entered in one account only. Compare **double entry. b** (*as modifier*): *a single-entry account.*

single file *n* a line of persons, animals, or things ranged one behind the other, either stationary or moving.

single-foot *n* **1** a rapid showy gait of a horse in which each foot strikes the ground separately, as in a walk. ◆ *vb* **2** to move or cause to move at this gait.

single-handed *adj, adv* **1** unaided or working alone: *a single-handed crossing of the Atlantic.* **2** having or operated by one hand or one person only. ▸ **ˌsingle-ˈhandedly** *adv* ▸ **ˌsingle-ˈhandedness** *n*

single-lens reflex *n* See **reflex camera.**

single market *n* a market consisting of a number of nations, esp. those of the European Union, in which goods, capital, and currencies can move freely across borders without tariffs or restrictions.

single-minded *adj* having but one aim or purpose; dedicated. ▸ **ˌsingle-ˈmindedly** *adv* ▸ **ˌsingle-ˈmindedness** *n*

single parent *n* **a** a person who has a dependent child or dependent children and who is widowed, divorced, or unmarried. **b** (*as modifier*): *a single-parent family.* Also called (N.Z.): **solo parent.**

single-phase *adj* (of a system, circuit, or device) having, generating, or using a single alternating voltage.

singles (ˈsɪŋɡᵊlz) *pl n Tennis, etc.* a match played with one person on each side.

singles bar *n* a bar or club that is a social meeting place for single people.

single-sex *adj* (of schools, etc.) admitting members of one sex only; not coeducational.

single sideband transmission *n* a method of transmitting radio waves in which either the upper or the lower sideband is transmitted, the carrier being either wholly or partially suppressed. This reduces the required bandwidth and improves the signal-to-noise ratio. Abbrev.: **SSB.**

single-space *vb* (*tr*) to type (copy) without leaving a space between the lines.

single-step *vb* **-steps, -stepping, -stepped.** (*tr*) *Computing.* to perform a single instruction on (a program), generally under the control of a debug program.

singlestick (ˈsɪŋɡᵊlˌstɪk) *n* **1** a wooden stick used instead of a sword for fencing. **2** fencing with such a stick. **3** any short heavy stick.

singlet (ˈsɪŋɡlɪt) *n* **1** *Chiefly Brit.* a man's sleeveless undergarment covering the body from the shoulders to the hips. **2** the Austral. name for **vest** (senses 1 and 2). **3** *Chiefly Brit.* a garment worn with shorts by athletes, boxers, etc. **4** *N.Z.* a black woollen outer garment worn by bushmen. **5** *Physics.* a multiplet that has only one member. **6** *Chem.* a chemical bond consisting of one electron. [C18: from SINGLE, on the model of *doublet*]

single tax *n U.S.* **1** a taxation system in which a tax on one commodity, usually land, is the only source of revenue. **2** such a tax.

single thread *n Computing.* the execution of an entire task from beginning to end without interruption.

single ticket *n Brit.* a ticket entitling a passenger to travel only to his destination, without returning. U.S. and Canadian equivalent: **one-way ticket.** Compare **return ticket.**

singleton (ˈsɪŋɡᵊltən) *n* **1** *Bridge, etc.* an original holding of one card only in a suit. **2** a single object, individual, etc., separated or distinguished from a pair or group. **3** *Maths.* a set containing only one member. [C19: from SINGLE, on the model of SIMPLETON]

single-tongue *vb Music.* to play (any nonlegato passage) on a wind instrument by obstructing and uncovering the air passage through the lips with the tongue. Compare **double-tongue, triple-tongue.** ▸ **single tonguing** *n*

single-track *adj* **1** (of a railway) having only a single pair of lines, so that trains can travel in only one direction at a time. **2** (of a road) only wide enough for one vehicle. **3** able to think about only one thing; one-track.

Single Transferable Vote *n* (*modifier*) of or relating to a system of voting in which voters list the candidates in order of preference. Any candidate achieving a predetermined proportion of the votes in a constituency is elected. Votes exceeding this amount and those cast for the bottom candidate are redistributed according to the stated preferences. Redistribution continues until all the seats are filled. Abbrev.: **STV.** See **proportional representation.**

singletree (ˈsɪŋɡᵊlˌtriː) *n* a variant, esp. U.S. and Austral., of **swingletree.**

singly (ˈsɪŋɡlɪ) *adv* **1** one at a time; one by one. **2** apart from others; separately; alone.

sing out *vb* (*tr, adv*) to call out in a loud voice; shout.

Sing Sing *n* a prison in New York State, in Ossining. [variant of *Ossining*]

singsong (ˈsɪŋˌsɒŋ) *n* **1** an accent, metre, or intonation that is characterized by an alternately rising and falling rhythm, as in a person's voice, piece of verse, etc. **2** *Brit.* an informal session of singing, esp. of popular or traditional songs. ◆ *adj* **3** having a regular or monotonous rising and falling rhythm: *a singsong accent.*

Singspiel *German.* (ˈzɪŋʃpiːl) *n* a type of comic opera in German with spoken dialogue, popular during the late 18th and early 19th centuries. [literally: singing play]

singular (ˈsɪŋɡjʊlə) *adj* **1** remarkable; exceptional; extraordinary: *a singular feat.* **2** unusual; odd: *a singular character.* **3** unique. **4** denoting a word or an inflected form of a word indicating that not more than one referent is being referred to or described. **5** *Logic.* of or referring to a specific thing or person as opposed to something general. ◆ *n* **6** *Grammar.* **6a** the singular number. **6b** a singular form of a word. [C14: from Latin *singulāris* SINGLE] ▸ **ˈsingularly** *adv* ▸ **ˈsingularness** *n*

singularity (ˌsɪŋɡjʊˈlærɪtɪ) *n, pl* **-ties. 1** the state, fact, or quality of being singular. **2** something distinguishing a person or thing from others. **3** something remarkable or unusual. **4** *Maths.* **4a** a point at which a function is not differentiable although it is differentiable in a neighbourhood of that point. See also **pole**[2] (sense 4). **4b** another word for **discontinuity. 5** *Astronomy.* a hypothetical point in space-time at which matter is infinitely compressed to infinitesimal volume.

singularize *or* **singularise** (ˈsɪŋɡjʊləˌraɪz) *vb* (*tr*) **1** to make (a word, etc.) singular. **2** to make conspicuous. ▸ **ˌsingulariˈzation** *or* **ˌsingulariˈsation** *n*

singulary (ˈsɪŋɡjʊlərɪ) *adj Logic, maths.* (of an operator) monadic.

singultus (sɪŋˈɡʌltəs) *n* a technical name for **hiccup.** [C18: from Latin, literally: a sob]

sinh (ʃaɪn, sɪnʃ) *n* hyperbolic sine; a hyperbolic function, $\sinh z = \frac{1}{2}(e^z - e^{-z})$, related to sine by the expression $\sinh iz = i \sin z$, where $i = \sqrt{-1}$. [C20: from SIN(E)[1] + H(YPERBOLIC)]

Sinhailien (ˈʃɪnˈhaɪˈljen) *n* a variant transliteration of the Chinese name for **Lianyungang.**

Sinhalese (ˌsɪnhəˈliːz) *or* **Singhalese** *n* **1** (*pl* **-leses** *or* **-lese**) a member of a people living chiefly in Sri Lanka, where they constitute the majority of the population. **2** the language of this people, belonging to the Indic branch of the Indo-European family: the official language of Sri Lanka. It is written in a script of Indian origin. ◆ *adj* **3** of or relating to this people or their language.

Sinicism (ˈsaɪnɪˌsɪzəm, ˈsɪn-) *n Rare.* a Chinese custom or idiom. [C19: from Medieval Latin *Sinicus* Chinese, from Late Latin *Sīnae* the Chinese, from Greek *Sinai,* from Arabic *Sīn* China]

Sining (ˈʃiːˈnɪŋ) *n* variant transliteration of the Chinese name for **Xining.**

sinister (ˈsɪnɪstə) *adj* **1** threatening or suggesting evil or harm; ominous: *a sinister glance.* **2** evil or treacherous, esp. in a mysterious way. **3** (*usually postpositive*) *Heraldry.* of, on, or starting from the left side from the bearer's point of view and therefore on the spectator's right. **4** *Archaic.* located on the left side. **5** *Archaic.* (of signs, omens, etc.) unfavourable. ◆ Compare **dexter**[1]. [C15: from Latin *sinister* on the left-hand side, considered by Roman augurs to be the unlucky one] ▸ **ˈsinisterly** *adv* ▸ **ˈsinisterness** *n*

sinistral (ˈsɪnɪstrəl) *adj* **1** of, relating to, or located on the left side, esp. the left side of the body. **2** a technical term for **left-handed. 3** (of the shells of certain gastropod molluscs) coiling in a clockwise direction from the apex. ◆ Compare **dextral.** [C15 (in the obsolete sense: adverse, evil); C19 (in current senses): from Medieval Latin *sinistrālis.* See SINISTER] ▸ 'sinistrally *adv*

sinistrodextral (ˌsɪnɪstrəʊ'dɛkstrəl) *adj* going or directed from left to right: *a sinistrodextral script.* [See SINISTER, DEXTER[1]]

sinistrorse ('sɪnɪˌstrɔːs, ˌsɪnɪ'strɔːs) *adj* (of some climbing plants) growing upwards in a spiral from right to left, or clockwise. Compare **dextrorse.** [C19: from Latin *sinistrōrsus* turned towards the left, from *sinister* on the left + *vertere* to turn] ▸ ˌsinis'trorsal *adj* ▸ 'sinisˌtrorsely *adv*

sinistrous ('sɪnɪstrəs) *adj Archaic.* **1** sinister or ill-omened. **2** sinistral. ▸ 'sinistrously *adv*

Sinitic (sɪ'nɪtɪk) *n* **1** a branch of the Sino-Tibetan family of languages, consisting of the various languages or dialects of Chinese. Compare **Tibeto-Burman.** ◆ *adj* **2** belonging or relating to this group of languages.

sink (sɪŋk) *vb* **sinks, sinking, sank; sunk** *or* **sunken. 1** to descend or cause to descend, esp. beneath the surface of a liquid or soft substance. **2** (*intr*) to appear to move down towards or descend below the horizon. **3** (*intr*) to slope downwards; dip. **4** (*intr; often foll. by in or into*) to pass into or gradually enter a specified lower state or condition: *to sink into apathy.* **5** to make or become lower in volume, pitch, etc. **6** to make or become lower in value, price, etc. **7** (*intr*) to become weaker in health, strength, etc. **8** to decline or cause to decline in moral value, worth, etc. **9** (*intr*) to seep or penetrate. **10** (*tr*) to suppress or conceal: *he sank his worries in drink.* **11** (*tr*) to dig, cut, drill, bore, or excavate (a hole, shaft, etc.). **12** (*tr*) to drive into the ground: *to sink a stake.* **13** (*tr; usually foll. by in or into*) **13a** to invest (money). **13b** to lose (money) in an unwise or unfortunate investment. **14** (*tr*) to pay (a debt). **15** (*intr*) to become hollow; cave in: *his cheeks had sunk during his illness.* **16** (*tr*) to hit, throw, or propel (a ball) into a hole, basket, pocket, etc.: *he sank a 15-foot putt.* **17** (*tr*) *Brit. informal.* to drink, esp. quickly: *he sank three pints in half an hour.* **18 sink or swim.** to take risks where the alternatives are loss and failure or security and success. ◆ *n* **19** a fixed basin, esp. in a kitchen, made of stone, earthenware, metal, etc., used for washing. **20** See **sinkhole. 21** another word for **cesspool. 22** a place of vice or corruption. **23** an area of ground below that of the surrounding land, where water collects. **24** *Physics.* a device or part of a system at which energy is removed from the system: *a heat sink.* ◆ *adj* **25** *Informal.* (of a housing estate or school) deprived or having low standards of achievement. [Old English *sincan;* related to Old Norse *sökkva* to sink, Gothic *siggan,* Old High German *sincan,* Swedish *sjunka*] ▸ 'sinkable *adj*

sinkage ('sɪŋkɪdʒ) *n Rare.* the act of sinking or degree to which something sinks or has sunk.

sinker ('sɪŋkə) *n* **1** a weight attached to a fishing line, net, etc., to cause it to sink in water. **2** a person who sinks shafts, etc. **3** *U.S.* an informal word for **doughnut. 4 hook, line, and sinker.** See **hook** (sense 18).

sinkhole ('sɪŋkˌhəʊl) *n* **1** Also called (esp. Brit.): **swallow hole.** a depression in the ground surface, esp. in limestone, where a surface stream disappears underground. **2** a place into which foul matter runs.

Sinkiang-Uighur Autonomous Region ('sɪn'kjæŋ 'wiːgʊə) *n* a variant transliteration of the Chinese name for the **Xinjiang Uygur Autonomous Region.**

sink in *vb* (*intr, adv*) to enter or penetrate the mind: *eventually the news sank in.*

sinking ('sɪŋkɪŋ) *n* **a** a feeling in the stomach caused by hunger or uneasiness. **b** (*as modifier*): *a sinking feeling.*

sinking fund *n* a fund accumulated out of a business enterprise's earnings or a government's revenue and invested to repay a long-term debt or meet a depreciation charge.

sinless ('sɪnlɪs) *adj* free from sin or guilt; innocent; pure. ▸ 'sinlessly *adv* ▸ 'sinlessness *n*

Sinn Féin ('ʃɪn 'feːn) *n* an Irish republican political movement founded about 1905 and linked to the revolutionary Irish Republican Army: divided into a Provisional and an Official movement since a similar split in the IRA in late 1969. [C20: from Irish: we ourselves] ▸ Sinn 'Féiner *n* ▸ Sinn 'Féinism *n*

Sino- *combining form.* Chinese: *Sino-Tibetan; Sinology.* [from French, from Late Latin *Sīnae* the Chinese, from Late Greek *Sinai,* from Arabic *Sīn* China, probably from Chinese *Ch'in*]

Sinology (saɪ'nɒlədʒɪ, sɪ-) *n* the study of Chinese history, language, culture, etc. ▸ **Sinological** (ˌsaɪnə'lɒdʒɪkᵊl, ˌsɪn-) *adj* ▸ Si'nologist *n* ▸ **Sinologue** ('saɪnəˌlɒg) *n*

Sinope (sə'nəʊpɪ) *n Astronomy.* a small outer satellite of the planet Jupiter.

Sino-Tibetan ('saɪnəʊ-) *n* **1** a family of languages that includes most of the languages of China, as well as Tibetan, Burmese, and possibly Thai. Their most noticeable phonological characteristic is the phonemic use of tones. ◆ *adj* **2** belonging or relating to this family of languages.

sinsemilla (ˌsɪnsə'miːljə) *n* **1** a type of marijuana with a very high narcotic content. **2** the plant from which it is obtained, a strain of *Cannabis sativa.* [C20: from American Spanish, literally: without seed]

sinter ('sɪntə) *n* **1** a whitish porous incrustation, usually consisting of silica, that is deposited from hot springs. **2** the product of a sintering process. **3** another name for **cinder** (sense 3). ◆ *vb* **4** (*tr*) to form large particles, lumps, or masses from (metal powders or powdery ores) by heating or pressure or both. [C18: German: CINDER]

Sint Maarten (sɪnt 'maːrtə) *n* the Dutch name for **Saint Martin.**

Sintra ('sɪntrə) *n* a town in central Portugal, near Lisbon, in the Sintra mountains: noted for its castles and palaces and the beauty of its setting: tourism. Former name: **Cintra.**

sinuate ('sɪnjʊɪt, -ˌeɪt) *or* **sinuated** *adj* **1** Also: **sinuous.** (of leaves) having a strongly waved margin. **2** another word for **sinuous.** [C17: from Latin *sinuātus* curved; see SINUS, -ATE[1]] ▸ 'sinuately *adv*

Sinŭiju (sɪˌnuːɪ'dʒuː) *n* a port in North Korea, on the Yalu River opposite Andong, China: developed by the Japanese during their occupation (1910–45); industrial centre. Pop.: 289 000 (1987 est.).

sinuosity (ˌsɪnjʊ'ɒsɪtɪ) *or* (*less commonly*) **sinuation** *n, pl* **-osities** *or* **-ations. 1** the quality of being sinuous. **2** a turn, curve, or intricacy.

sinuous ('sɪnjʊəs) *adj* **1** full of turns or curves; intricate. **2** devious; not straightforward. **3** supple; lithe. ◆ Also: **sinuate.** [C16: from Latin *sinuōsus* winding, from *sinus* a curve] ▸ 'sinuously *adv* ▸ 'sinuousness *n*

sinus ('saɪnəs) *n, pl* **-nuses. 1** *Anatomy.* **1a** any bodily cavity or hollow space. **1b** a large channel for venous blood, esp. between the brain and the skull. **1c** any of the air cavities in the cranial bones. **2** *Pathol.* a passage leading to a cavity containing pus. **3** *Botany.* a small rounded notch between two lobes of a leaf, petal, etc. **4** an irregularly shaped cavity. [C16: from Latin: a curve, bay]

sinusitis (ˌsaɪnə'saɪtɪs) *n* inflammation of the membrane lining a sinus, esp. a nasal sinus.

sinusoid ('saɪnəˌsɔɪd) *n* **1** any of the irregular terminal blood vessels that replace capillaries in certain organs, such as the liver, heart, spleen, and pancreas. **2** another name for **sine curve.** ◆ *adj* **3** resembling a sinus. [C19: from French *sinusoïde.* See SINUS, -OID]

sinusoidal (ˌsaɪnə'sɔɪdᵊl) *adj* **1** *Maths.* of or relating to a sine curve. **2** *Physics.* having a magnitude that varies as a sine curve. ▸ ˌsinus'oidally *adv*

sinusoidal projection *n* an equal-area map projection on which all parallels are straight lines and all except the prime meridian are sine curves, often used to show tropical latitudes. Also called: **Sanson-Flamsteed projection.**

Sion *n* **1** (*French* sjɔ̃). a town in SW Switzerland, capital of Valais canton, on the River Rhône. Pop.: 24 538 (1990). Latin name: **Sedunum. 2** ('saɪən). a variant of **Zion.**

Siouan ('suːən) *n* a family of North American Indian languages including Sioux, probably related to Iroquoian.

Sioux (suː) *n* **1** (*pl* **Sioux** (suː, suːz)) a member of a group of North American Indian peoples formerly ranging over a wide area of the Plains from Lake Michigan to the Rocky Mountains. **2** any of the Siouan languages. [from French, shortened from *Nadowessioux,* from Chippewa *Nadoweisiw*] ▸ 'Siouan *adj*

sip (sɪp) *vb* **sips, sipping, sipped. 1** to drink (a liquid) by taking small mouthfuls; drink gingerly or delicately. ◆ *n* **2** a small quantity of a liquid taken into the mouth and swallowed. **3** an act of sipping. [C14: probably from Low German *sippen*] ▸ 'sipper *n*

siphon *or* **syphon** ('saɪfᵊn) *n* **1** a tube placed with one end at a certain level in a vessel of liquid and the other end outside the vessel below this level, so that atmospheric pressure forces the liquid through the tube and out of the vessel. **2** See **soda siphon. 3** *Zoology.* any of various tubular organs in different aquatic animals, such as molluscs and elasmobranch fishes, through which a fluid, esp. water, passes. ◆ *vb* **4** (often foll. by *off*) to pass or draw off through or as if through a siphon. [C17: from Latin *sīphō,* from Greek *siphōn* siphon] ▸ 'siphonage *n* ▸ 'siphonal *or* siphonic (saɪ'fɒnɪk) *adj*

siphon bottle *n* another name (esp. U.S.) for **soda siphon.**

siphonophore ('saɪfənəˌfɔː, saɪ'fɒnə-) *n* any marine colonial hydrozoan of the order *Siphonophora,* including the Portuguese man-of-war. [C19: from New Latin *siphonophora,* from Greek *siphōnophoros* tube-bearing] ▸ **siphonophorous** (ˌsaɪfə'nɒfərəs) *adj*

siphonostele ('saɪfənəˌstiːl) *n Botany.* the cylinder of conducting tissue surrounding a central core of pith in certain stems. See also **stele** (sense 3). [C19: from SIPHON + STELE] ▸ **siphonostelic** (ˌsaɪfənə'stiːlɪk) *adj*

Siple ('saɪpᵊl) *n* **Mount.** a mountain in Antarctica, on the coast of Byrd Land. Height: 3100 m (10 171 ft.).

sipper ('sɪpə) *n U.S. informal.* a drinking straw.

sippet ('sɪpɪt) *n* a small piece of something, esp. a piece of toast or fried bread eaten with soup or gravy. [C16: used as diminutive of SOP; see -ET]

SIPS *abbrev. for* side impact protection system: bars built into certain cars to strengthen the bodywork.

Siqueiros (*Spanish* si'kejrɔs) *n* **David Alfaro** (da'βið al'faro). 1896–1974, Mexican painter, noted for his murals expressing a revolutionary message.

sir (sɜː) *n* **1** a formal or polite term of address for a man. **2** *Archaic.* a gentleman of high social status. [C13: variant of SIRE]

Sir (sɜː) *n* **1** a title of honour placed before the name of a knight or baronet: *Sir Walter Raleigh.* **2** *Archaic.* a title placed before the name of a figure from ancient history.

Siracusa (sira'kuːza) *n* the Italian name for **Syracuse.**

Siraj-ud-daula (sɪ'rɑːdʒʊd'daʊlə) *n* ?1728–57, Indian leader who became the Great Mogul's deputy in Bengal (1756); opponent of English colonization. He captured Calcutta (1756) from the English and many of his prisoners suffocated in a crowded room that became known as the Black Hole of Calcutta. He was defeated (1757) by a group of Indian nobles in alliance with Robert Clive.

sirdar ('sɜːdɑː) *n* **1** a general or military leader in Pakistan and India. **2** (formerly) the title of the British commander in chief of the Egyptian Army. **3** a variant spelling of **sardar.** [from Hindi *sardār,* from Persian, from *sar* head + *dār* possession]

sire (saɪə) *n* **1** a male parent, esp. of a horse or other domestic animal. **2** a respectful term of address, now used only in addressing a male monarch. **3** *Obsolete.* a man of high rank. ◆ *vb* **4** (*tr*) (esp. of a domestic animal) to father; beget. [C13: from Old French, from Latin *senior* an elder, from *senex* an old man]

siren ('saɪərən) *n* **1** a device for emitting a loud wailing sound, esp. as a warning or signal, typically consisting of a rotating perforated metal drum through which air or steam is passed under pressure. **2** (*sometimes cap.*) *Greek myth.* one of several sea nymphs whose seductive singing was believed to lure sailors to destruction on the rocks the nymphs inhabited. **3a** a woman considered to be dangerously alluring or seductive. **3b** (*as modifier*): *her siren charms.* **4** any aquatic eel-like salamander of the North American family *Sirenidae,* having external gills, no hind limbs, and reduced forelimbs. [C14: from Old French *sereine,* from Latin *sīrēn,* from Greek *seirēn*]

sirenian (saɪˈriːnɪən) *adj* **1** of, relating to, or belonging to the *Sirenia,* an order of aquatic herbivorous placental mammals having forelimbs modified as paddles, no hind limbs, and a horizontally flattened tail: contains only the dugong and manatees. ◆ *n* **2** any animal belonging to the order *Sirenia;* a sea cow.

Siret (sɪˈret) *n* a river in SE Europe, rising in the Ukraine and flowing southeast through E Romania to the Danube. Length: about 450 km (280 miles).

Sirius (ˈsɪrɪəs) *n* the brightest star in the sky, lying in the constellation Canis Major. It is a binary star whose companion, **Sirius B,** is a very faint white dwarf. Distance: 8.6 light years. Also called: the **Dog Star, Canicula, Sothis.** Related adjs: **canicular, cynic.** [C14: via Latin from Greek *Seirios,* of obscure origin]

sirloin (ˈsɜːˌlɔɪn) *n* a prime cut of beef from the loin, esp. the upper part. [C16 *surloyn,* from Old French *surlonge,* from *sur* above + *longe,* from *loigne* LOIN]

sirocco (sɪˈrɒkəʊ) *n, pl* **-cos. 1** a hot oppressive and often dusty wind usually occurring in spring, beginning in N Africa and reaching S Europe. **2** any hot southerly wind, esp. one moving to a low pressure centre. [C17: from Italian, from Arabic *sharq* east wind]

sironize *or* **sironise** (ˈsaɪrəˌnaɪz) *vb* (*tr*) *Austral.* to treat (a woollen fabric) chemically to prevent it wrinkling after being washed. [C20: from (C)SIRO + *-n-* + -IZE]

siroset (ˈsaɪrəʊˌset) *adj Austral.* of or relating to the chemical treatment of woollen fabrics to give a permanent-press effect, or a garment so treated.

sirrah (ˈsɪrə) *n Archaic.* a contemptuous term used in addressing a man or boy. [C16: probably variant of SIRE]

sirree (səˈriː) *interj* (*sometimes cap.*) *U.S. informal.* an emphatic exclamation used with *yes* or *no.*

sir-reverence *interj Obsolete.* an expression of apology used esp. to introduce taboo or vulgar words or phrases. [C16: short for *save your reverence*]

Sir Roger de Coverley *n* an English country dance performed to a traditional tune by two rows of dancers facing each other. [C18: alteration of *Roger of Coverley* influenced by *Sir Roger de Coverley,* a fictitious character appearing in the *Spectator* essays by Addison and Steele]

sirup (ˈsɪrəp) *n U.S.* a less common spelling of **syrup.**

sirvente (səˈvent) *n* a verse form employed by the troubadours of Provence to satirize moral or political themes. [C19: via French from Provençal *sirventes* song of a servant (that is, of a lover serving his mistress), from *sirvent* a servant, from Latin *servīre* to SERVE]

sis[1] (sɪs) *n Informal.* short for **sister.**

sis[2] *or* **sies** (sɪs, siːs) *interj S. African informal.* an exclamation of disgust. [Afrikaans, possibly from Khoi]

SIS *abbrev. for:* **1** (in Britain) Secret Intelligence Service. Also called: **MI6. 2** (in New Zealand) Security Intelligence Service.

sisal (ˈsaɪsᵊl) *n* **1** a Mexican agave plant, *Agave sisalana,* cultivated for its large fleshy leaves, which yield a stiff fibre used for making rope. **2** the fibre of this plant. **3** any of the fibres of certain similar or related plants. ◆ Also called: **sisal hemp.** [C19: from Mexican Spanish, named after *Sisal,* a port in Yucatán, Mexico]

Sisera (ˈsɪsərə) *n* a defeated leader of the Canaanites, who was assassinated by Jael (Judges 4:17–21).

siskin (ˈsɪskɪn) *n* **1** a yellow-and-black Eurasian finch, *Carduelis spinus.* **2 pine siskin.** a North American finch, *Spinus pinus,* having a streaked yellowish-brown plumage. [C16: from Middle Dutch *sīseken,* from Middle Low German *sīsek;* related to Czech *čížek,* Russian *chizh*]

Sisley (ˈsɪslɪ; *French* sislɛ) *n* **Alfred** (alfrɛd). 1839–99, French painter, esp. of landscapes; one of the originators of impressionism.

Sismondi (sɪsˈmɒndɪ; *French* sismɔ̃di) *n* **Jean Charles Léonard Simonde de** (ʒɑ̃ ʃarl leɔnar simɔ̃d də). 1773–1842, Swiss historian and economist. His *Histoire des républiques italiennes du moyen âge* (1807–18) contributed to the movement for Italian unification.

Sissinghurst Castle (ˈsɪsɪŋhɜːst) *n* a restored Elizabethan mansion near Cranbrook in Kent: noted for the gardens laid out in the 1930s by Victoria Sackville-West and Harold Nicolson.

sissy *or* **cissy** (ˈsɪsɪ) *n, pl* **-sies. 1** an effeminate, weak, or cowardly boy or man. ◆ *adj* **2** Also (informal or dialect): **ˈsissiˌfied** *or* **ˈcissiˌfied.** effeminate, weak, or cowardly.

sister (ˈsɪstə) *n* **1** a female person having the same parents as another person. **2** See **half-sister, stepsister. 3** a female person who belongs to the same group, trade union, etc., as another or others. **4** *Informal.* a form of address to a woman or girl, used esp. by Blacks in the U.S. **5** a senior nurse. **6** *Chiefly R.C. Church.* a nun or a title given to a nun. **7** a woman fellow member of a Church or religious body. **8** (*modifier*) belonging to the same class, fleet, etc., as another or others: *a sister ship.* **9** (*modifier*) *Biology.* denoting any of the cells or cell components formed by division of a parent cell or cell component: *sister nuclei.* [Old English *sweostor;* related to Old Norse *systir,* Old High German *swester,* Gothic *swistar*]

sisterhood (ˈsɪstəˌhʊd) *n* **1** the state of being related as a sister or sisters. **2** a religious body or society of sisters, esp. a community, order, or congregation of nuns. **3** the bond between women who support the Women's Movement.

sister-in-law *n, pl* **sisters-in-law. 1** the sister of one's husband or wife. **2** the wife of one's brother.

sisterly (ˈsɪstəlɪ) *adj* of, resembling, or suitable to a sister, esp. in showing kindness and affection. ▸ **ˈsisterliness** *n*

Sistine Chapel (ˈsɪstaɪn, -tiːn) *n* the chapel of the pope in the Vatican at Rome, built for Sixtus IV and decorated with frescoes by Michelangelo and others. [Sistine, from It. *Sistino* relating to *Sisto* Sixtus (Pope Sixtus IV)]

sistroid (ˈsɪstrɔɪd) *adj* contained between the convex sides of two intersecting curves. Compare **cissoid** (sense 2). [C20: from SISTRUM + -OID]

sistrum (ˈsɪstrəm) *n, pl* **-tra** (-trə). a musical instrument of ancient Egypt consisting of a metal rattle. [C14: via Latin from Greek *seistron,* from *seiein* to shake]

Sisyphean (ˌsɪsɪˈfiːən) *adj* **1** relating to Sisyphus. **2** actually or seemingly endless and futile.

Sisyphus (ˈsɪsɪfəs) *n Greek myth.* a king of Corinth, punished in Hades for his misdeeds by eternally having to roll a heavy stone up a hill: every time he approached the top, the stone escaped his grasp and rolled to the bottom.

sit (sɪt) *vb* **sits, sitting, sat.** (*mainly intr*) **1** (*also tr;* when *intr,* often foll. by *down, in,* or *on*) to adopt or rest in a posture in which the body is supported on the buttocks and thighs and the torso is more or less upright: *to sit on a chair; sit a horse.* **2** (*tr*) to cause to adopt such a posture. **3** (of an animal) to adopt or rest in a posture with the hindquarters lowered to the ground. **4** (of a bird) to perch or roost. **5** (of a hen or other bird) to cover eggs to hatch them; brood. **6** to be situated or located. **7** (of the wind) to blow from the direction specified. **8** to adopt and maintain a posture for one's portrait to be painted, etc. **9** to occupy or be entitled to a seat in some official capacity, as a judge, elected representative, etc. **10** (of a deliberative body) to be convened or in session. **11** to remain inactive or unused: *his car sat in the garage for a year.* **12** to rest or lie as specified: *the nut was sitting so awkwardly that he couldn't turn it.* **13** (of a garment) to fit or hang as specified: *that dress sits well on you.* **14** to weigh, rest, or lie as specified: *greatness sits easily on him.* **15** (*tr*) *Chiefly Brit.* to take (an examination): *he's sitting his bar finals.* **16** (usually foll. by *for*) *Chiefly Brit.* to be a candidate (for a qualification): *he's sitting for a BA.* **17** (*intr; in combination*) to look after a specified person or thing for someone else: *granny-sit.* **18** (*tr*) to have seating capacity for. **19 sitting pretty.** *Informal.* well placed or established financially, socially, etc. **20 sit tight. 20a** to wait patiently; bide one's time. **20b** to maintain one's position, stand, or opinion firmly. ◆ See also **sit back, sit down, sit-in, sit on, sit out, sit over, sit under, sit up.** [Old English *sittan;* related to Old Norse *sitja,* Gothic *sitan,* Old High German *sizzen,* Latin *sedēre* to sit, Sanskrit *sīdati* he sits]

Sita (ˈsiːtɑː) *n Hinduism.* goddess consort of the god Vishnu in the incarnation of Rama.

sitar (sɪˈtɑː, ˈsɪtɑː) *n* a stringed musical instrument, esp. of India, having a long neck, a rounded body, and movable frets. The main strings, three to seven in number, overlie other sympathetic strings, the tuning depending on the raga being performed. [from Hindi *sitār,* literally: three-stringed] ▸ **siˈtarist** *n*

sitatunga (ˌsɪtəˈtʊŋgə) *n* another name for **marshbuck.**

sit back *vb* (*intr, adv*) to relax, as when action should be taken: *many people just sit back and ignore the problems of today.*

sitcom (ˈsɪtˌkɒm) *n* an informal term for **situation comedy.**

sit down *vb* (*adv*) **1** to adopt or cause (oneself or another) to adopt a sitting posture. **2** (*intr;* foll. by *under*) to suffer (insults, etc.) without protests or resistance. ◆ *n* **sit-down. 3** a form of civil disobedience in which demonstrators sit down in a public place as a protest or to draw attention to a cause. **4** See **sit-down strike.** ◆ *adj* **sit-down. 5** (of a meal, etc.) eaten while sitting down at a table.

sit-down money *n Austral. informal.* social security benefits.

sit-down strike *n* a strike in which workers refuse to leave their place of employment until a settlement is reached.

site (saɪt) *n* **1a** the piece of land where something was, is, or is intended to be located: *a building site; archaeological site.* **1b** (*as modifier*): *site office.* **2** an Internet location where information relating to a specific subject or group of subjects can be accessed. ◆ *vb* **3** (*tr*) to locate, place, or install (something) in a specific place. [C14: from Latin *situs* situation, from *sinere* to be placed]

sitella (sɪˈtɛlə) *n Austral.* any of various small generally black-and-white birds of the genus *Neositta,* having a straight sharp beak and strong claws used to run up trees in search of insects: family *Sittidae* (nuthatches). Also called: **tree-runner.** [C19: from New Latin, the diminutive of *sitta,* from Greek *sittē* nuthatch]

sitfast (ˈsɪtˌfɑːst) *n* a sore on a horse's back caused by rubbing of the saddle. [C17: from SIT + FAST[1] (in the sense: secure, fixed)]

sith (sɪθ) *adv, conj, prep* an archaic word for **since.** [Old English *siththa,* short for *siththan* SINCE]

Sithole (sɪˈtəʊlɪ) *n* **Ndabaningi** (ᵊndabaˈnɪŋgɪ). born 1920, Zimbabwean clergyman and politician; leader of the Zimbabwe African National Union (1963–74). He was one of the negotiators of the internal settlement (1978) to pave the way for Black majority rule in Rhodesia (now Zimbabwe).

sit-in *n* **1** a form of civil disobedience in which demonstrators occupy seats in a public place and refuse to move as a protest. **2** another term for **sit-down strike.** ◆ *vb* **sit in.** (*intr, adv*) **3** (often foll. by *for*) to deputize (for). **4** (foll. by *on*) to take part (in) as a visitor or guest: *we sat in on Professor Johnson's seminar.* **5** to organize or take part in a sit-in.

Sitka (ˈsɪtkə) *n* a town in SE Alaska, in the Alexander Archipelago on W Baranof Island: capital of Russian America (1804–67) and of Alaska (1867–1906). Pop.: 8588 (1990).

sitkamer (ˈsɪtˌkɑːmə) *n S. African.* a sitting room; lounge. [from Afrikaans *sit* sitting + *kamer* room]

sitka spruce (ˈsɪtkə) *n* a tall North American spruce tree, *Picea sitchensis,* having yellowish-green needle-like leaves: yields valuable timber. [C19: from SITKA]

sitology (saɪˈtɒlədʒɪ) *n* the scientific study of food, diet, and nutrition. [C19: from Greek *sitos* food, grain + -LOGY]

sit on *vb* (*intr, prep*) **1** to be a member of (a committee, etc.). **2** *Informal.* to suppress. **3** *Informal.* to check or rebuke.

sitosterol (saɪˈtɒstəˌrɒl) *n* a white powder or waxy white solid extracted from soya beans, consisting of a mixture of isomers of the formula $C_{29}H_{50}O$ with other sterols: used in cosmetics and medicine. [C20: from Greek *sitos* food, grain + STEROL]

sit out *vb* (*adv*) **1** (*tr*) to endure to the end: *I sat out the play although it was terrible.* **2** (*tr*) to remain seated throughout (a dance, etc.). **3** (*intr*) *Chiefly Brit.* to lean backwards over the side of a light sailing boat in order to carry the centre of gravity as far to windward as possible to reduce heeling. U.S. and Canadian term: **hike out.**

sit over *vb* (*intr, prep*) *Cards.* to be seated in an advantageous position on the left of (the player).

Sitsang ('si:'tsæŋ) *n* a Chinese name for **Tibet.**

sitter ('sɪtə) *n* **1** a person or animal that sits. **2** a person who is posing for his or her portrait to be painted, carved, etc. **3** a broody hen or other bird that is sitting on its eggs to hatch them. **4** (*in combination*) a person who looks after a specified person or thing for someone else: *flat-sitter.* **5** short for **baby-sitter. 6** anyone, other than the medium, taking part in a seance. **7** anything that is extremely easy, such as an easy catch in cricket.

Sitter ('sɪtə) *n* **Willem de** ('wɪləm də). 1872–1934, Dutch astronomer, who calculated the size of the universe and conceived of it as expanding.

sitting ('sɪtɪŋ) *n* **1** a continuous period of being seated: *I read his novel at one sitting.* **2** such a period in a restaurant, canteen, etc., where space and other facilities are limited: *dinner will be served in two sittings.* **3** the act or period of posing for one's portrait to be painted, carved, etc. **4** a meeting, esp. of an official body, to conduct business. **5** the incubation period of a bird's eggs during which the mother sits on them to keep them warm. ◆ *adj* **6** in office: *a sitting Member of Parliament.* **7** (of a hen) brooding eggs. **8** seated: *in a sitting position.*

Sitting Bull *n* Indian name *Tatanka Yotanka.* ?1831–90, American Indian chief of the Teton Dakota Sioux. Resisting White encroachment on his people's hunting grounds, he led the Sioux tribes against the U.S. Army in the Sioux War (1876–77) in which Custer was killed. The hunger of the Sioux, whose food came from the diminishing buffalo, forced his surrender (1881). He was killed during renewed strife.

sitting room *n* a room in a private house or flat used for relaxation and entertainment of guests.

sitting target *n* a person or thing in a defenceless or vulnerable position. Also called (informal): **sitting duck.**

sitting tenant *n* a tenant occupying a house, flat, etc.

sitting trot *n* a horse's trot during which the rider sits still in the saddle. Compare **rising trot.**

situate ('sɪtjʊˌeɪt) *vb* **1** (*tr; often passive*) to allot a site to; place; locate. ◆ *adj* **2** (now used esp. in legal contexts) situated; located. [C16: from Late Latin *situāre* to position, from Latin *situs* a SITE]

situation (ˌsɪtjʊ'eɪʃən) *n* **1** physical placement, esp. with regard to the surroundings. **2a** state of affairs; combination of circumstances. **2b** a complex or critical state of affairs in a novel, play, etc. **3** social or financial status, position, or circumstances. **4** a position of employment; post. ► ˌ**situ'ational** *adj*

USAGE *Situation* is often used in contexts in which it is redundant or imprecise. Typical examples are: *the company is in a crisis situation* or *people in a job situation.* In the first example, *situation* does not add to the meaning and should be omitted. In the second example, it would be clearer and more concise to substitute a phrase such as *people at work.*

situation comedy *n* (on television or radio) a comedy series involving the same characters in various day-to-day situations which are developed as separate stories for each episode. Also called: **sitcom.**

situla ('sɪtjʊlə) *n, pl* **-lae** (-li:). **1** a bucket-shaped container, usually of metal or pottery and often richly decorated: typical of the N Italian Iron Age. ◆ *adj* **2** of or relating to the type of designs usually associated with these containers. [from Latin]

sit under *vb* (*intr, prep*) *Cards.* to be seated on the right of (the player).

sit up *vb* (*adv*) **1** to raise (oneself or another) from a recumbent to an upright or alert sitting posture. **2** (*intr*) to remain out of bed and awake, esp. until a late hour. **3** (*intr*) *Informal.* to become suddenly interested or alert: *devaluation of the dollar made the money market sit up.* ◆ *n* **sit-up. 4** a physical exercise in which the body is brought into a sitting position from one lying on the back.

situs ('saɪtəs) *n, pl* **-tus.** position or location, esp. the usual or right position of an organ or part of the body. [C18: from Latin: site, situation, position]

Sitwell ('sɪtwəl) *n* **1** Dame **Edith.** 1887–1964, English poet and critic, noted esp. for her collection *Façade* (1922). **2** her brother, Sir **Osbert.** 1892–1969, English writer, best known for his five autobiographical books (1944–50). **3** his brother, Sir **Sacheverell** (sə'ʃevərəl). 1897–1988, English poet and writer of books on art, architecture, music, and travel.

sitz bath (sɪts, zɪts) *n* a bath in which the buttocks and hips are immersed in hot water, esp. for therapeutic effects, as after perineal or pelvic surgery. [half translation of German *Sitzbad,* from *Sitz* SEAT + *Bad* BATH[1]]

sitzkrieg ('sɪtsˌkri:g, 'zɪts-) *n* a period during a war in which both sides change positions very slowly or not at all. [C20: from German, from *sitzen* to sit + *Krieg* war]

sitzmark ('sɪtsˌmɑ:k, 'zɪts-) *n Skiing.* a depression in the snow where a skier has fallen. [German, literally: seat mark]

SI unit *n* any of the units adopted for international use under the Système International d'Unités, now employed for all scientific and most technical purposes. There are seven fundamental units: the metre, kilogram, second, ampere, kelvin, candela, and mole; and two supplementary units: the radian and the steradian. All other units are derived by multiplication or division of these units without the use of numerical factors.

Siva ('si:və, 'sɪvə) *or* **Shiva** *n Hinduism.* the destroyer, one of the three chief divinities of the later Hindu pantheon, the other two being Brahma and Vishnu. Siva is also the god presiding over personal destinies. [from Sanskrit *Śiva,* literally: the auspicious (one)]

Sivaism ('si:vəˌɪzəm, 'sɪvə-) *n* the cult of Siva. ► '**Sivaist** *n* ► ˌ**Siva'istic** *adj*

Sivaji (sɪ'vɑ:ʒi) *n* 1627–80, Indian king (1674–80), who led an uprising of Hindus against Muslim rule and founded the Masatha kingdom.

Sivan (si:'vɑ:n) *n* (in the Jewish calendar) the third month of the year according to biblical reckoning and the ninth month of the civil year, usually falling within May and June. [from Hebrew]

Sivas (*Turkish* 'sivɑs) *n* a city in central Turkey, at an altitude of 1347 m (4420 ft.): one of the chief cities in Asia Minor in ancient times; scene of the national congress (1919) leading to the revolution that established modern Turkey. Pop.: 243 432 (1995 est.).

siwash ('saɪwɒʃ) *n* **1** another name for **Cowichan sweater.** ◆ *vb* **2** (*intr*) (in the Pacific Northwest) to camp out with only natural shelter. [see SIWASH]

Siwash ('saɪwɒʃ) (*sometimes not cap.*) *Slang, derogatory.* (in the Pacific Northwest) ◆ *n* **1** a North American Indian. ◆ *adj* **2** of, characteristic of, or relating to Indians. **3** worthless, stingy, or bad: *he's siwash.* [C19: from Chinook Jargon, from French *sauvage* SAVAGE]

six (sɪks) *n* **1** the cardinal number that is the sum of five and one. See also **number** (sense 1). **2** a numeral, 6, VI, etc., representing this number. **3** something representing, represented by, or consisting of six units, such as a playing card with six symbols on it. **4** Also called: **six o'clock.** six hours after noon or midnight. **5** Also called: **sixer.** *Cricket.* **5a** a stroke in which the ball crosses the boundary without bouncing. **5b** the six runs scored for such a stroke. **6** a division of a Brownie Guide or Cub Scout pack. **7 at sixes and sevens. 7a** in disagreement. **7b** in a state of confusion. **8 knock (someone) for six.** *Informal.* to upset or overwhelm (someone) completely; stun. **9 six of one and half a dozen of the other.** Also: **six and two threes.** a situation in which the alternatives are considered equivalent. ◆ *determiner* **10a** amounting to six: *six nations.* **10b** (*as pronoun*): *set the table for six.* ◆ Related prefixes: **hexa-, sex-.** [Old English *siex;* related to Old Norse *sex,* Gothic *saihs,* Old High German *sehs,* Latin *sex,* Greek *hex,* Sanskrit *sastha*]

Six (*French* sis) *n* **Les** (le). a group of six young composers in France, who from about 1916 formed a temporary association as a result of interest in neoclassicism and in the music of Satie and the poetry of Cocteau. Its members were Darius Milhaud, Arthur Honegger, Francis Poulenc, Georges Auric, Louis Durey, and Germaine Tailleferre.

sixain ('sɪkseɪn) *n* a stanza or poem of six lines. [from French]

Six Counties *pl n* the historic counties of Northern Ireland, which no longer have a local government function.

Six Day War *n* a war fought in the Middle East in June 1967, lasting six days. In it Israel defeated Egypt, Jordan, and Syria, occupying the Gaza Strip, the Sinai, Jerusalem, the West Bank of the Jordan, and the Golan Heights.

six-eight time *n Music.* a form of compound duple time in which there are six quaver beats to the bar, indicated by the time signature $\frac{6}{8}$. Often shortened to **six-eight.**

sixer ('sɪksə) *n* a leader of a Brownie Guide or Cub Scout six.

sixfold ('sɪksˌfəʊld) *adj* **1** equal to or having six times as many or as much. **2** composed of six parts. ◆ *adv* **3** by or up to six times as many or as much.

six-footer *n* a person who is at least six feet tall.

six-gun *n U.S. informal.* another word for **six-shooter.**

sixmo ('sɪksməʊ) *n, pl* **-mos. 1** Also called: **sexto.** a book size resulting from folding a sheet of paper into six leaves or twelve pages, each one sixth the size of the sheet. Often written: **6mo, 6°. 2** a book of this size.

Six Nations *pl n* (in North America) the Indian confederacy of the Cayugas, Mohawks, Oneidas, Onondagas, Senecas, and Tuscaroras. Also called: **Iroquois.** See also **Five Nations.**

six o'clock swill *n Austral. and N.Z. informal.* a period of heavy drinking, esp. during the years when hotels had to close their bars at 6.00 p.m.

six-pack *n Informal.* a package containing six units, esp. six cans of beer.

sixpence ('sɪkspəns) *n* a small British cupronickel coin with a face value of six pennies, worth 2½ (new) pence, not minted since 1970.

sixpenny ('sɪkspənɪ) *adj* (*prenominal*) (of a nail) two inches in length.

six-shooter *n U.S. informal.* a revolver with six chambers. Also called: **six-gun.**

sixte (sɪkst) *n* the sixth of eight basic positions from which a parry or attack can be made in fencing. [from French: (the) sixth (parrying position), from Latin *sextus* sixth]

sixteen ('sɪks'ti:n) *n* **1** the cardinal number that is the sum of ten and six. See also **number** (sense 1). **2** a numeral, 16, XVI, etc., representing this number. **3** *Music.* the numeral 16 used as the lower figure of a time signature to indicate that the beat is measured in semiquavers. **4** something represented by, representing, or consisting of 16 units. ◆ *determiner* **5a** amounting to sixteen: *sixteen tons.* **5b** (*as pronoun*): *sixteen are known to the police.*

sixteenmo ('sɪks'ti:nməʊ) *n, pl* **-mos. 1** Also called: **sextodecimo.** a book size resulting from folding a sheet of paper into 16 leaves or 32 pages, each one sixteenth the size of the sheet. Often written: **16mo, 16°. 2** a book of this size.

sixteenth ('sɪks'ti:nθ) *adj* **1** (*usually prenominal*) **1a** coming after the fifteenth in numbering or counting order, position, time, etc.; being the ordinal number of *sixteen:* often written 16th. **1b** (*as n*): *the sixteenth of the month.* ◆ *n* **2a** one of 16 equal or nearly equal parts of something. **2b** (*as modifier*): *a sixteenth part.* **3** the fraction that is equal to one divided by 16 (1/16).

sixteenth note *n* the usual U.S. and Canadian name for **semiquaver.**

sixth (sɪksθ) *adj* **1** (*usually prenominal*) **1a** coming after the fifth and before the seventh in numbering or counting order, position, time, etc.; being the ordinal number of *six:* often written 6th. **1b** (*as n*): *the sixth to go.* ◆ *n* **2a** one of six equal or nearly equal parts of an object, quantity, measurement, etc. **2b** (*as modifier*): *a sixth part.* **3** the fraction equal to one divided by six (1/6). **4**

Music. **4a** the interval between one note and another note six notes away from it counting inclusively along the diatonic scale. **4b** one of two notes constituting such an interval in relation to the other. See also **major** (sense 13), **minor** (sense 4), **interval** (sense 5). **4c** short for **sixth chord.** ◆ *adv* **5** Also: **sixthly.** after the fifth person, position, etc. ◆ *sentence connector.* **6** Also: **sixthly.** as the sixth point: linking what follows to the previous statements.

sixth chord *n* (in classical harmony) the first inversion of the triad, in which the note next above the root appears in the bass. See also **added sixth.**

sixth form *n* (in England and Wales) the most senior class in a secondary school to which pupils, usually above the legal leaving age, may proceed to take A levels, retake GCSEs, etc. ▸ **'sixth-,former** *n*

sixth-form college *n* (in England and Wales) a college offering A-level and other courses to pupils over sixteen from local schools, esp. from those that do not have sixth forms.

sixth sense *n* any supposed sense or means of perception, such as intuition or clairvoyance, other than the five senses of sight, hearing, touch, taste, and smell.

sixth year *n* (in Scotland) the most senior class in a secondary school to which pupils, usually above the legal leaving age, may proceed to take sixth-year studies, retake or take additional Highers, etc.

sixtieth ('sɪkstɪəθ) *adj* **1** (*usually prenominal*) **1a** being the ordinal number of *sixty* in numbering or counting order, position, time, etc.: often written 60th. **1b** (*as n*): *the sixtieth in a row.* ◆ *n* **2a** one of 60 approximately equal parts of something. **2b** (*as modifier*): *a sixtieth part.* **3** the fraction equal to one divided by 60 (1/60).

Sixtus IV ('sɪkstəs) *n* original name *Francesco della Rovere.* 1414–84, Italian ecclesiastic; pope (1471–84). Notorious for his nepotism and political intrigue, he was also a patron of the arts and commissioned the building (1473–81) of the Sistine Chapel.

Sixtus V *n* original name *Felice Peretti.* 1520–90, Italian ecclesiastic; pope (1585–90). He is noted for vigorous administrative reforms that contributed to the Counter-Reformation.

sixty ('sɪkstɪ) *n, pl* **-ties. 1** the cardinal number that is the product of ten and six. See also **number** (sense 1). **2** a numeral, 60, LX, etc., representing sixty. **3** something represented by, representing, or consisting of 60 units. ◆ *determiner* **4a** amounting to sixty: *sixty soldiers.* **4b** (*as pronoun*): *sixty are dead.* [Old English *sixtig*]

sixty-fourmo (,sɪkstɪ'fɔːməʊ) *n, pl* **-mos. 1** a book size resulting from folding a sheet of paper into 64 leaves or 128 pages, each one sixty-fourth the size of the sheet. Often written **64mo, 64°**. **2** a book of this size.

sixty-fourth note *n* the usual U.S. and Canadian name for **hemidemisemiquaver.**

sixty-four thousand dollar question *n* a crucial question or issue. [C20: an elaboration of the earlier *sixty-four dollar question,* so called from the top prize on the U.S. radio show *Take It or Leave It* (1941–48)]

sixty-nine *n* another term for **soixante-neuf.**

six-yard line *n Soccer.* the line marking the limits of the goal area.

sizable *or* **sizeable** ('saɪzəbᵊl) *adj* quite large. ▸ **'sizableness** *or* **'sizeableness** *n* ▸ **'sizably** *or* **'sizeably** *adv*

sizar ('saɪzə) *n Brit.* (at Peterhouse, Cambridge, and Trinity College, Dublin) an undergraduate receiving a maintenance grant from the college. [C16: from earlier *sizer,* from SIZE[1] (meaning "an allowance of food, etc.")] ▸ **'sizar,ship** *n*

size[1] (saɪz) *n* **1** the dimensions, proportions, amount, or extent of something. **2** large or great dimensions, etc. **3** one of a series of graduated measurements, as of clothing: *she takes size 4 shoes.* **4** *Informal.* state of affairs as summarized: *he's bankrupt, that's the size of it.* ◆ *vb* **5** to sort according to size. **6** (*tr*) to make or cut to a particular size or sizes. [C13: from Old French *sise,* shortened from *assise* ASSIZE] ▸ **'sizer** *n*

USAGE The use of *-size* and *-sized* after *large* or *small* is redundant, except when describing something which is made in specific sizes: *a large* (not *large-size*) *organization.* Similarly, *in size* is redundant in the expressions *large in size* and *small in size.*

size[2] (saɪz) *n* **1** Also called: **sizing.** a thin gelatinous mixture, made from glue, clay, or wax, that is used as a sealer or filler on paper, cloth, or plaster surfaces. ◆ *vb* **2** (*tr*) to treat or coat (a surface) with size. [C15: perhaps from Old French *sise;* see SIZE[1]] ▸ **'sizy** *adj*

sized (saɪzd) *adj* of a specified size: *medium-sized.*

USAGE See at **size**[1].

size up *vb* (*adv*) **1** (*tr*) to make an assessment of (a person, problem, etc.). **2** to conform to or make so as to conform to certain specifications of dimension.

size-weight illusion *n* a standard sense illusion that a small object is heavier than a large object of the same weight.

sizzle ('sɪzᵊl) *vb* (*intr*) **1** to make the hissing sound characteristic of frying fat. **2** *Informal.* to be very hot. **3** *Informal.* to be very angry. ◆ *n* **4** a hissing sound. [C17: of imitative origin. Compare *siss* (now dialect) to hiss, West Frisian *size, siizje.* See also FIZZ and FIZZLE] ▸ **'sizzling** *adj*

sizzler ('sɪzlə) *n* **1** something that sizzles. **2** *Informal.* a very hot day.

SJ *abbrev. for* Society of Jesus.

SJA *abbrev. for* Saint John's Ambulance (Brigade or Association).

Sjælland (*Danish* 'sjelan) *n* the Danish name for **Zealand.**

sjambok ('ʃæmbʌk, -bɒk) (in South Africa) ◆ *n* **1** a heavy whip of rhinoceros or hippopotamus hide. ◆ *vb* **-boks, -bokking, -bokked. 2** (*tr*) to strike or beat with such a whip. [C19: from Afrikaans, from Malay *samboq, chamboq,* from Urdu *chābuk*]

SJC (in the U.S.) *abbrev. for* Supreme Judicial Court.

SJD *abbrev. for* Doctor of Juridical Science. [from Latin *Scientiae Juridicae Doctor*]

sk *abbrev. for* sack.

SK **1** *abbrev. for* Saskatchewan. **2** *international car registration for* Slovakia.

ska (skɑː) *n* a type of West Indian pop music of the 1960s, accented on the second and fourth beats of a four-beat bar.

skag (skæg) *n* a variant spelling of **scag**[1].

Skagen ('skɑːgən) *n* **Cape.** another name for the **Skaw.**

Skagerrak ('skægə,ræk) *n* an arm of the North Sea between Denmark and Norway, merging with the Kattegat in the southeast.

skald *or* **scald** (skɔːld) *n* (in ancient Scandinavia) a bard or minstrel. [from Old Norse, of unknown origin] ▸ **'skaldic** *or* **'scaldic** *adj*

skank (skæŋk) *n* **1** a fast dance to reggae music. ◆ *vb* (*intr*) **2** to perform this dance.

Skara Brae ('skærə) *n* a neolithic village in NE Scotland, in the Orkney Islands: one of Europe's most perfectly preserved Stone Age villages, buried by a sand dune until uncovered by a storm in 1850.

skat (skæt) *n* a three-handed card game using 32 cards, popular in German-speaking communities. [C19: from German, from Italian *scarto* played cards, from *scartare* to discard, from *s-* EX-[1] + *carta,* from Latin *charta* CARD[1]]

skate[1] (skeɪt) *n* **1** See **roller skate, ice skate. 2** the steel blade or runner of an ice skate. **3** such a blade fitted with straps for fastening to a shoe. **4** a current collector on an electric railway train that collects its current from a third rail. Compare **bow collector. 5 get one's skates on.** to hurry. ◆ *vb* (*intr*) **6** to glide swiftly on skates. **7** to slide smoothly over a surface. **8 skate on thin ice.** to place oneself in a dangerous or delicate situation. [C17: via Dutch from Old French *éschasse* stilt, probably of Germanic origin]

skate[2] (skeɪt) *n, pl* **skate** *or* **skates.** any large ray of the family *Rajidae,* of temperate and tropical seas, having flat pectoral fins continuous with the head, two dorsal fins, a short spineless tail, and a long snout. [C14: from Old Norse *skata*]

skate[3] (skeɪt) *n U.S. slang.* a person; fellow. [from Scottish and northern English dialect *skate,* a derogatory term of uncertain origin]

skateboard ('skeɪt,bɔːd) *n* **1** a narrow board mounted on roller-skate wheels, usually ridden while standing up. ◆ *vb* **2** (*intr*) to ride on a skateboard. ▸ **'skate,boarder** *n* ▸ **'skate,boarding** *n*

skate over *vb* (*intr, prep*) **1** to cross on or as if on skates. **2** to avoid dealing with (a matter) fully.

skater ('skeɪtə) *n* **1** a person who skates. **2** See **pond-skater.**

skatole ('skætəʊl) *n* a white or brownish crystalline solid with a strong faecal odour, found in faeces, beetroot, and coal tar; B-methylindole. Formula: C_9H_9N. [C19: from Greek *skat-,* stem of *skōr* excrement + -OLE[1]]

Skaw (skɔː) *n* **the.** a cape at the N tip of Denmark. Also called: (Cape) **Skagen.**

skean (skiːn) *n* a kind of double-edged dagger formerly used in Ireland and Scotland. [from Irish and Scottish Gaelic *scian*]

skean-dhu ('skiːən'duː, 'skiːn-) *n Scot.* a variant of **sgian-dhu.**

skedaddle (skɪ'dædᵊl) *Informal.* ◆ *vb* **1** (*intr*) to run off hastily. ◆ *n* **2** a hasty retreat. [C19: of unknown origin]

skeet (skiːt) *n* a form of clay-pigeon shooting in which targets are hurled from two traps at varying speeds and angles. Also called: **skeet shooting.** [C20: changed from Old Norse *skeyti* a thrown object, from *skjōta* to shoot]

skeg (skɛg) *n Nautical.* **1** a reinforcing brace between the after end of a keel and the rudderpost. **2** a support at the bottom of a rudder. **3** a projection from the forefoot of a vessel for towing paravanes. **4** any short keel-like projection at the stern of a boat. **5** *Austral.* a rear fin on the underside of a surfboard. [C16: of Scandinavian origin; compare Icelandic *skegg* cutwater]

skein (skeɪn) *n* **1** a length of yarn, etc., wound in a long coil. **2** something resembling this, such as a lock of hair. **3** a flock of geese flying. Compare **gaggle** (sense 2). [C15: from Old French *escaigne,* of unknown origin]

skeleton ('skɛlɪtən) *n* **1** a hard framework consisting of inorganic material that supports and protects the soft parts of an animal's body and provides attachment for muscles: may be internal, as in vertebrates (see **endoskeleton**), or external, as in arthropods (see **exoskeleton**). **2** *Informal.* a very thin emaciated person or animal. **3** the essential framework of any structure, such as a building or leaf, that supports or determines the shape of the rest of the structure. **4** an outline consisting of bare essentials: *the skeleton of a novel.* **5** (*modifier*) reduced to a minimum: *a skeleton staff.* **6 skeleton in the cupboard** *or* (*U.S. and Canadian*) **closet.** a scandalous fact or event in the past that is kept secret. [C16: via New Latin from Greek: something desiccated, from *skellein* to dry up] ▸ **'skeletal** *adj* ▸ **'skeletally** *adv* ▸ **'skeleton-,like** *adj*

skeletonize *or* **skeletonise** ('skɛlɪtə,naɪz) *vb* (*tr*) **1** to reduce to a minimum framework, number, or outline. **2** to create the essential framework of.

skeleton key *n* a key with the serrated edge filed down so that it can open numerous locks. Also called: **passkey.** [C19: so called because it has been reduced to its essential parts]

skelf (skɛlf) *n Scot. and northern English dialect.* **1** a splinter of wood, esp. when embedded accidentally in the skin. **2** a thin or diminutive person. [from Scottish; see SHELF]

skellum ('skɛləm) *n Archaic and dialect.* a rogue. [C17: via Dutch from Old High German *skelmo* devil]

skelly[1] ('skɛlɪ) *n, pl* **-lies.** a whitefish, *Coregonus stigmaticus,* of certain lakes in the Lake District. [C18: perhaps from dialect *skell* a shell or scale, and so called because of its large scales]

skelly[2] ('skɛlɪ) *Scot. and northern English dialect.* ◆ *vb* **-lies, -lying, -lied.** (*intr*) **1** to look sideways or squint. ◆ *n, pl* **-lies. 2** a quick look; glance. ◆ *adj* **3** Also: **skelly-eyed.** cross-eyed. [probably from Old Norse, from *skjalgr* wry; related to Old English *sceolh* a squint]

skelm ('skɛlᵊm) *n S. African informal.* a villain or crook. [Afrikaans]

Skelmersdale ('skɛlməz,deɪl) *n* a town in NW England, in Lancashire: designated a new town in 1962. Pop.: 42 104 (1991).

skelp[1] (skɛlp) *Dialect.* ♦ *vb* **1** (*tr*) to slap. ♦ *n* **2** a slap. [C15: probably of imitative origin]
skelp[2] (skɛlp) *n* sheet or plate metal that has been curved and welded to form a tube. [C19: perhaps from Scottish Gaelic *sgealb* thin strip of wood]
Skelton ('skɛltən) *n* **John.** ?1460–1529, English poet celebrated for his short rhyming lines using the rhythms of colloquial speech. ► **Skel'tonic** *adj*
sken (skɛn) *vb* **skens, skenning, skenned.** (*intr*) *Northern English dialect.* to squint or stare. [of obscure origin]
skep (skɛp) *n* **1** a beehive, esp. one constructed of straw. **2** *Now chiefly dialect.* a large basket of wickerwork or straw. [Old English *sceppe,* from Old Norse *skeppa* bushel; related to Old High German *sceffil* bushel]
skeptic ('skɛptɪk) *n, adj* an archaic, and the usual U.S., spelling of **sceptic.** ► **'skeptical** *adj* ► **'skeptically** *adv* ► **'skepticalness** *n* ► **'skepticism** *n*
skerrick ('skɛrɪk) *n U.S., Austral., and N.Z.* a small fragment or amount (esp. in the phrase **not a skerrick**). [C20: northern English dialect, probably of Scandinavian origin]
skerry ('skɛrɪ) *n, pl* **-ries.** *Chiefly Scot.* **1** a small rocky island. **2** a reef. [C17: Orkney dialect, from Old Norse *sker* SCAR[2]]
sket (skɛt) *vb* **skets, sketting, sketted.** (*tr*) *South Wales dialect.* **1** to splash (water). **2** to splash (someone with water). [perhaps from Old Norse *skjóta* to shoot]
sketch (skɛtʃ) *n* **1** a rapid drawing or painting, often a study for subsequent elaboration. **2** a brief usually descriptive and informal essay or other literary composition. **3** a short play, often comic, forming part of a revue. **4** a short evocative piece of instrumental music, esp. for piano. **5** any brief outline. ♦ *vb* **6** to make a rough drawing (of). **7** (*tr;* often foll. by *out*) to make a brief description of. [C17: from Dutch *schets,* via Italian from Latin *schedius* hastily made, from Greek *skhedios* unprepared] ► **'sketchable** *adj* ► **'sketcher** *n*
sketchbook ('skɛtʃˌbʊk) *n* **1** a book of plain paper containing sketches or for making sketches in. **2** a book of literary sketches.
sketchy ('skɛtʃɪ) *adj* **sketchier, sketchiest. 1** characteristic of a sketch; existing only in outline. **2** superficial or slight. ► **'sketchily** *adv* ► **'sketchiness** *n*
skew (skjuː) *adj* **1** placed in or turning into an oblique position or course. **2** *Machinery.* having a component that is at an angle to the main axis of an assembly or is in some other way asymmetrical: *a skew bevel gear.* **3** *Maths.* **3a** composed of or being elements that are neither parallel nor intersecting as, for example, two lines not lying in the same plane in a three-dimensional space. **3b** (of a curve) not lying in a plane. **4** (of a statistical distribution) not having equal probabilities above and below the mean; non-normal. **5** distorted or biased. ♦ *n* **6** an oblique, slanting, or indirect course or position. **7** *Psychol.* the system of relationships in a family in which one parent is extremely dominating while the other parent tends to be meekly compliant. ♦ *vb* **8** to take or cause to take an oblique course or direction. **9** (*intr*) to look sideways; squint. **10** (*tr*) to place at an angle. **11** (*tr*) to distort or bias. [C14: from Old Norman French *escuer* to shun, of Germanic origin; compare Middle Dutch *schuwen* to avoid]
skew arch *n* an arch or vault, esp. one used in a bridge or tunnel, that is set at an oblique angle to the span.
skewback ('skjuːˌbæk) *n* **1** the sloping surface on both sides of a segmental arch that takes the thrust. **2** one or more stones that provide such a surface. ► **'skewˌbacked** *adj*
skewbald ('skjuːˌbɔːld) *adj* **1** marked or spotted in white and any colour except black. ♦ *n* **2** a horse with this marking. [C17: see SKEW, PIEBALD]
skewer ('skjʊə) *n* **1** a long pin for holding meat in position while being cooked, etc. **2** a similar pin having some other function. **3** *Chess.* a tactical manoeuvre in which an attacked man is made to move and expose another man to capture. ♦ *vb* **4** (*tr*) to drive a skewer through or fasten with a skewer. [C17: probably from dialect *skiver*]
skewness ('skjuːnɪs) *n* **1** the quality or condition of being skew. **2** *Statistics.* a measure of the symmetry of a distribution around its mean, esp. the statistic $B_1 = m_3/(m_2)^{3/2}$, where m_2 and m_3 are respectively the second and third moments of the distribution around the mean. In a normal distribution, $B_1 = 0$. Compare **kurtosis.**
skew symmetry *n* symmetry of top left with bottom right, and top right with bottom left.
skewwhiff ('skjuː'wɪf) *adj* (*postpositive*) *Brit. informal.* not straight; askew. [C18: probably influenced by ASKEW]
ski (skiː) *n, pl* **skis** *or* **ski. 1a** one of a pair of wood, metal, or plastic runners that are used for gliding over snow. Skis are commonly attached to shoes for sport, but may also be used as landing gear for aircraft, etc. **1b** (*as modifier*): *a ski boot.* **2** a water-ski. ♦ *vb* **skis, skiing; skied** *or* **ski'd. 3** (*intr*) to travel on skis. [C19: from Norwegian, from Old Norse *skíth* snowshoes; related to Old English *scīd* piece of split wood] ► **'skiable** *adj* ► **'skier** *n* ► **'skiing** *n*
skiamachy (skaɪ'æməkɪ) *n, pl* **-chies.** a variant of **sciamachy.**
skiascope ('skaɪəˌskəʊp) *n Med.* a medical instrument for examining the eye to detect errors of refraction. Also called: **retinoscope.** See also **retinoscopy.** [C19: from Greek *skia* a shadow + -SCOPE]
skiascopy (skaɪ'æskəpɪ) *n Med.* another name for **retinoscopy.**
skibob ('skiːbɒb) *n* a vehicle made of two short skis, the forward one having a steering handle and the rear one supporting a low seat, for gliding down snow slopes. [C20: from SKI + BOB[2]. See BOBSLEIGH] ► **'skibobber** *n* ► **'skibobbing** *n*
skid (skɪd) *vb* **skids, skidding, skidded. 1** to cause (a vehicle) to slide sideways or (of a vehicle) to slide sideways while in motion, esp. out of control. **2** (*intr*) to slide without revolving, as the wheel of a moving vehicle after sudden braking. **3** (*tr*) *U.S. and Canadian.* to put or haul on a skid, esp. along a special track. **4** to cause (an aircraft) to slide sideways away from the centre of a turn when insufficiently banked or (of an aircraft) to slide in this manner. ♦ *n* **5** an instance of sliding, esp. sideways. **6** *Chiefly U.S. and Canadian.* one of the logs forming a skidway. **7** a support on which heavy objects may be stored and moved short distances by sliding. **8** a shoe or drag used to apply pressure to the metal rim of a wheel to act as a brake. **9 on the skids.** in decline or about to fail. [C17: perhaps of Scandinavian origin; compare SKI] ► **'skiddy** *adj*
skidlid ('skɪdˌlɪd) *n* a slang word for **crash helmet.**
Skidoo (skɪ'duː) *n Canadian, Trademark.* another name for **snowmobile.**
skidpan ('skɪdˌpæn) *n Chiefly Brit.* an area made slippery so that vehicle drivers can practise controlling skids.
skidproof ('skɪdˌpruːf) *adj* (of a road surface, tyre, etc.) preventing or resistant to skidding.
skid road *n* (in the U.S. and Canada) **1** a track made of a set of logs laid transversely on which freshly cut timber can be hauled. **2a** (in the West) the part of a town frequented by loggers. **2b** another term for **skid row.**
skid row (rəʊ) *or* **skid road** *n Slang, chiefly U.S. and Canadian.* a dilapidated section of a city inhabited by vagrants, etc.
skidway ('skɪdˌweɪ) *n Chiefly U.S. and Canadian.* **1** a platform on which logs ready for sawing are piled. **2** a track made of logs for rolling objects along.
skied[1] (skaɪd) *vb* the past tense and past participle of **sky.**
skied[2] (skiːd) *vb* a past tense and past participle of **ski.**
Skien (*Norwegian* 'ʃeːən) *n* a port in S Norway, on the **Skien River:** one of the oldest towns in Norway; timber industry. Pop.: 47 870 (1990).
skiff (skɪf) *n* any of various small boats propelled by oars, sail, or motor. [C18: from French *esquif,* from Old Italian *schifo* a boat, of Germanic origin; related to Old High German *schif* SHIP]
skiffle[1] ('skɪfᵊl) *n* a style of popular music of the 1950s, played chiefly on guitars and improvised percussion instruments. [C20: of unknown origin]
skiffle[2] ('skɪfᵊl) *n Ulster dialect.* a drizzle: *a skiffle of rain.* [from Scottish *skiff,* from *skiff* to move lightly, probably changed from *skift,* from Old Norse *skipta* SHIFT]
skijoring (skiː'dʒɔːrɪŋ) *n* a sport in which a skier is pulled over snow or ice, usually by a horse. [Norwegian *skikjöring,* literally: ski-driving] ► **ski'jorer** *n*
ski jump *n* **1** a high ramp overhanging a slope from which skiers compete to make the longest jump. ♦ *vb* **ski-jump. 2** (*intr*) to perform a ski jump. ► **ski jumper** *n*
Skikda ('skɪkdɑː) *n* a port in NE Algeria, on an inlet of the Mediterranean: founded by the French in 1838 on the site of a Roman city. Pop.: 128 747 (1987). Former name: **Philippeville.**
skilful *or U.S.* **skillful** ('skɪlfʊl) *adj* **1** possessing or displaying accomplishment or skill. **2** involving or requiring accomplishment or skill. ► **'skilfully** *or U.S.* **'skillfully** *adv* ► **'skilfulness** *or U.S.* **'skillfulness** *n*
ski lift *n* any of various devices for carrying skiers up a slope, such as a chairlift.
skill (skɪl) *n* **1** special ability in a task, sport, etc., esp. ability acquired by training. **2** something, esp. a trade or technique, requiring special training or manual proficiency. **3** *Obsolete.* understanding. [C12: from Old Norse *skil* distinction; related to Middle Low German *schēle,* Middle Dutch *geschil* difference] ► **'skill-less** *or* **'skilless** *adj*
Skillcentre ('skɪlˌsɛntə) *n Brit.* any of a number of agencies attached to the Manpower Services Commission and funded by the Government to provide vocational training or retraining for employed or unemployed people.
skilled (skɪld) *adj* **1** possessing or demonstrating accomplishment, skill, or special training. **2** (*prenominal*) involving skill or special training: *a skilled job.*
skillet ('skɪlɪt) *n* **1** a small frying pan. **2** *Chiefly Brit.* a saucepan. [C15: probably from *skele* bucket, of Scandinavian origin; related to Old Norse *skjōla* bucket]
skilling ('skɪlɪŋ) *n* a former Scandinavian coin of low denomination. [C18: from Danish and Swedish; see SHILLING]
skillion ('skɪljən) *n Austral.* **a** a part of a building having a lower, esp. sloping, roof; lean-to. **b** (*as modifier*): *a skillion roof.* [C19: from English dialect *skilling* outhouse]
skilly ('skɪlɪ) *n Chiefly Brit.* a thin soup or gruel. [C19: shortened from *skilligallee,* probably a fanciful formation]
Skil Saw (skɪl) *n Trademark.* a portable electric saw.
skim (skɪm) *vb* **skims, skimming, skimmed. 1** (*tr*) to remove floating material from the surface of (a liquid), as with a spoon: *to skim milk.* **2** to glide smoothly or lightly over (a surface). **3** (*tr*) to throw (something) in a path over a surface, so as to bounce or ricochet: *to skim stones over water.* **4** (when *intr,* usually foll. by *through*) to read (a book) in a superficial or cursory manner. **5** to cover (a liquid) with a thin layer or (of liquid) to become coated in this way, as with ice, scum, etc. ♦ *n* **6** the act or process of skimming. **7** material skimmed off a liquid, esp. off milk. **8** the liquid left after skimming. **9** any thin layer covering a surface. ♦ See also **skim off.** [C15 *skimmen,* probably from *scumen* to skim; see SCUM]
skimble-scamble ('skɪmbᵊl'skæmbᵊl) *Archaic.* ♦ *adj* **1** rambling; confused. ♦ *n* **2** meaningless discourse. [C16: whimsical formation based on dialect *scamble* to struggle]
skimmed milk *n* milk from which the cream has been removed. Also called: **skim milk.** Compare **whole milk.**
skimmer ('skɪmə) *n* **1** a person or thing that skims. **2** any of several mainly tropical coastal aquatic birds of the genus *Rhynchops,* having long narrow wings and a bill with an elongated lower mandible for skimming food from the surface of the water: family *Rynchopidae,* order *Charadriiformes.* **3** a flat perforated spoon used for skimming fat from liquids.
skimmia ('skɪmɪə) *n* any rutaceous shrub of the S and SE Asian genus *Skimmia,* grown for their ornamental red berries and evergreen foliage. [C18: New Latin from Japanese (*mijama-*)*shikimi,* a native name of the plant]
skimmings ('skɪmɪŋz) *pl n* **1** material that is skimmed off a liquid. **2** the froth

containing concentrated ore removed during a flotation process. **3** slag, scum, or impurities removed from molten metals.

skim off *vb* (*tr, adv*) to take the best part of: *the teacher skimmed off the able pupils for his class.*

skimp (skɪmp) *vb* **1** to be extremely sparing or supply (someone) sparingly; stint. **2** to perform (work, etc.) carelessly, hastily, or with inadequate materials. [C17: perhaps a combination of SCANT and SCRIMP]

skimpy ('skɪmpɪ) *adj* **skimpier, skimpiest.** **1** (of clothes, etc.) made of too little material; scanty. **2** excessively thrifty; mean; stingy. ► **'skimpily** *adv* ► **'skimpiness** *n*

skin (skɪn) *n* **1a** the tissue forming the outer covering of the vertebrate body: it consists of two layers (see **dermis, epidermis**), the outermost of which may be covered with hair, scales, feathers, etc. It is mainly protective and sensory in function. **1b** (*as modifier*): *a skin disease.* Related adjs: **cutaneous, dermatoid.** **2** a person's complexion: *a fair skin.* **3** any similar covering in a plant or lower animal. **4** any coating or film, such as one that forms on the surface of a liquid. **5** unsplit leather made from the outer covering of various mammals, reptiles, etc. Compare **hide**[2] (sense 1). **6** the outer covering of a fur-bearing animal, dressed and finished with the hair on. **7** a container made from animal skin. **8** the outer covering surface of a vessel, rocket, etc. **9** a person's skin regarded as his life: *to save one's skin.* **10** (*often pl*) *Informal.* (in jazz or pop use) a drum. **11** *Informal.* short for **skinhead.** **12** *Slang.* a cigarette paper used for rolling a cannabis cigarette. **13** *Anglo-Irish slang.* a person; sort: *he's a good old skin.* **14 by the skin of one's teeth.** by a narrow margin; only just. **15 get under one's skin.** *Informal.* to irritate one. **16 jump out of one's skin.** to be very startled. **17 no skin off one's nose.** *Informal.* not a matter that affects one adversely. **18 thick** (*or* **thin**) **skin.** an insensitive (*or* sensitive) nature. ♦ *vb* **skins, skinning, skinned.** **19** (*tr*) to remove the outer covering from (fruit, etc.). **20** (*tr*) to scrape a small piece of skin from (a part of oneself) in falling, etc.: *he skinned his knee.* **21** (often foll. by *over*) to cover (something) with skin or a skinlike substance or (of something) to become covered in this way. **22** (*tr*) *Slang.* to strip of money; swindle. ♦ *adj* **23** relating to or for the skin: *skin cream.* **24** *Slang, chiefly U.S.* involving or depicting nudity: *skin magazines.* ♦ See also **skin up.** [Old English *scinn,* from Old Norse *skinn*] ► **'skinless** *adj* ► **'skin,like** *adj*

skin-deep *adj* **1** superficial; shallow. ♦ *adv* **2** superficially.

skin diving *n* the sport or activity of diving and underwater swimming without wearing a diver's costume. ► **'skin-,diver** *n*

skin effect *n* the tendency of alternating current to concentrate in the surface layer of a conductor, esp. at high frequencies, thus increasing its effective resistance.

skin flick *n Slang.* a film containing much nudity and explicit sex for sensational purposes.

skinflint ('skɪn,flɪnt) *n* an ungenerous or niggardly person; miser. [C18: referring to a person so avaricious that he would skin (swindle) a flint] ► **'skin,flinty** *adj*

skin food *n* a cosmetic cream for keeping the skin in good condition.

skin friction *n* the friction acting on a solid body when it is moving through a fluid.

skinful ('skɪn,fʊl) *n, pl* **-fuls.** *Slang.* sufficient alcoholic drink to make one drunk (esp. in the phrase **have a skinful**).

skin game *n Slang.* a swindling trick.

skin graft *n* a piece of skin removed from one part of the body and surgically grafted at the site of a severe burn or similar injury.

skinhead ('skɪn,hɛd) *n* **1** a member of a group of White youths, noted for their closely cropped hair, aggressive behaviour, and overt racism. **2** a closely cropped hairstyle.

skink (skɪŋk) *n* any lizard of the family *Scincidae,* commonest in tropical Africa and Asia, having reduced limbs and an elongated body covered with smooth scales. Related adj: **scincoid.** [C16: from Latin *scincus* a lizard, from Greek *skinkos*]

skinned (skɪnd) *adj* **1** stripped of the skin. **2a** having a skin as specified. **2b** (*in combination*): *thick-skinned.* **3 keep one's eyes skinned** (*or* **peeled**). to watch carefully (for).

skinner ('skɪnə) *n* a person who prepares or deals in animal skins.

Skinner ('skɪnə) *n* **B**(urrhus) **F**(rederic). 1904–90, U.S. behavioural psychologist. His "laws of learning", derived from experiments with animals, have been widely applied to education and behaviour therapy.

Skinner box *n* a device for studying the learning behaviour of animals, esp. rats and pigeons, consisting of a box in which the animal can move a lever to obtain a reward, such as a food pellet, or a punishment, such as an electric shock. [C20: named after B. F. SKINNER]

skinny ('skɪnɪ) *adj* **-nier, -niest.** **1** lacking in flesh; thin. **2** consisting of or resembling skin. ► **'skinniness** *n*

skinny-dip *vb* **-dips, -dipping, -dipped.** (*intr*) to swim in the nude. ► **skinny dipping** *n*

skin-pop *Slang.* ♦ *n* **1** the subcutaneous or intramuscular injection of a narcotic. ♦ *vb* **-pops, -popping, -popped.** **2** (*intr*) to take drugs in such a way.

skint (skɪnt) *adj* (*usually postpositive*) *Brit. slang.* without money. [variant of *skinned,* past participle of SKIN]

skin test *n Med.* any test to determine immunity to a disease or hypersensitivity by introducing a small amount of the test substance beneath the skin or rubbing it into a fresh scratch. See **scratch test.**

skintight ('skɪn'taɪt) *adj* (of garments) fitting tightly over the body; clinging.

skin up *vb* (*adv*) *Slang.* to roll (a cannabis cigarette).

skip[1] (skɪp) *vb* **skips, skipping, skipped.** **1** (when *intr,* often foll. by *over, along, into,* etc.) to spring or move lightly, esp. to move by hopping from one foot to the other. **2** (*intr*) to jump over a skipping-rope. **3** to cause (a stone, etc.) to bounce or skim over a surface or (of a stone) to move in this way. **4** to omit (intervening matter), as in passing from one part or subject to another: *he skipped a chapter of the book.* **5** (*intr;* foll. by *through*) *Informal.* to read or deal with quickly or superficially: *he skipped through the accounts before dinner.* **6 skip it!** *Informal.* it doesn't matter! **7** (*tr*) *Informal.* to miss deliberately: *to skip school.* **8** (*tr*) *Informal, chiefly U.S. and Canadian.* to leave (a place) in haste or secrecy: *to skip town.* ♦ *n* **9** a skipping movement or gait. **10** the act of passing over or omitting. **11** *Music, U.S. and Canadian.* another word for **leap** (sense 10). ♦ See also **skip off.** [C13: probably of Scandinavian origin; related to Old Norse *skopa* to take a run, obsolete Swedish *skuppa* to skip]

skip[2] (skɪp) *n, vb* **skips, skipping, skipped.** *Informal.* short for **skipper**[1].

skip[3] (skɪp) *n* **1** a large open container for transporting building materials, etc. **2** a cage used as a lift in mines, etc. [C19: variant of SKEP]

skip[4] (skɪp) *n* a college servant, esp. of Trinity College, Dublin. [C17: probably shortened from archaic *skip-kennel* a footman or lackey (from SKIP[1] + KENNEL[2])]

ski pants *pl n* trousers usually of stretch material and kept taut by a strap under the foot, worn for skiing or as a fashion garment.

skip distance *n* the shortest distance between a transmitter and a receiver that will permit reception of radio waves of a specified frequency by one reflection from the ionosphere.

skipjack ('skɪp,dʒæk) *n, pl* **-jack** *or* **-jacks.** **1** Also called: **skipjack tuna.** an important food fish, *Katsuwonus pelamis,* that has a striped abdomen and occurs in all tropical seas: family *Scombridae* (mackerels and tunas). **2 black skipjack.** a small spotted tuna, *Euthynnus yaito,* of Indo-Pacific seas. **3** any of several other unrelated fishes, such as the alewife and bonito. **4** *Nautical.* an American sloop used for oystering and as a yacht. **5** another name for a **click beetle.** [C18: from SKIP[1] + JACK[1]]

skiplane ('ski:,pleɪn) *n* an aircraft fitted with skis to enable it to land on and take off from snow.

skip off *vb* (*intr, adv*) *Brit. informal.* to leave work, school, etc., early or without authorization.

skipper[1] ('skɪpə) *n* **1** the captain of any vessel. **2** the captain of an aircraft. **3** a manager or leader, as of a sporting team. ♦ *vb* **4** to act as skipper (of). [C14: from Middle Low German, Middle Dutch *schipper* shipper]

skipper[2] ('skɪpə) *n* **1** a person or thing that skips. **2** any small butterfly of the family *Hesperiidae,* having a hairy mothlike body and erratic darting flight. **3** another name for the **saury** (a fish).

skippering ('skɪpərɪŋ) *n Slang.* the practice of sleeping rough. [C20: of unknown origin]

skippet ('skɪpɪt) *n* a small round box for preserving a document or seal. [C14: perhaps from *skeppe* SKEP]

skipping ('skɪpɪŋ) *n* the act of jumping over a rope that is held and swung either by the person jumping or by two other people, as a game or for exercise.

skipping-rope *n Brit.* a cord, usually having handles at each end, that is held in the hands and swung round and down so that the holder or others can jump over it.

Skipton ('skɪptən) *n* a market town in N England, in North Yorkshire: 11th-century castle. Pop.: 13 583 (1991).

skip-tooth saw *n* a saw with alternate teeth absent.

skip zone *n* a region surrounding a broadcasting station that cannot receive transmissions either directly or by reflection off the ionosphere.

skirl (skɜ:l; *Scot.* skɪrl) *vb* (*intr*) **1** *Scot. and northern English dialect.* (esp. of bagpipes) to emit a shrill sound. **2** to play the bagpipes. ♦ *n* **3** the sound of bagpipes. **4** a shrill sound. [C14: probably of Scandinavian origin; see SHRILL]

skirmish ('skɜ:mɪʃ) *n* **1** a minor short-lived military engagement. **2** any brisk clash or encounter, usually of a minor nature. ♦ *vb* **3** (*intr;* often foll. by *with*) to engage in a skirmish. [C14: from Old French *eskirmir,* of Germanic origin; related to Old High German *skirmen* to defend] ► **'skirmisher** *n*

Skíros ('skirɔs) *n* transliteration of the Modern Greek name for **Skyros.**

skirr (skɜ:) *vb* **1** (*intr;* usually foll. by *off, away,* etc.) to move, run, or fly rapidly. **2** (*tr*) *Archaic or literary.* to move rapidly over (an area, etc.), esp. in order to find or apprehend. ♦ *n* **3** a whirring or grating sound, as of the wings of birds in flight. [C16: variant of SCOUR[2]]

skirret ('skɪrɪt) *n* an umbelliferous Old World plant, *Sium sisarum,* cultivated in parts of Europe for its edible tuberous roots. [C14 *skirwhite,* perhaps from obsolete *skir* bright (see SHEER[1]) + WHITE]

skirt (skɜ:t) *n* **1** a garment hanging from the waist, worn chiefly by women and girls. **2** the part of a dress below the waist. **3** Also called: **apron.** a frieze or circular flap, as round the base of a hovercraft. **4** the flaps on a saddle that protect a rider's legs. **5** *Brit.* a cut of beef from the flank. **6** (*often pl*) a margin or outlying area. **7** *N.Z.* the lower part of a sheep's fleece. **8 bit of skirt.** *Slang.* a girl or woman. ♦ *vb* **9** (*tr*) to form the edge of. **10** (*tr*) to provide with a border. **11** (when *intr,* foll. by *around, along,* etc.) to pass (by) or be situated (near) the outer edge of (an area, etc.). **12** (*tr*) to avoid (a difficulty, etc.): *he skirted the issue.* **13** *Chiefly Austral. and N.Z.* to remove the trimmings or inferior wool from (a fleece). [C13: from Old Norse *skyrta* SHIRT] ► **'skirted** *adj*

skirter ('skɜ:tə) *n Austral.* a man who skirts fleeces. See **skirt** (sense 13).

skirting ('skɜ:tɪŋ) *n* **1** a border, esp. of wood or tiles, fixed round the base of an interior wall to protect it from kicks, dirt, etc. **2** material used or suitable for skirts.

skirting board *n* a skirting made of wood. U.S. and Canadian name: **baseboard.** U.S. name: **mopboard.**

skirtings ('skɜ:tɪŋz) *pl n* ragged edges trimmed from the fleece of a sheep.

ski run *n* a trail, slope, or course for skiing.

ski stick *or* **pole** *n* a stick, usually with a metal point and a disc to prevent it from sinking into the snow, used by skiers to gain momentum and maintain balance.

skit (skɪt) *n* **1** a brief satirical theatrical sketch. **2** a short satirical piece of writing.

3 a trick or hoax. [C18: related to earlier verb *skit* to move rapidly, hence to score a satirical hit, probably of Scandinavian origin; related to Old Norse *skjóta* to shoot]

skitch (skɪtʃ) *vb* (*tr*) *N.Z.* (of a dog) to attack; catch.

skite[1] (skəɪt) *Scot.* ◆ *vb* **1** (*intr*) to slide or slip, as on ice. **2** (*tr*) to strike with a sharp or glancing blow. ◆ *n* **3** an instance of sliding or slipping. **4** a sharp or glancing blow. **5 on the** (*or* **a**) **skite.** *Scot., Irish.* on a drinking spree. [C18: of uncertain origin]

skite[2] (skaɪt) *Austral. and N.Z. informal.* ◆ *vb* (*intr*) **1** to boast. ◆ *n* **2** boastful talk. **3** a person who boasts. [C19: from Scottish and northern English dialect; see SKATE[3]]

ski touring *n* long-distance hiking on skis over open, mountainous country; noncompetitive cross-country skiing.

ski tow *n* a device for pulling skiers uphill, usually a motor-driven rope grasped by the skier while riding on his skis.

skitter (ˈskɪtə) *vb* **1** (*intr;* often foll. by *off*) to move or run rapidly or lightly; scamper. **2** to skim or cause to skim lightly and rapidly, as across the surface of water. **3** (*intr*) *Angling.* to draw a bait lightly over the surface of water. [C19: probably from dialect *skite* to dash about; related to Old Norse *skjōta* to SHOOT]

skittish (ˈskɪtɪʃ) *adj* **1** playful, lively, or frivolous. **2** difficult to handle or predict. **3** *Now rare.* coy. [C15: probably of Scandinavian origin; compare Old Norse *skjōta* to SHOOT; see -ISH] ▸ **ˈskittishly** *adv* ▸ **ˈskittishness** *n*

skittle (ˈskɪtᵊl) *n* **1** a wooden or plastic pin, typically widest just above the base. **2** (*pl; functioning as sing*) Also called (esp. U.S.): **ninepins.** a bowling game in which players knock over as many skittles as possible by rolling a wooden ball at them. **3 beer and skittles.** (*often used with a negative*) *Informal.* an easy time; amusement. [C17: of obscure origin; perhaps related to Swedish, Danish *skyttel* shuttle]

skittle out *vb* (*tr, adv*) *Cricket.* to dismiss (batsmen) quickly.

skive[1] (skaɪv) *vb* (*tr*) to shave or remove the surface of (leather). [C19: from Old Norse *skifa;* related to English dialect *shive* a slice of bread]

skive[2] (skaɪv) *vb* (when *intr,* often foll. by *off*) *Brit. informal.* to evade (work or responsibility). [C20: of unknown origin]

skiver[1] (ˈskaɪvə) *n* **1** the tanned outer layer split from a skin. **2** a person, tool, or machine that skives.

skiver[2] (ˈskaɪvə) *n Brit. slang.* a person who persistently avoids work or responsibility.

skivvy[1] (ˈskɪvɪ) *n, pl* **-vies. 1** *Chiefly Brit., often contemptuous.* a servant, esp. a female, who does menial work of all kinds; drudge. ◆ *vb* **-vies, -vying, -vied. 2** (*intr*) *Brit.* to work as a skivvy. [C20: of unknown origin]

skivvy[2] (ˈskɪvɪ) *n, pl* **-vies. 1** *Slang, chiefly U.S.* a man's T-shirt or vest. **2** (*pl*) *Slang, chiefly U.S.* men's underwear. **3** *Austral. and N.Z.* a garment resembling a sweater with long sleeves and a polo neck, usually made of stretch cotton or cotton and polyester and worn by either sex. [of unknown origin]

skokiaan (ˈskɔːkɪˌɑːn) *n* (in South Africa) a potent alcoholic beverage drunk by Black Africans in shebeens. [C20: from Afrikaans, of unknown origin]

skol (skɒl) *or* **skoal** (skəʊl) *sentence substitute.* good health! (a drinking toast). [C16: from Danish *skaal* bowl, from Old Norse *skal;* see SCALE[2]]

skolly *or* **skollie** (ˈskɒlɪ) *n, pl* **-lies.** *S. African.* a Coloured hooligan, usually one of a gang. [C20: of unknown origin]

Skopje (ˈskɔːpjɛ) *n* the capital of (the Former Yugoslav Republic of) Macedonia, on the Vardar River: became capital of Serbia in 1346 and of Macedonia in 1945; suffered a severe earthquake in 1963; university (1949). Pop.: 541 280 (1994). Serbo-Croat name: **Skoplje** (ˈskɔpljɛ). Turkish name (1392–1913): **Üsküb.**

Skryabin *n* a variant spelling of **Scriabin.**

Skt *or* **Skr.** *abbrev. for* Sanskrit.

skua (ˈskjuːə) *n* any predatory gull-like bird of the family *Stercorariidae,* such as the **great skua** or **bonxie** (*Stercorarius skua*) or **arctic skua** (*S. parasiticus*) both of which harass terns or gulls into dropping or disgorging fish they have caught. [C17: from New Latin, from Faeroese *skūgvur,* from Old Norse *skūfr*]

skulduggery *or U.S.* **skullduggery** (skʌlˈdʌgərɪ) *n Informal.* underhand dealing; trickery. [C19: altered from earlier Scot. *sculduddery;* of obscure origin]

skulk (skʌlk) *vb* (*intr*) **1** to move stealthily so as to avoid notice. **2** to lie in hiding; lurk. **3** to shirk duty or evade responsibilities; malinger. ◆ *n* **4** a person who skulks. **5** *Obsolete.* a pack of foxes or other animals that creep about stealthily. [C13: of Scandinavian origin; compare Norwegian *skulka* to lurk, Swedish *skolka,* Danish *skulke* to shirk] ▸ **ˈskulker** *n*

skull (skʌl) *n* **1** the bony skeleton of the head of vertebrates. See **cranium.** Related adj: **cranial. 2** *Often derogatory.* the head regarded as the mind or intelligence: *to have a dense skull.* **3** a picture of a skull used to represent death or danger. [C13: of Scandinavian origin; compare Old Norse *skoltr,* Norwegian *skult,* Swedish dialect *skulle*]

skull and crossbones *n* a picture of the human skull above two crossed thighbones, formerly on the pirate flag, now used as a warning of danger or death.

skullcap (ˈskʌlˌkæp) *n* **1** a rounded brimless hat fitting the crown of the head. **2** the nontechnical name for **calvaria. 3** any of various perennial plants of the genus *Scutellaria,* esp. *S. galericulata,* that typically have helmet-shaped flowers: family *Labiatae* (labiates).

skunk (skʌŋk) *n, pl* **skunks** *or* **skunk. 1** any of various American musteline mammals of the subfamily *Mephitinae,* esp. *Mephitis mephitis* (**striped skunk**), typically having a black and white coat and bushy tail: they eject an unpleasant-smelling fluid from the anal gland when attacked. **2** *Informal.* a despicable person. **3** *Slang.* a strain of cannabis smoked for its exceptionally powerful psychoactive properties. ◆ *vb* **4** (*tr*) *U.S. and Canadian slang.* to defeat overwhelmingly in a game. [C17: from Algonquian; compare Abnaki *segākw* skunk]

skunk cabbage *n* **1** a low-growing fetid aroid swamp plant, *Symplocarpus foetidus* of E North America, having broad leaves and minute flowers enclosed in a mottled greenish or purple spathe. **2** a similar aroid plant, *Lysichitum americanum,* of the W coast of North America and N Asia. ◆ Also called: **skunkweed.**

sky (skaɪ) *n, pl* **skies. 1** (*sometimes pl*) the apparently dome-shaped expanse extending upwards from the horizon that is characteristically blue or grey during the day, red in the evening, and black at night. Related adjs: **celestial, empyrean. 2** outer space, as seen from the earth. **3** (*often pl*) weather, as described by the appearance of the upper air: *sunny skies.* **4** the source of divine power; heaven. **5** *Informal.* the highest level of attainment: *the sky's the limit.* **6 to the skies.** highly; extravagantly. ◆ *vb* **skies, skying, skied. 7** *Rowing.* to lift (the blade of an oar) too high before a stroke. **8** (*tr*) *Informal.* to hit (a ball) high in the air. [C13: from Old Norse *ský;* related to Old English *scio* cloud, Old Saxon *skio,* Old Norse *skjār* transparent skin] ▸ **ˈskyˌlike** *adj*

sky blue *n* **a** a light or pale blue colour. **b** (*as adj*): *a sky-blue jumper.*

sky-blue pink *n, adj* a jocular name for a nonexistent, unknown, or unimportant colour.

skydive (ˈskaɪˌdaɪv) *vb* **-dives, -diving, -dived** *or U.S.* **-dove; -dived.** (*intr*) to take part in skydiving. ▸ **ˈskyˌdiver** *n*

skydiving (ˈskaɪˌdaɪvɪŋ) *n* the sport of parachute jumping, in which participants perform manoeuvres before opening the parachute and attempt to land accurately.

Skye (skaɪ) *n* a mountainous island off the NW coast of Scotland, the largest island of the Inner Hebrides: tourist centre. Chief town: Portree. Pop.: 7500 (latest est.). Area: 1735 sq. km (670 sq. miles).

Skye terrier *n* a short-legged long-bodied breed of terrier with long wiry hair and erect ears.

sky-high *adj, adv* **1** at or to an unprecedented or excessive level: *prices rocketed sky-high.* ◆ *adv* **2** high into the air. **3 blow sky-high.** to destroy completely.

skyjack (ˈskaɪˌdʒæk) *vb* (*tr*) to commandeer (an aircraft), usually with a gun during flight, forcing the pilot to fly somewhere other than to its scheduled destination. [C20: from SKY + HIJACK] ▸ **ˈskyˌjacker** *n*

Skylab (ˈskaɪˌlæb) *n* a U.S. space station launched in May 1973 into an orbit inclined at 50° to the equatorial plane at a mean altitude of 430 kilometres (270 miles), the astronauts working there under conditions of zero gravity. It disintegrated, unmanned, in 1979, with some parts landing in the outback of Australia. [C20: from SKY + LAB(ORATORY)]

skylark (ˈskaɪˌlɑːk) *n* **1** an Old World lark, *Alauda arvensis,* noted for singing while hovering at a great height. ◆ *vb* **2** (*intr*) *Informal.* to romp or play jokes. ▸ **ˈskyˌlarker** *n*

skylight (ˈskaɪˌlaɪt) *n* a window placed in a roof or ceiling to admit daylight. Also called: **fanlight.**

skylight filter *n Photog.* a very slightly pink filter that absorbs ultraviolet light and reduces haze and excessive blueness.

skyline (ˈskaɪˌlaɪn) *n* **1** the line at which the earth and sky appear to meet; horizon. **2** the outline of buildings, mountains, trees, etc., seen against the sky.

sky marker *n* a parachute flare dropped to mark a target area.

sky pilot *n Slang.* a chaplain in one of the military services.

skyrocket (ˈskaɪˌrɒkɪt) *n* **1** another word for **rocket**[1] (sense 1). ◆ *vb* **2** (*intr*) *Informal.* to rise rapidly, as in price.

Skyros *or* **Scyros** (ˈskiːrɒs) *n* a Greek island in the Aegean, the largest island in the N Sporades. Pop.: 3000 (latest est.). Area: 199 sq. km (77 sq. miles). Modern Greek name: **Skíros.**

skysail (ˈskaɪˌseɪl) *n Nautical.* **1** a square sail set above the royal on a square-rigger. **2** a triangular sail set between the trucks of a racing schooner.

skyscape (ˈskaɪˌskeɪp) *n* a painting, drawing, photograph, etc., representing or depicting the sky.

skyscraper (ˈskaɪˌskreɪpə) *n* a very tall multistorey building.

skyward (ˈskaɪwəd) *adj* **1** directed or moving towards the sky. ◆ *adv* **2** Also: **skywards.** towards the sky.

sky wave *n* a radio wave reflected back to the earth by the ionosphere (**ionospheric wave**), permitting transmission around the curved surface of the earth. Compare **ground wave.**

skywriting (ˈskaɪˌraɪtɪŋ) *n* **1** the forming of words in the sky by the release of smoke or vapour from an aircraft. **2** the words so formed. ▸ **ˈskyˌwriter** *n*

sl *Bibliog. abbrev. for* sine loco. [Latin: without place (of publication)]

SL *abbrev. for* Solicitor at Law.

slab (slæb) *n* **1** a broad flat thick piece of wood, stone, or other material. **2** a thick slice of cake, etc. **3** any of the outside parts of a log that are sawn off while the log is being made into planks. **4** *Mountaineering.* a flat sheet of rock lying at an angle of between 30° and 60° from the horizontal. **5** a printer's ink table. **6** (*modifier*) *Austral. and N.Z.* made or constructed of coarse wooden planks: *a slab hut.* **7** *Informal, chiefly Brit.* an operating or mortuary table. ◆ *vb* **slabs, slabbing, slabbed.** (*tr*) **8** to cut or make into a slab or slabs. **9** to cover or lay with slabs. **10** to saw slabs from (a log). [C13: of unknown origin]

slabber (ˈslæbə) *vb, n* a dialect word for **slobber.** [C16: variant of SLOBBER]

slack[1] (slæk) *adj* **1** not tight, tense, or taut. **2** negligent or careless. **3** (esp. of water, etc.) moving slowly. **4** (of trade, etc.) not busy. **5** *Phonetics.* another term for **lax** (sense 4). ◆ *adv* **6** in a slack manner. ◆ *n* **7** a part of a rope, etc., that is slack: *take in the slack.* **8** a period of decreased activity. **9a** a patch of water without current. **9b** a slackening of a current. **10** *Prosody.* (in sprung rhythm) the unstressed syllable or syllables. ◆ *vb* **11** to neglect (one's duty, etc.). **12** (often foll. by *off*) to loosen; to make slack. **13** *Chem.* a less common word for **slake** (sense 3). ◆ See also **slacks.** [Old English *slæc, sleac;* related to Old High German *slah,* Old Norse *slākr* bad, Latin *laxus* LAX] ▸ **ˈslackly** *adv* ▸ **ˈslackness** *n*

slack[2] (slæk) *n* small pieces of coal with a high ash content. [C15: probably from Middle Low German *slecke;* related to Dutch *slak,* German *Schlacke* dross]

slacken ('slækən) *vb* (often foll. by *off*) **1** to make or become looser. **2** to make or become slower, less intense, etc.

slacker ('slækə) *n* **1** a person who evades work or duty; shirker. **2** *Informal.* **2a** an educated young adult characterized by cynicism and apathy. **2b** (*as modifier*): *slacker culture.*

slacks (slæks) *pl n* informal trousers worn by both sexes.

slack suit *n U.S.* casual male dress consisting of slacks and a matching shirt or jacket.

slack water *n* the period of still water around the turn of the tide, esp. at low tide.

slag (slæg) *n* **1** Also called: **cinder.** the fused material formed during the smelting or refining of metals by combining the flux with gangue, impurities in the metal, etc. It usually consists of a mixture of silicates with calcium, phosphorus, sulphur, etc. See also **basic slag. 2** the mass of rough fragments of rock derived from volcanic lava; scoria. **3** a mixture of shale, clay, coal dust, and other mineral waste produced during coal mining. **4** *Brit. slang.* a coarse or dissipated girl or woman. ◆ *vb* **slags, slagging, slagged. 5** to convert into or become slag. **6** (*tr;* sometimes foll. by *off*) *Slang.* to make disparaging comments about; slander. **7** (*intr*) *Austral. slang.* to spit. [C16: from Middle Low German *slagge,* perhaps from *slagen* to SLAY] ▸ '**slagging** *n* ▸ '**slaggy** *adj*

slag down *vb* (*tr, adv*) *Prison slang.* to give a verbal lashing to.

slag heap *n* a hillock of waste matter from coal mining, etc.

slain (sleɪn) *vb* the past participle of **slay.**

slàinte mhath (ˌslɑːndʒə 'va) *or* **slàinte** *Scot.;* **slàinte mhaith** (ˌslɑːntə 'va) *Irish. interj* a drinking toast; cheers. [Gaelic: good health]

slake (sleɪk) *vb* **1** (*tr*) *Literary.* to satisfy (thirst, desire, etc.). **2** (*tr*) *Poetic.* to cool or refresh. **3** Also: **slack.** to undergo or cause to undergo the process in which lime reacts with water or moist air to produce calcium hydroxide. **4** *Archaic.* to make or become less active or intense. [Old English *slacian,* from *slæc* SLACK[1]; related to Dutch *slaken* to diminish, Icelandic *slaka*] ▸ '**slakable** *or* '**slakeable** *adj* ▸ '**slaker** *n*

slaked lime *n* another name for **calcium hydroxide,** esp. when made by adding water to calcium oxide.

slalom ('slɑːləm) *n* **1** *Skiing.* a race, esp. one downhill, over a winding course marked by artificial obstacles. **2** a similar type of obstacle race in canoes. ◆ *vb* **3** (*intr*) to take part in a slalom. [Norwegian, from *slad* sloping + *lom* path]

slam[1] (slæm) *vb* **slams, slamming, slammed. 1** to cause (a door or window) to close noisily and with force or (of a door, etc.) to close in this way. **2** (*tr*) to throw (something) down noisily and violently. **3** (*tr*) *Slang.* to criticize harshly. **4** (*intr;* usually foll. by *into* or *out of*) *Informal.* to go (into or out of a room, etc.) in violent haste or anger. **5** (*tr*) to strike with violent force. **6** (*tr*) *Informal.* to defeat easily. ◆ *n* **7** the act or noise of slamming. **8** *Slang.* harsh criticism or abuse. [C17: of Scandinavian origin; compare Old Norse *slamra,* Norwegian *slemma,* Swedish dialect *slämma*]

slam[2] (slæm) *n* **1a** the winning of all (**grand slam**) or all but one (**little** or **small slam**) of the 13 tricks at bridge or whist. **1b** the bid to do so in bridge. **2** an old card game. [C17: of uncertain origin]

slam-bang *adv* **1** another word (esp. U.S.) for **slap-bang. 2** *U.S. informal.* carelessly; recklessly.

slam dance *vb* to hurl oneself repeatedly into or through a crowd at a rock-music concert.

slam dunk *Basketball.* ◆ *n* **1** a scoring shot in which a player jumps up and forces the ball down through the basket. ◆ *vb* **slam-dunk. 2** to jump up and force (a ball) through a basket.

slammer ('slæmə) *n* **the.** *Slang.* prison.

slander ('slɑːndə) *n* **1** *Law.* **1a** defamation in some transient form, as by spoken words, gestures, etc. **1b** a slanderous statement, etc. **2** any false or defamatory words spoken about a person; calumny. ◆ *vb* **3** to utter or circulate slander (about). [C13: via Anglo-French from Old French *escandle,* from Late Latin *scandalum* a cause of offence; see SCANDAL] ▸ '**slanderer** *n* ▸ '**slanderous** *adj* ▸ '**slanderously** *adv* ▸ '**slanderousness** *n*

slang (slæŋ) *n* **1a** vocabulary, idiom, etc., that is not appropriate to the standard form of a language or to formal contexts, may be restricted as to social status or distribution, and is characteristically more metaphorical and transitory than standard language. **1b** (*as modifier*): *a slang word.* **2** another word for **jargon.** ◆ *vb* **3** to abuse (someone) with vituperative language; insult. [C18: of unknown origin] ▸ '**slangy** *adj* ▸ '**slangily** *adv* ▸ '**slanginess** *n*

slanging match *n Brit.* a dispute in which insults and accusations are made by each party against the other.

slant (slɑːnt) *vb* **1** to incline or be inclined at an oblique or sloping angle. **2** (*tr*) to write or present (news, etc.) with a bias. **3** (*intr;* foll. by *towards*) (of a person's opinions) to be biased. ◆ *n* **4** an inclined or oblique line or direction; slope. **5** a way of looking at something. **6** a bias or opinion, as in an article. **7** a less technical name for **solidus. 8 on a** (*or* **the**) **slant.** sloping. ◆ *adj* **9** oblique, sloping. [C17: short for ASLANT, probably of Scandinavian origin] ▸ '**slanting** *adj* ▸ '**slantingly** *or* '**slantly** *adv*

slanter ('slæntə) *n Austral. obsolete, informal.* a variant of **slinter.**

slant rhyme *n Prosody.* another term for **half-rhyme.**

slantwise ('slɑːntˌwaɪz) *or* **slantways** ('slɑːntˌweɪz) *adv, adj* (*prenominal*) in a slanting or oblique direction.

slap (slæp) *n* **1** a sharp blow or smack, as with the open hand, something flat, etc. **2** the sound made by or as if by such a blow. **3** a sharp rebuke; reprimand. **4** (**a bit of**) **slap and tickle.** *Brit. informal.* sexual play. **5 a slap in the face.** an insult or rebuff. **6 a slap on the back.** congratulation. **7 a slap on the wrist.** a light punishment or reprimand. ◆ *vb* **slaps, slapping, slapped. 8** (*tr*) to strike (a person or thing) sharply, as with the open hand or something flat. **9** (*tr*) to bring down (the hand, something flat, etc.) sharply. **10** (when *intr,* usually foll. by *against*) to strike (something) with or as if with a slap. **11** (*tr*) *Informal, chiefly Brit.* to apply in large quantities, haphazardly, etc.: *she slapped butter on the bread.* **12 slap on the back.** to congratulate. ◆ *adv Informal.* **13** exactly; directly: *slap on time.* **14** forcibly or abruptly: *to fall slap on the floor.* [C17: from Low German *slapp,* German *Schlappe,* of imitative origin] ▸ '**slapper** *n*

slap-bang *adv Informal, chiefly Brit.* **1** in a violent, sudden, or noisy manner. U.S. equivalent: **slam-bang. 2** directly or immediately: *slap-bang in the middle.*

slapdash ('slæpˌdæʃ) *adv* **1** in a careless, hasty, or haphazard manner. ◆ *adj* **2** careless, hasty, or haphazard. ◆ *n* **3** slapdash activity or work. **4** another name for **roughcast** (sense 1). [C17: from SLAP + DASH[1]]

slap down *vb* (*tr, adv*) *Informal.* to rebuke sharply, as for impertinence.

slaphappy ('slæpˌhæpɪ) *adj* **-pier, -piest.** *Informal.* **1** cheerfully irresponsible or careless. **2** dazed or giddy from or as if from repeated blows; punch-drunk.

slaphead ('slæpˌhɛd) *n Derogatory slang.* a bald person. [C20: from SLAP + HEAD]

slapjack ('slæpˌdʒæk) *n* **1** a simple card game. **2** *U.S.* another word for **pancake.** [C19: from SLAP + JACK[1]]

slapped-cheek disease *n* another name for **fifth disease.**

slapper ('slæpə) *n Brit. slang.* a promiscuous woman.

slapshot ('slæpˌʃɒt) *n Ice hockey.* a hard, fast, often wild, shot executed with a powerful downward swing, and with the blade of the stick brushing firmly against the ice prior to striking the puck.

slapstick ('slæpˌstɪk) *n* **1a** comedy characterized by horseplay and physical action. **1b** (*as modifier*): *slapstick humour.* **2** a flexible pair of paddles bound together at one end, formerly used in pantomime to strike a blow to a person with a loud clapping sound but without injury.

slap-up *adj* (*prenominal*) *Brit. informal.* (esp. of meals) lavish; excellent; first-class.

slash (slæʃ) *vb* (*tr*) **1** to cut or lay about (a person or thing) with sharp sweeping strokes, as with a sword, knife, etc. **2** to lash with a whip. **3** to make large gashes in: *to slash tyres.* **4** to reduce (prices, etc.) drastically. **5** *Chiefly U.S.* to criticize harshly. **6** to slit (the outer fabric of a garment) so that the lining material is revealed. **7** to clear (scrub or undergrowth) by cutting. ◆ *n* **8** a sharp, sweeping stroke, as with a sword or whip. **9** a cut or rent made by such a stroke. **10** a decorative slit in a garment revealing the lining material. **11** *North American.* **11a** littered wood chips and broken branches that remain after trees have been cut down. **11b** an area so littered. **12** another name for **solidus. 13** *Brit. slang.* the act of urinating (esp. in the phrase **have a slash**). [C14 *slaschen,* perhaps from Old French *esclachier* to break]

slash-and-burn *adj* denoting a short-term method of cultivation in which land is cleared by destroying and burning trees and other vegetation for temporary agricultural use.

slasher ('slæʃə) *n* **1** a person or thing that slashes. **2** *Austral. and N.Z.* a wooden-handled cutting tool or tractor-drawn machine used for cutting scrub or undergrowth in the bush.

slasher movie *n Slang.* a film in which victims, usually women, are slashed with knives, razors, etc.

slashing ('slæʃɪŋ) *adj* aggressively or harshly critical (esp. in the phrase **slashing attack**). ▸ '**slashingly** *adv*

slash pocket *n* a pocket in which the opening is a slit in the seam of a garment.

Śląsk (ʃlɔ̃sk) *n* the Polish name for **Silesia.**

slat[1] (slæt) *n* **1** a narrow thin strip of wood or metal, as used in a Venetian blind, etc. **2** a movable or fixed auxiliary aerofoil attached to the leading edge of an aircraft wing to increase lift, esp. during landing and takeoff. ◆ *vb* **slats, slatting, slatted. 3** (*tr*) to provide with slats. [C14: from Old French *esclat* splinter, from *esclater* to shatter]

slat[2] (slæt) *Dialect.* ◆ *vb* **slats, slatting, slatted. 1** (*tr*) to throw violently; fling carelessly. **2** (*intr*) to flap violently. ◆ *n* **3** a sudden blow. [C13: of Scandinavian origin; related to Old Norse, Icelandic *sletta* to slap]

slat[3] (slæt) *n Irish.* a spent salmon. [C19: of uncertain origin]

slate[1] (sleɪt) *n* **1a** a compact fine-grained metamorphic rock formed by the effects of heat and pressure on shale. It can be split into thin layers along natural cleavage planes and is used as a roofing and paving material. **1b** (*as modifier*): *a slate tile.* **2** a roofing tile of slate. **3** (formerly) a writing tablet of slate. **4** a dark grey colour, often with a purplish or bluish tinge. **5** *Chiefly U.S. and Canadian.* a list of candidates in an election. **6** *Films.* **6a** the reference information written on a clapperboard. **6b** *Informal.* the clapperboard itself. **7 clean slate.** a record without dishonour. **8 have a slate loose.** *Brit. and Irish informal.* to be eccentric or crazy. **9 on the slate.** *Brit. informal.* on credit. **10 wipe the slate clean.** *Informal.* to make a fresh start, esp. by forgetting past differences. ◆ *vb* (*tr*) **11** to cover (a roof) with slates. **12** *Chiefly U.S.* to enter (a person's name) on a list, esp. on a political slate. **13** *U.S. and Canadian.* to choose or destine: *he was slated to go far.* ◆ *adj* **14** of the colour slate. [C14: from Old French *esclate,* from *esclat* a fragment; see SLAT[1]]

slate[2] (sleɪt) *vb* (*tr*) *Informal, chiefly Brit.* **1** to criticize harshly; censure. **2** to punish or defeat severely. [C19: probably from SLATE[1]]

slater ('sleɪtə) *n* **1** a person trained in laying roof slates. **2** *Dialect, Austral., and N.Z.* a woodlouse. See also **sea slater.**

slatey ('sleɪtɪ) *adj* **slatier, slatiest.** *Irish informal.* slightly mad; crazy.

slather ('slæðə) *n* **1** (*usually pl*) *Informal.* a large quantity. **2 open slather.** *Austral. and N.Z. slang.* a situation in which there are no restrictions; free-for-all. ◆ *vb* (*tr*) *U.S. and Canadian slang.* **3** to squander or waste. **4** to spread thickly or lavishly. [C19: of unknown origin]

slating[1] ('sleɪtɪŋ) *n* **1** the act or process of laying slates. **2** slates collectively, or material for making slates.

slating[2] ('sleɪtɪŋ) *n Informal, chiefly Brit.* a severe reprimand or critical attack.

slattern ('slætən) *n* a slovenly woman or girl; slut. [C17: probably from *slattering,* from dialect *slatter* to slop; perhaps from Scandinavian; compare Old Norse *sletta* to slap] ▸ **'slatternly** *adj* ▸ **'slatternliness** *n*

slaty ('sleɪtɪ) *adj* **slatier, slatiest. 1** consisting of or resembling slate. **2** having the colour of slate. ▸ **'slatiness** *n*

slaughter ('slɔːtə) *n* **1** the killing of animals, esp. for food. **2** the savage killing of a person. **3** the indiscriminate or brutal killing of large numbers of people, as in war; massacre. **4** *Informal.* a resounding defeat. ◆ *vb (tr)* **5** to kill (animals), esp. for food. **6** to kill in a brutal manner. **7** to kill indiscriminately or in large numbers. **8** *Informal.* to defeat resoundingly. [Old English *sleaht;* related to Old Norse *slāttar* hammering, *slātr* butchered meat, Old High German *slahta,* Gothic *slauhts,* German *Schlacht* battle] ▸ **'slaughterer** *n* ▸ **'slaughterous** *adj*

slaughterhouse ('slɔːtə,haʊs) *n* a place where animals are butchered for food; abattoir.

slaughterman ('slɔːtə,mæn) *n, pl* **-men.** a person employed to kill animals in a slaughterhouse.

Slav (slɑːv) *n* a member of any of the peoples of E Europe or NW Asia who speak a Slavonic language. [C14: from Medieval Latin *Sclāvus* a captive Slav; see SLAVE]

Slav. *abbrev. for* Slavonic *or* Slavic.

slave (sleɪv) *n* **1** a person legally owned by another and having no freedom of action or right to property. **2** a person who is forced to work for another against his will. **3** a person under the domination of another person or some habit or influence: *a slave to television.* **4** a person who works in harsh conditions for low pay. **5a** a device that is controlled by or that duplicates the action of another similar device (the master device). **5b** *(as modifier): slave cylinder.* ◆ *vb* **6** *(intr:* often foll. by *away)* to work like a slave. **7** *(tr)* an archaic word for **enslave.** [C13: via Old French from Medieval Latin *Sclāvus* a Slav, one held in bondage (from the fact that the Slavonic races were frequently conquered in the Middle Ages), from Late Greek *Sklabos* a Slav]

slave ant *n* any of various ants, esp. *Formica fusca,* captured and forced to do the work of a colony of ants of another species (**slave-making ants**). See also **amazon ant.**

Slave Coast *n* the coast of W Africa between the Volta River and Mount Cameroon, chiefly along the Bight of Benin: the main source of African slaves (16th–19th centuries).

slave cylinder *n* a small cylinder containing a piston that operates the brake shoes or pads in hydraulic brakes or the working part in any other hydraulically operated system. Compare **master cylinder.**

slave-driver *n* **1** (esp. formerly) a person forcing slaves to work. **2** an employer who demands excessively hard work from his employees.

slaveholder ('sleɪv,həʊldə) *n* a person who owns slaves. ▸ **'slave,holding** *n*

slaver[1] ('sleɪvə) *n* **1** an owner of or dealer in slaves. **2** another name for **slave ship.**

slaver[2] ('slævə) *vb (intr)* **1** to dribble saliva. **2** (often foll. by *over)* **2a** to fawn or drool (over someone). **2b** to show great desire (for); lust (after). ◆ *n* **3** saliva dribbling from the mouth. **4** *Informal.* drivel. [C14: probably of Low Dutch origin; related to SLOBBER] ▸ **'slaverer** *n*

Slave River *n* a river in W Canada, in the Northwest Territories and NE Alberta, flowing from Lake Athabaska northwest to Great Slave Lake. Length: about 420 km (260 miles). Also called: **Great Slave River.**

slavery ('sleɪvərɪ) *n* **1** the state or condition of being a slave; a civil relationship whereby one person has absolute power over another and controls his life, liberty, and fortune. **2** the subjection of a person to another person, esp. in being forced into work. **3** the condition of being subject to some influence or habit. **4** work done in harsh conditions for low pay.

slave ship *n* a ship used to transport slaves, esp. formerly from Africa to the New World.

Slave State *n U.S. history.* any of the 15 Southern states in which slavery was legal until the Civil War.

slave trade *n* the business of trading in slaves, esp. the transportation of Black Africans to America from the 16th to 19th centuries. ▸ **'slave-,trader** *n* ▸ **'slave-,trading** *n*

slavey ('sleɪvɪ) *n Brit. informal.* a female general servant. [C19: from SLAVE + -Y[2]]

Slavic ('slɑːvɪk) *n, adj* another word (esp. U.S.) for **Slavonic.**

slavish ('sleɪvɪʃ) *adj* **1** of or befitting a slave. **2** being or resembling a slave; servile. **3** unoriginal; imitative. **4** *Archaic.* ignoble. ▸ **'slavishly** *adv* ▸ **'slavishness** *n*

Slavism ('slɑːvɪzəm) *n* anything characteristic of, peculiar to, or associated with the Slavs or the Slavonic languages.

Slavkov ('slafkɔf) *n* the Czech name for **Austerlitz.**

slavocracy (sleɪ'vɒkrəsɪ) *n, pl* **-cies.** (esp. in the U.S. before the Civil War) **1** slaveholders as a dominant class. **2** domination by slaveholders.

Slavonia (slə'vəʊnɪə) *n* a region in Croatia, mainly between the Drava and Sava Rivers. ▸ **Sla'vonian** *adj, n*

Slavonic (slə'vɒnɪk) *or (esp U.S.)* **Slavic** *n* **1** a branch of the Indo-European family of languages, usually divided into three subbranches: **South Slavonic** (including Old Church Slavonic, Serbo-Croat, Bulgarian, etc.), **East Slavonic** (including Ukrainian, Russian, etc.), and **West Slavonic** (including Polish, Czech, Slovak, etc.). **2** the unrecorded ancient language from which all of these languages developed. ◆ *adj* **3** of, denoting, or relating to this group of languages. **4** of, denoting, or relating to the people who speak these languages. [C17: from Medieval Latin *Slavonicus, Sclavonicus,* from SLAVONIA]

Slavophile ('slɑːvəʊfɪl, -,faɪl) *or* **Slavophil** *n* **1** a person who admires the Slavs or their cultures. **2** *(sometimes not cap.)* (in 19th-century Russia) a person who believed in the superiority and advocated the supremacy of the Slavs. ◆ *adj* **3** admiring the Slavs and Slavonic culture, etc. **4** *(sometimes not cap.)* (in 19th-century Russia) of, characteristic of, or relating to the Slavophiles. ▸ **Slavophilism** (slə'vɒfɪ,lɪzəm, 'slɑːvəʊfɪ,lɪzəm) *n*

slaw (slɔː) *n Chiefly U.S. and Canadian.* short for **coleslaw.** [C19: from Danish *sla,* short for *salade* SALAD]

slay (sleɪ) *vb* **slays, slaying, slew, slain.** *(tr)* **1** *Archaic or literary.* to kill, esp. violently. **2** *Slang.* to impress (someone of the opposite sex). **3** *Obsolete.* to strike. [Old English *slēan;* related to Old Norse *slā,* Gothic, Old High German *slahan* to strike, Old Irish *slacaim* I beat] ▸ **'slayer** *n*

SLBM *abbrev. for* submarine-launched ballistic missile.

SLCM *abbrev. for* sea-launched cruise missile: a type of cruise missile that can be launched from either a submarine or a surface ship.

sld *abbrev. for:* **1** sailed. **2** sealed.

SLD *abbrev. for* Social and Liberal Democratic Party.

sleave (sliːv) *n* **1** a tangled thread. **2** a thin filament unravelled from a thicker thread. **3** *Chiefly poetic.* anything matted or complicated. ◆ *vb* **4** to disentangle (twisted thread, etc.). [Old English *slǣfan* to divide; related to Middle Low German *slēf,* Norwegian *sleiv* big spoon]

sleaze (sliːz) *n Informal.* **1** sleaziness. **2** dishonest, disreputable, or immoral behaviour, especially of public officials or employees: *political sleaze.*

sleazeball ('sliːz,bɔːl) *n Slang.* an odious and contemptible person.

sleazy ('sliːzɪ) *adj* **-zier, -ziest. 1** sordid; disreputable: *a sleazy nightclub.* **2** thin or flimsy, as cloth. [C17: origin uncertain] ▸ **'sleazily** *adv* ▸ **'sleaziness** *n*

sled dog *n* any of various hardy thick-coated breeds of dog, such as the Eskimo dog, the husky, and the malamute, developed for hauling sledges in various parts of the highest northern latitudes.

sledge[1] (slɛdʒ) *or (esp. U.S. and Canadian)* **sled** (slɛd) *n* **1** Also called: **sleigh.** a vehicle mounted on runners, drawn by horses or dogs, for transporting people or goods, esp. over snow. **2** a light wooden frame used, esp. by children, for sliding over snow; toboggan. **3** *N.Z.* a farm vehicle mounted on runners, for use on rough or muddy ground. ◆ *vb* **4** to convey, travel, or go by sledge. [C17: from Middle Dutch *sleedse;* C14 *sled,* from Middle Low German, from Old Norse *slethi,* related to SLIDE] ▸ **'sledger** *n*

sledge[2] (slɛdʒ) *n* short for **sledgehammer.**

sledge[3] (slɛdʒ) *vb (tr) Austral.* to bait (an opponent, esp. a batsman in cricket) in order to upset his concentration. [of uncertain origin; perhaps from SLEDGEHAMMER]

sledgehammer ('slɛdʒ,hæmə) *n* **1** a large heavy hammer with a long handle used with both hands for heavy work such as forging iron, breaking rocks, etc. **2** *(modifier)* resembling the action of a sledgehammer in power, ruthlessness, etc.: *a sledgehammer blow.* ◆ *vb* **3** *(tr)* to strike (something) with or as if with a sledgehammer. [C15 *sledge,* from Old English *slecg* a large hammer; related to Old Norse *sleggja,* Middle Dutch *slegge*]

sleek (sliːk) *adj* **1** smooth and shiny; polished. **2** polished in speech or behaviour; unctuous. **3** (of an animal or bird) having a shiny healthy coat or feathers. **4** (of a person) having a prosperous appearance. ◆ *vb (tr)* **5** to make smooth and glossy, as by grooming, etc. **6** (usually foll. by *over)* to cover (up), as by making more agreeable; gloss (over). [C16: variant of SLICK] ▸ **'sleekly** *adv* ▸ **'sleekness** *n* ▸ **'sleeky** *adj*

sleekit ('sliːkɪt) *adj Scot.* **1** smooth, glossy. **2** unctuous. **3** deceitful; crafty; sly. [Scottish, from past participle of SLEEK]

sleep (sliːp) *n* **1** a periodic state of physiological rest during which consciousness is suspended and metabolic rate is decreased. See also **paradoxical sleep. 2** *Botany.* the nontechnical name for **nyctitropism. 3** a period spent sleeping. **4** a state of quiescence or dormancy. **5** a poetic or euphemistic word for **death. 6** *Informal.* the dried mucoid particles often found in the corners of the eyes after sleeping. ◆ *vb* **sleeps, sleeping, slept. 7** *(intr)* to be in or as in the state of sleep. **8** *(intr)* (of plants) to show nyctitropism. **9** *(intr)* to be inactive or quiescent. **10** *(tr)* to have sleeping accommodation for (a certain number): *the boat could sleep six.* **11** *(tr;* foll. by *away)* to pass (time) sleeping. **12** *(intr)* to fail to pay attention. **13** *(intr) Poetic or euphemistic.* to be dead. **14 sleep on it.** to give (something) extended consideration, esp. overnight. ◆ See also **sleep around, sleep in, sleep off, sleep out, sleep with.** [Old English *slǣpan;* related to Old Frisian *slēpa,* Old Saxon *slāpan,* Old High German *slāfan,* German *schlaff* limp]

sleep apnoea *n* the temporary cessation of breathing during sleep, which in some cases is due to obstruction of the upper airway by enlarged tonsils, uvula, etc., causing the sufferer to snore loudly and fight for breath.

sleep around *vb (intr, adv) Informal.* to be sexually promiscuous.

sleeper ('sliːpə) *n* **1** a person, animal, or thing that sleeps. **2** a railway sleeping car or compartment. **3** *Brit.* one of the blocks supporting the rails on a railway track. U.S. and Canadian equivalent: **tie. 4** a heavy timber beam, esp. one that is laid horizontally on the ground. **5** *Chiefly Brit.* a small plain gold circle worn in a pierced ear lobe to prevent the hole from closing up. **6** a wrestling hold in which a wrestler presses the sides of his opponent's neck, causing him to pass out. **7** *U.S.* an unbranded calf. **8** Also called: **sleeper goby.** any gobioid fish of the family *Eleotridae,* of brackish or fresh tropical waters, resembling the gobies but lacking a ventral sucker. **9** *Informal.* a person or thing that achieves unexpected success after an initial period of obscurity. **10** a spy planted in advance for future use, but not currently active.

sleep in *vb (intr, adv)* **1** *Brit.* to sleep longer than usual. **2** to sleep at the place of one's employment.

sleeping bag *n* a large well-padded bag designed for sleeping in, esp. outdoors.

sleeping car *n* a railway car fitted with compartments containing bunks for people to sleep in.

sleeping draught *n* any drink containing a drug or agent that induces sleep.

sleeping partner *n* a partner in a business who does not play an active role, esp. one who supplies capital.

sleeping pill *n* a pill or tablet containing a sedative drug, such as a barbiturate, used to induce sleep.

sleeping policeman *n* a bump built across roads, esp. in housing estates, to deter motorists from speeding.

sleeping sickness *n* **1** Also called: **African sleeping sickness.** an African disease caused by infection with protozoans of the genus *Trypanosoma,* characterized by fever, wasting, and sluggishness. **2** Also called (esp. formerly): **sleepy sickness.** an epidemic viral form of encephalitis characterized by extreme drowsiness. Technical name: **encephalitis lethargica.**

sleepless ('sli:plɪs) *adj* **1** without sleep or rest: *a sleepless journey.* **2** unable to sleep. **3** always watchful or alert. **4** *Chiefly poetic.* always active or moving: *the sleepless tides.* ▸ **'sleeplessly** *adv* ▸ **'sleeplessness** *n*

sleep movement *n* the folding together of leaflets, petals, etc., that occurs at night in certain plants.

sleep off *vb* (*tr, adv*) *Informal.* to lose by sleeping: *to sleep off a hangover.*

sleep out *vb* (*intr, adv*) **1** (esp. of a tramp) to sleep in the open air. **2** to sleep away from the place of work. ◆ *n* **sleep-out. 3** *Austral. and N.Z.* an area of a veranda that has been glassed in or partitioned off so that it may be used as a bedroom.

sleepwalk ('sli:pˌwɔ:k) *vb* (*intr*) to walk while asleep. See also **somnambulism.** ▸ **'sleepˌwalker** *n* ▸ **'sleepˌwalking** *n, adj*

sleep with *vb* (*intr, prep*) to have sexual intercourse and (usually) spend the night with. Also: **sleep together.**

sleepy ('sli:pɪ) *adj* **sleepier, sleepiest. 1** inclined to or needing sleep; drowsy. **2** characterized by or exhibiting drowsiness, sluggishness, etc. **3** conducive to sleep; soporific. **4** without activity or bustle: *a sleepy town.* ▸ **'sleepily** *adv* ▸ **'sleepiness** *n*

sleepyhead ('sli:pɪˌhɛd) *n Informal.* a sleepy or lazy person. ▸ **'sleepyˌheaded** *adj*

sleet (sli:t) *n* **1** partly melted falling snow or hail or (esp. U.S.) partly frozen rain. **2** *Chiefly U.S.* the thin coat of ice that forms when sleet or rain freezes on cold surfaces. ◆ *vb* **3** (*intr*) to fall as sleet. [C13: from Germanic; compare Middle Low German *slōten* hail, Middle High German *slōze,* German *Schlossen* hailstones] ▸ **'sleety** *adj*

sleeve (sli:v) *n* **1** the part of a garment covering the arm. **2** a tubular piece that is forced or shrunk into a cylindrical bore to reduce the diameter of the bore or to line it with a different material; liner. **3** a tube fitted externally over two cylindrical parts in order to join them; bush. **4** a flat cardboard or plastic container to protect a gramophone record. U.S. name: **jacket. 5** (**have a few tricks**) **up one's sleeve.** (to have options, etc.) secretly ready. **6 roll up one's sleeves.** to prepare oneself for work, a fight, etc. ◆ *vb* **7** (*tr*) to provide with a sleeve or sleeves. [Old English *slīf, slēf;* related to Dutch *sloof* apron] ▸ **'sleeveless** *adj* ▸ **'sleeveˌlike** *adj*

sleeve board *n* a small ironing board for pressing sleeves, fitted onto an ironing board or table.

sleeveen ('sli:vi:n) *n Irish.* a sly obsequious smooth-tongued person. [from Irish Gaelic *slībhín*]

sleeve notes *pl n* the printed information on a record sleeve. U.S. equivalent: **liner notes.**

sleeve valve *n* (in an internal-combustion engine) a valve in the form of a thin steel sleeve fitted between the cylinder and piston and having a reciprocating and rotary oscillation movement.

sleeving ('sli:vɪŋ) *n Electronics, chiefly Brit.* tubular flexible insulation into which bare wire can be inserted. U.S. and Canadian name: **spaghetti.**

sleigh (sleɪ) *n* **1** another name for **sledge**[1] (sense 1). ◆ *vb* **2** (*intr*) to travel by sleigh. [C18: from Dutch *slee,* variant of *slede* SLEDGE[1]] ▸ **'sleigher** *n*

sleight (slaɪt) *n Archaic.* **1** skill; dexterity. See also **sleight of hand. 2** a trick or stratagem. **3** cunning; trickery. [C14: from Old Norse *slægth,* from *slægr* SLY]

sleight of hand *n* **1** manual dexterity used in performing conjuring tricks. **2** the performance of such tricks.

slender ('slɛndə) *adj* **1** of small width relative to length or height. **2** (esp. of a person's figure) slim and well-formed. **3** small or inadequate in amount, size, etc.: *slender resources.* **4** (of hopes, etc.) having little foundation; feeble. **5** very small: *a slender margin.* **6** (of a sound) lacking volume. **7** *Phonetics.* (now only in Irish phonology) relating to or denoting a close front vowel, such as *i* or *e.* [C14 *slendre,* of unknown origin] ▸ **'slenderly** *adv* ▸ **'slenderness** *n*

slenderize *or* **slenderise** ('slɛndəˌraɪz) *vb Chiefly U.S. and Canadian.* to make or become slender.

slept (slɛpt) *vb* the past tense and past participle of **sleep.**

Slesvig ('sle:svi) *n* the Danish name for **Schleswig.**

sleuth (slu:θ) *n* **1** an informal word for **detective. 2** short for **sleuthhound** (sense 1). ◆ *vb* **3** (*tr*) to track or follow. [C19: short for *sleuthhound,* from C12 *sleuth* trail, from Old Norse *sloth;* see SLOT[2]]

sleuthhound ('slu:θˌhaʊnd) *n* **1** a dog trained to track people, esp. a bloodhound. **2** an informal word for **detective.**

S level *n Brit.* the Special level of a subject taken for the General Certificate of Education: usually taken at the same time as A levels as an additional qualification.

slew[1] (slu:) *vb* the past tense of **slay.**

slew[2] *or* (*esp. U.S.*) **slue** (slu:) *vb* **1** to twist or be twisted sideways, esp. awkwardly: *he slewed around in his chair.* **2** *Nautical.* to cause (a mast) to rotate in its step or (of a mast) to rotate in its step. ◆ *n* **3** the act of slewing. [C18: of unknown origin]

slew[3] (slu:) *n* a variant spelling (esp. U.S.) of **slough**[1] (sense 2).

slew[4] *or* **slue** (slu:) *n Informal, chiefly U.S. and Canadian.* a great number or amount; a lot. [C20: from Irish Gaelic *sluagh;* related to Old Irish *slōg* army]

slewed (slu:d) *adj* (*postpositive*) *Brit. slang.* intoxicated; drunk. [C19: from SLEW[2]]

slew rate *n Electronics.* the rate at which an electronic amplifier can respond to an abrupt change of input level.

Slezsko ('slɛskɔ) *n* the Czech name for **Silesia.**

slice (slaɪs) *n* **1** a thin flat piece cut from something having bulk: *a slice of pork.* **2** a share or portion: *a slice of the company's revenue.* **3** any of various utensils having a broad flat blade and resembling a spatula. **4** (in golf, tennis, etc.) **4a** the flight of a ball that travels obliquely because it has been struck off centre. **4b** the action of hitting such a shot. **4c** the shot so hit. ◆ *vb* **5** to divide or cut (something) into parts or slices. **6** (when *intr,* usually foll. by *through*) to cut in a clean and effortless manner. **7** (when *intr,* foll. by *through*) to move or go (through something) like a knife: *the ship sliced through the water.* **8** (usually foll. by *off, from, away,* etc.) to cut or be cut (from) a larger piece. **9** (*tr*) to remove by use of a slicing implement. **10** to hit (a ball) with a slice. **11** (*tr*) *Rowing.* to put the blade of the oar into (the water) slantwise. [C14: from Old French *esclice* a piece split off, from *esclicier* to splinter] ▸ **'sliceable** *adj* ▸ **'slicer** *n*

slice bar *n* an iron bar used for raking out furnaces.

slicer ('slaɪsə) *n* a machine that slices bread, etc., usually with an electrically driven band knife or circular knife.

slick (slɪk) *adj* **1** flattering and glib: *a slick salesman.* **2** adroitly devised or executed: *a slick show.* **3** *Informal, chiefly U.S. and Canadian.* shrewd; sly. **4** *Informal.* superficially attractive: *a slick publication.* **5** *Chiefly U.S. and Canadian.* smooth and glossy; slippery. ◆ *n* **6** a slippery area, esp. a patch of oil floating on water. **7** a chisel or other tool used for smoothing or polishing a surface. **8** the tyre of a racing car that has worn treads. ◆ *vb* (*tr*) **9** *Chiefly U.S. and Canadian.* to make smooth or sleek. **10** *U.S. and Canadian informal.* (usually foll. by *up*) to smarten or tidy (oneself). **11** (often foll. by *up*) to make smooth or glossy. [C14: probably of Scandinavian origin; compare Icelandic, Norwegian *slikja* to be or make smooth] ▸ **'slickly** *adv* ▸ **'slickness** *n*

slickenside ('slɪkənˌsaɪd) *n* a rock surface with a polished appearance and fine parallel scratches caused by displacement of the rock during a fault. [C18: from dialect *slicken,* variant of SLICK + SIDE]

slicker ('slɪkə) *n* **1** *Informal.* a sly or untrustworthy person (esp. in the phrase **city slicker**). **2** *U.S. and Canadian.* a shiny raincoat, esp. an oilskin. **3** a small trowel used for smoothing the surfaces of a mould. ▸ **'slickered** *adj*

slide (slaɪd) *vb* **slides, sliding, slid** (slɪd); **slid** *or* **slidden** ('slɪdᵊn). **1** to move or cause to move smoothly along a surface in continual contact with it: *doors that slide open; children sliding on the ice.* **2** (*intr*) to lose grip or balance: *he slid on his back.* **3** (*intr;* usually foll. by *into, out of, away from,* etc.) to pass or move gradually and unobtrusively: *she slid into the room.* **4** (*intr;* usually foll. by *into*) to go (into a specified condition) by degrees, unnoticeably, etc.: *he slid into loose living.* **5** (foll. by *in, into,* etc.) to move (an object) unobtrusively or (of an object) to move in this way: *he slid the gun into his pocket.* **6** (*intr*) *Music.* to execute a portamento. **7 let slide.** to allow to follow a natural course, esp. one leading to deterioration: *to let things slide.* ◆ *n* **8** the act or an instance of sliding. **9** a smooth surface, as of ice or mud, for sliding on. **10** a construction incorporating an inclined smooth slope for sliding down in playgrounds, etc. **11** *Rowing.* a sliding seat in a boat or its runners. **12** a small glass plate on which specimens are mounted for microscopic study. **13** Also called: **transparency.** a positive photograph on a transparent base, mounted in a cardboard or plastic frame or between glass plates, that can be viewed by means of a slide projector. **14** Also called: **hair slide.** *Chiefly Brit.* an ornamental clip to hold hair in place. U.S. and Canadian name: **barrette. 15** *Machinery.* **15a** a sliding part or member. **15b** the track, guide, or channel on or in which such a part slides. **16** *Music.* **16a** the sliding curved tube of a trombone that is moved in or out to allow the production of different harmonic series and a wider range of notes. **16b** a portamento. **17** *Music.* **17a** a metal or glass tube placed over a finger held against the frets of a guitar to produce a portamento. **17b** the style of guitar playing using a slide. See also **bottleneck** (sense 3). **18** *Geology.* **18a** the downward movement of a large mass of earth, rocks, etc., caused by erosion, faulting, etc. **18b** the mass of material involved in this descent. See also **landslide.** [Old English *slīdan;* related to *slidor* slippery, *sliderian* to SLITHER, Middle High German *slīten*] ▸ **'slidable** *adj* ▸ **'slider** *n*

slide-action *adj* (of a shoulder firearm) ejecting the empty case and reloading by means of a sliding lever.

slide fastener *n Chiefly U.S. and Canadian.* another name for **zip** (sense 1).

slide guitar *n* a technique of guitar playing derived from bottleneck, using a steel or glass tube on one finger across the frets.

slide over *vb* (*intr, prep*) **1** to cross by or as if by sliding. **2** to avoid dealing with (a matter) fully.

slide rest *n Engineering.* a stack of platforms that sits on a lathe saddle and carries a tool post, and is adjustable in rotation and at right angles by a lathe operator.

slide rule *n* a mechanical calculating device consisting of two strips, one sliding along a central groove in the other, each strip graduated in two or more logarithmic scales of numbers, trigonometric functions, etc. It employs the same principles as logarithm tables.

slide trombone *n* See **trombone.**

slide valve *n* **1** a valve that slides across an aperture to expose the port or opening. **2** (*modifier*) fitted with slide valves: *a slide-valve engine.*

sliding ('slaɪdɪŋ) *adj* **1** rising or falling in accordance with given specifications: *fees were charged as a sliding percentage of income.* **2** regulated or moved by sliding.

sliding fit *n Engineering.* a fit that enables one part to be inserted into another by sliding or pushing, rather than by hammering. Also called: **push fit.**

sliding friction *n Engineering.* frictional resistance to relative movement of surfaces on loaded contact. Compare **rolling friction.**

sliding scale *n* a variable scale according to which specified wages, tariffs, prices, etc., fluctuate in response to changes in some other factor, standard, or conditions.

sliding seat *n Rowing.* a seat that slides forwards and backwards with the oarsman, lengthening his stroke.

slier ('slaɪə) *adj* a comparative of **sly.**

sliest ('slaɪɪst) *adj* a superlative of **sly.**

Slieve Donard (sliːv 'dɒnɑːd) *n* a mountain in SE Northern Ireland, in the Mourne Mountains: highest peak in Northern Ireland. Height: 853 m (2798 ft.).

slight (slaɪt) *adj* **1** small in quantity or extent. **2** of small importance; trifling. **3** slim and delicate. **4** lacking in strength or substance. ◆ *vb (tr)* **5** to show indifference or disregard for (someone); snub. **6** to treat as unimportant or trifling. **7** *U.S.* to devote inadequate attention to (work, duties, etc.). ◆ *n* **8** an act or omission indicating supercilious neglect or indifference. **[C13:** from Old Norse *slēttr* smooth; related to Old High German *slehtr,* Gothic *slaihts,* Middle Dutch *slecht* simple**]** ▸ **'slightness** *n*

slighting ('slaɪtɪŋ) *adj* characteristic of a slight; disparaging; disdainful: *in a slighting manner.* ▸ **'slightingly** *adv*

slightly ('slaɪtlɪ) *adv* in small measure or degree.

Sligo ('slaɪgəʊ) *n* **1** a county of NW Republic of Ireland, on the Atlantic: has a deeply indented low-lying coast; livestock and dairy farming. County town: Sligo. Pop.: 56 000 (1996). Area: 1795 sq. km (693 sq. miles). **2** a port in NW Republic of Ireland, county town of Co. Sligo on **Sligo Bay.** Pop.: 17 300 (1991).

slily ('slaɪlɪ) *adv* a variant spelling of **slyly.**

slim (slɪm) *adj* **slimmer, slimmest. 1** small in width relative to height or length. **2** small in amount or quality: *slim chances of success.* ◆ *vb* **slims, slimming, slimmed. 3** to make or become slim, esp. by diets and exercise. **4** to reduce or decrease or cause to be reduced or decreased. ◆ See also **slim down. [C17:** from Dutch: crafty, from Middle Dutch *slimp* slanting; compare Old High German *slimbi* obliquity**]** ▸ **'slimly** *adv* ▸ **'slimmer** *n* ▸ **'slimness** *n*

Slim[1] (slɪm) *n* the E African name for **AIDS. [**from its wasting effects**]**

Slim[2] (slɪm) *n* **William Joseph,** 1st Viscount. 1891–1970, British field marshal, who commanded (1943–45) the 14th Army in the reconquest of Burma (now called Myanmar) from the Japanese; governor general of Australia (1953–60).

slim down *vb (adv)* **1** to make or become slim, esp. intentionally. **2** to make (an organization) more efficient or (of an organization) to become more efficient, esp. by cutting staff. ◆ *n* **slimdown. 3** an instance of an organization slimming down.

slime (slaɪm) *n* **1** soft thin runny mud or filth. **2** any moist viscous fluid, esp. when noxious or unpleasant. **3** a mucous substance produced by various organisms, such as fish, slugs, and fungi. ◆ *vb (tr)* **4** to cover with slime. **5** to remove slime from (fish) before canning. **[**Old English *slīm;* related to Old Norse *slīm,* Old High German *slīmen* to smooth, Russian *slimák* snail, Latin *līmax* snail**]**

slime mould *n* any of various simple spore-producing organisms typically found as slimy masses on rotting vegetation, where they engulf food particles by amoeboid movements. Formerly regarded as fungi, they are now classified as protoctists of the phyla *Myxomycota* (true, or cellular slime moulds) or *Acrasiomycota* (plasmodial slime moulds).

slimline ('slɪm,laɪn) *adj* slim; giving the appearance of or conducive to slimness.

slimming ('slɪmɪŋ) *n* **a** the process of or concern with becoming slim or slimmer as by losing weight. **b** *(as modifier): slimming aids.*

slimsy ('slɪmzɪ) *adj* **-sier, -siest.** *U.S. informal.* frail. **[C19:** from SLIM + FLIMSY**]**

slimy ('slaɪmɪ) *adj* **slimier, slimiest. 1** characterized by, covered with, containing, secreting, or resembling slime. **2** offensive or repulsive. **3** *Chiefly Brit.* characterized by servility. ▸ **'slimily** *adv* ▸ **'sliminess** *n*

sling[1] (slɪŋ) *n* **1** a simple weapon consisting of a loop of leather, etc., in which a stone is whirled and then let fly. **2** a rope or strap by which something may be secured or lifted. **3** a rope net swung from a crane, used for loading and unloading cargo. **4** *Nautical.* **4a** a halyard for a yard. **4b** *(often pl)* the part of a yard where the sling is attached. **5** *Med.* a wide piece of cloth suspended from the neck for supporting an injured hand or arm across the front of the body. **6** a loop or band attached to an object for carrying. **7** *Mountaineering.* a loop of rope or tape used for support in belays, abseils, etc. **8** the act of slinging. ◆ *vb* **slings, slinging, slung. 9** *(tr)* to hurl with or as if with a sling. **10** to attach a sling or slings to (a load, etc.). **11** *(tr)* to carry or hang loosely from or as if from a sling: *to sling washing from the line.* **12** *Informal.* to throw. **13** *(intr) Austral. informal.* to pay a part of one's wages or profits as a bribe or tip. **[C13:** perhaps of Scandinavian origin; compare Old Norse *slyngva* to hurl, Old High German *slingan***]** ▸ **'slinger** *n*

sling[2] (slɪŋ) *n* a mixed drink with a spirit base, usually sweetened. **[C19:** of uncertain origin**]**

slingback ('slɪŋ,bæk) *n* **a** a shoe with a strap instead of a full covering for the heel. **b** *(as modifier): slingback shoes.*

slinger ring *n* a tubular ring around the hub of an aircraft propeller through which antifreeze solution is spread over the propeller blades by centrifugal force.

sling off *vb (intr, adv;* often foll. by *at) Austral. and N.Z. informal.* to laugh or jeer (at).

slingshot ('slɪŋ,ʃɒt) *n* **1** the U.S. and Canadian name for **catapult** (sense 1). **2** another name for **sling**[1] (sense 1).

slink (slɪŋk) *vb* **slinks, slinking, slunk. 1** *(intr)* to move or act in a furtive or cringing manner from or as if from fear, guilt, etc. **2** *(intr)* to move in a sinuous alluring manner. **3** *(tr)* (of animals, esp. cows) to give birth to prematurely. ◆ *n* **4a** an animal, esp. a calf, born prematurely. **4b** *(as modifier): slink veal.* **[**Old English *slincan;* related to Middle Low German *slinken* to shrink, Old Swedish *slinka* to creep, Danish *slunken* limp**]**

slinky ('slɪŋkɪ) *adj* **slinkier, slinkiest.** *Informal.* **1** moving in a sinuously graceful or provocative way. **2** (of clothes) figure-hugging; clinging. **3** characterized by furtive movements. ▸ **'slinkily** *adv* ▸ **'slinkiness** *n*

slinter ('slɪntə) *n N.Z. informal and Austral. obsolete, informal.* a dodge, trick, or stratagem. Also (Austral. obsolete): **slanter, slenter. [**from Dutch *slenter,* perhaps via S. African *schlenter***]**

sliotar ('ʃlɪtər) *n* the ball used in hurling. **[**Irish Gaelic**]**

slip[1] (slɪp) *vb* **slips, slipping, slipped. 1** to move or cause to move smoothly and easily. **2** *(tr)* to place, insert, or convey quickly or stealthily. **3** *(tr)* to put on or take off easily or quickly: *to slip on a sweater.* **4** *(intr)* to lose balance and slide unexpectedly: *he slipped on the ice.* **5** to let loose or be let loose. **6** to be released from (something); escape. **7** *(tr)* to let go (mooring or anchor lines) over the side. **8** (when *intr,* often foll. by *from* or *out of)* to pass out of (the mind or memory). **9** *(tr)* to overlook, neglect, or miss: *to slip an opportunity.* **10** *(intr)* to move or pass swiftly or unperceived: *to slip quietly out of the room.* **11** *(intr;* sometimes foll. by *up)* to make a mistake. **12** Also: **sideslip.** to cause (an aircraft) to slide sideways or (of an aircraft) to slide sideways. **13** *(intr)* to decline in health, mental ability, etc. **14** *(intr)* (of an intervertebral disc) to become displaced from the normal position. **15** *(tr)* to dislocate (a bone). **16** (of animals) to give birth to (offspring) prematurely. **17** *(tr)* to pass (a stitch) from one needle to another without knitting it. **18a** *(tr)* to operate (the clutch of a motor vehicle) so that it partially disengages. **18b** *(intr)* (of the clutch of a motor vehicle) to fail to engage, esp. as a result of wear. **19 let slip. 19a** to allow to escape. **19b** to say unintentionally. **20 slip one over on.** *Slang.* to hoodwink or trick. ◆ *n* **21** the act or an instance of slipping. **22** a mistake or oversight: *a slip of the pen.* **23** a moral lapse or failing. **24** a woman's sleeveless undergarment, worn as a lining for and to give support to a dress. **25** *U.S. and Canadian.* a narrow space between two piers in which vessels may dock. **26** See **slipway. 27** a kind of dog lead that allows for the quick release of the dog. **28** a small block of hard steel of known thickness used for measurement, usually forming one of a set. **29** the ratio between output speed and input speed of a transmission device when subtracted from unity, esp. of a drive belt or clutch that is not transmitting full power. **30** *Cricket.* **30a** the position of the fielder who stands a little way behind and to the offside of the wicketkeeper. **30b** the fielder himself. **31** the relative movement of rocks along a fault plane. **32** a landslide, esp. one blocking a road or railway line. **33** *Metallurgy, crystallog.* the deformation of a metallic crystal caused when one part glides over another part along a plane. **34** the deviation of a propeller from its helical path through a fluid, expressed as the difference between its actual forward motion and its theoretical forward motion in one revolution. **35** another name for **sideslip** (sense 1). **36 give someone the slip.** to elude or escape from someone. ◆ See also **slip up. [C13:** from Middle Low German or Dutch *slippen***]** ▸ **'slipless** *adj*

slip[2] (slɪp) *n* **1** a narrow piece; strip. **2** a small piece of paper: *a receipt slip.* **3** a part of a plant that, when detached from the parent, will grow into a new plant; cutting; scion. **4** a young slender person: *a slip of a child.* **5** *Dialect.* a young pig. **6** *Printing.* **6a** a long galley. **6b** a less common name for a **galley proof. 7** *Chiefly U.S.* a pew or similar long narrow seat. **8** a small piece of abrasive material of tapering section used in honing. ◆ *vb* **slips, slipping, slipped. 9** *(tr)* to detach (portions of stem, etc.) from (a plant) for propagation. **[C15:** probably from Middle Low German, Middle Dutch *slippe* to cut, strip**]**

slip[3] (slɪp) *n* clay mixed with water to a creamy consistency, used for decorating or patching a ceramic piece. **[**Old English *slyppe* slime; related to Norwegian *slipa* slime on fish; see SLOP[1]**]**

slipcase ('slɪp,keɪs) *n* a protective case for a book or set of books that is open at one end so that only the spines of the books are visible.

slipcover ('slɪp,kʌvə) *n* **1** the U.S. and Canadian word for a **loose cover. 2** *U.S. and Canadian.* a book jacket; dust cover.

slipe (slaɪp) *n N.Z.* **a** wool removed from the pelt of a slaughtered sheep by immersion in a chemical bath. **b** *(as modifier): slipe wool.* **[**from English dialect**]**

slip flow *n Physics.* gas flow occurring at hypersonic speeds in which molecular shearing occurs.

slip gauge *n* a very accurately ground block of hardened steel used to measure a gap with close accuracy: used mainly in tool-making and inspection.

slipknot ('slɪp,nɒt) *n* **1** Also called: **running knot.** a nooselike knot tied so that it will slip along the rope round which it is made. **2** a knot that can be easily untied by pulling one free end.

slipnoose ('slɪp,nuːs) *n* a noose made with a slipknot, so that it tightens when pulled.

slip-on *adj* **1** (of a garment or shoe) made so as to be easily and quickly put on or off. ◆ *n* **2** a slip-on garment or shoe.

slipover ('slɪp,əʊvə) *adj* **1** of or denoting a garment that can be put on easily over the head. ◆ *n* **2** such a garment, esp. a sleeveless pullover.

slippage ('slɪpɪdʒ) *n* **1** the act or an instance of slipping. **2** the amount of slipping or the extent to which slipping occurs. **3a** an instance of not reaching a norm, target, etc. **3b** the extent of this. **4** the power lost in a mechanical device or system as a result of slipping.

slipped disc *n Pathol.* a herniated intervertebral disc, often resulting in pain because of pressure on the spinal nerves.

slipper ('slɪpə) *n* **1** a light shoe of some soft material, for wearing around the house. **2** a woman's evening or dancing shoe. ◆ *vb* **3** *(tr) Informal.* to hit or beat with a slipper. ▸ **'slippered** *adj* ▸ **'slipper-,like** *adj*

slipper bath *n* **1** a bath in the shape of a slipper, with a covered end. **2** *History.* *(pl)* an establishment where members of the public paid to have a bath.

slipper satin *n* a fine satin fabric with a mat finish.

slipperwort ('slɪpəˌwɜːt) *n* another name for **calceolaria.** [C19: so called because of the slipper-like shape of the flower]

slippery ('slɪpərɪ, -prɪ) *adj* **1** causing or tending to cause objects to slip: *a slippery road.* **2** liable to slip from the grasp, a position, etc. **3** not to be relied upon; cunning and untrustworthy: *a slippery character.* **4** (esp. of a situation) liable to change; unstable. **5 slippery slope.** a course of action that will lead to disaster or failure. [C16: probably coined by Coverdale to translate German *schlipfferig* in Luther's Bible (Psalm 35:6); related to Old English *slipor* slippery] ▸ **'slipperily** *adv* ▸ **'slipperiness** *n*

slippery dip *n Austral. informal.* a long slide at a playground or funfair.

slippery elm *n* **1** a tree, *Ulmus fulva,* of E North America, having oblong serrated leaves, notched winged fruits, and a mucilaginous inner bark. **2** the bark of this tree, used medicinally as a demulcent. ◆ Also called: **red elm.**

slippy ('slɪpɪ) *adj* **-pier, -piest. 1** *Informal or dialect.* another word for **slippery** (senses 1, 2). **2** *Brit. informal.* alert; quick. ▸ **'slippiness** *n*

slip rail *n Austral. and N.Z.* a rail in a fence that can be slipped out of place to make an opening.

slip ring *n Electrical engineering.* a metal ring, mounted on but insulated from a rotating shaft of a motor or generator, by means of which current can be led through stationary brushes into or out of a winding on the shaft.

slip road *n Brit.* a short road connecting a motorway, etc., to another road.

slipsheet ('slɪpˌʃiːt) *n* **1** a sheet of paper that is interleaved between freshly printed sheets to prevent set-off. ◆ *vb* **2** to interleave (printed sheets) with slipsheets.

slipshod ('slɪpˌʃɒd) *adj* **1** (of an action) negligent; careless. **2** (of a person's appearance) slovenly; down-at-heel. [C16: from SLIP[1] + SHOD] ▸ **'slipˌshoddiness** *or* **'slipˌshodness** *n*

slipslop ('slɪpˌslɒp) *n* **1** *Archaic.* weak or unappetizing food or drink. **2** *Informal.* maudlin or trivial talk or writing.

slip step *n* a dance step made by moving the left foot one step sideways and closing the right foot to the left foot: used when dancing in a circle during Scottish reels and jigs.

slip stitch *n* **1** a sewing stitch for securing hems, etc., in which only two or three threads of the material are caught up by the needle each time, so that the stitches are nearly invisible from the right side. ◆ *vb* **2** (*tr*) to join (two edges) using slip stitches. [C19: from SLIP[1]]

slipstream ('slɪpˌstriːm) *n* **1** Also called: **airstream, race. 1a** the stream of air forced backwards by an aircraft propeller. **1b** a stream of air behind any moving object. ◆ *vb* **2** *Motor racing.* to follow (another car, etc.) closely in order to take advantage of the decreased wind resistance immediately behind it.

slip up *vb* (*intr, adv*) **1** *Informal.* to make a blunder or mistake; err. **2** to fall over: *he slipped up in the street.* ◆ *n* **slip-up. 3** *Informal.* a mistake, blunder, or mishap.

slipware ('slɪpˌwɛə) *n* pottery that has been decorated with slip.

slipway ('slɪpˌweɪ) *n* **1** the sloping area in a shipyard, containing the ways. **2** Also called: **marine railway.** the ways on which a vessel is launched. **3** the ramp of a whaling factory ship. **4** a pillowcase; pillowslip.

slit (slɪt) *vb* **slits, slitting, slit.** (*tr*) **1** to make a straight long incision in; split open. **2** to cut into strips lengthwise. **3** to sever. ◆ *n* **4** a long narrow cut. **5** a long narrow opening. [Old English *slītan* to slice; related to Old Norse *slita,* Old High German *slīzen*] ▸ **'slitter** *n*

slither ('slɪðə) *vb* **1** to move or slide or cause to move or slide unsteadily, as on a slippery surface. **2** (*intr*) to travel with a sliding motion. ◆ *n* **3** a slithering motion. [Old English *slidrian,* from *slīdan* to SLIDE] ▸ **'slithery** *adj*

slit pocket *n* a pocket on the underside of a garment, reached through a vertical opening.

slit trench *n Military.* a narrow trench dug for the protection of a small number of people.

sliver ('slɪvə) *n* **1** a thin piece that is cut or broken off lengthwise; splinter. **2** a loose strand or fibre obtained by carding. ◆ *vb* **3** to divide or be divided into splinters; split. **4** (*tr*) to form (wool, etc.) into slivers. [C14: from *sliven* to split] ▸ **'sliver-ˌlike** *adj*

slivovitz ('slɪvəvɪts, 'sliːvə-) *n* a plum brandy from E Europe. [from Serbo-Croat *šljivovica,* from *sljiva* plum]

Sloan (sləʊn) *n* **John.** 1871–1951, U.S. painter and etcher, a leading member of the group of realistic painters known as the Ash Can School. His pictures of city scenes include *McSorley's Bar* (1912) and *Backyards, Greenwich Village* (1914).

Sloane Ranger (sləʊn) *n* (in Britain) *Informal.* a young upper-class or upper-middle-class person, esp. a woman, having a home in London and in the country, characterized typically as wearing expensive informal country clothes. Also called: **Sloane.** [C20: coined by Peter York, punning on *Sloane* Square, London SW1, and *Lone Ranger,* television cowboy character]

slob (slɒb) *n* **1** *Informal.* a slovenly, unattractive, and lazy person. **2** *Irish.* mire. [C19: from Irish *slab* mud; compare SLAB] ▸ **'slobbish** *adj*

slobber ('slɒbə) *or* **slabber** *vb* **1** to dribble (saliva, food, etc.) from the mouth. **2** (*intr*) to speak or write mawkishly. **3** (*tr*) to smear with matter dribbling from the mouth. ◆ *n* **4** liquid or saliva spilt from the mouth. **5** maudlin language or behaviour. [C15: from Middle Low German, Middle Dutch *slubberen;* see SLAVER[2]] ▸ **'slobberer** *or* **'slabberer** *n* ▸ **'slobbery** *or* **'slabbery** *adj*

slob ice *n Canadian.* sludgy masses of floating ice. [see SLOB]

sloe (sləʊ) *n* **1** the small sour blue-black fruit of the blackthorn. **2** another name for **blackthorn.** [Old English *slāh;* related to Old High German *slēha,* Middle Dutch *sleeuwe*]

sloe-eyed *adj* having dark slanted or almond-shaped eyes.

sloe gin *n* gin flavoured with sloe juice.

slog (slɒg) *vb* **slogs, slogging, slogged. 1** to hit with heavy blows, as in boxing. **2** (*intr*) to work hard; toil. **3** (*intr;* foll. by *down, up, along,* etc.) to move with difficulty; plod. **4** *Cricket.* to score freely by taking large swipes at the ball. ◆ *n* **5** a tiring hike or walk. **6** long exhausting work. **7** a heavy blow or swipe. [C19: of unknown origin] ▸ **'slogger** *n*

slogan ('sləʊgən) *n* **1** a distinctive or topical phrase used in politics, advertising, etc. **2** *Scottish history.* a Highland battle cry. [C16: from Gaelic *sluagh-ghairm* war cry, from *sluagh* army + *gairm* cry]

sloganeer (ˌsləʊgə'nɪə) ◆ *n* **1** a person who coins or employs slogans frequently. ◆ *vb* **2** (*intr*) to coin or employ slogans so as to sway opinion.

slo-mo ('sləʊˌməʊ) *n, adj Informal.* a variant spelling of **slow-mo,** see **slow motion.**

sloop (sluːp) *n* a single-masted sailing vessel, rigged fore-and-aft, with the mast stepped about one third of the overall length aft of the bow. Compare **cutter** (sense 2). [C17: from Dutch *sloep;* related to French *chaloupe* launch, Old English *slūpan* to glide]

sloop of war *n* (formerly) a small fast sailing warship mounting some 10 to 30 small calibre guns on one deck.

sloop-rigged *adj Nautical.* rigged as a sloop, typically with a jib and a mainsail.

sloot (sluːt) *n S. African.* a ditch for irrigation or drainage. [from Afrikaans, from Dutch *sluit, sluis* SLUICE]

slop[1] (slɒp) *vb* **slops, slopping, slopped. 1** (when *intr,* often foll. by *about*) to cause (liquid) to splash or spill or (of liquid) to splash or spill. **2** (*tr*) to splash liquid upon. **3** (*intr;* foll. by *along, through,* etc.) to tramp (through) mud or slush. **4** (*tr*) to feed slop or swill to: *to slop the pigs.* **5** (*tr*) to ladle or serve, esp. clumsily. **6** (*intr;* foll. by *over*) *Informal, chiefly U.S. and Canadian.* to be unpleasantly effusive. ◆ *n* **7** a puddle of spilt liquid. **8** (*pl*) wet feed, esp. for pigs, made from kitchen waste, etc. **9** (*pl*) waste food or liquid refuse. **10** (*pl*) the beer, cider, etc., spilt from a barrel while being drawn. **11** (*often pl*) the residue left after spirits have been distilled. **12** (*often pl*) *Informal.* liquid or semiliquid food of low quality. **13** soft mud, snow, etc. **14** *Informal.* gushing speech or writing. [C14: probably from Old English *-sloppe* in *cūsloppe* COWSLIP; see SLIP[3]]

slop[2] (slɒp) *n* **1** (*pl*) sailors' clothing and bedding issued from a ship's stores. **2** any loose article of clothing, esp. a smock. **3** (*pl*) men's wide knee breeches worn in the 16th century. **4** (*pl*) shoddy manufactured clothing. [Old English *oferslop* surplice; related to Old Norse *slopps* gown, Middle Dutch *slop*]

slop around *vb* (*intr*) to move around in a casual and idle way: *he slops around the house in old slippers.* Also: **slop about.**

slop basin *n* a bowl or basin into which the dregs from teacups are emptied at the table.

slop chest *n* a stock of merchandise, such as clothing, tobacco, etc., maintained aboard merchant ships for sale to the crew. Compare **small stores.**

slope (sləʊp) *vb* **1** to lie or cause to lie at a slanting or oblique angle. **2** (*intr*) (esp. of natural features) to follow an inclined course: *many paths sloped down the hillside.* **3** (*intr;* foll. by *off, away,* etc.) to go furtively. **4** (*tr*) *Military.* (formerly) to hold (a rifle) in the slope position (esp. in the command **slope arms**). ◆ *n* **5** an inclined portion of ground. **6** (*pl*) hills or foothills. **7** any inclined surface or line. **8** the degree or amount of such inclination. **9** *Maths.* **9a** (of a line) the tangent of the angle between the line and another line parallel to the *x*-axis. **9b** the first derivative of the equation of a curve at a given point. **10** (formerly) the position adopted for British military drill when the rifle is rested on the shoulder. [C15: short for *aslope,* perhaps from the past participle of Old English *āslūpan* to slip away, from *slūpan* to slip] ▸ **'sloper** *n* ▸ **'sloping** *adj* ▸ **'slopingly** *adv* ▸ **'slopingness** *n*

slop out *vb* (*intr, adv*) (of prisoners) to empty chamber pots and collect water for washing.

sloppy ('slɒpɪ) *adj* **-pier, -piest. 1** (esp. of ground conditions, etc.) wet; slushy. **2** *Informal.* careless; untidy. **3** *Informal.* mawkishly sentimental. **4** (of food or drink) watery and unappetizing. **5** splashed with slops. **6** (of clothes) loose; baggy. ▸ **'sloppily** *adv* ▸ **'sloppiness** *n*

sloppy joe (dʒəʊ) *n Informal.* a long baggy thin sweater.

slopwork ('slɒpˌwɜːk) *n* **1** the manufacture of cheap shoddy clothing or the clothes so produced. **2** any work of low quality. ▸ **'slopˌworker** *n*

slosh (slɒʃ) *n* **1** watery mud, snow, etc. **2** *Brit. slang.* a heavy blow. **3** the sound of splashing liquid. **4** a popular dance with a traditional routine of steps, kicks, and turns performed in lines. ◆ *vb* **5** (*tr;* foll. by *around, on, in,* etc.) *Informal.* to throw or pour (liquid). **6** (when *intr,* often foll. by *about* or *around*) *Informal.* **6a** to shake or stir (something) in a liquid. **6b** (of a person) to splash (around) in water, etc. **7** (*tr*) *Brit. slang.* to deal a heavy blow to. **8** (usually foll. by *about* or *around*) *Informal.* to shake (a container of liquid) or (of liquid within a container) to be shaken. [C19: variant of SLUSH, influenced by SLOP[1]] ▸ **'sloshy** *adj*

sloshed (slɒʃt) *adj Chiefly Brit.* a slang word for **drunk.**

slot[1] (slɒt) *n* **1** an elongated aperture or groove, such as one in a vending machine for inserting a coin. **2** an air passage in an aerofoil to direct air from the lower to the upper surface, esp. the gap formed behind a slat. **3** a vertical opening between the leech of a foresail and a mast or the luff of another sail through which air spills from one against the other to impart forward motion. **4** *Informal.* a place in a series or scheme. ◆ *vb* **slots, slotting, slotted. 5** (*tr*) to furnish with a slot or slots. **6** (usually foll. by *in* or *into*) to fit or adjust in a slot. **7** *Informal.* to situate or be situated in a series or scheme. [C13: from Old French *esclot* the depression of the breastbone, of unknown origin] ▸ **'slotter** *n*

slot[2] (slɒt) *n* the trail of an animal, esp. a deer. [C16: from Old French *esclot* horse's hoof-print, probably of Scandinavian origin; compare Old Norse *sloth* track; see SLEUTH]

slot aerial *or* **antenna** *n Radio.* a transmitting aerial in which the radiating elements are open slots in a surrounding metal sheet.

sloth (sləʊθ) *n* **1** any of several shaggy-coated arboreal edentate mammals of the family *Bradypodidae,* esp. *Bradypus tridactylus* (**three-toed sloth** or **ai**) or *Choloepus didactylus* (**two-toed sloth** or **unau**), of Central and South America. They are slow-moving, hanging upside down by their long arms and feeding on vegetation. **2** reluctance to work or exert oneself. [Old English *slǣwth;* from *slǣw,* variant of *slāw* SLOW]

sloth bear *n* a bear, *Melursus ursinus,* of forests of S India and Sri Lanka, having a shaggy coat and an elongated snout specialized for feeding on termites.

slothful ('sləʊθfʊl) *adj* indolent. ▸ **'slothfully** *adv* ▸ **'slothfulness** *n*

slot machine *n* a machine, esp. one for selling small articles or for gambling, activated by placing a coin or metal disc in a slot.

slouch (slaʊtʃ) *vb* **1** (*intr*) to sit or stand with a drooping bearing. **2** (*intr*) to walk or move with an awkward slovenly gait. **3** (*tr*) to cause (the shoulders) to droop. ◆ *n* **4** a drooping carriage. **5** (*usually used in negative constructions*) *Informal.* an incompetent or slovenly person: *he's no slouch at football.* [C16: of unknown origin] ▸ **'sloucher** *n* ▸ **'slouchy** *adj* ▸ **'slouchily** *adv* ▸ **'slouchiness** *n* ▸ **'slouching** *adj* ▸ **'slouchingly** *adv*

slouch hat *n* any soft hat with a brim that can be pulled down over the ears, esp. an Australian army hat with the left side of the brim turned up.

slough[1] (slaʊ) *n* **1** a hollow filled with mud; bog. **2** (sluː) *North American.* **2a** (in the prairies) a large hole where water collects or the water in such a hole. **2b** (in the northwest) a sluggish side channel of a river. **2c** (on the Pacific coast) a marshy saltwater inlet. **3** despair or degradation. [Old English *slōh;* related to Middle High German *sluoche* ditch, Swedish *slaga* swamp] ▸ **'sloughy** *adj*

slough[2] (slʌf) *n* **1** any outer covering that is shed, such as the dead outer layer of the skin of a snake, the cellular debris in a wound, etc. **2** Also: **sluff.** *Bridge.* a discarded card. ◆ *vb* **3** (often foll. by *off*) to shed (a skin, etc.) or (of a skin, etc.) to be shed. **4** Also: **sluff.** *Bridge.* to discard (a card or cards). [C13: of Germanic origin; compare Middle Low German *slū* husk, German *Schlauch* hose, Norwegian *slō* fleshy part of a horn] ▸ **'sloughy** *adj*

Slough (slaʊ) *n* an industrial town and unitary authority in SE central England. Pop.: 110 708 (1991).

slough off (slʌf) *vb* (*tr, adv*) to cast off (cares, etc.).

Slovak ('sləʊvæk) *adj* **1** of, relating to, or characteristic of Slovakia, its people, or their language. ◆ *n* **2** the official language of Slovakia, belonging to the West Slavonic branch of the Indo-European family. Slovak is closely related to Czech, they are mutually intelligible. **3** a native or inhabitant of Slovakia.

Slovakia (sləʊ'vækɪə) *n* a country in central Europe: part of Hungary from the 11th century until 1918, when it united with Bohemia and Moravia to form Czechoslovakia; it became independent in 1993. Official language: Slovak. Religion: Roman Catholic majority. Currency: koruna. Capital: Bratislava. Pop.: 5 425 000 (1998 est.). Area: 49 036 sq. km (18 940 sq. miles). ▸ **Slo'vakian** *adj, n*

sloven ('slʌvᵊn) *n* a person who is habitually negligent in appearance, hygiene, or work. [C15: probably related to Flemish *sloef* dirty, Dutch *slof* negligent]

Slovene (sləʊ'viːn) *adj also* **Slovenian. 1** of, relating to, or characteristic of Slovenia, its people, or their language. ◆ *n* **2** Also: **Slovenian.** a South Slavonic language spoken in Slovenia, closely related to Serbo-Croat. **3a** a native or inhabitant of Slovenia. **3b** a speaker of Slovene.

Slovenia (sləʊ'viːnɪə) *n* a republic in S central Europe: settled by the Slovenes in the 6th century; joined Yugoslavia in 1918 and became an autonomous republic in 1946; became fully independent in 1992; rises over 2800 m (9000 ft.) in the Julian Alps. Official language: Slovene. Religion: Roman Catholic majority. Currency: tolar. Capital: Ljubljana. Pop.: 1 985 000 (1998 est.). Area: 20 251 sq. km (7819 sq. miles).

slovenly ('slʌvənlɪ) *adj* **1** frequently or habitually unclean or untidy. **2** negligent and careless; slipshod: *slovenly manners.* ◆ *adv* **3** in a negligent or slovenly manner. ▸ **'slovenliness** *n*

slow (sləʊ) *adj* **1** performed or occurring during a comparatively long interval of time. **2** lasting a comparatively long time: *a slow journey.* **3** characterized by lack of speed: *a slow walker.* **4** (*prenominal*) adapted to or productive of slow movement: *the slow lane of a motorway.* **5** (of a clock, etc.) indicating a time earlier than the correct time. **6** given to or characterized by a leisurely or lazy existence: *a slow town.* **7** not readily responsive to stimulation; intellectually unreceptive: *a slow mind.* **8** dull or uninteresting: *the play was very slow.* **9** not easily aroused: *a slow temperament.* **10** lacking promptness or immediacy: *a slow answer.* **11** unwilling to perform an action or enter into a state: *slow to anger.* **12** behind the times. **13** (of trade, etc.) unproductive; slack. **14** (of a fire) burning weakly. **15** (of an oven) cool. **16** *Photog.* requiring a relatively long time of exposure to produce a given density: *a slow lens.* **17** *Sport.* (of a track, etc.) tending to reduce the speed of the ball or the competitors. **18** *Cricket.* (of a bowler, etc.) delivering the ball slowly, usually with spin. ◆ *adv* **19** in a manner characterized by lack of speed; slowly. ◆ *vb* **20** (often foll. by *up* or *down*) to decrease or cause to decrease in speed, efficiency, etc. [Old English *slāw* sluggish; related to Old High German *slēo* dull, Old Norse *slǣr,* Dutch *sleeuw* slow] ▸ **'slowly** *adv* ▸ **'slowness** *n*

slow burn *n* a steadily penetrating show of anger or contempt.

slowcoach ('sləʊˌkəʊtʃ) *n Brit. informal.* a person who moves, acts, or works slowly. U.S. and Canadian equivalent: **slowpoke.**

slowdown ('sləʊˌdaʊn) *n* **1** the usual U.S. and Canadian word for **go-slow. 2** any slackening of pace.

slow handclap *n Brit.* slow rhythmic clapping, esp. used by an audience to indicate dissatisfaction or impatience.

slow march *n Military.* a march in slow time.

slow match *n* a match or fuse that burns slowly without flame, esp. a wick impregnated with potassium nitrate.

slow-mo *or* **slo-mo** ('sləʊˌməʊ) *n, adj Informal.* short for **slow motion.**

slow motion *n* **1** *Films, television, etc.* action that is made to appear slower than normal by passing the film through the taking camera at a faster rate than normal or by replaying a video tape recording more slowly. ◆ *adj* **slow-motion. 2** of or relating to such action. **3** moving or functioning at less than usual speed.

slow neutron *n Physics.* a neutron having a kinetic energy of less than 100 electronvolts.

slowpoke ('sləʊˌpəʊk) *n Informal.* the usual U.S. and Canadian word for **slowcoach.**

slow time *n Military.* a slow marching pace, usually 65 or 75 paces to the minute: used esp. in funeral ceremonies.

slow virus *n* any of a class of virus-like disease-causing agents that are present in the body for a long time before becoming active or infectious and are very resistant to radiation and similar factors: believed to be the cause of BSE and scrapie.

slow-witted *adj* slow in comprehension; unintelligent.

slowworm ('sləʊˌwɜːm) *n* a Eurasian legless lizard, *Anguis fragilis,* with a brownish-grey snakelike body: family *Anguidae.* Also called: **blindworm.**

SLR *abbrev. for* single-lens reflex. See **reflex camera.**

SLSC *Austral. abbrev. for* Surf Life Saving Club.

slub (slʌb) *n* **1** a lump in yarn or fabric, often made intentionally to give a knobbly effect. **2** a loosely twisted roll of fibre prepared for spinning. ◆ *vb* **slubs, slubbing, slubbed. 3** (*tr*) to draw out and twist (a sliver of fibre) preparatory to spinning. ◆ *adj* **4** (of material) having an irregular appearance. [C18: of unknown origin]

slubberdegullion (ˌslʌbədɪ'gʌlɪən) *n Archaic.* a slovenly or worthless person. [C17: from *slubber* (chiefly dialect variant of SLOBBER) + invented ending]

sludge (slʌdʒ) *n* **1** soft mud, snow, etc. **2** any deposit or sediment. **3** a surface layer of ice that has a slushy appearance. **4** (in sewage disposal) the solid constituents of sewage that precipitate during treatment and are removed for subsequent purification. [C17: probably related to SLUSH] ▸ **'sludgy** *adj*

slue[1] (sluː) *n, vb* a variant spelling (esp. U.S.) of **slew**[2].

slue[2] (sluː) *n* a variant spelling of **slough**[1] (sense 2).

slue[3] (sluː) *n U.S. informal.* a variant spelling of **slew**[4].

sluff (slʌf) *n, vb Bridge.* a variant spelling of **slough**[2].

slug[1] (slʌg) *n* **1** any of various terrestrial gastropod molluscs of the genera *Limax, Arion,* etc., in which the body is elongated and the shell is absent or very much reduced. Compare **sea slug.** Related adj: **limacine. 2** any of various other invertebrates having a soft slimy body, esp. the larvae of certain sawflies. **3** *Informal, chiefly U.S. and Canadian.* a slow-moving or lazy person or animal. [C15 (in the sense: a slow person or animal): probably of Scandinavian origin; compare Norwegian (dialect) *sluggje*]

slug[2] (slʌg) *n* **1** an fps unit of mass; the mass that will acquire an acceleration of 1 foot per second per second when acted upon by a force of 1 pound. 1 slug is approximately equal to 32.17 pounds. **2** *Metallurgy.* a metal blank from which small forgings are worked. **3** a bullet or pellet larger than a pellet of buckshot. **4** *Chiefly U.S. and Canadian.* a metal token for use in slot machines, etc. **5** *Printing.* **5a** a thick strip of type metal that is less than type-high and is used for spacing. **5b** a similar strip carrying a type-high letter, used as a temporary mark by compositors. **5c** a metal strip containing a line of characters as produced by a linecaster. **6** a draught of a drink, esp. an alcoholic one. **7** a magnetic core that is screwed into or out of an inductance coil to adjust the tuning of a radio frequency amplifier. [C17 (bullet), C19 (printing): perhaps from SLUG[1], with allusion to the shape of the animal]

slug[3] (slʌg) *vb* **slugs, slugging, slugged. 1** to hit very hard and solidly, as in boxing. **2** (*intr*) *U.S. and Canadian.* to plod as if through snow. **3** (*tr*) *Austral. and N.Z. informal.* to charge (someone) an exorbitant price. **4 slug it out.** *Informal.* to fight, compete, or struggle with fortitude. ◆ *n* **5** an act of slugging; heavy blow. **6** *Austral. and N.Z. informal.* an exorbitant charge or price. [C19: perhaps from SLUG[2] (bullet)]

slugabed ('slʌgəˌbɛd) *n* a person who remains in bed through laziness. [C16: from SLUG(GARD) + ABED]

sluggard ('slʌgəd) *n* **1** a person who is habitually indolent. ◆ *adj* **2** lazy. [C14 *slogarde;* related to SLUG[1]] ▸ **'sluggardly** *adj* ▸ **'sluggardliness** *n* ▸ **'sluggardness** *n*

slugger ('slʌgə) *n* (esp. in boxing, baseball, etc.) a person who strikes hard.

sluggish ('slʌgɪʃ) *adj* **1** lacking energy; inactive; slow-moving. **2** functioning at below normal rate or level. **3** exhibiting poor response to stimulation. ▸ **'sluggishly** *adv* ▸ **'sluggishness** *n*

sluice (sluːs) *n* **1** Also called: **sluiceway.** a channel that carries a rapid current of water, esp. one that has a sluicegate to control the flow. **2** the body of water controlled by a sluicegate. **3** See **sluicegate. 4** *Mining.* an inclined trough for washing ore, esp. one having riffles on the bottom to trap particles. **5** an artificial channel through which logs can be floated. **6** *Informal.* a brief wash in running water. ◆ *vb* **7** (*tr*) to draw out or drain (water, etc.) from (a pond, etc.) by means of a sluice. **8** (*tr*) to wash or irrigate with a stream of water. **9** (*tr*) *Mining.* to wash in a sluice. **10** (*tr*) to send (logs, etc.) down a sluice. **11** (*intr;* often foll. by *away* or *out*) (of water, etc.) to run or flow from or as if from a sluice. **12** (*tr*) to provide with a sluice. [C14: from Old French *escluse,* from Late Latin *exclūsa aqua* water shut out, from Latin *exclūdere* to shut out, EXCLUDE] ▸ **'sluiceˌlike** *adj*

sluicegate ('sluːsˌgeɪt) *n* a valve or gate fitted to a sluice to control the rate of flow of water. Sometimes shortened to **sluice.** See also **floodgate** (sense 1).

slum (slʌm) *n* **1** a squalid overcrowded house, etc. **2** (*often pl*) a squalid section of a city, characterized by inferior living conditions and usually by overcrowding. **3** (*modifier*) of, relating to, or characteristic of slums: *slum conditions.* ◆ *vb* **slums, slumming, slummed.** (*intr*) **4** to visit slums, esp. for curiosity. **5** Also: **slum it.** to suffer conditions below those to which one is accustomed. [C19: originally slang, of obscure origin] ▸ **'slummer** *n* ▸ **'slummy** *adj*

slumber ('slʌmbə) *vb* **1** (*intr*) to sleep, esp. peacefully. **2** (*intr*) to be quiescent or dormant. 3 (*tr*; foll. by *away*) to spend (time) sleeping. ◆ *n* 4 (*sometimes pl*) sleep. 5 a dormant or quiescent state. [Old English *slūma* sleep (n); related to Middle High German *slummeren*, Dutch *sluimeren*] ► **ˈslumberer** *n* ► **ˈslumberless** *adj*

slumberous (ˈslʌmbərəs, -brəs) *adj Chiefly poetic.* 1 sleepy; drowsy. 2 inducing sleep. 3 characteristic of slumber. ► **ˈslumberously** *adv* ► **ˈslumberousness** *n*

slumber party *n U.S. and Canadian.* a party attended by girls who dress in night clothes and pass the night eating and talking.

slumgullion (slʌmˈgʌljən, ˈslʌmˌgʌl-) *n U.S. and Canadian.* 1 *Slang.* an inexpensive stew. 2 offal, esp. the refuse from whale blubber. 3 a reddish mud deposited in mine sluices. [C19: from *slum* in U.S. sense slime + *gullion*, perhaps variant of *cullion* testicles]

slumlord (ˈslʌmˌlɔːd) *n Informal, chiefly U.S. and Canadian.* an absentee landlord of slum property, esp. one who profiteers.

slump (slʌmp) *vb* (*intr*) 1 to sink or fall heavily and suddenly. 2 to relax ungracefully. 3 (of business activity, etc.) to decline suddenly; collapse. 4 (of health, interest, etc.) to deteriorate or decline suddenly or markedly. 5 (of soil or rock) to slip down a slope, esp. a cliff, usually with a rotational movement. ◆ *n* 6 a sudden or marked decline or failure, as in progress or achievement; collapse. 7 a decline in commercial activity, prices, etc. 8 *Economics.* another word for **depression.** 9 the act of slumping. 10 a slipping of earth or rock; landslide. [C17: probably of Scandinavian origin; compare Low German *slump* bog, Norwegian *slumpa* to fall]

Slump (slʌmp) *n* **the.** another name for the **Depression.**

slumpflation (slʌmpˈfleɪʃən) *n* a situation in which economic depression is combined with increasing inflation. [C20: blend of SLUMP + INFLATION]

slump test *n Brit.* a test to determine the relative water content of concrete, depending on the loss in height (slump) of a sample obtained from a cone-shaped mould.

slung (slʌŋ) *adj* the past tense and past participle of **sling**[1].

slung shot *n* a weight attached to the end of a cord and used as a weapon.

slunk (slʌŋk) *vb* the past tense and past participle of **slink.**

slur (slɜː) *vb* **slurs, slurring, slurred.** (*mainly tr*) 1 (often foll. by *over*) to treat superficially, hastily, or without due deliberation; gloss. 2 (*also intr*) to pronounce or utter (words, etc.) indistinctly. 3 to speak disparagingly of or cast aspersions on. 4 *Music.* to execute (a melodic interval of two or more notes) smoothly, as in legato performance. 5 (*also intr*) to blur or smear. 6 *Archaic.* to stain or smear; sully. ◆ *n* 7 an indistinct sound or utterance. 8 a slighting remark; aspersion. 9 a stain or disgrace, as upon one's reputation; stigma. 10 *Music.* **10a** a performance or execution of a melodic interval of two or more notes in a part. **10b** the curved line (⌒ or ‿) indicating this. 11 a blur or smear. [C15: probably from Middle Low German; compare Middle Low German *slūren* to drag, trail, Middle Dutch *sloren*, Dutch *sleuren*]

slurp (slɜːp) *Informal.* ◆ *vb* 1 to eat or drink (something) noisily. ◆ *n* 2 a sound produced in this way. [C17: from Middle Dutch *slorpen* to sip; related to German *schlürfen*]

slurry (ˈslʌrɪ) *n, pl* **-ries.** a suspension of solid particles in a liquid, as in a mixture of cement, clay, coal dust, manure, meat, etc. with water. [C15 *slory*; see SLUR]

slush (slʌʃ) *n* 1 any watery muddy substance, esp. melting snow. 2 *Informal.* sloppily sentimental language. 3 *Nautical.* waste fat from the galley of a ship. ◆ *vb* 4 (*intr*; often foll. by *along*) to make one's way through or as if through slush. 5 (*intr*) to make a slushing sound. [C17: related to Danish *slus* sleet, Norwegian *slusk* slops; see SLUDGE, SLOSH]

slush fund *n* 1 a fund for financing political or commercial corruption. 2 *U.S. nautical.* a fund accumulated from the sale of slush from the galley.

slushy (ˈslʌʃɪ) *adj* **slushier, slushiest.** 1 of, resembling, or consisting of slush. ◆ *n, pl* **slushies.** 2 *Austral. slang.* an unskilled kitchen assistant. ► **ˈslushiness** *n*

slut (slʌt) *n* 1 a dirty slatternly woman. 2 an immoral woman. 3 *Archaic.* a female dog. [C14: of unknown origin] ► **ˈsluttish** *adj* ► **ˈsluttishly** *adv* ► **ˈsluttishness** *n*

Sluter (*Dutch* ˈslyːtər) *n* **Claus** (klaus). ?1345–1406, Dutch sculptor, working in Burgundy, whose realism influenced many sculptors and painters in 15th-century Europe. He is best known for the portal sculptures and the *Well of Moses* in the Carthusian monastery at Champnol.

sly (slaɪ) *adj* **slyer, slyest** *or* **slier, sliest.** 1 crafty; artful: *a sly dodge.* 2 insidious; furtive: *a sly manner.* 3 playfully mischievous; roguish: *sly humour.* ◆ *n* **4 on the sly.** in a secretive manner. [C12: from Old Norse *slægr* clever, literally: able to strike, from *slā* to SLAY] ► **ˈslyly** *or* **ˈslily** *adv* ► **ˈslyness** *n*

slyboots (ˈslaɪˌbuːts) *pl n* (*functioning as sing*) a person who is sly.

sly grog *n Austral. and N.Z. old-fashioned.* illicitly sold liquor.

slype (slaɪp) *n* a covered passageway in a cathedral or church that connects the transept to the chapterhouse. [C19: probably from Middle Flemish *slijpen* to slip]

Sm *the chemical symbol for* samarium.

SM *abbrev. for* 1 sergeant major. 2 sadomasochism.

smack[1] (smæk) *n* 1 a smell or flavour that is distinctive though faint. 2 a distinctive trace or touch: *the smack of corruption.* 3 a small quantity, esp. a mouthful or taste. 4 a slang word for **heroin.** ◆ *vb* (*intr*; foll. by *of*) 5 to have the characteristic smell or flavour (of something): *to smack of the sea.* 6 to have an element suggestive (of something): *his speeches smacked of bigotry.* [Old English *smæc*; related to Old High German *smoc*, Icelandic *smekkr* a taste, Dutch *smaak*]

smack[2] (smæk) *vb* 1 (*tr*) to strike or slap smartly, with or as if with the open hand. 2 to strike or send forcibly or loudly or to be struck or sent forcibly or loudly. 3 to open and close (the lips) loudly, esp. to show pleasure. 4 (*tr*) to kiss noisily. ◆ *n* 5 a sharp resounding slap or blow with something flat, or the sound of such a blow. 6 a loud kiss. 7 a sharp sound made by the lips, as in enjoyment. **8 have a smack at.** *Informal, chiefly Brit.* to attempt. **9 smack in the eye.** *Informal, chiefly Brit.* a snub or setback. ◆ *adv Informal.* 10 directly; squarely. 11 with a smack; sharply and unexpectedly. [C16: from Middle Low German or Middle Dutch *smacken*, probably of imitative origin]

smack[3] (smæk) *n* 1 a sailing vessel, usually sloop-rigged, used in coasting and fishing along the British coast. 2 a fishing vessel equipped with a well for keeping the catch alive. [C17: from Low German *smack* or Dutch *smak*, of unknown origin]

smacker (ˈsmækə) *n Slang.* 1 a loud kiss; smack. 2 a pound note or dollar bill.

smacking (ˈsmækɪŋ) *adj* brisk; lively: *a smacking breeze.*

small (smɔːl) *adj* 1 comparatively little; limited in size, number, importance, etc. 2 of little importance or on a minor scale: *a small business.* 3 lacking in moral or mental breadth or depth: *a small mind.* 4 modest or humble: *small beginnings.* 5 of low or inferior status, esp. socially. 6 (of a child or animal) young; not mature. 7 unimportant, trivial: *a small matter.* 8 not outstanding: *a small actor.* 9 of, relating to, or designating the ordinary modern minuscule letter used in printing and cursive writing. Compare **capital**[1] (sense 13). See also **lower case.** 10 lacking great strength or force: *a small effort.* 11 in fine particles: *small gravel.* 12 *Obsolete.* (of beer, etc.) of low alcoholic strength. ◆ *adv* 13 into small pieces: *cut it small.* 14 in a small or soft manner. **15 feel small.** to be humiliated or inferior. ◆ *n* 16 (often preceded by *the*) an object, person, or group considered to be small: *the small or the large?* 17 a small slender part, esp. of the back. 18 (*pl*) *Informal, chiefly Brit.* items of personal laundry, such as underwear. [Old English *smæl*; related to Old High German *smal*, Old Norse *smali* small cattle] ► **ˈsmallish** *adj* ► **ˈsmallness** *n*

small advertisement *or* **small ad** *n* a short, simply designed advertisement in a newspaper or magazine, usually set entirely in a small size of type. See **display advertisement.**

smallage (ˈsmɔːlɪdʒ) *n* an archaic name for **wild celery.** [C13: from earlier *smalache*, from *smal* SMALL + *ache* wild celery, from Old French, from Latin *apium*]

small arms *pl n* portable firearms of relatively small calibre.

small beer *n Informal, chiefly Brit.* people or things of no importance.

small-bore *adj* (of a firearm) having a small bore, especially one of less than .22 calibre.

smallboy (ˈsmɔːlˌbɔɪ) *n* the steward's assistant or deputy steward in European households in W Africa.

small calorie *n* another name for **calorie.**

small capital *n* a letter having the form of an upper-case letter but the same height as a lower-case letter.

small change *n* 1 coins, esp. those of low value. 2 a person or thing that is not outstanding or important.

small chop *pl n W African.* cocktail snacks.

small circle *n* a circular section of a sphere that does not contain the centre of the sphere. Compare **great circle.**

small claims court *n Brit. and Canadian.* a local court with jurisdiction to try civil actions involving small claims.

smallclothes (ˈsmɔːlˌkləuz, -ˌkləuðz) *pl n* men's close-fitting knee breeches of the 18th and 19th centuries.

small fry *pl n* 1 people or things regarded as unimportant. 2 young children. 3 young or small fishes.

small game *n Brit.* small animals that are hunted for sport.

small goods *pl n Austral. and N.Z.* meats bought from a delicatessen, such as sausages.

smallholding (ˈsmɔːlˌhəuldɪŋ) *n* a holding of agricultural land smaller than a small farm. ► **ˈsmallˌholder** *n*

small hours *pl n* **the.** the early hours of the morning, after midnight and before dawn.

small intestine *n* the longest part of the alimentary canal, consisting of the duodenum, jejunum, and ileum, in which digestion is completed. Compare **large intestine.**

small letter *n* a lower-case letter.

small-minded *adj* narrow-minded; petty; intolerant; mean. ► **ˌsmall-ˈmindedly** *adv* ► **ˌsmall-ˈmindedness** *n*

smallmouth bass (ˈsmɔːlˌmauθ ˈbæs) *n* a North American freshwater black bass, *Micropterus dolomieu*, that is a popular game fish.

small pica *n* (formerly) a size of printer's type approximately equal to 11 point.

small potatoes *n* (*functioning as sing or pl*) *Informal, chiefly U.S. and Canadian.* someone or something of little significance or value, esp. a small amount of money.

smallpox (ˈsmɔːlˌpɒks) *n* an acute highly contagious viral disease characterized by high fever, severe prostration, and a pinkish rash changing in form from papules to pustules, which dry up and form scabs that are cast off, leaving pitted depressions. Technical name: **variola.** Related adj: **variolous.** [C16: from SMALL + POX. So called to distinguish it from *the Great Pox*, an archaic name for syphilis]

small print *n* matter in a contract, etc., printed in small type, esp. when considered to be a trap for the unwary.

small-scale *adj* 1 of limited size or scope. 2 (of a map, model, etc.) giving a relatively small representation of something, usually missing out details.

small screen *n* an informal name for **television.**

small slam *n Bridge.* another name for **little slam.**

small stores *pl n Navy.* personal items, such as clothing, sold aboard ship or at a naval base. Compare **slop chest.**

small stuff *n Nautical.* any light twine or yarn used aboard ship for serving lines, etc.

smallsword ('smɔːlˌsɔːd) *n* a light sword used in the 17th and 18th centuries: formerly a fencing weapon.
small talk *n* light conversation for social occasions.
small-time *adj Informal.* insignificant; minor: *a small-time criminal.* ► 'small-'timer *n*
small white *n* a small white butterfly, *Artogeia rapae,* with scanty black markings, the larvae of which feed on brassica leaves.
smalt (smɔːlt) *n* **1** a type of silica glass coloured deep blue with cobalt oxide. **2** a pigment made by crushing this glass, used in colouring enamels. **3** the blue colour of this pigment. [C16: via French from Italian SMALTO, of Germanic origin; related to SMELT[1]]
smaltite ('smɔːltaɪt) *n* a silver-white to greyish mineral consisting chiefly of cobalt arsenide with nickel in cubic crystalline form. It occurs in veins associated with silver, nickel, and copper minerals, and is an important ore of cobalt and nickel. Formula: $(Co,Ni)As_2$. [C19: from SMALT + -ITE[1]]
smalto ('smɑːltəʊ) *n, pl* **-tos** *or* **-ti** (-tiː). coloured glass, etc., used in mosaics. [C18: from Italian; see SMALT]
smaragd ('smærægd) *n Archaic.* any green gemstone, such as the emerald. [C13: via Latin from Greek *smaragdos;* see EMERALD] ► **smaragdine** (smə'rægdɪn) *adj*
smaragdite (smə'rægdaɪt) *n* a green fibrous amphibole mineral.
smarm (smɑːm) *Brit. informal.* ♦ *vb* **1** (*tr;* often foll. by *down*) to flatten (the hair, etc.) with cream or grease. **2** (when *intr,* foll. by *up to*) to ingratiate oneself (with). ♦ *n* **3** obsequious flattery. [C19: of unknown origin]
smarmy ('smɑːmɪ) *adj* **smarmier, smarmiest.** *Brit. informal.* obsequiously flattering or unpleasantly suave. ► **'smarmily** *adv* ► **'smarminess** *n*
smart (smɑːt) *adj* **1** astute, as in business; clever or bright. **2** quick, witty, and often impertinent in speech: *a smart talker.* **3** fashionable; chic: *a smart hotel.* **4** well-kept; neat. **5** causing a sharp stinging pain. **6** vigorous or brisk. **7** *Dialect.* considerable or numerous: *a smart price.* **8** (of systems) operating as if by human intelligence by using automatic computer control. **9** (of a projectile or bomb) containing a device that allows it to be guided to its target. ♦ *vb* (*mainly intr*) **10** to feel, cause, or be the source of a sharp stinging physical pain or keen mental distress: *a nettle sting smarts; he smarted under their abuse.* **11** (often foll. by *for*) to suffer a harsh penalty. ♦ *n* **12** a stinging pain or feeling. ♦ *adv* **13** in a smart manner. [Old English *smeortan;* related to Old High German *smerzan,* Latin *mordēre* to bite, Greek *smerdnos* terrible] ► **'smartish** *adj* ► **'smartly** *adv* ► **'smartness** *n*
Smart (smɑːt) *n* **Christopher.** 1722–71, British poet, author of *A Song to David* (1763) and *Jubilate Agno* (written 1758–63, published 1939). He was confined (1756–63) for religious mania and died in a debtors' prison.
smart aleck ('ælɪk) *n, pl* **smart alecks.** *Informal.* an irritatingly oversmart person. [C19: from *Aleck, Alec,* short for *Alexander*] ► **'smart-ˌaleck** *or* **'smart-ˌalecky** *adj*
smartarse ('smɑːtˌɑːs) *n Derogatory slang.* **a** a clever person, esp. one who parades his knowledge offensively. **b** (*as modifier*): *smartarse guidebooks.* ► **'smartˌarsed** *adj*
smart card *n* a plastic card with integrated circuits used for storing and processing computer data. Also called: **laser card, intelligent card.**
smarten ('smɑːtᵊn) *vb* (usually foll. by *up*) **1** (*intr*) to make oneself neater. **2** (*tr*) to make quicker or livelier.
smart money *n* **1a** money bet or invested by experienced gamblers or investors, esp. with inside information. **1b** the gamblers or investors themselves. **2** money paid in order to extricate oneself from an unpleasant situation or agreement, esp. from military service. **3** money paid by an employer to someone injured while working for him. **4** *U.S. Law.* damages awarded to a plaintiff where the wrong was aggravated by fraud, malice, etc.
smarts (smɑːts) *pl n Slang, chiefly U.S.* know-how, intelligence, or wits: *street smarts.*
smart set *n* (*functioning as sing or pl*) fashionable sophisticated people considered as a group.
smarty *or* **smartie** ('smɑːtɪ) *n Informal.* a would-be clever person.
smarty-pants ('smɑːtɪˌpænts) *or* **smarty-boots** ('smɑːtɪˌbuːts) *n* (*functioning as sing*) *Informal.* a would-be clever person.
smash (smæʃ) *vb* **1** to break into pieces violently and usually noisily. **2** (when *intr,* foll. by *against, through, into,* etc.) to throw or crash (against) vigorously, causing shattering: *he smashed the equipment; it smashed against the wall.* **3** (*tr*) to hit forcefully and suddenly. **4** (*tr*) *Tennis, etc.* to hit (the ball) fast and powerfully, esp. with an overhead stroke. **5** (*tr*) to defeat or wreck (persons, theories, etc.). **6** (*tr*) to make bankrupt. **7** (*intr*) to collide violently; crash. **8** (*intr;* often foll. by *up*) to go bankrupt. **9 smash someone's face in.** *Informal.* to beat someone severely. ♦ *n* **10** an act, instance, or sound of smashing or the state of being smashed. **11** a violent collision, esp. of vehicles. **12** a total failure or collapse, as of a business. **13** *Tennis, etc.* a fast and powerful overhead stroke. **14** *Informal.* **14a** something having popular success. **14b** (*in combination*): *smash-hit.* **15** *Slang.* loose change; coins. ♦ *adv* **16** with a smash. [C18: probably from SM(ACK[2] + M)ASH] ► **'smashable** *adj*
smash-and-grab *adj Informal.* of or relating to a robbery in which a shop window is broken and the contents removed.
smashed (smæʃt) *adj Slang.* **1** completely intoxicated with alcohol. **2** noticeably under the influence of a drug.
smasher ('smæʃə) *n Informal, chiefly Brit.* a person or thing that is very attractive or outstanding.
smashing ('smæʃɪŋ) *adj Informal, chiefly Brit.* excellent or first-rate; wonderful: *we had a smashing time.*
smash-up *Informal.* ♦ *n* **1** a bad collision, esp. of cars. ♦ *vb* **smash up. 2** (*tr, adv*) to damage to the point of complete destruction: *they smashed the place up.*
smatch (smætʃ) *n* a less common word for **smack**[1].
smatter ('smætə) *n* **1** a smattering. ♦ *vb* **2** (*intr*) *Rare.* to prattle. **3** (*tr*) *Archaic.* to dabble in. [C14 (in the sense: to prattle): of uncertain origin; compare Middle High German *smetern* to gossip] ► **'smatterer** *n*
smattering ('smætərɪŋ) *n* **1** a slight or superficial knowledge. **2** a small amount. ► **'smatteringly** *adv*
SMATV *abbrev. for* (originally) small master antenna television; now more commonly, satellite master antenna television: a system for relaying broadcast television signals, embodying a master receiving antenna with distribution by cable to a small group of dwellings, such as a block of flats.
smaze (smeɪz) *n U.S.* a smoky haze, less damp than fog. [C20: from SM(OKE + H)AZE[1]]
SMD *Electronics. abbrev. for* surface-mounted device: a device such as resistor, capacitor, or integrated circuit on a printed circuit board.
SME *international car registration for* Surinam.
smear (smɪə) *vb* (*mainly tr*) **1** to bedaub or cover with oil, grease, etc. **2** to rub over or apply thickly. **3** to rub so as to produce a smudge. **4** to slander. **5** *U.S. slang.* to defeat completely. **6** (*intr*) to be or become smeared or dirtied. ♦ *n* **7** a dirty mark or smudge. **8a** a slanderous attack. **8b** (*as modifier*): *smear tactics.* **9** a preparation of blood, secretions, etc., smeared onto a glass slide for examination under a microscope. [Old English *smeoru* (n); related to Old Norse *smjör* fat, Old High German *smero,* Greek *muron* ointment] ► **'smearer** *n* ► **'smeary** *adj* ► **'smearily** *adv* ► **'smeariness** *n*
smear test *n Med.* another name for **Pap test.**
smectic ('smɛktɪk) *adj Chem.* (of a substance) existing in or having a mesomorphic state in which the molecules are oriented in layers. Compare **nematic.** See also **liquid crystal.** [C17: via Latin from Greek *smēktikos,* from *smēkhein* to wash; from the soaplike consistency of a smectic substance]
smectite ('smɛktaɪt) *n* any of a group of clay minerals of which montmorillonite and saponite are members.
smeddum ('smɛdəm) *n Scot.* **1** any fine powder. **2** spirit or mettle; vigour. [Old English *smedema* fine flour]
smegma ('smɛgmə) *n Physiol.* a whitish sebaceous secretion that accumulates beneath the prepuce. [C19: via Latin from Greek *smēgma* detergent, from *smekhein* to wash]
smell (smɛl) *vb* **smells, smelling, smelt** *or* **smelled. 1** (*tr*) to perceive the scent or odour of (a substance) by means of the olfactory nerves. **2** (*copula*) to have a specified smell; appear to the sense of smell to be: *the beaches smell of seaweed; some tobacco smells very sweet.* **3** (*intr;* often foll. by *of*) to emit an odour (of): *the park smells of flowers.* **4** (*intr*) to emit an unpleasant odour; stink. **5** (*tr;* often foll. by *out*) to detect through shrewdness or instinct. **6** (*intr*) to have or use the sense of smell; sniff. **7** (*intr;* foll. by *of*) to give indications (of): *he smells of money.* **8** (*intr;* foll. by *around, about,* etc.) to search, investigate, or pry. **9** (*copula*) to be or seem to be untrustworthy or corrupt. **10 smell a rat.** to detect something suspicious. ♦ *n* **11** that sense (olfaction) by which scents or odours are perceived. Related adj: **olfactory. 12** anything detected by the sense of smell; odour; scent. **13** a trace or indication. **14** the act or an instance of smelling. [C12: of uncertain origin; compare Middle Dutch *smölen* to scorch] ► **'smeller** *n*
smelling salts *pl n* a pungent preparation containing crystals of ammonium carbonate that has a stimulant action when sniffed in cases of faintness, headache, etc.
smelly ('smɛlɪ) *adj* **smellier, smelliest.** having a strong or nasty smell. ► **'smelliness** *n*
smelt[1] (smɛlt) *vb* (*tr*) to extract (a metal) from (an ore) by heating. [C15: from Middle Low German, Middle Dutch *smelten;* related to Old High German *smelzan* to melt]
smelt[2] (smɛlt) *n, pl* **smelt** *or* **smelts.** any marine or freshwater salmonoid food fish of the family *Osmeridae,* such as *Osmerus eperlanus* of Europe, having a long silvery body and occurring in temperate and cold northern waters. [Old English *smylt;* related to Dutch, Danish *smelt,* Norwegian *smelta,* German *Schmelz*]
smelt[3] (smɛlt) *vb* a past tense and past participle of **smell.**
smelter ('smɛltə) *n* **1** a person engaged in smelting. **2** Also called: **smeltery** ('smɛltərɪ). an industrial plant in which smelting is carried out.
Smetana (*Czech* 'smɛtana) *n* **Bedřich** ('bɛdrʒix). 1824–84, Czech composer, founder of his country's national school of music. His works include *My Fatherland* (1874–79), a cycle of six symphonic poems, and the opera *The Bartered Bride* (1866).
smew (smjuː) *n* a merganser, *Mergus albellus,* of N Europe and Asia, having a male plumage of white with black markings. [C17: of uncertain origin]
smidgen *or* **smidgin** ('smɪdʒən) *n Informal.* a very small amount or part. [C20: of obscure origin]
smilacaceous (ˌsmaɪlə'keɪʃəs) *adj* of, relating to, or belonging to the *Smilacaceae,* a temperate and tropical family of monocotyledonous flowering plants, most of which are climbing shrubs with prickly stems: includes smilax. [C19: via New Latin from Latin SMILAX]
smilax ('smaɪlæks) *n* **1** any typically climbing shrub of the smilacaceous genus *Smilax,* of warm and tropical regions, having slightly lobed leaves, small greenish or yellow flowers, and berry-like fruits: includes the sarsaparilla plant and greenbrier. **2** a fragile, much branched liliaceous vine, *Asparagus asparagoides,* of southern Africa: cultivated by florists for its glossy bright green foliage. [C17: via Latin from Greek: bindweed]
smile (smaɪl) *n* **1** a facial expression characterized by an upturning of the corners of the mouth, usually showing amusement, friendliness, etc., but sometimes scorn, etc. **2** favour or blessing: *the smile of fortune.* **3** an agreeable appearance. ♦ *vb* **4** (*intr*) to wear or assume a smile. **5** (*intr;* foll. by *at*) **5a** to look (at) with a kindly or amused expression. **5b** to look derisively (at) instead of being an-

noyed. **5c** to bear (troubles, etc.) patiently. **6** (*intr;* foll. by *on* or *upon*) to show approval; bestow a blessing. **7** (*tr*) to express by means of a smile: *she smiled a welcome.* **8** (*tr;* often foll. by *away*) to drive away or change by smiling: *smile away one's tears.* **9 come up smiling.** to recover cheerfully from misfortune. [C13: probably of Scandinavian origin; compare Swedish *smila,* Danish *smile;* related to Middle High German *smielen*] ▸ **'smiler** *n* ▸ **'smiling** *adj* ▸ **'smilingly** *adv* ▸ **'smilingness** *n*

Smiles (smaɪlz) *n* **Samuel.** 1812–1904, British writer: author of the didactic work *Self-Help* (1859).

smiley ('smaɪlɪ) *adj* **1** given to smiling; cheerful. **2** depicting a smile: *a smiley badge.* ◆ *n* **3** any of a group of symbols depicting a smile, or other facial expression, used in electronic mail.

smir, smirr (smɪr), *or* **smur** *Scot.* ◆ *n* **1** drizzly rain. ◆ *vb* **smirs** *or* **smirrs, smirring, smirred.** (*intr*) **2** to drizzle lightly. [C19: of uncertain origin; compare Dutch *smoor* mist]

smirch (smɜːtʃ) *vb* (*tr*) **1** to dirty; soil. ◆ *n* **2** the act of smirching or state of being smirched. **3** a smear or stain. [C15 *smorchen,* of unknown origin] ▸ **'smircher** *n*

smirk (smɜːk) *n* **1** a smile expressing scorn, smugness, etc., rather than pleasure. ◆ *vb* **2** (*intr*) to give such a smile. **3** (*tr*) to express with such a smile. [Old English *smearcian;* related to *smer* derision, Old High German *bismer* contempt, *bismerōn* to scorn] ▸ **'smirker** *n* ▸ **'smirking** *adj* ▸ **'smirkingly** *adv*

smit (smɪt) *n* **the.** *Scot. and northern English dialect.* an infection: *he's got the smit.* [Old English *smitte* a spot, and *smittian* to smear; related to Old High German *smiz,* whence Middle High German *smitz*]

smite (smaɪt) *vb* **smites, smiting, smote; smitten** *or* **smit.** (*mainly tr*) *Now archaic in most senses.* **1** to strike with a heavy blow or blows. **2** to damage with or as if with blows. **3** to afflict or affect severely: *smitten with flu.* **4** to afflict in order to punish. **5** (*intr;* foll. by *on*) to strike forcibly or abruptly: *the sun smote down on him.* [Old English *smītan;* related to Old High German *smīzan* to smear, Gothic *bismeitan,* Old Swedish *smēta* to daub] ▸ **'smiter** *n*

smith (smɪθ) *n* **1a** a person who works in metal, esp. one who shapes metal by hammering. **1b** (*in combination*): *a silversmith.* **2** See **blacksmith.** [Old English; related to Old Norse *smithr,* Old High German *smid,* Middle Low German *smīde* jewellery, Greek *smilē* carving knife]

Smith (smɪθ) *n* **1 Adam.** 1723–90, Scottish economist and philosopher, whose influential book *The Wealth of Nations* (1776) advocated free trade and private enterprise and opposed state interference. **2 Bessie,** known as *Empress of the Blues.* 1894–1937, U.S. blues singer and songwriter. **3 Delia.** born 1941, British cookery writer and broadcaster: her publications include *The Complete Cookery Course* (1982). **4 F. E.** See (1st Earl of) **Birkenhead. 5 Harvey.** born 1938, British showjumper. **6 Ian** (**Douglas**). born 1919, Zimbabwean statesman; prime minister of Rhodesia (1964–79). He declared independence from Britain unilaterally (1965). **7 John.** ?1580–1631, English explorer and writer, who helped found the North American colony of Jamestown, Virginia. He was reputedly saved by the Indian chief's daughter Pocahontas from execution by her tribe. Among his works is a *Description of New England* (1616). **8 John.** 1938–94, British Labour politician; leader of the Labour Party 1992–94. **9 Joseph.** 1805–44, U.S. religious leader; founder of the Mormon Church. **10** Dame **Maggie.** born 1934, British actress. Her films include *The VIPs* (1963), *The Prime of Miss Jean Brodie* (1969), *The Lonely Passion of Judith Hearne* (1988), and *The Secret Garden* (1993). **11 Stevie,** real name *Florence Margaret Smith.* 1902–71, British poet. Her works include *Novel on Yellow Paper* (1936), and the poems 'A Good Time was had by All' (1937) and 'Not Waving but Drowning' (1957). **12 Sydney.** 1771–1845, British clergyman and writer, noted for *The Letters of Peter Plymley* (1807–08), in which he advocated Catholic emancipation. **13 William.** 1769–1839, English geologist, who founded the science of stratigraphy by proving that rock strata could be dated by the fossils they contained.

smithereens (ˌsmɪðəˈriːnz) *pl n* little shattered pieces or fragments. [C19: from Irish Gaelic *smidirīn,* from *smiodar*]

smithery ('smɪθərɪ) *n, pl* **-eries. 1** the trade or craft of a blacksmith. **2** a rare word for **smithy.**

Smithson ('smɪθsən) *n* **James.** original name *James Lewes Macie.* 1765–1829, English chemist and mineralogist, who left a bequest to found the Smithsonian Institution.

Smithsonian Institution (smɪθ'səʊnɪən) *n* a national museum and institution in Washington, D.C., founded in 1846 from a bequest by James Smithson, primarily concerned with ethnology, zoology, and astrophysics.

smithsonite ('smɪθsəˌnaɪt) *n* a white mineral consisting of zinc carbonate in hexagonal crystalline form: occurs chiefly in dry limestone regions and is a source of zinc. Formula: $ZnCO_3$. Also called (U.S.): **calamine.** [C19: named after James SMITHSON]

smithy ('smɪðɪ) *n, pl* **smithies.** a place in which metal, usually iron or steel, is worked by heating and hammering; forge. [Old English *smiththe;* related to Old Norse *smithja,* Old High German *smidda,* Middle Dutch *smisse*]

smitten ('smɪtᵊn) *vb* a past participle of **smite.**

smock (smɒk) *n* **1** any loose protective garment, worn by artists, laboratory technicians, etc. **2** a woman's loose blouse-like garment, reaching to below the waist, worn over slacks, etc. **3** Also called: **smock frock.** a loose protective overgarment decorated with smocking, worn formerly esp. by farm workers. **4** *Archaic.* a woman's loose undergarment, worn from the 16th to the 18th centuries. ◆ *vb* **5** to ornament (a garment) with smocking. [Old English *smocc;* related to Old High German *smocco,* Old Norse *smokkr* blouse, Middle High German *gesmuc* decoration] ▸ **'smockˌlike** *adj*

smocking ('smɒkɪŋ) *n* ornamental needlework used to gather and stitch material in a honeycomb pattern so that the part below the gathers hangs in even folds.

smock mill *n* a type of windmill having a revolving top.

smog (smɒg) *n* a mixture of smoke, fog, and chemical fumes. [C20: from SM(OKE + F)OG[1]] ▸ **'smoggy** *adj*

smoke (sməʊk) *n* **1** the product of combustion, consisting of fine particles of carbon carried by hot gases and air. **2** any cloud of fine particles suspended in a gas. **3a** the act of smoking tobacco or other substances, esp. in a pipe or as a cigarette or cigar. **3b** the duration of smoking such substances. **4** *Informal.* **4a** a cigarette or cigar. **4b** a substance for smoking, such as pipe tobacco or marijuana. **5** something with no concrete or lasting substance: *everything turned to smoke.* **6** a thing or condition that obscures. **7** any of various colours similar to that of smoke, esp. a dark grey with a bluish, yellowish, or greenish tinge. **8 go** *or* **end up in smoke. 8a** to come to nothing. **8b** to burn up vigorously. **8c** to flare up in anger. ◆ *vb* **9** (*intr*) to emit smoke or the like, sometimes excessively or in the wrong place. **10** to draw in on (a burning cigarette, etc.) and exhale the smoke. **11** (*intr*) *Slang.* to use marijuana for smoking. **12** (*tr*) to bring (oneself) into a specified state by smoking. **13** (*tr*) to subject or expose to smoke. **14** (*tr*) to cure (meat, fish, cheese, etc.) by treating with smoke. **15** (*tr*) to fumigate or purify the air of (rooms, etc.). **16** (*tr*) to darken (glass, etc.) by exposure to smoke. **17** (*intr*) *Slang.* to move, drive, ride, etc., very fast. **18** (*tr*) *Obsolete.* to tease or mock. **19** (*tr*) *Archaic.* to suspect or detect. ◆ See also **smoke out.** [Old English *smoca* (n); related to Middle Dutch *smieken* to emit smoke] ▸ **'smokable** *or* **'smokeable** *adj*

Smoke (sməʊk) *n* **the.** short for **Big Smoke.**

smoke bomb *n* a device that emits large quantities of smoke when ignited.

smoke-dried *adj* (of fish, meat, etc.) cured in smoke.

smoked rubber *n* a type of crude natural rubber in the form of brown sheets obtained by coagulating latex with an acid, rolling it into sheets, and drying over open wood fires. It is the main raw material for natural rubber products. Also called: **ribbed and smoked sheet.** Compare **crepe rubber.**

smokeho ('sməʊkəʊ) *n* a variant spelling of **smoko.**

smokehouse ('sməʊkˌhaʊs) *n* a building or special construction for curing meat, fish, etc., by smoking.

smokejack ('sməʊkˌdʒæk) *n* a device formerly used for turning a roasting spit, operated by the movement of ascending gases in a chimney. [C17: from SMOKE + JACK[1]]

smokeless ('sməʊklɪs) *adj* having or producing little or no smoke: *smokeless fuel.*

smokeless powder *n* any one of a number of explosives that burn with relatively little smoke. They consist mainly of nitrocellulose and are used as propellants.

smokeless zone *n* an area designated by the local authority where only smokeless fuels are permitted.

smoke out *vb* (*tr, adv*) **1** to subject to smoke in order to drive out of hiding. **2** to bring into the open; expose to the public: *they smoked out the plot.*

smoker ('sməʊkə) *n* **1** a person who habitually smokes tobacco. **2** Also called: **smoking compartment.** a compartment of a train where smoking is permitted. **3** an informal social gathering, as at a club.

smoke screen *n* **1** *Military.* a cloud of smoke produced by artificial means to obscure movements or positions. **2** something said or done in order to hide the truth.

smokestack ('sməʊkˌstæk) *n* a tall chimney that conveys smoke into the air. Sometimes shortened to **stack.**

smokestack industry *n Informal.* any of the traditional British industries, esp. heavy engineering or manufacturing, as opposed to such modern industries as electronics.

smoke tree *n* **1** an anacardiaceous shrub, *Cotinus coggygria,* of S Europe and Asia, having clusters of yellowish feathery flowers. **2** a related tree, *Cotinus americanus,* of the southern U.S. [C19: so named because of the similarity between its flower clusters and a cloud of smoke]

smoking gun *n Chiefly U.S. and Canadian.* a piece of irrefutable incriminating evidence.

smoking jacket *n* a man's comfortable jacket of velvet, etc., closed by a tie belt or fastenings, worn at home. [so called because it was formerly worn for smoking]

smoking room *or* (*esp. Brit.*) **smoke room** *n* a room, esp. in a hotel or club, for those who wish to smoke.

smoko *or* **smokeho** ('sməʊkəʊ) *n, pl* **-kos** *or* **-hos.** *Austral. and N.Z. informal.* a short break from work for tea, a cigarette, etc. [C19: from SMOKE + -O]

smoky ('sməʊkɪ) *adj* **smokier, smokiest. 1** emitting, containing, or resembling smoke. **2** emitting smoke excessively or in the wrong place: *a smoky fireplace.* **3** of or tinged with the colour smoke: *a smoky cat.* **4** having the flavour of having been cured by smoking. **5** made dark, dirty, or hazy by smoke. ▸ **'smokily** *adv* ▸ **'smokiness** *n*

Smoky Mountains *pl n* See **Great Smoky Mountains.**

smoky quartz *n* another name for **cairngorm.** [so named because of its colour]

smolder ('sməʊldə) *vb, n* the U.S. spelling of **smoulder.**

Smolensk (*Russian* smaˈljensk; *English* ˈsmɒlɛnsk) *n* a city in W Russia, on the Dnieper River: a major commercial centre in medieval times; scene of severe fighting (1941 and 1943) in World War II. Pop.: 353 000 (1995 est.).

Smollett ('smɒlɪt) *n* **Tobias George.** 1721–71, Scottish novelist, whose picaresque satires include *Roderick Random* (1748), *Peregrine Pickle* (1751), and *Humphry Clinker* (1771).

smolt (sməʊlt) *n* a young salmon at the stage when it migrates from fresh water to the sea. [C14: Scottish, of uncertain origin; perhaps related to SMELT[2]]

smooch (smuːtʃ) *Informal.* ◆ *vb* (*intr*) **1** Also (Austral. and N.Z.): **smoodge, smooge.** (of two people) to kiss and cuddle. **2** *Brit.* to dance very slowly and amorously with one's arms around another person, or (of two people) to dance together in such a way. ◆ *n* 3 the act of smooching. 4 *Brit.* a piece of music played for dancing to slowly and amorously. [C20: variant of dialect *smouch,* of imitative origin]

smoodge *or* **smooge** (smu:dʒ) *vb Austral. and N.Z.* variants of **smooch** (sense 1).

smooth (smu:ð) *adj* 1 resting in the same plane; without bends or irregularities. 2 silky to the touch: *smooth velvet.* 3 lacking roughness of surface; flat. 4 tranquil or unruffled: *smooth temper.* 5 lacking obstructions or difficulties. 6a suave or persuasive, esp. as suggestive of insincerity. 6b (*in combination*): *smooth-tongued.* 7 (of the skin) free from hair. 8 of uniform consistency: *smooth batter.* 9 not erratic; free from jolts: *smooth driving.* 10 not harsh or astringent: *a smooth wine.* 11 having all projections worn away: *smooth tyres.* 12 *Maths.* (of a curve) differential at every point. 13 *Phonetics.* without preliminary or simultaneous aspiration. 14 gentle to the ear; flowing. 15 *Physics.* (of a plane, surface, etc.) regarded as being frictionless. ◆ *adv* 16 in a calm or even manner; smoothly. ◆ *vb* (*mainly tr*) 17 (*also intr;* often foll. by *down*) to make or become flattened or without roughness or obstructions. 18 (often foll. by *out* or *away*) to take or rub (away) in order to make smooth: *she smoothed out the creases in her dress.* 19 to make calm; soothe. 20 to make easier: *smooth his path.* 21 *Electrical engineering.* to remove alternating current ripple from the output of a direct current power supply. 22 *Obsolete.* to make more polished or refined. ◆ *n* 23 the smooth part of something. 24 the act of smoothing. 25 *Tennis, etc.* the side of a racket on which the binding strings form a continuous line. Compare **rough** (sense 27). ◆ See also **smooth over.** [Old English *smōth;* related to Old Saxon *māthmundi* gentle-minded, *smōthi* smooth] ▸ ˈ**smoothable** *adj* ▸ ˈ**smoother** *n* ▸ ˈ**smoothly** *adv* ▸ ˈ**smoothness** *n*

smoothbore (ˈsmu:ð,bɔ:) *n* 1 (*modifier*) (of a firearm) having an unrifled bore: *a smoothbore musket.* 2 such a firearm. ▸ ˈ**smooth,bored** *adj*

smooth breathing *n* (in Greek) the sign (ʼ) placed over an initial vowel, indicating that (in ancient Greek) it was not pronounced with an *h.* Compare **rough breathing.**

smoothen (ˈsmu:ðən) *vb* to make or become smooth.

smooth hound *n* any of several small sharks of the genus *Mustelus,* esp. *M. mustelus,* a species of North Atlantic coastal regions: family *Triakidae.* See also **dogfish** (sense 3). [C17: from HOUND(FISH); so called because it has no dorsal spines]

smoothie *or* **smoothy** (ˈsmu:ðɪ) *n, pl* **smoothies.** *Slang, usually derogatory.* a person, esp. a man, who is suave or slick, esp. in speech, dress, or manner.

smoothing circuit *n Electrical engineering.* a circuit used to remove ripple from the output of a direct current power supply.

smoothing iron *n* a former name for **iron** (senses 2, 3).

smooth muscle *n* muscle that is capable of slow rhythmic involuntary contractions: occurs in the walls of the blood vessels, alimentary canal, etc. Compare **striped muscle.** [so called because there is no cross-banding on the muscle]

smooth over *vb* (*tr*) to ease or gloss over: *to smooth over a situation.*

smooth snake *n* any of several slender nonvenomous colubrid snakes of the European genus *Coronella,* esp. *C. austriaca,* having very smooth scales and a reddish-brown coloration.

smooth-spoken *adj* speaking or spoken in a gently persuasive or competent manner.

smooth-tongued *adj* suave or persuasive in speech.

smorgasbord (ˈsmɔ:gəs,bɔ:d, ˈsmɜ:-) *n* a variety of cold or hot savoury dishes, such as pâté, smoked salmon, etc., served in Scandinavia as hors d'oeuvres or as a buffet meal. [Swedish, from *smörgås* sandwich + *bord* table]

smørrebrød (*Danish* ˈsmœrə,brœð) *n* small open savoury sandwiches, served esp. in Denmark as hors d'oeuvres, etc. [Danish, from *smør* butter + *brød* bread]

smote (sməʊt) *vb* the past tense of **smite.**

smother (ˈsmʌðə) *vb* 1 to suffocate or stifle by cutting off or being cut off from the air. 2 (*tr*) to surround (with) or envelop (in): *he smothered her with love.* 3 (*tr*) to extinguish (a fire) by covering so as to cut it off from the air. 4 to be or cause to be suppressed or stifled: *smother a giggle.* 5 (*tr*) to cook or serve (food) thickly covered with sauce, etc. ◆ *n* 6 anything, such as a cloud of smoke, that stifles. 7 a profusion or turmoil. 8 *Archaic.* a state of smouldering or a smouldering fire. [Old English *smorian* to suffocate; related to Middle Low German *smōren*] ▸ ˈ**smothery** *adj*

smothered mate *n Chess.* checkmate given by a knight when the king is prevented from moving by surrounding men.

smoulder *or U.S.* **smolder** (ˈsməʊldə) *vb* (*intr*) 1 to burn slowly without flame, usually emitting smoke. 2 (esp. of anger, etc.) to exist in a suppressed or half-suppressed state. 3 to have strong repressed or half repressed feelings, esp. anger. ◆ *n* 4 dense smoke, as from a smouldering fire. 5 a smouldering fire. [C14: from *smolder* (n), of obscure origin]

smout *or* **smowt** (smaʊt) *n Scot.* 1 a variant of **smolt.** 2 a child or undersized person. [C16: a variant of SMOLT]

SMP *abbrev. for* statutory maternity pay.

smriti (ˈsmrɪtɪ) *n* a class of Hindu sacred literature derived from the Vedas, containing social, domestic, and religious teaching. [from Sanskrit *smrti* what is remembered, from *samarati* he remembers]

smudge (smʌdʒ) *vb* 1 to smear, blur, or soil or cause to do so. 2 (*tr*) *Chiefly U.S. and Canadian.* to fill (an area) with smoke in order to drive insects away or guard against frost. ◆ *n* 3 a smear or dirty mark. 4 a blurred form or area: *that smudge in the distance is a quarry.* 5 *Chiefly U.S. and Canadian.* a smoky fire for driving insects away or protecting fruit trees or plants from frost. [C15: of uncertain origin] ▸ ˈ**smudgeless** *adj* ▸ ˈ**smudgy** *adj* ▸ ˈ**smudgily** *or* ˈ**smudgedly** *adv* ▸ ˈ**smudginess** *n*

smug (smʌg) *adj* **smugger, smuggest.** 1 excessively self-satisfied or complacent. 2 *Archaic.* trim or neat. [C16: of Germanic origin; compare Low German *smuck* neat] ▸ ˈ**smugly** *adv* ▸ ˈ**smugness** *n*

smuggle (ˈsmʌgᵊl) *vb* 1 to import or export (prohibited or dutiable goods) secretly. 2 (*tr;* often foll. by *into* or *out of*) to bring or take secretly, as against the law or rules. 3 (*tr;* foll. by *away*) to conceal; hide. [C17: from Low German *smukkelen* and Dutch *smokkelen,* perhaps from Old English *smūgen* to creep; related to Old Norse *smjūga*] ▸ ˈ**smuggler** *n* ▸ ˈ**smuggling** *n*

smur (smʌr) *n, vb Scot.* a variant of **smir.**

smut (smʌt) *n* 1 a small dark smudge or stain, esp. one caused by soot. 2 a speck of soot or dirt. 3 something obscene or indecent. 4a any of various fungal diseases of flowering plants, esp. cereals, in which black sooty masses of spores cover the affected parts. 4b any parasitic basidiomycetous fungus of the order *Ustilaginales* that causes such a disease. 5 *Angling.* a minute midge or other insect relished by trout. ◆ *vb* **smuts, smutting, smutted.** 6 to mark or become marked or smudged, as with soot. 7 to affect (grain) or (of grain) to be affected with smut. 8 (*tr*) to remove smut from (grain). 9 (*tr*) to make obscene. 10 (*intr*) to emit soot or smut. 11 (*intr*) *Angling.* (of trout) to feed voraciously on smuts. [Old English *smitte;* related to Middle High German *smitze;* associated with SMUDGE, SMUTCH] ▸ ˈ**smutty** *adj* ▸ ˈ**smuttily** *adv* ▸ ˈ**smuttiness** *n*

smutch (smʌtʃ) *vb* 1 (*tr*) to smudge; mark. ◆ *n* 2 a mark; smudge. 3 soot; dirt. [C16: probably from Middle High German *smutzen* to soil; see SMUT] ▸ ˈ**smutchy** *adj*

Smuts (smʌts) *n* **Jan Christiaan** (jan ˈkristi,an). 1870–1950, South African statesman; prime minister (1919–24; 1939–48). He fought for the Boers during the Boer War, then worked for Anglo-Boer reconciliation and served the Allies during World Wars I and II.

Smyrna (ˈsmɜ:nə) *n* an ancient city on the W coast of Asia Minor: a major trading centre in the ancient world; a centre of early Christianity. Modern name: **Izmir.**

Smyth (smaɪð) *n* Dame **Ethel** (**Mary**). 1858–1944, British composer, best known for her operas, such as *The Wreckers* (1906). She was imprisoned for supporting the suffragette movement.

Sn *the chemical symbol for* tin. [from New Latin *stannum*]

SN *international car registration for* Senegal.

snack (snæk) *n* 1 a light quick meal eaten between or in place of main meals. 2 a sip or bite. 3 *Rare.* a share. 4 *Austral. informal.* a very easy task. ◆ *vb* 5 (*intr*) to eat a snack. [C15: probably from Middle Dutch *snacken,* variant of *snappen* to SNAP]

snack bar *n* a place where light meals or snacks can be obtained, often with a self-service system.

snackette (ˈsnækɛt) *n* a Caribbean name for **snack bar.**

snaffle (ˈsnæfᵊl) *n* 1 Also called: **snaffle bit.** a simple jointed bit for a horse. ◆ *vb* (*tr*) 2 *Brit. informal.* to steal or take for oneself. 3 to equip or control with a snaffle. [C16: of uncertain origin; compare Old Frisian *snavel* mouth, Old High German *snabul* beak]

snafu (snæˈfu:) *Slang, chiefly military.* ◆ *n* 1 confusion or chaos regarded as the normal state. ◆ *adj* 2 (*postpositive*) confused or muddled up, as usual. ◆ *vb* **-fues, -fuing, -fued.** 3 (*tr*) *U.S. and Canadian.* to throw into chaos. [C20: from *s(ituation) n(ormal): a(ll) f(ucked) u(p)*]

snag (snæg) *n* 1 a difficulty or disadvantage: *the snag is that I have nothing suitable to wear.* 2 a sharp protuberance, such as a tree stump. 3 a small loop or hole in a fabric caused by a sharp object. 4 *Engineering.* a projection that brings to a stop a sliding or rotating component. 5 *Chiefly U.S. and Canadian.* a tree stump in a riverbed that is dangerous to navigation. 6 *U.S. and Canadian.* a standing dead tree, esp. one used as a perch by an eagle. 7 (*pl*) *Austral. slang.* sausages. ◆ *vb* **snags, snagging, snagged.** 8 (*tr*) to hinder or impede. 9 (*tr*) to tear or catch (fabric). 10 (*intr*) to develop a snag. 11 (*intr*) *Chiefly U.S. and Canadian.* (of a boat) to strike or be damaged by a snag. 12 (*tr*) *Chiefly U.S. and Canadian.* to clear (a stretch of water) of snags. 13 (*tr*) *U.S.* to seize (an opportunity, benefit, etc.). [C16: of Scandinavian origin; compare Old Norse *snaghyrndr* sharp-pointed, Norwegian *snage* spike, Icelandic *snagi* peg] ▸ ˈ**snaggy** *adj* ▸ ˈ**snag,like** *adj*

snaggletooth (ˈsnægᵊl,tu:θ) *n, pl* **-teeth.** a tooth that is broken or projecting. ▸ ˈ**snaggle,toothed** *adj*

snail (sneɪl) *n* 1 any of numerous terrestrial or freshwater gastropod molluscs with a spirally coiled shell, esp. any of the family *Helicidae,* such as *Helix aspersa* (**garden snail**). 2 any other gastropod with a spirally coiled shell, such as a whelk. 3 a slow-moving or lazy person or animal. [Old English *snægl;* related to Old Norse *snigill,* Old High German *snecko*] ▸ ˈ**snail-,like** *adj*

snail cam *n Mechanical engineering.* a cam with spiral cross section used for progressive lifting of a lever as the cam revolves.

snailfish (ˈsneɪl,fɪʃ) *n, pl* **-fish** *or* **-fishes.** another name for **sea snail.**

snail mail *Informal.* *n* 1 the conventional postal system, as opposed to electronic mail. ◆ *vb* **snail-mail.** 2 (*tr*) to send by the conventional postal system, rather than by electronic mail. [C20: so named because of the relative slowness of the conventional postal system]

snail's pace *n* a very slow or sluggish speed or rate.

snake (sneɪk) *n* 1 any reptile of the suborder *Ophidia* (or *Serpentes*), typically having a scaly cylindrical limbless body, fused eyelids, and a jaw modified for swallowing large prey: includes venomous forms such as cobras and rattlesnakes, large nonvenomous constrictors (boas and pythons), and small harmless types such as the grass snake. Related adjs: **colubrine, ophidian.** 2 Also called: **snake in the grass.** a deceitful or treacherous person. 3 anything resembling a snake in appearance or action. 4 (in the European Union) a former system of managing a group of currencies by allowing the exchange rate of each of them only to fluctuate within narrow limits. 5 a tool in the form of a long flexible wire for unblocking drains. ◆ *vb* 6 (*intr*) to glide or move like a snake. 7

(*tr*) *U.S.* to haul (a heavy object, esp. a log) by fastening a rope around one end of it. **8** (*tr*) *U.S.* (often foll. by *out*) to pull jerkily. **9** (*tr*) to move in or follow (a sinuous course). [Old English *snaca;* related to Old Norse *snākr* snake, Old High German *snahhan* to crawl, Norwegian *snōk* snail] ► **'snake,like** *adj*

snakebird ('sneɪk,bɜːd) *n* another name for **darter** (the bird).

snakebite ('sneɪk,baɪt) *n* **1** a bite inflicted by a snake, esp. a venomous one. **2** a drink of cider and lager.

snake charmer *n* an entertainer, esp. in Asia, who charms or appears to charm snakes by playing music and by rhythmic body movements.

snake dance *n* **1** a ceremonial dance, performed by the priests of the American Hopi Indians, in which live snakes are held in the mouth. **2a** the swaying movements of snakes responding to a snake charmer. **2b** a Hindu dance in which performers imitate such snake movements.

snake fly *n* any of various neuropterous insects of the family *Raphidiidae,* having an elongated thorax: order *Megaloptera.*

snake juice *n Austral. slang.* any strong alcoholic drink, esp. when homemade. [C19: perhaps so called from its poisonous effects]

snakemouth ('sneɪk,maʊθ) *n* a terrestrial orchid, *Pogonia ophioglossoides,* of E North America, having solitary fragrant pinkish-purple flowers. [so called because of the alleged similarity between the shape of the flower and a snake's mouth]

Snake River *n* a river in the northwestern U.S., rising in NW Wyoming and flowing west through Idaho, turning north as part of the border between Idaho and Oregon, and flowing west to the Columbia River near Pasco, Washington. Length: 1670 km (1038 miles).

snakeroot ('sneɪk,ruːt) *n* **1** any of various North American plants, such as *Aristolochia serpentaria* (**Virginia snakeroot**) and *Eupatorium urticaefolium* (**white snakeroot**), the roots or rhizomes of which have been used as a remedy for snakebite. **2** the rhizome or root of any such plant. **3** another name for **bistort** (senses 1, 2). ◆ Also called: **snakeweed.**

snakes and ladders *n* (*functioning as sing*) a board game in which players move counters along a series of squares according to throws of a dice. A ladder provides a short cut to a square nearer the finish and a snake obliges a player to return to a square nearer the start.

snake's head *n* a European fritillary plant, *Fritillaria meleagris,* of damp meadows, having purple-and-white chequered flowers. [C19: so called because its buds are claimed to resemble a snake's head]

snakeskin ('sneɪk,skɪn) *n* the skin of a snake, esp. when made into a leather valued for handbags, shoes, etc.

snaky ('sneɪkɪ) *adj* **snakier, snakiest. 1** of or like a snake; sinuous. **2** treacherous or insidious. **3** infested with snakes. **4** *Austral. and N.Z. informal.* angry or bad-tempered. ► **'snakily** *adv* ► **'snakiness** *n*

snap (snæp) *vb* **snaps, snapping, snapped. 1** to break or cause to break suddenly, esp. with a sharp sound. **2** to make or cause to make a sudden sharp cracking sound. **3** (*intr*) to give way or collapse suddenly, esp. from strain. **4** to move, close, etc., or cause to move, close, etc., with a sudden sharp sound. **5** to move or cause to move in a sudden or abrupt way. **6** (*intr;* often foll. by *at* or *up*) to seize something suddenly or quickly. **7** (when *intr,* often foll. by *at*) to bite at (something) bringing the jaws rapidly together. **8** to speak (words) sharply or abruptly. **9** (*intr*) (of eyes) to flash or sparkle. **10** to take a snapshot of (something). **11** (*intr*) *Hunting.* to fire a quick shot without taking deliberate aim. **12** (*tr*) *American football.* to put (the ball) into play by sending it back from the line of scrimmage to a teammate. **13 snap one's fingers at.** *Informal.* **13a** to dismiss with contempt. **13b** to defy. **14 snap out of it.** *Informal.* to recover quickly, esp. from depression, anger, or illness. ◆ *n* **15** the act of breaking suddenly or the sound produced by a sudden breakage. **16** a sudden sharp sound, esp. of bursting, popping, or cracking. **17** a catch, clasp, or fastener that operates with a snapping sound. **18** a sudden grab or bite. **19** the sudden release of something such as elastic thread. **20** a brisk movement of the thumb against one or more fingers. **21** a thin crisp biscuit: *ginger snaps.* **22** *Informal.* See **snapshot. 23** *Informal.* vigour, liveliness, or energy. **24** *Informal.* a task or job that is easy or profitable to do. **25** a short spell or period, esp. of cold weather. **26** *Brit. dialect.* food, esp. a packed lunch taken to work. **27** *Brit.* a card game in which the word *snap* is called when two cards of equal value are turned up on the separate piles dealt by each player. **28** *American football.* the start of each play when the centre passes the ball back from the line of scrimmage to a teammate. **29** (*modifier*) done on the spur of the moment, without consideration: *a snap decision.* **30** (*modifier*) closed or fastened with a snap. ◆ *adv* **31** with a snap. ◆ *interj* **32a** *Cards.* the word called while playing snap. **32b** an exclamation used to draw attention to the similarity of two things. ◆ See also **snap up.** [C15: from Middle Low German or Middle Dutch *snappen* to seize; related to Old Norse *snapa* to snuffle] ► **'snapless** *adj* ► **'snappable** *adj*

snapback ('snæp,bæk) *n* a sudden rebound or change in direction.

snap bean *n U.S. and Canadian.* **1** any of various bean plants that are cultivated in the U.S. for their crisp edible unripe pods. **2** the pod of such a plant. ◆ See also **string bean.** [C19: so called because the pods are broken into pieces for eating]

snapdragon ('snæp,drægən) *n* any of several scrophulariaceous chiefly Old World plants of the genus *Antirrhinum,* esp. *A. majus,* of the Mediterranean region, having spikes of showy white, yellow, pink, red, or purplish flowers. Also called: **antirrhinum.** [C16: so named because the flowers, which are claimed to look like a dragon's head, have a "mouth" which snaps shut if squeezed open and then released]

snap fastener *n* another name for **press stud.**

snapper ('snæpə) *n, pl* **-per** *or* **-pers. 1** any large sharp-toothed percoid food fish of the family *Lutjanidae* of warm and tropical coastal regions. See also **red snapper. 2** a sparid food fish, *Chrysophrys auratus,* of Australia and New Zealand, that has a pinkish body covered with blue spots. **3** another name for the **bluefish** or the **snapping turtle. 4** a person or thing that snaps. **5** *Informal.* a person who take snapshots; photographer. ◆ Also called (senses 1, 2): **schnapper.**

snapper up *n* a person who snaps up bargains, etc.

snapping beetle *n* another name for the **click beetle.**

snapping turtle *n* any large aggressive North American river turtle of the family *Chelydridae,* esp. *Chelydra serpentina* (**common snapping turtle**), having powerful hooked jaws and a rough shell. Also called: **snapper.**

snappy ('snæpɪ) *adj* **-pier, -piest. 1** Also: **snappish.** apt to speak sharply or irritably. **2** Also: **snappish.** apt to snap or bite. **3** crackling in sound: *a snappy fire.* **4** brisk, sharp, or chilly: *a snappy pace; snappy weather.* **5** smart and fashionable: *a snappy dresser.* **6 make it snappy.** *Slang.* be quick! hurry up! ► **'snappily** *adv* ► **'snappiness** *n*

snap ring *n Mountaineering.* another name for **karabiner.**

snap roll *n* a manoeuvre in which an aircraft makes a fast roll.

snapshot ('snæp,ʃɒt) *n* an informal photograph taken with a simple camera. Often shortened to **snap.**

snap shot *n Sports.* a sudden, fast shot at goal.

snap up *vb* (*tr, adv*) **1** to avail oneself of eagerly and quickly: *she snapped up the bargains.* **2** to interrupt abruptly.

snare[1] (snɛə) *n* **1** a device for trapping birds or small animals, esp. a flexible loop that is drawn tight around the prey. **2** a surgical instrument for removing certain tumours, consisting of a wire loop that may be drawn tight around their base to sever or uproot them. **3** anything that traps or entangles someone or something unawares. ◆ *vb* (*tr*) **4** to catch (birds or small animals) with a snare. **5** to catch or trap in or as if in a snare; capture by trickery. [Old English *sneare,* from Old Norse *snara;* related to Old High German *snaraha*] ► **'snareless** *adj* ► **'snarer** *n*

snare[2] (snɛə) *n Music.* a set of gut strings wound with wire fitted against the lower drumhead of a snare drum. They produce a rattling sound when the drum is beaten. See **snare drum.** [C17: from Middle Dutch *snaer* or Middle Low German *snare* string; related to Gothic *snōrjō* basket]

snare drum *n Music.* a cylindrical drum with two drumheads, the upper of which is struck and the lower fitted with a snare. See **snare**[2].

snarl[1] (snɑːl) *vb* **1** (*intr*) (of an animal) to growl viciously, baring the teeth. **2** to speak or express (something) viciously or angrily. ◆ *n* **3** a vicious growl, utterance, or facial expression. **4** the act of snarling. [C16: of Germanic origin; compare Middle Low German *snarren,* Middle Dutch *snarren* to drone] ► **'snarling** *adj* ► **'snarlingly** *adv* ► **'snarly** *adj*

snarl[2] (snɑːl) *n* **1** a tangled mass of thread, hair, etc. **2** a complicated or confused state or situation. **3** a knot in wood. ◆ *vb* **4** (often foll. by *up*) to be, become, or make tangled or complicated. **5** (*tr;* often foll. by *up*) to confuse mentally. **6** (*tr*) to flute or emboss (metal) by hammering on a tool held against the under surface. [C14: of Scandinavian origin; compare Old Swedish *snarel* noose, Old Norse *snara* SNARE[1]] ► **'snarler** *n* ► **'snarly** *adj*

snarler[1] ('snɑːlə) *n* **1** an animal or a person that snarls. **2** *N.Z. informal.* a sausage.

snarl-up *n Informal, chiefly Brit.* a confusion, obstruction, or tangle, esp. a traffic jam.

snatch (snætʃ) *vb* **1** (*tr*) to seize or grasp (something) suddenly or peremptorily: *he snatched the chocolate out of my hand.* **2** (*intr;* usually foll. by *at*) to seize or attempt to seize suddenly. **3** (*tr*) to take hurriedly: *to snatch some sleep.* **4** (*tr*) to remove suddenly: *she snatched her hand away.* **5** (*tr*) to gain, win, or rescue, esp. narrowly: *they snatched victory in the closing seconds.* **6** (*tr*) (in weightlifting) to lift (a weight) with a snatch. **7 snatch one's time.** *Austral. informal.* to leave a job, taking whatever pay is due. ◆ *n* **8** an act of snatching. **9** a fragment or small incomplete part: *snatches of conversation.* **10** a brief spell: *snatches of time off.* **11** *Weightlifting.* a lift in which the weight is raised in one quick motion from the floor to an overhead position. **12** *Slang, chiefly U.S.* an act of kidnapping. **13** *Brit. slang.* a robbery: *a diamond snatch.* [C13 *snacchen;* related to Middle Dutch *snakken* to gasp, Old Norse *snaka* to sniff around] ► **'snatcher** *n*

snatch block *n Nautical.* a block that can be opened so that a rope can be inserted from the side, without threading it through from the end. [C17: so called because the rope can be inserted quickly: figuratively, the block snatches it. See SNATCH]

snatch squad *n Brit.* a squad of soldiers or police trained to deal with demonstrations by picking out and arresting the alleged ringleaders.

snatchy ('snætʃɪ) *adj* **snatchier, snatchiest.** disconnected or spasmodic. ► **'snatchily** *adv*

snath (snæθ) *or* **snathe** (sneɪð) *n* the handle of a scythe. [C16: variant of earlier *snead,* from Old English *snǣd,* of obscure origin]

snazzy ('snæzɪ) *adj* **-zier, -ziest.** *Informal.* (esp. of clothes) stylishly and often flashily attractive. [C20: perhaps from SN(APPY + J)AZZY] ► **'snazzily** *adv* ► **'snazziness** *n*

SNCC (snɪk) *n* (in the U.S.) *acronym for* Student Nonviolent Coordinating Committee (1960–69) and Student National Coordinating Committee (from 1969); a civil-rights organization.

SNCF *abbrev. for* Société Nationale des Chemins de Fer: the French national railway system.

sneak (sniːk) *vb* **1** (*intr;* often foll. by *along, off, in,* etc.) to move furtively. **2** (*intr*) to behave in a cowardly or underhand manner. **3** (*tr*) to bring, take, or put stealthily. **4** (*intr*) *Informal, chiefly Brit.* to tell tales (esp. in schools). **5** (*tr*) *Informal.* to steal. **6** (*intr;* foll. by *off, out, away,* etc.) *Informal.* to leave unobtrusively. ◆ *n* **7** a person who acts in an underhand or cowardly manner, esp. as an informer. **8a** a stealthy act or movement. **8b** (*as modifier*): *a sneak attack.* **9** *Brit. informal.* an unobtrusive departure. [Old English *snīcan* to creep; from

Old Norse *snīkja* to hanker after] ▸ 'sneaky *adj* ▸ 'sneakily *adv* ▸ 'sneakiness *n*

sneakers ('sni:kəz) *pl n Chiefly U.S. and Canadian.* canvas shoes with rubber soles worn for sports or informally.

sneaking ('sni:kɪŋ) *adj* **1** acting in a furtive or cowardly way. **2** secret: *a sneaking desire to marry a millionaire.* **3** slight but nagging (esp. in the phrase **a sneaking suspicion**). ▸ 'sneakingly *adv* ▸ 'sneakingness *n*

sneak preview *n* a screening of a film at an unexpected time to test audience reaction before its release.

sneak thief *n* a person who steals paltry articles from premises, which he enters through open doors, windows, etc.

sneck[1] (snɛk) *n* **1** a small squared stone used in a rubble wall to fill spaces between stones of different height. **2** *Dialect, chiefly Scot. and northern English.* the latch or catch of a door or gate. ◆ *vb* **3** *Dialect, chiefly Scot. and northern English.* to fasten (a latch). [C15 *snekk*, of uncertain origin]

sneck[2] (snɛk) *n, vb* a Scot. word for **snick**.

sneer (snɪə) *n* **1** a facial expression of scorn or contempt, typically with the upper lip curled. **2** a scornful or contemptuous remark or utterance. ◆ *vb* **3** (*intr*) to assume a facial expression of scorn or contempt. **4** to say or utter (something) in a scornful or contemptuous manner. [C16: perhaps from Low Dutch; compare North Frisian *sneere* contempt] ▸ 'sneerer *n* ▸ 'sneerful *adj* ▸ 'sneering *adj, n* ▸ 'sneeringly *adv*

sneeze (sni:z) *vb* **1** (*intr*) to expel air from the nose involuntarily, esp. as the result of irritation of the nasal mucous membrane. ◆ *n* **2** the act or sound of sneezing. [Old English *fnēosan* (unattested); related to Old Norse *fnȳsa*, Middle High German *fnūsen*, Greek *pneuma* breath] ▸ 'sneezeless *adj* ▸ 'sneezer *n* ▸ 'sneezy *adj*

sneeze at *vb* (*intr, prep;* usually with a negative) *Informal.* to dismiss lightly: *his offer is not to be sneezed at.*

sneezewood ('sni:z,wʊd) *n* **1** a tree, *Ptaeroxylon utile*, native to southern Africa: family *Ptaeroxylaceae.* **2** the tough wood of this tree, which has a peppery smell and is used for bridges, piers, fencing posts, etc.

sneezewort ('sni:z,wɜ:t) *n* a Eurasian plant, *Achillea ptarmica*, having daisy-like flowers and long grey-green leaves, which cause sneezing when powdered: family *Compositae* (composites). See also **yarrow.**

snell (snɛl) *adj Scot.* biting; bitter; sharp. [Old English *snel* quick, active]

Snell's law (snɛlz) *n Physics.* the principle that the ratio of the sine of the angle of incidence to the sine of the angle of refraction is constant when a light ray passes from one medium to another. [C17: named after Willebrord *Snell* (1591–1626), Dutch physicist]

SNG *abbrev. for* synthetic natural gas.

snib (snɪb) *Scot.* ◆ *n* **1** the bolt or fastening of a door, window, etc. ◆ *vb* **snibs, snibbing, snibbed.** (*tr*) **2** to bolt or fasten (a door). [C19: of uncertain origin; perhaps from Low German *snibbe* beak]

snick (snɪk) *n* **1** a small cut; notch. **2** a knot in thread, etc. **3** *Cricket.* **3a** a glancing blow off the edge of the bat. **3b** the ball so hit. ◆ *vb* (*tr*) **4** to cut a small corner or notch in (material, etc.). **5** *Cricket.* to hit (the ball) with a snick. [C18: probably of Scandinavian origin; compare Old Norse *snikka* to whittle, Swedish *snicka*]

snicker ('snɪkə) *n, vb* **1** another word, esp. U.S. and Canadian, for **snigger.** ◆ *vb* **2** (of a horse) to whinny. [C17: probably of imitative origin]

snickersnee ('snɪkə,sni:) *n Archaic.* **1** a knife for cutting or thrusting. **2** a fight with knives. [C17 *stick or snee*, from Dutch *steken* to STICK[2] + *snijen* to cut]

snicket ('snɪkɪt) *n Northern English dialect.* a passageway between walls or fences. [of obscure origin]

snide (snaɪd) *adj* **1** Also: **snidey** ('snaɪdɪ). (of a remark, etc.) maliciously derogatory; supercilious. **2** counterfeit; sham. ◆ *n* **3** *Slang.* sham jewellery. [C19: of unknown origin] ▸ 'snidely *adv* ▸ 'snideness *n*

sniff (snɪf) *vb* **1** to inhale through the nose, usually in short rapid audible inspirations, as for the purpose of identifying a scent, for clearing a congested nasal passage, or for taking a drug or intoxicating fumes. **2** (when *intr*, often foll. by *at*) to perceive or attempt to perceive (a smell) by inhaling through the nose. ◆ *n* **3** the act or sound of sniffing. **4** a smell perceived by sniffing, esp. a faint scent. [C14: probably related to *snivelen* to SNIVEL] ▸ 'sniffer *n* ▸ 'sniffing *n, adj*

sniff at *vb* (*intr, prep*) to express contempt or dislike for.

sniffer dog *n* a police dog trained to detect drugs or explosives by smell.

sniffle ('snɪf^əl) *vb* **1** (*intr*) to breathe audibly through the nose, as when the nasal passages are congested. ◆ *n* **2** the act, sound, or an instance of sniffling. ▸ 'sniffler *n* ▸ 'sniffly *adj*

sniffles ('snɪf^əlz) *or* **snuffles** *pl n Informal.* **1 the.** a cold in the head. **2** the sniffling that sometimes accompanies weeping or prolonged crying.

sniff out *vb* (*tr, adv*) to detect through shrewdness or instinct.

sniffy ('snɪfɪ) *adj* **-fier, -fiest.** *Informal.* contemptuous or disdainful. ▸ 'sniffily *adv* ▸ 'sniffiness *n*

snifter ('snɪftə) *n* **1** a pear-shaped glass with a short stem and a bowl that narrows towards the top so that the aroma of brandy or a liqueur is retained. **2** *Informal.* a small quantity of alcoholic drink. [C19: perhaps from dialect *snifter* to sniff, perhaps of Scandinavian origin; compare Danish *snifta* (obsolete) to sniff]

snig (snɪg) *vb* (*tr*) **snigs, snigging, snigged.** *Austral. and N.Z.* to drag (a log) along the ground by a chain fastened at one end. [from English dialect]

snigger ('snɪgə) *or U.S. and Canadian* **snicker** ('snɪkə) *n* **1** a sly or disrespectful laugh, esp. one partly stifled. ◆ *vb* (*intr*) **2** to utter such a laugh. [C18: variant of SNICKER]

snigging chain *n Austral. and N.Z.* a chain attached to a log when being hauled out of the bush.

sniggle ('snɪg^əl) *vb* **1** (*intr*) to fish for eels by dangling or thrusting a baited hook into cavities. **2** (*tr*) to catch (eels) by sniggling. ◆ *n* **3** the baited hook used for sniggling eels. [C17: from C15 *snig* young eel] ▸ 'sniggler *n*

snip (snɪp) *vb* **snips, snipping, snipped.** **1** to cut or clip with a small quick stroke or a succession of small quick strokes, esp. with scissors or shears. ◆ *n* **2** the act of snipping. **3** the sound of scissors or shears closing. **4** Also called: **snipping.** a small piece of anything, esp. one that has been snipped off. **5** a small cut made by snipping. **6** *Chiefly Brit.* an informal word for **bargain.** **7** *Informal.* something easily done; cinch. **8** *U.S. and Canadian informal.* a small or insignificant person or thing, esp. an irritating or insolent one. ◆ *interj* **9** (*often reiterated*) a representation of the sound of scissors or shears closing. ◆ See also **snips.** [C16: from Low German, Dutch *snippen;* related to Middle High German *snipfen* to snap the fingers]

snipe (snaɪp) *n, pl* **snipe** *or* **snipes.** **1** any of various birds of the genus *Gallinago* (or *Capella*) and related genera, such as *G. gallinago* (**common** or **Wilson's snipe**), of marshes and river banks, having a long straight bill: family *Scolopacidae* (sandpipers, etc.), order *Charadriiformes.* **2** any of various similar related birds, such as certain sandpipers and curlews. **3** a shot, esp. a gunshot, fired from a place of concealment. ◆ *vb* **4** (when *intr*, often foll. by *at*) to attack (a person or persons) with a rifle from a place of concealment. **5** (*intr;* often foll. by *at*) to criticize adversely a person or persons from a position of security. **6** (*intr*) to hunt or shoot snipe. [C14: from Old Norse *snīpa;* related to Old High German *snepfa* Middle Dutch *snippe*] ▸ 'snipe,like *adj*

snipefish ('snaɪp,fɪʃ) *n, pl* **-fish** *or* **-fishes.** any teleost fish of the family *Macrorhamphosidae*, of tropical and temperate seas, having a deep body, long snout, and a single long dorsal fin: order *Solenichthyes* (sea horses, etc.). Also called: **bellows fish.** [C17: so called because of the resemblance between its snout and a snipe's bill]

snipe fly *n* any of various predatory dipterous flies of the family *Leptidae* (or *Rhagionidae*), such as *Rhagio scolopacea* of Europe, having an elongated body and long legs. [named after the snipe because its flight resembles that of the bird]

sniper ('snaɪpə) *n* a rifleman who fires from a concealed place, esp. a military marksman who fires from cover usually at long ranges at individual enemy soldiers.

sniperscope ('snaɪpə,skəʊp) *n* a telescope with crosshairs mounted on a sniper's rifle.

snippet ('snɪpɪt) *n* a small scrap or fragment. [C17: from SNIP + -ET] ▸ 'snippetiness *n* ▸ 'snippety *adj*

snippy ('snɪpɪ) *adj* **-pier, -piest.** **1** scrappy; fragmentary. **2** *Informal.* fault-finding. **3** *Dialect.* mean; stingy. ▸ 'snippily *adv* ▸ 'snippiness *n*

snips (snɪps) *pl n* a small pair of shears used for cutting sheet metal. Also called: **tin snips.**

snit (snɪt) *n U.S. and Austral.* a fit of temper. [C20: of unknown origin]

snitch (snɪtʃ) *Slang.* ◆ *vb* **1** (*tr*) to steal; take, esp. in an underhand way. **2** (*intr*) to act as an informer. ◆ *n* **3** an informer; telltale. **4** the nose. [C17: of unknown origin] ▸ 'snitcher *n*

snitchy ('snɪtʃɪ) *adj* **snitchier, snitchiest.** *N.Z. informal.* bad-tempered or irritable.

snivel ('snɪv^əl) *vb* **-els, -elling, -elled** *or U.S.* **-els, -eling, -eled.** **1** (*intr*) to sniffle as a sign of distress, esp. contemptibly. **2** to utter (something) tearfully; whine. **3** (*intr*) to have a runny nose. ◆ *n* **4** an instance of snivelling. [C14 *snivelen;* related to Old English *snyflung* mucus, Dutch *snuffelen* to smell out, Old Norse *snoppa* snout] ▸ 'sniveller *n* ▸ 'snivelling *adj, n* ▸ 'snivelly *adj*

snob (snɒb) *n* **1a** a person who strives to associate with those of higher social status and who behaves condescendingly to others. Compare **inverted snob.** **1b** (*as modifier*): *snob appeal.* **2** a person having similar pretensions with regard to his tastes, etc.: *an intellectual snob.* [C18 (in the sense: shoemaker; hence, C19: a person who flatters those of higher station, etc.): of unknown origin] ▸ 'snobbery *n* ▸ 'snobbish *adj* ▸ 'snobbishly *adv* ▸ 'snobbishness *or* 'snobbism *n* ▸ 'snobby *adj*

SNOBOL ('snəʊbɒl) *n* String Oriented Symbolic Language: a computer-programming language for handling strings of symbols.

Sno-Cat ('snəʊ,kæt) *n Trademark.* a type of snowmobile.

snoek (snʊk) *n* a South African edible marine fish, *Thyrsites atun.* [Afrikaans, from Dutch *snoek* pike]

snoep (snʊp) *adj S. African informal.* mean or tight-fisted. [Afrikaans *snoep* greedy]

snog (snɒg) *Brit. slang.* ◆ *vb* **snogs, snogging, snogged.** **1** to kiss and cuddle (someone). ◆ *n* **2** the act of kissing and cuddling. [of obscure origin]

snood (snu:d) *n* **1** a pouchlike hat, often of net, loosely holding a woman's hair at the back. **2** a headband, esp. one formerly worn by young unmarried women in Scotland. ◆ *vb* **3** (*tr*) to confine (the hair) in a snood. [Old English *snōd;* of obscure origin]

snook[1] (snu:k) *n, pl* **snook** *or* **snooks.** **1** any of several large game fishes of the genus *Centropomus*, esp. *C. undecimalis* of tropical American marine and fresh waters: family *Centropomidae* (robalos). **2** *Austral.* the sea pike *Australuzza novaehollandiae.* [C17: from Dutch *snoek* pike]

snook[2] (snu:k) *n Brit.* **cock a snook.** **a** to make a rude gesture by putting one thumb to the nose with the fingers of the hand outstretched. **b** to show contempt by being insulting or offensive. [C19: of obscure origin]

snooker ('snu:kə) *n* **1** a game played on a billiard table with 15 red balls, six balls of other colours, and a white cue ball. The object is to pot the balls in a certain order. **2** a shot in which the cue ball is left in a position such that another ball blocks the object ball. The opponent is then usually forced to play the cue ball off a cushion. ◆ *vb* (*tr*) **3** to leave (an opponent) in an unfavourable position by playing a snooker. **4** to place (someone) in a difficult situation. **5** (*often passive*) to thwart; defeat. [C19: of unknown origin]

snoop (snu:p) *Informal.* ◆ *vb* **1** (*intr;* often foll. by *about* or *around*) to pry into the private business of others. ◆ *n* **2** a person who pries into the business of others. **3** an act or instance of snooping. [C19: from Dutch *snoepen* to eat furtively] ▸ **'snoopy** *adj*

snooper ('snu:pə) *n* **1** a person who snoops. **2** *Brit. informal.* a person employed by the DSS to spy on claimants to make sure that they are not infringing the conditions of their eligibility for benefit.

snooperscope ('snu:pə,skəʊp) *n Military, U.S.* an instrument that enables the user to see objects in the dark by illuminating the object with infrared radiation and converting the reflected radiation to a visual image.

snoot (snu:t) *n* **1** *Slang.* the nose. **2** *Photog., films, television.* a cone-shaped fitment on a studio light to control the scene area illuminated. [C20: variant of SNOUT]

snooty ('snu:tɪ) *adj* **snootier, snootiest.** *Informal.* **1** aloof or supercilious. **2** snobbish or exclusive: *a snooty restaurant.* ▸ **'snootily** *adv* ▸ **'snootiness** *n*

snooze (snu:z) *Informal.* ◆ *vb* **1** (*intr*) to take a brief light sleep. ◆ *n* **2** a nap. [C18: of unknown origin] ▸ **'snoozer** *n* ▸ **'snoozy** *adj*

snore (snɔ:) *vb* **1** (*intr*) to breathe through the mouth and nose while asleep with snorting sounds caused by the soft palate vibrating. ◆ *n* **2** the act or sound of snoring. [C14: of imitative origin; related to Middle Low German, Middle Dutch *snorken;* see SNORT] ▸ **'snorer** *n*

snorkel ('snɔ:kᵊl) *n* **1** a device allowing a swimmer to breathe while face down on the surface of the water, consisting of a bent tube fitting into the mouth and projecting above the surface. **2** (on a submarine) a retractable vertical device containing air-intake and exhaust pipes for the engines and general ventilation: its use permits extended periods of submergence at periscope depth. **3** *Military.* a similar device on a tank, enabling it to cross shallow water obstacles. **4** a type of parka or anorak with a hood that projects beyond the face. ◆ *vb* **-kels, -kelling, -kelled** *or U.S.* **-kels, -keling, -keled. 5** (*intr*) to swim with a snorkel. [C20: from German *Schnorchel;* related to German *schnarchen* to SNORE]

Snorri Sturluson ('snɔ:rɪ 'stɜ:ləsᵊn) *n* 1179–1241, Icelandic historian and poet; author of *Younger* or *Prose Edda* (?1222), containing a collection of Norse myths and a treatise on poetry, and the *Heimskringla* sagas of the Norwegian kings from their mythological origins to the 12th century.

snort (snɔ:t) *vb* **1** (*intr*) to exhale forcibly through the nostrils, making a characteristic noise. **2** (*intr*) (of a person) to express contempt or annoyance by such an exhalation. **3** (*tr*) to utter in a contemptuous or annoyed manner. **4** *Slang.* to inhale (a powdered drug) through the nostrils. ◆ *n* **5** a forcible exhalation of air through the nostrils, esp. (of persons) as a noise of contempt or annoyance. **6** *Slang.* an instance of snorting a drug. **7** Also called: **snorter.** *Slang.* a short drink, esp. an alcoholic one. **8** *Slang.* the snorkel on a submarine. [C14 *snorten;* probably related to *snoren* to SNORE] ▸ **'snorting** *n, adj* ▸ **'snortingly** *adv*

snorter ('snɔ:tə) *n* **1** a person or animal that snorts. **2** *Brit. slang.* something outstandingly impressive or difficult. **3** *Brit. slang.* something or someone ridiculous.

snot (snɒt) *n* (*usually considered vulgar*) **1** nasal mucus or discharge. **2** *Slang.* a contemptible person. [Old English *gesnot;* related to Old High German *snuzza,* Norwegian, Danish *snot,* German *schneuzen* to blow one's nose]

snotter ('snɒtər) *Scot.* ◆ *n* **1** (*often pl*) another word for **snot.** ◆ *vb* (*intr*) **2** to breathe through obstructed nostrils. **3** to snivel or blubber.

snotty ('snɒtɪ) (*considered vulgar*) ◆ *adj* **-tier, -tiest. 1** dirty with nasal discharge. **2** *Slang.* contemptible; nasty. **3** snobbish; conceited. ◆ *n, pl* **-ties. 4** a slang word for **midshipman.** ▸ **'snottily** *adv* ▸ **'snottiness** *n*

snout (snaʊt) *n* **1** the part of the head of a vertebrate, esp. a mammal, consisting of the nose, jaws, and surrounding region, esp. when elongated. **2** the corresponding part of the head of such insects as weevils. **3** anything projecting like a snout, such as a nozzle or the lower end of a glacier. **4** *Slang.* a person's nose. **5** Also called: **snout moth.** a brownish noctuid moth, *Hypena proboscidalis,* that frequents nettles: named from the palps that project prominently from the head at rest. **6** *Brit. slang.* a cigarette or tobacco. **7** *Slang.* an informer. [C13: of Germanic origin; compare Old Norse *snyta,* Middle Low German, Middle Dutch *snūte*] ▸ **'snouted** *adj* ▸ **'snoutless** *adj* ▸ **'snout,like** *adj*

snout beetle *n* another name for **weevil** (sense 1). [C19: so named because of its long proboscis]

snow (snəʊ) *n* **1** precipitation from clouds in the form of flakes of ice crystals formed in the upper atmosphere. Related adj: **niveous. 2** a layer of snowflakes on the ground. **3** a fall of such precipitation. **4** anything resembling snow in whiteness, softness, etc. **5** the random pattern of white spots on a television or radar screen, produced by noise in the receiver and occurring when the signal is weak or absent. **6** *Slang.* cocaine. **7** See **carbon dioxide snow.** ◆ *vb* **8** (*intr;* with *it* as subject) to be the case that snow is falling. **9** (*tr;* usually passive, foll. by *over, under, in,* or *up*) to cover or confine with a heavy fall of snow. **10** (often with *it* as subject) to fall or cause to fall as or like snow. **11** (*tr*) *U.S. and Canadian slang.* to deceive or overwhelm with elaborate often insincere talk. See **snow job. 12 be snowed under.** to be overwhelmed, esp. with paperwork. [Old English *snāw;* related to Old Norse *snjōr,* Gothic *snaiws,* Old High German *snēo,* Greek *nipha*] ▸ **'snowless** *adj* ▸ **'snow,like** *adj*

Snow (snəʊ) *n* **C(harles) P(ercy),** Baron. 1905–80, British novelist and physicist. His novels include the series *Strangers and Brothers* (1949–70).

snowball ('snəʊ,bɔ:l) *n* **1** snow pressed into a ball for throwing, as in play. **2** a drink made of advocaat and lemonade. **3** *Slang.* a mixture of heroin and cocaine. **4** a dance started by one couple who separate and choose different partners. The process continues until all present are dancing. ◆ *vb* **5** (*intr*) to increase rapidly in size, importance, etc. **6** (*tr*) to throw snowballs at.

snowball tree *n* any of several caprifoliaceous shrubs of the genus *Viburnum,* esp. *V. opulus* var. *roseum,* a sterile cultivated variety with spherical clusters of white or pinkish flowers.

snowberry ('snəʊbərɪ, -brɪ) *n, pl* **-ries. 1** any of several caprifoliaceous shrubs of the genus *Symphoricarpos,* esp. *S. albus,* cultivated for their small pink flowers and white berries. **2** Also called: **waxberry.** any of the berries of such a plant. **3** any of various other white-berried plants.

snowbird ('snəʊ,bɜ:d) *n* **1** another name for the **snow bunting. 2** *U.S. slang.* a person addicted to cocaine, or sometimes heroin.

snow-blind *adj* temporarily unable to see or having impaired vision because of the intense reflection of sunlight from snow. ▸ **snow blindness** *n*

snowblink ('snəʊ,blɪŋk) *n* a whitish glare in the sky reflected from snow. Compare **iceblink.**

snowblower ('snəʊ,bləʊə) *n* a snow-clearing machine that sucks in snow and blows it away to one side.

snowboard ('snəʊ,bɔ:d) *n* a shaped board, resembling a skateboard without wheels, on which a person can stand to slide across snow. [C20: on the model of SURFBOARD]

snowboarding ('snəʊ,bɔ:dɪŋ) *n* the sport of moving across snow on a snowboard.

snowbound ('snəʊ,baʊnd) *adj* confined to one place by heavy falls or drifts of snow; snowed-in.

snow bridge *n Mountaineering.* a mass of snow bridging a crevasse, sometimes affording a risky way across it.

snow bunting *n* a bunting, *Plectrophenax nivalis,* of northern and arctic regions, having a white plumage with dark markings on the wings, back, and tail.

snowcap ('snəʊ,kæp) *n* a cap of snow, as on the top of a mountain. ▸ **'snow,capped** *adj*

snow cave *n Mountaineering.* another name for **snow hole.**

snow devil *n Canadian.* a whirling column of snow.

Snowdon[1] ('snəʊdᵊn) *n* a mountain in NW Wales, in Gwynedd: the highest peak in Wales. Height: 1085 m (3560 ft.).

Snowdon[2] ('snəʊdən) *n* **1st Earl of,** title of *Antony Armstrong-Jones.* born 1930, British photographer, whose work includes television documentaries, photographic books, and the design of the Snowdon Aviary, London Zoo (1965). His marriage (1960–78) to Princess Margaret ended in divorce.

Snowdonia (snəʊ'dəʊnɪə) *n* **1** a massif in NW Wales, in Gwynedd, the highest peak being Snowdon. **2** a national park in NW Wales, in Gwynedd and Conwy: includes the Snowdonia massif in the north. Area: 2189 sq. km (845 sq. miles).

snowdrift ('snəʊ,drɪft) *n* a bank of deep snow driven together by the wind.

snowdrop ('snəʊ,drɒp) *n* any of several amaryllidaceous plants of the Eurasian genus *Galanthus,* esp. *G. nivalis,* having drooping white bell-shaped flowers that bloom in early spring.

snowdrop tree *n* another name for **silver bell.**

snowfall ('snəʊ,fɔ:l) *n* **1** a fall of snow. **2** *Meteorol.* the amount of snow received in a specified place and time.

snow fence *n* a portable wire-and-paling fence erected to prevent snow from drifting across a road, drive, ski run, etc.

snowfield ('snəʊ,fi:ld) *n* a large area of permanent snow.

snowflake ('snəʊ,fleɪk) *n* **1** one of the mass of small thin delicate arrangements of ice crystals that fall as snow. **2** any of various European amaryllidaceous plants of the genus *Leucojum,* such as *L. vernum* (**spring snowflake**), that have white nodding bell-shaped flowers.

snow goose *n* a North American goose, *Anser hyperboreus* (or *Chen hyperborea* or *A. caerulescens*), having a white plumage with black wing tips.

snow grass *n* **1** *Austral.* any of various grey-green grasses of the genus *Poa,* of SE Australian mountain regions. **2** *N.Z.* any of various hill and high-country grasses of the genus *Danthonia.*

snow gum *n* another name for **sallee.** [so called because it grows at high altitude]

snow hole *n Mountaineering.* a shelter dug in deep usually drifted snow. Also called: **snow cave.**

snow-in-summer *n* another name for **dusty miller** (sense 1). [C19: so called from the appearance of its flowers]

snow job *n Slang, chiefly U.S. and Canadian.* an instance of deceiving or overwhelming someone with elaborate often insincere talk.

snow leopard *n* a large feline mammal, *Panthera uncia,* of mountainous regions of central Asia, closely related to the leopard but having a long pale brown coat marked with black rosettes. Also called: **ounce.**

snow line *n* the altitudinal or latitudinal limit of permanent snow.

snowman ('snəʊ,mæn) *n, pl* **-men.** a figure resembling a man, made of packed snow.

snowmobile ('snəʊmə,bi:l) *n* **a** a small open motor vehicle for travelling on snow, steered by two skis at the front and driven by a caterpillar track underneath. **b** Also called: **bombardier.** a larger closed motor vehicle with two skis at the front and a track at each side.

snow-on-the-mountain *n* a North American euphorbiaceous plant, *Euphorbia marginata,* having white-edged leaves and showy white bracts surrounding small flowers.

snow plant *n* a saprophytic plant, *Sarcodes sanguinea,* of mountain pine forests of W North America, having a fleshy scaly reddish stalk, no leaves, and pendulous scarlet flowers that are often produced before the snow melts: family *Monotropaceae.*

snowplough ('snəʊ,plaʊ) *n* **1** an implement or vehicle for clearing away snow. **2** *Skiing.* a technique of turning the points of the skis inwards to turn or stop.

snowshed ('snəʊ,ʃɛd) *n* a shelter built over an exposed section of railway track to prevent its blockage by snow.

snowshoe ('snəʊ,ʃu:) *n* **1** a device to facilitate walking on snow, esp. a racket-shaped frame with a network of thongs stretched across it. ◆ *vb* **-shoes, -shoeing, -shoed. 2** (*intr*) to walk or go using snowshoes. ▸ ˈ**snow,shoer** *n*

snowshoe hare *or* **rabbit** *n* a N North American hare, *Lepus americanus,* having brown fur in summer, white fur in winter, and heavily furred feet.

snowstorm (ˈsnəʊˌstɔːm) *n* a storm with heavy snow.

snow tyre *n* a motor vehicle tyre with deep treads and ridges to give improved grip on snow and ice.

snow-white *adj* **1** white as snow. **2** pure as white snow.

snowy (ˈsnəʊɪ) *adj* **snowier, snowiest. 1** covered with or abounding in snow: *snowy hills.* **2** characterized by snow: *snowy weather.* **3** resembling snow in whiteness, purity, etc. ▸ ˈ**snowily** *adv* ▸ ˈ**snowiness** *n*

snowy egret *n* a small American egret, *Egretta thula,* having a white plumage, yellow legs, and a black bill.

Snowy Mountains *pl n* a mountain range in SE Australia, part of the Australian Alps: famous hydroelectric scheme. Also called (Austral. informal): **the Snowy, the Snowies.** ▸ **Snowy Mountain** *adj*

snowy owl *n* a large owl, *Nyctea scandiaca,* of tundra regions, having a white plumage flecked with brown.

Snowy River *n* a river in SE Australia, rising in SE New South Wales: waters diverted through a system of dams and tunnels across the watershed into the Murray and Murrumbidgee Rivers for hydroelectric power and to provide water for irrigation. Length: 426 km (265 miles).

SNP *abbrev. for* Scottish National Party.

Snr *or* **snr** *abbrev. for* senior.

snub (snʌb) *vb* **snubs, snubbing, snubbed.** (*tr*) **1** to insult (someone) deliberately. **2** to stop or check the motion of (a boat, horse, etc.) by taking turns of a rope or cable around a post or other fixed object. ◆ *n* **3** a deliberately insulting act or remark. **4a** *Nautical.* an elastic shock absorber attached to a mooring line. **4b** (*as modifier*): *a snub rope.* ◆ *adj* **5** short and blunt. See also **snub-nosed.** [C14: from Old Norse *snubba* to scold; related to Norwegian, Swedish dialect *snubba* to cut short, Danish *snubbe*] ▸ ˈ**snubber** *n* ▸ ˈ**snubby** *adj*

snub-nosed *adj* **1** having a short turned-up nose. **2** (of a pistol) having an extremely short barrel.

snuck (snʌk) *vb U.S. and Canadian, not standard.* a past tense and past participle of **sneak.**

snuff[1] (snʌf) *vb* **1** (*tr*) to inhale through the nose. **2** (when *intr,* often foll. by *at*) (esp. of an animal) to examine by sniffing. ◆ *n* **3** an act or the sound of snuffing. [C16: probably from Middle Dutch *snuffen* to snuffle, ultimately of imitative origin] ▸ ˈ**snuffer** *n*

snuff[2] (snʌf) *n* **1** finely powdered tobacco for sniffing up the nostrils or less commonly for chewing. **2** a small amount of this. **3** any powdered substance, esp. one for sniffing up the nostrils. **4 up to snuff.** *Informal.* **4a** in good health or in good condition. **4b** *Chiefly Brit.* not easily deceived. ◆ *vb* **5** (*intr*) to use or inhale snuff. [C17: from Dutch *snuf,* shortened from *snuftabale,* literally: tobacco for snuffing; see SNUFF[1]]

snuff[3] (snʌf) *vb* (*tr*) **1** (often foll. by *out*) to extinguish (a light from a naked flame, esp. a candle). **2** to cut off the charred part of (the wick of a candle, etc.). **3** (usually foll. by *out*) *Informal.* to suppress; put an end to. **4 snuff it.** *Brit. informal.* to die. ◆ *n* **5** the burned portion of the wick of a candle. [C14 *snoffe,* of obscure origin]

snuffbox (ˈsnʌfˌbɒks) *n* a container, often of elaborate ornamental design, for holding small quantities of snuff.

snuff-dipping *n* the practice of absorbing nicotine by holding in one's mouth, between the cheek and the gum, a small amount of tobacco, either loose or enclosed in a sachet.

snuffer (ˈsnʌfə) *n* **1** a cone-shaped implement for extinguishing candles. **2** (*pl*) an instrument resembling a pair of scissors for trimming the wick or extinguishing the flame of a candle. **3** *Rare.* a person who takes snuff.

snuffle (ˈsnʌfᵊl) *vb* **1** (*intr*) to breathe noisily or with difficulty. **2** to say or speak in a nasal tone. **3** (*intr*) to snivel. ◆ *n* **4** an act or the sound of snuffling. **5** a nasal tone or voice. **6 the snuffles.** a condition characterized by snuffling. [C16: from Low German or Dutch *snuffelen;* see SNUFF[1], SNIVEL] ▸ ˈ**snuffler** *n* ▸ ˈ**snuffly** *adj*

snuff movie *or* **film** *n Slang.* a pornographic film in which an unsuspecting actress or actor is murdered as the climax of the film.

snuffy (ˈsnʌfɪ) *adj* **snuffier, snuffiest. 1** of, relating to, or resembling snuff. **2** covered with or smelling of snuff. **3** unpleasant; disagreeable. ▸ ˈ**snuffiness** *n*

snug (snʌg) *adj* **snugger, snuggest. 1** comfortably warm and well-protected; cosy: *the children were snug in bed during the blizzard.* **2** small but comfortable: *a snug cottage.* **3** well-ordered; compact: *a snug boat.* **4** sheltered and secure: *a snug anchorage.* **5** fitting closely and comfortably. **6** offering safe concealment. ◆ *n* **7** (in Britain and Ireland) one of the bars in certain pubs, offering intimate seating for only a few persons. **8** *Engineering.* a small peg under the head of a bolt engaging with a slot in the bolted component to prevent the bolt turning when the nut is tightened. ◆ *vb* **snugs, snugging, snugged. 9** to make or become comfortable and warm. **10** (*tr*) *Nautical.* to make (a vessel) ready for a storm by lashing down gear. [C16 (in the sense: prepared for storms (used of a ship)): related to Old Icelandic *snöggr* short-haired, Swedish *snygg* tidy, Low German *snögger* smart] ▸ ˈ**snugly** *adv* ▸ ˈ**snugness** *n*

snuggery (ˈsnʌgərɪ) *n, pl* **-geries. 1** a cosy and comfortable place or room. **2** another name for **snug** (sense 7).

snuggle (ˈsnʌgᵊl) *vb* **1** (*usually intr;* usually foll. by *down, up,* or *together*) to nestle into or draw close to (somebody or something) for warmth or from affection. ◆ *n* **2** the act of snuggling. [C17: frequentative SNUG (vb)]

snye (snaɪ) *n Canadian.* a side channel of a river. [from Canadian French *chenail,* from French *chenal* CHANNEL[1]]

so[1] (səʊ) *adv* **1** (foll. by an adjective or adverb and a correlative clause often introduced by *that*) to such an extent: *the river is so dirty that it smells.* **2** (*used with a negative;* it replaces the first *as* in an equative comparison) to the same extent as: *she is not so old as you.* **3** (intensifier): *it's so lovely; I love you so.* **4** in the state or manner expressed or implied: *they're happy and will remain so.* **5** (*not used with a negative;* foll. by an auxiliary verb or *do, have,* or *be* used as main verbs) also; likewise: *I can speak Spanish and so can you.* **6** *Dialect and U.S.* indeed: used to contradict a negative statement: *You didn't tell the truth. I did so!* **7** *Archaic.* provided that. **8 and so on** *or* **forth.** and continuing similarly. **9 just so.** See **just** (sense 19). **10 or so.** approximately: *fifty or so people came to see me.* **11 quite so.** I agree; exactly. **12 so be it.** used to express agreement or resignation. **13 so much. 13a** a certain degree or amount (of). **13b** a lot (of): *it's just so much nonsense.* **14 so much for. 14a** no more can or need be said about. **14b** used to express contempt for something that has failed: *so much for your bright idea.* ◆ *conj* (subordinating; often foll. by *that*) **15** in order (that): *to die so that you might live.* **16** with the consequence (that): *he was late home, so that there was trouble.* **17 so as.** (*takes an infinitive*) in order (to): *to slim so as to lose weight.* ◆ *sentence connector.* **18** in consequence; hence: *she wasn't needed, so she left.* **19** used to introduce a sentence expressing resignation, amazement, or sarcasm: *so you're publishing a book!* **20** thereupon; and then: *and so we ended up in France.* **21** used to introduce a sentence or clause to add emphasis: *he's crazy, so he is.* **22 so what!** *Informal.* what importance does that have? ◆ *pron* **23** used to substitute for a clause or sentence, which may be understood: *you'll stop because I said so.* ◆ *adj* **24** (used with *is, was,* etc.) factual; true: *it can't be so.* ◆ *interj* **25** an exclamation of agreement, surprise, etc. [Old English *swā;* related to Old Norse *svā,* Old High German *sō,* Dutch *zoo*]

USAGE In formal English, *so* is not used as a conjunction, to indicate either purpose (*he left by a back door so he could avoid photographers*) or result (*the project was abandoned so his services were no longer needed*). In the former case *to* or *in order to* should be used instead, and in the latter case *and so* or *and therefore* would be more acceptable. The expression *so therefore* should not be used.

so[2] (səʊ) *n Music.* a variant spelling of **soh.**

SO (in Britain) *abbrev. for* Stationery Office.

So. *abbrev. for* south(ern).

s.o. *abbrev. for:* **1** seller's option. **2** shipping order.

soak (səʊk) *vb* **1** to make, become, or be thoroughly wet or saturated, esp. by immersion in a liquid. **2** (when *intr,* usually foll. by *in* or *into*) (of a liquid) to penetrate or permeate. **3** (*tr;* usually foll. by *in* or *up*) (of a permeable solid) to take in (a liquid) by absorption: *the earth soaks up rainwater.* **4** (*tr;* foll. by *out* or *out of*) to remove by immersion in a liquid: *she soaked the stains out of the dress.* **5** (*tr*) *Metallurgy.* to heat (a metal) prior to working. **6** *Informal.* to drink excessively or make or become drunk. **7** (*tr*) *U.S. and Canadian slang.* to overcharge. **8** (*tr*) *Brit. slang.* to put in pawn. ◆ *n* **9** the act of immersing in a liquid or the period of immersion. **10** the liquid in which something may be soaked, esp. a solution containing detergent. **11** another name for **soakage** (sense 3). **12** *Brit. informal.* a heavy rainfall. **13** *Slang.* a person who drinks to excess. [Old English *sōcian* to cook; see SUCK] ▸ ˈ**soaker** *n* ▸ ˈ**soaking** *n, adj*

soakage (ˈsəʊkɪdʒ) *n* **1** the process or a period in which a permeable substance is soaked in a liquid. **2** liquid that has been soaked up or has seeped out. **3** Also called: **soak.** *Austral.* a small pool of water or swampy patch.

soakaway (ˈsəʊkəˌweɪ) *n* a pit filled with rubble, etc., into which rain or waste water drains.

so-and-so *n, pl* **so-and-sos.** *Informal.* **1** a person whose name is forgotten or ignored: *so-and-so came to see me.* **2** *Euphemistic.* a person or thing regarded as unpleasant or difficult: *which so-and-so broke my razor?*

Soane (səʊn) *n* Sir **John.** 1753–1837, British architect. His work includes Dulwich College Art Gallery (1811–14) and his own house in Lincoln's Inn Fields, London (1812–13), which is now the Sir John Soane's Museum.

soap (səʊp) *n* **1** a cleaning or emulsifying agent made by reacting animal or vegetable fats or oils with potassium or sodium hydroxide. Soaps often contain colouring matter and perfume and act by emulsifying grease and lowering the surface tension of water, so that it more readily penetrates open materials such as textiles. See also **detergent.** Related adj: **saponaceous. 2** any metallic salt of a fatty acid, such as palmitic or stearic acid. See also **metallic soap. 3** *Slang.* flattery or persuasive talk (esp. in the phrase **soft soap**). **4** *Informal.* short for **soap opera. 5** *U.S. and Canadian slang.* money, esp. for bribery. **6 no soap.** *U.S. and Canadian slang.* not possible or successful. ◆ *vb* **7** (*tr*) to apply soap to. **8** (*tr;* often foll. by *up*) *Slang.* **8a** to flatter or talk persuasively to. **8b** *U.S. and Canadian.* to bribe. [Old English *sāpe;* related to Old High German *seipfa,* Old French *savon,* Latin *sāpō*] ▸ ˈ**soapless** *adj* ▸ ˈ**soap,like** *adj*

soapbark (ˈsəʊpˌbɑːk) *n* **1** Also called: **quillai.** a W South American rosaceous tree, *Quillaja saponaria,* with undivided evergreen leaves and small white flowers. **2** Also called: **quillai bark.** the inner bark of this tree, formerly used as soap and as a source of saponin. **3** any of several trees or shrubs that have a bark similar to this.

soapberry (ˈsəʊpˌberɪ) *n, pl* **-ries. 1** any of various chiefly tropical American sapindaceous trees of the genus *Sapindus,* esp. *S. saponaria* (or *S. marginatus*), having pulpy fruit containing saponin. **2** a related plant, *S. drummondii,* of the southwestern U.S. **3** the fruit of any of these trees. ◆ Also called: **chinaberry.**

soap boiler *n* a manufacturer of soap. ▸ **soap boiling** *n*

soapbox (ˈsəʊpˌbɒks) *n* **1** a box or crate for packing soap. **2** a crate used as a platform for speech-making. **3** a child's homemade racing cart consisting of a wooden box set on a wooden frame with wheels and a steerable front axle.

soap bubble *n* **1** a bubble formed from soapy water. **2** something that is ephemeral but attractive.

soapolallie ('səʊpəˌlælɪ) *n Canadian.* a drink made by crushing soapberries. [from SOAP(BERRY) + *lallie* (compare *-lolly* as in LOBLOLLY)]

soap opera *n* a serialized drama, usually dealing with domestic themes and characterized by sentimentality, broadcast on radio or television. [C20: so called because manufacturers of soap were typical sponsors]

soapstone ('səʊpˌstəʊn) *n* a massive compact soft variety of talc, used for making tabletops, hearths, ornaments, etc. Also called: **steatite.** [C17: so called because it has a greasy feel and was sometimes used as soap]

soapsuds ('səʊpˌsʌdz) *pl n* foam or lather made from soap. ▸ **'soapˌsudsy** *adj*

soapwort ('səʊpˌwɜːt) *n* a Eurasian caryophyllaceous plant, *Saponaria officinalis,* having rounded clusters of fragrant pink or white flowers and leaves that were formerly used as a soap substitute. Also called: **bouncing Bet.**

soapy ('səʊpɪ) *adj* **soapier, soapiest. 1** containing or covered with soap: *soapy water.* **2** resembling or characteristic of soap. **3** *Slang.* flattering or persuasive. ▸ **'soapily** *adv* ▸ **'soapiness** *n*

soar (sɔː) *vb* (*intr*) **1** to rise or fly upwards into the air. **2** (of a bird, aircraft, etc.) to glide while maintaining altitude by the use of ascending air currents. **3** to rise or increase in volume, size, etc.: *soaring prices.* ◆ *n* **4** the act of soaring. **5** the altitude attained by soaring. [C14: from Old French *essorer,* from Vulgar Latin *exaurāre* (unattested) to expose to the breezes, from Latin EX-[1] + *aura* a breeze] ▸ **'soarer** *n*

Soares (*Portuguese* 'swarɪʃ) *n* **Mário** ('marju). born 1924, Portuguese statesman; prime minister of Portugal (1976–77; 1978–80; 1983–86); president of Portugal (1986–96).

Soave ('swɑːveɪ) *n* a dry white wine from the Veneto region of NE Italy. [C20: named after a town near Verona where it is produced]

Soay ('səʊeɪ) *n* a breed of small horned sheep having long legs and dark brown wool that is plucked rather than shorn; found mainly on St Kilda where they were probably introduced by the Vikings. [named after *Soay,* an island in the St Kilda group, where they were first found]

sob (sɒb) *vb* **sobs, sobbing, sobbed. 1** (*intr*) to weep with convulsive gasps. **2** (*tr*) to utter with sobs. **3** to cause (oneself) to be in a specified state by sobbing: *to sob oneself to sleep.* ◆ *n* **4** a convulsive gasp made in weeping. [C12: probably from Low German; compare Dutch *sabben* to suck] ▸ **'sobber** *n*

s.o.b. *Slang, chiefly U.S. and Canadian. abbrev. for* son of a bitch.

sobeit (səʊ'biːɪt) *conj Archaic.* provided that. [C16: from SO[1] + BE + IT: originally three words]

sober ('səʊbə) *adj* **1** not drunk. **2** not given to excessive indulgence in drink or any other activity. **3** sedate and rational: *a sober attitude to a problem.* **4** (of colours) plain and dull or subdued. **5** free from exaggeration or speculation: *he told us the sober truth.* ◆ *vb* **6** (usually foll. by *up*) to make or become less intoxicated, reckless, etc. [C14 *sobre,* from Old French, from Latin *sōbrius*] ▸ **'sobering** *adj* ▸ **'soberingly** *adv* ▸ **'soberly** *adv* ▸ **'soberness** *n*

Sobers ('səʊbəz) *n* Sir **Garfield St. Auburn,** known as *Garry.* born 1936, West Indian (Barbadian) cricketer; one of the finest all-rounders of all time.

sobersides ('səʊbəˌsaɪdz) *n* (*functioning as sing*) a solemn and sedate person. ▸ **'soberˌsided** *adj*

sobole ('səʊbəʊl) *n, pl* **soboles** (-liːz). a creeping underground stem that produces roots and buds; a sucker. [back formation from *soboles* (originally a sing), from Latin *soboles* a shoot, from *subolescere* to grow]

Sobranje (səʊ'brɑːnjɪ) *n* the legislature of Bulgaria.

sobriety (səʊ'braɪətɪ) *n* **1** the state or quality of being sober. **2** the quality of refraining from excess. **3** the quality of being serious or sedate.

sobriquet *or* **soubriquet** ('səʊbrɪˌkeɪ) *n* a humorous epithet, assumed name, or nickname. [C17: from French *soubriquet,* of uncertain origin]

sob sister *n* a journalist, esp. a woman, on a newspaper or magazine who writes articles of sentimental appeal.

sob story *n* a tale of personal distress intended to arouse sympathy, esp. one offered as an excuse or apology.

sob stuff *n* material such as films, stories, etc., that play upon the emotions by the overuse of pathos and sentiment.

Soc. *or* **soc.** *abbrev. for:* **1** socialist. **2** society.

soca ('səʊkə) *n* a mixture of soul and calypso music typical of the E Caribbean. [C20: a blend of *soul* and *calypso*]

socage ('sɒkɪdʒ) *n* **1** *English legal history.* the tenure of land by certain services, esp. of an agricultural nature. **2** *English law.* the freehold tenure of land. [C14: from Anglo-French, from *soc* SOKE] ▸ **'socager** *n*

so-called *adj* **a** (*prenominal*) designated or styled by the name or word mentioned, esp. (in the speaker's opinion) incorrectly: *a so-called genius.* **b** (also used parenthetically after a noun): *these experts, so-called, are no help.*

soccer ('sɒkə) *n* **a** a game in which two teams of eleven players try to kick or head a ball into their opponent's goal, only the goalkeeper on either side being allowed to touch the ball with his hands and arms except in the case of throw-ins. **b** (*as modifier*): *a soccer player.* ◆ Also called: **Association Football.** [C19: from (*as*)*soc.* + *-er*]

Socceroos (ˌsɒkə'ruːz) *pl n Informal.* the Australian national soccer team. [from SOCCER + (KANGAR)OO]

Soche *or* **So-ch'e** ('səʊ'tʃe) *n* a variant transliteration of the Chinese name for **Shache.**

Sochi (*Russian* 'sɔtʃi) *n* a city and resort in SW Russia, in the Krasnodar Territory on the Black Sea: hot mineral springs. Pop.: 355 000 (1995 est.).

sociable ('səʊʃəbᵊl) *adj* **1** friendly or companionable. **2** (of an occasion) providing the opportunity for friendliness and conviviality. ◆ *n* **3** *Chiefly U.S.* another name for **social** (sense 9). **4** a type of open carriage with two seats facing each other. [C16: via French from Latin *sociābilis,* from *sociāre* to unite, from *socius* an associate] ▸ **ˌsocia'bility** *or* **'sociableness** *n* ▸ **'sociably** *adv*

social ('səʊʃəl) *adj* **1** living or preferring to live in a community rather than alone. **2** denoting or relating to human society or any of its subdivisions. **3** of, relating to, or characteristic of the experience, behaviour, and interaction of persons forming groups. **4** relating to or having the purpose of promoting companionship, communal activities, etc.: *a social club.* **5** relating to or engaged in social services: *a social worker.* **6** relating to or considered appropriate to a certain class of society, esp. one thought superior. **7** (esp. of certain species of insects) living together in organized colonies: *social bees.* Compare **solitary** (sense 6). **8** (of plant species) growing in clumps, usually over a wide area. ◆ *n* **9** an informal gathering, esp. of an organized group, to promote companionship, communal activity, etc. [C16: from Latin *sociālis* companionable, from *socius* a comrade] ▸ **'socially** *adv* ▸ **'socialness** *n*

social accounting *n* the analysis of the economy by sectors leading to the calculation and publication of economic statistics, such as gross national product and national income. Also called: **national accounting.**

Social and Liberal Democratic Party *n* (in Britain) a centrist political party formed in 1988 by the merging of the Liberal Party and part of the Social Democratic Party. In 1989 it changed its name to the Liberal Democrats.

social anthropology *n* the branch of anthropology that deals with cultural and social phenomena such as kinship systems or beliefs, esp. of nonliterate peoples.

social assistance *n* a former name for **social security.**

Social Chapter *n* the section of the **Maastricht Treaty** concerning working conditions, consultation of workers, employment rights, and social security. In 1993 the UK government negotiated an opt-out clause from this section of the treaty.

Social Charter *n* a declaration of the rights, minimum wages, maximum hours, etc., of workers in the European Union.

social climber *n* a person who seeks advancement to a higher social class, esp. by obsequious behaviour. Sometimes shortened to **climber.** ▸ **social climbing** *n*

social contract *or* **compact** *n* (in the theories of Locke, Hobbes, Rousseau, and others) an agreement, entered into by individuals, that results in the formation of the state or of organized society, the prime motive being the desire for protection, which entails the surrender of some or all personal liberties.

Social Credit *n* (esp. in Canada) a right-wing Populist political party, movement, or doctrine based on the socioeconomic theories of Major C. H. Douglas. ▸ **Social Crediter** *n*

social democracy *n* (*sometimes cap.*) the beliefs, principles, practices, or programme of a Social Democratic Party or of social democrats. ▸ **social democratic** *adj*

social democrat *n* **1** any socialist who believes in the gradual transformation of capitalism into democratic socialism. **2** (*usually cap.*) a member of a Social Democratic Party.

Social Democratic and Labour Party *n* a Northern Irish political party, which advocates peaceful union with the Republic of Ireland.

Social Democratic Party *n* **1** (in Britain 1981–90) a centre political party founded by ex-members of the Labour Party. It formed an alliance with the Liberal Party and continued in a reduced form after many members left to join the Social and Liberal Democratic Party in 1988. **2** one of the two major political parties in Germany (formerly in West Germany), favouring gradual reform. **3** any of the parties in many other countries similar to that of Germany.

Social Education Centre *n* a daycentre, run by a local authority, for mentally handicapped people and sometimes also for physically handicapped or mentally ill adults.

social engineering *n* the manipulation of the social position and function of individuals in order to manage change in a society.

social evolution *n Sociol.* the process of social development from an early simple type of social organization to one that is complex and highly specialized.

social fund *n* (in Britain) a social security fund from which loans or payments may be made to people in cases of extreme need.

social housing *n* accommodation provided by the state for renting.

social inquiry report *n* (in Britain) a report on a person and his or her circumstances, which may be required by a court before sentencing and is made by a probation officer or a social worker from a local authority social services department.

social insurance *n* government insurance providing coverage for the unemployed, the injured, the old, etc.: usually financed by contributions from employers and employees, as well as general government revenue. See also **social security, national insurance, social assistance.**

socialism ('səʊʃəˌlɪzəm) *n* **1** an economic theory or system in which the means of production, distribution, and exchange are owned by the community collectively, usually through the state. It is characterized by production for use rather than profit, by equality of individual wealth, by the absence of competitive economic activity, and, usually, by government determination of investment, prices, and production levels. Compare **capitalism. 2** any of various social or political theories or movements in which the common welfare is to be achieved through the establishment of a socialist economic system. **3** (in Leninist theory) a transitional stage after the proletarian revolution in the development of a society from capitalism to communism: characterized by the distribution of income according to work rather than need.

socialist ('səʊʃəlɪst) *n* **1** a supporter or advocate of socialism or any party promoting socialism (**socialist party**). ◆ *adj* **2** of, characteristic of, implementing, or relating to socialism. **3** (*sometimes cap.*) of, characteristic of, or relating to socialists or a socialist party.

socialistic (ˌsəʊʃə'lɪstɪk) *adj* resembling or sympathizing with socialism. ▸ **ˌsocial'istically** *adv*

Socialist International *n* an international association of largely anti-Communist Social Democratic Parties founded in Frankfurt in 1951.
Socialist Labor Party *n* (in the U.S.) a minor Marxist party founded in 1876.
socialist realism *n* (in Communist countries, esp. formerly) the doctrine that art, literature, etc. should present an idealized portrayal of reality, which glorifies the achievements of the Communist Party.
socialite ('səʊʃə,laɪt) *n* a person who is or seeks to be prominent in fashionable society.
sociality (,səʊʃɪ'ælɪtɪ) *n, pl* **-ties. 1** the tendency of groups and persons to develop social links and live in communities. **2** the quality or state of being social.
socialization *or* **socialisation** (,səʊʃəlaɪ'zeɪʃən) *n* **1** *Psychol.* the modification from infancy of an individual's behaviour to conform with the demands of social life. **2** the act of socializing or the state of being socialized.
socialize *or* **socialise** ('səʊʃə,laɪz) *vb* **1** (*intr*) to behave in a friendly or sociable manner. **2** (*tr*) to prepare for life in society. **3** (*tr*) *Chiefly U.S.* to alter or create so as to be in accordance with socialist principles, as by nationalization. ► **'social,izable** *or* **'social,isable** *adj* ► **'social,izer** *or* **'social,iser** *n*
social market *n* **a** an economic system in which industry and commerce are run by private enterprise within limits set by the government to ensure equality of opportunity and social and environmental responsibility. **b** (*as modifier*): *a social-market economy.*
social organization *n Sociol.* the formation of a stable structure of relations inside a group, which provides a basis for order and patterns relationships for new members.
social psychology *n Psychol.* the area of psychology concerned with the interaction between individuals and groups and the effect of society on behaviour.
social realism *n* **1** the use of realist art, literature, etc. as a medium for social or political comment. **2** another name for **socialist realism.**
social science *n* **1** the study of society and of the relationship of individual members within society, including economics, history, political science, psychology, anthropology, and sociology. **2** any of these subjects studied individually. ► **social scientist** *n*
social secretary *n* **1** a member of an organization who arranges its social events. **2** a personal secretary who deals with private correspondence, etc.
social security *n* **1** public provision for the economic, and sometimes social, welfare of the aged, unemployed, etc., esp. through pensions and other monetary assistance. **2** (*often cap.*) a government programme designed to provide such assistance.
social services *pl n* welfare activities organized by the state or a local authority and carried out by trained personnel.
social stratification *n Sociol.* the hierarchical structures of class and status in any society.
social studies *n (functioning as sing)* the study of how people live and organize themselves in society, embracing geography, history, economics, and other subjects.
social welfare *n* **1** the various social services provided by a state for the benefit of its citizens. **2** (*caps.*) (in New Zealand) a government department concerned with pensions and benefits for the elderly, the sick, etc.
social work *n* any of various social services designed to alleviate the conditions of the poor and aged and to increase the welfare of children. ► **social worker** *n*
societal (sə'saɪətᵊl) *adj* of or relating to society, esp. human society or social relations. ► **so'cietally** *adv*
societal marketing *n* **1** marketing that takes into account society's long-term welfare. **2** the marketing of a social or charitable cause, such as an environmental campaign.
society (sə'saɪətɪ) *n, pl* **-ties. 1** the totality of social relationships among organized groups of human beings or animals. **2** a system of human organizations generating distinctive cultural patterns and institutions and usually providing protection, security, continuity, and a national identity for its members. **3** such a system with reference to its mode of social and economic organization or its dominant class: *middle-class society.* **4** those with whom one has companionship. **5** an organized group of people associated for some specific purpose or on account of some common interest: *a learned society.* **6a** the privileged class of people in a community, esp. as considered superior or fashionable. **6b** (*as modifier*): *a society woman.* **7** the social life and intercourse of such people: *to enter society as a debutante.* **8** companionship; the fact or state of being together with someone else: *I enjoy her society.* **9** *Ecology.* a small community of plants within a larger association. [C16: via Old French *societé* from Latin *societās,* from *socius* a comrade]
Society Islands *pl n* a group of islands in the S Pacific: administratively part of French Polynesia; consists of the Windward Islands and the Leeward Islands; became a French protectorate in 1843 and a colony in 1880. Pop.: 162 573 (1988). Area: 1595 sq. km (616 sq. miles).
Society of Jesus *n* the religious order of the Jesuits, founded by Ignatius Loyola.
Socinian (səʊ'sɪnɪən) *n* **1** a supporter of the beliefs of Faustus and Laelius Socinus, who rejected such traditional Christian doctrines as the divinity of Christ, the Trinity, and original sin, and held that those who follow Christ's virtues will be granted salvation. ◆ *adj* **2** of or relating to the Socinians or their beliefs. ► **So'cinian,ism** *n*
Socinus (səʊ'saɪnəs) *n* **Faustus** ('fɔːstəs), Italian name *Fausto Sozzini,* 1539–1604, and his uncle, **Laelius** ('liːlɪəs), Italian name *Lelio Sozzini,* 1525–62, Italian Protestant theologians and reformers.
socio- *combining form.* denoting social or society: *socioeconomic; sociopolitical; sociology.*
sociobiology (,səʊsɪəʊbaɪ'ɒlədʒɪ) *n* the study of social behaviour in animals and humans, esp. in relation to its survival value and evolutionary origins. ► **,sociobi'ologist** *n*
socioeconomic (,səʊsɪəʊ,iːkə'nɒmɪk, -,ɛkə-) *adj* of, relating to, or involving both economic and social factors. ► **,socio,eco'nomically** *adv*
sociol. *abbrev. for* sociology.
sociolinguistics (,səʊsɪəʊlɪŋ'gwɪstɪks) *n (functioning as sing)* the study of language in relation to its social context. ► **,socio'linguist** *n* ► **,sociolin'guistic** *adj*
sociology (,səʊsɪ'ɒlədʒɪ) *n* the study of the development, organization, functioning, and classification of human societies. ► **sociological** (,səʊsɪə'lɒdʒɪkᵊl) *adj* ► **,socio'logically** *adv* ► **,soci'ologist** *n*
sociometry (,səʊsɪ'ɒmɪtrɪ) *n* the study of sociological relationships, esp. of preferences, within social groups. ► **sociometric** (,səʊsɪə'mɛtrɪk) *adj* ► **,soci'ometrist** *n*
sociopath ('səʊsɪə,pæθ) *n Psychiatry.* another name for **psychopath.** ► **,socio'pathic** *adj* ► **sociopathy** (,səʊsɪ'ɒpəθɪ) *n*
sociopolitical (,səʊsɪəʊpə'lɪtɪkᵊl) *adj* of, relating to, or involving both political and social factors.
sock[1] (sɒk) *n* **1** a cloth covering for the foot, reaching to between the ankle and knee and worn inside a shoe. **2** an insole put in a shoe, as to make it fit better. **3** a light shoe worn by actors in ancient Greek and Roman comedy, sometimes taken to allude to comic drama in general (as in the phrase **sock and buskin**). See **buskin. 4** another name for **windsock. 5 pull one's socks up.** *Brit. informal.* to make a determined effort, esp. in order to regain control of a situation. **6 put a sock in it.** *Brit. slang.* be quiet! ◆ *vb* **7** (*tr*) to provide with socks. **8 socked in.** *U.S. and Canadian slang.* (of an airport) closed by adverse weather conditions. [Old English *socc* a light shoe, from Latin *soccus,* from Greek *sukkhos*]
sock[2] (sɒk) *Slang.* ◆ *vb* **1** (*usually tr*) to hit with force. **2 sock it to.** to make a forceful impression on. ◆ *n* **3** a forceful blow. [C17: of obscure origin]
sock away *vb (tr) U.S., Canadian, and N.Z. informal.* to save up.
sockdologer *or* **sockdolager** (sɒk'dɒlədʒə) *n Slang, chiefly U.S.* **1** a decisive blow or remark. **2** an outstanding person or thing. [C19: of uncertain origin; perhaps from SOCK[2] + DOXOLOGY (in the sense: the closing act of a church service) + -ER[1]]
socket ('sɒkɪt) *n* **1** a device into which an electric plug can be inserted in order to make a connection in a circuit. **2** *Chiefly Brit.* such a device mounted on a wall and connected to the electricity supply. Informal Brit. names: **point, plug.** U.S. and Canadian name: **outlet. 3** a part with an opening or hollow into which some other part, such as a pipe, probe, etc., can be fitted. **4** a spanner head having a recess suitable to be fitted over the head of a bolt. **5** *Anatomy.* **5a** a bony hollow into which a part or structure fits: *a tooth socket; an eye socket.* **5b** the receptacle of a ball-and-socket joint. ◆ *vb* **6** (*tr*) to furnish with or place into a socket. [C13: from Anglo-Norman *soket* a little ploughshare, from *soc,* of Celtic origin; compare Cornish *soch* ploughshare]
socket wrench *n* a wrench having a handle onto which socketed heads of various sizes can be fitted.
sockeye ('sɒk,aɪ) *n* a Pacific salmon, *Oncorhynchus nerka,* having red flesh and valued as a food fish. Also called: **red salmon.** [by folk etymology from Salishan *sukkegh*]
socle ('səʊkᵊl) *n* another name for **plinth** (sense 1). [C18: via French from Italian *zoccolo,* from Latin *socculus* a little shoe, from *soccus* a SOCK[1]]
socman ('sɒkmən, 'səʊk-) *or* **sokeman** ('səʊkmən) *n, pl* **-men.** *English history.* a tenant holding land by socage. [C16: from Anglo-Latin *socmannus;* see SOKE]
Socotra, Sokotra, *or* **Suqutra** (sə'kəʊtrə) *n* an island in the Indian Ocean, about 240 km (150 miles) off Cape Guardafui, Somalia: administratively part of Yemen. Capital: Tamrida. Area: 3100 sq. km (1200 sq. miles).
Socrates ('sɒkrə,tiːz) *n* ?470–399 B.C., Athenian philosopher, whose beliefs are known only through the writings of his pupils Plato and Xenophon. He taught that virtue was based on knowledge, which was attained by a dialectical process that took into account many aspects of a stated hypothesis. He was indicted for impiety and corruption of youth (399) and was condemned to death. He refused to flee and died by drinking hemlock.
Socratic (sɒ'krætɪk) *adj* **1** of or relating to Socrates, his methods, etc. ◆ *n* **2** a person who follows the teachings of Socrates. ► **So'cratically** *adv* ► **So'crati,cism** *n* ► **Socratist** ('sɒkrətɪst) *n*
Socratic irony *n Philosophy.* a means by which the pretended ignorance of a skilful questioner leads the person answering to expose his own ignorance.
Socratic method *n Philosophy.* the method of instruction by question and answer used by Socrates in order to elicit from his pupils truths he considered to be implicitly known by all rational beings. Compare **maieutic.**
Socred ('səʊkrɛd) *Canadian.* ◆ *n* **1** a supporter or member of a Social Credit movement or party. ◆ *adj* **2** of or relating to Social Credit.
sod[1] (sɒd) *n* **1** a piece of grass-covered surface soil held together by the roots of the grass; turf. **2** *Poetic.* the ground. ◆ *vb* **sods, sodding, sodded. 3** (*tr*) to cover with sods. [C15: from Low German; compare Middle Low German, Middle Dutch *sode;* related to Old Frisian *sātha*]
sod[2] (sɒd) *Slang, chiefly Brit.* ◆ *n* **1** a person considered to be obnoxious. **2** a jocular word for a person: *the poor sod hasn't been out for weeks.* **3 sod all.** *Slang.* nothing. ◆ *interj* **4 sod it.** a strong exclamation of annoyance. See also **sod off.** [C19: shortened from SODOMITE] ► **'sodding** *adj*
soda ('səʊdə) *n* **1** any of a number of simple inorganic compounds of sodium, such as sodium carbonate (**washing soda**), sodium bicarbonate (**baking soda**), and sodium hydroxide (**caustic soda**). **2** See **soda water. 3** *U.S. and Canadian.* a fizzy drink. **4** the top card of the pack in faro. **5 a soda.** *Austral. slang.* something easily done; a pushover. [C16: from Medieval Latin, from

sodanum barilla, a plant that was burned to obtain a type of sodium carbonate, perhaps of Arabic origin]

soda ash *n* the anhydrous commercial form of sodium carbonate.

soda biscuit *n* a biscuit leavened with sodium bicarbonate.

soda bread *n* a type of bread leavened with sodium bicarbonate combined with milk and cream of tartar.

soda fountain *n U.S. and Canadian.* **1** a counter that serves drinks, snacks, etc. **2** an apparatus dispensing soda water.

soda jerk *n U.S. slang.* a person who serves at a soda fountain.

soda lake *n* a salt lake that has a high content of sodium salts, esp. chlorides and sulphates.

soda lime *n* a solid mixture of sodium and calcium hydroxides used to absorb carbon dioxide and to dry gases.

sodalite ('səʊdəˌlaɪt) *n* a blue, grey, yellow, or colourless mineral consisting of sodium aluminium silicate and sodium chloride in cubic crystalline form. It occurs in basic igneous rocks. Formula: $Na_4Al_3Si_3O_{12}Cl$. [C19: from SODA + -LITE]

sodality (səʊ'dælɪtɪ) *n, pl* **-ties. 1** *R.C. Church.* a religious or charitable society. **2** fraternity; fellowship. [C16: from Latin *sodālitās* fellowship, from *sodālis* a comrade]

sodamide ('səʊdəˌmaɪd) *n* a white crystalline compound used as a dehydrating agent, as a chemical reagent, and in making sodium cyanide. Formula: $NaNH_2$. Also called: **sodium amide.** [C19: from SOD(IUM) + AMIDE]

soda nitre *n* another name for **Chile saltpetre.**

soda pop *n U.S. informal.* a fizzy drink.

soda siphon *n* a sealed bottle containing and dispensing soda water. The water is forced up a tube reaching to the bottom of the bottle by the pressure of gas above the water. Also called (esp. U.S.): **siphon bottle.**

soda water *n* an effervescent beverage made by charging water with carbon dioxide under pressure. Sometimes shortened to **soda.**

sodden ('sɒdᵊn) *adj* **1** completely saturated. **2a** dulled, esp. by excessive drinking. **2b** (*in combination*): *a drink-sodden mind.* **3** heavy or doughy, as bread is when improperly cooked. ◆ *vb* **4** to make or become sodden. [C13 *soden,* past participle of SEETHE] ▸ **'soddenly** *adv* ▸ **'soddenness** *n*

Soddy ('sɒdɪ) *n* **Frederick.** 1877–1956, English chemist, whose work on radioactive disintegration led to the discovery of isotopes: Nobel prize for chemistry 1921.

sodger ('sɒdʒər) *n, vb* a dialect variant of **soldier.**

sodium ('səʊdɪəm) *n* **a** a very reactive soft silvery-white element of the alkali metal group occurring principally in common salt, Chile saltpetre, and cryolite. Sodium and potassium ions maintain the essential electrolytic balance in living cells. It is used in the production of chemicals, in metallurgy, and, alloyed with potassium, as a cooling medium in nuclear reactors. Symbol: Na; atomic no.: 11; atomic wt.: 22.989768; valency: 1; relative density: 0.971; melting pt.: 97.81±0.03°C; boiling pt.: 892.9°C. **b** (*as modifier*): *sodium light.* [C19: New Latin, from SODA + -IUM]

sodium amytal *n* another name for **Amytal.**

sodium benzoate *n* a white crystalline soluble compound used as an antibacterial and antifungal agent in preserving food (**E211**), as an antiseptic, and in making dyes and pharmaceuticals. Formula: $Na(C_6H_5COO)$. Also called: **benzoate of soda.**

sodium bicarbonate *n* a white crystalline soluble compound usually obtained by the Solvay process and used in effervescent drinks, baking powders, fire extinguishers, and in medicine as an antacid; sodium hydrogen carbonate. Formula: $NaHCO_3$. Also called: **bicarbonate of soda, baking soda.**

sodium carbonate *n* a colourless or white odourless soluble crystalline compound existing in several hydrated forms and used in the manufacture of glass, ceramics, soap, and paper and as an industrial and domestic cleansing agent. It is made by the Solvay process and commonly obtained as the decahydrate (**washing soda** or **sal soda**) or a white anhydrous powder (**soda ash**). Formula: Na_2CO_3.

sodium chlorate *n* a colourless crystalline soluble compound used as a bleaching agent, weak antiseptic, and weedkiller. Formula: $NaClO_3$.

sodium chloride *n* common table salt; a soluble colourless crystalline compound occurring naturally as halite and in sea water: widely used as a seasoning and preservative for food and in the manufacture of chemicals, glass, and soap. Formula: NaCl. Also called: **salt.**

sodium cyanide *n* a white odourless crystalline soluble poisonous compound with an odour of hydrogen cyanide when damp. It is used for extracting gold and silver from their ores and for case-hardening steel. Formula: NaCN.

sodium dichromate *n* a soluble crystalline solid compound, usually obtained as red or orange crystals and used as an oxidizing agent, corrosion inhibitor, and mordant. Formula $Na_2Cr_2O_7$. Also called (not in technical usage): **sodium bichromate.**

sodium fluoroacetate (ˌflʊərəʊ'æsɪˌteɪt) *n* a white crystalline odourless poisonous compound, used as a rodenticide. Formula: $Na(CH_2FCOO)$.

sodium glutamate ('gluːtəˌmeɪt) *n* another name for **monosodium glutamate.**

sodium hydroxide *n* a white deliquescent strongly alkaline solid used in the manufacture of rayon, paper, aluminium, soap, and sodium compounds. Formula: NaOH. Also called: **caustic soda.** See also **lye.**

sodium hyposulphite *n* another name (not in technical usage) for **sodium thiosulphate.**

sodium lamp *n* another name for **sodium-vapour lamp.**

sodium nitrate *n* a white crystalline soluble solid compound occurring naturally as Chile saltpetre and caliche and used in matches, explosives, and rocket propellants, as a fertilizer, and as a curing salt for preserving food such as bacon, ham, and cheese (**E251**). Formula: $NaNO_3$.

Sodium Pentothal *n Trademark.* another name for **thiopentone sodium.**

sodium perborate *n* a white odourless crystalline compound used as an antiseptic and deodorant. It is sodium metaborate with both water and hydrogen peroxide of crystallization. Formula: $NaBO_2.H_2O_2.3H_2O$.

sodium peroxide *n* a yellowish-white odourless soluble powder formed when sodium reacts with an excess of oxygen: used as an oxidizing agent in chemical preparations, a bleaching agent, an antiseptic, and in removing carbon dioxide from air in submarines, etc. Formula: Na_2O_2.

sodium phosphate *n* any sodium salt of any phosphoric acid, esp. one of three salts of orthophosphoric acid having formulas NaH_2PO_4 (**monosodium dihydrogen orthophosphate**), Na_2HPO_4 (**disodium monohydrogen orthophosphate**), and Na_3PO_4 (**trisodium orthophosphate**).

sodium propionate *n* a transparent crystalline soluble substance used as a medical fungicide and to prevent the growth of moulds, esp. to retard spoilage in packed foods. Formula: $Na(C_2H_5COO)$.

sodium silicate *n* **1** Also called: **soluble glass.** a substance having the general formula, $Na_2O.xSiO_2$, where x varies between 3 and 5, existing as an amorphous powder or present in a usually viscous aqueous solution. See **water glass. 2** any sodium salt of orthosilicic acid or metasilicic acid.

sodium sulphate *n* a solid white substance that occurs naturally as thenardite and is usually used as the white anhydrous compound (**salt cake**) or the white crystalline decahydrate (**Glauber's salt**) in making glass, detergents, and pulp. Formula: Na_2SO_4.

sodium thiosulphate *n* a white soluble substance used, in the pentahydrate form, in photography as a fixer to dissolve unchanged silver halides and also to remove excess chlorine from chlorinated water. Formula: $Na_2S_2O_3$. Also called (not in technical usage): **sodium hyposulphite, hypo.**

sodium-vapour lamp *n* a type of electric lamp consisting of a glass tube containing neon and sodium vapour at low pressure through which an electric current is passed to give an orange light. They are used in street lighting.

sod off *vb (intr, adv; usually imperative) Taboo slang, chiefly Brit.* to go away; depart.

Sodom ('sɒdəm) *n* **1** *Old Testament.* a city destroyed by God for its wickedness that, with Gomorrah, traditionally typifies depravity (Genesis 19:24). **2** this city as representing homosexuality. **3** any place notorious for depravity.

sodomite ('sɒdəˌmaɪt) *n* a person who practises sodomy.

sodomize *or* **sodomise** ('sɒdəˌmaɪz) *vb* (*tr*) to have anal intercourse with (a person).

sodomy ('sɒdəmɪ) *n* anal intercourse committed by a man with another man or a woman. Compare **buggery.** [C13: via Old French *sodomie* from Latin (Vulgate) *Sodoma* Sodom]

Sod's law (sɒdz) *n Informal.* a humorous or facetious precept stating that if something can go wrong or turn out inconveniently it will. Also called: **Murphy's Law.**

Soekarno (suː'kɑːnəʊ) *n* a variant spelling of (Achmed) **Sukarno.**

Soemba ('suːmbə) *n* a variant spelling of **Sumba.**

Soembawa (suːm'bɑːwə) *n* a variant spelling of **Sumbawa.**

Soenda Islands ('suːndə) *pl n* a variant spelling of **Sunda Islands.**

Soenda Strait *n* a variant spelling of **Sunda Strait.**

Soerabaja (ˌsʊərə'baɪə) *n* a variant spelling of **Surabaya.**

soever (səʊ'evə) *adv* in any way at all: used to emphasize or make less precise a word or phrase, usually in combination with *what, where, when, how,* etc., or else separated by intervening words. Compare **whatsoever.**

sofa ('səʊfə) *n* an upholstered seat with back and arms for two or more people. [C17 (in the sense: dais upholstered as a seat): from Arabic *suffah*]

sofa bed *n* a sofa that can be converted into a bed.

sofar ('səʊfɑː) *n* a system for determining a position at sea, esp. that of survivors of a disaster, by exploding a charge underwater at that point. The times taken for the shock waves to travel through the water to three widely separated shore stations are used to calculate their position. [C20: from *so(und) f(ixing) a(nd) r(anging)*]

soffit ('sɒfɪt) *n* **1** the underside of a part of a building or a structural component, such as an arch, beam, stair, etc. **2** the upper inner surface of a drain or sewer. Compare **invert** (sense 6). [C17: via French from Italian *soffitto,* from Latin *suffixus* something fixed underneath, from *suffigere,* from *sub-* under + *figere* to fasten]

Sofia ('səʊfɪə) *n* the capital of Bulgaria, in the west: colonized by the Romans in 29 A.D.; became capital of Bulgaria in 1879; university (1880). Pop.: 1 116 823 (1996 est.). Ancient name: **Serdica.** Bulgarian name: **Sofiya** ('sɔfiˌja).

S. of Sol. *Bible. abbrev. for* Song of Solomon.

soft (sɒft) *adj* **1** easy to dent, work, or cut without shattering; malleable. **2** not hard; giving little or no resistance to pressure or weight. **3** fine, light, smooth, or fluffy to the touch. **4** gentle; tranquil. **5** (of music, sounds, etc.) low and pleasing. **6** (of light, colour, etc.) not excessively bright or harsh. **7** (of a breeze, climate, etc.) temperate, mild, or pleasant. **8** *Dialect.* drizzly or rainy: *a soft day; the weather has turned soft.* **9** slightly blurred; not sharply outlined: *soft focus.* **10** (of a diet) consisting of easily digestible foods. **11** kind or lenient, often excessively so. **12** easy to influence or impose upon. **13** prepared to compromise; not doctrinaire: *the soft left.* **14** *Informal.* feeble or silly; simple (often in the phrase **soft in the head**). **15** unable to endure hardship, esp. through too much pampering. **16** physically out of condition; flabby: *soft muscles.* **17** loving; tender: *soft words.* **18** *Informal.* requiring little exertion; easy: *a soft job.* **19** *Chem.* (of water) relatively free of mineral salts and therefore easily able to make soap lather. **20** (of a drug such as cannabis) nonaddictive or only mildly addictive. Compare **hard** (sense 19). **21** *Phonetics.* **21a** an older word for **lenis. 21b** (not in technical usage) denoting the consonants *c* and *g* in English when they are pronounced as palatal or alveolar fricatives or affricates (s, dʒ, ʃ, ð, tʃ) before *e* and *i,* rather than as velar stops (k, g). **21c** (in the Slavonic languages) palatalized before a front vowel or a special character (**soft sign**) written as b. **22a** unprotected against attack: *a soft target.* **22b** *Military.* unarmoured, esp. as applied to a truck by comparison with a tank. **23** *Finance, chiefly U.S.* (of prices, a market, etc.) unstable and tending to decline. **24** (of a currency) in relatively little demand, esp. because of a weak balance of payments situation. **25** (of radiation, such as X-rays and ultraviolet radiation) having low energy and not capable of deep penetration of materials. **26** *Physics.* (of valves or tubes) only partially evacuated. **27 soft on** *or* **about. 27a** gentle, sympathetic, or lenient towards. **27b** feeling affection or infatuation for. ◆ *adv* **28** in a soft manner: *to speak soft.* ◆ *n* **29** a soft object, part, or piece. **30** *Informal.* See **softie.** ◆ *interj Archaic.* **31** quiet! **32** wait! [Old English *sōfte;* related to Old Saxon *sāfti,* Old High German *semfti* gentle] ► **'softly** *adv*

softa ('sɒftə) *n* a Muslim student of divinity and jurisprudence, esp. in Turkey. [C17: from Turkish, from Persian *sōkhtah* aflame (with love of learning)]

softball ('sɒft,bɔːl) *n* **1** a variation of baseball using a larger softer ball, pitched underhand. **2** the ball used. **3** *Cookery.* the stage in the boiling of a sugar syrup at which it may be rubbed into balls after dipping in cold water.

soft-boiled *adj* **1** (of an egg) boiled for a short time so that the yolk is still soft. **2** *Informal.* softhearted.

soft-centred *adj* (of a chocolate or boiled sweet) having a centre consisting of cream, jelly, etc.

soft chancre *n Pathol.* a venereal ulcer caused by an infection that is not syphilitic. Also called: **chancroid.**

soft clam *n* another name for the **soft-shell clam.**

soft coal *n* another name for **bituminous coal.**

soft commodities *pl n* nonmetal commodities such as cocoa, sugar, and grains, bought and sold on a futures market. Also called: **softs.**

soft-core *adj* (of pornography) suggestive and titillating through not being totally explicit or detailed.

soft-cover *adj* a less common word for **paperback.**

soft drink *n* a nonalcoholic drink, usually cold.

soften ('sɒfᵊn) *vb* **1** to make or become soft or softer. **2** to make or become gentler. **3** (*intr*) *Commerce.* **3a** (of demand, a market, etc.) to weaken. **3b** (of a price) to fall.

softener ('sɒfᵊnə) *n* **1** a substance added to another substance to increase its softness, pliability, or plasticity. **2** a substance, such as a zeolite, for softening water.

softening of the brain *n* an abnormal softening of the tissues of the cerebrum characterized by various degrees of mental impairment.

soften up *vb* (*adv*) **1** to make or become soft. **2** (*tr*) to weaken (an enemy's defences) by shelling, bombing, etc. **3** (*tr*) to weaken the resistance of (a person) by persuasive talk, advances, etc.

soft-finned *adj* (of certain teleost fishes) having fins that are supported by flexible cartilaginous rays. See also **malacopterygian.** Compare **spiny-finned.**

soft-focus lens *n Photog.* a lens designed to produce an image that is uniformly very slightly out of focus: typically used for portrait work.

soft fruit *n Brit.* any of various types of small edible stoneless fruit, such as strawberries, raspberries, and currants, borne mainly on low-growing plants or bushes.

soft furnishings *pl n Brit.* curtains, hangings, rugs, etc.

soft goods *pl n* textile fabrics and related merchandise.

soft-headed *adj Informal.* feeble-minded; stupid; simple. ► **,soft-'headedness** *n*

softhearted (,sɒft'hɑːtɪd) *adj* easily moved to pity. ► **,soft'heartedly** *adv* ► **,soft'heartedness** *n*

soft hyphen *n* a hyphen, used in word processing to divide a word, which prints only when it appears at the end of a line. Also called: **optional hyphen.**

softie *or* **softy** ('sɒftɪ) *n, pl* **softies.** *Informal.* a person who is sentimental, weakly foolish, or lacking in physical endurance.

soft iron *n* **a** iron that has a low carbon content and is easily magnetized and demagnetized with a small hysteresis loss. **b** (*as modifier*): *a soft-iron core.*

soft landing *n* **1** a landing by a spacecraft on the moon or a planet at a sufficiently low velocity for the equipment or occupants to remain unharmed. **2** a painless resolution of a problem, esp. an economic problem. ◆ Compare **hard landing.**

soft lens *n* a flexible hydrogel lens worn on the surface of the eye to correct defects of vision. Compare **hard lens, gas-permeable lens.**

soft line *n* a moderate flexible attitude or policy. ► **,soft-'liner** *n*

soft loan *n* a loan on which interest is not charged, such as a loan made to an undeveloped country.

softly-softly *adj* gradual, cautious, and discreet.

softness ('sɒftnɪs) *n* **1** the quality or an instance of being soft. **2** *Metallurgy.* the tendency of a metal to distort easily. Compare **brittleness** (sense 2), **toughness** (sense 2).

soft option *n* in a number of choices, the one considered to be easy or the easiest to do, involving the least difficulty or exertion.

soft palate *n* the posterior fleshy portion of the roof of the mouth. It forms a movable muscular flap that seals off the nasopharynx during swallowing and speech.

soft paste *n* **a** artificial porcelain made from clay, bone ash, etc. **b** (*as modifier*): *softpaste porcelain.* [C19: from PASTE[1] (in the sense: the mixture from which porcelain is made); so called because of its consistency]

soft-pedal *vb* **-als, -alling, -alled** *or U.S.* **-als, -aling, -aled.** (*tr*) **1** to mute the tone of (a piano) by depressing the soft pedal. **2** *Informal.* to make (something, esp. something unpleasant) less obvious by deliberately failing to emphasize or allude to it. ◆ *n* **soft pedal. 3** a foot-operated lever on a piano, the left one of two, that either moves the whole action closer to the strings so that the hammers strike with less force or causes fewer of the strings to sound. Compare **sustaining pedal.** See **piano**[1].

soft porn *n Informal.* soft-core pornography.

soft rot *n* any of various bacterial or fungal plant diseases characterized by watery disintegration of fruits, roots, etc.

softs (sɒfts) *pl n* another name for **soft commodities.**

soft sell *n* a method of selling based on indirect suggestion or inducement. Compare **hard sell.**

soft-shell clam *n* any of several marine clams of the genus *Mya,* esp. *M. arenaria,* an edible species of coastal regions of the U.S. and Europe, having a thin brittle shell. Sometimes shortened to **soft-shell.** Compare **quahog.**

soft-shell crab *n* a crab, esp. of the edible species *Cancer pagurus,* that has recently moulted and has not yet formed its new shell. Compare **hard-shell crab.**

soft-shelled turtle *n* any freshwater turtle of the family *Trionychidae,* having a flattened soft shell consisting of bony plates covered by a leathery skin.

soft-shoe *n* (*modifier*) relating to a type of tap dancing performed wearing soft-soled shoes: *the soft-shoe shuffle.*

soft shoulder *or* **verge** *n* a soft edge along the side of a road that is unsuitable for vehicles to drive on.

soft soap *n* **1** *Med.* another name for **green soap. 2** *Informal.* flattering, persuasive, or cajoling talk. ◆ *vb* **soft-soap. 3** *Informal.* to use such talk on (a person).

soft-spoken *adj* **1** speaking or said with a soft gentle voice. **2** able to persuade or impress by glibness of tongue.

soft spot *n* a sentimental fondness (esp. in the phrase **have a soft spot for**).

soft tissue *n* the soft parts of the human body as distinct from bone and cartilage.

soft top *n* a convertible car with a roof made of fabric rather than metal.

soft touch *n Informal.* a person easily persuaded or imposed on, esp. to lend money.

software ('sɒft,wɛə) *n* **1** *Computing.* the programs that can be used with a particular computer system. Compare **hardware** (sense 2). **2** video cassettes and discs for use with a particular video system.

software house *n* a commercial organization that specializes in the production of computer software packages.

soft wheat *n* a type of wheat with soft kernels and a high starch content.

softwood ('sɒft,wʊd) *n* **1** the open-grained wood of any of numerous coniferous trees, such as pine and cedar, as distinguished from that of a dicotyledonous tree. **2** any tree yielding this wood. ◆ Compare **hardwood.**

SOGAT ('səʊgæt) *n* (in Britain, formerly) *acronym for* Society of Graphical and Allied Trades.

Sogdian ('sɒgdɪən) *n* **1** a member of the people who lived in Sogdiana. **2** the language of this people, now almost extinct, belonging to the East Iranian branch of the Indo-European family. ◆ *adj* **3** of or relating to Sogdiana, its people, or their language.

Sogdiana (,sɒgdɪ'ɑːnə) *n* a region of ancient central Asia. Its chief city was Samarkand.

soggy ('sɒgɪ) *adj* **-gier, -giest. 1** soaked with liquid. **2** (of bread, pastry, etc.) moist and heavy. **3** *Informal.* lacking in spirit or positiveness. [C18: probably from dialect *sog* marsh, of obscure origin] ► **'soggily** *adv* ► **'sogginess** *n*

soh *or* **so** (səʊ) *n Music.* (in tonic sol-fa) the name used for the fifth note or dominant of any scale. [C13: see GAMUT]

soho (səʊ'həʊ) *interj* **1** *Hunting.* an exclamation announcing the sighting of a hare. **2** an exclamation announcing the discovery of something unexpected. [an Anglo-French hunting call, probably of exclamatory origin]

Soho ('səʊhəʊ) *n* a district of central London, in the City of Westminster: a foreign quarter since the late 17th century, now chiefly known for restaurants, nightclubs, striptease clubs, etc.

soi-disant *French.* (swadizɑ̃) *adj* so-called; self-styled. [literally: calling oneself]

soigné *or* (*fem*) **soignée** ('swɑːnjeɪ; *French* swaɲe) *adj* well-groomed; elegant. [French, from *soigner* to take good care of, of Germanic origin; compare Old Saxon *sunnea* care]

soil[1] (sɔɪl) *n* **1** the top layer of the land surface of the earth that is composed of disintegrated rock particles, humus, water, and air. See **zonal soil, azonal soil, intrazonal soil, horizon** (senses 4, 5). Related adj: **telluric. 2** a type of this material having specific characteristics: *loamy soil.* **3** land, country, or region: *one's native soil.* **4 the soil.** life and work on a farm; land: *he belonged to the soil, as his forefathers had.* **5** any place or thing encouraging growth or development. [C14: from Anglo-Norman, from Latin *solium* a seat, but confused with Latin *solum* the ground]

soil[2] (sɔɪl) *vb* **1** to make or become dirty or stained. **2** (*tr*) to pollute with sin or disgrace; sully; defile: *he soiled the family honour by his cowardice.* ◆ *n* **3** the state or result of soiling. **4** refuse, manure, or excrement. [C13: from Old French *soillier* to defile, from *soil* pigsty, probably from Latin *sūs* a swine]

soil[3] (sɔɪl) *vb* (*tr*) to feed (livestock) freshly cut green fodder either to fatten or purge them. [C17: perhaps from obsolete vb (C16) *soil* to manure, from SOIL[2] (n)]

soilage ('sɔɪlɪdʒ) *n* green fodder, esp. when freshly cut and fed to livestock in a confined area.

soil bank *n* (in the U.S.) a federal programme by which farmers are paid to divert land to soil-enriching crops.

soil conservation *n* the preservation of soil against deterioration or erosion, and the maintenance of the fertilizing elements for crop production.

soil creep *n* the gradual downhill movement, under the force of gravity, of soil and loose rock material on a slope.

soil mechanics *n* (*functioning as sing*) the study of the physical properties of soil, esp. those properties that affect its ability to bear weight, such as water content, density, strength, etc.

soil pipe *n* a pipe that conveys sewage or waste water from a toilet, etc., to a soil drain or sewer.

soilure ('sɔɪljə) *n Archaic.* **1** the act of soiling or the state of being soiled. **2** a stain or blot. [C13: from Old French *soilleure,* from *soillier* to SOIL[2]]

soiree ('swɑːreɪ) *n* an evening party or other gathering given usually at a private house, esp. where guests are invited to listen to, play, or dance to music. [C19: from French, from Old French *soir* evening, from Latin *sērum* a late time, from *sērus* late]

Soissons (*French* swasɔ̃) *n* a city in N France, on the Aisne River: has Roman remains and an 11th-century abbey. Pop.: 32 144 (1990).

soixante-neuf *French.* (swasɑ̃tnœf) *n* a sexual activity in which two people simultaneously stimulate each other's genitalia with their mouths. Also called: **sixty-nine.** [literally: sixty-nine, from the position adopted by the participants]

sojourn ('sɒdʒɜːn, 'sʌdʒ-) *n* **1** a temporary stay. ◆ *vb* **2** (*intr*) to stay or reside temporarily. [C13: from Old French *sojorner,* from Vulgar Latin *subdiurnāre* (unattested) to spend a day, from Latin *sub-* during + Late Latin *diurnum* day] ► **'sojourner** *n*

soke (səʊk) *n English legal history.* **1** the right to hold a local court. **2** the territory under the jurisdiction of a particular court. [C14: from Medieval Latin *sōca,* from Old English *sōcn* a seeking; see SEEK]

sokeman ('səʊkmən) *n, pl* **-men.** (in the Danelaw) a freeman enjoying extensive rights, esp. over his land.

Sokoto ('səʊkəˌtəʊ) *n* **1** a state of NW Nigeria. Capital: Sokoto. Pop.: 4 524 162 (1992 est.). Area: 65 735 sq. km (25 380 sq. miles). **2** a town in NW Nigeria, capital of Sokoto state: capital of the Fulah Empire in the 19th century; Muslim place of pilgrimage. Pop.: 204 900 (1997 est.).

Sokotra (sə'kəʊtrə) *n* a variant spelling of **Socotra.**

sol[1] (sɒl) *n Music.* another name for **soh.** [C14: see GAMUT]

sol[2] (səʊl) *n* **1** short for **new sol. 2** a former French copper or silver coin, usually worth 12 deniers. [C16: from Old French, from Late Latin: SOLIDUS]

sol[3] (sɒl) *n* a colloid that has a continuous liquid phase, esp. one in which a solid is suspended in a liquid. [C20: shortened from HYDROSOL]

Sol (sɒl) *n* **1** the Roman god personifying the sun. Greek counterpart: **Helios. 2** a poetic word for the **sun.**

sol. *abbrev. for:* **1** soluble. **2** solution.

Sol. *abbrev. for:* **1** Also: **Solr** solicitor. **2** *Bible.* Solomon.

sola *Latin.* ('səʊlə) *adj* the feminine form of **solus.**

solace ('sɒlɪs) *n* **1** comfort in misery, disappointment, etc. **2** something that gives comfort or consolation. ◆ *vb* (*tr*) **3** to give comfort or cheer to (a person) in time of sorrow, distress, etc. **4** to alleviate (sorrow, misery, etc.). [C13: from Old French *solas,* from Latin *sōlātium* comfort, from *sōlārī* to console] ► **'solacer** *n*

solan *or* **solan goose** ('səʊlən) *n* an archaic name for the **gannet.** [C15 *soland,* of Scandinavian origin; compare Old Norse *sūla* gannet, *ōnd* duck]

solanaceous (ˌsɒlə'neɪʃəs) *adj* of, relating to, or belonging to the *Solanaceae,* a family of plants having typically tubular flowers with reflexed petals, protruding anthers, and often poisonous or narcotic properties: includes the potato, tobacco, henbane, mandrake, and several nightshades. [C19: from New Latin *Sōlānāceae,* from Latin *sōlānum* nightshade]

solander (sə'lændə) *n* a box for botanical specimens, maps, colour plates, etc., made in the form of a book, the front cover being the lid. [C18: named after D. D. *Solander* (1736–82), Swedish botanist]

solanine ('səʊləˌnaɪn) *n* a poisonous alkaloid found in various solanaceous plants, including potatoes which have gone green through exposure to light. [C19: from SOLAN(UM) + -INE[2]]

solanum (səʊ'leɪnəm) *n* any tree, shrub, or herbaceous plant of the mainly tropical solanaceous genus *Solanum:* includes the potato, aubergine, and certain nightshades. [C16: from Latin: nightshade]

solar ('səʊlə) *adj* **1** of or relating to the sun: *solar eclipse.* **2** operating by or utilizing the energy of the sun: *solar cell.* **3** *Astronomy.* determined from the motion of the earth relative to the sun: *solar year.* **4** *Astrology.* subject to the influence of the sun. [C15: from Latin *sōlāris,* from *sōl* the sun]

solar apex *n* another name for **apex** (sense 4).

solar cell *n* a photovoltaic cell that produces electricity from the sun's rays, used esp. in spacecraft.

solar constant *n* the rate at which the sun's energy is received per unit area at the top of the earth's atmosphere when the sun is at its mean distance from the earth and atmospheric absorption has been corrected for. Its value is 1367 watts per square metre.

solar day *n* See under **day** (sense 6).

solar eclipse *n* See under **eclipse** (sense 1).

solar energy *n* energy obtained from solar power.

solar flare *n* a brief powerful eruption of intense high-energy radiation from the sun's surface, associated with sunspots and causing radio and magnetic disturbances on earth. Sometimes shortened to **flare.** See also **solar wind.**

solar furnace *n* a furnace utilizing the sun as a heat source, sunlight being concentrated at the focus of a system of concave mirrors.

solar heating *n* heat radiation from the sun collected by heat-absorbing panels through which water is circulated: used for domestic hot water, central heating, and heating swimming pools.

solarimeter (ˌsəʊlə'rɪmɪtə) *n* any of various instruments for measuring solar radiation, as by use of a bolometer or thermopile. Also called: **pyranometer.**

solarism ('səʊləˌrɪzəm) *n* the explanation of myths in terms of the movements and influence of the sun. ► **'solarist** *n*

solarium (səʊ'lɛərɪəm) *n, pl* **-lariums** *or* **-laria** (-'lɛərɪə). **1** a room built largely of glass to afford exposure to the sun. **2** a bed equipped with ultraviolet lights used for acquiring an artificial suntan. **3** an establishment offering such facilities. [C19: from Latin: a terrace, from *sōl* sun]

solarize *or* **solarise** ('səʊləˌraɪz) *vb* (*tr*) **1** to treat by exposure to the sun's rays. **2** *Photog.* to reverse some of the tones of (a negative or print) and introduce pronounced outlines of highlights, by exposing it briefly to light after developing and washing, and then redeveloping. **3** to expose (a patient) to the therapeutic effects of solar or ultraviolet light. ► ˌ**solari'zation** *or* ˌ**solari'sation** *n*

solar mass *n* an astronomical unit of mass equal to the sun's mass, 1.981×10^{30} kilograms. Symbol: $M_\odot$

solar month *n* See under **month** (sense 4).

solar myth *n* a myth explaining or allegorizing the origin or movement of the sun.

solar panel *n* a panel exposed to radiation of heat from the sun, used to heat water or, when mounted with solar cells, to produce electricity direct, esp. for powering instruments in satellites.

solar plexus *n* **1** *Anatomy.* the network of sympathetic nerves situated behind the stomach that supply the abdominal organs. **2** (*not in technical usage*) the part of the stomach beneath the diaphragm; pit of the stomach. [C18: referring to resemblance between the radial network of nerves and ganglia and the rays of the sun]

solar power *n* heat radiation from the sun converted into electrical power.

solar system *n* the system containing the sun and the bodies held in its gravitational field, including the planets (Mercury, Venus, Earth, Mars, Jupiter, Saturn, Uranus, Neptune, Pluto), the asteroids, and comets.

solar wind (wɪnd) *n* the stream of charged particles, such as protons, emitted by the sun at high velocities, its intensity increasing during periods of solar activity. It affects terrestial magnetism, some of the particles being trapped by the magnetic lines of force, and causes auroral displays. See also **Van Allen belt, magnetosphere.**

solar year *n* See under **year** (sense 4).

solation (səʊ'leɪʃən) *n Chem.* the liquefaction of a gel.

solatium (səʊ'leɪʃɪəm) *n, pl* **-tia** (-ʃɪə). *Law, chiefly U.S. and Scot.* compensation awarded to a party for injury to the feelings as distinct from physical suffering and pecuniary loss. [C19: from Latin: see SOLACE]

sold (səʊld) *vb* **1** the past tense and past participle of **sell.** ◆ *adj* **2 sold on.** *Slang.* uncritically attached to or enthusiastic about.

soldan ('səʊldən, 'sɒl-) *n* an archaic word for **sultan.** [C13: via Old French from Arabic: SULTAN]

solder ('sɒldə; *U.S.* 'sɒdər) *n* **1** an alloy for joining two metal surfaces by melting the alloy so that it forms a thin layer between the surfaces. **Soft solders** are alloys of lead and tin; **brazing solders** are alloys of copper and zinc. **2** something that joins things together firmly; a bond. ◆ *vb* **3** to join or mend or be joined or mended with or as if with solder. [C14: via Old French from Latin *solidāre* to strengthen, from *solidus* SOLID] ► **'solderable** *adj* ► **'solderer** *n*

soldering iron *n* a hand tool consisting of a handle fixed to a copper tip that is heated, electrically or in a flame, and used to melt and apply solder.

soldier ('səʊldʒə) *n* **1a** a person who serves or has served in an army. **1b** Also called: **common soldier.** a noncommissioned member of an army as opposed to a commissioned officer. **2** a person who works diligently for a cause. **3** *Zoology.* **3a** an individual in a colony of social insects, esp. ants, that has powerful jaws adapted for defending the colony, crushing large food particles, etc. **3b** (*as modifier*): *soldier ant.* **4** *Informal.* a strip of bread or toast that is dipped into a soft-boiled egg. ◆ *vb* (*intr*) **5** to serve as a soldier. **6** *Obsolete slang.* to malinger or shirk. [C13: from Old French *soudier,* from *soude* (army) pay, from Late Latin *solidus* a gold coin, from Latin: firm]

soldier beetle *n* a yellowish-red cantharid beetle, *Rhagonycha fulva,* having a somewhat elongated body.

soldierly ('səʊldʒəlɪ) *adj* of or befitting a good soldier. ► **'soldierliness** *n*

soldier of fortune *n* a man who seeks money or adventure as a soldier; mercenary.

soldier on *vb* (*intr, adv*) to persist in one's efforts in spite of difficulties, pressure, etc.

soldier orchid *n* a European orchid, *Orchis militaris,* having pale purple flowers with a four-lobed lower lip. Also called: **military orchid.** [from an imagined resemblance to a soldier]

soldier settlement *n Austral.* the allocation of Crown land for farming to ex-servicemen. ► **soldier settler** *n*

soldiery ('səʊldʒərɪ) *n, pl* **-dieries. 1** soldiers collectively. **2** a group of soldiers. **3** the profession of being a soldier.

soldo ('sɒldəʊ; *Italian* 'soldo) *n, pl* **-di** (-diː; *Italian* -di). a former Italian copper coin worth one twentieth of a lira. [C16: from Italian, from Late Latin *solidum* a gold coin; see SOLDIER]

sole[1] (səʊl) *adj* **1** (*prenominal*) being the only one; only. **2** (*prenominal*) of or relating to one individual or group and no other: *sole rights on a patent.* **3** *Law.* having no wife or husband. See also **feme sole. 4** an archaic word for **solitary.** [C14: from Old French *soule,* from Latin *sōlus* alone] ► **'soleness** *n*

sole[2] (səʊl) *n* **1** the underside of the foot. Related adjs: **plantar, volar. 2** the underside of a shoe. **3a** the bottom of a furrow. **3b** the bottom of a plough. **4** the underside of a golf-club head. **5** the bottom of an oven, furnace, etc. ◆ *vb* (*tr*) **6** to provide (a shoe) with a sole. **7** *Golf.* to rest (the club) on the ground, as when preparing to make a stroke. [C14: via Old French from Latin *solea* sandal; probably related to *solum* the ground] ► **'soleless** *adj*

sole[3] (səʊl) *n, pl* **sole** *or* **soles. 1** any tongue-shaped flatfish of the family *Soleidae,* esp. *Solea solea* (**European sole**): most common in warm seas and highly valued as food fishes. **2** any of certain other similar fishes. [C14: via Old French from Vulgar Latin *sola* (unattested), from Latin *solea* a sandal (from the fish's shape)]

solecism ('sɒlɪˌsɪzəm) *n* **1a** the nonstandard use of a grammatical construction. **1b** any mistake, incongruity, or absurdity. **2** a violation of good manners. [C16: from Latin *soloecismus,* from Greek *soloikismos,* from *soloikos* speaking incorrectly, from *Soloi* an Athenian colony of Cilicia where the inhabitants spoke a corrupt form of Greek] ▸ **'solecist** *n* ▸ **ˌsole'cistic** *or* **ˌsole'cistical** *adj* ▸ **ˌsole'cistically** *adv*

solely ('səʊllɪ) *adv* **1** only; completely; entirely. **2** without another or others; singly; alone. **3** for one thing only.

solemn ('sɒləm) *adj* **1** characterized or marked by seriousness or sincerity: *a solemn vow.* **2** characterized by pomp, ceremony, or formality. **3** serious, glum, or pompous. **4** inspiring awe: *a solemn occasion.* **5** performed with religious ceremony. **6** gloomy or sombre: *solemn colours.* [C14: from Old French *solempne,* from Latin *sōllemnis* appointed, perhaps from *sollus* whole] ▸ **'solemnly** *adv* ▸ **'solemnness** *or* **'solemness** *n*

solemnify (sə'lɛmnɪˌfaɪ) *vb* **-fies, -fying, -fied.** (*tr*) to make serious or grave. ▸ **soˌlemnifi'cation** *n*

solemnity (sə'lɛmnɪtɪ) *n, pl* **-ties. 1** the state or quality of being solemn. **2** (*often pl*) solemn ceremony, observance, celebration, etc. **3** *Law.* a formality necessary to validate a deed, act, contract, etc.

solemnize *or* **solemnise** ('sɒləmˌnaɪz) *vb* (*tr*) **1** to celebrate or observe with rites or formal ceremonies, as a religious occasion. **2** to celebrate or perform the ceremony of (marriage). **3** to make solemn or serious. **4** to perform or hold (ceremonies, etc.) in due manner. ▸ **ˌsolemni'zation** *or* **ˌsolemni'sation** *n* ▸ **'solemˌnizer** *or* **'solemˌniser** *n*

Solemn League and Covenant *n* See **Covenant.**

solenette ('səʊləˌnɛt, 'səʊlˌnɛt) *n* a small European sole, *Buglossidium luteum,* up to 13 cm (5 in.) in length; not caught commercially. [SOLE[3] + -ETTE]

solenodon (sə'lɛnədən) *n* either of two rare shrewlike nocturnal mammals of the Caribbean, *Atopogale cubana* (**Cuban solenodon**) or *Solenodon paradoxus* (**Haitian solenodon**), having a long hairless tail and an elongated snout: family *Solenodontidae,* order *Insectivora* (insectivores). [C19: from New Latin, from Latin *sōlēn* sea mussel, razor-shell (from Greek: pipe) + Greek *odōn* tooth]

solenoid ('səʊlɪˌnɔɪd) *n* **1** a coil of wire, usually cylindrical, in which a magnetic field is set up by passing a current through it. **2** a coil of wire, partially surrounding an iron core, that is made to move inside the coil by the magnetic field set up by a current: used to convert electrical to mechanical energy, as in the operation of a switch. **3** such a device used as a relay, as in a motor vehicle for connecting the battery directly to the starter motor when activated by the ignition switch. [C19: from French *solénoïde,* from Greek *sōlēn* a pipe, tube] ▸ **ˌsole'noidal** *adj* ▸ **ˌsole'noidally** *adv*

Solent ('səʊlənt) *n* **the.** a strait of the English Channel between the coast of Hampshire, on the English mainland, and the Isle of Wight. Width: up to 6 km (4 miles).

Soleure (sɔlœr) *n* the French name for **Solothurn.**

sol-fa ('sɒl'fɑː) *n* **1** short for **tonic sol-fa.** ◆ *vb* **-fas, -faing, -faed. 2** *U.S.* to use tonic sol-fa syllables in singing (a tune). [C16: see GAMUT]

solfatara (ˌsɒlfə'tɑːrə) *n* a volcanic vent emitting only sulphurous gases and water vapour or sometimes hot mud. [C18: from Italian: a sulphurous volcano near Naples, from *solfo* SULPHUR] ▸ **ˌsolfa'taric** *adj*

solfeggio (sɒl'fɛdʒɪəʊ) *or* **solfège** (sɒl'fɛʒ) *n, pl* **-feggi** (-'fɛdʒiː), **-feggios,** *or* **-fèges.** *Music.* **1** a voice exercise in which runs, scales, etc., are sung to the same syllable or syllables. **2** solmization, esp. the French or Italian system, in which the names correspond to the notes of the scale of C major. [C18: from Italian *solfeggiare* to use the syllables sol-fa; see GAMUT]

solferino (ˌsɒlfə'riːnəʊ) *n* **a** a moderate purplish-red colour. **b** (*as adj*): *a solferino suit.* [C19: from a dye discovered in 1859, the year a battle was fought at *Solferino,* a town in Italy]

soli ('səʊlɪ) *adj, adv Music.* (of a piece or passage) to be performed by or with soloists. Compare **tutti.** [plural of SOLO]

solicit (sə'lɪsɪt) *vb* **-its, -iting, -ited. 1** (when *intr,* foll. by *for*) to make a request, application, or entreaty to (a person for business, support, etc.). **2** to accost (a person) with an offer of sexual relations in return for money. **3** to provoke or incite (a person) to do something wrong or illegal. [C15: from Old French *solliciter* to disturb, from Latin *sollicitāre* to harass, from *sollicitus* agitated, from *sollus* whole + *citus,* from *ciēre* to excite] ▸ **soˌlici'tation** *n*

solicitor (sə'lɪsɪtə) *n* **1** (in Britain) a lawyer who advises clients on matters of law, draws up legal documents, prepares cases for barristers, etc., and who may plead in certain courts. Compare **barrister. 2** (in the U.S.) an officer responsible for the legal affairs of a town, city, etc. **3** a person who solicits. ▸ **so'licitorship** *n*

Solicitor General *n, pl* **Solicitors General. 1** (in Britain) the law officer of the Crown ranking next to the Attorney General (in Scotland to the Lord Advocate) and acting as his assistant. **2** (in New Zealand) the government's chief lawyer: head of the Crown Law Office and prosecutor for the Crown.

solicitous (sə'lɪsɪtəs) *adj* **1** showing consideration, concern, attention, etc. **2** keenly anxious or willing; eager. [C16: from Latin *sollicitus* anxious; see SOLICIT] ▸ **so'licitously** *adv* ▸ **so'licitousness** *n*

solicitude (sə'lɪsɪˌtjuːd) *n* **1** the state or quality of being solicitous. **2** (*often pl*) something that causes anxiety or concern. **3** anxiety or concern.

solid ('sɒlɪd) *adj* **1** of, concerned with, or being a substance in a physical state in which it resists changes in size and shape. Compare **liquid** (sense 1), **gas** (sense 1). **2** consisting of matter all through. **3** of the same substance all through: *solid rock.* **4** sound; proved or provable: *solid facts.* **5** reliable or sensible; upstanding: *a solid citizen.* **6** firm, strong, compact, or substantial: *a solid table; solid ground.* **7** (of a meal or food) substantial. **8** (*often postpositive*) without interruption or respite; continuous: *solid bombardment.* **9** financially sound or solvent: *a solid institution.* **10** strongly linked or consolidated: *a solid relationship.* **11** *Geometry.* having or relating to three dimensions: *a solid figure; solid geometry.* **12** (of a word composed of two or more other words or elements) written or printed as a single word without a hyphen. **13** *Printing.* with no space or leads between lines of type. **14 solid for.** unanimously in favour of. **15** (of a writer, work, performance, etc.) adequate; sensible. **16** of or having a single uniform colour or tone. **17** *N.Z. informal.* excessive; unreasonably expensive. ◆ *n* **18** *Geometry.* **18a** a closed surface in three-dimensional space. **18b** such a surface together with the volume enclosed by it. **19** a solid substance, such as wood, iron, or diamond. [C14: from Old French *solide,* from Latin *solidus* firm; related to Latin *sollus* whole] ▸ **solidity** (sə'lɪdɪtɪ) *n* ▸ **'solidly** *adv* ▸ **'solidness** *n*

solidago (ˌsɒlɪ'deɪgəʊ) *n, pl* **-gos.** any plant of the chiefly American genus *Solidago,* which includes the goldenrods: family *Compositae* (composites). [C18: via New Latin from Medieval Latin *soldago* a plant reputed to have healing properties, from *soldāre* to strengthen, from Latin *solidāre,* from *solidus* SOLID]

solid angle *n* a geometric surface consisting of lines originating from a common point (the vertex) and passing through a closed curve or polygon: measured in steradians.

solidarity (ˌsɒlɪ'dærɪtɪ) *n, pl* **-ties.** unity of interests, sympathies, etc., as among members of the same class.

Solidarity (ˌsɒlɪ'dærɪtɪ) *n* the organization of free trade unions in Poland: recognized in 1980; outlawed in 1982; legalized and led the new noncommunist government in 1989. [C20: from Polish *solidarność:* solidarity]

solidary ('sɒlɪdərɪ, -drɪ) *adj* marked by unity of interests, responsibilities, etc. [C19: from French *solidaire,* from *solide* SOLID]

solid fuel *n* **1** a domestic or industrial fuel, such as coal or coke, that is a solid rather than an oil or gas. **2** Also called: **solid propellant.** a rocket fuel that is a solid rather than a liquid or a gas.

solid geometry *n* the branch of geometry concerned with the properties of three-dimensional geometric figures.

solidify (sə'lɪdɪˌfaɪ) *vb* **-fies, -fying, -fied. 1** to make or become solid or hard. **2** to make or become strong, united, determined, etc. ▸ **so'lidiˌfiable** *adj* ▸ **soˌlidifi'cation** *n* ▸ **so'lidiˌfier** *n*

solid injection *n* injection of fuel directly into the cylinder of an internal-combustion engine without the assistance of an air blast to atomize the fuel. Also called (in a petrol engine): **direct injection.** Compare **blast injection.**

solid solution *n Chem.* a crystalline material in which two or more elements or compounds share a common lattice.

solid-state *n* **1** (*modifier*) (of an electronic device) activated by a semiconductor component in which current flow is through solid material rather than in a vacuum. **2** (*modifier*) of, concerned with, characteristic of, or consisting of solid matter.

solid-state physics *n* (*functioning as sing*) the branch of physics concerned with experimental and theoretical investigations of the properties of solids, such as superconductivity, photoconductivity, and ferromagnetism.

solidus ('sɒlɪdəs) *n, pl* **-di** (-ˌdaɪ). **1** Also called: **diagonal, separatrix, shilling mark, slash, stroke, virgule.** a short oblique stroke used in text to separate items of information, such as days, months, and years in dates (*18/7/80*), alternative words (*and/or*), numerator from denominator in fractions (*55/103*), etc. **2** a gold coin of the Byzantine empire. [C14: from Late Latin *solidus* (*nummus*) a gold coin (from *solidus* solid); in Medieval Latin, *solidus* referred to a shilling and was indicated by a long *s,* which ultimately became the virgule]

solifidian (ˌsɒlɪ'fɪdɪən) *n Christianity.* a person who maintains that man is justified by faith alone. [C16: from New Latin *sōlifidius,* from Latin *sōlus* sole + *fides* faith] ▸ **ˌsoli'fidianˌism** *n*

solifluction *or* **solifluxion** ('sɒlɪˌflʌkʃən, 'səʊlɪ-) *n* slow downhill movement of soil, saturated with meltwater, over a permanently frozen subsoil in tundra regions. [C20: from Latin *solum* soil + *fluctio* act of flowing]

Solihull (ˌsəʊlɪ'hʌl) *n* **1** a town in central England, in Solihull unitary authority in the S West Midlands near Birmingham: mainly residential. Pop.: 94 531 (1991). **2** a unitary authority in central England, in the West Midlands. Pop.: 202 900 (1995 est.). Area: 180 sq. km (70 sq. miles).

soliloquize *or* **soliloquise** (sə'lɪləˌkwaɪz) *vb* (*intr*) to utter a soliloquy. ▸ **soliloquist** (sə'lɪləkwɪst) *or* **so'liloˌquizer** *or* **so'liloˌquiser** *n*

soliloquy (sə'lɪləkwɪ) *n, pl* **-quies. 1** the act of speaking alone or to oneself, esp. as a theatrical device. **2** a speech in a play that is spoken in soliloquy: *Hamlet's first soliloquy.* [C17: via Late Latin *sōliloquium,* from Latin *sōlus* sole + *loquī* to speak]

USAGE *Soliloquy* is sometimes wrongly used where *monologue* is meant. Both words refer to a long speech by one person, but a *monologue* can be addressed to other people, whereas in a *soliloquy* the speaker is always talking to himself or herself.

Soliman ('sɒlɪmən) *n* a variant spelling of **Suleiman I.**

Solimões (suli'mõəʃ) *n* **the.** the Brazilian name for the Amazon from the Peruvian border to the Rio Negro.

Solingen (*German* 'zoːlɪŋən) *n* a city in W Germany, in North Rhine-Westphalia: a major European centre of the cutlery industry. Pop.: 165 735 (1996 est.).

solipsism ('sɒlɪpˌsɪzəm) *n Philosophy.* the extreme form of scepticism which denies the possibility of any knowledge other than of one's own existence. [C19: from Latin *sōlus* alone + *ipse* self] ▸ **'solipsist** *n, adj* ▸ **ˌsolip'sistic** *adj*

solitaire ('sɒlɪˌtɛə, ˌsɒlɪ'tɛə) *n* **1** Also called: **pegboard.** a game played by one person, esp. one involving moving and taking pegs in a pegboard or marbles on an indented circular board with the object of being left with only one. **2** the U.S. name for **patience** (the card game). **3** a gem, esp. a diamond, set alone in a ring. **4** any of several extinct birds of the genus *Pezophaps,* related to the dodo.

5 any of several dull grey North American songbirds of the genus *Myadestes:* subfamily *Turdinae* (thrushes). [C18: from Old French: SOLITARY]

solitary ('sɒlɪtərɪ, -trɪ) *adj* **1** following or enjoying a life of solitude: *a solitary disposition.* **2** experienced or performed alone: *a solitary walk.* **3** (of a place) unfrequented. **4** (*prenominal*) single; sole: *a solitary speck in the sky.* **5** having few companions; lonely. **6** (of animals) not living in organized colonies or large groups: *solitary bees; a solitary elephant.* Compare **social** (sense 7), **gregarious** (sense 2). **7** (of flowers) growing singly. ◆ *n, pl* **-taries. 8** a person who lives in seclusion; hermit; recluse. **9** *Informal.* short for **solitary confinement.** [C14: from Latin *sōlitārius,* from *sōlus* SOLE[1]] ► **'solitarily** *adv* ► **'solitariness** *n*

solitary confinement *n* isolation imposed on a prisoner, as by confinement in a special cell.

soliton ('sɒlɪ,tɒn) *n Physics.* an isolated particle-like wave that is a solution of certain equations for propagation, occurring when two solitary waves do not change their form after collision and subsequently travelling for considerable distances. [C20: from *solitary* + -ON]

solitude ('sɒlɪ,tjuːd) *n* **1** the state of being solitary or secluded. **2** *Poetic.* a solitary place. [C14: from Latin *sōlitūdō,* from *sōlus* alone, SOLE[1]] ► **,soli'tudinous** *adj*

solleret (,sɒlə'rɛt) *n* a protective covering for the foot consisting of riveted plates of armour. [C19: from French, diminutive of Old French *soller* shoe, from Late Latin *subtēl* arch beneath the foot, from SUB- + *tālus* ankle]

sollicker ('sɒlɪkə) *n Austral. slang.* something very large. [C19: from English dialect]

solmization *or* **solmisation** (,sɒlmɪ'zeɪʃən) *n Music.* a system of naming the notes of a scale by syllables instead of letters derived from the 11th-century hexachord system of Guido d'Arezzo, which assigns the names *ut* (or *do*), *re, mi, fa, sol, la, si* (or *ti*) to the degrees of the major scale of C (**fixed system**) or (excluding the syllables *ut* and *si*) to the major scale in any key (**movable system**). See also **tonic sol-fa.** [C18: from French *solmisation,* from *solmiser* to use the sol-fa syllables, from SOL[1] + MI]

solo ('səʊləʊ) *n, pl* **-los. 1** (*pl* **-los** *or* **-li** (-liː)) a musical composition for one performer with or without accompaniment. **2** any of various card games in which each person plays on his own instead of in partnership with another, such as solo whist. **3** a flight in which an aircraft pilot is unaccompanied. **4a** any performance, mountain climb, or other undertaking carried out by an individual without assistance from others. **4b** (*as modifier*): *a solo attempt.* ◆ *adj* **5** *Music.* unaccompanied: *a sonata for cello solo.* ◆ *adv* **6** by oneself; alone: *to fly solo.* ◆ *vb* **7** to undertake a venture alone, esp. to operate an aircraft alone or climb alone. [C17: via Italian from Latin *sōlus* alone, SOLE[1]]

soloist ('səʊləʊɪst) *n* a person who performs a solo.

Solo man *n* a type of early man, *Homo soloensis,* of late Pleistocene times, having a skull resembling that of Neanderthal man but with a smaller cranial capacity. [C20: after *Solo,* site in central Java where remains were found]

Solomon ('sɒləmən) *n* 10th century B.C., king of Israel, son of David and Bathsheba, credited with great wisdom. ► **Solomonic** (,sɒlə'mɒnɪk) *or* **Solomonian** (,sɒlə'məʊnɪən) *adj*

Solomon Islands *pl n* an independent state in the SW Pacific comprising an archipelago extending for almost 1450 km (900 miles) in a northwest–southeast direction: the northernmost islands of the archipelago (Buka and Bougainville) form part of Papua New Guinea; the main islands are Guadalcanal, Malaita, San Cristobal, New Georgia, Santa Isabel, and Choiseul: a member of the Commonwealth. Official language: English. Religion: Christian majority. Currency: Solomon Islands dollar. Capital: Honiara. Pop.: 426 000 (1998 est.). Area: 29 785 sq. km (11 500 sq. miles).

Solomon Islands Pidgin *n* the variety of Neo-Melanesian spoken in the Solomon Islands and neighbouring islands.

Solomon's seal *n* **1** another name for **Star of David. 2** any of several liliaceous plants of the genus *Polygonatum* of N temperate regions, having greenish or yellow paired flowers, long narrow waxy leaves, and a thick underground stem with prominent leaf scars. [C16: translation of Medieval Latin *sigillum Solomonis,* perhaps referring to the resemblance of the leaf scars to seals]

solo mother *n N.Z.* a mother with a dependent child or dependent children and no husband.

Solon ('səʊlɒn) *n* ?638–?559 B.C., Athenian statesman, who introduced economic, political, and legal reforms. ► **Solonian** (səʊ'ləʊnɪən) *or* **Solonic** (səʊ'lɒnɪk) *adj*

solonchak (,sɒlən'tʃæk) *n* a type of intrazonal soil of arid regions with a greyish surface crust: contains large quantities of soluble salts. [Russian, literally: salt marsh]

solonetz *or* **solonets** (,sɒlə'nɛts) *n* a type of intrazonal soil with a high saline content characterized by leaching. [Russian *solonets* salt not obtained through decoction]

so long *sentence substitute. Informal.* farewell; goodbye.

solo parent *n N.Z.* the usual name for **single parent.**

solo stop *n* any of various organ stops designed to imitate a solo performance on a particular musical instrument.

Solothurn (*German* 'zoːlotʊrn) *n* **1** a canton of NW Switzerland. Capital: Solothurn. Pop.: 239 264 (1996 est.). Area: 793 sq. km (306 sq. miles). **2** a town in NW Switzerland, capital of Solothurn canton, on the Aare River. Pop.: 15 480 (1990 est.). ◆ French name: **Soleure.**

solo whist *n* a version of whist for four players acting independently, each of whom may bid to win or lose a fixed number of tricks before play starts, trumps having usually been decided by cutting.

solstice ('sɒlstɪs) *n* **1** either the shortest day of the year (**winter solstice**) or the longest day of the year (**summer solstice**). **2** either of the two points on the ecliptic at which the sun is overhead at the tropic of Cancer or Capricorn at the summer and winter solstices. [C13: via Old French from Latin *sōlstitium,* literally: the (apparent) standing still of the sun, from *sōl* sun + *sistere* to stand still] ► **solstitial** (sɒl'stɪʃəl) *adj*

Solti ('ʃɒltɪ) *n* Sir **Georg** ('geːɔrk). 1912–97, British conductor, born in Hungary.

solubility (,sɒljʊ'bɪlɪtɪ) *n, pl* **-ties. 1** the ability of a substance to dissolve; the quality of being soluble. **2** a measure of this ability for a particular substance in a particular solvent, equal to the quantity of substance dissolving in a fixed quantity of solvent to form a saturated solution under specified temperature and pressure. It is expressed in grams per cubic decametre, grams per hundred grams of solvent, moles per mole, etc.

solubilize *or* **solubilise** ('sɒljʊbɪ,laɪz) *vb* to make or become soluble, as in the addition of detergents to fats to make them dissolve in water.

soluble ('sɒljʊb[ə]l) *adj* **1** (of a substance) capable of being dissolved, esp. easily dissolved in some solvent, usually water. **2** capable of being solved or answered. [C14: from Late Latin *solūbilis,* from Latin *solvere* to dissolve] ► **'solubleness** *n* ► **'solubly** *adv*

soluble glass *n* another name for **sodium silicate** (sense 1).

soluble RNA *n* another name for **transfer RNA.**

solum ('səʊləm) *n, pl* **-lums** *or* **-la** (-lə). the upper layers of the soil profile, affected by climate and vegetation. [C19: New Latin from Latin: the ground]

solus ('səʊləs) *adj* **1** alone; separate. **2** of or denoting the position of an advertising poster or press advertisement that is separated from competing advertisements: *a solus position.* **3** of or denoting a retail outlet, such as a petrol station, that sells the products of one company exclusively: *a solus site.* **4** (*fem* **sola**) alone; by oneself (formerly used in stage directions). [C17: from Latin *sōlus* alone]

solute (sɒ'ljuːt) *n* **1** the component of a solution that changes its state in forming the solution or the component that is not present in excess; the substance that is dissolved in another substance. Compare **solvent.** ◆ *adj* **2** *Botany.* loose or unattached; free. [C16: from Latin *solūtus* free, unfettered, from *solvere* to release]

solution (sə'luːʃən) *n* **1** a homogeneous mixture of two or more substances in which the molecules or atoms of the substances are completely dispersed. The constituents can be solids, liquids, or gases. **2** the act or process of forming a solution. **3** the state of being dissolved (esp. in the phrase **in solution**). **4** a mixture of two or more substances in which one or more components are present as small particles with colloidal dimension; colloid: *a colloidal solution.* **5** a specific answer to or way of answering a problem. **6** the act or process of solving a problem. **7** *Maths.* **7a** the unique set of values that yield a true statement when substituted for the variables in an equation. **7b** a member of a set of assignments of values to variables under which a given statement is satisfied; a member of a solution set. **8** the stage of a disease, following a crisis, resulting in its termination. **9** *Law.* the payment, discharge, or satisfaction of a claim, debt, etc. [C14: from Latin *solūtiō* an unloosing, from *solūtus;* see SOLUTE]

solution set *n* another name for **truth set.**

Solutrean (sə'luːtrɪən) *adj* of or relating to an Upper Palaeolithic culture of Europe that was characterized by leaf-shaped flint blades. [C19: named after *Solutré,* village in central France where traces of this culture were originally found]

solvable ('sɒlvəb[ə]l) *adj* another word for **soluble** (sense 2). ► **,solva'bility** *or* **'solvableness** *n*

solvate ('sɒlveɪt) *vb Chem.* to undergo, cause to undergo, or partake in solvation. [C20: from SOLVENT]

solvation (sɒl'veɪʃən) *n* the process in which there is some chemical association between the molecules of a solute and those of the solvent. An example is an aqueous solution of copper sulphate which contains complex ions of the type $[Cu(H_2O)_4]^{2+}$.

Solvay process ('sɒlveɪ) *n* an industrial process for manufacturing sodium carbonate. Carbon dioxide is passed into a solution of sodium chloride saturated with ammonia. Sodium bicarbonate is precipitated and heated to form the carbonate. [C19: named after Ernest *Solvay* (1838–1922), Belgian chemist who invented it]

solve (sɒlv) *vb* (*tr*) **1** to find the explanation for or solution to (a mystery, problem, etc.). **2** *Maths.* **2a** to work out the answer to (a problem). **2b** to obtain the roots of (an equation). [C15: from Latin *solvere* to loosen, release, free from debt] ► **'solver** *n*

solvency ('sɒlvənsɪ) *n* ability to pay all debts.

solvent ('sɒlvənt) *adj* **1** capable of meeting financial obligations. **2** (of a substance, esp. a liquid) capable of dissolving another substance. ◆ *n* **3** a liquid capable of dissolving another substance: *water is a solvent for salt.* **4** the component of a solution that does not change its state in forming the solution or the component that is present in excess. Compare **solute. 5** something that solves. [C17: from Latin *solvēns* releasing, from *solvere* to free, SOLVE] ► **'solvently** *adv*

solvent abuse *n* the deliberate inhaling of intoxicating fumes given off by certain solvents such as toluene. See also **glue-sniffing.**

solvolysis (sɒl'vɒlɪsɪs) *n* a chemical reaction occurring between a dissolved substance and its solvent. See also **hydrolysis.** [from SOLV(ENT) + -LYSIS]

Solway Firth ('sɒlweɪ) *n* an inlet of the Irish Sea between SW Scotland and NW England. Length: about 56 km (35 miles).

Solyman ('sɒlɪmən) *n* a variant spelling of **Suleiman I.**

Solzhenitsyn (,sɒlʒə'nɪtsɪn; *Russian* səlʒə'nitsin) *n* **Alexander Isayevich** (alɪk'sandr i'sajɪvitʃ). born 1918, Russian novelist. His books include *One Day in the Life of Ivan Denisovich* (1962), *The First Circle* (1968), *Cancer Ward* (1968), *August 1914* (1971), *The Gulag Archipelago* (1974), and *October 1916* (1985). His works criticize the Soviet regime and he was imprisoned (1945–53) and exiled to Siberia (1953–56). He was deported to the West from the Soviet

Union in 1974; all charges against him were dropped in 1991 and he returned to Russia in 1994. Nobel prize for literature 1970.

som (sɒm) *n* the standard monetary unit of Kyrgyzstan, divided into 100 tyiyn.

Som. *abbrev. for* Somerset.

soma[1] ('səʊmə) *n, pl* **-mata** (-mətə) *or* **-mas.** the body of an organism, esp. an animal, as distinct from the germ cells. [C19: via New Latin from Greek *sōma* the body]

soma[2] ('səʊmə) *n* an intoxicating plant juice drink used in Vedic rituals. [from Sanskrit]

somaesthesia, *U.S.* **somesthesia** (ˌsɒmɪs'θiːzɪə), *or* **somaesthesis,** *U.S.* **somesthesis** (ˌsɒmɪs'θiːsɪs) *n* sensory perception of bodily feelings like touch, pain, position of the limbs, etc. [C20: from Greek *sōma* body + AESTHESIA] ▸ **somaesthetic** *or U.S.* **somesthetic** (ˌsɒmɪs'θɛtɪk) *adj*

Somali (səʊ'mɑːlɪ) *n* **1** (*pl* **-lis** *or* **-li**) a member of a tall dark-skinned people inhabiting Somalia. **2** the language of this people, belonging to the Cushitic subfamily of the Afro-Asiatic family of languages. ◆ *adj* **3** of, relating to, or characteristic of Somalia, the Somalis, or their language.

Somalia (səʊ'mɑːlɪə) *n* a republic in NE Africa, on the Indian Ocean and the Gulf of Aden: the north became a British protectorate in 1884; the east and south were established as an Italian protectorate in 1889; gained independence and united as the Somali Republic in 1960. In 1991 the former British Somaliland region in the north unilaterally declared itself independent as the Republic of Somaliland but this has not been recognized officially. Official languages: Arabic and Somali. Official religion: (Sunni) Muslim. Currency: Somali shilling. Capital: Mogadishu. Pop.: 6 842 000 (1998 est.). Area: 637 541 sq. km (246 154 sq. miles). ▸ **So'malian** *adj, n*

Somaliland (səʊ'mɑːlɪˌlænd) *n* a former region of E Africa, between the equator and the Gulf of Aden: includes Somalia, Djibouti, and SE Ethiopia.

somatic (səʊ'mætɪk) *adj* **1** of or relating to the soma: *somatic cells.* **2** of or relating to an animal body or body wall as distinct from the viscera, limbs, and head. **3** of or relating to the human body as distinct from the mind: *a somatic disease.* [C18: from Greek *sōmatikos* concerning the body, from *sōma* the body] ▸ **so'matically** *adv*

somatic cell *n* any of the cells of a plant or animal except the reproductive cells. Compare **germ cell.**

somatic nervous system *n Physiol.* the section of the nervous system responsible for sensation and control of the skeletal muscles. Compare **autonomic nervous system.**

somato- *or before a vowel* **somat-** *combining form.* body: *somatoplasm.* [from Greek *sōma, sōmat-* body]

somatogenic (səˌmætəʊ'dʒɛnɪk) *adj Med.* originating in the cells of the body: of organic, rather than mental, origin: *a somatogenic disorder.*

somatology (ˌsəʊmə'tɒlədʒɪ) *n* **1** the branch of biology concerned with the structure and function of the body. **2** the branch of anthropology dealing with the physical characteristics of man. ▸ **somatologic** (ˌsəʊmətə'lɒdʒɪk) *or* ˌ**somato'logical** *adj* ▸ ˌ**somato'logically** *adv* ▸ ˌ**soma'tologist** *n*

somatomedin (ˌsəʊmətə'miːdɪn) *n* a protein hormone that promotes tissue growth under the influence of growth hormone. [C20: from SOMATO- + Latin *medius* middle + -IN]

somatoplasm ('səʊmətəˌplæzəm) *n Biology.* **a** the protoplasm of a somatic cell. **b** the somatic cells collectively. Compare **germ plasm.** ▸ ˌ**somato'plastic** *adj*

somatopleure ('səʊmətəˌpluə, -ˌplɜː) *n* a mass of tissue in embryo vertebrates that is formed by fusion of the ectoderm with the outer layer of mesoderm: develops into the amnion, chorion, and part of the body wall. [C19: from New Latin *somatopleura,* from SOMATO- + Greek *pleura* a side] ▸ ˌ**somato'pleural** *or* ˌ**somato'pleuric** *adj*

somatostatin (ˌsəʊmətə'stætɪn) *n* a peptide hormone that prevents the release of growth hormone from the pituitary gland. [C20: from SOMATO- + -STAT + -IN]

somatotonia (ˌsəʊmətəʊ'təʊnɪə) *n* a personality type characterized by assertiveness and energy: said to be correlated with a mesomorph body type. Compare **cerebrotonia, viscerotonia.**

somatotrophin (ˌsəʊmətəʊ'trəʊfɪn) *or* **somatotropin** (ˌsəʊmətəʊ'trəʊpɪn) *n* other names for **growth hormone.** ▸ ˌ**somato'trophic** *or* ˌ**somato'tropic** *adj*

somatotype ('səʊmətəˌtaɪp) *n* a type or classification of physique or body build. See **endomorph, mesomorph, ectomorph.**

sombre *or U.S.* **somber** ('sɒmbə) *adj* **1** dismal; melancholy: *a sombre mood.* **2** dim, gloomy, or shadowy. **3** (of colour, clothes, etc.) sober, dull, or dark. [C18: from French, from Vulgar Latin *subumbrāre* (unattested) to shade, from Latin *sub* beneath + *umbra* shade] ▸ **'sombrely** *or U.S.* **'somberly** *adv* ▸ **'sombreness** *or U.S.* **'somberness** *n* ▸ **sombrous** ('sɒmbrəs) *adj*

sombrero (sɒm'brɛərəʊ) *n, pl* **-ros.** a felt or straw hat with a wide brim, as worn by men in Mexico. [C16: from Spanish, from *sombrero de sol* shade from the sun]

some (sʌm; *unstressed* səm) *determiner* **1a** (a) certain unknown or unspecified: *some lunatic drove into my car; some people never learn.* **1b** (*as pronoun; functioning as sing or pl*): *some can teach and others can't.* **2a** an unknown or unspecified quantity or amount of: *there's some rice on the table; he owns some horses.* **2b** (*as pronoun; functioning as sing or pl*): *we'll buy some.* **3a** a considerable number or amount of: *he lived some years afterwards.* **3b** a little: *show him some respect.* **4** (*usually stressed*) *Informal.* an impressive or remarkable: *that was some game!* **5** a certain amount (more) (in the phrases **some more** and (informal) **and then some**). **6** about; approximately: *he owes me some thirty pounds.* ◆ *adv* **7** *U.S., not standard.* to a certain degree or extent: *I guess I like him some.* [Old English *sum;* related to Old Norse *sumr,* Gothic *sums,* Old High German *sum* some, Sanskrit *samá* any, Greek *hamē* somehow]

-some[1] *suffix forming adjectives.* characterized by; tending to: *awesome; tiresome.* [Old English *-sum;* related to Gothic *-sama,* German *-sam*]

-some[2] *suffix forming nouns.* indicating a group of a specified number of members: *threesome.* [Old English *sum,* special use of SOME (determiner)]

-some[3] (-səʊm) *n combining form.* a body: *chromosome.* [from Greek *sōma* body]

somebody ('sʌmbədɪ) *pron* **1** some person; someone. ◆ *n, pl* **-bodies. 2** a person of greater importance than others: *he is somebody in this town.*

USAGE See at **everyone.**

someday ('sʌmˌdeɪ) *adv* at some unspecified time in the (distant) future.

somehow ('sʌmˌhaʊ) *adv* **1** in some unspecified way. **2** Also: **somehow or other.** by any means that are necessary.

someone ('sʌmˌwʌn, -wən) *pron* some person; somebody.

USAGE See at **everyone.**

someplace ('sʌmˌpleɪs) *adv U.S. and Canadian informal.* in, at, or to some unspecified place or region.

somersault *or* **summersault** ('sʌməˌsɔːlt) *n* **1a** a forward roll in which the head is placed on the ground and the trunk and legs are turned over it. **1b** a similar roll in a backward direction. **2** an acrobatic feat in which either of these rolls are performed in midair, as in diving or gymnastics. **3** a complete reversal of opinion, policy, etc. ◆ *vb* **4** (*intr*) to perform a somersault. [C16: from Old French *soubresault,* probably from Old Provençal *sobresaut,* from *sobre* over (from Latin *super*) + *saut* a jump, leap (from Latin *saltus*)]

Somerset[1] ('sʌməsɪt, -ˌset) *n* a county of SW England, on the Bristol Channel: the Mendip Hills lie in the north and Exmoor in the west: the geographical and ceremonial county includes the unitary authorities of North Somerset and Bath and North East Somerset (both part of Avon county from 1975 until 1996): mainly agricultural (esp. dairying and fruit). Administrative centre: Taunton. Pop. (including unitary authorities): 680 925 (1996 est.). Area (including unitary authorities: 4196 sq. km (1620 sq. miles).

Somerset[2] ('sʌməset) *n* **1st Duke of,** title of *Edward Seymour.* ?1500–52, English statesman, protector of England (1547–49) during Edward VI's minority. He defeated the Scots (1547) and furthered the Protestant Reformation: executed.

Somerset House *n* a building in London, in the Strand, built (1776–86) by Sir William Chambers; formerly housed the General Register Office of births, marriages, and deaths: contains (from 1990) the art collections of the Courtauld Institute.

Somerville ('sʌməvɪl) *n* **Mary,** original name *Mary Fairfax.* 1780–1872, British scientific writer, author of *Physical Geography* (1848) and other textbooks. Somerville College, Oxford, was named after her.

something ('sʌmθɪŋ) *pron* **1** an unspecified or unknown thing; some thing: *he knows something you don't; take something warm with you.* **2 something or other.** one unspecified thing or an alternative thing. **3** an unspecified or unknown amount; bit: *something less than a hundred.* **4** an impressive or important person, thing, or event: *isn't that something?* ◆ *adv* **5** to some degree; a little; somewhat: *to look something like me.* **6** (*foll. by an adj*) *Informal.* (intensifier): *it hurts something awful.*

-something *n combining form.* **a** a person whose age can be approximately expressed by a specified decade. **b** (*as modifier*): *the thirtysomething market.* [C20: from the U.S. television series *thirtysomething*]

sometime ('sʌmˌtaɪm) *adv* **1** at some unspecified point of time. ◆ *adj* **2** (*prenominal*) having been at one time; former: *the sometime President.* **3** (*prenominal*) *Archaic or U.S.* occasional; infrequent.

USAGE The form *sometime* should not be used to refer to a fairly long period of time: *he has been away for some time* (not *for sometime*).

sometimes ('sʌmˌtaɪmz) *adv* **1** now and then; from time to time; occasionally. **2** *Obsolete.* formerly; sometime.

someway ('sʌmˌweɪ) *adv* in some unspecified manner.

somewhat ('sʌmˌwɒt) *adv* (*not used with a negative*) rather; a bit: *she found it somewhat less easy than he.*

somewhere ('sʌmˌwɛə) *adv* **1** in, to, or at some unknown or unspecified place or point: *somewhere in England; somewhere between 3 and 4 o'clock.* **2 get somewhere.** *Informal.* to make progress.

somewise ('sʌmˌwaɪz) *adv* in some way or to some degree; somehow (archaic, except in the phrase **in somewise**). [C15: from SOME + -WISE]

somite ('səʊmaɪt) *n* **1** *Embryol.* any of a series of dorsal paired segments of mesoderm occurring along the notochord in vertebrate embryos. It develops into muscle and bone in the adult animal. **2** *Zoology.* another name for **metamere.** [C19: from Greek *sōma* a body] ▸ **somital** ('səʊmɪtᵊl) *or* **somitic** (səʊ'mɪtɪk) *adj*

Somme (*French* sɔm) *n* **1** a department of N France, in Picardy region. Capital: Amiens. Pop.: 553 100 (1995). Area: 6277 sq. km (2448 sq. miles). **2** a river in N France, rising in Aisne department and flowing west to Amiens, then northwest to the English Channel: scene of heavy fighting in World War I. Length: 245 km (152 miles).

sommelier ('sʌməlˌjeɪ) *n* a wine steward in a restaurant or hotel. [French: butler, via Old French from Old Provençal *saumalier* pack-animal driver, from Late Latin *sagma* a packsaddle, from Greek]

somnambulate (sɒm'næmbjuˌleɪt) *vb* (*intr*) to walk while asleep. [C19: from Latin *somnus* sleep + *ambulāre* to walk] ▸ **som'nambulance** *n* ▸ **som'nambulant** *adj, n* ▸ **somˌnambu'lation** *n* ▸ **som'nambuˌlator** *n*

somnambulism (sɒm'næmbjuˌlɪzəm) *n* a condition that is characterized by walking while asleep or in a hypnotic trance. Also called: **noctambulism.** ▸ **som'nambulist** *n* ▸ **somˌnambu'listic** *adj*

somni- *or before a vowel* **somn-** *combining form.* sleep: *somniferous.* [from Latin *somnus*]

somniferous (sɒmˈnɪfərəs) *or* **somnific** *adj Rare.* tending to induce sleep. [C17: from Latin *somnifer* (from *somnus* sleep + *ferre* to do) + -OUS] ▸ **somˈniferously** *adv*

somniloquy (sɒmˈnɪləkwɪ) *n, pl* **-quies.** *Rare.* the act of talking in one's sleep. [C19: from Latin *somnus* sleep + *loqui* to speak; compare SOLILOQUY] ▸ **somˈniloquist** *n* ▸ **somˈniloquous** *adj*

somnolent (ˈsɒmnələnt) *adj* **1** drowsy; sleepy. **2** causing drowsiness. [C15: from Latin *somnus* sleep] ▸ **ˈsomnolence** *or* **ˈsomnolency** *n* ▸ **ˈsomnolently** *adv*

Somnus (ˈsɒmnəs) *n* the Roman god of sleep. Greek counterpart: **Hypnos.**

son (sʌn) *n* **1** a male offspring; a boy or man in relation to his parents. **2** a male descendant. **3** (*often cap.*) a familiar term of address for a boy or man. **4** a male from a certain country, place, etc., or one closely connected with a certain environment: *a son of the circus.* ◆ Related adj: **filial.** [Old English *sunu;* related to Old Norse *sunr,* Gothic *sunus,* Old High German *sunu,* Lithuanian *sūnus,* Sanskrit *sūnu*] ▸ **ˈsonless** *adj* ▸ **ˈsonˌlike** *adj*

Son (sʌn) *n Christianity.* the second person of the Trinity, Jesus Christ.

sonant (ˈsəʊnənt) *adj* **1** *Phonetics.* denoting a voiced sound capable of forming a syllable or syllable nucleus. **2** inherently possessing, exhibiting, or producing a sound. ◆ *n* **3** *Phonetics.* a voiced sound belonging to the class of frictionless continuants or nasals (l, r, m, n, ŋ) considered from the point of view of being a vowel and, in this capacity, able to form a syllable or syllable nucleus. [C19: from Latin *sonāns* sounding, from *sonāre* to make a noise, resound] ▸ **ˈsonance** *n* ▸ **sonantal** (səʊˈnæntᵊl) *or* **soˈnantic** *adj*

sonar (ˈsəʊnɑː) *n* a communication and position-finding device used in underwater navigation and target detection using echolocation. [C20: from *so(und) na(vigation and) r(anging)*]

sonata (səˈnɑːtə) *n* **1** an instrumental composition, usually in three or more movements, for piano alone (**piano sonata**) or for any other instrument with or without piano accompaniment (**violin sonata, cello sonata,** etc.). See also **sonata form, symphony** (sense 1), **concerto** (sense 1). **2** a one-movement keyboard composition of the baroque period. [C17: from Italian, from *sonare* to sound, from Latin]

sonata form *n* a musical structure consisting of an expanded ternary form whose three sections (exposition, development, and recapitulation), followed by a coda, are characteristic of the first movement in a sonata, symphony, string quartet, concerto, etc.

sonatina (ˌsɒnəˈtiːnə) *n* a short sonata. [C19: from Italian]

sondage (sɒnˈdɑːʒ) *n, pl* **-dages** (-ˈdɑːʒɪz, -ˈdɑːʒ). *Archaeology.* a deep trial trench for inspecting stratigraphy. [C20: from French: a sounding, from *sonder* to sound]

sonde (sɒnd) *n* a rocket, balloon, or probe used for observing in the upper atmosphere. [C20: from French: plummet, plumb line; see SOUND[3]]

Sondheim (ˈsɒndhaɪm) *n* **Stephen (Joshua).** born 1930, U.S. songwriter. He wrote the lyrics for *West Side Story* (1957), the score for *Company* (1971), and both for *A Little Night Music* (1973) and *Into the Woods* (1987).

sone (səʊn) *n* a unit of loudness equal to 40 phons. [C20: from Latin *sonus* a sound]

son et lumière (ˈsɒn eɪ ˈluːmɪˌɛə; *French* sɔ̃n e lymjɛr) *n* an entertainment staged at night at a famous building, historical site, etc., whereby the history of the location is presented by means of lighting effects, sound effects, and narration. [French, literally: sound and light]

song (sɒŋ) *n* **1a** a piece of music, usually employing a verbal text, composed for the voice, esp. one intended for performance by a soloist. **1b** the whole repertory of such pieces. **1c** (*as modifier*): *a song book.* **2** poetical composition; poetry. **3** the characteristic tuneful call or sound made by certain birds or insects. **4** the act or process of singing: *they raised their voices in song.* **5 for a song.** at a bargain price. **6 on song.** *Brit. informal.* performing at peak efficiency or ability. [Old English *sang;* related to Gothic *saggws,* Old High German *sang;* see SING] ▸ **ˈsongˌlike** *adj*

Song (sʊŋ) *n* the Pinyin transliteration of the Chinese name for **Sung.**

song and dance *n Informal.* **1** *Brit.* a fuss, esp. one that is unnecessary. **2** *U.S. and Canadian.* a long or elaborate story or explanation, esp. one that is evasive.

songbird (ˈsɒŋˌbɜːd) *n* **1** any passerine bird of the suborder *Oscines,* having highly developed vocal organs and, in most, a musical call. Related adj: **oscine. 2** any bird having a musical call.

song cycle *n* any of several groups of songs written by composers during and after the Romantic period, each series employing texts, usually by one poet, relating a story or grouped around a central motif.

song form *n* another name for **ternary form.**

songful (ˈsɒŋfʊl) *adj* tuneful; melodious. ▸ **ˈsongfully** *adv* ▸ **ˈsongfulness** *n*

Songhai (sɒŋˈgaɪ) *n* **1** (*pl* **-ghai** *or* **-ghais**) a member of a Nilotic people of W Africa, living chiefly in Mali and Niger in the central Niger valley. **2** the language or group of dialects spoken by this people, now generally regarded as forming a branch of the Nilo-Saharan family.

Songhua (ˈsʌŋˈwɑː) *n* a river in NE China, rising in SE Jilin province and flowing north and northeast to the Amur River near Tongjiang: the chief river of Manchuria and largest tributary of the Amur; frozen from November to April. Length: over 1300 km (800 miles). Also called: **Sungari.**

Song Koi *or* **Song Coi** (ˈsɒŋ ˈkɔɪ) *n* transliteration of the Vietnamese name for the **Red River** (sense 3).

songkok (ˈsɒŋkɒ) *n* (in Malaysia and Indonesia) a kind of oval brimless hat, resembling a skull. [from Malay]

Song of Solomon *n* **the.** a book of the Old Testament consisting of a collection of dramatic love poems traditionally ascribed to Solomon. Also called: **Song of Songs, Canticle of Canticles.**

songololo (ˌsɒŋgəˈləʊləʊ) *n, pl* **-los.** *S. African.* a millipede, *Jurus terrestris,* having a hard shiny dark brown segmented exoskeleton. [from Nguni *ukusonga* to roll up]

songsmith (ˈsaɒŋˌsmɪθ) *n* a person who writes songs.

song sparrow *n* a common North American finch, *Melospiza melodia,* having brown-and-white plumage and a melodious song.

songster (ˈsɒŋstə) *n* **1** a singer or poet. **2** a singing bird; songbird. ▸ **ˈsongstress** *fem n*

song thrush *n* a common Old World thrush, *Turdus philomelos,* that has a brown back and spotted breast and is noted for its song.

songwriter (ˈsɒŋˌraɪtə) *n* a person who composes the words or music for songs in a popular idiom.

sonic (ˈsɒnɪk) *adj* **1** of, involving, or producing sound. **2** having a speed about equal to that of sound in air: 332 metres per second (743 miles per hour). [C20: from Latin *sonus* sound]

sonic barrier *n* another name for **sound barrier.**

sonic boom *n* a loud explosive sound caused by the shock wave of an aircraft, etc., travelling at supersonic speed.

sonic depth finder *n* an instrument for detecting the depth of water or of a submerged object by means of sound waves; Fathometer. See also **sonar.**

sonics (ˈsɒnɪks) *n* (*functioning as sing*) *Physics.* the study of mechanical vibrations in matter.

soniferous (sɒˈnɪfərəs) *adj* carrying or producing sound.

son-in-law *n, pl* **sons-in-law.** the husband of one's daughter.

sonnet (ˈsɒnɪt) *Prosody.* ◆ *n* **1** a verse form of Italian origin consisting of 14 lines in iambic pentameter with rhymes arranged according to a fixed scheme, usually divided either into octave and sestet or, in the English form, into three quatrains and a couplet. ◆ *vb* **2** (*intr*) to compose sonnets. **3** (*tr*) to celebrate in a sonnet. [C16: via Italian from Old Provençal *sonet* a little poem, from *son* song, from Latin *sonus* a sound]

sonneteer (ˌsɒnɪˈtɪə) *n* a writer of sonnets.

sonny (ˈsʌnɪ) *n, pl* **-nies.** *Often patronizing.* a familiar term of address to a boy or man. [C19: from SON + -Y[2]]

sonobuoy (ˈsəʊnəˌbɔɪ) *n* a buoy equipped to detect underwater noises and transmit them by radio. [from SONIC + BUOY]

son of a bitch *n, pl* **sons of bitches.** *Slang, chiefly U.S. and Canadian.* **1** a worthless or contemptible person: used as an insult. **2** a humorous or affectionate term for a person, esp. a man: *a lucky son of a bitch.*

son of a gun *n, pl* **sons of guns.** *Slang, chiefly U.S. and Canadian.* a rogue or rascal: used as a jocular form of address.

son of God *n Bible.* **1** an angelic being. **2** a Christian believer.

Son of Man *n Bible.* a title of Jesus Christ.

sonogram (ˈsəʊnəˌgræm) *n Physics.* a three-dimensional representation of a sound signal, using coordinates of frequency, time, and intensity.

Sonora (*Spanish* soˈnora) *n* a state of NW Mexico, on the Gulf of California: consists of a narrow coastal plain rising inland to the Sierra Madre Occidental; an important mining area in colonial times. Capital: Hermosillo. Pop.: 2 083 630 (1995 est.). Area: 184 934 sq. km (71 403 sq. miles).

sonorant (ˈsɒnərənt) *n Phonetics.* **1** one of the frictionless continuants or nasals (l, r, m, n, ŋ) having consonantal or vocalic functions depending on its situation within the syllable. **2** either of the two consonants represented in English orthography by *w* or *y* and regarded as either consonantal or vocalic articulations of the vowels (iː) and (uː). [from Latin *sonor* a noise + -ANT]

sonorous (səˈnɔːrəs, ˈsɒnərəs) *adj* **1** producing or capable of producing sound. **2** (of language, sound, etc.) deep or resonant. **3** (esp. of speech) high-flown; grandiloquent. [C17: from Latin *sonōrus* loud, from *sonor* a noise] ▸ **sonority** (səˈnɒrɪtɪ) *n* ▸ **soˈnorously** *adv* ▸ **soˈnorousness** *n*

Sons of Freedom *pl n* a Doukhobor sect, located largely in British Columbia: notorious for its acts of terrorism in opposition to the government in the 1950s and 1960s. Also called: **Freedomites.**

sonsy *or* **sonsie** (ˈsɒnsɪ) *adj* **-sier, -siest.** *Scot., Irish, and English dialect.* **1** plump; buxom; comely. **2** cheerful; good-natured. **3** lucky. [C16: from Gaelic *sonas* good fortune]

Sontag (ˈsɒntæg) *n* **Susan.** born 1933, U.S. intellectual and essayist, noted esp. for her writings on modern culture. Her works include 'Notes on Camp' (1964), 'Against Interpretation' (1968), *On Photography* (1977), *Illness as Metaphor* (1978), and the novel *The Volcano Lover* (1992).

Soo Canals (suː) *pl n* **the.** the two ship canals linking Lakes Superior and Huron. There is a canal on the Canadian and on the U.S. side of the rapids of the St Mary's River. See also **Sault Sainte Marie.**

Soochow (ˈsuːˈtʃaʊ) *n* a variant transliteration of the Chinese name for **Suzhou.**

sook[1] (sʊk) *n* **1** *Southwest English dialect.* a baby. **2** *Derogatory.* a coward. **3** *N.Z. informal.* a calf. [perhaps from Old English *sūcan* to suck, influenced by Welsh *swci swead* tame]

sook[2] *or* **souk** (suːk) *Scot.* ◆ *vb* **1** to suck. ◆ *n* **2** the act or an instance of sucking. **3** a sycophant; toady. [Old English *sūcan*]

sool (suːl) *vb* (*tr*) to incite (a dog) to attack. [C17: from English dialect *sowl* (esp. of a dog) to pull or seize roughly]

soon (suːn) *adv* **1** in or after a short time; in a little while; before long: *the doctor will soon be here.* **2 as soon as.** at the very moment that: *she burst into tears as soon as she saw him.* **3 as soon…as.** used to indicate that the second alternative mentioned is not preferable to the first: *I'd just as soon go by train as drive.* [Old English *sōna;* related to Old High German *sāno,* Gothic *suns*]

sooner (ˈsuːnə) *adv* **1** the comparative of **soon:** *he came sooner than I thought.* **2** rather; in preference: *I'd sooner die than give up.* **3 no sooner…than.** immediately after or when: *no sooner had he got home than the rain stopped; no sooner said than done.* **4 sooner or later.** eventually; inevitably.

USAGE *When* is sometimes used instead of *than* after *no sooner,* but this use is generally regarded as incorrect: *no sooner had he arrived than* (not *when*) *the telephone rang.*

Soong *or* **Song** (sʊŋ) *n* an influential Chinese family, notably **Soong Ch'ing-ling** (1890–1981), who married **Sun Yat-sen** and became a vice-chairman of the People's Republic of China (1959); and **Soong Mei-ling** (born 1898), who married **Chiang Kai-shek.**

soot (sʊt) *n* **1** finely divided carbon deposited from flames during the incomplete combustion of organic substances such as coal. ◆ *vb* **2** (*tr*) to cover with soot. [Old English *sōt;* related to Old Norse, Middle Low German *sōt,* Lithuanian *sódis,* Old Slavonic *sažda,* Old Irish *sūide*]

sooth (suːθ) *Archaic or poetic.* ◆ *n* **1** truth or reality (esp. in the phrase **in sooth**). ◆ *adj* **2** true or real. **3** smooth. [Old English *sōth;* related to Old Norse *sathr* true, Old High German *sand,* Gothic *sunja* truth, Latin *sōns* guilty, *sonticus* critical] ▸ **'soothly** *adv*

soothe (suːð) *vb* **1** (*tr*) to make calm or tranquil. **2** (*tr*) to relieve or assuage (pain, longing, etc.). **3** (*intr*) to bring tranquillity or relief. [C16 (in the sense: to mollify): from Old English *sōthian* to prove; related to Old Norse *sanna* to assert; see SOOTH] ▸ **'soother** *n* ▸ **'soothing** *adj* ▸ **'soothingly** *adv* ▸ **'soothingness** *n*

soothfast ('suːθ,fɑːst) *adj Archaic.* **1** truthful. **2** loyal; true. [from Old English *sōthfæst;* see SOOTH, FAST[1]]

soothsay ('suːθ,seɪ) *vb* **-says, -saying, -said.** (*intr*) to predict the future. ▸ **'sooth,saying** *n*

soothsayer ('suːθ,seɪə) *n* a seer or prophet.

sooty ('sʊtɪ) *adj* **sootier, sootiest. 1** covered with soot. **2** resembling or consisting of soot. ▸ **'sootily** *adv* ▸ **'sootiness** *n*

sooty mould *n* **1** a fungal plant disease characterized by a blackish growth covering the surface of leaves, fruits, etc. **2** any of various fungi, such as species of *Meliola* or *Capnodium,* that cause this disease.

sop (sɒp) *n* **1** (*often pl*) food soaked in a liquid before being eaten. **2** a concession, bribe, etc., given to placate or mollify: *a sop to one's feelings.* **3** *Informal.* a stupid or weak person. ◆ *vb* **sops, sopping, sopped. 4** (*tr*) to dip or soak (food) in liquid. **5** (when *intr,* often foll. by *in*) to soak or be soaked. ◆ See also **sop up.** [Old English *sopp;* related to Old Norse *soppa* SOUP, Old High German *sopfa* milk with bread; see SUP[2]]

SOP *abbrev. for* standard operating procedure.

sop. *abbrev. for* soprano.

Soper ('səʊpə) *n* **Donald (Oliver),** Baron. 1903–98, British Methodist minister and publicist, noted esp. for his pacifist convictions. His books include *All His Grace* (1953) and *Calling for Action* (1984).

Sophia (səʊ'faɪə) *n* 1630–1714, electress of Hanover (1658–1714), in whom the Act of Settlement (1701) vested the English Crown. She was a granddaughter of James I of England and her son became George I of Great Britain and Ireland.

sophism ('sɒfɪzəm) *n* an instance of sophistry. Compare **paralogism.** [C14: from Latin *sophisma,* from Greek: ingenious trick, from *sophizesthai* to use clever deceit, from *sophos* wise, clever]

sophist ('sɒfɪst) *n* **1** (*often cap.*) one of the pre-Socratic philosophers who were itinerant professional teachers of oratory and argument and who were prepared to enter into debate on any matter however specious. **2** a person who uses clever or quibbling arguments that are fundamentally unsound. [C16: from Latin *sophista,* from Greek *sophistēs* a wise man, from *sophizesthai* to act craftily]

sophister ('sɒfɪstə) *n* **1** (esp. formerly) a second-year undergraduate at certain British universities. **2** *Rare.* another word for **sophist.**

sophistic (sə'fɪstɪk) *or* **sophistical** *adj* **1** of or relating to sophists or sophistry. **2** consisting of sophisms or sophistry; specious. ▸ **so'phistically** *adv*

sophisticate *vb* (sə'fɪstɪ,keɪt). **1** (*tr*) to make (someone) less natural or innocent, as by education. **2** to pervert or corrupt (an argument, etc.) by sophistry. **3** (*tr*) to make more complex or refined. **4** *Rare.* to falsify (a text, etc.) by alterations. ◆ *n* (sə'fɪstɪ,keɪt, -kɪt). **5** a sophisticated person. [C14: from Medieval Latin *sophisticāre,* from Latin *sophisticus* sophistic] ▸ **so,phisti'cation** *n* ▸ **so'phisti,cator** *n*

sophisticated (sə'fɪstɪ,keɪtɪd) *adj* **1** having refined or cultured tastes and habits. **2** appealing to sophisticates: *a sophisticated restaurant.* **3** unduly refined or cultured. **4** pretentiously or superficially wise. **5** (of machines, methods, etc.) complex and refined. ▸ **so'phisti,catedly** *adv*

sophistry ('sɒfɪstrɪ) *n, pl* **-ries. 1a** a method of argument that is seemingly plausible though actually invalid and misleading. **1b** the art of using such arguments. **2** subtle but unsound or fallacious reasoning. **3** an instance of this; sophism.

Sophocles ('sɒfə,kliːz) *n* ?496–406 B.C., Greek dramatist; author of seven extant tragedies: *Ajax, Antigone, Oedipus Rex, Trachiniae, Electra, Philoctetes,* and *Oedipus at Colonus.* ▸ **Sophoclean** (,sɒfə'kliːən) *adj*

sophomore ('sɒfə,mɔː) *n Chiefly U.S. and Canadian.* a second-year student at a secondary (high) school or college. [C17: perhaps from earlier *sophumer,* from *sophum,* variant of SOPHISM + -ER[1]]

Sophy *or* **Sophi** ('səʊfɪ) *n, pl* **-phies.** (formerly) a title of the Persian monarchs. [C16: from Latin *sophī* wise men, from Greek *sophos* wise]

-sophy *n combining form.* indicating knowledge or an intellectual system: *philosophy; theosophy.* [from Greek *-sophia,* from *sophia* wisdom, from *sophos* wise] ▸ **-sophic** *or* **-sophical** *adj combining form.*

sopor ('səʊpə) *n* an abnormally deep sleep; stupor. [C17: from Latin: a deep sleep, death; related to *somnus* sleep]

soporific (,sɒpə'rɪfɪk) *adj also* (*archaic*) **soporiferous. 1** inducing sleep. **2** drowsy; sleepy. ◆ *n* **3** a drug or other agent that induces sleep. ▸ **,sopo'rifically** *adv*

sopping ('sɒpɪŋ) *adj* completely soaked; wet through. Also: **sopping wet.**

soppy ('sɒpɪ) *adj* **-pier, -piest. 1** wet or soggy. **2** *Brit. informal.* silly or sentimental. ▸ **'soppily** *adv* ▸ **'soppiness** *n*

sopranino (,sɒprə'niːnəʊ) *n, pl* **-nos. a** the instrument with the highest possible pitch in a family of instruments. **b** (*as modifier*): *a sopranino recorder.* [Italian, diminutive of SOPRANO]

soprano (sə'prɑːnəʊ) *n, pl* **-pranos** *or* **-prani** (-'prɑːniː). **1** the highest adult female voice, having a range approximately from middle C to the A a thirteenth above it. **2** the voice of a young boy before puberty. **3** a singer with such a voice. **4** the highest part of a piece of harmony. **5a** the highest or second highest instrument in a family of instruments. **5b** (*as modifier*): *a soprano saxophone.* ◆ See also **treble.** [C18: from Italian, from *sopra* above, from Latin *suprā*]

soprano clef *n* the clef that establishes middle C as being on the bottom line of the staff. See also **C clef.**

sop up *vb* (*tr, adv*) to mop or take up (spilt water, etc.) with or as if with a sponge.

Sopwith ('sɒpwɪθ) *n* Sir **Thomas Octave Murdoch.** 1888–1989, British aircraft designer, who built the Sopwith Camel biplane used during World War I. He was chairman (1935–63) of the Hawker Siddeley Group, which developed the Hurricane fighter and Lancaster bomber.

sora ('sɔːrə) *n* a North American rail, *Porzana carolina,* with a greyish-brown plumage and yellow bill. [C18: of unknown origin]

Sorata (*Spanish* so'rata) *n* **Mount.** a mountain in W Bolivia, in the Andes: the highest mountain in the Cordillera Real, with two peaks, Ancohuma, 6550 m (21 490 ft.), and Illampu, 6485 m (21 276 ft.).

sorb (sɔːb) *n* **1** another name for **service tree** (sense 1). **2** any of various related trees, esp. the mountain ash. **3** Also called: **sorb apple.** the fruit of any of these trees. [C16: from Latin *sorbus* the sorb, service tree] ▸ **'sorbic** *adj*

Sorb (sɔːb) *n* a member of a Slavonic people living chiefly in the rural areas of E Germany between the upper reaches of the Oder and Elbe rivers (Lusatia). Also called: **Wend, Lusatian.**

sorbefacient (,sɔːbɪ'feɪʃənt) *adj* **1** inducing absorption. ◆ *n* **2** a sorbefacient drug. [C19: from Latin *sorbē(re)* to absorb + -FACIENT]

sorbet ('sɔːbeɪ, -bɪt) *n* **1** a water ice made from fruit juice, egg whites, milk, etc. **2** a U.S. word for **sherbet** (sense 1). [C16: from French, from Old Italian *sorbetto,* from Turkish *şerbet,* from Arabic *sharbah* a drink]

Sorbian ('sɔːbɪən) *n* **1** a West Slavonic language spoken in the rural areas of E Germany between the upper reaches of the Oder and Elbe rivers; modern Wendish. ◆ *adj* **2** of or relating to the Sorbs or their language.

sorbic acid *n* a white crystalline unsaturated carboxylic acid found in berries of the mountain ash and used to inhibit the growth of moulds and as an additive for certain synthetic coatings, as of cheese (**E200**); 2,4-hexadienoic acid. It exists as *cis-* and *trans-* isomers, the latter being the one usually obtained. Formula: $CH_3CH{:}CHCH{:}CHCOOH$. [C19: from SORB (the tree), from its discovery in the berries of the mountain ash]

sorbitol ('sɔːbɪ,tɒl) *n* a white water-soluble crystalline alcohol with a sweet taste, found in certain fruits and berries and manufactured by the catalytic hydrogenation of sucrose: used as a sweetener (**E420**) and in the manufacture of ascorbic acid and synthetic resins. Formula: $C_6H_8(OH)_6$. [C19: from SORB + -ITOL]

Sorbonne (*French* sɔrbɔn) *n* **the.** a part of the University of Paris containing the faculties of science and literature: founded in 1253 by Robert de Sorbon as a theological college; given to the university in 1808.

sorbo rubber ('sɔːbəʊ) *n Brit.* a spongy form of rubber. [C20: from ABSORB]

sorbose ('sɔːbəʊs) *n Biochem.* a sweet-tasting hexose sugar derived from the berries of the mountain ash by bacterial action: used in the synthesis of ascorbic acid. Formula: $CH_2OH(CHOH)_3COCH_2OH$. [C19: from SORB + -OSE[2]]

sorcerer ('sɔːsərə) *or* (*fem*) **sorceress** ('sɔːsərɪs) *n* a person who seeks to control and use magic powers; a wizard or magician. [C16: from Old French *sorcier,* from Vulgar Latin *sortiārius* (unattested) caster of lots, from Latin *sors* lot]

sorcery ('sɔːsərɪ) *n, pl* **-ceries.** the art, practices, or spells of magic, esp. black magic, by which it is sought to harness occult forces or evil spirits in order to produce preternatural effects in the world. [C13: from Old French *sorcerie,* from *sorcier* SORCERER] ▸ **'sorcerous** *adj*

Sordello (*Italian* sor'dɛllo) *n* born ?1200, Italian troubadour.

sordes ('sɔːdiːz) *pl n Med.* dark incrustations on the lips and teeth of patients with prolonged fever. [C18: from Latin *sordēs* filth]

sordid ('sɔːdɪd) *adj* **1** dirty, foul, or squalid. **2** degraded; vile; base: *a sordid affair.* **3** selfish and grasping: *sordid avarice.* [C16: from Latin *sordidus,* from *sordēre* to be dirty] ▸ **'sordidly** *adv* ▸ **'sordidness** *n*

sordino (sɔː'diːnəʊ) *n, pl* **-ni** (-niː). **1** a mute for a stringed or brass musical instrument. **2** any of the dampers that arrest the vibrations of piano strings. **3 con sordino** *or* **sordini.** a musical direction to play with a mute. **4 senza sordino** *or* **sordini.** a musical direction to remove or play without the mute or (on the piano) with the sustaining pedal pressed down. ◆ See also **sourdine.** [Italian: from *sordo* deaf, from Latin *surdus*]

sore (sɔː) *adj* **1** (esp. of a wound, injury, etc.) painfully sensitive; tender. **2** causing annoyance: *a sore point.* **3** resentful; irked: *he was sore that nobody believed him.* **4** urgent; pressing: *in sore need.* **5** (*postpositive*) grieved; distressed. **6** causing grief or sorrow. ◆ *n* **7** a painful or sensitive wound, injury, etc. **8** any cause of distress or vexation. ◆ *adv* **9** *Archaic.* direly; sorely (now only in such phrases as **sore pressed, sore afraid**). [Old English *sār;* related to Old Norse *sārr,* Old High German *sēr,* Gothic *sair* sore, Latin *saevus* angry] ▸ **'soreness** *n*

soredium (sɔː'riːdɪəm) *n* an organ of vegetative reproduction in lichens consisting of a cluster of algal cells enclosed in fungal hyphae: dispersed by wind, insects, or other means. [C19: New Latin, from Greek *sōros* a heap]

sorehead ('sɔː,hɛd) *n Informal, chiefly U.S. and Canadian.* a peevish or disgruntled person. ▸ **,sore'headedly** *adv* ▸ **,sore'headedness** *n*

Sorel (*French* sɔrɛl) *n* **Georges** (**Eugène**) (ʒɔrʒ). 1847–1922, French social philosopher, who advocated revolutionary syndicalism and preached the creative role of violence and myth.

sorely ('sɔːlɪ) *adv* **1** painfully or grievously: *sorely wounded.* **2** pressingly or greatly: *to be sorely taxed.*

sorghum ('sɔːgəm) *n* any grass of the Old World genus *Sorghum,* having solid stems, large flower heads, and glossy seeds: cultivated for grain, hay, and as a source of syrup. See also **kaffir corn, durra.** [C16: from New Latin, from Italian *sorgo,* probably from Vulgar Latin *Syricum grānum* (unattested) Syrian grain]

sorgo *or* **sorgho** ('sɔːgəʊ) *n, pl* **-gos** *or* **-ghos.** any of several varieties of sorghum that have watery sweet juice and are grown for fodder, silage, or syrup. [Italian]

sori ('sɔːraɪ) *n* the plural of **sorus.**

soricine ('sɒrɪˌsaɪn) *adj* of, relating to, or resembling the shrews or the family (*Soricidae*) to which they belong. [C18: from Latin *sōricīnus,* from *sōrex* a shrew]

sorites (sɒ'raɪtiːz) *n Logic.* **a** a polysyllogism in which the premises are arranged so that intermediate conclusions are omitted, being understood, and only the final conclusion is stated. **b** a paradox of the form: *these few grains of sand do not constitute a heap, and the addition of a single grain never makes what is not yet a heap into a heap; so no matter how many single grains one adds it never becomes a heap.* [C16: via Latin from Greek *sōreitēs,* literally: heaped, from *sōros* a heap] ► **soritical** (sɒ'rɪtɪkᵊl) *or* **so'ritic** *adj*

sorn (sɔːn) *vb* (*intr,* often foll. by *on* or *upon*) *Scot.* to obtain food, lodging, etc., from another person by presuming on his generosity. [C16: from earlier *sorren* a feudal obligation requiring vassals to offer free hospitality to their lord and his men, from obsolete Irish *sorthan* free quarters]

Sorocaba (*Portuguese* soro'kaba) *n* a city in S Brazil, in São Paulo state: industrial centre. Pop.: 348 952 (1991).

Soroptimist (sə'rɒptɪmɪst) *n* a member of an organization of clubs (**Soroptimist International**) for professional and executive businesswomen. [C20: from Latin *soror* sister + OPTIMIST]

sororate ('sɒrəˌreɪt) *n* the custom in some societies of a widower marrying his deceased wife's younger sister. [C20: from Latin *soror* a sister]

sororicide (sə'rɒrɪˌsaɪd) *n* **1** the act of killing one's own sister. **2** a person who kills his or her sister. [C17: from Latin *sorōricīda* one who murders his sister, from *soror* sister + *caedere* to slay] ► **soˌrori'cidal** *adj*

sorority (sə'rɒrɪtɪ) *n, pl* **-ties.** *Chiefly U.S.* a social club or society for university women. [C16: from Medieval Latin *sorōritās,* from Latin *soror* sister]

sorosis (sə'rəʊsɪs) *n, pl* **-ses** (-siːz). a fleshy multiple fruit, such as that of the pineapple and mulberry, formed from flowers that are crowded together on a fleshy stem. [C19: from New Latin, from Greek *sōros* a heap]

sorption ('sɔːpʃən) *n* the process in which one substance takes up or holds another; adsorption or absorption. [C20: back formation from ABSORPTION, ADSORPTION]

sorrel[1] ('sɒrəl) *n* **1a** a light brown to brownish-orange colour. **1b** (*as adj*)*: a sorrel carpet.* **2** a horse of this colour. [C15: from Old French *sorel,* from *sor* a reddish brown, of Germanic origin; related to Middle Dutch *soor* desiccated]

sorrel[2] ('sɒrəl) *n* **1** any of several polygonaceous plants of the genus *Rumex,* esp. *R. acetosa,* of Eurasia and North America, having acid-tasting leaves used in salads and sauces. See also **dock**[4], **sheep sorrel. 2** short for **wood sorrel.** [C14: from Old French *surele,* from *sur* sour, of Germanic origin; related to Old High German *sūr* SOUR]

sorrel tree *n* a deciduous ericaceous tree, *Oxydendrum arboreum,* of E North America, having deeply fissured bark, sour-tasting leaves, and small white flowers. Also called: **sourwood.** [C17: so called because the bitter flavour of the leaves is reminiscent of sorrel]

Sorrento (sə'rɛntəʊ; *Italian* sor'rɛnto) *n* a port in SW Italy, in Campania on a mountainous peninsula between the Bay of Naples and the Gulf of Salerno: a resort since Roman times. Pop.: 17 500 (1990).

sorrow ('sɒrəʊ) *n* **1** the characteristic feeling of sadness, grief, or regret associated with loss, bereavement, sympathy for another's suffering, for an injury done, etc. **2** a particular cause or source of regret, grief, etc. **3** Also called: **sorrowing.** the outward expression of grief or sadness. ◆ *vb* **4** (*intr*) to mourn or grieve. [Old English *sorg;* related to Old Norse *sorg,* Gothic *saurga,* Old High German *sworga*] ► **'sorrower** *n* ► **'sorrowful** *adj* ► **'sorrowfully** *adv* ► **'sorrowfulness** *n*

sorry ('sɒrɪ) *adj* **-rier, -riest. 1** (*usually postpositive;* often foll. by *for*) feeling or expressing pity, sympathy, remorse, grief, or regret: *I feel sorry for him.* **2** pitiful, wretched, or deplorable: *a sorry sight.* **3** poor; paltry: *a sorry excuse.* **4** affected by sorrow; sad. **5** causing sorrow or sadness. ◆ *interj* **6** an exclamation expressing apology, used esp. at the time of the misdemeanour, offence, etc. [Old English *sārig;* related to Old High German *sērag;* see SORE] ► **'sorrily** *adv* ► **'sorriness** *n*

sort (sɔːt) *n* **1** a class, group, kind, etc., as distinguished by some common quality or characteristic. **2** *Informal.* type of character, nature, etc.: *he's a good sort.* **3** a more or less definable or adequate example: *it's a sort of review.* **4** (*often pl*) *Printing.* any of the individual characters making up a fount of type. **5** *Archaic.* manner; way: *in this sort we struggled home.* **6 after a sort.** to some extent. **7 of sorts** *or* **of a sort. 7a** of an inferior kind. **7b** of an indefinite kind. **8 out of sorts.** not in normal good health, temper, etc. **9 sort of.** in some way or other; as it were; rather. ◆ *vb* **10** (*tr*) to arrange according to class, type, etc. **11** (*tr*) to put (something) into working order. **12** (*tr*) to arrange (computer information) by machine in an order convenient to the computer user. **13** (*tr;* foll. by *with*) *Informal.* to supply, esp. with drugs. **14** (*intr;* foll. by *with, together,* etc.) *Archaic or dialect.* to associate, as on friendly terms. **15** (*intr*) *Archaic.* to agree; accord. [C14: from Old French, from Medieval Latin *sors* kind, from Latin: fate] ► **'sortable** *adj* ► **'sortably** *adv* ► **'sorter** *n*

USAGE See at **kind**[2].

sortal ('sɔːtəl) *n Logic, linguistics.* **1** a concept grasp of which includes knowledge of criteria of individuation and reidentification, such as *dog* or *concerto,* but not *flesh* or *music.* **2** a count noun representing such a concept.

sorted ('sɔːtɪd) *Slang.* ◆ *interj* **1** an exclamation of satisfaction, approval, etc. ◆ *adj* **2** possessing the desired recreational drugs.

sortie ('sɔːtɪ) *n* **1a** (of troops, etc.) the act of emerging from a contained or besieged position. **1b** the troops doing this. **2** an operational flight made by one aircraft. ◆ *vb* **-ties, -tieing, -tied. 3** (*intr*) to make a sortie. [C17: from French: a going out, from *sortir* to go out]

sortilege ('sɔːtɪlɪdʒ) *n* **1** the act or practice of divination by drawing lots. **2** magic or sorcery. [C14: via Old French from Medieval Latin *sortilegium,* from Latin *sortilegus* a soothsayer, from *sors* fate + *legere* to select]

sortition (sɔː'tɪʃən) *n* the act of casting lots. [C16: from Latin *sortitio,* from *sortiri* to cast lots]

sort out *vb* (*tr, adv*) **1** to find a solution to (a problem, etc.), esp. to make clear or tidy: *it took a long time to sort out the mess.* **2** to take or separate, as from a larger group: *he sorted out the most likely ones.* **3** to organize into an orderly and disciplined group. **4** *Informal.* to beat or punish.

sorus ('sɔːrəs) *n, pl* **-ri** (-raɪ). **1** a cluster of sporangia on the undersurface of certain fern leaves. **2** any of various similar spore-producing structures in some lichens and fungi. [C19: via New Latin from Greek *sōros* a heap]

SOS *n* **1** an internationally recognized distress signal in which the letters SOS are repeatedly spelt out, as by radio-telegraphy: used esp. by ships and aircraft. **2** a message broadcast in an emergency for people otherwise unobtainable. **3** *Informal.* a call for help. [C20: letters chosen as the simplest to transmit and receive in Morse code; by folk etymology taken to be abbrev. for *save our souls*]

sosatie (sə'sɑːtɪ) *n S. African.* a skewer of curried meat pieces. [Afrikaans]

Sosnowiec (*Polish* sɔs'nɔvjɛts) *n* an industrial town in S Poland. Pop.: 249 000 (1996 est.).

so-so *Informal.* ◆ *adj* **1** (*postpositive*) neither good nor bad. ◆ *adv* **2** in an average or indifferent manner.

sostenuto (ˌsɒstə'nuːtəʊ) *adj, adv Music.* (preceded by a tempo marking) to be performed in a smooth sustained manner. [C18: from Italian, from *sostenere* to sustain, from Latin *sustinēre* to uphold]

sostenuto pedal *n* another word for **sustaining pedal.**

sot[1] (sɒt) *n* **1** a habitual or chronic drunkard. **2** a person stupefied by or as if by drink. [Old English, from Medieval Latin *sottus;* compare French *sot* a fool] ► **'sottish** *adj*

sot[2] (sɒt) *adv Scot.* indeed: used to contradict a negative statement: *I am not! —You are sot!* [a variant of so[1], altered to rhyme with *not*]

soteriology (sɒˌtɪərɪ'ɒlədʒɪ) *n Theol.* the doctrine of salvation. [C19: from Greek *sōtēria* deliverance (from *sōtēr* a saviour) + -LOGY] ► **soteriologic** (sɒˌtɪərɪə'lɒdʒɪk) *or* **soˌterio'logical** *adj*

Sothic ('səʊθɪk, 'sɒθ-) *adj* relating to the star Sirius or to the rising of this star. [C19: from Greek *Sōthis,* from Egyptian, name of Sirius]

Sothic year *n* the fixed year of the ancient Egyptians, 365 days 6 hours long, beginning with the appearance of the star Sirius on the eastern horizon at dawn, which heralded the yearly flooding of the Nile. A **Sothic cycle** contained 1460 such years.

Sothis ('səʊθɪs) *n* another name for **Sirius.** [Greek; see SOTHIC]

Sotho ('suːtuː, 'səʊtəʊ) *n* **1** (*pl* **-tho** *or* **-thos**) a member of a large grouping of Negroid peoples of southern Africa, living chiefly in Botswana, South Africa, and Lesotho. **2** the group of mutually intelligible languages of this people, including Lesotho, Tswana, and Pedi. It belongs to the Bantu group of the Niger-Congo family. **3** (*pl* **-tho** *or* **-thos**) *S. African.* a member of the Basotho people; a Mosotho. **4** *S. African.* the dialect of Sotho spoken by the Basotho; Sesotho. It is an official language of Lesotho along with English. ◆ Former name (for senses 3, 4): **Basuto.**

Soto[1] (soto) *n* a Zen Buddhist school of Japan, characterized by the practice of sitting meditation leading to gradual enlightenment.

Soto[2] *n* See (Hernando) **De Soto.**

sotto voce ('sɒtəʊ 'vəʊtʃɪ) *adv* in an undertone. [C18: from Italian: under (one's) voice]

sou (suː) *n* **1** a former French coin of low denomination. **2** a very small amount of money: *I haven't a sou to my name.* [C19: from French, from Old French *sol,* from Latin: SOLIDUS]

soubise (suː'biːz) *n* a purée of onions mixed into a thick white sauce and served over eggs, fish, etc. Also called: **soubise sauce.** [C18: named after Charles de Rohan *Soubise* (1715–87), marshal of France]

soubrette (suː'brɛt) *n* **1** a minor female role in comedy, often that of a pert lady's maid. **2** any pert or flirtatious girl. [C18: from French: maidservant, from Provençal *soubreto,* from *soubret* conceited, from *soubra* to exceed, from Latin *superāre* to surmount, from *super* above] ► **sou'brettish** *adj*

soubriquet ('səʊbrɪˌkeɪ) *n* a variant spelling of **sobriquet.**

souchong ('suː'ʃɒŋ, -'tʃɒŋ) *n* a black tea with large leaves. [C18: from Chinese *hsiao-chung* small kind]

Soudan (sudɑ̃) *n* the French name for the **Sudan.**

souffle ('suːfᵊl) *n Med.* a blowing sound or murmur heard in auscultation. [C19: from French, from *souffler* to blow]

soufflé ('suːfleɪ) *n* **1** a very light fluffy dish made with egg yolks and stiffly beaten egg whites combined with cheese, fish, etc. **2** a similar sweet or savoury cold dish, set with gelatine. ◆ *adj, also* **souffléed. 3** made light and puffy, as by beating and cooking. [C19: from French, from *souffler* to blow, from Latin *sufflāre*]

Soufrière (*French* sufrjɛr) *n* **1** a volcano in the Caribbean, on N St Vincent:

erupted in 1902, killing about 2000 people. Height: 1234 m (4048 ft.). **2** a volcano in the Caribbean, on S Montserrat: the highest point on the island. Height: 915 m (3002 ft.). **3** a volcano in the Caribbean, on Guadeloupe. Height: 1484 m (4869 ft.).

sough[1] (saʊ) *vb* **1** (*intr*) (esp. of the wind) to make a characteristic sighing sound. ◆ *n* **2** a soft continuous murmuring sound. [Old English *swōgan* to resound; related to Gothic *gaswogjan* to groan, Lithuanian *svageti* to sound, Latin *vāgīre* to lament]

sough[2] (sʌf) *n Northern English dialect.* a sewer or drain or an outlet channel. [of obscure origin]

sought (sɔːt) *vb* the past tense and past participle of **seek**.

sought-after *adj* in demand; wanted.

souk[1] *or* **suq** (suːk) *n* (in Muslim countries, esp. North Africa and the Middle East) an open-air marketplace. [C20: from Arabic *sūq*]

souk[2] (suːk) *vb, n Scot.* a variant spelling of **sook**[2].

soukous (ˈsuːkʊs) *n* a style of African popular music that originated in Zaïre (now the Democratic Republic of the Congo), characterized by syncopated rhythms and intricate contrasting guitar melodies. [C20: perhaps from French *secouer* to shake]

soul (səʊl) *n* **1** the spirit or immaterial part of man, the seat of human personality, intellect, will, and emotions, regarded as an entity that survives the body after death. Related adj: **pneumatic**. **2** *Christianity.* the spiritual part of a person, capable of redemption from the power of sin through divine grace. **3** the essential part or fundamental nature of anything. **4** a person's feelings or moral nature as distinct from other faculties. **5a** Also called: **soul music**. a type of Black music resulting from the addition of jazz, gospel, and pop elements to the urban blues style. **5b** (*as modifier*): *a soul singer.* **6** (*modifier*) of or relating to Black Americans and their culture: *soul brother; soul food.* **7** nobility of spirit or temperament: *a man of great soul and courage.* **8** an inspiring spirit or leading figure, as of a cause or movement. **9 the life and soul.** See **life** (sense 28). **10** a person regarded as typifying some characteristic or quality: *the soul of discretion.* **11** a person; individual: *an honest soul.* **12 upon my soul!** an exclamation of surprise. [Old English *sāwol;* related to Old Frisian *sēle,* Old Saxon *sēola,* Old High German *sēula* soul] ▸ ˈ**soul-ˌlike** *adj*

Soul (səʊl) *n Christian Science.* another word for **God**.

soul-destroying *adj* (of an occupation, situation, etc.) unremittingly monotonous.

soul food *n Informal.* food, such as chitterlings or yams, traditionally eaten by Black people in the southern U.S.

soulful (ˈsəʊlfʊl) *adj Sometimes ironic.* expressing profound thoughts or feelings: *soulful music.* ▸ ˈ**soulfully** *adv* ▸ ˈ**soulfulness** *n*

soulless (ˈsəʊllɪs) *adj* **1** lacking any humanizing qualities or influences; dead; mechanical: *soulless work.* **2** (of a person) lacking in sensitivity or nobility. **3** heartless; cruel. ▸ ˈ**soullessly** *adv* ▸ ˈ**soullessness** *n*

soul mate *n* a person for whom one has a deep affinity, esp. a lover, wife, husband, etc.

soul-searching *n* **1** deep or critical examination of one's motives, actions, beliefs, etc. ◆ *adj* **2** displaying the characteristics of deep or painful self-analysis.

Soult (*French* sult) *n* **Nicolas Jean de Dieu** (nikɔla ʒɑ̃ də djø). 1769–1851, French marshal under Napoleon I. Under Louis-Philippe he was minister of war (1830–34; 1840–44).

sou marqué (ˈsuː mɑːˈkeɪ; *French* su marke) *n, pl* **sous marqués** (ˈsu mɑːˈkeɪz; *French* su marke). a French copper coin of the 18th century. [French, literally: a marked sou]

sound[1] (saʊnd) *n* **1a** a periodic disturbance in the pressure or density of a fluid or in the elastic strain of a solid, produced by a vibrating object. It has a velocity in air at sea level at 0°C of 332 metres per second (743 miles per hour) and travels as longitudinal waves. **1b** (*as modifier*): *a sound wave.* **2** (*modifier*) of or relating to radio as distinguished from television: *sound broadcasting; sound radio.* **3** the sensation produced by such a periodic disturbance in the organs of hearing. **4** anything that can be heard. **5** a particular instance, quality, or type of sound: *the sound of running water.* **6** volume or quality of sound: *a radio with poor sound.* **7** the area or distance over which something can be heard: *to be born within the sound of Big Ben.* **8** the impression or implication of something: *I don't like the sound of that.* **9** *Phonetics.* the auditory effect produced by a specific articulation or set of related articulations. **10** (*often pl*) *Slang.* music, esp. rock, jazz, or pop. ◆ *vb* **11** to cause (something, such as an instrument) to make a sound or (of an instrument, etc.) to emit a sound. **12** to announce or be announced by a sound: *to sound the alarm.* **13** (*intr*) (of a sound) to be heard. **14** (*intr*) to resonate with a certain quality or intensity: *to sound loud.* **15** (*copula*) to give the impression of being as specified when read, heard, etc.: *to sound reasonable.* **16** (*tr*) to pronounce distinctly or audibly: *to sound one's consonants.* **17** (*intr;* usually foll. by *in*) *Law.* to have the essential quality or nature (of): *an action sounding in damages.* ◆ See also **sound off**. [C13: from Old French *soner* to make a sound, from Latin *sonāre,* from *sonus* a sound] ▸ ˈ**soundable** *adj*

sound[2] (saʊnd) *adj* **1** free from damage, injury, decay, etc. **2** firm; solid; substantial: *a sound basis.* **3** financially safe or stable: *a sound investment.* **4** showing good judgment or reasoning; sensible; wise: *sound advice.* **5** valid, logical, or justifiable: *a sound argument.* **6** holding approved beliefs; ethically correct; upright; honest. **7** (of sleep) deep; peaceful; unbroken. **8** thorough; complete: *a sound examination.* **9** *Law.* (of a title, etc.) free from defect; legally valid. **10** constituting a valid and justifiable application of correct principles; orthodox: *sound theology.* **11** *Logic.* **11a** (of a deductive argument) valid. **11b** (of an inductive argument) according with whatever principles ensure the high probability of the truth of the conclusion given the truth of the premises. **11c** another word for **consistent** (sense 5b). ◆ *adv* **12** soundly; deeply: now archaic except when applied to sleep. [Old English *sund;* related to Old Saxon *gisund,* Old High German *gisunt*] ▸ ˈ**soundly** *adv* ▸ ˈ**soundness** *n*

sound[3] (saʊnd) *vb* **1** to measure the depth of (a well, the sea, etc.) by lowering a plumb line, by sonar, etc. **2** to seek to discover (someone's views, etc.), as by questioning. **3** (*intr*) (of a whale, etc.) to dive downwards swiftly and deeply. **4** *Med.* **4a** to probe or explore (a bodily cavity or passage) by means of a sound. **4b** to examine (a patient) by means of percussion and auscultation. ◆ *n* **5** *Med.* an instrument for insertion into a bodily cavity or passage to dilate strictures, dislodge foreign material, etc. ◆ See also **sound out**. [C14: from Old French *sonder,* from *sonde* sounding line, probably of Germanic origin; related to Old English *sundgyrd* sounding pole, Old Norse *sund* strait, SOUND[4]; see SWIM]

sound[4] (saʊnd) *n* **1** a relatively narrow channel between two larger areas of sea or between an island and the mainland. **2** an inlet or deep bay of the sea. **3** the air bladder of a fish. [Old English *sund* swimming, narrow sea; related to Middle Low German *sunt* strait; see SOUND[3]]

Sound (saʊnd) *n* **the.** a strait between SW Sweden and Sjælland (Denmark), linking the Kattegat with the Baltic: busy shipping lane. Length: 113 km (70 miles). Narrowest point: 5 km (3 miles). Swedish and Danish name: **Øresund**.

soundalike (ˈsaʊndəˌlaɪk) *n* **a** a person or thing that sounds like another, often well known, person or thing. **b** (*as modifier*): *a soundalike band.*

sound barrier *n* (*not in technical usage*) a hypothetical barrier to flight at or above the speed of sound, when a sudden large increase in drag occurs. Also called: **sonic barrier, transonic barrier.**

sound bite *n* a short pithy sentence or phrase extracted from a longer speech for use on radio or television.

sound bow (bəʊ) *n* the thick part of a bell against which the hammer strikes.

soundbox (ˈsaʊndˌbɒks) *n* the resonating chamber of the hollow body of a violin, guitar, etc.

sound check *n* an on-the-spot rehearsal by a band before a gig to enable the sound engineer to set up the mixer.

sound effect *n* any sound artificially produced, reproduced from a recording, etc., to create a theatrical effect, such as the bringing together of two halves of a hollow coconut shell to simulate a horse's gallop; used in plays, films, etc.

sounder[1] (ˈsaʊndə) *n* an electromagnetic device formerly used in telegraphy to convert electric signals sent over wires into audible sounds.

sounder[2] (ˈsaʊndə) *n* a person or device that measures the depth of water, etc.

sound head *n* the part of a film projector that reproduces the sound in a film.

sound hole *n* any of variously shaped apertures in the sounding board of certain stringed instruments, such as the *'f'* shaped holes of a violin.

sounding[1] (ˈsaʊndɪŋ) *adj* **1** resounding; resonant. **2** having an imposing sound and little content; pompous: *sounding phrases.* ▸ ˈ**soundingly** *adv*

sounding[2] (ˈsaʊndɪŋ) *n* **1** (*sometimes pl*) the act or process of measuring depth of water or examining the bottom of a river, lake, etc., as with a sounding line. **2** an observation or measurement of atmospheric conditions, as made using a radiosonde or rocketsonde. **3** (*often pl*) measurements taken by sounding. **4** (*pl*) a place where a sounding line will reach the bottom, esp. less than 100 fathoms in depth. **5 on** (*or* **off**) **soundings.** in waters less than (or more than) 100 fathoms in depth.

sounding board *n* **1** Also called: **soundboard**. a thin wooden board in a piano or comprising the upper surface of a resonating chamber in a violin, cello, etc., serving to amplify the vibrations produced by the strings passing across it. See also **belly** (sense 6). **2** Also called: **soundboard**. a thin screen suspended over a pulpit, stage, etc., to reflect sound towards an audience. **3** a person, group, experiment, etc., used to test a new idea, policy, etc., for acceptance or applicability.

sounding lead (lɛd) *n* a lead weight, usually conical and having a depression in the base for a dab of grease so that, when dropped to the bottom on a sounding line, a sample of sand, gravel, etc., can be retrieved.

sounding line *n* a line marked off to indicate its length and having a sounding lead at one end. It is dropped over the side of a vessel to determine the depth of the water.

soundless[1] (ˈsaʊndlɪs) *adj* extremely still or silent. ▸ ˈ**soundlessly** *adv* ▸ ˈ**soundlessness** *n*

soundless[2] (ˈsaʊndlɪs) *adj Chiefly poetic.* extremely deep.

sound mixer *n Films, radio, etc.* **1** the person who mixes various sound sources into a composite programme. **2** a piece of equipment designed for mixing sound.

sound off *vb* (*intr, adv*) **1** to proclaim loudly, as in venting one's opinions, grievances, etc. **2** to speak angrily.

sound out *vb* (*tr, adv*) to question (someone) in order to discover (opinions, facts, etc.).

soundpost (ˈsaʊndˌpəʊst) *n Music.* a small post, usually of pine, on guitars, violins, etc., that joins the front surface to the back, helps to support the bridge, and allows the whole body of the instrument to vibrate.

soundproof (ˈsaʊndˌpruːf) *adj* **1** not penetrable by sound. ◆ *vb* **2** (*tr*) to render soundproof.

sound ranging *n* the determination of the location of a source of sound waves by measuring the time lapse between their transmission and their reception at microphones situated at three or more known positions.

sound shift *n* a gradual alteration or series of alterations in the pronunciation of a set of sounds, esp. of vowels. See also **Great Vowel Shift**.

sound spectrograph *n* an electronic instrument that produces a record (**sound spectrogram**) of the way in which the frequencies and intensities of the components of a sound, such as a spoken word, vary with time.

sound stage *n* a soundproof room or building in which cinematic films are shot.

sound system *n* **1** any system of sounds, as in the speech of a language. **2** integrated equipment for producing amplified sound, as in a hi-fi or a mobile disco, or as a public-address system on stage.

soundtrack ('saund,træk) *n* **1** the recorded sound accompaniment to a film. Compare **commentary** (sense 2). **2** a narrow strip along the side of a spool of film, which carries the sound accompaniment.

sound truck *n* the U.S. and Canadian name for a **loudspeaker van.**

sound wave *n* a wave that propagates sound.

Souness ('su:nɪs) *n* **Graeme.** born 1953, Scottish footballer and manager.

soup (su:p) *n* **1** a liquid food made by boiling or simmering meat, fish, vegetables, etc., usually served hot at the beginning of a meal. **2** *Informal.* a photographic developer. **3** *Informal.* anything resembling soup in appearance or consistency, esp. thick fog. See also **peasouper. 4** a slang name for **nitroglycerine. 5 in the soup.** *Informal.* in trouble or difficulties. [C17: from Old French *soupe,* from Late Latin *suppa,* of Germanic origin; compare Middle High German *suppe,* Old Norse *soppa* soup]

soupçon *French.* (supsɔ̃) *n* a slight amount; dash. [C18: from French, ultimately from Latin *suspicio* SUSPICION]

soupfin *or* **soupfin shark** ('su:p,fɪn) *n* a Pacific requiem shark, *Galeorhinus zyopterus,* valued for its fins, which are used to make soup.

Souphanouvong (,su:fænu:'vɒŋ) *n* **Prince.** 1902–95, Laotian statesman; president of Laos (1975–86).

soup kitchen *n* **1** a place or mobile stall where food and drink, esp. soup, is served to destitute people. **2** *Military.* a mobile kitchen.

soup plate *n* a deep plate with a wide rim, used esp. for drinking soup.

soup up *Informal.* ◆ *vb* (*tr, adv*) **1** to modify (a vehicle or vehicle engine) in order to increase its power. **2** to make (something) more exciting or interesting. Also: **hot up** *or* (esp. U.S. and Canadian) **hop up.** ◆ *adj* **souped-up. 3** (of a vehicle or vehicle engine) modified so as to be more powerful: *a souped-up scooter.* **4** more exciting or interesting: *a souped-up version of their last single.*

soupy ('su:pɪ) *adj* **soupier, soupiest. 1** having the appearance or consistency of soup. **2** *Informal, chiefly U.S. and Canadian.* emotional or sentimental.

sour ('sauə) *adj* **1** having or denoting a sharp biting taste like that of lemon juice or vinegar. Compare **bitter** (sense 1). **2** made acid or bad, as in the case of milk or alcohol, by the action of microorganisms. **3** having a rancid or unwholesome smell. **4** (of a person's temperament) sullen, morose, or disagreeable. **5** (esp. of the weather or climate) harsh and unpleasant. **6** disagreeable; distasteful: *a sour experience.* **7** (of land, etc.) lacking in fertility, esp. due to excessive acidity. **8** (of oil, gas, or petrol) containing a relatively large amount of sulphur compounds. **9 go** *or* **turn sour.** to become unfavourable or inharmonious: *his marriage went sour.* ◆ *n* **10** something sour. **11** *Chiefly U.S.* any of several iced drinks usually made with spirits, lemon juice, and ice: *a whiskey sour.* **12** an acid used in laundering and bleaching clothes or in curing animal skins. ◆ *vb* **13** to make or become sour. [Old English *sūr;* related to Old Norse *sūrr,* Lithuanian *suras* salty, Old Slavonic *syrŭ* wet, raw, *surovu* green, raw, Sanskrit *surā* brandy] ► **'sourish** *adj* ► **'sourly** *adv* ► **'sourness** *n*

Sour (suə) *n* a variant spelling of **Sur.**

source (sɔ:s) *n* **1** the point or place from which something originates. **2a** a spring that forms the starting point of a stream; headspring. **2b** the area where the headwaters of a river rise: *the source of the Nile.* **3** a person, group, etc., that creates, issues, or originates something: *the source of a complaint.* **4a** any person, book, organization, etc., from which information, evidence, etc., is obtained. **4b** (*as modifier*): *source material.* **5** anything, such as a story or work of art, that provides a model or inspiration for a later work. **6** *Electronics.* the electrode region in a field-effect transistor from which majority carriers flow into the interelectrode conductivity channel. **7 at source.** at the point of origin. ◆ *vb* **8** (*tr;* foll. by *from*) to originate from. **9** (*tr*) to establish an originator or source of (a product, piece of information, etc.). [C14: from Old French *sors,* from *sourdre* to spring forth, from Latin *surgere* to rise]

source document *n* a document that has been or will be transcribed to a word processor or to the memory bank of a computer.

source program *n* an original computer program written by a programmer that is converted into the equivalent object program, written in machine language, by the compiler or assembler.

sour cherry *n* **1** a Eurasian rosaceous tree, *Prunus cerasus,* with white flowers: cultivated for its tart red fruits. **2** the fruit of this tree. Compare **sweet cherry.** See also **morello, amarelle.**

sour cream *n* cream soured by lactic acid bacteria, used in making salads, dips, etc. Also called: **soured cream.**

sourdine (suə'di:n) *n Music.* **1** a soft stop on an organ or harmonium. **2** another word for **sordino.** [C17 (meaning: a muted trumpet): from French: a mute, from Italian; see SORDINO]

sourdough ('sauə,dəu) *adj* **1** *Dialect.* (of bread) made with fermented dough used as a leaven. ◆ *n* **2** (in Western U.S., Canada, and Alaska) an old-time prospector or pioneer.

sour gourd *n* **1** a large bombacaceous tree, *Adansonia gregorii,* of N Australia, having gourdlike fruit. **2** the acid-tasting fruit of this tree, which has a woody rind and large seeds. **3** the fruit of the baobab tree.

sour grapes *n* (*functioning as sing*) the attitude of affecting to despise something because one cannot or does not have it oneself. [from a fable by Aesop]

sour gum *n* a cornaceous tree, *Nyssa sylvatica,* of the eastern U.S., having glossy leaves, soft wood, and sour purplish fruits. Also called: **black gum, pepperidge.** See also **tupelo.** Compare **sweet gum.**

sour mash *n U.S.* **1** a grain mash for use in distilling certain whiskeys, consisting of a mixture of new and old mash. **2** any whiskey distilled from such a mash.

sourpuss ('sauə,pus) *n Informal.* a person whose facial expression or nature is habitually gloomy or sullen. [C20: from SOUR + PUSS[2]]

soursop ('sauə,sɒp) *n* **1** a small West Indian tree, *Annona muricata,* having large spiny fruit: family *Annonaceae.* **2** the fruit of this tree, which has a tart edible pulp. Compare **sweetsop.** [C19: so called because of the flavour and consistency of the pulp]

sourwood ('sauə,wud) *n* another name for **sorrel tree.**

Sousa ('su:zə) *n* **John Philip.** 1854–1932, U.S. bandmaster and composer of military marches, such as *The Stars and Stripes Forever* (1897) and *The Liberty Bell* (1893).

sousaphone ('su:zə,fəun) *n Music.* a large tuba that encircles the player's body and has a bell facing forwards. [C20: named after J. P. SOUSA] ► **'sousa,phonist** *n*

souse[1] (saus) *vb* **1** to plunge (something, oneself, etc.) into water or other liquid. **2** to drench or be drenched. **3** (*tr*) to pour or dash (liquid) over (a person or thing). **4** to steep or cook (food) in a marinade. **5** (*tr; usually passive*) *Slang.* to make drunk. ◆ *n* **6** the liquid or brine used in pickling. **7** the act or process of sousing. **8** *Slang.* a habitual drunkard. [C14: from Old French *sous,* of Germanic origin; related to Old High German *sulza* brine]

souse[2] (saus) *Falconry.* (of hawks or falcons) ◆ *vb* (*intr*) **1** (often foll. by *on* or *upon*) to swoop suddenly downwards (on a prey). ◆ *n* **2** a sudden downward swoop. [C16: perhaps a variant of obsolete vb sense of SOURCE]

souslik ('su:slɪk) *n* a variant spelling of **suslik.**

sou-sou *or* **susu** ('su:su:) *n Caribbean.* an arrangement made among friends whereby each person makes regular contributions to a fund, the money being drawn out periodically by each individual in turn. [probably of W African origin, influenced by French *sou* small coin, via Creole]

Sousse (su:s), **Susa,** *or* **Susah** *n* a port in E Tunisia, on the Mediterranean: founded by the Phoenicians in the 9th century B.C. Pop.: 125 000 (1994). Ancient name: **Hadrumetum** (,hædrə'mi:təm).

soutache (su:'tæʃ) *n* a narrow braid used as a decorative trimming. [C19: from French, from Hungarian *sujtas*]

soutane (su:'tæn) *n R.C. Church.* a priest's cassock. [C19: from French, from Old Italian *sottana,* from Medieval Latin *subtanus* (adj) (worn) beneath, from Latin *subtus* below]

souter *or* **soutar** ('su:tər) *n Scot. and northern English.* a shoemaker or cobbler. [Old English *sūtere,* from Latin *sutor,* from *suere* to sew]

souterrain ('su:tə,reɪn) *n Archaeol.* an underground chamber or passage. [C18: from French]

south (sauθ) *n* **1** one of the four cardinal points of the compass, at 180° from north and 90° clockwise from east and anticlockwise from west. **2** the direction along a meridian towards the South Pole. **3 the south.** (*often cap.*) any area lying in or towards the south. Related adjs: **meridional, austral. 4** (*usually cap.*) *Cards.* the player or position at the table corresponding to south on the compass. ◆ *adj* **5** situated in, moving towards, or facing the south. **6** (esp. of the wind) from the south. ◆ *adv* **7** in, to, or towards the south. **8** *Archaic.* (of the wind) from the south. ◆ Symbol: **S** [Old English *sūth;* related to Old Norse *suthr* southward, Old High German *sundan* from the south]

South (sauθ) *n* **the. 1** the southern part of England, generally regarded as lying to the south of an imaginary line between the Wash and the Severn. **2** (in the U.S.) **2a** the area approximately south of Pennsylvania and the Ohio River, esp. those states south of the Mason-Dixon line that formed the Confederacy during the Civil War. **2b** the Confederacy itself. **3** the countries of the world that are not economically and technically advanced. ◆ *adj* **4a** of or denoting the southern part of a specified country, area, etc. **4b** (*cap. as part of a name*): *the South Pacific.*

South Africa *n* **Republic of.** a republic occupying the southernmost part of the African continent: the Dutch Cape Colony (1652) was acquired by Britain in 1806 and British victory in the Boer War resulted in the formation of the Union of South Africa in 1910, which became a republic in 1961; implementation of the apartheid system began in 1948 and was abolished, following an intense civil rights campaign, in 1993 with multiracial elections held in 1994; a member of the Commonwealth, it withdrew in 1961 but was re-admitted in 1994. Mainly plateau with mountains in the south and east. Mineral production includes gold, diamonds, coal, and copper. Official languages: Afrikaans; English; Ndebele; Pedi; South Sotho; Swazi; Tsonga; Tswana; Venda; Xhosa; Zulu. Religion: Christian majority. Currency: rand. Capitals: Cape Town (legislative), Pretoria (administrative), Bloemfontein (judicial). Pop.: 42 835 000 (1998 est.). Area: 1 221 044 sq. km (471 445 sq. miles). Former name (1910–61): **Union of South Africa.**

South African *adj* **1** of or relating to the Republic of South Africa, its inhabitants, or any of their languages. ◆ *n* **2** a native or inhabitant of the Republic of South Africa.

South African Dutch *n* (not used in South Africa) another name for **Afrikaans.**

South America *n* the fourth largest of the continents, bordering on the Caribbean in the north, the Pacific in the west, and the Atlantic in the east and joined to Central America by the Isthmus of Panama. It is dominated by the Andes Mountains, which extend over 7250 km (4500 miles) and include many volcanoes; ranges from dense tropical jungle, desert, and temperate plains to the cold wet windswept region of Tierra del Fuego. It comprises chiefly developing countries undergoing great changes. Pop.: 317 846 000 (1996). Area: 17 816 600 sq. km (6 879 000 sq. miles). ► **South American** *adj, n*

South American trypanosomiasis *n Pathol.* another name for **Chagas' disease.**

Southampton[1] (sauθ'æmptən, -'hæmp-) *n* **1** a port in S England, in Southampton unitary authority, Hampshire on **Southampton Water** (an inlet of the English Channel): chief English passenger port; university (1952); shipyards and oil refinery. Pop.: 210 138 (1991). **2** a unitary authority in S England, in Hampshire. Pop.: 213 500 (1995 est.). Area: 49 sq. km (19 sq. miles).

Southampton[2] (sauθ'æmptən, -'hæmp-) *n* **3rd Earl of,** title of *Henry Wriothesley.* 1573–1624, English courtier and patron of Shakespeare, who dedicated *Venus and Adonis* (1593) and *The Rape of Lucrece* (1594) to him: sentenced to death (1601) for his part in the Essex rebellion but reprieved.

Southampton Island *n* an island in N Canada, in the Northwest Territories at the entrance to Hudson Bay: inhabited chiefly by Inuit. Area: 49 470 sq. km (19 100 sq. miles).

South Arabia *n* **Federation of.** the former name (1963–67) of **South Yemen** (excluding Aden). ▸ **South Arabian** *adj, n*

South Australia *n* a state of S central Australia, on the Great Australian Bight: generally arid, with the Great Victoria Desert in the west central part, the Lake Eyre basin in the northeast, and the Flinders Ranges, Murray River basin, and salt lakes in the southeast. Capital: Adelaide. Pop.: 1 477 700 (1996 est.). Area: 984 395 sq. km (380 070 sq. miles). ▸ **South Australian** *adj, n*

South Bend *n* a city in the U.S., in N Indiana: university (1842). Pop.: 102 100 (1996 est.).

southbound ('saʊθˌbaʊnd) *adj* going or leading towards the south.

south by east *n* **1** one point on the compass east of south; 168° 45′ clockwise from north. ◆ *adj, adv* **2** in, from, or towards this direction.

south by west *n* **1** one point on the compass west of south; 191° 15′ clockwise from north. ◆ *adj, adv* **2** in, from, or towards this direction.

South Carolina *n* a state of the southeastern U.S., on the Atlantic: the first state to secede from the Union in 1860; consists largely of low-lying coastal plains, rising in the northwest to the Blue Ridge Mountains; the largest U.S. textile producer. Capital: Columbia. Pop.: 3 760 181 (1997 est.). Area: 78 282 sq. km (30 225 sq. miles). Abbrev. (and zip code): **SC** ▸ **South Carolinian** *adj, n*

South China Sea *n* part of the Pacific surrounded by SE China, Vietnam, the Malay Peninsula, Borneo, and the Philippines.

Southcott ('saʊθkɒt) *n* **Joanna.** 1750–1814, British religious fanatic, who claimed that she would give birth to the second Messiah.

South Dakota *n* a state of the western U.S.: lies mostly in the Great Plains; the chief U.S. producer of gold and beryl. Capital: Pierre. Pop.: 737 973 (1997 est.). Area: 196 723 sq. km (75 955 sq. miles). Abbrevs.: **S. Dak.** or (with zip code) **SD** ▸ **South Dakotan** *adj, n*

Southdown ('saʊθˌdaʊn) *n* an English breed of sheep with short wool and a greyish-brown face and legs. **[C18:** so called because it was originally bred on the SOUTH DOWNS**]**

South Downs *pl n* a range of low hills in S England, extending from E Hampshire to East Sussex.

southeast (ˌsaʊθ'iːst; *Nautical* ˌsaʊ'iːst) *n* **1** the point of the compass or the direction midway between south and east, 135° clockwise from north. ◆ *adj also* **southeastern. 2** (*sometimes cap.*) of or denoting the southeastern part of a specified country, area, etc. **3** situated in, proceeding towards, or facing the southeast. **4** (esp. of the wind) from the southeast. ◆ *adv* **5** in, to, towards, or (esp. of the wind) from the southeast. ◆ Symbol: **SE** ▸ **ˌsouth'easternmost** *adj*

Southeast (ˌsaʊθ'iːst) *n* (usually preceded by *the*) the southeastern part of Britain, esp. the London area.

Southeast Asia *n* a region including Brunei, Cambodia, Indonesia, Laos, Malaysia, Myanmar, the Philippines, Thailand, and Vietnam. ▸ **Southeast Asian** *adj, n*

Southeast Asia Treaty Organization *n* the full name of **SEATO.**

southeast by east *n* **1** one point on the compass north of southeast; 123° 45′ clockwise from north. ◆ *adj, adv* **2** in, from, or towards this direction.

southeast by south *n* **1** one point on the compass south of southeast; 146° 15′ clockwise from north. ◆ *adj, adv* **2** in, from, or towards this direction.

southeaster (ˌsaʊθ'iːstə; *Nautical* ˌsaʊ'iːstə) *n* a strong wind or storm from the southeast.

southeasterly (ˌsaʊθ'iːstəlɪ; *Nautical* ˌsaʊ'iːstəlɪ) *adj, adv* **1** in, towards, or (esp. of a wind) from the southeast. ◆ *n, pl* **-lies. 2** a strong wind or storm from the southeast.

southeastward (ˌsaʊθ'iːstwəd; *Nautical* ˌsaʊ'iːstwəd) *adj* **1** towards or (esp. of a wind) from the southeast. ◆ *n* **2** a direction towards or area in the southeast. ◆ *adv* **3** a variant of **southeastwards.**

southeastwards (ˌsaʊθ'iːstwədz; *Nautical* ˌsaʊ'iːstwədz) *or* **southeastward** *adv* to the southeast.

Southend-on-Sea (ˌsaʊθ'end-) *n* a town and from 1998 a unitary authority in SE England, in SE Essex on the Thames estuary: one of England's largest resorts, extending for about 11 km (7 miles) along the coast. Pop.: 171 200 (1995 est.). Area: 42 sq. km (16 sq. miles).

souther ('saʊðə) *n* a strong wind or storm from the south.

southerly ('sʌðəlɪ) *adj* **1** of, relating to, or situated in the south. ◆ *adv, adj* **2** towards or in the direction of the south. **3** from the south: *a southerly wind.* ◆ *n, pl* **-lies. 4** a wind from the south. ▸ **'southerliness** *n*

southerly buster *n* (*sometimes caps.*) a sudden violent cold wind on the SE coast of Australia causing a rapid drop in temperature. Sometimes shortened to **southerly.**

southern ('sʌðən) *adj* **1** situated in or towards the south. **2** (of a wind, etc.) coming from the south. **3** native to, inhabiting, or growing in the south. **4** (*sometimes cap.*) *Astronomy.* south of the celestial equator.

Southern ('sʌðən) *adj* of, relating to, or characteristic of the south of a particular region or country.

Southern Alps *pl n* a mountain range in New Zealand, on South Island: the highest range in Australasia. Highest peak: Mount Cook, 3764 m (12 349 ft.).

Southern British English *n* the dialect of spoken English regarded as standard in England and considered as having high social status in comparison with other British English dialects. Historically, it is derived from the S East Midland dialect of Middle English. Abbrev.: **SBE.** See also **Received Pronunciation.**

Southern Cross *n* **1** a small conspicuous constellation in the S hemisphere lying in the Milky Way near Centaurus. The four brightest stars form a cross the longer arm of which points to the south celestial pole. Formal names: **Crux, Crux Australis. 2** *Austral.* the flag flown at the Eureka Stockade.

Southerner ('sʌðənə) *n* (*sometimes not cap.*) a native or inhabitant of the south of any specified region, esp. the South of England or the Southern states of the U.S.

southern hemisphere *n* (*often caps.*) **1** that half of the earth lying south of the equator. **2** *Astronomy.* that half of the celestial sphere lying south of the celestial equator. ◆ Abbrev.: **S hemisphere.**

Southern Ireland *n* See **Ireland**[1] (sense 2).

southern lights *pl n* another name for **aurora australis.**

southernly ('sʌðənlɪ) *adj, adv* a less common word for **southerly.**

southernmost ('sʌðənˌməʊst) *adj* situated or occurring farthest south.

Southern Ocean *n* another name for the **Antarctic Ocean.**

Southern Rhodesia *n* the former name (until 1964) of **Zimbabwe.** ▸ **Southern Rhodesian** *adj, n*

Southern Sotho *n* another name for **Sesotho.**

Southern Uplands *pl n* a hilly region extending across S Scotland: includes the Lowther, Moorfoot, and Lammermuir hills.

southernwood ('sʌðənˌwʊd) *n* an aromatic shrubby wormwood, *Artemisia abrotanum*, of S Europe, having finely dissected leaves and small drooping heads of yellowish flowers. Also called: **old man, lad's love. [**Old English. See SOUTHERN, WOOD**]**

Southey ('saʊðɪ, 'sʌðɪ) *n* **Robert.** 1774–1843, English poet, a friend of Wordsworth and Coleridge, attacked by Byron; poet laureate (1813–43).

South Georgia *n* an island in the S Atlantic, about 1300 km (800 miles) southeast of the Falkland Islands, part of the UK Overseas Territory of **South Georgia and the South Sandwich Islands.** Area: 3755 sq. km (1450 sq. miles). ▸ **South Georgian** *adj*

South Glamorgan *n* a former county of S Wales, formed in 1974 from parts of Glamorgan and Monmouthshire plus the county borough of Cardiff: replaced in 1996 by the county boroughs of Cardiff and Vale of Glamorgan.

South Gloucestershire *n* a unitary authority of SW England, in Gloucestershire: formerly (1975–96) part of the county of Avon. Pop.: 220 000 (1996 est.). Area: 510 sq. km (197 sq. miles).

South Holland *n* a province of the SW Netherlands, on the North Sea: lying mostly below sea level, it has a coastal strip of dunes and is drained chiefly by distributaries of the Rhine, with large areas of reclaimed land; the most densely populated province in the country, intensively cultivated and industrialized. Capital: The Hague. Pop.: 3 332 900 (1996 est.). Area: 3196 sq. km (1234 sq. miles). Dutch name: **Zuidholland.**

southing ('saʊðɪŋ) *n* **1** *Navigation.* movement, deviation, or distance covered in a southerly direction. **2** *Astronomy.* a south or negative declination.

South Island *n* **the.** the largest island of New Zealand, separated from the North Island by Cook Strait. Pop.: 926 350 (1996). Area: 153 947 sq. km (59 439 sq. miles).

South Korea *n* a republic in NE Asia: established as a republic in 1948; invaded by North Korea and Chinese Communists in 1950 but division remained unchanged at the end of the war (1953); includes over 3000 islands; rapid industrialization. Language: Korean. Religions: Buddhist, Confucianist, Shamanist, and Chondokyo. Currency: won. Capital: Seoul. Pop.: 46 451 000 (1998 est.). Area: 98 477 sq. km (38 022 sq. miles). Korean name: **Hanguk.** ▸ **South Korean** *adj, n*

South Lanarkshire ('lænəkˌʃɪə, -ʃə) *n* a council area of S Scotland, comprising the S part of the historical county of Lanarkshire: included within Strathclyde Region from 1975 to 1996: has uplands in the S and part of the Glasgow conurbation in the N: mainly agricultural. Administrative centre: Hamilton. Pop.: 307 450 (1996 est.). Area: 1771 sq. km (684 sq. miles).

South Orkney Islands *pl n* a group of islands in the S Atlantic, southeast of Cape Horn: formerly a dependency of the Falkland Islands; part of British Antarctic Territory since 1962. Area: 621 sq. km (240 sq. miles).

South Ossetia (ə'siːʃə) *n* an administrative division in Georgia on the S slopes of the Caucasus Mountains. Capital: Tskhinvali. Pop.: 99 800 (1990). Area: 3900 sq. km (1500 sq. miles). Georgian name: **Tskhinvali.** Also called: **South Ossetian Autonomous Region.**

southpaw ('saʊθˌpɔː) *Informal.* ◆ *n* **1** a boxer who leads with his right hand and off his right foot as opposed to the orthodox style of leading with the left. **2** any left-handed person. ◆ *adj* **3** of or relating to a southpaw. **[C20:** from PAW (in the sense: hand): originally a term applied to a left-handed baseball player: perhaps so called because baseball pitchers traditionally face west, so that a left-handed pitcher would throw with the hand on the south side of his body**]**

South Pole *n* **1** the southernmost point on the earth's axis, at the latitude of 90°S. **2** *Astronomy.* the point of intersection, in the constellation Octans, of the earth's extended axis and the southern half of the celestial sphere. **3** (*usually not caps.*) the south-seeking pole of a freely suspended magnet.

Southport ('saʊθˌpɔːt) *n* a town and resort in NW England, in Sefton unitary authority, Merseyside on the Irish Sea. Pop.: 90 959 (1991).

Southron ('sʌðrən) *n* **1** *Chiefly Scot.* a Southerner, esp. an Englishman. **2** *Scot.* the English language as spoken in England. **3** *Dialect, chiefly southern U.S.* an inhabitant of the South, esp. at the time of the Civil War. ◆ *adj* **4** *Chiefly Scot.* of or relating to the South or to England. **[C15:** Scottish variant of SOUTHERN**]**

South Saskatchewan *n* a river in S central Canada, rising in S Alberta and flowing east and northeast to join the North Saskatchewan River, forming the Saskatchewan River. Length: 1392 km (865 miles).

South Sea Bubble *n Brit. history.* the financial crash that occurred in 1720 after the **South Sea Company** had taken over the national debt in return for a monopoly of trade with the South Seas, causing feverish speculation in their stocks. **[**so named because the rapid expansion and sudden collapse of investment resembled the blowing up and bursting of a bubble**]**

South Sea Islands *pl n* the islands in the S Pacific that constitute Oceania.

South Seas *pl n* the seas south of the equator.

South Shetland Islands *pl n* a group of islands in the S Atlantic, north of the Antarctic Peninsula: formerly a dependency of the Falkland Islands; part of British Antarctic Territory since 1962. Area: 4662 sq. km (1800 sq. miles).

South Shields *n* a port in NE England, in South Tyneside unitary authority, Tyne and Wear on the Tyne estuary opposite North Shields. Pop.: 83 704 (1991).

south-southeast *n* **1** the point on the compass or the direction midway between southeast and south; 157° 30′ clockwise from north. ◆ *adj, adv* **2** in, from, or towards this direction. ◆ Symbol: **SSE**

south-southwest *n* **1** the point on the compass or the direction midway between south and southwest; 202° 30′ clockwise from north. ◆ *adj, adv* **2** in, from, or towards this direction. ◆ Symbol: **SSW**

South Tyneside ('taɪn,saɪd) *n* a unitary authority of NE England, in Tyne and Wear. Pop.: 156 700 (1994 est.). Area: 64 sq. km (25 sq. miles).

South Tyrol *or* **Tirol** *n* a former part of the Austrian state of Tyrol: ceded to Italy in 1919, becoming the Bolzano and Trento provinces of the Trentino-Alto Adige Autonomous Region. Area: 14 037 sq. km (5420 sq. miles).

South Vietnam *n* a former republic (1955–76) occupying the S of present-day Vietnam on the South China Sea and the Gulf of Siam. ► **South Vietnamese** *adj, n*

southward ('saʊθwəd; *Nautical* 'sʌðəd) *adj* **1** situated, directed, or moving towards the south. ◆ *n* **2** the southward part, direction, etc.; the south. ◆ *adv* **3** a variant of **southwards.** ► **'southwardly** *adj, adv*

southwards ('saʊθwədz; *Nautical* 'sʌðədz) *or* **southward** *adv* towards the south.

Southwark ('sʌðək) *n* a borough of S central Greater London, on the River Thames: site of the Globe Theatre; docks and warehouses. Pop.: 228 800 (1994 est.). Area: 29 sq. km (11 sq. miles).

Southwell ('saʊθwɛl) *n* **Saint Robert.** ?1561–95, English poet and Roman Catholic martyr, who was imprisoned, tortured, and executed for his Jesuit activities. His best known poem is 'The Burning Babe'.

southwest (,saʊθ'wɛst; *Nautical* ,saʊ'wɛst) *n* **1** the point of the compass or the direction midway between west and south, 225° clockwise from north. ◆ *adj also* **southwestern. 2** (*sometimes cap.*) of or denoting the southwestern part of a specified country, area, etc.: *southwest Italy.* **3** situated in or towards the southwest. **4** (esp. of the wind) from the southwest. ◆ *adv* **5** in, to, towards, or (esp. of the wind) from the southwest. ◆ Symbol: **SW** ► **,south'westernmost** *adj*

Southwest (,saʊθ'wɛst) *n* (usually preceded by *the*) the southwestern part of Britain, esp. Cornwall, Devon, and Somerset.

South West Africa *n* another name for **Namibia.**

southwest by south *n* **1** one point on the compass south of southwest; 213° 45′ clockwise from north. ◆ *adj, adv* **2** in, from, or towards this direction.

southwest by west *n* **1** one point on the compass north of southwest, 236° 15′ clockwise from north. ◆ *adj, adv* **2** in, from, or towards this direction.

southwester (,saʊθ'wɛstə; *Nautical* ,saʊ'wɛstə) *n* a strong wind or storm from the southwest.

southwesterly (,saʊθ'wɛstəlɪ; *Nautical* ,saʊ'wɛstəlɪ) *adj, adv* **1** in, towards, or (esp. of a wind) from the southwest. ◆ *n, pl* **-lies. 2** a wind or storm from the southwest.

southwestward (,saʊθ'wɛstwəd; *Nautical* ,saʊ'wɛstwəd) *adj* **1** from or towards the southwest. ◆ *adv* **2** a variant of **southwestwards.** ◆ *n* **3** a direction towards or area in the southwest. ► **,south'westwardly** *adj, adv*

southwestwards (,saʊθ'wɛstwədz; *Nautical* ,saʊ'wɛstwədz) *or* **southwestward** *adv* to the southwest.

South Yemen *n* a former republic in SW Arabia, on the Gulf of Aden; now a part of Yemen: became a republic in 1967; merged with North Yemen in 1990. Official name (1967–90): **People's Democratic Republic of Yemen.** Name from 1963 to 1967 (excluding Aden): (Federation of) **South Arabia.** See also **Yemen, North Yemen.**

South Yorkshire *n* a metropolitan county of N England, administered since 1986 by the unitary authorities of Barnsley, Doncaster, Sheffield, and Rotherham. Area: 1560 sq. km (602 sq. miles).

Soutine (*French* sutin) *n* **Chaim** ('xaɪɪm). 1893–1943, French expressionist painter, born in Russia; noted for his portraits and still lifes, esp. of animal carcasses.

souvenir (,suːvə'nɪə, 'suːvə,nɪə) *n* **1** an object that recalls a certain place, occasion, or person; memento. ◆ *vb* (*tr*) **2** *Austral. and N.Z., euphemistic slang.* to steal or keep (something, esp. a small article) for one's own use; purloin. [C18: from French, from (*se*) *souvenir* to remember, from Latin *subvenīre* to come to mind, from *sub-* up to + *venīre* to come]

souvlakia (suː'vlækɪə) *n* a Greek dish of kebabs, esp. made with lamb. [C20: from Modern Greek]

sou'wester (saʊ'wɛstə) *n* a waterproof hat having a very broad rim behind, worn esp. by seamen. [C19: a contraction of SOUTHWESTER]

sovereign ('sɒvrɪn) *n* **1** a person exercising supreme authority, esp. a monarch. **2** a former British gold coin worth one pound sterling. ◆ *adj* **3** supreme in rank or authority: *a sovereign lord.* **4** excellent or outstanding: *a sovereign remedy.* **5** of, relating to, or characteristic of a sovereign. **6** independent of outside authority: *a sovereign state.* [C13: from Old French *soverain,* from Vulgar Latin *superānus* (unattested), from Latin *super* above; also influenced by REIGN] ► **'sovereignly** *adv*

sovereigntist ('sɒvrəntɪst) *n* (in Canada) a supporter of sovereignty association.

sovereignty ('sɒvrəntɪ) *n, pl* **-ties. 1** supreme and unrestricted power, as of a state. **2** the position, dominion, or authority of a sovereign. **3** an independent state.

sovereignty association *n* (in Canada) a proposed arrangement by which Quebec would become independent but would maintain a formal association with Canada.

Sovetsk (*Russian* sa'vjɛtsk) *n* a town in W Russia, in the Kaliningrad Region on the Neman River: scene of the signing of the treaty (1807) between Napoleon I and Tsar Alexander I; passed from East Prussia to the Soviet Union in 1945. Former name (until 1945): **Tilsit.**

soviet ('səʊvɪət, 'sɒv-) *n* **1** (in the former Soviet Union) an elected government council at the local, regional, and national levels, which culminated in the Supreme Soviet. **2** (in prerevolutionary Russia) a local revolutionary council. ◆ *adj* **3** of or relating to a soviet. [C20: from Russian *sovyet* council, from Old Russian *sŭvětŭ*]

Soviet ('səʊvɪət, 'sɒv-) *adj* of, characteristic of, or relating to the former Soviet Union, its people, or its government.

Soviet Central Asia *n* the region of the former Soviet Union now occupied by Kazakhstan, Kyrgyzstan, Tajikistan, Turkmenistan, and Uzbekistan. Also called: **Russian Turkestan, West Turkestan.**

sovietism ('səʊvɪɪ,tɪzəm, 'sɒv-) *n* (*sometimes cap.*) **1** the principle or practice of government through soviets, esp. as practised in the former Soviet Union. **2** any characteristic deemed representative of Soviet ideology. ► **'sovietist** *n, adj* ► **,soviet'istic** *adj*

sovietize *or* **sovietise** ('səʊvɪɪ,taɪz,'sɒv-) *vb* (*tr*) (*often cap.*) **1** to bring (a country, person, etc.) under Soviet control or influence. **2** to cause (a country) to conform to the Soviet model in its social, political, and economic structure. ► **,sovieti'zation** *or* **,sovieti'sation** *n*

Sovietologist (,səʊvɪə'tɒlədʒɪst, ,sɒv-) *n* a person who has studied the political policies and developments of the former Soviet government.

Soviet Russia *n* (formerly) another name for the **Russian Soviet Federative Socialist Republic** or the **Soviet Union.**

Soviets ('səʊvɪəts, 'sɒv-) *n* the people or government of the former Soviet Union.

Soviet Union *n* a former federal republic in E Europe and central and N Asia: the revolution of 1917 achieved the overthrow of the monarchy and the USSR was established in 1922 as a Communist state. In 1991 the Soviet Union broke up following a failed coup by Communist opponents of reform and declarations of independence by many of its constituent republics. It was the largest country in the world, occupying a seventh of the total land surface. Official name: **Union of Soviet Socialist Republics.** Also called: **Russia, Soviet Russia.** Abbrev.: **USSR.**

Soviet Zone *n* that part of Germany occupied by Soviet forces in 1945–49: transformed into the German Democratic Republic in 1949–50. Also called: **Russian Zone.**

sovkhoz (sɒf'kɒz; *Russian* saf'xɔs) *n, pl* **sovkhozy** (sɒf'kɒzɪ; *Russian* saf'xɔzi). (in the former Soviet Union) a large mechanized farm owned by the state. [C20: Russian, from *sovetskoe khozyaistvo* soviet economy]

sovran ('sɒvrən) *n, adj* a literary word for **sovereign.** ► **'sovranly** *adv* ► **'sovranty** *n*

sow[1] (səʊ) *vb* **sows, sowing, sowed; sown** *or* **sowed. 1** to scatter or place (seed, a crop, etc.) in or on (a piece of ground, field, etc.) so that it may grow: *to sow wheat; to sow a strip of land.* **2** (*tr*) to implant or introduce: *to sow a doubt in someone's mind.* [Old English *sāwan;* related to Old Norse *sā,* Old High German *sāen,* Old Slavonic *seja,* Latin *serere* to sow] ► **'sowable** *adj* ► **'sower** *n*

sow[2] (saʊ) *n* **1** a female adult pig. **2** the female of certain other animals, such as the mink. **3** *Metallurgy.* **3a** the channels for leading molten metal to the moulds in casting pig iron. **3b** iron that has solidified in these channels. [Old English *sugu;* related to Old Norse *sȳr,* Old High German *sū,* Latin *sūs,* Norwegian *sugga,* Dutch *zeug:* see SWINE]

sowback ('saʊ,bæk) *n* another name for **hogback** (sense 1).

sowbread ('saʊ,brɛd) *n* a S European primulaceous plant, *Cyclamen hederifolium,* with heart-shaped leaves and pink nodding flowers. See also **cyclamen** (sense 1). [C16: from SOW[2] + BREAD, based on Medieval Latin *panis porcinus;* the tuberous roots are eaten by swine]

sow bug (saʊ) *n U.S. and Canadian.* any of various woodlice, esp. any of the genera *Oniscus* and *Porcellio.* [C18: from its resemblance to a pig in shape]

sowens ('səʊənz, 'suː-) *n Scot.* a pudding made from oatmeal husks steeped and boiled. [C16: from Scottish Gaelic *sūghan,* from *sūgh* sap; related to Old High German *sūgan* to SUCK]

Soweto (sə'wɛtəʊ, -'weɪtəʊ) *n* a contiguous group of Black African townships southwest of Johannesburg, South Africa: the largest purely Black African urban settlement in southern Africa: scene of riots (1976) following protests against the use of Afrikaans in schools for Black African children. Area: 62 sq. km (24 sq. miles). Pop.: 596 632 (1991). [C20: from *so(uth) we(st) to(wnship)*]

sown (səʊn) *vb* a past participle of **sow**[1].

sow thistle (saʊ) *n* any of various plants of the Old World genus *Sonchus,* esp. *S. oleraceus,* having milky juice, prickly leaves, and heads of yellow flowers: family *Compositae* (composites). Also called: **milk thistle,** (N.Z.) **puha,** (N.Z.) **rauriki.** [C13: from *sugethistel,* perhaps variant of Old English *thugethistel, thuthistel* thowthistle, a dialect name of the sow thistle. See SOW[2], THISTLE]

soya bean ('sɔɪə) *or U.S. and Canadian* **soybean** ('sɔɪ,biːn) *n* **1** an Asian bean plant, *Glycine max* (or *G. soja*), cultivated for its nutritious seeds, for forage, and to improve the soil. **2** the seed of this plant, used as food, forage, and as the source of an oil. [C17 *soya,* via Dutch *soya* from Japanese *shōyu,* from Chinese *chiang yu,* from *chiang* paste + *yu* sauce]

Soyinka (sɔ'jɪŋkə) *n* **Wole** ('wɔːle). born 1934, Nigerian dramatist, novelist, poet, and literary critic. His works include the plays *The Strong Breed* (1963), *The Road* (1965), and *Kongi's Harvest* (1966), the novel *The Interpreters* (1965), and the political essays *The Burden of Memory, the Muse of Forgiveness*

(1999); forced into exile by the military regime (1993–98). Nobel prize for literature 1986.

soy sauce (sɔɪ) *n* a salty dark brown sauce made from fermented soya beans, used esp. in Japanese and Chinese cookery. Also called: **soya sauce.**

Soyuz (sɔɪˈjuz) *n* any of a series of Russian spacecraft used to ferry crew to and from space stations. [C20: Russian: union]

sozzled (ˈsɒzəld) *adj* an informal word for **drunk.** [C19: perhaps from obsolete *sozzle* stupor; related to SOUSE[1]]

sp *abbrev. for* without issue. [from Latin *sine prole*]

SP *abbrev. for:* **1** standard play: the standard recording speed on a VCR. **2** starting price. ◆ *n* **3** *Brit. slang.* latest information.

sp. *abbrev. for:* **1** special. **2** (*pl* **spp.**) species. **3** specific. **4** specimen. **5** spelling.

Sp. *abbrev. for:* **1** Spain. **2** Spaniard. **3** Spanish.

spa (spɑː) *n* a mineral spring or a place or resort where such a spring is found. [C17: named after SPA, Belgium]

Spa (spɑː) *n* a town in E Belgium, in Liège province: a resort with medicinal mineral springs (discovered in the 14th century). Pop.: 10 140 (1991).

SpA *abbrev. for* Società per Azioni. [Italian: limited company]

SPA *abbrev. for* Special Protection Area: an area designated by the European Union in order to protect endangered species, esp. of birds.

Spaak (spɑːk) *n* **Paul Henri** (pɔl ɑ̃ri). 1899–1972, Belgian statesman, first socialist premier of Belgium (1937–38); a leading advocate of European unity, he was president of the consultative assembly of the Council of Europe (1949–51) and secretary-general of NATO (1957–61).

space (speɪs) *n* **1** the unlimited three-dimensional expanse in which all material objects are located. Related adj: **spatial. 2** an interval of distance or time between two points, objects, or events. **3** a blank portion or area. **4a** unoccupied area or room: *there is no space for a table.* **4b** (*in combination*): *space-saving.* Related adj: **spacious. 5a** the region beyond the earth's atmosphere containing the other planets of the solar system, stars, galaxies, etc.; universe. **5b** (*as modifier*): *a space probe; space navigation.* **6a** the region beyond the earth's atmosphere occurring between the celestial bodies of the universe. The density is normally negligible although cosmic rays, meteorites, gas clouds, etc., can occur. It can be divided into **cislunar space** (between the earth and moon), **interplanetary space, interstellar space,** and **intergalactic space. 6b** (*as modifier*): *a space station; a space simulator.* **7** a seat or place, as on a train, aircraft, etc. **8** *Printing.* **8a** a piece of metal, less than type-high, used to separate letters or words in hot-metal printing. **8b** any of the gaps used to separate letters, words or lines in photocomposition, desktop publishing, etc. **9** *Music.* any of the gaps between the lines that make up the staff. **10** *Maths.* a collection of unspecified points having properties that obey a specified set of axioms: *Euclidean space.* **11** Also called: **spacing.** *Telegraphy.* the period of time that separates complete letters, digits, and other characters in Morse code. ◆ *vb* (*tr*) **12** to place or arrange at intervals or with spaces between. **13** to divide into or by spaces: *to space one's time evenly.* **14** *Printing.* to separate (letters, words, or lines) by the insertion of spaces. [C13: from Old French *espace,* from Latin *spatium*] ▸ **ˈspacer** *n*

space age *n* **1** the period in which the exploration of space has become possible. ◆ *adj* **space-age. 2** (*usually prenominal*) futuristic or ultramodern, esp. when suggestive of space technology.

spaceband (ˈspeɪsˌbænd) *n Printing.* a device on a linecaster for evening up the spaces between words.

space-bar *n* a horizontal bar on a typewriter that is depressed in order to leave a space between words, letters, etc.

space blanket *n* a plastic insulating body wrapping coated on one or both sides with aluminium foil which reflects back most of the body heat lost by radiation: carried by climbers, mountaineers, etc., for use in cases of exposure or exhaustion. [C20: material originally developed as part of the U.S. space programme]

space cadet *n Slang.* a person who is eccentric or out of touch with reality, as if affected by drugs.

space capsule *n* a vehicle, sometimes carrying people or animals, designed to obtain scientific information from space, planets, etc., and be recovered on returning to earth.

space character *n Computing.* a keyed space in text or data.

spacecraft (ˈspeɪsˌkrɑːft) *n* a manned or unmanned vehicle designed to orbit the earth or travel to celestial objects for the purpose of research, exploration, etc.

spaced out *adj Slang.* intoxicated through or as if through taking a drug. Often shortened to **spaced.**

space heater *n* a heater used to warm the air in an enclosed area, such as a room or office.

Space Invaders *n Trademark.* a video or computer game, the object of which is to destroy attacking alien spacecraft.

spacelab (ˈspeɪsˌlæb) *n* a laboratory in space where scientific experiments are performed, esp. one developed by the European Space Agency and carried on a space shuttle.

space lattice *n Crystallog.* the more formal name for **lattice** (sense 4).

spaceless (ˈspeɪslɪs) *adj Chiefly literary.* **1** having no limits in space; infinite or boundless. **2** occupying no space.

spaceman (ˈspeɪsˌmæn) *or* (*fem*) **spacewoman** *n, pl* **-men** *or* (*fem*) **-women.** a person who travels in outer space, esp. one trained to participate in a space flight.

space medicine *n* the branch of medicine concerned with the effects on man of flight outside the earth's atmosphere. Compare **aviation medicine.**

space opera *n* a science fiction drama, such as a film or television programme, esp. one dealing with interplanetary flight.

space platform *n* another name for **space station.**

spaceport (ˈspeɪsˌpɔːt) *n* a base equipped to launch, maintain, and test spacecraft.

space probe *n* a vehicle, such as a satellite, equipped to obtain scientific information, normally transmitted back to earth by radio, about the atmosphere, surface, and temperature of a planet, conditions in space, etc.

spaceship (ˈspeɪsˌʃɪp) *n* a manned spacecraft.

space shuttle *n* any of a series of reusable U.S. space vehicles (*Columbia, Challenger* (exploded 1986), *Discovery, Atlantis, Endeavour*) that can be launched into earth orbit transporting astronauts and equipment for a period of observation, research, etc., before re-entry and an unpowered landing on a runway; the first operational flight occurred in 1982.

space station *n* any large manned artificial satellite designed to orbit the earth during a long period of time thus providing a base for scientific and medical research in space and a construction site, launch pad, and docking arrangements for spacecraft. Also called: **space platform, space laboratory.**

spacesuit (ˈspeɪsˌsuːt, -ˌsjuːt) *n* any of various types of sealed and pressurized suits worn by astronauts or cosmonauts that provide an artificial atmosphere, acceptable temperature, radiocommunication link, and protection from radiation for work outside a spacecraft.

space-time *or* **space-time continuum** *n Physics.* the four-dimensional continuum having three spatial coordinates and one time coordinate that together completely specify the location of a particle or an event.

spacewalk (ˈspeɪsˌwɔːk) *n* **1** the act or an instance of floating and manoeuvring in space, outside but attached by a lifeline to a spacecraft. Technical name: **extravehicular activity.** ◆ *vb* **2** (*intr*) to float and manoeuvre in space while outside but attached to a spacecraft.

space writer *n* a writer paid by the area of his copy.

spacey (ˈspeɪsɪ) *adj* **spacier, spaciest.** *Slang.* vague and dreamy, as if under the influence of drugs. [C20: SPACE + -EY]

spacial (ˈspeɪʃəl) *adj* a variant spelling of **spatial.**

spacing (ˈspeɪsɪŋ) *n* **1** the arrangement of letters, words, etc., on a page in order to achieve legibility or aesthetic appeal. **2** the arrangement of objects in a space.

spacious (ˈspeɪʃəs) *adj* having a large capacity or area. [C14: from Latin *spātiosus,* from *spatium* SPACE] ▸ **ˈspaciously** *adv* ▸ **ˈspaciousness** *n*

spade[1] (speɪd) *n* **1** a tool for digging, typically consisting of a flat rectangular steel blade attached to a long wooden handle. **2a** an object or part resembling a spade in shape. **2b** (*as modifier*): *a spade beard.* **3** a heavy metallic projection attached to the trail of a gun carriage that embeds itself into the ground and so reduces recoil. **4** a type of oar blade that is comparatively broad and short. Compare **spoon** (sense 6). **5** a cutting tool for stripping the blubber from a whale or skin from a carcass. **6 call a spade a spade.** to speak plainly and frankly. ◆ *vb* **7** (*tr*) to use a spade on. [Old English *spadu;* related to Old Norse *spathi,* Old High German *spato,* Greek *spathē* blade] ▸ **ˈspader** *n*

spade[2] (speɪd) *n* **1a** the black symbol on a playing card resembling a heart-shaped leaf with a stem. **1b** a card with one or more of these symbols or (*when pl*) the suit of cards so marked, usually the highest ranking of the four. **2** a derogatory word for a Black. **3 in spades.** *Informal.* in an extreme or emphatic way. [C16: from Italian *spada* sword, used as an emblem on playing cards, from Latin *spatha,* from Greek *spathē* blade, broadsword]

spadefish (ˈspeɪdˌfɪʃ) *n, pl* **-fish** *or* **-fishes.** any spiny-finned food fish of the family *Ephippidae,* esp. *Chaetodipterus faber* of American Atlantic coastal waters, having a deeply compressed body.

spade foot *n* a spadelike projection at the end of a chair leg.

spade guinea *n Brit. history.* a guinea decorated with a spade-shaped shield, coined during the reign of George III.

spadework (ˈspeɪdˌwɜːk) *n* dull or routine preparatory work.

spadiceous (speɪˈdɪʃəs) *adj* **1** *Botany.* producing or resembling a spadix. **2** of a bright brown colour. [C17: from New Latin *spādīceus,* from Latin *spādix* palm branch; see SPADIX]

spadille (spəˈdɪl) *n Cards.* (in ombre and quadrille) the ace of spades. [C18: from French, from Spanish *espadilla,* diminutive of *espada* sword; see SPADE[2]]

spadix (ˈspeɪdɪks) *n, pl* **spadices** (speɪˈdaɪsiːz). a racemose inflorescence having many small sessile flowers borne on a fleshy stem, the whole being enclosed in a spathe: occurs in aroid plants. [C18: from Latin: pulled-off branch of a palm, with its fruit, from Greek: torn-off frond; related to Greek *span* to pull off]

spae (speɪ) *vb Scot.* to foretell (the future). [C14: from Old Norse]

spaewife (ˈspeˌwəɪf) *n, pl* **-wives.** *Scot.* a woman who can supposedly foretell the future.

spag[1] (spæg) *vb* **spags, spagging, spagged.** (*tr*) *South Wales dialect.* (of a cat) to scratch (a person) with the claws. [of uncertain origin]

spag[2] (spæg) *n Austral. offensive slang.* an Italian. [from SPAGHETTI]

spaghetti (spəˈgetɪ) *n* pasta in the form of long strings. [C19: from Italian: little cords, from *spago* a cord]

spaghetti junction *n* an interchange, usually between motorways, in which there are a large number of underpasses and overpasses and intersecting roads used by a large volume of high-speed traffic. [C20: from the nickname of the Gravelly Hill Interchange, Birmingham, where the M6, A38M, A38, and A5127 intersect]

spaghetti western *n* a cowboy film about the American West made, esp. by an Italian director, in Europe.

spagyric (spəˈdʒɪrɪk) *or* **spagyrical** *adj Rare.* of or relating to alchemy. [C16: from New Latin *spagiricus,* probably coined by Paracelsus, of obscure origin] ▸ **spaˈgyrically** *adv*

spahi *or* **spahee** (ˈspɑːhiː, ˈspɑːiː) *n, pl* **-his** *or* **-hees. 1** (formerly) an irregular cavalryman in the Turkish armed forces. **2** a member of a body of native Algerian cavalrymen in the French armed forces: disbanded after Algerian independence. [C16: from Old French, from Turkish *sipahi*, from Persian *sipāhī* soldier; see SEPOY]

Spain (spein) *n* a kingdom of SW Europe, occupying the Iberian peninsula between the Mediterranean and the Atlantic: a leading European power in the 16th century, with many overseas possessions, esp. in the New World; became a republic in 1931; under the fascist dictatorship of Franco following the Civil War (1936–39) until his death in 1975; a member of the European Union. It consists chiefly of a central plateau (the Meseta), with the Pyrenees and the Cantabrian Mountains in the north and the Sierra Nevada in the south. Official language: Castilian Spanish, with Catalan, Galician, and Basque official regional languages. Religion: Roman Catholic majority. Currency: euro and peseta. Capital: Madrid. Pop.: 39 371 000 (1998 est.). Area: 504 748 sq. km (194 883 sq. miles). Spanish name: **España.**

spake (speik) *vb Archaic or dialect.* a past tense of **speak.**

Spalato ('spa:lato) *n* the Italian name for **Split.**

Spalding ('spɔ:ldɪŋ) *n* a town in E England, in S Lincolnshire: noted for its bulbfields. Pop.: 18 731 (1991).

spall (spɔ:l) *n* **1** a splinter or chip of ore, rock, or stone. ◆ *vb* **2** to split or cause to split into such fragments. [C15: of unknown origin]

Spallanzani (,spælənt'sɑ:nɪ) *n* **Lazzaro.** 1729–99, Italian physiologist, noted esp. for his experimental studies of microorganisms and his work on animal reproduction and digestion.

spallation (spə'leɪʃən) *n Physics.* a type of nuclear reaction in which a photon or particle hits a nucleus and causes it to emit other particles or photons. [C20: from SPALL + -ATION]

spalpeen ('spælpi:n) *n Irish.* **1** an itinerant seasonal labourer. **2** a rascal or layabout. [C18: from Irish Gaelic *spailpīn* itinerant labourer]

spam (spæm) *vb* **spams, spamming, spammed.** *Computing., slang.* to send unsolicited electronic mail simultaneously to a number of newsgroups on the Internet. [C20: from the repeated use of the word *Spam* in a popular sketch from the British television show *Monty Python's Flying Circus,* first broadcast in 1969]

Spam (spæm) *n Trademark.* a kind of tinned luncheon meat, made largely from pork.

span[1] (spæn) *n* **1** the interval, space, or distance between two points, such as the ends of a bridge or arch. **2** the complete duration or extent: *the span of his life.* **3** *Psychol.* the amount of material that can be processed in a single mental act: *apprehension span; span of attention.* **4** short for **wingspan. 5** a unit of length based on the width of an expanded hand, usually taken as nine inches. ◆ *vb* **spans, spanning, spanned.** (*tr*) **6** to stretch or extend across, over, or around. **7** to provide with something that extends across or around: *to span a river with a bridge.* **8** to measure or cover, esp. with the extended hand. [Old English *spann;* related to Old Norse *sponn,* Old High German *spanna*]

span[2] (spæn) *n* a team of horses or oxen, esp. two matched animals. [C16 (in the sense: yoke): from Middle Dutch: something stretched, from *spannen* to stretch; see SPAN[1]]

span[3] (spæn) *vb Archaic or dialect.* a past tense of **spin.**

Span. *abbrev. for* Spanish.

spancel ('spænsᵊl) *n* **1** a length of rope for hobbling an animal, esp. a horse or cow. ◆ *vb* **-cels, -celling, -celled** *or U.S.* **-cels, -celing, -celed. 2** (*tr*) to hobble (an animal) with a loose rope. [C17: from Low German *spansel,* from *spannen* to stretch; see SPAN[2]]

spandex ('spændeks) *n* a type of synthetic stretch fabric made from polyurethane fibre. [C20: coined from an anagram of *expands*]

spandrel *or* **spandril** ('spændrəl) *n Architect.* **1** an approximately triangular surface bounded by the outer curve of an arch and the adjacent wall. **2** the surface area between two adjacent arches and the horizontal cornice above them. [C15 *spaundrell,* from Anglo-French *spaundre* spandrel, from Old French *spandre* to spread, EXPAND]

spang (spæŋ) *adv U.S. and Canadian informal.* exactly, firmly, or straight: *spang on target.* [C19: of unknown origin]

spangle ('spæŋgᵊl) *n* **1** a small thin piece of metal or other shiny material used as a decoration, esp. on clothes; sequin. **2** any glittering or shiny spot or object. ◆ *vb* **3** (*intr*) to glitter or shine with or like spangles. **4** (*tr*) to decorate or cover with spangles. [C15: diminutive of *spange,* perhaps from Middle Dutch: clasp; compare Old Norse *spöng*] ► **'spangly** *adj*

Spaniard ('spænjəd) *n* **1** a native or inhabitant of Spain. **2** *N.Z.* short for **wild Spaniard.**

spaniel ('spænjəl) *n* **1** any of several breeds of gundog with long drooping ears, a silky coat, and the tail usually docked. See **clumber spaniel, cocker spaniel, field spaniel, springer spaniel, Sussex spaniel, water spaniel. 2** either of two toy breeds of spaniel: see **King Charles spaniel. 3** an obsequiously devoted person. [C14: from Old French *espaigneul* Spanish (dog), from Old Provençal *espanhol,* ultimately from Latin *Hispānīolus* Spanish]

Spanish ('spænɪʃ) *n* **1** the official language of Spain, Mexico, and most countries of South and Central America except Brazil: also spoken in Africa, the Far East, and elsewhere. It is the native language of approximately 200 million people throughout the world. Spanish is an Indo-European language belonging to the Romance group. **2 the Spanish.** (*functioning as pl*) Spaniards collectively. ◆ *adj* **3** of or relating to the Spanish language or its speakers. **4** of or relating to Spain or Spaniards.

Spanish America *n* the parts of America colonized by Spaniards from the 16th century onwards and now chiefly Spanish-speaking: includes all of South America (except Brazil, Guyana, French Guiana, and Surinam), Central America (except Belize), Mexico, Cuba, Puerto Rico, the Dominican Republic, and a number of small Caribbean islands.

Spanish-American *adj* **1** of or relating to any of the Spanish-speaking countries or peoples of the Americas. ◆ *n* **2** a native or inhabitant of Spanish America. **3** a Spanish-speaking person in the U.S.

Spanish-American War *n* the war between the U.S. and Spain (1898) resulting in Spain's withdrawal from Cuba and its cession of Guam, the Philippines, and Puerto Rico.

Spanish Armada *n* the great fleet sent by Philip II of Spain against England in 1588: defeated in the Channel by the English fleets and almost completely destroyed by storms off the Hebrides. Also called: (the) **Armada.**

Spanish bayonet *n* any of several American liliaceous plants of the genus *Yucca,* esp. *Y. aloifolia,* that have a tall woody stem, stiff pointed leaves, and large clusters of white flowers: cultivated for ornament. See also **Adam's-needle.**

Spanish cedar *n* a tall meliaceous tree, *Cedrela odorata,* of tropical America, the East Indies, and Australia, having smooth bark, pinnate leaves, yellow flowers, and light-coloured aromatic wood.

Spanish Civil War *n* the civil war in Spain from 1936 to 1939 in which insurgent nationalists, led by General Franco, succeeded in overthrowing the republican government. During the war Spain became an ideological battleground for fascists and socialists from all countries.

Spanish customs *or* **practices** *pl n Informal.* irregular practices among a group of workers to gain increased financial allowances, reduced working hours, etc. Also called: **old Spanish customs** *or* **practices.**

Spanish fly *n* **1** a European blister beetle, *Lytta vesicatoria* (family *Meloidae*), the dried bodies of which yield the pharmaceutical product cantharides. **2** another name for **cantharides.**

Spanish Guinea *n* the former name (until 1964) of **Equatorial Guinea.**

Spanish guitar *n* the classic form of the guitar; a six-stringed instrument with a waisted body and a central sound hole.

Spanish Inquisition *n* the institution that guarded the orthodoxy of Catholicism in Spain, chiefly by the persecution of heretics, Jews, etc., esp. from the 15th to 17th centuries. See also **Inquisition.**

Spanish mackerel *n* **1** Also called: **kingfish.** any scombroid food fish of the genus *Scomberomorus,* esp. *S. maculatus,* of American coastal regions of the Atlantic: family *Scombridae* (mackerels, tunnies, etc.). **2** a mackerel, *Scomber colias,* of European and E North American coasts that is similar to the common Atlantic mackerel.

Spanish Main *n* **1** the mainland of Spanish America, esp. the N coast of South America from the Isthmus of Panama to the mouth of the Orinoco River, Venezuela. **2** the Caribbean Sea, the S part of which in colonial times was the route of Spanish treasure galleons and the haunt of pirates.

Spanish Morocco *n* a former Spanish colony on the N coast of Morocco: part of the kingdom of Morocco since 1956. ► **Spanish Moroccan** *adj, n*

Spanish moss *n* **1** an epiphytic bromeliaceous plant, *Tillandsia usneoides,* growing in tropical and subtropical regions as long bluish-grey strands suspended from the branches of trees. **2** a tropical lichen, *Usnea longissima,* growing as long trailing green threads from the branches of trees. ◆ Also called: **long moss.**

Spanish omelette *n* an omelette made by adding green peppers, onions, tomato, etc., to the eggs.

Spanish onion *n* any of several varieties of large mild-flavoured onions.

Spanish paprika *n* a mild seasoning made from a variety of red pepper grown in Spain.

Spanish rice *n* rice cooked with tomatoes, onions, green peppers, etc., and often flavoured with saffron.

Spanish Sahara *n* the former name (until 1975) of **Western Sahara.**

Spanish topaz *n* an orange-brown form of quartz, used as a gemstone.

Spanish West Africa *n* a former overseas territory of Spain in NW Africa: divided in 1958 into the overseas provinces of Ifni and Spanish Sahara. ► **Spanish West African** *adj, n*

Spanish windlass *n* a stick used as a device for twisting and tightening a rope or cable.

spank[1] (spæŋk) *vb* **1** (*tr*) to slap or smack with the open hand, esp. on the buttocks. ◆ *n* **2** a slap or series of slaps with the flat of the hand. [C18: probably of imitative origin]

spank[2] (spæŋk) *vb* (*intr*) to go at a quick and lively pace. [C19: back formation from SPANKING[2]]

spanker ('spæŋkə) *n* **1** *Nautical.* a fore-and-aft sail or a mast that is aftermost in a sailing vessel. **2** *Informal.* a person or animal that moves at a quick smart pace. **3** *Informal.* something outstandingly fine or large.

spanking[1] ('spæŋkɪŋ) *n* a series of spanks, esp. on the buttocks, usually as a punishment for children.

spanking[2] ('spæŋkɪŋ) *adj* (*prenominal*) **1** *Informal.* outstandingly fine, smart, large, etc. **2** quick and energetic; lively. **3** (esp. of a breeze) fresh and brisk. [C17: of uncertain origin. Compare Danish *spanke* to strut]

spanner ('spænə) *n* **1** a steel hand tool with a handle carrying jaws or a hole of particular shape designed to grip a nut or bolt head. **2 spanner in the works.** *Brit. informal.* a source of impediment or annoyance (esp. in the phrase **throw a spanner in the works**). [C17: from German, from *spannen* to stretch, SPAN[1]]

span-new *adj Archaic or dialect.* absolutely new. [C14: from Old Norse *spānnýr,* from *spānn* chip + *nýr* NEW]

span of apprehension *n Psychol.* the maximum number of objects that can be correctly assessed after a brief presentation.

span roof *n* a roof consisting of two equal sloping sides.

span saw *n Building trades.* another name for **frame saw.**

spanspek ('spɑn,spek) *n S. African.* a sweet rough-skinned melon; a cantaloupe: family *Cucurbitaceae.* [C19: possibly from Afrikaans: literally, Spanish bacon]

spansule ('spænsjuːl) *n* a time-release capsule of a drug.

spar[1] (spɑː) *n* **1a** any piece of nautical gear resembling a pole and used as a mast, boom, gaff, etc. **1b** (*as modifier*): *a spar buoy.* **2** a principal supporting structural member of an aerofoil that runs from tip to tip or root to tip. [C13: from Old Norse *sperra* beam; related to Old High German *sparro,* Old French *esparre*]

spar[2] (spɑː) *vb* **spars, sparring, sparred.** (*intr*) **1** *Boxing, martial arts.* to fight using light blows, as in training. **2** to dispute or argue. **3** (of gamecocks) to fight with the feet or spurs. ◆ *n* **4** an unaggressive fight. **5** an argument or wrangle. [Old English, perhaps from SPUR]

spar[3] (spɑː) *n* any of various minerals, such as feldspar or calcite, that are light-coloured, microcrystalline, transparent to translucent, and easily cleavable. Related adj: **spathic.** [C16: from Middle Low German *spar;* related to Old English *spærstān;* see FELDSPAR]

sparable ('spærəbᵊl) *n* a small nail with no head, used for fixing the soles and heels of shoes. [C17: changed from *sparrow-bill,* referring to the nail's shape]

sparaxis (spə'ræksɪs) *n* any plant of the cormous S African genus *Sparaxis,* esp. *S. grandiflora* and *S. tricolor,* grown for their dainty spikes of star-shaped purple, red, or orange flowers: family *Iridaceae.* [New Latin, from Greek *sparassein* to tear (from the appearance of the spathes)]

spar buoy *n Nautical.* a buoy resembling a vertical log.

spare (speə) *vb* **1** (*tr*) to refrain from killing, punishing, harming, or injuring. **2** (*tr*) to release or relieve, as from pain, suffering, etc. **3** (*tr*) to refrain from using: *spare the rod, spoil the child.* **4** (*tr*) to be able to afford or give: *I can't spare the time.* **5** (*usually passive*) (esp. of Providence) to allow to survive: *I'll see you again next year if we are spared.* **6** (*intr*) *Now rare.* to act or live frugally. **7** (*intr*) *Rare.* to show mercy. **8 not spare oneself.** to exert oneself to the full. **9 to spare.** more than is required: *two minutes to spare.* ◆ *adj* **10** (*often immediately postpositive*) in excess of what is needed; additional: *are there any seats spare?* **11** able to be used when needed: *a spare part.* **12** (of a person) thin and lean. **13** scanty or meagre. **14** (*postpositive*) *Brit. slang.* upset, angry, or distracted (esp. in the phrase **go spare**). ◆ *n* **15** a duplicate kept as a replacement in case of damage or loss. **16** a spare tyre. **17** *Tenpin bowling.* **17a** the act of knocking down all the pins with the two bowls of a single frame. **17b** the score thus made. Compare **strike** (sense 40). [Old English *sparian* to refrain from injuring; related to Old Norse *spara,* Old High German *sparōn*] ▸ **'sparely** *adv* ▸ **'spareness** *n* ▸ **'sparer** *n*

spare part *n* a duplicate or replacement component for a machine or other equipment.

spare-part surgery *n* surgical replacement of defective or damaged organs by transplant or insertion of artificial devices.

sparerib (ˌspeə'rɪb) *n* a cut of pork ribs with most of the meat trimmed off.

spare tyre *n* **1** an additional tyre, usually mounted on a wheel, carried by a motor vehicle in case of puncture. **2** *Brit. slang, jocular.* a deposit of fat just above the waist.

sparge (spɑːdʒ) *vb Rare.* to sprinkle or scatter (something). [C16: from Latin *spargere* to sprinkle] ▸ **'sparger** *n*

sparid ('spærɪd) *or* **sparoid** *n* **1** any marine percoid fish of the chiefly tropical and subtropical family *Sparidae,* having a deep compressed body and well-developed teeth: includes the sea breams and porgies. ◆ *adj* **2** of, relating to, or belonging to the family *Sparidae.* [C20: from New Latin *Sparidae,* from Latin *sparus* a sea bream, from Greek *sparos*]

sparing ('speərɪŋ) *adj* **1** (sometimes foll. by *with* or *of*) economical or frugal (with). **2** scanty; meagre. **3** merciful or lenient. ▸ **'sparingly** *adv* ▸ **'sparingness** *n*

spark[1] (spɑːk) *n* **1** a fiery particle thrown out or left by burning material or caused by the friction of two hard surfaces. **2a** a momentary flash of light accompanied by a sharp crackling noise, produced by a sudden electrical discharge through the air or some other insulating medium between two points. **2b** the electrical discharge itself. **2c** (*as modifier*): *a spark gap.* **3** anything that serves to animate, kindle, or excite. **4** a trace or hint: *she doesn't show a spark of interest.* **5** vivacity, enthusiasm, or humour. **6** a small piece of diamond, as used in the cutting of glass. ◆ *vb* **7** (*intr*) to give off sparks. **8** (*intr*) (of the sparking plug or ignition system of an internal-combustion engine) to produce a spark. **9** (*tr;* often foll. by *off*) to kindle, excite, or animate. ◆ See also **spark off, sparks.** [Old English *spearca;* related to Middle Low German *sparke,* Middle Dutch *spranke,* Lettish *spirgsti* cinders, Latin *spargere* to strew]

spark[2] (spɑːk) *Rare* (*except for sense 2*). ◆ *n* **1** a fashionable or gallant young man. **2 bright spark.** *Brit., usually ironic.* a person who appears clever or witty: *some bright spark left the papers next to the open window.* ◆ *vb* **3** to woo (a person). [C16 (in the sense: beautiful or witty woman): perhaps of Scandinavian origin; compare Old Norse *sparkr* vivacious] ▸ **'sparkish** *adj*

Spark (spɑːk) *n* Dame **Muriel** (**Sarah**). born 1918, British novelist and writer; her novels include *Memento Mori* (1959), *The Prime of Miss Jean Brodie* (1961), *The Takeover* (1976), *A Far Cry from Kensington* (1988), *Symposium* (1990), and *Reality and Dreams* (1996).

spark chamber *n Physics.* a device for detecting ionizing radiation, consisting of two oppositely charged metal plates in a chamber containing inert gas, so that a particle passing through the chamber ionizes the gas and causes a spark to jump between the electrodes.

spark coil *n* an induction coil used to produce spark discharges.

spark erosion *n Engineering.* a method of machining using a shaped electrode which erodes the workpiece by an electric spark discharge between itself and the workpiece.

spark gap *n* the space between two electrodes across which a spark can jump. Sometimes shortened to **gap.**

sparking plug *n* a device screwed into the cylinder head of an internal-combustion engine to ignite the explosive mixture by means of an electric spark which jumps across a gap between a point earthed to the body of the plug and the tip of a central insulated rod. Also called: **spark plug.**

sparkle ('spɑːkᵊl) *vb* **1** to issue or reflect or cause to issue or reflect bright points of light. **2** (*intr*) (of wine, mineral water, etc.) to effervesce. **3** (*intr*) to be vivacious or witty. ◆ *n* **4** a point of light, spark, or gleam. **5** vivacity or wit. [C12 *sparklen,* frequentative of *sparken* to SPARK[1]]

sparkler ('spɑːklə) *n* **1** a type of firework that throws out showers of sparks. **2** *Informal.* a sparkling gem.

sparkling wine *n* a wine made effervescent by carbon dioxide gas, introduced artificially or produced naturally by secondary fermentation.

spark off *vb* (*tr, adv*) to bring into being or action; activate or initiate: *to spark off an argument.*

spark plug *n* another name for **sparking plug.**

sparks (spɑːks) *n* (*functioning as sing*) *Informal.* **1** an electrician. **2** a radio officer, esp. on a ship.

spark transmitter *n* an early type of radio transmitter in which power is generated by discharging a capacitor through an inductor in series with a spark gap.

sparky ('spɑːkɪ) *adj* **sparkier, sparkiest.** lively; vivacious; spirited.

sparling ('spɑːlɪŋ) *n, pl* **-lings** *or* **-ling. 1** another name for the **European smelt** (see **smelt** (the fish)). **2** a young herring. [C14 *sperlynge,* from Old French *esperling,* from Middle Dutch *spierlinc,* from *spier* young shoot]

sparoid ('spærɔɪd) *adj, n* another word for **sparid.** [C19: from New Latin *Sparoīdēs;* see SPARID]

sparring partner ('spɑːrɪŋ) *n* **1** a person who practises with a boxer during training. **2** a person with whom one has friendly arguments.

sparrow ('spærəʊ) *n* **1** any weaverbird of the genus *Passer* and related genera, esp. the house sparrow, having a brown or grey plumage and feeding on seeds or insects. **2** *U.S. and Canadian.* any of various North American finches, such as the chipping sparrow (*Spizella passerina*), that have a dullish streaked plumage. ◆ See also **hedge sparrow, tree sparrow, song sparrow.** ◆ Related adj: **passerine.** [Old English *spearwa;* related to Old Norse *spörr,* Old High German *sparo*] ▸ **'sparrow-ˌlike** *adj*

sparrowgrass ('spærəʊˌgrɑːs) *n* a dialect or popular name for **asparagus.** [C17: variant of ASPARAGUS, associated by folk etymology with SPARROW and GRASS]

sparrowhawk ('spærəʊˌhɔːk) *n* any of several small hawks, esp. *Accipiter nisus,* of Eurasia and N Africa that prey on smaller birds.

sparrow hawk *n* a very small North American falcon, *Falco sparverius,* that is closely related to the kestrels.

sparry ('spɑːrɪ) *adj Geology.* containing, relating to, or resembling spar: *sparry coal.*

sparse (spɑːs) *adj* scattered or scanty; not dense. [C18: from Latin *sparsus,* from *spargere* to scatter] ▸ **'sparsely** *adv* ▸ **'sparseness** *or* **'sparsity** *n*

Sparta ('spɑːtə) *n* an ancient Greek city in the S Peloponnese, famous for the discipline and military prowess of its citizens and for their austere way of life.

Spartacist ('spɑːtəsɪst) *n* a member of a group of German radical socialists formed in 1916 and in 1919 becoming the German Communist Party, led by Karl Liebknecht and Rosa Luxemburg. [C20: from the pen name SPARTACUS adopted by Karl Liebknecht]

Spartacus ('spɑːtəkəs) *n* died 71 B.C., Thracian slave, who led an ultimately unsuccessful revolt of gladiators against Rome (73–71 B.C.).

Spartan ('spɑːtᵊn) *adj* **1** of or relating to Sparta or its citizens. **2** (*sometimes not cap.*) very strict or austere: *a Spartan upbringing.* **3** (*sometimes not cap.*) possessing courage and resolve. ◆ *n* **4** a citizen of Sparta. **5** (*sometimes not cap.*) a disciplined or brave person. ▸ **'Spartanism** *n*

sparteine ('spɑːtɪˌiːn, -ɪn) *n* a viscous oily alkaloid extracted from the broom plant and lupin seeds. It has been used in medicine to treat heart arrhythmias. [C19: from New Latin *Spartium,* from Greek *spartos* broom]

spasm ('spæzəm) *n* **1** an involuntary muscular contraction, esp. one resulting in cramp or convulsion. **2** a sudden burst of activity, emotion, etc. [C14: from Latin *spasmus,* from Greek *spasmos* a cramp, from *span* to tear]

spasmodic (spæz'mɒdɪk) *or* (*rarely*) **spasmodical** *adj* **1** taking place in sudden brief spells. **2** of or characterized by spasms. [C17: New Latin, from Greek *spasmos* SPASM] ▸ **spas'modically** *adv*

Spassky ('spæskɪ; *Russian* 'spaskij) *n* **Boris** (ba'ris). born 1937, Russian chess player; world champion (1969–72).

spastic ('spæstɪk) *n* **1** a person who is affected by spasms or convulsions, esp. one who has cerebral palsy. **2** *Offensive slang.* a clumsy, incapable, or incompetent person. ◆ *adj* **3** affected by or resembling spasms. **4** *Offensive slang.* clumsy, incapable or incompetent. [C18: from Latin *spasticus,* from Greek *spastikos,* from *spasmos* SPASM] ▸ **'spastically** *adv* ▸ **spas'ticity** (spæs'tɪsɪtɪ) *n*

spat[1] (spæt) *n* **1** *Now rare.* a slap or smack. **2** a slight quarrel. ◆ *vb* **spats, spatting, spatted. 3** *Now rare.* to slap (someone). **4** (*intr*) *U.S., Canadian, and* (*rarely*) *N.Z.* to have a slight quarrel. [C19: probably imitative of the sound of quarrelling]

spat[2] (spæt) *vb* a past tense and past participle of **spit**[1].

spat[3] (spæt) *n* another name for **gaiter** (sense 2). [C19: short for SPATTERDASH]

spat[4] (spæt) *n* **1** a larval oyster or similar bivalve mollusc, esp. when it settles to the sea bottom and starts to develop a shell. **2** such oysters or other molluscs collectively. [C17: from Anglo-Norman *spat;* perhaps related to SPIT[1]]

spatchcock ('spætʃˌkɒk) *n* **1** a chicken or game bird split down the back and grilled. Compare **spitchcock.** ◆ *vb* (*tr*) **2** to interpolate (words, a story, etc.) into a sentence, narrative, etc., esp. inappropriately. [C18: perhaps variant of *spitchcock* eel when prepared and cooked]

spate (speɪt) *n* **1** a fast flow, rush, or outpouring: *a spate of words.* **2** *Chiefly Brit.* a sudden flood: *the rivers were in spate.* **3** *Chiefly Brit.* a sudden heavy downpour. [C15 (Northern and Scottish): of unknown origin]

spathe (speɪð) *n* a large bract, often coloured, that encloses the inflorescence of any of several members of the lily family. [C18: from Latin *spatha,* from Greek *spathē* a blade] ▸ **spathaceous** (spəˈθeɪʃəs) *adj* ▸ **spathed** *adj*
spathic (ˈspæθɪk) *or* **spathose** (ˈspæθəʊs) *adj* (of minerals) resembling spar, esp. in having good cleavage. [C18: from German *spat, spath* SPAR[3]; related to Old High German *spān* chip; see SPOON]
spathulate (ˈspæθjʊlɪt) *adj* another word for **spatulate** (sense 2).
spatial *or* **spacial** (ˈspeɪʃəl) *adj* **1** of or relating to space. **2** existing or happening in space. ▸ **spatiality** (ˌspeɪʃɪˈælɪtɪ) *n* ▸ **ˈspatially** *adv*
spatial frequency *n Television.* the measure of fine detail in an optical image in terms of cycles per millimetre.
spatiotemporal (ˌspeɪʃɪəʊˈtɛmpərəl, -ˈtɛmprəl) *adj* **1** of or existing in both space and time. **2** of or concerned with space-time. [C20: from Latin *spatium* space + *temporālis,* from *tempus* time] ▸ **ˌspatioˈtemporally** *adv*
Spätlese (ˈʃpetˌleɪsə) *n* a wine, usually white, produced in Germany from grapes which have been allowed to ripen for longer than usual. [C20: from German, from *spät* late + *Lese* harvest, vintage]
spatter (ˈspætə) *vb* **1** to scatter or splash (a substance, esp. a liquid) or (of a substance) to splash (something) in scattered drops: *to spatter mud on the car; mud spattered in her face.* **2** (*tr*) to sprinkle, cover, or spot (with a liquid). **3** (*tr*) to slander or defame. **4** (*intr*) to shower or rain down: *bullets spattered around them.* ◆ *n* **5** the sound of something spattering. **6** something spattered, such as a spot or splash. **7** the act or an instance of spattering. [C16: of imitative origin; related to Low German, Dutch *spatten* to spout, Frisian *spatteren* to splash]
spatterdash (ˈspætəˌdæʃ) *n* **1** *U.S.* another name for **roughcast. 2** (*pl*) long leather leggings worn in the 18th century, as to protect from mud when riding. [C17: see SPATTER, DASH[1]]
spatula (ˈspætjʊlə) *n* a utensil with a broad flat, often flexible blade, used for lifting, spreading, or stirring foods, etc. [C16: from Latin: a broad piece, from *spatha* a flat wooden implement; see SPATHE] ▸ **ˈspatular** *adj*
spatulate (ˈspætjʊlɪt) *adj* **1** shaped like a spatula. **2** Also: **spathulate.** *Botany.* having a narrow base and a broad rounded apex: *a spatulate leaf.*
spavin (ˈspævɪn) *n Vet. science.* enlargement of the hock of a horse by a bony growth (**bony spavin**) or distension of the ligament (**bog spavin**), usually caused by inflammation or injury, and often resulting in lameness. [C15: from Old French *espavin,* of unknown origin]
spavined (ˈspævɪnd) *adj* **1** *Vet. science.* affected with spavin; lame. **2** decrepit or worn out.
spawn (spɔːn) *n* **1** the mass of eggs deposited by fish, amphibians, or molluscs. **2** *Often derogatory.* offspring, product, or yield. **3** *Botany.* the nontechnical name for **mycelium.** ◆ *vb* **4** (of fish, amphibians, etc.) to produce or deposit (eggs). **5** *Often derogatory.* (of people) to produce (offspring). **6** (*tr*) to produce or engender. [C14: from Anglo-Norman *espaundre,* from Old French *spandre* to spread out, EXPAND] ▸ **ˈspawner** *n*
spay (speɪ) *vb* (*tr*) to remove the ovaries from (a female animal). [C15: from Old French *espeer* to cut with the sword, from *espee* sword, from Latin *spatha*]
SPCK (in Britain) *abbrev. for* Society for Promoting Christian Knowledge.
SPD *abbrev. for* Sozialdemokratische Partei Deutschlands. [German: Social Democratic Party of Germany]
speak (spiːk) *vb* **speaks, speaking, spoke, spoken. 1** to make (verbal utterances); utter (words). **2** to communicate or express (something) in or as if in words: *I speak the truth.* **3** (*intr*) to deliver a speech, discourse, etc. **4** (*tr*) to know how to talk in (a language or dialect): *he does not speak German.* **5** (*intr*) to make a characteristic sound: *the clock spoke.* **6** (*intr*) (of dogs, esp. hounds used in hunting) to give tongue; bark. **7** (*tr*) *Nautical.* to hail and converse or communicate with (another vessel) at sea. **8** (*intr*) (of a musical instrument) to produce a sound. **9** (*intr;* foll. by *for*) to be a representative or advocate (of): *he speaks for all the members.* **10 on speaking terms.** on good terms; friendly. **11 so to speak.** in a manner of speaking; as it were. **12 speak one's mind.** to express one's opinions frankly and plainly. **13 to speak of.** of a significant or worthwhile nature: *we have had no support to speak of.* ◆ See also **speak for, speak out, speak to, speak up.** [Old English *specan;* related to Old High German *spehhan,* Middle High German *spechten* to gossip, Middle Dutch *speken;* see SPEECH] ▸ **ˈspeakable** *adj*
-speak *suffix forming nouns. Informal.* the language or jargon of a specific group, organization, or field: *computerspeak.* [C20: formed on the pattern of NEWSPEAK]
speakeasy (ˈspiːkˌiːzɪ) *n, pl* **-easies.** *U.S.* a place where alcoholic drink was sold illicitly during Prohibition. [C19: from SPEAK + EASY (in the sense: gently, quietly)]
speaker (ˈspiːkə) *n* **1** a person who speaks, esp. at a formal occasion. **2** See **loudspeaker.** ▸ **ˈspeakership** *n*
Speaker (ˈspiːkə) *n* the presiding officer in any of numerous legislative bodies, including the House of Commons in Britain and Canada and the House of Representatives in the U.S., Australia, and New Zealand.
speak for *vb* (*intr, prep*) **1** to speak as a representative of (other people). **2 speak for itself.** to be so evident that no further comment is necessary. **3 speak for yourself.** *Informal.* (used as an imperative) do not presume that other people agree with you.
speaking (ˈspiːkɪŋ) *adj* **1** (*prenominal*) eloquent, impressive, or striking. **2a** able to speak. **2b** (*in combination*) able to speak a particular language: *French-speaking.*
speaking clock *n Brit.* a telephone service that gives a precise verbal statement of the correct time.
speaking in tongues *n* another term for **gift of tongues.**
speaking trumpet *n* a trumpet-shaped instrument used to carry the voice a great distance or held to the ear by a deaf person to aid his hearing.
speaking tube *n* a tube or pipe for conveying a person's voice from one room, area, or building to another.
speak out *vb* (*intr, adv*) **1** to state one's beliefs, objections, etc., bravely and firmly. **2** to speak more loudly and clearly.
speak to *vb* (*intr, prep*) **1** to address (a person). **2** to reprimand: *your father will speak to you later.* **3** *Formal.* to give evidence of or comments on (a subject): *who will speak to this item?*
speak up *vb* (*intr, adv*) **1** to speak more loudly. **2** to state one's beliefs, objections, etc., bravely and firmly.
spear[1] (spɪə) *n* **1** a weapon consisting of a long shaft with a sharp pointed end of metal, stone, or wood that may be thrown or thrust. **2** a similar implement used to catch fish. **3** another name for **spearman.** ◆ *vb* **4** to pierce (something) with or as if with a spear. [Old English *spere;* related to Old Norse *spjör* spears, Greek *sparos* gilthead] ▸ **ˈspearer** *n*
spear[2] (spɪə) *n* a shoot, slender stalk or blade, as of grass, asparagus, or broccoli. [C16: probably variant of SPIRE[1], influenced by SPEAR[1]]
spearfish (ˈspɪəˌfɪʃ) *n, pl* **-fish** *or* **-fishes.** another name for **marlin.** [so named because of its long pointed jaw]
spear grass *n N.Z.* **1** another name for **wild Spaniard. 2** any of various grasses with sharp stiff blades or seeds.
spear gun *n* a device for shooting spears underwater.
spearhead (ˈspɪəˌhɛd) *n* **1** the pointed head of a spear. **2** the leading force in a military attack. **3** any person or thing that leads or initiates an attack, a campaign, etc. ◆ *vb* **4** (*tr*) to lead or initiate (an attack, a campaign, etc.).
spearman (ˈspɪəmən) *n, pl* **-men.** a soldier armed with a spear.
Spearman's rank-order coefficient (ˈspɪəmənz) *n* a statistic measuring the extent to which two sets of discrete data place the distinct items in the same order, given by $r_S = 1 - 6\Sigma d^2/n(n^2 - 1)$, where Σd^2 is the sum of the squares of the differences of ranks between the two orderings and *n* is the number of items in each. Also called: **Spearman's rank-order correlation coefficient.** [named after Charles E. *Spearman* (1863–1945), English mathematician and statistician]
spearmint (ˈspɪəmɪnt) *n* a purple-flowered mint plant, *Mentha spicata,* of S and central Europe, cultivated for its leaves, which yield an oil used for flavouring. [C16: so called because of its long narrow leaves]
spear side *n* the male side or branch of a family. Compare **distaff side.**
spearwort (ˈspɪəˌwɜːt) *n* any of several Eurasian ranunculaceous plants of the genus *Ranunculus,* such as *R. flammula* (**lesser spearwort**) and *R. lingua* (**great spearwort**), which grow in wet places and have long narrow leaves and yellow flowers. See also **buttercup.**
spec (spɛk) *Informal.* ◆ *n* **1 on spec.** as a speculation or gamble: *all the tickets were sold so I went to the theatre on spec.* ◆ *adj* **2** (*prenominal*) *Austral. and N.Z.* speculative: *a spec developer.* [C19: short for SPECULATION OR SPECULATIVE]
spec. *abbrev. for:* **1** special. **2** specification. **3** speculation.
special (ˈspɛʃəl) *adj* **1** distinguished, set apart from, or excelling others of its kind. **2** (*prenominal*) designed or reserved for a particular purpose: *a special tool for working leather.* **3** not usual or commonplace. **4** (*prenominal*) particular or primary: *his special interest was music.* **5** denoting or relating to the education of physically or mentally handicapped children: *a special school.* ◆ *n* **6** a special person or thing, such as an extra edition of a newspaper or a train reserved for a particular purpose. **7** a dish or meal given prominence, esp. at a low price, in a café, etc. **8** *Austral. history, slang.* a convict given special treatment on account of his education, social class, etc. **9** short for **special constable. 10** *Austral., N.Z., U.S. and Canadian informal.* an item in a store that is advertised at a reduced price; a loss leader. ◆ *vb* **-cials, -cialling, -cialled.** (*tr*) **11** *N.Z. informal.* to advertise and sell (an item) at a reduced price: *we are specialling butter this week.* [C13: from Old French *especial,* from Latin *speciālis* individual, special, from *speciēs* appearance, SPECIES] ▸ **ˈspecially** *adv* ▸ **ˈspecialness** *n*

USAGE See at **especial.**

Special Air Service *n* a regiment in the British Army specializing in clandestine operations.
special assessment *n* (in the U.S.) a special charge levied on property owners by a county or municipality to help pay the costs of a civic improvement that increases the value of their property.
Special Boat Service *n* a unit of the Royal Marines specializing in reconnaissance and sabotage.
Special Branch *n* (in Britain) the department of the police force that is concerned with political security.
special case *n Law.* an agreed written statement of facts submitted by litigants to a court for a decision on a point of law.
special clearing *n Banking.* (in Britain) the clearing of a cheque through a bank in less than the usual three days, for an additional charge.
special constable *n* a person recruited for temporary or occasional police duties, esp. in time of emergency.
special delivery *n* the delivery of a piece of mail outside the time of a scheduled delivery.
special drawing rights *pl n* (*sometimes caps.*) the reserve assets of the International Monetary Fund on which member nations may draw in proportion to their contribution to the Fund. Abbrev.: **SDRs.**
special effects *pl n Films.* techniques used in the production of scenes that cannot be achieved by normal techniques.
specialism (ˈspɛʃəˌlɪzəm) *n* the act or process of specializing in something, or the thing itself.
specialist (ˈspɛʃəlɪst) *n* **1a** a person who specializes in or devotes himself to a particular area of activity, field of research, etc. **1b** (*as modifier*): *specialist knowledge.* **2** an enlisted rank in the U.S. Army denoting technical qualifications that entitle the holder to a noncommissioned officer's pay. **3** *Ecology.* an

organism that has special nutritional requirements and lives in a restricted habitat that provides these. Compare **generalist.** ► ˌ**special'istic** *adj*

speciality (ˌspɛʃɪ'ælɪtɪ) *or chiefly U.S. and Canadian* **specialty** *n, pl* **-ties. 1** a special interest or skill. **2a** a service or product specialized in, as at a restaurant: *roast beef was a speciality of the house.* **2b** (*as modifier*): *a speciality dish.* **3** a special or distinguishing feature or characteristic.

specialize *or* **specialise** ('spɛʃəˌlaɪz) *vb* **1** (*intr*) to train in or devote oneself to a particular area of study, occupation, or activity. **2** (*usually passive*) to cause (organisms or their parts) to develop in a way most suited to a particular environment or way of life or (of organisms, etc.) to develop in this way. **3** (*tr*) to modify or make suitable for a special use or purpose. **4** (*tr*) to mention specifically; specify. **5** (*tr*) to endorse (a commercial paper) to a specific payee. ► ˌ**speciali'zation** *or* ˌ**speciali'sation** *n*

special jury *n* (formerly) a jury whose members were drawn from some profession or rank of society as well as possessing the usual qualifications for jury service.

special licence *n Brit.* a licence permitting a marriage to take place by dispensing with the usual legal conditions.

special pleading *n Law.* **1** a pleading that alleges new facts that offset those put forward by the other side rather than directly admitting or denying those facts. **2** a pleading that emphasizes the favourable aspects of a case while omitting the unfavourable.

special privilege *n* a legally endorsed privilege granted exclusively to some individual or group.

special school *n Brit.* a school for children who are unable to benefit from ordinary schooling because they have learning difficulties, physical or mental handicaps, etc.

special sort *n Printing.* a character, such as an accented letter, that is not a usual member of any fount. Also called: **peculiar, arbitrary.**

special team *n American football.* any of several predetermined permutations of the players within a team that play in situations, such as kick offs and attempts at field goals, where the standard offensive and defensive formations are not appropriate.

special theory of relativity *n* the theory proposed in 1905 by Einstein, which assumes that the laws of physics are equally valid in all nonaccelerated frames of reference and that the speed of electromagnetic radiation in free space has the same value for all inertial observers. It leads to the idea of a space-time continuum and the equivalence of mass and energy. In combination with quantum mechanics it forms the basis of the theory of elementary particles. Also called: **special relativity.** See also **general theory of relativity, Einstein's law** (sense 1).

specialty ('spɛʃəltɪ) *n, pl* **-ties. 1** *Law.* a formal contract or obligation expressed in a deed. **2** another word, chiefly U.S. and Canadian, for **speciality.**

speciate ('spiːsɪˌeɪt) *vb* to form or develop into a new biological species. **[C20:** back formation from SPECIATION**]**

speciation (ˌspiːʃɪ'eɪʃən) *n* the evolutionary development of a biological species, as by geographical isolation of a group of individuals from the main stock. **[C20:** from SPECIES + -ATION**]**

specie ('spiːʃiː) *n* **1** coin money, as distinguished from bullion or paper money. **2 in specie. 2a** (of money) in coin. **2b** in kind. **2c** *Law.* in the actual form specified. **[C16:** from the Latin phrase *in speciē* in kind**]**

specie point *n* another name for **gold point.**

species ('spiːʃiːz; *Latin* 'spiːʃɪˌiːz) *n, pl* **-cies. 1** *Biology.* **1a** any of the taxonomic groups into which a genus is divided, the members of which are capable of interbreeding: often containing subspecies, varieties, or races. A species is designated in italics by the genus name followed by the specific name, for example *Felis domesticus* (the domestic cat). Abbrev.: **sp. 1b** the animals of such a group. **1c** any group of related animals or plants not necessarily of this taxonomic rank. **2** (*modifier*) denoting a plant that is a natural member of a species rather than a hybrid or cultivar: *a species clematis.* **3** *Logic.* a group of objects or individuals, all sharing at least one common attribute, that forms a subdivision of a genus. **4** a kind, sort, or variety: *a species of treachery.* **5** *Chiefly R.C. Church.* the outward form of the bread and wine in the Eucharist. **6** *Obsolete.* an outward appearance or form. **7** *Obsolete.* specie. **[C16:** from Latin: appearance, from *specere* to look**]**

speciesism ('spiːʃiːzˌɪzəm) *n* a belief by humans that all other species of animals are inferior and may therefore be used for human benefit without regard to the suffering inflicted. **[C20:** from SPECIES + -ISM**]**

specif. *abbrev. for* specifically.

specifiable ('spɛsɪˌfaɪəbᵊl) *adj* able to be specified.

specific (spɪ'sɪfɪk) *adj* **1** explicit, particular, or definite: *please be more specific.* **2** relating to a specified or particular thing: *a specific treatment for arthritis.* **3** of or relating to a biological species: *specific differences.* **4** (of a disease) caused by a particular pathogenic agent. **5** *Physics.* **5a** characteristic of a property of a particular substance, esp. in relation to the same property of a standard reference substance: *specific gravity.* **5b** characteristic of a property of a particular substance per unit mass, length, area, volume, etc.: *specific heat.* **5c** (of an extensive physical quantity) divided by mass: *specific heat capacity; specific volume.* **6** Also (rare): **specifical.** *International trade.* denoting a tariff levied at a fixed sum per unit of weight, quantity, volume, etc., irrespective of value. ♦ *n* **7** (*sometimes pl*) a designated quality, thing, etc. **8** *Med.* any drug used to treat a particular disease. **[C17:** from Medieval Latin *specificus,* from Latin SPECIES**]** ► **spe'cifically** *adv* ► **specificity** (ˌspɛsɪ'fɪsɪtɪ) *n*

specification (ˌspɛsɪfɪ'keɪʃən) *n* **1** the act or an instance of specifying. **2** (in patent law) a written statement accompanying an application for a patent that describes the nature of an invention. **3** a detailed description of the criteria for the constituents, construction, appearance, performance, etc., of a material, apparatus, etc., or of the standard of workmanship required in its manufacture. **4** an item, detail, etc., specified.

specific charge *n Physics.* the charge-to-mass ratio of an elementary particle.

specific gravity *n* the ratio of the density of a substance to that of water. See **relative density.**

specific heat capacity *n* the heat required to raise unit mass of a substance by unit temperature interval under specified conditions, such as constant pressure: usually measured in joules per kelvin per kilogram. Symbol: c_p (for constant pressure). Also called: **specific heat.**

specific humidity *n* the mass of water vapour in a sample of moist air divided by the mass of the sample.

specific impulse *n* the ratio of the thrust produced by a rocket engine to the rate of fuel consumption: it has units of time and is the length of time that unit weight of propellant would last if used to produce one unit of thrust continuously.

specific performance *n Law.* a remedy awarded by a court where damages are an insufficient remedy.

specific resistance *n* the former name for **resistivity.**

specific viscosity *n Physics.* a measure of the resistance to flow of a fluid, expressed as the ratio of the absolute viscosity of the fluid to that of a reference fluid (usually water in the case of liquids).

specific volume *n Physics.* the volume of matter per unit mass; the reciprocal of the density. Symbol: v

specify ('spɛsɪˌfaɪ) *vb* **-fies, -fying, -fied.** (*tr; may take a clause as object*) **1** to refer to or state specifically. **2** to state as a condition. **3** to state or include in the specification of. **[C13:** from Medieval Latin *specificāre* to describe**]** ► **specificative** ('spɛsɪfɪˌkeɪtɪv) *adj* ► **'speciˌfier** *n*

specimen ('spɛsɪmɪn) *n* **1a** an individual, object, or part regarded as typical of the group or class to which it belongs. **1b** (*as modifier*): *a specimen signature; a specimen page.* **2** *Med.* a sample of tissue, blood, urine, etc., taken for diagnostic examination or evaluation. **3** the whole or a part of an organism, plant, rock, etc., collected and preserved as an example of its class, species, etc. **4** *Informal, often derogatory.* a person. **[C17:** from Latin: mark, evidence, proof, from *specere* to look at**]**

speciosity (ˌspiːʃɪ'ɒsɪtɪ) *n, pl* **-ties. 1** a thing or person that is deceptively attractive or plausible. **2** the state of being specious. **3** *Obsolete.* the state of being beautiful.

specious ('spiːʃəs) *adj* **1** apparently correct or true, but actually wrong or false. **2** deceptively attractive in appearance. **[C14** (originally: fair): from Latin *speciōsus* plausible, from *speciēs* outward appearance, from *specere* to look at**]** ► **'speciously** *adv* ► **'speciousness** *n*

speck (spɛk) *n* **1** a very small mark or spot. **2** a small or tiny piece of something. ♦ *vb* **3** (*tr*) to mark with specks or spots. **[**Old English *specca;* related to Middle Dutch *spekelen* to sprinkle**]**

speckle ('spɛkᵊl) *n* **1** a small or slight mark usually of a contrasting colour, as on the skin, a bird's plumage, or eggs. ♦ *vb* **2** (*tr*) to mark with or as if with speckles. **[C15:** from Middle Dutch *spekkel;* see SPECK**]** ► **'speckled** *adj*

speckled trout *n* another name for **brook trout.**

speckled wood *n* a common woodland brown satyrid butterfly, *Pararge aegeria,* marked with pale orange or yellowish-white spots.

speckle interferometry *n Astronomy.* a technique to increase the resolution of photographs taken by telescopes that are impaired by atmospheric turbulence, in which the information from a number of exposures of very short duration are combined.

specs (spɛks) *pl n Informal.* **1** short for **spectacles. 2** short for **specifications.**

spectacle ('spɛktəkᵊl) *n* **1** a public display or performance, esp. a showy or ceremonial one. **2** a thing or person seen, esp. an unusual or ridiculous one: *he makes a spectacle of himself.* **3** a strange or interesting object or phenomenon. ♦ See also **spectacles. [C14:** via Old French from Latin *spectaculum* a show, from *spectāre* to watch, from *specere* to look at**]**

spectacled ('spɛktəkᵊld) *adj* **1** wearing glasses. **2** (of an animal) having markings around the eyes resembling a pair of glasses.

spectacles ('spɛktəkᵊlz) *pl n* **1** a pair of glasses for correcting defective vision. Often (informal) shortened to **specs. 2 pair of spectacles.** *Cricket.* a score of 0 in each innings of a match.

spectacular (spɛk'tækjʊlə) *adj* **1** of or resembling a spectacle; impressive, grand, or dramatic. **2** unusually marked or great: *a spectacular increase in spending.* ♦ *n* **3** a lavishly produced performance. ► **spec'tacularly** *adv*

spectate (spɛk'teɪt) *vb* (*intr*) to be a spectator; watch. **[C20:** back formation from SPECTATOR**]**

spectator (spɛk'teɪtə) *n* a person viewing anything; onlooker; observer. **[C16:** from Latin, from *spectāre* to watch; see SPECTACLE**]**

spectator sport *n* a sport that attracts more people as spectators than as participants.

Spector ('spɛktə) *n* **Phil.** born 1940, U.S. record producer and songwriter, noted for the densely orchestrated "Wall of Sound" in his work with groups such as the Ronettes and the Crystals.

spectra ('spɛktrə) *n* the plural of **spectrum.**

spectral ('spɛktrəl) *adj* **1** of or like a spectre. **2** of or relating to a spectrum: *spectral colours.* **3** *Physics.* (of a physical quantity) relating to a single wavelength of radiation: *spectral luminous efficiency.* ► **spectrality** (spɛk'trælɪtɪ) *or* **'spectralness** *n* ► **'spectrally** *adv*

spectral luminous efficiency *n* a measure of the efficiency of radiation of a given wavelength in producing a visual sensation. It is equal to the ratio of the radiant flux at a standard wavelength to that at the given wavelength when the standard wavelength is chosen so that the maximum value of this ratio is unity. Symbol: $V(\lambda)$ (for photopic vision) or $V'(\lambda)$ (for scotopic vision).

spectral type *or* **class** *n* any of various groups into which stars are classified according to characteristic spectral lines and bands. The most important classification (**Harvard classification**) has a series of classes O, B, A, F, G, K, M, the series also being a scale of diminishing surface temperature.

spectre *or U.S.* **specter** ('spɛktə) *n* **1** a ghost; phantom; apparition. **2** a mental image of something unpleasant or menacing: *the spectre of redundancy.* [C17: from Latin *spectrum,* from *specere* to look at]

spectrin ('spɛktrɪn) *n* any one of a class of fibrous proteins found in the membranes of red blood cells, the brain, the intestine, etc. [C20: from SPECTR(E) + -IN, referring to the ghosts (isolated cell membranes) of red blood cells, the source of the first known member of the class]

spectro- *combining form.* indicating a spectrum: *spectrogram.*

spectrobolometer (ˌspɛktrəʊbəʊ'lɒmɪtə) *n* a combined spectroscope and bolometer for determining the wavelength distribution of radiant energy emitted by a source. ▸ **spectrobolometric** (ˌspɛktrəˌbəʊlə'mɛtrɪk) *adj*

spectrofluorimeter (ˌspɛktrəʊflʊə'rɪmɪtə) *or* **spectrofluorometer** *n* an instrument for recording fluorescence emission and absorption spectra.

spectrograph ('spɛktrəʊˌgrɑːf, -ˌgræf) *n* a spectroscope or spectrometer that produces a photographic record (**spectrogram**) of a spectrum. See also **sound spectrograph.** ▸ ˌ**spectro'graphic** *adj* ▸ ˌ**spectro'graphically** *adv* ▸ **spec'trography** *n*

spectroheliograph (ˌspɛktrəʊ'hiːlɪəˌgrɑːf, -ˌgræf) *n* an instrument used to photograph the sun in light of a particular wavelength, usually that of calcium or hydrogen, to show the distribution of the element over the surface and in the atmosphere. The photograph obtained is a **spectroheliogram.** [C19: from SPECTRO- + HELIO- + -GRAPH] ▸ ˌ**spectroˌhelio'graphic** *adj*

spectrohelioscope (ˌspɛktrəʊ'hiːlɪəʊˌskəʊp) *n* an instrument, similar to the spectroheliograph, used for observing solar radiation at one particular wavelength. ▸ **spectrohelioscopic** (ˌspɛktrəʊˌhiːlɪəʊ'skɒpɪk) *adj*

spectrometer (spɛk'trɒmɪtə) *n* any instrument for producing a spectrum, esp. one in which wavelength, energy, intensity, etc., can be measured. See also **mass spectrometer.** ▸ **spectrometric** (ˌspɛktrəʊ'mɛtrɪk) *adj* ▸ **spec'trometry** *n*

spectrophotometer (ˌspɛktrəʊfəʊ'tɒmɪtə) *n* an instrument for producing or recording a spectrum and measuring the photometric intensity of each wavelength present, esp. such an instrument used for infrared, visible, and ultraviolet radiation. See also **spectrometer.** [C19: from SPECTRO- + PHOTO- + -METER] ▸ **spectrophotometric** (ˌspɛktrəʊˌfəʊtə'mɛtrɪk) *adj* ▸ ˌ**spectropho'tometry** *n*

spectroscope ('spɛktrəˌskəʊp) *n* any of a number of instruments for dispersing electromagnetic radiation and thus forming or recording a spectrum. See also **spectrometer.** [C19: from SPECTRO- + -SCOPE; from French, or on the model of German *Spektroskop*] ▸ **spectroscopic** (ˌspɛktrə'skɒpɪk) *or* ˌ**spectro'scopical** *adj* ▸ ˌ**spectro'scopically** *adv*

spectroscopic analysis *n* the use of spectroscopy in determining the chemical or physical constitution of substances.

spectroscopy (spɛk'trɒskəpɪ) *n* the science and practice of using spectrometers and spectroscopes and of analysing spectra, the methods employed depending on the radiation being examined. The techniques are widely used in chemical analysis and in studies of the properties of atoms, molecules, ions, etc. ▸ **spec'troscopist** *n*

spectrum ('spɛktrəm) *n, pl* **-tra** (-trə). **1** the distribution of colours produced when white light is dispersed by a prism or diffraction grating. There is a continuous change in wavelength from red, the longest wavelength, to violet, the shortest. Seven colours are usually distinguished: violet, indigo, blue, green, yellow, orange, and red. **2** the whole range of electromagnetic radiation with respect to its wavelength or frequency. **3** any particular distribution of electromagnetic radiation often showing lines or bands characteristic of the substance emitting the radiation or absorbing it. See also **absorption spectrum, emission spectrum. 4** any similar distribution or record of the energies, velocities, masses, etc., of atoms, ions, electrons, etc.: *a mass spectrum.* **5** any range or scale, as of capabilities, emotions, or moods. **6** another name for an **afterimage.** [C17: from Latin: appearance, image, from *spectāre* to observe, from *specere* to look at]

spectrum analyser *n* an instrument that splits an input waveform into its frequency components, which are then displayed.

spectrum analysis *n* the analysis of a spectrum to determine the properties of its source, such as the analysis of the emission spectrum of a substance to determine the electron distribution in its molecules.

specular ('spɛkjʊlə) *adj* **1** of, relating to, or having the properties of a mirror: *specular reflection.* **2** of or relating to a speculum. [C16: from Latin *speculāris,* from *speculum* a mirror, from *specere* to look at] ▸ **'specularly** *adv*

speculate ('spɛkjʊˌleɪt) *vb* **1** (when *tr, takes a clause as object*) to conjecture without knowing the complete facts. **2** (*intr*) to buy or sell securities, property, etc., in the hope of deriving capital gains. **3** (*intr*) to risk loss for the possibility of considerable gain. **4** (*intr*) *N.Z. rugby.* to make an emergency forward kick of the ball without taking any particular aim. [C16: from Latin *speculārī* to spy out, from *specula* a watchtower, from *specere* to look at]

speculation (ˌspɛkjʊ'leɪʃən) *n* **1** the act or an instance of speculating. **2** a supposition, theory, or opinion arrived at through speculating. **3** investment involving high risk but also the possibility of high profits.

speculative ('spɛkjʊlətɪv) *adj* relating to or characterized by speculation, esp. financial speculation. ▸ **'speculatively** *adv* ▸ **'speculativeness** *n*

speculator ('spɛkjʊˌleɪtə) *n* **1** a person who speculates. **2** *N.Z. rugby.* an undirected kick of the ball.

speculum ('spɛkjʊləm) *n, pl* **-la** (-lə) *or* **-lums. 1** a mirror, esp. one made of polished metal for use in a telescope, etc. **2** *Med.* an instrument for dilating a bodily cavity or passage to permit examination of its interior. **3** a patch of distinctive colour on the wing of a bird, esp. in certain ducks. [C16: from Latin: mirror, from *specere* to look at]

speculum metal *n* a white hard brittle corrosion-resistant alloy of copper (55–70 per cent) and tin with smaller amounts of other metals. It takes a high polish and is used for mirrors, lamp reflectors, ornamental ware, etc.

sped (spɛd) *vb* a past tense and past participle of **speed.**

speech (spiːtʃ) *n* **1a** the act or faculty of speaking, esp. as possessed by persons: *to have speech with somebody.* **1b** (*as modifier*): *speech therapy.* **2** that which is spoken; utterance. **3** a talk or address delivered to an audience. **4** a person's characteristic manner of speaking. **5** a national or regional language or dialect. **6** *Linguistics.* another word for **parole** (sense 5). [Old English *spēc;* related to *specan* to SPEAK]

speech act *n Philosophy.* **1** an utterance that constitutes some act in addition to the mere act of uttering. **2** an act or type of act capable of being so performed. ♦ See also **performative.**

speech community *n* a community consisting of all the speakers of a particular language or dialect.

speech day *n Brit.* (in schools) an annual day on which prizes are presented, speeches are made by guest speakers, etc.

speech from the throne *n* (in Britain and the dominions of the Commonwealth) the speech at the opening of each session of Parliament in which the Government outlines its legislative programme. It is read by the sovereign or his or her representative. Also called (esp. Brit.): **Queen's** (*or* **King's**) **speech.**

speechify ('spiːtʃɪˌfaɪ) *vb* **-fies, -fying, -fied.** (*intr*) **1** to make a speech or speeches. **2** to talk pompously and boringly. ▸ ˌ**speechifi'cation** *n* ▸ **'speechiˌfier** *n*

speechless ('spiːtʃlɪs) *adj* **1** not able to speak. **2** temporarily deprived of speech. **3** not expressed or able to be expressed in words: *speechless fear.* ▸ **'speechlessly** *adv* ▸ **'speechlessness** *n*

speech-reading *n* another name for **lip-reading.**

speech recognition *n* the understanding of continuous speech by a computer.

speech therapy *n* treatment to improve the speech of children who have difficulty in learning to speak, for example because of partial deafness or brain damage, or to help restore the power of speech to adults who have lost it or partly lost it through accident or illness. ▸ **speech therapist** *n*

speed (spiːd) *n* **1** the act or quality of acting or moving fast; rapidity. **2** the rate at which something moves, is done, or acts. **3** *Physics.* **3a** a scalar measure of the rate of movement of a body expressed either as the distance travelled divided by the time taken (**average speed**) or the rate of change of position with respect to time at a particular point (**instantaneous speed**). It is measured in metres per second, miles per hour, etc. **3b** another word for **velocity** (sense 2). **4** a rate of rotation, usually expressed in revolutions per unit time. **5a** a gear ratio in a motor vehicle, bicycle, etc. **5b** (*in combination*): *a three-speed gear.* **6** *Photog.* a numerical expression of the sensitivity to light of a particular type of film, paper, or plate. See also **ISO rating. 7** *Photog.* a measure of the ability of a lens to pass light from an object to the image position, determined by the aperture and also the transmitting power of the lens. It increases as the f-number is decreased and vice versa. **8** a slang word for **amphetamine. 9** *Archaic.* prosperity or success. **10 at speed.** quickly. **11 up to speed. 11a** operating at an acceptable or competitive level. **11b** in possession of all the relevant or necessary information. ♦ *vb* **speeds, speeding; sped** *or* **speeded. 12** to move or go or cause to move or go quickly. **13** (*intr*) to drive (a motor vehicle) at a high speed, esp. above legal limits. **14** (*tr*) to help further the success or completion of. **15** (*intr*) *Slang.* to take or be under the influence of amphetamines. **16** (*intr*) to operate or run at a high speed. **17** *Archaic.* **17a** (*intr*) to prosper or succeed. **17b** (*tr*) to wish success to. ♦ See also **speed up.** [Old English *spēd* (originally in the sense: success); related to *spōwan* to succeed, Latin *spēs* hope, Old Slavonic *spěti* to be lucky] ▸ **'speeder** *n*

speedball ('spiːdˌbɔːl) *n Slang.* a mixture of heroin with amphetamine or cocaine.

speedboat ('spiːdˌbəʊt) *n* a high-speed motorboat having either an inboard or outboard motor.

speed chess *n* a form of chess in which each player's game is limited to a total stipulated time, usually half an hour; the first player to exceed the time limit loses.

speedfreak ('spiːdˌfriːk) *n Slang.* an amphetamine addict.

speed limit *n* the maximum permitted speed at which a vehicle may travel on certain roads.

speedo ('spiːdəʊ) *n, pl* **speedos.** an informal name for **speedometer** or (Austral.) **odometer.**

speedometer (spɪ'dɒmɪtə) *n* a device fitted to a vehicle to measure and display the speed of travel. See also **mileometer.**

speed skating *n* a form of ice skating in which contestants race against each other or the clock over various distances.

speedster ('spiːdstə) *n* a fast car, esp. a sports model.

speed trap *n* a section of road on which the police check the speed of vehicles, often using radar.

speed up *vb* (*adv*) **1** to increase or cause to increase in speed or rate; accelerate. ♦ *n* **speed-up. 2** an instance of this; acceleration.

USAGE The past tense and past participle of *speed up* is *speeded up* not *sped up.*

speedway ('spiːdˌweɪ) *n* **1a** the sport of racing on light powerful motorcycles round cinder tracks. **1b** (*as modifier*): *a speedway track.* **2** the track or stadium where such races are held. **3** *U.S. and Canadian.* **3a** a racetrack for cars. **3b** a road on which fast driving is allowed.

speedwell ('spiːdˌwɛl) *n* any of various temperate scrophulariaceous plants of the genus *Veronica,* such as *V. officinalis* (**common speedwell**) and *V. cha-*

maedrys (**germander speedwell**), having small blue or pinkish white flowers. [C16: from SPEED + WELL[1]]

Speedwriting ('spi:d,raɪtɪŋ) *n Trademark.* a form of shorthand in which alphabetic combinations are used to represent groups of sounds or short common words.

speedy ('spi:dɪ) *adj* **speedier, speediest. 1** characterized by speed of motion. **2** done or decided without delay; quick. ▸ **'speedily** *adv* ▸ **'speediness** *n*

speel (spi:l) *n Manchester dialect.* a splinter of wood. [probably from Old Norse; compare Norwegian *spela, spila,* Swedish *spjela, spjele* SPILL[2]]

speir *or* **speer** (spi:r) *vb Scot.* to ask; inquire. [Old English *spyrian* to seek after, search for]

speiss (spaɪs) *n* the arsenides and antimonides that form when ores containing arsenic or antimony are smelted. [C18: from German *Speise* food]

spek (spek) *n S. African.* bacon, fat, or fatty pork used for larding venison or other game. [Afrikaans]

spelaean *or* **spelean** (spɪ'li:ən) *adj* of, found in, or inhabiting caves: *spelaean animals.* [C19: via New Latin, from Latin *spēlaeum* a cave, from Greek *spēlaion*]

speleology *or* **spelaeology** (,spi:lɪ'ɒlədʒɪ) *n* **1** the scientific study of caves, esp. in respect of their geological formation, flora and fauna, etc. **2** the sport or pastime of exploring caves. [C19: from Latin *spēlaeum* cave] ▸ **speleological** *or* **spelaeological** (,spi:lɪə'lɒdʒɪk[ə]l) *adj* ▸ **,spele'ologist** *or* **,spelae'ologist** *n*

spelk (spelk) *n Scot. and northern English dialect.* a splinter of wood. [from Old English *spelc, spilc* surgical splint; related to Old Norse *spelkur* splints]

spell[1] (spel) *vb* **spells, spelling; spelt** *or* **spelled. 1** to write or name in correct order the letters that comprise the conventionally accepted form of (a word or part of a word). **2** (*tr*) (of letters) to go to make up the conventionally established form of (a word) when arranged correctly: *d-o-g spells dog.* **3** (*tr*) to indicate or signify: *such actions spell disaster for our cause.* ◆ See also **spell out.** [C13: from Old French *espeller,* of Germanic origin; related to Old Norse *spialla* to talk, Middle High German *spellen*] ▸ **'spellable** *adj*

spell[2] (spel) *n* **1** a verbal formula considered as having magical force. **2** any influence that can control the mind or character; fascination. **3** a state induced by or as if by the pronouncing of a spell; trance: *to break the spell.* **4 under a spell.** held in or as if in a spell. ◆ *vb* **5** (*tr*) *Rare.* to place under a spell. [Old English *spell* speech; related to Old Norse *spjall* tale, Gothic *spill,* Old High German *spel*]

spell[3] (spel) *n* **1** an indeterminate, usually short, period of time: *a spell of cold weather.* **2** a period or tour of duty after which one person or group relieves another. **3** *Scot., Austral., and N.Z.* a period or interval of rest. ◆ *vb* **4** (*tr*) to take over from (a person) for an interval of time; relieve temporarily. **5 spell a paddock.** *N.Z.* to give a field a rest period by letting it lie fallow. [Old English *spelian* to take the place of, of obscure origin]

spellbind ('spel,baɪnd) *vb* **-binds, -binding, -bound.** (*tr*) to cause to be spellbound; entrance or enthral.

spellbinder ('spel,baɪndə) *n* **1** a person capable of holding others spellbound, esp. a political speaker. **2** a novel, play, etc., that holds one enthralled.

spellbound ('spel,baʊnd) *adj* having one's attention held as though one is bound by a spell: *a spellbound audience.*

spellchecker ('spel,tʃɛkə) *n Computing.* a program that highlights any word in a word-processed document that is not recognized as being correctly spelt.

speller ('spelə) *n* **1** a person who spells words in the manner specified: *a bad speller.* **2** a book designed to teach or improve spelling.

spellican ('spelɪkən) *n* a variant spelling of **spillikin.**

spelling ('spelɪŋ) *n* **1** the act or process of writing words by using the letters conventionally accepted for their formation; orthography. **2** the art or study of orthography. **3** the actual way in which a word is spelt. **4** the ability of a person to spell: *John's spelling is good.*

spelling bee *n* a contest in which players are required to spell words according to orthographic conventions. [C19: from BEE[2]]

spelling pronunciation *n* a pronunciation of a word that is influenced by the word's orthography and often comes about as the modification of an earlier or original rendering, such as the pronunciation of the British name *Mainwaring,* usually ('mænərɪŋ), as ('meɪn,wɛərɪŋ).

spell out *vb* (*tr, adv*) **1** to make clear, distinct, or explicit; clarify in detail: *let me spell out the implications.* **2** to read laboriously or with difficulty, working out each word letter by letter. **3** to discern by study; puzzle out.

spelt[1] (spelt) *vb* a past tense and past participle of **spell**[1].

spelt[2] (spelt) *n* a species of wheat, *Triticum spelta,* that was formerly much cultivated and was used to develop present-day cultivated wheats. [Old English; related to Old Saxon *spelta,* Old High German *spelza*]

spelter ('speltə) *n* impure zinc, usually containing about 3 per cent of lead and other impurities. [C17: probably from Middle Dutch *speauter,* of obscure origin; compare Old French *peautre* pewter, Italian *peltro* PEWTER]

spelunker (spɪ'lʌŋkə) *n* a person whose hobby is the exploration and study of caves. [C20: from Latin *spēlunca,* from Greek *spēlunx* a cave] ▸ **spe'lunking** *n*

spence (spens) *n Dialect.* **a** a larder or pantry. **b** any monetary allowance. **c** a parlour, esp. in a cottage. [C14: from Old French *despense,* from Latin *dispendere* to distribute; see DISPENSE]

Spence (spens) *n* Sir **Basil** (**Unwin**). 1907–76, Scottish architect, born in India; designed Coventry Cathedral (1951).

spencer[1] ('spensə) *n* **1** a short fitted coat or jacket. **2** a woman's knitted vest. [C18: named after Earl *Spencer* (1758–1834)]

spencer[2] ('spensə) *n Nautical.* a large loose-footed gaffsail on a square-rigger or barque. [C19: perhaps after the surname *Spencer*]

Spencer ('spensə) *n* **1 Herbert.** 1820–1903, English philosopher, who applied evolutionary theory to the study of society, favouring laissez-faire doctrines. **2** Sir **Stanley.** 1891–1959, English painter, noted esp. for his paintings of Christ in a contemporary English setting.

Spencer Gulf *n* an inlet of the Indian Ocean in S Australia, between the Eyre and Yorke Peninsulas. Length: about 320 km (200 miles). Greatest width: about 145 km (90 miles).

spend (spend) *vb* **spends, spending, spent. 1** to pay out (money, wealth, etc.). **2** (*tr*) to concentrate (time, effort, thought, etc.) upon an object, activity, etc. **3** (*tr*) to pass (time) in a specific way, activity, place, etc. **4** (*tr*) to use up completely: *the hurricane spent its force.* **5** (*tr*) to give up (one's blood, life, etc.) in a cause. **6** (*intr*) *Obsolete.* to be used up or exhausted. **7 spend a penny.** *Brit. informal.* to urinate. ◆ *n* **8** an amount of money spent, esp. regularly, or allocated to be spent. ◆ See also **spends.** [Old English *spendan,* from Latin *expendere;* influenced also by Old French *despendre* to spend, from Latin *dispendere;* see EXPEND, DISPENSE] ▸ **'spendable** *adj*

spender ('spendə) *n* a person who spends money in a manner specified: *a big spender.*

Spender ('spendə) *n* Sir **Stephen.** 1909–95, English poet and critic, who played an important part in the left-wing literary movement of the 1930s: co-editor of *Horizon* (1939–41) and of *Encounter* (1953–67). His works include *Journals 1939–83* (1985), *Collected Poems* (1985), and the novel *The Temple* (1988).

spending money *n* an allowance for small personal expenses; pocket money.

spends (spendz) *pl n Lancashire dialect.* a child's pocket money.

spendthrift ('spend,θrɪft) *n* **1** a person who spends money in an extravagant manner. ◆ *adj* **2** (*usually prenominal*) of or like a spendthrift: *spendthrift economies.* [C17: from SPEND + THRIFT]

Spengler ('speŋlə; *German* 'ʃpeŋlər) *n* **Oswald** ('ɔsvalt). 1880–1936, German philosopher of history, noted for *The Decline of the West* (1918–22), which argues that civilizations go through natural cycles of growth and decay.

Spenser ('spensə) *n* **Edmund.** ?1552–99, English poet celebrated for *The Faerie Queene* (1590; 1596), an allegorical romance. His other verse includes the collection of eclogues *The Shepheardes Calendar* (1579) and the marriage poem *Epithalamion* (1594).

Spenserian (spen'sɪərɪən) *adj* **1** relating to, in the style of, or characteristic of Edmund Spenser or his poetry. ◆ *n* **2** a student or imitator of Edmund Spenser.

Spenserian sonnet *n Prosody.* a sonnet form used by the poet Spenser having the rhyme scheme a b a b b c b c c d c d e e.

Spenserian stanza *n Prosody.* the stanza form used by the poet Spenser in his poem *The Faerie Queene,* consisting of eight lines in iambic pentameter and a concluding Alexandrine, rhyming a b a b b c b c c.

spent (spent) *vb* **1** the past tense and past participle of **spend.** ◆ *adj* **2** used up or exhausted; consumed. **3** (of a fish) exhausted by spawning.

spent gnat *n* an angler's name for the spinner of various mayflies, esp. *Ephemeris danica* and *E. vulgata,* particularly when lying spent on the water surface after mating and egg-laying.

speos ('spi:ɒs) *n* (esp. in ancient Egypt) a temple or tomb cut into a rock face. [C19: Greek, literally: a cave, grotto]

Speranski (spe'rænskɪ) *n* **Mikhail Mikhailovich** (mixɑ'il). 1772–1839, Russian statesman, chief adviser (1807–12) to Alexander I. His greatest achievement was the codification of Russian law (begun 1826).

sperm[1] (spɜ:m) *n, pl* **sperms** *or* **sperm. 1** another name for **semen. 2** a male reproductive cell; male gamete. [C14: from Late Latin *sperma,* from Greek; related to Greek *speirein* to sow]

sperm[2] (spɜ:m) *n* short for **sperm whale, spermaceti,** or **sperm oil.**

-sperm *n combining form.* (in botany) a seed: *gymnosperm.* ▸ **-spermous** *or* **-spermal** *adj combining form.*

spermaceti (,spɜ:mə'setɪ, -'si:tɪ) *n* a white waxy substance obtained from oil from the head of the sperm whale: used in cosmetics, candles, ointments, etc. [C15: from Medieval Latin *sperma cētī* whale's sperm, from *sperma* SPERM[1] + Latin *cētus* whale, from Greek *kētos*]

spermary ('spɜ:mərɪ) *n, pl* **-maries.** any organ in which spermatozoa are produced, esp. a testis.

spermatheca (,spɜ:mə'θi:kə) *n* a sac or cavity within the body of many female invertebrates, esp. insects, used for storing spermatozoa before fertilization takes place. [C19: see SPERM[1], THECA] ▸ **,sperma'thecal** *adj*

spermatic (spɜ:'mætɪk), **spermic** ('spɜ:mɪk), *or* **spermous** ('spɜ:məs) *adj* **1** of or relating to spermatozoa: *spermatic fluid.* **2** of or relating to the testis: *the spermatic artery.* **3** of or relating to a spermary. [C16: from Late Latin *spermaticus,* from Greek *spermatikos* concerning seed, from *sperma* seed, SPERM[1]] ▸ **sper'matically** *adv*

spermatic cord *n* a cord in many male mammals that passes from each testis to the abdominal cavity and contains the spermatic artery and vein, vas deferens, and lymphatics.

spermatic fluid *n* another name for **semen.**

spermatid ('spɜ:mətɪd) *n Zoology.* any of four immature male gametes that are formed from a spermatocyte, each of which develops into a spermatozoon.

spermatium (spɜ:'meɪtɪəm) *n, pl* **-tia** (-tɪə). a nonmotile male reproductive cell in red algae and some fungi. [C19: New Latin, from Greek *spermation* a little seed; see SPERM[1]]

spermato-, spermo- *or before a vowel* **spermat-, sperm-** *combining form.* **1** indicating sperm: *spermatogenesis.* **2** indicating seed: *spermatophyte.* [from Greek *sperma, spermat-,* seed; see SPERM[1]]

spermatocide ('spɜ:mətəʊ,saɪd) *n* a less common word for **spermicide.** ▸ **,spermato'cidal** *adj*

spermatocyte ('spɜ:mətəʊ,saɪt) *n* **1** *Zoology.* an immature male germ cell, developed from a spermatogonium, that gives rise, by meiosis, to four spermatids. **2** *Botany.* a male germ cell that develops into an antherozoid.

spermatogenesis (ˌspɜːmətəʊˈdʒɛnɪsɪs) *n* the formation and maturation of spermatozoa in the testis. See also **spermatocyte** (sense 1). ▸ **spermatogenetic** (ˌspɜːmətəʊdʒəˈnɛtɪk) *adj*

spermatogonium (ˌspɜːmətəˈgəʊnɪəm) *n, pl* **-nia** (-nɪə). *Zoology.* an immature male germ cell that divides to form many spermatocytes. [C19: from SPERMATO- + -GONIUM] ▸ **ˌspermatoˈgonial** *adj*

spermatophore (ˈspɜːmətəʊˌfɔː) *n* a capsule of spermatozoa extruded by some molluscs, crustaceans, annelids, and amphibians. ▸ **spermatophoral** (ˌspɜːməˈtɒfərəl) *adj*

spermatophyte (ˈspɜːmətəʊˌfaɪt) *or* **spermophyte** *n* (in traditional classifications) any plant of the major division *Spermatophyta,* which includes all seed-bearing plants: an angiosperm or a gymnosperm. Former name: **phanerogam.** ▸ **spermatophytic** (ˌspɜːmətəʊˈfɪtɪk) *adj*

spermatorrhoea *or esp. U.S.* **spermatorrhea** (ˌspɜːmətəʊˈrɪə) *n* involuntary emission of semen.

spermatozoid (ˌspɜːmətəʊˈzəʊɪd) *n Botany.* another name for **antherozoid.**

spermatozoon (ˌspɜːmətəʊˈzəʊɒn) *n, pl* **-zoa** (-ˈzəʊə). any of the male reproductive cells released in the semen during ejaculation, consisting of a flattened egg-shaped head, a long neck, and a whiplike tail by which it moves to fertilize the female ovum. Also called: **sperm, zoosperm.** ▸ **ˌspermatoˈzoal, ˌspermatoˈzoan,** *or* **ˌspermatoˈzoic** *adj*

sperm bank *n* a place in which semen is stored until it is required for artificial insemination.

spermic (ˈspɜːmɪk) *adj* another word for **spermatic.**

spermicide (ˈspɜːmɪˌsaɪd) *n* any drug or other agent that kills spermatozoa. ▸ **ˌspermiˈcidal** *adj*

spermine (ˈspɜːmiːn, -mɪn) *n* a white or colourless basic water-soluble amine that is found in semen, sputum, and animal tissues; diaminopropyltetramethylenediamine. Formula: $C_{10}H_{26}N_4$.

spermiogenesis (ˌspɜːmɪəʊˈdʒɛnɪsɪs) *n* the stage in spermatogenesis in which spermatozoa are formed from spermatids. ▸ **spermiogenetic** (ˌspɜːmɪəʊdʒəˈnɛtɪk) *adj*

spermogonium (ˌspɜːməˈgəʊnɪəm) *n, pl* **-nia** (-nɪə). a reproductive body in some fungi and lichens, in which spermatia are formed.

sperm oil *n* an oil obtained from the head of the sperm whale, used as a lubricant.

spermophile (ˈspɜːməʊˌfaɪl) *n* any of various North American ground squirrels of the genera *Citellus, Spermophilopsis,* etc., regarded as pests in many regions. [C19: from SPERM(AT)O- + -PHILE, on the model of New Latin *spermophilus* a seed-lover]

spermophyte (ˈspɜːməʊˌfaɪt) *n* a variant spelling of **spermatophyte.**

spermous (ˈspɜːməs) *adj* **1** of or relating to the sperm whale or its products. **2** another word for **spermatic.**

sperm whale *n* a large toothed whale, *Physeter catodon,* having a square-shaped head and hunted for sperm oil, spermaceti, and ambergris: family *Physeteridae.* Also called: **cachalot.** [C19: short for SPERMACETI *whale*]

Sperrin Mountains (ˈspɛrɪn) *n* a mountain range in NW Northern Ireland.

sperrylite (ˈspɛrɪˌlaɪt) *n* a white metallic mineral consisting of platinum arsenide in cubic crystalline form. Formula: $PtAs_2$. [C19: named after F. L. *Sperry,* Canadian chemist]

spessartite (ˈspɛsəˌtaɪt) *n* a brownish red garnet that consists of manganese aluminium silicate and is used as a gemstone. Formula: $Mn_3Al_2(SiO_4)_3$. [C19: named after *Spessart,* mountain range in Germany]

speug (spjʌg) *n Scot.* a sparrow. [of unknown origin]

spew (spjuː) *vb* **1** to eject (the contents of the stomach) involuntarily through the mouth; vomit. **2** to spit (spittle, phlegm, etc.) out of the mouth. **3** (usually foll. by *out*) to send or be sent out in a stream: *flames spewed out.* ◆ *n* **4** something ejected from the mouth. ◆ Also (archaic): **spue.** [Old English *spīwan;* related to Old Norse *spȳja,* Gothic *speiwan,* Old High German *spīwan,* Latin *spuere,* Lithuanian *spiauti*] ▸ **ˈspewer** *n*

Spey (speɪ) *n* a river in E Scotland, flowing generally northeast through the Grampian Mountains to the Moray Firth: salmon fishing. Length: 172 km (107 miles).

Speyer (*German* ˈʃpaiər) *n* a port in SW Germany, in Rhineland-Palatinate on the Rhine: the scene of 50 imperial diets. Pop.: 47 450 (1991). English name: **Spires.**

sp. gr. *abbrev. for* specific gravity.

sphagnum (ˈsfægnəm) *n* any moss of the genus *Sphagnum,* of temperate bogs, having leaves capable of holding much water: layers of these mosses decay to form peat. Also called: **peat moss, bog moss.** [C18: from New Latin, from Greek *sphagnos* a variety of moss] ▸ **ˈsphagnous** *adj*

sphairee (sfaɪˈriː) *n Austral.* a game resembling tennis played with wooden bats and a perforated plastic ball, devised by F. A. Beck in 1961. [from Greek *sphaira* a ball]

sphalerite (ˈsfæləˌraɪt, ˈsfeɪlə-) *n* a yellow to brownish-black mineral consisting of zinc sulphide in cubic crystalline form with varying amounts of iron, manganese, cadmium, gallium, and indium: the chief source of zinc. Formula: ZnS. Also called: **zinc blende.** [C19: from Greek *sphaleros* deceitful, from *sphallein* to cause to stumble]

sphene (sfiːn) *n* a brown, yellow, green, or grey lustrous mineral consisting of calcium titanium silicate in monoclinic crystalline form. It occurs in metamorphic and acid igneous rocks and is used as a gemstone. Formula: $CaTiSiO_5$. Also called: **titanite.** [C19: from French *sphène,* from Greek *sphēn* a wedge, alluding to its crystals]

sphenic (ˈsfiːnɪk) *adj* having the shape of a wedge. [from Greek *sphēn* a wedge]

spheno- *or before a vowel* **sphen-** *combining form.* having the shape of a wedge: *sphenogram.* [from Greek *sphēn* wedge]

sphenodon (ˈsfiːnəˌdɒn) *n* the technical name for the **tuatara.** [C19: from Greek *sphēn* a wedge + *odōn* a tooth]

sphenogram (ˈsfiːnəˌgræm) *n* a character used in cuneiform script.

sphenoid (ˈsfiːnɔɪd) *adj also* **sphenoidal. 1** wedge-shaped. **2** of or relating to the sphenoid bone. ◆ *n* **3** See **sphenoid bone.**

sphenoid bone *n* the large butterfly-shaped compound bone at the base of the skull, containing a protective depression for the pituitary gland.

spheral (ˈsfɪərəl) *adj* **1** of or shaped like a sphere; spherical. **2** perfectly rounded; symmetrical.

sphere (sfɪə) *n* **1** *Maths.* **1a** a three-dimensional closed surface such that every point on the surface is equidistant from a given point, the centre. **1b** the solid figure bounded by this surface or the space enclosed by it. Equation: $(x-a)^2 + (y-b)^2 + (z-c)^2 = r^2$, where *r* is the radius and (*a, b, c*) are the coordinates of the centre; surface area: $4\pi r^2$; volume: $4\pi r^3/3$. **2** any object having approximately this shape; globe. **3** the night sky considered as a vaulted roof; firmament. **4** any heavenly object such as a planet, natural satellite, or star. **5** (in the Ptolemaic or Copernican systems of astronomy) one of a series of revolving hollow globes, arranged concentrically, on whose transparent surfaces the sun (or in the Copernican system the earth), the moon, the planets, and fixed stars were thought to be set, revolving around the earth (or in the Copernican system the sun). **6** particular field of activity; environment: *that's out of my sphere.* **7** a social class or stratum of society. ◆ *vb* (*tr*) *Chiefly poetic.* **8** to surround or encircle. **9** to place aloft or in the heavens. [C14: from Late Latin *sphēra,* from Latin *sphaera* globe, from Greek *sphaira*]

-sphere *n combining form.* **1** having the shape or form of a sphere: *bathysphere.* **2** indicating a spherelike enveloping mass: *atmosphere.* ▸ **-spheric** *adj combining form.*

sphere of influence *n* a region of the world in which one state is dominant.

spherical (ˈsfɛrɪkᵊl) *or* **spheric** *adj* **1** shaped like a sphere. **2** of or relating to a sphere: *spherical geometry.* **3** *Geom.* formed on the surface of or inside a sphere: *a spherical triangle.* **4a** of or relating to heavenly bodies. **4b** of or relating to the spheres of the Ptolemaic or the Copernican system. ▸ **ˈspherically** *adv* ▸ **ˈsphericalness** *n*

spherical aberration *n Physics.* a defect of optical systems that arises when light striking a mirror or lens near its edge is focused at different points on the axis to the light striking near the centre. The effect occurs when the mirror or lens has spherical surfaces. See also **aberration** (sense 4).

spherical angle *n* an angle formed at the intersection of two great circles of a sphere.

spherical coordinates *pl n* three coordinates that define the location of a point in three-dimensional space in terms of its radius vector, *r,* the angle, θ, which this vector makes with one axis, and the angle, ϕ, which the plane of this vector makes with a mutually perpendicular axis. Usually written (*r,* θ, ϕ).

spherical geometry *n* the branch of geometry concerned with the properties of figures formed on the surface of a sphere.

spherical polygon *n* a closed geometric figure formed on the surface of a sphere that is bounded by three or more arcs of great circles.

spherical triangle *n* a closed geometric figure formed on the surface of a sphere that is bounded by arcs of three great circles.

spherical trigonometry *n* the branch of trigonometry concerned with the measurement of the angles and sides of spherical triangles.

sphericity (sfɪˈrɪsɪtɪ) *n* the state or form of being spherical.

spherics[1] (ˈsfɛrɪks) *n* (*functioning as sing*) the geometry and trigonometry of figures on the surface of a sphere.

spherics[2] *or U.S.* **sferics** (ˈsfɛrɪks, ˈsfɪər-) *n* (*functioning as sing*) short for **atmospherics.**

spheroid (ˈsfɪərɔɪd) *n Maths.* another name for **ellipsoid of revolution.**

spheroidal (sfɪəˈrɔɪdᵊl) *adj* **1** shaped like an ellipsoid of revolution; approximately spherical. **2** of or relating to an ellipsoid of revolution. ▸ **spheˈroidally** *or* **spheˈroidically** *adv*

spheroidicity (ˌsfɪərɔɪˈdɪsɪtɪ) *n* the state or form of being spheroidal.

spherometer (sfɪəˈrɒmɪtə) *n* an instrument for measuring the curvature of a surface.

spherule (ˈsfɛruːl) *n* a very small sphere or globule. [C17: from Late Latin *sphaerula* a little SPHERE] ▸ **ˈspherular** *adj*

spherulite (ˈsfɛrʊˌlaɪt) *n* any of several spherical masses of radiating needle-like crystals of one or more minerals occurring in rocks such as obsidian. ▸ **spherulitic** (ˌsfɛrʊˈlɪtɪk) *adj*

sphery (ˈsfɪərɪ) *adj Poetic.* **1** resembling a sphere. **2** resembling a celestial body or bodies; starlike.

sphincter (ˈsfɪŋktə) *n Anatomy.* a ring of muscle surrounding the opening of a hollow organ or body and contracting to close it. [C16: from Late Latin, from Greek *sphinktēr,* from *sphingein* to grip tightly] ▸ **ˈsphincteral** *adj*

sphingomyelin (ˌsfɪŋgəʊˈmaɪəlɪn) *n Biochem.* any of a group of phospholipids, derived from sphingosine, that occur in biological membranes, being especially abundant in the brain. [from *sphingo-,* from Greek *sphingein* to bind + MYELIN]

sphingosine (ˈsfɪŋgəsɪn, -ˌsiːn) *n Biochem.* a long-chain compound occurring in sphingomyelins and cerebrosides, and from which it can be released by hydrolysis. Formula: $CH_3(CH_2)_{12}CH{:}CHCH(OH)CH(NH_2)CH_2OH$. [from *sphingos-,* from Greek *sphingein* to hold fast + -INE[2]]

sphinx (sfɪŋks) *n, pl* **sphinxes** *or* **sphinges** (ˈsfɪndʒiːz). **1** any of a number of huge stone statues built by the ancient Egyptians, having the body of a lion and the head of a man. **2** an inscrutable person.

Sphinx (sfɪŋks) *n* **the. 1** *Greek myth.* a monster with a woman's head and a lion's body. She lay outside Thebes, asking travellers a riddle and killing them when they failed to answer it. Oedipus answered the riddle and the Sphinx then killed herself. **2** the huge statue of a sphinx near the pyramids at El Gîza in

Egypt, of which the head is a carved portrait of the fourth-dynasty Pharaoh, Chephrēn. [C16: via Latin from Greek, apparently from *sphingein* to hold fast]
sphinxlike ('sfɪŋks,laɪk) *adj* like the Sphinx; enigmatic or inscrutable.
sphinx moth *n U.S. and Canadian.* another name for the **hawk moth.**
sphragistics (sfrə'dʒɪstɪks) *n (functioning as sing)* the study of seals and signet rings. [C19: from Greek *sphragistikos,* from *sphragizein* to seal, from *sphragis* a seal] ▸ **sphra'gistic** *adj*
sp. ht *abbrev. for* specific heat.
sphygmic ('sfɪgmɪk) *adj Physiol.* of or relating to the pulse.
sphygmo- *or before a vowel* **sphygm-** *combining form.* indicating the pulse: *sphygmometer.* [from Greek *sphugmos* pulsation, from *sphuzein* to throb]
sphygmograph ('sfɪgməʊ,grɑːf, -,græf) *n Med.* an instrument for making a recording (**sphygmogram**) of variations in blood pressure and pulse. ▸ **sphygmographic** (,sfɪgməʊ'græfɪk) *adj* ▸ **sphygmography** (sfɪg'mɒgrəfɪ) *n*
sphygmoid ('sfɪgmɔɪd) *adj Physiol.* resembling the pulse.
sphygmomanometer (,sfɪgməʊmə'nɒmɪtə) *n Med.* an instrument for measuring arterial blood pressure. [C19: from SPHYGMO- + MANOMETER, on the model of French *sphygmomanomètre*]
spic, spick, *or* **spik** (spɪk) *n U.S. slang.* a derogatory word for a person from a Spanish-speaking country in South or Central America or a Spanish-speaking community in the U.S. [C20: perhaps alluding to a foreigner's mispronunciation of *speak*]
spica ('spaɪkə) *n, pl* **-cae** (-siː) *or* **-cas. 1** *Med.* a spiral bandage formed by a series of overlapping figure-of-eight turns. **2** *Botany.* another word for **spike**[2] (sense 1). [C15: from Latin: ear of corn]
Spica ('spiːkə) *n* the brightest star in the constellation Virgo. Distance: 220 light years.
spicate ('spaɪkeɪt) *adj Botany.* having, arranged in, or relating to spikes: *a spicate inflorescence.* [C17: from Latin *spīcātus* having spikes, from *spīca* a point]
spiccato (spɪ'kɑːtəʊ) *Music.* ♦ *n* **1** a style of playing a bowed stringed instrument in which the bow bounces lightly off the strings. ♦ *adj, adv* **2** to be played in this manner. [Italian: detached, from *spiccare* to make distinct]
spice (spaɪs) *n* **1a** any of a variety of aromatic vegetable substances, such as ginger, cinnamon, nutmeg, used as flavourings. **1b** these substances collectively. **2** something that represents or introduces zest, charm, or gusto. **3** *Rare.* a small amount. **4** *Yorkshire dialect.* confectionery. ♦ *vb (tr)* **5** to prepare or flavour (food) with spices. **6** to introduce charm or zest into. [C13: from Old French *espice,* from Late Latin *speciēs* (pl) spices, from Latin *speciēs* (sing) kind; also associated with Late Latin *spīcea* (unattested) fragrant herb, from Latin *spīceus* having spikes of foliage; see SPICA] ▸ **'spicer** *n*
spiceberry ('spaɪsbərɪ, -brɪ) *n, pl* **-ries. 1** a myrtaceous tree, *Eugenia rhombea,* of the Caribbean and Florida, with orange or black edible fruits. **2** the fruit of this tree. **3** any of various other aromatic plants or shrubs having spicy edible berries, such as wintergreen.
spicebush ('spaɪs,bʊʃ) *n* a North American lauraceous shrub, *Lindera benzoin,* having yellow flowers and aromatic leaves and bark.
Spice Islands *pl n* the former name of the **Moluccas.**
spicery ('spaɪsərɪ) *n, pl* **-eries. 1** spices collectively. **2** the piquant or fragrant quality associated with spices. **3** *Obsolete.* a place to store spices.
spick-and-span *or* **spic-and-span** ('spɪkən'spæn) *adj* **1** extremely neat and clean. **2** new and fresh. [C17: shortened from *spick-and-span-new,* from obsolete *spick* spike, nail + SPAN-NEW]
spicule ('spɪkjuːl) *n* **1** Also called: **spiculum.** a small slender pointed structure or crystal, esp. any of the calcareous or siliceous elements of the skeleton of sponges, corals, etc. **2** *Astronomy.* a spiked ejection of hot gas occurring over 5000 kilometres above the sun's surface (in its atmosphere) and having a diameter of about 1000 kilometres. [C18: from Latin: SPICULUM] ▸ **spiculate** ('spɪkjʊ,leɪt, -lɪt) *adj*
spiculum ('spɪkjʊləm) *n, pl* **-la** (-lə). another word for **spicule** (sense 1). [C18: from Latin: small sharp point, from SPICA]
spicy ('spaɪsɪ) *adj* **spicier, spiciest. 1** seasoned with or containing spice. **2** highly flavoured; pungent. **3** *Informal.* suggestive of scandal or sensation. **4** producing or yielding spices. ▸ **'spicily** *adv* ▸ **'spiciness** *n*
spider ('spaɪdə) *n* **1** any predatory silk-producing arachnid of the order *Araneae,* having four pairs of legs and a rounded unsegmented body consisting of abdomen and cephalothorax. See also **wolf spider, trap-door spider, tarantula, black widow. 2** any of various similar or related arachnids. **3** a hub fitted with radiating spokes or arms that serve to transmit power or support a load. **4** *Agriculture.* an instrument used with a cultivator to pulverize soil. **5** any implement or tool having the shape of a spider. **6** *Nautical.* a metal frame fitted at the base of a mast to which halyards are tied when not in use. **7** any part of a machine having a number of radiating spokes, tines, or arms. **8** Also called: **octopus.** *Brit.* a cluster of elastic straps fastened at a central point and used to hold a load on a car rack, motorcycle, etc. **9** *Snooker, etc.* a rest having long legs, used to raise the cue above the level of the height of the ball. **10** *Angling.* an artificial fly tied with a hackle and no wings, perhaps originally thought to imitate a spider. **11** short for **spider phaeton.** [Old English *spīthra;* related to Danish *spinder,* German *Spinne;* see SPIN]
spider crab *n* any of various crabs of the genera *Macropodia, Libinia,* etc., having a small triangular body and very long legs.
spider hole *n Military.* a small hole in the ground in which a sniper hides.
spider-hunting wasp *n* any solitary wasp of the superfamily *Pompiloidea,* having a slender elongated body: the fast-running female hunts spiders as a food store for her larvae.
spiderman ('spaɪdə,mæn) *n, pl* **-men.** *Informal.* **1** *Chiefly Brit.* a person who erects the steel structure of a building. **2** another name for a **steeplejack.**
spider mite *n* any of various plant-feeding mites of the family *Tetranychidae,* esp. *Panonychus ulmi* (**red spider mite**), which is a serious orchard pest.
spider monkey *n* **1** any of several arboreal New World monkeys of the genus *Ateles,* of Central and South America, having very long legs, a long prehensile tail, and a small head. **2 woolly spider monkey.** a rare related monkey, *Brachyteles arachnoides,* of SE Brazil. [C18: so called because its long limbs resemble the legs of a spider]
spider orchid *n* any of several European orchids of the genus *Ophrys,* esp. *O. sphegodes,* having a flower with yellow, green, or pink sepals and a broad brown velvety lip.
spider phaeton *n* (formerly) a light horse-drawn carriage with a high body and large slender wheels. Sometimes shortened to **spider.**
spider plant *n* a name for various house plants, esp. for *Chlorophytum elatum:* see **chlorophytum.**
spiderwort ('spaɪdə,wɜːt) *n* **1** any of various plants of the American genus *Tradescantia,* esp. *T. virginiana,* having blue, purplish, or pink flowers and widely grown as house plants: family *Commelinaceae.* See also **tradescantia. 2** any of various similar or related plants. [C17: so called because of the spidery shape of its stamens]
spidery ('spaɪdərɪ) *adj* thin and angular like a spider's legs: *spidery handwriting.*
spiegeleisen ('spiːgᵊl,aɪzᵊn) *n* a type of pig iron that is rich in manganese and carbon. [C19: German, from *Spiegel* mirror + *Eisen* IRON]
spiel (ʃpiːl) *n* **1** a glib plausible style of talk, associated esp. with salesmen. ♦ *vb* **2** *(intr)* to deliver a prepared spiel. **3** *(tr; usually foll. by off)* to recite (a prepared oration). [C19: from German *Spiel* play] ▸ **'spieler** *n*
Spielberg ('spiːlbɜːg) *n* **Steven.** born 1947, U.S. film director, noted esp. for the commercial success of such films as *Jaws* (1975), *Close Encounters of the Third Kind* (1977), *Raiders of the Lost Ark* (1981) and its sequels, *E.T.* (1982), and *Jurassic Park* (1993). Other films include *The Color Purple* (1986), *Empire of the Sun* (1988), *Schindler's List* (1993), and *Saving Private Ryan* (1998).
spif (spɪf) *n Informal, chiefly Brit.* a postage stamp perforated with the initials of a firm to avoid theft by employees. Former name: **perfin.** [C20: from *s(tamp) p(erforated with) i(nitials of) f(irm)*]
spiffing ('spɪfɪŋ) *adj Brit. slang, old-fashioned.* excellent; splendid. [C19: probably from dialect *spiff* spruce, smartly dressed]
spiffy ('spɪfɪ) *adj* **-fier, -fiest.** *U.S. and Canadian slang.* smart; stylish. [C19: from dialect *spiff*] ▸ **'spiffily** *adv* ▸ **'spiffiness** *n*
spiflicate *or* **spifflicate** ('spɪflɪ,keɪt) *vb (tr) Brit. school slang.* to destroy; annihilate. [C18: a humorous coinage]
spignel ('spɪgnəl) *n* a European umbelliferous plant, *Meum athamanticum,* of mountain regions, having white flowers and finely divided aromatic leaves. Also called: **baldmoney, meu.** [C16: of uncertain origin]
spigot ('spɪgət) *n* **1** a stopper for the vent hole of a cask. **2** a tap, usually of wood, fitted to a cask. **3** a U.S. name for **tap**[2] (sense 1). **4** a short cylindrical projection on one component designed to fit into a hole on another, esp. the male part of a joint (**spigot and socket joint**) between two pipes. [C14: probably from Old Provençal *espiga* a head of grain, from Latin *spīca* a point]
spik (spɪk) *n* a variant spelling of **spic.**
spike[1] (spaɪk) *n* **1** a sharp point. **2** any sharp-pointed object, esp. one made of metal. **3** a long metal nail. **4** *Physics.* **4a** a transient variation in voltage or current in an electric circuit. **4b** a graphical recording of this, such as one of the peaks on an electroencephalogram. **5** *(pl)* shoes with metal projections on the sole and heel for greater traction, as used by athletes. **6** the straight unbranched antler of a young deer. **7** *Brit. slang.* another word for **dosshouse.** ♦ *vb (tr)* **8** to secure or supply with or as with spikes. **9** to render ineffective or block the intentions of; thwart. **10** to impale on a spike. **11** to add alcohol to (a drink). **12** *Journalism.* to reject (a news story). **13** *Volleyball.* to hit (a ball) sharply downwards with an overarm motion from the front of one's own court into the opposing court. **14** (formerly) to render (a cannon) ineffective by blocking its vent with a spike. **15 spike (someone's) guns.** to thwart (someone's) purpose. [C13 *spyk;* related to Old English *spīcing* nail, Old Norse *spīk* splinter, Middle Low German *spīker* spike, Norwegian *spīk* SPOKE[2], Latin *spīca* sharp point; see SPIKE[2]]
spike[2] (spaɪk) *n Botany.* **1** an inflorescence consisting of a raceme of sessile flowers, as in the gladiolus. **2** an ear of wheat, barley, etc. [C14: from Latin *spīca* ear of corn]
spike heel *n* a very high heel on a woman's shoe, tapering to a very narrow tip. Often shortened to: **spike.** Also called (esp. Brit.): **stiletto, stiletto heel.**
spike lavender *n* a Mediterranean lavender plant, *Lavandula latifolia,* having pale purple flowers and yielding an oil used in paints. [C17: from dialect *spick* lavender, via Old French and Old Provençal from Latin *spīca* SPIKE[2]]
spikelet ('spaɪklɪt) *n Botany.* a small spike, esp. the inflorescence characteristic of most grasses and sedges.
spikenard ('spaɪknɑːd, 'spaɪkə,nɑːd) *n* **1** an aromatic Indian valerianaceous plant, *Nardostachys jatamans,* having rose-purple flowers. **2** an aromatic ointment obtained from this plant. **3** any of various similar or related plants. **4** a North American araliaceous plant, *Aralia racemosa,* having small green flowers and an aromatic root. ♦ Also called (for senses 1, 2): **nard.** [C14: from Medieval Latin *spīca nardī;* see SPIKE[2], NARD]
spike-rush *n* any perennial plant of the temperate cyperaceous genus *Eleocharis,* occurring esp. by ponds, and having underground stems, narrow leaves, and small flowers.
spiky ('spaɪkɪ) *adj* **spikier, spikiest. 1** resembling a spike. **2** having a spike or spikes. **3** *Brit. informal.* ill-tempered. ▸ **'spikily** *adv* ▸ **'spikiness** *n*
spile (spaɪl) *n* **1** a heavy timber stake or pile. **2** *U.S. and Canadian.* a spout for

tapping sap from the sugar maple tree. **3** a plug or spigot. ♦ *vb* (*tr*) **4** to provide or support with a spile. **5** *U.S.* to tap (a tree) with a spile. [C16: probably from Middle Dutch *spile* peg; related to Icelandic *spila* skewer, Latin *spīna* thorn]

spill[1] (spɪl) *vb* **spills, spilling; spilt** *or* **spilled.** (*mainly tr*) **1** (when *intr*, usually foll. by *from, out of*, etc.) to fall or cause to fall from or as from a container, esp. unintentionally. **2** to disgorge (contents, occupants, etc.) or (of contents, occupants, etc.) to be disgorged: *the car spilt its passengers onto the road; the crowd spilt out of the theatre.* **3** to shed (blood). **4** Also: **spill the beans.** *Informal.* to disclose something confidential. **5** *Nautical.* to let (wind) escape from a sail or (of the wind) to escape from a sail. ♦ *n* **6** *Informal.* a fall or tumble. **7** short for **spillway. 8** a spilling of liquid, etc., or the amount spilt. **9** *Austral.* the declaring of several political jobs vacant when one higher up becomes so: *the Prime Minister's resignation could mean a Cabinet spill.* [Old English *spillan* to destroy; related to *spildan*, Old High German *spaltan* to split; see SPOIL] ▸ **'spiller** *n*

spill[2] (spɪl) *n* **1** a splinter of wood or strip of twisted paper with which pipes, fires, etc., are lit. **2** a small peg or rod made of metal. [C13: of Germanic origin; compare Old High German *spilla*, Middle Dutch *spile* stake]

spillage ('spɪlɪdʒ) *n* **1** an instance or the process of spilling. **2** something spilt or the amount spilt.

Spillane (spɪ'leɪn) *n* **Mickey**, original name *Frank Morrison Spillane.* born 1918, U.S. detective-story writer, best known for his books featuring the detective Mike Hammer, for example *I, the Jury* (1947) and *The Twisted Thing* (1966).

spillikin, spilikin ('spɪlɪkɪn), *or* **spellican** ('spɛlɪkən) *n* a thin strip of wood, cardboard, or plastic, esp. one used in spillikins.

spillikins ('spɪlɪkɪnz) *n* (*functioning as sing*) *Brit.* a game in which players try to pick each spillikin from a heap without moving any of the others. Also called: **jackstraws.** [C18: from SPILL[2] + diminutive ending. See -KIN]

spill over *vb* **1** (*intr, adv*) to overflow or be forced out of an area, container, etc. ♦ *n* **spillover. 2** *Chiefly U.S. and Canadian.* the act of spilling over. **3** *Chiefly U.S. and Canadian.* the excess part of something. **4** *Economics.* any indirect effect of public expenditure.

spillway ('spɪl,weɪ) *n* a channel that carries away surplus water, as from a dam. Also called: **wasteweir, spill.**

spilt (spɪlt) *vb* a past tense and past participle of **spill**[1].

spin (spɪn) *vb* **spins, spinning, spun. 1** to rotate or cause to rotate rapidly, as on an axis. **2a** to draw out and twist (natural fibres, as of silk or cotton) into a long continuous thread. **2b** to make such a thread or filament from (synthetic resins, etc.), usually by forcing through a nozzle. **3** (of spiders, silkworms, etc.) to form (webs, cocoons, etc.) from a silky fibre exuded from the body. **4** (*tr*) to shape (metal) into a rounded form on a lathe. **5** (*tr*) *Informal.* to tell (a tale, story, etc.) by drawing it out at great length (esp. in the phrase **spin a yarn**). **6** to bowl, pitch, hit, or kick (a ball) so that it rotates in the air and changes direction or speed on bouncing, or (of a ball) to be projected in this way. **7** (*intr*) (of wheels) to revolve rapidly without causing propulsion. **8** to cause (an aircraft) to dive in a spiral descent or (of an aircraft) to dive in a spiral descent. **9** (*intr;* foll. by *along*) to drive or travel swiftly. **10** (*tr*) Also: **spin-dry.** to rotate (clothes) in a washing machine in order to extract surplus water. **11** (*intr*) to reel or grow dizzy, as from turning around: *my head is spinning.* **12** (*intr*) to fish by drawing a revolving lure through the water. **13** (*intr*) *Informal.* to present news or information in a way that creates a favourable impression. ♦ *n* **14** a swift rotating motion; instance of spinning. **15** *Physics.* **15a** the intrinsic angular momentum of an elementary particle or atomic nucleus, as distinguished from any angular momentum resulting from its motion. **15b** a quantum number determining values of this angular momentum in units of the Dirac constant, having integral or half-integral values. Symbol: *S* or *s* **16** a condition of loss of control of an aircraft or an intentional flight manoeuvre in which the aircraft performs a continuous spiral descent because the angle of maximum lift is less than the angle of incidence. **17** a spinning motion imparted to a ball, etc. **18** (in skating) any of various movements involving spinning rapidly on the spot. **19** *Informal.* a short or fast drive, ride, etc., esp. in a car, for pleasure. **20 flat spin.** *Informal, chiefly Brit.* a state of agitation or confusion. **21** *Austral. and N.Z. informal.* a period of time or an experience; chance or luck; fortune: *a bad spin.* **22** *Commerce, informal.* a sudden downward trend in prices, values, etc. **23** *Informal.* the practice of presenting news or information in a way that creates a favourable impression. ♦ See also **spin out.** [Old English *spinnan;* related to Old Norse *spinna*, Old High German *spinnan* to spin, Lithuanian *pinu* to braid]

spina bifida ('spaɪnə 'bɪfɪdə) *n* a congenital condition in which the meninges of the spinal cord protrude through a gap in the backbone, sometimes causing enlargement of the skull (due to accumulation of cerebrospinal fluid) and paralysis. [New Latin; see SPINE, BIFID]

spinach ('spɪnɪdʒ, -ɪtʃ) *n* **1** a chenopodiaceous annual plant, *Spinacia oleracea*, cultivated for its dark green edible leaves. **2** the leaves of this plant, eaten as a vegetable. [C16: from Old French *espinache*, from Old Spanish *espinaca*, from Arabic *isfānākh*, from Persian]

spinal ('spaɪnᵊl) *adj* **1** of or relating to the spine or the spinal cord. **2** denoting a laboratory animal in which the spinal cord has been severed: *a spinal rat.* ♦ *n* **3** short for **spinal anaesthesia.** ▸ **'spinally** *adv*

spinal anaesthesia *n* **1** *Surgery.* anaesthesia of the lower half of the body produced by injecting an anaesthetic beneath the arachnoid membrane surrounding the spinal cord. See also **epidural** (sense 2). **2** *Pathol.* loss of sensation in some part of the body as the result of injury of the spinal cord.

spinal canal *n* the natural passage through the centre of the spinal column that contains the spinal cord.

spinal column *n* a series of contiguous or interconnecting bony or cartilaginous segments that surround and protect the spinal cord. Also called: **spine, vertebral column.** Nontechnical name: **backbone.**

spinal cord *n* the thick cord of nerve tissue within the spinal canal, which in man gives rise to 31 pairs of spinal nerves, and together with the brain forms the central nervous system.

spin bowler *n Cricket.* a bowler who specializes in bowling balls with a spinning motion.

spindle ('spɪndᵊl) *n* **1** a rod or stick that has a notch in the top, used to draw out natural fibres for spinning into thread, and a long narrow body around which the thread is wound when spun. **2** one of the thin rods or pins bearing bobbins upon which spun thread is wound in a spinning wheel or machine. **3** any of various parts in the form of a rod, esp. a rotating rod that acts as an axle, mandrel, or arbor. **4** a piece of wood that has been turned, such as a baluster or table leg. **5** a small square metal shaft that passes through the lock of a door and to which the door knobs or handles are fixed. **6** a measure of length of yarn equal to 18 hanks (15 120 yards) for cotton or 14 400 yards for linen. **7** *Biology.* a spindle-shaped structure formed from microtubules during mitosis or meiosis which draws the duplicated chromosomes apart as the cell divides. **8** a less common name for a **hydrometer. 9** a tall pole with a marker at the top, fixed to an underwater obstruction as an aid to navigation. **10** a device consisting of a sharp upright spike on a pedestal on which bills, order forms, etc., are impaled. ♦ *vb* **11** (*tr*) to form into a spindle or equip with spindles. **12** (*intr*) *Rare.* (of a plant, stem, shoot, etc.) to grow rapidly and become elongated and thin. [Old English *spinel;* related to *spinnan* to SPIN, Old Saxon *spinnila* spindle, Old High German *spinnala*]

spindle-legged *or* **spindle-shanked** *adj* having long thin legs.

spindlelegs ('spɪndᵊl,legz) *or* **spindleshanks** *pl n* **1** long thin legs. **2** (*functioning as sing*) a person who has long thin legs.

spindle tree *n* any of various shrubs or trees of the genus *Euonymus*, esp. *E. europaeus*, of Europe and W Asia, typically having red fruits and yielding a hard wood formerly used in making spindles: family *Celastraceae.*

spindling ('spɪndlɪŋ) *adj* **1** long and slender, esp. disproportionately so. **2** (of stalks, shoots, etc.) becoming long and slender. ♦ *n* **3** a spindling person or thing.

spindly ('spɪndlɪ) *adj* **-dlier, -dliest.** tall, slender, and frail; attenuated.

spin doctor *n Informal.* a person who provides a favourable slant to an item of news, potentially unpopular policy, etc., esp. on behalf of a political personality or party. [C20: from the spin given to a ball in various sports to make it go in the desired direction]

spindrift ('spɪn,drɪft) *n* **1** spray blown up from the surface of the sea. **2** powdery snow blown off a mountain. ♦ Also called: **spoondrift.** [C17: of Scottish origin, possibly from a variant of obsolete *spoon* to scud + DRIFT]

spin-dry *vb* **-dries, -drying, -dried.** (*tr*) to dry (clothes, linen, etc.) in a spin-dryer.

spin-dryer *n* a device that extracts water from clothes, linen, etc., by spinning them in a perforated drum.

spine (spaɪn) *n* **1** the spinal column. **2** the sharply pointed tip or outgrowth of a leaf, stem, etc. **3** *Zoology.* a hard pointed process or structure, such as the ray of a fin, the quill of a porcupine, or the ridge on a bone. **4** the back of a book, record sleeve, etc. **5** a ridge, esp. of a hill. **6** strength of endurance, will, etc. **7** anything resembling the spinal column in function or importance; main support or feature. [C14: from Old French *espine* spine, from Latin *spīna* thorn, backbone] ▸ **spined** *adj*

spine-bashing *n Austral. informal.* loafing or resting. ▸ **'spine-,basher** *n*

spine-chiller *n* a book, film, etc., that arouses terror. ▸ **'spine-,chilling** *adj*

spinel (spɪ'nɛl) *n* any of a group of hard glassy minerals of variable colour consisting of oxides of aluminium, magnesium, iron, zinc, or manganese and occurring in the form of octahedral crystals: used as gemstones. Formula: $MgAl_2O_4$. [C16: from French *spinelle*, from Italian *spinella*, diminutive of *spina* a thorn, from Latin; so called from the shape of the crystals]

spineless ('spaɪnlɪs) *adj* **1** lacking a backbone; invertebrate. **2** having no spiny processes: *spineless stems.* **3** lacking strength of character, resolution, or courage. ▸ **'spinelessly** *adv* ▸ **'spinelessness** *n*

spinescent (spaɪ'nɛsᵊnt) *adj Biology.* **1** having or resembling a spine or spines. **2** becoming spiny. [C18: from Late Latin *spīnēscere* to become thorny, from Latin *spīna* a thorn] ▸ **spi'nescence** *n*

spinet (spɪ'nɛt, 'spɪnɪt) *n* a small type of harpsichord having one manual. [C17: from Italian *spinetta*, perhaps from Giovanni *Spinetti*, 16th-century Italian maker of musical instruments and its supposed inventor]

spine-tingling *adj* causing a sensation of fear or excitement.

spiniferous (spaɪ'nɪfərəs) *or* **spinigerous** (spaɪ'nɪdʒərəs) *adj* (esp. of plants) bearing spines or thorns. [C17: from Late Latin *spīnifer* having spines, from Latin *spīna* a thorn, spine + *ferre* to bear]

spinifex ('spɪnɪ,fɛks) *n* **1** any Australian grass of the genus *Spinifex*, having pointed leaves and spiny seed heads: often planted to bind loose sand. **2** Also called: **porcupine grass.** *Austral.* any of various coarse spiny-leaved inland grasses of the genus *Triodia.* [C19: from New Latin, from Latin *spīna* a thorn + *-fex* maker, from *facere* to make]

spinnaker ('spɪnəkə; *Nautical* 'spæŋkə) *n* a large light triangular racing sail set from the foremast of a yacht when running or on a broad reach. [C19: probably from SPIN + (MO)NIKER, but traditionally derived from *Sphinx*, the yacht that first adopted this type of sail]

spinner ('spɪnə) *n* **1** a person or thing that spins. **2** *Cricket.* **2a** a ball that is bowled with a spinning motion. **2b** a bowler who specializes in bowling such balls. **3** a streamlined fairing that fits over and revolves with the hub of an aircraft propeller. **4** a fishing lure with a fin or wing that revolves when drawn through the water. **5** an angler's name for the mature adult form (imago) of various flies, especially the mayflies. Compare **dun**[2] (sense 3).

spinneret ('spɪnə,rɛt) *n* **1** any of several organs in spiders and certain insects through which silk threads are exuded. **2** a finely perforated dispenser through which a viscous liquid is extruded in the production of synthetic fibres. [C18: from SPINNER + -ET]

spinney ('spɪnɪ) *n Chiefly Brit.* a small wood or copse. [C16: from Old French *espinei,* from *espine* thorn, from Latin *spīna*]

spinning ('spɪnɪŋ) *n* **1a** the act or process of spinning. **1b** (*as modifier*): *spinning yarn.* **2** the act or technique of casting and drawing a revolving lure through the water so as to imitate the movement of a live fish, etc.

spinning jenny *n* an early type of spinning frame with several spindles, invented by James Hargreaves in 1764. [C18: see JENNY; the reason for the adoption of the woman's name is unclear]

spinning mule *n Textiles.* See **mule**[1] (sense 3).

spinning top *n* another name for **top**[2] (the toy).

spinning wheel *n* a wheel-like machine for spinning at home, having one hand- or foot-operated spindle.

spinode ('spaɪnəʊd) *n Maths.* another name for **cusp** (sense 4). [C19: from Latin *spīna* spine + NODE]

spin-off *n* **1** any product or development derived incidentally from the application of existing knowledge or enterprise. **2** a book, film, or television series derived from a similar successful book, film, or television series.

spinose ('spaɪnəʊs, spaɪ'nəʊs) *adj* (esp. of plants) bearing many spines. [C17: from Latin *spīnōsus* prickly, from *spīna* a thorn] ▸ **'spinosely** *adv* ▸ **spinosity** (spaɪ'nɒsɪtɪ) *n*

spinous ('spaɪnəs) *adj Biology.* **1** resembling a spine or thorn: *the spinous process of a bone.* **2** having spines or spiny projections. **3** another word for **spinose.**

spin out *vb* (*tr, adv*) **1** to extend or protract (a story, etc.) by including superfluous detail; prolong. **2** to spend or pass (time). **3** to contrive to cause (money, etc.) to last as long as possible. ◆ *n* **spinout. 4** a spinning skid in a car that causes it to run off the road.

Spinoza (spɪ'nəʊzə) *n* **Baruch** (bə'ruːk). 1632–77, Dutch philosopher who constructed a holistic metaphysical system derived from a series of hypotheses that he judged self-evident. His chief work is *Ethics* (1677).

Spinozism (spɪ'nəʊzɪzəm) *n* the philosophical system of Spinoza, esp. the concept of God as the unique reality possessing an infinite number of attributes of which we can know at least thought and extension. ▸ **Spi'nozist** *n*

spin stabilization *n* a technique by which a bullet, rocket, etc., is made to spin around its longitudinal axis to assist it in maintaining a steady flight path.

spinster ('spɪnstə) *n* **1** an unmarried woman regarded as being beyond the age of marriage. **2** *Law.* (in legal documents) a woman who has never married. Compare **feme sole. 3** (formerly) a woman who spins thread for her living. [C14 (in the sense: a person, esp. a woman, whose occupation is spinning; C17: a woman still unmarried): from SPIN + -STER] ▸ **'spinster,hood** *n* ▸ **'spinsterish** *adj*

spinthariscope (spɪn'θærɪ,skəʊp) *n* a device for observing ionizing radiation, consisting of a tube with a magnifying lens at one end and a phosphorescent screen at the other. A particle hitting the screen produces a scintillation. [C20: from Greek *spintharis* a little spark + -SCOPE]

spinule ('spaɪnjuːl) *n Biology.* a very small spine, thorn, or prickle. [C18: from Late Latin *spīnula*] ▸ **spinulose** ('spaɪnju,ləʊs) *adj*

spiny ('spaɪnɪ) *adj* **spinier, spiniest. 1** (of animals) having or covered with quills or spines. **2** (of plants) covered with spines; thorny. **3** troublesome to handle; puzzling. **4** shaped like a spine. ▸ **'spininess** *n*

spiny anteater *n* another name for **echidna.**

spiny-finned *adj* (of certain fishes) having fins that are supported by stiff bony spines. See also **acanthopterygian.** Compare **soft-finned.**

spiny lobster *n* any of various large edible marine decapod crustaceans of the genus *Palinurus* and related genera, having a very tough spiny carapace. Also called: **rock lobster, crawfish, langouste.**

spiracle ('spaɪərək^{ə}l, 'spaɪrə-) *n* **1** any of several paired apertures in the cuticle of an insect, by which air enters and leaves the trachea. **2** a small paired rudimentary gill slit just behind the head in skates, rays, and related fishes. **3** any similar respiratory aperture, such as the blowhole in whales. **4** *Geology.* a small vent in a lava flow, formed by escaping gases. [C14 (originally: breath): from Latin *spīrāculum* vent, from *spīrāre* to breathe] ▸ **spiracular** (spɪ'rækjʊlə) *adj* ▸ **spi'raculate** *adj*

spiraea *or esp. U.S.* **spirea** (spaɪ'rɪə) *n* any rosaceous plant of the genus *Spiraea,* having sprays of small white or pink flowers. See also **meadowsweet** (sense 2), **hardhack.** [C17: via Latin from Greek *speiraia,* from *speira* SPIRE[2]]

spiral ('spaɪərəl) *n* **1** *Geometry.* one of several plane curves formed by a point winding about a fixed point at an ever-increasing distance from it. Polar equation of **Archimedes spiral:** $r = a\theta$; of **logarithmic spiral:** $\log r = a\theta$; of **hyperbolic spiral:** $r\theta = a$, (where *a* is a constant). **2** another name for **helix** (sense 1). **3** something that pursues a winding, usually upward, course or that displays a twisting form or shape. **4** a flight manoeuvre in which an aircraft descends describing a helix of comparatively large radius with the angle of attack within the normal flight range. Compare **spin** (sense 16). **5** *Economics.* a continuous upward or downward movement in economic activity or prices, caused by interaction between prices, wages, demand, and production. ◆ *adj* **6** having the shape of a spiral. ◆ *vb* **-rals, -ralling, -ralled** *or U.S.* **-rals, -raling, -raled. 7** to assume or cause to assume a spiral course or shape. **8** (*intr*) to increase or decrease with steady acceleration: *wages and prices continue to spiral.* [C16: via French from Medieval Latin *spīrālis,* from Latin *spīra* a coil; see SPIRE[2]] ▸ **'spirally** *adv*

spiral binding *n Bookbinding.* a method of securing the pages of a publication by passing a coil of wire through small holes punched at the back edge of the covers and individual pages.

spiral galaxy *n* a galaxy consisting of an ellipsoidal nucleus of old stars from opposite sides of which arms, containing younger stars, spiral outwards around the nucleus. In a **barred spiral** the arms originate at the ends of a bar-shaped nucleus.

spiral of Archimedes *n Maths.* a spiral having the equation $r = a\theta$, where *a* is a constant. It is the locus of a point moving to or from the origin at a constant speed along a line rotating around that origin at a constant speed.

spiral staircase *n* a staircase constructed around a central axis.

spirant ('spaɪrənt) *adj* **1** *Phonetics.* another word for **fricative.** ◆ *n* **2** a fricative consonant. [C19: from Latin *spīrāns* breathing, from *spīrāre* to breathe]

spire[1] (spaɪə) *n* **1** Also called: **steeple.** a tall structure that tapers upwards to a point, esp. one on a tower or roof or one that forms the upper part of a steeple. **2** a slender tapering shoot or stem, such as a blade of grass. **3** the apical part of any tapering formation; summit. ◆ *vb* **4** (*intr*) to assume the shape of a spire; point up. **5** (*tr*) to furnish with a spire or spires. [Old English *spīr* blade; related to Old Norse *spīra* stalk, Middle Low German *spīr* shoot, Latin *spīna* thorn] ▸ **'spiry** *adj*

spire[2] (spaɪə) *n* **1** any of the coils or turns in a spiral structure. **2** the apical part of a spiral shell. [C16: from Latin *spīra* a coil, from Greek *speira*] ▸ **spiriferous** (spaɪə'rɪfərəs) *adj*

spirelet ('spaɪəlɪt) *n* another name for **flèche** (sense 1).

spireme ('spaɪriːm) *n Cytology.* the tangled mass of chromatin threads into which the nucleus of a cell is resolved at the start of mitosis. [C19: from Greek *speirēma* a coil, from *speira* a coil, SPIRE[2]]

Spires (spaɪəz) *n* the English name for **Speyer.**

spirillum (spaɪ'rɪləm) *n, pl* **-la** (-lə). **1** any bacterium having a curved or spirally twisted rodlike body. Compare **coccus** (sense 1), **bacillus** (sense 1). **2** any bacterium of the genus *Spirillum,* such as *S. minus,* which causes ratbite fever. [C19: from New Latin, literally: a little coil, from *spīra* a coil] ▸ **spi'rillar** *adj*

spirit[1] ('spɪrɪt) *n* **1** the force or principle of life that animates the body of living things. **2** temperament or disposition: *truculent in spirit.* **3** liveliness; mettle: *they set to it with spirit.* **4** the fundamental, emotional, and activating principle of a person; will: *the experience broke his spirit.* **5** a sense of loyalty or dedication: *team spirit.* **6** the prevailing element; feeling: *a spirit of joy pervaded the atmosphere.* **7** state of mind or mood; attitude: *he did it in the wrong spirit.* **8** (*pl*) an emotional state, esp. with regard to exaltation or dejection: *in high spirits.* **9** a person characterized by some activity, quality, or disposition: *a leading spirit of the movement.* **10** the deeper more significant meaning as opposed to a pedantic interpretation: *the spirit of the law.* **11** that which constitutes a person's intangible being as contrasted with his physical presence: *I shall be with you in spirit.* **12a** an incorporeal being, esp. the soul of a dead person. **12b** (*as modifier*): *spirit world.* ◆ *vb* (*tr*) **13** (usually foll. by *away* or *off*) to carry off mysteriously or secretly. **14** (often foll. by *up*) to impart animation or determination to. [C13: from Old French *esperit,* from Latin *spīritus* breath, spirit; related to *spīrāre* to breathe]

spirit[2] ('spɪrɪt) *n* **1** (*often pl*) any distilled alcoholic liquor such as brandy, rum, whisky, or gin. **2** *Chem.* **2a** an aqueous solution of ethanol, esp. one obtained by distillation. **2b** the active principle or essence of a substance, extracted as a liquid, esp. by distillation. **3** *Pharmacol.* **3a** a solution of a volatile substance, esp. a volatile oil, in alcohol. **3b** (*as modifier*): *a spirit burner.* **4** *Alchemy.* any of the four substances sulphur, mercury, sal ammoniac, or arsenic. [C14: special use of SPIRIT[1], name applied to alchemical substances (as in sense 4), hence extended to distilled liquids]

Spirit ('spɪrɪt) *n* **the. 1a** another name for the **Holy Ghost. 1b** God, esp. when regarded as transcending material limitations. **2** the influence of God or divine things upon the soul. **3** *Christian Science.* God or divine substance.

spirited ('spɪrɪtɪd) *adj* **1** displaying animation, vigour, or liveliness. **2** (*in combination*) characterized by mood, temper, or disposition as specified: *high-spirited; public-spirited.* ▸ **'spiritedly** *adv* ▸ **'spiritedness** *n*

spirit gum *n* a glue made from gum dissolved in ether used to stick a false beard, etc., onto the face.

spiritism ('spɪrɪ,tɪzəm) *n* a less common word for **spiritualism.** ▸ **'spiritist** *n* ▸ **,spirit'istic** *adj*

spirit lamp *n* a lamp that burns methylated or other spirits instead of oil.

spiritless ('spɪrɪtlɪs) *adj* lacking courage or liveliness; melancholic. ▸ **'spiritlessly** *adv* ▸ **'spiritlessness** *n*

spirit level *n* a device for setting horizontal surfaces, consisting of an accurate block of material in which a sealed slightly curved tube partially filled with liquid is set so that the air bubble rests between two marks on the tube when the block is horizontal.

spiritoso (,spɪrɪ'təʊsəʊ) *adj, adv Music.* (often preceded by a tempo marking) to be played in a spirited or animated manner: *allegro spiritoso.* [Italian, from *spirito* spirit, from Latin *spīritus* breath; see SPIRIT[1]]

spiritous ('spɪrɪtəs) *adj* **1** a variant spelling of **spirituous. 2** *Archaic.* high-spirited. **3** *Archaic.* ethereal; pure.

spirits of ammonia *n* (*functioning as sing or pl*) another name for **sal volatile** (sense 2).

spirits of hartshorn *n* (*functioning as sing or pl*) another name for **aqueous ammonia.** See **ammonium hydroxide.**

spirits of salt *n* (*functioning as sing or pl*) a solution of hydrochloric acid in water.

spirits of turpentine *n* (*functioning as sing or pl*) another name for **turpentine** (sense 3).

spirits of wine *n* (*functioning as sing or pl*) another name for **alcohol** (sense 1).

spiritual ('spɪrɪtjʊəl) *adj* **1** relating to the spirit or soul and not to physical nature or matter; intangible. **2** of, relating to, or characteristic of sacred things, the Church, religion, etc. **3** standing in a relationship based on communication between the souls or minds of the persons involved: *a spiritual father.* **4** having a mind or emotions of a high and delicately refined quality. ◆ *n* **5** See **Negro**

spiritual. 6 (*often pl*) the sphere of religious, spiritual, or ecclesiastical matters, or such matters in themselves. 7 **the.** the realm of spirits. ▸ **'spiritually** *adv* ▸ **'spiritualness** *n*

spiritual bouquet *n R.C. Church.* a collection of private devotional acts and prayers chosen and performed by one person for the benefit of another.

spiritual incest *n R.C. Church.* 1 marriage or a sexual relationship between persons related by spiritual affinity or with a person under a solemn vow of chastity. 2 the holding of two benefices by the same priest or bishop.

spiritualism ('spɪrɪtjʊə,lɪzəm) *n* 1 the belief that the disembodied spirits of the dead, surviving in another world, can communicate with the living in this world, esp. through mediums. 2 the doctrines and practices associated with this belief. 3 *Philosophy.* the belief that because reality is to some extent immaterial it is therefore spiritual. 4 any doctrine (in philosophy, religion, etc.) that prefers the spiritual to the material. 5 the condition or quality of being spiritual. ▸ **'spiritualist** *n* ▸ **,spiritua'listic** *adj*

spirituality (,spɪrɪtjʊ'ælɪtɪ) *n, pl* **-ties.** 1 the state or quality of being dedicated to God, religion, or spiritual things or values, esp. as contrasted with material or temporal ones. 2 the condition or quality of being spiritual. 3 a distinctive approach to religion or prayer: *the spirituality of the desert Fathers.* 4 (*often pl*) Church property or revenue or a Church benefice.

spiritualize *or* **spiritualise** ('spɪrɪtjʊə,laɪz) *vb* (*tr*) to make spiritual or infuse with spiritual content. ▸ **,spirituali'zation** *or* **,spirituali'sation** *n* ▸ **'spiritual,izer** *or* **'spiritual,iser** *n*

spiritualty ('spɪrɪtjʊəltɪ) *n, pl* **-ties.** *Archaic.* 1 the clergy collectively. 2 another word for **spirituality.**

spirituel (,spɪrɪtjʊ'ɛl) *adj* having a refined and lively mind or wit. Also (fem): **spirituelle** (,spɪrɪtjʊ'ɛl). [C17: from French]

spirituous ('spɪrɪtjʊəs) *adj* 1 characterized by or containing alcohol. 2 (of a drink) being a spirit. ▸ **spirituosity** (,spɪrɪtjʊ'ɒsɪtɪ) *or* **'spirituousness** *n*

spiritus asper ('spɪrɪtəs 'æspə) *n* another term for **rough breathing.** [Latin: rough breath]

spiritus lenis *n* another term for **smooth breathing.** [Latin: gentle breath]

spirit varnish *n* a varnish consisting of a gum or resin, such as shellac or copal, dissolved in alcohol.

spirketting ('spɜːkɪtɪŋ) *n Nautical.* 1 deck planking near the bulwarks. 2 the interior lining between ports and the overhead interior surface of the cabin. [C18: from obsolete *spirket* space between floor timbers in a ship]

spiro-[1] *combining form.* indicating breath or respiration: *spirograph.* [from Latin *spīrāre* to breathe]

spiro-[2] *combining form.* spiral; coil: *spirochaete.* [from Latin *spīra,* from Greek *speira* a coil]

spirochaete *or U.S.* **spirochete** ('spaɪrəʊ,kiːt) *n* any of a group of spirally coiled rodlike bacteria that includes the causative agent of syphilis. See **treponema.** [C19: from New Latin *spīrochaeta;* see SPIRO-[2], CHAETA]

spirochaetosis *or U.S.* **spirochetosis** (,spaɪrəʊkɪ'təʊsɪs) *n* any disease caused by a spirochaete.

spirograph ('spaɪrə,grɑːf, -,græf) *n Med.* an instrument for recording the movements of breathing. ▸ **,spiro'graphic** *adj*

spirogyra (,spaɪrə'dʒaɪərə) *n* any green freshwater multicellular alga of the genus *Spirogyra,* consisting of minute filaments containing spirally coiled chloroplasts. [C20: from New Latin, from SPIRO-[2] + Greek *guros* a circle]

spiroid ('spaɪrɔɪd) *adj* resembling a spiral or displaying a spiral form. [C19: from New Latin *spīroīdēs,* from Greek *speiroeidēs,* from *speira* a coil]

spirometer (spaɪ'rɒmɪtə) *n* an instrument for measuring the air capacity of the lungs. Compare **pneumatometer.** ▸ **spirometric** (,spaɪrə'metrɪk) *adj* ▸ **spi'rometry** *n*

spironolactone (,spaɪrənəʊ'læktəʊn) *n* a diuretic that increases water loss from the kidneys and is much used to treat oedema in heart and kidney failure. [C20: from SPIRO-[2] + linking syllable *-no-* + LACTONE]

spirt (spɜːt) *n* a variant spelling of **spurt.**

spirula ('spaɪrʊlə) *n* a tropical cephalopod mollusc, *Spirula peronii,* having prominent eyes, short arms, and a small flattened spirally coiled internal shell: order *Decapoda* (cuttlefish and squids). [C19: via New Latin from Late Latin: a small twisted cake, from Latin *spīra* a coil]

spiry ('spaɪərɪ) *adj Poetic.* of spiral form; helical.

spit[1] (spɪt) *vb* **spits, spitting, spat** *or* **spit.** 1 (*intr*) to expel saliva from the mouth; expectorate. 2 (*intr*) *Informal.* to show disdain or hatred by spitting. 3 (of a fire, hot fat, etc.) to eject (fragments of coal, sparks, etc.) violently and with an explosive sound; splutter. 4 (*intr*) to rain very lightly. 5 (*tr;* often foll. by *out*) to eject or discharge (something) from the mouth: *he spat the food out; to spit blood.* 6 (*tr;* often foll. by *out*) to utter (short sharp words or syllables), esp. in a violent manner. 7 **spit chips.** Also (N.Z.): **spit tacks.** *Austral. slang.* to be very angry. 8 **spit it out!** *Brit. informal.* a command given to someone that he should speak forthwith. ◆ *n* 9 another name for **spittle.** 10 a light or brief fall of rain, snow, etc. 11 the act or an instance of spitting. 12 *Informal, chiefly Brit.* another word for **spitting image.** [Old English *spittan;* related to *spǣtan* to spit, German dialect *spitzen*] ▸ **'spitter** *n*

spit[2] (spɪt) *n* 1 a pointed rod on which meat is skewered and roasted before or over an open fire. 2 Also called: **rotisserie, rotating spit.** a similar device rotated by electricity or clockwork, fitted onto a cooker. 3 an elongated often hooked strip of sand or shingle projecting from the shore, deposited by longshore drift, and usually above water. ◆ *vb* **spits, spitting, spitted.** 4 (*tr*) to impale on or transfix with or as if with a spit. [Old English *spitu;* related to Old High German *spiz* spit, Norwegian *spit* tip]

spit[3] (spɪt) *n* the depth of earth cut by a spade; a spade's depth. [C16: from Middle Dutch and Middle Low German *spit*]

spital ('spɪtᵊl) *n Obsolete.* 1 a hospital, esp. for the needy sick. 2 a highway shelter. [C13 *spitel,* changed from Medieval Latin *hospitāle* HOSPITAL]

spit and polish *n Informal.* punctilious attention to neatness, discipline, etc., esp. in the armed forces.

spitchcock ('spɪtʃ,kɒk) *n* an eel split and grilled or fried. Compare **spatchcock.** [C16: of unknown origin; see SPATCHCOCK]

spit curl *n* the U.S. and Canadian name for **kiss curl.** [perhaps so called because it is sometimes plastered down with spittle]

spite (spaɪt) *n* 1 maliciousness involving the desire to harm another; venomous ill will. 2 an instance of such malice; grudge. 3 *Archaic.* something that induces vexation. 4 **in spite of.** (*prep*) in defiance of; regardless of; notwithstanding. ◆ *vb* (*tr*) 5 to annoy in order to vent spite. 6 *Archaic.* to offend. [C13: variant of DESPITE]

spiteful ('spaɪtfʊl) *adj* full of or motivated by spite; vindictive. ▸ **'spitefully** *adv* ▸ **'spitefulness** *n*

spitfire ('spɪt,faɪə) *n* a person given to outbursts of spiteful temper and anger, esp. a woman or girl.

Spithead (,spɪt'hɛd) *n* an extensive anchorage between the mainland of England and the Isle of Wight, off Portsmouth.

Spitsbergen ('spɪts,bɜːgən) *n* another name for **Svalbard.**

spitsticker ('spɪt,stɪkə) *n* a wood-engraving tool with a fine prow-shaped point for cutting curved lines.

spitting distance *n* a short space or distance.

spitting image *n Informal.* a person who bears a strong physical resemblance to another, esp. to a relative. Also called: **spit, spit and image.** [C19: modification of *spit and image,* from SPIT[1] (as in the phrase *the very spit of,* the exact likeness of (someone))]

spitting snake *n* another name for the **rinkhals.**

spittle ('spɪtᵊl) *n* 1 the fluid secreted in the mouth; saliva or spit. 2 Also called: **cuckoo spit, frog spit.** the frothy substance secreted on plants by the larvae of certain froghoppers. [Old English *spǣtl* saliva; see SPIT[1]]

spittle insect *or* **spittlebug** ('spɪtᵊl,bʌg) *n* other names for the **froghopper.**

spittoon (spɪ'tuːn) *n* a receptacle for spit, usually in a public place. [C19: from SPIT[1] + *-oon:* see SALOON, BALLOON, etc.]

spitz (spɪts) *n* any of various breeds of dog characterized by very dense hair, a stocky build, a pointed muzzle, erect ears, and a tightly curled tail. [C19: from German, from *spitz* pointed]

Spitz (spɪts) *n* **Mark.** born 1950, U.S. swimmer, who won seven gold medals at the 1972 Olympic Games.

spiv (spɪv) *n Brit. slang.* a person who makes a living by underhand dealings or swindling; black marketeer. [C20: back formation from dialect *spiving* smart; compare SPIFFY, SPIFFING] ▸ **'spivvy** *adj*

splake (spleɪk) *n* a type of hybrid trout bred by Canadian zoologists. [from *sp(eckled)* + *lake (trout)*]

splanchnic ('splæŋknɪk) *adj* of or relating to the viscera; visceral: *a splanchnic nerve.* [C17: from New Latin *splanchnicus,* from Greek *splankhnikos* concerning the entrails, from *splankhna* the entrails]

splash (splæʃ) *vb* 1 to scatter (liquid) about in blobs; spatter. 2 to descend or cause to descend upon in blobs: *he splashed his jacket.* 3 to make (one's way) by or as if by splashing: *he splashed through the puddle.* 4 (*tr*) to print (a story or photograph) prominently in a newspaper. ◆ *n* 5 an instance or sound of splashing. 6 an amount splashed. 7 a patch created by or as if by splashing: *a splash of colour.* 8 *Informal.* an extravagant display, usually for effect (esp. in the phrase **make a splash**). 9 a small amount of soda water, water, etc., added to an alcoholic drink. [C18: alteration of PLASH[1]]

splashback ('splæʃ,bæk) *n* a sheet of glass, plastic, etc., attached to a wall above a basin to protect the wall against splashing.

splashboard ('splæʃ,bɔːd) *n* 1 a guard on a vehicle to protect people from splashing water, mud, etc. 2 *Nautical.* another word for **washboard** (sense 4b).

splashdown ('splæʃ,daʊn) *n* 1 the controlled landing of a spacecraft on water at the end of a space flight. 2 the time scheduled for this event. ◆ *vb* **splash down.** 3 (*intr, adv*) (of a spacecraft) to make a splashdown.

splasher ('splæʃə) *n* anything used for protection against splashes.

splash out *vb* (*adv;* often foll. by *on*) *Informal, chiefly Brit.* to spend (money) freely or extravagantly (on something).

splashy ('splæʃɪ) *adj* **splashier, splashiest.** 1 having irregular marks. 2 *Informal.* done to attract attention or make a sensation; showy. 3 making a splash or splashes. ▸ **'splashily** *adv* ▸ **'splashiness** *n*

splat[1] (splæt) *n* a wet slapping sound. [C19: of imitative origin]

splat[2] (splæt) *n* a wide flat piece of wood, esp. one that is the upright central part of a chair back. [C19: perhaps related to Old English *splātan* to SPLIT]

splatter ('splætə) *vb* 1 to splash with small blobs; spatter. ◆ *n* 2 a splash of liquid, mud, etc.

splatter movie *n Slang.* a film in which the main feature is the graphic and gory murder of numerous victims.

splatterpunk ('splætə,pʌŋk) *n* a literary genre characterized by graphically described scenes of an extremely gory nature. [C20: from SPLATTER + PUNK[1]]

splay (spleɪ) *adj* 1 spread out; broad and flat. 2 turned outwards in an awkward manner. ◆ *vb* 3 to spread out; turn out or expand. 4 (*tr*) *Vet. science.* to dislocate (a bone). ◆ *n* 5 a surface of a wall that forms an oblique angle to the main flat surfaces, esp. at a doorway or window opening. 6 enlargement. [C14: short for DISPLAY]

Splayd (spleɪd) *n Austral. trademark.* an implement combining the functions of knife, fork, and spoon. [from SP(OON) + (BL)ADE]

splayfoot ('spleɪ,fʊt) *n, pl* **-feet.** 1 *Pathol.* another word for **flatfoot** (sense 1). 2 a foot of which the toes are spread out, as in certain breeds of dog used in hunting waterfowl. ▸ **'splay,footed** *adj* ▸ **'splay,footedly** *adv*

spleen (spliːn) *n* 1 a spongy highly vascular organ situated near the stomach in man. It forms lymphocytes, produces antibodies, aids in destroying worn-out red blood cells, and filters bacteria and foreign particles from the blood. Related adjs: **lienal, splenetic, splenic. 2** the corresponding organ in other animals. **3** spitefulness or ill humour; peevishness: *to vent one's spleen.* **4** *Archaic.* the organ in the human body considered to be the seat of the emotions. **5** *Archaic.* another word for **melancholy. 6** *Obsolete.* whim; mood. [C13: from Old French *esplen,* from Latin *splēn,* from Greek; related to Latin *lien* spleen] ▸ **'spleenish** *or* **'spleeny** *adj*

spleenful ('spli:nfʊl) *adj* affected by spleen; bad-tempered or irritable. ▸ **'spleenfully** *adv*

spleenwort ('spli:nˌwɜ:t) *n* any of various ferns of the genus *Asplenium,* esp. *A. trichomanes,* that often grows on walls, having linear or oblong sori on the undersurface of the fronds. See also **asplenium.**

splendent ('splɛndənt) *adj Archaic.* **1** shining brightly; lustrous: *a splendent sun.* **2** famous; illustrious. [C15: from Latin *splendēns* brilliant, from *splendēre* to shine]

splendid ('splɛndɪd) *adj* **1** brilliant or fine, esp. in appearance. **2** characterized by magnificence; imposing. **3** glorious or illustrious: *a splendid reputation.* **4** brightly gleaming; radiant: *her splendid face; splendid colours.* **5** very good or satisfactory: *a splendid time.* [C17: from Latin *splendidus,* from *splendēre* to shine] ▸ **'splendidly** *adv* ▸ **'splendidness** *n*

splendiferous (splɛn'dɪfərəs) *adj Facetious.* grand; splendid: *a really splendiferous meal.* [C15: from Medieval Latin *splendiferus,* from Latin *splendor* radiance + *ferre* to bring] ▸ **splen'diferously** *adv* ▸ **splen'diferousness** *n*

splendour *or U.S.* **splendor** ('splɛndə) *n* **1** the state or quality of being splendid. **2 sun in splendour.** *Heraldry.* a representation of the sun with rays and a human face. ▸ **'splendorous** *or* **splendrous** ('splɛndrəs) *adj*

splenectomy (splɪ'nɛktəmɪ) *n, pl* **-mies.** surgical removal of the spleen.

splenetic (splɪ'nɛtɪk) *adj* **1** of or relating to the spleen. **2** spiteful or irritable; peevish. **3** *Obsolete.* full of melancholy. ◆ *n* **4** a spiteful or irritable person. [C16: from Late Latin *splēnēticus,* from Latin *splēn* SPLEEN] ▸ **sple'netically** *adv*

splenic ('splɛnɪk, 'spli:-) *adj* **1** of, relating to, or in the spleen. **2** having a disease or disorder of the spleen.

splenitis (splɪ'naɪtɪs) *n* inflammation of the spleen.

splenius ('spli:nɪəs) *n, pl* **-nii** (-nɪˌaɪ). *Anatomy.* either of two flat muscles situated at the back of the neck that rotate, flex, and extend the head and neck. [C18: via New Latin from Greek *splēnion* a plaster] ▸ **'splenial** *adj*

splenomegaly (ˌspli:nəʊ'mɛgəlɪ) *n Pathol.* abnormal enlargement of the spleen. [C20: from Greek *splēno-,* from *splēn* SPLEEN + *megalo-,* from *megas* large + -Y³]

splice (splaɪs) *vb (tr)* **1** to join (two ropes) by intertwining the strands. **2** to join up the trimmed ends of (two pieces of wire, film, magnetic tape, etc.) with solder or an adhesive material. **3** to join (timbers) by overlapping and binding or bolting the ends together. **4** *(passive) Informal.* to enter into marriage: *the couple got spliced last Saturday.* **5 splice the mainbrace.** *Nautical history.* to issue and partake of an extra allocation of alcoholic spirits. ◆ *n* **6** a join made by splicing. **7** the place where such a join occurs. **8** the wedge-shaped end of a cricket-bat handle or similar instrument that fits into the blade. [C16: probably from Middle Dutch *splissen;* related to German *spleissen,* Swedish *splitsa;* see SPLIT] ▸ **'splicer** *n*

spliff (splɪf) *n Slang.* a cannabis cigarette.

spline (splaɪn) *n* **1** any one of a series of narrow keys (**external splines**) formed longitudinally around the circumference of a shaft that fit into corresponding grooves (**internal splines**) in a mating part: used to prevent movement between two parts, esp. in transmitting torque. **2** a long narrow strip of wood, metal, etc.; slat. **3** a thin narrow strip made of wood, metal, or plastic fitted into a groove in the edge of a board, tile, etc., to connect it to another. ◆ *vb* **4** *(tr)* to provide (a shaft, part, etc.) with splines. [C18: East Anglian dialect; perhaps related to Old English *splin* spindle; see SPLINT]

splint (splɪnt) *n* **1** a rigid support for restricting movement of an injured part, esp. a broken bone. **2** a thin sliver of wood, esp. one that is used to light cigars, a fire, etc. **3** a thin strip of wood woven with others to form a chair seat, basket, etc. **4** *Vet. science.* a bony enlargement of the cannon bone of a horse. **5** one of the overlapping metal plates used in armour after about 1330. **6** another word for **splinter.** ◆ *vb* **7** to apply a splint to (a broken arm, etc.). [C13: from Middle Low German *splinte;* related to Middle Dutch *splinte* splint, Old High German *spaltan* to split] ▸ **'splintˌlike** *adj*

splint bone *n* one of the rudimentary metacarpal or metatarsal bones in horses and similar animals, occurring on each side of the cannon bone.

splinter ('splɪntə) *n* **1** a very small sharp piece of wood, glass, metal, etc., characteristically long and thin, broken off from a whole. **2** a metal fragment, from the container of a shell, bomb, etc., thrown out during an explosion. ◆ *vb* **3** to reduce or be reduced to sharp fragments; shatter. **4** to break or be broken off in small sharp fragments. [C14: from Middle Dutch *splinter;* see SPLINT] ▸ **'splintery** *adj*

splinter group *n* a number of members of an organization, political party, etc., who split from the main body and form an independent association, usually as the result of dissension.

split (splɪt) *vb* **splits, splitting, split. 1** to break or cause to break, esp. forcibly, by cleaving into separate pieces, often into two roughly equal pieces: *to split a brick.* **2** to separate or be separated from a whole: *he split a piece of wood from the block.* **3** to separate or be separated into factions, usually through discord. **4** (often foll. by *up*) to separate or cause to separate through a disagreement. **5** (when *tr,* often foll. by *up*) to divide or be divided among two or more persons: *split up the pie among the three of us.* **6** *Slang.* to depart; leave: *let's split; we split the scene.* **7** *(tr)* to separate (something) into its components by interposing something else: *to split a word with hyphens.* **8** *(intr;* usually foll. by *on) Slang.* to betray the trust, plans, etc. (of); inform: *he split on me to the cops.* **9** *(tr) U.S. politics.* to mark (a ballot, etc.) so as to vote for the candidates of more than one party: *he split the ticket.* **10** *(tr)* to separate (an animal hide or skin) into layers. **11 split hairs.** to make a fine but needless distinction. **12 split one's sides.** to laugh very heartily. **13 split the difference. 13a** to settle a dispute by effecting a compromise in which both sides give way to the same extent. **13b** to divide a remainder equally. ◆ *n* **14** the act or process of splitting. **15** a gap or rift caused or a piece removed by the process of splitting. **16** a breach or schism in a group or the faction resulting from such a breach. **17** a dessert of sliced fruit and ice cream, covered with whipped cream, nuts, etc.: *banana split.* **18** See **Devonshire split. 19a** a separated layer of an animal hide or skin other than the outer layer. **19b** leather made from such a layer. **20** *Tenpin bowling.* a formation of the pins after the first bowl in which there is a large gap between two pins or groups of pins. **21** *Informal.* an arrangement or process of dividing up loot or money. ◆ *adj* **22** having been split; divided: *split logs.* **23** having a split or splits: *hair with split ends.* ◆ See also **splits, split up.** [C16: from Middle Dutch *splitten* to cleave; related to Middle High German *splīzen;* see SPLICE] ▸ **'splitter** *n*

Split (*Serbo-Croat* split) *n* a port and resort in W Croatia on the Adriatic: remains of the palace of Diocletian (295–305). Pop.: 200 459 (1991). Italian name: **Spalato.**

split brain *n* a brain in which the tracts connecting the two halves of the cerebral cortex have been surgically split or are missing from birth.

split cane *n Angling.* bamboo split into strips of triangular section, tapered, and glued to form a stiff but flexible hexagonal rod: used, esp. formerly, for making fishing rods.

split decision *n Boxing.* the award of a fight on a majority verdict of the judges as opposed to a unanimous decision.

split infinitive *n* (in English grammar) an infinitive used with another word between *to* (the infinitive marker) and the verb itself, as in *I want to really finish it this time.*

USAGE The traditional rule against placing an adverb between *to* and its verb is gradually disappearing. Although it is true that a split infinitive may result in a clumsy sentence (*he decided to firmly and definitively deal with the problem*), this is not enough to justify the absolute condemnation that this practice has attracted. Indeed, very often the most natural position of the adverb is between *to* and the verb (*he decided to really try next time*) and to change it would result in an artificial and awkward construction (*he decided really to try next time*). The current view is therefore that the split infinitive is not a grammatical error. Nevertheless, many writers prefer to avoid splitting infinitives in formal written English, since readers with a more traditional point of view are likely to interpret this type of construction as incorrect.

split keyboarding *n Computing.* the act or practice of editing data from one terminal on another terminal.

split-level *adj* (of a house, room, etc.) having the floor level of one part about half a storey above or below the floor level of an adjoining part.

split-new *adj Scot.* brand-new.

split pea *n* a pea dried and split and used in soups, pease pudding, or as a vegetable.

split personality *n* **1** the tendency to change rapidly in mood or temperament. **2** a nontechnical term for **multiple personality.**

split pin *n* a metal pin made by bending double a wire, often of hemispherical section, so that it can be passed through a hole in a nut, shaft, etc., to secure another part by bending back the ends of the wire.

split ring *n* a steel ring having two helical turns, often used as a key ring.

splits (splɪts) *n (functioning as sing)* (in gymnastics, etc.) the act of sinking to the floor to achieve a sitting position in which both legs are straight, pointing in opposite directions, and at right angles to the body.

split-screen technique *n* a cinematic device by which two or more complete images are projected simultaneously onto separate parts of the screen. Also called: **split screen.**

split second *n* **1** an extremely small period of time; instant. ◆ *adj* **split-second.** *(prenominal)* **2** made or arrived at in an infinitely short time: *a split-second decision.* **3** depending upon minute precision: *split-second timing.*

split shift *n* a work period divided into two parts that are separated by an interval longer than a normal rest period.

split ticket *n* See **split** (sense 9). See also **straight ticket.**

split tin *n Brit.* a long loaf of bread split on top, giving a greater crust area.

splitting ('splɪtɪŋ) *adj* **1** (of a headache) intolerably painful; acute. **2** (of the head) assailed by an overpowering unbearable pain. ◆ *n* **3** *Psychoanal.* the Freudian defence mechanism in which an object or idea (or, alternatively, the ego) is separated into two or more parts in order to remove its threatening meaning.

split up *vb (adv)* **1** *(tr)* to separate out into parts; divide. **2** *(intr)* to become separated or parted through disagreement: *they split up after years of marriage.* **3** to break down or be capable of being broken down into constituent parts: *I have split up the question into three parts.* ◆ *n* **split-up. 4** the act or an instance of separating.

split wings *pl n Angling.* **a** wings (of an artificial fly) that are dressed cocked up and separated into a V shape. **b** *(as modifier): a split-wing pattern.*

splodge (splɒdʒ) *n* **1** a large irregular spot or blot. ◆ *vb* **2** *(tr)* to mark (something) with such a blot or blots. [C19: alteration of earlier SPLOTCH] ▸ **'splodgy** *adj*

splore (splɔ:r) *n Scot.* a revel; binge; escapade. [C18: of obscure origin]

splosh (splɒʃ) *vb* **1** to scatter (liquid) vigorously about in blobs: *visitors can splosh in the world's largest man-made waterfall.* ◆ *n* **2** an instance or sound of sploshing.

splotch (splɒtʃ) *n, vb* the usual U.S. word for **splodge.** [C17: perhaps a blend of SPOT + BLOTCH] ▸ **'splotchy** *adj*

splurge (splɜːdʒ) *n* **1** an ostentatious display, esp. of wealth. **2** a bout of unrestrained extravagance. ♦ *vb* **3** (often foll. by *on*) to spend (money) unrestrainedly or extravagantly. [C19: of uncertain origin]

splutter (ˈsplʌtə) *vb* **1** to spit out (saliva, food particles, etc.) from the mouth in an explosive manner, as through choking or laughing. **2** to utter (words) with spitting sounds, as through rage or choking. **3** to eject or be ejected in an explosive manner: *sparks spluttered from the fire.* **4** (*tr*) to bespatter (a person) with tiny particles explosively ejected: *he spluttered the boy next to him with ink.* ♦ *n* **5** the process or noise of spluttering. **6** spluttering incoherent speech, esp. in argument. **7** anything ejected through spluttering. [C17: variant of SPUTTER, influenced by SPLASH] ► **ˈsplutterer** *n*

Spock (spɒk) *n* **Benjamin**, known as *Dr Spock.* 1903–98, U.S. paediatrician, whose *The Common Sense Book of Baby and Child Care* (1946) has influenced the upbringing of children throughout the world.

spode (spəud) *n* (*sometimes cap.*) china or porcelain manufactured by Josiah Spode, English potter (1754–1827), or his company.

spodumene (ˈspɒdjuˌmiːn) *n* a greyish-white, green, or lilac pyroxene mineral consisting of lithium aluminium silicate in monoclinic crystalline form. It is an important ore of lithium and is used in the manufacture of glass and ceramics and as a gemstone. Formula: $LiAlSi_2O_6$. [C19: from French *spodumène,* from German *Spodumen,* from Greek *spodoumenos,* from *spodousthai* to be burnt to ashes, from *spodos* wood ash]

spoil (spɔɪl) *vb* **spoils, spoiling, spoilt** *or* **spoiled. 1** (*tr*) to cause damage to (something), in regard to its value, beauty, usefulness, etc. **2** (*tr*) to weaken the character of (a child) by complying unrestrainedly with its desires. **3** (*intr*) (of perishable substances) to become unfit for consumption or use: *the fruit must be eaten before it spoils.* **4** (*intr*) *Sport.* to disrupt the play or style of an opponent, as to prevent him from settling into a rhythm. **5** *Archaic.* to strip (a person or place) of (property or goods) by force or violence. **6 be spoiling for.** to have an aggressive desire for (a fight, etc). ♦ *n* **7** waste material thrown up by an excavation. **8** any treasure accumulated by a person: *this gold ring was part of the spoil.* **9** *Obsolete.* **9a** the act of plundering. **9b** a strategically placed building, city, etc., captured as plunder. ♦ See also **spoils.** [C13: from Old French *espoillier,* from Latin *spoliāre* to strip, from *spolium* booty]

spoilage (ˈspɔɪlɪdʒ) *n* **1** the act or an instance of spoiling or the state or condition of being spoilt. **2** an amount of material that has been wasted by being spoilt: *the spoilage of corn was considerable.*

spoiled priest *n Irish.* a person who was a student for the priesthood but who has withdrawn or been dismissed.

spoiler (ˈspɔɪlə) *n* **1** plunderer or robber. **2** a person or thing that causes spoilage or corruption. **3** a device fitted to an aircraft wing to increase drag and reduce lift. It is usually extended into the airflow to assist descent and banking. Compare **air brake** (sense 2). **4** a similar device fitted to a car. **5** *Sport.* a competitor who adopts spoiling tactics, as in boxing. **6** a magazine, newspaper, etc. produced specifically to coincide with the production of a rival magazine, newspaper, etc. in order to divert public interest and reduce its sales.

spoilfive (ˈspɔɪlˌfaɪv) *n* a card game for two or more players with five cards each.

spoils (spɔɪlz) *pl n* **1** (*sometimes sing*) valuables seized by violence, esp. in war. **2** *Chiefly U.S.* the rewards and benefits of public office regarded as plunder for the winning party or candidate. See also **spoils system.**

spoilsman (ˈspɔɪlzmən) *n, pl* **-men.** *U.S. politics.* a person who shares in the spoils of office or advocates the spoils system.

spoilsport (ˈspɔɪlˌspɔːt) *n Informal.* a person who spoils the pleasure of other people by his actions or attitudes.

spoils system *n Chiefly U.S.* the practice of filling appointive public offices with friends and supporters of the ruling political party. Compare **merit system.**

spoilt (spɔɪlt) *vb* a past tense and past participle of **spoil.**

Spokane (spəuˈkæn) *n* a city in E Washington: commercial centre of an agricultural region. Pop.: 186 562 (1996 est.).

spoke[1] (spəuk) *vb* **1** the past tense of **speak. 2** *Archaic or dialect.* a past participle of **speak.**

spoke[2] (spəuk) *n* **1** a radial member of a wheel, joining the hub to the rim. **2** a radial projection from the rim of a wheel, as in a ship's wheel. **3** a rung of a ladder. **4 put a spoke in someone's wheel.** *Brit.* to thwart someone's plans. ♦ *vb* **5** (*tr*) to equip with or as if with spokes. [Old English *spāca*]

spoken (ˈspəukən) *vb* **1** the past participle of **speak.** ♦ *adj* **2** uttered through the medium of speech. Compare **written. 3** (*in combination*) having speech as specified: *soft-spoken.* **4 spoken for.** engaged, reserved, or allocated.

spokeshave (ˈspəukˌʃeɪv) *n* a small plane with two handles, one on each side of its blade, used for shaping or smoothing cylindrical wooden surfaces, such as spokes.

spokesman (ˈspəuksmən), **spokesperson** (ˈspəuksˌpɜːsᵊn), *or* (*fem*) **spokeswoman** (ˈspəuksˌwumən) *n, pl* **-men, -persons** *or* **-people,** *or* **-women.** a person authorized to speak on behalf of another person, group of people, or organization.

spoliate (ˈspəulɪˌeɪt) *vb* a less common word for **despoil.**

spoliation (ˌspəulɪˈeɪʃən) *n* **1** the act or an instance of despoiling or plundering. **2** the authorized seizure or plundering of neutral vessels on the seas by a belligerent state in time of war. **3** *Law.* the material alteration of a document so as to render it invalid. **4** *English ecclesiastical law.* the taking of the fruits of a benefice by a person not entitled to them. [C14: from Latin *spoliātiō,* from *spoliāre* to SPOIL] ► **ˈspoliatory** *adj*

spondaic (spɒnˈdeɪɪk) *adj Prosody.* of, relating to, or consisting of spondees.

spondee (ˈspɒndiː) *n Prosody.* a metrical foot consisting of two long syllables (¯¯). [C14: from Old French *spondée,* from Latin *spondēus,* from Greek *spondeios,* from *spondē* a ritual libation; from the use of spondee in the music that characteristically accompanied such ceremonies]

spondulix *or* **spondulicks** (spɒnˈdjuːlɪks) *n Slang.* money. [C19: of obscure origin]

spondylitis (ˌspɒndɪˈlaɪtɪs) *n* inflammation of the vertebrae. [C19: from New Latin, from Greek *spondulos* vertebra; see -ITIS]

sponge (spʌndʒ) *n* **1** any multicellular typically marine animal of the phylum *Porifera,* usually occurring in complex sessile colonies in which the porous body is supported by a fibrous, calcareous, or siliceous skeletal framework. **2** a piece of the light porous highly absorbent elastic skeleton of certain sponges, used in bathing, cleaning, etc. See also **spongin. 3** any of a number of light porous elastic materials resembling a sponge. **4** another word for **sponger** (sense 1). **5** *Informal.* a person who indulges in heavy drinking. **6** leavened dough, esp. before kneading. **7** See **sponge cake. 8** Also called: **sponge pudding.** *Brit.* a light steamed or baked pudding, spongy in texture, made with various flavourings or fruit. **9** porous metal produced by electrolysis or by reducing a metal compound without fusion or sintering and capable of absorbing large quantities of gas: *platinum sponge.* **10** a rub with a sponge. **11 throw in the sponge.** See **throw in** (sense 4). ♦ *vb* **12** (*tr;* often foll. by *off* or *down*) to clean (something) by wiping or rubbing with a damp or wet sponge. **13** (*tr;* usually foll. by *off, away, out,* etc.) to remove (marks, etc.) by rubbing with a damp or wet sponge or cloth. **14** (when *tr,* often foll. by *up*) to absorb (liquids, esp. when spilt) in the manner of a sponge. **15** (*tr;* often foll. by *off*) to get (something) from (someone) by presuming on his generosity: *to sponge a meal off someone.* **16** (*intr;* often foll. by *off* or *on*) to obtain one's subsistence, welfare, etc., unjustifiably (from): *he sponges off his friends.* **17** (*intr*) to go collecting sponges. ♦ See also **sponge down.** [Old English, from Latin *spongia,* from Greek] ► **ˈspongeˌlike** *adj*

sponge bag *n* a small bag made of plastic, etc., that holds toilet articles, used esp. when travelling.

sponge bath *n* a washing of the body with a wet sponge or cloth, but without immersion in water.

sponge cake *n* a light porous cake, made of eggs, sugar, flour, and flavourings traditionally without any fat.

sponge cloth *n* any of various porous fabrics, usually made in a loose honeycomb weave.

sponge down *vb* (*tr, adv*) **1** to wipe clean with a damp sponge or cloth. ♦ *n* **sponge-down. 2** the act or instance of sponging down.

sponger (ˈspʌndʒə) *n* **1** *Informal.* a person who lives off other people by continually taking advantage of their generosity; parasite or scrounger. **2** a person or ship employed in collecting sponges.

spongiform (ˈspʌndʒɪˌfɔːm) *adj* **1** resembling a sponge in appearance, esp. in having many holes. **2** denoting diseases characterized by this appearance of affected tissues.

spongin (ˈspʌndʒɪn) *n* a fibrous horny protein that forms the skeletal framework of the bath sponge and related sponges. [C19: from German, from Latin *spongia* SPONGE + -IN]

spongioblast (ˈspʌndʒɪəuˌblɑːst) *n* any of numerous columnar epithelial cells in the brain and spinal cord that develop into neuroglia. [C20: from Greek *spongia* SPONGE + -BLAST] ► **spongioblastic** (ˌspʌndʒɪəuˈblæstɪk) *adj*

spongy (ˈspʌndʒɪ) *adj* **-gier, -giest. 1** of or resembling a sponge, esp. in texture, porosity, elasticity, or compressibility: *spongy bread; spongy bone.* **2** of or like a sponge in respect of its capacity to absorb fluid and yield it when compressed. ► **ˈspongily** *adv* ► **ˈsponginess** *n*

sponsion (ˈspɒnʃən) *n* **1** the act or process of becoming surety; sponsorship. **2** (*often pl*) *International law.* an unauthorized agreement made by a public officer, esp. an admiral or general in time of war, requiring ratification by the government of the state concerned. **3** any act or promise, esp. one made on behalf of someone else. [C17: from Latin *sponsiō,* from *spondēre* to pledge]

sponson (ˈspɒnsən) *n* **1** *Naval.* an outboard support for a gun enabling it to fire fore and aft. **2** a semicircular gun turret on the side of a tank. **3** a float or flotation chamber along the gunwale of a boat or ship. **4** a structural projection from the side of a paddle steamer for supporting a paddle wheel. **5** a structural unit attached to a helicopter fuselage by fixed struts, housing the main landing gear and inflatable flotation bags. [C19: perhaps from EXPANSION]

sponsor (ˈspɒnsə) *n* **1** a person or group that provides funds for an activity, esp.: **1a** a commercial organization that pays all or part of the cost of putting on a concert, sporting event, etc. **1b** a person who donates money to a charity when the person requesting the donation has performed a specified activity as part of an organized fund-raising effort. **2** *Chiefly U.S. and Canadian.* a person or business firm that pays the costs of a radio or television programme in return for advertising time. **3** a legislator who presents and supports a bill, motion, etc. **4** Also called: **godparent. 4a** an authorized witness who makes the required promises on behalf of a person to be baptized and thereafter assumes responsibility for his Christian upbringing. **4b** a person who presents a candidate for confirmation. **5** *Chiefly U.S.* a person who undertakes responsibility for the actions, statements, obligations, etc., of another, as during a period of apprenticeship; guarantor. ♦ *vb* **6** (*tr*) to act as a sponsor for. [C17: from Latin, from *spondēre* to promise solemnly] ► **sponsorial** (spɒnˈsɔːrɪəl) *adj* ► **ˈsponsorˌship** *n*

sponsored (ˈspɒnsəd) *adj* denoting an activity organized to raise money for a charity in which sponsors agree to donate money on completion of the activity, or a specified period or amount of it, by participants: *a sponsored walk.*

spontaneity (ˌspɒntəˈniːɪtɪ, -ˈneɪ-) *n, pl* **-ties. 1** the state or quality of being spontaneous. **2** (*often pl*) the exhibiting of actions, impulses, or behaviour that are stimulated by internal processes.

spontaneous (spɒnˈteɪnɪəs) *adj* **1** occurring, produced, or performed through natural processes without external influence: *spontaneous movement.* **2** arising from an unforced personal impulse; voluntary; unpremeditated: *a spontaneous comment.* **3** (of plants) growing naturally; indigenous. [C17: from Late Latin *spontāneus,* from Latin *sponte* voluntarily] ▸ **spon'taneously** *adv* ▸ **spon'taneousness** *n*

spontaneous combustion *n* the ignition of a substance or body as a result of internal oxidation processes, without the application of an external source of heat, occurring in finely powdered ores, coal, straw, etc.

spontaneous generation *n* another name for **abiogenesis.**

spontaneous recovery *n Psychol.* the reappearance of a response after its extinction has been followed by a period of rest.

spontoon (spɒn'tu:n) *n* a form of halberd carried by some junior infantry officers in the 18th and 19th centuries. **[C18:** from French *esponton,* from Italian *spuntone,* from *punto* POINT**]**

spoof (spu:f) *Informal.* ◆ *n* **1** a mildly satirical mockery or parody; lampoon: *a spoof on party politics.* **2** a good-humoured deception or trick; prank. ◆ *vb* **3** to indulge in a spoof of (a person or thing). **[C19:** coined by A. Roberts (1852–1933), English comedian, to designate a game of his own invention**]** ▸ **'spoofer** *n*

spook (spu:k) *Informal.* ◆ *n* **1** a ghost or a person suggestive of this. **2** *U.S. and Canadian.* a spy. ◆ *vb (tr) U.S. and Canadian.* **3** to frighten: *to spook horses; to spook a person.* **4** (of a ghost) to haunt. **[C19:** Dutch *spook,* from Middle Low German *spōk* ghost**]** ▸ **'spookish** *adj*

spooky ('spu:kɪ) *adj* **spookier, spookiest.** *Informal.* **1** ghostly or eerie: *a spooky house.* **2** resembling or appropriate to a ghost. **3** *U.S.* easily frightened; highly strung. ▸ **'spookily** *adv* ▸ **'spookiness** *n*

spool (spu:l) *n* **1** a device around which magnetic tape, film, cotton, etc., can be automatically wound, with plates at top and bottom to prevent it from slipping off. **2** anything round which other materials, esp. thread, are wound. ◆ *vb* **3** (sometimes foll. by *up*) to wind or be wound onto a spool or reel. **[C14:** of Germanic origin; compare Old High German *spuolo,* Middle Dutch *spoele***]**

spoon (spu:n) *n* **1** a metal, wooden, or plastic utensil having a shallow concave part, usually elliptical in shape, attached to a handle, used in eating or serving food, stirring, etc. **2** Also called: **spoonbait.** an angling lure for spinning or trolling, consisting of a bright piece of metal which swivels on a trace to which are attached a hook or hooks. **3** *Golf.* a former name for a No. 3 wood. **4 be born with a silver spoon in one's mouth.** to inherit wealth or social standing. **5 wooden spoon.** *Brit.* another name for **booby prize. 6** *Rowing.* a type of oar blade that is curved at the edges and tip to gain a firm grip on the water. Compare **spade**[1] (sense 4). ◆ *vb* **7** *(tr)* to scoop up or transfer (food, liquid, etc.) from one container to another with or as if with a spoon. **8** *(intr) Slang, old-fashioned.* to kiss and cuddle. **9** to hollow out (a cavity or spoon-shaped bowl) (in something). **10** *Sport.* to hit (a ball) with a weak lifting motion, as in golf, cricket, etc. **[**Old English *spōn* splinter; related to Old Norse *spōnn* spoon, chip, Old High German *spān***]**

spoonbill ('spu:n,bɪl) *n* any of several wading birds of warm regions, such as *Platalea leucorodia* (**common spoonbill**) and *Ajaia ajaja* (**roseate spoonbill**), having a long horizontally flattened bill: family *Threskiornithidae,* order *Ciconiiformes.*

spoondrift ('spu:n,drɪft) *n* a less common spelling of **spindrift.**

spoonerism ('spu:nə,rɪzəm) *n* the transposition of the initial consonants or consonant clusters of a pair of words, often resulting in an amusing ambiguity of meaning, such as *hush my brat* for *brush my hat.* **[C20:** named after W. A. *Spooner* (1844–1930), English clergyman renowned for slips of this kind**]**

spoon-feed *vb* **-feeds, -feeding, -fed.** *(tr)* **1** to feed with a spoon. **2** to overindulge or spoil. **3** to provide (a person) with ready-made opinions, judgments, etc., depriving him of original thought or action.

spoonful ('spu:n,fʊl) *n, pl* **-fuls. 1** the amount that a spoon is able to hold. **2** a small quantity.

spoony *or* **spooney** ('spu:nɪ) *Slang, rare, old-fashioned.* ◆ *adj* **spoonier, spooniest. 1** foolishly or stupidly amorous. ◆ *n, pl* **spoonies. 2** a fool or silly person, esp. one in love.

spoor (spʊə, spɔ:) *n* **1** the trail of an animal or person, esp. as discernible to the human eye. ◆ *vb* **2** to track (an animal) by following its trail. **[C19:** from Afrikaans, from Middle Dutch *spor;* related to Old English *spor* track, Old High German *spor;* see SPUR**]** ▸ **'spoorer** *n*

Sporades ('spɒrə,di:z) *pl n* two groups of Greek islands in the Aegean: the **Northern Sporades,** lying northeast of Euboea, and the **Southern Sporades,** which include the Dodecanese and lie off the SW coast of Turkey.

sporadic (spə'rædɪk) *adj* **1** occurring at irregular points in time; intermittent: *sporadic firing.* **2** scattered; isolated: *a sporadic disease.* **[C17:** from Medieval Latin *sporadicus,* from Greek *sporadikos,* from *sporas* scattered; related to Greek *speirein* to sow; see SPORE**]** ▸ **spo'radically** *adv* ▸ **spo'radicalness** *n*

sporangium (spə'rændʒɪəm) *n, pl* **-gia** (-dʒɪə). any organ, esp. in fungi, in which asexual spores are produced. **[C19:** from New Latin, from SPORO- + Greek *angeion* receptacle**]** ▸ **spo'rangial** *adj*

spore (spɔ:) *n* **1** a reproductive body, produced by bacteria, fungi, various plants and some protozoans, that develops into a new individual. A **sexual spore** is formed after the fusion of gametes and an **asexual spore** is the result of asexual reproduction. **2** a germ cell, seed, dormant bacterium, or similar body. ◆ *vb* **3** *(intr)* to produce, carry, or release spores. **[C19:** from New Latin *spora,* from Greek: a sowing; related to Greek *speirein* to sow**]**

spore case *n* the nontechnical name for **sporangium.**

spore print *n Botany.* the pattern produced by placing the cap of a mushroom on a piece of paper and allowing the spores to fall.

sporo- *or before a vowel* **spor-** *combining form.* (in botany) spore: *sporophyte.* **[**from New Latin *spora***]**

sporocarp ('spɔ:rəʊ,kɑ:p, 'spɒ-) *n* **1** a specialized leaf branch in certain aquatic ferns that encloses the sori. **2** the spore-producing structure in certain algae, lichens, and fungi.

sporocyst ('spɔ:rəʊ,sɪst, 'spɒ-) *n* **1** a thick-walled rounded structure produced by sporozoan protozoans, in which sporozoites are formed. **2** the saclike larva of a trematode worm that produces redia larvae by asexual reproduction. **3** any similar structure containing spores.

sporocyte ('spɔ:rəʊ,saɪt, 'spɒ-) *n* a diploid cell that divides by meiosis to produce four haploid spores.

sporogenesis (,spɔ:rəʊ'dʒenɪsɪs, ,spɒ-) *n* the process of spore formation in plants and animals. ▸ **sporogenous** (spɔ:'rɒdʒɪnəs, spɒ-) *adj*

sporogonium (,spɔ:rəʊ'gəʊnɪəm, ,spɒ-) *n, pl* **-nia** (-nɪə). a structure in mosses and liverworts consisting of a spore-bearing capsule on a short stalk that arises from the parent plant (the sporophyte). ▸ **,sporo'gonial** *adj*

sporogony (spɔ:'rɒgənɪ, -'rɒdʒ-, spɒ-) *n* the process in sporozoans by which sporozoites are formed from an encysted zygote by multiple fission.

sporophore ('spɔ:rəʊ,fɔ:, 'spɒ-) *n* an organ in fungi that produces or carries spores, esp. the massive spore-bearing body of mushrooms, etc.

sporophyll *or* **sporophyl** ('spɔ:rəʊfɪl, 'spɒ-) *n* a leaf in mosses, ferns, and related plants that bears the sporangia. See also **megasporophyll, microsporophyll.**

sporophyte ('spɔ:rəʊ,faɪt, 'spɒ-) *n* the diploid form of plants that have alternation of generations. It develops from a zygote and produces asexual spores. Compare **gametophyte.** ▸ sporophytic (,spɔ:rə'fɪtɪk, ,spɒ-) *adj*

-sporous *adj combining form.* (in botany) having a specified type or number of spores: *homosporous.*

sporozoan (,spɔ:rə'zəʊən, ,spɒ-) *n* **1** any parasitic protozoan of the phylum *Apicomplexa* (or *Sporozoa*), characterized by a complex life cycle, part of which is passed in the cells of the host, and the production of asexual spores: includes the malaria parasite. See **plasmodium** (sense 2). ◆ *adj* **2** of or relating to sporozoans.

sporozoite (,spɔ:rə'zəʊaɪt, ,spɒ-) *n* any of numerous small mobile usually infective individuals produced in sporozoans by sporogony.

sporran ('spɒrən) *n* a large pouch, usually of fur, worn hanging from a belt in front of the kilt in men's Scottish Highland dress. **[C19:** from Scottish Gaelic *sporan* purse; compare Irish Gaelic *sparān* purse, Late Latin *bursa* bag**]**

sport (spɔ:t) *n* **1** an individual or group activity pursued for exercise or pleasure, often involving the testing of physical capabilities and taking the form of a competitive game such as football, tennis, etc. **2** such activities considered collectively. **3** any particular pastime indulged in for pleasure. **4** the pleasure derived from a pastime, esp. hunting, shooting, or fishing: *we had good sport today.* **5** playful or good-humoured joking: *to say a thing in sport.* **6** derisive mockery or the object of such mockery: *to make sport of someone.* **7** someone or something that is controlled by external influences: *the sport of fate.* **8** *Informal.* (sometimes qualified by *good, bad,* etc.) a person who reacts cheerfully in the face of adversity, esp. a good loser. **9** *Informal.* a person noted for being scrupulously fair and abiding by the rules of a game. **10** *Informal.* a person who leads a merry existence, esp. a gambler: *he's a bit of a sport.* **11** *Austral. and N.Z. informal.* a form of address used esp. between males. **12** *Biology.* **12a** an animal or plant that differs conspicuously in one or more aspects from other organisms of the same species, usually because of a mutation. **12b** an anomalous characteristic of such an organism. ◆ *vb* **13** *(tr) Informal.* to wear or display in an ostentatious or proud manner: *she was sporting a new hat.* **14** *(intr)* to skip about or frolic happily. **15** to amuse (oneself), esp. in outdoor physical recreation. **16** *(intr;* often foll. by *with)* to dally or trifle (with). **17** *(tr;* often foll. by *away) Rare.* to squander (time or money): *sporting one's life away.* **18** *(intr;* often foll. by *with) Archaic.* to make fun (of). **19** *(intr) Biology.* to produce or undergo a mutation. ◆ See also **sports. [C15** *sporten,* variant of *disporten* to DISPORT**]** ▸ **'sporter** *n* ▸ **'sportful** *adj* ▸ **'sportfully** *adv* ▸ **'sportfulness** *n*

sporting ('spɔ:tɪŋ) *adj* **1** *(prenominal)* of, relating to, or used or engaged in a sport or sports: *several sporting interests.* **2** relating or conforming to sportsmanship; fair. **3** of, relating to, or characterized by an interest in gambling. **4** willing to take a risk. ▸ **'sportingly** *adv*

sporting house *n* **1** *U.S., rare.* a euphemistic word for **brothel. 2** *Archaic.* a tavern or inn frequented by gamblers or other sportsmen.

sportive ('spɔ:tɪv) *adj* **1** playful or joyous. **2** done in jest rather than seriously. **3** of, relating to, or interested in sports. **4** *Obsolete.* wanton or amorous: *a sportive wench.* ▸ **'sportively** *adv* ▸ **'sportiveness** *n*

sports (spɔ:ts) *n* **1** *(modifier)* relating to, concerned with, or used in sports: *sports equipment.* **2** Also called: **sports day.** *Brit.* a meeting held at a school or college for competitions in various athletic events.

sports car *n* a production car designed for speed, high acceleration, and manoeuvrability, having a low body and usually adequate seating for only two persons.

sportscast ('spɔ:ts,kɑ:st) *n* a radio or television broadcast consisting of sports news. ▸ **'sports,caster** *n*

sports coat *n U.S., Austral., and N.Z.* another name for **sports jacket.**

sports jacket *n* a man's informal jacket, made esp. of tweed: worn with trousers of different material. Also called (U.S., Austral., and N.Z.): **sports coat.**

sportsman ('spɔ:tsmən) *n, pl* **-men. 1** a man who takes part in sports, esp. of the outdoor type. **2** a person who exhibits qualities highly regarded in sport, such as fairness, generosity, observance of the rules, and good humour when losing. ▸ **'sportsman-,like** *or* **'sportsmanly** *adj* ▸ **'sportsman,ship** *n*

sports medicine *n* the branch of medicine concerned with injuries sustained through sport.

sportsperson ('spɔ:ts,pɜ:sən) *n* a person who takes part in sports, esp. of the outdoor type.

sports shirt *n* a man's informal shirt, sometimes of knitted wool or cotton, which may be worn outside the trousers.

sportswear ('spɔ:ts,weə) *n* clothes worn for sport or outdoor leisure wear.

sportswoman ('spɔːtsˌwʊmən) *n, pl* **-women.** a woman who takes part in sports, esp. of the outdoor type.

sporty ('spɔːtɪ) *adj* **sportier, sportiest. 1** (of a person) fond of sport or outdoor activities. **2** (of clothes) having the appearance of sportswear. **3** (of a car) having the performance or appearance of a sports car. ▸ **'sportily** *adv* ▸ **'sportiness** *n*

sporulate ('spɒrjʊˌleɪt) *vb* (*intr*) to produce spores, esp. by multiple fission. ▸ **ˌsporu'lation** *n*

sporule ('spɒruːl) *n* a spore, esp. a very small spore. [C19: from New Latin *sporula* a little SPORE]

spot (spɒt) *n* **1** a small mark on a surface, such as a circular patch or stain, differing in colour or texture from its surroundings. **2** a geographical area that is restricted in extent: *a beauty spot.* **3** a location: *this is the exact spot on which he died.* **4** a blemish of the skin, esp. a pimple or one occurring through some disease. **5** a blemish on the character of a person; moral flaw. **6** *Informal.* a place of entertainment: *we hit all the night spots.* **7** *Informal, chiefly Brit.* a small quantity or amount: *a spot of lunch.* **8** *Informal.* an awkward situation: *that puts me in a bit of a spot.* **9** a short period between regular television or radio programmes that is used for advertising. **10** a position or length of time in a show assigned to a specific performer. **11** short for **spotlight. 12** (in billiards) **12a** Also called: **spot ball.** the white ball that is distinguished from the plain by a mark or spot. **12b** the player using this ball. **13** *Billiards, snooker, etc.* one of several small black dots on a table that mark where a ball is to be placed. **14** (*modifier*) **14a** denoting or relating to goods, currencies, or securities available for immediate delivery and payment: *spot goods.* See also **spot market, spot price. 14b** involving immediate cash payment: *spot sales.* **15 change one's spots.** (*used mainly in negative constructions*) to reform one's character. **16 high spot.** an outstanding event: *the high spot of the holiday was the visit to the winery.* **17 knock spots off.** to outstrip or outdo with ease. **18 on the spot. 18a** immediately. **18b** at the place in question. **18c** in the best possible position to deal with a situation. **18d** in an awkward predicament. **18e** without moving from the place of one's location, etc. **18f** (*as modifier*): *our on-the-spot reporter.* **19 soft spot.** a special sympathetic affection or weakness for a person or thing. **20 tight spot.** a serious, difficult, or dangerous situation. **21 weak spot. 21a** some aspect of a character or situation that is susceptible to criticism. **21b** a flaw in a person's knowledge: *classics is my weak spot.* ◆ *vb* **spots, spotting, spotted. 22** (*tr*) to observe or perceive suddenly, esp. under difficult circumstances; discern. **23** to put stains or spots upon (something). **24** (*intr*) (of some fabrics) to be susceptible to spotting by or as if by water: *silk spots easily.* **25** (*tr*) to place here and there: *they spotted observers along the border.* **26** to look out for and note (trains, talent, etc.). **27** (*intr*) to rain slightly; spit. **28** (*tr*) *Billiards.* to place (a ball) on one of the spots. **29** *Military.* to adjust fire in order to correct deviations from (the target) by observation. **30** (*tr*) *U.S. informal.* to yield (an advantage or concession) to (one's opponent): *to spot someone a piece in chess.* [C12 (in the sense: moral blemish): of German origin; compare Middle Dutch *spotte,* Old Norse *spotti*] ▸ **'spottable** *adj*

spot check *n* **1** a quick random examination. **2** a check made without prior warning. ◆ *vb* **spot-check. 3** (*tr*) to perform a spot check on.

spot height *n* a mark on a map indicating the height of a hill, mountain, etc.

spotless ('spɒtlɪs) *adj* **1** free from stains; immaculate. **2** free from moral impurity; unsullied: *a spotless character.* ▸ **'spotlessly** *adv* ▸ **'spotlessness** *n*

spotlight ('spɒtˌlaɪt) *n* **1** a powerful light focused so as to illuminate a small area, usually mounted so that it can be directed at will. **2 the.** the focus of attention. ◆ *vb* **-lights, -lighting, -lit** *or* **-lighted.** (*tr*) **3** to direct a spotlight on. **4** to focus attention on.

spot market *n Commerce.* a market in which commodities, currencies, or securities are traded for immediate delivery. Compare **forward market.**

spot-on *adj Informal.* absolutely correct; very accurate.

spot price *n* the price of goods, currencies, or securities that are offered for immediate delivery and payment.

spotted ('spɒtɪd) *adj* **1** characterized by spots or marks, esp. in having a pattern of spots. **2** stained or blemished; soiled or bespattered.

spotted crake *n* a Eurasian rail, *Porzana porzana,* of swamps and marshes, having a buff speckled plumage and dark brown wings.

spotted dick *n Brit.* a steamed or boiled suet pudding containing dried fruit. [C19: perhaps from the man's name *Dick* (short for *Richard*), or from dialect *dick* pudding. The dried fruit gives it a speckled appearance]

spotted dog *n* **1** an informal name for a **Dalmatian. 2** another name for **spotted dick.**

spotted fever *n* any of various severe febrile diseases characterized by small irregular spots on the skin, as in Rocky Mountain spotted fever or tick fever.

spotted flycatcher *n* a European woodland songbird, *Muscicapa striata,* with a greyish-brown streaked plumage: family *Muscicapidae* (Old World flycatchers).

spotted gum *n* **1** an Australian eucalyptus tree, *Eucalyptus maculata.* **2** the wood of this tree, used for shipbuilding, sleepers, etc.

spotted orchid *n* **1** any of various common Eurasian orchids, esp. the **heath** and **common spotted orchids** (*Dactylorchis maculata* and *D. fuchsii*). The flowers are variable but usually have dark blotches. **2** a tall orchid, *Dipodium punctatum,* with white pink-spotted flowers, found in Australia.

spotted sandpiper *n* a North American sandpiper, *Actitis macularia,* having a spotted breast in its breeding plumage. Also called (U.S.): **peetweet.**

spotter ('spɒtə) *n* **1a** a person or thing that watches or observes. **1b** (*as modifier*): *a spotter plane.* **2** a person who makes a hobby of watching for and noting numbers or types of trains, buses, etc.: *a train spotter.* **3** *Military.* a person who orders or advises adjustment of fire on a target by observations. **4** a person, esp. one engaged in civil defence, who watches for enemy aircraft. **5** *U.S. informal.* an employee assigned to spy on his colleagues in order to check on their honesty. **6** *Films.* **6a** a person who checks against irregularities and inconsistencies. **6b** a person who searches for new material, performers, etc.

spottie ('spɒtɪ) *n N.Z.* a young deer of up to three months of age.

spotty ('spɒtɪ) *adj* **-tier, -tiest. 1** abounding in or characterized by spots or marks, esp. on the skin: *a spotty face.* **2** not consistent or uniform; irregular or uneven, often in quality. ▸ **'spottily** *adv* ▸ **'spottiness** *n*

spot-weld *vb* **1** (*tr*) to join (two pieces of metal, esp. in the form of wire or sheet) by one or more small circular welds by means of heat, usually electrically generated, and pressure. ◆ *n* **2** a weld so formed. ▸ **'spot-ˌwelder** *n*

spousal ('spaʊzᵊl) *n* **1** (*often pl*) **1a** the marriage ceremony. **1b** a wedding. ◆ *adj* **2** of or relating to marriage. ▸ **'spousally** *adv*

spouse *n* (spaʊs, spaʊz). **1** a person's partner in marriage. Related adj: **spousal.** ◆ *vb* (spaʊz, spaʊs). **2** (*tr*) *Obsolete.* to marry. [C12: from Old French *spus* (masculine), *spuse* (feminine), from Latin *sponsus, sponsa* betrothed man or woman, from *spondēre* to promise solemnly]

spout (spaʊt) *vb* **1** to discharge (a liquid) in a continuous jet or in spurts, esp. through a narrow gap or under pressure, or (of a liquid) to gush thus. **2** (of a whale, etc.) to discharge air through the blowhole, so that it forms a spray at the surface of the water. **3** *Informal.* to utter (a stream of words) on a subject, often at length. ◆ *n* **4** a tube, pipe, chute, etc., allowing the passage or pouring of liquids, grain, etc. **5** a continuous stream or jet of liquid. **6** short for **waterspout. 7 up the spout.** *Slang.* **7a** ruined or lost: *any hope of rescue is right up the spout.* **7b** pregnant. [C14: perhaps from Middle Dutch *spouten,* from Old Norse *spyta* to spit] ▸ **'spouter** *n*

spouting ('spaʊtɪŋ) *n N.Z.* **a** a rainwater downpipe on the exterior of a building. **b** such pipes collectively.

spp. *abbrev. for* species (plural).

SPQR *abbrev. for* Senatus Populusque Romanus. [Latin: the Senate and People of Rome].

SPR *abbrev. for* Society for Psychical Research.

sprag (spræg) *n* **1** a chock or steel bar used to prevent a vehicle from running backwards on an incline. **2** a support or post used in mining. **3** *N.Z. mining.* a steel bar inserted into the wheels of a box to act as a brake. [C19: of uncertain origin]

sprain (spreɪn) *vb* **1** (*tr*) to injure (a joint) by a sudden twisting or wrenching of its ligaments. ◆ *n* **2** the resulting injury to such a joint, characterized by swelling and temporary disability. [C17: of uncertain origin]

spraint (spreɪnt) *n* (*often pl*) a piece of otter's dung. [C15 *sprayntes* (pl), from Medieval French *espraintes* otter's dung, from *espreindre* to press out: compare EXPRESS]

sprang (spræŋ) *vb* the past tense of **spring.**

sprat (spræt) *n* **1** a small marine food fish, *Clupea sprattus,* of the NE Atlantic Ocean and North Sea: family *Clupeidae* (herrings). See also **brisling. 2** any of various small or young herrings. [C16: variant of Old English *sprott;* related to Middle Low German *sprott,* Norwegian *sprot* small rod]

sprawl (sprɔːl) *vb* **1** (*intr*) to sit or lie in an ungainly manner with one's limbs spread out. **2** to fall down or knock down with the limbs spread out in an ungainly way. **3** to spread out or cause to spread out in a straggling fashion: *his handwriting sprawled all over the paper.* ◆ *n* **4** the act or an instance of sprawling. **5** a sprawling posture or arrangement of items. **6a** the urban area formed by the expansion of a town or city into surrounding countryside: *the urban sprawl.* **6b** the process by which this has happened. [Old English *spreawlian;* related to Old English *spryttan* to sprout, SPURT, Greek *speirein* to scatter] ▸ **'sprawler** *n* ▸ **'sprawly** *adj*

spray[1] (spreɪ) *n* **1** fine particles of a liquid. **2a** a liquid, such as perfume, paint, etc., designed to be discharged from an aerosol or atomizer: *hair spray.* **2b** the aerosol or atomizer itself. **3** a quantity of small objects flying through the air: *a spray of bullets.* ◆ *vb* **4** to scatter (liquid) in the form of fine particles. **5** to discharge (a liquid) from an aerosol or atomizer. **6** (*tr*) to treat or bombard with a spray: *to spray the lawn.* [C17: from Middle Dutch *sprāien;* related to Middle High German *spræjen*] ▸ **'sprayer** *n*

spray[2] (spreɪ) *n* **1** a single slender shoot, twig, or branch that bears buds, leaves, flowers, or berries, either growing on or detached from a plant. **2** a small decorative bouquet or corsage of flowers and foliage. **3** a piece of jewellery designed to resemble a spray of flowers, leaves, etc. [C13: of Germanic origin; compare Old English *spræc* young shoot, Old Norse *sprek* brittle wood, Old High German *sprahhula* splinter]

spray gun *n* a device that sprays a fluid in a finely divided form by atomizing the fluid in an air jet.

spread (spred) *vb* **spreads, spreading, spread. 1** to extend or unfold or be extended or unfolded to the fullest width: *she spread the map on the table.* **2** to extend or cause to extend over a larger expanse of space or time: *the milk spread all over the floor; the political unrest spread over several years.* **3** to apply or be applied in a coating: *butter does not spread very well when cold.* **4** to distribute or be distributed over an area or region. **5** to display or be displayed in its fullest extent: *the landscape spread before us.* **6** (*tr*) to prepare (a table) for a meal. **7** (*tr*) to lay out (a meal) on a table. **8** to send or be sent out in all directions; disseminate or be disseminated: *someone has been spreading rumours; the disease spread quickly.* **9** (of rails, wires, etc.) to force or be forced apart. **10** to increase the breadth of (a part), esp. to flatten the head of a rivet by pressing, hammering, or forging. **11** (*tr*) *Agriculture.* **11a** to lay out (hay) in a relatively thin layer to dry. **11b** to scatter (seed, manure, etc.) over a relatively wide area. **12** (*tr;* often foll. by *around*) *Informal.* to make (oneself) agreeable to a large number of people, often of the opposite sex. **13** *Phonetics.* to narrow and lengthen the aperture of (the lips) as for the articulation of a front vowel, such as (iː) in English *see* (siː). ◆ *n* **14** the act or process of spreading; diffusion, dispersal, expansion, etc.: *the spread of the Christian religion.* **15** *Informal.* the wingspan of an aircraft. **16** an extent of space or time; stretch: *a spread of 50* *years.* **17** *Informal, chiefly U.S. and Canadian.* a ranch or relatively large tract of land. **18** the limit of something fully extended: *the spread of a bird's wings.* **19** a covering for a table or bed. **20** *Informal.* a large meal or feast, esp. when it is laid out on a table. **21** a food which can be spread on bread, etc.: *salmon spread.* **22** two facing pages in a book or other publication. **23** a widening of the hips and waist: *middle-age spread.* **24** *Stock Exchange.* **24a** the difference between the bid and offer prices quoted by a market maker. **24b** the excess of the price at which stock is offered for public sale over the price paid for the same stock by an underwriter. **24c** *Chiefly U.S.* a double option. Compare **straddle** (sense 9). **25** *Jewellery.* the apparent size of a gemstone when viewed from above expressed in carats: *a diamond with a spread of four carats.* ◆ *adj* **26** extended or stretched out, esp. to the fullest extent. **27** (of a gem) shallow and flat. **28** *Phonetics.* **28a** (of the lips) forming a long narrow aperture. **28b** (of speech sounds) articulated with spread lips: (iː) *in English "feel" is a spread vowel.* [Old English *sprǣdan;* related to Old High German *spreiten* to spread, Old Lithuanian *sprainas* stiff] ▸ **ˌspreadaˈbility** *n* ▸ **ˈspreadable** *adj*

spread betting *n* a form of gambling in which stakes are placed not on the results of contests but on the number of points scored, etc. Winnings and losses are calculated according to the accuracy or inaccuracy of the prediction.

spread eagle *n* **1** the representation of an eagle with outstretched wings, used as an emblem of the U.S. **2** an acrobatic skating figure.

spread-eagle *adj also* **spread-eagled. 1** lying or standing with arms and legs outstretched. ◆ *vb* **2** to assume or cause to assume the shape of a spread eagle. **3** (*intr*) *Skating.* to execute a spread eagle.

spreader (ˈsprɛdə) *n* **1** a machine or device used for scattering bulk materials, esp. manure or fertilizer, over a relatively wide area. **2** a device for keeping apart or spacing parallel objects, such as electric wires.

spread sampling *n* the selection of a corpus for statistical analysis by selecting a number of short passages at random throughout the work and considering their aggregation. Compare **block sampling.**

spreadsheet (ˈsprɛdˌʃiːt) *n* a computer program that allows easy entry and manipulation of figures, equations, and text, used esp. for financial planning and budgeting.

spreathed (spriːðd) *adj Southwestern English and south Wales dialect.* sore; chapped. [from *spreathe* to make sore: of obscure origin]

sprechgesang (*German* ˈʃprɛçgəzaŋ) *n Music.* a type of vocalization between singing and recitation in which the voice sings the beginning of each note and then falls rapidly from the notated pitch. It was originated by Arnold Schoenberg, who used it in *Pierrot Lunaire* (1912). [C20: from German, literally: speaking-song]

sprechstimme (*German* ˈʃprɛçʃtɪmə) *n Music.* a vocal part employing sprechgesang. [C20: from German: speaking voice]

spree (spriː) *n* **1** a session of considerable overindulgence, esp. in drinking, squandering money, etc. **2** a romp. [C19: perhaps changed from Scottish *spreath* plundered cattle, ultimately from Latin *praeda* booty]

sprekelia (sprəˈkiːlɪə) *n* a bulbous plant, *Sprekelia formosissima,* from Mexico and Guatemala, related to hippeastrum and grown for its striking crimson or white pendent flowers, in the form of a cross: family *Amaryllidaceae.* [named after J. H. von *Sprekelsen* (died 1764), German botanist]

sprig (sprɪg) *n* **1** a shoot, twig, or sprout of a tree, shrub, etc.; spray. **2** an ornamental device resembling a spray of leaves or flowers. **3** a small wire nail without a head. **4** *Informal, rare.* a youth. **5** *Informal, rare.* a person considered as the descendant of an established family, social class, etc. **6** *N.Z.* another name for **stud**[1] (sense 7). ◆ *vb* **sprigs, sprigging, sprigged.** (*tr*) **7** to fasten or secure with sprigs. **8** to ornament (fabric, wallpaper, etc.) with a design of sprigs. **9** to make sprays from (twigs and branches). [C15: probably of Germanic origin; compare Low German *sprick,* Swedish *sprygg*] ▸ **ˈsprigger** *n* ▸ **ˈspriggy** *adj*

sprightly (ˈspraɪtlɪ) *adj* **-lier, -liest. 1** full of vitality; lively. ◆ *adv* **2** *Obsolete.* in a lively manner. [C16: from *spright,* variant of SPRITE + -LY[1]] ▸ **ˈsprightliness** *n*

spring (sprɪŋ) *vb* **springs, springing, sprang** *or* **sprung; sprung. 1** to move or cause to move suddenly upwards or forwards in a single motion. **2** to release or be released from a forced position by elastic force: *the bolt sprang back.* **3** (*tr*) to leap or jump over. **4** (*intr*) to come, issue, or arise suddenly. **5** (*intr*) (of a part of a mechanism, etc.) to jump out of place. **6** to make (wood, etc.) warped or split or (of wood, etc.) to become warped or split. **7** to happen or cause to happen unexpectedly: *to spring a surprise; the boat sprung a leak.* **8** (*intr*) to develop or originate: *the idea sprang from a chance meeting.* **9** (*intr;* usually foll. by *from*) to be descended: *he sprang from peasant stock.* **10** (*intr;* often foll. by *up*) to come into being or appear suddenly: *factories springing up.* **11** (*tr*) (of a gun dog) to rouse (game) from cover. **12** (*intr*) (of game or quarry) to start or rise suddenly from cover. **13** (*intr*) to appear to have a strong upward movement: *the beam springs away from the pillar.* **14** to explode (a mine) or (of a mine) to explode. **15** (*tr*) to provide with a spring or springs. **16** (*tr*) *Informal.* to arrange the escape of (someone) from prison. **17** (*intr*) *Archaic or poetic.* (of daylight or dawn) to begin to appear. ◆ *n* **18** the act or an instance of springing. **19** a leap, jump, or bound. **20a** the quality of resilience; elasticity. **20b** (*as modifier*): *spring steel.* **21** the act or an instance of moving rapidly back from a position of tension. **22a** a natural outflow of ground water, as forming the source of a stream. **22b** (*as modifier*): *spring water.* **23a** a device, such as a coil or strip of steel, that stores potential energy when it is compressed, stretched, or bent and releases it when the restraining force is removed. **23b** (*as modifier*): *a spring mattress.* **24** a structural defect such as a warp or bend. **25a** (*sometimes cap.*) the season of the year between winter and summer, astronomically from the March equinox to the June solstice in the N hemisphere and from the September equinox to the December solstice in the S hemisphere. **25b** (*as modifier*): *spring showers.* Related adj: **vernal. 26** the earliest or freshest time of something. **27** a source or origin. **28** one of a set of strips of rubber, steel, etc., running down the inside of the handle of a cricket bat, hockey stick, etc. **29** Also called: **spring line.** *Nautical.* a mooring line, usually one of a pair that cross amidships. **30** a flock of teal. **31** *Architect.* another name for **springing.** [Old English *springan;* related to Old Norse *springa,* Old High German *springan,* Sanskrit *sprhayati* he desires, Old Slavonic *pragu* grasshopper] ▸ **ˈspringless** *adj* ▸ **ˈspringˌlike** *adj*

spring balance *or esp. U.S.* **spring scale** *n* a device in which an object to be weighed is attached to the end of a helical spring, the extension of which indicates the weight of the object on a calibrated scale.

spring beauty *n* a pale green annual plant (*Claytonia perfoliata*) of the purslane family, originally North American, having small white flowers above fused leaves that encircle the stem.

springboard (ˈsprɪŋˌbɔːd) *n* **1** a flexible board, usually projecting low over the water, used for diving. **2** a similar board used for gaining height or momentum in gymnastics. **3** *Austral. and N.Z.* a board inserted into the trunk of a tree at some height above the ground on which a lumberjack stands to chop down the tree. **4** anything that serves as a point of departure or initiation.

springbok *or* (*less commonly*) **springbuck** (ˈsprɪŋˌbʌk) *n, pl* **-bok, -boks** *or* **-buck, -bucks.** an antelope, *Antidorcas marsupialis,* of semidesert regions of southern Africa, which moves in leaps exposing a patch of white erectile hairs on the rump that are usually covered by a fold of skin. [C18: from Afrikaans, from Dutch *springen* to SPRING + *bok* goat, BUCK[1]]

Springbok (ˈsprɪŋˌbʌk, -ˌbɒk) *n* a person who has represented South Africa in a national sports team.

spring chicken *n* **1** Also called: **springer.** *Chiefly U.S. and Canadian.* a young chicken, tender for cooking, esp. one from two to ten months old. **2 he** *or* **she is no spring chicken.** *Informal.* he or she is no longer young.

spring-clean *vb* **1** to clean (a house) thoroughly: traditionally at the end of the winter. ◆ *n* **2** an instance of spring-cleaning. ▸ **ˌspring-ˈcleaning** *n*

springe (sprɪndʒ) *n* **1** a snare set to catch small wild animals or birds and consisting of a loop attached to a bent twig or branch under tension. ◆ *vb* **2** (*intr*) to set such a snare. **3** (*tr*) to catch (small wild animals or birds) with such a snare. [C13: related to Old English *springan* to SPRING]

springer (ˈsprɪŋə) *n* **1** short for **springer spaniel. 2** Also called: **springing cow.** a cow about to give birth. **3** a person or thing that springs. **4** *Architect.* **4a** the first and lowest stone of an arch. **4b** the impost of an arch.

springer spaniel *n* either of two breeds of large quick-moving spaniels bred to spring game, having a slightly domed head and ears of medium length. The **English springer spaniel** is the larger and can be of various colours; the **Welsh springer spaniel** is always a rich red and white.

spring fever *n* the feeling of restlessness experienced by many people at the onset of spring.

Springfield (ˈsprɪŋˌfiːld) *n* **1** a city in S Massachusetts, on the Connecticut River: the site of the U.S. arsenal and armoury (1794–1968), which developed the Springfield and Garand rifles. Pop.: 149 948 (1996 est.). **2** a city in SW Missouri. Pop.: 143 407 (1996 est.). **3** a city in central Illinois, capital of the state: the home and burial place of Abraham Lincoln. Pop.: 112 921 (1996 est.).

Springfield rifle *n* a magazine-fed bolt-action breech-loading .30 calibre rifle formerly used by the U.S. Army. [from SPRINGFIELD, Massachusetts]

springhaas (ˈsprɪŋˌhɑːs) *n, pl* **-haas** *or* **-hase** (-ˌhɑːzə). a S and E African nocturnal rodent, *Pedetes capensis,* resembling a small kangaroo: family *Pedetidae.* [from Afrikaans: spring hare]

springhalt (ˈsprɪŋˌhɔːlt) *n Vet. science.* another name for **stringhalt.** [C17: probably an alteration, influenced by SPRING, of STRINGHALT]

springhead (ˈsprɪŋˌhɛd) *n* the source of a stream; spring.

springhouse (ˈsprɪŋˌhaʊs) *n* a storehouse built over a spring for keeping dairy products and meat cool and fresh.

springing (ˈsprɪŋɪŋ) *n* the level where an arch or vault rises from a support. Also called: **spring, springing line, springing point.**

springlet (ˈsprɪŋlɪt) *n* a small spring; brooklet or rill.

spring lock *n* a type of lock having a spring-loaded bolt, a key being required only to unlock it.

spring mattress *n* a mattress containing an arrangement of spiral springs.

spring onion *n* an immature form of the onion (*Allium cepa*), widely cultivated for its tiny bulb and long green leaves which are eaten in salads, etc. Also called: **green onion, scallion.**

spring roll *n* a Chinese dish consisting of a savoury mixture of vegetables and meat rolled up in a thin pancake and fried.

Springs (sprɪŋz) *n* a city in E South Africa: developed around a coal mine established in 1885 and later became a major world gold-mining centre, now with uranium extraction. Pop.: 68 235 (1985).

Springsteen (ˈsprɪŋˌstiːn) *n* **Bruce.** born 1949, U.S. rock singer, songwriter, and guitarist. His albums with the E Street Band include *Born to Run* (1975), *Darkness on the Edge of Town* (1978), and *Born in the U.S.A.* (1984).

springtail (ˈsprɪŋˌteɪl) *n* any primitive wingless insect of the order *Collembola,* having a forked springing organ with which it projects itself forward.

spring tide *n* **1** either of the two tides that occur at or just after new moon and full moon when the tide-generating force of the sun acts in the same direction as that of the moon, reinforcing it and causing the greatest rise and fall in tidal level. The highest spring tides (**equinoctial springs**) occur at the equinoxes. Compare **neap tide. 2** any great rush or flood.

springtime (ˈsprɪŋˌtaɪm) *n* **1** Also called: **springtide** (ˈsprɪŋˌtaɪd). the season of spring. **2** the earliest, usually the most attractive, period of the existence of something.

springwood (ˈsprɪŋˌwʊd) *n* the wood that is produced by a plant in the spring and early summer and consists of large thin-walled xylem cells. Compare **summerwood.**

springy (ˈsprɪŋɪ) *adj* **springier, springiest. 1** possessing or characterized by resilience or bounce. **2** (of a place) having many wells or springs of water. ▸ **'springily** *adv* ▸ **'springiness** *n*

sprinkle ('sprɪŋkᵊl) *vb* **1** to scatter (liquid, powder, etc.) in tiny particles or droplets over (something). **2** (*tr*) to distribute over (something): *the field was sprinkled with flowers.* **3** (*intr*) to drizzle slightly. ♦ *n* **4** the act or an instance of sprinkling or a quantity that is sprinkled. **5** a slight drizzle. [C14: probably from Middle Dutch *sprenkelen;* related to Old English *spearca* SPARK[1]]

sprinkler ('sprɪŋklə) *n* **1** a device perforated with small holes that is attached to a garden hose or watering can and used to spray plants, lawns, etc., with water. **2** a person or thing that sprinkles. **3** See **sprinkler system.**

sprinkler system *n* a fire-extinguishing system that releases water from overhead pipes through nozzles opened automatically by a rise in temperature.

sprinkling ('sprɪŋklɪŋ) *n* a small quantity or amount: *a sprinkling of commonsense.*

sprint (sprɪnt) *n* **1** *Athletics.* a short race run at top speed, such as the 100 metres. **2** a fast finishing speed at the end of a longer race, as in running or cycling, etc. **3** any quick run. ♦ *vb* (*intr*) **4** to go at top speed, as in running, cycling, etc. [C16: from Scandinavian; related to Old English *gesprintan* to emit, Old Norse *spretta* to jump up, Old High German *sprinzan* to jump up, Swedish *sprata* to kick] ▸ **'sprinter** *n*

sprit (sprɪt) *n Nautical.* a light spar pivoted at the mast and crossing a fore-and-aft quadrilateral sail diagonally to the peak. [Old English *spreot;* related to Old High German *spriuzen* to support, Dutch *spriet* sprit, Norwegian *sprȳta*]

sprite (spraɪt) *n* **1** (in folklore) a nimble elflike creature, esp. one associated with water. **2** a small dainty person. **3** an icon in a computer game which can be manoeuvred around the screen by means of a joystick, etc. [C13: from Old French *esprit,* from Latin *spīritus* SPIRIT[1]]

spritsail ('sprɪt,seɪl; *Nautical* 'sprɪtsəl) *n Nautical.* **1** a rectangular sail mounted on a sprit in some 19th century small vessels. **2** (in medieval rigging) a square sail mounted on a yard on the bowsprit.

spritzer ('sprɪtsə) *n* a drink, usually white wine, with soda water added. [from German *spritzen* to splash]

spritzig ('sprɪtsɪg; *German* 'ʃprɪtsɪç) *adj* (of wine) sparkling. [German, from *spritzen* to splash]

sprocket ('sprɒkɪt) *n* **1** Also called: **sprocket wheel.** a relatively thin wheel having teeth projecting radially from the rim, esp. one that drives or is driven by a chain. **2** an individual tooth on such a wheel. **3** a cylindrical wheel with teeth on one or both rims for pulling film through a camera or projector. **4** a small wedge-shaped piece of wood used to extend a roof over the eaves. [C16: of unknown origin]

sprog (sprɒg) *n Slang.* **1** a child; baby. **2** (esp. in RAF) a recruit.

sprout (spraʊt) *vb* **1** (of a plant, seed, etc.) to produce (new leaves, shoots, etc.). **2** (*intr;* often foll. by *up*) to begin to grow or develop: *new office blocks are sprouting up all over the city.* ♦ *n* **3** a newly grown shoot or bud. **4** something that grows like a sprout. **5** See **Brussels sprout.** [Old English *sprūtan;* related to Middle High German *sprūzen* to sprout, Lettish *sprausties* to jostle]

spruce[1] (spru:s) *n* **1** any coniferous tree of the N temperate genus *Picea,* cultivated for timber and for ornament: family *Pinaceae.* They grow in a pyramidal shape and have needle-like leaves and light-coloured wood. See also **Norway spruce, blue spruce, white spruce, black spruce. 2** the wood of any of these trees. [C17: short for *Spruce fir,* from C14 *Spruce* Prussia, changed from *Pruce,* via Old French from Latin *Prussia*]

spruce[2] (spru:s) *adj* neat, smart, and trim. [C16: perhaps from *Spruce leather* a fashionable leather imported from Prussia; see SPRUCE[1]] ▸ **'sprucely** *adv* ▸ **'spruceness** *n*

spruce beer *n* an alcoholic drink made of fermented molasses flavoured with spruce twigs and cones.

spruce pine *n* **1** a large pine tree, *Pinus glabra,* of the southeastern U.S. **2** any of several similar plants, such as certain pines, hemlocks, and spruces.

spruce up *vb* (*adv*) to make (oneself, a person, or thing) smart and neat.

sprue[1] (spru:) *n* **1** a vertical channel in a mould through which plastic or molten metal is introduced or out of which it flows when the mould is filled. **2** plastic or metal that solidifies in a sprue. [C19: of unknown origin]

sprue[2] (spru:) *n* a chronic disease, esp. of tropical climates, characterized by flatulence, diarrhoea, frothy foul-smelling stools, and emaciation. [C19: from Dutch *spruw;* related to Middle Low German *sprüwe* tumour]

sprue[3] (spru:) *n London dialect.* an inferior type of asparagus. [C19: of unknown origin]

spruik ('spru:ɪk) *vb* (*intr*) *Austral. archaic slang.* to speak in public (used esp. of a showman or salesman). [C20: of unknown origin] ▸ **'spruiker** *n*

spruit (spreɪt) *n S. African.* a small tributary stream or watercourse. [Afrikaans *spruit* offshoot, tributary]

sprung (sprʌŋ) *vb* the past participle and a past tense of **spring.**

sprung rhythm *n Prosody.* a type of poetic rhythm characterized by metrical feet of irregular composition, each having one strongly stressed syllable, often the first, and an indefinite number of unstressed syllables.

spry (spraɪ) *adj* **spryer, spryest** *or* **sprier, spriest.** active and brisk; nimble. [C18: perhaps of Scandinavian origin; compare Swedish dialect *spragg* SPRIG] ▸ **'spryly** *adv* ▸ **'spryness** *n*

spt *abbrev. for* seaport.

SPUC (spʌk) *n acronym for* Society for the Protection of the Unborn Child.

spud (spʌd) *n* **1** an informal word for **potato** (sense 1). **2** a narrow-bladed spade for cutting roots, digging up weeds, etc. **3** Also called: **spudder.** a tool, resembling a chisel, for removing bark from trees. ♦ *vb* **spuds, spudding, spudded. 4** (*tr*) to remove (bark) or eradicate (weeds) with a spud. **5** (*intr*) to drill the first foot of an oil-well. [C15 *spudde* short knife, of unknown origin; applied later to a digging tool, and hence to a potato]

spud-bashing *n Brit. slang, chiefly military.* the task of peeling potatoes, given as a punishment.

Spud Island *n* a slang name for **Prince Edward Island.**

spue (spju:) *vb* **spues, spuing, spued.** an archaic spelling of **spew.** ▸ **'spuer** *n*

spuggy ('spʊgɪ) *or* **spug** (spʊg) *n, pl* **spuggies** *or* **spugs.** *Northeast English dialect.* a house sparrow. Compare **speug.** [variant of Scottish *sprug,* of obscure origin]

spume (spju:m) *n* **1** foam or surf, esp. on the sea; froth. ♦ *vb* **2** (*intr*) to foam or froth. [C14: from Old French *espume,* from Latin *spūma;* related to *spuere* to SPEW] ▸ **'spumous** *or* **'spumy** *adj*

spumescent (spju:'mɛsᵊnt) *adj* producing or resembling foam or froth. ▸ **spu'mescence** *n*

spumone *or* **spumoni** (spu:'məʊnɪ; *Italian* spu'mo:ne) *n, pl* **-ni** (-nɪ). a creamy Italian ice cream, made in sections of different colouring, usually containing candied fruit and nuts. [Italian, from *spuma* foam, SPUME]

spun (spʌn) *vb* **1** the past tense and past participle of **spin.** ♦ *adj* **2** formed or manufactured by spinning: *spun gold; spun glass.*

spunk (spʌŋk) *n* **1** *Informal.* courage or spirit. **2** *Taboo, Brit.* a slang word for **semen. 3** touchwood or tinder, esp. originally made from various spongy types of fungus. **4** *Austral. informal.* a person, esp. male, who is attractive to the opposite sex. [C16 (in the sense: a spark): from Scottish Gaelic *spong* tinder, sponge, from Latin *spongia* sponge] ▸ **'spunky** *adj* ▸ **'spunkily** *adv*

spun silk *n* yarn or fabric made from silk waste.

spun sugar *n U.S.* another term for **candyfloss.**

spun yarn *n Nautical.* small stuff made from rope yarns twisted together.

spur (spɜ:) *n* **1** a pointed device or sharp spiked wheel fixed to the heel of a rider's boot to enable him to urge his horse on. **2** anything serving to urge or encourage: *the increase in salary was a spur to their production.* **3** a sharp horny projection from the leg just above the claws in male birds, such as the domestic cock. **4** a pointed process in any of various animals; calcar. **5** a tubular extension at the base of the corolla in flowers such as larkspur. **6** a short or stunted branch of a tree. **7** a ridge projecting laterally from a mountain or mountain range. **8** a wooden prop or a masonry reinforcing pier. **9** another name for **groyne. 10** Also called: **spur track.** a railway branch line or siding. **11** a short side road leading off a main road: *a motorway spur.* **12** a sharp cutting instrument attached to the leg of a gamecock. **13 on the spur of the moment.** on impulse. **14 win one's spurs. 14a** *History.* to earn knighthood. **14b** to prove one's ability; gain distinction. ♦ *vb* **spurs, spurring, spurred. 15** (*tr*) to goad or urge with or as if with spurs. **16** (*intr*) to go or ride quickly; press on. **17** (*tr*) to injure or strike with a spur. **18** (*tr*) to provide with a spur or spurs. [Old English *spura;* related to Old Norse *spori,* Old High German *sporo*]

spurge (spɜ:dʒ) *n* any of various euphorbiaceous plants of the genus *Euphorbia* that have milky sap and small flowers typically surrounded by conspicuous bracts. Some species have purgative properties. [C14: from Old French *espurge,* from *espurgier* to purge, from Latin *expurgāre* to cleanse, from EX-[1] + *purgāre* to PURGE]

spur gear *or* **wheel** *n* a gear having involuted teeth either straight or helically cut on a cylindrical surface. Two such gears are used to transmit power between parallel shafts.

spurge laurel *n* See **laurel** (sense 4).

spurious ('spjʊərɪəs) *adj* **1** not genuine or real. **2** (of a plant part or organ) having the appearance of another part but differing from it in origin, development, or function; false: *a spurious fruit.* **3** (of radiation) produced at an undesired frequency by a transmitter, causing interference, etc. **4** *Rare.* illegitimate. [C17: from Latin *spurius* of illegitimate birth] ▸ **'spuriously** *adv* ▸ **'spuriousness** *n*

spurn (spɜ:n) *vb* **1** to reject (a person or thing) with contempt. **2** (when *intr,* often foll. by *against*) *Archaic.* to kick (at). ♦ *n* **3** an instance of spurning. **4** *Archaic.* a kick or thrust. [Old English *spurnan;* related to Old Norse *sporna,* Old High German *spurnan,* Latin *spernere* to despise, Lithuanian *spiriu* to kick] ▸ **'spurner** *n*

spurrier ('spʌrɪə) *n* a maker of spurs.

spurry *or* **spurrey** ('spʌrɪ) *n, pl* **-ries.** any of several low-growing caryophyllaceous plants of the European genus *Spergula,* esp. *S. arvensis,* having whorled leaves and small white flowers. [C16: from Dutch *spurrie,* perhaps from Medieval Latin *spergula;* related to German *Spergel*]

spurt *or* **spirt** (spɜ:t) *vb* **1** to gush or cause to gush forth in a sudden stream or jet. **2** to make a sudden effort. ♦ *n* **3** a sudden forceful stream or jet. **4** a short burst of activity, speed, or energy. [C16: perhaps related to Middle High German *sprützen* to squirt]

Sputnik ('spʊtnɪk, 'spʌt-) *n* any of a series of Soviet artificial satellites, **Sputnik 1** (launched in 1957) being the first man-made satellite to orbit the earth. [C20: from Russian, literally: fellow traveller, from *s-* with + *put* path + *-nik* suffix indicating agent]

sputter ('spʌtə) *vb* **1** another word for **splutter** (senses 1-3). **2** *Physics.* **2a** to undergo or cause to undergo a process in which atoms of a solid are removed from its surface by the impact of high-energy ions, as in a discharge tube. **2b** to coat (a film of a metal) onto (a solid surface) by using this process. ♦ *n* **3** the process or noise of sputtering. **4** incoherent stammering speech. **5** something that is ejected while sputtering. [C16: from Dutch *sputteren,* of imitative origin] ▸ **'sputterer** *n*

sputum ('spju:təm) *n, pl* **-ta** (-tə). **1** a mass of salivary matter ejected from the mouth. **2** saliva ejected from the mouth mixed with mucus or pus exuded from the respiratory passages, as in bronchitis or bronchiectasis. [C17: from Latin: spittle, from *spuere* to spit out]

spy (spaɪ) *n, pl* **spies. 1** a person employed by a state or institution to obtain secret information from rival countries, organizations, companies, etc. **2** a person who keeps secret watch on others. **3** *Obsolete.* a close view. ◆ *vb* **spies, spying, spied. 4** (*intr;* usually foll. by *on*) to keep a secret or furtive watch (on). **5** (*intr*) to engage in espionage. **6** (*tr*) to catch sight of; descry. [C13 *spien,* from Old French *espier,* of Germanic origin; related to Old High German *spehōn,* Middle Dutch *spien*]

spyglass ('spaɪˌglɑːs) *n* a small telescope.

spyhole ('spaɪˌhəʊl) *n* a small hole in a door, etc. through which one may watch secretly; peephole.

spy out *vb* (*tr, adv*) **1** to discover by careful observation: *to spy out a route.* **2** to make a close scrutiny of: *to spy out the land.*

Spy Wednesday *n* (in Ireland) the Wednesday before Easter, named for Judas' becoming a spy for the Sanhedrin.

sq. *abbrev. for:* **1** sequence. **2** square. **3** (*pl* **sqq.**) the following one. [from Latin *sequens*]

Sq. *abbrev. for:* **1** Squadron. **2** (in place names) Square.

SQA (in Britain) *abbrev. for* Scottish Qualifications Agency.

SQL *abbrev. for* structured query language: a computer programming language used for database management.

sqn *abbrev. for* squadron.

Sqn Ldr *abbrev. for* squadron leader.

sqq. *abbrev. for* the following ones. [from Latin *sequentia*]

squab (skwɒb) *n, pl* **squabs** *or* **squab. 1** a young unfledged bird, esp. a pigeon. **2** a short fat person. **3a** a well-stuffed bolster or cushion. **3b** a sofa. ◆ *adj* **4** (of birds) recently hatched and still unfledged. **5** short and fat. [C17: probably of Germanic origin; compare Swedish dialect *sqvabb* flabby skin, *sqvabba* fat woman, German *Quabbe* soft mass, Norwegian *kvabb* mud] ▸ **'squabby** *adj*

squabble ('skwɒbᵊl) *vb* **1** (*intr*) to quarrel over a small matter. ◆ *n* **2** a petty quarrel. [C17: probably of Scandinavian origin; related to Swedish dialect *sqvabbel* to quarrel] ▸ **'squabbler** *n*

squacco ('skwækəʊ) *n, pl* **-cos.** a S European heron, *Ardeola ralloides,* with a short thick neck and a buff-coloured plumage with white wings. [C17: Italian dialect]

squad (skwɒd) *n* **1** the smallest military formation, typically comprising a dozen soldiers, used esp. as a drill formation. **2** any small group of people engaged in a common pursuit. **3** *Sport.* a number of players from which a team is to be selected. [C17: from Old French *esquade,* from Old Spanish *escuadra,* from *escuadrar* to SQUARE, from the square formations used]

squaddie *or* **squaddy** ('skwɒdɪ) *n, pl* **-dies.** *Brit. slang.* a private soldier. Compare **swaddy.** [C20: from SQUAD]

squadron ('skwɒdrən) *n* **1a** a subdivision of a naval fleet detached for a particular task. **1b** a number of naval units usually of similar type and consisting of two or more divisions. **2** a cavalry unit comprising two or more troops, headquarters, and supporting arms. **3** the basic tactical and administrative air force unit comprising two or more flights. ◆ Abbrev.: **sqn.** [C16: from Italian *squadrone* soldiers drawn up in square formation, from *squadro* SQUARE]

squadron leader *n* an officer holding commissioned rank, between flight lieutenant and wing commander in the air forces of Britain and certain other countries.

squalene ('skweɪˌliːn) *n Biochem.* a terpene first found in the liver of sharks but also present in the livers of most higher animals: an important precursor of cholesterol. [C20: from New Latin *squalus* genus name of the shark]

squalid ('skwɒlɪd) *adj* **1** dirty and repulsive, esp. as a result of neglect or poverty. **2** sordid. [C16: from Latin *squālidus,* from *squālēre* to be stiff with dirt] ▸ **squalidity** (skwɒ'lɪdɪtɪ) *or* **'squalidness** *n* ▸ **'squalidly** *adv*

squall[1] (skwɔːl) *n* **1** a sudden strong wind or brief turbulent storm. **2** any sudden commotion or show of temper. ◆ *vb* **3** (*intr*) to blow in a squall. [C18: perhaps a special use of SQUALL[2]] ▸ **'squallish** *adj* ▸ **'squally** *adj*

squall[2] (skwɔːl) *vb* **1** (*intr*) to cry noisily; yell. ◆ *n* **2** a shrill or noisy yell or howl. [C17: probably of Scandinavian origin; compare Icelandic *skvala* to shout; see SQUEAL] ▸ **'squaller** *n*

squall line *n* a narrow zone along a cold front along which squalls occur. See also **line squall.**

squalor ('skwɒlə) *n* the condition or quality of being squalid; disgusting dirt and filth. [C17: from Latin]

squama ('skweɪmə) *n, pl* **-mae** (-miː). *Biology.* a scale or scalelike structure. [C18: from Latin] ▸ **squamate** ('skweɪmeɪt) *adj*

squamation (skweɪ'meɪʃən) *n* **1** the condition of having or forming scales or squamae. **2** the arrangement of scales in fishes or reptiles.

squamiform ('skweɪmɪˌfɔːm) *adj Biology.* resembling a scale: *squamiform cells.*

squamosal (skwə'məʊsᵊl) *n* **1** a thin platelike paired bone in the skull of vertebrates: in mammals it forms part of the temporal bone. ◆ *adj* **2** of or relating to this bone. **3** a less common word for **squamous.**

squamous ('skweɪməs) *or* **squamose** ('skweɪməʊs) *adj Biology.* **1** (of epithelium) consisting of a single layer of flat platelike cells. **2** covered with, formed of, or resembling scales. [C16: from Latin *squāmōsus,* from *squāma* a scale] ▸ **'squamously** *or* **'squamosely** *adv* ▸ **'squamousness** *or* **'squamoseness** *n*

squamulose ('skwæmjʊˌləʊs, -ˌləʊz, 'skweɪ-) *adj* (esp. of plants or their parts) covered with minute scales. [C19: from Latin *squāmula* diminutive of *squāma* a scale]

squander ('skwɒndə) *vb* (*tr*) **1** to spend wastefully or extravagantly; dissipate. **2** an obsolete word for **scatter.** ◆ *n* **3** *Rare.* extravagance or dissipation. [C16: of unknown origin] ▸ **'squanderer** *n*

square (skweə) *n* **1** a plane geometric figure having four equal sides and four right angles. Compare **rectangle, rhombus. 2** any object, part, or arrangement having this or a similar shape: *a square of carpet; a square on a chess board.* **3** (*cap. when part of name*) an open area in a town, sometimes including the surrounding buildings, which may form a square. **4** *Maths.* the product of two equal factors; the second power: *9 is the square of 3, written* 3^2. **5** an instrument having two strips of wood, metal, etc., set in the shape of a T or L, used for constructing or testing right angles. **6** *Cricket.* the closely-cut area in the middle of a ground on which wickets are prepared. **7** a body of soldiers drawn up in the form of a square. **8** *Rowing.* the position of the blade of an oar perpendicular to the surface of the water just before and during a stroke. **9** *Informal.* a person who is old-fashioned in views, customs, appearance, etc. **10** *Astrology.* an aspect of about 90° between two planets, etc. Compare **conjunction** (sense 5), **opposition** (sense 9), **trine** (sense 1). **11** *Obsolete.* a standard, pattern, or rule. **12 back to square one.** indicating a return to the starting-point of an investigation, experiment, etc., because of failure, lack of progress, etc. **13 on the square. 13a** at right angles. **13b** on equal terms. **13c** *Informal.* honestly and openly. **13d** *Slang.* a phrase identifying someone as a Freemason: *he is on the square.* **14 out of square. 14a** not at right angles or not having a right angle. **14b** not in order or agreement. ◆ *adj* **15** being a square in shape. **16** having or forming one or more right angles or being at right angles to something. **17** square or rectangular in section: *a square bar.* **18a** (*prenominal*) denoting a measure of area of any shape: *a circle of four square feet.* **18b** (*immediately postpositive*) denoting a square having a specified length on each side: *a board four feet square contains 16 square feet.* **19** fair and honest (esp. in the phrase **a square deal**). **20** straight, even, or level: *a square surface.* **21** *Cricket.* at right angles to the wicket: *square leg.* **22** *Soccer, hockey, etc.* in a straight line across the pitch: *a square pass.* **23** *Nautical.* (of the sails of a square-rigger) set at right angles to the keel. **24** *Informal.* old-fashioned in views, customs, appearance, etc. **25** stocky or sturdy: *square shoulders.* **26** (*postpositive*) having no remaining debts or accounts to be settled. **27** (of a horse's gait) sound, steady, or regular. **28** (*prenominal*) unequivocal or straightforward: *a square contradiction.* **29** (*postpositive*) neat and tidy. **30** *Maths.* (of a matrix) having the same number of rows and columns. **31 all square.** on equal terms; even in score. **32 square peg (in a round hole).** *Informal.* a person or thing that is a misfit, such as an employee in a job for which he is unsuited. ◆ *vb* (*mainly tr*) **33** to make into a square or similar shape. **34** *Maths.* to raise (a number or quantity) to the second power. **35** to test or adjust for deviation with respect to a right angle, plane surface, etc. **36** (sometimes foll. by *off*) to divide into squares. **37** to position so as to be rectangular, straight, or level: *square the shoulders.* **38** (sometimes foll. by *up*) to settle (debts, accounts, etc.). **39** to level (the score) in a game, etc. **40** (*also intr;* often foll. by *with*) to agree or cause to agree: *your ideas don't square with mine.* **41** *Rowing.* to turn (an oar) perpendicular to the surface of the water just before commencing a stroke. **42** (in canoeing) to turn (a paddle) perpendicular to the direction of the canoe at the commencement of a stroke. Compare **feather** (sense 15). **43** to arrange (something), esp. by a corrupt method or come to an arrangement with (someone), as by bribery. **44 square the circle.** to attempt the impossible (in reference to the insoluble problem of constructing a square having exactly the same area as a given circle). ◆ *adv* **45** in order to be square. **46** at right angles. **47** *Soccer, hockey, etc.* in a straight line across the pitch: *pass the ball square.* **48** *Informal.* squarely. ◆ See also **square away, square off, square up.** [C13: from Old French *esquare,* from Vulgar Latin *exquadra* (unattested), from Latin EX-[1] + *quadrāre* to make square; see QUADRANT] ▸ **'squareness** *n* ▸ **'squarer** *n* ▸ **'squarish** *adj*

square away *vb* (*adv*) **1** to set the sails of (a square-rigger) at right angles to the keel. **2** (*tr*) *U.S. and Canadian.* to make neat and tidy.

square-bashing *n Brit. military slang.* drill on a barrack square.

square bracket *n* **1** either of a pair of characters [ ], used to enclose a section of writing or printing to separate it from the main text. **2** Also called: **bracket.** either of these characters used as a sign of aggregation in mathematical or logical expressions indicating that the expression contained in the brackets is to be evaluated first and treated as a unit in the evaluation of the whole.

square dance *n* **1** *Chiefly U.S. and Canadian.* any of various formation dances, such as a quadrille, in which the couples form squares. ◆ *vb* **square-dance. 2** (*intr*) to perform such a dance. ▸ **'square-ˌdancer** *n*

square knot *n* another name for **reef knot.**

square leg *n Cricket.* **1** a fielding position on the on side approximately at right angles to the batsman. **2** a person who fields in this position.

squarely ('skweəlɪ) *adv* **1** in a direct way; straight: *he hit me squarely on the nose.* **2** in an honest, frank, and just manner. **3** at right angles.

square matrix *n Maths.* a matrix in which the number of rows is equal to the number of columns.

square meal *n* a substantial meal consisting of enough food to satisfy.

square measure *n* a unit or system of units for measuring areas.

square number *n* an integer, such as 1, 4, 9, or 16, that is the square of an integer.

square off *vb* (*intr, adv*) to assume a posture of offence or defence, as in boxing.

square of opposition *n* See **opposition** (sense 10b).

square piano *n Music.* an obsolete form of piano, horizontally strung and with an oblong frame.

square-rigged *adj Nautical.* rigged with square sails.

square-rigger *n Nautical.* a square-rigged ship.

square root *n* a number or quantity that when multiplied by itself gives a given number or quantity: *2 is the square root of 4, usually written* $\sqrt{4}$, $\sqrt[]{4}$, $4^{1/2}$.

square sail *n Nautical.* a rectangular or square sail set on a horizontal yard rigged more or less athwartships.

square shooter *n Informal, chiefly U.S.* an honest or frank person. ▸ **square shooting** *n*

square tin *n Brit.* a medium-sized loaf having a crusty top, baked in a tin with a square base.

square up *vb (adv)* **1** to pay or settle (bills, debts, etc.). **2** *Informal.* to arrange or be arranged satisfactorily. **3** *(intr; foll. by to)* to prepare to be confronted (with), esp. courageously. **4** *(tr; foll. by to)* to adopt a position of readiness to fight (an opponent). **5** *(tr)* to transfer (a drawing) by aid of a network of squares.

square wave *n* an oscillation, for example in voltage pulse, that alternates between two fixed values with a negligible transition time between the two, giving a rectangular waveform.

squarrose ('skwærəʊz, 'skwɒ-) *adj* **1** *Biology.* having a rough surface, caused by the presence of projecting hairs, scales, etc. **2** *Botany.* having or relating to overlapping parts that are pointed or recurved: *squarrose bracts.* [C18: from Latin *squarrōsus* scabby]

squash[1] (skwɒʃ) *vb* **1** to press or squeeze or be pressed or squeezed in or down so as to crush, distort, or pulp. **2** *(tr)* to suppress or overcome. **3** *(tr)* to humiliate or crush (a person), esp. with a disconcerting retort. **4** *(intr)* to make a sucking, splashing, or squelching sound. **5** (often foll. by *in* or *into*) to enter or insert in a confined space. ◆ *n* **6** *Brit.* a still drink made from fruit juice or fruit syrup diluted with water. **7** a crush, esp. of people in a confined space. **8** something that is squashed. **9** the act or sound of squashing or the state of being squashed. **10** Also called: **squash rackets, squash racquets.** a game for two or four players played in an enclosed court with a small rubber ball and light long-handled rackets. The ball may be hit against any of the walls but must hit the facing wall at a point above a horizontal line. See also **rackets. 11** Also called: **squash tennis.** a similar game played with larger rackets and a larger pneumatic ball. [C16: from Old French *esquasser,* from Vulgar Latin *exquassāre* (unattested), from Latin EX-[1] + *quassāre* to shatter] ▸ **'squasher** *n*

squash[2] (skwɒʃ) *n, pl* **squashes** *or* **squash.** *U.S. and Canadian.* **1** any of various marrow-like cucurbitaceous plants of the genus *Cucurbita,* esp. *C. pepo* and *C. moschata,* the fruits of which have a hard rind surrounding edible flesh. **2** the fruit of any of these plants, eaten as a vegetable. [C17: from Narraganset *askutasquash,* literally: green vegetable eaten green]

squash bug *n* any of various heteropterous insects of the family *Coreidae,* esp. a North American species, *Anasa tristis,* which is a pest of squash, pumpkin, and related plants.

squash ladder *n* a list showing the relative order of merit of a set of squash players determined by the winning player in each match taking the higher of the two players' positions.

squashy ('skwɒʃɪ) *adj* **squashier, squashiest. 1** easily squashed; pulpy: *a squashy peach.* **2** soft and wet; marshy: *squashy ground.* **3** having a squashed appearance: *a squashy face.* ▸ **'squashily** *adv* ▸ **'squashiness** *n*

squat (skwɒt) *vb* **squats, squatting, squatted.** *(intr)* **1** to rest in a crouching position with the knees bent and the weight on the feet. **2** to crouch down, esp. in order to hide. **3** *Law.* to occupy land or property to which the occupant has no legal title. ◆ *adj* **4** Also: **squatty** ('skwɒtɪ). short and broad: *a squat chair.* ◆ *n* **5** a squatting position. **6** a house occupied by squatters. [C13: from Old French *esquater,* from *es-* EX-[1] + *catir* to press together, from Vulgar Latin *coactīre* (unattested), from Latin *cōgere* to compress, from CO- + *agere* to drive] ▸ **'squatly** *adv* ▸ **'squatness** *n*

squatter ('skwɒtə) *n* **1** a person who occupies property or land to which he has no legal title. **2** (in Australia) **2a** (formerly) a person who occupied a tract of land, esp. pastoral land, as tenant of the Crown. **2b** a farmer of sheep or cattle on a large scale. **3** (in New Zealand) a 19th-century settler who took up large acreage on a Crown lease.

squatter sovereignty *n* a contemptuous term for **popular sovereignty,** used by its critics.

squat thrust *n* an exercise in which the hands are kept on the floor with the arms held straight while the legs are straightened out behind and quickly drawn in towards the body again.

squattocracy (skwɒ'tɒkrəsɪ) *n Chiefly Austral.* squatters collectively, regarded as rich and influential. See **squatter** (sense 2b). [C19: from SQUATTER + -CRACY]

squaw (skwɔː) *n* **1** *Offensive.* a North American Indian woman. **2** *Slang, usually facetious.* a woman or wife. [C17: of Algonquian origin; compare Natick *squa* female creature]

squawk (skwɔːk) *n* **1** a loud raucous cry; screech. **2** *Informal.* a loud complaint or protest. ◆ *vb* **3** to utter a squawk or with a squawk. **4** *(intr) Informal.* to complain loudly. [C19: of imitative origin] ▸ **'squawker** *n*

squaw man *n Derogatory.* a White or other non-Indian married to a North American Indian woman.

squeak (skwiːk) *n* **1** a short shrill cry or high-pitched sound. **2** *Informal.* an escape (esp. in the phrases **narrow squeak, near squeak**). ◆ *vb* **3** to make or cause to make a squeak. **4** *(intr; usually foll. by through or by)* to pass with only a narrow margin: *to squeak through an examination.* **5** *(intr) Informal.* to confess information about oneself or another. **6** *(tr)* to utter with a squeak. [C17: probably of Scandinavian origin; compare Swedish *skväka* to croak] ▸ **'squeaker** *n* ▸ **'squeaky** *adj* ▸ **'squeakily** *adv* ▸ **'squeakiness** *n*

squeaky-clean *adj* **1** (of hair) washed so clean that wet strands squeak when rubbed. **2** completely clean.

squeal (skwiːl) *n* **1** a high shrill yelp, as of pain. **2** a screaming sound, as of tyres when a car brakes suddenly. ◆ *vb* **3** to utter a squeal or with a squeal. **4** *(intr) Slang.* to confess information about another. **5** *(intr) Informal, chiefly Brit.* to complain or protest loudly. [C13 *squelen,* of imitative origin] ▸ **'squealer** *n*

squeamish ('skwiːmɪʃ) *adj* **1** easily sickened or nauseated, as by the sight of blood. **2** easily shocked; fastidious or prudish. **3** easily frightened: *squeamish about spiders.* [C15: from Anglo-French *escoymous,* of unknown origin] ▸ **'squeamishly** *adv* ▸ **'squeamishness** *n*

squeegee ('skwiːdʒiː) *or (less commonly)* **squilgee** *n* **1** an implement with a rubber blade used for wiping away surplus water from a surface, such as a windowpane. **2** any of various similar devices used in photography for pressing the water out of wet prints or negatives or for squeezing prints onto a glazing surface. ◆ *vb* **-gees, -geeing, -geed. 3** to remove (water or other liquid) from (something) by use of a squeegee. **4** *(tr)* to press down (a photographic print, etc.) with a squeegee. [C19: probably of imitative origin, influenced by SQUEEZE]

squeeze (skwiːz) *vb (mainly tr)* **1** to grip or press firmly, esp. so as to crush or distort; compress. **2** to crush or press (something) so as to extract (a liquid): *to squeeze the juice from an orange; to squeeze an orange.* **3** to apply gentle pressure to, as in affection or reassurance: *he squeezed her hand.* **4** to push or force in a confined space: *to squeeze six lettuces into one box; to squeeze through a crowd.* **5** to hug closely. **6** to oppress with exacting demands, such as excessive taxes. **7** to exert pressure on (someone) in order to extort (something): *to squeeze money out of a victim by blackmail.* **8** *(intr)* to yield under pressure. **9** to make an impression of (a coin, etc.) in a soft substance. **10** *Bridge, whist.* to lead a card that forces (opponents) to discard potentially winning cards. ◆ *n* **11** the act or an instance of squeezing or of being squeezed. **12** a hug or handclasp. **13** a crush of people in a confined space. **14** *Chiefly Brit.* a condition of restricted credit imposed by a government to counteract price inflation. **15** an impression, esp. of a coin, etc., made in a soft substance. **16** an amount extracted by squeezing: *add a squeeze of lemon juice.* **17** *Commerce.* any action taken by a trader or traders on a market that forces buyers to make purchases and prices to rise. **18** *Informal.* pressure brought to bear in order to extort something (esp. in the phrase **put the squeeze on**). **19** Also called: **squeeze play.** *Bridge, whist.* a manoeuvre that forces opponents to discard potentially winning cards. **20** *Informal.* a person with whom one is having a romantic relationship. [C16: from Middle English *queysen* to press, from Old English *cwӯsan*] ▸ **'squeezable** *adj* ▸ **'squeezer** *n*

squeeze-box *n* an informal name for **concertina, accordion.**

squelch (skweltʃ) *vb* **1** *(intr)* to walk laboriously through soft wet material or with wet shoes, making a sucking noise. **2** *(intr)* to make such a noise. **3** *(tr)* to crush completely; squash. **4** *(tr) Informal.* to silence, as by a crushing retort. ◆ *n* **5** a squelching sound. **6** something that has been squelched. **7** *Electronics.* a circuit that cuts off the audio-frequency amplifier of a radio receiver in the absence of an input signal, in order to suppress background noise. **8** *Informal.* a crushing remark. [C17: of imitative origin] ▸ **'squelcher** *n* ▸ **'squelching** *adj* ▸ **'squelchy** *adj*

squeteague (skwɪ'tiːg) *n, pl* **-teague** *or* **-teagues.** any of various sciaenid food fishes of the genus *Cynoscion,* esp. *C. regalis,* of the North American coast of the Atlantic Ocean. [C19: from Narraganset *pesukwiteag,* literally: they give glue; so called because glue is made from them]

squib (skwɪb) *n* **1** a firework, usually having a tube filled with gunpowder, that burns with a hissing noise and culminates in a small explosion. **2** a firework that does not explode because of a fault; dud. **3** a short witty attack; lampoon. **4** an electric device for firing a rocket engine. **5** *Obsolete.* an insignificant person. **6** *Austral. and N.Z. slang.* a coward. **7 damp squib.** something intended but failing to impress. ◆ *vb* **squibs, squibbing, squibbed. 8** *(intr)* to sound, move, or explode like a squib. **9** *(intr)* to let off or shoot a squib. **10** to write a squib against (someone). **11** *(intr)* to move in a quick irregular fashion. **12** *(intr) Austral. slang.* to behave in a cowardly fashion. [C16: probably imitative of a quick light explosion]

squid (skwɪd) *n, pl* **squid** *or* **squids. 1** any of various fast-moving pelagic cephalopod molluscs of the genera *Loligo, Ommastrephes,* etc., of most seas, having a torpedo-shaped body ranging from about 10 centimetres to 16.5 metres long and a pair of triangular tail fins: order *Decapoda* (decapods). See also **cuttlefish.** ◆ *vb* **squids, squidding, squidded. 2** *(intr)* (of a parachute) to assume an elongated squidlike shape owing to excess air pressure. [C17: of unknown origin]

squidgy ('skwɪdʒɪ) *adj* **squidgier, squidgiest.** soft, moist, and squashy. [of imitative origin]

squiffy ('skwɪfɪ) *adj* **-fier, -fiest.** *Brit. informal.* slightly drunk. Also: **squiffed.** [C19: of unknown origin]

squiggle ('skwɪgᵊl) *n* **1** a mark or movement in the form of a wavy line; curlicue. **2** an illegible scrawl. ◆ *vb* **3** *(intr)* to wriggle. **4** *(intr)* to form or draw squiggles. **5** *(tr)* to make into squiggles. [C19: perhaps a blend of SQUIRM + WIGGLE] ▸ **'squiggler** *n* ▸ **'squiggly** *adj*

squilgee ('skwɪldʒiː) *n* a variant of **squeegee.** [C19: perhaps from SQUEEGEE, influenced by SQUELCH]

squill (skwɪl) *n* **1** See **sea squill. 2** the bulb of the sea squill, which is sliced, dried, and used medicinally, as an expectorant. **3** any Old World liliaceous plant of the genus *Scilla,* such as *S. verna* (**spring squill**) of Europe, having small blue or purple flowers. [C14: from Latin *squilla* sea onion, from Greek *skilla,* of obscure origin]

squilla ('skwɪlə) *n, pl* **-las** *or* **-lae** (-liː). any mantis shrimp of the genus *Squilla.* [C16: from Latin *squilla* shrimp, of obscure origin]

squillion ('skwɪljən) *Informal.* ◆ *n, pl* **-lions** *or* **-lion. 1** *(often pl)* an extremely large but unspecified number, quantity, or amount. ◆ *determiner* **2a** amounting to a squillion. **2b** *(as pronoun): there were squillions of them everywhere.*

squinch (skwɪntʃ) *n* a small arch, corbelling, etc., across an internal corner of a tower, used to support a superstructure such as a spire. Also called: **squinch arch.** [C15: from obsolete *scunch,* from Middle English *sconcheon,* from Old French *escoinson,* from *es-* EX-[1] + *coin* corner]

squint (skwɪnt) *vb* **1** *(usually intr)* to cross or partly close (the eyes). **2** *(intr)* to have a squint. **3** *(intr)* to look or glance sideways or askance. ◆ *n* **4** the nontechnical name for **strabismus. 5** the act or an instance of squinting; glimpse. **6** Also called: **hagioscope.** a narrow oblique opening in a wall or pillar of a church to permit a view of the main altar from a side aisle or transept. **7** *Informal.* a quick look; glance. ◆ *adj* **8** having a squint. **9** *Informal.* crooked; askew. [C14: short for ASQUINT] ▸ **'squinter** *n* ▸ **'squinty** *adj*

squint-eyed *adj* **1** having a squint. **2** looking sidelong.

squire (skwaɪə) *n* **1** a country gentleman in England, esp. the main landowner in a rural community. **2** *Feudal history.* a young man of noble birth, who attended upon a knight. **3** *Rare.* a man who courts or escorts a woman. **4** *Informal, chiefly Brit.* a term of address used by one man to another, esp., unless ironic, to a member of a higher social class. **5** *Austral.* an immature snapper (see **snapper** (sense 2)). ◆ *vb* **6** (*tr*) (of a man) to escort (a woman). **[C13:** from Old French *esquier;* see ESQUIRE**]**

squirearchy *or* **squirarchy** ('skwaɪə,rɑːkɪ) *n, pl* **-chies. 1** government by squires. **2** squires collectively, esp. as a political or social force. **[C19:** from SQUIRE + -ARCHY, on the model of HIERARCHY, MONARCHY, etc.**]** ▸ **squire'archal, squir'archal** *or* **squire'archical, squir'archical** *adj*

squireen (skwaɪ'riːn) *or* **squireling** ('skwaɪəlɪŋ) *n Rare.* a petty squire. **[C19:** from SQUIRE + *-een,* Anglo-Irish diminutive suffix, from Irish Gaelic *-ín***]**

squirm (skwɜːm) *vb* (*intr*) **1** to move with a wriggling motion; writhe. **2** to feel deep mental discomfort, guilt, embarrassment, etc. ◆ *n* **3** a squirming movement. **[C17:** of imitative origin (perhaps influenced by WORM)**]** ▸ **'squirmer** *n* ▸ **'squirming** *adj* ▸ **'squirmingly** *adv* ▸ **'squirmy** *adj*

squirrel ('skwɪrəl; *U.S.* 'skwɜːrəl, 'skwʌr-) *n, pl* **-rels** *or* **-rel. 1** any arboreal sciurine rodent of the genus *Sciurus,* such as *S. vulgaris* (**red squirrel**) or *S. carolinensis* (**grey squirrel**), having a bushy tail and feeding on nuts, seeds, etc. Related adj: **sciurine. 2** any other rodent of the family *Sciuridae,* such as a ground squirrel or a marmot. **3** the fur of such an animal. **4** *Informal.* a person who hoards things. ◆ *vb* **-rels, -relling, -relled** *or* (esp. U.S.) **-rels, -reling, -reled. 5** (*tr;* usually foll. by *away*) *Informal.* to store for future use; hoard. **[C14:** from Old French *esquireul,* from Late Latin *sciūrus,* from Greek *skiouros,* from *skia* shadow + *oura* tail**]** ▸ **'squirrel-,like** *adj*

squirrel cage *n* **1** a cage consisting of a cylindrical framework that is made to rotate by a small animal running inside the framework. **2** a repetitive purposeless task, way of life, etc. **3** Also called: **squirrel-cage motor.** *Electrical engineering.* the rotor of an induction motor with a cylindrical winding having copper bars around the periphery parallel to the axis. **4** an electric fan with many long narrow blades arranged in parallel so as to form a cylinder about an axis around which they spin.

squirrel corn *n* a North American plant, *Dicentra canadensis,* having yellow flowers and tubers resembling grains of corn: family *Fumariaceae.* Also called: **colicweed.**

squirrelfish ('skwɪrəl,fɪʃ) *n, pl* **-fish** *or* **-fishes.** any tropical marine brightly coloured teleost fish of the family *Holocentridae.* **[C18:** so called because it can make a squirrel-like noise**]**

squirrel monkey *n* **1** a small New World monkey, *Saimiri sciureus,* of N South American forests, having a yellowish-green coat and orange feet and limbs. **2 red-backed squirrel monkey.** a related species, *Saimiri oerstedi,* of Central America, having a reddish coat and dark brown limbs. **[C18:** so called because it is small and tree-dwelling**]**

squirrel-tail grass *n* an annual grass, *Hordeum marinum,* of salt marsh margins of Europe, having bushy awns.

squirt (skwɜːt) *vb* **1** to force (a liquid) or (of a liquid) to be forced out of a narrow opening. **2** (*tr*) to cover or spatter with liquid so ejected. ◆ *n* **3** a jet or amount of liquid so ejected. **4** the act or an instance of squirting. **5** an instrument used for squirting. **6** *Informal.* **6a** a person regarded as insignificant or contemptible. **6b** a short person. **[C15:** of imitative origin**]** ▸ **'squirter** *n*

squirt gun *n U.S. and Canadian.* another name for **water pistol.**

squirting cucumber *n* a hairy cucurbitaceous plant, *Ecballium elaterium,* of the Mediterranean region, having a fruit that discharges its seeds explosively when ripe.

squish (skwɪʃ) *vb* **1** (*tr*) to crush, esp. so as to make a soft splashing noise. **2** (*intr*) (of mud, etc.) to make a splashing noise: *the ground squishes as you tread.* ◆ *n* **3** a soft squashing sound: *the ripe peach fell with a squish.* **[C17:** of imitative origin**]** ▸ **'squishy** *adj*

squit (skwɪt) *n Brit. slang.* **1** an insignificant person. **2** nonsense; rubbish. **[C19:** dialectal variant of SQUIRT**]**

squiz (skwɪz) *n, pl* **squizzes.** *Austral. and N.Z. slang.* a look or glance, esp. an inquisitive one. **[C20:** perhaps a blend of SQUINT and QUIZ**]**

sr *symbol for* steradian.

Sr *abbrev. for:* **1** (after a name) senior. **2** Señor. **3** Sir. **4** Sister (religious). **5** *the chemical symbol for* strontium.

Sra *abbrev. for* Señora.

Srbija ('s[ə]rbija) *n* the Serbian name for **Serbia.**

SRCN (in Britain) *abbrev. for* State Registered Children's Nurse.

S-R connection *n Psychol.* stimulus-response connection; the basic unit of learning according to behaviourist learning theory. See also **reflex arc.**

Sri (ʃriː) *n Hinduism.* **1** the consort of Vishnu. **2** a title of honour used when addressing a distinguished Hindu. **[**literally: majesty, holiness**]**

Sri Lanka (,sriː 'læŋkə) *n* a republic in S Asia, occupying the island of Ceylon: settled by the Sinhalese from S India in about 550 B.C.; became a British colony 1802; gained independence in 1948, becoming a republic within the Commonwealth in 1972. Exports include tea, cocoa, cinnamon, and copra. Official languages: Sinhalese and Tamil; English is also widely spoken. Religion: Hinayana Buddhist majority. Currency: Sri Lanka rupee. Capital: Colombo (administrative), Sri Jayewardenepura Kotte (legislative). Pop.: 18 729 000 (1998 est.). Area: 65 610 sq. km (25 332 sq. miles). Official name (since 1978): **Democratic Socialist Republic of Sri Lanka.** Former name (until 1972): **Ceylon.** ▸ **Sri Lankan** *adj, n*

Srinagar (sriː'nʌgə) *n* a city in N India, the summer capital of the state of Jammu and Kashmir, at an altitude of 1600 m (5250 ft.) on the Jhelum River: seat of the University of Jammu and Kashmir (1948). Pop.: 586 038 (1991).

SRN (formerly in Britain) *abbrev. for* State Registered Nurse.

SRO *abbrev. for:* **1** standing room only. **2** *Brit.* Statutory Rules and Orders. **3** self-regulatory organization.

Srta *abbrev. for* Señorita.

SS *abbrev. for:* **1** a paramilitary organization within the Nazi party that provided Hitler's bodyguard, security forces including the Gestapo, concentration camp guards, and a corp of combat troops (the Waffen-SS) in World War II. **[**German *Schutzstaffel* protection squad**] 2** steamship. **3** Sunday school.

ss. *abbrev. for* sections.

SS. *abbrev. for* Saints.

SSB *abbrev. for* single sideband (transmission).

SSC *abbrev. for:* **1** (in India) Secondary School Certificate. **2** (in Scotland) solicitor to the Supreme Court.

SSD (in Britain) *abbrev. for* Social Services Department.

SSE *symbol for* south-southeast.

SSHA *abbrev. for* Scottish Special Housing Association.

SSM *abbrev. for* surface-to-surface missile.

SSN *abbrev. for* severely subnormal; used of a person of very limited intelligence who needs special schooling.

SSP (in Britain) *abbrev. for* statutory sick pay.

ssp. (*pl* **sspp.**) *Biology. abbrev. for* subspecies.

SSR *abbrev. for* (formerly) Soviet Socialist Republic.

SSRC *abbrev. for* (formerly, in Britain) Social Science Research Council.

SSRI *abbrev. for* selective serotonin reuptake inhibitor; any of a class of drugs, including fluvoxamine, paroxetine, and Prozac, that increase levels of serotonin in the bloodstream by inhibiting its reabsorption in the brain: used in the treatment of depression.

SSSI (in Britain) *abbrev. for* site of special scientific interest: an area identified by the Nature Conservancy Council or its successors as having flora, fauna, or geological features of special interest.

SST *abbrev. for* supersonic transport.

SSTA *abbrev. for* Scottish Secondary Teachers' Association.

Ssu-ma Ch'ien ('suːmɑː 'tʃɪən) *n* a variant transliteration of **Si-ma Qian.**

SSW *symbol for* south-southwest.

st *abbrev. for* short ton.

St *abbrev. for* Saint (all entries that are usually preceded by *St* are in this dictionary listed alphabetically under **Saint**).

st. *abbrev. for:* **1** stanza. **2** statute. **3** *Cricket.* stumped by.

St. *abbrev. for:* **1** statute. **2** Strait. **3** Street.

-st *suffix.* a variant of **-est**[2].

Sta (in the names of places or churches) *abbrev. for* Saint (female). **[**Italian *Santa***]**

sta. *abbrev. for:* **1** station. **2** stationary.

stab (stæb) *vb* **stabs, stabbing, stabbed. 1** (*tr*) to pierce or injure with a sharp pointed instrument. **2** (*tr*) (of a sharp pointed instrument) to pierce or wound: *the knife stabbed her hand.* **3** (when *intr,* often foll. by *at*) to make a thrust (at); jab: *he stabbed at the doorway.* **4** (*tr*) to inflict with a sharp pain. **5 stab in the back. 5a** (*vb*) to do damage to the reputation of (a person, esp. a friend) in a surreptitious way. **5b** (*n*) a treacherous action or remark that causes the downfall of or injury to a person. ◆ *n* **6** the act or an instance of stabbing. **7** an injury or rift made by stabbing. **8** a sudden sensation, esp. an unpleasant one: *a stab of pity.* **9** *Informal.* an attempt (esp. in the phrase **make a stab at**). **[C14:** from *stabbe* stab wound; probably related to Middle English *stob* stick**]** ▸ **'stabber** *n*

Stabat Mater ('stɑːbæt 'mɑːtə) *n* **1** *R.C. Church.* a Latin hymn, probably of the 13th century, commemorating the sorrows of the Virgin Mary at the crucifixion and used in the Mass and various other services. **2** a musical setting of this hymn. **[**from the opening words, literally: the mother was standing**]**

stabile ('steɪbaɪl) *n* **1** *Arts.* a stationary abstract construction, usually of wire, metal, wood, etc. Compare **mobile** (sense 6a). ◆ *adj* **2** fixed; stable. **3** resistant to chemical change. **[C18:** from Latin *stabilis***]**

stability (stə'bɪlɪtɪ) *n, pl* **-ties. 1** the quality of being stable. **2** the ability of an aircraft to resume its original flight path after inadvertent displacement. **3** *Meteorol.* **3a** the condition of an air mass characterized by no upward movement. **3b** the degree of susceptibility of an air mass to disturbance by convection currents. **4** *Ecology.* the ability of an ecosystem to resist change. **5** *Electrical engineering.* the ability of an electrical circuit to cope with changes in the operational conditions. **6** a vow taken by every Benedictine monk attaching him perpetually to the monastery where he is professed.

stabilize *or* **stabilise** ('steɪbɪ,laɪz) *vb* **1** to make or become stable or more stable. **2** to keep or be kept stable. **3** to put or keep (an aircraft, vessel, etc.) in equilibrium by one or more special devices, or (of an aircraft, vessel, etc.) to become stable. ▸ **,stabili'zation** *or* **,stabili'sation** *n*

stabilizer *or* **stabiliser** ('steɪbɪ,laɪzə) *n* **1** any device for stabilizing an aircraft. See also **horizontal stabilizer, vertical stabilizer. 2** a substance added to something to maintain it in a stable or unchanging state, such as an additive to food to preserve its texture during distribution and storage. **3** *Nautical.* **3a** a system of one or more pairs of fins projecting from the hull of a ship and controllable to counteract roll. **3b** See **gyrostabilizer. 4** either of a pair of brackets supporting a small wheel that can be fitted to the back wheel of a bicycle to help an inexperienced cyclist to maintain balance. **5** an electronic device for producing a direct current supply of constant voltage. **6** *Economics.* a measure, such as progressive taxation, interest-rate control, or unemployment benefit, used to restrict swings in prices, employment, production, etc., in a free economy. **7** a person or thing that stabilizes.

stab kick *n Australian Rules football.* a rapid kick of the ball from one player to another member of his team. Also called: **stab pass.**

stable[1] ('steɪb[ə]l) *n* **1** a building, usually consisting of stalls, for the lodging of horses or other livestock. **2** the animals lodged in such a building, collectively.

3a the racehorses belonging to a particular establishment or owner. **3b** the establishment itself. **3c** (*as modifier*): *stable companion.* **4** *Informal.* a source of training, such as a school, theatre, etc.: *the two athletes were out of the same stable.* **5** a number of people considered as a source of a particular talent: *a stable of writers.* **6** (*modifier*) of, relating to, or suitable for a stable: *stable manners.* ◆ *vb* **7** to put, keep, or be kept in a stable. [C13: from Old French *estable* cowshed, from Latin *stabulum* shed, from *stāre* to stand]

stable[2] ('steɪbᵊl) *adj* **1** steady in position or balance; firm. **2** lasting or permanent: *a stable relationship.* **3** steadfast or firm of purpose. **4** (of an elementary particle, atomic nucleus, etc.) not undergoing decay; not radioactive: *a stable nuclide.* **5** (of a chemical compound) not readily partaking in a chemical change. **6** (of electronic equipment) with no tendency to self-oscillation. [C13: from Old French *estable,* from Latin *stabilis* steady, from *stāre* to stand] ▸ **'stableness** *n* ▸ **'stably** *adv*

stableboy ('steɪbᵊl,bɔɪ) *or* **stableman** ('steɪbᵊl,mæn, -mən) *n, pl* **-boys** *or* **-men.** a boy or man who works in a stable.

stable door *n* a door with an upper and lower leaf that may be opened separately. U.S. and Canadian equivalent: **Dutch door.**

stable fly *n* a blood-sucking muscid fly, *Stomoxys calcitrans,* that attacks man and domestic animals.

Stableford ('steɪbᵊlfəd) *n Golf.* **a** a scoring system in which points are awarded according to the number of strokes taken at each hole, whereby a hole completed in one stroke over par counts as one point, a hole completed in level par counts as two points, etc. **b** (*as modifier*): *a Stableford competition.* ◆ Compare **match play, stroke play.** [C20: named after its inventor, Dr Frank *Stableford* (1870–1959), English amateur golfer]

stable lad *n* a person who looks after the horses in a racing stable.

stabling ('steɪblɪŋ) *n* stable buildings or accommodation.

stablish ('stæblɪʃ) *vb* an archaic variant of **establish.**

Stabroek (*Dutch* 'sta:bru:k) *n* the former name (until 1812) of **Georgetown** (sense 1).

stacc. *Music. abbrev. for* staccato.

staccato (stə'kɑ:təʊ) *adj* **1** *Music.* (of notes) short, clipped, and separate. **2** characterized by short abrupt sounds, as in speech: *a staccato command.* ◆ *adv* **3** (esp. used as a musical direction) in a staccato manner. [C18: from Italian, from *staccare* to detach, shortened from *distaccare*]

stachys ('steɪkɪs) *n* any plant of the genus *Stachys,* esp. *S. lanata* (lamb's ears) and *S. officinalis* (betony). [New Latin, from Greek *stachys* ear of corn, used as a plant name]

stack (stæk) *n* **1** an ordered pile or heap. **2** a large orderly pile of hay, straw, etc., for storage in the open air. **3** (*often pl*) *Library science.* compactly spaced bookshelves, used to house collections of books in an area usually prohibited to library users. **4** a number of aircraft circling an airport at different altitudes, awaiting their signal to land. **5** a large amount: *a stack of work.* **6** *Military.* a pile of rifles or muskets in the shape of a cone. **7** *Brit.* a measure of coal or wood equal to 108 cubic feet. **8** See **chimney stack, smokestack. 9** a vertical pipe, such as the funnel of a ship or the soil pipe attached to the side of a building. **10** a high column of rock, esp. one isolated from the mainland by the erosive action of the sea. **11** an area in a computer memory for temporary storage. ◆ *vb* (*tr*) **12** to place in a stack; pile: *to stack bricks on a lorry.* **13** to load or fill up with piles of something: *to stack a lorry with bricks.* **14** to control (a number of aircraft waiting to land at an airport) so that each flies at a different altitude. **15 stack the cards.** to prearrange the order of a pack of cards secretly so that the deal will benefit someone. [C13: from Old Norse *stakkr* haystack, of Germanic origin; related to Russian *stog*] ▸ **'stackable** *adj* ▸ **'stacker** *n*

stacked (stækt) *adj Slang.* a variant of **well-stacked.**

stacking ('stækɪŋ) *n* the arrangement of aircraft traffic in busy flight lanes, esp. while waiting to land at an airport, with a minimum vertical separation for safety of 1000 feet below 29 000 feet and 2000 feet above 29 000 feet.

stacking truck *n* another name for **pallet truck.**

stacte ('stækti:) *n Old Testament.* one of several sweet-smelling spices used in incense (Exodus 30:34). [C14: via Latin from Greek *staktē* oil of myrrh, from *staktos* distilling a drop at a time, from *stazein* to flow, drip]

staddle ('stædᵊl) *n* **1** a support or prop, esp. a low flat-topped stone structure for supporting hay or corn stacks about two feet above ground level. **2** a supporting frame for such a stack. **3** the lower part of a hay or corn stack. [Old English *stathol* base; related to Old Norse *stothull* cow pen, Old High German *stadal* barn]

staddlestone ('stædᵊl,stəʊn) *n* (formerly) one of several supports for a hayrick, consisting of a truncated conical stone surmounted by a flat circular stone.

stadholder *or* **stadtholder** ('stæd,həʊldə) *n* **1** the chief magistrate of the former Dutch republic or of any of its provinces (from about 1580 to 1802). **2** a viceroy or governor of a province. [C16: partial translation of Dutch *stad houder,* from *stad* city (see STEAD) + *houder* holder] ▸ **'stad,holder,ate, 'stad,holdership** *or* **'stadt,holder,ate, 'stadt,holdership** *n*

stadia[1] ('steɪdɪə) *n* **1a** tacheometry that makes use of a telescopic surveying instrument and a graduated staff calibrated to correspond with the distance from the observer. **1b** (*as modifier*): *stadia surveying.* **2** the two parallel cross hairs or **stadia hairs** in the eyepiece of the instrument used. **3** the staff used. [C19: probably from STADIA[2]]

stadia[2] ('steɪdɪə) *n* a plural of **stadium.**

stadiometer (,steɪdɪ'ɒmɪtə) *n* an instrument that measures the length of curves, dashes, etc., by running a toothed wheel along them. [C19: from *stadio-,* from STADIUM + -METER]

stadium ('steɪdɪəm) *n, pl* **-diums** *or* **-dia** (-dɪə). **1** a sports arena with tiered seats for spectators. **2** (in ancient Greece) a course for races, usually located between two hills providing natural slopes for tiers of seats. **3** an ancient Greek measure of length equivalent to about 607 feet or 184 metres. **4** (in many arthropods) the interval between two consecutive moultings. **5** a particular period or stage in the development of a disease. [C16: via Latin from Greek *stadion,* changed from *spadion* a racecourse, from *spān* to pull; also influenced by Greek *stadios* steady]

Staël (*French* stal) *n* **Madame de.** full name *Baronne Anne Louise Germaine* (née *Necker*) *de Staël-Holstein.* 1766–1817, French writer, whose works, esp. *De l'Allemagne* (1810), anticipated French romanticism.

staff[1] (stɑ:f) *n, pl* **staffs** *for senses 1, 3, 4;* **staffs** *or* **staves** (steɪvz) *for senses 5–9.* **1** a group of people employed by a company, individual, etc., for executive, clerical, sales work, etc. **2** (*modifier*) attached to or provided for the staff of an establishment: *a staff doctor.* **3** the body of teachers or lecturers of an educational institution, as distinct from the students. **4** the officers appointed to assist a commander, service, or central headquarters organization in establishing policy, plans, etc. **5** a stick with some special use, such as a walking stick or an emblem of authority. **6** something that sustains or supports: *bread is the staff of life.* **7** a pole on which a flag is hung. **8** *Chiefly Brit.* a graduated rod used in surveying, esp. for sighting to with a levelling instrument. Usual U.S. name: **rod. 9** Also called: **stave.** *Music.* **9a** the system of horizontal lines grouped into sets of five (four in the case of plainsong) upon which music is written. The spaces between them are also used, being employed in conjunction with a clef in order to give a graphic indication of pitch. **9b** any set of five lines in this system together with its clef: *the treble staff.* ◆ *vb* **10** (*tr*) to provide with a staff. [Old English *stæf;* related to Old Frisian *stef,* Old Saxon *staf,* German *Stab,* Old Norse *stafr,* Gothic *Stafs;* see STAVE]

staff[2] (stɑ:f) *n U.S.* a mixture of plaster and hair used to cover the external surface of temporary structures and for decoration. [C19: of unknown origin]

Staffa ('stæfə) *n* an island in W Scotland, in the Inner Hebrides west of Mull: site of Fingal's Cave.

staff association *n* an association of employees that performs some of the functions of a trade union, such as representing its members in discussions with the management, and may also have other social and professional purposes.

staff college *n* a training centre for executive military personnel.

staff corporal *n* a noncommissioned rank in the British Army above that of staff sergeant and below that of warrant officer.

staffer ('stɑ:fə) *n Informal.* a member of staff, esp., in journalism, of editorial staff.

staffman ('stɑ:f,mæn) *n, pl* **-men.** *Brit.* a person who holds the levelling staff when a survey is being made.

staff nurse *n* a qualified nurse ranking immediately below a sister.

staff of Aesculapius *n* an emblem consisting of a staff with a serpent entwined around it, used by the Royal Medical Corps and the American Medical Association. Compare **caduceus** (sense 2).

staff officer *n* a commissioned officer serving on the staff of a commander, service, or central headquarters.

Stafford[1] ('stæfəd) *n* a market town in central England, administrative centre of Staffordshire. Pop.: 61 885 (1991).

Stafford[2] ('stæfəd) *n* Sir **Edward William.** 1819–1901, New Zealand statesman, born in Scotland: prime minister of New Zealand (1856–61; 1865–69; 1872).

Staffordshire ('stæfəd,ʃɪə, -ʃə) *n* a county of central England: formerly important coalfields lie in the east and south and the Pennine uplands in the north; important in the history of industry, coal and iron worked at least as early as the 13th century. Administrative centre: Stafford. Pop. (including Stoke-on-Trent): 1 054 400 (1994 est.). Area (including Stoke-on-Trent): 2716 sq. km (1048 sq. miles).

Staffordshire bull terrier *n* a breed of smooth-coated terrier with a stocky frame and generally a pied or brindled coat. See also **bull terrier.**

Staffs (stæfs) *abbrev. for* Staffordshire.

staff sergeant *n Military.* **1** *Brit.* a noncommissioned officer holding a rank between sergeant and warrant officer and employed on administrative duties. **2** *U.S.* a noncommissioned officer who ranks: **2a** (in the Army) above sergeant and below sergeant first class. **2b** (in the Air Force) above airman first class and below technical sergeant. **2c** (in the Marine Corps) above sergeant and below gunnery sergeant.

stag (stæg) *n* **1** the adult male of a deer, esp. a red deer. **2** a man unaccompanied by a woman at a social gathering. **3** *Stock Exchange. Brit.* **3a** a speculator who applies for shares in a new issue in anticipation of a rise in price when trading commences in order to make a quick profit on resale. **3b** (*as modifier*): *stag operations.* **4** (*modifier*) (of a social gathering) attended by men only. **5** (*modifier*) pornographic in content: *a stag show.* ◆ *adv* **6** without a female escort. ◆ *vb* (*tr*) **7** *Stock Exchange.* to apply for (shares in a new issue) with the intention of selling them for a quick profit when trading commences. [Old English *stagga* (unattested); related to Old Norse *steggr* male bird]

stag beetle *n* any lamellicorn beetle of the family *Lucanidae,* the males of which have large branched mandibles.

stage (steɪdʒ) *n* **1** a distinct step or period of development, growth, or progress: *a child at the toddling stage.* **2** a raised area or platform. **3** the platform in a theatre where actors perform. **4 the.** the theatre as a profession. **5** any scene regarded as a setting for an event or action. **6** a portion of a journey or a stopping place after such a portion. **7** short for **stagecoach. 8** *Brit.* a division of a bus route for which there is a fixed fare. **9** one of the separate propulsion units of a rocket that can be jettisoned when it has burnt out. See also **multistage** (sense 1). **10** any of the various distinct periods of growth or development in the life of an organism, esp. an insect: *a larval stage; pupal stage.* **11** the organism itself at such a period of growth. **12** a small stratigraphical unit; a subdivision of a rock series or system. **13** the platform on a microscope on which the specimen is mounted for examination. **14** *Electronics.* a part of a complex circuit, esp. one of a number of transistors with the associated elements required to amplify a signal in an amplifier. **15** a university subject studied for one academic year: *Stage II French.* **16 by** *or* **in easy stages.** not hurriedly: *he learned French by easy stages.* ♦ *vb* **17** *(tr)* to perform (a play), esp. on a stage: *we are going to stage "Hamlet".* **18** *(tr)* to set the action of (a play) in a particular time or place. **19** *(tr)* to plan, organize, and carry out (an event). **20** *(intr) Obsolete.* to travel by stagecoach. **[C13:** from Old French *estage* position, from Vulgar Latin *staticum* (unattested), from Latin *stāre* to stand**]**

stagecoach ('steɪdʒˌkəʊtʃ) *n* a large four-wheeled horse-drawn vehicle formerly used to carry passengers, mail, etc., on a regular route between towns and cities.

stagecraft ('steɪdʒˌkrɑːft) *n* skill in or the art of writing or staging plays.

stage direction *n Theatre.* an instruction to an actor or director, written into the script of a play.

stage door *n* a door at a theatre leading backstage.

stage effect *n* a special effect created on the stage by lighting, sound, etc.

stage fright *n* nervousness or panic that may beset a person about to appear in front of an audience.

stagehand ('steɪdʒˌhænd) *n* a person who sets the stage, moves props, etc., in a theatrical production.

stage left *n* the part of the stage to the left of a performer facing the audience.

stage-manage *vb* **1** to work as stage manager for (a play, etc.). **2** *(tr)* to arrange, present, or supervise from behind the scenes: *to stage-manage a campaign.*

stage manager *n* a person who supervises the stage arrangements of a theatrical production.

stager ('steɪdʒə) *n* **1** a person of experience; veteran (esp. in the phrase **old stager**). **2** an archaic word for **actor.**

stage right *n* the part of the stage to the right of a performer facing the audience.

stage-struck *adj* infatuated with the glamour of theatrical life, esp. with the desire to act.

stage whisper *n* **1** a loud whisper from one actor to another onstage intended to be heard by the audience. **2** any loud whisper that is intended to be overheard.

stagey ('steɪdʒɪ) *adj* **stagier, stagiest.** a variant spelling (in the U.S.) of **stagy.** ▸ **'stagily** *adv* ▸ **'staginess** *n*

stagflation (stæg'fleɪʃən) *n* a situation in which inflation is combined with stagnant or falling output and employment. **[C20:** blend of STAGNATION + INFLATION**]**

staggard ('stægəd) *n* a male red deer in the fourth year of life. **[C15:** see STAG, -ARD**]**

stagger ('stægə) *vb* **1** *(usually intr)* to walk or cause to walk unsteadily as if about to fall. **2** *(tr)* to astound or overwhelm, as with shock: *I am staggered by his ruthlessness.* **3** *(tr)* to place or arrange in alternating or overlapping positions or time periods to prevent confusion or congestion: *a staggered junction; to stagger holidays.* **4** *(intr)* to falter or hesitate: *his courage staggered in the face of the battle.* **5** *(tr)* to set (the wings of a biplane) so that the leading edge of one extends beyond that of the other. ♦ *n* **6** the act or an instance of staggering. **7** a staggered arrangement on a biplane, etc. ♦ See also **staggers. [C13** dialect *stacker,* from Old Norse *staka* to push**]** ▸ **'staggerer** *n* ▸ **'staggering** *adj* ▸ **'staggeringly** *adv*

staggerbush ('stægəˌbʊʃ) *n* an ericaceous deciduous shrub, *Lyonia mariana,* of E North America, having white or pinkish flowers: it is poisonous to livestock. **[C19:** so named because it was believed to cause STAGGERS in sheep**]**

staggered directorships *pl n Business.* a defence against unwelcome takeover bids in which a company resolves that its directors should serve staggered terms of office and that no director can be removed from office without just cause, thus preventing a bidder from controlling the board for some years.

staggered hours *pl n* a system of working in which the employees of an organization do not all arrive and leave at the same time, but have large periods of overlap.

staggers ('stægəz) *n (functioning as sing or pl)* **1** a form of vertigo associated with decompression sickness. **2** Also called: **blind staggers.** a disease of horses and some other domestic animals characterized by a swaying unsteady gait, caused by infection or lesions of the central nervous system.

staghound ('stægˌhaʊnd) *n* a breed of hound similar in appearance to the foxhound but larger.

staging ('steɪdʒɪŋ) *n* any temporary structure used in the process of building, esp. the horizontal platforms supported by scaffolding. **[C14:** from STAGE + -ING[1]**]**

staging area *n* a general locality used as a checkpoint or regrouping area for military formations in transit.

staging post *n* a place where a journey is usually broken, esp. a stopover on a flight.

Stagira (stə'dʒaɪrə) *n* an ancient city on the coast of Chalcidice in Macedonia: the birthplace of Aristotle.

Stagirite ('stædʒɪˌraɪt) *n* **1** an inhabitant or native of Stagira. **2** an epithet of Aristotle.

stagnant ('stægnənt) *adj* **1** (of water, etc.) standing still; without flow or current. **2** brackish and foul from standing still. **3** stale, sluggish, or dull from inaction. **4** not growing or developing; static. **[C17:** from Latin *stagnāns,* from *stagnāre* to be stagnant, from *stagnum* a pool**]** ▸ **'stagnancy** *or* **'stagnance** *n* ▸ **'stagnantly** *adv*

stagnate (stæg'neɪt, 'stægˌneɪt) *vb (intr)* to be or to become stagnant. ▸ **stag'nation** *n*

stag night *or* **party** *n* a party for men only, esp. one held for a man before he is married. Compare **hen night, hen party.**

stag's horn *or* **staghorn** ('stægˌhɔːn) *n* **1** the antlers of a stag used as a material for carved implements. **2** a creeping variety of club moss, *Lycopodium clavatum,* growing on moors and mountains, having silvery hair points on its leaves.

stagy *or U.S.* **stagey** ('steɪdʒɪ) *adj* **stagier, stagiest.** excessively theatrical or dramatic. ▸ **'stagily** *adv* ▸ **'staginess** *n*

staid (steɪd) *adj* **1** of a settled, sedate, and steady character. **2** *Now rare.* permanent. **[C16:** obsolete past participle of STAY[1]**]** ▸ **'staidly** *adv* ▸ **'staidness** *n*

stain (steɪn) *vb (mainly tr)* **1** to mark or discolour with patches of something that dirties: *the dress was stained with coffee.* **2** to dye with a penetrating dyestuff or pigment. **3** to bring disgrace or shame on: *to stain someone's honour.* **4** to colour (specimens) for microscopic study by treatment with a dye or similar reagent. **5** *(intr)* to produce indelible marks or discoloration: *does ink stain?* ♦ *n* **6** a spot, mark, or discoloration. **7** a moral taint; blemish or slur. **8** a dye or similar reagent, used to colour specimens for microscopic study. **9** a solution or liquid used to penetrate the surface of a material, esp. wood, and impart a rich colour without covering up the surface or grain. **10** any dye that is made into a solution and used to colour textiles and hides. **[C14** *steynen* (vb), shortened from *disteynen* to remove colour from, from Old French *desteindre* to discolour, from *des-* DIS-[1] + *teindre,* from Latin *tingere* to TINGE**]** ▸ **'stainable** *adj* ▸ **ˌstaina'bility** *n* ▸ **'stainer** *n*

stained glass *n* **a** glass that has been coloured in any of various ways, as by fusing with a film of metallic oxide or burning pigment into the surface, used esp. for church windows. **b** *(as modifier): a stained-glass window.*

Stainer ('steɪnə) *n* Sir **John.** 1840–1901, British composer and organist, noted for his sacred music, esp. the oratorio *The Crucifixion* (1887).

Staines (steɪnz) *n* a town in SE England, in N Surrey on the River Thames. Pop.: 51 167 (1991).

stainless ('steɪnlɪs) *adj* **1** resistant to discoloration, esp. discoloration resulting from corrosion; rust-resistant: *stainless steel.* **2** having no blemish: *a stainless reputation.* ♦ *n* **3** stainless steel. ▸ **'stainlessly** *adv*

stainless steel *n* **a** a type of steel resistant to corrosion as a result of the presence of large amounts of chromium (12–15 per cent). The carbon content depends on the application, being 0.2–0.4 per cent for steel used in cutlery, etc., and about 1 per cent for use in scalpels and razor blades. **b** *(as modifier): stainless-steel cutlery.*

stair (stɛə) *n* **1** one of a flight of stairs. **2** a series of steps: *a narrow stair.* ♦ See also **stairs. [**Old English *stæger;* related to *stīg* narrow path, *stīgan* to ascend, descend, Old Norse *steigurligr* upright, Middle Dutch *steiger* ladder**]**

staircase ('stɛəˌkeɪs) *n* a flight of stairs, its supporting framework, and, usually, a handrail or banisters.

stairhead ('stɛəˌhɛd) *n* the top of a flight of stairs.

stair rod *n* any of a series of rods placed in the angles between the steps of a carpeted staircase, used to hold the carpet in position.

stairs (stɛəz) *pl n* **1** a flight of steps leading from one storey or level to another, esp. indoors. **2 below stairs.** *Brit.* in the servants' quarters; in domestic service.

stairway ('stɛəˌweɪ) *n* a means of access consisting of stairs; staircase or flight of steps.

stairwell ('stɛəˌwɛl) *n* a vertical shaft or opening that contains a staircase.

stake[1] (steɪk) *n* **1** a stick or metal bar driven into the ground as a marker, part of a fence, support for a plant, etc. **2** one of a number of vertical posts that fit into sockets around a flat truck or railway wagon to hold the load in place. **3** a method or the practice of executing a person by binding him to a stake in the centre of a pile of wood that is then set on fire. **4** *Mormon Church.* an administrative district consisting of a group of wards under the jurisdiction of a president. **5 pull up stakes.** to leave one's home or temporary resting place and move on. ♦ *vb (tr)* **6** to tie, fasten, or tether with or to a stake. **7** (often foll. by *out* or *off*) to fence or surround with stakes. **8** (often foll. by *out*) to lay (a claim) to land, rights, etc. **9** to support with a stake. **[**Old English *staca* pin; related to Old Frisian *staka,* Old High German *stehho,* Old Norse *stjaki;* see STICK[1]**]**

stake[2] (steɪk) *n* **1** the money or valuables that a player must hazard in order to buy into a gambling game or make a bet. **2** an interest, often financial, held in something: *a stake in the company's future.* **3** *(often pl)* the money that a player has available for gambling. **4** *(often pl)* a prize in a race, etc., esp. one made up of contributions from contestants or owners. **5** *(pl) Horse racing.* a race in which all owners of competing horses contribute to the prize money. **6** *U.S. and Canadian informal.* short for **grubstake** (sense 1). **7 at stake.** at risk: *two lives are at stake.* **8 raise the stakes. 8a** to increase the amount of money or valuables hazarded in a gambling game. **8b** to increase the costs, risks, or considerations involved in taking an action or reaching a conclusion: *the Libyan allegations raised the stakes in the propaganda war between Libya and the United States.* ♦ *vb (tr)* **9** to hazard (money, etc.) on a result. **10** to invest in or support by supplying with money, etc.: *to stake a business enterprise.* **[C16:** of uncertain origin**]**

Staked Plain *n* another name for the **Llano Estacado.**

stakeholder ('steɪkˌhəʊldə) *n* **1** a person or group owning a significant percentage of a company's shares. **2** a person or group not owning shares in an enterprise but affected by or having an interest in its operations, such as the employees, customers, local community, etc. ♦ *adj* **3** of or relating to policies intended to allow people to participate in and benefit from decisions made by enterprises in which they have a stake: *a stakeholder economy.*

stakeout ('steɪkaʊt) *Slang, chiefly U.S. and Canadian.* ♦ *n* **1** a police surveillance of an area, house, or criminal suspect. **2** an area or house kept under such surveillance. ♦ *vb* **stake out. 3** *(tr, adv)* to keep under surveillance.

Stakhanovism (stæ'kænəˌvɪzəm) *n* (in the former Soviet Union) a system designed to raise production by offering incentives to efficient workers. **[C20:** named after A. G. *Stakhanov* (1906–77), Soviet coal miner, the worker first awarded benefits under the system in 1935**]** ▸ **Sta'khanovˌite** *n*

stalactite ('stæləkˌtaɪt) *n* a cylindrical mass of calcium carbonate hanging from the roof of a limestone cave: formed by precipitation from continually dripping water. Compare **stalagmite.** [C17: from New Latin *stalactites,* from Greek *stalaktos* dripping, from *stalassein* to drip] ▸ **stalactiform** (stəˈlæktɪˌfɔːm) *adj* ▸ **stalactitic** (ˌstæləkˈtɪtɪk) *or* ˌ**stalacˈtitical** *adj*

stalag (ˈstælæg; *German* ˈʃtalak) *n* a German prisoner-of-war camp in World War II, esp. for noncommissioned officers and other ranks. [short for *Stammlager* base camp, from *Stamm* base (related to STEM[1]) + *Lager* camp]

stalagmite (ˈstæləgˌmaɪt) *n* a cylindrical mass of calcium carbonate projecting upwards from the floor of a limestone cave: formed by precipitation from continually dripping water. Compare **stalactite.** [C17: from New Latin *stalagmites,* from Greek *stalagmos* dripping; related to Greek *stalassein* to drip; compare STALACTITE] ▸ **stalagmitic** (ˌstæləgˈmɪtɪk) *or* ˌ**stalagˈmitical** *adj*

stale[1] (steɪl) *adj* **1** (esp. of food) hard, musty, or dry from being kept too long. **2** (of beer, etc.) flat and tasteless from being kept open too long. **3** (of air) stagnant; foul. **4** uninteresting from overuse; hackneyed: *stale clichés.* **5** no longer new: *stale news.* **6** lacking in energy or ideas through overwork or lack of variety. **7** *Banking* (of a cheque) not negotiable by a bank as a result of not having been presented within six months of being written. **8** *Law.* (of a claim, etc.) having lost its effectiveness or force, as by failure to act or by the lapse of time. ◆ *vb* **9** to make or become stale. [C13 (originally applied to liquor in the sense: well matured): probably via Norman French from Old French *estale* (unattested) motionless, of Frankish origin; related to STALL[1], INSTALL] ▸ ˈ**stalely** *adv* ▸ ˈ**staleness** *n*

stale[2] (steɪl) *vb* **1** (*intr*) (of livestock) to urinate. ◆ *n* **2** the urine of horses or cattle. [C15: perhaps from Old French *estaler* to stand in one position; see STALL[1]; compare Middle Low German *stallen* to urinate, Greek *stalassein* to drip]

stale bull *n Business.* a dealer or speculator who holds unsold commodities after a rise in market prices but who cannot trade because there are no buyers at the new levels and because his financial commitments prevent him from making further purchases.

stalemate (ˈsteɪlˌmeɪt) *n* **1** a chess position in which any of a player's possible moves would place his king in check: in this position the game ends in a draw. **2** a situation in which two opposing forces find that further action is impossible or futile; deadlock. ◆ *vb* **3** (*tr*) to subject to a stalemate. [C18: from obsolete *stale,* from Old French *estal* STALL[1] + MATE[2]]

Stalin[1] (ˈstɑːlɪn) *n* **1** Also called: **Stalino.** a former name (from after the Revolution until 1961) of **Donetsk. 2** the former name (1950–61) of **Braşov. 3** the former name (1949–56) of **Varna.**

Stalin[2] (ˈstɑːlɪn) *n* **Joseph.** original name *Iosif Vissarionovich Dzhugashvili.* 1879–1953, Soviet leader; general secretary of the Communist Party of the Soviet Union (1922–53). He succeeded Lenin as head of the party and created a totalitarian state, crushing all opposition, esp. in the great purges of 1934–37. He instigated rapid industrialization and the collectivization of agriculture and established the Soviet Union as a world power.

Stalinabad (*Russian* stəlinaˈbat) *n* the former name (1929–61) of **Dushanbe.**

Stalingrad (ˈstɑːlɪnˌgræd; *Russian* stəlinˈgrat) *n* the former name (1925–61) of **Volgograd.**

Stalinism (ˈstɑːlɪˌnɪzəm) *n* the theory and form of government associated with Stalin: a variant of Marxism-Leninism characterized by totalitarianism, rigid bureaucracy, and loyalty to the state. ▸ ˈ**Stalinist** *n, adj*

Stalinogrod (*Polish* staliˈnɔgrɔt) *n* the former name (1953–56) for **Katowice.**

Stalin Peak *n* a former name for **Kommunizma Peak.**

Stalinsk (*Russian* ˈstalinsk) *n* the former name (1932–61) of **Novokuznetsk.**

stalk[1] (stɔːk) *n* **1** the main stem of a herbaceous plant. **2** any of various subsidiary plant stems, such as a leafstalk (petiole) or flower stalk (peduncle). **3** a slender supporting structure in animals such as crinoids and certain protozoans, coelenterates, and barnacles. **4** any long slender supporting shaft or column. [C14: probably a diminutive formed from Old English *stalu* upright piece of wood; related to Old Frisian *staal* handle] ▸ **stalked** *adj* ▸ ˈ**stalkless** *adj* ▸ ˈ**stalkˌlike** *adj*

stalk[2] (stɔːk) *vb* **1** to follow or approach (game, prey, etc.) stealthily and quietly. **2** to pursue persistently and, sometimes, attack (a person with whom one is obsessed, often a celebrity). **3** to spread over (a place) in a menacing or grim manner: *fever stalked the camp.* **4** (*intr*) to walk in a haughty, stiff, or threatening way: *he stalked out in disgust.* **5** to search or draw (a piece of land) for prey. ◆ *n* **6** the act of stalking. **7** a stiff or threatening stride. [Old English *bestealcian* to walk stealthily; related to Middle Low German *stolkeren,* Danish *stalke*] ▸ ˈ**stalker** *n*

stalking-horse *n* **1** a horse or an imitation one used by a hunter to hide behind while stalking his quarry. **2** something serving as a means of concealing plans; pretext. **3** a candidate put forward by one group to divide the opposition or mask the candidacy of another person for whom the stalking-horse would then withdraw.

stalky (ˈstɔːkɪ) *adj* **stalkier, stalkiest. 1** like a stalk; slender and tall. **2** having or abounding in stalks. ▸ ˈ**stalkily** *adv* ▸ ˈ**stalkiness** *n*

stall[1] (stɔːl) *n* **1a** a compartment in a stable or shed for confining or feeding a single animal. **1b** another name for **stable**[1] (sense 1). **2** a small often temporary stand or booth for the display and sale of goods. **3** (in a church) **3a** one of a row of seats, usually divided from the others by armrests or a small screen, for the use of the choir or clergy. **3b** a pen. **4** an instance of an engine stalling. **5** a condition of an aircraft in flight in which a reduction in speed or an increase in the aircraft's angle of attack causes a sudden loss of lift resulting in a downward plunge. **6** any small room or compartment. **7** *Brit.* **7a** a seat in a theatre or cinema that resembles a chair, usually fixed to the floor. **7b** (*pl*) the area of seats on the ground floor of a theatre or cinema nearest to the stage or screen. **8** a tubelike covering for a finger, as in a glove. **9** (*pl*) short for **starting stalls. 10 set out one's stall.** *Brit.* to make the necessary arrangements for the achievement of something and show that one is determined to achieve it. ◆ *vb* **11** to cause (a motor vehicle or its engine) to stop, usually by incorrect use of the clutch or incorrect adjustment of the fuel mixture, or (of an engine or motor vehicle) to stop, usually for these reasons. **12** to cause (an aircraft) to go into a stall or (of an aircraft) to go into a stall. **13** to stick or cause to stick fast, as in mud or snow. **14** (*tr*) to confine (an animal) in a stall. [Old English *steall* a place for standing; related to Old High German *stall,* and *stellen* to set]

stall[2] (stɔːl) *vb* **1** to employ delaying tactics towards (someone); be evasive. **2** (*intr*) *Sport, chiefly U.S.* to play or fight below one's best in order to deceive. ◆ *n* **3** an evasive move; pretext. [C16: from Anglo-French *estale* bird used as a decoy, influenced by STALL[1]]

stall-feed *vb* **-feeds, -feeding, -fed.** (*tr*) to keep and feed (an animal) in a stall, esp. as an intensive method of fattening it for slaughter.

stallholder (ˈstɔːlˌhəʊldə) *n* a person who sells goods at a market stall.

stalling angle *n* the angle between the chord line of an aerofoil and the undisturbed relative airflow at which stalling occurs. Also called: **stall angle, critical angle.**

stallion (ˈstæljən) *n* an uncastrated male horse, esp. one used for breeding. [C14: *staloun,* from Old French *estalon,* of Germanic origin; related to Old High German *stal* STALL[1]]

stalwart (ˈstɔːlwət) *adj* **1** strong and sturdy; robust. **2** solid, dependable, and courageous: *stalwart citizens.* **3** resolute and firm. ◆ *n* **4** a stalwart person, esp. a supporter. [Old English *stǣlwirthe* serviceable, from *stǣl,* shortened from *stathol* support + *wierthe* WORTH[1]] ▸ ˈ**stalwartly** *adv* ▸ ˈ**stalwartness** *n*

Stambul *or* **Stamboul** (stæmˈbuːl) *n* the old part of Istanbul, Turkey, south of the Golden Horn: the site of ancient Byzantium; sometimes used as a name for the whole city.

stamen (ˈsteɪmen) *n, pl* **stamens** *or* **stamina** (ˈstæmɪnə). the male reproductive organ of a flower, consisting of a stalk (filament) bearing an anther in which pollen is produced. [C17: from Latin: the warp in an upright loom, from *stāre* to stand] ▸ **staminal** (ˈstæmɪnᵊl) *adj* ▸ **staminiferous** (ˌstæmɪˈnɪfərəs) *adj*

Stamford (ˈstæmfəd) *n* a city in SW Connecticut, on Long Island Sound: major chemical research laboratories. Pop.: 110 056 (1996 est.).

Stamford Bridge *n* a village in N England, east of York: site of a battle (1066) in which King Harold of England defeated his brother Tostig and King Harald Hardrada of Norway, three weeks before the Battle of Hastings.

stamina[1] (ˈstæmɪnə) *n* enduring energy, strength, and resilience. [C19: identical with STAMINA[2], from Latin *stāmen* thread, hence the threads of life spun out by the Fates, hence energy, etc.] ▸ ˈ**staminal** *adj*

stamina[2] (ˈstæmɪnə) *n* a plural of **stamen.**

staminate (ˈstæmɪnɪt, -ˌneɪt) *adj* (of plants) having stamens, esp. having stamens but no carpels; male. [C19: from Latin *stāminātus* consisting of threads. See STAMEN, -ATE[1]]

staminode (ˈstæmɪˌnəʊd) *or* **staminodium** (ˌstæmɪˈnəʊdɪəm) *n, pl* **-nodes** *or* **-nodia** (-ˈnəʊdɪə). a vestigial stamen that produces no pollen. [C19: from STAMEN + -ODE[1]]

staminody (ˈstæmɪˌnəʊdɪ) *n* the development of any of various plant organs, such as petals or sepals, into stamens.

stammel (ˈstæməl) *n* **1** a coarse woollen cloth in former use for undergarments, etc., and usually dyed red. **2** the bright red colour of this cloth. [C16: from Old French *estamin,* from Latin *stāmineus* made of threads, from *stāmen* a thread; see STAMEN]

stammer (ˈstæmə) *vb* **1** to speak or say (something) in a hesitant way, esp. as a result of a speech disorder or through fear, stress, etc. ◆ *n* **2** a speech disorder characterized by involuntary repetitions and hesitations. [Old English *stamerian;* related to Old Saxon *stamarōn,* Old High German *stamm*] ▸ ˈ**stammerer** *n* ▸ ˈ**stammering** *n, adj* ▸ ˈ**stammeringly** *adv*

stamp (stæmp) *vb* **1** (when *intr,* often foll. by *on*) to bring (the foot) down heavily (on the ground, etc.). **2** (*intr*) to walk with heavy or noisy footsteps. **3** (*intr;* foll. by *on*) to repress, extinguish, or eradicate: *he stamped on any criticism.* **4** (*tr*) to impress or mark (a particular device or sign) on (something). **5** to mark (something) with an official impress, seal, or device: *to stamp a passport.* **6** (*tr*) to fix or impress permanently: *the date was stamped on her memory.* **7** (*tr*) to affix a postage stamp to. **8** (*tr*) to distinguish or reveal: *that behaviour stamps him as a cheat.* **9** to pound or crush (ores, etc.). ◆ *n* **10** the act or an instance of stamping. **11a** See **postage stamp. 11b** a mark applied to postage stamps for cancellation purposes. **12** a similar piece of gummed paper used for commercial or trading purposes. **13** a block, die, etc., used for imprinting a design or device. **14** a design, device, or mark that has been stamped. **15** a characteristic feature or trait; hallmark: *the story had the stamp of authenticity.* **16** a piece of gummed paper or other mark applied to official documents to indicate payment of a fee, validity, ownership, etc. **17** *Brit. informal.* a national insurance contribution, formerly recorded by means of a stamp on an official card. **18** type or class: *we want to employ men of his stamp.* **19** an instrument or machine for crushing or pounding ores, etc., or the pestle in such a device. ◆ See also **stamp out.** [Old English *stampe;* related to Old High German *stampfōn* to stamp, Old Norse *stappa*] ▸ ˈ**stamper** *n*

Stamp Act *n* a law passed by the British Parliament requiring all publications and legal and commercial documents in the American colonies to bear a tax stamp (1765): a cause of unrest in the colonies.

stamp collecting *n* another name for **philately.** ▸ **stamp collector** *n*

stamp duty *or* **tax** *n* a tax on legal documents, publications, etc., the payment of which is certified by the attaching or impressing of official stamps.

stampede (stæmˈpiːd) *n* **1** an impulsive headlong rush of startled cattle or horses. **2** headlong rush of a crowd: *a stampede of shoppers.* **3** any sudden large-scale movement or other action, such as a rush of people to support a candidate. **4** *Western U.S. and Canadian.* a rodeo event featuring fairground and social elements. ◆ *vb* **5** to run away or cause to run away in a stampede. [C19:

from American Spanish *estampida,* from Spanish: a din, from *estampar* to stamp, of Germanic origin; see STAMP] ▸ **stam'peder** *n*

stamping ground *n* a habitual or favourite meeting or gathering place.

stamp mill *n Metallurgy.* a machine for crushing ore.

stamp out *vb (tr, adv)* **1** to put out or extinguish by stamping: *to stamp out a fire.* **2** to crush or suppress by force: *to stamp out a rebellion.*

stance (stæns, stɑːns) *n* **1** the manner and position in which a person or animal stands. **2** *Sport.* the posture assumed when about to play the ball, as in golf, cricket, etc. **3** general emotional or intellectual attitude: *a leftist stance.* **4** *Scot.* a place where buses or taxis wait. **5** *Mountaineering.* a place at the top of a pitch where a climber can stand and belay. [C16: via French from Italian *stanza* place for standing, from Latin *stāns,* from *stāre* to stand]

stanch (stɑːntʃ) *or* **staunch** (stɔːntʃ) *vb* **1** to stem the flow of (a liquid, esp. blood) or (of a liquid) to stop flowing. **2** to prevent the flow of a liquid, esp. blood, from (a hole, wound, etc.). **3** an archaic word for **assuage.** ♦ *n* **4** a primitive form of lock in which boats are carried over shallow parts of a river in a rush of water released by the lock. [C14: from Old French *estanchier,* from Vulgar Latin *stanticāre* (unattested) to cause to stand, from Latin *stāre* to stand, halt] ▸ **'stanchable** *or* **'staunchable** *adj* ▸ **'stancher** *or* **'stauncher** *n*

stanchion ('stɑːnʃən) *n* **1** any vertical pole, beam, rod, etc., used as a support. ♦ *vb* **2** *(tr)* to provide or support with a stanchion or stanchions. [C14: from Old French *estanchon,* from *estance,* from Vulgar Latin *stantia* (unattested) a standing, from Latin *stāre* to stand]

stand (stænd) *vb* **stands, standing, stood.** *(mainly intr)* **1** *(also tr)* to be or cause to be in an erect or upright position. **2** to rise to, assume, or maintain an upright position. **3** *(copula)* to have a specified height when standing: *to stand six feet.* **4** to be situated or located: *the house stands in the square.* **5** to be or exist in a specified state or condition: *to stand in awe of someone.* **6** to adopt or remain in a resolute position or attitude. **7** *(may take an infinitive)* to be in a specified position: *I stand to lose money in this venture; he stands high in the president's favour.* **8** to remain in force or continue in effect: *whatever the difficulties, my orders stand.* **9** to come to a stop or halt, esp. temporarily. **10** (of water, etc.) to collect and remain without flowing. **11** (often foll. by *at*) (of a score, account, etc.) to indicate the specified position of the parties involved: *the score stands at 20 to 1.* **12** *(also tr;* when *intr,* foll. by *for)* to tolerate or bear: *I won't stand for your nonsense any longer; I can't stand spiders.* **13** *(tr)* to resist; survive: *to stand the test of time.* **14** *(tr)* to submit to: *to stand trial.* **15** (often foll. by *for*) *Chiefly Brit.* to be or become a candidate: *will he stand for Parliament?* **16** to navigate in a specified direction: *we were standing for Madeira when the storm broke.* **17** (of a gun dog) to point at game. **18** to halt, esp. to give action, repel attack, or disrupt an enemy advance when retreating. **19** (of a male domestic animal, esp. a stallion) to be available as a stud. **20** *(also tr) Printing.* to keep (type that has been set) or (of such type) to be kept, for possible use in future printings. **21** *(tr) Informal.* to bear the cost of; pay for: *to stand someone a drink.* **22 stand a chance.** to have a hope or likelihood of winning, succeeding, etc. **23 stand fast.** to maintain one's position firmly. **24 stand one's ground.** to maintain a stance or position in the face of opposition. **25 stand still. 25a** to remain motionless. **25b** (foll. by *for*) *U.S.* to tolerate: *I won't stand still for your threats.* **26 stand to (someone).** *Irish informal.* to be useful to (someone): *your knowledge of English will stand to you.* ♦ *n* **27** the act or an instance of standing. **28** an opinion, esp. a resolutely held one: *he took a stand on capital punishment.* **29** a halt or standstill. **30** a place where a person or thing stands. **31** *Austral. and N.Z.* **31a** a position on the floor of a shearing shed allocated to one shearer. **31b** the shearing equipment belonging to such a position. **32** a structure, usually of wood, on which people can sit or stand. **33** a frame or rack on which such articles as coats and hats may be hung. **34** a small table or piece of furniture where articles may be placed or stored: *a music stand.* **35** a supporting framework, esp. for a tool or instrument. **36** a stall, booth, or counter from which goods may be sold. **37** an exhibition area in a trade fair. **38** a halt to give action, etc., esp. one taken during a retreat and having some duration or some success. **39** *Cricket.* an extended period at the wicket by two batsmen. **40** a growth of plants in a particular area, esp. trees in a forest or a crop in a field. **41** a stop made by a touring theatrical company, pop group, etc., to give a performance (esp. in the phrase **one-night stand**). **42** *S. African.* a plot or site earmarked for the erection of a building. **43** (of a gun dog) the act of pointing at game. **44** a complete set, esp. of arms or armour for one man. **45 stand of colours.** *Military.* the flags of a regiment. ♦ See also **stand by, stand down, stand for, stand in, standoff, stand on, stand out, stand over, stand pat, stand to, stand up.** [Old English *standan;* related to Old Norse *standa,* Old High German *stantan,* Latin *stāre* to stand; see STEAD] ▸ **'stander** *n*

stand-alone *adj Computing.* (of a device or system) capable of operating independently of any other device or system.

standard ('stændəd) *n* **1** an accepted or approved example of something against which others are judged or measured. **2** *(often pl)* a principle of propriety, honesty, and integrity: *she has no standards.* **3** a level of excellence or quality: *a low standard of living.* **4** any distinctive flag, device, etc., as of a nation, sovereign, or special cause. **5a** any of a variety of naval or military flags. **5b** the colours of a cavalry regiment. **6** a flag or emblem formerly used to show the central or rallying point of an army in battle. **7** a large tapering flag ending in two points, originally borne by a sovereign or high-ranking noble. **8** the commodity or commodities in which is stated the value of a basic monetary unit: *the gold standard.* **9** an authorized model of a unit of measure or weight. **10** a unit of board measure equal to 1980 board feet. **11** (in coinage) the prescribed proportion by weight of precious metal and base metal that each coin must contain. **12** an upright pole or beam, esp. one used as a support. **13a** a piece of furniture consisting of an upright pole or beam on a base or support. **13b** *(as modifier): a standard lamp.* **14a** a plant, esp. a fruit tree, that is trained so that it has an upright stem free of branches. **14b** *(as modifier): a standard cherry.* **15** a song or piece of music that has remained popular for many years. **16** the largest petal of a papilionaceous flower, such as a sweetpea. **17** (in New Zealand and, formerly, in England and Wales) a class or level of attainment in an elementary school. ♦ *adj* **18** of the usual, regularized, medium, or accepted kind: *a standard size.* **19** of recognized authority, competence, or excellence: *the standard work on Greece.* **20** denoting or characterized by idiom, vocabulary, etc., that is regarded as correct and acceptable by educated native speakers. Compare **nonstandard, informal. 21** *Brit.* (formerly) (of eggs) of a size that is smaller than *large* and larger than *medium.* [C12: from Old French *estandart* gathering place, flag to mark such a place, probably of Germanic origin; compare Old High German *stantan* to stand, Old High German *ort* place]

standard amenities *pl n* (in Britain) *Social welfare.* the sanitary facilities recommended for all dwellings by the housing law: a fixed bath or shower, wash-hand basin, and sink, all supplied with hot and cold water, and a flush toilet.

standard assessment tasks *pl n Brit. Education.* externally devised assessments in core subjects which complement those carried out by teachers. Abbrev.: **SATS** ('sæts).

standard-bearer *n* **1** an officer or man who carries a standard. **2** a leader of a cause or party.

standard-bred *n* a U.S. and Canadian breed of trotting and pacing horse, used esp. for harness-racing. [C19: so called because they are bred to attain a prescribed standard of speed]

standard candle *n* another name for **candela:** not in scientific usage because of possible confusion with the former **international candle.**

standard cell *n* a voltaic cell producing a constant and accurately known electromotive force that can be used to calibrate voltage-measuring instruments.

standard cost *n Accounting.* the predetermined budgeted cost of a regular manufacturing process against which actual costs are compared.

standard deviation *n Statistics.* a measure of dispersion obtained by extracting the square root of the mean of the squared deviations of the observed values from their mean in a frequency distribution.

standard error *n Statistics.* the estimated standard deviation of a parameter, the value of which is not known exactly.

standard function *n Computing.* a subprogram provided by a translator that carries out a task, for example the computation of a mathematical function, such as sine, square root, etc.

standard gauge *n* **1** a railway track with a distance of 4 ft. 8½ in. (1.435 m) between the lines; used on most railways. See also **narrow gauge, broad gauge.** ♦ *adj* **standard-gauge** *or* **standard-gauged. 2** of, relating to, or denoting a railway with a standard gauge.

Standard Grade *n* (in Scotland) a type of examination designed to test skills and the application of knowledge, replaced O grade.

standard housing benefit *n* (in Britain) *Social welfare.* a rebate of a proportion of a person's eligible housing costs paid by a local authority and calculated on the basis of level of income and family size.

standardize *or* **standardise** ('stændəˌdaɪz) *vb* **1** to make or become standard. **2** *(tr)* to test by or compare with a standard. ▸ **ˌstandardi'zation** *or* **ˌstandardi'sation** *n* ▸ **'standardˌizer** *or* **'standardˌiser** *n*

standard model *n Physics.* a theory of fundamental interactions in which the electromagnetic, weak, and strong interactions are described in terms of the exchange of virtual particles.

standard normal distribution *n Statistics.* a normal distribution with mean zero and variance 1, with probability density function $[\exp(-\frac{1}{2}x^2)]/\sqrt{2\pi}$.

standard of living *n* a level of subsistence or material welfare of a community, class, or person.

standard scratch score *n Golf.* the number of strokes a scratch player would need to go round a particular course, based on the length of each hole to the green and allowing 36 putts for the round.

standard time *n* the official local time of a region or country determined by the distance from Greenwich of a line of longitude passing through the area.

stand by *vb* **1** *(intr, adv)* to be available and ready to act if needed or called upon. **2** *(intr, adv)* to be present as an onlooker or without taking any action: *he stood by at the accident.* **3** *(intr, prep)* to be faithful to: *to stand by one's principles.* **4** *(tr, adv) English law.* (of the Crown) to challenge (a juror) without needing to show cause. ♦ *n* **stand-by. 5a** a person or thing that is ready for use or can be relied on in an emergency. **5b** *(as modifier): stand-by provisions.* **6 on stand-by.** in a state of readiness for action or use. ♦ *adj* **7** (of an airline passenger, fare, or seat) not booked in advance but awaiting or subject to availability.

stand down *vb (adv)* **1** *(intr)* to resign or withdraw, esp. in favour of another. **2** *(intr)* to leave the witness box in a court of law after giving evidence. **3** *Chiefly Brit.* to go or be taken off duty.

standee (stæn'diː) *n* a person who stands, esp. when there are no vacant seats.

standfirst ('stændˌfɜːst) *n Journalism.* an introductory paragraph in an article, printed in larger or bolder type or in capitals, which summarizes the article.

stand for *vb (intr, prep)* **1** to represent or mean. **2** *Chiefly Brit.* to be or become a candidate for. **3** to support or recommend. **4** *Informal.* to tolerate or bear: *he won't stand for any disobedience.*

stand in *vb* **1** *(intr, adv;* usually foll. by *for)* to act as a substitute. **2 stand (someone) in good stead.** to be of benefit or advantage to (someone). ♦ *n* **stand-in. 3a** a person or thing that serves as a substitute. **3b** *(as modifier): a stand-in teacher.* **4** a person who substitutes for an actor during intervals of waiting or in dangerous stunts.

standing ('stændɪŋ) *n* **1** social or financial position, status, or reputation: *a man of some standing.* **2** length of existence, experience, etc. **3** *(modifier)* used to stand in or on: *standing room.* ♦ *adj* **4** *Athletics.* **4a** (of the start of a race) begun from a standing position without the use of starting blocks. **4b** (of a jump, leap, etc.) performed from a stationary position without a run-up. **5** *(pre-*

nominal) permanent, fixed, or lasting. **6** (*prenominal*) still or stagnant: *a standing pond.* **7** *Printing.* (of type) set and stored for future use. Compare **dead** (sense 17).

standing army *n* a permanent army of paid soldiers maintained by a nation.

standing chop *n N.Z.* (in an axemen's competition) a chop with the log standing upright. Compare **underhand chop.**

standing committee *n* a permanent committee appointed to deal with a specified subject.

standing order *n* **1** Also called: **banker's order.** an instruction to a bank by a depositor to pay a stated sum at regular intervals. Compare **direct debit. 2** a rule or order governing the procedure, conduct, etc., of a legislative body. **3** *Military.* one of a number of orders which have or are likely to have long-term validity.

standing rigging *n* the stays, shrouds, and other more or less fixed, though adjustable, wires and ropes that support the masts of a sailing vessel. Compare **running rigging.**

standing wave *n Physics.* the periodic disturbance in a medium resulting from the combination of two waves of equal frequency and intensity travelling in opposite directions. There are generally two kinds of displacement, and the maximum value of the amplitude of one of these occurs at the same points as the minimum value of the amplitude of the other. Thus in the case of electromagnetic radiation the amplitude of the oscillations of the electric field has its greatest value at the points where the magnetic oscillation is zero, and vice versa. Also called: **stationary wave.** Compare **node, antinode.**

standish ('stændɪʃ) *n* a stand, usually of metal, for pens, ink bottles, etc. **[C15:** of unknown origin**]**

Standish ('stændɪʃ) *n* **Myles** (or **Miles**). ?1584–1656, English military leader of the Pilgrim Fathers at Plymouth, New England.

standoff ('stænd,ɒf) *n* **1** *U.S. and Canadian.* the act or an instance of standing off or apart. **2** a deadlock or stalemate. **3** any situation or disposition of forces that counterbalances or neutralizes. **4** *Rugby.* short for **stand-off half.** ◆ *vb* **stand off** (*adv*) **5** (*intr*) to navigate a vessel so as to avoid the shore, an obstruction, etc. **6** (*tr*) to keep or cause to keep at a distance. **7** (*intr*) to reach a deadlock or stalemate. **8** (*tr*) to dismiss (workers), esp. temporarily.

stand-off half *n Rugby.* **1** a player who acts as a link between his scrum half and three-quarter backs. **2** this position in a team. ◆ Also called: **fly half.**

standoffish (,stænd'ɒfɪʃ) *adj* reserved, haughty, or aloof. ▸ **,stand'offishly** *adv* ▸ **,stand'offishness** *n*

standoff missile *n* a missile capable of striking a distant target after launch by an aircraft outside the range of missile defences.

stand oil *n* a thick drying oil made by heating linseed, tung, or soya to over 300°C: used in oil enamel paints.

stand on *vb* (*intr*) **1** (*adv*) to continue to navigate a vessel on the same heading. **2** (*prep*) to insist on: *to stand on ceremony.* **3 stand on one's own** (**two**) **feet.** *Informal.* to be independent or self-reliant.

stand out *vb* (*intr, adv*) **1** to be distinctive or conspicuous. **2** to refuse to agree, consent, or comply: *they stood out for a better price.* **3** to protrude or project. **4** to navigate a vessel away from a port, harbour, anchorage, etc. ◆ *n* **standout. 5** *Informal.* **5a** a person or thing that is distinctive or outstanding. **5b** (*as modifier*): *the standout track from the album.* **6** a person who refuses to agree or consent.

stand over *vb* **1** (*intr, prep*) to watch closely; keep tight control over. **2** (*adv*) to postpone or be postponed. **3** (*intr, prep*) *Austral. and N.Z. informal.* to threaten or intimidate (a person). ◆ *n* **standover. 4** *Austral. and N.Z. informal.* a threatening or intimidating act.

standover man ('stænd,əʊvə) *n Austral. informal.* a person who extorts money by intimidation.

stand pat *vb* (*intr*) **1** *Poker.* to refuse the right to change any of one's cards; keep one's hand unchanged. **2** to resist change or remain unchanged. ▸ **'stand'patter** *n*

standpipe ('stænd,paɪp) *n* **1** a vertical pipe, open at the upper end, attached to a pipeline or tank serving to limit the pressure head to that of the height of the pipe. **2** a temporary freshwater outlet installed in a street during a period when household water supplies are cut off.

standpoint ('stænd,pɔɪnt) *n* a physical or mental position from which things are viewed.

standstill ('stænd,stɪl) *n* a complete cessation of movement; stop; halt: *the car came to a standstill.*

standstill agreement *n* an agreement that preserves the status quo, esp. one between two countries when one country cannot pay its debts to the other that a certain fixed extension of time will be given to repay the debts.

stand to *vb* **1** (*adv*) *Military.* to assume positions or cause to assume positions to resist a possible attack. **2 stand to reason.** to conform with the dictates of reason: *it stands to reason that pigs can't fly.*

stand up *vb* (*adv*) **1** (*intr*) to rise to the feet. **2** (*intr*) to resist or withstand wear, criticism, etc. **3** (*tr*) *Informal.* to fail to keep an appointment with, esp. intentionally. **4 stand up for. 4a** to support, side with, or defend. **4b** *U.S.* to serve as best man for (the groom) at a wedding. **5 stand up to. 5a** to confront or resist courageously. **5b** to withstand or endure (wear, criticism, etc.). ◆ *adj* **stand-up.** (*prenominal*) **6** having or being in an erect position: *a stand-up collar.* **7** done, performed, taken, etc., while standing: *a stand-up meal.* **8** (of comedy or a comedian) performed or performing solo. **9** *Informal.* (of a boxer) having an aggressive style without much leg movement: *a stand-up fighter.* ◆ *n* **stand-up. 10** a stand-up comedian. **11** stand-up comedy.

stane (steɪn) *n* a Scot. word for **stone.**

Stanford ('stænfəd) *n* Sir **Charles** (**Villiers**). 1852–1924, Anglo-Irish composer and conductor, who as a teacher at the Royal College of Music had much influence on the succeeding generation of composers: noted esp. for his church music, oratorios, and cantatas.

Stanford-Binet test ('stænfədbɪ'neɪ) *n Psychol.* a revision, esp. for U.S. use, of the Binet-Simon scale designed to measure mental ability by comparing the performance of an individual with the average performance for his age group. See also **Binet-Simon scale, intelligence test. [C20:** named after *Stanford University,* California, and Alfred *Binet* (1857–1911), French psychologist**]**

stang (stæŋ) *vb Archaic or dialect.* a past tense of **sting.**

stanhope ('stænəp) *n* a light one-seater carriage with two or four wheels. **[C18:** named after Fitzroy *Stanhope* (1787–1864), English clergyman for whom it was first built**]**

Stanhope ('stænəp) *n* **1 Charles,** 3rd Earl. 1753–1816, British radical politician and scientist. His inventions included two calculating machines, a microscope lens, and a stereotyping machine. **2** his grandfather, **James,** 1st Earl. 1673–1721, British soldier and statesman; George I's chief minister (1717–21). He fought under Marlborough in the War of the Spanish Succession (1701–14) and negotiated the Triple Alliance with France and Holland (1717).

Stanislavsky *or* **Stanislavski** (,stænɪ'slævskɪ; *Russian* stənɪ'slafskij) *n* **Konstantin** (kənstan'tin). 1863–1938, Russian actor and director, cofounder of the Moscow Art Theatre (1897). He is famous for his theory of acting, known as the Method, which directs the actor to find the truth within himself about the role he is playing.

Stanisław (*Polish* 'stanɪswaf) *or* **Stanislaus** *n* **Saint.** 1030–79, the patron saint of Poland. As Bishop of Cracow (1072–79) he excommunicated King Bolesław II, who arranged his murder. Feast day: May 11.

Stanisław II *n* surnamed *Poniatowski.* 1732–98, the last king of Poland (1764–95), during whose reign Poland was repeatedly invaded and partitioned (1772, 1791, 1795) by its neighbours: abdicated.

stank[1] (stæŋk) *vb* a past tense of **stink.**

stank[2] (stæŋk) *n* **1** a small cofferdam, esp. one of timber made watertight with clay. **2** *Scot. and northern English dialect.* a pond or pool. ◆ *vb* **3** (*tr*) to make (a stream, cofferdam, etc.) watertight, esp. with clay. **[C13:** from Old French *estanc,* probably from *estancher* to stanch**]**

stank[3] (stæŋk) *n Dialect.* **1** a drain, as in a roadway. **2** a draining board adjacent to a sink unit. **[**special use of STANK[2] (in the sense: pool, pond)**]**

Stanley[1] ('stænlɪ) *n* **1** the capital of the Falkland Islands, in NE East Falkland Island: scene of fighting in the Falklands War of 1982. Pop.: 1557 (1991). **2** a town in NE England, in N Durham. Pop.: 18 905 (1991). **3 Mount.** a mountain in central Africa, between Uganda and the Democratic Republic of the Congo (formerly Zaïre): the highest peak of the Ruwenzori range. Height: 5109 m (16 763 ft.). Congolese name: **Ngaliema Mountain.**

Stanley[2] ('stænlɪ) *n* Sir **Henry Morton.** 1841–1904, British explorer and journalist, who led an expedition to Africa in search of Livingstone, whom he found on Nov. 10, 1871. He led three further expeditions in Africa (1874–77; 1879–84; 1887–89) and was instrumental in securing Belgian sovereignty over the Congo Free State.

Stanley Falls *pl n* the former name of **Boyoma Falls.**

Stanley knife *n Trademark.* a type of knife used for carpet fitting, etc., consisting of a thick hollow metal handle with a short, very sharp, replaceable blade inserted at one end. **[C19:** named after F.T. *Stanley,* U.S. businessman and founder of the Stanley Rule and Level Company**]**

Stanley Pool *n* a lake between the Democratic Republic of the Congo (formerly Zaïre) and the Congo, formed by a widening of the River Congo. Area: 829 sq. km (320 sq. miles). Congolese name: **Pool Malebo.**

Stanleyville ('stænlɪ,vɪl) *n* the former name (until 1966) of **Kisangani.**

stann- *combining form.* denoting tin: *stannite.* **[**from Late Latin *stannum* tin**]**

Stannaries ('stænərɪz) *n* **the.** a tin-mining district of Devon and Cornwall, under the jurisdiction of special courts.

stannary ('stænərɪ) *n, pl* **-ries.** a place or region where tin is mined or worked. **[C15:** from Medieval Latin *stannāria,* from Late Latin: STANNUM, tin**]**

stannic ('stænɪk) *adj* of or containing tin, esp. in the tetravalent state. **[C18:** from Late Latin *stannum* tin**]**

stannic sulphide *n* an insoluble solid compound of tin usually existing as golden crystals or as a yellowish-brown powder: used as a pigment. Formula: SnS_2. See also **mosaic gold.**

stanniferous (stə'nɪfərəs) *adj* containing tin; tin-bearing. **[C18:** from Late Latin *stannum* tin + -FEROUS**]**

stannite ('stænaɪt) *n* a grey metallic mineral that consists of a sulphide of tin, copper, and iron and is a source of tin. Formula: Cu_2FeSnS_4. **[C19:** from STANNUM + -ITE[1]**]**

stannous ('stænəs) *adj* of or containing tin, esp. in the divalent state.

stannum ('stænəm) *n* an obsolete name for **tin** (the metal). **[C18:** from Late Latin: tin, from Latin: alloy of silver and lead, perhaps of Celtic origin; compare Welsh *ystaen* tin**]**

Stanovoi Range *or* **Stanovoy Range** (*Russian* stəna'vɔj) *n* a mountain range in SE Russia; forms part of the watershed between rivers flowing to the Arctic and the Pacific. Highest peak: Mount Skalisty, 2482 m (8143 ft.).

Stans (*German* ʃtans) *n* a town in central Switzerland, capital of Nidwalden demicanton, 11 km (7 miles) southeast of Lucerne: tourist centre. Pop.: 5700 (latest est.).

stanza ('stænzə) *n* **1** *Prosody.* a fixed number of verse lines arranged in a definite metrical pattern, forming a unit of a poem. **2** *U.S. and Austral.* a half or a quarter in a football match. **[C16:** from Italian: halting place, from Vulgar Latin *stantia* (unattested) station, from Latin *stāre* to stand**]** ▸ **'stanzaed** *adj* ▸ **stanzaic** (stæn'zeɪɪk) *adj*

stapelia (stə'piːlɪə) *n* any fleshy cactus-like leafless African plant of the asclepiadaceous genus *Stapelia,* having thick four-angled stems and large typically fetid mottled flowers. [C18: from New Latin, named after J. B. van *Stapel,* (died 1636), Dutch botanist]

stapes ('steɪpi:z) *n, pl* **stapes** *or* **stapedes** (stæ'pi:di:z). the stirrup-shaped bone that is the innermost of three small bones in the middle ear of mammals. Nontechnical name: **stirrup bone.** Compare **incus, malleus.** [C17: via New Latin from Medieval Latin, perhaps a variant of *staffa, stapeda* stirrup, influenced in form by Latin *stāre* to stand + *pēs* a foot] ► **stapedial** (stæ'pi:dɪəl) *adj*

staphylo- *combining form.* **1** uvula: *staphyloplasty.* **2** resembling a bunch of grapes: *staphylococcus.* [from Greek *staphulē* bunch of grapes, uvula]

staphylococcus (ˌstæfɪləʊ'kɒkəs) *n, pl* **-cocci** (-'kɒkaɪ; *U.S.* -'kɒksaɪ). any spherical Gram-positive bacterium of the genus *Staphylococcus,* typically occurring in clusters and including many pathogenic species, causing boils, infection in wounds, and septicaemia: family *Micrococcaceae.* Often shortened to **staph.** [C19: from STAPHYLO- (in the sense: like a bunch of grapes) + COCCUS so called because of their shape] ► **staphylococcal** (ˌstæfɪləʊ'kɒkᵊl) *or* **staphylococcic** (ˌstæfɪləʊ'kɒkɪk; *U.S.* -'kɒksɪk) *adj*

staphyloplasty ('stæfɪləʊˌplæstɪ) *n* plastic surgery or surgical repair involving the soft palate or the uvula. [C19: from STAPHYLO- + -PLASTY] ► **ˌstaphylo'plastic** *adj*

staphylorrhaphy (ˌstæfɪ'lɒrəfɪ) *n* repair of a cleft palate by means of staphyloplasty and suturing. [C19: from STAPHYLO- (in the sense: uvula) + Greek *raphē* a sewing or suture] ► **staphylorrhaphic** (ˌstæfɪlɒ'ræfɪk) *adj*

staple[1] ('steɪpᵊl) *n* **1** a short length of thin wire bent into a square U-shape, used to fasten papers, cloth, etc. **2** a short length of stiff wire formed into a U-shape with pointed ends, used for holding a hasp to a post, securing electric cables, etc. ◆ *vb* **3** (*tr*) to secure (papers, wire, etc.) with a staple or staples. [Old English *stapol* prop, of Germanic origin; related to Middle Dutch *stapel* step, Old High German *staffal*]

staple[2] ('steɪpᵊl) *adj* **1** of prime importance; principal: *staple foods.* **2** (of a commodity) forming a predominant element in the product, consumption, or trade of a nation, region, etc. ◆ *n* **3** a staple commodity. **4** a main constituent; integral part. **5** *Chiefly U.S. and Canadian.* a principal raw material produced or grown in a region. **6** the fibre of wool, cotton, etc., graded as to length and fineness. **7** (in medieval Europe) a town appointed to be the exclusive market for one or more major exports of the land. ◆ *vb* **8** (*tr*) to arrange or sort (wool, cotton, etc.) according to length and fineness. [C15: from Middle Dutch *stapel* warehouse; see STAPLE[1]]

staple gun *n* a mechanism that fixes staples to a surface.

stapler ('steɪplə) *n* a machine that inserts staples into sheets of paper, etc., to hold them together.

star (stɑ:) *n* **1** any of a vast number of celestial objects that are visible in the clear night sky as points of light. **2a** a hot gaseous mass, such as the sun, that radiates energy, esp. as light and infrared radiation, usually derived from thermonuclear reactions in the interior, and in some cases as ultraviolet, radio waves, and X-rays. The surface temperature can range from about 2100 to 40 000°C. See also **Hertzsprung-Russell diagram, giant star, white dwarf, neutron star, black hole. 2b** (*as modifier*): *a star catalogue.* Related adjs: **astral, sidereal, stellar. 3** *Astrology.* **3a** a celestial body, esp. a planet, supposed to influence events, personalities, etc. **3b** (*pl*) another name for **horoscope** (sense 1). **4** an emblem shaped like a conventionalized star, usually with five or more points, often used as a symbol of rank, an award, etc. **5** a small white blaze on the forehead of an animal, esp. a horse. **6** Also called: **star facet.** any of the eight triangular facets cut in the crown of a brilliant. **7a** a distinguished or glamorous celebrity, often from the entertainment world. **7b** (*as modifier*): *star quality.* **8** another word for **asterisk. 9** *Prison slang.* a convict serving his first prison sentence. **10 see stars.** to see or seem to see bright moving pinpoints of light, as from a blow on the head, increased blood pressure, etc. ◆ *vb* **stars, starring, starred. 11** (*tr*) to mark or decorate with a star or stars. **12** to feature or be featured as a star: *"Greed" starred Erich von Stroheim; Olivier starred in "Hamlet".* [Old English *steorra;* related to Old Frisian *stēra,* Old Norse *stjarna,* German *Stern,* Latin *stella*] ► **'starless** *adj* ► **'starˌlike** *adj*

star-apple *n* **1** a West Indian sapotaceous tree, *Chrysophyllum cainito,* with smooth-skinned edible greenish-purple fruit. **2** the fruit of this tree which, when cut across, reveals a star-shaped arrangement of seeds.

Stara Zagora (*Bulgarian* 'stara za'gɔra) *n* a city in central Bulgaria: ceded to Bulgaria by Turkey in 1877. Pop.: 149 666 (1996 est.).

starboard ('stɑ:bəd, -ˌbɔ:d) *n* **1** the right side of an aeroplane or vessel when facing the nose or bow. Compare **port**[2]. ◆ *adj* **2** relating to or on the starboard. ◆ *vb* **3** to turn or be turned towards the starboard. [Old English *stēorbord,* literally: steering side, from *stēor* steering paddle + *bord* side; see STEER[1], BOARD; from the fact that boats were formerly steered by a paddle held over the right-hand side]

starch (stɑ:tʃ) *n* **1** a polysaccharide composed of glucose units that occurs widely in plant tissues in the form of storage granules, consisting of amylose and amylopectin. Related adj: **amylaceous. 2** Also called: **amylum.** a starch obtained from potatoes and some grain: it is fine white powder that forms a translucent viscous solution on boiling with water and is used to stiffen fabric and in many industrial processes. **3** any food containing a large amount of starch, such as rice and potatoes. **4** stiff or pompous formality of manner or conduct. ◆ *vb* **5** (*tr*) to stiffen with or soak in starch. ◆ *adj* **6** (of a person) formal; stiff. [Old English *stercan* (unattested except by the past participle *sterced*) to stiffen; related to Old Saxon *sterkian,* Old High German *sterken* to strengthen, Dutch *sterken;* see STARK] ► **'starcher** *n* ► **'starchˌlike** *adj*

Star Chamber *n* **1** *English history.* the Privy Council sitting as a court of equity, esp. powerful under the Tudor monarchs; abolished 1641. **2** (*sometimes not caps.*) any arbitrary tribunal dispensing summary justice. **3** (*sometimes not caps.*) (in Britain, in a Conservative government) a group of senior ministers who make the final decision on the public spending of each government department.

starch-reduced *adj* (of food, esp. bread) having the starch content reduced, as in proprietary slimming products.

starchy ('stɑ:tʃɪ) *adj* **starchier, starchiest. 1** of, relating to, or containing starch: *starchy foods.* **2** extremely formal, stiff, or conventional: *a starchy manner.* **3** stiffened with starch. ► **'starchily** *adv* ► **'starchiness** *n*

star connection *n* a connection used in a polyphase electrical device or system of devices in which the windings each have one end connected to a common junction, the **star point,** and the other end to a separate terminal. See also **Y connection.** Compare **delta connection.**

star-crossed *adj* dogged by ill luck; destined to misfortune. [C16: from CROSS (in the sense: thwart): so called because of the astrological belief that the stars affect people's destinies]

stardom ('stɑ:dəm) *n* **1** the fame and prestige of being a star in films, sport, etc. **2** the world of celebrities.

stardust ('stɑ:ˌdʌst) *n* **1** a large number of distant stars appearing to the observer as a cloud of dust. **2** a dreamy romantic or sentimental quality or feeling.

stare[1] (stɛə) *vb* **1** (*intr*) (often foll. by *at*) to look or gaze fixedly, often with hostility or rudeness. **2** (*intr*) (of an animal's fur, bird's feathers, etc.) to stand on end because of fear, ill health, etc. **3** (*intr*) to stand out as obvious; glare. **4 stare one in the face.** to be glaringly obvious or imminent. ◆ *n* **5** the act or an instance of staring. [Old English *starian;* related to Old Norse *stara,* Old High German *starēn* to stare, Greek *stereos* stiff, Latin *consternāre* to confuse] ► **'starer** *n*

stare[2] (stɛə) *n Dialect.* a starling. [Old English *stær*]

stare out *or* **down** *vb* (*tr, adv*) to look at (a person or animal) fixedly until his gaze is turned away.

starfish ('stɑ:ˌfɪʃ) *n, pl* **-fish** *or* **-fishes.** any echinoderm of the class *Asteroidea,* such as *Asterias rubens,* typically having a flattened body covered with a flexible test and five arms radiating from a central disc.

starflower ('stɑ:ˌflaʊə) *n* any of several plants with starlike flowers, esp. the star-of-Bethlehem.

star fruit *n* another name for **carambola.**

stargaze ('stɑ:ˌgeɪz) *vb* (*intr*) **1** to observe the stars. **2** to daydream. ► **'starˌgazer** *n* ► **'starˌgazing** *n, adj*

star grass *n* any of various temperate and tropical plants of the amaryllidaceous genus *Hypoxis,* having long grasslike leaves and yellow star-shaped flowers.

stark (stɑ:k) *adj* **1** (*usually prenominal*) devoid of any elaboration; blunt: *the stark facts.* **2** grim; desolate: *a stark landscape.* **3** (*usually prenominal*) utter; absolute: *stark folly.* **4** *Archaic.* severe; violent. **5** *Archaic or poetic.* rigid, as in death (esp. in the phrases **stiff and stark, stark dead**). **6** short for **stark-naked.** ◆ *adv* **7** completely: *stark mad.* [Old English *stearc* stiff; related to Old Norse *sterkr,* Gothic *gastaurknan* to stiffen] ► **'starkly** *adv* ► **'starkness** *n*

Stark *n* **1** (stɑ:k). Dame **Freya** (**Madeline**) ('freɪə). 1893–1993, British traveller and writer, whose many books include *The Southern Gates of Arabia* (1936), *Beyond Euphrates* (1951), and *The Journey's Echo* (1963). **2** (*German* ʃtark). **Johannes** (jo'hanəs). 1874–1957, German physicist, who discovered the splitting of the lines of a spectrum when the source of light is subjected to a strong electrostatic field (**Stark effect,** 1913): Nobel prize for physics 1919.

stark-naked *adj* completely naked. Informal word (*postpositive*): **starkers** ('stɑ:kəz). [C13 *stert naket,* literally: tail naked; *stert,* from Old English *steort* tail; related to Old Norse *stertr* tail + NAKED]

starlet ('stɑ:lɪt) *n* **1** a young and inexperienced actress who is projected as a potential star. **2** a small star.

starlight ('stɑ:ˌlaɪt) *n* **1** the light emanating from the stars. ◆ *adj also* **starlighted. 2** of or like starlight. **3** Also: **starlit** ('stɑ:ˌlɪt). illuminated by starlight.

starling[1] ('stɑ:lɪŋ) *n* any gregarious passerine songbird of the Old World family *Sturnidae,* esp. *Sturnus vulgaris,* which has a blackish plumage and a short tail. [Old English *stærlinc,* from *stær* starling (related to Icelandic *stari*) + *-linc* -LING[1]]

starling[2] ('stɑ:lɪŋ) *n* an arrangement of piles that surround a pier of a bridge to protect it from debris, etc. [C17: probably changed from *staddling,* from STADDLE]

Starling ('stɑ:lɪŋ) *n* **Ernest Henry.** 1866–1927, British physiologist, who contributed greatly to the understanding of many bodily functions and with William Bayliss (1860–1924) discovered the hormone secretin (1902).

star-nosed mole *n* an E North American amphibious mole, *Condylura cristata,* having a ring of pink fleshy tentacles around the nose.

star-of-Bethlehem *n* **1** Also called: **starflower.** a Eurasian liliaceous plant, *Ornithogalum umbellatum,* naturalized in the eastern U.S., having narrow leaves and starlike white flowers. **2** any of several similar and related plants.

Star of Bethlehem *n* the star that is supposed to have appeared above Bethlehem at the birth of Christ.

Star of Courage *n* a Canadian award for bravery.

Star of David *n* an emblem symbolizing Judaism and consisting of a six-pointed star formed by superimposing one inverted equilateral triangle upon another of equal size. Also called: **Magen David.**

Starr (stɑ:) *n* **1** (**Myra**) **Belle.** 1848–89, U.S. outlaw, a famous rustler of horses and cattle. **2 Ringo,** original name *Richard Starkey.* born 1940, British rock musician; drummer (1962–70) with the Beatles.

starred (stɑ:d) *adj* **a** having luck or fortune as specified. **b** (*in combination*): *ill-starred.*

star ruby *n* a ruby that resembles a starlike figure in reflected light because of its crystalline structure.

starry ('stɑ:rɪ) *adj* **-rier, -riest. 1** filled, covered with, or illuminated by stars. **2** of, like, or relating to a star or stars. ► **'starrily** *adv* ► **'starriness** *n*

starry-eyed *adj* given to naive wishes, judgments, etc.; full of unsophisticated optimism; gullible.

Stars and Bars *n (functioning as sing)* **the.** the flag of the Confederate States of America.

Stars and Stripes *n (functioning as sing)* **the.** the national flag of the United States of America, consisting of 50 white stars representing the present states on a blue field and seven red and six white horizontal stripes representing the original states. Also called: the **Star-Spangled Banner.**

star sapphire *n* a sapphire showing a starlike figure in reflected light because of its crystalline structure.

star shell *n* an artillery shell containing a flare or other illuminant: often containing a parachute to prolong the descent of the illuminating material.

star-spangled *adj* marked or decorated with stars.

Star-Spangled Banner *n* **the. 1** the national anthem of the United States of America. **2** another term for the **Stars and Stripes.**

star stream *n* one of two main streams of stars that, because of the rotation of the Milky Way, appear to move in opposite directions, one towards Orion, the other towards Ara.

star-studded *adj* featuring a large proportion of well-known actors or other performers: *a star-studded cast.*

star system *n* **1** *Astronomy.* a group of celestial bodies that are associated as a result of natural laws. **2** the practice of casting one or two famous actors or actresses in a film, play, etc., so that their popularity ensures its success. **3** a design for laying cables for cable television in which each house is fed by an individual cable from a local central distribution point.

start (stɑːt) *vb* **1** to begin or cause to begin (something or to do something); come or cause to come into being, operation, etc.: *he started a quarrel; they started to work.* **2** (when *intr*, sometimes foll. by *on*) to make or cause to make a beginning of (a process, series of actions, etc.): *they started on the project.* **3** (sometimes foll. by *up*) to set or be set in motion: *he started up the machine.* **4** (*intr*) to make a sudden involuntary movement of one's body, from or as if from fright; jump. **5** (*intr;* sometimes foll. by *up, away,* etc.) to spring or jump suddenly from a position or place. **6** to establish or be established; set up: *to start a business.* **7** (*tr*) to support (someone) in the first part of a venture, career, etc. **8** to work or cause to work loose. **9** to enter or be entered in a race. **10** (*intr*) to flow violently from a source: *wine started from a hole in the cask.* **11** (*tr*) to rouse (game) from a hiding place, lair, etc. **12** (*intr*) (esp. of eyes) to bulge; pop. **13** an archaic word for **startle. 14** (*intr*) *Brit. informal.* to commence quarrelling or causing a disturbance. **15 to start with.** in the first place. ◆ *n* **16** the first or first part of a series of actions or operations, a journey, etc. **17** the place or time of starting, as of a race or performance. **18** a signal to proceed, as in a race. **19** a lead or advantage, either in time or distance and usually of specified extent, in a competitive activity: *he had an hour's start on me.* **20** a slight involuntary movement of the body, as through fright, surprise, etc.: *she gave a start as I entered.* **21** an opportunity to enter a career, undertake a project, etc. **22** *Informal.* a surprising incident. **23** a part that has come loose or been disengaged. **24 by fits and starts.** spasmodically; without concerted effort. **25 for a start.** in the first place. ◆ See also **start in, start off, start on, start out, start up.** [Old English *styrtan;* related to Old Norse *sterta* to crease, Old High German *sturzen* to rush]

START (stɑːt) *n acronym for* Strategic Arms Reduction Talks.

starter ('stɑːtə) *n* **1** Also called: **self-starter.** a device for starting an internal-combustion engine, usually consisting of a powerful electric motor that engages with the flywheel. **2** *U.S.* a person who organizes the timely departure of buses, trains, etc. **3** a person who supervises and signals the start of a race. **4** a competitor who starts in a race or contest. **5** *Informal, chiefly Austral. and N.Z.* an acceptable or practicable proposition, plan, idea, etc. **6** *Austral. and N.Z. informal.* a person who is willing to engage in a particular activity. **7** a culture of bacteria used to start fermentation, as in making cheese or yogurt. **8** *Chiefly Brit.* the first course of a meal. **9** (*modifier*) designed to be used by a novice: *a starter kit.* **10 for starters.** *Slang.* in the first place. **11 under starter's orders. 11a** (of horses in a race) awaiting the start signal. **11b** (of a person) eager or ready to begin.

starter home *n* a compact flat or house marketed by price and size specifications to suit the requirements of first-time home buyers.

star thistle *n* any of several plants of the genus *Centaurea,* esp. *C. calcitrapa,* of Eurasia, which has spiny purplish flower heads: family *Compositae* (composites). See also **centaury** (sense 2). [C16: so called because it has a thistle-shaped flower surrounded by radiating spines]

start in *vb* (*adv*) to undertake (something or doing something); commence or begin.

starting block *n* one of a pair of adjustable devices with pads or blocks against which a sprinter braces his feet in crouch starts.

starting gate *n* **1** a movable barrier so placed on the starting line of a racecourse that the raising of it releases all the contestants simultaneously. **2** the U.S. name for **starting stalls.**

starting grid *n Motor racing.* a marked section of the track at the start where the cars line up according to their times in practice, the fastest occupying the front position.

starting price *n* (esp. in horse racing) the latest odds offered by bookmakers at the start of a race.

starting stalls *pl n Brit.* a line of stalls in which horses are enclosed at the start of a race and from which they are released by the simultaneous springing open of retaining barriers at the front of each stall.

startle ('stɑːtᵊl) *vb* to be or cause to be surprised or frightened, esp. so as to start involuntarily. [Old English *steartlian* to stumble; related to Middle High German *starzen* to strut, Norwegian *sterta* to strain oneself] ▸ **'startler** *n* ▸ **'startling** *adj* ▸ **'startlingly** *adv*

startle colour *n Zoology.* a bright region of an animal's coloration, normally hidden from view and often part of a design resembling birds' eyes, etc., exposed when the animal is disturbed by a predator.

start off *vb* (*adv*) **1** (*intr*) to set out on a journey. **2** to be or make the first step in an activity; initiate: *he started the show off with a lively song.* **3** (*tr*) to cause (a person) to act or do something, such as to laugh, to tell stories, etc.

start on *vb* (*intr, prep*) *Brit. informal.* to pick a quarrel with (someone).

start out *vb* (*intr, adv*) **1** to set out on a journey. **2** to take the first steps, as in life, one's career, etc.: *he started out as a salesman.* **3** to take the first actions in an activity in a particular way or specified aim: *they started out wanting a house, but eventually bought a flat.*

start up *vb* (*adv*) **1** to come or cause to come into being for the first time; originate. **2** (*intr*) to spring or jump suddenly from a position or place. **3** to set in or go into motion, activity, etc.: *he started up the engine; the orchestra started up.* ◆ *adj* **start-up. 4** of or relating to input, usually financial, made to establish a new project or business: *a start-up mortgage.*

starvation (stɑː'veɪʃən) *n* **a** the act or an instance of starving or state of being starved. **b** (*as modifier*): *a starvation diet; starvation wages.*

starve (stɑːv) *vb* **1** to die or cause to die from lack of food. **2** to deprive (a person or animal) or (of a person, etc.) to be deprived of food. **3** (*intr*) *Informal.* to be very hungry. **4** (foll. by *of* or *for*) to deprive or be deprived (of something necessary), esp. so as to cause suffering or malfunctioning: *the engine was starved of fuel.* **5** (*tr;* foll. by *into*) to bring (to) a specified condition by starving: *to starve someone into submission.* **6** *Archaic or Brit. dialect.* to be or cause to be extremely cold. [Old English *steorfan* to die; related to Old Frisian *sterva* to die, Old High German *sterban* to die] ▸ **'starver** *n*

starveling ('stɑːvlɪŋ) *Archaic.* ◆ *n* **1a** a starving or poorly fed person, animal, etc. **1b** (*as modifier*): *a starveling child.* ◆ *adj* **2** insufficient; meagre; scant. [C16: from STARVE + -LING[1]]

Star Wars *n (functioning as sing)* **1** (in the U.S.) a proposed system of artificial satellites armed with lasers to destroy enemy missiles in space. Formal name: **Strategic Defense Initiative.** Abbrev.: **SDI. 2** (modifier) (*sometimes not caps.*) of, relating to, or denoting this system: *Star Wars defence; star wars policy.* [C20: popularly named after the science fiction film *Star Wars* (1977) by George Lucas]

starwort ('stɑːˌwɜːt) *n* **1** any of several plants with star-shaped flowers, esp. the stitchwort. **2 water starwort.** any of several aquatic plants of the genus *Callitriche,* having a star-shaped rosette of floating leaves: family *Callitrichaceae.*

stash (stæʃ) *vb* **1** (*tr;* often foll. by *away*) *Informal.* to put or store (money, valuables, etc.) in a secret place, as for safekeeping. ◆ *n* **2** *Informal.* a secret store or the place where this is hidden. **3** *Slang.* drugs kept for personal consumption. [C20: origin unknown]

stashie ('stæʃɪ) *n Scot.* a variant of **stushie.**

Stasi ('stɑːzɪ) *n* formerly, the secret police in East Germany. [from German *Sta(ats)si(cherheitsdienst),* literally: state security service]

stasis ('steɪsɪs) *n* **1** *Pathol.* a stagnation in the normal flow of bodily fluids, such as the blood or urine. **2** *Literature.* a state or condition in which there is no action or progress; static situation: *dramatic stasis.* [C18: via New Latin from Greek: a standing, from *histanai* to cause to stand; related to Latin *stāre* to stand]

stat. *abbrev. for:* **1** (in prescriptions) immediately. [from Latin *statim*] **2** stationary. **3** statue. **4** statutary. **5** statute.

-stat *n combining form.* indicating a device that causes something to remain stationary or constant: *thermostat.* [from Greek *-statēs,* from *histanai* to cause to stand]

statant ('steɪtᵊnt) *adj Heraldry.* (of an animal) in profile with all four feet on the ground. [C15: from Latin, apparently from irregularly formed present participle of *stāre* to stand]

state (steɪt) *n* **1** the condition of a person, thing, etc., with regard to main attributes. **2** the structure, form, or constitution of something: *a solid state.* **3** any mode of existence. **4** position in life or society; estate. **5** ceremonious style, as befitting wealth or dignity: *to live in state.* **6** a sovereign political power or community. **7** the territory occupied by such a community. **8** the sphere of power in such a community: *affairs of state.* **9** (*often cap.*) one of a number of areas or communities having their own governments and forming a federation under a sovereign government, as in the U.S. **10** (*often cap.*) the body politic of a particular sovereign power, esp. as contrasted with a rival authority such as the Church. **11** *Obsolete.* a class or order; estate. **12** *Informal.* a nervous, upset, or excited condition (esp. in the phrase **in a state**). **13 lie in state.** (of a body) to be placed on public view before burial. **14 state of affairs.** a situation; present circumstances or condition. **15 state of play.** the current situation. ◆ *modifier.* **16** controlled or financed by a state: *state university.* **17** of, relating to, or concerning the State: *State trial.* **18** involving ceremony or concerned with a ceremonious occasion: *state visit.* ◆ *vb (tr; may take a clause as object)* **19** to articulate in words; utter. **20** to declare formally or publicly: *to state one's innocence.* **21** to resolve. [C13: from Old French *estat,* from Latin *status* a standing, from *stāre* to stand] ▸ **'statable** *or* **'stateable** *adj* ▸ **'statehood** *n*

state bank *n* (in the U.S.) a commercial bank incorporated under a State charter and not required to be a member of the Federal Reserve System. Compare **national bank.**

state capitalism *n* a form of capitalism in which the state owns or controls most of the means of production and other capital: often very similar to state socialism.

statecraft ('steɪtˌkrɑːft) *n* the art of conducting public affairs; statesmanship.

stated ('steɪtɪd) *adj* **1** (esp. of a sum) determined by agreement; fixed. **2** explicitly formulated or narrated: *a stated argument.*

stated case *n* another term for **case stated.**

State Department *n* the U.S. government department in charge of foreign affairs.

state duma *n* another name for **duma** (sense 3).

State Enrolled Nurse *n* (in Britain) a nurse who has had training and passed examinations enabling him or her to perform many nursing services. Abbrev.: **SEN.**

state function *n Physics.* a thermodynamic quantity that has definite values for given states of a system, such as entropy, enthalpy, free energy, etc.

state house *n N.Z.* a house built by the government for renting.

Statehouse ('steɪt,haʊs) *n* **1** (in the U.S.) the building which houses a state legislature; State capitol. **2** a building in which public affairs or state ceremonies are conducted.

stateless ('steɪtlɪs) *adj* **1** without nationality: *stateless persons.* **2** without a state or states. **3** *Chiefly Brit.* without ceremonial dignity. ▸ **'statelessness** *n*

statelet ('steɪtlɪt) *n* a small state: *the Gaza Strip statelet.*

stately ('steɪtlɪ) *adj* **-lier, -liest. 1** characterized by a graceful, dignified, and imposing appearance or manner. ◆ *adv* **2** in a stately manner. ▸ **'stateliness** *n*

stately home *n Brit.* a large mansion, esp. one open to the public.

statement ('steɪtmənt) *n* **1** the act of stating. **2** something that is stated, esp. a formal prepared announcement or reply. **3** *Law.* a declaration of matters of fact, esp. in a pleading. **4** an account containing a summary of bills or invoices and displaying the total amount due. **5** an account prepared by a bank for each of its clients, usually at regular intervals, to show all credits and debits since the last account and the balance at the end of the period. **6** *Music.* the presentation of a musical theme or idea, such as the subject of a fugue or sonata. **7** a computer instruction written in a source language, such as FORTRAN, which is converted into one or more machine code instructions by a compiler. **8** *Logic.* the content of a sentence that affirms or denies something and may be true or false; what is thereby affirmed or denied abstracted from the act of uttering it. Thus *I am warm* said by me and *you are warm* said to me make the same statement. Compare **proposition** (sense 2b). **9** *Brit. Education.* a legally binding account of the provisions that will be made to meet the needs of a pupil with special educational needs.

statement of claim *n Law.* (in England) the first pleading made by the plaintiff in a High Court action showing the facts upon which he relies in support of his claim and the relief asked for.

Staten Island ('stætᵊn) *n* an island in SE New York State, in New York Harbor: a borough of New York city; heavy industry. Pop.: 378 977 (1990). Area: 155 sq. km (60 sq. miles).

state of the art *n* **1** the level of knowledge and development achieved in a technique, science, etc., esp. at present. ◆ *adj* (*prenominal*) **state-of-the-art. 2** the most recent and therefore considered the best; up-to-the-minute: *a state-of-the-art amplifier.*

state of war *n* **1** a period of armed conflict between states, regardless of whether or not war has been officially declared. **2** a legal condition begun by a declaration of war and ended formally, during which the rules of international law applicable to warfare may be invoked.

state prayers *pl n Church of England.* prayers for the Sovereign, the royal family, the clergy, and Parliament said at matins and evensong.

State prison *n* (in the U.S.) a prison where persons convicted of serious crimes are confined.

stater ('steɪtə) *n* any of various usually silver coins of ancient Greece. [C14: via Late Latin from Greek *statēr* a standard of weight, from *histanai* to stand]

State Registered Nurse *n* (formerly in Britain) a nurse who had extensive training and passed examinations enabling him or her to perform all nursing services. Abbrev.: **SRN.** See **Registered General Nurse.**

stateroom ('steɪt,ruːm, -,rʊm) *n* **1** a private cabin or room on a ship, train, etc. **2** *Chiefly Brit.* a large room in a palace or other building for use on state occasions.

States (steɪts) *n* (*functioning as sing or pl*) **the.** an informal name for the **United States of America.**

state school *n* any school maintained by the state, in which education is free.

state services *pl n Church of England.* services appointed to commemorate days of national celebration or deliverance such as the accession of a sovereign.

State Services Commission *n* (in New Zealand) a government-appointed body in charge of the public service.

state's evidence *n* (in the U.S.) **1** the evidence for the prosecution given on behalf of a state in a criminal prosecution. **2** evidence given for the state by an accomplice against his former associates in crime (esp. in the phrase **turn state's evidence**). Brit. equivalent: **queen's** (or **king's**) **evidence.**

States General *pl n* **1** the bicameral legislature of the Netherlands. **2** *History.* **2a** an assembly of the estates of an entire country in contrast to those of a single province. **2b** Also called: **Estates General.** the assembly of the estates of all France, last meeting in 1789. **2c** the sovereign body of the Dutch republic from the 16th to 18th century.

stateside ('steɪt,saɪd) *adj, adv U.S.* of, in, to, or towards the U.S.

statesman ('steɪtsmən) *n, pl* **-men. 1** a political leader whose wisdom, integrity, etc., win great respect. **2** a person active and influential in the formulation of high government policy, such as a cabinet member. **3** a politician. ▸ **'statesman-,like** *or* **'statesmanly** *adj* ▸ **'statesmanship** *n* ▸ **'states-,woman** *fem n*

state socialism *n* a variant of socialism in which the power of the state is employed for the purpose of creating an egalitarian society by means of public control of major industries, banks, etc., coupled with economic planning and a social security system. ▸ **state socialist** *n*

States of the Church *pl n* another name for the **Papal States.**

states' rights *pl n* (*often caps.*) (in the U.S.) **1** the rights and powers generally conceded to the states, or all those powers claimed for the states under some interpretations of the Constitution. **2** a doctrine advocating the severe curtailment of Federal powers by such an interpretation of the Constitution. ▸ **states' righter** *n*

state trooper *n U.S.* a state policeman.

static ('stætɪk) *adj also* **statical. 1** not active or moving; stationary. **2** (of a weight, force, or pressure) acting but causing no movement. **3** of or concerned with forces that do not produce movement. Compare **dynamic** (sense 1). **4** relating to or causing stationary electric charges; electrostatic. **5** of or relating to interference in the reception of radio or television transmissions. **6** of or concerned with statics. **7** *Sociol.* characteristic of or relating to a society that has reached a state of equilibrium so that no changes are taking place. **8** *Computing.* (of a memory) not needing its contents refreshed periodically. Compare **dynamic** (sense 5). ◆ *n* **9** random hissing or crackling or a speckled picture caused by the interference of electrical disturbances in the reception of radio or television transmissions. **10** electric sparks or crackling produced by friction. ◆ See also **statics.** [C16: from New Latin *staticus,* from Greek *statikos* causing to stand, from *histanai* to stand, put on the scales] ▸ **'statically** *adv*

statice ('stætɪsɪ) *n* a plant name formerly held to include both *Armeria* (see **thrift**) and *Limonium* (see **sea lavender**). The gardener's statice comprises various species of the latter, esp. those whose flowers can be dried and kept: family *Plumbaginaceae.* [Latin: thrift, from Greek *statikē,* from *statikos* astringent (from a medicinal use of thrift)]

static line *n* a line attaching the pack of a parachute to an aircraft, so that the parachute is opened when it has fallen clear of the aircraft.

statics ('stætɪks) *n* (*functioning as sing*) the branch of mechanics concerned with the forces that produce a state of equilibrium in a system of bodies. Compare **dynamics** (sense 1).

static tube *n* an open-ended tube used to measure the static pressure at a point in a moving fluid and positioned in such a way that it is unaffected by the fluid's motion.

station ('steɪʃən) *n* **1** the place or position at which a thing or person stands or is supposed to stand. **2a** a place along a route or line at which a bus, train, etc., stops for fuel or to pick up or let off passengers or goods, esp. one with ancillary buildings and services: *railway station.* **2b** (*as modifier*): *a station buffet.* **3a** the headquarters or local offices of an official organization such as the police or fire services. **3b** (*as modifier*): *a station sergeant.* See **police station, fire station. 4** a building, depot, etc., with special equipment for some particular purpose: *power station; petrol station; television station.* **5** *Military.* a place of duty: *an action station.* **6** *Navy.* **6a** a location to which a ship or fleet is assigned for duty. **6b** an assigned location for a member of a ship's crew. **7** a radio or television channel. **8** a position or standing, as in a particular society or organization. **9** the type of one's occupation; calling. **10** (in British India) a place where the British district officials or garrison officers resided. **11** *Biology.* the type of habitat occupied by a particular animal or plant. **12** *Austral. and N.Z.* a large sheep or cattle farm. **13** *Surveying.* a point at which a reading is made or which is used as a point of reference. **14** (*often cap.*) *R.C. Church.* **14a** one of the Stations of the Cross. **14b** any of the churches (**station churches**) in Rome that have been used from ancient times as points of assembly for religious processions and ceremonies on particular days (**station days**). **15** (*pl*) (in rural Ireland) mass, preceded by confessions, held annually in a parishioner's dwelling and attended by other parishioners. ◆ *vb* **16** (*tr*) to place in or assign to a station. [C14: via Old French from Latin *statiō* a standing still, from *stāre* to stand]

stationary ('steɪʃənərɪ) *adj* **1** not moving; standing still. **2** not able to be moved. **3** showing no change: *the doctors said his condition was stationary.* **4** tending to remain in one place. [C15: from Latin *statiōnārius,* from *statiō* STATION] ▸ **'stationarily** *adv* ▸ **'stationariness** *n*

USAGE Avoid confusion with **stationery.**

stationary engine *n* an engine that remains in a fixed position, esp. one in a building that drives generators or other machinery. ▸ **stationary engineer** *n*

stationary orbit *n Astronautics.* a synchronous orbit lying in or approximately in the plane of the equator.

stationary point *n* **1** a point on a curve at which the tangent is either horizontal or vertical, such as a maximum, a minimum, or a point of inflection. **2** *Astronomy.* a point in the apparent path of a planet when it reverses direction.

stationary wave *n* another name for **standing wave.**

stationer ('steɪʃənə) *n* **1** a person who sells stationery or a shop where stationery is sold. **2** *Obsolete.* a publisher or bookseller. [C14: from Medieval Latin *stationarius* a person having a regular station, hence a shopkeeper (esp. a bookseller) as distinguished from an itinerant tradesman; see STATION]

Stationers' Company *n* a guild, established by Royal Charter from Queen Mary in 1557, composed of booksellers, printers, etc.

stationery ('steɪʃənərɪ) *n* any writing materials, such as paper, envelopes, pens, ink, rulers, etc.

USAGE Avoid confusion with **stationary.**

Stationery Office *n* **the.** (in the UK) the company that supplies the civil service with all its office supplies, machinery, printing and binding, etc.

station house *n Chiefly U.S.* a house that is situated by or serves as a station, esp. as a police or fire station.

stationmaster ('steɪʃən,mɑːstə) *or* **station manager** *n* the senior official in charge of a railway station.

Stations of the Cross *pl n R.C. Church.* **1** a series of 14 crosses, often accompanied by 14 pictures or carvings, arranged in order around the walls of a church, to commemorate 14 supposed stages in Christ's journey to Calvary. **2** a devotion consisting of 14 prayers relating to each of these stages.

station wagon *n* a U.S., Canadian, Austral., and N.Z. name for **estate car.**

statism ('steɪtɪzəm) *n* the theory or practice of concentrating economic and political power in the state, resulting in a weak position for the individual or community with respect to the government.

statist ('steɪtɪst) *n* **1** an advocate of statism. **2** a less common name for a **statistician**. **3** *Archaic.* a politician or statesman. ◆ *adj* **4** of, characteristic of, advocating, or relating to statism.

statistic (stə'tɪstɪk) *n* any function of a number of random variables, usually identically distributed, that may be used to estimate a population parameter. See also **sampling statistic, estimator** (sense 2), **parameter** (sense 3). ▸ **sta'tistical** *adj* ▸ **sta'tistically** *adv*

statistical dependence *n* a condition in which two random variables are not independent. *X* and *Y* are **positively dependent** if the conditional probability, $P(X|Y)$, of *X* given *Y* is greater than the probability, $P(X)$, of *X*, or equivalently if $P(X\&Y) > P(X).P(Y)$. They are **negatively dependent** if the inequalities are reversed.

statistical inference *n* the theory, methods, and practice of forming judgments about the parameters of a population, usually on the basis of random sampling. Also called: **inferential statistics.** Compare **hypothesis testing.**

statistical mechanics *n* (*functioning as sing*) the study of the properties of physical systems as predicted by the statistical behaviour of their constituent particles.

statistical tables *pl n* tables showing the values of the cumulative distribution functions, probability functions, or probability density functions of certain common distributions for different values of their parameters, and used esp. to determine whether or not a particular statistical result exceeds the required significance level. See **hypothesis testing.**

statistician (ˌstætɪ'stɪʃən) *n* **1** a person who specializes in or is skilled at statistics. **2** a person who compiles statistics.

statistics (stə'tɪstɪks) *n* **1** (*functioning as pl*) quantitative data on any subject, esp. data comparing the distribution of some quantity for different subclasses of the population: *statistics for earnings by different age groups.* **2** (*functioning as sing*) **2a** the classification and interpretation of such data in accordance with probability theory and the application of methods such as hypothesis testing to them. **2b** the mathematical study of the theoretical nature of such distributions and tests. See also **descriptive statistics, statistical inference.** [C18 (originally "science dealing with facts of a state"): via German *Statistik,* from New Latin *statisticus* concerning state affairs, from Latin *status* STATE]

Statius ('steɪʃɪəs) *n* **Publius Papinius** ('pʌblɪəs pə'pɪnɪəs). ?45–96 A.D., Roman poet; author of the collection *Silvae* and of two epics, *Thebais* and the unfinished *Achilleis.*

stative ('steɪtɪv) *Grammar.* ◆ *adj* **1** denoting a verb describing a state rather than an activity, act, or event, such as *know* and *want* as opposed to *leave* and *throw*. Compare **nonstative.** ◆ *n* **2** a stative verb. [C19: from New Latin *stativus,* from Latin *stāre* to stand]

stato- *combining form.* static; standing; fixed: *statolith.* [from Greek *statos* standing, set]

statoblast ('stætəʊˌblɑːst) *n Zoology.* an encapsulated bud produced asexually by certain bryozoans that can survive adverse conditions and that gives rise to a new colony.

statocyst ('stætəʊsɪst) *n* an organ of balance in some invertebrates, such as crustaceans, that consists of a sensory vesicle containing small granules (see **statolith**).

statolatry (steɪ'tɒlətrɪ) *n Rare.* the act or practice of idolizing the state. [C19: from STATE + -LATRY]

statolith ('stætəʊlɪθ) *n* **1** Also called: **otolith.** any of the granules of calcium carbonate occurring in a statocyst: movement of statoliths, caused by a change in position of the animal, stimulates hair cells, which convey the information to the brain by nerve fibres. **2** any of various movable inclusions, such as starch grains, that occur in plant cells and are thought to function in geotropic responses. ▸ ˌ**stato'lithic** *adj*

stator ('steɪtə) *n* **1** the stationary part of a rotary machine or device, esp. of a motor or generator. **2** a system of nonrotating radially arranged parts within a rotating assembly, esp. the fixed blades of an axial flow compressor in a gas turbine. ◆ Compare **rotor** (sense 1). [C20: from Latin: one who stands (by), from *stāre* to stand]

statoscope ('stætəˌskəʊp) *n* a very sensitive form of aneroid barometer used to detect and measure small variations in atmospheric pressure, such as one used in an aircraft to indicate small changes in altitude.

statuary ('stætjʊərɪ) *n* **1** statues collectively. **2** the art of making statues. ◆ *adj* **3** of, relating to, or suitable for statues. [C16: from Latin *statuārius*]

statue ('stætjuː) *n* a wooden, stone, metal, plaster, or other kind of sculpture of a human or animal figure, usually life-size or larger. [C14: via Old French from Latin *statua,* from *statuere* to set up; compare STATUTE]

statued ('stætjuːd) *adj* decorated with or portrayed in a statue or statues.

Statue of Liberty *n* a monumental statue personifying liberty, in New York Harbor, on Liberty Island: a gift from France, erected in 1885. Official name: **Liberty Enlightening the World.**

statuesque (ˌstætjʊ'ɛsk) *adj* like a statue, esp. in possessing great formal beauty or dignity. [C19: from STATUE + -ESQUE, on the model of PICTURESQUE] ▸ ˌ**statu'esquely** *adv* ▸ ˌ**statu'esqueness** *n*

statuette (ˌstætjʊ'ɛt) *n* a small statue.

stature ('stætʃə) *n* **1** the height of something, esp. a person or animal when standing. **2** the degree of development of a person: *the stature of a champion.* **3** intellectual or moral greatness: *a man of stature.* [C13: via Old French from Latin *statūra,* from *stāre* to stand]

status ('steɪtəs) *n, pl* **-tuses. 1** a social or professional position, condition, or standing to which varying degrees of responsibility, privilege, and esteem are attached. **2** the relative position or standing of a person or thing. **3** a high position or standing; prestige: *he has acquired a new status since he has been in that job.* **4** the legal standing or condition of a person. **5** a state of affairs. [C17: from Latin: posture, from *stāre* to stand]

status quo (kwəʊ) *n* (usually preceded by *the*) the existing state of affairs. [literally: the state in which]

status symbol *n* a possession which is regarded as proof of the owner's social position, wealth, prestige, etc.

statutable ('stætjʊtəbᵊl) *adj* a variant of **statutory** (senses 2, 3). ▸ **'statutably** *adv*

statute ('stætjuːt) *n* **1a** an enactment of a legislative body expressed in a formal document. **1b** this document. **2** a permanent rule made by a body or institution for the government of its internal affairs. [C13: from Old French *estatut,* from Late Latin *statūtum,* from Latin *statuere* to set up, decree, ultimately from *stāre* to stand]

statute book *n Chiefly Brit.* a register of enactments passed by the legislative body of a state, usually made up of a series of volumes that form a complete official record: *not on the statute book.*

statute law *n* **1** a law enacted by a legislative body. **2** a particular example of this. ◆ Compare **common law, equity.**

statute mile *n* a legal or formal name for **mile** (sense 1).

statute of limitations *n* a legislative enactment prescribing the period of time within which proceedings must be instituted to enforce a right or bring an action at law. See also **laches.**

Statute of Westminster *n* the act of Parliament (1931) that formally recognized the independence of the dominions within the Empire.

statutory ('stætjʊtərɪ, -trɪ) *adj* **1** of, relating to, or having the nature of a statute. **2** prescribed or authorized by statute. **3** (of an offence) **3a** recognized by statute. **3b** subject to a punishment or penalty prescribed by statute. ▸ **'statutorily** *adv*

statutory declaration *n Law.* a declaration made under statutory authority before a justice of the peace or commissioner for oaths which may in certain cases be substituted for a statement on oath.

statutory order *n* a statute that applies further legislation to an existing act.

statutory rape *n* (in the U.S.) the criminal offence of having sexual intercourse with a girl who has not reached the age of consent.

Stauffenberg ('ʃtaʊfənˌbɜːg) *n* **Claus** (klaus), Graf von. 1907–44, German army officer, who tried to assassinate Hitler (1944). He and his fellow conspirators were executed.

staun (stɔːn) *vb, n* a Scot. word for **stand.**

staunch[1] (stɔːntʃ) *adj* **1** loyal, firm, and dependable: *a staunch supporter.* **2** solid or substantial in construction. **3** *Rare.* (of a ship, etc.) watertight; seaworthy. [C15: (originally: watertight): from Old French *estanche,* from *estanchier* to STANCH] ▸ **'staunchly** *adv* ▸ **'staunchness** *n*

staunch[2] (stɔːntʃ) *vb, n* a variant spelling of **stanch.**

staurolite ('stɔːrəˌlaɪt) *n* a brown glassy mineral consisting of iron aluminium silicate in the form of prismatic crystals: used as a gemstone. Formula: $FeAl_4Si_2O_{10}(OH)_2$. [C19: from Greek *stauros* a cross + -LITE] ▸ **staurolitic** (ˌstɔːrə'lɪtɪk) *adj*

stauroscope ('stɔːrəˌskəʊp) *n* an optical instrument for studying the crystal structure of minerals under polarized light. [C19: from Greek *stauros* a cross + -SCOPE] ▸ **stauroscopic** (ˌstɔːrə'skɒpɪk) *adj* ▸ ˌ**stauro'scopically** *adv*

Stavanger (*Norwegian* sta'vaŋər) *n* a port in SW Norway: canning and shipbuilding industries. Pop.: 104 322 (1996).

stave (steɪv) *n* **1** any one of a number of long strips of wood joined together to form a barrel, bucket, boat hull, etc. **2** any of various bars, slats, or rods, usually of wood, such as a rung of a ladder or a crosspiece bracing the legs of a chair. **3** any stick, staff, etc. **4** a stanza or verse of a poem. **5** *Music.* **5a** *Brit.* an individual group of five lines and four spaces used in staff notation. **5b** another word for **staff**[1] (sense 9). ◆ *vb* **staves, staving, staved** *or* **stove. 6** (often foll. by *in*) to break or crush (the staves of a boat, barrel, etc.) or (of the staves of a boat) to be broken or crushed. **7** (*tr;* usually foll. by *in*) to burst or force (a hole in something). **8** (*tr*) to provide (a ladder, chair, etc.) with a stave or staves. **9** (*tr*) *Scot.* to sprain (a finger, toe, etc.). [C14: back formation from *staves,* plural of STAFF[1]]

stave off *vb* (*tr, adv*) to avert or hold off (something undesirable or harmful), esp. temporarily: *to stave off hunger.*

staves (steɪvz) *n* a plural of **staff**[1] or **stave.**

stavesacre ('steɪvzˌeɪkə) *n* **1** a Eurasian ranunculaceous plant, *Delphinium staphisagria,* having purple flowers and poisonous seeds. **2** the seeds of this plant, which have strong emetic and cathartic properties. [C14 *staphisagre,* from Latin *staphis agria,* from Greek, from *staphis* raisin + *agria* wild]

Stavropol (*Russian* 'stavrəpəlj) *n* **1** a city in SW Russia: founded as a fortress in 1777. Pop.: 342 000 (1995 est.). Former name (1940–44): **Voroshilovsk. 2** the former name (until 1964) of **Togliatti.**

stay[1] (steɪ) *vb* **1** (*intr*) to continue or remain in a certain place, position, etc.: *to stay outside.* **2** (*copula*) to continue to be; remain: *to stay awake.* **3** (*intr;* often foll. by *at*) to reside temporarily, esp. as a guest: *to stay at a hotel.* **4** (*tr*) to remain for a specified period: *to stay the weekend.* **5** (*intr*) *Scot. and S. African.* to reside permanently or habitually; live. **6** *Archaic.* to stop or cause to stop. **7** (*intr*) to wait, pause, or tarry. **8** (*tr*) to delay or hinder. **9** (*tr*) **9a** to discontinue or suspend (a judicial proceeding). **9b** to hold in abeyance or restrain from enforcing (an order, decree, etc.). **10** to endure (something testing or difficult, such as a race): *a horse that stays the course.* **11** (*intr;* usually foll. by *with*) to keep pace (with a competitor in a race, etc.). **12** (*intr*) *Poker.* to raise one's stakes enough to stay in a round. **13** (*tr*) to hold back or restrain: *to stay one's anger.* **14** (*tr*) to satisfy or appease (an appetite, etc.) temporarily. **15** (*tr*) *Archaic.* to quell or suppress. **16** (*intr*) *Archaic.* to stand firm. **17 stay put.** See **put** (sense 18). ◆ *n* **18** the act of staying or sojourning in a place or the period during which one stays. **19** the act of stopping or restraining or state of being stopped, etc. **20** the suspension of a judicial proceeding, etc.: *stay of execution.*

◆ See also **stay out.** [C15 *staien,* from Anglo-French *estaier* to stay, from Old French *ester* to stay, from Latin *stāre* to stand]

stay[2] (steɪ) *n* **1** anything that supports or steadies, such as a prop or buttress. **2** a thin strip of metal, plastic, bone, etc., used to stiffen corsets, etc. ◆ *vb* (*tr*) *Archaic.* **3** (often foll. by *up*) to prop or hold. **4** (often foll. by *up*) to comfort or sustain. **5** (foll. by *on* or *upon*) to cause to rely or depend. ◆ See also **stays** (sense 1). [C16: from Old French *estaye,* of Germanic origin; compare STAY[3]]

stay[3] (steɪ) *n* a rope, cable, or chain, usually one of a set, used for bracing uprights, such as masts, funnels, flagpoles, chimneys, etc.; guy. ◆ See also **stays** (senses 2, 3). [Old English *stæg;* related to Old Norse *stag,* Middle Low German *stach,* Norwegian *stagle* wooden post]

stay-at-home *adj* **1** (of a person) enjoying a quiet, settled, and unadventurous use of leisure. ◆ *n* **2** a stay-at-home person.

stayer ('steɪə) *n* **1** a person or thing that stays. **2** *Informal.* **2a** a persistent or tenacious person. **2b** *Horse racing.* a persistent horse.

staying power *n* endurance; stamina.

Stayman ('steɪmən) *n* (in contract bridge) a conventional response in clubs to a partner's opening no-trump bid, as a request for the partner to show any four-card major. [C20: named after Samuel M. *Stayman* (1909–94), U.S. bridge expert]

stay out *vb* (*adv*) **1** (*intr*) to remain away from home: *the cat stayed out all night.* **2** (*tr*) to remain beyond the end of: *to stay out a welcome.* **3** (*tr*) to remain throughout: *to stay the night out.*

stays (steɪz) *pl n* **1** *Now rare.* corsets with bones in them. **2** a position of a sailing vessel relative to the wind so that the sails are luffing or aback. Compare **irons** (sense 2). **3 miss stays.** Also: **refuse stays.** (of a sailing vessel) to fail to come about.

staysail ('steɪˌseɪl; *Nautical* 'steɪsᵊl) *n* an auxiliary sail, often triangular, set to catch the wind, as between the masts of a yawl (**mizzen staysail**), aft of a spinnaker (**spinnaker staysail**), etc.

stay stitching *n* a line of stitches made in the seam allowance to prevent the edges from stretching.

stbd *abbrev. for* starboard.

STC (in India) *abbrev. for* State Trading Corporation.

std *abbrev. for* standard.

STD *abbrev. for:* **1** subscriber trunk dialling. **2** *N.Z.* subscriber toll dialling. **3** sexually transmitted disease. **4** Doctor of Sacred Theology.

STD code *n Brit.* a code of four or more digits, other than those comprising a subscriber's local telephone number, that determines the routing of a call. [C20: *s(ubscriber) t(runk) d(ialling)*]

Ste *abbrev. for* Saint (female). [French *Sainte*]

stead (stɛd) *n* **1** (preceded by *in*) *Rare.* the place, function, or position that should be taken by another: *to come in someone's stead.* **2 stand (someone) in good stead.** to be useful or of good service to (someone). ◆ *vb* **3** (*tr*) *Archaic.* to help or benefit. [Old English *stede;* related to Old Norse *stathr* place, Old High German *stat* place, Latin *statiō* a standing, *statim* immediately]

Stead (stɛd) *n* **Christina (Ellen).** 1902–83, Australian novelist. Her works include *Seven Poor Men of Sydney* (1934), *The Man who Loved Children* (1940), and *Cotters' England* (1966).

steadfast *or* **stedfast** ('stɛdfəst, -ˌfɑːst) *adj* **1** (esp. of a person's gaze) fixed in intensity or direction; steady. **2** unwavering or determined in purpose, loyalty, etc.: *steadfast resolve.* ▸ **'steadfastly** *or* **'stedfastly** *adv* ▸ **'steadfastness** *or* **'stedfastness** *n*

Steadicam ('stɛdɪˌkæm) *n Trademark.* a mechanism for steadying a hand-held camera, consisting of a shock-absorbing arm to which the camera is attached and a harness worn by the camera operator.

steading ('stɛdɪŋ) *n Brit.* **1** a farmstead. **2** the outbuildings of a farm. [C15: from STEAD + -ING[1]]

steady ('stɛdɪ) *adj* **steadier, steadiest. 1** not able to be moved or disturbed easily; stable. **2** free from fluctuation: *the level stayed steady.* **3** not easily excited; imperturbable. **4** staid; sober. **5** regular; habitual: *a steady drinker.* **6** continuous: *a steady flow.* **7** *Nautical.* (of a vessel) keeping upright, as in heavy seas. ◆ *vb* **steadies, steadying, steadied. 8** to make or become steady. ◆ *adv* **9** in a steady manner. **10 go steady.** *Informal.* to date one person regularly. ◆ *n, pl* **steadies. 11** *Informal.* one's regular boyfriend or girlfriend. ◆ *interj* **12** *Nautical.* an order to the helmsman to stay on a steady course. **13** a warning to keep calm, be careful, etc. **14** *Brit.* a command to get set to start, as in a race: *ready, steady, go!* [C16: from STEAD + -Y[1]; related to Old High German *stātīg,* Middle Dutch *stēdig*] ▸ **'steadier** *n* ▸ **'steadily** *adv* ▸ **'steadiness** *n*

steady state *n Physics.* the condition of a system when some or all of the quantities describing it are independent of time but not necessarily in thermodynamic or chemical equilibrium. See also **equilibrium** (sense 6).

steady-state theory *n* a cosmological theory postulating that the universe exists throughout time in a steady state such that the average density of matter does not vary with distance or time. Matter is continuously created in the space left by the receding stars and galaxies of the expanding universe. Compare **big-bang theory.**

steak (steɪk) *n* **1** See **beefsteak. 2** any of various cuts of beef of varying quality, used for braising, stewing, etc. **3** a thick slice of pork, veal, etc., or of a large fish, esp. cod or salmon. **4** minced meat prepared in the same way as steak: *hamburger steak.* [C15: from Old Norse *steik* roast; related to *steikja* to roast on a spit; see STICK[1]]

steakhouse ('steɪkˌhaʊs) *n* a restaurant that has steaks as its speciality.

steak tartare *or* **tartar** *n* raw minced steak, mixed with onion, seasonings, and raw egg. Also called: **tartare steak, tartar steak.**

steal (stiːl) *vb* **steals, stealing, stole, stolen. 1** to take (something) from someone, etc. without permission or unlawfully, esp. in a secret manner. **2** (*tr*) to obtain surreptitiously. **3** (*tr*) to appropriate (ideas, etc.) without acknowledgment, as in plagiarism. **4** to move or convey stealthily: *they stole along the corridor.* **5** (*intr*) to pass unnoticed: *the hours stole by.* **6** (*tr*) to win or gain by strategy or luck, as in various sports: *to steal a few yards.* **7 steal a march on.** to obtain an advantage over, esp. by a secret or underhand measure. **8 steal someone's thunder.** to detract from the attention due to another by forestalling him. **9 steal the show.** to be looked upon as the most interesting, popular, etc., esp. unexpectedly. ◆ *n Informal.* **10** the act of stealing. **11** something stolen or acquired easily or at little cost. [Old English *stelan;* related to Old Frisian, Old Norse *stela,* Gothic *stilan,* German *stehlen*] ▸ **'stealer** *n*

stealth (stɛlθ) *n* **1** the act or characteristic of moving with extreme care and quietness, esp. so as to avoid detection: *the stealth of a cat.* **2** cunning or underhand procedure or dealing. **3** *Archaic.* the act of stealing. [C13 *stelthe;* see STEAL, -TH[1]] ▸ **'stealthful** *adj*

Stealth (stɛlθ) *n* (*modifier*) *Informal.* denoting or referring to technology that aims to reduce the radar, thermal, and acoustic recognizability of aircraft and missiles.

Stealth bomber *or* **plane** *n* a type of U.S. military aircraft using advanced technology to render it virtually undetectable to sight, radar, or infrared sensors. Also called: **B-2.**

stealthy ('stɛlθɪ) *adj* **stealthier, stealthiest.** characterized by great caution, secrecy, etc.; furtive. ▸ **'stealthily** *adv* ▸ **'stealthiness** *n*

steam (stiːm) *n* **1** the gas or vapour into which water is changed when boiled. **2** the mist formed when such gas or vapour condenses in the atmosphere. **3** any vaporous exhalation. **4** *Informal.* power, energy, or speed. **5 get up steam. 5a** (of a ship, etc.) to work up a sufficient head of steam in a boiler to drive an engine. **5b** *Informal.* to go quickly. **6 let off steam.** *Informal.* to release pent-up energy or emotions. **7 under one's own steam.** without the assistance of others. **8** *Austral. slang.* cheap wine. **9** (*modifier*) driven, operated, heated, powered, etc., by steam: *a steam radiator.* **10** (*modifier*) treated by steam: *steam ironed; steam cleaning.* **11** (*modifier*) *Humorous.* old-fashioned; outmoded: *steam radio.* ◆ *vb* **12** to emit or be emitted as steam. **13** (*intr*) to generate steam, as a boiler, etc. **14** (*intr*) to move or travel by steam power, as a ship, etc. **15** (*intr*) *Informal.* to proceed quickly and sometimes forcefully. **16** to cook or be cooked in steam. **17** (*tr*) to treat with steam or apply steam to, as in cleaning, pressing clothes, etc. ◆ See also **steam up.** [Old English; related to Dutch *stoom* steam, perhaps to Old High German *stioban* to raise dust, Gothic *stubjus* dust]

steam bath *n* **1** a room or enclosure that can be filled with steam in which people bathe to induce sweating and refresh or cleanse themselves. **2** an act of taking such a bath. **3** an enclosure through which steam can be passed continuously, used in laboratories for sterilizing equipment, maintaining a constant temperature, etc.

steamboat ('stiːmˌbəʊt) *n* a boat powered by a steam engine.

steam-boiler *n* a vessel in which water is boiled to generate steam. An industrial boiler usually consists of a system of parallel tubes through which water passes, suspended above a furnace.

steam-chest *n* a chamber that encloses the slide valve of a steam engine and forms a manifold for the steam supply to the valve.

steam coal *n* coal suitable for use in producing steam, as in a steam-boiler.

steam-engine *n* an engine that uses the thermal energy of steam to produce mechanical work, esp. one in which steam from a boiler is expanded in a cylinder to drive a reciprocating piston.

steamer ('stiːmə) *n* **1** a boat or ship driven by steam engines. **2** Also called: **steam box.** an apparatus for steaming wooden beams and planks to make them pliable for shipbuilding. **3** a vessel used to cook food by steam. **4** *Austral. slang.* a clash of sporting teams characterized by rough play.

steam-generating heavy-water reactor *n* a nuclear reactor using heavy water as the moderator, light water (H_2O) as the coolant, and uranium oxide cased in zirconium alloy as the fuel. Abbrev.: **SGHWR.**

steamie ('stiːmɪ) *n Scot. urban dialect.* a public wash house.

steaming ('stiːmɪŋ) *adj* **1** very hot. **2** *Informal.* angry. **3** *Slang.* drunk. ◆ *n* **4** *Informal.* robbery, esp. of passengers in a railway carriage or bus, by a large gang of armed youths.

steam iron *n* an electric iron that emits steam from channels in the iron face to facilitate the pressing and ironing of clothes, etc., the steam being produced from water contained within the iron.

steam jacket *n Engineering.* a jacket containing steam that surrounds and heats a cylinder.

steam organ *n* a type of organ powered by steam, once common at fairgrounds, in which the pipes are sounded either by a keyboard or in a sequence determined by a moving punched card. U.S. name: **calliope.**

steam point *n* the temperature at which the maximum vapour pressure of water is equal to one atmosphere (1.01325×10^5 N/m^2). It has the value of 100° on the Celsius scale. Compare **ice point.**

steam reforming *n Chem.* a process in which methane from natural gas is heated, with steam, usually with a catalyst, to produce a mixture of carbon monoxide and hydrogen used in organic synthesis and as a fuel.

steamroller ('stiːmˌrəʊlə) *n* **1a** a steam-powered vehicle with heavy rollers at the front and rear used for compressing road surfaces during road-making. **1b** another word for **roadroller. 2a** an overpowering force or a person with such force that overcomes all opposition. **2b** (*as modifier*): *steamroller tactics.* ◆ *vb* **3** (*tr*) to crush (opposition, etc.) by overpowering force.

steam room *n* a room that can be filled with steam for use as a steam bath.

steamship ('stiːmˌʃɪp) *n* a ship powered by one or more steam engines.

steam-shovel *n* a steam-driven mechanical excavator, esp. one having a large bucket or grab on a beam slung from a revolving jib.

steamtight ('stiːmˌtaɪt) *adj* (of joints, cylinders, etc.) being sealed in such a way that steam cannot leak out. ▸ **'steamˌtightness** *n*

steam trap *n* a device in a steam pipe that collects and discharges condensed water.
steam turbine *n* a turbine driven by steam.
steam up *vb* (*adv*) **1** to cover (windows, etc.) or (of windows, etc.) to become covered with a film of condensed steam. **2** (*tr; usually passive*) *Slang.* to excite or make angry: *he's all steamed up about the delay.*
steam whistle *n* a type of whistle sounded by a blast of steam, as used formerly in factories, on locomotives, etc.
steamy ('stiːmɪ) *adj* **steamier, steamiest. 1** of, resembling, full of, or covered with steam. **2** *Informal.* lustful or erotic: *steamy nightlife.* ► **'steamily** *adv* ► **'steaminess** *n*
steapsin (stɪ'æpsɪn) *n Biochem.* a pancreatic lipase. [C19: from Greek *stear* fat + PEPSIN]
stearate ('stɪəˌreɪt) *n* any salt or ester of stearic acid.
stearic (stɪ'ærɪk) *adj* **1** of or relating to suet or fat. **2** of, consisting of, containing, or derived from stearic acid. [C19: from French *stéarique,* from Greek *stear* fat, tallow]
stearic acid *n* a colourless odourless insoluble waxy carboxylic acid used for making candles and suppositories; octadecanoic acid. Formula: $CH_3(CH_2)_{16}$-COOH. See also **stearin** (sense 2).
stearin *or* **stearine** ('stɪərɪn) *n* **1** Also called: **tristearin.** a colourless crystalline ester of glycerol and stearic acid, present in fats and used in soap and candles; glycerol tristearate; glycerol trioctadecanoate. Formula: $(C_{17}H_{35}COO)_3C_3H_5$. **2** another name for **stearic acid,** esp. a commercial grade containing other fatty acids. **3** fat in its solid form. [C19: from French *stéarine,* from Greek *stear* fat, tallow + -IN]
stearoptene (ˌstɪə'rɒptiːn) *n* the part of an essential oil that separates out as a solid on cooling or standing. [C19: from New Latin *stearoptenum,* from Greek *stear* fat + *-ptenum,* from *ptēnos* winged (volatile)]
steatite ('stɪəˌtaɪt) *n* another name for **soapstone.** [C18: from Latin *steatītēs,* from Greek *stear* fat + -ITE[1]] ► **steatitic** (ˌstɪə'tɪtɪk) *adj*
steato- *combining form.* denoting fat. [from Greek *stear, steat-* fat, tallow]
steatolysis (ˌstɪə'tɒlɪsɪs) *n Physiol.* **1** the digestive process whereby fats are emulsified and then hydrolysed to fatty acids and glycerine. **2** the breaking down of fat.
steatopygia (ˌstɪətəʊ'pɪdʒɪə, -'paɪ-) *or* **steatopyga** (ˌstɪətəʊ'paɪgə) *n* excessive fatness of the buttocks. [C19: from New Latin, from STEATO- + Greek *pugē* the buttocks] ► **steatopygic** (ˌstɪətəʊ'pɪdʒɪk) *or* **steatopygous** (ˌstɪə'tɒpɪgəs) *adj*
steatorrhoea *or esp. U.S.* **steatorrhea** (ˌstɪətə'rɪə) *n Pathol.* **1** a condition in which the stools are abnormally fatty. **2** another word for **seborrhoea.**
Stębark ('stɛmbark) *n* the Polish name for **Tannenberg.**
stedfast ('stɛdfəst, -ˌfɑːst) *adj* a less common spelling of **steadfast.**
steed (stiːd) *n Archaic or literary.* a horse, esp. one that is spirited or swift. [Old English *stēda* stallion; related to German *Stute* female horse; see STUD[2]]
steel (stiːl) *n* **1a** any of various alloys based on iron containing carbon (usually 0.1–1.7 per cent) and often small quantities of other elements such as phosphorus, sulphur, manganese, chromium, and nickel. Steels exhibit a variety of properties, such as strength, machinability, malleability, etc., depending on their composition and the way they have been treated. **1b** (*as modifier*): *steel girders.* See also **stainless steel. 2** something that is made of steel. **3** a steel stiffener in a corset, etc. **4** a ridged steel rod with a handle used for sharpening knives. **5** the quality of hardness, esp. with regard to a person's character or attitudes. **6** *Stock Exchange.* the quotation for steel shares. See also **steels. 7** (*modifier*) resembling steel: *steel determination.* ◆ *vb* (*tr*) **8** to fit, plate, edge, or point with steel. **9** to make hard and unfeeling: *he steeled his heart against her sorrow; he steeled himself for the blow.* [Old English *stēli;* related to Old High German *stehli,* Middle Dutch *stael*] ► **'steely** *adj* ► **'steeliness** *n*
Steel (stiːl) *n* Baron **David** (**Martin Scott**). born 1938, British politician; leader of the Liberal Party (1976–88).
steel band *n Music.* a type of instrumental band, popular in the Caribbean Islands, consisting mainly of tuned percussion instruments made chiefly from the heads of oil drums, hammered or embossed to obtain different notes.
steel blue *n* **a** a dark bluish-grey colour. **b** (*as adj*): *steel-blue eyes.*
Steele (stiːl) *n* Sir **Richard.** 1672–1729, British essayist and dramatist, born in Ireland; with Joseph Addison he was the chief contributor to the periodicals *The Tatler* (1709–11) and *The Spectator* (1711–12).
steel engraving *n* **a** a method or art of engraving (letters, etc.) on a steel plate. **b** a print made from such a plate.
steel grey *n* **a** a dark grey colour, usually slightly purple. **b** (*as adj*): *a steel-grey suit.*
steel guitar *n* See **Hawaiian guitar, pedal steel guitar.**
steelhead ('stiːlˌhɛd) *n, pl* **-heads** *or* **-head.** a silvery North Pacific variety of the rainbow trout (*Salmo gairdneri*).
steels (stiːlz) *pl n Stock Exchange.* shares and bonds of steel companies.
steel wool *n* a tangled or woven mass of fine steel fibres, used for cleaning or polishing.
steelwork ('stiːlˌwɜːk) *n* a frame, foundation, building, or article made of steel: *the steelwork of a skyscraper.* ► **'steelˌworking** *n*
steelworks ('stiːlˌwɜːks) *n* (*functioning as sing or pl*) a plant in which steel is made from iron ore and rolled or forged into blooms, billets, bars, or sheets. ► **'steelˌworker** *n*
steelyard ('stiːlˌjɑːd) *n* a portable balance consisting of a pivoted bar with two unequal arms. The load is suspended from the shorter one and the bar is returned to the horizontal by adding weights to the longer one. [C17: from STEEL + YARD[1] (in the archaic sense: a rod or pole]
steen (stɪən) *n S. African.* **1** a red grape variety of South Africa. **2** any of the red wines made from this grape. [Afrikaans]
Steen (steɪn) *n* **Jan** (jɑn). 1626–79, Dutch genre painter.
steenbok ('stiːnˌbɒk) *n, pl* **-boks** *or* **-bok.** a small antelope, *Raphicerus campestris,* of central and southern Africa, having a reddish-brown coat and straight smooth horns. Also called: **steinbok.** [C18: from Afrikaans, from Dutch *steen* stone + *bok* BUCK[1]; Compare STEINBOCK]
steep[1] (stiːp) *adj* **1a** having or being a slope or gradient approaching the perpendicular. **1b** (*as n*): *the steep.* **2** *Informal.* (of a fee, price, demand, etc.) unduly high; unreasonable (esp. in the phrase **that's a bit steep**). **3** *Informal.* excessively demanding or ambitious: *a steep task.* **4** *Brit. informal.* (of a statement) extreme or far-fetched. **5** *Obsolete.* elevated. [Old English *steap;* related to Old Frisian *stāp,* Old High German *stouf* cliff, Old Norse *staup*] ► **'steeply** *adv* ► **'steepness** *n*
steep[2] (stiːp) *vb* **1** to soak or be soaked in a liquid in order to soften, cleanse, extract an element, etc. **2** (*tr; usually passive*) to saturate; imbue: *steeped in ideology.* ◆ *n* **3** an instance or the process of steeping or the condition of being steeped. **4** a liquid or solution used for the purpose of steeping something. [Old English *stēpan;* related to *steap* vessel, cup, Old High German *stouf,* Old Norse *staup,* Middle Dutch *stōp*] ► **'steeper** *n*
steepen ('stiːpᵊn) *vb* to become or cause to become steep or steeper.
steeple ('stiːpᵊl) *n* **1** a tall ornamental tower that forms the superstructure of a church, temple, etc. **2** such a tower with the spire above it. **3** any spire or pointed structure. [Old English *stēpel;* see STEEP[1]] ► **'steepled** *adj*
steeplebush ('stiːpᵊlˌbʊʃ) *n* another name for **hardhack.** [C19: so called because of the shape of its flower clusters]
steeplechase ('stiːpᵊlˌtʃeɪs) *n* **1** a horse race over a course equipped with obstacles to be jumped, esp. artificial hedges, ditches, water jumps, etc. **2** a track race, usually of 3000 metres, in which the runners have to leap hurdles, a water jump, etc. **3** *Archaic.* **3a** a horse race across a stretch of open countryside including obstacles to be jumped. **3b** a rare word for **point-to-point.** ◆ *vb* **4** (*intr*) to take part in a steeplechase. [C19: so called because it originally took place cross-country, with a church tower serving as a landmark to guide the riders] ► **'steepleˌchaser** *n* ► **'steepleˌchasing** *n*
steeplejack ('stiːpᵊlˌdʒæk) *n* a person trained and skilled in the construction and repair of steeples, chimneys, etc. [C19: from STEEPLE + JACK[1] (in the sense: a man or fellow)]
steer[1] (stɪə) *vb* **1** to direct the course of (a vehicle or vessel) with a steering wheel, rudder, etc. **2** (*tr*) to guide with tuition: *his teachers steered him through his exams.* **3** (*tr*) to direct the movements or course of (a person, conversation, etc.). **4** to pursue (a specified course). **5** (*intr*) (of a vessel, vehicle, etc.) to admit of being guided in a specified fashion: *this boat does not steer properly.* **6 steer clear of.** to keep away from; shun. ◆ *n* **7** *Chiefly U.S.* information; guidance (esp. in the phrase **a bum steer**). [Old English *stieran;* related to Old Frisian *stiūra,* Old Norse *stȳra,* German *stevern;* see STARBOARD, STERN[2]] ► **'steerable** *adj* ► **'steerer** *n*
steer[2] (stɪə) *n* a castrated male ox or bull; bullock. [Old English *stēor;* related to Old Norse *stjōrr,* Gothic *stiur,* Old High German *stior,* Middle Dutch *stēr*]
steerage ('stɪərɪdʒ) *n* **1** the cheapest accommodation on a passenger ship, originally the compartments containing the steering apparatus. **2** an instance or the practice of steering and the effect of this on a vessel or vehicle.
steerageway ('stɪərɪdʒˌweɪ) *n Nautical.* enough forward movement to allow a vessel to be steered.
steering column *n* (in a motor vehicle) the shaft on which a steering wheel is mounted and by which it is connected with the steering gear.
steering committee *n* a committee set up to prepare and arrange topics to be discussed, the order of business, etc., for a legislative assembly or other body.
steering gear *n* any mechanism used for steering a vehicle, ship, aircraft, etc.
steering wheel *n* a wheel turned by the driver of a motor vehicle, ship, etc., when he wishes to change direction. It is connected to the front wheels, rudder, etc.
steersman ('stɪəzmən) *n, pl* **-men.** the helmsman of a vessel.
steeve[1] (stiːv) *n* **1** a spar having a pulley block at one end, used for stowing cargo on a ship. ◆ *vb* **2** (*tr*) to stow (cargo) securely in the hold of a ship. [C15 *steven,* probably from Spanish *estibar* to pack tightly, from Latin *stīpāre* to cram full]
steeve[2] (stiːv) *Nautical.* ◆ *vb* **1** to incline (a bowsprit or other spar) upwards or (of a bowsprit) to incline upwards at an angle from the horizontal. ◆ *n* **2** such an angle. [C17: of uncertain origin]
Stefan Dušan ('stɛfən 'duːʃæn) *n* 1308–55, king of Serbia (1331–55), who conquered Albania (1343) and large parts of the Byzantine empire, into which he introduced legal and administrative reforms.
Stefan's law ('stɛfənz) *n* the principle that the energy radiated per second by unit area of a black body at thermodynamic temperature T is directly proportional to T^4. The constant of proportionality is the **Stefan constant,** equal to 5.6697×10^{-8} Wm^{-2} K^{-4}. Also called: **Stefan-Boltzmann law.** [C19: named after Josef *Stefan* (1835–93), Austrian physicist]
Stefansson ('stɛfənsən) *n* **Vilhjalmur** ('vɪlˌhjaʊmɛr) 1879–1962, Canadian explorer, noted for his books on the Inuit.
Steffens ('stɛfənz) *n* (**Joseph**) **Lincoln.** 1866–1936, U.S. political analyst, known for his exposure of political corruption.
stegodon ('stɛgəˌdɒn) *or* **stegodont** ('stɛgəˌdɒnt) *n* any proboscidean mammal of the genus *Stegodon,* of Pliocene to Pleistocene times, similar to the mastodons. [C19: New Latin (literally: ridge-toothed), from Greek *stegos* roof, from *stegein* to cover + *odōn* tooth]
stegomyia (ˌstɛgə'maɪə) *n* a former name for **aedes.** [C19: from Greek *stegos* roof + *-myia,* from *muia* a fly]
stegosaur ('stɛgəˌsɔː) *or* **stegosaurus** (ˌstɛgə'sɔːrəs) *n* any quadrupedal herbivorous ornithischian dinosaur of the suborder *Stegosauria,* esp. any of the

genus *Stegosaurus,* of Jurassic and early Cretaceous times, having an armour of bony plates. [C19: from Greek *stegos* roof + -SAUR]

Steier (*German* 'ʃtaiər) *n* a variant spelling of **Steyr**.

Steiermark ('ʃtaiərˌmark) *n* the German name for **Styria**.

stein (staɪn) *n* **1** an earthenware beer mug, esp. of a German design. **2** the quantity contained in such a mug. [German, literally: STONE]

Stein *n* **1** (staɪn). **Gertrude**. 1874–1946, U.S. writer, resident in Paris (1903–1946). Her works include *Three Lives* (1908) and *The Autobiography of Alice B. Toklas* (1933). **2** (*German* ʃtain). **Heinrich Friedrich Carl** ('hainrɪç 'friːdrɪç karl), Baron Stein. 1757–1831, Prussian statesman, who contributed greatly to the modernization of Prussia and played a major role in the European coalition against Napoleon (1813–15). **3** (stiːn) **Jock**, real name *John.* 1922–85, Scottish footballer and manager: managed Celtic (1965–78) and Scotland (1978–85).

Steinbeck ('staɪnbɛk) *n* **John** (**Ernst**). 1902–68, U.S. writer, noted for his novels about agricultural workers, esp. *The Grapes of Wrath* (1939): Nobel prize for literature 1962.

steinbock ('staɪnˌbɒk) *n* another name for **ibex**. [C17: from German *Steinbock;* compare STEENBOK]

steinbok ('staɪnˌbɒk) *n, pl* **-boks** *or* **-bok**. a variant spelling of **steenbok**.

Steiner ('staɪnə; *German* 'ʃtainər) *n* **Rudolf** ('ruːdɔlf). 1861–1925, Austrian philosopher, founder of anthroposophy. He was particularly influential in education. See also **anthroposophy**.

Steinitz ('staɪnɪts; *German* 'ʃtainɪts) *n* **Wilhelm** ('vɪlhɛlm). 1836–1900, U.S. chess player, born in Prague; world champion (1866–94).

Steinway ('staɪnweɪ) *n* **Henry** (**Engelhard**), original name *Heinrich Engelhardt Steinweg.* 1797–1871, U.S. piano maker, born in Germany.

stele ('stiːlɪ, stiːl) *n, pl* **stelae** ('stiːliː) *or* **steles** ('stiːlɪz, stiːlz). **1** an upright stone slab or column decorated with figures or inscriptions, common in prehistoric times. **2** a prepared vertical surface that has a commemorative inscription or design, esp. one on the face of a building. **3** the conducting tissue of the stems and roots of plants, which is in the form of a cylinder, principally containing xylem, phloem, and pericycle. See also **protostele, siphonostele.** ◆ Also called (for senses 1, 2): **stela** ('stiːlə). [C19: from Greek *stēlē;* related to Greek *histanai* to stand, Latin *stāre*] ▸ **stelar** ('stiːlə) *adj*

stellar ('stɛlə) *adj* **1** of, relating to, involving, or resembling a star or stars. **2** of or relating to star entertainers. **3** *Informal.* outstanding or immense: *companies are registering stellar profits.* [C17: from Late Latin *stellāris,* from Latin *stella* star]

stellarator ('stɛləˌreɪtə) *n Physics.* an apparatus used in research into thermonuclear reactions, consisting of a toroidal vessel designed so that a plasma may be contained within it by a magnetic field. [C20: from STELLAR + (GENER)ATOR]

stellar evolution *n Astronomy.* the sequence of changes that occurs in a star as it ages.

stellate ('stɛlɪt, -eɪt) *or* **stellated** *adj* resembling a star in shape; radiating from the centre: *a stellate arrangement of petals.* [C16: from Latin *stellātus* starry, from *stellāre* to stud with stars, from *stella* a star] ▸ **'stellately** *adv*

stelliferous (stɛ'lɪfərəs) *adj* full of stars. [C16: from Latin *stellifer* star-bearing, from *stella* star; see -FEROUS]

stelliform ('stɛlɪˌfɔːm) *adj* star-shaped. [C18: from New Latin *stelliformis,* from Latin *stella* star + *forma* shape]

stellify ('stɛlɪˌfaɪ) *vb* **-fies, -fying, -fied.** to change or be changed into a star. [C14: from Latin *stella* a star]

Stellite ('stɛlaɪt) *n Trademark.* any of various alloys containing cobalt, chromium, carbon, tungsten, and molybdenum: characteristically very hard and wear resistant, they are used as castings or hard surface-coatings.

stellular ('stɛljʊlə) *adj* **1** displaying or abounding in small stars: *a stellular pattern.* **2** resembling a little star or little stars. [C18: from Late Latin *stellula,* diminutive of Latin *stella* star] ▸ **'stellularly** *adv*

stem[1] (stɛm) *n* **1** the main axis of a plant, which bears the leaves, axillary buds, and flowers and contains a hollow cylinder of vascular tissue. **2** any similar subsidiary structure in such plants that bears a flower, fruit, or leaf. **3** a corresponding structure in algae and fungi. **4** any long slender part, such as the hollow part of a tobacco pipe that lies between the bit and the bowl, or the support between the base and the bowl of a wineglass, goblet, etc. **5** a banana stalk with several bunches attached. **6** the main line of descent or branch of a family. **7** a round pin in some locks on which a socket in the end of a key fits and about which it rotates. **8** any shank or cylindrical pin or rod, such as the pin that carries the winding knob on a watch. **9** *Linguistics.* the form of a word that remains after removal of all inflectional affixes; the root of a word, esp. as occurring together with a thematic element. Compare **root**[1] (sense 9). **10** the main, usually vertical, stroke of a letter or of a musical note such as a minim. **11** *Electronics.* the tubular glass section projecting from the base of a light bulb or electronic valve, on which the filament or electrodes are mounted. **12a** the main upright timber or structure at the bow of a vessel. **12b** the very forward end of a vessel (esp. in the phrase **from stem to stern**). ◆ *vb* **stems, stemming, stemmed. 13** (*intr;* usually foll. by *from*) to be derived; originate. **14** (*tr*) to make headway against (a tide, wind, etc.). **15** (*tr*) to remove or disengage the stem or stems from. **16** (*tr*) to supply (something) with a stem or stems. [Old English *stemn;* related to Old Norse *stafn* stem of a ship, German *Stamm* tribe, Gothic *stōma* basis, Latin *stāmen* thread] ▸ **'stemˌlike** *adj* ▸ **'stemmer** *n*

stem[2] (stɛm) *vb* **stems, stemming, stemmed. 1** (*tr*) to restrain or stop (the flow of something) by or as if by damming up. **2** (*tr*) to pack tightly or stop up. **3** *Skiing.* to manoeuvre (a ski or skis), as in performing a stem. ◆ *n* **4** *Skiing.* a technique in which the heel of one ski or both skis is forced outwards from the direction of movement in order to slow down or turn. [C15 *stemmen,* from Old Norse *stemma;* related to Old Norse *stamr* blocked, stammering, German *stemmen* to prop; see STAMMER] ▸ **'stemmer** *n*

stem-and-leaf diagram *n Statistics.* a histogram in which the data points falling within each class interval are listed in order.

stem cell *n Histology.* an undifferentiated cell that gives rise to specialized cells, such as blood cells.

stem ginger *n* the choice pieces of the underground stem of the ginger plant, which are crystallized or preserved in syrup and eaten as a sweetmeat.

stemhead ('stɛmˌhɛd) *n Nautical.* the head of the stem of a vessel.

stemma ('stɛmə) *n* a family tree; pedigree. [C19: via Latin from Greek *stemma* garland, wreath, from *stephein* to crown, wreathe]

stemmed (stɛmd) *adj* **1a** having a stem. **1b** (*in combination*): *a thin-stemmed plant; a long-stemmed glass.* **2** having had the stem or stems removed.

stemson ('stɛmsən) *n Nautical.* a curved timber scarfed into or bolted to the stem and keelson at the bow of a wooden vessel. Compare **sternson.** [C18: from STEM[1] + (KEEL)SON]

stem turn *n Skiing.* a turn in which the heel of one ski is stemmed and the other ski is brought parallel. Also called: **stem.**

stemware ('stɛmˌwɛə) *n* a collective term for glasses, goblets, etc., with stems.

stem-winder *n* a watch wound by an expanded crown on the bar projecting outside the case, as opposed to one wound by a separate key. Also called: **stem-winding watch.**

stench (stɛntʃ) *n* a strong and extremely offensive odour; stink. [Old English *stenc;* related to Old Saxon, Old High German *stank;* see STINK]

stench trap *n* a trap in a sewer that by means of a water seal prevents the upward passage of foul-smelling gases. Also called: **stink trap.**

stencil ('stɛnsᵊl) *n* **1** a device for applying a design, characters, etc., to a surface, consisting of a thin sheet of plastic, metal, cardboard, etc. in which the design or characters have been cut so that ink or paint can be applied through the incisions onto the surface. **2** a decoration, design, or characters produced in this way. ◆ *vb* **-cils, -cilling, -cilled** *or U.S.* **-cils, -ciling, -ciled.** (*tr*) **3** to mark (a surface) with a stencil. **4** to produce (characters or a design) with a stencil. [C14 *stanselen* to decorate with bright colours, from Old French *estenceler,* from *estencele* a spark, from Latin *scintilla*] ▸ **'stenciller** *n*

Stendhal (*French* stɛ̃dal) *n* original name *Marie Henri Beyle.* 1783–1842, French writer, who anticipated later novelists in his psychological analysis of character. His two chief novels are *Le Rouge et le noir* (1830) and *La Chartreuse de Parme* (1839).

stengah ('stɛŋgə) *n* another name for **stinger** (sense 3). [from Malay *sa tengah* one half]

Sten gun (stɛn) *n* a light 9 mm sub-machine-gun formerly used in the British Army and Commonwealth forces. [C20: from *s* and *t* (initials of Shepherd and Turpin, the inventors) + *-en,* as in BREN GUN]

steno ('stɛnəʊ) *n, pl* **stenos.** *U.S. and Canadian informal.* short for **stenographer.**

steno- *or before a vowel* **sten-** *combining form.* indicating narrowness or contraction: *stenography; stenosis.* [from Greek *stenos* narrow]

stenograph ('stɛnəˌgræf, -ˌgrɑːf) *n* **1** any of various keyboard machines for writing in shorthand. **2** any character used in shorthand. ◆ *vb* **3** (*tr*) to record (speeches, minutes, letters, etc.) in shorthand.

stenographer (stə'nɒgrəfə) *n* the U.S. and Canadian name for **shorthand typist.**

stenography (stə'nɒgrəfɪ) *n* **1** the act or process of writing in shorthand by hand or machine. **2** matter written in shorthand. ▸ **stenographic** (ˌstɛnə'græfɪk) *or* **ˌsteno'graphical** *adj* ▸ **ˌsteno'graphically** *adv*

stenohaline (ˌstɛnəʊ'heɪliːn, -laɪn) *adj* (of certain aquatic animals) able to exist only within a narrow range of salinity. Compare **euryhaline.** [C20: from STENO- + *haline,* from Greek *hals* salt + -INE[1]]

stenopetalous (ˌstɛnəʊ'petᵊləs) *adj* (of flowers) having narrow petals.

stenophagous (stə'nɒfəgəs) *adj* (of animals) feeding on a single type or limited variety of food. [C17: from STENO- + *-phagous* (via Latin from Greek *phagos* eating)]

stenophyllous (ˌstɛnəʊ'fɪləs) *adj* (of plants) having narrow leaves.

stenosis (stɪ'nəʊsɪs) *n, pl* **-ses** (-siːz). *Pathol.* an abnormal narrowing of a bodily canal or passage. [C19: via New Latin from Greek *stenōsis,* from *stenoun* to constrict, from *stenos* narrow] ▸ **stenotic** (stɪ'nɒtɪk) *adj*

stenothermal (ˌstɛnə'θɜːməl) *adj* (of animals or plants) able to exist only within a narrow range of temperature. Compare **eurythermal.**

stenotopic (ˌstɛnəʊ'tɒpɪk) *adj Ecology.* (of a species, group, etc.) able to tolerate only a narrow range of environmental changes. Also (sometimes (influenced by -TROPIC)): **stenotropic.** Compare **eurytopic.** [from STENO- + *top* from Greek *topos* place + -IC]

Stenotype ('stɛnəˌtaɪp) *n* **1** *Trademark.* a machine with a keyboard for recording speeches, etc., in a phonetic shorthand. **2** any machine resembling this. **3** the phonetic symbol typed in one stroke of such a machine.

stenotypy ('stɛnəˌtaɪpɪ) *n* a form of shorthand in which alphabetic combinations are used to represent groups of sounds or short common words. [C19: from STENO- + TYPE + -Y[3], on the model of STENOGRAPHY] ▸ **stenotypic** (ˌstɛnə'tɪpɪk) *adj* ▸ **'stenoˌtypist** *n*

stentor ('stɛntɔː) *n* **1** a person with an unusually loud voice. **2** any trumpet-shaped protozoan of the genus *Stentor,* having a ciliated spiral feeding funnel at the wider end: phylum *Ciliophora* (ciliates). [C19: after STENTOR]

Stentor ('stɛntɔː) *n Greek myth.* a Greek herald with a powerful voice who died after he lost a shouting contest with Hermes, herald of the gods.

stentorian (stɛn'tɔːrɪən) *adj* (of the voice, etc.) uncommonly loud: *stentorian tones.*

step (stɛp) *n* **1** the act of motion brought about by raising the foot and setting it down again in coordination with the transference of the weight of the body. **2** the distance or space covered by such a motion. **3** the sound made by such a movement. **4** the impression made by such movement of the foot; footprint. **5**

the manner of walking or moving the feet; gait: *he received his prize with a proud step.* **6** a sequence of foot movements that make up a particular dance or part of a dance: *I have mastered the steps of the waltz.* **7** any of several paces or rhythmic movements in marching, dancing, etc.: *the goose step.* **8** (*pl*) a course followed by a person in walking or as walking: *they followed in their leader's steps.* **9** one of a sequence of separate consecutive stages in the progression towards some goal: *another step towards socialism.* **10** a rank or grade in a series or scale: *he was always a step behind.* **11** an object or device that offers support for the foot when ascending or descending. **12** (*pl*) a flight of stairs, esp. out of doors. **13** (*pl*) another name for **stepladder. 14** a very short easily walked distance: *it is only a step to my place.* **15** *Music.* a melodic interval of a second. See **whole tone, half-step. 16** an offset or change in the level of a surface similar to the step of a stair. **17** a strong block or frame bolted onto the keel of a vessel and fitted to receive the base of a mast. **18** a ledge cut in mining or quarrying excavations. **19 break step.** to cease to march in step. **20 keep step.** to remain walking, marching, dancing, etc., in unison or in a specified rhythm. **21 in step. 21a** marching, dancing, etc., in conformity with a specified pace or moving in unison with others. **21b** *Informal.* in agreement or harmony. **22 out of step. 22a** not moving in conformity with a specified pace or in accordance with others. **22b** *Informal.* not in agreement; out of harmony. **23 step by step.** with care and deliberation; gradually. **24 take steps.** to undertake measures (to do something) with a view to the attainment of some end. **25 watch one's step. 25a** *Informal.* to conduct oneself with caution and good behaviour. **25b** to walk or move carefully. ◆ *vb* **steps, stepping, stepped. 26** (*intr*) to move by raising the foot and then setting it down in a different position, transferring the weight of the body to this foot and repeating the process with the other foot. **27** (*intr;* often foll. by *in, out,* etc.) to move or go on foot, esp. for a short distance: *step this way, ladies.* **28** (*intr*) *Informal, chiefly U.S.* to move, often in an attractive graceful manner, as in dancing: *he can really step around.* **29** (*intr;* usually foll. by *on* or *upon*) to place or press the foot; tread: *to step on the accelerator.* **30** (*intr;* usually foll. by *into*) to enter (into a situation) apparently with ease: *she stepped into a life of luxury.* **31** (*tr*) to walk or take (a number of paces, etc.): *to step ten paces.* **32** (*tr*) to perform the steps of: *they step the tango well.* **33** (*tr*) to set or place (the foot). **34** (*tr;* usually foll. by *off* or *out*) to measure (some distance of ground) by stepping. **35** (*tr*) to arrange in or supply with a series of steps so as to avoid coincidence or symmetry. **36** (*tr*) to raise (a mast) and fit it into its step. ◆ See also **step down, step in, step on, step out, step up.** [Old English *stepe, stæpe;* related to Old Frisian *stap, stepe,* Old High German *stapfo* (German *Stapfe* footprint), Old Norse *stapi* high rock] ► **'step,like** *adj*

Step (stɛp) *n* **a** a set of aerobic exercises designed to improve the cardiovascular system, which consists of stepping on and off a special box of adjustable height. **b** (*as modifier*): *Step aerobics.*

STEP (stɛp) *n acronym for* Special Temporary Employment Programme.

step- *combining form.* indicating relationship through the previous marriage of a spouse or parent rather than by blood: *stepson; stepfather.* [Old English *stēop-;* compare *āstȳpan* to bereave]

stepbrother ('stɛp,brʌðə) *n* a son of one's stepmother or stepfather by a union with someone other than one's father or mother respectively.

stepchild ('stɛp,tʃaɪld) *n, pl* **-children.** a stepson or stepdaughter.

stepdame ('stɛp,deɪm) *n* an archaic word for **stepmother.** [C14: from STEP- + DAME (in the archaic sense: mother; see DAM[2])]

step dance *n* a dance in which a display of steps is more important than gesture or posture, esp. a solo dance.

stepdaughter ('stɛp,dɔːtə) *n* a daughter of one's husband or wife by a former union.

step down *vb* (*adv*) **1** (*tr*) to reduce gradually. **2** (*intr*) *Informal.* to resign or abdicate (from a position). **3** (*intr*) *Informal.* to assume an inferior or less senior position. ◆ *adj* **step-down.** (*prenominal*) **4** (of a transformer) reducing a high voltage applied to the primary winding to a lower voltage on the secondary winding. Compare **step-up** (sense 3). **5** decreasing or falling by stages. ◆ *n* **step-down. 6** *Informal.* a decrease in quantity or size.

stepfather ('stɛp,fɑːðə) *n* a man who has married one's mother after the death or divorce of one's father.

step function *n* an electrical waveform that rises or falls instantly from one level to another.

stephanotis (,stɛfə'nəʊtɪs) *n* any climbing asclepiadaceous shrub of the genus *Stephanotis,* esp. *S. floribunda,* of Madagascar and Malaya: cultivated for their fragrant white waxy flowers. [C19: via New Latin from Greek: fit for a crown, from *stephanos* a crown]

Stephen ('stiːvᵊn) *n* **1** ?1097–1154, king of England (1135–54); grandson of William the Conqueror. He seized the throne on the death of Henry I, causing civil war with Henry's daughter Matilda. He eventually recognized her son (later Henry II) as his successor. **2 Saint.** died ?35 A.D., the first Christian martyr. Feast day: Dec. 26 or 27. **3 Saint,** Hungarian name *István.* ?975–1038 A.D., first king of Hungary as Stephen I (997–1038). Feast day: Aug. 16 or 20. **4** Sir **Leslie.** 1832–1904, English biographer, critic, and first editor of the *Dictionary of National Biography;* father of the novelist Virginia Woolf.

Stephenson ('stiːvənsən) *n* **1 George.** 1781–1848, British inventor of the first successful steam locomotive (1814); constructed the first railway line to carry passengers, the Stockton and Darlington Railway (opened 1825). **2** his son, **Robert.** 1803–59, British engineer, noted for his construction of railway bridges and viaducts, esp. the tubular bridge over the Menai Strait.

step in *vb* **1** (*intr, adv*) *Informal.* to intervene or involve oneself, esp. dramatically or at a senior level. ◆ *adj* **step-in. 2** (*prenominal*) (of garments, etc.) put on by being stepped into; without fastenings. **3** (of a ski binding) engaging automatically when the boot is positioned on the ski. ◆ *n* **step-in. 4** (*often pl*) a step-in garment, esp. underwear.

stepladder ('stɛp,lædə) *n* a folding portable ladder that is made of broad flat steps fixed to a supporting frame hinged at the top to another supporting frame.

stepmother ('stɛp,mʌðə) *n* a woman who has married one's father after the death or divorce of one's mother.

step on *vb* (*intr, prep*) **1** to place or press the foot on. **2** *Informal.* to behave harshly or contemptuously towards. **3** *Drugs slang.* to adulterate. **4 step on it.** *Informal.* to go more quickly, hurry up.

step out *vb* (*intr, adv*) **1** to go outside or leave a room, building, etc., esp. briefly. **2** to begin to walk more quickly and take longer strides. **3** *U.S. and Canadian informal.* to withdraw from involvement; bow out.

step-parent ('stɛp,pɛərənt) *n* a stepfather or stepmother. ► **'step-,parenting** *n*

steppe (stɛp) *n* (*often pl*) an extensive grassy plain usually without trees. Compare **prairie, pampas.** [C17: from Old Russian *step* lowland]

stepper ('stɛpə) *n* a person who or animal that steps, esp. a horse or a dancer.

Steppes (stɛps) *pl n* **the. 1** the huge grasslands of Eurasia, chiefly in the Ukraine and Russia. **2** another name for **Kyrgyz Steppe.**

stepping stone *n* **1** one of a series of stones acting as footrests for crossing streams, marshes, etc. **2** a circumstance that assists progress towards some goal.

stepsister ('stɛp,sɪstə) *n* a daughter of one's stepmother or stepfather by a union with someone other than one's father or mother respectively.

stepson ('stɛp,sʌn) *n* a son of one's husband or wife by a former union.

step up *vb* (*adv*) *Informal.* **1** (*tr*) to increase or raise by stages; accelerate. **2** (*intr*) to make progress or effect an advancement; be promoted. ◆ *adj* **step-up.** (*prenominal*) **3** (of a transformer) increasing a low voltage applied to the primary winding to a higher voltage on the secondary winding. Compare **step-down** (sense 4). **4** *Informal.* involving a rise by stages. ◆ *n* **step-up. 5** *Informal.* an increment in quantity, size, etc.

stepwise ('stɛp,waɪz) *adj* **1** arranged in the manner of or resembling steps. **2** *Music, U.S.* proceeding by melodic intervals of a second. ◆ *adv* **3** with the form or appearance of steps; step by step. **4** *Music, U.S.* in a stepwise motion.

ster. *abbrev. for* sterling.

-ster *suffix forming nouns.* **1** indicating a person who is engaged in a certain activity: *prankster; songster.* Compare **-stress. 2** indicating a person associated with or being something specified: *mobster; youngster.* [Old English *-estre*]

steradian (stə'reɪdɪən) *n* an SI unit of solid angle; the angle that, having its vertex in the centre of a sphere, cuts off an area of the surface of the sphere equal to the square of the length of the radius. Symbol: sr [C19: from STEREO- + RADIAN]

stercoraceous (,stɜːkə'reɪʃəs) *adj* of, relating to, or consisting of dung or excrement. [C18: from Latin *stercus* dung + -ACEOUS]

stercoricolous (,stɜːkə'rɪkələs) *adj* (of organisms) living in dung. [C19: from Latin *stercus* dung + *colere* to live]

sterculiaceous (stɜː,kjuːlɪ'eɪʃəs) *adj* of, relating to, or belonging to the *Sterculiaceae,* a chiefly tropical family of plants that includes cacao and cola. [C18: via New Latin from Latin *Sterculius* god of manuring, from *stercus* dung, alluding to the odour of some species]

stere (stɪə) *n* a unit used to measure volumes of stacked timber equal to one cubic metre (35.315 cubic feet). [C18: from French *stère,* from Greek *stereos* solid]

stereo ('stɛrɪəʊ, 'stɪər-) *adj* **1** short for **stereophonic** or **stereoscopic.** ◆ *n, pl* **stereos. 2** stereophonic sound: *to broadcast in stereo.* **3** a stereophonic record player, tape recorder, etc. **4** *Photog.* **4a** stereoscopic photography. **4b** a stereoscopic photograph. **5** *Printing.* short for **stereotype.** [C20: shortened form]

stereo- *or sometimes before a vowel* **stere-** *combining form.* indicating three-dimensional quality or solidity: *stereoscope.* [from Greek *stereos* solid]

stereobate ('stɛrɪəʊ,beɪt, 'stɪər-) *n* **1** another name for **stylobate. 2** a foundation of a building in the form of a platform of masonry. [C19: via Latin, from Greek *stereobatēs* from *stereos* solid + *-batēs* base, from *bainein* to walk]

stereochemistry (,stɛrɪəʊ'kɛmɪstrɪ, ,stɪər-) *n* the study of the spatial arrangement of atoms in molecules and the effect of spatial arrangement on chemical properties.

stereochrome ('stɛrɪəʊ,krəʊm, 'stɪər-) *n* **1** a picture made by stereochromy. ◆ *vb* **2** (*tr*) to produce (a picture) by the process of stereochromy.

stereochromy ('stɛrɪə,krəʊmɪ, 'stɪər-) *n* a method of wall painting in which water glass is used either as a painting medium or as a final fixative coat. [C19: via German *Stereochromie,* from STEREO- + Greek *khrōma* colour]

stereognosis (,stɛrɪɒg'nəʊsɪs, ,stɪər-) *n* the perception of depth or three-dimensionality through any of the senses. [C20: STEREO- + GNOSIS]

stereogram ('stɛrɪə,græm, 'stɪər-) *n* **1** *Brit.* a stereo radiogram. **2** another name for **stereograph.**

stereograph ('stɛrɪə,græf, -,grɑːf, 'stɪər-) *n* two almost identical pictures, or one special picture, that when viewed through special glasses or a stereoscope form a single three-dimensional image. Also called: **stereogram.**

stereography (,stɛrɪ'ɒgrəfɪ, ,stɪər-) *n* **1** the study and construction of geometrical solids. **2** the art of drawing a solid figure on a flat surface. ► **stereographic** (,stɛrɪə'græfɪk, ,stɪər-) *or* **,stereo'graphical** *adj* ► **,stereo'graphically** *adv*

stereoisomer (,stɛrɪəʊ'aɪsəmə, ,stɪər-) *n Chem.* one of the isomers of a compound that exhibits stereoisomerism.

stereoisomerism (,stɛrɪəʊaɪ'sɒmə,rɪzəm, ,stɪər-) *n Chem.* isomerism caused by differences in the spatial arrangement of atoms in molecules. ► **stereoisometric** (,stɛrɪəʊ,aɪsə'mɛtrɪk, ,stɪər-) *adj*

stereome ('stɛrɪ,əʊm) *n Botany.* the tissue of a plant that provides mechanical support.

stereometry (,stɛrɪ'ɒmɪtrɪ, ,stɪər-) *n* the measurement of volume. ► **stereometric** (,stɛrɪəʊ'mɛtrɪk, ,stɪər-) *or* **,stereo'metrical** *adj*

stereophonic (,stɛrɪə'fɒnɪk, ,stɪər-) *adj* (of a system for recording, reproducing, or broadcasting sound) using two or more separate microphones to feed two or more loudspeakers through separate channels in order to give a spatial effect to the sound. Often shortened to **stereo.** Compare **monophonic, quadraphonics.** ▸ **ˌstereoˈphonically** *adv* ▸ **stereophony** (ˌstɛrɪˈɒfənɪ, ˌstɪər-) *n*

stereopsis (ˌstɛrɪˈɒpsɪs, ˌstɪər-) *n* stereoscopic vision. [from STEREO- + Greek *opsis* vision]

stereopticon (ˌstɛrɪˈɒptɪkᵊn, ˌstɪər-) *n* a type of projector with two complete units arranged so that one picture dissolves as the next is forming. [C19: from STEREO- + Greek *optikon,* neuter form of *optikos* OPTIC]

stereoscope (ˈstɛrɪəˌskəʊp, ˈstɪər-) *n* an optical instrument for viewing two-dimensional pictures and giving them an illusion of depth and relief. It has a binocular eyepiece through which two slightly different pictures of the same object are viewed, one with each eye.

stereoscopic (ˌstɛrɪəˈskɒpɪk, ˌstɪər-) *adj* **1** of, concerned with, or relating to seeing space three-dimensionally as a result of binocular disparity: *stereoscopic vision.* **2** of, relating to, or formed by a stereoscope. ▸ **ˌstereoˈscopically** *adv*

stereoscopy (ˌstɛrɪˈɒskəpɪ, ˌstɪər-) *n* **1** the viewing or appearance of objects in or as if in three dimensions. **2** the study and use of the stereoscope. ▸ **ˌstereˈoscopist** *n*

stereospecific (ˌstɛrɪəʊspɪˈsɪfɪk, ˌstɪər-) *adj Chem.* relating to or having fixed position in space, as in the spatial arrangements of atoms in certain polymers.

stereospecific catalyst *n Chem.* a catalyst for stereospecific chemical reactions. See also **Ziegler catalyst.**

stereospecific polymer *n* an organic polymer in which the steric arrangements of groups on assymetric carbon atoms occur in a regular sequence. Many natural and synthetic rubbers are stereospecific polymers.

stereotactic (ˌstɛrɪəˈtæktɪk, ˌstɪər-) *adj* **1** of or relating to stereotaxis. **2** *Med.* of or relating to precise localization of a tissue, esp. in the brain: *stereotactic surgery.* ▸ **ˌstereoˈtactically** *adv*

stereotaxis (ˌstɛrɪəˈtæksɪs, ˌstɪər-) *n* the movement of an organism in response to the stimulus of contact with a solid object. [C20: from STEREO- + -TAXIS]

stereotomy (ˌstɛrɪˈɒtəmɪ, ˌstɪər-) *n* the art of cutting three-dimensional solids into particular shapes. [C18: from French *stéréotomie.* See STEREO-, -TOMY]

stereotropism (ˌstɛrɪˈɒtrəˌpɪzəm, ˌstɪər-) *n* another name for **thigmotropism.** ▸ **stereotropic** (ˌstɛrɪəˈtrɒpɪk, ˌstɪər-) *adj*

stereotype (ˈstɛrɪəˌtaɪp, ˈstɪər-) *n* **1a** a method of producing cast-metal printing plates from a mould made from a forme of type matter in papier-mâché or some other material. **1b** the plate so made. **2** another word for **stereotypy. 3** an idea, trait, convention, etc., that has grown stale through fixed usage. **4** *Sociol.* a set of inaccurate, simplistic generalizations about a group that allows others to categorize them and treat them accordingly. ◆ *vb (tr)* **5a** to make a stereotype of. **5b** to print from a stereotype. **6** to impart a fixed usage or convention to. ▸ **ˈstereoˌtyper** *or* **ˈstereoˌtypist** *n* ▸ **stereotypic** (ˌstɛrɪəˈtɪpɪk, ˌstɪər-) *or* **ˌstereoˈtypical** *adj*

stereotyped (ˈstɛrɪəˌtaɪpt, ˈstɪər-) *adj* **1** lacking originality or individuality; conventional; trite. **2** reproduced from or on a stereotype printing plate.

stereotypy (ˈstɛrɪəˌtaɪpɪ, ˈstɪər-) *n* **1** the act or process of making stereotype printing plates. **2** a tendency to think or act in rigid, repetitive, and often meaningless patterns.

stereovision (ˈstɛrɪəʊˌvɪʒən, ˈstɪər-) *n* the perception or exhibition of three-dimensional objects in three dimensions.

steric (ˈstɛrɪk, ˈstɪər-) *or* **sterical** *adj Chem.* of, concerned with, or caused by the spatial arrangement of atoms in a molecule. [C19: from STEREO- + -IC] ▸ **ˈsterically** *adv*

sterigma (stəˈrɪgmə) *n Biology.* a minute stalk bearing a spore or chain of spores in certain fungi. [C19: New Latin from Greek *stērigma* support, from *stērizein* to sustain]

sterilant (ˈstɛrɪlənt) *n* any substance or agent used in sterilization.

sterile (ˈstɛraɪl) *adj* **1** unable to produce offspring; infertile. **2** free from living, esp. pathogenic, microorganisms; aseptic. **3** (of plants or their parts) not producing or bearing seeds, fruit, spores, stamens, or pistils. **4** lacking inspiration or vitality; fruitless. **5** *Economics, U.S.* (of gold) not being used to support credit creation or an increased money supply. [C16: from Latin *sterilis*] ▸ **ˈsterilely** *adv* ▸ **sterility** (stɛˈrɪlɪtɪ) *n*

sterilization *or* **sterilisation** (ˌstɛrɪlaɪˈzeɪʃən) *n* **1** the act or procedure of sterilizing or making sterile. **2** the state of being sterile; sterilized condition.

sterilize *or* **sterilise** (ˈstɛrɪˌlaɪz) *vb (tr)* to render sterile; make infertile or barren. ▸ **ˈsteriˌlizable** *or* **ˈsteriˌlisable** *adj* ▸ **ˈsteriˌlizer** *or* **ˈsteriˌliser** *n*

sterlet (ˈstɜːlɪt) *n* a small sturgeon, *Acipenser ruthenus,* of seas and rivers in N Asia and E Europe: used as a food fish and a source of caviar. [C16: from Russian *sterlyad,* of Germanic origin; compare Old High German *sturio* sturgeon]

sterling (ˈstɜːlɪŋ) *n* **1a** British money: *pound sterling.* **1b** (*as modifier*): *sterling reserves.* **2** the official standard of fineness of British coins: for gold 0.91666 and for silver 0.925. **3a** short for **sterling silver. 3b** (*as modifier*): *a sterling bracelet.* **4** an article or articles manufactured from sterling silver. **5** a former British silver penny. ◆ *adj* **6** (*prenominal*) genuine and reliable; first-class: *sterling quality.* [C13: probably from Old English *steorra* STAR + -LING[1]; referring to a small star on early Norman pennies; related to Old French *esterlin*]

Sterling (ˈstɜːlɪŋ) *n* **Peter.** born 1960, Australian rugby league player.

sterling area *n* a group of countries that use sterling as a medium of international payments and sometimes informally as a currency against which to peg their own currencies. For these purposes they deposit sterling balances and hold gold and dollar reserves in the Bank of England. Also called: **sterling bloc, scheduled territories.**

sterling silver *n* **1** an alloy containing not less than 92.5 per cent of silver, the remainder usually being copper. **2** sterling-silver articles collectively.

Sterlitamak (*Russian* stjerlitaˈmak) *n* an industrial city in W Russia, in the Bashkir Republic. Pop.: 259 000 (1995 est.).

stern[1] (stɜːn) *adj* **1** showing uncompromising or inflexible resolve; firm, strict, or authoritarian. **2** lacking leniency or clemency; harsh or severe. **3** relentless; unyielding: *the stern demands of parenthood.* **4** having an austere or forbidding appearance or nature. [Old English *styrne;* related to Old High German *stornēn* to alarm, Latin *sternāx* stubborn, Greek *stereos* hard] ▸ **ˈsternly** *adv* ▸ **ˈsternness** *n*

stern[2] (stɜːn) *n* **1** the rear or after part of a vessel, opposite the bow or stem. **2** the rear part of any object. **3** the tail of certain breeds of dog, such as the foxhound or beagle. ◆ *adj* **4** relating to or located at the stern. [C13: from Old Norse *stjōrn* steering; see STEER[1]]

Stern (stɜːn) *n* **Isaac.** born 1920, U.S. concert violinist, born in Russia.

Sternberg (ˈstɜːnˌbɜːg, ˈʃtɜːn-) *n* See (Joseph) **von Sternberg.**

stern-chaser *n* a gun mounted at the stern of a vessel for firing aft at a pursuing vessel.

Sterne (stɜːn) *n* **Laurence.** 1713–68, English novelist, born in Ireland, author of *The Life and Opinions of Tristram Shandy, Gentleman* (1759–67) and *A Sentimental Journey through France and Italy* (1768).

sternforemost (ˈstɜːnˈfɔːməʊst) *adv Nautical.* backwards.

sternmost (ˈstɜːnˌməʊst) *adj Nautical.* **1** farthest to the stern; aftmost. **2** nearest the stern.

sternpost (ˈstɜːnˌpəʊst) *n Nautical.* the main upright timber or structure at the stern of a vessel.

stern sheets *pl n Nautical.* the part of an open boat near the stern.

sternson (ˈstɜːnsᵊn) *n Nautical.* a timber scarfed into or bolted to the sternpost and keelson at the stern of a wooden vessel. Compare **stemson.** [C19: from STERN[2] + *-son,* on the model of KEELSON]

sternum (ˈstɜːnəm) *n, pl* **-na** (-nə) *or* **-nums. 1** (in man) a long flat vertical bone, situated in front of the thorax, to which are attached the collarbone and the first seven pairs of ribs. Nontechnical name: **breastbone. 2** the corresponding part in many other vertebrates. **3** a cuticular plate covering the ventral surface of a body segment of an arthropod. Compare **tergum.** [C17: via New Latin from Greek *sternon* breastbone] ▸ **ˈsternal** *adj*

sternutation (ˌstɜːnjuˈteɪʃən) *n* a sneeze or the act of sneezing. [C16: from Late Latin *sternūtāre* to sneeze, from *sternuere* to sputter (of a light)]

sternutator (ˈstɜːnjuˌteɪtə) *n* a substance that causes sneezing, coughing, and tears; used in chemical warfare.

sternutatory (stɜːˈnjuːtətərɪ, -trɪ) *adj also* **sternutative. 1** causing or having the effect of sneezing. ◆ *n, pl* **-tories. 2** an agent or substance that causes sneezing.

sternwards (ˈstɜːnwədz) *or* **sternward** *adv Nautical.* towards the stern; astern.

sternway (ˈstɜːnˌweɪ) *n Nautical.* movement of a vessel sternforemost.

stern-wheeler *n* a vessel, esp. a riverboat, propelled by a large paddle wheel at the stern. Compare **sidewheeler.**

steroid (ˈstɪərɔɪd, ˈstɛr-) *n Biochem.* any of a large group of fat-soluble organic compounds containing a characteristic chemical ring system. The majority, including the sterols, bile acids, many hormones, and the D vitamins, have important physiological action. [C20: from STEROL + -OID] ▸ **steˈroidal** *adj*

sterol (ˈstɛrɒl) *n Biochem.* any of a group of natural steroid alcohols, such as cholesterol and ergosterol, that are waxy insoluble substances. [C20: shortened from CHOLESTEROL, ERGOSTEROL, etc.]

stertor (ˈstɜːtə) *n* laborious or noisy breathing caused by obstructed air passages. [C17: from New Latin, from Latin *stertere* to snore]

stertorous (ˈstɜːtərəs) *adj* **1** marked or accompanied by heavy snoring. **2** breathing in this way. ▸ **ˈstertorously** *adv* ▸ **ˈstertorousness** *n*

stet (stɛt) *n* **1** a word or mark indicating that certain deleted typeset or written matter is to be retained. Compare **dele.** ◆ *vb* **stets, stetting, stetted. 2** *(tr)* to mark (matter to be retained) with a stet. [Latin, literally: let it stand]

stethoscope (ˈstɛθəˌskəʊp) *n Med.* an instrument for listening to the sounds made within the body, typically consisting of a hollow disc that transmits the sound through hollow tubes to earpieces. [C19: from French, from Greek *stēthos* breast + -SCOPE] ▸ **stethoscopic** (ˌstɛθəˈskɒpɪk) *adj* ▸ **stethoscopy** (stɛˈθɒskəpɪ) *n*

Stetson (ˈstɛtsᵊn) *n Trademark.* a type of felt hat with a broad brim and high crown, worn mainly by cowboys. [C20: named after John *Stetson* (1830–1906), American hatmaker who designed it]

Stettin (ʃtɛˈtiːn) *n* the German name for **Szczecin.**

stevedore (ˈstiːvɪˌdɔː) *n* **1** a person employed to load or unload ships. ◆ *vb* **2** to load or unload (a ship, ship's cargo, etc.). [C18: from Spanish *estibador* a packer, from *estibar* to load (a ship), from Latin *stīpāre* to pack full]

stevedore's knot *n* a knot forming a lump in a line, used by stevedores to secure ropes passing through holes.

Stevenage (ˈstiːvənɪdʒ) *n* a town in SE England, in N Hertfordshire on the Great North Road: developed chiefly as the first of the new towns (1946). Pop.: 76 064 (1991).

Stevengraph (ˈstiːvᵊnˌgrɑːf) *or* **Stevensgraph** *n* a picture, usually small, woven in silk. [named after Thomas *Stevens* (1828–88), English weaver]

Stevens (ˈstiːvᵊnz) *n* **1 Thaddeus** (ˈθædɪəs). 1792–1868, U.S. Radical Republican politician. An opponent of slavery, he supported Reconstruction and entered the resolution calling for the impeachment of President Andrew Johnson. **2 Wallace.** 1879–1955, U.S. poet, whose books include the collections *Harmonium* (1923), *The Man with the Blue Guitar* (1937), and *Transport to Summer* (1947).

Stevenson (ˈstiːvənsən) *n* **1 Adlai Ewing** (ˈædleɪ ˈjuːɪŋ). 1900–68, U.S. statesman: twice defeated as Democratic presidential candidate (1952; 1956); U.S. delegate at the United Nations (1961–65). **2 Robert Louis (Balfour).** 1850–94,

Scottish writer: his novels include *Treasure Island* (1883), *Kidnapped* (1886), and *The Master of Ballantrae* (1889).

stew[1] (stju:) *n* **1a** a dish of meat, fish, or other food, cooked by stewing. **1b** (*as modifier*): *stew pot.* **2** *Informal.* a difficult or worrying situation or a troubled state (esp. in the phrase **in a stew**). **3** a heterogeneous mixture: *a stew of people of every race.* **4** (*usually pl*) *Archaic.* a brothel. **5** *Obsolete.* a public room for hot steam baths. ◆ *vb* **6** to cook or cause to cook by long slow simmering. **7** (*intr*) *Informal.* to be troubled or agitated. **8** (*intr*) *Informal.* to be oppressed with heat or crowding. **9** to cause (tea) to become bitter or (of tea) to become bitter through infusing for too long. **10 stew in one's own juice.** to suffer unaided the consequences of one's actions. [C14 *stuen* to take a very hot bath, from Old French *estuver,* from Vulgar Latin *extūfāre* (unattested), from EX-[1] + (unattested) *tūfus* vapour, from Greek *tuphos*]

stew[2] (stju:) *n Brit.* **1** a fishpond or fishtank. **2** an artificial oyster bed. [C14: from Old French *estui,* from *estoier* to shut up, confine, ultimately from Latin *studium* STUDY]

steward ('stjuəd) *n* **1** a person who administers the property, house, finances, etc., of another. **2** a person who manages the eating arrangements, staff, or service at a club, hotel, etc. **3** a waiter on a ship or aircraft. **4** a mess attendant in a naval mess afloat or ashore. **5** a person who helps to supervise some event or proceedings in an official capacity. **6** short for **shop steward.** ◆ *vb* **7** to act or serve as a steward (of something). [Old English *stigweard,* from *stig* hall (see STY) + *weard* WARD] ▸ **'steward,ship** *n*

stewardess ('stjuədɪs, ˌstjuə'dɛs) *n* a woman who performs a steward's job on an aircraft or ship.

Stewart ('stjuət) *n* **1** the usual spelling for the royal house of **Stuart** before the reign of Mary Queen of Scots (Mary Stuart). **2 Jackie,** full name *John Young Stewart.* born 1939, Scottish motor-racing driver: world champion 1969, 1971, and 1973. **3 James** (**Maitland**). 1908–97, U.S. film actor, known for his distinctive drawl; appeared in many films including *Destry Rides Again* (1939), *The Glenn Miller Story* (1953), *Shenandoah* (1965), and *Airport 77* (1977). **4 Rod.** born 1945, British rock singer: vocalist with the Faces (1969–75). His albums include *Gasoline Alley* (1970), *Every Picture Tells a Story* (1971), and *Atlantic Crossing* (1975).

Stewart Island *n* the third largest island of New Zealand, in the SW Pacific off the S tip of South Island. Pop.: 450 (1989 est.). Area: 1735 sq. km (670 sq. miles).

stewed (stju:d) *adj* **1** (of meat, fruit, etc.) cooked by stewing. **2** *Brit.* (of tea) having a bitter taste through having been left to infuse for too long. **3** a slang word for **drunk** (sense 1).

St. Ex. *abbrev. for* stock exchange.

Steyr *or* **Steier** (*German* 'ʃtaiər) *n* an industrial city in N central Austria, in Upper Austria. Pop.: 39 542 (1991).

stg *abbrev. for* sterling.

stge *abbrev. for* storage.

Sth *abbrev. for* South.

sthenic ('sθɛnɪk) *adj* abounding in energy or bodily strength; active or strong. [C18: from New Latin *sthenicus,* from Greek *sthenos* force, on the model of *asthenic*]

Stheno ('sθi:nəu, 'sθɛnəu) *n Greek myth.* one of the three Gorgons.

stibine ('stɪbaɪn) *n* **1** a colourless slightly soluble poisonous gas with an offensive odour: made by the action of hydrochloric acid on an alloy of antimony and zinc. Formula: SbH_3. **2** any one of a class of stibine derivatives in which one or more hydrogen atoms have been replaced by organic groups. [C19: from Latin STIBIUM + -INE[2]]

stibium ('stɪbɪəm) *n* an obsolete name for **antimony.** [C14: from Latin: antimony (used as a cosmetic in ancient Rome), via Greek from Egyptian *stm*] ▸ **'stibial** *adj*

stibnite ('stɪbnaɪt) *n* a soft greyish mineral consisting of antimony sulphide in orthorhombic crystalline form. It occurs in quartz veins and is the chief ore of antimony. Formula: Sb_2S_3. [C19: from obsolete *stibine* stibnite + -ITE[1]]

stich (stɪk) *n* a line of poetry; verse. [C18: from Greek *stikhos* row, verse; related to *steikhein* to walk] ▸ **'stichic** *adj* ▸ **'stichically** *adv*

stichometry (stɪ'kɒmɪtrɪ) *n Prosody.* the practice of writing out a prose text in lines that correspond to the sense units and indicate the phrasal rhythms. [C18: from Late Greek *stikhometria.* See STICH, -METRY] ▸ **stichometric** (ˌstɪkəu'mɛtrɪk) *or* **ˌsticho'metrical** *adj*

stichomythia (ˌstɪkəu'mɪθɪə) *or* **stichomythy** (stɪ'kɒmɪθɪ) *n* a form of dialogue originating in Greek drama in which single lines are uttered by alternate speakers. [C19: from Greek *stikhomuthein* to speak alternate lines, from *stikhos* line + *muthos* speech; see MYTH] ▸ **ˌsticho'mythic** *adj*

-stichous *adj combining form.* having a certain number of rows: *distichous.* [from Late Latin *-stichus,* from Greek *-stikhos,* from *stikhos* line, row; see STICH]

stick[1] (stɪk) *n* **1** a small thin branch of a tree. **2a** any long thin piece of wood. **2b** such a piece of wood having a characteristic shape for a special purpose: *a walking stick; a hockey stick.* **2c** a baton, wand, staff, or rod. **3** an object or piece shaped like a stick: *a stick of celery; a stick of dynamite.* **4** See **control stick. 5** *Informal.* the lever used to change gear in a motor vehicle. **6** *Nautical.* a mast or yard. **7** *Printing.* See **composing stick. 8a** a group of bombs arranged to fall at intervals across a target. **8b** a number of paratroops jumping in sequence. **9** *Slang.* **9a** verbal abuse, criticism: *I got some stick for that blunder.* **9b** physical power, force (esp. in the phrase **give it some stick**). **10** (*usually pl*) a piece of furniture: *these few sticks are all I have.* **11** (*pl*) *Informal.* a rural area considered remote or backward (esp. in the phrase **in the sticks**). **12** (*pl*) *W and NW Canadian informal.* the wooded interior part of the country. **13** (*pl*) *Hockey.* a declaration made by the umpire if a player's stick is above the shoulders. **14** (*pl*) goalposts. **15** *U.S. obsolete.* a cannabis cigarette. **16** a means of coercion. **17** *Informal.* a dull boring person. **18** (usually preceded by *old*) *Informal.* a familiar name for a person: *not a bad old stick.* **19 in a cleft stick.** in a difficult position. **20 wrong end of the stick.** a complete misunderstanding of a situation, explanation, etc. ◆ *vb* **sticks, sticking, sticked. 21** to support (a plant) with sticks; stake. [Old English *sticca;* related to Old Norse *stikka,* Old High German *stecca*]

stick[2] (stɪk) *vb* **sticks, sticking, stuck. 1** (*tr*) to pierce or stab with or as if with something pointed. **2** to thrust or push (a sharp or pointed object) or (of a sharp or pointed object) to be pushed into or through another object. **3** (*tr*) to fasten in position by pushing or forcing a point into something: *to stick a peg in a hole.* **4** (*tr*) to fasten in position by or as if by pins, nails, etc.: *to stick a picture on the wall.* **5** (*tr*) to transfix or impale on a pointed object. **6** (*tr*) to cover with objects piercing or set in the surface. **7** (when *intr,* foll. by *out, up, through,* etc.) to put forward or be put forward; protrude or cause to protrude: *to stick one's head out of the window.* **8** (*tr*) *Informal.* to place or put in a specified position: *stick your coat on this chair.* **9** to fasten or be fastened by or as if by an adhesive substance: *stick the pages together; they won't stick.* **10** (*tr*) *Informal.* to cause to become sticky. **11** (when *tr, usually passive*) to come or cause to come to a standstill: *we were stuck for hours in a traffic jam; the wheels stuck.* **12** (*intr*) to remain for a long time: *the memory sticks in my mind.* **13** (*tr*) *Slang, chiefly Brit.* to tolerate; abide: *I can't stick that man.* **14** (*intr*) to be reluctant. **15** (*tr; usually passive*) *Informal.* to cause to be at a loss; baffle, puzzle, or confuse: *I was totally stuck for an answer.* **16** (*tr*) *Slang.* to force or impose something unpleasant on: *they stuck me with the bill for lunch.* **17** (*tr*) to kill by piercing or stabbing. **18 stick in one's throat** (*or* **craw**). *Informal.* to be difficult, or against one's conscience, for one to accept, utter, or believe. **19 stick one's nose into.** See **nose** (sense 17). **20 stick to the ribs.** *Informal.* (of food) to be hearty and satisfying. ◆ *n* **21** the state or condition of adhering. **22** *Informal.* a substance causing adhesion. **23** *Obsolete.* something that causes delay or stoppage. ◆ See also **stick around, stick at, stick by, stick down, stick out, stick to, stick together, stick-up, stick with, stuck.** [Old English *stician;* related to Old High German *stehhan* to sting, Old Norse *steikja* to roast on a spit]

stick around *or* **about** *vb* (*intr, adv*) *Informal.* to remain in a place, esp. awaiting something.

stick at *vb* (*intr, prep*) **1** to continue constantly at: *to stick at one's work.* **2 stick at nothing.** to be prepared to do anything; be unscrupulous or ruthless.

stick by *vb* (*intr, prep*) to remain faithful to; adhere to.

stick down *vb* (*tr, adv*) *Informal.* to write: *stick your name down here.*

sticker ('stɪkə) *n* **1** an adhesive label, poster, or paper. **2** a person or thing that sticks. **3** a persevering or industrious person. **4** something prickly, such as a thorn, that clings to one's clothing, etc. **5** *Informal.* something that perplexes. **6** *Informal.* a knife used for stabbing or piercing.

stick float *n Angling.* a float attached at the top and bottom to the line.

stickhandle ('stɪkˌhændᵊl) *vb Ice hockey.* to manoeuvre (the puck) deftly. ▸ **'stickˌhandler** *n*

sticking plaster *n* a thin cloth with an adhesive substance on one side, used for covering slight or superficial wounds. Usual U.S. term: **adhesive tape.**

sticking point *n* a problem or point on which agreement cannot be reached, preventing progress from being made.

stick insect *n* any of various mostly tropical insects of the family *Phasmidae* that have an elongated cylindrical body and long legs and resemble twigs: order *Phasmida.* Also called (U.S. and Canadian): **walking stick.** See also **leaf insect.**

stick-in-the-mud *n Informal.* a staid or predictably conservative person who lacks initiative or imagination.

stickle ('stɪkᵊl) *vb* (*intr*) **1** to dispute stubbornly, esp. about minor points. **2** to refuse to agree or concur, esp. by making petty stipulations. [C16 *stightle* (in the sense: to arbitrate): frequentative of Old English *stihtan* to arrange; related to Old Norse *stētta* to support]

stickleback ('stɪkᵊlˌbæk) *n* any small teleost fish of the family *Gasterosteidae,* such as *Gasterosteus aculeatus* (**three-spined stickleback**) of rivers and coastal regions and *G. pungitius* (**ten-spined stickleback**) confined to rivers. They have a series of spines along the back and occur in cold and temperate northern regions. [C15: from Old English *stickel* prick, sting + BACK[1]]

stickler ('stɪklə) *n* **1** (usually foll. by *for*) a person who makes insistent demands: *a stickler for accuracy.* **2** a problem or puzzle: *the investigation proved to be a stickler.*

stick out *vb* (*adv*) **1** to project or cause to project. **2** (*tr*) *Informal.* to endure (something disagreeable) (esp. in the phrase **stick it out**). **3 stick out a mile** *or* **like a sore thumb.** *Informal.* to be extremely obvious. **4 stick out for** (*intr*) to insist on (a demand), refusing to yield until it is met: *the unions stuck out for a ten per cent wage rise.*

stick pin *n* the U.S. name for **tiepin.**

stickseed ('stɪkˌsi:d) *n* any of various Eurasian and North American plants of the boraginaceous genus *Lappula,* having red-and-blue flowers and small prickly fruits. Also called: **beggar's-lice.** [C19: from STICK[2]; so called because its seeds have adhesive hooks on them]

stick shift *n U.S. and Canadian.* **1a** a manually operated transmission system in a motor vehicle. **1b** a motor vehicle having manual transmission. **2** a gear lever.

sticktight ('stɪkˌtaɪt) *n* any of various plants, esp. the bur marigold, that have barbed clinging fruits.

stick to *vb* (*prep, mainly intr*) **1** (*also tr*) to adhere or cause to adhere to. **2** to continue constantly at. **3** to remain faithful to. **4** not to move or digress from: *the speaker stuck closely to his subject.* **5 stick to someone's fingers.** *Informal.* to be stolen by someone.

stick together *vb (intr, adv) Informal.* to remain loyal or friendly to one another.

stick-up *n* **1** *Slang, chiefly U.S.* a robbery at gunpoint; hold-up. ♦ *vb* **stick up.** *(adv)* **2** *(tr) Slang, chiefly U.S.* to rob, esp. at gunpoint. **3** *(intr;* foll. by *for) Informal.* to support or defend: *stick up for oneself.*

stickweed ('stɪk,wiːd) *n* any of several plants that have clinging fruits or seeds, esp. the ragweed.

stick with *vb (intr, prep) Informal.* to persevere with; remain faithful to.

sticky ('stɪkɪ) *adj* **stickier, stickiest. 1** covered or daubed with an adhesive or viscous substance: *sticky fingers.* **2** having the property of sticking to a surface. **3** (of weather or atmosphere) warm and humid; muggy. **4** (of prices) tending not to fall in deflationary conditions. **5** *Informal.* difficult, awkward, or painful: *a sticky business.* **6** *U.S. informal.* sentimental. ♦ *vb* **stickies, stickying, stickied. 7** *(tr) Informal.* to make sticky. ♦ *n, pl* **stickies.** *Austral. informal.* **8** short for **stickybeak. 9** an inquisitive look or stare (esp. in the phrase **have a sticky at**). ▸ **'stickily** *adv* ▸ **'stickiness** *n*

stickybeak ('stɪkɪ,biːk) *Austral. and N.Z. informal.* ♦ *n* **1** an inquisitive person. ♦ *vb* **2** *(intr)* to pry. [from STICKY + BEAK[1] (in the slang sense: a human nose)]

sticky end *n Informal.* an unpleasant finish or death (esp. in the phrase **come to** *or* **meet a sticky end**).

sticky-fingered *adj Informal.* given to thieving.

sticky wicket *n* **1** a cricket pitch that is rapidly being dried by the sun after rain and is particularly conducive to spin. **2** *Informal.* a difficult or awkward situation (esp. in the phrase **on a sticky wicket**).

sticky willie *n* another name for **cleavers.**

stiction ('stɪkʃən) *n* the frictional force to be overcome to set one object in motion when it is in contact with another. [C20: blend of STATIC + FRICTION]

Stieglitz ('stiːglɪts) *n* **Alfred.** 1864–1946, U.S. photographer, whose work helped to develop photography as an art: among his best photographs are those of his wife Georgia O'Keeffe. He was also well known as a promoter of modern art.

stiff (stɪf) *adj* **1** not easily bent; rigid; inflexible. **2** not working or moving easily or smoothly: *a stiff handle.* **3** difficult to accept in its severity or harshness: *a stiff punishment.* **4** moving with pain or difficulty; not supple: *a stiff neck.* **5** difficult; arduous: *a stiff climb.* **6** unrelaxed or awkward; formal. **7** firmer than liquid in consistency; thick or viscous. **8** powerful; strong: *a stiff breeze; a stiff drink.* **9** excessively high: *a stiff price.* **10** *Nautical.* (of a sailing vessel) relatively resistant to heeling or rolling. Compare **tender**[1] (sense 11). **11** lacking grace or attractiveness. **12** stubborn or stubbornly maintained: *a stiff fight.* **13** *Obsolete.* tightly stretched; taut. **14** *Slang, chiefly Austral.* unlucky. **15** *Slang.* intoxicated. **16 stiff upper lip.** See **lip** (sense 9). **17 stiff with.** *Informal.* amply provided with. ♦ *n* **18** *Slang.* a corpse. **19** *Slang.* anything thought to be a loser or a failure; flop. ♦ *adv* **20** completely or utterly: *bored stiff; frozen stiff.* ♦ *vb* **21** *(intr) Slang.* to fail: *the film stiffed.* **22** *(tr) Slang, chiefly U.S.* to cheat or swindle. [Old English *stīf;* related to Old Norse *stīfla* to dam up, Middle Low German *stīf* stiff, Latin *stīpēs* wooden post, *stīpāre* to press] ▸ **'stiffish** *adj* ▸ **'stiffly** *adv* ▸ **'stiffness** *n*

stiffen ('stɪfᵊn) *vb* **1** to make or become stiff or stiffer. **2** *(intr)* to become suddenly tense or unyielding. ▸ **'stiffener** *n*

stiff-necked *adj* haughtily stubborn or obstinate.

stifle[1] ('staɪfᵊl) *vb* **1** *(tr)* to smother or suppress: *stifle a cough.* **2** to feel or cause to feel discomfort and difficulty in breathing. **3** to prevent or be prevented from breathing so as to cause death. **4** *(tr)* to crush or stamp out. [C14: variant of *stuflen,* probably from Old French *estouffer* to smother] ▸ **'stifler** *n*

stifle[2] ('staɪfᵊl) *n* the joint in the hind leg of a horse, dog, etc., between the femur and tibia. [C14: of unknown origin]

stifling ('staɪflɪŋ) *adj* oppressively hot or stuffy: *a stifling atmosphere.* ▸ **'stiflingly** *adv*

stigma ('stɪgmə) *n, pl* **stigmas** *or* (for sense 7) **stigmata** ('stɪgmətə, stɪg'mɑːtə) **1** a distinguishing mark of social disgrace: *the stigma of having been in prison.* **2** a small scar or mark such as a birthmark. **3** *Pathol.* **3a** any mark on the skin, such as one characteristic of a specific disease. **3b** any sign of a mental deficiency or emotional upset. **4** *Botany.* the terminal part of the ovary, at the end of the style, where deposited pollen enters the gynoecium. **5** *Zoology.* **5a** a pigmented eyespot in some protozoans and other invertebrates. **5b** the spiracle of an insect. **6** *Archaic.* a mark branded on the skin. **7** *(pl) Christianity.* marks resembling the wounds of the crucified Christ, believed to appear on the bodies of certain individuals. [C16: via Latin from Greek: brand, from *stizein* to tattoo]

stigmasterol (stɪg'mæstə,rɒl) *n Biochem.* a sterol obtained from Calabar beans and soya beans and used in the manufacture of progesterone. Formula: $C_{29}H_{47}OH$. [C20: from New Latin *(physo)stigma* genus name of the Calabar bean + STEROL; see PHYSOSTIGMINE]

stigmatic (stɪg'mætɪk) *adj* **1** relating to or having a stigma or stigmata. **2** another word for **anastigmatic.** ♦ *n also* **stigmatist** ('stɪgmətɪst). **3** *Chiefly R.C. Church.* a person marked with the stigmata.

stigmatism ('stɪgmə,tɪzəm) *n* **1** *Physics.* the state or condition of being anastigmatic. **2** *Pathol.* the condition resulting from or characterized by stigmata.

stigmatize *or* **stigmatise** ('stɪgmə,taɪz) *vb (tr)* **1** to mark out or describe (as something bad). **2** to mark with a stigma or stigmata. ▸ **,stigmati'zation** *or* **,stigmati'sation** *n* ▸ **'stigma,tizer** *or* **'stigma,tiser** *n*

Stijl (staɪl) *n* **De.** See **De Stijl.**

stilb (stɪlb) *n Physics.* a unit of luminance equal to 1 candela per square centimetre. Symbol: sb [C20: from Greek *stilbē* lamp]

stilbene ('stɪlbiːn) *n* a colourless or slightly yellow crystalline water-insoluble unsaturated hydrocarbon used in the manufacture of dyes; *trans-1,2*-diphenylethene. Formula: $C_6H_5CH{:}CHC_6H_5$. [C19: from Greek *stilbos* glittering + -ENE]

stilbite ('stɪlbaɪt) *n* a white or yellow zeolite mineral consisting of hydrated calcium sodium aluminium silicate, often in the form of sheaves of monoclinic crystals. Formula: $(Na_2Ca)Al_2Si_6O_{16}.6H_2O$. [C19: from Greek *stilbos* glittering (from *stilbein* to shine) + -ITE[1]]

stilboestrol *or U.S.* **stilbestrol** (stɪl'biːstrəl) *n* a synthetic hormone having derivatives with oestrogenic properties. Formula: $OHC_6H_4CH{:}CHC_6H_4OH$. Also called: **diethylstilboestrol.** [C20: from STILBENE + OESTRUS + -OL[1]]

stile[1] (staɪl) *n* **1** a set of steps or rungs in a wall or fence to allow people, but not animals, to pass over. **2** short for **turnstile.** [Old English *stigel;* related to *stīgan* to climb, Old High German *stigilla;* see STAIR]

stile[2] (staɪl) *n* a vertical framing member in a door, window frame, or piece of panelling. Compare **rail**[1] (sense 3). [C17: probably from Dutch *stijl* pillar, ultimately from Latin *stilus* writing instrument; see STYLE]

stiletto (stɪ'lɛtəʊ) *n, pl* **-tos. 1** a small dagger with a slender tapered blade. **2** a sharply pointed tool used to make holes in leather, cloth, etc. **3** Also called: **spike heel, stiletto heel.** a very high heel on a woman's shoe, tapering to a very narrow tip. ♦ *vb* **-toes, -toeing, -toed. 4** *(tr)* to stab with a stiletto. [C17: from Italian, from *stilo* a dagger, from Latin *stilus* a stake, pen; see STYLUS]

Stilicho ('stɪlɪkəʊ) *n* **Flavius** ('fleɪvɪəs). ?365–408 A.D., Roman general and statesman, born a Vandal. As the guardian of Emperor Theodosius' son Honorius, he was effective ruler of the Western Roman Empire (395–408), which he defended against the Visigoths.

still[1] (stɪl) *adj* **1** *(usually predicative)* motionless; stationary. **2** undisturbed or tranquil; silent and calm. **3** not sparkling or effervescent: *a still wine.* **4** gentle or quiet; subdued. **5** *Obsolete.* (of a child) dead at birth. ♦ *adv* **6** continuing now or in the future as in the past: *do you still love me?* **7** up to this or that time; yet: *I still don't know your name.* **8** (often used with a comparative) even or yet: *still more insults.* **9** quiet or without movement: *sit still.* **10** *Poetic and dialect.* always. ♦ *n* **11** *Poetic.* silence or tranquillity: *the still of the night.* **12a** a still photograph, esp. of a scene from a motion-picture film. **12b** *(as modifier): a still camera.* ♦ *vb* **13** to make or become still, quiet, or calm. **14** *(tr)* to allay or relieve: *her fears were stilled.* ♦ *sentence connector.* **15** even then; nevertheless: *the child has some new toys and still cries.* [Old English *stille;* related to Old Saxon, Old High German *stilli,* Dutch *stollen* to curdle, Sanskrit *sthānús* immobile] ▸ **'stillness** *n*

still[2] (stɪl) *n* **1** an apparatus for carrying out distillation, consisting of a vessel in which a mixture is heated, a condenser to turn the vapour back to liquid, and a receiver to hold the distilled liquid, used esp. in the manufacture of spirits. **2** a place where spirits are made; distillery. [C16: from Old French *stiller* to drip, from Latin *stillāre,* from *stilla* a drip; see DISTIL]

stillage ('stɪlɪdʒ) *n* **1** a frame or stand for keeping things off the ground, such as casks in a brewery. **2** a container in which goods, machinery, etc., are transported. [C16: probably from Dutch *stillagie* frame, scaffold, from *stellen* to stand; see -AGE]

stillbirth ('stɪl,bɜːθ) *n* **1** birth of a dead fetus or baby. **2** a stillborn fetus or baby.

stillborn ('stɪl,bɔːn) *adj* **1** (of a fetus) dead at birth. **2** (of an idea, plan, etc.) fruitless; abortive; unsuccessful. ♦ *n* **3** a stillborn fetus or baby.

still frame *n* continuous display of a single frame of a film or of a single picture from a television signal.

still hunt *n* **1** the hunting of game by stalking or ambushing. ♦ *vb* **still-hunt. 2** to hunt (quarry) in this way.

stillicide ('stɪlɪ,saɪd) *n Law.* a right or duty relating to the drainage of water from the eaves of a roof onto adjacent land. [C17: from Latin *stillicidium,* from *stilla* drop + *-cidium,* from *cadere* to fall]

stilliform ('stɪlɪ,fɔːm) *adj Rare.* having the shape of a drop or globule. [C20: from Latin *stilla* a drop + -FORM]

still life *n, pl* **still lifes. 1a** a painting or drawing of inanimate objects, such as fruit, flowers, etc. **1b** *(as modifier): a still-life painting.* **2** the genre of such paintings.

still room *n Brit.* **1** a room in which distilling is carried out. **2** a pantry or storeroom, as in a large house.

Stillson wrench ('stɪlsᵊn) *n Trademark.* a large wrench having adjustable jaws that tighten as the pressure on the handle is increased.

stilly *adv* ('stɪllɪ). **1** *Archaic or literary.* quietly or calmly. ♦ *adj* ('stɪlɪ). **2** *Poetic.* still, quiet, or calm.

stilt (stɪlt) *n* **1** either of a pair of two long poles with footrests on which a person stands and walks, as used by circus clowns. **2** a long post or column that is used with others to support a building above ground level. **3** any of several shore birds of the genera *Himantopus* and *Cladorhynchus,* similar to the avocets but having a straight bill. ♦ *vb* **4** *(tr)* to raise or place on or as if on stilts. [C14 (in the sense: crutch, handle of a plough): related to Low German *stilte* pole, Norwegian *stilta*]

stilted ('stɪltɪd) *adj* **1** (of speech, writing, etc.) formal, pompous, or bombastic. **2** not flowing continuously or naturally: *stilted conversation.* **3** *Architect.* (of an arch) having vertical piers between the impost and the springing. ▸ **'stiltedly** *adv* ▸ **'stiltedness** *n*

Stilton ('stɪltən) *n Trademark.* either of two rich cheeses made from whole milk, blue-veined (**blue Stilton**) or white (**white Stilton**), both very strong in flavour. [C18: named after *Stilton,* Cambridgeshire, where it was originally sold]

Stilwell ('stɪlwɛl) *n* **Joseph W(arren),** known as *Vinegar Joe.* 1883–1946, U.S. general, who was (1941–44) Chiang Kai-shek's chief of staff and commander of all U.S. forces in China, Burma (Myanmar), and India.

stim (stɪm) *n Irish. (used with a negative)* a very small amount: *I couldn't see a stim; she hasn't a stim of sense.* [of uncertain origin]

stimulant ('stɪmjʊlənt) *n* **1** a drug or similar substance that increases physiological activity, esp. of a particular organ. **2** any stimulating agent or thing.

♦ *adj* **3** increasing physiological activity; stimulating. [C18: from Latin *stimulāns* goading, from *stimulāre* to urge on; see STIMULUS]

stimulate ('stɪmjʊˌleɪt) *vb* **1** (*tr; usually passive*) to fill (a person) with ideas or enthusiasm: *he was stimulated by the challenge.* **2** (*tr*) *Physiol.* to excite (a nerve, organ, etc.) with a stimulus. **3** to encourage (something) to start or progress further: *a cut in interest rates should help stimulate economic recovery.* [C16: from Latin *stimulāre;* see STIMULANT] ▸ **'stimulable** *adj* ▸ **ˌstimu'lation** *n* ▸ **'stimulative** *adj, n* ▸ **'stimuˌlator** *or* **'stimuˌlater** *n*

stimulating ('stɪmjʊˌleɪtɪŋ) *adj* **1** inspiring new ideas or enthusiasm. **2** (of a physical activity) making one feel refreshed and energetic. ▸ **'stimuˌlatingly** *adv*

stimulus ('stɪmjʊləs) *n, pl* **-li** (-ˌlaɪ, -ˌliː). **1** something that stimulates or acts as an incentive. **2** any drug, agent, electrical impulse, or other factor able to cause a response in an organism. **3** an object or event that is apprehended by the senses. **4** *Med.* another word for a **stimulant.** [C17: from Latin: a cattle goad]

sting (stɪŋ) *vb* **stings, stinging, stung. 1** (of certain animals and plants) to inflict a wound on (an organism) by the injection of poison. **2** to feel or cause to feel a sharp mental or physical pain. **3** (*tr*) to goad or incite (esp. in the phrase **sting into action**). **4** (*tr*) *Informal.* to cheat, esp. by overcharging. ♦ *n* **5** a skin wound caused by the poison injected by certain insects or plants. **6** pain caused by or as if by the sting of a plant or animal. **7** a mental pain or pang: *a sting of conscience.* **8** a sharp pointed organ, such as the ovipositor of a wasp, by which poison can be injected into the prey. **9** the ability to sting: *a sharp sting in his criticism.* **10** something as painful or swift of action as a sting: *the sting of death.* **11** a sharp stimulus or incitement. **12** *Botany.* another name for **stinging hair. 13** *Slang.* a swindle or fraud. **14** *Slang.* a trap set up by the police to entice a person to commit a crime and thereby produce evidence. **15 sting in the tail.** an unexpected and unpleasant ending. [Old English *stingan;* related to Old Norse *stinga* to pierce, Gothic *usstangan* to pluck out, Greek *stakhus* ear of corn] ▸ **'stinging** *adj* ▸ **'stingingly** *adv* ▸ **'stingingness** *n*

stingaree ('stɪŋəˌriː, ˌstɪŋə'riː) *n U.S., Canadian, and Austral.* a popular name for the **stingray.** [C19: variant of STINGRAY]

stinger ('stɪŋə) *n* **1** a person, plant, animal, etc., that stings or hurts. **2** *Austral.* any marine creature that stings its victims, esp. the box jellyfish. **3** Also called: **stengah.** a whisky and soda with crushed ice.

stinging hair *n* a multicellular hair in plants, such as the stinging nettle, that injects an irritant fluid when in contact with an animal.

stinging nettle *n* See **nettle** (sense 1).

stingray ('stɪŋˌreɪ) *n* any ray of the family *Dasyatidae,* having a whiplike tail bearing a serrated venomous spine capable of inflicting painful weals on man.

stingy[1] ('stɪndʒɪ) *adj* **-gier, -giest. 1** unwilling to spend or give. **2** insufficient or scanty. [C17 (perhaps in the sense: ill-tempered): perhaps from *stinge,* dialect variant of STING] ▸ **'stingily** *adv* ▸ **'stinginess** *n*

stingy[2] ('stɪŋɪ) *adj* **stingier, stingiest. 1** *Informal.* stinging or capable of stinging. ♦ *n, pl* **stingies. 2** *South Wales dialect.* a stinging nettle: *I put my hand on a stingy.*

stink (stɪŋk) *n* **1** a strong foul smell; stench. **2** *Slang.* a great deal of trouble (esp. in the phrase **to make** *or* **raise a stink**). **3 like stink.** intensely; furiously. ♦ *vb* **stinks, stinking, stank** *or* **stunk; stunk.** (*mainly intr*) **4** to emit a foul smell. **5** *Slang.* to be thoroughly bad or abhorrent: *this town stinks.* **6** *Informal.* to have a very bad reputation: *his name stinks.* **7** to be of poor quality. **8** (foll. by *of* or *with*) *Slang.* to have or appear to have an excessive amount (of money). **9** (*tr;* usually foll. by *up*) *Informal.* to cause to stink. ♦ See also **stink out.** [Old English *stincan;* related to Old Saxon *stinkan,* German *stinken,* Old Norse *stökkva* to burst; see STENCH] ▸ **'stinky** *adj*

stink ball *n* another name for **stinkpot** (sense 4).

stink bomb *n* a small glass globe, used by practical jokers: it releases a liquid with an offensive smell when broken.

stinker ('stɪŋkə) *n* **1** a person or thing that stinks. **2** *Slang.* a difficult or very unpleasant person or thing. **3** *Slang.* something of very poor quality. **4** *Informal.* any of several fulmars or related birds that feed on carrion.

stinkhorn ('stɪŋkˌhɔːn) *n* any of various basidiomycetous saprotrophic fungi of the genus *Phallus,* such as *P. impudicus,* having an offensive odour.

stinking ('stɪŋkɪŋ) *adj* **1** having a foul smell. **2** *Informal.* unpleasant or disgusting. **3** (*postpositive*) *Slang.* very drunk. ♦ *adv* **4** *Informal.* (intensifier, expressing contempt for the person referred to): *stinking rich.* ▸ **'stinkingly** *adv* ▸ **'stinkingness** *n*

stinking badger *n* another name for **teledu.**

stinking iris *n* an iris plant, *Iris foetidissima,* of W Europe and N Africa, having purplish flowers and a strong unpleasant smell when bruised. Also called: **gladdon.**

stinking smut *n* a smut that affects wheat and is caused by the fungus *Tilletia caries.* Also called: **bunt.**

stinko ('stɪŋkəʊ) *adj* (*postpositive*) a slang word for **drunk.**

stink out *vb* (*tr, adv*) **1** to drive out or away by a foul smell. **2** *Brit.* to cause to stink: *the smell of orange peel stinks out the room.*

stinkpot ('stɪŋkˌpɒt) *n* **1** *Slang.* a person or thing that stinks. **2** *Slang.* a person considered to be unpleasant. **3** another name for **musk turtle. 4** Also called: **stink ball.** *Military.* (formerly) a container filled with material that gives off noxious or suffocating vapours.

stinkstone ('stɪŋkˌstəʊn) *n* any of various rocks producing a fetid odour when struck, esp. certain limestones.

stink trap *n* another name for **stench trap.**

stinkweed ('stɪŋkˌwiːd) *n* **1** Also called: **wall mustard.** a cruciferous plant, *Diplotaxis muralis,* naturalized in Britain and S and central Europe, having pale yellow flowers, cylindrical seed pods, and a disagreeable smell when bruised. **2** any of various other ill-smelling plants, such as mayweed.

stinkwood ('stɪŋkˌwʊd) *n* **1** any of various trees having offensive-smelling wood, esp. *Ocotea bullata,* a southern African lauraceous tree yielding a hard wood used for furniture. **2** the heavy durable wood of any of these trees.

stint[1] (stɪnt) *vb* **1** to be frugal or miserly towards (someone) with (something). **2** *Archaic.* to stop or check (something). ♦ *n* **3** an allotted or fixed amount of work. **4** a limitation or check. **5** *Obsolete.* a pause or stoppage. [Old English *styntan* to blunt; related to Old Norse *stytta* to cut short; see STUNT[1]] ▸ **'stinter** *n*

stint[2] (stɪnt) *n* any of various small sandpipers of the chiefly northern genus *Calidris* (or *Erolia*), such as *C. minuta* (**little stint**). [Old English; related to Middle High German *stinz* small salmon, Swedish dialect *stinta* teenager; see STUNT[1]]

stipe (staɪp) *n* **1** a stalk in plants that bears reproductive structures, esp. the stalk bearing the cap of a mushroom. **2** the stalk that bears the leaflets of a fern or the thallus of a seaweed. **3** *Zoology.* any stalklike part; stipes. [C18: via French from Latin *stīpes* tree trunk; related to Latin *stīpāre* to pack closely; see STIFF]

stipel ('staɪpᵊl) *n* a small paired leaflike structure at the base of certain leaflets; secondary stipule. [C19: via New Latin from Latin *stipula,* diminutive of *stīpes* a log] ▸ **stipellate** (staɪ'pɛlɪt, -eɪt) *adj*

stipend ('staɪpɛnd) *n* a fixed or regular amount of money paid as a salary or allowance, as to a clergyman. [C15: from Old French *stipende,* from Latin *stīpendium* tax, from *stips* a contribution + *pendere* to pay out]

stipendiary (staɪ'pɛndɪərɪ) *adj* **1** receiving or working for regular pay: *a stipendiary magistrate.* **2** paid for by a stipend. ♦ *n, pl* **-aries. 3** a person who receives regular payment. [C16: from Latin *stīpendiārius* concerning tribute, from *stīpendium* STIPEND]

stipes ('staɪpiːz) *n, pl* **stipites** ('stɪpɪˌtiːz). *Zoology.* **1** the second maxillary segment in insects and crustaceans. **2** the eyestalk of a crab or similar crustacean. **3** any similar stemlike structure. [C18: from Latin; see STIPE] ▸ **stipiform** ('staɪpɪˌfɔːm) *or* **stipitiform** ('stɪpɪtɪˌfɔːm) *adj*

stipitate ('stɪpɪˌteɪt) *adj Botany.* possessing or borne on the end of a stipe. [C18: from New Latin *stīpitātus* having a stalk, from Latin *stīpes;* see STIPE]

stipple ('stɪpᵊl) *vb* (*tr*) **1** to draw, engrave, or paint using dots or flecks. **2** to apply paint, powder, etc., to (something) with many light dabs. **3** to give (wet paint, cement, etc.) a granular effect. ♦ *n also* **stippling. 4** the technique of stippling or a picture produced by or using stippling. [C18: from Dutch *stippelen,* from *stippen* to prick, from *stip* point] ▸ **'stippler** *n*

stipulate[1] ('stɪpjʊˌleɪt) *vb* **1** (*tr; may take a clause as object*) to specify, often as a condition of an agreement. **2** (*intr;* foll. by *for*) to insist (on) as a term of an agreement. **3** *Roman law.* to make (an oral contract) in the form of question and answer necessary to render it legally valid. **4** (*tr; may take a clause as object*) to guarantee or promise. [C17: from Latin *stipulārī,* probably from Old Latin *stipulus* firm, but perhaps from *stipula* a stalk, from the convention of breaking a straw to ratify a promise] ▸ **stipulable** ('stɪpjʊləbᵊl) *adj* ▸ **ˌstipu'lation** *n* ▸ **'stipuˌlator** *n* ▸ **stipulatory** ('stɪpjʊlətərɪ, -trɪ) *adj*

stipulate[2] ('stɪpjʊlɪt, -ˌleɪt) *adj* (of a plant) having stipules.

stipule ('stɪpjuːl) *n* a small paired usually leaflike outgrowth occurring at the base of a leaf or its stalk. [C18: from Latin; see STIPE, STIPES] ▸ **stipular** ('stɪpjʊlə) *adj*

stir[1] (stɜː) *vb* **stirs, stirring, stirred. 1** to move an implement such as a spoon around in (a liquid) so as to mix up the constituents: *she stirred the porridge.* **2** to change or cause to change position; disturb or be disturbed: *he stirred in his sleep.* **3** (*intr;* often foll. by *from*) to venture or depart (from one's usual or preferred place): *he won't stir from the fireside.* **4** (*intr*) to be active after a rest; be up and about. **5** (*tr*) to excite or stimulate, esp. emotionally. **6** to move (oneself) briskly or vigorously; exert (oneself). **7** (*tr*) to rouse or awaken: *to stir someone from sleep; to stir memories.* **8** *Informal.* (when *tr,* foll. by *up*) to cause or incite others to cause (trouble, arguments, etc.). **9 stir one's stumps.** *Informal.* to move or become active. ♦ *n* **10** the act or an instance of stirring or the state of being stirred. **11** a strong reaction, esp. of excitement: *his publication caused a stir.* **12** a slight movement. **13** *N.Z. informal.* a noisy party. ♦ See also **stir up.** [Old English *styrian;* related to Middle High German *stürn* to poke, stir, Norwegian *styrja* to cause a commotion; see STORM, STURGEON] ▸ **'stirrable** *adj*

stir[2] (stɜː) *n* a slang word for **prison:** *in stir.* [C19: perhaps from Romany *stariben* prison]

Stir. *abbrev. for* Stirlingshire.

stirabout ('stɜːrəˌbaʊt) *n* **1** a kind of porridge orginally made in Ireland. **2** a bustling person.

stir-crazy *adj Slang.* mentally disturbed as a result of being in prison or otherwise confined.

stir-fry ('stɜː'fraɪ) *vb* **-fries, -frying, -fried. 1** to cook (small pieces of meat, vegetables, etc.) rapidly by stirring them in a wok or frying pan over a high heat: used esp. for Chinese food. ♦ *n, pl* **-fries. 2** a dish cooked in this way.

stirk (stɜːk) *n* **1** a heifer of 6 to 12 months old. **2** a yearling heifer or bullock. [Old English *stierc;* related to Middle Low German *sterke,* Old High German *stero* ram, Latin *sterilis* sterile, Greek steira; see STEER[2]]

Stirling ('stɜːlɪŋ) *n* **1** a town in central Scotland, in Stirling council area on the River Forth: its castle was a regular residence of many Scottish monarchs between the 12th century and 1603. Pop.: 30 515 (1991). **2** a council area of central Scotland, created from part of Central Region in 1996; includes most of the historical county of Stirlingshire: the Forth valley rises to the Grampian Mountains in the N. Administrative centre: Stirling. Pop.: 82 750 (1996 est.). Area: 2173 sq. km (839 sq. miles).

Stirling engine *n* an external-combustion engine that uses air or an inert gas as the working fluid operating on a highly efficient thermodynamic cycle (the **Stirling cycle**). [named after Robert *Stirling* (1790–1878), Scottish minister who invented it]

Stirling's formula *n* a formula giving the approximate value of the factorial of a large number *n*, as *n*! ≅ $(n/e)^n\sqrt{2\pi n}$ [named after James *Stirling* (1692–1770), Scottish mathematician]

Stirlingshire ('stɜːlɪŋˌʃɪə, -ʃə) *n* a former county of central Scotland: became part of Central Region in 1975: now covered by the council areas of Stirling and Falkirk.

stirps (stɜːps) *n, pl* **stirpes** ('stɜːpiːz). **1** *Genealogy.* a line of descendants from an ancestor; stock or strain. **2** *Botany.* a race or variety, esp. one in which the characters are maintained by cultivation. [C17: from Latin: root, family origin]

stirrer ('stɜːrə) *n* **1** a person or thing that stirs. **2** *Informal.* a person who deliberately causes trouble. **3** *Austral. and N.Z. informal.* a political activist or agitator.

stirring ('stɜːrɪŋ) *adj* **1** exciting the emotions; stimulating. **2** active, lively, or busy. ▸ **'stirringly** *adv*

stirrup ('stɪrəp) *n* **1** Also called: **stirrup iron.** either of two metal loops on a riding saddle, with a flat footpiece through which a rider puts his foot for support. They are attached to the saddle by **stirrup leathers. 2** a U-shaped support or clamp made of metal, wood, leather, etc. **3** *Nautical.* one of a set of ropes fastened to a yard at one end and having a thimble at the other through which a footrope is rove for support. **4** the usual U.S. name for **étrier.** [Old English *stigrāp*, from *stīg* path, step (related to Old High German *stīgan* to move up) + *rāp* ROPE; related to Old Norse *stigreip*, Old High German *stegareif*]

stirrup bone *n* the nontechnical name for **stapes.** [C17: so called because of its stirrup-like shape]

stirrup cup *n* a cup containing an alcoholic drink offered to a horseman ready to ride away.

stirrup pump *n* a hand-operated reciprocating pump, the base of the cylinder of which is placed in a bucket of water: used in fighting fires.

stir up *vb (tr, adv)* to set in motion; instigate: *he stirred up trouble.*

stishie ('stɪʃɪ) *n Scot.* a variant of **stushie.**

stitch (stɪtʃ) *n* **1** a link made by drawing a thread through material by means of a needle. **2** a loop of yarn formed around an implement used in knitting, crocheting, etc. **3** a particular method of stitching or shape of stitch. **4** a sharp spasmodic pain in the side resulting from running or exercising. **5** *(usually used with a negative) Informal.* the least fragment of clothing: *he wasn't wearing a stitch.* **6** *Agriculture.* the ridge between two furrows. **7 in stitches.** *Informal.* laughing uncontrollably. **8 drop a stitch.** to allow a loop of wool to fall off a knitting needle accidentally while knitting. ◆ *vb* **9** *(tr)* to sew, fasten, etc., with stitches. **10** *(intr)* to be engaged in sewing. **11** *(tr)* to bind together (the leaves of a book, pamphlet, etc.) with wire staples or thread. ◆ *n, vb* **12** an informal word for **suture** (senses 1b, 6). ◆ *See also* **stitch up.** [Old English *stice* sting; related to Old Frisian *steke*, Old High German *stih*, Gothic *stiks*, Old Norse *tikta* sharp] ▸ **'stitcher** *n*

stitchery ('stɪtʃərɪ) *n* needlework, esp. modern embroidery.

stitch up *vb (tr, adv)* **1** to join or mend by means of stitches or sutures. **2** *Slang.* **2a** to incriminate (someone) on a false charge by manufacturing evidence. **2b** to betray, cheat, or defraud. **3** *Slang.* to prearrange (something) in a clandestine manner. ◆ *n* **stitch-up. 4** *Slang.* a matter that has been prearranged clandestinely.

stitch wheel *n* a notched wheel used by a harness maker to mark out the spacing for stitching.

stitchwort ('stɪtʃˌwɜːt) *n* any of several low-growing N temperate herbaceous plants of the caryophyllaceous genus *Stellaria*, having small white star-shaped flowers. [C13: so named because it was once thought to be a remedy for stitches in the side]

stithy ('stɪðɪ) *n, pl* **stithies. 1** *Archaic or dialect.* a forge or anvil. ◆ *vb* **stithies, stithying, stithied. 2** *(tr) Obsolete.* to forge on an anvil. [C13: from Old Norse *stedhi*]

stiver ('staɪvə) *n* **1** a former Dutch coin worth one twentieth of a guilder. **2** a small amount, esp. of money. [C16: from Dutch *stuiver*; related to Middle Low German *stüver*, Danish *styver*]

St John ('sɪndʒən) *n* **Henry.** See (1st Viscount) **Bolingbroke.**

stk *abbrev. for* stock.

stoa ('stəʊə) *n, pl* **stoae** ('stəʊiː) *or* **stoas.** a covered walk that has a colonnade on one or both sides, esp. as used in ancient Greece. [C17: from Greek]

stoat (stəʊt) *n* a small Eurasian musteline mammal, *Mustela erminea*, closely related to the weasels, having a brown coat and a black-tipped tail: in the northern parts of its range it has a white winter coat and is then known as an ermine. [C15: of unknown origin]

stob (stɒb) *n Scot., Northern English, and U.S. dialect.* a post or stump. [C14: variant of STUB]

stochastic (stɒ'kæstɪk) *adj* **1** *Statistics.* **1a** (of a random variable) having a probability distribution, usually with finite variance. **1b** (of a process) involving a random variable the successive values of which are not independent. **1c** (of a matrix) square with non-negative elements that add to unity in each row. **2** *Rare.* involving conjecture. [C17: from Greek *stokhastikos* capable of guessing, from *stokhazesthai* to aim at, conjecture, from *stokhos* a target] ▸ **sto'chastically** *adv*

stock (stɒk) *n* **1a** *(sometimes pl)* the total goods or raw material kept on the premises of a shop or business. **1b** *(as modifier): a stock clerk; stock book.* **2** a supply of something stored for future use: *he keeps a good stock of whisky.* **3** *Finance.* **3a** the capital raised by a company through the issue and subscription of shares entitling their holders to dividends, partial ownership, and usually voting rights. **3b** the proportion of such capital held by an individual shareholder. **3c** the shares of a specified company or industry. **3d** (formerly) the part of an account or tally given to a creditor. **3e** the debt represented by this. **4** standing or status. **5a** farm animals, such as cattle and sheep, bred and kept for their meat, skins, etc. **5b** *(as modifier): stock farming.* **6** the trunk or main stem of a tree or other plant. **7** *Horticulture.* **7a** a rooted plant into which a scion is inserted during grafting. **7b** a plant or stem from which cuttings are taken. See also **rootstock. 8** the original type from which a particular race, family, group, etc., is derived. **9** a race, breed, or variety of animals or plants. **10** *(often pl)* a small pen in which a single animal can be confined. **11** a line of descent. **12** any of the major subdivisions of the human species; race or ethnic group. **13** the part of a rifle, sub-machine-gun, etc., into which the barrel and firing mechanism is set: held by the firer against the shoulder. **14** the handle of something, such as a whip or fishing rod. **15** the main body of a tool, such as the block of a plane. **16** short for **diestock, gunstock,** or **rolling stock. 17** (formerly) the part of a plough to which the irons and handles were attached. **18** the main upright part of a supporting structure. **19** a liquid or broth in which meat, fish, bones, or vegetables have been simmered for a long time. **20** film material before exposure and processing. **21** *Metallurgy.* **21a** a portion of metal cut from a bar upon which a specific process, such as forging, is to be carried out. **21b** the material that is smelted in a blast furnace. **22** Also called: **gillyflower.** any of several cruciferous plants of the genus *Matthiola*, such as *M. incana* and *M. bicornis* (**evening** or **night-scented stock**), of the Mediterranean region: cultivated for their brightly coloured flowers. **23 Virginian stock.** a similar and related North American plant, *Malcomia maritima.* **24** a long usually white neckcloth wrapped around the neck, worn in the 18th century and as part of modern riding dress. **25** *Cards.* a pile of cards left after the deal in certain games, from which players draw. **26a** the repertoire of plays available to a repertory company. **26b** *(as modifier): a stock play.* **27** (on some types of anchors) a crosspiece at the top of the shank under the ring. **28** the centre of a wheel. **29** an exposed mass of igneous rock that is the uppermost part of an underlying batholith. **30** a log or block of wood. **31** See **laughing stock. 32** an archaic word for **stocking. 33 in stock. 33a** stored on the premises or available for sale or use. **33b** supplied with goods of a specified kind. **34 out of stock. 34a** not immediately available for sale or use. **34b** not having goods of a specified kind immediately available. **35 take stock. 35a** to make an inventory. **35b** to make a general appraisal, esp. of prospects, resources, etc. **36 take stock in.** to attach importance to. **37 lock, stock, and barrel.** See **lock**[1] (sense 7). ◆ *adj* **38** staple, standard: *stock sizes in clothes.* **39** *(prenominal)* being a cliché; hackneyed: *a stock phrase.* ◆ *vb* **40** *(tr)* to keep (goods) for sale. **41** *(intr; usually foll. by up or up on)* to obtain a store of (something) for future use or sale: *to stock up on beer.* **42** *(tr)* to supply with live animals, fish, etc.: *to stock a farm.* **43** *(intr)* (of a plant) to put forth new shoots. **44** *(tr) Obsolete.* to punish by putting in the stocks. ◆ See also **stocks.** [Old English *stocc* trunk (of a tree), stem, stick (the various senses developed from these meanings, as trunk of a tree, hence line of descent; structures made of timber; a store of timber or other goods for future use, hence an aggregate of goods, animals, etc.); related to Old Saxon, Old High German *stock* stick, stump] ▸ **'stocker** *n*

stockade (stɒ'keɪd) *n* **1** an enclosure or barrier of stakes and timbers. **2** *U.S.* a military prison or detention area. ◆ *vb* **3** *(tr)* to surround with a stockade. [C17: from Spanish *estacada*, from *estaca* a stake, post, of Germanic origin; see STAKE[1]]

stock and station agent *n Austral. and N.Z.* a firm dealing in and financing farm activities.

stockbreeder ('stɒkˌbriːdə) *n* a person who breeds or rears livestock as an occupation. ▸ **'stockˌbreeding** *n*

stockbroker ('stɒkˌbrəʊkə) *n* a person who buys and sells securities on a commission basis for customers. Often shortened to **broker.** ▸ **stockbrokerage** ('stɒkˌbrəʊkərɪdʒ) *or* **'stockˌbroking** *n*

stockbroker belt *n Brit. informal.* the area outside a city, esp. London, in which rich commuters live. Compare **exurbia.**

stock car *n* **1a** a car, usually a production saloon, strengthened and modified for a form of racing in which the cars often collide. **1b** *(as modifier): stock-car racing.* **2** the U.S. and Canadian term for **cattle truck.**

stock certificate *n* the U.S. equivalent of **share certificate.**

stock company *n* **1** *U.S.* a business enterprise the capital of which is divided into transferable shares. **2** a U.S. term for **repertory company.**

stock dove *n* a European dove, *Columba oenas*, smaller than the wood pigeon and having a uniformly grey plumage. [C14: so called because it lives in tree trunks. See STOCK]

stock exchange *n (often caps.)* **1** Also called: **stock market. 1a** a highly organized market facilitating the purchase and sale of securities and operated by professional stockbrokers and market makers according to fixed rules. **1b** a place where securities are regularly traded. **1c** *(as modifier): a stock-exchange operator; stock-exchange prices.* **2** the prices or trading activity of a stock exchange: *the stock exchange fell heavily today.*

stock farm *n* a farm on which livestock is bred. ▸ **stock farmer** *n* ▸ **stock farming** *n*

stockfish ('stɒkˌfɪʃ) *n, pl* **-fish** *or* **-fishes.** fish, such as cod or haddock, cured by splitting and drying in the air. [C13: of uncertain origin. Perhaps from STOCK (in the sense: stem, tree trunk) because it was dried on wooden racks. Compare Middle Dutch *stocvisch*]

Stockhausen (*German* 'ʃtɔkhauzən) *n* **Karlheinz** (karl'haints). born 1928, German composer, whose avant-garde music exploits advanced serialization, electronic sounds, group improvization, and vocal and instrumental timbres and techniques. Works include *Gruppen* (1959) for three orchestras, *Stimmung* (1968) for six vocalists, and *Ylem* (1972) for instrumental ensemble and tape.

stockholder ('stɒkˌhəʊldə) *n* **1** an owner of corporate capital stock. **2** *Austral.* a person who keeps livestock. ▸ **'stockˌholding** *n*

Stockholm ('stɒkhəʊm; *Swedish* 'stɔkhɔlm) *n* the capital of Sweden, a port in the E central part at the outflow of Lake Mälar into the Baltic: situated partly on the mainland and partly on islands; traditionally founded about 1250; university (1877). Pop.: 718 462 (1997 est.).

Stockholm syndrome *n* a psychological condition in which hostages or kidnap victims become sympathetic towards their captors. [C20: after a group of hostages in Stockholm in 1973]

stockhorse ('stɒk,hɔːs) *n Austral.* a horse trained in the handling of stock.

stockinet (,stɒkɪ'nɛt) *n* a machine-knitted elastic fabric used, esp. formerly, for stockings, undergarments, etc. [C19: perhaps changed from earlier *stocking-net*]

stocking ('stɒkɪŋ) *n* **1** one of a pair of close-fitting garments made of knitted yarn to cover the foot and part or all of the leg. **2** something resembling this in position, function, appearance, etc. **3 in (one's) stocking** *or* **stockinged feet.** wearing stockings or socks but no shoes. [C16: from dialect *stock* stocking + -ING[1]] ▸ **'stockinged** *adj*

stocking cap *n* a conical knitted cap, often with a tassel.

stockinger ('stɒkɪŋə) *n* a person who knits on a stocking frame.

stocking filler *n Brit.* a present, esp. a toy, of a size suitable for inclusion in a child's Christmas stocking.

stocking frame *n* a type of knitting machine. Also called: **stocking loom, stocking machine.**

stocking mask *n* a nylon stocking worn over the face by a criminal to disguise the features.

stocking stitch *n* a pattern of stitches in knitting consisting of alternate rows of plain and purl stitch. [C19: so named because of its use in hosiery]

stock in trade *n* **1** goods in stock necessary for carrying on a business. **2** anything constantly used by someone as a part of his profession, occupation, or trade: *friendliness is the salesman's stock in trade.*

stockish ('stɒkɪʃ) *adj* stupid or dull. ▸ **'stockishly** *adv* ▸ **'stockishness** *n*

stockist ('stɒkɪst) *n Commerce, Brit.* a dealer who undertakes to maintain stocks of a specified product at or above a certain minimum in return for favourable buying terms granted by the manufacturer of the product.

stockjobber ('stɒk,dʒɒbə) *n* **1** *Brit.* (formerly) a wholesale dealer on a stock exchange who sold securities to brokers without transacting directly with the public. Often shortened to **jobber**. See also **market maker. 2** *U.S., disparaging.* a stockbroker, esp. one dealing in worthless securities. ▸ **'stock,jobbery** *or* **'stock,jobbing** *n*

stock lock *n* a lock that is enclosed in a wooden case.

stockman ('stɒkmən, -,mæn) *n, pl* **-men. 1a** a man engaged in the rearing or care of farm livestock, esp. cattle. **1b** an owner of cattle or other livestock. **2** *U.S. and Canadian.* a man employed in a warehouse or stockroom.

stock market *n* **1** another name for **stock exchange** (sense 1). **2** the usual U.S. name for **stock exchange** (sense 2).

stockpile ('stɒk,paɪl) *vb* **1** to acquire and store a large quantity of (something). ♦ *n* **2** a large store or supply accumulated for future use. ▸ **'stock,piler** *n*

Stockport ('stɒk,pɔːt) *n* **1** a town in NW England, in Stockport unitary authority, Greater Manchester: an early textile centre and scene of several labour disturbances in the early 19th century. Pop.: 132 813 (1991). **2** a unitary authority in NW England, in Greater Manchester. Pop.: 290 600 (1995 est.). Area: 126 sq. km (49 sq. miles).

stockpot ('stɒk,pɒt) *n Chiefly Brit.* a pot in which stock for soup, etc., is made or kept.

stockroom ('stɒk,ruːm, -,rʊm) *n* a room in which a stock of goods is kept, as in a shop or factory.

stockroute ('stɒk,ruːt) *n Austral. and N.Z.* a route designated for droving sheep or cattle.

stocks (stɒks) *pl n* **1** *History.* an instrument of punishment consisting of a heavy wooden frame with holes in which the feet, hands, or head of an offender were locked. **2** a frame in which an animal is held while receiving veterinary attention or while being shod. **3** a frame used to support a boat while under construction. **4** *Nautical.* a vertical post or shaft at the forward edge of a rudder, extended upwards for attachment to the steering controls. **5 on the stocks.** in preparation or under construction.

stock saddle *n Chiefly U.S.* a cowboy's saddle, esp. an ornamental one.

stock-still *adv* absolutely still; motionless.

stocktaking ('stɒk,teɪkɪŋ) *n* **1** the examination, counting, and valuing of goods on hand in a shop or business. **2** a reassessment of one's current situation, progress, prospects, etc.

Stockton[1] ('stɒktən) *n* an inland port in central California, on the San Joaquin River: seat of the University of the Pacific (1851). Pop.: 232 660 (1996 est.).

Stockton[2] ('stɒktən) *n* **1st Earl of.** title of (Maurice Harold) **Macmillan.**

Stockton-on-Tees *n* **1** a port in NE England, in Stockton unitary authority, Co. Durham, on the River Tees: industrial centre, famous for the **Stockton-Darlington Railway** (1825), the first passenger-carrying railway in the world. Pop.: 83 576 (1991). **2** a unitary authority in NE England, in Co. Durham and North Yorkshire: created in 1996 from part of Cleveland county. Pop.: 176 600 (1996 est.). Area: 195 sq. km (75 sq. miles).

stock unit *n N.Z.* **a** the tax basis for evaluating farmers' stock. Cattle, sheep, and deer are each given differing stock-unit values, the basic measure being the ewe equivalent. **b** (*as modifier*): *stock-unit values.*

stock watering *n Business.* the creation of more new shares in a company than is justified by its assets.

stock whip *n* a whip with a long lash and a short handle, as used to herd cattle.

Stockwood ('stɒkwʊd) *n* (**Arthur**) **Mervyn.** 1913–95, British Anglican prelate; bishop of Southwark (1959–80).

stocky ('stɒkɪ) *adj* **stockier, stockiest.** (usually of a person) thickset; sturdy. ▸ **'stockily** *adv* ▸ **'stockiness** *n*

stockyard ('stɒk,jɑːd) *n* a large yard with pens or covered buildings where farm animals are assembled, sold, etc.

stodge (stɒdʒ) *Informal.* ♦ *n* **1** heavy filling starchy food. **2** *Dialect, chiefly southern English.* baked or steamed pudding. **3** a dull person or subject. ♦ *vb* **4** to stuff (oneself or another) with food. [C17: perhaps a blend of STUFF + PODGE]

stodgy ('stɒdʒɪ) *adj* **stodgier, stodgiest. 1** (of food) heavy or uninteresting. **2** excessively formal and conventional. [C19: from STODGE] ▸ **'stodgily** *adv* ▸ **'stodginess** *n*

stoep (stup) *n S. African.* a veranda. [Afrikaans from Dutch]

stogy *or* **stogey** ('stəʊgɪ) *n, pl* **-gies.** *U.S.* any long cylindrical inexpensive cigar. [C19: from *stoga,* short for *Conestoga,* a town in Pennsylvania]

stoic ('stəʊɪk) *n* **1** a person who maintains stoical qualities. ♦ *adj* **2** a variant of **stoical.**

Stoic ('stəʊɪk) *n* **1** a member of the ancient Greek school of philosophy founded by Zeno, holding that virtue and happiness can be attained only by submission to destiny and the natural law. ♦ *adj* **2** of or relating to the doctrines of the Stoics. [C16: via Latin from Greek *stōikos,* from *stoa* the porch in Athens where Zeno taught]

stoical ('stəʊɪkᵊl) *adj* characterized by impassivity or resignation. ▸ **'stoically** *adv* ▸ **'stoicalness** *n*

stoichiology, stoicheiology, *or* **stoechiology** (,stɔɪkɪ'ɒlədʒɪ) *n* the branch of biology concerned with the study of the cellular components of animal tissues. [C19: from Greek *stoikheion* element + -LOGY] ▸ **stoichiological, stoicheiological,** *or* **stoechiological** (,stɔɪkɪə'lɒdʒɪkᵊl) *adj*

stoichiometric, stoicheiometric, *or* **stoechiometric** (,stɔɪkɪə'metrɪk) *adj Chem.* **1** concerned with, involving, or having the exact proportions for a particular chemical reaction: *a stoichiometric mixture.* **2** (of a compound) having its component elements present in the exact proportions indicated by its formula. **3** of or concerned with stoichiometry. [C19: see STOICHIOMETRY]

stoichiometry, stoicheiometry, *or* **stoechiometry** (,stɔɪkɪ'ɒmɪtrɪ) *n* the branch of chemistry concerned with the proportions in which elements are combined in compounds and the quantitative relationships between reactants and products in chemical reactions. [C19: from Greek *stoikheion* element + -METRY]

stoicism ('stəʊɪ,sɪzəm) *n* **1** indifference to pleasure and pain. **2** (*cap.*) the philosophy of the Stoics.

stoke (stəʊk) *vb* **1** to feed, stir, and tend (a fire, furnace, etc.). **2** (*tr*) to tend the furnace of; act as a stoker for. ♦ See also **stoke up.** [C17: back formation from STOKER]

stokehold ('stəʊk,həʊld) *n Nautical.* **1** a coal bunker for a ship's furnace. **2** the hold for a ship's boilers; fire room.

stokehole ('stəʊk,həʊl) *n* **1** another word for **stokehold. 2** a hole in a furnace through which it is stoked.

Stoke-on-Trent *n* **1** a city in central England, in Stoke-on-Trent unitary authority, Staffordshire on the River Trent: a centre of the pottery industry. Pop.: 266 543 (1991). **2** a unitary authority in central England, in N Staffordshire. Pop.: 254 300 (1995 est.). Area: 93 sq. km (36 sq. miles).

stoker ('stəʊkə) *n* a person employed to tend a furnace, as on a steamship. [C17: from Dutch, from *stoken* to STOKE]

Stoker ('stəʊkə) *n* **Bram,** original name *Abraham Stoker.* 1847–1912, Irish novelist, author of *Dracula* (1897).

stokes (stəʊks) *or* **stoke** *n* the cgs unit of kinematic viscosity, equal to the viscosity of a fluid in poise divided by its density in grams per cubic centimetre. 1 stokes is equivalent to 10^{-4} square metre per second. Symbol: St [C20: named after Sir George *Stokes* (1819–1903), British physicist]

Stokesay Castle ('stəʊksɪ) *n* a fortified manor house near Craven Arms in Shropshire: built in the 12th century, with a 16th-century gatehouse.

stoke up *vb* (*adv*) **1** to feed and tend (a fire, etc.) with fuel. **2** (*intr*) to fill oneself with food.

Stokowski (stə'kɒfskɪ) *n* **Leopold.** 1887–1977, U.S. conductor, born in Britain. He did much to popularize classical music with orchestral transcriptions and film appearances, esp. in *Fantasia* (1940).

STOL (stɒl) *n* **1** a system in which an aircraft can take off and land in a short distance. **2** an aircraft using this system. Compare **VTOL.** [C20: *s*(*hort*) *t*(*ake*) *o*(*ff and*) *l*(*anding*)]

stole[1] (stəʊl) *vb* the past tense of **steal.**

stole[2] (stəʊl) *n* **1** a long scarf or shawl, worn by women. **2** a long narrow scarf worn by various officiating clergymen. [Old English *stole,* from Latin *stola,* Greek *stolē* clothing; related to *stellein* to array]

stolen ('stəʊlən) *vb* the past participle of **steal.**

stolid ('stɒlɪd) *adj* showing little or no emotion or interest. [C17: from Latin *stolidus* dull; compare Latin *stultus* stupid; see STILL[1]] ▸ **stolidity** (stɒ'lɪdɪtɪ) *or* **'stolidness** *n* ▸ **'stolidly** *adv*

stollen ('stəʊlən; *German* 'ʃtɔlən) *n* a rich sweet bread containing nuts, raisins, etc. [German, from *Stollen* wooden post, prop; so called from its shape; see STALL[1]]

stolon ('stəʊlən) *n* **1** another name for **runner** (sense 13). **2** a branching structure in lower animals, esp. the anchoring rootlike part of colonial organisms, such as hydroids, on which the polyps are borne. [C17: from Latin *stolō* shoot] ▸ **stoloniferous** (,stəʊlə'nɪfərəs) *adj*

Stolypin (,stʌlɪ'pjɪn) *n* **Petr Arkadievich.** 1863–1911, Russian conservative statesman: prime minister (1906–11). He instituted agrarian reforms but was ruthless in suppressing rebellion: assassinated.

stoma ('stəʊmə) *n, pl* **stomata** ('stəʊmətə, 'stɒm-, stəʊ'mɑːtə). **1** *Botany.* an epidermal pore, present in large numbers in plant leaves, that controls the passage of gases into and out of a plant. **2** *Zoology, anatomy.* a mouth or mouthlike part. **3** *Surgery.* an artificial opening made in a tubular organ, esp. the colon or ileum. See **colostomy, ileostomy.** [C17: via New Latin from Greek: mouth]

stomach ('stʌmək) *n* **1** (in vertebrates) the enlarged muscular saclike part of the alimentary canal in which food is stored until it has been partially digested and rendered into chyme. Related adj: **gastric. 2** the corresponding digestive organ in invertebrates. **3** the abdominal region. **4** desire, appetite, or inclination: *I* *have no stomach for arguments.* **5** an archaic word for **temper. 6** an obsolete word for **pride.** ◆ *vb (tr; used mainly in negative constructions)* **7** to tolerate; bear: *I can't stomach his bragging.* **8** to eat or digest: *he cannot stomach oysters.* [C14: from Old French *stomaque,* from Latin *stomachus* (believed to be the seat of the emotions), from Greek *stomakhos,* from *stoma* mouth]

stomachache ('stʌmək,eɪk) *n* pain in the stomach or abdominal region, as from acute indigestion. Technical name: **gastralgia.** Also called: **stomach upset, upset stomach.**

stomacher ('stʌməkə) *n* a decorative V-shaped panel of stiff material worn over the chest and stomach by men and women in the 16th century, later only by women.

stomachic (stə'mækɪk) *adj also* **stomachical. 1** stimulating gastric activity. **2** of or relating to the stomach. ◆ *n* **3** a stomachic medicine.

stomach pump *n Med.* a suction device for removing stomach contents by a tube inserted through the mouth.

stomach worm *n* any of various nematode worms that are parasitic in the stomach of mammals, esp. *Haemonchus contortus,* which infests sheep: family *Trichostrongylidae.*

stomachy ('stʌmækɪ) *adj* **1** having a large belly; paunchy. **2** *Dialect.* easily angered; irritable.

stomack ('stʌmək) *n* **have a stomack.** *E African informal.* to be pregnant.

stomata ('stəumətə, 'stɒm-, stəu'mɑːtə) *n* the plural of **stoma.**

stomatal ('stəumətᵊl, 'stɒm-) *or* **stomatous** ('stɒmətəs, 'stəu-) *adj* of, relating to, or possessing stomata or a stoma.

stomatic (stəu'mætɪk) *adj* of or relating to a mouth or mouthlike part.

stomatitis (,stəumə'taɪtɪs, ,stɒm-) *n* inflammation of the mouth. ▸ **stomatitic** (,stəumə'tɪtɪk, ,stɒm-) *adj*

stomato- *or before a vowel* **stomat-** *combining form.* indicating the mouth or a mouthlike part: *stomatology.* [from Greek *stoma, stomat-*]

stomatology (,stəumə'tɒlədʒɪ) *n* the branch of medicine or dentistry concerned with the structures, functions, and diseases of the mouth. ▸ **stomatological** (,stəumətə'lɒdʒɪkᵊl) *adj*

stomatoplasty ('stɒmətə,plæstɪ, 'stəu-) *n* plastic surgery or surgical repair involving the mouth.

stomatopod ('stɒmətə,pɒd, 'stəu-) *n* any marine crustacean of the order *Stomatopoda,* having abdominal gills: subclass *Malacostraca.* The group includes the mantis shrimp. [C19: via New Latin from Greek *stoma* mouth + *-podos, pous* foot]

-stome *n combining form.* indicating a mouth or opening resembling a mouth: *peristome.* [from Greek *stoma* mouth, and *stomion* little mouth]

stomodaeum *or* **stomodeum** (,stəumə'diːəm,,stɒm-) *n, pl* **daea** *or* **dea** (-'diːə). the oral cavity of a vertebrate embryo, which is formed from an invagination of the ectoderm and develops into the part of the alimentary canal between the mouth and stomach. [C19: from New Latin, from Greek *stoma* mouth + *hodaios* on the way, from *hodos* way] ▸ **,stomo'daeal** *or* **,stomo'deal** *adj*

-stomous *adj combining form.* having a specified type of mouth: *monostomous.*

stomp (stɒmp) *vb (intr)* **1** *Informal.* to tread or stamp heavily. ◆ *n* **2** a rhythmic stamping jazz dance. [variant of STAMP] ▸ **'stomper** *n*

stompie ('stɒmpɪ) *n S. African slang.* **1** a cigarette butt. **2** a short man. [from Afrikaans *stomp* stump]

-stomy *n combining form.* indicating a surgical operation performed to make an artificial opening into or for a specified part: *cytostomy.* [from Greek *-stomia,* from *stoma* mouth]

stone (stəun) *n* **1** the hard compact nonmetallic material of which rocks are made. Related adj: **lithic. 2** a small lump of rock; pebble. **3** *Jewellery.* short for **gemstone. 4a** a piece of rock designed or shaped for some particular purpose. **4b** *(in combination): gravestone; millstone.* **5a** something that resembles a stone. **5b** *(in combination): hailstone.* **6** the woody central part of such fruits as the peach and plum, that contains the seed; endocarp. **7** any similar hard part of a fruit, such as the stony seed of a date. **8** *(pl* **stone**) *Brit.* a unit of weight, used esp. to express human body weight, equal to 14 pounds or 6.350 kilograms. **9** Also called: **granite.** the rounded heavy mass of granite or iron used in the game of curling. **10** *Pathol.* a nontechnical name for **calculus. 11** *Printing.* a table with a very flat iron or stone surface upon which hot-metal pages are composed into formes; imposition table. **12** *Rare.* (in certain games) a piece or man. **13a** any of various dull grey colours. **13b** *(as adj): stone paint.* **14** *(modifier)* relating to or made of stone: *a stone house.* **15** *(modifier)* made of stoneware: *a stone jar.* **16 cast a stone (at).** cast aspersions (upon). **17 heart of stone.** an obdurate or unemotional nature. **18 leave no stone unturned.** to do everything possible to achieve an end. ◆ *adv* **19** *(in combination)* completely: *stone-cold; stone-deaf.* ◆ *vb (tr)* **20** to throw stones at, esp. to kill. **21** to remove the stones from. **22** to furnish or provide with stones. **23 stone the crows.** *Brit. and Austral. slang.* an expression of surprise, dismay, etc. [Old English *stān;* related to Old Saxon *stēn,* German *Stein,* Old Norse *steinn,* Gothic *stains,* Greek *stion* pebble] ▸ **'stonable** *or* **'stoneable** *adj* ▸ **'stoneless** *adj* ▸ **'stonelessness** *n* ▸ **'stone,like** *adj* ▸ **'stoner** *n*

Stone (stəun) *n* **1 Oliver.** born 1946, U.S. film director and screenwriter: his films include *Platoon* (1986), *Born on the Fourth of July* (1989), *JFK* (1991), and *Nixon* (1995). **2 Sharon.** born 1958, U.S. film actress: her films include *Basic Instinct* (1991) and *Casino* (1995).

Stone Age *n* **1** a period in human culture identified by the use of stone implements and usually divided into the Palaeolithic, Mesolithic, and Neolithic stages. ◆ *modifier.* **Stone-Age. 2** *(sometimes not caps.)* of or relating to this period: *stone-age man.*

stone axe *n* **1** a primitive axe made of chipped stone. **2** a blunt axe used for cutting stone.

stone bass (bæs) *n* a large sea perch, *Polyprion americanus,* of the Atlantic and Mediterranean. Also called: **wreckfish.**

stone-blind *adj* completely blind. Compare **sand-blind.**

stoneboat ('stəun,bəut) *n U.S. and Canadian.* a type of sleigh used for moving rocks from fields, for hauling milk cans, etc.

stone boiling *n* a primitive method of boiling liquid with heated stones.

stone bramble *n* a herbaceous Eurasian rosaceous plant, *Rubus saxatilis,* of stony places, having white flowers and berry-like scarlet fruits (drupelets). See also **bramble** (sense 1). [C18: so called because it grows in stony places]

stonecast ('stəun,kɑːst) *n* a less common name for **stone's throw.**

stonechat ('stəun,tʃæt) *n* an Old World songbird, *Saxicola torquata,* having a black plumage with a reddish-brown breast: subfamily *Turdinae* (thrushes). [C18: so called from its cry, which sounds like clattering pebbles]

stone-cold *adj* **1** completely cold. ◆ *adv* **2** (intensifier): *stone-cold sober.*

stonecrop ('stəun,krɒp) *n* **1** any of various N temperate crassulaceous plants of the genus *Sedum,* having fleshy leaves and typically red, yellow, or white flowers. **2** any of various similar or related plants. [Old English: so named because it grows on rocks and walls]

stone curlew *n* any of several brownish shore birds of the family *Burhinidae,* esp. *Burhinus oedicnemus,* having a large head and eyes: order *Charadriiformes.* Also called: **thick-knee.** [C17: so called because it is found in stony habitats and resembles a curlew]

stonecutter ('stəun,kʌtə) *n* **1** a person who is skilled in cutting and carving stone. **2** a machine used to dress stone. ▸ **'stone,cutting** *n*

stoned (stəund) *adj Slang.* under the influence of drugs or alcohol.

stone-dead *adj* completely lifeless.

stone-deaf *adj* completely deaf.

stonefish ('stəun,fɪʃ) *n, pl* **-fish** *or* **-fishes.** a venomous tropical marine scorpaenid fish, *Synanceja verrucosa,* that resembles a piece of rock on the seabed.

stonefly ('stəun,flaɪ) *n, pl* **-flies.** any insect of the order *Plecoptera,* in which the larvae are aquatic, living beneath stones, and the adults have long antennae and two pairs of large wings and occur near water. [C15: so called because its larvae live under stones in rivers]

stone fruit *n* the nontechnical name for **drupe.**

stoneground ('stəun,graund) *adj* (of flour) ground with millstones.

Stonehenge (,stəun'hɛndʒ) *n* a prehistoric ruin in S England, in Wiltshire on Salisbury Plain: constructed over the period of roughly 2500–1500 B.C.; one of the most important megalithic monuments in Europe; believed to have had religious and astronomical purposes.

stone-lily *n* the fossil of any of several species of sea lily or other crinoid.

stone marten *n* **1** a marten, *Martes foina,* of Eurasian woods and forests, having a brown coat with a pale underfur. **2** the highly valued fur of this animal.

stonemason ('stəun,meɪsᵊn) *n* a person who is skilled in preparing stone for building. ▸ **'stone,masonry** *n*

stone parsley *n* a roadside umbelliferous plant, *Sison amomum,* of W Europe and the Mediterranean region, having clusters of small white flowers and aromatic seeds.

stone pine *n* a Mediterranean pine tree, *Pinus pinea,* having a short bole and radiating branches forming an umbrella shape. Also called: **umbrella pine.**

stone pit *n* a less common name for **quarry**[1].

stone roller *n* a small silvery freshwater cyprinid fish, *Campostoma anomalum,* of the eastern U.S., having a narrow black stripe on the dorsal and anal fins. [C19: so called because it pushes stones about in building its nest]

Stones (stəunz) *pl n* **the.** See **Rolling Stones.**

stone saw *n* an untoothed iron saw used to cut stone.

stone shoot *n Mountaineering.* a long steeply sloping line of loose boulder-strewn scree.

stone's throw *n* a short distance. Also called: **stonecast.**

stonewall (,stəun'wɔːl) *vb* **1** *(intr) Cricket.* (of a batsman) to play defensively. **2** to obstruct or hinder (parliamentary business). ▸ **,stone'waller** *n*

stoneware ('stəun,wɛə) *n* **1** a hard opaque pottery, fired at a very high temperature. ◆ *adj* **2** made of stoneware.

stonewashed ('stəun,wɒʃt) *adj* (of new clothes or fabric, esp. denim jeans) given a worn faded look by being subjected to the abrasive action of many small pieces of pumice.

stonework ('stəun,wɜːk) *n* **1** any structure or part of a building made of stone. **2** the process of dressing or setting stones. ▸ **'stone,worker** *n*

stonewort ('stəun,wɜːt) *n* any of various green algae of the genus *Chara,* which grow in brackish or fresh water and have jointed fronds encrusted with lime.

stonk (stɒŋk) *vb (tr)* **1** to bombard (soldiers, buildings, etc.) with artillery. ◆ *n* **2** a concentrated bombardment by artillery. [C20: from *st(andard) (linear) (c)onc(entration)*]

stonkered ('stɒŋkəd) *adj Slang.* completely exhausted or beaten; whacked. [C20: from *stonker* to beat, of unknown origin]

stony *or* **stoney** ('stəunɪ) *adj* **stonier, stoniest. 1** of or resembling stone. **2** abounding in stone or stones. **3** unfeeling, heartless, or obdurate. **4** short for **stony-broke.** ▸ **'stonily** *adv* ▸ **'stoniness** *n*

stony-broke *adj Brit. slang.* completely without money; penniless. U.S. and Canadian term: **stone-broke.**

stony coral *n* any coral of the order *Madreporaria,* having a calcareous skeleton, aggregations of which form reefs and islands.

stony-hearted *adj* unfeeling; hardhearted. ▸ **,stony'heartedness** *n*

stony meteorite *n* a meteorite composed mainly of silicates.

stood (stud) *vb* the past tense and past participle of **stand.**

stooge (stuːdʒ) *n* **1** an actor who feeds lines to a comedian or acts as his foil or butt. **2** *Slang.* someone who is taken advantage of by another. ◆ *vb (intr)* **3** *Slang.* to act as a stooge. **4** (foll. by *about* or *around*) *Slang.* (esp. in the RAF) to fly or move about aimlessly. [C20: of unknown origin]

stook (stu:k) *n* **1** a number of sheaves set upright in a field to dry with their heads together. ◆ *vb* **2** (*tr*) to set up (sheaves) in stooks. [C15: variant of *stouk*, of Germanic origin; compare Middle Low German *stūke*, Old High German *stūhha* sleeve] ▸ **'stooker** *n*

stookie ('stʊkɪ) *n Scot.* **1** stucco. **2** plaster; plaster of Paris. **3** a statue: *he stood there like a stookie.*

stool (stu:l) *n* **1** a backless seat or footrest consisting of a small flat piece of wood, etc., resting on three or four legs, a pedestal, etc. **2** a rootstock or base of a plant from which shoots, etc., are produced. **3** a cluster of shoots growing from such a base. **4** *Chiefly U.S.* a decoy used in hunting. **5** waste matter evacuated from the bowels. **6** a lavatory seat. **7** (in W Africa, esp. Ghana) a chief's throne. **8 fall between two stools. 8a** to fail through vacillation between two alternatives. **8b** to be in an unsatisfactory situation through not belonging to either of two categories or groups. ◆ *vb* (*intr*) **9** (of a plant) to send up shoots from the base of the stem, rootstock, etc. **10** to lure wildfowl with a decoy. [Old English *stōl;* related to Old Norse *stōll*, Gothic *stōls*, Old High German *stuol* chair, Greek *stulos* pillar]

stool ball *n* a game resembling cricket, still played by girls and women in Sussex, England.

stool pigeon *n* **1** a living or dummy pigeon used to decoy others. **2** an informer for the police; nark. **3** *U.S. slang.* a person acting as a decoy.

stoop[1] (stu:p) *vb* (*mainly intr*) **1** (*also tr*) to bend (the body or the top half of the body) forward and downward. **2** to carry oneself with head and shoulders habitually bent forward. **3** (often foll. by *to*) to abase or degrade oneself. **4** (often foll. by *to*) to condescend; deign. **5** (of a bird of prey) to swoop down. **6** *Archaic.* to give in. ◆ *n* **7** the act, position, or characteristic of stooping. **8** a lowering from a position of dignity or superiority. **9** a downward swoop, esp. of a bird of prey. [Old English *stūpan;* related to Middle Dutch *stupen* to bow, Old Norse *stūpa*, Norwegian *stupa* to fall; see STEEP[1]] ▸ **'stooper** *n* ▸ **'stooping** *adj* ▸ **'stoopingly** *adv*

stoop[2] (stu:p) *n U.S. and Canadian.* a small platform with steps up to it at the entrance to a building. [C18: from Dutch *stoep*, of Germanic origin; compare Old High German *stuofa* stair, Old English *stōpel* footprint; see STEP]

stoop[3] (stu:p) *n Archaic or northern Brit. dialect.* a pillar or post. [C15: variant of dialect *stulpe*, probably from Old Norse *stolpe;* see STELE]

stoop[4] (stu:p) *n* a less common spelling of **stoup.**

stoor (stu:r) *n Scot.* a variant of **stour.**

stop (stɒp) *vb* **stops, stopping, stopped. 1** to cease from doing or being (something); discontinue: *stop talking.* **2** to cause (something moving) to halt or (of something moving) to come to a halt: *to stop a car; the car stopped.* **3** (*tr*) to prevent the continuance or completion of: *to stop a show.* **4** (*tr;* often foll. by *from*) to prevent or restrain: *to stop George from fighting.* **5** (*tr*) to keep back: *to stop supplies to the navy.* **6** (*tr*) to intercept or hinder in transit: *to stop a letter.* **7** (*tr;* often foll. by *up*) to block or plug, esp. so as to close: *to stop up a pipe.* **8** (*tr;* often foll. by *up*) to fill a hole or opening in: *to stop up a wall.* **9** (*tr*) to staunch or stem: *to stop a wound.* **10** (*tr*) to instruct a bank not to honour (a cheque). **11** (*tr*) to deduct (money) from pay. **12** (*tr*) *Brit.* to provide with punctuation. **13** (*tr*) *Boxing.* to beat (an opponent) either by a knockout or a technical knockout. **14** (*tr*) *Informal.* to receive (a blow, hit, etc.). **15** (*intr*) to stay or rest: *we stopped at the Robinsons' for three nights.* **16** (*tr*) *Rare.* to defeat, beat, or kill. **17** (*tr*) *Music.* **17a** to alter the vibrating length of (a string on a violin, guitar, etc.) by pressing down on it at some point with the finger. **17b** to alter the vibrating length of an air column in a wind instrument by closing (a finger hole, etc.). **17c** to produce (a note) in this manner. **18** (*tr*) to place a hand inside (the bell of a French horn) to alter the tone colour and pitch or play (a note) on a French horn in such a manner. **19** *Bridge.* to have a protecting card or winner in (a suit in which one's opponents are strong). **20 stop at nothing.** to be prepared to do anything; be unscrupulous or ruthless. ◆ *n* **21** an arrest of movement or progress. **22** the act of stopping or the state of being stopped. **23** a place where something halts or pauses: *a bus stop.* **24** a stay in or as if in the course of a journey. **25** the act or an instance of blocking or obstructing. **26** a plug or stopper. **27** a block, screw, or other device or object that prevents, limits, or terminates the motion of a mechanism or moving part. **28** *Brit.* a punctuation mark, esp. a full stop. **29** Also called: **stop thrust.** *Fencing.* a counterthrust made without a parry in the hope that one's blade will touch before one's opponent's blade. **30** short for **stop payment** or **stop order. 31** *Music.* **31a** the act of stopping the string, finger hole, etc., of an instrument. **31b** a set of organ pipes or harpsichord strings that may be allowed to sound as a group by muffling or silencing all other such sets. **31c** a knob, lever, or handle on an organ, etc., that is operated to allow sets of pipes to sound. **31d** an analogous device on a harpsichord or other instrument with variable registers, such as an electrophonic instrument. **32 pull out all the stops. 32a** to play at full volume. **32b** to spare no effort. **33** *Austral.* a stud on a football boot. **34** the angle between the forehead and muzzle of a dog or cat, regarded as a point in breeding. **35** *Nautical.* a short length of line or small stuff used as a tie, esp. for a furled sail. **36** Also called: **stop consonant.** *Phonetics.* any of a class of consonants articulated by first making a complete closure at some point of the vocal tract and then releasing it abruptly with audible plosion. Stops include the labials (p, b), the alveolars or dentals (t, d), the velars (k, g). Compare **continuant. 37** Also called: **f-stop.** *Photog.* **37a** a setting of the aperture of a camera lens, calibrated to the corresponding f-number. **37b** another name for **diaphragm** (sense 4). **38** a block or carving used to complete the end of a moulding. **39** Also called: **stopper.** *Bridge.* a protecting card or winner in a suit in which one's opponents are strong. ◆ See also **stop down, stop off, stop out, stopover, stops.** [C14: from Old English *stoppian* (unattested), as in *forstoppian* to plug the ear, ultimately from Late Latin *stuppāre* to stop with a tow, from Latin *stuppa* tow, from Greek *stuppē*] ▸ **'stoppable** *adj*

stopbank ('stɒp,bæŋk) *n N.Z.* an embankment to prevent flooding.

stop bath *n* a weakly acidic solution used in photographic processing to stop the action of a developer on a film, plate, or paper before the material is immersed in fixer.

stop chorus *n Jazz.* a solo during which the rhythm section plays only the first beat of each phrase of music.

stopcock ('stɒp,kɒk) *n* a valve used to control or stop the flow of a fluid in a pipe.

stop down *vb* (*adv*) to reduce the size of the aperture of (a camera lens).

stope (stəʊp) *n* **1** a steplike excavation made in a mine to extract ore. ◆ *vb* **2** to mine (ore, etc.) by cutting stopes. [C18: probably from Low German *stope;* see STOOP[2]]

Stopes (stəʊps) *n* **Marie Carmichael.** 1880–1958, English pioneer of birth control, who established the first birth-control clinic in Britain (1921).

stop-frame *adj Films.* of or relating to animated films involving models, puppets, etc., in which each frame is photographed individually: *stop-frame photography.*

stopgap ('stɒp,gæp) *n* **a** a temporary substitute for something else. **b** (*as modifier*): *a stopgap programme.*

stop-go *adj Brit.* (of economic policy) characterized by deliberate alternate expansion and contraction of aggregate demand in an effort to curb inflation and eliminate balance of payments deficits, and yet maintain full employment.

stoping ('stəʊpɪŋ) *n Geology.* the process by which country rock is broken up and engulfed by the upward movement of magma. Also called: **magmatic stoping.** See also **stope.**

stoplight ('stɒp,laɪt) *n* **1** a red light on a traffic signal indicating that vehicles or pedestrians coming towards it should stop. **2** another word for **brake light.**

stop-loss *adj Business.* of or relating to an order to a broker in a commodity or security market to close an open position at a specified price in order to limit any loss.

stop off, stop in, *or esp. U.S.* **stop by** *vb* **1** (*intr, adv;* often foll. by *at*) to halt and call somewhere, as on a visit or errand, esp. en route to another place. ◆ *n* **stopoff. 2a** a break in a journey. **2b** (*as modifier*): *stopoff point.*

stop order *n Stock Exchange.* an instruction to a broker to sell one or more shares when the price offered for them falls below a stipulated level. Also called: **stop-loss order.**

stop out *vb* (*tr, adv*) to cover (part of the area) of a piece of cloth, printing plate, etc., to prevent it from being dyed, etched, etc.

stopover ('stɒp,əʊvə) *n* **1** a stopping place on a journey. ◆ *vb* **stop over. 2** (*intr, adv*) to make a stopover.

stoppage ('stɒpɪdʒ) *n* **1** the act of stopping or the state of being stopped. **2** something that stops or blocks. **3** a deduction of money, as from pay. **4** an organized cessation of work, as during a strike.

stoppage time *n Soccer, rugby, etc.* another name for **injury time.**

Stoppard ('stɒpɑ:d) *n* Sir **Tom.** born 1937, British playwright, born in Czechoslovakia: his works include *Rosencrantz and Guildenstern are Dead* (1967), *Travesties* (1974), *Hapgood* (1988), and *Invention of Love* (1997).

stop payment *n* an instruction to a bank by the drawer of a cheque to refuse payment on it.

stopped (stɒpt) *adj* (of a pipe or tube, esp. an organ pipe) closed at one end and thus sounding an octave lower than an open pipe of the same length.

stopper ('stɒpə) *n* **1** Also called: **stopple** ('stɒp[ə]l). a plug or bung for closing a bottle, pipe, duct, etc. **2** a person or thing that stops or puts an end to something. **3** *Bridge.* another name for **stop** (sense 39). ◆ *vb* **4** (*tr*) Also: **stopple.** to close or fit with a stopper.

stopping ('stɒpɪŋ) *n* **1** *Brit. informal.* a dental filling. **2** a solid barrier in a mine tunnel to seal off harmful gases, fire, fresh air from used air, etc. ◆ *adj* **3** *Chiefly Brit.* making many stops in a journey: *a stopping train.*

stopping power *n Physics.* a measure of the effect a substance has on the kinetic energy of a particle passing through it.

stop press *n Brit.* **1** news items inserted into a newspaper after the printing has been started. **2** the space regularly left blank for this.

stops (stɒps) *n* (*functioning as sing*) any one of several card games in which players must play their cards in certain sequences.

stop thrust *n Fencing.* another name for **stop** (sense 29).

stop time *n Jazz.* a passage where the beat stops temporarily.

stopwatch ('stɒp,wɒtʃ) *n* a type of watch used for timing events, such as sporting events, accurately, having a device for stopping the hand or hands instantly.

storage ('stɔ:rɪdʒ) *n* **1** the act of storing or the state of being stored. **2** space or area reserved for storing. **3** a charge made for storing. **4** *Computing.* **4a** the act or process of storing information in a computer memory or on a magnetic tape, disk, etc. **4b** (*as modifier*): *a storage device; storage capacity.*

storage battery *n* another name (esp. U.S.) for **accumulator** (sense 1).

storage capacity *n* the maximum number of bits, bytes, words, or items that can be held in a memory system such as that of a computer or of the brain.

storage device *n* a piece of computer equipment, such as a magnetic tape, disk, etc., in or on which data and instructions can be stored, usually in binary form.

storage heater *n* an electric device capable of accumulating and radiating heat generated by off-peak electricity.

storage tube *n Electronics.* an electron tube in which information is stored as charges for a predetermined time.

storax ('stɔ:ræks) *n* **1** any of numerous styracaceous trees or shrubs of the genus *Styrax*, of tropical and subtropical regions, having drooping showy white flowers. **2** a vanilla-scented solid resin obtained from one of these trees, *Styrax officinalis* of the Mediterranean region and SW Asia, formerly used as incense and in perfumery and medicine. **3** a liquid aromatic balsam obtained from liquidambar trees, esp. *Liquidambar orientalis* of SW Asia, and used in perfumery and medicine. [C14: via Late Latin from Greek, variant of STYRAX]

store (stɔː) *vb* **1** (*tr*) to keep, set aside, or accumulate for future use. **2** (*tr*) to place in a warehouse, depository, etc., for safekeeping. **3** (*tr*) to supply, provide, or stock. **4** (*intr*) to be put into storage. **5** *Computing.* to enter or retain (information) in a storage device. ♦ *n* **6a** an establishment for the retail sale of goods and services. **6b** (*in combination*): *storefront.* **7a** a large supply or stock kept for future use. **7b** (*as modifier*): *store ship.* **8** short for **department store. 9a** a storage place such as a warehouse or depository. **9b** (*in combination*): *storeman.* **10** the state of being stored (esp. in the phrase **in store**). **11** a large amount or quantity. **12** *Computing., chiefly Brit.* another name for **memory** (sense 7). **13** Also called: **store pig.** a pig that has not yet been weaned and weighs less than 40 kg. **14a** an animal bought lean to be fattened up for market. **14b** (*as modifier*): *store cattle.* **15 in store.** forthcoming or imminent. **16 lay, put,** *or* **set store by.** to value or reckon as important. ♦ See also **stores.** [C13: from Old French *estor,* from *estorer* to restore, from Latin *instaurāre* to refresh; related to Greek *stauros* stake] ▸ **'storable** *adj*

store and forward *vb* to store (information) in a computer for later forward transmission through a telecommunication network.

Store Bælt ('sdoːrə 'bɛld) *n* the Danish name for the **Great Belt.**

store card *n* another name for **charge card.**

storehouse ('stɔːˌhaus) *n* a place where things are stored.

storekeeper ('stɔːˌkiːpə) *n* a manager, owner, or keeper of a store. ▸ **'store,keeping** *n*

store of value *n Economics.* the function of money that enables goods and services to be paid for a considerable time after they have been acquired.

storeroom ('stɔːˌruːm, -ˌrum) *n* **1** a room in which things are stored. **2** room for storing.

stores (stɔːz) *pl n* **1** a supply or stock of something, esp. essentials, for a specific purpose: *the ship's stores.* **2** specifically, munitions slung externally on a military aircraft airframe.

storey *or U.S.* **story** ('stɔːrɪ) *n, pl* **-reys** *or* **-ries. 1** a floor or level of a building. **2** a set of rooms on one level. [C14: from Anglo-Latin *historia,* picture, from Latin: narrative, probably arising from the pictures on medieval windows]

Storey ('stɔːrɪ) *n* **David** (**Malcolm**). born 1933, British novelist and dramatist. His best-known works include the novel *This Sporting Life* (1960), and the plays *In Celebration* (1969), *Home* (1970), *The March on Russia* (1989), and *Stages* (1992).

storeyed *or U.S.* **storied** ('stɔːrɪd) *adj* **a** having a storey or storeys. **b** (*in combination*): *a two-storeyed house.*

storey house *n* (in W Africa) a house having more than one storey.

storiated ('stɔːrɪˌeɪtɪd) *adj* another word for **historiated** or **storied** (sense 2).

storied ('stɔːrɪd) *adj* **1** recorded in history or in a story; fabled. **2** decorated with narrative scenes or pictures.

stork (stɔːk) *n* **1** any large wading bird of the family *Ciconiidae,* chiefly of warm regions of the Old World, having very long legs and a long stout pointed bill, and typically having a white-and-black plumage: order *Ciconiiformes.* **2** (*sometimes cap.*) a variety of domestic fancy pigeon resembling the fairy swallow. [Old English *storc;* related to Old High German *storah,* Old Norse *storkr,* Old English *stearc* stiff; from the stiff appearance of its legs; see STARK]

storksbill ('stɔːksˌbɪl) *n* any of various geraniaceous plants of the genus *Erodium,* esp. *E. cicutarium* (**common storksbill**), having pink or reddish-purple flowers and fruits with a beaklike process.

storm (stɔːm) *n* **1a** a violent weather condition of strong winds, rain, hail, thunder, lightning, blowing sand, snow, etc. **1b** (*as modifier*): *storm signal; storm sail.* **1c** (*in combination*): *stormproof.* **2** *Meteorol.* a violent gale of force 10 on the Beaufort scale reaching speeds of 55 to 63 mph. **3** a strong or violent reaction: *a storm of protest.* **4** a direct assault on a stronghold. **5** a heavy discharge or rain, as of bullets or missiles. **6** short for **storm window** (sense 1). **7 storm in a teacup.** *Brit.* a violent fuss or disturbance over a trivial matter. U.S. equivalent: **tempest in a teapot. 8 take by storm. 8a** to capture or overrun by a violent assault. **8b** to overwhelm and enthral. ♦ *vb* **9** to attack or capture (something) suddenly and violently. **10** (*intr*) to be vociferously angry. **11** (*intr*) to move or rush violently or angrily. **12** (*intr; with* it *as subject*) to rain, hail, or snow hard and be very windy, often with thunder or lightning. [Old English, related to Old Norse *stormr,* German *Sturm;* see STIR[1]] ▸ **'storm,like** *adj*

storm belt *n* an area of the earth's surface in which storms are frequent.

stormbound ('stɔːmˌbaund) *adj* detained or harassed by storms.

storm centre *n* **1** the centre of a cyclonic storm, etc., where pressure is lowest. **2** the centre of any disturbance or trouble.

storm cloud *n* **1** a heavy dark cloud presaging rain or a storm. **2** a herald of disturbance, anger, or violence: *the storm clouds of war.*

storm-cock *n* another name for **missel thrush.** [C18: so called because it was believed to give forewarning of bad weather]

storm collar *n* a high collar on a coat.

storm cone *n Brit.* a canvas cone hoisted as a warning of high winds.

storm door *n* an extra outer door for protection in bad weather.

stormer ('stɔːmə) *n Informal.* an outstanding example of its kind: *that film was a real stormer.*

storm glass *n* a sealed tube containing a solution supposed to change in appearance according to the weather.

storming ('stɔːmɪŋ) *adj Informal.* characterized by or displaying dynamism, speed, and energy: *a storming performance.*

storm lantern *n* another name for **hurricane lamp.**

Stormont ('stɔːmənt) *n* a suburb of Belfast: site of Parliament House (1928–30), formerly the seat of the parliament of Northern Ireland (1922–72); Stormont House, formerly the residence of the prime minister of Northern Ireland; and Stormont Castle.

storm petrel *n* any small petrel, such as the northern *Hydrobates pelagicus,* of the family *Hydrobatidae,* typically having a dark plumage with paler underparts. Also called: **Mother Carey's chicken, stormy petrel.** [C19: so named because it was thought to be a harbinger of rough weather]

stormproof ('stɔːmˌpruːf) *adj* withstanding or giving protection against storms.

storm trooper *n* **1** a member of the Nazi SA. **2** a member of a force of shock troops.

storm warning *n* **1** a pattern of lights, flags, etc., displayed at certain ports as a warning to shipping of an approaching storm. **2** an announcement on radio or television of an approaching storm. **3** any warning of approaching danger or trouble.

storm window *n* **1** an additional window fitted to the outside of an ordinary window to provide insulation against wind, cold, rain, etc. **2** a type of dormer window.

stormy ('stɔːmɪ) *adj* **stormier, stormiest. 1** characterized by storms. **2** subject to, involving, or characterized by violent disturbance or emotional outburst. ▸ **'stormily** *adv* ▸ **'storminess** *n*

stormy petrel *n* **1** another name for **storm petrel. 2** a person who brings or portends trouble.

Stornoway ('stɔːnəˌweɪ) *n* a port in NW Scotland, on the E coast of Lewis in the Outer Hebrides, administrative centre of the Western Isles. Pop.: 5975 (1991).

Storting *or* **Storthing** ('stɔːtɪŋ) *n* the parliament of Norway. See also **Lagting, Odelsting.** [C19: Norwegian, from *stor* great + *thing* assembly]

story[1] ('stɔːrɪ) *n, pl* **-ries. 1** a narration of a chain of events told or written in prose or verse. **2** Also called: **short story.** a piece of fiction, briefer and usually less detailed than a novel. **3** Also called: **story line.** the plot of a book, film, etc. **4** an event that could be the subject of a narrative. **5** a report or statement on a matter or event. **6** the event or material for such a report. **7** *Informal.* a lie, fib, or untruth. **8 cut** (*or* **make**) **a long story short.** to leave out details in a narration. **9** *Informal.* **the same old story.** the familiar or regular course of events. **10 the story goes.** it is commonly said or believed. ♦ *vb* **-ries, -rying, -ried.** (*tr*) **11** to decorate (a pot, wall, etc.) with scenes from history or legends. [C13: from Anglo-French *estorie,* from Latin *historia;* see HISTORY]

story[2] ('stɔːrɪ) *n, pl* **-ries.** another spelling (esp. U.S.) of **storey.**

storyboard ('stɔːrɪˌbɔːd) *n* (in films, television, advertising, etc.) a series of sketches or photographs showing the sequence of shots or images planned for a film.

storybook ('stɔːrɪˌbuk) *n* **1** a book containing stories, esp. for children. ♦ *adj* **2** unreal or fantastic: *a storybook world.*

story line *n* the plot of a book, film, play, etc.

storyteller ('stɔːrɪˌtɛlə) *n* **1** a person who tells stories. **2** *Informal.* a liar. ▸ **'story,telling** *n, adj*

stoss (stɒs; *German* ʃtoːs) *adj* (of the side of a hill, crag, etc.) facing the onward flow of a glacier or the direction in which a former glacier flowed. [German, from *stossen* to thrust]

Stoss (*German* ʃtoːs) *n* **Viet** (faɪət). ?1445–1533, German Gothic sculptor and woodcarver. His masterpiece is the high altar in the Church of St Mary, Cracow (1477–89).

stot[1] (stɒt) *n Dialect.* **1** a bullock. **2** a castrated male ox. [Old English]

stot[2] (stɒt, stot) *vb* **stots, stotting, stotted.** *Scot. and northern English dialect.* **1** to bounce or cause to bounce. **2** (*intr*) Also: **stotter.** to stagger. [of obscure origin]

stotinka (stɒ'tɪŋkə) *n, pl* **-ki** (-kɪ). a Bulgarian monetary unit worth one hundredth of a lev. [from Bulgarian; related to *suto* hundred]

stotious ('stəuʃəs) *adj Now chiefly Irish, dialect.* drunk; inebriated. [of obscure origin; perhaps from STOT[2]]

stotter ('stɒtə; *Scot.* 'stotər) *Scot. dialect, chiefly Glasgow.* ♦ *vb* (*intr*) **1** to stagger. ♦ *n* **2** anything outstanding, esp. a good-looking person. [from STOT[2]]

stottie ('stɒtɪ) *n Northeast English.* a wedge of bread cut from a flat round loaf (**stottie cake**) that has been split and filled with meat, cheese, etc. [origin unknown]

stound (staund) *n Obsolete or Brit. dialect.* **1** a short while; instant. **2** a pang or pain. [Old English *stund;* related to Old High German *stunta* period of time, hour]

stoup *or* **stoop** (stuːp) *n* **1** a small basin for holy water. **2** *Scot. and northern English dialect.* Also: **stowp.** a bucket or drinking vessel. [C14 (in the sense: bucket): of Scandinavian origin; compare Old Norse *staup* beaker, Old English *stēap* flagon; see STEEP[1]]

stour (stauə) *or Scot.* **stoor** (stuːr) *n Archaic or Scot. and northern English dialect.* **1** turmoil or conflict. **2** dust; a cloud of dust. [C14: from Old French *estour* armed combat, of Germanic origin; related to Old High German *sturm* STORM]

Stour (stauə) *n* **1** Also called: **Great Stour.** a river in S England, in Kent, rising in the Weald and flowing N to the North Sea: separates the Isle of Thanet from the mainland. **2** any of several smaller rivers in England.

Stourbridge ('stauəˌbrɪdʒ) *n* an industrial town in W central England, in Dudley unitary authority, West Midlands. Pop.: 55 624 (1991).

Stourhead ('stauəˌhɛd) *n* a Palladian mansion near Mere in Wiltshire: built (1722) for Henry Hoare; famous for its landscaped gardens laid out (1741) by Flitcroft.

stoush (stauʃ) *Austral. and N.Z. slang.* ♦ *vb* **1** (*tr*) to hit or punch. ♦ *n* **2** fighting, violence, or a fight. [C19: of uncertain origin]

stout (staut) *adj* **1** solidly built or corpulent. **2** (*prenominal*) resolute or valiant: *stout fellow.* **3** strong, substantial, and robust. **4 a stout heart.** courage; resolution. ♦ *n* **5** strong porter highly flavoured with malt. [C14: from Old French *estout* bold, of Germanic origin; related to Middle High German *stolz* proud, Middle Dutch *stolt* brave] ▸ **'stoutish** *adj* ▸ **'stoutly** *adv* ▸ **'stoutness** *n*

Stout (staʊt) *n* Sir **Robert.** 1844–1930, New Zealand statesman, born in Scotland: prime minister of New Zealand (1884–87).

stouthearted (ˌstaʊtˈhɑːtɪd) *adj* valiant; brave. ▶ ˌ**stoutˈheartedly** *adv* ▶ ˌ**stoutˈheartedness** *n*

stove[1] (stəʊv) *n* **1** another word for **cooker** (sense 1). **2** any heating apparatus, such as a kiln. ◆ *vb* (*tr*) **3** to process (ceramics, metalwork, etc.) by heating in a stove. **4** *Scot.* to stew (meat, vegetables, etc.). [Old English *stofa* bathroom; related to Old High German *stuba* steam room, Greek *tuphos* smoke]

stove[2] (stəʊv) *vb* a past tense and past participle of **stave.**

stove enamel *n* a type of enamel made heatproof by treatment in a stove.

stovepipe (ˈstəʊvˌpaɪp) *n* **1** a pipe that serves as a flue to a stove. **2** Also called: **stovepipe hat.** a man's tall silk hat.

stovepipes (ˈstəʊvˌpaɪps) *pl n Informal.* tight trousers with narrow legs.

stover (ˈstəʊvə) *n* **1** *Chiefly Brit.* fodder. **2** *U.S.* cornstalks used as fodder. [C14: shortened from ESTOVERS]

stovies (ˈstovɪz, ˈstəʊ-) *pl n Scot.* potatoes stewed with onions. [from STOVE[1]]

stow (stəʊ) *vb* (*tr*) **1** (often foll. by *away*) to pack or store. **2** to fill by packing. **3** *Nautical.* to pack or put away (cargo, sails and other gear, etc.). **4** to have enough room for. **5** (*usually imperative*) *Brit. slang.* to cease from: *stow your noise! stow it!* [Old English *stōwian* to keep, hold back, from *stōw* a place; related to Old High German *stouwen* to accuse, Gothic *stōjan* to judge, Old Slavonic *staviti* to place]

Stow (stəʊ) *n* **John.** 1525–1605, English antiquary, noted for his *Survey of London and Westminster* (1598; 1603).

stowage (ˈstəʊɪdʒ) *n* **1** space, room, or a charge for stowing goods. **2** the act or an instance of stowing or the state of being stowed. **3** something that is stowed.

stowaway (ˈstəʊəˌweɪ) *n* **1** a person who hides aboard a vehicle, ship, or aircraft in order to gain free passage. ◆ *vb* **stow away. 2** (*intr, adv*) to travel in such a way.

Stowe[1] (stəʊ) *n* a mansion near Buckingham in N Buckinghamshire: built and decorated in the 17th and 18th centuries by Vanbrugh, Robert Adam, Grinling Gibbons, and William Kent; formerly the seat of the Dukes of Buckingham; fine landscaped gardens: now occupied by a public school.

Stowe[2] (stəʊ) *n* **Harriet Elizabeth Beecher.** 1811–96, U.S. writer, whose best-selling novel *Uncle Tom's Cabin* (1852) contributed to the antislavery cause.

stowp (staʊp) *n Scot.* a variant of **stoup** (sense 2).

STP *abbrev. for:* **1** *Trademark.* scientifically treated petroleum: an oil substitute promising renewed power for an internal-combustion engine. **2** Also: **NTP.** standard temperature and pressure: standard conditions of 0°C temperature and 101.325 kPa (760 mmHg) pressure. **3** Professor of Sacred Theology. [from Latin: *Sanctae Theologiae Professor*] ◆ *n* **4** a synthetic hallucinogenic drug related to mescaline. [from humorous reference to the extra power resulting from scientifically treated petroleum]

str *abbrev. for* steamer.

str. *abbrev. for:* **1** straight. **2** *Music.* **2a** strings. **2b** stringed. **3** strait. **4** street. **5** stroke oar.

Strabane (strəˈbæn) *n* a district of W Northern Ireland, in Co. Tyrone. Pop.: 36 141 (1991). Area: 862 sq. km (333 sq. miles)

strabismus (strəˈbɪzməs) *n* abnormal alignment of one or both eyes, characterized by a turning inwards or outwards from the nose thus preventing parallel vision: caused by paralysis of an eye muscle, etc. Also called: **squint.** [C17: via New Latin from Greek *strabismos,* from *strabizein* to squint, from *strabos* cross-eyed] ▶ **straˈbismal, straˈbismic,** *or* **straˈbismical** *adj*

Strabo (ˈstreɪbəʊ) *n* ?63 B.C.–?23 A.D., Greek geographer and historian, noted for his *Geographica.*

strabotomy (strəˈbɒtəmɪ) *n, pl* **-mies.** a former method of treating strabismus by surgical division of one or more muscles of the eye. [C19: from French *strabotomie,* from Greek *strabos* squinting + -TOMY]

Strachey (ˈstreɪtʃɪ) *n* (**Giles**) **Lytton.** 1880–1932, English biographer and critic, best known for *Eminent Victorians* (1918) and *Queen Victoria* (1921).

straddle (ˈstrædᵊl) *vb* **1** (*tr*) to have one leg, part, or support on each side of. **2** (*tr*) *U.S. and Canadian informal.* to be in favour of both sides of (something). **3** (*intr*) to stand, walk, or sit with the legs apart. **4** (*tr*) to spread (the legs) apart. **5** *Gunnery.* to fire a number of shots slightly beyond and slightly short of (a target) to determine the correct range. **6** (*intr*) (in poker, of the second player after the dealer) to double the ante before looking at one's cards. ◆ *n* **7** the act or position of straddling. **8** a noncommittal attitude or stand. **9** *Business.* a contract or option permitting its purchaser to either sell or buy securities or commodities within a specified period of time at specified prices. It is a combination of a put and a call option. Compare **spread** (sense 24c). **10** *Athletics.* a high-jumping technique in which the body is parallel with the bar and the legs straddle it at the highest point of the jump. **11** (in poker) the stake put up after the ante in poker by the second player after the dealer. **12** *Irish.* a wooden frame placed on a horse's back to which panniers are attached. [C16: frequentative formed from obsolete *strad-* (Old English *strode*), past stem of STRIDE] ▶ **ˈstraddler** *n*

Stradivari (ˌstrædɪˈvɑːrɪ) *n* **Antonio** (anˈtɔːnjo). ?1644–1737, Italian violin, viola, and cello maker.

Stradivarius (ˌstrædɪˈvɛərɪəs) *n* any of a number of violins manufactured by Antonio Stradivari or his family. Often shortened to (informal) **Strad.**

strafe (streɪf, strɑːf) *vb* (*tr*) **1** to machine-gun (troops, etc.) from the air. **2** *Slang.* to punish harshly. ◆ *n* **3** an act or instance of strafing. [C20: from German *strafen* to punish] ▶ **ˈstrafer** *n*

Strafford (ˈstræfəd) *n* **Thomas Wentworth,** Earl of. 1593–1641, English statesman. As lord deputy of Ireland (1632–39) and a chief adviser to Charles I, he was a leading proponent of the king's absolutist rule. He was impeached by Parliament and executed.

straggle (ˈstrægᵊl) *vb* (*intr*) **1** to go, come, or spread in a rambling or irregular way; stray. **2** to linger behind or wander from a main line or part. [C14: of uncertain origin; perhaps related to STRAKE and STRETCH] ▶ **ˈstraggler** *n* ▶ **ˈstraggling** *adj* ▶ **ˈstragglingly** *adv* ▶ **ˈstraggly** *adj*

straight (streɪt) *adj* **1** not curved or crooked; continuing in the same direction without deviating. **2** straightforward, outright, or candid: *a straight rejection.* **3** even, level, or upright in shape or position. **4** in keeping with the facts; accurate. **5** honest, respectable, or reliable. **6** accurate or logical: *straight reasoning.* **7** continuous; uninterrupted. **8** (esp. of an alcoholic drink) undiluted; neat. **9** not crisp, kinked, or curly: *straight hair.* **10** correctly arranged; orderly. **11** (of a play, acting style, etc.) straightforward or serious. **12** *Journalism.* (of a story, article, etc.) giving the facts without unnecessary embellishment. **13** *U.S.* sold at a fixed unit price irrespective of the quantity sold. **14** *Boxing.* (of a blow) delivered with an unbent arm: *a straight left.* **15** (of the cylinders of an internal-combustion engine) in line, rather than in a V-formation or in some other arrangement: *a straight eight.* **16** a slang word for **heterosexual. 17** *Informal.* no longer owing or being owed something: *if you buy the next round we'll be straight.* **18** *Slang.* conventional in views, customs, appearance, etc. **19** *Slang.* not using narcotics; not addicted. ◆ *adv* **20** in a straight line or direct course. **21** immediately; at once: *he came straight back.* **22** in an even, level, or upright position. **23** without cheating, lying, or unreliability: *tell it to me straight.* **24** continuously; uninterruptedly. **25** *U.S.* without discount regardless of the quantity sold. **26** (often foll. by *out*) frankly; candidly: *he told me straight out.* **27 go straight.** *Informal.* to reform after having been dishonest or a criminal. ◆ *n* **28** the state of being straight. **29** a straight line, form, part, or position. **30** *Brit.* a straight part of a racetrack. U.S. name: **straightaway. 31** *Poker.* **31a** five cards that are in sequence irrespective of suit. **31b** a hand containing such a sequence. **31c** (*as modifier*): *a straight flush.* **32** *Slang.* a conventional person. **33** *Slang.* a heterosexual. **34** *Slang.* a cigarette containing only tobacco, without marijuana, etc. [C14: from the past participle of Old English *streccan* to STRETCH] ▶ **ˈstraightly** *adv* ▶ **ˈstraightness** *n*

straight and narrow *n Informal.* the proper, honest, and moral path of behaviour. [perhaps an alteration of *strait and narrow,* an allusion to Matthew 7:14: "strait is the gate, and narrow is the way, which leadeth unto life"]

straight angle *n* an angle of 180°.

straight-arm *adj* **1** *Rugby.* (of a tackle) performed with the arm fully extended. ◆ *vb* **2** (*tr*) to ward off (an opponent) with the arm outstretched.

straight arm lift *n* a wrestling attack, in which a wrestler twists his opponent's arm against the joint and lifts him by it, often using his shoulder as a fulcrum.

straight arrow *n Informal, chiefly U.S.* **a** a clean-living and honest person. **b** (*as modifier*): *a straight-arrow cop.*

straightaway (ˌstreɪtəˈweɪ) *adv also* **straight away. 1** at once. ◆ *n* **2** the U.S. word for **straight** (sense 30).

straight bat *n* **1** *Cricket.* a bat held vertically. **2** *Brit. informal.* honest or honourable behaviour.

straight chain *n* **a** an open chain of atoms in a molecule with no attached side chains. **b** (*as modifier*): *a straight-chain hydrocarbon.* ◆ Compare **branched chain.**

straight chair *n* a straight-backed side chair.

straightedge (ˈstreɪtˌedʒ) *n* a stiff strip of wood or metal that has one edge straight and true and is used for ruling and testing straight lines. ▶ **ˈstraightˌedged** *adj*

straighten (ˈstreɪtᵊn) *vb* (sometimes foll. by *up* or *out*) **1** to make or become straight. **2** (*tr*) to make neat or tidy: *straighten your desk.* ▶ **ˈstraightener** *n*

straighten out *vb* (*adv*) **1** to make or become less complicated or confused: *the situation will straighten out.* **2** *U.S. and Canadian.* to reform or become reformed.

straighten up *vb* (*adv*) **1** to become or cause to become erect. **2** *Chiefly U.S.* to reform or become reformed.

straight face *n* a serious facial expression, esp. one that conceals the impulse to laugh. ▶ **ˈstraight-ˈfaced** *adj*

straight fight *n* a contest between two candidates only.

straight flush *n* (in poker) five consecutive cards of the same suit.

straightforward (ˌstreɪtˈfɔːwəd) *adj* **1** (of a person) honest, frank, or simple. **2** *Chiefly Brit.* (of a task, etc.) simple; easy. ◆ *adv, adj* **3** in a straight course. ▶ ˌ**straightˈforwardly** *adv* ▶ ˌ**straightˈforwardness** *n*

straightjacket (ˈstreɪtˌdʒækɪt) *n* a less common spelling of **straitjacket.**

straight joint *n* a vertical joint in brickwork that is directly above a vertical joint in the course below.

straight-laced *adj* a variant spelling of **strait-laced.**

straight-line *n* (*modifier*) **1** (of a machine) having components that are arranged in a row or that move in a straight line when in operation. **2** of or relating to a method of depreciation whereby equal charges are made against gross profit for each year of an asset's expected life.

straight man *n* a subsidiary actor who acts as stooge to a comedian.

straight off *adv Informal.* without deliberation or hesitation: *tell me the answer straight off.*

straight-out *adj Informal.* **1** complete; thoroughgoing. **2** frank or honest.

straight razor *n* another name for **cut-throat** (sense 2).

straight ticket *n U.S.* a ballot for all the candidates of one and only one political party. Compare **split ticket.**

straight up *sentence substitute. Brit. slang.* honestly; truly; exactly.

straightway (ˈstreɪtˌweɪ) *adv Archaic.* at once.

strain[1] (streɪn) *vb* **1** to draw or be drawn taut; stretch tight. **2** to exert, tax, or use (resources) to the utmost extent. **3** to injure or damage or be injured or damaged by overexertion: *he strained himself.* **4** to deform or be deformed as a result of a stress. **5** (*intr*) to make intense or violent efforts; strive. **6** to subject or be subjected to mental tension or stress. **7** to pour or pass (a substance) or (of a substance) to be poured or passed through a sieve, filter, or strainer. **8** (*tr*) to draw off or remove (one part of a substance or mixture from another) by or as if by filtering. **9** (*tr*) to clasp tightly; hug. **10** (*tr*) *Obsolete.* to force or constrain. **11** (*intr;* foll. by *at*) **11a** to push, pull, or work with violent exertion (upon). **11b** to strive (for). **11c** to balk or scruple (from). ◆ *n* **12** the act or an instance of straining. **13** the damage resulting from excessive exertion. **14** an intense physical or mental effort. **15** *Music.* (*often pl*) a theme, melody, or tune. **16** a great demand on the emotions, resources, etc. **17** a feeling of tension and tiredness resulting from overwork, worry, etc.; stress. **18** a particular style or recurring theme in speech or writing. **19** *Physics.* the change in dimension of a body under load expressed as the ratio of the total deflection or change in dimension to the original unloaded dimension. It may be a ratio of lengths, areas, or volumes. [C13: from Old French *estreindre* to press together, from Latin *stringere* to bind tightly]

strain[2] (streɪn) *n* **1** the main body of descendants from one ancestor. **2** a group of organisms within a species or variety, distinguished by one or more minor characteristics. **3** a variety of bacterium or fungus, esp. one used for a culture. **4** a streak; trace. **5** *Archaic.* a kind, type, or sort. [Old English *strēon;* related to Old High German *gistriuni* gain, Latin *struere* to CONSTRUCT]

strained (streɪnd) *adj* **1** (of an action, performance, etc.) not natural or spontaneous. **2** (of an atmosphere, relationship, etc.) not relaxed; tense.

strainer ('streɪnə) *n* **1** a sieve used for straining sauces, vegetables, tea, etc. **2** a gauze or simple filter used to strain liquids. **3** *Austral. and N.Z.* a self-locking device or a tool for tightening fencing wire. **4** *Austral. and N.Z.* the main post in a wire fence, often diagonally braced.

strain gauge *n* a device for measuring strain in a machine or other structure, usually consisting of a metal filament that is attached to it and receives the same strain. The strain can be measured by the change in the electrical properties of the filament.

strain hardening *n* a process in which a metal is permanently deformed in order to increase its resistance to further deformation.

straining piece *or* **beam** *n* a horizontal tie beam that connects the top of two queen posts of a roof truss.

strait (streɪt) *n* **1** (*often pl*) **1a** a narrow channel of the sea linking two larger areas of sea. **1b** (*cap. as part of a name*): *the Strait of Gibraltar.* **2** (*often pl*) a position of acute difficulty (often in the phrase **in dire** *or* **desperate straits**). **3** *Archaic.* a narrow place or passage. ◆ *adj Archaic.* **4** (of spaces, etc.) affording little room. **5** (of circumstances, etc.) limiting or difficult. **6** severe, strict, or scrupulous. [C13: from Old French *estreit* narrow, from Latin *strictus* constricted, from *stringere* to bind tightly] ▶ **'straitly** *adv* ▶ **'straitness** *n*

straiten ('streɪtᵊn) *vb* **1** (*tr; usually passive*) to embarrass or distress, esp. financially. **2** (*tr*) to limit, confine, or restrict. **3** *Archaic.* to make or become narrow.

straitjacket ('streɪt,dʒækɪt) *n* **1** Also called: **straightjacket** a jacket made of strong canvas material with long sleeves for binding the arms of violent prisoners or mental patients. **2** a severe restriction or limitation. ◆ *vb* **3** (*tr*) to confine in or as if in a straitjacket.

strait-laced *or* **straight-laced** *adj* prudish or puritanical.

Straits Settlements (streɪts) *n* (formerly) a British crown colony of SE Asia that included Singapore, Penang, Malacca, Labuan, and some smaller islands.

strake (streɪk) *n* **1a** a curved metal plate forming part of the metal rim on a wooden wheel. **1b** any metal plate let into a rubber tyre. **2** Also called: **streak.** *Nautical.* one of a continuous range of planks or plates forming the side of a vessel. **3** a profiled piece of wood carried on an arm that rotates round a fixed post: used to sweep the internal shape of a mould, as for a bell or a ship's propeller blade, in sand or loam. [C14: related to Old English *streccan* to STRETCH]

Stralsund (*German* 'ʃtraːlzʊnt) *n* a port in NE Germany, in Mecklenburg-West Pomerania on a strait of the Baltic: one of the leading towns of the Hanseatic League. Pop.: 71 620 (1991).

stramash (strə'mæʃ) *Scot.* ◆ *n* **1** an uproar; tumult; brawl. ◆ *vb* (*tr*) **2** to destroy; smash. [C18: perhaps expanded from SMASH]

stramonium (strə'məʊnɪəm) *n* **1** a preparation of the dried leaves and flowers of the thorn apple, containing hyoscyamine and used as a drug to treat nervous disorders. **2** another name for **thorn apple** (sense 1). [C17: from New Latin, of uncertain origin]

strand[1] (strænd) *vb* **1** to leave or drive (ships, fish, etc.) aground or ashore or (of ships, fish, etc.) to be left or driven ashore. **2** (*tr; usually passive*) to leave helpless, as without transport or money, etc. ◆ *n Chiefly poetic.* **3** a shore or beach. **4** a foreign country. [Old English; related to Old Norse *strönd* side, Middle High German *strant* beach, Latin *sternere* to spread]

strand[2] (strænd) *n* **1** a set of or one of the individual fibres or threads of string, wire, etc., that form a rope, cable, etc. **2** a single length of string, hair, wool, wire, etc. **3** a string of pearls or beads. **4** a constituent element in a complex whole: *one strand of her argument.* ◆ *vb* **5** (*tr*) to form (a rope, cable, etc.) by winding strands together. [C15: of uncertain origin]

Strand (strænd) *n* **the.** a street in W central London, parallel to the Thames: famous for its hotels and theatres.

Strandloper ('strant,luəpə) *n* a member of an extinct tribe of Khoikhoi or Bushmen who lived on sea food gathered on the beaches of southern Africa. [C17: from Afrikaans *strand* beach + *loper* walker]

strandwolf ('strænd,wʊlf; *Afrikaans* 'strant,vɔlf) *n, pl* **-wolves.** a species of hyena (*Hyaena brunnea*) that scavenges on shores of southern Africa. Also called: **brown hyena.** [C19: Afrikaans, from Dutch *strand* beach + Afrikaans *wolf* hyena]

strange (streɪndʒ) *adj* **1** odd, unusual, or extraordinary in appearance, effect, manner, etc.; peculiar. **2** not known, seen, or experienced before; unfamiliar: *a strange land.* **3** not easily explained: *a strange phenomenon.* **4** (usually foll. by *to*) inexperienced (in) or unaccustomed (to): *strange to a task.* **5** not of one's own kind, locality, etc.; alien; foreign. **6** shy; distant; reserved. **7 strange to say.** it is unusual or surprising that. **8** *Physics.* **8a** denoting a particular flavour of quark. **8b** denoting or relating to a hypothetical form of matter composed of such quarks: *strange matter; a strange star.* ◆ *adv* **9** *Not standard.* in a strange manner. [C13: from Old French *estrange,* from Latin *extrāneus* foreign; see EXTRANEOUS] ▶ **'strangely** *adv*

strange attractor *n Maths.* a pattern existing in abstract mathematical space, representing the path traced by a point that expresses the essential parameters of a chaotic system.

strangeness ('streɪndʒnɪs) *n* **1** the state or quality of being strange. **2** *Physics.* a property of certain elementary particles, characterized by a quantum number (**strangeness number**) conserved in strong but not in weak interactions. This number is equivalent to the hypercharge minus the baryon number.

stranger ('streɪndʒə) *n* **1** any person whom one does not know. **2** a person who is new to a particular locality, from another region, town, etc. **3** a guest or visitor. **4** (foll. by *to*) a person who is unfamiliar (with) or new (to) something: *he is no stranger to computers.* **5** *Law.* a person who is neither party nor privy to a transaction.

stranger's gallery *n* another name for **public gallery.**

strangle ('stræŋgᵊl) *vb* **1** (*tr*) to kill by compressing the windpipe; throttle. **2** (*tr*) to prevent or inhibit the growth or development of: *to strangle originality.* **3** (*tr*) to suppress (an utterance) by or as if by swallowing suddenly: *to strangle a cry.* ◆ See also **strangles.** [C13: via Old French, ultimately from Greek *strangalē* a halter] ▶ **'strangler** *n*

stranglehold ('stræŋgᵊl,həʊld) *n* **1** a wrestling hold in which a wrestler's arms are pressed against his opponent's windpipe. See also **Japanese stranglehold. 2** complete power or control over a person or situation.

strangles ('stræŋgᵊlz) *n* (*functioning as sing*) an acute bacterial disease of horses caused by infection with *Streptococcus equi,* characterized by inflammation of the mucous membranes of the respiratory tract. Also called: **equine distemper.** [C18: from STRANGLE]

strangulate ('stræŋgjʊ,leɪt) *vb* (*tr*) **1** to constrict (a hollow organ, vessel, etc.) so as to stop the natural flow of air, blood, etc., through it. **2** another word for **strangle.** [C18: from Latin *strangulāt-,* past participle stem of *strangulāre* to STRANGLE] ▶ **,strangu'lation** *n*

strangury ('stræŋgjʊrɪ) *n Pathol.* painful excretion of urine, drop by drop, caused by muscular spasms of the urinary tract. [C14: from Latin *strangūria,* from Greek, from *stranx* a drop squeezed out + *ouron* urine]

Stranraer (stræn'rɑː) *n* a market town in SW Scotland, in W Dumfries and Galloway: fishing port with a ferry service to Northern Ireland. Pop.: 11 348 (1991).

strap (stræp) *n* **1** a long strip of leather or similar material, for binding trunks, baggage, or other objects. **2** a strip of leather or similar material used for carrying, lifting, or holding. **3** a loop of leather, rubber, etc., suspended from the roof in a bus or train for standing passengers to hold on to. **4** a razor strop. **5** *Business.* a triple option on a security or commodity consisting of one put option and two call options at the same price and for the same period. Compare **strip**[2] (sense 5). **6** *Irish, derogatory slang.* a shameless or promiscuous woman. **7 the strap.** a beating with a strap as a punishment. **8** short for **shoulder strap.** ◆ *vb* **straps, strapping, strapped.** (*tr*) **9** to tie or bind with a strap. **10** to beat with a strap. **11** to sharpen with a strap or strop. [C16: variant of STROP]

straphanger ('stræp,hæŋə) *n Informal.* a passenger in a bus, train, etc., who has to travel standing, esp. by holding on to a strap. ▶ **'strap,hanging** *n*

strap hinge *n* a hinge with a long leaf or flap attached to the face of a door, gate, etc.

strapless ('stræplɪs) *adj* (of a woman's formal dress, brassiere, etc.) without straps over the shoulders.

strapline ('stræp,laɪn) *n* a subheading in a newspaper or magazine article or in any advertisement.

strap-oil *n Slang.* a beating.

strappado (strə'peɪdəʊ, -'pɑː-) *n, pl* **-does.** a system of torture in which a victim was hoisted by a rope tied to his wrists and then allowed to drop until his fall was suddenly checked by the rope. [C16: from French *strapade,* from Italian *strappare* to tug sharply, probably of Germanic origin; related to German (dialect) *strapfen* to make taut]

strapped (stræpt) *adj* (*postpositive;* often foll. by *for*) *Slang.* badly in need (of money, manpower, etc.); short of.

strapper ('stræpə) *n Informal.* a strapping person.

strapping ('stræpɪŋ) *adj* (*prenominal*) tall and sturdy. [C17: from STRAP (in the archaic sense: to work vigorously)]

strap work *n Architect.* decorative work resembling interlacing straps.

Strasbourg (*French* strasbur; *English* 'stræzbɜːg) *n* a city in NE France, on the Rhine: the chief French inland port; under German rule (1870–1918); university (1567); seat of the Council of Europe and of the European Parliament. Pop.: 255 937 (1990). German name: **Strassburg** ('ʃtraːsbʊrk).

strass (stræs) *n Jewellery.* another word for **paste**[1] (sense 6). [C19: German, named after J. *Strasser,* 18th-century German jeweller who invented it]

strata ('strɑːtə) *n* a plural of **stratum.**

USAGE *Strata* is sometimes wrongly used as a singular noun: *this stratum* (not *strata*) *of society is often disregarded.*

stratagem ('strætɪdʒəm) *n* a plan or trick, esp. one to deceive an enemy. [C15: ultimately from Greek *stratēgos* a general, from *stratos* an army + *agein* to lead]

strata title *n Austral.* a system of registered ownership of space in multistorey buildings, to be equivalent to the ownership of the land of a single-storey building. N.Z. equivalent: **stratum title.**

strategic (strə'tiːdʒɪk) *or* **strategical** *adj* **1** of, relating to, or characteristic of strategy. **2** important to a strategy or to strategy in general. **3** (of weapons, attacks, etc.) directed against an enemy's homeland rather than used on a battlefield: *a strategic missile: strategic bombing.* ► **stra'tegically** *adv*

strategics (strə'tiːdʒɪks) *n* (*functioning as sing*) strategy, esp. in a military sense.

strategist ('strætɪdʒɪst) *n* a specialist or expert in strategy.

strategy ('strætɪdʒɪ) *n, pl* **-gies. 1** the art or science of the planning and conduct of a war; generalship. **2** a particular long-term plan for success, esp. in business or politics. Compare **tactics** (sense 2). **3** a plan or stratagem. **[C17**: from French *stratégie,* from Greek *stratēgia* function of a general; see STRATAGEM**]**

Stratford-on-Avon *or* **Stratford-upon-Avon** ('strætfəd) *n* a market town in central England, in SW Warwickshire on the River Avon: the birthplace and burial place of William Shakespeare and home of the Royal Shakespeare Company; tourist centre. Pop.: 22 231 (1991).

strath (stræθ) *n Scot.* a broad flat river valley. **[C16**: from Scot. and Irish Gaelic *srath,* Welsh *ystrad***]**

Strathclyde Region (ˌstræθ'klaɪd) *n* a former local government region in W Scotland: formed in 1975 from Glasgow, Renfrewshire, Lanarkshire, Buteshire, Dunbartonshire, and parts of Argyllshire, Ayrshire, and Stirlingshire; replaced in 1996 by the council areas of Glasgow, Renfrewshire, East Renfrewshire, Inverclyde, North Lanarkshire, South Lanarkshire, Argyll and Bute, Dunbartonshire, West Dunbartonshire, North Ayrshire, South Ayrshire, and East Ayrshire.

strathspey (ˌstræθ'speɪ) *n* **1** a Scottish dance with gliding steps, slower than a reel. **2** a piece of music in four-four time composed for this dance.

strati- *combining form.* indicating stratum or strata: *stratiform; stratigraphy.*

straticulate (strə'tɪkjulɪt, -ˌleɪt) *adj* (of a rock formation) composed of very thin even strata. **[C19**: from New Latin *strāticulum* (unattested), diminutive of Latin *strātum* something strewn; see STRATUS**]** ► **straˌticu'lation** *n*

stratification (ˌstrætɪfɪ'keɪʃən) *n* **1** the arrangement of sedimentary rocks in distinct layers (strata), each layer representing the sediment deposited over a specific period. **2** the act of stratifying or state of being stratified. **3** *Sociol.* See **social stratification. [C17** (in the obsolete sense: the act of depositing in layers) and **C18** (in the current senses): from New Latin *strātificātiōnem,* from *stratificāre* to STRATIFY**]** ► ˌ**stratifi'cational** *adj*

stratificational grammar *n Linguistics.* a theory of grammar analysing language in terms of several structural strata or layers with different syntactic rules.

stratified sample *n Statistics.* a sample that is not drawn at random from the whole population, but separately from a number of disjoint strata of the population in order to ensure a more representative sample. See also **frame** (sense 13).

stratiform ('strætɪˌfɔːm) *adj* **1** (of rocks) occurring as or arranged in strata. **2** *Meteorol.* resembling a stratus cloud.

stratify ('strætɪˌfaɪ) *vb* **-fies, -fying, -fied. 1** to form or be formed in layers or strata. **2** (*tr*) to preserve or render fertile (seeds) by storing between layers of sand or earth. **3** *Sociol.* to divide (a society) into horizontal status groups or (of a society) to develop such groups. **[C17**: from French *stratifier,* from New Latin *stratificāre,* from Latin STRATUM**]**

stratigraphy (strə'tɪgrəfɪ) *n* **1** the study of the composition, relative positions, etc., of rock strata in order to determine their geological history. Abbrev.: **stratig. 2** *Archaeol.* a vertical section through the earth showing the relative positions of the human artefacts and therefore the chronology of successive levels of occupation. ► **stratigrapher** (strə'tɪgrəfə) *or* **stratigraphist** (strə'tɪgrəfɪst) *n* ► **stratigraphic** (ˌstrætɪ'græfɪk) *or* ˌ**strati'graphical** *adj*

strato- *combining form.* **1** denoting stratus: *stratocumulus.* **2** denoting the stratosphere: *stratopause.*

stratocracy (strə'tɒkrəsɪ) *n, pl* **-cies.** military rule. **[C17**: from Greek *stratos* an army + -CRACY**]** ► **stratocrat** ('strætəˌkræt) *n* ► **stratocratic** (ˌstrætə'krætɪk) *adj*

stratocumulus (ˌstrætəʊ'kjuːmjʊləs, ˌstreɪtəʊ-) *n, pl* **-li** (-ˌlaɪ). *Meteorol.* a uniform stretch of cloud containing dark grey globular masses.

stratopause ('strætəˌpɔːz) *n Meteorol.* the transitional zone of maximum temperature between the stratosphere and the mesosphere.

stratosphere ('strætəˌsfɪə) *n* the atmospheric layer lying between the troposphere and the mesosphere, in which temperature generally increases with height. ► **stratospheric** (ˌstrætə'sferɪk) *or* ˌ**strato'spherical** *adj*

stratum ('strɑːtəm) *n, pl* **-ta** (-tə) *or* **-tums. 1** (*usually pl*) any of the distinct layers into which sedimentary rocks are divided. **2** *Biology.* a single layer of tissue or cells. **3** a layer of any material, esp. one of several parallel layers. **4** a layer of ocean or atmosphere either naturally or arbitrarily demarcated. **5** a level of a social hierarchy that is distinguished according to such criteria as educational achievement or caste status. **[C16**: via New Latin from Latin: something strewn, from *sternere* to scatter**]** ► **'stratal** *adj*

stratum title *n* the N.Z. name for **strata title.**

stratus ('streɪtəs) *n, pl* **-ti** (-taɪ). a grey layer cloud. Compare **cirrus** (sense 1), **cumulus. [C19**: via New Latin from Latin: strewn, from *sternere* to extend**]**

Straus (straus) *n* **Oscar** (ɔskar). 1870–1954, French composer, born in Austria, noted for such operettas as *Waltz Dream* (1907) and *The Chocolate Soldier* (1908).

Strauss (straus; *German* ʃtraus) *n* **1 David Friedrich** ('daːfɪt 'friːdrɪç). 1808–74, German Protestant theologian: in his *Life of Jesus* (1835–36) he treated the supernatural elements of the story as myth. **2 Johann** (jo'han). 1804–49, Austrian composer, noted for his waltzes. **3** his son, **Johann,** called the *Waltz King.* 1825–99, Austrian composer, whose works include *The Blue Danube Waltz* (1867) and the operetta *Die Fledermaus* (1874). **4 Richard** ('rɪçart). 1864–1949, German composer, noted esp. for his symphonic poems, including *Don Juan* (1889) and *Till Eulenspiegel* (1895), his operas, such as *Elektra* (1909) and *Der Rosenkavalier* (1911), and his *Four Last Songs* (1948).

stravaig (strə'veɪg) *vb* (*intr*) *Scot. and northern English dialect.* to wander aimlessly. **[C19**: perhaps a variant of obsolete *extravage,* from Medieval Latin *extrāvagārī,* from *vagārī* to wander**]**

Stravinsky (*Russian* stra'vinskij) *n* **Igor Fyodorovich** ('igərj 'fjɔdərəvitʃ). 1882–1971, U.S. composer, born in Russia. He created ballet scores, such as *The Firebird* (1910), *Petrushka* (1911), and *The Rite of Spring* (1913), for Diaghilev. These were followed by neoclassical works, including *Oedipus Rex* (1927) and the *Symphony of Psalms* (1930). The 1950s saw him reconciled to serial techniques, which he employed in such works as the *Canticum Sacrum* (1955), the ballet *Agon* (1957), and *Requiem Canticles* (1966).

straw[1] (strɔː) *n* **1a** stalks of threshed grain, esp. of wheat, rye, oats, or barley, used in plaiting hats, baskets, etc., or as fodder. **1b** (*as modifier*): *a straw hat.* **2** a single dry or ripened stalk, esp. of a grass. **3** a long thin hollow paper or plastic tube or stem of a plant, used for sucking up liquids into the mouth. **4** (*usually used with a negative*) anything of little value or importance: *I wouldn't give a straw for our chances.* **5** a measure or remedy that one turns to in desperation (esp. in the phrases **clutch** *or* **grasp at a straw** *or* **straws**). **6a** a pale yellow colour. **6b** (*as adj*): *straw hair.* **7 the last straw.** a small incident, setback, etc. that, coming after others, proves intolerable. **8 straw in the wind.** a hint or indication. ◆ *adj* **9** *Chiefly U.S.* having little value or substance. ◆ See also **man of straw. [**Old English *streaw;* related to Old Norse *strā,* Old Frisian *strē,* Old High German *strō;* see STREW**]** ► **'strawˌlike** *adj* ► **'strawy** *adj*

straw[2] (strɔː) *vb Archaic.* another word for **strew.**

Straw (strɔː) *n* **Jack,** full name *John Whitaker Straw.* born 1946, British Labour politician; Home Secretary from 1997.

strawberry ('strɔːbərɪ, -brɪ) *n, pl* **-ries. 1a** any of various low-growing rosaceous plants of the genus *Fragaria,* such as *F. vesca* (**wild strawberry**) and *F. ananassa* (**garden strawberry**), which have white flowers and red edible fruits and spread by runners. **1b** (*as modifier*): *a strawberry patch.* **2a** the fruit of any of these plants, consisting of a sweet fleshy receptacle bearing small seedlike parts (the true fruits). **2b** (*as modifier*): *strawberry ice cream.* **3 barren strawberry.** a related Eurasian plant, *Potentilla sterilis,* that does not produce edible fruit. **4a** a purplish-red colour. **4b** (*as adj*): *strawberry shoes.* **[**Old English *streawberige;* perhaps from the strawlike appearance of the runners**]**

strawberry blonde *adj* **1** (of hair) reddish blonde. ◆ *n* **2** a woman with such hair.

strawberry bush *n* **1** an E North American shrub or small tree, *Euonymus americanus,* having pendulous capsules that split when ripe to reveal scarlet seeds: family *Celastraceae.* **2** any of various similar or related plants.

strawberry mark *n* a soft vascular red birthmark. Technical name: **haemangioma simplex.** Also called: **strawberry.**

strawberry tomato *n* **1** a tropical solanaceous annual plant, *Physalis peruviana,* having bell-shaped whitish-yellow flowers and small edible round yellow berries. **2** a similar and related plant, *Physalis pubescens.* **3** the fruit of either of these plants, eaten fresh or made into preserves and pickles. ◆ Also called: **Cape gooseberry.**

strawberry tree *n* a S European evergreen tree, *Arbutus unedo,* having white or pink flowers and red strawberry-like berries. See also **arbutus.**

strawboard ('strɔːˌbɔːd) *n* a board made of compressed straw and adhesive, used esp. in book covers.

strawflower ('strɔːˌflauə) *n* an Australian plant, *Helichrysum bracteatum,* in which the coloured bracts retain their colour when the plant is dried: family *Compositae* (composites). See also **immortelle.**

straw man *n Chiefly U.S.* **1** a figure of a man made from straw. **2** another term for **man of straw.**

straw poll *or* (*chiefly U.S., Canadian, and N.Z.*) **vote** *n* an unofficial poll or vote taken to determine the opinion of a group or the public on some issue.

Strawson ('strɔːsən) *n* Sir **Peter** (**Frederick**). born 1919, British philosopher. His early work deals with the relationship between language and logic, his later work with metaphysics. His books include *The Bounds of Sense* (1966) and *Freedom and Resentment* (1974).

strawweight ('strɔːˌweɪt) *n* **a** a professional boxer weighing not more than 47.6 kg (105 pounds). **b** (*as modifier*): *the strawweight title.* ◆ Also called: **mini-flyweight.**

straw wine *n* any of several wines made from grapes dried on straw mats to increase their sugar strength.

strawworm ('strɔːˌwɜːm) *n* another name for a **caddis worm.**

stray (streɪ) *vb* (*intr*) **1** to wander away, as from the correct path or from a given area. **2** to wander haphazardly. **3** to digress from the point, lose concentration, etc. **4** to deviate from certain moral standards. ◆ *n* **5a** a domestic animal, fowl, etc., that has wandered away from its place of keeping and is lost. **5b** (*as modifier*): *stray dogs.* **6** a lost or homeless person, esp. a child: *waifs and strays.* **7** an isolated or random occurrence, specimen, etc., that is out of place or outside the usual pattern. ◆ *adj* **8** scattered, random, or haphazard: *a stray bullet grazed his thigh.* **[C14**: from Old French *estraier,* from Vulgar Latin *estragāre* (unattested), from Latin *extrā-* outside + *vagārī* to roam; see ASTRAY, EXTRAVAGANT, STRAVAIG**]** ► **'strayer** *n*

Strayhorn ('streɪˌhɔːn) *n* **Billy,** full name *William Strayhorn.* 1915–67, U.S. jazz composer and pianist, noted esp. for his association (1939–67) with Duke Ellington.

strays (streɪz) *pl n* **1** Also called: **stray capacitance.** *Electronics.* undesired capacitance in equipment, occurring between the wiring, between the wiring and the chassis, or between components and the chassis. **2** *Telecomm.* another word for **static** (sense 9).

streak[1] (striːk) *n* **1** a long thin mark, stripe, or trace of some contrasting colour. **2a** (of lightning) a sudden flash. **2b** (*as modifier*): *streak lightning.* **3** an element or trace, as of some quality or characteristic. **4** a strip, vein, or layer: *fatty streaks.* **5** a short stretch or run, esp. of good or bad luck. **6** *Mineralogy.* the powdery mark made by a mineral when rubbed on a hard or rough surface: its colour is an important distinguishing characteristic. **7** *Bacteriol.* the inoculation of a culture medium by drawing a wire contaminated with the microorganisms across the surface of the medium. **8** *Informal.* an act or the practice of running naked through a public place. ◆ *vb* **9** (*tr*) to mark or daub with a streak or streaks. **10** (*intr*) to form streaks or become streaked. **11** (*intr*) to move rapidly in a straight line. **12** (*intr*) *Informal.* to run naked through a crowd of people in a public place in order to shock or amuse them. [Old English *strica,* related to Old Frisian *strike,* Old High German *strih,* Norwegian, Swedish *strika*] ▸ **streaked** *adj* ▸ **'streaker** *n* ▸ **'streak,like** *adj*

streak[2] (stri:k) *n* a variant spelling of **strake** (sense 2).

streaking ('stri:kɪŋ) *n* **1** an act or instance of running naked through a public place. **2** *Television.* light or dark streaks to the right of a bright object in a television picture, caused by distortion in the transmission chain.

streaky ('stri:kɪ) *adj* **streakier, streakiest. 1** marked with streaks. **2** occurring in streaks. **3** (of bacon) having alternate layers of meat and fat. **4** of varying or uneven quality. ▸ **'streakily** *adv* ▸ **'streakiness** *n*

stream (stri:m) *n* **1** a small river; brook. **2** any steady flow of water or other fluid. **3** something that resembles a stream in moving continuously in a line or particular direction. **4** a rapid or unbroken flow of speech, etc.: *a stream of abuse.* **5** *Brit.* any of several parallel classes of schoolchildren, or divisions of children within a class, grouped together because of similar ability. **6 go** (*or* **drift**) **with the stream.** to conform to the accepted standards. **7 off stream.** (of an industrial plant, manufacturing process, etc.) shut down or not in production. **8 on stream.** (of an industrial plant, manufacturing process, etc.) in or about to go into operation or production. ◆ *vb* **9** to emit or be emitted in a continuous flow: *his nose streamed blood.* **10** (*intr*) to move in unbroken succession, as a crowd of people, vehicles, etc. **11** (*intr*) to float freely or with a waving motion: *bunting streamed in the wind.* **12** (*tr*) to unfurl (a flag, etc.). **13** (*intr*) to move causing a trail of light, condensed gas, etc., as a jet aircraft. **14** (when *intr,* often foll. by *for*) *Mining.* to wash (earth, gravel, etc.) in running water in prospecting (for gold, etc.), to expose the particles of ore or metal. **15** *Brit. education.* to group or divide (children) in streams. [Old English; related to Old Frisian *strām,* Old Norse *straumr,* Old High German *stroum,* Greek *rheuma*] ▸ **'streamlet** *n* ▸ **'stream,like** *adj*

streamer ('stri:mə) *n* **1** a long narrow flag or part of a flag. **2** a long narrow coiled ribbon of coloured paper that becomes unrolled when tossed. **3** a stream of light, esp. one appearing in some forms of the aurora. **4** *Journalism.* a large heavy headline printed across the width of a page of a newspaper. **5** *Computing.* another word for **tape streamer.**

streamline ('stri:m,laɪn) *n* **1** a contour on a body that offers the minimum resistance to a gas or liquid flowing around it. **2** a line in a fluid such that the tangent at any point indicates the direction of the velocity of a particle of the fluid at that point. ◆ *vb* (*tr*) **3** to make streamlined.

streamlined ('stri:m,laɪnd) *adj* **1** offering or designed to offer the minimum resistance to the flow of a gas or liquid. **2** made more efficient, esp. by simplifying.

streamline flow *n* flow of a fluid in which its velocity at any point is constant or varies in a regular manner. Also called: **viscous flow.** Compare **turbulent flow.** See also **laminar flow.**

stream of consciousness *n* **1** *Psychol.* the continuous flow of ideas, thoughts, and feelings forming the content of an individual's consciousness. The term was originated by William James. **2a** a literary technique that reveals the flow of thoughts and feelings of characters through long passages of soliloquy. **2b** (*as modifier*): *a stream-of-consciousness novel.*

streamy ('stri:mɪ) *adj* **streamier, streamiest.** *Chiefly poetic.* **1** (of an area, land, etc.) having many streams. **2** flowing or streaming. ▸ **'streaminess** *n*

streel (stri:l) *n Irish.* a slovenly woman. [from Irish Gaelic *straoill*]

Streep (stri:p) *n* **Meryl,** original name *Mary Louise Streep.* born 1949, U.S. actress. Her films include *The Deerhunter* (1978), *Kramer vs Kramer* (1979), *The French Lieutenant's Woman* (1981), *Sophie's Choice* (1982), *Out of Africa* (1986), and *Dancing at Lughnasa* (1999).

street (stri:t) *n* **1a** (*cap. when part of a name*) a public road that is usually lined with buildings, esp. in a town: *Oxford Street.* **1b** (*as modifier*): *a street directory.* **2** the buildings lining a street. **3** the part of the road between the pavements, used by vehicles. **4** the people living, working, etc., in a particular street. **5** (*modifier*) of or relating to the urban counterculture: *street style; street drug.* **6 man in the street.** an ordinary or average citizen. **7 on the streets. 7a** earning a living as a prostitute. **7b** homeless. **8** (**right**) **up one's street.** *Informal.* (just) what one knows or likes best. **9 streets ahead of.** *Informal.* superior to, more advanced than, etc. **10 streets apart.** *Informal.* markedly different. ◆ *vb* (*tr*) **11** *Austral.* to outdistance. [Old English *strǣt,* from Latin *via strāta* paved way (*strāta,* from *strātus,* past participle of *sternere* to stretch out); compare Old Frisian *strēte,* Old High German *strāza;* see STRATUS]

street Arab *n Literary and old-fashioned.* a homeless child, esp. one who survives by begging and stealing; urchin.

streetcar ('stri:t,kɑ:) *n* the usual U.S. and Canadian name for **tram**[1] (sense 1).

street credibility *n* a convincing command or display of the style, fashions, knowledge, etc., associated with urban counterculture. Often shortened to **street cred.** ▸ **,street-'credible** *adj*

street cry *n* (*often pl*) the cry of a street hawker.

street door *n* the door of a house that opens onto the street.

street furniture *n* pieces of equipment, such as streetlights and pillar boxes, placed in the street for the benefit of the public.

streetlight ('stri:t,laɪt) *or* **streetlamp** *n* a light, esp. one carried on a lamppost, that illuminates a road, etc.

street piano *n* another name for **barrel organ.**

street theatre *n* dramatic entertainments performed esp. in shopping precincts.

street value *n* the monetary worth of a commodity, usually an illicit commodity such as a drug, considered as the price it would fetch when sold to the ultimate user.

streetwalker ('stri:t,wɔ:kə) *n* a prostitute who solicits on the streets. ▸ **'street,walking** *n, adj*

streetwise ('stri:t,waɪz) *adj* attuned to and adept at surviving in an urban, poor and often criminal environment. Also: **street-smart.** ▸ **street wisdom** *n*

Streicher ('ʃtraɪkə) *n* **Julius.** 1885–1946, German Nazi journalist and politician, who spread anti-Semitic propaganda as editor of *Der Stürmer* (1923–45). He was hanged as a war criminal.

Streisand ('straɪsænd) *n* **Barbra.** born 1942, U.S. singer, actress, and film director: the films she has acted in include *Funny Girl* (1968) and *A Star is Born* (1976); her films as actress and director include *Yentl* (1983), *Prince of Tides* (1990), and *The Mirror has Two Faces* (1996).

strelitzia (strɛ'lɪtsɪə) *n* any southern African perennial herbaceous plant of the musaceous genus *Strelitzia,* cultivated for its showy flowers: includes the bird-of-paradise flower. [C18: named after Charlotte of Mecklenburg-*Strelitz* (1744–1818), queen of Great Britain and Ireland]

strength (strɛŋθ) *n* **1** the state or quality of being physically or mentally strong. **2** the ability to withstand or exert great force, stress, or pressure. **3** something that is regarded as being beneficial or a source of power: *their chief strength is technology.* **4** potency, as of a drink, drug, etc. **5** power to convince; cogency: *the strength of an argument.* **6** degree of intensity or concentration of colour, light, sound, flavour, etc. **7** the full or part of the full complement as specified: *at full strength; below strength.* **8** *Finance.* firmness of or a rising tendency in prices, esp. security prices. **9** *Archaic or poetic.* a stronghold or fortress. **10** *Austral. and N.Z. informal.* the general idea, the main purpose: *to get the strength of something.* **11 from strength to strength.** with ever-increasing success. **12 in strength.** in large numbers. **13 on the strength of.** on the basis of or relying upon. [Old English *strengthu;* related to Old High German *strengida;* see STRONG]

strengthen ('strɛŋθən) *vb* to make or become stronger. ▸ **'strengthener** *n*

strenuous ('strɛnjuəs) *adj* **1** requiring or involving the use of great energy or effort. **2** characterized by great activity, effort, or endeavour. [C16: from Latin *strēnuus* brisk, vigorous] ▸ **strenuosity** (,strɛnju'ɒsɪtɪ) *or* **'strenuousness** *n* ▸ **'strenuously** *adv*

strep (strɛp) *n Informal.* short for **streptococcus.**

strepitoso ('strɛpɪ'təʊsəʊ) *adj, adv Music.* (to be performed) boisterously. [Italian, literally; noisily]

strepitous ('strɛpɪtəs) *or* **strepitant** *adj Rare.* noisy; boisterous. [C17: from Latin *strepitus* a din]

strepto- *combining form.* **1** indicating a shape resembling a twisted chain: *streptococcus.* **2** indicating streptococcus: *streptolysin.* [from Greek *streptos* twisted, from *strephein* to twist]

streptocarpus (,strɛptə'kɑ:pəs) *n* any plant of the typically stemless subtropical perennial genus *Streptocarpus,* some species of which are grown as greenhouse plants for their tubular flowers in a range of bright colours: family *Gesneriaceae.* [New Latin, from Greek *streptos* twisted + *karpos* fruit (from the shape of the capsule)]

streptococcus (,strɛptəʊ'kɒkəs) *n, pl* **-cocci** (-'kɒkaɪ; *U.S.* -'kɒksaɪ). any Gram-positive spherical bacterium of the genus *Streptococcus,* typically occurring in chains and including many pathogenic species, such as *S. pyogenes,* which causes scarlet fever, sore throat, etc.: family *Lactobacillaceae.* Often shortened to **strep.** ▸ streptococcal (,strɛptəʊ'kɒkəl) *or* (*less commonly*) **streptococcic** (,strɛptəʊ'kɒkɪk; *U.S.* -'kɒksɪk) *adj*

streptokinase (,strɛptəʊ'kaɪneɪs) *n* an enzyme produced by streptococci that causes the fibrin of certain animal species to undergo lysis.

streptomycin (,strɛptəʊ'maɪsɪn) *n* an antibiotic obtained from the bacterium *Streptomyces griseus:* used in the treatment of tuberculosis and Gram-negative bacterial infections. Formula: $C_{21}H_{39}N_7O_{12}$. [from *Streptomyces,* genus name of bacteria (from STREPTO- + Greek *mukēs* fungus + -IN)]

streptothricin (,strɛptəʊ'θraɪsɪn) *n* an antibiotic active against bacteria and some fungi, produced by the bacterium *Streptomyces lavendulae.* [from *Streptothrix,* genus name of bacteria (from STREPTO- + Greek *thrix* hair + -IN)]

Stresemann (*German* 'ʃtreːzəman) *n* **Gustav.** 1878–1929, German statesman; chancellor (1923) and foreign minister (1923–29) of the Weimar Republic. He gained (1926) Germany's admission to the League of Nations and shared the Nobel peace prize (1926) with Aristide Briand.

stress (strɛs) *n* **1** special emphasis or significance attached to something. **2** mental, emotional, or physical strain or tension. **3** emphasis placed upon a syllable by pronouncing it more loudly than those that surround it. **4** such emphasis as part of a regular rhythmic beat in music or poetry. **5** a syllable so emphasized. **6** *Physics.* **6a** force or a system of forces producing deformation or strain. **6b** the force acting per unit area. ◆ *vb* (*tr*) **7** to give emphasis or prominence to. **8** to pronounce (a word or syllable) more loudly than those that surround it. **9** to subject to stress or strain. [C14: *stresse,* shortened from DISTRESS] ▸ **'stressful** *adj* ▸ **'stressfully** *adv* ▸ **'stressfulness** *n*

-stress *suffix forming nouns.* indicating a woman who performs or is engaged in a certain activity: *songstress; seamstress.* Compare **-ster** (sense 1). [from -ST(E)R + -ESS]

stressor ('strɛsə) *n* an event, experience, etc., that causes stress.

stretch (strɛtʃ) *vb* **1** to draw out or extend or be drawn out or extended in length, area, etc. **2** to extend or be extended to an undue degree, esp. so as to distort or lengthen permanently. **3** to extend (the limbs, body, etc.). **4** (*tr*) to reach or suspend (a rope, etc.) from one place to another. **5** (*tr*) to draw tight; tighten. **6** (often foll. by *out, forward,* etc.) to reach or hold (out); extend. **7** (*intr;* usually foll. by *over*) to extend in time: *the course stretched over three months.* **8** (*intr;* foll. by *for, over,* etc.) (of a region, etc.) to extend in length or area. **9** (*intr*) (esp. of a garment) to be capable of expanding, as to a larger size: *socks that will stretch.* **10** (*tr*) to put a great strain upon or extend to the limit. **11** to injure (a muscle, tendon, ligament, etc.) by means of a strain or sprain. **12** (*tr; often foll. by out*) to make do with (limited resources): *to stretch one's budget.* **13** (*tr*) *Informal.* to expand or elaborate (a story, etc.) beyond what is credible or acceptable: *that's stretching it a bit.* **14** (*tr; often passive*) to extend, as to the limit of one's abilities or talents. **15** *Archaic or slang.* to hang or be hanged by the neck. **16 stretch a point. 16a** to make a concession or exception not usually made. **16b** to exaggerate. **17 stretch one's legs.** to take a walk, esp. after a period of inactivity. ◆ *n* **18** the act of stretching or state of being stretched. **19** a large or continuous expanse or distance: *a stretch of water.* **20** extent in time, length, area, etc. **21a** capacity for being stretched, as in some garments. **21b** (*as modifier*): *stretch pants.* **22** *Horse racing.* the section or sections of a racecourse that are straight, esp. the final straight section leading to the finishing line. **23** *Slang.* a term of imprisonment. **24 at a stretch.** *Chiefly Brit.* **24a** with some difficulty; by making a special effort. **24b** if really necessary or in extreme circumstances. [Old English *streccan;* related to Old Frisian *strekka,* Old High German *strecken;* see STRAIGHT, STRAKE] ▸ **'stretchable** *adj* ▸ **,stretcha'bility** *n*

stretcher ('strɛtʃə) *n* **1** a device for transporting the ill, wounded, or dead, consisting of a frame covered by canvas or other material. **2** a strengthening often decorative member joining the legs of a chair, table, etc. **3** the wooden frame on which canvas is stretched and fixed for oil painting. **4** a tie beam or brace used in a structural framework. **5** a brick or stone laid horizontally with its length parallel to the length of a wall. Compare **header** (sense 4). **6** *Rowing.* a fixed board across a boat on which an oarsman braces his feet. **7** *Austral. and N.Z.* a camp bed. **8** *Slang.* an exaggeration or lie. ◆ *vb* (*tr*) **9** to transport (a sick or injured person) on a stretcher.

stretcher-bearer *n* a person who helps to carry a stretcher, esp. in wartime.

stretch limo *n Informal.* a limousine that has been lengthened to provide extra seating accommodation and more legroom. In full: **stretch limousine.**

stretchmarks ('strɛtʃ,mɑːks) *pl n* marks that remain visible on the abdomen after its distension in pregnancy.

stretchy ('strɛtʃɪ) *adj* **stretchier, stretchiest.** characterized by elasticity. ▸ **'stretchiness** *n*

Stretford ('strɛtfəd) *n* an industrial town in NW England, in Trafford unitary authority, Greater Manchester. Pop.: 43 953 (1991).

stretto ('strɛtəʊ) *n, pl* **-tos** *or* **-ti** (-tiː). **1** (in a fugue) the close overlapping of two parts or voices, the second one entering before the first has completed its statement of the subject. **2** Also called: **stretta** ('strɛtə). a concluding passage in a composition, played at a faster speed than the earlier material. [C17: from Italian, from Latin *strictus* tightly bound; see STRICT]

streusel ('struːsᵊl, 'strɔɪ-; *German* 'ʃtrɔyzəl) *n Chiefly U.S.* a crumbly topping for rich pastries. [German, from *streuen* to STREW]

strew (struː) *vb* **strews, strewing, strewed; strewn** *or* **strewed.** to spread or scatter or be spread or scattered, as over a surface or area. [Old English *streowian;* related to Old Norse *strā,* Old High German *streuwen,* Latin *struere* to spread] ▸ **'strewer** *n*

strewth (struːθ) *interj* an expression of surprise or dismay. [C19: alteration of *God's truth*]

stria ('straɪə) *n, pl* **striae** ('straɪiː). (*often pl*) **1** Also called: **striation.** *Geology.* any of the parallel scratches or grooves on the surface of a rock over which a glacier has flowed or on the surface of a crystal. **2** *Biology, anatomy.* a narrow band of colour or a ridge, groove, or similar linear mark, usually occurring in a parallel series. **3** *Architect.* a narrow channel, such as a flute on the shaft of a column. [C16: from Latin: a groove]

striate *adj* ('straɪɪt), *also* **striated. 1** marked with striae; striped. ◆ *vb* ('straɪeɪt). **2** (*tr*) to mark with striae. [C17: from Latin *striāre* to make grooves, from STRIA]

striation (straɪ'eɪʃən) *n* **1** an arrangement or pattern of striae. **2** the condition of being striate. **3** another word for **stria** (sense 1).

strick (strɪk) *n Textiles.* any bast fibres preparatory to being made into slivers. [C15 *stric,* perhaps of Low German origin; compare Middle Dutch *stric,* Middle Low German *strik* rope]

stricken ('strɪkən) *adj* **1** laid low, as by disease or sickness. **2** deeply affected, as by grief, love, etc. **3** *Archaic.* wounded or injured. [C14: past participle of STRIKE] ▸ **'strickenly** *adv*

strickle ('strɪkᵊl) *n* **1** Also called: **strike.** a board used for sweeping off excess material in a container. **2** a template used for shaping a mould. **3** a bar of abrasive material for sharpening a scythe. ◆ *vb* **4** (*tr*) to level, form, or sharpen with a strickle. [Old English *stricel;* related to Latin *strigilis* scraper, German *Striegel;* see STRIKE]

strict (strɪkt) *adj* **1** adhering closely to specified rules, ordinances, etc.: *a strict faith.* **2** complied with or enforced stringently; rigorous: *a strict code of conduct.* **3** severely correct in attention to rules of conduct or morality: *a strict teacher.* **4** (of a punishment, etc.) harsh; severe. **5** (*prenominal*) complete; absolute: *in strict secrecy.* **6** *Logic, maths.* (of a relation) **6a** applying more narrowly than some other relation often given the same name, as *strict inclusion,* which holds only between pairs of sets that are distinct, while *simple inclusion* permits the case in which they are identical. See also **proper** (sense 9), **ordering. 6b** distinguished from a relation of the same name that is not the subject of formal study. **7** *Botany, rare.* very straight, narrow, and upright: *strict panicles.* [C16: from Latin *strictus,* from *stringere* to draw tight] ▸ **'strictly** *adv* ▸ **'strictness** *n*

stricture ('strɪktʃə) *n* **1** a severe criticism; censure. **2** *Pathol.* an abnormal constriction of a tubular organ, structure, or part. **3** *Obsolete.* severity. [C14: from Latin *strictūra* contraction; see STRICT] ▸ **'strictured** *adj*

stride (straɪd) *n* **1** a long step or pace. **2** the space measured by such a step. **3** a striding gait. **4** an act of forward movement by an animal, completed when the legs have returned to their initial relative positions. **5** progress or development (esp. in the phrase **make rapid strides**). **6** a regular pace or rate of progress: *to get into one's stride; to be put off one's stride.* **7** *Rowing.* the distance covered between strokes. **8** Also called: **stride piano.** *Jazz.* a piano style characterized by single bass notes on the first and third beats and chords on the second and fourth. **9** (*pl*) *Informal, chiefly Austral.* men's trousers. **10 take (something) in one's stride.** to do (something) without difficulty or effort. ◆ *vb* **strides, striding, strode, stridden. 11** (*intr*) to walk with long regular or measured paces, as in haste, etc. **12** (*tr*) to cover or traverse by striding: *he strode thirty miles.* **13** (often foll. by *over, across,* etc.) to cross (over a space, obstacle, etc.) with a stride. **14** (*intr*) *Rowing.* to achieve the desired rhythm in a racing shell. [Old English *strīdan;* related to Old High German *strītan* to quarrel; see STRADDLE] ▸ **'strider** *n*

strident ('straɪdᵊnt) *adj* **1** (of a shout, voice, etc.) having or making a loud or harsh sound. **2** urgent, clamorous, or vociferous: *strident demands.* [C17: from Latin *strīdēns,* from *strīdēre* to make a grating sound] ▸ **'stridence** *or* **'stridency** *n* ▸ **'stridently** *adv*

stridor ('straɪdɔː) *n* **1** *Pathol.* a high-pitched whistling sound made during respiration, caused by obstruction of the air passages. **2** *Chiefly literary.* a harsh or shrill sound. [C17: from Latin; see STRIDENT]

stridulate ('strɪdjʊ,leɪt) *vb* (*intr*) (of insects such as the cricket) to produce sounds by rubbing one part of the body against another. [C19: back formation from *stridulation,* from Latin *strīdulus* creaking, hissing, from *strīdēre* to make a harsh noise] ▸ **,stridu'lation** *n* ▸ **'stridu,lator** *n* ▸ **stridulatory** ('strɪdjʊ,leɪtərɪ) *adj*

stridulous ('strɪdjʊləs) *or* **stridulant** *adj* **1** making a harsh, shrill, or grating noise. **2** *Pathol.* of, relating to, or characterized by stridor. [C17: from Latin *strīdulus,* from *strīdēre* to make a harsh noise. See STRIDENT] ▸ **'stridulously** *or* **'stridulantly** *adv* ▸ **'stridulousness** *or* **'stridulance** *n*

strife (straɪf) *n* **1** angry or violent struggle; conflict. **2** rivalry or contention, esp. of a bitter kind. **3** *Austral. and N.Z.* trouble or discord of any kind: *to get into strife.* **4** *Archaic.* striving. [C13: from Old French *estrif,* probably from *estriver* to STRIVE]

strigiform ('strɪdʒɪ,fɔːm) *adj* of, relating to, or belonging to the *Strigiformes,* an order of birds comprising the owls. [via New Latin from Latin *strix* a screech owl]

strigil ('strɪdʒɪl) *n* **1** a curved blade used by the ancient Romans and Greeks to scrape the body after bathing. **2** *Architect.* a decorative fluting, esp. one in the shape of the letter *S* as used in Roman architecture. [C16: from Latin *strigilis,* from *stringere* to graze]

strigose ('straɪɡəʊs) *adj* **1** *Botany.* bearing stiff hairs or bristles: *strigose leaves.* **2** *Zoology.* marked with fine closely set grooves or ridges. [C18: via New Latin *strigōsus,* from *striga* a bristle, from Latin: grain cut down]

strike (straɪk) *vb* **strikes, striking, struck. 1** to deliver (a blow or stroke) to (a person). **2** to come or cause to come into sudden or violent contact (with). **3** (*tr*) to make an attack on. **4** to produce (fire, sparks, etc.) or (of fire, sparks, etc.) to be produced by ignition. **5** to cause (a match) to light by friction or (of a match) to be lighted. **6** to press (the key of a piano, organ, etc.) or to sound (a specific note) in this or a similar way. **7** to indicate (a specific time) by the sound of a hammer striking a bell or by any other percussive sound. **8** (of a venomous snake) to cause injury by biting. **9** (*tr*) to affect or cause to affect deeply, suddenly, or radically, as if by dealing a blow: *her appearance struck him as strange; I was struck on his art.* **10** (*past participle* **struck** *or* **stricken**) (*tr; passive; usually foll. by with*) to render incapable or nearly so: *she was stricken with grief.* **11** (*tr*) to enter the mind of: *it struck me that he had become very quiet.* **12** (*past participle* **struck** *or* **stricken**) to render: *I was struck dumb.* **13** (*tr*) to be perceived by; catch: *the glint of metal struck his eye.* **14** to arrive at or come upon (something), esp. suddenly or unexpectedly: *to strike the path for home; to strike upon a solution.* **15** (*intr; sometimes foll. by out*) to set (out) or proceed, esp. upon a new course: *to strike for the coast.* **16** (*tr; usually passive*) to afflict with a disease, esp. unexpectedly: *he was struck with polio when he was six.* **17** (*tr*) to discover or come upon a source of (ore, petroleum, etc.). **18** (*tr*) (of a plant) to produce or send down (a root or roots). **19** (*tr*) to take apart or pack up; break (esp. in the phrase **strike camp**). **20** (*tr*) to take down or dismantle (a stage set, formwork, etc.). **21** (*tr*) *Nautical.* **21a** to lower or remove (a specified piece of gear). **21b** to haul down or dip (a flag, sail, etc.) in salute or in surrender. **21c** to lower (cargo, etc.) into the hold of a ship. **22** to attack (an objective) with the intention of causing damage to, seizing, or destroying it. **23** to impale the hook in the mouth of (a fish) by suddenly tightening or jerking the line after the bait or fly has been taken. **24** (*tr*) to form or impress (a coin, metal, etc.) by or as if by stamping. **25** to level (a surface) by use of a flat board. **26** (*tr*) to assume or take up (an attitude, posture, etc.). **27** (*intr*) (of workers in a factory, etc.) to cease work collectively as a protest against working conditions, low pay, etc. **28** (*tr*) to reach by agreement: *to strike a bargain.* **29** (*tr*) to form (a jury, esp. a special jury) by cancelling certain names among those nominated for jury service until only the requisite number remains. See also **special jury. 30** (*tr*) *Rowing.* to make (a certain number of strokes) per minute: *Oxford were striking 38.* **31** to make a stroke or kick in swimming. **32** (*tr*) (in Malaysia) to win (a lottery or raffle). **33 strike home. 33a** to deliver an effective blow. **33b** to achieve the intended effect. **34 strike (it) lucky.** to have some good luck. **35 strike it rich.** *Informal.* **35a** to discover an extensive deposit of a mineral, petroleum, etc. **35b** to have an unexpected financial success. ◆ *n* **36** an act or instance of striking. **37** a cessation of work by workers in a factory, industry, etc., as a protest against working conditions or low pay: *the workers are on strike again.* **38** a military attack, esp. an air attack on a surface target: *air strike.* **39** *Baseball.* a pitched ball judged good but missed or not swung at, three of which cause a batter to be out. **40** Also called: **ten-strike.** *Tenpin bowling.* **40a** the act or an instance of knocking down all the pins with the first bowl of a single frame. **40b** the score thus made. Compare **spare** (sense 17). **41** a sound made by striking. **42** the mechanism that makes a clock strike. **43** the discovery of a source of ore, petroleum, etc. **44** the horizontal direction of a fault, rock stratum, etc., which is perpendicular to the direction of the dip. **45** *Angling.* the act or an instance of striking. **46** the number of coins or medals made at one time. **47** another name for **strickle** (sense 1). **48** *Informal.* an unexpected or complete success, esp. one that brings financial gain. **49 take strike.** *Cricket.* (of a batsman) to prepare to play a ball delivered by the bowler. ◆ See also **strike down, strike off, strike out, strike through, strike up.** [Old English *strīcan;* related to Old Frisian *strīka* to stroke, Old High German *strīhhan* to smooth, Latin *stria* furrow] ► **'strikeless** *adj*

strikebound ('straɪk,baʊnd) *adj* (of a factory, etc.) closed or made inoperative by a strike.

strikebreaker ('straɪk,breɪkə) *n* a person who tries to make a strike ineffectual by working or by taking the place of those on strike. ► **'strike,breaking** *n, adj*

strike down *vb (tr, adv)* to cause to die, esp. suddenly: *he was struck down in his prime.*

strike fault *n* a fault that runs parallel to the strike of the affected rocks.

strike note *or esp. U.S.* **strike tone** *n* the note produced by a bell when struck, defining its musical pitch.

strike off *vb (tr)* **1** to remove or erase from (a list, record, etc.) by or as if by a stroke of the pen. **2** *(adv)* to cut off or separate by or as if by a blow: *she was struck off from the inheritance.*

strike out *vb (adv)* **1** *(tr)* to remove or erase. **2** *(intr)* to start out or begin: *to strike out on one's own.* **3** *Baseball.* to put out or be put out on strikes. **4** *(intr) U.S. and Canadian informal.* to fail utterly.

strike pay *n* money paid to strikers from the funds of a trade union.

striker ('straɪkə) *n* **1** a person who is on strike. **2** the hammer in a timepiece that rings a bell or alarm. **3** any part in a mechanical device that strikes something, such as the firing pin of a gun. **4** *Soccer, informal.* an attacking player, esp. one who generally positions himself near his opponent's goal in the hope of scoring. **5** *Cricket.* the batsman who is about to play a ball. **6a** a person who harpoons whales or fish. **6b** the harpoon itself.

strike-slip fault *n* a geological fault on which the movement is along the strike of the fault.

strike through *vb (tr)* to draw (a line) through (something) to delete it.

strike up *vb (adv)* **1** (of a band, orchestra, etc.) to begin to play or sing **2** *(tr)* to bring about; cause to begin: *to strike up a friendship.* **3** *(tr)* to emboss (patterns, etc.) on (metal).

striking ('straɪkɪŋ) *adj* **1** attracting attention; fine; impressive: *a striking beauty.* **2** conspicuous; noticeable: *a striking difference.* ► **'strikingly** *adv* ► **'strikingness** *n*

striking circle *n Hockey.* the semicircular area in front of each goal, which an attacking player must have entered before scoring a goal.

Strimmer ('strɪmə) *n Trademark.* an electrical tool for trimming the edges of lawns.

Strimon ('strimɔn) *n* a transliteration of the Greek name for the **Struma.**

Strindberg ('strɪndbɜːg; *Swedish* 'strɪndbærj) *n* **August** ('augʊst). 1849–1912, Swedish dramatist and novelist, whose plays include *The Father* (1887), *Miss Julie* (1888), and *The Ghost Sonata* (1907).

Strine (straɪn) *n* a humorous transliteration of Australian pronunciation, as in *Gloria Soame* for *glorious home.* [C20: a jocular rendering, coined by Alastair Morrison, of the Australian pronunciation of *Australian*]

string (strɪŋ) *n* **1** a thin length of cord, twine, fibre, or similar material used for tying, hanging, binding, etc. **2** a group of objects threaded on a single strand: *a string of beads.* **3** a series or succession of things, events, acts, utterances, etc.: *a string of oaths.* **4** a number, chain, or group of similar things, animals, etc., owned by or associated with one person or body: *a string of girlfriends.* **5** a tough fibre or cord in a plant: *the string of an orange; the string of a bean.* **6** *Music.* a tightly stretched wire, cord, etc., found on stringed instruments, such as the violin, guitar, and piano. **7** short for **bowstring. 8** *Architect.* short for **string course** or **stringer** (sense 1). **9** *Maths, linguistics.* a sequence of symbols or words. **10** *Linguistics.* a linear sequence, such as a sentence as it is spoken. **11** *Physics.* a one-dimensional entity postulated to be a fundamental component of matter in some theories of particle physics. See also **cosmic string. 12** *Billiards.* another word for **lag**[1] (sense 6). **13** a group of characters that can be treated as a unit by a computer program. **14** *(pl; usually preceded by the)* **14a** violins, violas, cellos, and double basses collectively. **14b** the section of a symphony orchestra constituted by such instruments. **15** *(pl)* complications or conditions (esp. in the phrase **no strings attached**). **16** *(modifier)* composed of stringlike strands woven in a large mesh: *a string bag; string vest.* **17 first (second,** *etc.***) string.** a person or thing regarded as a primary (secondary, etc.) source of strength. **18 keep on a string.** to have control or a hold over (a person), esp. emotionally. **19 pull strings.** *Informal.* to exert personal influence, esp. secretly or unofficially. **20 pull the strings.** to have real or ultimate control of something. ◆ *vb* **strings, stringing, strung** (strʌŋ). **21** *(tr)* to provide with a string or strings. **22** *(tr)* to suspend or stretch from one point to another. **23** *(tr)* to thread on a string. **24** *(tr)* to form or extend in a line or series. **25** (foll. by *out*) to space or spread out at intervals. **26** *(tr;* usually foll. by *up) Informal.* to kill (a person) by hanging. **27** *(tr)* to remove the stringy parts from (vegetables, esp. beans). **28** *(intr)* (esp. of viscous liquids) to become stringy or ropey. **29** *(tr;* often foll. by *up)* to cause to be tense or nervous. **30** *Billiards.* another word for **lag**[1] (sense 3). [Old English *streng;* related to Old High German *strang,* Old Norse *strengr;* see STRONG] ► **'string,like** *adj*

string along *vb (adv) Informal.* **1** *(intr;* often foll. by *with)* to agree or appear to be in agreement (with). **2** *(tr)* Also: **string on.** to deceive, fool, or hoax, esp. in order to gain time.

string band *n* **1** a band consisting of stringed instruments. **2** an informal name for **string orchestra.**

string bass (beɪs) *n* another name for **double bass.**

string bean *n* **1** any of several bean plants, such as the scarlet runner, cultivated for their edible unripe pods. See also **green bean, wax bean. 2** *Informal.* a tall thin person.

stringboard ('strɪŋ,bɔːd) *n* a skirting that covers the ends of the steps in a staircase. Also called: **stringer.**

string course *n* another name for **cordon** (sense 4).

stringed (strɪŋd) *adj* (of musical instruments) having or provided with strings.

stringed instrument *n* any musical instrument in which sound is produced by the vibration of a string across a soundboard or soundbox. Also called: **chordophone.**

stringendo (strɪn'dʒendəʊ) *adj, adv Music.* to be performed with increasing speed. [Italian, from *stringere* to compress, from Latin: to draw tight; see STRINGENT]

stringent ('strɪndʒənt) *adj* **1** requiring strict attention to rules, procedure, detail, etc. **2** *Finance.* characterized by or causing a shortage of credit, loan capital, etc. [C17: from Latin *stringere* to bind] ► **'stringency** *n* ► **'stringently** *adv*

stringer ('strɪŋə) *n* **1** *Architect.* **1a** a long horizontal beam that is used for structural purposes. **1b** another name for **stringboard. 2** *Nautical.* a longitudinal structural brace for strengthening the hull of a vessel. **3** a journalist retained by a newspaper or news service on a part-time basis to cover a particular town or area.

stringhalt ('strɪŋ,hɔːlt) *n Vet. science.* a sudden spasmodic lifting of the hind leg of a horse, resulting from abnormal contraction of the flexor muscles of the hock. Also called: **springhalt.** [C16: probably STRING + HALT[2]]

string line *n Billiards.* another name for **baulk line** (sense 1).

string orchestra *n* an orchestra consisting only of violins, violas, cellos, and double basses.

stringpiece ('strɪŋ,piːs) *n* a long horizontal timber beam used to strengthen or support a framework.

string quartet *n Music.* **1** an instrumental ensemble consisting of two violins, one viola, and one cello. **2** a piece of music written for such a group, usually having the form and commonest features of a sonata.

string tie *n* a very narrow tie, usually tied in a bow.

string variable *n Computer programming.* data on which arithmetical operations will not be performed.

stringy ('strɪŋɪ) *adj* **stringier, stringiest. 1** made of strings or resembling strings. **2** (of meat, etc.) fibrous. **3** (of a person's build) wiry; sinewy. **4** (of liquids) forming in strings. ► **'stringily** *adv* ► **'stringiness** *n*

stringy-bark *n Austral.* any of several eucalyptus trees having a fibrous bark.

strip[1] (strɪp) *vb* **strips, stripping, stripped. 1** to take or pull (the covering, clothes, etc.) off (oneself, another person, or thing): *to strip a wall; to strip a bed.* **2** *(intr)* **2a** to remove all one's clothes. **2b** to perform a striptease. **3** *(tr)* to denude or empty completely. **4** *(tr)* to deprive: *he was stripped of his pride.* **5** *(tr)* to rob or plunder. **6** *(tr)* to remove (paint, varnish, etc.) from (a surface, furniture, etc.) by sanding, with a solvent, etc.: *stripped pine.* **7** *(tr)* Also: **pluck.** to pull out the old coat of hair from (dogs of certain long- and wire-haired breeds). **8a** to remove the leaves from the stalks of (tobacco, etc.). **8b** to separate the two sides of a leaf from the stem of (tobacco, etc.). **9** *(tr) Agriculture.* to draw the last milk from each of the teats of (a cow). **10** to dismantle (an engine, mechanism, etc.). **11** to tear off or break (the thread) from (a screw, bolt, etc.) or (the teeth) from (a gear). **12** (often foll. by *down*) to remove the accessories from (a motor vehicle): *his car was stripped down.* **13** to remove (the most volatile constituent) from (a mixture of liquids) by boiling, evaporation, or distillation. **14** *Printing.* (usually foll. by *in*) to combine (pieces of film or paper) to form a composite sheet from which a plate can be made. **15** *(tr)* (in freight transport) to unpack (a container). See also **stuffing and stripping.** ◆ *n* **16** the act or an instance of undressing or of performing a striptease. ◆ See also **strip out.** [Old English *bestriepan* to plunder; related to Old High German *stroufen* to plunder, strip]

strip[2] (strɪp) *n* **1** a relatively long, flat, narrow piece of something. **2** short for **airstrip. 3** *Philately.* a horizontal or vertical row of three or more unseparated postage stamps. **4** the clothes worn by the members of a team, esp. a football team. **5** *Business.* a triple option on a security or commodity consisting of one call option and two put options at the same price and for the same period. Compare **strap** (sense 5). **6** *N.Z.* short for **dosing strip. 7 tear (someone) off a strip.** *Informal.* to rebuke (someone) angrily. ◆ *vb* **strips, stripping, stripped. 8** to cut or divide into strips. [C15: from Middle Dutch *strīpe* STRIPE[1]]

strip cartoon *n* another term for **comic strip.**

strip club *n* a small club in which striptease performances take place.

strip cropping *n* a method of growing crops in strips or bands arranged to serve as barriers against erosion.

stripe[1] (straɪp) *n* **1** a relatively long band of distinctive colour or texture that differs from the surrounding material or background. **2** a fabric having such bands. **3** a strip, band, or chevron of fabric worn on a military uniform, etc., esp. one that indicates rank. **4** *Chiefly U.S. and Canadian.* kind; sort; type: *a man of a certain stripe.* ◆ *vb* **5** *(tr)* to mark with a stripe or stripes. [C17: probably from Middle Dutch *strīpe;* related to Middle High German *strīfe,* of obscure origin]

stripe[2] (straɪp) *n* a stroke from a whip, rod, cane, etc. [C15: perhaps from Middle Low German *strippe;* related to STRIPE[1]]

striped (straɪpt) *adj* marked or decorated with stripes.

striped muscle *or* **striated muscle** *n* a type of contractile tissue that is marked by transverse striations; it is concerned with moving skeletal parts to which it is usually attached. Compare **smooth muscle.**

striper ('straɪpə) *n Military slang.* an officer who has a stripe or stripes on his uniform, esp. in the navy: *a two-striper* (lieutenant).

strip lighting *n* electric lighting by means of long glass tubes that are fluorescent lamps or that contain long filaments.

stripling ('strɪplɪŋ) *n* a lad. [C13: from STRIP[2] + -LING[1]]

strip mill *n* a mill in which steel slabs are rolled into strips.

strip mining *n* another term (esp. U.S.) for **opencast mining.**

strip out *vb* (*tr, adv*) to remove the working parts of (a machine).

stripped-down *adj* reduced to the bare essentials; spare.

stripper ('strɪpə) *n* **1** a striptease artist. **2** a person or thing that strips. **3** a device or substance for removing paint, varnish, etc.

strip poker *n* a card game in which a player's losses are paid by removing an article of clothing.

strip-search *vb* **1** (*tr*) (of police, customes officials, etc.) to strip (a prisoner or suspect) naked to search him or her for contraband, narcotics, etc. ♦ *n* **2** a search that involves stripping a person naked. ▸ **'strip-ˌsearching** *n*

striptease ('strɪpˌtiːz) *n* **a** a form of erotic entertainment in which a person gradually undresses to music. **b** (*as modifier*): *a striptease club.* [from STRIP[1] + TEASE] ▸ **'stripˌteaser** *n*

stripy *or* **stripey** ('straɪpɪ) *adj* **stripier, stripiest.** marked by or with stripes; striped.

strive (straɪv) *vb* **strives, striving, strove, striven** ('strɪvᵊn). **1** (*may take a clause as object or an infinitive*) to make a great and tenacious effort: *to strive to get promotion.* **2** (*intr*) to fight; contend. [C13: from Old French *estriver,* of Germanic origin; related to Middle High German *streben* to strive, Old Norse *strītha* to fight] ▸ **'striver** *n*

strobe (strəʊb) *n* **1** short for **strobe lighting** or **stroboscope.** ♦ *vb* **2** to give the appearance of arrested or slow motion by using intermittent illumination.

strobe lighting *n* **1** a high-intensity flashing beam of light produced by rapid electrical discharges in a tube or by a perforated disc rotating in front of an intense light source: used in discotheques, etc. **2** the use of or the apparatus for producing such light. Sometimes shortened to **strobe.**

strobe tuner *n* an electronic instrument tuner that uses stroboscopic light.

strobic ('strəʊbɪk) *adj* spinning or appearing to spin. [C19: from Greek *strobos* act of spinning]

strobila ('strəʊbɪlə) *n, pl* **-bilae** (-bɪliː). **1** the body of a tapeworm, consisting of a string of similar segments (proglottides). **2** a less common name for **scyphistoma.** [C19: from New Latin, from Greek *strobilē* plug of lint twisted into a cone shape, from *strobilos* a fir cone]

strobilaceous (ˌstrəʊbɪ'leɪʃəs) *adj Botany.* relating to or resembling a cone or cones.

strobilation (ˌstrəʊbɪ'leɪʃən) *n* asexual reproduction by division into segments, as in tapeworms and jellyfishes.

strobilus ('strəʊbɪləs) *or* **strobile** ('strəʊbaɪl) *n, pl* **-biluses, -bili** (-bɪlaɪ), *or* **-biles.** *Botany.* the technical name for **cone** (sense 3). [C18: via Late Latin from Greek *strobilos* a fir cone; see STROBILA]

stroboscope ('strəʊbəˌskəʊp) *n* **1** an instrument producing a flashing light, the frequency of which can be synchronized with some multiple of the frequency of rotation, vibration, or operation of an object, etc., making it appear stationary. It is used to determine speeds of rotation or vibration, or to adjust objects or parts. Sometimes shortened to **strobe. 2** a similar device synchronized with the opening of the shutter of a camera so that a series of still photographs can be taken of a moving object. [C19: from *strobo-,* from Greek *strobos* a twisting, whirling + -SCOPE] ▸ **stroboscopic** (ˌstrəʊbə'skɒpɪk) *or* **ˌstroboˈscopical** *adj* ▸ **ˌstroboˈscopically** *adv*

strode (strəʊd) *vb* the past tense of **stride.**

Stroessner ('strəʊsnə) *n* **Alfredo.** born 1912, Paraguayan soldier and politician; president (1954–89): deposed in a military coup.

stroganoff ('strɒgəˌnɒf) *n* short for **beef stroganoff.**

Stroheim ('strəʊˌhaɪm, 'ʃtrəʊ-) *n* See (Erich) **von Stroheim.**

stroke (strəʊk) *n* **1** the act or an instance of striking; a blow, knock, or hit. **2** a sudden action, movement, or occurrence: *a stroke of luck.* **3** a brilliant or inspired act or feat: *a stroke of genius.* **4** *Pathol.* apoplexy; rupture of a blood vessel in the brain resulting in loss of consciousness, often followed by paralysis, or embolism or thrombosis affecting a cerebral vessel. **5a** the striking of a clock. **5b** the hour registered by the striking of a clock: *on the stroke of three.* **6** a mark, flourish, or line made by a writing implement. **7** another name for **solidus,** used esp. when dictating or reading aloud. **8** a light touch or caress, as with the fingers. **9** a pulsation, esp. of the heart. **10** a single complete movement or one of a series of complete movements. **11** *Sport.* the act or manner of striking the ball with a racket, club, bat, etc. **12** any one of the repeated movements used by a swimmer to propel himself through the water. **13** a manner of swimming, esp. one of several named styles such as the crawl or butterfly. **14a** any one of a series of linear movements of a reciprocating part, such as a piston. **14b** the distance travelled by such a part from one end of its movement to the other. **15** a single pull on an oar or oars in rowing. **16** manner or style of rowing. **17** the oarsman who sits nearest the stern of a shell, facing the cox, and sets the rate of striking for the rest of the crew. **18** *U.S. informal.* a compliment or comment that enhances a persons self-esteem. **19** (*modifier*) *Slang, chiefly U.S.* pornographic; masturbatory: *stroke magazines.* **20 a stroke (of work).** (*usually used with a negative*) a small amount of work. **21 off one's stroke.** performing or working less well than usual. **22 on the stroke (of).** punctually (at). ♦ *vb* **23** (*tr*) to touch, brush, or caress lightly or gently. **24** (*tr*) to mark a line or a stroke on or through. **25** to act as the stroke of (a racing shell). **26** (*tr*) *Sport.* to strike (a ball) with a smooth swinging blow. **27** (*tr*) *U.S. and Canadian informal.* to handle or influence (someone) with care, using persuasion, flattery, etc. [Old English *strācian;* related to Middle Low German *strēken;* see STRIKE]

stroke play *n Golf.* **a** scoring by counting the number of strokes taken. **b** (*as modifier*): *a strokeplay tournament.* ♦ Also called: **medal play.** Compare **match play, Stableford.**

stroll (strəʊl) *vb* **1** to walk about in a leisurely manner. **2** (*intr*) to wander from place to place. ♦ *n* **3** a leisurely walk. [C17: probably from dialect German *strollen,* of obscure origin; compare German *Strolch* tramp]

stroller ('strəʊlə) *n* the usual U.S., Canadian, and Austral. word for **pushchair.**

stroma ('strəʊmə) *n, pl* **-mata** (-mətə). *Biology.* **1** the dense colourless framework of a chloroplast and certain cells. **2** the fibrous connective tissue forming the matrix of the mammalian ovary and testis. **3** a dense mass of hyphae that is produced by certain fungi and gives rise to spore-producing bodies. [C19: via New Latin from Late Latin: a mattress, from Greek; related to Latin *sternere* to strew] ▸ **stromatic** (strəʊ'mætɪk) *or* **'stromatous** *adj*

stromatolite (strəʊ'mætəˌlaɪt) *n* a rocky mass consisting of layers of calcareous material formed by the prolific growth of cyanobacteria: such structures date back to Precambrian times. [C20: from Greek, from *strōma* covering + -LITE] ▸ **stromatolitic** (strəʊˌmætə'lɪtɪk) *adj*

Stromboli ('strɒmbəlɪ) *n* an island in the Tyrrhenian Sea, in the Lipari Islands off the N coast of Sicily: famous for its active volcano, 927 m (3040 ft.) high.

Strombolian (strɒm'bəʊlɪən) *adj* relating to or denoting a type of volcanic eruption characterized by repeated small explosions caused by gas escaping through lava.

strong (strɒŋ) *adj* **stronger** ('strɒŋgə), **strongest** ('strɒŋgɪst). **1** involving or possessing physical or mental strength. **2** solid or robust in construction; not easily broken or injured. **3** having a resolute will or morally firm and incorruptible character. **4** intense in quality; not faint or feeble: *a strong voice; a strong smell.* **5** easily defensible; incontestable or formidable. **6** concentrated; not weak or diluted. **7a** (*postpositive*) containing or having a specified number: *a navy 40 000 strong.* **7b** (*in combination*): *a 40 000-strong navy.* **8** having an unpleasantly powerful taste or smell. **9** having an extreme or drastic effect: *strong discipline.* **10** emphatic or immoderate: *strong language.* **11** convincing, effective, or cogent. **12** (of a colour) having a high degree of saturation or purity; being less saturated than a vivid colour but more so than a moderate colour; produced by a concentrated quantity of colouring agent. **13** *Grammar.* **13a** denoting or belonging to a class of verbs, in certain languages including the Germanic languages, whose conjugation shows vowel gradation, as *sing, sang, sung.* **13b** belonging to any part-of-speech class, in any of various languages, whose inflections follow the less regular of two possible patterns. Compare **weak** (sense 10). **14** (of a wind, current, etc.) moving fast. **15** (of a syllable) accented or stressed. **16** (of an industry, market, currency, securities, etc.) firm in price or characterized by firm or increasing prices. **17** (of certain acids and bases) producing high concentrations of hydrogen or hydroxide ions in aqueous solution. **18** *Irish.* prosperous; well-to-do (esp. in the phrase **a strong farmer**). **19 have a strong stomach.** not to be prone to nausea. ♦ *adv* **20** *Informal.* in a strong way; effectively: *going strong.* **21 come on strong.** to make a forceful or exaggerated impression. [Old English *strang;* related to Old Norse *strangr,* Middle High German *strange,* Lettish *strans* courageous] ▸ **'strongish** *adj* ▸ **'strongly** *adv* ▸ **'strongness** *n*

strong-arm *Informal.* ♦ *n* **1** (*modifier*) relating to or involving physical force or violence: *strong-arm tactics.* ♦ *vb* **2** (*tr*) to show violence towards.

strongbox ('strɒŋˌbɒks) *n* a specially designed box or safe in which valuables are locked for safety.

strong breeze *n Meteorol.* a considerable wind of force six on the Beaufort scale, reaching speeds of 25–31 mph.

strong drink *n* alcoholic drink.

strong-eye dog *n N.Z.* a dog trained to control sheep by its gaze.

strong gale *n Meteorol.* a strong wind of force nine on the Beaufort scale, reaching speeds of 47–54 mph: capable of causing minor structural damage to buildings.

stronghold ('strɒŋˌhəʊld) *n* **1** a defensible place; fortress. **2** a major centre or area of predominance. [C15: from STRONG + HOLD[1] (in the archaic sense: a fortified place)]

strong interaction *or* **force** *n Physics.* an interaction between elementary particles responsible for the forces between nucleons in the nucleus. It operates at distances less than about 10^{-15} metres, and is about a hundred times more powerful than the electromagnetic interaction. Also called: **strong nuclear interaction** *or* **force.** See **interaction** (sense 2).

strongman ('strɒŋˌmæn) *n, pl* **-men. 1** a performer, esp. one in a circus, who performs feats of strength. **2** any person regarded as a source of power, capability, initiative, etc.

strong meat *n* anything arousing fear, anger, repulsion, etc., except among a tolerant or receptive minority: *some scenes in the film were strong meat.*

strong-minded *adj* having strength of mind; firm, resolute, and determined. ▸ **ˌstrong-'mindedly** *adv* ▸ **ˌstrong'mindedness** *n*

strong point *n* something at which one excels; forte: *tactfulness was never his strong point.*

strongpoint ('strɒŋˌpɔɪnt) *n Military.* **1** a location that is by its site and nature easily defended. **2** a spot in a defensive position that is heavily defended.

strongroom ('strɒŋˌruːm, -ˌrʊm) *n* a specially designed room in which valuables are locked for safety.

strong waters *pl n* an archaic name for alcoholic drink.

strong-willed *adj* having strength of will.

strongyle ('strɒndʒɪl) *or* **strongyl** ('strɒndʒəl) *n* any parasitic nematode worm of the family *Strongylidae,* chiefly occurring in the intestines of horses. [C19: via New Latin *Strongylus,* from Greek *strongulos* round]

strongyloidiasis (ˌstrɒndʒɪlɔɪ'daɪəsɪs) *or* **strongyloidosis** (-'dəʊsɪs) *n* an intestinal disease caused by infection with the nematode worm *Strongyloides stercoralis*.

strontia ('strɒntɪə) *n* another name for **strontium monoxide.** [C19: changed from STRONTIAN]

strontian ('strɒntɪən) *n* **1** another name for **strontianite. 2** another name for **strontium** or **strontium monoxide.** [C18: named after a parish in Argyll, where it was discovered]

strontianite ('strɒntɪəˌnaɪt) *n* a white, lightly coloured, or colourless mineral consisting of strontium carbonate in orthorhombic crystalline form: it is a source of strontium compounds. Formula: $SrCO_3$.

strontium ('strɒntɪəm) *n* a soft silvery-white element of the alkaline earth group of metals, occurring chiefly in celestite and strontianite. Its compounds burn with a crimson flame and are used in fireworks. The radioisotope **strontium-90,** with a half-life of 28.1 years, is used in nuclear power sources and is a hazardous nuclear fall-out product. Symbol: Sr; atomic no.: 38; atomic wt.: 87.62; valency: 2; relative density: 2.54; melting pt.: 769°C; boiling pt.: 1384°C. [C19: from New Latin, from STRONTIAN]

strontium monoxide *n* a white insoluble solid substance used in making strontium salts and purifying sugar. Formula: SrO. Also called: **strontium oxide, strontia.**

strontium unit *n* a unit expressing the concentration of strontium-90 in an organic medium, such as soil, milk, bone, etc., relative to the concentration of calcium in the same medium. Abbrev.: **SU.**

strop (strɒp) *n* **1** a leather strap or an abrasive strip for sharpening razors. **2** a rope or metal band around a block or deadeye for support. ♦ *vb* **strops, stropping, stropped. 3** (*tr*) to sharpen (a razor, etc.) on a strop. [C14 (in nautical use: a strip of rope): via Middle Low German or Middle Dutch *strop,* ultimately from Latin *stroppus,* from Greek *strophos* cord; see STROPHE]

strophanthin (strəʊ'fænθɪn) *n* a toxic glycoside or mixture of glycosides obtained from the ripe seeds of certain species of strophanthus: used as a cardiac stimulant.

strophanthus (strəʊ'fænθəs) *n* **1** any small tree or shrub of the apocynaceous genus *Strophanthus,* of tropical Africa and Asia, having strap-shaped twisted petals. The seeds of certain species yield the drug strophanthin. **2** the seeds of any of these plants. [C19: New Latin, from Greek *strophos* twisted cord + *anthos* flower]

strophe ('strəʊfɪ) *n Prosody.* **1** (in ancient Greek drama) **1a** the first of two movements made by a chorus during the performance of a choral ode. **1b** the first part of a choral ode sung during this movement. **2** (in classical verse) the first division of the threefold structure of a Pindaric ode. **3** the first of two metrical systems used alternately within a poem. ♦ See **antistrophe, epode.** [C17: from Greek: a verse, literally: a turning, from *strephein* to twist]

strophic ('strɒfɪk, 'strəʊ-) *or* (*less commonly*) **strophical** *adj* **1** of, relating to, or employing a strophe or strophes. **2** (of a song) having identical or related music in each verse. Compare **through-composed. 3** *Botany.* denoting the twisting growth of a plant organ in response to a directional stimulus.

stroppy ('strɒpɪ) *adj* **-pier, -piest.** *Brit. informal.* angry or awkward. [C20: changed and shortened from OBSTREPEROUS] ▸ **'stroppily** *adv* ▸ **'stroppiness** *n*

stroud (straʊd) *n* a coarse woollen fabric. [C17: perhaps named after *Stroud,* textile centre in Gloucestershire]

strove (strəʊv) *vb* the past tense of **strive.**

strow (strəʊ) *vb* **strows, strowing, strowed; strown** *or* **strowed.** an archaic variant of **strew.**

stroy (strɔɪ) *vb* an archaic variant of **destroy.** ▸ **'stroyer** *n*

struck (strʌk) *vb* **1** the past tense and past participle of **strike.** ♦ *adj* **2** *Chiefly U.S. and Canadian.* (of an industry, factory, etc.) shut down or otherwise affected by a labour strike.

struck measure *n* a measure of grain, etc., in which the contents are made level with the top of the container rather than being heaped.

structural ('strʌktʃərəl) *adj* **1** of, relating to, or having structure or a structure. **2** of, relating to, or forming part of the structure of a building. **3** of or relating to the structure of rocks and other features of the earth's crust. **4** of or relating to the structure of organisms; morphological. **5** *Chem.* of, concerned with, caused by, or involving the arrangement of atoms in molecules. ▸ **'structurally** *adv*

structural formula *n* a chemical formula showing the composition and structure of a molecule. The atoms are represented by symbols and the structure is indicated by showing the relative positions of the atoms in space and the bonds between them: *H–C≡C–H is the structural formula of acetylene.* See also **empirical formula, molecular formula.**

structuralism ('strʌktʃərəˌlɪzəm) *n* **1** an approach to anthropology and other social sciences and to literature that interprets and analyses its material in terms of oppositions, contrasts, and hierarchical structures, esp. as they might reflect universal mental characteristics or organizing principles. Compare **functionalism. 2** an approach to linguistics that analyses and describes the structure of language, as distinguished from its comparative and historical aspects. ▸ **'structuralist** *n, adj*

structural linguistics *n* (*functioning as sing*) a descriptive approach to a synchronic or diachronic analysis of language on the basis of its structure as reflected by irreducible units of phonological, morphological, and semantic features.

structural psychology *n* (formerly) a school of psychology using introspection to analyse experience into basic units.

structural steel *n* a strong mild steel used in construction work.

structural unemployment *n Economics.* unemployment resulting from changes in the structure of an industry as a result of changes in either technology or taste.

structure ('strʌktʃə) *n* **1** a complex construction or entity. **2** the arrangement and interrelationship of parts in a construction, such as a building. **3** the manner of construction or organization: *the structure of society.* **4** *Biology.* morphology; form. **5** *Chem.* the arrangement of atoms in a molecule of a chemical compound: *the structure of benzene.* **6** *Geology.* the way in which a mineral, rock, rock mass or stratum, etc., is made up of its component parts. **7** *Now rare.* the act of constructing. ♦ *vb* **8** (*tr*) to impart a structure to. [C15: from Latin *structūra,* from *struere* to build]

structured ('strʌktʃəd) *adj* **1** having a distinct physical shape or form, often provided by an internal structure. **2** planned in broad outline; organized: *structured play for preschoolers.* **3** having a definite predetermined pattern; rigid: *structured hierarchy.*

strudel ('struːdᵊl; *German* 'ʃtruːdəl) *n* a thin sheet of filled dough rolled up and baked: *apple strudel.* [German, from Middle High German *strodel* eddy, whirlpool, so called from the way the pastry is rolled]

struggle ('strʌgᵊl) *vb* **1** (*intr;* usually foll. by *for* or *against; may take an infinitive*) to exert strength, energy, and force; work or strive: *to struggle to obtain freedom.* **2** (*intr*) to move about strenuously so as to escape from something confining. **3** (*intr*) to contend, battle, or fight. **4** (*intr*) to go or progress with difficulty. ♦ *n* **5** a laboured or strenuous exertion or effort. **6** a fight or battle. **7** the act of struggling. [C14: of obscure origin] ▸ **'struggler** *n* ▸ **'struggling** *adj* ▸ **'strugglingly** *adv*

struggle for existence *n* (*not in technical usage*) competition between organisms of a population, esp. as a factor in the evolution of plants and animals. See also **natural selection.**

strum (strʌm) *vb* **strums, strumming, strummed. 1** to sound (the strings of a guitar, banjo, etc.) with a downward or upward sweep of the thumb or of a plectrum. **2** to play (chords, a tune, etc.) in this way. [C18: probably of imitative origin; see THRUM¹] ▸ **'strummer** *n*

struma ('struːmə) *n, pl* **-mae** (-miː). **1** *Pathol.* an abnormal enlargement of the thyroid gland; goitre. **2** *Botany.* a swelling, esp. one at the base of a moss capsule. **3** another word for **scrofula.** [C16: from Latin: a scrofulous tumour, from *struere* to heap up] ▸ **strumatic** (struː'mætɪk), **strumous** ('struːməs), *or* **strumose** ('struːməʊs) *adj*

Struma ('struːmə) *n* a river in S Europe, rising in SW Bulgaria near Sofia and flowing generally southeast through Greece to the Aegean. Length: 362 km (225 miles). Greek names: **Strimon, Strymon.**

strumpet ('strʌmpɪt) *n Archaic.* a prostitute or promiscuous woman. [C14: of unknown origin]

strung (strʌŋ) *vb* **1** a past tense and past participle of **string.** ♦ *adj* **2a** (of a piano, etc.) provided with strings, esp. of a specified kind or in a specified manner. **2b** (*in combination*)*: gut-strung.* **3 highly strung.** very nervous or volatile in character. Usual U.S. and Canadian phrase: **high-strung.**

strung out *adj Slang.* **1** addicted to a drug. **2** (of a drug addict) suffering or distressed because of the lack of a drug.

strung up *adj* (*postpositive*) *Informal.* tense or nervous.

strut (strʌt) *vb* **struts, strutting, strutted. 1** (*intr*) to walk in a pompous manner; swagger. **2** (*tr*) to support or provide with struts. **3 strut one's stuff.** *Informal.* to behave or perform in a proud and confident manner; show off. ♦ *n* **4** a structural member used mainly in compression, esp. as part of a framework. **5** an affected, proud, or stiff walk. [C14 *strouten* (in the sense: swell, stand out; C16: to walk stiffly), from Old English*strūtian* to stand stiffly; related to Low German *strutt* stiff] ▸ **'strutter** *n* ▸ **'strutting** *adj* ▸ **'struttingly** *adv*

struthious ('struːθɪəs) *adj* **1** (of birds) related to or resembling the ostrich. **2** of, relating to, or designating all flightless (ratite) birds. [C18: from Late Latin *strūthiō,* from Greek *strouthiōn,* from *strouthos* an ostrich]

Struve ('struːvə) *n* **Otto.** 1897–1963, U.S. astronomer, born in Russia, noted for his work in stellar spectroscopy and his discovery (1937) of interstellar hydrogen.

strychnic ('strɪknɪk) *adj* of, relating to, or derived from strychnine.

strychnine ('strɪkniːn) *n* a white crystalline very poisonous alkaloid, obtained from the plant nux vomica: formerly used in small quantities as a stimulant of the central nervous system and the appetite. Formula: $C_{21}H_{22}O_2N_2$. [C19: via French from New Latin *Strychnos,* from Greek *strukhnos* nightshade]

strychninism ('strɪknɪˌnɪzəm) *n Pathol.* poisoning caused by the excessive or prolonged use of strychnine.

Strymon ('straɪmən) *n* transliteration of the Greek name for the **Struma.**

Stuart ('stjʊət) *n* **1** the royal house that ruled in Scotland from 1371 to 1714 and in England from 1603 to 1714. See also **Stewart** (sense 1). **2 Charles Edward,** called *the Young Pretender* or *Bonnie Prince Charlie.* 1720–88, pretender to the British throne. He led the Jacobite Rebellion (1745–46) in an attempt to re-establish the Stuart succession. **3** his father, **James Francis Edward,** called *the Old Pretender.* 1688–1766, pretender to the British throne; son of James II (James VII of Scotland) and his second wife, Mary of Modena. He made two unsuccessful attempts to realize his claim to the throne (1708; 1715). **4 Mary.** See **Mary, Queen of Scots.**

stub (stʌb) *n* **1** a short piece remaining after something has been cut, removed, etc.: *a cigar stub.* **2** the residual piece or section of a receipt, ticket, cheque, etc. **3** the usual U.S. and Canadian word for **counterfoil. 4** any short projection or blunted end. **5** the stump of a tree or plant. ♦ *vb* **stubs, stubbing, stubbed.** (*tr*) **6** to strike (one's toe, foot, etc.) painfully against a hard surface. **7** (usually foll. by *out*) to put (out a cigarette or cigar) by pressing the end against a surface. **8** to clear (land) of stubs. **9** to dig up (the roots) of (a tree or bush). [Old English *stubb;* related to Old Norse *stubbi,* Middle Dutch *stubbe,* Greek *stupos* stem, stump]

stub axle *n* a short axle that carries one of the front steered wheels of a motor vehicle and is capable of limited angular movement about a kingpin.

stubbies ('stʌbɪz) *pl n Austral. trademark.* a type of shorts.

stubble ('stʌbᵊl) *n* **1a** the stubs of stalks left in a field where a crop has been cut and harvested. **1b** (*as modifier*): *a stubble field.* **2** any bristly growth or surface. [C13: from Old French *estuble,* from Latin *stupula,* variant of *stipula* stalk, stem, stubble] ▸ **'stubbled** *or* **'stubbly** *adj*

stubble-jumper *n Canadian slang.* a prairie grain farmer.

stubborn ('stʌbᵊn) *adj* **1** refusing to comply, agree, or give in; obstinate. **2** difficult to handle, treat, or overcome. **3** persistent and dogged: *a stubborn crusade.* [C14 *stoborne,* of obscure origin] ▸ **'stubbornly** *adv* ▸ **'stubbornness** *n*

Stubbs (stʌbz) *n* **George.** 1724–1806, English painter, noted esp. for his pictures of horses.

stubby ('stʌbɪ) *adj* **-bier, -biest. 1** short and broad; stumpy or thickset. **2** bristling and stiff. ◆ *n* **3** Also called: **stubbie.** *Austral. slang.* a small bottle of beer. ▸ **'stubbily** *adv* ▸ **'stubbiness** *n*

stub nail *n* **1** a short thick nail. **2** a worn nail in a horseshoe.

STUC *abbrev. for* Scottish Trades Union Congress.

stucco ('stʌkəʊ) *n, pl* **-coes** *or* **-cos. 1** a weather-resistant mixture of dehydrated lime, powdered marble, and glue, used in decorative mouldings on buildings. **2** any of various types of cement or plaster used for coating outside walls. **3** Also called: **stuccowork.** decorative work moulded in stucco. ◆ *vb* **-coes** *or* **-cos, -coing, -coed. 4** (*tr*) to apply stucco to. [C16: from Italian, of Germanic origin; compare Old High German *stukki* a fragment, crust, Old English *stycce*] ▸ **'stuccoer** *n*

stuck (stʌk) *vb* **1** the past tense and past participle of **stick**[2]. ◆ *adj* **2** *Informal.* baffled or nonplussed. **3** (foll. by *on*) *Slang.* keen (on) or infatuated (with). **4 get stuck in** *or* **into.** *Informal.* **4a** to perform (a task) with determination. **4b** to attack (a person) verbally or physically.

stuck-up *adj Informal.* conceited, arrogant, or snobbish. ▸ **'stuck-'upness** *n*

stud[1] (stʌd) *n* **1** a large-headed nail or other projection protruding from a surface, usually as decoration. **2** a type of fastener consisting of two discs at either end of a short shank, used to fasten shirtfronts, collars, etc. **3** *Building.* a vertical member made of timber, steel, etc., that is used with others to construct the framework of a wall. **4** a headless bolt that is threaded at both ends, the centre portion being unthreaded. **5** any short projection on a machine, such as the metal cylinder that forms a journal for the gears on a screw-cutting lathe. **6** the crossbar in the centre of a link of a heavy chain. **7** one of a number of rounded projections on the sole of a boot or shoe to give better grip, as on a football boot. ◆ *vb* **studs, studding, studded.** (*tr*) **8** to provide, ornament, or make with studs. **9** to dot or cover (with): *the park was studded with daisies.* **10** *Building.* to provide or support (a wall, partition, etc.) with studs. [Old English *studu;* related to Old Norse *stoth* post, Middle High German *stud* post]

stud[2] (stʌd) *n* **1** a group of pedigree animals, esp. horses, kept for breeding purposes. **2** any male animal kept principally for breeding purposes, esp. a stallion. **3** a farm or stable where a stud is kept. **4** the state or condition of being kept for breeding purposes: *at stud; put to stud.* **5** (*modifier*) of or relating to such animals or the place where they are kept: *a stud farm; a stud horse.* **6** *Slang.* a virile or sexually active man. **7** short for **stud poker.** [Old English *stōd;* related to Old Norse *stōth,* Old High German *stuot*]

studbook ('stʌd,bʊk) *n* a written record of the pedigree of a purebred stock, esp. of racehorses.

studding ('stʌdɪŋ) *n* **1** building studs collectively, esp. as used to form a wall or partition. See also **stud**[1] (sense 3). **2** material that is used to form studs or serve as studs.

studdingsail ('stʌdɪŋ,seɪl; *Nautical* 'stʌnsᵊl) *n Nautical.* a light auxiliary sail set outboard on spars on either side of a square sail. Also called: **stunsail, stuns'l.** [C16: *studding,* perhaps from Middle Low German, Middle Dutch *stōtinge,* from *stōten* to thrust; related to German *stossen*]

student ('stju:dᵊnt) *n* **1a** a person following a course of study, as in a school, college, university, etc. **1b** (*as modifier*): *student teacher.* **2** a person who makes a thorough study of a subject. [C15: from Latin *studēns* diligent, from *studēre* to be zealous; see STUDY]

student adviser *n* another word for **counsellor** (sense 6).

studentship ('stju:dᵊntʃɪp) *n* **1** the role or position of a student. **2** another word for **scholarship** (sense 3).

Student's t *n* a statistic often used to test the hypothesis that a random sample of normally distributed observations has a given mean, μ; given by $t = (\bar{x}-\mu)\sqrt{n}/s$ where $\bar{x}$ is the mean of the sample, *s* is its standard deviation, and *n* is the size of the sample. [after *Student,* the pen name of W. S. Gosset (1876–1937), English statistician and research scientist]

student teacher *n* a person who is teaching in a school for a limited period under supervision as part of a course to qualify as a teacher.

studhorse ('stʌd,hɔ:s) *n* another word for **stallion.**

studied ('stʌdɪd) *adj* **1** carefully practised, designed, or premeditated: *a studied reply.* **2** an archaic word for **learned.** ▸ **'studiedly** *adv* ▸ **'studiedness** *n*

studio ('stju:dɪ,əʊ) *n, pl* **-dios. 1** a room in which an artist, photographer, or musician works. **2** a room used to record television or radio programmes, make films, etc. **3** (*pl*) the premises of a radio, television, or film company. [C19: from Italian, literally: study, from Latin *studium* diligence]

studio couch *n* an upholstered couch, usually backless, convertible into a double bed.

studio flat *n* a flat with one main room.

studious ('stju:dɪəs) *adj* **1** given to study. **2** of a serious, thoughtful, and hardworking character. **3** showing deliberation, care, or precision. [C14: from Latin *studiōsus* devoted to, from *studium* assiduity] ▸ **'studiously** *adv* ▸ **'studiousness** *n*

stud poker *n* a variety of poker in which the first card is dealt face down before each player and the next four are dealt face up (**five-card stud**) or in which the first two cards and the last card are dealt face down and the intervening four cards are dealt face up (**seven-card stud**), with bets made after each round. Often shortened to **stud.** [C19: from STUD[2] + POKER[2]]

stud welding *n* the semiautomatic welding of a stud or similar piece of metal to a flat part, usually by means of an accurately timed electric arc.

studwork ('stʌd,wɜ:k) *n* **1** work decorated with studs. **2** the supporting framework of a wall or partition.

study ('stʌdɪ) *vb* **studies, studying, studied. 1** to apply the mind to the learning or understanding of (a subject), esp. by reading: *to study languages; to study all night.* **2** (*tr*) to investigate or examine, as by observation, research, etc.: *to study the effects of heat on metal.* **3** (*tr*) to look at minutely; scrutinize. **4** (*tr*) to give much careful or critical thought to. **5** to take a course in (a subject), as at a college. **6** (*tr*) to try to memorize: *to study a part for a play.* **7** (*intr*) to meditate or contemplate; reflect. ◆ *n, pl* **studies. 8a** the act or process of studying **8b** (*as modifier*): *study group.* **9** a room used for studying, reading, writing, etc. **10** (*often pl*) work relating to a particular discipline: *environmental studies.* **11** an investigation and analysis of a subject, situation, etc.: *a study of transport provision in rural districts.* **12** a product of studying, such as a written paper or book. **13** a drawing, sculpture, etc., executed for practice or in preparation for another work. **14** a musical composition intended to develop one aspect of performing technique: *a study in spiccato bowing.* **15** *Theatre.* a person who memorizes a part in the manner specified: *a quick study.* **16 in a brown study.** in a reverie or daydream. [C13: from Old French *estudie,* from Latin *studium* zeal, inclination, from *studēre* to be diligent]

stuff (stʌf) *vb* (*mainly tr*) **1** to pack or fill completely; cram. **2** (*intr*) to eat large quantities. **3** to force, shove, or squeeze: *to stuff money into a pocket.* **4** to fill (food such as poultry or tomatoes) with a stuffing. **5** to fill (an animal's skin) with material so as to restore the shape of the live animal. **6** *Taboo slang.* to have sexual intercourse with (a woman). **7** *Tanning.* to treat (an animal skin or hide) with grease. **8** *U.S. and Canadian.* to fill (a ballot box) with a large number of fraudulent votes. **9** (in marine transport) to pack (a container). See also **stuffing and stripping. 10** *Slang.* to ruin, frustrate, or defeat. ◆ *n* **11** the raw material or fabric of something. **12** woollen cloth or fabric. **13** any general or unspecified substance or accumulation of objects. **14** stupid or worthless actions, speech, ideas, etc. **15** subject matter, skill, etc.: *he knows his stuff.* **16** a slang word for **money. 17** *Slang.* a drug, esp. cannabis. **18** *Informal.* **do one's stuff.** to do what is expected of one. **19 that's the stuff.** that is what is needed. **20** *Brit. slang.* a girl or woman considered sexually (esp. in the phrase **bit of stuff**). [C14: from Old French *estoffe,* from *estoffer* to furnish, provide, of Germanic origin; related to Middle High German *stopfen* to cram full] ▸ **'stuffer** *n*

stuffed (stʌft) *adj* **1** filled with something, esp. (of poultry and other food) filled with stuffing. **2** (foll. by *up*) (of the nasal passages) blocked with mucus. **3 get stuffed!** *Brit. taboo slang.* an exclamation of contemptuous anger or annoyance, esp. against another person.

stuffed shirt *n Informal.* a pompous or formal person.

stuff gown *n Brit.* a woollen gown worn by a barrister who has not taken silk.

stuffing ('stʌfɪŋ) *n* **1** the material with which something is stuffed. **2** a mixture of chopped and seasoned ingredients with which poultry, meat, etc., is stuffed before cooking. **3 knock the stuffing out of (someone).** to defeat (someone) utterly.

stuffing and stripping *n* (in marine transport) the packing and unpacking of containers.

stuffing box *n* a small chamber in which an annular packing is compressed around a reciprocating or rotating rod or shaft to form a seal. Also called: **packing box.**

stuffing nut *n* a large nut that is tightened to compress the packing in a stuffing box.

stuffy ('stʌfɪ) *adj* **stuffier, stuffiest. 1** lacking fresh air. **2** excessively dull, staid, or conventional. **3** (of the nasal passages) blocked with mucus. ▸ **'stuffily** *adv* ▸ **'stuffiness** *n*

stull (stʌl) *n Mining.* a timber prop or platform in a stope. [C18: perhaps from German *Stollen,* from Old High German *stollo*]

stultify ('stʌltɪ,faɪ) *vb* **-fies, -fying, -fied.** (*tr*) **1** to make useless, futile, or ineffectual, esp. by routine. **2** to cause to appear absurd or inconsistent. **3** to prove (someone) to be of unsound mind and thus not legally responsible. [C18: from Latin *stultus* stupid + *facere* to make] ▸ **,stultifi'cation** *n* ▸ **'stulti,fier** *n*

stum (stʌm) (in wine-making) ◆ *n* **1** a less common word for **must**[2]. **2** partly fermented wine added to fermented wine as a preservative. ◆ *vb* **stums, stumming, stummed. 3** to preserve (wine) by adding stum. [C17: from Dutch *stom* dumb; related to German *stumm*]

stumble ('stʌmbᵊl) *vb* (*intr*) **1** to trip or fall while walking or running. **2** to walk in an awkward, unsteady, or unsure way. **3** to make mistakes or hesitate in speech or actions. **4** (foll. by *across* or *upon*) to come (across) by accident. **5** to commit a grave mistake or sin. ◆ *n* **6** a false step, trip, or blunder. **7** the act of stumbling. [C14: related to Norwegian *stumla,* Danish dialect *stumle;* see STAMMER] ▸ **'stumbler** *n* ▸ **'stumbling** *adj* ▸ **'stumblingly** *adv*

stumbling block *n* any impediment or obstacle.

stumer ('stju:mə) *n* **1** *Slang.* a forgery or cheat. **2** *Irish dialect.* a poor bargain. **3** *Scot.* a stupid person. **4 come a stumer.** *Austral. slang.* to crash financially. [of unknown origin]

stump (stʌmp) *n* **1** the base part of a tree trunk left standing after the tree has been felled or has fallen. **2** the part of something, such as a tooth, limb, or blade, that remains after a larger part has been removed. **3** *Informal, facetious.* **3a** (*often pl*) a leg. **3b stir one's stumps.** to move or become active. **4** *Cricket.* any of three upright wooden sticks that, with two bails laid across them, form a wicket (the **stumps**). **5** Also called: **tortillon.** a short sharply-pointed stick of cork or rolled paper or leather, used in drawing and shading. **6** a heavy tread or the sound of heavy footsteps. 7 a platform used by an orator when addressing a meeting. **8 on the stump.** *Chiefly U.S. and Canadian.* engaged in campaigning, esp. by political speech-making. 9 (*often pl*) *Austral.* a pile used to support a house. ◆ *vb* **10** (*tr*) to stop, confuse, or puzzle. **11** (*intr*) to plod or trudge heavily. **12** (*tr*) *Cricket.* (of a fielder, esp. a wicketkeeper) to dismiss (a batsman) by breaking his wicket with the ball or with the ball in the hand while he is out of his crease. **13** *Chiefly U.S. and Canadian.* to campaign or canvass (an area), esp. by political speech-making. **14** (*tr*) to reduce to a stump; lop. **15** (*tr*) to clear (land) of stumps. [C14: from Middle Low German *stump;* related to Dutch *stomp,* German *Stumpf;* see STAMP] ▸ **'stumper** *n*

stumpage ('stʌmpɪdʒ) *n* **1** *U.S. and Canadian.* standing timber or its value. **2** *U.S. and Canadian.* the right to fell timber on another person's land. **3** *Canadian.* a tax or royalty payable on each tree felled, esp. on crown land.

stump-jump plough *n Austral.* a plough designed for use on land not cleared of stumps.

stump ranch *or* **farm** *n Canadian informal.* (in British Columbia) an undeveloped ranch in the bush where animals graze among the stumps of felled trees.

stump up *vb* (*adv*) *Brit. informal.* to give (the money required).

stumpwork ('stʌmp,wɜːk) *n* a type of embroidery of the 15th to 17th centuries featuring raised or embossed figures, padded with cotton wool or hair.

stumpy ('stʌmpɪ) *adj* **stumpier, stumpiest. 1** short and thickset like a stump; stubby. **2** abounding in or full of stumps. ▸ **'stumpiness** *n*

stun (stʌn) *vb* **stuns, stunning, stunned.** (*tr*) **1** to render unconscious, as by a heavy blow or fall. **2** to shock or overwhelm. **3** to surprise or astound. ◆ *n* **4** the state or effect of being stunned. [C13 *stunen,* from Old French *estoner* to daze, stupefy, from Vulgar Latin *extonāre* (unattested), from Latin EX-[1] + *tonāre* to thunder]

stung (stʌŋ) *vb* **1** the past tense and past participle of **sting.** ◆ *adj* **2** *Austral. slang.* drunk; intoxicated.

stun gun *n* a device designed to immobilize an animal or person temporarily without inflicting serious injury.

stunk (stʌŋk) *vb* a past tense and past participle of **stink.**

stunner ('stʌnə) *n Informal.* a person or thing of great beauty, quality, size, etc.

stunning ('stʌnɪŋ) *adj Informal.* very attractive, impressive, astonishing, etc. ▸ **'stunningly** *adv*

stunsail *or* **stuns'l** ('stʌnsᵊl) *n* another word for **studdingsail.**

stunt[1] (stʌnt) *vb* **1** (*tr*) to prevent or impede (the growth or development) of (a plant, animal, etc.). ◆ *n* **2** the act or an instance of stunting. **3** a person, animal, or plant that has been stunted. [C17 (as vb: to check the growth of): perhaps from C15 *stont* of short duration, from Old English *stunt* simple, foolish; sense probably influenced by Old Norse *stuttr* short in stature, dwarfed] ▸ **'stunted** *adj* ▸ **'stuntedness** *n*

stunt[2] (stʌnt) *n* **1** an acrobatic or dangerous piece of action in a film, television programme, etc. **2** anything spectacular or unusual done to gain publicity. ◆ *vb* **3** (*intr*) to perform a stunt or stunts. [C19: U.S. student slang, of unknown origin]

stuntman ('stʌntmən) *or* (*fem*) **stuntwoman** *n, pl* **-men** *or* **-women.** a person who performs dangerous acts in a film, television programme, etc. in place of an actor.

stupa ('stuːpə) *n* a domed edifice housing Buddhist or Jain relics. Also called: **tope.** [C19: from Sanskrit: dome]

stupe[1] (stjuːp) *n Med.* a hot damp cloth, usually sprinkled with an irritant, applied to the body to relieve pain by counterirritation. [C14: from Latin *stuppa* flax, from Greek *stuppē*]

stupe[2] (stjuːp) *n U.S. slang.* a stupid person; clot.

stupefacient (,stjuːpɪ'feɪʃɪənt) *n* **1** a drug that causes stupor. ◆ *adj* **2** of, relating to, or designating this type of drug. [C17: from Latin *stupefacere* to make senseless, from *stupēre* to be stunned + *facere* to make]

stupefaction (,stjuːpɪ'fækʃən) *n* **1** astonishment. **2** the act of stupefying or the state of being stupefied.

stupefy ('stjuːpɪ,faɪ) *vb* **-fies, -fying, -fied.** (*tr*) **1** to render insensitive or lethargic. **2** to confuse or astound. [C16: from Old French *stupefier,* from Latin *stupefacere;* see STUPEFACIENT] ▸ **'stupe,fier** *n* ▸ **'stupe,fying** *adj* ▸ **'stupe,fyingly** *adv*

stupendous (stjuː'pendəs) *adj* astounding, wonderful, huge, etc. [C17: from Latin *stupēre* to be amazed] ▸ **stu'pendously** *adv* ▸ **stu'pendousness** *n*

stupid ('stjuːpɪd) *adj* **1** lacking in common sense, perception, or normal intelligence. **2** (*usually postpositive*) stunned, dazed, or stupefied: *stupid from lack of sleep.* **3** having dull mental responses; slow-witted. **4** trivial, silly, or frivolous. ◆ *n* **5** *Informal.* a stupid person. [C16: from French *stupide,* from Latin *stupidus* silly, from *stupēre* to be amazed] ▸ **'stupidly** *adv* ▸ **'stupidness** *n*

stupidity (stjuː'pɪdɪtɪ) *n, pl* **-ties. 1** the quality or state of being stupid. **2** a stupid act, remark, etc.

stupor ('stjuːpə) *n* **1** a state of unconsciousness. **2** mental dullness; torpor. [C17: from Latin, from *stupēre* to be aghast] ▸ **'stuporous** *adj*

sturdy[1] ('stɜːdɪ) *adj* **-dier, -diest. 1** healthy, strong, and vigorous. **2** strongly built; stalwart. [C13 (in the sense: rash, harsh): from Old French *estordi* dazed, from *estordir* to stun, perhaps ultimately related to Latin *turdus* a thrush (taken as representing drunkenness)] ▸ **'sturdily** *adv* ▸ **'sturdiness** *n*

sturdy[2] ('stɜːdɪ) *n Vet. science.* another name for **staggers** (sense 2). [C17: from STURDY[1] (in the obsolete sense: giddy)] ▸ **'sturdied** *adj*

sturgeon ('stɜːdʒən) *n* any primitive bony fish of the family *Acipenseridae,* of temperate waters of the N hemisphere, having an elongated snout and rows of spines along the body: valued as a source of caviar and isinglass. [C13: from Old French *estourgeon,* of Germanic origin; related to Old English *styria,* Old High German *sturio*]

Sturmabteilung *German.* ('ʃturm'aptailuŋ) *n* the full name of the Nazi **SA.** [literally: storm division]

Sturmer ('stɜːmə) *n* a variety of eating apple having a pale green skin and crisp tart flesh. [C19: named after *Sturmer,* Suffolk]

Sturm und Drang *German.* ('ʃturm unt 'draŋ) *n* a German literary movement of the latter half of the 18th century, characterized by a reaction against rationalism. [literally: storm and stress, from the title of a play by F. M. von Klinger (1752–1831), German dramatist]

Sturt (stɜːt) *n* **Charles.** 1795–1869, English explorer, who led three expeditions (1828–29; 1829; 1844–45) into the Australian interior, discovering the Darling River (1828).

stushie ('stuʃɪ), **stishie,** *or* **stashie** *n Scot.* **1** a commotion, rumpus, or row. **2** a state of excitement or anxiety; a tizzy. ◆ Also called: **stooshie, stoushie.** [C19: perhaps shortened from *ecstasy*]

stutter ('stʌtə) *vb* **1** to speak (a word, phrase, etc.) with recurring repetition of consonants, esp. initial ones. **2** to make (an abrupt sound) repeatedly: *the gun stuttered.* ◆ *n* **3** the act or habit of stuttering. **4** a stuttering sound. [C16: related to Middle Low German *stötern,* Old High German *stōzan* to push against, Latin *tundere* to beat] ▸ **'stutterer** *n* ▸ **'stuttering** *n, adj* ▸ **'stutteringly** *adv*

Stuttgart (*German* 'ʃtutgart) *n* an industrial city in W Germany, capital of Baden-Württemberg state, on the River Neckar: developed around a stud farm (*Stuotgarten*) of the Counts of Württemberg. Pop.: 585 604 (1996 est.).

Stuyvesant ('staɪvɪsᵊnt) *n* **Peter.** ?1610–72, Dutch colonial administrator of New Netherland (later New York) (1646–64).

STV *abbrev. for* **1** Scottish Television. **2** single transferable vote.

sty (staɪ) *n, pl* **sties. 1** a pen in which pigs are housed and fed. **2** any filthy or corrupt place. ◆ *vb* **sties, stying, stied. 3** to enclose or be enclosed in a sty. [Old English *stig;* related to Old Norse *stīa* pen, fold, Old High German *stīga,* Middle Dutch *stije*]

stye *or* **sty** (staɪ) *n, pl* **styes** *or* **sties.** inflammation of a sebaceous gland of the eyelid, usually caused by bacteria. [C15 *styanye* (mistakenly taken as *sty on eye*), from Old English *stīgend* rising, hence swelling, stye + *ye* eye]

Stygian ('stɪdʒɪən) *adj* **1** of or relating to the river Styx. **2** *Chiefly literary.* **2a** dark, gloomy, or hellish. **2b** completely inviolable, as a vow sworn by the river Styx. [C16: from Latin *Stygius,* from Greek *Stugios,* from *Stux* STYX; related to *stugein* to hate]

style (staɪl) *n* **1** a form of appearance, design, or production; type or make: *a new style of house.* **2** the way in which something is done: *good or bad style.* **3** the manner in which something is expressed or performed, considered as separate from its intrinsic content, meaning, etc. **4** a distinctive, formal, or characteristic manner of expression in words, music, painting, etc. **5** elegance or refinement of manners, dress, etc. **6** prevailing fashion in dress, looks, etc. **7** a fashionable or ostentatious mode of existence: *to live in style.* **8** the particular mode of orthography, punctuation, design, etc., followed in a book, journal, etc., or in a printing or publishing house. **9** *Chiefly Brit.* the distinguishing title or form of address of a person or firm. **10** *Botany.* the long slender extension of the ovary, bearing the stigma. **11** *Zoology.* a slender pointed structure, such as the piercing mouthparts of certain insects. **12** a method of expressing or calculating dates. See **Old Style, New Style. 13** another word for **stylus** (sense 1). **14** the arm of a sundial. ◆ *vb* (*mainly tr*) **15** to design, shape, or tailor: *to style hair.* **16** to adapt or make suitable (for). **17** to make consistent or correct according to a printing or publishing style. **18** to name or call; designate: *to style a man a fool.* **19** (*intr*) to decorate objects using a style or stylus. [C13: from Latin *stylus, stilus* writing implement, hence characteristics of the writing, style] ▸ **'stylar** *adj* ▸ **'styler** *n*

stylebook ('staɪl,bʊk) *n* a book containing rules and examples of punctuation, typography, etc., for the use of writers, editors, and printers.

stylet ('staɪlɪt) *n* **1** *Surgery.* **1a** a wire for insertion into a flexible cannula or catheter to maintain its rigidity or patency during passage. **1b** a slender probe. **2** *Zoology.* any small pointed bristle-like part. [C17: from French *stilet,* from Old Italian STILETTO; influenced in spelling by Latin *stylus* STYLE]

styliform ('staɪlɪ,fɔːm) *adj Zoology.* shaped like a stylus or bristle: *a styliform antenna.* [C16: from New Latin *stiliformis,* from Latin STYLUS]

styling mousse *n Hairdressing.* a light foamy substance applied to the hair before styling in order to retain the shape of the style.

stylish ('staɪlɪʃ) *adj* having style; smart; fashionable. ▸ **'stylishly** *adv* ▸ **'stylishness** *n*

stylist ('staɪlɪst) *n* **1** a person who performs, writes, or acts with attention to style. **2** a designer of clothes, décor, etc. **3** a hairdresser who styles hair. **4** a designer whose job is to coordinate the style of products, advertising material, etc.

stylistic (staɪ'lɪstɪk) *adj* of or relating to style, esp. artistic or literary style. ▸ **sty'listically** *adv*

stylistics (staɪ'lɪstɪks) *n* (*functioning as sing or pl*) a branch of linguistics concerned with the study of characteristic choices in use of language, esp. literary language, as regards sound, form, or vocabulary, made by different individuals or social groups in different situations of use.

stylite ('staɪlaɪt) *n Christianity.* one of a class of recluses who in ancient times lived on the top of high pillars. [C17: from Late Greek *stulitēs,* from Greek *stulos* a pillar] ▸ **stylitic** (staɪ'lɪtɪk) *adj*

stylize *or* **stylise** ('staɪlaɪz) *vb* (*tr*) to give a conventional or established stylistic form to. ▸ **,styli'zation** *or* **,styli'sation** *n* ▸ **'stylizer** *or* **'styliser** *n*

stylo- *or before a vowel* **styl-** *combining form.* **1** (in biology) a style: *stylopodium.* **2** indicating a column or point: *stylobate; stylograph.* [from Greek *stulos* column]

stylobate ('staɪlə,beɪt) *n* a continuous horizontal course of masonry that supports a colonnade. [C17: from Latin *stylobatēs,* from Greek *stulos* pillar + *-batēs,* from *bainein* to tread, walk]

stylograph ('staɪlə,græf, -,grɑːf) *n* a fountain pen having a fine hollow tube as the writing point instead of a nib. **[C19:** from STYL(US) + -GRAPH**]**

stylographic (,staɪlə'græfɪk) *or* **stylographical** *adj* of or relating to a stylograph or stylography. ► **,stylo'graphically** *adv*

stylography (staɪ'lɒgrəfɪ) *n* the art or method of writing, drawing, or engraving with a stylus or style.

styloid ('staɪlɔɪd) *adj* **1** resembling a stylus. **2** *Anatomy.* of or relating to a projecting process of the temporal bone. **[C18:** from New Latin *styloides,* from Greek *stuloeidēs* like a STYLUS; influenced also by Greek *stulos* pillar**]**

stylolite ('staɪlə,laɪt) *n* any of the small striated columnar structures within the strata of some limestones. **[C19:** from Greek *stulos* pillar + -LITE**]** ► **stylolitic** (,staɪlə'lɪtɪk) *adj*

stylophone ('staɪlə,fəʊn) *n* a type of battery-powered electronic instrument played with a steel-tipped penlike stylus. **[C20:** from STYL(US) + -PHONE**]**

stylopize *or* **stylopise** ('staɪlə,paɪz) *vb* (*tr*) (of a stylops) to parasitize (a host): *the bee was stylopized.*

stylopodium (,staɪlə'pəʊdɪəm) *n, pl* **-dia** (-dɪə). *Botany.* a swelling at the base of the style in umbelliferous plants. **[C19:** New Latin, from Greek *stulos* pillar + -PODIUM**]**

stylops ('staɪlɒps) *n, pl* **-lopes** (-lə,piːz). any insect of the order *Strepsiptera,* including the genus *Stylops,* living as a parasite in other insects, esp. bees and wasps: the females remain in the body of the host but the males move between hosts. **[C19:** New Latin, from Greek, from *stulos* a pillar + *ōps* an eye, from the fact that the male insect has stalked compound eyes**]**

stylostixis (,staɪləʊ'stɪksɪs) *n Med.* another name for **acupuncture.** **[C20:** New Latin, from Greek *stulos* style (pointed instrument) + *stixis* mark, spot**]**

stylus ('staɪləs) *n, pl* **-li** (-laɪ) *or* **-luses. 1** Also called: **style.** a pointed instrument for engraving, drawing, or writing. **2** a tool used in ancient times for writing on wax tablets, which was pointed at one end and blunt at the other for erasing mistakes. **3** a device attached to the cartridge in the pick-up arm of a record player that rests in the groove in the record, transmitting the vibrations to the sensing device in the cartridge. It consists of or is tipped with a hard material, such as diamond or sapphire. **[C18:** from Latin, variant of *stilus* writing implement; see STYLE**]** ► **'stylar** *adj*

stymie *or* **stymy** ('staɪmɪ) *vb* **-mies, -mieing, -mied** *or* **-mies, -mying, -mied.** (*tr; often passive*) **1** to hinder or thwart. **2** *Golf.* to impede with a stymie. ◆ *n, pl* **-mies. 3** *Golf.* (formerly) a situation on the green in which an opponent's ball is blocking the line between the hole and the ball about to be played: an obstructing ball may now be lifted and replaced by a marker. **4** a situation of obstruction. **[C19:** of uncertain origin**]**

stypsis ('stɪpsɪs) *n* the action, application, or use of a styptic. **[C19:** via New Latin from Late Latin: astringency, from Greek *stupsis,* from *stuphein* to contract**]**

styptic ('stɪptɪk) *adj* **1** contracting the blood vessels or tissues. ◆ *n* **2** a styptic drug. **[C14:** via Late Latin, from Greek *stuptikos* capable of contracting; see STYPSIS**]** ► **stypticity** (stɪp'tɪsɪtɪ) *n*

styptic pencil *n* a styptic agent in the form of a small stick, for application to razor nicks, etc.

styracaceous (,staɪrə'keɪʃəs) *adj* of, relating to, or belonging to the *Styracaceae,* a family of Asian and American trees and shrubs having leathery leaves: includes storax and silver bell. **[C19:** *styrac-,* from STYRAX**]**

styrax ('staɪræks) *n* any tropical or subtropical tree of the genus *Styrax,* which includes the storaxes. **[C16:** via Latin from Greek *sturax***]**

styrene ('staɪriːn) *n* a colourless oily volatile flammable water-insoluble liquid made from ethylene and benzene. It is an unsaturated compound and readily polymerizes: used in making synthetic plastics and rubbers. Formula: $C_6H_5CH{:}CH_2$. See also **polystyrene.** **[C20:** from STYR(AX) + -ENE**]**

Styria ('stɪərɪə) *n* a mountainous state of SE Austria: rich mineral resources. Capital: Graz. Pop.: 1 206 000 (1995 est.). Area: 16 384 sq. km (6326 sq. miles). German name: **Steiermark.**

Styx (stɪks) *n Greek myth.* a river in Hades across which Charon ferried the souls of the dead. **[**from Greek *Stux;* related to *stugein* to hate**]**

SU *abbrev. for:* **1** strontium unit. ◆ **2** (formerly) *international car registration for* Soviet Union.

suable ('sjuːəbᵊl) *adj* liable to be sued in a court. **[C17:** from SUE + -ABLE**]** ► **,sua'bility** *n*

Suakin ('suːɑːkɪn) *n* a port in the NE Sudan, on the Red Sea: formerly the chief port of the African Red Sea; now obstructed by a coral reef. Pop.: 5511 (latest est.).

Suárez (*Spanish* 'swareθ) *n* **Francisco de.** 1548–1617, Spanish theologian, considered the leading scholastic philosopher after Aquinas and the principal Jesuit theologian. His works include *Disputationes Metaphysicae* (1597) and *De Legibus* (1612).

suasion ('sweɪʒən) *n* a rare word for **persuasion.** **[C14:** from Latin *suāsiō,* from *suādēre* to PERSUADE**]** ► **'suasive** *adj*

suave (swɑːv) *adj* (esp. of a man) displaying smoothness and sophistication in manner or attitude; urbane. **[C16:** from Latin *suāvis* sweet**]** ► **'suavely** *adv* ► **suavity** ('swɑːvɪtɪ) *or* **'suaveness** *n*

sub (sʌb) *n* **1** short for several words beginning with *sub-,* such as **subaltern, subeditor, submarine, subordinate, subscription, substandard, substitute,** and **substratum** (in photography). **2** *Brit. informal.* an advance payment of wages or salary. Formal term: **subsistence allowance.** ◆ *vb* **subs, subbing, subbed. 3** (*intr*) to serve as a substitute. **4** (*intr*) *Informal.* to act as a substitute (for). **5** *Brit. informal.* to grant or receive (an advance payment of wages or salary). **6** (*tr*) *Informal.* short for **subedit. 7** (*tr*) *Photog.* to apply a substratum to (a film or plate base).

sub. *abbrev. for:* **1** subeditor. **2** subito (in music). **3** subscription. **4** substitute. **5** suburb(an). **6** subway.

sub- *prefix* **1** situated under or beneath: *subterranean.* **2** secondary in rank; subordinate: *subeditor.* **3** falling short of; less than or imperfectly: *subarctic; subhuman.* **4** forming a subdivision or subordinate part of a whole: *subcommittee.* **5** (in chemistry) **5a** indicating that a compound contains a relatively small proportion of a specified element: *suboxide.* **5b** indicating that a salt is basic salt: *subacetate.* **[**from Latin *sub***]**

subacetate (sʌb'æsɪ,teɪt) *n* any one of certain crystalline basic acetates containing hydroxide ions in addition to acetate ions. For example, the subacetate of aluminium is probably $Al_3(OH)_2(CH_3COO)$.

subacid (sʌb'æsɪd) *adj* (esp. of some fruits) moderately acid or sour. ► **subacidity** (,sʌbə'sɪdɪtɪ) *or* **sub'acidness** *n* ► **sub'acidly** *adv*

subacute (,sʌbə'kjuːt) *adj* intermediate between acute and chronic.

subadar *or* **subahdar** ('suːbə,dɑː) *n* (formerly) the chief native officer of a company of Indian soldiers in the British service. Also called: **subah.** **[C17:** via Urdu from Persian, from *sūba* province + *-dār* holding**]**

subah ('suːbɑː) *n* (in India) **1** a province in the Mogul empire. **2** another word for **subadar.** **[C18:** via Urdu and Persian from Arabic *sūba* province**]**

subalpine (sʌb'ælpaɪn) *adj* **1** situated in or relating to the regions at the foot of mountains. **2** (of plants) growing below the treeline in mountainous regions.

subaltern ('sʌbᵊltən) *n* **1** a commissioned officer below the rank of captain in certain armies, esp. the British. **2** a person of inferior rank or position. **3** *Logic.* **3a** the relation of one proposition to another when the first is implied by the second, esp. the relation of a particular to a universal proposition. **3b** (*as modifier*): *a subaltern relation.* ◆ *adj* **4** of inferior position or rank. **[C16:** from Late Latin *subalternus,* from Latin SUB- + *alternus* alternate, from *alter* the other**]**

subalternate (sʌb'ɔːltənɪt) *adj* **1** (of leaves) having an arrangement intermediate between alternate and opposite. **2** following in turn. **3** of lesser quality or status. ► **subalternation** (sʌb,ɔːltə'neɪʃən) *n*

subantarctic (,sʌbænt'ɑːktɪk) *adj* of or relating to latitudes immediately north of the Antarctic Circle.

subapostolic (,sʌbæpə'stɒlɪk) *adj Christianity.* of or relating to the era after that of the Apostles.

subaqua (,sʌb'ækwə) *adj* of or relating to underwater sport: *subaqua swimming; a subaqua club.* **[**from SUB- + Latin *aqua* water**]**

subaquatic (,sʌbə'kwætɪk, -'kwɒt-) *adj* **1** living or growing partly in water and partly on land. **2** of or relating to conditions, existence, or activities under water.

subaqueous (sʌb'eɪkwɪəs, -'ækwɪ-) *adj* occurring, appearing, formed, or used under water.

subarctic (sʌb'ɑːktɪk) *adj* of or relating to latitudes immediately south of the Arctic Circle.

subarid (sʌb'ærɪd) *adj* receiving slightly more rainfall than arid regions; moderately dry.

subassembly (,sʌbə'sɛmblɪ) *n, pl* **-blies.** a number of machine components integrated into a unit forming part of a larger assembly.

subastral (sʌb'æstrəl) *adj* a rare word for **terrestrial.**

subatomic (,sʌbə'tɒmɪk) *adj* **1** of, relating to or being a particle making up an atom or a process occurring within atoms: *the electron is a subatomic particle.* **2** having dimensions smaller than atomic dimensions.

subaudition (,sʌbɔː'dɪʃən) *n* **1** something that is not directly stated but implied. **2** the ability or act of understanding that which is only implied. **[C18:** from Late Latin *subaudīre,* from SUB- + Latin *audīre* to hear**]**

subauricular (,sʌbɔː'rɪkjʊlə) *adj Anatomy.* situated below the auricle of the ear.

subaxillary (,sʌb'æksɪlərɪ) *adj* **1** situated or growing beneath the axil of a plant: *subaxillary bracts.* **2** situated beneath the armpit.

subbase ('sʌb,beɪs) *n* the lowest part of a pedestal, base, or skirting. Compare **surbase.**

subbasement ('sʌb,beɪsmənt) *n* an underground storey of a building beneath the main basement.

subbass *or* **subbase** ('sʌb,beɪs) *n* another name for **bourdon.**

Subbuteo (sə'bjuːtɪəʊ) *n Trademark.* a football game played on a table, with toy players affixed to rounded bases which are flicked with the fingers. **[C20:** arbitrarily named, from Latin *subbuteo,* the specific name of the hobby hawk *Falco subbuteo***]**

subcalibre *or U.S.* **subcaliber** (sʌb'kælɪbə) *adj* **1** (of a projectile) having a calibre less than that of the firearm from which it is discharged and therefore either fitted with a disc or fired through a tube inserted into the barrel. **2** of, relating to, or firing subcalibre projectiles.

subcarrier ('sʌb,kærɪə) *n* a subsidiary carrier wave that is modulated with information and applied as modulation to a main carrier wave that is already modulated with other information.

subcartilaginous (sʌb,kɑːtɪ'lædʒɪnəs) *adj* **1** composed partly of cartilage: *a subcartilaginous skeleton.* **2** situated beneath a cartilage or a cartilaginous structure.

subcelestial (,sʌbsɪ'lɛstɪəl) *adj* **1** beneath the heavens; terrestrial. ◆ *n* **2** a subcelestial object.

'sub,branch *n*	**sub'category** *n, pl* **-ries.**

subception (səb'sɛpʃən) *n Psychol.* another word for **subliminal perception.**

subchloride (sʌb'klɔːraɪd) *n* a chloride of an element that contains less chlorine than its common chloride.

subclass ('sʌb,klɑːs) *n* **1** a principal subdivision of a class. **2** *Biology.* a taxonomic group that is a subdivision of a class. **3** *Maths.* another name for **subset** (sense 1). ◆ *vb* **4** *(tr)* to assign to a subclass.

subclavian (sʌb'kleɪvɪən) *adj Anatomy.* (of an artery, vein, area, etc.) situated below the clavicle. [C17: from New Latin *subclāvius,* from Latin SUB- + *clavis* key]

subclimax (sʌb'klaɪmæks) *n Ecology.* a community in which development has been arrested before climax has been attained. ▸ **subclimactic** (,sʌbklaɪ'mæktɪk) *adj*

subclinical (sʌb'klɪnɪk^{ə}l) *adj Med.* of or relating to the stage in the course of a disease before the symptoms are first noted. ▸ **sub'clinically** *adv*

subconscious (sʌb'kɒnʃəs) *adj* **1** acting or existing without one's awareness: *subconscious motive.* ◆ *n* **2** *Psychoanal.* that part of the mind which is on the fringe of consciousness and contains material of which it is possible to become aware by redirecting attention. Compare **preconscious** (sense 2), **unconscious** (sense 5). ▸ **sub'consciously** *adv* ▸ **sub'consciousness** *n*

subcontinent (sʌb'kɒntɪnənt) *n* a large land mass that is a distinct part of a continent, such as India is of Asia. ▸ **subcontinental** (,sʌbkɒntɪ'nent^{ə}l) *adj*

subcontract *n* (sʌb'kɒntrækt). **1** a subordinate contract under which the supply of materials, services, or labour is let out to someone other than a party to the main contract. ◆ *vb* (,sʌbkən'trækt). **2** *(intr; often foll. by for)* to enter into or make a subcontract. **3** *(tr)* to let out (work) on a subcontract.

subcontractor (,sʌbkən'træktə) *n* a person, company, etc., that enters into a subcontract, esp. a firm that undertakes to complete part of another's contract.

subcontrary (sʌb'kɒntrərɪ) *Logic.* ◆ *adj* **1** (of a pair of propositions) related such that they cannot both be false at once, although they may be true together. Compare **contrary** (sense 5), **contradictory** (sense 3). ◆ *n, pl* **-ries. 2** a statement that cannot be false when a given statement is false.

subcortex (sʌb'kɔːteks) *n, pl* **-tices** (-tɪ,siːz). *Anatomy.* the matter of the brain situated beneath the cerebral cortex. ▸ **subcortical** (sʌb'kɔːtɪk^{ə}l) *adj*

subcritical (sʌb'krɪtɪk^{ə}l) *adj Physics.* (of a nuclear reaction, power station, etc.) having or involving a chain reaction that is not self-sustaining; not yet critical.

subculture *n* ('sʌb,kʌltʃə). **1** a subdivision of a national culture or an enclave within it with a distinct integrated network of behaviour, beliefs, and attitudes. **2** a culture of microorganisms derived from another culture. ◆ *vb* (sʌb'kʌltʃə). **3** *(tr)* to inoculate (bacteria from one culture medium) onto another medium. ▸ **sub'cultural** *adj*

subcutaneous (,sʌbkjuː'teɪnɪəs) *adj Med.* situated, used, or introduced beneath the skin: *a subcutaneous injection.* [C17: from Late Latin *subcutāneus,* from SUB- + Latin *cutis* skin + -EOUS] ▸ **,subcu'taneously** *adv*

subdeacon (,sʌb'diːkən) *n Chiefly R.C. Church.* **1** a cleric who assists at High Mass. **2** (formerly) a person ordained to the lowest of the major orders. ▸ **subdeaconate** (sʌb'diːkənɪt) *n*

subdelirium (,sʌbdə'lɪrɪəm) *n, pl* **-liriums** *or* **-liria** (-'lɪrɪə). mild or intermittent delirium.

subdiaconate (,sʌbdaɪ'ækənɪt, -,neɪt) *n* the rank or office of a subdeacon. [C18: from Medieval Latin *subdiaconus* subdeacon + -ATE²; see DEACON] ▸ **,subdi'aconal** *adj*

subdivide (,sʌbdɪ'vaɪd, 'sʌbdɪ,vaɪd) *vb* **1** to divide (something) resulting from an earlier division. **2** *(tr) U.S. and Canadian.* to divide (land) into lots for sale. ▸ **,subdi'vider** *n*

subdivision ('sʌbdɪ,vɪʒən) *n* **1** the process, instance, or state of being divided again following upon an earlier division. **2** a portion that is the result of subdividing. **3** *U.S. and Canadian.* a tract of land for building resulting from subdividing land. **4** *Canadian.* a housing development built on such a tract. ▸ **,subdi'visional** *adj*

subdominant (sʌb'dɒmɪnənt) *Music.* ◆ *n* **1** the fourth degree of a major or minor scale. **2** a key or chord based on this. ◆ *adj* **3** of or relating to the subdominant.

subduct (səb'dʌkt) *vb (tr)* **1** *Physiol.* to draw or turn (the eye, etc.) downwards. **2** *Rare.* to take away; deduct. [C17: from Latin *subdūcere,* from SUB- + *dūcere* to lead, bring]

subduction (səb'dʌkʃən) *n* **1** the act of subducting, esp. of turning the eye downwards. **2** *Geology.* the process of one tectonic plate sliding under another, resulting in tensions in the earth's crust, with earthquakes and volcanic eruptions.

subduction zone *n Geology.* another name for **Benioff zone.**

subdue (səb'djuː) *vb* **-dues, -duing, -dued.** *(tr)* **1** to establish ascendancy over by force. **2** to overcome and bring under control, as by intimidation or persuasion. **3** to hold in check or repress (feelings, emotions, etc.). **4** to render less intense or less conspicuous. [C14 *sobdue,* from Old French *soduire* to mislead, from Latin *subdūcere* to remove; English sense influenced by Latin *subdere* to subject] ▸ **sub'duable** *adj* ▸ **sub'duably** *adv* ▸ **sub'dual** *n*

subdued (səb'djuːd) *adj* **1** cowed, passive, or shy. **2** gentle or quiet: *a subdued whisper.* **3** (of colours, etc.) not harsh or bright: *subdued lighting.* ▸ **sub'duedly** *adv* ▸ **sub'duedness** *n*

subdural (sʌb'djuərəl) *adj Anatomy.* between the dura mater and the arachnoid: *subdural haematoma.*

subedit (sʌb'ɛdɪt) *vb* to edit and correct (written or printed material).

subeditor (sʌb'ɛdɪtə) *n* a person who checks and edits copy, esp. on a newspaper.

subequatorial (sʌb,ɛkwə'tɔːrɪəl) *adj* situated in or characteristic of regions immediately north or south of equatorial regions.

suberic acid (sjuː'bɛrɪk) *n* another name for **octanedioic acid.** [C18: from French *subérique,* from Latin *sūber* cork (from which the acid is obtained)]

suberin ('sjuːbərɪn) *n* a fatty or waxy substance that is present in the walls of cork cells, making them impermeable to water and resistant to decay. [C19: from Latin *sūber* cork + -IN]

suberize *or* **suberise** ('sjuːbə,raɪz) *vb (tr) Botany.* to impregnate (cell walls) with suberin during the formation of corky tissue. ▸ **,suberi'zation** *or* **,suberi'sation** *n*

suberose ('sjuːbə,rəʊs), **subereous** (sjuː'bɛrɪəs), *or* **suberic** (sjuː'bɛrɪk) *adj Botany.* relating to, resembling, or consisting of cork; corky.

subfamily ('sʌb,fæmɪlɪ) *n, pl* **-lies. 1** *Biology.* a taxonomic group that is a subdivision of a family. **2** any analogous subdivision, as of a family of languages.

subfloor ('sʌb,flɔː) *n* a rough floor that forms a base for a finished floor.

subfusc ('sʌbfʌsk) *adj* **1** devoid of brightness or appeal; drab, dull, or dark. ◆ *n* **2** (at Oxford University) formal academic dress. [C18: from Latin *subfuscus* dusky, from *fuscus* dark]

subgenus (sʌb'dʒiːnəs, -'dʒen-; 'sʌb,dʒiːnəs, -,dʒen-) *n, pl* **-genera** (-'dʒenərə) *or* **-genuses.** *Biology.* a taxonomic group that is a subdivision of a genus but of higher rank than a species. ▸ **subgeneric** (,sʌbdʒə'nɛrɪk) *adj*

subglacial (sʌb'gleɪsɪəl) *adj* formed or occurring at the bottom of a glacier. ▸ **sub'glacially** *adv*

subgrade ('sʌb,greɪd) *n* the ground beneath a roadway or pavement.

subgroup ('sʌb,gruːp) *n* **1** a distinct and often subordinate division of a group. **2** a mathematical group whose members are members of another group, both groups being subject to the same rule of combination.

subha ('suːbaː) *n Islam.* a string of beads used in praying and meditating. [from Arabic]

subharmonic (,sʌbhɑː'mɒnɪk) *n* an integral submultiple of a frequency.

subheading ('sʌb,hɛdɪŋ) *or* **subhead** *n* **1** the heading or title of a subdivision or subsection of a printed work. **2** a division subordinate to a main heading or title.

subhuman (sʌb'hjuːmən) *adj* **1** of, relating to, or designating animals that are below man (*Homo sapiens*) in evolutionary development. **2** less than human.

subimago (,sʌbɪ'meɪgəʊ) *n, pl* **-imagoes** *or* **-imagines** (-ɪ'mædʒə,niːz). the first winged stage of the mayfly, with dull opaque wings, known to anglers as a **dun,** before it metamorphoses into the shiny gauzy imago or **spinner.**

subindex (sʌb'ɪndɛks) *n, pl* **-dices** (-dɪ,siːz) *or* **-dexes. 1** another word for **subscript** (sense 2). **2** *U.S.* an index to a subcategory.

subinfeudate (,sʌbɪn'fjuːdeɪt) *vb* to grant (lands) by subinfeudation.

subinfeudation (,sʌbɪnfjʊ'deɪʃən) *n* **1** (in feudal society) the granting of land by a vassal to another man who became his vassal. **2** the tenure or relationship so established.

subinfeudatory (,sʌbɪn'fjuːdətərɪ, -trɪ) (in feudal society) ◆ *n, pl* **-ries. 1** a man who held his fief by a subinfeudation. ◆ *adj* **2** of or relating to subinfeudation.

subirrigate (sʌb'ɪrɪ,geɪt) *vb* to irrigate (land) by means of an underground system of pipe lines or by natural moisture in the subsoil. ▸ **,subirri'gation** *n*

subitize *or* **subitise** ('sʌbɪ,taɪz) *vb Psychol.* to perceive the number of (a group of items) at a glance and without counting: *the maximum number of items that can be subitized is about five.* [C20: from Latin *subitus* sudden + -IZE]

subito ('suːbɪ,təʊ) *adv Music.* (preceding or following a dynamic marking, etc.) suddenly; immediately. Abbrev.: **sub.** [C18: via Italian from Latin: suddenly, from *subitus* sudden, from *subīre* to approach, from SUB- (indicating stealth) + *īre* to go]

subj. *abbrev. for:* **1** subject. **2** subjective(ly). **3** subjunctive.

subjacent (sʌb'dʒeɪs^{ə}nt) *adj* **1** forming a foundation; underlying. **2** lower than though not directly below: *tall peaks and their subjacent valley.* [C16: from Latin *subjacēre* to lie close, adjoin, be under, from SUB- + *jacēre* to lie] ▸ **sub'jacency** *n* ▸ **sub'jacently** *adv*

subject *n* ('sʌbdʒɪkt). **1a** the predominant theme or topic, as of a book, discussion, etc. **1b** *(in combination): subject-heading.* **2** any branch of learning considered as a course of study. **3** *Grammar, logic.* a word, phrase, or formal expression about which something is predicated or stated in a sentence; for example, *the cat* in the sentence *The cat catches mice.* **4** a person or thing that undergoes experiment, analysis, treatment, etc. **5** a person who lives under the rule of a monarch, government, etc. **6** an object, figure, scene, etc., as selected by an artist or photographer for representation. **7** *Philosophy.* **7a** that which thinks or feels as opposed to the object of thinking and feeling; the self or the mind. **7b** a substance as opposed to its attributes. **8** Also called: **theme.** *Music.* a melodic or thematic phrase used as the principal motif of a fugue, the basis from which the musical material is derived in a sonata-form movement, or the recurrent figure in a rondo. **9** *Logic.* **9a** the term of a categorial statement of which something is predicated. **9b** the reference or denotation of the subject term of a statement. The subject of *John is tall* is not the name *John,* but John himself. **10** an originating motive. **11 change the subject.** to select a new topic of conversation. ◆ *adj* ('sʌbdʒɪkt). *(usually postpositive* and foll. by *to)* **12** being under the power or sovereignty of a ruler, government, etc.: *subject peoples.* **13** showing a tendency (towards): *a child subject to indiscipline.* **14** exposed or vulnerable: *subject to ribaldry.* **15** conditional upon: *the results are*

'**sub,clan** *n*
'**sub,clause** *n*
'**subcom,mission** *n*
,**subcom'missioner** *n*
'**subcom,mittee** *n*
'**sub,district** *n*
sub'entry *n, pl* **-tries.**

subject to correction. ◆ *adv* **16 subject to.** (*prep*) under the condition that: *we accept, subject to her agreement.* ◆ *vb* (səb'dʒɛkt). (*tr*) **17** (foll. by *to*) to cause to undergo the application (of): *they subjected him to torture.* **18** (*often passive;* foll. by *to*) to expose or render vulnerable or liable (to some experience): *he was subjected to great danger.* **19** (foll. by *to*) to bring under the control or authority (of): *to subject a soldier to discipline.* **20** *Now rare.* to subdue or subjugate. **21** *Rare.* to present for consideration; submit. **22** *Obsolete.* to place below. ◆ Abbrev.: **subj.** [C14: from Latin *subjectus* brought under, from *subicere* to place under, from SUB- + *jacere* to throw] ▸ **sub'jectable** *adj* ▸ **sub,jecta'bility** *n* ▸ **'subjectless** *adj* ▸ **'subject-,like** *adj*

subject catalogue *n Library science.* a catalogue with entries arranged by subject in a classified sequence.

subjectify (səb'dʒɛktɪ,faɪ) *vb* **-fies, -fying, -fied.** (*tr*) to make subjective or interpret subjectively. ▸ **sub,jectifi'cation** *n*

subjection (səb'dʒɛkʃən) *n* the act or process of subjecting or the state of being subjected.

subjective (səb'dʒɛktɪv) *adj* **1** belonging to, proceeding from, or relating to the mind of the thinking subject and not the nature of the object being considered. **2** of, relating to, or emanating from a person's emotions, prejudices, etc.: *subjective views.* **3** relating to the inherent nature of a person or thing; essential. **4** existing only as perceived and not as a thing in itself. **5** *Med.* (of a symptom, condition, etc.) experienced only by the patient and incapable of being recognized or studied by anyone else. **6** *Grammar.* denoting a case of nouns and pronouns, esp. in languages having only two cases, that identifies the subject of a finite verb and (in formal use in English) is selected for predicate complements, as in *It is I.* See also **nominative** (sense 1). ◆ *n* **7** *Grammar.* **7a** the subjective case. **7b** a subjective word or speech element. ◆ Abbrev.: **subj.** Compare **objective.** ▸ **sub'jectively** *adv* ▸ **,subjec'tivity** *or* **sub'jectiveness** *n*

subjective idealism *n Philosophy.* the theory that all experience is of ideas in the mind.

subjective intension *n Logic.* the associations that an expression has for an individual; the intension he believes it to have.

subjectivism (səb'dʒɛktɪ,vɪzəm) *n* **1** the meta-ethical doctrine that there are no absolute moral values but that these are variable in the same way as taste is. **2** any similar philosophical theory, for example, about truth or perception. **3** any theological theory that attaches primary importance to religious experience. **4** the quality or condition of being subjective. ▸ **sub'jectivist** *n* ▸ **sub,jecti'vistic** *adj* ▸ **sub,jecti'vistically** *adv*

subject matter *n* the substance or main theme of a book, discussion, debate, etc.

subject-raising *n Transformational grammar.* a rule that moves the subject of a complement clause into the clause in which it is embedded, as in the derivation of *He is likely to be late* from *It is likely that he will be late.*

subjoin (sʌb'dʒɔɪn) *vb* (*tr*) to add or attach at the end of something spoken, written, etc. [C16: from French *subjoindre,* from Latin *subjungere* to add to, from *sub-* in addition + *jungere* to JOIN] ▸ **sub'joinder** *n* ▸ **subjunction** (sʌb'dʒʌŋkʃən) *n*

sub judice ('dʒu:dɪsɪ) *adj* (*usually postpositive*) before a court of law or a judge; under judicial consideration. [Latin]

subjugate ('sʌbdʒʊ,geɪt) *vb* (*tr*) **1** to bring into subjection. **2** to make subservient or submissive. [C15: from Late Latin *subjugāre* to subdue, from Latin SUB- + *jugum* yoke] ▸ **subjugable** ('sʌbdʒəgəbᵊl) *adj* ▸ **,subju'gation** *n* ▸ **'subju,gator** *n*

subjunctive (səb'dʒʌŋktɪv) *adj* **1** *Grammar.* denoting a mood of verbs used when the content of the clause is being doubted, supposed, feared true, etc., rather than being asserted. The rules for its use and the range of meanings it may possess vary considerably from language to language. In the following sentence, *were* is in the subjunctive: *I'd think very seriously about that if I were you.* Compare **indicative.** ◆ *n* **2** *Grammar.* **2a** the subjunctive mood. **2b** a verb in this mood. ◆ Abbrev.: **subj.** [C16: via Late Latin *subjunctīvus,* from Latin *subjungere* to SUBJOIN] ▸ **sub'junctively** *adv*

subkingdom (sʌb'kɪŋdəm) *n Biology.* a taxonomic group that is a subdivision of a kingdom.

sublapsarianism (,sʌblæp'sɛərɪə,nɪzəm) *n* another word for **infralapsarianism.** [C17 *sublapsarian,* via New Latin, from Latin SUB- + *lāpsus* a fall] ▸ **,sublap'sarian** *n, adj*

sublease *n* ('sʌb,li:s). **1** a lease of property made by a person who is himself a lessee or tenant of that property. ◆ *vb* (sʌb'li:s). **2** to grant a sublease of (property); sublet. **3** (*tr*) to take, obtain, or hold by sublease. ▸ **sublessee** (,sʌblɛ'si:) *n* ▸ **sublessor** (,sʌblɛ'sɔ:) *n*

sublet *vb* (sʌb'lɛt), **-lets, -letting, -let. 1** to grant a sublease of (property). **2** to let out (work, etc.) under a subcontract. ◆ *n* ('sʌb,lɛt). **3** *Informal, chiefly U.S.* a sublease.

sublieutenant (,sʌblə'tɛnənt) *n* the most junior commissioned officer in the Royal Navy and certain other navies. ▸ **,sublieu'tenancy** *n*

sublimate ('sʌblɪ,meɪt) *vb* **1** *Psychol.* to direct the energy of (a primitive impulse, esp. a sexual one) into activities that are considered to be socially more acceptable. **2** (*tr*) to make purer; refine. ◆ *n* **3** *Chem.* the material obtained when a substance is sublimed. ◆ *adj* **4** exalted or purified. [C16: from Latin *sublīmāre* to elevate, from *sublīmis* lofty; see SUBLIME] ▸ **sublimable** ('sʌbləməbᵊl) *adj*

sublimation (,sʌblɪ'meɪʃən) *n* **1** (in Freudian psychology) the diversion of psychic energy derived from sexual impulses into nonsexual activity, esp. of a creative nature. **2** the process or an instance of sublimating. **3** something sublimated. **4** *Chem.* the process or instance or subliming.

sublime (sə'blaɪm) *adj* **1** of high moral, aesthetic, intellectual, or spiritual value; noble; exalted. **2** inspiring deep veneration, awe, or uplifting emotion because of its beauty, nobility, grandeur, or immensity. **3** unparalleled; supreme: *a sublime compliment.* **4** *Poetic.* of proud bearing or aspect. **5** *Archaic.* raised up. ◆ *n* **the sublime. 6** something that is sublime. **7** the ultimate degree or perfect example: *the sublime of folly.* ◆ *vb* **8** (*tr*) to make higher or purer. **9** to change or cause to change directly from a solid to a vapour or gas without first melting: *to sublime iodine; many mercury salts sublime when heated.* **10** to undergo or cause to undergo this process followed by a reverse change directly from a vapour to a solid: *to sublime iodine onto glass.* [C14: from Latin *sublīmis* lofty, perhaps from *sub-* up to + *līmen* lintel] ▸ **sub'limely** *adv* ▸ **sublimity** (sə'blɪmɪtɪ) *n*

Sublime Porte *n* the full name of the **Porte.**

subliminal (sʌb'lɪmɪnᵊl) *adj* **1** resulting from processes of which the individual is not aware. **2** (of stimuli) less than the minimum intensity or duration required to elicit a response. [C19: from Latin SUB- below + *līmen* threshold] ▸ **sub'liminally** *adv*

subliminal advertising *n* a form of advertising on film or television that employs subliminal images to influence the viewer unconsciously.

subliminal perception *n Psychol.* perception of or reaction to a stimulus that occurs without awareness or consciousness. Also called: **subception.**

sublingual (sʌb'lɪŋgwəl) *adj Anatomy.* situated beneath the tongue.

sublittoral (sʌb'lɪtərəl) *adj* **1** (of marine organisms) growing, living, or situated close to the seashore: *a sublittoral plant.* **2** of or relating to the zone between the seashore and the edge of the continental shelf.

sublunary (sʌb'lu:nərɪ) *adj* **1** situated between the moon and the earth. **2** of or relating to the earth or world. [C16: via Late Latin, from Latin SUB- + *lūna* moon]

subluxate (sʌb'lʌkseɪt) *vb* (*tr*) *Pathol.* to partially dislocate. ▸ **,sublux'ation** *n*

sub-machine-gun *n* a portable automatic or semiautomatic light gun with a short barrel, firing pistol ammunition: designed to be fired from the hip or shoulder.

submarginal (sʌb'mɑ:dʒɪnᵊl) *adj* **1** below the minimum requirements. **2** situated close to the margin of an organ or part. **3** (of land) infertile and unprofitable for cultivation. ▸ **sub'marginally** *adv*

submarine ('sʌbmə,ri:n, ,sʌbmə'ri:n) *n* **1** a vessel, esp. one designed for warfare, capable of operating for protracted periods below the surface of the sea. Often shortened to **sub. 2** (*modifier*) **2a** of or relating to a submarine: *a submarine captain.* **2b** occurring or situated below the surface of the sea: *a submarine cable.*

submariner (sʌb'mærɪnə) *n* a crewman in a submarine.

submaxillary (,sʌbmæk'sɪlərɪ) *adj* of, relating to, or situated close to the lower jaw.

submaxillary gland *n* (in mammals) either of a pair of salivary glands situated on each side behind the lower jaw.

submediant (sʌb'mi:dɪənt) *Music.* ◆ *n* **1** the sixth degree of a major or minor scale. **2** a key or chord based on this. ◆ *adj* **3** of or relating to the submediant. ◆ Also (U.S. and Canadian): **superdominant.**

submental (sʌb'mɛntᵊl) *adj Anatomy.* situated beneath the chin. [from SUB- + Latin *mentum* chin]

submerge (səb'mɜ:dʒ) *or* **submerse** (səb'mɜ:s) *vb* **1** to plunge, sink, or dive or cause to plunge, sink, or dive below the surface of water, etc. **2** (*tr*) to cover with water or some other liquid. **3** (*tr*) to hide; suppress. **4** (*tr*) to overwhelm, as with work, difficulties, etc. [C17: from Latin *submergere,* from SUB- + *mergere* to immerse] ▸ **sub'mergence** *or* **submersion** (səb'mɜ:ʃᵊn) *n*

submerged (səb'mɜ:dʒd) *or* **submersed** (səb'mɜ:st) *adj* **1** (of plants or plant parts) growing beneath the surface of the water. **2** hidden; obscured. **3** overwhelmed or overburdened.

submerged arc welding *n* a type of heavy electric-arc welding using mechanically fed bare wire with the arc submerged in powdered flux to keep out oxygen.

submersible (səb'mɜ:səbᵊl) *or* **submergible** (səb'mɜ:dʒɪbᵊl) *adj* **1** able to be submerged. **2** capable of operating under water, etc. ◆ *n* **3** a vessel designed to operate under water for short periods. **4** a submarine taking one or more men that is designed and equipped to carry out work in deep water below the levels at which divers can work. ▸ **sub,mersi'bility** *or* **sub,mergi'bility** *n*

submicroscopic (,sʌbmaɪkrə'skɒpɪk) *adj* too small to be seen through an optical microscope. ▸ **,submicro'scopically** *adv*

subminiature (sʌb'mɪnɪətʃə) *adj* smaller than miniature.

subminiature camera *n* a pocket-sized camera, usually using 16 millimetre film with a very fine grain so that negatives can produce considerably enlarged prints.

subminiaturize *or* **subminiaturise** (sʌb'mɪnɪətʃə,raɪz) *vb* (*tr*) to make subminiature, as in the manufacture of electronic equipment, etc. ▸ **sub,miniaturi'zation** *or* **sub,miniaturi'sation** *n*

submiss (səb'mɪs) *adj Archaic or poetic.* **1** docile; submissive. **2** soft in tone. [C16: from Latin *submissus* lowered, gentle, from *submittere* to reduce, from SUB- + *mittere* to send]

submission (səb'mɪʃən) *n* **1** an act or instance of submitting. **2** something submitted; a proposal, argument, etc. **3** the quality or condition of being submissive to another. **4** the act of referring a document, etc., for the consideration of someone else. **5** *Law.* **5a** an agreement by the parties to a dispute to refer the matter to arbitration. **5b** the instrument referring a disputed matter to arbitration. **6** (in wrestling) the act of causing such pain to one's opponent that he submits. Compare **fall** (sense 48). **7** *Archaic.* a confession of error.

submissive (səb'mɪsɪv) *adj* of, tending towards, or indicating submission, humility, or servility. ▸ **sub'missively** *adv* ▸ **sub'missiveness** *n*

submit (səb'mɪt) *vb* **-mits, -mitting, -mitted. 1** (often foll. by *to*) to yield (oneself), as to the will of another person, a superior force, etc. **2** (foll. by *to*) to subject or be voluntarily subjected (to analysis, treatment, etc.). **3** (*tr;* often foll. by *to*) to refer (something to someone) for judgment or consideration: *to submit a claim.* **4** (*tr; may take a clause as object*) to state, contend, or propose deferentially. **5** (*intr; often foll. by to*) to defer or accede (to the decision, opinion, etc., of another). [C14: from Latin *submittere* to place under, from SUB- + *mittere* to send] ▸ **subˈmittable** *or* **subˈmissible** *adj* ▸ **subˈmittal** *n* ▸ **subˈmitter** *n*

submontane (sʌbˈmɒnteɪn) *adj* **1** situated on or characteristic of the lower slopes of a mountain. **2** beneath a mountain or mountain range. [C19: from Latin SUB- + *mōns* mountain] ▸ **subˈmontanely** *adv*

submucosa (ˌsʌbmjuːˈkəʊsə) *n, pl* **-cosae** (-ˈkəʊsiː). *Anatomy.* the connective tissue beneath a mucous membrane.

submultiple (sʌbˈmʌltɪpᵊl) *n* **1** a number that can be divided into another number an integral number of times without a remainder: *three is a submultiple of nine.* ◆ *adj* **2** being a submultiple of a quantity or number.

subnormal (sʌbˈnɔːməl) *adj* **1** less than the normal. **2** having a low intelligence, esp. having an IQ of less than 70. ◆ *n* **3** a subnormal person. ▸ **subnormality** (ˌsʌbnɔːˈmælɪtɪ) *n* ▸ **subˈnormally** *adv*

subnuclear (sʌbˈnjuːklɪə) *adj* **1** of or relating to particles within the nucleus of an atom. **2** of a lesser level of organization than the nucleus of an atom.

suboceanic (sʌbˌəʊʃɪˈænɪk) *adj* formed or situated beneath the ocean or ocean floor.

suborbital (sʌbˈɔːbɪtᵊl) *adj* **1** (of a rocket, missile, etc.) having a flight path that is less than one complete orbit of the earth or other celestial body. **2** *Anatomy.* situated beneath the orbit of the eye.

suborder (ˈsʌbˌɔːdə) *n Biology.* a taxonomic group that is a subdivision of an order. ▸ **subˈordinal** *adj*

subordinary (sʌbˈɔːdɪnərɪ, -dɪnrɪ) *n, pl* **-naries.** any of several heraldic bearings of secondary importance to the ordinary, such as the lozenge, the orle, and the fret.

subordinate *adj* (səˈbɔːdɪnɪt). **1** of lesser order or importance. **2** under the authority or control of another: *a subordinate functionary.* ◆ *n* (səˈbɔːdɪnɪt). **3** a person or thing that is subordinate. ◆ *vb* (səˈbɔːdɪˌneɪt). (*tr; usually foll. by to*) **4** to put in a lower rank or position (than). **5** to make subservient: *to subordinate mind to heart.* [C15: from Medieval Latin *subordināre,* from Latin SUB- + *ordō* rank] ▸ **subˈordinately** *adv* ▸ **subˌordiˈnation** *or* **subˈordinateness** *n* ▸ **subˈordinative** *adj*

subordinate clause *n Grammar.* a clause with an adjectival, adverbial, or nominal function, rather than one that functions as a separate sentence in its own right. Compare **coordinate clause, main clause.**

subordinated debt *n Commerce.* a debt that an unsecured creditor can only claim, in the event of a liquidation, after the claims of secured creditors have been paid.

subordinating conjunction *n* a conjunction that introduces subordinate clauses, such as *if, because, although,* and *until.* Compare **coordinating conjunction.**

subordinationism (səˌbɔːdɪˈneɪʃəˌnɪzəm) *n* either of two interpretations of the doctrine of the Trinity, often regarded as heretical, according to which the Son is subordinate to the Father or the Holy Ghost is subordinate to both. ▸ **subˌordiˈnationist** *n*

suborn (səˈbɔːn) *vb* (*tr*) **1** to bribe, incite, or instigate (a person) to commit a wrongful act. **2** *Criminal law.* to induce (a witness) to commit perjury. [C16: from Latin *subornāre,* from *sub-* secretly + *ornāre* to furnish] ▸ **subornation** (ˌsʌbɔːˈneɪʃən) *n* ▸ **subornative** (sʌˈbɔːnətɪv) *adj* ▸ **subˈorner** *n*

Subotica (*Serbo-Croat* ˈsubɔtitsa) *n* a town in NE Yugoslavia, in Serbia near the border with Hungary: agricultural and industrial centre. Pop.: 100 386 (1991). Hungarian name: **Szabadka.**

suboxide (sʌbˈɒksaɪd) *n* an oxide of an element containing less oxygen than the common oxide formed by the element: *carbon suboxide,* C_2O_3.

subphylum (sʌbˈfaɪləm) *n, pl* **-la** (-lə). *Biology.* a taxonomic group that is a subdivision of a phylum. ▸ **subˈphylar** *adj*

subplot (ˈsʌbˌplɒt) *n* a subordinate or auxiliary plot in a novel, play, film, etc.

subpoena (səbˈpiːnə) *n* **1** a writ issued by a court of justice requiring a person to appear before the court at a specified time. ◆ *vb* **-nas, -naing, -naed. 2** (*tr*) to serve with a subpoena. [C15: from Latin: under penalty]

subpopulation (ˌsʌbpɒpjuˈleɪʃən) *n Statistics.* a subgroup of a statistical population.

sub-post office *n* (in Britain) a post office run by a **sub-postmaster** or **sub-postmistress** as a self-employed agent for the Post Office.

subprincipal (sʌbˈprɪnsɪpᵊl) *n* a vice-principal in a college, etc.

subprogram (ˈsʌbˌprəʊgræm) *n Computing.* a part of a program that can be designed and tested independently.

subregion (sʌbˈriːdʒən) *n* a subdivision of a region, esp. a zoogeographical or ecological region. ▸ **subˈregional** *adj*

subreption (səbˈrepʃən) *n* **1** *Now rare.* the concealment of facts in order to obtain a benefit, esp. an ecclesiastical benefit or, in Scots Law, a grant from the Crown. Compare **obreption. 2** any deceitful misrepresentation or concealment of facts. [C17: from Latin *subreptiō* theft, from *subripere,* from *sub-* secretly + *rapere* to seize] ▸ **subreptitious** (ˌsʌbrepˈtɪʃəs) *adj*

subrogate (ˈsʌbrəˌgeɪt) *vb* (*tr*) *Law.* to put (one person or thing) in the place of another in respect of a right or claim. [C16: from Latin *subrogāre,* from *sub-* in place of + *rogāre* to ask]

subrogation (ˌsʌbrəˈgeɪʃən) *n Law.* the substitution of one person or thing for another, esp. the placing of a surety who has paid the debt in the place of the creditor, entitling him to payment from the original debtor.

sub rosa (ˈrəʊzə) *adv* in secret. [Latin, literally: under the rose; from the rose that, in ancient times, was hung over the council table, as a token of secrecy]

subroutine (ˈsʌbruːˌtiːn) *n* a section of a computer program that is stored only once but can be used when required at several different points in the program, thus saving space. Also called: **procedure.**

sub-Saharan *adj* in, of, or relating to Africa south of the Sahara desert.

subscapular (sʌbˈskæpjulə) *adj* **1** (of a muscle or artery) situated beneath the scapula. ◆ *n* **2** any subscapular muscle or artery.

subscribe (səbˈskraɪb) *vb* **1** (usually foll. by *to*) to pay or promise to pay (a sum of money) as a contribution (to a fund or charity, for a magazine, etc.), esp. at regular intervals. **2** to inscribe or sign (one's name, etc.) at the end of a contract, will, or other document. **3** (*intr; foll. by to*) to give support or approval: *to subscribe to the theory of transubstantiation.* [C15: from Latin *subscrībere* to write underneath, from SUB- + *scrībere* to write] ▸ **subˈscriber** *n*

subscriber trunk dialling *n Brit.* a service by which telephone subscribers can obtain trunk calls by dialling direct without the aid of an operator. Abbrev.: **STD.** U.S. and Canadian equivalent: **direct distance dialing.**

subscript (ˈsʌbskrɪpt) *adj* **1** *Printing.* (of a character) written or printed below the line. Compare **superscript.** ◆ *n* **2** Also called: **subindex.** a subscript character.

subscription (səbˈskrɪpʃən) *n* **1** a payment or promise of payment for consecutive issues of a magazine, newspaper, book, etc., over a specified period of time. **2a** the advance purchase of tickets for a series of concerts, operas, etc. **2b** (*as modifier*): *a subscription concert.* **3** an amount of money paid or promised, as to a charity, or the fund raised in this way. **4** an offer to buy shares or bonds issued by a company. **5** the act of signing one's name to a document, etc. **6** a signature or other appendage attached to the bottom of a document, etc. **7** agreement, consent, or acceptance expressed by or as if by signing one's name. **8** a signed document, statement, etc. **9** *Chiefly Brit.* the membership dues or fees paid to a society or club. **10** acceptance of a fixed body of articles of faith, doctrines, or principles laid down as universally binding upon all the members of a Church. **11** *Med.* that part of a written prescription directing the pharmacist how to mix and prepare the ingredients: rarely seen today as modern drugs are mostly prepackaged by the manufacturers. **12** an advance order for a new product. **13a** the sale of books, etc., prior to printing. **13b** (*as modifier*): *a subscription edition.* **14** *Archaic.* allegiance; submission. Abbrev.: **sub.** ▸ **subˈscriptive** *adj*

subscription library *n* a commercial lending library.

subscription television *n* another name for **pay television.**

subsellium (sʌbˈselɪəm) *n* a rare word for **misericord** (sense 1). [C19: from Latin, from SUB- + *sella* seat]

subsequence (ˈsʌbsɪkwəns; *for sense 3* ˌsʌbˈsiːkwəns) *n* **1** the fact or state of being subsequent. **2** a subsequent incident or occurrence. **3** *Maths.* a sequence derived from a given sequence by selecting certain of its terms and retaining their order. Thus, <a_2, a_3> is a subsequence of <a_1, a_2, a_3>, while <a_3, a_2> is not.

subsequent (ˈsʌbsɪkwənt) *adj* occurring after; succeeding. [C15: from Latin *subsequēns* following on, from *subsequī,* from *sub-* near + *sequī* to follow] ▸ **ˈsubsequently** *adv* ▸ **ˈsubsequentness** *n*

subsere (ˈsʌbˌsɪə) *n* a secondary sere arising when the progress of a sere towards its climax has been interrupted. [C20: SUB- + SERE[2]]

subserve (səbˈsɜːv) *vb* (*tr*) **1** to be helpful or useful to. **2** *Obsolete.* to be subordinate to. [C17: from Latin *subservīre* to be subject to, from SUB- + *servīre* to serve]

subservient (səbˈsɜːvɪənt) *adj* **1** obsequious in behaviour or attitude. **2** serving as a means to an end. **3** a less common word for **subordinate** (sense 2). [C17: from Latin *subserviēns* complying with, from *subservīre* to SUBSERVE] ▸ **subˈserviently** *adv* ▸ **subˈservience** *or* **subˈserviency** *n*

subset (ˈsʌbˌset) *n* **1** *Maths.* **1a** a set the members of which are all members of some given class: *A is a subset of B* is usually written A⊆B. **1b proper subset.** one that is strictly contained within a larger class and excludes some of its members. Symbol: A⊂B. **2** a set within a larger set.

subshrub (ˈsʌbˌʃrʌb) *n* a small bushy plant that is woody except for the tips of the branches. ▸ **ˈsubˌshrubby** *adj*

subside (səbˈsaɪd) *vb* (*intr*) **1** to become less loud, excited, violent, etc.; abate. **2** to sink or fall to a lower level. **3** (of the surface of the earth, etc.) to cave in; collapse. **4** (of sediment, etc.) to sink or descend to the bottom; settle. [C17: from Latin *subsīdere* to settle down, from *sub-* down + *sīdere* to settle] ▸ **subˈsider** *n*

subsidence (səbˈsaɪdᵊns, ˈsʌbsɪdᵊns) *n* **1** the act or process of subsiding or the condition of having subsided. **2** *Geology.* the gradual sinking of landforms to a lower level as a result of earth movements, mining operations, etc.

subsidiarity (səbˌsɪdɪˈærɪtɪ) *n* **1** (in the Roman Catholic Church) a principle of social doctrine that all social bodies exist for the sake of the individual so that what individuals are able to do, society should not take over, and what small societies can do, larger societies should not take over. **2** (in political systems) the principle of devolving decisions to the lowest practical level.

subsidiary (səbˈsɪdɪərɪ) *adj* **1** serving to aid or supplement; auxiliary. **2** of lesser importance; subordinate in function. ◆ *n, pl* **-aries. 3** a person who or thing that is subsidiary. **4** short for **subsidiary company.** [C16: from Latin *subsidiārius* supporting, from *subsidium* SUBSIDY] ▸ **subˈsidiarily** *adv* ▸ **subˈsidiariness** *n*

subsidiary coin *n* a coin of denomination smaller than that of the standard monetary unit.

subˈofficer *n*	**subˈparaˌgraph** *n*	**ˈsubˌsect** *n*	**ˈsubˌsection** *n*

subsidiary company *n* a company with at least half of its capital stock owned by another company.

subsidize *or* **subsidise** ('sʌbsɪˌdaɪz) *vb* (*tr*) **1** to aid or support with a subsidy. **2** to obtain the aid of by means of a subsidy. ► ˌ**subsi'dizable** *or* ˌ**subsi'disable** *adj* ► ˌ**subsidi'zation** *or* ˌ**subsidi'sation** *n* ► '**subsiˌdizer** *or* '**subsiˌdiser** *n*

subsidy ('sʌbsɪdɪ) *n, pl* **-dies. 1** a financial aid supplied by a government, as to industry, for reasons of public welfare, the balance of payments, etc. **2** *English history.* a financial grant made originally for special purposes by Parliament to the Crown. **3** any monetary aid, grant, or contribution. [C14: from Anglo-Norman *subsidie,* from Latin *subsidium* assistance, from *subsidēre* to remain, from *sub-* down + *sedēre* to sit]

subsist (səb'sɪst) *vb* (*mainly intr*) **1** (often foll. by *on*) to be sustained; manage to live: *to subsist on milk.* **2** to continue in existence. **3** (foll. by *in*) to lie or reside by virtue (of); consist. **4** *Philosophy.* **4a** to exist as a concept or relation rather than a fact. **4b** to be conceivable. **5** (*tr*) *Obsolete.* to provide with support. [C16: from Latin *subsistere* to stand firm, from *sub-* up + *sistere* to make a stand] ► **sub'sistent** *adj* ► **sub'sister** *n*

subsistence (səb'sɪstəns) *n* **1** the means by which one maintains life. **2** the act or condition of subsisting. **3** a thing that has real existence. **4** the state of being inherent. **5** *Philosophy.* an inferior mode of being ascribed to the references of general terms which do not in fact exist. See also **nonbeing.**

subsistence allowance *n Chiefly Brit.* **1** an advance paid to an employee before his pay begins. **2** a payment to an employee to reimburse expenses, as while on assignments.

subsistence farming *n* a type of farming in which most of the produce (**subsistence crop**) is consumed by the farmer and his family, leaving little or nothing to be marketed.

subsistence level *n* a standard of living barely adequate to support life.

subsistence wage *n* the lowest wage upon which a worker and his family can survive.

subsocial (sʌb'səʊʃəl) *adj* lacking a complex or definite social structure. ► **sub'socially** *adv*

subsoil ('sʌbˌsɔɪl) *n* **1a** Also called: **undersoil.** the layer of soil beneath the surface soil and overlying the bedrock. **1b** (*as modifier*): *a subsoil plough.* ◆ *vb* **2** (*tr*) to plough (land) to a depth below the normal ploughing level and so break up the subsoil. ► '**subˌsoiler** *n*

subsolar (sʌb'səʊlə) *adj* **1** (of a point on the earth) directly below the sun. **2** situated between the tropics; equatorial.

subsong ('sʌbˌsɒŋ) *n* a subdued form of birdsong modified from the full territorial song and used by some birds esp. in courtship.

subsonic (sʌb'sɒnɪk) *adj* being, having, or travelling at a velocity below that of sound: *a subsonic aircraft.*

subspecies ('sʌbˌspiːʃiːz) *n, pl* **-cies.** *Biology.* a taxonomic group that is a subdivision of a species: usually occurs because of isolation within a species. Abbrev.: **ssp.** ► **subspecific** (ˌsʌbspɪ'sɪfɪk) *adj* ► ˌ**subspe'cifically** *adv*

subst. *abbrev. for:* **1** substantive. **2** substitute.

substage ('sʌbˌsteɪdʒ) *n* the part of a microscope below the stage, usually consisting of an adjustable assembly holding a condenser lens for illuminating the specimen.

substance ('sʌbstəns) *n* **1** the tangible matter of which a thing consists. **2** a specific type of matter, esp. a homogeneous material with a definite composition. **3** the essence, meaning, etc., of a written or spoken thought. **4** solid or meaningful quality. **5** material density: *a vacuum has no substance.* **6** material possessions or wealth: *a man of substance.* **7** *Philosophy.* **7a** the supposed immaterial substratum that can receive modifications and in which attributes and accidents inhere. **7b** a thing considered as a continuing whole that survives the changeability of its properties. **8** *Christian Science.* that which is eternal. **9 in substance.** with regard to the salient points. [C13: via Old French from Latin *substantia,* from *substāre,* from SUB- + *stāre* to stand] ► '**substanceless** *adj*

substandard (sʌb'stændəd) *adj* **1** below an established or required standard. **2** another word for **nonstandard.**

substantial (səb'stænʃəl) *adj* **1** of a considerable size or value: *substantial funds.* **2** worthwhile; important: *a substantial reform.* **3** having wealth or importance. **4** (of food or a meal) sufficient and nourishing. **5** solid or strong in construction, quality, or character: *a substantial door.* **6** real; actual; true: *the evidence is substantial.* **7** of or relating to the basic or fundamental substance or aspects of a thing. **8** *Philosophy.* of or relating to substance rather than to attributes, accidents, or modifications. ► **substantiality** (səbˌstænʃɪ'ælɪtɪ) *or* **sub'stantialness** *n* ► **sub'stantially** *adv*

substantialism (səb'stænʃəˌlɪzəm) *n Philosophy.* **1** the doctrine that a substantial reality underlies phenomena. **2** the doctrine that matter is a real substance. ► **sub'stantialist** *n*

substantialize *or* **substantialise** (səb'stænʃəˌlaɪz) *vb* to make or become substantial or actual.

substantiate (səb'stænʃɪˌeɪt) *vb* (*tr*) **1** to establish as valid or genuine. **2** to give form or real existence to. [C17: from New Latin *substantiāre,* from Latin *substantia* SUBSTANCE] ► **subˌstanti'ation** *n* ► **sub'stantiative** *adj* ► **sub'stantiˌator** *n*

substantive ('sʌbstəntɪv) *n* **1** *Grammar.* a noun or pronoun used in place of a noun. ◆ *adj* **2** of, relating to, containing, or being the essential element of a thing. **3** having independent function, resources, or existence. **4** of substantial quantity. **5** solid in foundation or basis. **6** *Grammar.* denoting, relating to, or standing in place of a noun. **7** (səb'stæntɪv). relating to the essential legal principles administered by the courts, as opposed to practice and procedure. Compare **adjective** (sense 3). **8** (səb'stæntɪv). (of a dye or colour) staining the material directly without use of a mordant. ◆ Abbrevs.: **s., sb., subst.** [C15: from Late Latin *substantīvus,* from Latin *substāre* to stand beneath; see SUBSTANCE] ► **substantival** (ˌsʌbstən'taɪvᵊl) *adj* ► ˌ**substan'tivally** *adv* ► '**substantively** *adv* ► '**substantiveness** *n*

substantive agreements *pl n* collective agreements that regulate jobs, pay, and conditions.

substantive rank (səb'stæntɪv) *n* a permanent rank in the armed services obtained by length of service, selection, etc.

substantivize *or* **substantivise** ('sʌbstəntɪˌvaɪz) *vb* (*tr*) to make (a word other than a noun) play the grammatical role of a noun in a sentence. ► ˌ**substantivi'zation** *or* ˌ**substantivi'sation** *n*

substation ('sʌbˌsteɪʃən) *n* **1** a subsidiary station. **2** an installation at which electricity is received from one or more power stations for conversion from alternating to direct current, reducing the voltage, or switching before distribution by a low-tension network.

substituent (sʌb'stɪtjʊənt) *n* **1** *Chem.* an atom or group that replaces another atom or group in a molecule or can be regarded as replacing an atom in a parent compound. ◆ *adj* **2** substituted or substitutable. [C19: from Latin *substituere* to SUBSTITUTE]

substitute ('sʌbstɪˌtjuːt) *vb* **1** (often foll. by *for*) to serve or cause to serve in place of another person or thing. **2** *Chem.* to replace (an atom or group in a molecule) with (another atom or group). **3** *Logic, maths.* to replace (one expression) by (another) in the context of a third, as replacing $x + y$ for x in $3x = k$ gives $3x + 3y = k$. ◆ *n* **4a** a person or thing that serves in place of another, such as a player in a game who takes the place of an injured colleague. **4b** (*as modifier*): *a substitute goalkeeper.* Often shortened to **sub. 5** *Grammar.* another name for **pro-form. 6** *Canadian.* another name for **supply teacher. 7** *Nautical.* another word for **repeater** (sense 5). **8** (formerly) a person paid to replace another due for military service. [C16: from Latin *substituere,* from *sub-* in place of + *statuere* to set up] ► ˌ**substi'tutable** *adj* ► ˌ**substiˌtuta'bility** *n*

USAGE *Substitute* is sometimes wrongly used where *replace* is meant: *he replaced* (not *substituted*) *the worn tyre with a new one.*

substitution (ˌsʌbstɪ'tjuːʃən) *n* **1** the act of substituting or state of being substituted. **2** something or someone substituted. **3** *Maths.* the replacement of a term of an equation by another that is known to have the same value in order to simplify the equation. **4** *Maths, logic.* **4a** the uniform replacement of one expression by another. **4b substitution instance.** an expression so derived from another.

substitutive ('sʌbstɪˌtjuːtɪv) *adj* **1** acting or able to act as a substitute. **2** of or involving substitution. ► '**substiˌtutively** *adv*

substitutivity (ˌsʌbstɪtjuː'tɪvɪtɪ) *n Logic, philosophy.* the principle that expressions with the same reference can be substituted for one another without affecting the truth-value of any context in which they occur. See also **transparent context, opaque context.**

substrate ('sʌbstreɪt) *n* **1** *Biochem.* the substance upon which an enzyme acts. **2** another word for **substratum. 3** *Electronics.* the semiconductor base on which other material is deposited, esp. in the construction of integrated circuits.

substratum (sʌb'strɑːtəm, -'streɪ-) *n, pl* **-strata** (-'strɑːtə, -'streɪtə). **1** any layer or stratum lying underneath another. **2** a basis or foundation; groundwork. **3** the nonliving material on which an animal or plant grows or lives. **4** *Geology.* **4a** the solid rock underlying soils, gravels, etc.; bedrock. **4b** the layer of soil beneath the surface layer; subsoil. **5** *Sociol.* any of several subdivisions or grades within a stratum. **6** *Photog.* a binding layer by which an emulsion is made to adhere to a glass or film base. Sometimes shortened to **sub. 7** *Philosophy.* substance considered as that in which attributes and accidents inhere. **8** *Linguistics.* the language of an indigenous population when replaced by the language of a conquering or colonizing population, esp. as it influences the form of the dominant language or of any mixed languages arising from their contact. Compare **superstratum** (sense 2). [C17: from New Latin, from Latin *substrātus* strewn beneath, from *substernere* to spread under, from SUB- + *sternere* to spread] ► **sub'strative** *or* **sub'stratal** *adj*

substructure ('sʌbˌstrʌktʃə) *n* **1** a structure, pattern, etc., that forms the basis of anything. **2** a structure forming a foundation or framework for a building or other construction. ► **sub'structural** *adj*

subsume (səb'sjuːm) *vb* (*tr*) **1** to incorporate (an idea, proposition, case, etc.) under a comprehensive or inclusive classification or heading. **2** to consider (an instance of something) as part of a general rule or principle. [C16: from New Latin *subsumere,* from Latin SUB- + *sumere* to take] ► **sub'sumable** *adj*

subsumption (səb'sʌmpʃən) *n* the act of subsuming or the state of being subsumed. ► **sub'sumptive** *adj*

subtangent (sʌb'tændʒənt) *n Geometry.* a segment of the *x*-axis lying between the *x*-coordinate of the point at which a tangent is drawn to a curve and the intercept of the tangent with the axis; the projection of the tangent on the axis.

subteen (ˌsʌb'tiːn) *n U.S. and Canadian, rare.* a young person who has not yet become a teenager.

subtemperate (sʌb'tɛmpərɪt) *adj* of or relating to the colder temperate regions.

subtenant (sʌb'tɛnənt) *n* a person who rents or leases property from a tenant. ► **sub'tenancy** *n*

subtend (səb'tɛnd) *vb* (*tr*) **1** *Geometry.* to be opposite to and delimit (an angle

sub'surface *adj* '**subˌsystem** *n*

or side). **2** (of a bract, stem, etc.) to have (a bud or similar part) growing in its axil. **3** to mark off. **4** to underlie; be inherent in. [C16: from Latin *subtendere* to extend beneath, from SUB- + *tendere* to stretch out]

subterfuge (ˈsʌbtəˌfjuːdʒ) *n* a stratagem employed to conceal something, evade an argument, etc. [C16: from Late Latin *subterfugium,* from Latin *subterfugere* to escape by stealth, from *subter* secretly + *fugere* to flee]

subterminal (sʌbˈtɜːmɪnᵊl) *adj* almost at an end.

subternatural (ˌsʌbtəˈnætʃərəl, -ˈnætʃrəl) *adj Rare.* falling below what is accepted as natural; less than natural. [C19: from Latin *subter-* below + NATURAL]

subterranean (ˌsʌbtəˈreɪnɪən) *adj* **1** Also: **subterraneous, subterrestrial.** situated, living, or operating below the surface of the earth. **2** existing or operating in concealment. [C17: from Latin *subterrāneus,* from SUB- + *terra* earth] ▸ **ˌsubterˈraneanly** *or* **ˌsubterˈraneously** *adv*

subtext (ˈsʌbˌtɛkst) *n* **1** an underlying theme in a piece of writing. **2** a message which is not stated directly but can be inferred.

subtile (ˈsʌtᵊl) *adj* a rare spelling of **subtle.** ▸ **ˈsubtilely** *adv* ▸ **subtility** (sʌbˈtɪlɪtɪ) *or* **ˈsubtileness** *n* ▸ **ˈsubtilty** *n*

subtilize *or* **subtilise** (ˈsʌtɪˌlaɪz) *vb* **1** (*tr*) to bring to a purer state; refine. **2** to debate subtly. **3** (*tr*) to make (the mind, etc.) keener. ▸ **ˌsubtiliˈzation** *or* **ˌsubtiliˈsation** *n* ▸ **ˈsubtilˌizer** *or* **ˈsubtilˌiser** *n*

subtitle (ˈsʌbˌtaɪtᵊl) *n* **1** an additional subordinate title given to a literary or other work. **2** (*often pl*) Also called: **caption.** *Films.* **2a** a written translation superimposed on a film that has foreign dialogue. **2b** explanatory text on a silent film. ♦ *vb* **3** (*tr; usually passive*) to provide a subtitle for. ▸ **subtitular** (sʌbˈtɪtjʊlə, -ˈtɪtʃə-) *adj*

subtle (ˈsʌtᵊl) *adj* **1** not immediately obvious or comprehensible. **2** difficult to detect or analyse, often through being delicate or highly refined: *a subtle scent.* **3** showing or making or capable of showing or making fine distinctions of meaning. **4** marked by or requiring mental acuteness or ingenuity; discriminating. **5** delicate or faint: *a subtle shade.* **6** cunning or wily: *a subtle rogue.* **7** operating or executed in secret: *a subtle intrigue.* [C14: from Old French *soutil,* from Latin *subtīlis* finely woven] ▸ **ˈsubtleness** *n* ▸ **ˈsubtly** *adv*

subtlety (ˈsʌtᵊltɪ) *n, pl* **-ties. 1** the state or quality of being subtle; delicacy. **2** a fine distinction or the ability to make such a distinction. **3** something subtle.

subtonic (sʌbˈtɒnɪk) *n Music.* the seventh degree of a major or minor scale. Also called: **leading note.**

subtopia (sʌbˈtəʊpɪə) *n Brit.* suburban development that encroaches on rural areas yet appears to offer the attractions of country life to suburban dwellers. [C20: blend of SUBURB + UTOPIA] ▸ **subˈtopian** *adj*

subtorrid (sʌbˈtɒrɪd) *adj* a less common word for **subtropical.**

subtotal (sʌbˈtəʊtᵊl, ˈsʌbˌtəʊtᵊl) *n* **1** the total made up by a column of figures, etc., forming part of the total made up by a larger column or group. ♦ *vb* **-tals, -talling, -talled** *or U.S.* **-tals, -taling, -taled. 2** to establish or work out a subtotal for (a column, group, etc.).

subtract (səbˈtrækt) *vb* **1** to calculate the difference between (two numbers or quantities) by subtraction. **2** to remove (a part of a thing, quantity, etc.) from the whole. [C16: from Latin *subtractus* withdrawn, from *subtrahere* to draw away from beneath, from SUB- + *trahere* to draw] ▸ **subˈtracter** *n*

subtraction (səbˈtrækʃən) *n* **1** the act or process of subtracting. **2** a mathematical operation in which the difference between two numbers or quantities is calculated. Usually indicated by the symbol (−).

subtractive (səbˈtræktɪv) *adj* **1** able or tending to remove or subtract. **2** indicating or requiring subtraction; having a minus sign: *−x is a subtractive quantity.*

subtractive process *n* a photographic process in which all but the desired colours are removed by passing the illuminating light through subtractive filters. Compare **additive process.**

subtrahend (ˈsʌbtrəˌhɛnd) *n* the number to be subtracted from another number (the **minuend**). [C17: from Latin *subtrahendus,* from *subtrahere* to SUBTRACT]

subtreasury (sʌbˈtrɛʒərɪ) *n pl* **-uries.** *U.S.* a branch treasury. ▸ **subˈtreasurer** *n* ▸ **subˈtreasurership** *n*

subtropics (sʌbˈtrɒpɪks) *pl n* the region lying between the tropics and temperate lands. ▸ **subˈtropical** *adj*

subtype (ˈsʌbˌtaɪp) *n* a secondary or subordinate type or genre, esp. a specific one considered as falling under a general classification. ▸ **subtypical** (sʌbˈtɪpɪkᵊl) *adj*

subulate (ˈsuːbjʊlɪt, -ˌleɪt) *adj* (esp. of plant parts) tapering to a point; awl-shaped. [C18: from New Latin *subulatus* like an awl, from Latin *sūbula* awl]

suburb (ˈsʌbɜːb) *n* a residential district situated on the outskirts of a city or town. [C14: from Latin *suburbium,* from *sub-* close to + *urbs* a city] ▸ **ˈsuburbed** *adj*

suburban (səˈbɜːbᵊn) *adj* **1** of, relating to, situated in, or inhabiting a suburb or the suburbs. **2** characteristic of or typifying a suburb or the suburbs. **3** *Mildly derogatory.* narrow or unadventurous in outlook. ♦ *n* **4** another word for **suburbanite.**

suburbanite (səˈbɜːbəˌnaɪt) *n* a person who lives in a suburb.

suburbanize *or* **suburbanise** (sʌˈbɜːbəˌnaɪz) *vb* (*tr*) to make suburban.

suburbia (səˈbɜːbɪə) *n* **1** suburbs or the people living in them considered as an identifiable community or class in society. **2** the life, customs, etc., of suburbanites.

suburbicarian (səˌbɜːbɪˈkɛərɪən) *adj R.C. Church.* situated near the city of Rome: used esp. of the dioceses surrounding Rome. [C17: from Late Latin *suburbicārius,* from *suburbium* SUBURB]

subvene (səbˈviːn) *vb* (*intr*) *Rare.* to happen in such a way as to be of assistance, esp. in preventing something. [C18: from Latin *subvenīre,* from *venīre* to come]

subvention (səbˈvɛnʃən) *n* **1** a grant, aid, or subsidy, as from a government to an educational institution. **2** the act or process of providing aid or help of any sort. **3** *Sport.* a fee paid indirectly to a supposedly amateur athlete for appearing at a meeting. [C15: from Late Latin *subventiō* assistance, from Latin *subvenīre* to SUBVENE] ▸ **subˈventionary** *adj*

subversion (səbˈvɜːʃən) *n* **1** the act or an instance of subverting or overthrowing a legally constituted government, institution, etc. **2** the state of being subverted; destruction or ruin. **3** something that brings about an overthrow. [C14: from Late Latin *subversiō* destruction, from Latin *subvertere* to SUBVERT]

subversive (səbˈvɜːsɪv) *adj* **1** liable to subvert or overthrow a government, legally constituted institution, etc. ♦ *n* **2** a person engaged in subversive activities, etc. ▸ **subˈversively** *adv* ▸ **subˈversiveness** *n*

subvert (səbˈvɜːt) *vb* (*tr*) **1** to bring about the complete downfall or ruin of (something existing or established by a system of law, etc.). **2** to undermine the moral principles of (a person, etc.); corrupt. [C14: from Latin *subvertere* to overturn, from *sub-* from below + *vertere* to turn] ▸ **subˈverter** *n*

subviral (sʌbˈvaɪrəl) *adj* of, caused by, or denoting a part of the structure of a virus.

subway (ˈsʌbˌweɪ) *n* **1** *Brit.* an underground passage or tunnel enabling pedestrians to cross a road, railway, etc. **2** an underground passage or tunnel for traffic, electric power supplies, etc. **3** *Chiefly U.S. and Canadian.* an underground railway.

subzero (sʌbˈzɪərəʊ) *adj* (esp. of temperature) lower or less than zero.

succah (suˈkɑ, ˈsukɔ, ˈsukə) *n Judaism.* a variant spelling of **sukkah.**

succedaneum (ˌsʌksɪˈdeɪnɪəm) *n, pl* **-nea** (-nɪə). something that is used as a substitute, esp. any medical drug or agent that may be taken or prescribed in place of another. [C17: from Latin *succēdāneus* following after, from *succēdere* to SUCCEED] ▸ **ˌsucceˈdaneous** *adj*

succeed (səkˈsiːd) *vb* **1** (*intr*) to accomplish an aim, esp. in the manner desired: *he succeeded in winning.* **2** (*intr*) to happen in the manner desired: *the plan succeeded.* **3** (*intr*) to acquit oneself satisfactorily or do well, as in a specified field: *to succeed in publishing.* **4** (when *intr,* often foll. by *to*) to come next in order (after someone or something). **5** (when *intr,* often foll. by *to*) to take over an office, post, etc. (from a person): *he succeeded to the vice presidency.* **6** (*intr; usually foll. by to*) to come into possession (of property, etc.); inherit. **7** (*intr*) to have a result according to a specified manner: *the plan succeeded badly.* **8** (*intr*) to devolve upon: *the estate succeeded to his son.* [C15: from Latin *succēdere* to follow after, from *sub-* after + *cēdere* to go] ▸ **sucˈceedable** *adj* ▸ **sucˈceeder** *n* ▸ **sucˈceeding** *adj* ▸ **sucˈceedingly** *adv*

succentor (səkˈsɛntə) *n* the deputy of the precentor of a cathedral that has retained its statutes from pre-Reformation days. [C17: from Late Latin: one who accompanies singing, from *succinere* to accompany, from Latin *canere* to sing] ▸ **sucˈcentorship** *n*

succès de scandale *French.* (syksɛ də skɑ̃dal) *n, pl* ***succès de scandale.*** success of a play, book, etc., because of notoriety or its scandalous character. [literally: success of scandal]

succès d'estime *French.* (syksɛ dɛstim) *n, pl* ***succès d'estime.*** success, as of a book, play, etc., based on the appreciation of the critics rather than popular acclaim. [literally: success of esteem]

succès fou *French.* (syksɛ fu) *n, pl* ***succès fous*** (syksɛ fu). a fantastic success. [literally: mad success]

success (səkˈsɛs) *n* **1** the favourable outcome of something attempted. **2** the attainment of wealth, fame, etc. **3** an action, performance, etc., that is characterized by success. **4** a person or thing that is successful. **5** *Obsolete.* any outcome. [C16: from Latin *successus* an outcome, from *succēdere* to SUCCEED] ▸ **sucˈcessless** *adj*

successful (səkˈsɛsfʊl) *adj* **1** having succeeded in one's endeavours. **2** marked by a favourable outcome. **3** having obtained fame, wealth, etc. ▸ **sucˈcessfully** *adv* ▸ **sucˈcessfulness** *n*

succession (səkˈsɛʃən) *n* **1** the act or an instance of one person or thing following another. **2** a number of people or things following one another in order. **3** the act, process, or right by which one person succeeds to the office, etc., of another. **4** the order that determines how one person or thing follows another. **5** a line of descent to a title, etc. **6** *Ecology.* the sum of the changes in the composition of a community that occur during its development towards a stable climax community. **7 in succession.** in a manner such that one thing is followed uninterruptedly by another. [C14: from Latin *successio,* from *succēdere* to SUCCEED] ▸ **sucˈcessional** *adj* ▸ **sucˈcessionally** *adv*

succession state *n* any of a number of usually new states that are established in or expand over the territory formerly ruled by one large state: *Czechoslovakia was a succession state of the Austro-Hungarian monarchy.*

successive (səkˈsɛsɪv) *adj* **1** following another without interruption. **2** of or involving succession: *a successive process.* ▸ **sucˈcessively** *adv* ▸ **sucˈcessiveness** *n*

successor (səkˈsɛsə) *n* **1** a person or thing that follows, esp. a person who succeeds another in an office. **2** *Logic.* the element related to a given element by a serial ordering, esp. the natural number next larger to a given one. The successor of *n* is *n + 1,* usually written *Sn* or *n′*. ▸ **sucˈcessoral** *adj*

succinate (ˈsʌksɪˌneɪt) *n* any salt or ester of succinic acid. [C18: from SUCCIN(IC) + -ATE[2]]

succinct (səkˈsɪŋkt) *adj* **1** marked by brevity and clarity; concise. **2** compressed into a small area. **3** *Archaic.* **3a** encircled by or as if by a girdle. **3b** drawn up

ˈsubˌtribe *n* **ˈsubˌunit** *n*

tightly; closely fitting. [C15: from Latin *succinctus* girt about, from *succingere* to gird from below, from *sub-* from below + *cingere* to gird] ▸ **suc'cinctly** *adv* ▸ **suc'cinctness** *n*

succinic (sʌk'sɪnɪk) *adj* **1** of, relating to, or obtained from amber. **2** of, consisting of, containing, or derived from succinic acid. [C18: from French *succinique,* from Latin *succinum* amber]

succinic acid *n* a colourless odourless water-soluble dicarboxylic acid found in plant and animal tissues: used in making lacquers, dyes, perfumes, etc.; 1,4-butanedioic acid. Formula: $HOOCCH_2{:}CH_2COOH$.

succise (sək'saɪz) *adj Botany.* ending abruptly, as if cut off: *succise leaves.* [from Latin *succisus* cut below]

succory ('sʌkərɪ) *n, pl* **-cories.** another name for **chicory.** [C16: variant of *cicoree* CHICORY; related to Middle Low German *suckerie,* Dutch *suikerei*]

succotash ('sʌkə,tæʃ) *n U.S. and Canadian.* a mixture of cooked sweet corn kernels and lima beans, served as a vegetable. [C18: from Narraganset *msiquatash,* literally: broken pieces]

Succoth ('sʊkəʊt, -kəʊθ; *Hebrew* su:'kɔt) *n* a variant spelling of **Sukkoth.**

succour *or U.S.* **succor** ('sʌkə) *n* **1** help or assistance, esp. in time of difficulty. **2** a person or thing that provides help. ◆ *vb* **3** (*tr*) to give aid to. [C13: from Old French *sucurir,* from Latin *succurrere* to hurry to help, from *sub-* under + *currere* to run] ▸ **'succourable** *or U.S.* **'succorable** *adj* ▸ **'succourer** *or U.S.* **'succorer** *n* ▸ **'succourless** *or U.S.* **'succorless** *adj*

succubus ('sʌkjʊbəs) *n, pl* **-bi** (-,baɪ). **1** Also called: **succuba.** a female demon fabled to have sexual intercourse with sleeping men. Compare **incubus. 2** any evil demon. [C16: from Medieval Latin, from Late Latin *succuba* harlot, from Latin *succubāre* to lie beneath, from SUB- + *cubāre* to lie]

succulent ('sʌkjʊlənt) *adj* **1** abundant in juices; juicy. **2** (of plants) having thick fleshy leaves or stems. **3** *Informal.* stimulating interest, desire, etc. ◆ *n* **4** a plant that is able to exist in arid conditions by using water stored in its fleshy tissues. [C17: from Latin *succulentus,* from *sūcus* juice] ▸ **'succulence** *or* **'succulency** *n* ▸ **'succulently** *adv*

succumb (sə'kʌm) *vb* (*intr;* often foll. by *to*) **1** to give way in face of the overwhelming force (of) or desire (for). **2** to be fatally overwhelmed (by disease, old age, etc.); die (of). [C15: from Latin *succumbere* to be overcome, from SUB- + *-cumbere* from *cubāre* to lie down] ▸ **suc'cumber** *n*

succursal (sʌ'kɜ:sᵊl) *adj* **1** (esp. of a religious establishment) subsidiary. ◆ *n* **2** a subsidiary establishment. [C19: from French, from Medieval Latin *succursus,* from Latin *succurrere* to SUCCOUR]

succuss (sʌ'kʌs) *vb* **1** *Med.* to shake (a patient) to detect the sound of fluid in the thoracic or another bodily cavity. **2** *Rare.* to shake, esp. with sudden force. [C17: from Latin *succussus* flung aloft, from *succutere* to toss up, from *sub-* from below + *quatere* to shake] ▸ **succussion** (sʌ'kʌʃən) *n* ▸ **suc'cussive** *adj*

such (sʌtʃ) (often foll. by a corresponding subordinate clause introduced by *that* or *as*) ◆ *determiner* **1a** of the sort specified or understood: *such books shouldn't be sold here.* **1b** (*as pronoun*): *such is life; robbers, rapists, and such.* **2** so great; so much: *such a help; I've never seen such weeping.* **3a as such.** in the capacity previously specified or understood: *a judge as such hasn't so much power.* **3b** in itself or themselves: *intelligence as such can't guarantee success.* **4 such and such.** specific, but not known or named: *at such and such a time.* **5 such as. 5a** for example: *animals, such as elephants and tigers.* **5b** of a similar kind as; like: *people such as your friend John make me angry.* **5c** of the (usually small) amount, etc.: *the food, such as there was, was excellent.* **6 such that.** so that: used to express purpose or result: *power such that it was effortless.* ◆ *adv* **7** (intensifier): *such nice people; such a nice person that I gave him a present.* [Old English *swilc;* related to Old Frisian *sālik,* Old Norse *slīkr,* Gothic *swaleiks,* Old High German *sulih*]

suchlike ('sʌtʃ,laɪk) *adj* **1** (*prenominal*) of such a kind; similar: *John, Ken, and other suchlike idiots.* ◆ *n* **2** such or similar persons or things: *hyenas, jackals, and suchlike.*

Su-chou ('su:'tʃaʊ) *n* a variant transliteration of the Chinese name for **Suzhou.**

Süchow ('ʃu:'tʃaʊ) *n* a variant transliteration of the Chinese name for **Xuzhou.**

suck (sʌk) *vb* **1** to draw (a liquid or other substance) into the mouth by creating a partial vacuum in the mouth. **2** to draw in (fluid, etc.) by or as if by a similar action: *plants suck moisture from the soil.* **3** to drink milk from (a mother's breast); suckle. **4** (*tr*) to extract fluid content from (a solid food): *to suck a lemon.* **5** (*tr*) to take into the mouth and moisten, dissolve, or roll around with the tongue: *to suck one's thumb.* **6** (*tr;* often foll. by *down, in,* etc.) to draw by using irresistible force: *the whirlpool sucked him down.* **7** (*intr*) (of a pump) to draw in air because of a low supply level or leaking valves, pipes, etc. **8** (*tr*) to assimilate or acquire (knowledge, comfort, etc.). **9** (*intr*) *Slang.* to be contemptible or disgusting. ◆ *n* **10** the act or an instance of sucking. **11** something that is sucked, esp. milk from the mother's breast. **12 give suck to.** to give (a baby or young animal) milk from the breast or udder. **13** an attracting or sucking force: *the suck of the whirlpool was very strong.* **14** a sound caused by sucking. ◆ See also **suck in, suck off, sucks, suck up to.** [Old English *sūcan;* related to Old Norse *súga,* Middle Dutch *sūgen,* Latin *sūgere* to suck, exhaust; see SOAK] ▸ **'suckless** *adj*

sucker ('sʌkə) *n* **1** a person or thing that sucks. **2** *Slang.* a person who is easily deceived or swindled. **3** *Slang.* a person who cannot resist the attractions of a particular type of person or thing: *he's a sucker for blondes.* **4** a young animal that is not yet weaned, esp. a suckling pig. **5** *Zoology.* an organ that is specialized for sucking or adhering. **6** a cup-shaped device, generally made of rubber, that may be attached to articles allowing them to adhere to a surface by suction. **7** *Botany.* **7a** a strong shoot that arises in a mature plant from a root, rhizome, or the base of the main stem. **7b** a short branch of a parasitic plant that absorbs nutrients from the host. **8** a pipe or tube through which a fluid is drawn by suction. **9** any small mainly North American cyprinoid fish of the family *Catostomidae,* having toothless jaws and a large sucking mouth. **10** any of certain fishes that have sucking discs, esp. the clingfish or sea snail. **11** a piston in a suction pump or the valve in such a piston. ◆ *vb* **12** (*tr*) to strip off the suckers from (a plant). **13** (*intr*) (of a plant) to produce suckers.

suckerfish ('sʌkə,fɪʃ) *or* **suckfish** *n, pl* **-fish** *or* **-fishes.** other names for **remora.** [C18: so called because of the suction disc on its head]

sucker punch *n* **1** a sudden surprise punch, esp. from behind. **2** a sudden unexpected defeat or setback.

suck in *vb* (*adv*) **1** (*tr*) to attract by using an inexorable force, inducement, etc.: *the current sucked him in.* **2** to draw in (one's breath) sharply. **3** (*tr*) *Slang.* to deceive or defraud.

sucking ('sʌkɪŋ) *adj* **1** not yet weaned: *sucking pig.* **2** not yet fledged: *sucking dove.*

sucking louse *n* any insect of the order *Anoplura.* See **louse** (sense 1). [so named because it has a mouth adapted for sucking the body fluids of its host]

suckle ('sʌkᵊl) *vb* **1** to give (a baby or young animal) milk from the breast or (of a baby, etc.) to suck milk from the breast. **2** (*tr*) to bring up; nurture. [C15: probably back formation from SUCKLING] ▸ **'suckler** *n*

suckling ('sʌklɪŋ) *n* **1** an infant or young animal that is still taking milk from the mother. **2** a very young child. [C15: see SUCK, -LING[1]; related to Middle Dutch *sūgeling,* Middle High German *sōgelinc*]

Suckling ('sʌklɪŋ) *n* Sir **John.** 1609–42, English Cavalier poet and dramatist.

suck off *vb* (*tr, adv*) *Taboo slang.* to perform the act of fellatio or cunnilingus on.

sucks (sʌks) *interj Slang.* **1** an expression of disappointment. **2** an exclamation of defiance or derision (esp. in the phrase **yah boo sucks to you**).

suck up to *vb* (*intr, adv + prep*) *Informal.* to flatter for one's own profit; toady.

sucrase ('sju:kreɪz) *n* another name for **invertase.** [C19: from French *sucre* sugar + -ASE]

sucre (*Spanish* 'sukre) *n* the standard monetary unit of Ecuador, divided into 100 centavos. [C19: after Antonio José de SUCRE]

Sucre[1] (*Spanish* 'sukre) *n* the legal capital of Bolivia, in the south central part of the country in the E Andes: university (1624). Pop.: 144 994 (1993 est.). Former name (until 1839): **Chuquisaca.**

Sucre[2] (*Spanish* 'sukre) *n* **Antonio José de** (an'tonjo xo'se de). 1795–1830, South American liberator, born in Venezuela, who assisted Bolivar in the colonial revolt against Spain; first president of Bolivia (1826–28).

sucrose ('sju:krəʊz, -krəʊs) *n* the technical name for **sugar** (sense 1). [C19: from French *sucre* sugar + -OSE[2]]

suction ('sʌkʃən) *n* **1** the act or process of sucking. **2** the force or condition produced by a pressure difference, as the force holding a suction cap onto a surface. **3** the act or process of producing such a force or condition. [C17: from Late Latin *suctiō* a sucking, from Latin *sūgere* to suck] ▸ **'suctional** *adj*

suction pump *n* a pump for raising water or a similar fluid by suction. It usually consists of a cylinder containing a piston fitted with a flap valve.

suction stop *n Phonetics.* another word for **click** (sense 3).

suction valve *n* a nonreturn valve in a pump suction to prevent the pump draining or depriming when not in service. Also called: **foot valve.**

suctorial (sʌk'tɔ:rɪəl) *adj* **1** specialized for sucking or adhering: *the suctorial mouthparts of certain insects.* **2** relating to or possessing suckers or suction. [C19: from New Latin *suctōrius,* from Latin *sūgere* to suck]

Sudan (su:'dɑ:n, -'dæn) *n* **the. 1** a republic in NE Africa, on the Red Sea: the largest country in Africa; conquered by Mehemet Ali of Egypt (1820–22) and made an Anglo-Egyptian condominium in 1899 after joint forces defeated the Mahdist revolt; became a republic in 1956; civil war has been waged between separatists, in the mainly Christian south, and the government since independence, apart from a period of peace (1972–83). It consists mainly of a plateau, with the Nubian Desert in the north. Official language: Arabic. Official religion: Muslim; there are large Christian and animist minorities. Currency: Sudanese dinar. Capital: Khartoum. Pop.: 33 551 000 (1998 est.). Area: 2 505 805 sq. km (967 491 sq. miles). Former name (1899–1956): **Anglo-Egyptian Sudan.** French name: **Soudan. 2** a region stretching across Africa south of the Sahara and north of the tropical zone: inhabited chiefly by Negroid tribes rather than Arabs. ▸ **Sudanese** (,su:dᵊ'ni:z) *adj, n*

Sudanic (su:'dænɪk) *n* **1** a group of languages spoken in scattered areas of the Sudan, most of which are now generally assigned to the Chari-Nile branch of the Nilo-Saharan family. ◆ *adj* **2** relating to or belonging to this group of languages. **3** of or relating to the Sudan.

sudarium (sju'dɛərɪəm) *n, pl* **-daria** (-'dɛərɪə). another word for **sudatorium** or **veronica**[2]. [C17: from Latin, from *sūdāre* to sweat]

sudatorium (,sju:də'tɔ:rɪəm) *or* **sudatory** *n, pl* **-toria** (-'tɔ:rɪə) *or* **-tories.** a room, esp. in a Roman bathhouse, where sweating is induced by heat. [C18: from Latin, from *sūdāre* to sweat]

sudatory ('sju:dətərɪ, -trɪ) *adj* **1** relating to or producing sweating; sudorific. ◆ *n, pl* **-ries. 2** *Med.* a sudatory agent. **3** another word for **sudatorium.**

Sudbury ('sʌdbərɪ, -brɪ) *n* a city in central Canada, in Ontario: a major nickel-mining centre. Pop.: 92 884 (1991).

sudd (sʌd) *n* floating masses of reeds and weeds that occur on the White Nile and obstruct navigation. [C19: from Arabic, literally: obstruction]

sudden ('sʌdᵊn) *adj* **1** occurring or performed quickly and without warning. **2** marked by haste; abrupt. **3** *Rare.* rash; precipitate. ◆ *n* **4** *Archaic.* an abrupt occurrence or the occasion of such an occurrence (in the phrase **on a sudden**). **5 all of a sudden.** without warning; unexpectedly. ◆ *adv* **6** *Chiefly poetic.* without warning; suddenly. [C13: via French from Late Latin *subitāneus,* from Latin *subitus* unexpected, from *subīre* to happen unexpectedly, from *sub-* secretly + *īre* to go] ▸ **'suddenly** *adv* ▸ **'suddenness** *n*

sudden death *n* **1** (in sports, etc.) an extra game or contest to decide the winner of a tied competition. **2** an unexpected or quick death.

sudden infant death syndrome *n* a technical term for **cot death**. Abbrev.: **SIDS**.
Sudetenland (suːˈdeɪtᵊnˌlænd) *n* a mountainous region of the N Czech Republic: part of Czechoslovakia (1919–38; 1945–93); occupied by Germany (1938–45). Also called: **the Sudeten**.
Sudetes (suːˈdiːtiːz) *or* **Sudeten Mountains** *pl n* a mountain range in E central Europe, along the N border of the Czech Republic, extending into Germany and Poland: rich in minerals, esp. coal. Highest peak: Schneekoppe, 1603 m (5259 ft.).
sudor (ˈsjuːdɔː) *n* a technical name for **sweat**. [Latin] ▸ **sudoral** (ˈsjuːdərəl) *adj*
sudoriferous (ˌsjuːdəˈrɪfərəs) *adj* producing or conveying sweat. Also: **sudoriparous** (ˌsjuːdəˈrɪpərəs). [C16: via New Latin from SUDOR + Latin *ferre* to bear] ▸ **ˌsudorˈiferousness** *n*
sudorific (ˌsjuːdəˈrɪfɪk) *adj* **1** producing or causing sweating; sudatory. ◆ *n* **2** a sudorific agent. [C17: from New Latin *sūdōrificus*, from SUDOR + Latin *facere* to make]
Sudra (ˈsjuːdrə) *n* the lowest of the four main Hindu castes, the workers. [C17: from Sanskrit]
suds (sʌdz) *pl n* **1** the bubbles on the surface of water in which soap, detergents, etc., have been dissolved; lather. **2** soapy water. **3** *Slang, chiefly U.S. and Canadian.* beer or the bubbles floating on it. [C16: probably from Middle Dutch *sudse* marsh; related to Middle Low German *sudde* swamp; see SEETHE] ▸ **ˈsudsy** *adj*
sue (sjuː, suː) *vb* **sues, suing, sued. 1** to institute legal proceedings (against). **2** to make suppliant requests of (someone for something). **3** *Archaic.* to pay court (to). [C13: via Anglo-Norman from Old French *sivre*, from Latin *sequī* to follow] ▸ **ˈsuer** *n*
Sue (*French* sy) *n* **Eugène** (øʒɛn). original name *Marie-Joseph Sue*. 1804–57, French novelist, whose works, notably *Les mystères de Paris* (1842–43) and *Le juif errant* (1844–45), were among the first to reflect the impact of the industrial revolution on France.
suede (sweɪd) *n* **a** a leather finished with a fine velvet-like nap, usually on the flesh side of the skin or hide, produced by abrasive action. **b** (*as modifier*): *a suede coat.* [C19: from French *gants de Suède*, literally: gloves from Sweden]
suet (ˈsuːɪt, ˈsjuːɪt) *n* a hard waxy fat around the kidneys and loins in sheep, cattle, etc., used in cooking and making tallow. [C14: from Old French *seu*, from Latin *sēbum*] ▸ **ˈsuety** *adj*
Suetonius (swiːˈtəunɪəs) *n* full name *Gaius Suetonius Tranquillus*. 75–150 A.D., Roman biographer and historian, whose chief works were *Concerning Illustrious Men* and *The Lives of the Caesars* (from Julius Caesar to Domitian).
suet pudding *n Brit.* any of a variety of sweet or savoury puddings made with suet and steamed or boiled.
Suez (ˈsuːɪz) *n* **1** a port in NE Egypt, at the head of the Gulf of Suez at the S end of the Suez Canal: an ancient trading site and a major naval station under the Ottoman Empire; port of departure for pilgrims to Mecca; oil-refining centre. It suffered severely in the Arab–Israeli conflicts of 1967 and 1973. Pop.: 388 000 (1992 est.). **2 Isthmus of.** a strip of land in NE Egypt, between the Mediterranean and the Red Sea: links Africa and Asia and is crossed by the Suez Canal. **3 Gulf of.** the NW arm of the Red Sea: linked with the Mediterranean by the Suez Canal.
Suez Canal *n* a sea-level canal in NE Egypt, crossing the Isthmus of Suez and linking the Mediterranean with the Red Sea: built (1854–69) by de Lesseps with French and Egyptian capital; nationalized in 1956 by the Egyptians. Length: 163 km (101 miles).
suf. *abbrev. for* suffix.
suff. *abbrev. for:* **1** sufficient. **2** suffix.
Suff. *abbrev. for:* **1** Suffolk. **2** Suffragan.
suffer (ˈsʌfə) *vb* **1** to undergo or be subjected to (pain, punishment, etc.). **2** (*tr*) to undergo or experience (anything): *to suffer a change of management.* **3** (*intr*) to be set at a disadvantage: *this author suffers in translation.* **4** to be prepared to endure (pain, death, etc.): *he suffers for the cause of freedom.* **5** (*tr*) *Archaic.* to permit (someone to do something): *suffer the little children to come unto me.* **6 suffer from. 6a** to be ill with, esp. recurrently. **6b** to be given to: *he suffers from a tendency to exaggerate.* [C13: from Old French *soffrir*, from Latin *sufferre*, from SUB- + *ferre* to bear] ▸ **ˈsufferer** *n*
sufferable (ˈsʌfərəbᵊl, ˈsʌfrə-) *adj* able to be tolerated or suffered; endurable. ▸ **ˈsufferably** *adv*
sufferance (ˈsʌfərəns, ˈsʌfrəns) *n* **1** tolerance arising from failure to prohibit; tacit permission. **2** capacity to endure pain, injury, etc. **3** the state or condition of suffering. **4** *Archaic.* patient endurance. **5 on sufferance.** with reluctance. [C13: via Old French from Late Latin *sufferentia* endurance, from Latin *sufferre* to SUFFER]
suffering (ˈsʌfərɪŋ, ˈsʌfrɪŋ) *n* **1** the pain, misery, or loss experienced by a person who suffers. **2** the state or an instance of enduring pain, etc. ▸ **ˈsufferingly** *adv*
suffice (səˈfaɪs) *vb* **1** to be adequate or satisfactory for (something). **2 suffice it to say that.** (*takes a clause as object*) let us say no more than that; I shall just say that. [C14: from Old French *suffire*, from Latin *sufficere* from *sub-* below + *facere* to make] ▸ **sufˈficer** *n*
sufficiency (səˈfɪʃənsɪ) *n, pl* **-cies. 1** the quality or condition of being sufficient. **2** an adequate amount or quantity, as of income. **3** *Archaic.* efficiency.
sufficient (səˈfɪʃənt) *adj* **1** enough to meet a need or purpose; adequate. **2** *Logic.* (of a condition) assuring the truth of a statement; requiring but not necessarily required by some other state of affairs. Compare **necessary** (sense 3e). **3** *Archaic.* competent; capable. ◆ *n* **4** a sufficient quantity. [C14: from Latin *sufficiens* supplying the needs of, from *sufficere* to SUFFICE] ▸ **sufˈficiently** *adv*
sufficient reason *n Philosophy.* **1** the principle that nothing happens by pure chance, but that an explanation must always be available. **2** the view that such an explanation is a reason for God to have chosen one alternative rather than another.
suffix *n* (ˈsʌfɪks). **1** *Grammar.* an affix that follows the stem to which it is attached, as for example *-s* and *-ness* in *dogs* and *softness*. Compare **prefix** (sense 1). **2** anything that is added at the end of something else. ◆ *vb* (ˈsʌfɪks, səˈfɪks). **3** (*tr*) *Grammar.* to add (a morpheme) as a suffix to the end of a word. [C18: from New Latin *suffixum*, from Latin *suffixus* fastened below, from *suffīgere*, from SUB- + *fīgere* to fasten] ▸ **suffixal** (ˈsʌfɪksəl) *adj* ▸ **suffixion** (sʌˈfɪkʃən) *n*
sufflate (sʌˈfleɪt) *vb* an archaic word for **inflate**. [C17: from Latin *sufflāre* from SUB- + *flāre* blow] ▸ **sufˈflation** *n*
suffocate (ˈsʌfəˌkeɪt) *vb* **1** to kill or be killed by the deprivation of oxygen, as by obstruction of the air passage or inhalation of noxious gases. **2** to block the air passages or have the air passages blocked. **3** to feel or cause to feel discomfort from heat and lack of air. [C16: from Latin *suffōcāre*, from SUB- + *faucēs* throat] ▸ **ˈsuffoˌcating** *adj* ▸ **ˈsuffoˌcatingly** *adv* ▸ **ˌsuffoˈcation** *n* ▸ **ˈsuffoˌcative** *adj*
Suffolk[1] (ˈsʌfək) *n* a county of SE England, on the North Sea: its coast is flat and marshy, indented by broad tidal estuaries. Administrative centre: Ipswich. Pop.: 649 500 (1994 est.). Area: 3800 sq. km (1467 sq. miles).
Suffolk[2] (ˈsʌfək) *n* a black-faced breed of sheep.
Suffolk punch *n* a breed of draught horse with a chestnut coat and short legs. [C18: from dialect *punch* squat, short and thick]
Suffr. *abbrev. for* Suffragan.
suffragan (ˈsʌfrəgən) *adj* **1a** (of any bishop of a diocese) subordinate to and assisting his superior archbishop or metropolitan. **1b** (of any assistant bishop) having the duty of assisting the bishop of the diocese to which he is appointed but having no ordinary jurisdiction in that diocese. ◆ *n* **2** a suffragan bishop. [C14: from Medieval Latin *suffrāgāneus*, from *suffrāgium* assistance, from Latin: SUFFRAGE] ▸ **ˈsuffraganship** *n*
suffrage (ˈsʌfrɪdʒ) *n* **1** the right to vote, esp. in public elections; franchise. **2** the exercise of such a right; casting a vote. **3** a supporting vote. **4** a prayer, esp. a short intercessory prayer. [C14: from Latin *suffrāgium*]
suffragette (ˌsʌfrəˈdʒɛt) *n* a female advocate of the extension of the franchise to women, esp. a militant one, as in Britain at the beginning of the 20th century. [C20: from SUFFRAG(E) + -ETTE] ▸ **ˌsuffraˈgettism** *n*
suffragist (ˈsʌfrədʒɪst) *n* an advocate of the extension of the franchise, esp. to women. ▸ **ˈsuffragism** *n*
suffruticose (səˈfruːtɪˌkəuz) *adj* (of a plant) having a permanent woody base and herbaceous branches. [C18: from New Latin *suffruticōsus*, from Latin SUB- + *frutex* a shrub]
suffumigate (səˈfjuːmɪˌgeɪt) *vb* (*tr*) to fumigate from or as if from beneath. [C16: from Latin *suffūmigāre*, from SUB- + *fūmigāre* to FUMIGATE] ▸ **sufˌfumiˈgation** *n*
suffuse (səˈfjuːz) *vb* (*tr; usually passive*) to spread or flood through or over (something): *the evening sky was suffused with red.* [C16: from Latin *suffūsus* overspread with, from *suffundere*, from SUB- + *fundere* to pour] ▸ **suffusion** (səˈfjuːʒən) *n* ▸ **sufˈfusive** *adj*
Sufi (ˈsuːfɪ) *n, pl* **-fis.** an adherent of any of various Muslim mystical orders or teachings, which emphasize the direct personal experience of God. [C17: from Arabic *sūfīy*, literally: (man) of wool, from *sūf* wool; probably from the ascetic's woollen garments] ▸ **ˈSufic** *adj*
Sufism (ˈsuːfɪzəm) *n* the mystical doctrines of the Sufis. ▸ **Sufistic** (suːˈfɪstɪk) *adj*
Sufu (ˈʃuːˈfuː) *n* a variant spelling of **Shufu**.
súgán (ˈsuːgɑːn) *n Irish.* **1** a straw rope. **2 súgán chair.** a chair with a seat made from woven súgáns. [Irish Gaelic]
sugar (ˈʃugə) *n* **1** Also called: **sucrose, saccharose.** a white crystalline sweet carbohydrate, a disaccharide, found in many plants and extracted from sugar cane and sugar beet: it is used esp. as a sweetening agent in food and drinks. Formula: $C_{12}H_{22}O_{11}$. Related adj: **saccharine. 2** any of a class of simple water-soluble carbohydrates, such as sucrose, lactose, and fructose. **3** *Informal, chiefly U.S. and Canadian.* a term of affection, esp. for one's sweetheart. **4** *Rare.* a slang word for **money. 5** a slang name for **LSD.** ◆ *vb* **6** (*tr*) to add sugar to; make sweet. **7** (*tr*) to cover or sprinkle with sugar. **8** (*intr*) to produce sugar. **9 sugar the pill** *or* **medicine.** to make something unpleasant more agreeable by adding something pleasant: *the government stopped wage increases but sugared the pill by reducing taxes.* [C13 *suker*, from Old French *çucre*, from Medieval Latin *zuccārum*, from Italian *zucchero*, from Arabic *sukkar*, from Persian *shakar*, from Sanskrit *śarkarā*] ▸ **ˈsugarless** *adj* ▸ **ˈsugar-ˌlike** *adj*
sugarallie (ˈʃugərˈælɪ) *n Scot.* liquorice. [C19: from earlier *sugar alicreesh*]
sugar apple *n* another name for **sweetsop.**
sugar bag *n Austral. and N.Z.* a small hessian bag occasionally still used, esp. in rural areas, as a rough-and-ready measure for dry goods.
sugar beet *n* a variety of the plant *Beta vulgaris* that is cultivated for its white roots from which sugar is obtained. Compare **sugar cane.**
sugar bird *n* a South African nectar-eating bird, *Promerops cafer*, with a long curved bill and long tail: family *Meliphagidae* (honey-eaters).
sugar bush *n* an anacardiaceous evergreen shrub, *Rhus ovata*, of S California and Arizona, having pale oval leaves, spikes of yellow-tinged red flowers, and deep red fruits.
sugar candy *n* **1** Also called: **rock candy.** large crystals of sugar formed by suspending strings in a strong sugar solution that hardens on the strings, used chiefly for sweetening coffee. **2** *Chiefly U.S.* confectionery; sweets.

sugar cane *n* a coarse perennial grass, *Saccharum officinarum*, of Old World tropical regions, having tall stout canes that yield sugar: cultivated chiefly in the Caribbean and the southern U.S. Compare **sugar beet.**

sugar-coat *vb* (*tr*) **1** to coat or cover with sugar. **2** to cause to appear more attractive; make agreeable.

sugar corn *n* another name for **sweet corn** (sense 1).

sugar daddy *n Slang.* a rich usually middle-aged or old man who bestows expensive gifts on a young person in return for companionship or sexual favours.

sugar diabetes *n* an informal name for **diabetes mellitus** (see **diabetes**).

sugared ('ʃʊgəd) *adj* made sweeter or more appealing with or as with sugar.

sugar glider *n* a common Australian phalanger, *Petaurus breviceps,* that glides from tree to tree feeding on insects and nectar.

sugar gum *n Austral.* a small eucalyptus tree, *Eucalyptus cladocalyx,* having smooth bark and barrel-shaped fruits and grown for timber and ornament. It has sweet-tasting leaves which are often eaten by livestock.

sugar loaf *n* **1** a large conical mass of hard refined sugar. See also **loaf sugar. 2** something resembling this in shape.

Sugar Loaf Mountain *n* a mountain in SE Brazil, in Rio de Janeiro on Guanabara Bay. Height: 390 m (1280 ft.). Portuguese name: **Pão de Açúcar.**

sugar maple *n* a North American maple tree, *Acer saccharum,* that is grown as a source of sugar, which is extracted from the sap, and for its hard wood.

sugar of lead (lɛd) *n* another name for **lead acetate.**

sugar of milk *n* another name for **lactose.**

sugar pea *n* another name for **mangetout.**

sugar pine *n* a pine tree, *Pinus lambertiana,* of California and Oregon, having spreading pendulous branches, light brown cones, and sugary resin.

sugarplum ('ʃʊgə,plʌm) *n* a crystallized plum.

sugar soap *n* an alkaline compound used for cleaning or stripping paint.

sugary ('ʃʊgərɪ) *adj* **1** of, like, or containing sugar. **2** containing too much sugar; excessively sweet. **3** deceptively pleasant; insincere. ▸ **'sugariness** *n*

Suger (su:'ʒɛə) *n* 1081–1151, French ecclesiastic and statesman, who acted as adviser to Louis VI and regent (1147–49) to Louis VII. As abbot of Saint-Denis (1122–51) he influenced the development of Gothic architecture.

suggest (sə'dʒɛst; *U.S.* səg'dʒɛst) *vb* (*tr; may take a clause as object*) **1** to put forward (a plan, idea, etc.) for consideration: *I suggest Smith for the post; a plan suggested itself.* **2** to evoke (a person, thing, etc.) in the mind of someone by the association of ideas: *that painting suggests home to me.* **3** to give an indirect or vague hint of: *his face always suggests his peace of mind.* [C16: from Latin *suggerere* to bring up, from SUB- + *gerere* to bring] ▸ **sug'gester** *n*

suggestibility (sə,dʒɛstɪ'bɪlɪtɪ) *n Psychol.* a state, esp. under hypnosis, in which a person will accept the suggestions of another person and act accordingly.

suggestible (sə'dʒɛstɪbᵊl) *adj* **1** easily influenced by ideas provided by other persons. **2** characteristic of something that can be suggested. ▸ **sug'gestibleness** *n* ▸ **sug'gestibly** *adv*

suggestion (sə'dʒɛstʃən) *n* **1** something that is suggested. **2** a hint or indication: *a suggestion of the odour of violets.* **3** *Psychol.* the process whereby the mere presentation of an idea to a receptive individual leads to the acceptance of that idea. See also **autosuggestion.**

suggestive (sə'dʒɛstɪv) *adj* **1** (*postpositive;* foll. by *of*) conveying a hint (of something): *this painting is suggestive of a hot summer day.* **2** tending to suggest something improper or indecent. **3** able or liable to suggest an idea, plan, etc. ▸ **sug'gestively** *adv* ▸ **sug'gestiveness** *n*

Suharto (sʊ'hɑːtəʊ) *n* **T. N. J.** born 1921, Indonesian general and statesman; president (1968–98).

suicidal (,suːɪ'saɪdᵊl, ,sjuː-) *adj* **1** involving, indicating, or tending towards suicide. **2** liable to result in suicide: *a suicidal attempt.* **3** liable to destroy one's own interests or prospects; dangerously rash. ▸ **,sui'cidally** *adv*

suicide ('suːɪ,saɪd, 'sjuː-) *n* **1** the act or an instance of killing oneself intentionally. **2** the self-inflicted ruin of one's own prospects or interests: *a merger would be financial suicide.* **3** a person who kills himself intentionally. **4** (*modifier*) reckless; extremely dangerous: *a suicide mission.* **5** (*modifier*) (of an action) undertaken or (of a person) undertaking an action in the knowledge that it will result in the death of the person performing it in order that maximum damage may be inflicted on an enemy: *a suicide attack; suicide bomber.* [C17: from New Latin *suīcīdium,* from Latin *suī* of oneself + *-cīdium,* from *caedere* to kill]

sui generis (,suːaɪ 'dʒɛnərɪs) *adj* unique. [Latin, literally: of its own kind]

sui juris ('suːaɪ 'dʒʊərɪs) *adj* (*usually postpositive*) *Law.* of full age and not under disability; legally competent to manage one's own affairs; independent. [C17: from Latin, literally: of one's own right]

suint ('suːɪnt, swɪnt) *n* a water-soluble substance found in the fleece of sheep, consisting of peptides, organic acids, metal ions, and inorganic cations and formed from dried perspiration. [C18: from French *suer* to sweat, from Latin *sūdāre*]

Suisse (sɥis) *n* the French name for **Switzerland.**

suit (suːt, sjuːt) *n* **1** any set of clothes of the same or similar material designed to be worn together, now usually (for men) a jacket with matching trousers or (for women) a jacket with matching or contrasting skirt or trousers. **2** (*in combination*) any outfit worn for a specific purpose: *a spacesuit.* **3** any set of items, such as the full complement of sails of a vessel or parts of personal armour. **4** any of the four sets of 13 cards in a pack of playing cards, being spades, hearts, diamonds, and clubs. The cards in each suit are two to ten, jack, queen, and king in the usual order of ascending value, with ace counting as either the highest or lowest according to the game. **5** a civil proceeding; lawsuit. **6** the act or process of suing in a court of law. **7** a petition or appeal made to a person of superior rank or status or the act of making such a petition. **8** *Slang.* a business executive or white-collar manager. **9** a man's courting of a woman. **10 follow suit. 10a** to play a card of the same suit as the card played immediately before it. **10b** to act in the same way as someone else. **11 strong** *or* **strongest suit.** something that one excels in. ◆ *vb* **12** to make or be fit or appropriate for: *that dress suits you.* **13** to meet the requirements or standards (of). **14** to be agreeable or acceptable to (someone). **15 suit oneself.** to pursue one's own intentions without reference to others. [C13: from Old French *sieute* set of things, from *sivre* to follow; compare SUE] ▸ **'suit,like** *adj*

suitable ('suːtəbᵊl, 'sjuːt-) *adj* appropriate; proper; fit. ▸ **,suita'bility** *or* **'suitableness** *n* ▸ **'suitably** *adv*

suitcase ('suːt,keɪs, 'sjuːt-) *n* a portable rectangular travelling case, usually stiffened, for carrying clothing, etc.

suite (swiːt) *n* **1** a series of items intended to be used together; set. **2** a number of connected rooms in a hotel forming one living unit: *the presidential suite.* **3** a matching set of furniture, esp. of two armchairs and a settee. **4** a number of attendants or followers. **5** *Music.* **5a** an instrumental composition consisting of several movements in the same key based on or derived from dance rhythms, esp. in the baroque period. **5b** an instrumental composition in several movements less closely connected than a sonata. **5c** a piece of music containing movements based on or extracted from music already used in an opera, ballet, play, etc. [C17: from French, from Old French *sieute;* see SUIT]

suiting ('suːtɪŋ, 'sjuːt-) *n* a fabric used for suits.

suitor ('suːtə, 'sjuːt-) *n* **1** a man who courts a woman; wooer. **2** *Law.* a person who brings a suit in a court of law; plaintiff. **3** *Rare.* a person who makes a request or appeal for anything. [C13: from Anglo-Norman *suter,* from Latin *secūtor* follower, from *sequī* to follow]

Suiyüan ('swiː'jɑːn) *n* a former province in N China: now part of the Inner Mongolian Autonomous Region.

Sukarnapura (sʊ,kɑːnə'pʊərə) *n* a former name of **Jayapura.**

Sukarno *or* **Soekarno** (suː'kɑːnəʊ) *n* **Achmed** ('ɑːkmɛd). 1901–70, Indonesian statesman; first president of the Republic of Indonesia (1945–67).

Sukarno Peak *n* a former name of (Mount) **Jaya.**

Sukhumi (*Russian* su'xumi) *n* a port and resort in W Georgia, on the Black Sea: site of an ancient Greek colony. Pop.: 112 000 (1993).

sukiyaki (,suːkɪ'jɑːkɪ) *n* a Japanese dish consisting of very thinly sliced beef or other meat, vegetables, and seasonings cooked together quickly, usually at the table. [from Japanese]

sukkah *or* **succah** (sʊ'kɑ, 'sukɔ, 'sukə) *n* a temporary structure with a roof of branches in which orthodox Jews eat and, if possible, sleep during the festival of Sukkoth. Also called: **tabernacle.** [from Hebrew, literally: tabernacle]

Sukkoth *or* **Succoth** ('sʊkəʊt, -kəʊθ; *Hebrew* suː'kɔt) *n* an eight-day Jewish harvest festival beginning on Tishri 15, which commemorates the period when the Israelites lived in the wilderness. Also called: **Feast of Tabernacles.** [from Hebrew, literally: tabernacles]

Sulawesi (,suːlə'weɪsɪ) *n* an island in E Indonesia: mountainous and forested, with volcanoes and hot springs. Pop.: 12 520 711 (1990). Area (including adjacent islands): 229 108 sq. km (88 440 sq. miles). Also called: **Celebes.**

sulcate ('sʌlkeɪt) *adj Biology.* marked with longitudinal parallel grooves: *sulcate stems.* [C18: via Latin *sulcātus* from *sulcāre* to plough, from *sulcus* a furrow] ▸ **sul'cation** *n*

sulcus ('sʌlkəs) *n, pl* **-ci** (-saɪ). **1** a linear groove, furrow, or slight depression. **2** any of the narrow grooves on the surface of the brain that mark the cerebral convolutions. Compare **fissure.** [C17: from Latin]

Suleiman I (,suːlɪ'mɑːn, -leɪ-), **Soliman,** *or* **Solyman** *n* called *the Magnificent.* ?1495–1566, sultan of the Ottoman Empire (1520–66), whose reign was noted for its military power and cultural achievements.

sulf- *combining form.* a U.S. variant of **sulph-.**

sulfamethazine (,sʌlfə'mɛθə,ziːn) *n* U.S. name for **sulphadimidine.**

sulfur ('sʌlfə) *n* the U.S. preferred spelling of **sulphur.**

sulk (sʌlk) *vb* **1** (*intr*) to be silent and resentful because of a wrong done to one, esp. in order to gain sympathy; brood sullenly: *the child sulked in a corner after being slapped.* ◆ *n* **2** (*often pl*) a state or mood of feeling resentful or sullen: *he's in a sulk because he lost the game; he's got the sulks.* **3** Also: **sulker.** a person who sulks. [C18: perhaps a back formation from SULKY[1]]

sulky[1] ('sʌlkɪ) *adj* **sulkier, sulkiest. 1** sullen, withdrawn, or moody, through or as if through resentment. **2** dull or dismal: *sulky weather.* [C18: perhaps from obsolete *sulke* sluggish, probably related to Old English *āseolcan* to be lazy] ▸ **'sulkily** *adv* ▸ **'sulkiness** *n*

sulky[2] ('sʌlkɪ) *n, pl* **sulkies.** a light two-wheeled vehicle for one person, usually drawn by one horse. [C18: from SULKY[1], because it can carry only one person]

Sulla ('sʌlə) *n* full name *Lucius Cornelius Sulla Felix.* 138–78 B.C., Roman general and dictator (82–79). He introduced reforms to strengthen the power of the Senate.

sullage ('sʌlɪdʒ) *n* **1** filth or waste, esp. sewage. **2** sediment deposited by running water. [C16: perhaps from French *souiller* to sully; compare Old English *sol* mud]

sullen ('sʌlən) *adj* **1** unwilling to talk or be sociable; sulky; morose. **2** sombre; gloomy: *a sullen day.* **3** *Literary.* sluggish; slow: *a sullen stream.* **4** *Obsolete.* threatening. ◆ *n* **5** (*pl*) *Archaic.* a sullen mood. [C16: perhaps from Anglo-French *solain* (unattested), ultimately related to Latin *sōlus* alone] ▸ **'sullenly** *adv* ▸ **'sullenness** *n*

Sullivan ('sʌlɪvᵊn) *n* **1** Sir **Arthur** (**Seymour**). 1842–1900, English composer who wrote operettas, such as *H.M.S. Pinafore* (1878) and *The Mikado* (1885), with W. S. Gilbert as librettist. **2 Louis** (**Henri**). 1856–1924, U.S. pioneer of modern architecture: he coined the slogan "form follows function".

Sullom Voe ('sʌləm vəʊ) *n* a deep coastal inlet in the Shetland Islands, on the N coast of Mainland. It is used for the storage and transshipment of oil.

sully ('sʌlɪ) *vb* **-lies, -lying, -lied. 1** to stain or tarnish (a reputation, etc.) or (of a reputation) to become stained or tarnished. ◆ *n, pl* **-lies. 2** a stain. **3** the act of sullying. [C16: probably from French *souiller* to soil] ▸ **'sulliable** *adj*

Sully ('sʌlɪ; *French* sylli) *n* **Maximilien de Béthune** (maksimiljɛ̃ də betyn), Duc de Sully. 1559–1641, French statesman; minister of Henry IV. He helped restore the finances of France after the Wars of Religion.

Sully-Prudhomme (*French* sylli prydɔm) *n* **René François Armand** (rəne frɑ̃swa armɑ̃). 1839–1907, French poet: Nobel prize for literature 1901.

sulph- *or U.S.* **sulf-** *combining form.* containing sulphur: *sulphate; sulphonic acid.*

sulphadiazine (ˌsʌlfəˈdaɪəˌziːn) *n* an important sulpha drug used chiefly in combination with an antibiotic. Formula: $C_{10}H_{10}N_4O_2S$.

sulphadimidine (ˌsʌlfəˈdaɪmɪˌdiːn) *n* a sulpha drug used in human and veterinary medicine. There is concern that residues of the drug in pork products may cause cancer, but this has not yet been proved. U.S. name: **sulfamethazine.**

sulpha drug (ˈsʌlfə) *n* any of a group of sulphonamide compounds that inhibit the activity of bacteria and are used in medicine to treat bacterial infections.

sulphanilamide (ˌsʌlfəˈnɪləˌmaɪd) *n* a white odourless crystalline compound formerly used in medicine in the treatment of bacterial infections. Formula: $NH_2C_6H_4SO_2NH_2$. See also **sulpha drug.**

sulphate (ˈsʌlfeɪt) *n* **1** any salt or ester of sulphuric acid, such as sodium sulphate, Na_2SO_4, sodium hydrogen sulphate, or diethyl sulphate, $(C_2H_5)_2SO_4$. **2** *Slang.* amphetamine sulphate. Often shortened to **sulph.** ◆ *vb* **3** (*tr*) to treat with a sulphate or convert into a sulphate. **4** to undergo or cause to undergo the formation of a layer of lead sulphate on the plates of an accumulator. **[C18:** from New Latin *sulfātum;* see SULPHUR**]** ▸ **sulˈphation** *n*

sulphate-resisting cement *n* a type of cement that resists normal concentrations of sulphates: used in concrete for flues and underwater work.

sulphathiazole (ˌsʌlfəˈθaɪəˌzəʊl) *n* a sulpha drug used in veterinary medicine and formerly in clinical medicine. Formula: $C_9H_9N_3O_2S_2$.

sulphide (ˈsʌlfaɪd) *n* **1** a compound of sulphur with a more electropositive element. **2** another name for **thio-ether.**

sulphinyl (ˈsʌlfənɪl) *n* (*modifier*) another term (no longer in technical usage) for **thionyl. [C20:** from SULF- + -IN + -YL**]**

sulphisoxazole (ˌsʌlfɪˈsɒksəˌzəʊl) *n* a sulpha drug used in the treatment of meningitis and certain diseases of the eye, such as trachoma. Formula: $C_{11}H_{13}N_3O_3S$.

sulphite (ˈsʌlfaɪt) *n* any salt or ester of sulphurous acid, containing the ions SO_3^{2-} or HSO_3^- (**hydrogen sulphite**) or the groups SO_3 or HSO_3. The salts are usually soluble crystalline compounds. ▸ **sulphitic** (sʌlˈfɪtɪk) *adj*

sulphonamide (sʌlˈfɒnəˌmaɪd) *n* any of a class of organic compounds that are amides of sulphonic acids containing the group $-SO_2NH_2$ or a group derived from this. An important class of sulphonamides are the sulpha drugs.

sulphonate (ˈsʌlfəˌneɪt) *Chem.* ◆ *n* **1** a salt or ester of any sulphonic acid containing the ion RSO_2O^- or the group RSO_2O-, R being an organic group. ◆ *vb* **2** (*tr*) to introduce a sulphonic acid group, SO_2OH, into (a molecule).

sulphone (ˈsʌlfəʊn) *n* any of a class of organic compounds containing the divalent group SO_2 linked to two other organic groups. Certain sulphones are used in the treatment of leprosy and tuberculosis.

sulphonic acid (sʌlˈfɒnɪk) *n* any of a large group of strong organic acids that contain the group $-SO_2OH$ and are used in the manufacture of dyes and drugs.

sulphonium compound *or* **salt** (sʌlˈfəʊnɪəm) *n* any one of a class of salts derived by the addition of a proton to the sulphur atom of a thiol or thio-ether thus producing a positive ion (**sulphonium ion**).

sulphonmethane (ˌsʌlfɒnˈmiːθeɪn) *n* a colourless crystalline compound used medicinally as a hypnotic. Formula: $C_7H_{16}O_4S_2$.

sulphonyl (ˈsʌlfənɪl) *n* (*modifier*) another term for **sulphuryl.**

sulphur *or U.S.* **sulfur** (ˈsʌlfə) *n* **a** an allotropic nonmetallic element, occurring free in volcanic regions and in combined state in gypsum, pyrite, and galena. The stable yellow rhombic form converts on heating to monoclinic needles. It is used in the production of sulphuric acid, in the vulcanization of rubber, and in fungicides. Symbol: S; atomic no.: 16; atomic wt.: 32.066; valency: 2, 4, or 6; relative density: 2.07 (rhombic), 1.957 (monoclinic); melting pt.: 115.22°C (rhombic), 119.0°C (monoclinic); boiling pt.: 444.674°C. Related adj: **thionic. b** (*as modifier*): *sulphur springs.* **[C14** *soufre,* from Old French, from Latin *sulfur***]** ▸ **sulphuric** *or U.S.* **sulfuric** (sʌlˈfjʊərɪk) *adj*

sulphurate (ˈsʌlfjʊˌreɪt) *vb* (*tr*) to combine or treat with sulphur or a sulphur compound. ▸ ˌ**sulphuˈration** *n*

sulphur-bottom *n* another name for **blue whale.**

sulphur dioxide *n* a colourless soluble pungent gas produced by burning sulphur. It is both an oxidizing and a reducing agent and is used in the manufacture of sulphuric acid, the preservation of a wide range of foodstuffs (**E220**), bleaching, and disinfecting. Formula: SO_2. Systematic name: **sulphur(IV) oxide.**

sulphureous (sʌlˈfjʊərɪəs) *adj* **1** another word for **sulphurous** (sense 1). **2** of the yellow colour of sulphur. ▸ **sulˈphureously** *adv* ▸ **sulˈphureousness** *n*

sulphuret (ˈsʌlfjʊˌret) *vb* **-rets, -retting, -retted** *or U.S.* **-rets, -reting, -reted.** (*tr*) to treat or combine with sulphur.

sulphuretted hydrogen *n* another name for **hydrogen sulphide.**

sulphuric acid *n* a colourless dense oily corrosive liquid produced by the reaction of sulphur trioxide with water and used in accumulators and in the manufacture of fertilizers, dyes, and explosives. Formula: H_2SO_4. Systematic name: **sulphuric(VI) acid.**

sulphurize *or* **sulphurise** (ˈsʌlfjʊˌraɪz) *vb* (*tr*) to combine or treat with sulphur or a sulphur compound. ▸ ˌ**sulphuriˈzation** *or* ˌ**sulfuriˈsation** *n*

sulphurous (ˈsʌlfərəs) *adj* **1** Also: **sulphureous.** of, relating to, or resembling sulphur: *a sulphurous colour.* **2** of or containing sulphur with an oxidation state of 4: *sulphurous acid.* **3** of or relating to hellfire. **4** hot-tempered. ▸ **ˈsulphurously** *adv* ▸ **ˈsulphurousness** *n*

sulphurous acid *n* an unstable acid produced when sulphur dioxide dissolves in water: used as a preservative for food and a bleaching agent. Formula: H_2SO_3. Systematic name: **sulphuric(IV) acid.**

sulphur trioxide *n* a white corrosive substance existing in three crystalline forms of which the stable (*alpha-*) form is usually obtained as silky needles. It is produced by the oxidation of sulphur dioxide, and is used in the sulphonation of organic compounds. Formula: SO_3. Systematic name: **sulphur(VI) oxide.**

sulphur tuft *n* a poisonous basidiomycetous fungus, *Hypholoma fasciculare,* having a sulphurous yellow cap and found in clumps on and around broad-leaved trees.

sulphuryl (ˈsʌlfjʊrɪl, -fərɪl) *n* (*modifier*) of, consisting of, or containing the divalent group, $=SO_2$: *sulphuryl chloride.* Also: **sulphonyl** (ˈsʌlfəˌnɪl).

sultan (ˈsʌltən) *n* **1** the sovereign of a Muslim country, esp. of the former Ottoman Empire. **2** an arbitrary ruler; despot. **3** a small domestic fowl with a white crest and heavily feathered legs and feet: originated in Turkey. **[C16:** from Medieval Latin *sultānus,* from Arabic *sultān* rule, from Aramaic *salita* to rule**]** ▸ **sultanic** (sʌlˈtænɪk) *adj* ▸ **ˈsultan-ˌlike** *adj* ▸ **ˈsultanship** *n*

sultana (sʌlˈtɑːnə) *n* **1a** the dried fruit of a small white seedless grape, originally produced in SW Asia: used in cakes, curries, etc.; seedless raisin. **1b** the grape itself. **2** Also called: **sultaness.** a wife, concubine, or female relative of a sultan. **3** a mistress; concubine. **[C16:** from Italian, feminine of *sultano* SULTAN**]**

sultanate (ˈsʌltəˌneɪt) *n* **1** the territory or a country ruled by a sultan. **2** the office, rank, or jurisdiction of a sultan.

sultry (ˈsʌltrɪ) *adj* **-trier, -triest. 1** (of weather or climate) oppressively hot and humid. **2** characterized by or emitting oppressive heat. **3** displaying or suggesting passion; sensual: *sultry eyes.* **[C16:** from obsolete *sulter* to SWELTER + -Y[1]**]** ▸ **ˈsultrily** *adv* ▸ **ˈsultriness** *n*

Sulu Archipelago (ˈsuːluː) *n* a chain of over 500 islands in the SW Philippines, separating the Sulu Sea from the Celebes Sea: formerly a sultanate, ceded to the Philippines in 1940. Capital: Jolo. Pop.: 555 239 (1980). Area: 2686 sq. km (1037 sq. miles).

Sulu Sea *n* part of the W Pacific between Borneo and the central Philippines.

sum[1] (sʌm) *n* **1a** the result of the addition of numbers, quantities, objects, etc. **1b** the cardinality of the union of disjoint sets whose cardinalities are the given numbers. **2** one or more columns or rows of numbers to be added, subtracted, multiplied, or divided. **3** *Maths.* the limit of a series of sums of the first *n* terms of a converging infinite series as *n* tends to infinity. **4** (*pl*) another name for **number work. 5** a quantity, esp. of money: *he borrows enormous sums.* **6** the essence or gist of a matter (esp. in the phrases **in sum, in sum and substance**). **7** a less common word for **summary. 8** *Archaic.* the summit or maximum. **9** (*modifier*) complete or final (esp. in the phrase **sum total**). ◆ *vb* **sums, summing, summed. 10** (often foll. by *up*) to add or form a total of (something). **11** (*tr*) to calculate the sum of (the terms in a sequence). ◆ See also **sum up. [C13** *summe,* from Old French, from Latin *summa* the top, sum, from *summus* highest, from *superus* in a higher position; see SUPER**]**

sum[2] (sum) *n, pl* **sumy** (sumɪ). the standard monetary unit of Uzbekistan.

sumach *or U.S.* **sumac** (ˈsuːmæk, ˈʃuː-) *n* **1** any temperate or subtropical shrub or small tree of the anacardiaceous genus *Rhus,* having compound leaves, clusters of green flowers, and red hairy fruits. See also **poison sumach. 2** a preparation of powdered leaves of certain species of *Rhus,* esp. *R. coriaria,* used in dyeing and tanning. **3** the wood of any of these plants. **[C14:** via Old French from Arabic *summāq***]**

Sumatra (sʊˈmɑːtrə) *n* a mountainous island in W Indonesia, in the Greater Sunda Islands, separated from the Malay Peninsula by the Strait of Malacca: Dutch control began in the 16th century; joined Indonesia in 1945. Pop.: 22 706 200 (1995 est.). Area: 473 606 sq. km (182 821 sq. miles). ▸ **Suˈmatran** *adj, n*

Sumba *or* **Soemba** (ˈsuːmbə) *n* an island in Indonesia, in the Lesser Sunda Islands, separated from Flores by the **Sumba Strait:** formerly important for sandalwood exports. Pop.: 355 073 (1990). Area: 11 153 sq. km (4306 sq. miles). Former name: **Sandalwood Island.**

Sumbawa *or* **Soembawa** (suːmˈbɑːwə) *n* a mountainous island in Indonesia, in the Lesser Sunda Islands, between Lombok and Flores Islands. Pop.: 373 000 (1990 est.). Area: 14 750 sq. km (5695 sq. miles).

Sumer (ˈsuːmə) *n* the S region of Babylonia; seat of a civilization of city-states that reached its height in the 3rd millennium B.C.

Sumerian (suːˈmɪərɪən, -ˈmeər-) *n* **1** a member of a people who established a civilization in Sumer during the 4th millennium B.C. **2** the extinct language of this people, of no known relationship to any other language. ◆ *adj* **3** of or relating to ancient Sumer, its inhabitants, or their language or civilization.

summa (ˈsʊmɑː) *n, pl* **-mae** (-miː). **1** *Medieval Christianity theol.* a compendium of theology, philosophy, or canon law, or sometimes of all three together. The **Summa Theologica** of St Thomas Aquinas, written between 1265 and 1274, was the most famous of all such compendia. **2** *Rare.* a comprehensive work or survey. **[C15:** from Latin: SUM[1]**]**

summa cum laude (ˈsʊmɑː kʊm ˈlaʊdeɪ) *adv, adj Chiefly U.S.* with the utmost praise: the highest of three designations for above-average achievement in examinations. In Britain it is sometimes used to designate a first-class honours degree. Compare **cum laude, magna cum laude. [**from Latin**]**

summand (ˈsʌmænd, sʌˈmænd) *n* a number or quantity forming part of a sum. **[C19:** from Medieval Latin *summandus,* from Latin *summa* SUM[1]**]**

summarize *or* **summarise** (ˈsʌməˌraɪz) *vb* (*tr*) to make or be a summary of; express concisely. ▸ **ˈsummaˌrizable** *or* **ˈsummaˌrisable** *adj* ▸ ˌ**summariˈzation** *or* ˌ**summariˈsation** *n* ▸ **ˈsummaˌrizer, ˈsummaˌriser,** *or* **ˈsummarist** *n*

summary (ˈsʌmərɪ) *n, pl* **-maries. 1** a brief account giving the main points of something. ◆ *adj* (*usually prenominal*). **2** performed arbitrarily and quickly, without formality: *a summary execution.* **3** (of legal proceedings) short and free from the complexities and delays of a full trial. **4 summary jurisdiction.**

the right a court has to adjudicate immediately upon some matter arising during its proceedings. **5** giving the gist or essence. **[C15:** from Latin *summārium,* from *summa* SUM[1]**]** ▸ **'summarily** *adv* ▸ **'summariness** *n*

summary offence *n* an offence that is triable in a magistrates' court.

summation (sʌ'meɪʃən) *n* **1** the act or process of determining a sum; addition. **2** the result of such an act or process. **3** a summary. **4** *U.S. law.* the concluding statements made by opposing counsel in a case before a court. **[C18:** from Medieval Latin *summātiō,* from *summāre* to total, from Latin *summa* SUM[1]**]** ▸ **sum'mational** *adj* ▸ **'summative** *adj*

summative assessment ('sʌmətɪv) *n Brit. educ.* general assessment of a pupil's achievements over a range of subjects by means of a combined appraisal of formative assessments.

summer[1] ('sʌmə) *n* **1** (*sometimes cap.*) **1a** the warmest season of the year, between spring and autumn, astronomically from the June solstice to the September equinox in the N hemisphere and at the opposite time of year in the S hemisphere. **1b** (*as modifier*): *summer flowers; a summer dress.* Related adj: **aestival. 2** the period of hot weather associated with the summer. **3** a time of blossoming, greatest happiness, etc. **4** *Chiefly poetic.* a year represented by this season: *a child of nine summers.* ◆ *vb* **5** (*intr*) to spend the summer (at a place). **6** (*tr*) to keep or feed (farm animals) during the summer: *they summered their cattle on the mountain slopes.* **[**Old English *sumor;* related to Old Frisian *sumur,* Old Norse *sumar,* Old High German *sumar,* Sanskrit *samā* season**]** ▸ **'summerless** *adj* ▸ **'summer-,like** *adj* ▸ **'summerly** *adj, adv* ▸ **'summery** *adj* ▸ **'summeriness** *n*

summer[2] ('sʌmə) *n* **1** Also called: **summer tree.** a large horizontal beam or girder, esp. one that supports floor joists. **2** another name for **lintel. 3** a stone on the top of a column, pier, or wall that supports an arch or lintel. **[C14:** from Anglo-Norman *somer,* from Old French *somier* beam, packhorse, from Late Latin *sagmārius* (*equus*) pack(horse), from *sagma* a packsaddle, from Greek**]**

summer cypress *n* another name for **kochia.**

summerhouse ('sʌmə,haus) *n* a small building in a garden or park, used for shade or recreation in the summer.

summer pudding *n Brit.* a pudding made by filling a bread-lined basin with a purée of fruit, leaving it to soak, and then turning it out.

summersault ('sʌmə,sɔːlt) *n, vb* a variant spelling of **somersault.**

summer school *n* a school, academic course, etc., held during the summer.

summer solstice *n* **1** the time at which the sun is at its northernmost point in the sky (southernmost point in the S hemisphere), appearing at noon at its highest altitude above the horizon. It occurs about June 21 (December 22 in the S hemisphere). **2** *Astronomy.* the point on the celestial sphere, opposite the **winter solstice,** at which the ecliptic is furthest north from the celestial equator. Right ascension: 6 hours; declination: 23.5°.

summertime ('sʌmə,taɪm) *n* the period or season of summer.

summer time *n Brit.* any daylight-saving time, esp. British Summer Time.

summerweight ('sʌmə,weɪt) *adj* (of clothes) suitable in weight for wear in the summer; relatively light.

summerwood ('sʌmə,wud) *n* the wood that is produced by a plant near the end of the growing season: consists of small thick-walled xylem cells. Compare **springwood.**

summing-up *n* **1** a review or summary of the main points of an argument, speech, etc. **2** a direction regarding the law and a summary of the evidence, given by a judge in his address to the jury before they retire to consider their verdict.

summit ('sʌmɪt) *n* **1** the highest point or part, esp. of a mountain or line of communication; top. **2** the highest possible degree or state; peak or climax: *the summit of ambition.* **3** the highest level, importance, or rank: *a meeting at the summit.* **4a** a meeting of chiefs of governments or other high officials. **4b** (*as modifier*): *a summit conference.* **[C15:** from Old French *somet,* diminutive of *som,* from Latin *summum;* see SUM[1]**]** ▸ **'summital** *adj* ▸ **'summitless** *adj*

summitry ('sʌmɪtrɪ) *n Chiefly U.S.* the practice of conducting international negotiations by summit conferences.

summon ('sʌmən) *vb* (*tr*) **1** to order to come; send for, esp. to attend court, by issuing a summons. **2** to order or instruct (to do something) or call (to something): *the bell summoned them to their work.* **3** to call upon to meet or convene. **4** (often foll. by *up*) to muster or gather (one's strength, courage, etc.). **[C13:** from Latin *summonēre* to give a discreet reminder, from *monēre* to advise**]** ▸ **'summonable** *adj*

summons ('sʌmənz) *n, pl* **-monses. 1** a call, signal, or order to do something, esp. to appear in person or attend at a specified place or time. **2a** an official order requiring a person to attend court, either to answer a charge or to give evidence. **2b** the writ making such an order. Compare **warrant. 3** a call or command given to the members of an assembly to convene a meeting. ◆ *vb* **4** to take out a summons against (a person). **[C13:** from Old French *somonse,* from *somondre* to SUMMON**]**

summum bonum *Latin.* ('sʊmʊm 'bɒnʊm) *n* the principle of goodness in which all moral values are included or from which they are derived; highest or supreme good.

sumo ('suːməʊ) *n* the national style of wrestling of Japan, the object of which is to force one's opponent to touch the ground with any part of his body except the soles of his feet or to step out of the ring. **[**from Japanese *sumō***]**

sump (sʌmp) *n* **1** a receptacle, such as the lower part of the crankcase of an internal-combustion engine, into which liquids, esp. lubricants, can drain to form a reservoir. **2** another name for **cesspool. 3** *Mining.* **3a** a depression at the bottom of a shaft where water collects before it is pumped away. **3b** the front portion of a shaft or tunnel, ahead of the main bore. **4** *Brit. dialect.* a muddy pool or swamp. **[C17:** from Middle Dutch *somp* marsh; see SWAMP**]**

sumph (sʌmf) *n Scot.* a stupid person; simpleton. **[C18:** of uncertain origin**]**

sumpter ('sʌmptə) *n Archaic.* a packhorse, mule, or other beast of burden. **[C14:** from Old French *sometier* driver of a baggage horse, from Vulgar Latin *sagmatārius* (unattested), from Late Latin *sagma* packsaddle**]**

sumptuary ('sʌmptjʊərɪ) *adj* relating to or controlling expenditure or extravagance. **[C17:** from Latin *sumptuārius* concerning expense, from *sumptus* expense, from *sūmere* to spend**]**

sumptuary law *n* (formerly) a law imposing restraint on luxury, esp. by limiting personal expenditure or by regulating personal conduct in religious and moral spheres.

sumptuous ('sʌmptjʊəs) *adj* **1** expensive or extravagant: *sumptuous costumes.* **2** magnificent; splendid: *a sumptuous scene.* **[C16:** from Old French *somptueux,* from Latin *sumptuōsus* costly, from *sumptus;* see SUMPTUARY**]** ▸ **'sumptuously** *adv* ▸ **'sumptuousness** *or* **sumptuosity** (,sʌmptjʊ'ɒsɪtɪ) *n*

Sumter ('sʌmtə) *n* See **Fort Sumter.**

sum up *vb* (*adv*) **1** to summarize (feelings, the main points of an argument, etc.): *the judge began to sum up.* **2** (*tr*) to form a quick opinion of: *I summed him up in five minutes.*

Sumy (*Russian* 'sumi) *n* a city in the Ukraine, on the River Pysol: site of early Slav settlements. Pop.: 304 000 (1996 est.).

sun (sʌn) *n* **1** the star that is the source of heat and light for the planets in the solar system. It is a gaseous body having a highly compressed core, in which energy is generated by thermonuclear reactions (at about 15 million °C), surrounded by a less dense convective zone serving to transport the energy to the surface (the **photosphere**). The atmospheric layers (the **chromosphere** and **corona**) are normally invisible except during a total eclipse. Mass and diameter: 333 000 and 109 times that of earth respectively; mean distance from earth: 149.6 million km (1 astronomical unit). Related adj: **solar. 2** any star around which a planetary system revolves. **3** the sun as it appears at a particular time or place: *the winter sun.* **4** the radiant energy, esp. heat and light, received from the sun; sunshine. **5** a person or thing considered as a source of radiant warmth, glory, etc. **6** a pictorial representation of the sun, often depicted with a human face. **7** *Poetic.* a year or a day. **8** *Poetic.* a climate. **9** *Archaic.* sunrise or sunset (esp. in the phrase **from sun to sun**). **10 catch the sun.** to become slightly sunburnt. **11 place in the sun.** a prominent or favourable position. **12 take** *or* **shoot the sun.** *Nautical.* to measure the altitude of the sun in order to determine latitude. **13 touch of the sun.** slight sunstroke. **14 under** *or* **beneath the sun.** on earth; at all: *nobody under the sun eats more than you do.* ◆ *vb* **suns, sunning, sunned. 15** to expose (oneself) to the sunshine. **16** (*tr*) to expose to the sunshine in order to warm, tan, etc. **[**Old English *sunne;* related to Old High German *sunna,* Old Frisian *senne,* Gothic *sunno***]** ▸ **'sun,like** *adj*

Sun. *abbrev. for* Sunday.

sunbake ('sʌn,beɪk) *Austral. informal.* ◆ *vb* (*intr*) **1** to sunbathe, esp. in order to become tanned. ◆ *n* **2** a period of sunbaking.

sunbaked ('sʌn,beɪkt) *adj* **1** (esp. of roads, etc.) dried or cracked by the sun's heat. **2** baked hard by the heat of the sun: *sunbaked bricks.*

sun bath *n* the exposure of the body to the rays of the sun or a sun lamp, esp. in order to get a suntan.

sunbathe ('sʌn,beɪð) *vb* (*intr*) to bask in the sunshine, esp. in order to get a suntan. ▸ **'sun,bather** *n*

sunbeam ('sʌn,biːm) *n* **1** a beam, ray, or stream of sunlight. **2** *Austral. slang.* a piece of crockery or cutlery laid for a meal but remaining unused. ▸ **'sun,beamed** *or* **'sun,beamy** *adj*

sun bear *n* a small bear, *Helarctos malayanus,* of tropical forests in S and SE Asia, having a black coat and a yellowish snout and feeding mostly on honey and insects. Also called: **honey bear.**

Sunbelt ('sʌn,bɛlt) *n* the southern states of the U.S.A.

sunbird ('sʌn,bɜːd) *n* any small songbird of the family *Nectariniidae,* of tropical regions of the Old World, esp. Africa, having a long slender curved bill and a bright plumage in the males.

sun bittern *n* a cranelike bird, *Eurypyga helias,* of tropical American forests, having a greyish plumage with orange and brown wings: family *Eurypygidae,* order *Gruiformes* (cranes, rails, etc.).

sun blind *n Chiefly Brit.* a blind, such as a Venetian blind, that shades a room from the sun's glare.

sun block *n* a chemical, usually in the form of a cream, applied to exposed skin to block out all or almost all of the ultraviolet rays of the sun.

sunbonnet ('sʌn,bɒnɪt) *n* a hat that shades the face and neck from the sun, esp. one made of cotton with a projecting brim now worn esp. by babies. ▸ **'sun,bonneted** *adj*

sunbow ('sʌn,bəʊ) *n* a bow of prismatic colours similar to a rainbow, produced when sunlight shines through spray.

sunburn ('sʌn,bɜːn) *n* **1** inflammation of the skin caused by overexposure to the sun. Technical name: **erythema solare. 2** another word for **suntan.** ▸ **'sun,burnt** *or* **'sun,burned** *adj*

sunburst ('sʌn,bɜːst) *n* **1** a burst of sunshine, as through a break in the clouds. **2** a pattern or design resembling that of the sun. **3** a jewelled brooch with this pattern.

sunburst pleats *pl n* the U.S. term for **sunray pleats.**

Sunbury-on-Thames ('sʌnbərɪ, -brɪ) *n* a town in SE England, in N Surrey. Pop.: 27 392 (1991).

sun-cured *adj* cured or preserved by exposure to the sun.

sundae ('sʌndɪ, -deɪ) *n* ice cream topped with a sweet sauce, nuts, whipped cream, etc. **[C20:** of uncertain origin**]**

Sunda Islands ('sʌndə) *or* **Soenda Islands** *pl n* a chain of islands in the Malay Archipelago, consisting of the **Greater Sunda Islands** (chiefly Sumatra, Java, Borneo, and Sulawesi) and **Nusa Tenggara** (formerly the Lesser Sunda Islands).

sun dance *n* a North American Indian ceremony associated with the sun, performed at the summer solstice.

Sunda Strait *or* **Soenda Strait** *n* a strait between Sumatra and Java, linking the Java Sea with the Indian Ocean. Narrowest point: about 26 km (16 miles).

Sunday ('sʌndɪ) *n* the first day of the week and the Christian day of worship. [Old English *sunnandæg,* translation of Latin *diēs sōlis* day of the sun, translation of Greek *hēmera hēliou;* related to Old Norse *sunnu dagr,* German *Sonntag*]

Sunday best *n* one's best clothes, esp. regarded as those most suitable for churchgoing.

Sunday painter *n* a person who paints pictures as a hobby.

Sunday punch *n Informal, chiefly U.S.* **1** *Boxing.* a heavy blow intended to knock out one's opponent. **2** any manoeuvre or action intended to crush an opponent.

Sunday school *n* **1a** a school for the religious instruction of children on Sundays, usually held in a church hall and formerly also providing secular education. **1b** (*as modifier*): *a Sunday-school outing.* **2** the members of such a school.

sun deck *n* **1** an upper open deck on a passenger ship. **2** *Austral. and N.Z.* a balcony or deck attached to a house, used for sunbathing.

sunder ('sʌndə) *Archaic or literary.* ◆ *vb* **1** to break or cause to break apart or in pieces. ◆ *n* **2 in sunder.** into pieces; apart. [Old English *sundrian;* related to Old Norse *sundr* asunder, Gothic *sundrō* apart, Old High German *suntar,* Latin *sine* without] ▸ **'sunderable** *adj* ▸ **'sunderance** *n* ▸ **'sunderer** *n*

Sunderland ('sʌndələnd) *n* **1** a port in NE England, in Sunderland unitary authority, Tyne and Wear at the mouth of the River Wear: shipbuilding and marine engineering. Pop.: 183 310 (1991). **2** a unitary authority in NE England, in Tyne and Wear. Pop.: 295 800 (1995 est.). Area: 138 sq. km (53 sq. miles).

sundew ('sʌn,djuː) *n* any of several bog plants of the genus *Drosera,* having leaves covered with sticky hairs that trap and digest insects: family *Droseraceae.* [C16: translation of Latin *ros solis*]

sundial ('sʌn,daɪəl) *n* a device indicating the time during the hours of sunlight by means of a stationary arm (the **gnomon**) that casts a shadow onto a plate or surface marked in hours at right angles to the gnomon.

sun disc *n* a disc symbolizing the sun, esp. one flanked by two serpents and the extended wings of a vulture, used as a religious figure in ancient Egypt.

sundog ('sʌn,dɒg) *n* **1** another word for **parhelion. 2** a small rainbow or halo near the horizon.

sundown ('sʌn,daʊn) *n* another name for **sunset.**

sundowner ('sʌn,daʊnə) *n* **1** *Austral. and N.Z. obsolete slang.* a tramp, esp. one who seeks food and lodging at sundown when it is too late to work. **2** *Nautical.* a strict ship's officer. **3** *Informal, chiefly Brit.* an alcoholic drink taken at sunset. **4** *N.Z. slang.* a lazy sheepdog.

sundress ('sʌn,drɛs) *n* a dress for hot weather that exposes the shoulders, arms, and back, esp. one with straps over the shoulders.

sun-dried *adj* dried or preserved by exposure to the sun.

sundry ('sʌndrɪ) *determiner* **1** several or various; miscellaneous. ◆ *pron* **2 all and sundry.** all the various people, individually and collectively. ◆ *n, pl* **-dries. 3** (*pl*) miscellaneous unspecified items. **4** the Austral. name for **extra** (sense 6). [Old English *syndrig* separate; related to Old High German *suntarīg;* see SUNDER, -Y[1]]

sundry shop *n* (in Malaysia) a shop, similar to a delicatessen, that sells predominantly Chinese foodstuffs.

Sundsvall (*Swedish* 'sʊndsval) *n* a port in E Sweden, on the Gulf of Bothnia: icebound in winter; cellulose industries. Pop.: 94 815 (1994).

sunfast ('sʌn,fɑːst) *adj Chiefly U.S. and Canadian.* not fading in sunlight.

sunfish ('sʌn,fɪʃ) *n, pl* **-fish** *or* **-fishes. 1** any large plectognath fish of the family *Molidae,* of temperate and tropical seas, esp. *Mola mola,* which has a large rounded compressed body, long pointed dorsal and anal fins, and a fringelike tail fin. **2** any of various small predatory North American freshwater percoid fishes of the family *Centrarchidae,* typically having a compressed brightly coloured body.

sunflower ('sʌn,flaʊə) *n* **1** any of several American plants of the genus *Helianthus,* esp. *H. annuus,* having very tall thick stems, large flower heads with yellow rays, and seeds used as food, esp. for poultry: family *Compositae* (composites). See also **Jerusalem artichoke. 2 sunflower seed oil.** the oil extracted from sunflower seeds, used as a salad oil, in the manufacture of margarine, etc.

sung (sʌŋ) *vb* **1** the past participle of **sing.** ◆ *adj* **2** produced by singing: *a sung syllable.*

USAGE See at **ring**[2].

Sung *or* **Song** (sʊŋ) *n* an imperial dynasty of China (960–1279 A.D.), notable for its art, literature, and philosophy.

Sungari ('sʊŋgərɪ) *n* another name for the **Songhua.**

Sungkiang ('sʊŋ'kjæŋ, -kaɪ'æŋ) *n* a former province of NE China: now part of the Inner Mongolian AR.

sunglass ('sʌn,glɑːs) *n* a convex lens used to focus the sun's rays and thus produce heat or ignition; burning glass.

sunglasses ('sʌn,glɑːsɪz) *pl n* glasses with darkened or polarizing lenses that protect the eyes from the sun's glare.

sunglow ('sʌn,gləʊ) *n* a pinkish glow often seen in the sky before sunrise or after sunset. It is caused by scattering or diffraction of sunlight by particles in the atmosphere.

sun-god *n* **1** the sun considered as a personal deity. **2** a deity associated with the sun or controlling its movements.

sungrebe ('sʌn,griːb) *n* another name for **finfoot.**

sunhat ('sʌn,hæt) *n* a hat that shades the face and neck from the sun.

sunk (sʌŋk) *vb* **1** a past participle of **sink.** ◆ *adj* **2** *Informal.* with all hopes dashed; ruined: *if the police come while we're opening the safe, we'll be sunk.*

sunken ('sʌŋkən) *vb* **1** a past participle of **sink.** ◆ *adj* **2** unhealthily hollow: *sunken cheeks.* **3** situated at a lower level than the surrounding or usual one. **4** situated under water; submerged. **5** depressed; low: *sunken spirits.*

sunk fence *n* a ditch, one side of which is made into a retaining wall so as to enclose an area of land while remaining hidden in the total landscape. Also called: **ha-ha.**

Sun King *n* **the.** an epithet of **Louis XIV.**

sun lamp *n* **1** a lamp that generates ultraviolet rays, used for obtaining an artificial suntan, for muscular therapy, etc. **2** a lamp used in film studios, etc., to give an intense beam of light by means of parabolic mirrors.

sunless ('sʌnlɪs) *adj* **1** without sun or sunshine. **2** gloomy; depressing. ▸ **'sunlessly** *adv* ▸ **'sunlessness** *n*

sunlight ('sʌnlaɪt) *n* **1** the light emanating from the sun. **2** an area or the time characterized by sunshine. ▸ **'sunlit** *adj*

sun lounge *or U.S.* **sun parlor** *n* a room with large windows positioned to receive as much sunlight as possible.

sunn (sʌn) *n* **1** a leguminous plant, *Crotalaria juncea,* of the East Indies, having yellow flowers. **2** the hemplike fibre obtained from the inner bark of this plant, used in making rope, sacking, etc. [C18: from Hindi *san,* from Sanskrit *śāṇá* hempen]

Sunna ('sʌnə) *n* the body of traditional Islamic law accepted by most orthodox Muslims as based on the words and acts of Mohammed. [C18: from Arabic *sunnah* rule]

Sunni ('sʌnɪ) *n* **1** one of the two main branches of orthodox Islam (the other being the Shiah), consisting of those who acknowledge the authority of the Sunna. **2** (*pl* **-ni**) a less common word for **Sunnite.**

Sunnite ('sʌnaɪt) *n Islam.* an adherent of the Sunni.

sunny ('sʌnɪ) *adj* **-nier, -niest. 1** full of or exposed to sunlight. **2** radiating good humour. **3** of or resembling the sun. ▸ **'sunnily** *adv* ▸ **'sunniness** *n*

sunny side *n* **1** the cheerful aspect or point of view: *look on the sunny side of things.* **2 on the sunny side of.** *Informal.* younger than (a specified age).

sunny-side up *adj* (of eggs) fried on one side only.

sunray pleats ('sʌn,reɪ) *pl n Brit.* bias-cut knife pleats that are narrower at the top than at the bottom, producing a flared effect, used esp. for skirts. U.S. term: **sunburst pleats.**

sunrise ('sʌn,raɪz) *n* **1** the daily appearance of the sun above the horizon. **2** the atmospheric phenomena accompanying this appearance. **3** Also called (esp. U.S.): **sunup.** the time at which the sun rises at a particular locality. **4** (*modifier*) of or relating to sunrise industry: *sunrise technology; sunrise sector.*

sunrise industry *n* any of the high-technology industries, such as electronics, that hold promise of future development.

sunroof ('sʌn,ruːf) *or* **sunshine roof** *n* a panel, often translucent, that may be opened in the roof of a car.

sunset ('sʌn,sɛt) *n* **1** the daily disappearance of the sun below the horizon. **2** the atmospheric phenomena accompanying this disappearance. **3** Also called: **sundown.** the time at which the sun sets at a particular locality. **4** the final stage or closing period, as of a person's life.

sunshade ('sʌn,ʃeɪd) *n* a device, esp. a parasol or awning, serving to shade from the sun.

sunshine ('sʌn,ʃaɪn) *n* **1** the light received directly from the sun. **2** the warmth from the sun. **3** a sunny area. **4** a light-hearted or ironic term of address. ▸ **'sun,shiny** *adj*

sunspot ('sʌn,spɒt) *n* any of the dark cool patches, with a diameter of up to several thousand kilometres, that appear on the surface of the sun and last about a week. They occur in approximately 11-year cycles and possess a strong magnetic field. ▸ **'sun,spotted** *adj*

sunstar ('sʌn,stɑː) *n* any starfish of the genus *Solaster,* having up to 13 arms radiating from a central disc.

sunstone ('sʌn,stəʊn) *n* another name for **aventurine** (sense 2). [C17: so called because it contains red and gold flecks which reflect the light]

sunstroke ('sʌn,strəʊk) *n* heatstroke caused by prolonged exposure to intensely hot sunlight.

sunsuit ('sʌn,suːt, -,sjuːt) *n* a child's outfit consisting of a brief top and shorts or a short skirt.

suntan ('sʌn,tæn) *n* **a** a brownish colouring of the skin caused by the formation of the pigment melanin within the skin on exposure to the ultraviolet rays of the sun or a sunlamp. Often shortened to **tan. b** (*as modifier*): *suntan oil.* ▸ **'sun,tanned** *adj*

suntrap ('sʌn,træp) *n* a very sunny sheltered place.

sunup ('sʌn,ʌp) *n* another name (esp. U.S.) for **sunrise** (sense 3).

sunward ('sʌnwəd) *adj* **1** directed or moving towards the sun. ◆ *adv* **2** a variant of **sunwards.**

sunwards ('sʌnwədz) *or* **sunward** *adv* towards the sun.

sunwise ('sʌn,waɪz) *adv* moving in the same direction as the sun; clockwise.

Sun Yat-sen ('sʊn 'jɑːt'sɛn) *n* 1866–1925, Chinese statesman, who was instrumental in the overthrow of the Manchu dynasty and was the first president of the Republic of China (1911). He reorganized the Kuomintang.

suo jure ('suːəʊ 'dʒʊərɪ) *adv Chiefly law.* in one's own right. [Latin]

suo loco ('suːəʊ 'lɒkəʊ) *adv Chiefly law.* in a person or thing's own or rightful place. [Latin]

Suomi ('suɔmi) *n* the Finnish name for **Finland.**

sup[1] (sʌp) *vb* **sups, supping, supped. 1** (*intr*) *Archaic.* to have supper. **2** (*tr*) *Obsolete.* to provide with supper. [C13: from Old French *soper;* see SUP[2]]

sup[2] (sʌp) *vb* **sups, supping, supped. 1** to partake of (liquid) by swallowing a little at a time. **2** *Scot. and northern English dialect.* to drink. ◆ *n* **3** a sip. [Old

English *sūpan;* related to Old High German *sūfan,* German *saufen;* see also SUP[1]]

sup. *abbrev. for:* **1** above. [from Latin *supra*] **2** superior. **3** *Grammar.* superlative. **4** supine (noun). **5** supplement. **6** supplementary. **7** supply.

super ('suːpə) *adj* **1** *Informal.* outstanding; exceptionally fine. ◆ *n* **2** petrol with a high octane rating. **3** *Informal.* a superintendent or supervisor. **4** *Austral. and N.Z. informal.* superannuation benefits. **5** *Austral. and N.Z. informal.* superphosphate. ◆ *interj* **6** *Brit. informal.* an enthusiastic expression of approval or assent. [from Latin: above]

super. *abbrev. for:* **1** superfine. **2** superior. **3** supernumerary.

super- *prefix* **1** placed above or over: *superscript.* **2** of greater size, extent, quality, etc.: *supermarket.* **3** surpassing others; outstanding: *superstar.* **4** beyond a standard or norm; exceeding or exceedingly: *supersonic.* **5** indicating that a chemical compound contains a specified element in a higher proportion than usual: *superoxide.* [from Latin *super* above]

superable ('suːpərəbᵊl, -prəbᵊl) *adj* able to be surmounted or overcome. [C17: from Latin *superābilis,* from *superāre* to overcome] ▸ **ˌsuperaˈbility** *or* **ˈsuperableness** *n* ▸ **ˈsuperably** *adv*

superabound (ˌsuːpərəˈbaʊnd) *vb* **1** (*intr*) to abound abnormally; be in surplus. **2** *Rare.* to be more abundant than (something else). ▸ **superabundance** (ˌsuːpərəˈbʌndəns) *n* ▸ **ˌsuperaˈbundant** *adj*

superadd (ˌsuːpərˈæd) *vb* (*tr*) to add (something) to something that has already been added; add as extra. ▸ **ˌsuperadˈdition** *n* ▸ **ˌsuperadˈditional** *adj*

superaerodynamics (ˌsuːpəˌɛərəʊdaɪˈnæmɪks) *n* (*functioning as sing*) the study of aerodynamics at very high altitudes, where the air density is very low.

superaltar ('suːpərˌɔːltə) *n Christianity.* a consecrated portable stone slab for use on an unconsecrated altar.

superannuate (ˌsuːpərˈænjʊˌeɪt) *vb* (*tr*) **1** to pension off. **2** to discard as obsolete or old-fashioned.

superannuated (ˌsuːpərˈænjʊˌeɪtɪd) *adj* **1** discharged, esp. with a pension, owing to age or illness. **2** too old to serve usefully. **3** obsolete. [C17: from Medieval Latin *superannātus* aged more than one year, from Latin SUPER- + *annus* a year]

superannuation (ˌsuːpərˌænjʊˈeɪʃən) *n* **1a** the amount deducted regularly from employees' incomes in a contributory pension scheme. **1b** the pension finally paid to such employees. **2** the act or process of superannuating or the condition of being superannuated.

superb (sʊˈpɜːb, sjʊ-) *adj* **1** surpassingly good; excellent: *a superb actor.* **2** majestic or imposing: *a superb mansion.* **3** magnificently rich; luxurious: *the jubilee was celebrated with a superb banquet.* [C16: from Old French *superbe,* from Latin *superbus* distinguished, from *super* above] ▸ **suˈperbly** *adv* ▸ **suˈperbness** *n*

superbazaar *or* **superbazar** ('suːpəbəˈzɑː) *n* (in India) a large department store or supermarket, esp. one set up as a cooperative store by the government.

Super Bowl *n American football.* the main championship game of the sport, held annually in January between the champions of the American Football Conference and the National Football Conference.

superbug ('suːpəˌbʌg) *n Informal.* an infective microorganism that has become resistant to antibiotics.

supercalender (ˌsuːpəˈkæləndə) *n* **1** a calender with a number of rollers that gives a high gloss to paper. ◆ *vb* **2** (*tr*) to produce a glossy finish on (paper) by pressing in a supercalender. ▸ **ˌsuperˈcalendered** *adj*

supercargo (ˌsuːpəˈkɑːgəʊ) *n, pl* **-goes.** an officer on a merchant ship who supervises commercial matters and is in charge of the cargo. [C17: changed from Spanish *sobrecargo,* from *sobre* over (from Latin SUPER) + *cargo* CARGO]

supercharge ('suːpəˌtʃɑːdʒ) *vb* (*tr*) **1** to increase the intake pressure of (an internal-combustion engine) with a supercharger; boost. **2** to charge (the atmosphere, a remark, etc.) with an excess amount of (tension, emotion, etc.). **3** to apply pressure to (a fluid); pressurize.

supercharger ('suːpəˌtʃɑːdʒə) *n* a device, usually a fan or compressor, that increases the mass of air drawn into an internal-combustion engine by raising the intake pressure. Also called: **blower, booster.**

superciliary (ˌsuːpəˈsɪlɪərɪ) *adj* relating to or situated over the eyebrow or a corresponding region in lower animals. [C18: from New Latin *superciliaris,* from Latin *supercilium,* from SUPER- + *cilium* eyelid]

supercilious (ˌsuːpəˈsɪlɪəs) *adj* displaying arrogant pride, scorn, or indifference. [C16: from Latin *superciliōsus,* from *supercilium* eyebrow; see SUPERCILIARY] ▸ **ˌsuperˈciliously** *adv* ▸ **ˌsuperˈciliousness** *n*

superclass ('suːpəˌklɑːs) *n* a taxonomic group that is a subdivision of a subphylum.

supercolumnar (ˌsuːpəkəˈlʌmnə) *adj Architect.* **1** having one colonnade above another. **2** placed above a colonnade or a column. ▸ **ˌsupercolˌumniˈation** *n*

supercomputer (ˌsuːpəkəmˈpjuːtə) *n* a powerful computer that can process large quantities of data of a similar type very quickly.

superconductivity (ˌsuːpəˌkɒndʌkˈtɪvɪtɪ) *n Physics.* the property of certain substances that have no electrical resistance. In metals it occurs at very low temperatures, but higher temperature superconductivity occurs in some ceramic materials. ▸ **superconduction** (ˌsuːpəkənˈdʌkʃən) *n* ▸ **ˌsuperconˈductive** *or* **ˌsuperconˈducting** *adj* ▸ **ˌsuperconˈductor** *n*

supercontinent ('suːpəˌkɒntɪnənt) *n* a great landmass thought to have existed in the geological past and to have split into smaller landmasses, which drifted and formed the present continents.

supercool (ˌsuːpəˈkuːl) *vb Chem.* to cool or be cooled without freezing or crystallization to a temperature below that at which freezing or crystallization should occur. Supercooled liquids are not in equilibrium.

supercritical (ˌsuːpəˈkrɪtɪkᵊl) *adj* **1** *Physics.* (of a fluid) brought to a temperature and pressure higher than its critical temperature and pressure, so that its physical and chemical properties change. **2** *Nuclear physics.* of or containing more than the critical mass.

superdense theory (ˌsuːpəˈdɛns) *n Astronomy.* another name for the **big-bang theory.**

superdominant (ˌsuːpəˈdɒmɪnənt) *n U.S. and Canadian.* another word for **submediant.**

super-duper ('suːpəˈduːpə) *adj Informal.* extremely pleasing, impressive, etc.: often used as an exclamation.

superego (ˌsuːpərˈiːgəʊ, -ˈɛgəʊ) *n, pl* **-gos.** *Psychoanal.* that part of the unconscious mind that acts as a conscience for the ego, developing mainly from the relationship between a child and his parents. See also **id, ego.**

superelastic (ˌsuːpərɪˈlæstɪk) *adj Physics.* (of collisions) involving an overall increase in translational kinetic energy.

superelevation (ˌsuːpərˌɛlɪˈveɪʃən) *n* **1** another name for **bank**[2] (sense 7). **2** the difference between the heights of the sides of a road or railway track on a bend.

supereminent (ˌsuːpərˈɛmɪnənt) *adj* of distinction, dignity, or rank superior to that of others; pre-eminent. ▸ **ˌsuperˈeminence** *n*

supererogate (ˌsuːpərˈɛrəˌgeɪt) *vb* (*intr*) *Obsolete.* to do or perform more than is required. [C16: from Late Latin *superērogāre* to spend over and above, from Latin SUPER- + *ērogāre* to pay out] ▸ **ˌsuperˈeroˌgator** *n*

supererogation (ˌsuːpərˌɛrəˈgeɪʃən) *n* **1** the performance of work in excess of that required. **2** *R.C. Church.* supererogatory prayers, devotions, etc.

supererogatory (ˌsuːpərɛˈrɒgətərɪ, -trɪ) *adj* **1** performed to an extent exceeding that required or expected. **2** exceeding what is needed; superfluous. **3** *R.C. Church.* of, characterizing, or relating to prayers, good works, etc., performed over and above those prescribed as obligatory. [C16: from Medieval Latin *superērogātōrius;* see SUPEREROGATE] ▸ **ˌsupereˈrogatorily** *adv*

superette (ˌsuːpəˈrɛt) *n N.Z. informal.* a small store or dairy laid out along the lines of a supermarket.

superfamily ('suːpəˌfæmɪlɪ) *n, pl* **-lies.** **1** *Biology.* a taxonomic group that is a subdivision of a suborder. **2** any analogous group, such as a group of related languages.

superfecundation (ˌsuːpəˌfiːkənˈdeɪʃən) *n Physiol.* the fertilization of two or more ova, produced during the same menstrual cycle, by sperm ejaculated during two or more acts of sexual intercourse.

superfemale ('suːpəˌfiːmeɪl) *n* a former name for **metafemale.**

superfetation (ˌsuːpəfiːˈteɪʃən) *n Physiol.* the presence in the uterus of two fetuses developing from ova fertilized at different times. [C17 *superfetate,* from Latin *superfētāre* to fertilize when already pregnant, from SUPER- + *fētāre* to impregnate, from *fētus* offspring] ▸ **superfetate** (ˌsuːpəˈfiːteɪt) *adj*

superficial (ˌsuːpəˈfɪʃəl) *adj* **1** of, relating to, being near, or forming the surface: *superficial bruising.* **2** displaying a lack of thoroughness or care: *a superficial inspection.* **3** only outwardly apparent rather than genuine or actual: *the similarity was merely superficial.* **4** of little substance or significance; trivial: *superficial differences.* **5** lacking originality or profundity: *the film's plot was quite superficial.* **6** (of measurements) involving only the surface area. [C14: from Late Latin *superficiālis* of the surface, from Latin SUPERFICIES] ▸ **superficiality** (ˌsuːpəˌfɪʃɪˈælɪtɪ) *or* (*less commonly*) **ˌsuperˈficialness** *n* ▸ **ˌsuperˈficially** *adv*

superficies (ˌsuːpəˈfɪʃiːz) *n, pl* **-cies.** *Rare.* **1** a surface or outer face. **2** the outward form of a thing. [C16: from Latin: upper side, from SUPER- + *faciēs* face]

superfine (ˌsuːpəˈfaɪn) *adj* **1** of exceptional fineness or quality. **2** excessively refined. ▸ **ˌsuperˈfineness** *n*

superfix ('suːpəˌfɪks) *n Linguistics.* a suprasegmental feature distinguishing the meaning or grammatical function of one word or phrase from that of another, as stress does for example between the noun *conduct* and the verb *conduct.* [from SUPER- + *-fix,* on the model of PREFIX, SUFFIX]

superfluid (ˌsuːpəˈfluːɪd) *n* **1** *Physics.* a fluid in a state characterized by a very low viscosity, high thermal conductivity, high capillarity, etc. The only known example is that of liquid helium at temperatures close to absolute zero. ◆ *adj* **2** being or relating to a superfluid.

superfluidity (ˌsuːpəfluːˈɪdɪtɪ) *n Physics.* the state of being or property of becoming a superfluid.

superfluity (ˌsuːpəˈfluːɪtɪ) *n* **1** the condition of being superfluous. **2** a quantity or thing that is in excess of what is needed. **3** a thing that is not needed. [C14: from Old French *superfluité,* via Late Latin from Latin *superfluus* SUPERFLUOUS]

superfluous (suːˈpɜːfluəs) *adj* **1** exceeding what is sufficient or required. **2** not necessary or relevant; uncalled-for. **3** *Obsolete.* extravagant in expenditure or oversupplied with possessions. [C15: from Latin *superfluus* overflowing, from SUPER- + *fluere* to flow] ▸ **suˈperfluously** *adv* ▸ **suˈperfluousness** *n*

superfuse (ˌsuːpəˈfjuːz) *vb Obsolete.* to pour or be poured so as to cover something. [C17: from Latin *superfūsus* poured over, from *superfundere,* from SUPER- + *fundere* to pour] ▸ **ˌsuperˈfusion** *n*

Super-G *n Skiing.* a type of slalom in which the course is shorter than in a standard slalom and the obstacles are farther apart than in a giant slalom. [C20: from SUPER- + G(IANT)]

supergiant ('suːpəˌdʒaɪənt) *n* any of a class of extremely bright stars, such as Betelgeuse, which have expanded to a large diameter and are eventually likely to explode as supernovas. Compare **giant star, white dwarf.**

superglacial (ˌsuːpəˈgleɪsɪəl) *adj* on or originating from the surface of a glacier.

superglue ('suːpəˌgluː) *n* any of various impact adhesives that quickly make an exceptionally strong bond.

supergrass ('suːpəˌgrɑːs) *n* an informer whose information implicates a large number of people in terrorist activities or other major crimes.

supergravity (ˌsuːpəˈgrævɪtɪ) *n Physics.* any of various theories in which supersymmetry is applied to the theory of gravitation.

supergroup ('suːpəˌgruːp) *n* a rock band whose members are individually famous from previous groups.
superheat (ˌsuːpə'hiːt) *vb* (*tr*) **1** to heat (a vapour, esp. steam) to a temperature above its saturation point for a given pressure. **2** to heat (a liquid) to a temperature above its boiling point without boiling occurring. **3** to heat excessively; overheat. ▸ ˌ**super'heater** *n*
superheavy (ˌsuːpə'hɛvɪ) *n Physics.* denoting or relating to elements of high atomic number (above 109) postulated to exist with special stability as a consequence of the shell model of the nucleus.
superhero ('suːpəˌhɪərəʊ) *n, pl* **-roes.** any of various comic-strip characters with superhuman abilities or magical powers, wearing a distinctive costume, and fighting against evil.
superhet ('suːpəˌhɛt) *n* See **superheterodyne receiver.**
superheterodyne receiver (ˌsuːpə'hɛtərəˌdaɪn) *n* a radio receiver that combines two radio-frequency signals by heterodyne action, to produce a signal above the audible frequency limit. This signal is amplified and demodulated to give the desired audio-frequency signal. Sometimes shortened to **superhet.** [C20: from SUPER(SONIC) + HETERODYNE]
superhigh frequency ('suːpəˌhaɪ) *n* a radio-frequency band or radio frequency lying between 30 000 and 3000 megahertz. Abbrev.: **SHF.**
superhighway ('suːpəˌhaɪweɪ) *n Chiefly U.S.* a fast dual-carriageway road.
superhuman (ˌsuːpə'hjuːmən) *adj* **1** having powers above and beyond those of mankind. **2** exceeding normal human ability or experience. ▸ ˌ**superhu'manity** *or* ˌ**super'humanness** *n* ▸ ˌ**super'humanly** *adv*
superhumeral (ˌsuːpə'hjuːmərəl) *n* an ecclesiastical vestment worn over the shoulders. [C17: from Late Latin *superhumerāle;* see SUPER-, HUMERAL]
superimpose (ˌsuːpərɪm'pəʊz) *vb* (*tr*) **1** to set or place on or over something else. **2** (usually foll. by *on* or *upon*) to add (to). ▸ ˌ**superˌimpo'sition** *n*
superincumbent (ˌsuːpərɪn'kʌmbənt) *adj* **1** lying or being on top of something else. **2** situated or suspended above; overhanging. ▸ ˌ**superin'cumbence** *or* ˌ**superin'cumbency** *n* ▸ ˌ**superin'cumbently** *adv*
superinduce (ˌsuːpərɪn'djuːs) *vb* (*tr*) to introduce as an additional feature, factor, etc. ▸ ˌ**superin'ducement** *n* ▸ **superinduction** (ˌsuːpərɪn'dʌkʃən) *n*
superintend (ˌsuːpərɪn'tɛnd, ˌsuːprɪn-) *vb* to undertake the direction or supervision (of); manage. [C17: from Church Latin *superintendere,* from Latin SUPER- + *intendere* to give attention to] ▸ ˌ**superin'tendence** *n*
superintendency (ˌsuːpərɪn'tɛndənsɪ, ˌsuːprɪn-) *n, pl* **-cies. 1** the office or jurisdiction of a superintendent. **2** a district under the jurisdiction of a superintendent.
superintendent (ˌsuːpərɪn'tɛndənt, ˌsuːprɪn-) *n* **1** a person who directs and manages an organization, office, etc. **2** (in Britain) a senior police officer higher in rank than an inspector but lower than a chief superintendent. **3** (in the U.S.) the head of a police department. **4** *Chiefly U.S. and Canadian.* a caretaker, esp. of a block of apartments. ◆ *adj* **5** of or relating to supervision; superintending. [C16: from Church Latin *superintendens* overseeing]
superior (suː'pɪərɪə) *adj* **1** greater in quality, quantity, etc. **2** of high or extraordinary worth, merit, etc. **3** higher in rank or status: *a superior tribunal.* **4** displaying a conscious sense of being above or better than others; supercilious. **5** (*often postpositive;* foll. by *to*) not susceptible (to) or influenced (by). **6** placed higher up; situated further from the base. **7** *Astronomy.* **7a** (of a planet) having an orbit further from the sun than the orbit of the earth. **7b** (of a conjunction) occurring when the sun lies between the earth and an inferior planet. **8** (of a plant ovary) situated above the calyx and other floral parts. **9** *Anatomy.* (of one part in relation to another) situated above or higher. **10** *Printing.* (of a character) written or printed above the line; superscript. ◆ *n* **11** a person or thing of greater rank or quality. **12** *Printing.* a character set in a superior position. **13** (*often cap.*) the head of a community in a religious order. [C14: from Latin, from *superus* placed above, from *super* above] ▸ **su'perioress** *fem n* ▸ **superiority** (suːˌpɪərɪ'ɒrɪtɪ) *n* ▸ **su'periorly** *adv*
USAGE *Superior* should not be used with *than: he is a better* (not *a superior*) *poet than his brother; his poetry is superior to* (not *superior than*) *his brother's.*
Superior (suː'pɪərɪə, sjuː-) *n* **Lake.** a lake in the N central U.S. and S Canada: one of the largest freshwater lakes in the world and westernmost of the Great Lakes. Area: 82 362 sq. km (31 800 sq. miles).
superior court *n* **1** (in England) a higher court not subject to control by any other court except by way of appeal. See also **Supreme Court of Judicature. 2** *U.S.* (in several states) a court of general jurisdiction ranking above the inferior courts and below courts of last resort.
superiority complex *n Informal.* an inflated estimate of one's own merit, usually manifested in arrogance.
superior planet *n* any of the six planets (Mars, Jupiter, Saturn, Uranus, Neptune, and Pluto) whose orbit lies outside that of the earth.
superjacent (ˌsuːpə'dʒeɪsᵊnt) *adj* lying immediately above or upon. [C17: from Late Latin *superjacēre,* from Latin SUPER- + *jacēre* to lie]
superl. *abbrev. for* superlative.
superlative (suː'pɜːlətɪv) *adj* **1** of outstanding quality, degree, etc.; supreme. **2** *Grammar.* denoting the form of an adjective or adverb that expresses the highest or a very high degree of quality. In English the superlative degree is usually marked by the suffix *-est* or the word *most,* as in *loudest* or *most loudly.* Compare **positive** (sense 10), **comparative** (sense 3). **3** (of language or style) excessive; exaggerated. ◆ *n* **4** a thing that excels all others or is of the highest quality. **5** *Grammar.* the superlative form of an adjective. **6** the highest degree; peak. [C14: from Old French *superlatif,* via Late Latin from Latin *superlātus* extravagant, from *superferre* to carry beyond, from SUPER- + *ferre* to bear] ▸ **su'perlatively** *adv* ▸ **su'perlativeness** *n*
superload ('suːpəˌləʊd) *n* another name for **live load.**
superluminal (ˌsuːpə'luːmɪnəl) *adj Physics.* of or relating to a speed or velocity exceeding the speed of light.
superlunar (ˌsuːpə'luːnə) *adj* situated beyond the moon; celestial. ▸ ˌ**super'lunary** *adj*
supermale ('suːpəˌmeɪl) *n* a former name for **metamale.**
superman ('suːpəˌmæn) *n, pl* **-men. 1** (in the philosophy of Nietzsche) an ideal man who through integrity and creativity would rise above good and evil and who represents the goal of human evolution. **2** any man of apparently superhuman powers.
supermarket ('suːpəˌmɑːkɪt) *n* a large self-service store retailing food and household supplies.
supermembrane (ˌsuːpə'mɛmbreɪn) *n Physics.* a type of membrane postulated in certain theories of elementary particles that involve supersymmetry.
supermodel ('suːpəˌmɒdᵊl) *n* a very successful and well-known photographic or catwalk model.
supermundane (ˌsuːpə'mʌndeɪn) *adj* of or relating to what is elevated above earthly things.
supernal (suː'pɜːnᵊl, sjuː-) *adj Literary.* **1** of or from the world of the divine; celestial. **2** of or emanating from above or from the sky. [C15: from Medieval Latin *supernālis,* from Latin *supernus* that is on high, from *super* above] ▸ **su'pernally** *adv*
supernatant (ˌsuːpə'neɪtᵊnt) *adj* **1** floating on the surface or over something. **2** *Chem.* (of a liquid) lying above a sediment or settled precipitate. [C17: from Latin *supernatāre* to float, from SUPER- + *natāre* to swim] ▸ ˌ**superna'tation** *n*
supernational (ˌsuːpə'næʃnᵊl) *adj* a less common word for **supranational.** ▸ ˌ**super'nationalism** *n* ▸ ˌ**super'nationalist** *n* ▸ ˌ**super'nationally** *adv*
supernatural (ˌsuːpə'nætʃrəl, -'nætʃərəl) *adj* **1** of or relating to things that cannot be explained according to natural laws. **2** characteristic of or caused by or as if by a god; miraculous. **3** of, involving, or ascribed to occult beings. **4** exceeding the ordinary; abnormal. ◆ *n* **5 the.** supernatural forces, occurrences, and beings collectively or their realm. ▸ ˌ**super'naturally** *adv* ▸ ˌ**super'naturalness** *n*
supernaturalism (ˌsuːpə'nætʃrəlɪzəm, -'nætʃərə-)) *n* **1** the quality or condition of being supernatural. **2** a supernatural agency, the effects of which are felt to be apparent in this world. **3** belief in supernatural forces or agencies as producing effects in this world. ▸ ˌ**super'naturalist** *n, adj* ▸ ˌ**superˌnatural'istic** *adj*
supernormal (ˌsuːpə'nɔːməl) *adj* greatly exceeding the normal. ▸ **supernormality** (ˌsuːpənɔː'mælɪtɪ) *n* ▸ ˌ**super'normally** *adv*
supernova (ˌsuːpə'nəʊvə) *n, pl* **-vae** (-viː) *or* **-vas.** a star that explodes catastrophically owing to instabilities following the exhaustion of its nuclear fuel, becoming for a few days up to one hundred million times brighter than the sun. The expanding shell of debris (the **supernova remnant**) creates a nebula that radiates radio waves, X-rays, and light, for hundreds or thousands of years. Compare **nova.**
supernumerary (ˌsuːpə'njuːmərərɪ, -'njuːmrərɪ) *adj* **1** exceeding a regular or proper number; extra. **2** functioning as a substitute or assistant with regard to a regular body or staff. ◆ *n, pl* **-aries. 3** a person or thing that exceeds the normal, required, or regular number. **4** a person who functions as a substitute or assistant. **5** an actor who has no lines, esp. a nonprofessional one. [C17: from Late Latin *supernumerārius,* from Latin SUPER- + *numerus* number]
superorder ('suːpərˌɔːdə) *n Biology.* a taxonomic group that is a subdivision of a subclass.
superordinate *adj* (ˌsuːpər'ɔːdɪnɪt). **1** of higher status or condition. ◆ *n* (ˌsuːpər'ɔːdɪnɪt). **2** a person or thing that is superordinate. **3** a word the meaning of which includes the meaning of another word or words: *"red" is a superordinate of "scarlet", "vermilion", and "crimson".* Compare **hyponym, synonym, antonym.** ◆ *vb* (ˌsuːpər'ɔːdɪˌneɪt). **4** (*tr*) *Rare.* to make superordinate.
superorganic (ˌsuːpərɔː'gænɪk) *adj Sociol.* (no longer widely used) relating to those aspects of a culture that are conceived as being superior to the individual members of the society. ▸ ˌ**superor'ganicism** *n* ▸ ˌ**superor'ganicist** *n*
superoxide (ˌsuːpər'ɒksaɪd) *n* any of certain metal oxides that contain the O_2^- ion: *potassium superoxide,* KO_2.
superphosphate (ˌsuːpə'fɒsfeɪt) *n* **1** a mixture of the diacid calcium salt of orthophosphoric acid $Ca(H_2PO_4)_2$ with calcium sulphate and small quantities of other phosphates: used as a fertilizer. **2** a salt of phosphoric acid formed by incompletely replacing its acidic hydrogen atoms; acid phosphate; hydrogen phosphate.
superphysical (ˌsuːpə'fɪzɪkᵊl) *adj* not explained by the known physical laws and phenomena; supernatural.
superplastic (ˌsuːpə'plæstɪk) *adj* **1** (of a metal, alloy, etc.) very easily moulded at high temperatures without fracturing. ◆ *n* **2** such a metal, alloy, etc. ▸ ˌ**superplas'ticity** *n*
superpose (ˌsuːpə'pəʊz) *vb* (*tr*) **1** *Geometry.* to transpose (the coordinates of one geometric figure) to coincide with those of another. **2** a rare word for **superimpose** (sense 1). [C19: from French *superposer,* from Latin *superpōnere,* from SUPER- + *pōnere* to place] ▸ ˌ**super'posable** *adj*
superposition (ˌsuːpəpə'zɪʃən) *n* **1** the act of superposing or state of being superposed. **2** *Geology.* the principle that in any sequence of sedimentary rocks which has not been disturbed, the oldest strata lie at the bottom and the youngest at the top.
superpower ('suːpəˌpaʊə) *n* **1** an extremely powerful state, such as the U.S. **2** extremely high power, esp. electrical or mechanical. ▸ '**superˌpowered** *adj*
superrealism (ˌsuːpə'rɪəˌlɪzəm) *n* another name for **surrealism.** ▸ ˌ**super'realist** *n, adj*
supersaturated (ˌsuːpə'sætʃəˌreɪtɪd) *adj* **1** (of a solution) containing more solute than a saturated solution and therefore not in equilibrium. **2** (of a vapour)

containing more material than a saturated vapour and therefore not in equilibrium. ▸ ˌsuperˌsatuˈration *n*

superscribe (ˌsuːpəˈskraɪb) *vb* (*tr*) to write (an inscription, name, etc.) above, on top of, or outside. [C16: from Latin *superscrībere*, from SUPER- + *scrībere* to write]

superscript (ˈsuːpəˌskrɪpt) *adj* **1** *Printing.* (of a character) written or printed above the line; superior. Compare **subscript.** ◆ *n* **2** a superscript or superior character. **3** *Obsolete.* a superscription on a document, letter, etc. [C16: from Latin *superscriptus*; see SUPERSCRIBE]

superscription (ˌsuːpəˈskrɪpʃən) *n* **1** the act of superscribing. **2** a superscribed title, address, etc. **3** the symbol (**℞**) at the head of a medical prescription, which stands for the Latin word *recipe* (take).

supersede (ˌsuːpəˈsiːd) *vb* (*tr*) **1** to take the place of (something old-fashioned or less appropriate); supplant. **2** to replace in function, office, etc.; succeed. **3** to discard or set aside or cause to be set aside as obsolete or inferior. [C15: via Old French from Latin *supersedēre* to sit above, from SUPER- + *sedēre* to sit] ▸ ˌsuperˈsedable *adj* ▸ ˌsuperˈsedence *n* ▸ ˌsuperˈseder *n* ▸ **supersedure** (ˌsuːpəˈsiːdʒə) *n* ▸ **supersession** (ˌsuːpəˈsɛʃən) *n*

supersensible (ˌsuːpəˈsɛnsɪbᵊl) *or* **supersensory** (ˌsuːpəˈsɛnsərɪ) *adj* imperceptible to or beyond reach of the senses. ▸ ˌsuperˈsensibly *adv*

supersex (ˈsuːpəˌsɛks) *n Genetics.* a sterile organism in which the ratio between the sex chromosomes is disturbed. See **metafemale, metamale.**

supersonic (ˌsuːpəˈsɒnɪk) *adj* being, having, or capable of reaching a velocity in excess of the velocity of sound: *supersonic aircraft.* ▸ ˌsuperˈsonically *adv*

supersonics (ˌsuːpəˈsɒnɪks) *n* (*functioning as sing*) **1** the study of supersonic motion. **2** a less common name for **ultrasonics.**

superstar (ˈsuːpəˌstɑː) *n* a popular singer, film star, etc., who is idolized by fans and elevated to a position of importance in the entertainment industry. ▸ ˈsuperˌstardom *n*

superstate (ˈsuːpəˌsteɪt) *n* a large state, esp. created from a federation of states.

superstition (ˌsuːpəˈstɪʃən) *n* **1** irrational belief usually founded on ignorance or fear and characterized by obsessive reverence for omens, charms, etc. **2** a notion, act or ritual that derives from such belief. **3** any irrational belief, esp. with regard to the unknown. [C15: from Latin *superstitiō* dread of the supernatural, from *superstāre* to stand still by something (as in amazement)]

superstitious (ˌsuːpəˈstɪʃəs) *adj* **1** disposed to believe in superstition. **2** of or relating to superstition. ▸ ˌsuperˈstitiously *adv* ▸ ˌsuperˈstitiousness *n*

superstore (ˈsuːpəˌstɔː) *n* a very large supermarket, often selling household goods, clothes, etc., as well as food.

superstratum (ˌsuːpəˈstrɑːtəm, -ˈstreɪ-) *n, pl* **-ta** (-tə) *or* **-tums. 1** *Geology.* a layer or stratum overlying another layer or similar structure. **2** *Linguistics.* the language of a conquering or colonizing population as it supplants that of an indigenous population, as for example French and English in the Caribbean. Compare **substratum** (sense 8).

superstring (ˈsuːpəˌstrɪŋ) *n Physics.* a type of string (sense 11) postulated in certain theories of elementary particles that involve supersymmetry.

superstruct (ˌsuːpəˈstrʌkt) *vb* (*tr*) to erect upon a foundation or on top of another building or part.

superstructure (ˈsuːpəˌstrʌktʃə) *n* **1** the part of a building above its foundation. **2** any structure or concept erected on something else. **3** *Nautical.* any structure above the main deck of a ship with sides flush with the sides of the hull. **4** the part of a bridge supported by the piers and abutments. **5** (in Marxist theory) an edifice of interdependent agencies of the state, including legal and political institutions and ideologies, each possessing some autonomy but remaining products of the dominant mode of economic production. ▸ ˈsuperˌstructural *adj*

supersymmetry (ˌsuːpəˈsɪmɪtrɪ) *n Physics.* a symmetry of elementary particles having a higher order than that in the standard model, postulated to encompass the behaviour of both bosons and fermions.

supertanker (ˈsuːpəˌtæŋkə) *n* a large fast tanker of more than 275 000 tons capacity.

supertax (ˈsuːpəˌtæks) *n* a tax levied in addition to the basic tax, esp. a graduated surtax on incomes above a certain level.

supertonic (ˌsuːpəˈtɒnɪk) *n Music.* **1** the second degree of a major or minor scale. **2** a key or chord based on this.

Super Tuesday *n U.S. politics.* the Tuesday, typically in March, on which party members in over 20 states vote in primary elections to select their party's presidential candidate.

supervene (ˌsuːpəˈviːn) *vb* (*intr*) **1** to follow closely; ensue. **2** to occur as an unexpected or extraneous development. [C17: from Latin *supervenīre* to come upon, from SUPER- + *venīre* to come] ▸ ˌsuperˈvenience *or* **supervention** (ˌsuːpəˈvɛnʃən) *n*

supervenient (ˌsuːpəˈviːnɪənt) *adj* **1** supervening. **2** *Philosophy.* (of a property) inseparable from the other properties of something. Two objects may be identical except that one is red and the other not, but they cannot be identical except that one is beautiful and the other not; beauty is thus a supervenient property.

supervise (ˈsuːpəˌvaɪz) *vb* (*tr*) **1** to direct or oversee the performance or operation of. **2** to watch over so as to maintain order, etc. [C16: from Medieval Latin *supervidēre*, from Latin SUPER- + *vidēre* to see] ▸ **supervision** (ˌsuːpəˈvɪʒən) *n*

supervision order *n* (in Britain) *Social welfare.* an order by a juvenile court requiring a named probation officer or local-authority social worker to advise, assist, and befriend a child or young person who is the subject of care proceedings, over a period of up to three years.

supervisor (ˈsuːpəˌvaɪzə) *n* **1** a person who manages or supervises. **2** a foreman or forewoman. **3** (in some British universities) a tutor supervising the work, esp. research work, of a student. **4** (in some U.S. schools) an administrator running a department of teachers. **5** (in some U.S. states) the elected chief official of a township or other subdivision of a county. **6** *Obsolete.* a spectator. ▸ ˈsuperˌvisorship *n*

supervisory (ˈsuːpəˌvaɪzərɪ) *adj* of, involving, or limited to supervision: *a supervisory capacity.*

supervisory board *n* a board of management of which nonmanagerial workers are members, having supervisory powers over some aspects of management decision-making.

superwoman (ˈsuːpəˌwʊmən) *n, pl* **-women.** a woman who fulfils her many roles with apparently superhuman efficiency.

supinate (ˈsuːpɪˌneɪt, ˈsjuː-) *vb* to turn (the hand and forearm) so that the palm faces up or forwards. [C19: from Latin *supīnāre* to lay on the back, from *supīnus* SUPINE] ▸ ˌsupiˈnation *n*

supinator (ˈsuːpɪˌneɪtə, ˈsjuː-) *n Anatomy.* the muscle of the forearm that can produce the motion of supination.

supine *adj* (suːˈpaɪn, sjuː-; ˈsuːpaɪn, ˈsjuː-). **1** lying or resting on the back with the face, palm, etc., upwards. **2** displaying no interest or animation; lethargic. ◆ *n* (ˈsuːpaɪn, ˈsjuː-). **3** *Grammar.* a noun form derived from a verb in Latin, often used to express purpose with verbs of motion. Abbrev.: **sup.** [C15: from Latin *supīnus* related to *sub* under, up; (in grammatical sense) from Latin *verbum supīnum* supine word (the reason for this use is unknown)] ▸ suˈpinely *adv* ▸ suˈpineness *n*

suplex (ˈsuːplɛks) *n* a wrestling hold in which a wrestler grasps his opponent round the waist from behind and carries him backwards. [C20: of uncertain origin]

supp. *or* **suppl.** *abbrev. for* supplement(ary).

supper (ˈsʌpə) *n* **1** an evening meal, esp. a light one. **2** an evening social event featuring a supper. **3 sing for one's supper.** to obtain something by performing a service. ◆ *vb* **4** (*tr*) *Rare.* to give supper to. **5** (*intr*) *Rare.* to eat supper. [C13: from Old French *soper*; see SUP[1]] ▸ ˈsupperless *adj*

supper club *n U.S. and Canadian.* (formerly) a small expensive nightclub.

Suppiluliumas I (ˌsʌpɪlʌlɪˈuːməs) *n* king of the Hittites (?1375–?1335 B.C.); founder of the Hittite empire.

supplant (səˈplɑːnt) *vb* (*tr*) to take the place of, often by trickery or force: *he easily supplanted his rival.* [C13: via Old French from Latin *supplantāre* to trip up, from *sub-* from below + *planta* sole of the foot] ▸ **supplantation** (ˌsʌplɑːnˈteɪʃən) *n* ▸ supˈplanter *n*

supple (ˈsʌpᵊl) *adj* **1** bending easily without damage. **2** capable of or showing easy or graceful movement; lithe. **3** mentally flexible; responding readily. **4** disposed to agree, sometimes to the point of servility. ◆ *vb* **5** *Rare.* to make or become supple. [C13: from Old French *souple*, from Latin *supplex* bowed] ▸ ˈsuppleness *n*

supplejack (ˈsʌpᵊlˌdʒæk) *n* **1** a North American twining rhamnaceous woody vine, *Berchemia scandens*, that has greenish-white flowers and purple fruits. **2** a bush plant of New Zealand, *Rhipogonum scandens*, having tough climbing vines. **3** a tropical American woody sapindaceous vine, *Paullinia curassavica*, having strong supple wood. **4** any of various other vines with strong supple stems. **5** *U.S.* a walking stick made from the wood of *Paullinia curassavica.* [C18: from SUPPLE + JACK[1]]

supplement *n* (ˈsʌplɪmənt). **1** an addition designed to complete, make up for a deficiency, etc. **2** a section appended to a publication to supply further information, correct errors, etc. **3** a magazine or section inserted into a newspaper or periodical, such as one with colour photographs issued every week. **4** *Geometry.* **4a** either of a pair of angles whose sum is 180°. **4b** an arc of a circle that when added to another arc forms a semicircle. ◆ Abbrevs.: **sup., supp.** ◆ *vb* (ˈsʌplɪˌmɛnt). **5** (*tr*) to provide a supplement to, esp. in order to remedy a deficiency. [C14: from Latin *supplēmentum*, from *supplēre* to SUPPLY[1]] ▸ ˌsupplemenˈtation *n* ▸ ˈsuppleˌmenter *n*

supplementary (ˌsʌplɪˈmɛntərɪ, -trɪ) *adj* **1** Also (*less commonly*): **supplemental** (ˌsʌplɪˈmɛntᵊl). forming or acting as a supplement. ◆ *n, pl* **-ries. 2** a person or thing that is a supplement. ▸ ˌsuppleˈmentarily *or* (*less commonly*) ˌsuppleˈmentally *adv*

supplementary angle *n* either of two angles whose sum is 180°. Compare **complementary angle.**

suppletion (səˈpliːʃən) *n* the use of an unrelated word to complete the otherwise defective paradigm of a given word, as for example the use of *went* for the past tense of *go.* [C14: from Medieval Latin *supplētiō* a completing, from Latin *supplēre* to SUPPLY[1]] ▸ supˈpletive *n, adj*

suppletory (ˈsʌplɪtərɪ, -trɪ) *adj Archaic.* remedying deficiencies; supplementary. ▸ ˈsuppletorily *adv*

suppliant (ˈsʌplɪənt) *adj* **1** expressing entreaty or supplication. ◆ *n, adj* **2** another word for **supplicant.** [C15: from French *supplier* to beseech, from Latin *supplicāre* to kneel in entreaty; see SUPPLE] ▸ ˈsuppliantly *adv* ▸ ˈsuppliance *n*

supplicant (ˈsʌplɪkənt) *or* **suppliant** *n* **1** a person who supplicates. ◆ *adj* **2** entreating humbly; supplicating. [C16: from Latin *supplicāns* beseeching; see SUPPLE]

supplicate (ˈsʌplɪˌkeɪt) *vb* **1** to make a humble request to (someone); plead. **2** (*tr*) to ask for or seek humbly. [C15: from Latin *supplicāre* to beg on one's knees; see SUPPLE] ▸ ˈsuppliˌcatory *adj*

supplication (ˌsʌplɪˈkeɪʃən) *n* **1** the act of supplicating. **2** a humble entreaty or petition; prayer.

supply[1] (səˈplaɪ) *vb* **-plies, -plying, -plied. 1** (*tr*; often foll. by *with*) to furnish with something that is required: *to supply the community with good government.* **2** (*tr*; often foll. by *to* or *for*) to make available or provide (something that is desired or lacking): *to supply books to the library.* **3** (*tr*) to provide for adequately; make good; satisfy: *who will supply their needs?* **4** to serve as a substitute, usually temporary, in (another's position, etc.): *there are no clergymen to supply the pulpit.* **5** (*tr*) *Brit.* to fill (a vacancy, position, etc.). ◆ *n, pl* **-plies. 6a** the act of providing or something that is provided. **6b** (*as modifier*): *a supply dump.* **7** (*often pl*) an amount available for use; stock. **8** (*pl*) food, equipment, etc., needed for a campaign or trip. **9** *Economics.* **9a** willingness and ability to offer goods and services for sale. **9b** the amount of a commodity that producers are willing and able to offer for sale at a specified price. Compare **demand** (sense 9). **10** *Military.* **10a** the management and disposal of food and equipment. **10b** (*as modifier*): *supply routes.* **11** (*often pl*) a grant of money voted by a legislature for government expenses, esp. those not covered by other revenues. **12** (in Parliament and similar legislatures) the money voted annually for the expenses of the civil service and armed forces. **13a** a person who acts as a temporary substitute. **13b** (*as modifier*): *a supply vicar.* **14** a source of electrical energy, gas, etc. **15** *Obsolete.* aid or assistance. [C14: from Old French *souppleier,* from Latin *supplēre* to complete, from *sub-* up + *plēre* to fill] ▸ **sup'pliable** *adj* ▸ **sup'plier** *n*

supply[2] ('sʌplɪ) *or* **supplely** ('sʌpᵊlɪ) *adv* in a supple manner.

supply chain *n Marketing.* a channel of distribution beginning with the supplier of materials or components, extending through a manufacturing process to the distributor and retailer, and ultimately to the consumer.

supply-side economics *n* (*functioning as sing*) a school of economic thought that emphasizes the importance to a strong economy of policies that remove impediments to supply.

supply teacher *n* a teacher employed to replace other teachers when they are absent.

support (sə'pɔːt) *vb* (*tr*) **1** to carry the weight of. **2** to bear or withstand (pressure, weight, etc.). **3** to provide the necessities of life for (a family, person, etc.). **4** to tend to establish (a theory, statement, etc.) by providing new facts; substantiate. **5** to speak in favour of (a motion). **6** to give aid or courage to. **7** to give approval to (a cause, principle, etc.); subscribe to: *to support a political candidature.* **8** to endure with forbearance: *I will no longer support bad behaviour.* **9** to give strength to; maintain: *to support a business.* **10** (*tr*) (in a concert) to perform earlier than (the main attraction). **11** *Films, theatre.* **11a** to play a subordinate role to. **11b** to accompany (the feature) in a film programme. **12** to act or perform (a role or character). ◆ *n* **13** the act of supporting or the condition of being supported. **14** a thing that bears the weight or part of the weight of a construction. **15** a person who or thing that furnishes aid. **16** the means of maintenance of a family, person, etc. **17** a band or entertainer not topping the bill. **18** (often preceded by *the*) an actor or group of actors playing subordinate roles. **19** *Med.* an appliance worn to ease the strain on an injured bodily structure or part. **20** the solid material on which a painting is executed, such as canvas. **21** See **athletic support.** [C14: from Old French *supporter,* from Latin *supportāre* to bring, from *sub-* up + *portāre* to carry] ▸ **sup'portless** *adj*

supportable (sə'pɔːtəbᵊl) *adj* able to be supported or endured; bearable. ▸ **sup,porta'bility** *or* **sup'portableness** *n* ▸ **sup'portably** *adv*

support area *n Military.* an area containing concentrations of personnel and materiel ready to support a force in the field.

supporter (sə'pɔːtə) *n* **1** a person who or thing that acts as a support. **2** a person who backs a sports team, politician, etc. **3** a garment or device worn to ease the strain on or restrict the movement of a bodily structure or part. **4** *Heraldry.* a figure or beast in a coat of arms depicted as holding up the shield.

supporting (sə'pɔːtɪŋ) *adj* **1** (of a role) being a fairly important but not leading part, esp. in a play or film. **2** (of an actor or actress) playing a supporting role.

supportive (sə'pɔːtɪv) *adj* providing support, esp. moral or emotional support. ▸ **sup'portively** *adv* ▸ **sup'portiveness** *n*

supportive therapy *n* **1** *Med.* any treatment, such as the intravenous administration of certain fluids, designed to reinforce or sustain the physiological well-being of a patient. **2** *Psychol.* a form of therapy for mental disturbances employing guidance and encouragement to develop the patient's own resources.

suppose (sə'pəʊz) *vb* (*tr; may take a clause as object*) **1** to presume (something) to be true without certain knowledge: *I suppose he meant to kill her.* **2** to consider as a possible suggestion for the sake of discussion, elucidation, etc.; postulate: *suppose that he wins the election.* **3** (of theories, propositions, etc.) to imply the inference or assumption (of): *your policy supposes full employment.* [C14: from Old French *supposer,* from Medieval Latin *suppōnere,* from Latin: to substitute, from SUB- + *pōnere* to put] ▸ **sup'posable** *adj* ▸ **sup'poser** *n*

supposed (sə'pəʊzd, -'pəʊzɪd) *adj* **1** (*prenominal*) presumed to be true without certain knowledge: *his supposed date of birth.* **2** (*prenominal*) believed to be true on slight grounds; highly doubtful: *the supposed existence of ghosts.* **3** (sə'pəʊzd). (*postpositive;* foll. by *to*) expected or obliged (to): *I'm supposed to be there at nine.* **4** (*postpositive; used in negative;* foll. by *to*) expected or obliged not (to): *you're not supposed to walk on the grass.* ▸ **supposedly** (sə'pəʊzɪdlɪ) *adv*

supposition (,sʌpə'zɪʃən) *n* **1** the act of supposing. **2** a fact, theory, etc., that is supposed. ▸ **,suppo'sitional** *adj* ▸ **,suppo'sitionally** *adv* ▸ **,suppo'sitionless** *adj*

suppositious (,sʌpə'zɪʃəs) *adj* deduced from supposition; hypothetical. ▸ **,suppo'sitiously** *adv* ▸ **,suppo'sitiousness** *n*

supposititious (sə,pɒzɪ'tɪʃəs) *adj* substituted with intent to mislead or deceive. ▸ **sup,posi'titiously** *adv* ▸ **sup,posi'titiousness** *n*

suppositive (sə'pɒzɪtɪv) *adj* **1** of, involving, or arising out of supposition. **2** *Grammar.* denoting a conjunction introducing a clause expressing a supposition, as for example *if, supposing,* or *provided that.* ◆ *n* **3** *Grammar.* a suppositive conjunction. ▸ **sup'positively** *adv*

suppository (sə'pɒzɪtərɪ, -trɪ) *n, pl* **-ries.** *Med.* an encapsulated or solid medication for insertion into the vagina, rectum, or urethra, where it melts and releases the active substance. [C14: from Medieval Latin *suppositōrium,* from Latin *suppositus* placed beneath, from *suppōnere;* see SUPPOSE]

suppress (sə'prɛs) *vb* (*tr*) **1** to put an end to; prohibit. **2** to hold in check; restrain: *I was obliged to suppress a smile.* **3** to withhold from circulation or publication: *to suppress seditious pamphlets.* **4** to stop the activities of; crush: *to suppress a rebellion.* **5** *Electronics.* **5a** to reduce or eliminate (unwanted oscillations) in a circuit. **5b** to eliminate (a particular frequency or group of frequencies) in a signal. **6** *Psychiatry.* **6a** to resist consciously (an idea or a desire entering one's mind). **6b** to exercise self-control by preventing the expression of (certain desires). Compare **repress** (sense 3). [C14: from Latin *suppressus* held down, from *supprimere* to restrain, from *sub-* down + *premere* to press] ▸ **sup'presser** *n* ▸ **sup'pressible** *adj*

suppressant (sə'prɛsənt) *adj* **1** tending to suppress or restrain an action or condition. ◆ *n* **2** a suppressant drug or agent: *a cough suppressant.*

suppressed carrier modulation *n Radio.* an amplitude-modulated wave in which only the sidebands are transmitted, the carrier being removed.

suppression (sə'prɛʃən) *n* **1** the act or process of suppressing or the condition of being suppressed. **2** *Psychoanal.* the conscious avoidance of unpleasant thoughts. Compare **repression** (sense 2). **3** *Electronics.* the act or process of suppressing a frequency, oscillation, etc. **4** *Biology.* the failure of an organ or part to develop. **5** *Med.* the cessation of any physiological process.

suppressive (sə'prɛsɪv) *adj* **1** tending or acting to suppress; involving suppression. **2** *Psychiatry.* tending to prevent the expression of certain of one's desires or to resist the emergence of mental symptoms.

suppressor (sə'prɛsə) *n* **1** a person or thing that suppresses. **2** a device fitted to an electrical appliance to suppress unwanted electrical interference to audiovisual signals.

suppressor grid *n* an electrode placed between the screen grid and anode of a valve. Its negative potential, relative to both screen and anode, prevents secondary electrons from the anode reaching the screen.

suppurate ('sʌpjʊ,reɪt) *vb* (*intr*) *Pathol.* (of a wound, sore, etc.) to discharge pus; fester. [C16: from Latin *suppūrāre,* from SUB- + *pūs* PUS]

suppuration (,sʌpjʊ'reɪʃən) *n* **1** the discharging of pus from a wound, sore, etc. **2** the discharge itself.

suppurative ('sʌpjʊrətɪv) *adj* **1** causing suppuration. ◆ *n* **2** any suppurative drug.

supr. *abbrev. for* supreme.

supra ('suːprə) *adv* above, esp. referring to earlier parts of a book etc. [C15: from Latin; related to SUPER-]

supra- *prefix* over, above, beyond, or greater than: *supranational; supramolecular.* [from Latin *suprā* above]

supraglottal (,suːprə'glɒtᵊl, ,sjuː-) *adj Anatomy.* situated above the glottis: *supraglottal obstruction.*

supralapsarian (,suːprəlæp'sɛərɪən, ,sjuː-) *n Christian theol., chiefly Calvinist.* a person who believes that God decreed the election or nonelection of individuals to salvation even before the Fall. Compare **infralapsarian.** [C17: from New Latin *suprālapsārius,* from Latin SUPRA- + *lapsus* a fall] ▸ **,supra-lap'sarianism** *n*

supraliminal (,suːprə'lɪmɪnᵊl, ,sjuː-) *adj* of or relating to any stimulus that is above the threshold of sensory awareness. Compare **subliminal.** ▸ **,supra'liminally** *adv*

supramaxillary (,suːprəmæk'sɪlərɪ) *adj* of or relating to the upper jaw.

supramolecular (,suːprəmə'lɛkjʊlə, ,sjuː-) *adj* **1** more complex than a molecule. **2** consisting of more than one molecule.

supranational (,suːprə'næʃənᵊl, ,sjuː-) *adj* beyond the authority or jurisdiction of one national government: *the supranational institutions of the EU.* ▸ **,supra'nationalism** *n* ▸ **,supra'nationally** *adv*

supraorbital (,suːprə'ɔːbɪtᵊl, ,sjuː-) *adj Anatomy.* situated above the orbit.

suprarenal (,suːprə'riːnᵊl, ,sjuː-) *adj Anatomy.* situated above a kidney. [C19: from New Latin *suprārēnālis.* See SUPRA-, RENAL]

suprarenal gland *n* another name for **adrenal gland.**

suprasegmental (,suːprəsɛg'mɛntᵊl, ,sjuː-) *adj Linguistics.* denoting those features of a sound or sequence of sounds that accompany rather than form part of the consecutive segments of a word or sentence, as for example stress and pitch in English. ▸ **,supraseg'mentally** *adv*

supremacist (sʊ'prɛməsɪst, sjʊ-) *n* **1** a person who promotes or advocates the supremacy of any particular group. ◆ *adj* **2** characterized by belief in the supremacy of any particular group. ▸ **su'prematism** *n*

supremacy (sʊ'prɛməsɪ, sjʊ-) *n* **1** supreme power; authority. **2** the quality or condition of being supreme.

Suprematism (sʊ'prɛmə,tɪzəm, sjʊ-) *n* a form of pure cubist art, launched in Russia in 1913, and based on the principle that paintings should be composed only of rectangles, circles, triangles, or crosses. [C20: from *suprematist* a supporter of this theory, from French *suprémacie* SUPREMACY] ▸ **Su'prematist** *n, adj*

supreme (sʊ'priːm, sjʊ-) *adj* **1** of highest status or power: *a supreme tribunal.* **2** (*usually prenominal*) of highest quality, importance, etc.: *supreme endeavour.* **3** greatest in degree; extreme: *supreme folly.* **4** (*prenominal*) final or last, esp. being last in one's life or progress; ultimate: *the supreme judgment.* [C16: from Latin *suprēmus* highest, from *superus* that is above, from *super* above] ▸ **su'premely** *adv* ▸ **su'premeness** *n*

suprême (sʊ'priːm, -'prɛm, sjʊ-) *n* **1** Also called: **suprême sauce.** a rich velouté sauce made with a base of veal or chicken stock, with cream or egg yolks added. **2** the best or most delicate part of meat, esp. the breast and wing of chicken, cooked in suprême sauce. [French: SUPREME]

Supreme Being *n* the most exalted being; God.

supreme commander *n* the military officer in overall command of all forces in one theatre of operations.

Supreme Court *n* (in the U.S.) **1** the highest Federal court, possessing final appellate jurisdiction and exercising supervisory jurisdiction over the lower courts. **2** (in many states) the highest state court.

Supreme Court of Judicature *n* (in England) a court formed in 1873 by the amalgamation of several superior courts into two divisions, the High Court of Justice and the Court of Appeal.

supreme sacrifice *n* **the.** the sacrifice of one's life.

Supreme Soviet *n* (in the former Soviet Union) **1** the bicameral legislature, comprising the **Soviet of the Union** and the **Soviet of the Nationalities**; officially the highest organ of state power. **2** a similar legislature in each former Soviet republic.

supremo (sʊ'priːməʊ, sjʊ-) *n, pl* **-mos.** *Brit. informal.* a person in overall authority. [C20: from SUPREME]

Supt *or* **supt** *abbrev. for* superintendent.

suq (suːk) *n* a variant spelling of **souk**[1].

Suqutra (sə'kəʊtrə) *n* a variant spelling of **Socotra.**

Sur *or* **Sour** (sʊə) *n* transliteration of the Arabic name for **Tyre.**

sur-[1] *prefix* over; above; beyond: *surcharge; surrealism.* Compare **super-**. [from Old French, from Latin SUPER-]

sur-[2] *prefix* a variant of **sub-** before *r: surrogate.*

sura ('sʊərə) *n* any of the 114 chapters of the Koran. [C17: from Arabic *sūrah* section]

Surabaya, Surabaja, *or* **Soerabaja** (ˌsʊərə'baɪə) *n* a port in Indonesia, on E Java on the **Surabaya Strait:** the country's second port and chief naval base; university (1954); fishing and ship-building industries; oil refinery. Pop.: 2 701 300 (1995 est.).

surah ('sʊərə) *n* a twill-weave fabric of silk or rayon, used for dresses, blouses, etc. [C19: from the French pronunciation of SURAT]

Surakarta (ˌsʊərə'kɑːtə) *n* a town in Indonesia, on central Java: textile manufacturing. Pop.: 516 500 (1995 est.).

sural ('sjʊərəl) *adj Anatomy.* of or relating to the calf of the leg. [C17: via New Latin from Latin *sūra* calf]

surat (sjuː'ræt) *n* (formerly) a cotton fabric from the Surat area of India.

Surat (sʊ'ræt, 'sʊərət) *n* a port in W India, in W Gujarat: a major port in the 17th century; textile manufacturing. Pop.: 1 498 817 (1991).

surbase ('sɜːˌbeɪs) *n* the uppermost part, such as a moulding, of a pedestal, base, or skirting. Compare **subbase.** ► **sur'basement** *n*

surbased ('sɜːˌbeɪst) *adj Architect.* **1** having a surbase. **2** (of an arch) having a rise of less than half the span. [C18: from French *surbaisser* to depress, from *sur-* (intensive) + *baisser* to lower, from *bas* low; see BASE[1]]

surcease (sɜː'siːs) *Archaic.* ◆ *n* **1** cessation or intermission. ◆ *vb* **2** to desist from (some action). **3** to cease or cause to cease. [C16: from earlier *sursesen,* from Old French *surseoir,* from Latin *supersedēre;* see SUPERSEDE]

surcharge *n* ('sɜːˌtʃɑːdʒ). **1** a charge in addition to the usual payment, tax, etc. **2** an excessive sum charged, esp. when unlawful. **3** an extra and usually excessive burden or supply. **4** *Law.* the act or an instance of surcharging. **5** an overprint that alters the face value of a postage stamp. ◆ *vb* (sɜː'tʃɑːdʒ, 'sɜːˌtʃɑːdʒ). (*tr*) **6** to charge an additional sum, tax, etc. **7** to overcharge (a person) for something. **8** to put an extra physical burden upon; overload. **9** to fill to excess; overwhelm. **10** *Law.* to insert credits that have been omitted in (an account). **11** to overprint a surcharge on (a stamp). ► **sur'charger** *n*

surcingle ('sɜːˌsɪŋɡᵊl) *n* **1** a girth for a horse which goes around the body, used esp. with a racing saddle. **2** the belt worn with a cassock. ◆ *vb* **3** to put a surcingle on or over (a horse). [C14: from Old French *surcengle,* from *sur-* over + *cengle* a belt, from Latin *cingulum*]

surcoat ('sɜːˌkəʊt) *n* **1** a tunic, often embroidered with heraldic arms, worn by a knight over his armour during the Middle Ages. **2** an outer coat or other garment.

surculose ('sɜːkjʊˌləʊs) *adj* (of a plant) bearing suckers. [C19: from Latin *surculōsus* woody, from *surculus* twig, from *sūrus* a branch]

surd (sɜːd) *n* **1** *Maths.* an expression containing one or more irrational roots of numbers, such as $2\sqrt{3} + 3\sqrt{2} + 6$. **2** *Phonetics.* a voiceless consonant, such as (t). ◆ *adj* **3** of or relating to a surd. [C16: from Latin *surdus* muffled]

sure (ʃʊə, ʃɔː) *adj* **1** (sometimes foll. by *of*) free from hesitancy or uncertainty (with regard to a belief, conviction, etc.): *we are sure of the accuracy of the data; I am sure that he is lying.* **2** (foll. by *of*) having no doubt, as of the occurrence of a future state or event: *sure of success.* **3** always effective; unfailing: *a sure remedy.* **4** reliable in indication or accuracy: *a sure criterion.* **5** (of persons) worthy of trust or confidence: *a sure friend.* **6** not open to doubt: *sure proof.* **7** admitting of no vacillation or doubt: *he is very sure in his beliefs.* **8** bound to be or occur; inevitable: *victory is sure.* **9** (*postpositive*) bound inevitably (to be or do something); certain: *she is sure to be there tonight.* **10** physically secure or dependable: *a sure footing.* **11** *Obsolete.* free from exposure to harm or danger. **12 be sure.** (*usually imperative or dependent imperative; takes a clause as object or an infinitive,* sometimes with *to* replaced by *and*) to be careful or certain: *be sure and shut the door; I told him to be sure to shut the door.* **13 for sure.** without a doubt; surely. **14 make sure. 14a** (*takes a clause as object*) to make certain; ensure. **14b** (foll. by *of*) to establish or confirm power or possession (over). **15 sure enough.** *Informal.* as might have been confidently expected; definitely: often used as a sentence substitute. **16 to be sure. 16a** without doubt; certainly. **16b** it has to be acknowledged; admittedly. ◆ *adv* **17** (*sentence substitute*) *Informal.* willingly; yes. **18** (*sentence modifier*) *Informal, chiefly U.S. and Canadian.* without question; certainly. [C14: from Old French *seur,* from Latin *sēcūrus* SECURE] ► **'sureness** *n*

sure-fire *adj* (*usually prenominal*) *Informal.* certain to succeed or meet expectations; assured.

sure-footed *adj* **1** unlikely to fall, slip, or stumble. **2** not likely to err or fail, as in judgment. ► **ˌsure-'footedly** *adv* ► **ˌsure-'footedness** *n*

surely ('ʃʊəlɪ, 'ʃɔː-) *adv* **1** without doubt; assuredly: *things could surely not have been worse.* **2** without fail; inexorably (esp. in the phrase **slowly but surely**). **3** (*sentence modifier*) am I not right in thinking that?; I am sure that: *surely you don't mean it?* **4** *Rare.* in a sure manner. **5** *Archaic.* safely; securely. **6** (*sentence substitute*) *Chiefly U.S. and Canadian.* willingly; of course; yes.

sure thing *Informal.* **1** (*sentence substitute*) *Chiefly U.S.* all right! yes indeed! used to express enthusiastic assent. ◆ *n* **2** something guaranteed to be successful.

surety ('ʃʊətɪ, 'ʃʊərɪtɪ) *n, pl* **-ties. 1** a person who assumes legal responsibility for the fulfilment of another's debt or obligation and himself becomes liable if the other defaults. **2** security given against loss or damage or as a guarantee that an obligation will be met. **3** *Obsolete.* the quality or condition of being sure. **4** *Obsolete.* a means of assurance or safety. **5 stand surety.** to act as a surety. [C14: from Old French *seurte,* from Latin *sēcūritās* SECURITY] ► **'suretyˌship** *n*

surf (sɜːf) *n* **1** waves breaking on the shore or on a reef. **2** foam caused by the breaking of waves. ◆ *vb* **3** (*intr*) to take part in surfing. **4a** to move rapidly and easily through a particular medium: *surfing the Internet.* **4b** (*in combination*): *channelsurfing.* **5a** *Informal.* to be carried on top of something: *that guy's surfing the audience.* **5b** (*in combination*): *trainsurfing.* [C17: probably variant of SOUGH[1]] ► **'surfable** *adj* ► **'surfˌlike** *adj*

surface ('sɜːfɪs) *n* **1a** the exterior face of an object or one such face. **1b** (*as modifier*): *surface gloss.* **2a** the area or size of such a face. **2b** (*as modifier*): *surface measurements.* **3** material resembling such a face, with length and width but without depth. **4a** the superficial appearance as opposed to the real nature. **4b** (*as modifier*): *a surface resemblance.* **5** *Geom.* **5a** the complete boundary of a solid figure. **5b** a continuous two-dimensional configuration. **6a** the uppermost level of the land or sea. **6b** (*as modifier*): *surface transportation.* **7 come to the surface.** to emerge; become apparent. **8 on the surface.** to all appearances. ◆ *vb* **9** to rise or cause to rise to or as if to the surface (of water, etc.). **10** (*tr*) to treat the surface of, as by polishing, smoothing, etc. **11** (*tr*) to furnish with a surface. **12** (*intr*) *Mining.* **12a** to work at or near the ground surface. **12b** to wash surface ore deposits. **13** (*intr*) to become apparent; emerge. **14** (*intr*) *Informal.* **14a** to wake up. **14b** to get up. [C17: from French, from *sur* on + *face* FACE, probably on the model of Latin SUPERFICIES] ► **'surfaceless** *adj* ► **'surfacer** *n*

surface acoustic wave *n* an acoustic wave generated on the surface of a piezoelectric substrate: used as a filter in electronic circuits.

surface-active *adj* (of a substance, esp. a detergent) capable of lowering the surface tension of a liquid, usually water. See also **surfactant.**

surface condenser *n* a steam condenser usually associated with a steam turbine in which the steam is condensed on the surface of tubes through which water is passed. Compare **jet condenser.**

surface friction drag *n* the part of the drag on a body moving through a fluid that is dependent on the nature of the surface of the body. Also called: **skin friction.**

surface mail *n* mail transported by land or sea. Compare **airmail.**

surface noise *n* noise produced by the friction of the needle or stylus of a record player with the rotating record, caused by a static charge, dust, or irregularities on the surface of a record.

surface plate *n* another name for **faceplate** (sense 2).

surface structure *n Generative grammar.* a representation of a string of words or morphemes as they occur in a sentence, together with labels and brackets that represent syntactic structure. Compare **deep structure.**

surface tension *n* **1** a property of liquids caused by intermolecular forces near the surface leading to the apparent presence of a surface film and to capillarity, etc. **2** a measure of this property expressed as the force acting normal to one side of a line of unit length on the surface: measured in newtons per metre. Symbol: T, γ, or σ

surface-to-air *adj* of or relating to a missile launched from the surface of the earth against airborne targets.

surface-to-surface *adj* of or relating to a missile launched from the surface of the earth against surface targets.

surfactant (sɜː'fæktənt) *n* **1** Also called: **surface-active agent.** a substance, such as a detergent, that can reduce the surface tension of a liquid and thus allow it to foam or penetrate solids; a wetting agent. ◆ *adj* **2** having the properties of a surfactant. [C20: *surf(ace)-act(ive) a(ge)nt*]

surfbird ('sɜːfˌbɜːd) *n* an American shore bird, *Aphriza virgata,* having a spotted plumage, with a black and white tail: family *Scolopacidae* (sandpipers, etc.), order *Charadriiformes.*

surfboard ('sɜːfˌbɔːd) *n* a long narrow board used in surfing.

surfboat ('sɜːfˌbəʊt) *n* a boat with a high bow and stern and flotation chambers, equipped for use in rough surf.

surfcasting ('sɜːfˌkɑːstɪŋ) *n* fishing from the shore by casting into the surf. ► **'surfˌcaster** *n*

surfeit ('sɜːfɪt) *n* **1** (usually foll. by *of*) an excessive or immoderate amount. **2** overindulgence, esp. in eating or drinking. **3** disgust, nausea, etc., caused by such overindulgence. ◆ *vb* **4** (*tr*) to supply or feed excessively; satiate. **5** (*intr*) *Archaic.* to eat, drink, or be supplied to excess. **6** (*intr*) *Obsolete.* to feel uncomfortable as a consequence of overindulgence. [C13: from French *sourfait,* from *sourfaire* to overdo, from SUR-[1] + *faire,* from Latin *facere* to do] ► **'surfeiter** *n*

surfie ('sɜːfɪ) *n Austral. and N.Z. slang.* a young person whose main interest is in surfing, esp. when considered as a cult figure.

surfing ('sɜːfɪŋ) *n* the sport of riding towards shore on the crest of a wave by standing or lying on a surfboard. ► **'surfer** *or* **'surfˌrider** *n*

surf mat *n Austral. informal.* a small inflatable rubber mattress used to ride on waves.

surf music *n* a U.S. West Coast style of pop music of the early 1960s, characterized by high harmony vocals and strong trebly guitar riffs.

surf 'n' turf *n* a dish consisting of meat served with seafood.

surfperch ('sɜːf,pɜːtʃ) *n* any viviparous marine percoid fish of the family *Embiotocidae,* of North American Pacific coastal waters. Also called: **sea perch.**

surf scoter *or* **duck** *n* a North American scoter, *Melanitta perspicillata,* having white patches on the head.

surg. *abbrev. for:* **1** surgeon. **2** surgery. **3** surgical.

surge (sɜːdʒ) *n* **1** a strong rush or sweep; sudden increase: *a surge of anger.* **2** the rolling swell of the sea, esp. after the passage of a large wave. **3** a heavy rolling motion or sound: *the surge of the trumpets.* **4** an undulating rolling surface, as of hills. **5** a billowing cloud or volume. **6** *Nautical.* a temporary release or slackening of a rope or cable. **7** a large momentary increase in the voltage or current in an electric circuit. **8** an instability or unevenness in the power output of an engine. **9** *Astronomy.* a short-lived disturbance, occurring during the eruption of a solar flare. ◆ *vb* **10** (*intr*) (of waves, the sea, etc.) to rise or roll with a heavy swelling motion. **11** (*intr*) to move like a heavy sea. **12** *Nautical.* to slacken or temporarily release (a rope or cable) from a capstan or (of a rope, etc.) to be slackened or released and slip back. **13** (*intr*) (of an electric current or voltage) to undergo a large momentary increase. **14** (*tr*) *Rare.* to cause to move in or as if in a wave or waves. **[C15:** from Latin *surgere* to rise, from *sub-* up + *regere* to lead**]** ▸ **'surgeless** *adj* ▸ **'surger** *n*

surgeon ('sɜːdʒən) *n* **1** a medical practioner who specializes in surgery. **2** a medical officer in the Royal Navy. **[C14:** from Anglo-Norman *surgien,* from Old French *cirurgien;* see SURGERY**]**

surgeoncy ('sɜːdʒənsɪ) *n, pl* **-cies.** *Chiefly Brit.* the office, duties, or position of a surgeon, esp. in the army or navy.

surgeonfish ('sɜːdʒən,fɪʃ) *n, pl* **-fish** *or* **-fishes.** any tropical marine spiny-finned fish of the family *Acanthuridae,* having a compressed brightly coloured body with one or more knifelike spines at the base of the tail.

surgeon general *n, pl* **surgeons general. 1** (in the British, U.S., and certain other armies and navies) the senior officer of the medical service. **2** the head of the public health service in the U.S.

surgeon's knot *n* a knot used by surgeons in tying ligatures, etc.

surgery ('sɜːdʒərɪ) *n, pl* **-geries. 1** the branch of medicine concerned with treating disease, injuries, etc., by means of manual or operative procedures, esp. by incision into the body. **2** the performance of such procedures by a surgeon. **3** *Brit.* a place where a doctor, dentist, etc., can be consulted. **4** *Brit.* an occasion when an MP, lawyer, etc., is available for consultation. **5** *U.S. and Canadian.* an operating theatre where surgical operations are performed. **[C14:** via Old French from Latin *chirurgia,* from Greek *kheirurgia,* from *kheir* hand + *ergon* work**]**

surge tank *n Engineering.* a tank used to absorb surges in flow.

surgical ('sɜːdʒɪkᵊl) *adj* of, relating to, involving, or used in surgery. ▸ **'surgically** *adv*

surgical boot *n* a specially designed boot or shoe that compensates for deformities of the foot or leg.

surgical spirit *n* methylated spirit containing small amounts of oil of wintergreen and castor oil: used medically for sterilizing.

Suribachi (,sʊərɪ'bɑːtʃɪ) *n* **Mount.** a volcanic hill in the Volcano Islands, on Iwo Jima: site of a U.S. victory (1945) over the Japanese in World War II.

suricate ('sjʊərɪ,keɪt) *n* another name for **slender-tailed meerkat** (see **meerkat**). **[C18:** from French *surikate,* probably from a native South African word**]**

Surinam (,sʊərɪ'næm) *n* a republic in NE South America, on the Atlantic: became a self-governing part of the Netherlands in 1954 and fully independent in 1975. Official languages: Dutch; English is also widely spoken. Religion: Hindu, Christian, and Muslim. Currency: guilder. Capital: Paramaribo. Pop.: 418 000 (1998 est.). Area: 163 820 sq. km (63 251 sq. miles). Former names: **Dutch Guiana, Netherlands Guiana.**

Surinam toad *n* another name for **pipa.**

surjection (sɜː'dʒɛkʃən) *n* a mathematical function or mapping for which every element of the image space is a value for some members of the domain. See also **injection** (sense 5), **bijection. [C20:** from SUR-[1] + *-jection,* on the model of PROJECTION**]** ▸ **sur'jective** *adj*

surly ('sɜːlɪ) *adj* **-lier, -liest. 1** sullenly ill-tempered or rude. **2** (of an animal) ill-tempered or refractory. **3** dismal. **4** *Obsolete.* arrogant. **[C16:** from obsolete *sirly* haughty; see SIR**]** ▸ **'surlily** *adv* ▸ **'surliness** *n*

surmise *vb* (sɜː'maɪz). **1** (when *tr, may take a clause as object*) to infer (something) from incomplete or uncertain evidence. ◆ *n* (sɜː'maɪz, 'sɜːmaɪz). **2** an idea inferred from inconclusive evidence. **[C15:** from Old French, from *surmettre* to accuse, from Latin *supermittere* to throw over, from SUPER- + *mittere* to send**]** ▸ **sur'misable** *adj* ▸ **sur'miser** *n*

surmount (sɜː'maʊnt) *vb* (*tr*) **1** to prevail over; overcome: *to surmount tremendous difficulties.* **2** to ascend and cross to the opposite side of. **3** to lie on top of or rise above. **4** to put something on top of or above. **5** *Obsolete.* to surpass or exceed. **[C14:** from Old French *surmonter,* from SUR-[1] + *monter* to MOUNT[1]**]** ▸ **sur'mountable** *adj* ▸ **sur'mountableness** *n* ▸ **sur'mounter** *n*

surmullet (sɜː'mʌlɪt) *n* a U.S. name for the **red mullet. [C17:** from French *sormulet,* from *sor* brown + MULLET**]**

surname ('sɜː,neɪm) *n* **1** Also called: **last name, second name.** a family name as opposed to a first or Christian name. **2** (formerly) a descriptive epithet attached to a person's name to denote a personal characteristic, profession, etc.; nickname. ◆ *vb* **3** (*tr*) to furnish with or call by a surname. **[C14:** via Anglo-French from Old French *surnom.* See SUR-[1], NAME**]** ▸ **'sur,namer** *n*

surpass (sɜː'pɑːs) *vb* (*tr*) **1** to be greater than in degree, extent, etc. **2** to be superior to in achievement or excellence. **3** to overstep the limit or range of: *the theory surpasses my comprehension.* **[C16:** from French *surpasser,* from SUR-[1] + *passer* to PASS**]** ▸ **sur'passable** *adj*

surpassing (sɜː'pɑːsɪŋ) *adj* **1** exceptional; extraordinary. ◆ *adv* **2** *Obsolete or poetic.* (intensifier): *surpassing fair.* ▸ **sur'passingly** *adv*

surplice ('sɜːplɪs) *n* a loose wide-sleeved liturgical vestment of linen, reaching to the knees, worn over the cassock by clergymen, choristers, and acolytes. **[C13:** via Anglo-French from Old French *sourpelis,* from Medieval Latin *superpellīcium,* from SUPER- + *pellīcium* coat made of skins, from Latin *pellis* a skin**]** ▸ **'surpliced** *adj*

surplus ('sɜːpləs) *n, pl* **-pluses. 1** a quantity or amount in excess of what is required. **2** *Accounting.* **2a** an excess of total assets over total liabilities. **2b** an excess of actual net assets over the nominal value of capital stock. **2c** an excess of revenues over expenditures during a certain period of time. **3** *Economics.* **3a** an excess of government revenues over expenditures during a certain financial year. **3b** an excess of receipts over payments on the balance of payments. ◆ *adj* **4** being in excess; extra. **[C14:** from Old French, from Medieval Latin *superplūs,* from Latin SUPER- + *plūs* more**]**

surplusage ('sɜːpləsɪdʒ) *n* **1** *Law.* (in pleading, etc.) irrelevant matter, such as a superfluous allegation. **2** an excess of words. **3** a less common word for **surplus.**

surprint ('sɜː,prɪnt) *vb* **1** (*tr*) to print (additional matter) over something already printed; overprint. ◆ *n* **2** marks, printed matter, etc., that have been surprinted.

surprise (sə'praɪz) *vb* (*tr*) **1** to cause to feel amazement or wonder. **2** to encounter or discover unexpectedly or suddenly. **3** to capture or assault suddenly and without warning. **4** to present with something unexpected, such as a gift. **5** (foll. by *into*) to provoke (someone) to unintended action by a trick, etc.: *to surprise a person into an indiscretion.* **6** (often foll. by *from*) to elicit by unexpected behaviour or by a trick: *to surprise information from a prisoner.* ◆ *n* **7** the act or an instance of surprising; the act of taking unawares. **8** a sudden or unexpected event, gift, etc. **9** the feeling or condition of being surprised; astonishment. **10** (*modifier*) causing, characterized by, or relying upon surprise: *a surprise move.* **11 take by surprise. 11a** to come upon suddenly and without warning. **11b** to capture unexpectedly or catch unprepared. **11c** to astonish; amaze. **[C15:** from Old French, from *surprendre* to overtake, from SUR-[1] + *prendre* from Latin *prehendere* to grasp; see PREHENSILE**]** ▸ **sur'prisal** *n* ▸ **sur'prised** *adj* ▸ **surprisedly** (sə'praɪzɪdlɪ) *adv* ▸ **sur'priser** *n*

surprising (sə'praɪzɪŋ) *adj* causing surprise; unexpected or amazing. ▸ **sur'prisingly** *adv* ▸ **sur'prisingness** *n*

surra ('sʊərə) *n* a tropical febrile disease of cattle, horses, camels, and dogs, characterized by severe emaciation: caused by the protozoan *Trypanosoma evansi* and transmitted by fleas. **[**from Marathi**]**

surreal (sə'rɪəl) *adj* **1** suggestive of surrealism; dreamlike. ◆ *n* **2 the.** the atmosphere or qualities evoked by surrealism.

surrealism (sə'rɪə,lɪzəm) *n* (*sometimes cap.*) a movement in art and literature in the 1920s, which developed esp. from dada, characterized by the evocative juxtaposition of incongruous images in order to include unconscious and dream elements. **[C20:** from French *surréalisme,* from SUR-[1] + *réalisme* REALISM**]** ▸ **sur'realist** *n, adj* ▸ **sur,real'istic** *adj* ▸ **sur,real'istically** *adv*

surrebuttal (,sɜːrɪ'bʌtᵊl) *n Law.* (in pleading) the giving of evidence in support of a surrebutter.

surrebutter (,sɜːrɪ'bʌtə) *n Law.* (in pleading) the plaintiff's reply to the defendant's rebutter.

surrejoinder (,sɜːrɪ'dʒɔɪndə) *n Law.* (in pleading) the plaintiff's reply to the defendant's rejoinder.

surrender (sə'rɛndə) *vb* **1** (*tr*) to relinquish to the control or possession of another under duress or on demand: *to surrender a city.* **2** (*tr*) to relinquish or forego (an office, position, etc.), esp. as a voluntary concession to another: *he surrendered his place to a lady.* **3** to give (oneself) up physically, as or as if to an enemy. **4** to allow (oneself) to yield, as to a temptation, influence, etc. **5** (*tr*) to give up (hope, etc.) **6** (*tr*) *Law.* to give up or restore (an estate), esp. to give up a lease before expiration of the term. **7** (*tr*) *Obsolete.* to return or render (thanks, etc.). **8 surrender to bail.** to present oneself at court at the appointed time after having been on bail. ◆ *n* **9** the act or instance of surrendering. **10** *Insurance.* the voluntary discontinuation of a life policy by its holder in return for a consideration (the **surrender value**). **11** *Law.* **11a** the yielding up or restoring of an estate, esp. the giving up of a lease before its term has expired. **11b** the giving up to the appropriate authority of a fugitive from justice. **11c** the act of surrendering or being surrendered to bail. **11d** the deed by which a legal surrender is effected. **[C15:** from Old French *surrendre* to yield, from SUR-[1] + *rendre* to RENDER**]** ▸ **sur'renderer** *n*

surreptitious (,sʌrəp'tɪʃəs) *adj* **1** done, acquired, etc., in secret or by improper means. **2** operating by stealth. **3** characterized by fraud or misrepresentation of the truth. **[C15:** from Latin *surreptīcius* furtive, from *surripere* to steal, from *sub-* secretly + *rapere* to snatch**]** ▸ **,surrep'titiously** *adv* ▸ **,surrep'titiousness** *n*

surrey ('sʌrɪ) *n* a light four-wheeled horse-drawn carriage having two or four seats. **[C19:** shortened from *Surrey cart,* after SURREY[1], where it was originally made**]**

Surrey[1] ('sʌrɪ) *n* a county of SE England, on the River Thames: urban in the northeast; crossed from east to west by the North Downs and drained by tributaries of the Thames. Administrative centre: Kingston upon Thames. Pop.: 1 041 200 (1994 est.). Area: 1679 sq. km (648 sq. miles).

Surrey[2] ('sʌrɪ) *n* **Earl of,** title of *Henry Howard.* ?1517–47, English courtier and poet; one of the first in England to write sonnets. He was beheaded for high treason.

surrogate *n* ('sʌrəgɪt). **1** a person or thing acting as a substitute. **2** *Chiefly Brit.* a deputy, such as a clergyman appointed to deputize for a bishop in granting marriage licences. **3** *Psychiatry.* a person who is a substitute for someone else, esp. in childhood when different persons, such as a brother or teacher, can act as substitutes for the parents. **4** (in some U.S. states) a judge with jurisdiction over the probate of wills, etc. **5** (*modifier*) of, relating to, or acting as a surrogate: *a surrogate pleasure.* ◆ *vb* ('sʌrəˌgeɪt). (*tr*) **6** to put in another's position as a deputy, substitute, etc. **7** to appoint as a successor to oneself. [C17: from Latin *surrogāre* to substitute; see SUBROGATE] ▸ **'surrogateship** *n* ▸ **ˌsurro'gation** *n*

surrogate mother *n* a woman who bears a child on behalf of a couple unable to have a child, either by artificial insemination from the man or implantation of an embryo from the woman. ▸ **surrogacy** ('sʌrəgəsɪ) *n*

surround (sə'raʊnd) *vb* (*tr*) **1** to encircle or enclose or cause to be encircled or enclosed. **2** to deploy forces on all sides of (a place or military formation), so preventing access or retreat. **3** to exist around: *I dislike the people who surround her.* ◆ *n* **4** *Chiefly Brit.* a border, esp. the area of uncovered floor between the walls of a room and the carpet or around an opening or panel. **5** *Chiefly U.S.* **5a** a method of capturing wild beasts by encircling the area in which they are believed to be. **5b** the area so encircled. [C15 *surrounden* to overflow, from Old French *suronder,* from Late Latin *superundāre,* from Latin SUPER- + *undāre* to abound, from *unda* a wave] ▸ **sur'rounding** *adj*

surroundings (sə'raʊndɪŋz) *pl n* the conditions, scenery, etc., around a person, place, or thing; environment.

surround sound *n* a system of sound recording and reproduction that uses three or more independent recording channels and loudspeakers in order to give the impression that the listener is surrounded by the sound sources. Compare **quadraphonics.** See also **ambisonics.**

sursum corda ('sɜːsəm 'kɔːdə) *n* **1** *R.C. Church.* a Latin versicle meaning *Lift up your hearts,* said by the priest at Mass. **2** a cry of exhortation, hope, etc. [C16: Latin, literally: up hearts]

surtax ('sɜːˌtæks) *n* **1** a tax, usually highly progressive, levied on the amount by which a person's income exceeds a specific level. **2** an additional tax on something that has already been taxed. ◆ *vb* **3** (*tr*) to assess for liability to surtax; charge with an extra tax.

Surtees ('sɜːtiːz) *n* **1 John.** born 1934, British racing motorcyclist and motor-racing driver. He was motorcycling world champion (1956, 1958–60) and world champion motor-racing driver (1964), the only man to have been world champion in both sports. **2 Robert Smith.** 1803–64, British journalist and novelist, who satirized the sporting life of the English gentry in such works as *Jorrocks's Jaunts and Jollities* (1838).

surtitles ('sɜːˌtaɪtᵊlz) *pl n* brief translations of the text of an opera that is being sung in a foreign language, projected above the stage.

surtout ('sɜːtuː; *French* syrtu) *n* a man's overcoat resembling a frock coat, popular in the late 19th century. [C17: from French, from *sur* over + *tout* all]

surv. *abbrev. for:* **1** Also: **survey.** surveying. **2** surveyor.

surveillance (sɜː'veɪləns) *n* close observation or supervision maintained over a person, group, etc., esp. one in custody or under suspicion. [C19: from French, from *surveiller* to watch over, from SUR-[1] + *veiller* to keep watch (from Latin *vigilāre;* see VIGIL)] ▸ **sur'veillant** *adj, n*

survey *vb* (sɜː'veɪ, 'sɜːveɪ). **1** (*tr*) to view or consider in a comprehensive or general way: *to survey the situation.* **2** (*tr*) to examine carefully, as or as if to appraise value: *to survey oneself in a mirror.* **3** to plot a detailed map of (an area of land) by measuring or calculating distances and height. **4** *Brit.* to inspect a building to determine its condition and value. **5** to examine a vessel thoroughly in order to determine its seaworthiness. **6** (*tr*) to run a statistical survey on (incomes, opinions, etc.). ◆ *n* ('sɜːveɪ). **7** a comprehensive or general view: *a survey of English literature.* **8** a critical, detailed, and formal inspection: *a survey of the nation's hospitals.* **9** *Brit.* an inspection of a building to determine its condition and value. **10** a report incorporating the results of such an inspection. **11a** a body of surveyors. **11b** an area surveyed. **12** *Statistics.* a random sample. [C15: from French *surveoir,* from SUR-[1] + *veoir* to see, from Latin *vidēre*] ▸ **sur'veyable** *adj*

surveying (sɜː'veɪɪŋ) *n* **1** the study or practice of measuring altitudes, angles, and distances on the land surface so that they can be accurately plotted on a map. **2** the setting out on the ground of the positions of proposed construction or engineering works.

surveyor (sɜː'veɪə) *n* **1** a person whose occupation is to survey land or buildings. See also **quantity surveyor. 2** *Chiefly Brit.* a person concerned with the official inspection of something for purposes of measurement and valuation. **3** a person who carries out surveys, esp. of ships (**marine surveyor**) to determine seaworthiness, etc. **4** a customs official. **5** *Archaic.* a supervisor. ▸ **sur'veyorˌship** *n*

surveyor's chain *n* a measuring chain 22 yards in length; Gunter's chain. See **chain** (sense 7).

surveyor's level *n* another term for **level** (sense 19).

surveyor's measure *n* the system of measurement based on the chain (66 feet) as a unit.

survival (sə'vaɪvᵊl) *n* **1** a person or thing that survives, such as a custom. **2a** the act or fact of surviving or condition of having survived. **2b** (*as modifier*): *survival kit.*

survival bag *n* a large plastic bag carried by climbers for use in an emergency as protection against exposure.

survivalist (sə'vaɪvəlɪst) *n U.S.* **a** a person who believes in ensuring his personal survival of a catastrophic event by arming himself and often by living in the wild. **b** (*as modifier*): *survivalist weapons.* ▸ **sur'vivalˌism** *n*

survival of the fittest *n* a popular term for **natural selection.**

survive (sə'vaɪv) *vb* **1** (*tr*) to live after the death of (another): *he survived his wife by 12 years.* **2** to continue in existence or use after (a passage of time, an adversity, etc.). **3** *Informal.* to endure (something): *I don't know how I survive such an awful job.* [C15: from Old French *sourvivre,* from Latin *supervīvere,* from SUPER- + *vīvere* to live] ▸ **sur'vivable** *adj* ▸ **surˌviva'bility** *n*

survivor (sə'vaɪvə) *n* **1** a person or thing that survives. **2** *Property law.* one of two or more specified persons having joint interests in property who lives longer than the other or others and thereby becomes entitled to the whole property. ▸ **sur'vivorˌship** *n*

sus (sʌs) *Brit. slang.* ◆ *n* **1** suspicion. **2** a suspect. ◆ *adj* **3** suspicious. ◆ *vb* **4** a variant spelling of **suss** (sense 2). ◆ See also **sus laws.** [C20: shortened from SUSPICION]

Susa ('suːsə) *n* an ancient city north of the Persian Gulf: capital of Elam and of the Persian Empire; flourished as a Greek polis under the Seleucids and Parthians. Biblical name: **Shushan.**

Susah *or* **Susa** ('suːzə) *n* other names for **Sousse.**

Susanna (suː'zænə) *n Apocrypha.* **1** the wife of Joachim, who was condemned to death for adultery because of a false accusation, but saved by Daniel's sagacity. **2** the book of the Apocrypha containing this story.

susceptance (sə'sɛptəns) *n Physics.* the imaginary component of the admittance. [C19: from SUSCEPT(IBILITY) + -ANCE]

susceptibility (səˌsɛptə'bɪlɪtɪ) *n, pl* **-ties. 1** the quality or condition of being susceptible. **2** the ability or tendency to be impressed by emotional feelings; sensitivity. **3** (*pl*) emotional sensibilities; feelings. **4** *Physics.* **4a** Also called: **electric susceptibility.** (of a dielectric) the amount by which the relative permittivity differs from unity. Symbol: X **4b** Also called: **magnetic susceptibility.** (of a magnetic medium) the amount by which the relative permeability differs from unity. Symbol: K

susceptible (sə'sɛptəbᵊl) *adj* **1** (*postpositive;* foll. by *of* or *to*) yielding readily (to); capable (of): *hypotheses susceptible of refutation; susceptible to control.* **2** (*postpositive;* foll. by *to*) liable to be afflicted (by): *susceptible to colds.* **3** easily impressed emotionally. [C17: from Late Latin *susceptibilis,* from Latin *suscipere* to take up, from SUB- + *capere* to take] ▸ **sus'ceptibleness** *n* ▸ **sus'ceptibly** *adv*

susceptive (sə'sɛptɪv) *adj* **1** another word for **receptive. 2** a variant of **susceptible.** ▸ susceptivity (ˌsʌsɛp'tɪvɪtɪ) *or* **sus'ceptiveness** *n*

sushi ('suːʃɪ) *n* a Japanese dish consisting of small cakes of cold rice with a topping esp. of raw fish. [from Japanese]

Susian ('suːzɪən) *n, adj* another word for **Elamite.** [C16: from *Susiana,* a province of the ancient Persian Empire with its capital at SUSA]

sus laws *or* **suss laws** *pl n Brit. slang* laws authorizing the arrest and punishment of suspected persons frequenting, or loitering in, public places with criminal intent. In England, the sus law formed part of the Vagrancy Act of 1824, repealed in 1981.

suslik ('sʌslɪk) *or* **souslik** *n* a central Eurasian ground squirrel, *Citellus citellus,* of dry open areas, having large eyes and small ears. [from Russian]

suspect *vb* (sə'spɛkt). **1** (*tr*) to believe guilty of a specified offence without proof. **2** (*tr*) to think false, questionable, etc.: *she suspected his sincerity.* **3** (*tr; may take a clause as object*) to surmise to be the case; think probable: *to suspect fraud.* **4** (*intr*) to have suspicion. ◆ *n* ('sʌspɛkt). **5** a person who is under suspicion. ◆ *adj* ('sʌspɛkt). **6** causing or open to suspicion. [C14: from Latin *suspicere* to mistrust, from SUB- + *specere* to look] ▸ **sus'pecter** *n* ▸ **'suspectless** *adj*

suspend (sə'spɛnd) *vb* **1** (*tr*) to hang from above so as to permit free movement. **2** (*tr; passive*) to cause to remain floating or hanging: *a cloud of smoke was suspended over the town.* **3** (*tr*) to render inoperative or cause to cease, esp. temporarily: *to suspend interest payments.* **4** (*tr*) to hold in abeyance; postpone action on: *to suspend a decision.* **5** (*tr*) to debar temporarily from privilege, office, etc., as a punishment. **6** (*tr*) *Chem.* to cause (particles) to be held in suspension in a fluid. **7** (*tr*) *Music.* to continue (a note) until the next chord is sounded, with which it usually forms a dissonance. See **suspension** (sense 11). **8** (*intr*) to cease payment, as from incapacity to meet financial obligations. **9** (*tr*) *Obsolete.* to put or keep in a state of anxiety or wonder. **10** (*intr*) *Obsolete.* to be attached from above. [C13: from Latin *suspendere* from SUB- + *pendere* to hang] ▸ **sus'pendible** *or* **sus'pensible** *adj* ▸ **susˌpendi'bility** *n*

suspended animation *n* a temporary cessation of the vital functions, as by freezing an organism.

suspended sentence *n* a sentence of imprisonment that is not served by an offender unless he commits a further offence during its currency. Compare **deferred sentence.**

suspender (sə'spɛndə) *n* **1** (*often pl*) *Brit.* **1a** an elastic strap attached to a belt or corset having a fastener at the end, for holding up women's stockings. **1b** a similar fastener attached to a garter worn by men in order to support socks. U.S. and Canadian equivalent: **garter. 2** (*pl*) the U.S. and Canadian name for **braces. 3** a person or thing that suspends, such as one of the vertical cables in a suspension bridge.

suspender belt *n* a belt with suspenders hanging from it to hold up women's stockings. U.S. and Canadian name: **garter belt.**

suspense (sə'spɛns) *n* **1** the condition of being insecure or uncertain: *the matter of the succession remained in suspense for many years.* **2** mental uncertainty; anxiety: *their father's illness kept them in a state of suspense.* **3** excitement felt at the approach of the climax: *a play of terrifying suspense.* **4** the condition of being suspended. [C15: from Medieval Latin *suspensum* delay, from Latin *suspendere* to hang up; see SUSPEND] ▸ **sus'penseful** *adj*

suspense account *n Book-keeping.* an account in which entries are made until determination of their proper disposition.

suspension (sə'spɛnʃən) *n* **1** an interruption or temporary revocation: *the suspension of a law.* **2** a temporary debarment, as from position, privilege, etc. **3** a deferment, esp. of a decision, judgment, etc. **4** *Law.* **4a** a postponement of execution of a sentence or the deferring of a judgment, etc. **4b** a temporary extinguishment of a right or title. **5** cessation of payment of business debts, esp. as a result of insolvency. **6** the act of suspending or the state of being suspended. **7** a system of springs, shock absorbers, etc., that supports the body of a wheeled or tracked vehicle and insulates it and its occupants from shocks transmitted by the wheels. See also **hydraulic suspension. 8** a device or structure, usually a wire or spring, that serves to suspend or support something, such as the pendulum of a clock. **9** *Chem.* a dispersion of fine solid or liquid particles in a fluid, the particles being supported by buoyancy. See also **colloid. 10** the process by which eroded particles of rock are transported in a river. **11** *Music.* one or more notes of a chord that are prolonged until a subsequent chord is sounded, usually to form a dissonance.

suspension bridge *n* a bridge that has a deck suspended by cables or rods from other cables or chains that hang between two towers and are anchored at both ends.

suspension point *n Chiefly U.S.* one of a group of dots, usually three, used in written material to indicate the omission of a word or words. Compare **ellipsis** (sense 2).

suspensive (sə'spensɪv) *adj* **1** having the power of deferment; effecting suspension. **2** causing, characterized by, or relating to suspense. **3** inclined to defer judgment; undecided. ▸ **sus'pensively** *adv* ▸ **sus'pensiveness** *n*

suspensoid (sə'spensɔɪd) *n Chem.* a system consisting of a suspension of solid particles in a liquid.

suspensor (sə'spensə) *n* **1** another name for **suspensory** (sense 1). **2** *Botany.* (in a seed) a row of cells attached to the embryo plant, by means of which it is pushed into the endosperm.

suspensory (sə'spensərɪ) *n, pl* **-ries. 1** Also called: **suspensor.** *Anatomy.* a ligament or muscle that holds a structure or part in position. **2** *Med.* a bandage, sling, etc., for supporting a dependent part. **3** another name (esp. U.S.) for **athletic support.** ♦ *adj* **4** suspending or supporting. **5** *Anatomy.* (of a ligament or muscle) supporting or holding a structure or part in position.

suspicion (sə'spɪʃən) *n* **1** the act or an instance of suspecting; belief without sure proof, esp. that something is wrong. **2** the feeling of mistrust of a person who suspects. **3** the state of being suspected: *to be shielded from suspicion.* **4** a slight trace. **5 above suspicion.** in such a position that no guilt may be thought or implied, esp. through having an unblemished reputation. **6 on suspicion.** as a suspect. **7 under suspicion.** regarded with distrust. [C14: from Old French *sospeçon,* from Latin *suspīciō* distrust, from *suspicere* to mistrust; see SUSPECT] ▸ **sus'picional** *adj* ▸ **sus'picionless** *adj*

suspicious (sə'spɪʃəs) *adj* **1** exciting or liable to excite suspicion; questionable. **2** disposed to suspect something wrong. **3** indicative or expressive of suspicion. ▸ **sus'piciously** *adv* ▸ **sus'piciousness** *n*

suspire (sə'spaɪə) *vb Archaic or poetic.* **1** to sigh or utter with a sigh; yearn. **2** (*intr*) to breathe; respire. [C15: from Latin *suspīrāre* to take a deep breath, from SUB- + *spīrāre* to breathe] ▸ **suspiration** (ˌsʌspɪ'reɪʃən) *n*

Susquehanna (ˌsʌskwɪ'hænə) *n* a river in the eastern U.S., rising in Otsego Lake and flowing generally south to Chesapeake Bay at Havre de Grace: the longest river in the eastern U.S. Length: 714 km (444 miles).

suss (sʌs) *vb (tr) Slang.* **1** (often foll. by *out*) to attempt to work out (a situation, person's character, etc.), esp. using one's intuition. **2** Also: **sus.** to become aware of; suspect (esp. in the phrase **suss it**). ♦ *n* **3** sharpness of mind; social astuteness. ♦ See also **sus laws.** [C20: shortened from SUSPECT]

Sussex ('sʌsɪks) *n* **1** (until 1974) a county of SE England, now divided into the separate counties of East Sussex and West Sussex. **2** (in Anglo-Saxon England) the kingdom of the South Saxons, which became a shire of the kingdom of Wessex in the early 9th century A.D. **3** a breed of red beef cattle originally from Sussex. **4** a heavy and long-established breed of domestic fowl used principally as a table bird.

Sussex spaniel *n* a short-legged breed of spaniel with a golden-liver coloured coat. [so named because it was bred in Sussex, in the late 18th century]

sustain (sə'steɪn) *vb (tr)* **1** to hold up under; withstand: *to sustain great provocation.* **2** to undergo (an injury, loss, etc.); suffer: *to sustain a broken arm.* **3** to maintain or prolong: *to sustain a discussion.* **4** to support physically from below. **5** to provide for or give support to, esp. by supplying necessities: *to sustain one's family; to sustain a charity.* **6** to keep up the vitality or courage of. **7** to uphold or affirm the justice or validity of: *to sustain a decision.* **8** to establish the truth of; confirm. ♦ *n* **9** *Music.* the prolongation of a note, by playing technique or electronics. [C13: via Old French from Latin *sustinēre* to hold up, from SUB- + *tenēre* to hold] ▸ **sus'tained** *adj* ▸ **sustainedly** (sə'steɪnɪdlɪ) *adv* ▸ **sus'taining** *adj* ▸ **sus'tainingly** *adv* ▸ **sus'tainment** *n*

sustainable (sə'steɪnəb°l) *adj* **1** capable of being sustained. **2** (of economic development, energy sources, etc.) capable of being maintained at a steady level without exhausting natural resources or causing severe ecological damage: *sustainable development.* **3** (of economic growth) non-inflationary.

sustainer (sə'steɪnə) *n* a rocket engine that maintains the velocity of a space vehicle after the booster has been jettisoned.

sustaining pedal *n Music.* a foot-operated lever on a piano, usually the right one of two, that keeps the dampers raised from the strings when keys are released, allowing them to continue to vibrate. Compare **soft pedal.**

sustaining program *n U.S. and Canadian.* a television or radio programme promoted by the broadcasting network or station itself and not by a commercial sponsor.

sustenance ('sʌstənəns) *n* **1** means of sustaining health or life; nourishment. **2** means of maintenance; livelihood. **3** Also: **sustention** (sə'stenʃən). the act or process of sustaining or the quality of being sustained. [C13: from Old French *sostenance,* from *sustenir* to SUSTAIN]

sustentacular (ˌsʌsten'tækjʊlə) *adj Anatomy.* (of fibres, cells, etc.) supporting or forming a support. [C19: from Latin *sustentāculum* a stay, from *sustentāre* to support, from *sustinēre* to SUSTAIN]

sustentation (ˌsʌsten'teɪʃən) *n* a less common word for **sustenance.** [C14: from Latin *sustentātio,* from *sustentāre,* frequentative of *sustinēre* to SUSTAIN]

sustentation fund *n* a fund, esp. in the Church of Scotland, to augment the support of ministers.

susu ('su:su:) *n* a variant form of **sou-sou.**

Susu ('su:su:) *n* **1** (*pl* **-su** *or* **-sus**) a member of a Negroid people of W Africa, living chiefly in Guinea, the Sudan, and Sierra Leone. **2** the language of this people, belonging to the Mande branch of the Niger-Congo family.

susurrate ('sju:səˌreɪt) *vb (intr) Literary.* to make a soft rustling sound; whisper; murmur. [C17: from Latin *susurrāre* to whisper] ▸ **susurrant** (sju:'sʌrənt) *adj* ▸ **ˌsusur'ration** *or* **'susurrus** *n*

Sutcliffe ('sʌtˌklɪf) *n* **Herbert.** 1894–1978, English cricketer, who played for Yorkshire; scorer of 149 centuries and 1000 runs in a season 24 times.

Suth. *abbrev. for* Sutherland.

Sutherland[1] ('sʌðələnd) *n* (until 1975) a county of N Scotland, now part of Highland.

Sutherland[2] ('sʌðələnd) *n* **1 Graham.** 1903–80, English artist, noted for his work as an official war artist (1941–44), for his tapestry *Christ in Majesty* (1962) in Coventry Cathedral, and for his portraits. **2** Dame **Joan,** known as *La Stupenda.* born 1926, Australian operatic soprano.

Sutherland Falls *n* a waterfall in New Zealand, on SW South Island. Height: 580 m (1904 ft.).

Sutlej ('sʌtlɪdʒ) *n* a river in S Asia, rising in SW Tibet and flowing west through the Himalayas: crosses Himachal Pradesh and the Punjab (India), enters Pakistan, and joins the Chenab west of Bahawalpur: the longest of the five rivers of the Punjab. Length: 1368 km (850 miles).

sutler ('sʌtlə) *n* (formerly) a merchant who accompanied an army in order to sell provisions to the soldiers. [C16: from obsolete Dutch *soeteler,* from Middle Low German *suteler,* from Middle High German *sudelen* to do dirty work; related to SOOT, SEETHE] ▸ **'sutlerˌship** *n*

sutra ('su:trə) *n* **1** *Hinduism.* Sanskrit sayings or collections of sayings on Vedic doctrine dating from about 200 A.D. onwards. **2** (*modifier*) *Hinduism.* **2a** of or relating to the last of the Vedic literary periods, from about 500 to 100 B.C.: *the sutra period.* **2b** of or relating to the sutras or compilations of sutras of about 200 A.D. onwards. **3** *Buddhism.* collections of dialogues and discourses of classic Mahayana Buddhism dating from the 2nd to the 6th centuries A.D. [C19: from Sanskrit: list of rules]

suttee (sʌ'ti:, 'sʌti:) *n* **1** the former Hindu custom whereby a widow burnt herself to death on her husband's funeral pyre. **2** a Hindu widow who immolated herself in this way. [C18: from Sanskrit *satī* virtuous woman, from *sat* good] ▸ **sut'teeism** *n*

Sutton ('sʌt°n) *n* a borough of S Greater London. Pop.: 173 400 (1994 est.). Area: 43 sq. km (17 sq. miles).

Sutton Coldfield (-'kəʊldˌfi:ld) *n* a town in central England, in Birmingham unitary authority, West Midlands; a residential suburb of Birmingham. Pop.: 106 001 (1991).

Sutton Hoo (hu:) *n* a 7th-century site in Suffolk where a Saxon long boat containing rich grave goods, probably for an East Anglian king, was found in 1939.

Sutton-in-Ashfield (-'æʃˌfi:ld) *n* a market town in N central England, in W Nottinghamshire. Pop.: 37 890 (1991).

suture ('su:tʃə) *n* **1** *Surgery.* **1a** catgut, silk thread, or wire used to stitch together two bodily surfaces. **1b** the surgical seam formed after joining two surfaces. **2** *Anatomy.* a type of immovable joint, esp. between the bones of the skull (**cranial suture**). **3** a seam or joining, as in sewing. **4** *Zoology.* a line of junction in a mollusc shell, esp. the line between adjacent chambers of a nautiloid shell. **5** *Botany.* a line marking the point of dehiscence in a seed pod or capsule. ♦ *vb* **6** (*tr*) *Surgery.* to join (the edges of a wound, etc.) by means of sutures. [C16: from Latin *sūtūra,* from *suere* to SEW] ▸ **'sutural** *adj* ▸ **'suturally** *adv*

Suu Kyi *n* See **Aung San Suu Kyi.**

Suva ('su:və) *n* the capital and chief port of Fiji, on the SE coast of Viti Levu; popular tourist resort; University of the South Pacific (1968). Pop.: 167 421 (1996).

Suvorov (*Russian* su'vɔrəf) *n* **Aleksandr Vasilyevich** (alɪk'sandr va'siljɪvitʃ). 1729–1800, Russian field marshal, who fought successfully against the Turks (1787–91), the Poles (1794), and the French in Italy (1798–99).

Suwannee (sʊ'wɒnɪ) *or* **Swanee** *n* a river in the southeastern U.S., rising in SE Georgia and flowing across Florida to the Gulf of Mexico at **Suwannee Sound.** Length: about 400 km (250 miles).

suzerain ('su:zəˌreɪn) *n* **1a** a state or sovereign exercising some degree of dominion over a dependent state, usually controlling its foreign affairs. **1b** (*as modifier*): *a suzerain power.* **2a** a feudal overlord. **2b** (*as modifier*): *suzerain lord.* [C19: from French, from *sus* above (from Latin *sursum* turned upwards, from *sub-* up + *vertere* to turn) + *-erain,* as in *souverain* SOVEREIGN]

suzerainty ('su:zərəntɪ) *n, pl* **-ties. 1** the position, power, or dignity of a suzerain. **2** the relationship between suzerain and subject.

Suzhou ('su:'dʒəʊ), **Su-chou,** *or* **Soochow** *n* a city in E China, in S Jiangsu on the Grand Canal: noted for its gardens; produces chiefly silk. Pop.: 706 459 (1990 est.). Also called: **Wuhsien.**

sv *abbrev. for:* **1** sailing vessel. **2** side valve. **3** sub verbo *or* voce. [Latin: under the word *or* voice]

SV *abbrev. for:* **1** Sancta Virgo. [Latin: Holy Virgin] **2** Sanctitas Vestra. [Latin: Your Holiness]

Svalbard (*Norwegian* 'sva:lbar) *n* a Norwegian archipelago in the Arctic Ocean, about 650 km (400 miles) north of Norway: consists of the main group (Spitsbergen, North East Land, Edge Island, Barents Island, and Prince Charles Foreland) and a number of outlying islands; sovereignty long disputed but granted to Norway in 1920; coal mining. Administrative centre: Longyearbyen. Area: 62 050 sq. km (23 958 sq. miles). Also called: **Spitsbergen.**

svelte (svɛlt, sfɛlt) *adj* **1** attractively or gracefully slim; slender. **2** urbane or sophisticated. [C19: from French, from Italian *svelto*, from *svellere* to pull out, from Latin *ēvellere*, from EX-[1] + *vellere* to pull]

Svengali (svɛnˈɡɑːlɪ) *n* a person who controls another's mind, usually with sinister intentions. [after a character in George Du Maurier's novel *Trilby* (1894)]

Sverdlovsk (*Russian* svɪrˈdlɔfsk) *n* the former name (1924–91) of **Yekaterinburg.**

Sverige (ˈsværjə) *n* the Swedish name for **Sweden.**

Svevo (*Italian* ˈsvevo) *n* **Italo** (ɪˈtalo), original name *Ettore Schnitz*. 1861–1928, Italian novelist and short-story writer, best known for the novel *Confessions of Zeno* (1923).

Svizzera (ˈzvittsera) *n* the Italian name for **Switzerland.**

SVGA *abbrev. for* super video graphics array. See **VGA.**

SW **1** *symbol for* southwest(ern). **2** *abbrev. for* short wave.

Sw. *abbrev. for:* **1** Sweden. **2** Swedish.

swab (swɒb) *n* **1** *Med.* **1a** a small piece of cotton, gauze, etc., for use in applying medication, cleansing a wound, or obtaining a specimen of a secretion, etc. **1b** the specimen so obtained. **2** a mop for cleaning floors, decks, etc. **3** a brush used to clean a firearm's bore. **4** *Slang.* an uncouth or worthless fellow. ◆ *vb* **swabs, swabbing, swabbed. 5** (*tr*) to clean or medicate with or as if with a swab. **6** (*tr;* foll. by *up*) to take up with a swab. [C16: probably from Middle Dutch *swabbe* mop; related to Norwegian *svabba* to splash, Dutch *zwabberen* to mop, German *schwappen* to slop over]

swabber (ˈswɒbə) *n* **1** a person who uses a swab. **2** a device designed for swabbing. **3** *Slang.* an uncouth fellow.

Swabia (ˈsweɪbɪə) *n* a region and former duchy (from the 10th century to 1313) of S Germany, now part of Baden-Württemberg and Bavaria: part of West Germany until 1990. German name: **Schwaben** (ˈʃvaːbᵊn). ▸ **ˈSwabian** *adj, n*

swacked (swækt) *adj Slang.* in a state of intoxication, stupor, or euphoria induced by drugs or alcohol. [C20: perhaps from Scottish *swack* a heavy blow, of imitative origin]

swaddle (ˈswɒdᵊl) *vb* (*tr*) **1** to wind a bandage round. **2** to wrap (a baby) in swaddling clothes. **3** to restrain as if by wrapping with bandages; smother. ◆ *n* **4** *Chiefly U.S.* swaddling clothes. [C15: from Old English *swæthel* swaddling clothes; related to *swathian* to SWATHE]

swaddling clothes *pl n* **1** long strips of linen or other cloth formerly wrapped round a newly born baby. **2** restrictions or supervision imposed on the immature.

swaddy *or* **swaddie** (ˈswɒdɪ) *n, pl* **-dies.** *Brit. slang.* a private soldier. Compare **squaddie.** [C19: from dialect *swad* a country bumpkin]

Swadeshi (swəˈdeɪʃɪ) *adj* **1** (in present-day India) produced within the country; not imported. ◆ *n* **2** (in British India) the encouragement of domestic production and boycott of foreign goods as part of the campaign for independence. [C20: from Bengali *svadesī*, from Sanskrit *svadeśin*, from *sva* one's own + *deśa* country]

swag (swæɡ) *n* **1** *Slang.* property obtained by theft or other illicit means. **2** *Slang.* goods; valuables. **3** an ornamental festoon of fruit, flowers, or drapery or a representation of this. **4** a swaying movement; lurch. **5** *Midland England dialect.* a depression filled with water, resulting from mining subsidence. **6** *Austral. and N.Z. informal.* (formerly) a swagman's pack containing personal belongings. **7 go on the swag.** *Austral. and N.Z. informal.* to become a tramp. **8 swags of.** *Austral. and N.Z. informal.* lots of. ◆ *vb* **swags, swagging, swagged. 9** *Chiefly Brit.* to lurch or sag or cause to lurch or sag. **10** (*tr*) to adorn or arrange with swags. **11** (*intr*) *Austral. informal.* to tramp about carrying a pack of personal belongings. [C17: perhaps of Scandinavian origin; compare Norwegian *svagga* to SWAY]

swage (sweɪdʒ) *n* **1** a shaped tool or die used in forming cold metal by hammering, pressing, etc. **2** a decorative moulding. ◆ *vb* **3** (*tr*) to form (metal) with a swage. [C19: from French *souage,* of unknown origin] ▸ **ˈswager** *n*

swage block *n* an iron block cut with holes, recesses, and grooves to assist in the cold-working of metal.

swagger[1] (ˈswæɡə) *vb* **1** (*intr*) to walk or behave in an arrogant manner. **2** (*intr;* often foll. by *about*) to brag loudly. **3** (*tr*) *Rare.* to force, influence, etc., by blustering. ◆ *n* **4** arrogant gait, conduct, or manner. ◆ *adj* **5** *Brit. informal, rare.* elegantly fashionable. [C16: probably from SWAG] ▸ **ˈswaggerer** *n* ▸ **ˈswaggering** *adj* ▸ **ˈswaggeringly** *adv*

swagger[2] (ˈswæɡə) *or* **swaggie** (ˈswæɡɪ) *n* other names for **swagman.**

swagger stick *or esp. Brit.* **swagger cane** *n* a short cane or stick carried on occasion mainly by army officers.

swaggie (ˈswæɡɪ) *n Austral. and N.Z. slang.* short for **swagman.**

swagman (ˈswæɡˌmæn, -mən) *n, pl* **-men.** *Austral. and N.Z. informal.* a labourer who carries his personal possessions in a pack or swag while travelling about in search of work; vagrant worker. Also called: **swagger, swaggie.**

Swahili (swɑːˈhiːlɪ) *n* **1** Also called: **Kiswahili.** a language of E Africa that is an official language of Kenya and Tanzania and is widely used as a lingua franca throughout E and central Africa. It is a member of the Bantu group of the Niger-Congo family, originally spoken in Zanzibar, and has a large number of loan words taken from Arabic and other languages. **2** (*pl* **-lis** *or* **-li**) Also called: **Mswahili** (*pl* **Waswahili**). a member of a people speaking this language, living chiefly in Zanzibar. ◆ *adj* **3** of or relating to the Swahilis or their language. [C19: from Arabic *sawāhil* coasts] ▸ **Swaˈhilian** *adj*

swain (sweɪn) *n Archaic or poetic.* **1** a male lover or admirer. **2** a country youth. [Old English *swān* swineherd; related to Old High German *swein,* Old Norse *sveinn* boy; see SWINE] ▸ **ˈswainish** *adj*

swale (sweɪl) *n Chiefly U.S.* **a** a moist depression in a tract of land, usually with rank vegetation. **b** (*as modifier*): *swell and swale topography.* [C16: probably of Scandinavian origin; compare Old Norse *svala* to chill]

Swaledale (ˈsweɪlˌdeɪl) *n* a breed of small hardy sheep kept esp. in northern England for its coarse wool which is used for making tweeds and carpets. [from *Swaledale,* Yorkshire]

SWALK (swɔːlk) *acronym for* sealed with a loving kiss: sometimes written on the back of envelopes.

swallow[1] (ˈswɒləʊ) *vb* (*mainly tr*) **1** to pass (food, drink, etc.) through the mouth to the stomach by means of the muscular action of the oesophagus. **2** (often foll. by *up*) to engulf or destroy as if by ingestion: *Nazi Germany swallowed up several small countries.* **3** *Informal.* to believe gullibly: *he will never swallow such an excuse.* **4** to refrain from uttering or manifesting: *to swallow one's disappointment.* **5** to endure without retaliation. **6** to enunciate (words, etc.) indistinctly; mutter. **7** (often foll. by *down*) to eat or drink reluctantly. **8** (*intr*) to perform or simulate the act of swallowing, as in gulping. **9 swallow one's words.** to retract a statement, argument, etc., often in humiliating circumstances. ◆ *n* **10** the act of swallowing. **11** the amount swallowed at any single time; mouthful. **12** Also called: **crown, throat.** *Nautical.* the opening between the shell and the groove of the sheave of a block, through which the rope is passed. **13** *Rare.* another word for **throat** or **gullet. 14** *Rare.* a capacity for swallowing; appetite. [Old English *swelgan;* related to Old Norse *svelga,* Old High German *swelgan* to swallow, Swedish *svalg* gullet] ▸ **ˈswallowable** *adj* ▸ **ˈswallower** *n*

swallow[2] (ˈswɒləʊ) *n* **1** any passerine songbird of the family *Hirundinidae,* esp. *Hirundo rustica* (**common** or **barn swallow**), having long pointed wings, a forked tail, short legs, and a rapid flight. Related adj: **hirundine. 2** See **fairy swallow.** [Old English *swealwe;* related to Old Frisian *swale,* Old Norse *svala,* Old High German *swalwa*] ▸ **ˈswallow-ˌlike** *adj*

swallow dive *n* a type of dive in which the diver arches back while in the air, keeping his legs straight and together and his arms outstretched, finally entering the water headfirst. U.S. and Canadian equivalent: **swan dive.**

swallow hole *n Chiefly Brit.* another word for **sinkhole** (sense 1).

swallowtail (ˈswɒləʊˌteɪl) *n* **1** any of various butterflies of the genus *Papilio* and related genera, esp. *P. machaon* of Europe, having a tail-like extension of each hind wing: family *Papilionidae.* **2** the forked tail of a swallow or similar bird. **3** short for **swallow-tailed coat.**

swallow-tailed *adj* **1** (of a bird) having a deeply forked tail. **2** having a part resembling a swallow's tail.

swallow-tailed coat *n* another name for **tail coat.**

swallowwort (ˈswɒləʊˌwɜːt) *n* **1** any of several Eurasian vines of the genus *Cynanchum,* esp. *C. nigrum,* having small brownish-purple flowers: family *Asclepiadaceae.* **2** a related European herbaceous plant, *Vincetoxicum officinale* (or *Cynanchum vincetoxicum*), having an emetic root. **3** another name for **greater celandine.** [C16: so called because the shape of its pod is reminiscent of a flying swallow]

swam (swæm) *vb* the past tense of **swim.**

swami (ˈswɑːmɪ) *n, pl* **-mies** *or* **-mis.** (in India) a title of respect for a Hindu saint or religious teacher. [C18: from Hindi *svāmī,* from Sanskrit *svāmin* master, from *sva* one's own]

swamp (swɒmp) *n* **1a** permanently waterlogged ground that is usually overgrown and sometimes partly forested. Compare **marsh. 1b** (*as modifier*): *swamp fever.* ◆ *vb* **2** to drench or submerge or be drenched or submerged. **3** *Nautical.* to cause (a boat) to sink or fill with water or (of a boat) to sink or fill with water. **4** to overburden or overwhelm or be overburdened or overwhelmed, as by excess work or great numbers: *we have been swamped with applications.* **5** to sink or stick or cause to sink or stick in or as if in a swamp. **6** (*tr*) to render helpless. [C17: probably from Middle Dutch *somp;* compare Middle High German *sumpf,* Old Norse *svöppr* sponge, Greek *somphos* spongy] ▸ **ˈswampish** *adj* ▸ **ˈswampless** *adj* ▸ **ˈswampy** *adj*

swamp boat *n* a shallow-draught boat powered by an æroplane engine mounted on a raised structure for use in swamps. Also called: **airboat.**

swamp buggy *n* (esp. in the U.S. and Canada) a light aerofoil conveyance for use in regions with swamps, lakes, etc.

swamp cypress *n* a North American deciduous coniferous tree, *Taxodium distichum,* that grows in swamps and sends up aerial roots from its base. Also called: **bald cypress.**

swamper (ˈswɒmpə) *n U.S.* **a** a person who lives or works in a swampy region, esp. in the southern U.S. **b** a person who clears a swamp of trees and undergrowth or who clears a path in a forest for transporting logs.

swamp fever *n* **1** Also called: **equine infectious anaemia.** a viral disease of horses characterized by recurring fever, staggering gait, and general debility. **2** *U.S.* another name for **malaria.**

swampland (ˈswɒmpˌlænd) *n* a permanently waterlogged area; marshland.

swan (swɒn) *n* **1** any large aquatic bird of the genera *Cygnus* and *Coscoroba,* having a long neck and usually a white plumage: family *Anatidae,* order *Anseriformes.* **2** *Rare, literary.* **2a** a poet. **2b** (*cap. when part of a title or epithet*): *the Swan of Avon* (Shakespeare). ◆ *vb* **swans, swanning, swanned. 3** (*intr;* usually foll. by *around* or *about*) *Informal.* to wander idly. [Old English; related to Old Norse *svanr,* Middle Low German *swōn*] ▸ **ˈswanˌlike** *adj*

Swan[1] (swɒn) *n* a river in SW Western Australia, rising as the Avon northeast of Narrogin and flowing northwest and west to the Indian Ocean below Perth. Length: about 240 km (150 miles).

Swan[2] (swɒn) *n* Sir **Joseph Wilson.** 1828–1914, English physicist and chemist, who developed the incandescent electric light (1880) independently of Edison.

swan dive *n* the U.S. and Canadian name for **swallow dive.**

Swanee (ˈswɒnɪ) *n* a variant spelling of **Suwannee.**

swanherd (ˈswɒnˌhɜːd) *n* a person who herds swans.

swank (swæŋk) *Informal.* ◆ *vb* **1** (*intr*) to show off or swagger. ◆ *n* **2** Also called: **swankpot.** *Brit.* a swaggering or conceited person. **3** *Chiefly U.S.* elegance or style, esp. of a showy kind. **4** swagger; ostentation. ◆ *adj* **5** another word (esp.

U.S.) for **swanky**. [C19: perhaps from Middle High German *swanken* to sway; see SWAG]

swanky ('swæŋkɪ) *adj* **swankier, swankiest.** *Informal.* **1** expensive and showy; stylish: *a swanky hotel.* **2** boastful or conceited. ▸ **'swankily** *adv* ▸ **'swankiness** *n*

swan maiden *n* any of a group of maidens in folklore who by magic are transformed into swans.

Swanndri *or* **Swandri** ('swɒn,draɪ) *n, pl* **-dris.** *N.Z. trademark.* an all-weather heavy woollen shirt. Also called: **swannie** ('swɒnɪ).

swan neck *n* a tube, rail, etc., curved like a swan's neck.

swannery ('swɒnərɪ) *n, pl* **-neries.** a place where swans are kept and bred.

swan's-down *n* **1** the fine soft down feathers of a swan, used to trim powder puffs, clothes, etc. **2** a thick soft fabric of wool with silk, cotton, or rayon, used for infants' clothing, etc. **3** a cotton fabric with a heavy nap.

Swansea ('swɒnzɪ) *n* **1** a port in S Wales, in Swansea county on an inlet of the Bristol Channel (**Swansea Bay**); a metallurgical and oil-refining centre; university (1920). Pop.: 171 038 (1991). **2** a county of S Wales on the Bristol Channel, created in 1996 from part of West Glamorgan: includes the Swansea conurbation and the Gower peninsula. Administrative centre: Swansea. Pop.: 230 600 (1996 est.). Area: 378 sq. km (146 sq. miles).

swanskin ('swɒn,skɪn) *n* **1** the skin of a swan with the feathers attached. **2** a fine twill-weave flannel fabric.

swan song *n* **1** the last act, appearance, publication, or utterance of a person before retirement or death. **2** the song that a dying swan is said to sing

swan-upping *n Brit.* **1** the practice or action of marking nicks in swans' beaks as a sign of ownership. **2** the annual swan-upping of royal cygnets on the River Thames. [C16: from UP (in the archaic sense: to catch and mark a swan)]

swap *or* **swop** (swɒp) *vb* **swaps, swapping, swapped** *or* **swops, swopping, swopped. 1** to trade or exchange (something or someone) for another. ◆ *n* **2** an exchange. **3** something that is exchanged. **4** *Finance.* Also called: **swap option, swaption.** a contract in which the parties to it exchange liabilities on outstanding debts, often exchanging fixed interest-rate for floating-rate debts (**debt swap**), either as a means of debt management or in trading (**swap trading**). [C14 (in the sense: to shake hands on a bargain, strike): probably of imitative origin] ▸ **'swapper** *or* **'swopper** *n*

SWAPO *or* **Swapo** ('swɑːpəʊ) *n acronym for* South-West Africa People's Organization.

swap shop *n* a place or occasion at which articles no longer wanted may be exchanged for other articles.

swaption ('swɒpʃən) *n* another name for **swap** (sense 4).

swaraj (swəˈrɑːdʒ) *n* (in British India) self-government; independence. [C20: from Sanskrit *svarāj*, from *sva* self + *rājya* rule] ▸ **swa'rajism** *n* ▸ **swa'rajist** *n, adj*

sward (swɔːd) *n* **1** turf or grass or a stretch of turf or grass. ◆ *vb* **2** to cover or become covered with grass. [Old English *sweard* skin; related to Old Frisian *swarde* scalp, Middle High German *swart* hide]

swarf (swɔːf, swɑːf) *n* material removed by cutting or grinding tools in the machining of metals, stone, etc. [C16: of Scandinavian origin; related to Old Norse *svarf* metallic dust]

swarm[1] (swɔːm) *n* **1** a group of social insects, esp. bees led by a queen, that has left the parent hive in order to start a new colony. **2** a large mass of small animals, esp. insects. **3** a throng or mass, esp. when moving or in turmoil. ◆ *vb* **4** (*intr*) (of small animals, esp. bees) to move in or form a swarm. **5** (*intr*) to congregate, move about or proceed in large numbers. **6** (when *intr*, often foll. by *with*) to overrun or be overrun (with): *the house swarmed with rats.* **7** (*tr*) to cause to swarm. [Old English *swearm;* related to Old Norse *svarmr* uproar, Old High German *swaram* swarm]

swarm[2] (swɔːm) *vb* (when *intr*, usually foll. by *up*) to climb (a ladder, etc.) by gripping with the hands and feet: *the boys swarmed up the rigging.* [C16: of unknown origin]

swarm cell *or* **spore** *n* another name for **zoospore.**

swart (swɔːt) *or* **swarth** (swɔːθ) *adj Archaic or dialect.* swarthy. [Old English *sweart;* related to Old Frisian *swart*, Old Norse *svartr*, Old High German *swarz* black, Latin *sordēs* dirt; see SORDID] ▸ **'swartness** *or* **'swarthness** *n*

swarthy ('swɔːðɪ) *adj* **swarthier, swarthiest.** dark-hued or dark-complexioned. [C16: from obsolete *swarty*, from SWART + -Y[1]] ▸ **'swarthily** *adv* ▸ **'swarthiness** *n*

swash (swɒʃ) *vb* **1** (*intr*) (esp. of water or things in water) to wash or move with noisy splashing. **2** (*tr*) to dash (a liquid, esp. water) against or upon. **3** (*intr*) *Archaic.* to swagger or bluster. ◆ *n* **4** Also called: **send.** the dashing movement or sound of water, such as that of waves on a beach. Compare **backwash. 5** any other swashing movement or sound. **6** a sandbar washed by the waves. **7** Also called: **swash channel.** a channel of moving water cutting through or running behind a sandbank. **8** *Archaic.* **8a** swagger or bluster. **8b** a swashbuckler. [C16: probably of imitative origin]

swashbuckler ('swɒʃ,bʌklə) *n* a swaggering or flamboyant adventurer. [C16: from SWASH (in the archaic sense: to make the noise of a sword striking a shield) + BUCKLER]

swashbuckling ('swɒʃ,bʌklɪŋ) *adj* (*usually prenominal*) **1** of or characteristic of a swashbuckler. **2** (esp. of films in period costume) full of adventure and excitement.

swash letter *n Printing.* a decorative letter, esp. an ornamental italic capital. [C17 *swash* (n, in the sense: the decorative flourish of an ornamental letter) from *aswash* aslant]

swash plate *n Engineering.* a collar or face plate on a shaft that is inclined at an oblique angle to the axis of rotation and either imparts reciprocating motion to push rods parallel to the shaft axis as in a **swash plate pump** or, conversely, converts reciprocating motion to rotation as in a **swash plate motor.** Also called: **wobble plate.** [from *swash* (obsolete n) an oblique figure or ornament, from *aswash:* see SWASH LETTER]

swastika ('swɒstɪkə) *n* **1** a primitive religious symbol or ornament in the shape of a Greek cross, usually having the ends of the arms bent at right angles in either a clockwise or anticlockwise direction. **2** this symbol with clockwise arms, officially adopted in 1935 as the emblem of Nazi Germany. [C19: from Sanskrit *svastika*, from *svasti* prosperity; from the belief that it brings good luck]

swat[1] (swɒt) *vb* **swats, swatting, swatted.** (*tr*) **1** to strike or hit sharply: *to swat a fly.* ◆ *n* **2** another word (esp. Brit.) for **swatter** (sense 1). **3** a sharp or violent blow. ◆ Also: **swot.** [C17: northern English dialect and U.S. variant of SQUAT]

swat[2] (swɒt) *vb* **swats, swatting, swatted.** *n* a variant of **swot**[1].

Swat (swɒt) *n* **1** a former princely state of NW India: passed to Pakistan in 1947. **2** a river in Pakistan, rising in the north and flowing south to the Kabul River north of Peshawar. Length: about 640 km (400 miles).

SWAT (swɒt) *n acronym for* Special Weapons and Tactics: a military-like unit within the U.S. police force, trained to deal with specially dangerous situations, such as hostage-taking and riots.

swatch (swɒtʃ) *n* **1** a sample of cloth. **2** a number of such samples, usually fastened together in book form. **3** *Printing.* **3a** a small sample of colour supplied to the printer for matching during printing. **3b** a sample of ink spread on paper by a printer to check the accuracy of a required colour. [C16: Scottish and northern English, of uncertain origin]

swath (swɔːθ) *or* **swathe** (sweɪð) *n, pl* **swaths** (swɔːðz) *or* **swathes. 1** the width of one sweep of a scythe or of the blade of a mowing machine. **2** the strip cut by either of these in one course. **3** the quantity of cut grass, hay, or similar crop left in one course of such mowing. **4** a long narrow strip or belt. [Old English *swæth;* related to Old Norse *svath* smooth patch]

swathe (sweɪð) *vb* (*tr*) **1** to bandage (a wound, limb, etc.), esp. completely. **2** to wrap a band, garment, etc., around, esp. so as to cover completely; swaddle. **3** to envelop. ◆ *n* **4** a bandage or wrapping. **5** a variant spelling of **swath.** [Old English *swathian;* related to *swæthel* swaddling clothes, Old High German *swedil*, Dutch *zwadel;* see SWADDLE] ▸ **'swathable** *or* **'swatheable** *adj*

Swatow ('swɒ'taʊ) *n* a variant transliteration of the Chinese name for **Shantou.**

swatter ('swɒtə) *n* **1** a device for killing insects, esp. a meshed flat attached to a handle. **2** a person who swats.

sway (sweɪ) *vb* **1** (*usually intr*) to swing or cause to swing to and fro. **2** (*usually intr*) to lean or incline or cause to lean or incline to one side or in different directions in turn. **3** (*usually intr*) to vacillate or cause to vacillate between two or more opinions. **4** to be influenced or swerve or influence or cause to swerve to or from a purpose or opinion. **5** (*tr*) *Nautical.* to hoist (a yard, mast, or other spar). **6** *Archaic or poetic.* to rule or wield power (over). **7** (*tr*) *Archaic.* to wield (a weapon). ◆ *n* **8** control; power. **9** a swinging or leaning movement. **10** *Archaic.* dominion; governing authority. **11 hold sway.** to be master; reign. [C16: probably from Old Norse *sveigja* to bend; related to Dutch *zwaaien*, Low German *swājen*] ▸ **'swayable** *adj* ▸ **'swayer** *n* ▸ **'swayful** *adj*

sway-back *n Vet. science.* an abnormal sagging or concavity of the spine in horses. ▸ **'sway-,backed** *adj*

Swazi ('swɑːzɪ) *n* **1** (*pl* **-zis** *or* **-zi**) a member of a racially mixed people of southern Africa living chiefly in Swaziland, who first formed into a strong political group in the late 19th century. **2** the language of this people: an official language of Swaziland along with English. It belongs to the Niger-Congo family and is closely related to Xhosa and Zulu.

Swaziland ('swɑːzɪ,lænd) *n* a kingdom in southern Africa: made a protectorate of the Transvaal by Britain in 1894; gained independence in 1968; a member of the Commonwealth. Official languages: Swazi and English. Religion: Christian majority, traditional beliefs. Currency: lilangeni (plural emalangeni). Capital: Mbabane (administrative), Lobamba (legislative). Pop.: 966 000 (1998 est.). Area: 17 363 sq. km (6704 sq. miles).

Swazi Territory *n* the former name of **KaNgwane.**

swear (sweə) *vb* **swears, swearing, swore, sworn. 1** to declare or affirm (a statement) as true, esp. by invoking a deity, etc., as witness. **2** (foll. by *by*) **2a** to invoke (a deity, etc.) by name as a witness or guarantee to an oath. **2b** to trust implicitly; have complete confidence (in). **3** (*intr;* often foll. by *at*) to curse, blaspheme, or use swearwords. **4** (when *tr*, *may take a clause as object or an infinitive*) to promise solemnly on oath; vow. **5** (*tr*) to assert or affirm with great emphasis or earnestness. **6** (*intr*) to give evidence or make any statement or solemn declaration on oath. **7** to take an oath in order to add force or solemnity to (a statement or declaration). **8 swear blind.** *Informal.* to assert emphatically. ◆ *n* **9** a period of swearing. [Old English *swerian;* related to Old Norse *sverja*, Gothic *swaran*, Old Frisian *swera*, German *schwören*] ▸ **'swearer** *n*

swear in *vb* (*tr, adv*) to administer an oath to (a person) on his assuming office, entering the witness box to give evidence, etc.

swear off *vb* (*intr, prep*) to promise to abstain from something: *to swear off drink.*

swear out *vb* (*tr, adv*) *U.S.* to secure the issue of (a warrant for an arrest) by making a charge under oath.

swearword ('sweə,wɜːd) *n* a socially taboo word or phrase of a profane, obscene, or insulting character.

sweat (swet) *n* **1** the secretion from the sweat glands, esp. when profuse and visible, as during strenuous activity, from excessive heat, etc.; perspiration. Related adjs: **sudatory, sudorific. 2** the act or process of secreting this fluid. **3** the act of inducing the exudation of moisture. **4** drops of moisture given forth or gathered on the surface of something. **5** *Informal.* a state or condition of worry or eagerness (esp. in the phrase **in a sweat**). **6** *Slang.* drudgery or hard labour: *mowing lawns is a real sweat!* **7** *Chiefly U.S.* an exercise gallop given to a horse, esp. on the day of a race. **8** *Slang, chiefly Brit.* a soldier, esp. one who is old and experienced. **9 no sweat!** (*interj*) *Slang.* an expression suggesting that something can be done without problems or difficulty. ◆ *vb* **sweats, sweating; sweat** *or* **sweated. 10** to secrete (sweat) through the pores of the skin, esp. profusely; perspire. **11** (*tr*) to make wet or stain with perspiration. **12** to give forth or cause to give forth (moisture) in droplets: *a sweating cheese; the maple sweats sap.* **13** (*intr*) to collect and condense moisture on an outer surface: *a glass of beer sweating in the sun.* **14** (*intr*) (of a liquid) to pass through a porous surface in droplets. **15** (of tobacco leaves, cut and dried hay, etc.) to exude moisture and, sometimes, begin to ferment or to cause (tobacco leaves, etc.) to exude moisture. **16** (*tr*) to heat (food, esp. vegetables) slowly in butter in a tightly closed saucepan. **17** (*tr*) to join (pieces of metal) by pressing together and heating. **18** (*tr*) to heat (solder) until it melts. **19** (*tr*) to heat (a partially fused metal) to extract an easily fusible constituent. **20** to shake together (coins, esp. gold coins) so as to remove particles for illegal use. **21** *Informal.* to suffer anxiety, impatience, or distress. **22** *Informal.* to overwork or be overworked. **23** (*tr*) *Informal.* to employ at very low wages and under bad conditions. **24** (*tr*) *Informal.* to extort, esp. by torture: *to sweat information out of a captive.* **25** (*intr*) *Informal.* to suffer punishment: *you'll sweat for this!* **26 sweat blood.** *Informal.* **26a** to work very hard. **26b** to be filled with anxiety or impatience. ◆ See also **sweat off, sweat out.** [Old English *swætan* to sweat, from *swāt* sweat; related to Old Saxon *swēt*, Old Norse *sveiti*, Old High German *sweiz*, Latin *sūdor*, Sanskrit *svedas*] ▸ **'sweatless** *adj*

sweatband ('swɛt,bænd) *n* **1** a band of material set in a hat or cap to protect it from sweat. **2** a piece of cloth tied around the forehead to keep sweat out of the eyes or around the wrist to keep the hands dry, as in sports.

sweatbox ('swɛt,bɒks) *n* **1** a device for causing tobacco leaves, fruit, or hides to sweat. **2** a very small pen or cubicle where a pig is fattened intensively. **3** *Informal, chiefly U.S.* a narrow room or cell for a prisoner. **4** *Informal.* any place where a person sweats on account of confinement, heat, etc.

sweated ('swɛtɪd) *adj* **1** made by exploited labour: *sweated goods.* **2** (of workers, etc.) forced to work in poor conditions for low pay.

sweater ('swɛtə) *n* **1a** a garment made of knitted or crocheted material covering the upper part of the body, esp. a heavy one worn for warmth. **1b** (*as modifier*): *a sweater dress.* **2** a person or thing that sweats. **3** an employer who overworks and underpays his employees.

sweater girl *n Slang, now rare.* a young woman or girl with large breasts who wears tight sweaters.

sweat gland *n* any of the coiled tubular subcutaneous glands that secrete sweat by means of a duct that opens on to the skin.

sweating sickness *n* **1** the nontechnical name for **miliary fever. 2** an acute infectious febrile disease that was widespread in Europe during the late 15th century, characterized by profuse sweating. **3** a disease of cattle, esp. calves, prevalent in southern Africa and transmitted by ticks.

sweat off *or* **away** *vb* (*tr, adv*) *Informal.* to get rid of (weight) by strenuous exercise or sweating.

sweat out *vb* (*tr, adv*) **1** to cure or lessen the effects of (a cold, respiratory infection, etc.) by sweating. **2** *Informal.* to endure (hardships) for a time (often in the phrase **sweat it out**). **3 sweat one's guts out.** *Informal.* to work extremely hard.

sweats (swɛts) *pl n* sweatshirts and sweat-suit trousers: *jeans and sweats.*

sweatshirt ('swɛt,ʃɜːt) *n* a long-sleeved knitted cotton sweater worn by athletes, etc.

sweatshop ('swɛt,ʃɒp) *n* a workshop where employees work long hours under bad conditions for low wages.

sweat suit *n* a suit worn by athletes for training comprising knitted cotton trousers fitting closely at the ankle and a light cotton sweater.

sweaty ('swɛtɪ) *adj* **sweatier, sweatiest. 1** covered with perspiration; sweating. **2** smelling of or like sweat. **3** causing sweat. ▸ **'sweatily** *adv* ▸ **'sweatiness** *n*

swede (swiːd) *n* **1** a Eurasian cruciferous plant, *Brassica napobrassica*, cultivated for its bulbous edible root, which is used as a vegetable and as cattle fodder. **2** the root of this plant. **3** *N.Z.* a slang word for **head** (sense 1). ◆ Also called (for senses 1 and 2): **Swedish turnip.** U.S. and Canadian name: **rutabaga.** [C19: so called after being introduced into Scotland from Sweden in the 18th century]

Swede (swiːd) *n* a native, citizen, or inhabitant of Sweden.

Sweden ('swiːdᵊn) *n* a kingdom in NW Europe, occupying the E part of the Scandinavian Peninsula, on the Gulf of Bothnia and the Baltic: first united during the Viking period (8th–11th centuries); a member of the European Union. About 50 per cent of the total area is forest and 9 per cent lakes. Exports include timber, pulp, paper, iron ore, and steel. Official language: Swedish. Official religion: Church of Sweden (Lutheran). Currency: krona. Capital: Stockholm. Pop.: 8 860 000 (1998 est.). Area: 449 793 sq. km (173 665 sq. miles). Swedish name: **Sverige.**

Swedenborg ('swiːdᵊn,bɔːg; *Swedish* 'sveːdənbɔrj) *n* **Emanuel** (e'manuel). original surname *Svedberg.* 1688–1772, Swedish scientist and theologian, whose mystical ideas became the basis of a religious movement.

Swedenborgianism (,swiːdᵊn'bɔːdʒɪə,nɪzəm, -gɪ-) *or* **Swedenborgism** ('swiːdᵊn,bɔːdʒɪzəm, -gɪz-) *n* the system of philosophical and religious doctrines of Emanuel Swedenborg, emphasizing the spiritual structure of the universe, the possibility of direct contact with spirits, and the divinity of Christ. This provided the basis for the **New Jerusalem Church** (or **New Church**) founded by Swedenborg's followers. ▸ **,Sweden'borgian** *n, adj*

Swedish ('swiːdɪʃ) *adj* **1** of, relating to, or characteristic of Sweden, its people, or their language. ◆ *n* **2** the official language of Sweden, belonging to the North Germanic branch of the Indo-European family: one of the two official languages of Finland. **3 the Swedish.** (*functioning as pl*) the people of Sweden collectively.

Swedish massage *n* massage combined with a system (**Swedish movements** or **gymnastics**) of passive and active exercising of muscles and joints.

Swedish mile *n* a unit of length used in Sweden, equal to 10 kilometres.

Sweelinck (*Dutch* 'sweːlɪŋk) *n* **Jan Pieterszoon** (jɑn 'piːtər,zoːn). 1562–1621, Dutch composer and organist, whose organ works are important for being the first to incorporate independent parts for the pedals.

sweeny ('swiːnɪ) *n Vet. science.* a wasting of the shoulder muscles of a horse, esp. as the result of a nerve injury. [C19: probably from German dialect *Schweine* emaciation, atrophy]

sweep (swiːp) *vb* **sweeps, sweeping, swept. 1** to clean or clear (a space, chimney, etc.) with a brush, broom, etc. **2** (often foll. by *up*) to remove or collect (dirt, rubbish, etc.) with a brush, broom, etc. **3** to move in a smooth or continuous manner, esp. quickly or forcibly: *cars swept along the road.* **4** to move in a proud or dignified fashion: *she swept past.* **5** to spread or pass rapidly across, through, or along (a region, area, etc.): *the news swept through the town.* **6** (*tr*) to direct (the gaze, line of fire, etc.) over; survey. **7** (*tr;* foll. by *away* or *off*) to overwhelm emotionally: *she was swept away by his charm.* **8** (*tr*) to brush or lightly touch (a surface, etc.): *the dress swept along the ground.* **9** (*tr;* often foll. by *away*) to convey, clear, or abolish, esp. with strong or continuous movements: *the sea swept the sandcastle away; secondary modern schools were swept away.* **10** (*intr*) to extend gracefully or majestically, esp. in a wide circle: *the plains sweep down to the sea.* **11** to search (a body of water) for mines, etc., by dragging. **12** to search (a room, area, etc.) electronically to detect spying devices. **13** (*tr*) to win overwhelmingly, esp. in an election: *Labour swept the country.* **14** *Cricket.* to play (a ball) with a sweep. **15** (*tr*) to propel (a boat) with sweeps. **16 sweep the board. 16a** (in gambling) to win all the cards or money. **16b** to win every event or prize in a contest. **17 sweep (something) under the carpet.** to conceal (something, esp. a problem) in the hope that it will be overlooked by others. ◆ *n* **18** the act or an instance of sweeping; removal by or as if by a brush or broom. **19** a swift or steady movement, esp. in an arc: *with a sweep of his arms.* **20** the distance, arc, etc., through which something, such as a pendulum, moves. **21** a wide expanse or scope: *the sweep of the plains.* **22** any curving line or contour. **23** *Cards.* **23a** the winning of every trick in a hand of whist. **23b** the taking, by pairing, of all exposed cards in cassino. **24** short for **sweepstake. 25** *Cricket.* a shot in which the ball is hit more or less square on the leg side from a half-kneeling position with the bat held nearly horizontal. **26a** a long oar used on an open boat. **26b** *Austral.* a person steering a surf boat with such an oar. **27** any of the sails of a windmill. **28** *Electronics.* a steady horizontal or circular movement of an electron beam across or around the fluorescent screen of a cathode-ray tube. **29** *Agriculture.* **29a** a rakelike attachment for the front of a motor vehicle for pushing hay into piles. **29b** a triangular blade on a cultivator used to cut through roots below the surface of the soil. **30** a curving driveway. **31** *Chiefly Brit.* See **chimney sweep. 32** another name for **swipe** (sense 5). **33 clean sweep. 33a** an overwhelming victory or success. **33b** a complete change; purge: *to make a clean sweep.* [C13 *swepen;* related to Old English *swāpan*, Old Norse *sveipa;* see SWIPE, SWOOP] ▸ **'sweepy** *adj*

sweepback ('swiːp,bæk) *n* the rearward inclination of a component or surface, such as an aircraft wing, fin, etc.

sweeper ('swiːpə) *n* **1** a person employed to sweep, such as a roadsweeper. **2** any device for sweeping: *a carpet sweeper.* **3** *Informal, soccer.* a player who supports the main defenders, as by intercepting loose balls, etc.

sweep hand *n Horology.* a long hand that registers seconds or fractions of seconds on the perimeter of the dial.

sweeping ('swiːpɪŋ) *adj* **1** comprehensive and wide-ranging: *sweeping reforms.* **2** indiscriminate or without reservations: *sweeping statements.* **3** decisive or overwhelming: *a sweeping victory.* **4** taking in a wide area: *a sweeping glance.* **5** driving steadily onwards, esp. over a large area: *a sweeping attack.* ▸ **'sweepingly** *adv* ▸ **'sweepingness** *n*

sweepings ('swiːpɪŋz) *pl n* debris, litter, or refuse.

sweep-saw *n* a saw with a thin blade that can be used for cutting curved shapes.

sweepstake ('swiːp,steɪk) *or esp. U.S.* **sweepstakes** *n* **1a** a lottery in which the stakes of the participants constitute the prize. **1b** the prize itself. **2** any event involving a lottery, esp. a horse race in which the prize is the competitors' stakes. ◆ Often shortened to **sweep.** [C15: originally referring to someone who *sweeps* or takes all the stakes in a game]

sweer (swiːr) *vb Scot.* a variant spelling of **sweir**[1] and **sweir**[2].

sweet (swiːt) *adj* **1** having or denoting a pleasant taste like that of sugar. **2** agreeable to the senses or the mind: *sweet music.* **3** having pleasant manners; gentle: *a sweet child.* **4** (of wine, etc.) having a relatively high sugar content; not dry. **5** (of foods) not decaying or rancid: *sweet milk.* **6** not salty: *sweet water.* **7** free from unpleasant odours: *sweet air.* **8** containing no corrosive substances: *sweet soil.* **9** (of petrol) containing no sulphur compounds. **10** sentimental or unrealistic. **11** individual; particular: *the electorate went its own sweet way.* **12** *Jazz.* performed with a regular beat, with the emphasis on clearly outlined melody and little improvisation. **13** *Austral. slang.* satisfactory or in order; all right. **14** *Archaic.* respected; dear (used in polite forms of address): *sweet sir.* **15** smooth and precise; perfectly executed: *a sweet shot.* **16 sweet on.** fond of or infatuated with. **17 keep (someone) sweet.** to ingratiate oneself in order to ensure cooperation. ◆ *adv* **18** *Informal.* in a sweet manner. ◆ *n* **19** a sweet taste or smell; sweetness in general. **20** (*often pl*) *Brit.* any of numerous kinds of confectionery consisting wholly or partly of sugar, esp. of sugar boiled and crystallized (**boiled sweets**). **21** *Brit.* a pudding, fruit, or any sweet dish served as a dessert. **22** dear; sweetheart (used as a form of address). **23** anything that is sweet. **24** (*often pl*) a pleasurable experience, state, etc.: *the sweets of success.* **25** *U.S.* See **sweet potato.** [Old English *swēte;* related to Old Saxon *swōti*, Old High German *suozi*, Old Norse *sœtr*, Latin *suādus* persuasive, *suāvis* sweet, Greek *hēdus,* Sanskrit *svādu;* see PERSUADE, SUAVE] ▸ ˈ**sweetish** *adj* ▸ ˈ**sweetly** *adv* ▸ ˈ**sweetness** *n*

Sweet *n* **Henry.** 1845–1912, English philologist; a pioneer of modern phonetics. His books include *A History of English Sounds* (1874).

sweet alyssum *n* a Mediterranean cruciferous plant, *Lobularia maritima,* having clusters of small fragrant white or violet flowers: widely grown in gardens. See also **alyssum.**

sweet-and-sour *adj* (of food) cooked in a sauce made from sugar and vinegar and other ingredients.

sweet basil *n* See **basil** (sense 1).

sweet bay *n* a small tree, *Magnolia virginiana,* of SE North America, having large fragrant white flowers: family *Magnoliaceae* (magnolias). Sometimes shortened to **bay.**

sweetbread (ˈswiːtˌbrɛd) *n* the pancreas (**stomach sweetbread**) or the thymus gland (**neck** or **throat sweetbread**) of an animal, used for food. [C16: SWEET + BREAD, perhaps from Old English *brǣd* meat; related to Old Saxon *brādo* ham, Old High German *brāt,* Old Norse *brāth*]

sweetbrier (ˈswiːtˌbraɪə) *n* a Eurasian rose, *Rosa rubiginosa,* having a tall bristly stem, fragrant leaves, and single pink flowers. Also called: **eglantine.**

sweet cherry *n* **1** either of two types of cherry tree that are cultivated for their red edible sweet fruit, the gean having tender-fleshed fruit, the bigarreau having firm-fleshed fruit. **2** the fruit of any of these trees. See also **heart cherry.** ◆ Also called: **dessert cherry.** Compare **sour cherry.**

sweet chestnut *n* See **chestnut** (sense 1).

sweet cicely *n* **1** Also called: **myrrh.** an aromatic umbelliferous European plant, *Myrrhis odorata,* having compound leaves and clusters of small white flowers. **2** the leaves of this plant, formerly used in cookery for their flavour of aniseed. **3** any of various plants of the umbelliferous genus *Osmorhiza,* of Asia and America, having aromatic roots and clusters of small white flowers.

sweet cider *n* **1** *Brit.* cider having a high sugar content. **2** *U.S. and Canadian.* unfermented apple juice. Compare **hard cider.**

sweet clover *n* another name for **melilot.**

sweet corn *n* **1** Also called: **sugar corn, green corn.** a variety of maize, *Zea mays saccharata,* whose kernels are rich in sugar and eaten as a vegetable when young. **2** the unripe ears of maize, esp. the sweet kernels removed from the cob, cooked as a vegetable.

sweeten (ˈswiːtᵊn) *vb* (*mainly tr*) **1** (*also intr*) to make or become sweet or sweeter. **2** to mollify or soften (a person). **3** to make more agreeable. **4** (*also intr*) *Chem.* to free or be freed from unpleasant odours, acidic or corrosive substances, or the like. **5** *Finance, chiefly U.S.* to raise the value of (loan collateral) by adding more securities. **6** *Informal, poker.* to enlarge (the pot) by adding chips.

sweetener (ˈswiːtᵊnə) *n* **1** a sweetening agent, esp. one that does not contain sugar. **2** *Informal.* a bribe. **3** *Informal.* a financial inducement.

sweetening (ˈswiːtᵊnɪŋ) *n* something that sweetens.

sweet fern *n* a North American shrub, *Comptonia* (or *Myrica*) *asplenifolia,* having scented fernlike leaves and heads of brownish flowers: family *Myricaceae.*

sweet flag *n* an aroid marsh plant, *Acorus calamus,* having swordlike leaves, small greenish flowers, and aromatic roots. Also called: **calamus.** [C18: see FLAG[2]]

sweet gale *n* a shrub, *Myrica gale,* of northern swamp regions, having yellow catkin-like flowers and aromatic leaves: family *Myricaceae.* Also called: **bog myrtle.** Often shortened to **gale.** [C17: see GALE[2]]

sweet gum *n* **1** a North American liquidambar tree, *Liquidambar styraciflua,* having prickly spherical fruit clusters and fragrant sap: the wood (called **satin walnut**) is used to make furniture. Compare **sour gum. 2** the sap of this tree. ◆ Also called: **red gum.**

sweetheart (ˈswiːtˌhɑːt) *n* **1** a person loved by another. **2** *Informal.* a lovable, generous, or obliging person. **3** a term of endearment for a beloved or lovable person. ◆ *adj* **4** of or relating to a garment with a sweetheart neckline: *sweetheart cardigan.*

sweetheart agreement *n* **1** an industrial agreement made at a local level between an employer and employees, often with clauses advantageous to the employer, such as no strikes, but without the recognition of the national union representing the employees. **2** *Austral.* an industrial agreement negotiated directly between employers and employees, without resort to arbitration.

sweetheart neckline *n* a neckline on a woman's dress that is low at the front and shaped like the top of a heart.

sweetie (ˈswiːtɪ) *n Informal.* **1** sweetheart; darling: used as a term of endearment. **2** *Brit.* another word for **sweet** (sense 20). **3** *Chiefly Brit.* an endearing person. **4** a large seedless variety of grapefruit which has a green to yellow rind and juicy sweet pulp.

sweetiewife (ˈswiːtɪˌwaɪf) *n, pl* **-wives.** *Scot. dialect.* **1** a garrulous person. **2** (formerly) a woman selling sweets.

sweeting (ˈswiːtɪŋ) *n* **1** a variety of sweet apple. **2** an archaic word for **sweetheart.**

sweetman (ˈswiːtˌmæn) *n, pl* **-men.** (in the Caribbean) a man kept by a woman.

sweet marjoram *n* another name for **marjoram** (sense 1).

sweet marten *n* a name for the pine marten, referring to the fact that its scent glands produce a less offensive scent marker than that of the polecat (the foul marten or foumart).

sweetmeal (ˈswiːtˌmiːl) *adj* (of biscuits) sweet and wholemeal.

sweetmeat (ˈswiːtˌmiːt) *n* a sweetened delicacy, such as a preserve, sweet, or, formerly, a cake or pastry.

sweetness and light *n* an apparently affable reasonableness. [C19: adopted by Matthew Arnold from Swift's *Battle of the Books* (1704)]

sweet oil *n* another name for **olive oil.**

sweet pea *n* a climbing papilionaceous plant, *Lathyrus odoratus,* of S Europe, widely cultivated for its butterfly-shaped fragrant flowers of delicate pastel colours.

sweet pepper *n* **1** a pepper plant, *Capsicum frutescens grossum,* with large bell-shaped fruits that are eaten unripe (**green pepper**) or ripe (**red pepper**). **2** the fruit of this plant.

sweet potato *n* **1** a convolvulaceous twining plant, *Ipomoea batatas,* of tropical America, cultivated in the tropics for its edible fleshy yellow root. **2** the root of this plant. ◆ Also called (N.Z.): **kumera.**

sweet shop *n Chiefly Brit.* a shop solely or largely selling sweets, esp. boiled sweets.

sweetsop (ˈswiːtˌsɒp) *n* **1** a small West Indian tree, *Annona squamosa,* having yellowish-green fruit: family *Annonaceae.* **2** the fruit of this tree, which has a sweet edible pulp. ◆ Also called: **sugar apple, custard apple.** Compare **soursop.** [C19: so called because of the flavour and consistency of its pulp]

sweet spot *n Sport.* the centre area of a racquet, golf club, etc., from which the cleanest shots are made.

sweet-talk *Informal.* ◆ *vb* **1** to coax, flatter, or cajole (someone). ◆ *n* **sweet talk. 2** cajolery; coaxing.

sweet tooth *n* a strong liking for sweet foods.

sweet william *n* a widely cultivated Eurasian caryophyllaceous plant, *Dianthus barbatus,* with flat clusters of white, pink, red, or purple flowers.

sweet woodruff *n* a Eurasian and North African rubiaceous plant, *Galium odoratum* (or *Asperula odorata*), having whorls of leaves and clusters of fragrant white flowers.

sweir[1] (swiːr) *vb, n* a Scot. word for **swear.**

sweir[2] (swiːr) *adj Scot.* **1** lazy. **2** loath; disinclined. [Old English]

swell (swɛl) *vb* **swells, swelling, swelled; swollen** *or* **swelled. 1** to grow or cause to grow in size, esp. as a result of internal pressure. Compare **contract** (senses 1,3). **2** to expand or cause to expand at a particular point or above the surrounding level; protrude. **3** to grow or cause to grow in size, amount, intensity, or degree: *the party is swelling with new recruits.* **4** to puff or be puffed up with pride or another emotion. **5** (*intr*) (of seas or lakes) to rise in waves. **6** (*intr*) to well up or overflow. **7** (*tr*) to make (a musical phrase) increase gradually in volume and then diminish. ◆ *n* **8a** the undulating movement of the surface of the open sea. **8b** a succession of waves or a single large wave. **9** a swelling or being swollen; expansion. **10** an increase in quantity or degree; inflation. **11** a bulge; protuberance. **12** a gentle hill. **13** *Informal.* a person very fashionably dressed. **14** *Informal.* a man of high social or political standing. **15** *Music.* a crescendo followed by an immediate diminuendo. **16** Also called: **swell organ.** *Music.* **16a** a set of pipes on an organ housed in a box (**swell box**) fitted with a shutter operated by a pedal, which can be opened or closed to control the volume. **16b** the manual on an organ controlling this. Compare **choir** (sense 4), **great** (sense 21). ◆ *adj* **17** *Informal.* stylish or grand. **18** *Slang.* excellent; first-class. [Old English *swellan;* related to Old Norse *svella,* Old Frisian *swella,* German *schwellen*]

swelled head *or* **swollen head** *Informal.* ◆ *n* **1** an inflated view of one's own worth, often caused by sudden success. ◆ *adj* **swelled-headed, swell-headed,** *or* **swollen-headed. 2** conceited.

swellfish (ˈswɛlˌfɪʃ) *n, pl* **-fish** *or* **-fishes.** a popular name for **puffer** (sense 2).

swelling (ˈswɛlɪŋ) *n* **1** the act of expansion or inflation. **2** the state of being or becoming swollen. **3** a swollen or inflated part or area. **4** an abnormal enlargement of a bodily structure or part, esp. as the result of injury. Related adj: **tumescent.**

swelter (ˈswɛltə) *vb* **1** (*intr*) to suffer under oppressive heat, esp. to perspire and feel faint. **2** (*tr*) *Archaic.* to exude (venom). **3** (*tr*) *Rare.* to cause to suffer under oppressive heat. ◆ *n* **4** a sweltering condition (esp. in the phrase **in a swelter**). **5** oppressive humid heat. [C15 *swelten,* from Old English *sweltan* to die; related to Old Norse *svelta* to starve, Old High German *swelzan* to burn with passion; see SULTRY]

sweltering (ˈswɛltərɪŋ) *adj* oppressively hot and humid: *a sweltering day.* ▸ ˈ**swelteringly** *adv*

swept (swɛpt) *vb* the past tense of **sweep.**

sweptback (ˈswɛptˌbæk) *adj* (of an aircraft wing) having leading edge and trailing edges inclined backwards towards the rear of the fuselage.

swept volume *n* another term for **volumetric displacement.**

sweptwing (ˈswɛptˌwɪŋ) *adj* (of an aircraft, winged missile, etc.) having wings swept (usually) backwards.

swerve (swɜːv) *vb* **1** to turn or cause to turn aside, usually sharply or suddenly, from a course. ◆ *n* **2** the act, instance, or degree of swerving. [Old English *sweorfan* to scour; related to Old High German *swerban* to wipe off, Gothic *afswairban* to wipe off, Old Norse *sverfa* to file] ▸ ˈ**swervable** *adj* ▸ ˈ**swerver** *n*

sweven (ˈswɛvᵊn) *n Archaic.* a vision or dream. [Old English *swefn;* related to Old Norse *svefn* dream, sleep, Lithuanian *sāpnas,* Old Slavonic *sunu,* Latin *somnus*]

Sweyn (sweɪn) *n* known as *Sweyn Forkbeard.* died 1014, king of Denmark (?986–1014). He conquered England, forcing Ethelred II to flee (1013); father of Canute.

SWG Standard Wire Gauge; a notation for the diameters of metal rods or thickness of metal sheet ranging from 16 mm to 0.02 mm or from 0.5 inch to 0.001 inch.

swift (swɪft) *adj* **1** moving or able to move quickly; fast. **2** occurring or performed quickly or suddenly; instant: *a swift response.* **3** (*postpositive;* foll. by *to*) prompt to act or respond: *swift to take revenge.* ◆ *adv* **4a** swiftly or quickly. **4b** (*in combination*): *swift-moving.* ◆ *n* **5** any bird of the families *Apodidae* and *Hemiprocnidae,* such as *Apus apus* (**common swift**) of the Old World:

order *Apodiformes.* They have long narrow wings and spend most of the time on the wing. **6** (*sometimes cap.*) a variety of domestic fancy pigeon originating in Egypt and Syria and having an appearance somewhat similar to a swift. **7** short for **swift moth. 8** any of certain North American lizards of the genera *Sceloporus* and *Uta* that can run very rapidly: family *Iguanidae* (iguanas). **9** the main cylinder in a carding machine. **10** an expanding circular frame used to hold skeins of silk, wool, etc. [Old English, from *swīfan* to turn; related to Old Norse *svifa* to rove, Old Frisian *swīvia* to waver, Old High German *sweib* a reversal; see SWIVEL] ▸ **'swiftly** *adv* ▸ **'swiftness** *n*

Swift (swɪft) *n* **1 Graham Colin.** born 1949, British writer: his novels include *Waterland* (1983) and *Last Orders* (1996), which won the Booker prize. **2 Jonathan.** 1667–1745, Anglo-Irish satirist and churchman, who became dean of St. Patrick's, Dublin, in 1713. His works include *A Tale of a Tub* (1704) and *Gulliver's Travels* (1726). ▸ **'Swiftian** *adj*

swifter ('swɪftə) *n Nautical.* a line run around the ends of capstan bars to prevent their falling out of their sockets. [C17: related to the nautical term *swift* to fasten with tight-drawn ropes; probably Scandinavian in origin: compare Old Norse *svipta* to reef]

swift fox *n* a small fox, *Vulpes velox,* of the plains of W North America. Also called: **kit fox.**

swiftie *or* **swifty** ('swɪftɪ) *n Slang, chiefly Austral.* a trick, ruse, or deception.

swiftlet ('swɪftlɪt) *n* any of various small swifts of the Asian genus *Collocalia* that often live in caves and use echolocation: the nests, which are made of hardened saliva, are used in oriental cookery to make birds' nest soup.

swift moth *n* any of five species of fast-flying moths of the family *Hepialidae,* regarded as primitive in development, having forewings and hind wings similar in size and shape: the best known is the **ghost swift,** *Hepialus humili.* Often shortened to **swift.**

swig (swɪg) *Informal.* ♦ *n* **1** a large swallow or deep drink, esp. from a bottle. ♦ *vb* **swigs, swigging, swigged. 2** to drink (some liquid) deeply, esp. from a bottle. [C16: of unknown origin] ▸ **'swigger** *n*

swill (swɪl) *vb* **1** to drink large quantities of (liquid, esp. alcoholic drink); guzzle. **2** (*tr;* often foll. by *out*) *Chiefly Brit.* to drench or rinse in large amounts of water. **3** (*tr*) to feed swill to (pigs, etc.). ♦ *n* **4** wet feed, esp. for pigs, consisting of kitchen waste, skimmed milk, etc. **5** garbage or refuse, esp. from a kitchen. **6** a deep draught of drink, esp. beer. **7** any liquid mess. **8** the act of swilling. [Old English *swilian* to wash out] ▸ **'swiller** *n*

swim (swɪm) *vb* **swims, swimming, swam, swum. 1** (*intr*) to move along in water, etc., by means of movements of the body or parts of the body, esp. the arms and legs, or (in the case of fish) tail and fins. **2** (*tr*) to cover (a distance or stretch of water) in this way. **3** (*tr*) to compete in (a race) in this way. **4** (*intr*) to be supported by and on a liquid; float. **5** (*tr*) to use (a particular stroke) in swimming. **6** (*intr*) to move smoothly, usually through air or over a surface. **7** (*intr*) to reel or seem to reel: *my head swam; the room swam around me.* **8** (*intr;* often foll. by *in* or *with*) to be covered or flooded with water or other liquid. **9** (*intr;* often foll. by *in*) to be liberally supplied (with): *he's swimming in money.* **10** (*tr*) to cause to float or swim. **11** (*tr*) to provide (something) with water deep enough to float in. **12 swim with** (*or* **against**) **the stream** *or* **tide.** to conform to (or resist) prevailing opinion. ♦ *n* **13** the act, an instance, or period of swimming. **14** any graceful gliding motion. **15** a condition of dizziness; swoon. **16** a pool in a river good for fishing. **17 in the swim.** *Informal.* fashionable or active in social or political activities. [Old English *swimman;* related to Old Norse *svima,* German *schwimmen,* Gothic *swumsl* pond, Norwegian *svamla* to paddle] ▸ **'swimmable** *adj* ▸ **'swimmer** *n* ▸ **'swimming** *n, adj*

swim bladder *n Ichthyol.* another name for **air bladder** (sense 1).

swimfeeder ('swɪm,fiːdə) *n Angling.* a device containing bait, attached to the line to ensure the gradual baiting of the swim from under the surface.

swimmeret ('swɪmə,rɛt) *n* any of the small paired appendages on the abdomen of crustaceans, used chiefly in locomotion and reproduction. Also called: **pleopod.** [C19: from SWIM + -ER[1] + -ET]

swimmers (swɪməz) *pl n Austral.* a swimming costume.

swimming bath *n* (*often pl*) an indoor swimming pool.

swimming costume *or* **bathing costume** *n Chiefly Brit.* any apparel worn for swimming or sunbathing, such as a woman's one-piece garment covering most of the torso but not the limbs.

swimmingly ('swɪmɪŋlɪ) *adv* successfully, effortlessly, or well (esp. in the phrase **go swimmingly**).

swimming pool *n* an artificial pool for swimming.

swimsuit ('swɪm,suːt, -,sjuːt) *n* a woman's one-piece swimming garment that leaves the arms and legs bare.

Swinburne ('swɪn,bɜːn) *n* **Algernon Charles.** 1837–1909, English lyric poet and critic.

swindle ('swɪndəl) *vb* **1** to cheat (someone) of money, etc.; defraud. **2** (*tr*) to obtain (money, etc.) by fraud. ♦ *n* **3** a fraudulent scheme or transaction. [C18: back formation from German *Schwindler,* from *schwindeln,* from Old High German *swintilōn,* frequentative of *swintan* to disappear] ▸ **'swindler** *n*

swindle sheet *n* a slang term for **expense account.**

Swindon ('swɪndən) *n* a town and unitary authority in S England, in NE Wiltshire: railway workshops. Pop.: 173 500 (1994 est.). Area: 230 sq. km (89 sq. miles).

swine (swaɪn) *n* **1** (*pl* **swines**) a coarse or contemptible person. **2** (*pl* **swine**) another name for a **pig.** [Old English *swīn;* related to Old Norse *svīn,* Gothic *swein,* Latin *suīnus* relating to swine] ▸ **'swine,like** *adj* ▸ **'swinish** *adj* ▸ **'swinishly** *adv* ▸ **'swinishness** *n*

swine fever *n* an infectious viral disease of pigs, characterized by fever, refusal to eat, weight loss, and diarrhoea. U.S. term: **hog cholera.**

swineherd ('swaɪn,hɜːd) *n Archaic.* a person who looks after pigs.

swinepox ('swaɪn,pɒks) *n* **1** Also called: **variola porcina** (pɔː'saɪnə). an acute infectious viral disease of pigs characterized by skin eruptions. **2** a form of chickenpox in which the skin eruptions are not pitted.

swine's cress *n* another name for **wart cress.**

swine vesicular disease *n* a viral disease of swine characterized by vesicular lesions on the feet, legs, snout, and tongue.

swing (swɪŋ) *vb* **swings, swinging, swung. 1** to move or cause to move rhythmically to and fro, as a free-hanging object; sway. **2** (*intr*) to move, walk, etc., with a relaxed and swaying motion. **3** to pivot or cause to pivot, as on a hinge. **4** to move or cause to move in a curve: *the car swung around the bend.* **5** to move or cause to move by suspending or being suspended. **6** to hang or be hung so as to be able to turn freely. **7** (*intr*) *Slang.* to be hanged: *he'll swing for it.* **8** to alter or cause to alter habits, a course, etc. **9** (*tr*) *Informal.* to influence or manipulate successfully: *I hope he can swing the deal.* **10** (*tr;* foll. by *up*) to raise or hoist, esp. in a sweeping motion. **11** (*intr;* often foll. by *at*) to hit out or strike (at), esp. with a sweeping motion. **12** (*tr*) to wave (a weapon, etc.) in a sweeping motion; flourish. **13** to arrange or play (music) with the rhythmically flexible and compulsive quality associated with jazz. **14** (*intr*) (of popular music, esp. jazz, or of the musicians who play it) to have this quality. **15** *Slang.* to be lively and modern. **16** (*intr*) *Slang.* to swap sexual partners in a group, esp. habitually. **17** (*intr*) *Cricket.* to bowl (a ball) with swing or (of a ball) to move with a swing. **18** to turn (a ship or aircraft) in order to test compass error. **19 swing both ways.** *Slang.* to enjoy sexual partners of both sexes. **20 swing the lead.** *Informal.* to malinger or make up excuses. ♦ *n* **21** the act or manner of swinging or the distance covered while swinging: *a wide swing.* **22** a sweeping stroke or blow. **23** *Boxing.* a wide punch from the side similar to but longer than a hook. **24** *Cricket.* the lateral movement of a bowled ball through the air. **25** any free-swaying motion. **26** any curving movement; sweep. **27** something that swings or is swung, esp. a suspended seat on which a person may sit and swing back and forth. **28a** a kind of popular dance music influenced by jazz, usually played by big bands and originating in the 1930s. **28b** (*as modifier*): *swing music.* **29** *Prosody.* a steady distinct rhythm or cadence in prose or verse. **30** *Informal.* the normal round or pace: *get into the swing of things.* **31a** a fluctuation, as in some business activity, voting pattern etc. **31b** (*as modifier*) able to bring about a swing in a voting pattern: *swing party.* **32** *U.S. informal.* free scope; freedom of activity. **33** *Chiefly U.S.* a circular tour. **34** *Canadian.* a tour of a particular area or region. **35 go with a swing.** to go well; be successful. **36 in full swing.** at the height of activity. **37 swings and roundabouts.** equal advantages and disadvantages. [Old English *swingan;* related to Old Frisian *swinga,* Old High German *swingan*]

swingboat ('swɪŋ,bəʊt) *n* a piece of fairground equipment consisting of a boat-shaped carriage for swinging in.

swing bridge *n* **1** Also called: **pivot bridge, turn bridge.** a low bridge that can be rotated about a vertical axis, esp. to permit the passage of ships. Compare **drawbridge. 2** *N.Z.* a pedestrian bridge over a river, suspended by heavy wire cables.

swing door *or* **swinging door** *n* a door pivoted or hung on double-sided hinges so that it can open either way.

swinge (swɪndʒ) *vb* **swinges, swingeing** *or* **swinging, swinged.** (*tr*) *Archaic.* to beat, flog, or punish. [Old English *swengan;* related to Old Frisian *swenga* to drench, Gothic *afswaggwjan* to cause to sway; see SWING]

swingeing ('swɪndʒɪŋ) *adj Chiefly Brit.* punishing; severe.

swinger ('swɪŋə) *n Slang.* a person regarded as being modern and lively. ▸ **'swinging** *adj* ▸ **'swingingly** *adv*

swinging voter *n* an Austral. and N.Z. informal term for **floating voter.**

swingle ('swɪŋgəl) *n* **1** a flat-bladed wooden instrument used for beating and scraping flax or hemp to remove coarse matter from it. ♦ *vb* **2** (*tr*) to use a swingle on. [Old English *swingel* stroke; related to Middle High German *swüngel,* Middle Dutch *swinghel*]

swingletree ('swɪŋgəl,triː) *n* a crossbar in a horse's harness to which the ends of the traces are attached. Also called: **whippletree,** (esp. U.S.) **whiffletree.** [C15: from SWINGLE + TREE (in the sense: a post or bar)]

swingometer (swɪŋ'ɒmɪtə) *n* a device used in television broadcasting during a general election to indicate the swing of votes from one political party to another.

swing shift *n* the usual U.S. and Canadian term for **backshift.**

swing-wing *adj* **1** of or relating to a variable-geometry aircraft. ♦ *n* **2a** such an aircraft. **2b** either wing of such an aircraft.

swink (swɪŋk) *Archaic or Brit. dialect.* ♦ *vb* **1** (*intr*) to toil or drudge. ♦ *n* **2** toil or drudgery. [Old English *swinc,* from *swincan*] ▸ **'swinker** *n*

swipe (swaɪp) *vb* **1** (when *intr,* usually foll. by *at*) *Informal.* to hit hard with a sweeping blow. **2** (*tr*) *Slang.* to steal. **3** (*tr*) to pass a machine-readable card, such as a credit card, debit card, etc., through a machine that electronically interprets the information encoded, usu. in a magnetic strip, on the card. ♦ *n* **4** *Informal.* a hard blow. **5** Also called: **sweep.** a type of lever for raising and lowering a weight, such as a bucket in a well. [C19: perhaps related to SWEEP]

swipes (swaɪps) *pl n Brit. slang.* beer, esp. when poor or weak. [C18: probably related to SWEEP]

swipple *or* **swiple** ('swɪpəl) *n* the part of a flail that strikes the grain. [C15 *swipyl,* variant of *swepyl,* from *swep(en)* to SWEEP + *-yl,* suffix denoting an instrument]

swirl (swɜːl) *vb* **1** to turn or cause to turn in a twisting spinning fashion. **2** (*intr*) to be dizzy; swim: *my head was swirling.* ♦ *n* **3** a whirling or spinning motion, esp. in water. **4** a whorl; curl. **5** the act of swirling or stirring. **6** dizzy confusion. [C15: probably from Dutch *zwirrelen;* related to Norwegian *svirla,* German *schwirren*] ▸ **'swirling** *adj* ▸ **'swirlingly** *adv* ▸ **'swirly** *adj*

swish (swɪʃ) *vb* **1** to move with or make or cause to move with or make a whistling or hissing sound. **2** (*intr*) (esp. of fabrics) to rustle. **3** (*tr*) *Slang, now rare.* to whip; flog. **4** (*tr;* foll. by *off*) to cut with a swishing blow. ♦ *n* **5** a hissing or rustling sound or movement. **6** a rod for flogging or a blow from such a rod. **7** *U.S. slang.* an effeminate male homosexual. **8** a W African building material composed of mortar and mud or laterite, or more recently of cement and earth. ◆ *adj* **9** *Informal, chiefly Brit.* fashionable; smart. **10** *U.S. slang.* effeminate and homosexual. [C18: of imitative origin] ▸ **'swisher** *n* ▸ **'swishing** *adj* ▸ **'swishingly** *adv* ▸ **'swishy** *adj*

Swiss (swɪs) *adj* **1** of, relating to, or characteristic of Switzerland, its inhabitants, or their dialects of German, French, and Italian. ◆ *n* **2** a native, inhabitant, or citizen of Switzerland.

Swiss chard *n* another name for **chard.**

Swiss cheese *n* a hard white or pale yellow cheese with holes, such as Gruyère or Emmenthal.

Swiss cheese plant *n* See **monstera.**

Swiss Guard *n* **1** the bodyguard of the pope, recruited from Swiss nationals. **2** a member of this bodyguard. **3** one of a group of Swiss mercenaries who acted as bodyguards to the French kings: destroyed in the Revolution.

swiss muslin *n* a fine muslin dress fabric, usually having a raised or woven pattern of dolls or figures. [C19: so called because it was formerly imported from Switzerland]

swiss roll *n* a sponge cake spread with jam, cream, or some other filling, and rolled up.

Swiss tournament *n* (in certain games and sports) a tournament system in which players are paired in each round according to the scores they then have, playing a new opponent each time. More players can take part than in an all-play-all tournament of the same duration. [named from a chess tournament held in Zürich in 1895]

switch (swɪtʃ) *n* **1** a mechanical, electrical, or electronic device for opening or closing a circuit or for diverting a current from one part of a circuit to another. **2** a swift and usually sudden shift or change. **3** an exchange or swap. **4** a flexible rod or twig, used esp. for punishment. **5** the sharp movement or blow of such an instrument. **6** a tress of false hair used to give added length or bulk to a woman's own hairstyle. **7** the tassel-like tip of the tail of cattle and certain other animals. **8** any of various card games in which the suit is changed during play. **9** *U.S. and Canadian.* a railway siding. **10** *U.S. and Canadian.* a railway point. **11** *Austral. informal.* See **switchboard.** ◆ *vb* **12** to shift, change, turn aside, or change the direction of (something). **13** to exchange (places); replace (something by something else): *the battalions switched fronts.* **14** *Chiefly U.S. and Canadian.* to transfer (rolling stock) from one railway track to another. **15** (*tr*) to cause (an electric current) to start or stop flowing or to change its path by operating a switch. **16** to swing or cause to swing, esp. back and forth. **17** (*tr*) to lash or whip with or as if with a switch. ◆ See also **switch off, switch on.** [C16: perhaps from Middle Dutch *swijch* branch, twig] ▸ **'switcher** *n* ▸ **'switch,like** *adj*

switchback ('swɪtʃ,bæk) *n* **1** a mountain road, railway, or track which rises and falls sharply many times or a sharp rise and fall on such a road, railway, or track. **2** another word (esp. Brit.) for **big dipper.**

switchblade *or* **switchblade knife** ('swɪtʃ,bleɪd) *n* another name (esp. U.S. and Canadian) for **flick knife.**

switchboard ('swɪtʃ,bɔːd) *n* **1** an installation in a telephone exchange, office, hotel, etc., at which the interconnection of telephone lines is manually controlled. **2** an assembly of switchgear for the control of power supplies in an installation or building.

switched-star *adj* denoting or relating to a cable television system in which only one or two programme channels are fed to each subscriber, who can select other channels by remote control of a central switching point: *a switched-star network.* Compare **tree-and-branch.**

switcheroo (,swɪtʃə'ruː) *n U.S. slang.* a surprising or unexpected change or variation. [C20: from SWITCH]

switchgear ('swɪtʃ,gɪə) *n Electrical engineering.* any of several devices used for opening and closing electric circuits, esp. those that pass high currents.

switchgirl ('swɪtʃ,gɜːl) *n Informal, chiefly Austral.* a woman who operates a telephone switchboard.

switch-hitter *n U.S. and Canadian.* **1** *Baseball.* a batsman who can hit either right- or left-handed. **2** *Slang.* a bisexual person.

switchman ('swɪtʃmən) *n, pl* **-men.** the U.S. and Canadian name for **pointsman.**

switch off *vb* (*adv*) **1** to cause (a device) to stop operating by or as if by moving a switch, knob, or lever; turn off. **2** *Informal.* to cease to interest or be interested; make or become bored, alienated, etc.

switch on *vb* (*adv*) **1** to cause (a device) to operate by or as if by moving a switch, knob, or lever; turn on. **2** (*tr*) *Informal.* to produce (charm, tears, etc.) suddenly or automatically. **3** (*tr*) *Informal.* (now slightly dated) to make up-to-date, esp. regarding outlook, dress, etc. **4** (*tr*) *Slang.* to arouse emotionally or sexually. **5** (*intr*) *Slang.* to take or become intoxicated by drugs. **6** (*tr*) *Slang.* to introduce (someone) to drugs.

switch selling *n* a system of selling, now illegal in Britain, whereby potential customers are attracted by a special offer on some goods but the salesman's real aim is to sell other more expensive goods instead.

switch yard *n U.S. and Canadian.* an area in a railway system where rolling stock is shunted, as in forming trains.

swither ('swɪðər) *Scot.* ◆ *vb* (*intr*) **1** to hesitate; vacillate; be perplexed. ◆ *n* **2** hesitation; perplexity; agitation. [C16: of unknown origin]

Swithin *or* **Swithun** ('swɪðɪn, 'swɪθ-) *n* **Saint.** died 862 A.D., English ecclesiastic: bishop of Winchester (?852–862). Feast day: July 15.

Switz. *or* **Swit.** *abbrev. for* Switzerland.

Switzer ('swɪtsə) *n* **1** a less common word for **Swiss.** **2** a member of the Swiss Guard. [C16: from Middle High German, from *Swīz* Switzerland]

Switzerland ('swɪtsələnd) *n* a federal republic in W central Europe: the cantons of Schwyz, Uri, and Unterwalden formed a defensive league against the Hapsburgs in 1291, later joined by other cantons; gained independence in 1499; adopted a policy of permanent neutrality from 1516; a leading centre of the Reformation in the 16th century. It lies in the Jura Mountains and the Alps, with a plateau between the two ranges. Official languages: German, French, and Italian; Romansch minority. Religion: mostly Protestant and Roman Catholic. Currency: Swiss franc. Capital: Bern. Pop.: 7 118 000 (1998 est.). Area: 41 288 sq. km (15 941 sq. miles). German name: **Schweiz.** French name: **Suisse.** Italian name: **Svizzera.** Latin name: **Helvetia** (hɛl'viːʃə).

swive (swaɪv) *vb Archaic.* to have sexual intercourse with (a person). [Old English *swīfan* to revolve, SWIVEL]

swivel ('swɪvᵊl) *n* **1** a coupling device which allows an attached object to turn freely. **2** such a device made of two parts which turn independently, such as a compound link of a chain. **3a** a pivot on which is mounted a gun that may be swung from side to side in a horizontal plane. **3b** Also called: **swivel gun.** the gun itself. ◆ *vb* **-els, -elling, -elled** *or U.S.* **-els, -eling, -eled.** **4** to turn or swing on or as if on a pivot. **5** (*tr*) to provide with, secure by, or support with a swivel. [C14: from Old English *swīfan* to turn; see SWIFT] ▸ **'swivel-,like** *adj*

swivel chair *n* a chair, the seat of which is joined to the legs by a swivel and which thus may be spun round.

swivel pin *n* another name for **kingpin** (sense 3).

swiz *or* **swizz** (swɪz) *n Brit. informal.* a swindle or disappointment; swizzle.

swizzle ('swɪzᵊl) *n* **1** *U.S.* an unshaken cocktail. **2** a Caribbean drink of milk and rum. **3** *Brit. informal.* a swiz. ◆ *vb* **4** (*tr*) to stir a swizzle stick in (a drink). **5** *Brit. informal.* to swindle; cheat. [C19: of unknown origin]

swizzle stick *n* a small rod used to agitate an effervescent drink to facilitate the escape of carbon dioxide.

swob (swɒb) *n, vb,* **swobs, swobbing, swobbed.** a less common word for **swab.**

swollen ('swəʊlən) *vb* **1** a past participle of **swell.** ◆ *adj* **2** tumid or enlarged by or as if by swelling. **3** turgid or bombastic. ▸ **'swollenly** *adv* ▸ **'swollenness** *n*

swollen head *n* another term for **swelled head.**

swollen-headed *adj Informal.* conceited.

swoon (swuːn) *vb* (*intr*) **1** a literary word for **faint.** **2** to become ecstatic. ◆ *n* **3** an instance of fainting. ◆ Also (archaic or dialect): **swound.** [Old English *geswōgen* insensible, past participle of *swōgan* (unattested except in compounds) to suffocate] ▸ **'swooning** *adj* ▸ **'swooningly** *adv*

swoop (swuːp) *vb* **1** (*intr;* usually foll. by *down, on,* or *upon*) to sweep or pounce suddenly. **2** (*tr;* often foll. by *up, away,* or *off*) to seize or scoop suddenly. ◆ *n* **3** the act of swooping. **4** a swift descent. [Old English *swāpan* to sweep; related to Old High German *sweifan* to swing around, Old Norse *sveipa* to throw]

swoosh (swʊʃ) *vb* **1** to make or cause to make a rustling or swirling sound, esp. when moving or pouring out. ◆ *n* **2** a swirling or rustling sound or movement. [C20: of imitative origin (probably influenced by SWISH and SWOOP)]

swop (swɒp) *n, vb,* **swops, swopping, swopped.** a variant spelling of **swap.**

sword (sɔːd) *n* **1** a thrusting, striking, or cutting weapon with a long blade having one or two cutting edges, a hilt, and usually a crosspiece or guard. **2** such a weapon worn on ceremonial occasions as a symbol of authority. **3** something resembling a sword, such as the snout of a swordfish. **4** **cross swords.** to argue or fight. **5** **the sword.** **5a** violence or power, esp. military power. **5b** death; destruction: *to put to the sword.* [Old English *sweord;* related to Old Saxon *swerd,* Old Norse *sverth,* Old High German *swert*] ▸ **'swordless** *adj* ▸ **'sword,like** *adj*

sword bayonet *n* a bayonet with a swordlike blade and hilt, capable of use as a sword.

swordbearer ('sɔːd,bɛərə) *n* an official who carries a ceremonial sword.

sword belt *n* a belt with a sling or strap for a sword.

swordbill ('sɔːd,bɪl) *n* a South American hummingbird, *Ensifera ensifera,* having a bill as long as its body.

sword cane *n* another name for **swordstick.**

swordcraft ('sɔːd,krɑːft) *n* the art of using a sword.

sword dance *n* a dance in which the performers dance nimbly over swords on the ground or brandish them in the air. ▸ **sword dancer** *n* ▸ **sword dancing** *n*

sword fern *n* any of numerous ferns having sword-shaped fronds.

swordfish ('sɔːd,fɪʃ) *n, pl* **-fish** *or* **-fishes.** a large scombroid fish, *Xiphias gladius,* with a very long upper jaw: valued as a food and game fish: family *Xiphiidae.*

sword grass *n* any of various grasses and other plants having sword-shaped sharp leaves.

sword knot *n* a loop on the hilt of a sword by which it was attached to the wrist, now purely decorative.

sword lily *n* another name for **gladiolus** (sense 1). [C18: so called because of its sword-shaped leaves]

Sword of Damocles *n* a closely impending disaster. [see DAMOCLES]

swordplay ('sɔːd,pleɪ) *n* **1** the action or art of fighting with a sword. **2** verbal sparring. ▸ **'sword,player** *n*

swordsman ('sɔːdzmən) *n, pl* **-men.** one who uses or is skilled in the use of a sword. ▸ **'swordsman,ship** *n*

swordstick ('sɔːd,stɪk) *n* a hollow walking stick containing a short sword or dagger.

sword-swallower *n* a performer who simulates the swallowing of swords.

swordtail ('sɔːd,teɪl) *n* any of several small freshwater cyprinodont fishes of the genus *Xiphophorus,* esp. *X. helleri,* of Central America, having a long swordlike tail.

swore (swɔː) *vb* the past tense of **swear.**

sworn (swɔːn) *vb* **1** the past participle of **swear.** ◆ *adj* **2** bound, pledged, or made inveterate, by or as if by an oath: *a sworn statement; he was sworn to God.*

swot[1] (swɒt) *Brit. informal.* ♦ *vb* **swots, swotting, swotted. 1** (often foll. by *up*) to study (a subject) intensively, as for an examination; cram. ♦ *n* **2** Also called: **swotter** ('swɒtə). a person who works or studies hard. **3** hard work or grind. ♦ Also: **swat.** [C19: dialect variant of SWEAT (n)]

swot[2] (swɒt) *vb* **swots, swotting, swotted,** *n* a variant of **swat**[1].

SWOT *abbrev. for* strengths, weaknesses, opportunities, and threats: an analysis of a product made before it is marketed.

swound (swaʊnd) *n, vb* an archaic or dialect word for **swoon.**

swounds *or* **'swounds** (zwaʊndz, zaʊndz) *interj Archaic.* less common spellings of **zounds.**

swum (swʌm) *vb* the past participle of **swim.**

swung (swʌŋ) *vb* the past tense and past participle of **swing.**

swung dash *n* a mark, ~, traditionally used in text to indicate the omission of a word or part of a word.

swy (swaɪ) *n Austral.* another name for **two-up.** [C20: from German *zwei* two]

SY *international car registration for* Seychelles.

Sybaris ('sɪbərɪs) *n* a Greek colony in S Italy, on the Gulf of Taranto: notorious for its luxurious living, founded about 720 B.C. and sacked in 510. ▸ **'Sybarite** *n* ▸ **Sybaritic** (ˌsɪbə'rɪtɪk) *adj*

sybarite ('sɪbəˌraɪt) *n* **1** (*sometimes cap.*) a devotee of luxury and the sensual vices. ♦ *adj* **2** luxurious; sensuous. [C16: from Latin *Sybarīta,* from Greek *Subaritēs* inhabitant of SYBARIS] ▸ **sybaritic** (ˌsɪbə'rɪtɪk) *or* (*less commonly*) **ˌsyba'ritical** *adj* ▸ **ˌsyba'ritically** *adv* ▸ **'sybaritism** *n*

sybo, syboe, *or* **sybow** ('saɪbɪ, 'saɪ-, -bo) *n, pl* **syboes, sybows.** *Scot.* a spring onion. [C16: from *cibol,* from French *ciboule,* from Latin *cepulla* onion bed, from *cepa* onion]

sycamine ('sɪkəˌmaɪn) *n* a mulberry tree mentioned in the Bible, thought to be the black mulberry, *Morus nigra.* [C16: from Latin *sȳcamīnus,* from Greek *sukaminon,* from Hebrew *shiqmāh*]

sycamore ('sɪkəˌmɔː) *n* **1** a Eurasian maple tree, *Acer pseudoplatanus,* naturalized in Britain and North America, having five-lobed leaves, yellow flowers, and two-winged fruits. **2** *U.S. and Canadian.* an American plane tree, *Platanus occidentalis.* See **plane tree. 3** a moraceous tree, *Ficus sycomorus,* of N Africa and W Asia, having an edible figlike fruit. [C14: from Old French *sicamor,* from Latin *sȳcomorus,* from Greek *sukomoros,* from *sukon* fig + *moron* mulberry]

syce, sice, *or* **saice** (saɪs) *n* **1** (formerly, in India) a servant employed to look after horses, drive carriages, etc. **2** (in Malaysia) a driver or chauffeur. [C17: from Urdu *sā'is,* from Arabic, from *sāsa* to administer]

sycee *or* **sycee silver** (saɪ'siː) *n* silver ingots formerly used as a medium of exchange in China. [C18: from Chinese *saì sz* fine silk; so called because the silver can be made into threads as fine as silk]

syconium (saɪ'kəʊnɪəm) *n, pl* **-nia** (-nɪə). *Botany.* the fleshy fruit of the fig, consisting of a greatly enlarged receptacle. [C19: from New Latin, from Greek *sukon* fig]

sycophant ('sɪkəfənt) *n* a person who uses flattery to win favour from individuals wielding influence; toady. [C16: from Latin *sȳcophanta,* from Greek *sukophantēs,* literally: the person showing a fig, apparently referring to the fig sign used in making an accusation, from *sukon* fig + *phainein* to show; sense probably developed from "accuser" to "informer, flatterer"] ▸ **'sycophancy** *n* ▸ **sycophantic** (ˌsɪkə'fæntɪk) *adj* ▸ **ˌsyco'phantically** *adv*

sycosis (saɪ'kəʊsɪs) *n* chronic inflammation of the hair follicles, esp. those of the beard, caused by a staphylococcal infection. [C16: via New Latin from Greek *sukōsis,* from *sukon* fig]

Sydenham's chorea ('sɪdᵊnəmz) *n* a form of chorea affecting children, often associated with rheumatic fever. Nontechnical name: **Saint Vitus's dance.** [named after T. *Sydenham* (1624–89), English physician]

Sydney[1] ('sɪdnɪ) *n* **1** a port in SE Australia, capital of New South Wales, on an inlet of the S Pacific: the largest city in Australia and the first British settlement, established as a penal colony in 1788; developed rapidly after 1820 with the discovery of gold in its hinterland; large wool market; three universities. Pop.: 3 772 700 (1995 est.). **2** a port in SE Canada, in Nova Scotia on NE Cape Breton Island: capital of Cape Breton Island until 1820, when the island united administratively with Nova Scotia. Pop.: 26 063 (1991).

Sydney[2] ('sɪdnɪ) *n* a variant spelling of (Sir Philip) **Sidney.**

Sydneysider ('sɪdnɪˌsaɪdə) *n Chiefly Austral.* a resident of Sydney.

Sydney silky *n* a small silky-coated breed of terrier, originally from Australia.

Syene (saɪ'iːnɪ) *n* transliteration of the Ancient Greek name for **Aswan.**

syenite ('saɪəˌnaɪt) *n* a light-coloured coarse-grained plutonic igneous rock consisting of feldspars with hornblende or biotite. [C18: from French *syénite,* from Latin *syēnītēs lapis* stone from *Syene* (Aswan), where it was originally quarried] ▸ **syenitic** (ˌsaɪə'nɪtɪk) *adj*

SYHA *abbrev. for* Scottish Youth Hostels Association.

Syktyvkar (*Russian* siktif'kar) *n* a city in NW Russia, capital of the Komi Republic: timber industry. Pop.: 229 000 (1995 est.).

syl. *or* **syll.** *abbrev. for:* **1** syllable. **2** syllabus.

syllabary ('sɪləbərɪ) *n, pl* **-baries. 1** a table or list of syllables. **2** a set of symbols used in certain writing systems, such as one used for Japanese, in which each symbol represents a spoken syllable. [C16: from New Latin *syllabārium,* from Latin *syllaba* SYLLABLE]

syllabi ('sɪləˌbaɪ) *n* a plural of **syllabus.**

syllabic (sɪ'læbɪk) *adj* **1** of or relating to syllables or the division of a word into syllables. **2** denoting a kind of verse line based on a specific number of syllables rather than being regulated by stresses or quantities. **3** (of a consonant) constituting a syllable. **4** (of plainsong and similar chanting) having each syllable sung to a different note. ♦ *n* **5** a syllabic consonant. ▸ **syl'labically** *adv*

syllabify (sɪ'læbɪˌfaɪ) *or* **syllabicate** *vb* **-fies, -fying, -fied** *or* **-cates, -cating, -cated.** (*tr*) to divide (a word) into its constituent syllables. ▸ **sylˌlabifi'cation** *or* **sylˌlabi'cation** *n*

syllabism ('sɪləˌbɪzəm) *n* use of a writing system consisting of characters for syllables rather than for individual sounds or whole words. Also called: **syllabography.**

syllable ('sɪləbᵊl) *n* **1** a combination or set of one or more units of sound in a language that must consist of a sonorous element (a sonant or vowel) and may or may not contain less sonorous elements (consonants or semivowels) flanking it on either or both sides: for example "paper" has two syllables. See also **open** (sense 34b), **closed** (sense 6a). **2** (in the writing systems of certain languages, esp. ancient ones) a symbol or set of symbols standing for a syllable. **3** the least mention in speech or print: *don't breathe a syllable of it.* **4 in words of one syllable.** simply; bluntly. ♦ *vb* **5** to pronounce syllables of (a text); articulate. **6** (*tr*) to write down in syllables. [C14: via Old French from Latin *syllaba,* from Greek *sullabē,* from *sullambanein* to collect together, from *sul-* SYN- + *lambanein* to take]

syllabogram (sɪ'læbəʊˌgræm) *n* a written symbol representing a single syllable.

syllabography (ˌsɪlə'bɒgrəfɪ) *n* another word for **syllabism.** Compare **logography, phonography.**

syllabub *or* **sillabub** ('sɪləˌbʌb) *n* **1** a spiced drink made of milk with rum, port, brandy, or wine, often hot. **2** *Brit.* a cold dessert made from milk or cream beaten with sugar, wine, and lemon juice. [C16: of unknown origin]

syllabus ('sɪləbəs) *n, pl* **-buses** *or* **-bi** (-ˌbaɪ). **1** an outline of a course of studies, text, etc. **2** *Brit.* **2a** the subjects studied for a particular course. **2b** a document which lists these subjects and states how the course will be assessed. [C17: from Late Latin, erroneously from Latin *sittybus* parchment strip giving title and author, from Greek *sittuba*]

Syllabus ('sɪləbəs) *n R.C. Church.* **1** Also called: **Syllabus of Errors.** a list of 80 doctrinal theses condemned as erroneous by Pius IX in 1864. **2** a list of 65 Modernist propositions condemned as erroneous by Pius X in 1907.

syllepsis (sɪ'lɛpsɪs) *n, pl* **-ses** (-siːz). **1** (in grammar or rhetoric) the use of a single sentence construction in which a verb, adjective, etc. is made to cover two syntactical functions, as the verb form *have* in *she and they have promised to come.* **2** another word for **zeugma.** [C16: from Late Latin, from Greek *sullēpsis,* from *sul-* SYN- + *lēpsis* a taking, from *lambanein* to take] ▸ **syl'leptic** *adj* ▸ **syl'leptically** *adv*

syllogism ('sɪləˌdʒɪzəm) *n* **1** a deductive inference consisting of two premises and a conclusion, all of which are categorial propositions. The subject of the conclusion is the **minor term** and its predicate the **major term;** the **middle term** occurs in both premises but not the conclusion. There are 256 such arguments but only 24 are valid. *Some men are mortal; some men are angelic; so some mortals are angelic* is invalid, while *some temples are in ruins; all ruins are fascinating; so some temples are fascinating* is valid. Here *fascinating, in ruins,* and *temples* are respectively major, middle, and minor terms. **2** a deductive inference of certain other forms with two premises, such as the **hypothetical syllogism,** *if P then Q; if Q then R; so if P then R.* **3** a piece of deductive reasoning from the general to the particular. **4** a subtle or deceptive piece of reasoning. [C14: via Latin from Greek *sullogismos,* from *sullogizesthai* to reckon together, from *sul-* SYN- + *logizesthai* to calculate, from *logos* a discourse]

syllogistic (ˌsɪlə'dʒɪstɪk) *adj also* **syllogistical. 1** of, relating to or consisting of syllogisms. ♦ *n* (*often pl*) **2** the branch of logic concerned with syllogisms. **3** reasoning by means of syllogisms. ▸ **ˌsyllo'gistically** *adv*

syllogize *or* **syllogise** ('sɪləˌdʒaɪz) *vb* to reason or infer by using syllogisms. [C15: via Old French from Late Latin *syllogizāre,* from Greek *sullogizesthai;* see SYLLOGISM] ▸ **ˌsyllogi'zation** *or* **ˌsyllogi'sation** *n* ▸ **'sylloˌgizer** *or* **'sylloˌgiser** *n*

sylph (sɪlf) *n* **1** a slender graceful girl or young woman. **2** any of a class of imaginary beings assumed to inhabit the air. [C17: from New Latin *sylphus,* probably coined from Latin *silva* wood + Greek *numphē* NYMPH] ▸ **'sylphˌlike** *or* (*less commonly*) **'sylphic, 'sylphish,** *or* **'sylphy** *adj*

sylva *or* **silva** ('sɪlvə) *n, pl* **-vas** *or* **-vae** (-viː). the trees growing in a particular region. [C17: Latin *silva* a wood]

sylvan *or* **silvan** ('sɪlvən) *Chiefly poetic.* ♦ *adj* **1** of, characteristic of, or consisting of woods or forests. **2** living or located in woods or forests. **3** idyllically rural or rustic. ♦ *n* **4** an inhabitant of the woods, esp. a spirit. [C16: from Latin *silvānus,* from *silva* forest]

sylvanite ('sɪlvəˌnaɪt) *n* a silver-white mineral consisting of a telluride of gold and silver in the form of elongated striated crystals: a source of gold in Australia and North America. Formula: $(Au,Ag)Te_2$. [C18: from (TRAN)SYLVAN(IA) + -ITE[1], with reference to the region where it was first found]

Sylvanus (sɪl'veɪnəs) *n* a variant spelling of **Silvanus.**

sylvatic (sɪl'vætɪk) *adj* growing, living, or occurring in a wood or beneath a tree. Also: **sylvestral** (sɪl'vɛstrəl).

Sylvester II (sɪl'vɛstə) *n* original name *Gerbert of Aurillac. c.* 940–1003 A.D., French ecclesiastic and scholar; pope (909–1003): noted for his achievements in mathematics and astronomy.

sylviculture ('sɪlvɪˌkʌltʃə) *n* a variant spelling of **silviculture.**

sylvite ('sɪlvaɪt) *or* **sylvine** ('sɪlviːn) *n* a soluble colourless, white, or coloured mineral consisting of potassium chloride in cubic crystalline form with sodium impurities: it occurs chiefly in sedimentary beds and is an important ore of potassium. Formula: KCl. [C19: *sylvite,* alteration of *sylvine,* from New Latin *sal digestiva Sylvii* digestive salt of Sylvius, after Franciscus *Sylvius* (died 1672), German anatomist. See -ITE[1], -INE[2]]

sym. *abbrev. for:* **1** symbol. **2** *Chem.* symmetrical. **3** symphony. **4** symptom.

sym- *prefix* a variant of **syn-** before *b, p,* and *m.*

symbiont ('sɪmbɪˌɒnt) *n* an organism living in a state of symbiosis. [C19: from Greek *sumbioun* to live together, from *bioun* to live] ▸ **ˌsymbiˈontic** *adj* ▸ **ˌsymbiˈontically** *adv*

symbiosis (ˌsɪmbɪˈəʊsɪs, ˌsɪmbaɪˈəʊsɪs) *n* **1** a close association of two animal or plant species that are dependent on one another. **2** a similar relationship between interdependent persons or groups. [C19: via New Latin from Greek: a living together; see SYMBIONT] ▸ **ˌsymbiˈotic** *or (less commonly)* **ˌsymbiˈotical** *adj*

symbol ('sɪmbᵊl) *n* **1** something that represents or stands for something else, usually by convention or association, esp. a material object used to represent something abstract. **2** an object, person, idea, etc., used in a literary work, film, etc., to stand for or suggest something else with which it is associated either explicitly or in some more subtle way. **3** a letter, figure, or sign used in mathematics, science, music, etc. to represent a quantity, phenomenon, operation, function, etc. **4** *Psychoanal.* the end product, in the form of an object or act, of a conflict in the unconscious between repression processes and the actions and thoughts being repressed: *the symbols of dreams.* **5** *Psychol.* any mental process that represents some feature of external reality. ◆ *vb* **-bols, -bolling, -bolled** *or U.S.* **-bols, -boling, -boled. 6** (*tr*) another word for **symbolize.** [C15: from Church Latin *symbolum,* from Greek *sumbolon* sign, from *sumballein* to throw together, from SYN- + *ballein* to throw]

symbolic (sɪmˈbɒlɪk) *or* **symbolical** *adj* **1** of or relating to a symbol or symbols. **2** serving as a symbol. **3** characterized by the use of symbols or symbolism. ▸ **symˈbolically** *adv* ▸ **symˈbolicalness** *n*

symbolical books *pl n Christianity.* the books containing the creeds, beliefs, or doctrine of religious groups that have emerged since the Reformation.

symbolic logic *n* another term for **formal logic.**

symbolism ('sɪmbəˌlɪzəm) *n* **1** the representation of something in symbolic form or the attribution of symbolic meaning or character to something. **2** a system of symbols or symbolic representation. **3** a symbolic significance or quality. **4** (*often cap.*) a late 19th-century movement in art that sought to express mystical or abstract ideas through the symbolic use of images. See also **synthetism. 5** *Theol.* any symbolist interpretation of the Eucharist.

symbolist ('sɪmbəlɪst) *n* **1** a person who uses or can interpret symbols, esp. as a means to revealing aspects of truth and reality. **2** an artist or writer who practises symbolism in his work. **3** (*usually cap.*) a writer associated with the symbolist movement. **4** (*often cap.*) an artist associated with the movement of symbolism. **5** *Christian theol.* a person who rejects any interpretation of the Eucharist that suggests that Christ is really present in it, and who maintains that the bread and wine are only symbols of his body and blood. ◆ *adj* **6** of, relating to, or characterizing symbolism or symbolists. ▸ **ˌsymbolˈistic** *adj* ▸ **ˌsymbolˈistically** *adv*

symbolist movement *n* (*usually cap.*) a movement beginning in French and Belgian poetry towards the end of the 19th century with the verse of Mallarmé, Valéry, Verlaine, Rimbaud, Maeterlinck, and others, and seeking to express states of mind rather than objective reality by making use of the power of words and images to suggest as well as denote.

symbolize *or* **symbolise** ('sɪmbəˌlaɪz) *vb* **1** (*tr*) to serve as or be a symbol of. **2** (*tr;* usually foll. by *by*) to represent by a symbol or symbols. **3** (*intr*) to use symbols. **4** (*tr*) to treat or regard as symbolic or figurative. ▸ **ˌsymboliˈzation** *or* **ˌsymboliˈsation** *n*

symbology (sɪmˈbɒlədʒɪ) *n* the use, study, or interpretation of symbols. ▸ **symbological** (ˌsɪmbəˈlɒdʒɪkᵊl) *adj* ▸ **symˈbologist** *n*

symbol retailer *n* any member of a voluntary group of independent retailers, often using a common name or symbol, formed to obtain better prices from wholesalers or manufacturers in competition with supermarket chains. Also called: **voluntary retailer.**

symmetallism *or U.S.* **symmetalism** (sɪˈmɛtəˌlɪzəm) *n* **1** the use of an alloy of two or more metals in fixed relative value as the standard of value and currency. **2** the economic policies and doctrine supporting a symmetallic standard. [C19: from SYM- + *-metallism,* on the model of BIMETALLISM]

symmetric (sɪˈmɛtrɪk) *adj* **1** *Logic, maths.* (of a relation) holding between a pair of arguments *x* and *y* when and only when it holds between *y* and *x,* as ... *is a sibling of* ... but not ... *is a brother of* .... Compare **asymmetric** (sense 5), **antisymmetric, nonsymmetric. 2** another word for **symmetrical** (sense 5).

symmetrical (sɪˈmɛtrɪkᵊl) *adj* **1** possessing or displaying symmetry. Compare **asymmetric. 2** *Maths.* **2a** (of two points) capable of being joined by a line that is bisected by a given point or bisected perpendicularly by a given line or plane: *the points (x, y) and (–x,–y) are symmetrical about the origin.* **2b** (of a configuration) having pairs of points that are symmetrical about a given point, line, or plane: *a circle is symmetrical about a diameter.* **2c** (of an equation or function of two or more variables) remaining unchanged in form after an interchange of two variables: $x + y = z$ *is a symmetrical equation.* **3** *Chem.* (of a compound) having a molecular structure in which substituents are symmetrical about the molecule. **4** *Botany.* another word for **actinomorphic. 5** Also: **symmetric.** (of a disease, infection, etc.) affecting both sides of the body or corresponding parts, such as both legs. ▸ **symˈmetrically** *adv* ▸ **symˈmetricalness** *n*

symmetric matrix *n Maths.* a square matrix that is equal to its transpose, being symmetrical about its main diagonal. A **skew symmetric matrix** is equal to the negation of its transpose. Compare **orthogonal matrix.**

symmetrize *or* **symmetrise** ('sɪmɪˌtraɪz) *vb* (*tr*) to render symmetrical or perfectly balanced. ▸ **ˌsym..ıetriˈzation** *or* **ˌsymmetriˈsation** *n*

symmetry ('sɪmɪtrɪ) *n, pl* **-tries. 1** similarity, correspondence, or balance among systems or parts of a system. **2** *Maths.* an exact correspondence in position or form about a given point, line, or plane. See **symmetrical** (sense 2). **3** beauty or harmony of form based on a proportionate arrangement of parts. **4** *Physics.* the independence of a property with respect to direction; isotropy. [C16: from Latin *symmetria,* from Greek *summetria* proportion, from SYN- + *metron* measure]

Symonds ('sɪməndz) *n* **John Addington** ('ædɪŋtən). 1840–93, English writer, noted for his *Renaissance in Italy* (1875–86) and for studies of homosexuality.

Symons ('saɪmənz) *n* **Arthur.** 1865–1945, English poet and critic, who helped to introduce the French symbolists to England.

sympathectomy (ˌsɪmpəˈθɛktəmɪ) *n, pl* **-mies.** the surgical excision or chemical destruction (**chemical sympathectomy**) of one or more parts of the sympathetic nervous system. [C20: from SYMPATHETIC + -ECTOMY]

sympathetic (ˌsɪmpəˈθɛtɪk) *adj* **1** characterized by, feeling, or showing sympathy; understanding. **2** in accord with the subject's personality or mood; congenial: *a sympathetic atmosphere.* **3** (when *postpositive,* often foll. by *to* or *towards*) showing agreement (with) or favour (towards): *sympathetic to the proposals.* **4** *Anatomy, physiol.* of or relating to the division of the autonomic nervous system that acts in opposition to the parasympathetic system accelerating the heartbeat, dilating the bronchi, inhibiting the smooth muscles of the digestive tract, etc. Compare **parasympathetic. 5** relating to vibrations occurring as a result of similar vibrations in a neighbouring body: *sympathetic strings on a sitar.* ▸ **ˌsympaˈthetically** *adv*

sympathetic ink *n* another term for **invisible ink.**

sympathetic magic *n* a type of magic in which it is sought to produce a large-scale effect, often at a distance, by performing some small-scale ceremony resembling it, such as the pouring of water on an altar to induce rainfall.

sympathin ('sɪmpəθɪn) *n* a substance released at certain sympathetic nerve endings: thought to be identical with adrenaline. [C20: from SYMPATH(ETIC) + -IN]

sympathize *or* **sympathise** ('sɪmpəˌθaɪz) *vb* (*intr;* often foll. by *with*) **1** to feel or express compassion or sympathy (for); commiserate: *he sympathized with my troubles.* **2** to share or understand the sentiments or ideas (of); be in sympathy (with). ▸ **ˈsympaˌthizer** *or* **ˈsympaˌthiser** *n*

sympatholytic (ˌsɪmpəθəʊˈlɪtɪk) *Med.* ◆ *adj* **1a** inhibiting or antagonistic to nerve impulses of the sympathetic nervous system. **1b** of or relating to such inhibition. ◆ *n* **2** a sympatholytic drug. Compare **sympathomimetic.** [C20: from SYMPATH(ETIC) + -LYTIC]

sympathomimetic (ˌsɪmpəθəʊmɪˈmɛtɪk) *Med.* ◆ *adj* **1** causing a physiological effect similar to that produced by stimulation of the sympathetic nervous system. ◆ *n* **2** a sympathomimetic drug. Compare **sympatholytic.** [C20: from SYMPATH(ETIC) + MIMETIC]

sympathy ('sɪmpəθɪ) *n, pl* **-thies. 1** the sharing of another's emotions, esp. of sorrow or anguish; pity; compassion. **2** an affinity or harmony, usually of feelings or interests, between persons or things: *to be in sympathy with someone.* **3** mutual affection or understanding arising from such a relationship; congeniality. **4** the condition of a physical system or body when its behaviour is similar or corresponds to that of a different system that influences it, such as the vibration of sympathetic strings. **5** (*sometimes pl*) a feeling of loyalty, support, or accord, as for an idea, cause, etc. **6** *Physiol.* the mutual relationship between two organs or parts whereby a change in one has an effect on the other. [C16: from Latin *sympathīa,* from Greek *sumpatheia,* from *sumpathēs,* from SYN- + *pathos* suffering]

sympathy strike *n* a strike organized in support of another section of workers or a cause and not because of direct grievances. Also called: **sympathetic strike.**

sympatric (sɪmˈpætrɪk) *adj* (of biological speciation or species) taking place or existing in the same or overlapping geographical areas. Compare **allopatric.** [C20: from SYN- + *-patric,* from Greek *patra* native land, from *patēr* father] ▸ **symˈpatrically** *adv*

sympetalous (sɪmˈpɛtələs) *adj Botany.* another word for **gamopetalous.**

symphile ('sɪmfaɪl) *n* an insect or other organism that lives in the nests of social insects, esp. ants and termites, and is fed and reared by the inmates. Compare **synoekete.** [C20: from Greek *sumphilein* to love mutually; see SYN-, -PHILE]

symphonic poem *n Music.* an extended orchestral composition, originated by Liszt, based on nonmusical material, such as a work of literature or folk tale. Also called: **tone poem.**

symphonious (sɪmˈfəʊnɪəs) *adj Literary.* harmonious or concordant. ▸ **symˈphoniously** *adv*

symphonist ('sɪmfənɪst) *n* a person who composes symphonies.

symphony ('sɪmfənɪ) *n, pl* **-nies. 1** an extended large-scale orchestral composition, usually with several movements, at least one of which is in sonata form. The classical form of the symphony was fixed by Haydn and Mozart, but the innovations of subsequent composers have freed it entirely from classical constraints. It continues to be a vehicle for serious, large-scale orchestral music. **2** a piece of instrumental music in up to three very short movements, used as an overture to or interlude in a baroque opera. **3** any purely orchestral movement in a vocal work, such as a cantata or oratorio. **4** short for **symphony orchestra. 5** (in musical theory, esp. of classical Greece) **5a** another word for **consonance** (sense 3). Compare **diaphony** (sense 2). **5b** the interval of unison. **6** anything distinguished by a harmonious composition: *the picture was a symphony of green.* **7** *Archaic.* harmony in general; concord. [C13: from Old French *symphonie,* from Latin *symphōnia* concord, concert, from Greek *sumphōnia,* from SYN- + *phōnē* sound] ▸ **symphonic** (sɪmˈfɒnɪk) *adj* ▸ **symˈphonically** *adv*

symphony orchestra *n Music.* an orchestra capable of performing symphonies, esp. the large orchestra comprising strings, brass, woodwind, harp and percussion.

symphysis ('sɪmfɪsɪs) *n, pl* **-ses** (-ˌsiːz). **1** *Anatomy, botany.* a growing together of parts or structures, such as two bony surfaces joined by an intermediate layer of fibrous cartilage. **2** a line marking this growing together. **3** *Pathol.* an abnormal adhesion of two or more parts or structures. [C16: via New Latin from Greek *sumphusis*, from *sumphuein*, from SYN- + *phuein* to grow] ▸ **symphysial** or **symphyseal** (sɪm'fɪzɪəl) *adj* ▸ **symphystic** (sɪm'fɪstɪk) or **sym'phytic** *adj*

symplast ('sɪmplæst) *n Botany.* the continuous system of protoplasts, linked by plasmodesmata and bounded by the cell wall. ▸ **sym'plastic** *adj*

sympodium (sɪm'pəudɪəm) *n, pl* **-dia** (-dɪə). the main axis of growth in the grapevine and similar plants: a number of lateral branches that arise from just behind the apex of the main stem, which ceases to grow. Compare **monopodium.** [C19: from New Latin, from SYN- + Greek *podion* a little foot, from *pous* foot] ▸ **sym'podial** *adj* ▸ **sym'podially** *adv*

symposiac (sɪm'pəuzɪ,æk) *adj* **1** of, suitable for, or occurring at a symposium. ◆ *n* **2** an archaic word for **symposium.** [C17: from Latin *symposiacus;* see SYMPOSIUM]

symposiarch (sɪm'pəuzɪ,ɑ:k) *n* **1** the president of a symposium, esp. in classical Greece. **2** a rare word for **toastmaster.** [C17: from Greek; see SYMPOSIUM, -ARCH]

symposiast (sɪm'pəuzɪ,æst) *n* a person who takes part in a symposium.

symposium (sɪm'pəuzɪəm) *n, pl* **-siums** or **-sia** (-zɪə). **1** a conference or meeting for the discussion of some subject, esp. an academic topic or social problem. **2** a collection of scholarly contributions, usually published together, on a given subject. **3** (in classical Greece) a drinking party with intellectual conversation, music, etc. [C16: via Latin from Greek *sumposion,* from *sumpinein* to drink together, from *sum-* SYN- + *pinein* to drink]

symptom ('sɪmptəm) *n* **1** *Med.* any sensation or change in bodily function experienced by a patient that is associated with a particular disease. Compare **sign** (sense 9). **2** any phenomenon or circumstance accompanying something and regarded as evidence of its existence; indication. [C16: from Late Latin *symptōma,* from Greek *sumptōma* chance, from *sumpiptein* to occur, from SYN- + *piptein* to fall] ▸ **'symptomless** *adj*

symptomatic (,sɪmptə'mætɪk) *adj* **1** (often foll. by *of*) being a symptom; indicative: *symptomatic of insanity.* **2** of or relating to a symptom or symptoms. **3** according to symptoms: *a symptomatic analysis of a case.* ▸ **,sympto'matically** *adv*

symptomatology (,sɪmptəmə'tɒlədʒɪ) *n* the branch of medicine concerned with the study and classification of the symptoms of disease.

syn (saɪn, sɪn) *adv, prep, conj* a variant of **syne**[1], a Scot. word for **since.**

syn. *abbrev. for* synonym(ous).

syn- *prefix* **1** with or together: *synecology.* **2** fusion: *syngamy.* [from Greek *sun* together, with]

synaeresis (sɪ'nɪərɪsɪs) *n* a variant spelling of **syneresis.**

synaesthesia or *U.S.* **synesthesia** (,sɪni:s'θi:zɪə) *n* **1** *Physiol.* a sensation experienced in a part of the body other than the part stimulated. **2** *Psychol.* the subjective sensation of a sense other than the one being stimulated. For example, a sound may evoke sensations of colour. [from New Latin, from SYN- + *-esthesia,* from Greek *aisthēsis* sensation] ▸ **synaesthetic** or *U.S.* **synesthetic** (,sɪni:s'θetɪk) *adj*

synagogue ('sɪnə,gɒg) *n* **1a** a building for Jewish religious services and usually also for religious instruction. **1b** (*as modifier*): *synagogue services.* **2** a congregation of Jews who assemble for worship or religious study. **3** the religion of Judaism as organized in such congregations. [C12: from Old French *sinagogue,* from Late Latin *synagōga,* from Greek *sunagōgē* a gathering, from *sunagein* to bring together, from SYN- + *agein* to lead] ▸ **synagogical** (,sɪnə'gɒdʒɪk°l) or **synagogal** ('sɪnə,gɒg°l) *adj*

synalepha or **synaloepha** (,sɪnə'li:fə) *n Linguistics.* vowel elision, esp. as it arises when one word ends in a vowel and the following word begins with one. [C16: from Late Latin *synaloepha,* from Greek *sunaliphē,* from SYN- + *aleiphein* to melt, smear]

synapse ('saɪnæps) *n* the point at which a nerve impulse is relayed from the terminal portion of an axon to the dendrites of an adjacent neuron.

synapsis (sɪ'næpsɪs) *n, pl* **-ses** (-si:z). **1** *Cytology.* the association in pairs of homologous chromosomes at the start of meiosis. **2** another word for **synapse.** [C19: from New Latin, from Greek *sunapsis* junction, from *sunaptein* to join together, from SYN- + *haptein* to connect] ▸ **synaptic** (sɪ'næptɪk) or **syn'aptical** *adj* ▸ **syn'aptically** *adv*

synarchy ('sɪnəkɪ) *n, pl* **-chies.** joint rule. [C18: from Greek *sunarchia,* from *sunarchein* to rule jointly]

synarthrosis (,sɪnɑ:'θrəusɪs) *n, pl* **-ses** (-si:z). *Anatomy.* any of various joints which lack a synovial cavity and are virtually immovable; a fixed joint. [via New Latin from Greek *sunarthrōsis,* from *sunarthrousthai* to be connected by joints, from *sun-* SYN- + *arthron* a joint] ▸ **,synar'throdial** *adj* ▸ **,synar'throdially** *adv*

sync or **synch** (sɪŋk) *Films, television, computers, etc.* ◆ *vb* **1** an informal word for **synchronize.** ◆ *n* **2** an informal word for **synchronization** (esp. in the phrases **in** or **out of sync**).

syncarp ('sɪnkɑ:p) *n Botany.* a fleshy multiple fruit, formed from two or more carpels of one flower or the aggregated fruits of several flowers. [C19: from New Latin *syncarpium,* from SYN- + Greek *karpos* fruit]

syncarpous (sɪn'kɑ:pəs) *adj* **1** (of the ovaries of certain flowering plants) consisting of united carpels. Compare **apocarpous. 2** of or relating to a syncarp. ▸ **syncarpy** ('sɪnkɑ:pɪ) *n*

syncategorematic (sɪn,kætə,gɒ:rə'mætɪk) *adj Philosophy.* applying to expressions that are not in any of Aristotle's categories, but form meaningful expressions together with them, such as conjunctions and adverbs.

synchro ('sɪŋkrəu) *n, pl* **-chros. 1** any of a number of electrical devices in which the angular position of a rotating part is transformed into a voltage, or vice versa. Also called: **selsyn. 2** short for **synchronized swimming.**

synchro- *combining form.* indicating synchronization: *synchroflash.*

synchrocyclotron (,sɪŋkrəu'saɪklə,trɒn) *n* a type of cyclotron in which the frequency of the electric field is modulated to allow for relativistic effects at high velocities and thus produce higher energies.

synchroflash ('sɪŋkrəu,flæʃ) *n* a mechanism in a camera that enables the shutter to be fully open while the light from a flashbulb or electronic flash is at its brightest.

synchromesh ('sɪŋkrəu,meʃ) *adj* **1** (of a gearbox, etc.) having a system of clutches that synchronizes the speeds of the driving and driven members before engagement to avoid shock in gear changing and to reduce noise and wear. ◆ *n* **2** a gear system having these features. [C20: shortened from *synchronized mesh*]

synchronic (sɪn'krɒnɪk) *adj* **1** concerned with the events or phenomena at a particular period without considering historical antecedents: *synchronic linguistics.* Compare **diachronic. 2** synchronous. ▸ **syn'chronically** *adv*

synchronicity (,sɪnkrə'nɪsɪtɪ) *n* an apparently meaningful coincidence in time of two or more similar or identical events that are causally unrelated. [C20: coined by Carl Jung from SYNCHRONIC + -ITY]

synchronism ('sɪŋkrə,nɪzəm) *n* **1** the quality or condition of being synchronous. **2** a chronological usually tabular list of historical persons and events, arranged to show parallel or synchronous occurrence. **3** the representation in a work of art of one or more incidents that occurred at separate times. [C16: from Greek *sunkhronismos;* see SYNCHRONOUS, -ISM] ▸ **,synchro'nistic** *adj* ▸ **,synchro'nistically** *adv*

synchronize or **synchronise** ('sɪŋkrə,naɪz) *vb* **1** (when *intr,* usually foll. by *with*) to occur or recur or cause to occur or recur at the same time or in unison. **2** to indicate or cause to indicate the same time: *synchronize your watches.* **3** (*tr*) *Films.* to establish (the picture and soundtrack records) in their correct relative position. **4** (*tr*) to designate (events) as simultaneous. ▸ **,synchroni'zation** or **,synchroni'sation** *n* ▸ **'synchro,nizer** or **'synchro,niser** *n*

synchronized swimming *n* the art or sport of one or more swimmers moving in patterns in the water in time to music. Sometimes shortened to **synchro** or **synchro swimming.**

synchronous ('sɪŋkrənəs) *adj* **1** occurring at the same time; contemporaneous. **2** *Physics.* (of periodic phenomena, such as voltages) having the same frequency and phase. **3** occurring or recurring exactly together and at the same rate: *the synchronous flapping of a bird's wings.* [C17: from Late Latin *synchronus,* from Greek *sunkhronos,* from SYN- + *khronos* time] ▸ **'synchronously** *adv* ▸ **'synchronousness** *n*

synchronous converter *n* a synchronous machine that converts alternating current to direct current, or vice versa.

synchronous machine *n* an electrical machine, whose rotating speed is proportional to the frequency of the alternating-current supply and independent of the load.

synchronous motor *n* an alternating-current motor that runs at a speed that is equal to or is a multiple of the frequency of the supply.

synchronous orbit *n Astronautics.* an earth orbit in which a satellite makes one complete revolution in the period taken for the earth to rotate about its axis.

synchrony ('sɪŋkrənɪ) *n* the state of being synchronous; simultaneity.

synchroscope ('sɪŋkrə,skəup) or **synchronoscope** (sɪŋ'krɒnə,skəup) *n* an instrument used to indicate whether two periodic quantities or motions are synchronous.

synchrotron ('sɪŋkrə,trɒn) *n* a type of particle accelerator similar to a betatron but having an electric field of fixed frequency as well as a changing magnetic field. It is capable of producing very high energies in the GeV range. [C20: from SYNCHRO- + (ELEC)TRON]

synchrotron radiation *n* electromagnetic radiation emitted in narrow beams tangential to the orbit of very high energy charged particles, such as electrons, spiralling along the lines of force in a strong magnetic field. It occurs in synchrotron accelerators and in supernova remnants such as the Crab Nebula.

synclastic (sɪŋ'klæstɪk) *adj Maths.* (of a surface) having a curvature at a given point and in a particular direction that is of the same sign as the curvature at that point in perpendicular direction. Compare **anticlastic.** [C19: from SYN- (alike) + Greek *klastos* bent, from *klan* to bend]

syncline ('sɪŋklaɪn) *n* a downward fold of stratified rock in which the strata slope towards a vertical axis. Compare **anticline.** [C19: from SYN- + Greek *klīnein* to lean] ▸ **syn'clinal** *adj*

synclinorium (,sɪŋklɪ'nɔ:rɪəm) *n, pl* **-ria** (-rɪə). a vast elongated syncline with its strata further folded into anticlines and synclines. [C19: New Latin, from SYNCLINE + *-orium,* suffix indicating a place]

Syncom ('sɪn,kɒm) *n* a communications satellite in stationary orbit. [C20: from *syn(chronous) com(munication)*]

syncopate ('sɪŋkə,peɪt) *vb* (*tr*) **1** *Music.* to modify or treat (a beat, rhythm, note, etc.) by syncopation. **2** to shorten (a word) by omitting sounds or letters from the middle. [C17: from Medieval Latin *syncopāre* to omit a letter or syllable, from Late Latin *syncopa* SYNCOPE] ▸ **'synco,pator** *n*

syncopation (,sɪŋkə'peɪʃən) *n* **1** *Music.* **1a** the displacement of the usual rhythmic accent away from a strong beat onto a weak beat. **1b** a note, beat, rhythm, etc., produced by syncopation. **2** another word for **syncope** (sense 2).

syncope ('sɪŋkəpɪ) *n* **1** *Pathol.* a technical word for a **faint. 2** the omission of one or more sounds or letters from the middle of a word. [C16: from Late Latin *syncopa,* from Greek *sunkopē* a cutting off, from SYN- + *koptein* to cut] ▸ **syncopic** (sɪŋ'kɒpɪk) or **'syncopal** *adj*

syncretism ('sɪŋkrɪ,tɪzəm) *n* **1** the tendency to syncretize. **2** the historical tendency of languages to reduce their use of inflection, as in the development of Old English with all its case endings into Modern English. [C17: from New Latin *syncrētismus,* from Greek *sunkrētismos* alliance of Cretans, from *sunkrētizein* to join forces (in the manner of the Cretan towns), from SYN- + *Krēs* a Cretan] ▸ **syncretic** (sɪŋ'kretɪk) *or* **ˌsyncre'tistic** *adj* ▸ **'syncretist** *n*

syncretize *or* **syncretise** ('sɪŋkrɪˌtaɪz) *vb* to combine or attempt to combine the characteristic teachings, beliefs, or practices of (differing systems of religion or philosophy). ▸ **ˌsyncreti'zation** *or* **ˌsyncreti'sation** *n*

syncytium (sɪn'sɪtɪəm) *n, pl* **-cytia** (-'sɪtɪə). *Zoology.* a mass of cytoplasm containing many nuclei and enclosed in a cell membrane. [C19: New Latin; see SYN-, CYTO-, -IUM] ▸ **syn'cytial** *adj*

synd (səɪnd) *vb, n Scot.* a variant of **syne**².

synd. *abbrev. for* syndicate.

syndactyl (sɪn'dæktɪl) *adj* **1** (of certain animals) having two or more digits growing fused together. ◆ *n* **2** an animal with this arrangement of digits. ▸ **syn'dactylism** *n*

syndesis (sɪn'diːsɪs) *n Grammar.* **1** the use of syndetic constructions. **2** another name for **polysyndeton** (sense 2). [C20: from Greek, from *sundein* to bind together, from SYN- + *dein* to bind]

syndesmosis (ˌsɪndɛs'məʊsɪs) *n, pl* **-ses** (-siːz). *Anatomy.* a type of joint in which the articulating bones are held together by a ligament of connective tissue. [New Latin, from Greek *sundein* to bind together; see SYNDESIS] ▸ **syndesmotic** (ˌsɪndɛs'mɒtɪk) *adj*

syndetic (sɪn'dɛtɪk) *adj* denoting a grammatical construction in which two clauses are connected by a conjunction. Compare **asyndetic** (sense 2). [C17: from Greek *sundetikos,* from *sundetos* bound together; see SYNDESIS] ▸ **syn'detically** *adv*

syndeton (sɪn'diːtᵊn) *n Grammar.* a syndetic construction. Compare **asyndeton** (sense 2). [C20: from Greek *sundeton* a bond, from *sundein* to bind together; see SYNDESIS]

syndic ('sɪndɪk) *n* **1** *Brit.* a business agent of some universities or other bodies. **2** (in several countries) a government administrator or magistrate with varying powers. [C17: via Old French from Late Latin *syndicus,* from Greek *sundikos* defendant's advocate, from SYN- + *dikē* justice] ▸ **'syndicˌship** *n* ▸ **'syndical** *adj*

syndicalism ('sɪndɪkəˌlɪzəm) *n* **1** a revolutionary movement and theory advocating the seizure of the means of production and distribution by syndicates of workers through direct action, esp. a general strike. **2** an economic system resulting from such action. ▸ **'syndical** *adj* ▸ **'syndicalist** *adj, n* ▸ **ˌsyndical'istic** *adj*

syndicate *n* ('sɪndɪkɪt). **1** an association of business enterprises or individuals organized to undertake a joint project requiring considerable capital. **2** a news agency that sells articles, photographs, etc., to a number of newspapers for simultaneous publication. **3** any association formed to carry out an enterprise or enterprises of common interest to its members. **4** a board of syndics or the office of syndic. **5** (in Italy under the Fascists) a local organization of employers or employees. ◆ *vb* ('sɪndɪˌkeɪt). **6** (*tr*) to sell (articles, photographs, etc.) to several newspapers for simultaneous publication. **7** (*tr*) *U.S.* to sell (a programme or programmes) to several local commercial television or radio stations. **8** to form a syndicate of (people). [C17: from Old French *syndicat* office of a SYNDIC] ▸ **ˌsyndi'cation** *n*

syndiotactic (ˌsɪndɪəʊ'tæktɪk) *adj Chem.* (of a stereospecific polymer) having alternating stereochemical configurations of the groups on successive carbon atoms in the chain. Compare **isotactic.** [C20: from *syndyo,* from Greek *sunduo* two together + -TACTIC]

syndrome ('sɪndrəʊm) *n* **1** *Med.* any combination of signs and symptoms that are indicative of a particular disease or disorder. **2** a symptom, characteristic, or set of symptoms or characteristics indicating the existence of a condition, problem, etc. [C16: via New Latin from Greek *sundromē,* literally: a running together, from SYN- + *dramein* to run] ▸ **syndromic** (sɪn'drɒmɪk) *adj*

syne¹ *or* **syn** (saɪn) *adv, prep, conj* a Scot. word for **since.** [C14: probably related to Old English *sīth* since]

syne² (saɪn) *or* **synd** *Scot.* ◆ *vb* **1** (*tr*) to rinse; wash out. ◆ *n* **2** a rinse. [C14: of uncertain origin]

synecdoche (sɪn'ɛkdəkɪ) *n* a figure of speech in which a part is substituted for a whole or a whole for a part, as in *50 head of cattle* for *50 cows,* or *the army* for *a soldier.* [C14: via Latin from Greek *sunekdokhē,* from SYN- + *ekdokhē* interpretation, from *dekhesthai* to accept] ▸ **synecdochic** (ˌsɪnɛk'dɒkɪk) *or* **ˌsynec'dochical** *adj* ▸ **ˌsynec'dochically** *adv*

synecious (sɪ'niːʃəs) *adj* a variant spelling of **synoecious.**

synecology (ˌsɪnɪ'kɒlədʒɪ) *n* the ecological study of communities of plants and animals. Compare **autecology.** ▸ **synecologic** (sɪnˌɛkə'lɒdʒɪk) *or* **synˌeco'logical** *adj* ▸ **synˌeco'logically** *adv*

synectics (sɪ'nɛktɪks) *n* (*functioning as sing*) a method of identifying and solving problems that depends on creative thinking, the use of analogy, and informal conversation among a small group of individuals with diverse experience and expertise. [C20: from SYN- + ECTO- + -ICS, in the sense: working together from outside]

syneresis *or* **synaeresis** (sɪ'nɪərɪsɪs) *n* **1** *Chem.* the process in which a gel contracts on standing and exudes liquid, as in the separation of whey in cheese-making. **2** the contraction of two vowels into a diphthong. **3** another word for **synizesis.** [C16: via Late Latin from Greek *sunairesis* a shortening, from *sunairein* to draw together, from SYN- + *hairein* to take]

synergetic (ˌsɪnə'dʒɛtɪk) *or* **synergistic** (ˌsɪnə'dʒɪstɪk) *adj* acting together. [C17: from Greek *sunergētikos,* from SYN- + *-ergētikos,* from *ergon* work; see ENERGY] ▸ **ˌsyner'getically** *or* **ˌsyner'gistically** *adv*

synergism ('sɪnəˌdʒɪzəm, sɪ'nɜː-) *n* **1** Also called: **synergy.** the working together of two or more drugs, muscles, etc., to produce an effect greater than the sum of their individual effects. **2** another name for **synergy** (sense 1). **3** *Christian theol.* the doctrine or belief that the human will cooperates with the Holy Spirit and with divine grace, esp. in the act of conversion or regeneration. [C18: from New Latin *synergismus,* from Greek *sunergos,* from SYN- + *ergon* work]

synergist ('sɪnədʒɪst, sɪ'nɜː-) *n* **1** a drug, muscle, etc., that increases the action of another. **2** *Christian theol.* an upholder of synergism. ◆ *adj* **3** of or relating to synergism.

synergy ('sɪnədʒɪ) *n, pl* **-gies. 1** Also called: **synergism.** the potential ability of individual organizations or groups to be more successful or productive as a result of a merger. **2** another name for **synergism** (sense 1). [C19: from New Latin *synergia,* from Greek *sunergos;* see SYNERGISM] ▸ **synergic** (sɪ'nɜːdʒɪk) *adj*

synesis ('sɪnɪsɪs) *n* a grammatical construction in which the inflection or form of a word is conditioned by the meaning rather than the syntax, as for example the plural form *have* with the singular noun *group* in the sentence *the group have already assembled.* [via New Latin from Greek *sunesis* union, from *sunienai* to bring together, from SYN- + *hienai* to send]

synesthesia (ˌsɪniːs'θiːzɪə) *n* the usual U.S. spelling of **synaesthesia.** ▸ **synesthetic** (ˌsɪniːs'θɛtɪk) *adj*

syngamy ('sɪŋgəmɪ) *or* **syngenesis** (sɪn'dʒɛnɪsɪs) *n* other names for **sexual reproduction.** ▸ **syngamic** (sɪŋ'gæmɪk) *or* **syngamous** ('sɪŋgəməs) *adj*

Synge (sɪŋ) *n* **John Millington.** 1871–1909, Irish playwright. His plays, marked by vivid colloquial Irish speech, include *Riders to the Sea* (1904) and *The Playboy of the Western World,* produced amidst uproar at the Abbey Theatre, Dublin, in 1907.

synizesis (ˌsɪnɪ'ziːsɪs) *n* **1** *Phonetics.* the contraction of two vowels originally belonging to separate syllables into a single syllable, without diphthongization. Compare **syneresis. 2** *Cytology.* the contraction of chromatin towards one side of the nucleus during the prophase of meiosis. [C19: via Late Latin from Greek *sunizēsis* a collapse, from *sunizanein* to sink down, from SYN- + *hizein* to sit]

synkaryon (sɪn'kærɪˌɒn) *n Biology.* the nucleus of a fertilized egg. [C20: New Latin, from SYN- + Greek *karuon* a nut] ▸ **synˌkary'onic** *adj*

synod ('sɪnəd, 'sɪnɒd) *n* a local or special ecclesiastical council, esp. of a diocese, formally convened to discuss ecclesiastical affairs. [C14: from Late Latin *synodus,* from Greek *sunodos,* from SYN- + *hodos* a way] ▸ **'synodal** *or* (*less commonly*) **syn'odical** *adj*

synodic (sɪ'nɒdɪk) *adj* relating to or involving a conjunction or two successive conjunctions of the same star, planet, or satellite: *the synodic month.*

synodic month *n* See **month** (sense 6).

Synod of Whitby *n* the synod held in 664 at Whitby at which the Roman date for Easter was accepted and the Church in England became aligned with Rome.

synoecious, synecious (sɪ'niːʃəs), *or* **synoicous** (sɪ'nɔɪkəs) *adj* (of plants) having male and female organs on the same flower or corresponding structure. [C19: SYN- + *-oecious,* from Greek *oikion* diminutive of *oikos* house]

synoekete (sɪ'niːkiːt) *or* **synoecete** (sɪ'niːsiːt) *n* an insect that lives in the nests of social insects, esp. ants, without receiving any attentions from the inmates. Compare **symphile.** [C20: from Greek *sunoiketēs* house-fellow, from *sunoikia* community]

synonym ('sɪnənɪm) *n* **1** a word that means the same or nearly the same as another word, such as *bucket* and *pail.* **2** a word or phrase used as another name for something, such as *Hellene* for a *Greek.* **3** *Biology.* a taxonomic name that has been superseded or rejected. [C16: via Late Latin from Greek *sunōnumon,* from SYN- + *onoma* name] ▸ **ˌsyno'nymic** *or* **ˌsyno'nymical** *adj* ▸ **ˌsyno'nymity** *n*

synonymize *or* **synonymise** (sɪ'nɒnɪˌmaɪz) *vb* (*tr*) to analyse the synonyms of or provide with synonyms.

synonymous (sɪ'nɒnɪməs) *adj* **1** (often foll. by *with*) being a synonym (of). **2** (*postpositive;* foll. by *with*) closely associated (with) or suggestive (of): *his name was synonymous with greed.* ▸ **syn'onymously** *adv* ▸ **syn'onymousness** *n*

synonymy (sɪ'nɒnɪmɪ) *n, pl* **-mies. 1** the study of synonyms. **2** the character of being synonymous; equivalence. **3** a list or collection of synonyms, esp. one in which their meanings are discriminated. **4** *Biology.* a collection of the synonyms of a species or group.

synop. *abbrev. for* synopsis.

synopsis (sɪ'nɒpsɪs) *n, pl* **-ses** (-siːz). a condensation or brief review of a subject; summary. [C17: via Late Latin from Greek *sunopsis,* from SYN- + *opsis* view]

synopsize *or* **synopsise** (sɪ'nɒpsaɪz) *vb* (*tr*) **1** to make a synopsis of. **2** *U.S.* variants of **epitomize.**

synoptic (sɪ'nɒptɪk) *adj* **1** of or relating to a synopsis. **2** (*often cap.*) *Bible.* **2a** (of the Gospels of Matthew, Mark, and Luke) presenting the narrative of Christ's life, ministry, etc. from a point of view held in common by all three, and with close similarities in content, order, etc. **2b** of, relating to, or characterizing these three Gospels. **3** *Meteorol.* showing or concerned with the distribution of meteorological conditions over a wide area at a given time: *a synoptic chart.* ◆ *n* **4** (*often cap.*) *Bible.* **4a** any of the three synoptic Gospels. **4b** any of the authors of these three Gospels. [C18: from Greek *sunoptikos,* from SYNOPSIS] ▸ **syn'optically** *adv* ▸ **syn'optist** *n*

synovia (saɪ'nəʊvɪə, sɪ-) *n* a transparent viscid lubricating fluid, secreted by the membrane lining joints, tendon sheaths, etc. [C17: from New Latin, probably from SYN- + Latin *ōvum* egg] ▸ **syn'ovial** *adj* ▸ **syn'ovially** *adv*

synovitis (ˌsaɪnəʊ'vaɪtɪs, ˌsɪn-) *n* inflammation of the membrane surrounding a joint. ▸ **synovitic** (ˌsaɪnəʊ'vɪtɪk, ˌsɪn-) *adj*

synroc ('sɪnˌrɒk) *n* a titanium-ceramic substance that can incorporate nuclear waste in its crystals. [from *syn(thetic)* + *roc(k)*]

synsepalous (sɪn'sɛpələs) *adj* another word for **gamosepalous.**

syntactic (sɪn'tæktɪk) *adj* **1** Also: **syntactical.** relating to or determined by syntax. **2** *Logic, linguistics.* describable wholly with respect to the grammatical structure of an expression or the rules of well-formedness of a formal system. ▸ **syn'tactically** *adv*

syntactics (sɪn'tæktɪks) *n* (*functioning as sing*) the branch of semiotics that deals with the formal properties of symbol systems; proof theory.

syntagma (sɪn'tægmə) *or* **syntagm** ('sɪn,tæm) *n, pl* **-tagmata** (-'tægmətə) *or* **-tagms. 1** a syntactic unit or a word or phrase forming a syntactic unit. **2** a systematic collection of statements or propositions. [C17: from Late Latin, from Greek, from *suntassein* to put in order; see SYNTAX]

syntagmatic (,sɪntæg'mætɪk) *adj* **1** of or denoting a syntagma. **2** Also: **syntagmic** (sɪn'tægmɪk). *Linguistics.* denoting or concerning the relationship between a word and other members of a syntactic unit containing it.

syntax ('sɪntæks) *n* **1** the branch of linguistics that deals with the grammatical arrangement of words and morphemes in the sentences of a language or of languages in general. **2** the totality of facts about the grammatical arrangement of words in a language. **3** a systematic statement of the rules governing the grammatical arrangement of words and morphemes in a language. **4** *Logic.* a systematic statement of the rules governing the properly formed formulas of a logical system. **5** any orderly arrangement or system. [C17: from Late Latin *syntaxis,* from Greek *suntaxis,* from *suntassein* to put in order, from SYN- + *tassein* to arrange]

synth (sɪnθ) *n* short for **synthesizer.**

synthesis ('sɪnθɪsɪs) *n, pl* **-ses** (-,si:z). **1** the process of combining objects or ideas into a complex whole. Compare **analysis. 2** the combination or whole produced by such a process. **3** the process of producing a compound by a chemical reaction or series of reactions, usually from simpler or commonly available starting materials. **4** *Linguistics.* the use of inflections rather than word order and function words to express the syntactic relations in a language. Compare **analysis** (sense 5). **5** *Philosophy, archaic.* synthetic reasoning. **6** *Philosophy.* **6a** (in the writings of Kant) the unification of one concept with another not contained in it. Compare **analysis** (sense 7). **6b** the final stage in the Hegelian dialectic, that resolves the contradiction between thesis and antithesis. [C17: via Latin from Greek *sunthesis,* from *suntithenai* to put together, from SYN- + *tithenai* to place] ▸ **'synthesist** *n*

synthesis gas *n Chem.* **1** a mixture of carbon dioxide, carbon monoxide, and hydrogen formerly made by using water gas and reacting it with steam to enrich the proportion of hydrogen for use in the synthesis of ammonia. **2** a similar mixture of gases made by steam reforming natural gas, used for synthesizing organic chemicals and as a fuel.

synthesize ('sɪnθɪ,saɪz), **synthetize** *or* **synthesise, synthetise** *vb* **1** to combine or cause to combine into a whole. **2** (*tr*) to produce by synthesis. ▸ **,synthesi'zation, ,syntheti'zation** *or* **,synthesi'sation, ,syntheti'sation** *n*

synthesizer ('sɪnθɪ,saɪzə) *n* **1** an electrophonic instrument, usually operated by means of a keyboard and pedals, in which sounds are produced by voltage-controlled oscillators, filters, and amplifiers, with an envelope generator module that controls attack, decay, sustain, and release. **2** a person or thing that synthesizes.

synthetic (sɪn'θetɪk) *adj also* **synthetical. 1** (of a substance or material) made artificially by chemical reaction. **2** not genuine; insincere: *synthetic compassion.* **3** denoting languages, such as Latin, whose morphology is characterized by synthesis. Compare **polysynthetic, agglutinative** (sense 2), **analytic** (sense 3). **4** *Philosophy.* **4a** (of a proposition) having a truth-value that is not determined solely by virtue of the meanings of the words, as in *all men are arrogant.* **4b** contingent. Compare **a posteriori, empirical.** ◆ *n* **5** a synthetic substance or material. [C17: from New Latin *syntheticus,* from Greek *sunthetikos* expert in putting together, from *suntithenai* to put together; see SYNTHESIS] ▸ **syn'thetically** *adv*

synthetic resin *n* See **resin** (sense 2).

synthetic rubber *n* any of various synthetic materials, similar to natural rubber, made by polymerizing unsaturated hydrocarbons, such as isoprene and butadiene.

synthetism ('sɪnθɪ,tɪzəm) *n* (*often cap.*) the symbolism of Gauguin and the Nabis, who reacted against the impressionists and realists by seeking to produce brightly coloured abstractions of their inner experience. [C19: from Greek *sunthetos* composite; see SYNTHETIC] ▸ **'synthetist** *n*

syntonic (sɪn'tɒnɪk) *adj Psychol.* emotionally in harmony with one's environment. [C20: from Greek *suntonos* in harmony with; see SYN-, TONE] ▸ **syn'tonically** *adv*

Syon House ('saɪən) *n* a mansion near Brentford in London: originally a monastery, rebuilt in the 16th century, altered by Inigo Jones in the 17th century, and by Robert Adam in the 18th century; seat of the Dukes of Northumberland; gardens laid out by Capability Brown.

sypher ('saɪfə) *vb* (*tr*) to lap (a chamfered edge of one plank over that of another) in order to form a flush surface. [C19: variant of CIPHER] ▸ **'syphering** *n*

syphilis ('sɪfɪlɪs) *n* a venereal disease caused by infection with the microorganism *Treponema pallidum:* characterized by an ulcerating chancre, usually on the genitals and progressing through the lymphatic system to nearly all tissues of the body, producing serious clinical manifestations. [C18: from New Latin *Syphilis* (*sive Morbus Gallicus*) "Syphilis (or the French disease)", title of a poem (1530) by G. Fracastoro, Italian physician and poet, in which a shepherd *Syphilus* is portrayed as the first victim of the disease] ▸ **syphilitic** (,sɪfɪ'lɪtɪk) *adj* ▸ **,syphi'litically** *adv* ▸ **'syphi,loid** *adj*

syphilology (,sɪfɪ'lɒlədʒɪ) *n* the branch of medicine concerned with the study and treatment of syphilis. ▸ **,syphi'lologist** *n*

syphiloma (,sɪfɪ'ləʊmə) *n, pl* **-mas** *or* **-mata** (-mətə). *Pathol.* a tumour or gumma caused by infection with syphilis. [C19: from SYPHILIS + *-oma,* as in *sarcoma*]

syphon ('saɪfᵊn) *n* a variant spelling of **siphon.**

SYR *international car registration for* Syria.

Syr. *abbrev. for:* **1** Syria. **2** Syriac. **3** Syrian.

Syracuse *n* **1** ('saɪrə,kju:z). a port in SW Italy, in SE Sicily on the Ionian Sea: founded in 734 B.C. by Greeks from Corinth and taken by the Romans in 212 B.C., after a siege of three years. Pop.: 127 448 (1996 est.). Italian name: **Siracusa. 2** ('sɪrə,kju:s). a city in central New York State, on Lake Onondaga: site of the capital of the Iroquois Indian federation. Pop.: 155 865 (1996 est.).

Syrah ('sɪrrə) *n* **1** a red grape grown in France and Australia, used, often in a blend, for making wine. **2** any of various wines made from this grape. Australian name: **Shiraz.** [from SHIRAZ[1], the city in Iran where the wine supposedly originated]

Syr Darya (*Russian* sɨ darj'ja) *n* a river in central Asia, formed from two headstreams rising in the Tian Shan: flows generally west to the Aral Sea: the longest river in central Asia. Length: (from the source of the Naryn) 2900 km (1800 miles). Ancient name: **Jaxartes.**

Syria ('sɪrɪə) *n* **1** a republic in W Asia, on the Mediterranean: ruled by the Ottoman Turks (1516–1918); made a French mandate in 1920; became independent in 1944; joined Egypt in the United Arab Republic (1958–61). Official language: Arabic. Religion: Muslim majority. Currency: Syrian pound. Capital: Damascus. Pop.: 15 335 000 (1998 est.). Area: 185 180 sq. km (71 498 sq. miles). **2** (formerly) the region between the Mediterranean, the Euphrates, the Taurus, and the Arabian Desert.

Syriac ('sɪrɪ,æk) *n* a dialect of Aramaic spoken in Syria until about the 13th century A.D. and still in use as a liturgical language of certain Eastern churches.

Syrian ('sɪrɪən) *adj* **1** of, relating to, or characteristic of Syria, its people, or their dialect of Arabic. **2** *Eastern Church.* of or relating to Christians who belong to churches with Syriac liturgies. ◆ *n* **3** a native or inhabitant of Syria. **4** *Eastern Church.* a Syrian Christian.

syringa (sɪ'rɪŋgə) *n* another name for **mock orange** and **lilac** (sense 1). [C17: from New Latin, from Greek *surinx* tube, alluding to the use of its hollow stems for pipes]

syringe ('sɪrɪndʒ, sɪ'rɪndʒ) *n* **1** *Med.* an instrument, such as a hypodermic syringe or a rubber ball with a slender nozzle, for use in withdrawing or injecting fluids, cleaning wounds, etc. **2** any similar device for injecting, spraying, or extracting liquids by means of pressure or suction. ◆ *vb* **3** (*tr*) to cleanse, inject, or spray with a syringe. [C15: from Late Latin, from Latin: SYRINX]

syringomyelia (sə,rɪŋgəʊmaɪ'i:lɪə) *n* a chronic progressive disease of the spinal cord in which cavities form in the grey matter: characterized by loss of the sense of pain and temperature. [C19: *syringo-,* from Greek: SYRINX + *-myelia* from Greek *muelos* marrow] ▸ **syringomyelic** (sə,rɪŋgəʊmaɪ'elɪk) *adj*

syrinx ('sɪrɪŋks) *n, pl* **syringes** (sɪ'rɪndʒi:z) *or* **syrinxes. 1** the vocal organ of a bird, which is situated in the lower part of the trachea. **2** (in classical Greek music) a panpipe or set of panpipes. **3** *Anatomy.* another name for the **Eustachian tube.** [C17: via Latin from Greek *surinx* pipe] ▸ **syringeal** (sɪ'rɪndʒɪəl) *adj*

Syrinx ('sɪrɪŋks) *n Greek myth.* a nymph who was changed into a reed to save her from the amorous pursuit of Pan. From this reed Pan then fashioned his musical pipes.

Syro- ('saɪrəʊ-) *combining form.* **1** indicating Syrian and: *Syro-Lebanese.* **2** indicating Syriac and: *Syro-Aramaic.* [from Greek *Suro-,* from *Suros* a Syrian]

syrphid ('sɜ:fɪd) *n* any dipterous fly of the family *Syrphidae,* typically having a coloration mimicking that of certain bees and wasps: includes the hover flies. [C19: from Greek *surphos* gnat]

Syrtis Major ('sɜ:tɪs) *n* a conspicuous dark region visible in the N hemisphere of Mars.

syrup ('sɪrəp) *n* **1** a solution of sugar dissolved in water and often flavoured with fruit juice: used for sweetening fruit, etc. **2** any of various thick sweet liquids prepared for cooking or table use from molasses, sugars, etc. **3** a liquid medicine containing a sugar solution for flavouring or preservation. ◆ *vb* (*tr*) **4** to bring to the consistency of syrup. **5** to cover, fill, or sweeten with syrup. ◆ Also: **sirup.** [C15: from Medieval Latin *syrupus,* from Arabic *sharāb* a drink, from *shariba* to drink] ▸ **'syrup-,like** *adj*

syrupy ('sɪrəpɪ) *adj* **1** (of a liquid) thick or sweet. **2** cloyingly sentimental: *a syrupy version of the Blue Danube.*

syssarcosis (,sɪsɑ:'kəʊsɪs) *n, pl* **-ses** (-si:z). *Anatomy.* the union or articulation of bones by muscle. [C17: from New Latin, from Greek *sussarkōsis,* from *sussarkousthai,* from *sus-* SYN- + *sarkoun* to become fleshy, from *sarx* flesh] ▸ **syssarcotic** (,sɪsɑ:'kɒtɪk) *adj*

syst. *abbrev. for* system.

systaltic (sɪ'stæltɪk) *adj* (esp. of the action of the heart) of, relating to, or characterized by alternate contractions and dilations; pulsating. [C17: from Late Latin *systalticus,* from Greek *sustaltikos,* from *sustellein* to contract, from SYN- + *stellein* to place]

system ('sɪstəm) *n* **1** a group or combination of interrelated, interdependent, or interacting elements forming a collective entity; a methodical or coordinated assemblage of parts, facts, concepts, etc.: *a system of currency; the Copernican system.* **2** any scheme of classification or arrangement: *a chronological system.* **3** a network of communications, transportation, or distribution. **4** a method or complex of methods: *he has a perfect system at roulette.* **5** orderliness; an ordered manner. **6 the system.** (*often cap.*) society seen as an environment exploiting, restricting, and repressing individuals. **7** an organism considered as a functioning entity. **8** any of various bodily parts or structures that are anatomically or physiologically related: *the digestive system.* **9** one's physiological or psychological constitution: *get it out of your system.* **10** any assembly of electronic, electrical, or mechanical components with interdependent functions, usually forming a self-contained unit: *a brake system.* **11** a group of celestial bodies that are associated as a result of natural laws, esp. gravitational attraction: *the solar system.* **12** *Chem.* a sample of matter in which there are one or more substances in one or more phases. See also **phase rule.** **13** a point of view or doctrine used to interpret a branch of knowledge. **14** *Mineralogy.* one of a group of divisions into which crystals may be placed on the basis of the lengths and inclinations of their axes. **15** *Geology.* a stratigraphical unit for the rock strata formed during a period of geological time. It can be subdivided into series. **[C17:** from French *système,* from Late Latin *systēma,* from Greek *sustēma,* from SYN- + *histanai* to cause to stand**]** ▸ **'systemless** *adj*

systematic (ˌsɪstɪˈmætɪk) *adj* **1** characterized by the use of order and planning; methodical: *a systematic administrator.* **2** comprising or resembling a system: *systematic theology.* **3** Also: **systematical** (sɪstəˈmætɪkᵊl). *Biology.* of or relating to the taxonomic classification of organisms. ▸ **ˌsystemˈatically** *adv*

systematic desensitization *n Psychol.* a treatment of phobias in which the patient while relaxed is exposed, often only in imagination, to progressively more frightening aspects of the phobia.

systematics (ˌsɪstɪˈmætɪks) *n (functioning as sing)* the study of systems and the principles of classification and nomenclature.

systematism (ˈsɪstɪməˌtɪzəm) *n* **1** the practice of classifying or systematizing. **2** adherence to a system. **3** a systematic classification; systematized arrangement.

systematist (ˈsɪstɪmətɪst) *n* **1** a person who constructs systems. **2** an adherent of a system. **3** a taxonomist.

systematize (ˈsɪstɪməˌtaɪz), **systemize** *or* **systematise, systemise** *vb (tr)* to arrange in a system. ▸ **ˌsystematiˈzation, ˌsystematiˈsation** *or* **ˌsystemiˈzation, ˌsystemiˈsation** *n* ▸ **ˈsystemaˌtizer, ˈsystemaˌtiser** *or* **ˈsystemˌizer, ˈsystemˌiser** *n*

systematology (ˌsɪstɪməˈtɒlədʒɪ) *n* the study of the nature and formation of systems.

system building *n* a method of building in which prefabricated components are used to speed the construction of buildings. ▸ **system built** *adj*

Système International d'Unités *(French* sistɛm ɛ̃tɛrnasjɔnal dynite) *n* the International System of units. See **SI unit.**

systemic (sɪˈstɛmɪk, -ˈstiː-) *adj* **1** another word for **systematic** (senses 1, 2). **2** *Physiol.* (of a poison, disease, etc.) affecting the entire body. **3** (of a pesticide, fungicide, etc.) spreading through all the parts of a plant and making it toxic to pests or parasites without destroying it. ◆ *n* **4** a systemic pesticide, fungicide, etc. ▸ **sysˈtemically** *adv*

systemic grammar *n* a grammar in which description is founded on the relationships among the various units at different ranks of a language, and in which language is viewed as a system of meaning creating choices. Compare **transformational grammar, case grammar.**

systems analysis *n* the analysis of the requirements of a task and the expression of those requirements in a form that permits the assembly of computer hardware and software to perform the task. ▸ **systems analyst** *n*

systems disk *n* a disk used to store computer programs, esp. the basic operating programs of a computer.

systems engineering *n* the branch of engineering, based on systems analysis and information theory, concerned with the design of integrated systems.

systems theory *n* an approach to industrial relations which likens the enterprise to an organism with interdependent parts, each with its own specific function and interrelated responsibilities.

systole (ˈsɪstəlɪ) *n* contraction of the heart, during which blood is pumped into the aorta and the arteries that lead to the lungs. Compare **diastole.** **[C16:** via Late Latin from Greek *sustolē,* from *sustellein* to contract; see SYSTALTIC**]** ▸ **systolic** (sɪˈstɒlɪk) *adj*

syver *or* **siver** (ˈsaɪvər) *n Scot.* **1** a street drain or the grating over it. **2** a street gutter. **[C17:** of uncertain origin**]**

Syzran *(Russian* ˈsizrənj) *n* a port in W central Russia, on the Volga River: oil refining. Pop.: 177 000 (1995 est.).

syzygy (ˈsɪzɪdʒɪ) *n, pl* **-gies.** **1** either of the two positions (conjunction or opposition) of a celestial body when sun, earth, and the body lie in a straight line: *the moon is at syzygy when full.* **2** (in classical prosody) a metrical unit of two feet. **3** *Rare.* any pair, usually of opposites. **4** *Biology.* the aggregation in a mass of certain protozoans, esp. when occurring before sexual reproduction. **[C17:** from Late Latin *syzygia,* from Greek *suzugia,* from *suzugos* yoked together, from SYN- + *zugon* a yoke**]** ▸ **syzygial** (sɪˈzɪdʒɪəl), **syzygetic** (ˌsɪzɪˈdʒɛtɪk), *or* **syzygal** (ˈsɪzɪgᵊl) *adj* ▸ **ˌsyzyˈgetically** *adv*

Szabadka (ˈsɔbɔtkɔ) *n* the Hungarian name for **Subotica.**

Szczecin *(Polish* ˈʃtʃɛtʃin) *n* a port in NW Poland, on the River Oder: the busiest Polish port and leading coal exporter; shipbuilding. Pop.: 419 300 (1996 est.). German name: **Stettin.**

Szechwan (ˈseɪˈtʃwɑːn) *n* a variant transliteration of the Chinese name for **Sichuan.**

Szeged *(Hungarian* ˈsɛgɛd) *n* an industrial city in S Hungary, on the Tisza River. Pop.: 166 000 (1997 est.).

Szell (sɛl) *n* **George.** 1897–1970, U.S. conductor, born in Hungary.

Szent-Györgyi (sɛntˈdʒɜːdʒɪ) *n* **Albert (von Nagyrapolt).** 1893–1986, U.S. biochemist, born in Hungary, who isolated ascorbic acid and identified it as vitamin C. Nobel prize for physiology or medicine 1937.

Szilard (ˈsɪlɑːd) *n* **Leo.** 1898–1964, U.S. physicist, born in Hungary, who originated the idea of a self-sustaining nuclear chain reaction (1934). He worked on the atomic bomb during World War II but later pressed for the international control of nuclear weapons.

Szombathely *(Hungarian* ˈsombɔthɛj) *n* a city in W Hungary: site of the Roman capital of Pannonia. Pop.: 84 000 (1995 est.).

Szymanowski *(Polish* ʃimaˈnɔfski) *n* **Karol** (ˈkarɔl). 1882–1937, Polish composer, whose works include the opera *King Roger* (1926), two violin concertos, symphonies, piano music, and songs.

Tt

t *or* **T** (tiː) *n, pl* **t's, T's,** *or* **Ts. 1** the 20th letter and 16th consonant of the modern English alphabet. **2** a speech sound represented by this letter, usually a voiceless alveolar stop, as in *tame.* **3a** something shaped like a T. **3b** (*in combination*): *a T-junction.* **4 to a T.** in every detail; perfectly: *the work suited her to a T.*

t *symbol for:* **1** tonne(s). **2** troy (weight). **3** *Statistics.* distribution. **4** *Statistics.* See **Student's t.**

T *symbol for:* **1** absolute temperature. **2** tera-. **3** *Chem.* tritium. **4** *Biochem.* thymine. **5** tesla. **6** surface tension. ◆ **7** *international car registration for* Thailand.

t. *abbrev. for:* **1** *Commerce.* tare. **2** teaspoon(ful). **3** temperature. **4** *Music.* tempo. **5** tempore. [Latin: in the time of] **6** tenor. **7** *Grammar.* tense. **8** ton(s). **9** transitive.

T. *abbrev. for:* **1** tablespoon(ful). **2** territory. **3** time. **4** Tuesday. **5** Also: **Th.** Thursday.

't *contraction of* it.

T- *abbrev. for* trainer (aircraft): *T-37.*

ta (tɑː) *interj Brit. informal.* thank you. [C18: imitative of baby talk]

Ta *the chemical symbol for* tantalum.

TA (in Britain) *abbrev. for* Territorial Army (now superseded by **TAVR**).

taal (tɑːl) *n* **the.** *S. African.* language: usually, by implication, Afrikaans. [Afrikaans from Dutch]

Taal (tɑːˈɑːl) *n* an active volcano in the Philippines, on S Luzon on an island in the centre of **Lake Taal.** Height: 300 m (984 ft.). Area of lake: 243 sq. km (94 sq. miles).

taata (ˈtata) *n E African.* a child's word for **father.**

tab[1] (tæb) *n* **1** a small flap of material, esp. one on a garment for decoration or for fastening to a button. **2** any similar flap, such as a piece of paper attached to a file for identification. **3** a small auxiliary aerofoil on the trailing edge of a rudder, aileron, or elevator, etc., to assist in the control of the aircraft in flight. See also **trim tab. 4** *Brit. military.* the insignia on the collar of a staff officer. **5** *Chiefly U.S. and Canadian.* a bill, esp. one for a meal or drinks. **6** *Scot. and northern English dialect.* a cigarette. **7 keep tabs on.** *Informal.* to keep a watchful eye on. ◆ *vb* **tabs, tabbing, tabbed. 8** (*tr*) to supply (files, clothing, etc.) with a tab or tabs. [C17: of unknown origin]

tab[2] (tæb) *n* **1** short for **tabulator** or **tablet. 2** *Slang.* a portion of a drug, esp. LSD or ecstasy.

TAB *abbrev. for:* **1** typhoid-paratyphoid A and B (vaccine). **2** *Austral. and N.Z.* Totalizator Agency Board.

tab. *abbrev. for* table (list or chart).

tabanid (ˈtæbənɪd) *n* any stout-bodied fly of the dipterous family *Tabanidae,* the females of which have mouthparts specialized for sucking blood: includes the horseflies. [C19: from Latin *tabānus* horsefly]

tabard (ˈtæbəd) *n* a sleeveless or short-sleeved jacket, esp. one worn by a herald, bearing a coat of arms, or by a knight over his armour. [C13: from Old French *tabart,* of uncertain origin]

tabaret (ˈtæbərɪt) *n* a hard-wearing fabric of silk or similar cloth with stripes of satin or moire, used esp. for upholstery. [C19: perhaps from TABBY[1]]

Tabari (təˈbɑːrɪ) *n* **Muhammad ibn Jarir al-.** 838–923 A.D., Arab scholar, whose works include a history of the world from the Creation to 915 A.D. and a commentary on the Koran.

Tabasco[1] (təˈbæskəʊ) *n Trademark.* a very hot red sauce made from matured capsicums.

Tabasco[2] (*Spanish* taˈβasko) *n* a state in SE Mexico, on the Gulf of Campeche: mostly flat and marshy with extensive jungles; hot and humid climate. Capital: Villahermosa. Pop.: 1 748 664 (1995 est.). Area: 24 661 sq. km (9520 sq. miles).

tabbouleh *or* **tabbouli** (təˈbuːlɪ) *n* a kind of Middle Eastern salad made with cracked wheat, mint, parsley, and usually cucumber. [C20: from Arabic *tabbūla*]

tabby[1] (ˈtæbɪ) *n* a fabric with a watered pattern, esp. silk or taffeta. [C17: from Old French *tabis* silk cloth, from Arabic *al-'attabiya,* literally: the quarter of (Prince) 'Attab, the part of Baghdad where the fabric was first made]

tabby[2] (ˈtæbɪ) *adj* **1** (esp. of cats) brindled with dark stripes or wavy markings on a lighter background. **2** having a wavy or striped pattern, particularly in colours of grey and brown. ◆ *n, pl* **-bies. 3** a tabby cat. **4** any female domestic cat. **5** *Brit. informal.* a gossiping old woman. **6** *Austral. slang.* any girl or woman. [C17: from *Tabby,* pet form of the girl's name *Tabitha,* probably influenced by TABBY[1]]

tabernacle (ˈtæbəˌnækəl) *n* **1** (*often cap.*) *Old Testament.* **1a** the portable sanctuary in the form of a tent in which the ancient Israelites carried the Ark of the Covenant (Exodus 25–27). **1b** the Jewish Temple regarded as the shrine of the divine presence. **2** *Judaism.* an English word for **sukkah. 3** any place of worship that is not called a church. **4** a small ornamented cupboard or box used for the reserved sacrament of the Eucharist. **5** the human body regarded as the temporary dwelling of the soul. **6** *Chiefly R.C. Church.* a canopied niche or recess forming the shrine of a statue. **7** *Nautical.* a strong framework for holding the foot of a mast stepped on deck, allowing it to be swung down horizontally to pass under low bridges, etc. [C13: from Latin *tabernāculum* a tent, from *taberna* a hut; see TAVERN] ▸ **ˌtaberˈnacular** *adj*

Tabernacles (ˈtæbəˌnækəlz) *pl n Judaism.* an English name for **Sukkoth.**

tabes (ˈteɪbiːz) *n, pl* **tabes. 1** a wasting of a bodily organ or part. **2** short for **tabes dorsalis.** [C17: from Latin: a wasting away] ▸ **tabetic** (təˈbɛtɪk) *adj*

tabescent (təˈbɛsənt) *adj* **1** progressively emaciating; wasting away. **2** of, relating to, or having tabes. [C19: from Latin *tābēscere,* from TABES] ▸ **taˈbescence** *n*

tabes dorsalis (dɔːˈsɑːlɪs) *n* a form of late syphilis that attacks the spinal cord causing degeneration of the nerve fibres, pains in the legs, paralysis of the leg muscles, acute abdominal pain, etc. Also called: **locomotor ataxia.** [New Latin, literally: tabes of the back; see TABES, DORSAL]

tabla (ˈtʌblə, ˈtɑːblɑː) *n* a musical instrument of India consisting of a pair of drums whose pitches can be varied. [Hindu, from Arabic *tabla* drum]

tablature (ˈtæblətʃə) *n* **1** *Music.* any of a number of forms of musical notation, esp. for playing the lute, consisting of letters and signs indicating rhythm and fingering. **2** an engraved or painted tablet or other flat surface. [C16: from French, ultimately from Latin *tabulātum* wooden floor, from *tabula* a plank]

table (ˈteɪbəl) *n* **1** a flat horizontal slab or board, usually supported by one or more legs, on which objects may be placed. Related adj: **mensal. 2a** such a slab or board on which food is served: *we were six at table.* **2b** (*as modifier*): *table linen.* **2c** (*in combination*): *a tablecloth.* **3** food as served in a particular household or restaurant: *a good table.* **4** such a piece of furniture specially designed for any of various purposes: *a backgammon table; bird table.* **5a** a company of persons assembled for a meal, game, etc. **5b** (*as modifier*): *table talk.* **6** any flat or level area, such as a plateau. **7** a rectangular panel set below or above the face of a wall. **8** *Architect.* another name for **cordon** (sense 4). **9** an upper horizontal facet of a cut gem. **10** *Music.* the sounding board of a violin, guitar, or similar stringed instrument. **11a** an arrangement of words, numbers, or signs, usually in parallel columns, to display data or relations: *a table of contents.* **11b** See **multiplication table. 12** a tablet on which laws were inscribed by the ancient Romans, the Hebrews, etc. **13** *Palmistry.* an area of the palm's surface bounded by four lines. **14** *Printing.* a slab of smooth metal on which ink is rolled to its proper consistency. **15a** either of the two bony plates that form the inner and outer parts of the flat bones of the cranium. **15b** any thin flat plate, esp. of bone. **16 on the table.** put forward for discussion and acceptance: *we currently have our final offer on the table.* **17 turn the tables on (someone).** to cause a complete reversal of circumstances, esp. to defeat or get the better of (someone) who was previously in a stronger position. ◆ *vb* (*tr*) **18** to place on a table. **19** *Brit.* to submit (a bill, etc.) for consideration by a legislative body. **20** *U.S.* to suspend discussion of (a bill, etc.) indefinitely or for some time. **21** to enter in or form into a list; tabulate. [C12: via Old French from Latin *tabula* a writing tablet] ▸ **ˈtableful** *n* ▸ **ˈtableless** *adj*

tableau (ˈtæbləʊ) *n, pl* **-leaux** (-ləʊ, -ləʊz) *or* **-leaus. 1** See ***tableau vivant.*** **2** a pause during or at the end of a scene on stage when all the performers briefly freeze in position. **3** any dramatic group or scene. **4** *Logic.* short for **semantic tableau.** [C17: from French, from Old French *tablel* a picture, diminutive of TABLE]

tableau vivant *French.* (tablo vivɑ̃) *n, pl* ***tableaux vivants*** (tablo vivɑ̃). a representation of a scene, painting, sculpture, etc., by a person or group posed silent and motionless. [C19: literally: living picture]

Table Bay *n* the large bay on which Cape Town is situated, on the SW coast of South Africa.

tablecloth (ˈteɪbəlˌklɒθ) *n* a cloth for covering the top of a table, esp. during meals.

table d'hôte (ˈtɑːbəl ˈdəʊt; *French* tablə dot) *adj* **1** (of a meal) consisting of a set number of courses with limited choice of dishes offered at a fixed price. Compare **à la carte, prix fixe.** ◆ *n, pl* **tables d'hôte** (ˈtɑːbəlz ˈdəʊt; *French* tablə dot). **2** a table d'hôte meal or menu. [C17: from French, literally: the host's table]

tableland (ˈteɪbəlˌlænd) *n* flat elevated land; a plateau.

table licence *n* a licence authorizing the sale of alcoholic drinks with meals only.

table money *n* an allowance for official entertaining of visitors, clients, etc., esp. in the army.

Table Mountain *n* a mountain in SW South Africa, overlooking Cape Town and Table Bay: flat-topped and steep-sided. Height: 1087 m (3567 ft.).

table napkin *n* See **napkin** (sense 1).

table-rapping *n* the sounds of knocking or tapping made without any apparent physical agency while a group of people sit round a table, and attributed by spiritualists to the spirit of a dead person using this as a means of communication with the living.

table salt *n* salt that is used at table rather than for cooking.

tablespoon (ˈteɪbəlˌspuːn) *n* **1** a spoon, larger than a dessertspoon, used for serving food, etc. **2** Also called: **tablespoonful.** the amount contained in such a spoon. **3** a unit of capacity used in cooking, medicine, etc., equal to half a fluid ounce or three teaspoons.

tablet (ˈtæblɪt) *n* **1** a pill made of a compressed powdered medicinal substance. **2** a flattish cake of some substance, such as soap. **3** *Scot.* a sweet made of butter, sugar, and condensed milk, usually shaped in a flat oblong block. **4** a slab of stone, wood, etc., esp. one formerly used for inscriptions. **5a** a thinner rigid sheet, as of bark, ivory, etc., used for similar purposes. **5b** (*often pl*) a set or pair of these fastened together, as in a book. **6** a pad of writing paper. **7** *N.Z.* a token giving right of way to the driver of a train on a single line section. **[C14:** from Old French *tablete* a little table, from Latin *tabula* a board**]**

table talk *n* informal conversation on a range of topics, as that at table during and after a meal.

table tennis *n* a miniature form of tennis played on a table with small bats and a light hollow ball.

table-turning *n* **1** the movement of a table attributed by spiritualists to the power of spirits working through a group of persons placing their hands or fingers on the table top. **2** *Often derogatory.* spiritualism in general.

tableware ('teɪbᵊl,wɛə) *n* articles such as dishes, plates, knives, forks, etc., used at meals.

table wine *n* a wine considered suitable for drinking with a meal.

tabloid ('tæblɔɪd) *n* **1** a newspaper with pages about 30 cm (12 inches) by 40 cm (16 inches), usually characterized by an emphasis on photographs and a concise and often sensational style. Compare **broadsheet. 2** (*modifier*) designed to appeal to a mass audience or readership; sensationalist: *the tabloid press; tabloid television.* **[C20:** from earlier *Tabloid,* a trademark for a medicine in tablet form**]**

taboo *or* **tabu** (tə'buː) *adj* **1** forbidden or disapproved of; placed under a social prohibition or ban: *taboo words.* **2** (in Polynesia and other islands of the South Pacific) marked off as simultaneously sacred and forbidden. ◆ *n, pl* **-boos** *or* **-bus. 3** any prohibition resulting from social or other conventions. **4** ritual restriction or prohibition, esp. of something that is considered holy or unclean. ◆ *vb* **5** (*tr*) to place under a taboo. **[C18:** from Tongan *tapu***]**

tabor *or* **tabour** ('teɪbə) *n Music.* a small drum used esp. in the Middle Ages, struck with one hand while the other held a three-holed pipe. See **pipe**[1] (sense 7). **[C13:** from Old French *tabour,* perhaps from Persian *tabīr***]** ▸ **'taborer** *or* **'tabourer** *n*

Tabor ('teɪbə) *n* **Mount.** a mountain in N Israel, near Nazareth: traditionally regarded as the mountain where the Transfiguration took place. Height: 588 m (1929 ft.).

taboret *or* **tabouret** ('tæbərɪt) *n* **1** a low stool, originally in the shape of a drum. **2** a frame, usually round, for stretching out cloth while it is being embroidered. **3** Also called: **taborin, tabourin** ('tæbərɪn). a small tabor. **[C17:** from French *tabouret,* diminutive of TABOR**]**

Tabriz (tæ'briːz) *n* a city in NW Iran: an ancient city, situated in a volcanic region of hot springs; university (1947); carpet manufacturing. Pop.: 1 166 203 (1994 est.). Ancient name: **Tauris** ('tɔːrɪs).

tabular ('tæbjʊlə) *adj* **1** arranged in systematic or table form. **2** calculated from or by means of a table. **3** like a table in form; flat. **[C17:** from Latin *tabulāris* concerning boards, from *tabula* a board**]** ▸ **'tabularly** *adv*

tabula rasa ('tæbjʊlə 'rɑːsə) *n, pl* **tabulae rasae** ('tæbjʊliː 'rɑːsiː). **1** (esp. in the philosophy of Locke) the mind in its uninformed original state. **2** an opportunity for a fresh start; clean slate. **[**Latin: a scraped tablet (one from which the writing has been erased)**]**

tabulate *vb* ('tæbjʊ,leɪt). (*tr*) **1** Also: **tabularize** ('tæbjʊlə,raɪz). to set out, arrange, or write in tabular form. **2** to form or cut with a flat surface. ◆ *adj* ('tæbjʊlɪt, -,leɪt). **3** having a flat surface. **4** (of certain corals) having transverse skeletal plates. **[C18:** from Latin *tabula* a board**]** ▸ **'tabulable** *adj* ▸ **,tabu'lation** *n*

tabulator ('tæbjʊ,leɪtə) *n* **1** a device for setting the automatic stops that locate the column margins on a typewriter. **2** *Computing.* a machine that reads data from one medium, such as punched cards, producing lists, tabulations, or totals, usually on a continuous sheet of paper. **3** any machine that tabulates data.

tabun (tɑː'buːn) *n* an organic compound used in chemical warfare as a lethal nerve gas. Formula: $C_2H_5OP(O)(CN)N(CH_3)_2$. **[C20:** from German, of uncertain origin**]**

tacamahac ('tækəmə,hæk) *or* **tacmahack** *n* **1** any of several strong-smelling resinous gums obtained from certain trees, used in making ointments, incense, etc. **2** any tree yielding this resin, esp. the balsam poplar. **[C16:** from Spanish *tacamahaca,* from Nahuatl *tecomahca* aromatic resin**]**

Tacan ('tækən) *n* an electronic ultrahigh-frequency navigation system for aircraft which gives a continuous indication of bearing and distance from a transmitting station. **[C20:** *tac(tical) a(ir) n(avigation)***]**

tace (tæs, teɪs) *n* a less common word for **tasset.**

tacet ('teɪsɛt, 'tæs-) *vb* (*intr*) (on a musical score) a direction indicating that a particular instrument or singer does not take part in a movement or part of a movement. **[C18:** from Latin: it is silent, from *tacēre* to be quiet**]**

tache[1] (tæʃ, tɑːʃ) *n Archaic.* a buckle, clasp, or hook. **[C17:** from Old French, of Germanic origin; compare TACK[1]**]**

tache[2] (tæʃ) *n Informal.* short for **moustache.**

tacheo- *combining form.* a variant of **tachy-**.

tacheometer (,tækɪ'ɒmɪtə) *or* **tachymeter** *n Surveying.* a type of theodolite designed for the rapid measurement of distances, elevations, and directions.

tacheometry (,tækɪ'ɒmɪtrɪ) *or* **tachymetry** *n Surveying.* the measurement of distance, etc., using a tacheometer. ▸ **tacheometric** (,tækɪə'mɛtrɪk), **,tacheo'metrical** *or* **,tachy'metric, ,tachy'metrical** *adj* ▸ **,tacheo'metrically** *or* **,tachy'metrically** *adv*

tachina fly ('tækɪnə) *n* any bristly fly of the dipterous family *Tachinidae,* the larvae of which live parasitically in caterpillars, beetles, hymenopterans, and other insects. **[C19:** via New Latin *Tachina,* from Greek *takhinos* swift, from *takhos* fleetness**]**

tachisme ('tɑːʃɪzəm; *French* taʃism) *n* a type of action painting evolved in France in which haphazard dabs and blots of colour are treated as a means of instinctive or unconscious expression. **[C20:** French, from *tache* stain**]**

tachistoscope (tə'kɪstə,skəʊp) *n* an instrument, used mainly in experiments on perception and memory, for displaying visual images for very brief intervals, usually a fraction of a second. **[C20:** from Greek *takhistos* swiftest (see TACHY-) + -SCOPE**]** ▸ **tachistoscopic** (tə,kɪstə'skɒpɪk) *adj* ▸ **ta,chisto'scopically** *adv*

tacho- *combining form.* speed: *tachograph; tachometer.* **[**from Greek *takhos***]**

tachograph ('tækə,grɑːf, -,græf) *n* a tachometer that produces a graphical record (**tachogram**) of its readings, esp. a device for recording the speed of and distance covered by a heavy goods vehicle. Often shortened to **tacho.**

tachometer (tæ'kɒmɪtə) *n* any device for measuring speed, esp. the rate of revolution of a shaft. Tachometers (rev counters) are often fitted to cars to indicate the number of revolutions per minute of the engine. ▸ **tachometric** (,tækə'mɛtrɪk) *or* **,tacho'metrical** *adj* ▸ **,tacho'metrically** *adv* ▸ **ta'chometry** *n*

tachy- *or* **tacheo-** *combining form.* swift or accelerated: *tachycardia; tachygraphy; tachylyte; tachyon; tachyphylaxis.* **[**from Greek *takhus* swift**]**

tachycardia (,tækɪ'kɑːdɪə) *n Pathol.* abnormally rapid beating of the heart, esp. over 100 beats per minute. Compare **bradycardia.** ▸ **tachycardiac** (,tækɪ'kɑːdɪ,æk) *adj*

tachygraphy (tæ'kɪgrəfɪ) *n* shorthand, esp. as used in ancient Rome or Greece. ▸ **ta'chygrapher** *or* **ta'chygraphist** *n* ▸ **tachygraphic** (,tækɪ'græfɪk) *adj* ▸ **,tachy'graphically** *adv*

tachylyte *or* **tachylite** ('tækɪ,laɪt) *n* a black glassy basalt often found on the edges of intrusions of basalt. **[C19:** from German *tachylit,* from TACHY- + Greek *lutos* soluble, melting, from *luein* to release; so called because it fuses easily when heated. The form *tachylite* is influenced by -LITE stone**]** ▸ **tachylytic** (,tækɪ'lɪtɪk) *or* **,tachy'litic** *adj*

tachymeter (tæ'kɪmɪtə) *n* another name for **tacheometer.**

tachymetry (tæ'kɪmɪtrɪ) *n* another name for **tacheometry.**

tachyon ('tækɪ,ɒn) *n Physics.* a hypothetical elementary particle capable of travelling faster than the velocity of light. **[C20:** from TACHY- + -ON**]**

tachyphylaxis (,tækɪfɪ'læksɪs) *n* very rapid development of tolerance or immunity to the effects of a drug. **[**New Latin, from TACHY- + *phylaxis* on the model of *prophylaxis.* See PROPHYLACTIC**]**

tachypnoea *or U.S.* **tachypnea** (,tækɪp'nɪə) *n Pathol.* abnormally rapid breathing.

tacit ('tæsɪt) *adj* **1** implied or inferred without direct expression; understood: *a tacit agreement.* **2** created or having effect by operation of law, rather than by being directly expressed. **[C17:** from Latin *tacitus,* past participle of *tacēre* to be silent**]** ▸ **'tacitly** *adv* ▸ **'tacitness** *n*

taciturn ('tæsɪ,tɜːn) *adj* habitually silent, reserved, or uncommunicative; not inclined to conversation. **[C18:** from Latin *taciturnus,* from *tacitus* silent, from *tacēre* to be silent**]** ▸ **,taci'turnity** *n* ▸ **'taci,turnly** *adv*

Tacitus ('tæsɪtəs) *n* **Publius Cornelius** ('pʌblɪəs kɔː'niːljəs). ?55–?120 A.D., Roman historian and orator, famous as a prose stylist. His works include the *Histories,* dealing with the period 68–96, and the *Annals,* dealing with the period 14–68.

tack[1] (tæk) *n* **1** a short sharp-pointed nail, usually with a flat and comparatively large head. **2** *Brit.* a long loose temporary stitch used in dressmaking, etc. **3** See **tailor's-tack. 4** a temporary fastening. **5** stickiness, as of newly applied paint, varnish, etc. **6** *Nautical.* the heading of a vessel sailing to windward, stated in terms of the side of the sail against which the wind is pressing. **7** *Nautical.* **7a** a course sailed by a sailing vessel with the wind blowing from forward of the beam. **7b** one such course or a zigzag pattern of such courses. **8** *Nautical.* **8a** a sheet for controlling the weather clew of a course. **8b** the weather clew itself. **9** *Nautical.* the forward lower clew of a fore-and-aft sail. **10** a course of action differing from some previous course: *he went off on a fresh tack.* **11 on the wrong tack.** under a false impression. ◆ *vb* **12** (*tr*) to secure by a tack or series of tacks. **13** *Brit.* to sew (something) with long loose temporary stitches. **14** (*tr*) to attach or append: *tack this letter onto the other papers.* **15** *Nautical.* to change the heading of (a sailing vessel) to the opposite tack. **16** *Nautical.* to steer (a sailing vessel) on alternate tacks. **17** (*intr*) *Nautical.* (of a sailing vessel) to proceed on a different tack or to alternate tacks. **18** (*intr*) to follow a zigzag route; keep changing one's course of action. **[C14** *tak* fastening, nail; related to Middle Low German *tacke* pointed instrument**]** ▸ **'tacker** *n* ▸ **'tackless** *adj*

tack[2] (tæk) *n Informal.* food, esp. when regarded as inferior or distasteful. See also **hardtack. [C19:** of unknown origin**]**

tack[3] (tæk) *n* **a** riding harness for horses, such as saddles, bridles, etc. **b** (*as modifier*): *the tack room.* **[C20:** shortened from TACKLE**]**

tack[4] (tæk) *n Scot.* **1** a lease. **2** an area of land held on a lease. **[C15:** from *tak* a Scots word for *take***]**

tacket ('tækɪt) *n Scot. and northern English dialect.* a nail, esp. a hobnail. **[C14:** from TACK[1]**]** ▸ **'tackety** *adj*

tack hammer *n* a light hammer for driving tacks.

tackies *or* **takkies** ('tækɪz) *pl n, sing* **tacky.** *S. African informal.* tennis shoes or plimsolls. **[C20:** probably from TACKY[1], with reference to their nonslip rubber soles**]**

tackle ('tækᵊl; *Nautical often* 'teɪkᵊl) *n* **1** any mechanical system for lifting or pulling, esp. an arrangement of ropes and pulleys designed to lift heavy weights. **2** the equipment required for a particular occupation, etc.: *fishing tackle.* **3** *Nautical.* the halyards and other running rigging aboard a vessel. **4** *Sport.* a physical challenge to an opponent, as to prevent his progress with the ball. **5** *American football.* a defensive lineman. ◆ *vb* **6** (*tr*) to undertake (a task, problem, etc.). **7** (*tr*) to confront (a person, esp. an opponent) with a difficult proposition. **8** *Sport.* (esp. in football games) to challenge (an opponent) with a tackle. **[C13:** related to Middle Low German *takel* ship's rigging, Middle Dutch *taken* to TAKE**]** ▸ **'tackler** *n*

tack rag *n Building trades.* a cotton cloth impregnated with an oil, used to remove dust from a surface prior to painting.

tacksman ('tæksmən) *n, pl* **-men.** *Scot.* a leaseholder, esp. a tenant in the Highlands who sublets. **[C16:** from TACK[4]**]**

tack welding *n Engineering.* short intermittent welds made to hold components in place before full welding is begun.

tacky[1] *or* **tackey** ('tækɪ) *adj* **tackier, tackiest.** slightly sticky or adhesive: *the varnish was still tacky.* **[C18:** from TACK[1] (in the sense: stickiness)**]** ▸ **'tackily** *adv* ▸ **'tackiness** *n*

tacky[2] ('tækɪ) *adj* **tackier, tackiest.** *Informal.* **1** shabby or shoddy. **2** ostentatious and vulgar. **3** *U.S.* (of a person) dowdy; seedy. **[C19:** from dialect *tacky* an inferior horse, of unknown origin**]** ▸ **'tackiness** *n*

tacmahack ('tækmə,hæk) *n* a variant of **tacamahac.**

Tacna-Arica (*Spanish* 'taknaa'rika) *n* a coastal desert region of W South America, long disputed by Chile and Peru: divided in 1929 into the Peruvian department of Tacna and the Chilean department of Arica.

tacnode ('tæk,nəʊd) *n* another name for **osculation** (sense 1). **[C19:** from Latin *tactus* touch (from *tangere* to touch) + NODE**]**

taco ('tɑːkəʊ) *n, pl* **-cos.** *Mexican cookery.* a tortilla folded into a roll with a filling and usually fried. **[**from Mexican Spanish, from Spanish: literally, a snack, a bite to eat**]**

Tacoma (tə'kəʊmə) *n* a port in W Washington, on Puget Sound: industrial centre. Pop.: 179 114 (1996 est.).

taconite ('tækə,naɪt) *n* a fine-grained sedimentary rock containing magnetite, haematite, and silica, which occurs in the Lake Superior region: a low-grade iron ore. **[C20:** named after the *Taconic* Mountains in New England**]**

tact (tækt) *n* **1** a sense of what is fitting and considerate in dealing with others, so as to avoid giving offence or to win good will; discretion. **2** skill or judgment in handling difficult or delicate situations; diplomacy. **[C17:** from Latin *tactus* a touching, from *tangere* to touch**]** ▸ **'tactful** *adj* ▸ **'tactfully** *adv* ▸ **'tactfulness** *n* ▸ **'tactless** *adj* ▸ **'tactlessly** *adv* ▸ **'tactlessness** *n*

tactic ('tæktɪk) *n* a piece of tactics; tactical move. See also **tactics.**

-tactic *adj combining form.* having a specified kind of pattern or arrangement or having an orientation determined by a specified force: *syndiotactic; phototactic.* **[**from Greek *taktikos* relating to order or arrangement; see TACTICS**]**

tactical ('tæktɪkᵊl) *adj* **1** of, relating to, or employing tactics: *a tactical error.* **2** (of weapons, attacks, etc.) used in or supporting limited military operations: *a tactical missile; tactical bombing.* **3** skilful or diplomatic: *a tactical manoeuvre.* ▸ **'tactically** *adv*

tactical voting *n* (in an election) the practice of casting one's vote not for the party of one's choice but for the second strongest contender in order to defeat the likeliest winner.

tactics ('tæktɪks) *pl n* **1** (*functioning as sing*) *Military.* the art and science of the detailed direction and control of movement or manoeuvre of forces in battle to achieve an aim or task. **2** the manoeuvres used or plans followed to achieve a particular short-term aim. **[C17:** from New Latin *tactica,* from Greek *ta taktika* the matters of arrangement, neuter plural of *taktikos* concerning arrangement or order, from *taktos* arranged (for battle), from *tassein* to arrange**]** ▸ **tac'tician** *n*

tactile ('tæktaɪl) *adj* **1** of, relating to, affecting, or having a sense of touch: *a tactile organ; tactile stimuli.* **2** *Now rare.* capable of being touched; tangible. **[C17:** from Latin *tactilis,* from *tangere* to touch**]** ▸ **tactility** (tæk'tɪlɪtɪ) *n*

taction ('tækʃən) *n Obsolete.* the act of touching; contact. **[C17:** from Latin *tactiō* a touching, from *tangere* to touch**]**

tactual ('tæktjʊəl) *adj* **1** caused by touch; causing a tactile sensation. **2** of or relating to the tactile sense or the organs of touch. **[C17:** from Latin *tactus* a touching; see TACT**]** ▸ **'tactually** *adv*

tad (tæd) *n Informal.* **1** *U.S. and Canadian.* a small boy; lad. **2** *U.S. and Canadian.* a small bit or piece. **3 a tad.** a little; rather: *she may be a tad short but she got a top modelling job.* **[C20:** short for TADPOLE**]**

Tadmor ('tædmɔː) *n* the biblical name for **Palmyra.**

tadpole ('tæd,pəʊl) *n* the aquatic larva of frogs, toads, etc., which develops from a limbless tailed form with external gills into a form with internal gills, limbs, and a reduced tail. **[C15** *taddepol,* from *tadde* TOAD + *pol* head, POLL**]**

Tadzhik *or* **Tadjik** ('tɑːdʒɪk, tɑː'dʒiːk) *n, pl* **-dzhik, -djik,** *or* **-jik.** a variant spelling of **Tajik.**

Tadzhikistan (tɑː,dʒɪkɪ'stɑːn, -stæn) *n* a variant spelling of **Tajikistan.**

tae[1] (te) *prep, adv* a Scot. word for **to.**

tae[2] (te) *adv* a Scot. word for **too.**

tae[3] (te) *n* a Scot. word for **toe.**

taedium vitae ('tiːdɪəm 'viːtaɪ, 'vaɪtiː) *n* the feeling that life is boring and dull. **[**Latin, literally: weariness of life**]**

Taegu (te'guː) *n* a city in SE South Korea: textile and agricultural trading centre. Pop.: 2 449 139 (1995).

Taejon (te'dʒɒn) *n* a city in W South Korea: market centre of an agricultural region. Pop.: 1 272 143 (1995).

tae kwon do ('taɪ 'kwɒn 'dəʊ, 'teɪ) *n* a Korean martial art that resembles karate. **[C20:** Korean *tae* kick + *kwon* fist + *do* way, method**]**

tael (teɪl) *n* **1** a unit of weight, used in the Far East, having various values between one to two and a half ounces. **2** (formerly) a Chinese monetary unit equivalent in value to a tael weight of standard silver. **[C16:** from Portuguese, from Malay *tahil* weight, perhaps from Hindi *tolā* weight of a new rupee, from Sanskrit *tulā* weight**]**

ta'en (teɪn) *vb* a poetic contraction of **taken.**

taenia *or U.S.* **tenia** ('tiːnɪə) *n, pl* **-niae** (-nɪ,iː). **1** (in ancient Greece) a narrow fillet or headband for the hair. **2** *Architect.* the fillet between the architrave and frieze of a Doric entablature. **3** *Anatomy.* any bandlike structure or part. **4** any tapeworm of the genus *Taenia,* such as *T. soleum,* a parasite of man that uses the pig as its intermediate host. **[C16:** via Latin from Greek *tainia* narrow strip; related to Greek *teinein* to stretch**]**

taeniacide *or U.S.* **teniacide** ('tiːnɪə,saɪd) *n* a substance, esp. a drug, that kills tapeworms.

taeniafuge *or U.S.* **teniafuge** ('tiːnɪə,fjuːdʒ) *n* a substance, esp. a drug, that expels tapeworms from the body of their host.

taeniasis *or U.S.* **teniasis** (tiː'naɪəsɪs) *n Pathol.* infestation with tapeworms of the genus *Taenia.*

TAFE ('tæfɪ) *n* (in Australia) *acronym for* Technical and Further Education.

Tafelwein ('tɑːfəl,vaɪn) *n* German table wine. **[C20:** from German *Tafel* table + *Wein* wine**]**

taffeta ('tæfɪtə) *n* **1a** a crisp lustrous plain-weave silk, rayon, etc., used esp. for women's clothes. **1b** (*as modifier*)*: a taffeta petticoat.* **2** any of various similar fabrics. **[C14:** from Medieval Latin *taffata,* from Persian *tāftah* spun, from *tāftan* to spin**]**

taffrail ('tæf,reɪl) *n Nautical.* **1** a rail at the stern or above the transom of a vessel. **2** the upper part of the transom of a vessel, esp. a sailing vessel, often ornately decorated. **[C19:** changed (through influence of RAIL[1]) from earlier *tafferel,* from Dutch *taffereel* panel (hence applied to the part of a vessel decorated with carved panels), variant of *tafeleel* (unattested), from *tafel* TABLE**]**

taffy ('tæfɪ) *n, pl* **-fies. 1** *U.S. and Canadian.* a chewy sweet made of brown sugar or molasses and butter, boiled and then pulled so that it becomes glossy. **2** *Chiefly U.S. and Canadian.* a less common term for **toffee. [C19:** perhaps from TAFIA**]**

Taffy ('tæfɪ) *n, pl* **-fies.** a slang word or nickname for a Welshman. **[C17:** from the supposed Welsh pronunciation of *Davy* (from *David,* Welsh *Dafydd*), a common Welsh Christian name**]**

tafia *or* **taffia** ('tæfɪə) *n* a type of rum, esp. from Guyana or the Caribbean. **[C18:** from French, from West Indian Creole, probably from RATAFIA**]**

Tafilelt (tæ'fiːlɛlt) *or* **Tafilalet** (,tæfɪ'lɑːlɛt) *n* an oasis in SE Morocco, the largest in the Sahara. Area: about 1300 sq. km (500 sq. miles).

Taft (tæft) *n* **William Howard.** 1857–1930, U.S. statesman; 27th president of the U.S. (1909–13).

tag[1] (tæg) *n* **1** a piece or strip of paper, plastic, leather, etc., for attaching to something by one end as a mark or label: *a price tag.* **2** an electronic device worn, usually on the wrist or ankle, by an offender serving a noncustodial sentence, which monitors the offender's whereabouts by means of a link to a central computer through the telephone system. Also called: **electronic tag. 3** a small piece of material hanging from or loosely attached to a part or piece. **4** a point of metal or other hard substance at the end of a cord, lace, etc., to prevent it from fraying and to facilitate threading. **5** an epithet or verbal appendage, the refrain of a song, the moral of a fable, etc. **6** a brief quotation, esp. one in a foreign language: *his speech was interlarded with Horatian tags.* **7** *Grammar.* **7a** Also called: **tag question.** a clause added on to another clause to invite the hearer's agreement or conversational cooperation. Tags are usually in the form of a question with a pronoun as subject, the antecedent of which is the subject of the main clause; as *isn't it* in *the bread is on the table, isn't it?* **7b** a linguistic item added on to a sentence but not forming part of it, as *John* in *are you there, John?* **8** an ornamental flourish as at the end of a signature. **9** the contrastingly coloured tip to an animal's tail. **10** a matted lock of wool or hair. **11** *Angling.* a strand of tinsel, wire, etc., tied to the body of an artificial fly. ◆ *vb* **tags, tagging, tagged.** (*mainly tr*) **12** to mark with a tag. **13** to monitor the whereabouts of (an offender) by means of an electronic tag. **14** to add or append as a tag. **15** to supply (prose or blank verse) with rhymes. **16** (*intr; usually foll. by on or along*) to trail (behind): *many small boys tagged on behind the procession.* **17** to name or call (someone something): *they tagged him Lanky.* **18** to cut the tags of wool or hair from (an animal). **[C15:** of uncertain origin; related to Swedish *tagg* point, perhaps also to TACK[1]**]**

tag[2] (tæg) *n* **1** Also called: **tig.** a children's game in which one player chases the others in an attempt to catch one of them who will then become the chaser. **2** the act of tagging one's partner in tag wrestling. **3** (*modifier*) denoting or relating to a wrestling contest between two teams of two wrestlers, in which only one from each team may be in the ring at one time. The contestant outside the ring may change places with his team-mate inside the ring after touching his hand. ◆ *vb* **tags, tagging, tagged.** (*tr*) **4** to catch (another child) in the game of tag. **5** (in tag wrestling) to touch the hand of (one's partner). **[C18:** perhaps from TAG[1]**]**

Tagalog (tə'gɑːlɒg) *n* **1** (*pl* **-logs** *or* **-log**) a member of a people of the Philippines, living chiefly in the region around Manila. **2** the language of this people, belonging to the Malayo-Polynesian family: the official language of the Philippines. ◆ *adj* **3** of or relating to this people or their language.

Taganrog (*Russian* təgan'rɔk) *n* a port in SW Russia, on the **Gulf of Taganrog** (an inlet of the Sea of Azov): founded in 1698 as a naval base and fortress by Peter the Great: industrial centre. Pop.: 292 000 (1995 est.).

tag end *n* **1** the last part of something: *the tag end of the day.* **2** a loose end of cloth, thread, etc.

tagetes (tæ'dʒiːtiːz) *n* See **marigold** (sense 1).

taggers ('tægəz) *pl n* very thin iron or steel sheet coated with tin. **[C19:** perhaps so called because it was used to make tags for laces**]**

tagliatelle (,tæljə'tɛlɪ) *n* a form of pasta made in narrow strips. **[**Italian, from *tagliare* to cut**]**

Taglioni (*Italian* ta'ʎoni) *n* **Marie.** 1804–84, Italian ballet dancer, whose romantic style greatly influenced ballet in the 19th century.

tagma ('tægmə) *n, pl* **-mata** (-mətə). *Zoology.* a distinct region of the body of an arthropod, such as the head, thorax, or abdomen of an insect. **[C19:** from Greek: something arranged, from *tassein* to put in order**]**

tagmeme ('tægmiːm) *n Linguistics.* a class of speech elements all of which may fulfil the same grammatical role in a sentence; the minimum unit of analysis in tagmemics. [C20: from Greek *tagma* order, from *tassein* to put in order + -EME] ▸ **tag'memic** *adj*

tagmemics (tæg'mi:mɪks) *pl n* (*functioning as sing*) *Linguistics.* a type of grammatical analysis based on the concept of function in sentence slots and the determination of classes of words that can fill each slot.

Tagore (tə'gɔ:) *n* **Rabindranath** (rə'bi:ndrə,nɑ:t). 1861–1941, Indian poet and philosopher. His verse collections, written in Bengali and English, include *Gitanjali* (1910; 1912): Nobel prize for literature 1913.

taguan ('tæg,wæn) *n* a large nocturnal flying squirrel, *Petaurista petaurista,* of high forests in the East Indies that uses its long tail as a rudder. [C19: its Filipino name]

Tagus ('teɪgəs) *n* a river in SW Europe, rising in E central Spain and flowing west to the border with Portugal, then southwest to the Atlantic at Lisbon: the longest river of the Iberian Peninsula. Length: 1007 km (626 miles). Portuguese name: **Tejo.** Spanish name: **Tajo.**

tahini (tə'hi:nɪ) *or* **tahina** (tə'hi:nə) *n* a paste made from sesame seeds originating in the Middle East, often used as an ingredient of hummus and other dips. [from Arabic]

Tahiti (tə'hi:tɪ) *n* an island in the S Pacific, in the Windward group of the Society Islands: the largest and most important island in French Polynesia; became a French protectorate in 1842 and a colony in 1880. Capital: Papeete. Pop.: 115 820 (1988). Area: 1005 sq. km (388 sq. miles). ▸ **Tahitian** (tə'hi:tɪən, tə'hi:ʃɪən) *adj, n*

Tahltan ('tæltən) *n* **1** a member of a North American Indian people inhabiting NW British Columbia. **2** the language of this people, belonging to the Athapascan group of the Na-Dene phylum.

Tahoe ('tɑ:həʊ, 'teɪ-) *n* **Lake.** a lake between E California and W Nevada, in the Sierra Nevada Mountains at an altitude of 1899 m (6229 ft.). Area: about 520 sq. km (200 sq. miles).

tahr *or* **thar** (tɑ:) *n* any of several goatlike bovid mammals of the genus *Hemitragus,* such as *H. jemlahicus* (**Himalayan tahr**), of mountainous regions of S and SW Asia, having a shaggy coat and curved horns. [from Nepali *thār*]

tahsil (tə'si:l) *n* an administrative division of a zila in certain states in India. [Urdu, from Arabic: collection]

tahsildar (tə'si:ldɑ:) *n* the officer in charge of the collection of revenues, etc., in a tahsil. [C18: via Hindi from Persian, from TAHSIL + Persian *-dār* having]

Tai (taɪ) *adj, n* a variant spelling of **Thai.**

taiaha ('taɪə,hɑ:) *n N.Z.* a carved weapon in the form of a staff, now used in Maori ceremonial oratory. [Maori]

t'ai chi ch'uan ('taɪ dʒi: 'tʃwɑ:n) *n* a Chinese system of callisthenics characterized by coordinated and rhythmic movements. Often shortened to **t'ai chi** ('taɪ 'dʒi:). [Chinese, literally: great art of boxing]

Taichung *or* **T'ai-chung** ('taɪ'tʃʊŋ) *n* a city in W Taiwan (Republic of China): commercial centre of an agricultural region. Pop.: 881 870 (1997 est.).

taig (teɪg) *n Ulster dialect, often derogatory.* a Roman Catholic. [variant of the Irish name *Tadhg,* originally signifying any Irishman]

taiga ('taɪgə) *n* the coniferous forests extending across much of subarctic North America and Eurasia, bordered by tundra to the north and steppe to the south. [from Russian, of Turkic origin; compare Turkish *dağ* mountain]

taihoa ('taɪhəʊə) *interj N.Z.* hold on! no hurry! [Maori]

tail[1] (teɪl) *n* **1** the region of the vertebrate body that is posterior to or above the anus and contains an elongation of the vertebral column, esp. forming a flexible movable appendage. Related adj: **caudal. 2** anything resembling such an appendage in form or position; the bottom, lowest, or rear part: *the tail of a shirt.* **3** the last part or parts: *the tail of the storm.* **4** the rear part of an aircraft including the fin, tail plane, and control surfaces; empennage. **5** *Astronomy.* the luminous stream of gas and dust particles, up to 200 million kilometres long, driven from the head of a comet, when close to the sun, under the effect of the solar wind. **6** the rear portion of a bomb, rocket, missile, etc., usually fitted with guiding or stabilizing vanes. **7** a line of people or things. **8** a long braid or tress of hair: *a ponytail; a pigtail.* **9** *Angling.* Also called: **'tail,fly.** the lowest fly on a wet-fly cast. **10** a final short line in a stanza. **11** *Informal.* a person employed to follow and spy upon another or others. **12** an informal word for **buttocks. 13** *Taboo slang.* **13a** the female genitals. **13b** a woman considered sexually (esp. in the phrases **piece of tail, bit of tail**). **14** *Printing.* **14a** the margin at the foot of a page. **14b** the bottom edge of a book. **15** the lower end of a pool or part of a stream. **16** *Informal.* the course or track of a fleeing person or animal: *the police are on my tail.* **17** (*modifier*) coming from or situated in the rear: *a tail wind.* **18 turn tail.** to run away; escape. **19 with one's tail between one's legs.** in a state of utter defeat or confusion. ◆ *vb* **20** to form or cause to form the tail. **21** to remove the tail of (an animal); dock. **22** (*tr*) to remove the stalk of: *to top and tail the gooseberries.* **23** (*tr*) to connect (objects, ideas, etc.) together by or as if by the tail. **24** (*tr*) *Informal.* to follow stealthily. **25** (*tr*) *Austral.* to tend (cattle) on foot. **26** (*intr*) (of a vessel) to assume a specified position, as when at a mooring. **27** to build the end of (a brick, joist, etc.) into a wall or (of a brick, etc.) to have one end built into a wall. ◆ See also **tail off, tail out, tails.** [Old English *tægel;* related to Old Norse *tagl* horse's tail, Gothic *tagl* hair, Old High German *zagal* tail] ▸ **'tailless** *adj* ▸ **'taillessly** *adv* ▸ **'taillessness** *n* ▸ **'tail-,like** *adj*

tail[2] (teɪl) *Property law.* ◆ *n* **1** the limitation of an estate or interest to a person and the heirs of his body. See also **entail.** ◆ *adj* **2** (*immediately postpositive*) (of an estate or interest) limited in this way. [C15: from Old French *taille* a division; see TAILOR, TALLY] ▸ **'tailless** *adj*

tailback ('teɪl,bæk) *n* a queue of traffic stretching back from an obstruction.

tailboard ('teɪl,bɔ:d) *n* a board at the rear of a lorry, wagon, etc., that can be removed or let down on a hinge.

tail coat *n* **1** Also called: **tails.** a man's black coat having a horizontal cut over the hips and a tapering tail with a vertical slit up to the waist: worn as part of full evening dress. **2** Also called: **swallow-tailed coat.** another name for **morning coat.**

tail covert *n* any of the covert feathers of a bird covering the bases of the tail feathers.

tail end *n* the last, endmost, or final part.

tail fan *n* the fanned structure at the hind end of a lobster or related crustacean, formed from the telson and uropods.

tailgate ('teɪl,geɪt) *n* **1** another name for **tailboard. 2** a door at the rear of a hatchback vehicle. ◆ *vb* **3** to drive very close behind (a vehicle). ▸ **'tail,gater** *n*

tail gate *n* a gate that is used to control the flow of water at the lower end of a lock. Compare **head gate.**

tail-heavy *adj* (of an aircraft) having too much weight at the rear because of overloading or poor design.

tailing ('teɪlɪŋ) *n* the part of a beam, rafter, projecting brick or stone, etc., embedded in a wall.

tailings ('teɪlɪŋz) *pl n* waste left over after certain processes, such as from an ore-crushing plant or in milling grain.

taille (taɪ; *French* tɑj) *n, pl* **tailles** (taɪ, taɪz; *French* tɑj). (in France before 1789) a tax levied by a king or overlord on his subjects. [C17: from French, from Old French *taillier* to shape; see TAILOR]

tail-light *or* **tail lamp** *n* other names for **rear light.**

tail off *or* **away** *vb* (*adv, usually intr*) to decrease or cause to decrease in quantity, degree, etc., esp. gradually: *his interest in collecting stamps tailed off over the years.*

tailor ('teɪlə) *n* **1** a person who makes, repairs, or alters outer garments, esp. menswear. Related adj: **sartorial. 2** a voracious and active marine food fish, *Pomatomus saltator,* of Australia with scissor-like teeth. ◆ *vb* **3** to cut or style (material, clothes, etc.) to satisfy certain requirements. **4** (*tr*) to adapt so as to make suitable for something specific: *he tailored his speech to suit a younger audience.* **5** (*intr*) to follow the occupation of a tailor. [C13: from Anglo-Norman *taillour,* from Old French *taillier* to cut, from Latin *tālea* a cutting; related to Greek *talis* girl of marriageable age]

tailorbird ('teɪlə,bɜ:d) *n* any of several tropical Asian warblers of the genus *Orthotomus,* which build nests by sewing together large leaves using plant fibres.

tailor-made *adj* **1** made by a tailor to fit exactly: *a tailor-made suit.* **2** perfectly meeting a particular purpose: *a girl tailor-made for him.* ◆ *n* **3** a tailor-made garment. **4** *Slang.* a cigarette made in a factory rather than rolled by hand.

tailor's chalk *n* pipeclay used by tailors and dressmakers to mark seams, darts, etc., on material.

tailor's-tack *n* one of a series of loose looped stitches used to transfer markings for seams, darts, etc., from a paper pattern to material.

tail out *vb* (*tr, adv*) to guide (timber) as it emerges from a power saw.

tailpiece ('teɪl,pi:s) *n* **1** an extension or appendage that lengthens or completes something. **2** *Printing.* a decorative design at the foot of a page or end of a chapter. **3** *Music.* a piece of wood to which the strings of a violin, etc., are attached at their lower end. It is suspended between the taut strings and the bottom of the violin by a piece of gut or metal. **4** Also called: **tail beam.** *Architect.* a short beam or rafter that has one end embedded in a wall.

tailpipe ('teɪl,paɪp) *n* a pipe from which the exhaust gases from an internal-combustion engine are discharged, esp. the terminal pipe of the exhaust system of a motor vehicle.

tailplane ('teɪl,pleɪn) *n* a small horizontal wing at the tail of an aircraft to provide longitudinal stability. Also called (esp. U.S.): **horizontal stabilizer.**

tailrace ('teɪl,reɪs) *n* **1** a channel that carries water away from a water wheel, turbine, etc. Compare **headrace. 2** *Mining.* the channel for removing tailings in water.

tail rotor *n* a small propeller fitted to the rear of a helicopter to counteract the torque reaction of the main rotor and thus prevent the body of the helicopter from rotating in an opposite direction.

tails (teɪlz) *pl n* **1** an informal name for **tail coat.** ◆ *interj, adv* **2** with the reverse side of a coin uppermost: used as a call before tossing a coin. Compare **heads.**

tailskid ('teɪl,skɪd) *n* **1** a runner under the tail of an aircraft. **2** a rear-wheel skid of a motor vehicle.

tailspin ('teɪl,spɪn) *n* **1** *Aeronautics.* another name for **spin** (sense 16). **2** *Informal.* a state of confusion or panic.

tailstock ('teɪl,stɒk) *n* a casting that slides on the bed of a lathe in alignment with the headstock and is locked in position to support the free end of a workpiece.

tail wheel *n* a wheel fitted to the rear of a vehicle, esp. the landing wheel under the tail of an aircraft.

tailwind ('teɪl,wɪnd) *n* a wind blowing in the same direction as the course of an aircraft or ship. Compare **headwind.**

Taimyr Peninsula (*Russian* taj'mir) *n* a large peninsula of N central Russia, between the Kara Sea and the Laptev Sea. Also called: **Taymyr Peninsula.**

tain (teɪn) *n* tinfoil used in backing mirrors. [from French, from *étain* tin, from Old French *estain,* from Latin *stagnum* alloy of silver and lead; see STANNUM]

Tainan *or* **T'ai-nan** ('taɪ'næn) *n* a city in the SW Republic of China (Taiwan): an early centre of Chinese emigration from the mainland; largest city and capital of the island (1638–1885); Chengkung University. Pop.: 712 172 (1997 est.).

Taínaron ('tɛnarɔn) *n* transliteration of the Modern Greek name for (Cape) **Matapan.**

Taine (*French* tɛn) *n* **Hippolyte Adolphe** (ipɔlit adɔlf). 1828–93, French literary critic and historian. He applied determinist criteria to the study of literature, art, history, and psychology, regarding them as products of environment and race. His works include *Histoire de la littérature anglaise* (1863–64) and *Les Origines de la France contemporaine* (1875–93).

Taino ('taɪnəʊ) *n* **1** (*pl* **-nos** *or* **-no**) a member of an extinct American Indian people of the Greater Antilles and the Bahamas. **2** the language of this people, belonging to the Arawakan family.

taint (teɪnt) *vb* **1** to affect or be affected by pollution or contamination: *oil has tainted the water.* **2** to tarnish (someone's reputation, etc.). ◆ *n* **3** a defect or flaw: *a taint on someone's reputation.* **4** a trace of contamination or infection. [C14: (influenced by *attaint* infected, from ATTAIN) from Old French *teindre* to dye, from Latin *tingere* to dye] ► ˈ**taintless** *adj*

taipan[1] (ˈtaɪˌpæn) *n* a large highly venomous elapid snake, *Oxyuranus scutellatus,* of NE Australia. [C20: from a native Australian language]

taipan[2] (ˈtaɪˌpæn) *n* the foreign head of a business in China. [C19: from dialectal form of Chinese *da* great + *ban* company, class]

Taipei *or* **T'ai-pei** (ˈtaɪˈpeɪ) *n* the capital of the Republic of China (Taiwan), at the N tip of the island: became capital in 1885; industrial centre; two universities. Pop.: 2 595 699 (1997 est.).

Taiping (ˈtaɪˈpɪŋ) *n History.* a person who supported or took part in the movement of religious mysticism and agrarian unrest in China between 1850 and 1864 (**Taiping rebellion**), which weakened the Manchu dynasty but was eventually suppressed with foreign aid. [C19: from Chinese, from *t'ai* great + *p'ing* peace]

Taisho (taɪˈʃəʊ) *n* **1** the period of Japanese history and artistic style associated with the reign of Emperor Yoshihito (1912–26). **2** the throne name of Yoshihito (1879–1926), emperor of Japan (1912–26).

Taiwan (ˈtaɪˈwɑːn) *n* an island in SE Asia between the East China Sea and the South China Sea, off the SE coast of the People's Republic of China: the principal territory of the Republic of China. Pop.: 21 843 000 (1998 est.). Former name: **Formosa.** ► ˌ**Taiwanˈese** *adj, n*

Taiwan Strait *n* another name for **Formosa Strait.**

Taiyuan *or* **T'ai-yüan** (ˈtaɪjuːˈɑːn) *n* a city in N China, capital of Shanxi: founded before 450 A.D.; an industrial centre, surrounded by China's largest reserves of high-grade bituminous coal. Pop.: 1 500 000 (1991 est.).

Ta'izz (tæˈɪz, teɪˈiːz) *n* a town in SW Yemen, formerly in North Yemen: agricultural trading centre. Pop.: 178 043 (1995 est.).

taj (tɑːdʒ) *n* a tall conical cap worn as a mark of distinction by Muslims. [via Arabic from Persian: crown, crest]

Tajik (ˈtɑːdʒɪk, tɑːˈdʒiːk) *n, pl* **-jik.** a member of a Persian-speaking Muslim people inhabiting Tajikistan and parts of Sinkiang in W China.

Tajiki, Tadzhiki (tɑːˈdʒɪkiː, -ˈdʒiː-) **Tajik,** *or* **Tadzhik** *n* **1** the language of the Tajik, belonging to the West Iranian subbranch of the Indo-European family. ◆ *adj* **2** of or relating to the Tajik or their language.

Tajikistan, Tadzhikistan, *or* **Tadjikistan** (tɑːˌdʒɪkɪˈstɑːn, -stæn) *n* a republic in central Asia: under Uzbek rule from the 15th century until taken over by Russia in the 1860s, it became an autonomous Soviet republic in 1929 and gained full independence from the Soviet Union in 1991; it is mainly mountainous. Official language: Tajiki. Religion: believers are mainly Muslim. Currency: rouble. Capital: Dushanbe. Pop.: 6 112 000 (1998 est.). Area: 143 100 sq. km (55 240 sq. miles).

Taj Mahal (ˈtɑːdʒ məˈhɑːl) *n* a white marble mausoleum in central India, in Agra on the Jumna River: built (1632–43) by the emperor Shah Jahan in memory of his beloved wife, Mumtaz Mahal; regarded as the finest example of Mogul architecture. [Urdu, literally: crown of buildings]

Tajo (ˈtaxo) *n* the Spanish name for the **Tagus.**

taka (ˈtɑːkɑː) *n* the standard monetary unit of Bangladesh, divided into 100 paise. [from Bengali]

takahe (ˈtɑːkəˌhiː) *n* a very rare flightless New Zealand rail, *Notornis mantelli.* [from Maori, of imitative origin]

Takamatsu (ˌtækəˈmætsuː) *n* a port in SW Japan, on NE Shikoku on the Inland Sea. Pop.: 330 997 (1995).

Takao (tæˈkaʊ) *n* the Japanese name for **Kaohsiung.**

take (teɪk) *vb* **takes, taking, took, taken.** (*mainly tr*) **1** (*also intr*) to gain possession of (something) by force or effort. **2** to appropriate or steal: *to take other people's belongings.* **3** to receive or accept into a relationship with oneself: *to take a wife.* **4** to pay for or buy. **5** to rent or lease: *to take a flat in town.* **6** to receive or obtain by regular payment: *we take a newspaper every day.* **7** to obtain by competing for; win: *to take first prize.* **8** to obtain or derive from a source: *he took his good manners from his older brother.* **9** to assume the obligations of: *to take office.* **10** to endure, esp. with fortitude: *to take punishment.* **11** to adopt as a symbol of duty, obligation, etc.: *to take the veil.* **12** to receive or react to in a specified way: *she took the news very well.* **13** to adopt as one's own: *to take someone's part in a quarrel.* **14** to receive and make use of: *to take advice.* **15** to receive into the body, as by eating, inhaling, etc.: *to take a breath.* **16** to eat, drink, etc., esp. habitually: *to take sugar in one's tea.* **17** to have or be engaged in for one's benefit or use: *to take a rest.* **18** to work at or study: *to take economics at college.* **19** to make, do, or perform (an action): *to take a leap.* **20** to make use of: *to take an opportunity.* **21** to put into effect; adopt: *to take measures.* **22** (*also intr*) to make a photograph of or admit of being photographed. **23** to act or perform: *she takes the part of the Queen.* **24** to write down or copy: *to take notes.* **25** to experience or feel: *to take pride in one's appearance; to take offence.* **26** to consider, believe, or regard: *I take him to be honest.* **27** to consider or accept as valid: *I take your point.* **28** to hold or maintain in the mind: *his father took a dim view of his career.* **29** to deal or contend with: *the tennis champion took her opponent's best strokes without difficulty.* **30** to use as a particular case: *take hotels for example.* **31** (*intr; often foll. by from*) to diminish or detract: *the actor's bad performance took from the effect of the play.* **32** to confront successfully: *the horse took the jump at the third attempt.* **33** (*intr*) to have or produce the intended effect; succeed: *her vaccination took; the glue is taking well.* **34** (*intr*) (of seeds, plants, etc.) to start growing successfully. **35** to aim or direct: *he took a swipe at his opponent.* **36** to deal a blow to in a specified place. **37** *Archaic.* to have sexual intercourse with. **38** to carry off or remove from a place. **39** to carry along or have in one's possession: *don't forget to take your umbrella.* **40** to convey or transport: *the train will take us out of the city.* **41** to use as a means of transport: *I shall take the bus.* **42** to conduct or lead: *this road takes you to the station.* **43** to escort or accompany: *may I take you out tonight?* **44** to bring or deliver to a state, position, etc.: *his ability took him to the forefront in his field.* **45** to go to look for; seek: *to take cover.* **46** to ascertain or determine by measuring, computing, etc.: *to take a pulse; take a reading from a dial.* **47** (*intr*) (of a mechanism) to catch or engage (a part). **48** to put an end to; destroy: *she took her own life.* **49** to come upon unexpectedly; discover. **50** to contract: *he took a chill.* **51** to affect or attack: *the fever took him one night.* **52** (*copula*) to become suddenly or be rendered (ill): *he took sick; he was taken sick.* **53** (*also intr*) to absorb or become absorbed by something: *to take a polish.* **54** (*usually passive*) to charm or captivate: *she was very taken with the puppy.* **55** (*intr*) to be or become popular; win favour. **56** to require or need: *this job will take a lot of attention; that task will take all your time.* **57** to subtract or deduct: *to take six from ten leaves four.* **58** to hold or contain: *the suitcase won't take all your clothes.* **59** to quote or copy: *he has taken several paragraphs from the book for his essay.* **60** to proceed to occupy: *to take a seat.* **61** (often foll. by *to*) to use or employ: *to take steps to ascertain the answer.* **62** to win or capture (a trick, counter, piece, etc.). **63** (*also intr*) to catch as prey or catch prey. **64** *Slang.* to cheat, deceive, or victimize. **65 take amiss.** to be annoyed or offended by. **66 take at one's word.** See **word** (sense 17). **67 take care.** to pay attention; be heedful. **68 take care of.** to assume responsibility for; look after. **69 take chances** *or* **a chance.** to behave in a risky manner. **70 take five** (*or* **ten**). *Informal, chiefly U.S. and Canadian.* to take a break of five (or ten) minutes. **71 take heart.** to become encouraged. **72 take it. 72a** to assume; believe: *I take it you'll be back later.* **72b** *Informal.* to stand up to or endure criticism, abuse, harsh treatment, etc. **73 take one's time.** to use as much time as is needed; not rush. **74 take place.** to happen or occur. **75 take (someone's) name in vain. 75a** to use a name, esp. of God, disrespectfully or irreverently. **75b** *Jocular.* to say (someone's) name. **76 take (something) upon oneself.** to assume the right to do or responsibility for (something). ◆ *n* **77** the act of taking. **78** the number of quarry killed or captured on one occasion. **79** *Informal, chiefly U.S.* the amount of anything taken, esp. money. **80** *Films, music.* **80a** one of a series of recordings from which the best will be selected for release. **80b** the process of taking one such recording. **80c** a scene or part of a scene photographed without interruption. **81** *Informal.* **81a** any objective indication of a successful vaccination, such as a local skin reaction. **81b** a successful skin graft. **82** *Printing.* a part of an article, story, etc., given to a compositor or keyboard operator for setting in type. **83** *Informal.* a try or attempt. **84** *Informal, chiefly U.S.* a version or interpretation: *Cronenberg's harsh take on the sci-fi story.* ◆ See also **take aback, take after, take against, take apart, take away, take back, take down, take for, take in, take off, take on, take out, take over, take to, take up.** [Old English *tacan,* from Old Norse *taka;* related to Gothic *tekan* to touch] ► ˈ**takable** *or* ˈ**takeable** *adj*

take aback *vb* (*tr, adv*) to astonish or disconcert.

take after *vb* (*intr, prep*) **1** to resemble in appearance, character, behaviour, etc. **2** to follow as an example.

take against *vb* (*intr, prep*) to start to dislike, esp. without good reason.

take apart *vb* (*tr, adv*) **1** to separate (something) into component parts. **2** to criticize or punish severely: *the reviewers took the new play apart.*

take away *vb* (*tr, adv*) **1** to deduct; subtract: *take away four from nine to leave five.* ◆ *prep* **2** minus: *nine take away four is five.* ◆ *adj* **takeaway.** *Brit., Austral., and N.Z.* **3** sold for consumption away from the premises on which it is prepared: *a takeaway meal.* **4** preparing and selling food for consumption away from the premises: *a takeaway Indian restaurant.* ◆ *n* **takeaway.** *Brit., Austral., and N.Z.* **5** a shop or restaurant that sells such food: *let's go to the Chinese takeaway.* **6** a meal bought at such a shop or restaurant: *we'll have a Chinese takeaway tonight to save cooking.* ◆ Scot. word (for senses 3–6) **carry-out.** U.S. and Canadian word (for senses 3–6) **takeout.**

take back *vb* (*adv, mainly tr*) **1** to retract or withdraw (something said, written, promised, etc.). **2** to regain possession of. **3** to return for exchange: *to take back a substandard garment.* **4** to accept (someone) back (into one's home, affections, etc.). **5** to remind one of the past; cause one to reminisce: *that tune really takes me back.* **6** (*also intr*) *Printing.* to move (copy) to the previous line.

take down *vb* (*tr, adv*) **1** to record in writing. **2** to dismantle or tear down: *to take down an old shed.* **3** to lower or reduce in power, arrogance, etc. (esp. in the phrase **to take down a peg**). ◆ *adj* **take-down. 4** made or intended to be disassembled.

take for *vb* (*tr, prep*) *Informal.* to consider or suppose to be, esp. mistakenly: *the fake coins were taken for genuine; who do you take me for?*

take-home pay *n* the remainder of one's pay after all income tax and other compulsory deductions have been made.

take in *vb* (*tr, adv*) **1** to comprehend or understand. **2** to include or comprise: *his thesis takes in that point.* **3** to receive into one's house in exchange for payment: *to take in washing; take in lodgers.* **4** to make (an article of clothing, etc.) smaller by altering seams. **5** to include: *the tour takes in the islands as well as the mainland.* **6** *Informal.* to cheat or deceive. **7** to go to; visit: *let's take in a movie tonight.* ◆ *n* **take-in. 8** *Informal.* the act or an instance of cheating or deceiving.

taken (ˈteɪkən) *vb* **1** the past participle of **take.** ◆ *adj* **2** (*postpositive;* foll. by *with*) enthusiastically impressed (by); infatuated (with).

take off *vb* (*adv*) **1** (*tr*) to remove or discard (a garment). **2** (*intr*) (of an aircraft) to become airborne. **3** *Informal.* to set out or cause to set out on a journey: *they took off for Spain.* **4** (*tr*) (of a disease) to prove fatal to; kill. **5** (*tr*) *Informal.* to mimic or imitate, esp. in an amusing or satirical manner. **6** (*intr*) *Informal.* to become successful or popular, esp. suddenly. ◆ *n* **takeoff. 7** the act or process of making an aircraft airborne. **8** the stage of a country's economic development when rapid and sustained economic growth is first achieved. **9** *Informal.* an act of mimicry; imitation.

take on *vb* (*adv, mainly tr*) **1** to employ or hire: *to take on new workmen.* **2** to assume or acquire: *his voice took on a plaintive note.* **3** to agree to do; undertake: *I'll take on that job for you.* **4** to compete against, oppose, or fight: *I will take him on at tennis; I'll take him on any time.* **5** (*intr*) *Informal.* to exhibit great emotion, esp. grief.

take out *vb* (*tr, adv*) **1** to extract or remove. **2** to obtain or secure (a licence, patent, etc.) from an authority. **3** to go out with; escort: *George is taking Susan out next week.* **4** *Bridge.* to bid a different suit from (one's partner) in order to rescue him from a difficult contract. **5** *Slang.* to kill or destroy. **6** *Austral. informal.* to win, esp. in sport: *he took out the tennis championship.* **7 take it** *or* **a lot out of.** *Informal.* to sap the energy or vitality of. **8 take out on.** *Informal.* to vent (anger, frustration, etc.) on (esp. an innocent person). **9 take someone out of himself.** *Informal.* to make someone forget his anxieties, problems, etc. ◆ *adj* **takeout. 10** *Bridge.* of or designating a conventional informatory bid, asking one's partner to bid another suit. ◆ *adj, n* **11** an informal word (chiefly U.S. and Canadian) for **takeaway** (senses 3–6).

take over *vb* (*adv*) **1** to assume the control or management of. **2** *Printing.* to move (copy) to the next line. ◆ *n* **takeover. 3a** the act of seizing or assuming power, control, etc. **3b** (*as modifier*): *takeover bid.* **4** *Sport.* another word for **changeover** (sense 3).

taker ('teɪkə) *n* a person who takes something, esp. a bet, wager, or offer of purchase.

take to *vb* (*intr, prep*) **1** to make for; flee to: *to take to the hills.* **2** to form a liking for, esp. after a short acquaintance: *I took to him straightaway.* **3** to have recourse to: *to take to the bottle.* **4 take to heart.** to regard seriously.

take up *vb* (*adv, mainly tr*) **1** to adopt the study, practice, or activity of: *to take up gardening.* **2** *Austral. and N.Z.* to occupy and break in (uncultivated land): *he took up some hundreds of acres in the back country.* **3** to shorten (a garment or part of a garment): *she took all her skirts up three inches.* **4** to pay off (a note, mortgage, etc.). **5** to agree to or accept (an invitation, etc.). **6** to pursue further or resume (something): *he took up French where he left off.* **7** to absorb (a liquid). **8** to adopt as a protégé; act as a patron to. **9** to occupy or fill (space or time). **10** to interrupt, esp. in order to contradict or criticize. **11 take up on. 11a** to argue or dispute with (someone): *can I take you up on two points in your talk?* **11b** to accept what is offered by (someone): *let me take you up on your invitation.* **12 take up with. 12a** to discuss with (someone); refer to: *to take up a fault with the manufacturers.* **12b** (*intr*) to begin to keep company or associate with. ◆ *n* **take-up. 13a** the claiming or acceptance of something, esp. a state benefit, that is due or available. **13b** (*as modifier*): *take-up rate.* **14** *Machinery.* the distance through which a part must move to absorb the free play in a system. **15** (*modifier*) denoting the part of a mechanism on which film, tape, or wire is wound up: *a take-up spool on a tape recorder.*

takin ('tɑːkiːn) *n* a massive bovid mammal, *Budorcas taxicolor,* of mountainous regions of S Asia, having a shaggy coat, short legs, and horns that point backwards and upwards. **[C19: from Mishmi]**

taking ('teɪkɪŋ) *adj* **1** charming, fascinating, or intriguing. **2** *Informal.* infectious; catching. ◆ *n* **3** something taken. **4** (*pl*) receipts; earnings. ▸ **'takingly** *adv* ▸ **'takingness** *n*

takkies ('tækɪz) *pl n S. African informal.* a variant spelling of **tackies.**

Takoradi (ˌtɑːkəˈrɑːdɪ) *n* the chief port of Ghana, in the southwest on the Gulf of Guinea: modern harbour opened in 1928. Pop. (with Sekondi): 103 600 (1988 est.).

tala ('tɑːlə) *n* the standard monetary unit of Western Samoa, divided into 100 sene.

Talaing (tɑːˈlaɪŋ) *n* another name for **Mon.**

talapoin ('tæləˌpɔɪn) *n* **1** the smallest of the guenon monkeys, *Cercopithecus talapoin,* of swampy central W African forests, having olive-green fur and slightly webbed digits. **2a** (in Myanmar and Thailand) a Buddhist monk. **2b** a title of respect used in addressing such a monk. **[C16:** from French, literally: Buddhist monk, from Portuguese *talapão,* from Mon *tala pōi* our lord; originally jocular, from the appearance of the monkey**]**

talaria (təˈlɛərɪə) *pl n Greek myth.* winged sandals, such as those worn by Hermes. **[C16:** from Latin, from *tālāris* belonging to the ankle, from *tālus* ankle**]**

Talavera de la Reina (*Spanish* talaˈβera ðe la ˈreina) *n* a walled town in central Spain, on the Tagus River: scene of the defeat of the French by British and Spanish forces (1809) during the Peninsular War; agricultural processing centre. Pop.: 68 640 (1991).

talbot ('tɔːlbət) *n* (formerly) an ancient breed of large hound, usually white or light-coloured, having pendulous ears and strong powers of scent. **[C16:** supposed to have been brought to England by the *Talbot* family**]**

Talbot ('tɒlbət) *n* (**William Henry**) **Fox.** 1800–77, British scientist, a pioneer of photography, who developed the calotype process.

talc (tælk) *n also* **talcum. 1** See **talcum powder. 2** a white, grey, brown, or pale green mineral, found in metamorphic rocks. It is used in the manufacture of talcum powder and electrical insulators. Composition: hydrated magnesium silicate. Formula: $Mg_3Si_4O_{10}(OH)_2$. Crystal structure: monoclinic. ◆ *vb* **talcs, talcking, talcked** *or* **talcs, talcing, talced. 3** (*tr*) to apply talc to. **[C16:** from Medieval Latin *talcum,* from Arabic *talq* mica, from Persian *talk***]** ▸ **'talcose** *or* **'talcous** *adj*

Talca (*Spanish* 'talka) *n* a city in central Chile: scene of the declaration of Chilean independence (1818). Pop.: 169 448 (1995 est.).

Talcahuano (*Spanish* talkaˈwano) *n* a port in S central Chile, near Concepción on an inlet of the Pacific: oil refinery. Pop.: 260 915 (1995 est.).

talcum powder ('tælkəm) *n* a powder made of purified talc, usually scented, used for perfuming the body and for absorbing excess moisture. Often shortened to **talc.**

tale (teɪl) *n* **1** a report, narrative, or story. **2** one of a group of short stories connected by an overall narrative framework. **3a** a malicious or meddlesome rumour or piece of gossip: *to bear tales against someone.* **3b** (*in combination*): *talebearer; taleteller.* **4** a fictitious or false statement. **5 tell tales. 5a** to tell fanciful lies. **5b** to report malicious stories, trivial complaints, etc., esp. to someone in authority. **6 tell a tale.** to reveal something important. **7 tell its own tale.** to be self-evident. **8** *Archaic.* **8a** a number; amount. **8b** computation or enumeration. **9** an obsolete word for **talk. [**Old English *talu* list; related to Old Frisian *tele* talk, Old Saxon, Old Norse *tala* talk, number, Old High German *zala* number**]**

talent ('tælənt) *n* **1** innate ability, aptitude, or faculty, esp. when unspecified; above average ability: *a talent for cooking; a child with talent.* **2** a person or persons possessing such ability. **3** any of various ancient units of weight and money. **4** *Informal.* members of the opposite sex collectively, esp. those living in a particular place: *the local talent.* **5** an obsolete word for **inclination. [**Old English *talente,* from Latin *talenta,* pl. of *talentum* sum of money, from Greek *talanton* unit of money or weight; in Medieval Latin the sense was extended to ability through the influence of the parable of the talents (Matthew 25:14–30)**]** ▸ **'talented** *adj*

talent scout *n* a person whose occupation is the search for talented artists, sportsmen, performers, etc., for engagements as professionals.

taler ('tɑːlə) *n, pl* **-ler** *or* **-lers.** a variant spelling of **thaler.**

tales ('teɪliːz) *n Law.* **1** (*functioning as pl*) a group of persons summoned from among those present in court or from bystanders to fill vacancies on a jury panel. **2** (*functioning as sing*) the writ summoning such jurors. **[C15:** from Medieval Latin phrase *tālēs dē circumstantibus* such men from among the bystanders, from Latin *tālis* such**]** ▸ **'talesman** *n*

Taliban, Taleban, *or* **Talibaan** ('tælɪbæn) *n* (in Afghanistan) a fundamentalist Islamic army: in 1996 it defeated the ruling mujaheddin factions and seized control of the country. **[C20:** from Arabic *tālibān* seekers**]**

Taliesin (ˌtælɪˈɛsɪn) *n* 6th century A.D., Welsh bard; supposed author of 12 heroic poems in the *Book of Taliesin.*

taligrade ('tælɪˌgreɪd) *adj* (of mammals) walking on the outer side of the foot. **[C20:** from New Latin, from Latin *tālus* ankle, heel + -GRADE**]**

talion ('tælɪən) *n* the system or legal principle of making the punishment correspond to the crime; retaliation. **[C15:** via Old French from Latin *tāliō,* from *tālis* such**]**

taliped ('tælɪˌpɛd) *adj* **1** *Pathol.* having a club foot. ◆ *n* **2** a club-footed person. **[C19:** see TALIPES**]**

talipes ('tælɪˌpiːz) *n* **1** a congenital deformity of the foot by which it is twisted in any of various positions. **2** a technical name for **club foot. [C19:** New Latin, from Latin *tālus* ankle + *pēs* foot**]**

talipot *or* **talipot palm** ('tælɪˌpɒt) *n* a palm tree, *Corypha umbraculifera,* of the East Indies, having large leaves that are used for fans, thatching houses, etc. **[C17:** from Bengali: palm leaf, from Sanskrit *tālī* fan palm + *pattra* leaf**]**

talisman ('tælɪzmən) *n, pl* **-mans. 1** a stone or other small object, usually inscribed or carved, believed to protect the wearer from evil influences. **2** anything thought to have magical or protective powers. **[C17:** via French or Spanish from Arabic *tilsam,* from Medieval Greek *telesma* ritual, from Greek: consecration, from *telein* to perform a rite, complete, from *telos* end, result**]** ▸ **talismanic** (ˌtælɪzˈmænɪk) *adj*

talk (tɔːk) *vb* **1** (*intr;* often foll. by *to* or *with*) to express one's thoughts, feelings, or desires by means of words (to); speak (to). **2** (*intr*) to communicate or exchange thoughts by other means: *lovers talk with their eyes.* **3** (*intr;* usually foll. by *about*) to exchange ideas, pleasantries, or opinions (about): *to talk about the weather.* **4** (*intr*) to articulate words; verbalize: *his baby can talk.* **5** (*tr*) to give voice to; utter: *to talk rubbish.* **6** (*tr*) to hold a conversation about; discuss: *to talk business.* **7** (*intr*) to reveal information: *the prisoner talked after torture.* **8** (*tr*) to know how to communicate in (a language or idiom): *he talks English.* **9** (*intr*) to spread rumours or gossip: *we don't want the neighbours to talk.* **10** (*intr*) to make sounds suggestive of talking. **11** (*intr*) to be effective or persuasive: *money talks.* **12 now you're talking.** *Informal.* at last you're saying something agreeable. **13 talk big.** to boast or brag. **14 talk shop.** to speak about one's work, esp. when meeting socially, sometimes with the effect of excluding those not similarly employed. **15 you can talk.** *Informal.* you don't have to worry about doing a particular thing yourself. **16 you can** *or* **can't talk.** *Informal.* you yourself are guilty of offending in the very matter you are upholding or decrying. ◆ *n* **17** a speech or lecture: *a talk on ancient Rome.* **18** an exchange of ideas or thoughts: *a business talk with a colleague.* **19** idle chatter, gossip, or rumour: *there has been a lot of talk about you two.* **20** a subject of conversation; theme: *our talk was of war.* **21** (*often pl*) a conference, discussion, or negotiation: *talks about a settlement.* **22** a specific manner of speaking: *children's talk.* ◆ See also **talk about, talk at, talk back, talk down, talk into, talk out, talk round, talk through, talk up. [C13** *talkien* to talk; related to Old English *talu* TALE, Frisian *talken* to talk**]** ▸ **'talkable** *adj* ▸ **ˌtalkaˈbility** *n* ▸ **'talker** *n*

talk about *vb* (*intr, prep*) **1** to discuss. **2** used informally and often ironically to add emphasis to a statement: *all his plays have such ridiculous plots —talk about good drama!* **3 know what one is talking about.** to have thorough or specialized knowledge.

talk at *vb* (*intr, prep*) to speak to (a person) in a way that indicates a response is not really wanted: *I wish he'd talk to me rather than at me.*

talkative ('tɔːkətɪv) *adj* given to talking a great deal. ▸ **'talkatively** *adv* ▸ **'talkativeness** *n*

talk back *vb* (*intr, adv*) **1** to answer boldly or impudently. **2** *N.Z.* to conduct a telephone dialogue for immediate transmission over the air. ◆ *n* **talkback. 3**

Television, radio. a system of telephone links enabling spoken directions to be given during the production of a programme. **4** *N.Z.* **4a** a broadcast telephone dialogue. **4b** (*as modifier*): *a talkback show.*

talkbox ('tɔːkˌbɒks) *n* another name for **voice box** (sense 2).

talk down *vb* (*adv*) **1** (*intr;* often foll. by *to*) to behave (towards) in a superior or haughty manner. **2** (*tr*) to override (a person or argument) by continuous or loud talking. **3** (*tr*) to give instructions to (an aircraft) by radio to enable it to land.

talkie ('tɔːkɪ) *n Informal.* an early film with a soundtrack. Full name: **talking picture.**

Talking Book *n Trademark.* a recording of a book, designed to be used by the blind.

talking head *n* (on television) a person, such as a newscaster, who is shown only from the shoulders up, and speaks without the use of any illustrative material.

talking shop *n Informal.* a group or committee that has discussions that never result in action.

talking-to *n Informal.* a session of criticism, as of the work or attitude of a subordinate by a person in authority.

talk into *vb* (*tr, prep*) to persuade to by talking: *I talked him into buying the house.*

talk out *vb* (*adv*) **1** (*tr*) to resolve or eliminate by talking: *they talked out their differences.* **2** (*tr*) *Brit.* to block (a bill, etc.) in a legislative body by lengthy discussion. **3 talk out of.** to dissuade from by talking: *she was talked out of marriage.*

talk round *vb* **1** (*tr, adv*) Also: **talk over.** to persuade to one's opinion: *I talked him round to buying a car.* **2** (*intr, prep*) to discuss the arguments relating to (a subject), esp. without coming to a conclusion: *to talk round the problem of the human condition.* **3** (*intr, prep*) to discuss (a subject) vaguely without considering basic facts: *they talked round the idea of moving house quite forgetting they hadn't enough money.*

talk show *n* another name for **chat show.**

talk through *vb* (*tr*) **1** (*adv*) to discuss (a problem or situation) in detail. **2** (*prep*) to explain to (a person) all the stages of a process: *ask a friend to talk you through the exercise.*

talk up *vb* (*tr, adv*) to speak of or discuss favourably in order to arouse interest or support.

talky ('tɔːkɪ) *adj* **talkier, talkiest.** *U.S. and Canadian.* containing too much dialogue or inconsequential talk: *a talky novel.*

tall (tɔːl) *adj* **1** of more than average height. **2a** (*postpositive*) having a specified height: *a woman five feet tall.* **2b** (*in combination*): *a twenty-foot-tall partition.* **3** *Informal.* exaggerated or incredible: *a tall story.* **4** *Informal.* difficult to accomplish: *a tall order.* **5** an archaic word for **excellent.** [**C14** (in the sense: big, comely, valiant); related to Old English *getæl* prompt, Old High German *gizal* quick, Gothic *untals* foolish] ▸ '**tallness** *n*

tallage ('tælɪdʒ) *English history.* ◆ *n* **1a** a tax levied by the Norman and early Angevin kings on their Crown lands and royal towns. **1b** a toll levied by a lord upon his tenants or by a feudal lord upon his vassals. ◆ *vb* **2** (*tr*) to levy a tax (upon); impose a tax (upon). [**C13**: from Old French *taillage,* from *taillier* to cut; see TAILOR]

Tallahassee (ˌtælə'hæsɪ) *n* a city in N Florida, capital of the state: two universities. Pop.: 136 812 (1996 est.).

tallboy ('tɔːlˌbɔɪ) *n* **1** a high chest of drawers made in two sections and placed one on top of the other; chest-on-chest. **2** a fitting on the top of a chimney to prevent downdraughts. [**C18**: from TALL + BOY]

Talleyrand-Périgord ('tælɪˌrænd'perɪgɔː; *French* talɛrɑ̃perigɔr) *n* **Charles Maurice** (ʃarl mɔris). 1754–1838, French statesman; foreign minister (1797–1807; 1814–15). He secretly negotiated with the Allies against Napoleon I from 1808 and was France's representative at the Congress of Vienna (1815).

Tallinn *or* **Tallin** ('tælɪn) *n* the capital of Estonia, on the Gulf of Finland: founded by the Danes in 1219; a port and naval base. Pop.: 427 500 (1996 est.). German name: **Reval.**

tallis ('tɑlis) *or* **tallith** (tɑ'lit) *n Judaism.* a fringed shawl worn by Jewish men during morning prayers. [from Hebrew, literally: a cover]

Tallis ('tælɪs) *n* **Thomas.** ?1505–85, English composer and organist; noted for his music for the Anglican liturgy.

tallit ('tælɪθ; *Hebrew* ta'liːt) *n, pl* **tallaisim** (tæ'leɪsɪm), **tallites,** *or* **tallitot** (*Hebrew* -liː'tɔt). **1** a white shawl with fringed corners worn over the head and shoulders by Jewish males during religious services. **2** a smaller form of this worn under the outer garment during waking hours by some Jewish males. [**C17**: from Hebrew *tallīt*]

tall oil *n* any of various oily liquid mixtures obtained by acidifying the liquor resulting from the treatment of wood pulp with sodium hydroxide: it contains chiefly rosin acids and fatty acids and is used in making soaps and lubricants. [**C20**: partial translation of German *Tallöl,* from Swedish *tallolja,* from *tall* pine + *olja* OIL]

tallow ('tæləʊ) *n* **1** a fatty substance consisting of a mixture of glycerides, including stearic, palmitic, and oleic acids and extracted chiefly from the suet of sheep and cattle: used for making soap, candles, food, etc. ◆ *vb* **2** (*tr*) to cover or smear with tallow. [Old English *tælg,* a dye; related to Middle Low German *talch* tallow, Dutch *talk,* Icelandic *tólg*] ▸ '**tallowy** *adj*

tallow wood *n Austral.* a tall eucalyptus tree, *Eucalyptus microcorys,* of coastal regions, having soft fibrous bark and conical fruits and yielding a greasy timber.

tall poppy *n Austral. informal.* a person who has a high salary or is otherwise prominent. [perhaps from Tarquin's decapitation of the tallest poppies in his garden, to indicate the fate of the most prominent citizens of Gabii]

tall poppy syndrome *n Austral. informal.* a tendency to disparage any person who has achieved great prominence or wealth.

tall ship *n* any square-rigged sailing ship.

tally ('tælɪ) *vb* **-lies, -lying, -lied. 1** (*intr*) to correspond one with the other: *the two stories don't tally.* **2** (*tr*) to supply with an identifying tag. **3** (*intr*) to keep score. **4** (*tr*) *Obsolete.* to record or mark. ◆ *n, pl* **-lies. 5** any record of debit, credit, the score in a game, etc. **6** a ticket, label, or mark, used as a means of identification, classification, etc. **7** a counterpart or duplicate of something, such as the counterfoil of a cheque. **8** a stick used (esp. formerly) as a record of the amount of a debt according to the notches cut in it. **9** a notch or mark cut in or made on such a stick. **10** a mark or number of marks used to represent a certain number in counting. **11** *Austral. and N.Z.* the total number of sheep shorn by one shearer in a specified period of time. [**C15**: from Medieval Latin *tālea,* from Latin: a stick; related to Latin *tālus* heel] ▸ '**tallier** *n*

tally clerk *n* a person, esp. on a wharf or dock or in an airport, who checks the count of goods being loaded or unloaded.

tally-ho (ˌtælɪ'həʊ) *interj* **1** the cry of a participant at a hunt to encourage the hounds when the quarry is sighted. ◆ *n, pl* **-hos. 2** an instance of crying tally-ho. **3** another name for a **four-in-hand** (sense 1). ◆ *vb* **-hos, -hoing, -hoed** *or* **-ho'd. 4** (*intr*) to make the cry of tally-ho. [**C18**: perhaps from French *taïaut* cry used in hunting]

tallyman ('tælɪmən) *n, pl* **-men. 1** a scorekeeper or recorder. **2** *Dialect.* a travelling salesman for a firm specializing in hire-purchase. ▸ '**tallyˌwoman** *fem n*

Talmud ('tælmʊd) *n Judaism.* **1** the primary source of Jewish religious law, consisting of the Mishnah and the Gemara. **2** either of two recensions of this compilation, the Palestinian Talmud of about 375 A.D., or the longer and more important Babylonian Talmud of about 500 A.D. [**C16**: from Hebrew *talmūdh,* literally: instruction, from *lāmadh* to learn] ▸ **Tal'mudic** *or* **Tal'mudical** *adj* ▸ '**Talmudism** *n*

Talmudist ('tælmʊdɪst) *n* **1** a scholar specializing in the study of the Talmud. **2** any of the writers of or contributors to the Talmud.

talon ('tælən) *n* **1** a sharply hooked claw, esp. of a bird of prey. **2** anything resembling a bird's claw. **3** the part of a lock that the key presses on when it is turned. **4** *Piquet, etc.* the pile of cards left after the deal. **5** *Architect.* another name for **ogee. 6** *Stock Exchange.* a printed slip attached to some bearer bonds to enable the holder to apply for a new sheet of coupons. [**C14**: from Old French: heel, from Latin *tālus* heel] ▸ '**taloned** *adj*

Talos ('teɪlɒs) *n Greek myth.* the nephew and apprentice of Daedalus, who surpassed his uncle as an inventor and was killed by him out of jealousy.

taluk ('tɑːlʊk, tɑː'lʊk), **taluka,** *or* **talooka** (tɑː'luːkə) *n* (in India) **1** a subdivision of a district; a group of several villages organized for revenue purposes. **2** a hereditary estate. [**C18**: from Urdu *ta' alluk* estate, ultimately from Arabic]

talus[1] ('teɪləs) *n, pl* **-li** (-laɪ). the bone of the ankle that articulates with the leg bones to form the ankle joint. Nontechnical name: **anklebone.** [**C18**: from Latin: ankle]

talus[2] ('teɪləs) *n, pl* **-luses. 1** *Geology.* another name for **scree. 2** *Fortifications.* the sloping side of a wall. [**C17**: from French, from Latin *talūtium* slope, perhaps of Iberian origin]

talweg ('tɑːlvɛg) *n* a variant spelling of **thalweg.**

tam (tæm) *n* short for **tam-o'-shanter.**

tamale (tə'mɑːlɪ) *n* a Mexican dish made of minced meat mixed with crushed maize and seasonings, wrapped in maize husks and steamed. [**C19**: erroneously for *tamal,* from Mexican Spanish, from Nahuatl *tamalli*]

tamandua (ˌtæmən'duə) *or* **tamandu** ('tæmənˌduː) *n* a small arboreal edentate mammal, *Tamandua tetradactyla,* of Central and South America, having a prehensile tail and tubular mouth specialized for feeding on termites: family *Myrmecophagidae.* Also called: **lesser anteater.** [**C17**: via Portuguese from Tupi: ant trapper, from *taixi* ant + *mondê* to catch]

tamarack ('tæməˌræk) *n* **1** any of several North American larches, esp. *Larix laricina,* which has reddish-brown bark, bluish-green needle-like leaves, and shiny oval cones. **2** the wood of any of these trees. [**C19**: from Algonquian]

tamarau *or* **tamarao** ('tæməˌraʊ) *n* a small rare member of the cattle tribe, *Anoa mindorensis,* of lowland areas of Mindoro in the Philippines. Compare **anoa.** [from Tagalog *tamaráw*]

tamari (tə'mɒːrɪ) *n* a Japanese variety of soy sauce. [Japanese]

tamarillo (ˌtæmə'rɪləʊ) *n, pl* **-los.** another name for **tree tomato.**

tamarin ('tæmərɪn) *n* any of numerous small monkeys of the genera *Saguinus* (or *Leontocebus*) and *Leontideus,* of South and Central American forests; similar to the marmosets: family *Callithricidae.* [**C18**: via French from Galibi]

tamarind ('tæmərɪnd) *n* **1** a caesalpiniaceous tropical evergreen tree, *Tamarindus indica,* having pale yellow red-streaked flowers and brown pulpy pods, each surrounded by a brittle shell. **2** the acid fruit of this tree, used as a food and to make beverages and medicines. **3** the wood of this tree. [**C16**: from Medieval Latin *tamarindus,* ultimately from Arabic *tamr hindī* Indian date, from *tamr* date + *hindī* Indian, from *Hind* India]

tamarisk ('tæmərɪsk) *n* any of various ornamental trees and shrubs of the genus *Tamarix,* of the Mediterranean region and S and SE Asia, having scalelike leaves, slender branches, and feathery clusters of pink or whitish flowers: family *Tamaricaceae.* [**C15**: from Late Latin *tamariscus,* from Latin *tamarix*]

tamasha (tə'mɑːʃə) *n* (in India) a show; entertainment. [**C17**: via Urdu from Arabic: a stroll, saunter]

Tamatave (*French* tamatav) *n* the former name (until 1979) of **Toamasina.**

Tamaulipas (*Spanish* tamau'lipas) *n* a state of NE Mexico, on the Gulf of Mexico. Capital: Ciudad Victoria. Pop.: 2 526 387 (1995 est.). Area: 79 829 sq. km (30 822 sq. miles).

tambac ('tæmbæk) *n* a variant spelling of **tombac.**

Tambo ('tæmbəʊ) *n* **Oliver.** 1917–93, South African politician; president

(1977–91) of the African National Congress. He was arrested (1956) with Nelson Mandela but released (1957).

Tambora ('tæmbəˌrɑː) *n* a volcano in Indonesia, on N Sumbawa: violent eruption of 1815 reduced its height from about 4000 m (13 000 ft.) to 2850 m (9400 ft.).

tambour ('tæmbʊə) *n* **1** *Real Tennis.* the sloping buttress on one side of the receiver's end of the court. **2** a small round embroidery frame, consisting of two concentric hoops over which the fabric is stretched while being worked. **3** embroidered work done on such a frame. **4** a sliding door on desks, cabinets, etc., made of thin strips of wood glued side by side onto a canvas backing. **5** *Architect.* a wall that is circular in plan, esp. one that supports a dome or one that is surrounded by a colonnade. **6** a drum. ◆ *vb* **7** to embroider (fabric or a design) on a tambour. [C15: from French, from *tabour* TABOR]

tamboura (tæm'bʊərə) *n* an instrument with a long neck, four strings, and no frets, used in Indian music to provide a drone. [from Persian *tanbūr,* from Arabic *tunbūr*]

tambourin ('tæmbʊrɪn) *n* **1** an 18th-century Provençal folk dance. **2** a piece of music composed for or in the rhythm of this dance. **3** a small drum. [C18: from French: a little drum, from TAMBOUR]

tambourine (ˌtæmbə'riːn) *n Music.* a percussion instrument consisting of a single drumhead of skin stretched over a circular wooden frame hung with pairs of metal discs that jingle when it is struck or shaken. [C16: from Middle Flemish *tamborijn* a little drum, from Old French: TAMBOURIN] ▸ ˌ**tambou'rinist** *n*

Tambov (*Russian* tam'bɔf) *n* an industrial city in W Russia: founded in 1636 as a Muscovite fort; a major engineering centre. Pop.: 316 000 (1995 est.).

Tamburlaine ('tæmbəˌleɪn) *n* a variant of **Tamerlane.**

tame (teɪm) *adj* **1** changed by man from a naturally wild state into a tractable, domesticated, or cultivated condition. **2** (of animals) not fearful of human contact. **3** lacking in spirit or initiative; meek or submissive: *a tame personality.* **4** flat, insipid, or uninspiring: *a tame ending to a book.* **5** slow-moving: *a tame current.* ◆ *vb* (*tr*) **6** to make tame; domesticate. **7** to break the spirit of, subdue, or curb. **8** to tone down, soften, or mitigate. [Old English *tam;* related to Old Norse *tamr,* Old High German *zam*] ▸ '**tamable** *or* '**tameable** *adj* ▸ ˌ**tama'bility**, ˌ**tamea'bility** *or* '**tamableness**, '**tameableness** *n* ▸ '**tameless** *adj* ▸ '**tamely** *adv* ▸ '**tameness** *n* ▸ '**tamer** *n*

Tamerlane ('tæməˌleɪn) *or* **Tamburlaine** *n* Turkic name *Timur* (tiː'mʊə). ?1336–1405, Mongol conqueror of the area from Mongolia to the Mediterranean; ruler of Samarkand (1369–1405). He defeated the Turks at Angora (1402) and died while invading China.

Tameside ('teɪmˌsaɪd) *n* a unitary authority of NW England, in Greater Manchester. Pop.: 221 500 (1995 est.). Area: 103 sq. km (40 sq. miles).

Tamil ('tæmɪl) *n* **1** (*pl* **-ils** *or* **-il**) a member of a mixed Dravidian and Caucasoid people of S India and Sri Lanka. **2** the language of this people: the state language of Tamil Nadu, also spoken in Sri Lanka and elsewhere, belonging to the Dravidian family of languages. ◆ *adj* **3** of or relating to this people or their language.

Tamil Nadu ('tæmɪl nɑː'duː) *n* a state of SE India, on the Coromandel Coast: reorganized in 1956 and 1960 and made smaller; consists of a coastal plain backed by hills, including the Nilgiri Hills in the west. Capital: Madras. Pop.: 58 840 000 (1994 est.). Area: 130 058 sq. km (50 216 sq. miles). Former name (until 1968): **Madras.**

tamis ('tæmɪ, -ɪs) *n, pl* **-ises** (-ɪz, -ɪsɪz). a less common word for **tammy**[3] (sense 1).

Tammany Hall ('tæmənɪ) *n U.S. politics.* the central organization of the Democratic Party in New York county. Originally founded as a benevolent society (**Tammany Society**) in 1789, Tammany Hall was notorious for the corruption in city and state politics that it fostered in the 19th and early 20th centuries. Also called: **Tammany.** ▸ '**Tammanyism** *n* ▸ '**Tammanyite** *n*

tammar ('tæmə) *n* a small scrub wallaby, *Macropus eugenii,* of Australia, having a thick dark-coloured coat. [C19: from a native Australian language]

Tammerfors (tamər'fɔrs) *n* the Swedish name for **Tampere.**

Tammuz ('tæmuːz, -ʊz) *n* (in the Jewish calendar) the fourth month of the year according to biblical reckoning and the tenth month of the civil year, usually falling within June and July. [from Hebrew]

tammy[1] ('tæmɪ) *n, pl* **-mies.** a glazed woollen or mixed fabric, used for linings, undergarments, etc. [C17: of unknown origin]

tammy[2] ('tæmɪ) *n, pl* **-mies.** another word for **tam-o'-shanter.**

tammy[3] ('tæmɪ) *n, pl* **-mies. 1** Also called: **tammy cloth, tamis.** (esp. formerly) a rough-textured woollen cloth used for straining sauces, soups, etc. ◆ *vb* **-mies, -mying, -mied. 2** (*tr*) (esp. formerly) to strain (sauce, soup, etc.) through a tammy. [C18: changed (through influence of TAMMY[1]) from French *tamis,* perhaps of Celtic origin; compare Breton *tamouez* strainer]

tam-o'-shanter (ˌtæmə'ʃæntə) *n* a Scottish brimless wool cap with a bobble in the centre, usually worn pulled down at one side. Also called: **tam, tammy.** [C19: named after the hero of Burns' poem *Tam o' Shanter* (1790)]

tamoxifen (tə'mɒksɪfen) *n* a drug that antagonizes the action of oestrogen and is used to treat breast cancer and some types of infertility in women. [C20: altered from T(RANS-) + AM(INE) + OXY-[2] + PHEN(OL)]

tamp[1] (tæmp) *vb* (*tr*) **1** to force or pack down firmly by repeated blows. **2** to pack sand, earth, etc. into (a drill hole) over an explosive. [C17: probably a back formation from *tampin* (obsolete variant of TAMPION), which was taken as being a present participle *tamping*]

tamp[2] (tæmp) *vb South Wales dialect.* **1** (*tr*) to bounce (a ball). **2** (*intr;* usually foll. by *down*) to pour with rain. [probably special use of TAMP[1]]

Tampa ('tæmpə) *n* a port and resort in W Florida, on **Tampa Bay** (an arm of the Gulf of Mexico): two universities. Pop.: 285 206 (1996 est.).

tamper[1] ('tæmpə) *vb* (*intr*) **1** (usually foll. by *with*) to interfere or meddle. **2** to use corrupt practices such as bribery or blackmail. **3** (usually foll. by *with*) to attempt to influence or corrupt, esp. by bribery: *to tamper with the jury.* [C16: alteration of TEMPER (vb)] ▸ '**tamperer** *n*

tamper[2] ('tæmpə) *n* **1** a person or thing that tamps, esp. an instrument for packing down tobacco in a pipe. **2** a casing around the core of a nuclear weapon to increase its efficiency by reflecting neutrons and delaying the expansion.

Tampere (*Finnish* 'tampɛrɛ) *n* a city in SW Finland: the second largest town in Finland; textile manufacturing. Pop.: 186 026 (1997 est.). Swedish name: **Tammerfors.**

Tampico (*Spanish* tam'piko) *n* a port and resort in E Mexico, in Tamaulipas on the Pánuco River: oil refining. Pop.: 272 690 (1990).

tamping *or* **tamping mad** ('tæmpɪŋ) *adj* (*postpositive*) *South Wales dialect.* very angry. [see TAMP[1]]

tampion ('tæmpɪən) *or* **tompion** *n* a plug placed in a gun's muzzle when the gun is not in use to keep out moisture and dust. [C15: from French: TAMPON]

tampon ('tæmpɒn) *n* **1** a plug of lint, cotton wool, cotton, etc., inserted into an open wound or body cavity to stop the flow of blood, absorb secretions, etc., esp. one inserted into the vagina to absorb menstrual blood. ◆ *vb* **2** (*tr*) to plug (a wound, etc.) with a tampon. [C19: via French from Old French *tapon* a little plug, from *tape* a plug, of Germanic origin] ▸ '**tamponage** *n*

tam-tam *n* another name for **gong** (sense 1). [from Hindi: see TOM-TOM]

tamworth ('tæmwəθ) *n* (*often cap.*) any of a hardy breed of long-bodied reddish pigs. [named after TAMWORTH, England, where it was developed]

Tamworth ('tæmwəθ) *n* **1** a market town in W central England, in SE Staffordshire. Pop.: 68 440 (1991). **2** a city in SE Australia, in E central New South Wales: industrial centre of an agricultural region. Pop.: 33 900 (1985 est.).

tan[1] (tæn) *n* **1** the brown colour produced by the skin after intensive exposure to ultraviolet rays, esp. those of the sun. **2** a light or moderate yellowish-brown colour. **3** short for **tanbark.** ◆ *vb* **tans, tanning, tanned. 4** to go brown or cause to go brown after exposure to ultraviolet rays: *she tans easily.* **5** to convert (a skin or hide) into leather by treating it with a tanning agent, such as vegetable tannins, chromium salts, fish oils, or formaldehyde. **6** (*tr*) *Slang.* to beat or flog. ◆ *adj* **tanner, tannest. 7** of the colour tan: *tan gloves.* **8** used in or relating to tanning. [Old English *tannian* (unattested as infinitive, attested as *getanned,* past participle), from Medieval Latin *tannāre,* from *tannum* tanbark, perhaps of Celtic origin; compare Irish *tana* thin] ▸ '**tannable** *adj* ▸ '**tannish** *adj*

tan[2] (tæn) *abbrev. for* tangent (sense 2).

tana ('tɑːnə) *n* **1** a small Madagascan lemur, *Phaner furcifer.* **2** a large tree shrew, *Tupaia tana,* of Sumatra and Borneo. [C19: from Malay *tūpai tana* ground squirrel]

Tana ('tɑːnə) *n* **1 Lake.** Also called: (Lake) **Tsana.** a lake in NW Ethiopia, on a plateau 1800 m (6000 ft.) high: the largest lake of Ethiopia; source of the Blue Nile. Area: 3673 sq. km (1418 sq. miles). **2** a river in E Kenya, rising in the Aberdare Range and flowing in a wide curve east to the Indian Ocean: the longest river in Kenya. Length: 708 km (440 miles). **3** a river in NE Norway, flowing generally northeast as part of the border between Norway and Finland to the Arctic Ocean by Tana Fjord. Length: about 320 km (200 miles). Finnish name: **Teno.**

Tanach *Hebrew.* (ta'nax) *n* the Hebrew Bible as used by Jews, divided into the Torah, Prophets, and Hagiographa. [from Hebrew, acronym formed from *torāh* (the Pentateuch), *nebi'im* (the prophets), and *ketūbim* (the Hagiographa)]

tanager ('tænədʒə) *n* any American songbird of the family *Thraupidae,* having a short thick bill and a brilliantly coloured male plumage. [C19: from New Latin *tanagra,* based on Tupi *tangara*]

Tanagra ('tænəgrə) *n* a town in ancient Boeotia, famous for terracotta figurines of the same name, first discovered in its necropolis.

Tanana ('tænənɑː) *n* a river in central Alaska, rising in the Wrangell Mountains and flowing northwest to the Yukon River. Length: about 765 km (475 miles).

Tananarive (*French* tananariv) *n* the former name of **Antananarivo.**

tanbark ('tænˌbɑːk) *n* the bark of certain trees, esp. the oak and hemlock, used as a source of tannin. Often shortened to **tan.**

Tancred ('tæŋkrɪd) *n* died 1112, Norman hero of the First Crusade, who played a prominent part in the capture of Jerusalem (1099).

tandem ('tændəm) *n* **1** a bicycle with two sets of pedals and two saddles, arranged one behind the other for two riders. **2** a two-wheeled carriage drawn by two horses harnessed one behind the other. **3** a team of two horses so harnessed. **4** any arrangement of two things in which one is placed behind the other. **5 in tandem.** together or in conjunction. ◆ *adj* **6** *Brit.* used as, used in, or routed through an intermediate automatic telephone exchange: *a tandem exchange.* ◆ *adv* **7** one behind the other: *to ride tandem.* [C18: whimsical use of Latin *tandem* at length, to indicate a vehicle of elongated appearance]

tandem roller *n* a type of road roller in which the front and back wheels consist of rollers of about the same diameter.

T & G *abbrev. for* Transport and General Workers' Union.

Tandjungpriok *or* **Tanjungpriok** (ˌtændʒʊŋ'priːɒk) *n* a port in Indonesia, on the NW coast of Java adjoining the capital, Jakarta: a major shipping and distributing centre for the whole archipelago.

tandoori (tæn'dʊərɪ) *n* **a** an Indian method of cooking meat or vegetables on a spit in a clay oven. **b** (*as modifier*): *tandoori chicken.* [from Urdu, from *tandoor* an oven]

tang (tæŋ) *n* **1** a strong taste or flavour: *the tang of the sea.* **2** a pungent or characteristic smell: *the tang of peat fires.* **3** a trace, touch, or hint of something: *a tang of cloves in the apple pie.* **4** the pointed end of a tool, such as a chisel, file, knife, etc., which is fitted into a handle, shaft, or stock. [C14: from Old Norse *tangi* point; related to Danish *tange* point, spit]

Tang (tæŋ) *n* the imperial dynasty of China from 618–907 A.D.

tanga ('tæŋgə) *n* a type of very brief bikini.

Tanga ('tæŋgə) *n* a port in N Tanzania, on the Indian Ocean: Tanzania's second port. Pop.: 187 155 (1988).

Tanganyika (,tæŋgə'nji:kə) *n* **1** a former state in E Africa: became part of German East Africa in 1884; ceded to Britain as a League of Nations mandate in 1919 and as a UN trust territory in 1946; gained independence in 1961 and united with Zanzibar in 1964 as the United Republic of Tanzania. **2 Lake.** a lake in central Africa between Tanzania and the Democratic Republic of the Congo (formerly Zaïre), bordering also on Burundi and Zambia, in the Great Rift Valley: the longest freshwater lake in the world. Area: 32 893 sq. km (12 700 sq. miles). Length: 676 km (420 miles). ▸ **,Tangan'yikan** *adj, n*

Tange ('tæŋgə) *n* **Kenzo.** born 1913, Japanese architect. His buildings include the Kurashiki city hall (1960) and St Mary's Cathedral in Tokyo (1962–64).

tangelo ('tændʒə,ləʊ) *n, pl* **-los. 1** a hybrid produced by crossing a tangerine tree with a grapefruit tree. **2** the fruit of this hybrid, having orange acid-tasting flesh. [C20: from TANG(ERINE) + (POM)ELO]

tangent ('tændʒənt) *n* **1** a geometric line, curve, plane, or curved surface that touches another curve or surface at one point but does not intersect it. **2** (of an angle) a trigonometric function that in a right-angled triangle is the ratio of the length of the opposite side to that of the adjacent side; the ratio of sine to cosine. Abbrev.: **tan. 3** the straight part on a survey line between curves. **4** *Music.* a part of the action of a clavichord consisting of a small piece of metal that strikes the string to produce a note. **5 on** *or* **at a tangent.** on a completely different or divergent course, esp. of thought: *to go off at a tangent.* ◆ *adj* **6a** of or involving a tangent. **6b** touching at a single point. **7** touching. **8** almost irrelevant. [C16: from Latin phrase *līnea tangēns* the touching line, from *tangere* to touch] ▸ **'tangency** *n*

tangent galvanometer *n* a type of galvanometer having a vertical coil of wire with a horizontal magnetic needle at its centre. The current to be measured is passed through the coil and produces a proportional magnetic field which deflects the needle.

tangential (tæn'dʒenʃəl) *adj* **1** of, being, relating to, or in the direction of a tangent. **2** Also: **transverse.** *Astronomy.* (of velocity) in a direction perpendicular to the line of sight of a celestial object. Compare **radial** (sense 6). **3** of superficial relevance only; digressive. ▸ **tan,genti'ality** *n* ▸ **tan'gentially** *or* **tan'gentally** *adv*

tangerine (,tændʒə'ri:n) *n* **1** an Asian citrus tree, *Citrus reticulata*, cultivated for its small edible orange-like fruits. **2** the fruit of this tree, having a loose rind and sweet spicy flesh. **3a** a reddish-orange colour. **3b** (*as adj*): *a tangerine door.* [C19: from TANGIER]

tangi ('tʌŋi:) *n, pl* **-gis.** *N.Z.* **1** a Maori funeral ceremony. **2** *Informal.* a lamentation. [Maori]

tangible ('tændʒəbᵊl) *adj* **1** capable of being touched or felt; having real substance: *a tangible object.* **2** capable of being clearly grasped by the mind; substantial rather than imaginary: *tangible evidence.* **3** having a physical existence; corporeal: *tangible assets.* ◆ *n* **4** (*often pl*) a tangible thing or asset. [C16: from Late Latin *tangibilis*, from Latin *tangere* to touch] ▸ **,tangi'bility** *or* **'tangibleness** *n* ▸ **'tangibly** *adv*

Tangier (tæn'dʒɪə) *n* a port in N Morocco, on the Strait of Gibraltar: a Phoenician trading post in the 15th century B.C.; a neutral international zone (1923–56); made the summer capital of Morocco and a free port in 1962; commercial and financial centre. Pop.: 307 000 (1993 est.). ▸ **,Tange'rine** *n, adj*

tangle[1] ('tæŋgᵊl) *n* **1** a confused or complicated mass of hairs, lines, fibres, etc., knotted or coiled together. **2** a complicated problem, condition, or situation. ◆ *vb* **3** to become or cause to become twisted together in a confused mass. **4** (*intr*; often foll. by *with*) to come into conflict; contend: *to tangle with the police.* **5** (*tr*) to involve in matters which hinder or confuse: *to tangle someone in a shady deal.* **6** (*tr*) to ensnare or trap, as in a net. [C14 *tangilen*, variant of *tagilen*, probably of Scandinavian origin; related to Swedish dialect *taggla* to entangle] ▸ **'tanglement** *n* ▸ **'tangler** *n* ▸ **'tangly** *adj*

tangle[2] *or* **tangle weed** ('tæŋgᵊl) *n* alternative names (esp. Scot.) for **oarweed.** [C16: of Scandinavian origin: compare Danish *tang* seaweed]

tango ('tæŋgəʊ) *n, pl* **-gos. 1** a Latin American dance in duple time, characterized by long gliding steps and sudden pauses. **2** a piece of music composed for or in the rhythm of this dance. ◆ *vb* **-goes, -going, -goed. 3** (*intr*) to perform this dance. [C20: from American Spanish, probably of Niger-Congo origin; compare Ibibio *tamgu* to dance] ▸ **'tangoist** *n*

Tango ('tæŋgəʊ) *n Communications.* a code word for the letter *t.*

tangram ('tæŋgræm) *n* a Chinese puzzle in which a square, cut into a parallelogram, a square, and five triangles, is formed into figures. [C19: perhaps from Chinese *t'ang* Chinese + -GRAM]

Tangshan ('tæŋ'ʃæn) *n* an industrial city in NE China, in Hebei province. Pop.: 1 500 000 (1991 est.).

Tanguy (*French* tãgi) *n* **Yves** (iv). 1900–55, U.S. surrealist painter, born in France.

tangy ('tæŋɪ) *adj* **tangier, tangiest.** having a pungent, fresh, or briny flavour or aroma: *a tangy sea breeze.*

tanh (θæn, tænʃ) *n* hyperbolic tangent; a hyperbolic function that is the ratio of sinh to cosh. [C20: from TAN(GENT) + H(YPERBOLIC)]

Tanis ('teɪnɪs) *n* an ancient city located in the E part of the Nile delta: abandoned after the 6th century B.C.; at one time the capital of Egypt. Biblical name: **Zoan.**

tanist ('tænɪst) *n History.* the heir apparent of a Celtic chieftain chosen by election during the chief's lifetime: usually the worthiest of his kin. [C16: from Irish Gaelic *tánaiste*, literally: the second person] ▸ **'tanistry** *n*

taniwha ('tʌni:fɑ:, 'tænəwɑ:) *n N.Z.* a legendary Maori monster. [Maori]

Tanizaki Jun-ichiro (,tɑ:ni:'zɑ:ki: ,dʒu:ni:'tʃi:rɔ:) *n* 1886–1965, Japanese novelist, whose works, such as *Some Prefer Nettles* (1929) and *The Makioka Sisters* (1943–48), reflect the tension between Western values and Japanese traditions.

Tanjore (tæn'dʒɔ:) *n* the former name of **Thanjavur.**

Tanjungpriok (,tændʒʊŋ'pri:ɒk) *n* a variant spelling of **Tandjungpriok.**

tank (tæŋk) *n* **1** a large container or reservoir for the storage of liquids or gases: *tanks for storing oil.* **2a** an armoured combat vehicle moving on tracks and armed with guns, etc. **2b** (*as modifier*): *a tank commander; a tank brigade.* **3** *Brit. or U.S. dialect.* a reservoir, lake, or pond. **4** *Photog.* **4a** a light-tight container inside which a film can be processed in daylight, the solutions and rinsing waters being poured in and out without light entering. **4b** any large dish or container used for processing a number of strips or sheets of film. **5** *Slang, chiefly U.S.* **5a** a jail. **5b** a jail cell. **6** Also called: **tankful.** the quantity contained in a tank. **7** *Austral.* a dam formed by excavation. ◆ *vb* **8** (*tr*) to put or keep in a tank. **9** (*intr*) to move like a tank, esp. heavily and rapidly. **10** *Slang.* to defeat heavily. ◆ See also **tank up.** [C17: from Gujarati *tānkh* artificial lake, but influenced also by Portuguese *tanque*, from *estanque* pond, from *estancar* to dam up, from Vulgar Latin *stanticāre* (unattested) to block, STANCH] ▸ **'tankless** *adj* ▸ **'tank,like** *adj*

tanka ('tɑ:ŋkə) *n, pl* **-kas** *or* **-ka.** a Japanese verse form consisting of five lines, the first and third having five syllables, the others seven. [C19: from Japanese, from *tan* short + *ka* verse]

tankage ('tæŋkɪdʒ) *n* **1** the capacity or contents of a tank or tanks. **2** the act of storing in a tank or tanks, or a fee charged for such storage. **3** *Agriculture.* **3a** fertilizer consisting of the dried and ground residues of animal carcasses. **3b** a protein supplement feed for livestock.

tankard ('tæŋkəd) *n* **a** a large one-handled drinking vessel, commonly made of silver, pewter, or glass, sometimes fitted with a hinged lid. **b** the quantity contained in a tankard. [C14: related to Middle Dutch *tankaert*, French *tanquart*]

tank engine *or* **locomotive** *n* a steam locomotive that carries its water supply in tanks mounted around its boiler.

tanker ('tæŋkə) *n* a ship, lorry, or aeroplane designed to carry liquid in bulk, such as oil.

tank farming *n* another name for **hydroponics.** ▸ **tank farmer** *n*

tank top *n* a sleeveless upper garment with wide shoulder straps and a low neck, usually worn over a shirt, blouse, or jumper. [C20: named after *tank suits*, one-piece bathing costumes of the 1920s worn in tanks or swimming pools]

tank trap *n* any obstacle, such as a number of concrete stumps set in the ground, designed to stop a military tank.

tank up *vb* (*adv*) *Chiefly Brit.* **1** to fill the tank of (a vehicle) with petrol. **2** *Slang.* to imbibe or cause to imbibe a large quantity of alcoholic drink.

tank wagon *or esp. U.S. and Canadian* **tank car** *n* a form of railway wagon carrying a tank for the transport of liquids.

tannage ('tænɪdʒ) *n* **1** the act or process of tanning. **2** a skin or hide that has been tanned.

tannate ('tæneɪt) *n* any salt or ester of tannic acid.

Tannenberg (*German* 'tanənbɛrk) *n* a village in N Poland, formerly in East Prussia: site of a decisive defeat of the Teutonic Knights by the Poles in 1410 and of a decisive German victory over the Russians in 1914. Polish name: **Stębark.**

tanner[1] ('tænə) *n* a person who tans skins and hides.

tanner[2] ('tænə) *n Brit.* (formerly) an informal word for **sixpence.** [C19: of unknown origin]

tannery ('tænərɪ) *n, pl* **-neries.** a place or building where skins and hides are tanned.

Tannhäuser ('tæn,hɔɪzə) *n* 13th-century German minnesinger, commonly identified with a legendary knight who sought papal absolution after years spent in revelry with Venus. The legend forms the basis of an opera by Wagner.

tannic ('tænɪk) *adj* of, relating to, containing, or produced from tan, tannin, or tannic acid.

tannie ('tʌnɪ) *n S. African.* a title of respect used to refer to an elderly woman. [Afrikaans; literally: aunt]

tannin ('tænɪn) *n* any of a class of yellowish or brownish solid compounds found in many plants and used as tanning agents, mordants, medical astringents, etc. Tannins are derivatives of gallic acid with the approximate formula $C_{76}H_{52}O_{46}$. Also called: **tannic acid.** [C19: from French *tanin*, from TAN[1]]

Tannoy ('tænɔɪ) *n Trademark.* a sound-amplifying apparatus used as a public-address system esp. in a large building, such as a university.

Tans (tænz) *pl n* **the.** *Irish informal.* short for the **Black and Tans.**

tansy ('tænzɪ) *n, pl* **-sies. 1** any of numerous plants of the genus *Tanacetum*, esp. *T. vulgare*, having yellow flowers in flat-topped clusters and formerly used in medicine and for seasoning: family *Compositae* (composites). **2** any of various similar plants. [C15: from Old French *tanesie*, from Medieval Latin *athanasia* tansy (with reference to its alleged power to prolong life), from Greek: immortality]

Tanta ('tæntə) *n* a city in N Egypt, on the Nile delta: noted for its Muslim festivals. Pop.: 380 000 (1992 est.).

tantalate ('tæntə,leɪt) *n* any of various salts of tantalic acid formed when the pentoxide of tantalum dissolves in an alkali.

tantalic (tæn'tælɪk) *adj* of or containing tantalum, esp. in the pentavalent state.

tantalic acid *n* a white gelatinous substance produced by hydrolysis of tantalic halides. It dissolves in strong bases to give tantalates.

tantalite ('tæntə,laɪt) *n* a heavy brownish mineral consisting of a tantalum oxide of iron and manganese in orthorhombic crystalline form: it occurs in coarse granite, often with columbite, and is an ore of tantalum. Formula: $(Fe,Mn)(Ta,Nb)_2O_6$. [C19: from TANTALUM + -ITE[1]]

tantalize *or* **tantalise** ('tæntə,laɪz) *vb* (*tr*) to tease or make frustrated, as by tormenting with the sight of something greatly desired but inaccessible. [C16: from the punishment of TANTALUS] ▸ **,tantali'zation** *or* **,tantali'sation**

n ▸ 'tanta,lizer *or* 'tanta,liser *n* ▸ 'tanta,lizing *or* 'tanta,lising *adj* ▸ 'tanta,lizingly *or* 'tanta,lisingly *adv*

tantalous ('tæntələs) *adj* of or containing tantalum in the trivalent state. [C19: from TANTAL(UM) + -OUS]

tantalum ('tæntələm) *n* a hard greyish-white metallic element that occurs with niobium in tantalite and columbite: used in electrolytic components and in alloys to increase hardness and chemical resistance, esp. in surgical instruments. Symbol: Ta; atomic no.: 73; atomic wt.: 180.9479; valency: 2, 3, 4, or 5; relative density: 16.654; melting pt.: 3020°C; boiling pt.: 5458±100°C. [C19: named after TANTALUS, with reference to the metal's incapacity to absorb acids]

tantalus ('tæntələs) *n Brit.* a case in which bottles may be locked with their contents tantalizingly visible.

Tantalus ('tæntələs) *n Greek myth.* a king, the father of Pelops, punished in Hades for his misdeeds by having to stand in water that recedes when he tries to drink it and under fruit that moves away as he reaches for it.

tantamount ('tæntə,maʊnt) *adj* (*postpositive;* foll. by *to*) as good (as); equivalent in effect (to): *his statement was tantamount to an admission of guilt.* [C17: basically from Anglo-French *tant amunter* to amount to as much, from *tant* so much + *amunter* to AMOUNT]

tantara ('tæntərə, tæn'tɑːrə) *n* a blast, as on a trumpet or horn. [C16: from Latin *taratantara,* imitative of the sound of the tuba]

tantivy (tæn'tɪvɪ) *adv* **1** at full speed; rapidly. ◆ *n, pl* **-tivies,** *interj* **2** a hunting cry, esp. at full gallop. [C17: perhaps imitative of galloping hooves]

tant mieux *French.* (tɑ̃ mjø) so much the better.

tanto ('tæntəʊ; *Italian* 'tanto) *adv* too much: *allegro ma non tanto.* See **non troppo.** [C19: from Italian, from Latin *tantum* so much]

tant pis *French.* (tɑ̃ pi) so much the worse.

Tantra ('tæntrə, 'tʌn-) *n Hinduism, Buddhism.* the sacred books of Tantrism, written between the 7th and 17th centuries A.D., mainly in the form of a dialogue between Siva and his wife. [C18: from Sanskrit: warp, hence underlying principle, from *tanoti* he weaves]

Tantrism ('tæntrɪzəm) *n* **1** a movement within Hinduism combining magical and mystical elements and with sacred writings of its own. **2** a similar movement within Buddhism. [C18: from Sanskrit *tantra,* literally: warp, hence, doctrine] ▸ **'Tantric** *adj* ▸ **'Tantrist** *n*

tantrum ('tæntrəm) *n* (*often pl*) a childish fit of rage; outburst of bad temper. [C18: of unknown origin]

Tan-tung ('tæn'tʊŋ) *n* a variant transliteration of the Chinese name for **Andong.**

Tanzania (,tænzə'nɪə) *n* a republic in E Africa, on the Indian Ocean: formed by the union of the independent states of Tanganyika and Zanzibar in 1964; a member of the Commonwealth. Exports include coffee, tea, sisal, and cotton. Official languages: Swahili and English. Religions: Christian, Muslim, and animist. Currency: Tanzanian shilling. Capital: Dodoma. Pop.: 30 609 000 (1998 est.). Area: 945 203 sq. km (364 943 sq. miles). ▸ **,Tanza'nian** *adj, n*

Tao (taʊ) *n* (in the philosophy of Taoism) **1** that in virtue of which all things happen or exist. **2** the rational basis of human conduct. **3** the course of life and its relation to eternal truth. [Chinese, literally: path, way]

Taoiseach ('tiːʃæx) *n* the prime minister of the Republic of Ireland. [from Irish Gaelic, literally: leader]

Taoism ('taʊɪzəm) *n* **1** the philosophy of Lao Zi that advocates a simple honest life and noninterference with the course of natural events. **2** a popular Chinese system of religion and philosophy claiming to be teachings of Lao Zi but also incorporating pantheism and sorcery. ▸ **'Taoist** *n, adj* ▸ **Tao'istic** *adj*

taonga (tɑ'ɔŋə) *n N.Z.* treasure; anything highly prized. [Maori]

tap[1] (tæp) *vb* **taps, tapping, tapped. 1** to strike (something) lightly and usually repeatedly: *to tap the table; to tap on the table.* **2** (*tr*) to produce by striking in this way: *to tap a rhythm.* **3** (*tr*) to strike lightly with (something): *to tap one's finger on the desk.* **4** (*intr*) to walk with a tapping sound: *she tapped across the floor.* **5** (*tr*) to attach metal or leather reinforcing pieces to (the toe or heel of a shoe). ◆ *n* **6** a light blow or knock, or the sound made by it. **7** the metal piece attached to the toe or heel of a shoe used for tap-dancing. **8** short for **tap-dancing. 9** *Phonetics.* the contact made between the tip of the tongue and the alveolar ridge as the tongue is flicked upwards in the execution of a flap or vibrates rapidly in the execution of a trill or roll. ◆ See also **taps.** [C13 *tappen,* probably from Old French *taper,* of Germanic origin; related to Middle Low German *tappen* to pluck, Swedish dialect *täpa* to tap] ▸ **'tappable** *adj*

tap[2] (tæp) *n* **1** a valve by which a fluid flow from a pipe can be controlled by opening and closing an orifice. U.S. name: **faucet. 2** a stopper to plug a cask or barrel and enable the contents to be drawn out in a controlled flow. **3** a particular quality of alcoholic drink, esp. when contained in casks: *an excellent tap.* **4** *Brit.* short for **taproom. 5** the surgical withdrawal of fluid from a bodily cavity: *a spinal tap.* **6** Also called: **screw tap.** a tool for cutting female screw threads, consisting of a threaded steel cylinder with longitudinal grooves forming cutting edges. Compare **die**[2] (sense 2). **7** *Electronics, chiefly U.S. and Canadian.* a connection made at some point between the end terminals of an inductor, resistor, or some other component. Usual Brit. name: **tapping. 8** *Stock Exchange.* **8a** an issue of a government security released slowly onto the market when its market price reaches a predetermined level. **8b** (*as modifier*): *tap stock; tap issue.* **9** a concealed listening or recording device connected to a telephone or telegraph wire for the purpose of obtaining information secretly. **10 on tap. 10a** *Informal.* ready for immediate use. **10b** (of drinks) on draught. ◆ *vb* **taps, tapping, tapped.** (*tr*) **11** to furnish with a tap. **12** to draw off with or as if with a tap. **13** to cut into (a tree) and draw off sap from it. **14** *Brit. informal.* to ask or beg (someone) for money: *he tapped me for a fiver.* **15a** to connect a tap to (a telephone or telegraph wire). **15b** to listen in secret to (a telephone message, etc.) by means of a tap. **16** to make a connection to (a pipe, drain, etc.). **17** to cut a female screw thread in (an object or material) by use of a tap. **18** to withdraw (fluid) from (a bodily cavity). **19** *Informal.* (of a sports team or an employer) to make an illicit attempt to recruit (a player or employee bound by an existing contract). [Old English *tæppa;* related to Old Norse *tappi* tap, Old High German *zapfo*] ▸ **'tappable** *adj* ▸ **'tapper** *n*

tap[3] (tæp) *n, vb* a Scot. word for **top**[1].

tapa ('tɑːpə) *n* **1** the inner bark of the paper mulberry. **2** a paper-like cloth made from this in the Pacific islands. [C19: from Marquesan and Tahitian]

tapadera (,tæpə'dɛərə) *n* the leather covering for the stirrup on an American saddle. [via American Spanish from Spanish: cover, from *tapar* to cover, of Germanic origin; compare TAMPON, TAP[2]]

Tapajós (*Portuguese* tapa'ʒɔs) *n* a river in N Brazil, rising in N central Mato Grosso and flowing northeast to the Amazon. Length: about 800 km (500 miles).

tapas ('tæpəs) *pl n* **a** light snacks or appetizers, usually eaten with drinks. **b** (*as modifier*): *a tapas bar.* [from Spanish *tapa* cover, lid]

tap dance *n* **1** a step dance in which the performer wears shoes equipped with taps that make a rhythmic sound on the stage as he dances. ◆ *vb* **tap-dance.** (*intr*) **2** to perform a tap dance. ▸ **'tap-,dancer** *n* ▸ **'tap-,dancing** *n*

tape (teɪp) *n* **1** a long thin strip, made of cotton, linen, etc., used for binding, fastening, etc. **2** any long narrow strip of cellulose, paper, metal, etc., having similar uses. **3** a string stretched across the track at the end of a race course. **4** *Military slang, chiefly Brit.* another word for **stripe**[1] (sense 3). **5** See **magnetic tape, ticker tape, paper tape, tape recording.** ◆ *vb* (*mainly tr*) **6** (*also intr*) Also: **tape-record.** to record (speech, music, etc.). **7** to furnish with tapes. **8** to bind, measure, secure, or wrap with tape. **9** (*usually passive*) *Brit. informal.* to take stock of (a person or situation); sum up: *he's got the job taped.* [Old English *tæppe;* related to Old Frisian *tapia* to pull, Middle Dutch *tapen* to tear] ▸ **'tape,like** *adj* ▸ **'taper** *n*

tape deck *n* **1** a tape recording unit in a hi-fi system. **2** the platform supporting the spools, cassettes, or cartridges of a tape recorder, incorporating the motor or motors that drive them and the playback, recording, and erasing heads. ◆ Sometimes shortened to **deck.**

tape echo *n* a means of delaying the repeat of a sound by adjusting the time lapse between the recording and playback heads of a tape recorder. Also called: **tape slap.**

tape grass *n* any of several submerged freshwater plants of the genus *Vallisneria,* esp. *V. spiralis,* of warm temperate regions, having ribbon-like leaves: family *Hydrocharitaceae.*

tape machine *n* **1** another word for **tape recorder. 2** a telegraphic receiving device that records messages electronically or on ticker tape. U.S. equivalent: **ticker.**

tape measure *n* a tape or length of metal marked off in inches, centimetres, etc., used principally for measuring and fitting garments. Also called (esp. U.S.): **'tape,line.**

taper ('teɪpə) *vb* **1** to become or cause to become narrower towards one end: *the spire tapers to a point.* **2** (often foll. by *off*) to become or cause to become smaller or less significant. ◆ *n* **3** a thin candle. **4** a thin wooden or waxed strip for transferring a flame; spill. **5** a narrowing. **6** *Engineering.* (in conical parts) the amount of variation in the diameter per unit of length. **7** any feeble source of light. [Old English *tapor,* probably from Latin *papȳrus* PAPYRUS (from its use as a wick)] ▸ **'taperer** *n* ▸ **'tapering** *adj* ▸ **'taperingly** *adv*

tape-record *vb* to make a tape recording (of).

tape recorder *n* an electrical device used for recording sounds on magnetic tape and usually also for reproducing them, consisting of a tape deck and one or more amplifiers and loudspeakers.

tape recording *n* **1** the act or process of recording on magnetic tape. **2** the magnetized tape used in making such a recording. **3** the speech, music, etc., so recorded.

tapered roller bearing *n Engineering.* a rolling bearing that uses tapered rollers running in coned races and is able to accept axial thrust as well as providing shaft location. Compare **thrust bearing.**

taper pin *n* a short round metal rod having a small amount of taper so that when driven into a hole it tightens on the taper so that it can act as a stop or wedge.

tape slap *n* another term for **tape echo.**

tape streamer *n Computing.* an electromechanical device that enables data to be copied byte by byte from a hard disk onto magnetic tape for security or storage.

tapestry ('tæpɪstrɪ) *n, pl* **-tries. 1** a heavy ornamental fabric, often in the form of a picture, used for wall hangings, furnishings, etc., and made by weaving coloured threads into a fixed warp. **2** another word for **needlepoint. 3** a colourful and complicated situation: *the rich tapestry of London life.* [C15: from Old French *tapisserie* carpeting, from Old French *tapiz* carpet; see TAPIS] ▸ **'tapestried** *adj* ▸ **'tapestry-,like** *adj*

tapestry moth *n* one of the larger tineid moths, *Trichophaga tapetzella,* the larvae of which devour animal fibres. It is brown, with white-tipped forewings, and prefers damp environments.

tape transport *n* the motorized mechanism that moves tape evenly across the recording and playback heads of a tape recorder or cassette player.

tapetum (tə'piːtəm) *n, pl* **-ta** (-tə). **1** a layer of nutritive cells in the sporangia of ferns and anthers of flowering plants that surrounds developing spore cells. **2a** a membranous reflecting layer of cells in the choroid of the eye of nocturnal vertebrates. **2b** a similar structure in the eyes of certain nocturnal insects. **3** *Anatomy.* a covering layer of cells. [C18: from New Latin, from Medieval Latin: covering, from Latin *tapēte* carpet, from Greek *tapēs* carpet] ▸ **ta'petal** *adj*

tapeworm ('teɪp,wɜːm) *n* any parasitic ribbon-like flatworm of the class *Cestoda,* having a body divided into many egg-producing segments and lacking a mouth and gut. The adults inhabit the intestines of vertebrates. See also **echinococcus, taenia.**

taphephobia (ˌtæfɪ'fəʊbɪə) *n Med.* a pathological fear of being buried alive. [from Greek *taphos* grave + -PHOBIA] ▸ ˌ**tapheˈphobic** *adj*

taphole ('tæpˌhəʊl) *n* a hole in a furnace for running off molten metal or slag.

taphonomy (tə'fɒnəmɪ) *n* the study of the processes affecting an organism after death that result in its fossilization. [C20: from Greek *taphos* grave + -NOMY] ▸ **taphonomic** (ˌtæfə'nɒmɪk) *or* ˌ**taphoˈnomical** *adj*

taphouse ('tæpˌhaʊs) *n Now rare.* an inn or bar.

taphrogenesis (ˌtæfrəʊ'dʒɛnɪsɪs) *n Geology.* vertical movement of the earth's crust, resulting in major faults. [C20: from German *tafrogenese,* from Greek *taphros* pit + -GENESIS]

tapioca (ˌtæpɪ'əʊkə) *n* a beadlike starch obtained from cassava root, used in cooking as a thickening agent, esp. in puddings. [C18: via Portuguese from Tupi *tipioca* pressed-out juice, from *tipi* residue + *ok* to squeeze out]

tapir ('teɪpə) *n, pl* **-pirs** *or* **-pir.** any perissodactyl mammal of the genus *Tapirus,* such as *T. indicus* (**Malayan tapir**), of South and Central America and SE Asia, having an elongated snout, three-toed hind legs, and four-toed forelegs: family *Tapiridae.* [C18: from Tupi *tapiira*]

tapis ('tæpiː, 'tæpɪ; *French* tapi) *n, pl* **tapis.** tapestry or carpeting, esp. as formerly used to cover a table in a council chamber. [C17: from French, from Old French *tapiz,* from Greek *tapētion* rug, from *tapēs* carpet]

tappet ('tæpɪt) *n* a mechanical part that reciprocates to receive or transmit intermittent motion, esp. the part of an internal-combustion engine that transmits motion from the camshaft to the push rods or valves. [C18: from TAP[1] + -ET]

tappit-hen ('tæpɪt'hɛn) *n Scot.* **1** a hen with a crest. **2** a pewter tankard, usually with a distinctive knob on the lid. [C18: from Scottish *tappit* topped, crested + HEN]

taproom ('tæpˌruːm, -ˌrʊm) *n* a bar, as in a hotel or pub.

taproot ('tæpˌruːt) *n* the large single root of plants such as the dandelion, which grows vertically downwards and bears smaller lateral roots. [C17: from TAP[2] + ROOT[1]] ▸ **'tapˌrooted** *adj*

taps (tæps) *n* (*functioning as sing*) **1** *Chiefly U.S.* **1a** (in army camps, etc.) a signal given on a bugle, drum, etc., indicating that lights are to be put out. **1b** any similar signal, as at a military funeral. **2** (in the Guide movement) a closing song sung at an evening camp fire or at the end of a meeting. [C19: from TAP[1]]

tapsalteerie ('tæpsᵊl'tiːrɪ) *adj, adv, n Scot.* topsy-turvy. [C17: of uncertain origin]

tapster ('tæpstə) *n* **1** *Rare.* a barman. **2** (in W Africa) a man who taps palm trees to collect and sell palm wine. [Old English *tæppestre,* feminine of *tæppere,* from *tappian* to TAP[2]] ▸ **'tapstress** *fem n*

tapu ('tɑːpuː) *adj N.Z.* sacred; forbidden. [Maori, from Tongan]

tap water *n* water drawn off through taps from pipes in a house, as distinguished from distilled water, mineral water, etc.

tar[1] (tɑː) *n* **1** any of various dark viscid substances obtained by the destructive distillation of organic matter such as coal, wood, or peat. **2** another name for **coal tar.** ◆ *vb* **tars, tarring, tarred.** (*tr*) **3** to coat with tar. **4 tar and feather.** to punish by smearing tar and feathers over (someone). **5 tarred with the same brush.** regarded as having the same faults. [Old English *teoru;* related to Old Frisian *tera,* Old Norse *tjara,* Middle Low German *tere* tar, Gothic *triu* tree] ▸ **'tarry** *adj* ▸ **'tarriness** *n*

tar[2] (tɑː) *n* an informal word for **seaman.** [C17: short for TARPAULIN]

Tara ('tærə, 'tɑːrə) *n* a village in Co. Meath near Dublin, by the **Hill of Tara,** the historic seat of the ancient Irish kings.

Tarabulus el Gharb (tə'rɑːbələs ɛl 'gɑːb) *n* transliteration of the Arabic name for **Tripoli** (Libya).

Tarabulus esh Sham (tə'rɑːbələs ɛʃ 'ʃæm) *n* transliteration of the Arabic name for **Tripoli** (Lebanon).

taradiddle ('tærəˌdɪdᵊl) *n* another spelling of **tarradiddle.**

tarakihi ('tærəˌkiːhiː) *or* **terakihi** *n, pl* **-kihis.** a common edible sea fish of New Zealand waters.

taramasalata (ˌtærəməsə'lɑːtə) *n* a creamy pale pink pâté, made from the roe of grey mullet or smoked cod and served as an hors d'oeuvre. [C20: from Modern Greek, from *tarama* cod's roe]

Taranaki gate (ˌtærə'nækiː) *n N.Z.* a rough-and-ready gate in a fence made from wire and battens. [first used on dairy farms in *Taranaki,* province of N.Z.]

tarantass (ˌtɑːrən'tæs) *n* a large horse-drawn four-wheeled Russian carriage without springs. [C19: from Russian *tarantas,* from Kazan Tatar *taryntas*]

tarantella (ˌtærən'tɛlə) *n* **1** a peasant dance from S Italy. **2** a piece of music composed for or in the rhythm of this dance, in fast six-eight time. [C18: from Italian, from *Taranto* TARANTO; associated with TARANTISM]

tarantism ('tærənˌtɪzəm) *n* a nervous disorder marked by uncontrollable bodily movement, widespread in S Italy during the 15th to 17th centuries: popularly thought to be caused by the bite of a tarantula. [C17: from New Latin *tarantismus,* from TARANTO; see TARANTULA]

Taranto (tə'ræntəʊ; *Italian* 'taranto) *n* a port in SE Italy, in Apulia on the **Gulf of Taranto** (an inlet of the Ionian Sea): the chief city of Magna Graecia; taken by the Romans in 272 B.C. Pop.: 212 650 (1996 est.). Latin name: **Tarentum.**

tarantula (tə'ræntjʊlə) *n, pl* **-las** *or* **-lae** (-ˌliː). **1** any of various large hairy mostly tropical spiders of the American family *Theraphosidae.* **2** a large hairy spider, *Lycosa tarentula* of S Europe, the bite of which was formerly thought to cause tarantism. [C16: from Medieval Latin, from Old Italian *tarantola,* from TARANTO]

Tarantula nebula *n* a huge bright emission nebula located in the S hemisphere in the Large Magellanic Cloud.

Tararua biscuit ('tɑːrɑːˌruːə) *n N.Z. informal.* a tramper's home-made biscuit with a high calorie content.

Tarawa (tə'rɑːwə) *n* an atoll in Kiribati, occupying a chain of islets surrounding a lagoon in the W central Pacific: the capital of Kiribati, Bairiki, is on this atoll. Pop.: 29 028 (1990).

taraxacum (tə'ræksəkəm) *n* **1** any perennial plant of the genus *Taraxacum,* such as the dandelion, having dense heads of small yellow flowers and seeds with a feathery attachment: family *Compositae* (composites). **2** the dried root of the dandelion, used as a laxative, diuretic, and tonic. [C18: from Medieval Latin, from Arabic *tarakhshaqūn* wild chicory, possibly of Persian origin]

Tarbes (*French* tarb) *n* a town in SW France: noted for the breeding of Anglo-Arab horses. Pop.: 50 228 (1990).

tarboosh, tarbush, *or* **tarbouche** (tɑː'buːʃ) *n* a felt or cloth brimless cap resembling the fez, usually red and often with a silk tassel, worn alone or as part of a turban by Muslim men. [C18: from Arabic *tarbūsh*]

tar boy *n Austral. and N.Z. informal.* a boy who applies tar to the skin of sheep cut during shearing.

Tardenoisian (ˌtɑːdə'nɔɪzɪən) *adj* of or referring to a Mesolithic culture characterized by small flint instruments. [C20: after *Tardenois,* France, where implements were found]

tardigrade ('tɑːdɪˌgreɪd) *n* **1** any minute aquatic segmented eight-legged invertebrate of the phylum *Tardigrada,* related to the arthropods, occurring in soil, ditches, etc. Popular name: **water bear.** ◆ *adj* **2** of, relating to, or belonging to the *Tardigrada.* [C17: via Latin *tardigradus,* from *tardus* sluggish + *gradī* to walk]

tardy ('tɑːdɪ) *adj* **-dier, -diest. 1** occurring later than expected: *tardy retribution.* **2** slow in progress, growth, etc.: *a tardy reader.* [C15: from Old French *tardif,* from Latin *tardus* slow] ▸ **'tardily** *adv* ▸ **'tardiness** *n*

tare[1] (tɛə) *n* **1** any of various vetch plants, such as *Vicia hirsuta* (**hairy tare**) of Eurasia and N Africa. **2** the seed of any of these plants. **3** *Bible.* a troublesome weed, thought to be the darnel. [C14: of unknown origin]

tare[2] (tɛə) *n* **1** the weight of the wrapping or container in which goods are packed. **2** a deduction from gross weight to compensate for this. **3** the weight of a vehicle without its cargo, passengers, etc. **4** an empty container used as a counterbalance in determining net weight. ◆ *vb* **5** (*tr*) to weigh (a package, etc.) in order to calculate the amount of tare. [C15: from Old French: waste, from Medieval Latin *tara,* from Arabic *tarhah* something discarded, from *taraha* to reject]

Tarentum (tə'rɛntəm) *n* the Latin name of **Taranto.**

targe (tɑːdʒ) *n* an archaic word for **shield.** [C13: from Old French, of Germanic origin; related to Old High German *zarga* rim, frame, Old Norse *targa* shield]

target ('tɑːgɪt) *n* **1a** an object or area at which an archer or marksman aims, usually a round flat surface marked with concentric rings. **1b** (*as modifier*): *target practice.* **2a** any point or area aimed at; the object of an attack or a takeover bid. **2b** (*as modifier*): *target area; target company.* **3** a fixed goal or objective: *the target for the appeal is £10 000.* **4** a person or thing at which an action or remark is directed or the object of a person's feelings: *a target for the teacher's sarcasm.* **5** a joint of lamb consisting of the breast and neck. **6** *Surveying.* a marker on which sights are taken, such as the sliding marker on a levelling staff. **7** (formerly) a small round shield. **8** *Physics, electronics.* **8a** a substance, object, or system subjected to bombardment by electrons or other particles, or to irradiation. **8b** an electrode in a television camera tube whose surface, on which image information is stored, is scanned by the electron beam. **9** *Electronics.* an object detected by the reflection of a radar or sonar signal, etc. **10 on target.** on the correct course to meet a target or objective. ◆ *vb* **-gets, -geting, -geted.** (*tr*) **11** to make a target of. **12** to direct or aim: *to target benefits at those most in need.* [C14: from Old French *targette* a little shield, from Old French TARGE] ▸ **'targetless** *adj*

target language *n* **1** the language into which a text, document, etc., is translated. **2** a language that is being or is to be learnt.

target man *n Soccer.* an attacking player to whom high crosses and centres are played, esp. a tall forward.

Targum ('tɑːgəm; *Hebrew* tar'gum) *n* an Aramaic translation, usually in the form of an expanded paraphrase, of various books or sections of the Old Testament. [C16: from Aramaic: interpretation] ▸ **Targumic** (tɑː'guːmɪk) *or* **Tar'gumical** *adj* ▸ **'Targumist** *n*

tariff ('tærɪf) *n* **1a** a tax levied by a government on imports or occasionally exports for purposes of protection, support of the balance of payments, or the raising of revenue. **1b** a system or list of such taxes. **2** any schedule of prices, fees, fares, etc. **3** *Chiefly Brit.* **3a** a method of charging for the supply of services, esp. public services, such as gas and electricity: *block tariff.* **3b** a schedule of such charges. **4** *Chiefly Brit.* a bill of fare with prices listed; menu. ◆ *vb* (*tr*) **5** to set a tariff on. **6** to set a price on according to a schedule of tariffs. [C16: from Italian *tariffa,* from Arabic *ta'rīfa* to inform] ▸ **'tariffless** *adj*

tariff office *n Insurance.* a company whose premiums are based on a tariff agreed with other insurance companies.

Tarim ('tɑː'riːm) *n* a river in NW China, in Xinjiang Uygur AR: flows east along the N edge of the Taklimakan Shama desert, dividing repeatedly and forming lakes among the dunes, finally disappearing in the Lop Nor depression; the chief river of Xinjiang Uygur AR; drains the great **Tarim Basin** between the Tian Shan and Kunlun mountain systems of central Asia, an area of about 906 500 sq. km (350 000 sq. miles). Length: 2190 km (1360 miles).

Tarkington ('tɑːkɪŋtən) *n* (**Newton**) **Booth.** 1869–1946, U.S. novelist. His works include the historical romance *Monsieur Beaucaire* (1900), tales of the Middle West, such as *The Magnificent Ambersons* (1918) and *Alice Adams* (1921), and the series featuring the character Penrod.

Tarkovsky (*Russian* 'tɑkɔfskij) *n* **Andrei** ('ɑndrej). 1932–86, Soviet film director, whose films include *Andrei Rublev* (1966), *Solaris* (1971), *Nostalgia* (1983), and *The Sacrifice* (1986).

tarlatan ('tɑːlətən) *n* an open-weave cotton fabric, used for stiffening garments. [C18: from French *tarlatane,* variant of *tarnatane* type of muslin, perhaps of Indian origin]

Tarmac ('tɑːmæk) *n* **1** *Trademark.* *(often not cap.)* a paving material that consists of crushed stone rolled and bound with a mixture of tar and bitumen, esp. as used for a road, airport runway etc. Full name: **Tarmacadam** (ˌtɑːmə'kædəm). See also **macadam.** ◆ *vb* **-macs, -macking, -macked.** *(tr)* **2** *(usually not cap.)* to apply Tarmac to.

tarn (tɑːn) *n* a small mountain lake or pool. [C14: of Scandinavian origin; related to Old Norse *tjörn* pool]

Tarn (*French* tarn) *n* **1** a department of S France, in Midi-Pyrénées region. Capital: Albi. Pop.: 341 700 (1995). Area: 5780 sq. km (2254 sq. miles). **2** a river in SW France, rising in the Massif Central and flowing generally west to the Garonne River. Length: 375 km (233 miles).

tarnal ('tɑːnᵊl) *U.S. dialect.* ◆ *adj* **1** *(prenominal)* damned. ◆ *adv* **2** (intensifier): *tarnal lucky!* [C18: aphetic dialect pronunciation of ETERNAL] ▸ **'tarnally** *adv*

tarnation (tɑː'neɪʃən) *n* a euphemism for **damnation.**

Tarn-et-Garonne (*French* tarnegarɔn) *n* a department of SW France, in Midi-Pyrénées region. Capital: Montauban. Pop.: 205 200 (1995). Area: 3731 sq. km (1455 sq. miles).

tarnish ('tɑːnɪʃ) *vb* **1** to lose or cause to lose the shine, esp. by exposure to air or moisture resulting in surface oxidation; discolour: *silver tarnishes quickly.* **2** to stain or become stained; taint or spoil: *a fraud that tarnished his reputation.* ◆ *n* **3** a tarnished condition, surface, or film. [C16: from Old French *ternir* to make dull, from *terne* lustreless of Germanic origin; related to Old High German *tarnen* to conceal, Old English *dierne* hidden] ▸ **'tarnishable** *adj* ▸ **'tarnisher** *n*

Tarnopol (tar'nɔpɔl) *n* the Polish name for **Ternopol.**

Tarnów (*Polish* 'tarnuf) *n* an industrial city in SE Poland. Pop.: 121 500 (1996 est.).

taro ('tɑːrəʊ) *n, pl* **-ros. 1** an aroid plant, *Colocasia esculenta,* cultivated in the tropics for its large edible rootstock. **2** the rootstock of this plant. ◆ Also called: **elephant's-ear, dasheen, eddo, Chinese eddo.** [C18: from Tahitian and Maori]

tarot ('tærəʊ) *n* **1** one of a special pack of cards, now used mainly for fortune-telling, consisting of 78 cards (4 suits of 14 cards each (the minor arcana), and 22 other cards (the major arcana)). **2** a card in a tarot pack with distinctive symbolic design, such as the Wheel of Fortune. ◆ *adj* **3** relating to tarot cards. [C16: from French, from Old Italian *tarocco,* of unknown origin]

tarp (tɑːp) *n U.S., Austral., and N.Z.* an informal word for **tarpaulin.**

tarpan ('tɑːpæn) *n* a European wild horse, *Equus caballus gomelini,* common in prehistoric times but now extinct. [from Kirghiz Tatar]

tarpaulin (tɑː'pɔːlɪn) *n* **1** a heavy hard-wearing waterproof fabric made of canvas or similar material coated with tar, wax, or paint, for outdoor use as a protective covering against moisture. **2** a sheet of this fabric. **3** a hat of or covered with this fabric, esp. a sailor's hat. **4** a rare word for **seaman.** [C17: probably from TAR[1] + PALL[1] + -ING[1]]

Tarpeia (tɑː'piːə) *n* (in Roman legend) a vestal virgin, who betrayed Rome to the Sabines and was killed by them when she requested a reward.

Tarpeian Rock (tɑː'piːən) *n* (in ancient Rome) a cliff on the Capitoline hill from which traitors were hurled.

tarpon ('tɑːpən) *n, pl* **-pons** *or* **-pon. 1** a large silvery clupeoid game fish, *Tarpon atlanticus,* of warm Atlantic waters, having a compressed body covered with large scales: family *Elopidae.* **2** any similar related fish. [C17: perhaps from Dutch *tarpoen,* of unknown origin]

Tarquin ('tɑːkwɪn) *n* **1** Latin name *Lucius Tarquinius Priscus.* fifth legendary king of Rome (616–578 B.C.). **2** Latin name *Lucius Tarquinius Superbus.* seventh and last legendary king of Rome (534–510 B.C.).

tarradiddle ('tærəˌdɪdᵊl) *n* **1** a trifling lie. **2** nonsense; twaddle. [of unknown origin]

tarragon ('tærəgən) *n* **1** an aromatic perennial plant, *Artemisia dracunculus,* of the Old World, having whitish flowers and small toothed leaves, which are used as seasoning: family *Compositae* (composites). **2** the leaves of this plant. ◆ Also called: **estragon.** [C16: from Old French *targon,* from Medieval Latin *tarcon, from Arabic tarkhūn,* perhaps from Greek *drakontion* adderwort]

Tarragona (*Spanish* tarra'yona) *n* a port in NE Spain, on the Mediterranean: one of the richest seaports of the Roman Empire; destroyed by the Moors (714). Pop.: 114 931 (1995 est.). Latin name: **Tarraco** (tə'rɑːkəʊ).

Tarrasa (*Spanish* ta'rrasa) *n* a city in NE Spain: textile centre. Pop.: 161 428 (1994 est.).

tarriance ('tærɪəns) *n* an archaic word for **delay.**

tarry ('tærɪ) *vb* **-ries, -rying, -ried. 1** *(intr)* to delay in coming or going; linger. **2** *(intr)* to remain temporarily or briefly. **3** *(intr)* to wait or stay. **4** *(tr) Archaic or poetic.* to await. ◆ *n, pl* **-ries. 5** *Rare.* a stay. [C14 *tarien,* of uncertain origin] ▸ **'tarrier** *n*

tarsal ('tɑːsᵊl) *adj* **1** of, relating to, or constituting the tarsus or tarsi. ◆ *n* **2** a tarsal bone.

tar sand *n* a sandstone in which hydrocarbons have been trapped; the lighter compounds evaporate, leaving a residue of asphalt in the rock pores.

tarseal ('tɑːˌsiːl) *n N.Z.* **1** the bitumen surface of a road. **2 the.** the main highway.

Tarshish ('tɑːʃɪʃ) *n Old Testament.* an ancient port, mentioned in I Kings 10:22, situated in Spain or in one of the Phoenician colonies in Sardinia.

tarsia ('tɑːsɪə) *n* another term for **intarsia.** [C17: from Italian, from Arabic *tarsī';* see INTARSIA]

tarsier ('tɑːsɪə) *n* any of several nocturnal arboreal prosimian primates of the genus *Tarsius,* of Indonesia and the Philippines, having huge eyes, long hind legs, and digits ending in pads to facilitate climbing: family *Tarsiidae.* [C18: from French, from *tarse* the flat of the foot; see TARSUS]

tarsometatarsus (ˌtɑːsəʊˌmetə'tɑːsəs) *n, pl* **-si** (-saɪ). a bone in the lower part of a bird's leg consisting of the metatarsal bones and some of the tarsal bones fused together. [C19: *tarso-,* from TARSUS + METATARSUS] ▸ **ˌtarsoˌmeta'tarsal** *adj*

tarsus ('tɑːsəs) *n, pl* **-si** (-saɪ). **1** the bones of the ankle and heel, collectively. **2a** the corresponding part in other mammals and in amphibians and reptiles. **2b** another name for **tarsometatarsus. 3** the dense connective tissue supporting the free edge of each eyelid. **4** the part of an insect's leg that lies distal to the tibia. [C17: from New Latin, from Greek *tarsos* flat surface, instep]

Tarsus ('tɑːsəs) *n* **1** a city in SE Turkey, on the Tarsus River: site of ruins of ancient Tarsus, capital of Cilicia, and birthplace of St. Paul. Pop.: 229 518 (1995 est.). **2** a river in SE Turkey, in Cilicia, rising in the Taurus Mountains and flowing south past Tarsus to the Mediterranean. Ancient name: **Cydnus.** Length: 153 km (95 miles).

tart[1] (tɑːt) *n* a pastry case often having no top crust, with a sweet filling of fruit, jam, custard, etc. [C14: from Old French *tarte,* of uncertain origin; compare Medieval Latin *tarte*]

tart[2] (tɑːt) *adj* **1** (of a flavour, food, etc.) sour, acid, or astringent. **2** cutting, sharp, or caustic: *a tart remark.* [Old English *teart* rough; related to Dutch *tarten* to defy, Middle High German *traz* defiance] ▸ **'tartish** *adj* ▸ **'tartishly** *adv* ▸ **'tartly** *adv* ▸ **'tartness** *n*

tart[3] (tɑːt) *n Informal.* a promiscuous woman, esp. a prostitute: often a term of abuse. See also **tart up.** [C19: shortened from SWEETHEART] ▸ **'tarty** *adj*

tartan[1] ('tɑːtᵊn) *n* **1a** a design of straight lines, crossing at right angles to give a chequered appearance, esp. the distinctive design or designs associated with each Scottish clan: *the Buchanan tartan.* **1b** *(as modifier): a tartan kilt.* **2** a woollen fabric or garment with this design. **3 the tartan.** Highland dress. [C16: perhaps from Old French *tertaine* linsey-woolsey, from Old Spanish *tiritaña* a fine silk fabric, from *tiritar* to rustle] ▸ **'tartaned** *adj*

tartan[2] ('tɑːtᵊn) *n* a single-masted vessel used in the Mediterranean, usually with a lateen sail. [C17: from French, perhaps from Provençal *tartana* falcon, buzzard, since a ship was frequently given the name of a bird]

tartanry ('tɑːtᵊnrɪ) *n Derogatory.* the excessive use of tartan and other Scottish imagery to produce a distorted sentimental view of Scotland and its history. [C20: TARTAN[1] + -RY]

tartar[1] ('tɑːtə) *n* **1** *Dentistry.* a hard crusty deposit on the teeth, consisting of food, cellular debris, and mineral salts. **2** Also called: **argol.** a brownish-red substance consisting mainly of potassium hydrogen tartrate, present in grape juice and deposited during the fermentation of wine. [C14: from Medieval Latin *tartarum,* from Medieval Greek *tartaron*]

tartar[2] ('tɑːtə) *n (sometimes cap.)* a fearsome or formidable person. [C16: special use of TARTAR]

Tartar ('tɑːtə) *n, adj* a variant spelling of **Tatar.** ▸ **Tartarian** (tɑː'tɛərɪən) *or* **Tartaric** (tɑː'tærɪk) *adj*

tartare *or* **tartar sauce** *n* a mayonnaise sauce mixed with hard-boiled egg yolks, chopped herbs, capers, and gherkins. [from French *sauce tartare,* from TARTAR]

Tartarean (tɑː'tɛərɪən, -'tɑːrɪ-) *adj Literary.* of or relating to Tartarus; infernal.

tartar emetic *n* another name for **antimony potassium tartrate.**

tartaric (tɑː'tærɪk) *adj* of, concerned with, containing, or derived from tartar or tartaric acid. Systematic name: **2,3-dihydroxybutanedioic acid.**

tartaric acid *n* a colourless or white odourless crystalline water-soluble dicarboxylic acid existing in four stereoisomeric forms, the commonest being the dextrorotatory (*d*-) compound which is found in many fruits: used as a food additive (**E334**) in soft drinks, confectionery, and baking powders and in tanning and photography. Formula: HOOCCH(OH)CH(OH)COOH.

tartarize *or* **tartarise** ('tɑːtəˌraɪz) *vb (tr)* to impregnate or treat with tartar or tartar emetic. ▸ **ˌtartari'zation** *or* **ˌtartari'sation** *n*

tartarous ('tɑːtərəs) *adj* consisting of, containing, or resembling tartar.

tartar steak *n* a variant term for **steak tartare.**

Tartarus ('tɑːtərəs) *n Greek myth.* **1** an abyss under Hades where the Titans were imprisoned. **2** a part of Hades reserved for evildoers. **3** the underworld; Hades. **4** a primordial god who became the father of the monster Typhon. [C16: from Latin, from Greek *Tartaros,* of obscure origin]

Tartary ('tɑːtərɪ) *n* a variant spelling of **Tatary.**

tartlet ('tɑːtlɪt) *n Brit.* an individual pastry case with a filling of fruit or other sweet or savoury mixture.

tartrate ('tɑːtreɪt) *n* any salt or ester of tartaric acid.

tartrated ('tɑːtreɪtɪd) *adj* being in the form of a tartrate.

tartrazine ('tɑːtrəˌziːn, -zɪn) *n* an azo dye that produces a yellow colour: widely used as a food additive (**E102**) in convenience foods, soft drinks, sweets, etc., and in drugs, and also to dye textiles.

Tartu (*Russian* 'tartu) *n* a city in SE Estonia: became Russian in 1704 after successive Russian, Polish, and Swedish rule; became part of independent Estonia in 1991; university (1632). Pop.: 103 400 (1996 est.). Former name (11th century until 1918): **Yurev.** German name: **Dorpat.**

Tartuffe *or* **Tartufe** (tɑː'tuf, -'tuːf) *n* a person who hypocritically pretends to be deeply pious. [from the character in Molière's comedy *Tartuffe* (1664)] ▸ **Tar'tuffian** *or* **Tar'tufian** *adj*

tart up *vb (tr, adv) Brit. informal.* **1** to dress and make (oneself) up in a provocative or promiscuous way. **2** *Informal.* to decorate or improve the appearance of: *to tart up a bar.*

tarwhine ('tɑːˌwaɪn) *n* a bream, *Rhabdosargus sarba,* of E Australia, silver in colour with gold streaks. [from a native Australian language]

Tarzan ('tɑːzən) *n* (*sometimes not cap.*) *Informal, often ironical.* a man with great physical strength, agility, and virility. [C20: after the hero of a series of stories by E. R. BURROUGHS]

Tas. *abbrev. for* Tasmania.

Tashi Lama ('tɑːʃɪ 'lɑːmə) *n* another name for the **Panchen Lama.** [from *Tashi (Lumpo)*, name of Tibetan monastery over which this Lama presides]

Tashkent (*Russian* taʃ'kjɛnt) *n* the capital of Uzbekistan: one of the oldest and largest cities in central Asia; cotton textile manufacturing. Pop.: 2 106 000 (1994 est.).

tasimeter (tə'sɪmɪtə) *n* a device for measuring small temperature changes. It depends on the changes of pressure resulting from expanding or contracting solids. [C19 *tasi-*, from Greek *tasis* tension + -METER] ▸ **tasimetric** (ˌtæsɪ'metrɪk) *adj* ▸ **ta'simetry** *n*

task (tɑːsk) *n* **1** a specific piece of work required to be done as a duty or chore. **2** an unpleasant or difficult job or duty. **3** any piece of work. **4 take to task.** to criticize or reprove. ♦ *vb* (*tr*) **5** to assign a task to. **6** to subject to severe strain; tax. [C13: from Old French *tasche*, from Medieval Latin *tasca*, from *taxa* tax, from Latin *taxāre* to TAX] ▸ **'tasker** *n* ▸ **'taskless** *adj*

task force *n* **1** a temporary grouping of military units formed to undertake a specific mission. **2** any semipermanent organization set up to carry out a continuing task.

taskmaster ('tɑːskˌmɑːstə) *n* a person, discipline, etc., that enforces work, esp. hard or continuous work: *his teacher is a hard taskmaster.* ▸ **'taskˌmistress** *fem n*

taskwork ('tɑːskˌwɜːk) *n* **1** hard or unpleasant work. **2** a rare word for **piecework.**

Tasman ('tæzmən) *n* **Abel Janszoon** ('abəl 'jansuːn). 1603–59, Dutch navigator, who discovered Tasmania, New Zealand, and the Tonga and Fiji Islands (1642–43).

Tasmania (tæz'meɪnɪə) *n* an island in the S Pacific, south of mainland Australia: forms, with offshore islands, the smallest state of Australia; discovered by the Dutch explorer Tasman in 1642; used as a penal colony by the British (1803–53); mostly forested and mountainous. Capital: Hobart. Pop.: 473 200 (1996 est.). Area: 68 332 sq. km (26 383 sq. miles). Former name (1642–1855): **Van Diemen's Land.** ▸ **Tas'manian** *adj, n*

Tasmanian devil *n* a small ferocious carnivorous marsupial, *Sarcophilus harrisi,* of Tasmania, having black fur with pale markings, strong jaws, and short legs: family *Dasyuridae*. Also called: **ursine dasyure.**

Tasmanian wolf *or* **tiger** *n* other names for **thylacine.**

Tasman Sea *n* the part of the Pacific between SE Australia and NW New Zealand.

tass (tæs) *or* **tassie** ('tæsɪ) *n Scot. and northern English dialect.* **1** a cup, goblet, or glass. **2** the contents of such a vessel. [C15: from Old French *tasse* cup, from Arabic *tassah* basin, from Persian *tast*]

Tass (tæs) *n* (formerly) the principal news agency of the Soviet Union: replaced in 1992 by **Itar Tass.** [*T(elegrafnoye) a(genstvo) S(ovetskovo) S(oyuza)* Telegraphic Agency of the Soviet Union]

tassel ('tæsᵊl) *n* **1** a tuft of loose threads secured by a knot or ornamental knob, used to decorate soft furnishings, clothes, etc. **2** anything resembling this tuft, esp. the tuft of stamens at the tip of a maize inflorescence. ♦ *vb* **-sels, -selling, -selled** *or U.S.* **-sels, -seling, -seled. 3** (*tr*) to adorn with a tassel or tassels. **4** (*intr*) (of maize) to produce stamens in a tuft. **5** (*tr*) to remove the tassels from. [C13: from Old French, from Vulgar Latin *tassellus* (unattested), changed from Latin *taxillus* a small die, from *tālus* gaming die] ▸ **'tasselly** *adj*

tasset ('tæsɪt), **tasse** (tæs), *or* (*less commonly*) **tace** *n* a piece of armour consisting of one or more plates fastened on to the bottom of a cuirass to protect the thigh. [C19: from French *tassette* small pouch, from Old French *tasse* purse]

Tassie *or* **Tassy** ('tæzɪ) *n, pl* **-sies.** *Austral. informal.* **1** Tasmania. **2** a native or inhabitant of Tasmania.

Tasso (*Italian* 'tasso) *n* **Torquato** (tor'kwaːto). 1544–95, Italian poet, noted for his pastoral idyll *Aminta* (1573) and for *Jerusalem Delivered* (1581), dealing with the First Crusade.

taste (teɪst) *n* **1** the sense by which the qualities and flavour of a substance are distinguished by the taste buds. **2** the sensation experienced by means of the taste buds. **3** the act of tasting. **4** a small amount eaten, drunk, or tried on the tongue. **5** a brief experience of something: *a taste of the whip.* **6** a preference or liking for something; inclination: *to have a taste for danger.* **7** the ability to make discerning judgments about aesthetic, artistic, and intellectual matters; discrimination: *to have taste.* **8** judgment of aesthetic or social matters according to a generally accepted standard: *bad taste.* **9** discretion; delicacy: *that remark lacks taste.* **10** *Obsolete.* the act of testing. ♦ *vb* **11** to distinguish the taste of (a substance) by means of the taste buds. **12** (*usually tr*) to take a small amount of (a food, liquid, etc.) into the mouth, esp. in order to test the quality: *to taste the wine.* **13** (often foll. by *of*) to have a specific flavour or taste: *the tea tastes of soap; this apple tastes sour.* **14** (when *intr*, usually foll. by *of*) to have an experience of (something): *to taste success.* **15** (*tr*) an archaic word for **enjoy. 16** (*tr*) *Obsolete.* to test by touching. [C13: from Old French *taster*, ultimately from Latin *taxāre* to appraise] ▸ **'tastable** *adj*

taste bud *n* any of the elevated oval-shaped sensory end organs on the surface of the tongue, by means of which the sensation of taste is experienced.

tasteful ('teɪstfʊl) *adj* **1** indicating good taste: *a tasteful design.* **2** a rare word for **tasty.** ▸ **'tastefully** *adv* ▸ **'tastefulness** *n*

tasteless ('teɪstlɪs) *adj* **1** lacking in flavour; insipid. **2** lacking social or aesthetic taste. **3** *Rare.* unable to taste. ▸ **'tastelessly** *adv* ▸ **'tastelessness** *n*

taster ('teɪstə) *n* **1** a person who samples food or drink for quality. **2** any device used in tasting or sampling. **3** a person employed, esp. formerly, to taste food and drink prepared for a king, etc., to test for poison. **4** a sample or preview of a product, experience, etc., intended to stimulate interest in the product, experience, etc., itself: *the single serves as a taster for the band's new album.*

tasty ('teɪstɪ) *adj* **tastier, tastiest. 1** having a pleasant flavour. **2** *Brit. informal.* attractive: used chiefly by men when talking of women. ▸ **'tastily** *adv* ▸ **'tastiness** *n*

tat[1] (tæt) *vb* **tats, tatting, tatted.** to make (something) by tatting. [C19: of unknown origin]

tat[2] (tæt) *n* **1** tatty articles or a tatty condition. **2** tasteless articles. **3** a tangled mass. [C20: back formation from TATTY]

tat[3] (tæt) *n* See **tit for tat.**

ta-ta (tæ'tɑː) *sentence substitute. Brit. informal.* goodbye; farewell. [C19: of unknown origin]

tatami (tə'tɑːmɪ, tæ'tæmɪ) *n, pl* **-mi** *or* **-mis.** a thick rectangular mat of woven straw, used as a standard to measure a Japanese room. [Japanese]

Tatar *or* **Tartar** ('tɑːtə) *n* **1a** a member of a Mongoloid people who under Genghis Khan established a vast and powerful state in central Asia from the 13th century until conquered by Russia in 1552. **1b** a descendant of this people, now scattered throughout Russia but living chiefly in the Tatar Republic. **2** any of the languages spoken by the present-day Tatars, belonging to various branches of the Turkic family of languages, esp. Kazan Tatar. ♦ *adj* **3** of, relating to, or characteristic of the Tatars. [C14: from Old French *Tartare*, from Medieval Latin *Tartarus* (associated with Latin *Tartarus* the underworld), from Persian *Tātār*] ▸ **Tatarian** (tɑː'teərɪən), **Tar'tarian** *or* **Tataric** (tɑː'tærɪk), **Tar'taric** *adj*

Tatar Republic *n* a constituent republic of W Russia, around the confluence of the Volga and Kama Rivers. Capital: Kazan. Pop.: 3 755 000 (1995 est.) Area: 68 000 sq. km (26 250 sq. miles).

Tatar Strait *n* an arm of the Pacific between the mainland of SE Russia and Sakhalin Island, linking the Sea of Japan with the Sea of Okhotsk. Length: about 560 km (350 miles). Also called: **Gulf of Tatary.**

Tatary *or* **Tartary** ('tɑːtərɪ) *n* **1** a historical region (with indefinite boundaries) in E Europe and Asia, inhabited by Bulgars until overrun by the Tatars in the mid-13th century: extended as far east as the Pacific under Genghis Khan. **2 Gulf of.** another name for the **Tatar Strait.**

Tate (teɪt) *n* **1 (John Orley) Allen.** 1899–1979, U.S. poet and critic. **2 Sir Henry.** 1819–99, British sugar refiner and philanthropist; founder of the Tate Gallery. **3 Nahum** ('neɪʊm). 1652–1715, British poet, dramatist, and hymn-writer, born in Ireland: poet laureate (1692–1715). He is best known for writing a version of *King Lear* with a happy ending.

Tate Gallery *n* an art gallery in London, built in 1897.

tater ('teɪtə) *n* a dialect word for **potato.**

Tati (*French* tati) *n* **Jacques** (ʒak), real name *Jacques Tatischeff.* 1908–82, French film director, pantomimist, and comic actor, creator of the character Monsieur Hulot.

tatouay ('tætʊˌeɪ, ˌtɑːtʊ'aɪ) *n* a large armadillo, *Cabassous tatouay*, of South America. [C16: from Spanish *tatuay*, from Guarani *tatu ai*, from *tatu* armadillo + *ai* worthless (because inedible)]

Tatra Mountains ('tɑːtrə, 'tæt-) *pl n* a mountain range along the border between Slovakia and Poland, extending for about 64 km (40 miles): the highest range of the central Carpathians. Highest peak: Gerlachovka, 2663 m (8737 ft.). Also called: **High Tatra.**

tatter ('tætə) *vb* **1** to make or become ragged or worn to shreds. ♦ *n* **2** (*pl*) torn or ragged pieces, esp. of material. **3 in tatters. 3a** torn to pieces; in shreds. **3b** destroyed or ruined. [C14: of Scandinavian origin; compare Icelandic *tötturr* rag, Old English *tættec*, Old High German *zæter* rag]

tatterdemalion (ˌtætədɪ'meɪljən, -'mæl-) *n Rare.* **a** a person dressed in ragged clothes. **b** (*as modifier*): *a tatterdemalion dress.* [C17: from TATTER + *-demalion*, of uncertain origin]

tattered ('tætəd) *adj* **1** ragged or worn: *a tattered old book.* **2** wearing ragged or torn clothing: *tattered refugees.* **3** damaged, defeated, or in disarray: *he believes he can bring the tattered party together.*

tattersall ('tætəˌsɔːl) *n* **a** a fabric, sometimes brightly coloured, having stripes or bars in a checked or squared pattern. **b** (*as modifier*): *a tattersall coat.* [C19: after TATTERSALL'S; the horse blankets at the market originally had this pattern]

Tattersall's ('tætəˌsɔːlz) *n* **1** a large horse market in London founded in the eighteenth century. **2** *Austral.* a large-scale lottery based in Melbourne. Also (informal) **Tatt's. 3** a name used for sportsmen's clubs in Australia. [named after Richard *Tattersall* (died 1795), English horseman, who founded the market]

tattie *or* **tatty** ('tætɪ) *n, pl* **-ties.** a Scot. or dialect word for **potato.**

tattie-bogle (ˌtætɪ'bogᵊl) *n Scot.* a scarecrow. [TATTIE + BOGLE[1]]

tattie-peelin ('tætɪ'piːlɪn) *adj Central Scot. dialect* (esp. of speech) highfalutin, affected, or pretentious. [from *potato-peeling;* sense development obscure]

tatting ('tætɪŋ) *n* **1** an intricate type of lace made by looping a thread of cotton or linen by means of a hand shuttle. **2** the act or work of producing this. [C19: of unknown origin]

tattle ('tætᵊl) *vb* **1** (*intr*) to gossip about another's personal matters or secrets. **2** (*tr*) to reveal by gossiping: *to tattle a person's secrets.* **3** (*intr*) to talk idly; chat. ♦ *n* **4** the act or an instance of tattling. **5** a scandalmonger or gossip. [C15 (in the sense: to stammer, hesitate): from Middle Dutch *tatelen* to prate, of imitative origin]

tattler ('tætlə) *n* **1** a person who tattles; gossip. **2** any of several sandpipers of the genus *Heteroscelus*, such as *H. incanus* (**Polynesian tattler**), of Pacific coastal regions.

tattletale ('tætᵊlˌteɪl) *Chiefly U.S. and Canadian.* ♦ *n* **1** a scandalmonger or gossip. **2** another word for **telltale** (sense 1).

tattoo[1] (tæ'tuː) *n, pl* **-toos. 1** (formerly) a signal by drum or bugle ordering the military to return to their quarters. **2** a military display or pageant, usually at night. **3** any similar beating on a drum, etc. [C17: from Dutch *taptoe*, from the command *tap toe!* turn off the taps! from *tap* tap of a barrel + *toe* to shut]

tattoo[2] (tæ'tuː) *vb* **-toos, -tooing, -tooed. 1** to make (pictures or designs) on (the skin) by pricking and staining with indelible colours. ◆ *n, pl* **-toos. 2** a design made by this process. **3** the practice of tattooing. [C18: from Tahitian *tatau*] ► **tat'tooer** *or* **tat'tooist** *n*

tatty ('tætɪ) *adj* **-tier, -tiest.** *Chiefly Brit.* worn out, shabby, tawdry, or unkempt. [C16: of Scottish origin, probably related to Old English *tættec* a tatter] ► **'tattily** *adv* ► **'tattiness** *n*

Tatum ('teɪtəm) *n* **1 Art,** full name *Arthur Tatum.* 1910–56, U.S. jazz pianist. **2 Edward Lawrie.** 1909–75, U.S. biochemist, who showed how genes regulate biochemical processes in an organism and demonstrated that bacteria reproduce sexually; Nobel prize for physiology or medicine (1958) with Beadle and Lederberg.

tau (tɔː, taʊ) *n* the 19th letter in the Greek alphabet (Τ or τ), a consonant, transliterated as *t.* [C13: via Latin from Greek, of Semitic origin; see TAV]

tau cross *n* a cross shaped like the Greek letter tau. Also called: **Saint Anthony's cross.**

taught (tɔːt) *vb* the past tense and past participle of **teach.**

tau neutrino *n Physics.* a type of neutrino associated with the decay of tau particles.

taunt[1] (tɔːnt) *vb* (*tr*) **1** to provoke or deride with mockery, contempt, or criticism. **2** to tease; tantalize. ◆ *n* **3** a jeering remark. **4** *Archaic.* the object of mockery. [C16: from French phrase *tant pour tant* like for like, rejoinder] ► **'taunter** *n* ► **'taunting** *adj* ► **'tauntingly** *adv*

taunt[2] (tɔːnt) *adj Nautical.* (of the mast or masts of a sailing vessel) unusually tall. [C15: of uncertain origin]

Taunton ('tɔːntən) *n* a market town in SW England, administrative centre of Somerset: scene of Judge Jeffreys' "Bloody Assize" (1685) after the Battle of Sedgemoor. Pop.: 55 855 (1991).

tauon ('taʊɒn) *n Physics.* a negatively charged elementary particle of high mass classed as a lepton, with an associated antiparticle and neutrino. [C20: from Greek letter TAU + -ON]

tau particle *n Physics.* a type of elementary particle classified as a lepton.

taupe (təʊp) *n* **a** a brownish-grey colour. **b** (*as adj*): *a taupe coat.* [C20: from French, literally: mole, from Latin *talpa*]

Taupo ('taʊpəʊ) *n* **Lake.** a lake in New Zealand, on central North Island: the largest lake of New Zealand. Area: 616 sq. km (238 sq. miles).

Tauranga (taʊ'ræŋə) *n* a port in New Zealand, on NE North Island on the Bay of Plenty: exports dairy produce, meat, and timber. Pop.: 76 100 (1994).

taurine[1] ('tɔːraɪn) *adj* of, relating to, or resembling a bull. [C17: from Latin *taurīnus*, from *taurus* a bull]

taurine[2] ('tɔːriːn, -rɪn) *n* a derivative of the amino acid, cysteine, obtained from the bile of animals; 2-aminoethanesulphonic acid. Formula: $NH_2CH_2CH_2SO_3H$. [C19: from TAURO- (as in *taurocholic* acid, so called because discovered in ox bile) + -INE[2]]

tauro- *or before a vowel* **taur-** *combining form.* denoting a bull: *tauromachy.* [from Latin *taurus* bull, Greek *tauros*]

tauromachy (tɔː'rɒməkɪ) *n* the art or act of bullfighting. [C19: Greek *tauromakhia*, from TAURO- + *makhē* fight] ► **tauromachian** (ˌtɔːrə'meɪkɪən) *adj*

Taurus ('tɔːrəs) *n, Latin genitive* **Tauri** ('tɔːraɪ). **1** *Astronomy.* a zodiacal constellation in the N hemisphere lying close to Orion and between Aries and Gemini. It contains the star Aldebaran, the star clusters Hyades and Pleiades, and the Crab Nebula. **2** *Astrology.* **2a** Also called: the **Bull.** the second sign of the zodiac, symbol ♉, having a fixed earth classification and ruled by the planet Venus. The sun is in this sign between about April 20 and May 20. **2b** a person born when the sun is in this sign. ◆ *adj* **3** born under or characteristic of Taurus. ◆ Also (for senses 2b, 3): **Taurean** ('tɔːrɪən, tɔː'rɪən). [C14: from Latin: bull]

Taurus Mountains *pl n* a mountain range in S Turkey, parallel to the Mediterranean coast: crossed by the Cilician Gates; continued in the northeast by the Anti-Taurus range. Highest peak: Kaldi Dağ, 3734 m (12 251 ft.).

taut (tɔːt) *adj* **1** tightly stretched; tense. **2** showing nervous strain; stressed. **3** *Chiefly nautical.* in good order; neat. [C14 *tought*; probably related to Old English *togian* to TOW[1]] ► **'tautly** *adv* ► **'tautness** *n*

tauten ('tɔːtᵊn) *vb* to make or become taut or tense.

tauto- *or before a vowel* **taut-** *combining form.* identical or same: *tautology; tautonym.* [from Greek *tauto*, from *to auto*]

tautog (tɔː'tɒg) *n* a large dark-coloured wrasse, *Tautoga onitis*, of the North American coast of the Atlantic Ocean: used as a food fish. Also called: **blackfish.** [C17: from Narraganset *tautauog*, plural of *tautau* sheepshead]

tautologize *or* **tautologise** (tɔː'tɒləˌdʒaɪz) *vb* (*intr*) to express oneself tautologically. ► **tau'tologist** *n*

tautology (tɔː'tɒlədʒɪ) *n, pl* **-gies. 1** the use of words that merely repeat elements of the meaning already conveyed, as in the sentence *Will these supplies be adequate enough?* in place of *Will these supplies be adequate?* **2** *Logic.* a statement that is always true, esp. a truth-functional expression that takes the value true for all combinations of values of its components, as in *either the sun is out or the sun is not out.* Compare **inconsistency** (sense 3), **contingency** (sense 5). [C16: from Late Latin *tautologia*, from Greek, from *tautologos*] ► **tautological** (ˌtɔːtᵊ'lɒdʒɪkᵊl), **ˌtauto'logic,** *or* **tau'tologous** *adj* ► **ˌtauto'logically** *or* **tau'tologously** *adv*

tautomer ('tɔːtəmə) *n* either of the two forms of a chemical compound that exhibits tautomerism.

tautomerism (tɔː'tɒməˌrɪzəm) *n* the ability of certain chemical compounds to exist as a mixture of two interconvertible isomers in equilibrium. See also **keto-enol tautomerism.** [C19: from TAUTO- + ISOMERISM] ► **tautomeric** (ˌtɔːtə'merɪk) *adj*

tautonym ('tɔːtənɪm) *n Biology.* a taxonomic name in which the generic and specific components are the same, as in *Rattus rattus* (black rat). [C20: from Greek *tautonymos.* See TAUTO-, -ONYM] ► **ˌtauto'nymic** *or* **tautonymous** (tɔː'tɒnɪməs) *adj* ► **tau'tonymy** *n*

tav *or* **taw** (tɑːv, tɑːf; *Hebrew* tav, taf) *n* the 23rd and last letter in the Hebrew alphabet (ת), transliterated as *t* or when final *th.* [from Hebrew: cross, mark]

Tavel (tɑː'vel) *n* a fine rosé wine produced in the Rhône valley near the small town of Tavel in S France.

Tavener ('tævənə) *n* **John (Kenneth).** born 1944, British composer, whose works include the cantata *The Whale* (1966), the opera *Thérèse* (1979), and the choral work *The Last Discourse* (1998); many of his later works are inspired by the liturgy of the Russian Orthodox Church.

tavern ('tævən) *n* **1** a less common word for **pub. 2** *U.S., Eastern Canadian, and N.Z.* a place licensed for the sale and consumption of alcoholic drink. [C13: from Old French *taverne*, from Latin *taberna* hut]

taverna (tə'vɜːnə) *n* **1** (in Greece) a guesthouse that has its own bar. **2** a Greek restaurant. [C20: Modern Greek, from Latin *taberna*]

taverner ('tævənə) *n* **1** *Archaic.* a keeper of a tavern. **2** *Obsolete.* a constant frequenter of taverns.

Taverner ('tævənə) *n* **John.** ?1495–1545, English composer, esp. of church music; best known for the mass *Western Wynde*, based on a secular song.

TAVR *abbrev. for* Territorial and Army Volunteer Reserve.

taw[1] (tɔː) *n* **1** the line from which the players shoot in marbles. **2 back to taws.** *Austral. informal.* back to the beginning. **3** a large marble used for shooting. **4** a game of marbles. [C18: of unknown origin]

taw[2] (tɔː) *vb* (*tr*) **1** to convert (skins) into white leather by treatment with mineral salts, such as alum and salt, rather than by normal tanning processes. **2** *Archaic or dialect.* to flog; beat. [Old English *tawian*; compare Old High German *zouwen* to prepare, Gothic *taujan* to make] ► **'tawer** *n*

tawa ('tɑːwə) *n* a tall timber tree, *Beilschmiedia tawa*, of New Zealand, having edible purple berries. [Maori]

tawai ('tɑːˌwaɪ) *or* **tawhai** ('tɑːˌhwaɪ) *n* any of various species of beech of the genus *Nothofagus* of New Zealand, originally called "birches" by the settlers. [Maori]

tawdry ('tɔːdrɪ) *adj* **-drier, -driest.** cheap, showy, and of poor quality: *tawdry jewellery.* [C16 *tawdry lace*, shortened and altered from *Seynt Audries lace*, finery sold at the fair of St *Audrey* (Etheldrida), 7th-century queen of Northumbria and patron saint of Ely, Cambridgeshire] ► **'tawdrily** *adv* ► **'tawdriness** *n*

Tawney ('tɔːnɪ) *n* **R(ichard) H(enry).** 1880–1962, British economic historian, born in India. His chief works are *The Acquisitive Society* (1920), *Religion and the Rise of Capitalism* (1926), and *Equality* (1931).

tawny *or* **tawney** ('tɔːnɪ) *n* **a** a light brown to brownish-orange colour. **b** (*as adj*): *tawny port.* [C14: from Old French *tané*, from *taner* to TAN[1]] ► **'tawniness** *n*

tawny owl *n* a European owl, *Strix aluco*, having a reddish-brown or grey plumage, black eyes, and a round head. Also called: **brown owl, wood owl.**

Tawny Owl *n* a name (no longer in official use) for an assistant Brownie Guider.

tawny pipit *n* a small sandy-brown European bird of the wagtail family; an irregular migrant to some parts of Britain.

tawse *or* **taws** (tɔːz) *Chiefly Scot.* ◆ *n* **1** a leather strap having one end cut into thongs, formerly used as an instrument of punishment by a schoolteacher. ◆ *vb* **2** to punish (someone) with or as if with a tawse; whip. [C16: probably plural of obsolete *taw* strip of leather; see TAW[2]]

tax (tæks) *n* **1** a compulsory financial contribution imposed by a government to raise revenue, levied on the income or property of persons or organizations, on the production costs or sales prices of goods and services, etc. **2** a heavy demand on something; strain: *a tax on our resources.* ◆ *vb* (*tr*) **3** to levy a tax on (persons, companies, etc., or their incomes, etc.). **4** to make heavy demands on; strain: *to tax one's intellect.* **5** to accuse, charge, or blame: *he was taxed with the crime.* **6** to determine (the amount legally chargeable or allowable to a party to a legal action), as by examining the solicitor's bill of costs: *to tax costs.* [C13: from Old French *taxer*, from Latin *taxāre* to appraise, from *tangere* to touch] ► **'taxer** *n* ► **'taxless** *adj*

taxable ('tæksəbᵊl) *adj* **1** capable of being taxed; able to bear tax. **2** subject to tax. ◆ *n* **3** (*often pl*) *U.S.* a person, income, property, etc., that is subject to tax. ► **ˌtaxa'bility** *or* **'taxableness** *n* ► **'taxably** *adv*

taxaceous (tæk'seɪʃəs) *adj* of, relating to, or belonging to the *Taxaceae*, a family of coniferous trees that includes the yews. [C19: from New Latin *taxāceus*, from Latin *taxus* a yew]

taxation (tæk'seɪʃən) *n* **1** the act or principle of levying taxes or the condition of being taxed. **2a** an amount assessed as tax. **2b** a tax rate. **3** revenue from taxes. ► **tax'ational** *adj*

tax avoidance *n* reduction or minimization of tax liability by lawful methods. Compare **tax evasion.**

tax-deductible *adj* (of an expense, loss, etc.) legally deductible from income or wealth before tax assessment.

tax disc *n* a paper disc displayed on the windscreen of a motor vehicle showing that the tax due on it has been paid.

taxeme ('tæksiːm) *n Linguistics.* any element of speech that may differentiate one utterance from another with a different meaning, such as the occurrence of a particular phoneme, the presence of a certain intonation, or a distinctive word order. [C20: from Greek *taxis* order, arrangement + -EME] ► **tax'emic** *adj*

tax evasion *n* reduction or minimization of tax liability by illegal methods. Compare **tax avoidance.**

tax-exempt *adj* **1** (of an income or property) exempt from taxation. **2** (of an asset) earning income that is not subject to taxation.

tax exile *n* a person having a high income who chooses to live abroad so as to avoid paying high taxes.

tax-free *adj* not needing to have tax paid on it: *tax-free savings schemes.*

tax haven *n* a country or state having a lower rate of taxation than elsewhere.

tax holiday *n* a period during which tax concessions are made for some reason; examples include an export incentive or an incentive to start a new business given by some governments, in which a company is excused all or part of its tax liability.

taxi ('tæksɪ) *n, pl* **taxis** *or* **taxies. 1** Also called: **cab, taxicab.** a car, usually fitted with a taximeter, that may be hired, along with its driver, to carry passengers to any specified destination. ◆ *vb* **taxies, taxiing** *or* **taxying, taxied. 2** to cause (an aircraft) to move along the ground under its own power, esp. before takeoff and after landing, or (of an aircraft) to move along the ground in this way. **3** (*intr*) to travel in a taxi. [C20: shortened from *taximeter cab*]

taxi dancing *n* a system, as in a dance hall or hotel, whereby a person pays to get a partner (**taxi dancer**) for a dance, payment being required for each individual dance during an evening.

taxidermy ('tæksɪˌdɜːmɪ) *n* the art or process of preparing, stuffing, and mounting animal skins so that they have a lifelike appearance. [C19: from Greek *taxis* arrangement + *-dermy,* from Greek *derma* skin] ▸ **ˌtaxi'dermal** *or* **ˌtaxi'dermic** *adj* ▸ **'taxiˌdermist** *n*

taximeter ('tæksɪˌmiːtə) *n* a meter fitted to a taxi to register the fare, based on the length of the journey. [C19: from French *taximètre;* see TAX, -METER]

taxing ('tæksɪŋ) *adj* demanding, onerous, and wearing. ▸ **'taxingly** *adv*

taxiplane ('tæksɪˌpleɪn) *n U.S.* an aircraft that is available for hire.

taxi rank *n* a place where taxis wait to be hired.

taxis ('tæksɪs) *n* **1** the movement of a cell or organism in a particular direction in response to an external stimulus. **2** *Surgery.* the repositioning of a displaced organ or part by manual manipulation only. [C18: via New Latin from Greek: arrangement, from *tassein* to place in order]

-taxis *or* **-taxy** *n combining form.* **1** indicating movement towards or away from a specified stimulus: *thermotaxis.* **2** order or arrangement: *phyllotaxis.* [from New Latin, from Greek *taxis* order] ▸ **-tactic** *or* **-taxic** *adj combining form.*

taxi truck *n Austral.* a truck with a driver that can be hired.

taxiway ('tæksɪˌweɪ) *n* a marked path along which aircraft taxi to or from a runway, parking area, etc. Also called: **taxi strip, peritrack.**

tax loss *n* a loss sustained by a company that can be set against future profits for tax purposes.

taxman ('tæksˌmæn) *n, pl* **-men. 1** a collector of taxes. **2** *Informal.* a tax-collecting body personified: *he was convicted of conspiring to cheat the taxman of five million pounds.*

taxon ('tæksɒn) *n, pl* **taxa** ('tæksə). *Biology.* any taxonomic group or rank. [C20: back formation from TAXONOMY]

taxonomy (tæk'sɒnəmɪ) *n* **1a** the branch of biology concerned with the classification of organisms into groups based on similarities of structure, origin, etc. **1b** the practice of arranging organisms in this way. **2** the science or practice of classification. [C19: from French *taxonomie,* from Greek *taxis* order + -NOMY] ▸ **taxonomic** (ˌtæksə'nɒmɪk) *or* **ˌtaxo'nomical** *adj* ▸ **ˌtaxo'nomically** *adv* ▸ **tax'onomist** *or* **tax'onomer** *n*

taxpayer ('tæksˌpeɪə) *n* a person or organization that pays taxes or is liable to taxation. ▸ **'taxˌpaying** *adj*

tax rate *n* the percentage of income, wealth, etc., assessed as payable in taxation.

tax relief *n* a reduction in the amount of tax a person or company has to pay.

tax return *n* a declaration of personal income made annually to the tax authorities and used as a basis for assessing an individual's liability for taxation.

tax shelter *n Commerce.* a form into which business or financial activities may be organized to minimize taxation.

-taxy *n combining form.* a variant of **-taxis.**

tax year *n* a period of twelve months used by a government as a basis for calculating taxes.

tay (teɪ) *n* an Irish dialect word for **tea.**

Tay (teɪ) *n* **1 Firth of.** the estuary of the River Tay on the North Sea coast of Scotland. Length: 40 km (25 miles). **2** a river in central Scotland, flowing northeast through Loch Tay, then southeast to the Firth of Tay: the longest river in Scotland; noted for salmon fishing. Length: 193 km (120 miles). **3 Loch.** a lake in central Scotland, in Stirling council area. Length: 23 km (14 miles).

tayberry ('teɪbərɪ) *n, pl* **-ries. 1** a hybrid shrub produced by crossing a blackberry, raspberry, and loganberry. **2** the large sweet red fruit of this plant. [C20: so named because first grown at Blairgowrie on *Tayside,* Scotland]

Taylor ('teɪlə) *n* **1 A(lan) J(ohn) P(ercivale).** 1906–90, British historian whose many works include *The Origins of the Second World War* (1961). **2 Brook.** 1685–1731, English mathematician, who laid the foundations of differential calculus. **3 Elizabeth.** born 1932, U.S. film actress, born in England: films include *National Velvet* (1944), *Cat on a Hot Tin Roof* (1958), *Suddenly Last Summer* (1959), and *Butterfield 8* (1960) and *Who's Afraid of Virginia Woolf?* (1966), for both of which she won Oscars. **4 Frederick Winslow.** 1856–1915, U.S. engineer, who pioneered the use of time and motion studies to increase efficiency in industry. **5 Jeremy.** 1613–67, English cleric, best known for his devotional manuals *Holy Living* (1650) and *Holy Dying* (1651). **6 Zachary.** 1784–1850, 12th president of the U.S. (1849–50); hero of the Mexican War.

Taylor's series *n Maths.* an infinite sum giving the value of a function f(z) in the neighbourhood of a point a in terms of the derivatives of the function evaluated at a. Under certain conditions, the series has the form $f(z) = f(a) + [f'(a)(z-a)]/1! + [f''(a)(z-a)^2]/2! + \ldots$. See also **Maclaurin's series.** [C18: named after B. TAYLOR]

Taymyr Peninsula (taɪ'mɪə) *n* a variant spelling of **Taimyr Peninsula.**

tayra ('taɪrə) *n* a large arboreal musteline mammal, *Eira barbara,* of Central and South America, having a dark brown body and paler head. [C19: from Tupi *taira*]

Tay-Sachs disease (ˌteɪ'sæks) *n* an inherited disorder, caused by a faulty recessive gene, in which lipids accumulate in the brain, leading to mental retardation and blindness. It occurs mostly in Ashkenazi Jews. [C20: named after W. *Tay* (1843–1927), British physician, and B. *Sachs* (1858–1944), U.S. neurologist]

Tayside Region ('teɪˌsaɪd) *n* a former local government region in E Scotland: formed in 1975 from Angus, Kinross-shire, and most of Perthshire; replaced in 1996 by the council areas of Angus, City of Dundee, and Perth and Kinross.

tazza ('tætsə) *n* a wine cup with a shallow bowl and a circular foot. [C19: from Italian, probably from Arabic *tassah* bowl]

tb *abbrev. for:* **1** trial balance. **2** Also: **TB.** tuberculosis.

Tb *the chemical symbol for* terbium.

TB *abbrev. for:* **1** torpedo boat. **2** Also: **tb.** tuberculosis.

T-bar *n* **1** a T-shaped wrench for use with a socket. **2** a metal bar having a T-shaped cross section. **3** a T-shaped bar on a ski tow which skiers hold on to while being pulled up slopes. **4** (*modifier*) another term for **T-strap.**

Tbilisi (dbɪ'liːsɪ) *n* the capital of Georgia, on the Kura River: founded in 458; taken by the Russians in 1801; university (1918); a major industrial centre. Pop.: 1 253 100 (1994). Russian name: **Tiflis.**

T-bone steak *n* a large choice steak cut from the sirloin of beef, containing a T-shaped bone.

tbs. *or* **tbsp.** *abbrev. for* tablespoon(ful).

TBT *abbrev. for* tri-*n*-butyl tin: a biocide used in marine paints to prevent fouling.

Tc *the chemical symbol for* technetium.

TC (on cars, etc.) *abbrev. for* twin carburettors.

TCA cycle *abbrev. for* tricarboxylic acid cycle: another name for **Krebs cycle.**

T-cell *n* another name for **T-lymphocyte.**

Tchad (tʃad) *n* the French name for **Chad.**

Tchaikovsky (tʃaɪ'kɒfskɪ; *Russian* tʃɪj'kɔfskij) *n* **Pyotr Ilyich** (pjɔtr ilj'jitʃ). 1840–93, Russian composer. His works, which are noted for their expressive melodies, include the *Sixth Symphony* (the *Pathétique;* 1893), ballets, esp. *Swan Lake* (1876) and *The Sleeping Beauty* (1889), and operas, including *Eugene Onegin* (1879) and *The Queen of Spades* (1890), both based on works by Pushkin.

Tchebychev's inequality (ˌtʃebɪ'ʃɒfs) *n* See **Chebyshev's inequality.**

TCP *n Trademark.* a mild disinfectant used for cleansing minor wounds, gargling, etc. [abbrev. for *t(ri)c(hloro)p(henylmethyliodisalicyl)*]

TD *abbrev. for:* **1** (in Ireland) Teachta Dála. [Irish Gaelic: member of the Dáil]. **2** technical drawing. **3** (in Britain) Territorial Decoration. **4** Also: **td.** touchdown.

t.d.c. *abbrev. for* top dead-centre.

t distribution *n* See **Student's t.**

tdm *abbrev. for* time-division multiplex. See **multiplex** (sense 1).

te *or* **ti** (tiː) *n Music.* (in tonic sol-fa) the syllable used for the seventh note or subtonic of any scale. [see GAMUT]

Te *the chemical symbol for* tellurium.

tea (tiː) *n* **1** an evergreen shrub or small tree, *Camellia sinensis,* of tropical and subtropical Asia, having toothed leathery leaves and white fragrant flowers: family *Theaceae.* **2a** the dried shredded leaves of this shrub, used to make a beverage by infusion in boiling water. **2b** such a beverage, served hot or iced. **2c** (*as modifier*): *tea caddy; tea urn.* **3a** any of various plants that are similar to *Camellia sinensis* or are used to make a tealike beverage. **3b** any such beverage. **4** *Chiefly Brit.* **4a** Also called: **afternoon tea.** a light meal eaten in mid-afternoon, usually consisting of tea and cakes, biscuits, or sandwiches. **4b** (*as modifier*): *a tea party.* **4c** Also called: **high tea.** afternoon tea that also includes a light cooked dish. **5** *Brit., Austral., and N.Z.* the main evening meal. **6** *U.S. and Canadian dated slang.* marijuana. **7 tea and sympathy.** *Informal.* a caring attitude, esp. to someone in trouble. [C17: from Chinese (Amoy) *t'e,* from Ancient Chinese *d'a*]

tea bag *n* a small bag of paper or cloth containing tea leaves, infused in boiling water to make tea.

tea ball *n Chiefly U.S.* a perforated metal ball filled with tea leaves and put in boiling water to make tea.

teaberry ('tiːbərɪ, -brɪ) *n, pl* **-ries. 1** the berry of the wintergreen (*Gaultheria procumbens*). **2** another name for **wintergreen** (sense 1). [C19: so called because its dried leaves have been used as a substitute for tea]

tea biscuit *n Brit.* any of various semisweet biscuits.

teabread ('tiːˌbrɛd) *n* **1** a loaf-shaped cake that contains dried fruit which has been steeped in cold tea before baking: served sliced and buttered. **2** any of a variety of loaf-shaped, usually light, cakes: *banana teabread.*

tea break *n Brit.* a short rest period during working hours during which tea, coffee, etc. is drunk.

teacake ('tiːˌkeɪk) *n Brit.* a flat cake made from a yeast dough with raisins in it, usually eaten toasted and buttered.

teacart ('tiːˌkɑːt) *n* a U.S. and Canadian word for **tea trolley.**

teach (tiːtʃ) *vb* **teaches, teaching, taught. 1** (*tr; may take a clause as object or an infinitive;* often foll. by *how*) to help to learn; tell or show (how): *to teach someone to paint; to teach someone how to paint.* **2** to give instruction or lessons in (a subject) to (a person or animal): *to teach French; to teach children; she teaches.* **3** (*tr; may take a clause as object or an infinitive*) to cause to learn or understand: *experience taught him that he could not be a journalist.* **4** Also: **teach (someone) a lesson.** *Informal.* to cause (someone) to suffer the unpleasant consequences of some action or behaviour. **[**Old English *tǣcan;* related to *tācen* TOKEN, Old Frisian *tēken,* Old Saxon *tēkan,* Old High German *zeihhan,* Old Norse *teikn* sign**]** ▸ **ˈteachable** *adj*

Teach (tiːtʃ) *n* **Edward,** known as *Blackbeard.* died 1718, English pirate, active in the West Indies and on the Atlantic coast of North America.

teacher (ˈtiːtʃə) *n* **1** a person whose occupation is teaching others, esp. children. **2** a personified concept that teaches: *nature is a good teacher.* ▸ **ˈteacherless** *adj*

teachers' centre *n* (in Britain) a place that provides a central store of educational aids, such as films and display material, and also in-service training, and is available for use to all the teachers within a particular area.

teach-in *n* an informal conference, esp. on a topical subject, usually held at a university or college and involving a panel of visiting speakers, lecturers, students, etc.

teaching (ˈtiːtʃɪŋ) *n* **1** the art or profession of a teacher. **2** (*sometimes pl*) something taught; precept. **3** (*modifier*) denoting a person or institution that teaches: *a teaching hospital.* **4** (*modifier*) used in teaching: *teaching aids.*

teaching aid *n* any device, object, or machine used by a teacher to clarify or enliven a subject.

teaching fellow *n* a postgraduate student who is given tuition, accommodation, expenses, etc., in return for some teaching duties. ▸ **teaching fellowship** *n*

teaching hospital *n* a hospital that is affiliated to a medical school and provides the students with teaching and supervised practical experience.

teaching machine *n* a machine that presents information and questions to the user, registers the answers, and indicates whether these are correct or acceptable.

teaching practice *n* a temporary period of teaching in a school undertaken under supervision by a person who is training to become a teacher.

tea cloth *n* another name for **tea towel.**

tea cosy *n* a covering for a teapot to keep the contents hot, often having holes for the handle and spout.

teacup (ˈtiːˌkʌp) *n* **1** a cup out of which tea may be drunk, larger than a coffee cup. **2** Also called: **teacupful.** the amount a teacup will hold, about four fluid ounces.

tea dance *n* a dance held in the afternoon at which tea is served.

tea garden *n* **1** an open-air restaurant that serves tea and light refreshments. **2** a tea plantation.

tea gown *n* (formerly) a long loose decorative dress worn esp. when entertaining guests to afternoon tea.

teahouse (ˈtiːˌhaʊs) *n* a restaurant, esp. in Japan or China, where tea and light refreshments are served.

teak (tiːk) *n* **1** a large verbenaceous tree, *Tectona grandis,* of the East Indies, having white flowers and yielding a valuable wood. **2** the hard resinous yellowish-brown wood of this tree, used for furniture making, etc. **3** any of various similar trees or their wood. **4** a brown or yellowish-brown colour. **[C17:** from Portuguese *teca,* from Malayalam *tēkka***]**

teakettle (ˈtiːˌketᵊl) *n* a kettle for boiling water to make tea.

teal (tiːl) *n, pl* **teals** *or* **teal. 1** any of various small ducks, such as the Eurasian *Anas crecca* (**common teal**) that are related to the mallard and frequent ponds, lakes, and marshes. **2** a greenish-blue colour. **[C14:** related to Middle Low German *tēlink,* Middle Dutch *tēling***]**

tea lady *n* a woman employed in a factory, office, etc. to make tea during a tea break.

tea leaf *n* **1** the dried leaf of the tea shrub, used to make tea. **2** (*usually pl*) shredded parts of these leaves, esp. after infusion. **3** *Brit. and Austral. slang.* a thief. **[**sense 3 rhyming slang**]**

team (tiːm) *n* (*sometimes functioning as pl*) **1** a group of people organized to work together. **2** a group of players forming one of the sides in a sporting contest. **3** two or more animals working together to pull a vehicle or agricultural implement. **4** such animals and the vehicle: *the coachman riding his team.* **5** *Dialect.* a flock, herd, or brood. **6** *Obsolete.* ancestry. ◆ *vb* **7** (when *intr,* often foll. by *up*) to make or cause to make a team: *he teamed George with Robert.* **8** (*tr*) *U.S. and Canadian.* to drag or transport in or by a team. **9** (*intr*) *U.S. and Canadian.* to drive a team. **[**Old English *team* offspring; related to Old Frisian *tām* bridle, Old Norse *taumr* chain yoking animals together, Old High German *zoum* bridle**]**

tea-maker *n* a spoon with a perforated cover used to infuse tea in a cup of boiling water. Also called (esp. Brit.): **infuser, tea egg.**

team-mate *n* a fellow member of a team.

team spirit *n* willingness to cooperate as part of a team.

teamster (ˈtiːmstə) *n* **1** a driver of a team of horses used for haulage. **2** *U.S. and Canadian.* the driver of a lorry.

team teaching *n* a system whereby two or more teachers pool their skills, knowledge, etc., to teach combined classes.

teamwork (ˈtiːmˌwɜːk) *n* **1** the cooperative work done by a team. **2** the ability to work efficiently as a team.

tea party *n* a social gathering in the afternoon at which tea is served.

teapot (ˈtiːˌpɒt) *n* a container with a lid, spout, and handle, in which tea is made and from which it is served.

teapoy (ˈtiːpɔɪ) *n* **1** a small table or stand with a tripod base. **2** a tea caddy on such a table or stand. **[C19:** from Hindi *tipāī,* from Sanskrit *tri* three + *pāda* foot; compare Persian *sīpæ* three-legged stand**]**

tear[1] (tɪə) *n* **1** a drop of the secretion of the lacrimal glands. See **tears. 2** something shaped like a hanging drop: *a tear of amber.* ◆ Also called: **teardrop.** **[**Old English *tēar,* related to Old Frisian, Old Norse *tār,* Old High German *zahar,* Greek *dakri***]** ▸ **ˈtearless** *adj*

tear[2] (tɛə) *vb* **tears, tearing, tore, torn. 1** to cause (material, paper, etc.) to come apart or (of material, etc.) to come apart; rip. **2** (*tr*) to make (a hole or split) in (something): *to tear a hole in a dress.* **3** (*intr;* often foll. by *along*) to hurry or rush: *to tear along the street.* **4** (*tr;* usually foll. by *away* or *from*) to remove or take by force. **5** (when *intr,* often foll. by *at*) to cause pain, distress, or anguish (to): *it tore at my heartstrings to see the starving child.* **6 tear one's hair.** *Informal.* to be angry, frustrated, very worried, etc. ◆ *n* **7** a hole, cut, or split. **8** the act of tearing. **9** a great hurry; rush. ◆ See also **tear away, tear down, tear into, tear off, torn. [**Old English *teran;* related to Old Saxon *terian,* Gothic *gatairan* to destroy, Old High German *zeran* to destroy**]** ▸ **ˈtearable** *adj* ▸ **ˈtearer** *n*

tear away (tɛə) *vb* **1** (*tr, adv*) to persuade (oneself or someone else) to leave: *I couldn't tear myself away from the television.* ◆ *n* **tearaway. 2** *Brit.* **2a** a reckless impetuous unruly person. **2b** (*as modifier*): *a tearaway young man.*

tear down (tɛə) *vb* (*tr, adv*) to destroy or demolish: *to tear a wall down; to tear down an argument.*

tear duct (tɪə) *n* the nontechnical name for **lacrimal duct.**

tearful (ˈtɪəfʊl) *adj* **1** about to cry. **2** accompanying or indicative of weeping: *a tearful expression.* **3** tending to produce tears; sad. ▸ **ˈtearfully** *adv* ▸ **ˈtearfulness** *n*

tear gas (tɪə) *n* any one of a number of gases or vapours that make the eyes smart and water, causing temporary blindness; usually dispersed from grenades and used in warfare and to control riots. Also called: **lacrimator.**

tearing (ˈtɛərɪŋ) *adj* violent or furious (esp. in the phrase **tearing hurry** *or* **rush**).

tear into (tɛə) *vb* (*intr, prep*) *Informal.* to attack vigorously and damagingly.

tear-jerker (ˈtɪəˌdʒɜːkə) *n Informal.* an excessively sentimental film, play, book, etc.

tear off (tɛə) *vb* **1** (*tr*) to separate by tearing. **2** (*intr, adv*) to rush away; hurry. **3** (*tr, adv*) to produce in a hurry; do quickly and carelessly: *to tear off a letter.* **4 tear (someone) off a strip.** *Brit. informal.* to reprimand or rebuke (someone) forcibly. ◆ *adj* **tear-off. 5** (of paper, etc.) produced in a roll or block and marked with perforations so that one section at a time can be torn off.

tearoom (ˈtiːˌruːm, -ˌrʊm) *n* another name for **teashop.**

tea rose *n* **1** any of several varieties of hybrid rose that are derived from *Rosa odorata* and have pink or yellow flowers with a scent resembling that of tea. **2a** a yellowish-pink colour. **2b** (*as adj*): *tea-rose walls.*

tears (tɪəz) *pl n* **1** the clear salty solution secreted by the lacrimal glands that lubricates and cleanses the surface of the eyeball and inner surface of the eyelids. Related adj: **lachrymal. 2** a state of intense frustration (esp. in the phrase **bored to tears**). **3 in tears.** weeping. **4 without tears.** presented so as to be easily assimilated: *reading without tears.*

tear sheet (tɛə) *n* a page in a newspaper or periodical that is cut or perforated so that it can be easily torn out.

tease (tiːz) *vb* **1** to annoy (someone) by deliberately offering something with the intention of delaying or withdrawing the offer. **2** to arouse sexual desire in (someone) with no intention of satisfying it. **3** to vex (someone) maliciously or playfully, esp. by ridicule. **4** (*tr*) to separate the fibres of; comb; card. **5** (*tr*) to raise the nap of (a fabric) with a teasel. **6** another word (esp. U.S. and Canadian) for **backcomb. 7** (*tr*) to loosen or pull apart (biological tissues, etc.) by delicate agitation or prodding with an instrument. ◆ *n* **8** a person or thing that teases. **9** the act of teasing. ◆ See also **tease out. [**Old English *tǣsan;* related to Old High German *zeisan* to pick**]** ▸ **ˈteasing** *adj* ▸ **ˈteasingly** *adv*

teasel, teazel, *or* **teazle** (ˈtiːzəl) *n* **1** any of various stout biennial plants of the genus *Dipsacus,* of Eurasia and N Africa, having prickly leaves and prickly heads of yellow or purple flowers: family *Dipsacaceae.* See also **fuller's teasel. 2a** the prickly dried flower head of the fuller's teasel, used for teasing. **2b** any manufactured implement used for the same purpose. ◆ *vb* **-sels, -selling, -selled** *or U.S.* **-sels, -seling, -seled. 3** (*tr*) to tease (a fabric). **[**Old English *tǣsel;* related to Old High German *zeisala* teasel, Norwegian *tīsl* undergrowth, *tīsla* to tear to bits; see TEASE**]** ▸ **ˈteaseller** *n*

tease out *vb* (*tr, adv*) to extract (information) with difficulty.

teaser (ˈtiːzə) *n* **1** a person who teases. **2** a preliminary advertisement in a campaign that attracts attention by making people curious to know what product is being advertised. **3** a difficult question.

tea service *or* **set** *n* the china or pottery articles used in serving tea, including a teapot, cups, saucers, etc.

teashop (ˈtiːˌʃɒp) *n Brit.* a restaurant where tea and light refreshments are served. Also called: **tearoom.**

teaspoon (ˈtiːˌspuːn) *n* **1** a small spoon used for stirring tea, eating certain desserts, etc. **2** Also called: **teaspoonful** (ˈtiːˌspuːnfʊl). the amount contained in such a spoon. **3** a unit of capacity used in cooking, medicine, etc., equal to about one fluid dram.

teat (tiːt) *n* **1a** the nipple of a mammary gland. **1b** (in cows, etc.) any of the projections from the udder through which milk is discharged. See **nipple. 2** something resembling a teat in shape or function, such as the rubber mouthpiece of a feeding bottle. **[C13:** from Old French *tete,* of Germanic origin; compare Old English *titt,* Middle High German *zitze***]**

tea towel *or* **cloth** *n* a towel for drying dishes and kitchen utensils. U.S. name: **dishtowel.**

tea tree *n* any of various myrtaceous trees of the genus *Leptospermum,* of Australia and New Zealand, that yield an oil used as an antiseptic.

tea trolley *n Brit.* a trolley from which tea is served.

tea wagon *n* a U.S. and Canadian name for **tea trolley.**

Tebet (teˈvet) *n* a variant spelling of **Tevet.**

TEC (tɛk) *n acronym for* Training and Enterprise Council. See **Training Agency.**

tech (tɛk) *n Informal.* short for **technical college.**

tech. *abbrev. for:* **1** technical. **2** technology.

technetium (tɛk'niːʃɪəm) *n* a silvery-grey metallic element, artificially produced by bombardment of molybdenum by deuterons: used to inhibit corrosion in steel. The radioisotope **technetium-99m,** with a half-life of six hours, is used in radiotherapy. Symbol: Tc; atomic no.: 43; half-life of most stable isotope, ^{97}Tc: 2.6 × 10^6 years; valency: 0, 2, 4, 5, 6, or 7; relative density: 11.50 (calculated); melting pt.: 2204°C; boiling pt.: 4265°C. [C20: New Latin, from Greek *tekhnētos* manmade, from *tekhnasthai* to devise artificially, from *tekhnē* skill]

technic *n* **1** (tɛk'niːk). another word for **technique. 2** ('tɛknɪk). another word for **technics.** [C17: from Latin *technicus,* from Greek *tekhnikos,* from *tekhnē* art, skill]

technical ('tɛknɪk^{ə}l) *adj* **1** of, relating to, or specializing in industrial, practical, or mechanical arts and applied sciences: *a technical institute.* **2** skilled in practical and mechanical arts rather than theoretical or abstract thinking. **3** relating to or characteristic of a particular field of activity: *the technical jargon of linguistics.* **4** existing by virtue of a strict application of the rules or a strict interpretation of the wording: *a technical loophole in the law; a technical victory.* **5** of, derived from, or showing technique: *technical brilliance.* **6** (of a financial market) having prices determined by internal speculative or manipulative factors rather than by general or economic conditions: *a technical rally.* ► **'technically** *adv* ► **'technicalness** *n*

technical college *n Brit.* an institution for further education that provides courses in technology, art, secretarial skills, agriculture, etc. Sometimes shortened to (informal) **tech.**

technical drawing *n* the study and practice, esp. as a subject taught in school, of the basic techniques of draughtsmanship, as employed in mechanical drawing, architecture, etc. Abbrev.: **TD.**

technical institute *n N.Z.* a higher-education institution. Sometimes shortened to (informal): **tech.**

technicality (ˌtɛknɪ'kælɪtɪ) *n, pl* **-ties. 1** a petty formal point arising from a strict interpretation of rules, etc.: *the case was dismissed on a technicality.* **2** the state or quality of being technical. **3** technical methods and vocabulary.

technical knockout *n Boxing.* a judgment of a knockout given when a boxer is in the referee's opinion too badly beaten to continue without risk of serious injury.

technical sergeant *n* a noncommissioned officer in the U.S. Marine Corps or Air Force ranking immediately subordinate to a master sergeant.

technician (tɛk'nɪʃən) *n* **1** a person skilled in mechanical or industrial techniques or in a particular technical field. **2** a person employed in a laboratory, technical college, or scientific establishment to do practical work. **3** a person having specific artistic or mechanical skill, esp. if lacking original flair or genius.

Technicolor ('tɛknɪˌkʌlə) *n Trademark.* the process of producing colour film by means of superimposing synchronized films of the same scene, each of which has a different colour filter, to obtain the desired mix of colour.

technicolour ('tɛknɪˌkʌlə) *or* **technicoloured** ('tɛknɪˌkʌləd) *adj* brightly, showily, or garishly coloured; vividly noticeable.

technics ('tɛknɪks) *n* (*functioning as sing*) the study or theory of industry and industrial arts; technology.

technikon ('tɛknɪ'kɒn) *n S. African.* a technical college.

technique *or* **technic** (tɛk'niːk) *n* **1** a practical method, skill, or art applied to a particular task. **2** proficiency in a practical or mechanical skill. **3** special facility; knack: *he had the technique of turning everything to his advantage.* [C19: from French, from *technique* (adj) TECHNIC]

techno ('tɛknəʊ) *n* a type of very fast disco music, using electronic sounds and having a strong technological influence.

techno- *combining form.* **1** craft or art: *technology; technography.* **2** technological or technical: *technocracy.* **3** relating to or using technology: *technophobia.* [from Greek *tekhnē* skill]

technocracy (tɛk'nɒkrəsɪ) *n, pl* **-cies. 1** a theory or system of society according to which government is controlled by scientists, engineers, and other experts. **2** a body of such experts. **3** a state considered to be governed or organized according to these principles. ► **technocrat** ('tɛknəˌkræt) *n* ► ˌ**techno'cratic** *adj*

technography (tɛk'nɒgrəfɪ) *n* the study and description of the historical development of the arts and sciences in the context of their ethnic and geographical background.

technol. *abbrev. for:* **1** technological. **2** technology.

technology (tɛk'nɒlədʒɪ) *n, pl* **-gies. 1** the application of practical sciences to industry or commerce. **2** the methods, theory, and practices governing such application: *a highly developed technology.* **3** the total knowledge and skills available to any human society for industry, art, science, etc. [C17: from Greek *tekhnologia* systematic treatment, from *tekhnē* art, skill] ► **technological** (ˌtɛknə'lɒdʒɪk^{ə}l) *adj* ► ˌ**techno'logically** *adv* ► **tech'nologist** *n*

technology agreement *n* a framework designed by trade unions for negotiating changes in employment caused by the introduction of new technology.

technophobia (ˌtɛknəʊ'fəʊbɪə) *n* **1** fear of the effects of technological developments on society or the environment. **2** fear of using technological devices, such as computers. ► **technophobe** ('tɛknəˌfəʊb) *n*

technostructure ('tɛknəʊˌstrʌktʃə) *n* the people who control the technology of a society, such as professional administrators, experts in business management, etc.

techy ('tɛtʃɪ) *adj* **techier, techiest.** a variant spelling of **tetchy.** ► **'techily** *adv* ► **'techiness** *n*

tectibranch ('tɛktɪˌbræŋk) *n* a mollusc of the suborder *Tectibranchia* (or *Tectibranchiata*) (order: *Opisthobranchia*) which includes the sea slugs and sea hares. [C19: New Latin, from *tectus* covered, from *tegere* to cover + *branchia:* see -BRANCH]

tectonic (tɛk'tɒnɪk) *adj* **1** denoting or relating to construction or building. **2** *Geology.* **2a** (of landforms, rock masses, etc.) resulting from distortion of the earth's crust due to forces within it. **2b** (of processes, movements, etc.) occurring within the earth's crust and causing structural deformation. [C17: from Late Latin *tectonicus,* from Greek *tektonikos* belonging to carpentry, from *tektōn* a builder] ► **tec'tonically** *adv*

tectonics (tɛk'tɒnɪks) *n* (*functioning as sing*) **1** the art and science of construction or building. **2** the study of the processes by which the earth's surface has attained its present structure. See also **plate tectonics.**

tectorial membrane (tɛk'tɔːrɪəl) *n* the membrane in the inner ear that covers the organ of Corti. [C19: *tectorial,* from Latin *tectōrium* a covering, from *tegere* to cover]

tectrix ('tɛktrɪks) *n, pl* **tectrices** ('tɛktrɪˌsiːz, tɛk'traɪsiːz). (*usually pl*) *Ornithol.* another name for **covert** (sense 6). [C19: New Latin, from Latin *tector* plasterer, from *tegere* to cover] ► **tectricial** (tɛk'trɪʃəl) *adj*

Tecumseh (tɪ'kʌmsə) *n* ?1768–1813, American Indian chief of the Shawnee tribe. He attempted to unite western Indian tribes against the Whites, but was defeated at Tippecanoe (1811). He was killed while fighting for the British in the War of 1812.

ted[1] (tɛd) *vb* **teds, tedding, tedded.** to shake out and loosen (hay), so as to dry it. [C15: from Old Norse *tethja;* related to *tad* dung, Old High German *zetten* to spread]

ted[2] (tɛd) *n Informal.* short for **teddy boy.**

tedder ('tɛdə) *n* **1** a machine equipped with a series of small rotating forks for tedding hay. **2** a person who teds.

Tedder ('tɛdə) *n* **Arthur William,** 1st Baron Tedder of Glenguin. 1890–1967, British marshal of the Royal Air Force; deputy commander under Eisenhower of the Allied Expeditionary Force (1944–45).

teddy ('tɛdɪ) *n, pl* **-dies.** a woman's one-piece undergarment, incorporating a chemise top and panties.

teddy bear *n* a stuffed toy bear made from soft or fluffy material. Often shortened to **teddy.** [C20: from *Teddy,* from *Theodore,* after Theodore ROOSEVELT, who was well known as a hunter of bears]

teddy boy *n* **1** (in Britain, esp. in the mid-1950s) one of a cult of youths who wore mock Edwardian fashions, such as tight narrow trousers, pointed shoes, and long sideboards. Often shortened to **ted. 2** any tough or delinquent youth. [C20: from *Teddy,* from *Edward,* referring to the Edwardian dress]

teddy girl *n* a girl companion to a teddy boy.

Te Deum (ˌtiː 'diːəm) *n* **1** an ancient Latin hymn in rhythmic prose, sung or recited at matins in the Roman Catholic Church and in English translation at morning prayer in the Church of England and used by both Churches as an expression of thanksgiving on special occasions. **2** a musical setting of this hymn. **3** a service of thanksgiving in which the recital of this hymn forms a central part. [from the Latin canticle beginning *Tē Deum laudāmus,* literally: Thee, God, we praise]

tedious ('tiːdɪəs) *adj* **1** causing fatigue or tedium; monotonous. **2** *Obsolete.* progressing very slowly. ► **'tediously** *adv* ► **'tediousness** *n*

tedium ('tiːdɪəm) *n* the state of being bored or the quality of being boring; monotony. [C17: from Latin *taedium,* from *taedēre* to weary]

tee[1] (tiː) *n* **1** a pipe fitting in the form of a letter T, used to join three pipes. **2** a metal section with a cross section in the form of a letter T, such as a rolled-steel joist. **3** any part or component shaped like a T.

tee[2] (tiː) *Golf.* ◆ *n* **1** Also called: **teeing ground.** an area, often slightly elevated, from which the first stroke of a hole is made. **2** a support for a golf ball, usually a small wooden or plastic peg, used when teeing off or in long grass, etc. ◆ *vb* **tees, teeing, teed. 3** (when *intr,* often foll. by *up*) to position (the ball) ready for striking, on or as if on a tee. ◆ See also **tee off.** [C17 *teaz,* of unknown origin]

tee[3] (tiː) *n* a mark used as a target in certain games such as curling and quoits. [C18: perhaps from T-shaped marks, which may have originally been used in curling]

tee-hee *or* **te-hee** ('tiː'hiː) *interj* **1** an exclamation of laughter, esp. when mocking. ◆ *n* **2** a chuckle. ◆ *vb* **-hees, -heeing, -heed. 3** (*intr*) to snigger or laugh, esp. derisively. [C14: of imitative origin]

tee-joint *n* a variant spelling of **T-joint.**

teem[1] (tiːm) *vb* **1** (*intr;* usually foll. by *with*) to be prolific or abundant (in); abound (in). **2** *Obsolete.* to bring forth (young). [Old English *tēman* to produce offspring; related to West Saxon *tīeman;* see TEAM]

teem[2] (tiːm) *vb* **1** (*intr;* often foll. by *down* or *with rain*) to pour in torrents: *it's teeming down.* **2** (*tr*) to pour or empty out. [C15 *temen* to empty, from Old Norse *tœma;* related to Old English *tōm,* Old High German *zuomīg* empty] ► **'teemer** *n*

teen[1] (tiːn) *adj Informal.* another word for **teenage.**

teen[2] (tiːn) *n Obsolete.* affliction or woe. [Old English *tēona;* related to Old Saxon *tiono,* Old Frisian *tiona* injury]

-teen *n combining form.* ten: added to modified forms of the numbers 3 to 9 to form the numbers 13 to 19. [Old English *-tēne, -tȳne*] ► **-teenth** *adj combining form.*

teenage ('tiːnˌeɪdʒ) *adj also* **teenaged. 1** (*prenominal*) of or relating to the time in a person's life between the ages of 13 and 19 inclusive. ◆ *n* **2** this period of time.

teenager ('tiːnˌeɪdʒə) *n* a person between the ages of 13 and 19 inclusive.

teens (tiːnz) *pl n* **1** the years of a person's life between the ages of 13 and 19 inclusive. **2** all the numbers that end in *-teen.*

teeny ('ti:nɪ) *adj* **-nier, -niest.** *Informal.* extremely small; tiny. Also: **teeny-weeny** ('ti:nɪ'wi:nɪ) *or* **teensy-weensy** ('ti:nzɪ'wi:nzɪ). [C19: variant of TINY]

teenybopper ('ti:nɪ,bɒpə) *n Slang.* a young teenager, usually a girl, who avidly follows fashions in clothes and pop music. [C20: *teeny,* from TEENAGE + *-bopper* see BOP[1]]

tee off *vb* (*adv*) **1** *Golf.* to strike (the ball) from a tee, as when starting a hole. **2** *Informal.* to begin; start.

teepee ('ti:pi:) *n* a variant spelling of **tepee.**

tee-piece *n* a variant spelling of **T-piece.**

tee-plate *n* a variant spelling of **T-plate.**

Tees (ti:z) *n* a river in N England, rising in the N Pennines and flowing southeast and east to the North Sea at Middlesbrough. Length: 113 km (70 miles).

tee shirt *n* a variant of **T-shirt.**

tee-square *n* a variant spelling of **T-square.**

Teesside ('ti:z,saɪd) *n* the industrial region around the lower Tees valley and estuary: a county borough, containing Middlesbrough, from 1968 to 1974.

teeter ('ti:tə) *vb* **1** to move or cause to move unsteadily; wobble. ◆ *n, vb* **2** another word for **seesaw.** [C19: from Middle English *titeren,* related to Old Norse *titra* to tremble, Old High German *zittarōn* to shiver]

teeth (ti:θ) *n* **1** the plural of **tooth. 2** the most violent part: *the teeth of the gale.* **3** the power to produce a desired effect: *that law has no teeth.* **4 by the skin of one's teeth.** See **skin** (sense 14). **5 get one's teeth into.** to become engrossed in. **6 in the teeth of.** in direct opposition to; against: *in the teeth of violent criticism he went ahead with his plan.* **7 to the teeth.** to the greatest possible degree: *armed to the teeth.* **8 show one's teeth.** to threaten, esp. in a defensive manner.

teethe (ti:ð) *vb* (*intr*) to cut one's baby (deciduous) teeth.

teething ring *n* a plastic, hard rubber, or bone ring on which babies may bite while teething.

teething troubles *pl n* the difficulties or problems that arise during the initial stages of a project, enterprise, etc.

teetotal (ti:'təʊtᵊl) *adj* **1** of, relating to, or practising abstinence from alcoholic drink. **2** *Dialect.* complete. [C19: allegedly coined in 1833 by Richard Turner, English advocate of total abstinence from alcoholic liquors; probably from TOTAL, with emphatic reduplication] ▸ **tee'totaller** *n* ▸ **tee'totally** *adv* ▸ **tee'totalism** *n*

teetotum (ti:'təʊtəm) *n Archaic.* **1** a spinning top bearing letters of the alphabet on its four sides. **2** such a top used as a die in gambling games. [C18: from *T totum,* from *T* initial inscribed on one of the faces + *totum* the name of the toy, from Latin *tōtum* the whole]

tef *or* **teff** (tɛf) *n* an annual grass, *Eragrostis abyssinica,* of NE Africa, grown for its grain. [C18: from Amharic *tēf*]

tefillah *or* **tephillah** (tə'filə) *n, pl* **-lin** (-lin). *Judaism.* another name for **phylactery** (sense 1). [from Hebrew]

TEFL ('tɛfᵊl) *acronym for* Teaching (of) English as a Foreign Language.

Teflon ('tɛflɒn) *n* **1** a trademark for **polytetrafluoroethylene** when used in nonstick cooking vessels. ◆ *adj* **2** *Facetious.* denoting the ability to evade blame: *the Teflon president.*

teg (tɛg) *n* **1** a two-year-old sheep. **2** the fleece of a two-year-old sheep. [C16: of unknown origin]

tegmen ('tɛgmən) *n, pl* **-mina** (-mɪnə). **1** either of the leathery forewings of the cockroach and related insects. **2** the delicate inner covering of a seed. **3** any similar covering or layer. [C19: from Latin: a cover, variant of *tegimen,* from *tegere* to cover] ▸ **'tegminal** *adj*

Tegucigalpa (*Spanish* teɣuθi'ɣalpa) *n* the capital of Honduras, in the south on the Choluteca River: founded about 1579; university (1847). Pop.: 813 900 (1995 est.).

tegular ('tɛgjʊlə) *adj* **1** of, relating to, or resembling a tile or tiles. **2** *Biology.* overlapping like a series of tiles: *tegular scales.* [C18: from Latin *tēgula* a tile, from *tegere* to cover] ▸ **'tegularly** *adv*

tegument ('tɛgjʊmənt) *n* a less common word for **integument.** [C15: from Latin *tegumentum* a covering, from *tegere* to cover] ▸ **tegumental** (,tɛgjʊ'mɛntᵊl) *or* **,tegu'mentary** *adj*

te-hee ('ti:'hi:) *interj, n, vb* a variant spelling of **tee-hee.**

Tehran *or* **Teheran** (tɛə'rɑ:n, -'ræn) *n* the capital of Iran, at the foot of the Elburz Mountains: built on the site of the ancient capital Ray, destroyed by Mongols in 1220; became capital in the 1790s; three universities. Pop.: 11 000 000 (1994 est.).

Tehuantepec (tə'wɑ:ntə,pɛk) *n* **Isthmus of.** the narrowest part of S Mexico, with the Bay of Campeche on the north coast and the **Gulf of Tehuantepec** (an inlet of the Pacific) on the south coast.

Teide *or* **Teyde** (*Spanish* 'teiðe) *n* **Pico de** ('piko de). a volcanic mountain in the Canary Islands, on Tenerife. Height: 3718 m (12 198 ft.).

te igitur *Latin.* (teɪ 'ɪgɪ,tʊə; *English* teɪ 'ɪdʒɪ,tʊə) *n R.C. Church.* the first prayer of the canon of the Mass, which begins *Te igitur clementissime Pater* (*Thee, therefore, most merciful Father*).

Teilhard de Chardin (*French* tɛjar də ʃardɛ̃) *n* **Pierre** (pjɛr). 1881–1955, French Jesuit priest, palaeontologist, and philosopher. *The Phenomenon of Man* (1938–40), uses scientific evolution to prove the existence of God.

teind (ti:nd) *n, vb* a Scot. and northern English word for **tithe.**

Tejo ('təʒu) *n* the Portuguese name for the **Tagus.**

Te Kanawa (teɪ 'kɑ:nəwə) *n* Dame **Kiri** ('kɪrɪ). born 1944, New Zealand operatic soprano.

tektite ('tɛktaɪt) *n* a small dark glassy object found in several areas around the world, thought to be a product of meteorite impact. See also **moldavite.** [C20: from Greek *tēktos* molten]

tel. *abbrev. for:* **1** telegram. **2** telegraph(ic). **3** telephone.

tel- *combining form.* a variant of **tele-** and **telo-** before a vowel.

tela ('ti:lə) *n, pl* **-lae** (-li:). *Anatomy.* any delicate tissue or weblike structure. [from New Latin, from Latin: a web]

telaesthesia *or U.S.* **telesthesia** (,tɛlɪs'θi:zɪə) *n* the alleged perception of events that are beyond the normal range of perceptual processes. Compare **telegnosis, clairvoyance.** ▸ **telaesthetic** *or U.S.* **telesthetic** (,tɛlɪs'θɛtɪk) *adj*

telamon ('tɛləmən) *n, pl* **telamones** (,tɛlə'məʊni:z) *or* **-mons.** a column in the form of a male figure, used to support an entablature. Also called: **atlas.** Compare **caryatid.** [C18: via Latin from Greek, from *tlēnai* to bear]

Telamon ('tɛləmən, -,mɒn) *n Greek myth.* a king of Salamis; brother of Peleus and father of Teucer and Ajax.

Telanaipura (,tɛlənaɪ'pʊərə) *n* another name for **Jambi.**

telangiectasis (tɪ,lændʒɪ'ɛktəsɪs) *or* **telangiectasia** (tɪ,lændʒɪɛk'teɪzɪə) *n, pl* **-ses** (-,si:z). *Pathol.* an abnormal dilation of the capillaries or terminal arteries producing blotched red spots, esp. on the face or thighs. [C19: New Latin, from Greek *telos* end + *angeion* vessel + *ektasis* dilation] ▸ **telangiectatic** (tɪ,lændʒɪɛk'tætɪk) *adj*

Telautograph (tɛl'ɔ:tə,græf, -,grɑ:f) *n Trademark.* a telegraphic device for reproducing handwriting, drawings, etc., the movements of an electromagnetically controlled pen at one end being transmitted along a line to a similar pen at the receiving end. ▸ **tel,auto'graphic** *adj* ▸ **telautography** (,tɛlɔ:'tɒgrəfɪ) *n*

Tel Aviv ('tɛl ə'vi:v) *n* a city in W Israel, on the Mediterranean: the largest city and chief financial centre in Israel; incorporated the city of Jaffa in 1950; university (1953): the capital of Israel according to the UN and international law. Pop.: 355 900 (1997 est.). Official name: **Tel Aviv-Jaffa** ('tɛlə'vi:v'dʒæfə).

tele- *or before a vowel* **tel-** *combining form.* **1** at or over a distance; distant: *telescope; telegony; telekinesis; telemeter.* **2** television: *telecast.* **3** by means of or via telephone or television. [from Greek *tele* far]

telecast ('tɛlɪ,kɑ:st) *vb* **-casts, -casting, -cast** *or* **-casted. 1** to broadcast (a programme) by television. ◆ *n* **2** a television broadcast. ▸ **'tele,caster** *n*

telecine ('tɛlɪ,sɪnɪ) *n* apparatus for producing a television signal from cinematograph film.

telecom ('tɛlɪ,kɒm) *or* **telecoms** ('tɛlɪ,kɒmz) *n* (*functioning as sing*) short for **telecommunications.**

telecommunication (,tɛlɪkə,mju:nɪ'keɪʃən) *n* the telegraphic or telephonic communication of audio, video, or digital information over a distance by means of radio waves, optical signals, etc., or along a transmission line.

telecommunications (,tɛlɪkə,mju:nɪ'keɪʃənz) *n* (*functioning as sing*) the science and technology of communications by telephony, radio, television, etc.

telecommuting ('tɛlɪkə,mju:tɪŋ) *n* another name for **teleworking.** ▸ **'telecom,muter** *n*

teleconference ('tɛlɪ,kɒnfərəns) *n* a conference in which the participants communicate from different places via a telephone or video network.

telecottage ('tɛlɪ,kɒtɪdʒ) *n* a communal workplace, situated in a rural area, which contains computers and other facilities linked into a communications network, thereby enabling people to work from remote locations.

teledu ('tɛlɪ,du:) *n* a badger, *Mydaus javanensis,* of SE Asia and Indonesia, having dark brown hair with a white stripe along the back and producing a fetid secretion from the anal glands when attacked. [C19: from Malay]

téléférique (teɪleɪfeɪ'ri:k) *n* a variant spelling of **téléphérique.**

teleg. *abbrev. for:* **1** telegram. **2** telegraph(ic). **3** telegraphy.

telega (tɛ'leɪgə) *n* a rough four-wheeled cart used in Russia. [C16: from Russian]

telegenic (,tɛlɪ'dʒɛnɪk) *adj* having or showing a pleasant television image. [C20: from TELE(VISION) + (PHOTO)GENIC] ▸ **,tele'genically** *adv*

telegnosis (,tɛlə'nəʊsɪs, ,tɛləg-) *n* knowledge about distant events alleged to have been obtained without the use of any normal sensory mechanism. Compare **clairvoyance.** [C20: from TELE- + *-gnosis,* from Greek *gnōsis* knowledge] ▸ **telegnostic** (,tɛlə'nɒstɪk, ,tɛləg-) *adj*

Telegonus (tɪ'lɛgənəs) *n Greek myth.* a son of Odysseus and Circe, who sought his father and mistakenly killed him, later marrying Odysseus' widow Penelope.

telegony (tɪ'lɛgənɪ) *n Genetics.* the supposed influence of a previous sire on offspring borne by a female to other sires. [C19: from TELE- + -GONY. Compare Greek *tēlegonos* "born far from one's homeland"] ▸ **telegonic** (,tɛlɪ'gɒnɪk) *or* **te'legonous** *adj*

telegram ('tɛlɪ,græm) *n* a communication transmitted by telegraph. See also **cable** (sense 5), **Telemessage.** ▸ **telegrammatic** (,tɛlɪgrə'mætɪk) *or* **,tele'grammic** *adj*

telegraph ('tɛlɪ,græf, -,grɑ:f) *n* **1a** a device, system, or process by which information can be transmitted over a distance, esp. using radio signals or coded electrical signals sent along a transmission line connected to a transmitting and a receiving instrument. **1b** (*as modifier*): *telegraph pole.* **2** a message transmitted by such a device, system, or process; telegram. ◆ *vb* **3** to send a telegram to (a person or place); wire. **4** (*tr*) to transmit or send by telegraph. **5** (*tr*) *Boxing, informal.* to prepare to deliver (a punch) so obviously that one's opponent has ample time to avoid it. **6** (*tr*) to give advance notice of (anything), esp. unintentionally. **7** (*tr*) *Canadian informal.* to cast (votes) illegally by impersonating registered voters. ▸ **telegraphist** (tɪ'lɛgrəfɪst) *or* **te'legrapher** *n*

telegraphic (,tɛlɪ'græfɪk) *adj* **1** used in or transmitted by telegraphy. **2** of or relating to a telegraph. **3** having a concise style; clipped: *telegraphic speech.* ▸ **,tele'graphically** *adv*

telegraph plant *n* a small tropical Asian leguminous shrub, *Desmodium gyrans,* having small leaflets that turn in various directions during the day and droop at night.

telegraphy (tɪ'lɛgrəfɪ) *n* **1** a system of telecommunications involving any process providing reproduction at a distance of written, printed, or pictorial matter. See also **facsimile** (sense 2). **2** the skill or process of operating a telegraph.

Telegu ('tɛləˌguː) *n, adj* a variant spelling of **Telugu.**

telekinesis (ˌtɛlɪkɪ'niːsɪs, -kaɪ-) *n* **1** the movement of a body caused by thought or willpower without the application of a physical force. **2** the ability to cause such movement. ► **telekinetic** (ˌtɛlɪkɪ'nɛtɪk, -kaɪ-) *adj*

Telemachus (tɪ'lɛməkəs) *n Greek myth.* the son of Odysseus and Penelope, who helped his father slay his mother's suitors.

Telemann (*German* 'teːləman) *n* **Georg Philipp** ('geːɔrk 'fiːlɪp). 1681–1767, German composer, noted for his prolific output.

telemark ('tɛlɪˌmɑːk) *n* **1** *Skiing.* a turn in which one ski is placed far forward of the other and turned gradually inwards. **2** a step in ballroom dancing involving a heel pivot. [C20: named after *Telemark,* county in Norway]

telemarketing ('tɛlɪˌmɑːkɪtɪŋ) *n* another name for **telesales.** [C20: short for TELE(PHONE) MARKETING] ► '**teleˌmarketer** *n*

telemedicine ('tɛlɪˌmɛdɪsɪn, -ˌmɛdsɪn) *n* the treatment of disease or injury by consultation with a specialist in a distant place, esp. by means of a computer or satellite link.

Telemessage ('tɛlɪˌmɛsɪdʒ) *n Trademark.* a message sent by telephone or telex and delivered in printed form; in Britain, it has replaced the telegram.

telemeter (tɪ'lɛmɪtə) *n* **1** any device for recording or measuring a distant event and transmitting the data to a receiver or observer. **2** any device or apparatus used to measure a distance without directly comparing it with a measuring rod, etc., esp. one that depends on the measurement of angles. ◆ *vb* **3** (*tr*) to obtain and transmit (data) from a distant source, esp. from a spacecraft. ► **telemetric** (ˌtɛlɪ'mɛtrɪk) *or* ˌ**tele'metrical** *adj* ► ˌ**tele'metrically** *adv*

telemetry (tɪ'lɛmɪtrɪ) *n* **1** the use of radio waves, telephone lines, etc., to transmit the readings of measuring instruments to a device on which the readings can be indicated or recorded. See also **radiotelemetry. 2** the measurement of linear distance using a tellurometer.

telencephalon (ˌtɛlɛn'sɛfəˌlɒn) *n* the cerebrum together with related parts of the hypothalamus and the third ventricle. ► **telencephalic** (ˌtɛlɛnsɪ'fælɪk) *adj*

teleological argument *n Philosophy.* the argument purporting to prove the existence of God from empirical facts, the premise being that the universe shows evidence of order and hence design. Also called: **argument from design.** Compare **ontological argument, cosmological argument.**

teleology (ˌtɛlɪ'ɒlədʒɪ, ˌtiːlɪ-) *n* **1** *Philosophy.* **1a** the doctrine that there is evidence of purpose or design in the universe, and esp. that this provides proof of the existence of a Designer. **1b** the belief that certain phenomena are best explained in terms of purpose rather than cause. **1c** the systematic study of such phenomena. ◆ See also **final cause. 2** *Biology.* the belief that natural phenomena have a predetermined purpose and are not determined by mechanical laws. [C18: from New Latin *teleologia,* from Greek *telos* end + -LOGY] ► **teleological** (ˌtɛlɪə'lɒdʒɪkᵊl, ˌtiːlɪ-) *or* ˌ**teleo'logic** *adj* ► ˌ**teleo'logically** *adv* ► ˌ**tele'ologism** *n* ► ˌ**tele'ologist** *n*

teleost ('tɛlɪˌɒst, 'tiːlɪ-) *n* **1** any bony fish of the subclass *Teleostei,* having rayed fins and a swim bladder: the group contains most of the bony fishes, including the herrings, carps, eels, cod, perches, etc. ◆ *adj* **2** of, relating to, or belonging to the *Teleostei.* [C19: from New Latin *teleosteī* (pl) creatures having complete skeletons, from Greek *teleos* complete + *osteon* bone]

telepath ('tɛlɪˌpæθ) *n* **1** a person who is telepathic. ◆ *vb* (*intr*) **2** to practise telepathy.

telepathize *or* **telepathise** (tɪ'lɛpəˌθaɪz) *vb* (*intr*) to practise telepathy.

telepathy (tɪ'lɛpəθɪ) *n Psychol.* the communication between people of thoughts, feelings, desires, etc., involving mechanisms that cannot be understood in terms of known scientific laws. Also called: **thought transference.** Compare **telegnosis, clairvoyance.** [C19: from TELE- + Greek *patheia* feeling, perception: see -PATHY] ► **telepathic** (ˌtɛlɪ'pæθɪk) *adj* ► ˌ**tele'pathically** *adv* ► **te'lepathist** *n*

téléphérique *or* **téléférique** (teɪleɪfeɪ'riːk) *n* **1** a mountain cable car. **2** a cableway. [C20: from French]

telephone ('tɛlɪˌfəʊn) *n* **1a** Also called: **telephone set.** an electrical device for transmitting speech, consisting of a microphone and receiver mounted on a handset. **1b** (*as modifier*): *a telephone receiver.* **2a** a worldwide system of communications using telephones. The microphone in one telephone converts sound waves into electrical signals that are transmitted along a telephone wire or by radio to one or more distant sets, the receivers of which reconvert the incoming signal into the original sound. **2b** (*as modifier*): *a telephone exchange; a telephone call.* **3** See **telephone box.** ◆ *vb* **4** to call or talk to (a person) by telephone. **5** to transmit (a recorded message, radio or television programme, or other information) by telephone, using special transmitting and receiving equipment. ◆ Often shortened to **phone.** ► '**teleˌphoner** *n* ► **telephonic** (ˌtɛlɪ'fɒnɪk) *adj* ► ˌ**tele'phonically** *adv*

telephone answering machine *n* the full name for **answering machine.**

telephone banking *n* a facility enabling customers to make use of banking services, such as oral payment instructions, account movements, raising loans, etc., over the telephone rather than by personal visit.

telephone box *n* an enclosure from which a paid telephone call can be made. Also called: **telephone kiosk, telephone booth.**

telephone directory *n* a book listing the names, addresses, and telephone numbers of subscribers in a particular area.

telephone number *n* **1** a set of figures identifying the telephone of a particular subscriber, and used in making connections to that telephone. **2** (*pl*) extremely large numbers, esp. in reference to salaries or prices.

telephone selling *n* another name for **telesales.**

telephonist (tɪ'lɛfənɪst) *n Brit.* a person who operates a telephone switchboard. Also called (esp. U.S.): **telephone operator.**

telephony (tɪ'lɛfənɪ) *n* a system of telecommunications for the transmission of speech or other sounds.

telephotography (ˌtɛlɪfə'tɒgrəfɪ) *n* the process or technique of photographing distant objects using a telephoto lens. ► **telephotographic** (ˌtɛlɪˌfəʊtə'græfɪk) *adj*

telephoto lens ('tɛlɪˌfəʊtəʊ) *n* a compound camera lens in which the focal length is greater than that of a simple lens of the same dimensions and thus produces a magnified image of a distant object. See also **zoom lens.**

teleport ('tɛlɪˌpɔːt) *vb* (*tr*) to move by means of telekinesis. [C20: from TELE- + PORT[5]]

teleprinter ('tɛlɪˌprɪntə) *n* **1** a telegraph apparatus consisting of a keyboard transmitter, which converts a typed message into coded pulses for transmission along a wire or cable, and a printing receiver, which converts incoming signals and prints out the message. U.S. name: **teletypewriter.** See also **telex, radioteletype. 2** a network of such devices, formerly used for communicating information, etc. **3** a similar device used for direct input/output of data into a computer at a distant location.

teleprocessing (ˌtɛlɪ'prəʊsɛsɪŋ) *n* the use of remote computer terminals connected to a central computer to process data.

Teleprompter ('tɛlɪˌprɒmptə) *n Trademark.* the U.S. and Canadian name for **Autocue.**

Teleran ('tɛləˌræn) *n Trademark.* an electronic navigational aid in which the image of a ground-based radar system is televised to aircraft in flight so that a pilot can see the position of his aircraft in relation to others. [C20: from *Tele(vision) R(adar) A(ir) N(avigation)*]

telerecording (ˌtɛlɪrɪ'kɔːdɪŋ) *n* the recording of television signals on tape or, more usually, on film.

telesales ('tɛlɪˌseɪlz) *n* (*functioning as sing*) the selling or attempted selling of a particular commodity or service by a salesman who makes his initial approach by telephone. Also called: **telemarketing, telephone selling.**

telescience ('tɛlɪˌsaɪəns) *n Astronautics.* the investigation of remotely controlled scientific experiments.

telescope ('tɛlɪˌskəʊp) *n* **1** an optical instrument for making distant objects appear closer by use of a combination of lenses (**refracting telescope**) or lenses and curved mirrors (**reflecting telescope**). See also **terrestrial telescope, astronomical telescope, Cassegrain telescope, Galilean telescope, Newtonian telescope. 2** any instrument, such as a radio telescope, for collecting, focusing, and detecting electromagnetic radiation from space. ◆ *vb* **3** to crush together or be crushed together, as in a collision: *the front of the car was telescoped by the impact.* **4** to fit together like a set of cylinders that slide into one another, thus allowing extension and shortening. **5** to make or become smaller or shorter: *the novel was telescoped into a short play.* [C17: from Italian *telescopio* or New Latin *telescopium,* literally: far-seeing instrument; see TELE-, -SCOPE]

telescopic (ˌtɛlɪ'skɒpɪk) *adj* **1** of or relating to a telescope. **2** seen through or obtained by means of a telescope. **3** visible only with the aid of a telescope. **4** able to see far. **5** having or consisting of parts that telescope: *a telescopic umbrella.* ► ˌ**tele'scopically** *adv*

telescopic sight *n* a telescope mounted on a rifle, etc., used for sighting.

Telescopium (ˌtɛlɪ'skəʊpɪəm) *n, Latin genitive* **Telescopii** (ˌtɛlɪ'skəʊpɪˌaɪ). an inconspicuous constellation in the S hemisphere, close to Sagittarius and Ara. [New Latin; see TELESCOPE]

telescopy (tɪ'lɛskəpɪ) *n* the branch of astronomy concerned with the use and design of telescopes.

telesis ('tɛlɪsɪs) *n* the purposeful use of natural and social processes to obtain specific social goals. [C19: from Greek: event, from *telein* to fulfil, from *telos* end]

telesoftware (ˌtɛlɪ'sɒftwɛə) *n* the transmission of computer programs on a teletext system.

telespectroscope (ˌtɛlɪ'spɛktrəˌskəʊp) *n* a combination of a telescope and a spectroscope, used for spectroscopic analysis of radiation from stars and other celestial bodies.

telestereoscope (ˌtɛlɪ'stɪərɪəˌskəʊp, -'stɛrɪə-) *n* an optical instrument for obtaining stereoscopic images of distant objects.

telesthesia (ˌtɛlɪs'θiːzɪə) *n* the usual U.S. spelling of **telaesthesia.** ► **telesthetic** (ˌtɛlɪs'θɛtɪk) *adj*

telestich (tɪ'lɛstɪk, 'tɛlɪˌstɪk) *n* a short poem in which the last letters of each successive line form a word. [C17: from Greek *telos* end + STICH]

teletex ('tɛlɪˌtɛks) *n* an international means of communicating text between a variety of terminals.

Teletext ('tɛlɪˌtɛkst) *n Trademark.* a form of Videotex in which information is broadcast by a television station and received on an adapted television set. **Ceefax** is provided by the BBC and **Oracle** by ITV.

telethon ('tɛləˌθɒn) *n* a lengthy television programme to raise charity funds, etc. [C20: from TELE- + MARATHON]

Teletype ('tɛlɪˌtaɪp) *n* **1** *Trademark.* a type of teleprinter. **2** (*sometimes not cap.*) a network of such devices, used for communicating messages, information, etc. ◆ *vb* **3** (*sometimes not cap.*) to transmit (a message) by Teletype.

Teletypesetter (ˌtɛlɪ'taɪpˌsɛtə, 'tɛlɪˌtaɪp-) *n Trademark, printing.* a keyboard device whose output can either be punched tape, which can be used directly to operate a line-casting machine, or be transmitted by cable or wire to operate such a machine indirectly. ► ˌ**tele'typeˌsetting** *n*

teletypewriter (ˌtɛlɪ'taɪpˌraɪtə, 'tɛlɪˌtaɪp-) *n* a U.S. name for **teleprinter.**

teleutospore (tɪ'luːtəˌspɔː) *n* another name for **teliospore.** [C19: from Greek *teleutē,* from *telos* end + SPORE] ► **teˌleuto'sporic** *adj*

televangelist (ˌtɛlɪ'vændʒəlɪst) *n U.S.* an evangelical preacher who appears regularly on television, preaching the gospel and appealing for donations from viewers. [C20: from TELE(VISION + E)VANGELIST]

televise ('tɛlɪˌvaɪz) *vb* **1** to put (a programme) on television. **2** (*tr*) to transmit (a programme, signal, etc.) by television.

television ('tɛlɪˌvɪʒən) *n* **1** the system or process of producing on a distant screen a series of transient visible images, usually with an accompanying sound signal. Electrical signals, converted from optical images by a camera tube, are transmitted by UHF or VHF radio waves or by cable and reconverted into optical images by means of a television tube inside a television set. **2** Also called: **television set.** a device designed to receive and convert incoming electrical signals into a series of visible images on a screen together with accompanying sound. **3** the content, etc., of television programmes. **4** the occupation or profession concerned with any aspect of the broadcasting of television programmes: *he's in television.* **5** (*modifier*) of, relating to, or used in the transmission or reception of video and audio UHF or VHF radio signals: *a television transmitter.* ◆ Abbrev.: **TV** [C20: from TELE- + VISION] ► **ˌtele'visional** *adj* ► **ˌtele'visionally** *adv* ► **ˌtele'visionary** *adj*

television tube *n* a cathode-ray tube designed for the reproduction of television pictures. Sometimes shortened to **tube.** Also called: **picture tube.**

televisual (ˌtɛlɪ'vɪʒuəl, -zju-) *adj* relating to, shown on, or suitable for production on television. ► **ˌtele'visually** *adv*

teleworking ('tɛlɪˌwɜːkɪŋ) *n* the use of home computers, telephones, etc., to enable a person to work from home while maintaining contact with colleagues, customers, or a central office. Also called: **telecommuting.** ► **'teleˌworker** *n*

telewriter ('tɛlɪˌraɪtə) *n* a telegraphic device for reproducing handwriting by converting the manually controlled movements of a pen into signals that, after transmission, control the movements of a similar pen.

telex ('tɛlɛks) *n* **1** an international telegraph service in which teleprinters are rented out to subscribers for the purpose of direct communication. **2** a teleprinter used in such a service. **3** a message transmitted or received by telex. ◆ *vb* **4** to transmit (a message) to (a person, office, etc.) by telex. [C20: from *tel(eprinter) ex(change)*]

telfer ('tɛlfə) *n* a variant spelling of **telpher.**

telferage ('tɛlfərɪdʒ) *n* a variant spelling of **telpherage.**

Telford[1] ('tɛlfəd) *n* a town in W central England, in Shropshire: designated a new town in 1963. Pop.: 119 340 (1991).

Telford[2] ('tɛlfəd) *n* **Thomas.** 1757–1834, Scottish civil engineer, known esp. for his roads and such bridges as the Menai suspension bridge (1825).

Telford and Wrekin *n* a unitary authority in W Central England, in Shropshire. Pop.: 144 200 (1996 est.). Area: 289 sq. km (112 sq. miles).

telic ('tɛlɪk) *adj* **1** directed or moving towards some goal; purposeful. **2** (of a clause or phrase) expressing purpose. [C19: from Greek *telikos* final, from *telos* end]

Telidon ('tɛlɪˌdɒn) *n Trademark.* a Canadian interactive viewdata service.

teliospore ('tiːlɪəˌspɔː) *n* any of the dark noninfective spores that are produced in each telium of the rust fungi and remain dormant during the winter. Also called: **teleutospore.** [C20: from TELIUM + SPORE]

telium ('tiːlɪəm, 'tɛl-) *n, pl* **telia** ('tiːlɪə, 'tɛlɪə). the spore-producing body of some rust fungi in which the teliospores are formed. [C20: New Latin, from Greek *teleion,* from *teleios* complete, from *telos* end] ► **'telial** *adj*

tell[1] (tɛl) *vb* **tells, telling, told. 1** (when *tr, may take a clause as object*) to let know or notify: *he told me that he would go.* **2** (*tr*) to order or instruct (someone to do something): *I told her to send the letter airmail.* **3** (when *intr,* usually foll. by *of*) to give an account or narration (of something): *she told me her troubles.* **4** (*tr*) to communicate by words; utter: *to tell the truth.* **5** (*tr*) to make known; disclose: *to tell fortunes.* **6** (*intr;* often foll. by *of*) to serve as an indication: *her blush told of her embarrassment.* **7** (*tr;* used with *can,* etc.; *may take a clause as object*) to comprehend, discover, or discern: *I can tell what is wrong.* **8** (*tr;* used with *can,* etc.) to distinguish or discriminate: *he couldn't tell chalk from cheese.* **9** (*intr*) to have or produce an impact, effect, or strain: *every step told on his bruised feet.* **10** (*intr;* sometimes foll. by *on*) *Informal.* to reveal secrets or gossip (about): *don't tell! she told on him.* **11** (*tr*) to assure: *I tell you, I've had enough!* **12** (*tr*) to count (votes). **13** (*intr*) *Dialect.* to talk or chatter. **14 tell it like it is.** *Informal, chiefly U.S.* to tell the truth no matter how unpleasant it is. **15 tell the time.** to read the time from a clock. **16 you're telling me.** *Slang.* I know that very well. ◆ See also **tell apart, tell off.** [Old English *tellan;* related to Old Saxon *tellian,* Old High German *zellen* to tell, count, Old Norse *telja*] ► **'tellable** *adj*

tell[2] (tɛl) *n* a large mound resulting from the accumulation of rubbish on a long-settled site, esp. one with mudbrick buildings, particularly in the Middle East. [C19: from Arabic *tall*]

Tell (tɛl) *n* **William,** German name *Wilhelm Tell.* a legendary Swiss patriot, who, traditionally, lived in the early 14th century and was compelled by an Austrian governor to shoot an apple from his son's head with one shot of his crossbow. He did so without mishap.

tell apart *vb* (*tr, adv*) to distinguish between; discern: *can you tell the twins apart?*

Tell el Amarna ('tɛl ɛl ə'mɑːnə) *n* a group of ruins and rock tombs in Upper Egypt, on the Nile below Asyut: site of the capital of Amenhotep IV, built about 1375 B.C.; excavated from 1891 onwards.

teller ('tɛlə) *n* **1** another name for **cashier**[1] (sense 2). **2** a person appointed to count votes in a legislative body, assembly, etc. **3** a person who tells; narrator. ► **'tellerˌship** *n*

Teller ('tɛlə) *n* **Edward.** born 1908, U.S. nuclear physicist, born in Hungary: a major contributor to the development of the hydrogen bomb (1952).

tellin ('tɛlɪn) *n* any of various slim marine bivalve molluscs of the genus *Tellina* (or *Macoma*) that live in intertidal sand, esp. the smooth oval delicately tinted *T. tenuis.* [from New Latin *tellina,* from Greek *tellinē* a shellfish]

telling ('tɛlɪŋ) *adj* **1** having a marked effect or impact: *a telling blow.* **2** revealing: *a telling smile.* ► **'tellingly** *adv*

tell off *vb* (*tr, adv*) **1** *Informal.* to reprimand; scold: *they told me off for stealing apples.* **2** to count and dismiss: *he told off four more soldiers.* ► **telling off** *or* **telling-off** *n*

telltale ('tɛlˌteɪl) *n* **1** a person who tells tales about others. **2a** an outward indication of something concealed. **2b** (*as modifier*): *a telltale paw mark.* **3** any of various indicators or recording devices used to monitor a process, machine, etc. **4** *Nautical.* **4a** another word for **dogvane. 4b** one of a pair of light vanes mounted on the main shrouds of a sailing boat to indicate the apparent direction of the wind.

tellurate ('tɛljuˌreɪt) *n* any salt or ester of telluric acid.

tellurian (tɛ'lʊərɪən) *adj* **1** of or relating to the earth. ◆ *n* **2** (esp. in science fiction) an inhabitant of the earth. [C19: from Latin *tellūs* the earth]

telluric[1] (tɛ'lʊərɪk) *adj* **1** of, relating to, or originating on or in the earth or soil; terrestrial. **2** *Astronomy.* (of spectral lines or bands) observed in the spectra of celestial objects and caused by oxygen, water vapour, and carbon dioxide in the earth's atmosphere. [C19: from Latin *tellūs* the earth]

telluric[2] (tɛ'lʊərɪk) *adj* of or containing tellurium, esp. in a high valence state. [C20: from TELLUR(IUM) + -IC]

telluric acid *n* a white crystalline dibasic acid produced by the oxidation of tellurium by hydrogen peroxide. Formula: H_6TeO_6.

telluride ('tɛljuˌraɪd) *n* any compound of tellurium, esp. one formed between tellurium and a more electropositive element or group.

tellurion *or* **tellurian** (tɛ'lʊərɪən) *n* an instrument that shows how day and night and the seasons result from the tilt of the earth, its rotation on its axis, and its revolution around the sun. [C19: from Latin *tellūs* the earth]

tellurite ('tɛljuˌraɪt) *n* any salt or ester of tellurous acid.

tellurium (tɛ'lʊərɪəm) *n* a brittle silvery-white nonmetallic element occurring both uncombined and in combination with metals: used in alloys of lead and copper and as a semiconductor. Symbol: Te; atomic no.: 52; atomic wt.: 127.60; valency: 2, 4, or 6; relative density: 6.24; melting pt.: 449.57±0.3°C; boiling pt.: 988°C. [C19: New Latin, from Latin *tellūs* the earth, formed by analogy with URANIUM]

tellurize *or* **tellurise** ('tɛljuˌraɪz) *vb* (*tr*) to mix or combine with tellurium.

tellurometer (ˌtɛlju'rɒmɪtə) *n Surveying.* an electronic instrument for measuring distances of up to about 30 miles that consists of two units, one at each end of the distance to be measured, between which radio waves are transmitted. [C20: from Latin *tellūs* the earth + -METER]

tellurous ('tɛljurəs, tɛ'lʊərəs) *adj* of or containing tellurium, esp. in a low valence state.

Tellus ('tɛləs) *n* the Roman goddess of the earth; protectress of marriage, fertility, and the dead.

telly ('tɛlɪ) *n, pl* **-lies.** *Informal, chiefly Brit.* short for **television.**

telo- *or before a vowel* **tel-** *combining form.* **1** complete; final; perfect: *telophase.* **2** end; at the end: *telencephalon.* [from Greek *telos* end]

telocentric (ˌtɛlə'sɛntrɪk) *adj Genetics.* (of a chromosome) having the centromere at or close to the end.

telomerization *or* **telomerisation** (tɛˌlɒmərar'zeɪʃən) *n Chem.* polymerization in the presence of a chain transfer agent to yield a series of products of low molecular weight. [C20: from TELO- + -MER]

telophase ('tɛləˌfeɪz) *n* **1** the final stage of mitosis, during which the chromosomes at each end of the cell are dispersed into nuclear material and a nuclear membrane forms around the two new nuclei. See also **prophase, metaphase, anaphase. 2** the corresponding stage of the first division of meiosis. ► **ˌtelo'phasic** *adj*

telpher *or* **telfer** ('tɛlfə) *n* **1** a load-carrying car in a telpherage. **2a** another word for **telpherage. 2b** (*as modifier*): *a telpher line; a telpher system.* ◆ *vb* **3** (*tr*) to transport (a load) by means of a telpherage. [C19: changed from *telephore,* from TELE- + -PHORE] ► **'telpheric** *or* **'telferic** *adj*

telpherage *or* **telferage** ('tɛlfərɪdʒ) *n* an overhead transport system in which an electrically driven truck runs along a single rail or cable, the load being suspended in a separate car beneath. Also called: **telpher line, telpher.**

telson ('tɛlsən) *n* the last segment or an appendage on the last segment of the body of crustaceans and arachnids. [C19: from Greek: a boundary; probably related to *telos* end] ► **telsonic** (tɛl'sɒnɪk) *adj*

Telstar ('tɛlˌstɑː) *n* either of two low-altitude active communications satellites launched in 1962 and 1963 by the U.S. and used in the transmission of television programmes, telephone messages, etc.

Telugu *or* **Telegu** ('tɛləˌguː) *n* **1** a language of SE India, belonging to the Dravidian family of languages: the state language of Andhra Pradesh. **2** (*pl* **-gus** *or* **-gu**) a member of the people who speak this language. ◆ *adj* **3** of or relating to this people or their language.

Telukbetung *or* **Teloekbetoeng** (təˌlukbə'tuŋ) *n* a port in Indonesia, in S Sumatra on the Sunda Strait. Pop.: 284 275 (1980).

Tema ('tiːmə) *n* a port in SE Ghana on the Atlantic: new harbour opened in 1962; oil-refining. Pop.: 110 000 (1988 est.).

temazepam (tə'mæzəˌpæm) *n* a sedative in the form of a gel-like capsule, which is taken orally or melted and injected by drug users.

Témbi ('tɛmbiː) *n* transliteration of the Modern Greek name for **Tempe.**

temblor ('tɛmblə, -blɔː) *n, pl* **temblors** *or* **temblores** (tɛm'blɔːreɪz). *Chiefly U.S.* an earthquake or earth tremor. [C19: American Spanish, from Spanish *temblar* to shake, tremble]

temerity (tɪ'mɛrɪtɪ) *n* rashness or boldness. [C15: from Latin *temeritās* accident, from *temere* at random] ► **temerarious** (ˌtɛmə'rɛərɪəs) *adj*

Temesvár ('tɛmɛʃvaːr) *n* the Hungarian name for **Timişoara.**

Temne ('tɛmnɪ, 'tɪm-) *n* **1** (*pl* **-nes** *or* **-ne**) a member of a Negroid people of N Sierra Leone. **2** the language of this people, closely related to Bantu.

temp (tɛmp) *Informal.* ◆ *n* **1** a person, esp. a typist or other office worker, employed on a temporary basis. ◆ *vb* (*intr*) **2** to work as a temp.

temp. *abbrev. for:* **1** temperate. **2** temperature. **3** temporary. **4** tempore. [Latin: in the time of]

Tempe ('tɛmpɪ) *n* **Vale of.** a wooded valley in E Greece, in Thessaly between the mountains Olympus and Ossa. Modern Greek name: **Témbi.**

temper ('tɛmpə) *n* **1** a frame of mind; mood or humour: *a good temper.* **2** a sudden outburst of anger; tantrum. **3** a tendency to exhibit uncontrolled anger; irritability. **4** a mental condition of moderation and calm (esp. in the phrases **keep one's temper, lose one's temper, out of temper**). **5** the degree of hardness, elasticity, or a similar property of a metal or metal object. ◆ *vb* (*tr*) **6** to make more temperate, acceptable, or suitable by adding something else; moderate: *he tempered his criticism with kindly sympathy.* **7** to strengthen or toughen (a metal or metal article) by heat treatment, as by heating and quenching. **8** *Music.* **8a** to adjust the frequency differences between the notes of a scale on (a keyboard instrument) in order to allow modulation into other keys. **8b** to make such an adjustment to the pitches of notes in (a scale). **9** a rare word for **adapt. 10** an archaic word for **mix.** [Old English *temprian* to mingle, (influenced by Old French *temprer*), from Latin *temperāre* to mix, probably from *tempus* time] ► **'temperable** *adj* ► **,tempera'bility** *n* ► **'temperer** *n*

tempera ('tɛmpərə) *n* **1** a painting medium for powdered pigments, consisting usually of egg yolk and water. **2a** any emulsion used as a painting medium, with casein, glue, wax, etc., as a base. **2b** the paint made from mixing this with pigment. **3** the technique of painting with tempera. [C19: from Italian phrase *pingere a tempera* painting in tempera, from *temperare* to mingle; see TEMPER]

temperament ('tɛmpərəmənt, -prəmənt) *n* **1** an individual's character, disposition, and tendencies as revealed in his reactions. **2** excitability, moodiness, or anger, esp. when displayed openly: *an actress with temperament.* **3** the characteristic way an individual behaves, esp. towards other people. See also **character, personality. 4a** an adjustment made to the frequency differences between notes on a keyboard instrument to allow modulation to other keys. **4b** any of several systems of such adjustment, such as **just temperament,** a system not practically possible on keyboard instruments (see **just intonation**), **meantone temperament,** a system giving an approximation to natural tuning, and **equal temperament,** the system commonly used in keyboard instruments, giving a scale based on an octave divided into twelve exactly equal semitones. **5** *Obsolete.* the characteristic way an individual behaves, viewed as the result of the influence of the four humours (blood, phlegm, yellow bile, and black bile). **6** *Archaic.* compromise or adjustment. **7** an obsolete word for **temperature.** [C15: from Latin *temperāmentum* a mixing in proportion, from *temperāre* to TEMPER]

temperamental (,tɛmpərə'mɛntəl, -prə'mɛntəl) *adj* **1** easily upset or irritated; excitable; volatile. **2** of, relating to, or caused by temperament. **3** *Informal.* working erratically and inconsistently; unreliable: *a temperamental sewing machine.* ► **,tempera'mentally** *adv*

temperance ('tɛmpərəns) *n* **1** restraint or moderation, esp. in yielding to one's appetites or desires. **2** abstinence from alcoholic drink. [C14: from Latin *temperantia,* from *temperāre* to regulate]

temperate ('tɛmpərɪt, 'tɛmprɪt) *adj* **1** having a climate intermediate between tropical and polar; moderate or mild in temperature. **2** mild in quality or character; exhibiting temperance. [C14: from Latin *temperātus*] ► **'temperately** *adv* ► **'temperateness** *n*

Temperate Zone *n* those parts of the earth's surface lying between the Arctic Circle and the tropic of Cancer and between the Antarctic Circle and the tropic of Capricorn.

temperature ('tɛmprɪtʃə) *n* **1** the degree of hotness of a body, substance, or medium; a physical property related to the average kinetic energy of the atoms or molecules of a substance. **2** a measure of this degree of hotness, indicated on a scale that has one or more fixed reference points. **3** *Informal.* a body temperature in excess of the normal. **4** *Archaic.* **4a** compromise. **4b** temperament. **4c** temperance. [C16 (originally: a mingling): from Latin *temperātūra* proportion, from *temperāre* to TEMPER]

temperature gradient *n* the rate of change in temperature in a given direction, esp. in altitude.

temperature-humidity index *n* an index of the effect on human comfort of temperature and humidity levels, 65 being the highest comfortable level.

temperature inversion *n Meteorol.* an abnormal increase in temperature with height in the troposphere.

tempered ('tɛmpəd) *adj* **1** *Music.* **1a** (of a scale) having the frequency differences between notes adjusted in accordance with the system of equal temperament. See **temperament. 1b** (of an interval) expanded or contracted from the state of being pure. **2** (*in combination*) having a temper or temperament as specified: *ill-tempered.*

tempest ('tɛmpɪst) *n* **1** *Chiefly literary.* a violent wind or storm. **2** a violent commotion, uproar, or disturbance. ◆ *vb* **3** (*tr*) *Poetic.* to agitate or disturb violently. [C13: from Old French *tempeste,* from Latin *tempestās* storm, from *tempus* time]

tempestuous (tɛm'pɛstjuəs) *adj* **1** of or relating to a tempest. **2** violent or stormy: *a tempestuous love affair.* ► **tem'pestuously** *adv* ► **tem'pestuousness** *n*

tempi ('tɛmpiː) *n* (in musical senses) the plural of **tempo.**

Templar ('tɛmplə) *n* **1** a member of a military religious order (**Knights of the Temple of Solomon**) founded by Crusaders in Jerusalem around 1118 to defend the Holy Sepulchre and Christian pilgrims; suppressed in 1312. **2** (*sometimes not cap.*) *Brit.* a lawyer, esp. a barrister, who lives or has chambers in the Inner or Middle Temple in London. [C13: from Medieval Latin *templārius* of the temple, from Latin *templum* TEMPLE[1]; first applied to the knightly order because their house was near the site of the Temple of Solomon]

template *or* **templet** ('tɛmplɪt) *n* **1** a gauge or pattern, cut out in wood or metal, used in woodwork, etc., to help shape something accurately. **2** a pattern cut out in card or plastic, used in various crafts to reproduce shapes. **3** a short beam, made of metal, wood, or stone, that is used to spread a load, as over a doorway. **4** *Biochem.* the molecular structure of a compound that serves as a pattern for the production of the molecular structure of another specific compound in a reaction. [C17 *templet* (later spelling influenced by PLATE), probably from French, diminutive of TEMPLE[3]]

temple[1] ('tɛmpəl) *n* **1** a building or place dedicated to the worship of a deity or deities. **2** a Mormon church. **3** *U.S.* another name for a **synagogue. 4** any Christian church, esp. a large or imposing one. **5** any place or object regarded as a shrine where God makes himself present, esp. the body of a person who has been sanctified or saved by grace. **6** a building regarded as the focus of an activity, interest, or practice: *a temple of the arts.* [Old English *tempel,* from Latin *templum;* probably related to Latin *tempus* TIME, Greek *temenos* sacred enclosure, literally: a place cut off, from *temnein* to cut] ► **'templed** *adj* ► **'temple-,like** *adj*

temple[2] ('tɛmpəl) *n* the region on each side of the head in front of the ear and above the cheek bone. Related adj: **temporal.** [C14: from Old French *temple,* from Latin *tempora* the temples, from *tempus* temple of the head]

temple[3] ('tɛmpəl) *n* the part of a loom that keeps the cloth being woven stretched to the correct width. [C15: from French, from Latin *templum* a small timber]

Temple[1] ('tɛmpəl) *n* **1** either of two buildings in London and Paris that belonged to the Templars. The one in London now houses two of the chief law societies. **2** any of three buildings or groups of buildings erected by the Jews in ancient Jerusalem for the worship of Jehovah.

Temple[2] ('tɛmpəl) *n* **1 Shirley,** married name *Shirley Temple Black.* born 1928, U.S. film actress and politician. Her films as a child star include *Little Miss Marker* (1934), *Wee Willie Winkie* (1937), and *Heidi* (1937). She was U.S. ambassador to Ghana (1974–76) and to Czechoslovakia (1989–92). **2** Sir **William.** 1628–99, English diplomat and essayist. He negotiated the Triple Alliance (1668) and the marriage of William of Orange to Mary II. **3 William.** 1881–1944, English prelate and advocate of social reform; archbishop of Canterbury (1942–44).

Temple of Artemis *n* the large temple at Ephesus, on the W coast of Asia Minor: one of the Seven Wonders of the World.

tempo ('tɛmpəʊ) *n, pl* **-pos** *or* **-pi** (-piː). **1** the speed at which a piece or passage of music is meant to be played, usually indicated by a musical direction (**tempo marking**) or metronome marking. **2** rate or pace. [C18: from Italian, from Latin *tempus* time]

tempolabile (,tɛmpəʊ'leɪbaɪl) *adj Chem.* changing irregularly with time.

temporal[1] ('tɛmpərəl, 'tɛmprəl) *adj* **1** of or relating to time. **2** of or relating to secular as opposed to spiritual or religious affairs: *the lords spiritual and temporal.* **3** lasting for a relatively short time. **4** *Grammar.* of or relating to tense or the linguistic expression of time in general: *a temporal adverb.* [C14: from Latin *temporālis,* from *tempus* time] ► **'temporally** *adv* ► **'temporalness** *n*

temporal[2] ('tɛmpərəl, 'tɛmprəl) *adj Anatomy.* of, relating to, or near the temple or temples. [C16: from Late Latin *temporālis* belonging to the temples; see TEMPLE[2]]

temporal bone *n* either of two compound bones forming part of the sides and base of the skull: they surround the organs of hearing.

temporality (,tɛmpə'rælɪtɪ) *n, pl* **-ties. 1** the state or quality of being temporal. **2** something temporal. **3** (*often pl*) a secular possession or revenue belonging to a Church, a group within the Church, or the clergy.

temporal lobe *n* the laterally protruding portion of each cerebral hemisphere, situated below the parietal lobe and associated with sound perception and interpretation: it is thought to be the centre for memory recall.

temporary ('tɛmpərərɪ, 'tɛmprərɪ) *adj* **1** not permanent; provisional: *temporary accommodation.* **2** lasting only a short time; transitory: *temporary relief from pain.* ◆ *n, pl* **-raries. 3** a person, esp. a secretary or other office worker, employed on a temporary basis. Often shortened to **temp.** [C16: from Latin *temporārius,* from *tempus* time] ► **'temporarily** *adv* ► **'temporariness** *n*

temporary hardness *n Chem.* hardness of water due to the presence of magnesium and calcium hydrogencarbonates, which can be precipitated as carbonates by boiling.

temporize *or* **temporise** ('tɛmpə,raɪz) *vb* (*intr*) **1** to delay, act evasively, or protract a discussion, negotiation, etc., esp. in order to gain time or effect a compromise. **2** to adapt oneself to the circumstances or occasion, as by temporary or apparent agreement. [C16: from French *temporiser,* from Medieval Latin *temporizāre,* from Latin *tempus* time] ► **,tempori'zation** *or* **,tempori'sation** *n* ► **'tempo,rizer** *or* **'tempo,riser** *n*

tempt (tɛmpt) *vb* (*tr*) **1** to attempt to persuade or entice to do something, esp. something morally wrong or unwise. **2** to allure, invite, or attract. **3** to give rise to a desire in (someone) to do something; dispose: *their unfriendliness tempted me to leave the party.* **4** to risk provoking (esp. in the phrase **tempt fate**). [C13: from Old French *tempter,* from Latin *temptāre* to test] ► **'temptable** *adj* ► **'tempter** *n*

temptation (tɛmp'teɪʃən) *n* **1** the act of tempting or the state of being tempted. **2** a person or thing that tempts.

Tempter ('tɛmptə) *n* **the.** Satan regarded as trying to lead men into sin.

tempting ('tɛmptɪŋ) *adj* attractive or inviting: *a tempting meal.* ► **'temptingly** *adv* ► **'temptingness** *n*

temptress ('tɛmptrɪs) *n* a woman who sets out to allure or seduce a man or men; seductress.

tempura ('tɛmpərə) *n* a Japanese dish of seafood or vegetables dipped in batter and deep-fried, often at the table. [from Japanese: fried food]

tempus fugit *Latin.* ('tɛmpəs 'fjuːdʒɪt, -gɪt) time flies.

Temuco (*Spanish* te'muko) *n* a city in S Chile: agricultural trading centre. Pop.: 239 340 (1995 est.).

ten (tɛn) *n* **1** the cardinal number that is the sum of nine and one. It is the base of the decimal number system and the base of the common logarithm. See also **number** (sense 1). **2** a numeral, 10, X, etc., representing this number. **3** something representing, represented by, or consisting of ten units, such as a playing card with ten symbols on it. **4** Also called: **ten o'clock.** ten hours after noon or midnight. ◆ *determiner* **5a** amounting to ten: *ten tigers.* **5b** (*as pronoun*): *to sell only ten.* ◆ Related adj: **decimal.** Related prefixes: **deca-, deci-.** [Old English *tēn;* related to Old Saxon *tehan,* Old High German *zehan,* Gothic *taihun,* Latin *decem,* Greek *deka,* Sanskrit *dasa*]

ten. *Music. abbrev. for:* **1** tenor. **2** tenuto.

ten- *combining form.* a variant of **teno-** before a vowel.

tenable ('tɛnəbᵊl) *adj* able to be upheld, believed, maintained, or defended. [C16: from Old French, from *tenir* to hold, from Latin *tenēre*] ▸ ˌ**tena'bility** *or* '**tenableness** *n* ▸ '**tenably** *adv*

tenace ('tɛneɪs) *n Bridge, whist.* a holding of two nonconsecutive high cards of a suit, such as the ace and queen. [C17: from French, from Spanish *tenaza* forceps, ultimately from Latin *tenāx* holding fast, from *tenēre* to hold]

tenacious (tɪ'neɪʃəs) *adj* **1** holding or grasping firmly; forceful: *a tenacious grip.* **2** retentive: *a tenacious memory.* **3** stubborn or persistent: *a tenacious character.* **4** holding together firmly; tough or cohesive: *tenacious cement.* **5** tending to stick or adhere: *tenacious mud.* [C16: from Latin *tenāx,* from *tenēre* to hold] ▸ **te'naciously** *adv* ▸ **te'naciousness** *or* **tenacity** (tɪ'næsɪtɪ) *n*

ten-acre block *n N.Z.* a block of subdivided farming land, usually within commuting distance of a city, that provides a semirural way of life.

tenaculum (tɪ'nækjʊləm) *n, pl* **-la** (-lə). a surgical or dissecting instrument for grasping and holding parts, consisting of a slender hook mounted in a handle. [C17: from Late Latin, from Latin *tenēre* to hold]

tenaille (tɛ'neɪl) *n Fortifications.* a low outwork in the main ditch between two bastions. [C16: from French, literally: tongs, from Late Latin *tenācula,* pl. of TENACULUM]

tena koe (tə'nɑː 'kwɔɪ) *interj N.Z.* a Maori greeting to one person.

tenancy ('tɛnənsɪ) *n, pl* **-cies. 1** the temporary possession or holding by a tenant of lands or property owned by another. **2** the period of holding or occupying such property. **3** the period of holding office, a position, etc. **4** property held or occupied by a tenant.

tenant ('tɛnənt) *n* **1** a person who holds, occupies, or possesses land or property by any kind of right or title, esp. from a landlord under a lease. **2** a person who has the use of a house, flat, etc., subject to the payment of rent. **3** any holder or occupant. ◆ *vb* **4** (*tr*) to hold (land or property) as a tenant. **5** (*intr;* foll. by *in*) *Rare.* to dwell. [C14: from Old French, literally: (one who is) holding, from *tenir* to hold, from Latin *tenēre*] ▸ '**tenantable** *adj* ▸ '**tenantless** *adj* ▸ '**tenant-**ˌ**like** *adj*

tenant farmer *n* a person who farms land rented from another, the rent usually taking the form of part of the crops grown or livestock reared.

tenant-in-chief *n* (in feudal society) a tenant who held some or all of his lands directly from the king.

tenantry ('tɛnəntrɪ) *n* **1** tenants collectively, esp. those with the same landlord. **2** the status or condition of being a tenant.

tenants association *n* an organization of tenants, usually with a written constitution and charitable status, whose aim is to improve the housing conditions, amenities, community life, and contractual positions of its members. See also **community association, residents association.**

tenants' charter *n* (in Britain) a package of legal rights to which tenants of local authorities, new towns, and housing associations are entitled, including security of tenure, and the rights to buy the dwelling cheaply, to take in lodgers, and to sublet.

tench (tɛntʃ) *n* a European freshwater cyprinid game fish, *Tinca tinca,* having a thickset dark greenish body with a barbel at each side of the mouth. [C14: from Old French *tenche,* from Late Latin *tinca*]

Ten Commandments *pl n* **the.** *Old Testament.* the commandments summarizing the basic obligations of man towards God and his fellow men, delivered to Moses on Mount Sinai engraved on two tables of stone (Exodus 20:1–17). Also called: the **Decalogue.**

tend[1] (tɛnd) *vb* (when *intr,* usually foll. by *to* or *towards*) **1** (when *tr, takes an infinitive*) to have a general disposition (to do something); be inclined: *children tend to prefer sweets to meat.* **2** (*intr*) to have or be an influence (towards a specific result); be conducive: *the party atmosphere tends to hilarity.* **3** (*intr*) to go or move (in a particular direction): *to tend to the south.* [C14: from Old French *tendre,* from Latin *tendere* to stretch]

tend[2] (tɛnd) *vb* **1** (*tr*) to care for: *to tend wounded soldiers.* **2** (when *intr,* often foll. by *to*) to attend (to): *to tend to someone's needs.* **3** (*tr*) to handle or control: *to tend a fire.* **4** (*intr;* often foll. by *to*) *Informal, chiefly U.S. and Canadian.* to pay attention. [C14: variant of ATTEND]

tendance ('tɛndəns) *n* **1** *Rare.* care and attention; ministration. **2** *Obsolete.* attendants collectively.

tendency ('tɛndənsɪ) *n, pl* **-cies. 1** (often foll. by *to*) an inclination, predisposition, propensity, or leaning: *she has a tendency to be frivolous; a tendency to frivolity.* **2** the general course, purport, or drift of something, esp. a written work. **3** a faction, esp. one within a political party: *the militant tendency.* [C17: from Medieval Latin *tendentia,* from Latin *tendere* to TEND[1]]

tendentious *or* **tendencious** (tɛn'dɛnʃəs) *adj* having or showing an intentional tendency or bias, esp. a controversial one. [C20: from TENDENCY] ▸ **ten'dentiously, ten'denciously** *or* **ten'dentially, ten'dencially** *adv* ▸ **ten'dentiousness** *or* **ten'denciousness** *n*

tender[1] ('tɛndə) *adj* **1** easily broken, cut, or crushed; soft; not tough: *a tender steak.* **2** easily damaged; vulnerable or sensitive: *a tender youth; at a tender age.* **3** having or expressing warm and affectionate feelings: *a tender smile.* **4** kind, merciful, or sympathetic: *a tender heart.* **5** arousing warm feelings; touching: *a tender memory.* **6** gentle and delicate: *a tender breeze.* **7** requiring care in handling; ticklish: *a tender question.* **8** painful or sore: *a tender wound.* **9** sensitive to moral or spiritual feelings: *a tender conscience.* **10** (*postpositive;* foll. by *of*) careful or protective: *tender of one's emotions.* **11** (of a sailing vessel) easily keeled over by a wind; crank. Compare **stiff** (sense 10). ◆ *vb* **12** (*tr*) *Rare.* **12a** to make tender. **12b** to treat tenderly. [C13: from Old French *tendre,* from Latin *tener* delicate] ▸ '**tenderly** *adv* ▸ '**tenderness** *n*

tender[2] ('tɛndə) *vb* **1** (*tr*) to give, present, or offer: *to tender one's resignation; tender a bid.* **2** (*intr;* foll. by *for*) to make a formal offer or estimate for (a job or contract). **3** (*tr*) *Law.* to offer (money or goods) in settlement of a debt or claim. ◆ *n* **4** the act or an instance of tendering; offer. **5** *Commerce.* a formal offer to supply specified goods or services at a stated cost or rate. **6** something, esp. money, used as an official medium of payment: *legal tender.* [C16: from Anglo-French *tendre,* from Latin *tendere* to extend; see TEND[1]] ▸ '**tenderable** *adj* ▸ '**tenderer** *n*

tender[3] ('tɛndə) *n* **1** a small boat, such as a dinghy, towed or carried by a yacht or ship. **2** a vehicle drawn behind a steam locomotive to carry the fuel and water. **3** an ancillary vehicle used to carry supplies, spare parts, etc., for a mobile operation, such as an outside broadcast. **4** a person who tends. [C15: variant of *attender*]

tenderfoot ('tɛndəˌfʊt) *n, pl* **-foots** *or* **-feet. 1** a newcomer, esp. to the mines or ranches of the southwestern U.S. **2** (formerly) a beginner in the Scouts or Guides.

tenderhearted (ˌtɛndə'hɑːtɪd) *adj* having a compassionate, kindly, or sensitive disposition. ▸ ˌ**tender'heartedly** *adv* ▸ ˌ**tender'heartedness** *n*

tenderize *or* **tenderise** ('tɛndəˌraɪz) *vb* (*tr*) to make (meat) tender by pounding it to break down the fibres, by steeping it in a marinade, or by treating it with a tenderizer. ▸ ˌ**tenderi'zation** *or* ˌ**tenderi'sation** *n*

tenderizer *or* **tenderiser** ('tɛndəˌraɪzə) *n* a substance, such as the plant enzyme papain, rubbed onto meat to soften the fibres and make it more tender.

tenderloin ('tɛndəˌlɔɪn) *n* **1** a tender cut of pork or other meat from between the sirloin and ribs. **2** *U.S.* a district of a city that is particularly noted for vice and corruption. [sense 2 from *Tenderloin,* former district of New York City, regarded as an easy source of bribes for a corrupt policeman]

tendinous ('tɛndɪnəs) *adj* of, relating to, possessing, or resembling tendons; sinewy. [C17: from New Latin *tendinōsus,* from Medieval Latin *tendō* TENDON]

tendon ('tɛndən) *n* a cord or band of white inelastic collagenous tissue that attaches a muscle to a bone or some other part; sinew. [C16: from Medieval Latin *tendō,* from Latin *tendere* to stretch; related to Greek *tenōn* sinew]

tendril ('tɛndrɪl) *n* **1** a specialized threadlike leaf or stem that attaches climbing plants to a support by twining or adhering. **2** something resembling a tendril, such as a wisp of hair. [C16: perhaps from Old French *tendron* tendril (confused with Old French *tendron* bud), from Medieval Latin *tendō* TENDON] ▸ '**tendrillar** *or* '**tendrilous** *adj*

Tenebrae ('tɛnəˌbreɪ) *n* (*functioning as sing or pl*) *R.C. Church.* (formerly) the matins and lauds for Thursday, Friday, and Saturday of Holy Week, usually sung in the evenings or at night. [C17: from Latin: darkness]

tenebrism ('tɛnəˌbrɪzəm) *n* (*sometimes cap.*) a school, style, or method of painting, adopted chiefly by 17th-century Spanish and Neapolitan painters, esp. Caravaggio, characterized by large areas of dark colours, usually relieved with a shaft of light. ▸ '**tenebrist** *n, adj*

tenebrous ('tɛnəbrəs) *or* **tenebrious** (tə'nɛbrɪəs) *adj* gloomy, shadowy, or dark. [C15: from Latin *tenebrōsus* from *tenebrae* darkness] ▸ **tenebrosity** (ˌtɛnə'brɒsɪtɪ), '**tenebrousness,** *or* **te'nebriousness** *n*

Tenedos ('tɛnɪˌdɒs) *n* an island in the NE Aegean, near the entrance to the Dardanelles: in Greek legend the base of the Greek fleet during the siege of Troy. Modern Turkish name: **Bozcaada.**

tenement ('tɛnəmənt) *n* **1** Also called: **tenement building.** (now esp. in Scotland) a large building divided into separate flats. **2** a dwelling place or residence, esp. one intended for rent. **3** *Chiefly Brit.* a room or flat for rent. **4** *Property law.* any form of permanent property, such as land, dwellings, offices, etc. [C14: from Medieval Latin *tenementum,* from Latin *tenēre* to hold] ▸ **tenemental** (ˌtɛnə'mɛntᵊl) *or* ˌ**tene'mentary** *adj* ▸ '**tene**ˌ**mented** *adj*

Tenerife (ˌtɛnə'riːf; *Spanish* tene'rife) *n* a Spanish island in the Atlantic, off the NW coast of Africa: the largest of the Canary Islands; volcanic and mountainous; tourism and agriculture. Capital: Santa Cruz. Pop.: 560 000 (latest est.). Area: 2058 sq. km (795 sq. miles).

tenesmus (tɪ'nɛzməs, -'nɛs-) *n Pathol.* an ineffective painful straining to empty the bowels or bladder. [C16: from Medieval Latin, from Latin *tēnesmos,* from Greek *teinesmos,* from *teinein* to strain] ▸ **te'nesmic** *adj*

tenet ('tɛnɪt, 'tiːnɪt) *n* a belief, opinion, or dogma. [C17: from Latin, literally: he (it) holds, from *tenēre* to hold]

tenfold ('tɛnˌfəʊld) *adj* **1** equal to or having 10 times as many or as much: *a tenfold increase in population.* **2** composed of 10 parts. ◆ *adv* **3** by or up to 10 times as many or as much: *the population increased tenfold.*

ten-gallon hat *n* (in the U.S. and Canada) a cowboy's broad-brimmed felt hat with a very high crown. [C20: so called because of its large size]

tenge (tɛŋ'geɪ) *n* the standard monetary unit of Kazakhstan, divided into 100 tiyn.

Teng Hsiao-ping ('tɛŋ sjaʊ 'pɪŋ) *n* a variant transliteration of the Chinese name for **Deng Xiaoping.**

Tengri Khan ('tɛŋgrɪ 'kɑːn) *n* a mountain in central Asia, on the border between Kyrgyzstan and the Xinjiang Uygur Autonomous Region of W China. Height: 6995 m (22 951 ft.).

Tengri Nor ('tɛŋgrɪ 'nɔː) *n* another name for **Nam Co.**

Ten Gurus *pl n* the ten leaders of the Sikh religion from the founder of Sikhism **Guru Nanak** to Guru Govind Singh (1666–1708), who ended the line of gurus by calling on Sikhs to rely on the holy text of the Granth to guide them.

tenia ('tiːnɪə) *n, pl* **-niae** (-nɪˌiː). the U.S. spelling of **taenia.**

teniacide ('tiːnɪəˌsaɪd) *n* the U.S. spelling of **taeniacide.**

teniafuge ('tiːnɪəˌfjuːdʒ) *n* the U.S. spelling of **taeniafuge.**

teniasis (tiː'naɪəsɪs) *n* the U.S. spelling of **taeniasis.**

Teniers ('tɛnɪəz) *n* **David** ('dɑːvɪt), called *the Elder,* 1582–1649, and his son **David,** called *the Younger,* 1610–90, Flemish painters.

Tenn. *abbrev. for* Tennessee.

tenner ('tɛnə) *n Informal.* **1** *Brit.* **1a** a ten-pound note. **1b** the sum of ten pounds. **2** *U.S.* a ten-dollar bill.

Tennessee (ˌtɛnɪ'siː) *n* **1** a state of the E central U.S.: consists of a plain in the west, rising to the Appalachians and the Cumberland Plateau in the east. Capital: Nashville. Pop.: 5 368 198 (1997 est.). Area: 109 412 sq. km (42 244 sq. miles). Abbrevs.: **Tenn.** or (with zip code) **TN** **2** a river in the E central U.S., flowing southwest from E Tennessee into N Alabama, then west and north to the Ohio River at Paducah: the longest tributary of the Ohio; includes a series of dams and reservoirs under the Tennessee Valley Authority. Length: 1049 km (652 miles). ▸ ˌ**Tennes'sean** *adj, n*

Tennessee Walking Horse *n* an American breed of horse, marked by its stamina and trained to move at a fast running walk. Often shortened to **Walking Horse.**

Tenniel ('tɛnjəl) *n* Sir **John.** 1820–1914, English caricaturist, noted for his illustrations to Lewis Carroll's *Alice* books and for his political cartoons in *Punch* (1851–1901).

tennis ('tɛnɪs) *n* **a** a racket game played between two players or pairs of players who hit a ball to and fro over a net on a rectangular court of grass, asphalt, clay, etc. See also **lawn tennis, real tennis, court tennis, table tennis. b** (*as modifier*): *tennis court; tennis racket.* [C14: probably from Anglo-French *tenetz* hold (imperative), from Old French *tenir* to hold, from Latin *tenēre*]

tennis ball *n* a hollow rubber ball covered with felt, used in tennis.

tennis elbow *n* a painful inflammation of the elbow caused by exertion in playing tennis and similar games.

tennis shoe *n* a rubber-soled canvas shoe tied with laces.

tenno ('tɛnəʊ) *n, pl* **-no** *or* **-nos.** the formal title of the Japanese emperor, esp. when regarded as a divine religious leader. [from Japanese *tennō*]

Tennyson ('tɛnɪsᵊn) *n* **Alfred,** Lord Tennyson. 1809–92, English poet; poet laureate (1850–92). His poems include *The Lady of Shalott* (1832), *Morte d'Arthur* (1842), the collection *In Memoriam* (1850), *Maud* (1855), and *Idylls of the King* (1859). ▸ **Tennysonian** (ˌtɛnɪ'səʊnɪən) *adj, n*

Teno ('tɛnɔ) *n* the Finnish name for **Tana** (sense 3).

teno- *or before a vowel* **ten-** *combining form.* tendon: *tenosynovitis.* [from Greek *tenōn*]

Tenochtitlán (tɛˌnɔːtʃtiː'tlɑːn) *n* an ancient city and capital of the Aztec empire on the present site of Mexico City; razed by Cortés in 1521.

tenon ('tɛnən) *n* **1** the projecting end of a piece of wood formed to fit into a corresponding mortise in another piece. ◆ *vb* (*tr*) **2** to form a tenon on (a piece of wood). **3** to join with a tenon and mortise. [C15: from Old French, from *tenir* to hold, from Latin *tenēre*] ▸ '**tenoner** *n*

tenon saw *n* a small fine-toothed saw with a strong back, used esp. for cutting tenons.

tenor ('tɛnə) *n* **1** *Music.* **1a** the male voice intermediate between alto and baritone, having a range approximately from the B a ninth below middle C to the G a fifth above it. **1b** a singer with such a voice. **1c** a saxophone, horn, recorder, etc., intermediate in compass and size between the alto and baritone or bass. **1d** (*as modifier*): *a tenor sax.* **2** general drift of thought; purpose: *to follow the tenor of an argument.* **3a** (in early polyphonic music) the part singing the melody or the cantus firmus. **3b** (in four-part harmony) the second lowest part lying directly above the bass. **4** *Change-ringing.* **4a** the heaviest and lowest-pitched bell in a ring. **4b** (*as modifier*): *a tenor bell.* **5** a settled course of progress. **6** *Archaic.* general tendency. **7** *Finance.* the time required for a bill of exchange or promissory note to become due for payment. **8** *Law.* **8a** the exact words of a deed, etc., as distinct from their effect. **8b** an exact copy or transcript. [C13 (originally: general meaning or sense): from Old French *tenour,* from Latin *tenor* a continuous holding to a course, from *tenēre* to hold; musical sense via Italian *tenore,* referring to the voice part that was continuous, that is, to which the melody was assigned] ▸ '**tenorless** *adj*

tenor clef *n* the clef that establishes middle C as being on the fourth line of the staff, used for the writing of music for the bassoon, cello, or tenor trombone. See also **C clef.**

tenorite ('tɛnəˌraɪt) *n* a black mineral found in copper deposits and consisting of copper oxide in the form of either metallic scales or earthy masses. Formula: CuO. [C19: named after G. *Tenore* (died 1861), Italian botanist]

tenorrhaphy (tɪ'nɒrəfɪ) *n, pl* **-phies.** *Surgery.* the union of torn or divided tendons by means of sutures. [C19: from TENO- + Greek *raphē* a sewing or suture]

tenosynovitis ('tɛnəʊˌsaɪnəʊ'vaɪtɪs) *n* painful swelling and inflammation of tendons, usually of the wrist, often the result of repetitive movements such as typing.

tenotomy (tə'nɒtəmɪ) *n, pl* **-mies.** surgical division of a tendon. ▸ **te'notomist** *n*

tenpenny ('tɛnpənɪ) *adj* (*prenominal*) *U.S. and Canadian.* (of a nail) three inches in length.

tenpin ('tɛnˌpɪn) *n* one of the pins used in tenpin bowling. See also **tenpins.**

tenpin bowling *n* a bowling game in which heavy bowls are rolled down a long lane to knock over the ten target pins at the other end. Also called (esp. U.S. and Canadian): **tenpins.**

tenpins ('tɛnˌpɪnz) *n* (*functioning as sing*) the U.S. and Canadian name for **tenpin bowling.**

tenrec ('tɛnrɛk) *n* any small mammal, such as *Tenrec ecaudatus* (**tailless tenrec**), of the Madagascan family *Tenrecidae,* resembling hedgehogs or shrews: order *Insectivora* (insectivores). [C18: via French from Malagasy *tràndraka*]

tense[1] (tɛns) *adj* **1** stretched or stressed tightly; taut or rigid. **2** under mental or emotional strain. **3** producing mental or emotional strain: *a tense day.* **4** (of a speech sound) pronounced with considerable muscular effort and having relatively precise accuracy of articulation and considerable duration: *in English the vowel* (iː) *in "beam" is tense.* Compare **lax** (sense 4). ◆ *vb* **5** (often foll. by *up*) to make or become tense. [C17: from Latin *tensus* taut, from *tendere* to stretch] ▸ '**tensely** *adv* ▸ '**tenseness** *n*

tense[2] (tɛns) *n Grammar.* a category of the verb or verbal inflections, such as present, past, and future, that expresses the temporal relations between what is reported in a sentence and the time of its utterance. [C14: from Old French *tens* time, from Latin *tempus*] ▸ '**tenseless** *adj*

tense logic *n Logic.* the study of the logical properties of tense operators, and of the logical relations between sentences having tense, by means of consideration of appropriate formal systems.

tensible ('tɛnsəbᵊl) *adj* capable of being stretched; tensile. ▸ ˌ**tensi'bility** *or* '**tensibleness** *n* ▸ '**tensibly** *adv*

tensile ('tɛnsaɪl) *adj* **1** of or relating to tension. **2** sufficiently ductile to be stretched or drawn out. [C17: from New Latin *tensilis,* from Latin *tendere* to stretch] ▸ '**tensilely** *adv* ▸ **tensility** (tɛn'sɪlɪtɪ) *or* '**tensileness** *n*

tensile strength *n* a measure of the ability of a material to withstand a longitudinal stress, expressed as the greatest stress that the material can stand without breaking.

tensimeter (tɛn'sɪmɪtə) *n* a device that measures differences in vapour pressures. It is used to determine transition points by observing changes of vapour pressure with temperature. [C20: from TENSI(ON) + -METER]

tensiometer (ˌtɛnsɪ'ɒmɪtə) *n* **1** an instrument for measuring the tensile strength of a wire, beam, etc. **2** an instrument used to compare the vapour pressures of two liquids, usually consisting of two sealed bulbs containing the liquids, each being connected to one limb of a manometer. **3** an instrument for measuring the surface tension of a liquid, usually consisting of a sensitive balance for measuring the force needed to pull a wire ring from the surface of the liquid. **4** an instrument for measuring the moisture content of soil.

tension ('tɛnʃən) *n* **1** the act of stretching or the state or degree of being stretched. **2** mental or emotional strain; stress. **3** a situation or condition of hostility, suspense, or uneasiness. **4** *Physics.* a force that tends to produce an elongation of a body or structure. **5** *Physics.* **5a** voltage, electromotive force, or potential difference. **5b** (*in combination*): *high-tension; low-tension.* **6** a device for regulating the tension in a part, string, thread, etc., as in a sewing machine. **7** *Knitting.* the degree of tightness or looseness with which a person knits. [C16: from Latin *tensiō,* from *tendere* to strain] ▸ '**tensional** *adj* ▸ '**tensionless** *adj*

tensity ('tɛnsɪtɪ) *n* a rare word for **tension** (senses 1–3).

tensive ('tɛnsɪv) *adj* of or causing tension or strain.

tensor ('tɛnsə, -sɔː) *n* **1** *Anatomy.* any muscle that can cause a part to become firm or tense. **2** *Maths.* a set of components, functions of the coordinates of any point in space, that transform linearly between coordinate systems. For three dimensional space there are 3^r components, where *r* is the rank. A tensor of zero rank is a scalar, of rank one, a vector. [C18: from New Latin, literally: a stretcher] ▸ **tensorial** (tɛn'sɔːrɪəl) *adj*

ten-strike *n Tenpin bowling.* another word for **strike** (sense 40).

tent[1] (tɛnt) *n* **1a** a portable shelter of canvas, plastic, or other waterproof material supported on poles and fastened to the ground by pegs and ropes. **1b** (*as modifier*): *tent peg.* **2** something resembling this in function or shape. ◆ *vb* **3** (*intr*) to camp in a tent. **4** (*tr*) to cover with or as if with a tent or tents. **5** (*tr*) to provide with a tent as shelter. [C13: from Old French *tente,* from Latin *tentōrium* something stretched out, from *tendere* to stretch] ▸ '**tented** *adj* ▸ '**tentless** *adj* ▸ '**tent**ˌ**like** *adj*

tent[2] (tɛnt) *Med.* ◆ *n* **1** a plug of soft material for insertion into a bodily canal, etc., to dilate it or maintain its patency. ◆ *vb* **2** (*tr*) to insert such a plug into (a bodily canal, etc.). [C14 (in the sense: a probe): from Old French *tente* (n), ultimately from Latin *temptāre* to try; see TEMPT]

tent[3] (tɛnt) *n Obsolete.* a red table wine from Alicante, Spain. [C16: from Spanish *tinto* dark-coloured; see TINT]

tent[4] (tɛnt) *Scot.* ◆ *n* **1** heed; attention. ◆ *vb* (*tr*) **2** to pay attention to; take notice of. **3** to attend to. [C14: from *attent* ATTEND and INTENT] ▸ '**tenter** *n*

tentacle ('tɛntəkᵊl) *n* **1** any of various elongated flexible organs that occur near the mouth in many invertebrates and are used for feeding, grasping, etc. **2** any of the hairs on the leaf of an insectivorous plant that are used to capture prey. **3** something resembling a tentacle, esp. in its ability to reach out or grasp. [C18: from New Latin *tentāculum,* from Latin *tentāre,* variant of *temptāre* to feel] ▸ '**tentacled** *adj* ▸ '**tentacle-**ˌ**like** *or* **tentaculoid** (tɛn'tækjʊˌlɔɪd) *adj* ▸ **tentacular** (tɛn'tækjʊlə) *adj*

tentage ('tɛntɪdʒ) *n* **1** tents collectively. **2** a supply of tents or tenting equipment.

tentation (tɛn'teɪʃən) *n* a method of achieving the correct adjustment of a mechanical device by a series of trials. [C14: from Latin *tentātiō,* variant of *temptātiō* TEMPTATION]

tentative ('tɛntətɪv) *adj* **1** provisional or experimental; conjectural. **2** hesitant, uncertain, or cautious. [C16: from Medieval Latin *tentātīvus,* from Latin *tentāre* to test] ▸ '**tentatively** *adv* ▸ '**tentativeness** *n*

tent caterpillar *n* the larva of various moths of the family *Lasiocampidae,* esp. *Malacosoma americana* of North America, which build communal webs in trees.

tent dress *n* a very full tent-shaped dress, having no darts, waistline, etc.
tenter ('tɛntə) *n* **1** a frame on which cloth is stretched during the manufacturing process in order that it may retain its shape while drying. **2** a person who stretches cloth on a tenter. ◆ *vb* **3** (*tr*) to stretch (cloth) on a tenter. [C14: from Medieval Latin *tentōrium,* from Latin *tentus* stretched, from *tendere* to stretch]
tenterhook ('tɛntəˌhʊk) *n* **1** one of a series of hooks or bent nails used to hold cloth stretched on a tenter. **2 on tenterhooks.** in a state of tension or suspense.
tenth (tɛnθ) *adj* **1** (*usually prenominal*) **1a** coming after the ninth in numbering or counting order, position, time, etc.; being the ordinal number of *ten:* often written 10th. **1b** (*as n*): *see you on the tenth; tenth in line.* ◆ *n* **2a** one of 10 approximately equal parts of something. **2b** (*as modifier*): *a tenth part.* **3** one of 10 equal divisions of a particular measurement, etc. Related prefix: **deci-**: *decibel.* **4** the fraction equal to one divided by ten (1/10). **5** *Music.* **5a** an interval of one octave plus a third. **5b** one of two notes constituting such an interval in relation to the other. ◆ *adv* **6** Also: **tenthly.** after the ninth person, position, event, etc. ◆ *sentence connector.* **7** Also: **tenthly.** as the 10th point: linking what follows with the previous statements, as in a speech or argument. [C12 *tenthe,* from Old English *tēotha;* see TEN, -TH[2]]
tent stitch *n* another term for **petit point** (sense 1). [C17: of uncertain origin]
tenuis ('tɛnjʊɪs) *n, pl* **tenues** ('tɛnjʊˌiːz). (in the grammar of classical Greek) any of the voiceless stops as represented by kappa, pi, or tau (k, p, t). [C17: from Latin: thin]
tenuous ('tɛnjʊəs) *adj* **1** insignificant or flimsy: *a tenuous argument.* **2** slim, fine, or delicate: *a tenuous thread.* **3** diluted or rarefied in consistency or density: *a tenuous fluid.* [C16: from Latin *tenuis*] ▸ **tenuity** (tɛ'njuːɪtɪ) *or* **'tenuousness** *n* ▸ **'tenuously** *adv*
tenure ('tɛnjʊə, 'tɛnjə) *n* **1** the possession or holding of an office or position. **2** the length of time an office, position, etc., lasts; term. **3** *Chiefly U.S. and Canadian.* the improved security status of a person after having been in the employ of the same company or institution for a specified period. **4** the right to permanent employment until retirement, esp. for teachers, lecturers, etc. **5** *Property law.* **5a** the holding or occupying of property, esp. realty, in return for services rendered, etc. **5b** the duration of such holding or occupation. [C15: from Old French, from Medieval Latin *tenitūra,* ultimately from Latin *tenēre* to hold] ▸ **ten'urial** *adj* ▸ **ten'urially** *adv*
tenured ('tɛnjʊəd, 'tɛnjəd) *adj Chiefly U.S. and Canadian.* **a** having tenure of office: *a tenured professor.* **b** guaranteeing tenure of office: *a tenured post.*
tenuto (tɪ'njuːtəʊ) *adj, adv Music.* (of a note) to be held for or beyond its full time value. Symbol: ⁻ (written above a note). [from Italian, literally: held, from *tenere* to hold, from Latin *tenēre*]
Tenzing Norgay ('tɛnsɪŋ 'nɔːgeɪ) *n* 1914–86, Nepalese mountaineer. With Sir Edmund Hillary, he was the first to reach the summit of Mount Everest (1953).
teocalli (ˌtiːəʊ'kælɪ) *n, pl* **-lis.** any of various truncated pyramids built by the Aztecs as bases for their temples. [C17: from Nahuatl, from *teotl* god + *calli* house]
teosinte (ˌtiːəʊ'sɪntɪ) *n* a tall Central American annual grass, *Euchlaena mexicana,* resembling maize and grown for forage in the southern U.S. [C19: from Nahuatl *teocentli,* from *teotl* god + *centli* dry ear of corn]
tepal ('tiːpᵊl, 'tɛpᵊl) *n* any of the subdivisions of a perianth that is not clearly differentiated into calyx and corolla. [C20: from French *tépale* changed (on analogy with *sépale* sepal) from *pétale* PETAL]
tepee *or* **teepee** ('tiːpiː) *n* a cone-shaped tent of animal skins used by certain North American Indians. [C19: from Siouan *tīpī,* from *ti* to dwell + *pi* used for]
tepefy ('tɛpɪˌfaɪ) *vb* **-fies, -fying, -fied.** to make or become tepid. [C17: from Latin *tepēre*] ▸ **tepefaction** (ˌtɛpɪ'fækʃən) *n*
tephra ('tɛfrə) *n Chiefly U.S.* solid matter ejected during a volcanic eruption. [C20: Greek, literally: ashes]
tephrite ('tɛfraɪt) *n* a variety of basalt containing augite, nepheline, or leucite. [C17: from Greek *tephros,* from *tephra* ashes; see -ITE[1]] ▸ **tephritic** (tɪ'frɪtɪk) *adj*
Tepic (*Spanish* te'pik) *n* a city in W central Mexico, capital of Nayarit state: agricultural, trading and processing centre. Pop.: 206 967 (1990).
tepid ('tɛpɪd) *adj* **1** slightly warm; lukewarm. **2** relatively unenthusiastic or apathetic: *the play had a tepid reception.* [C14: from Latin *tepidus,* from *tepēre* to be lukewarm] ▸ **te'pidity** *or* **'tepidness** *n* ▸ **'tepidly** *adv*
tequila (tɪ'kiːlə) *n* **1** a spirit that is distilled in Mexico from an agave plant and forms the basis of many mixed drinks. **2** the plant, *Agave tequilana,* from which this drink is made. [C19: from Mexican Spanish, from *Tequila,* region of Mexico]
ter. *abbrev. for:* **1** terrace. **2** territory.
ter- *combining form.* three, third, or three times: *tercentenary.* [from Latin *ter* thrice; related to *trēs* THREE]
tera- *prefix* denoting 10^{12}: *terameter.* Symbol: T [from Greek *teras* monster]
teraflop ('tɛrəˌflɒp) *n Computing.* a measure of processing speed, consisting of a thousand billion floating-point operations a second. [C20: from TERA- + *flo(ating) p(oint)*]
teraglin (tə'ræglən) *n* an edible marine fish, *Zeluco atelodus,* of Australia which has fine scales and is blue in colour. [from a native Australian language]
Terai (tə'raɪ) *n* **1** (in India) a belt of marshy land at the foot of mountains, esp. at the foot of the Himalayas in Uttar Pradesh. **2** a felt hat with a wide brim worn in subtropical regions.
terakihi (ˌtɛrə'kiːhiː) *n, pl* **-kihis.** See **tarakihi.**
teraph ('tɛrəf) *n, pl* **-aphim** (-əfɪm). *Old Testament.* any of various small household gods or images venerated by ancient Semitic peoples. (Genesis 31:19–21; I Samuel 19:13–16). [C14: from Hebrew, of uncertain origin]
terat- *or* **terato-** *combining form.* indicating a monster or something abnormal: *teratism; teratoid.* [from Greek *terat-, teras* monster, prodigy]
teratism ('tɛrəˌtɪzəm) *n* a malformed animal or human, esp. in the fetal stage; monster.
teratogen ('tɛrətədʒən, tɪ'rætə-) *n* any substance, organism, or process that causes malformations in a fetus. Teratogens include certain drugs (such as thalidomide), infections (such as German measles), and ionizing radiation. ▸ **ˌterato'genic** *adj*
teratoid ('tɛrəˌtɔɪd) *adj Biology.* resembling a monster.
teratology (ˌtɛrə'tɒlədʒɪ) *n* **1** the branch of medical science concerned with the development of physical abnormalities during the fetal or early embryonic stage. **2** the branch of biology that is concerned with the structure, development, etc., of monsters. **3** a collection of tales about mythical or fantastic creatures, monsters, etc. ▸ **teratologic** (ˌtɛrətə'lɒdʒɪk) *or* **ˌterato'logical** *adj* ▸ **ˌtera'tologist** *n*
teratoma (ˌtɛrə'təʊmə) *n, pl* **-mata** (-mətə) *or* **-mas.** a tumour or group of tumours composed of tissue foreign to the site of growth.
teratophobia (ˌtɛrətəʊ'fəʊbɪə) *n Psychiatry.* fear of giving birth to a monster.
terbia ('tɜːbɪə) *n* another name (not in technical usage) for **terbium oxide.**
terbium ('tɜːbɪəm) *n* a soft malleable silvery-grey element of the lanthanide series of metals, occurring in gadolinite and monazite and used in lasers and for doping solid-state devices. Symbol: Tb; atomic no.: 65; atomic wt.: 158.92534; valency: 3 or 4; relative density: 8.230; melting pt.: 1356°C; boiling pt.: 3230°C. [C19: from New Latin, named after *Ytterby,* Sweden, village where it was discovered] ▸ **'terbic** *adj*
terbium metal *n Chem.* any of a group of related lanthanides, including terbium, europium, and gadolinium.
terbium oxide *n* an amorphous white insoluble powder. Formula: Tb_2O_3. Also called: **terbia.**
Ter Borch *or* **Terborch** (*Dutch* tɛr 'bɔrx) *n* **Gerard** ('xeːrɑrt). 1617–81, Dutch genre and portrait painter.
Terbrugghen ('tɑbruˌgən) *n* **Hendrik.** 1588–1629, Dutch painter of the Utrecht school, who specialized in religious subjects, for example the *Incredulity of St Thomas* and the *Calling of St Matthew.*
terce (tɜːs) *or* **tierce** *n Chiefly R.C. Church.* the third of the seven canonical hours of the divine office, originally fixed at the third hour of the day, about 9 a.m. [a variant of TIERCE]
Terceira (*Portuguese* tər'sairə) *n* an island in the N Atlantic, in the Azores: NATO military air base. Pop.: 60 000 (latest est.). Area: 397 sq. km (153 sq. miles).
tercel ('tɜːsᵊl) *or* **tiercel** *n* a male falcon or hawk, esp. as used in falconry. [C14: from Old French, from Vulgar Latin *tertiolus* (unattested), from Latin *tertius* third, referring to the tradition that only one egg in three hatched a male chick]
tercentenary (ˌtɜːsɛn'tiːnərɪ) *or* **tercentennial** *adj* **1** of or relating to a period of 300 years. **2** of or relating to a 300th anniversary or its celebration. ◆ *n, pl* **-tenaries** *or* **-tennials. 3** an anniversary of 300 years or its celebration. ◆ Also: **tricentennial.**
tercet ('tɜːsɪt, tɜː'sɛt) *n* a group of three lines of verse that rhyme together or are connected by rhyme with adjacent groups of three lines. [C16: from French, from Italian *terzetto,* diminutive of *terzo* third, from Latin *tertius*]
terebene ('tɛrəˌbiːn) *n* a mixture of hydrocarbons prepared from oil of turpentine and sulphuric acid, used to make paints and varnishes and medicinally as an expectorant and antiseptic. [C19: from TEREB(INTH) + -ENE]
terebic acid (tɛ'rɛbɪk) *n* a white crystalline carboxylic acid produced by the action of nitric acid on turpentine. Formula: $C_7H_{10}O_4$. [C19: from TEREB(INTH) + -IC]
terebinth ('tɛrɪbɪnθ) *n* a small anacardiaceous tree, *Pistacia terebinthus,* of the Mediterranean region, having winged leafstalks and clusters of small flowers, and yielding a turpentine. [C14: from Latin *terebinthus,* from Greek *terebinthos* turpentine tree]
terebinthine (ˌtɛrɪ'bɪnθaɪn) *adj* **1** of or relating to terebinth or related plants. **2** of, consisting of, or resembling turpentine.
terebrate ('tɛrɪˌbreɪt) *adj* (of animals, esp. insects) having a boring or penetrating organ, such as a sting. [C20: from Latin *terebra* borer + -ATE[1]]
teredo (tɛ'riːdəʊ) *n, pl* **-dos** *or* **-dines** (-dɪˌniːz). any marine bivalve mollusc of the genus *Teredo.* See **shipworm.** [C17: via Latin from Greek *terēdōn* wood-boring worm; related to Greek *tetrainein* to pierce]
Terence ('tɛrəns) *n* Latin name *Publius Terentius Afer.* ?190–159 B.C., Roman comic dramatist. His six comedies, *Andria, Hecyra, Heauton Timoroumenos, Eunuchus, Phormio,* and *Adelphoe,* are based on Greek originals by Menander.
Terengganu (tɛrɛŋ'gɑːnuː) *n* a variant spelling of **Trengganu.**
te reo (teɪ 'reɪəʊ) *n N.Z.* the Maori language. [Maori, literally: the language]
terephthalic acid (ˌtɛrɛf'θælɪk) *n* a white crystalline water-insoluble carboxylic acid used in making polyester resins such as Terylene; 1,4-benzenedicarboxylic acid. Formula: $C_6H_4(COOH)_2$. [C20: from TEREBENE + PHTHALIC ACID]
Teresa *or* **Theresa** (tə'riːzə; *Spanish* te'resa) *n* **1 Saint,** known as *Teresa of Avila.* 1515–82, Spanish nun and mystic. She reformed the Carmelite order and founded 17 convents. Her writings include a spiritual autobiography and *The Way to Perfection.* Feast day: Oct. 15. **2 Mother,** original name *Agnes Gonxha Bojaxhiu.* 1910–97, Indian Roman Catholic missionary, born in Skopje, now in the Former Yugoslav Republic of Macedonia, of Albanian parents: noted for her work among the starving in Calcutta; Nobel peace prize 1979. ◆ See also **Thérèse de Lisieux.**
Tereshkova (*Russian* tɪrɪʃ'kɔvə) *n* **Valentina Vladimirovna** (vəlɪn'tinə vla'dimirəvnə). born 1937, Soviet cosmonaut; first woman in space (1963).

Teresina (*Portuguese* tere'zina) *n* an inland port in NE Brazil, capital of Piauí state, on the Parnaíba River: chief commercial centre of the Parnaíba valley. Pop.: 556 073 (1991). Former name: **Therezina.**

terete ('tɛri:t) *adj* (esp. of plant parts) cylindrical and tapering. [C17: from Latin *teres* smooth, from *terere* to rub]

Tereus ('tɪərɪəs) *n Greek myth.* a prince of Thrace, who raped Philomela, sister of his wife Procne, and was punished by being turned into a hoopoe.

tergiversate ('tɜ:dʒɪvəˌseɪt) *vb* (*intr*) **1** to change sides or loyalties; apostatize. **2** to be evasive or ambiguous; equivocate. [C17: from Latin *tergiversārī* to turn one's back, from *tergum* back + *vertere* to turn] ▸ ˌ**tergiver'sation** *n* ▸ '**tergiverˌsator** *or* **tergiversant** ('tɜ:dʒɪˌvɜ:sᵊnt) *n* ▸ ˌ**tergi'versatory** *adj*

tergum ('tɜ:gəm) *n, pl* **-ga** (-gə). a cuticular plate covering the dorsal surface of a body segment of an arthropod. Compare **sternum** (sense 3). [C19: from Latin: the back] ▸ '**tergal** *adj*

teriyaki (ˌtɛrɪ'jækɪ) *adj* **1** *Japanese cookery.* basted with soy sauce and rice wine and broiled over an open fire. ◆ *n* **2** a dish prepared in this way. [from Japanese, from *teri* glaze + *yaki* to broil]

term (tɜ:m) *n* **1** a name, expression, or word used for some particular thing, esp. in a specialized field of knowledge: *a medical term.* **2** any word or expression. **3** a limited period of time: *his second term of office; a prison term.* **4** any of the divisions of the academic year during which a school, college, etc., is in session. **5** a point in time determined for an event or for the end of a period. **6** Also called: **full term.** the period at which childbirth is imminent. **7** *Law.* **7a** an estate or interest in land limited to run for a specified period: *a term of years.* **7b** the duration of an estate, etc. **7c** (formerly) a period of time during which sessions of courts of law were held. **7d** time allowed to a debtor to settle. **8** *Maths.* either of the expressions the ratio of which is a fraction or proportion, any of the separate elements of a sequence, or any of the individual addends of a polynomial or series. **9** *Logic.* **9a** the word or phrase that forms either the subject or predicate of a proposition. **9b** a name or variable, as opposed to a predicate. **9c** one of the relata of a relation. **9d** any of the three subjects or predicates occurring in a syllogism. **10** Also called: **terminal, terminus, terminal figure.** *Architect.* a sculptured post, esp. one in the form of an armless bust or an animal on the top of a square pillar. **11** *Australian Rules football.* the usual word for **quarter** (sense 10). **12** *Archaic.* a boundary or limit. ◆ *vb* **13** (*tr*) to designate; call: *he was termed a thief.* ◆ See also **terms.** [C13: from Old French *terme,* from Latin *terminus* end] ▸ '**termly** *adv*

term. *abbrev. for:* **1** terminal. **2** termination.

termagant ('tɜ:məgənt) *n* **a** a shrewish woman; scold. **b** (*as modifier*): *a termagant woman.* [C13: from earlier *Tervagaunt,* from Old French *Tervagan,* from Italian *Trivigante;* after an arrogant character in medieval mystery plays who was supposed to be a Muslim deity] ▸ '**termagancy** *n* ▸ '**termagantly** *adv*

termer ('tɜ:mə) *n* a variant spelling of **termor.**

-termer *n* (*in combination*) a person serving a specified length of time in prison: *a short-termer.*

terminable ('tɜ:mɪnəbᵊl, 'tɜ:mnəbᵊl) *adj* **1** able to be terminated. **2** terminating after a specific period or event: *a terminable annuity.* ▸ ˌ**termina'bility** *or* '**terminableness** *n* ▸ '**terminably** *adv*

terminal ('tɜ:mɪnᵊl) *adj* **1** of, being, or situated at an end, terminus, or boundary: *a terminal station; terminal buds.* **2** of, relating to, or occurring after or in a term: *terminal leave.* **3** (of a disease) terminating in death: *terminal cancer.* **4** *Informal.* extreme: *terminal boredom.* **5** of or relating to the storage or delivery of freight at a warehouse: *a terminal service.* ◆ *n* **6** a terminating point, part, or place. **7a** a point at which current enters or leaves an electrical device, such as a battery or a circuit. **7b** a conductor by which current enters or leaves at such a point. **8** *Computing.* a device having input/output links with a computer but situated at a distance from the computer. **9** *Architect.* **9a** an ornamental carving at the end of a structure. **9b** another name for **term** (sense 10). **10a** a point or station usually at the end of the line of a railway, serving as an important access point for passengers or freight. **10b** a less common name for **terminus. 11** a purpose-built reception and departure structure at the terminus of a bus, sea, or air transport route. **12** a site where raw material is unloaded, stored, in some cases reprocessed, and reloaded for further transportation, esp. an onshore installation designed to receive offshore oil or gas from tankers or a pipeline. **13** *Physiol.* **13a** the smallest arteriole before its division into capillaries. **13b** either of two veins that collect blood from the thalamus and surrounding structures and empty it into the internal cerebral vein. **13c** the portion of a bronchiole just before it subdivides into the air sacs of the lungs. [C15: from Latin *terminālis,* from *terminus* end] ▸ '**terminally** *adv*

terminal market *n* a commodity market in a trading centre rather than at a producing centre.

terminal platform *n* (in the oil industry) an offshore platform from which oil or gas is pumped ashore through a pipeline.

terminal velocity *n* **1** the constant maximum velocity reached by a body falling under gravity through a fluid, esp. the atmosphere. **2** the velocity of a missile or projectile when it reaches its target. **3** the maximum velocity attained by a rocket, missile, or shell flying in a parabolic flight path. **4** the maximum velocity that an aircraft can attain, as determined by its total drag.

terminate ('tɜ:mɪˌneɪt) *vb* **1** (when *intr,* often foll. by *in* or *with*) to form, be, or put an end (to); conclude: *to terminate a pregnancy; their relationship terminated amicably.* **2** (*tr*) to connect (suitable circuitry) to the end of an electrical transmission line to absorb the energy and avoid reflections. **3** (*intr*) *Maths.* (of a decimal expansion) to have only a finite number of digits. [C16: from Latin *terminātus* limited, from *termināre* to set boundaries, from *terminus* end] ▸ '**terminative** *adj* ▸ '**terminatory** *adj*

termination (ˌtɜ:mɪ'neɪʃən) *n* **1** the act of terminating or the state of being terminated. **2** something that terminates. **3** a final result. ▸ ˌ**termi'national** *adj*

terminator ('tɜ:mɪˌneɪtə) *n* the line dividing the illuminated and dark part of the moon or a planet.

terminology (ˌtɜ:mɪ'nɒlədʒɪ) *n, pl* **-gies. 1** the body of specialized words relating to a particular subject. **2** the study of terms. [C19: from Medieval Latin *terminus* term, from Latin: end] ▸ **terminological** (ˌtɜ:mɪnə'lɒdʒɪkᵊl) *adj* ▸ ˌ**termino'logically** *adv* ▸ ˌ**termi'nologist** *n*

term insurance *n* life assurance, usually low in cost and offering no cash value, that provides for the payment of a specified sum of money only if the insured dies within a stipulated period of time.

terminus ('tɜ:mɪnəs) *n, pl* **-ni** (-naɪ) *or* **-nuses. 1** the last or final part or point. **2** either end of a railway, bus route, etc., or a station or town at such a point. **3** a goal aimed for. **4** a boundary or boundary marker. **5** *Architect.* another name for **term** (sense 10). [C16: from Latin: end; related to Greek *termōn* boundary]

Terminus ('tɜ:mɪnəs) *n* the Roman god of boundaries.

terminus ad quem *Latin.* ('tɜ:mɪˌnʊs æd 'kwɛm) *n* the aim or terminal point. [literally: the end to which]

terminus a quo *Latin.* ('tɜ:mɪˌnʊs ɑ: 'kwəʊ) *n* the starting point; beginning. [literally: the end from which]

termitarium (ˌtɜ:mɪ'tɛərɪəm) *n, pl* **-ia** (-ɪə). the nest of a termite colony. [C20: from TERMITE + -ARIUM]

termite ('tɜ:maɪt) *n* any whitish ant-like social insect of the order *Isoptera,* of warm and tropical regions. Some species feed on wood, causing damage to furniture, buildings, trees, etc. Also called: **white ant.** [C18: from New Latin *termitēs* white ants, pl of *termes,* from Latin: a woodworm; related to Greek *tetrainein* to bore through] ▸ **termitic** (tɜ:'mɪtɪk) *adj*

termless ('tɜ:mlɪs) *adj* **1** without limit or boundary. **2** unconditional. **3** an archaic word for **indescribable.**

termor *or* **termer** ('tɜ:mə) *n Property law.* a person who holds an estate for a term of years or until he dies. [C14: from Anglo-French *termer,* from *terme* TERM]

terms (tɜ:mz) *pl n* **1** (usually specified prenominally) the actual language or mode of presentation used: *he described the project in loose terms.* **2** conditions of an agreement: *you work here on our terms.* **3** a sum of money paid for a service or credit; charges. **4** (usually preceded by *on*) mutual relationship or standing: *they are on affectionate terms.* **5 in terms of.** as expressed by; regarding: *in terms of money he was no better off.* **6 come to terms.** to reach acceptance or agreement: *to come to terms with one's failings.*

terms of trade *pl n Economics, Brit.* the ratio of export prices to import prices. It measures a nation's trading position, which improves when export prices rise faster or fall slower than import prices.

tern[1] (tɜ:n) *n* any aquatic bird of the subfamily *Sterninae,* having a forked tail, long narrow wings, a pointed bill, and a typically black-and-white plumage: family *Laridae* (gulls, etc.), order *Charadriiformes.* [C18: from Old Norse *therna;* related to Norwegian *terna,* Swedish *tärna*]

tern[2] (tɜ:n) *n* **1** a three-masted schooner. **2** *Rare.* a group of three. [C14: from Old French *terne,* from Italian *terno,* from Latin *ternī* three each; related to Latin *ter* thrice, *trēs* three]

ternary ('tɜ:nərɪ) *adj* **1** consisting of three or groups of three. **2** *Maths.* **2a** (of a number system) to the base three. **2b** involving or containing three variables. **3** (of an alloy, mixture, or chemical compound) having three different components or composed of three different elements. ◆ *n, pl* **-ries. 4** a group of three. [C14: from Latin *ternārius,* from *ternī* three each]

ternary form *n* a musical structure consisting of two contrasting sections followed by a repetition of the first; the form *aba.* Also called: **song form.**

ternate ('tɜ:nɪt, -neɪt) *adj* **1** (esp. of a leaf) consisting of three leaflets or other parts. **2** (esp. of plants) having groups of three members. [C18: from New Latin *ternātus,* from Medieval Latin *ternāre* to increase threefold] ▸ '**ternately** *adv*

terne (tɜ:n) *n* **1** Also called: **terne metal.** an alloy of lead containing tin (10–20 per cent) and antimony (1.5–2 per cent). **2** Also called: **terne plate.** steel plate coated with this alloy. [C16: perhaps from French *terne* dull, from Old French *ternir* to TARNISH]

Terni (*Italian* 'tɛrni) *n* an industrial city in central Italy, in Umbria: site of waterfalls created in Roman times. Pop.: 108 435 (1996 est.).

ternion ('tɜ:nɪən) *n Rare.* a group of three. [C16: from Latin *terniō* triad, from *ternī* three each; related to *ter* thrice]

Ternopol (*Russian* tɪr'nɔpəlj) *n* a town in the W Ukraine, on the River Seret: formerly under Polish rule. Pop.: 235 000 (1996 est.). Polish name: **Tarnopol.**

terotechnology (ˌtɪərəʊtɛk'nɒlədʒɪ, ˌtɛr-) *n* a branch of technology that utilizes management, financial, and engineering expertise in the installation and efficient operation and maintenance of equipment and machinery. [C20: from Greek *tērein* to care for + TECHNOLOGY]

terpene ('tɜ:pi:n) *n* any one of a class of unsaturated hydrocarbons, such as limonene, pinene, and the carotenes, that are found in the essential oils of many plants, esp. conifers. Their molecules contain isoprene units and have the general formula $(C_5H_8)_n$. [C19: *terp-* from obsolete *terpentine* TURPENTINE + -ENE] ▸ **ter'penic** *adj*

terpineol (tɜ:'pɪnɪˌɒl) *n* a terpene alcohol with an odour of lilac, existing in three isomeric forms that occur in several essential oils. A mixture of the isomers is used as a solvent and in flavourings and perfumes. Formula: $C_{10}H_{17}OH$. [C20: from TERPENE + -INE[2] + -OL[1]]

Terpsichore (tɜ:p'sɪkərɪ) *n* the Muse of the dance and of choral song. [C18: via Latin from Greek, from *terpsikhoros* delighting in the dance, from *terpein* to delight + *khoros* dance; see CHORUS]

Terpsichorean (ˌtɜ:psɪkə'rɪən, -'kɔ:rɪən) *Often used facetiously.* ◆ *adj also* **Terpsichoreal. 1** of or relating to dancing or the art of dancing. ◆ *n* **2** a dancer.

terr. *abbrev. for:* **1** terrace. **2** territory.
terra ('tɛrə) *n* (in legal contexts) earth or land. [from Latin]
terra alba ('ælbə) *n* **1** a white finely powdered form of gypsum, used to make paints, paper, etc. **2** any of various other white earthy substances, such as kaolin, pipeclay, and magnesia. [from Latin, literally: white earth]
terrace ('tɛrəs) *n* **1** a horizontal flat area of ground, often one of a series in a slope. **2a** a row of houses, usually identical and having common dividing walls, or the street onto which they face. **2b** (*cap. when part of a street name*): *Grosvenor Terrace.* **3** a paved area alongside a building, serving partly as a garden. **4** a balcony or patio. **5** the flat roof of a house built in a Spanish or Oriental style. **6** a flat area bounded by a short steep slope formed by the down-cutting of a river or by erosion. **7** (*usually pl*) **7a** unroofed tiers around a football pitch on which the spectators stand. **7b** the spectators themselves. ♦ *vb* **8** (*tr*) to make into or provide with a terrace or terraces. [C16: from Old French *terrasse,* from Old Provençal *terrassa* pile of earth, from *terra* earth, from Latin] ▸ **'terraceless** *adj*
terraced house *n Brit.* a house that is part of a terrace. U.S. and Canadian names: **row house, town house.** ▸ **terraced housing** *n*
terracing ('tɛrəsɪŋ) *n* **1** a series of terraces, esp. one dividing a slope into a step-like system of flat narrow fields. **2** the act of making a terrace or terraces. **3** another name for **terrace** (sense 7a).
terracotta (ˌtɛrə'kɒtə) *n* **1** a hard unglazed brownish-red earthenware, or the clay from which it is made. **2** something made of terracotta, such as a sculpture. **3** a strong reddish-brown to brownish-orange colour. ♦ *adj* **4** made of terracotta: *a terracotta urn.* **5** of the colour terracotta: *a terracotta carpet.* [C18: from Italian, literally: baked earth]
terra firma ('fɜːmə) *n* the solid earth; firm ground. [C17: from Latin]
terrain (tə'reɪn, 'tɛreɪn) *n* **1** ground or a piece of ground, esp. with reference to its physical character or military potential: *radio reception can be difficult in mountainous terrain; a rocky terrain.* **2** a variant spelling of **terrane.** [C18: from French, ultimately from Latin *terrēnum* ground, from *terra* earth]
terra incognita *Latin.* ('tɛrə ɪn'kɒgnɪtə) *n* an unexplored or unknown land, region, or area for study.
Terramycin (ˌtɛrə'maɪsɪn) *n Trademark.* a broad-spectrum antibiotic used in treating various infections.
terrane *or* **terrain** ('tɛreɪn) *n* a series of rock formations, esp. one having a prevalent type of rock. [C19: see TERRAIN]
terrapin ('tɛrəpɪn) *n* any of various web-footed chelonian reptiles that live on land and in fresh water and feed on small aquatic animals: family *Emydidae.* Also called: **water tortoise.** [C17: of Algonquian origin; compare Delaware *torope* turtle]
terrarium (tɛ'rɛərɪəm) *n, pl* **-rariums** *or* **-raria** (-'rɛərɪə). **1** an enclosure for keeping small land animals. **2** a glass container, often a globe, in which plants are grown. [C19: New Latin, from Latin *terra* earth]
terra sigillata ('tɛrə ˌsɪdʒɪ'lɑːtə) *n* **1** a reddish-brown clayey earth found on the Aegean island of Lemnos: formerly used as an astringent and in the making of earthenware pottery. **2** any similar earth resembling this. **3** earthenware pottery made from this or a similar earth, esp. Samian ware. [from Latin: sealed earth]
terrazzo (tɛ'rætsəʊ) *n* a floor or wall finish made by setting marble or other stone chips into a layer of mortar and polishing the surface. [C20: from Italian: TERRACE]
Terre Adélie (*French* tɛr adeli) *n* the French name for **Adélie Land.**
terrene (tɛ'riːn) *adj* **1** of or relating to the earth; worldly; mundane. **2** *Rare.* of earth; earthy. ♦ *n* **3** a land. **4** a rare word for **earth.** [C14: from Anglo-Norman, from Latin *terrēnus,* from *terra* earth] ▸ **ter'renely** *adv*
terreplein ('tɛəˌpleɪn) *n* **1** the top of a rampart where guns are placed behind the parapet. **2** an embankment with a level top surface. [C16: from French, from Medieval Latin phrase *terrā plēnus* filled with earth]
terrestrial (tə'rɛstrɪəl) *adj* **1** of or relating to the earth. **2** of or belonging to the land as opposed to the sea or air. **3** (of animals and plants) living or growing on the land. **4** earthly, worldly, or mundane. **5** (of television signals) sent over the earth's surface from a transmitter on land, rather than by satellite. ♦ *n* **6** an inhabitant of the earth. [C15: from Latin *terrestris,* from *terra* earth] ▸ **ter'restrially** *adv* ▸ **ter'restrialness** *n*
terrestrial guidance *n* a method of missile or rocket guidance in which the flight path is controlled by reference to the strength and direction of the earth's gravitational or magnetic field. Compare **inertial guidance.**
terrestrial telescope *n* a telescope for use on earth rather than for making astronomical observations. Such telescopes contain an additional lens or prism system to produce an erect image. Compare **astronomical telescope.**
terret ('tɛrɪt) *n* **1** either of the two metal rings on a harness saddle through which the reins are passed. **2** the ring on a dog's collar for attaching the lead. [C15: variant of *toret,* from Old French, diminutive of *tor* loop; see TOUR]
terre-verte ('tɛəˌvɜːt) *n* **1** a greyish-green pigment used in paints, consisting of powdered glauconite. ♦ *adj* **2** of a greyish-green colour. [C17: from French, literally: green earth]
terrible ('tɛrəbᵊl) *adj* **1** very serious or extreme: *a terrible cough.* **2** *Informal.* of poor quality; unpleasant or bad: *a terrible meal; a terrible play.* **3** causing terror. **4** causing awe: *the terrible nature of God.* [C15: from Latin *terribilis,* from *terrēre* to terrify] ▸ **'terribleness** *n*
terribly ('tɛrəblɪ) *adv* **1** in a terrible manner. **2** (intensifier): *you're terribly kind.*
terricolous (tɛ'rɪkələs) *adj* living on or in the soil. [C19: from Latin *terricola,* from *terra* earth + *colere* to inhabit]
terrier[1] ('tɛrɪə) *n* any of several usually small, active, and short-bodied breeds of dog, originally trained to hunt animals living underground. [C15: from Old French *chien terrier* earth dog, from Medieval Latin *terrārius* belonging to the earth, from Latin *terra* earth]
terrier[2] ('tɛrɪə) *n English legal history.* a register or survey of land. [C15: from Old French, from Medieval Latin *terrārius* of the land, from Latin *terra* land]
Terrier ('tɛrɪə) *n Informal.* a member of the British Army's Territorial and Volunteer Reserve.
terrific (tə'rɪfɪk) *adj* **1** very great or intense: *a terrific noise.* **2** *Informal.* very good; excellent: *a terrific singer.* **3** very frightening. [C17: from Latin *terrificus,* from *terrēre* to frighten; see -FIC] ▸ **ter'rifically** *adv*
terrify ('tɛrɪˌfaɪ) *vb* **-fies, -fying, -fied.** (*tr*) to inspire fear or dread in; frighten greatly. [C16: from Latin *terrificāre,* from *terrēre* to alarm + *facere* to cause] ▸ **'terriˌfier** *n* ▸ **'terriˌfying** *adj* ▸ **'terriˌfyingly** *adv*
terrigenous (tɛ'rɪdʒɪnəs) *adj* **1** of or produced by the earth. **2** (of geological deposits) formed in the sea from material derived from the land by erosion. [C17: from Latin *terrigenus,* from *terra* earth + *gignere* to beget]
terrine (tɛ'riːn) *n* **1** an oval earthenware cooking dish with a tightly fitting lid used for pâtés, etc. **2** the food cooked or served in such a dish, esp. pâté. **3** another word for **tureen.** [C18: earlier form of TUREEN]
territorial (ˌtɛrɪ'tɔːrɪəl) *adj* **1** of or relating to a territory or territories. **2** restricted to or owned by a particular territory: *the Indian territorial waters.* **3** local or regional. **4** pertaining to a territorial army, providing a reserve of trained men for use in emergency. ▸ **ˌterri'torially** *adv*
Territorial (ˌtɛrɪ'tɔːrɪəl) *n* a member of a territorial army, esp. the British Army's Territorial and Volunteer Reserve.
Territorial Army *n* (in Britain) a standing reserve army originally organized between 1907 and 1908. Full name: **Territorial and Volunteer Reserve.**
territorialism (ˌtɛrɪ'tɔːrɪəlɪzəm) *n* **1** a social system under which the predominant force in the state is the landed class. **2** a former Protestant theory that the civil government has the right to determine the religious beliefs of the subjects of a state. ▸ **ˌterri'torialist** *n*
territoriality (ˌtɛrɪˌtɔːrɪ'ælɪtɪ) *n* **1** the state or rank of being a territory. **2** the behaviour shown by an animal when establishing and defending its territory.
territorialize *or* **territorialise** (ˌtɛrɪ'tɔːrɪəˌlaɪz) *vb* (*tr*) **1** to make a territory of. **2** to place on a territorial basis: *the militia was territorialized.* **3** to enlarge (a country) by acquiring more territory. **4** to make territorial. ▸ **ˌterriˌtoriali'zation** *or* **ˌterriˌtoriali'sation** *n*
territorial waters *pl n* the waters over which a nation exercises jurisdiction and control.
Territorian (ˌtɛrɪ'tɔːrɪən) *n Austral.* an inhabitant of the Northern Territory.
territory ('tɛrɪtərɪ, -trɪ) *n, pl* **-ries. 1** any tract of land; district. **2** the geographical domain under the jurisdiction of a political unit, esp. of a sovereign state. **3** the district for which an agent, etc., is responsible: *a salesman's territory.* **4** an area inhabited and defended by an individual animal or a breeding pair of animals. **5** an area of knowledge: *science isn't my territory.* **6** (in football, hockey, etc.) the area defended by a team. **7** (*often cap.*) a region of a country, esp. of a federal state, that enjoys less autonomy and a lower status than most constituent parts of the state. **8** (*often cap.*) a protectorate or other dependency of a country. [C15: from Latin *territōrium* land surrounding a town, from *terra* land]
Territory ('tɛrɪtərɪ, -trɪ) *n* **the.** *Austral.* See **Northern Territory.**
terror ('tɛrə) *n* **1** great fear, panic, or dread. **2** a person or thing that inspires great dread. **3** *Informal.* a troublesome person or thing, esp. a child. **4** terrorism. [C14: from Old French *terreur,* from Latin *terror,* from *terrēre* to frighten; related to Greek *trein* to run away in terror] ▸ **'terrorful** *adj* ▸ **'terrorless** *adj*
terrorism ('tɛrəˌrɪzəm) *n* **1** systematic use of violence and intimidation to achieve some goal. **2** the act of terrorizing. **3** the state of being terrorized.
terrorist ('tɛrərɪst) *n* **a** a person who employs terror or terrorism, esp. as a political weapon. **b** (*as modifier*): *terrorist tactics.* ▸ **ˌterror'istic** *adj*
terrorize *or* **terrorise** ('tɛrəˌraɪz) *vb* (*tr*) **1** to coerce or control by violence, fear, threats, etc. **2** to inspire with dread; terrify. ▸ **ˌterrori'zation** *or* **ˌterrori'sation** *n* ▸ **'terrorˌizer** *or* **'terrorˌiser** *n*
terror-stricken *or* **terror-struck** *adj* in a state of terror.
terry ('tɛrɪ) *n, pl* **-ries. 1** an uncut loop in the pile of towelling or a similar fabric. **2a** a fabric with such a pile on both sides. **2b** (*as modifier*): *a terry towel.* [C18: perhaps variant of TERRET]
Terry ('tɛrɪ) *n* **1** Dame **Ellen.** 1847–1928, British actress, noted for her Shakespearean roles opposite Sir Henry Irving and for her correspondence with George Bernard Shaw. **2** (**John**) **Quinlan** ('kwɪnlən). born 1937, British architect, noted for his works in neoclassical style, such as the Richmond riverside project (1984).
terse (tɜːs) *adj* **1** neatly brief and concise. **2** curt; abrupt. [C17: from Latin *tersus* precise, from *tergēre* to polish] ▸ **'tersely** *adv* ▸ **'terseness** *n*
tertial ('tɜːʃəl) *adj, n* another word for **tertiary** (senses 5, 6). [C19: from Latin *tertius* third, from *ter* thrice, from *trēs* three]
tertian ('tɜːʃən) *adj* **1** (of a fever or the symptoms of a disease, esp. malaria) occurring every other day. ♦ *n* **2** a tertian fever or symptoms. [C14: from Latin *febris tertiāna* fever occurring every third day, reckoned inclusively, from *tertius* third]
tertiary ('tɜːʃərɪ) *adj* **1** third in degree, order, etc. **2** (of an industry) involving services as opposed to extraction or manufacture, such as transport, finance, etc. Compare **primary** (sense 8b), **secondary** (sense 7). **3** *R.C. Church.* of or relating to a Third Order. **4** *Chem.* **4a** (of an organic compound) having a functional group attached to a carbon atom that is attached to three other groups. **4b** (of an amine) having three organic groups attached to a nitrogen atom. **4c** (of a salt) derived from a tribasic acid by replacement of all its acidic hydrogen atoms with metal atoms or electropositive groups. **5** Also: **tertial.** *Ornithol., rare.* of, relating to, or designating any of the small flight feathers attached to the part of the humerus nearest to the body. ♦ *n, pl* **-tiaries. 6** Also called: **tertial.** *Ornithol., rare.* any of the tertiary feathers. **7** *R.C. Church.* a member of a

Third Order. [C16: from Latin *tertiārius* containing one third, from *tertius* third]

Tertiary ('tɜːʃərɪ) *adj* **1** of, denoting, or formed in the first period of the Cenozoic era, which lasted for 69 million years, during which mammals became dominant. ◆ *n* **2 the.** the Tertiary period or rock system, divided into Palaeocene, Eocene, Oligocene, Miocene, and Pliocene epochs or series.

tertiary bursary *n N.Z.* a noncompetitive award granted to all pupils who have passed a university entrance examination.

tertiary college *n Brit.* a college system incorporating the secondary school sixth form and vocational courses.

tertiary colour *n* a colour formed by mixing two secondary colours.

tertium quid ('tɜːtɪəm 'kwɪd) *n* an unknown or indefinite thing related in some way to two known or definite things, but distinct from both: *there is either right or wrong, with no tertium quid.* [C18: from Late Latin, rendering Greek *triton ti* some third thing]

Tertullian (tɜː'tʌlɪən) *n* Latin name *Quintus Septimius Florens Tertullianus.* ?160–?220 A.D., Carthaginian Christian theologian, who wrote in Latin rather than Greek and originated much of Christian terminology.

Teruel (*Spanish* te'rwel) *n* a city in E central Spain: 15th-century cathedral; scene of fierce fighting during the Spanish Civil War. Pop.: 31 000 (1991).

tervalent (tɜː'veɪlənt) *adj Chem.* another word for **trivalent.** ▸ **ter'valency** *n*

Terylene ('tɛrɪ,liːn) *n Trademark.* a synthetic polyester fibre or fabric based on terephthalic acid, characterized by lightness and crease resistance and used for clothing, sheets, ropes, sails, etc. U.S. name (trademark): **Dacron.**

terza rima ('tɛətsə 'riːmə) *n, pl* **terze rime** ('tɛətseɪ 'riːmeɪ). a verse form of Italian origin consisting of a series of tercets in which the middle line of one tercet rhymes with the first and third lines of the next. [C19: from Italian, literally: third rhyme]

terzetto (tɜː'tsetəʊ) *n, pl* **-tos** *or* **-ti** (-tɪ). *Music.* a trio, esp. a vocal one. [C18: Italian: trio; see TERCET]

TES *abbrev. for* Times Educational Supplement.

TESL ('tɛsᵊl) *acronym for* Teaching (of) English as a Second Language.

tesla ('tɛslə) *n* the derived SI unit of magnetic flux density equal to a flux of 1 weber in an area of 1 square metre. Symbol: T [C20: named after Nikola TESLA]

Tesla ('tɛslə) *n* **Nikola** ('nɪkələ). 1857–1943, U.S. electrical engineer and inventor, born in Smiljan, now in Croatia. His inventions include a transformer, generators, and dynamos.

tesla coil *n* a step-up transformer with an air core, used for producing high voltages at high frequencies. The secondary circuit is tuned to resonate with the primary winding. [C20: named after Nikola TESLA]

TESSA ('tɛsə) *n* (in Britain) *acronym for* Tax Exempt Special Savings Account; a former (available 1991–99) tax-free savings scheme.

tessellate ('tɛsɪ,leɪt) *vb* **1** (*tr*) to construct, pave, or inlay with a mosaic of small tiles. **2** (*intr*) (of identical shapes) to fit together exactly: *triangles will tessellate but octagons will not.* [C18: from Latin *tessellātus* checked, from *tessella* small stone cube, from TESSERA]

tessellation (,tɛsɪ'leɪʃən) *n* **1** the act of tessellating. **2** the form or a specimen of tessellated work.

tessera ('tɛsərə) *n, pl* **-serae** (-sə,riː). **1** a small square tile of stone, glass, etc., used in mosaics. **2** a die, tally, etc., used in classical times, made of bone or wood. [C17: from Latin, from Ionic Greek *tesseres* four] ▸ **'tesseral** *adj*

Tessin (tɛ'siːn) *n* the German name for **Ticino.**

tessitura (,tɛsɪ'tʊərə) *n Music.* **1** the general pitch level of a piece of vocal music: *an uncomfortably high tessitura.* **2** the compass or range of a voice. [Italian: texture, from Latin *textura;* see TEXTURE]

test[1] (tɛst) *vb* **1** to ascertain (the worth, capability, or endurance) of (a person or thing) by subjection to certain examinations; try. **2** (often foll. by *for*) to carry out an examination on (a substance, material, or system) by applying some chemical or physical procedure designed to indicate the presence of a substance or the possession of a property: *to test food for arsenic; to test for magnetization.* **3** (*intr*) to achieve a specified result in a test: *a quarter of the patients at the clinic tested positive for the AIDS virus.* **4** (*tr*) to put under severe strain: *the long delay tested my patience.* **5 test the water.** to make an exploratory or initial approach; sound out. ◆ *n* **6** a method, practice, or examination designed to test a person or thing. **7** a series of questions or problems designed to test a specific skill or knowledge: *an intelligence test.* **8** a standard of judgment; criterion. **9a** a chemical reaction or physical procedure for testing a substance, material, etc. **9b** a chemical reagent used in such a procedure: *litmus is a test for acids.* **9c** the result of the procedure or the evidence gained from it: *the test for alcohol was positive.* **10** *Sport.* See **test match. 11** *Archaic.* a declaration or confirmation of truth, loyalty, etc.; oath. **12** (*modifier*) performed as a test: *test drive; test flight.* [C14 (in the sense: vessel used in treating metals): from Latin *testum* earthen vessel] ▸ **'testable** *adj* ▸ **,testa'bility** *n* ▸ **'testing** *adj*

test[2] (tɛst) *n* **1** the hard or tough outer covering of certain invertebrates and tunicates. **2** a variant of **testa.** [C19: from Latin *testa* shell]

testa ('tɛstə) *n, pl* **-tae** (-tiː). a hard protective outer layer of the seeds of flowering plants; seed coat. [C18: from Latin: shell; see TEST[2]]

testaceous (tɛ'steɪʃəs) *adj Biology.* **1** of, relating to, or possessing a test or testa. **2** of the reddish-brown colour of terra cotta. [C17: from Latin *testācens,* from TESTA]

Test Act *n* a law passed in 1673 in England to exclude Catholics from public life by requiring all persons holding offices under the Crown, such as army officers, to take the Anglican Communion and perform other acts forbidden to a Catholic: repealed in 1828.

testament ('tɛstəmənt) *n* **1** *Law.* a will setting out the disposition of personal property (esp. in the phrase **last will and testament**). **2** a proof, attestation, or tribute: *his success was a testament to his skills.* **3a** a covenant instituted between God and man, esp. the covenant of Moses or that instituted by Christ. **3b** a copy of either the Old or the New Testament, or of the complete Bible. [C14: from Latin: a will, from *testārī* to bear witness, from *testis* a witness] ▸ **,testa'mental** *adj*

Testament ('tɛstəmənt) *n* **1** either of the two main parts of the Bible; the Old Testament or the New Testament. **2** the New Testament as distinct from the Old.

testamentary (,tɛstə'mentərɪ) *adj* **1** of or relating to a will or testament. **2** derived from, bequeathed, or appointed by a will. **3** contained or set forth in a will.

testate ('testeɪt, 'tɛstɪt) *adj* **1** having left a legally valid will at death. ◆ *n* **2** a person who dies testate. ◆ Compare **intestate.** [C15: from Latin *testārī* to make a will; see TESTAMENT] ▸ **testacy** ('tɛstəsɪ) *n*

testator (tɛ'steɪtə) *or* (*fem*) **testatrix** (tɛ'steɪtrɪks) *n* a person who makes a will, esp. one who dies testate. [C15: from Anglo-French *testatour,* from Late Latin *testātor,* from Latin *testārī* to make a will; see TESTAMENT]

test ban *n* an agreement among nations to forgo tests of some or all types of nuclear weapons.

test-bed *n Engineering.* an area equipped with instruments, etc., used for testing machinery, engines, etc., under working conditions.

test card *or* **pattern** *n* a complex pattern used to test the characteristics of a television transmission system.

test case *n* a legal action that serves as a precedent in deciding similar succeeding cases.

test-drive *vb* (*tr*) **-drives, -driving, -drove, -driven.** to drive (a car or other motor vehicle) for a limited period in order to assess its capabilities and limitations.

tester[1] ('tɛstə) *n* a person or thing that tests or is used for testing.

tester[2] ('tɛstə) *n* (in furniture) a canopy, esp. the canopy over a four-poster bed. [C14: from Medieval Latin *testerium,* from Late Latin *testa* a skull, from Latin: shell]

tester[3] ('tɛstə) *n* another name for **teston** (sense 2).

testes ('tɛstiːz) *n* the plural of **testis.**

testicle ('tɛstɪkᵊl) *n* either of the two male reproductive glands, in most mammals enclosed within the scrotum, that produce spermatozoa and the hormone testosterone. Also called: **testis.** [C15: from Latin *testiculus,* diminutive of *testis* testicle] ▸ **testicular** (tɛ'stɪkjʊlə) *adj*

testiculate (tɛ'stɪkjʊlɪt) *adj Botany.* having an oval shape: *the testiculate tubers of certain orchids.* [C18: from Late Latin *testiculātus;* see TESTICLE]

testify ('tɛstɪ,faɪ) *vb* **-fies, -fying, -fied. 1** (when *tr, may take a clause as object*) to state (something) formally as a declaration of fact: *I testify that I know nothing about him.* **2** *Law.* to declare or give (evidence) under oath, esp. in court. **3** (when *intr,* often foll. by *to*) to be evidence (of); serve as witness (to): *the money testified to his good faith.* **4** (*tr*) to declare or acknowledge openly. [C14: from Latin *testificārī,* from *testis* witness] ▸ **,testifi'cation** *n* ▸ **'testi,fier** *n*

testimonial (,tɛstɪ'məʊnɪəl) *n* **1a** a recommendation of the character, ability, etc., of a person or of the quality of a consumer product or service, esp. by a person whose opinion is valued. **1b** (*as modifier*): *testimonial advertising.* **2** a formal statement of truth or fact. **3** a tribute given for services or achievements. **4** a sports match to raise money for a particular player. ◆ *adj* **5** of or relating to a testimony or testimonial.

USAGE *Testimonial* is sometimes wrongly used where *testimony* is meant: *his re-election is a testimony* (not *a testimonial*) *to his popularity with his constituents.*

testimony ('tɛstɪmənɪ) *n, pl* **-nies. 1** a declaration of truth or fact. **2** *Law.* evidence given by a witness, esp. orally in court under oath or affirmation. **3** evidence testifying to something: *her success was a testimony to her good luck.* **4** *Old Testament.* **4a** the Ten Commandments, as inscribed on the two stone tables. **4b** the Ark of the Covenant as the receptacle of these (Exodus 25:16; 16:34). [C15: from Latin *testimōnium,* from *testis* witness]

testing station *n N.Z.* an establishment licensed to issue warrants of fitness for motor vehicles.

testis ('tɛstɪs) *n, pl* **-tes** (-tiːz). another word for **testicle.** [C17: from Latin, literally: witness (to masculinity)]

test marketing *n* the use of a representative segment of a total market for experimental purposes, as to test a new product about to be launched or a price change.

test match *n* (in various sports, esp. cricket) an international match, esp. one of a series.

teston ('tɛstən) *or* **testoon** (tɛ'stuːn) *n* **1** a French silver coin of the 16th century. **2** Also called: **tester.** an English silver coin of the 16th century, originally worth one shilling, bearing the head of Henry VIII. [C16: from Italian *testone,* from *testa* head, from Late Latin: skull, from Latin: shell]

testosterone (tɛ'stɒstə,rəʊn) *n* a potent steroid hormone secreted mainly by the testes. It can be extracted from the testes of animals or synthesized and used to treat androgen deficiency or promote anabolism. Formula: $C_{19}H_{28}O_2$. [C20: from TESTIS + STEROL + -ONE]

test paper *n* **1** *Chem.* paper impregnated with an indicator for use in chemical tests. See also **litmus. 2** *Brit. education.* **2a** the question sheet of a test. **2b** the paper completed by a test candidate.

test pilot *n* a pilot who flies aircraft of new design to test their performance in the air.

test tube *n* **1** a cylindrical round-bottomed glass tube open at one end: used in scientific experiments. **2** (*modifier*) made synthetically in, or as if in, a test tube: *a test-tube product.*

test-tube baby *n* **1** a fetus that has developed from an ovum fertilized in an artificial womb. **2** a baby conceived by artificial insemination.

testudinal (tɛ'stjuːdɪnᵊl) *or* **testudinary** *adj* of, relating to, or resembling a tortoise or turtle or the shell of either of these animals. [C19: from Latin TESTUDO]

testudo (tɛˈstjuːdəʊ) *n, pl* **-dines** (-dɪˌniːz). a form of shelter used by the ancient Roman Army for protection against attack from above, consisting either of a mobile arched structure or of overlapping shields held by the soldiers over their heads. [C17: from Latin: a tortoise, from *testa* a shell]

testy (ˈtɛstɪ) *adj* **-tier, -tiest.** irritable or touchy. [C14: from Anglo-Norman *testif* headstrong, from Old French *teste* head, from Late Latin *testa* skull, from Latin: shell] ► **ˈtestily** *adv* ► **ˈtestiness** *n*

Tet (tɛt) *n* the New Year as celebrated in Vietnam during the first seven days of the first lunar month of the year. [Vietnamese]

tetanic (təˈtænɪk) *adj* **1** of, relating to, or producing tetanus or the spasms of tetanus. ◆ *n* **2** a tetanic drug or agent. ► **teˈtanically** *adv*

tetanize *or* **tetanise** (ˈtɛtəˌnaɪz) *vb (tr)* to induce tetanus in (a muscle); affect (a muscle) with tetanic spasms. ► **ˌtetaniˈzation** *or* **ˌtetaniˈsation** *n*

tetanus (ˈtɛtənəs) *n* **1** Also called: **lockjaw.** an acute infectious disease in which sustained muscular spasm, contraction, and convulsion are caused by the release of exotoxins from the bacterium, *Clostridium tetani:* infection usually occurs through a contaminated wound. **2** *Physiol.* any tense contraction of a muscle, esp. when produced by electric shocks. [C16: via Latin from Greek *tetanos,* from *tetanos* taut, from *teinein* to stretch] ► **ˈtetanal** *adj* ► **ˈtetaˌnoid** *adj*

tetany (ˈtɛtənɪ) *n Pathol.* an abnormal increase in the excitability of nerves and muscles resulting in spasms of the arms and legs, caused by a deficiency of parathyroid secretion. [C19: from French *tétanie.* See TETANUS]

tetartohedral (tɪˌtɑːtəʊˈhiːdrəl) *adj* (of a crystal) having one quarter of the number of faces necessary for the full symmetry of its crystal system. [C19: from Greek *tetartos* one fourth + -HEDRAL] ► **teˌtartoˈhedrally** *adv* ► **teˌtartoˈhedralism** *or* **teˌtartoˈhedrism** *n*

tetchy (ˈtɛtʃɪ) *adj* **tetchier, tetchiest.** being or inclined to be cross, irritable, or touchy. [C16: probably from obsolete *tetch* defect, from Old French *tache* spot, of Germanic origin] ► **ˈtetchily** *adv* ► **ˈtetchiness** *n*

tête-à-tête (ˌteɪtəˈteɪt) *n, pl* **-têtes** *or* **-tête. 1a** a private conversation between two people. **1b** *(as modifier)*: *a tête-à-tête conversation.* **2** a small sofa for two people, esp. one that is S-shaped in plan so that the sitters are almost face to face. ◆ *adv* **3** intimately; in private. [C17: from French, literally: head to head]

tête-bêche (tɛtˈbɛʃ) *adj Philately.* (of an unseparated pair of stamps) printed so that one is inverted in relation to the other. [C19: from French, from *tête* head + *bêche,* from obsolete *béchevet* double-headed (originally of a bed)]

teth (tɛs; *Hebrew* tɛt) *n* the ninth letter of the Hebrew alphabet (ט) transliterated as *t* and pronounced more or less like English *t* with pharyngeal articulation.

tether (ˈtɛðə) *n* **1** a restricting rope, chain, etc., by which an animal is tied to a particular spot. **2** the range of one's endurance, etc. **3 at the end of one's tether.** distressed or exasperated to the limit of one's endurance. ◆ *vb (tr)* **4** to tie or limit with or as if with a tether. [C14: from Old Norse *tjothr;* related to Middle Dutch *tūder* tether, Old High German *zeotar* pole of a wagon]

Tethys[1] (ˈtiːθɪs, ˈtɛθ-) *n Greek myth.* a Titaness and sea goddess, wife of Oceanus.

Tethys[2] (ˈtiːθɪs, ˈtɛθ-) *n* a large satellite of the planet Saturn.

Tethys[3] (ˈtiːθɪs, ˈtɛθ-) *n* the sea that lay between Laurasia and Gondwanaland, the two supercontinents formed by the first split of the larger supercontinent Pangaea. The Tethys Sea can be regarded as the predecessor of today's smaller Mediterranean. See also **Pangaea.**

Teton Range (ˈtiːtᵊn) *n* a mountain range in the N central U.S., mainly in NW Wyoming. Highest peak: Grand Teton, 4196 m (13 766 ft.).

tetra (ˈtɛtrə) *n, pl* **-ra** *or* **-ras.** any of various brightly coloured tropical freshwater fishes of the genus *Hemigrammus* and related genera: family *Characidae* (characins). [C20: short for New Latin *tetragonopterus* (former genus name), from TETRAGON + -O- + *-pterous,* from Greek*pteron* wing]

tetra- *or before a vowel* **tetr-** *combining form.* four: *tetrameter.* [from Greek]

tetrabasic (ˌtɛtrəˈbeɪsɪk) *adj* (of an acid) containing four replaceable hydrogen atoms. ► **tetrabasicity** (ˌtɛtrəbeɪˈsɪsɪtɪ) *n*

tetrabrach (ˈtɛtrəˌbræk) *n* (in classical prosody) a word or metrical foot composed of four short syllables (⏑⏑⏑⏑). [C19: from Greek *tetrabrakhus,* from TETRA- + *brakhus* short]

tetrabranchiate *adj* (ˌtɛtrəˈbræŋkɪɪt, -ˌeɪt). **1** of, relating to, or belonging to the *Tetrabranchiata,* a former order of cephalopod molluscs having four gills and including the pearly nautilus. ◆ *n* (ˌtɛtrəˈbræŋkɪˌeɪt). **2** any mollusc belonging to the *Tetrabranchiata.*

tetrachloride (ˌtɛtrəˈklɔːraɪd) *n* any compound that contains four chlorine atoms per molecule: *carbon tetrachloride,* CCl_4.

tetrachloromethane (ˈtɛtrəklɔːrəʊˌmiːθeɪn) *n* the systematic name for **carbon tetrachloride.**

tetrachord (ˈtɛtrəˌkɔːd) *n* (in musical theory, esp. of classical Greece) any of several groups of four notes in descending order, in which the first and last notes form a perfect fourth. [C17: from Greek *tetrakhordos* four-stringed, from TETRA- + *khordē* a string] ► **ˌtetraˈchordal** *adj*

tetracid (tɛˈtræsɪd) *adj* (of a base) capable of reacting with four molecules of a monobasic acid.

tetracyclic (ˌtɛtrəˈsaɪklɪk) *adj Chem.* (of a compound) containing four rings in its molecular structure.

tetracycline (ˌtɛtrəˈsaɪklaɪn, -klɪn) *n* an antibiotic synthesized from chlortetracycline or derived from the bacterium *Streptomyces viridifaciens:* used in treating rickettsial infections and various bacterial and viral infections. Formula: $C_{22}H_{24}N_2O_8$. [C20: from TETRA- + CYCL(IC) + -INE[2]]

tetrad (ˈtɛtræd) *n* **1** a group or series of four. **2** the number four. **3** *Botany.* a group of four cells formed by meiosis from one diploid cell. **4** *Genetics.* a four-stranded structure, formed during the pachytene stage of meiosis, consisting of paired homologous chromosomes that have each divided into two chromatids. **5** *Chem.* an element, atom, group, or ion with a valency of four. **6** *Ecology.* a square of 2 × 2 km used in distribution mapping. [C17: from Greek *tetras,* from *tettares* four]

tetradactyl (ˌtɛtrəˈdæktɪl) *n* **1** a four-toed animal. ◆ *adj also* **ˌtetraˈdactylous. 2** having four toes or fingers. [C19: from Greek *tetradaktulos,* from TETRA- + *dactulos* finger]

tetradymite (tɛˈtrædɪˌmaɪt) *n* a grey metallic mineral consisting of a telluride and sulphide of bismuth. Formula: Bi_2Te_2S. [C19: from Late Greek *tetradumos* fourfold, from Greek TETRA- + *didumos* double]

tetradynamous (ˌtɛtrəˈdaɪnəməs, -ˈdɪn-) *adj* (of plants) having six stamens, two of which are shorter than the others. [C19: from TETRA- + Greek *dunamis* power]

tetraethyl lead (ˌtɛtrəˈiːθaɪl lɛd) *n* a colourless oily insoluble liquid used in petrol to prevent knocking. Formula: $Pb(C_2H_5)_4$. Systematic name: **lead tetraethyl.**

tetrafluoroethene (ˈtɛtrəˌflʊərəʊˈɛθiːn) *n Chem.* a dense colourless gas that is polymerized to make polytetrafluorethene (PTFE). Formula: $F_2C{:}CF_2$. Also called: **tetrafluoroethylene.** [C20: from TETRA- + FLUORO- + ETHENE]

tetragon (ˈtɛtrəˌgɒn) *n* a less common name for **quadrilateral** (sense 2). [C17: from Greek *tetragōnon;* see TETRA-, -GON]

tetragonal (tɛˈtrægənᵊl) *adj* **1** Also: **dimetric.** *Crystallog.* relating or belonging to the crystal system characterized by three mutually perpendicular axes of which only two are equal. **2** of, relating to, or shaped like a quadrilateral. ► **teˈtragonally** *adv* ► **teˈtragonalness** *n*

tetragram (ˈtɛtrəˌgræm) *n* any word of four letters.

Tetragrammaton (ˌtɛtrəˈgræmətᵊn) *n Bible.* the Hebrew name for God revealed to Moses on Mount Sinai (Exodus 3), consisting of the four consonants Y H V H (or Y H W H) and regarded by Jews as too sacred to be pronounced. It is usually transliterated as *Jehovah* or *Yahweh.* Sometimes shortened to **Tetragram.** [C14: from Greek, from *tetragrammatos* having four letters, from TETRA- + *gramma* letter]

tetrahedrite (ˌtɛtrəˈhiːdraɪt) *n* a grey metallic mineral consisting of a sulphide of copper, iron, and antimony, often in the form of tetrahedral crystals: it is a source of copper. Formula: $(Cu,Fe)_{12}Sb_4S_{13}$.

tetrahedron (ˌtɛtrəˈhiːdrən) *n, pl* **-drons** *or* **-dra** (-drə). **1** a solid figure having four plane faces. A **regular tetrahedron** has faces that are equilateral triangles. See also **polyhedron. 2** any object shaped like a tetrahedron. [C16: from New Latin, from Late Greek *tetraedron;* see TETRA-, -HEDRON] ► **ˌtetraˈhedral** *adj* ► **ˌtetraˈhedrally** *adv*

tetralogy (tɛˈtrælədʒɪ) *n, pl* **-gies. 1** a series of four related works, as in drama or opera. **2** (in ancient Greece) a group of four dramas, the first three tragic and the last satiric. [C17: from Greek *tetralogia;* see TETRA-, -LOGY]

tetramerous (tɛˈtræmərəs) *adj* **1** (esp. of animals or plants) having or consisting of four parts. **2** (of certain flowers) having parts arranged in whorls of four members. [C19: from New Latin *tetramerus,* from Greek *tetramerēs*] ► **teˈtramerism** *n*

tetrameter (tɛˈtræmɪtə) *n Prosody.* **1** a line of verse consisting of four metrical feet. **2** a verse composed of such lines. **3** (in classical prosody) a line of verse composed of four dipodies.

tetramethyldiarsine (ˌtɛtrəˌmiːθaɪldaɪˈɑːsiːn) *n* an oily slightly water-soluble poisonous liquid with garlic-like odour. Its derivatives are used as accelerators for rubber. Also called (not in technical usage): **cacodyl, dicacodyl.**

tetraplegia (ˌtɛtrəˈpliːdʒɪə) *n* another name for **quadriplegia.** [from TETRA- + Greek *plegē* a blow, from *plēssein* to strike] ► **ˌtetraˈplegic** *adj*

tetraploid (ˈtɛtrəˌplɔɪd) *Genetics.* ◆ *adj* **1** having four times the haploid number of chromosomes in the nucleus. ◆ *n* **2** a tetraploid organism, nucleus, or cell.

tetrapod (ˈtɛtrəˌpɒd) *n* **1** any vertebrate that has four limbs. **2** Also called: **caltrop.** a device consisting of four arms radiating from a central point, each at about 109° to the others, so that regardless of its position on a surface, three arms form a supporting tripod and the fourth is vertical. **3** *Engineering.* a very large cast concrete structure of a similar shape piled in large numbers round breakwaters and sea defence systems to dissipate the energy of the waves.

tetrapody (tɛˈtræpədɪ) *n, pl* **-dies.** *Prosody.* a metrical unit consisting of four feet. ► **tetrapodic** (ˌtɛtrəˈpɒdɪk) *adj*

tetrapterous (tɛˈtræptərəs) *adj* **1** (of certain insects) having four wings. **2** *Biology.* having four winglike extensions or parts. [C19: from New Latin *tetrapterus,* from Greek *tetrapteros,* from TETRA- + *pteron* wing]

tetrarch (ˈtɛtrɑːk) *n* **1** the ruler of one fourth of a country. **2** a subordinate ruler, esp. of Syria under the Roman Empire. **3** the commander of one of the smaller subdivisions of a Macedonian phalanx. **4** any of four joint rulers. [C14: from Greek *tetrarkhēs;* see TETRA-, -ARCH] ► **tetrarchate** (tɛˈtrɑːˌkeɪt, -kɪt) *n* ► **teˈtrarchic** *or* **teˈtrarchical** *adj* ► **ˈtetrarchy** *n*

tetraspore (ˈtɛtrəˌspɔː) *n* any of the asexual spores that are produced in groups of four in the sporangium (**tetrasporangium**) of any of the red algae. ► **tetrasporic** (ˌtɛtrəˈspɒrɪk) *or* **tetrasporous** (ˌtɛtrəˈspɔːrəs, tɪˈtræspərəs) *adj*

tetrastich (ˈtɛtrəˌstɪk) *n* a poem, stanza, or strophe that consists of four lines. [C16: via Latin from Greek *tetrastikhon,* from TETRA- + *stikhos* row] ► **tetrastichic** (ˌtɛtrəˈstɪkɪk) *or* **tetrastichal** (tɛˈtræstɪkᵊl) *adj*

tetrastichous (tɛˈtræstɪkəs) *adj* (of flowers or leaves on a stalk) arranged in four vertical rows.

tetrasyllable (ˌtɛtrəˈsɪləbᵊl) *n* a word of four syllables. ► **tetrasyllabic** (ˌtɛtrəsɪˈlæbɪk) *or* **ˌtetrasylˈlabical** *adj*

tetratomic (ˌtɛtrəˈtɒmɪk) *adj* composed of four atoms or having four atoms per molecule: *phosgene has tetratomic molecules.*

tetravalent (ˌtɛtrəˈveɪlənt) *adj Chem.* **1** having a valency of four. **2** Also: **quadrivalent.** having four valencies. ► **ˌtetraˈvalency** *n*

Tetrazzini (*Italian* tetrat'tsi:ni) *n* **Luisa** (lu'i:za). 1871–1940, Italian coloratura soprano.

tetrode ('tɛtrəud) *n* **1** an electronic valve having four electrodes, namely a cathode, control grid, screen grid, and anode. **2** (*modifier*) (of a transistor) having two terminals on the base or gate to improve the performance at high frequencies.

tetroxide (tɛ'trɒksaɪd) *or* **tetroxid** (tɛ'trɒksɪd) *n* any oxide that contains four oxygen atoms per molecule: *osmium tetroxide,* OsO_4.

tetryl ('tɛtrɪl) *n* a yellow crystalline explosive solid used in detonators; trinitrophenylmethylnitramine. Formula: $(NO_2)_3C_6H_2N(NO_2)CH_3$. Also called: **nitramine.**

tetter ('tɛtə) *n* **1** a blister or pimple. **2** *Informal.* any of various skin eruptions, such as eczema. [Old English *teter;* related to Old High German *zitaroh,* Sanskrit *dadru,* Late Latin *derbita*]

Tetuán (tɛ'twɑ:n) *n* a city in N Morocco: capital of Spanish Morocco (1912–56). Pop.: 272 000 (1993 est.).

Tetzel *or* **Tezel** ('tɛts^əl) *n* **Johann** (jo'han). ?1465–1519, German Dominican monk. His preaching on papal indulgences provoked Luther's 95 theses at Wittenberg (1517).

Teucer ('tju:sə) *n Greek myth.* **1** a Cretan leader, who founded Troy. **2** a son of Telamon and Hesione, who distinguished himself by his archery on the side of the Greeks in the Trojan War.

teuchter ('tju:xtər) *n Scot.* (*sometimes cap.*) **a** a derogatory word used by Lowlanders for a Highlander. **b** (*as modifier*): *teuchter music.* [C20: of uncertain origin]

Teucrian ('tju:krɪən) *n, adj* another word for **Trojan.**

Teut. *abbrev. for* Teuton(ic).

Teutoburger Wald (*German* 'tɔytoburgər valt) *n* a low wooded mountain range in N Germany: possible site of the annihilation of three Roman legions by Germans under Arminius in 9 A.D.

Teuton ('tju:tən) *n* **1** a member of an ancient Germanic people from Jutland who migrated to S Gaul in the 2nd century B.C.: annihilated by a Roman army in 102 B.C. **2** a member of any people speaking a Germanic language, esp. a German. ◆ *adj* **3** Teutonic. [C18: from Latin *Teutonī* the Teutons, of Germanic origin]

Teutonic (tju:'tɒnɪk) *adj* **1** characteristic of or relating to the German people: *Teutonic thoroughness.* **2** of or relating to the ancient Teutons. **3** (not used in linguistics) of or relating to the Germanic languages. ◆ *n* **4** an obsolete name for **Germanic.** ▸ **Teu'tonically** *adv*

Teutonic order *n* a military and religious order of German knights, priests, and serving brothers founded about 1190 during the Third Crusade, later conquering large parts of the Baltic provinces and Russia. Also called: **Teutonic Knights.**

Teutonism ('tju:tə,nɪzəm) *n* **1** a German idiom, custom, or characteristic. **2** German society or civilization.

Teutonize *or* **Teutonise** ('tju:tə,naɪz) *vb* to make or become German or Germanic; Germanize. ▸ **,Teutoni'zation** *or* **,Teutoni'sation** *n*

Tevere ('te:vere) *n* the Italian name for the **Tiber.**

Tevet *or* **Tebet** (te'vet) *n* (in the Jewish calendar) the tenth month of the year according to biblical reckoning and the fourth month of the civil year, usually falling within December and January. [from Hebrew]

Tewkesbury ('tju:ksbərɪ, -brɪ) *n* a town in W England, in N Gloucestershire at the confluence of the Rivers Severn and Avon: scene of a decisive battle (1471) of the Wars of the Roses in which the Yorkists defeated the Lancastrians; 12th-century abbey. Pop.: 9488 (1991).

tex *n* a unit of weight used to measure the density of textiles. It is equal to 1 gram per 1000 metres. [C20: from French, from *textile* TEXTILE]

Tex. *abbrev. for:* **1** Texan. **2** Texas.

Texas ('tɛksəs) *n* a state of the southwestern U.S., on the Gulf of Mexico: the second largest state; part of Mexico from 1821 to 1836, when it was declared an independent republic; joined the U.S. in 1845; consists chiefly of a plain, with a wide flat coastal belt rising up to the semiarid Sacramento and Davis Mountains of the southwest; a major producer of cotton, rice, and livestock; the chief U.S. producer of oil and gas; a leading world supplier of sulphur. Capital: Austin. Pop.: 19 439 337 (1997 est.). Area: 678 927 sq. km (262 134 sq. miles). Abbrevs.: **Tex.** or (with zip code) **TX** ▸ **'Texan** *n, adj*

Texas fever *n* an infectious disease of cattle caused by the protozoan *Babesia bigemina* and transmitted by the bite of a tick.

Texas hedge *n Finance.* the opposite of a normal hedging operation, in which risk is increased by buying more than one financial instrument of the same kind.

Texas Rangers *pl n* the state police of Texas, originally formed in the 19th century to defend outlying regions against Indians and Mexicans and to fight lawlessness.

Texel ('tɛks^əl) *n* a breed of sheep originating from the Netherlands having a heavy white fleece: kept for the production of lean lambs. [C20: named after *Texel,* one of the West Frisian Islands off the Netherlands]

Tex-Mex ('tɛks,mɛks) *adj* of, relating to, or denoting the Texan version of something Mexican, such as music, food, or language.

text (tɛkst) *n* **1** the main body of a printed or written work as distinct from commentary, notes, illustrations, etc. **2** the words of something printed or written. **3** (*often pl*) a book prescribed as part of a course of study. **4** *Computing.* the words printed, written, or displayed on a visual display unit. **5** the original exact wording of a work, esp. the Bible, as distinct from a revision or translation. **6** a short passage of the Bible used as a starting point for a sermon or adduced as proof of a doctrine. **7** the topic or subject of a discussion or work. **8** *Printing.* any one of several styles of letters or types. **9** short for **textbook.** [C14: from Medieval Latin *textus* version, from Latin *textus* texture, from *texere* to compose] ▸ **'textless** *adj*

textbook ('tɛkst,bʊk) *n* **a** a book used as a standard source of information on a particular subject. **b** (*as modifier*): *a textbook example.* ▸ **'text,bookish** *adj*

textile ('tɛkstaɪl) *n* **1** any fabric or cloth, esp. woven. **2** raw material suitable to be made into cloth; fibre or yarn. ◆ *adj* **3** of or relating to fabrics or the making of fabrics. [C17: from Latin *textilis* woven, from *texere* to weave]

text processing *n* the handling of alphabetic characters by a computer.

textual ('tɛkstjʊəl) *adj* **1** of or relating to a text or texts. **2** based on or conforming to a text. ▸ **'textually** *adv*

textual criticism *n* **1** the scholarly study of manuscripts, esp. of the Bible, in an effort to establish the original text. **2** literary criticism emphasizing a close analysis of the text. ▸ **textual critic** *n*

textualism ('tɛkstjʊə,lɪzəm) *n* **1** doctrinaire adherence to a text, esp. of the Bible. **2** textual criticism, esp. of the Bible. ▸ **'textualist** *n, adj*

textuary ('tɛkstjʊərɪ) *adj* **1** of, relating to, or contained in a text. ◆ *n, pl* **-aries. 2** a textual critic.

texture ('tɛkstʃə) *n* **1** the surface of a material, esp. as perceived by the sense of touch: *a wall with a rough texture.* **2** the structure, appearance, and feel of a woven fabric. **3** the general structure and disposition of the constituent parts of something: *the texture of a cake.* **4** the distinctive character or quality of something: *the texture of life in America.* **5** the nature of a surface other than smooth: *woollen cloth has plenty of texture.* **6** *Art.* the representation of the nature of a surface: *the painter caught the grainy texture of the sand.* **7a** music considered as the interrelationship between the horizontally presented aspects of melody and rhythm and the vertically represented aspect of harmony: *a contrapuntal texture.* **7b** the nature and quality of the instrumentation of a passage, piece, etc. ◆ *vb* **8** (*tr*) to give a distinctive usually rough or grainy texture to. [C15: from Latin *textūra* web, from *texere* to weave] ▸ **'textural** *adj* ▸ **'texturally** *adv* ▸ **'textureless** *adj*

Teyde (*Spanish* 'teiðe) *n* a variant spelling of **Teide.**

Tezel ('tɛts^əl) *n* a variant spelling of (Johann) **Tetzel.**

tg *Biology. abbrev. for* type genus.

TG 1 *abbrev. for* transformational grammar. ◆ **2** *international car registration for* Togo.

TGAT ('ti:gæt) *n* (in Britain) *acronym for* Task Group on Assessment and Testing: a group which advises on assessment and testing within the National Curriculum.

T-group *n Psychol.* a group that meets for educational or therapeutic purposes to study its own communication. [C20: from (*Sensitivity*) *T*(*raining*) *Group*]

TGV (*French* teʒeve) (in France) *abbrev. for* train à grande vitesse: a high-speed passenger train.

TGWU (in Britain) *abbrev. for* Transport and General Workers' Union.

Th *the chemical symbol for* thorium.

Th. *abbrev. for* Thursday.

-th[1] *suffix forming nouns.* **1** (*from verbs*) indicating an action or its consequence: *growth.* **2** (*from adjectives*) indicating a quality: *width.* [from Old English *-thu, -tho*]

-th[2] *or* **-eth** *suffix.* forming ordinal numbers: *fourth; thousandth.* [from Old English -(*o*)*tha,* -(*o*)*the*]

Thabana-Ntlenyana (tɑ:'bɑ:nə^ən'tleɪnjənə) *n* a mountain in Lesotho: the highest peak of the Drakensberg Mountains. Height: 3482 m (11 425 ft.). Also called: **Thadentsonyane, Thabantshonyana.**

Thackeray ('θækərɪ) *n* **William Makepeace.** 1811–63, English novelist, born in India. His novels, originally serialized, include *Vanity Fair* (1848), *Pendennis* (1850), *Henry Esmond* (1852), and *The Newcomes* (1855).

Thaddeus *or* **Thadeus** ('θædɪəs) *n New Testament.* one of the 12 apostles (Matthew 10:3; Mark 3:18), traditionally identified with Jude.

Thadentsonyane (,tɑ:dən'tsɒnjənə) *n* another name for **Thabana-Ntlenyana.**

Thai (taɪ) *adj* **1** of, relating to, or characteristic of Thailand, its people, or their language. ◆ *n* **2** (*pl* **Thais** *or* **Thai**) a native or inhabitant of Thailand. **3** the language of Thailand, sometimes classified as belonging to the Sino-Tibetan family. ◆ Also called: **Siamese.**

Thailand ('taɪ,lænd) *n* a kingdom in SE Asia, on the Andaman Sea and the Gulf of Siam: united as a kingdom in 1350 and became a major SE Asian power; consists chiefly of a central plain around the Chao Phraya river system, mountains rising over 2400 m (8000 ft.) in the northwest, and rainforest the length of the S peninsula. Official language: Thai. Official religion: (Hinayana) Buddhist. Currency: baht. Capital: Bangkok. Pop.: 61 201 000 (1998 est.). Area: 513 998 sq. km (198 455 sq. miles). Former name (until 1939 and 1945–49): **Siam.**

Thaïs ('θeɪɪs) *n* 4th-century B.C. Athenian courtesan; mistress of Alexander the Great.

thalamencephalon (,θæləmɛn'sɛfə,lɒn) *n, pl* **-lons** *or* **-la** (-lə). *Anatomy.* **1** the part of the diencephalon of the brain that includes the thalamus, pineal gland, and adjacent structures. **2** another name for **diencephalon.** ▸ **thalamencephalic** (,θælə,mɛnsə'fælɪk) *adj*

thalamus ('θæləməs) *n, pl* **-mi** (-,maɪ). **1** either of the two contiguous egg-shaped masses of grey matter at the base of the brain. **2** both of these masses considered as a functional unit. **3** the receptacle or torus of a flower. [C18: from Latin, Greek *thalamos* inner room; probably related to Greek *tholos* vault] ▸ **thalamic** (θə'læmɪk) *adj* ▸ **tha'lamically** *adv*

thalassaemia *or U.S.* **thalassemia** (,θælə'si:mɪə) *n* a hereditary disease, common in many parts of the world, resulting from defects in the synthesis of the red blood pigment haemoglobin. Also called: **Cooley's anaemia** ('ku:lɪz). [New Latin, from Greek *thalassa* sea + -AEMIA, from it being esp. prevalent round the eastern Mediterranean Sea]

thalassic (θə'læsɪk) *adj* **1** of or relating to the sea. **2** of or relating to small or inland seas, as opposed to open waters. **3** inhabiting or growing in the sea; marine: *thalassic fauna.* [C19: from French *thalassique,* from Greek *thalassa* sea]

thalassocracy (ˌθæləˈsɒkrəsɪ) *or* **thalattocracy** *n* the government of a nation having dominion over large expanses of the seas. [C19: from Attic Greek *thalassocratia,* from *thalassa* sea + -CRACY]

thalassotherapy (ˌθæləsəʊˈθɛrəpɪ) *n* the use of sea water and marine products as a therapeutic treatment. [C20: from Greek *thalassa* sea + THERAPY]

thaler *or* **taler** (ˈtɑːlə) *n, pl* **-ler** *or* **-lers.** a former German, Austrian, or Swiss silver coin. [from German; see DOLLAR]

Thales (ˈθeɪliːz) *n* ?624–?546 B.C., Greek philosopher, mathematician, and astronomer, born in Miletus. He held that water was the origin of all things and he predicted the solar eclipse of May 28, 585 B.C.

thali (ˈtɑːlɪ) *n Indian cookery.* a meal consisting of several small meat or vegetable dishes accompanied by rice, bread, etc., and sometimes by a starter or a sweet. [C20: from Hindi *thālī* a plate or tray on which food is served]

Thalia (θəˈlaɪə) *n Greek myth.* **1** the Muse of comedy and pastoral poetry. **2** one of the three Graces. [C17: via Latin from Greek, from *thaleia* blooming]

thalidomide (θəˈlɪdəˌmaɪd) *n* **a** a synthetic drug formerly used as a sedative and hypnotic but withdrawn from the market when found to cause abnormalities in developing fetuses. Formula: $C_{13}H_{10}N_2O_4$. **b** (*as modifier*): *a thalidomide baby.* [C20: from THALLIC + *-id-* (from IMIDE) + IMIDE]

thallic (ˈθælɪk) *adj* of or containing thallium, esp. in the trivalent state.

thallium (ˈθælɪəm) *n* a soft malleable highly toxic white metallic element used as a rodent and insect poison and in low-melting glass. Its compounds are used as infrared detectors and in photoelectric cells. Symbol: Tl; atomic no.: 81; atomic wt.: 204.3833; valency: 1 or 3; relative density: 11.85; melting pt.: 304°C; boiling pt.: 1473±10°C. [C19: from New Latin, from Greek *thallos* a green shoot; referring to the green line in its spectrum]

thallophyte (ˈθæləˌfaɪt) *n Obsolete.* any organism of the former division *Thallophyta,* lacking true stems, leaves, and roots: includes the algae, fungi, lichens, and bacteria, all now regarded as separate phyla. [C19: from New Latin *thallophyta,* from Greek *thallos* a young shoot + *phuton* a plant] ▸ **thallophytic** (ˌθæləˈfɪtɪk) *adj*

thallous (ˈθæləs) *adj* of or containing thallium, esp. in the monovalent state.

thallus (ˈθæləs) *n, pl* **thalli** (ˈθælaɪ) *or* **thalluses.** the undifferentiated vegetative body of algae, fungi, and lichens. [C19: from Latin, from Greek *thallos* green shoot, from *thallein* to bloom] ▸ ˈ**thalloid** *adj*

thalweg *or* **talweg** (ˈtɑːlvɛg) *n Geography, rare.* **1** the longitudinal outline of a riverbed from source to mouth. **2** the line of steepest descent from any point on the land surface. [C19: from German, from *Thal* valley + *Weg* way, path]

Thames *n* **1** (tɛmz). a river in S England, rising in the Cotswolds in several headstreams and flowing generally east through London to the North Sea by a large estuary. Length: 346 km (215 miles). Ancient name: **Tamesis** (ˈtæməsɪs). **2** (teɪmz, θeɪmz). a river in SE Canada, in Ontario, flowing south to London, then southwest to Lake St Clair. Length: 217 km (135 miles).

Thammuz (ˈtæmuːz, -uz) *n* a variant spelling of **Tammuz.**

than (ðæn; *unstressed* ðən) *conj* (*coordinating*), *prep* **1** used to introduce the second element of a comparison, the first element of which expresses difference: *shorter than you; couldn't do otherwise than love him; he swims faster than I run.* **2** used after adverbs such as *rather* or *sooner* to introduce a rejected alternative in an expression of preference: *rather than be imprisoned, I shall die.* **3 other than.** besides; in addition to. [Old English *thanne;* related to Old Saxon, Old High German *thanna;* see THEN]

USAGE In formal English, *than* is usually regarded as a conjunction governing an unexpressed verb: *he does it far better than I (do).* The case of any pronoun therefore depends on whether it is the subject or object of the unexpressed verb: *she likes him more than I (like him); she likes him more than (she likes) me.* However in ordinary speech and writing *than* is usually treated as a preposition and is followed by the object form of a pronoun: *my brother is younger than me.*

thanatology (ˌθænəˈtɒlədʒɪ) *n* the scientific study of death and the phenomena and practices relating to it. [C19: from Greek *thanatos* death + -LOGY]

thanatopsis (ˌθænəˈtɒpsɪs) *n* a meditation on death, as in a poem. [C19: from Greek *thanatos* death + *opsis* a view]

Thanatos (ˈθænəˌtɒs) *n* the Greek personification of death: son of Nyx, goddess of night. Roman counterpart: **Mors.** Thanatos was the name chosen by Freud to represent a universal death instinct. Compare **Eros**[1]. ▸ **Thanatotic** (ˌθænəˈtɒtɪk) *adj*

thane *or* (*less commonly*) **thegn** (θeɪn) *n* **1** (in Anglo-Saxon England) a member of an aristocratic class, ranking below an ealdorman, whose status was hereditary and who held land from the king or from another nobleman in return for certain services. **2** (in medieval Scotland) **2a** a person of rank, often the chief of a clan, holding land from the king. **2b** a lesser noble who was a Crown official holding authority over an area of land. [Old English *thegn;* related to Old Saxon, Old High German *thegan* thane] ▸ **thanage** (ˈθeɪnɪdʒ) *n*

Thanet (ˈθænɪt) *n* **Isle of.** an island in SE England, in NE Kent, separated from the mainland by two branches of the River Stour: scene of many Norse invasions. Area: 109 sq. km (42 sq. miles).

Thanjavur (ˌtʌndʒəˈvʊə) *n* a city in SE India, in E Tamil Nadu: headquarters of the earliest Protestant missions in India. Pop.: 202 013 (1991). Former name: **Tanjore.**

thank (θæŋk) *vb* (*tr*) **1** to convey feelings of gratitude to. **2** to hold responsible; *he has his creditors to thank for his bankruptcy.* **3** used in exclamations of relief: *thank goodness; thank God.* **4 I'll thank you to.** used ironically to intensify a command, request, etc.: *I'll thank you to mind your own business.* [Old English *thancian;* related to Old Frisian *thankia,* Old Norse *thakka,* Old Saxon, Old High German *thancōn*]

thankful (ˈθæŋkfʊl) *adj* grateful and appreciative. ▸ ˈ**thankfulness** *n*

thankfully (ˈθæŋkfʊlɪ) *adv* **1** showing gratitude or appreciation. **2** *Informal.* fortunately: *thankfully she was not injured.*

USAGE The use of *thankfully* to mean *fortunately* was formerly considered incorrect by many people, but has now become acceptable in informal contexts.

thankless (ˈθæŋklɪs) *adj* **1** receiving no thanks or appreciation: *a thankless job.* **2** ungrateful: *a thankless pupil.* ▸ ˈ**thanklessly** *adv* ▸ ˈ**thanklessness** *n*

thanks (θæŋks) *pl n* **1** an expression of appreciation or gratitude or an acknowledgment of services or favours given. **2 thanks to.** because of: *thanks to him we lost the match.* ◆ *interj* **3** *Informal.* an exclamation expressing acknowledgment, gratitude, or appreciation.

thanksgiving (ˈθæŋksˌgɪvɪŋ; *U.S.* θæŋksˈgɪvɪŋ) *n* **1** the act of giving thanks. **2a** an expression of thanks to God. **2b** a public act of religious observance or a celebration in acknowledgment of divine favours.

Thanksgiving Day *n* an annual day of holiday celebrated in thanksgiving to God on the fourth Thursday of November in the United States, and on the second Monday of October in Canada. Often shortened to **Thanksgiving.**

thank you *interj, n* a conventional expression of gratitude.

Thant (θænt) *n* **U** (uː). 1909–74, Burmese diplomat; secretary-general of the United Nations (1962–71).

Thapsus (ˈθæpsəs) *n* an ancient town near Carthage in North Africa: site of Caesar's victory over Pompey in 46 B.C.

thar (tɑː) *n* a variant spelling of **tahr.**

Thar Desert (tɑː) *n* a desert in NW India, mainly in NW Rajasthan state and extending into Pakistan. Area: over 260 000 sq. km (100 000 sq. miles). Also called: **Indian Desert, Great Indian Desert.**

Thásos (ˈθæsɒs) *n* a Greek island in the N Aegean: colonized by Greeks from Paros in the 7th century B.C. as a gold-mining centre; under Turkish rule (1455–1912). Pop.: 13 110 (1981). Area: 379 sq. km (146 sq. miles).

that (ðæt; *unstressed* ðət) *determiner* (*used before a singular n*) **1a** used preceding a noun that has been mentioned at some time or is understood: *that idea of yours.* **1b** (*as pronoun*): *don't eat that; that's what I mean.* **2a** used preceding a noun that denotes something more remote or removed: *that dress is cheaper than this one; that building over there is for sale.* **2b** (*as pronoun*): *that is John and this is his wife; give me that.* Compare **this. 3** used to refer to something that is familiar: *that old chap from across the street.* **4 and (all) that.** *Informal.* everything connected with the subject mentioned: *he knows a lot about building and that.* **5 at that.** (*completive-intensive*) additionally, all things considered, or nevertheless: *he's a pleasant fellow at that; I might decide to go at that.* **6 like that. 6a** with ease; effortlessly: *he gave me the answer just like that.* **6b** of such a nature, character, etc.: *he paid for all our tickets —he's like that.* **7 that is. 7a** to be precise. **7b** in other words. **7c** for example. **8 that's more like it.** that is better, an improvement, etc. **9 that's that.** there is no more to be done, discussed, etc. **10 with** (*or* **at**) **that.** thereupon; having said or done that. ◆ *conj* (*subordinating*) **11** used to introduce a noun clause: *I believe that you'll come.* **12** Also: **so that, in order that.** used to introduce a clause of purpose: *they fought that others might have peace.* **13** used to introduce a clause of result: *he laughed so hard that he cried.* **14** used to introduce a clause after an understood sentence expressing desire, indignation, or amazement: *oh, that I had never lived!* ◆ *adv* **15** used with adjectives or adverbs to reinforce the specification of a precise degree already mentioned: *go just that fast and you should be safe.* **16** Also: **all that.** (*usually used with a negative*) *Informal.* (intensifier): *he wasn't that upset at the news.* **17** *Dialect.* (intensifier): *the cat was that weak after the fight.* ◆ *pron* **18** used to introduce a restrictive relative clause: *the book that we want.* **19** used to introduce a clause with the verb *to be* to emphasize the extent to which the preceding noun is applicable: *genius that she is, she outwitted the computer.* [Old English *thæt;* related to Old Frisian *thet,* Old Norse, Old Saxon *that,* Old High German *daz,* Greek *to,* Latin *istud,* Sanskrit *tad*]

USAGE Precise stylists maintain a distinction between *that* and *which: that* is used as a relative pronoun in restrictive clauses and *which* in nonrestrictive clauses. In *the book that is on the table is mine,* the clause *that is on the table* is used to distinguish one particular book (the one on the table) from another or others (which may be anywhere, but not on the table). In *the book, which is on the table, is mine,* the *which* clause is merely descriptive or incidental. The more formal the level of language, the more important it is to preserve the distinction between the two relative pronouns; but in informal or colloquial usage, the words are often used interchangeably.

thatch (θætʃ) *n* **1a** Also called: **thatching.** a roofing material that consists of straw, reed, etc. **1b** a roof made of such a material. **2** anything resembling this, such as the hair of the head. **3** Also called: **thatch palm.** any of various palms with leaves suitable for thatching. ◆ *vb* **4** to cover (a roof) with thatch. [Old English *theccan* to cover; related to *thæc* roof, Old Saxon *thekkian* to thatch, Old High German *decchen,* Old Norse *thekja*] ▸ ˈ**thatcher** *n* ▸ ˈ**thatchless** *adj* ▸ ˈ**thatchy** *adj*

Thatcher (ˈθætʃə) *n* **Margaret** (**Hilda**), Baroness (*née Roberts*). born 1925, British stateswoman; leader of the Conservative Party (1975–90); prime minister (1979–90).

Thatcherism (ˈθætʃəˌrɪzəm) *n* the policies of monetarism, privatization, and self-help promoted by Margaret Thatcher. ▸ **Thatcherite** (ˈθætʃəˌraɪt) *n, adj*

thaumato- *or before a vowel* **thaumat-** *combining form.* miracle; marvel: *thaumaturge.* [from Greek *thauma, thaumat-* a marvel]

thaumatology (ˌθɔːməˈtɒlədʒɪ) *n* the study of or a treatise on miracles.

thaumatrope (ˈθɔːməˌtrəʊp) *n* a toy in which partial pictures on the two sides of a card appear to merge when the card is twirled rapidly. [C19: from THAUMATO- + -TROPE] ▸ **thaumatropical** (ˌθɔːməˈtrɒpɪkᵊl) *adj*

thaumaturge (ˈθɔːməˌtɜːdʒ) *n Rare.* a performer of miracles; magician. [C18:

from Medieval Latin *thaumaturgus,* from Greek *thaumatourgos* miracle-working, from THAUMATO- + *-ourgos* working, from *ergon* work] ► 'thauma,turgy *n* ► ,thauma'turgic *adj*

thaw (θɔː) *vb* **1** to melt or cause to melt from a solid frozen state: *the snow thawed.* **2** to become or cause to become unfrozen; defrost. **3** (*intr*) to be the case that the ice or snow is melting: *it's thawing fast.* **4** (*intr*) to become more sociable, relaxed, or friendly. ◆ *n* **5** the act or process of thawing. **6** a spell of relatively warm weather, causing snow or ice to melt. **7** an increase in relaxation or friendliness. [Old English *thawian;* related to Old High German *douwen* to thaw, Old Norse *theyja* to thaw, Latin *tabēre* to waste away] ► '**thawer** *n* ► '**thawless** *adj*

ThB *abbrev. for* Bachelor of Theology.

THC *abbrev. for:* **1** tetrahydrocannabinol: the main active principle in cannabis. **2** (in New Zealand) Tourist Hotel Corporation.

ThD *abbrev. for* Doctor of Theology.

the[1] (*stressed or emphatic* ðiː; *unstressed before a consonant* ðə; *unstressed before a vowel* ðɪ) *determiner (article)* **1** used preceding a noun that has been previously specified: *the pain should disappear soon; the man then opened the door.* Compare: **a**[1]. **2** used with a qualifying word or phrase to indicate a particular person, object, etc., as distinct from others: *ask the man standing outside; give me the blue one.* Compare **a**[1]. **3** used preceding certain nouns associated with one's culture, society, or community: *to go to the doctor; listen to the news; watch the television.* **4** used preceding present participles and adjectives when they function as nouns: *the singing is awful; the dead salute you.* **5** used preceding titles and certain uniquely specific or proper nouns, such as place names: *the United States; the Honourable Edward Brown; the Chairman; the moon.* **6** used preceding a qualifying adjective or noun in certain names or titles: *William the Conqueror; Edward the First.* **7** used preceding a noun to make it refer to its class generically: *the white seal is hunted for its fur; this is good for the throat; to play the piano.* **8** used instead of *my, your, her,* etc., with parts of the body: *take me by the hand.* **9** (usually stressed) the best, only, or most remarkable: *Harry's is* the *club in this town.* **10** used with proper nouns when qualified: *written by the young Hardy.* **11** another word for **per,** esp. with nouns or noun phrases of cost: *fifty pence the pound.* **12** *Often facetious or derogatory.* my; our: *the wife goes out on Thursdays.* **13** used preceding a unit of time in phrases or titles indicating an outstanding person, event, etc.: *match of the day; housewife of the year.* [Middle English, from Old English *thē,* a demonstrative adjective that later superseded *sē* (masculine singular) and *sēo, sio* (feminine singular); related to Old Frisian *thi,* thin, Old High German *der, diu*]

the[2] (ðə, ðɪ) *adv* **1** (often foll. by *for*) used before comparative adjectives or adverbs for emphasis: *she looks the happier for her trip.* **2** used correlatively before each of two comparative adjectives or adverbs to indicate equality: *the sooner you come, the better; the more I see you, the more I love you.* [Old English *thī, thȳ,* instrumental case of THE[1] and THAT; related to Old Norse *thī,* Gothic *thei*]

the- *combining form.* a variant of **theo-** before a vowel.

theaceous (θiːˈeɪʃəs) *adj* of, relating to, or belonging to the *Theaceae,* a family of evergreen trees and shrubs of tropical and warm regions: includes the tea plant.

theanthropism (θiːˈænθrə,pɪzəm) *n* **1** the ascription of human traits or characteristics to a god or gods. **2** *Christian theol.* the doctrine of the hypostatic union of the divine and human natures in the single person of Christ. [C19: from Ecclesiastical Greek *theanthrōpos* (from *theos* god + *anthrōpos* man) + -ISM] ► ,**thean'thropic** *adj* ► **the'anthropist** *n*

thearchy (ˈθiːɑːkɪ) *n, pl* **-chies.** rule or government by God or gods; theocracy. [C17: from Church Greek *thearkhia;* see THEO-, -ARCHY] ► **the'archic** *adj*

theatre *or U.S.* **theater** (ˈθɪətə) *n* **1a** a building designed for the performance of plays, operas, etc. **1b** (*as modifier*): *a theatre ticket.* **1c** (*in combination*): *a theatregoer.* **2** a large room or hall, usually with a raised platform and tiered seats for an audience, used for lectures, film shows, etc. **3** Also called: **operating theatre.** a room in a hospital or other medical centre equipped for surgical operations. **4** plays regarded collectively as a form of art. **5 the theatre.** the world of actors, theatrical companies, etc.: *the glamour of the theatre.* **6** a setting for dramatic or important events. **7** writing that is suitable for dramatic presentation: *a good piece of theatre.* **8** *U.S., Austral., N.Z.* the usual word for **cinema** (sense 1). **9** a major area of military activity: *the theatre of operations.* **10** a circular or semicircular open-air building with tiers of seats. [C14: from Latin *theātrum,* from Greek *theatron* place for viewing, from *theasthai* to look at; related to Greek *thauma* miracle]

theatre-in-the-round *n, pl* **theatres-in-the-round. 1** a theatre with seats arranged around a central acting area. **2** drama written or designed for performance in such a theatre. ◆ Also called: **arena theatre.**

theatre of cruelty *n* a type of theatre advocated by Antonin Artaud in *Le Théâtre et son double* that seeks to communicate to its audience a sense of pain, suffering, and evil, using gesture, movement, sound, and symbolism rather than language.

theatre of the absurd *n* drama in which normal conventions and dramatic structure are ignored or modified in order to present life as irrational or meaningless.

theatrical (θɪˈætrɪkᵊl) *adj* **1** of or relating to the theatre or dramatic performances. **2** exaggerated and affected in manner or behaviour; histrionic. ► **the,atri'cality** *or* **the'atricalness** *n* ► **the'atrically** *adv*

theatricals (θɪˈætrɪkᵊlz) *pl n* dramatic performances and entertainments, esp. as given by amateurs.

theatrics (θɪˈætrɪks) *n* (*functioning as sing*) **1** the art of staging plays. **2** exaggerated mannerisms or displays of emotions.

Thebaid (ˈθiːbeɪɪd, -bɪ-) *n* the territory around ancient Thebes in Egypt, or sometimes around Thebes in Greece.

thebaine (ˈθiːbə,iːn, θɪˈbeɪiːn, -aɪn) *n* a poisonous white crystalline alkaloid, extracted from opium and used in medicine. Formula: $C_{19}H_{21}NO_3$. Also called: **paramorphine.** [C19: from New Latin *thebaia* opium of Thebes (with reference to Egypt as a chief source of opium) + -INE[2]]

Thebe (ˈθiːbɪ) *n Astronomy.* an inner satellite of Jupiter discovered in 1979. [C20: named after *Thebe,* mythical queen of THEBES]

Thebes (θiːbz) *n* **1** (in ancient Greece) the chief city of Boeotia, destroyed by Alexander the Great (336 B.C.). **2** (in ancient Egypt) a city on the Nile: at various times capital of Upper Egypt or of the entire country. ► **Thebaic** (θɪˈbeɪɪk) *adj* ► '**Theban** *adj, n*

theca (ˈθiːkə) *n, pl* **-cae** (-siː). **1** *Botany.* an enclosing organ, cell, or spore case, esp. the capsule of a moss. **2** *Zoology.* a hard outer covering, such as the cup-shaped container of a coral polyp. [C17: from Latin *thēca,* from Greek *thēkē* case; related to Greek *tithenai* to place] ► '**thecal** *or* '**thecate** *adj*

thecodont (ˈθiːkə,dɒnt) *adj* **1** (of mammals and certain reptiles) having teeth that grow in sockets. **2** of or relating to teeth of this type. ◆ *n* **3** any extinct reptile of the order *Thecodontia,* of Triassic times, having teeth set in sockets: they gave rise to the dinosaurs, crocodiles, pterodactyls, and birds. [C20: New Latin *Thecondontia,* from Greek *thēkē* case + -ODONT]

thé dansant *French.* (te dɑ̃sɑ̃) *n, pl* ***thés dansant*** (te dɑ̃sɑ̃). a dance held while afternoon tea is served, popular in the 1920s and 1930s. [literally: dancing tea]

thee (ðiː) *pron* **1** the objective form of **thou**[1]. **2** (*subjective*) *Rare.* refers to the person addressed: used mainly by members of the Society of Friends. [Old English *thē;* see THOU[1]]

theft (θɛft) *n* **1** *Criminal law.* the dishonest taking of property belonging to another person with the intention of depriving the owner permanently of its possession. **2** *Rare.* something stolen. [Old English *thēofth;* related to Old Norse *thȳfth,* Old Frisian *thiūvethe,* Middle Dutch *dūfte;* see THIEF] ► '**theftless** *adj*

thegn (θeɪn) *n* a variant spelling of **thane.**

Theiler (ˈtaɪlə) *n* **Max.** 1899–1972, U.S. virologist, born in South Africa, who developed a vaccine against yellow fever. Nobel prize for physiology or medicine 1951.

theine (ˈθiːiːn, -ɪn) *n* another name for **caffeine,** esp. when present in tea. [C19: from New Latin *thea* tea + -INE[2]]

their (ðɛə) *determiner* **1** of, belonging to, or associated in some way with them: *their finest hour; their own clothes; she tried to combat their mocking her.* **2** belonging to or associated in some way with people in general not including the speaker or people addressed: *in many countries they wash their clothes in the river.* **3** belonging to or associated in some way with an indefinite antecedent such as *one, whoever,* or *anybody: everyone should bring their own lunch.* [C12: from Old Norse *theira* (genitive plural); see THEY, THEM]

USAGE See at **they.**

theirs (ðɛəz) *pron* **1** something or someone belonging to or associated in some way with them: *theirs is difficult.* **2** *Not standard.* something or someone belonging to or associated in some way with an indefinite antecedent such as *one, whoever,* or *anybody: everyone thinks theirs is best.* **3 of theirs.** belonging to or associated with them.

theism (ˈθiːɪzəm) *n* **1** the form of the belief in one God as the transcendent creator and ruler of the universe that does not necessarily entail further belief in divine revelation. Compare **deism. 2** the belief in the existence of a God or gods. Compare **atheism.** [C17: from Greek *theos* god + -ISM] ► '**theist** *n, adj* ► **the'istic** *or* **the'istical** *adj* ► **the'istically** *adv*

them (ðɛm; *unstressed* ðəm) *pron* **1** (*objective*) refers to things or people other than the speaker or people addressed: *I'll kill them; what happened to them?* **2** *Chiefly U.S.* a dialect word for **themselves** when used as an indirect object: *they got them a new vice president.* ◆ *determiner* **3** a nonstandard word for **those:** *three of them oranges.* [Old English *thǣm,* influenced by Old Norse *theim;* related to Old Frisian *thām,* Old Saxon, Old High German *thēm,* Old Norse *theimr,* Gothic *thaim*]

USAGE See at **me, they.**

thematic (θɪˈmætɪk) *adj* **1** of, relating to, or consisting of a theme or themes. **2** *Linguistics.* denoting a word that is the theme of a sentence. **3** *Grammar.* **3a** denoting a vowel or other sound or sequence of sounds that occurs between the root of a word and any inflectional or derivational suffixes. **3b** of or relating to the stem or root of a word. ◆ *n* **4** *Grammar.* a thematic vowel: *"-o-" is a thematic in the combining form "psycho-".* ► **the'matically** *adv*

thematic apperception test *n Psychol.* a projective test in which drawings of interacting people are shown and the person being tested is asked to make up a story about them.

thematization *or* **thematisation** (,θiːmətaɪˈzeɪʃən) *n Linguistics.* the mental act or process of selecting particular topics as themes in discourse or words as themes in sentences.

theme (θiːm) *n* **1** an idea or topic expanded in a discourse, discussion, etc. **2** (in literature, music, art, etc.) a unifying idea, image, or motif, repeated or developed throughout a work. **3** *Music.* a group of notes forming a recognizable melodic unit, often used as the basis of the musical material in a composition. **4** a short essay, esp. one set as an exercise for a student. **5** *Linguistics.* the first major constituent of a sentence, usually but not necessarily the subject. In the sentence *history I do like,* "history" is the theme of the sentence, even though it is the object of the verb. **6** *Grammar.* another word for **root**[1] (sense 9) or **stem**[1] (sense 9). **7** (in the Byzantine Empire) a territorial unit consisting of several provinces under a military commander. **8** (*modifier*) planned or designed round one unifying subject, image, etc.: *a theme holiday.* ◆ *vb* (*tr*) **9** to design, decorate, arrange, etc., in accordance with a theme. [C13: from Latin *thema,* from Greek: deposit, from *tithenai* to lay down] ► '**themeless** *adj*

theme park *n* an area planned as a leisure attraction, in which all the displays, buildings, activities, etc., are based on or relate to one particular subject.

theme song *n* **1** a melody used, esp. in a film score, to set a mood, introduce a character, etc. **2** another term for **signature tune.**

Themis ('θi:mɪs) *n Greek myth.* a goddess of order and justice.

Themistocles (θə'mɪstə,kli:z) *n* ?527–?460 B.C., Athenian statesman, who was responsible for the Athenian victory against the Persians at Salamis (480). He was ostracized in 470.

themselves (ðəm'sɛlvz) *pron* **1a** the reflexive form of *they* or *them.* **1b** (intensifier): *the team themselves voted on it.* **2** (*preceded by a copula*) their normal or usual selves: *they don't seem themselves any more.* **3** Also: **themself.** *Not standard.* a reflexive form of an indefinite antecedent such as *one, whoever,* or *anybody: everyone has to look after themselves.*

then (ðɛn) *adv* **1** at that time; over that period of time. **2** (*sentence modifier*) in that case; that being so: *then why don't you ask her? if he comes, then you'll have to leave; go on then, take it.* **3 then and there.** a variant of **there and then**: see **there** (sense 6). ◆ *sentence connector.* **4** after that; with that: *then John left the room and didn't return.* ◆ *n* **5** that time: *before then; from then on.* ◆ *adj* **6** (*prenominal*) existing, functioning, etc., at that time: *the then prime minister.* [Old English *thenne;* related to Old Saxon, Old High German *thanna;* see THAN]

thenar ('θi:nɑ:) *Anatomy.* ◆ *n* **1** the palm of the hand. **2** the fleshy area of the palm at the base of the thumb. ◆ *adj* **3** of or relating to the palm or the region at the base of the thumb. [C17: via New Latin from Greek; related to Old High German *tenar* palm of the hand]

thenardite (θɪ'nɑ:daɪt, tɪ-) *n* a whitish vitreous mineral that consists of anhydrous sodium sulphate and occurs in saline residues. Formula: Na_2SO_4. [C19: named after Baron L. J. *Thénard* (1777–1857), French chemist; see -ITE[1]]

Thénard's blue ('teɪnɑ:z, -nɑ:dz) *n* another name for **cobalt blue.** [C19: named after Baron L. J. *Thénard;* see THENARDITE]

thence (ðɛns) *adv* **1** from that place. **2** Also: **thenceforth** ('ðɛns'fɔ:θ). from that time or event; thereafter. **3** therefore. [C13: *thannes,* from *thanne,* from Old English *thanon;* related to Gothic *thanana,* Old Norse *thanan*]

thenceforward ('ðɛns'fɔ:wəd) *or* **thenceforwards** *adv* from that time or place on; thence.

theo- *or before a vowel* **the-** *combining form.* indicating God or gods: *theology.* [from Greek *theos* god]

theobromine (,θi:əʊ'brəʊmi:n, -mɪn) *n* a white crystalline slightly water-soluble alkaloid that occurs in many plants, such as tea and cacao: used to treat coronary heart disease and headaches. Formula: $C_7H_8N_4O_2$. See also **xanthine** (sense 2). [C18: from New Latin *theobroma* genus of trees, literally: food of the gods, from THEO- + Greek *brōma* food + -INE[2]]

theocentric (,θɪə'sɛntrɪk) *adj Theol.* having God as the focal point of attention. ▸ ,**theocen'tricity** *n* ▸ ,**theo'centrism** *or* **theocentricism** (,θi:əʊ-'sɛntrɪ,sɪzəm) *n*

theocracy (θɪ'ɒkrəsɪ) *n, pl* **-cies. 1** government by a deity or by a priesthood. **2** a community or political unit under such government. ▸ **'theo,crat** *n* ▸ ,**theo'cratic** *or* ,**theo'cratical** *adj* ▸ ,**theo'cratically** *adv*

theocrasy (θɪ'ɒkrəsɪ) *n* **1** a mingling into one of deities or divine attributes previously regarded as distinct. **2** the union of the soul with God in mysticism. [C19: from Greek *theokrasia,* from THEO- + *-krasia* from *krasis* a blending]

Theocritus (θɪ'ɒkrɪtəs) *n* ?310–?250 B.C., Greek poet, born in Syracuse. He wrote the first pastoral poems in Greek literature and was closely imitated by Virgil. ▸ **The'ocritan** *or* **Theocritean** (θɪ,ɒkrɪ'ti:ən) *adj, n*

theodicy (θɪ'ɒdɪsɪ) *n, pl* **-cies.** the branch of theology concerned with defending the attributes of God against objections resulting from physical and moral evil. [C18: coined by Leibnitz in French as *théodicée,* from THEO- + Greek *dikē* justice] ▸ **the,odi'cean** *adj*

theodolite (θɪ'ɒdə,laɪt) *n* a surveying instrument for measuring horizontal and vertical angles, consisting of a small tripod-mounted telescope that is free to move in both the horizontal and vertical planes. Also called (in the U.S. and Canada): **transit.** [C16: from New Latin *theodolitus,* of uncertain origin] ▸ **theodolitic** (θɪ,ɒdə'lɪtɪk) *adj*

Theodora (,θɪə'dɔ:rə) *n* ?500–548 A.D., Byzantine empress; wife and counsellor of Justinian I.

Theodorakis (*Greek* θεɔðɔ'rakis) *n* **Mikis** ('mikis). born 1925, Greek composer, who wrote the music for the film *Zorba the Greek* (1965): imprisoned (1967–70) for his opposition to the Greek military government.

Theodore I ('θi:ədɔ:) *n* called *Lascaris.* ?1175–1222, Byzantine ruler, who founded a Byzantine state in exile at Nicaea after Constantinople fell to the Crusaders (1204).

Theodoric *or* **Theoderic** (θɪ'ɒdərɪk) *n* called *the Great.* ?454–526 A.D., king of the Ostrogoths and founder of the Ostrogothic kingdom in Italy after his murder of Odoacer (493).

Theodosius I (,θɪə'dəʊsɪəs) *n* called *the Great.* ?346–395 A.D., Roman emperor of the Eastern Roman Empire (379–95) and of the Western Roman Empire (392–95).

theogony (θɪ'ɒgənɪ) *n, pl* **-nies. 1** the origin and descent of the gods. **2** an account of this, often recited in epic poetry. [C17: from Greek *theogonia;* see THEO-, -GONY] ▸ **theogonic** (,θɪə'gɒnɪk) *adj* ▸ **the'ogonist** *n*

theol. *abbrev. for:* **1** theologian. **2** theological. **3** theology.

theologian (,θɪə'ləʊdʒɪən) *n* a person versed in or engaged in the study of theology, esp. Christian theology.

theological (,θɪə'lɒdʒɪk[ə]l) *adj* **1** of, relating to, or based on theology. **2** based on God's revelation to man of his nature, his designs, and his will. ▸ ,**theo'logically** *adv*

theological virtues *pl n* (esp. among the scholastics) those virtues that are infused into man by a special grace of God, specifically faith, hope, and charity. Compare **natural virtues.**

theologize *or* **theologise** (θɪ'ɒlə,dʒaɪz) *vb* **1** (*intr*) to speculate upon theological subjects, engage in theological study or discussion, or formulate theological arguments. **2** (*tr*) to render theological or treat from a theological point of view. ▸ **the,ologi'zation** *or* **the,ologi'sation** *n* ▸ **the'olo,gizer** *or* **the'olo,giser** *n*

theology (θɪ'ɒlədʒɪ) *n, pl* **-gies. 1** the systematic study of the existence and nature of the divine and its relationship to and influence upon other beings. **2** a specific branch of this study, undertaken from the perspective of a particular group: *feminist theology.* **3** the systematic study of Christian revelation concerning God's nature and purpose, esp. through the teaching of the Church. **4** a specific system, form, or branch of this study, esp. for those preparing for the ministry or priesthood. [C14: from Late Latin *theologia,* from Latin; see THEO-, -LOGY] ▸ **the'ologist** *n*

theomachy (θɪ'ɒməkɪ) *n, pl* **-chies.** a battle among the gods or against them. [C16: from Greek *theomakhia,* from THEO- + *makhē* battle]

theomancy ('θi:əʊmænsɪ) *n* divination or prophecy by an oracle or by people directly inspired by a god. [C17: from THEO- + -MANCY]

theomania (,θɪə'meɪnɪə) *n* religious madness, esp. when it takes the form of believing oneself to be a god. ▸ ,**theo'mani,ac** *n*

theomorphic (,θɪə'mɔ:fɪk) *adj* of or relating to the conception or representation of man as having the form of God or a deity. [C19: from Greek *theomorphos,* from THEO- + *morphē* form] ▸ ,**theo'morphism** *n*

theonomy (θɪ'ɒnəmɪ) *n* the state of being governed by God.

theopathy (θɪ'ɒpəθɪ) *n* religious emotion engendered by the contemplation of or meditation upon God. [C18: from THEO- + *-pathy,* from SYMPATHY] ▸ **theopathetic** (,θɪəpə'θɛtɪk) *or* **theopathic** (,θɪə'pæθɪk) *adj*

theophagy (θɪ'ɒfədʒɪ) *n, pl* **-gies.** the sacramental eating of a god.

theophany (θɪ'ɒfənɪ) *n, pl* **-nies.** *Theol.* a manifestation of a deity to man in a form that, though visible, is not necessarily material. [C17: from Late Latin *theophania,* from Late Greek *theophaneia,* from THEO- + *phainein* to show] ▸ **theophanic** (θɪə'fænɪk) *or* **the'ophanous** *adj*

Theophilus[1] (θɪ'ɒfɪləs) *n* a conspicuous crater in the SE quadrant of the moon, 100 kilometres in diameter.

Theophilus[2] (θɪ'ɒfɪləs) *n* died 842 A.D., Byzantine emperor (829–42); a patron of learning and supporter of iconoclasm.

theophobia (,θɪə'fəʊbɪə) *n* morbid fear or hatred of God. ▸ ,**theo'phobi,ac** *n*

Theophrastus (,θɪə'fræstəs) *n* ?372–?287 B.C., Greek Peripatetic philosopher, noted esp. for his *Characters,* a collection of sketches of moral types.

theophylline (,θɪə'fɪli:n, -ɪn; θɪ'ɒfɪlɪn) *n* a white crystalline slightly water-soluble alkaloid that is an isomer of theobromine: it occurs in plants such as tea and is used to treat heart disease and headaches. Formula: $C_7H_8N_4O_2$. See also **xanthine** (sense 2). [C19: from THEO(BROMINE) + PHYLLO- + -INE[2]]

theorbo (θɪ'ɔ:bəʊ) *n, pl* **-bos.** *Music.* an obsolete form of the lute, having two necks, one above the other, the second neck carrying a set of unstopped sympathetic bass strings. [C17: from Italian *teorba,* probably from Venetian, variant of *tuorba* travelling bag, ultimately from Turkish *torba* bag] ▸ **the'orbist** *n*

theorem ('θɪərəm) *n Maths, logic.* a statement or formula that can be deduced from the axioms of a formal system by means of its rules of inference. [C16: from Late Latin *theōrēma,* from Greek: something to be viewed, from *theōrein* to view] ▸ **theorematic** (,θɪərə'mætɪk) *or* **theoremic** (,θɪə'rɛmɪk) *adj* ▸ ,**theore'matically** *adv*

theoretic (,θɪə'rɛtɪk) *adj* **1** another word for **theoretical.** ◆ *n* **2** another word for **theoretics.**

theoretical (,θɪə'rɛtɪk[ə]l) *or* **theoretic** *adj* **1** of or based on theory. **2** lacking practical application or actual existence; hypothetical. **3** using or dealing in theory; impractical. ▸ ,**theo'retically** *adv*

theoretician (,θɪərɪ'tɪʃən) *n* a student or user of the theory rather than the practical aspects of a subject.

theoretics (,θɪə'rɛtɪks) *n* (*functioning as sing or pl*) the theory of a particular subject. Also called (less commonly): **theoretic.**

theorize *or* **theorise** ('θɪə,raɪz) *vb* (*intr*) to produce or use theories; speculate. ▸ **'theorist** *n* ▸ ,**theori'zation** *or* ,**theori'sation** *n* ▸ **'theo,rizer** *or* **'theo,riser** *n*

theory ('θɪərɪ) *n, pl* **-ries. 1** a system of rules, procedures, and assumptions used to produce a result. **2** abstract knowledge or reasoning. **3** a speculative or conjectural view or idea: *I have a theory about that.* **4** an ideal or hypothetical situation (esp. in the phrase **in theory**). **5** a set of hypotheses related by logical or mathematical arguments to explain and predict a wide variety of connected phenomena in general terms: *the theory of relativity.* **6** a nontechnical name for **hypothesis** (sense 1). [C16: from Late Latin *theōria,* from Greek: a sight, from *theōrein* to gaze upon]

theory-laden *adj* (of an expression) capable of being understood only within the context of a specific theory, as for example *superego,* which requires the apparatus of Freudian theory in explanation.

theory of games *n* another name for **game theory.**

theos. *abbrev. for:* **1** theosophical. **2** theosophy.

theosophy (θɪ'ɒsəfɪ) *n* **1** any of various religious or philosophical systems claiming to be based on or to express an intuitive insight into the divine nature. **2** the system of beliefs of the Theosophical Society founded in 1875, claiming to be derived from the sacred writings of Brahmanism and Buddhism, but denying the existence of any personal God. [C17: from Medieval Latin *theosophia,* from Late Greek; see THEO-, -SOPHY] ▸ **theosophical** (,θɪə'sɒfɪk[ə]l) *or* ,**theo'sophic** *adj* ▸ ,**theo'sophically** *adv* ▸ **the'osophism** *n* ▸ **the'osophist** *n*

Thera ('θɪərə) *n* a Greek island in the Aegean Sea, in the Cyclades: site of a Minoan settlement and of the volcano that ended Minoan civilization on Crete. Pop.: 7000 (latest est.). Also called: **Santoríni.** Modern Greek name: **Thíra.**

therap. *or* **therapeut.** *abbrev. for:* **1** therapeutic. **2** therapeutics.

therapeutic (ˌθɛrəˈpjuːtɪk) *adj* **1** of or relating to the treatment of disease; curative. **2** serving or performed to maintain health: *therapeutic abortion.* [C17: from New Latin *therapeuticus,* from Greek *therapeutikos,* from *therapeuein* to minister to, from *theraps* an attendant] ▸ **ˌtheraˈpeutically** *adv*

therapeutics (ˌθɛrəˈpjuːtɪks) *n* (*functioning as sing*) the branch of medicine concerned with the treatment of disease.

therapist (ˈθɛrəpɪst) *n* a person skilled in a particular type of therapy: *a physical therapist.*

therapsid (θəˈræpsɪd) *n* any extinct reptile of the order *Therapsida,* of Permian to Triassic times: considered to be the ancestors of mammals. [C20: from New Latin *Therapsida,* from Greek *theraps* attendant]

therapy (ˈθɛrəpɪ) *n, pl* **-pies. a** the treatment of physical, mental, or social disorders or disease. **b** (*in combination*): *physiotherapy; electrotherapy.* [C19: from New Latin *therapia,* from Greek *therapeia* attendance; see THERAPEUTIC]

Theravada (ˌθɛrəˈvɑːdə) *n* the southern school of Buddhism, the name preferred by Hinayana Buddhists for their doctrines. [from Pali: doctrine of the elders]

there (ðɛə) *adv* **1** in, at, or to that place, point, case, or respect: *we never go there; I'm afraid I disagree with you there.* ◆ *pron* **2** used as a grammatical subject with some verbs, esp. *be,* when the true subject is an indefinite or mass noun phrase following the verb as complement: *there is a girl in that office; there doesn't seem to be any water left.* ◆ *adj* **3** (*postpositive*) who or which is in that place or position: *that boy there did it.* **4 all there.** (*predicative*) having his wits about him; of normal intelligence. **5 so there.** an exclamation that usually follows a declaration of refusal or defiance: *you can't have any more, so there!* **6 there and then.** on the spot; immediately; instantly. **7 there it is.** that is the state of affairs. **8 there you are. 8a** an expression used when handing a person something requested or desired. **8b** an exclamation of triumph: *there you are, I knew that would happen!* ◆ *n* **9** that place: *near there; from there.* ◆ *interj* **10** an expression of sympathy, as in consoling a child. [Old English *thǣr;* related to Old Frisian *thēr,* Old Saxon, Old High German *thār,* Old Norse, Gothic *thar*]

USAGE In correct usage, the verb should agree with the number of the subject in such constructions as *there is a man waiting* and *there are several people waiting.* However, where the subject is compound, it is common in speech to use the singular as in *there's a police car and an ambulance outside.*

thereabouts (ˈðɛərəˌbaʊts) *or U.S.* **thereabout** *adv* near that place, time, amount, etc.: *fifty or thereabouts.*

thereafter (ˌðɛərˈɑːftə) *adv* from that time on or after that time: *thereafter, he ceased to pay attention.*

thereat (ˌðɛərˈæt) *adv Rare.* **1** at that point or time. **2** for that reason.

thereby (ˌðɛəˈbaɪ, ˈðɛəˌbaɪ) *adv* **1** by that means; because of that. **2** *Archaic.* by or near that place; thereabouts.

therefor (ˌðɛəˈfɔː) *adv Archaic or law.* for this, that, or it: *he will be richer therefor.*

therefore (ˈðɛəˌfɔː) *sentence connector.* **1** thus; hence: used to mark an inference on the speaker's part: *those people have their umbrellas up; therefore, it must be raining.* **2** consequently; as a result: *they heard the warning on the radio and therefore took another route.*

therefrom (ˌðɛəˈfrɒm) *adv Archaic.* from that or there: *the roads that lead therefrom.*

therein (ˌðɛərˈɪn) *adv Formal or law.* in or into that place, thing, etc.

thereinafter (ˌðɛərɪnˈɑːftə) *adv Formal or law.* from this point on in that document, statement, etc.

thereinto (ˌðɛərˈɪntuː) *adv Formal or law.* into that place, circumstance, etc.

thereof (ˌðɛərˈɒv) *adv Formal or law.* **1** of or concerning that or it. **2** from or because of that.

thereon (ˌðɛərˈɒn) *adv* an archaic word for **thereupon.**

Theresa (təˈriːzə; *Spanish* teˈresa) *n* See (Saint) **Teresa.**

Thérèse de Lisieux (*French* terez də lizjø) *n* **Saint,** known as *the Little Flower of Jesus.* 1873–97, French Carmelite nun, noted for her autobiography, *The Story of a Soul* (1897). Feast day: Oct. 3.

thereto (ˌðɛəˈtuː) *adv* **1** *Formal or law.* to that or it: *the form attached thereto.* **2** *Obsolete.* in addition to that.

theretofore (ˌðɛətuˈfɔː) *adv Formal or law.* before that time; previous to that.

thereunder (ˌðɛərˈʌndə) *adv Formal or law.* **1** (in documents, etc.) below that or it; subsequently in that; thereafter. **2** under the terms or authority of that.

thereupon (ˌðɛərəˈpɒn) *adv* **1** immediately after that; at that point: *thereupon, the whole class applauded.* **2** *Formal or law.* upon that thing, point, subject, etc.

therewith (ˌðɛəˈwɪθ, -ˈwɪð) *or* **therewithal** *adv* **1** *Formal or law.* with or in addition to that. **2** a less common word for **thereupon** (sense 1). **3** *Archaic.* by means of or on account of that.

Therezina (*Portuguese* tereˈzina) *n* the former name of **Teresina.**

therianthropic (ˌθɪərɪænˈθrɒpɪk) *adj* **1** (of certain mythical creatures or deities) having a partly animal, partly human form. **2** of or relating to such creatures or deities. [C19: from Greek *thērion* wild animal + *anthrōpos* man] ▸ **therianthropism** (ˌθɪərɪˈænθrəˌpɪzəm) *n*

theriomorphic (ˌθɪərɪəʊˈmɔːfɪk) *or* **theriomorphous** *adj* (esp. of a deity) possessing or depicted in the form of a beast. [C19: from Greek *thēriomorphos,* from *thērion* wild animal + *morphē* shape] ▸ **ˈtherioˌmorph** *n*

therm (θɜːm) *n Brit.* a unit of heat equal to 100 000 British thermal units. One therm is equal to 1.055 056 × 10^8 joules. [C19: from Greek *thermē* heat]

thermae (ˈθɜːmiː) *pl n* public baths or hot springs, esp. in ancient Greece or Rome. [C17: from Latin, from Greek *thermai,* pl. of *thermē* heat]

thermaesthesia *or U.S.* **thermesthesia** (ˌθɜːmɪsˈθiːzɪə) *n* sensitivity to various degrees of heat and cold. [C19: from New Latin, from THERM- + Greek *aisthēsis* feeling]

thermal (ˈθɜːməl) *adj* **1** Also: **thermic** (ˈθɜːmɪk). of, relating to, caused by, or generating heat or increased temperature. **2** hot or warm: *thermal baths; thermal spring.* **3** (of garments or fabrics) specially designed so as to have exceptional heat-retaining properties. ◆ *n* **4** *Meteorol.* a column of rising air caused by local unequal heating of the land surface, and used by gliders and birds to gain height. **5** (*pl*) thermal garments, esp. underclothes. ▸ **ˈthermally** *adv*

thermal barrier *n* an obstacle to flight at very high speeds as a result of the heating effect of air friction. Also called: **heat barrier.**

thermal conductivity *n* a measure of the ability of a substance to conduct heat, determined by the rate of heat flow normally through an area in the substance divided by the area and by minus the component of the temperature gradient in the direction of flow: measured in watts per metre per kelvin. Symbol: λ or *k* Sometimes shortened to **conductivity.**

thermal efficiency *n* the ratio of the work done by a heat engine to the energy supplied to it. Compare **efficiency.**

thermal equator *n* an imaginary line round the earth running through the point on each meridian with the highest average temperature. It lies mainly to the north because of the larger landmasses and therefore greater summer heating.

thermalize *or* **thermalise** (ˈθɜːməˌlaɪz) *vb Physics.* to undergo or cause to undergo a process in which neutrons lose energy in a moderator and become thermal neutrons. ▸ **ˌthermaliˈzation** *or* **ˌthermaliˈsation** *n*

thermal neutrons *pl n* slow neutrons that are approximately in thermal equilibrium with a moderator. They have a distribution of speeds similar to that of the molecules of a gas at the temperature of the moderator. Data concerning nuclear interactions are often given for standard thermal neutrons of speed 2200 metres per second, which is approximately the most probable speed at normal laboratory temperatures.

thermal noise *n* electrical noise caused by thermal agitation of conducting electrons.

thermal printer *n Computing.* another name for **electrothermal printer.**

thermal reactor *n* a nuclear reactor in which most of the fission is caused by thermal neutrons.

thermal shock *n* a fluctuation in temperature causing stress in a material. It often results in fracture, esp. in brittle materials such as ceramics.

thermette (θɜːˈmɛt) *n N.Z.* a device, used outdoors, for boiling water rapidly.

Thermidor *French.* (tɛrmidɔr) *n* the month of heat: the eleventh month of the French revolutionary calendar, extending from July 20 to Aug. 18. Also called: **Fervidor.** [C19: from French, from Greek *thermē* heat + *dōron* gift]

thermion (ˈθɜːmɪən) *n Physics.* an electron or ion emitted by a body at high temperature.

thermionic (ˌθɜːmɪˈɒnɪk) *adj* of, relating to, or operated by electrons emitted from materials at high temperatures: *a thermionic valve.*

thermionic current *n* an electric current produced between two electrodes as a result of electrons emitted by thermionic emission.

thermionic emission *n* the emission of electrons from very hot solids or liquids: used for producing electrons in valves, electron microscopes, X-ray tubes, etc.

thermionics (ˌθɜːmɪˈɒnɪks) *n* (*functioning as sing*) the branch of electronics concerned with the emission of electrons by hot bodies and with devices based on this effect, esp. the study and design of thermionic valves.

thermionic valve *or esp. U.S. and Canadian* **tube** *n* an electronic valve in which electrons are emitted from a heated rather than a cold cathode.

thermistor (θɜːˈmɪstə) *n* a semiconductor device having a resistance that decreases rapidly with an increase in temperature. It is used for temperature measurement, to compensate for temperature variations in a circuit, etc. [C20: from THERMO- + (RES)ISTOR]

Thermit (ˈθɜːmɪt) *or* **Thermite** (ˈθɜːmaɪt) *n Trademark.* a mixture of aluminium powder and a metal oxide, such as iron oxide, which when ignited reacts with the evolution of heat to yield aluminium oxide and molten metal: used for welding and in some types of incendiary bombs.

thermite process *n* another name for **aluminothermy.**

thermo- *or before a vowel* **therm-** *combining form.* related to, caused by, or measuring heat: *thermodynamics; thermophile.* [from Greek *thermos* hot, *thermē* heat]

thermobarograph (ˌθɜːməʊˈbærəˌgrɑːf, -ˌgræf) *n* a device that simultaneously records the temperature and pressure of the atmosphere.

thermobarometer (ˌθɜːməʊbəˈrɒmɪtə) *n* an apparatus that provides an accurate measurement of pressure by observation of the change in the boiling point of a fluid.

thermochemistry (ˌθɜːməʊˈkɛmɪstrɪ) *n* the branch of chemistry concerned with the study and measurement of the heat evolved or absorbed during chemical reactions. ▸ **ˌthermoˈchemical** *adj* ▸ **ˌthermoˈchemically** *adv* ▸ **ˌthermoˈchemist** *n*

thermochromism (ˌθɜːməʊˈkrəʊmɪzəm) *n* a phenomenon in which certain dyes made from liquid crystals change colour reversibly when their temperature is changed. ▸ **ˈthermochromy** *n* ▸ **ˌthermoˈchromic** *adj*

thermocline (ˈθɜːməʊˌklaɪn) *n* a temperature gradient in a thermally stratified body of water, such as a lake.

thermocouple (ˈθɜːməʊˌkʌpᵊl) *n* **1** a device for measuring temperature consisting of a pair of wires of different metals or semiconductors joined at both ends. One junction is at the temperature to be measured, the second at a fixed temperature. The electromotive force generated depends upon the temperature difference. **2** a similar device with only one junction between two dissimilar metals or semiconductors. [C19: from THERMO- + COUPLE]

thermodynamic (ˌθɜːməʊdaɪˈnæmɪk) *or* **thermodynamical** *adj* **1** of or concerned with thermodynamics. **2** determined by or obeying the laws of thermodynamics. ▸ **ˌthermodyˈnamically** *adv*

thermodynamic equilibrium *n* the condition of a system in which the quantities that specify its properties, such as pressure, temperature, etc., all remain unchanged. Sometimes shortened to **equilibrium.**

thermodynamics (ˌθɜːməudaɪˈnæmɪks) *n* (*functioning as sing*) the branch of physical science concerned with the interrelationship and interconversion of different forms of energy and the behaviour of systems in terms of certain basic quantities, such as pressure, temperature, etc. See also **law of thermodynamics.**

thermodynamic temperature *n* temperature defined in terms of the laws of thermodynamics and not in terms of the properties of any real material. It is usually expressed on the Kelvin scale. Also called: **absolute temperature.**

thermoelectric (ˌθɜːməuɪˈlɛktrɪk) *or* **thermoelectrical** *adj* **1** of, relating to, used in, or operated by the generation of an electromotive force by the Seebeck effect or the Thomson effect: *a thermoelectric thermometer.* **2** of, relating to, used in, or operated by the production or absorption of heat by the Peltier effect: *a thermoelectric cooler.* ► **ˌthermoeˈlectrically** *adv*

thermoelectric effect *n* another name for the **Seebeck effect** or **Peltier effect.**

thermoelectricity (ˌθɜːməuɪlɛkˈtrɪsɪtɪ) *n* **1** electricity generated by a thermocouple. **2** the study of the relationship between heat and electrical energy. See also **Seebeck effect, Peltier effect.**

thermoelectron (ˌθɜːməuɪˈlɛktrɒn) *n* an electron emitted at high temperature, such as one produced in a thermionic valve.

thermogenesis (ˌθɜːməuˈdʒɛnɪsɪs) *n* the production of heat by metabolic processes. ► **thermogenous** (θɜːˈmɒdʒɪnəs) *or* **thermogenetic** (ˌθɜːməudʒɪˈnɛtɪk) *adj*

thermogram (ˈθɜːməuˌgræm) *n* **1** *Med.* a picture produced by thermography, using photographic film sensitive to infrared radiation. **2** the record produced by a thermograph.

thermograph (ˈθɜːməuˌgrɑːf, -ˌgræf) *n* a type of thermometer that produces a continuous record of a fluctuating temperature.

thermography (θɜːˈmɒgrəfɪ) *n* **1** any writing, printing, or recording process involving the use of heat. **2** a printing process which produces raised characters by heating special powder or ink placed on the paper. **3** *Med.* the measurement and recording of heat produced by a part of the body: used in the diagnosis of tumours, esp. of the breast (**mammothermography**), which have an increased blood supply and therefore generate more heat than normal tissue. See also **thermogram.** ► **therˈmographer** *n* ► **thermographic** (ˌθɜːməuˈgræfɪk) *adj*

thermojunction (ˌθɜːməuˈdʒʌŋkʃən) *n* a point of electrical contact between two dissimilar metals across which a voltage appears, the magnitude of which depends on the temperature of the contact and the nature of the metals. See also **Seebeck effect.**

thermolabile (ˌθɜːməuˈleɪbɪl) *adj* (of certain biochemical and chemical compounds) easily decomposed or subject to a loss of characteristic properties by the action of heat: *a thermolabile enzyme.* Compare **thermostable** (sense 1). [C20: from THERMO- + LABILE]

thermoluminescence (ˌθɜːməuˌluːmɪˈnɛsəns) *n* phosphorescence of certain materials or objects as a result of heating. It is caused by pre-irradiation of the material inducing defects which are removed by the heat, the energy released appearing as light: used in archaeological dating. ► **ˌthermoˌlumiˈnescent** *adj*

thermolysis (θɜːˈmɒlɪsɪs) *n* **1** *Physiol.* loss of heat from the body. **2** the dissociation of a substance as a result of heating. ► **thermolytic** (ˌθɜːməuˈlɪtɪk) *adj*

thermomagnetic (ˌθɜːməumægˈnɛtɪk) *adj* of or concerned with the relationship between heat and magnetism, esp. the change in temperature of a body when it is magnetized or demagnetized. Former term: **pyromagnetic.**

thermometer (θəˈmɒmɪtə) *n* an instrument used to measure temperature, esp. one in which a thin column of liquid, such as mercury, expands and contracts within a graduated sealed tube. See also **clinical thermometer, gas thermometer, resistance thermometer, thermocouple, pyrometer.**

thermometry (θəˈmɒmɪtrɪ) *n* the branch of physics concerned with the measurement of temperature and the design and use of thermometers and pyrometers. ► **thermometric** (ˌθɜːməˈmɛtrɪk) *or* **ˌthermoˈmetrical** *adj* ► **ˌthermoˈmetrically** *adv*

thermomotor (ˌθɜːməuˈməutə) *n* an engine that produces force from the expansion of a heated fluid.

thermonasty (ˈθɜːməuˌnæstɪ) *n Botany.* a nastic movement in response to a temperature change, as occurs in the opening of certain flowers.

thermonuclear (ˌθɜːməuˈnjuːklɪə) *adj* **1** involving nuclear fusion: *a thermonuclear reaction; thermonuclear energy.* **2** involving thermonuclear weapons: *a thermonuclear war.*

thermonuclear bomb *n* another name for **fusion bomb.**

thermonuclear reaction *n* a nuclear fusion reaction occurring at a very high temperature: responsible for the energy produced in the sun, nuclear weapons, and fusion reactors. See **nuclear fusion, hydrogen bomb.**

thermoperiodism (ˌθɜːməuˈpɪərɪədɪzəm) *or* **thermoperiodicity** (ˌθɜːməuˌpɪərɪəˈdɪsɪtɪ) *n Botany.* the response of a plant to cycles of temperature fluctuation. ► **ˌthermoˌperiˈodic** *adj*

thermophile (ˈθɜːməuˌfaɪl) *or* **thermophil** (ˈθɜːməuˌfɪl) *n* **1** an organism, esp. a bacterium or plant, that thrives under warm conditions. ◆ *adj* **2** thriving under warm conditions. ► **ˌthermoˈphilic** *or* **thermophilous** (θɜːˈmɒfɪləs) *adj*

thermophyllous (ˌθɜːməuˈfɪləs) *adj* (of plants) having leaves only in the warmer part of the year; deciduous.

thermopile (ˈθɜːməuˌpaɪl) *n* an instrument for detecting and measuring heat radiation or for generating a thermoelectric current. It consists of a number of thermocouple junctions, usually joined together in series. [C19: from THERMO- + PILE[1] (in the sense: voltaic pile)]

thermoplastic (ˌθɜːməuˈplæstɪk) *adj* **1** (of a material, esp. a synthetic plastic or resin) becoming soft when heated and rehardening on cooling without appreciable change of properties. Compare **thermosetting.** ◆ *n* **2** a synthetic plastic or resin, such as polystyrene, with these properties. ► **thermoplasticity** (ˌθɜːməuplæˈstɪsɪtɪ) *n*

Thermopylae (θəˈmɒpəˌliː) *n* (in ancient Greece) a narrow pass between the mountains and the sea linking Locris and Thessaly: a defensible position on a traditional invasion route from N Greece; scene of a famous battle (480 B.C.) in which a greatly outnumbered Greek army under Leonidas fought to the death to delay the advance of the Persians during their attempted conquest of Greece.

Thermos *or* **Thermos flask** (ˈθɜːməs) *n Trademark.* a type of stoppered vacuum flask used to preserve the temperature of its contents. See also **Dewar flask.**

thermoscope (ˈθɜːməˌskəup) *n* a device that indicates a change in temperature, esp. one that does not measure the actual temperature. ► **thermoscopic** (ˌθɜːməˈskɒpɪk) *or* **ˌthermoˈscopical** *adj* ► **ˌthermoˈscopically** *adv*

thermosetting (ˌθɜːməuˈsɛtɪŋ) *adj* (of a material, esp. a synthetic plastic or resin) hardening permanently after one application of heat and pressure. Thermosetting plastics, such as phenol-formaldehyde, cannot be remoulded. Compare **thermoplastic.**

thermosiphon (ˌθɜːməuˈsaɪfən) *n* a system in which a coolant is circulated by convection caused by a difference in density between the hot and cold portions of the liquid.

thermosphere (ˈθɜːməˌsfɪə) *n* an atmospheric layer lying between the mesosphere and the exosphere, reaching an altitude of about 400 kilometres where the temperature is over 1000°C.

thermostable (ˌθɜːməuˈsteɪbᵊl) *adj* **1** (of certain chemical and biochemical compounds) capable of withstanding moderate heat without loss of characteristic properties: *a thermostable plastic.* Compare **thermolabile. 2** not affected by high temperatures. ► **thermostability** (ˌθɜːməustəˈbɪlɪtɪ) *n*

thermostat (ˈθɜːməˌstæt) *n* **1** a device that maintains a system at a constant temperature. It often consists of a bimetallic strip that bends as it expands and contracts with temperature, thus breaking and making contact with an electrical power supply. **2** a similar device that actuates equipment, such as a sprinkler, when a certain temperature is reached. ► **ˌthermoˈstatic** *adj* ► **ˌthermoˈstatically** *adv*

thermostatics (ˌθɜːməˈstætɪks) *n* (*functioning as sing*) the branch of science concerned with thermal equilibrium.

thermotaxis (ˌθɜːməuˈtæksɪs) *n* the directional movement of an organism in response to the stimulus of a source of heat. ► **ˌthermoˈtaxic** *adj*

thermotensile (ˌθɜːməuˈtɛnsaɪl) *adj* of or relating to tensile strength in so far as it is affected by temperature.

thermotherapy (ˌθɜːməuˈθɛrəpɪ) *n Med.* treatment of a bodily structure or part by the application of heat.

thermotolerant (ˌθɜːməuˈtɒlərənt) *adj* (of plants) able to tolerate, but not thriving in, high temperatures.

thermotropism (ˌθɜːməuˈtrəupɪzəm) *n* the directional growth of a plant in response to the stimulus of heat. ► **ˌthermoˈtropic** *adj*

-thermy *n combining form.* indicating heat: *diathermy.* [from New Latin *-thermia,* from Greek *thermē*] ► **-thermic** *or* **-thermal** *adj combining form.*

theroid (ˈθɪərɔɪd) *adj* of, relating to, or resembling a beast. [C19: from Greek *thēroeidēs,* from *thēr* wild animal; see -OID]

therophyte (ˈθɪərəˌfaɪt) *n* a plant that overwinters as a seed. [from Greek *theros* summer + -PHYTE]

theropod (ˈθɪərəpɒd) *n* any bipedal carnivorous saurischian dinosaur of the suborder *Theropoda,* having strong hind legs and grasping hands. They lived in Triassic to Cretaceous times and included tyrannosaurs and megalosaurs. [C19: from New Latin *theropoda,* from Greek *thēr* beast + *pous* foot] ► **theropodan** (θɪˈrɒpədᵊn) *n, adj*

Theroux (θəˈruː) *n* **Paul** (**Edward**). born 1941, U.S. novelist and travel writer. His novels include *Picture Palace* (1978), *The Mosquito Coast* (1981), and *My Other Life* (1996); travel writings include *The Great Railway Bazaar* (1975).

Thersites (θəˈsaɪtiːz) *n* the ugliest and most evil-tongued fighter on the Greek side in the Trojan War, killed by Achilles when he mocked him.

thersitical (θəˈsɪtɪkᵊl) *adj Rare.* abusive and loud. [C17: from THERSITES]

thesaurus (θɪˈsɔːrəs) *n, pl* **-ruses** *or* **-ri** (-raɪ). **1** a book containing systematized lists of synonyms and related words. **2** a dictionary of selected words or topics. **3** *Rare.* a treasury. [C18: from Latin, Greek: TREASURE]

these (ðiːz) *determiner* **a** the form of **this** used before a plural noun: *these men.* **b** (*as pronoun*): *I don't much care for these.*

Theseus (ˈθiːsɪəs) *n Greek myth.* a hero of Attica, noted for his many great deeds, among them the slaying of the Minotaur, the conquest of the Amazons, whose queen he married, participation in the Calydonian hunt, and the search for the Golden Fleece. ► **Thesean** (θɪˈsiːən) *adj*

Thesiger (ˈθɛsɪdʒə) *n* **Wilfred** (**Patrick**). born 1910, British writer, who explored the Empty Quarter of Arabia (1945–50) and lived with the Iraqi marsh Arabs (1950–58). His books include *Arabian Sands* (1958), *The Marsh Arabs* (1964), and *My Kenya Days* (1994).

thesis (ˈθiːsɪs) *n, pl* **-ses** (-siːz). **1** a dissertation resulting from original research, esp. when submitted by a candidate for a degree or diploma. **2** a doctrine maintained or promoted in argument. **3** a subject for a discussion or essay. **4** an unproved statement, esp. one put forward as a premise in an argument. **5** *Music.* the downbeat of a bar, as indicated in conducting. **6** (in classical prosody) the syllable or part of a metrical foot not receiving the ictus. Compare **arsis. 7** *Philosophy.* the first stage in the Hegelian dialectic, that is challenged by the antithesis. [C16: via Late Latin from Greek: a placing, from *tithenai* to place]

Thespian ('θɛspɪən) *adj* 1 of or relating to Thespis. 2 *(usually not cap.)* of or relating to drama and the theatre; dramatic. ◆ *n (usually not cap.)* 3 *Often facetious.* an actor or actress.

Thespis ('θɛspɪs) *n* 6th century B.C., Greek poet, regarded as the founder of tragic drama.

Thess. *Bible. abbrev. for* Thessalonians.

Thessalonian (ˌθɛsəˈləʊnɪən) *adj* 1 of or relating to ancient Thessalonica (modern Salonika). ◆ *n* 2 an inhabitant of ancient Thessalonica.

Thessalonians (ˌθɛsəˈləʊnɪənz) *n (functioning as sing)* either of two books of the New Testament (in full **The First and Second Epistles of Paul the Apostle to the Thessalonians**).

Thessaloníki (*Greek* θesalɔˈniki) *n* a port in NE Greece, in central Macedonia at the head of the **Gulf of Salonika** (an inlet of the Aegean): capital of the Roman province of Macedonia; university (1926). Pop.: 377 951 (1991). Latin name: **Thessalonica** (ˌθɛsəˈlɒnɪkə). English name: **Salonika** or **Salonica.**

Thessaly ('θɛsəlɪ) *n* a region of E Central Greece, on the Aegean: an extensive fertile plain, edged with mountains. Pop.: 734 846 (1991). Area: 14 037 sq. km (5418 sq. miles). Modern Greek name: **Thessalía** (ˌθɛsaˈlija). ▸ **Thessalian** (θɛˈseɪlɪən) *adj, n*

theta ('θiːtə) *n* 1 the eighth letter of the Greek alphabet (Θ, θ), a consonant, transliterated as *th.* 2 the lower-case form of this letter used in phonetic transcription to represent the voiceless dental fricative *th* as in *thick, both.* Compare **edh.** [C17: from Greek, of Semitic origin; compare Hebrew *tēth*]

Thetford Mines ('θɛtfəd) *n* a city in SE Canada, in S Quebec: asbestos industry. Pop.: 17 273 (1991).

thetic ('θɛtɪk) *adj* 1 (in classical prosody) of, bearing, or relating to a metrical stress. 2 positive and arbitrary; prescriptive. [C17: from Greek *thetikos,* from *thetos* laid down, from *tithenai* to place] ▸ **'thetically** *adv*

Thetis ('θiːtɪs) *n* one of the Nereids and mother of Achilles by Peleus.

theurgy ('θiːˌɜːdʒɪ) *n, pl* **-gies. 1a** the intervention of a divine or supernatural agency in the affairs of man. **1b** the working of miracles by such intervention. **2** beneficent magic as taught and performed by Egyptian Neoplatonists and others. [C16: from Late Latin *theūrgia,* from Late Greek *theourgia* the practice of magic, from *theo-* THEO- + *-urgia,* from *ergon* work] ▸ **the'urgic** *or* **the'urgical** *adj* ▸ **the'urgically** *adv* ▸ **'theurgist** *n*

thew (θjuː) *n* 1 muscle, esp. if strong or well-developed. 2 (*pl*) muscular strength. [Old English *thēaw;* related to Old Saxon, Old High German *thau* discipline, Latin *tuērī* to observe, *tūtus* secure] ▸ **'thewy** *adj* ▸ **'thewless** *adj*

they (ðeɪ) *pron (subjective)* 1 refers to people or things other than the speaker or people addressed: *they fight among themselves.* 2 refers to unspecified people or people in general not including the speaker or people addressed: *in Australia they have Christmas in the summer.* 3 *Not standard.* refers to an indefinite antecedent such as *one, whoever,* or *anybody: if anyone objects, they can go.* 4 an archaic word for **those:** *blessed are they that mourn.* [C12: *thei* from Old Norse *their,* masculine nominative plural, equivalent to Old English *thā*]

USAGE It was formerly considered correct to use *he, him,* or *his* after pronouns such as *everyone, no-one, anyone,* or *someone* as in *everyone did his best,* but it is now more common to use *they, them,* or *their,* and this use has become acceptable in all but the most formal contexts: *everyone did their best.*

they'd (ðeɪd) *contraction of* they would *or* they had.

they'll (ðeɪl) *contraction of* they will *or* they shall.

they're (ðɛə, 'ðeɪə) *contraction of* they are.

they've (ðeɪv) *contraction of* they have.

THI *abbrev. for* temperature-humidity index.

thi- *combining form.* a variant of **thio-.**

thiamine ('θaɪəˌmiːn, -mɪn) *or* **thiamin** ('θaɪəmɪn) *n Biochem.* a soluble white crystalline vitamin that occurs in the outer coat of rice and other grains. It forms part of the vitamin B complex and is essential for carbohydrate metabolism: deficiency leads to nervous disorders and to the disease beriberi. Formula: $C_{12}H_{17}ON_4SCl.H_2O$. Also called: **vitamin B_1, aneurin.** [C20: THIO- + (VIT)AMIN]

thiazine ('θaɪəˌziːn, -ˌzaɪn) *n* any of a group of organic compounds containing a ring system composed of four carbon atoms, a sulphur atom, and a nitrogen atom.

thiazole ('θaɪəˌzəʊl) *or* **thiazol** ('θaɪəˌzɒl) *n* 1 a colourless liquid with a pungent smell that contains a ring system composed of three carbon atoms, a sulphur atom, and a nitrogen atom. It is used in dyes and fungicides. Formula: C_3H_3NS. 2 any of a group of compounds derived from this substance that are used in dyes.

thick (θɪk) *adj* 1 of relatively great extent from one surface to the other; fat, broad, or deep: *a thick slice of bread.* **2a** (*postpositive*) of specific fatness: *ten centimetres thick.* **2b** (*in combination*): *a six-inch-thick wall.* 3 having a relatively dense consistency; not transparent: *thick soup.* 4 abundantly covered or filled: *a piano thick with dust.* 5 impenetrable; dense: *a thick fog.* 6 stupid, slow, or insensitive: *a thick person.* 7 throaty or badly articulated: *a voice thick with emotion.* 8 (of accents, etc.) pronounced. 9 *Informal.* very friendly (esp. in the phrase **thick as thieves**). **10 a bit thick.** *Brit.* unfair or excessive. **11 a thick ear.** *Informal.* a blow on the ear delivered as punishment, in anger, etc. ◆ *adv* 12 in order to produce something thick: *to slice bread thick.* 13 profusely; in quick succession (esp. in the phrase **thick and fast**). **14 lay it on thick.** *Informal.* **14a** to exaggerate a story, statement, etc. **14b** to flatter excessively. ◆ *n* 15 a thick piece or part. **16 the thick.** the busiest or most intense part. **17 through thick and thin.** in good times and bad. [Old English *thicce;* related to Old Saxon, Old High German *thikki,* Old Norse *thykkr*] ▸ **'thickish** *adj* ▸ **'thickly** *adv*

thicken ('θɪkən) *vb* 1 to make or become thick or thicker: *thicken the soup by adding flour.* 2 (*intr*) to become more involved: *the plot thickened.* ▸ **'thickener** *n*

thickening ('θɪkənɪŋ) *n* 1 something added to a liquid to thicken it. 2 a thickened part or piece.

thicket ('θɪkɪt) *n* a dense growth of small trees, shrubs, and similar plants. [Old English *thiccet;* see THICK]

thickhead ('θɪkˌhɛd) *n* 1 a stupid or ignorant person; fool. 2 Also called: **whistler.** any of various Australian and SE Asian songbirds of the family *Muscicapidae* (flycatchers, etc.). ▸ **ˌthick'headed** *adj* ▸ **ˌthick'headedness** *n*

thickie *or* **thicky** ('θɪkɪ) *n, pl* **-ies.** *Brit. slang.* a variant of **thicko.**

thick-knee *n* another name for **stone curlew.** [C19: so called because it has thick knee joints]

thickleaf ('θɪkˌliːf) *n, pl* **-leaves.** any of various succulent plants of the crassulaceous genus *Crassula,* having sessile or short-stalked fleshy leaves.

thickness ('θɪknɪs) *n* 1 the state or quality of being thick. 2 the dimension through an object, as opposed to length or width. 3 a layer of something. 4 a thick part.

thicko ('θɪkəʊ) *n, pl* **thickos** *or* **thickoes.** *Brit. slang.* a slow-witted unintelligent person. Also: **thickie, thicky.**

thickset (ˌθɪkˈsɛt) *adj* 1 stocky in build; sturdy. 2 densely planted or placed. ◆ *n* 3 a rare word for **thicket.**

thick-skinned *adj* insensitive to criticism or hints; not easily upset or affected.

thick-witted *or* **thick-skulled** *adj* stupid, dull, foolish, or slow to learn. ▸ **ˌthick-'wittedly** *adv* ▸ **ˌthick-'wittedness** *n*

thief (θiːf) *n, pl* **thieves** (θiːvz). 1 a person who steals something from another. 2 *Criminal law.* a person who commits theft. [Old English *thēof;* related to Old Frisian *thiāf,* Old Saxon *thiof,* Old High German *diob,* Old Norse *thjōfr,* Gothic *thiufs*] ▸ **'thievish** *adj* ▸ **'thievishly** *adv* ▸ **'thievishness** *n*

Thiers (*French* tjɛr) *n* **Louis Adolphe** (lwi adɔlf). 1797–1877, French statesman and historian. After the Franco-Prussian war, he suppressed the Paris Commune and became first president of the Third Republic (1871–73). His policies made possible the paying off of the war indemnity exacted by Germany.

thieve (θiːv) *vb* to steal (someone's possessions). [Old English *thēofian,* from *thēof* THIEF] ▸ **'thievery** *n* ▸ **'thieving** *adj*

thigh (θaɪ) *n* 1 the part of the leg between the hip and the knee in man. 2 the corresponding part in other vertebrates and insects. ◆ Related adjs: **crural, femoral.** [Old English *thēh;* related to Old Frisian *thiāch,* Old High German *dioh* thigh, Old Norse *thjō* buttock, Old Slavonic *tyku* fat]

thighbone ('θaɪˌbəʊn) *n* a nontechnical name for the **femur.**

thigmotaxis (ˌθɪgməˈtæksɪs) *n* another name for **stereotaxis.** [C19: from Greek *thigma* touch + -TAXIS] ▸ **ˌthigmo'tactic** *adj* ▸ **ˌthigmo'tactically** *adv*

thigmotropism (ˌθɪgməʊˈtrəʊpɪzəm) *n* the directional growth of a plant, in response to the stimulus of direct contact. Also called: **haptotropism, stereotropism.** [C19: from Greek *thigma* touch + -TROPISM] ▸ **ˌthigmo'tropic** *adj*

thill (θɪl) *n Archaic.* another word for **shaft** (sense 6). [C14: perhaps related to Old English *thille* board, planking, Old High German *dilla* plank, Old Norse *thili*]

thimble ('θɪmbᵊl) *n* 1 a cap of metal, plastic, etc., used to protect the end of the finger when sewing. 2 any small metal cap resembling this. 3 *Nautical.* a loop of metal having a groove at its outer edge for a rope or cable, for lining the inside of an eye. 4 short for **thimbleful.** [Old English *thȳmel* thumbstall, from *thūma* THUMB]

thimbleful ('θɪmbᵊlˌfʊl) *n* a very small amount, esp. of a liquid.

thimblerig ('θɪmbᵊlˌrɪg) *n* 1 a game in which the operator rapidly moves about three inverted thimbles, often with sleight of hand, one of which conceals a token, the other player betting on which thimble the token is under. ◆ *vb* **-rigs, -rigging, -rigged.** (*tr*) 2 to cheat or swindle, as in this game. [C19: from THIMBLE + *rig* (in obsolete sense: a trick, scheme)] ▸ **'thimbleˌrigger** *n*

thimbleweed ('θɪmbᵊlˌwiːd) *n U.S.* any of various plants having a thimble-shaped fruit, esp. an American anemone, *Anemone virginiana,* and a rudbeckia, *Rudbeckia laciniata.*

thimblewit ('θɪmbᵊlˌwɪt) *n Chiefly U.S.* a silly or dimwitted person; dunce. ▸ **'thimbleˌwitted** *adj*

Thimbu ('θɪmbuː) *or* **Thimphu** ('θɪmfuː) *n* the capital of Bhutan, in the west in the foothills of the E Himalayas: became the official capital in 1962. Pop.: 30 340 (1993 est.).

thimerosal (θaɪˈmɛrəˌsæl) *n* a creamy white crystalline compound of mercury, used in solution as an antiseptic. Formula: $C_9H_9HgNaO_2S$. [C20: from THIO- + MER(CURY) + SAL(ICYLATE)]

thin (θɪn) *adj* **thinner, thinnest.** 1 of relatively small extent from one side or surface to the other; fine or narrow. 2 slim or lean. 3 sparsely placed; meagre: *thin hair.* 4 of relatively low density or viscosity: *a thin liquid.* 5 weak; poor; insufficient: *a thin disguise.* 6 (of a photographic negative) having low density, usually insufficient to produce a satisfactory positive. 7 *Mountaineering.* a climb or pitch on which the holds are few and small. **8 thin on the ground.** few in number; scarce. ◆ *adv* 9 in order to produce something thin: *to cut bread thin.* ◆ *vb* **thins, thinning, thinned.** 10 to make or become thin or sparse. [Old English *thynne;* related to Old Frisian *thenne,* Old Saxon, Old High German *thunni,* Old Norse *thunnr,* Latin *tenuis* thin, Greek *teinein* to stretch] ▸ **'thinly** *adv* ▸ **'thinness** *n*

thine (ðaɪn) *determiner Archaic.* **a** (*preceding a vowel*) of, belonging to, or associated in some way with you (thou): *thine eyes.* **b** (*as pronoun*): *thine is the greatest burden.* ◆ Compare **thy.** [Old English *thīn;* related to Old High German *dīn,* Gothic *theina*]

thin-film *adj* (of an electronic component, device, or circuit) composed of one or more extremely thin layers of metal, semiconductor, etc., deposited on a ceramic or glass substrate: *thin-film capacitor.*

thing[1] (θɪŋ) *n* **1** an object, fact, affair, circumstance, or concept considered as being a separate entity. **2** any inanimate object. **3** an object or entity that cannot or need not be precisely named. **4** *Informal.* a person or animal regarded as the object of pity, contempt, etc.: *you poor thing.* **5** an event or act. **6** a thought or statement. **7** *Law.* any object or right that may be the subject of property (as distinguished from a person). **8** a device, means, or instrument. **9** (*often pl*) a possession, article of clothing, etc. **10** *Informal.* a mental attitude, preoccupation or obsession (esp. in the phrase **have a thing about**). **11** an activity or mode of behaviour satisfying to one's personality (esp. in the phrase **do one's (own) thing**). **12 the done thing.** acceptable or normal behaviour. **13 the thing.** the latest fashion. **14 be on to a good thing.** to be in a profitable situation or position. **15 make a thing of.** to make a fuss about; exaggerate the importance of. [Old English *thing* assembly; related to Old Norse *thing* assembly, Old High German *ding* assembly]

thing[2] (θɪŋ, tɪŋ) *n* (*often cap.*) a law court or public assembly in the Scandinavian countries. Also: **ting**[2]. [C19: from Old Norse *thing* assembly (the same word as THING[1])]

thing-in-itself *n* (in the philosophy of Kant) an element of the noumenal rather than the phenomenal world, of which the senses give no knowledge but whose bare existence can be inferred from the nature of experience.

thingumabob *or* **thingamabob** (ˈθɪŋəmə,bɒb) *n Informal.* a person or thing the name of which is unknown, temporarily forgotten, or deliberately overlooked. Also: **thingumajig, thingamajig** (ˈθɪŋəmə,dʒɪg), *or* **thingummy** (ˈθɪŋəmɪ). [C18: from THING[1], with humorous suffix]

think (θɪŋk) *vb* **thinks, thinking, thought. 1** (*tr; may take a clause as object*) to consider, judge, or believe: *he thinks my ideas impractical.* **2** (*intr;* often foll. by *about*) to exercise the mind as in order to make a decision; ponder. **3** (*intr*) to be capable of conscious thought: *man is the only animal that thinks.* **4** to remember; recollect: *I can't think what his name is.* **5** (*intr;* foll. by *of*) to make the mental choice (of): *think of a number.* **6** (*may take a clause as object or an infinitive*) **6a** to expect; suppose: *I didn't think to see you here.* **6b** to be considerate or aware enough (to do something): *he did not think to thank them.* **7** (*intr;* foll. by *of*) to consider; regard: *she thinks of herself as a poet.* **8** (*intr*) to focus the attention on being: *think thin; think big.* **9** (*tr*) to bring into or out of a specified condition by thinking: *to think away one's fears.* **10 I don't think.** *Slang.* a phrase added to an ironical statement: *you're the paragon of virtue, I don't think.* **11 think again.** to reconsider one's decision, opinion, etc. **12 think better of. 12a** to change one's mind about (a course of action, decision, etc.). **12b** to have a more favourable opinion of (a person). **13 think much of.** (*usually negative*) to have a high opinion of. **14 think nothing of. 14a** to regard as routine, easy, or natural. **14b** to have no compunction or hesitation about. **14c** to have a very low opinion of. **15 think twice.** to consider carefully before deciding (about something). ◆ *n* **16** *Informal.* a careful, open-minded assessment: *let's have a fresh think about this problem.* **17** (*modifier*) *Informal.* characterized by or involving thinkers, thinking, or thought: *a think session.* **18 you've (he's, she's,** etc.) **got another think coming.** *Slang.* you (etc.) are mistaken and will soon have to alter your opinion. ◆ See also **think out, think over, think up.** [Old English *thencan;* related to Old Frisian *thenza,* Old Saxon *thenkian,* Old High German *denken,* Old Norse *thekkja,* Gothic *thagkjan*] ▸ **ˈthinker** *n*

thinkable (ˈθɪŋkəbᵊl) *adj* able to be conceived or considered; possible; feasible.

thinking (ˈθɪŋkɪŋ) *n* **1** opinion or judgment. **2** the process of thought. ◆ *adj* **3** (*prenominal*) using or capable of using intelligent thought: *thinking people.* **4 put on one's thinking cap.** to ponder a matter or problem.

think out *or* **through** *vb* (*tr, adv*) to consider carefully and rationally in order to reach a conclusion.

think over *vb* (*tr, adv*) to ponder or consider: *to think over a problem.*

think-tank *n Informal.* a group of specialists organized by a business enterprise, governmental body, etc., and commissioned to undertake intensive study and research into specified problems.

think up *vb* (*tr, adv*) to invent or devise: *to think up a plan.*

thin-layer chromatography *n* a form of chromatography in which components of a liquid mixture are separated by means of a thin layer of adsorbent material coated on a glass, plastic, or foil sheet. Abbrev.: **TLC.**

thinner (ˈθɪnə) *n* (*often pl, functioning as sing*) a solvent, such as turpentine, added to paint or varnish to dilute it, reduce its opacity or viscosity, or increase its penetration into the ground.

thin-skinned *adj* sensitive to criticism or hints; easily upset or affected.

thio- *or before a vowel* **thi-** *combining form.* indicating that a chemical compound contains sulphur, esp. denoting that a compound is derived from a specified compound by the replacement of an oxygen atom with a sulphur atom: *thiol; thiosulphate.* [from Greek *theion* sulphur]

thioalcohol (,θaɪəʊˈælkə,hɒl) *n* another name for a **thiol.**

thiocarbamide (,θaɪəʊˈkɑːbə,maɪd) *n* another name for **thiourea.**

thiocyanate (,θaɪəʊˈsaɪə,neɪt) *n* any salt or ester of thiocyanic acid.

thiocyanic acid (,θaɪəʊsaɪˈænɪk) *n* an unstable acid known in the form of thiocyanate salts. Formula: HSCN.

thio-ether (,θaɪəʊˈiːθə) *n* any of a class of organic compounds in which a sulphur atom is bound to two hydrocarbon groups.

thiofuran (,θaɪəʊˈfjʊəræn) *n* another name for **thiophen.** [C20: from THIO- + FURAN]

thiol (ˈθaɪɒl) *n* any of a class of sulphur-containing organic compounds with the formula RSH, where R is an organic group. Also called (not in technical usage): **mercaptan.**

thionate (ˈθaɪə,neɪt) *n* any salt or ester of thionic acid.

thionic (θaɪˈɒnɪk) *adj* of, relating to, or containing sulphur.

thionine (ˈθaɪəʊ,niːn, -,naɪn) *or* **thionin** (ˈθaɪənɪn) *n* **1** a crystalline derivative of thiazine used as a violet dye to stain microscope specimens. **2** any of a class of related dyes. [C19: by shortening, from *ergothioneine,* a crystalline betaine found in ergot and blood]

thionyl (ˈθaɪənɪl) *n* (*modifier*) of, consisting of, or containing the divalent group SO: *a thionyl group or radical; thionyl chloride.* Also: **sulphinyl.** [C19 *thion-,* from Greek *theion* sulphur + -YL]

thiopentone sodium (,θaɪəʊˈpɛntəʊn) *or* **thiopental sodium** (,θaɪəʊˈpɛntæl) *n* a barbiturate drug used in medicine as an intravenous general anaesthetic. Formula: $C_{11}H_{17}NaN_2O_2S$. Also called: **Sodium Pentothal.** See also **truth drug.**

thiophen (ˈθaɪəʊ,fɛn) *or* **thiophene** (ˈθaɪəʊ,fiːn) *n* a colourless liquid heterocyclic compound found in the benzene fraction of coal tar and manufactured from butane and sulphur. It has an odour resembling that of benzene and is used as a solvent and in the manufacture of dyes, pharmaceuticals, and resins. Formula: C_4H_4S. Also called: **thiofuran.**

thiosinamine (,θaɪəʊˈsɪnə,miːn, -sɪˈnæmɪn) *n* a white crystalline bitter-tasting compound with a slight garlic-like odour, occurring in mustard oil and used in organic synthesis; 1-allyl-2-thiourea. Formula: $CH_2{:}CHCH_2NHCSNH_2$. [C19: from THIO- + *sin-* (from Latin *sināpis* mustard) + AMINE]

thiosulphate (,θaɪəʊˈsʌlfeɪt) *n* any salt of thiosulphuric acid.

thiosulphuric acid (,θaɪəʊsʌlˈfjʊərɪk) *n* an unstable acid known only in solutions and in the form of its salts. Formula: $H_2S_2O_3$.

thiouracil (,θaɪəʊˈjʊərəsɪl) *n* a white crystalline water-insoluble substance with an intensely bitter taste, used in medicine to treat hyperthyroidism; 2-thio-4-oxypyrimidine. Formula: $C_4H_4N_2OS$. [from THIO- + *uracil* (URO-[1] + AC(ETIC) + -*il* -ILE)]

thiourea (,θaɪəʊˈjʊərɪə) *n* a white water-soluble crystalline substance with a bitter taste that forms addition compounds with metal ions and is used in photographic fixing, rubber vulcanization, and the manufacture of synthetic resins. Formula: H_2NCSNH_2.

third (θɜːd) *adj* (*usually prenominal*) **1a** coming after the second and preceding the fourth in numbering or counting order, position, time, etc.; being the ordinal number of *three:* often written 3rd. **1b** (*as n*): *he arrives on the third; the third got a prize.* **2** rated, graded, or ranked below the second level. **3** denoting the third from lowest forward ratio of a gearbox in a motor vehicle. ◆ *n* **4a** one of three equal or nearly equal parts of an object, quantity, etc. **4b** (*as modifier*): *a third part.* **5** the fraction equal to one divided by three (1/3). **6** the forward ratio above second of a gearbox in a motor vehicle. In some vehicles it is the top gear. **7a** the interval between one note and another three notes away from it counting inclusively along the diatonic scale. **7b** one of two notes constituting such an interval in relation to the other. See also **interval** (sense 5), **major** (sense 13a), **minor** (sense 4d). **8** *Brit.* an honours degree of the third and usually the lowest class. Full term: **third class honours degree. 9** (*pl*) goods of a standard lower than that of seconds. ◆ *adv* **10** Also: **thirdly.** in the third place. ◆ *sentence connector.* **11** Also: **thirdly.** as the third point: linking what follows with the previous statements as in a speech or argument. [Old English *thirda,* variant of *thridda;* related to Old Frisian *thredda,* Old Saxon *thriddio,* Old High German *drittio,* Old Norse *thrithi,* Latin *tertius*] ▸ **ˈthirdly** *adv*

Third Age *n* **the.** old age, esp. when viewed as an opportunity for travel, further education, etc.

third class *n* **1** the class or grade next in value, quality, etc., to the second. ◆ *adj* (**third-class** *when prenominal*). **2** of the class or grade next in value, quality, etc., to the second. **3** of or denoting the class of accommodation in a hotel, on a ship, etc., next in quality and price to the second: usually the cheapest. **4** (in the U.S. and Canada) of or relating to a class of mail consisting largely of unsealed printed matter. **5** *Brit.* See **third** (sense 8). ◆ *adv* **6** by third-class mail, transport, etc.

third degree *n Informal.* torture or bullying, esp. used to extort confessions or information.

third-degree burn *n Pathol.* See **burn**[1] (sense 22).

third dimension *n* the additional dimension by which a solid object may be distinguished from a two-dimensional drawing or picture of it or from any planar object.

third estate *n* the third order or class in a country or society divided into estates, esp. for representation in a parliament; the commons, townsmen, or middle class.

third eyelid *n* another name for **nictitating membrane.**

third house *n U.S.* a political lobby for a special interest.

Third International *n* another name for **Comintern.**

third man *n Cricket.* **a** a fielding position on the off side near the boundary behind the batsman's wicket. **b** a fielder in this position.

third man argument *n* (in the philosophy of Aristotle) the argument against the existence of Platonic Forms that since the Form of Man is itself a perfect man, a further form (the "third" man) would be required to explain this, and so ad infinitum.

Third Market *n* a market established by the London Stock Exchange in 1987 to trade in shares in companies required to provide less detailed information than that required by the main market or the unlisted securities market.

Third Order *n R.C. Church.* a religious society of laymen affiliated to one of the religious orders and following a mitigated form of religious rule.

third party *n* **1** a person who is involved by chance or only incidentally in a legal proceeding, agreement, or other transaction, esp. one against whom a defendant claims indemnity. ◆ *adj* **2** *Insurance.* providing protection against liability caused by accidental injury or death of other persons or damage to their property.

third person *n* a grammatical category of pronouns and verbs used when referring to objects or individuals other than the speaker or his addressee(s).

third rail *n* an extra rail from which an electric train picks up current by means of a sliding collector to feed power to its motors.

third-rate *adj* not of high quality; mediocre or inferior. ► **'third-'rater** *n*

third reading *n* (in a legislative assembly) **1** *Brit.* the process of discussing the committee's report on a bill. **2** *U.S.* the final consideration of a bill.

Third Reich *n* See **Reich**[1] (sense 4).

Third Republic *n* (in France) **1** the governmental system established after the fall of Napoleon III in the Franco-Prussian War and lasting until the German occupation of 1940. **2** the period during which this governmental system functioned (1870–1940).

thirdstream ('θɜːdˌstriːm) *adj* **1** (of music) combining jazz and classical elements. ◆ *n* **2** such music.

Third Way *n* **a** a political ideology that seeks to combine egalitarian and individualist policies, and elements of socialism and capitalism. **b** (*as modifier*): *Third Way government.*

Third World *n* the less economically advanced countries of Africa, Asia, and Latin America collectively, esp. when viewed as underdeveloped and as neutral in the East-West alignment. Also called: **developing world.**

thirl[1] (θɜːl) *vb* (*tr*) *Dialect.* **a** to bore or drill. **b** to thrill. [Old English *thyrelian,* from *thyrel* hole; see NOSTRIL]

thirl[2] (θɪrl, θɜːl) *vb* (*tr*) *Chiefly Scot.* to enslave; bind. [C16: variant of earlier *thrill* THRALL]

thirlage ('θɜːlɪdʒ) *n Scots Law.* (formerly) **1** an obligation imposed upon tenants of certain lands requiring them to have their grain ground at a specified mill. **2** the fee paid for grinding the grain. [C16: variant of earlier *thrillage,* from *thrill,* Scottish variant of THRALL]

Thirlmere ('θɜːlmɪə) *n* a lake in NW England, in Cumbria in the Lake District: provides part of Manchester's water supply. Length: 6 km (4 miles).

thirst (θɜːst) *n* **1** a craving to drink, accompanied by a feeling of dryness in the mouth and throat. **2** an eager longing, craving, or yearning: *a thirst for knowledge.* ◆ *vb* (*intr*) **3** to feel a thirst: *to thirst for a drink; to thirst after righteousness.* [Old English *thyrstan,* from *thurst* thirst; related to Old Norse *thyrsta* to thirst, Old High German *dursten* to thirst, Latin *torrēre* to parch] ► **'thirster** *n*

thirsty ('θɜːstɪ) *adj* **thirstier, thirstiest. 1** feeling a desire to drink. **2** dry; arid: *the thirsty soil.* **3** (foll. by *for*) feeling an eager desire: *thirsty for information.* **4** causing thirst: *thirsty work.* ► **'thirstily** *adv* ► **'thirstiness** *n*

thirteen ('θɜː'tiːn) *n* **1** the cardinal number that is the sum of ten and three and is a prime number. See also **number** (sense 1). **2** a numeral, 13, XIII, etc., representing this number. **3** the amount or quantity that is three more than ten; baker's dozen. **4** something represented by, representing, or consisting of 13 units. ◆ *determiner* **5a** amounting to thirteen: *thirteen buses.* **5b** (*as pronoun*): *thirteen of them fell.* [Old English *threotēne;* see THREE, -TEEN]

thirteenth ('θɜː'tiːnθ) *adj* **1** (*usually prenominal*) **1a** coming after the twelfth in numbering or counting order, position, time, etc.; being the ordinal number of *thirteen:* often written 13th. **1b** (*as n*): *Friday the thirteenth.* ◆ *n* **2a** one of 13 equal or nearly equal parts of something. **2b** (*as modifier*): *a thirteenth part.* **3** the fraction equal to one divided by 13 (1/13). **4** *Music.* **4a** an interval of one octave plus a sixth. See also **interval** (sense 5). **4b** short for **thirteenth chord.**

thirteenth chord *n* a chord much used in jazz and pop, consisting of a major or minor triad upon which are superimposed the seventh, ninth, eleventh, and thirteenth above the root. Often shortened to **thirteenth.**

thirtieth ('θɜːtɪɪθ) *adj* **1** (*usually prenominal*) **1a** being the ordinal number of *thirty* in counting order, position, time, etc.: often written 30th. **1b** (*as n*): *the thirtieth of the month.* ◆ *n* **2a** one of 30 approximately equal parts of something. **2b** (*as modifier*): *a thirtieth part.* **3** the fraction equal to one divided by 30 (1/30).

thirty ('θɜːtɪ) *n, pl* **-ties. 1** the cardinal number that is the product of ten and three. See also **number** (sense 1). **2** a numeral, 30, XXX, etc., representing this number. **3** (*pl*) the numbers 30-39, esp. the 30th to the 39th year of a person's life or of a century. **4** the amount or quantity that is three times as big as ten. **5** something representing, represented by, or consisting of 30 units. ◆ *determiner* **6a** amounting to thirty: *thirty trees.* **6b** (*as pronoun*): *thirty are broken.* [Old English *thrītig;* see THREE, -TY[1]]

Thirty-nine Articles *pl n* a set of formulas defining the doctrinal position of the Church of England, drawn up in the 16th century, to which the clergy are required to give general consent.

thirty-second note *n* the usual U.S. and Canadian name for **demisemiquaver.**

thirty-three *n* a former name for **LP**[1]. [C20: so called because it is played at thirty-three and a third revolutions per minute]

thirty-twomo (ˌθɜːtɪ'tuːməʊ) *n, pl* **-mos.** a book size resulting from folding a sheet of paper into 32 leaves or 64 pages. Often written: **32mo, 32°.**

Thirty Years' War *n* a major conflict involving principally Austria, Denmark, France, Holland, the German states, Spain, and Sweden, that devastated central Europe, esp. large areas of Germany (1618–48). It began as a war between Protestants and Catholics but was gradually transformed into a struggle to determine whether the German emperor could assert more than nominal authority over his princely vassals. The Peace of Westphalia gave the German states their sovereignty and the right of religious toleration and confirmed French ascendancy.

Thiruvananthapuram (ˌθɪruːvə'næntæˌpuːrɑːm) *n* the official name of **Trivandrum.**

this (ðɪs) *determiner* (*used before a singular n*) **1a** used preceding a noun referring to something or someone that is closer: distinct from **that:** *this dress is cheaper than that one; look at this picture.* **1b** (*as pronoun*): *this is Mary and that is her boyfriend; take this.* **2a** used preceding a noun that has just been mentioned or is understood: *this plan of yours won't work.* **2b** (*as pronoun*): *I first saw this on Sunday.* **3a** used to refer to something about to be said, read, etc.: *consider this argument.* **3b** (*as pronoun*): *listen to this.* **4a** the present or immediate: *this time you'll know better.* **4b** (*as pronoun*): *before this, I was mistaken.* **5** *Informal.* an emphatic form of **a**[1] or **the**[1]: used esp. on relating a story: *I saw this big brown bear.* **6 this and that.** various unspecified and trivial actions, matters, objects, etc. **7 this here.** *U.S., not standard.* an emphatic form of **this** (senses 1–3). **8 with** (*or* **at**) **this.** after this; thereupon. ◆ *adv* **9** used with adjectives and adverbs to specify a precise degree that is about to be mentioned: *go just this fast and you'll be safe.* [Old English *thēs, thēos, this* (masculine, feminine, neuter singular); related to Old Saxon *thit,* Old High German *diz,* Old Norse *thessi*]

Thisbe ('θɪzbɪ) *n* See **Pyramus and Thisbe.**

thistle ('θɪsᵊl) *n* **1** any of numerous plants of the genus *Cirsium,* having prickly-edged leaves, pink, purple, yellow, or white dense flower heads, and feathery hairs on the seeds: family *Compositae* (composites). **2** any of various similar or related plants, such as the star thistle. **3** a thistle, or a representation of one, as the national emblem of Scotland. [Old English *thīstel,* related to Old Saxon, Old High German *thīstil,* Old Norse *thīstill*] ► **'thistly** *adj*

Thistle ('θɪsᵊl) *n* **the. 1** See **Order of the Thistle. 2** (*sometimes not cap.*) **2a** the emblem of this Order. **2b** membership of this Order.

thistledown ('θɪsᵊlˌdaʊn) *n* **1** the mass of feathery plumed seeds produced by a thistle. **2** anything resembling this.

thither ('ðɪðə) *or* **thitherward** *adv Obsolete or formal.* to or towards that place; in that direction. [Old English *thider,* variant of *thæder,* influenced by *hider* HITHER; related to Old Norse *thathra* there]

thitherto (ˌðɪðə'tuː, 'ðɪðəˌtuː) *adv Obsolete or formal.* until that time.

thixotropic (ˌθɪksə'trɒpɪk) *adj* (of fluids and gels) having a reduced viscosity when stress is applied, as when stirred: *thixotropic paints.* [C20: from Greek *thixis* the act of touching + -TROPIC] ► **thixotropy** (θɪk'sɒtrəpɪ) *n* ► **thixotrope** ('θɪksəˌtrəʊp) *n*

tho' *or* **tho** (ðəʊ) *conj, adv U.S. or poetic.* a variant spelling of **though.**

thole[1] (θəʊl) *or* **tholepin** ('θəʊlˌpɪn) *n* a wooden pin or one of a pair, set upright in the gunwales of a rowing boat to serve as a fulcrum in rowing. [Old English *tholl,* related to Middle Low German *dolle,* Norwegian *toll,* Icelandic *thollr*]

thole[2] (θəʊl) *vb* **1** (*tr*) *Scot. and northern English dialect.* to put up with; bear. **2** an archaic word for **suffer.** [Old English *tholian;* related to Old Saxon, Old High German *tholōn,* Old Norse *thola* to endure: compare Latin *tollere* to bear up]

tholos ('θəʊlɒs) *n, pl* **-loi** (-lɔɪ). a dry-stone beehive-shaped tomb associated with the Mycenaean culture of Greece in the 16th to the 12th century B.C. [C17: from Greek]

Thomas ('tɒməs) *n* **1 Saint.** Also called: **doubting Thomas.** one of the twelve apostles, who refused to believe in Christ's resurrection until he had seen his wounds (John 20:24–29). Feast day: July 3 or Dec. 21 or Oct. 6. **2** (*French* tɔmɑ). **Ambroise** (ɑ̃brwaz). 1811–96, French composer of light operas, including *Mignon* (1866). **3 Dylan** (**Marlais**) ('dɪlən). 1914–53, Welsh poet and essayist. His works include the prose *Portrait of the Artist as a Young Dog* (1940), the verse collection *Deaths and Entrances* (1946), and his play for voices *Under Milk Wood* (1954). **4** (**Philip**) **Edward,** pen name *Edward Eastaway.* 1878–1917, British poet and critic: killed in World War I. **5 R**(**onald**) **S**(**tuart**). born 1913, Welsh poet and clergyman. His collections include *Song at the Year's Turning* (1955), *Not that He Brought Flowers* (1968), and *Laboratories of the Spirit* (1975).

Thomas à Kempis *n* See (Thomas à) **Kempis.**

Thomas Becket *n* **Saint.** See (Saint Thomas) **Becket.**

Thomas of Erceldoune ('ɜːsəlˌduːn) *n* called *Thomas the Rhymer.* ?1220–?97, Scottish seer and poet; reputed author of a poem on the Tristan legend.

Thomas of Woodstock *n* 1355–97, youngest son of Edward III, who led opposition to his nephew Richard II (1386–89); arrested in 1397, he died in prison.

Thomism ('təʊmɪzəm) *n* the comprehensive system of philosophy and theology developed by Saint Thomas Aquinas in the 13th century and since taught and maintained by his followers, esp. in the Dominican order. ► **'Thomist** *n, adj* ► **Tho'mistic** *or* **Tho'mistical** *adj*

Thompson ('tɒmpsən, 'tɒmsən) *n* **1 Benjamin,** Count Rumford. 1753–1814, Anglo-American physicist, noted for his work on the nature of heat. **2 Daley.** born 1958, British athlete: Olympic decathlon champion (1980, 1984). **3 Emma.** born 1959, British actress: her films include *Howards End* (1991), *Remains of the Day* (1993), and *Sense and Sensibility* (1996; also wrote screenplay). **4 Flora** (**Jane**). 1876–1947, British writer, author of the autobiographical *Lark Rise to Candleford* (1945). **5 Francis.** 1859–1907, British poet, best known for the mystical poem *The Hound of Heaven* (1893).

Thompson sub-machine-gun *n Trademark.* a .45 calibre sub-machine-gun. Also called: **Tommy gun.** [C20: after John T. *Thompson* (1860–1940), U.S. Army Officer, its coinventor]

Thomson ('tɒmsən) *n* **1** Sir **George Paget,** son of Joseph John Thomson. 1892–1975, British physicist, who discovered (1927) the diffraction of electrons by crystals: shared the Nobel prize for physics 1937. **2 James.** 1700–48, Scottish poet. He anticipated the romantics' feeling for nature in *The Seasons* (1726–30). **3 James,** pen name *B.V.* 1834–82, British poet, born in Scotland, noted esp. for *The City of Dreadful Night* (1874), reflecting man's isolation and despair. **4** Sir **Joseph John.** 1856–1940, British physicist. He discovered the electron (1897) and his work on the nature of positive rays led to the discovery of isotopes: Nobel prize for physics 1906. **5 Roy,** 1st Baron Thomson of Fleet. 1894–1976, British newspaper proprietor, born in Canada. **6 Virgil.** 1896–1989, U.S. composer, music critic, and conductor, whose works include two operas, *Four Saints in Three Acts* (1928) and *The Mother of Us All* (1947), piano sonatas, a cello concerto, songs, and film music. 7 Sir **William.** See (1st Baron) **Kelvin.**

Thomson effect *n Physics.* the phenomenon in which a temperature gradient along a metallic (or semiconductor) wire or strip causes an electric potential gradient to form along its length. [named after Sir William THOMSON]

thon (ðɒn) *determiner* a Scot. word for **yon.** [C19: of uncertain origin]

-thon *suffix forming nouns.* indicating a large-scale event or operation of a specified kind: *telethon.* [C20: on the pattern of MARATHON]

Thonburi (ˌtɒnbuˈriː) *n* a city in central Thailand, part of Bankok Metropolis on the Chao Phraya River; the national capital (1767–82).

thonder (ˈðɒndər) *adv, determiner.* a Scot. word for **yonder.** [C19: of uncertain origin]

thong (θɒŋ) *n* **1** a thin strip of leather or other material, such as one used for lashing things together. **2** a whip or whiplash, esp. one made of leather. **3** *U.S., Canadian, Austral., and N.Z.* the usual name for **flip-flop** (sense 5). **4** a skimpy article of beachwear, worn by men or women, consisting of thin strips of leather or cloth attached to a piece of material that covers the genitals while leaving the buttocks bare. [Old English *thwang;* related to Old High German *dwang* reins, Old Norse *thvengr* strap]

Thor (θɔː) *n Norse myth.* the god of thunder, depicted as wielding a hammer, emblematic of the thunderbolt. [Old English *Thōr,* from Old Norse *thōrr* THUNDER]

thoracentesis (ˌθɔːrəsɛnˈtiːsɪs) *or* **thoracocentesis** (ˌθɔːrəkəʊsɛnˈtiːsɪs) *n Med.* the surgical puncture of the pleural cavity using a hollow needle, in order to withdraw fluid, drain blood, etc. Also called: **pleurocentesis.**

thoracic (θɔːˈræsɪk) *adj* of, near, or relating to the thorax.

thoracic duct *n* the major duct of the lymphatic system, beginning below the diaphragm and ascending in front of the spinal column to the base of the neck.

thoraco- *or before a vowel* **thorac-** *combining form.* thorax: *thoracotomy.*

thoracoplasty (ˈθɔːrəkəʊˌplæstɪ) *n, pl* **-ties. 1** plastic surgery of the thorax. **2** surgical removal of several ribs or a part of them to permit the collapse of a diseased lung, used in cases of pulmonary tuberculosis and bronchiectasis.

thoracoscope (ˈθɔːrəkəʊˌskəʊp) *n Med.* an instrument used for examining the pleural cavity.

thoracotomy (ˌθɔːrəˈkɒtəmɪ) *n, pl* **-mies.** surgical incision into the chest wall.

thorax (ˈθɔːræks) *n, pl* **thoraxes** *or* **thoraces** (ˈθɔːrəˌsiːz, θɔːˈreɪsiːz). **1** the part of the human body enclosed by the ribs. **2** the corresponding part in other vertebrates. **3** the part of an insect's body between the head and abdomen, which bears the wings and legs. [C16: via Latin from Greek *thōrax* breastplate, chest]

Thoreau (ˈθɔːrəʊ, θɔːˈrəʊ) *n* **Henry David.** 1817–62, U.S. writer, noted esp. for *Walden, or Life in the Woods* (1854), an account of his experiment in living in solitude. A powerful social critic, his essay *Civil Disobedience* (1849) influenced such dissenters as Gandhi.

thoria (ˈθɔːrɪə) *n* another name for **thorium dioxide.** [C19: THORIUM + *-a,* on the model of *magnesia*]

thorianite (ˈθɔːrɪəˌnaɪt) *n* a rare black mineral consisting of thorium and uranium oxides. Formula: $ThO_2.U_3O_8$.

thorite (ˈθɔːraɪt) *n* a yellow, brownish, or black radioactive mineral consisting of tetragonal thorium silicate. It occurs in coarse granite and is a source of thorium. Formula: $ThSiO_4$.

thorium (ˈθɔːrɪəm) *n* a soft ductile silvery-white metallic element. It is radioactive and occurs in thorite and monazite: used in gas mantles, magnesium alloys, electronic equipment, and as a nuclear power source. Symbol: Th; atomic no.: 90; atomic wt.: 232.0381; half-life of most stable isotope, ^{232}Th: 1.41×10^{10} years; valency: 4; relative density: 11.72; melting pt.: 1755°C; boiling pt.: 4788°C. [C19: New Latin, from THOR + -IUM] ▸ ˈ**thoric** *adj*

thorium dioxide *n* a heavy insoluble white powder used in incandescent mantles. Formula: ThO_2. Also called: **thoria.**

thorium series *n* a radioactive series that starts with thorium-232 and ends with lead-208.

thorn (θɔːn) *n* **1** a sharp pointed woody extension of a stem or leaf. Compare **prickle** (sense 1). **2a** any of various trees or shrubs having thorns, esp. the hawthorn. **2b** the wood of any of these plants. **3** short for **thorn moth. 4** a Germanic character of runic origin (Þ) used in Old and Modern Icelandic to represent the voiceless dental fricative sound of *th,* as in *thin, bath.* Its use in phonetics for the same purpose is now obsolete. See **theta. 5** this same character as used in Old and Middle English as an alternative to *edh,* but indistinguishable from it in function or sound. Compare **edh. 6** *Zoology.* any of various sharp spiny parts. **7** a source of irritation (esp. in the phrases **a thorn in one's side** *or* **flesh**). [Old English; related to Old High German *dorn,* Old Norse *thorn*] ▸ ˈ**thornless** *adj*

Thorn (tɔrn) *n* the German name for **Toruń.**

thorn apple *n* **1** a poisonous solanaceous plant, *Datura stramonium,* of the N hemisphere, having white funnel-shaped flowers and spiny capsule fruits. U.S. name: **jimson weed.** See also **stramonium. 2** any other plant of the genus *Datura.* **3** the fruit of certain types of hawthorn.

thornback (ˈθɔːnˌbæk) *n* **1** a European ray, *Raja clavata,* having a row of spines along the back and tail. **2** a similar fish, *Platyrhinoidis triseriata,* of the Pacific Ocean.

thornbill (ˈθɔːnˌbɪl) *n* **1** any of various South American hummingbirds of the genera *Chalcostigma, Ramphomicron,* etc., having a thornlike bill. **2** Also called: **thornbill warbler.** any of various Australasian wrens of the genus *Acanthiza* and related genera: family *Muscicapidae.* **3** any of various other birds with thornlike bills.

Thorndike (ˈθɔːnˌdaɪk) *n* **1 Edward Lee.** 1874–1949, U.S. psychologist, who worked on animals and proposed that all learnt behaviour is regulated by rewards and punishments (**Thorndike's law** *or* **law of effect**). **2** Dame (**Agnes**) **Sybil.** 1882–1976, British actress.

Thornhill (ˈθɔːnˌhɪl) *n* Sir **James.** 1675–1734, English baroque painter. He is best known for decorating the Painted Hall, Greenwich Hospital (1708–27) and the interior of the dome of St Paul's Cathedral (1715–17).

thorn moth *n* any of various woodland geometrid moths, typified by the **large thorn** (*Ennomos autumnaria*), having wings set somewhat at an angle and held up when at rest. Often shortened to **thorn.**

thorny (ˈθɔːnɪ) *adj* **thornier, thorniest. 1** bearing or covered with thorns. **2** difficult or unpleasant: *a thorny problem.* **3** sharp. ▸ ˈ**thornily** *adv* ▸ ˈ**thorniness** *n*

thoron (ˈθɔːrɒn) *n* a radioisotope of radon that is a decay product of thorium. Symbol: Tn or ^{220}Rn; atomic no.: 86; half-life: 54.5s. [C20: from THORIUM + -ON]

thorough (ˈθʌrə) *adj* **1** carried out completely and carefully: *a thorough search.* **2** (*prenominal*) utter: *a thorough bore.* **3** painstakingly careful: *my work is thorough.* [Old English *thurh;* related to Old Frisian *thruch,* Old Saxon *thuru,* Old High German *duruh;* see THROUGH] ▸ ˈ**thoroughly** *adv* ▸ ˈ**thoroughness** *n*

Thorough (ˈθʌrə) *n* thoroughgoing policy, as adopted in England by Strafford and Laud during the reign of Charles I.

thorough bass (beɪs) *n* **a** Also called: **basso continuo, continuo.** (esp. during the baroque period) a bass part underlying a piece of concerted music. It is played on a keyboard instrument, usually supported by a cello, viola da gamba, etc. See also **figured bass. b** (*as adj*): *a thorough-bass part; thorough-bass technique.*

thorough brace *n Chiefly U.S.* either of two strong leather straps upon which the body of certain types of carriage is supported. ▸ ˈ**thorough-ˌbraced** *adj*

thoroughbred (ˈθʌrəˌbrɛd) *adj* **1** purebred. ◆ *n* **2** a pedigree animal; purebred. **3** a person regarded as being of good breeding.

Thoroughbred (ˈθʌrəˌbrɛd) *n* a British breed of horse the ancestry of which can be traced to English mares and Arab sires; most often used as a racehorse.

thoroughfare (ˈθʌrəˌfɛə) *n* **1** a road from one place to another, esp. a main road. **2** way through or access: *no thoroughfare.*

thoroughgoing (ˈθʌrəˌgəʊɪŋ) *adj* **1** extremely thorough. **2** (*usually prenominal*) absolute; complete: *thoroughgoing incompetence.* ▸ ˈ**thoroughˌgoingly** *adv* ▸ ˈ**thoroughˌgoingness** *n*

thoroughpaced (ˈθʌrəˌpeɪst) *adj* **1** (of a horse) showing performing ability in all paces. **2** thoroughgoing.

thoroughpin (ˈθʌrəˌpɪn) *n* an inflammation and swelling on both sides of the hock joint of a horse affecting the sheath of the deep flexor tendon. [C18: so called because it makes the leg look as if it has a pin stuck through it]

thorp *or* **thorpe** (θɔːp) *n Obsolete except in place names.* a small village. [Old English; related to Old Norse *thorp* village, Old High German *dorf,* Gothic *thaurp*]

Thorpe (θɔːp) *n* **1 James Francis.** 1888–1953, American football player and athlete: Olympic pentathlon and decathlon champion (1912). **2 Jeremy.** born 1929, British politician; leader of the Liberal party (1967–76).

Thorshavn (*Danish* ˈtɔːrshaun) *n* the capital of the Faeroe Islands, a port on the northernmost island. Pop.: 13 757 (1980).

Thorvaldsen *or* **Thorwaldsen** (*Danish* ˈtɔrvalsən) *n* **Bertel** (ˈbertəl). 1770–1884, Danish neoclassical sculptor.

those (ðəʊz) *determiner* the form of **that** used before a plural noun. [Old English *thās,* plural of THIS]

Thoth (θəʊθ, təʊt) *n* (in Egyptian mythology) a moon deity, scribe of the gods and protector of learning and the arts.

thou[1] (ðaʊ) *pron* (*subjective*) **1** *Archaic or Brit. dialect.* refers to the person addressed: used mainly in familiar address or to a younger person or inferior. **2** (*usually cap.*) refers to God when addressed in prayer, etc. [Old English *thū;* related to Old Saxon *thū,* Old High German *du,* Old Norse *thū,* Latin *tū,* Doric Greek *tu*]

thou[2] (θaʊ) *n, pl* **thous** *or* **thou. 1** one thousandth of an inch. 1 thou is equal to 0.0254 millimetre. **2** *Informal.* short for **thousand.**

though (ðəʊ) *conj* (*subordinating*) **1** (sometimes preceded by *even*) despite the fact that: *though he tries hard, he always fails; poor though she is, her life is happy.* **2 as though.** as if: *he looked as though he'd seen a ghost.* ◆ *adv* **3** nevertheless; however: *he can't dance; he sings well, though.* [Old English *theah;* related to Old Frisian *thāch,* Old Saxon, Old High German *thōh* Old Norse *thō*]

thought (θɔːt) *vb* **1** the past tense and past participle of **think.** ◆ *n* **2** the act or process of thinking; deliberation, meditation, or reflection. **3** a concept, opinion, or idea. **4** philosophical or intellectual ideas typical of a particular time or place: *German thought in the 19th century.* **5** application of mental attention; consideration: *he gave the matter some thought.* **6** purpose or intention: *I have no thought of giving up.* **7** expectation: *no thought of reward.* **8** a small amount; trifle: *you could be a thought more enthusiastic.* **9** kindness or regard: *he has no thought for his widowed mother.* [Old English *thōht;* related to Old Frisian *thochta,* Old Saxon, Old High German *githāht*]

thought disorder *n Psychiatry.* a cognitive disorder in which the patient's thoughts or conversations are characterized by irrationality or sudden changes of subject.

thoughtful (ˈθɔːtfʊl) *adj* **1** considerate in the treatment of other people. **2** showing careful thought. **3** pensive; reflective. ▸ ˈ**thoughtfully** *adv* ▸ ˈ**thoughtfulness** *n*

thoughtless (ˈθɔːtlɪs) *adj* **1** inconsiderate: *a thoughtless remark.* **2** having or showing lack of thought: *a thoughtless essay.* **3** unable to think; not having the power of thought. ▸ ˈ**thoughtlessly** *adv* ▸ ˈ**thoughtlessness** *n*

thought-out *adj* conceived and developed by careful thought: *a well thought-out scheme.*

thought police *n* a group of people with totalitarian views on a given subject, who constantly monitor others for any deviation from prescribed thinking. [C20: from the *Thought Police* described by George Orwell in his novel *Nineteen Eighty-Four* (1949)]

thought transference *n Psychol.* another name for **telepathy.**

thousand ('θaʊzənd) *n* **1** the cardinal number that is the product of 10 and 100. See also **number** (sense 1). **2** a numeral, 1000, 10^3, M, etc., representing this number. **3** (*often pl*) a very large but unspecified number, amount, or quantity: *they are thousands of miles away.* **4** (*pl*) the numbers 2000–9999: *the price of the picture was in the thousands.* **5** the amount or quantity that is one hundred times greater than ten. **6** something represented by, representing, or consisting of 1000 units. **7** *Maths.* the position containing a digit representing that number followed by three zeros: *in 4760, 4 is in the thousand's place.* ◆ *determiner* **8a** amounting to a thousand: *a thousand ships.* **8b** (*as pronoun*): *a thousand is hardly enough.* **9** amounting to 1000 times a particular scientific unit. Related prefix: **kilo-.** ◆ Related adj: **millenary.** [Old English *thūsend;* related to Old Saxon *thūsind,* Old High German *thūsunt,* Old Norse *thūsund*]

Thousand and One Nights *n* See **Arabian Nights' Entertainments.**

Thousand Guineas *n* (*functioning as sing*), usually written **1,000 Guineas.** an annual horse race, restricted to fillies, run at Newmarket since 1814. Also called: **One Thousand Guineas.**

Thousand Island dressing *n* a salad dressing made from mayonnaise with ketchup, chopped gherkins, etc. [probably from the THOUSAND ISLANDS]

Thousand Islands *pl n* a group of about 1500 islands between the U.S. and Canada, in the upper St Lawrence River: administratively divided between the U.S. and Canada. ▸ **Thousand Island** *adj*

thousandth ('θaʊzənθ) *adj* **1** (*usually prenominal*) **1a** being the ordinal number of 1000 in numbering or counting order, position, time, etc. **1b** (*as n*): *the thousandth in succession.* ◆ *n* **2a** one of 1000 approximately equal parts of something. **2b** (*as modifier*): *a thousandth part.* **3** one of 1000 equal divisions of a particular scientific quantity. Related prefix: **milli-:** *millivolt.* **4** the fraction equal to one divided by 1000 (1/1000).

Thrace (θreɪs) *n* **1** an ancient country in the E Balkan Peninsula: successively under the Persians, Macedonians, and Romans. **2** a region of SE Europe, corresponding to the S part of the ancient country: divided by the Maritsa River into **Western Thrace** (Greece) and **Eastern Thrace** (Turkey).

Thracian ('θreɪʃɪən) *n* **1** a member of an ancient Indo-European people who lived in the SE corner of the Balkan Peninsula. **2** the ancient language spoken by this people, belonging to the Thraco-Phrygian branch of the Indo-European family: extinct by the early Middle Ages. ◆ *adj* **3** of or relating to Thrace, its inhabitants, or the extinct Thracian language.

Thraco-Phrygian (ˌθreɪkəʊ'frɪdʒɪən) *n* **1** a branch of the Indo-European family of languages, all members of which are extinct except for Armenian. ◆ *adj* **2** relating to or belonging to this group of languages. [from *Thraco-,* from Greek *Thraikē* Thrace; see PHRYGIAN]

Thrale (θreɪl) *n* **Hester Lynch,** known as *Mrs Thrale* or (later) *Mrs Piozzi* (née *Salusbury*). 1741–1821, English writer of memoirs, noted for her friendship with Dr Johnson. Her works include *Anecdotes of the late Samuel Johnson* (1786) and *Letters to and from the late Samuel Johnson* (1788).

thrall (θrɔːl) *n* **1** Also called: **thraldom** or (U.S.) **thralldom** ('θrɔːldəm). the state or condition of being in the power of another person. **2** a person who is in such a state. **3** a person totally subject to some need, desire, appetite, etc. ◆ *vb* **4** (*tr*) to enslave or dominate. [Old English *thrǣl* slave, from Old Norse *thrǣll*]

thrang (θræŋ) *Scot.* ◆ *n* **1** a throng; crowd. ◆ *vb* **2** to throng; crowd. ◆ *adj* **3** crowded; busy. **4** engaged or occupied; busy. [Scot. variant of THRONG]

thrapple ('θræpᵊl) *Scot.* ◆ *n* **1** the throat or windpipe. ◆ *vb* **2** to throttle. [C18: a variant of earlier *thropple,* of uncertain origin]

thrash (θræʃ) *vb* **1** (*tr*) to beat soundly, as with a whip or stick. **2** (*tr*) to defeat totally; overwhelm. **3** (*intr*) to beat or plunge about in a wild manner. **4** (*intr*) to move the legs up and down in the water, as in certain swimming strokes. **5** to sail (a boat) against the wind or tide or (of a boat) to sail in this way. **6** another word for **thresh.** ◆ *n* **7** the act of thrashing; blow; beating. **8** *Informal.* a party or similar social gathering. [Old English *threscan;* related to Old High German *dreskan,* Old Norse *thriskja*]

thrasher[1] ('θræʃə) *n* another name for **thresher** (the shark).

thrasher[2] ('θræʃə) *n* any of various brown thrushlike American songbirds of the genus *Toxostoma* and related genera, having a long downward-curving bill and long tail: family *Mimidae* (mockingbirds). [C19: perhaps from English dialect *thresher, thrusher* a thrush]

thrashing ('θræʃɪŋ) *n* a physical assault; flogging.

thrash metal *n* a type of very fast, very loud rock music that combines elements of heavy metal and punk rock. Often shortened to **thrash.**

thrash out *vb* (*tr, adv*) to discuss fully or vehemently, esp. in order to come to a solution or agreement.

thrasonical (θrə'sɒnɪkᵊl) *adj Rare.* bragging; boastful. [C16: from Latin *Thrasō* name of boastful soldier in *Eunuchus,* a play by Terence, from Greek *Thrasōn,* from *thrasus* forceful] ▸ **thra'sonically** *adv*

thrave (θreɪv) *n Scot. and northern English dialect.* twenty-four sheaves of corn. [Old English *threfe,* of Scandinavian origin]

thrawn (θrɔːn) *adj Scot. and northern English dialect.* **1** crooked or twisted. **2** stubborn; perverse. [Northern English dialect, variant of THROWN, from Old English *thrāwan* to twist about, THROW]

thread (θrɛd) *n* **1** a fine strand, filament or fibre of some material. **2** a fine cord of twisted filaments, esp. of cotton, used in sewing, weaving, etc. **3** any of the filaments of which a spider's web is made. **4** any fine line, stream, mark, or piece: *from the air, the path was a thread of white.* **5** a helical groove in a cylindrical hole (**female thread**), formed by a tap or lathe tool, or a helical ridge on a cylindrical bar, rod, shank, etc. (**male thread**), formed by a die or lathe tool. **6** a very thin seam of coal or vein of ore. **7** something acting as the continuous link or theme of a whole: *the thread of the story.* **8** the course of an individual's life believed in Greek mythology to be spun, measured, and cut by the Fates. ◆ *vb* **9** (*tr*) to pass (thread, film, magnetic tape, etc.) through (something): *to thread a needle; to thread cotton through a needle.* **10** (*tr*) to string on a thread: *she threaded the beads.* **11** to make (one's way) through or over (something). **12** (*tr*) to produce a screw thread by cutting, rolling, tapping, or grinding. **13** (*tr*) to pervade: *hysteria threaded his account.* **14** (*intr*) (of boiling syrup) to form a fine thread when poured from a spoon. ◆ See also **threads.** [Old English *thrǣd;* related to Old Frisian *thrēd,* Old High German *drāt,* Old Norse *thrāthr* thread] ▸ **'threader** *n* ▸ **'threadless** *adj* ▸ **'thread,like** *adj*

threadbare ('θrɛd,bɛə) *adj* **1** (of cloth, clothing, etc.) having the nap worn off so that the threads are exposed. **2** meagre or poor: *a threadbare existence.* **3** hackneyed: *a threadbare argument.* **4** wearing threadbare clothes; shabby. ▸ **'thread,bareness** *n*

threadfin ('θrɛd,fɪn) *n, pl* **-fin** *or* **-fins.** any spiny-finned tropical marine fish of the family *Polynemidae,* having pectoral fins consisting partly of long threadlike rays.

thread mark *n* a mark put into paper money to prevent counterfeiting, consisting of a pattern of silk fibres.

Threadneedle Street (ˌθrɛd'niːdᵊl, 'θrɛd,niːdᵊl) *n* a street in the City of London famous for its banks, including the Bank of England, known as **The Old Lady of Threadneedle Street.**

thread rolling *n Engineering.* the production of a screw thread by a rolling swaging process using hardened profiled rollers. Rolled threads are stronger than threads machined by a cutting tool.

threads (θrɛdz) *pl n* a slang word for **clothes.**

threadworm ('θrɛd,wɜːm) *n* any of various nematodes, esp. the pinworm.

thready ('θrɛdɪ) *adj* **threadier, threadiest. 1** of, relating to, or resembling a thread or threads. **2** *Med.* (of the pulse) barely perceptible; weak; fine. **3** sounding thin, weak, or reedy: *a thready tenor.* ▸ **'threadiness** *n*

threap *or* **threep** (θriːp) *vb* (*tr*) *Scot. and northern English dialect.* **1** to scold. **2** to contradict. [Old English *thrēapian* to blame; related to Old Frisian *thrūwa,* Old High German *threwen,* Old Norse *threa*] ▸ **'threaper** *or* **'threeper** *n*

threat (θrɛt) *n* **1** a declaration of the intention to inflict harm, pain, or misery. **2** an indication of imminent harm, danger, or pain. **3** a person or thing that is regarded as dangerous or likely to inflict pain or misery. ◆ *vb* **4** an archaic word for **threaten.** [Old English; related to Old Norse *thraut,* Middle Low German *drōt*]

threaten ('θrɛtᵊn) *vb* **1** (*tr*) to be a threat to. **2** to be a menacing indication of (something); portend: *dark clouds threatened rain.* **3** (when *tr, may take a clause as object*) to express a threat to (a person or people). ▸ **'threatener** *n* ▸ **'threatening** *adj* ▸ **'threateningly** *adv*

three (θriː) *n* **1** the cardinal number that is the sum of two and one and is a prime number. See also **number** (sense 1). **2** a numeral, 3, III, (iii), representing this number. **3** the amount or quantity that is one greater than two. **4** something representing, represented by, or consisting of three units such as a playing card with three symbols on it. **5** Also called: **three o'clock.** three hours after noon or midnight. ◆ *determiner* **6a** amounting to three: *three ships.* **6b** (*as pronoun*): *three were killed.* ◆ Related adjs: **ternary, tertiary, treble, triple.** Related prefixes: **tri-, ter-.** [Old English *thrēo;* related to Old Norse *thrīr,* Old High German *drī,* Latin *trēs,* Greek *treis*]

three-card trick *n* a game in which players bet on which of three inverted playing cards is the queen.

three-colour *adj* of, relating to, or comprising a colour print or a photomechanical process in which a picture is reproduced by superimposing three prints from half-tone plates in inks corresponding to the three primary colours.

three-D *or* **3-D** *n* a three-dimensional effect.

three-day event *n* See **eventing.**

three-day measles *n Pathol.* an informal name for **rubella.**

three-decker *n* **1a** anything having three levels or layers. **1b** (*as modifier*): *a three-decker sandwich.* **2** a warship with guns on three decks.

three-dimensional, three-D, *or* **3-D** *adj* **1** of, having, or relating to three dimensions: *three-dimensional space.* **2** (of a film, transparency, etc.) simulating the effect of depth by presenting slightly different views of a scene to each eye. **3** having volume. **4** lifelike or real.

threefold ('θriː,fəʊld) *adj* **1** equal to or having three times as many or as much; triple: *a threefold decrease.* **2** composed of three parts: *a threefold purpose.* ◆ *adv* **3** by or up to three times as many or as much.

three-four time *n Music.* a form of simple triple time in which there are three crotchet beats to the bar, indicated by the time signature $\frac{3}{4}$. Often shortened to **three-four.** Also called (esp. U.S. and Canadian): **three-quarter time.**

three-gaited *adj Chiefly U.S.* (of a horse) having the three usual paces, the walk, trot, and canter.

three-legged race *n* a race in which pairs of competitors run with their adjacent legs tied together.

three-line whip *n* See **whip** (sense 20c).

three-mile limit *n International law.* the range of a nation's territorial waters, extending to three nautical miles from shore.

threep (θriːp) *vb* a variant spelling of **threap.**

threepenny bit *or* **thrupenny bit** ('θrʌpnɪ, -ənɪ, 'θrɛp-) *n* a twelve-sided British coin of nickel-brass, valued at three old pence, obsolete since 1971.

three-phase *adj* (of an electrical system, circuit, or device) having, generating, or using three alternating voltages of the same frequency, displaced in phase by 120°.

three-piece *adj* **1** having three pieces, esp. (of a suit, suite, etc.) consisting of three matching parts. ◆ *n* **2** a three-piece suite, suit, etc.

three-ply *adj* **1** having three layers or thicknesses. **2a** (of knitting wool, etc.) three-stranded. **2b** (*as n*): *the sweater was knitted in three-ply.*

three-point landing *n* **1** an aircraft landing in which the two main wheels and the nose or tail wheel all touch the ground simultaneously. **2** a successful conclusion.

three-point turn *n* a turn reversing the direction of motion of a motor vehicle using forward and reverse gears alternately, and completed after only three movements.

three-quarter *adj* **1** being three quarters of something: *a three-quarter turn.* **2** being of three quarters the normal length: *a three-quarter coat.* ◆ *n* **3** *Rugby.* **3a** any of the four players between the fullback and the halfbacks. **3b** this position. **3c** (*as modifier*): *three-quarter play.*

three-quarter binding *n* a bookbinding style in which the spine and much of the sides are in a different material (esp. leather) from the rest of the covers.

three-ring circus *n U.S. and Canadian.* **1** a circus with three rings in which separate performances are carried on simultaneously. **2** a situation of confusion, characterized by a bewildering variety of events or activities.

Three Rivers *n* the English name for **Trois Rivières.**

three Rs *pl n* **the.** the three skills regarded as the fundamentals of education; reading, writing, and arithmetic. [from the humorous spelling *reading, 'riting,* and *'rithmetic*]

threescore ('θriːˈskɔː) *determiner* an archaic word for **sixty.**

threesome ('θriːsəm) *n* **1** a group of three. **2** *Golf.* a match in which a single player playing his own ball competes against two others playing alternate strokes on the same ball. **3** any game, etc., for three people. **4** (*modifier*) performed by three: *a threesome game.*

three-square *adj* having a cross section that is an equilateral triangle: *a three-square file.*

three-way *adj* **1** providing connections to three routes from a central point. **2** involving three things or people.

three-wheeler *n* a light car that has three wheels.

thremmatology (ˌθreməˈtɒlədʒɪ) *n* the science of breeding domesticated animals and plants. [C19: from Greek *thremma* nursling + -LOGY]

threnody ('θrɛnədɪ, 'θriː-) *or* **threnode** ('θriːnəʊd, 'θrɛn-) *n, pl* **threnodies** *or* **threnodes.** an ode, song, or speech of lamentation, esp. for the dead. [C17: from Greek *thrēnōidia,* from *thrēnos* dirge + *ōidē* song] ▸ **threnodial** (θrɪˈnəʊdɪəl) *or* **threnodic** (θrɪˈnɒdɪk) *adj* ▸ **threnodist** ('θrɛnədɪst, 'θriː-) *n*

threonine ('θriːəˌniːn, -nɪn) *n* an essential amino acid that occurs in certain proteins. [C20: *threon-,* probably from Greek *eruthron,* from *eruthros* red (see ERYTHRO-) + -INE[2]]

thresh (θrɛʃ) *vb* **1** to beat or rub stalks of ripe corn or a similar crop either with a hand implement or a machine to separate the grain from the husks and straw. **2** (*tr*) to beat or strike. **3** (*intr; often foll. by about*) to toss and turn; thrash. ◆ *n* **4** the act of threshing. [Old English *threscan;* related to Gothic *thriskan,* Old Norse *thriskja;* see THRASH]

thresher ('θrɛʃə) *n* **1** a person who threshes. **2** short for **threshing machine. 3** Also called: **thrasher, thresher shark.** any of various large sharks of the genus *Alopias,* esp. *A. vulpinus,* occurring in tropical and temperate seas: family *Alopiidae.* They have a very long whiplike tail with which they are thought to round up the small fish on which they feed.

threshing machine *n* a machine for threshing crops.

threshold ('θrɛʃəʊld, 'θrɛʃˌhəʊld) *n* **1** Also called: **doorsill.** a sill, esp. one made of stone or hardwood, placed at a doorway. **2** any doorway or entrance. **3** the starting point of an experience, event, or venture: *on the threshold of manhood.* **4** *Psychol.* the strength at which a stimulus is just perceived: *the threshold of consciousness.* Compare **absolute threshold, difference threshold. 5a** a level or point at which something would happen, would cease to happen, or would take effect, become true, etc. **5b** (*as modifier*): *threshold price; threshold effect.* **6a** the minimum intensity or value of a signal, etc., that will produce a response or specified effect: *a frequency threshold.* **6b** (*as modifier*): *a threshold current.* **7** (*modifier*) designating or relating to a pay agreement, clause, etc., that raises wages to compensate for increases in the cost of living. ◆ Related adj: **liminal.** [Old English *therscold;* related to Old Norse *threskoldr,* Old High German *driscubli,* Old Swedish *thriskuldi*]

threshold agreement *n* an agreement between an employer and employees or their union to increase wages by a specified sum if inflation exceeds a specified level in a specified time.

thresh out *vb* another term for **thrash out.**

threw (θruː) *vb* the past tense of **throw.**

thrice (θraɪs) *adv* **1** three times. **2** in threefold degree. **3** *Archaic.* greatly. [Old English *thrīwa, thrīga;* see THREE]

thrift (θrɪft) *n* **1** wisdom and caution in the management of money. **2** Also called: **sea pink.** any of numerous perennial plumbaginaceous low-growing plants of the genus *Armeria,* esp. *A. maritima,* of Europe, W Asia, and North America, having narrow leaves and round heads of pink or white flowers. **3** *Rare.* vigorous thriving or growth, as of a plant. **4** an obsolete word for **prosperity.** [C13: from Old Norse: success; see THRIVE] ▸ **'thriftless** *adj* ▸ **'thriftlessly** *adv* ▸ **'thriftlessness** *n*

thrifty ('θrɪftɪ) *adj* **thriftier, thriftiest. 1** showing thrift; economical or frugal. **2** *Rare.* thriving or prospering. ▸ **'thriftily** *adv* ▸ **'thriftiness** *n*

thrill (θrɪl) *n* **1** a sudden sensation of excitement and pleasure: *seeing his book for sale gave him a thrill.* **2** a situation producing such a sensation: *it was a thrill to see Rome for the first time.* **3** a trembling sensation caused by fear or emotional shock. **4** *Pathol.* an abnormal slight tremor associated with a heart or vascular murmur, felt on palpation. ◆ *vb* **5** to feel or cause to feel a thrill. **6** to tremble or cause to tremble; vibrate or quiver. [Old English *thyrlian* to pierce, from *thyrel* hole; see NOSTRIL, THROUGH]

thriller ('θrɪlə) *n* **1** a book, film, play, etc., depicting crime, mystery, or espionage in an atmosphere of excitement and suspense. **2** a person or thing that thrills.

thrilling ('θrɪlɪŋ) *adj* **1** very exciting or stimulating. **2** vibrating or trembling. ▸ **'thrillingly** *adv*

thrips (θrɪps) *n, pl* **thrips.** any of various small slender-bodied insects of the order *Thysanoptera,* typically having piercing mouthparts and narrow feathery wings and feeding on plant sap. Some species are serious plant pests. [C18: via New Latin from Greek: woodworm]

thrive (θraɪv) *vb* **thrives, thriving; thrived** *or* **throve; thrived** *or* **thriven** ('θrɪvᵊn). (*intr*) **1** to grow strongly and vigorously. **2** to do well; prosper. [C13: from Old Norse *thrīfask* to grasp for oneself, reflexive of *thrīfa* to grasp, of obscure origin] ▸ **'thriver** *n* ▸ **'thriving** *adj* ▸ **'thrivingly** *adv*

thro' *or* **thro** (θruː) *prep, adv Informal or poetic.* variant spellings of **through.**

throat (θrəʊt) *n* **1a** that part of the alimentary and respiratory tracts extending from the back of the mouth (nasopharynx) to just below the larynx. **1b** the front part of the neck. **2** something resembling a throat, esp. in shape or function: *the throat of a chimney.* **3** *Botany.* the gaping part of a tubular corolla or perianth. **4** *Informal.* a sore throat. **5 cut one's (own) throat.** to bring about one's own ruin. **6 have by the throat.** to have compete control over (a person or thing). **7 jump down someone's throat.** See **jump** (sense 24). **8 ram** *or* **force (something) down someone's throat.** to insist that someone listen to or accept (something): *he rammed his own opinions down my throat.* **9 stick in one's throat** (*or* **craw**). *Informal.* to be difficult, or against one's conscience, for one to accept, utter, or believe. ◆ Related adjs: **gular, guttural, jugular, laryngeal.** [Old English *throtu;* related to Old High German *drozza* throat, Old Norse *throti* swelling]

throatlash ('θrəʊtˌlæʃ) *or* **throatlatch** *n* the strap that holds a bridle in place, fastening under the horse's jaw.

throat microphone *n* a type of microphone that is held against the throat to pick up voice vibrations. Also called: **throat mike.**

throaty ('θrəʊtɪ) *adj* **throatier, throatiest. 1** indicating a sore throat; hoarse: *a throaty cough.* **2** of, relating to, or produced in or by the throat. **3** deep, husky, or guttural. ▸ **'throatily** *adv* ▸ **'throatiness** *n*

throb (θrɒb) *vb* **throbs, throbbing, throbbed.** (*intr*) **1** to pulsate or beat repeatedly, esp. with increased force: *to throb with pain.* **2** (of engines, drums, etc.) to have a strong rhythmic vibration or beat. ◆ *n* **3** the act or an instance of throbbing, esp. a rapid pulsation as of the heart: *a throb of pleasure.* [C14: perhaps of imitative origin] ▸ **'throbbing** *adj* ▸ **'throbbingly** *adv*

Throckmorton ('θrɒkˌmɔːtən) *or* **Throgmorton** ('θrɒgˌmɔːtən) *n* **Francis.** 1554–84, English conspirator, who with French and Spanish support plotted (1583) to depose Elizabeth I in favour of Mary, Queen of Scots: executed.

throe (θrəʊ) *n Rare.* a pang or pain. [Old English *thrāwu* threat; related to Old High German *drawa* threat, Old Norse *thrā* desire, *thrauka* to endure]

throes (θrəʊz) *pl n* **1** a condition of violent pangs, pain, or convulsions: *death throes.* **2 in the throes of.** struggling with great effort with: *a country in the throes of revolution.*

thrombin ('θrɒmbɪn) *n Biochem.* an enzyme that acts on fibrinogen in blood causing it to clot.

thrombo- *or sometimes before a vowel* **thromb-** *combining form.* indicating a blood clot: *thromboembolism.* [from Greek *thrombos* lump, clot]

thrombocyte ('θrɒmbəˌsaɪt) *n* another name for **platelet.** ▸ **thrombocytic** (ˌθrɒmbəˈsɪtɪk) *adj*

thrombocytopenia (ˌθrɒmbəʊˌsaɪtəʊˈpiːnɪə) *n Pathol.* an abnormal decrease in the number of platelets in the blood. [C20: from German *thrombocytopenie* from THROMBOCYTE + Greek *penia* poverty]

thromboembolism (ˌθrɒmbəʊˈɛmbəˌlɪzəm) *n Pathol.* the obstruction of a blood vessel by a thrombus that has become detached from its original site.

thrombogen ('θrɒmbəˌdʒɛn) *n* a protein present in blood that is essential for the formation of thrombin.

thrombokinase (ˌθrɒmbəʊˈkaɪneɪs) *n* another name for **thromboplastin.**

thrombolytic (ˌθrɒmbəˈlɪtɪk) *adj* **1** causing the break-up of a blood clot. ◆ *n* **2** a thrombolytic drug.

thrombophlebitis (ˌθrɒmbəʊflɪˈbaɪtɪs) *n* inflammation of a vein associated with the formation of a thrombus.

thromboplastic (ˌθrɒmbəʊˈplæstɪk) *adj* causing or enhancing the formation of a blood clot.

thromboplastin (ˌθrɒmbəʊˈplæstɪn) *n* any of a group of substances that are liberated from damaged blood platelets and other tissues and convert prothrombin to thrombin. Also called: **thrombokinase.**

thrombose ('θrɒmbəʊz) *vb* to become or affect with a thrombus. [C19: back formation from THROMBOSIS]

thrombosis (θrɒmˈbəʊsɪs) *n, pl* **-ses** (siːz). **1** the formation or presence of a thrombus. **2** *Informal.* short for **coronary thrombosis.** [C18: from New Latin, from Greek: curdling, from *thrombousthai* to clot, from *thrombos* THROMBUS] ▸ **thrombotic** (θrɒmˈbɒtɪk) *adj*

thrombus ('θrɒmbəs) *n, pl* **-bi** (-baɪ). a clot of coagulated blood that forms within a blood vessel or inside the heart and remains at the site of its formation, often impeding the flow of blood. Compare **embolus.** [C17: from New Latin, from Greek *thrombos* lump, of obscure origin]

throne (θrəʊn) *n* **1** the ceremonial seat occupied by a monarch, bishop, etc. on occasions of state. **2** the power, duties, or rank ascribed to a royal person. **3** a person holding royal rank. **4** (*pl; often cap.*) the third of the nine orders into which the angels are traditionally divided in medieval angelology. ◆ *vb* **5** to place or be placed on a throne. [C13: from Old French *trone,* from Latin *thronus,* from Greek *thronos* throne] ▸ **'throneless** *adj*

throng (θrɒŋ) *n* **1** a great number of people or things crowded together. ◆ *vb* **2** to gather in or fill (a place) in large numbers; crowd. **3** (*tr*) to hem in (a person);

jostle. ◆ *adj* 4 *Yorkshire dialect.* (*postpositive*) busy. [Old English *gethrang;* related to Old Norse *throug,* Old High German *drangōd*]

throstle ('θrɒsᵊl) *n* 1 a poetic name for **thrush**[1], esp. the song thrush. 2 a spinning machine for wool or cotton in which the fibres are twisted and wound continuously. [Old English; related to Old Saxon *throsla,* Old Norse *thröstr,* Middle High German *drostel*]

throttle ('θrɒtᵊl) *n* 1 Also called: **throttle valve.** any device that controls the quantity of fuel or fuel and air mixture entering an engine. 2 an informal or dialect word for **throat.** ◆ *vb* (*tr*) 3 to kill or injure by squeezing the throat. 4 to suppress: *to throttle the press.* 5 to control or restrict (a flow of fluid) by means of a throttle valve. [C14: *throtelen,* from *throte* THROAT] ▸ **'throttler** *n*

through (θruː) *prep* 1 going in or starting at one side and coming out or stopping at the other side of: *a path through the wood.* 2 occupying or visiting several points scattered around in (an area). 3 as a result of; by means of: *the thieves were captured through his vigilance.* 4 *Chiefly U.S.* up to and including: *Monday through Friday.* 5 during: *through the night.* 6 at the end of; having (esp. successfully) completed. 7 **through with.** having finished with (esp. when dissatisfied with). ◆ *adj* 8 (*postpositive*) having successfully completed some specified activity. 9 (on a telephone line) connected. 10 (*postpositive*) no longer able to function successfully in some specified capacity: *as a journalist, you're through.* 11 (*prenominal*) (of a route, journey, etc.) continuous or unbroken: *a through train.* ◆ *adv* 12 through some specified thing, place, or period of time. 13 **through and through.** thoroughly; completely. ◆ Also: **thro'** *or* **thro** (informal or poetic), **thru** (chiefly U.S.). [Old English *thurh;* related to Old Frisian *thruch,* Old Saxon *thuru,* Old High German *duruh*]

through bridge *n Civil engineering.* a bridge in which the track is carried by the lower horizontal members.

through-composed *adj Music.* of or relating to a song in stanzaic form, in which different music is provided for each stanza. Compare **strophic** (sense 2).

throughly ('θruːlɪ) *adv Archaic.* thoroughly; completely.

through-other *adj Scot.* 1 untidy or dishevelled. 2 mixed up; in disorder. [a literal translation of Irish Gaelic *trí n-a chéile* through each other, hence, mixed up with each other]

throughout (θruː'aʊt) *prep* 1 right through; through the whole of (a place or a period of time): *throughout the day.* ◆ *adv* 2 through the whole of some specified period or area.

throughput ('θruːˌpʊt) *n* the quantity of raw material or information processed or communicated in a given period, esp. by a computer.

throughway ('θruːˌweɪ) *n U.S.* a thoroughfare, esp. a motorway.

throve (θrəʊv) *vb* a past tense of **thrive.**

throw (θrəʊ) *vb* **throws, throwing, threw, thrown.** (*mainly tr*) 1 (*also intr*) to project or cast (something) through the air, esp. with a rapid motion of the arm and wrist. 2 (foll. by *in, on, onto,* etc.) to put or move suddenly, carelessly, or violently: *she threw her clothes onto the bed.* 3 to bring to or cause to be in a specified state or condition, esp. suddenly or unexpectedly: *the news threw the family into a panic.* 4 to direct or cast (a shadow, light, etc.). 5 to project (the voice) so as to make it appear to come from other than its source. 6 to give or hold (a party). 7 to cause to fall or be upset; dislodge: *the horse soon threw his rider.* 8a to tip (dice) out onto a flat surface. 8b to obtain (a specified number) in this way. 9 to shape (clay) on a potter's wheel. 10 to move (a switch or lever) to engage or disengage a mechanism. 11 to be subjected to (a fit). 12 to turn (wood, etc.) on a lathe. 13 *Informal.* to baffle or astonish; confuse: *the last question on the test paper threw me.* 14 *Boxing.* to deliver (a punch). 15 *Wrestling.* to hurl (an opponent) to the ground. 16 *Informal.* to lose (a contest, fight, etc.) deliberately, esp. in boxing. 17a to play (a card). 17b to discard (a card). 18 (of a female animal, esp. a cow) to give birth to (young). 19 to twist or spin (filaments) into thread. 20 **throw cold water on (something).** *Informal.* to be unenthusiastic about or discourage (something). 21 **throw oneself at.** to strive actively to attract the attention or affection of. 22 **throw oneself into.** to involve oneself enthusiastically in. 23 **throw oneself on.** to rely entirely upon: *he threw himself on the mercy of the police.* ◆ *n* 24 the act or an instance of throwing. 25 the distance or extent over which anything may be thrown: *a stone's throw.* 26 *Informal.* a chance, venture, or try. 27 an act or result of throwing dice. 28a the eccentricity of a cam. 28b the radial distance between the central axis of a crankshaft and the axis of a crankpin forming part of the shaft. 29 a decorative light blanket or cover, as thrown over a chair. 30 a sheet of fabric used for draping over an easel or unfinished painting, etc., to keep the dust off. 31 *Geology.* the vertical displacement of rock strata at a fault. 32 *Physics.* the deflection of a measuring instrument as a result of a sudden fluctuation. ◆ See also **throw about, throwaway, throwback, throw in, throw off, throw out, throw over, throw together, throw up.** [Old English *thrāwan* to turn, torment; related to Old High German *drāen* to twist, Latin *terere* to rub] ▸ **'thrower** *n*

throw about *vb* (*tr, adv*) 1 to spend (one's money) in a reckless and flaunting manner. 2 **throw one's weight about.** *Informal.* to act in an authoritarian or aggressive manner.

throwaway ('θrəʊəˌweɪ) *adj* (*prenominal*) 1 said or done incidentally, esp. for rhetorical effect; casual: *a throwaway remark.* 2a anything designed to be discarded after use rather than reused, refilled, etc.; disposable. 2b (*as modifier*): *a throwaway carton.* ◆ *n* 3 *Chiefly U.S. and Canadian.* a handbill or advertisement distributed in a public place. ◆ *vb* **throw away.** (*tr, adv*) 4 to get rid of; discard. 5 to fail to make good use of; waste: *to throw away all one's money on horses.*

throwback ('θrəʊˌbæk) *n* 1a a person, animal, or plant that has the characteristics of an earlier or more primitive type. 1b a reversion to such an organism. ◆ *vb* **throw back.** (*adv*) 2 (*intr*) to revert to an earlier or more primitive type. 3 (*tr;* foll. by *on*) to force to depend (on): *the crisis threw her back on her faith in God.*

throw in *vb* (*tr, adv*) 1 to add (something extra) at no additional cost. 2 to contribute or interpose (a remark, argument, etc.), esp. in a discussion. 3 **throw in one's hand.** 3a (in cards) to concede defeat by putting one's cards down. 3b to give in and accept defeat; discontinue a venture. 4 **throw in the towel** (*or* **sponge**). 4a (in boxing) to concede defeat by the throwing of a towel (or sponge) into the ring by a second. 4b to give in and accept defeat; discontinue a venture. ◆ *n* **throw-in.** 5 *Soccer.* the method of putting the ball into play after it has gone into touch by throwing it two-handed from behind the head to a teammate, both feet being kept on the ground.

throwing stick *n* a primitive device for hurling a spear with greater leverage, consisting of a rod with a groove in it and a hook or projection at the back end to hold the weapon until its release.

thrown (θrəʊn) *vb* the past participle of **throw.**

throw off *vb* (*mainly tr, adv*) 1 to free oneself of; discard. 2 to produce or utter in a casual manner: *to throw off a witty remark.* 3 to escape from or elude: *the fox rapidly threw off his pursuers.* 4 to confuse or disconcert: *the interruption threw the young pianist off.* 5 (*intr,* often foll. by *at*) *Austral. and N.Z. informal.* to deride or ridicule.

throw out *vb* (*tr, adv*) 1 to discard or reject. 2 to expel or dismiss, esp. forcibly. 3 to construct (something projecting or prominent, such as a wing of a building). 4 to put forward or offer: *the chairman threw out a new proposal.* 5 to utter in a casual or indirect manner: *to throw out a hint.* 6 to confuse or disconcert: *the noise threw his concentration out.* 7 to give off or emit. 8 *Cricket.* (of a fielder) to put (the batsman) out by throwing the ball to hit the wicket. 9 *Baseball.* to make a throw to a teammate who in turn puts out (a base runner).

throw over *vb* (*tr, adv*) to forsake or abandon; jilt.

throwster ('θrəʊstə) *n* a person who twists silk or other fibres into yarn. [C15 *throwestre,* from THROW + -STER]

throw together *vb* (*tr, adv*) 1 to assemble hurriedly. 2 to cause to become casually acquainted.

throw up *vb* (*adv, mainly tr*) 1 to give up; abandon, relinquish. 2 to build or construct hastily. 3 to reveal; produce: *every generation throws up its own leaders.* 4 (*also intr*) *Informal.* to vomit.

throw weight *n* the maximum weight of supplementary mechanisms that can be lifted by the boost stages of a particular missile.

thru (θruː) *prep, adv, adj Chiefly U.S.* a variant spelling of **through.**

thrum[1] (θrʌm) *vb* **thrums, thrumming, thrummed.** 1 to strum rhythmically but without expression on (a musical instrument). 2 (*intr*) to drum incessantly: *rain thrummed on the roof.* 3 to repeat (something) monotonously. ◆ *n* 4 a repetitive strumming or recitation. [C16: of imitative origin] ▸ **'thrummer** *n*

thrum[2] (θrʌm) *Textiles.* ◆ *n* 1a any of the unwoven ends of warp thread remaining on the loom when the web has been removed. 1b such ends of thread collectively. 2 a fringe or tassel of short unwoven threads. ◆ *vb* **thrums, thrumming, thrummed.** 3 (*tr*) to trim with thrums. [C14: from Old English; related to Old High German *drum* remnant, Dutch *dreum*]

thrum-eyed *adj* (of flowers, esp. primulas) having the stigma on a short style below the anthers, which lie in the mouth of the corolla on big stamens. Compare **pin-eyed.** [C19: from THRUM[2], because of the ring of anthers visible at the neck of the corolla]

thrupenny bit ('θrʌpnɪ, -ənɪ, 'θrɛp-) *n* a variant spelling of **threepenny bit.**

thrush[1] (θrʌʃ) *n* any songbird of the subfamily *Turdinae,* esp. those having a brown plumage with a spotted breast, such as the mistle thrush and song thrush: family *Muscicapidae.* Compare **water thrush.** Related adj: **turdine.** [Old English *thrȳsce;* related to Old High German *drōsca;* see THROSTLE, THROAT]

thrush[2] (θrʌʃ) *n* 1a a fungal disease of the mouth, esp. of infants, and the genitals, characterized by the formation of whitish spots and caused by infection with the fungus *Candida albicans.* 1b another word for **sprue**[2]. 2 a softening of the frog of a horse's hoof characterized by inflammation and a thick foul discharge. [C17: related to Old Danish *törsk,* Danish *troske*]

thrust (θrʌst) *vb* **thrusts, thrusting, thrust.** 1 (*tr*) to push (someone or something) with force or sudden strength: *she thrust him away; she thrust it into the fire.* 2 (*tr*) to force or impose upon (someone) or into (some condition or situation): *they thrust extra responsibilities upon her; she was thrust into the limelight.* 3 (*tr;* foll. by *through*) to pierce; stab. 4 (*intr;* usually foll. by *through* or *into*) to force a passage or entrance. 5 (*intr*) to push forwards, upwards, or outwards. 6 (*intr;* foll. by *at*) to make a stab or lunge at (a person or thing). ◆ *n* 7 a forceful drive, push, stab, or lunge. 8 a force, esp. one that produces motion. 9a a propulsive force produced by the fluid pressure or the change of momentum of the fluid in a jet engine, rocket engine, etc. 9b a similar force produced by a propeller. 10 a pressure that is exerted continuously by one part of an object, structure, etc., against another. 11 *Geology.* 11a the compressive force in the earth's crust that produces recumbent folds. 11b See **thrust fault.** 12 *Civil engineering.* a force exerted in a downwards and outwards direction, as by an arch or a rafter. 13 force, impetus, or drive: *a man with thrust and energy.* 14 the essential or most forceful part: *the thrust of the argument.* [C12: from Old Norse *thrysta;* related to Latin *trūdere;* see INTRUDE]

thrust bearing *n Engineering* a low-friction bearing on a rotating shaft that resists axial thrust in the shaft. Usually it consists of a collar which bears against a ring of well lubricated stationary and sometimes tilting pads. Compare **tapered roller bearing.**

thruster ('θrʌstə) *n* 1 a person or thing that thrusts. 2 Also called: **vernier rocket.** a small rocket engine, esp. one used to correct the altitude or course of a spacecraft. 3 an auxiliary propeller on a ship, capable of acting athwartships.

thrust fault *n* a fault in which the rocks on the lower side of an inclined fault plane have been displaced downwards, usually by compression; a reverse fault.

thrusting (θrʌstɪŋ) *adj* ambitious and having great drive: *a thrusting young executive.*

Thucydides (θuː'sɪdɪˌdiːz) *n* ?460–?395 B.C., Greek historian and politician, distinguished for his *History of the Peloponnesian War.* ▸ **Thuˌcydi'dean** *adj*

thud (θʌd) *n* **1** a dull heavy sound: *the book fell to the ground with a thud.* **2** a blow or fall that causes such a sound. ◆ *vb* **thuds, thudding, thudded. 3** to make or cause to make such a sound. [Old English *thyddan* to strike; related to *thoddettan* to beat, perhaps of imitative origin]

thug (θʌg) *n* **1** a tough and violent man, esp. a criminal. **2** (*sometimes cap.*) (formerly) a member of an organization of robbers and assassins in India who typically strangled their victims. [C19: from Hindi *thag* thief, from Sanskrit *sthaga* scoundrel, from *sthagati* to conceal] ▸ **'thuggery** *n* ▸ **'thuggish** *adj*

thuggee (θʌ'gi:) *n History.* the methods and practices of the thugs of India. [C19: from Hindi *thagī;* see THUG]

thuja *or* **thuya** ('θu:jə) *n* any of various coniferous trees of the genus *Thuja,* of North America and East Asia, having scalelike leaves, small cones, and an aromatic wood: family *Pinaceae.* See also **arbor vitae.** [C18: from New Latin, from Medieval Latin *thuia,* ultimately from Greek *thua* name of an African tree]

Thule ('θju:lɪ) *n* **1** Also called: **ultima Thule.** a region believed by ancient geographers to be the northernmost land in the inhabited world: sometimes thought to have been Iceland, Norway, or one of the Shetland Islands. **2** an Eskimo settlement in NW Greenland: a Danish trading post, founded in 1910, and U.S. air force base.

thulium ('θju:lɪəm) *n* a malleable ductile silvery-grey element occurring principally in monazite. The radioisotope **thulium-170** is used as an electron source in portable X-ray units. Symbol: Tm; atomic no.: 69; atomic wt.: 168.93421; valency: 3; relative density: 9.321; melting pt.: 1545°C; boiling pt.: 1950°C. [C19: New Latin, from THULE + -IUM]

thumb (θʌm) *n* **1** the first and usually shortest and thickest of the digits of the hand, composed of two short bones. Technical name: **pollex.** Related adj: **pollical. 2** the corresponding digit in other vertebrates. **3** the part of a glove shaped to fit the thumb. **4** *Architect.* another name for **ovolo. 5 all thumbs.** clumsy. **6 thumbs down.** an indication of refusal, disapproval, or negation: *he gave the thumbs down on our proposal.* **7 thumbs up.** an indication of encouragement, approval, or acceptance. **8 under someone's thumb.** at someone's mercy or command. ◆ *vb* **9** (*tr*) to touch, mark, or move with the thumb. **10** to attempt to obtain (a lift or ride) by signalling with the thumb. **11** (when *intr,* often foll. by *through*) to flip the pages of (a book, magazine, etc.) perfunctorily in order to glance at the contents. **12 thumb one's nose at.** to deride or mock, esp. by placing the thumb on the nose with fingers extended. [Old English *thūma;* related to Old Saxon *thūma,* Old High German *thūmo,* Old Norse *thumall* thumb of a glove, Latin *tumēre* to swell] ▸ **'thumbless** *adj* ▸ **'thumb,like** *adj*

thumb index *n* **1** a series of indentations cut into the fore edge of a book to facilitate quick reference. ◆ *vb* **thumb-index. 2** (*tr*) to furnish with a thumb index.

thumb knot *n* another name for **overhand knot.**

thumbnail ('θʌm,neɪl) *n* **1** the nail of the thumb. **2** (*modifier*) concise and brief: *a thumbnail sketch.*

thumbnut ('θʌm,nʌt) *n* a nut with projections enabling it to be turned by the thumb and forefinger; wing nut.

thumb piano *n* another name for **mbira.**

thumbprint ('θʌm,prɪnt) *n* an impression of the upper part of the thumb, used esp. for identification purposes. See **fingerprint.**

thumbscrew ('θʌm,skru:) *n* **1** an instrument of torture that pinches or crushes the thumbs. **2** a screw with projections on its head enabling it to be turned by the thumb and forefinger.

thumbstall ('θʌm,stɔ:l) *n* a protective sheathlike cover for the thumb.

thumbtack ('θʌm,tæk) *n* the U.S. and Canadian name for **drawing pin.**

Thummim ('θʌmɪm) *n Old Testament.* See **Urim and Thummim.**

thump (θʌmp) *n* **1** the sound of a heavy solid body hitting or pounding a comparatively soft surface. **2** a heavy blow with the hand: *he gave me a thump on the back.* ◆ *vb* **3** (*tr*) to strike or beat heavily; pound. **4** (*intr*) to throb, beat, or pound violently: *his heart thumped with excitement.* [C16: related to Icelandic, Swedish dialect *dumpa* to thump; see THUD, BUMP] ▸ **'thumper** *n*

thumping ('θʌmpɪŋ) *adj* (*prenominal*) *Slang.* huge or excessive: *a thumping loss.* ▸ **'thumpingly** *adv*

Thun (*German* tu:n) *n* **1** a town in central Switzerland, in Bern canton on Lake Thun. Pop.: 36 700 (1990 est.). **2 Lake.** a lake in central Switzerland, formed by a widening of the Aar River. Length: about 17 km (11 miles). Width: 3 km (2 miles). German name: **Thuner See.**

thunbergia (θʊn'bɜ:dʒɪə) *n* any plant of the typically climbing tropical genus *Thunbergia* such as black-eyed Susan: family *Acanthaceae.* [named after K. P. *Thunberg* (1743–1822), Swedish traveller and botanist]

thunder ('θʌndə) *n* **1** a loud cracking or deep rumbling noise caused by the rapid expansion of atmospheric gases which are suddenly heated by lightning. **2** any loud booming sound. **3** *Rare.* a violent threat or denunciation. **4 steal someone's thunder.** to detract from the attention due to another by forestalling him. ◆ *vb* **5** to make (a loud sound) or utter (words) in a manner suggesting thunder. **6** (*intr;* with *it* as subject) to be the case that thunder is being heard. **7** (*intr*) to move fast and heavily: *the bus thundered downhill.* **8** (*intr*) to utter vehement threats or denunciation; rail. [Old English *thunor;* related to Old Saxon *thunar,* Old High German *donar,* Old Norse *thōrr;* see THOR, THURSDAY] ▸ **'thunderer** *n* ▸ **'thundery** *adj*

Thunder Bay *n* a port in central Canada, in Ontario on Lake Superior: formed in 1970 by the amalgamation of Fort William and Port Arthur; the head of the St Lawrence Seaway for Canada. Pop.: 113 746 (1991).

thunderbird ('θʌndə,bɜ:d) *n* a legendary bird that produces thunder, lightning, and rain according to the folk belief of several North American Indian peoples.

thunderbolt ('θʌndə,bəʊlt) *n* **1** a flash of lightning accompanying thunder. **2** the imagined agency of destruction produced by a flash of lightning. **3** (in mythology) the destructive weapon wielded by several gods, esp. the Greek god Zeus. See also **Thor. 4** something very startling.

thunderbox ('θʌndə,bɒks) *n Slang.* **1** a portable boxlike lavatory seat that can be placed over a hole in the ground. **2** any portable lavatory.

thunderclap ('θʌndə,klæp) *n* **1** a loud outburst of thunder. **2** something as violent or unexpected as a clap of thunder.

thundercloud ('θʌndə,klaʊd) *n* **1** a towering electrically charged cumulonimbus cloud associated with thunderstorms. **2** anything that is threatening.

thunderhead ('θʌndə,hɛd) *n Chiefly U.S. and Canadian.* the anvil-shaped top of a cumulonimbus cloud.

thundering ('θʌndərɪŋ) *adj* (*prenominal*) *Slang.* very great or excessive: *a thundering idiot.* ▸ **'thunderingly** *adv*

thunderous ('θʌndərəs) *adj* **1** resembling thunder, esp. in loudness: *thunderous clapping.* **2** threatening and extremely angry: *she gave him a thunderous look.* ▸ **'thunderously** *adv*

thunder sheet *n* a large sheet of metal that can be shaken to produce a noise resembling thunder as a sound effect for a theatrical production.

thundershower ('θʌndə,ʃaʊə) *n* a heavy shower during a thunderstorm.

thunderstone ('θʌndə,stəʊn) *n* **1** a long tapering stone, fossil, or similar object, formerly thought to be a thunderbolt. **2** an archaic word for **thunderbolt.**

thunderstorm ('θʌndə,stɔ:m) *n* a storm caused by strong rising air currents and characterized by thunder and lightning and usually heavy rain or hail.

thunderstruck ('θʌndə,strʌk) *or* **thunderstricken** ('θʌndə,strɪkən) *adj* **1** completely taken aback; amazed or shocked. **2** *Rare.* struck by lightning.

Thurber ('θɜ:bə) *n* **James (Grover).** 1894–1961, U.S. humorist and illustrator. He contributed drawings and stories to the *New Yorker* and his books include *Is Sex Necessary?* (1929), written with E. B. White.

Thurgau (*German* 'tu:rgau) *n* a canton of NE Switzerland, on Lake Constance: annexed by the confederated Swiss states in 1460. Capital: Frauenfeld. Pop.: 223 372 (1996 est.). Area: 1007 sq. km (389 sq. miles). French name: **Thurgovie** (tyrgɔvi).

thurible ('θjʊərɪbᵊl) *n* another word for **censer.** [C15: from Latin *tūribulum* censer, from *tūs* incense]

thurifer ('θjʊərɪfə) *n* a person appointed to carry the censer at religious ceremonies. [C19: from Latin, from *tūs* incense + *ferre* to carry]

Thuringia (θjʊ'rɪndʒɪə) *n* a state of central Germany, formerly in East Germany. Pop.: 2 503 800 (1996 est.). German name: **Thüringen** ('ty:rɪŋən). ▸ **Thu'ringian** *adj, n*

Thuringian Forest *n* a forested mountainous region in E central Germany, rising over 900 m (3000 ft.). German name: **Thüringer Wald** ('ty:rɪŋər 'valt).

Thurrock ('θʌrək) *n* a unitary authority in SE England, in Essex. Pop.: 132 300 (1996 est.). Area: 163 sq. km (63 sq. miles).

Thurs. *abbrev. for* Thursday.

Thursday ('θɜ:zdɪ) *n* the fifth day of the week; fourth day of the working week. [Old English *Thursdæg,* literally: Thor's day; related to Old High German *Donares tag;* see THOR, THUNDER, DAY]

Thursday Island *n* an island in Torres Strait, between NE Australia and New Guinea: administratively part of Queensland, Australia. Area: 4 sq. km (1.5 sq. miles).

thus (ðʌs) *adv* **1** in this manner: *do it thus.* **2** to such a degree: *thus far and no further.* ◆ *sentence connector.* **3** therefore: *We have failed. Thus we have to take the consequences.* [Old English; related to Old Frisian, Old Saxon *thus*]

Thutmose I (θʊt'məʊsə, -məʊs) *n* died *c.* 1500 B.C., king of Egypt of the 18th dynasty, who extended his territory in Nubia and Syria and enlarged the Temple of Amon at Karnak.

Thutmose III *n* died *c.* 1450 B.C., king of Egypt of the 18th dynasty, who completed the conquest of Syria and dominated the Middle East. He was also a patron of the arts and a famous athlete.

thuya ('θu:jə) *n* a variant spelling of **thuja.**

thwack (θwæk) *vb* **1** to beat, hit, or flog, esp. with something flat. ◆ *n* **2a** a blow with something flat. **2b** the sound made by it. ◆ *interj* **3** an exclamation imitative of this sound. [C16: of imitative origin] ▸ **'thwacker** *n*

thwaite (θweɪt) *n Obsolete except in place names.* a piece of land cleared from forest or reclaimed from wasteland. [from Old Norse *thveit* paddock]

thwart (θwɔ:t) *vb* **1** to oppose successfully or prevent; frustrate: *they thwarted the plan.* **2** *Obsolete.* to be or move across. ◆ *n* **3** *Nautical.* **3a** a seat lying across a boat and occupied by an oarsman. **3b** a crosspiece that spreads the gunwales of a boat. ◆ *adj* **4** passing or being situated across. **5** *Archaic.* perverse or stubborn. ◆ *prep, adv* **6** *Obsolete.* across. [C13: from Old Norse *thvert,* from *thverr* transverse; related to Old English *thweorh* crooked, Old High German *twerh* transverse] ▸ **'thwartedly** *adv* ▸ **'thwarter** *n*

thy (ðaɪ) *determiner* (*usually preceding a consonant*) *Archaic or Brit. dialect.* belonging to or associated in some way with you (thou): *thy goodness and mercy.* Compare **thine.** [C12: variant of THINE]

Thyestes (θaɪ'ɛsti:z) *n Greek myth.* son of Pelops and brother of Atreus, with whose wife he committed adultery. In revenge, Atreus killed Thyestes' sons and served them to their father at a banquet. ▸ **Thyestean** *or* **Thyestian** (θaɪ'ɛstɪən, ,θaɪɛ'sti:ən) *adj*

thylacine ('θaɪlə,saɪn) *n* an extinct or very rare doglike carnivorous marsupial, *Thylacinus cynocephalus,* of Tasmania, having greyish-brown fur with dark vertical stripes on the back: family *Dasyuridae.* Also called: **Tasmanian wolf.** [C19: from New Latin *thȳlacīnus,* from Greek *thulakos* pouch, sack]

thyme (taɪm) *n* any of various small shrubs of the temperate genus *Thymus,* having a strong mintlike odour, small leaves, and white, pink, or red flowers: family *Labiatae* (labiates). [C14: from Old French *thym,* from Latin *thymum,* from Greek *thumon,* from *thuein* to make a burnt offering] ▸ **'thymy** *adj*

thymectomy (θaɪˈmɛktəmɪ) *n pl* **-mies.** surgical removal of the thymus.
thymelaeaceous (ˌθɪmɪlɪˈeɪʃəs) *adj* of, relating to, or belonging to the *Thymelaeaceae,* a family of trees and shrubs having tough acrid bark and simple leaves: includes spurge laurel, leatherwood, and mezereon. [C19: via New Latin, from Greek *thumelaia,* from *thumon* THYME + *elaia* olive]
-thymia *n combining form.* indicating a certain emotional condition, mood, or state of mind: *cyclothymia.* [New Latin, from Greek *thumos* temper]
thymic (ˈθaɪmɪk) *adj* of or relating to the thymus.
thymidine (ˈθaɪmɪˌdiːn) *n* the crystalline nucleoside of thymine, found in DNA. Formula: $C_{10}H_{14}N_2O_5$. [C20: from THYM(INE) + -IDE + -INE[2]]
thymidylic acid (ˌθaɪmɪˈdɪlɪk) *n* a nucleotide consisting of thymine, deoxyribose, and a phosphate group. It is a constituent of DNA. Also called: **thymidine monophosphate.**
thymine (ˈθaɪmiːn) *n* a white crystalline pyrimidine base found in DNA. Formula: $C_5H_6N_2O_2$. [C19: from THYMIC (see THYMUS) + -INE[2]]
thymocyte (ˈθaɪməsaɪt) *n* a lymphocyte found in the thymus.
thymol (ˈθaɪmɒl) *n* a white crystalline substance with an aromatic odour, obtained from the oil of thyme and used as a fungicide, antiseptic, and anthelmintic and in perfumery and embalming; 2-isopropylphenol. Formula: $(CH_3)_2CHC_6H_3(CH_3)OH$. [C19: from THYME + -OL[2]]
thymus (ˈθaɪməs) *n, pl* **-muses** *or* **-mi** (-maɪ). a glandular organ of vertebrates, consisting in man of two lobes situated below the thyroid. In early life it produces lymphocytes and is thought to influence certain immunological responses. It atrophies with age and is almost nonexistent in the adult. [C17: from New Latin, from Greek *thumos* sweetbread]
thyratron (ˈθaɪrəˌtrɒn) *n Electronics.* a gas-filled tube that has three electrodes and can be switched between an 'off' state and an 'on' state. It has been superseded by the thyristor. [C20: originally a trademark, from Greek *thura* door, valve + -TRON]
thyristor (θaɪˈrɪstə) *n* any of a group of semiconductor devices, such as the silicon-controlled rectifier, that can be switched between two states. [C20: from THYR(ATRON) + (TRANS)ISTOR]
thyro- *or before a vowel* **thyr-** *combining form.* thyroid: *thyrotoxicosis; thyrotropin.*
thyrocalcitonin (ˌθaɪrəʊˌkælsɪˈtəʊnɪn) *n* another name for **calcitonin.** [C20: from THYRO- + CALCITONIN]
thyroid (ˈθaɪrɔɪd) *adj* **1** of or relating to the thyroid gland. **2** of or relating to the largest cartilage of the larynx. ◆ *n* **3** see **thyroid gland. 4** the powdered preparation made from the thyroid gland of certain animals, used to treat hypothyroidism. [C18: from New Latin *thyroidēs,* from Greek *thureoeidēs,* from *thureos* oblong (literally: door-shaped) shield, from *thura* door]
thyroidectomy (ˌθaɪrɔɪˈdɛktəmɪ) *n, pl* **-mies.** surgical removal of all or part of the thyroid gland.
thyroid gland *n* an endocrine gland of vertebrates, consisting in man of two lobes near the base of the neck. It secretes hormones that control metabolism and body growth.
thyroiditis (ˌθaɪrɔɪˈdaɪtɪs) *n* inflammation of the thyroid gland.
thyroid-stimulating hormone *n* another name for **thyrotropin.** Abbrev.: **TSH.**
thyrotoxicosis (ˌθaɪrəʊˌtɒksɪˈkəʊsɪs) *n* another name for **hyperthyroidism.**
thyrotropin (ˌθaɪrəʊˈtrəʊpɪn) *or* **thyrotrophin** *n* a glycoprotein hormone secreted by the anterior lobe of the pituitary gland: it stimulates the activity of the thyroid gland. Also called: **thyroid-stimulating hormone.** [C20: from THYRO- + -TROPE + -IN]
thyroxine (θaɪˈrɒksiːn, -sɪn) *or* **thyroxin** (θaɪˈrɒksɪn) *n* the principal hormone produced by the thyroid gland: it increases the metabolic rate of tissues and also controls growth, as in amphibian metamorphosis. It can be synthesized or extracted from the thyroid glands of animals and used to treat hypothyroidism. Chemical name: tetra-iodothyronine; formula: $C_{15}H_{11}I_4NO_4$. [C19: from THYRO- + OXY-[2] + -INE[2]]
thyrse (θɜːs) *or* **thyrsus** (ˈθɜːsəs) *n, pl* **thyrses** *or* **thyrsi** (ˈθɜːsaɪ). *Botany.* a type of inflorescence, occurring in the lilac and grape, in which the main branch is racemose and the lateral branches cymose. [C17: from French: THYRSUS] ▸ **ˈthyrsoid** *adj*
thyrsus (ˈθɜːsəs) *n, pl* **-si** (-saɪ). **1** *Greek myth.* a staff, usually one tipped with a pine cone, borne by Dionysus (Bacchus) and his followers. **2** a variant spelling of **thyrse.** [C18: from Latin, from Greek *thursos* stalk]
thysanuran (ˌθɪsəˈnjʊərən) *n* **1** any primitive wingless insect of the order *Thysanura,* which comprises the bristletails. ◆ *adj* **2** of, relating to, or belonging to the order *Thysanura.* [C19: from New Latin, from Greek *thusanos* fringe + *oura* tail] ▸ ˌ**thysaˈnurous** *adj*
thyself (ðaɪˈsɛlf) *pron Archaic.* **a** the reflexive form of *thou* or *thee.* **b** (intensifier): *thou, thyself, wouldst know.*
ti[1] (tiː) *n Music.* a variant spelling of **te.**
ti[2] (tiː) *n, pl* **tis. 1** a woody palmlike agave plant, *Cordyline terminalis,* of the East Indies, having white, mauve, or reddish flowers. The sword-shaped leaves are used for garments, fodder, thatch, etc., and the root for food and liquor. **2** a similar and related plant, *Cordyline australis,* of New Zealand. [of Polynesian origin]
Ti *the chemical symbol for* titanium.
TIA *Med. abbrev. for* transient ischaemic attack; a minor and temporary stroke.
Tia Juana (ˈtɪə ˈwɑːnə; *Spanish* ˈtia ˈxwana) *n* a variant spelling of **Tijuana.**
Tia Maria (ˈtɪə məˈrɪə) *n Trademark.* a coffee-flavoured liqueur from the Caribbean.
Tianjin (ˈtjɛnˈdʒɪn), **Tientsin,** *or* **T'ien-ching** *n* an industrial city in NE China, in Hebei province, on the Grand Canal, 51 km (32 miles) from the Yellow Sea: the third largest city in China; seat of Nankai University (1919). Pop.: 5 770 000 (1991 est.).
Tian Shan *or* **Tien Shan** (ˈtjɛnˈʃɑːn) *n* a great mountain system of central Asia, in Kyrgyzstan and the Xinjiang Uygur Autonomous Region of W China, extending for about 2500 km (1500 miles). Highest peak: Pobeda Peak, 7439 m (24 406 ft.). Russian name: **Tyan-Shan.**
tiara (tɪˈɑːrə) *n* **1** a woman's semicircular jewelled headdress for formal occasions. **2** a high headdress worn by Persian kings in ancient times. **3** *R.C. Church.* **3a** a headdress worn by the pope, consisting of a beehive-shaped diadem surrounded by three coronets. **3b** the office or rank of pope. [C16: via Latin from Greek, of Oriental origin] ▸ **tiˈaraed** *adj*
Tiber (ˈtaɪbə) *n* a river in central Italy, rising in the Tuscan Apennines and flowing south through Rome to the Tyrrhenian Sea. Length: 405 km (252 miles). Ancient name: **Tiberis** (ˈtiːbərɪs). Italian name: **Tevere.**
Tiberias (taɪˈbɪərɪˌæs) *n* **1** a resort in N Israel, on the Sea of Galilee: an important Jewish centre after the destruction of Jerusalem by the Romans. Pop.: 35 400 (1989 est.). **2 Lake.** another name for the (Sea of) **Galilee.**
Tiberius (taɪˈbɪərɪəs) *n* full name *Tiberius Claudius Nero Caesar Augustus.* 42 B.C.–37 A.D., Roman emperor (14–37 A.D.). He succeeded his father-in-law Augustus after a brilliant military career. He became increasingly tyrannical.
Tibesti *or* **Tibesti Massif** (tɪˈbɛstɪ) *n* a mountain range of volcanic origin in NW Chad, in the central Sahara extending for about 480 km (300 miles). Highest peak: Emi Koussi, 3415 m (11 204 ft.).
Tibet (tɪˈbɛt) *n* an autonomous region of SW China: Europeans strictly excluded in the 19th century; invaded by China in 1950; rebellion (1959) against Chinese rule suppressed and the Dalai Lama fled to India; military rule imposed (1989–90) after continued demands for independence; consists largely of a vast high plateau between the Himalayas and Kunlun Mountains; formerly a theocracy and the centre of Lamaism. Capital: Lhasa. Pop.: 2 400 000 (1996 est.). Area: 1 221 601 sq. km (471 660 sq. miles). Chinese names: **Xizang Autonomous Region, Sitsang.**
Tibetan (tɪˈbɛtᵊn) *adj* **1** of, relating to, or characteristic of Tibet, its people, or their language. ◆ *n* **2** a native or inhabitant of Tibet. **3** the language of Tibet, belonging to the Sino-Tibetan family.
Tibetan terrier *n* a breed of dog with a long dense shaggy coat: it resembles a small Old English sheepdog.
Tibeto-Burman (tɪˈbɛtəʊˈbɜːmən) *n* **1** a branch of the Sino-Tibetan family of languages, sometimes regarded as a family in its own right. Compare **Sinitic.** ◆ *adj* **2** belonging or relating to this group of languages.
tibia (ˈtɪbɪə) *n, pl* **tibiae** (ˈtɪbɪˌiː) *or* **tibias. 1** Also called: **shinbone.** the inner and thicker of the two bones of the human leg between the knee and ankle. Compare **fibula. 2** the corresponding bone in other vertebrates. **3** the fourth segment of an insect's leg, lying between the femur and the tarsus. [C16: from Latin: leg, pipe] ▸ **ˈtibial** *adj*
tibiotarsus (ˌtɪbɪəʊˈtɑːsəs) *n* the bone in the leg of a bird formed by fusion of the tibia and some of the tarsal bones. [C19: from *tibio-* (combining form of TIBIA) + TARSUS]
Tibullus (tɪˈbʌləs) *n* **Albius** (ˈælbɪəs). ?54–?19 B.C., Roman elegiac poet.
Tibur (ˈtaɪbə) *n* the ancient name for **Tivoli.**
tic (tɪk) *n Pathol.* **1** spasmodic twitching of a particular group of muscles. **2** See **tic douloureux.** [C19: from French, of uncertain origin; compare Italian *ticche*]
tical (tɪˈkɑːl, -ˈkɔːl; ˈtiːkᵊl) *n, pl* **-cals** *or* **-cal. 1** the former standard monetary unit of Thailand, replaced by the baht in 1928. **2** a unit of weight, formerly used in Thailand, equal to about half an ounce or 14 grams. [C17: via Siamese and Portuguese from Malay *tikal* monetary unit]
tic douloureux (ˈtɪk ˌduːləˈruː) *n* a condition of momentary stabbing pain along the trigeminal nerve. Also called: **trigeminal neuralgia.** [C19: from French, literally: painful tic]
tichy (ˈtɪtʃɪ) *adj* **tichier, tichiest.** a variant spelling of **titchy.**
Ticino (*Italian* tiˈtʃiːno) *n* **1** a canton in S Switzerland: predominantly Italian-speaking and Roman Catholic; mountainous. Capital: Bellinzona. Pop.: 305 199 (1996 est.). Area: 2810 sq. km (1085 sq. miles). German name: **Tessin. 2** a river in S central Europe, rising in S central Switzerland and flowing south-east and west to Lake Maggiore, then southeast to the River Po. Length: 248 km (154 miles).
tick[1] (tɪk) *n* **1** a recurrent metallic tapping or clicking sound, such as that made by a clock or watch. **2** *Brit. informal.* a moment or instant. **3** a mark (✓) or dash used to check off or indicate the correctness of something. **4** *Commerce.* the smallest increment of a price fluctuation in a commodity exchange. Tick size is usually 0.01% of the nominal value of the trading unit. ◆ *vb* **5** to produce a recurrent tapping sound or indicate by such a sound: *the clock ticked the minutes away.* **6** (when *tr,* often foll. by *off*) to mark or check (something, such as a list) with a tick. **7 what makes someone tick.** *Informal.* the basic drive or motivation of a person. ◆ See also **tick off, tick over.** [C13: from Low German *tikk* touch; related to Old High German *zekōn* to pluck, Norwegian *tikke* to touch]
tick[2] (tɪk) *n* **1** any of various small parasitic arachnids of the families *Ixodidae* (**hard ticks**) and *Argasidae,* (**soft ticks**), typically living on the skin of warm-blooded animals and feeding on the blood and tissues of their hosts: order *Acarina* (mites and ticks). See also **sheep tick** (sense 1). Related adj: **acaroid. 2** any of certain other arachnids of the order *Acarina.* **3** any of certain insects of the dipterous family *Hippoboscidae* that are ectoparasitic on horses, cattle, sheep, etc., esp. the sheep ked. [Old English *ticca;* related to Middle High German *zeche* tick, Middle Irish *dega* stag beetle]
tick[3] (tɪk) *n* **1** the strong covering of a pillow, mattress, etc. **2** *Informal.* short for **ticking.** [C15: probably from Middle Dutch *tīke;* related to Old High German *ziecha* pillow cover, Latin *tēca* case, Greek *thēkē*]
tick[4] (tɪk) *n Brit. informal.* account or credit (esp. in the phrase **on tick**). [C17: shortened from TICKET]
tick-bird *n* another name for **oxpecker.** [C19: so called because it eats insects off animals' backs]

tick-borne typhus *n* another name for **Rocky Mountain spotted fever.**

ticker ('tɪkə) *n* **1** *Slang.* **1a** the heart. **1b** a watch. **2** a person or thing that ticks. **3** *Stock Exchange.* the U.S. word for **tape machine** (sense 2).

ticker tape *n* **1** *Stock Exchange.* a continuous paper ribbon on which a tape machine automatically prints current stock quotations. **2 ticker-tape reception** (*or* **parade**). (mainly in New York) the showering of the motorcade of a distinguished politician, visiting head of state, etc., with ticker tape as a sign of welcome.

ticket ('tɪkɪt) *n* **1a** a piece of paper, cardboard, etc., showing that the holder is entitled to certain rights, such as travel on a train or bus, entry to a place of public entertainment, etc. **1b** (*modifier*) concerned with or relating to the issue, sale, or checking of tickets: *a ticket office; ticket collector.* **2** a piece of card, cloth, etc., attached to an article showing information such as its price, size, or washing instructions. **3** a summons served for a parking offence or violation of traffic regulations. **4** *Informal.* the certificate of competence issued to a ship's captain or an aircraft pilot. **5** *Chiefly U.S. and N.Z.* the group of candidates nominated by one party in an election; slate. **6** *Chiefly U.S.* the declared policy of a political party at an election. **7** *Brit. informal.* a certificate of discharge from the armed forces. **8** *Informal.* the right or appropriate thing: *that's the ticket.* **9 have (got) tickets on oneself.** *Austral. informal.* to be conceited. ◆ *vb* **-ets, -eting, -eted.** (*tr*) **10** to issue or attach a ticket or tickets to. **11** *Informal.* to earmark for a particular purpose. [C17: from Old French *etiquet,* from *estiquier* to stick on, from Middle Dutch *steken* to STICK²]

ticket day *n* (on the London Stock Exchange) the day on which selling brokers receive from buying brokers the names of investors who have made purchases during the previous account. Also called: **name day.** Compare **account day.**

ticket of leave *n* (formerly in Britain) a permit allowing a convict (**ticket-of-leave man**) to leave prison, after serving only part of his sentence, with certain restrictions placed on him.

tickets ('tɪkɪts) *pl n S. African informal.* the end; that was it. [of unknown origin]

ticket tout *n* See **tout** (sense 6).

tickety-boo (ˌtɪkɪtɪ'buː) *adj Brit. old-fashioned informal.* as it should be; correct; satisfactory. [C20: of obscure origin]

tickey ('tɪkɪ) *n* a South African threepenny piece, which was replaced by the five-cent coin in 1961. [of uncertain origin]

tick fever *n* **1** any acute infectious febrile disease caused by the bite of an infected tick. **2** another name for **Rocky Mountain spotted fever.**

ticking ('tɪkɪŋ) *n* a strong cotton fabric, often striped, used esp. for mattress and pillow covers. [C17: from TICK³]

tickle ('tɪkᵊl) *vb* **1** to touch, stroke, or poke (a person, part of the body, etc.) so as to produce pleasure, laughter, or a twitching sensation. **2** (*tr*) to excite pleasurably; gratify. **3** (*tr*) to delight or entertain (often in the phrase **tickle one's fancy**). **4** (*intr*) to itch or tingle. **5** (*tr*) to catch (a fish, esp. a trout) by grasping it with the hands and gently moving the fingers into its gills. **6 tickle pink** *or* **to death.** *Informal.* to please greatly: *he was tickled pink to be elected president.* ◆ *n* **7** a sensation of light stroking or itching. **8** the act of tickling. [C14: related to Old English *tinclian,* Old High German *kizziton,* Old Norse *kitla,* Latin *titillāre* to TITILLATE] ▸ **'tickly** *adj*

tickler ('tɪklə) *n* **1** *Informal, chiefly Brit.* a difficult or delicate problem. **2** Also called: **tickler file.** *U.S.* a memorandum book or file. **3** *Accounting, U.S.* a single-entry business journal. **4** a person or thing that tickles.

tickler coil *n* a small inductance coil connected in series in the anode circuit of a valve and magnetically coupled to a coil in the grid circuit to provide feedback.

ticklish ('tɪklɪʃ) *adj* **1** susceptible and sensitive to being tickled. **2** delicate or difficult: *a ticklish situation.* **3** easily upset or offended. ▸ **'ticklishly** *adv* ▸ **'ticklishness** *n*

tick off *vb* (*tr, adv*) **1** to mark with a tick. **2** *Informal, chiefly Brit.* to scold; reprimand. ▸ **ticking off** *or* **ticking-off** *n*

tick over *vb* (*intr, adv*) **1** Also: **idle.** *Brit.* (of an engine) to run at low speed with the throttle control closed and the transmission disengaged. **2** to run smoothly without any major changes: *keep the firm ticking over until I get back.* ◆ *n* **tick-over. 3** *Brit.* **3a** the speed of an engine when it is ticking over. **3b** (*as modifier*): *tick-over speed.*

ticktack ('tɪkˌtæk) *n* **1** *Brit.* a system of sign language, mainly using the hands, by which bookmakers transmit their odds to each other at racecourses. **2** *U.S.* a ticking sound, as made by a clock. [from TICK¹]

tick-tack-toe (ˌtɪktæk'təʊ) *or* **tick-tack-too** (ˌtɪktæk'tuː) *n* the usual U.S. and Canadian term for **noughts and crosses.** [C19: from TICKTACK (meaning: an obsolete variety of backgammon)]

ticktock ('tɪkˌtɒk) *n* **1** a ticking sound as made by a clock. ◆ *vb* **2** (*intr*) to make a ticking sound.

tick trefoil *n* any of various tropical and subtropical leguminous plants of the genus *Desmodium,* having trifoliate leaves, clusters of small purplish or white flowers, and sticky jointed seed pods, which separate into segments that cling to animals. Also called: **beggar-ticks.**

Ticonderoga (ˌtaɪkɒndə'rəʊgə) *n* a village in NE New York State, on Lake George: site of Fort Ticonderoga, scene of battles between the British and French (1758–59) and a strategic point in the War of American Independence.

t.i.d. (in prescriptions) *abbrev. for* ter in die. [Latin: three times a day]

tidal ('taɪdᵊl) *adj* **1** relating to, characterized by, or affected by tides: *a tidal estuary.* **2** dependent on the state of the tide: *a tidal ferry.* **3** (of a glacier) reaching the sea and discharging floes or icebergs. ▸ **'tidally** *adv*

tidal basin *n* a basin for vessels that is filled at high tide.

tidal energy *n* energy obtained by harnessing tidal power.

tidal power *n* the use of the rise and fall of tides involving very large volumes of water at low heads to generate electric power.

tidal volume *n* **1** the volume of water associated with a rising tide. **2** *Physiol.* the amount of air passing into and out of the lungs during normal breathing.

tidal wave *n* **1** a name (not accepted in technical usage) for **tsunami. 2** an unusually large incoming wave, often caused by high winds and spring tides. **3** a forceful and widespread movement in public opinion, action, etc.

tidbit ('tɪdˌbɪt) *n* the usual U.S. spelling of **titbit.**

tiddler ('tɪdlə) *n Brit. informal.* **1** a very small fish or aquatic creature, esp. a stickleback, minnow, or tadpole. **2** a small child, esp. one undersized for its age. [C19: from dialectal *tittlebat,* childish variant of STICKLEBACK, influenced by TIDDLY¹]

tiddly¹ ('tɪdlɪ) *adj* **-dlier, -dliest.** *Brit.* small; tiny. [C19: childish variant of LITTLE]

tiddly² ('tɪdlɪ) *adj* **-dlier, -dliest.** *Slang, chiefly Brit.* slightly drunk. [C19 (meaning: a drink): of unknown origin]

tiddlywink ('tɪdlɪˌwɪŋk) *n* any of the discs used in the game of tiddlywinks.

tiddlywinks ('tɪdlɪˌwɪŋks) *n* (*functioning as sing*) a game in which players try to flick discs of plastic into a cup by pressing them sharply on the side with other larger discs. [C19: probably from TIDDLY¹ + dialect *wink,* variant of WINCH¹]

tide¹ (taɪd) *n* **1** the cyclic rise and fall of sea level caused by the gravitational pull of the sun and moon. There are usually two high tides and two low tides in each lunar day. See also **tide-generating force, neap tide, spring tide. 2** the current, ebb, or flow of water at a specified place resulting from these changes in level: *the tide is coming in.* **3** See **ebb** (sense 3) and **flood** (sense 3). **4** a widespread tendency or movement: *the tide of resentment against the government.* **5** a critical point in time; turning point: *the tide of his fortunes.* **6** *Northern English dialect.* a fair or holiday. **7** *Archaic except in combination.* a season or time: *Christmastide.* **8** *Rare.* any body of mobile water, such as a stream. **9** *Archaic.* a favourable opportunity. ◆ *vb* **10** to carry or be carried with or as if with the tide. **11** (*intr*) to ebb and flow like the tide. [Old English *tīd* time; related to Old High German *zīt,* Old Norse *tīthr* time] ▸ **'tideless** *adj* ▸ **'tideˌlike** *adj*

tide² (taɪd) *vb* (*intr*) *Archaic.* to happen. [Old English *tīdan;* related to Old Frisian *tīdia* to proceed to, Middle Low German *tīden* to hurry, Old Norse *tītha* to desire]

tide-gauge *n* a gauge used to measure extremes or the present level of tidal movement.

tide-generating force *n* the difference between the force of gravity exerted by the moon or the sun on a particle of water in the ocean and that exerted on an equal mass of matter at the centre of the earth. The lunar tide-generating forces are about 2.2 times greater than are the solar ones. See also **neap tide, spring tide, tide¹.**

tideland ('taɪdˌlænd) *n U.S.* land between high-water and low-water marks.

tidemark ('taɪdˌmɑːk) *n* **1** a mark left by the highest or lowest point of a tide. **2** a marker indicating the highest or lowest point reached by a tide. **3** *Chiefly Brit.* a mark showing a level reached by a liquid: *a tidemark on the bath.* **4** *Informal, chiefly Brit.* a dirty mark on the skin, indicating the extent to which someone has washed.

tide over *vb* (*tr*) to help to get through (a period of difficulty, distress, etc.): *the money tided him over until he got a job.*

tide race *n* a fast-running tidal current.

tide-rip *n* another word for **riptide** (sense 1).

tide table *n* a table showing the height of the tide at different times of day over a period at a particular place.

tidewaiter ('taɪdˌweɪtə) *n* (formerly) a customs officer who boarded and inspected incoming ships.

tidewater ('taɪdˌwɔːtə) *n* **1** water that advances and recedes with the tide. **2** water that covers land that is dry at low tide. **3** *U.S.* **3a** coastal land drained by tidal streams. **3b** (*as modifier*): *tidewater regions.*

tideway ('taɪdˌweɪ) *n* a strong tidal current or its channel, esp. the tidal part of a river.

tidings ('taɪdɪŋz) *pl n* information or news. [Old English *tīdung;* related to Middle Low German *tīdinge* information, Old Norse *tidhendi* events; see TIDE²]

tidy ('taɪdɪ) *adj* **-dier, -diest. 1** characterized by or indicating neatness and order. **2** *Informal.* considerable: *a tidy sum of money.* ◆ *vb* **-dies, -dying, -died. 3** (when *intr,* usually foll. by *up*) to put (things) in order; neaten. ◆ *n, pl* **-dies. 4a** a small container in which odds and ends are kept. **4b sink tidy.** a container with holes in the bottom, kept in the sink to retain rubbish that might clog the plug hole. **5** *Chiefly U.S. and Canadian.* an ornamental protective covering for the back or arms of a chair. [C13 (in the sense: timely, seasonable, excellent): from TIDE¹ + -Y¹; related to Dutch *tijdig*timely] ▸ **'tidily** *adv* ▸ **'tidiness** *n*

tie (taɪ) *vb* **ties, tying, tied. 1** (when *tr,* often foll. by *up*) to fasten or be fastened with string, thread, etc. **2** to make (a knot or bow) in (something): *to tie a knot; tie a ribbon.* **3** (*tr*) to restrict or secure. **4** to equal the score of a competitor or fellow candidate. **5** (*tr*) *Informal.* to unite in marriage. **6** *Music.* **6a** to execute (two successive notes of the same pitch) as though they formed one note of composite time value. **6b** to connect (two printed notes) with a tie. **7 fit to be tied.** *Slang.* very angry or upset. ◆ *n* **8** a bond, link, or fastening. **9** a restriction or restraint. **10** a string, wire, ribbon, etc., with which something is tied. **11** a long narrow piece of material worn, esp. by men, under the collar of a shirt, tied in a knot close to the throat with the ends hanging down the front. U.S. name: **necktie. 12a** an equality in score, attainment, etc., in a contest. **12b** the match or competition in which such a result is attained. **13** a structural member such as a tie beam or tie rod. **14** *Sport, Brit.* a match or game in an eliminating competition: *a cup tie.* **15** (*usually pl*) a shoe fastened by means of laces. **16** the U.S. and Canadian name for **sleeper** (on a railway track). **17** *Music.* a slur connecting two notes of the same pitch indicating that the sound is to be prolonged for their joint time value. **18** *Surveying.* one of two measurements running from two points on a survey line to a point of detail to fix its position. **19** *Lacemaking.* another name for **bride**[2]. ◆ See also **tie in, tie up.** [Old English *tīgan* to tie; related to Old Norse *teygja* to draw, stretch out, Old English *tēon* to pull; see TUG, TOW[1], TIGHT]

tieback ('taɪˌbæk) *n* **a** a length of cord, ribbon, or other fabric used for tying a curtain to one side. **b** a curtain having such a device.

tie beam *n* a horizontal beam that serves to prevent two other structural members from separating, esp. one that connects two corresponding rafters in a roof or roof truss.

tie-break *or* **tie-breaker** ('taɪˌbreɪkə) *n* **1** *Tennis.* a method of deciding quickly the result of a set drawn at six-all, usually involving the playing of one deciding game for the best of twelve points in which the service changes after every two points. **2** any contest or game played to decide a winner when contestants have tied scores.

Tieck (*German* tiːk) *n* **Ludwig** ('luːtvɪç). 1773–1853, German romantic writer, noted esp. for his fairy tales.

tie clasp *n* a clip, often ornamental, which holds a tie in place against a shirt. Also called: **tie clip.**

tied (taɪd) *adj Brit.* **1** (of a public house, retail shop, etc.) obliged to sell only the beer, products, etc. of a particular producer: *a tied house; tied outlet.* **2** (of a house or cottage) rented out to the tenant for as long as he is employed by the owner. **3** (of a loan) made by one nation to another on condition that the money is spent on goods or services provided by the lending nation.

tie-dyeing *n* a method of dyeing textiles to produce patterns by tying sections of the cloth together so that they will not absorb the dye. Also called: **tie-and-dye.** ▸ **'tie-ˌdyed** *adj*

tie in *vb* (*adv*) **1** to come or bring into a certain relationship; coordinate. ◆ *n* **tie-in. 2** a link, relationship, or coordination. **3** publicity material, a book, tape, etc., linked to a film or broadcast programme or series. **4** *U.S.* **4a** a sale or advertisement offering products of which a purchaser must buy one or more in addition to his purchase. **4b** an item sold or advertised in this way, esp. the extra item. **4c** (*as modifier*): *a tie-in sale.*

tie line *n* a telephone line between two private branch exchanges or private exchanges that may or may not pass through a main exchange.

tiemannite ('tiːməˌnaɪt) *n* a grey mineral consisting of mercury selenide. Formula: HgSe. [C19: named after J. C. W. F. *Tiemann* (1848–99), German scientist]

Tien Shan ('tjɛn'ʃɑːn) *n* a variant transliteration of the Chinese name for the **Tian Shan.**

Tientsin ('tjɛn'tsɪn) *n* a variant transliteration of the Chinese name for **Tianjin.**

tiepin ('taɪˌpɪn) *n* an ornamental pin of various shapes used to pin the two ends of a tie to a shirt.

Tiepolo (*Italian* 'tjɛːpolo; *English* tiː'ɛpəˌləʊ) *n* **Giovanni Battista** (dʒo'vanni bat'tista). 1696–1770, Italian rococo painter, esp. of frescoes as in the Residenz at Würzburg.

tier[1] (tɪə) *n* **1** one of a set of rows placed one above and behind the other, such as theatre seats. **2a** a layer or level. **2b** (*in combination*): *a three-tier cake.* **3** a rank, order, or row. ◆ *vb* **4** to be or arrange in tiers. [C16: from Old French *tire* rank, of Germanic origin; compare Old English *tīr* embellishment]

tier[2] ('taɪə) *n* a person or thing that ties.

tierce (tɪəs) *n* **1** a variant of **terce. 2** the third of eight basic positions from which a parry or attack can be made in fencing. **3** (tɜːs). *Piquet, etc.* a sequence of three cards in the same suit. **4** an obsolete measure of capacity equal to 42 wine gallons. [C15: from Old French, feminine of *tiers* third, from Latin *tertius*]

tierce de Picardie (*French* tjɛrs də pikardi) *n* another term for **Picardy third.**

tiercel ('tɪəsᵊl) *n* a variant of **tercel.**

tie rod *n* any rod or bar designed to prevent the separation of two parts, as in a vehicle.

Tierra del Fuego (*Spanish* 'tjɛrra ðel 'fweɣo) *n* an archipelago at the S extremity of South America, separated from the mainland by the Strait of Magellan: the west and south belong to Chile, the east to Argentina, and several islands are disputed. Area: 73 643 sq. km (28 434 sq. miles).

tie up *vb* (*adv*) **1** (*tr*) to attach or bind securely with or as if with string, rope, etc. **2** to moor (a vessel). **3** (*tr; often passive*) to engage the attentions of: *he's tied up at the moment and can't see you.* **4** (*tr; often passive*) to conclude (the organization of something): *the plans for the trip were tied up well in advance.* **5** to come or bring to a complete standstill. **6** (*tr*) to invest or commit (funds, etc.) and so make unavailable for other uses. **7** (*tr*) to subject (property) to conditions that prevent sale, alienation, or other action. ◆ *n* **tie-up. 8** a link or connection. **9** *Chiefly U.S. and Canadian.* a standstill. **10** *Chiefly U.S. and Canadian.* an informal term for **traffic jam.**

tiff[1] (tɪf) *n* **1** a petty quarrel. **2** a fit of ill humour. ◆ *vb* **3** (*intr*) to have or be in a tiff. [C18: of unknown origin]

tiff[2] (tɪf) *n Archaic.* a small draught of alcoholic drink; dram. [C18: see TIFFIN]

tiffany ('tɪfənɪ) *n, pl* **-nies.** a sheer fine gauzy fabric. [C17: (in the sense: a fine dress worn on Twelfth Night): from Old French *tifanie,* from ecclesiastical Latin *theophania* Epiphany; see THEOPHANY]

Tiffany ('tifənɪ) *n* **Louis Comfort.** 1848–1933, U.S. glass-maker and Art-Nouveau craftsman, best known for creating the Favrile style of stained glass.

Tiffany glass *n* another term for **Favrile glass.**

tiffin ('tɪfɪn) *n* (in India) a light meal, esp. one taken at midday. [C18: probably from obsolete *tiffing,* from *tiff* to sip]

Tiflis (tɪf'liːs) *n* transliteration of the Russian name for **Tbilisi.**

tig (tɪg) *n, vb* **tigs, tigging, tigged.** another name for **tag**[2] (senses 1, 4).

tiger ('taɪgə) *n* **1** a large feline mammal, *Panthera tigris,* of forests in most of Asia, having a tawny yellow coat with black stripes. **2** (*not in technical use*) any of various other animals, such as the jaguar, leopard, and thylacine. **3** a dynamic, forceful, or cruel person. **4a** a country, esp. in E Asia, that is achieving rapid economic growth. **4b** (*as modifier*): *a tiger economy.* **5** *Archaic.* a servant in livery, esp. a page or groom. **6** short for **tiger moth. 7 have a tiger by the tail.** *Informal.* to find oneself in a situation that has turned out to be much more difficult to control than one had expected. [C13: from Old French *tigre,* from Latin *tigris,* from Greek, of Iranian origin] ▸ **'tigerish** *or* **'tigrish** *adj* ▸ **'tigerishly** *adv* ▸ **'tigerishness** *n* ▸ **'tiger-like** *adj*

Tiger ('taɪgə) *n* See **TIGR.**

Tiger balm *n Trademark.* (in Malaysia) a mentholated ointment widely used as a panacea.

tiger beetle *n* any active predatory beetle of the family *Cicindelidae,* chiefly of warm dry regions, having powerful mandibles and long legs. [C19: so called because it has patterned, sometimes striped, wing covers]

tiger cat *n* **1** a medium-sized feline mammal, *Felis tigrina,* of Central and South America, having a dark-striped coat. **2** any similar feline with tiger-like markings, such as the margay.

tiger lily *n* **1** a lily plant, *Lilium tigrinum,* of China and Japan, cultivated for its flowers, which have black-spotted orange reflexed petals. **2** any of various similar lilies.

tiger market *n Informal.* any of the four most important markets on the Pacific rim after Japan: Hong Kong, South Korea, Singapore, and Taiwan. Compare **dragon market.**

tiger moth *n* any of a group of arctiid moths, mostly boldly marked, often in black, orange, and yellow, of the genera *Arctia Parasemia, Euplagia,* etc., producing woolly bear larvae and typified by the **garden tiger** (*Arctia caja*). Often shortened to **tiger.**

tiger's-eye ('taɪgəzˌaɪ) *or* **tigereye** ('taɪgərˌaɪ) *n* **1** a golden brown silicified variety of crocidolite, used as an ornamental stone. **2** a glaze resembling this, used on pottery.

tiger shark *n* **1** a voracious omnivorous requiem shark, *Galeocerdo cuvieri,* chiefly of tropical waters, having a striped or spotted body. **2** any of certain other spotted sharks, such as *Stegostoma tigrinum,* of the Indian Ocean.

tiger snake *n* a highly venomous brown-and-yellow elapid snake, *Notechis scutatus,* of Australia.

tight (taɪt) *adj* **1** stretched or drawn so as not to be loose; taut: *a tight cord.* **2** fitting or covering in a close manner: *a tight dress.* **3** held, made, fixed, or closed firmly and securely: *a tight knot.* **4a** of close and compact construction or organization, esp. so as to be impervious to water, air, etc. **4b** (*in combination*): *watertight; airtight.* **5** unyielding or stringent: *to keep a tight hold on resources.* **6** cramped or constricted: *a tight fit.* **7** mean or miserly. **8** difficult and problematic: *a tight situation.* **9** hardly profitable: *a tight bargain.* **10** *Economics.* **10a** (of a commodity) difficult to obtain; in excess demand. **10b** (of funds, money, etc.) difficult and expensive to borrow because of high demand or restrictive monetary policy. **10c** (of markets) characterized by excess demand or scarcity with prices tending to rise. Compare **easy** (sense 8). **11** (of a match or game) very close or even. **12** (of a team or group, esp. of a pop group) playing well together, in a disciplined coordinated way. **13** *Informal.* drunk. **14** *Informal.* (of a person) showing tension. **15** *Archaic or dialect.* neat. ◆ *adv* **16** in a close, firm, or secure way: *pull it tight.* **17 sit tight. 17a** to wait patiently; bide one's time. **17b** to maintain one's position, stand, or opinion firmly. **18 sleep tight.** to sleep soundly. [C14: probably variant of *thight,* from Old Norse *thēttr* close; related to Middle High German *dīhte* thick] ▸ **'tightly** *adv* ▸ **'tightness** *n*

tightass ('taɪtˌæs) *n Slang, chiefly U.S.* an inhibited or excessively self-controlled person. ▸ **'tightˌassed** *adj*

tighten ('taɪtᵊn) *vb* **1** to make or become tight or tighter. **2 tighten one's belt.** to economize. ▸ **'tightener** *n*

tightfisted (ˌtaɪt'fɪstɪd) *adj* mean; miserly.

tight head *n Rugby.* the prop on the hooker's right in the front row of a scrum. Compare **loose head.**

tightknit (ˌtaɪt'nɪt) *adj* **1** closely integrated: *a tightknit community.* **2** organized carefully and concisely.

tight-lipped *adj* **1** reticent, secretive, or taciturn. **2** with the lips pressed tightly together, as through anger.

tightrope ('taɪtˌrəʊp) *n* **1** a rope or cable stretched taut above the ground on which acrobats walk or perform balancing feats. **2 walk a tightrope.** to be in a difficult situation that demands careful and considered behaviour.

tightrope walker *n* an acrobat who performs on a tightrope. ▸ **tightrope walking** *n*

tights (taɪts) *pl n* **1a** Also called (U.S., Canadian, Austral., and N.Z.): **pantihose.** a one-piece clinging garment covering the body from the waist to the feet, worn by women in place of stockings. **1b** *U.S. and Canadian.* Also called: **leotards.** a similar, tight-fitting garment worn instead of trousers by either sex. **2** a similar garment formerly worn by men, as in the 16th century with a doublet.

tightwad ('taɪtˌwɒd) *n Slang, chiefly U.S. and Canadian.* a stingy person; miser.

Tiglath-pileser I ('tɪglæθpɪ'liːzə, -paɪ-) *n* king of Assyria (?1116–?1093 B.C.), who extended his kingdom to the upper Euphrates and defeated the king of Babylonia.

Tiglath-pileser III *n* known as *Pulu.* died ?727 B.C., king of Assyria (745–727), who greatly extended his empire, subjugating Syria and Palestine.

tiglic acid ('tɪglɪk) *n* a syrupy liquid or crystalline colourless unsaturated carboxylic acid, with the *trans*-configuration, found in croton oil and used in perfumery; *trans*-2-methyl-2-butenoic acid. Formula: $CH_3CH{:}C(CH_3)COOH$. [C19 *tiglic,* from New Latin phrase *Croton tiglium* (name of the croton plant), of uncertain origin]

tigon ('taɪgən) *or* **tiglon** ('tɪglɒn) *n* the hybrid offspring of a male tiger and a female lion.

TIGR *abbrev. for* Treasury Investment Growth Receipts: a bond denominated in dollars and linked to U.S. treasury bonds, the yield on which is taxed in the UK as income when it is cashed or redeemed. Also called: **Tiger**.

Tigré *or* **Tigray** ('ti:greɪ) *n* **1** an autonomous region of N Ethiopia, bordering on Eritrea: formerly a separate kingdom. Capital: Mekele. Pop.: 2 999 948 (1993 est.). Area: 53 498 sq. km (20 656 sq. miles). **2** a language of NE Ethiopia, belonging to the SE Semitic subfamily of the Afro-Asiatic family.

tigress ('taɪgrɪs) *n* **1** a female tiger. **2** a fierce, cruel, or wildly passionate woman.

tigridia (taɪ'grɪdɪə) *n* any plant of the bulbous genus *Tigridia,* native to subtropical and tropical America, esp. *T. pavonia,* the tiger flower or peacock tiger flower, grown for its large strikingly marked red, white, or yellow concave flowers: family *Iridaceae*. [New Latin, from Greek *tigris, tigridis* tiger]

Tigrinya (tɪ'gri:njə) *n* a language of N Ethiopia, belonging to the SE Semitic subfamily of the Afro-Asiatic family.

Tigris ('taɪgrɪs) *n* a river in SW Asia, rising in E Turkey and flowing southeast through Baghdad to the Euphrates in SE Iraq, forming the delta of the Shatt-al-Arab, which flows into the Persian Gulf: part of a canal and irrigation system as early as 2400 B.C., with many ancient cities (including Nineveh) on its banks. Length: 1900 km (1180 miles).

TIG welding (tɪg) *n* tungsten-electrode inert gas welding: a method of welding in which the arc is maintained by a tungsten electrode and shielded from the access of air by an inert gas. Compare **MIG welding**.

Tihwa *or* **Tihua** ('ti:'hwɑ:) *n* a former name for **Urumchi**.

Tijuana (ti:'wɑ:nə; *Spanish* ti'xwana) *or* **Tia Juana** *n* a city and resort in NW Mexico, in Baja California. Pop.: 698 752 (1990).

tike (taɪk) *n* a variant spelling of **tyke**.

tiki ('ti:kɪ) *n* an amulet or figurine in the form of a carved representation of an ancestor, worn in some Maori cultures. [from Maori]

tikka ('ti:kə) *adj* (*immediately postpositive*) *Indian cookery*. (of meat, esp. chicken or lamb) marinated in spices then dry-roasted, usu. in a clay oven.

tikoloshe (,tɪkɒ'lɒʃ, -'lɒʃɪ) *n* a variant of **tokoloshe**.

til (tɪl, ti:l) *n* another name for **sesame**, esp. a variety grown in India. [C19: from Hindi, from Sanskrit *tilá* sesame]

tilak ('tɪlək) *n, pl* **-ak** *or* **-aks**. a coloured spot or mark worn by Hindus, esp. on the forehead, often indicating membership of a religious sect, caste, etc., or (in the case of a woman) marital status. [from Sanskrit *tilaka*]

Tilak ('tɪlək) *n* **Bal Gangadhar** ('bæl 'gæŋədɑ:), also called *Lokamanya*. 1856–1920, Indian nationalist leader, educationalist, and scholar, who founded (1914) the Indian Home Rule League.

tilapia (tɪ'læpɪə, -'leɪ-) *n* any mouthbrooding cichlid fish of the African freshwater genus *Tilapia:* used as food fishes. [C18: from New Latin]

Tilburg ('tɪlbɜ:g; *Dutch* 'tɪlbyrx) *n* a city in the S Netherlands, in North Brabant: textile industries. Pop.: 164 380 (1996 est.).

tilbury ('tɪlbərɪ, -brɪ) *n, pl* **-buries**. a light two-wheeled horse-drawn open carriage, seating two people. [C19: probably named after the inventor]

Tilbury ('tɪlbərɪ, -brɪ) *n* an area in Essex, on the River Thames: extensive docks; principal container port of the Port of London.

tilde ('tɪldə) *n* the diacritical mark (~) placed over a letter to indicate a palatal nasal consonant, as in Spanish *señor*. This symbol is also used in the International Phonetic Alphabet to represent any nasalized vowel. [C19: from Spanish, from Latin *titulus* title, superscription]

Tilden ('tɪldᵊn) *n* **Bill**, full name *William Tatem Tilden,* known as *Big Bill*. 1893–1953, U.S. tennis player: won the U.S. singles championship (1920–25, 1929) and the British singles championship (1920–21, 1930).

tile (taɪl) *n* **1** a flat thin slab of fired clay, rubber, linoleum, etc., usually square or rectangular and sometimes ornamental, used with others to cover a roof, floor, wall, etc. Related adj: **tegular**. **2** a short pipe made of earthenware, concrete, or plastic, used with others to form a drain. **3** tiles collectively. **4** a rectangular block used as a playing piece in mah jong and other games. **5** *Brit. old-fashioned slang*. a hat. **6 on the tiles**. *Informal*. on a spree, esp. of drinking or debauchery. ◆ *vb* **7** (*tr*) to cover with tiles. [Old English *tīgele,* from Latin *tēgula;* related to German *Ziegel*] ▸ **'tiler** *n*

tilefish ('taɪl,fɪʃ) *n, pl* **-fish** *or* **-fishes**. a large brightly coloured deep-sea percoid food fish, *Lopholatilus chamaeleonticeps,* of warm and tropical seas, esp. the North American coast of the Atlantic: family *Branchiostegidae*. [C19: from New Latin *-tilus,* ending of genus name *Lopholatilus;* perhaps also from a resemblance between its colours and patterning and ornamental tiles]

tiliaceous (,tɪlɪ'eɪʃəs) *adj* of, relating to, or belonging to the *Tiliaceae,* a family of flowering plants, mostly trees and shrubs of warm and tropical regions: includes linden and jute. [C19: from Late Latin *tiliāceus,* from Latin *tilia* linden]

tiling ('taɪlɪŋ) *n* **1** tiles collectively. **2** something made of or surfaced with tiles.

till[1] (tɪl) *conj, prep* **1** short for **until**. Also (not standard): **'til**. **2** *Scot*. to; towards. **3** *Dialect*. in order that: *come here till I tell you*. [Old English *til;* related to Old Norse *til* to, Old High German *zil* goal, aim]

USAGE *Till* is a variant of *until* that is acceptable at all levels of language. *Until* is, however, often preferred at the beginning of a sentence in formal writing: *until his behaviour improves, he cannot become a member*.

till[2] (tɪl) *vb* (*tr*) **1** to cultivate and work (land) for the raising of crops. **2** another word for **plough**. [Old English *tilian* to try, obtain; related to Old Frisian *tilia* to obtain, Old Saxon *tilōn* to obtain, Old High German *zilōn* to hasten towards] ▸ **'tillable** *adj* ▸ **'tiller** *n*

till[3] (tɪl) *n* a box, case, or drawer into which the money taken from customers is put, now usually part of a cash register. [C15 *tylle,* of obscure origin]

till[4] (tɪl) *n* an unstratified glacial deposit consisting of rock fragments of various sizes. The most common is boulder clay. [C17: of unknown origin]

tillage ('tɪlɪdʒ) *n* **1** the act, process, or art of tilling. **2** tilled land.

tillandsia (tɪ'lændzɪə) *n* any bromeliaceous epiphytic plant of the genus *Tillandsia,* such as Spanish moss, of tropical and subtropical America. [C18: New Latin, named after Elias *Tillands* (died 1693), Finno-Swedish botanist]

tiller[1] ('tɪlə) *n Nautical*. a handle fixed to the top of a rudderpost to serve as a lever in steering it. [C14: from Anglo-French *teiler* beam of a loom, from Medieval Latin *tēlārium,* from Latin *tēla* web] ▸ **'tillerless** *adj*

tiller[2] ('tɪlə) *n* **1** a shoot that arises from the base of the stem in grasses. **2** a less common name for **sapling**. ◆ *vb* **3** (*intr*) (of a plant) to produce tillers. [Old English *telgor* twig; related to Icelandic *tjalga* branch]

Till Eulenspiegel ('tɪl 'ɔɪlən,ʃpi:gᵊl) *n* ?14th century, legendary German peasant, whose pranks became the subject of many tales.

Tilley ('tɪlɪ) *n* **Vesta** ('vɛstə), original name *Matilda Alice Powles*. 1864–1952, British music-hall entertainer, best known as a male impersonator.

Tillich ('tɪlɪk) *n* **Paul Johannes**. 1886–1965, U.S. Protestant theologian and philosopher, born in Germany. His works include *The Courage to Be* (1952) and *Systematic Theology* (1951–63).

tillicum ('tɪlɪkəm) *n North American informal*. (in the Pacific Northwest) a friend. [from Chinook Jargon, from Chinook *tlxam* kin, esp. as distinguished from chiefs]

Tilly ('tɪlɪ) *n* Count **Johan Tserclaes von** (jo'hɑn tser'klas fɔn). 1559–1632, Flemish soldier, who commanded the army of The Catholic League (1618–32) and the imperial forces (1630–32) in the Thirty Years' War.

Tilsit ('tɪlzɪt) *n* the former name (until 1945) of **Sovetsk**.

tilt[1] (tɪlt) *vb* **1** to incline or cause to incline at an angle. **2** (*usually intr*) to attack or overthrow (a person or people) in a tilt or joust. **3** (when *intr,* often foll. by *at*) to aim or thrust: *to tilt a lance*. **4** (*tr*) to work or forge with a tilt hammer. ◆ *n* **5** a slope or angle: *at a tilt*. **6** the act of tilting. **7** (esp. in medieval Europe) **7a** a jousting contest. **7b** a thrust with a lance or pole delivered during a tournament. **8** an attempt to win a contest. **9** See **tilt hammer**. **10** (**at**) **full tilt**. at full speed or force. [Old English *tealtian;* related to Dutch *touteren* to totter, Norwegian *tylta* to tiptoe, *tylten* unsteady] ▸ **'tilter** *n*

tilt[2] (tɪlt) *n* **1** an awning or canopy, usually of canvas, for a boat, booth, etc. ◆ *vb* **2** (*tr*) to cover or provide with a tilt. [Old English *teld;* related to Old High German *zelt* tent, Old Norse *tjald* tent]

tilth (tɪlθ) *n* **1** the act or process of tilling land. **2** the condition of soil or land that has been tilled, esp. with respect to suitability for promoting plant growth. [Old English *tilthe;* see TILL[2]]

tilt hammer *n* a drop hammer consisting of a heavy head moving at the end of a pivoted arm; used in forging.

tiltyard ('tɪlt,jɑ:d) *n* (formerly) an enclosed area for tilting.

Tim. *Bible. abbrev. for* Timothy.

Timaru ('tɪmə,ru:) *n* a port and resort in S New Zealand, on E South Island. Pop.: 15 350 (1995 est.).

timbal *or* **tymbal** ('tɪmbᵊl) *n Music*. a type of kettledrum. [C17: from French *timbale,* from Old French *tamballe,* (associated also with *cymbale* cymbal), from Old Spanish *atabal,* from Arabic *at-tabl* the drum]

timbale (tæm'bɑ:l; *French* tɛ̃bal) *n* **1** a mixture of meat, fish, etc., in a rich sauce, cooked in a mould lined with potato or pastry. **2** a plain straight-sided mould in which such a dish is prepared. [C19: from French: kettledrum]

timber ('tɪmbə) *n* **1a** wood, esp. when regarded as a construction material. Usual U.S. and Canadian word: **lumber**. **1b** (*as modifier*): *a timber cottage*. **2a** trees collectively. **2b** *Chiefly U.S*. woodland. **3** a piece of wood used in a structure. **4** *Nautical*. a frame in a wooden vessel. **5** potential material, for a post, rank, etc.: *he is managerial timber*. ◆ *vb* **6** (*tr*) to provide with timbers. ◆ *interj* **7** a lumberjack's shouted warning when a tree is about to fall. [Old English; related to Old High German *zimbar* wood, Old Norse *timbr* timber, Latin *domus* house]

timbered ('tɪmbəd) *adj* **1** made of or containing timber or timbers. **2** covered with trees; wooded.

timberhead ('tɪmbə,hɛd) *n Nautical*. a timber, the top of which rises above deck level and is used as a bollard.

timber hitch *n* a knot used for tying a rope round a spar, log, etc., for haulage.

timbering ('tɪmbərɪŋ) *n* **1** timbers collectively. **2** work made of timber.

timberland ('tɪmbə,lænd) *n U.S. and Canadian*. land covered with trees grown for their timber.

timber line *n* the altitudinal or latitudinal limit of normal tree growth. See also **tree line**.

timberman ('tɪmbəmən) *n, pl* **-men**. any of various longicorn beetles that have destructive wood-eating larvae. Also called: **timberman beetle**.

timber wolf *n* a variety of the wolf, *Canis lupus,* having a grey brindled coat and occurring in forested northern regions, esp. of North America. Also called: **grey wolf**.

timberwork ('tɪmbə,wɜ:k) *n* a structure made of timber.

timberyard ('tɪmbə,jɑ:d) *n Brit*. an establishment where timber and sometimes other building materials are stored or sold. U.S. and Canadian word: **lumberyard**.

timbre ('tɪmbə, 'tæmbə; *French* tɛ̃brə) *n* **1** *Phonetics*. the distinctive tone quality differentiating one vowel or sonant from another. **2** *Music*. tone colour or quality of sound, esp. a specific type of tone colour. [C19: from French: note of a bell, from Old French: drum, from Medieval Greek *timbanon,* from Greek *tumpanon* drum]

timbrel ('tɪmbrəl) *n Chiefly biblical*. another word for **tambourine**. [C16: from Old French; see TIMBRE]

Timbuktu (,tɪmbʌk'tu:) *n* **1** a town in central Mali, on the River Niger: terminus of a trans-Saharan caravan route; a great Muslim centre (14th–16th centuries). Pop.: 31 925 (1987). French name: **Tombouctou**. **2** any distant or outlandish place: *from here to Timbuktu*.

time (taɪm) *n* **1a** the continuous passage of existence in which events pass from a state of potentiality in the future, through the present, to a state of finality in the past. **1b** (*as modifier*): *time travel.* Related adj: **temporal. 2** *Physics.* a quantity measuring duration, usually with reference to a periodic process such as the rotation of the earth or the vibration of electromagnetic radiation emitted from certain atoms (see **caesium clock, second**[2] (sense 1)). In classical mechanics, time is absolute in the sense that the time of an event is independent of the observer. According to the theory of relativity it depends on the observer's frame of reference. Time is considered as a fourth coordinate required, along with three spatial coordinates, to specify an event. See **space-time continuum. 3** a specific point on this continuum expressed in terms of hours and minutes: *the time is four o'clock.* **4** a system of reckoning for expressing time: *Greenwich mean time.* **5a** a definite and measurable portion of this continuum. **5b** (*as modifier*): *time limit.* **6a** an accepted period such as a day, season, etc. **6b** (*in combination*): *springtime.* **7** an unspecified interval; a while: *I was there for a time.* **8** (*often pl*) a period or point marked by specific attributes or events: *the Victorian times; time for breakfast.* **9** a sufficient interval or period: *have you got time to help me?* **10** an instance or occasion: *I called you three times.* **11** an occasion or period of specified quality: *have a good time; a miserable time.* **12** the duration of human existence. **13** the heyday of human life: *in her time she was a great star.* **14** a suitable period or moment: *it's time I told you.* **15** the expected interval in which something is done: *the flying time from New York to London was seven hours.* **16** a particularly important moment, esp. childbirth or death: *her time had come.* **17** (*pl*) indicating a degree or amount calculated by multiplication with the number specified: *ten times three is thirty; he earns four times as much as me.* **18** (*often pl*) the fashions, thought, etc., of the present age (esp. in the phrases **ahead of one's time, behind the times**). **19** *Brit.* (in bars, pubs, etc.) short for **closing time. 20** *Informal.* a term in jail (esp. in the phrase **do time**). **21a** a customary or full period of work. **21b** the rate of pay for this period. **22** Also (esp. U.S.): **metre. 22a** the system of combining beats or pulses in music into successive groupings by which the rhythm of the music is established. **22b** a specific system having a specific number of beats in each grouping or bar: *duple time.* **23** *Music.* short for **time value. 24** *Prosody.* a unit of duration used in the measurement of poetic metre; mora. **25 against time.** in an effort to complete something in a limited period. **26 ahead of time.** before the deadline. **27 all in good time.** in due course. **28 all the time.** continuously. **29 at one time. 29a** once; formerly. **29b** simultaneously. **30 at the same time. 30a** simultaneously. **30b** nevertheless; however. **31 at times.** sometimes. **32 beat time.** (of a conductor, etc.) to indicate the tempo or pulse of a piece of music by waving a baton or a hand, tapping out the beats, etc. **33 before one's time.** prematurely. **34 for the time being.** for the moment; temporarily. **35 from time to time.** at intervals; occasionally. **36 gain time.** See **gain**[1] (sense 9). **37 have no time for.** to have no patience with; not tolerate. **38 in good time. 38a** early. **38b** quickly. **39 in no time.** very quickly; almost instantaneously. **40 in one's own time. 40a** outside paid working hours. **40b** at one's own rate. **41 in time. 41a** early or at the appointed time. **41b** eventually. **41c** *Music.* at a correct metrical or rhythmic pulse. **42 keep time.** to observe correctly the accent or rhythmic pulse of a piece of music in relation to tempo. **43 lose time.** (of a timepiece) to operate too slowly. **44 lose no time.** to do something without delay. **45 make time. 45a** to find an opportunity. **45b** (often foll. by *with*) *U.S. informal.* to succeed in seducing. **46 mark time.** See **mark** (sense 35). **47 in the nick of time.** at the last possible moment; at the critical moment. **48 on time. 48a** at the expected or scheduled time. **48b** *U.S.* payable in instalments. **49 pass the time of day.** to exchange casual greetings (with an acquaintance). **50 time about.** *Scot.* alternately; turn and turn about. **51 time and again.** frequently. **52 time off.** a period when one is absent from work for a holiday, through sickness, etc. **53 time on.** the Austral. equivalent of **extra time. 54 time out of mind.** from time immemorial. **55 time of one's life.** a memorably enjoyable time. **56** (*modifier*) operating automatically at or for a set time, for security or convenience: *time lock; time switch.* ◆ *vb* (*tr*) **57** to ascertain or calculate the duration or speed of. **58** to set a time for. **59** to adjust to keep accurate time. **60** to pick a suitable time for. **61** *Sport.* to control the execution or speed of (an action, esp. a shot or stroke) so that it has its full effect at the right moment. ◆ *interj* **62** the word called out by a publican signalling that it is closing time. [Old English *tīma;* related to Old English *tīd* time, Old Norse *tīmi,* Alemannic *zīme;* see TIDE[1]]

time and a half *n* the rate of pay equalling one and a half times the normal rate, often offered for overtime work.

time and motion study *n* the analysis of industrial or work procedures to determine the most efficient methods of operation. Also: **time and motion, time study, motion study.**

time bomb *n* a bomb containing a timing mechanism that determines the time at which it will detonate.

time capsule *n* a container holding articles, documents, etc., representative of the current age, buried in the earth or in the foundations of a new building for discovery in the future.

timecard (ˈtaɪm,kɑːd) *n* a card used with a time clock.

time charter *n* the hire of a ship or aircraft for a specified period. Compare **voyage charter.**

time clock *n* a clock which records, by punching or stamping cards inserted into it, the time of arrival or departure of people, such as employees in a factory.

time code *n* (on video or audio tape) a separate track on which time references are continually recorded in digital form as an aid to editing.

time constant *n Electronics.* the time required for the current or voltage in a circuit to rise or fall exponentially through approximately 63 per cent of its amplitude.

time-consuming *adj* taking up or involving a great deal of time.

time deposit *n* a bank deposit from which withdrawals may be made only after advance notice or at a specified future date. Compare **demand deposit.**

time dilation *or* **dilatation** *n* the principle predicted by relativity that time intervals between events in a system have larger values measured by an observer moving with respect to the system than those measured by an observer at rest with respect to it.

time-division multiplex *n* See **multiplex** (sense 1).

time exposure *n* **1** an exposure of a photographic film for a relatively long period, usually a few seconds. **2** a photograph produced by such an exposure.

time-honoured *adj* having been observed for a long time and sanctioned by custom.

time immemorial *n* **1** the distant past beyond memory or record. **2** *Law.* time beyond legal memory, fixed by English statute as before the reign of Richard I (1189).

timekeeper (ˈtaɪm,kiːpə) *n* **1** a person or thing that keeps or records time. **2** an employee who maintains a record of the hours worked by the other employees. **3** a device for indicating time; timepiece. **4** an employee with respect to his record of punctuality: *a good timekeeper.* ▸ ˈ**time,keeping** *n*

time-lag *n* an interval between two connected events.

time-lapse photography *n* the technique of recording a very slow process, such as the withering of a flower, by taking a large number of photographs on a strip of film at regular intervals. The film is then projected at normal speed.

timeless (ˈtaɪmlɪs) *adj* **1** unaffected or unchanged by time; ageless. **2** eternal. **3** an archaic word for **untimely.** ▸ ˈ**timelessly** *adv* ▸ ˈ**timelessness** *n*

time loan *n* a loan repayable before or at a specified future date. Compare **call loan.**

timely (ˈtaɪmlɪ) *adj* **-lier, -liest,** *adv* **1** at the right or an opportune or appropriate time. **2** an archaic word for **early.** ▸ ˈ**timeliness** *n*

time machine *n* (in science fiction) a machine in which people or objects can be transported into the past or the future.

timeous (ˈtaɪməs) *adj Scot.* in good time; sufficiently early: *a timeous warning.* [C15: Scottish; see TIME, -OUS] ▸ ˈ**timeously** *adv*

time-out *n* **1** *Sport.* an interruption in play during which players rest, discuss tactics, or make substitutions. **2** a break taken during working hours. **3** *Computing.* a condition occurring when the amount of time a computer has been instructed to wait for another device to perform a task has expired, usually indicated by an error message. ◆ *vb* (*intr*) **time out. 4** (of a computer) to stop operating because of a time-out.

timepiece (ˈtaɪm,piːs) *n* **1** any of various devices, such as a clock, watch, or chronometer, which measure and indicate time. **2** a device which indicates the time but does not strike or otherwise audibly mark the hours.

timer (ˈtaɪmə) *n* **1** a device for measuring, recording, or indicating time. **2** a switch or regulator that causes a mechanism to operate at a specific time or at predetermined intervals. **3** a person or thing that times.

time-saving (ˈtaɪm,seɪvɪŋ) *adj* shortening the length of time required for an operation, activity, etc. ▸ ˈ**time-,saver** *n*

timescale (ˈtaɪm,skeɪl) *n* the span of time within which certain events occur or are scheduled to occur considered in relation to any broader period of time.

time series *n Statistics.* a series of values of a variable taken in successive periods of time.

time-served *adj* (of a craftsman or tradesman) having completed an apprenticeship; fully trained and competent: *a time-served mechanic.*

timeserver (ˈtaɪm,sɜːvə) *n* a person who compromises and changes his opinions, way of life, etc., to suit the current fashions. ▸ ˈ**time,serving** *adj, n*

time-share *adj* denoting, relating to, or forming part of time sharing of property: *time-share villas.*

time sharing *n* **1a** a system of part ownership of a property, such as a flat or villa, for use as a holiday home, whereby each participant buys the right to use the property for the same fixed period annually. **1b** (*as modifier*): *a time-sharing system.* **2a** a system by which users at different terminals of a computer can, because of its high speed, apparently communicate with it at the same time. Compare **batch processing. 2b** (*as modifier*): *a time-sharing computer.*

time sheet *n* a card on which are recorded the hours spent working by an employee or employees.

time signal *n* an announcement of the correct time, esp. on radio or television.

time signature *n Music.* a sign usually consisting of two figures, one above the other, the upper figure representing the number of beats per bar and the lower one the time value of each beat. This sign is placed after the key signature at the outset of a piece or section of a piece.

Times Square *n* a square formed by the intersection of Broadway and Seventh Avenue in New York City, extending from 42nd to 45th Street.

time study *n* short for **time and motion study.**

time switch *n* an electric switch that can be set to operate an appliance, such as a light or an oven, at a particular time.

timetable (ˈtaɪm,teɪbᵊl) *n* **1** a list or table of events arranged according to the time when they take place; schedule. ◆ *vb* **2** (*tr*) to include in or arrange according to a timetable. **3** (*intr*) to draw up a timetable.

time trial *n* (esp. in cycling) a race in which the competitors compete against the clock over a specified course. ▸ ˈ**time-,trialling** *n*

time value *n Music.* the duration of a given printed note relative to other notes in a composition or section and considered in relation to the basic tempo. Often shortened to **time.** Also called: **note value, time.**

time warp *n* **1** any distortion of space-time. **2** a hypothetical distortion of time in which people and events from one age can be imagined to exist in another age. **3** *Informal.* an illusion in which time appears to stand still: *he is living in a time warp.*

timework (ˈtaɪm,wɜːk) *n* work paid for by the length of time taken, esp. by the hour or the day. Compare **piecework.** ▸ ˈ**time,worker** *n*

timeworn ('taɪm,wɔːn) *adj* **1** showing the adverse effects of overlong use or of old age. **2** hackneyed; trite.

time zone *n* a region throughout which the same standard time is used. There are 24 time zones in the world, demarcated approximately by meridians at 15° intervals, an hour apart. See also **zonetime.**

timid ('tɪmɪd) *adj* **1** easily frightened or upset, esp. by human contact; shy. **2** indicating shyness or fear. [C16: from Latin *timidus,* from *timēre* to fear] ▸ **ti'midity** *or* **'timidness** *n* ▸ **'timidly** *adv*

timing ('taɪmɪŋ) *n* the process or art of regulating actions or remarks in relation to others to produce the best effect, as in music, the theatre, sport, etc.

timing gear *n* (in an internal-combustion engine) the drive between the crankshaft and the camshaft, usually giving a ratio of 2 : 1.

Timişoara (*Romanian* timi'ʃwara) *n* a city in W Romania: formerly under Turkish and then Hapsburg rule, being allotted to Romania in 1920; scene of violence during the revolution of 1989. Pop.: 327 830 (1994 est.). Hungarian name: **Temesvár.**

timocracy (taɪ'mɒkrəsɪ) *n, pl* **-cies. 1** a political unit or system in which possession of property serves as the first requirement for participation in government. **2** a political unit or system in which love of honour is deemed the guiding principle of government. [C16: from Old French *tymocracie,* ultimately from Greek *timokratia,* from *timē* worth, honour, price + -CRACY] ▸ **timocratic** (,taɪmə'krætɪk) *or* **,timo'cratical** *adj*

Timor ('tiːmɔː, 'taɪ-) *n* an island in Indonesia in the Malay Archipelago, the largest and easternmost of the Lesser Sunda Islands: the east, together with an enclave on the NW coast, was held by Portugal until 1975, when it declared independence but was immediately invaded by Indonesia. In 1999 a referendum showed majority support for the independence movement, but anti-independence militias attacked, killing many Timorese and a UN peacekeeping force was sent in. Area: 30 775 sq. km (11 883 sq. miles).

timorous ('tɪmərəs) *adj* **1** fearful or timid. **2** indicating fear or timidity. [C15: from Old French *temoros,* from Medieval Latin *timōrōsus,* from Latin *timor* fear, from *timēre* to be afraid] ▸ **'timorously** *adv* ▸ **'timorousness** *n*

Timor Sea *n* an arm of the Indian Ocean between Australia and Timor. Width: about 480 km (300 miles).

Timoshenko (,tɪmə'ʃɛŋkəʊ; *Russian* tima'ʃɛnkə) *n* **Semyon Konstantinovich** (sɪ'mjɔn kənstan'tinəvitʃ). 1895–1970, Soviet general in World War II.

Timothy ('tɪməθɪ) *n New Testament.* **1 Saint.** a disciple of Paul, who became leader of the Christian community at Ephesus. Feast day: Jan. 26 or 22. **2** either of the two books addressed to him (in full **The First and Second Epistles of Paul the Apostle to Timothy**), containing advice on pastoral matters.

timothy grass *or* **timothy** ('tɪməθɪ) *n* a perennial grass, *Phleum pratense,* of temperate regions, having erect stiff stems and cylindrical flower spikes: grown for hay and pasture. [C18: apparently named after a *Timothy Hanson,* who brought it to colonial Carolina]

timpani *or* **tympani** ('tɪmpənɪ) *pl n* (*sometimes functioning as sing*) a set of kettledrums, two or more in number. Often shortened to **timps** (informal). [from Italian, pl of *timpano* kettledrum, from Latin: TYMPANUM] ▸ **'timpanist** *or* **'tympanist** *n*

Timur *or* **Timour** (tiː'mʊə) *n* See **Tamerlane.**

tin (tɪn) *n* **1** a metallic element, occurring in cassiterite, that has several allotropes; the ordinary malleable silvery-white metal slowly changes below 13.2°C to a grey powder. It is used extensively in alloys, esp. bronze and pewter, and as a noncorroding coating for steel. Symbol: Sn; atomic no.: 50; atomic wt.: 118.710; valency: 2 or 4; relative density: 5.75 (grey), 7.31 (white); melting pt.: 231.9°C; boiling pt.: 2603°C. Related adjs: **stannic, stannous. 2** Also called (esp. U.S. and Canadian): **can.** an airtight sealed container of thin sheet metal coated with tin, used for preserving and storing food or drink. **3** any container made of metallic tin. **4 fill her tins.** *N.Z.* to complete a home baking of cakes, biscuits, etc. **5** Also called: **tinful.** the contents of a tin or the amount a tin will hold. **6** *Brit., Austral., and N.Z.* corrugated or galvanized iron: *a tin roof.* **7** any metal regarded as cheap or flimsy. **8** *Brit.* a loaf of bread with a rectangular shape, baked in a tin. **9** *Slang.* money. ♦ *vb* **tins, tinning, tinned.** (*tr*) **10** to put (food, etc.) into a tin or tins; preserve in a tin. **11** to plate or coat with tin. **12** to prepare (a metal) for soldering or brazing by applying a thin layer of solder to the surface. [Old English; related to Old Norse *tin,* Old High German *zin*] ▸ **'tin,like** *adj*

tinamou ('tɪnə,muː) *n* any bird of the order *Tinamiformes* of Central and South America, having small wings, a heavy body, and an inconspicuous plumage. [C18: via French from Carib (Galibi) *tinamu*]

Tinbergen ('tɪn,bɜːgən) *n* **1 Jan** (jæn). 1903–94, Dutch economist, noted for his work on econometrics. He shared (1969) the first Nobel prize for economics with Ragnar Frisch. **2** his brother, **Nikolaas** ('nɪkələs). 1907–88, British zoologist, born in the Netherlands; studied animal behaviour, esp. instincts, and was one of the founders of ethology; Nobel prize for physiology or medicine 1973.

tincal ('tɪŋkᵊl) *n* another name for **borax** (sense 1). [C17: from Malay *tingkal,* from Sanskrit *tankana*]

tin can *n* a metal food container, esp. when empty.

tinct (tɪŋkt) *n, vb* **1** an obsolete word for **tint.** ♦ *adj* **2** *Poetic.* tinted or coloured. [C15: from Latin *tinctus,* from *tingere* to colour]

tinct. *abbrev. for* tincture.

tinctorial (tɪŋk'tɔːrɪəl) *adj* **1** of or relating to colouring, staining, or dyeing. **2** imbuing with colour. [C17: from Latin *tinctōrius,* from *tingere* to tinge] ▸ **tinc'torially** *adv*

tincture ('tɪŋktʃə) *n* **1** *Pharmacol.* a medicinal extract in a solution of alcohol. **2** a tint, colour, or tinge. **3** a slight flavour, aroma, or trace. **4** any one of the colours or either of the metals used on heraldic arms. **5** *Obsolete.* a dye or pigment. ♦ *vb* **6** (*tr*) to give a tint or colour to. [C14: from Latin *tinctūra* a dyeing, from *tingere* to dye]

Tindal *or* **Tindale** ('tɪndᵊl) *n* variant spellings of (William) **Tyndale.**

tinder ('tɪndə) *n* **1** dry wood or other easily combustible material used for lighting a fire. **2** anything inflammatory or dangerous: *his speech was tinder to the demonstrators' unrest.* [Old English *tynder;* related to Old Norse *tundr,* Old High German *zuntara*] ▸ **'tindery** *adj*

tinderbox ('tɪndə,bɒks) *n* **1** a box used formerly for holding tinder, esp. one fitted with a flint and steel. **2** a person or thing that is particularly touchy or explosive.

tine (taɪn) *n* **1** a slender prong, esp. of a fork. **2** any of the sharp terminal branches of a deer's antler. [Old English *tind;* related to Old Norse *tindr,* Old High German *zint*] ▸ **tined** *adj*

tinea ('tɪnɪə) *n* any fungal skin disease, esp. ringworm. [C17: from Latin: worm] ▸ **'tineal** *adj*

tineid ('tɪnɪɪd) *n* **1** any moth of the family *Tineidae,* which includes the clothes moths. ♦ *adj* **2** of, relating to, or belonging to the family *Tineidae.* [C19: from New Latin *Tineidae,* from Latin: TINEA]

tinfoil ('tɪn,fɔɪl) *n* **1** thin foil made of tin or an alloy of tin and lead. **2** thin foil made of aluminium; used for wrapping foodstuffs.

ting[1] (tɪŋ) *n* **1** a high metallic sound such as that made by a small bell. ♦ *vb* **2** to make or cause to make such a sound. [C15: of imitative origin]

ting[2] (tɪŋ) *n* (*often cap.*) a variant spelling of **thing**[2].

Ting (tɪŋ) *n* **Samuel Chao Chung.** U.S. physicist, who discovered the J/psi particle independently of Burton Richter, with whom he shared (1976) the Nobel prize for physics.

ting-a-ling ('tɪŋə'lɪŋ) *n* the sound of a small bell.

tinge (tɪndʒ) *n* **1** a slight tint or colouring: *her hair had a tinge of grey.* **2** any slight addition. ♦ *vb* **tinges, tingeing** *or* **tinging, tinged.** (*tr*) **3** to colour or tint faintly. **4** to impart a slight trace to: *her thoughts were tinged with nostalgia.* [C15: from Latin *tingere* to colour]

tingle ('tɪŋgᵊl) *vb* **1** (*usually intr*) to feel or cause to feel a prickling, itching, or stinging sensation of the flesh, as from a cold plunge or electric shock. ♦ *n* **2** a sensation of tingling. [C14: perhaps a variant of TINKLE] ▸ **'tingler** *n* ▸ **'tingling** *adj* ▸ **'tinglingly** *adv* ▸ **'tingly** *adj*

tin god *n* **1** a self-important dictatorial person. **2** a person erroneously regarded as holy or venerable.

tin hat *n Informal.* a steel helmet worn by military personnel for protection against small metal fragments.

tinhorn ('tɪn,hɔːn) *U.S. slang.* ♦ *n* **1** a cheap pretentious person, esp. a gambler with extravagant claims. ♦ *adj* **2** cheap and showy.

tinker ('tɪŋkə) *n* **1** (esp. formerly) a travelling mender of pots and pans. **2** a clumsy worker. **3** the act of tinkering. **4** *Scot. and Irish.* another name for a **Gypsy. 5** *Brit. informal.* a mischievous child. **6** any of several small mackerels that occur off the North American coast of the Atlantic. ♦ *vb* **7** (*intr; foll. by with*) to play, fiddle, or meddle (with machinery, etc.), esp. while undertaking repairs. **8** to mend (pots and pans) as a tinker. [C13 *tinkere,* perhaps from *tink* tinkle, of imitative origin] ▸ **'tinkerer** *n*

tinker's damn *or* **cuss** *n Slang.* the slightest heed (esp. in the phrase **not give a tinker's damn** *or* **cuss**).

tinkle ('tɪŋkᵊl) *vb* **1** to ring or cause to ring with a series of high tinny sounds, like a small bell. **2** (*tr*) to announce or summon by such a ringing. **3** (*intr*) *Brit. informal.* to urinate. ♦ *n* **4** a high clear ringing sound. **5** the act of tinkling. **6** *Brit. informal.* a telephone call. [C14: of imitative origin] ▸ **'tinkling** *adj, n* ▸ **'tinkly** *adj*

tin lizzie ('lɪzɪ) *n Informal.* an old or decrepit car; jalopy. [originally a nickname for the Model T Ford]

tinned (tɪnd) *adj* **1** plated, coated, or treated with tin. **2** *Chiefly Brit.* preserved or stored in airtight tins: *tinned soup.* **3** coated with a layer of solder.

tinner ('tɪnə) *n* **1** a tin miner. **2** a worker in tin; tinsmith. **3** a person or organization that puts food, etc., into tins; canner.

tinnitus (tɪ'naɪtəs) *n Pathol.* a ringing, hissing, or booming sensation in one or both ears, caused by infection of the middle or inner ear, a side effect of certain drugs, etc. [C19: from Latin, from *tinnīre* to ring]

tinny ('tɪnɪ) *adj* **-nier, -niest. 1** of, relating to, or resembling tin. **2** cheap, badly made, or shoddy. **3** (of a sound) high, thin, and metallic. **4** (of food or drink) flavoured with metal, as from a container. **5** *Austral. informal.* lucky. ♦ *n, pl* **-nies. 6** *Austral. slang.* a can of beer. **7** *Austral. informal.* Also: **tinnie.** a small fishing or pleasure boat with an aluminium hull. ▸ **'tinnily** *adv* ▸ **'tinniness** *n*

tin-opener *n* a small tool for opening tins.

Tin Pan Alley *n* **1** a district in a city concerned with the production of popular music, originally a small district in New York. **2** *Derogatory.* the strictly commercial side of show business and pop music.

tin plate *n* **1** thin steel sheet coated with a layer of tin that protects the steel from corrosion. ♦ *vb* **tin-plate. 2** (*tr*) to coat (a metal or object) with a layer of tin, usually either by electroplating or by dipping in a bath of molten tin. ▸ **'tin-,plater** *n*

tinpot ('tɪn,pɒt) *adj* (*prenominal*) *Brit. informal.* **1** inferior, cheap, or worthless. **2** paltry; unimportant.

tinsel ('tɪnsəl) *n* **1** a decoration consisting of a piece of string with thin strips of metal foil attached along its length. **2** a yarn or fabric interwoven with strands of glittering thread. **3** anything cheap, showy, and gaudy. ♦ *vb* **-sels, -selling, -selled** *or U.S.* **-sels, -seling, -seled.** (*tr*) **4** to decorate with or as if with tinsel: *snow tinsels the trees.* **5** to give a gaudy appearance to. ♦ *adj* **6** made of or decorated with tinsel. **7** showily but cheaply attractive; gaudy. [C16: from Old French *estincele* a spark, from Latin *scintilla;* compare STENCIL] ▸ **'tinsel-,like** *adj* ▸ **'tinselly** *adj*

Tinseltown ('tɪnsəl,taʊn) *n* an informal name for **Hollywood.** [C20: from the insubstantial glitter of the film world]

tinsmith ('tɪnˌsmɪθ) *n* a person who works with tin or tin plate.

tin soldier *n* **1** a miniature toy soldier, usually made of lead. **2** a person who enjoys playing at being a soldier.

tinstone ('tɪnˌstəʊn) *n* another name for **cassiterite.**

tint (tɪnt) *n* **1** a shade of a colour, esp. a pale one. **2** a colour that is softened or desaturated by the addition of white. **3** a tinge. **4** a semipermanent dye for the hair. **5** a trace or hint: *a tint of jealousy in his voice.* **6** *Engraving.* uniform shading, produced esp. by hatching. **7** *Printing.* a panel of colour serving as a background to letters or other matter. ♦ *vb* **8** (*tr*) to colour or tinge. **9** (*tr*) to change or influence slightly: *his answer was tinted by his prior knowledge.* **10** (*intr*) to acquire a tint. [C18: from earlier TINCT] ▸ **'tinter** *n*

Tintagel Head (tɪn'tædʒəl) *n* a promontory in SW England, on the W coast of Cornwall: ruins of **Tintagel Castle,** legendary birthplace of King Arthur.

tintinnabulation (ˌtɪntɪˌnæbjʊ'leɪʃən) *n* the act or an instance of the ringing or pealing of bells. ▸ ˌ**tintin'nabular,** ˌ**tintin'nabulary,** *or* ˌ**tintin'nabulous** *adj*

tintinnabulum (ˌtɪntɪ'næbjʊləm) *n, pl* **-la** (-lə). a small high-pitched bell. [C16: from Latin, from *tintinnāre* to tinkle, from *tinnīre* to ring; see TINNITUS]

tintometer (tɪn'tɒmɪtə) *n* another name for **colorimeter** (sense 1).

Tintoretto (ˌtɪntə'rɛtəʊ; *Italian* tinto'retto) *n* **Il** (il). original name *Jacopo Robusti.* 1518–94, Italian painter of the Venetian school. His works include *Susanna bathing* (?1550) and the fresco cycle in the Scuola di San Rocco, Venice (from 1564).

tint tool *n* a kind of burin used in wood engraving for carving lines of even thickness, as in hatching.

tintype ('tɪnˌtaɪp) *n* another name for **ferrotype** (senses 1, 2).

tinware ('tɪnˌwɛə) *n* objects made of tin plate.

tin whistle *n* another name for **penny whistle.**

tinwork ('tɪnˌwɜːk) *n* objects made of tin.

tinworks ('tɪnˌwɜːks) *n* (*functioning as sing or pl*) a place where tin is mined, smelted, or rolled.

tiny ('taɪnɪ) *adj* **tinier, tiniest.** very small; minute. [C16 *tine,* of uncertain origin] ▸ **'tinily** *adv* ▸ **'tininess** *n*

-tion *suffix forming nouns.* indicating state, condition, action, process, or result: *election; prohibition.* Compare **-ation, -ion.** [from Old French, from Latin *-tiō, -tiōn-*]

tip[1] (tɪp) *n* **1** the extreme end of something, esp. a narrow or pointed end. **2** the top or summit. **3** a small piece forming an extremity or end: *a metal tip on a cane.* ♦ *vb* **tips, tipping, tipped.** (*tr*) **4** to adorn or mark the tip of. **5** to cause to form a tip. [C15: from Old Norse *typpa;* related to Middle Low German, Middle Dutch *tip*] ▸ **'tipless** *adj*

tip[2] (tɪp) *vb* **tips, tipping, tipped. 1** to tilt or cause to tilt. **2** (usually foll. by *over* or *up*) to tilt or cause to tilt, so as to overturn or fall. **3** *Brit.* to dump (rubbish, etc.). **4 tip one's hat.** to take off, raise, or touch one's hat in salutation. ♦ *n* **5** the act of tipping or the state of being tipped. **6** *Brit.* a dump for refuse, etc. [C14: of uncertain origin; related to TOP[1], TOPPLE] ▸ **'tippable** *adj*

tip[3] (tɪp) *n* **1** a payment given for services in excess of the standard charge; gratuity. **2** a helpful hint, warning, or other piece of information. **3** a piece of inside information, esp. in betting or investing. ♦ *vb* **tips, tipping, tipped. 4** to give a tip to (a person). [C18: perhaps from TIP[4]]

tip[4] (tɪp) *vb* **tips, tipping, tipped.** (*tr*) **1** to hit or strike lightly. **2** to hit (a ball) indirectly so that it glances off the bat in cricket. ♦ *n* **3** a light blow. **4** a glancing hit in cricket. [C13: perhaps from Low German *tippen*]

tip and run *n* **1** a form of cricket in which the batsman must run if his bat touches the ball. ♦ *adj* **tip-and-run. 2** (*prenominal*) characterized by a rapid departure immediately after striking: *a tip-and-run raid.*

tipcat ('tɪpˌkæt) *n* a game in which a short sharp-ended piece of wood (the cat) is tipped in the air with a stick.

tipi ('tiːpɪ) *n, pl* **-pis.** a variant spelling of **tepee.**

tip-off *n* **1** a warning or hint, esp. given confidentially and based on inside information. **2** *Basketball.* the act or an instance of putting the ball in play by a jump ball. ♦ *vb* **tip off. 3** (*tr, adv*) to give a hint or warning to.

tipper ('tɪpə) *n* **1** a person who gives or leaves a tip: *he is a generous tipper.* **2** short for **tipper truck.**

Tipperary (ˌtɪpə'rɛərɪ) *n* a county of S Republic of Ireland, in Munster province; divided into the North Riding and South Riding: mountainous. County town: Clonmel. Pop.: 133 000 (1996). Area: 4255 sq. km (1643 sq. miles).

tipper truck *or* **lorry** *n* a truck or lorry the rear platform of which can be raised at the front end to enable the load to be discharged by gravity. Also called: **tip truck.**

tippet ('tɪpɪt) *n* **1** a woman's fur cape for the shoulders, often consisting of the whole fur of a fox, marten, etc. **2** the long stole of Anglican clergy worn during a service. **3** a long streamer-like part to a sleeve, hood, etc., esp. in the 16th century. **4** the ruff of a bird. **5** a tippet feather or something similar used in dressing some artificial angling flies. [C14: perhaps from TIP[1]]

Tippett ('tɪpɪt) *n* Sir **Michael.** 1905–98, English composer, whose works include the oratorio *A Child of Our Time* (1941) and the operas *The Midsummer Marriage* (1952), *King Priam* (1961), *The Knot Garden* (1970), *The Ice Break* (1976), and *New Year* (1989).

tipple[1] ('tɪpᵊl) *vb* **1** to make a habit of taking (alcoholic drink), esp. in small quantities. ♦ *n* **2** alcoholic drink. [C15: back formation from obsolete *tippler* tapster, of unknown origin] ▸ **'tippler** *n*

tipple[2] ('tɪpᵊl) *n* **1** a device for overturning ore trucks, mine cars, etc., so that they discharge their load. **2** a place at which such trucks are tipped and unloaded. ♦ *vb* **3** *Northern English dialect.* to fall or cause to fall. [C19: from *tipple* to overturn, from TIP[2]]

tippler ('tɪplə) *n* (*sometimes cap.*) **1** a variety of domestic pigeon bred mainly for flying. Also called: **high-flying tippler. 2** a domestic fancy pigeon of a smaller rounder type kept mainly for exhibition. Usual name: **show tippler.** [C19: from TIPPLE[2] + -ER[1]]

tipstaff ('tɪpˌstɑːf) *n* **1** a court official having miscellaneous duties, mostly concerned with the maintenance of order in court. **2** a metal-tipped staff formerly used as a symbol of office. [C16 *tipped staff;* see TIP[1], STAFF[1]]

tipster ('tɪpstə) *n* a person who sells tips on horse racing, the stock market, etc.

tipsy ('tɪpsɪ) *adj* **-sier, -siest. 1** slightly drunk. **2** slightly tilted or tipped; askew. [C16: from TIP[2]] ▸ **'tipsily** *adv* ▸ **'tipsiness** *n*

tipsy cake *n Brit.* a kind of trifle made from a sponge cake soaked with white wine or sherry and decorated with almonds and crystallized fruit.

tip-tilted *adj* (of a nose) slightly turned up.

tiptoe ('tɪpˌtəʊ) *vb* **-toes, -toeing, -toed.** (*intr*) **1** to walk with the heels off the ground and the weight supported by the ball of the foot and the toes. **2** to walk silently or stealthily. ♦ *n* **3 on tiptoe. 3a** on the tips of the toes or on the ball of the foot and the toes. **3b** eagerly anticipating something. **3c** stealthily or silently. ♦ *adv* **4** on tiptoe. ♦ *adj* **5** walking or standing on tiptoe. **6** stealthy or silent.

tiptop (ˌtɪp'tɒp) *adj, adv* **1** at the highest point of health, excellence, etc. **2** at the topmost point. ♦ *n* **3** the best in quality. **4** the topmost point.

tip truck *n* another name for **tipper truck.**

tip-up *adj* (*prenominal*) able to be turned upwards around a hinge or pivot: *a tip-up seat.*

Tipu Sahib *or* **Tippoo Sahib** ('tɪpuː 'sɑːɪb) *n* ?1750–99, sultan of Mysore (1782–99): killed fighting the British.

TIR (on continental lorries) *abbrev. for* Transports Internationaux Routiers. [French: International Road Transport]

tirade (taɪ'reɪd) *n* **1** a long angry speech or denunciation. **2** *Prosody, rare.* a speech or passage dealing with a single theme. [C19: from French, literally: a pulling, from Italian *tirata,* from *tirare* to pull, of uncertain origin]

tiramisu (ˌtiːrəmiː'suː) *n* an Italian dessert made with sponge soaked in coffee and Marsala, topped with soft cheese and powdered chocolate. [C20: from Italian *tira!* pull! + *mi* me + *su* up]

Tiran (tɪ'rɑːn) *n* **Strait of.** a strait between the Gulf of Aqaba and the Red Sea. Length: 16 km (10 miles). Width: 8 km (5 miles).

Tirana (tɪ'rɑːnə) *or* **Tiranë** (*Albanian* ti'ranə) *n* the capital of Albania, in the central part 32 km (20 miles) from the Adriatic: founded in the early 17th century by Turks; became capital in 1920; the country's largest city and industrial centre. Pop.: 270 000 (1995 est.).

tire[1] ('taɪə) *vb* **1** (*tr*) to reduce the energy of, esp. by exertion; weary. **2** (*tr; often passive*) to reduce the tolerance of; bore or irritate: *I'm tired of the children's chatter.* **3** (*intr*) to become wearied or bored; flag. [Old English *tēorian,* of unknown origin] ▸ **'tiring** *adj*

tire[2] ('taɪə) *n, vb* the U.S. spelling of **tyre.**

tire[3] ('taɪə) *vb, n* an archaic word for **attire.**

tired ('taɪəd) *adj* **1** weary; fatigued. **2** (foll. by *of*) **2a** having lost interest in; bored: *I'm tired of playing cards.* **2b** having lost patience with; exasperated by: *I'm tired of his eternal excuses.* **3** hackneyed; stale: *the same tired old jokes.* **4 tired and emotional.** a euphemism for slightly drunk. ▸ **'tiredly** *adv* ▸ **'tiredness** *n*

Tiree (taɪ'riː) *n* an island off the W coast of Scotland, in the Inner Hebrides. Pop.: 1054 (latest est.). Area: 78 sq. km (30 sq. miles).

tireless ('taɪəlɪs) *adj* unable to be tired; indefatigable. ▸ **'tirelessly** *adv* ▸ **'tirelessness** *n*

Tiresias (taɪ'riːsɪˌæs) *n Greek myth.* a blind soothsayer of Thebes, who revealed to Oedipus that the latter had murdered his father and married his mother.

tiresome ('taɪəsəm) *adj* boring and irritating; irksome. ▸ **'tiresomely** *adv* ▸ **'tiresomeness** *n*

tirewoman ('taɪəˌwʊmən) *n, pl* **-women.** an obsolete term for **lady's maid.** [C17: see TIRE[3]]

Tîrgu Mureş (*Romanian* 'tirgu 'mureʃ) *n* a city in central Romania: manufacturing and cultural centre. Pop.: 166 315 (1994 est.).

Tirich Mir ('tɪərɪtʃ 'mɪə) *n* a mountain in N Pakistan: highest peak of the Hindu Kush. Height: 7690 m (25 230 ft.).

tiring room *n Archaic.* a dressing room in a theatre.

tiro ('taɪrəʊ) *n, pl* **-ros.** a variant spelling of **tyro.**

Tirol (tɪ'rəʊl, 'tɪrəʊl; *German* ti'roːl) *n* a variant spelling of **Tyrol.** ▸ **Tirolese** (ˌtɪrə'liːz) *or* ˌ**Tiro'lean** *adj, n*

Tiros ('taɪrəʊs) *n* one of a series of U.S. weather satellites carrying infrared and television camera equipment for transmitting meteorological data to the earth. [C20: from *T(elevision and) I(nfra-)R(ed) O(bservation) S(atellite)*]

Tirpitz (*German* 'tɪrpɪts) *n* **Alfred von** ('alfreːt fɔn). 1849–1930, German admiral: as secretary of state for the Imperial Navy (1897–1916), he created the modern German navy, which challenged British supremacy at sea.

Tirso de Molina (*Spanish* 'tirso ðe mo'lina) *n* pen name of *Gabriel Téllez.* ?1571–1648, Spanish dramatist; author of the first dramatic treatment of the Don Juan legend *El Burlador de Sevilla* (1630).

Tiruchirapalli (ˌtɪrətʃɪrə'pʌlɪ, tɪˌruːtʃɪ'rɑːpəlɪ) *or* **Trichinopoly** *n* an industrial city in S India, in central Tamil Nadu on the Cauvery River: dominated by a rock fortress 83 m (273 ft.) high. Pop.: 387 223 (1991).

Tirunelveli (ˌtɪrʊ'nɛlvəlɪ) *n* a city in S India, in Tamil Nadu: site of St Francis Xavier's first preaching in India; textile manufacturing. Pop.: 135 825 (1991).

'tis (tɪz) *Poetic or dialect. contraction of* it is.

Tisa ('tisa) *n* the Slavonic and Romanian name for the **Tisza.**

tisane (tɪ'zæn) *n* an infusion of dried or fresh leaves or flowers, as camomile. [C19: from French, from Latin *ptisana* barley water; see PTISAN]

Tishah b'Av (ti'ʃa bə'av) *n Judaism.* the ninth day of the month of Av observed as a fast day in memory of the destruction of the First and Second Temples.

Tishri (tɪʃ'riː) *n* (in the Jewish calendar) the seventh month of the year according to biblical reckoning and the first month of the civil year, usually falling within September and October. [from Hebrew]

Tisiphone (tɪˈsɪfənɪ) *n Greek myth.* one of the three Furies; the others are Alecto and Megaera.

Tissot (ˈtɪsəʊ) *n* **James Joseph Jacques.** 1836–1902, French painter and etcher, best known for scenes of fashionable Victorian life painted in England.

tissue (ˈtɪsjuː, ˈtɪʃuː) *n* **1** a part of an organism consisting of a large number of cells having a similar structure and function: *connective tissue; nerve tissue.* **2** a thin piece of soft absorbent paper, usually of two or more layers, used as a disposable handkerchief, towel, etc. **3** See **tissue paper. 4** an interwoven series: *a tissue of lies.* **5** a woven cloth, esp. of a light gauzy nature, originally interwoven with threads of gold or silver. ♦ *vb (tr)* **6** *Rare.* to weave into tissue. **7** to decorate or clothe with tissue or tissue paper. [C14: from Old French *tissu* woven cloth, from *tistre* to weave, from Latin *texere*]

tissue culture *n* **1** the growth of small pieces of animal or plant tissue in a sterile controlled medium. **2** the tissue produced as a result of this process.

tissue paper *n* very thin soft delicate paper used to wrap breakable goods, as decoration, etc.

tissue type *n* the inherited chemical characteristics of the bodily tissue of an individual that are recognized and, when grafted, are accepted or rejected by the immune system of another individual. The tissue type is determined by the histocompatibility antigens.

Tisza (*Hungarian* ˈtiso) *n* a river in S central Europe, rising in the W Ukraine and flowing west, forming part of the border between the Ukraine and Romania, then southwest across Hungary into Yugoslavia to join the Danube north of Belgrade. Slavonic and Romanian name: **Tisa.**

tit[1] (tɪt) *n* **1** any of numerous small active Old World songbirds of the family *Paridae* (titmice), esp. those of the genus *Parus* (bluetit, great tit, etc.). They have a short bill and feed on insects and seeds. **2** any of various similar small birds. **3** *Archaic or dialect.* a worthless or worn-out horse; nag. [C16: perhaps of imitative origin, applied to small animate or inanimate objects; compare Icelandic *tittr* pin]

tit[2] (tɪt) *n* **1** *Slang.* a female breast. **2** a teat or nipple. **3** *Derogatory.* a girl or young woman. **4** *Taboo slang.* a despicable or unpleasant person: often used as a term of address. [Old English *titt;* related to Middle Low German *title,* Norwegian *titta*]

Tit. *Bible. abbrev. for* Titus.

titan (ˈtaɪtᵊn) *n* a person of great strength or size. [C17: from TITAN[1]]

Titan[1] (ˈtaɪtᵊn) *or (fem)* **Titaness** *n Greek myth.* **1** any of a family of primordial gods, the sons and daughters of Uranus (sky) and Gaea (earth). **2** any of the offspring of the children of Uranus and Gaea.

Titan[2] (ˈtaɪtᵊn) *n* the largest satellite of the planet Saturn, having a thick atmosphere consisting mainly of nitrogen. Diameter: 5150 km.

titanate (ˈtaɪtəˌneɪt) *n* any salt or ester of titanic acid.

Titanesque (ˌtaɪtəˈnɛsk) *adj* resembling a Titan; gigantic.

titania (taɪˈteɪnɪə) *n* another name for **titanium dioxide.**

Titania[1] (tɪˈtɑːnɪə) *n* **1** (in medieval folklore) the queen of the fairies and wife of Oberon. **2** (in classical antiquity) a poetic epithet used variously to characterize Circe, Diana, Latona, or Pyrrha.

Titania[2] (tɪˈtɑːnɪə) *n* the largest of the satellites of Uranus and the second furthest from the planet.

titanic[1] (taɪˈtænɪk) *adj* of or containing titanium, esp. in the tetravalent state.

titanic[2] (taɪˈtænɪk) *adj* possessing or requiring colossal strength: *a titanic battle.* ▸ **tiˈtanically** *adv*

Titanic (taɪˈtænɪk) *n* **the.** a luxury British liner that struck an iceberg near Newfoundland on its maiden voyage on the night of April 14–15, 1912, with the loss of 1513 lives.

titanic acid *n* any of various white substances regarded as hydrated forms of titanium dioxide, typical formulas being H_4TiO_4 and H_2TiO_3.

titanic oxide *n* another name for **titanium dioxide.**

titaniferous (ˌtaɪtəˈnɪfərəs) *adj* of or containing titanium; bearing titanium: *a titaniferous ore.*

Titanism (ˈtaɪtəˌnɪzəm) *n* a spirit of defiance of and rebellion against authority, social convention, etc.

titanite (ˈtaɪtəˌnaɪt) *n* another name for **sphene.** [C19: from German *Titanit,* so named because it contained TITANIUM]

titanium (taɪˈteɪnɪəm) *n* a strong malleable white metallic element, which is very corrosion-resistant and occurs in rutile and ilmenite. It is used in the manufacture of strong lightweight alloys, esp. aircraft parts. Symbol: Ti; atomic no.: 22; atomic wt.: 47.88; valency: 2, 3, or 4; relative density: 4.54; melting pt.: 1670±10°C; boiling pt.: 3289°C. [C18: New Latin; see TITAN, -IUM]

titanium dioxide *n* a white insoluble powder occurring naturally as rutile and used chiefly as a pigment of high covering power and durability. Formula: TiO_2. Also called: **titanium oxide, titanic oxide, titania.**

Titanomachy (ˌtaɪtəˈnɒməkɪ) *n Greek myth.* the unsuccessful revolt of the family of the Titan Iapetus against Zeus. [C19: from Greek *titanomakhia,* from TITAN + *makhē* a battle]

titanosaur (taɪˈtænəˌsɔː) *n* any of various herbivorous quadrupedal dinosaurs of the family *Titanosauridae,* of Jurassic and Cretaceous times: suborder *Sauropoda* (sauropods). [C19: from New Latin *Tītānosaurus,* from Greek TITAN + -SAUR]

titanothere (taɪˈtænəˌθɪə) *n* any of various very large horse-like perissodactyl mammals of the genera *Menodus, Brontotherium,* etc., that lived in Eocene and Oligocene times in North America. See also **chalicothere.** [C19: from New Latin *Tītānotherium* giant animal, from Greek TITAN + *thēr* wild beast]

titanous (taɪˈtænəs) *adj* of or containing titanium, esp. in the trivalent state.

titarakura (ˈtiːtɑːrəˌkuːrə) *n N.Z.* another name for **bully**[2].

titbit (ˈtɪtˌbɪt) *or esp. U.S.* **tidbit** *n* **1** a tasty small piece of food; dainty. **2** a pleasing scrap of anything, such as scandal. [C17: perhaps from dialect *tid* tender, of obscure origin]

titchy *or* **tichy** (ˈtɪtʃɪ) *adj* **titchier, titchiest.** *Brit. slang.* very small; tiny. [C20: from *tich* or *titch* a small person, from *Little Tich,* the stage name of Harry Relph (1867–1928), English actor noted for his small stature]

titer (ˈtaɪtə, ˈtiː-) *n* the usual U.S. spelling of **titre.**

titfer (ˈtɪtfə) *n Brit. slang.* a hat. [from rhyming slang *tit for tat* hat]

tit for tat *n* an equivalent given in return or retaliation; blow for blow. [C16: from earlier *tip for tap*]

tithable (ˈtaɪðəbᵊl) *adj* **1** (until 1936) liable to pay tithes. **2** (of property, etc.) subject to the payment of tithes.

tithe (taɪð) *n* **1** *(often pl) Christianity.* a tenth part of agricultural or other produce, personal income, or profits, contributed either voluntarily or as a tax for the support of the church or clergy or for charitable purposes. **2** any levy, esp. of one tenth. **3** a tenth or very small part of anything. ♦ *vb* **4** *(tr)* **4a** to exact or demand a tithe or tithes from (an individual or group). **4b** to levy a tithe upon (a crop or amount of produce, etc.). **5** *(intr)* to pay a tithe or tithes. [Old English *teogoth;* related to Old Frisian *tegotha,* Old Saxon *tegotho,* Old High German *zehando,* Old Norse *tīundi,* Gothic *taihunda*] ▸ **ˈtither** *n*

tithe barn *n* a large barn where, formerly, the agricultural tithe of a parish was stored.

tithing (ˈtaɪðɪŋ) *n English history.* **1a** a tithe; tenth. **1b** the exacting or paying of tithes. **2** a company of ten householders in the system of frankpledge. **3** a rural division, originally regarded as a tenth of a hundred.

Tithonus (tɪˈθəʊnəs) *n Greek myth.* the son of Laomedon of Troy who was loved by the goddess Eos. She asked that he be made immortal but forgot to ask that he be made eternally young. When he aged she turned him into a grasshopper.

titi[1] (ˈtiːtiː) *n, pl* **-tis.** any of several small omnivorous New World monkeys of the genus *Callicebus,* of South America, having long beautifully coloured fur and a long nonprehensile tail. [via Spanish from Aymaran, literally: little cat]

titi[2] (ˈtiːtiː) *n, pl* **-tis.** any of various evergreen shrubs or small trees of the family *Cyrillaceae* of the southern U.S., esp. the leatherwood and *Cliftonia monophyllia,* which has white or pinkish fragrant flowers. [C19: of American Indian origin]

Titian[1] (ˈtɪʃən) *n* original name *Tiziano Vecellio.* ?1490–1576, Italian painter of the Venetian school, noted for his religious and mythological works, such as *Bacchus and Ariadne* (1523), and his portraits. ▸ **ˌTitianˈesque** *adj*

Titian[2] (ˈtɪʃən) *adj (sometimes not cap.)* reddish-gold, like the hair colour used in many of the works of Titian. Also called: **Titian red.**

Titicaca (*Spanish* titiˈkaka) *n* **Lake.** a lake between S Peru and W Bolivia, in the Andes: the highest large lake in the world; drained by the Desaguadero River flowing into Lake Poopó. Area: 8135 sq. km (3141 sq. miles). Altitude: 3809 m (12 497 ft.). Depth: 370 m (1214 ft.).

titillate (ˈtɪtɪˌleɪt) *vb (tr)* **1** to arouse, tease, interest, or excite pleasurably and often superficially. **2** to cause a tickling or tingling sensation in, esp. by touching. [C17: from Latin *tītillāre*] ▸ **ˈtitilˌlating** *adj* ▸ **ˈtitilˌlatingly** *adv* ▸ **ˌtitilˈlation** *n* ▸ **ˈtitilˌlative** *adj*

titivate *or* **tittivate** (ˈtɪtɪˌveɪt) *vb* **1** to smarten up (oneself or another), as by making up, doing the hair, etc. **2** *(tr)* to smarten up (a thing): *to titivate a restaurant.* [C19: earlier *tidivate,* perhaps based on TIDY and CULTIVATE] ▸ **ˌtitiˈvation** *or* **ˌtittiˈvation** *n* ▸ **ˈtitiˌvator** *or* **ˈtittiˌvator** *n*

titlark (ˈtɪtˌlɑːk) *n* another name for **pipit,** esp. the meadow pipit (*Anthus pratensis*). [C17: from TIT[1] + LARK[1]]

title (ˈtaɪtᵊl) *n* **1** the distinctive name of a work of art, musical or literary composition, etc. **2** a descriptive name, caption, or heading of a section of a book, speech, etc. **3** See **title page. 4** a name or epithet signifying rank, office, or function. **5** a formal designation, such as *Mr, Mrs,* or *Miss.* **6** an appellation designating nobility. **7** *Films.* **7a** short for **subtitle** (sense 2). **7b** written material giving credits in a film or television programme. **8** *Sport.* a championship. **9** *Property law.* **9a** the legal right to possession of property, esp. real property. **9b** the basis of such right. **9c** the documentary evidence of such right: *title deeds.* **10** *Law.* **10a** the heading or a division of a statute, book of law, etc. **10b** the heading of a suit or action at law. **11a** any customary or established right. **11b** a claim based on such a right. **12** a definite spiritual charge or office in the church, without appointment to which a candidate for holy orders cannot lawfully be ordained. **13** *R.C. Church.* a titular church. ♦ *vb* **14** *(tr)* to give a title to. [C13: from Old French, from Latin *titulus*]

titled (ˈtaɪtᵊld) *adj* having a title: *the titled classes.*

title deed *n* a deed or document evidencing a person's legal right or title to property, esp. real property.

titleholder (ˈtaɪtᵊlˌhəʊldə) *n* a person who holds a title, esp. a sporting championship. ▸ **ˈtitleˌholding** *adj*

title page *n* the page in a book that bears the title, author's name, publisher's imprint, etc.

title role *n* the role of the character after whom a play, etc., is named.

titman (ˈtɪtmən) *n, pl* **-men.** (of pigs) the runt of a litter. [*tit-* (as in TITMOUSE) + MAN]

titmouse (ˈtɪtˌmaʊs) *n, pl* **-mice.** *(usually pl)* any small active songbird of the family *Paridae,* esp. those of the genus *Parus* (see **tit**[1]). [C14 *titemous,* from *tite* (see TIT[1]) + MOUSE]

Tito (ˈtiːtəʊ) *n* **Marshal.** original name *Josip Broz.* 1892–1980, Yugoslav statesman, who led the communist guerrilla resistance to German occupation during World War II; prime minister of Yugoslavia (1945–53) and president (1953–80).

Titograd (*Serbo-Croat* ˈtitɔgraːd) *n* the former name (1946–92) of **Podgorica.**

Titoism (ˈtiːtəʊˌɪzəm) *n* **1** the variant of Communism practised by Tito in the former Yugoslavia, characterized by independence from the Soviet bloc and neutrality in East-West controversies, a considerable amount of decentralization, and a large degree of worker control of industries. **2** any variant of Communism resembling Titoism. ▸ **'Titoist** *n, adj*

titrant ('taɪtrənt) *n* the solution in a titration that is added from a burette to a measured quantity of another solution.

titrate ('taɪtreɪt) *vb* (*tr*) to measure the volume or concentration of (a solution) by titration. [C19: from French *titrer;* see TITRE] ▸ **ti'tratable** *adj*

titration (taɪ'treɪʃən) *n* an operation, used in volumetric analysis, in which a measured amount of one solution is added to a known quantity of another solution until the reaction between the two is complete. If the concentration of one solution is known, that of the other can be calculated.

titre *or U.S.* **titer** ('taɪtə, 'tiː-) *n* **1a** the concentration of a solution as determined by titration. **1b** the minimum quantity of a solution required to complete a reaction in a titration. **2** the quantity of antibody present in an organism. [C19: from French *titre* proportion of gold or silver in an alloy, from Old French *title* TITLE]

titter ('tɪtə) *vb* **1** (*intr*) to snigger, esp. derisively or in a suppressed way. **2** (*tr*) to express by tittering. ◆ *n* **3** a suppressed laugh, chuckle, or snigger. [C17: of imitative origin] ▸ **'titterer** *n* ▸ **'tittering** *adj* ▸ **'titteringly** *adv*

tittivate ('tɪtɪˌveɪt) *vb* a less common spelling of **titivate.**

tittle ('tɪt^{ə}l) *n* **1** a small mark in printing or writing, esp. a diacritic. **2** a jot; particle. [C14: from Medieval Latin *titulus* label, from Latin: TITLE]

tittle-tattle *n* **1** idle chat or gossip. ◆ *vb* **2** (*intr*) to chatter or gossip. ▸ **'tittle-ˌtattler** *n*

tittup ('tɪtəp) *vb* **-tups, -tupping, -tupped** *or U.S.* **-tups, -tuping, -tuped. 1** (*intr*) to prance or frolic. ◆ *n* **2** a caper. **3** the sound made by high-heeled shoes. [C18 (in the sense: a horse's gallop): probably imitative]

titubation (ˌtɪtjʊ'beɪʃən) *n Pathol.* **1** a disordered gait characterized by stumbling or staggering, often caused by a lesion of the cerebellum. **2** Also called: **lingual titubation.** stuttering or stammering. [C17: from Latin *titubātiō,* from *titubāre* to reel]

titular ('tɪtjʊlə) *or* **titulary** ('tɪtjʊlərɪ) *adj* **1** of, relating to, or of the nature of a title. **2** in name only. **3** bearing a title. **4** giving a title. **5** *R.C. Church.* designating any of certain churches in Rome to whom cardinals or bishops are attached as their nominal incumbents. ◆ *n, pl* **-lars** *or* **-laries. 6** the bearer of a title. **7** the bearer of a nominal office. [C18: from French *titulaire,* from Latin *titulus* TITLE] ▸ **'titularly** *adv*

Titus ('taɪtəs) *n* **1** *New Testament.* **1a Saint.** a Greek disciple and helper of Saint Paul. Feast day: Jan. 26 or Aug. 25. **1b** the book written to him (in full **The Epistle of Paul the Apostle to Titus**), containing advice on pastoral matters. **2** full name *Titus Flavius Sabinus Vespasianus.* ?40–81 A.D., Roman emperor (78–81 A.D.).

Tiu ('tiːuː) *n* (in Anglo-Saxon mythology) the god of war and the sky. Norse counterpart: **Tyr.**

Tiv (tɪv) *n* **1** (*pl* **Tivs** *or* **Tiv**) a member of a Negroid people of W Africa, living chiefly in the savanna of the Benue area of S Nigeria and noted by anthropologists for having no chiefs. **2** the language of this people, belonging to the Benue-Congo branch of the Niger-Congo family.

Tivoli ('tɪvəlɪ; *Italian* 'tiːvoli) *n* a town in central Italy, east of Rome: a summer resort in Roman times; contains the Renaissance Villa d'Este and the remains of Hadrian's Villa. Pop.: 55 030 (1990). Ancient name: **Tibur.**

Tizard ('tɪzɑːd) *n* Sir **Henry (Thomas).** 1885–1959, British chemist and scientific administrator, who specialized in the military application of science and backed the development of radar.

tizzy ('tɪzɪ) *n, pl* **-zies.** *Informal.* a state of confusion, anxiety, or excitement. Also called: **tizz, tiz-woz** ('tɪzˌwɒz). [C19: of unknown origin]

Tjirebon *or* **Cheribon** ('tʃɪərəˌbɒn) *n* a port in S central Indonesia, on N Java on the Java Sea: scene of the signing of the **Tjirebon Agreement** of Indonesian independence (1946) by the Netherlands. Pop.: 245 307 (1990).

T-joint *n* a right-angled joint, esp. one in wood, making the shape of the letter T.

T-junction *n* a road junction in which one road joins another at right angles but does not cross it.

TKO *Boxing. abbrev. for* technical knockout.

Tl *the chemical symbol for* thallium.

Tlaxcala (*Spanish* tlas'kala) *n* **1** a state of S central Mexico: the smallest Mexican state; formerly an Indian principality, the chief Indian ally of Cortés in the conquest of Mexico. Capital: Tlaxcala. Pop.: 883 630 (1995 est.). Area: 3914 sq. km (1511 sq. miles). **2** a city in E central Mexico, on the central plateau, capital of Tlaxcala state: the church of San Francisco (founded 1521 by Cortés) is the oldest in the Americas. Pop.: 25 000 (1990 est.). Official name: **Tlaxcala de Xicohténcatl.**

TLC *Informal. abbrev. for:* **1** tender loving care. **2** thin-layer chromatography.

Tlemcen (*French* tsɛn) *n* a city in NW Algeria: capital of an Arab kingdom from the 12th to the late 14th century. Pop.: 107 632 (1987).

Tlingit ('tlɪŋgɪt) *n* **1** (*pl* **-gits** *or* **-git**) a member of a seafaring group of North American Indian peoples inhabiting S Alaska and N British Columbia. **2** the language of these peoples, belonging to the Na-Dene phylum.

TLS *abbrev. for* Times Literary Supplement.

T-lymphocyte *n* a type of lymphocyte that matures in the thymus gland and has an important role in the immune response. There are several subclasses: **killer T-cells** are responsible for killing cells that are infected by a virus; **helper T-cells** induce other cells (**B-lymphocytes**) to produce antibodies. Also called: **T-cell.**

Tm *the chemical symbol for* thulium.

TM *abbrev. for* transcendental meditation.

T-man *n, pl* **-men.** *U.S.* a law-enforcement agent of the U.S. Treasury.

tmesis (tə'miːsɪs, 'miːsɪs) *n* interpolation of a word or group of words between the parts of a compound word. [C16: via Latin from Greek, literally: a cutting, from *temnein* to cut]

TN 1 *abbrev. for* Tennessee. ◆ **2** *international car registration for* Tunisia.

tng *abbrev. for* training.

TNT *n* 2,4,6-trinitrotoluene; a yellow solid: used chiefly as a high explosive and is also an intermediate in the manufacture of dyestuffs. Formula: $CH_3C_6H_2(NO_2)_3$.

T-number *or* **T number** *n Photog.* a function of the f-number of a camera lens that takes into account the amount of light actually transmitted by the lens. [from *T(otal Light Transmission) Number*]

to (tuː; *unstressed before vowels* tʊ; *unstressed before consonants* tə) *prep* **1** used to indicate the destination of the subject or object of an action: *he climbed to the top.* **2** used to mark the indirect object of a verb in a sentence: *telling stories to children.* **3** used to mark the infinitive of a verb: *he wanted to go.* **4** as far as; until: *working from Monday to Friday.* **5** used to indicate equality: *16 ounces to the pound.* **6** against; upon; onto: *put your ear to the wall.* **7** before the hour of: *five minutes to four.* **8** accompanied by: *dancing to loud music.* **9** as compared with, as against: *the score was eight to three.* **10** used to indicate a resulting condition: *he tore her dress to shreds; they starved to death.* **11** a dialect word for **at**[1]: *he's to town; where's it to.* ◆ *adv* **12** towards a fixed position, esp. (of a door) closed. [Old English *tō;* related to Old Frisian, Old Saxon *to,* Old High German *zuo,* Latin *do-* as in *dōnec* until]

toad (təʊd) *n* **1** any anuran amphibian of the class *Bufonidae,* such as *Bufo bufo* (**common toad**) of Europe. They are similar to frogs but are more terrestrial, having a drier warty skin. Related adj: **batrachian. 2** any of various similar amphibians of different families. **3** a loathsome person. [Old English *tādige,* of unknown origin; see TADPOLE] ▸ **'toadish** *or* **'toadˌlike** *adj*

toadeater ('təʊdˌiːtə) *n* a rare word for **toady** (sense 1). [C17: originally a mountebank's assistant who would pretend to eat toads (believed to be poisonous), hence a servile flatterer, toady]

toadfish ('təʊdˌfɪʃ) *n, pl* **-fish** *or* **-fishes.** any spiny-finned bottom-dwelling marine fish of the family *Batrachoididae,* of tropical and temperate seas, having a flattened tapering body and a wide mouth.

toadflax ('təʊdˌflæks) *n* any of various scrophulariaceous plants of the genus *Linaria,* esp. *L. vulgaris,* having narrow leaves and spurred two-lipped yellow-orange flowers. Also called: **butter-and-eggs.**

toad-in-the-hole *n Brit. and Austral.* a dish made of sausages baked in a batter.

toad spit *or* **spittle** *n* another name for **cuckoo spit.**

toadstone ('təʊdˌstəʊn) *n* an amygdaloidal basalt occurring in the limestone regions of Derbyshire. [C18: perhaps from a supposed resemblance to a toad's spotted skin]

toadstool ('təʊdˌstuːl) *n* (*not in technical use*) any basidiomycetous fungus with a capped spore-producing body that is poisonous. Compare **mushroom** (sense 1a). [C14: from TOAD + STOOL]

toady ('təʊdɪ) *n, pl* **toadies. 1** a person who flatters and ingratiates himself in a servile way; sycophant. ◆ *vb* **toadies, toadying, toadied. 2** to fawn on and flatter (someone). [C19: shortened from TOADEATER] ▸ **'toadyish** *adj* ▸ **'toadyism** *n*

Toamasina (*Portuguese* tõʊma'sinə) *n* a port in E Madagascar, on the Indian Ocean: the country's chief commercial centre. Pop.: 127 441 (1993). Former name (until 1979): **Tamatave.**

to and fro *adj, adv* **to-and-fro 1** back and forth. **2** here and there. ▸ **'toing and 'froing** *n*

toast[1] (təʊst) *n* **1** sliced bread browned by exposure to heat, usually under a grill, over a fire, or in a toaster. ◆ *vb* **2** (*tr*) to brown under a grill or over a fire: *to toast cheese.* **3** to warm or be warmed in a similar manner: *to toast one's hands by the fire.* [C14: from Old French *toster,* from Latin *tōstus* parched, baked from *torrēre* to dry with heat; see THIRST, TORRID] ▸ **'toasty** *adj*

toast[2] (təʊst) *n* **1** a tribute or proposal of health, success, etc., given to a person or thing by a company of people and marked by raising glasses and drinking together. **2** a person or thing honoured by such a tribute or proposal. **3** (esp. formerly) an attractive woman to whom such tributes are frequently made: *she was the toast of the town.* ◆ *vb* **4** to propose or drink a toast to (a person or thing). **5** (*intr*) to add vocal effects to a prerecorded track: a disc-jockey technique. See also **rap**[1] (sense 6). [C17 (in the sense: a lady to whom the company is asked to drink): from TOAST[1],from the idea that the name of the lady would flavour the drink like a piece of spiced toast] ▸ **'toaster** *n*

toaster ('təʊstə) *n* a device for toasting bread, usually electric, and often equipped with an automatic timer.

toastmaster ('təʊstˌmɑːstə) *n* a person who introduces after-dinner speakers, proposes or announces toasts, etc., at public or formal dinners. ▸ **'toastˌmistress** *fem n*

toast rack *n* a small stand consisting of a usually oblong base with a number of open-sided partitions between which pieces of toast may be stood upright.

toasty *or* **toastie** ('təʊstɪ) *n, pl* **toasties.** a toasted sandwich.

Tob. *abbrev. for* Tobit.

tobacco (tə'bækəʊ) *n, pl* **-cos** *or* **-coes. 1** any of numerous solanaceous plants of the genus *Nicotiana,* having mildly narcotic properties, tapering hairy leaves, and tubular or funnel-shaped fragrant flowers. The species *N. tabacum* is cultivated as the chief source of commercial tobacco. **2** the leaves of certain of these plants dried and prepared for snuff, chewing, or smoking. [C16: from Spanish *tabaco,* perhaps from Taino: leaves rolled for smoking, assumed by the Spaniards to be the name of the plant] ▸ **to'baccoless** *adj*

tobacco mosaic virus *n* the virus that causes mosaic disease in tobacco and related plants: its discovery in 1892 provided the first evidence of the existence of viruses. Abbrev.: **TMV.**

tobacconist (təˈbækənɪst) *n Chiefly Brit.* a person or shop that sells tobacco, cigarettes, pipes, etc.

Tobago (təˈbeɪgəʊ) *n* an island in the SE Caribbean, northeast of Trinidad: ceded to Britain in 1814; joined with Trinidad in 1888 as a British colony; part of the independent republic of Trinidad and Tobago. Pop.: 46 400 (1990). ▸ **Tobagonian** (ˌtəʊbəˈgəʊnɪən) *adj, n*

-to-be *adj* (*in combination*) about to be; future: *a mother-to-be; the bride-to-be.*

Tobey (ˈtəʊbɪ) *n* **Mark.** 1890–1976, U.S. painter. Influenced by Chinese calligraphy, he devised a style of improvisatory abstract painting called "white writing".

Tobit (ˈtəʊbɪt) *n Old Testament.* **1** a pious Jew who was released from blindness through the help of the archangel Raphael. **2** a book of the Apocrypha relating this story.

toboggan (təˈbɒgən) *n* **1** a light wooden frame on runners used for sliding over snow and ice. **2** a long narrow sledge made of a thin board curved upwards and backwards at the front. ◆ *vb* **-gans, -ganing, -ganed.** (*intr*) **3** to ride on a toboggan. [C19: from Canadian French, from Algonquian; related to Abnaki *udābāgan*] ▸ **toˈbogganer** *or* **toˈbogganist** ~

Tobol (*Russian* taˈbɔl) *n* a river in central Asia, rising in N Kazakhstan and flowing northeast into Russia to join the Irtysh River. Length: about 1300 km (800 miles).

Tobolsk (*Russian* taˈbɔljsk) *n* a town in central Russia, at the confluence of the Irtysh and Tobol Rivers: the chief centre for the early Russian colonization of Siberia. Pop.: 83 000 (1988 est.).

Tobruk (təˈbrʊk, təʊ-) *n* a small port in NE Libya, in E Cyrenaica on the Mediterranean coast road: scene of severe fighting in World War II: taken from the Italians by the British in January 1941, from the British by the Germans in June 1942, and finally taken by the British in November 1942.

toby (ˈtəʊbɪ) *n, pl* **-bies.** *N.Z.* a water stopcock at the boundary of a street and house section.

toby jug (ˈtəʊbɪ) *n* a beer mug or jug typically in the form of a stout seated man wearing a three-cornered hat and smoking a pipe. Also called: **toby.** [C19: from the familiar form of the Christian name *Tobias*]

Tocantins (*Portuguese* tokãˈtĩs) *n* **1** a state of N Brazil, created from the northern part of Goiás state in 1988. Capital: Palmas. Pop.: 1 007 000 (1995 est.). Area: 278 421 sq. km (107 499 sq. miles). **2** a river in E Brazil, rising in S central Goiás state and flowing generally north to the Pará River. Length: about 2700 km (1700 miles).

toccata (təˈkɑːtə) *n* a rapid keyboard composition for organ, harpsichord, etc., dating from the baroque period, usually in a rhythmically free style. [C18: from Italian, literally: touched, from *toccare* to play (an instrument), TOUCH]

Toc H (ˈtɒk ˈeɪtʃ) *n* a society formed in England after World War I to fight loneliness and hate and to encourage Christian comradeship. [C20: from the obsolete telegraphic code for *T.H.*, initials of *Talbot House,* Poperinge, Belgium, the original headquarters of the society]

Tocharian *or* **Tokharian** (tɒˈkɑːrɪən) *n* **1** a member of an Asian people with a complex material culture, sometimes thought to be of European origin, who lived in the Tarim Basin until overcome by the Uighurs around 800 A.D. **2** the language of this people, known from records in a N Indian script of the 7th and 8th centuries A.D. It belongs to the Indo-European family, is regarded as forming an independent branch, and shows closer affinities with the W or European group than with the E or Indo-Iranian group. The language is recorded in two dialects, known as **Tocharian A** and **Tocharian B.** [C20: ultimately from Greek *Tokharoi,* name of uncertain origin]

tocher (ˈtɒxər) *Scot.* ◆ *n* **1** a dowry. ◆ *vb* (*tr*) **2** to give a dowry to. [C15: from Irish Gaelic *tochar;* Scot. Gaelic *tochradh*]

tocology *or* **tokology** (tɒˈkɒlədʒɪ) *n* the branch of medicine concerned with childbirth; obstetrics. [C19: from Greek *tokos* childbirth, from *tiktein* to bear]

tocopherol (tɒˈkɒfəˌrɒl) *n Biochem.* any of a group of fat-soluble alcohols that occur in wheat-germ oil, watercress, lettuce, egg yolk, etc. They are thought to be necessary for healthy human reproduction. Also called: **vitamin E.** [C20: from *toco-,* from Greek *tokos* offspring (see TOCOLOGY) + *-pher-,* from *pherein* to bear + -OL[1]]

Tocqueville (ˈtəʊkvɪl, ˈtɒk-; *French* tɔkvil) *n* **Alexis Charles Henri Maurice Clérel de** (aleksi ʃarl ɑ̃ri mɔris klerɛl də). 1805–59, French politician and political writer. His chief works are *De la Démocratie en Amérique* (1835–40) and *L'Ancien régime et la révolution* (1856).

tocsin (ˈtɒksɪn) *n* **1** an alarm or warning signal, esp. one sounded on a bell. **2** an alarm bell. [C16: from French, from Old French *toquassen,* from Old Provençal *tocasenh,* from *tocar* to TOUCH + *senh* bell, from Latin *signum*]

tod[1] (tɒd) *n Brit.* a unit of weight, used for wool, etc., usually equal to 28 pounds. [C15: probably related to Frisian *todde* rag, Old High German *zotta* tuft of hair]

tod[2] (tɒd) *n* **on one's tod.** *Brit. slang.* on one's own. [C19: rhyming slang *Tod Sloan/alone,* after *Tod* Sloan, a jockey]

tod[3] (tɒd) *n* a Scot. and northern English dialect word for a **fox.** [C12: of unknown origin]

today (təˈdeɪ) *n* **1** this day, as distinct from yesterday or tomorrow. **2** the present age: *children of today.* ◆ *adv* **3** during or on this day. **4** nowadays. [Old English *tō dæge,* literally: on this day, from TO + *dæge,* dative of *dæg* DAY]

Todd (tɒd) *n* Baron **Alexander Robertus.** 1907–97, Scottish chemist, noted for his research into the structure of nucleic acids: Nobel prize for chemistry 1957.

toddle (ˈtɒdᵊl) *vb* (*intr*) **1** to walk with short unsteady steps, as a child does when learning to walk. **2** (foll. by *off*) *Jocular.* to depart. **3** (foll. by *round, over,* etc.) *Jocular.* to stroll; amble. ◆ *n* **4** the act or an instance of toddling. [C16 (Scottish and northern English): of obscure origin]

toddler (ˈtɒdlə) *n* **1** a young child, usually one between the ages of one and two and a half. **2** (*modifier*) designed or suitable for a toddler: *toddler suits.*

toddy (ˈtɒdɪ) *n, pl* **-dies. 1** a drink made from spirits, esp. whisky, with hot water, sugar, and usually lemon juice. **2a** the sap of various palm trees (**toddy** or **wine palms**), used as a beverage. **2b** the liquor prepared from this sap. **3** (in Malaysia) a milky-white sour alcoholic drink made from fermented coconut milk, drunk chiefly by Indians. [C17: from Hindi *tāṛī* juice of the palmyra palm, from *tār* palmyra palm, from Sanskrit *tāra,* probably of Dravidian origin]

to-do (təˈduː) *n, pl* **-dos.** a commotion, fuss, or quarrel.

tody (ˈtəʊdɪ) *n, pl* **-dies.** any small bird of the family *Todidae* of the Caribbean, having a red-and-green plumage and long straight bill: order *Coraciiformes* (kingfishers, etc.). [C18: from French *todier,* from Latin *todus* small bird]

toe (təʊ) *n* **1** any one of the digits of the foot. **2** the corresponding part in other vertebrates. **3** the part of a shoe, sock, etc., covering the toes. **4** anything resembling a toe in shape or position. **5** the front part of the head of a golf club, hockey stick, etc. **6** the lower bearing of a vertical shaft assembly. **7** the tip of a cam follower that engages the cam profile. **8 dip one's toe** (*or* **toes**) **in.** *Informal.* to begin doing or try something new or unfamiliar. **9 on one's toes.** alert. **10 tread on someone's toes.** to offend or insult a person, esp. by trespassing on his field of responsibility. **11 turn up one's toes.** *Informal.* to die. **12** *Austral. slang.* speed: *a player with plenty of toe.* ◆ *vb* **toes, toeing, toed. 13** (*tr*) to touch, kick, or mark with the toe. **14** (*tr*) *Golf.* to strike (the ball) with the toe of the club. **15** (*tr*) to drive (a nail, spike, etc.) obliquely. **16** (*intr*) to walk with the toes pointing in a specified direction: *to toe inwards.* **17 toe the line.** to conform to expected standards, attitudes, etc. [Old English *tā;* related to Old Frisian *tāne,* Old Norse *tā,* Old High German *zēha,* Latin *digitus* finger] ▸ **ˈtoeˌlike** *adj*

toea (ˈtəʊɑː) *n* a monetary unit of Papua New Guinea, worth one-hundredth of a kina. [from a Papuan language]

toe and heel *n* a technique used by racing drivers while changing gear on sharp bends, in which the brake is operated by the toe (or heel) of the right foot while the heel (or toe) simultaneously operates the accelerator.

toecap (ˈtəʊˌkæp) *n* a reinforced covering for the toe of a boot or shoe.

toe crack *n Vet. science.* a sand crack occurring on the forepart of the hind foot of a horse.

toe-curling *adj Informal.* causing feelings of acute embarrassment.

toed (təʊd) *adj* **1** having a part resembling a toe. **2** (of a vertical or oblique member of a timber frame) fixed by nails driven in at the foot. **3** (*in combination*) having a toe or toes as specified: *five-toed.*

toe dance *n* **1** a dance performed on tiptoe. ◆ *vb* **toe-dance. 2** (*intr*) *Ballet.* to dance on pointes. ▸ **toe dancer** *n*

toehold (ˈtəʊˌhəʊld) *n* **1** a small foothold to facilitate climbing. **2** any means of gaining access, support, etc.: *the socialist party gained a toehold in the local elections.* **3** a wrestling hold in which the opponent's toe is held and his leg twisted against the joints.

toe-in *n* a slight forward convergence given to the wheels of motor vehicles to improve steering and equalize tyre wear.

toenail (ˈtəʊˌneɪl) *n* **1** a thin horny translucent plate covering part of the dorsal surface of the end joint of each toe. Related adjs: **ungual, ungular. 2** *Carpentry.* a nail driven obliquely, as in joining one beam at right angles to another. **3** *Printers' slang.* a parenthesis. ◆ *vb* **4** (*tr*) *Carpentry.* to join (beams) by driving nails obliquely.

toerag (ˈtəʊˌræg) *n Brit. slang.* a contemptible or despicable person. [C20: originally, a beggar, tramp: from the pieces of rag they wrapped round their feet]

toetoe (ˈtɔɪtɔɪ, ˈtəuiːˌtəuiː, ˌtəuiːˈtəuiː) *n* See **toitoi**[1].

toey (ˈtəʊɪ) *adj Austral. slang.* **1** (of a person) nervous or anxious. **2** *Rare.* (of a horse) eager to race.

toff (tɒf) *n Brit. slang.* a rich, well-dressed, or upper-class person, esp. a man. [C19: perhaps variant of TUFT, nickname for a titled student at Oxford University, wearing a cap with a gold tassel]

toffee *or* **toffy** (ˈtɒfɪ) *n, pl* **-fees** *or* **-fies. 1** a sweet made from sugar or treacle boiled with butter, nuts, etc. **2 for toffee.** (preceded by *can't*) *Informal.* to be incompetent at a specified activity: *he can't sing for toffee.* [C19: variant of earlier TAFFY]

toffee-apple *n* an apple fixed on a stick and coated with a thin layer of toffee.

toffee-nosed *adj Slang, chiefly Brit.* pretentious or supercilious; used esp. of snobbish people. [C20: perhaps coined as a pun on *toffy* stylish, grand: see TOFF]

toft (tɒft) *n Brit. history.* **1** a homestead. **2** an entire holding, consisting of a homestead and the attached arable land. [Old English, from Old Norse *topt*]

tofu (ˈtəʊˌfuː) *n* unfermented soya-bean curd, a food with a soft cheeselike consistency made from soya-bean milk. [from Japanese]

tog[1] (tɒg) *Informal.* ◆ *vb* **togs, togging, togged. 1** (often foll. by *up* or *out*) to dress oneself, esp. in smart clothes. ◆ *n* **2** See **togs.** [C18: probably short for obsolete cant *togemans* coat, from Latin *toga* TOGA + *-mans,* of uncertain origin]

tog[2] (tɒg) *n* **a** a unit of thermal resistance used to measure the power of insulation of a fabric, garment, quilt, etc. The tog-value of an article is equal to ten times the temperature difference between its two faces, in degrees Celsius, when the flow of heat across it is equal to one watt per m^2. **b** (*as modifier*): *tog-rating.* [C20: arbitrary coinage from TOG[1] (n)]

toga (ˈtəʊgə) *n* **1** a garment worn by citizens of ancient Rome, consisting of a piece of cloth draped around the body. **2** the official vestment of certain offices. [C16: from Latin, related to *tegere* to cover] ▸ **togaed** (ˈtəʊgəd) *adj*

toga praetexta (priːˈtɛkstə) *n* (in ancient Rome) a toga with a broad purple border worn by certain magistrates and priests and by boys until they assumed the toga virilis. [Latin, literally: bordered toga]

toga virilis (vɪˈraɪlɪs) *n* (in ancient Rome) the toga assumed by a youth at the age of 14 as a symbol of manhood and citizenship. [Latin, literally: manly (i.e., man's) toga]

together (tə'geðə) *adv* **1** with cooperation and interchange between constituent elements, members, etc.: *we worked together.* **2** in or into contact or union with each other: *to stick papers together.* **3** in or into one place or assembly; with each other: *the people are gathered together.* **4** at the same time: *we left school together.* **5** considered collectively or jointly: *all our wages put together couldn't buy that car.* **6** continuously: *working for eight hours together.* **7** closely, cohesively, or compactly united or held: *water will hold the dough together.* **8** mutually or reciprocally: *to multiply seven and eight together.* **9** *Informal.* organized: *to get things together.* **10 together with.** in addition to. ◆ *adj* **11** *Slang.* self-possessed and well-organized; mentally and emotionally stable: *she's a very together lady.* [Old English *tōgædre;* related to Old Frisian *togadera,* Middle High German *gater;* see GATHER]

USAGE See at **plus.**

togetherness (tə'geðənɪs) *n* a feeling of closeness or affection from being united with other people.

toggery ('tɒgərɪ) *n Informal.* clothes; togs.

toggle ('tɒgᵊl) *n* **1** a wooden peg or metal rod fixed crosswise through an eye at the end of a rope, chain, or cable, for fastening temporarily by insertion through an eye in another rope, chain, etc. **2** a wooden or plastic bar-shaped button inserted through a loop for fastening. **3** a pin inserted into a nautical knot to keep it secure. **4** *Machinery.* a toggle joint or a device having such a joint. ◆ *vb* **5** *(tr)* to supply or fasten with a toggle or toggles. [C18: of unknown origin] ▸ **'toggler** *n*

toggle iron *n* a whaling harpoon with a pivoting barb near its head to prevent a harpooned whale pulling free. Also called: **toggle harpoon.**

toggle joint *n* a device consisting of two arms pivoted at a common joint and at their outer ends and used to apply pressure by straightening the angle between the two arms.

toggle switch *n* **1** an electric switch having a projecting lever that is manipulated in a particular way to open or close a circuit. **2** a computer device that is used to turn a feature on or off.

Toghril Beg ('tɒgrɪl 'bɛg) *n* ?990–1063 A.D., Sultan of Turkey (1055–63), who founded the Seljuq dynasty and conquered Baghdad (1055).

Togliatti[1] (ˌtɒlɪ'ætɪ) *n* a city in W central Russia, on the Volga River: automobile industry: renamed in honour of Palmiro Togliatti, an Italian communist. Pop.: 702 000 (1995 est.). Former name (until 1964): **Stavropol.** Russian name: **Tol'yatti.**

Togliatti[2] (*Italian* to'ʎatti) *n* **Palmiro** (pal'miro). 1893–1964, Italian politician; leader of the Italian Communist Party (1926–64). After Mussolini's fall he became a minister (1944) and vice premier (1945).

Togo[1] ('təʊgəʊ) *n* a republic in West Africa, on the Gulf of Guinea: became French Togoland (a League of Nations mandate) after the division of German Togoland in 1922; independent since 1960. Official language: French. Religion: animist majority. Currency: franc. Capital: Lomé. Pop.: 4 906 000 (1998 est.). Area: 56 700 sq. km (20 900 sq. miles). ▸ **Togolese** (ˌtəʊgə'liːz) *adj, n*

Togo[2] ('təʊgəʊ) *n* Marquis **Heihachiro** (ˌheɪhɑː'tʃiːrəʊ). 1847–1934, Japanese admiral, who commanded the Japanese fleet in the war with Russia (1904–05).

Togoland ('təʊgəʊˌlænd) *n* a former German protectorate in West Africa on the Gulf of Guinea: divided in 1922 into the League of Nations mandates of British Togoland (west) and French Togoland (east); the former joined Ghana in 1957; the latter became independent as Togo in 1960. ▸ **'Togoˌlander** *n*

togs (tɒgz) *pl n Informal.* **1** clothes. **2** *Austral., N.Z., and Irish.* a swimming costume. [from TOG[1]]

toheroa (ˌtəʊə'rəʊə) *n* **1** a bivalve mollusc, *Amphidesma* (or *Semele*) *ventricosum,* of New Zealand. **2** a greenish soup made of this. [from Maori]

tohunga ('tɒhʊŋə, tɒ'hʊŋə) *n N.Z.* a Maori priest, the repository of traditional lore.

toil[1] (tɔɪl) *n* **1** hard or exhausting work. **2** an obsolete word for **strife.** ◆ *vb* **3** *(intr)* to labour. **4** *(intr)* to progress with slow painful movements: *to toil up a hill.* **5** *(tr) Archaic.* to achieve by toil. [C13: from Anglo-French *toiler* to struggle, from Old French *toeillier* to confuse, from Latin *tudiculāre* to stir, from *tudicula* machine for bruising olives, from *tudes* a hammer, from *tundere* to beat] ▸ **'toiler** *n*

toil[2] (tɔɪl) *n* **1** *(often pl)* a net or snare: *the toils of fortune had ensnared him.* **2** *Archaic.* a trap for wild beasts. [C16: from Old French *toile,* from Latin *tēla* loom]

toile (twɑːl) *n* **1** a transparent linen or cotton fabric. **2** a garment of exclusive design made up in cheap cloth so that alterations and experiments can be made. [C19: from French, from Latin *tēla* a loom]

toilet ('tɔɪlɪt) *n* **1** another word for **lavatory. 2** *Old-fashioned.* the act of dressing and preparing oneself: *to make one's toilet.* **3** *Old-fashioned.* a dressing table or the articles used when making one's toilet. **4** *Rare.* costume. **5** the cleansing of a wound, etc., after an operation or childbirth. [C16: from French *toilette* dress, from TOILE]

toilet paper *or* **tissue** *n* thin absorbent paper, often wound in a roll round a cardboard cylinder (**toilet roll**), used for cleaning oneself after defecation or urination.

toiletry ('tɔɪlɪtrɪ) *n, pl* **-ries.** an object or cosmetic used in making up, dressing, etc.

toilet set *n* a matching set consisting of a hairbrush, comb, mirror, and clothes brush.

toilet soap *n* a mild soap, often coloured and scented, used for washing oneself.

toilette (twɑː'lɛt; *French* twalɛt) *n Usually literary or affected.* another word for **toilet** (sense 2). [C16: from French; see TOILET]

toilet training *n* the process of teaching young children to control the timing of bladder and bowel movements and to use the lavatory.

toilet water *n* a form of liquid perfume lighter than cologne. Compare **cologne.** Also called: **eau de toilette.**

toilsome ('tɔɪlsəm) *or* **toilful** *adj* laborious. ▸ **'toilsomely** *adv* ▸ **'toilsomeness** *n*

toitoi[1] ('tɔɪtɔɪ) *or* **toetoe** *n, pl* **-tois** *or* **-toes.** any of various tall grasses of the genus *Cortaderia* of New Zealand, with feathery fronds. [Maori]

toitoi[2] ('tɔɪtɔɪ) *n N.Z.* another name for **bully**[2].

Tojo ('təʊdʒəʊ) *n* **Hideki** ('hiːdɛˌkiː). 1885–1948, Japanese soldier and statesman; minister of war (1940–41) and premier (1941–44); hanged as a war criminal.

tokamak ('tɒkəˌmæk) *n Physics.* a toroidal reactor used in thermonuclear experiments, in which strong axial magnetic fields keep the plasma from contacting the external walls. [C20: from Russian *to(roidál'naya) kám(era s) ak(siál'nym magnitnym pólem),* toroidal chamber with magnetic field]

tokay ('təʊkeɪ) *n* a small gecko, *Gekko gecko,* of S and SE Asia, having a retractile claw at the tip of each digit. [from Malay *toke,* of imitative origin]

Tokay (təʊ'keɪ) *n* **1** a fine sweet wine made near Tokaj, Hungary. **2** a variety of large sweet grape used to make this wine. **3** a similar wine made elsewhere.

toke (təʊk) *Slang.* ◆ *n* **1** a draw on a cannabis cigarette. ◆ *vb (intr)* **2** to take a draw on a cannabis cigarette.

Tokelau Islands ('təʊkəˌlaʊ) *pl n* an island group in the South Pacific composed of three atolls, Nukunono, Atafu, and Fakaofo, which in 1948 was included within the territorial boundaries of New Zealand. Pop.: 1577 (1991). Area: about 11 sq. km (4 sq. miles).

token ('təʊkən) *n* **1** an indication, warning, or sign of something. **2** a symbol or visible representation of something. **3** something that indicates authority, proof, or authenticity. **4** a metal or plastic disc, such as a substitute for currency for use in slot machines. **5** a memento. **6** a gift voucher that can be used as payment for goods of a specified value. **7** *(modifier)* as a matter of form only; nominal: *a token increase in salary.* **8** *Linguistics.* a symbol regarded as an individual concrete mark, not as a class of identical symbols. Compare **type** (sense 11). **9** *Philosophy.* an individual instance: if the same sentence has different truth-values on different occasions of utterance the truth-value may be said to attach to the sentence-token. Compare **type** (sense 13). **10 by the same token.** moreover and for the same or a similar reason. ◆ *vb* **11** *(tr)* to act or serve as a warning or symbol of; betoken. [Old English *tācen;* related to Old Frisian *tēken,* Old Saxon *tēkan,* Old High German *zeihhan,* Old Norse *teikn;* see TEACH]

token economy *n* a type of psychotherapy in which the inmates of an institution are rewarded for good behaviour with tokens that can be exchanged for privileges.

tokenism ('təʊkəˌnɪzəm) *n* the practice of making only a token effort or doing no more than the minimum, esp. in order to comply with a law. ▸ **ˌtoken'istic** *adj*

token money *n* coins of the regular issue having greater face value than the value of their metal content.

token payment *n* a small payment made in acknowledgment of the existence of debt.

token strike *n* a brief strike intended to convey strength of feeling on a disputed issue.

token vote *n* a Parliamentary vote of money in which the amount quoted to aid discussion is not intended to be binding.

Tokharian (tɒ'kɑːrɪən) *n* a variant spelling of **Tocharian.**

tokology (tɒ'kɒlədʒɪ) *n* a variant spelling of **tocology.**

tokoloshe (ˌtɒkɒ'lɒʃ, -'lɒʃɪ) *n* (in Bantu folklore) a malevolent mythical man-like animal of short stature. Also called: **tikoloshe.** [from Xhosa *uthikoloshe*]

Tokugawa Iyeyasu (ˌtəʊkuː'gɑːwə ˌiːjeɪ'jɑːsuː) *n* See (Tokugawa) **Iyeyasu.**

Tokyo ('təʊkjəʊ, -kɪˌəʊ) *n* the capital of Japan, a port on SE Honshu on **Tokyo Bay** (an inlet of the Pacific): part of the largest conurbation in the world (the Tokyo-Yukohama metropolitan area) of over 25 million people; major industrial centre and the chief cultural centre of Japan. Pop.: 7 966 195 (1995).

tola ('təʊlə) *n* a unit of weight, used in India, equal to 180 ser or 180 grains. [C17: from Hindi *tolā,* from Sanskrit *tulā* scale, from *tul* to weigh]

tolan ('təʊlæn) *or* **tolane** ('təʊleɪn) *n* a white crystalline derivative of acetylene; diphenylacetylene; diphenylethyne. Formula: $C_6H_5C{:}CC_6H_5$. [C19: from TOL(UENE) + *-an* (see -ANE)]

tolar ('tɒlɑː) *n* the standard monetary unit of Slovenia, divided into 100 stotinas.

tolbooth ('təʊlˌbuːθ, -ˌbuːð, 'tɒl-) *n* **1** *Chiefly Scot.* a town hall. **2** a variant spelling of **tollbooth.**

tolbutamide (tɒl'bjuːtəˌmaɪd) *n* a synthetic crystalline compound administered orally in the treatment of diabetes to lower blood glucose levels. Formula: $C_{12}H_{18}N_2O_3S$. [C20: from TOL(UYL) + BUT(YRIC ACID) + AMIDE]

told (təʊld) *vb* **1** the past tense and past participle of **tell**[1]. ◆ *adj* **2** See **all told.**

tole (təʊl) *n* enamelled or lacquered metal ware, usually gilded, popular in the 18th century. [from French *tôle* sheet metal, from French (dialect): table, from Latin *tabula* table]

Toledo *n* **1** (tɒ'leɪdəʊ; *Spanish* to'leðo). a city in central Spain, on the River Tagus: capital of Visigothic Spain, and of Castile from 1087 to 1560; famous for steel and swords since the first century. Pop.: 63 560 (1991). Ancient name: **Toletum** (tə'liːtəm). **2** (tə'liːdəʊ). an inland port in NW Ohio, on Lake Erie: one of the largest coal-shipping ports in the world; transportation and industrial centre; university (1872). Pop.: 317 606 (1996 est.). **3** a fine-tapered sword or sword blade.

tolerable ('tɒlərəbᵊl) *adj* **1** able to be tolerated; endurable. **2** permissible. **3** *Informal.* fairly good. ▸ **'tolerableness** *or* **ˌtolera'bility** *n* ▸ **'tolerably** *adv*

tolerance ('tɒlərəns) *n* **1** the state or quality of being tolerant. **2** capacity to endure something, esp. pain or hardship. **3** the permitted variation in some measurement or other characteristic of an object or workpiece. **4** *Physiol.* the capacity of an organism to endure the effects of a poison or other substance, esp. after it has been taken over a prolonged period.

tolerant ('tɒlərənt) *adj* **1** able to tolerate the beliefs, actions, opinions, etc., of others. **2** permissive. **3** able to withstand extremes, as of heat and cold. **4** *Med.* (of a patient) exhibiting tolerance to a drug. ▸ **'tolerantly** *adv*

tolerate ('tɒlə,reɪt) *vb* (*tr*) **1** to treat with indulgence, liberality, or forbearance. **2** to permit. **3** to be able to bear; put up with. **4** *Med.* to have tolerance for (a drug, poison, etc.). [C16: from Latin *tolerāre* sustain; related to THOLE[2]] ▸ **'tolerative** *adj* ▸ **'toler,ator** *n*

toleration (,tɒlə'reɪʃən) *n* **1** the act or practice of tolerating. **2** freedom to hold religious opinions that differ from the established or prescribed religion of a country. ▸ **,toler'ationism** *n* ▸ **,toler'ationist** *n*

tolidine ('tɒlɪ,di:n) *n* any of several isomeric compounds, esp. the *ortho-* isomer, which is a white or reddish crystalline substance used in the manufacture of dyes and resins. Formula: $(C_6H_3NH_2CH_3)_2$. [C19: from TOL(UENE) + -ID[3] + -INE[2]]

Tolima (*Spanish* to'lima) *n* a volcano in W Colombia, in the Andes. Height: 5215 m (17 110 ft.).

Tolkien ('tɒlki:n) *n* **J(ohn) R(onald) R(euel).** 1892–1973, British philologist and writer, born in South Africa. He is best known for *The Hobbit* (1937), the trilogy *The Lord of the Rings* (1954–55), and the posthumously published *The Silmarillion* (1977).

toll[1] (təʊl) *vb* **1** to ring or cause to ring slowly and recurrently. **2** (*tr*) to summon, warn, or announce by tolling. **3** *U.S. and Canadian.* to decoy (game, esp. ducks). ♦ *n* **4** the act or sound of tolling. [C15: perhaps related to Old English *-tyllan*, as in *fortyllan* to attract]

toll[2] (təʊl, tɒl) *n* **1a** an amount of money levied, esp. for the use of certain roads, bridges, etc., to cover the cost of maintenance. **1b** (*as modifier*): *toll road; toll bridge.* **2** loss or damage incurred through an accident, disaster, etc.: *the war took its toll of the inhabitants.* **3** Also called: **'tollage.** (formerly) the right to levy a toll. **4** Also called: **toll charge.** *N.Z.* a charge for a telephone call beyond a free-dialling area. [Old English *toln*; related to Old Frisian *tolene*, Old High German *zol* toll, from Late Latin *telōnium* customs house, from Greek *telōnion*, ultimately from *telos* tax]

tollbooth *or* **tolbooth** ('təʊl,bu:θ, -,bu:ð, 'tɒl-) *n* a booth or kiosk at which a toll is collected.

toll call *n* **1** *Brit. obsolete.* a short-distance trunk call. **2** *U.S.* a long-distance telephone call at a rate higher than that for a local call. **3** *N.Z.* a telephone call beyond a free-dialling area for which a charge is made.

Toller (*German* 'tɔlər) *n* **Ernst** (ɛrnst). 1893–1939, German dramatist and revolutionary, noted particularly for his expressionist plays, esp. *Masse Mensch* (1921).

tollgate ('təʊl,geɪt, 'tɒl-) *n* a gate across a toll road or bridge at which travellers must stop and pay.

tollhouse ('təʊl,haʊs, 'tɒl-) *n* a small house at a tollgate occupied by a toll collector.

tolly *or* **tollie** ('tɒlɪ) *n, pl* **-lies.** *S. African.* a castrated calf. [C19: from Xhosa *ithole* calf on which the horns have begun to appear]

Tolpuddle Martyrs ('tɒl,pʌdᵊl) *n* six farm workers sentenced to transportation for seven years in 1834 for administering an unlawful oath to form a trade union in the village of Tolpuddle, Dorset.

Tolstoy ('tɒlstɔɪ; *Russian* tal'stɔj) *n* **Leo,** Russian name *Count Lev Nikolayevich Tolstoy.* 1828–1910, Russian novelist, short-story writer, and philosopher; author of the two monumental novels *War and Peace* (1865–69) and *Anna Karenina* (1875–77). Following a spiritual crisis in 1879, he adopted a form of Christianity based on a doctrine of nonresistance to evil.

Toltec ('tɒltɛk) *n, pl* **-tecs** *or* **-tec. 1** a member of a Central American Indian people who dominated the valley of Mexico from their capital Tula from about 950 to 1160 A.D., when the valley was overrun by the Aztecs. ♦ *adj also* **Toltecan. 2** of or relating to this people. [C19: from Spanish *tolteca*, of American Indian origin]

tolu (tɒ'lu:) *n* an aromatic balsam obtained from a South American tree, *Myroxylon balsamum.* See **balsam** (sense 1). [C17: after *Santiago de Tolu*, Colombia, from which it was exported]

toluate ('tɒlju,eɪt) *n* any salt or ester of any of the three isomeric forms of toluic acid. [C19: from TOLU(IC ACID) + -ATE[1]]

Toluca (*Spanish* to'luka) *n* **1** a city in S central Mexico, capital of Mexico state, at an altitude of 2640 m (8660 ft.). Pop.: 327 865 (1990). Official name: **Toluca de Lerdo** (de'lɛrðo). **2 Nevado de** (ne'βaðo de). a volcano in central Mexico, in Mexico state near Toluca: crater partly filled by a lake. Height: 4577 m (15 017 ft.).

toluene ('tɒlju,i:n) *n* a colourless volatile flammable liquid with an odour resembling that of benzene, obtained from petroleum and coal tar and used as a solvent and in the manufacture of many organic chemicals. Formula: $C_6H_5CH_3$. [C19: from TOLU + -ENE, since it was previously obtained from tolu]

toluic acid (tɒ'lu:ɪk) *n* a white crystalline derivative of toluene existing in three isomeric forms; methylbenzoic acid. The *ortho-* and *para-* isomers are used in synthetic resins and the *meta-* isomer is used as an insect repellent. Formula: $C_6H_4CH_3COOH$. [C19: from TOLU(ENE) + -IC]

toluidine (tɒ'lju:ɪ,di:n) *n* an amine derived from toluene existing in three isomeric forms; aminotoluene. The *ortho-* and *meta-* isomers are liquids and the *para-* isomer is a crystalline solid. All three are used in making dyes. Formula: $C_6H_4CH_3NH_2$. [C19: from TOLU(ENE) + -IDE + -INE[2]]

toluol ('tɒlju,ɒl) *n* another name for **toluene.**

toluyl ('tɒljuɪl) *n* (*modifier*) of, consisting of, or containing any of three isomeric groups $CH_3C_6H_4CO$-, derived from a toluic acid by removal of the hydroxyl group: *toluyl group or radical.* [C19: from TOLU(ENE) + -YL]

tolyl ('tɒlɪl) *n* **1** (*modifier*) of, consisting of, or containing any of three isomeric groups, $CH_3C_6H_4$-, derived from toluene: *tolyl group or radical.* **2** (*modifier*) another word for **benzyl.** Also called: **α-tolyl.** [C19: from TOLU (see TOLUENE) + -YL]

tom[1] (tɒm) *n* **a** the male of various animals, esp. the cat. **b** (*as modifier*): *a tom turkey.* **c** (*in combination*): *a tomcat.* [C16: special use of the shortened form of *Thomas*, applied to any male, often implying a common or ordinary type of person, etc.]

tom[2] (tɒm) *n Austral. and N.Z.* a temporary supporting post. [from a specialized use of TOM[1]]

tomahawk ('tɒmə,hɔ:k) *n* **1** a fighting axe, with a stone or later an iron head, used by the North American Indians. **2** *Chiefly Austral.* the usual word for **hatchet.** [C17: from Virginia Algonquian *tamahaac*]

tomalley ('tɒmælɪ) *n* fat from a lobster, called "liver", and eaten as a delicacy. [C17: of Caribbean origin; compare Galibi *tumali* sauce of crab or lobster liver]

toman (tə'ma:n) *n* a gold coin formerly issued in Persia. [C16: from Persian, of Mongolian origin]

Tom and Jerry *n U.S.* a hot mixed drink containing rum, brandy, egg, nutmeg, and sometimes milk.

tomato (tə'ma:təʊ) *n, pl* **-toes. 1** a solanaceous plant, *Lycopersicon* (or *Lycopersicum*) *esculentum*, of South America, widely cultivated for its red fleshy many-seeded edible fruits. **2** the fruit of this plant, which has slightly acid-tasting flesh and is eaten in salads, as a vegetable, etc. **3** *U.S. and Canadian slang.* a girl or woman. [C17 *tomate*, from Spanish, from Nahuatl *tomatl*]

tomb (tu:m) *n* **1** a place, esp. a vault beneath the ground, for the burial of a corpse. **2** a stone or other monument to the dead. **3 the tomb.** a poetic term for **death. 4** anything serving as a burial place: *the sea was his tomb.* ♦ *vb* **5** (*tr*) *Rare.* to place in a tomb; entomb. [C13: from Old French *tombe*, from Late Latin *tumba* burial mound, from Greek *tumbos*; related to Latin *tumēre* to swell, Middle Irish *tomm* hill] ▸ **'tomb,like** *adj*

tombac ('tɒmbæk) *or* **tambac** ('tæmbæk) *n* any of various brittle alloys containing copper and zinc and sometimes tin and arsenic: used for making cheap jewellery, etc. [C17: from French, from Dutch *tombak*, from Malay *tambâga* copper, apparently from Sanskrit *tāmraka*, from *tāmra* dark coppery red]

Tombaugh ('tɒmbaʊ) *n* **Clyde William.** 1906–97, U.S. astronomer, who discovered (1930) the planet Pluto.

tombola (tɒm'bəʊlə) *n Brit.* a type of lottery, esp. at a fête, in which tickets are drawn from a revolving drum. [C19: from Italian, from *tombolare* to somersault; see TUMBLE]

tombolo ('tɒmbə,ləʊ) *n, pl* **-los.** a narrow sand or shingle bar linking a small island with another island or the mainland. [C20: from Italian, from Latin *tumulus* mound; see TUMULUS]

Tombouctou (tɔ̃buktu) *n* the French name for **Timbuktu.**

tomboy ('tɒm,bɔɪ) *n* a girl who acts or dresses in a boyish way, liking rough outdoor activities. ▸ **'tom,boyish** *adj* ▸ **'tom,boyishly** *adv* ▸ **'tom,boyishness** *n*

tombstone ('tu:m,stəʊn) *n* another word for **gravestone.**

Tombstone ('tu:m,stəʊn) *n* a town in the U.S., in Arizona: scene of the gunfight at the OK Corral in 1881. Pop.: 1220 (1990).

Tom Collins *n* a long drink consisting of gin, lime or lemon juice, sugar or syrup, and soda water.

Tom, Dick, and (**or**) **Harry** *n* an ordinary, undistinguished, or common person (esp. in the phrases **every Tom, Dick, and Harry; any Tom, Dick, or Harry**).

tome (təʊm) *n* **1** a large weighty book. **2** one of the several volumes of a work. [C16: from French, from Latin *tomus* section of larger work, from Greek *tomos* a slice, from *temnein* to cut; related to Latin *tondēre* to shear]

-tome *n combining form.* indicating an instrument for cutting: *osteotome.* [from Greek *tomē* a cutting, *tomos* a slice, from *temnein* to cut]

tomentum (tə'mɛntəm) *n, pl* **-ta** (-tə). **1** a feltlike covering of downy hairs on leaves and other plant parts. **2** a network of minute blood vessels occurring in the human brain between the pia mater and cerebral cortex. [C17: New Latin, from Latin: stuffing for cushions; related to Latin *tumēre* to swell] ▸ **tomentose** (tə'mɛntəʊs) *adj*

tomfool (,tɒm'fu:l) *n* **a** a fool. **b** (*as modifier*): *tomfool ideas.* [C14: from TOM[1] + FOOL[1]] ▸ **,tom'foolish** *adj* ▸ **,tom'foolishness** *n*

tomfoolery (,tɒm'fu:lərɪ) *n, pl* **-eries. 1** foolish behaviour. **2** utter nonsense; rubbish.

tommy ('tɒmɪ) *n, pl* **-mies.** (*often cap.*) *Brit. informal.* a private in the British Army. Also called: **Tommy Atkins** ('ætkɪnz). [C19: originally *Thomas Atkins*, a name representing a typical private in specimen forms; compare TOM[1]]

tommy bar *n* a short bar used as a lever to provide torque for tightening a box spanner or key.

Tommy gun *n* an informal name for **Thompson sub-machine-gun.**

tommyrot ('tɒmɪ,rɒt) *n* utter nonsense; tomfoolery.

tomography (tə'mɒgrəfɪ) *n* any of a number of techniques used to obtain an X-ray photograph of a selected plane section of the human body or some other solid object. [C20: from Greek *tomē* a cutting + -GRAPHY]

tomorrow (tə'mɒrəʊ) *n* **1** the day after today. **2** the future. ♦ *adv* **3** on the day after today. **4** at some time in the future. [Old English *tō morgenne*, from TO (at, on) + *morgenne*, dative of *morgen* MORNING; see MORROW]

tompion ('tɒmpɪən) *n* a variant of **tampion.**

Tomsk (*Russian* tɔmsk) *n* a city in central Russia: formerly an important gold-mining town and administrative centre for a large area of Siberia; university (1888); engineering industries. Pop.: 470 000 (1995 est.).

Tom Thumb *n* **1 General,** stage name of *Charles Stratton.* 1838–83, U.S.

midget, exhibited in P. T. Barnum's circus. **2** a dwarf; midget. [after *Tom Thumb,* the tiny hero of several English folk tales]

tomtit ('tɒm,tɪt) *n Brit.* any of various tits, esp. the bluetit.

tom-tom *n* **1** a drum associated either with the American Indians or with Eastern cultures, usually beaten with the hands as a signalling instrument. **2** a standard cylindrical drum, normally with one drumhead. **3** a monotonous drumming or beating sound. [C17: from Hindi *tamtam,* of imitative origin]

-tomy *n combining form.* indicating a surgical cutting of a specified part or tissue: *lobotomy.* [from Greek *-tomia;* see -TOME]

ton[1] (tʌn) *n* **1** Also called: **long ton.** *Brit.* a unit of weight equal to 2240 pounds or 1016.046 909 kilograms. **2** Also called: **short ton, net ton.** *U.S.* a unit of weight equal to 2000 pounds or 907.184 kilograms. **3** Also called: **metric ton, tonne.** a unit of weight equal to 1000 kilograms. **4** Also called: **freight ton.** a unit of volume or weight used for charging or measuring freight in shipping. It depends on the type of material being shipped but is often taken as 40 cubic feet, 1 cubic metre, or 1000 kilograms: *freight is charged at £40 per ton of 1 cubic metre.* **5** Also called: **measurement ton, shipping ton.** a unit of volume used in shipping freight, equal to 40 cubic feet, irrespective of the commodity shipped. **6** Also called: **displacement ton.** a unit used for measuring the displacement of a ship, equal to 35 cubic feet of sea water or 2240 pounds. **7** Also called: **register ton.** a unit of internal capacity of ships equal to 100 cubic feet. ◆ *adv* **8 tons.** (intensifier): *the new flat is tons better than the old one.* [C14: variant of TUN]

ton[2] *French.* (tɔ̃) *n* style, fashion, or distinction. [C18: from French, from Latin *tonus* TONE]

ton[3] (tʌn) *n Slang, chiefly Brit.* a score or achievement of a hundred, esp. a hundred miles per hour, as on a motorcycle. [C20: special use of TON[1] applied to quantities of one hundred]

tonal ('təʊnᵊl) *adj* **1** of or relating to tone. **2** of, relating to, or utilizing the diatonic system; having an established key. Compare **atonal. 3a** (of an answer in a fugue) not having the same melodic intervals as the subject, so as to remain in the original key. **3b** denoting a fugue as having such an answer. Compare **real**[1] (sense 11). ▸ **'tonally** *adv*

tonality (təʊ'nælɪtɪ) *n, pl* **-ties. 1** *Music.* **1a** the actual or implied presence of a musical key in a composition. **1b** the system of major and minor keys prevalent in Western music since the decline of modes. Compare **atonality. 2** the overall scheme of colours and tones in a painting.

to-name *n Scot.* a nickname used to distinguish one person from others of the same name.

Tonbridge ('tʌn,brɪdʒ) *n* a market town in SE England, in SW Kent on the River Medway. Pop.: 34 260 (1991).

tondo ('tɒndəʊ) *n, pl* **-di** (-di:). a circular easel painting or relief carving. [C19: from Italian: a circle, shortened from *rotondo* round]

tone (təʊn) *n* **1** sound with reference to quality, pitch, or volume. **2** short for **tone colour. 3** *U.S. and Canadian.* another word for **note** (sense 10). **4** (in acoustic analysis) a sound resulting from periodic or regular vibrations, composed either of a simple sinusoidal waveform (**pure tone**) or of several such waveforms superimposed upon one main one (**compound tone**). **5** an interval of a major second; whole tone. **6** Also called: **Gregorian tone.** any of several plainsong melodies or other chants used in the singing of psalms. **7** *Linguistics.* any of the pitch levels or pitch contours at which a syllable may be pronounced, such as high tone, falling tone, etc. **8** the quality or character of a sound: *a nervous tone of voice.* **9** general aspect, quality, or style: *I didn't like the tone of his speech.* **10** high quality or style: *to lower the tone of a place.* **11** the quality of a given colour, as modified by mixture with white or black; shade; tint: *a tone of red.* **12** *Physiol.* **12a** the normal tension of a muscle at rest. **12b** the natural firmness of the tissues and normal functioning of bodily organs in health. **13** the overall effect of the colour values and gradations of light and dark in a picture. **14** *Photog.* a colour or shade of colour, including black or grey, of a particular area on a negative or positive that can be distinguished from surrounding lighter or darker areas. ◆ *vb* **15** (*intr;* often foll. by *with*) to be of a matching or similar tone (to): *the curtains tone with the carpet.* **16** (*tr*) to give a tone to or correct the tone of. **17** (*tr*) *Photog.* to soften or change the colour of the tones of (a photographic image) by chemical means. **18** an archaic word for **intone.** ◆ See also **tone down, tone up.** [C14: from Latin *tonus,* from Greek *tonos* tension, tone, from *teinein* to stretch]

Tone (təʊn) *n* (**Theobald**) **Wolfe.** 1763–98, Irish nationalist, who founded (1791) the Society of United Irishmen and led (1798) French military forces to Ireland. He was captured and sentenced to death but committed suicide.

tone arm *n* another name for **pick-up** (sense 1).

tone cluster *n Music.* a group of adjacent notes played simultaneously, either in an orchestral score or, on the piano, by depressing a whole set of adjacent keys.

tone colour *n* the quality of a musical sound that is conditioned or distinguished by the upper partials or overtones present in it. Often shortened to **tone.** See also **timbre** (sense 2).

tone control *n* a device in a radio, etc., by which the relative intensities of high and low frequencies may be varied.

tone-deaf *adj* unable to distinguish subtle differences in musical pitch. ▸ **tone deafness** *n*

tone down *vb* (*adv*) to moderate or become moderated in tone: *to tone down an argument; to tone down a bright colour.*

tone language *n* a language, such as Chinese or certain African languages, in which differences in tone may make differences in meaning.

toneless ('təʊnlɪs) *adj* **1** having no tone. **2** lacking colour or vitality. ▸ **'tonelessly** *adv* ▸ **'tonelessness** *n*

toneme ('təʊni:m) *n Linguistics.* a phoneme that is distinguished from another phoneme only by its tone. [C20: from TONE + -EME] ▸ **to'nemic** *adj*

tone poem *n* another term for **symphonic poem.**

toner ('təʊnə) *n* **1** a person or thing that tones or produces tones, esp. a concentrated pure organic pigment. **2** a cosmetic preparation that is applied to produce a required effect, such as one that softens or alters hair colour or one that reduces the oiliness of the skin. **3** *Photog.* a chemical solution that softens or alters the colour of the tones of a photographic image. **4** a powdered chemical used in photocopying machines and laser printers, which is transferred onto paper to form the printed image.

tone row *or* **series** *n Music.* a group of notes having a characteristic pattern or order that forms the basis of the musical material in a serial composition, esp. one consisting of the twelve notes of the chromatic scale. Also called: **note row.** See also **serialism, twelve-tone.**

tonetic (təʊ'nɛtɪk) *adj* (of a language) distinguishing words semantically by distinction of tone as well as by other sounds. See **tone language.** [C20: from TONE + *-etic,* as in PHONETIC] ▸ **to'netically** *adv*

tone up *vb* (*adv*) to make or become more vigorous, healthy, etc.: *exercise tones up the muscles.*

tong[1] (tɒŋ) *vb* (*tr*) **1** to gather or seize with tongs. **2** to curl or style (hair) with curling tongs.

tong[2] (tɒŋ) *n* (formerly) a Chinese secret society or association, esp. one popularly assumed to engage in criminal activities. [C20: from Chinese (Cantonese) *t'ong* meeting place]

tonga ('tɒŋgə) *n* a light two-wheeled vehicle used in rural areas of India. [C19: from Hindi *tāngā*]

Tonga[1] ('tɒŋgə, 'tɒŋə) *n* **1** (*pl* **-gas** *or* **-ga**) a member of a Negroid people of S central Africa, living chiefly in Zambia and Zimbabwe. **2** the language of this people, belonging to the Bantu group of the Niger-Congo family.

Tonga[2] ('tɒŋə, 'tɒŋgə) *n* a kingdom occupying an archipelago of more than 150 volcanic and coral islands in the SW Pacific, east of Fiji: inhabited by Polynesians; became a British protectorate in 1900 and gained independence in 1970; a member of the Commonwealth. Official languages: Tongan and English. Religion: Christian majority. Currency: pa'anga. Capital: Nuku'alofa. Pop.: 97 900 (1998 est.). Area: 750 sq. km (290 sq. miles). Also called: **Friendly Islands.**

Tongan ('tɒŋən) *adj* **1** of or relating to the kingdom of Tonga, its inhabitants, or their language. ◆ *n* **2** a member of the people that inhabits Tonga. **3** the language of this people, belonging to the Polynesian family.

tongs (tɒŋz) *pl n* a tool for grasping or lifting, consisting of a hinged, sprung, or pivoted pair of arms or levers, joined at one end. Also called: **pair of tongs.** [plural of Old English *tange;* related to Old Saxon *tanga,* Old High German *zanga,* Old Norse *tong*]

tongue (tʌŋ) *n* **1** a movable mass of muscular tissue attached to the floor of the mouth in most vertebrates. It is the organ of taste and aids the mastication and swallowing of food. In man it plays an important part in the articulation of speech sounds. Related adjs: **glottic, lingual. 2** an analogous organ in invertebrates. **3** the tongue of certain animals used as food. **4** a language, dialect, or idiom: *the English tongue.* **5** the ability to speak: *to lose one's tongue.* **6** a manner of speaking: *a glib tongue.* **7** utterance or voice (esp. in the phrase **give tongue**). **8** (*pl*) See **gift of tongues. 9** anything which resembles a tongue in shape or function: *a tongue of flame; a tongue of the sea.* **10** a promontory or spit of land. **11** a flap of leather on a shoe, either for decoration or under the laces or buckles to protect the instep. **12** *Music.* the reed of an oboe or similar instrument. **13** the clapper of a bell. **14** the harnessing pole of a horse-drawn vehicle. **15** a long and narrow projection on a machine part that serves as a guide for assembly or as a securing device. **16** a projecting strip along an edge of a board that is made to fit a corresponding groove in the edge of another board. **17 hold one's tongue.** to keep quiet. **18 on the tip of one's tongue.** about to come to mind: *her name was on the tip of his tongue.* **19 with** (**one's**) **tongue in** (**one's**) **cheek.** Also: **tongue in cheek.** with insincere or ironical intent. ◆ *vb* **tongues, tonguing, tongued. 20** to articulate (notes played on a wind instrument) by the process of tonguing. **21** (*tr*) to lick, feel, or touch with the tongue. **22** (*tr*) *Carpentry.* to provide (a board) with a tongue. **23** (*intr*) (of a piece of land) to project into a body of water. **24** (*tr*) *Obsolete.* to reproach; scold. [Old English *tunge;* related to Old Saxon, Old Norse *tunga,* Old High German *zunga,* Latin *lingua*] ▸ **'tongueless** *adj* ▸ **'tongue,like** *adj*

tongue-and-groove joint *n* a joint made between two boards by means of a tongue along the edge of one board that fits into a groove along the edge of the other board.

tongued (tʌŋd) *adj* **1a** having a tongue or tongues. **1b** (*in combination*): *long-tongued.* **2** (*in combination*) having a manner of speech as specified: *sharp-tongued.*

tongue-lash *vb* (*tr*) to reprimand severely; scold. ▸ **'tongue-,lashing** *n, adj*

tongue-tie *n* a congenital condition in which the tongue has restricted mobility as the result of an abnormally short frenulum.

tongue-tied *adj* **1** speechless, esp. with embarrassment or shyness. **2** having a condition of tongue-tie.

tongue twister *n* a sentence or phrase that is difficult to articulate clearly and quickly, such as *Peter Piper picked a peck of pickled pepper.*

tonguing ('tʌŋɪŋ) *n* a technique of articulating notes on a wind instrument. See **single-tongue, double-tongue, triple-tongue.**

tonic ('tɒnɪk) *n* **1** a medicinal preparation that improves and strengthens the functioning of the body or increases the feeling of wellbeing. **2** anything that enlivens or strengthens: *his speech was a tonic to the audience.* **3** Also called: **tonic water.** a mineral water, usually carbonated and containing quinine and often mixed with gin or other alcoholic drinks. **4** *Music.* **4a** the first degree of a major or minor scale and the tonal centre of a piece composed in a particular key. **4b** a key or chord based on this. **5** a stressed syllable in a word. ◆ *adj* **6** serving to enliven and invigorate: *a tonic wine.* **7** of or relating to a tone or tones. **8** *Music.* of or relating to the first degree of a major or minor scale. **9** of or denoting the general effect of colour and light and shade in a picture. **10** *Physiol.* of, relating to, characterized by, or affecting normal muscular or bodily tone: *a tonic spasm.* **11** of or relating to stress or the main stress in a word. **12** denoting a tone language. **[**C17: from New Latin *tonicus,* from Greek *tonikos* concerning tone, from *tonos* TONE**]** ▸ **ˈtonically** *adv*

tonic accent *n* **1** emphasis imparted to a note by virtue of its having a higher pitch, rather than greater stress or long duration relative to other notes. **2** another term for **pitch accent.**

tonicity (təʊˈnɪsɪtɪ) *n* **1** the state, condition, or quality of being tonic. **2** *Physiol.* another name for **tonus.**

tonic sol-fa *n* a method of teaching music, esp. singing, used mainly in Britain, by which the syllables of a movable system of solmization are used as names for the notes of the major scale in any key. In this system *sol* is usually replaced by *so* as the name of the fifth degree. See **solmization.**

tonight (təˈnaɪt) *n* **1** the night or evening of this present day. ◆ *adv* **2** in or during the night or evening of this day. **3** *Obsolete or western Brit. dialect.* last night. **[**Old English *tōniht,* from TO (at) + NIGHT**]**

tonk[1] (tɒŋk) *vb Informal.* to strike with a heavy blow. **[**C20: of imitative origin**]**

tonk[2] (tɒŋk) *n Austral. slang.* an effete or effeminate man. **[**C20: origin unknown**]**

tonka bean (ˈtɒŋkə) *n* **1** a tall leguminous tree, *Coumarouna odorata,* of tropical America, having fragrant black almond-shaped seeds. **2** the seeds of this tree, used in the manufacture of perfumes, snuff, etc. **[**C18: probably from Tupi *tonka***]**

Tonkin (ˈtɒnˈkɪn) *or* **Tongking** (ˈtɒŋˈkɪŋ) *n* **1** a former state of N French Indochina (1883–1946), on the Gulf of Tonkin: forms the largest part of N Vietnam. **2 Gulf of.** an arm of the South China Sea, bordered by N Vietnam, the Leizhou Peninsula of SW China, and Hainan Island. Length: about 500 km (300 miles).

Tonle Sap (ˈtɒnlɪ ˈsæp) *n* a lake in W central Cambodia, linked with the Mekong River by the **Tonle Sap River.** Area: (dry season) about 2600 sq. km (1000 sq. miles); (rainy season) about 10 000 sq. km (3860 sq. miles).

tonnage *or* **tunnage** (ˈtʌnɪdʒ) *n* **1** the capacity of a merchant ship expressed in tons, for which purpose a ton is considered as 40 cubic feet of freight or 100 cubic feet of bulk cargo, unless such an amount would weigh more than 2000 pounds in which case the actual weight is used. **2** the weight of the cargo of a merchant ship. **3** the total amount of shipping of a port or nation, estimated by the capacity of its ships. **4** a duty on ships based either on their capacity or their register tonnage. **[**C15: from Old French, from *tonne* barrel**]**

tonne (tʌn) *n* a unit of mass equal to 1000 kg or 2204.6 pounds. Also called (not in technical use): **metric ton.** **[**from French**]**

tonneau (ˈtɒnəʊ) *n, pl* **-neaus** *or* **-neaux** (-nəʊ, -nəʊz). **1** Also called: **tonneau cover. 1a** a detachable cover to protect the rear part of an open car when it is not carrying passengers. **1b** a similar cover that fits over all the passenger seats, but not the driver's, in an open vehicle. **2** *Rare.* the part of an open car in which the rear passengers sit. **[**C20: from French: special type of vehicle body, from Old French *tonnel* cask, from *tonne* tun**]**

tonometer (təʊˈnɒmɪtə) *n* **1** an instrument for measuring the pitch of a sound, esp. one consisting of a set of tuning forks. **2** any of various types of instrument for measuring pressure or tension, such as the blood pressure, vapour pressure, etc. **[**C18: from Greek *tonos* TONE + -METER**]** ▸ **tonometric** (ˌtɒnəˈmɛtrɪk, ˌtəʊ-) *adj* ▸ **toˈnometry** *n*

tonoplast (ˈtəʊnəˌplæst) *n Botany.* the membrane enclosing a vacuole in a plant cell. **[**C20: from Greek *tonos* tone + -PLAST**]**

tonsil (ˈtɒnsəl) *n* **1** Also called: **palatine tonsil.** either of two small masses of lymphatic tissue situated one on each side of the back of the mouth. Related adj: **amygdaline. 2** *Anatomy.* any small rounded mass of tissue, esp. lymphatic tissue. **[**C17: from Latin *tōnsillae* (pl) tonsils, of uncertain origin**]** ▸ **ˈtonsillar** *or* **ˈtonsillary** *adj*

tonsillectomy (ˌtɒnsɪˈlɛktəmɪ) *n, pl* **-mies.** surgical removal of the palatine tonsils.

tonsillitis (ˌtɒnsɪˈlaɪtɪs) *n* inflammation of the palatine tonsils, causing enlargement, occasionally to the extent that they nearly touch one another. ▸ **tonsillitic** (ˌtɒnsɪˈlɪtɪk) *adj*

tonsillotomy (ˌtɒnsɪˈlɒtəmɪ) *n, pl* **-mies.** surgical incision into one or both of the palatine tonsils, usually followed by removal (tonsillectomy).

tonsorial (tɒnˈsɔːrɪəl) *adj Often facetious.* of or relating to barbering or hairdressing. **[**C19: from Latin *tōnsōrius* concerning shaving, from *tondēre* to shave**]**

tonsure (ˈtɒnʃə) *n* **1** (in certain religions and monastic orders) **1a** the shaving of the head or the crown of the head only. **1b** the part of the head left bare by shaving. **1c** the state of being shaven thus. ◆ *vb* **2** (*tr*) to shave the head of. **[**C14: from Latin *tōnsūra* a clipping, from *tondēre* to shave**]** ▸ **ˈtonsured** *adj*

tontine (ˈtɒntiːn, tɒnˈtiːn) *n* **1a** an annuity scheme by which several subscribers accumulate and invest a common fund out of which they receive an annuity that increases as subscribers die until the last survivor takes the whole. **1b** the subscribers to such a scheme collectively. **1c** the share of each subscriber. **1d** the common fund accumulated. **1e** (*as modifier*): *a tontine fund.* **2** a system of mutual life assurance by which benefits are received by those participants who survive and maintain their policies throughout a stipulated period (the **tontine period**). **[**C18: from French, named after Lorenzo *Tonti,* Neapolitan banker who devised the scheme**]**

ton-up *Brit. informal.* ◆ *adj* (*prenominal*) **1** (esp. of a motorcycle) capable of speeds of a hundred miles per hour or more. **2** liking to travel at such speeds: *a ton-up boy.* ◆ *n* **3** a person who habitually rides at such speeds.

tonus (ˈtəʊnəs) *n Physiol.* the normal tension of a muscle at rest; tone. **[**C19: from Latin, from Greek *tonos* TONE**]**

tony (ˈtəʊnɪ) *adj* **tonier, toniest.** *U.S. and Canadian informal.* stylish or distinctive; classy. **[**C20: from TONE**]**

Tony (ˈtəʊnɪ) *n, pl* **Tonies** *or* **Tonys.** any of several medallions awarded annually in the United States by a professional school for the performing arts for outstanding achievement in the theatre. **[**from *Tony,* the nickname of Antoinette Perry (died 1946), U.S. actress and producer**]**

too (tuː) *adv* **1** as well; in addition; also: *can I come too?* **2** in or to an excessive degree; more than a fitting or desirable amount: *I have too many things to do.* **3** extremely: *you're too kind.* **4** *U.S. and Canadian informal.* indeed: used to reinforce a command: *you will too do it!* **5 too right!** *Brit., Austral., and N.Z.* certainly; indeed. **[**Old English *tō;* related to Old Frisian, Old Saxon *to,* Old High German *zou;* see TO**]**

USAGE See at **very.**

toodle-oo (ˌtuːdəˈluː) *or* **toodle-pip** *sentence substitute. Brit. informal, rare.* goodbye. **[**C20: perhaps imitative of the horn of a car**]**

took (tʊk) *vb* the past tense of **take.**

Tooke (tʊk) *n* **John Horne,** original name *John Horne.* 1736–1812, British radical, who founded (1771) the Constitutional Society to press for parliamentary reform: acquitted (1794) of high treason. He also wrote the philological treatise *The Diversions of Purley* (1786).

tool (tuːl) *n* **1a** an implement, such as a hammer, saw, or spade, that is used by hand. **1b** a power-driven instrument; machine tool. **1c** (*in combination*): *a toolkit.* **2** the cutting part of such an instrument. **3a** any of the instruments used by a bookbinder to impress a design on a book cover. **3b** a design so impressed. **4** anything used as a means of performing an operation or achieving an end: *he used his boss's absence as a tool for gaining influence.* **5** a person used to perform dishonourable or unpleasant tasks for another. **6** a necessary medium for or adjunct to one's profession: *numbers are the tools of the mathematician's trade.* **7** *Taboo slang.* another word for **penis. 8** *Brit.* an underworld slang word for **gun.** ◆ *vb* **9** to work, cut, shape, or form (something) with a tool or tools. **10** (*tr*) to decorate (a book cover) with a bookbinder's tool. **11** (*tr;* often foll. by *up*) to furnish with tools. **12** (when *intr,* often foll. by *along*) to drive (a vehicle) or (of a vehicle) to be driven, esp. in a leisurely or casual style. **[**Old English *tōl;* related to Old Norse *tōl* weapon, Old English *tawian* to prepare; see TAW[2]**]** ▸ **ˈtooler** *n* ▸ **ˈtool-less** *adj*

tooled up *adj Slang.* equipped with a weapon, esp. a gun.

tooling (ˈtuːlɪŋ) *n* **1** any decorative work done with a tool, esp. a design stamped onto a book cover, piece of leatherwork, etc. **2** the selection, provision, and setting up of tools, esp. for a machining operation.

tool-maker (ˈtuːlˌmeɪkə) *n* a person who specializes in the production or reconditioning of precision tools, cutters, etc. ▸ **ˈtool-ˌmaking** *n*

tool post *n* the rigid holding device which holds the cutting tool on a lathe and some other machine tools.

tool pusher *n* a foreman who supervises drilling operations on an oil rig.

toolroom (ˈtuːlruːm, -rʊm) *n* a room, as in a machine shop, where tools are made or stored.

tool shed *n* a small shed in the garden or yard of a house used for storing tools, esp. those for gardening.

tool steel *n* any of various steels whose hardness and ability to retain a cutting edge make them suitable for use in tools for cutting wood and metal.

toon (tuːn) *n* **1** a large meliaceous tree, *Cedrela toona,* of the East Indies and Australia, having clusters of flowers from which a dye is obtained. **2** the close-grained red wood of this tree, used for furniture, carvings, etc. **[**from Hindi *tūn,* from Sanskrit *tunna***]**

toorie *or* **tourie** (ˈtʊrɪ) *n Scot.* **1** a tassel or bobble on a bonnet. **2** Also: **toorie bonnet.** a bonnet with a toorie. **[**C19: from Scot. *toor* tower**]**

toot[1] (tuːt) *vb* **1** to give or cause to give (a short blast, hoot, or whistle): *to toot a horn; to toot a blast; the train tooted.* ◆ *n* **2** the sound made by or as if by a horn, whistle, etc. **3** *Slang.* any drug for snorting, esp. cocaine. **4** *U.S. and Canadian slang.* a drinking spree. **5** (tʊt). *Austral. slang.* a lavatory. **[**C16: from Middle Low German *tuten,* of imitative origin**]** ▸ **ˈtooter** *n*

toot[2] (tuːt) *n N.Z.* an informal name for **tutu**[2].

tooth (tuːθ) *n, pl* **teeth** (tiːθ). **1** any of various bonelike structures set in the jaws of most vertebrates and modified, according to the species, for biting, tearing, or chewing. Related adj: **dental. 2** any of various similar structures in invertebrates, occurring in the mouth or alimentary canal. **3** anything resembling a tooth in shape, prominence, or function: *the tooth of a comb.* **4** any of the various small indentations occurring on the margin of a leaf, petal, etc. **5** any one of a number of uniform projections on a gear, sprocket, rack, etc., by which drive is transmitted. **6** taste or appetite (esp. in the phrase **sweet tooth**). **7 long in the tooth.** old or ageing: used originally of horses, because their gums recede with age. **8 tooth and nail.** with ferocity and force: *we fought tooth and nail.* ◆ *vb* (tuːð, tuːθ). **9** (*tr*) to provide with a tooth or teeth. **10** (*intr*) (of two gearwheels) to engage. **[**Old English *tōth;* related to Old Saxon *tand,* Old High German *zand,* Old Norse *tonn,* Gothic *tunthus,* Latin *dens***]** ▸ **ˈtoothless** *adj* ▸ **ˈtoothˌlike** *adj*

toothache (ˈtuːθˌeɪk) *n* a pain in or about a tooth. Technical name: **odontalgia.**

toothache tree *n* another name for **prickly ash.**

toothbrush (ˈtuːθˌbrʌʃ) *n* a small brush, usually with a long handle, for cleaning the teeth.

toothed (tuːθt) *adj* **a** having a tooth or teeth. **b** (*in combination*): *sabre-toothed; six-toothed.*

toothed whale *n* any whale belonging to the cetacean suborder *Odontoceti,* having a single blowhole and numerous simple teeth and feeding on fish, smaller mammals, molluscs, etc.: includes dolphins and porpoises. Compare **whalebone whale.**

toothpaste (ˈtuːθˌpeɪst) *n* a paste used for cleaning the teeth, applied with a toothbrush.

toothpick (ˈtuːθˌpɪk) *n* **1** a small sharp sliver of wood, plastic, etc., used for extracting pieces of food from between the teeth. **2** a slang word for **bowie knife.**

tooth powder *n* a powder used for cleaning the teeth, applied with a toothbrush.

tooth shell *n* another name for the **tusk shell.**

toothsome (ˈtuːθsəm) *adj* **1** of delicious or appetizing appearance, flavour, or smell. **2** attractive; alluring. ▸ **ˈtoothsomely** *adv* ▸ **ˈtoothsomeness** *n*

toothwort (ˈtuːθˌwɜːt) *n* **1** an orobanchaceous European plant, *Lathraea squamaria,* having scaly cream or pink stems and pinkish flowers and a rhizome covered with toothlike scales. **2** any cruciferous North American or Eurasian plant of the genus *Dentaria,* having creeping rhizomes covered with toothlike projections. See also **crinkleroot.**

toothy (ˈtuːθɪ) *adj* **toothier, toothiest.** having or showing numerous, large, or projecting teeth: *a toothy grin.* ▸ **ˈtoothily** *adv* ▸ **ˈtoothiness** *n*

tootle[1] (ˈtuːtᵊl) *vb* **1** to toot or hoot softly or repeatedly: *the flute tootled quietly.* ◆ *n* **2** a soft hoot or series of hoots. [C19: from TOOT[1]] ▸ **ˈtootler** *n*

tootle[2] (ˈtuːtᵊl) *Brit. informal.* ◆ *vb* **1** (*intr*) to go, esp. by car. ◆ *n* **2** a drive, esp. a short pleasure trip. [C19: from TOOTLE[1], imitative of the horn of a car]

toots (tʊts) *or* **tootsy** *n, pl* **tootses** *or* **tootsies.** *Informal, chiefly U.S.* darling; sweetheart. [C20: perhaps related to earlier dialect *toot* worthless person, of obscure origin]

tootsy *or* **tootsie** (ˈtʊtsɪ), *n, pl* **-sies.** a child's word for **toe.**

Toowoomba (təˈwʊmbə) *n* a city in E Australia, in SE Queensland: agricultural and industrial centre. Pop.: 75 060 (latest est.).

top[1] (tɒp) *n* **1** the highest or uppermost part of anything: *the top of a hill.* **2** the most important or successful position: *to be at the top of the class; the top of the table.* **3** the part of a plant that is above ground: *carrot tops.* **4** a thing that forms or covers the uppermost part of anything, esp. a lid or cap: *put the top on the saucepan.* **5** the highest degree or point: *at the top of his career.* **6** the most important person: *he's the top of this organization.* **7** the best or finest part of anything: *we've got the top of this year's graduates.* **8** the loudest or highest pitch (esp. in the phrase **top of one's voice**). **9** short for **top gear. 10** *Cards.* the highest card of a suit in a player's hand. **11** *Sport.* **11a** a stroke that hits the ball above its centre. **11b** short for **topspin. 12** a platform around the head of a lower mast of a sailing vessel, the edges of which serve to extend the topmast shrouds. **13** *Chem.* the part of a volatile liquid mixture that distils first. **14** a garment, esp. for a woman, that extends from the shoulders to the waist or hips. **15a** the high-frequency content of an audio signal. **15b** (*as modifier*): *this amplifier has a good top response.* **16 blow one's top.** *Informal.* to lose one's temper. **17 on top of. 17a** in addition to: *on top of his accident, he caught pneumonia.* **17b** *Informal.* in complete control of (a difficult situation, job, etc.). **18 off the top of one's head.** with no previous preparation; extempore. **19 over the top. 19a** over the parapet or leading edge of a trench. **19b** over the limit; excessive(ly); lacking restraint or a sense of proportion. **20 the top of the morning.** a morning greeting regarded as characteristic of Irishmen. ◆ *adj* **21** of, relating to, serving as, or situated on the top: *the top book in a pile.* ◆ *vb* **tops, topping, topped.** (*mainly tr*) **22** to form a top on (something): *to top a cake with whipped cream.* **23** to remove the top of or from: *to top carrots.* **24** to reach or pass the top of: *we topped the mountain.* **25** to be at the top of: *he tops the team.* **26** to exceed or surpass. **27** *Slang.* to kill, esp. by hanging. **28** (*also intr*) *Sport.* **28a** to hit (a ball) above the centre. **28b** to make (a stroke) by hitting the ball in this way. **29** *Chem.* to distil off (the most volatile part) from a liquid mixture. **30** to add other colorants to (a dye) in order to modify the shade produced. **31 top and tail. 31a** to trim off the ends of (fruit or vegetables) before cooking them. **31b** to wash a baby's face and bottom without immersion in a bath. ◆ See also **top off, top out, tops, top up.** [Old English *topp;* related to Old High German *zopf* plait, Old Norse *toppr* tuft]

top[2] (tɒp) *n* **1** a toy that is spun on its pointed base by a flick of the fingers, by pushing a handle at the top up and down, etc. **2** anything that spins or whirls around. **3 sleep like a top.** to sleep very soundly. [Old English, of unknown origin]

top- *combining form.* a variant of **topo-** before a vowel.

topagnosia (ˌtɒpægˈnəʊzɪə) *or* **topagnosis** (ˌtɒpægˈnəʊsɪs) *n* a symptom of disease of or damage to the brain in which a person cannot identify a part of the body that has been touched.

topalgia (tɒˈpældʒɪə) *n* pain restricted to a particular spot: a neurotic or hysterical symptom.

toparch (ˈtɒpɑːk) *n* the ruler of a small state or realm. [C17: from Greek *toparchēs,* from *topos* a place + -ARCH] ▸ **ˈtoparchy** *n*

topaz (ˈtəʊpæz) *n* **1** a white or colourless mineral often tinted by impurities, found in cavities in igneous rocks and in quartz veins. It is used as a gemstone. Composition: hydrated aluminium silicate. Formula: $Al_2SiO_4(F,OH)_2$. Crystal structure: orthorhombic. **2 oriental topaz.** a yellowish-brown variety of sapphire. **3 false topaz.** another name for **citrine. 4a** a yellowish-brown colour, as in some varieties of topaz. **4b** (*as adj*): *topaz eyes.* **5** either of two South American hummingbirds, *Topaza pyra* and *T. pella.* [C13: from Old French *topaze,* from Latin *topazus,* from Greek *topazos*]

topazolite (təʊˈpæzəˌlaɪt) *n* a yellowish-green variety of andradite garnet. [C19: from TOPAZ + -LITE; so called because it is the same colour as some topaz]

top banana *n Slang, chiefly U.S.* **1** the leading comedian in vaudeville, burlesque, etc. **2** the leader; boss.

top boot *n* a high boot, often with a decorative or contrasting upper section.

top brass *n* (*functioning as pl*) *Informal.* the most important or high-ranking officials or leaders, as in politics, industry, etc. See also **brass** (sense 5).

topcoat (ˈtɒpˌkəʊt) *n* an outdoor coat worn over a suit, etc.

top dead-centre *n Engineering.* the position of the crank of a reciprocating engine or pump when the piston is at the top of its stroke. Abbrev.: **t.d.c.**

top dog *n Informal.* the leader or chief of a group.

top-down *adj* controlled, directed, or organized from the top.

top drawer *n* people of the highest standing, esp. socially (esp. in the phrase **out of the top drawer**).

top dollar *n Informal.* the highest level of payment.

top-dress *vb* (*tr*) to spread manure or fertilizer on the surface of (land) without working it into the soil.

top dressing *n* **1** a surface application of manure or fertilizer to land. **2** a thin layer of loose gravel that covers the top of a road surface.

tope[1] (təʊp) *vb* to consume (alcoholic drink) as a regular habit, usually in large quantities. [C17: from French *toper* to keep an agreement, from Spanish *topar* to take a bet; probably because a wager was generally followed by a drink] ▸ **ˈtoper** *n*

tope[2] (təʊp) *n* **1** a small grey requiem shark, *Galeorhinus galeus,* of European coastal waters. **2** any of various other small sharks. [C17: of uncertain origin; compare Norfolk dialect *toper* dogfish]

tope[3] (təʊp) *n* another name for a **stupa.** [C19: from Hindi *tōp;* compare Sanskrit *stūpa* STUPA]

topee *or* **topi** (ˈtəʊpiː, -pɪ) *n, pl* **-pees** *or* **-pis.** another name for **pith helmet.** [C19: from Hindi *topī* hat]

Topeka (təˈpiːkə) *n* a city in E central Kansas, capital of the state, on the Kansas River: university (1865). Pop.: 119 658 (1996 est.).

top end *n* (in vertical engines) another name for **little end** (sense 1).

Top End *n* **the.** *Austral.* the northern part of the Northern Territory.

top-flight *adj* of superior or excellent quality; outstanding.

topfull (ˈtɒpˌfʊl) *adj Rare.* full to the top.

topgallant (ˌtɒpˈgælənt; *Nautical* təˈgælənt) *n* **1** Also called: **topgallant mast.** a mast on a square-rigger above a topmast or an extension of a topmast. **2** Also called: **topgallant sail.** a sail set on a yard of a topgallant mast. **3** (*modifier*) of or relating to a topgallant. [C16: from TOP[1] + GALLANT]

top gear *n* the highest gear in a motor vehicle, often shortened to **top.**

top hat *n* a man's hat with a tall cylindrical crown and narrow brim, often made of silk, now worn for some formal occasions. Also called: **high hat.**

top-hat scheme *n Informal.* a pension scheme for the senior executives of an organization.

top-heavy *adj* **1** unstable or unbalanced through being overloaded at the top. **2** *Finance.* (of an enterprise or its capital structure) characterized by or containing too much debt capital in relation to revenue or profit so that too little is left over for dividend distributions; overcapitalized. **3** (of a business enterprise) having too many executives. ▸ **ˌtop-ˈheavily** *adv* ▸ **ˌtopˈheaviness** *n*

Tophet *or* **Topheth** (ˈtəʊfɛt) *n Old Testament.* a place in the valley immediately to the southwest of Jerusalem; the Shrine of Moloch, where human sacrifices were offered. [from Hebrew *Tōpheth*]

top-hole *interj, adj Brit. informal.* excellent; splendid.

tophus (ˈtəʊfəs) *n, pl* **-phi** (-faɪ). *Pathol.* a deposit of sodium urate in the helix of the ear or surrounding a joint: a diagnostic of advanced or chronic gout. Also called: **chalkstone.** [C16: from Latin, variant of *tōfus* TUFA, TUFF] ▸ **tophaceous** (təʊˈfeɪʃəs) *adj*

topi *n, pl* **-pis. 1** (ˈtəʊpɪ). an antelope, *Damaliscus korrigum,* of grasslands and semideserts of Africa, having angular curved horns and an elongated muzzle. **2** (ˈtəʊpiː, -pɪ). another name for **pith helmet.** [C19: from Hindi: hat]

topiary (ˈtəʊpɪərɪ) *adj* **1** of, relating to, or characterized by the trimming or training of trees or bushes into artificial decorative animal, geometric, or other shapes. ◆ *n* **2** (*pl* **-aries**) **2a** topiary work. **2b** a topiary garden. **3** the art of topiary. [C16: from French *topiaire,* from Latin *topia* decorative garden work, from Greek *topion* little place, from *topos* place] ▸ **topiarian** (ˌtəʊpɪˈɛərɪən) *adj* ▸ **ˈtopiarist** *n*

topic (ˈtɒpɪk) *n* **1** a subject or theme of a speech, essay, book, etc. **2** a subject of conversation; item of discussion. **3** (in rhetoric, logic, etc.) a category or class of arguments or ideas which may be drawn on to furnish proofs. [C16: from Latin *topica* translating Greek *ta topika,* literally: matters relating to commonplaces, title of a treatise by Aristotle, from *topoi,* pl. of *topos* place, commonplace]

topical (ˈtɒpɪkᵊl) *adj* **1** of, relating to, or constituting current affairs. **2** relating to a particular place; local. **3** of or relating to a topic or topics. **4** (of a drug, ointment, etc.) for application to the body surface; local. ▸ **topicality** (ˌtɒpɪˈkælɪtɪ) *n* ▸ **ˈtopically** *adv*

topic sentence *n* a sentence in a paragraph that expresses the main idea or point of the whole paragraph.

topknot (ˈtɒpˌnɒt) *n* **1** a crest, tuft, decorative bow, chignon, etc., on the top of the head. **2** any of several European flatfishes of the genus *Zeugopterus* and related genera, esp. *Z. punctatus,* which has an oval dark brown body marked with darker blotches: family *Bothidae* (turbot, etc.).

topless (ˈtɒplɪs) *adj* **1** having no top. **2a** denoting a costume which has no covering for the breasts. **2b** wearing such a costume. **3** *Archaic.* immeasurably high. ▸ **ˈtoplessness** *n*

top-level *n* (*modifier*) of, involving, or by those on the highest level of influence or authority: *top-level talks.*

toplofty (ˈtɒpˌlɒftɪ) *adj Informal.* haughty or pretentious. ▸ **ˈtopˌloftily** *adv* ▸ **ˈtopˌloftiness** *n*

top management *or* **senior management** *n* the most senior staff of an organization or business, including the heads of various divisions or departments led by the chief executive. Compare **middle management.**

topmast (ˈtɒpˌmɑːst; *Nautical* ˈtɒpməst) *n* the mast next above a lower mast on a sailing vessel.

topminnow (ˈtɒpˌmɪnəʊ) *n, pl* **-now** *or* **-nows.** any of various small American freshwater cyprinodont fishes that are either viviparous (genera *Heterandria, Gambusia,* etc.) or egg-laying (genus *Fundulus*). [from TOP[1] + MINNOW; so called because they are small and swim near the surface of the water]

topmost ('tɒp,məʊst) *adj* highest; at or nearest the top.

top-notch ('tɒp'nɒtʃ) *adj Informal.* excellent; superb. ► **'top-'notcher** *n*

topo ('tɒpəʊ) *n Mountaineering.* a picture of a mountain with details of climbing routes superimposed on it. [C20: shortened from *topographical picture*]

topo- *or before a vowel* **top-** *combining form.* indicating place or region: *topography; topology; toponym; topotype.* [from Greek *topos* a place, commonplace]

topochemistry ('tɒpə,kɛmɪstrɪ) *n Chem.* the study of reactions that only occur at specific regions in a system.

top off *vb (tr, adv)* to finish or complete, esp. with some decisive action: *he topped off the affair by committing suicide.*

topog. *abbrev. for:* **1** topographical. **2** topography.

topography (tə'pɒgrəfɪ) *n, pl* **-phies. 1** the study or detailed description of the surface features of a region. **2** the detailed mapping of the configuration of a region. **3** the land forms or surface configuration of a region. **4** the surveying of a region's surface features. **5** the study or description of the configuration of any object. ► **to'pographer** *n* ► **topographic** (,tɒpə'græfɪk) *or* **,topo'graphical** *adj* ► **,topo'graphically** *adv*

topological group *n Maths.* a group, such as the set of all real numbers, that constitutes a topological space and in which multiplication and inversion are continuous.

topological space *n Maths.* a set *S* with an associated family of subsets τ that is closed under set union and finite intersection. *S* and the empty set are members of τ.

topology (tə'pɒlədʒɪ) *n* **1** the branch of mathematics concerned with generalization of the concepts of continuity, limit, etc. **2** a branch of geometry describing the properties of a figure that are unaffected by continuous distortion, such as stretching or knotting. Former name: **analysis situs. 3** *Maths.* a family of subsets of a given set *S,* such that *S* is a topological space. **4** the arrangement and interlinking of computers in a computer network. **5** the study of the topography of a given place, esp. as far as it reflects its history. **6** the anatomy of any specific bodily area, structure, or part. ► **topologic** (,tɒpə'lɒdʒɪk) *or* **,topo'logical** *adj* ► **,topo'logically** *adv* ► **to'pologist** *n*

Topolski (to'pɒlskɪ) *n* **Feliks** (fi:lɪks). 1907–89, British painter, born in Poland; best known for his sketches and murals, esp. for *Memoir of the Century* (1975–89) painted on viaduct arches on London's South Bank.

toponym ('tɒpənɪm) *n* **1** the name of a place. **2** any name derived from a place name.

toponymy (tə'pɒnɪmɪ) *n* **1** the study of place names. **2** *Rare.* the anatomical nomenclature of bodily regions, as distinguished from that of specific organs or structures. ► **toponymic** (,tɒpə'nɪmɪk) *or* **,topo'nymical** *adj*

topos ('tɒpɒs) *n, pl* **-oi** (-ɔɪ). a basic theme or concept, esp. a stock topic in rhetoric. [C20: Greek, literally: place]

topotype ('tɒpə,taɪp) *n* a specimen plant or animal taken from an area regarded as the typical habitat.

top out *vb (adv)* to place the highest stone on (a building) or perform a ceremony on this occasion.

topper ('tɒpə) *n* **1** an informal name for **top hat. 2** a person or thing that tops. **3** *Informal.* a remark that caps the one before.

topping ('tɒpɪŋ) *n* **1** something that tops something else, esp. a sauce or garnish for food. **2** *Angling.* part of a brightly-coloured feather, usually from a golden pheasant crest, used to top some artificial flies. ♦ *adj* **3** high or superior in rank, degree, etc. **4** *Brit. slang.* excellent; splendid.

topping lift *n Nautical.* a line or cable for raising the end of a boom that is away from the mast.

topple ('tɒp^{ə}l) *vb* **1** to tip over or cause to tip over, esp. from a height. **2** *(intr)* to lean precariously or totter. **3** *(tr)* to overthrow; oust. [C16: frequentative of TOP[1] (vb)]

tops (tɒps) *Slang.* ♦ *n* **1 the tops.** a person or thing of top quality. ♦ *adj* **2** *(postpositive)* excellent; superb.

TOPS (tɒps) *n* (in Britain) *acronym for* Training Opportunities Scheme.

topsail ('tɒp,seɪl; *Nautical* 'tɒps^{ə}l) *n* a square sail carried on a yard set on a topmast.

top-secret *adj* containing information whose disclosure would cause exceedingly grave damage to the nation and therefore classified as needing the highest level of secrecy and security.

top-shell *n* any marine gastropod mollusc of the mainly tropical Old World family *Trochidae,* having a typically brightly coloured top-shaped or conical shell.

topside ('tɒp,saɪd) *n* **1** the uppermost side of anything. **2** *Brit. and N.Z.* a lean cut of beef from the thigh containing no bone. **3** *(often pl)* **3a** the part of a ship's sides above the waterline. **3b** the parts of a ship above decks.

top slicing *n* the act or process of using a specific part of a sum of money for a special purpose, such as assessing a taxable gain.

topsoil ('tɒp,sɔɪl) *n* **1** the surface layer of soil. ♦ *vb* **2** *(tr)* to spread topsoil on (land). **3** *(tr)* to remove the topsoil from (land).

topspin ('tɒp,spɪn) *n Tennis, etc.* spin imparted to make a ball bounce or travel exceptionally far, high, or quickly, as by hitting it with a sharp forward and upward stroke. Compare **backspin.**

topsy-turvy ('tɒpsɪ'tɜ:vɪ) *adj* **1** upside down. **2** in a state of confusion. ♦ *adv* **3** in a topsy-turvy manner. ♦ *n* **4** a topsy-turvy state. [C16: probably from *tops,* plural of TOP[1] + obsolete *tervy* to turn upside down; perhaps related to Old English *tearflian* to roll over]

top up *vb (tr, adv) Brit.* **1** to raise the level of (a liquid, powder, etc.) in (a container), usually bringing it to the brim of the container: *top up the sugar in those bowls.* **2a** to increase the benefits from (an insurance scheme), esp. to increase a pension when a salary rise enables higher premiums to be paid. **2b** to add money to (a loan, bank account, etc.) in order to keep it at a constant or acceptable level. ♦ *n* **top-up. 3a** an amount added to something in order to raise it to or maintain it at a desired level. **3b** *(as modifier): a top-up loan; a top-up policy.*

toque (təʊk) *n* **1** a woman's small round brimless hat, popular esp. in Edwardian times. **2** a hat with a small brim and a pouched crown, popular in the 16th century. **3** *Canadian.* same as **tuque** (sense 2). **4** a chef's tall white hat. [C16: from French, from Old Spanish *toca* headdress, probably from Basque *tauka* hat]

tor (tɔ:) *n* **1** a high hill, esp. a bare rocky one. **2** *Chiefly southwestern Brit.* a prominent rock or heap of rocks, esp. on a hill. [Old English *torr,* probably of Celtic origin; compare Scottish Gaelic *torr* pile, Welsh *twr*]

Torah ('təʊrə; *Hebrew* tɔ'ra) *n* **1a** the Pentateuch. **1b** the scroll on which this is written, used in synagogue services. **2** the whole body of traditional Jewish teaching, including the Oral Law. **3** *(modifier)* promoting or according with traditional Jewish Law. [C16: from Hebrew: precept, from *yārāh* to instruct]

Torbay (,tɔ:'beɪ) *n* **1** a resort and from 1998 a unitary authority in SW England, in Devon, formed in 1968 by the amalgamation of Torquay with two neighbouring coastal towns. Pop.: 102 576 (1991). Area: 63 sq. km (24 sq. miles). **2** Also: **Tor Bay.** an inlet of the English Channel on the coast of SW England, near Torquay.

torbernite ('tɔ:bə,naɪt) *n* a green secondary mineral consisting of hydrated copper uranium phosphate in the form of square platelike crystals. Formula: $Cu(UO_2)(PO_4)_2.12H_2O$. [C19: named after *Torbern* O. Bergman (1735–84), Swedish chemist; see -ITE[1]]

torc (tɔ:k) *n* another spelling of **torque** (sense 1).

torch (tɔ:tʃ) *n* **1** a small portable electric lamp powered by one or more dry batteries. U.S. and Canadian word: **flashlight. 2** a wooden or tow shaft dipped in wax or tallow and set alight. **3** anything regarded as a source of enlightenment, guidance, etc.: *the torch of evangelism.* **4** any apparatus that burns with a hot flame for welding, brazing, or soldering. **5 carry a torch for.** to be in love with, esp. unrequitedly. **6 put to the torch.** to set fire to; burn down: *the looted monastery was put to the torch.* ♦ *vb* **7** *(tr) Slang.* to set fire to, esp. deliberately as an act of arson. [C13: from Old French *torche* handful of twisted straw, from Vulgar Latin *torca* (unattested), from Latin *torquēre* to twist] ► **'torch,like** *adj*

torchbearer ('tɔ:tʃ,bɛərə) *n* **1** a person or thing that carries a torch. **2** a person who leads or inspires.

torchère (tɔ:'ʃɛə) *n* a tall narrow stand for holding a candelabrum. [C20: from French, from *torche* TORCH]

torchier *or* **torchiere** ('tɔ:tʃɪə) *n* a standing lamp with a bowl for casting light upwards and so giving all-round indirect illumination. [C20: from TORCHÈRE]

torchon lace ('tɔ:ʃən; *French* tɔrʃɔ̃) *n* a coarse linen or cotton lace with a simple openwork pattern. [C19 *torchon,* from French: a cleaning cloth, from *torcher* to wipe, from Old French *torche* bundle of straw; see TORCH]

torch song *n* a sentimental or romantic popular song, usually sung by a woman. [C20: from the phrase *to carry a torch for (someone)*] ► **torch singer** *n*

torchwood ('tɔ:tʃ,wʊd) *n* **1** any of various rutaceous trees or shrubs of the genus *Amyris,* esp. *A. balsamifera,* of Florida and the Caribbean, having hard resinous wood used for torches. **2** any of various similar trees the wood of which is used for torches. **3** the wood of any of these trees.

tore[1] (tɔ:) *vb* the past tense of **tear**[2].

tore[2] (tɔ:) *n Architect.* another name for **torus** (sense 1). [C17: from French, from Latin: TORUS]

toreador ('tɒrɪə,dɔ:) *n* a bullfighter. [C17: from Spanish, from *torear* to take part in bullfighting, from *toro* a bull, from Latin *taurus;* compare STEER[2]]

toreador pants *pl n* tight-fitting women's trousers reaching to midcalf or above the ankle.

torero (tɒ'rɛərəʊ) *n, pl* **-ros.** a bullfighter, esp. one who fights on foot. [C18: from Spanish, from Late Latin *taurārius,* from Latin *taurus* a bull]

toreutics (tə'ru:tɪks) *n (functioning as sing or pl)* the art of making detailed ornamental reliefs, esp. in metal, by embossing and chasing. [C19: from Greek *toreutikos* concerning work in relief, from *toreuein* to bore through, from *toreus* tool for boring] ► **to'reutic** *adj*

Torfaen ('tɔ:,væn) *n* a county borough of SE Wales, created in 1996 from part of Gwent. Administrative centre: Pontypool. Pop.: 90 527 (1996 est.). Area: 290 sq. km (112 sq. miles).

tori ('tɔ:raɪ) *n* the plural of **torus.**

toric ('tɒrɪk) *adj* of, relating to, or having the form of a torus.

toric lens *n* a lens used to correct astigmatism, having one of its surfaces shaped like part of a torus so that its focal lengths are different in different meridians.

torii ('tɔ:rɪ,i:) *n, pl* **-rii.** a gateway, esp. one at the entrance to a Japanese Shinto temple. [C19: from Japanese, literally: a perch for birds]

Torino (to'ri:no) *n* the Italian name for **Turin.**

torment *vb* (tɔ:'mɛnt). *(tr)* **1** to afflict with great pain, suffering, or anguish; torture. **2** to tease or pester in an annoying way: *stop tormenting the dog.* ♦ *n* ('tɔ:mɛnt). **3** physical or mental pain. **4** a source of pain, worry, annoyance, etc. **5** *Archaic.* an instrument of torture. **6** *Archaic.* the infliction of torture. [C13: from Old French, from Latin *tormentum,* from *torquēre*] ► **tor'mented** *adj* ► **tor'mentedly** *adv* ► **tor'menting** *adj* ► **tor'mentingly** *adv*

tormentil ('tɔ:məntɪl) *n* a rosaceous downy perennial plant, *Potentilla erecta,* of Europe and W Asia, having serrated leaves, four-petalled yellow flowers, and an astringent root used in medicine, tanning, and dyeing. Also called: **bloodroot.** [C15: from Old French *tormentille,* from Medieval Latin *tormentilla,* from Latin *tormentum* agony; referring to its use in relieving pain; see TORMENT]

tormentor *or* **tormenter** (tɔ:'mɛntə) *n* **1** a person or thing that torments. **2** a curtain or movable piece of stage scenery at either side of the proscenium arch, used to mask lights or exits and entrances. **3** *Films.* a panel of sound-insulating material placed outside the field of the camera to control the acoustics on the sound stage.

torn (tɔːn) *vb* **1** the past participle of **tear**[2]. **2 that's torn it.** *Brit. slang.* an unexpected event or circumstance has upset one's plans. ♦ *adj* **3** split or cut. **4** divided or undecided, as in preference: *he was torn between staying and leaving.*

tornado (tɔːˈneɪdəʊ) *n, pl* **-does** *or* **-dos. 1** Also called: **cyclone** or (U.S. and Canadian informal) **twister.** a violent storm with winds whirling around a small area of extremely low pressure, usually characterized by a dark funnel-shaped cloud causing damage along its path. **2** a small but violent squall or whirlwind, such as those occurring on the West African coast. **3** any violently active or destructive person or thing. **[C16:** probably alteration of Spanish *tronada* thunderstorm (from *tronar* to thunder, from Latin *tonāre*), through influence of *tornar* to turn, from Latin *tornāre* to turn in a lathe**]** ▸ **tornadic** (tɔːˈnædɪk) *adj* ▸ **torˈnado-ˌlike** *adj*

toroid (ˈtɔːrɔɪd) *n* **1** *Geometry.* a surface generated by rotating a closed plane curve about a coplanar line that does not intersect the curve. **2** the solid enclosed by such a surface. See also **torus.** ▸ **toˈroidal** *adj*

Toronto (təˈrɒntəʊ) *n* a city in S central Canada, capital of Ontario, on Lake Ontario: the major industrial centre of Canada; two universities. Pop.: 635 395 (1991), with a metropolitan area of 4 338 400 (1995). ▸ **Toronˈtonian** *adj, n*

torose (ˈtɔːrəʊz, tɔːˈrəʊz) *or* **torous** (ˈtɔːrəs) *adj Biology.* (of a cylindrical part) having irregular swellings; knotted. **[C18:** from Latin *torōsus* muscular, from *torus* a swelling**]** ▸ **torosity** (tɔːˈrɒsɪtɪ) *n*

torpedo (tɔːˈpiːdəʊ) *n, pl* **-does. 1** a cylindrical self-propelled weapon carrying explosives that is launched from aircraft, ships, or submarines and follows an underwater path to hit its target. **2** *Obsolete.* a submarine mine. **3** *U.S. and Canadian.* a firework containing gravel and a percussion cap that explodes when dashed against a hard surface. **4** *U.S. and Canadian.* a detonator placed on a railway line as a danger signal. **5** any of various electric rays of the genus *Torpedo.* ♦ *vb* **-does, -doing, -doed.** (*tr*) **6** to hit (a ship, etc.) with one or a number of torpedoes. **7** to render ineffective; destroy or wreck: *to torpedo the administration's plan.* **[C16:** from Latin: crampfish (whose electric discharges can cause numbness), from *torpēre* to be inactive; see TORPID**]** ▸ **torˈpedo-ˌlike** *adj*

torpedo boat *n* (formerly) a small high-speed warship designed to carry out torpedo attacks in coastal waters.

torpedo-boat destroyer *n* (formerly) a large powerful high-speed torpedo boat designed to destroy enemy torpedo boats: a forerunner of the modern destroyer, from which the name is derived.

torpedo tube *n* the tube from which a torpedo is discharged from submarines or surface ships.

torpid (ˈtɔːpɪd) *adj* **1** apathetic, sluggish, or lethargic. **2** (of a hibernating animal) dormant; having greatly reduced metabolic activity. **3** unable to move or feel. **[C17:** from Latin *torpidus,* from *torpēre* to be numb, motionless**]** ▸ **torˈpidity** *n* ▸ **ˈtorpidly** *adv*

torpor (ˈtɔːpə) *n* a state of torpidity. **[C17:** from Latin: inactivity, from *torpēre* to be motionless**]** ▸ **ˌtorporˈific** *adj*

Torquay (ˌtɔːˈkiː) *n* a town and resort in SW England, in S Devon: administratively part of Torbay since 1968.

torque (tɔːk) *n* **1** Also: **torc.** a necklace or armband made of twisted metal, worn esp. by the ancient Britons and Gauls. **2** any force or system of forces that causes or tends to cause rotation. **3** the ability of a shaft to cause rotation. **[C19:** from Latin *torquēs* necklace, and *torquēre* to twist**]**

torque converter *n* a hydraulic device for the smooth transmission of power in which an engine-driven impeller transmits its momentum to a fluid held in a sealed container, which in turn drives a rotor. Also called: **hydraulic coupling.**

Torquemada (*Spanish* torkeˈmaða) *n* **Tomás de** (toˈmas de). 1420–98, Spanish Dominican monk. As first Inquisitor-General of Spain (1483–98), he was responsible for the burning of some 2000 heretics.

torque meter *n Engineering.* a device designed to determine the torque or torsion in a shaft, usually by measuring the twist in a calibrated length of shafting. Also called: **torsion meter.**

torques (ˈtɔːkwiːz) *n* a distinctive band of hair, feathers, skin, or colour around the neck of an animal; a collar. **[C17:** from Latin: necklace, from *torquēre* to twist**]** ▸ **torquate** (ˈtɔːkwɪt, -kweɪt) *adj*

torque spanner *n* a spanner having a torque-limiting mechanism which can be set to a predetermined value.

torque wrench *n* a type of wrench with a gauge attached to indicate the torque applied to the workpiece.

torr (tɔː) *n, pl* **torr.** a unit of pressure equal to one millimetre of mercury (133.322 newtons per square metre). **[C20:** named after E. TORRICELLI**]**

Torrance (ˈtɒrəns) *n* a city in SW California, southwest of Los Angeles: developed rapidly with the discovery of oil. Pop.: 136 183 (1996 est.).

Torre del Greco (*Italian* ˈtorre del ˈgreːko) *n* a city in SW Italy, in Campania near Vesuvius on the Bay of Naples: damaged several times by eruptions. Pop.: 100 688 (1992).

torrefy (ˈtɒrɪˌfaɪ) *vb* **-fies, -fying, -fied.** (*tr*) to dry (drugs, ores, etc.) by subjection to intense heat; roast. **[C17:** from French *torréfier,* from Latin *torrefacere,* from *torrēre* to parch + *facere* to make**]** ▸ **torrefaction** (ˌtɒrɪˈfækʃən) *n*

Torrens (ˈtɒrənz) *n* **Lake.** a shallow salt lake in E central South Australia, about 8 m (25 ft.) below sea level. Area: 5776 sq. km (2230 sq. miles).

Torrens title *n Austral.* legal title to land based on record of registration rather than on title deeds. **[**from Sir Robert Richard *Torrens* (1814–84), who introduced the system as premier of South Australia in 1857**]**

torrent (ˈtɒrənt) *n* **1** a fast, voluminous, or violent stream of water or other liquid. **2** an overwhelming flow of thoughts, words, sound, etc. ♦ *adj* **3** *Rare.* like or relating to a torrent. **[C17:** from French, from Latin *torrēns* (n), from *torrēns* (adj) burning, from *torrēre* to burn**]**

torrential (tɒˈrenʃəl, tə-) *adj* **1** of or relating to a torrent. **2** pouring or flowing fast, violently, or heavily: *torrential rain.* **3** abundant, overwhelming, or irrepressible: *torrential abuse.* ▸ **torˈrentially** *adv*

Torreón (*Spanish* torreˈɔn) *n* an industrial city in N Mexico, in Coahuila state. Pop.: 439 436 (1990).

Torres Strait (ˈtɔːrɪz, ˈtɒr-) *n* a strait between NE Australia and S New Guinea, linking the Arafura Sea with the Coral Sea. Width: about 145 km (90 miles).

Torricelli (ˌtɒrɪˈtʃelɪ) *n* **Evangelista** (evandʒeˈlista). 1608–47, Italian physicist and mathematician, who discovered the principle of the barometer.

Torricellian tube (ˌtɒrɪˈselɪən) *n* a vertical glass tube partly evacuated and partly filled with mercury, the height of which is used as a measure of atmospheric pressure. **[C17:** named after E. TORRICELLI**]**

Torricellian vacuum *n* the vacuum at the top of a Torricellian tube. **[C17:** named after E. TORRICELLI**]**

torrid (ˈtɒrɪd) *adj* **1** so hot and dry as to parch or scorch. **2** arid or parched. **3** highly charged emotionally: *a torrid love scene.* **[C16:** from Latin *torridus,* from *torrēre* to scorch**]** ▸ **torˈridity** *or* **ˈtorridness** *n* ▸ **ˈtorridly** *adv*

Torrid Zone *n Rare.* that part of the earth's surface lying between the tropics of Cancer and Capricorn.

torsade (tɔːˈseɪd) *n* an ornamental twist or twisted cord, as on hats. **[C19:** from French, from obsolete *tors* twisted, from Late Latin *torsus,* from Latin *torquēre* to twist**]**

torsi (ˈtɔːsɪ) *n Rare.* a plural of **torso.**

torsibility (ˌtɔːsəˈbɪlɪtɪ) *n* **1** the ability to be twisted. **2** the degree of resistance to or the capacity of recovering from being twisted.

torsion (ˈtɔːʃən) *n* **1a** the twisting of a part by application of equal and opposite torques. **1b** the condition of twist and shear stress produced by a torque on a part or component. **2** the act of twisting or the state of being twisted. **[C15:** from Old French, from medical Latin *torsiō* griping pains, from Latin *torquēre* to twist, torture**]** ▸ **ˈtorsional** *adj* ▸ **ˈtorsionally** *adv*

torsion balance *n* an instrument used to measure small forces, esp. electric or magnetic forces, by the torsion they produce in a thin wire, thread, or rod.

torsion bar *n* a metal bar acting as a torsional spring, esp. as used in the suspensions of some motor vehicles.

torsion meter *n* another name for **torque meter.**

torsk (tɔːsk) *n, pl* **torsks** *or* **torsk.** a gadoid food fish, *Brosmius brosme,* of northern coastal waters, having a single long dorsal fin. Usual U.S. and Canadian name: **cusk. [C17:** of Scandinavian origin; related to Old Norse *thorskr* codfish, Danish *torsk***]**

torso (ˈtɔːsəʊ) *n, pl* **-sos** *or* **-si** (-sɪ). **1** the trunk of the human body. **2** a statue of a nude human trunk, esp. without the head or limbs. **3** something regarded as incomplete or truncated. **[C18:** from Italian: stalk, stump, from Latin: THYRSUS**]**

tort (tɔːt) *n Law.* a civil wrong or injury arising out of an act or failure to act, independently of any contract, for which an action for damages may be brought. **[C14:** from Old French, from Medieval Latin *tortum,* literally: something twisted, from Latin *torquēre* to twist**]**

torte (tɔːt; *German* ˈtɔrtə) *n* a rich cake, originating in Austria, usually decorated or filled with cream, fruit, nuts, and jam. **[C16:** ultimately perhaps from Late Latin *tōrta* a round loaf, of uncertain origin**]**

Tortelier (*French* tɔrtəlje) *n* **Paul** (pɔl). 1914–90, French cellist and composer.

tortellini (ˌtɔːtəˈliːnɪ) *n* pasta cut into small rounds, folded about a filling, and boiled. **[**from Italian, diminutive of *tortelli* a type of pie, ultimately from Late Latin *tōrta* a round loaf or cake; see TORTE**]**

tort-feasor (ˈtɔːtˈfiːzə) *n Law.* a person guilty of tort. **[C17:** from Old French, literally: wrongdoer, from TORT + *faiseur,* from *faire* to do**]**

torticollis (ˌtɔːtɪˈkɒlɪs) *n Pathol.* an abnormal position of the head, usually with the neck bent to one side, caused congenitally by contracture of muscles, muscular spasm, etc. **[C19:** New Latin, from Latin *tortus* twisted (from *torquēre* to twist) + *collum* neck**]** ▸ **ˌtortiˈcollar** *adj*

tortile (ˈtɔːtaɪl) *adj Rare.* twisted or coiled. **[C17:** from Latin *tortilis* winding, from *tortus* twisted, from *torquēre* to twist**]** ▸ **tortility** (tɔːˈtɪlɪtɪ) *n*

tortilla (tɔːˈtiːə) *n Mexican cookery.* a kind of thin pancake made from corn meal and cooked on a hot griddle until dry. **[C17:** from Spanish: a little cake, from *torta* a round cake, from Late Latin; see TORTE**]**

tortillon (ˌtɔːtiːˈɒn, -ˈəʊn; *French* tɔrtijɔ̃) *n* another word for **stump** (sense 5). **[**from French: something twisted, from Old French *tortiller* to twist**]**

tortious (ˈtɔːʃəs) *adj Law.* having the nature of or involving a tort; wrongful. **[C14:** from Anglo-French *torcious,* from *torcion,* literally: a twisting, from Late Latin *tortiō* torment, from Latin *torquēre* to twist; influenced in meaning by TORT**]** ▸ **ˈtortiously** *adv*

tortoise (ˈtɔːtəs) *n* **1** any herbivorous terrestrial chelonian reptile of the family *Testudinidae,* of most warm regions, having a heavy dome-shaped shell and clawed limbs. Related adjs: **chelonian, testudinal. 2 water tortoise.** another name for **terrapin. 3** a slow-moving person. **4** another word for **testudo.** ♦ See also **giant tortoise. [C15:** probably from Old French *tortue* (influenced by Latin *tortus* twisted), from Medieval Latin *tortūca,* from Late Latin *tartarūcha* coming from Tartarus, from Greek *tartaroukhos;* referring to the belief that the tortoise originated in the underworld**]**

tortoise beetle *n* a metallic-coloured leaf beetle of the genus *Cassida,* in which the elytra and terga cover the body like a shell.

tortoiseshell (ˈtɔːtəsˌʃel) *n* **1** a horny translucent yellow-and-brown mottled substance obtained from the outer layer of the shell of the hawksbill turtle: used for making ornaments, jewellery, etc. **2** a similar synthetic substance, esp. plastic or celluloid, now more widely used than the natural product. **3** a breed of domestic cat, usually female, having black, cream, and brownish markings. **4**

any of several nymphalid butterflies of the genus *Nymphalis,* and related genera, having orange-brown wings with black markings. **5 tortoiseshell turtle** another name for **hawksbill turtle. 6a** a yellowish-brown mottled colour. **6b** (*as adj*)*: a tortoiseshell décor.* **7** (*modifier*) made of tortoiseshell: *a tortoiseshell comb.*

Tortola (tɔːˈtəʊlə) *n* an island in the NE Caribbean, in the Leeward Islands group: chief island of the British Virgin Islands. Pop.: 13 568 (1991). Area: 62 sq. km (24 sq. miles).

tortoni (tɔːˈtəʊnɪ) *n* a rich ice cream often flavoured with sherry. **[**from Italian: probably from the name of a 19th-century Italian caterer in Paris**]**

tortricid (ˈtɔːtrɪsɪd) *n* **1** any small moth of the chiefly temperate family *Tortricidae,* the larvae of which live concealed in leaves, which they roll or tie together, and are pests of fruit and forest trees: includes the codling moth. ♦ *adj* **2** of, relating to, or belonging to the family *Tortricidae.* **[C19:** from New Latin *Tortrīcidae,* from *tortrix,* feminine of *tortor,* literally: twister, referring to the leaf-rolling of the larvae, from *torquēre* to twist**]**

Tortuga (tɔːˈtuːgə) *n* an island in the Caribbean, off the NW coast of Haiti: haunt of pirates in the 17th century. Area: 180 sq. km (70 sq. miles). French name: **La Tortue** (la tɔrty).

tortuosity (ˌtɔːtjuˈɒsɪtɪ) *n, pl* **-ties. 1** the state or quality of being tortuous. **2** a twist, turn, or coil.

tortuous (ˈtɔːtjʊəs) *adj* **1** twisted or winding: *a tortuous road.* **2** devious or cunning: *a tortuous mind.* **3** intricate. ▸ **ˈtortuously** *adv* ▸ **ˈtortuousness** *n*

torture (ˈtɔːtʃə) *vb* (*tr*) **1** to cause extreme physical pain to, esp. in order to extract information, break resistance, etc.: *to torture prisoners.* **2** to give mental anguish to. **3** to twist into a grotesque form. ♦ *n* **4** physical or mental anguish. **5** the practice of torturing a person. **6** a cause of mental agony or worry. **[C16:** from Late Latin *tortūra* a twisting, from *torquēre* to twist**]** ▸ **ˈtortured** *adj* ▸ **ˈtorturedly** *adv* ▸ **ˈtorturer** *n* ▸ **ˈtorturesome** *or* **ˈtorturous** *adj* ▸ **ˈtorturing** *adj* ▸ **ˈtorturingly** *adv* ▸ **ˈtorturously** *adv*

USAGE The adjective *torturous* is sometimes confused with *tortuous.* One speaks of a *torturous* experience, i.e. one that involves pain or suffering, but of a *tortuous* road, i.e. one that winds or twists.

Toruń (*Polish* ˈtɔrunj) *n* an industrial city in N Poland, on the River Vistula: developed around a castle that was founded by the Teutonic Knights in 1230; under Prussian rule (1793–1919). Pop.: 204 300 (1996 est.). German name: **Thorn.**

torus (ˈtɔːrəs) *n, pl* **-ri** (-raɪ). **1** Also called: **tore.** a large convex moulding approximately semicircular in cross section, esp. one used on the base of a classical column. **2** *Geom.* a ring-shaped surface generated by rotating a circle about a coplanar line that does not intersect the circle. Area: $4\pi^2 Rr$; volume: $2\pi^2 Rr^2$, where *r* is the radius of the circle and *R* is the distance from the line to the centre of the circle. **3** *Botany.* another name for **receptacle** (sense 2). **4** *Anatomy.* a ridge, fold, or similar linear elevation. **[C16:** from Latin: a swelling, of obscure origin**]**

Torvill and Dean (ˈtɔːvɪl) *n* two British ice dancers, **Jayne Torvill,** born 1957, and **Christopher Dean,** born 1958. They won the world championships in 1981–84, the European championships in 1981–82, 1984, and 1994, and the gold medal in the 1984 Olympic Games.

Tory (ˈtɔːrɪ) *n, pl* **-ries. 1** a member or supporter of the Conservative Party in Great Britain or Canada. **2** a member of the English political party that opposed the exclusion of James, Duke of York from the royal succession (1679–80). Tory remained the label for subsequent major conservative interests until they gave birth to the Conservative Party in the 1830s. **3** an American supporter of the British cause; loyalist. Compare **Whig. 4** (*sometimes not cap.*) an ultraconservative or reactionary. **5** (in the 17th century) an Irish Roman Catholic, esp. an outlaw who preyed upon English settlers. ♦ *adj* **6** of, characteristic of, or relating to Tories. **7** (*sometimes not cap.*) ultraconservative or reactionary. **[C17:** from Irish *tōraidhe* outlaw, from Middle Irish *tōir* pursuit**]** ▸ **ˈToryish** *adj* ▸ **ˈToryism** *n*

tosa (ˈtəʊsə) *n* a large dog, usually red in colour, which is a cross between a mastiff and a Great Dane: originally developed for dog-fighting; it is not recognized as a breed by kennel clubs outside Japan. **[C20:** from the name of a province of the island of Skikoku, Japan**]**

Toscana (tosˈkaːna) *n* the Italian name for **Tuscany.**

Toscanini (ˌtɒskəˈniːnɪ) *n* **Arturo** (arˈtuːro). 1867–1957, Italian conductor; musical director of La Scala, Milan, and of the NBC symphony orchestra (1937–57) in New York.

tosh (tɒʃ) *n Slang, chiefly Brit.* nonsense; rubbish. **[C19:** of unknown origin**]**

toss (tɒs) *vb* **1** (*tr*) to throw lightly or with a flourish, esp. with the palm of the hand upwards. **2** to fling or be flung about, esp. constantly or regularly in an agitated or violent way: *a ship tosses in a storm.* **3** to discuss or put forward for discussion in an informal way. **4** (*tr*) (of an animal such as a horse) to throw (its rider). **5** (*tr*) (of an animal) to butt with the head or the horns and throw into the air: *the bull tossed the matador.* **6** (*tr*) to shake, agitate, or disturb. **7** to toss up a coin with (someone) in order to decide or allot something: *I'll toss you for it; let's toss for it.* **8** (*intr*) to move away angrily or impatiently: *she tossed out of the room.* ♦ *n* **9** an abrupt movement. **10** a rolling or pitching motion. **11** the act or an instance of tossing. **12** the act of tossing up a coin. See **toss-up. 13 argue the toss.** to wrangle or dispute at length. **14** a fall from a horse or other animal. **15 give a toss.** *Slang.* to be concerned or interested (esp. in the phrase **not give a toss**). **[C16:** of Scandinavian origin; related to Norwegian, Swedish *tossa* to strew**]**

tosser (ˈtɒsə) *n Brit. slang.* a stupid or despicable person. **[C20:** probably from TOSS OFF (to masturbate)**]**

toss off *vb* (*adv*) **1** (*tr*) to perform, write, consume, etc., quickly and easily: *he tossed off a letter to Jim.* **2** (*tr*) to drink quickly at one draught. **3** (*intr*) *Brit. taboo.* to masturbate.

tosspot (ˈtɒsˌpɒt) *n* **1** *Archaic or literary.* a habitual drinker. **2** *Brit. slang.* a stupid or contemptible person.

toss up *vb* (*adv*) **1** to spin (a coin) in the air in order to decide between alternatives by guessing which side will fall uppermost. **2** (*tr*) to prepare (food) quickly. ♦ *n* **toss-up. 3** an instance of tossing up a coin. **4** *Informal.* an even chance or risk; gamble.

Tostig (ˈtɒstɪg) *n* died 1066, earl of Northumbria (1055–65), brother of King Harold II. He joined the Norwegian forces that invaded England in 1066 and died at Stamford Bridge.

tot[1] (tɒt) *n* **1** a young child; toddler. **2** *Chiefly Brit.* a small amount of anything. **3** a small measure of spirits. **[C18:** perhaps short for *totterer;* see TOTTER**]**

tot[2] (tɒt) *vb* **tots, totting, totted.** (usually foll. by *up*) *Chiefly Brit.* to total; add. **[C17:** shortened from TOTAL or from Latin *totum* all**]**

total (ˈtəʊtᵊl) *n* **1** the whole, esp. regarded as the complete sum of a number of parts. ♦ *adj* **2** complete; absolute: *the evening was a total failure; a total eclipse.* **3** (*prenominal*) being or related to a total: *the total number of passengers.* ♦ *vb* **-tals, -talling, -talled** *or U.S.* **-tals, -taling, -taled. 4** (when *intr,* sometimes foll. by *to*) to amount: *to total six pounds.* **5** (*tr*) to add up: *to total a list of prices.* **6** (*tr*) *Slang.* to kill or destroy. **[C14:** from Old French, from Medieval Latin *tōtālis,* from Latin *tōtus* all**]** ▸ **ˈtotally** *adv*

total allergy syndrome *n* a condition in which a person suffers from a large number of symptoms that are claimed to be caused by allergies to various substances used or encountered in modern life.

total depravity *n Chiefly Calvinist theol.* the doctrine that man's nature is totally corrupt as a result of the Fall.

total eclipse *n* an eclipse as seen from a particular area of the earth's surface where the eclipsed body is completely hidden. Compare **annular eclipse, partial eclipse.**

total football *n* an attacking style of play, popularized by the Dutch national team of the 1970s, in which there are no fixed positions and every outfield player can join in the attack.

total heat *n* another term for **enthalpy.**

total internal reflection *n Physics.* the complete reflection of a light ray at the boundary of two media, when the ray is in the medium with greater refractive index.

totalitarian (təʊˌtælɪˈtɛərɪən) *adj* **1** of, denoting, relating to, or characteristic of a dictatorial one-party state that regulates every realm of life. ♦ *n* **2** a person who advocates or practises totalitarian policies. **[**from TOTALITY + -ARIAN**]** ▸ **toˌtaliˈtarianism** *n*

totality (təʊˈtælɪtɪ) *n, pl* **-ties. 1** the whole amount. **2** the state of being total. **3** the state or period of an eclipse when light from the eclipsed body is totally obscured.

totalizator (ˈtəʊtᵊlaɪˌzeɪtə), **totalizer** *or* **totalisator, totaliser** *n* **1** a system of betting on horse races in which the aggregate stake, less an administration charge and tax, is paid out to winners in proportion to their stake. **2** the machine that records bets in this system and works out odds, pays out winnings, etc. **3** an apparatus for registering totals, as of a particular function or measurement. ♦ U.S. and Canadian term (for senses 1, 2): **pari-mutuel.**

totalize *or* **totalise** (ˈtəʊtᵊˌlaɪz) *vb* to combine or make into a total. ▸ **ˌtotaliˈzation** *or* **ˌtotaliˈsation** *n*

totalizer *or* **totaliser** (ˈtəʊtᵊˌlaɪzə) *n* **1** a variant of **totalizator. 2** *Chiefly U.S.* an adding machine.

total quality management *n* an approach to the management of an organization that integrates the needs of customers with a deep understanding of the technical details, costs, and human-resource relationships of the organization. Abbrev.: **TQM.**

total recall *n Psychol.* the faculty or an instance of complete and clear recall of every detail of something.

total serialism *or* **serialization** *n* (in some music after 1945) the use of serial techniques applied to such elements as rhythm, dynamics, and tone colour, as found in the early works of Stockhausen, Boulez, etc.

totaquine (ˈtəʊtəˌkwiːn, -kwɪn) *n* a mixture of quinine and other alkaloids derived from cinchona bark, used as a substitute for quinine in treating malaria. **[C20:** from New Latin *tōtaquīna,* from TOTA(L) + Spanish *quina* cinchona bark; see QUININE**]**

totara (ˈtəʊtərə) *n* a tall coniferous forest tree, *Podocarpus totara,* of New Zealand, having a hard durable wood. **[**Maori**]**

tote[1] (təʊt) *Informal.* ♦ *vb* **1** (*tr*) to carry, convey, or drag. ♦ *n* **2** the act of or an instance of toting. **3** something toted. **[C17:** of obscure origin**]** ▸ **ˈtoter** *n*

tote[2] (təʊt) *n* (usually preceded by *the*) *Informal.* short for **totalizator** (senses 1, 2).

tote bag *n* a large roomy handbag or shopping bag.

totem (ˈtəʊtəm) *n* **1** (in some societies, esp. among North American Indians) an object, species of animal or plant, or natural phenomenon symbolizing a clan, family, etc., often having ritual associations. **2** a representation of such an object. **[C18:** from Ojibwa *nintōtēm* mark of my family**]** ▸ **totemic** (təʊˈtɛmɪk) *adj* ▸ **toˈtemically** *adv*

totemism (ˈtəʊtəˌmɪzəm) *n* **1** the belief in kinship of groups or individuals having a common totem. **2** the rituals, taboos, and other practices associated with such a belief. ▸ **ˈtotemist** *n* ▸ **ˌtotemˈistic** *adj*

totem pole *n* a pole carved or painted with totemic figures set up by certain North American Indians, esp. those of the NW Pacific coast, within a village as a tribal symbol or, sometimes, in memory of a dead person.

tother *or* **t'other** (ˈtʌðə) *adj, n Archaic or dialect.* the other. **[C13** *the tother,* by mistaken division from *thet other* (*thet,* from Old English *thæt,* neuter of THE[1])**]**

totipalmate (ˌtəʊtɪˈpælmɪt, -ˌmeɪt) *adj* (of certain birds) having all four toes webbed. [C19: from Latin *tōtus* entire + *palmate,* from Latin *palmātus* shaped like a hand, from *palma* PALM[1]] ▸ ˌ**totipal'mation** *n*

totipotent (təʊ'tɪpətənt) *adj* (of an animal cell) capable of differentiation and so forming a new individual, tissue, organ, etc. [C20: from Latin *tōtus* entire + POTENT[1]] ▸ **to'tipotency** *n*

totter ('tɒtə) *vb* (*intr*) **1** to walk or move in an unsteady manner, as from old age. **2** to sway or shake as if about to fall. **3** to be failing, unstable, or precarious. ◆ *n* **4** the act or an instance of tottering. [C12: perhaps from Old English *tealtrian* to waver, and Middle Dutch *touteren* to stagger] ▸ '**totterer** *n* ▸ '**tottering** *adj* ▸ '**totteringly** *adv* ▸ '**tottery** *adj*

tottie *or* **totty** ('tɒtɪ) *adj Chiefly Scot.* very small; tiny. [from TOT[1]]

totting ('tɒtɪŋ) *n Brit.* the practice of searching through rubbish for usable or saleable items. [C19: of unknown origin]

totty ('tɒtɪ) *n Brit. informal.* women collectively considered as sexual objects. [C19: diminutive of TOT[1]]

toucan ('tu:kən) *n* any tropical American arboreal fruit-eating bird of the family *Ramphastidae,* having a large brightly coloured bill with serrated edges and a bright plumage. [C16: from French, from Portuguese *tucano,* from Tupi *tucana,* probably imitative of its cry]

touch (tʌtʃ) *n* **1** the sense by which the texture and other qualities of objects can be experienced when they come in contact with a part of the body surface, esp. the tips of the fingers. Related adjs: **haptic, tactile, tactual. 2** the quality of an object as perceived by this sense; feel; feeling. **3** the act or an instance of something coming into contact with the body. **4** a gentle push, tap, or caress. **5** a small amount; hint: *a touch of sarcasm.* **6** a noticeable effect; influence: *the house needed a woman's touch.* **7** any slight stroke or mark: *with a touch of his brush he captured the scene.* **8** characteristic manner or style: *the artist had a distinctive touch.* **9** a detail of some work, esp. a literary or artistic work: *she added a few finishing touches to the book.* **10** a slight attack, as of a disease: *a touch of bronchitis.* **11** a specific ability or facility: *the champion appeared to have lost his touch.* **12** the state of being aware of a situation or in contact with someone: *to get in touch with someone.* **13** the state of being in physical contact. **14** a trial or test (esp. in the phrase **put to the touch**). **15** *Rugby, soccer, etc.* the area outside the touchlines, beyond which the ball is out of play (esp. in the phrase **in touch**). **16** *Archaic.* **16a** an official stamp on metal indicating standard purity. **16b** the die stamp used to apply this mark. Now usually called: **hallmark. 17** a scoring hit in competitive fencing. **18** an estimate of the amount of gold in an alloy as obtained by use of a touchstone. **19** the technique of fingering a keyboard instrument. **20** the quality of the action of a keyboard instrument with regard to the relative ease with which the keys may be depressed: *this piano has a nice touch.* **21** *Bell-ringing.* any series of changes where the permutations are fewer in number than for a peal. **22** *Slang.* **22a** the act of asking for money as a loan or gift, often by devious means. **22b** the money received in this way. **22c** a person asked for money in this way: *he was an easy touch.* ◆ *vb* **23** (*tr*) to cause or permit a part of the body to come into contact with. **24** (*tr*) to tap, feel, or strike, esp. with the hand: *don't touch the cake!* **25** to come or cause (something) to come into contact with (something else): *their hands touched briefly; he touched the match to the fuse.* **26** (*intr*) to be in contact. **27** (*tr; usually used with a negative*) to take hold of (a person or thing), esp. in violence: *don't touch the baby!* **28** to be adjacent to (each other): *the two properties touch.* **29** (*tr*) to move or disturb by handling: *someone's touched my desk.* **30** (*tr*) to have an effect on: *the war scarcely touched our town.* **31** (*tr*) to produce an emotional response in: *his sad story touched her.* **32** (*tr*) to affect; concern. **33** (*tr; usually used with a negative*) to partake of, eat, or drink. **34** (*tr; usually used with a negative*) to handle or deal with: *I wouldn't touch that business.* **35** (when *intr,* often foll. by *on*) to allude (to) briefly or in passing: *the speech touched on several subjects.* **36** (*tr*) to tinge or tint slightly: *brown hair touched with gold.* **37** (*tr*) to spoil or injure slightly: *blackfly touched the flowers.* **38** (*tr*) to mark, as with a brush or pen. **39** (*tr*) to compare to in quality or attainment; equal or match: *there's no-one to touch him.* **40** (*tr*) to reach or attain: *he touched the high point in his career.* **41** (*intr*) to dock or stop briefly: *the ship touches at Tenerife.* **42** (*tr*) *Slang.* to ask for a loan or gift of money from. **43** *Rare.* **43a** to finger (the keys or strings of an instrument). **43b** to play (a tune, piece of music, etc.) in this way. ◆ See also **touchdown, touch off, touch up.** [C13: from Old French *tochier,* from Vulgar Latin *toccāre* (unattested) to strike, ring (a bell), probably imitative of a tapping sound] ▸ '**touchable** *adj* ▸ '**touchableness** *n* ▸ '**toucher** *n* ▸ '**touchless** *adj*

touch and go *adj* (**touch-and-go** *when prenominal*) risky or critical: *a touch-and-go situation.*

touchback ('tʌtʃˌbæk) *n American football.* a play in which the ball is put down by a player behind his own goal line when the ball has been put across the goal line by an opponent. Compare **safety** (sense 4b.).

touchdown ('tʌtʃˌdaʊn) *n* **1** the moment at which a landing aircraft or spacecraft comes into contact with the landing surface. **2** *Rugby.* the act of placing or touching the ball on the ground behind the goal line, as in scoring a try. **3** *American football.* a scoring play worth six points, achieved by being in possession of the ball in the opposing team's end zone. Abbrev.: **TD.** See also **field goal.** ◆ *vb* **touch down.** (*intr, adv*) **4** (of a space vehicle, aircraft, etc.) to land. **5** *Rugby.* to place the ball behind the goal line, as when scoring a try.

touché (tu:'ʃeɪ) *interj* **1** an acknowledgment that a scoring hit has been made in a fencing competition. **2** an acknowledgment of the striking home of a remark or the capping of a witticism. [from French, literally: touched]

touched (tʌtʃt) *adj* (*postpositive*) **1** moved to sympathy or emotion; affected. **2** showing slight insanity.

touch football *n* an informal version of American football chiefly characterized by players being touched rather than tackled.

touchhole ('tʌtʃˌhəʊl) *n* a hole in the breech of early cannon and firearms through which the charge was ignited.

touching ('tʌtʃɪŋ) *adj* **1** evoking or eliciting tender feelings: *your sympathy is touching.* ◆ *prep* **2** on the subject of; relating to. ▸ '**touchingly** *adv* ▸ '**touchingness** *n*

touch-in goal *n Rugby.* the area at each end of a pitch between the goal line and the dead-ball line.

touch judge *n* one of the two linesmen in rugby.

touchline ('tʌtʃˌlaɪn) *n* either of the lines marking the side of the playing area in certain games, such as rugby.

touchmark ('tʌtʃˌmɑ:k) *n* a maker's mark stamped on pewter objects.

touch-me-not *n* any of several balsaminaceous plants of the genus *Impatiens,* esp. *I. noli-me-tangere,* having yellow spurred flowers and seed pods that burst open at a touch when ripe. Also called: **noli-me-tangere.**

touch off *vb* (*tr, adv*) **1** to cause to explode, as by touching with a match. **2** to cause (a disturbance, violence, etc.) to begin: *the marchers' action touched off riots.*

touchpaper ('tʌtʃˌpeɪpə) *n* **1** paper soaked in saltpetre and used for firing gunpowder. **2 light the (blue) touchpaper.** to do something that will cause much anger or excitement.

touchstone ('tʌtʃˌstəʊn) *n* **1** a criterion or standard by which judgment is made. **2** a hard dark siliceous stone, such as basalt or jasper, that is used to test the quality of gold and silver from the colour of the streak they produce on it.

touch system *n* a typing system in which the fingers are trained to find the correct keys, permitting the typist to read and type copy without looking at the keyboard.

touch-tone *adj* of or relating to a telephone dialling system in which each of the buttons pressed generates a tone of a different pitch, which is transmitted to the exchange.

touch-type *vb* (*intr*) to type without having to look at the keys of the typewriter. ▸ '**touch-ˌtypist** *n*

touch up *vb* (*tr, adv*) **1** to put extra or finishing touches to. **2** to enhance, renovate, or falsify by putting extra touches to: *to touch up a photograph.* **3** to stimulate or rouse as by a tap or light blow. **4** *Brit. slang.* to touch or caress (someone), esp. to arouse sexual feelings. ◆ *n* **touch-up. 5** a renovation or retouching, as of a painting.

touchwood ('tʌtʃˌwʊd) *n* something, esp. dry wood or fungus material such as amadou, used as tinder. [C16: TOUCH (in the sense: to kindle) + WOOD[1]]

touchy ('tʌtʃɪ) *adj* **touchier, touchiest. 1** easily upset or irritated; oversensitive. **2** extremely risky. **3** easily ignited. ▸ '**touchily** *adv* ▸ '**touchiness** *n*

touchy-feely ('tʌtʃɪ'fi:lɪ) *adj Informal, sometimes derogatory.* sensitive and caring.

tough (tʌf) *adj* **1** strong or resilient; durable: *a tough material.* **2** not tender: *he could not eat the tough steak.* **3** having a great capacity for endurance; hardy and fit: *a tough mountaineer.* **4** rough or pugnacious: *a tough gangster.* **5** resolute or intractable: *a tough employer.* **6** difficult or troublesome to do or deal with: *a tough problem.* **7** *Informal.* unfortunate or unlucky: *it's tough on him.* ◆ *n* **8** a rough, vicious, or pugnacious person. ◆ *adv* **9** *Informal.* violently, aggressively, or intractably: *to treat someone tough.* ◆ *vb* (*tr*) **10** *Slang.* to stand firm, hold out against (a difficulty or difficult situation) (esp. in **tough it out**). [Old English *tōh;* related to Old High German *zāhi* tough, Old Norse *tā* trodden ground in front of a house] ▸ '**toughish** *adj* ▸ '**toughly** *adv*

toughen ('tʌfən) *vb* to make or become tough or tougher.

tough love *n* the practice of taking a stern attitude towards a relative or friend suffering from an addiction, etc., to help the addict overcome the problem.

tough-minded *adj* practical, unsentimental, stern, or intractable. ▸ ˌ**tough-'mindedly** *adv* ▸ ˌ**tough-'mindedness** *n*

toughness ('tʌfnɪs) *n* **1** the quality or an instance of being tough. **2** *Metallurgy.* the ability of a metal to withstand repeated twisting and bending, measured by the energy in kilojoules needed to break it. Compare **brittleness** (sense 2), **softness** (sense 2).

Toul (tu:l) *n* a town in NE France: a leading episcopal see in the Middle Ages. Pop.: 17 406 (1982).

Toulon (*French* tulɔ̃) *n* a fortified port and naval base in SE France, on the Mediterranean: naval arsenal developed by Henry IV and Richelieu, later fortified by Vauban. Pop.: 170 167 (1990).

Toulouse (tu:'lu:z) *n* a city in S France, on the Garonne River: scene of severe religious strife in the early 13th and mid-16th centuries; university (1229). Pop.: 365 933 (1990). Ancient name: **Tolosa** (tə'ləʊsə).

Toulouse-Lautrec (*French* tuluzlotrɛk) *n* **Henri** (**Marie Raymond**) **de** (ɑ̃ri də). 1864–1901, French painter and lithographer, noted for his paintings and posters of the life of Montmartre, Paris.

toun (tu:n) *n Scot.* **1** a town. **2** a farmstead.

toupee ('tu:peɪ) *n* **1** a wig or hairpiece worn, esp. by men, to cover a bald or balding place. **2** (formerly) a prominent lock on a periwig, esp. in the 18th century. [C18: apparently from French *toupet* forelock, from Old French *toup* top, of Germanic origin; see TOP[1]]

tour (tʊə) *n* **1** an extended journey, usually taken for pleasure, visiting places of interest along the route. **2** *Military.* a period of service, esp. in one place of duty. **3** a short trip, as for inspection. **4** a trip made by a theatre company, orchestra, etc., to perform in several different places: *a concert tour.* **5** an overseas trip made by a cricket or rugby team, etc., to play in several places. ◆ *vb* **6** to make a tour of (a place). [C14: from Old French: a turn, from Latin *tornus* a lathe, from Greek *tornos;* compare TURN]

touraco *or* **turaco** ('tʊərəˌkəʊ) *n, pl* **-cos.** any brightly coloured crested arboreal African bird of the family *Musophagidae:* order *Cuculiformes* (cuckoos, etc.). [C18: of West African origin]

Touraine (*French* turɛn) *n* a former province of NW central France: at its height in the 16th century as an area of royal residences, esp. along the Loire. Chief town: Tours.

Tourane (tu:'rɑ:n) *n* the former name of **Da Nang.**

tourbillion (tʊə'bɪljən) *n* a rare word for **whirlwind.** [C15: from French *tourbillon,* ultimately from Latin *turbō* something that spins, from *turbāre* to confuse]

Tourcoing (*French* turkwɛ̃) *n* a town in NE France: textile manufacturing. Pop.: 93 765 (1990).

tour de force *French.* (tur də fɔrs; *English* 'tʊə də 'fɔ:s) *n, pl* ***tours de force*** (tur; *English* 'tʊə). a masterly or brilliant stroke, creation, effect, or accomplishment. [literally: feat of skill or strength]

Touré ('tʊəreɪ) *n* (**Ahmed**) **Sékou** ('seɪku:). 1922–84, president of the Republic of Guinea (1958–84).

tourer ('tʊərə) *n* a large open car with a folding top, usually seating a driver and four passengers. Also called (esp. U.S.): **touring car.**

Tourette syndrome (tʊə'rɛt) *n* a brain disorder characterized by involuntary outbursts of swearing, spitting, barking, etc., and sudden involuntary movements. Also called: **Gilles de la Tourette syndrome, Tourette's syndrome, Tourette's.** [C20: named after Georges Gilles de la *Tourette* 1857–1904, French neurologist]

tourie ('tʊrɪ) *n Scot.* a variant spelling of **toorie.**

tourism ('tʊərɪzəm) *n* tourist travel and the services connected with it, esp. when regarded as an industry.

tourist ('tʊərɪst) *n* **1a** a person who travels for pleasure, usually sightseeing and staying in hotels. **1b** (*as modifier*): *tourist attractions.* **2** a person on an excursion or sightseeing tour. **3** a person travelling abroad as a member of a sports team that is playing a series of usually international matches. **4** Also called: **tourist class.** the lowest class of accommodation on a passenger ship. ◆ *adj* **5** of or relating to tourist accommodation. ► **tour'istic** *adj*

touristy ('tʊərɪstɪ) *adj Informal, often derogatory.* abounding in or designed for tourists.

tourmaline ('tʊəmə,li:n) *n* any of a group of hard glassy minerals of variable colour consisting of complex borosilicates of aluminium with quantities of lithium, sodium, potassium, iron, and magnesium in hexagonal crystalline form: used in optical and electrical equipment and in jewellery. [C18: from German *Turmalin,* from Sinhalese *toramalli* carnelian] ► **tourmalinic** (,tʊəmə'lɪnɪk) *adj*

Tournai (*French* turnɛ) *n* a city in W Belgium, in Hainaut province on the River Scheldt: under several different European rulers until 1814. Pop.: 68 086 (1995 est.). Flemish name: **Doornik.**

tournament ('tʊənəmənt, 'tɔ:-, 'tɜ:-) *n* **1** a sporting competition in which contestants play a series of games to determine an overall winner. **2** a meeting for athletic or other sporting contestants: *an archery tournament.* **3** *Medieval history* **3a** (originally) a martial sport or contest in which mounted combatants fought for a prize. **3b** (later) a meeting for knightly sports and exercises. [C13: from Old French *torneiement,* from *torneier* to fight on horseback, literally: to turn, from the constant wheeling round of the combatants; see TOURNEY]

tournedos ('tʊənə,dəʊ) *n, pl* **-dos** (-,dəʊz). a thick round steak of beef cut from the fillet or undercut of sirloin. [from French, from *tourner* to TURN + *dos* back]

Tourneur ('tɜ:nə) *n* **Cyril.** ?1575–1626, English dramatist; author of *The Atheist's Tragedy* (1611) and, reputedly, of *The Revenger's Tragedy* (1607).

tourney ('tʊənɪ, 'tɔ:-) *Medieval history.* ◆ *n* **1** a knightly tournament. ◆ *vb* **2** (*intr*) to engage in a tourney. [C13: from Old French *torneier,* from Vulgar Latin *tornidiāre* (unattested) to turn constantly, from Latin *tornāre* to TURN (in a lathe); see TOURNAMENT] ► **'tourneyer** *n*

tourniquet ('tʊənɪ,keɪ, 'tɔ:-) *n Med.* any instrument or device for temporarily constricting an artery of the arm or leg to control bleeding. [C17: from French: device that operates by turning, from *tourner* to TURN]

tour operator *n* a person or company that provides package holidays.

Tours (*French* tur) *n* a town in W central France, on the River Loire: nearby is the scene of the defeat of the Arabs in 732, which ended the advance of Islam in W Europe. Pop.: 133 403 (1990).

tousle ('taʊzᵊl) *vb* (*tr*) **1** to tangle, ruffle, or disarrange. **2** to treat roughly. ◆ *n* **3** a disorderly, tangled, or rumpled state. **4** a dishevelled or disordered mass, esp. of hair. [C15: from Low German *tūsen* to shake; related to Old High German *zirzūsōn* to tear to pieces]

tous-les-mois (,tu:leɪ'mwɑ:) *n* **1** a large widely cultivated plant, *Canna edulis,* of the Caribbean and South America, having purplish stems and leaves, bright red flowers and edible tubers: family *Cannaceae.* **2** the tuber of this plant, used as a source of starch. [C19: from French, literally: all the months, probably an attempt to give phonetic reproduction of *tolomane,* from native West Indian name]

Toussaint L'Ouverture (*French* tusɛ̃ luvɛrtyr) *n* **Pierre Dominique** (pjɛr dɔminik). ?1743–1803, Haitian revolutionary leader. He was made governor of the island by the French Revolutionary government (1794) and expelled the Spanish and British but when Napoleon I proclaimed the re-establishment of slavery he was arrested. He died in prison in France.

tout (taʊt) *vb* **1** to solicit (business, customers, etc.) or hawk (merchandise), esp. in a brazen way. **2** (*intr*) **2a** to spy on racehorses being trained in order to obtain information for betting purposes. **2b** to sell, or attempt to sell, such information or to take bets, esp. in public places. **3** (*tr*) *Informal.* to recommend flatteringly or excessively. ◆ *n* **4a** a person who spies on racehorses so as to obtain betting information to sell. **4b** a person who sells information obtained by such spying. **5** a person who solicits business in a brazen way. **6** Also called: **ticket tout.** a person who sells tickets unofficially for a heavily booked sporting event, concert, etc., at greatly inflated prices. **7** *Northern Ireland.* a police informer. [C14 (in the sense: to peer, look out): related to Old English *tȳtan* to peep out] ► **'touter** *n*

tout à fait *French.* (tut a fɛ) *adv* completely; absolutely.

tout court *French.* (tu kur) *adv* simply; briefly.

tout de suite *French.* (tud sɥit) *adv* at once; immediately.

tout ensemble *French.* (tut ɑ̃sɑ̃blə) *adv* **1** everything considered; all in all. ◆ *n* **2** the total impression or effect.

tout le monde *French.* (tu lə mɔ̃d) *n* all the world; everyone.

touzle ('taʊzᵊl) *vb, n* a rare spelling of **tousle.**

tovarisch, tovarich, *or* **tovarish** (tə'vɑ:rɪʃ; *Russian* ta'varjɪʃtʃ) *n* comrade: a term of address. [from Russian]

tow[1] (təʊ) *vb* **1** (*tr*) to pull or drag (a vehicle, boat, etc.), esp. by means of a rope or cable. ◆ *n* **2** the act or an instance of towing. **3** the state of being towed (esp. in the phrases **in tow, under tow, on tow**). **4** something towed. **5** something used for towing. **6 in tow.** in one's charge or under one's influence. **7** *Informal.* (in motor racing, etc.) the act of taking advantage of the slipstream of another car (esp. in the phrase **get a tow**). **8** short for **ski tow.** [Old English *togian;* related to Old Frisian *togia,* Old Norse *toga,* Old High German *zogōn*] ► **'towable** *adj*

tow[2] (təʊ) *n* **1** the fibres of hemp, flax, jute, etc., in the scutched state. **2** synthetic fibres preparatory to spinning. **3** the coarser fibres discarded after combing. [Old English *tōw;* related to Old Saxon *tou,* Old Norse *tō* tuft of wool, Dutch *touwen* to spin] ► **'towy** *adj*

towage ('təʊɪdʒ) *n* **1** a charge made for towing. **2** the act of towing or the state of being towed.

toward *adj* ('təʊəd). **1** *Now rare.* in progress; afoot. **2** *Obsolete.* about to happen; imminent. **3** *Obsolete.* promising or favourable. ◆ *prep* (tə'wɔ:d, tɔ:d). **4** a variant of **towards.** [Old English *tōweard;* see TO, -WARD]

towardly ('təʊədlɪ) *adj Archaic.* **1** compliant. **2** propitious or suitable. ► **'towardliness** *or* **'towardness** *n*

towards (tə'wɔ:dz, tɔ:dz) *prep* **1** in the direction or vicinity of: *towards London.* **2** with regard to: *her feelings towards me.* **3** as a contribution or help to: *money towards a new car.* **4** just before: *towards one o'clock.* **5** *Irish.* in comparison with: *it's no work towards having to do it by hand.* ◆ Also: **toward.**

towbar ('təʊ,bɑ:) *n* a rigid metal bar or frame used for towing vehicles. Compare **towrope, towline.**

towboat ('təʊ,bəʊt) *n* another word for **tug** (the boat).

tow-coloured *adj* pale yellow; flaxen.

towel ('taʊəl) *n* **1** a square or rectangular piece of absorbent cloth or paper used for drying the body. **2** a similar piece of cloth used for drying plates, cutlery, etc. **3 throw in the towel.** See **throw in** (sense 4). ◆ *vb* **-els, -elling, -elled** *or U.S.* **-els, -eling, -eled. 4** (*tr*) to dry or wipe with a towel. **5** (*tr;* often foll. by *up*) *Austral. slang.* to assault or beat (a person). [C13: from Old French *toaille,* of Germanic origin; related to Old High German *dwahal* bath, Old Saxon *twahila* towel, Gothic *thwahan* to wash]

towelling ('taʊəlɪŋ) *n* an absorbent fabric, esp. with a nap, used for making towels, bathrobes, etc.

towel rail *n* a rail or frame in a bathroom, etc., for hanging towels on.

tower ('taʊə) *n* **1** a tall, usually square or circular structure, sometimes part of a larger building and usually built for a specific purpose: *a church tower; a control tower.* **2** a place of defence or retreat. **3** a mobile structure used in medieval warfare to attack a castle, etc. **4 tower of strength.** a person who gives support, comfort, etc. ◆ *vb* **5** (*intr*) to be or rise like a tower; loom. [C12: from Old French *tur,* from Latin *turris,* from Greek]

tower crane *n* a rotatable cantilever jib on top of a steelwork tower used on building sites where the operator needs to command a good view of the site.

towered ('taʊəd) *adj* **a** having a tower or towers. **b** (*in combination*): *four-towered; high-towered.*

Tower Hamlets *n* a borough of E Greater London, on the River Thames: contains the main part of the East End. Pop.: 159 000 (1994 est.). Area: 20 sq. km (8 sq. miles).

towering ('taʊərɪŋ) *adj* **1** very tall; lofty. **2** outstanding, as in importance or stature. **3** (*prenominal*) very intense: *a towering rage.* ► **'toweringly** *adv*

Tower of London *n* a fortress in the City of London, on the River Thames: begun 1078; later extended and used as a palace, the main state prison, and now as a museum containing the crown jewels.

tow-haired (,təʊ'hɛəd) *adj* having blond and sometimes tousled hair.

towhead ('təʊ,hɛd) *n Often disparaging.* **1** a person with blond or yellowish hair. **2** a head of such hair. [from TOW[2] (flax)] ► **,tow'headed** *adj*

towhee ('taʊhɪ, 'təʊ-) *n* any of various North American brownish-coloured sparrows of the genera *Pipilo* and *Chlorura.* [C18: imitative of its note]

towing path *n* another name for **towpath.**

towkay (taʊ'keɪ) *n* sir; master: used as a form of address. [of Chinese origin]

towline ('təʊ,laɪn) *n* another name for **towrope.**

town (taʊn) *n* **1a** a densely populated urban area, typically smaller than a city and larger than a village, having some local powers of government and a fixed boundary. **1b** (*as modifier*): *town life.* Related adj: **urban. 2** a city, borough, or other urban area. **3** (in the U.S.) a territorial unit of local government that is smaller than a county; township. **4** the nearest town or commercial district. **5** London or the chief city of an area. **6** the inhabitants of a town. **7** the permanent residents of a university town as opposed to the university staff and students. Compare **gown** (sense 3). **8 go to town. 8a** to make a supreme or unrestricted effort; go all out. **8b** *Austral. and N.Z. informal.* to lose one's temper. **9 on the town.** seeking out entertainments and amusements. [Old English *tūn* village; related to Old Saxon, Old Norse *tūn,* Old High German *zūn* fence, Old Irish *dūn*] ► **'townish** *adj* ► **'townless** *adj*

town clerk *n* **1** (in Britain until 1974) the secretary and chief administrative officer of a town or city. **2** (in the U.S.) the official who keeps the records of a town.

town crier *n* (formerly) a person employed by a town to make public announcements in the streets.

Townes (taʊnz) *n* **Charles Hard.** born 1915, U.S. physicist, noted for his research in quantum electronics leading to the invention of the maser and the laser; shared the Nobel prize for physics in 1964.

town gas *n* coal gas manufactured for domestic and industrial use.

town hall *n* the chief building in which municipal business is transacted, often with a hall for public meetings.

townhall clock (ˈtaʊn,hɔːl) *n Brit.* another name for **moschatel.**

town house *n* **1** a terraced house in an urban area, esp. a fashionable one, often having the main living room on the first floor with an integral garage on the ground floor. **2** a person's town residence as distinct from his country residence. **3** another name (now chiefly Scot.) for **town hall. 4** a U.S. and Canadian name for **terraced house.**

townie (ˈtaʊnɪ) *or* **townee** (taʊˈniː) *n Informal, often disparaging.* a permanent resident in a town, esp. as distinct from country dwellers or students.

townland (ˈtaʊnlænd) *n Irish.* a division of land of various sizes.

town meeting *n U.S.* **1** an assembly of the inhabitants of a town. **2** (esp. in New England) an assembly of the qualified voters of a town. Such a meeting may exercise all the powers of local government.

town milk *n N.Z.* milk treated by pasteurization for direct consumption, as opposed to dairy factory milk for the production of butter, cheese, etc.

town planning *n* the comprehensive planning of the physical and social development of a town, including the construction of facilities. U.S. term: **city planning.** ▸ **town planner** *n*

townscape (ˈtaʊnskeɪp) *n* a view of an urban scene.

Townshend (ˈtaʊnzɛnd) *n* **1 Charles,** 2nd Viscount, nicknamed *Turnip Townshend.* 1674–1738, English politician and agriculturist. **2 Pete.** born 1945, British rock guitarist, singer, and songwriter: member of the Who (1964–83) and composer of much of their material.

township (ˈtaʊnʃɪp) *n* **1** a small town. **2** (in the Scottish Highlands and islands) a small crofting community. **3** (in the U.S. and Canada) a territorial area, esp. a subdivision of a county: often organized as a unit of local government. **4** (formerly, in South Africa) a planned urban settlement of Black Africans or Coloured people. Compare **location** (sense 4). **5** *English history.* **5a** any of the local districts of a large parish, each division containing a village or small town. **5b** the particular manor or parish itself as a territorial division. **5c** the inhabitants of a township collectively.

townsman (ˈtaʊnzmən) *n, pl* **-men. 1** an inhabitant of a town. **2** a person from the same town as oneself. ▸ **ˈtowns,woman** *fem n*

townspeople (ˈtaʊnz,piːpᵊl) *or* **townsfolk** *n* the inhabitants of a town; citizens.

Townsville (ˈtaʊnzvɪl) *n* a port in E Australia, in NE Queensland on the Coral Sea: centre of a vast agricultural and mining hinterland. Pop.: 124 900 (1995 est.).

towpath (ˈtəʊ,pɑːθ) *n* a path beside a canal or river, used by people or animals towing boats. Also called: **towing path.**

towrope (ˈtəʊ,rəʊp) *n* a rope or cable used for towing a vehicle or vessel. Also called: **towline.**

tow truck *n* a U.S. and Canadian name for **breakdown van.**

tox. *or* **toxicol.** *abbrev. for* toxicology.

tox-, toxic- *or before a consonant* **toxo-, toxico-** *combining form.* indicating poison: *toxalbumin.* [from Latin *toxicum*]

toxaemia *or U.S.* **toxemia** (tɒkˈsiːmɪə) *n* **1** a condition characterized by the presence of bacterial toxins in the blood. **2** the condition in pregnancy of pre-eclampsia or eclampsia. [C19: from TOX- + -AEMIA] ▸ **toxˈaemic** *or U.S.* **toxˈemic** *adj*

toxalbumin (,tɒksælˈbjuːmɪn) *n Biochem.* any of a group of toxic albumins that occur in certain plants, such as toadstools, and in snake venom.

toxaphene (ˈtɒksə,fiːn) *n* an amber waxy solid with a pleasant pine odour, consisting of chlorinated terpenes, esp. chlorinated camphene: used as an insecticide.

toxic (ˈtɒksɪk) *adj* **1** of, relating to, or caused by a toxin or poison; poisonous. **2** harmful or deadly. [C17: from medical Latin *toxicus,* from Latin *toxicum* poison, from Greek *toxikon* (*pharmakon*) (poison) used on arrows, from *toxon* arrow] ▸ **ˈtoxically** *adv*

toxicant (ˈtɒksɪkənt) *n* **1** a toxic substance; poison. **2** a rare word for **intoxicant.** ◆ *adj* **3** poisonous; toxic. [C19: from Medieval Latin *toxicāre* to poison; see TOXIC]

toxicity (tɒkˈsɪsɪtɪ) *n* **1** the degree of strength of a poison. **2** the state or quality of being poisonous.

toxicogenic (,tɒksɪkəʊˈdʒɛnɪk) *adj* **1** producing toxic substances or effects. **2** caused or produced by a toxin.

toxicology (,tɒksɪˈkɒlədʒɪ) *n* the branch of science concerned with poisons, their nature, effects, and antidotes. ▸ **toxicological** (,tɒksɪkəˈlɒdʒɪkᵊl) *or* **,toxicoˈlogic** *adj* ▸ **,toxicoˈlogically** *adv* ▸ **,toxiˈcologist** *n*

toxicosis (,tɒksɪˈkəʊsɪs) *n* any disease or condition caused by poisoning. [C19: from New Latin, from TOXIC + -OSIS]

toxic shock syndrome *n* a potentially fatal condition in women, characterized by fever, stomachache, a painful rash, and a drop in blood pressure, that is caused by staphylococcal blood poisoning, most commonly from a retained tampon during menstruation.

toxin (ˈtɒksɪn) *n* **1** any of various poisonous substances produced by microorganisms that stimulate the production of neutralizing substances (antitoxins) in the body. See also **endotoxin, exotoxin. 2** any other poisonous substance of plant or animal origin.

toxin-antitoxin *n* a mixture of a specific toxin and antitoxin. The diphtheria toxin-antitoxin was formerly used in the U.S. for active immunization.

toxocariasis (,tɒksəkəˈraɪəsɪs) *n* the infection of humans with the larvae of a genus of roundworms, *Toxocara,* of dogs and cats. It can cause swelling of the liver and, sometimes, damage to the eyes.

toxoid (ˈtɒksɔɪd) *n* a toxin that has been treated to reduce its toxicity and is used in immunization to stimulate production of antitoxins.

toxophilite (tɒkˈsɒfɪ,laɪt) *Formal.* ◆ *n* **1** an archer. ◆ *adj* **2** of or relating to archery. [C18: from *Toxophilus,* the title of a book (1545) by Ascham, designed to mean: a lover of the bow, from Greek *toxon* bow + *philos* loving] ▸ **toxˈophily** *n*

toxoplasmosis (,tɒksəʊplæzˈməʊsɪs) *n* a protozoal disease characterized by jaundice, enlarged liver and spleen, and convulsions, caused by infection with *Toxoplasma gondii.* ▸ **,toxoˈplasmic** *adj*

toy (tɔɪ) *n* **1** an object designed to be played with. **2a** something that is a non-functioning replica of something else, esp. a miniature one. **2b** (*as modifier*): *a toy guitar.* **3** any small thing of little value; trifle. **4a** something small or miniature, esp. a miniature variety of a breed of dog. **4b** (*as modifier*): *a toy poodle.* ◆ *vb* **5** (*intr;* usually foll. by *with*) to play, fiddle, or flirt. [C16 (in the sense: amorous dalliance): of uncertain origin] ▸ **ˈtoyer** *n* ▸ **ˈtoyless** *adj* ▸ **ˈtoy,like** *adj*

Toyama (ˈtəujɑː,mɑː) *n* a city in central Japan, on W Honshu on **Toyama Bay** (an inlet of the Sea of Japan): chemical and textile centre. Pop.: 325 303 (1995).

toy boy *n* the much younger male lover of an older woman.

Toynbee (ˈtɔɪnbɪ) *n* **1 Arnold.** 1852–83, British economist and social reformer, after whom **Toynbee Hall**, a residential settlement in East London, is named. **2** his nephew, **Arnold Joseph.** 1889–1975, British historian. In his chief work, *A Study of History* (1934–61), he attempted to analyse the principles determining the rise and fall of civilizations.

toy-toy or **toyi-toyi** (tɔɪtɔɪ) *S. African.* ◆ *n* **1** a dance expressing defiance and protest. ◆ *vb* **2** (*intr*) to dance in this way. [of uncertain origin]

TPI *abbrev. for* tax and price index: a measure of the increase in taxable income needed to compensate for an increase in retail prices.

T-piece *n* a strut or part shaped like a T.

T-plate *n* a metal plate shaped like a T used to strengthen or effect a right-angled joint between two beams, etc.

TPN *n Biochem.* triphosphopyridine nucleotide; a former name for **NADP.**

Tpr *abbrev. for* Trooper.

TQM *abbrev. for* total quality management.

tr *abbrev. for* treasurer.

TR *international car registration for* Turkey.

tr. *abbrev. for:* **1** transitive. **2** translated. **3** translator. **4** *Music.* trill. **5** trustee.

trabeated (ˈtreɪbɪ,eɪtɪd) *or* **trabeate** (ˈtreɪbɪɪt, -,eɪt) *adj Architect.* constructed with horizontal beams as opposed to arches. Compare **arcuate.** [C19: back formation from *trabeation,* from Latin *trabs* a beam] ▸ **,trabeˈation** *n*

trabecula (trəˈbɛkjulə) *n, pl* **-lae** (-,liː). *Anatomy, botany.* **1** any of various rod-shaped structures that support other organs. **2** any of various rod-shaped cells or structures that bridge a cavity, as within the capsule of a moss. [C19: via New Latin from Latin: a little beam, from *trabs* a beam] ▸ **traˈbecular** *or* **traˈbeculate** *adj*

Trabzon (ˈtrɑːbzɔːn) *or* **Trebizond** *n* a port in NE Turkey, on the Black Sea: founded as a Greek colony in the 8th century B.C. at the terminus of an important trade route from central Europe to Asia. Pop.: 143 573 (1995 est.).

tracasserie (trəˈkæsərɪ) *n* a turmoil; annoyance. [from French, from *tracasser* to fuss about]

trace[1] (treɪs) *n* **1** a mark or other sign that something has been in a place; vestige. **2** a tiny or scarcely detectable amount or characteristic. **3** a footprint or other indication of the passage of an animal or person. **4** any line drawn by a recording instrument or a record consisting of a number of such lines. **5** something drawn, such as a tracing. **6** *Chiefly U.S.* a beaten track or path. **7** the postulated alteration in the cells of the nervous system that occurs as the result of any experience or learning. See also **memory trace, engram. 8** *Geom.* the intersection of a surface with a coordinate plane. **9** *Maths.* the sum of the diagonal entries of a square matrix. **10** *Linguistics.* a symbol inserted in the constituent structure of a sentence to mark the position from which a constituent has been moved in a generative process. **11** *Meteorol.* an amount of precipitation that is too small to be measured. **12** *Archaic.* a way taken; route. ◆ *vb* **13** (*tr*) to follow, discover, or ascertain the course or development of (something): *to trace the history of China.* **14** (*tr*) to track down and find, as by following a trail. **15** to copy (a design, map, etc.) by drawing over the lines visible through a superimposed sheet of transparent paper or other material. **16** (*tr;* often foll. by *out*) **16a** to draw or delineate a plan or diagram of: *she spent hours tracing the models one at a time.* **16b** to outline or sketch (an idea, policy, etc.): *he traced out his scheme for the robbery.* **17** (*tr*) to decorate with tracery. **18** (*tr*) to imprint (a design) on cloth, etc. **19** (usually foll. by *back*) to follow or be followed to source; date back: *his ancestors trace back to the 16th century.* **20** *Archaic.* to make one's way over, through, or along (something). [C13: from French *tracier,* from Vulgar Latin *tractiāre* (unattested) to drag, from Latin *tractus,* from *trahere* to drag] ▸ **ˈtraceable** *adj* ▸ **,traceaˈbility** *or* **ˈtraceableness** *n* ▸ **ˈtraceably** *adv* ▸ **ˈtraceless** *adj* ▸ **ˈtracelessly** *adv*

trace[2] (treɪs) *n* **1** either of the two side straps that connect a horse's harness to the swingletree. **2** *Angling.* a length of nylon or, formerly, gut attaching a hook or fly to a line. **3 kick over the traces.** to escape or defy control. [C14 *trais,* from Old French *trait,* ultimately from Latin *trahere* to drag]

trace element *n* any of various chemical elements, such as iron, manganese, zinc, copper, and iodine, that occur in very small amounts in organisms and are essential for many physiological and biochemical processes.

trace fossil *n* the fossilized remains of a track, trail, footprint, burrow, etc., of an organism.

tracer (ˈtreɪsə) *n* **1** a person or thing that traces. **2a** a projectile that can be observed when in flight by the burning of chemical substances in its base. **2b** ammunition consisting of such projectiles. **2c** (*as modifier*): *tracer fire.* **3** *Med.* any radioactive isotope introduced into the body to study metabolic processes, absorption, etc., by following its progress through the body with a gamma camera or other detector. **4** an investigation to trace missing cargo, mail, etc.

tracer bullet *n* a round of small arms ammunition containing a tracer.

tracery ('treɪsərɪ) *n, pl* **-eries. 1** a pattern of interlacing ribs, esp. as used in the upper part of a Gothic window, etc. **2** any fine pattern resembling this. ▸ **'traceried** *adj*

trachea (trə'kiːə) *n, pl* **-cheae** (-'kiːiː). **1** *Anatomy, zoology.* the membranous tube with cartilaginous rings that conveys inhaled air from the larynx to the bronchi. Nontechnical name: **windpipe. 2** any of the tubes in insects and related animals that convey air from the spiracles to the tissues. **3** *Botany.* another name for **vessel** (sense 5). [C16: from Medieval Latin, from Greek *trakheia,* shortened from (*artēria*) *trakheia* rough (artery), from *trakhus* rough] ▸ **tra'cheal** *or* **tra'cheate** *adj*

tracheid ('treɪkɪɪd) *or* **tracheide** *n Botany.* an element of xylem tissue consisting of an elongated lignified cell with tapering ends. [C19: from TRACHEA (in the sense: a vessel in a plant) + -ID[2]] ▸ **tracheidal** (trə'kiːɪdᵊl, ˌtreɪkɪ'aɪdᵊl) *adj*

tracheitis (ˌtreɪkɪ'aɪtɪs) *n* inflammation of the trachea.

tracheo- *or before a vowel* **trache-** *combining form.* denoting the trachea: *tracheotomy.*

tracheophyte ('treɪkɪəʊˌfaɪt) *n* any plant that has a conducting system of xylem and phloem elements; a vascular plant.

tracheostomy (ˌtrækɪ'ɒstəmɪ) *n, pl* **-mies.** the surgical formation of a temporary or permanent opening into the trachea following tracheotomy.

tracheotomy (ˌtrækɪ'ɒtəmɪ) *n, pl* **-mies.** surgical incision into the trachea, usually performed when the upper air passage has been blocked.

trachoma (trə'kəʊmə) *n* a chronic contagious disease of the eye characterized by inflammation of the conjunctiva and cornea and the formation of scar tissue, caused by infection with the virus-like bacterium *Chlamydia trachomatis.* [C17: from New Latin, from Greek *trakhōma* roughness, from *trakhus* rough] ▸ **trachomatous** (trə'kɒmətəs, -'kəʊ-) *adj*

trachyte ('treɪkaɪt, 'træ-) *n* a light-coloured fine-grained volcanic rock of rough texture consisting of feldspars with small amounts of pyroxene or amphibole. [C19: from French, from Greek *trakhutēs,* from *trakhus* rough] ▸ **trachytoid** ('trækɪˌtɔɪd, 'treɪ-) *adj*

trachytic (trə'kɪtɪk) *adj* (of the texture of certain igneous rocks) characterized by a parallel arrangement of crystals, which mark the flow of the lava when still molten.

tracing ('treɪsɪŋ) *n* **1** a copy made by tracing. **2** the act of making a trace. **3** a record made by an instrument.

tracing paper *n* strong transparent paper used for tracing.

track (træk) *n* **1** the mark or trail left by something that has passed by: *the track of an animal.* **2** any road or path affording passage, esp. a rough one. **3** a rail or pair of parallel rails on which a vehicle, such as a locomotive, runs, esp. the rails together with the sleepers, ballast, etc., on a railway. **4** a course of action, thought, etc.: *don't start on that track again!* **5** a line of motion or travel, such as flight. **6** an endless jointed metal band driven by the wheels of a vehicle such as a tank or tractor to enable it to move across rough or muddy ground. **7** *Physics.* the path of a particle of ionizing radiation as observed in a cloud chamber, bubble chamber, or photographic emulsion. **8a** a course for running or racing. **8b** (*as modifier*): *track events.* **9** *U.S. and Canadian.* **9a** sports performed on a track. **9b** track and field events as a whole. **10** a path on a magnetic recording medium, esp. magnetic tape, on which information, such as music or speech, from a single input channel is recorded. **11** any of a number of separate sections in the recording on a record, CD, or cassette. **12** the distance between the points of contact with the ground of a pair of wheels, such as the front wheels of a motor vehicle or the paired wheels of an aircraft undercarriage. **13** a hypothetical trace made on the surface of the earth by a point directly below an aircraft in flight. **14 keep** (*or* **lose**) **track of.** to follow (or fail to follow) the passage, course, or progress of. **15 off the beaten track.** See **beaten** (sense 4). **16 off the track.** away from what is correct or true. **17 on the track of.** on the scent or trail of; pursuing. **18 the right** (*or* **wrong**) **track.** pursuing the correct (or incorrect) line of investigation, inquiry, etc. ◆ *vb* **19** to follow the trail of (a person, animal, etc.). **20** to follow the flight path of (a satellite, spacecraft, etc.) by picking up radio or radar signals transmitted or reflected by it. **21** *U.S. railways.* **21a** to provide with a track. **21b** to run on a track of (a certain width). **22** (of a camera or camera operator) to follow (a moving object) in any direction while operating. **23** to move (a camera) towards the scene (**track in**) or away from the scene (**track out**). **24** to follow a track through (a place): *to track the jungles.* **25** (*intr*) (of the pick-up, stylus, etc., of a record player) to follow the groove of a record: *the pick-up tracks badly.* ◆ See also **tracks.** [C15: from Old French *trac,* probably of Germanic origin; related to Middle Dutch *tracken* to pull, Middle Low German *trecken;* compare Norwegian *trakke* to trample] ▸ **'trackable** *adj* ▸ **'tracker** *n*

trackball ('trækˌbɔːl) *or* **trackerball** ('trækəˌbɔːl) *n Computing.* a device consisting of a small ball, mounted in a cup, which can be rotated to move the cursor around the screen.

track down *vb* (*tr, adv*) to find by tracking or pursuing.

tracker dog *n* a dog specially trained to hunt fugitives or to search for missing people.

track event *n* a competition in athletics, such as relay running or sprinting, that takes place on a running track.

tracker fund *n Finance.* an investment fund that is administered so that its value changes in line with the average value of shares in a market.

tracking ('trækɪŋ) *n* **1** the act or process of following something or someone. **2** *Electrical engineering.* a leakage of electric current between two insulated points caused by dirt, carbon particles, moisture, etc.

tracking radar *n* a radar system emitting a narrow beam which oscillates about the target, thus compensating for abrupt changes of direction.

tracking shot *n* a camera shot in which the cameraman follows a specific person or event in the action.

tracking station *n* a station that can use a radio or radar beam to determine and follow the path of an object, esp. a spacecraft or satellite, in space or in the atmosphere.

tracklaying ('trækˌleɪɪŋ) *adj* (of a vehicle) having an endless jointed metal band around the wheels.

trackless ('træklɪs) *adj* **1** having or leaving no trace or trail: *a trackless jungle.* **2** (of a vehicle) using or having no tracks. ▸ **'tracklessly** *adv* ▸ **'tracklessness** *n*

trackman ('trækmən) *n, pl* **-men.** the U.S. and Canadian name for **platelayer.**

track meet *n U.S. and Canadian.* an athletics meeting.

track record *n Informal.* the past record of the accomplishments and failures of a person, business, etc.

track rod *n* the rod connecting the two front wheels of a motor vehicle ensuring that they turn at the same angle.

tracks (træks) *pl n* **1** (*sometimes sing*) marks, such as footprints, tyre impressions, etc., left by someone or something that has passed. **2 in one's tracks.** on the very spot where one is standing (esp. in the phrase **stop in one's tracks**). **3 make tracks.** to leave or depart. **4 make tracks for.** to go or head towards. **5 the wrong side of the tracks.** the unfashionable or poor district or stratum of a community.

track shoe *n* either of a pair of light running shoes fitted with steel spikes for better grip. Also called: **spike.**

tracksuit ('trækˌsuːt, -ˌsjuːt) *n* a warm suit worn by athletes, etc. usually over the clothes, esp. during training.

tract[1] (trækt) *n* **1** an extended area, as of land. **2** *Anatomy.* a system of organs, glands, or other tissues that has a particular function: *the digestive tract.* **3** a bundle of nerve fibres having the same function, origin, and termination: *the optic tract.* **4** *Archaic.* an extended period of time. [C15: from Latin *tractus* a stretching out, from *trahere* to drag]

tract[2] (trækt) *n* a treatise or pamphlet, esp. a religious or moralistic one. [C15: from Latin *tractātus* TRACTATE]

tract[3] (trækt) *n R.C. Church.* an anthem in some Masses. [C14: from Medieval Latin *tractus cantus* extended song; see TRACT[1]]

tractable ('træktəbᵊl) *adj* **1** easily controlled or persuaded. **2** readily worked; malleable. [C16: from Latin *tractābilis,* from *tractāre* to manage, from *trahere* to draw] ▸ **ˌtracta'bility** *or* **'tractableness** *n* ▸ **'tractably** *adv*

Tractarianism (træk'tɛərɪəˌnɪzəm) *n* another name for the **Oxford Movement.** ▸ **Trac'tarian** *n, adj*

tractate ('trækteɪt) *n* **1** a short tract; treatise. **2** *Judaism.* one of the volumes of the Talmud. [C15: from Latin *tractātus,* from *tractāre* to handle; see TRACTABLE]

tractile ('træktaɪl) *adj* capable of being drawn out; ductile. [C17: from Latin *trahere* to drag] ▸ **tractility** (træk'tɪlɪtɪ) *n*

traction ('trækʃən) *n* **1** the act of drawing or pulling, esp. by motive power. **2** the state of being drawn or pulled. **3** *Med.* the application of a steady pull on a part during healing of a fractured or dislocated bone, using a system of weights and pulleys or splints. **4** the adhesive friction between a wheel and a surface, as between a driving wheel of a motor vehicle and the road. [C17: from Medieval Latin *tractiō,* from Latin *tractus* dragged; see TRACTILE] ▸ **'tractional** *adj* ▸ **tractive** ('træktɪv) *adj*

traction engine *n* a steam-powered locomotive used, esp. formerly, for drawing heavy loads along roads or over rough ground. It usually has two large rear wheels and a rope drum for haulage purposes.

traction load *n Geology.* the solid material that is carried along the bed of a river.

tractive force *n* the force measured in the drawbar of a locomotive or tractor.

tractor ('træktə) *n* **1** a motor vehicle used to pull heavy loads, esp. farm machinery such as a plough or harvester. It usually has two large rear wheels with deeply treaded tyres. **2** a short motor vehicle with a powerful engine and a driver's cab, used to pull a trailer, as in an articulated lorry. **3** an aircraft with its propeller or propellers mounted in front of the engine. [C18: from Late Latin: one who pulls, from *trahere* to drag]

tractorfeed ('træktəˌfiːd) *n Computing.* the automatic movement of a continuous roll of edge-perforated paper through the platen of the printer.

Tracy ('treɪsɪ) *n* **Spencer.** 1900–67, U.S. film actor. His films include *The Power and the Glory* (1933), *Captains Courageous* (1937) and *Boys' Town* (1938), for both of which he won Oscars, *Adam's Rib* (1949), and *Bad Day at Black Rock* (1955).

trad (træd) *n* **1** *Chiefly Brit.* traditional jazz, as revived in the 1950s. ◆ *adj* **2** short for **traditional.**

trade (treɪd) *n* **1** the act or an instance of buying and selling goods and services either on the domestic (wholesale and retail) markets or on the international (import, export, and entrepôt) markets. Related adj: **mercantile. 2** a personal occupation, esp. a craft requiring skill. **3** the people and practices of an industry, craft, or business. **4** exchange of one thing for something else. **5** the regular clientele of a firm or industry. **6** amount of custom or commercial dealings; business. **7** a specified market or business: *the tailoring trade.* **8** an occupation in commerce, as opposed to a profession. **9** commercial customers, as opposed to the general public: *trade only; trade advertising.* **10** *Homosexual slang.* a sexual partner or sexual partners collectively. **11** *Archaic.* a custom or habit. ◆ *vb* **12** (*tr*) to buy and sell (commercial merchandise). **13** to exchange (one thing) for another. **14** (*intr*) to engage in trade. **15** (*intr*) to deal or do business (with): *we trade with them regularly.* ◆ *adj* **16** intended for or available only to people in industry or business: *trade prices.* ◆ See also **trade-in, trade on.** [C14 (in the sense: track, hence, a regular business): related to Old Saxon *trada,* Old High German *trata* track; see TREAD] ▸ **'tradable** *or* **'tradeable** *adj* ▸ **'tradeless** *adj*

trade agreement *n* a commercial treaty between two or more nations.

trade association *n* an association of organizations in the same trade formed to further their collective interests, esp. in negotiating with governments, trade unions, etc.

trade bill *n* a bill of exchange drawn on and accepted (**trade acceptance**) by a trader in payment for goods.

trade book *or* **edition** *n* an ordinary edition of a book sold in the normal way in shops, as opposed to a de luxe or mail-order edition.

trade cycle *n* the recurrent fluctuation between boom and depression in the economic activity of a capitalist country. Also called (esp. U.S. and Canadian): **business cycle.**

trade discount *n* a sum or percentage deducted from the list price of a commodity allowed by a manufacturer, distributor, or wholesaler to a retailer or by one enterprise to another in the same trade.

traded option *n Stock Exchange.* an option that can itself be bought and sold on a stock exchange. Compare **traditional option.**

trade down *vb* (*intr, adv*) to sell a large or relatively expensive house, car, etc., and replace it with a smaller or less expensive one.

trade gap *n* the amount by which the value of a country's visible imports exceeds that of visible exports; an unfavourable balance of trade.

trade-in *n* **1a** a used article given in part payment for the purchase of a new article. **1b** a transaction involving such part payment. **1c** the valuation put on the article traded in. **1d** (*as modifier*): *a trade-in dealer.* ◆ *vb* **trade in. 2** (*tr, adv*) to give (a used article) as part payment for the purchase of a new article.

trade journal *n* a periodical containing new developments, discussions, etc., concerning a trade or profession.

trade-last *n U.S. informal.* a compliment that one has heard about someone, which one offers to tell to that person in exchange for a compliment heard about oneself.

trademark ('treɪd,mɑːk) *n* **1** the name or other symbol used to identify the goods produced by a particular manufacturer or distributed by a particular dealer and to distinguish them from products associated with competing manufacturers or dealers. A trademark that has been officially registered and is therefore legally protected is known as a **Registered Trademark. 2** any distinctive sign or mark of the presence of a person or animal. ◆ *vb* (*tr*) **3** to label with a trademark. **4** to register as a trademark.

trade name *n* **1** the name used by a trade to refer to a commodity, service, etc. **2** the name under which a commercial enterprise operates in business.

trade-off *n* an exchange, esp. as a compromise.

trade on *vb* (*intr, prep*) to exploit or take advantage of: *he traded on her endless patience.*

trade plate *n* a numberplate attached temporarily to a vehicle by a dealer, etc., before the vehicle has been registered.

trader ('treɪdə) *n* **1** a person who engages in trade; dealer; merchant. **2** a vessel regularly employed in foreign or coastal trade. **3** *Stock Exchange, U.S.* a member who operates mainly on his own account rather than for customers' accounts. ▸ **'trader,ship** *n*

trade reference *n* a reference in which one trader gives his opinion as to the credit worthiness of another trader in the same trade, esp. to a supplier.

Tradescant ('trædəskaent) *n* **1 John.** 1570–1638, English botanist and gardener to Charles I. He introduced many plants from overseas into Britain. **2** his son, **John.** 1608–62, English naturalist and gardener, who continued his father's work.

tradescantia (,trædəs'kænʃɪə) *n* any plant of the American genus *Tradescantia,* widely cultivated for their striped variegated leaves: family *Commelinaceae.* See also **wandering Jew, spiderwort.** [C18: New Latin, named after John TRADESCANT]

trade school *n* a school or teaching unit organized by an industry or large company to provide trade training, apprentice education, and similar courses.

Trades Council *n* (in Britain) an association of the different trade unions in one town or area.

trade secret *n* a secret formula, technique, process, etc., known and used to advantage by only one manufacturer.

tradesman ('treɪdzmən) *n, pl* **-men. 1** a man engaged in trade, esp. a retail dealer. **2** a skilled worker. ▸ **'trades,woman** *fem n*

tradespeople ('treɪdz,piːpᵊl) *or* **tradesfolk** ('treɪdz,fəuk) *pl n Chiefly Brit.* people engaged in trade, esp. shopkeepers.

Trades Union Congress *n* the major association of British trade unions, which includes all the larger unions. Abbrev.: **TUC.**

trade union *or* **trades union** *n* an association of employees formed to improve their incomes and working conditions by collective bargaining with the employer or employer organizations. ▸ **trade unionism** *or* **trades unionism** *n* ▸ **trade unionist** *or* **trades unionist** *n*

trade up *vb* (*intr, adv*) to sell a small or relatively inexpensive house, car, etc., and replace it with a larger or more expensive one.

trade wind (wɪnd) *n* a wind blowing obliquely towards the equator either from the northeast in the N hemisphere or the southeast in the S hemisphere, approximately between latitudes 30° N and S, forming part of the planetary wind system. [C17: from *to blow trade* to blow steadily in one direction, from TRADE in the obsolete sense: a track]

trading estate *n Chiefly Brit.* a large area in which a number of commercial or industrial firms are situated. Also called: **industrial estate.**

trading post *n* **1** a general store established by a trader in an unsettled or thinly populated region. **2** *Stock Exchange.* a booth or location on an exchange floor at which a particular security is traded.

trading stamp *n* (esp. formerly) a stamp of stated value given by some retail organizations to customers, according to the value of their purchases and redeemable for articles offered on a premium list.

tradition (trə'dɪʃən) *n* **1** the handing down from generation to generation of the same customs, beliefs, etc., esp. by word of mouth. **2** the body of customs, thought, practices, etc., belonging to a particular country, people, family, or institution over a relatively long period. **3** a specific custom or practice of long standing. **4** *Christianity.* a doctrine or body of doctrines regarded as having been established by Christ or the apostles though not contained in Scripture. **5** (*often cap.*) *Judaism.* a body of laws regarded as having been handed down from Moses orally and only committed to writing in the 2nd century A.D. **6** the beliefs and customs of Islam supplementing the Koran, esp. as embodied in the Sunna. **7** *Law, chiefly Roman and Scots.* the act of formally transferring ownership of movable property; delivery. [C14: from Latin *trāditiō* a handing down, surrender, from *trādere* to give up, transmit, from TRANS- + *dāre* to give] ▸ **tra'ditionless** *adj* ▸ **tra'ditionist** *n*

traditional (trə'dɪʃənᵊl) *adj* **1** of, relating to, or being a tradition. **2** of or relating to the style of jazz originating in New Orleans, characterized by collective improvisation by a front line of trumpet, trombone, and clarinet accompanied by various rhythm instruments. ▸ **traditionality** (trə,dɪʃə'nælɪtɪ) *n* ▸ **tra'ditionally** *adv*

traditionalism (trə'dɪʃənᵊ,lɪzəm) *n* **1** the doctrine that all knowledge originates in divine revelation and is perpetuated by tradition. **2** adherence to tradition, esp. in religion. ▸ **tra'ditionalist** *n, adj* ▸ **tra,ditional'istic** *adj*

traditional option *n Stock Exchange.* an option that once purchased cannot be resold. Compare **traded option.**

traditional policy *n* a life assurance policy in which the policyholder's premiums are paid into a general fund and his investment benefits are calculated according to actuarial formulae. Compare **unit-linked policy.**

traditional weapon *n S. African.* a weapon having ceremonial tribal significance, such as an assegai or knobkerrie.

traditor ('trædɪtə) *n, pl* **traditores** (,trædɪ'tɔːriːz) *or* **traditors.** *Early Church.* a Christian who betrayed his fellow Christians at the time of the Roman persecutions. [C15: from Latin: traitor, from *trādere* to hand over]

traduce (trə'djuːs) *vb* (*tr*) to speak badly of. [C16: from Latin *trādūcere* to lead over, transmit, disgrace, from TRANS- + *dūcere* to lead] ▸ **tra'ducement** *n* ▸ **tra'ducer** *n* ▸ **tra'ducible** *adj*

traducianism (trə'djuːʃə,nɪzəm) *n* the theory that the soul is transmitted to a child in the act of generation or concomitantly with its body. Compare **creationism.** [C18: from Church Latin *trādūciānus,* from *trādux* transmission; see TRADUCE] ▸ **tra'ducianist** *or* **tra'ducian** *n, adj* ▸ **tra,ducian'istic** *adj*

Trafalgar (trə'fælgə; *Spanish* trafal'ɣar) *n* **Cape.** a cape on the SW coast of Spain, south of Cádiz: scene of the decisive naval battle (1805) in which the French and Spanish fleets were defeated by the English under Nelson, who was mortally wounded.

traffic ('træfɪk) *n* **1a** the vehicles coming and going in a street, town, etc. **1b** (*as modifier*): *traffic lights.* **2** the movement of vehicles, people, etc., in a particular place or for a particular purpose: *sea traffic.* **3a** the business of commercial transportation by land, sea, or air. **3b** the freight, passengers, etc., transported. **4** (usually foll. by *with*) dealings or business: *have no traffic with that man.* **5** trade, esp. of an illicit or improper kind: *drug traffic.* **6** the aggregate volume of messages transmitted through a communications system in a given period. **7** *Chiefly U.S.* the number of customers patronizing a commercial establishment in a given time period. ◆ *vb* **-fics, -ficking, -ficked.** (*intr*) **8** (often foll. by *in*) to carry on trade or business, esp. of an illicit kind. **9** (usually foll. by *with*) to have dealings. [C16: from Old French *trafique,* from Old Italian *traffico,* from *trafficare* to engage in trade] ▸ **'trafficker** *n* ▸ **'trafficless** *adj*

trafficator ('træfɪ,keɪtə) *n* (formerly) an illuminated arm on a motor vehicle that was raised to indicate a left or right turn. Compare **indicator** (sense 5).

traffic calming *n* the use of a series of devices, such as bends and humps in the road, to slow down traffic, esp. in residential areas.

traffic circle *n* the U.S. and Canadian name for **roundabout** (sense 2).

traffic cop *n Informal.* a policeman who supervises road traffic.

traffic court *n Law.* a magistrates' court dealing with traffic offences.

traffic engineering *n* a discipline which includes the design of highways and pedestrian ways, the study and application of traffic statistics, and the environmental aspects of the transportation of goods and people.

traffic island *n* a raised area in the middle of a road, designed as a guide for traffic and to provide a stopping place for pedestrians.

traffic jam *n* a number of vehicles so obstructed that they can scarcely move. ▸ **'traffic-,jammed** *adj*

traffic light *or* **signal** *n* one of a set of coloured lights placed at crossroads, junctions, etc., to control the flow of traffic. A red light indicates that traffic must stop and a green light that it may go: usually an amber warning light is added between the red and the green.

traffic pattern *n* a pattern of permitted lanes in the air around an airport to which an aircraft is restricted.

traffic warden *n Brit.* a person who is appointed to supervise road traffic and report traffic offences.

Trafford ('træfəd) *n* a unitary authority in NW England, in Greater Manchester. Pop.: 218 300 (1995 est.). Area: 106 sq. km (41 sq. miles).

tragacanth ('trægə,kænθ) *n* **1** any of various spiny leguminous plants of the genus *Astragalus,* esp. *A. gummifer,* of Asia, having clusters of white, yellow, or purple flowers, and yielding a substance that is made into a gum. **2** the gum obtained from any of these plants, used in the manufacture of pills and lozenges, etc. [C16: from French *tragacante,* from Latin *tragacantha* goat's thorn, from Greek *tragakantha,* from *tragos* goat + *akantha* thorn]

tragedian (trəˈdʒiːdɪən) *or (fem)* **tragedienne** (trəˌdʒiːdɪˈɛn) *n* **1** an actor who specializes in tragic roles. **2** a writer of tragedy.

tragedy (ˈtrædʒɪdɪ) *n, pl* **-dies. 1** (esp. in classical and Renaissance drama) a play in which the protagonist, usually a man of importance and outstanding personal qualities, falls to disaster through the combination of a personal failing and circumstances with which he cannot deal. **2** (in later drama, such as that of Ibsen) a play in which the protagonist is overcome by a combination of social and psychological circumstances. **3** any dramatic or literary composition dealing with serious or sombre themes and ending with disaster. **4** (in medieval literature) a literary work in which a great person falls from prosperity to disaster, often through no fault of his own. **5** the branch of drama dealing with such themes. **6** the unfortunate aspect of something. **7** a shocking or sad event; disaster. ◆ Compare **comedy.** [C14: from Old French *tragédie,* from Latin *tragoedia,* from Greek *tragōidia,* from *tragos* goat + *ōidē* song; perhaps a reference to the goat-satyrs of Peloponnesian plays]

tragic (ˈtrædʒɪk) *or (less commonly)* **tragical** *adj* **1** of, relating to, or characteristic of tragedy. **2** mournful or pitiable: *a tragic face.* ► **ˈtragically** *adv*

tragic flaw *n* a failing of character in the hero of a tragedy that brings about his downfall.

tragic irony *n* the use of dramatic irony in a tragedy (originally, in Greek tragedy), so that the audience is aware that a character's words or actions will bring about a tragic or fatal result, while the character himself is not.

tragicomedy (ˌtrædʒɪˈkɒmɪdɪ) *n, pl* **-dies. 1a** a drama in which aspects of both tragedy and comedy are found. **1b** the dramatic genre of works of this kind. **2** an event or incident having both comic and tragic aspects. [C16: from French, ultimately from Late Latin *tragicōmoedia;* see TRAGEDY, COMEDY] ► **ˌtragiˈcomic** *or* **ˌtragiˈcomical** *adj* ► **ˌtragiˈcomically** *adv*

tragopan (ˈtræɡəˌpæn) *n* any pheasant of the genus *Tragopan,* of S and SE Asia, having a brilliant plumage and brightly coloured fleshy processes on the head. [C19: via Latin from Greek, from *tragos* goat + PAN]

tragus (ˈtreɪɡəs) *n, pl* **-gi** (-dʒaɪ). **1** the cartilaginous fleshy projection that partially covers the entrance to the external ear. **2** any of the hairs that grow just inside this entrance. [C17: from Late Latin, from Greek *tragos* hairy projection of the ear, literally: goat] ► **ˈtragal** *adj*

Traherne (trəˈhɜːn) *n* **Thomas.** 1637–74, English mystical prose writer and poet. His prose works include *Centuries of Meditations,* which was discovered in manuscript in 1896 and published in 1908.

trail (treɪl) *vb* **1** to drag or stream, or permit to drag or stream along a surface, esp. the ground: *her skirt trailed; she trailed her skipping rope.* **2** to make (a track or path) through (a place): *to trail a way; to trail a jungle.* **3** to chase, follow, or hunt (an animal or person) by following marks or tracks. **4** (when *intr,* often foll. by *behind*) to lag or linger behind (a person or thing). **5** (*intr*) to be falling behind in a race or competition: *the favourite is trailing at the last fence.* **6** (*tr*) to tow (a boat, caravan, etc.) behind a motor vehicle. **7** (*tr*) to carry (a rifle) at the full length of the right arm in a horizontal position, with the muzzle to the fore. **8** (*intr*) to move wearily or slowly: *we trailed through the city.* **9** (*tr*) (on television or radio) to advertise (a future programme) with short extracts. **10 trail one's coat.** to invite a quarrel by deliberately provocative behaviour. ◆ *n* **11** a print, mark, or marks made by a person, animal, or object. **12** the act or an instance of trailing. **13** the scent left by a moving person or animal that is followed by a hunting animal. **14** a path, track, or road, esp. one roughly blazed. **15** something that trails behind or trails in loops or strands. **16** the part of a towed gun carriage and limber that connects the two when in movement and rests on the ground as a partial support when unlimbered. **17** *Engineering.* the distance between the point of contact of a steerable wheel and a line drawn from the swivel pin axis to the ground. [C14: from Old French *trailler* to draw, tow, from Vulgar Latin *tragulāre* (unattested), from Latin *trāgula* dragnet, from *trahere* to drag; compare Middle Dutch *traghelen* to drag] ► **ˈtrailless** *adj*

trail away *or* **off** *vb* (*intr, adv*) to become fainter, quieter, or weaker: *his voice trailed off.*

trail bike *n* a motorcycle adapted for riding on rough tracks.

trailblazer (ˈtreɪlˌbleɪzə) *n* **1** a leader or pioneer in a particular field. **2** a person who blazes a trail. ► **ˈtrailˌblazing** *adj, n*

trailer (ˈtreɪlə) *n* **1** a road vehicle, usually two-wheeled, towed by a motor vehicle: used for transporting boats, etc. **2** the part of an articulated lorry that is drawn by the cab. **3** a series of short extracts from a film, used to advertise it in a cinema or on television. **4** a person or thing that trails. **5** the U.S. and Canadian name for **caravan** (sense 1).

trailing (ˈtreɪlɪŋ) *adj* (of a plant) having a long stem which spreads over the ground or hangs loosely: *trailing ivy.*

trailing arbutus *n* a creeping evergreen ericaceous plant, *Epigaea repens,* of E North America, having clusters of fragrant pink or white flowers. Also called: **mayflower.**

trailing edge *n* **1** the rear edge of a propeller blade or aerofoil. Compare **leading edge. 2** *Physics.* the edge of a pulse signal as its amplitude falls.

trailing vortex drag *n* drag arising from vortices that occur behind a body moving through a gas or liquid. Often shortened to **vortex drag.** Former name: **induced drag.**

trail rope *n* **1** another name for **dragrope** (sense 2). **2** a long rope formerly used for various military purposes, esp. to allow a vehicle, horses, or men to pull a gun carriage.

train (treɪn) *vb* **1** (*tr*) to guide or teach (to do something), as by subjecting to various exercises or experiences: *to train a man to fight.* **2** (*tr*) to control or guide towards a specific goal: *to train a plant up a wall.* **3** (*intr*) to do exercises and prepare for a specific purpose: *the athlete trained for the Olympics.* **4** (*tr*) to improve or curb by subjecting to discipline: *to train the mind.* **5** (*tr*) to focus or bring to bear (on something): *to train a telescope on the moon.* ◆ *n* **6a** a line of coaches or wagons coupled together and drawn by a railway locomotive. **6b** (*as modifier*): *a train ferry.* **7** a sequence or series, as of events, thoughts, etc.: *a train of disasters.* **8** a procession of people, vehicles, etc., travelling together, such as one carrying supplies of ammunition or equipment in support of a military operation. **9** a series of interacting parts through which motion is transmitted: *a train of gears.* **10** a fuse or line of gunpowder to an explosive charge, etc. **11** something drawn along, such as the long back section of a dress that trails along the floor behind the wearer. **12** a retinue or suite. **13** proper order or course. [C14: from Old French *trahiner,* from Vulgar Latin *tragīnāre* (unattested) to draw; related to Latin *trahere* to drag] ► **ˈtrainable** *adj* ► **ˈtrainless** *adj*

trainband (ˈtreɪnˌbænd) *n* a company of English militia from the 16th to the 18th century. [C17: altered from *trained band*]

trainbearer (ˈtreɪnˌbɛərə) *n* an attendant in a procession who holds up the train of a dignitary's robe.

trainee (treɪˈniː) *n* **a** a person undergoing training. **b** (*as modifier*): *a trainee journalist.*

trainer (ˈtreɪnə) *n* **1** a person who trains athletes in a sport. **2** a piece of equipment employed in training, such as a simulated aircraft cockpit. **3** *Horse racing.* a person who schools racehorses and prepares them for racing. **4** (*pl*) an informal name for **training shoes.**

training (ˈtreɪnɪŋ) *n* **1a** the process of bringing a person, etc., to an agreed standard of proficiency, etc., by practice and instruction: *training for the priesthood; physical training.* **1b** (*as modifier*): *training college.* **2 in training. 2a** undergoing physical training. **2b** physically fit. **3 out of training.** physically unfit.

Training Agency *n* (in Britain) an organization established in 1989 to replace the **Training Commission,** which itself replaced the Manpower Services Commission; it provides training and retraining for adult workers and operates the Youth Training Scheme, in England and Wales working through the local **Training and Enterprise Councils** (TECs) and in Scotland through the **Local Enterprise Companies** (LECs) set up in 1990.

training shoes *pl n* **1** running shoes for sports training, esp. in contrast to studded or spiked shoes worn for the sport itself. **2** shoes in the style of those used for sports training. ◆ Also called: **trainers.**

train oil *n* oil obtained from the blubber of various marine animals, esp. the whale. [C16: from earlier *train* or *trane,* from Middle Low German *trān* or Middle Dutch *traen* tear, exudation]

train spotter *n* **1** a person who collects the numbers of railway locomotives. **2** *Informal.* a person who is obsessed with trivial details, esp. of a subject generally considered uninteresting.

traipse *or* **trapes** (treɪps) *Informal.* ◆ *vb* **1** (*intr*) to walk heavily or tiredly. ◆ *n* **2** a long or tiring walk; trudge. [C16: of unknown origin]

trait (treɪt, treɪ) *n* **1** a characteristic feature or quality distinguishing a particular person or thing. **2** *Rare.* a touch or stroke. [C16: from French, from Old French: a pulling, from Latin *tractus,* from *trahere* to drag]

traitor (ˈtreɪtə) *n* a person who is guilty of treason or treachery, in betraying friends, country, a cause or trust, etc. [C13: from Old French *traitour,* from Latin *trāditor* TRADITOR] ► **ˈtraitorous** *adj* ► **ˈtraitorously** *adv* ► **ˈtraitorˌship** *n* ► **ˈtraitress** *fem n*

Trajan (ˈtreɪdʒən) *n* Latin name *Marcus Ulpius Traianus.* ?53–117 A.D., Roman emperor (98–117). He extended the empire to the east and built many roads, bridges, canals, and towns.

traject (trəˈdʒɛkt) *vb* (*tr*) *Archaic.* to transport or transmit. [C17: from Latin *trājectus* cast over, from *trāicere* to throw across, from TRANS- + *iacere* to throw] ► **traˈjection** *n*

trajectory (trəˈdʒɛktərɪ, -trɪ) *n, pl* **-ries. 1** the path described by an object moving in air or space under the influence of such forces as thrust, wind resistance, and gravity, esp. the curved path of a projectile. **2** *Geometry.* a curve that cuts a family of curves or surfaces at a constant angle. ► **trajectile** (trəˈdʒɛktaɪl) *adj*

Trakl (ˈtrɑːkᵊl) *n* **Georg.** 1887–1914, Austrian poet, noted for his expressionist style: died of a drug overdose while serving as a medical officer in World War I.

tra-la *or* **tra-la-la** a set of nonsensical syllables used in humming music, esp. for a melody or refrain.

Tralee (trəˈliː) *n* a market town in SW Republic of Ireland, county town of Kerry, near **Tralee Bay** (an inlet of the Atlantic). Pop.: 17 200 (1991).

tram[1] (træm) *n* **1** Also called: **tramcar.** an electrically driven public transport vehicle that runs on rails let into the surface of the road, power usually being taken from an overhead wire. U.S. and Canadian names: **streetcar, trolley car. 2** a small vehicle on rails for carrying loads in a mine; tub. [C16 (in the sense: shaft of a cart): probably from Low German *traam* beam; compare Old Norse *thrömr,* Middle Dutch *traem* beam, tooth of a rake] ► **ˈtramless** *adj*

tram[2] (træm) *n* **1** *Machinery.* a fine adjustment that ensures correct function or alignment. ◆ *vb* **trams, tramming, trammed. 2** (*tr*) to adjust (a mechanism) to a fine degree of accuracy. [C19: short for TRAMMEL]

tram[3] (træm) *n* (in weaving) a weft yarn of two or more twisted strands of silk. [C17: from French *trame,* from Latin *trāma;* related to Latin *trāns* across, *trāmes* footpath]

tramline (ˈtræmˌlaɪn) *n* **1** (*often pl*) Also called: **tramway.** the tracks on which a tram runs. **2** the route taken by a tram. **3** (*often pl*) the outer markings along the sides of a tennis or badminton court. **4** (*pl*) a set of guiding principles.

trammel (ˈtræməl) *n* **1** (*often pl*) a hindrance to free action or movement. **2** Also called: **trammel net.** a fishing net in three sections, the two outer nets having a large mesh and the middle one a fine mesh. **3** *Rare.* a fowling net. **4** *U.S.* a fetter or shackle, esp. one used in teaching a horse to amble. **5** a device for drawing ellipses consisting of a flat sheet of metal, plastic, or wood having a cruciform slot in which run two pegs attached to a beam. The free end of the beam describes an ellipse. **6** (*sometimes pl*) another name for **beam compass. 7** Also called: **tram.** a gauge for setting up machines correctly. **8** a device set in a fireplace to support cooking pots. ◆ *vb* **-els, -elling, -elled** *or U.S.* **-els, -eling, -eled.** (*tr*) **9** to hinder or restrain. **10** to catch or ensnare. **11** to produce an accurate setting of (a machine adjustment), as with a trammel. **[C14:** from Old French *tramail* three-mesh net, from Late Latin *trēmaculum,* from Latin *trēs* three + *macula* hole, mesh in a net**]** ▸ **'trammeler** *or U.S.* **'trammeler** *n*

trammie ('træmɪ) *n Austral. informal.* the conductor or driver of a tram.

tramontane (trə'mɒnteɪn) *adj also* **transmontane. 1** being or coming from the far side of the mountains, esp. from the other side of the Alps as seen from Italy. **2** foreign or barbarous. **3** (of a wind) blowing down from the mountains. ◆ *n* **4** an inhabitant of a tramontane country. **5** Also called: **tramontana.** a cold dry wind blowing south or southwest from the mountains in Italy and the W Mediterranean. **6** *Rare.* a foreigner or barbarian. **[C16:** from Italian *tramontano,* from Latin *trānsmontānus,* from TRANS- + *montānus,* from *mōns* mountain**]**

tramp (træmp) *vb* **1** (*intr*) to walk long and far; hike. **2** to walk heavily or firmly across or through (a place); march or trudge. **3** (*intr*) to wander about as a vagabond or tramp. **4** (*tr*) to make (a journey) or traverse (a place) on foot, esp. laboriously or wearily: *to tramp the streets in search of work.* **5** (*tr*) to tread or trample. **6** (*intr*) *N.Z.* to walk for sport or recreation, esp. in the bush. ◆ *n* **7** a person who travels about on foot, usually with no permanent home, living by begging or doing casual work. **8** a long hard walk; hike. **9** a heavy or rhythmic step or tread. **10** the sound of heavy treading. **11** Also called: **tramp steamer.** a merchant ship that does not run between ports on a regular schedule but carries cargo wherever the shippers desire. **12** *Slang, chiefly U.S. and Canadian.* a prostitute or promiscuous girl or woman. **13** an iron plate on the sole of a boot. **[C14:** probably from Middle Low German *trampen;* compare Gothic *anatrimpan* to press heavily upon, German *trampen* to hitchhike**]** ▸ **'tramper** *n* ▸ **'tramping** *n* ▸ **'trampish** *adj*

tramping club *n N.Z.* an organization of bush walkers.

tramping hut *n N.Z.* a hut in the bush for the use of trampers.

trample ('træmpᵊl) *vb* (when *intr,* usually foll. by *on, upon,* or *over*) **1** to stamp or walk roughly (on): *to trample the flowers.* **2** to encroach (upon) so as to violate or hurt: *to trample on someone's feelings.* ◆ *n* **3** the action or sound of trampling. **[C14:** frequentative of TRAMP; compare Middle High German *trampeln***]** ▸ **'trampler** *n*

trampoline ('træmpəlɪn, -,liːn) *n* **1** a tough canvas sheet suspended by springs or elasticated cords from a frame, used by acrobats, gymnasts, etc. ◆ *vb* **2** (*intr*) to exercise on a trampoline. **[C18:** via Spanish from Italian *trampolino,* from *trampoli* stilts, of Germanic origin; compare TRAMPLE**]** ▸ **'trampoliner** *or* **'trampolinist** *n*

tramway ('træm,weɪ) *n* **1** another name for **tramline** (sense 1). **2** *Brit.* **2a** a public transportation system using trams. **2b** the company owning or running such a system. **3** Also called (esp. U.S.): **tramroad.** a small or temporary railway for moving freight along tracks, as in a quarry.

trance (trɑːns) *n* **1** a hypnotic state resembling sleep. **2** any mental state in which a person is unaware or apparently unaware of the environment, characterized by loss of voluntary movement, rigidity, and lack of sensitivity to external stimuli. **3** a dazed or stunned state. **4** a state of ecstasy or mystic absorption so intense as to cause a temporary loss of consciousness at the earthly level. **5** *Spiritualism.* a state in which a medium, having temporarily lost consciousness, can supposedly be controlled by an intelligence from without as a means of communication with the dead. ◆ *vb* **6** (*tr*) to put into or as into a trance. **[C14:** from Old French *transe,* from *transir* to faint, pass away, from Latin *trānsīre* to go over, from TRANS- + *īre* to go**]** ▸ **'trance,like** *adj*

tranche (trɑːnʃ) *n* a portion or instalment, esp. of a loan or share issue. **[**from French, literally: a slice**]**

trannie *or* **tranny** ('trænɪ) *n, pl* **-nies.** *Informal, chiefly Brit.* **1** a transistor radio. **2** a transvestite.

tranquil ('træŋkwɪl) *adj* calm, peaceful or quiet. **[C17:** from Latin *tranquillus***]** ▸ **'tranquilly** *adv* ▸ **'tranquilness** *n*

tranquillity *or U.S.* (*sometimes*) **tranquility** (træŋ'kwɪlɪtɪ) *n* a state of calm or quietude.

tranquillize, tranquillise, *or U.S.* **tranquilize** ('træŋkwɪ,laɪz) *vb* to make or become calm or calmer. ▸ **,tranquilli'zation, ,tranquilli'sation,** *or U.S.* **,tranquili'zation** *n*

tranquillizer, tranquilliser, *or U.S.* **tranquilizer** ('træŋkwɪ,laɪzə) *n* **1** a drug that calms a person without affecting clarity of consciousness. **2** anything that tranquillizes.

trans. *abbrev. for:* **1** transaction. **2** transferred. **3** transitive. **4** translated. **5** translator. **6** transport(ation). **7** transparent. **8** transpose. **9** transverse.

trans- *or sometimes before* s- **tran-** *prefix* **1** across, beyond, crossing, on the other side: *transoceanic; trans-Siberian; transatlantic.* **2** changing thoroughly: *transliterate.* **3** transcending: *transubstantiation.* **4** transversely: *transect.* **5** (*often in italics*) indicating that a chemical compound has a molecular structure in which two identical groups or atoms are on opposite sides of a double bond: *trans*-butadiene. Compare **cis-** (sense 2). **[**from Latin *trāns* across, through, beyond**]**

transact (træn'zækt) *vb* to do, conduct, or negotiate (business, a deal, etc.). **[C16:** from Latin *trānsactus,* from *trānsigere,* literally: to drive through, from TRANS- + *agere* to drive**]** ▸ **trans'actor** *n*

transactinide (,træns'æktɪ,naɪd) *n* any artificially produced element with an atomic number greater than 103. **[C20:** from TRANS- + ACTINIDE**]**

transaction (træn'zækʃən) *n* **1** something that is transacted, esp. a business deal or negotiation. **2** the act of transacting or the state of being transacted. **3** (*pl*) the published records of the proceedings of a society, conference, etc. **4** (in business computing) the act of obtaining and paying for an item or service. **5** (in general computing) the transmission and processing of an item of data. ▸ **trans'actional** *adj* ▸ **trans'actionally** *adv*

transactional analysis *n Psychol.* a form of psychotherapy that attributes neuroses to lack of balance in the personality between the conflicting ego-states of child, adult, and parent.

transalpine (trænz'ælpaɪn) *adj* (*prenominal*) **1** situated in or relating to places beyond the Alps, esp. from Italy. **2** passing over the Alps. ◆ *n* **3** a transalpine person.

Transalpine Gaul *n* (in the ancient world) that part of Gaul northwest of the Alps.

transaminase (trænz'æmɪ,neɪz, -,neɪs) *n Biochem.* an enzyme that catalyses the transfer of an amino group from one molecule, esp. an amino acid, to another, esp. a keto acid, in the process of **transamination.**

transatlantic (,trænzət'læntɪk) *adj* **1** on or from the other side of the Atlantic. **2** crossing the Atlantic.

transcalent (træns'keɪlənt) *adj Rare.* permitting the passage of heat. **[C19:** TRANS- + *-calent,* from Latin *calēre* to be hot**]** ▸ **trans'calency** *n*

Transcaucasia (,trænskɔː'keɪzjə) *n* a region in central Asia, south of the Caucasus Mountains between the Black and Caspian Seas in Georgia, Armenia, and Azerbaijan: a constituent republic of the Soviet Union from 1918 until 1936. ▸ **,Transcau'casian** *adj, n*

transceiver (træn'siːvə) *n* a device which transmits and receives radio or electronic signals. **[C20:** from TRANS(MITTER) + (RE)CEIVER**]**

transcend (træn'send) *vb* **1** to go above or beyond (a limit, expectation, etc.), as in degree or excellence. **2** (*tr*) to be superior to. **3** *Philosophy, theol.* (esp. of the Deity) to exist beyond (the material world). **[C14:** from Latin *trānscendere* to climb over, from TRANS- + *scandere* to climb**]** ▸ **trans'cendingly** *adv*

transcendent (træn'sendənt) *adj* **1** exceeding or surpassing in degree or excellence. **2a** (in the philosophy of Kant) beyond or before experience; a priori. **2b** (of a concept) falling outside a given set of categories. **2c** beyond consciousness or direct apprehension. **3** *Theol.* (of God) having continuous existence outside the created world. **4** free from the limitations inherent in matter. ◆ *n* **5** *Philosophy.* a transcendent thing. ▸ **tran'scendence** *n* ▸ **tran'scendency** *n* ▸ **tran'scendently** *adv* ▸ **tran'scendentness** *n*

transcendental (,trænsen'dentᵊl) *adj* **1** transcendent, superior, or surpassing. **2** (in the philosophy of Kant) **2a** (of a judgment or logical deduction) being both synthetic and a priori. **2b** of or relating to knowledge of the presuppositions of thought. **3** *Philosophy.* beyond our experience of phenomena, although not beyond potential knowledge. **4** *Theol.* surpassing the natural plane of reality or knowledge; supernatural or mystical. ▸ **,transcenden'tality** *n* ▸ **,transcen'dentally** *adv*

transcendental argument *n Philosophy.* an argument designed to make explicit the conditions under which a certain kind of knowledge is possible, esp. those of Kant.

transcendental function *n Maths.* a function that is not capable of expression in terms of a finite number of arithmetical operations, such as sin *x.*

transcendental idealism *n Philosophy.* the Kantian doctrine that reality consists not of appearances, but of some other order of being whose existence can be inferred from the nature of human reason.

transcendentalism (,trænsen'dentə,lɪzəm) *n* **1a** any system of philosophy, esp. that of Kant, holding that the key to knowledge of the nature of reality lies in the critical examination of the processes of reason on which depends the nature of experience. **1b** any system of philosophy, esp. that of Emerson, that emphasizes intuition as a means to knowledge or the importance of the search for the divine. **2** vague philosophical speculation. **3** the state of being transcendental. **4** something, such as thought or language, that is transcendental. ▸ **,transcen'dentalist** *n, adj*

transcendental meditation *n* a technique, based on Hindu traditions, for relaxing and refreshing the mind and body through the silent repetition of a mantra.

transcendental number *n Maths.* a number or quantity that is real but nonalgebraic, that is, one that is not a root of any polynomial with rational coefficients such as π or *e.*

transcontinental (,trænzkɒntɪ'nentᵊl) *adj* **1** crossing a continent. **2** on or from the far side of a continent. ▸ **,transconti'nentally** *adv*

transcribe (træn'skraɪb) *vb* (*tr*) **1** to write, type, or print out fully from speech, notes, etc. **2** to make a phonetic transcription of. **3** to transliterate or translate. **4** to make an electrical recording of (a programme or speech) for a later broadcast. **5** *Music.* to rewrite (a piece of music) for an instrument or medium other than that originally intended; arrange. **6** *Computing.* **6a** to transfer (information) from one storage device, such as punched cards, to another, such as magnetic tape. **6b** to transfer (information) from a computer to an external storage device. **7** (*usually passive*) *Biochem.* to convert the genetic information in (a strand of DNA) into a strand of RNA, esp. messenger RNA. See also **genetic code, translate** (sense 6). **[C16:** from Latin *transcrībere,* from TRANS- + *scrībere* to write**]** ▸ **tran'scribable** *adj* ▸ **tran'scriber** *n*

transcript ('trænskrɪpt) *n* **1** a written, typed, or printed copy or manuscript made by transcribing. **2** *Education, chiefly U.S. and Canadian.* an official record of a student's school progress and achievements. **3** any reproduction or copy. **[C13:** from Latin *transcriptum,* from *transcrībere* to TRANSCRIBE**]**

transcriptase (træn'skrɪpteɪz) *n* See **reverse transcriptase.**

transcription (træn'skrɪpʃən) *n* **1** the act or an instance of transcribing or the state of being transcribed. **2** something transcribed. **3** a representation in writing of the actual pronunciation of a speech sound, word, or piece of continuous text, using not a conventional orthography but a symbol or set of symbols specially designated as standing for corresponding phonetic values. ▸ **tran'scriptional** *or* **tran'scriptive** *adj* ▸ **tran'scriptionally** *or* **tran'scriptively** *adv*

transculturation (ˌtrænzkʌltʃʊˈreɪʃən) *n* the introduction of foreign elements into an established culture.

transcurrent (trænzˈkʌrənt) *adj* running across; transverse.

transdermal (trænzˈdɜːməl) *adj* (of a medicine) entering the bloodstream by absorption through the skin. [C20: from TRANS- + DERMAL]

Transdniestria (ˈtrænsdnɪˌɛstrɪə) *n* a region of E Moldova: unilaterally declared itself independent and was the scene of fighting between government troops and separatists in 1992.

transducer (trænzˈdjuːsə) *n* any device, such as a microphone or electric motor, that converts one form of energy into another. [C20: from Latin *transducere* to lead across, from TRANS- + *ducere* to lead]

transduction (trænzˈdʌkʃən) *n Genetics.* the transfer by a bacteriophage of genetic material from one bacterium to another. [C17: from Latin *transductiō*, variant of *trāductiō* a leading along, from *trādūcere* to lead over; see TRADUCE]

transect *vb (tr)* (trænˈsɛkt) **1** to cut or divide crossways. ♦ *n* (ˈtrænsɛkt). **2** a sample strip of land used to monitor plant distribution, animal populations, etc., within a given area. [C17: from Latin TRANS- + *secāre* to cut] ▸ **tranˈsection** *n*

transept (ˈtrænsɛpt) *n* either of the two wings of a cruciform church at right angles to the nave. [C16: from Anglo-Latin *transeptum*, from Latin TRANS- + *saeptum* enclosure] ▸ **tranˈseptal** *adj*

transeunt (ˈtrænsɪənt) *or* **transient** *adj Philosophy.* (of a mental act) causing effects outside the mind. Compare **immanent** (sense 2). [C17: from Latin *transiēns* going over, from *transīre* to pass over; see TRANCE]

transf. *abbrev. for* transferred.

trans-fatty acid *n* a polyunsaturated fatty acid that has been converted from the cis-form by hydrogenation: used in the manufacture of margarine.

transfect (trænsˈfɛkt) *vb (tr)* to bring about transfection in. [from TRANS- + (IN)FECT]

transfection (trænsˈfɛkʃən) *n* the transfer into another cell of genetic material isolated from a cell or virus.

transfer *vb* (trænsˈfɜː), **-fers, -ferring, -ferred. 1** to change or go or cause to change or go from one thing, person, or point to another: *they transferred from the Park Hotel to the Imperial; she transferred her affections to her dog.* **2** to change (buses, trains, etc.). **3** *Law.* to make over (property, etc.) to another; convey. **4** to displace (a drawing, design, etc.) from one surface to another. **5** (of a football player, esp. a professional) to change clubs or (of a club, manager, etc.) to sell or release (a player) to another club. **6** to leave one school, college, etc., and enrol at another. **7** to change (the meaning of a word, etc.), esp. by metaphorical extension. ♦ *n* (ˈtrænsfɜː). **8** the act, process, or system of transferring, or the state of being transferred. **9a** a person or thing that transfers or is transferred. **9b** (*as modifier*): *a transfer student.* **10** a design or drawing that is transferred from one surface to another, as by ironing a printed design onto cloth. **11** *Law.* the passing of title to property or other right from one person to another by act of the parties or by operation of law; conveyance. **12** *Finance.* **12a** the act of transferring the title of ownership to shares or registered bonds in the books of the issuing enterprise. **12b** (*as modifier*): *transfer deed; transfer form.* **13** any document or form effecting or regulating a transfer. **14** *Chiefly U.S. and Canadian.* a ticket that allows a passenger to change routes. [C14: from Latin *transferre*, from TRANS- + *ferre* to carry] ▸ **transˈferable** *or* **transˈferrable** *adj* ▸ **ˌtransferaˈbility** *n*

transferable vote *n* a vote that is transferred to a second candidate indicated by the voter if the first is eliminated from the ballot.

transferase (ˈtrænsfəˌreɪs) *n* any enzyme that catalyses the transfer of a chemical group from one substance to another.

transfer characteristic *n Electronics.* the relationship between output and input of an electronic or electromechanical system, esp. as depicted graphically.

transferee (ˌtrænsfəˈriː) *n* **1** *Property law.* a person to whom property is transferred. **2** a person who is transferred.

transference (ˈtrænsfərəns, -frəns) *n* **1** the act or an instance of transferring or the state of being transferred. **2** *Psychoanal.* the redirection of attitudes and emotions towards a substitute, such as towards the analyst during therapy. ▸ **transferential** (ˌtrænsfəˈrɛnʃəl) *adj*

transfer fee *n* a sum of money paid by one football club to another for a transferred player.

transfer list *n* a list of football players available for transfer.

transferor *or* **transferrer** (trænsˈfɜːrə) *n Property law.* a person who makes a transfer, as of property.

transfer payment *n* (*usually pl*) money received by an individual or family from the state or other body, often a pension or unemployment benefit. It is not reckoned when calculating the national income as it is money transferred rather than paid for merchandise or a service rendered.

transfer pricing *n* the setting of a price for the transfer of raw materials, components, products, or services between the trading units of a large organization.

transferrin (trænsˈfɜːrɪn) *n Biochem.* any of a group of blood glycoproteins that transport iron. Also called: **beta globulin, siderophilin.** [C20: from TRANS- + FERRO- + -IN]

transfer RNA *n Biochem.* any of several soluble forms of RNA of low molecular weight, each of which transports a specific amino acid to a ribosome during protein synthesis. Sometimes shortened to **t-RNA.** Also called: **soluble RNA.** See also **messenger RNA, genetic code.**

transfiguration (ˌtrænsfɪgjʊˈreɪʃən) *n* the act or an instance of transfiguring or the state of being transfigured.

Transfiguration (ˌtrænsfɪgjʊˈreɪʃən) *n* **1** *New Testament.* the change in the appearance of Christ that took place before three disciples (Matthew 17:1–9). **2** the Church festival held in commemoration of this on Aug. 6.

transfigure (trænsˈfɪgə) *vb* (*usually tr*) **1** to change or cause to change in appearance. **2** to become or cause to become more exalted. [C13: from Latin *transfigūrāre*, from TRANS- + *figūra* appearance] ▸ **transˈfigurement** *n*

transfinite (trænsˈfaɪnaɪt) *adj* extending beyond the finite.

transfinite number *n* a cardinal or ordinal number used in the comparison of infinite sets for which several types of infinity can be classified: *the set of integers and the set of real numbers have different transfinite numbers.*

transfix (trænsˈfɪks) *vb* **-fixes, -fixing, -fixed** *or* **-fixt.** (*tr*) **1** to render motionless, esp. with horror or shock. **2** to impale or fix with a sharp weapon or other device. **3** *Med.* to cut through (a limb or other organ), as in amputation. [C16: from Latin *transfīgere* to pierce through, from TRANS- + *fīgere* to thrust in] ▸ **transfixion** (trænsˈfɪkʃən) *n*

transform *vb* (trænsˈfɔːm). **1** to alter or be altered radically in form, function, etc. **2** (*tr*) to convert (one form of energy) to another form. **3** (*tr*) *Maths.* to change the form of (an equation, expression, etc.) by a mathematical transformation. **4** (*tr*) to increase or decrease (an alternating current or voltage) using a transformer. ♦ *n* (ˈtrænsˌfɔːm). **5** *Maths.* the result of a mathematical transformation, esp. (of a matrix or an element of a group) another related to the given one by $B=X^{-1}AX$ for some appropriate X. [C14: from Latin *transformāre*, from TRANS- + *formāre* to FORM] ▸ **transˈformable** *adj* ▸ **transˈformative** *adj*

transformation (ˌtrænsfəˈmeɪʃən) *n* **1** a change or alteration, esp. a radical one. **2** the act of transforming or the state of being transformed. **3** *Maths.* **3a** a change in position or direction of the reference axes in a coordinate system without an alteration in their relative angle. **3b** an equivalent change in an expression or equation resulting from the substitution of one set of variables by another. **4** *Physics.* a change in an atomic nucleus to a different nuclide as the result of the emission of either an alpha-particle or a beta-particle. Compare **transition** (sense 5). **5** *Linguistics.* another word for **transformational rule. 6** an apparently miraculous change in the appearance of a stage set. ▸ **ˌtransforˈmational** *adj*

transformational grammar *n* a grammatical description of a language making essential use of transformational rules. Such grammars are usually but not necessarily generative grammars. Compare **systemic grammar, case grammar.**

transformational rule *n* **1** *Generative grammar.* a rule that converts one phrase marker into another. Taken together, these rules, which form the **transformational component** of the grammar, convert the deep structures of sentences into their surface structures. **2** (*pl*) *Logic.* a rule that specifies in purely syntactic terms a method by which theorems may be derived from the axioms of a formal system.

transformer (trænsˈfɔːmə) *n* **1** a device that transfers an alternating current from one circuit to one or more other circuits, usually with an increase (**step-up transformer**) or decrease (**step-down transformer**) of voltage. The input current is fed to a primary winding, the output being taken from a secondary winding or windings inductively linked to the primary. **2** a person or thing that transforms.

transformism (trænsˈfɔːmɪzəm) *n* a less common word for **evolution**, esp. the theory of evolution. ▸ **transˈformist** *n*

transfuse (trænsˈfjuːz) *vb (tr)* **1** to permeate or infuse: *a blush transfused her face.* **2a** to inject (blood, etc.) into a blood vessel. **2b** to give a transfusion to (a patient). **3** *Rare.* to transfer from one vessel to another, esp. by pouring. [C15: from Latin *transfundere* to pour out, from TRANS- + *fundere* to pour] ▸ **transˈfuser** *n* ▸ **transˈfusible** *or* **transˈfusable** *adj* ▸ **transˈfusive** *adj*

transfusion (trænsˈfjuːʒən) *n* **1** the act or an instance of transfusing. **2** the injection of blood, blood plasma, etc., into the blood vessels of a patient.

transgenic (trænzˈdʒɛnɪk) *adj* (of an animal or plant) containing genetic material artificially transferred from another species.

transgress (trænzˈgrɛs) *vb* **1** to break (a law, rule, etc.). **2** to go beyond or overstep (a limit). [C16: from Latin *transgredī*, from TRANS- + *gradī* to step] ▸ **transˈgressive** *adj* ▸ **transˈgressively** *adv* ▸ **transˈgressor** *n*

transgression (trænzˈgrɛʃən) *n* **1** a breach of a law, etc.; sin or crime. **2** the act or an instance of transgressing.

tranship (trænˈʃɪp) *vb* **-ships, -shipping, -shipped.** a variant spelling of **transship.** ▸ **tranˈshipment** *n*

transhumance (trænsˈhjuːməns) *n* the seasonal migration of livestock to suitable grazing grounds. [C20: from French, from *transhumer* to change one's pastures, from Spanish *trashumar*, from Latin TRANS- + *humus* ground] ▸ **transˈhumant** *adj*

transient (ˈtrænzɪənt) *adj* **1** for a short time only; temporary or transitory. **2** *Philosophy.* a variant of **transeunt.** ♦ *n* **3** a transient person or thing. **4** *Physics.* a brief change in the state of a system, such as a sudden short-lived oscillation in the current flowing through a circuit. [C17: from Latin *transiēns* going over, from *transīre* to pass over, from TRANS- + *īre* to go] ▸ **ˈtransiently** *adv* ▸ **ˈtransience** *or* **ˈtransiency** *n*

transilient (trænˈsɪlɪənt) *adj* passing quickly from one thing to another. [C19: from Latin *transilīre* to jump over, from TRANS- + *salīre* to leap] ▸ **tranˈsilience** *n*

transilluminate (ˌtrænzɪˈluːmɪˌneɪt) *vb (tr) Med.* to pass a light through the wall of (a bodily cavity, membrane, etc.) in order to detect fluid, lesions, etc. ▸ **ˌtransilˌlumiˈnation** *n* ▸ **ˌtransilˈlumiˌnator** *n*

transistor (trænˈzɪstə) *n* **1** a semiconductor device, having three or more terminals attached to electrode regions, in which current flowing between two electrodes is controlled by a voltage or current applied to one or more specified electrodes. The device is capable of amplification, etc., and has replaced the valve in most circuits since it is much smaller, more robust, and works at a much lower voltage. See also **junction transistor, field-effect transistor. 2** *Informal.* a transistor radio. [C20: originally a trademark, from TRANSFER + RESISTOR, referring to the transfer of electric signals across a resistor]

transistorize *or* **transistorise** (træn'zɪstəˌraɪz) *vb* **1** to convert (a system, device, industry, etc.) to the use or manufacture of or operation by transistors and other solid-state components. **2** to equip (a device or circuit) with transistors and other solid-state components.

transit ('trænsɪt, 'trænz-) *n* **1a** the passage or conveyance of goods or people. **1b** (*as modifier*): *a transit visa.* **2** a change or transition. **3** a route. **4** *Astronomy.* **4a** the passage of a celestial body or satellite across the face of a relatively larger body as seen from the earth. **4b** the apparent passage of a celestial body across the meridian, caused by the earth's diurnal rotation. **5** *Astrology.* the passage of a planet across some special point on the zodiac. **6 in transit.** while being conveyed; during passage. ◆ *vb* **7** to make a transit through or over (something). **8** *Astronomy.* to make a transit across (a celestial body or the meridian). **9** to cause (the telescope of a surveying instrument) to turn over or (of such a telescope) to be turned over in a vertical plane so that it points in the opposite direction. [C15: from Latin *transitus* a going over, from *transīre* to pass over; see TRANSIENT] ▸ **'transitable** *adj*

transit camp *n* a camp in which refugees, soldiers, etc., live temporarily before moving to another destination.

transit instrument *n* an astronomical instrument, mounted on an E-W axis, in which the reticle of a telescope is always in the plane of the meridian. It is used to time the transit of a star, etc., across the meridian.

transition (træn'zɪʃən) *n* **1** change or passage from one state or stage to another. **2** the period of time during which something changes from one state or stage to another. **3** *Music.* **3a** a movement from one key to another; modulation. **3b** a linking passage between two divisions in a composition; bridge. **4** Also called: **transitional.** a style of architecture that was used in western Europe in the late 11th and early 12th century, characterized by late Romanesque forms combined with early Gothic details. **5** *Physics.* a change in the configuration of an atomic nucleus, involving either a change in energy level resulting from the emission of a gamma-ray photon or a transformation to another element or isotope. **6** a sentence, passage, etc., that connects a topic to one that follows or that links sections of a written work. [C16: from Latin *transitio;* see TRANSIENT] ▸ **tran'sitional** *or* (*rarely*) **tran'sitionary** *adj* ▸ **tran'sitionally** *adv*

transition element *or* **metal** *n Chem.* any element belonging to one of three series of elements with atomic numbers between 21 and 30, 39 and 48, and 57 and 80. They have an incomplete penultimate electron shell and tend to exhibit more than one valency and to form complexes.

transition point *n* **1** the point in a stream of fluid flow at which laminar flow changes to turbulent flow. **2** See **transition temperature.**

transition temperature *n* the temperature at which a sudden change of physical properties occurs, such as a change of phase, crystalline structure, or conductivity.

transitive ('trænsɪtɪv) *adj* **1** *Grammar.* **1a** denoting an occurrence of a verb when it requires a direct object or denoting a verb that customarily requires a direct object: *"to find" is a transitive verb.* **1b** (*as n*): *these verbs are transitives.* **2** *Grammar.* denoting an adjective, such as *fond,* or a noun, such as *husband,* that requires a noun phrase and cannot be used without some implicit or explicit reference to such a noun phrase. **3** *Logic, maths.* having the property that if one object bears a relationship to a second object that also bears the same relationship to a third object, then the first object bears this relationship to the third object: *mathematical equality is transitive, since if* $x = y$ *and* $y = z$ *then* $x = z$. ◆ Compare **intransitive.** [C16: from Late Latin *transitīvus,* from Latin *transitus* a going over; see TRANSIENT] ▸ **'transitively** *adv* ▸ **ˌtransi'tivity** *or* **'transitiveness** *n*

transitory ('trænsɪtərɪ, -trɪ) *adj* of short duration; transient or ephemeral. [C14: from Church Latin *transitōrius* passing, from Latin *transitus* a crossing over; see TRANSIENT] ▸ **'transitorily** *adv* ▸ **'transitoriness** *n*

transitory action *n Law.* an action that can be brought in any country regardless of where it originated.

transit theodolite *n* a theodolite the telescope of which can be rotated completely about its horizontal axis.

Trans-Jordan *n* the former name (1922–49) of **Jordan.** ▸ **ˌTrans-Jor'danian** *adj, n*

Transkei (træn'skaɪ) *n* a former Bantu homeland in South Africa: the largest of South Africa's Bantu homelands and the first Bantu self-governing territory (1963); declared an independent state in 1976 but this status was not recognized outside South Africa; abolished in 1993 when South African citizenship was restored to its inhabitants. Capital: Umtata. ▸ **Trans'keian** *adj, n*

transl. *abbrev. for:* **1** translated. **2** translator.

translate (træns'leɪt, trænz-) *vb* **1** to express or be capable of being expressed in another language or dialect: *he translated Shakespeare into Afrikaans; his books translate well.* **2** (*intr*) to act as translator. **3** (*tr*) to express or explain in simple or less technical language. **4** (*tr*) to interpret or infer the significance of (gestures, symbols, etc.). **5** (*tr*) to transform or convert: *to translate hope into reality.* **6** (*tr; usually passive*) *Biochem.* to transform the molecular structure of (messenger RNA) into a polypeptide chain by means of the information stored in the genetic code. See also **transcribe** (sense 7). **7** to move or carry from one place or position to another. **8** (*tr*) **8a** to transfer (a cleric) from one ecclesiastical office to another. **8b** to transfer (a see) from one place to another. **9** (*tr*) *R.C. Church.* to transfer (the body or the relics of a saint) from one resting place to another. **10** (*tr*) *Theol.* to transfer (a person) from one place or plane of existence to another, as from earth to heaven. **11** *Maths, physics.* to move (a figure or body) laterally, without rotation, dilation, or angular displacement. **12** (*intr*) (of an aircraft, missile, etc.) to fly or move from one position to another. **13** (*tr*) *Archaic.* to bring to a state of spiritual or emotional ecstasy. [C13: from Latin *translātus* transferred, carried over, from *transferre* to TRANSFER] ▸ **trans'latable** *adj* ▸ **ˌtranslata'bility** *n*

translation (træns'leɪʃən, trænz-) *n* **1** something that is or has been translated, esp. a written text. **2** the act of translating or the state of being translated. **3** *Maths.* a transformation in which the origin of a coordinate system is moved to another position so that each axis retains the same direction or, equivalently, a figure or curve is moved so that it retains the same orientation to the axes. ▸ **trans'lational** *adj*

translator (træns'leɪtə, trænz-) *n* **1** a person or machine that translates speech or writing. **2** *Radio.* a relay transmitter that retransmits a signal on a carrier frequency different from that on which it was received. **3** *Computing.* a computer program that converts a program from one language to another. ▸ **ˌtransla'torial** *adj*

transliterate (trænz'lɪtəˌreɪt) *vb* (*tr*) to transcribe (a word, etc., in one alphabet) into corresponding letters of another alphabet: *the Greek word* λογος *can be transliterated as "logos".* [C19: TRANS- + *-literate,* from Latin *līttera* LETTER] ▸ **ˌtransliter'ation** *n* ▸ **trans'literˌator** *n*

translocate (ˌtrænzləʊ'keɪt) *vb* (*tr*) to move; displace.

translocation (ˌtrænzləʊ'keɪʃən) *n* **1** *Genetics.* the transfer of one part of a chromosome to another part of the same or a different chromosome, resulting in rearrangement of the genes. **2** *Botany.* the transport of minerals, sugars, etc., in solution within a plant. **3** a movement from one position or place to another.

translucent (trænz'luːsᵊnt) *adj* allowing light to pass through partially or diffusely; semitransparent. [C16: from Latin *translūcēre* to shine through, from TRANS- + *lūcēre* to shine] ▸ **trans'lucence** *or* **trans'lucency** *n* ▸ **trans'lucently** *adv*

translunar (trænz'luːnə) *or* **translunary** (trænz'luːnərɪ) *adj* **1** lying beyond the moon. Compare **cislunar. 2** unworldly or ethereal.

transmarine (ˌtrænzmə'riːn) *adj* a less common word for **overseas.** [C16: from Latin *transmarīnus,* from TRANS- + *marīnus,* from *mare* sea]

transmigrant (trænz'maɪgrənt, 'trænzmɪgrənt) *n* **1** an emigrant on the way to the country of immigration. ◆ *adj* **2** passing through from one place or stage to another.

transmigrate (ˌtrænzmaɪ'greɪt) *vb* (*intr*) **1** to move from one place, state, or stage to another. **2** (of souls) to pass from one body into another at death. ▸ **ˌtransmi'gration** *n* ▸ **ˌtransmi'grational** *adj* ▸ **trans'migrative** *adj* ▸ **ˌtransmi'grator** *n* ▸ **trans'migratory** *adj*

transmissible spongiform encephalopathy *n* the full name for **TSE.**

transmission (trænz'mɪʃən) *n* **1** the act or process of transmitting. **2** something that is transmitted. **3** the extent to which a body or medium transmits light, sound, or some other form of energy. **4** the transference of motive force or power. **5** a system of shafts, gears, torque converters, etc., that transmits power, esp. the arrangement of such parts that transmits the power of the engine to the driving wheels of a motor vehicle. **6** the act or process of sending a message, picture, or other information from one location to one or more other locations by means of radio waves, electrical signals, light signals, etc. **7** a radio or television broadcast. [C17: from Latin *transmissiō* a sending across; see TRANSMIT] ▸ **trans'missible** *adj* ▸ **transˌmissi'bility** *n* ▸ **trans'missive** *adj* ▸ **trans'missively** *adv* ▸ **trans'missiveness** *n*

transmission density *n Physics.* a measure of the extent to which a substance transmits light or other electromagnetic radiation, equal to the logarithm to base ten of the reciprocal of the transmittance. Symbol: τ Former name: **optical density.**

transmission line *n* a coaxial cable, waveguide, or other system of conductors that transfers electrical signals from one location to another. Sometimes shortened to **line.**

transmissivity (ˌtrænzmɪ'sɪvɪtɪ) *n Physics.* a measure of the ability of a material to transmit radiation, equal to the internal transmittance of the material under conditions in which the path of the radiation has unit length.

transmit (trænz'mɪt) *vb* **-mits, -mitting, -mitted. 1** (*tr*) to pass or cause to go from one place or person to another; transfer. **2** (*tr*) to pass on or impart (a disease, infection, etc.). **3** (*tr*) to hand down to posterity. **4** (*tr; usually passive*) to pass (an inheritable characteristic) from parent to offspring. **5** to allow the passage of (particles, energy, etc.): *radio waves are transmitted through the atmosphere.* **6a** to send out (signals) by means of radio waves or along a transmission line. **6b** to broadcast (a radio or television programme). **7** (*tr*) to transfer (a force, motion, power, etc.) from one part of a mechanical system to another. [C14: from Latin *transmittere* to send across, from TRANS- + *mittere* to send] ▸ **trans'mittable** *or* **trans'mittible** *adj* ▸ **trans'mittal** *n*

transmittance (trænz'mɪtᵊns) *n* **1** the act of transmitting. **2** Also called: **transmission factor.** *Physics.* a measure of the ability of anything to transmit radiation, equal to the ratio of the transmitted flux to the incident flux; the reciprocal of the opacity. For a plate of material the ratio of the flux leaving the entry surface to that reaching the exit surface is the **internal transmittance.** Symbol: τ Compare **reflectance, absorptance.**

transmittancy (trænz'mɪtᵊnsɪ) *n Physics.* a measure of the extent to which a solution transmits radiation. It is equal to the ratio of the transmittance of the solution to the transmittance of a pure solvent of the same dimensions.

transmitter (trænz'mɪtə) *n* **1** a person or thing that transmits. **2** the equipment used for generating and amplifying a radio-frequency carrier, modulating the carrier with information, and feeding it to an aerial for transmission. **3** the microphone in a telephone that converts sound waves into audio-frequency electrical signals. **4** a device that converts mechanical movements into coded electrical signals transmitted along a telegraph circuit. **5** *Physiol.* a substance released by nerve endings that transmits impulses across synapses.

transmittivity (ˌtrænzmɪ'tɪvɪtɪ) *n Physics.* the transmittance of unit thickness of a substance, neglecting any scattering effects.

transmogrify (trænz'mɒgrɪˌfaɪ) *vb* **-fies, -fying, -fied.** (*tr*) *Jocular.* to change or transform into a different shape, esp. a grotesque or bizarre one. [C17: of unknown origin] ► **trans,mogrifi'cation** *n*

transmontane (ˌtrænzmɒn'teɪn) *adj, n* another word for **tramontane.**

transmundane (trænz'mʌndeɪn) *adj* beyond this world or worldly considerations.

transmutation (ˌtrænzmjuː'teɪʃən) *n* **1** the act or an instance of transmuting. **2** the change of one chemical element into another by a nuclear reaction. **3** the attempted conversion, by alchemists, of base metals into gold or silver. ► **ˌtransmu'tational** *or* **trans'mutative** *adj* ► **ˌtransmu'tationist** *n, adj*

transmute (trænz'mjuːt) *vb (tr)* **1** to change the form, character, or substance of. **2** to alter (an element, metal, etc.) by alchemy. [C15: via Old French from Latin *transmūtāre* to shift, from TRANS- + *mūtāre* to change] ► **trans,mut-a'bility** *n* ► **trans'mutable** *adj* ► **trans'mutably** *adv* ► **trans'muter** *n*

transnational (trænz'næʃənəl) *adj* extending beyond the boundaries, interests, etc., of a single nation.

Trans-New Guinea phylum *n* the largest grouping of the non-Austronesian languages of Papua and New Guinea and the surrounding regions. Older term: **New Guinea Macrophylum.**

transoceanic ('trænzˌəʊʃɪ'ænɪk) *adj* **1** on or from the other side of an ocean. **2** crossing an ocean.

transom ('trænsəm) *n* **1** Also called: **traverse.** a horizontal member across a window. Compare **mullion. 2** a horizontal member that separates a door from a window over it. **3** the usual U.S. name for **fanlight. 4** *Nautical.* **4a** a surface forming the stern of a vessel, either vertical or canted either forwards (**reverse transom**) or aft at the upper side. **4b** any of several transverse beams used for strengthening the stern of a vessel. [C14: earlier *traversayn,* from Old French *traversin,* from TRAVERSE] ► **'transomed** *adj*

transonic (træn'sɒnɪk) *adj* of or relating to conditions when travelling at or near the speed of sound.

transonic barrier *n* another name for **sound barrier.**

transp. *abbrev. for* transport(ation).

transpacific (ˌtrænzpə'sɪfɪk) *adj* **1** crossing the Pacific. **2** on or from the other side of the Pacific.

transpadane ('trænzpəˌdeɪn, træns'peɪdeɪn) *adj (prenominal)* on or from the far (or north) side of the River Po, as viewed from Rome. Compare **cispadane.** [C17: from Latin *Transpadānus,* from TRANS- + *Padus* the River Po]

transparency (træns'pærənsɪ, -'pɛər-) *n, pl* **-cies. 1** Also called: **transparence.** the state of being transparent. **2** Also called: **slide.** a positive photograph on a transparent base, usually mounted in a frame or between glass plates. It can be viewed by means of a slide projector.

transparent (træns'pærənt, -'pɛər-) *adj* **1** permitting the uninterrupted passage of light; clear: *a window is transparent.* **2** easy to see through, understand, or recognize; obvious. **3** (of a substance or object) permitting the free passage of electromagnetic radiation: *a substance that is transparent to X-rays.* **4** candid, open, or frank. [C15: from Medieval Latin *transpārēre* to show through, from Latin TRANS- + *pārēre* to appear] ► **trans'parently** *adv* ► **trans'parentness** *n*

transparent context *n Philosophy, logic.* an expression in which any term may be replaced by another with the same reference without changing its truth-value. Compare **opaque context.**

transpicuous (træn'spɪkjʊəs) *adj* a less common word for **transparent.** [C17: from Medieval Latin *transpicuus,* from Latin *transpicere* to look through, from TRANS- + *specere* to look] ► **tran'spicuously** *adv*

transpierce (træns'pɪəs) *vb (tr)* to pierce through.

transpire (træn'spaɪə) *vb* **1** *(intr)* to come to light; be known. **2** *(intr) Informal.* to happen or occur. **3** *Physiol.* to give off or exhale (water or vapour) through the skin, a mucous membrane, etc. **4** (of plants) to lose (water in the form of water vapour), esp. through the stomata of the leaves. [C16: from Medieval Latin *transpīrāre,* from Latin TRANS- + *spīrāre* to breathe] ► **tran'spirable** *adj* ► **transpiration** (ˌtrænspə'reɪʃən) *n* ► **tran'spiratory** *adj*

USAGE It is often maintained that *transpire* should not be used to mean happen or occur, as in *the event transpired late in the evening,* and that the word is properly used to mean become known, as in *it transpired later that the thief had been caught.* The word is, however, widely used in the former sense, esp. in spoken English.

transplant *vb* (træns'plɑːnt). **1** *(tr)* to remove or transfer (esp. a plant) from one place to another. **2** *(intr)* to be capable of being transplanted. **3** *Surgery.* to transfer (an organ or tissue) from one part of the body to another or from one person or animal to another during a grafting or transplant operation. ◆ *n* ('trænsˌplɑːnt). **4** *Surgery.* **4a** the procedure involved in such a transfer. **4b** the organ or tissue transplanted. ► **trans'plantable** *adj* ► **ˌtransplan'tation** *n* ► **trans'planter** *n*

transpolar (trænz'pəʊlə) *adj* crossing a polar region.

transponder *or* **transpondor** (træn'spɒndə) *n* **1** a type of radio or radar transmitter-receiver that transmits signals automatically when it receives predetermined signals. **2** the receiver and transmitter in a communications or broadcast satellite, relaying received signals back to earth. [C20: from TRANSMITTER + RESPONDER]

transpontine (trænz'pɒntaɪn) *adj* **1** on or from the far side of a bridge. **2** *Archaic.* on or from the south side of the Thames in London. [C19: TRANS- + *-pontine,* from Latin *pōns* bridge]

transport *vb* (træns'pɔːt). *(tr)* **1** to carry or cause to go from one place to another, esp. over some distance. **2** to deport or exile to a penal colony. **3** *(usually passive)* to have a strong emotional effect on. ◆ *n* ('trænsˌpɔːt). **4a** the business or system of transporting goods or people. **4b** *(as modifier): a modernized transport system.* **5** *Brit.* freight vehicles generally. **6a** a vehicle used to transport goods or people, esp. lorries or ships used to convey troops. **6b** *(as modifier): a transport plane.* **7** the act of transporting or the state of being transported. **8** ecstasy, rapture, or any powerful emotion. **9** a convict sentenced to be transported. [C14: from Latin *transportāre,* from TRANS- + *portāre* to carry] ► **trans'portable** *adj* ► **ˌtransporta'bility** *n* ► **trans'porter** *n* ► **trans'portive** *adj*

transportation (ˌtrænspɔː'teɪʃən) *n* **1** a means or system of transporting. **2** the act of transporting or the state of being transported. **3** (esp. formerly) deportation to a penal colony. **4** *Chiefly U.S.* a ticket or fare.

transport café *n Brit.* an inexpensive eating place on a main route, used mainly by long-distance lorry drivers.

transporter bridge *n* a bridge consisting of a movable platform suspended from cables, for transporting vehicles, etc., across a body of water.

transpose (træns'pəʊz) *vb* **1** *(tr)* to alter the positions of; interchange, as words in a sentence; put into a different order. **2** *Music.* **2a** to play (notes, music, etc.) in a different key from that originally intended. **2b** to move (a note or series of notes) upwards or downwards in pitch. **3** *(tr) Maths.* to move (a term) from one side of an equation to the other with a corresponding reversal in sign. ◆ *n* **4** *Maths.* the matrix resulting from interchanging the rows and columns of a given matrix. [C14: from Old French *transposer,* from Latin *transpōnere* to remove, from TRANS- + *pōnere* to place] ► **trans'posable** *adj* ► **trans,pos-a'bility** *n* ► **trans'posal** *n* ► **trans'poser** *n*

transposing instrument *n* a musical instrument, esp. a horn or clarinet, pitched in a key other than C major, but whose music is written down as if its basic scale were C major. A piece of music in the key of F intended to be played on a horn pitched in F is therefore written down a fourth lower than an ordinary part in that key and has the same key signature as a part written in C.

transposition (ˌtrænspə'zɪʃən) *n* **1** the act of transposing or the state of being transposed. **2** something transposed. ► **ˌtranspo'sitional** *or* **transpositive** (træns'pɒzɪtɪv) *adj*

transposon (træns'pəʊzɒn) *n Genetics.* a fragment of bacterial nucleic acid that can move from one site in a chromosome to another site in the same or a different chromosome and thus alter the genetic constitution of the bacterium. [C20: TRANSPOS(E) + -ON]

transputer (trænz'pjuːtə) *n Computing.* a type of fast, powerful microchip that is the equivalent of a 32-bit microprocessor with its own RAM facility. [C20: from TRANS(ISTOR) + (COM)PUTER]

transsexual *or* **transexual** (trænz'sɛksjʊəl) *n* **1** a person who permanently acts the part of and completely identifies with the opposite sex. **2** a person who has undergone medical and surgical procedures to alter external sexual characteristics to those of the opposite sex.

transsexualism *or* **transexualism** (trænz'sɛksjʊəˌlɪzəm) *n* a strong desire to change sex.

transship (træns'ʃɪp) *or* **tranship** *vb* **-ships, -shipping, -shipped.** to transfer or be transferred from one vessel or vehicle to another. ► **trans'shipment** *or* **tran'shipment** *n*

Trans-Siberian Railway *n* a railway in S Russia, extending from Moscow to Vladivostok on the Pacific: constructed between 1891 and 1916, making possible the settlement and industrialization of sparsely inhabited regions. Length: 9335 km (5800 miles).

transubstantiate (ˌtrænsəb'stænʃɪˌeɪt) *vb* **1** *(intr) R.C. theol.* (of the Eucharistic bread and wine) to undergo transubstantiation. **2** *(tr)* to change (one substance) into another; transmute. [C16: from Medieval Latin *transsubstantiāre,* from Latin TRANS- + *substantia* SUBSTANCE] ► **ˌtransub'stantial** *adj* ► **ˌtransub'stantially** *adv*

transubstantiation (ˌtrænsəbˌstænʃɪ'eɪʃən) *n* **1** (esp. in Roman Catholic theology) **1a** the doctrine that the whole substance of the bread and wine changes into the substance of the body and blood of Christ when consecrated in the Eucharist. **1b** the mystical process by which this is believed to take place during consecration. Compare **consubstantiation. 2** a substantial change; transmutation. ► **ˌtransubˌstanti'ationalist** *n*

transudate ('trænsʊˌdeɪt) *n* **1** *Physiol.* any fluid that passes through a membrane, esp. through the wall of a capillary. **2** anything that has been transuded.

transude (træn'sjuːd) *vb* (of a fluid) to ooze or pass through interstices, pores, or small holes. [C17: from New Latin *transūdāre,* from Latin TRANS- + *sūdāre* to sweat] ► **transudation** (ˌtrænsjʊ'deɪʃən) *n* ► **tran'sudatory** *adj*

transuranic (ˌtrænzjʊ'rænɪk), **transuranian** (ˌtrænzjʊ'reɪnɪən), *or* **transuranium** *adj* **1** (of an element) having an atomic number greater than that of uranium. **2** of, relating to, or having the behaviour of transuranic elements. [C20: from TRANS- + *uranic,* from URANIUM]

Transvaal ('trænzvɑːl) *n* former province of NE South Africa: colonized by the Boers after the Great Trek (1836); became a British colony in 1902; joined South Africa in 1910; replaced in 1994. Capital: Pretoria. ► **Trans'vaalian** *adj*

transvalue (trænz'væljuː) *vb* **-ues, -uing, -ued.** *(tr)* to evaluate by a principle that varies from the accepted standards. ► **trans,valu'ation** *n* ► **trans'valuer** *n*

transversal (trænz'vɜːsəl) *n* **1** *Geometry.* a line intersecting two or more other lines. ◆ *adj* **2** a less common word for **transverse.** ► **trans'versally** *adv*

transverse (trænz'vɜːs) *adj* **1** crossing from side to side; athwart; crossways. **2** *Geometry.* denoting the axis that passes through the foci of a hyperbola. **3** (of a flute, etc.) held almost at right angles to the player's mouth, so that the breath passes over a hole in the side to create a vibrating air column within the tube of the instrument. **4** *Astronomy.* another word for **tangential** (sense 2). ◆ *n* **5** a transverse piece or object. [C16: from Latin *transversus,* from *transvertere* to turn across, from TRANS- + *vertere* to turn] ► **trans'versely** *adv* ► **trans'verseness** *n*

transverse colon *n Anatomy.* the part of the large intestine passing transversely in front of the liver and stomach.

transverse flute *n* the normal orchestral flute, as opposed to the recorder (or **fipple flute**).

transverse process *n Anatomy.* either of the projections that arise from either side of a vertebra and provide articulation for the ribs.

transverse wave *n* a wave, such as an electromagnetic wave, that is propagated in a direction perpendicular to the direction of displacement of the transmitting field or medium. Compare **longitudinal wave.**

transverter (trænzˈvɜːtə) *n* a piece of equipment attached to a radio transceiver to enable it to transmit and receive on additional frequencies.

transvestite (trænzˈvɛstaɪt) *n* a person who seeks sexual pleasure from wearing clothes that are normally associated with the opposite sex. [C19: from German *Transvestit,* from TRANS- + Latin *vestītus* clothed, from *vestīre* to clothe] ▸ **transˈvestism** *or* **transˈvestitism** *n*

Transylvania (ˌtrænsɪlˈveɪnɪə) *n* a region of central and NW Romania: belonged to Hungary from the 11th century until 1918; restored to Romania in 1947.

Transylvanian Alps (ˌtrænsɪlˈveɪnɪən) *pl n* a mountain range in S Romania; a SW extension of the Carpathian Mountains. Highest peak: Mount Negoiu, 2548 m (8360 ft.).

trap[1] (træp) *n* **1** a mechanical device or enclosed place or pit in which something, esp. an animal, is caught or penned. **2** any device or plan for tricking a person or thing into being caught unawares. **3** anything resembling a trap or prison. **4** a fitting for a pipe in the form of a U-shaped or S-shaped bend that contains standing water to prevent the passage of gases. **5** any similar device. **6** a device that hurls clay pigeons into the air to be fired at by trapshooters. **7** *Greyhound racing.* any one of a line of boxlike stalls in which greyhounds are enclosed before the start of a race. **8** See **trap door. 9** a light two-wheeled carriage. **10** a slang word for **mouth. 11** *Golf.* an obstacle or hazard, esp. a bunker. **12** (*pl*) *Jazz slang.* percussion instruments. **13** (*usually pl*) *Austral. obsolete slang.* a policeman. ◆ *vb* **traps, trapping, trapped. 14** (*tr*) to catch, take, or pen in or as if in a trap; entrap. **15** (*tr*) to ensnare by trickery; trick. **16** (*tr*) to provide (a pipe) with a trap. **17** to set traps in (a place), esp. for animals. [Old English *træppe;* related to Middle Low German *trappe,* Medieval Latin *trappa*] ▸ **ˈtrapˌlike** *adj*

trap[2] (træp) *n* **1** an obsolete word for **trappings** (sense 2). ◆ *vb* **traps, trapping, trapped. 2** (*tr;* often foll. by *out*) to dress or adorn. ◆ See also **traps.** [C11: probably from Old French *drap* cloth]

trap[3] (træp) *or* **traprock** *n* **1** any fine-grained often columnar dark igneous rock, esp. basalt. **2** any rock in which oil or gas has accumulated. [C18: from Swedish *trappa* stair (from its steplike formation); see TRAP[1]]

trapan (trəˈpæn) *vb* **-pans, -panning, -panned,** *n* a variant spelling of **trepan**[2]. ▸ **traˈpanner** *n*

Trapani (*Italian* ˈtraːpani) *n* a port in S Italy, in NW Sicily: Carthaginian naval base, ceded to the Romans after the First Punic War. Pop.: 72 840 (1990).

trap door *n* **1** a door or flap flush with and covering an opening, esp. in a ceiling. **2** the opening so covered.

trap-door spider *n* any of various spiders of the family *Ctenizidae* that construct a silk-lined hole in the ground closed by a hinged door of earth and silk.

trapes (treɪps) *vb, n* a less common spelling of **traipse.**

trapeze (trəˈpiːz) *n* **1** a free-swinging bar attached to two ropes, used by circus acrobats, etc. **2** a sling like a bosun's chair at one end of a line attached to the masthead of a light racing sailing boat, used in sitting out. [C19: from French *trapèze,* from New Latin; see TRAPEZIUM]

trapeziform (trəˈpiːzɪˌfɔːm) *adj Rare.* shaped like a trapezium: *a trapeziform part.*

trapezium (trəˈpiːzɪəm) *n, pl* **-ziums** *or* **-zia** (-zɪə). **1** *Chiefly Brit.* a quadrilateral having two parallel sides of unequal length. Usual U.S. and Canadian name: **trapezoid. 2** *Now chiefly U.S. and Canadian.* a quadrilateral having neither pair of sides parallel. **3** a small bone of the wrist near the base of the thumb. [C16: via Late Latin from Greek *trapezion,* from *trapeza* table] ▸ **traˈpezial** *adj*

trapezius (trəˈpiːzɪəs) *n, pl* **-uses.** either of two flat triangular muscles, one covering each side of the back and shoulders, that rotate the shoulder blades. [C18: from New Latin *trapezius* (*musculus*) trapezium-shaped (muscle)]

trapezohedron (trəˌpiːzəʊˈhiːdrən) *n, pl* **-drons** *or* **-dra** (-drə). *Crystallog.* a crystal form in which all the crystal's faces are trapeziums. [C19: from *trapezo-* combining form of TRAPEZIUM + -HEDRON, on the model of TETRAHEDRON] ▸ **traˌpezoˈhedral** *adj*

trapezoid (ˈtræpɪˌzɔɪd) *n* **1** a quadrilateral having neither pair of sides parallel. **2** the usual U.S. and Canadian name for **trapezium. 3** a small bone of the wrist near the base of the index finger. [C18: from New Latin *trapezoidēs,* from Late Greek *trapezoeidēs* trapezium-shaped, from *trapeza* table]

trappean (ˈtræpɪən, trəˈpɪən) *adj Rare.* of, relating to, or consisting of igneous rock, esp. a basalt. [C19: from TRAP[3]]

trapper (ˈtræpə) *n* a person who traps animals, esp. for their furs or skins.

trappings (ˈtræpɪŋz) *pl n* **1** the accessories and adornments that characterize or symbolize a condition, office, etc.: *the visible trappings of success.* **2** ceremonial harness for a horse or other animal, including bridles, saddles, etc. [C16: from TRAP[2]]

Trappist (ˈtræpɪst) *n* **a** a member of a branch of the Cistercian order of Christian monks, the **Reformed Cistercians of the Strict Observance,** which originated at La Trappe in France in 1664. They are noted for their rule of silence. **b** (*as modifier*): *a Trappist monk.*

traprock (ˈtræpˌrɒk) *n* another name for **trap**[3].

traps (træps) *pl n* belongings; luggage. [C19: probably shortened from TRAPPINGS]

trapshooting (ˈtræpˌʃuːtɪŋ) *n* the sport of shooting at clay pigeons thrown up by a trap. ▸ **ˈtrapˌshooter** *n*

trapunto (trəˈpuntəʊ) *n, pl* **-tos.** a type of quilting that is only partly padded, in a design. [Italian, from *trapungere* to embroider, from *pungere* to prick (from Latin)]

trash[1] (træʃ) *n* **1** foolish ideas or talk; nonsense. **2** *Chiefly U.S. and Canadian.* useless or unwanted matter or objects. **3** a literary or artistic production of poor quality. **4** *Chiefly U.S. and Canadian.* a poor or worthless person or a group of such people. **5** bits that are broken or lopped off, esp. the trimmings from trees or plants. **6** the dry remains of sugar cane after the juice has been extracted. ◆ *vb* **7** to remove the outer leaves and branches from (growing plants, esp. sugar cane). **8** *Slang.* to attack or destroy (someone or something) wilfully or maliciously. [C16: of obscure origin; perhaps related to Norwegian *trask*] ▸ **ˈtrashery** *n*

trash[2] (træʃ) *Archaic.* ◆ *vb* **1** (*tr*) to restrain with or as if with a lead. ◆ *n* **2** a lead for a dog. [C17: perhaps from obsolete French *tracier* to track, TRACE[1]]

trash can *n* a U.S. name for **dustbin.** Also called: **ash can, garbage can.**

trash farming *n U.S.* cultivation by leaving stubble, etc., on the surface of the soil to serve as a mulch.

trashy (ˈtræʃɪ) *adj* **trashier, trashiest.** cheap, worthless, or badly made. ▸ **ˈtrashily** *adv* ▸ **ˈtrashiness** *n*

Trasimene (ˈtræzɪˌmiːn) *n* **Lake.** a lake in central Italy, in Umbria: the largest lake in central Italy; scene of Hannibal's victory over the Romans in 217 B.C. Area: 128 sq. km (49 sq. miles). Italian name: **Trasimeno.** Also called: (Lake) **Perugia.**

trass (træs) *n* a variety of the volcanic rock tuff, used to make a hydraulic cement. [from Dutch *tras, tarasse,* from Italian *terrazza* worthless earth; see TERRACE]

trattoria (ˌtrætəˈrɪə) *n* an Italian restaurant. [C19: from Italian, from *trattore* innkeeper, from French *traiteur,* from Old French *tretier* to TREAT]

trauma (ˈtrɔːmə) *n, pl* **-mata** (-mətə) *or* **-mas. 1** *Psychol.* a powerful shock that may have long-lasting effects. **2** *Pathol.* any bodily injury or wound. [C18: from Greek: a wound] ▸ **traumatic** (trɔːˈmætɪk) *adj* ▸ **trauˈmatically** *adv*

traumatism (ˈtrɔːməˌtɪzəm) *n* **1** any abnormal bodily condition caused by injury, wound, or shock. **2** (not in technical usage) another name for **trauma** (sense 2).

traumatize *or* **traumatise** (ˈtrɔːməˌtaɪz) *vb* **1** (*tr*) to wound or injure (the body). **2** to subject or be subjected to mental trauma. ▸ **ˌtraumatiˈzation** *or* **ˌtraumatiˈsation** *n*

travail (ˈtræveɪl) *Literary.* ◆ *n* **1** painful or excessive labour or exertion. **2** the pangs of childbirth; labour. ◆ *vb* **3** (*intr*) to suffer or labour painfully, esp. in childbirth. [C13: from Old French *travaillier,* from Vulgar Latin *tripaliāre* (unattested) to torture, from Late Latin *trepālium* instrument of torture, from Latin *tripālis* having three stakes, from *trēs* three + *pālus* stake]

Travancore (ˌtrævənˈkɔː) *n* a former princely state of S India which joined with Cochin in 1949 to form **Travancore-Cochin:** part of Kerala state since 1956.

trave (treɪv) *n* **1** a stout wooden cage in which difficult horses are shod. **2** another name for **crossbeam. 3** a bay formed by crossbeams. [C15: from Old French *trave* beam, from Latin *trabs*]

travel (ˈtrævᵊl) *vb* **-els, -elling, -elled** *or U.S.* **-els, -eling, -eled.** (*mainly intr*) **1** to go, move, or journey from one place to another: *he travels to improve his mind; she travelled across France.* **2** (*tr*) to go, move, or journey through or across (an area, region, etc.): *he travelled the country.* **3** to go, move, or cover a specified or unspecified distance. **4** to go from place to place as a salesman: *to travel in textiles.* **5** (esp. of perishable goods) to withstand a journey. **6** (of light, sound, etc.) to be transmitted or move: *the sound travelled for miles.* **7** to progress or advance. **8** *Basketball.* to take an excessive number of steps while holding the ball. **9** (of part of a mechanism) to move in a fixed predetermined path. **10** *Informal.* to move rapidly: *that car certainly travels.* **11** (often foll. by *with*) *Informal.* to be in the company (of); associate. ◆ *n* **12a** the act of travelling. **12b** (*as modifier*): *a travel brochure.* Related adj: **itinerant. 13** (*usually pl*) a tour or journey. **14** the distance moved by a mechanical part, such as the stroke of a piston. **15** movement or passage. [C14 *travaillen* to make a journey, from Old French *travaillier* to TRAVAIL]

travel agency *or* **bureau** *n* an agency that arranges and negotiates flights, holidays, etc., for travellers. ▸ **travel agent** *n*

travelator (ˈtrævəˌleɪtə) *n* a variant spelling of **travolator.**

travelled *or U.S.* **traveled** (ˈtrævəld) *adj* having experienced or undergone much travelling: *a travelled urbane epicure.*

traveller *or U.S.* **traveler** (ˈtrævələ, ˈtrævlə) *n* **1** a person who travels, esp. habitually. **2** See **travelling salesman. 3** (*sometimes cap.*) a member of the travelling people. **4** a part of a mechanism that moves in a fixed course. **5** *Nautical.* **5a** a thimble fitted to slide freely on a rope, spar, or rod. **5b** the fixed rod on which such a thimble slides. **6** *Austral.* a swagman.

traveller's cheque *n* a cheque in any of various denominations sold for use abroad by a bank, etc., to the bearer, who signs it on purchase and can cash it by signing it again.

traveller's joy *n* a ranunculaceous Old World climbing plant, *Clematis vitalba,* having white flowers and heads of feathery plumed fruits. Also called: **old man's beard.**

travelling people *or* **folk** *pl n* (*sometimes caps.*) *Brit.* Gypsies or other itinerant people: a term used esp. by such people of themselves.

travelling salesman *n* a salesman who travels within an assigned territory in order to sell merchandise or to solicit orders for the commercial enterprise he represents by direct personal contact with customers and potential customers. Also called: **commercial traveller, traveller.**

travelling wave *n* **a** a wave carrying energy away from its source. **b** (*as modifier*): *a travelling-wave aerial.*

travelling-wave tube *n* an electronic tube in which an electron beam interacts with a high-frequency magnetic field so that energy is transferred from the beam to the field.

travelogue *or U.S. (sometimes)* **travelog** ('trævəˡlɒg) *n* a film, lecture, or brochure on travels and travelling. [C20: from TRAVEL + -LOGUE]

travel-sick *adj* nauseated from riding in a moving vehicle. ▸ **'travel-,sickness** *n*

Traven ('trɑːvən) *n* **B(en)**, original name *Albert Otto Max Feige.* ?1882–1969, U.S. novelist, born in Germany and living in Mexico from 1920, who kept his identity secret. His novels, originally written in German, include *The Treasure of Sierra Madre* (1934).

Travers ('trævɜːz) *n* **Ben(jamin)**. 1886–1980, British dramatist, best known for such farces as *Rookery Nook* (1926), *Thark* (1927), and *Plunder* (1928).

traverse ('trævɜːs, trə'vɜːs) *vb* **1** to pass or go over or back and forth over (something); cross. **2** (*tr*) to go against; oppose; obstruct. **3** to move or cause to move sideways or crosswise. **4** (*tr*) to extend or reach across. **5** to turn (an artillery gun) laterally on its pivot or mount or (of an artillery gun) to turn laterally. **6** (*tr*) to look over or examine carefully. **7** (*tr*) *Law.* to deny (an allegation of fact), as in pleading. **8** (*intr*) *Fencing.* to slide one's blade towards an opponent's hilt while applying pressure against his blade. **9** *Mountaineering.* to move across (a face) horizontally. **10** (*tr*) *Nautical.* to brace (a yard) fore and aft. ◆ *n* **11** something being or lying across, such as a transom. **12** a gallery or loft inside a building that crosses it. **13** *Maths.* another name for **transversal** (sense 1). **14** an obstruction or hindrance. **15** *Fortifications.* a protective bank or other barrier across a trench or rampart. **16** a railing, screen, or curtain. **17** the act or an instance of traversing or crossing. **18** a path or road across. **19** *Nautical.* the zigzag course of a vessel tacking frequently. **20** *Law.* the formal denial of a fact alleged in the opposite party's pleading. **21** *Surveying.* a survey consisting of a series of straight lines, the length of each and the angle between them being measured. **22** *Mountaineering.* a horizontal move across a face. ◆ *adj* **23** being or lying across; transverse. ◆ *adv* **24** an archaic word for **across.** [C14: from Old French *traverser,* from Late Latin *trānsversāre,* from Latin *trānsversus* TRANSVERSE] ▸ **'traversable** *adj* ▸ **tra'versal** *n* ▸ **'traverser** *n*

travertine *or* **travertin** ('trævətɪn) *n* a porous rock consisting of calcium carbonate, used for building. Also called: **calc-sinter.** [C18: from Italian *travertino* (influenced by *tra-* TRANS-), from Latin *lapis Tīburtīnus* Tiburtine stone, from *Tībur*s the district around Tibur (now Tivoli)]

travesty ('trævɪstɪ) *n, pl* **-ties. 1** a farcical or grotesque imitation; mockery; parody. ◆ *vb* **-ties, -tying, -tied.** (*tr*) **2** to make or be a travesty of. [C17: from French *travesti* disguised, from *travestir* to disguise, from Italian *travestire,* from *tra-* TRANS- + *vestire* to clothe]

travois (trə'vɔɪ) *n, pl* **-vois** (-'vɔɪz). a sled formerly used by the Plains Indians of North America, consisting of two poles joined by a frame and dragged by an animal. [from Canadian French, from French *travail* TRAVE]

travolator *or* **travelator** ('trævə,leɪtə) *n* a moving pavement for transporting pedestrians, as in a shopping precinct or an airport. [C20: coined on the model of ESCALATOR]

trawl (trɔːl) *n Sea fishing.* **1** Also called: **trawl net.** a large net, usually in the shape of a sock or bag, drawn at deep levels behind special boats (trawlers). **2** Also called: **trawl line.** a long line to which numerous shorter hooked lines are attached, suspended between buoys. See also **setline, trotline. 3** the act of trawling. ◆ *vb* **4** *Sea fishing.* to catch or try to catch (fish) with a trawl net or trawl line. **5** *Sea fishing.* (*tr*) to drag (a trawl net) or suspend (a trawl line). **6** (*intr;* foll. by *for*) to seek or gather (something, such as information, or someone, such as a likely appointee) from a wide variety of sources. ◆ *n, vb* **7** *Angling.* another word for **troll**[1]. [C17: from Middle Dutch *traghelen* to drag, from Latin *trāgula* dragnet; see TRAIL]

trawler ('trɔːlə) *n* **1** a vessel used for trawling. **2** a person who trawls.

tray (treɪ) *n* **1** a thin flat board or plate of metal, plastic, etc., usually with a raised edge, on which things can be carried. **2** a shallow receptacle for papers, etc., sometimes forming a drawer in a cabinet or box. [Old English *trieg;* related to Old Swedish *trö* corn measure, Old Norse *treyja* carrier, Greek *driti* tub, German *Trog* TROUGH]

traymobile ('treɪmə,biːl) *n Austral. informal.* a small table on casters used for conveying food, drink, etc.

treacherous ('tretʃərəs) *adj* **1** betraying or likely to betray faith or confidence. **2** unstable, unreliable, or dangerous: *treacherous weather; treacherous ground.* ▸ **'treacherously** *adv* ▸ **'treacherousness** *n*

treachery ('tretʃərɪ) *n, pl* **-eries. 1** the act or an instance of wilful betrayal. **2** the disposition to betray. [C13: from Old French *trecherie,* from *trechier* to cheat; compare TRICK]

treacle ('triːkəˡl) *n* **1** Also called: **black treacle.** *Brit.* a dark viscous syrup obtained during the refining of sugar. **2** *Brit.* another name for **golden syrup. 3** anything sweet and cloying. **4** *Obsolete.* any of various preparations used as an antidote to poisoning. [C14: from Old French *triacle,* from Latin *thēriaca* antidote to poison] ▸ **'treacly** *adj* ▸ **'treacliness** *n*

treacle mustard *n* a N temperate cruciferous annual plant, *Erysimum cheiranthoides,* having small yellow flowers. It is a common weed in cultivated ground. [C16: so called because of its alleged medicinal properties. See TREACLE]

tread (trɛd) *vb* **treads, treading, trod, trodden** *or* **trod. 1** to walk or trample in, on, over, or across (something). **2** (when *intr,* foll. by *on*) to crush or squash by or as if by treading: *to tread grapes; to tread on a spider.* **3** (*intr;* sometimes foll. by *on*) to subdue or repress, as by doing injury (to): *to tread on one's inferiors.* **4** (*tr*) to do by walking or dancing: *to tread a measure.* **5** (*tr*) (of a male bird) to copulate with (a female bird). **6 tread lightly.** to proceed with delicacy or tact. **7 tread on (someone's) toes.** to offend or insult (someone), esp. by infringing on his sphere of action, etc. **8 tread water.** to stay afloat in an upright position by moving the legs in a walking motion. ◆ *n* **9** a manner or style of walking, dancing, etc.: *a light tread.* **10** the act of treading. **11** the top surface of a step in a staircase. **12** the outer part of a tyre or wheel that makes contact with the road, esp. the grooved surface of a pneumatic tyre. **13** the part of a rail that wheels touch. **14** the part of a shoe that is generally in contact with the ground. **15** a rare word for **footprint.** [Old English *tredan;* related to Old Norse *trotha,* Old High German *tretan,* Swedish *träda*] ▸ **'treader** *n*

treadle ('trɛdəˡl) *n* **1a** a rocking lever operated by the foot to drive a machine. **1b** (*as modifier*): *a treadle sewing machine.* ◆ *vb* **2** to work (a machine) with a treadle. [Old English *tredel,* from *trǣde* something firm, from *tredan* to TREAD] ▸ **'treadler** *n*

treadmill ('trɛd,mɪl) *n* **1** Also called: **treadwheel.** (formerly) an apparatus used to produce rotation, in which the weight of men or animals climbing steps on or around the periphery of a cylinder or wheel caused it to turn. **2** a dreary round or routine. **3** an exercise machine that consists of a continuous moving belt on which to walk or jog.

treas. *abbrev. for:* **1** treasurer. **2** treasury.

treason ('triːzəˡn) *n* **1** violation or betrayal of the allegiance that a person owes his sovereign or his country, esp. by attempting to overthrow the government; high treason. **2** any treachery or betrayal. [C13: from Old French *traïson,* from Latin *trāditiō* a handing over; see TRADITION, TRADITOR] ▸ **'treasonable** *or* **'treasonous** *adj* ▸ **'treasonableness** *n* ▸ **'treasonably** *adv*

treasure ('trɛʒə) *n* **1** wealth and riches, usually hoarded, esp. in the form of money, precious metals, or gems. **2** a thing or person that is highly prized or valued. ◆ *vb* (*tr*) **3** to prize highly as valuable, rare, or costly. **4** to store up and save; hoard. [C12: from Old French *tresor,* from Latin *thēsaurus* anything hoarded, from Greek *thēsauros*] ▸ **'treasurable** *adj* ▸ **'treasureless** *adj*

treasure flower *n* another name for **gazania.**

treasure hunt *n* a game in which players act upon successive clues and are eventually directed to a prize.

treasurer ('trɛʒərə) *n* a person appointed to look after the funds of a society, company, city, or other governing body. ▸ **'treasurership** *n*

Treasurer ('trɛʒərə) *n* (in the Commonwealth of Australia and each of the Australian states) the minister of finance.

treasure-trove *n* (in Britain) **1** *Law.* valuable articles, such as coins, bullion, etc., found hidden in the earth or elsewhere and of unknown ownership. Such articles become the property of the Crown, which compensates the finder if the treasure is declared. In 1996 treasure was defined as any item over 300 years old and containing more than 5% precious metal. **2** anything similarly discovered that is of value. [C16: from Anglo-French *tresor trové* treasure found, from Old French *tresor* TREASURE + *trover* to find]

treasury ('trɛʒərɪ) *n, pl* **-uries. 1** a storage place for treasure. **2** the revenues or funds of a government, private organization, or individual. **3** a place where funds are kept and disbursed. **4** Also: **treasure house.** a collection or source of valuable items: *a treasury of information.* [C13: from Old French *tresorie,* from *tresor* TREASURE]

Treasury ('trɛʒərɪ) *n* (in various countries) the government department in charge of finance. In Britain the Treasury is also responsible for economic strategy.

Treasury Bench *n* (in Britain) the front bench to the right of the Speaker in the House of Commons, traditionally reserved for members of the Government.

Treasury bill *n* a short-term noninterest-bearing obligation issued by the Treasury, payable to bearer and maturing usually in three months, within which it is tradable on a discount basis on the open market.

treasury bond *n* a long-term interest-bearing bond issued by the U.S. Treasury.

treasury certificate *n* a short-term obligation issued by the U.S. Treasury, maturing in 12 months with interest payable by coupon redemption.

treasury note *n* a note issued by a government treasury and generally receivable as legal tender for any debt, esp.: **a** a medium-term interest-bearing obligation issued by the U.S. Treasury, maturing in from one to five years. **b** Also called: **currency note.** a note issued by the British Treasury in 1914 to the value of £1 or ten shillings: amalgamated with banknotes in 1928.

treasury tag *n* a short piece of cord having metal ends one of which can be slotted inside the other: used for holding papers together or fastening them into a file.

treat (triːt) *n* **1** a celebration, entertainment, gift, or feast given for or to someone and paid for by another. **2** any delightful surprise or specially pleasant occasion. **3** the act of treating. ◆ *vb* **4** (*tr*) to deal with or regard in a certain manner: *she treats school as a joke.* **5** (*tr*) to apply treatment to: *to treat a patient for malaria.* **6** (*tr*) to subject to a process or to the application of a substance: *to treat photographic film with developer.* **7** (often foll. by *to*) to provide (someone) (with) as a treat: *he treated the children to a trip to the zoo.* **8** (*intr;* usually foll. by *of*) *Formal.* to deal (with), as in writing or speaking. **9** (*intr*) *Formal.* to discuss settlement; negotiate. [C13: from Old French *tretier,* from Latin *tractāre* to manage, from *trahere* to drag] ▸ **'treatable** *adj* ▸ **'treater** *n*

treatise ('triːtɪz) *n* **1** a formal work on a subject, esp. one that deals systematically with its principles and conclusions. **2** an obsolete word for **narrative.** [C14: from Anglo-French *tretiz,* from Old French *tretier* to TREAT]

treatment ('triːtmənt) *n* **1** the application of medicines, surgery, psychotherapy, etc., to a patient or to a disease or symptom. **2** the manner of handling or dealing with a person or thing, as in a literary or artistic work. **3** the act, practice, or manner of treating. **4** *Films.* an expansion of a script into sequence form, indicating camera angles, dialogue, etc. **5 the treatment.** *Slang.* the usual manner of dealing with a particular type of person (esp. in the phrase **give someone the (full) treatment**).

treaty ('triːtɪ) *n, pl* **-ties. 1a** a formal agreement or contract between two or more states, such as an alliance or trade arrangement. **1b** the document in which such a contract is written. **2** any international agreement. **3** any pact or agreement. **4** an agreement between two parties concerning the purchase of property at a price privately agreed between them. **5** *Archaic.* negotiation towards an agreement. **6** (in Canada) **6a** any of the formal agreements between Indian bands and the federal government by which the Indians surrender their land rights in return for various forms of aid. **6b** (*as modifier*): *treaty Indians; treaty money.* **7** an obsolete word for **entreaty.** [C14: from Old French *traité,* from Medieval Latin *tractātus* treaty, from Latin: discussion, from *tractāre* to manage; see TREAT] ▸ **ˈtreatyless** *adj*

treaty port *n* (in China, Japan, and Korea during the last half of the 19th and first half of the 20th century) a city, esp. a port, in which foreigners, esp. Westerners, were allowed by treaty to conduct trade.

Trebizond (ˈtrɛbɪˌzɒnd) *n* a variant of **Trabzon.**

treble (ˈtrɛbəl) *adj* **1** threefold; triple. **2** of, relating to, or denoting a soprano voice or part or a high-pitched instrument. ◆ *n* **3** treble the amount, size, etc. **4** a soprano voice or part or a high-pitched instrument. **5** the highest register of a musical instrument. **6a** the high-frequency response of an audio amplifier, esp. in a record player or tape recorder. **6b** a control knob on such an instrument by means of which the high-frequency gain can be increased or decreased. **7** *Change-ringing.* the lightest and highest bell in a ring. **8a** the narrow inner ring on a dartboard. **8b** a hit on this ring. ◆ *vb* **9** to make or become three times as much. [C14: from Old French, from Latin *triplus* threefold, TRIPLE] ▸ **ˈtrebleness** *n* ▸ **ˈtrebly** *adv, adj*

treble chance *n* a method of betting in football pools in which the chances of winning are related to the number of draws and the number of home and away wins forecast by the competitor.

treble clef *n Music.* the clef that establishes G a fifth above middle C as being on the second line of the staff. Symbol: 𝄞

Treblinka (trɛˈblɪŋkə) *n* a Nazi concentration camp in central Poland, on the Bug River northeast of Warsaw: chiefly remembered as the place where the Jews of the Warsaw ghetto were put to death.

trebuchet (ˈtrɛbjʊˌʃɛt) *or* **trebucket** (ˈtriːbʌkɪt) *n* a large medieval siege engine for hurling missiles consisting of a sling on a pivoted wooden arm set in motion by the fall of a weight. [C13: from Old French, from *trebuchier* to stumble, from *tre-* TRANS- + *-buchier,* from *buc* trunk of the body, of Germanic origin; compare Old High German *būh* belly, Old English *buc*]

trecento (treɪˈtʃɛntəʊ) *n* the 14th century, esp. with reference to Italian art and literature. [C19: shortened from Italian *mille trecento* one thousand three hundred] ▸ **treˈcentist** *n*

tree (triː) *n* **1** any large woody perennial plant with a distinct trunk giving rise to branches or leaves at some distance from the ground. Related adj: **arboreal. 2** any plant that resembles this but has a trunk not made of wood, such as a palm tree. **3** a wooden post, bar, etc. **4** See **family tree, shoetree, saddletree. 5** *Chem.* a treelike crystal growth; dendrite. **6a** a branching diagrammatic representation of something, such as the grammatical structure of a sentence. **6b** (*as modifier*): *a tree diagram.* **7** an archaic word for **gallows. 8** *Archaic.* the cross on which Christ was crucified. **9 at the top of the tree.** in the highest position of a profession, etc. **10 up a tree.** *U.S. and Canadian informal.* in a difficult situation; trapped or stumped. ◆ *vb* **trees, treeing, treed.** (*tr*) **11** to drive or force up a tree. **12** to shape or stretch (a shoe) on a shoetree. [Old English *treo;* related to Old Frisian, Old Norse *trē,* Old Saxon *trio,* Gothic *triu,* Greek *doru* wood, *drus* tree] ▸ **ˈtreeless** *adj* ▸ **ˈtreelessness** *n* ▸ **ˈtreeˌlike** *adj*

Tree (triː) *n* Sir **Herbert Beerbohm.** 1853–1917, English actor and theatre manager; half-brother of Sir Max Beerbohm. He was noted for his lavish productions of Shakespeare.

tree-and-branch *adj* denoting a cable television system in which all available programme channels are fed to each subscriber. Compare **switched-star.**

tree creeper *n* any small songbird of the family *Certhiidae* of the N hemisphere, having a brown-and-white plumage and slender downward-curving bill. They creep up trees to feed on insects.

tree farm *n* an area of forest in which the growth of the trees is managed on a commercial basis.

tree fern *n* any of numerous large tropical ferns, mainly of the family *Cyatheaceae,* having a trunklike stem bearing fronds at the top.

tree frog *n* **1** any arboreal frog of the family *Hylidae,* chiefly of SE Asia, Australia, and America. They are strong jumpers and have long toes ending in adhesive discs, which assist in climbing. **2** any of various other arboreal frogs of different families.

tree heath *n* another name for **briar**[1] (sense 1).

treehopper (ˈtriːˌhɒpə) *n* any homopterous insect of the family *Membracidae,* which live among trees and other plants and typically have a large hoodlike thoracic process curving backwards over the body.

tree kangaroo *n* any of several arboreal kangaroos of the genus *Dendrolagus,* of New Guinea and N Australia, having hind and forelegs of a similar length and a long tail.

tree layer *n* See **layer** (sense 2).

tree line *n* the zone, at high altitudes or high latitudes, beyond which no trees grow. Trees growing between the timber line and the tree line are typically stunted.

tree mallow *n* a malvaceous treelike plant, *Lavatera arborea,* of rocky coastal areas of Europe and N Africa, having a woody stem, rounded leaves, and red-purple flowers.

treen (ˈtriːən) *adj* **1** made of wood; wooden. ◆ *n* **2** another name for **treenware. 3** the art of making treenware. [Old English *trēowen,* from *trēow* TREE]

treenail, trenail (ˈtriːneɪl, ˈtrɛnəl), *or* **trunnel** (ˈtrʌnəl) *n* a dowel used for pinning planks or timbers together.

treenware (ˈtriːənˌwɛə) *n* dishes and other household utensils made of wood, as by pioneers in North America. [from TREEN + WARE[1]]

tree of heaven *n* another name for **ailanthus.**

tree of knowledge of good and evil *n Old Testament.* the tree in the Garden of Eden bearing the forbidden fruit that Adam and Eve ate, thus incurring loss of primal innocence (Genesis 2:9; 3:2–7).

tree of life *n* **1** *Old Testament.* a tree in the Garden of Eden, the fruit of which had the power of conferring eternal life (Genesis 2:9; 3:22). **2** *New Testament.* a tree in the heavenly Jerusalem, for the healing of the nations (Revelation 22:2).

tree ring *n* another name for **annual ring.**

tree runner *n Austral.* another name for **sitella.**

tree shrew *n* any of numerous small arboreal mammals of the family *Tupaiidae* and order *Scandentia,* of SE Asia, having large eyes and resembling squirrels.

tree snake *n* any of various slender arboreal colubrid snakes of the genera *Chlorophis* (**green tree snakes**), *Chrysopelea* (**golden tree snakes**), etc.

tree sparrow *n* **1** a small European weaverbird, *Passer montanus,* similar to the house sparrow but having a brown head. **2** a small North American finch, *Spizella arborea,* having a reddish-brown head, grey underparts, and brown striped back and wings.

tree surgery *n* the treatment of damaged trees by filling cavities, applying braces, etc. ▸ **tree surgeon** *n*

tree toad *n* a less common name for **tree frog.**

tree tomato *n* **1** an arborescent shrub, *Cyphomandra betacea* or *C. crassifolia,* native to South America but widely cultivated, bearing red egg-shaped edible fruit: family *Solanaceae.* **2** the fruit of this plant. ◆ Also called: **tamarillo.**

tref, treif (treɪf), *or* **treifa** (ˈtreɪfə) *adj Judaism.* ritually unfit to be eaten; not kosher. [Yiddish, from Hebrew *terēphāh,* literally: torn (i.e., animal meat torn by beasts), from *tāraf* to tear]

trefoil (ˈtrɛfɔɪl) *n* **1** any of numerous leguminous plants of the temperate genus *Trifolium,* having leaves divided into three leaflets and dense heads of small white, yellow, red, or purple flowers. **2** any of various related plants having leaves divided into three leaflets, such as bird's-foot trefoil. **3** a flower or leaf having three lobes. **4** *Architect.* an ornament in the form of three arcs arranged in a circle. [C14: from Anglo-French *trifoil,* from Latin *trifolium* three-leaved herb, from TRI- + *folium* leaf] ▸ **ˈtrefoiled** *adj*

trehala (trɪˈhɑːlə) *n* an edible sugary substance obtained from the pupal cocoon of an Asian weevil, *Larinus maculatus.* [C19: from Turkish *tīgāla,* from Persian *tīghāl*]

trehalose (ˈtriːhəˌləʊs, -ˌləʊz) *n* a white crystalline disaccharide that occurs in yeast and certain fungi. Formula: $C_{12}H_{22}O_{11}$. [C19: from TREHALA]

treillage (ˈtreɪlɪdʒ) *n* latticework; trellis. [C17: from French, from Old French *treille* bower, from Latin *trichila;* see -AGE]

Treitschke (*German* ˈtraitʃkə) *n* **Heinrich von** (ˈhainrɪç fɔn). 1834–96, German historian, noted for his highly nationalistic views.

trek (trɛk) *n* **1** a long and often difficult journey. **2** *S. African.* a journey or stage of a journey, esp. a migration by ox wagon. ◆ *vb* **treks, trekking, trekked. 3** (*intr*) to make a trek. **4** (*tr*) *S. African.* (of an ox, etc.) to draw (a load). [C19: from Afrikaans, from Middle Dutch *trekken* to travel; related to Old Frisian *trekka*] ▸ **ˈtrekker** *n*

trellis (ˈtrɛlɪs) *n* **1** a structure or pattern of latticework, esp. one used to support climbing plants. **2** an arch made of latticework. ◆ *vb* (*tr*) **3** to interweave (strips of wood, etc.) to make a trellis. **4** to provide or support with a trellis. [C14: from Old French *treliz* fabric of open texture, from Late Latin *trilīcius* woven with three threads, from Latin TRI- + *līcium* thread] ▸ **ˈtrellis-ˌlike** *adj*

trelliswork (ˈtrɛlɪsˌwɜːk) *n* **a** work or patterns of trellis; latticework. **b** (*as modifier*): *a trelliswork fence.*

trematode (ˈtrɛməˌtəʊd, ˈtriː-) *n* any parasitic flatworm of the class *Trematoda,* which includes the flukes. [C19: from New Latin *Trematoda,* from Greek *trēmatōdēs* full of holes, from *trēma* a hole]

tremble (ˈtrɛmbəl) *vb* (*intr*) **1** to vibrate with short slight movements; quiver. **2** to shake involuntarily, as with cold or fear; shiver. **3** to experience fear or anxiety. ◆ *n* **4** the act or an instance of trembling. [C14: from Old French *trembler,* from Medieval Latin *tremulāre,* from Latin *tremulus* quivering, from *tremere* to quake] ▸ **ˈtrembling** *adj* ▸ **ˈtremblingly** *adv* ▸ **ˈtrembly** *adj*

trembler (ˈtrɛmblə) *n Electrical engineering.* a device that vibrates to make or break an electrical circuit.

trembles (ˈtrɛmbəlz) *n* (*functioning as sing*) **1** Also called: **milk sickness.** a disease of cattle and sheep characterized by muscular incoordination and tremor, caused by ingestion of white snakeroot or rayless goldenrod. **2** a nontechnical name for **Parkinson's disease.**

trembling poplar *n* another name for **aspen.**

tremendous (trɪˈmɛndəs) *adj* **1** vast; huge. **2** *Informal.* very exciting or unusual. **3** *Informal.* (intensifier): *a tremendous help.* **4** *Archaic.* terrible or dreadful. [C17: from Latin *tremendus* terrible, literally: that is to be trembled at, from *tremere* to quake] ▸ **treˈmendously** *adv* ▸ **treˈmendousness** *n*

tremie (ˈtrɛmɪ) *n Civil engineering.* a large metal hopper and pipe used to distribute freshly mixed concrete over an underwater site. [C20: from French, from Italian *tramoggia,* from Latin *trimodia* a three-peck measure]

tremolite (ˈtrɛməˌlaɪt) *n* a white or pale green mineral of the amphibole group consisting of calcium magnesium silicate and used as a form of asbestos. Formula: $Ca_2(Mg,Fe)_5Si_8O_{22}(OH)_2$. [C18: from *Tremola,* name of Swiss valley where it was found + -ITE[1]]

tremolo (ˈtrɛməˌləʊ) *n, pl* **-los.** *Music.* **1a** (in playing the violin, cello, etc.) the rapid repetition of a single note produced by a quick back-and-forth movement of the bow. **1b** the rapid reiteration of two notes usually a third or greater interval apart (**fingered tremolo**). Compare **trill**[1] (sense 1). **2** (in singing) a fluctuation in pitch. Compare **vibrato. 3** a vocal ornament of late renaissance music consisting of the increasingly rapid reiteration of a single note. **4** another word for **tremulant.** [C19: from Italian: quavering, from Medieval Latin *tremulāre* to TREMBLE]

tremolo arm *n* a metal lever attached to the bridge of an electric guitar, used to vary the pitch of a played note.

tremor ('trɛmə) *n* **1** an involuntary shudder or vibration, as from illness, fear, shock, etc. **2** any trembling or quivering movement. **3** a vibrating or trembling effect, as of sound or light. **4** Also called: **earth tremor.** a minor earthquake. ◆ *vb (intr)* **5** to tremble. [C14: from Latin: a shaking, from *tremere* to tremble, quake] ▸ **'tremorless** *adj* ▸ **'tremorous** *adj*

tremulant ('trɛmjulənt) *n Music.* **a** a device on an organ by which the wind stream is made to fluctuate in intensity producing a tremolo effect. **b** a device on an electrophonic instrument designed to produce a similar effect. [C19: from Medieval Latin *tremulāre* to TREMBLE]

tremulous ('trɛmjuləs) *adj* **1** vibrating slightly; quavering; trembling: *a tremulous voice.* **2** showing or characterized by fear, anxiety, excitement, etc. [C17: from Latin *tremulus* quivering, from *tremere* to shake] ▸ **'tremulously** *adv* ▸ **'tremulousness** *n*

trenail ('tri:neɪl, 'trɛn°l) *n* a variant spelling of **treenail.**

trench (trɛntʃ) *n* **1** a deep ditch or furrow. **2** a ditch dug as a fortification, having a parapet of the excavated earth. ◆ *vb* **3** to make a trench in (a place). **4** *(tr)* to fortify with a trench or trenches. **5** to slash or be slashed. **6** *(intr;* foll. by *on* or *upon)* to encroach or verge. ◆ See also **trenches.** [C14: from Old French *trenche* something cut, from *trenchier* to cut, from Latin *truncāre* to cut off]

trenchant ('trɛntʃənt) *adj* **1** keen or incisive: *trenchant criticism.* **2** vigorous and effective: *a trenchant foreign policy.* **3** distinctly defined: *a trenchant outline.* **4** *Archaic or poetic.* sharp: *a trenchant sword.* [C14: from Old French *trenchant* cutting, from *trenchier* to cut; see TRENCH] ▸ **'trenchancy** *n* ▸ **'trenchantly** *adv*

Trenchard ('trɛntʃɑ:d) *n* **Hugh Montague,** 1st Viscount. 1873–1956, British air marshal, who as chief of air staff (1918, 1919–27) and marshal of the RAF (1927–29) established the RAF as a fully independent service. As commissioner of the Metropolitan Police (1931–35) he founded the police college at Hendon.

trench coat *n* a belted double-breasted waterproof coat of gabardine, etc., resembling a military officer's coat.

trencher[1] ('trɛntʃə) *n* **1** (esp. formerly) a wooden board on which food was served or cut. **2** Also called: **trencher cap.** another name for **mortarboard** (sense 1). [C14 *trenchour* knife, plate for carving on, from Old French *trencheoir,* from *trenchier* to cut; see TRENCH]

trencher[2] ('trɛntʃə) *n* a person or thing that digs trenches.

trencherman ('trɛntʃəmən) *n, pl* **-men. 1** a person who enjoys food; hearty eater. **2** *Archaic.* a person who sponges on others; parasite. [C16: from TRENCHER[1] + MAN]

trenches ('trɛntʃɪz) *pl n* a system of excavations used for the protection of troops, esp. those **(the Trenches)** used at the front line in World War I.

trench fever *n* an acute infectious disease characterized by fever and muscular aches and pains, caused by the microorganism *Rickettsia quintana* and transmitted by the bite of a body louse.

trench foot *n* a form of frostbite affecting the feet of persons standing for long periods in cold water.

trench knife *n* a double-edged steel knife for close combat. [C20: so called because such knives were carried by patrols in the Trenches during World War I]

trench mortar *n* a portable mortar used in trench warfare to shoot projectiles at a high trajectory over a short range.

trench mouth *n* a bacterial ulcerative disease characterized by inflammation of the tonsils, gums, etc. [C20: so called because it was prevalent in soldiers in the Trenches during World War I]

trench warfare *n* a type of warfare in which opposing armies face each other in entrenched positions.

trend (trɛnd) *n* **1** general tendency or direction. **2** fashion; mode. ◆ *vb* **3** *(intr)* to take a certain trend. [Old English *trendan* to turn; related to Middle Low German *trenden*]

trendsetter ('trɛnd,sɛtə) *n* a person or thing that creates, or may create, a new fashion. ▸ **'trend,setting** *adj*

trendy ('trɛndɪ) *Brit. informal, often derogatory.* ◆ *adj* **trendier, trendiest. 1** consciously fashionable. ◆ *n, pl* **trendies. 2** a trendy person. ▸ **'trendily** *adv* ▸ **'trendiness** *n*

Trengganu *or* **Terengganu** (trɛŋ'gɑ:nu:, tərɛŋ-) *n* a state of E Peninsular Malaysia, on the South China Sea: under Thai suzerainty until becoming a British protectorate in 1909; joined the Federation of Malaya in 1948; an isolated forested region; mainly agricultural. Capital: Kuala Trengganu. Pop.: 752 030 (1993 est.). Area: 13 020 sq. km (5027 sq. miles).

Trent (trɛnt) *n* **1** a river in central England, rising in Staffordshire and flowing generally northeast into the Humber: the chief river of the Midlands. Length: 270 km (170 miles). **2** Also: **Trient.** the German name for **Trento.**

trente et quarante *(French* trɑ̃t e karɑ̃t) *n* another name for **rouge et noir.** [C17: French, literally: thirty and forty; referring to the rule that forty is the maximum number that may be dealt and the winning colour is the one closest to thirty-one]

Trentino-Alto Adige (trɛn'ti:nəʊ'ɑ:ltəʊ 'ɑ:dɪ,dʒeɪ) *n* a region of N Italy: consists of the part of the Tyrol south of the Brenner Pass, ceded by Austria after World War I. Pop.: 913 169 (1996 est.). Area: 13 613 sq. km (5256 sq. miles). Former name (until 1947): **Venezia Tridentina.**

Trento *(Italian* 'trɛnto) *n* a city in N Italy, in Trentino-Alto Adige region on the Adige River: Roman military base; seat of the Council of Trent. Pop.: 103 181 (1996 est.). Latin name: **Tridentum.** German name: **Trent.**

Trenton ('trɛntən) *n* a city in W New Jersey, capital of the state, on the Delaware River: settled by English Quakers in 1679; scene of the defeat of the British by Washington (1776) during the War of American Independence. Pop.: 85 437 (1996 est.).

trepan[1] (trɪ'pæn) *n* **1** *Surgery.* an instrument resembling a carpenter's brace and bit formerly used to remove circular sections of bone (esp. from the skull). Compare **trephine. 2** a tool for cutting out circular blanks or for making grooves around a fixed centre. **3a** the operation of cutting a hole with such a tool. **3b** the hole so produced. ◆ *vb* **-pans, -panning, -panned.** *(tr)* **4** to cut (a hole or groove) with a trepan. **5** *Surgery.* another word for **trephine.** [C14: from Medieval Latin *trepanum* rotary saw, from Greek *trupanon* auger, from *trupan* to bore, from *trupa* a hole] ▸ **trepanation** (,trɛpə'neɪʃən) *n* ▸ **tre'panner** *n*

trepan[2] (trɪ'pæn) *or* **trapan** (trə'pæn) *Archaic.* ◆ *vb* **-pans, -panning, -panned.** *(tr)* **1** to entice, ensnare, or entrap. **2** to swindle or cheat. ◆ *n* **3** a person or thing that traps. [C17: of uncertain origin]

trepang (trɪ'pæŋ) *n* any of various large sea cucumbers of tropical Oriental seas, the body walls of which are used as food by the Japanese and Chinese. Also called: **bêche-de-mer.** [C18: from Malay *tĕripang*]

trephine (trɪ'fi:n) *n* **1** a surgical sawlike instrument for removing circular sections of bone, esp. from the skull. ◆ *vb* **2** *(tr)* to remove a circular section of bone from (esp. the skull). ◆ Also called: **trepan.** [C17: from French *tréphine,* from obsolete English *trefine* TREPAN[1], allegedly from Latin *trēs fīnēs* literally: three ends; influenced also by English *trepane* TREPAN[1]] ▸ **trephination** (,trɛfɪ'neɪʃən) *n*

trepidation (,trɛpɪ'deɪʃən) *n* **1** a state of fear or anxiety. **2** a condition of quaking or palpitation, esp. one caused by anxiety. [C17: from Latin *trepidātiō,* from *trepidāre* to be in a state of alarm; compare INTREPID]

treponema (,trɛpə'ni:mə) *or* **treponeme** ('trɛpəni:m) *n, pl* **-nemas, -nemata** (-'ni:mətə), *or* **-nemes.** any anaerobic spirochaete bacterium of the genus *Treponema,* such as *T. pallidum* which causes syphilis. [C19: from New Latin, from Greek *trepein* to turn + *nēma* thread] ▸ **treponematous** (,trɛpə'nɛmətəs) *adj*

trespass ('trɛspəs) *vb (intr)* **1** (often foll. by *on* or *upon)* to go or intrude (on the property, privacy, or preserves of another) with no right or permission. **2** *Law.* to commit trespass, esp. to enter wrongfully upon land belonging to another. **3** *Archaic.* (often foll. by *against)* to sin or transgress. ◆ *n* **4** *Law.* **4a** any unlawful act committed with force or violence, actual or implied, which causes injury to another person, his property, or his rights. **4b** a wrongful entry upon another's land. **4c** an action to recover damages for such injury or wrongful entry. **5** an intrusion on another's privacy or preserves. **6** a sin or offence. [C13: from Old French *trespas* a passage, from *trespasser* to pass through, from *tres-* TRANS- + *passer,* ultimately from Latin *passus* a PACE[1]] ▸ **'trespasser** *n*

tress (trɛs) *n* **1** *(often pl)* a lock of hair, esp. a long lock of woman's hair. **2** a plait or braid of hair. ◆ *vb (tr)* **3** to arrange in tresses. [C13: from Old French *trece,* of uncertain origin] ▸ **'tressy** *adj*

tressed (trɛst) *adj (in combination)* having a tress or tresses as specified: *gold-tressed; long-tressed.*

tressure ('trɛʃə, 'trɛsjʊə) *n Heraldry.* a narrow inner border on a shield, usually decorated with fleurs-de-lys. [C14: from Old French *tressour,* from *trecier* to plait, from *trece* TRESS] ▸ **'tressured** *adj*

trestle ('trɛs°l) *n* **1** a framework in the form of a horizontal member supported at each end by a pair of splayed legs, used to carry scaffold boards, a table top, etc. **2a** a braced structural tower-like framework of timber, metal, or reinforced concrete that is used to support a bridge or ropeway. **2b** a bridge constructed of such frameworks. [C14: from Old French *trestel,* ultimately from Latin *trānstrum* TRANSOM]

trestletree ('trɛs°l,tri:) *n Nautical.* either of a pair of fore-and-aft timbers fixed horizontally on opposite sides of a lower masthead to support an upper mast.

trestlework ('trɛs°l,wɜ:k) *n* an arrangement of trestles, esp. one that supports or makes a bridge.

tret (trɛt) *n Commerce.* (formerly) an allowance according to weight granted to purchasers for waste due to transportation. It was calculated after deduction for tare. [C15: from Old French *trait* pull, tilt of the scale; see TRAIT]

trevally (trɪ'vælɪ) *n, pl* **-lies.** *Austral. and N.Z.* any of various marine food and game fishes of the genus *Caranx:* family *Carangidae.* [C19: probably alteration of *cavally;* see CAVALLA]

Trevelyan (trɪ'vɛljən, -'vɪl-) *n* **1 George Macaulay.** 1876–1962, British historian, noted for his *English Social History* (1944). **2** his father, Sir **George Otto.** 1838–1928, British historian and biographer. His works include a biography of his uncle Lord Macaulay (1876).

Trèves (trɛv) *n* the French name for **Trier.**

Trevino (trə'vi:nəʊ) *n* **Lee.** born 1939, U.S. professional golfer: winner of the U.S. Open Championship (1968; 1971) and the British Open Championship (1971; 1972).

Treviso *(Italian* tre'vi:zo) *n* a city in N Italy, in Veneto region: agricultural market centre. Pop.: 84 066 (1990).

Trevithick (trə'vɪθɪk) *n* **Richard.** 1771–1833, British engineer, who built the first steam-driven passenger carriage (1801) and the first locomotive to run on smooth wheels on smooth rails (1804).

Trevor ('trɛvə) *n* **William,** real name *William Trevor Cox.* born 1928, Irish novelist and short-story writer. His novels include *The Old Boys* (1964), *The Children of Dynmouth* (1977), *Felicia's Journey* (1994), and *Death in Summer* (1998).

trews (tru:z) *pl n Chiefly Brit.* close-fitting trousers, esp. of tartan cloth and worn by certain Scottish soldiers. [C16: from Scottish Gaelic *triubhas,* from Old French *trebus;* see TROUSERS]

trey (treɪ) *n* any card or dice throw with three spots. [C14: from Old French *treis* three, from Latin *trēs*]

TRH *abbrev. for* Their Royal Highnesses.

tri- *prefix* **1** three or thrice: *triaxial; trigon; trisect.* **2** occurring every three: *trimonthly.* [from Latin *trēs,* Greek *treis*]

triable ('traɪəbᵊl) *adj* **1a** liable to be tried judicially. **1b** subject to examination or determination by a court of law. **2** *Rare.* able to be tested. ▸ **'triableness** *n*

triacid (traɪ'æsɪd) *adj* (of a base) capable of reacting with three molecules of a monobasic acid.

triad ('traɪæd) *n* **1** a group of three; trio. **2** *Chem.* an atom, element, group, or ion that has a valency of three. **3** *Music.* a three-note chord consisting of a note and the third and fifth above it. **4** an aphoristic literary form used in medieval Welsh and Irish literature. **5** the U.S. strategic nuclear force, consisting of intercontinental ballistic missiles, submarine-launched ballistic missiles, and bombers. [C16: from Late Latin *trias,* from Greek; related to Greek *treis* three] ▸ **tri'adic** *adj* ▸ **'triadism** *n*

Triad ('traɪæd) *n* any of several Chinese secret societies, esp. one involved in criminal activities, such as drug trafficking.

triage ('traɪɪdʒ) *n* **1** the principle or practice of sorting casualties in battle or disaster or other patients into categories of priority for treatment. **2** the principle or practice of allocating limited resources, as of food or foreign aid, on a basis of expediency rather than according to moral principles or the needs of the recipients. [C18 (in the sense: sorting (goods) according to quality): from French; see TRY, -AGE]

trial[1] ('traɪəl, traɪl) *n* **1a** the act or an instance of trying or proving; test or experiment. **1b** (*as modifier*): *a trial run.* **2** *Law.* **2a** the judicial examination of the issues in a civil or criminal cause by a competent tribunal and the determination of these issues in accordance with the law of the land. **2b** the determination of an accused person's guilt or innocence after hearing evidence for the prosecution and for the accused and the judicial examination of the issues involved. **2c** (*as modifier*): *trial proceedings.* **3** an effort or attempt to do something: *we had three trials at the climb.* **4** trouble or grief. **5** an annoying or frustrating person or thing. **6** (*often pl*) a competition for individuals: *sheepdog trials.* **7** a motorcycling competition in which the skills of the riders are tested over rough ground. **8** *Ceramics.* a piece of sample material used for testing the heat of a kiln and its effects. **9 on trial. 9a** undergoing trial, esp. before a court of law. **9b** being tested, as before a commitment to purchase. ◆ *vb* **trials, trialling, trialled.** (*tr*) **10** to test or make experimental use of (something): *the idea has been trialled in several schools.* [C16: from Anglo-French, from *trier* to TRY] ▸ **'trialling** *n*

trial[2] ('traɪəl) *n Grammar.* **1** a grammatical number occurring in some languages for words in contexts where exactly three of their referents are described or referred to. **2** (*modifier*) relating to or inflected for this number. [C19: from TRI- + -AL[1]]

trial and error *n* a method of discovery, solving problems, etc., based on practical experiment and experience rather than on theory: *he learned to cook by trial and error.*

trial balance *n Book-keeping.* a statement of all the debit and credit balances in the ledger of a double-entry system, drawn up to test their equality.

trial balloon *n* a tentative action or statement designed to test public opinion on a controversial matter. Compare **ballon d'essai.**

trial by battle *or* **trial by combat** *n History.* a method of trying an accused person or of settling a dispute by a personal fight between the two parties involved or, in some circumstances, their permitted champions, in the presence of a judge. It was introduced to England after the Norman Conquest and abolished in 1819.

trial court *n Law.* the first court before which the facts of a case are decided.

triallist *or* **trialist** ('traɪəlɪst, 'traɪlɪst) *n* **1** a person who takes part in a competition, esp. a motorcycle trial. **2** *Sport.* a person who takes part in a preliminary match or heat held to determine selection for an event, a team, etc.

trial run *n* **1** a test drive in a vehicle to assess its performance. **2** a test or rehearsal of something new or untried to assess its effectiveness.

triangle ('traɪ,æŋgᵊl) *n* **1** *Geometry.* a three-sided polygon that can be classified by angle, as in an acute triangle, or by side, as in an equilateral triangle. Sum of interior angles: 180°; area: ½ base × height. **2** any object shaped like a triangle. **3** any situation involving three parties or points of view. See also **eternal triangle.** **4** *Music.* a percussion instrument consisting of a sonorous metal bar bent into a triangular shape, beaten with a metal stick. **5** a group of three. [C14: from Latin *triangulum* (n), from *triangulus* (adj), from TRI- + *angulus* corner] ▸ **'tri,angled** *adj*

triangle of forces *n Physics.* a triangle whose sides represent the magnitudes and directions of three forces in equilibrium whose resultant is zero and which are therefore in equilibrium.

triangular (traɪ'æŋgjʊlə) *adj* **1** Also: **trigonal.** of, shaped like, or relating to a triangle; having three corners or sides. **2** of or involving three participants, pieces, or units. **3** *Maths.* having a base shaped like a triangle. ▸ **triangularity** (traɪ,æŋgjʊ'lærɪtɪ) *n* ▸ **tri'angularly** *adv*

triangulate *vb* (traɪ'æŋgjʊ,leɪt). (*tr*) **1a** to survey by the method of triangulation. **1b** to calculate trigonometrically. **2** to divide into triangles. **3** to make triangular. ◆ *adj* (traɪ'æŋgjʊlɪt, -,leɪt). **4** marked with or composed of triangles. ▸ **tri'angulately** *adv*

triangulation (traɪ,æŋgjʊ'leɪʃən) *n* **1** a method of surveying in which an area is divided into triangles, one side (the base line) and all angles of which are measured and the lengths of the other lines calculated trigonometrically. **2** the network of triangles so formed. **3** the fixing of an unknown point, as in navigation, by making it one vertex of a triangle, the other two being known. **4** *Chess.* a key manoeuvre in the endgame in which the king moves thrice in a triangular path to leave the opposing king with the move and at a disadvantage.

triangulation station *n* a point used in triangulation as a basis for making maps. Triangulation stations are marked in a number of ways, such as by a tapering stone pillar on a hilltop. Also called (informal): **trig point,** (Austral. and N.Z.) **trig.**

Triangulum (traɪ'æŋgjʊləm) *n, Latin genitive* **Trianguli** (traɪ'æŋgjʊ,laɪ). a small triangular constellation in the N hemisphere, close to Perseus and Aries.

Triangulum Australe (ɒ'streɪlɪ) *n, Latin genitive* **Trianguli Australis** (ɒ'streɪlɪs). a small bright triangular constellation in the S hemisphere, lying between Ara and the Southern Cross, that contains an open star cluster. [New Latin: southern triangle]

triarchy ('traɪɑːkɪ) *n, pl* **-chies. 1** government by three people; a triumvirate. **2** a country ruled by three people. **3** an association of three territories each governed by its own ruler. **4** any of the three such territories.

Triassic (traɪ'æsɪk) *adj* **1** of, denoting, or formed in the first period of the Mesozoic era that lasted for 45 million years and during which reptiles flourished. ◆ *n* **2 the.** Also called: **Trias.** the Triassic period or rock system. [C19: from Latin *trias* triad, with reference to the three subdivisions]

triathlon (traɪ'æθlɒn) *n* an athletic contest in which each athlete competes in three different events, swimming, cycling, and running. [C20: from TRI- + Greek *athlon* contest] ▸ **,tri'athlete** *n*

triatomic (,traɪə'tɒmɪk) *adj Chem.* having three atoms in the molecule. ▸ **,tria'tomically** *adv*

triaxial (traɪ'æksɪəl) *adj* having three axes.

triazine ('traɪə,ziːn, -zɪn; traɪ'æziːn, -zɪn) *or* **triazin** ('traɪəzɪn, traɪ'æzɪn) *n* **1** any of three azines that contain three nitrogen atoms in their molecules. Formula: $C_3H_3N_3$. **2** any substituted derivative of any of these compounds.

triazole ('traɪə,zɒl, -,zəʊl; traɪ'æzɒl, -zəʊl) *n* **1** any of four heterocyclic compounds having a five-membered ring with the formula $C_2H_3N_3$. **2** any substituted derivative of any of these compounds. [C19: from TRI- + AZOLE] ▸ **triazolic** (,traɪə'zɒlɪk) *adj*

tribade ('trɪbəd) *n* a lesbian, esp. one who practises tribadism. [C17: from Latin *tribas,* from Greek *tribein* to rub] ▸ **tribadic** (trɪ'bædɪk) *adj*

tribadism ('trɪbəd,ɪzəm) *n* a lesbian practice in which one partner lies on top of the other and simulates the male role in heterosexual intercourse.

tribalism ('traɪbə,lɪzəm) *n* **1** the state of existing as a separate tribe or tribes. **2** the customs and beliefs of a tribal society. **3** loyalty to a tribe or tribal values. ▸ **'tribalist** *n, adj* ▸ **,tribal'istic** *adj*

tribasic (traɪ'beɪsɪk) *adj* **1** (of an acid) containing three replaceable hydrogen atoms in the molecule. **2** (of a molecule) containing three monovalent basic atoms or groups in the molecule.

tribe (traɪb) *n* **1** a social division of a people, esp. of a preliterate people, defined in terms of common descent, territory, culture, etc. **2** an ethnic or ancestral division of ancient cultures, esp. of one of the following: **2a** any of the three divisions of the ancient Romans, the Latins, Sabines, and Etruscans. **2b** one of the later political divisions of the Roman people. **2c** any of the 12 divisions of ancient Israel, each of which was named after and believed to be descended from one of the 12 patriarchs. **2d** a phyle of ancient Greece. **3** *Informal, often jocular.* **3a** a large number of persons, animals, etc. **3b** a specific class or group of persons. **3c** a family, esp. a large one. **4** *Biology.* a taxonomic group that is a subdivision of a subfamily. **5** *Stockbreeding.* a strain of animals descended from a common female ancestor through the female line. [C13: from Latin *tribus;* probably related to Latin *trēs* three] ▸ **'tribal** *adj* ▸ **'tribally** *adv* ▸ **'tribeless** *adj*

tribesman ('traɪbzmən) *n, pl* **-men.** a member of a tribe.

triblet ('trɪblɪt) *n* a spindle or mandrel used in making rings, tubes, etc. [C17: from French *triboulet,* of unknown origin]

tribo- *combining form.* indicating friction: *triboelectricity.* [from Greek *tribein* to rub]

triboelectricity (,traɪbəʊɪlɛk'trɪsɪtɪ, -,iːlɛk-) *n* electricity generated by friction. Also called: **frictional electricity.** ▸ **,triboe'lectric** *adj*

tribology (traɪ'bɒlədʒɪ) *n* the study of friction, lubrication, and wear between moving surfaces.

triboluminescence (,traɪbəʊ,luːmɪ'nɛsəns) *n* luminescence produced by friction, such as the emission of light when certain crystals are crushed. ▸ **,tribo,lumi'nescent** *adj*

tribrach[1] ('traɪbræk, 'trɪb-) *n Prosody.* a metrical foot of three short syllables (˘˘˘). [C16: from Latin *tribrachys,* from Greek *tribrakhus,* from TRI- + *brakhus* short] ▸ **tri'brachic** *or* **tri'brachial** *adj*

tribrach[2] ('trɪbræk) *n Archaeol.* a three-armed object, esp. a flint implement. [C19: from TRI- + Greek *brakhiōn* arm]

tribromoethanol (traɪ,brəʊməʊ'ɛθə,nɒl) *n* a soluble white crystalline compound with a slight aromatic odour, used as a general anaesthetic; 2,2,2-tribromoethanol. Formula: CBr_3CH_2OH.

tribulation (,trɪbjʊ'leɪʃən) *n* **1** a cause of distress. **2** a state of suffering or distress. [C13: from Old French, from Church Latin *trībulātiō,* from Latin *trībulāre* to afflict, from *trībulum* a threshing board, from *terere* to rub]

tribunal (traɪ'bjuːnᵊl, trɪ-) *n* **1** a court of justice or any place where justice is administered. **2** (in England) a special court, convened by the government to inquire into a specific matter. **3** a raised platform containing the seat of a judge or magistrate, originally that in a Roman basilica. [C16: from Latin *tribūnus* TRIBUNE[1]]

tribunate ('trɪbjʊnɪt) *or* **tribuneship** *n* the office or rank of a tribune.

tribune[1] ('trɪbjuːn) *n* **1** (in ancient Rome) **1a** an officer elected by the plebs to protect their interests. Originally there were two of these officers but finally there were ten. **1b** a senior military officer. **2** a person or institution that upholds public rights; champion. [C14: from Latin *tribunus,* probably from *tribus* TRIBE] ▸ **'tribunary** *adj*

tribune[2] ('trɪbjuːn) *n* **1a** the apse of a Christian basilica that contains the bishop's throne. **1b** the throne itself. **2** a gallery or raised area in a church. **3** *Rare.* a raised platform from which a speaker may address an audience; dais.

[C17: via French from Italian *tribuna,* from Medieval Latin *tribūna,* variant of Latin *tribūnal* TRIBUNAL]

Tribune Group *n* (in Britain) a group made up of left-wing Labour Members of Parliament: founded 1966. [named after the *Tribune* newspaper, with which it is associated] ▸ **'Tribun,ite** *n, adj*

tributary ('trɪbjʊtərɪ, -trɪ) *n, pl* **-taries. 1** a stream, river, or glacier that feeds another larger one. **2** a person, nation, or people that pays tribute. ◆ *adj* **3** (of a stream, etc.) feeding a larger stream. **4** given or owed as a tribute. **5** paying tribute. ▸ **'tributarily** *adv*

tribute ('trɪbjuːt) *n* **1** a gift or statement made in acknowledgment, gratitude, or admiration. **2a** a payment by one ruler or state to another, usually as an acknowledgment of submission. **2b** any tax levied for such a payment. **3** (in feudal society) homage or a payment rendered by a vassal to his lord. **4** the obligation to pay tribute. [C14: from Latin *tribūtum,* from *tribuere* to grant (originally: to distribute among the tribes), from *tribus* TRIBE]

tricarboxylic acid cycle (traɪˌkɑːbɒk'sɪlɪk) *n Biochem.* another name for **Krebs cycle.** Abbrev.: **TCA cycle.**

trice[1] (traɪs) *n* moment; instant (esp. in the phrase **in a trice**). [C15 (in the phrase *at* or *in a trice,* in the sense: at one tug): apparent substantive use of TRICE[2]]

trice[2] (traɪs) *vb* (*tr;* often foll. by *up*) *Nautical.* to haul up or secure. [C15: from Middle Dutch *trīsen,* from *trīse* pulley]

tricentenary (ˌtraɪsɛn'tiːnərɪ) *or* **tricentennial** (ˌtraɪsɛn'tɛnɪəl) *adj* **1** of or relating to a period of 300 years. **2** of or relating to a 300th anniversary or its celebration. ◆ *n* **3** an anniversary of 300 years or its celebration. ◆ Also: **tercentenary, tercentennial.**

triceps ('traɪsɛps) *n, pl* **-cepses** (-sɛpsɪz) *or* **-ceps.** any muscle having three heads, esp. the one (*triceps brachii*) that extends the forearm. [C16: from Latin, from TRI- + *caput* head]

triceratops (traɪ'sɛrəˌtɒps) *n* any rhinoceros-like herbivorous dinosaur of the ornithischian genus *Triceratops,* of Cretaceous times, having a heavily armoured neck and three horns on the skull. [C19: from New Latin, from TRI- + Greek *kerat-, keras* horn + *ōps* eye]

trich- *combining form.* a variant of **tricho-** before a vowel.

trichiasis (trɪ'kaɪəsɪs) *n Pathol.* **1** an abnormal position of the eyelashes that causes irritation when they rub against the eyeball. **2** the presence of hairlike filaments in the urine. [C17: via Late Latin from Greek *trikhiasis,* from *thrix* a hair + -IASIS]

trichina (trɪ'kaɪnə) *n, pl* **-nae** (-niː). a parasitic nematode worm, *Trichinella spiralis,* occurring in the intestines of pigs, rats, and man and producing larvae that form cysts in skeletal muscle. [C19: from New Latin, from Greek *trikhinos* relating to hair, from *thrix* a hair]

trichinize *or* **trichinise** ('trɪkɪˌnaɪz) *vb* (*tr*) to infest (an organism) with trichinae. ▸ **ˌtrichini'zation** *or* **ˌtrichini'sation** *n*

Trichinopoly (ˌtrɪkɪ'nɒpəlɪ) *n* another name for **Tiruchirapalli.**

trichinosis (ˌtrɪkɪ'nəʊsɪs) *n* a disease characterized by nausea, fever, diarrhoea, and swelling of the muscles, caused by ingestion of pork infected with trichina larvae. Also called: **trichiniasis** (ˌtrɪkɪ'naɪəsɪs). [C19: from New Latin TRICHINA]

trichinous ('trɪkɪnəs) *adj* **1** of, relating to, or having trichinosis. **2** infested with trichinae.

trichite ('trɪkaɪt) *n* **1** any of various needle-shaped crystals that occur in some glassy volcanic rocks. **2** *Botany.* any of numerous long slender crystals assumed to be present in a starch grain. ▸ **trichitic** (trɪ'kɪtɪk) *adj*

trichloride (traɪ'klɔːraɪd) *n* any compound that contains three chlorine atoms per molecule.

trichloroacetic acid (traɪˌklɔːrəʊə'siːtɪk, -'sɛtɪk) *n* a corrosive deliquescent crystalline acid with a characteristic odour, used as a veterinary astringent and antiseptic. Formula: CCl_3COOH.

trichloroethane (traɪˌklɔːrəʊ'iːθeɪn) *n* a volatile nonflammable colourless liquid with low toxicity used for cleaning electrical apparatus and as a solvent; 1,2,3-trichloroethane. Formula: CH_3CCl_3. Also called: **methyl chloroform.**

trichloroethylene (traɪˌklɔːrəʊ'ɛθɪˌliːn) *or* **trichlorethylene** *n* a volatile nonflammable mobile colourless liquid with an odour resembling that of chloroform. It is a good solvent for certain organic materials and is also an inhalation anaesthetic. Formula $CHCl{:}CCl_2$.

trichlorophenoxyacetic acid (traɪ'klɔːrəʊfəˌnɒksɪə'siːtɪk) *n* an insoluble crystalline solid; 2,4,5-trichlorophenoxyacetic acid. It is a plant hormone and is used as a weedkiller. Formula: $C_8H_5Cl_3O_3$. Also called: **2,4,5-T.**

tricho- *or before a vowel* **trich-** *combining form.* indicating hair or a part resembling hair: *trichocyst.* [from Greek *thrix* (genitive *trikhos*) hair]

trichocyst ('trɪkəˌsɪst) *n* any of various cavities on the surface of some ciliate protozoans, each containing a sensory thread that can be ejected. ▸ **ˌtricho'cystic** *adj*

trichogyne ('trɪkəˌdʒaɪn, -dʒɪn) *n* a hairlike projection of the female reproductive organs of certain algae, fungi, and lichens, which receives the male gametes before fertilization takes place. [C19: from TRICHO- + Greek *gunē* woman] ▸ **ˌtricho'gynial** *or* **ˌtricho'gynic** *adj*

trichoid ('trɪkɔɪd) *adj Zoology.* resembling a hair; hairlike.

trichology (trɪ'kɒlədʒɪ) *n* the branch of medicine concerned with the hair and its diseases. ▸ **trichological** (ˌtrɪkə'lɒdʒɪkᵊl) *adj* ▸ **tri'chologist** *n*

trichome ('traɪkəʊm, 'trɪk-) *n* **1** any hairlike outgrowth from the surface of a plant. **2** any of the threadlike structures that make up the filaments of blue-green algae. [C19: from Greek *trikhōma,* from *trikhoun* to cover with hair, from *thrix* a hair] ▸ **trichomic** (trɪ'kɒmɪk) *adj*

trichomonad (ˌtrɪkəʊ'mɒnæd) *n* any parasitic flagellate protozoan of the genus *Trichomonas,* occurring in the digestive and reproductive systems of man and animals. ▸ **trichomonadal** (ˌtrɪkəʊ'mɒnədəl) *or* **trichomonal** (ˌtrɪkə'mɒnᵊl, -'məʊ-; trɪ'kɒmənᵊl) *adj*

trichomoniasis (ˌtrɪkəʊmə'naɪəsɪs) *n* **1** inflammation of the vagina characterized by a frothy discharge, caused by infection with parasitic protozoa (*Trichomonas vaginalis*). **2** any infection caused by parasitic protozoa of the genus *Trichomonas.* [C19: New Latin; see TRICHOMONAD, -IASIS]

trichopteran (traɪ'kɒptərən) *n* **1** any insect of the order *Trichoptera,* which comprises the caddis flies. ◆ *adj* **2** Also: **trichopterous** (trɪ'kɒptərəs). of, relating to, or belonging to the order *Trichoptera.* [C19: from New Latin *Trichoptera,* literally: having hairy wings, from Greek *thrix* a hair + *pteron* wing]

trichosis (trɪ'kəʊsɪs) *n* any abnormal condition or disease of the hair. [C19: via New Latin from Greek *trikhōsis* growth of hair]

trichotomy (traɪ'kɒtəmɪ) *n, pl* **-mies. 1** division into three categories. **2** *Theol.* the division of man into body, spirit, and soul. [C17: probably from New Latin *trichotomia,* from Greek *trikhotomein* to divide into three, from *trikha* triple + *temnein* to cut] ▸ **trichotomic** (ˌtrɪkə'tɒmɪk) *or* **tri'chotomous** *adj* ▸ **tri'chotomously** *adv*

trichroism ('traɪkrəʊˌɪzəm) *n* a property of biaxial crystals as a result of which they show a perceptible difference in colour when viewed along three different axes. See **pleochroism.** [C19: from Greek *trikhroos* three-coloured, from TRI- + *khrōma* colour] ▸ **tri'chroic** *adj*

trichromat ('traɪkrəʊˌmæt) *n* any person with normal colour vision, who can therefore see the three primary colours.

trichromatic (ˌtraɪkrəʊ'mætɪk) *or* **trichromic** (traɪ'krəʊmɪk) *adj* **1** *Photog., printing.* involving the combination of three primary colours in the production of any colour. **2** of, relating to, or having normal colour vision. **3** having or involving three colours.

trichromatism (traɪ'krəʊməˌtɪzəm) *n* **1** the use or combination of three primary colours for colour reproduction in photography, printing, television, etc. **2** *Rare.* the state of being trichromatic.

trichuriasis (ˌtrɪkjʊə'raɪəsɪs) *n* infection of the large intestine with the whipworm *Trichuris trichiura,* resulting in anaemia, weakness, etc.

trick (trɪk) *n* **1** a deceitful, cunning, or underhand action or plan. **2a** a mischievous, malicious, or humorous action or plan; joke: *the boys are up to their tricks again.* **2b** (*as modifier*): *a trick spider.* **3** an illusory or magical feat or device. **4** a simple feat learned by an animal or person. **5** an adroit or ingenious device; knack: *a trick of the trade.* **6** a behavioural trait, habit, or mannerism. **7** a turn or round of duty or work. **8** *Cards.* **8a** a batch of cards containing one from each player, usually played in turn and won by the player or side that plays the card with the highest value. **8b** a card that can potentially win a trick. **9 can't take a trick.** *Austral. slang.* to be consistently unsuccessful or unlucky. **10 do the trick.** *Informal.* to produce the right or desired result. **11 how's tricks?** *Slang.* how are you? **12 turn a trick.** *Slang.* (of a prostitute) to gain a customer. ◆ *vb* **13** to defraud, deceive, or cheat (someone), esp. by means of a trick. [C15: from Old Northern French *trique,* from *trikier* to deceive, from Old French *trichier,* ultimately from Latin *trīcārī* to play tricks] ▸ **'tricker** *n* ▸ **'trickless** *adj*

trick cyclist *n* a slang term for **psychiatrist.**

trickery ('trɪkərɪ) *n, pl* **-eries.** the practice or an instance of using tricks: *he obtained the money by trickery.*

trickle ('trɪkᵊl) *vb* **1** to run or cause to run in thin or slow streams: *she trickled the sand through her fingers.* **2** (*intr*) to move, go, or pass gradually: *the crowd trickled away.* ◆ *n* **3** a thin, irregular, or slow flow of something. **4** the act of trickling. [C14: perhaps of imitative origin] ▸ **'trickling** *adj* ▸ **'tricklingly** *adv* ▸ **'trickly** *adj*

trickle charger *n* a small mains-operated battery charger, esp. one that delivers less than 5 amperes and is used by car owners.

trickle-down *adj* of or concerning the theory that granting concessions such as tax cuts to the rich will benefit all levels of society by stimulating the economy.

trick or treat *sentence substitute. Chiefly U.S. and Canadian.* the cry by children at Halloween when they call at houses, indicating that they want a present or money or else they will play a trick on the householder.

trick out *or* **up** *vb* (*tr, adv*) to dress up; deck out: *tricked out in frilly dresses.*

trickster ('trɪkstə) *n* a person who deceives or plays tricks.

tricksy ('trɪksɪ) *adj* **-sier, -siest. 1** playing tricks habitually; mischievous. **2** crafty or difficult to deal with. **3** *Archaic.* well-dressed; spruce; smart. ▸ **'tricksiness** *n*

tricktrack ('trɪkˌtræk) *n* a variant spelling of **trictrac.**

tricky ('trɪkɪ) *adj* **trickier, trickiest. 1** involving snags or difficulties: *a tricky job.* **2** needing careful and tactful handling: *a tricky situation.* **3** characterized by tricks; sly; wily: *a tricky dealer.* ▸ **'trickily** *adv* ▸ **'trickiness** *n*

triclinic (traɪ'klɪnɪk) *adj* relating to or belonging to the crystal system characterized by three unequal axes, no pair of which are perpendicular. Also: **anorthic.**

triclinium (traɪ'klɪnɪəm) *n, pl* **-ia** (-ɪə). (in ancient Rome) **1** an arrangement of three couches around a table for reclining upon while dining. **2** a dining room, esp. one containing such an arrangement of couches. [C17: from Latin, from Greek *triklinion,* from TRI- + *klinē* a couch]

tricolour *or U.S.* **tricolor** ('trɪkələ, 'traɪˌkʌlə) *adj also* **tricoloured** *or U.S.* **tricolored** ('traɪˌkʌləd). **1** having or involving three colours. ◆ *n* **2** (*often cap.*) the French national flag, having three equal vertical stripes in blue, white, and red. **3** any flag, badge, ribbon, etc., with three colours.

tricorn ('traɪˌkɔːn) *n also* **tricorne. 1** a cocked hat with opposing brims turned back and caught in three places. **2** an imaginary animal having three horns. ◆ *adj also* **tricornered. 3** having three horns or corners. [C18: from Latin *tricornis,* from TRI- + *cornu* HORN]

tricostate (traɪ'kɒsteɪt) *adj Biology.* having three ribs or riblike parts: *tricostate leaves.* [C19: from TRI- + COSTATE]

tricot ('trɪkəʊ, 'triː-) *n* **1** a thin rayon or nylon fabric knitted or resembling knitting, used for dresses, etc. **2** a type of ribbed dress fabric. [C19: from French, from *tricoter* to knit, of unknown origin]

tricotine (ˌtrɪkə'tiːn, ˌtriː-) *n* a twill-weave woollen fabric resembling gabardine. [C20: from French; see TRICOT]

tricrotic (traɪ'krɒtɪk) *adj Physiol.* (of the pulse) having a tracing characterized by three elevations with each beat. [C19: from Greek *trikrotos* having three beats, from TRI- + *krotos* a beat] ▸ **tricrotism** ('traɪkrəˌtɪzəm, 'trɪk-) *n*

trictrac *or* **tricktrack** ('trɪkˌtræk) *n* a game similar to backgammon. [C17: from French, imitative]

tricuspid (traɪ'kʌspɪd) *Anatomy.* ◆ *adj also* **tricuspidal. 1a** having three points, cusps, or segments: *a tricuspid tooth; a tricuspid valve.* **1b** of or relating to such a tooth or valve. ◆ *n* **2** a tooth having three cusps.

tricycle ('traɪsɪk^əl) *n* **1** a three-wheeled cycle, esp. one driven by pedals. **2** a three-wheeler for invalids. ◆ *vb* **3** (*intr*) to ride a tricycle. ▸ **'tricyclist** *n*

tricyclic (traɪ'saɪklɪk) *adj* **1** (of a chemical compound) containing three rings in the molecular structure. ◆ *n* **2** an antidepressant drug having a tricyclic molecular structure.

tridactyl (traɪ'dækt^əl) *or* **tridactylous** *adj* having three digits on one hand or foot.

trident ('traɪd^ənt) *n* **1** a three-pronged spear, originally from the East. **2** (in Greek and Roman mythology) the three-pronged spear that the sea god Poseidon (Neptune) is represented as carrying. **3** a three-pronged instrument, weapon, or symbol. ◆ *adj* **4** having three prongs. [C16: from Latin *tridēns* three-pronged, from TRI- + *dēns* tooth]

Trident ('traɪd^ənt) *n* a type of U.S. submarine-launched ballistic missile with independently targetable warheads.

tridentate (traɪ'dɛnteɪt) *or* **tridental** *adj Anatomy, botany.* having three prongs, teeth, or points.

Tridentine (traɪ'dɛntaɪn) *adj* **1** *History.* **1a** of or relating to the Council of Trent. **1b** in accord with Tridentine doctrine. ◆ *n* **2** an orthodox Roman Catholic. [C16: from Medieval Latin *Tridentīnus,* from *Tridentum* TRENT]

Tridentum (traɪ'dɛntəm) *n* the Latin name for **Trento.**

tridimensional (ˌtraɪdɪ'mɛnʃən^əl, -daɪ-) *adj* a less common word for **three-dimensional.** ▸ ˌ**tridiˌmension'ality** *n* ▸ ˌ**tridi'mensionally** *adv*

triduum ('trɪdjʊəm, 'traɪ-) *n R.C. Church.* a period of three days for prayer before a feast. [C19: Latin, perhaps from *triduum spatium* a space of three days]

triecious (traɪ'iːʃəs) *adj* a variant spelling of **trioecious.**

tried (traɪd) *vb* the past tense and past participle of **try.**

triella (traɪ'ɛlə) *n Austral.* three nominated horse races in which the punter bets on selecting the three winners.

triene ('traɪˌiːn) *n* a chemical compound containing three double bonds.

triennial (traɪ'ɛnɪəl) *adj* **1** relating to, lasting for, or occurring every three years. ◆ *n* **2** a third anniversary. **3** a triennial period, thing, or occurrence. [C17: from Latin TRIENNIUM] ▸ **tri'ennially** *adv*

triennium (traɪ'ɛnɪəm) *n, pl* **-niums** *or* **-nia** (-nɪə). a period or cycle of three years. [C19: from Latin, from TRI- + *annus* a year]

Trient (tri'ɛnt) *n* the German name for **Trento.** Also: **Trent.**

trier ('traɪə) *n* a person or thing that tries.

Trier (*German* triːr) *n* a city in W Germany, in the Rhineland-Palatinate on the Moselle River: one of the oldest towns of central Europe, ancient capital of a Celto-Germanic tribe (the **Treveri**); an early centre of Christianity, ruled by powerful archbishops until the 18th century; wine trade; important Roman remains. Pop.: 98 750 (1991). Latin name: **Augusta Treverorum** (aʊ'guːstə ˌtrɛvə'rəʊrəm). French name: **Trèves.**

trierarch ('traɪəˌrɑːk) *n Greek history.* **1** a citizen responsible for fitting out a state trireme, esp. in Athens. **2** the captain of a trireme. [C17: from Latin, from Greek *triērarkhos,* from *triērēs* equipped with three banks of oars + *arkhein* to command]

trierarchy ('traɪəˌrɑːkɪ) *n, pl* **-chies.** *Greek history.* **1** the responsibility for fitting out a state trireme, esp. in Athens. **2** the office of a trierarch. **3** trierarchs collectively.

Trieste (triː'ɛst; *Italian* tri'ɛste) *n* **1** a port in NE Italy, capital of Friuli-Venezia Giulia region, on the **Gulf of Trieste** at the head of the Adriatic Sea: under Austrian rule (1382–1918); capital of the Free Territory of Trieste (1947–54); important transit port for central Europe. Pop.: 223 611 (1996 est.). Slovene and Serbo-Croat name: **Trst. 2 Free Territory of.** a former territory on the N Adriatic: established by the UN in 1947; most of the N part passed to Italy and the remainder to Yugoslavia in 1954.

trifacial (traɪ'feɪʃəl) *adj* another word for **trigeminal.**

trifecta (traɪ'fɛktə) *n* a form of betting in which the punter selects the first three place-winners in a horse race in the correct order. [from TRI- + (*per*)*fecta,* a U.S. system of betting]

triffid ('trɪfɪd) *n* any of a species of fictional plants that supposedly grew to a gigantic size, were capable of moving about, and could kill humans. [from the science fiction novel *The Day of the Triffids* (1951) by John Wyndham]

trifid ('traɪfɪd) *adj* divided or split into three parts or lobes. [C18: from Latin *trifidus* from TRI- + *findere* to split]

trifle ('traɪf^əl) *n* **1** a thing of little or no value or significance. **2** a small amount; bit: *a trifle more enthusiasm.* **3** *Brit.* a cold dessert made with sponge cake spread with jam or fruit, soaked in wine or sherry, covered with a custard sauce and cream, and decorated. **4** a type of pewter of medium hardness. **5** articles made from this pewter. ◆ *vb* **6** (*intr;* usually foll. by *with*) to deal (with) as if worthless; dally: *to trifle with a person's affections.* **7** to waste (time) frivolously. [C13: from Old French *trufle* mockery, from *trufler* to cheat] ▸ **'trifler** *n*

trifling ('traɪflɪŋ) *adj* **1** insignificant or petty. **2** frivolous or idle. ▸ **'triflingly** *adv* ▸ **'triflingness** *n*

trifocal *adj* (traɪ'fəʊk^əl). **1** having three focuses. **2** having three focal lengths. ◆ *n* (traɪ'fəʊk^əl, 'traɪˌfəʊk^əl). **3** (*pl*) glasses that have trifocal lenses.

trifold ('traɪˌfəʊld) *adj* a less common word for **triple.**

trifoliate (traɪ'fəʊlɪɪt, -ˌeɪt) *or* **trifoliated** *adj* having three leaves, leaflike parts, or (of a compound leaf) leaflets.

trifolium (traɪ'fəʊlɪəm) *n* any leguminous plant of the temperate genus *Trifolium,* having leaves divided into three leaflets and dense heads of small white, yellow, red, or purple flowers: includes the clovers and trefoils. [C17: from Latin, from TRI- + *folium* leaf]

triforium (traɪ'fɔːrɪəm) *n, pl* **-ria** (-rɪə). an arcade above the arches of the nave, choir, or transept of a church. [C18: from Anglo-Latin, apparently from Latin TRI- + *foris* a doorway; referring to the fact that each bay characteristically had three openings] ▸ **tri'forial** *adj*

trifurcate ('traɪfɜːkɪt, -ˌkeɪt) *or* **trifurcated** *adj* having three branches or forks. [from Latin *trifurcus,* from TRI- + *furca* a fork] ▸ ˌ**trifur'cation** *n*

trig[1] (trɪg) *Archaic or dialect.* ◆ *adj* **1** neat or spruce. ◆ *vb* **trigs, trigging, trigged. 2** to make or become trim or spruce. [C12 (originally: trusty): of Scandinavian origin; related to Old Norse *tryggr* true] ▸ **'trigly** *adv* ▸ **'trigness** *n*

trig[2] (trɪg) *Chiefly dialect.* ◆ *n* **1** a wedge or prop. ◆ *vb* **trigs, trigging, trigged.** (*tr*) **2** to block or stop. **3** to prop or support. [C16: probably of Scandinavian origin; compare Old Norse *tryggja* to make secure; see TRIG[1]]

trig. *abbrev. for:* **1** trigonometry. **2** trigonometrical.

trigeminal (traɪ'dʒɛmɪn^əl) *adj Anatomy.* of or relating to the trigeminal nerve. [C19: from Latin *trigeminus* triplet, from TRI- + *geminus* twin]

trigeminal nerve *n* either one of the fifth pair of cranial nerves, which supply the muscles of the mandible and maxilla. Their ophthalmic branches supply the area around the orbit of the eye, the nasal cavity, and the forehead.

trigeminal neuralgia *n Pathol.* another name for **tic douloureux.**

trigger ('trɪgə) *n* **1** a small projecting lever that activates the firing mechanism of a firearm. **2** *Machinery.* a device that releases a spring-loaded mechanism or a similar arrangement. **3** any event that sets a course of action in motion. ◆ *vb* (*tr*) **4** (usually foll. by *off*) to give rise (to); set off. **5** to fire or set in motion by or as by pulling a trigger. [C17 *tricker,* from Dutch *trekker,* from *trekken* to pull; see TREK] ▸ **'triggered** *adj* ▸ **'triggerless** *adj*

triggerfish ('trɪgəˌfɪʃ) *n, pl* **-fish** *or* **-fishes.** any plectognath fish of the family *Balistidae,* of tropical and temperate seas. They have a compressed body with erectile spines in the first dorsal fin.

trigger-happy *adj Informal.* **1** tending to resort to the use of firearms or violence irresponsibly. **2** tending to act rashly or without due consideration.

trigger plant *n Austral.* any of several small grasslike plants of the genus *Stylidium,* having sensitive stamens that are erected when disturbed: family *Stylidiaceae.*

triglyceride (traɪ'glɪsəˌraɪd) *n* any ester of glycerol and one or more carboxylic acids, in which each glycerol molecule has combined with three carboxylic acid molecules. Most natural fats and oils are triglycerides.

triglyph ('traɪˌglɪf) *n Architect.* a stone block in a Doric frieze, having three vertical channels. [C16: via Latin from Greek *trigluphos* three-grooved, from *tri-* TRI- + *gluphē* carving. See GLYPH] ▸ **tri'glyphic** *adj*

trigon ('traɪgɒn) *n* **1** (in classical Greece or Rome) a triangular harp or lyre. **2** an archaic word for **triangle.** [C17: via Latin from Greek *trigōnon* triangle. See TRI-, -GON]

trigonal ('trɪgən^əl) *adj* **1** another word for **triangular** (sense 1). **2** Also: **rhombohedral.** relating or belonging to the crystal system characterized by three equal axes that are equally inclined and not perpendicular to each other.

trigonometric function *n* **1** Also called: **circular function.** any of a group of functions of an angle expressed as a ratio of two of the sides of a right-angled triangle containing the angle. The group includes sine, cosine, tangent, secant, cosecant, and cotangent. **2** any function containing only sines, cosines, etc., and constants.

trigonometry (ˌtrɪgə'nɒmɪtrɪ) *n* the branch of mathematics concerned with the properties of trigonometric functions and their application to the determination of the angles and sides of triangles. Used in surveying, navigation, etc. Abbrev.: **trig.** [C17: from New Latin *trigōnometria,* from Greek *trigōnon* triangle] ▸ **trigonometric** (ˌtrɪgənə'mɛtrɪk) *or* ˌ**trigono'metrical** *adj* ▸ ˌ**trigono'metrically** *adv*

trigonous ('trɪgənəs) *adj* (of stems, seeds, and similar parts) having a triangular cross section.

trig point *n* an informal name for **triangulation station.** Also called (Austral. and N.Z.): **trig.**

trigraph ('traɪˌgrɑːf, -ˌgræf) *n* a combination of three letters used to represent a single speech sound or phoneme, such as *eau* in French *beau.* ▸ **trigraphic** (traɪ'græfɪk) *adj*

trihalomethane (traɪˌheɪləʊ'miːθeɪn) *n* a type of chemical compound in which three of the hydrogen atoms in a methane molecule have been replaced by halogen atoms, esp. by chlorine in drinking water. Trihalomethanes are thought to be carcinogenic.

trihedral (traɪ'hiːdrəl) *adj* **1** having or formed by three plane faces meeting at a point. ◆ *n* **2** a figure formed by the intersection of three lines in different planes. [C18: from TRI- + Greek *hedra* base, seat + -AL[1]]

trihedron (traɪ'hiːdrən) *n, pl* **-drons** *or* **-dra** (-drə). a figure determined by the intersection of three planes.

trihydrate (traɪ'haɪdreɪt) *n Chem.* a substance that contains three molecules of water. ▸ **tri'hydrated** *adj*

trihydric (traɪ'haɪdrɪk) *or* **trihydroxy** (ˌtraɪhaɪ'drɒksɪ) *adj* (of an alcohol or similar compound) containing three hydroxyl groups.

triiodomethane (ˌtraɪaɪˌəʊdəʊ'miːθeɪn) *n* another name for **iodoform.**

triiodothyronine (ˌtraɪaɪˌəʊdəʊ'θaɪrəˌniːn) *n* an amino acid hormone that contains iodine and is secreted by the thyroid gland with thyroxine, to which it has a similar action. Formula: $C_{15}H_{12}I_3NO_4$. [C20: from TRI- + IODO- + THYRO- + -INE[2]]

trike (traɪk) *n* **1** short for **tricycle**. **2** short for **trichloroethylene.**

trilateral (traɪ'lætərəl) *adj* having three sides. ▸ **tri'laterally** *adv*

trilateration (ˌtraɪlætə'reɪʃən) *n* a method of surveying in which a whole area is divided into triangles, the sides of which are measured, usually by electromagnetic distance measuring for geodetic control or by chain survey for a detailed survey.

trilby ('trɪlbɪ) *n, pl* **-bies. 1** *Chiefly Brit.* a man's soft felt hat with an indented crown. **2** *(pl) Slang.* feet. [C19: named after *Trilby,* the heroine of a dramatized novel (1893) of that title by George du Maurier]

trilemma (traɪ'lemə) *n* **1** a quandary posed by three alternative courses of action. **2** an argument one of the premises of which is the disjunction of three statements from each of which the same conclusion is derived. [C17: formed on the model of DILEMMA, from TRI- + Greek *lēmma* assumption]

trilinear (traɪ'lɪnɪə) *adj* consisting of, bounded by, or relating to three lines.

trilingual (traɪ'lɪŋgwəl) *adj* **1** able to speak three languages fluently. **2** expressed or written in three languages. ▸ **tri'lingualism** *n* ▸ **tri'lingually** *adv*

triliteral (traɪ'lɪtərəl) *adj* **1** having three letters. **2** (of a word root in Semitic languages) consisting of three consonants. ◆ *n* **3** a word root of three consonants.

trilithon (traɪ'lɪθɒn, 'traɪlɪˌθɒn) *or* **trilith** ('traɪlɪθ) *n* a structure consisting of two upright stones with a third placed across the top, such as those of Stonehenge. [C18: from Greek; see TRI-, -LITH] ▸ **trilithic** (traɪ'lɪθɪk) *adj*

trill[1] (trɪl) *n* **1** *Music.* a melodic ornament consisting of a rapid alternation between a principal note and the note a whole tone or semitone above it. Usual symbol: *tr.* or *tr~* (written above a note). **2** a shrill warbling sound, esp. as made by some birds. **3** *Phonetics.* **3a** the articulation of an (r) sound produced by holding the tip of the tongue close to the alveolar ridge, allowing the tongue to make a succession of taps against the ridge. **3b** the production of a similar effect using the uvula against the back of the tongue. ◆ *vb* **4** to sound, sing, or play (a trill or with a trill). **5** *(tr)* to pronounce (an (r) sound) by the production of a trill. [C17: from Italian *trillo,* from *trillare,* apparently from Middle Dutch *trillen* to vibrate]

trill[2] (trɪl) *vb, n* an archaic or poetic word for **trickle.** [C14: probably of Scandinavian origin; related to Norwegian *trilla* to roll; see TRILL[1]]

Trilling ('trɪlɪŋ) *n* **Lionel.** 1905–75, U.S. literary critic, whose works include *The Liberal Imagination* (1950) and *Sincerity and Authenticity* (1974).

trillion ('trɪljən) *n* **1** the number represented as one followed by twelve zeros (10^{12}); a million million. **2** (formerly, in Britain) the number represented as one followed by eighteen zeros (10^{18}); a million million million. **3** *(often pl)* an exceptionally large but unspecified number. ◆ *determiner* **4** (preceded by *a* or a numeral) **4a** amounting to a trillion: *a trillion stars.* **4b** *(as pronoun): there are three trillion.* [C17: from French, on the model of *million*] ▸ **'trillionth** *n, adj*

trillium ('trɪljəm) *n* any herbaceous plant of the genus *Trillium,* of Asia and North America, having a whorl of three leaves at the top of the stem with a single central white, pink, or purple three-petalled flower: family *Trilliaceae.* [C18: from New Latin, modification by Linnaeus of Swedish *trilling* triplet]

trilobate (traɪ'ləʊbeɪt, 'traɪləˌbeɪt) *adj* (esp. of a leaf) consisting of or having three lobes or parts.

trilobite ('traɪləˌbaɪt) *n* any extinct marine arthropod of the group *Trilobita,* abundant in Palaeozoic times, having a segmented exoskeleton divided into three parts. [C19: from New Latin *Trilobītēs,* from Greek *trilobos* having three lobes; see TRI-, LOBE] ▸ **trilobitic** (ˌtraɪlə'bɪtɪk) *adj*

trilocular (traɪ'lɒkjʊlə) *adj* (esp. of a plant ovary or anther) having or consisting of three chambers or cavities. [C18: from TRI- + Latin *loculus* compartment (from *locus* place) + -AR]

trilogy ('trɪlədʒɪ) *n, pl* **-gies. 1** a series of three related works, esp. in literature, etc. **2** (in ancient Greece) a series of three tragedies performed together at the Dionysian festivals. [C19: from Greek *trilogia;* see TRI-, -LOGY]

trim (trɪm) *adj* **trimmer, trimmest. 1** neat and spruce in appearance. **2** slim; slender. **3** in good condition. ◆ *vb* **trims, trimming, trimmed.** *(mainly tr)* **4** to put in good order, esp. by cutting or pruning. **5** to shape and finish (timber). **6** to adorn or decorate. **7** (sometimes foll. by *off* or *away)* to cut so as to remove: *to trim off a branch.* **8** to cut down to the desired size or shape: *to trim material to a pattern.* **9** *Dialect.* to decorate: *to trim a Christmas tree.* **10** *Nautical.* **10a** *(also intr)* to adjust the balance of (a vessel) or (of a vessel) to maintain an even balance, by distribution of ballast, cargo, etc. **10b** *(also intr)* to adjust (a vessel's sails) to take advantage of the wind. **10c** to stow (cargo). **11** to balance (an aircraft) before flight by adjusting the position of the load or in flight by the use of trim tabs, fuel transfer, etc. **12** *(also intr)* to modify (one's opinions, etc.) to suit opposing factions or for expediency. **13** *Informal.* to thrash or beat. **14** *Informal.* to rebuke. **15** *Obsolete.* to furnish or equip. ◆ *n* **16** a decoration or adornment. **17** the upholstery and decorative facings, as on the door panels, of a car's interior. **18** proper order or fitness; good shape: *in trim.* **19** a haircut that neatens but does not alter the existing hairstyle. **20** *Nautical.* **20a** the general set and appearance of a vessel. **20b** the difference between the draught of a vessel at the bow and at the stern. **20c** the fitness of a vessel. **20d** the position of a vessel's sails relative to the wind. **20e** the relative buoyancy of a submarine. **21** dress or equipment. **22** *U.S.* window-dressing. **23** the attitude of an aircraft in flight when the pilot allows the main control surfaces to take up their own positions. **24** *Films.* a section of shot cut out during editing. **25** material that is trimmed off. **26** decorative mouldings, such as architraves, picture rails, etc. [Old English *trymman* to strengthen; related to *trum* strong, Old Irish *druma* tree, Russian *drom* thicket] ▸ **'trimly** *adv* ▸ **'trimness** *n*

Trim (trɪm) *n* the county town of Meath, Republic of Ireland; 12th-century castle, medieval cathedral; textiles and machinery. Pop.: 18 120 (1991).

trimaran ('traɪməˌræn) *n* a vessel, usually of shallow draught, with two hulls flanking the main hull. [C20: from TRI- + (CATA)MARAN]

Trimble ('trɪmbᵊl) *n* **(William) David.** born 1944, Northern Irish politician; leader of the Ulster Unionist party from 1995, First Minister of Northern Ireland from 1998; Nobel peace prize jointly with John Hume in 1998.

trimer ('traɪmə) *n* a polymer or a molecule of a polymer consisting of three identical monomers. ▸ **trimeric** (traɪ'merɪk) *adj*

trimerous ('trɪmərəs) *adj* **1** (of plants) having parts arranged in groups of three. **2** consisting of or having three parts.

trimester (traɪ'mestə) *n* **1** a period of three months. **2** (in some U.S. and Canadian universities or schools) any of the three academic sessions. [C19: from French *trimestre,* from Latin *trimēstris* of three months, from TRI- + *mēnsis* month] ▸ **tri'mestral** *or* **tri'mestrial** *adj*

trimeter ('trɪmɪtə) *Prosody.* ◆ *n* **1** a verse line consisting of three metrical feet. ◆ *adj* **2** designating such a line.

trimethadione (ˌtraɪmeθə'daɪəʊn) *n* a crystalline compound with a bitter taste and camphor-like odour, used in the treatment of epilepsy. Formula: $C_6H_9NO_3$. [from TRI- + METH(YL) + DI-[1] + -ONE]

trimetric (traɪ'metrɪk) *or* **trimetrical** *adj* **1** *Prosody.* of, relating to, or consisting of a trimeter or trimeters. **2** *Crystallog.* another word for **orthorhombic.**

trimetric projection *n* a geometric projection, used in mechanical drawing, in which the three axes are at arbitrary angles, often using different linear scales.

trimetrogon (traɪ'metrəˌgɒn) *n* **a** a method of aerial photography for rapid topographic mapping, in which one vertical and two oblique photographs are taken simultaneously. **b** *(as modifier): trimetrogon photography.* [from TRI- + *metro-,* from Greek *metron* measure + -GON]

trimmer ('trɪmə) *n* **1** Also called: **trimmer joist.** a beam in a floor or roof structure attached to truncated joists in order to leave an opening for a staircase, chimney, etc. **2** a machine for trimming timber. **3** Also called: **trimming capacitor.** *Electronics.* a variable capacitor of small capacitance used for making fine adjustments, etc. **4** a person who alters his opinions on the grounds of expediency. **5** a person who fits out motor vehicles.

trimming ('trɪmɪŋ) *n* **1** an extra piece used to decorate or complete. **2** *(pl)* usual or traditional accompaniments: *roast turkey with all the trimmings.* **3** *(pl)* parts that are cut off. **4** *(pl) Dialect.* ornaments; decorations: *Christmas trimmings.* **5** *Informal.* a reproof, beating, or defeat.

trimolecular (ˌtraɪmə'lekjʊlə) *adj Chem.* of, concerned with, formed from, or involving three molecules.

trimonoecious (ˌtraɪmə'niːʃəs) *adj* (of a plant) having separate male, female, and hermaphrodite flowers on the same plant.

trimonthly (traɪ'mʌnθlɪ) *adj, adv* every three months.

trimorph ('traɪmɔːf) *n* **1** a substance, esp. a mineral, that exists in three distinct forms. **2** any of the forms in which such a structure exists.

trimorphism (traɪ'mɔːfɪzəm) *n* **1** *Biology.* the property exhibited by certain species of having or occurring in three different forms. **2** the property of certain minerals of existing in three crystalline forms. [C19: from Greek *trimorphos* (from TRI- + *morphē* form) + -ISM] ▸ **tri'morphic** *or* **tri'morphous** *adj*

trim size *n* the size of a book or a page of a book after all excess material has been trimmed off.

trim tab *n* a small control surface attached to the trailing edge of a main control surface to enable the pilot to trim an aircraft.

Trimurti (trɪ'mʊətɪ) *n* the triad of the three chief gods of later Hinduism, consisting of Brahma the Creator, Vishnu the Sustainer, and Siva the Destroyer. [from Sanskrit, from *tri* three + *mūrti* form]

Trinacria (trɪ'neɪkrɪə, traɪ-) *n* the Latin name for **Sicily.** ▸ **Tri'nacrian** *adj*

trinary ('traɪnərɪ) *adj* **1** made up of three parts; ternary. **2** going in threes. [C15: from Late Latin *trīnārius* of three sorts, from Latin *trīnī* three each, from *trēs* three]

Trincomalee (ˌtrɪŋkəʊmə'liː) *n* a port in NE Sri Lanka, on the **Bay of Trincomalee** (an inlet of the Bay of Bengal); British naval base until 1957. Pop.: 51 000 (latest est.).

trine (traɪn) *n* **1** *Astrology.* an aspect of 120° between two planets, an orb of 8° being allowed. Compare **conjunction** (sense 5), **opposition** (sense 9), **square** (sense 10). **2** anything comprising three parts. ◆ *adj* **3** of or relating to a trine. **4** threefold; triple. [C14: from Old French *trin,* from Latin *trīnus* triple, from *trēs* three] ▸ **'trinal** *adj*

Trinidad ('trɪnɪˌdæd) *n* an island in the West Indies, off the NE coast of Venezuela: colonized by the Spanish in the 17th century and ceded to Britain in 1802; joined with Tobago in 1888 as a British colony; now part of the independent republic of Trinidad and Tobago. Pop.: 1 184 106 (1990). ▸ **ˌTrini'dadian** *adj, n*

Trinidad and Tobago *n* an independent republic in the Caribbean, occupying the two southernmost islands of the Lesser Antilles: became a British colony in 1888 and gained independence in 1962; became a republic in 1976; a member of the Commonwealth. Official language: English. Religion: Christian majority, with a large Hindu minority. Currency: Trinidad and Tobago dollar. Capital: Port of Spain. Pop.: 1 275 000 (1998 est.). Area: 5128 sq. km (1980 sq. miles).

Trinil man ('triːnɪl) *n* another name for **Java man.** [C20: named after the village in Java where remains were found]

Trinitarian (ˌtrɪnɪ'teərɪən) *n* **1** a person who believes in the doctrine of the Trinity. **2** a member of the Holy Trinity. See **Trinity** (sense 3). ◆ *adj* **3** of or relating to the doctrine of the Trinity or those who uphold it. **4** of or relating to the Holy Trinity. ▸ **ˌTrini'tarianˌism** *n*

trinitrobenzene (traɪˌnaɪtrəʊ'benziːn, -ben'ziːn) *n* any of three explosive crystalline isomeric compounds with the formula $C_6H_3(NO_2)_3$. They are less sensitive to impact than TNT but more powerful in their explosive force.

trinitrocresol (traɪˌnaɪtrəʊˈkriːsɒl) *n* a yellow crystalline highly explosive compound. Formula: $CH_3C_6H(OH)(NO_2)_3$.
trinitroglycerine (traɪˌnaɪtrəʊˈglɪsəˌriːn) *n* the full name for **nitroglycerine.**
trinitrophenol (traɪˌnaɪtrəʊˈfiːnɒl) *n* another name for **picric acid.**
trinitrotoluene (traɪˌnaɪtrəʊˈtɒljuˌiːn) *or* **trinitrotoluol** (traɪˌnaɪtrəʊˈtɒljuˌɒl) *n* the full name for **TNT.**
trinity (ˈtrɪnɪtɪ) *n, pl* **-ties. 1** a group of three. **2** the state of being threefold. [C13: from Old French *trinite,* from Late Latin *trīnitās,* from Latin *trīnus* triple]
Trinity (ˈtrɪnɪtɪ) *n* **1** Also called: **Holy Trinity, Blessed Trinity.** *Christian theol.* the union of three persons, the Father, Son, and Holy Ghost, in one Godhead. **2** See **Trinity Sunday. 3 Holy Trinity.** a religious order founded in 1198.
Trinity Brethren *pl n* the members of Trinity House.
Trinity House *n* an association that provides lighthouses, buoys, etc., around the British coast.
Trinity Sunday *n* the Sunday after Whit Sunday.
Trinity term *n* the summer term at the Inns of Court and some educational establishments.
trinket (ˈtrɪŋkɪt) *n* **1** a small or worthless ornament or piece of jewellery. **2** a trivial object; trifle. [C16: perhaps from earlier *trenket* little knife, via Old Northern French, from Latin *truncāre* to lop] ▸ **ˈtrinketry** *n*
trinocular (traɪˈnɒkjʊlə) *adj* of or relating to a binocular microscope having a lens for photographic recording while direct visual observation is taking place. [C20: from TRI- + (BI)NOCULAR]
trinomial (traɪˈnəʊmɪəl) *adj* **1** *Maths.* consisting of or relating to three terms. **2** *Biology.* denoting or relating to the three-part name of an organism that incorporates its genus, species, and subspecies. ◆ *n* **3** *Maths.* a polynomial consisting of three terms, such as $ax^2 + bx + c$. **4** *Biology.* the third word in the trinomial name of an organism, which distinguishes between subspecies. [C18: TRI- + *-nomial* on the model of *binomial*] ▸ **triˈnomially** *adv*
trio (ˈtriːəʊ) *n, pl* **trios. 1** a group of three people or things. **2** *Music.* **2a** a group of three singers or instrumentalists or a piece of music composed for such a group. **2b** a subordinate section in a scherzo, minuet, etc., that is contrastive in style and often in a related key. **3** *Piquet.* three cards of the same rank. [C18: from Italian, ultimately from Latin *trēs* three; compare DUO]
triode (ˈtraɪəʊd) *n* **1** an electronic valve having three electrodes, a cathode, an anode, and a grid, the potential of the grid controlling the flow of electrons between the cathode and anode. It has been replaced by the transistor. **2** any electronic device, such as a thyratron, having three electrodes. [C20: TRI- + ELECTRODE]
trioecious *or* **triecious** (traɪˈiːʃəs) *adj* (of a plant species) having male, female, and hermaphrodite flowers in three different plants. [C18: from New Latin *trioecia,* from Greek TRI- + *oikos* house]
triol (ˈtraɪɒl) *n* any of a class of alcohols that have three hydroxyl groups per molecule. Also called: **trihydric alcohol.** [from TRI- + -OL[1]]
triolein (traɪˈəʊlɪɪn) *n* a naturally occurring glyceride of oleic acid, found in fats and oils. Formula: $(C_{17}H_{33}COO)_3C_3H_5$. Also called: **olein.**
triolet (ˈtriːəʊˌlɛt) *n* a verse form of eight lines, having the first line repeated as the fourth and seventh and the second line as the eighth, rhyming a b a a a b a b. [C17: from French: a little TRIO]
triose (ˈtraɪəʊz, -əʊs) *n* a simple monosaccharide produced by the oxidation of glycerol. Formula: $CH_2OHCHOHCHO$.
trio sonata *n* **1** a type of baroque composition in several movements scored for two upper parts and a bass part. **2** a similar type of composition played on a keyboard instrument, esp. an organ.
trioxide (traɪˈɒksaɪd) *n* any oxide that contains three oxygen atoms per molecule: *sulphur trioxide,* SO_3.
trip (trɪp) *n* **1** an outward and return journey, often for a specific purpose. **2** any tour, journey, or voyage. **3** a false step; stumble. **4** any slip or blunder. **5** a light step or tread. **6** a manoeuvre or device to cause someone to trip. **7** Also called: **tripper. 7a** any catch on a mechanism that acts as a switch. **7b** (*as modifier*): *trip button.* **8** *Informal.* a hallucinogenic drug experience. **9** *Informal.* any stimulating, profound, etc., experience. ◆ *vb* **trips, tripping, tripped. 10** (often foll. by *up,* or when *intr,* by *on* or *over*) to stumble or cause to stumble. **11** to make or cause to make a mistake or blunder. **12** (*tr;* often foll. by *up*) to trap or catch in a mistake. **13** (*intr*) to go on a short tour or journey. **14** (*intr*) to move or tread lightly. **15** (*intr*) *Informal.* to experience the effects of LSD or any other hallucinogenic drug. **16** (*tr*) **16a** to activate (a mechanical trip). **16b trip a switch.** to switch electric power off by moving the switch armature to disconnect the supply. ◆ See also **trip out.** [C14: from Old French *triper* to tread, of Germanic origin; related to Low German *trippen* to stamp, Middle Dutch *trippen* to walk trippingly, *trepelen* to trample] ▸ **ˈtrippingly** *adv*
tripalmitin (traɪˈpælmɪtɪn) *n* another name for **palmitin.**
tripartite (traɪˈpɑːtaɪt) *adj* **1** divided into or composed of three parts. **2** involving three participants. **3** (esp. of leaves) consisting of three parts formed by divisions extending almost to the base. ▸ **triˈpartitely** *adv*
tripartition (ˌtraɪpɑːˈtɪʃən) *n* division into or among three.
tripe (traɪp) *n* **1** the stomach lining of an ox, cow, or other ruminant, prepared for cooking. **2** *Informal.* something silly; rubbish. **3** (*pl*) *Archaic, informal.* intestines; belly. [C13: from Old French, of unknown origin]
tripersonal (traɪˈpɜːsənᵊl) *adj Christian theol.* (of God) existing as the Trinity. Compare **unipersonal.** ▸ **ˌtripersonˈality** *n*
triphammer (ˈtrɪpˌhæmə) *n* a power hammer that is raised or tilted by a cam and allowed to fall under gravity.
triphenylmethane (traɪˌfiːnaɪlˈmiːθeɪn, -ˌfɛn-) *n* a colourless crystalline solid used for the preparation of many dyes. Formula: $(C_6H_5)_3CH$.
triphibious (traɪˈfɪbɪəs) *adj* (esp. of military operations) occurring on land, at sea, and in the air. [C20: from TRI- + (AM)PHIBIOUS]
trip-hop (ˈtrɪpˌhɒp) *n* a type of British electronic dance music of the 1990s, influenced by drug culture. [C20: TRIP (in the sense: drug experience) + HIP-HOP]
triphthong (ˈtrɪfθɒŋ, ˈtrɪp-) *n* **1** a composite vowel sound during the articulation of which the vocal organs move from one position through a second, ending in a third. **2** a trigraph representing a composite vowel sound such as this. [C16: via New Latin from Medieval Greek *triphthongos,* from TRI- + *phthongos* sound; compare DIPHTHONG] ▸ **triphˈthongal** *adj*
triphylite (ˈtrɪfɪˌlaɪt) *n* a bluish-grey rare mineral that consists of lithium iron phosphate in orthorhombic crystalline form and occurs in pegmatites. Formula: $LiFePO_4$. [C19: from TRI- + *phyl-,* from Greek *phulon* family + -ITE[1], referring to its three bases]
tripinnate (traɪˈpɪnɪt, -eɪt) *adj* (of a leaf) having pinnate leaflets that are bipinnately arranged. ▸ **triˈpinnately** *adv*
Tripitaka (ˌtrɪpɪˈtɑːkə) *n Buddhism.* the three collections of books making up the Buddhist canon of scriptures. [from Pali *tri* three + *pitaka* basket]
tripl. *abbrev. for* triplicate.
triplane (ˈtraɪˌpleɪn) *n* an aeroplane having three wings arranged one above the other.
triple (ˈtrɪpᵊl) *adj* **1** consisting of three parts; threefold. **2** (of musical time or rhythm) having three beats in each bar. **3** three times as great or as much. ◆ *n* **4** a threefold amount. **5** a group of three. ◆ *vb* **6** to increase or become increased threefold; treble. [C16: from Latin *triplus*] ▸ **ˈtriply** *adv*
triple A *n Military.* anti-aircraft artillery: written as **AAA.**
Triple Alliance *n* **1** the secret alliance between Germany, Austria-Hungary, and Italy formed in 1882 and lasting until 1914. **2** the alliance of France, the Netherlands, and Britain against Spain in 1717. **3** the alliance of England, Sweden, and the Netherlands against France in 1668.
triple bond *n* a type of chemical bond consisting of three distinct covalent bonds linking two atoms in a molecule.
triple crown *n* **1** *R.C. Church.* the Pope's tiara. **2** *Horse racing.* the winning of three important races in one season. **3** (*often cap.*) *Rugby Union.* a victory by Scotland, England, Wales, or Ireland in all three games against the others in the annual Five Nations Championship. Compare **grand slam** (sense 3).
Triple Entente *n* the understanding between Britain, France, and Russia that developed between 1894 and 1907 and counterbalanced the Triple Alliance of 1882. The Entente became a formal alliance on the outbreak of World War I and was ended by the Russian Revolution in 1917.
triple expansion engine *n* (formerly) a steam engine in which the steam is expanded in three stages in cylinders of increasing diameter to accommodate the increasing volume of the steam.
triple jump *n* an athletic event in which the competitor has to perform successively a hop, a step, and a jump in continuous movement. Also called: **hop, step, and jump.**
triple-nerved *adj* (of a leaf) having three main veins.
triple point *n Chem.* the temperature and pressure at which the three phases of a substance are in equilibrium. The triple point of water, 273.16 K at a pressure of 611.2 Pa, is the basis of the definition of the kelvin.
triplet (ˈtrɪplɪt) *n* **1** a group or set of three similar things. **2** one of three offspring born at one birth. **3** *Music.* a group of three notes played in a time value of two, four, etc. **4** *Chem.* a state of a molecule or free radical in which there are two unpaired electrons. [C17: from TRIPLE, on the model of *doublet*]
tripletail (ˈtrɪpᵊlˌteɪl) *n, pl* **-tail** *or* **-tails.** any percoid fish of the family *Lobotidae,* esp. *Lobotes surinamensis,* of brackish waters of SE Asia, having tail-like dorsal and anal fins.
triple time *n* musical time with three beats in each bar.
triple-tongue *vb Music.* to play (very quick staccato passages of notes grouped in threes) on a wind instrument by a combination of single- and double-tonguing. Compare **single-tongue, double-tongue.** ▸ **triple tonguing** *n*
triplex (ˈtrɪplɛks) *adj* a less common word for **triple.** [C17: from Latin: threefold, from TRI- + *-plex* -FOLD]
Triplex (ˈtrɪplɛks) *n Brit. trademark.* a laminated safety glass, as used in car windows.
triplicate *adj* (ˈtrɪplɪkɪt). **1** triple. ◆ *vb* (ˈtrɪplɪˌkeɪt). **2** to multiply or be multiplied by three. ◆ *n* (ˈtrɪplɪkɪt). **3a** a group of three things. **3b** one of such a group. **4 in triplicate.** written out three times. [C15: from Latin *triplicāre* to triple, from TRIPLEX] ▸ **ˌtripliˈcation** *n*
triplicity (trɪˈplɪsɪtɪ) *n, pl* **-ties. 1** a group of three things. **2** the state of being three. **3** *Astrology.* any of four groups, earth, air, fire, and water, each consisting of three signs of the zodiac that are thought to have something in common in their nature. [C14: from Late Latin *triplicitās,* from Latin *triplex* threefold; see TRIPLEX]
triploblastic (ˌtrɪpləʊˈblæstɪk) *adj* (of all multicellular animals except coelenterates) having a body developed from all three germ layers. Compare **diploblastic.** [C19: from *triplo-* threefold (from Greek *triploos*) + -BLAST]
triploid (ˈtrɪplɔɪd) *adj* **1** having or relating to three times the haploid number of chromosomes: *a triploid organism.* ◆ *n* **2** a triploid organism. [C19: from Greek *tripl(oos)* triple + (HAPL)OID]
tripod (ˈtraɪpɒd) *n* **1** an adjustable and usually collapsible three-legged stand to which a camera, etc., can be attached to hold it steady. **2** a stand or table having three legs. [C17: via Latin from Greek *tripod-, tripous* three-footed, from TRI- + *pous* foot] ▸ **tripodal** (ˈtrɪpədᵊl) *adj*
tripody (ˈtrɪpədɪ) *n, pl* **-dies.** *Prosody.* a metrical unit consisting of three feet.
tripoli (ˈtrɪpəlɪ) *n* a lightweight porous siliceous rock derived by weathering and used in a powdered form as a polish, filter, etc. [C17: named after TRIPOLI, in Libya or in Lebanon]
Tripoli (ˈtrɪpəlɪ) *n* **1** the capital and chief port of Libya, in the northwest on the Mediterranean: founded by Phoenicians in about the 7th century B.C.; the only city that has survived of the three (Oea, Leptis Magna, and Sabratha) that

formed the African Tripolis ("three cities"); fishing and manufacturing centre. Pop.: 591 062 (1988 est.). Ancient name: **Oea** ('iːə). Arabic name: **Tarabulus el Gharb. 2** a port in N Lebanon, on the Mediterranean: the second largest town in Lebanon; taken by the Crusaders in 1109 after a siege of five years; oil-refining and manufacturing centre. Pop.: 240 000 (1991 est.). Ancient name: **Tripolis.** Arabic name: **Tarabulus esh Sham.**

Tripolitania (ˌtrɪpəlɪ'teɪnɪə) *n* the NW part of Libya: established as a Phoenician colony in the 7th century B.C.; taken by the Turks in 1551 and became one of the Barbary states; under Italian rule from 1912 until World War II. ▸ **ˌTripoli'tanian** *adj, n*

tripos ('traɪpɒs) *n Brit.* the final honours degree examinations in all subjects at Cambridge University. **[C16:** from Latin *tripūs,* influenced by Greek noun ending *-os***]**

trip out *vb* (*adv*) (of an electrical circuit) to disconnect or be disconnected or (of a machine) to stop or be stopped by means of a trip switch or trip button.

tripper ('trɪpə) *n* **1** a person who goes on a trip. **2** *Chiefly Brit.* a tourist; excursionist. **3** another word for **trip** (sense 7). **4a** any device that generates a signal causing a trip to operate. **4b** the signal so generated.

trippet ('trɪpɪt) *n* any mechanism that strikes or is struck at regular intervals, as by a cam. **[C15** (in the sense: a piece of wood used in a game): from *trippen* to TRIP**]**

trippy ('trɪpɪ) *adj* **-pier, -piest.** *Informal.* suggestive of or resembling the effect produced by a hallucinogenic drug.

trip switch *n* an electric switch arranged to interrupt a circuit suddenly and disconnect power from a running machine so that the machine is stopped.

triptane ('trɪpteɪn) *n* a colourless highly flammable liquid alkane hydrocarbon, isomeric with heptane, used in aviation fuel; 2,2,3-trimethylbutane. Formula: $CH_3C(CH_3)_2CH(CH_3)CH_3$. **[C20:** shortened and altered from *trimethylbutane;* see TRI-, METHYL, BUTANE**]**

tripterous ('trɪptərəs) *adj* (of fruits, seeds, etc.) having three winglike extensions or parts. **[C19:** from TRI- + Greek *-pteros,* from *pteron* wing**]**

Triptolemus (trɪp'tɒlɪməs) *n Greek myth.* a favourite of Demeter, sent by her to teach men agriculture.

triptych ('trɪptɪk) *n* **1** a set of three pictures or panels, usually hinged so that the two wing panels fold over the larger central one: often used as an altarpiece. **2** a set of three hinged writing tablets. **[C18:** from Greek *triptukhos,* from TRI- + *ptux* plate; compare DIPTYCH**]**

triptyque (trɪp'tiːk) *n* a customs permit for the temporary importation of a motor vehicle. **[**from French: TRIPTYCH (referring to its three sections)**]**

Tripura ('trɪpurə) *n* a state of NE India: formerly a princely state, ruled by the Maharajahs for over 1300 years; became a union territory in 1956 and a state in 1972; extensive jungles. Capital: Agartala. Pop.: 3 055 000 (1994 est.). Area: 10 486 sq. km (4051 sq. miles).

tripwire ('trɪpˌwaɪə) *n* a wire that activates a trap, mine, etc., when tripped over.

triquetrous (traɪ'kwiːtrəs, -'kwɛ-) *adj* triangular, esp. in cross section: *a triquetrous stem.* **[C17:** from Latin *triquetrus* having three corners**]**

triradiate (traɪ'reɪdɪɪt, -ˌeɪt) *adj Biology.* having or consisting of three rays or radiating branches. ▸ **tri'radiately** *adv*

trireme ('traɪriːm) *n* a galley, developed by the ancient Greeks as a warship, with three banks of oars on each side. **[C17:** from Latin *trirēmis,* from TRI- + *rēmus* oar**]**

trisaccharide (traɪ'sækəˌraɪd) *n* an oligosaccharide whose molecules have three linked monosaccharide molecules.

trisect (traɪ'sɛkt) *vb* (*tr*) to divide into three parts, esp. three equal parts. **[C17:** TRI- + *-sect* from Latin *secāre* to cut**]** ▸ **trisection** (traɪ'sɛkʃən) *n* ▸ **tri'sector** *n*

triserial (traɪ'sɪərɪəl) *adj* arranged in three rows or series.

trishaw ('traɪˌʃɔː) *n* another name for **rickshaw** (sense 2). **[C20:** from TRI- + RICKSHAW**]**

triskaidekaphobia (ˌtrɪskaɪˌdekə'fəubɪə) *n* an abnormal fear of the number thirteen. **[C20:** from Greek *triskaideka* thirteen + -PHOBIA**]** ▸ **ˌtriskaiˌdeka'phobic** *adj, n*

triskelion (trɪ'skelɪˌɒn, -ən) *or* **triskele** ('trɪskiːl) *n, pl* **triskelia** (trɪ'skelɪə) *or* **triskeles.** a symbol consisting of three bent limbs or lines radiating from a centre. **[C19:** from Greek *triskelēs* three-legged, from TRI- + *skelos* leg**]**

Trismegistus (ˌtrɪsmɪ'dʒɪstəs) *n* See **Hermes Trismegistus.**

trismus ('trɪzməs) *n Pathol.* the state or condition of being unable to open the mouth because of sustained contractions of the jaw muscles, caused by a form of tetanus. Nontechnical name: **lockjaw. [C17:** from New Latin, from Greek *trismos* a grinding**]** ▸ **'trismic** *adj*

trisoctahedron (trɪsˌɒktə'hiːdrən) *n, pl* **-drons** *or* **-dra** (-drə). a solid figure having 24 identical triangular faces, groups of three faces being formed on an underlying octahedron. **[C19:** from Greek *tris* three times + OCTAHEDRON**]** ▸ **trisˌocta'hedral** *adj*

trisomy ('traɪsəumɪ) *n* the condition of having one chromosome of the set represented three times in an otherwise diploid organism, cell, etc. Trisomy of chromosome 21 results in Down's syndrome. **[C20:** from TRI- + (CHROMO)SOM(E) + -Y[3]**]** ▸ **trisomic** (traɪ'səumɪk) *adj*

Tristan ('trɪstən) *or* **Tristram** ('trɪstrəm) *n* (in medieval romance) the nephew of King Mark of Cornwall who fell in love with his uncle's bride, Iseult, after they mistakenly drank a love potion.

Tristan da Cunha ('trɪstən də 'kuːnjə) *n* a group of four small volcanic islands in the S Atlantic, about halfway between South Africa and South America: comprises the main island of Tristan and the uninhabited islands of Gough, Inaccessible, and Nightingale; discovered in 1506 by the Portuguese admiral Tristão da Cunha; annexed to Britain in 1816; whole population of Tristan evacuated for two years after the volcanic eruption of 1961. Pop.: 313 (1988). Area: about 100 sq. km (40 sq. miles).

tristate ('traɪˌsteɪt) *adj* (of a digital computer chip) having high, low, and floating output states.

triste (triːst) *or* **tristful** ('trɪstfʊl) *adj* archaic words for **sad. [**from French**]** ▸ **'tristfully** *adv* ▸ **'tristfulness** *n*

tristearin (traɪ'stɪərɪn) *n* another name for **stearin.**

tristich ('trɪstɪk) *n Prosody.* a poem, stanza, or strophe that consists of three lines. **[C19:** from Greek, from TRI- + *stikhos* STICH, on the model of DISTICH**]** ▸ **tris'tichic** *adj*

tristichous ('trɪstɪkəs) *adj* arranged in three rows, esp. (of plants) having three vertical rows of leaves.

tristimulus values (traɪ'stɪmjuləs) *pl n* three values that together are used to describe a colour and are the amounts of three reference colours that can be mixed to give the same visual sensation as the colour considered. Symbol: X, Y, Z. See also **chromaticity coordinates.**

trisulphide (traɪ'sʌlfaɪd) *n* any sulphide containing three sulphur atoms per molecule.

trisyllable (traɪ'sɪləbᵊl) *n* a word of three syllables. ▸ **trisyllabic** (ˌtraɪsɪ'læbɪk) *adj* ▸ **ˌtrisyl'labically** *adv*

tritanopia (ˌtraɪtə'nəupɪə, ˌtrɪt-) *n* a form of colour blindness in which there is a tendency to confuse blues and greens and in which sensitivity to blue is reduced. **[C19/20:** from New Latin, from Greek *tritos* third + New Latin *anopia* blindness; signifying that only two thirds of the spectrum can be distinguished**]** ▸ **tritanopic** (ˌtraɪtə'nɒpɪk, ˌtrɪt-) *adj*

trite (traɪt) *adj* **1** hackneyed; dull: *a trite comment.* **2** *Archaic.* frayed or worn out. **[C16:** from Latin *trītus* worn down, from *terere* to rub**]** ▸ **'tritely** *adv* ▸ **'triteness** *n*

tritheism ('traɪθɪˌɪzəm) *n Theol.* belief in three gods, esp. in the Trinity as consisting of three distinct gods. ▸ **'tritheist** *n, adj* ▸ **ˌtrithe'istic** *or* **ˌtrithe'istical** *adj*

tritiate ('trɪtɪˌeɪt) *vb* (*tr*) to replace normal hydrogen atoms in (a compound) by those of tritium. **[C20:** from TRITI(UM) + -ATE[1]**]** ▸ **ˌtriti'ation** *n*

triticale (ˌtrɪtɪ'kɑːlɪ) *n* a fertile hybrid cereal, a cross between wheat (*Triticum*) and rye (*Secale*), produced by polyploidy. **[C20:** from *Tritic(um)* + *(Sec)ale***]**

triticum ('trɪtɪkəm) *n* any annual cereal grass of the genus *Triticum,* which includes the wheats. **[C19:** Latin, literally: wheat, probably from *tritum,* supine of *terere* to grind**]**

tritium ('trɪtɪəm) *n* a radioactive isotope of hydrogen, occurring in trace amounts in natural hydrogen and produced in a nuclear reactor. Tritiated compounds are used as tracers. Symbol: T or ^{3}H; half-life: 12.5 years. **[C20:** New Latin, from Greek *tritos* third**]**

triton[1] ('traɪtᵊn) *n* any of various chiefly tropical marine gastropod molluscs of the genera *Charonia, Cymatium,* etc., having large beautifully-coloured spiral shells. **[C16:** via Latin from Greek *tritōn***]**

triton[2] ('traɪtɒn) *n Physics.* a nucleus of an atom of tritium, containing two neutrons and one proton. **[C20:** from TRIT(IUM) + -ON**]**

Triton[1] ('traɪtᵊn) *n Greek myth.* **1** a sea god, son of Poseidon and Amphitrite, depicted as having the upper parts of a man with a fish's tail and holding a trumpet made from a conch shell. **2** one of a class of minor sea deities.

Triton[2] ('traɪtᵊn) *n* the largest satellite of the planet Neptune. Diameter: 2700 km.

tritone ('traɪˌtəun) *n* a musical interval consisting of three whole tones; augmented fourth.

tritonia (traɪ'təunɪə) *n* any plant of the perennial cormous S. African genus *Tritonia,* with typically scarlet or orange flowers. The gardener's montbretia is a cross between *Tritonia* and the related *Crocosmia:* family *Iridaceae.* **[**New Latin, from Greek *Tritōn* TRITON[1]**]**

triturate ('trɪtjuˌreɪt) *vb* **1** (*tr*) to grind or rub into a fine powder or pulp; masticate. ◆ *n* **2** the powder or pulp resulting from this grinding. **[C17:** from Late Latin *trītūrāre* to thresh, from Latin *trītūra* a threshing, from *terere* to grind**]** ▸ **'triturable** *adj* ▸ **'trituˌrator** *n*

trituration (ˌtrɪtju'reɪʃən) *n* **1** the act of triturating or the state of being triturated. **2** *Pharmacol.* a mixture of one or more finely ground powdered drugs.

triumph ('traɪəmf) *n* **1** the feeling of exultation and happiness derived from a victory or major achievement. **2** the act or condition of being victorious; victory. **3** (in ancient Rome) a ritual procession to the Capitoline Hill held in honour of a victorious general. **4** *Obsolete.* a public display or celebration. **5** *Cards.* an obsolete word for **trump**[1]. ◆ *vb* (*intr*) **6** (often foll. by *over*) to win a victory or control: *to triumph over one's weaknesses.* **7** to rejoice over a victory. **8** to celebrate a Roman triumph. **[C14:** from Old French *triumphe,* from Latin *triumphus,* from Old Latin *triumpus;* probably related to Greek *thriambos* Bacchic hymn**]** ▸ **'triumpher** *n*

triumphal (traɪ'ʌmfəl) *adj* **1** celebrating a triumph: *a triumphal procession.* **2** resembling triumph.

triumphal arch *n* an arch built to commemorate a victory.

triumphalism (traɪ'ʌmfəlɪzəm) *n* excessive celebration of the defeat of one's enemies or opponents. ▸ **tri'umphalist** *adj*

triumphant (traɪ'ʌmfənt) *adj* **1** experiencing or displaying triumph. **2** exultant through triumph. **3** *Obsolete.* **3a** magnificent. **3b** triumphal. ▸ **tri'umphantly** *adv*

triumvir (traɪ'ʌmvə) *n, pl* **-virs** *or* **-viri** (-vɪˌriː). (esp. in ancient Rome) a member of a triumvirate. **[C16:** from Latin: one of three administrators, from *trium virōrum* of three men, from *trēs* three + *vir* man**]** ▸ **tri'umviral** *adj*

triumvirate (traɪ'ʌmvɪrɪt) *n* **1** (in ancient Rome) **1a** a board of three officials jointly responsible for some task. **1b** the political alliance of Caesar, Crassus, and Pompey, formed in 60 B.C. (**First Triumvirate**). **1c** the coalition and joint rule of the Roman Empire by Antony, Lepidus, and Octavian, begun in 43 B.C.

(**Second Triumvirate**). **2** any joint rule by three men. **3** any group of three men associated in some way. **4** the office of a triumvir.

triune ('traɪjuːn) *adj* **1** constituting three in one, esp. the three persons in one God of the Trinity. ◆ *n* **2** a group of three. **3** (*often cap.*) another word for **Trinity.** [C17: TRI- + *-une,* from Latin *ūnus* one] ▸ **tri'unity** *n*

Triunitarian (traɪˌjuːnɪ'tɛərɪən) *n, adj* a less common word for **Trinitarian.**

trivalent (traɪ'veɪlənt, 'trɪvələnt) *adj Chem.* **1** having a valency of three. **2** having three valencies. ◆ Also: **tervalent.** ▸ **tri'valency** *n*

Trivandrum (trɪ'vændrəm) *n* a city in S India, capital of Kerala, on the Malabar Coast: made capital of the kingdom of Travancore in 1745; University of Kerala (1937). Pop.: 524 006 (1991). Official name: **Thiruvananthapuram.**

trivet ('trɪvɪt) *n* **1** a stand, usually three-legged and metal, on which cooking vessels are placed over a fire. **2** a short metal stand on which hot dishes are placed on a table. **3 as right as a trivet.** *Old-fashioned.* in perfect health. [Old English *trefet* (influenced by Old English *thrifēte* having three feet), from Latin *tripēs* having three feet]

trivia ('trɪvɪə) *n* (*functioning as sing or pl*) petty details or considerations; trifles; trivialities. [from New Latin, plural of Latin *trivium* junction of three roads; for meaning, see TRIVIAL]

trivial ('trɪvɪəl) *adj* **1** of little importance; petty or frivolous: *trivial complaints.* **2** ordinary or commonplace; trite: *trivial conversation.* **3** *Maths.* (of the solutions of a set of homogeneous equations) having zero values for all the variables. **4** *Biology.* denoting the specific name of an organism in binomial nomenclature. **5** *Biology, chemistry.* denoting the popular name of an organism or substance, as opposed to the scientific one. **6** of or relating to the trivium. [C15: from Latin *triviālis* belonging to the public streets, common, from *trivium* crossroads, junction of three roads, from TRI- + *via* road] ▸ **'trivially** *adv* ▸ **'trivialness** *n*

triviality (ˌtrɪvɪ'ælɪtɪ) *n, pl* **-ties. 1** the state or quality of being trivial. **2** something, such as a remark, that is trivial. ◆ Also called: **trivialism** ('trɪvɪəˌlɪzəm).

trivialize *or* **trivialise** ('trɪvɪəˌlaɪz) *vb* (*tr*) to cause to seem trivial or more trivial; minimize: *he trivialized his injuries.* ▸ **ˌtriviali'zation** *or* **ˌtriviali'sation** *n*

trivium ('trɪvɪəm) *n, pl* **-ia** (-ɪə). (in medieval learning) the lower division of the seven liberal arts, consisting of grammar, rhetoric, and logic. Compare **quadrivium.** [C19: from Medieval Latin, from Latin: crossroads; see TRIVIAL]

triweekly (traɪ'wiːklɪ) *adj, adv* **1** every three weeks. **2** three times a week. ◆ *n, pl* **-lies. 3** a triweekly publication.

-trix *suffix forming nouns.* indicating a feminine agent, corresponding to nouns ending in *-tor: executrix.* [from Latin]

t-RNA *abbrev. for* **transfer RNA.**

Troas ('trəuæs) *n* the region of NW Asia Minor surrounding the ancient city of Troy. Also called: **the Troad** ('trəuæd).

troat (trəut) *vb* (*intr*) (of a rutting buck) to call or bellow. [C17: probably related to Old French *trout, trut,* a cry used by hunters to urge on the dogs]

Trobriand Islands ('trəubrɪˌænd) *pl n* a group of coral islands in the Solomon Sea, north of the E part of New Guinea: part of Papua New Guinea. Area: about 440 sq. km (170 sq. miles). ▸ **Trobriand Islander** *n*

trocar ('trəukɑː) *n* a surgical instrument for removing fluid from bodily cavities, consisting of a puncturing device situated inside a tube. [C18: from French *trocart* literally: with three sides, from *trois* three + *carre* side]

trochaic (trəu'keɪɪk) *Prosody.* ◆ *adj* **1** of, relating to, or consisting of trochees. ◆ *n* **2** another word for **trochee. 3** a verse composed of trochees. ▸ **tro'chaically** *adv*

trochal ('trəuk^{ə}l) *adj Zoology.* shaped like a wheel: *the trochal disc of a rotifer.* [C19: from Greek *trokhos* wheel]

trochanter (trəu'kæntə) *n* **1** any of several processes on the upper part of the vertebrate femur, to which muscles are attached. **2** the third segment of an insect's leg. [C17: via French from Greek *trokhantēr,* from *trekhein* to run]

troche (trəuʃ) *n Med.* another name for **lozenge** (sense 1). [C16: from French *trochisque,* from Late Latin *trochiscus,* from Greek *trokhiskos* little wheel, from *trokhos* wheel]

trochee ('trəukiː) *n Prosody.* a metrical foot of two syllables, the first long and the second short (¯˘). Compare **iamb.** [C16: via Latin from Greek *trokhaios pous,* literally: a running foot, from *trekhein* to run]

trochelminth ('trɒk^{ə}lˌmɪnθ) *n* any invertebrate of the former taxonomic group *Trochelminthes,* which included the rotifers and gastrotrichs, now classed as separate phyla. [C19: from New Latin *trochelminthes,* from Greek *trokhos* wheel, from *trekhein* to run + HELMINTH]

trochilus ('trɒkɪləs) *n, pl* **-li** (-ˌlaɪ). **1** another name for **hummingbird. 2** any of several Old World warblers, esp. *Phylloscopus trochilus* (willow warbler). [C16: via Latin from Greek *trokhilos* name of a small Egyptian bird said by ancient writers to pick the teeth of crocodiles, from *trekhein* to run]

trochlea ('trɒklɪə) *n, pl* **-leae** (-lɪˌiː). any bony or cartilaginous part with a grooved surface over which a bone, tendon, etc., may slide or articulate. [C17: from Latin, from Greek *trokhileia* a sheaf of pulleys; related to *trokhos* wheel, *trekhein* to run]

trochlear ('trɒklɪə) *adj* **1** of or relating to a trochlea or trochlear nerve. **2** *Botany.* shaped like a pulley. ◆ *n* **3** See **trochlear nerve.**

trochlear nerve *n* either one of the fourth pair of cranial nerves, which supply the superior oblique muscle of the eye.

trochoid ('trəukɔɪd) *n* **1** the curve described by a fixed point on the radius or extended radius of a circle as the circle rolls along a straight line. ◆ *adj also* **trochoidal. 2** rotating or capable of rotating about a central axis. **3** *Anatomy.* (of a structure or part) resembling or functioning as a pivot or pulley. [C18: from Greek *trokhoeidēs* circular, from *trokhos* wheel] ▸ **tro'choidally** *adv*

trochophore ('trɒkəˌfɔː) *or* **trochosphere** ('trɒkəsˌfɪə) *n* the ciliated planktonic larva of many invertebrates, including polychaete worms, molluscs, and rotifers. [C19: from Greek *trokhos* wheel + -PHORE]

trod (trɒd) *vb* the past tense and a past participle of **tread.**

trodden ('trɒd^{ə}n) *vb* a past participle of **tread.**

trode (trəud) *vb Archaic.* a past tense of **tread.**

trog (trɒg) *vb* **trogs, trogging, trogged.** (*intr;* often foll. by *along*) *Brit. informal.* to walk, esp. aimlessly or heavily; stroll. [C20: perhaps a blend of TRUDGE and SLOG]

troglodyte ('trɒgləˌdaɪt) *n* **1** a cave dweller, esp. one of the prehistoric peoples thought to have lived in caves. **2** *Informal.* a person who lives alone and appears eccentric. [C16: via Latin from Greek *trōglodutēs* one who enters caves, from *trōglē* hole + *duein* to enter] ▸ **troglodytic** (ˌtrɒglə'dɪtɪk) *or* **ˌtroglo'dytical** *adj*

trogon ('trəugɒn) *n* any bird of the order *Trogoniformes* of tropical and subtropical regions of America, Africa, and Asia. They have a brilliant plumage, short hooked bill, and long tail. See also **quetzal.** [C18: from New Latin, from Greek *trōgōn,* from *trōgein* to gnaw]

troika ('trɔɪkə) *n* **1** a Russian vehicle drawn by three horses abreast. **2** three horses harnessed abreast. **3** a triumvirate. [C19: from Russian, from *troe* three]

troilism ('trɔɪlɪzəm) *n* sexual activity involving three people. [C20: perhaps from French *trois* three (compare MÉNAGE À TROIS) + *-l-,* as in DUALISM] ▸ **'troilist** *adj*

Troilus ('trɔɪləs, 'trəuɪləs) *n Greek myth.* the youngest son of King Priam and Queen Hecuba, slain at Troy. In medieval romance he is portrayed as the lover of Cressida.

Trois Rivières (*French* trwɑ rivjɛr) *n* a port in central Canada, in Quebec on the St Lawrence River: one of the world's largest centres of newsprint production. Pop.: 49 426 (1991), with a metropolitan area of 136 300 (1991). English name: **Three Rivers.**

Trojan ('trəudʒən) *n* **1** a native or inhabitant of ancient Troy. **2** a person who is hard-working and determined. ◆ *adj* **3** of or relating to ancient Troy or its inhabitants.

Trojan asteroid *n* one of a number of asteroids that have the same mean motion and orbit as Jupiter, preceding or following the planet by a longitude of 60°.

Trojan Horse *n* **1** Also called: the **Wooden Horse.** *Greek myth.* the huge wooden hollow figure of a horse left outside Troy by the Greeks when they feigned retreat and dragged inside by the Trojans. The men concealed inside it opened the city to the final Greek assault. **2** a trap intended to undermine an enemy. **3** *Computing.* a bug inserted into a program or system designed to be activated after a certain time or a certain number of operations.

Trojan War *n Greek myth.* a war fought by the Greeks against the Trojans to avenge the abduction of Helen from her Greek husband Menelaus by Paris, son of the Trojan king. It lasted ten years and ended in the sack of Troy.

troll[1] (trəul) *vb* **1** *Angling.* **1a** to draw (a baited line, etc.) through the water, often from a boat. **1b** to fish (a stretch of water) by trolling. **1c** to fish (for) by trolling. **2** to roll or cause to roll. **3** *Archaic.* to sing (a refrain, chorus, etc.) or (of a refrain, etc.) to be sung in a loud hearty voice. **4** (*intr*) *Brit. informal.* to walk or stroll. **5** (*intr*) *Homosexual slang.* to stroll around looking for sexual partners; cruise. ◆ *n* **6** the act or an instance of trolling. **7** *Angling.* a bait or lure used in trolling, such as a spinner. [C14: from Old French *troller* to run about; related to Middle High German *trollen* to run with short steps] ▸ **'troller** *n*

troll[2] (trəul) *n* (in Scandinavian folklore) one of a class of supernatural creatures that dwell in caves or mountains and are depicted either as dwarfs or as giants. [C19: from Old Norse: demon; related to Danish *trold*]

trolley ('trɒlɪ) *n* **1** *Brit.* a small table on casters used for conveying food, drink, etc. **2** *Brit.* a wheeled cart or stand pushed by hand and used for moving heavy items, such as shopping in a supermarket or luggage at a railway station. **3** *Brit.* (in a hospital) a bed mounted on casters and used for moving patients who are unconscious, immobilized, etc. **4** *Brit.* See **trolley-bus. 5** *U.S. and Canadian.* See **trolley car. 6** a device that collects the current from an overhead wire (**trolley wire**), third rail, etc., to drive the motor of an electric vehicle. **7** a pulley or truck that travels along an overhead wire in order to support a suspended load. **8** *Chiefly Brit.* a low truck running on rails, used in factories, mines, etc., and on railways. **9** a truck, cage, or basket suspended from an overhead track or cable for carrying loads in a mine, quarry, etc. **10 off one's trolley.** *Slang.* **10a** mentally confused or disorganized. **10b** insane. [C19: probably from TROLL[1]]

trolleybus ('trɒlɪˌbʌs) *n* an electrically driven public-transport vehicle that does not run on rails but takes its power from an overhead wire through a trolley.

trolley car *n* a U.S. and Canadian name for **tram**[1] (sense 1).

trollius ('trɒlɪəs) *n* See **globeflower.** [New Latin, from German *Trollblume* globeflower]

trollop ('trɒləp) *n* **1** a promiscuous woman, esp. a prostitute. **2** an untidy woman; slattern. [C17: perhaps from German dialect *Trolle* prostitute; perhaps related to TRULL] ▸ **'trollopy** *adj*

Trollope ('trɒləp) *n* **1 Anthony.** 1815–82, English novelist. His most successful novels, such as *The Warden* (1855), *Barchester Towers* (1857), and *Dr Thorne* (1858), are those in the Barsetshire series of studies of English provincial life. The Palliser series of political novels includes *Phineas Redux* (1874) and *The Prime Minister* (1876). **2 Joanna.** born 1943, British novelist: her works include *The Choir* (1988), *A Village Affair* (1989), *The Rector's Wife* (1991), *The Best of Friends* (1995), and *Next of Kin* (1996).

tromba marina ('trɒmbə mə'riːnə) *n* an obsolete viol with a long thin body and a single string. It resembled the natural trumpet in its range of notes (limited to harmonics) and its tone. [from Italian, literally: marine trumpet]

trombidiasis (ˌtrɒmbɪˈdaɪəsɪs) *n Pathol.* infestation with mites of the family *Trombiculidae.* [C20: New Latin, from *Trombid(ium)* genus name + -IASIS]

trombone (trɒmˈbəʊn) *n* **1** a brass instrument, a low-pitched counterpart of the trumpet, consisting of a tube the effective length of which is varied by means of a U-shaped slide. The usual forms of this instrument are the **tenor trombone** (range: about two and a half octaves upwards from E) and the **bass trombone** (pitched a fourth lower). **2** a person who plays this instrument in an orchestra. [C18: from Italian, from *tromba* a trumpet, from Old High German *trumba*] ▸ **tromˈbonist** *n*

trommel (ˈtrɒməl) *n* a revolving cylindrical sieve used to screen crushed ore. [C19: from German: a drum]

Tromp (*Dutch* tromp) *n* **1 Cornelis** (**Martenszoon**) (korˈneːlɪs). 1629–91, Dutch admiral, who fought during the 2nd and 3rd Anglo-Dutch Wars. **2** his father, **Maarten** (**Harpertszoon**) (ˈmartən). 1598–1653, Dutch admiral, who fought in the 1st Anglo-Dutch War: killed in action.

trompe (trɒmp) *n* an apparatus for supplying the blast of air in a forge, consisting of a thin column down which water falls, drawing in air through side openings. [C19: from French, literally: trumpet]

trompe l'oeil (*French* trɔ̃p lœj) *n, pl* **trompe l'oeils** (trɔ̃p lœj). **1** a painting or decoration giving a convincing illusion of reality. **2** an effect of this kind. [from French, literally: deception of the eye]

Tromsø (ˈtrɒmsəʊ; *Norwegian* ˈtrumsø) *n* a port in N Norway, on a small island between Kvaløy and the mainland: fishing and sealing centre. Pop.: 51 218 (1990).

tron (trɒn) *n* **1** a public weighing machine. **2** the place where a tron is set up; marketplace. [C15: from Old French *trone,* from Latin *trutina,* from Greek *trutanē* balance, set of scales]

-tron *suffix forming nouns.* **1** indicating a vacuum tube: *magnetron.* **2** indicating an instrument for accelerating atomic or subatomic particles: *synchrotron.* [from Greek, suffix indicating instrument]

trona (ˈtrəʊnə) *n* a greyish mineral that consists of hydrated sodium carbonate and occurs in salt deposits. Formula: $Na_2CO_3NaHCO_3.2H_2O$. [C18: from Swedish, probably from Arabic *natrūn* NATRON]

tronc (trɒŋk) *n* a pool into which waiters, waitresses, hotel workers, etc., pay their tips and into which some managements pay service charges for later distribution to staff by a **tronc master**, according to agreed percentages. [C20: from French: collecting box]

Trondheim (ˈtrɒndˌhaɪm; *Norwegian* ˈtrɔnheim) *n* a port in central Norway, on **Trondheim Fjord** (an inlet of the Norwegian Sea): national capital until 1380; seat of the Technical University of Norway. Pop.: 143 746 (1996). Former name (until the 16th century and from 1930 to 1931): **Nidaros.**

tronk (trɒŋk) *n S. African informal.* jail. [Afrikaans]

troop (truːp) *n* **1** a large group or assembly; flock: *a troop of children.* **2** a subdivision of a cavalry squadron or artillery battery of about platoon size. **3** (*pl*) armed forces; soldiers. **4** a large group of Scouts comprising several patrols. **5** an archaic spelling of **troupe.** ◆ *vb* **6** (*intr*) to gather, move, or march in or as if in a crowd. **7** (*tr*) *Military, chiefly Brit.* to parade (the colour or flag) ceremonially: *trooping the colour.* **8** (*tr*) *Brit. military slang.* (formerly) to report (a serviceman) for a breach of discipline. **9** (*intr*) an archaic word for **consort** (sense 1). [C16: from French *troupe,* from *troupeau* flock, of Germanic origin]

troop carrier *n* a vehicle, aircraft, or ship designed for the carriage of troops.

trooper (ˈtruːpə) *n* **1** a soldier in a cavalry regiment. **2** *U.S. and Austral.* a mounted policeman. **3** *U.S.* a state policeman. **4** a cavalry horse. **5** *Informal, chiefly Brit.* a troopship.

troopship (ˈtruːpˌʃɪp) *n* a ship, usually a converted merchant ship, used to transport military personnel.

troostite (ˈtruːstaɪt) *n* a reddish or greyish mineral that is a variety of willemite in which some of the zinc is replaced by manganese. [C19: named after Gerard *Troost* (died 1850), U.S. geologist]

trop. *abbrev. for* tropic(al).

tropaeolin (trəʊˈpiːəlɪn) *n* any of certain yellow and orange azo dyes of complex structure. [C19: see TROPAEOLUM, -IN]

tropaeolum (trəʊˈpiːələm) *n, pl* **-lums** *or* **-la** (-lə). any garden plant of the genus *Tropaeolum,* esp. the nasturtium. [C18: from New Latin, from Latin *tropaeum* TROPHY; referring to the shield-shaped leaves and helmet-shaped flowers]

trope (trəʊp) *n* **1** *Rhetoric.* a word or expression used in a figurative sense. **2** an interpolation of words or music into the plainsong settings of the Roman Catholic liturgy. [C16: from Latin *tropus* figurative use of a word, from Greek *tropos* style, turn; related to *trepein* to turn]

-trope *n combining form.* indicating a turning towards, development in the direction of, or affinity to: *heliotrope.* [from Greek *tropos* a turn]

trophallaxis (ˌtrɒfəˈlæksɪs) *n* the exchange of regurgitated food that occurs between adults and larvae in colonies of social insects. [C19/20: from New Latin, from TROPHO- + Greek *allaxis* exchange, from *allassein* to change, from *allos* other] ▸ ˌ**trophalˈlactic** *adj*

trophic (ˈtrɒfɪk) *adj* of or relating to nutrition: *the trophic levels of a food chain.* [C19: from Greek *trophikos,* from *trophē* food, from *trephein* to feed] ▸ ˈ**trophically** *adv*

tropho- *or before a vowel* **troph-** *combining form.* indicating nourishment or nutrition: *trophozoite.* [from Greek *trophē* food, from *trephein* to feed]

trophoblast (ˈtrɒfəˌblæst) *n* a membrane that encloses the embryo of placental mammals, becoming attached to the uterus wall and absorbing nourishment from the uterine fluids. [C19: from TROPHO- + -BLAST] ▸ ˌ**trophoˈblastic** *adj*

trophoplasm (ˈtrɒfəˌplæzəm) *n Biology.* the cytoplasm that is involved in the nutritive processes of a cell.

trophozoite (ˌtrɒfəˈzəʊaɪt) *n* the form of a sporozoan protozoan in the feeding stage. In the malaria parasite this stage occurs in the human red blood cell. Compare **merozoite.**

trophy (ˈtrəʊfɪ) *n, pl* **-phies. 1** an object such as a silver or gold cup that is symbolic of victory in a contest, esp. a sporting contest; prize. **2** a memento of success, esp. one taken in war or hunting. **3** (in ancient Greece and Rome) **3a** a memorial to a victory, usually consisting of captured arms raised on the battlefield or in a public place. **3b** a representation of such a memorial. **4** an ornamental carving that represents a group of weapons, etc. **5** (*modifier*) *Informal.* highly desirable and regarded as a symbol of wealth or success: *a trophy wife.* [C16: from French *trophée,* from Latin *tropaeum,* from Greek *tropaion,* from *tropē* a turning, defeat of the enemy; related to Greek *trepein* to turn]

-trophy *n combining form.* indicating a certain type of nourishment or growth: *dystrophy.* [from Greek *-trophia,* from *trophē* nourishment] ▸ **-trophic** *adj combining form.*

tropic (ˈtrɒpɪk) *n* **1** (*sometimes cap.*) either of the parallel lines of latitude at about 23½°N (**tropic of Cancer**) and 23½°S (**tropic of Capricorn**) of the equator. **2 the tropics.** (*often cap.*) that part of the earth's surface between the tropics of Cancer and Capricorn; the Torrid Zone. **3** *Astronomy.* either of the two parallel circles on the celestial sphere having the same latitudes and names as the corresponding lines on the earth. ◆ *adj* **4** a less common word for **tropical.** [C14: from Late Latin *tropicus* belonging to a turn, from Greek *tropikos,* from *tropos* a turn; from the ancient belief that the sun turned back at the solstices]

-tropic *adj combining form.* turning or developing in response to a certain stimulus: *heliotropic.* [from Greek *tropos* a turn; see TROPE]

tropical (ˈtrɒpɪkᵊl) *adj* **1** situated in, used in, characteristic of, or relating to the tropics. **2** (of weather) very hot, esp. when humid. **3** *Rhetoric.* of or relating to a trope. ▸ ˌ**tropiˈcality** *n* ▸ ˈ**tropically** *adv*

tropicalize *or* **tropicalise** (ˈtrɒpɪkᵊˌlaɪz) *vb* (*tr*) to adapt to tropical use, temperatures, etc. ▸ ˌ**tropicaliˈzation** *or* ˌ**tropicaliˈsation** *n*

tropical year *n* another name for **solar year.** See **year** (sense 4).

tropicbird (ˈtrɒpɪkˌbɜːd) *n* any aquatic bird of the tropical family *Phaethontidae,* having long slender tail feathers and a white plumage with black markings: order *Pelecaniformes* (pelicans, cormorants, etc.). [C17: so called because it is found in the tropical regions]

tropine (ˈtrəʊpiːn, -pɪn) *n* a white crystalline poisonous hygroscopic alkaloid obtained by heating atropine or hyoscyamine with barium hydroxide. Formula: $C_8H_{15}NO$. [C19: shortened from ATROPINE]

tropism (ˈtrəʊpɪzəm) *n* the response of an organism, esp. a plant, to an external stimulus by growth in a direction determined by the stimulus. [from Greek *tropos* a turn] ▸ ˌ**tropisˈmatic** *adj* ▸ **tropistic** (trəʊˈpɪstɪk) *adj*

-tropism *or* **-tropy** *n combining form.* indicating a tendency to turn or develop in response to a certain stimulus: *phototropism.* [from Greek *tropos* a turn]

tropo- *combining form.* indicating change or a turning: *tropophyte.* [from Greek *tropos* a turn]

tropology (trɒˈpɒlədʒɪ) *n, pl* **-gies. 1** *Rhetoric.* the use of figurative language in speech or writing. **2** *Christian theol.* the educing of moral or figurative meanings from the Scriptures. **3** a treatise on tropes or figures of speech. [C16: via Late Latin from Greek *tropalogia;* see TROPE, -LOGY] ▸ ˌ**tropoˈlogic** *or* ˌ**tropoˈlogical** *adj*

tropopause (ˈtrɒpəˌpɔːz) *n Meteorol.* the plane of discontinuity between the troposphere and the stratosphere, characterized by a sharp change in the lapse rate and varying in altitude from about 18 kilometres (11 miles) above the equator to 6 km (4 miles) at the Poles.

tropophilous (trɒˈpɒfɪləs) *adj* (of plants) able to adapt to seasonal changes in temperature, rainfall, etc.

tropophyte (ˈtrɒpəˌfaɪt) *n* a plant that is able to adapt to seasonal changes in temperature, rainfall, etc. ▸ **tropophytic** (ˌtrɒpəˈfɪtɪk) *adj*

troposphere (ˈtrɒpəˌsfɪə) *n* the lowest atmospheric layer, about 18 kilometres (11 miles) thick at the equator to about 6 km (4 miles) at the Poles, in which air temperature decreases normally with height at about 6.5°C per km. Most meteorological phenomena occur in this layer. ▸ ˌ**tropoˈspheric** *adj*

-tropous *adj combining form.* indicating a turning away: *anatropous.* [from Greek *-tropos* concerning a turn]

troppo[1] (ˈtrɒpəʊ) *adv Music.* too much; excessively. See **non troppo.** [Italian]

troppo[2] (ˈtrɒpəʊ) *adj Austral. slang.* mentally affected by a tropical climate.

Trossachs (ˈtrɒsəks) *n* (*functioning as pl or sing*) **the. 1** a narrow wooded valley in central Scotland, between Loch Achray and Loch Katrine: made famous by Sir Walter Scott's descriptions. **2** (popularly) the area extending northwards from Loch Ard and Aberfoyle to Lochs Katrine, Achray, and Venachar.

trot (trɒt) *vb* **trots, trotting, trotted. 1** to move or cause to move at a trot. **2** *Angling.* to fish (a fast-moving stream or river) by using a float and weighted line that carries the baited hook just above the bottom. ◆ *n* **3** a gait of a horse or other quadruped, faster than a walk, in which diagonally opposite legs come down together. See also **jog trot, rising trot, sitting trot. 4** a steady brisk pace. **5** (in harness racing) a race for horses that have been trained to trot fast. **6** *Angling.* **6a** one of the short lines attached to a trotline. **6b** the trotline. **7** *Austral. and N.Z. informal.* a run of luck: *a good trot.* **8** *Chiefly Brit.* a small child; tot. **9** *U.S. slang.* a student's crib. **10 on the trot.** *Informal.* **10a** one after the other: *to read two books on the trot.* **10b** busy, esp. on one's feet. **11 the trots.** *Informal.* **11a** diarrhoea. **11b** *N.Z.* trotting races. [C13: from Old French *trot,* from *troter* to trot, of Germanic origin; related to Middle High German *trotten* to run]

Trot (trɒt) *n Informal.* a follower of Trotsky; Trotskyist.

troth (trəʊθ) *n Archaic.* **1** a pledge or oath of fidelity, esp. a betrothal. **2** truth (esp. in the phrase **in troth**). 3 loyalty; fidelity. [Old English *trēowth;* related to Old High German *gitriuwida* loyalty; see TRUTH]

trothplight ('trəuθ,plaɪt) *Archaic.* ◆ *n* 1 a betrothal. ◆ *vb* 2 (*tr*) to betroth. ◆ *adj* 3 betrothed; engaged. [C14: from TROTH + PLIGHT[2]]

trotline ('trɒt,laɪn) *n Angling.* a long line suspended across a stream, river, etc., to which shorter hooked and baited lines are attached. Compare **trawl** (sense 2). See also **setline.**

trot out *vb* (*tr, adv*) *Informal.* to bring forward, as for approbation or admiration, esp. repeatedly: *he trots out the same excuses every time.*

Trotsky *or* **Trotski** ('trɒtskɪ) *n* **Leon,** original name *Lev Davidovich Bronstein.* 1879–1940, Russian revolutionary and Communist theorist. He was a leader of the November Revolution (1917) and, as commissar of foreign affairs and war (1917–24), largely created the Red Army. He was ousted by Stalin after Lenin's death and deported from Russia (1929); assassinated by a Stalinist agent.

Trotskyism ('trɒtskɪ,ɪzəm) *n* Trotsky's theory of communism, in which he called for immediate worldwide revolution by the proletariat. ▸ **'Trotskyist** *or* **'Trotskyite** *n, adj*

Trotskyist International *n* any of several international Trotskyist organizations that have developed from the international federation of anti-Stalinist Communists founded by Trotsky in 1936.

trotter ('trɒtə) *n* 1 a person or animal that trots, esp. a horse that is specially trained to trot fast. 2 (*usually pl*) the foot of certain animals, esp. of pigs.

trotting race *n* the N.Z. term for **harness race.**

trotyl ('trəutɪl, -ti:l) *n* another name for **TNT.** [C20: from (TRINI)TROT(OLUENE) + -YL]

troubadour ('tru:bə,duə) *n* 1 any of a class of lyric poets who flourished principally in Provence and N Italy from the 11th to the 13th centuries, writing chiefly on courtly love in complex metric form. 2 a singer. [C18: from French, from Old Provençal *trobador,* from *trobar* to write verses, perhaps ultimately from Latin *tropus* TROPE]

trouble ('trʌbᵊl) *n* 1 a state or condition of mental distress or anxiety. 2 a state or condition of disorder or unrest: *industrial trouble.* 3 a condition of disease, pain, or malfunctioning: *she has liver trouble.* 4 a cause of distress, disturbance, or pain; problem: *what is the trouble?* 5 effort or exertion taken to do something: *he took a lot of trouble over this design.* 6 liability to suffer punishment or misfortune (esp. in the phrase **be in trouble**): *he's in trouble with the police.* 7 a personal quality that is regarded as a weakness, handicap, or cause of annoyance: *his trouble is that he's too soft.* 8 (*pl*) 8a political unrest or public disturbances. 8b **the Troubles.** political violence in Ireland during the 1920s or in Northern Ireland since the late 1960s. 9 the condition of an unmarried girl who becomes pregnant (esp. in the phrase **in trouble**). ◆ *vb* 10 (*tr*) to cause trouble to; upset, pain, or worry. 11 (*intr;* usually with a negative and foll. by *about*) to put oneself to inconvenience; be concerned: *don't trouble about me.* 12 (*intr;* usually with a negative) to take pains; exert oneself: *please don't trouble to write everything down.* 13 (*tr*) to cause inconvenience or discomfort to: *does this noise trouble you?* 14 (*tr; usually passive*) to agitate or make rough: *the seas were troubled.* 15 (*tr*) *Caribbean.* to interfere with: *he wouldn't like anyone to trouble his new bicycle.* [C13: from Old French *troubler,* from Vulgar Latin *turbulāre* (unattested), from Late Latin *turbidāre,* from *turbidus* confused, from *turba* commotion] ▸ **'troubled** *adj* ▸ **'troubler** *n*

troublemaker ('trʌbᵊl,meɪkə) *n* a person who makes trouble, esp. between people. ▸ **'trouble,making** *adj, n*

troubleshooter ('trʌbᵊl,ʃu:tə) *n* a person who locates the cause of trouble and removes or treats it. ▸ **'trouble,shooting** *n, adj*

troublesome ('trʌbᵊlsəm) *adj* 1 causing a great deal of trouble; worrying, upsetting, or annoying. 2 characterized by violence; turbulent. ▸ **'troublesomely** *adv* ▸ **'troublesomeness** *n*

trouble spot *n* a place of recurring trouble, esp. of political unrest.

troublous ('trʌbləs) *adj Archaic or literary.* unsettled; agitated. ▸ **'troublously** *adv* ▸ **'troublousness** *n*

trou-de-loup (,tru:dᵊ'lu:) *n, pl* **trous-de-loup** (,tru:dᵊ'lu:). *Military.* any of a series of conical-shaped pits with a stake fixed in the centre, formerly used as protection against enemy cavalry. [C18: from French, literally: wolf's hole]

trough (trɒf) *n* 1 a narrow open container, esp. one in which food or water for animals is put. 2 a narrow channel, gutter, or gulley. 3 a narrow depression either in the land surface, ocean bed, or between two successive waves. 4 *Meteorol.* an elongated area of low pressure, esp. an extension of a depression. Compare **ridge** (sense 6). 5 a single or temporary low point; depression. 6 *Physics.* the portion of a wave, such as a light wave, in which the amplitude lies below its average value. 7 *Economics.* the lowest point or most depressed stage of the trade cycle. [Old English *trōh;* related to Old Saxon, Old Norse *trog* trough, Dutch *trügge* ladle] ▸ **'trough,like** *adj*

trounce (trauns) *vb* (*tr*) to beat or defeat utterly; thrash. [C16: of unknown origin]

troupe (tru:p) *n* 1 a company of actors or other performers, esp. one that travels. ◆ *vb* 2 (*intr*) (esp. of actors) to move or travel in a group. [C19: from French; see TROOP]

trouper ('tru:pə) *n* 1 a member of a troupe. 2 an experienced or dependable worker or associate.

troupial ('tru:pɪəl) *n* any of various American orioles of the genus *Icterus,* esp. *I. icterus,* a bright orange-and-black South American bird. [C19: from French *troupiale,* from *troupe* flock; referring to its gregarious habits]

trouse (trauz) *pl n Brit.* close-fitting breeches worn in Ireland. [from Irish and Scot. Gaelic *triubhas:* compare TREWS]

trouser ('trauzə) *n* (*modifier*) of or relating to trousers: *trouser buttons.*

trousers ('trauzəz) *pl n* 1 a garment shaped to cover the body from the waist to the ankles or knees with separate tube-shaped sections for both legs. 2 **wear the trousers.** *Brit. informal.* to have control, esp. in a marriage. U.S. equivalent: **wear the pants.** [C17: from earlier *trouse,* a variant of TREWS, influenced by DRAWERS] ▸ **'trousered** *adj* ▸ **'trouserless** *adj*

trouser suit *n Chiefly Brit.* a woman's suit of a jacket or top and trousers. Also called (esp. U.S. and Canadian): **pant suit.**

trousseau ('tru:səu) *n, pl* **-seaux** *or* **-seaus** (-səuz). the clothes, linen, etc., collected by a bride for her marriage. [C19: from Old French, literally: a little bundle, from *trusse* a bundle; see TRUSS]

trout (traut) *n, pl* **trout** *or* **trouts.** 1 any of various game fishes, esp. *Salmo trutta* and related species, mostly of fresh water in northern regions: family *Salmonidae* (salmon). They resemble salmon but are smaller and spotted. 2 any of various similar or related fishes, such as a sea trout. 3 *Brit. informal.* a person, esp. an unattractive woman. [Old English *trūht,* from Late Latin *tructa,* from Greek *troktēs* sharp-toothed fish]

trouvère (tru:'vɛə; *French* truvɛr) *or* **trouveur** (*French* truvœr) *n* any of a group of poets of N France during the 12th and 13th centuries who composed chiefly narrative works. [C19: from French, from Old French *troveor,* from *trover* to compose; related to TROUBADOUR]

trove (trəuv) *n* See **treasure-trove.**

trover ('trəuvə) *n Law.* (formerly) the act of wrongfully assuming proprietary rights over personal goods or property belonging to another. [C16: from Old French, from *trover* to find; see TROUVÈRE, TROUBADOUR]

trow (trəu) *vb Archaic.* to think, believe, or trust. [Old English *treow;* related to Old Frisian *triūwe,* Old Saxon *treuwa,* Old High German *triuwa;* see TROTH, TRUE]

Trowbridge ('trəu,brɪdʒ) *n* a market town in SW England, administrative centre of Wiltshire: woollen manufacturing. Pop.: 29 334 (1991).

trowel ('trauəl) *n* 1 any of various small hand tools having a flat metal blade attached to a handle, used for scooping or spreading plaster or similar materials. 2 a similar tool with a curved blade used by gardeners for lifting plants, etc. ◆ *vb* **-els, -elling, -elled** *or U.S.* **-els, -eling, -eled.** 3 (*tr*) to use a trowel on (plaster, soil, etc.). [C14: from Old French *truele,* from Latin *trulla* a scoop, from *trua* a stirring spoon] ▸ **'troweller** *or U.S.* **'troweler** *n*

Troy (trɔɪ) *n* any of nine ancient cities in NW Asia Minor, each of which was built on the ruins of its predecessor. The seventh was the site of the Trojan War (mid-13th century B.C.). Greek name: **Ilion.** Latin name: **Ilium.** Related adj: **Trojan.**

Troyes (*French* trwa) *n* an industrial city in NE France: became prosperous through its great fairs in the early Middle Ages. Pop.: 59 271 (1990).

troy weight *or* **troy** (trɔɪ) *n* a system of weights used for precious metals and gemstones, based on the grain, which is identical to the avoirdupois grain. 24 grains = 1 pennyweight; 20 pennyweights = 1 (troy) ounce; 12 ounces = 1 (troy) pound. [C14: named after the city of *Troyes,* France, where it was first used]

trs *Printing. abbrev. for* transpose.

Trst (trst) *n* the Slovene and Serbo-Croat name for **Trieste.**

truant ('tru:ənt) *n* 1 a person who is absent without leave, esp. from school. ◆ *adj* 2 being or relating to a truant. ◆ *vb* 3 (*intr*) to play truant. [C13: from Old French: vagabond, probably of Celtic origin; compare Welsh *truan* miserable, Old Irish *trōg* wretched] ▸ **'truancy** *n*

truce (tru:s) *n* 1 an agreement to stop fighting, esp. temporarily. 2 temporary cessation of something unpleasant. [C13: from the plural of Old English *treow* TROW; see TRUE, TRUST]

Trucial States ('tru:ʃəl) *pl n* a former name (until 1971) of the **United Arab Emirates.** Also called: **Trucial Sheikdoms, Trucial Oman, Trucial Coast.**

truck[1] (trʌk) *n* 1 *Brit.* a vehicle for carrying freight on a railway; wagon. 2 another name (esp. U.S., Canadian, and Austral.) for **lorry** (sense 1). 3 a frame carrying two or more pairs of wheels and usually springs and brakes, attached under an end of a railway coach, etc. 4 *Nautical.* 4a a disc-shaped block fixed to the head of a mast having sheave holes for receiving signal halyards. 4b the head of a mast itself. 5 any wheeled vehicle used to move goods. ◆ *vb* 6 to convey (goods) in a truck. 7 (*intr*) *Chiefly U.S. and Canadian.* to drive a truck. [C17: perhaps shortened from TRUCKLE[2]]

truck[2] (trʌk) *n* 1 commercial goods. 2 dealings (esp. in the phrase **have no truck with**). 3 commercial exchange. 4 *Archaic.* payment of wages in kind. 5 miscellaneous articles. 6 *Informal.* rubbish. 7 *U.S. and Canadian.* vegetables grown for market. ◆ *vb* 8 *Archaic.* to exchange (goods); barter. 9 (*intr*) to traffic or negotiate. [C13: from Old French *troquer* (unattested) to barter, equivalent to Medieval Latin *trocare,* of unknown origin]

truckage ('trʌkɪdʒ) *n U.S.* 1 conveyance of cargo by truck. 2 the charge for this.

trucker[1] ('trʌkə) *n Chiefly U.S. and Canadian.* 1 a lorry driver. 2 a person who arranges for the transport of goods by lorry.

trucker[2] ('trʌkə) *n U.S. and Canadian.* 1 a market gardener. 2 another word for **hawker**[1].

truck farm *n U.S. and Canadian.* a market garden. ▸ **truck farmer** *n* ▸ **truck farming** *n*

truckie ('trʌkɪ) *n Austral. informal.* a truck driver.

trucking[1] ('trʌkɪŋ) *n Chiefly U.S. and Canadian.* the transportation of goods by lorry.

trucking[2] ('trʌkɪŋ) *n* 1 the usual U.S. and Canadian term for **market gardening.** 2 commercial exchange; barter.

truckle[1] ('trʌkᵊl) *vb* (*intr;* usually foll. by *to*) to yield weakly; give in. [C17: from obsolete *truckle* to sleep in a truckle bed; see TRUCKLE[2]] ▸ **'truckler** *n*

truckle[2] ('trʌkᵊl) *n* 1 a small wheel; caster. 2 a small barrel-shaped cheese. ◆ *vb* 3 (*intr*) to roll on truckles. 4 (*tr*) to push (a piece of furniture) along on truckles. [C15 *trokel,* from Anglo-Norman *trocle,* from Latin *trochlea* sheaf of a pulley; see TROCHLEA]

truckle bed *n* a low bed on wheels, stored under a larger bed, used esp. formerly by a servant.

truckload ('trʌk,ləud) *n* the amount carried by a truck.

truck system *n* a system during the early years of the Industrial Revolution of forcing workers to accept payment of wages in kind, usually to the employer's advantage. [C19: from TRUCK[2]]

truculent ('trʌkjulənt) *adj* **1** defiantly aggressive, sullen, or obstreperous. **2** *Archaic.* savage, fierce, or harsh. [C16: from Latin *truculentus,* from *trux* fierce] ▸ **'truculence** *or* **'truculency** *n* ▸ **'truculently** *adv*

Trudeau (tru:'dəu) *n* **Pierre Elliott.** born 1919, Canadian statesman; Liberal prime minister (1968–79; 1980–84).

trudge (trʌdʒ) *vb* **1** (*intr*) to walk or plod heavily or wearily. **2** (*tr*) to pass through or over by trudging. ◆ *n* **3** a long tiring walk. [C16: of obscure origin] ▸ **'trudger** *n*

trudgen ('trʌdʒən) *n* a type of swimming stroke that uses overarm action, as in the crawl, and a scissors kick. [C19: named after John *Trudgen,* English swimmer, who introduced it]

true (tru:) *adj* **truer, truest. 1** not false, fictional, or illusory; factual or factually accurate; conforming with reality. **2** (*prenominal*) being of real or natural origin; genuine; not synthetic: *true leather.* **3a** unswervingly faithful and loyal to friends, a cause, etc.: *a true follower.* **3b** (*as collective n;* preceded by *the*): *the loyal and the true.* **4** faithful to a particular concept of truth, esp. of religious truth: *a true believer.* **5** conforming to a required standard, law, or pattern: *a true aim; a true fit.* **6** exactly in tune: *a true note.* **7** (of a compass bearing) according to the earth's geographical rather than magnetic poles: *true north.* **8** *Biology.* conforming to the typical structure of a designated type: *sphagnum moss is a true moss, Spanish moss is not.* **9** *Physics.* not apparent or relative; taking into account all complicating factors: *the true expansion of a liquid takes into account the expansion of the container.* Compare **apparent** (sense 3). **10 not true.** *Informal.* unbelievable; remarkable: *she's got so much money it's not true.* **11 true to life.** exactly comparable with reality. ◆ *n* **12** correct alignment (esp. in the phrases **in true, out of true**). ◆ *adv* **13** truthfully; rightly. **14** precisely or unswervingly: *he shot true.* **15** *Biology.* without variation from the ancestral type: *to breed true.* ◆ *vb* **trues, truing, trued. 16** (*tr*) to adjust so as to make true. [Old English *triewe;* related to Old Frisian *triūwe,* Old Saxon, Old High German *triuwi* loyal, Old Norse *tryggr;* see TROW, TRUST] ▸ **'trueness** *n*

true bill *n Criminal law.* (formerly in Britain; now only U.S.) the endorsement made on a bill of indictment by a grand jury certifying it to be supported by sufficient evidence to warrant committing the accused to trial.

true-blue *adj* **1** unwaveringly or staunchly loyal, esp. to a person, a cause, etc. ◆ *n* **true blue. 2** *Chiefly Brit.* a staunch royalist or Conservative.

true-born *adj* being such by birth: *a true-born Japanese.*

true level *n* a hypothetical surface that is perpendicular at every point to the plumb line, such as the mean sea level or geoid: *a still liquid surface is at true level.*

true-life *adj* directly comparable to reality: *a true-life romance.*

truelove ('tru:ˌlʌv) *n* **1** someone truly loved; sweetheart. **2** another name for **herb Paris.**

truelove knot *or* **true-lovers' knot** *n* a complicated bowknot that is hard to untie, symbolizing ties of love.

Trueman ('tru:mən) *n* **Freddy,** full name *Frederick Sewards Trueman.* born 1931, English cricketer, a fast bowler for Yorkshire and England.

true north *n* the direction from any point along a meridian towards the North Pole. Also called: **geographic north.** Compare **magnetic north.**

true rib *n* any of the upper seven pairs of ribs in man.

true time *n* the time shown by a sundial; solar time. When the sun is at the highest point in its daily path, the true time is exactly noon. Compare **mean time.**

Truffaut (*French* tryfo) *n* **François** (frɑ̃swa). 1932–84, French film director of the New Wave. His films include *Les Quatre cents coups* (1959), *Jules et Jim* (1961), *Baisers volés* (1968), and *Le Dernier Métro* (1980).

truffle ('trʌfᵊl) *n* **1** Also called: **earthnut.** any of various edible saprotrophic ascomycetous subterranean fungi of the European genus *Tuber.* They have a tuberous appearance and are regarded as a delicacy. **2** Also called: **rum truffle.** *Chiefly Brit.* a sweet resembling this fungus in shape, flavoured with chocolate or rum. [C16: from French *truffe,* from Old Provençal *trufa,* ultimately from Latin *tūber*]

trug (trʌg) *n Brit.* a long shallow basket made of curved strips of wood and used for carrying flowers, fruit, etc. [C16: perhaps dialect variant of TROUGH]

trugo ('tru:gəu) *n Austral.* a game similar to croquet, originally improvised in Victoria from the rubber discs used as buffers on railway carriages. [from *true go,* when the wheel is hit between the goalposts]

truism ('tru:ɪzəm) *n* an obvious truth; platitude. [C18: from TRUE + -ISM] ▸ **tru'istic** *adj*

Trujillo[1] (*Spanish* tru'xijo) *n* a city in NW Peru: founded 1535; university (1824); centre of a district producing rice and sugar cane. Pop.: 627 553 (1995).

Trujillo[2] (*Spanish* tru'xijo) *n* **Rafael (Léonidas)** (ˌrafa'el), original name *Rafael Léonidas Trujillo Molina.* 1891–1961, Dominican dictator, who governed the Dominican Republic (1930–61) with the help of a powerful police force: assassinated.

Truk Islands (trʌk) *pl n* a group of islands in the W Pacific, in the E Caroline Islands: administratively part of the U.S. Trust Territory of the Pacific Islands from 1947; became self-governing in 1979 as part of the Federated States of Micronesia; consists of 11 chief islands; a major Japanese naval base during World War II. Pop.: 52 870 (1994). Area: 130 sq. km (50 sq. miles).

trull (trʌl) *n Archaic.* a prostitute; harlot. [C16: from German *Trulle;* see TROLLOP]

truly ('tru:lɪ) *adv* **1** in a true, just, or faithful manner. **2** (intensifier): *a truly great man.* **3** indeed; really. ◆ See also **yours truly.**

Truman ('tru:mən) *n* **Harry S.** 1884–1972, U.S. Democratic statesman; 33rd president of the U.S. (1945–53). He approved the dropping of the two atomic bombs on Japan (1945), advocated the postwar loan to Britain, and involved the U.S. in the Korean War.

trumeau (tru'məu) *n, pl* **-meaux** (-məuz). *Architect.* a section of a wall or pillar between two openings. [from French]

trump[1] (trʌmp) *n* **1** Also called: **trump card. 1a** any card from the suit chosen as trumps. **1b** this suit itself; trumps. **2** Also called: **trump card.** a decisive or advantageous move, resource, action, etc. **3** *Informal.* a fine or reliable person. ◆ *vb* **4** to play a trump card on (a suit, or a particular card of a suit, that is not trumps). **5** (*tr*) to outdo or surpass. ◆ See also **trumps, trump up.** [C16: variant of TRIUMPH] ▸ **'trumpless** *adj*

trump[2] (trʌmp) *Archaic or literary.* ◆ *n* **1** a trumpet or the sound produced by one. **2 the last trump.** the final trumpet call that according to the belief of some will awaken and raise the dead on the Day of Judgment. ◆ *vb* **3** (*intr*) to produce a sound upon or as if upon the trumpet. **4** (*tr*) to proclaim or announce with or as if with a fanfare. [C13: from Old French *trompe,* from Old High German *trumpa* trumpet; compare TROMBONE]

trumpery ('trʌmpərɪ) *n, pl* **-eries. 1** foolish talk or actions. **2** a useless or worthless article; trinket. ◆ *adj* **3** useless or worthless. [C15: from Old French *tromperie* deceit, from *tromper* to cheat]

trumpet ('trʌmpɪt) *n* **1** a valved brass instrument of brilliant tone consisting of a narrow tube of cylindrical bore ending in a flared bell, normally pitched in B flat. Range: two and a half octaves upwards from F sharp on the fourth line of the bass staff. **2** any instrument consisting of a valveless tube ending in a bell, esp. a straight instrument used for fanfares, signals, etc. **3** a person who plays a trumpet in an orchestra. **4** a loud sound such as that of a trumpet, esp. when made by an animal: *the trumpet of the elephants.* **5** an eight-foot reed stop on an organ. **6** something resembling a trumpet in shape, esp. in having a flared bell. **7** short for **ear trumpet. 8 blow one's own trumpet.** to boast about oneself; brag. ◆ *vb* **-pets, -peting, -peted. 9** to proclaim or sound loudly. [C13: from Old French *trompette* a little TRUMP[2]] ▸ **'trumpet-ˌlike** *adj*

trumpeter ('trʌmpɪtə) *n* **1** a person who plays the trumpet, esp. one whose duty it is to play fanfares, signals, etc. **2** any of three birds of the genus *Psophia* of the forests of South America, having a rounded body, long legs, and a glossy blackish plumage: family *Psophiidae,* order *Gruiformes* (cranes, rails, etc.). **3** (*sometimes cap.*) a breed of domestic fancy pigeon with a long ruff.

trumpeter swan *n* a large swan, *Cygnus buccinator,* of W North America, having a white plumage and black bill.

trumpet flower *n* **1** any of various plants having trumpet-shaped flowers. **2** the flower of any of these plants.

trumpet honeysuckle *n* a North American honeysuckle shrub, *Lonicera sempervirens,* having orange, scarlet, or yellow trumpet-shaped flowers.

trumpetweed ('trʌmpɪtˌwi:d) *n U.S.* any of various eupatorium plants, esp. joe-pye weed. [C19: so called because it has a hollow stem which children sometimes use as imitation trumpets]

trumps (trʌmps) *pl n* **1** (*sometimes sing*) *Cards.* any one of the four suits, decided by cutting or bidding, that outranks all the other suits for the duration of a deal or game. **2 turn up trumps.** (of a person) to bring about a happy or successful conclusion (to an event, problem, etc.), esp. unexpectedly.

trump up *vb* (*tr, adv*) to concoct or invent (a charge, accusation, etc.) so as to deceive or implicate someone.

truncate *vb* (trʌŋ'keɪt, 'trʌŋkeɪt). **1** (*tr*) to shorten by cutting off a part, end, or top. ◆ *adj* ('trʌŋkeɪt). **2** cut short; truncated. **3** *Biology.* having a blunt end, as though cut off at the tip: *a truncate leaf.* [C15: from Latin *truncāre* to lop] ▸ **'truncately** *adv* ▸ **trun'cation** *n*

truncated (trʌŋ'keɪtɪd) *adj* **1** *Maths.* (of a cone, pyramid, prism, etc.) having an apex or end removed by a plane intersection that is usually nonparallel to the base. **2** (of a crystal) having edges or corners cut off. **3** shortened by or as if by cutting off; truncate.

truncheon ('trʌntʃən) *n* **1** *Chiefly Brit.* a short thick club or cudgel carried by a policeman. **2** a baton of office: *a marshal's truncheon.* **3** *Archaic.* a short club or cudgel. **4** the shaft of a spear. ◆ *vb* **5** (*tr*) to beat with a truncheon. [C16: from Old French *tronchon* stump, from Latin *truncus* trunk; see TRUNCATE]

trundle ('trʌndᵊl) *vb* **1** to move heavily on or as if on wheels: *the bus trundled by.* **2** (*tr*) *Archaic.* to rotate or spin. ◆ *n* **3** the act or an instance of trundling. **4** a small wheel or roller. **5a** the pinion of a lantern. **5b** any of the bars in a lantern pinion. **6** a small truck with low wheels. [Old English *tryndel;* related to Middle High German *trendel* disc]

trundle bed *n* a less common word for **truckle bed.**

trundler ('trʌndlə) *n N.Z.* **1** a golf bag or shopping trolley. **2** a child's pushchair.

trunk (trʌŋk) *n* **1** the main stem of a tree, usually thick and upright, covered with bark and having branches at some distance from the ground. **2** a large strong case or box used to contain clothes and other personal effects when travelling and for storage. **3** *Anatomy.* the body excluding the head, neck, and limbs; torso. **4** the elongated prehensile nasal part of an elephant; proboscis. **5** the U.S. and Canadian name for **boot**[1] (sense 2). **6** *Anatomy.* the main stem of a nerve, blood vessel, etc. **7** *Nautical.* a watertight boxlike cover within a vessel with its top above the waterline, such as one used to enclose a centreboard. **8** an enclosed duct or passageway for ventilation, etc. **9** (*modifier*) of or relating to a main road, railway, etc., in a network: *a trunk line.* ◆ See also **trunks.** [C15: from Old French *tronc,* from Latin *truncus,* from *truncus* (adj) lopped] ▸ **'trunkˌful** *n* ▸ **'trunkless** *adj*

trunk cabin *n Nautical.* a long relatively low cabin above the deck of a yacht.

trunk call *n Chiefly Brit.* a long-distance telephone call.

trunk curl *n* another name for **sit-up.**

trunkfish ('trʌŋkˌfɪʃ) *n, pl* **-fish** *or* **-fishes.** any tropical plectognath fish of the family *Ostraciidae,* having the body encased in bony plates with openings for the fins, eyes, mouth, etc. Also called: **boxfish, cowfish.**

trunk hose *n* a man's puffed-out breeches reaching to the thighs and worn with tights in the 16th century. [C17: of uncertain origin; perhaps from the obsolete *trunk* to truncate]

trunking ('trʌŋkɪŋ) *n* **1** *Telecomm.* the cables that take a common route through an exchange building linking ranks of selectors. **2** plastic housing used to conceal wires, etc.; casing. **3** the delivery of goods over long distances, esp. by road vehicles to local distribution centres, from which deliveries and collections are made.

trunk line *n* **1** a direct link between two telephone exchanges or switchboards that are a considerable distance apart. **2** the main route or routes on a railway.

trunk road *n Brit.* a main road, esp. one that is suitable for heavy vehicles.

trunks (trʌŋks) *pl n* **1** Also called: **swimming trunks.** a man's garment worn for swimming, either fairly loose and extending from the waist to the thigh or briefer and close-fitting. **2** shorts worn for some sports. **3** *Chiefly Brit.* men's underpants with legs that reach midthigh.

trunnel ('trʌnᵊl) *n* a variant spelling of **treenail.**

trunnion ('trʌnjən) *n* **1** one of a pair of coaxial projections attached to opposite sides of a container, cannon, etc., to provide a support about which it can turn in a vertical. **2** the structure supporting such a projection. [C17: from Old French *trognon* trunk] ► **'trunnioned** *adj*

Truro ('trʊərəʊ) *n* a market town in SW England, administrative centre of Cornwall. Pop.: 18 966 (1991).

truss (trʌs) *vb (tr)* **1** (sometimes foll. by *up*) to tie, bind, or bundle: *to truss up a prisoner.* **2** to fasten or bind the wings and legs of (a fowl) before cooking to keep them in place. **3** to support or stiffen (a roof, bridge, etc.) with structural members. **4** *Informal.* to confine (the body or a part of it) in tight clothes. **5** *Falconry.* (of falcons) to hold (the quarry) in the stoop without letting go. **6** *Med.* to supply or support with a truss. ◆ *n* **7** a structural framework of wood or metal, esp. one arranged in triangles, used to support a roof, bridge, etc. **8** *Med.* a device for holding a hernia in place, typically consisting of a pad held in position by a belt. **9** *Horticulture.* a cluster of flowers or fruit growing at the end of a single stalk. **10** *Nautical.* a metal fitting fixed to a yard at its centre for holding it to a mast while allowing movement. **11** *Architect.* another name for **corbel.** **12** a bundle or pack. **13** *Chiefly Brit.* a bundle of hay or straw, esp. one having a fixed weight of 36, 56, or 60 pounds. [C13: from Old French *trousse,* from *trousser,* apparently from Vulgar Latin *torciāre* (unattested), from *torca* (unattested) a bundle, TORCH] ► **'trusser** *n*

truss bridge *n* a bridge that is constructed of trusses.

trussing ('trʌsɪŋ) *n Engineering.* **1** a system of trusses, esp. for strengthening or reinforcing a structure. **2** the parts or members that form a truss.

trust (trʌst) *n* **1** reliance on and confidence in the truth, worth, reliability, etc., of a person or thing; faith. Related adj: **fiducial.** **2** a group of commercial enterprises combined to monopolize and control the market for any commodity: illegal in the U.S. **3** the obligation of someone in a responsible position: *a position of trust.* **4** custody, charge, or care: *a child placed in my trust.* **5** a person or thing in which confidence or faith is placed. **6** commercial credit. **7a** an arrangement whereby a person to whom the legal title to property is conveyed (the trustee) holds such property for the benefit of those entitled to the beneficial interest. **7b** property that is the subject of such an arrangement. **7c** the confidence put in the trustee. Related adj: **fiduciary.** **8** (in the British National Health Service) a self-governing hospital, group of hospitals, or other body providing health-care services, which operates as an independent commercial unit within the NHS. **9** See **trust company, trust account** (sense 2). **10** (*modifier*) of or relating to a trust or trusts: *trust property.* ◆ *vb* **11** (*tr; may take a clause as object*) to expect, hope, or suppose: *I trust that you are well.* **12** (when *tr, may take an infinitive;* when *intr,* often foll. by *in* or *to*) to place confidence in (someone to do something); have faith (in); rely (upon): *I trust him to tell her.* **13** (*tr*) to consign for care: *the child was trusted to my care.* **14** (*tr*) to allow (someone to do something) with confidence in his or her good sense or honesty: *I trust my daughter to go.* **15** (*tr*) to extend business credit to. [C13: from Old Norse *traust;* related to Old High German *Trost* solace] ► **'trustable** *adj* ► **,trusta'bility** *n* ► **'truster** *n*

trust account *n* **1** Also called: **trustee account.** a savings account deposited in the name of a trustee who controls it during his lifetime, after which the balance is payable to a prenominated beneficiary. **2** property under the control of a trustee or trustees.

trustbuster ('trʌst,bʌstə) *n U.S. informal.* a person who seeks the dissolution of corporate trusts, esp. a federal official who prosecutes trusts under the antitrust laws. ► **'trust,busting** *n*

trust company *n* a commercial bank or other enterprise organized to perform trustee functions. Also called: **trust corporation.**

trust deed *n* a document that transfers the legal title to property to a trustee.

trustee (trʌ'stiː) *n* **1** a person to whom the legal title to property is entrusted to hold or use for another's benefit. **2** a member of a board that manages the affairs and administers the funds of an institution or organization.

trustee in bankruptcy *n* a person entrusted with the administration of a bankrupt's affairs and with realizing his assets for the benefit of the creditors.

trustee investment *n Stock Exchange.* an investment in which trustees are authorized to invest money belonging to a trust fund.

trusteeship (trʌ'stiːʃɪp) *n* **1** the office or function of a trustee. **2a** the administration or government of a territory by a foreign country under the supervision of the **Trusteeship Council** of the United Nations. **2b** (*often cap.*) any such dependent territory; trust territory.

trustful ('trʌstfʊl) *or* **trusting** *adj* characterized by a tendency or readiness to trust others. ► **'trustfully** *or* **'trustingly** *adv* ► **'trustfulness** *or* **'trustingness** *n*

trust fund *n* money, securities, etc., held in trust.

trust hotel *or* **tavern** *n N.Z.* a licensed hotel or a bar owned by a publicly elected committee as trustees, the profits of which go to public amenities.

trustless ('trʌstlɪs) *adj Archaic or literary.* **1** untrustworthy; deceitful. **2** distrusting; suspicious; wary. ► **'trustlessly** *adv* ► **'trustlessness** *n*

trust territory *n* (*sometimes cap.*) another name for a **trusteeship** (sense 2).

trustworthy ('trʌst,wɜːðɪ) *adj* worthy of being trusted; honest, reliable, or dependable. ► **'trust,worthily** *adv* ► **'trust,worthiness** *n*

trusty ('trʌstɪ) *adj* **trustier, trustiest.** **1** faithful or reliable. **2** *Archaic.* trusting. ◆ *n, pl* **trusties.** **3** someone who is trusted, esp. a convict to whom special privileges are granted. ► **'trustily** *adv* ► **'trustiness** *n*

truth (truːθ) *n* **1** the quality of being true, genuine, actual, or factual: *the truth of his statement was attested.* **2** something that is true as opposed to false: *you did not tell me the truth.* **3** a proven or verified principle or statement; fact: *the truths of astronomy.* **4** (*usually pl*) a system of concepts purporting to represent some aspect of the world: *the truths of ancient religions.* **5** fidelity to a required standard or law. **6** faithful reproduction or portrayal: *the truth of a portrait.* **7** an obvious fact; truism; platitude. **8** honesty, reliability, or veracity: *the truth of her nature.* **9** accuracy, as in the setting, adjustment, or position of something, such as a mechanical instrument. **10** the state or quality of being faithful; allegiance. ◆ Related adjs: **veritable, veracious.** [Old English *triewth;* related to Old High German *gitriuwida* fidelity, Old Norse *tryggr* true] ► **'truthless** *adj*

truth-condition *n Logic, philosophy.* **1** the circumstances under which a statement is true. **2** a statement of these circumstances: sometimes identified with the meaning of the statement.

truth drug *or* **serum** *n Informal.* any of various drugs supposed to have the property of making people tell the truth, as by relaxing them.

truthful ('truːθfʊl) *adj* **1** telling or expressing the truth; honest or candid. **2** realistic: *a truthful portrayal of the king.* ► **'truthfully** *adv* ► **'truthfulness** *n*

truth-function *n Logic.* **1** a function that determines the truth-value of a complex sentence solely in terms of the truth-values of the component sentences without reference to their meaning. **2** a complex sentence whose truth-value is so determined, such as a negation or conjunction.

truth set *n* **1** *Logic, maths.* Also called: **solution set.** the set of values that satisfy an open sentence, equation, inequality, etc., having no unique solution. **2** *Logic.* the set of possible worlds in which a statement is true.

truth table *n* **1** a table, used in logic, indicating the truth-value of a compound statement for every truth-value of its component propositions. **2** a similar table, used in transistor technology, to indicate the value of the output signal of a logic circuit for every value of input signal.

truth-value *n Logic.* **a** either of the values, true or false, that may be taken by a statement. **b** by analogy, any of the values that a semantic theory may accord to a statement.

truth-value gap *n Logic.* the possibility in certain semantic systems of a statement being neither true nor false while also not being determinately of any third truth-value, as *all my children are asleep* uttered by a childless person.

try (traɪ) *vb* **tries, trying, tried.** **1** (when *tr, may take an infinitive,* sometimes with *to* replaced by *and*) to make an effort or attempt: *he tried to climb a cliff.* **2** (*tr;* often foll. by *out*) to sample, test, or give experimental use to (something) in order to determine its quality, worth, etc.: *try her cheese flan.* **3** (*tr*) to put strain or stress on: *he tries my patience.* **4** (*tr; often passive*) to give pain, affliction, or vexation to: *I have been sorely tried by those children.* **5a** to examine and determine the issues involved in (a cause) in a court of law. **5b** to hear evidence in order to determine the guilt or innocence of (an accused). **5c** to sit as judge at the trial of (an issue or person). **6** (*tr*) to melt (fat, lard, etc.) in order to separate out impurities. **7** (*tr;* usually foll. by *out*) *Obsolete.* to extract (a material) from an ore, mixture, etc., usually by heat; refine. ◆ *n, pl* **tries.** **8** an experiment or trial. **9** an attempt or effort. **10** *Rugby.* the act of an attacking player touching the ball down behind the opposing team's goal line, scoring five or, in Rugby League, four points. **11** Also called: **try for a point.** *American football.* an attempt made after a touchdown to score an extra point by kicking a goal or, for two extra points, by running the ball or completing a pass across the opponents' goal line. [C13: from Old French *trier* to sort, sift, of uncertain origin]

USAGE The use of *and* instead of *to* after *try* is very common, but should be avoided in formal writing: *we must try to prevent* (not *try and prevent*) *this happening.*

trying ('traɪɪŋ) *adj* upsetting, difficult, or annoying: *a trying day at the office.* ► **'tryingly** *adv* ► **'tryingness** *n*

trying plane *n* a plane with a long body for planing the edges of long boards.

tryma ('traɪmə) *n, pl* **-mata** (-mətə). *Botany.* a drupe produced by the walnut and similar plants, in which the endocarp is a hard shell and the epicarp is dehiscent. [C19: from New Latin, from Greek *truma* a hole (referring to the hollow drupe), from *truein* to wear away]

try on *vb (tr, adv)* **1** to put on (an article of clothing) to find out whether it fits or is suitable. **2 try it on.** *Informal.* to attempt to deceive or fool someone. ◆ *n* **try-on.** **3** *Brit. informal.* an action or statement made to test out a person's gullibility, tolerance, etc.

try out *vb (adv)* **1** (*tr*) to test or put to experimental use: *I'm going to try the new car out.* **2** (when *intr,* usually foll. by *for*) *U.S. and Canadian.* (of an athlete, actor, etc.) to undergo a test or to submit (an athlete, actor, etc.) to a test to determine suitability for a place in a team, an acting role, etc. ◆ *n* **tryout.** **3** *Chiefly U.S. and Canadian.* a trial or test, as of an athlete or actor.

trypan blue ('trɪpən, 'trɪpæn, trɪ'pæn) *n* a dye obtained from tolidine that is absorbed by the macrophages of the reticuloendothelial system and is therefore used for staining cells in biological research. [so called because it is *trypanocidal:* see TRYPANOSOME, -CIDE]

trypanosome ('trɪpənə,səʊm) *n* any parasitic flagellate protozoan of the genus

Trypanosoma, which lives in the blood of vertebrates, is transmitted by certain insects, and causes sleeping sickness and certain other diseases. [C19: from New Latin *Trypanosoma*, from Greek *trupanon* borer + *sōma* body] ▸ ˌ**trypano'somal** *or* **trypanosomic** (ˌtrɪpənə'sɒmɪk) *adj*

trypanosomiasis (ˌtrɪpənəsə'maɪəsɪs) *n* any infection of an animal or human with a trypanosome. See also **sleeping sickness, Chagas' disease.**

tryparsamide (trɪ'pɑːsəmɪd) *n* a synthetic crystalline compound of arsenic used in the treatment of trypanosomal and other protozoan infections. Formula: $C_8H_{10}AsN_2O_4Na.½H_2O$. [C20: from a trademark]

trypsin ('trɪpsɪn) *n* an enzyme occurring in pancreatic juice: it catalyses the hydrolysis of proteins to peptides and is secreted from the pancreas in the form of trypsinogen. See also **chymotrypsin.** [C19 *tryp-*, from Greek *tripsis* a rubbing, from *tribein* to rub + -IN; referring to the fact that it was originally produced by rubbing the pancreas with glycerine] ▸ **tryptic** ('trɪptɪk) *adj*

trypsinogen (trɪp'sɪnədʒən) *n* the inactive precursor of trypsin that is converted to trypsin by the enzyme enterokinase.

tryptophan ('trɪptəˌfæn) *n* an essential amino acid; a component of proteins necessary for growth. [C20: from TRYPT(IC) + -O- + *-phan*, variant of -PHANE]

trysail ('traɪˌseɪl; *Nautical* 'traɪsᵊl) *n* a small fore-and-aft sail, triangular or square, set on the mainmast of a sailing vessel in foul weather to help keep her head to the wind. Also called: **storm trysail.**

try square *n* a device for testing or laying out right angles, usually consisting of a metal blade fixed at right angles to a wooden handle.

tryst (trɪst, traɪst) *Archaic or literary.* ♦ *n* **1** an appointment to meet, esp. secretly. **2** the place of such a meeting or the meeting itself. ♦ *vb* **3** (*intr*) to meet at or arrange a tryst. [C14: from Old French *triste* lookout post, apparently of Scandinavian origin; compare Old Norse *traust* trust] ▸ '**tryster** *n*

tsade ('tsɑːdiː, 'sɑː-; *Hebrew* 'tsadi) *n* a variant spelling of **sadhe.**

Tsana ('tsɑːnə) *n* **Lake.** another name for (Lake) **Tana.**

tsar *or* **czar** (zɑː) *n* **1** (until 1917) the emperor of Russia. **2** a tyrant; autocrat. **3** *Informal.* a person in authority; leader. **4** (formerly) any of several S Slavonic rulers, such as any of the princes of Serbia in the 14th century. ♦ Also (less commonly) **tzar.** [from Russian *tsar*, via Gothic *kaisar* from Latin: CAESAR] ▸ '**tsardom** *or* '**czardom** *n*

tsarevitch *or* **czarevitch** ('zɑːrəvɪtʃ) *n* a son of a Russian tsar, esp. the eldest son. [from Russian *tsarevich*, from TSAR + *-evich*, masculine patronymic suffix]

tsarevna *or* **czarevna** (zɑː'revnə) *n* **1** a daughter of a Russian tsar. **2** the wife of a Russian tsarevitch. [from Russian, from TSAR + *-evna*, feminine patronymic suffix]

tsarina, czarina (zɑː'riːnə) *or* **tsaritsa, czaritza** (zɑː'rɪtsə) *n* the wife of a Russian tsar; Russian empress. [from Italian, Spanish *czarina*, from German *Czarin*]

tsarism *or* **czarism** ('zɑːrɪzəm) *n* **1** a system of government by a tsar, esp. in Russia until 1917. **2** absolute rule; dictatorship. ▸ '**tsarist** *or* '**czarist** *n, adj*

Tsaritsyn (*Russian* tsa'ritsin) *n* a former name (until 1925) of **Volgograd.**

TSB *abbrev. for* Trustee Savings Bank, now known as the T.S.B. Group plc.

TSE *abbrev. for* transmissible spongiform encephalopathy: any of a group of degenerative brain diseases, including BSE in cattle, that can be transmitted from one individual or species to another.

Tselinograd (*Russian* tsəlɪna'grat) *n* a former name (1961–94) for **Akmola.**

tsetse fly *or* **tzetze fly** ('tsetsɪ) *n* any of various bloodsucking African dipterous flies of the genus *Glossina*, which transmit the pathogens of various diseases: family *Muscidae*. [C19: via Afrikaans from Tswana]

TSH *abbrev. for* thyroid-stimulating hormone; another name for **thyrotropin.**

Tshiluba (tʃɪ'luːbə) *n* the language of the Luba people, used as a trade language in the Democratic Republic of the Congo (formerly Zaïre). See **Luba.**

T-shirt *or* **tee shirt** *n* a lightweight simple garment for the upper body, usually short-sleeved. [so called because of its shape]

Tshombe ('tʃɒmbɪ) *n* **Moise** (məʊ'iːz). 1919–69, Congolese statesman. He led the secession of Katanga (1960) from the newly independent Congo; forced into exile (1963) but returned (1964–65) as premier of the Congo; died in exile.

Tsinan ('tsiː'næn) *n* a variant transliteration of the Chinese name for **Jinan.**

Tsinghai ('tsɪŋ'haɪ) *n* **1** a variant transliteration of the Chinese name for **Qinghai. 2** a variant transliteration of the Chinese name for **Koko Nor.**

Tsingtao ('tsɪŋ'taʊ) *n* a variant transliteration of the Chinese name for **Qingdao.**

Tsingyuan ('tsɪŋ'jwɑːn) *or* **Ch'ing-yüan** *n* the former name of **Baoding.**

Tsiolkovski (*Russian* tsʌl'kofskjɪ) *n* **Konstantin Eduardovich** (kənstʌn'tjin edu'adəvɪtʃ). 1857–1935, Russian aeronautical engineer, a pioneer of rocket and space research. His work on liquid-fuelled rockets anticipated the ideas of Robert Goddard.

Tsitsihar ('tsɪtsɪˌhɑː) *n* a variant transliteration of the Chinese name for **Qiqihar.**

tsitsith ('tsɪtsɪs, tsiː'tsiːt) *n* (*functioning as sing or pl*) *Judaism.* the tassels or fringes of thread attached to the four corners of the tallith. [from Hebrew *sīsīth*]

Tskhinvali ('tskɪnˌvɑːlɪ) *n* the Georgian name for **South Ossetia.**

Tsonga ('tsɒŋgə) *n* **1** (*pl* **-ga** *or* **-gas**) a member of a Negroid people of S Mozambique, Swaziland, and South Africa. **2** the language of this people, belonging to the Bantu group of the Niger-Congo family.

tsotsi ('tsɒtsɪ, 'tsɔː-) *n, pl* **-tsis.** *S. African informal.* a Black street thug or gang member; wide boy. [C20: perhaps from Nguni *tsotsa* to dress flashily]

tsotsitaal 'tsɔːtsɪˌtɑːl) *n S. African.* a type of street slang used by tsotsis. [C20: from Nguni *tsotsi* thug + Afrikaans *taal* language]

tsp. *abbrev. for* teaspoon.

T-square *n* a T-shaped ruler used in mechanical drawing, consisting of a short crosspiece, which slides along the edge of the drawing board, and a long horizontal piece: used for drawing horizontal lines and to support set squares when drawing vertical and inclined lines.

T-stop *n* a setting of the lens aperture on a camera calibrated photometrically and assigned a T-number.

T-strap *n* (*modifier*) denoting a type of woman's shoe fastened with a T-shaped strap having one part passing across the ankle and the other attached to it in the middle and lying along the length of the foot. Also called: **T-bar.**

Tsugaru Strait ('tsugɑˌru) *n* a channel between N Honshu and S Hokkaido islands, Japan. Width: about 30 km (20 miles).

tsunami (tsʊ'næmɪ) *n, pl* **-mis** *or* **-mi.** a large, often destructive, sea wave produced by a submarine earthquake, subsidence, or volcanic eruption. Sometimes incorrectly called a tidal wave. [from Japanese, from *tsu* port + *nami* wave]

Tsushima ('tsuːʃiːˌmɑː) *n* a group of five rocky islands between Japan and South Korea, in the Korea Strait: administratively part of Japan; scene of a naval defeat for the Russians (1905) during the Russo-Japanese war. Pop.: 50 810 (1980). Area: 698 sq. km (269 sq. miles).

tsutsugamushi disease (ˌtsutsugə'muʃɪ) *n* **1** one of the five major groups of acute infectious rickettsial diseases affecting man, common in Asia and including scrub typhus. It is caused by the microorganism *Rickettsia tsutsugamushi*, transmitted by the bite of mites. **2** another name for **scrub typhus.** [from Japanese, from *tsutsuga* disease + *mushi* insect]

Tsvetaeva (tsfɛtə'jervə) *n* **Marina (Ivanovna).** 1892–1941, Russian poet. Opposed to the Revolution, she left Russia (1922) and lived in Paris: when she returned (1939) her husband was shot and she committed suicide.

Tswana ('tswɑːnə) *n* **1** (*pl* **-na** *or* **-nas**) a member of a mixed Negroid and Bushman people of the Sotho group of southern Africa, living chiefly in Botswana. **2** the language of this people, belonging to the Bantu group of the Niger-Congo family: the principal language of Botswana.

TT *abbrev. for:* **1** teetotal. **2** teetotaller. **3** telegraphic transfer: a method of sending money abroad by cabled transfer between banks. **4** Tourist Trophy (annual motorcycle races held in the Isle of Man). **5** tuberculin-tested. ♦ **6** *international car registration for* Trinidad and Tobago.

TTL *abbrev. for:* **1** transistor transistor logic: a method of constructing electronic logic circuits. **2** through-the-lens: denoting a system of light metering in cameras.

TU *abbrev. for* trade union.

Tu. *abbrev. for* Tuesday.

Tuamotu Archipelago (ˌtuːə'məʊtuː) *n* a group of about 80 coral islands in the S Pacific, in French Polynesia. Pop.: 11 793 (1983). Area: 860 sq. km (332 sq. miles). Also called: **Low Archipelago, Paumotu Archipelago.**

tuan[1] ('tuːɑːn) *n* (in Malay-speaking countries) sir; lord: a form of address used as a mark of respect. [Malay]

tuan[2] ('tuːən, 'tjuː-) *n* a flying phalanger, *Phascogale tapoatafa*, of Australia. It is about the size of a rat, bluish grey in colour, brush-tailed, arboreal, and nocturnal. Also called: **wambenger, brush-tailed phascogale.** [C19: from a native Australian language]

Tuareg ('twɑːrɛg) *n* **1** (*pl* **-reg** *or* **-regs**) a member of a nomadic Berber people of the Sahara. **2** the dialect of Berber spoken by this people.

tuart ('tuːɑːt) *n* a eucalyptus tree, *Eucalyptus gomphocephala*, of Australia, yielding a very durable light-coloured timber. [from a native Australian language]

tuatara (ˌtuːə'tɑːrə) *n* a greenish-grey lizard-like rhynchocephalian reptile, *Sphenodon punctatus*, occurring only on certain small islands near New Zealand: it is the sole surviving member of a group common in Mesozoic times. [C19: from Maori, from *tua* back + *tara* spine]

tub (tʌb) *n* **1** a low wide open container, typically round, originally one made of wood and used esp. for washing: now made of wood, plastic, metal, etc., and used in a variety of domestic and industrial situations. **2** a small plastic or cardboard container of similar shape for ice cream, margarine, etc. **3** Also called: **bathtub.** another word (esp. U.S. and Canadian) for **bath**[1] (sense 1). **4** Also called: **tubful.** the amount a tub will hold. **5** a clumsy slow boat or ship. **6** *Informal.* (in rowing) a heavy wide boat used for training novice oarsmen. **7a** Also called: **tram, hutch.** a small vehicle on rails for carrying loads in a mine. **7b** a container for lifting coal or ore up a mine shaft; skip. ♦ *vb* **tubs, tubbing, tubbed. 8** *Brit. informal.* to wash (oneself or another) in a tub. **9** (*tr*) to keep or put in a tub. [C14: from Middle Dutch *tubbe*] ▸ '**tubbable** *adj* ▸ '**tubber** *n*

tuba ('tjuːbə) *n, pl* **-bas** *or* **-bae** (-biː). **1** a valved brass instrument of bass pitch, in which the bell points upwards and the mouthpiece projects at right angles. The tube is of conical bore and the mouthpiece cup-shaped. **2** any other bass brass instrument such as the euphonium, helicon, etc. **3** a powerful reed stop on an organ. **4** a form of trumpet of ancient Rome. [Latin]

tubal ('tjuːbᵊl) *adj* **1** of or relating to a tube. **2** of, relating to, or developing in a Fallopian tube: *a tubal pregnancy.*

Tubal-cain ('tjuːbᵊlˌkeɪn) *n Old Testament.* a son of Lamech, said in Genesis 4:22 to be the first artificer of metals.

tubate ('tjuːbeɪt) *adj* a less common word for **tubular.**

tubby ('tʌbɪ) *adj* **-bier, -biest. 1** plump. **2** shaped like a tub. **3** *Rare.* having little resonance. ▸ '**tubbiness** *n*

tube (tjuːb) *n* **1** a long hollow and typically cylindrical object, used for the passage of fluids or as a container. **2** a collapsible cylindrical container of soft metal or plastic closed with a cap, used to hold viscous liquids or pastes. **3** *Anatomy.* **3a** short for **Eustachian tube** or **Fallopian tube. 3b** any hollow cylindrical structure. **4** *Botany.* **4a** the lower part of a gamopetalous corolla or gamosepalous calyx, below the lobes. **4b** any other hollow structure in a plant. **5** (*sometimes cap.*) *Brit.* **5a the tube.** Also called: **the underground.** an underground railway system, esp. that in London. U.S. and Canadian equivalent: **subway. 5b** the tunnels through which the railway runs. **5c** the train itself. **6** *Electron-*

ics. **6a** another name for **valve** (sense 3). **6b** See **electron tube, cathode-ray tube, television tube.** **7** (preceded by *the*) *Slang.* a television set. **8** *Austral. slang.* a bottle or can of beer. **9** *Surfing.* the cylindrical passage formed when a wave breaks and the crest tips forward. **10** an archaic word for **telescope.** ◆ *vb* (*tr*) **11** to fit or supply with a tube or tubes. **12** to carry or convey in a tube. **13** to shape like a tube. [C17: from Latin *tubus*] ▸ **'tube-like** *adj*

tube fly *n Angling.* an artificial fly with the body tied on a hollow tube that can slide up the leader when a fish takes.

tube foot *n* any of numerous tubular outgrowths of the body wall of most echinoderms that are used as organs of locomotion and respiration and to aid ingestion of food.

tubeless tyre *n* a pneumatic tyre in which the outer casing makes an airtight seal with the rim of the wheel so that an inner tube is unnecessary.

tuber ('tju:bə) *n* **1** a fleshy underground stem (as in the potato) or root (as in the dahlia) that is an organ of vegetative reproduction and food storage. **2** *Anatomy.* a raised area; swelling. [C17: from Latin *tūber* hump]

tubercle ('tju:bək[ə]l) *n* **1** any small rounded nodule or elevation, esp. on the skin, on a bone, or on a plant. **2** any small rounded pathological lesion of the tissues, esp. one characteristic of tuberculosis. [C16: from Latin *tūberculum* a little swelling, diminutive of TUBER]

tubercle bacillus *n* a rodlike Gram-positive bacterium, *Mycobacterium tuberculosis,* that causes tuberculosis: family *Mycobacteriaceae.*

tubercular (tjʊ'bɜ:kjʊlə) *adj* **1** of, relating to, or symptomatic of tuberculosis. **2** of or relating to a tubercle or tubercles. **3** characterized by the presence of tubercles. ◆ *n* **4** a person with tuberculosis. ▸ **tu'bercularly** *adv*

tuberculate (tjʊ'bɜ:kjʊlɪt) *adj* covered with tubercles. ▸ **tu'berculately** *adv* ▸ **tu,bercu'lation** *n*

tuberculin (tjʊ'bɜ:kjʊlɪn) *n* a sterile liquid prepared from cultures of attenuated tubercle bacillus and used in the diagnosis of tuberculosis.

tuberculin-tested *adj* (of milk) produced by cows that have been certified as free of tuberculosis.

tuberculosis (tjʊ,bɜ:kjʊ'ləʊsɪs) *n* a communicable disease caused by infection with the tubercle bacillus, most frequently affecting the lungs (**pulmonary tuberculosis**). Also called: **consumption, phthisis.** Abbrev.: **TB.** [C19: from New Latin; see TUBERCLE, -OSIS]

tuberculous (tjʊ'bɜ:kjʊləs) *adj* of or relating to tuberculosis or tubercles; tubercular. ▸ **tu'berculously** *adv*

tuberose *n* ('tju:bə,rəʊz) **1** a perennial Mexican agave plant, *Polianthes tuberosa,* having a tuberous root and spikes of white fragrant lily-like flowers. ◆ *adj* ('tju:bə,rəʊs). **2** a variant of **tuberous.** [C17: from Latin *tūberōsus* full of lumps; referring to its root]

tuberosity (,tju:bə'rɒsɪtɪ) *n, pl* **-ties.** any protuberance on a bone, esp. for the attachment of a muscle or ligament.

tuberous ('tju:bərəs) *or* **tuberose** ('tju:bə,rəʊs) *adj* **1** (of plants or their parts) forming, bearing, or resembling a tuber or tubers: *a tuberous root.* **2** *Anatomy.* of, relating to, or having warty protuberances or tubers. [C17: from Latin *tūberōsus* full of knobs; see TUBER]

tube worm *n* any of various polychaete worms that construct and live in a tube made of sand, lime, etc.

tubicolous (tju:'bɪkələs) *adj* (of certain invertebrate animals) living in a self-constructed tube.

tubifex ('tju:bɪ,fɛks) *n, pl* **-fex** *or* **-fexes.** any small reddish freshwater oligochaete worm of the genus *Tubifex;* it characteristically lives in a tube in sand and is used as food for aquarium fish. [C19: from New Latin, from Latin *tubus* tube + *facere* to make, do]

tubing ('tju:bɪŋ) *n* **1** tubes collectively. **2** a length of tube. **3** a system of tubes. **4** fabric in the form of a tube, used for pillowcases and some cushions; piping.

Tübingen ('tju:bɪŋən) *n* a town in SW Germany, in Baden-Württemberg: university (1477). Pop.: 76 040 (1989 est.).

Tubman ('tʌbmən) *n* **William Vacanarat Shadrach** (və'kænə,ræt 'ʃædræk). 1895–1971, Liberian statesman; president of Liberia (1944–71).

tub-thumper *n* a noisy, violent, or ranting public speaker. ▸ **'tub-,thumping** *adj, n*

Tubuai Islands (,tu:bu:'aɪ) *pl n* a chain of small islands extending about 1400 km (850 miles) in the S Pacific, in French Polynesia; discovered by Captain Cook in 1777; annexed by France in 1880. Pop.: 6509 (1988). Area: 173 sq. km (67 sq. miles). Also called: **Austral Islands.**

tubular ('tju:bjʊlə) *adj* **1** Also: **tubiform** ('tju:bɪ,fɔ:m). having the form of a tube or tubes. **2** of or relating to a tube or tubing. ▸ **,tubu'larity** *n* ▸ **'tubularly** *adv*

tubular bells *pl n Music.* an orchestral percussion instrument of 18 chromatically tuned metal tubes suspended vertically and struck near the top.

tubulate *vb* ('tju:bjʊ,leɪt). (*tr*) **1** to form or shape into a tube. **2** to fit or furnish with a tube. ◆ *adj* ('tju:bjʊlɪt, -,leɪt). **3** a less common word for **tubular.** [C18: from Latin *tubulātus,* from *tubulus* a little pipe, from *tubus* pipe] ▸ **,tubu'lation** *n* ▸ **'tubu,lator** *n*

tubule ('tju:bju:l) *n* any small tubular structure, esp. one in an animal, as in the kidney, testis, etc. [C17: from Latin *tubulus* a little TUBE]

tubuliflorous (,tju:bjʊlɪ'flɔ:rəs) *adj* (of plants) having flowers or florets with tubular corollas. [C19: from TUBULE + -FLOROUS]

tubulous ('tju:bjʊləs) *adj* **1** tube-shaped; tubular. **2** characterized by or consisting of small tubes. [C17: from New Latin *tubulōsus*] ▸ **'tubulously** *adv*

TUC (in Britain) *abbrev. for* Trades Union Congress.

Tucana (tu:'kɑ:nə) *n, Latin genitive* **Tucanae** (tu:'kɑ:ni:). a faint extensive constellation in the S hemisphere close to Hydrus and Eridanus, containing most of the Small Magellanic Cloud. [probably from Tupi: toucan]

tuchun (tu:'tʃu:n) *n* (formerly) a Chinese military governor or warlord. [from Chinese, from *tu* to superintend + *chün* troops]

tuck[1] (tʌk) *vb* **1** (*tr*) to push or fold into a small confined space or concealed place or between two surfaces: *to tuck a letter into an envelope.* **2** (*tr*) to thrust the loose ends or sides of (something) into a confining space, so as to make neat and secure: *to tuck the sheets under the mattress.* **3** to make a tuck or tucks in (a garment). **4** (*usually tr*) to draw together, contract, or pucker. ◆ *n* **5** a tucked object or part. **6** a pleat or fold in a part of a garment, usually stitched down so as to make it a better fit or as decoration. **7** the part of a vessel where the after ends of the planking or plating meet at the sternpost. **8** *Brit.* **8a** an informal or schoolchild's word for **food,** esp. cakes and sweets. **8b** (*as modifier*): *a tuck box.* **9** a position of the body in certain dives in which the legs are bent with the knees drawn up against the chest and tightly clasped. ◆ See also **tuck away, tuck in.** [C14: from Old English *tūcian* to torment; related to Middle Dutch *tucken* to tug, Old High German *zucchen* to twitch]

tuck[2] (tʌk) *n Archaic.* a rapier. [C16: from French *estoc* sword, from Old French: tree trunk, sword, of Germanic origin]

tuck[3] (tʌk) *Dialect.* ◆ *n* **1** a touch, blow, or stroke. ◆ *vb* **2** (*tr*) to touch or strike. **3** (*intr*) to throb or bump. [C16: from Middle English *tukken* to beat a drum, from Old Northern French *toquer* to TOUCH; compare TUCKET]

Tuck (tʌk) *n* **Friar.** See **Friar Tuck.**

tuck away *vb* (*tr, adv*) *Informal.* **1** to eat (a large amount of food). **2** to store, esp. in a place difficult to find.

tucker[1] ('tʌkə) *n* **1** a person or thing that tucks. **2** a detachable yoke of lace, linen, etc., often white, worn over the breast, as of a low-cut dress. **3** an attachment on a sewing machine used for making tucks at regular intervals. **4** *Austral. and N.Z. old-fashioned.* an informal word for **food.**

tucker[2] ('tʌkə) *vb* (*tr; often passive;* usually foll. by *out*) *Informal, chiefly U.S. and Canadian.* to weary or tire completely.

tucker-bag *or* **tuckerbox** ('tʌkə,bɒks) *n Austral. informal, old-fashioned.* a bag or box used for carrying food.

tucket ('tʌkɪt) *n Archaic.* a flourish on a trumpet. [C16: from Old Northern French *toquer* to sound (on a drum)]

tuck in *vb* (*adv*) **1** (*tr*) Also: **tuck into.** to put to bed and make snug. **2** (*tr*) to thrust the loose ends or sides of (something) into a confining space: *tuck the blankets in.* **3** (*intr*) Also: **tuck into.** *Informal.* to eat, esp. heartily. ◆ *n* **tuck-in. 4** *Brit. informal.* a meal, esp. a large one.

tuck shop *n Chiefly Brit.* a shop, esp. one in or near a school, where food such as cakes and sweets are sold.

tucotuco (,tu:kəʊ'tu:kəʊ) *or* **tucutucu** (,tu:ku:'tu:ku:) *n* any of various colonial burrowing South American hystricomorph rodents of the genus *Ctenomys,* having long-clawed feet and a stocky body: family *Ctenomyidae.* [C19: of South American Indian origin]

Tucson ('tu:sɒn) *n* a city in SE Arizona, at an altitude of 700m (2400 ft.): resort and seat of the University of Arizona (1891). Pop.: 449 002 (1996 est.).

Tucumán (*Spanish* tuku'man) *n* a city in NW Argentina: scene of the declaration (1816) of Argentinian independence from Spain; university (1914). Pop.: 642 473 (1992 est.).

-tude *suffix forming nouns.* indicating state or condition: *plenitude.* [from Latin *-tūdō*]

Tudor ('tju:də) *n* **1** an English royal house descended from a Welsh squire, **Owen Tudor** (died 1461), and ruling from 1485 to 1603. Monarchs of the Tudor line were Henry VII, Henry VIII, Edward VI, Mary I, and Elizabeth I. ◆ *adj* **2** denoting a style of architecture of the late perpendicular period and characterized by half-timbered houses.

Tues. *abbrev. for* Tuesday.

Tuesday ('tju:zdɪ) *n* the third day of the week; second day of the working week. [Old English *tīwesdæg,* literally: day of Tiw, representing Latin *diēs Martis* day of Mars; compare Old Norse *tȳsdagr,* Old High German *zīostag;* see TIU, DAY]

tufa ('tju:fə) *n* a soft porous rock consisting of calcium carbonate deposited from springs rich in lime. Also called: **calc-tufa.** [C18: from Italian *tufo,* from Late Latin *tōfus*] ▸ **tufaceous** (tju:'feɪʃəs) *adj*

tuff (tʌf) *n* a rock formed by the fusing together on the ground of small rock fragments (less than 2 mm across) ejected from a volcano. [C16: from Old French *tuf,* from Italian *tufo;* see TUFA] ▸ **tuffaceous** (tʌ'feɪʃəs) *adj*

tuffet ('tʌfɪt) *n* a small mound or low seat. [C16: alteration of TUFT]

tuft (tʌft) *n* **1** a bunch of feathers, grass, hair, etc., held together at the base. **2** a cluster of threads drawn tightly through upholstery, a mattress, a quilt, etc., to secure and strengthen the padding. **3** a small clump of trees or bushes. **4** (formerly) a gold tassel on the cap worn by titled undergraduates at English universities. **5** a person entitled to wear such a tassel. ◆ *vb* **6** (*tr*) to provide or decorate with a tuft or tufts. **7** to form or be formed into tufts. **8** to secure and strengthen (a mattress, quilt, etc.) with tufts. [C14: perhaps from Old French *tufe,* of Germanic origin; compare TOP[1]] ▸ **'tufter** *n* ▸ **'tufty** *adj*

tufted ('tʌftɪd) *adj* **1** having a tuft or tufts. **2** (of plants or plant parts) having or consisting of one or more groups of short branches all arising at the same level.

tufted duck *n* a European lake-dwelling duck, *Aythya fuligula,* the male of which has a black plumage with white underparts and a long black drooping crest.

Tu Fu ('du: 'fu:) *n* a variant transliteration of the Chinese name for **Du Fu.**

tug (tʌg) *vb* **tugs, tugging, tugged. 1** (when *intr,* sometimes foll. by *at*) to pull or drag with sharp or powerful movements: *the boy tugged at the door handle.* **2** (*tr*) to tow (a vessel) by means of a tug. **3** (*intr*) to work; toil. ◆ *n* **4** a strong pull or jerk: *he gave the rope a tug.* **5** Also called: **tugboat.** a boat with a powerful engine, used for towing barges, ships, etc. **6** a hard struggle or fight. **7** a less common word for **trace**[2] (sense 1). [C13: related to Old English *tēon* to TOW[1]] ▸ **'tugger** *n*

Tugela (tu:'geɪlə) *n* a river in E South Africa, rising in the Drakensberg where it forms the **Tugela Falls,** 856 m (2810 ft.) high, before flowing east to the Indian

Ocean: scene of battles during the Zulu War (1879) and the Boer War (1899–1902). Length: about 500 km (312 miles).

tug-of-love *n* a conflict over custody of a child between divorced parents or between natural parents and foster or adoptive parents.

tug-of-war *n* **1** a contest in which two people or teams pull opposite ends of a rope in an attempt to drag the opposition over a central line. **2** any hard struggle, esp. between two equally matched factions.

tugrik *or* **tughrik** ('tu:,gri:k) *n* the standard monetary unit of Mongolia, divided into 100 mongos. [from Mongolian]

tui ('tu:ɪ) *n, pl* **tuis.** a New Zealand honeyeater, *Prosthemadera novaeseelandiae,* having a glossy bluish-green plumage with white feathers at the throat: it mimics human speech and the songs of other birds. [from Maori]

Tuileries ('twi:lərɪ; *French* tɥilri) *n* a former royal residence in Paris: begun in 1564 by Catherine de' Medici and burned in 1871 by the Commune; site of the **Tuileries Gardens** (a park near the Louvre).

tuition (tju:'ɪʃən) *n* **1** instruction, esp. that received in a small group or individually. **2** the payment for instruction, esp. in colleges or universities. [C15: from Old French *tuicion,* from Latin *tuitiō* a guarding, from *tuērī* to watch over] ▸ **tu'itional** *adj*

tuktu *or* **tuktoo** ('tʌk,tu:) *n* (in Canada) another name for **caribou.** [from Eskimo]

Tula (*Russian* 'tulə) *n* an industrial city in W central Russia. Pop.: 532 000 (1995 est.).

tularaemia *or U.S.* **tularemia** (,tu:lə'ri:mɪə) *n* an acute infectious bacterial disease of rodents, transmitted to man by infected ticks or flies or by handling contaminated flesh. It is characterized by fever, chills, and inflammation of the lymph glands. Also called: **rabbit fever.** [C19/20: from New Latin, from *Tulare,* county in California where it was first observed; see -AEMIA] ▸ **,tula'raemic** *or* **,tula'remic** *adj*

tulip ('tju:lɪp) *n* **1** any spring-blooming liliaceous plant of the temperate Eurasian genus *Tulipa,* having tapering bulbs, long broad pointed leaves, and single showy bell-shaped flowers. **2** the flower or bulb of any of these plants. [C17: from New Latin *tulipa,* from Turkish *tülbend* turban, which the opened bloom was thought to resemble] ▸ **'tulip-,like** *adj*

tulip tree *n* **1** Also called: **tulip poplar, yellow poplar.** a North American magnoliaceous forest tree, *Liriodendron tulipifera,* having tulip-shaped greenish-yellow flowers and long conelike fruits. **2** any of various other trees with tulip-shaped flowers, such as the magnolia.

tulipwood ('tju:lɪp,wʊd) *n* **1** Also called: **white poplar, yellow poplar.** the light soft wood of the tulip tree, used in making furniture and veneer. **2** any of several woods having stripes or streaks of colour, esp. that of *Dalbergia variabilis,* a tree of tropical South America.

Tull (tʌl) *n* **Jethro** ('dʒɛθrəʊ). 1674–1741, English agriculturalist, who invented the seed drill.

Tullamore (tʌlə'mɔ:) *n* the county town of Offaly, Republic of Ireland; food processing and brewing. Pop.: 8484 (1986).

tulle (tju:l) *n* a fine net fabric of silk, rayon, etc., used for evening dresses, as a trimming for hats, etc. [C19: from French, from *Tulle,* city in S central France, where it was first manufactured]

Tully ('tʌlɪ) *n* the former English name for (Marcus Tullius) **Cicero.**

Tulsa ('tʌlsə) *n* a city in NE Oklahoma, on the Arkansas River: a major oil centre; two universities. Pop.: 378 491 (1996 est.).

tum (tʌm) *n* an informal or childish word for **stomach.**

tumble ('tʌmbᵊl) *vb* **1** to fall or cause to fall, esp. awkwardly, precipitately, or violently. **2** (*intr; usually foll. by about*) to roll or twist, esp. in playing: *the kittens tumbled about on the floor.* **3** (*intr*) to perform leaps, somersaults, etc. **4** to go or move in a heedless or hasty way. **5** (*tr*) to polish (gemstones) in a tumbler. **6** (*tr*) to disturb, rumple, or toss around: *to tumble the bedclothes.* ◆ *n* **7** the act or an instance of tumbling. **8** a fall or toss. **9** an acrobatic feat, esp. a somersault. **10** a state of confusion. **11** a confused heap or pile: *a tumble of clothes.* [Old English *tumbian,* from Old French *tomber;* related to Old High German *tūmōn* to turn]

tumbledown ('tʌmbᵊl,daʊn) *adj* falling to pieces; dilapidated; crumbling.

tumble-dry *vb* **-dries, -drying, -dried.** (*tr*) to dry (laundry) in a tumble dryer.

tumble dryer *or* **tumble drier** *n* a machine that dries wet laundry by rotating it in warmed air inside a metal drum. Also called: **tumbler dryer, tumbler.**

tumblehome ('tʌmbᵊl,həʊm) *n* the inward curvature of the upper parts of the sides of a vessel at or near the stern.

tumbler ('tʌmblə) *n* **1a** a flat-bottomed drinking glass with no handle or stem. Originally, a tumbler had a round or pointed base and so could not stand upright. **1b** Also called: **tumblerful.** the contents or quantity such a glass holds. **2** a person, esp. a professional entertainer, who performs somersaults and other acrobatic feats. **3** another name for **tumble dryer. 4** Also called: **tumbling box.** a pivoted box or drum rotated so that the contents (usually inferior gemstones) tumble about and become smooth and polished. **5** the part of a lock that retains or releases the bolt and is moved by the action of a key. **6** a lever in a gunlock that receives the action of the mainspring when the trigger is pressed and thus forces the hammer forwards. **7a** a part that moves a gear in a train of gears into and out of engagement. **7b** a single cog or cam that transmits motion to the part with which it engages. **8** a toy, often a doll, that is so weighted that it rocks when touched. **9** (*often cap.*) a breed of domestic pigeon kept for exhibition or flying. The performing varieties execute backward somersaults in flight.

tumbler gear *n* a train of gears in which the gear-selection mechanism is operated by tumblers.

tumbler switch *n* a switch that is turned over to connect or disconnect an electric current.

tumble to *vb* (*intr, prep*) *Informal.* to understand; become aware of: *she tumbled to his plan quickly.*

tumbleweed ('tʌmbᵊl,wi:d) *n* any densely branched plant that breaks off near the ground on withering and is rolled about by the wind, esp. one of several amaranths of the western U.S. and Australia.

tumbrel *or* **tumbril** ('tʌmbrəl) *n* **1** a farm cart for carrying dung, esp. one that tilts backwards to deposit its load. A cart of this type was used to take condemned prisoners to the guillotine during the French Revolution. **2** (formerly) a covered cart that accompanied artillery in order to carry ammunition, tools, etc. **3** an obsolete word for a **ducking stool.** [C14 *tumberell* ducking stool, from Medieval Latin *tumbrellum,* from Old French *tumberel* dump cart, from *tomber* to tumble, of Germanic origin]

tumefacient (,tju:mɪ'feɪʃɪənt) *adj* producing or capable of producing swelling: *a tumefacient drug.* [C16: from Latin *tumefacere* to cause to swell, from *tumēre* to swell + *facere* to cause]

tumefaction (,tju:mɪ'fækʃən) *n* **1** the act or process of swelling. **2** a puffy or swollen structure or part.

tumefy ('tju:mɪ,faɪ) *vb* **-fies, -fying, -fied.** to make or become tumid; swell or puff up. [C16: from French *tuméfier,* from Latin *tumefacere;* see TUMEFACIENT]

tumescent (tju:'mɛsənt) *adj* swollen or becoming swollen. [C19: from Latin *tumescere* to begin to swell, from *tumēre*] ▸ **tu'mescence** *n*

tumid ('tju:mɪd) *adj* **1** (of an organ or part) enlarged or swollen. **2** bulging or protuberant. **3** pompous or fulsome in style: *tumid prose.* [C16: from Latin *tumidus,* from *tumēre* to swell] ▸ **tu'midity** *or* **'tumidness** *n* ▸ **'tumidly** *adv*

tummy ('tʌmɪ) *n, pl* **-mies.** an informal or childish word for **stomach.**

tummy tuck *n Informal.* the surgical removal of abdominal fat and skin for cosmetic purposes.

tumour *or U.S.* **tumor** ('tju:mə) *n* **1** *Pathol.* **1a** any abnormal swelling. **1b** a mass of tissue formed by a new growth of cells, normally independent of the surrounding structures. **2** *Obsolete.* pompous style or language. [C16: from Latin, from *tumēre* to swell] ▸ **'tumorous** *or* **'tumoral** *adj*

tump (tʌmp) *n Western English dialect.* a small mound or clump. [C16: of unknown origin]

tumpline ('tʌmp,laɪn) *n* (in the U.S. and Canada, esp. formerly) a leather or cloth band strung across the forehead or chest and attached to a pack or load in order to support it. Also called: **tump.** [C19: from *tump,* of Algonquian origin + LINE[1]; compare Abnaki *mádûmbi* pack strap]

tumular ('tju:mjʊlə) *adj* of, relating to, or like a mound.

tumulose ('tju:mjʊləʊs) *or* **tumulous** ('tju:mjʊləs) *adj* **1** abounding in small hills or mounds. **2** being or resembling a mound. [C18: from Latin *tumulōsus,* from *tumulus* a hillock] ▸ **tumulosity** (,tju:mjʊ'lɒsɪtɪ) *n*

tumult ('tju:mʌlt) *n* **1** a loud confused noise, as of a crowd; commotion. **2** violent agitation or disturbance. **3** great emotional or mental agitation. [C15: from Latin *tumultus,* from *tumēre* to swell up]

tumultuous (tju:'mʌltjʊəs) *adj* **1** uproarious, riotous, or turbulent: *a tumultuous welcome.* **2** greatly agitated, confused, or disturbed: *a tumultuous dream.* **3** making a loud or unruly disturbance: *tumultuous insurgents.* ▸ **tu'multuously** *adv* ▸ **tu'multuousness** *n*

tumulus ('tju:mjʊləs) *n, pl* **-li** (-li:). *Archaeol.* (no longer in technical usage) another word for **barrow**[2]. [C17: from Latin: a hillock, from *tumēre* to swell up]

tun (tʌn) *n* **1** a large beer cask. **2** a measure of capacity, usually equal to 252 wine gallons. **3** a cask used during the manufacture of beer: *a mash tun.* ◆ *vb* **tuns, tunning, tunned. 4** (*tr*) to put into or keep in tuns. [Old English *tunne;* related to Old High German, Old Norse *tunna,* Medieval Latin *tunna*]

tuna[1] ('tju:nə) *n, pl* **-na** *or* **-nas.** another name for **tunny** (sense 1). [C20: from American Spanish, from Spanish *atún,* from Arabic *tūn,* from Latin *thunnus* tunny, from Greek]

tuna[2] ('tju:nə) *n* **1** any of various tropical American prickly pear cacti, esp. *Opuntia tuna,* that are cultivated for their sweet edible fruits. **2** the fruit of any of these cacti. [C16: via Spanish from Taino]

tunable *or* **tuneable** ('tju:nəbᵊl) *adj* **1** able to be tuned. **2** *Archaic or poetic.* melodious or tuneful.

Tunbridge Wells ('tʌn,brɪdʒ) *n* a town and resort in SE England, in SW Kent: chalybeate spring discovered in 1606; an important social centre in the 17th and 18th centuries. Pop.: 60 272 (1991). Official name: **Royal Tunbridge Wells.**

tundra ('tʌndrə) *n* **a** a vast treeless zone lying between the ice cap and the timber line of North America and Eurasia and having a permanently frozen subsoil. **b** (*as modifier*): *tundra vegetation.* [C19: from Russian, from Lapp *tundar* hill; related to Finnish *tunturi* treeless hill]

tune (tju:n) *n* **1** a melody, esp. one for which harmony is not essential. **2** the most important part in a musical texture: *the cello has the tune at that point.* **3** the condition of producing accurately pitched notes, intervals, etc. (esp. in the phrases **in tune, out of tune**): *he can't sing in tune.* **4** accurate correspondence of pitch and intonation between instruments (esp. in the phrases **in tune, out of tune**): *the violin is not in tune with the piano.* **5** the correct adjustment of a radio, television, or some other electronic circuit with respect to the required frequency (esp. in the phrases **in tune, out of tune**). **6** a frame of mind; disposition or mood. **7** *Obsolete.* a musical sound; note. **8 call the tune.** to be in control of the proceedings. **9 change one's tune** *or* **sing another** (*or* **a different**) **tune.** to alter one's attitude or tone of speech. **10 to the tune of.** *Informal.* to the amount or extent of: *costs to the tune of a hundred pounds.* ◆ *vb* **11** to adjust (a musical instrument or a changeable part of one) to a certain pitch. **12** to adjust (a note, etc.) so as to bring it into harmony or concord. **13** (*tr*) to adapt or adjust (oneself); attune: *to tune oneself to a slower life.* **14** (*tr; often foll. by up*) to make fine adjustments to (an engine, machine, etc.) to obtain optimum performance. **15** *Electronics.* to adjust (one or more circuits) for resonance at a desired frequency. **16** *Obsolete.* to utter (something) musically or in the form of a melody; sing ◆ See also **tune in, tune up.** [C14: variant of TONE]

tuneful ('tju:nfʊl) *adj* **1** having a pleasant or catchy tune; melodious. **2** producing a melody or music: *a tuneful blackbird.* ▸ **'tunefully** *adv* ▸ **'tunefulness** *n*

tune in *vb* (*adv; often foll. by to*) **1** to adjust (a radio or television) to receive (a station or programme). **2** *Slang.* to make or become more aware, knowledgeable, etc. (about).

tuneless ('tju:nlɪs) *adj* **1** having no melody or tune. **2** *Chiefly poetic.* not producing or able to produce music; silent. ▸ **'tunelessly** *adv* ▸ **'tunelessness** *n*

tuner ('tju:nə) *n* **1** a person who tunes instruments, esp. pianos. **2** the part of a radio or television receiver for selecting only those signals having a particular frequency.

tunesmith ('tju:nˌsmɪθ) *n Informal.* a composer of light or popular music and songs.

tune up *vb* (*adv*) **1** to adjust (a musical instrument) to a particular pitch, esp. a standard one. **2** (esp. of an orchestra or other instrumental ensemble) to tune (instruments) to a common pitch. **3** (*tr*) to adjust (an engine) in (a car, etc.) to improve performance. ◆ *n* **tune-up. 4** adjustments made to an engine to improve its performance.

tung oil (tʌŋ) *n* a fast-drying oil obtained from the seeds of a central Asian euphorbiaceous tree, *Aleurites fordii*, used in paints, varnishes, etc., as a drying agent and to give a water-resistant finish. Also called: **Chinese wood oil.** [partial translation of Chinese *yu t'ung* tung tree oil, from *yu* oil + *t'ung* tung tree]

tungstate ('tʌŋsteɪt) *n* a salt of tungstic acid. [C20: from TUNGST(EN) + -ATE[1]]

tungsten ('tʌŋstən) *n* a hard malleable ductile greyish-white element. It occurs principally in wolframite and scheelite and is used in lamp filaments, electrical contact points, X-ray targets, and, alloyed with steel, in high-speed cutting tools. Symbol: W; atomic no.: 74; atomic wt.: 183.85; valency: 2–6; relative density: 19.3; melting pt.: 3422±20°C; boiling pt.: 5555°C. Also called: **wolfram.** [C18: from Swedish *tung* heavy + *sten* STONE]

tungsten carbide *n* a fine very hard crystalline grey powder produced by heating tungsten and carbon to a very high temperature: used in the manufacture of drill bits, dies, etc. Symbol: WC; melting pt.: 2870°C.

tungsten lamp *n* a lamp in which light is produced by a tungsten filament heated to incandescence by an electric current. The glass bulb enclosing the filament contains a low pressure of inert gas, usually argon. Sometimes small amounts of a halogen, such as iodine, are added to improve the intensity (**tungsten-halogen lamp**).

tungsten steel *n* any of various hard steels containing tungsten (1–20 per cent) and traces of carbon. They are resistant to wear at high temperatures and are used in tools.

tungstic ('tʌŋstɪk) *adj* of or containing tungsten, esp. in a high valence state. [C18: from TUNGST(EN) + -IC]

tungstic acid *n* any of various oxyacids of tungsten obtained by neutralizing alkaline solutions of tungstates. They are often polymeric substances, typical examples being H_2WO_4 (**orthotungstic acid**), $H_2W_4O_{13}$ (**metatungstic acid**), and $H_{10}W_{12}O_{14}$ (**paratungstic acid**).

tungstite ('tʌŋstaɪt) *n* a yellow earthy rare secondary mineral that consists of tungsten oxide and occurs with tungsten ores. Formula: WO_3. [C20: from TUNGST(EN) + -ITE[1]]

tungstous ('tʌŋstəs) *adj* of or containing tungsten in a low valence state.

Tungting *or* **Tung-t'ing** (ˌtʊŋ'tɪŋ) *n* a variant transliteration of the Chinese name for the **Dongting.**

Tungus ('tʊŋgʊs) *n* **1** (*pl* **-guses** *or* **-gus**) a member of a formerly nomadic Mongoloid people of E Siberia. **2** Also called: **Evenki.** the language of this people, belonging to the Tungusic branch of the Altaic family.

Tungusic (tʊŋ'gʊsɪk) *n* **1** a branch or subfamily of the Altaic family of languages, including Tungus and Manchu. ◆ *adj also* **Tungusian. 2** of or relating to these languages or their speakers.

Tunguska (*Russian* tun'guskə) *n* any of three rivers in Russia, in central Siberia, all tributaries of the Yenisei: the **Lower** (Nizhnyaya) **Tunguska,** 2690 km (1670 miles) long; the **Stony** (Podkamennaya) **Tunguska,** 1550 km (960 miles) long; the **Upper** (Verkhnyaya) **Tunguska,** which is the lower course of the Angara.

tunic ('tju:nɪk) *n* **1** any of various hip-length or knee-length garments, such as the loose sleeveless garb worn in ancient Greece or Rome, the jacket of some soldiers, or a woman's hip-length garment, worn with a skirt or trousers. **2** Also called: **tunica.** *Anatomy, botany, zoology.* a covering, lining, or enveloping membrane of an organ or part. **3** *Chiefly R.C. Church.* another word for **tunicle.** [Old English *tunice* (unattested except in the accusative case), from Latin *tunica*]

tunicate ('tju:nɪkɪt, -ˌkeɪt) *n* **1** any minute primitive marine chordate animal of the subphylum *Tunicata* (or *Urochordata, Urochorda*). The adults have a saclike unsegmented body enclosed in a cellulose-like outer covering (tunic) and only the larval forms have a notochord: includes the sea squirts. See also **ascidian.** ◆ *adj also* **tunicated. 2** of, relating to, or belonging to the subphylum *Tunicata.* **3** (esp. of a bulb) having or consisting of concentric layers of tissue. [C18: from Latin *tunicātus* clad in a TUNIC]

tunicle ('tju:nɪkᵊl) *n Chiefly R.C. Church.* the liturgical vestment worn by the subdeacon and bishops at High Mass and other religious ceremonies. [C14: from Latin *tunicula* a little TUNIC]

tuning ('tju:nɪŋ) *n Music.* **1** a set of pitches to which the open strings of a guitar, violin, etc., are tuned: *the normal tuning on a violin is G, D, A, E.* **2** the accurate pitching of notes and intervals by a choir, orchestra, etc.; intonation.

tuning fork *n* a two-pronged metal fork that when struck produces a pure note of constant specified pitch. It is used to tune musical instruments and in acoustics.

tuning key *n* a device that may be placed over a wrest pin on a piano, etc., and turned to alter the tension and pitch of a string.

Tunis ('tju:nɪs) *n* the capital and chief port of Tunisia, in the northeast on the **Gulf of Tunis** (an inlet of the Mediterranean): dates from Carthaginian times, the ruins of ancient Carthage lying to the northeast; university (1960). Pop.: 674 100 (1994).

Tunisia (tju:'nɪzɪə, -'nɪsɪə) *n* a republic in N Africa, on the Mediterranean: settled by the Phoenicians in the 12th century B.C.; made a French protectorate in 1881 and gained independence in 1955. It consists chiefly of the Sahara in the south, a central plateau, and the Atlas Mountains in the north. Exports include petroleum, phosphates, and iron ore. Official language: Arabic; French is also widely spoken. Official religion: Muslim. Currency: dinar. Capital: Tunis. Pop.: 9 380 000 (1998 est.). Area: 164 150 sq. km (63 380 sq. miles). ▸ **Tu'nisian** *adj, n*

tunnage ('tʌnɪdʒ) *n* a variant spelling of **tonnage.**

tunnel ('tʌnᵊl) *n* **1** an underground passageway, esp. one for trains or cars that passes under a mountain, river, or a congested urban area. **2** any passage or channel through or under something. **3** a dialect word for **funnel. 4** *Obsolete.* the flue of a chimney. ◆ *vb* **-nels, -nelling, -nelled** *or U.S.* **-nels, -neling, -neled. 5** (*tr*) to make or force (a way) through or under (something): *to tunnel a hole in the wall; to tunnel the cliff.* **6** (*intr;* foll. by *through, under,* etc.) to make or force a way (through or under something): *he tunnelled through the bracken.* [C15: from Old French *tonel* cask, from *tonne* tun, from Medieval Latin *tonna* barrel, of Celtic origin] ▸ **'tunneller** *or U.S.* **'tunneler** *n*

tunnel diode *n* an extremely stable semiconductor diode, having a very narrow highly doped p-n junction, in which electrons travel across the junction by means of the tunnel effect. Also called: **Esaki diode.**

tunnel disease *n* another name (esp. formerly) for **decompression sickness.** [so called because it used to be common among people who were digging tunnels]

tunnel effect *n Physics.* the phenomenon in which an object, usually an elementary particle, tunnels through a potential barrier even though it does not have sufficient energy to surmount the barrier. It is explained by wave mechanics and is the cause of alpha decay, field emission, and certain conduction processes in semiconductors.

tunnel vault *n* another name for **barrel vault.**

tunnel vision *n* **1** a condition in which peripheral vision is greatly restricted. **2** narrowness of viewpoint resulting from concentration on a single idea, opinion, etc., to the exclusion of others.

Tunney ('tʌnɪ) *n* **Gene,** original name *James Joseph Tunney.* 1897–1978, U.S. boxer; world heavyweight champion (1926–28).

tunny ('tʌnɪ) *n, pl* **-nies** *or* **-ny. 1** Also called: **tuna.** any of various large marine spiny-finned fishes of the genus *Thunnus,* esp. *T. thynnus,* chiefly of warm waters: family *Scombridae.* They have a spindle-shaped body and widely forked tail, and are important food fishes. **2** any of various similar and related fishes. [C16: from Old French *thon,* from Old Provençal *ton,* from Latin *thunnus,* from Greek]

tup (tʌp) *n* **1** *Chiefly Brit.* an uncastrated male sheep; ram. **2** the head of a pile-driver or steam hammer. ◆ *vb* **tups, tupping, tupped.** (*tr*) **3** to cause (a ram) to mate with a ewe, or (of a ram) to mate with (a ewe). **4** *Lancashire dialect.* to butt (someone), as in a fight. [C14: of unknown origin]

Tupamaro (ˌtu:pə'mɑ:rəʊ) *n, pl* **-ros.** any of a group of Marxist urban guerrillas in Uruguay. [C20: after *Tupac Amaru,* 18th-century Peruvian Indian who led a rebellion against the Spaniards]

tupelo ('tju:pɪˌləʊ) *n, pl* **-los. 1** any of several cornaceous trees of the genus *Nyssa,* esp. *N. aquatica,* a large tree of deep swamps and rivers of the southern U.S. **2** the light strong wood of any of these trees. [C18: from Creek *ito opilwa,* from *ito* tree + *opilwa* swamp]

Tupi (tu:'pi:) *n* **1** (*pl* **-pis** *or* **-pi**) a member of a South American Indian people of Brazil and Paraguay. **2** the language of this people, belonging to the Tupi-Guarani family. ▸ **Tu'pian** *adj*

Tupi-Guarani *n* a family of South American Indian languages spoken in Brazil, Paraguay, and certain adjacent regions: possibly distantly related to Quechua. ▸ **'Tupi,-Guara'nian** *adj*

tupik *or* **tupek** ('tu:pək) *n Canadian.* (esp. in the Arctic) a tent of animal skins, a traditional type of Inuit summer dwelling. [from Eskimo *tupiq*]

-tuple *n and adj combining form.* indicating a set of the number specified.

Tupolev (*Russian* tu'pəljif) *n* **Andrei Nikolaievich** (un'drjeɪ njɪkə'lajɪvjɪtʃ). 1888–1972, Soviet aircraft designer, who designed the first supersonic passenger aircraft, the TU-144 (tested 1969). He also designed supersonic bombers and the TU-104, one of the first passenger jet aircraft (1955).

tuppence ('tʌpəns) *n Brit.* a variant spelling of **twopence.**

tuppenny ('tʌpənɪ) *adj* a variant spelling of **twopenny.**

Tupperware ('tʌpəweə) *n Trademark.* a range of plastic containers used for storing food. [C20: *Tupper,* U.S. manufacturing company + WARE[1]]

Tupungato (*Spanish* tupuŋ'gato) *n* a mountain on the border between Argentina and Chile, in the Andes. Height: 6550 m (21 484 ft.).

tuque (tu:k) *n Canadian.* **1** a knitted cap with a long tapering end. **2** Also called: **toque.** a close-fitting knitted hat often with a tassel or pompom. [C19: from Canadian French, from French: TOQUE]

tu quoque *Latin.* (tju: 'kwəʊkwɪ) *interj* you likewise: a retort made by a person accused of a crime implying that the accuser is also guilty of the same crime.

turaco ('tʊərəˌkəʊ) *n, pl* **-cos.** a variant spelling of **touraco.**

Turanian (tjʊ'reɪnɪən) *n* **1** a member of any of the peoples inhabiting ancient Turkestan, or their descendants. **2** another name for **Ural-Altaic.** ◆ *adj* **3** of or relating to the Ural-Altaic languages or any of the peoples who speak them. **4** of or relating to Turkestan or its people.

turban ('tɜːbᵊn) *n* **1** a man's headdress, worn esp. by Muslims, Hindus, and Sikhs, made by swathing a length of linen, silk, etc., around the head or around a caplike base. **2** a woman's brimless hat resembling this. **3** any headdress resembling this. [C16: from Turkish *tülbend,* from Persian *dulband*] ▸ **'turbaned** *adj* ▸ **'turban-ˌlike** *adj*

turbary ('tɜːbərɪ) *n, pl* **-ries. 1** land where peat or turf is cut or has been cut. **2** Also called: **common of turbary.** (in England) the legal right to cut peat for fuel on a common. [C14: from Old French *turbarie,* from Medieval Latin *turbāria,* from *turba* peat, TURF]

turbellarian (ˌtɜːbɪ'lɛərɪən) *n* **1** any typically aquatic free-living flatworm of the class *Turbellaria,* having a ciliated epidermis and a simple life cycle: includes the planarians. ◆ *adj* **2** of, relating to, or belonging to the class *Turbellaria.* [C19: from New Latin *Turbellāria,* from Latin *turbellae* (pl) bustle, from *turba* brawl, referring to the swirling motion created in the water]

turbid ('tɜːbɪd) *adj* **1** muddy or opaque, as a liquid clouded with a suspension of particles. **2** dense, thick, or cloudy: *turbid fog.* **3** in turmoil or confusion. [C17: from Latin *turbidus,* from *turbāre* to agitate, from *turba* crowd] ▸ **tur'bidity** *or* **'turbidness** *n* ▸ **'turbidly** *adv*

turbidimeter (ˌtɜːbɪ'dɪmɪtə) *n* a device that measures the turbidity of a liquid.

turbidite ('tɜːbɪˌdaɪt) *n* a sediment deposited by a turbidity current. [C20: from TURBID + -ITE[1]]

turbidity current *n* a swirling mass of water and suspended material stirred up by a tsunami, a storm, a river in flood, etc.

turbinate ('tɜːbɪnɪt, -ˌneɪt) *or* **turbinal** ('tɜːbɪnᵊl) *adj also* **turbinated. 1** *Anatomy.* of or relating to any of the thin scroll-shaped bones situated on the walls of the nasal passages. **2** shaped like a spiral or scroll. **3** (esp. of the shells of certain molluscs) shaped like an inverted cone. ◆ *n* **4** Also called: **nasal concha.** a turbinate bone. **5** a turbinate shell. [C17: from Latin *turbō* spinning top] ▸ **ˌturbi'nation** *n*

turbine ('tɜːbɪn, -baɪn) *n* any of various types of machine in which the kinetic energy of a moving fluid is converted into mechanical energy by causing a bladed rotor to rotate. The moving fluid may be water, steam, air, or combustion products of a fuel. See also **reaction turbine, impulse turbine, gas turbine.** [C19: from French, from Latin *turbō* whirlwind, from *turbāre* to throw into confusion]

turbine blade *n* any of a number of bladelike vanes assembled around the periphery of a turbine rotor to guide the steam or gas flow.

turbit ('tɜːbɪt) *n* a crested breed of domestic pigeon. [C17: from Latin *turbō* spinning top, with reference to the bird's shape; compare TURBOT]

turbo- *combining form.* of, relating to, or driven by a turbine: *turbofan.*

turbocar ('tɜːbəʊˌkɑː) *n* a car driven by a gas turbine.

turbocharger ('tɜːbəʊˌtʃɑːdʒə) *n* a centrifugal compressor which boosts the intake pressure of an internal-combustion engine, driven by an exhaust-gas turbine fitted to the engine's exhaust manifold.

turbo-electric (ˌtɜːbəʊɪ'lɛktrɪk) *adj* of, relating to, or using an electric generator driven by a turbine: *turbo-electric propulsion.*

turbofan (ˌtɜːbəʊ'fæn) *n* **1** Also called: **high bypass ratio engine.** a type of by-pass engine in which a large fan driven by a turbine and housed in a short duct forces air rearwards around the exhaust gases in order to increase the propulsive thrust. **2** an aircraft driven by one or more turbofans. **3** the ducted fan in such an engine. ◆ Also called (for senses 1, 2): **fanjet.**

turbogenerator (ˌtɜːbəʊ'dʒɛnəˌreɪtə) *n* a large electrical generator driven by a steam turbine.

turbojet (ˌtɜːbəʊ'dʒɛt) *n* **1** short for **turbojet engine. 2** an aircraft powered by one or more turbojet engines.

turbojet engine *n* a gas turbine in which the exhaust gases provide the propulsive thrust to drive an aircraft.

turboprop (ˌtɜːbəʊ'prɒp) *n* **1** an aircraft propulsion unit where a propeller is driven by a gas turbine. **2** an aircraft powered by turboprops.

turbosupercharger (ˌtɜːbəʊ'suːpəˌtʃɑːdʒə) *n Obsolete.* a supercharging device for an internal-combustion engine, consisting of a turbine driven by the exhaust gases.

turbot ('tɜːbət) *n, pl* **-bot** *or* **-bots. 1** a European flatfish, *Scophthalmus maximus,* having a pale brown speckled scaleless body covered with tubercles: family *Bothidae.* It is highly valued as a food fish. **2** any of various similar or related fishes. [C13: from Old French *tourbot,* from Medieval Latin *turbō,* from Latin: spinning top, from a fancied similarity in shape; see TURBIT, TURBINE]

turbulence ('tɜːbjʊləns) *or* (*rarely*) **turbulency** *n* **1** a state or condition of confusion, movement, or agitation; disorder. **2** *Meteorol.* instability in the atmosphere causing considerable gusty air currents and cumulonimbus clouds. **3** turbulent flow in a liquid or gas.

turbulent ('tɜːbjʊlənt) *adj* **1** being in a state of turbulence. **2** wild or insubordinate; unruly. [C16: from Latin *turbulentus,* from *turba* confusion] ▸ **'turbulently** *adv*

turbulent flow *n* flow of a fluid in which its velocity at any point varies rapidly in an irregular manner. Compare **laminar flow.** See also **streamline flow.**

Turco ('tɜːkəʊ) *n, pl* **-cos.** (formerly) an Algerian serving in the light infantry of the French army. [C19: via French from Italian: a Turk]

Turco- *or* **Turko-** *combining form.* indicating Turkey or Turkish: *Turco-Greek.*

turd (tɜːd) *n Taboo.* **1** a lump of dung; piece of excrement. **2** *Slang.* an unpleasant or contemptible person or thing. [Old English *tord;* related to Old Norse *tordy fill* dung beetle, Dutch *tort* dung]

turdine ('tɜːdaɪn, -dɪn) *adj* of, relating to, or characteristic of thrushes. [C19: from Latin *turdus* thrush]

tureen (tə'riːn) *n* a large deep usually rounded dish with a cover, used for serving soups, stews, etc. [C18: from French *terrine* earthenware vessel, from *terrin* made of earthenware, from Vulgar Latin *terrīnus* (unattested) earthen, from Latin *terra* earth]

Turenne (*French* tyrɛn) *n* **Vicomte de,** title of *Henri de la Tour d'Auvergne.* 1611–75, French marshal. He commanded armies during the Thirty Years' War and the wars of the Fronde.

turf (tɜːf) *n, pl* **turfs** *or* **turves** (tɜːvz). **1** the surface layer of fields and pastures, consisting of earth containing a dense growth of grasses with their roots; sod. **2** a piece cut from this layer, used to form lawns, verges, etc. **3 the turf. 3a** a track, usually of grass or dirt, where horse races are run. **3b** horse racing as a sport or industry. **4** *U.S. slang.* the territory or area of activity over which a person or group claims exclusive rights. **5** an area of knowledge or influence: *he's on home turf when it comes to music.* **6** another term for **peat.** ◆ *vb* **7** (*tr*) to cover with pieces of turf. [Old English; related to Old Norse *torfa,* Old High German *zurba,* Sanskrit *darbha* tuft of grass]

turf accountant *n Brit.* a formal name for a **bookmaker.**

turfman ('tɜːfmən) *n, pl* **-men.** *Chiefly U.S.* a person devoted to horse racing. Also called: **turfite** ('tɜːfaɪt).

turf out *vb* (*tr, adv*) *Brit. informal.* to throw out or dismiss; eject: *we were turfed out of the club.*

turfy ('tɜːfɪ) *adj* **turfier, turfiest. 1** of, covered with, or resembling turf. **2** relating to or characteristic of horse racing or persons connected with it. ▸ **'turfiness** *n*

Turgenev (*Russian* tur'gjenɪf) *n* **Ivan Sergeyevich** (i'van sɪr'gjejɪvitʃ). 1818–83, Russian novelist and dramatist. In *A Sportsman's Sketches* (1852) he pleaded for the abolition of serfdom. His novels, such as *Rudin* (1856) and *Fathers and Sons* (1862), are noted for their portrayal of country life and of the Russian intelligentsia. His plays include *A Month in the Country* (1850).

turgent ('tɜːdʒənt) *adj* an obsolete word for **turgid.** [C15: from Latin *turgēre* to swell] ▸ **'turgently** *adv*

turgescent (tɜː'dʒɛsᵊnt) *adj* becoming or being swollen; inflated; tumid. ▸ **tur'gescence** *or* **tur'gescency** *n*

turgid ('tɜːdʒɪd) *adj* **1** swollen and distended; congested. **2** (of style or language) pompous and high-flown; bombastic. [C17: from Latin *turgidus,* from *turgēre* to swell] ▸ **tur'gidity** *or* **'turgidness** *n* ▸ **'turgidly** *adv*

turgite ('tɜːdʒaɪt) *n* a red or black mineral consisting of hydrated ferric oxide. Formula: $Fe_2O_3.nH_2O$.

turgor ('tɜːgə) *n* the normal rigid state of a cell, caused by pressure of the cell contents against the cell wall or membrane. [C19: from Late Latin: a swelling, from Latin *turgēre* to swell]

Turgot (*French* tyrgo) *n* **Anne Robert Jacques** (ɑn rɔbɛr ʒak). 1727–81, French economist and statesman. As controller general of finances (1774–76), he attempted to abolish feudal privileges, incurring the hostility of the aristocracy and his final dismissal.

Turin (tjʊə'rɪn) *n* a city in NW Italy, capital of Piedmont region, on the River Po: became capital of the Kingdom of Sardinia in 1720; first capital (1861–65) of united Italy; university (1405); a major industrial centre, producing most of Italy's cars. Pop.: 923 106 (1996 est.). Italian name: **Torino.**

Turing ('tjʊərɪŋ) *n* **Alan Mathison.** 1912–54, English mathematician, who was responsible for formal description of abstract automata, and speculation on computer imitation of humans.

Turing machine *n* a hypothetical universal computing machine able to modify its original instructions by reading, erasing, or writing a new symbol on a moving tape of fixed length that acts as its program. The concept was instrumental in the early development of computer systems.

Turing test *n* a proposed test of a computer's ability to think, requiring that the covert substitution of the computer for one of the participants in a keyboard and screen dialogue should be undetectable by the remaining human participant.

turion ('tʊərɪən) *n* a perennating bud produced by many aquatic plants: it detaches from the parent plant and remains dormant until the following spring. [C17: from French *turion,* from Latin *turio* shoot]

Turishcheva (*Russian* tu'riʃtʃəvə) *n* **Ludmilla** (lud'mɪlə). born 1952, Soviet gymnast: world champion 1970, 1972 (at the Olympic Games), and 1974.

Turk (tɜːk) *n* **1** a native, inhabitant, or citizen of Turkey. **2** a native speaker of any Turkic language, such as an inhabitant of Turkmenistan or Kyrgyzstan. **3** *Obsolete, derogatory.* a violent, brutal, or domineering person.

Turk. *abbrev. for:* **1** Turkey. **2** Turkish.

Turkana (tɜː'kɑːnə) *n* **Lake.** a long narrow lake in E Africa, in the Great Rift Valley. Area: 7104 sq. km (2743 sq. miles). Former name: (Lake) **Rudolf.**

Turkestan *or* **Turkistan** (ˌtɜːkɪ'stɑːn) *n* an extensive region of central Asia between Siberia in the north and Tibet, India, Afghanistan, and Iran in the south: formerly divided into **West** (**Russian**) **Turkestan** (also called Soviet Central Asia), comprising present-day Turkmenistan, Uzbekistan, Tajikistan, and Kyrgyzstan and the S part of Kazakhstan, and **East** (**Chinese**) **Turkestan,** consisting of the Xinjiang Uygur Autonomous Region. ▸ **ˌTurke'stani** *adj, n*

turkey ('tɜːkɪ) *n, pl* **-keys** *or* **-key. 1** a large gallinaceous bird, *Meleagris gallopavo,* of North America, having a bare wattled head and neck and a brownish iridescent plumage. The male is brighter and has a fan-shaped tail. A domestic variety is widely bred for its flesh. **2** the flesh of the turkey used as food. **3** a similar and related bird, *Agriocharis ocellata* (**ocellated turkey**), of Central and N South America. **4** *Slang, chiefly U.S. and Canadian.* **4a** a dramatic production that fails; flop. **4b** a thing or person that fails; dud. **5** *Slang, chiefly U.S. and Canadian.* a stupid, incompetent, or unappealing person. **6** *Slang.* (in tenpin bowling) three strikes in a row. **7** See **cold turkey. 8 talk turkey.** *Informal, chiefly U.S. and Canadian.* to discuss frankly and practically. [C16: shortened from *Turkey cock* (*hen*), used at first to designate the African guinea fowl (apparently because the bird was brought through Turkish territory), later applied by mistake to the American bird]

Turkey ('tɜːkɪ) *n* a republic in W Asia and SE Europe, between the Black Sea, the Mediterranean, and the Aegean: one of the oldest inhabited regions of the world; the centre of the Ottoman Empire; became a republic in 1923. The major Asian part, consisting mainly of an arid plateau, is separated from European Turkey by the Bosporus, Sea of Marmara, and Dardanelles. Official languages: Turkish; Kurdish and Arabic minority languages. Religion: Muslim majority. Currency: lira. Capital: Ankara. Pop.: 64 567 000 (1998 est.). Area: 780 576 sq. km (301 380 sq. miles).

turkey brown *n* an angler's name for a species of mayfly, *Paraleptophlebia submarginata.*

turkey buzzard *or* **vulture** *n* a New World vulture, *Cathartes aura,* having a dark plumage and naked red head.

Turkey carpet *n* a wool carpet made in one piece and having a deep velvety pile and rich glowing colours.

turkey cock *n* **1** a male turkey. **2** an arrogant person.

turkey nest *n Austral.* a small earth dam adjacent to, and higher than, a larger earth dam, to feed water by gravity to a cattle trough, etc.

Turkey oak *n* an oak tree, *Quercus cerris,* of W and S Europe, with deeply lobed hairy leaves. **[**C18: so called because its acorns are often eaten by turkeys**]**

Turkey red *n* **1a** a moderate or bright red colour. **1b** *(as adj): a Turkey-red fabric.* **2** a cotton fabric of a bright red colour.

turkey trot *n* an early ragtime one-step, popular in the period of World War I.

Turki ('tɜːkɪ) *adj* **1** of or relating to the Turkic languages, esp. those of central Asia. **2** of or relating to speakers of these languages. ◆ *n* **3** these languages collectively; esp. Eastern Turkic.

Turkic ('tɜːkɪk) *n* a branch or subfamily of the Altaic family of languages, including Turkish, Turkmen, Kirghiz, Tatar, etc., members of which are found from Turkey to NE China, esp. in central Asia.

Turkish ('tɜːkɪʃ) *adj* **1** of, relating to, or characteristic of Turkey, its people, or their language. ◆ *n* **2** the official language of Turkey, belonging to the Turkic branch of the Altaic family. See also **Osmanli.** ▸ **'Turkishness** *n*

Turkish bath *n* **1** a type of bath in which the bather sweats freely in hot dry air, is then washed, often massaged, and has a cold plunge or shower. **2** *(sometimes pl)* an establishment where such a bath is obtainable.

Turkish coffee *n* very strong black coffee made with finely ground coffee beans.

Turkish delight *n* a jelly-like sweet flavoured with flower essences, usually cut into cubes and covered in icing sugar.

Turkish Empire *n* another name for the **Ottoman Empire.**

Turkish tobacco *n* a fragrant dark tobacco cultivated in E Europe, esp. Turkey and Greece.

Turkish towel *n* a rough loose-piled towel; terry towel.

Turkism ('tɜːkɪzəm) *n Rare.* **1** the culture, beliefs, and customs of the Turks. **2** a Turkish word, fashion, etc.

Turkmen ('tɜːkmɛn) *n* the language of the Turkomans, belonging to the Turkic branch of the Altaic family.

Turkmenistan (ˌtɜːkmɛnɪ'stɑːn) *n* a republic in central Asia; the area has been occupied by a succession of empires; a Turkmen state was established in the 15th century but suffered almost continual civil strife and was gradually conquered by Russia; in 1918 it became a Soviet republic and gained independence from the Soviet Union in 1991: deserts including the **Kara Kum** cover most of the region; agricultural communities are concentrated around oases; there are rich mineral deposits. Official language: Turkmen. Religion: believers are mainly Muslim. Currency: manat. Capital: Ashkhabad. Pop.: 4 731 000 (1998 est.). Area: 488 100 sq. km (186 400 sq. miles).

Turko- *combining form.* a variant spelling of **Turco-.**

Turkoman ('tɜːkəmən) *or* **Turkman** *n* **1** *(pl* **-mans** *or* **-men)** a member of a formerly nomadic people of central Asia, now living chiefly in Turkmenistan and in NE Iran. **2** the Turkmen language. ◆ *adj* **3** of or relating to this people or their language. **[**C16: from Medieval Latin *Turcomannus,* from Persian *turkumān* resembling a Turk, from *turk* Turk + *māndan* to be like**]**

Turks and Caicos Islands *pl n* a UK Overseas Territory in the Caribbean, southeast of the Bahamas: consists of the eight **Turks Islands,** separated by the **Turks Island Passage** from the Caicos group, which has six main islands. Capital: Grand Turk. Pop.: 14 000 (1993 est.). Area: 430 sq. km (166 sq. miles).

Turk's-cap lily *n* any of several cultivated lilies, such as *Lilium martagon* and *L. superbum,* that have brightly coloured flowers with reflexed petals. See also **martagon. [**C17: so called because of a resemblance between its flowers and a turban**]**

Turk's-head *n* an ornamental turban-like knot made by weaving small cord around a larger rope.

Turku *(Finnish* 'turku) *n* a city and port in SW Finland, on the Gulf of Bothnia: capital of Finland until 1812. Pop.: 166 929 (1997 est.). Swedish name: **Åbo.**

turlough ('tɜːlɒx) *n* a seasonal lake or pond: a low-lying area on limestone, esp. in Ireland, that becomes flooded in wet weather by the upsurge of underlying ground water. **[**C17: from Irish *tur* dry + LOUGH**]**

turmeric ('tɜːmərɪk) *n* **1** a tropical Asian zingiberaceous plant, *Curcuma longa,* having yellow flowers and an aromatic underground stem. **2** the powdered stem of this plant, used as a condiment and as a yellow dye. **3** any of several other plants with similar roots. **[**C16: from Old French *terre merite,* from Medieval Latin *terra merita,* literally: meritorious earth, name applied for obscure reasons to curcuma**]**

turmeric paper *n Chem.* paper impregnated with turmeric used as a test for alkalis, which turn it brown, and for boric acid, which turns it reddish brown.

turmoil ('tɜːmɔɪl) *n* **1** violent or confused movement; agitation; tumult. ◆ *vb* **2** *Archaic.* to make or become turbulent. **[**C16: perhaps from TURN + MOIL**]**

turn (tɜːn) *vb* **1** to move or cause to move around an axis: *a wheel turning; to turn a knob.* **2** (sometimes foll. by *round*) to change or cause to change positions by moving through an arc of a circle: *he turned the chair to face the light.* **3** to change or cause to change in course, direction, etc.: *he turned left at the main road.* **4** (of soldiers, ships, etc.) to alter the direction of advance by changing direction simultaneously or (of a commander) to cause the direction of advance to be altered simultaneously. **5** to go or pass to the other side of (a corner, etc.). **6** to assume or cause to assume a rounded, curved, or folded form: *the road turns here.* **7** to reverse or cause to reverse position. **8** *(tr)* to pass round (an enemy or enemy position) so as to attack it from the flank or rear: *the Germans turned the Maginot line.* **9** *(tr)* to perform or do by a rotating movement: *to turn a somersault.* **10** *(tr)* to shape or cut a thread in (a workpiece, esp. one of metal, wood, or plastic) by rotating it on a lathe against a fixed cutting tool. **11** (when *intr,* foll. by *into* or *to*) to change or convert or be changed or converted: *the alchemists tried to turn base metals into gold.* **12** (foll. by *into*) to change or cause to change in nature, character, etc.: *the frog turned into a prince.* **13** *(copula)* to change so as to become: *he turned nasty when he heard the price.* **14** to cause (foliage, etc.) to change colour or (of foliage, etc.) to change colour: *frost turned the trees a vivid orange.* **15** to cause (milk, etc.) to become rancid or sour or (of milk, etc.) to become rancid or sour. **16** to change or cause to change in subject, trend, etc.: *the conversation turned to fishing.* **17** to direct or apply or be directed or applied: *he turned his attention to the problem.* **18** *(intr;* usually foll. by *to)* to appeal or apply (to) for help, advice, etc.: *she was very frightened and didn't know where to turn.* **19** to reach, pass, or progress beyond in age, time, etc.: *she has just turned twenty.* **20** *(tr)* to cause or allow to go: *to turn an animal loose.* **21** to affect or be affected with nausea: *the sight of the dead body turned his stomach.* **22** to affect or be affected with giddiness: *my head is turning.* **23** *(tr)* to affect the mental or emotional stability of (esp. in the phrase **turn (someone's) head)**. **24** *(tr)* to release from a container: *she turned the fruit into a basin.* **25** *(tr)* to render into another language. **26** (usually foll. by *against* or *from*) to transfer or reverse or cause to transfer or reverse (one's loyalties, affections, etc.). **27** *(tr)* to cause (an enemy agent) to become a double agent working for one's own side: *the bureau turned some of the spies it had caught.* **28** *(tr)* to bring (soil) from lower layers to the surface. **29** to blunt (an edge) or (of an edge) to become blunted. **30** *(tr)* to give a graceful form to: *to turn a compliment.* **31** *(tr)* to reverse (a cuff, collar, etc.) in order to hide the outer worn side. **32** *(intr) U.S.* to be merchandised as specified: *shirts are turning well this week.* **33** *Cricket.* to spin (the ball) or (of the ball) to spin. **34 turn one's hand to.** to undertake (something, esp. something practical). **35 turn tail.** to run away; flee. **36 turn the tables (on someone)**. See **table** (sense 17). **37 turn the tide.** to reverse the general course of events. ◆ *n* **38** an act or instance of turning or the state of being turned or the material turned: *a turn of a rope around a bollard.* **39** a movement of complete or partial rotation. **40** a change or reversal of direction or position. **41** direction or drift: *his thoughts took a new turn.* **42** a deviation or departure from a course or tendency. **43** the place, point, or time at which a deviation or change occurs. **44** another word for **turning** (sense 1). **45** the right or opportunity to do something in an agreed order or succession: *we'll take turns to play; now it's George's turn; you must not play out of turn.* **46** a change in nature, condition, etc.: *his illness took a turn for the worse.* **47** a period of action, work, etc. **48** a short walk, ride, or excursion: *to take a turn in the park.* **49** natural inclination: *he is of a speculative turn of mind; she has a turn for needlework.* **50** distinctive form or style: *a neat turn of phrase.* **51** requirement, need, or advantage: *to serve someone's turn.* **52** a deed performed that helps or hinders someone: *to do an old lady a good turn.* **53** a twist, bend, or distortion in shape. **54** *Music.* a melodic ornament that makes a turn around a note, beginning with the note above, in a variety of sequences. **55** *Theatre, chiefly Brit.* a short theatrical act, esp. in music hall, cabaret, etc. **56** *Stock Exchange.* **56a** *Brit.* the difference between a market maker's bid and offer prices, representing the market maker's profit. **56b** a transaction including both a purchase and a sale. **57** a military manoeuvre in which men or ships alter their direction of advance together. **58** *Austral. slang.* a party. **59** *Informal.* a shock or surprise: *the bad news gave her quite a turn.* **60 at every turn.** on all sides or occasions. **61 by turns.** one after another; alternately. **62 on the turn.** *Informal.* **62a** at the point of change. **62b** about to go rancid. **63 out of turn. 63a** not in the correct or agreed order of succession. **63b** improperly, inappropriately, or inopportunely. **64 turn and turn about.** one after another; alternately. **65 to a turn.** to the proper amount; perfectly: *cooked to a turn.* ◆ See also **turn against, turn away, turn down, turn in, turn off, turn on, turn out, turn over, turn to, turn up.** **[**Old English *tyrnian,* from Old French *torner,* from Latin *tornāre* to turn in a lathe, from *tornus* lathe, from Greek *tornos* dividers**]** ▸ **'turnable** *adj*

turnabout ('tɜːnəˌbaʊt) *n* **1** the act of turning so as to face a different direction. **2** a change or reversal of opinion, attitude, etc.

turn against *vb (prep)* to change or cause to change one's attitude so as to become hostile or to retaliate.

turnaround ('tɜːnəˌraʊnd) *n* **1a** the act or process in which a ship, aircraft, etc., unloads passengers and freight at the end of a trip and reloads for the next trip. **1b** the time taken for this. **2** the total time taken by a ship, aircraft, or other vehicle in a round trip. **3** a complete reversal of a situation or set of circumstances. ◆ Also called: **turnround.**

turnaround time *n Computing.* the total time taken between the submission of a program for execution and the return of the complete output to the customer.

turn away *vb (adv)* **1** to move or cause to move in a different direction so as not to face something: *one of the children turned away while the others hid.* **2** *(tr)* to refuse admittance or assistance to: *dozens of people were turned away from the hostel.*

turn bridge *n* another name for **swing bridge.**

turnbuckle ('tɜːnˌbʌkᵊl) *n* an open mechanical sleeve usually having a swivel at one end and a thread at the other to enable a threaded wire or rope to be tightened. **[**C19: from TURN + BUCKLE**]**

turncoat ('tɜːnˌkəʊt) *n* a person who deserts one cause or party for the opposite faction; renegade.

turncock ('tɜːnˌkɒk) *n* (formerly) an official employed to turn on the water for the mains supply.

turn down *vb* (*tr, adv*) **1** to reduce (the volume or brightness) of (something): *turn the radio down.* **2** to reject or refuse. **3** to fold down (a collar, sheets on a bed, etc.). ◆ *adj* **turndown. 4** (*prenominal*) capable of being or designed to be folded or doubled down.

turner ('tɜːnə) *n* **1** a person or thing that turns, esp. a person who operates a lathe. **2** *U.S.* a member of a society of gymnasts.

Turner ('tɜːnə) *n* **1 J(oseph) M(allord) W(illiam).** 1775–1851, British landscape painter; a master of water colours. He sought to convey atmosphere by means of an innovative use of colour and gradations of light. **2 Nat.** 1800–31, U.S. rebel slave, who led (1831) Turner's Insurrection, the only major slave revolt in U.S. history: executed. **3 Tina,** real name *Annie Mae Bullock.* born 1940, U.S. rock singer who performed (1958–75) with her then husband Ike Turner (born 1931) and later as a solo act. Her recordings include "River Deep, Mountain High" (1966) and *Simply the Best* (1991).

turnery ('tɜːnərɪ) *n, pl* **-eries. 1** objects made on a lathe. **2** Also called: **turning.** the process or skill of turning objects on a lathe. **3** the workshop of a lathe operator.

turn in *vb* (*adv*) *Informal.* **1** (*intr*) to go to bed for the night. **2** (*tr*) to hand in; deliver: *to turn in an essay.* **3** (*tr*) to deliver (someone accused of a crime) into police custody. **4** to give up or conclude (something): *we turned in the game when it began to rain.* **5** (*tr*) to record (a score, etc.). **6 turn in on oneself.** to withdraw or cause to withdraw from contact with others and become preoccupied with one's own problems.

turning ('tɜːnɪŋ) *n* **1** Also called: **turn.** a road, river, or path that turns off the main way: *the fourth turning on the right.* **2** the point where such a way turns off. **3** a bend in a straight course. **4** an object made on a lathe. **5** another name for **turnery** (sense 2). **6** (*pl*) the waste produced in turning on a lathe.

turning circle *n* the smallest circle in which a vehicle can turn.

turning point *n* **1** a moment when the course of events is changed: *the turning point of his career.* **2** a point at which there is a change in direction or motion. **3** *Maths.* a stationary point at which the first derivative of a function changes sign, so that typically its graph does not cross a horizontal tangent. **4** *Surveying.* a point to which a foresight and a backsight are taken in levelling; change point.

turnip ('tɜːnɪp) *n* **1** a widely cultivated cruciferous plant, *Brassica rapa,* of the Mediterranean region, with a large yellow or white edible root. **2** the root of this plant, which is eaten as a vegetable. **3** any of several similar or related plants. **4 turnip cabbage.** another name for **kohlrabi.** ◆ Also called (for senses 1, 2): **navew.** **[C16:** from earlier *turnepe,* perhaps from TURN (indicating its rounded shape) + *nepe,* from Latin *nāpus* turnip; see NEEP**]**

turnip moth *n* a common noctuid moth, *Agrotis segetum,* drab grey-brown in colour, the larvae of which feed on root crops and brassica stems.

turnkey ('tɜːnˌkiː) *n* **1** *Archaic.* a keeper of the keys, esp. in a prison; warder or jailer. ◆ *adj* **2** denoting a project, as in civil engineering, in which a single contractor has responsibility for the complete job from the start to the time of installation or occupancy.

turnkey project *n Engineering.* a complete project usually including many major units of plant completed under one overall contract, such as a chemical works or power station complex. **[C20:** from use of *turnkey* in the construction industry to describe the day a job will be completed and the owner able to turn the key in the door**]**

turnkey system *n* a computer or computer system supplied to a customer in such a complete form that it can be put to immediate use.

turn off *vb* **1** (*intr*) to leave (a road, pathway, etc.). **2** (*intr*) (of a road, pathway, etc.) to deviate from (another road, etc.). **3** (*tr, adv*) to cause (something) to cease operating by turning a knob, pushing a button, etc.: *to turn off the radio.* **4** (*tr*) *Informal.* to cause (a person, etc.) to feel dislike or distaste for (something): *this music turns me off.* **5** (*tr, adv*) *Brit. informal.* to dismiss from employment. ◆ *n* **turn-off. 6** a road or other way branching off from the main thoroughfare. **7** *Informal.* a person or thing that elicits dislike or distaste.

turn on *vb* **1** (*tr, adv*) to cause (something) to operate by turning a knob, etc.: *to turn on the light.* **2** (*intr, prep*) to depend or hinge on: *the success of the party turns on you.* **3** (*prep*) to change or cause to change one's attitude so as to become hostile or to retaliate: *the dog turned on the children.* **4** (*tr, adv*) *Informal.* to produce (charm, tears, etc.) suddenly or automatically. **5** (*tr, adv*) *Slang.* to arouse emotionally or sexually. **6** (*intr, adv*) *Slang.* to take or become intoxicated by drugs. **7** (*tr, adv*) *Slang.* to introduce (someone) to drugs. ◆ *n* **turn-on. 8** *Slang.* a person or thing that causes emotional or sexual arousal.

turn out *vb* (*adv*) **1** (*tr*) to cause (something, esp. a light) to cease operating by or as if by turning a knob, etc. **2** (*tr*) to produce by an effort or process: *she turned out 50 units per hour.* **3** (*tr*) to dismiss, discharge, or expel: *the family had been turned out of their home.* **4** (*tr*) to empty the contents of, esp. in order to clean, tidy, or rearrange: *to turn out one's pockets.* **5** (*copula*) **5a** to prove to be: *her work turned out to be badly done.* **5b** to end up; result: *it all turned out well.* **6** (*tr*) to fit as with clothes: *that woman turns her children out well.* **7** (*intr*) to assemble or gather: *a crowd turned out for the fair.* **8** (of a soldier) to parade or to call (a soldier) to parade. **9** (*intr*) *Informal.* to get out of bed. **10** (*intr;* foll. by *for*) *Informal.* to make an appearance, esp. in a sporting competition: *he was asked to turn out for Liverpool.* ◆ *n* **turnout. 11** the body of people appearing together at a gathering. **12** the quantity or amount produced. **13** an array of clothing or equipment. **14** the manner in which a person or thing is arrayed or equipped.

turn over *vb* (*adv*) **1** to change or cause to change position, esp. so as to reverse top and bottom. **2** to start (an engine), esp. with a starting handle, or (of an engine) to start or function correctly. **3** to shift or cause to shift position, as by rolling from side to side. **4** (*tr*) to deliver; transfer. **5** (*tr*) to consider carefully: *he turned over the problem for hours.* **6** (*tr*) **6a** to sell and replenish (stock in trade). **6b** to transact business and so generate gross revenue of (a specified sum). **7** (*tr*) to invest and recover (capital). **8** (*tr*) *Slang.* to rob. **9 turn over a new leaf.** to reform; resolve to improve one's behaviour. ◆ *n* **turnover. 10a** the amount of business, usually expressed in terms of gross revenue, transacted during a specified period. **10b** (*as modifier*): *a turnover tax.* **11** the rate at which stock in trade is sold and replenished. **12** a change or reversal of position. **13** a small semicircular or triangular pastry case filled with fruit, jam, etc. **14a** the number of workers employed by a firm in a given period to replace those who have left. **14b** the ratio between this number and the average number of employees during the same period. **15** *Banking.* the amount of capital funds loaned on call during a specified period. ◆ *adj* **16** (*prenominal*) able or designed to be turned or folded over: *a turnover collar.*

turnpike ('tɜːnˌpaɪk) *n* **1** (between the mid-16th and late 19th centuries) **1a** gates or some other barrier set across a road to prevent passage until a toll had been paid. **1b** a road on which a turnpike was operated. **2** an obsolete word for **turnstile** (sense 1). **3** *U.S.* a motorway for use of which a toll is charged. **[C15:** from TURN + PIKE[2]**]**

turnround ('tɜːnˌraʊnd) *n* another word for **turnaround.**

turnsole ('tɜːnˌsəʊl) *n* **1** any of various plants having flowers that are said to turn towards the sun. **2** a euphorbiaceous plant, *Croton tinctoria,* of the Mediterranean region that yields a purple dye. **3** the dye extracted from this plant. **[C14:** from Old French *tournesole,* from Old Italian *tornasole,* from *tornare* to TURN + *sole* sun, from Latin *sōl* sun**]**

turnspit ('tɜːnˌspɪt) *n* **1** (formerly) a servant or small dog whose job was to turn the spit on which meat, poultry, etc., was roasting. **2** a spit that can be so turned.

turnstile ('tɜːnˌstaɪl) *n* **1** a mechanical gate or barrier with metal arms that are turned to admit one person at a time, usually in one direction only. **2** any similar device that admits foot passengers but no large animals or vehicles. **3** *Logic.* Also called: **gatepost.** a symbol of the form ⊢, ⊨, or ⊩, used to represent logical consequence when inserted between expressions to form a sequent, or when prefixed to a single expression to indicate its status as a theorem.

turnstone ('tɜːnˌstəʊn) *n* either of two shore birds of the genus *Arenaria,* esp. *A. interpres* (**ruddy turnstone**). They are related and similar to plovers and sandpipers. **[C17:** so called because it turns over stones in search of food**]**

turntable ('tɜːnˌteɪbᵊl) *n* **1** the circular horizontal platform that rotates a gramophone record while it is being played. **2** a flat circular platform that can be rotated about its centre, used for turning locomotives and cars. **3** the revolvable platform on a microscope on which specimens are examined.

turntable ladder *n Brit.* a power-operated extending ladder mounted on a fire engine. U.S. and Canadian name: **aerial ladder.**

turn to *vb* (*intr, adv*) to set about a task: *we must turn to and finish our work.*

turn up *vb* (*adv*) **1** (*intr*) to arrive or appear: *he turned up late at the party.* **2** to find or be found, esp. by accident: *his book turned up in the cupboard.* **3** (*tr*) to increase the flow, volume, etc., of: *to turn up the radio.* **4** (*tr*) *Informal.* to cause to vomit. ◆ *n* **turn-up. 5** (*often pl*) *Brit.* the turned-up fold at the bottom of some trouser legs. U.S. and Canadian name: **cuff. 6** *Informal.* an unexpected or chance occurrence.

turpentine ('tɜːpᵊnˌtaɪn) *n* **1** Also called: **gum turpentine.** any of various viscous oleoresins obtained from various coniferous trees, esp. from the longleaf pine, and used as the main source of commercial turpentine. **2** a brownish-yellow sticky viscous oleoresin that exudes from the terebinth tree. **3** Also called: **oil of turpentine, spirits of turpentine.** a colourless flammable volatile liquid with a pungent odour, distilled from turpentine oleoresin. It is an essential oil containing a mixture of terpenes and is used as a solvent for paints and in medicine as a rubefacient and expectorant. Sometimes shortened (esp. Brit.) to **turps. 4** Also called: **turpentine substitute, white spirit.** (*not in technical usage*) any one of a number of thinners for paints and varnishes, consisting of fractions of petroleum. Related adj: **terebinthine.** ◆ *vb* (*tr*) **5** to treat or saturate with turpentine. **6** to extract crude turpentine from (trees). **[C14** *terebentyne,* from Medieval Latin *terbentīna,* from Latin *terebinthīna* turpentine, from *terebinthus* the turpentine tree, TEREBINTH**]**

turpentine tree *n* **1** a tropical African leguminous tree, *Copaifera mopane,* yielding a hard dark wood and a useful resin. **2** either of two Australian evergreen myrtaceous trees, *Syncarpia lilli* or *S. glomulifera,* that have durable wood and are sometimes planted as shade trees.

turpeth ('tɜːpɪθ) *n* **1** a convolvulaceous plant, *Operculina turpethum,* of the East Indies, having roots with purgative properties. **2** the root of this plant or the drug obtained from it. **[C14:** from Medieval Latin *turbithum,* ultimately from Arabic *turbid***]**

Turpin ('tɜːpɪn) *n* **Dick.** 1706–39, English highwayman.

turpitude ('tɜːpɪˌtjuːd) *n* base character or action; depravity. **[C15:** from Latin *turpitūdō* ugliness, from *turpis* base**]**

turps (tɜːps) *n* (*functioning as sing*) **1** *Brit.* short for **turpentine** (sense 3). **2** *Austral. and N.Z. slang.* alcoholic drink, esp. beer (esp. in the phrase **on the turps**).

turquoise ('tɜːkwɔɪz, -kwɑːz) *n* **1** a greenish-blue fine-grained secondary mineral consisting of hydrated copper aluminium phosphate. It occurs in igneous rocks rich in aluminium and is used as a gemstone. Formula: $CuAl_6(PO_4)_4(OH)_8.4H_2O$. **2a** the colour of turquoise. **2b** (*as adj*): *a turquoise dress.* **[C14:** from Old French *turqueise* Turkish (stone)**]**

turret ('tʌrɪt) *n* **1** a small tower that projects from the wall of a building, esp. a medieval castle. **2a** a self-contained structure, capable of rotation, in which weapons are mounted, esp. in tanks and warships. **2b** a similar structure on an aircraft that houses one or more guns and sometimes a gunner. **3** a tall wooden tower on wheels used formerly by besiegers to scale the walls of a fortress. **4** (on a machine tool) a turret-like steel structure with tools projecting radially that can be indexed round to bring each tool to bear on the work. [C14: from Old French *torete,* from *tor* tower, from Latin *turris*]

turreted ('tʌrɪtɪd), **turriculate** (tʌ'rɪkjʊlɪt, -ˌleɪt), *or* **turriculated** *adj* **1** having or resembling a turret or turrets. **2** (of a gastropod shell) having the shape of a long spiral.

turret lathe *n* another name for **capstan lathe.**

turtle[1] ('tɜːtᵊl) *n* **1** any of various aquatic chelonian reptiles, esp. those of the marine family *Chelonidae,* having a flattened shell enclosing the body and flipper-like limbs adapted for swimming. Related adjs: **chelonian, testudinal. 2** *U.S. and Canadian.* any of the chelonian reptiles, including the tortoises and terrapins. **3** *Nautical.* a zip bag made as part of a spinnaker for holding the sail so that it can be set rapidly. **4 turn turtle.** to capsize. ♦ *vb* **5** (*intr*) to catch or hunt turtles. [C17: from French *tortue* TORTOISE (influenced by TURTLE[2])] ▸ **'turtler** *n*

turtle[2] ('tɜːtᵊl) *n* an archaic name for **turtledove.** [Old English *turtla,* from Latin *turtur,* of imitative origin; related to German *Turteltaube*]

turtleback ('tɜːtᵊlˌbæk) *n* **1** an arched projection over the upper deck of a ship at the bow and sometimes at the stern for protection in heavy seas. **2** (*now obsolete in archaeological usage*) a crude convex stone axe.

turtledove ('tɜːtᵊlˌdʌv) *n* **1** any of several Old World doves of the genus *Streptopelia,* having a brown plumage with speckled wings and a long dark tail. **2** a gentle or loving person. [see TURTLE[2]]

turtleneck ('tɜːtᵊlˌnɛk) *n* **a** a round high close-fitting neck on a sweater or the sweater itself. **b** (*as modifier*): *a turtleneck sweater.*

turves (tɜːvz) *n* a plural of **turf.**

Tuscan ('tʌskən) *adj* **1** of or relating to Tuscany, its inhabitants, or their dialect of Italian. **2** of, denoting, or relating to one of the five classical orders of architecture: characterized by a column with an unfluted shaft and a capital and base with mouldings but no decoration. See also **Ionic, Composite, Doric, Corinthian.** ♦ *n* **3** a native or inhabitant of Tuscany. **4** any of the dialects of Italian spoken in Tuscany, esp. the dialect of Florence: the standard form of Italian.

Tuscany ('tʌskənɪ) *n* a region of central Italy, on the Ligurian and Tyrrhenian Seas: corresponds roughly to ancient Etruria; a region of numerous small states in medieval times; united in the 15th and 16th centuries under Florence; united with the rest of Italy in 1861. Capital: Florence. Pop.: 3 523 238 (1996 est.). Area: 22 990 sq. km (8876 sq. miles). Italian name: **Toscana.**

Tuscarora (ˌtʌskə'rɔːrə) *n* **1** (*pl* **-ras** *or* **-ra**) a member of a North American Indian people formerly living in North Carolina, who later moved to New York State and joined the Iroquois. **2** the language of this people, belonging to the Iroquoian family.

tusche (tʊʃ) *n* a substance used in lithography for drawing the design and as a resist in silk-screen printing and lithography. [from German, from *tuschen* to touch up with colour or ink, from French *toucher* to TOUCH]

Tusculum ('tʌskjʊləm) *n* an ancient city in Latium near Rome. ▸ **'Tusculan** *adj*

tush[1] (tʌʃ) *interj Archaic.* an exclamation of disapproval or contempt. [C15: Middle English, of imitative origin]

tush[2] (tʌʃ) *n Rare.* a tusk. [Old English *tūsc;* see TUSK]

tush[3] (tʊʃ) *n U.S. slang.* the buttocks. [C20: from Yiddish *tokhes,* from Hebrew *tahath* beneath]

tushery ('tʌʃərɪ) *n Literary.* the use of affectedly archaic language in novels, etc. [coined by R. L. STEVENSON from TUSH[1] + -ERY]

tusk (tʌsk) *n* **1** a pointed elongated usually paired tooth in the elephant, walrus, and certain other mammals that is specialized for fighting. **2** the canine tooth of certain animals, esp. horses. **3** a sharp pointed projection. **4** Also called: **tusk tenon.** *Building trades.* a tenon shaped with an additional oblique shoulder to make a stronger joint. ♦ *vb* **5** to stab, tear, or gore with the tusks. [Old English *tūsc;* related to Old Frisian *tosk;* see TOOTH] ▸ **tusked** *adj* ▸ **'tuskˌlike** *adj*

tusker ('tʌskə) *n* any animal with prominent tusks, esp. a wild boar or elephant.

tusk shell *n* any of various burrowing seashore molluscs of the genus *Dentalium* and related genera that have a long narrow tubular shell open at both ends: class *Scaphopoda.* Also called: **tooth shell.**

Tussaud (*French* tyso) *n* **Marie** (mari). 1760–1850, Swiss modeller in wax, who founded a permanent exhibition in London of historical and contemporary figures.

tussis ('tʌsɪs) *n* the technical name for a **cough.** See **pertussis.** [Latin: cough] ▸ **'tussal** *adj* ▸ **'tussive** *adj*

tussle ('tʌsᵊl) *vb* **1** (*intr*) to fight or wrestle in a vigorous way; struggle. ♦ *n* **2** a vigorous fight; scuffle; struggle. [C15: related to Old High German *zūsen;* see TOUSLE]

tussock ('tʌsək) *n* **1** a dense tuft of vegetation, esp. of grass. **2** *Austral. and N.Z.* **2a** short for **tussock grass. 2b the.** country where tussock grass grows. [C16: perhaps related to TUSK] ▸ **'tussocky** *adj*

tussock grass *n Austral. and N.Z.* any of several pasture grasses of the genus *Poa.*

tussock moth *n* any of various pale or dull-coloured moths of the family *Lymantriidae* (or *Laparidae*), the hairy caterpillars of which are pests of many trees. See also **gipsy moth, brown-tail moth, goldtail moth.** [C19: so named because of the tufts of hair on the caterpillars]

tussore (tʊ'sɔː, 'tʌsə), **tusser** ('tʌsə), *or* (*chiefly U.S.*) **tussah** ('tʌsə) *n* **1** a strong coarse brownish Indian silk obtained from the cocoons of an Oriental saturniid silkworm, *Antheraea paphia.* **2** a fabric woven from this silk. **3** the silkworm producing this silk. [C17: from Hindi *tasar* shuttle, from Sanskrit *tasara* a wild silkworm]

tut *interj* (*pronounced as an alveolar click; spelling pron* tʌt), *n, vb* **tuts, tutting, tutted.** short for **tut-tut.**

Tutankhamen (ˌtuːtən'kɑːmen, -mən) *or* **Tutankhamun** (ˌtuːtənkɑː'muːn) *n* king (1361–1352 B.C.) of the 18th dynasty of Egypt. His tomb near Luxor, discovered in 1922, contained many material objects.

tutee (tjuː'tiː) *n* one who is tutored, esp. in a university.

tutelage ('tjuːtɪlɪdʒ) *n* **1** the act or office of a guardian or tutor. **2** instruction or guidance, esp. by a tutor. **3** the condition of being under the supervision of a guardian or tutor. [C17: from Latin *tūtēla* a caring for, from *tuērī* to watch over; compare TUITION]

tutelary ('tjuːtɪlərɪ) *or* **tutelar** ('tjuːtɪlə) *adj* **1** invested with the role of guardian or protector. **2** of or relating to a guardian or guardianship. ♦ *n, pl* **-laries** *or* **-lars. 3** a tutelary person, deity, or saint.

tutiorism ('tjuːtɪəˌrɪzəm) *n* (in Roman Catholic moral theology) the doctrine that in cases of moral doubt it is best to follow the safer course or that in agreement with the law. [C19: from Latin *tutior* safer, comparative of *tutus* safe] ▸ **'tutiorist** *n*

tutor ('tjuːtə) *n* **1** a teacher, usually instructing individual pupils and often engaged privately. **2** (at universities, colleges, etc.) a member of staff responsible for the teaching and supervision of a certain number of students. **3** *Scots Law.* the guardian of a pupil. See **pupil**[1] (sense 2). ♦ *vb* **4** to act as a tutor to (someone); instruct. **5** (*tr*) to act as guardian to; have care of. **6** (*intr*) *Chiefly U.S.* to study under a tutor. **7** (*tr*) *Rare.* to admonish, discipline, or reprimand. [C14: from Latin: a watcher, from *tuērī* to watch over] ▸ **'tutorage** *or* **'tutorˌship** *n*

tutorial (tjuː'tɔːrɪəl) *n* **1** a period of intensive tuition given by a tutor to an individual student or to a small group of students. ♦ *adj* **2** of or relating to a tutor.

tutorial system *n* a system, mainly in universities, in which students receive guidance in academic or personal matters from tutors.

tutsan ('tʌtsən) *n* a woodland shrub, *Hypericum androsaemum,* of Europe and W Asia, having yellow flowers and reddish-purple fruits: family *Hypericaceae.* See also **Saint John's wort.** [C15: from Old French *toute-saine* (unattested), literally: all healthy]

Tutsi ('tuːtsɪ) *n, pl* **-si** *or* **-sis.** a member of a people of Rwanda and Burundi, probably a Nilotic people.

tutti ('tʊtɪ) *adj, adv Music.* to be performed by the whole orchestra, choir, etc. Compare **soli.** [C18: from Italian, pl of *tutto* all, from Latin *tōtus*]

tutti-frutti ('tuːtɪ'fruːtɪ) *n* **1** (*pl* **-fruttis**) an ice cream or a confection containing small pieces of candied or fresh fruits. **2** a preserve of chopped mixed fruits, often with brandy syrup. **3** a flavour like that of many fruits combined. ♦ *adj* **4** having such a flavour. [from Italian, literally: all the fruits]

tut-tut *interj* (*pronounced as alveolar clicks; spelling pron* 'tʌt'tʌt). **1** an exclamation of mild reprimand, disapproval, or surprise. ♦ *vb* **-tuts, -tutting, -tutted. 2** (*intr*) to express disapproval by the exclamation of "tut-tut." ♦ *n* **3** the act of tut-tutting. ♦ Often shortened to **tut.**

tutty ('tʌtɪ) *n* finely powdered impure zinc oxide obtained from the flues of zinc-smelting furnaces and used as a polishing powder. [C14: from Old French *tutie,* from Arabic *tūtiyā,* probably from Persian, from Sanskrit *tuttha*]

tutu[1] ('tuːtuː) *n* a very short skirt worn by ballerinas, made of projecting layers of stiffened sheer material. [from French, changed from the nursery word *cucu* backside, from *cul,* from Latin *cūlus* the buttocks]

tutu[2] ('tuːtuː) *n* a shrub, *Coriaria arborea,* of New Zealand, having seeds that are poisonous to farm animals. [Maori]

Tutu ('tuːtuː) *n* **Desmond.** born 1931, South African clergyman, noted for his opposition to apartheid: Anglican Bishop of Johannesburg (1984–86) and Archbishop of Cape Town (1986–96); in 1995 he became leader of the Truth and Reconciliation Commission, established to investigate human rights violations during the apartheid era. Nobel peace prize 1984.

Tutuila (ˌtuːtuː'iːlə) *n* the largest island of American Samoa, in the SW Pacific. Chief town and port: Pago Pago. Pop.: 30 226 (latest est.). Area: 135 sq. km (52 sq. miles).

Tutuola ('tuːtuːˌəʊlə) *n* **Amos.** 1920–97, Nigerian writer: his books include *The Palm-Wine Drinkard* (1952) and *Pauper, Brawler and Slanderer* (1987).

Tuva Republic ('tuːvə) *n* a constituent republic of S Russia: mountainous. Capital: Kizyl. Pop.: 308 000 (1995 est.). Area: 170 500 sq. km (65 800 sq. miles). Also called: **Tuvinian Autonomous Republic.**

Tuvalu (ˌtuːvə'luː) *n* a country in the SW Pacific, comprising a group of nine coral islands: established as a British protectorate in 1892. From 1915 until 1975 the islands formed part of the British colony of the Gilbert and Ellice Islands; achieved full independence in 1978; a special member of the Commonwealth (not represented at meetings of Commonwealth heads of state). Languages: English and Tuvaluan. Religion: Christian majority. Currency: Australian dollar; Tuvalu dollars are also used. Capital: Funafuti. Pop.: 10 400 (1998 est.). Area: 26 sq. km (10 sq. miles). Former names: **Lagoon Islands, Ellice Islands.** ▸ ˌ**Tuva'luan** *adj, n*

tu-whit tu-whoo (tə'wɪt tə'wuː) *interj* an imitation or representation of the sound made by an owl.

tuxedo (tʌk'siːdəʊ) *n, pl* **-dos.** the usual U.S. and Canadian name for **dinner jacket,** often shortened to **tux.** [C19: named after a country club in *Tuxedo Park,* New York]

Tuxtla Gutiérrez (*Spanish* 'tustla gu'tjerreθ) *n* a city in SE Mexico, capital of Chiapas state: agricultural centre. Pop.: 289 626 (1990).

tuyère ('twiːɛə, 'twaɪə; *French* tyjɛr) *or* **twyer** ('twaɪə) *n* a water-cooled nozzle through which air is blown into a cupola, blast furnace, or forge. [C18: from French, from *tuyau* pipe, from Old French *tuel,* probably of Germanic origin]

TV *abbrev. for* television.

TVEI (in Britain) *abbrev. for* technical and vocational educational initiative: a national educational scheme in which pupils gain practical experience in technology and industry often through work placement.

Tver (*Russian* tvjerj) *n* a city in central Russia, at the confluence of the Volga and Tversta Rivers: chief port of the upper Volga, linked by canal with Moscow. Pop.: 454 000 (1994 est.). Former name (1932–91) **Kalinin**[1].

TVP *abbrev. for* textured vegetable protein: a protein obtained from soya beans or other vegetables that have been spun into fibres and flavoured: used esp. as a substitute for meat.

TVR *abbrev. for* television rating: a measurement of the popularity of a TV programme based on a survey.

TVRO *abbrev. for* television receive only: an antenna and associated apparatus for reception from a broadcasting satellite.

twa (twɔː) *or* **twae** (twe) *n, determiner.* a Scot. word for **two.**

twaddle ('twɒdᵊl) *n* **1** silly, trivial, or pretentious talk or writing; nonsense. ◆ *vb* **2** to talk or write (something) in a silly or pretentious way. [C16 *twattle,* variant of *twittle* or *tittle;* see TITTLE-TATTLE] ► **'twaddler** *n*

twain (tweɪn) *determiner, n* an archaic word for **two.** [Old English *twēgen;* related to Old Saxon *twēne,* Old High German *zwēne,* Old Norse *tveir,* Gothic *twai*]

Twain (tweɪn) *n* **Mark,** pen name of *Samuel Langhorne Clemens.* 1835–1910, U.S. novelist and humorist, famous for his classics *The Adventures of Tom Sawyer* (1876) and *The Adventures of Huckleberry Finn* (1885).

twang (twæŋ) *n* **1** a sharp ringing sound produced by or as if by the plucking of a taut string: *the twang of a guitar.* **2** the act of plucking a string to produce such a sound. **3** a strongly nasal quality in a person's speech, esp. in certain dialects. ◆ *vb* **4** to make or cause to make a twang: *to twang a guitar.* **5** to strum (music, a tune, etc.): *to twang on a guitar.* **6** to speak or utter with a sharp nasal voice. **7** (*intr*) to be released or move with a twang: *the arrow twanged away.* [C16: of imitative origin] ► **'twangy** *adj*

'twas (twɒz; *unstressed* twəz) *Poetic or dialect. contraction of* it was.

twat (twæt, twɒt) *n Taboo slang.* **1** the female genitals. **2** a girl or woman considered sexually. **3** a foolish or despicable person. [of unknown origin]

twattle ('twɒtᵊl) *n* a rare word for **twaddle.**

twayblade ('tweɪ,bleɪd) *n* any of various terrestrial orchids of the genera *Listera, Liparis, Ophrys,* etc., having a basal pair of oval unstalked leaves arranged opposite each other. [C16: translation of Medieval Latin *bifolium* having two leaves, from obsolete *tway* TWO + BLADE]

tweak (twiːk) *vb* (*tr*) **1** to twist, jerk, or pinch with a sharp or sudden movement: *to tweak someone's nose.* **2** *Motor racing slang.* to tune (a car or engine) for peak performance. **3** *Informal.* to make a minor alteration. ◆ *n* **4** an instance of tweaking. **5** *Informal.* a minor alteration. [Old English *twiccian;* related to Old High German *zwecchōn;* see TWITCH] ► **'tweaky** *adj*

tweaker ('twiːkə) *n Slang.* an engineer's small screwdriver, used for fine adjustments.

twee (twiː) *adj Brit.* excessively sentimental, sweet, or pretty. [C19: from *tweet,* mincing or affected pronunciation of SWEET] ► **'tweely** *adv*

tweed (twiːd) *n* **1a** a thick woollen often knobbly cloth produced originally in Scotland. **1b** (*as modifier*): *a tweed coat.* **2** (*pl*) clothes made of this cloth, esp. a man's or woman's suit. **3** (*pl*) *Austral. informal.* trousers. [C19: probably from *tweel,* a Scottish variant of TWILL, influenced by TWEED]

Tweed (twiːd) *n* a river in SE Scotland and NE England, flowing east and forming part of the border between Scotland and England, then crossing into England to enter the North Sea at Berwick. Length: 156 km (97 miles).

Tweeddale ('twiːd,deɪl) *n* another name for **Peeblesshire.**

Tweedledum and Tweedledee (,twiːdᵊl'dʌm; ,twiːdᵊl'diː) *n* any two persons or things that differ only slightly from each other; two of a kind. [C19: from the proverbial names of HANDEL and the musician Buononcini, who were supported by rival factions though it was thought by some that there was nothing to choose between them. The names were popularized by Lewis Carroll's use of them in *Through the Looking Glass* (1872)]

Tweedsmuir ('twiːdzmjuə) *n* **Baron.** title of (John) **Buchan.**

tweedy ('twiːdɪ) *adj* **tweedier, tweediest. 1** of, made of, or resembling tweed. **2** showing a fondness for a hearty outdoor life, usually associated with wearers of tweeds. ► **'tweediness** *n*

'tween (twiːn) *Poetic or dialect. contraction of* between.

'tween deck *or* **decks** *n Nautical.* a space between two continuous decks of a vessel.

tweeny ('twiːnɪ) *n, pl* **tweenies.** *Brit. informal, obsolete.* a maid who assists both cook and housemaid. [C19: shortened from BETWEEN (that is, a maid between cook and housemaid)]

tweet (twiːt) *interj* **1** (*often reiterated*) an imitation or representation of the thin chirping sound made by small or young birds. ◆ *vb* **2** (*intr*) to make this sound. [C19: of imitative origin]

tweeter ('twiːtə) *n* a loudspeaker used in high-fidelity systems for the reproduction of high audio frequencies. It is usually employed in conjunction with a woofer and a crossover network. [C20: from TWEET]

tweeze (twiːz) *vb Chiefly U.S.* to take hold of or pluck (hair, small objects, etc.) with or as if with tweezers. [C17: back formation from TWEEZERS]

tweezers ('twiːzəz) *pl n* a small pincer-like instrument for handling small objects, plucking out hairs, etc. Also called: **pair of tweezers, tweezer** (esp. U.S.). [C17: plural of *tweezer* (on the model of *scissors,* etc.), from *tweeze* case of instruments, from French *étuis* cases (of instruments), from Old French *estuier* to preserve, from Vulgar Latin *studiāre* (unattested) to keep, from Latin *studēre* to care about]

twelfth (twelfθ) *adj* **1** (*usually prenominal*) **1a** coming after the eleventh in number or counting order, position, time, etc.; being the ordinal number of *twelve:* often written 12th. **1b** (*as n*): *the twelfth of the month.* ◆ *n* **2a** one of 12 equal or nearly equal parts of an object, quantity, measurement, etc. **2b** (*as modifier*): *a twelfth part.* **3** the fraction equal to one divided by 12 (1/12). **4** *Music.* **4a** an interval of one octave plus a fifth. **4b** one of two notes constituting such an interval in relation to the other. **4c** an organ stop sounding a note one octave and a fifth higher than that normally produced by the key depressed. [from Old English *twelfta*]

Twelfth Day *n* **a** Jan. 6, the twelfth day after Christmas and the feast of the Epiphany, formerly observed as the final day of the Christmas celebrations. **b** (*as modifier*): *Twelfth-Day celebrations.*

twelfth man *n* a reserve player in a cricket team.

Twelfth Night *n* **a** the evening of Jan. 5, the eve of Twelfth Day, formerly observed with various festal celebrations. **b** the evening of Twelfth Day itself. **c** (*as modifier*): *Twelfth-Night customs.*

Twelfthtide ('twelfθ,taɪd) *n* **a** the season of Epiphany. **b** (*as modifier*): *the Twelfthtide celebrations.*

twelve (twɛlv) *n* **1** the cardinal number that is the sum of ten and two. See also **number** (sense 1). **2** a numeral, 12, XII, etc., representing this number. **3** something represented by, representing, or consisting of 12 units. **4** Also called: **twelve o'clock.** noon or midnight. ◆ *determiner* **5a** amounting to twelve: *twelve loaves.* **5b** (*as pronoun*): *twelve have arrived.* ◆ Related adj: **duodecimal.** Related prefix: **dodeca-.** See also **dozen.** [Old English *twelf;* related to Old Frisian *twelif,* Old High German *zwelif,* Old Norse *tolf,* Gothic *twalif*]

twelve-inch *n* a gramophone record 12 inches in diameter and played at 45 revolutions per minute, usually containing an extended remix of a single.

twelve-mile limit *n* the offshore boundary 12 miles from the coast claimed by some states as marking the extent of their territorial jurisdiction.

twelvemo ('twɛlvməʊ) *n, pl* **-mos.** *Bookbinding.* another word for **duodecimo.**

twelvemonth ('twɛlv,mʌnθ) *n Chiefly Brit.* an archaic or dialect word for a **year.**

twelve pitch *n* another name for **elite** (sense 2).

Twelve Tables *pl n* **the.** the earliest code of Roman civil, criminal, and religious law, promulgated in 451–450 B.C.

twelve-tone *adj* of, relating to, or denoting the type of serial music invented and developed by Arnold Schoenberg, which uses as musical material a tone row formed by the 12 semitones of the chromatic scale, together with its inverted and retrograde versions. The technique has been applied in various ways by different composers and usually results in music in which there are few, if any, tonal centres. See **serialism.**

twentieth ('twɛntɪɪθ) *adj* **1** (*usually prenominal*) **1a** coming after the nineteenth in numbering or counting order, position, time, etc.; being the ordinal number of *twenty:* often written 20th. **1b** (*as n*): *he left on the twentieth.* ◆ *n* **2a** one of 20 approximately equal parts of something. **2b** (*as modifier*): *a twentieth part.* **3** the fraction that is equal to one divided by 20 (1/20). [from Old English *twentigotha*]

twenty ('twɛntɪ) *n, pl* **-ties. 1** the cardinal number that is the product of ten and two; a score. See also **number** (sense 1). **2** a numeral, 20, XX, etc., representing this number. **3** something representing, represented by, or consisting of 20 units. ◆ *determiner* **4a** amounting to twenty: *twenty questions.* **4b** (*as pronoun*): *to order twenty.* ◆ Related adjs: **vicenary, vigesimal.** Related prefix: **icosa-.** [Old English *twēntig;* related to Old High German *zweinzug,* German *zwanzig*]

twenty-one *n* another name (esp. U.S.) for **pontoon**[2] (sense 1).

twenty-six counties *pl n* the counties of the Republic of Ireland.

twenty-twenty *adj Med.* (of vision) being of normal acuity: usually written 20/20.

'twere (twɜː; *unstressed* twə) *Poetic or dialect. contraction of* it were.

twerp *or* **twirp** (twɜːp) *n Informal.* a silly, weak-minded, or contemptible person. [C20: of unknown origin]

Twi (twiː) *n* **1** a language of S Ghana: one of the two chief dialects of Akan. Formerly called: **Ashanti.** Compare **Fanti. 2** (*pl* **Twi** *or* **Twis**) a member of the Negroid people who speak this language.

twibill *or* **twibil** ('twaɪ,bɪl) *n* **1** a mattock with a blade shaped like an adze at one end and like an axe at the other. **2** *Archaic.* a double-bladed battle-axe. [Old English, from *twi-* two, double + *bill* sword, BILL[3]]

twice (twaɪs) *adv* **1** two times; on two occasions or in two cases: *he coughed twice.* **2** double in degree or quantity: *twice as long.* [Old English *twiwa;* related to Old Norse *tvisvar,* Middle Low German *twiges*]

twice-laid *adj* **1** made from strands of used rope. **2** made from old or used material or retwisted yarn. [C16: from LAY[1] (in the sense: to twist together)]

twice-told *adj* hackneyed through repeated use.

Twickenham ('twɪkənəm) *n* a former town in SE England, on the River Thames: part of the Greater London borough of Richmond-upon-Thames since 1965; contains the English Rugby Football Union ground.

twiddle ('twɪdᵊl) *vb* **1** (when *intr,* often foll. by *with*) to twirl or fiddle (with), often in an idle way. **2 twiddle one's thumbs.** to do nothing; be unoccupied. **3** (*intr*) to turn, twirl, or rotate. **4** (*intr*) *Rare.* to be occupied with trifles. ◆ *n* **5** an act or instance of twiddling. [C16: probably a blend of TWIRL + FIDDLE] ► **'twiddler** *n*

twig[1] (twɪg) *n* **1** any small branch or shoot of a tree or other woody plant. **2** something resembling this, esp. a minute branch of a blood vessel. [Old English *twigge;* related to Old Norse *dvika* consisting of two, Old High German *zwīg* twig, Old Danish *tvige* fork] ► **'twig,like** *adj*

twig[2] (twɪg) *vb* **twigs, twigging, twigged.** *Brit. informal.* **1** to understand (something). **2** to find out or suddenly comprehend (something): *he hasn't twigged yet.* **3** (*tr*) *Rare.* to perceive (something). [C18: perhaps from Scottish Gaelic *tuig* I understand]

twiggy ('twɪgɪ) *adj* **-gier, -giest. 1** of or relating to a twig or twigs. **2** covered with twigs. **3** slender or fragile.

twilight ('twaɪ,laɪt) *n* **1** the soft diffused light occurring when the sun is just below the horizon, esp. following sunset. Related adj: **crepuscular. 2** the period in which this light occurs. **3** the period of time during which the sun is a specified angular distance below the horizon (6°, 12°, and 18° for **civil twilight, nautical twilight,** and **astronomical twilight,** respectively). **4** any faint light. **5** a period in which strength, importance, etc., are waning: *the twilight of his life.* **6** (*modifier*) **6a** of or relating to the period towards the end of the day: *the twilight shift.* **6b** of or relating to the final phase of a particular era: *the twilight days of the Bush presidency.* **6c** denoting irregularity and obscurity: *a twilight existence.* [C15: literally: half-light (between day and night), from Old English *twi-* half + LIGHT[1]] ▸ **twilit** (ˈtwaɪˌlɪt) *adj*

Twilight of the Gods *n* another term for **Götterdämmerung** or **Ragnarök.**

twilight sleep *n Med.* a state of partial anaesthesia in which the patient retains a slight degree of consciousness.

twilight zone *n* **1** any indefinite or transitional condition or area. **2** an area of a city or town, usually surrounding the central business district, where houses have become dilapidated. **3** the lowest level of the ocean to which light can penetrate.

twill (twɪl) *adj* **1** (in textiles) of or designating a weave in which the weft yarns are worked around two or more warp yarns to produce an effect of parallel diagonal lines or ribs. ◆ *n* **2** any fabric so woven. ◆ *vb* **3** (*tr*) to weave in this fashion. [Old English *twilic* having a double thread; related to Old High German *zwilīth* twill, Latin *bilīx* two-threaded]

'twill (twɪl) *Poetic or dialect. contraction of* it will.

twin (twɪn) *n* **1a** either of two persons or animals conceived at the same time. **1b** (*as modifier*): *a twin brother.* See also **identical** (sense 3), **fraternal** (sense 3). **2a** either of two persons or things that are identical or very similar; counterpart. **2b** (*as modifier*): *twin carburettors.* **3** Also called: **macle.** a crystal consisting of two parts each of which has a definite orientation to the other. ◆ *vb* **twins, twinning, twinned. 4** to pair or be paired together; couple. **5** (*intr*) to bear twins. **6** (*intr*) (of a crystal) to form into a twin. **7** (*intr*) *Archaic.* to be born as a twin. **8a** (*tr*) to create a reciprocal relation between (two towns in different countries); pair (a town) with another in a different country. **8b** (*intr*) (of a town) to be paired with a town in a different country. [Old English *twinn;* related to Old High German *zwiniling* twin, Old Norse *tvinnr* double] ▸ **'twinning** *n*

twin bed *n* one of a pair of matching single beds.

twinberry (ˈtwɪnbərɪ, -brɪ) *n, pl* **-ries.** another name for **partridgeberry** (sense 1).

twin bill *n U.S.* an informal name for **double feature** or **double-header** (sense 2).

twine (twaɪn) *n* **1** string made by twisting together fibres of hemp, cotton, etc. **2** the act or an instance of twining. **3** something produced or characterized by twining. **4** a twist, coil, or convolution. **5** a knot, tangle, or snarl. ◆ *vb* **6** (*tr*) to twist together; interweave: *she twined the wicker to make a basket.* **7** (*tr*) to form by or as if by twining: *to twine a garland.* **8** (when *intr*, often foll. by *around*) to wind or cause to wind, esp. in spirals: *the creeper twines around the tree.* [Old English *twīn;* related to Old Frisian *twīne,* Dutch *twijn* twine, Lithuanian *dvynu* twins; see TWIN] ▸ **'twiner** *n*

twinflower (ˈtwɪnˌflaʊə) *n* an evergreen caprifoliaceous trailing shrub, *Linnaea borealis,* of North America, having round leaves, white or pink fragrant bell-shaped flowers arranged in pairs, and yellow fruits.

twinge (twɪndʒ) *n* **1** a sudden brief darting or stabbing pain. **2** a sharp emotional pang: *a twinge of conscience.* ◆ *vb* **3** to have or cause to have a twinge. **4** (*tr*) *Obsolete.* to pinch; tweak. [Old English *twengan* to pinch; related to Old High German *zwengen*]

twinkle (ˈtwɪŋkᵊl) *vb* (*mainly intr*) **1** to emit or reflect light in a flickering manner; shine brightly and intermittently; sparkle: *twinkling stars.* **2** (of the eyes) to sparkle, esp. with amusement or delight. **3** *Rare.* to move about quickly. **4** (*also tr*) *Rare.* to wink (the eyes); blink. ◆ *n* **5** an intermittent gleam of light; flickering brightness; sparkle or glimmer. **6** an instant. **7** a rare word for **wink**[1]. [Old English *twinclian;* related to Middle High German *zwinken* to blink] ▸ **'twinkler** *n*

twinkling (ˈtwɪŋklɪŋ) *or* **twink** (twɪŋk) *n* a very short time; instant; moment. Also called: **twinkling of an eye.**

twin-lens reflex *n* See **reflex camera.**

twin paradox *n* a phenomenon predicted by relativity. One of a pair of identical twins is supposed to live normally in an inertial system whilst the other is accelerated to a high speed in a spaceship, travels for a long time, and finally returns to rest beside his twin. The travelled twin will be found to be younger than his brother.

Twins (twɪnz) *pl n* **the.** the constellation Gemini, the third sign of the zodiac.

twin-screw *adj* (of a vessel) having two propellers.

twinset (ˈtwɪnˌsɛt) *n Brit.* a matching jumper and cardigan.

twin town *n Brit.* a town that has civic associations, such as reciprocal visits and cultural exchanges, with a foreign town, usually of similar size and sometimes with other similarities, as in commercial activities.

twin-tub *n* a type of washing machine that has two revolving drums, one for washing and the other for spin-drying.

twirl (twɜːl) *vb* **1** to move or cause to move around rapidly and repeatedly in a circle. **2** (*tr*) to twist, wind, or twiddle, often idly: *she twirled her hair around her finger.* **3** (*intr;* often foll. by *around* or *about*) to turn suddenly to face another way: *she twirled around angrily to face him.* ◆ *n* **4** an act of rotating or being rotated; whirl or twist. **5** something wound around or twirled; coil. **6** a written flourish or squiggle. [C16: perhaps a blend of TWIST + WHIRL] ▸ **'twirler** *n*

twirp (twɜːp) *n* a variant spelling of **twerp.**

twist (twɪst) *vb* **1** to cause (one end or part) to turn or (of one end or part) to turn in the opposite direction from another; coil or spin. **2** to distort or be distorted; change in shape. **3** to wind or cause to wind; twine, coil, or intertwine: *to twist flowers into a wreath.* **4** to force or be forced out of the natural form or position: *to twist one's ankle.* **5** (*usually passive*) to change or cause to change for the worse in character, meaning, etc.; pervert: *his ideas are twisted; she twisted the statement.* **6** to revolve or cause to revolve; rotate. **7** (*tr*) to wrench with a turning action: *to twist something from someone's grasp.* **8** (*intr*) to follow a winding course. **9** (*intr*) to squirm, as with pain. **10** (*intr*) to dance the twist. **11** (*tr*) *Brit. informal.* to cheat; swindle. **12 twist someone's arm.** to persuade or coerce someone. ◆ *n* **13** the act or an instance of twisting. **14** something formed by or as if by twisting: *a twist of hair.* **15** a decisive change of direction, aim, meaning, or character. **16** (in a novel, play, etc.) an unexpected event, revelation, or other development. **17** a bend: *a twist in the road.* **18** a distortion of the original or natural shape or form. **19** a jerky pull, wrench, or turn. **20** a strange personal characteristic, esp. a bad one. **21** a confused mess, tangle, or knot made by twisting. **22** a twisted thread used in sewing where extra strength is needed. **23** (in weaving) a specified direction of twisting the yarn. **24 the twist.** a modern dance popular in the 1960s, in which couples vigorously twist the hips in time to rhythmic music. **25** a bread loaf or roll made of one or more pieces of twisted dough. **26** a thin sliver of peel from a lemon, lime, etc., twisted and added to a drink. **27a** a cigar made by twisting three cigars around one another. **27b** chewing tobacco made in the form of a roll by twisting the leaves together. **28** *Physics.* torsional deformation or shear stress or strain. **29** *Sport, chiefly U.S. and Canadian.* spin given to a ball in various games, esp. baseball. **30** the extent to which the grooves in the bore of a rifled firearm are spiralled. **31 round the twist.** *Brit. slang.* mad; eccentric. [Old English; related to German dialect *Zwist* a quarrel, Dutch *twisten* to quarrel] ▸ **'twistable** *adj* ▸ **ˌtwistaˈbility** *n* ▸ **'twisted** *adj* ▸ **'twisting** *adj* ▸ **'twisty** *adj*

twist drill *n* a drill bit having two helical grooves running from the point along the shank to clear swarf and cuttings.

twister (ˈtwɪstə) *n* **1** *Brit.* a swindling or dishonest person. **2** a person or thing that twists, such as a device used in making ropes. **3** *U.S. and Canadian.* an informal name for **tornado. 4** a ball moving with a twisting motion.

twist grip *n* a handlebar control in the form of a ratchet-controlled rotating grip, used on some bicycles and motorcycles as a gear-change control and on motorcycles as an accelerator.

twit[1] (twɪt) *vb* **twits, twitting, twitted. 1** (*tr*) to tease, taunt, or reproach, often in jest. ◆ *n* **2** *U.S. and Canadian informal.* a nervous or excitable state. **3** *Rare.* a reproach; taunt. [Old English *ætwītan,* from *æt* against + *wītan* to accuse; related to Old High German *wīzan* to punish]

twit[2] (twɪt) *n Informal, chiefly Brit.* a foolish or stupid person; idiot. [C19: from TWIT[1] (originally in the sense: a person given to twitting)]

twitch (twɪtʃ) *vb* **1** to move or cause to move in a jerky spasmodic way. **2** (*tr*) to pull or draw (something) with a quick jerky movement. **3** (*intr*) to hurt with a sharp spasmodic pain. **4** (*tr*) *Rare.* to nip. ◆ *n* **5** a sharp jerking movement. **6** a mental or physical twinge. **7** a sudden muscular spasm, esp. one caused by a nervous condition. Compare **tic. 8** a loop of cord used to control a horse by drawing it tight about its upper lip. [Old English *twiccian* to pluck; related to Old High German *zwecchōn* to pinch, Dutch *twicken*] ▸ **'twitching** *adj, n*

twitcher (ˈtwɪtʃə) *n* **1** a person or thing that twitches. **2** *Informal.* a birdwatcher who tries to spot as many rare species as possible.

twitch grass *n* another name for **couch grass.** Sometimes shortened to **twitch.** [C16: a variant of QUITCH GRASS]

twitchy (ˈtwɪtʃɪ) *adj* nervous, worried, and ill-at-ease: *he was twitchy with anticipation.*

twite (twaɪt) *n* a N European finch, *Acanthis flavirostris,* with a brown streaked plumage. [C16: imitative of its cry]

twitter (ˈtwɪtə) *vb* **1** (*intr*) (esp. of a bird) to utter a succession of chirping sounds. **2** (*intr*) to talk or move rapidly and tremulously. **3** (*intr*) to giggle: *her schoolmates twittered behind their desks.* **4** (*tr*) to utter in a chirping way. ◆ *n* **5** a twittering sound, esp. of a bird. **6** the act of twittering. **7** a state of nervous excitement (esp. in the phrase **in a twitter**). [C14: of imitative origin] ▸ **'twitterer** *n* ▸ **'twittery** *adj*

'twixt *or* **twixt** (twɪkst) *Poetic contraction of* betwixt.

two (tuː) *n* **1** the cardinal number that is the sum of one and one. It is a prime number. See also **number** (sense 1). **2** a numeral, 2, II, (ii), etc., representing this number. **3** *Music.* the numeral 2 used as the lower figure in a time signature, indicating that the beat is measured in minims. **4** something representing, represented by, or consisting of two units, such as a playing card with two symbols on it. **5** Also called: **two o'clock.** two hours after noon or midnight. **6 in two.** in or into two parts: *break the bread in two.* **7 put two and two together.** to make an inference from available evidence, esp. an obvious inference. **8 that makes two of us.** the same applies to me. ◆ *determiner* **9a** amounting to two: *two nails.* **9b** (*as pronoun*): *he bought two.* ◆ Related adjs: **binary, double, dual.** Related prefixes: **di-, bi-.** [Old English *twā* (feminine); related to Old High German *zwā,* Old Norse *tvau,* Latin, Greek *duo*]

Two-and-a-half International *n* another name for the **Vienna Union.**

two-bit *adj* (*prenominal*) *Slang, chiefly U.S. and Canadian.* worth next to nothing; cheap. [C20: from the phrase *two bits* a small sum]

two-by-four *n* **1** a length of untrimmed timber with a cross section that measures 2 inches by 4 inches. **2** a trimmed timber joist with a cross section that measures 1½ inches by 3½ inches.

twoccing *or* **twocking** (ˈtwɒkɪŋ) *n Brit. slang.* the act of breaking into a motor vehicle and driving it away. [C20: from *T(aking) W(ithout) O(wner's) C(onsent),* the legal offence with which car thieves may be charged] ▸ **'twoccer** *or* **'twocker** *n*

two-cycle *adj* the U.S. and Canadian word for **two-stroke.**

two-dimensional *adj* **1** of, having, or relating to two dimensions, usually describable in terms of length and breadth or length and height. **2** lying on a plane; having an area but not enclosing any volume. **3** lacking in depth, as characters in a literary work. **4** (of painting or drawing) lacking the characteristics of form or depth. ▸ **'two-di,mension'ality** *n* ▸ **'two-di'mensionally** *adv*

two-edged *adj* **1** having two cutting edges. **2** (esp. of a remark) having two interpretations, such as *she looks nice when she smiles.*

two-faced *adj* deceitful; insincere; hypocritical. ▸ **two-facedly** ('tu:'feɪsɪdlɪ, -'feɪst-) *adv* ▸ **'two-'facedness** *n*

twofold ('tu:,fəʊld) *adj* **1** equal to twice as many or twice as much; double: *a twofold increase.* **2** composed of two parts; dual: *a twofold reason.* ◆ *adv* **3** doubly.

two-four time *n Music.* a form of simple duple time in which there are two crotchet beats in each bar.

two-handed *adj* **1** requiring the use of both hands. **2** ambidextrous. **3** requiring the participation or cooperation of two people. ▸ **'two-'handedly** *adv*

two-hander (,tu:'hændə) *n* a play for two actors.

two-line *n* (*modifier*) (formerly) denoting double the normal size of printer's type: *two-line pica* (24 point).

two-name paper *n U.S. finance.* a commercial paper signed by two persons both of whom accept full liability.

two-pack *adj* (of a paint, filler, etc.) supplied as two separate components, for example a base and a catalyst, that are mixed together immediately before use.

two-party system *n* a condition or system in which two major parties dominate a political unit.

twopence *or* **tuppence** ('tʌpəns) *n Brit.* **1** the sum of two pennies. **2** (*used with a negative*) something of little value (in the phrase **not care** *or* **give twopence**). **3** a former British silver coin, now only coined as Maundy money.

twopenny *or* **tuppenny** ('tʌpənɪ) *adj Chiefly Brit.* **1** Also: **twopenny-halfpenny.** cheap or tawdry. **2** (intensifier): *a twopenny damn.* **3** worth two pence.

two-phase *adj* (of an electrical circuit, device, etc.) generating or using two alternating voltages of the same frequency, displaced in phase by 90°. Also: **quarter-phase.**

two-piece *adj* **1** consisting of two separate parts, usually matching, as of a garment. ◆ *n* **2** such an outfit.

two-ply *adj* **1** made of two thicknesses, layers, or strands. ◆ *n, pl* **-plies. 2** a two-ply wood, knitting yarn, etc.

two-pot screamer *n Austral. slang.* a person easily influenced by alcohol.

two-seater *n* a vehicle providing seats for two people.

Two Sicilies *pl n* **the.** a former kingdom of S Italy, consisting of the kingdoms of Sicily and Naples (1061–1860).

two-sided *adj* **1** having two sides or aspects. **2** controversial; debatable: *a two-sided argument.*

twosome ('tu:səm) *n* **1** two together, esp. two people. **2** a match between two people. **3** (*modifier*) consisting of or played by two: *a twosome performance.*

two-spot *n* a card with two pips; two; deuce.

two-step *n* **1** an old-time dance in duple time. **2** a piece of music composed for or in the rhythm of such a dance.

two-stroke *adj* relating to or designating an internal-combustion engine whose piston makes two strokes for every explosion. U.S. and Canadian word: **two-cycle.** Compare **four-stroke.**

two-tailed *adj Statistics.* (of a significance test) concerned with the hypothesis that an observed value of a sampling statistic differs significantly from a given value, where an error in either direction is relevant: for instance, in testing the fairness of scales, an inspector will seek to exclude both overweight and underweight goods. Compare **one-tailed.**

two-tailed pasha *n* a distinctive vanessid butterfly of S Europe, *Charaxes jasius,* having mottled brown wings with a yellow-orange margin and frilled hind edges.

Two Thousand Guineas *n* (*functioning as sing*), *usually written* **2000 Guineas. the.** an annual horse race run at Newmarket since 1809.

two-tier *adj* involving or comprising two levels of structure, policy, etc.

two-time *vb Informal.* to deceive (someone, esp. a lover) by carrying on a relationship with another. ▸ **,two-'timer** *n*

two-tone *adj* **1** of two colours or two shades of the same colour. **2** (esp. of sirens, car horns, etc.) producing or consisting of two notes.

two-tooth *n, pl* **-tooths.** *Austral. and N.Z.* a sheep between one and two years old with two permanent incisor teeth.

'twould (twʊd) *Poetic or dialect. contraction of* it would.

two-up *n Chiefly Austral.* a gambling game in which two coins are tossed or spun. Bets are made on both coins landing with the same face uppermost.

two-way *adj* **1** moving, permitting movement, or operating in either of two opposite directions: *two-way traffic; a two-way valve.* **2** involving two participants: *a two-way agreement.* **3** involving reciprocal obligation or mutual action: *a two-way process.* **4** (of a radio, telephone, etc.) allowing communications in two directions using both transmitting and receiving equipment.

two-way mirror *n* a half-silvered sheet of glass that functions as a mirror when viewed from one side but is translucent from the other.

twp (tʊp) *adj* (*predicative*) *South Wales dialect.* stupid; daft. [Welsh]

twyer ('twaɪə) *n* a variant of **tuyère.**

TX *abbrev. for* Texas.

-ty[1] *suffix of numerals.* denoting a multiple of ten: *sixty; seventy.* [from Old English *-tig* TEN]

-ty[2] *suffix forming nouns.* indicating state, condition, or quality: *cruelty.* [from Old French *-te, -tet,* from Latin *-tās, -tāt-;* related to Greek *-tēs*]

Tyan-Shan ('tjan'ʃan) *n* transliteration of the Russian name for the **Tian Shan.**

Tyburn ('taɪbɜ:n) *n* (formerly) a place of execution in London, on the **River Tyburn** (a tributary of the Thames, now entirely below ground).

Tyche ('taɪkɪ) *n Greek myth.* the goddess of fortune. Roman counterpart: **Fortuna.**

tychism ('taɪkɪzəm) *n Philosophy.* the theory that chance is an objective reality at work in the universe, esp. in evolutionary adaptations. [from Greek *tukhē* chance]

Tycho ('taɪkəʊ) *n* a relatively young crater in the SW quadrant of the moon, 4 km deep and 84 kilometres in diameter, with a central peak. It is the centre of a conspicuous system of rays. [named after *Tycho* BRAHE]

tycoon (taɪ'ku:n) *n* **1** a business man of great wealth and power. **2** an archaic name for a **shogun.** [C19: from Japanese *taikun,* from Chinese *ta* great + *chün* ruler]

tyke *or* **tike** (taɪk) *n* **1** a dog, esp. a mongrel. **2** *Informal.* a small or cheeky child: used esp. in affectionate reproof. **3** *Brit. dialect.* a rough ill-mannered person. **4** Also called: **Yorkshire tyke.** *Brit. slang, often offensive.* a person from Yorkshire. **5** *Austral. slang, offensive.* a Roman Catholic. [C14: from Old Norse *tīk* bitch]

Tyler ('taɪlə) *n* **1 John.** 1790–1862, U.S. statesman; tenth president of the U.S. (1841–45). **2 Wat** (wɒt). died 1381, English leader of the Peasants' Revolt (1381).

tylopod ('taɪləʊ,pɒd) *n* any artiodactyl mammal of the suborder *Tylopoda,* having padded, rather than hoofed, digits: includes the camels and llamas. [C19: from New Latin, from Greek *tulos* knob or *tulē* cushion + -POD]

Tylor ('taɪlə) *n* Sir **Edward Burnett.** 1832–1917, British anthropologist; first professor of anthropology at Oxford (1896). His *Primitive Culture* (1871) became a standard work.

tylosis (taɪ'ləʊsɪs) *n Botany.* a bladder-like outgrowth from certain cells in woody tissue that extends into and blocks adjacent conducting xylem cells. [C19: from Greek *tulōsis,* from *tulos* knob or *tulē* callus + -OSIS]

tymbal ('tɪmbᵊl) *n* a variant spelling of **timbal.**

tympan ('tɪmpən) *n* **1** a membrane stretched over a frame or resonating cylinder, bowl, etc. **2** *Printing.* packing interposed on a hand-operated text between the platen and the paper to be printed in order to provide an even impression. **3** *Architect.* another name for **tympanum** (sense 3). [Old English *timpana,* from Latin; see TYMPANUM]

tympani ('tɪmpənɪ) *pl n* a variant spelling of **timpani.**

tympanic (tɪm'pænɪk) *adj* **1** *Anatomy, architect.* of, relating to, or having a tympanum. **2** of, relating to, or resembling a drumhead.

tympanic bone *n* the part of the temporal bone in the mammalian skull that surrounds the auditory canal.

tympanic membrane *n* the thin translucent oval membrane separating the external ear from the middle ear. It transmits vibrations produced by sound waves, via the ossicles, to the cochlea. Also called: **tympanum.** Nontechnical name: **eardrum.**

tympanist ('tɪmpənɪst) *n* a person who plays a drum, now specifically the kettledrum.

tympanites (,tɪmpə'naɪti:z) *n* distension of the abdomen caused by an abnormal accumulation of gas in the intestinal or peritoneal cavity, as in peritonitis. Also called: **meteorism, tympany.** [C14: from Late Latin, from Greek *tumpanitēs* concerning a drum, from *tumpanon* drum] ▸ **tympanitic** (,tɪmpə'nɪtɪk) *adj*

tympanitis (,tɪmpə'naɪtɪs) *n* inflammation of the eardrum. Also called: **otitis media.**

tympanum ('tɪmpənəm) *n, pl* **-nums** *or* **-na** (-nə). **1a** the cavity of the middle ear. **1b** another name for **tympanic membrane. 2** any diaphragm resembling that in the middle ear in function. **3** Also called: **tympan.** *Architect.* **3a** the recessed space bounded by the cornices of a pediment, esp. one that is triangular in shape and ornamented. **3b** the recessed space bounded by an arch and the lintel of a doorway or window below it. **4** *Music.* a tympan or drum. **5** a scoop wheel for raising water. [C17: from Latin, from Greek *tumpanon* drum; related to Greek *tuptein* to beat]

tympany ('tɪmpənɪ) *n, pl* **-nies. 1** another name for **tympanites. 2** *Obsolete.* excessive pride or arrogance.

Tyndale, Tindal, *or* **Tindale** ('tɪndᵊl) *n* **William.** ?1492–1536, English Protestant and humanist, who translated the New Testament (1525), the Pentateuch (1530), and the Book of Jonah (1531) into English. He was burnt at the stake as a heretic.

Tyndall ('tɪndᵊl) *n* **John.** 1820–93, Irish physicist, noted for his work on the radiation of heat by gases, the transmission of sound through the atmosphere, and the scattering of light.

Tyndall effect *n* the phenomenon in which light is scattered by particles of matter in its path. It enables a beam of light to become visible by illuminating dust particles, etc. [C19: named after John TYNDALL]

tyndallimetry (,tɪndᵊl'ɪmətrɪ) *n Chem.* the determination of the concentration of suspended material in a liquid by measuring the amount of light scattered. [C20: from TYNDALL EFFECT + -METRY]

Tyndareus (tɪn'dærɪəs) *n Greek myth.* a Spartan king; the husband of Leda.

Tyne (taɪn) *n* a river in N England, flowing east to the North Sea. Length: 48 km (30 miles).

Tyne and Wear *n* a metropolitan county of NE England, administered since 1986 by the unitary authorities of Newcastle upon Tyne, North Tyneside, Gateshead, South Tyneside, and Sunderland. Area: 540 sq. km (208 sq. miles).

Tynemouth ('taɪn,maʊθ) *n* a port in NE England, in North Tyneside unitary authority, Tyne and Wear, at the mouth of the River Tyne: includes the port and industrial centre of North Shields; fishing, ship-repairing, and marine engineering. Pop.: 20 716 (1991).

Tyneside ('taɪn,saɪd) *n* the conurbation on the banks of the Tyne from Newcastle to the coast. Related word: **Geordie.**

Tynwald ('tɪnwəld, 'taɪn-) *n* **the.** the Parliament of the Isle of Man, consisting of the crown, lieutenant governor, House of Keys, and legislative council. Full name: **Tynwald Court.** [C15: from Old Norse *thingvollr*, from *thing* assembly + *vollr* field]

typ., typo., *or* **typog.** *abbrev. for:* **1** typographer. **2** typographic(al). **3** typography.

typal ('taɪpᵊl) *adj* a rare word for **typical.**

type (taɪp) *n* **1** a kind, class, or category, the constituents of which share similar characteristics. **2** a subdivision of a particular class of things or people; sort: *what type of shampoo do you use?* **3** the general form, plan, or design distinguishing a particular group. **4** *Informal.* a person who typifies a particular quality: *he's the administrative type.* **5** *Informal.* a person, esp. of a specified kind: *he's a strange type.* **6a** a small block of metal or more rarely wood bearing a letter or character in relief for use in printing. **6b** such pieces collectively. **7** characters printed from type; print. **8** *Biology.* **8a** the taxonomic group the characteristics of which are used for defining the next highest group, for example *Rattus norvegicus* (brown rat) is the type species of the rat genus *Rattus.* **8b** (*as modifier*): *a type genus; a type species.* **9** See **type specimen. 10** the characteristic device on a coin. **11** *Linguistics.* a symbol regarded as standing for the class of all symbols identical to it. Compare **token** (sense 8). **12** *Logic.* a class of expressions or of the entities they represent that can all enter into the same syntactic relations. The **theory of types** was advanced by Bertrand Russell to avoid the liar paradox, Russell's paradox, etc. **13** *Philosophy.* a universal. If a sentence always has the same meaning whenever it is used, the meaning is said to be a property of the sentence-type. Compare **token** (sense 9). **14** *Chiefly Christian theol.* a figure, episode, or symbolic factor resembling some future reality in such a way as to foreshadow or prefigure it. **15** *Rare.* a distinctive sign or mark. ◆ *vb* **16** to write (copy) on a typewriter. **17** (*tr*) to be a symbol of; typify. **18** (*tr*) to decide the type of; clarify into a type. **19** (*tr*) *Med.* to determine the blood group of (a blood sample). **20** (*tr*) *Chiefly Christian theol.* to foreshadow or serve as a symbol of (some future reality). [C15: from Latin *typus* figure, from Greek *tupos* image, from *tuptein* to strike]

-type *n combining form.* **1** type or form: *archetype.* **2** printing type or photographic process: *collotype.* [from Latin *-typus*, from Greek *-typos*, from *tupos* TYPE]

typebar ('taɪp,bɑː) *n* one of the bars in a typewriter that carry the type and are operated by keys.

typecase ('taɪp,keɪs) *n* a compartmental tray for storing printer's type.

typecast ('taɪp,kɑːst) *vb* **-casts, -casting, -cast.** (*tr*) to cast (an actor) in the same kind of role continually, esp. because of his physical appearance or previous success in such roles. ▸ **'type,caster** *n*

typeface ('taɪp,feɪs) *n* another name for **face** (sense 17).

type founder *n* a person who casts metallic printer's type. ▸ **type founding** *n* ▸ **type foundry** *n*

type-high *adj* having the height of a piece of type, standardized as 0.918 inches.

type metal *n Printing.* an alloy of tin, lead, and antimony, from which type is cast.

type I error *n Statistics.* the error of rejecting the null hypothesis when it is true, the probability of which is the significance level of a result.

typescript ('taɪp,skrɪpt) *n* **1** a typed copy of a document, literary script, etc. **2** any typewritten material.

typeset ('taɪp,sɛt) *vb* **-sets, -setting, -set.** (*tr*) *Printing.* to set (textual matter) in type.

typesetter ('taɪp,sɛtə) *n* **1** a person who sets type; compositor. **2** a typesetting machine.

type specimen *n Biology.* the original specimen from which a description of a new species is made. Also called: **holotype.**

type II error *n Statistics.* the error of not rejecting the null hypothesis when it is false. The probability of avoiding such an error is the power of the test and is a function of the alternative hypothesis.

typewrite ('taɪp,raɪt) *vb* **-writes, -writing, -wrote, -written.** to write by means of a typewriter; type.

typewriter ('taɪp,raɪtə) *n* **1** a keyboard machine for writing mechanically in characters resembling print. It may be operated entirely by hand (**manual typewriter**) or be powered by electricity (**electric typewriter**). **2** *Printing.* a style of type resembling typescript.

typewriting ('taɪp,raɪtɪŋ) *n* **1** the act or skill of using a typewriter. **2** copy produced by a typewriter; typescript.

typhlitis (tɪf'laɪtɪs) *n* **1** inflammation of the caecum. **2** an obsolete name for **appendicitis.** [C19: from New Latin, from Greek *tuphlon* the caecum, from *tuphlos* blind] ▸ **typhlitic** (tɪf'lɪtɪk) *adj*

typhlology (tɪf'lɒlədʒɪ) *n* the branch of science concerned with blindness and the care of the blind. [C19: from Greek *tuphlos* blind]

Typhoeus (taɪ'fiːəs) *n Greek myth.* the son of Gaea and Tartarus who had a hundred dragon heads, which spurted fire, and a bellowing many-tongued voice. He created the whirlwinds and fought with Zeus before the god hurled him beneath Mount Etna. ▸ **Ty'phoean** *adj*

typhogenic (,taɪfəʊ'dʒɛnɪk) *adj* causing typhus or typhoid fever.

typhoid ('taɪfɔɪd) *Pathol.* ◆ *adj also* **typhoidal. 1** resembling typhus. ◆ *n* **2** short for **typhoid fever.**

typhoid fever *n* an acute infectious disease characterized by high fever, rose-coloured spots on the chest or abdomen, abdominal pain, and occasionally intestinal bleeding. It is caused by the bacillus *Salmonella typhosa* ingested with food or water. Also called: **enteric fever.** [C19: from TYPHUS + -OID; so called because the symptoms resemble those of typhus]

typhoidin (taɪ'fɔɪdɪn) *n Med.* a culture of dead typhoid bacillus for injection into the skin to test for typhoid fever.

Typhon ('taɪfɒn) *n Greek myth.* a monster and one of the whirlwinds: later confused with his father Typhoeus.

typhoon (taɪ'fuːn) *n* **1** a small violent tropical storm or cyclone, esp. in the China seas and W Pacific. **2** a violent storm of India. [C16: from Chinese *tai fung* great wind, from *tai* great + *fung* wind; influenced by Greek *tuphōn* whirlwind] ▸ **typhonic** (taɪ'fɒnɪk) *adj*

typhus ('taɪfəs) *n* any one of a group of acute infectious rickettsial diseases characterized by high fever, skin rash, and severe headache. Also called: **typhus fever.** [C18: from New Latin *tȳphus*, from Greek *tuphos* fever; related to *tuphein* to smoke] ▸ **'typhous** *adj*

typical ('tɪpɪkᵊl) *adj* **1** being or serving as a representative example of a particular type; characteristic: *the painting is a typical Rembrandt.* **2** considered to be an example of some undesirable trait: *that is typical of you!* **3** of or relating to a representative specimen or type. **4** conforming to a type. **5** *Biology.* having most of the characteristics of a particular taxonomic group: *a typical species of a genus.* ◆ Also (poetic) **typic.** [C17: from Medieval Latin *typicālis*, from Late Latin *typicus* figurative, from Greek *tupikos*, from *tupos* TYPE] ▸ **'typically** *adv* ▸ **'typicalness** *or* **,typi'cality** *n*

typify ('tɪpɪ,faɪ) *vb* **-fies, -fying, -fied.** (*tr*) **1** to be typical of; characterize. **2** to symbolize or represent completely, by or as if by a type. [C17: from Latin *typus* TYPE + -IFY] ▸ **,typifi'cation** *n* ▸ **'typi,fier** *n*

typing ('taɪpɪŋ) *n* **1** the work or activity of using a typewriter or word processor. **2** the skill of using a typewriter quickly and accurately.

typist ('taɪpɪst) *n* a person who types, esp. for a living.

typo ('taɪpəʊ) *n, pl* **-pos.** *Informal.* a typographical error. Also called (Brit.): **literal.**

typo. *or* **typog.** *abbrev.* variants of **typ.**

typographer (taɪ'pɒgrəfə) *n* **1** a person skilled in typography. **2** another name for **compositor.**

typography (taɪ'pɒgrəfɪ) *n* **1** the art, craft, or process of composing type and printing from it. **2** the selection and planning of type for printed publications. ▸ **typographical** (,taɪpə'græfɪkᵊl) *or* **,typo'graphic** *adj* ▸ **,typo'graphically** *adv*

typology (taɪ'pɒlədʒɪ) *n Chiefly Christian theol.* the doctrine or study of types or of the correspondence between them and the realities which they typify. ▸ **typological** (,taɪpə'lɒdʒɪkᵊl) *or* **,typo'logic** *adj* ▸ **,typo'logically** *adv* ▸ **ty'pologist** *n*

typothetae (taɪ'pɒθɪ,tiː, ,taɪpə'θiːtiː) *pl n U.S.* printers collectively; used in the names of organized associations, as of master printers. [C19: New Latin: typesetters, from Greek *tupos* TYPE + *thetēs* one who places, from *tithenai* to place]

typw. *abbrev. for:* **1** typewriter. **2** typewritten.

Tyr *or* **Tyrr** (tjʊə, tɪə) *n Norse myth.* the god of war, son of Odin. Anglo-Saxon counterpart: **Tiu.**

tyramine ('taɪrə,miːn, 'tɪ-) *n* a colourless crystalline amine derived from phenol and found in ripe cheese, ergot, decayed animal tissue, and mistletoe and used for its sympathomimetic action; 4-hydroxyphenethylamine. Formula: $(C_2H_4NH_2)C_6H_4OH$. [C20: from TYR(OSINE) + AMINE]

tyrannical (tɪ'rænɪkᵊl) *or* **tyrannic** *adj* characteristic of or relating to a tyrant or to tyranny; oppressive. ▸ **ty'rannically** *adv* ▸ **ty'rannicalness** *n*

tyrannicide (tɪ'rænɪ,saɪd) *n* **1** the killing of a tyrant. **2** a person who kills a tyrant. ▸ **tyr,ranni'cidal** *adj*

tyrannize *or* **tyrannise** ('tɪrə,naɪz) *vb* (when *intr*, often foll. by *over*) to rule or exercise power (over) in a cruel or oppressive manner. ▸ **'tyran,nizer** *or* **'tyran,niser** *n*

tyrannosaurus (tɪ,rænə'sɔːrəs) *or* **tyrannosaur** (tɪ'rænə,sɔː) *n* any large carnivorous bipedal dinosaur of the genus *Tyrannosaurus*, common in North America in upper Jurassic and Cretaceous times: suborder *Theropoda* (theropods). [C19: from New Latin, from Greek *turannos* TYRANT + *sauros* lizard]

tyranny ('tɪrənɪ) *n, pl* **-nies. 1a** government by a tyrant or tyrants; despotism. **1b** similarly oppressive and unjust government by more than one person. **2** arbitrary, unreasonable, or despotic behaviour or use of authority: *the teacher's tyranny.* **3** any harsh discipline or oppression: *the tyranny of the clock.* **4** a political unit ruled by a tyrant. **5** (esp. in ancient Greece) government by a usurper. **6** a tyrannical act. [C14: from Old French *tyrannie*, from Medieval Latin *tyrannia*, from Latin *tyrannus* TYRANT] ▸ **'tyrannous** *adj* ▸ **'tyrannously** *adv* ▸ **'tyrannousness** *n*

tyrant ('taɪrənt) *n* **1** a person who governs oppressively, unjustly, and arbitrarily; despot. **2** any person who exercises authority in a tyrannical manner. **3** anything that exercises tyrannical influence. **4** (esp. in ancient Greece) a ruler whose authority lacked the sanction of law or custom; usurper. [C13: from Old French *tyrant*, from Latin *tyrannus*, from Greek *turannos*]

tyrant flycatcher *n* any passerine bird of the American family *Tyrannidae.* Often shortened to **flycatcher.**

tyre *or U.S.* **tire** ('taɪə) *n* **1** a rubber ring placed over the rim of a wheel of a road vehicle to provide traction and reduce road shocks, esp. a hollow inflated ring (**pneumatic tyre**) consisting of a reinforced outer casing enclosing an inner tube. See also **tubeless tyre, cross-ply, radial-ply. 2** a ring of wear-resisting steel shrunk thermally onto a cast-iron railway wheel. **3** a metal band or hoop attached to the rim of a wooden cartwheel. ◆ *vb* **4** (*tr*) to fit a tyre or tyres to (a wheel, vehicle, etc.). [C18: variant of C15 *tire*, probably from TIRE[3]]

Tyre *or* **Tyr** ('taɪə) *n* a port in S Lebanon, on the Mediterranean: founded about the 15th century B.C.; for centuries a major Phoenician seaport, famous for silks and its Tyrian-purple dye; now a small market town. Pop.: 70 000 (1991 est.). Arabic name: **Sur.**

Tyrian ('tɪrɪən) *n* **1** a native or inhabitant of ancient Tyre. **2** short for **Tyrian purple** (sense 2). ◆ *adj* **3** of or relating to ancient Tyre.

Tyrian purple *n* **1** a deep purple dye obtained from molluscs of the genus *Murex* and highly prized in antiquity. **2a** a vivid purplish-red colour. **2b** (*as adj*): *a Tyrian-purple robe.* Sometimes shortened to **Tyrian.**

tyro *or* **tiro** ('taɪrəʊ) *n, pl* **-ros.** a novice or beginner. [C17: from Latin *tīrō* recruit] ▸ **tyronic** *or* **tironic** (taɪ'rɒnɪk) *adj*

tyrocidine (ˌtaɪrəʊ'saɪdiːn) *n* an antibiotic that is the main constituent of tyrothricin. [C20: from TYRO(SINE) + -CID(E) + -INE[1]]

Tyrol *or* **Tirol** (tɪ'rəʊl, 'tɪrəʊl; *German* ti'roːl) *n* a mountainous state of W Austria: passed to the Hapsburgs in 1363; S part transferred to Italy in 1919. Capital: Innsbruck. Pop.: 658 000 (1995 est.). Area: 12 648 sq. km (4883 sq. miles). ▸ **Tyrolese** (ˌtɪrə'liːz) *or* ˌ**Tyro'lean** *adj, n*

Tyrolienne (tɪˌrəʊlɪ'ɛn) *n* **1** a lively peasant dance from the Tyrol. **2** a song composed for or in the style of this dance, characterized by the yodel. [French: of the TYROL]

Tyrone (tɪ'rəʊn) *n* a historical county of W Northern Ireland, occupying almost a quarter of the total area of Northern Ireland; it has no local government function.

tyropitta (tɪ'rɒpɪtə) *n* a Greek cheese pie. [C20: from Modern Greek]

tyrosinase (ˌtaɪrəʊsɪ'neɪz, ˌtɪrəʊ-) *n* an enzyme occurring in many organisms that is a catalyst in the conversion of tyrosine to the pigment melanin; inactivity of this enzyme results in albinism.

tyrosine ('taɪrəˌsiːn, -sɪn, 'tɪrə-) *n* an aromatic nonessential amino acid; a component of proteins. It is a metabolic precursor of thyroxine, the pigment melanin, and other biologically important compounds. [C19: from Greek *turos* cheese + -INE[2]]

tyrothricin (ˌtaɪrəʊ'θraɪsɪn) *n* an antibiotic, obtained from the soil bacterium *Bacillus brevis,* consisting of tyrocidine and gramicidin and active against Gram-positive bacteria such as staphylococci and streptococci: applied locally for the treatment of ulcers and abscesses. [C20: from New Latin *Tyrothrix* (genus name), from Greek *turos* cheese + *thrix* hair]

Tyrr (tjʊə, tɪə) *n* a variant spelling of **Tyr.**

Tyrrhenian Sea (tɪ'riːnɪən) *n* an arm of the Mediterranean between Italy and the islands of Corsica, Sardinia, and Sicily.

Tyson ('taɪsᵊn) *n* **Mike.** born 1966, U.S. boxer. World heavyweight champion (1986–90, and 1996): jailed for rape (1992–95); banned from professional boxing in 1997 after biting off part of his opponent's ear.

Tyumen (*Russian* tju'mjenj) *n* a port in S central Russia, on the Tura River: one of the oldest Russian towns in Siberia; industrial centre with nearby oil and natural gas reserves. Pop.: 494 000 (1995 est.).

tzar (zɑː) *n* a less common spelling of **tsar.** ▸ **'tzarism** *n*

Tzara ('zɑːrə) *n* **Tristan,** original name *Samuel Rosenstock.* 1896–1963, French poet and essayist, born in Romania, best known as the founder of Dada: author of *The Approximate Man* (1931).

tzatziki (tsæt'sɪkɪ) *n* a Greek dip made from yogurt, chopped cucumber, and mint. [C20: from Modern Greek]

tzitzit ('tsɪtzɪt; *Hebrew* tsit'siːt) *pl n* the fringes or tassels on the corners of the tallit. [from Hebrew, literally: tassel]

Tzekung ('tsɛ'kʊŋ) *or* **Tzu-kung** ('tsuː'kʊŋ) *n* a variant transliteration of the Chinese name for **Zigong.**

tzetze fly ('tsɛtsɪ) *n* a variant spelling of **tsetse fly.**

Tzigane (tsɪ'gɑːn, sɪ-) *n* **a** a Gypsy, esp. a Hungarian one. **b** (*as modifier*): *Tzigane music.* [C19: via French from Hungarian *czigány* Gypsy, of uncertain origin]

Tzu-po ('tsuː'pəʊ) *or* **Tzepo** ('tse'pəʊ) *n* a variant transliteration of the Chinese name for **Zibo.**

Uu

u *or* **U** (juː) *n, pl* **u's, U's,** *or* **Us. 1** the 21st letter and fifth vowel of the modern English alphabet. **2** any of several speech sounds represented by this letter, in English as in *mute, cut, hurt, sure, pull,* or *minus.* **3a** something shaped like a U. **3b** (*in combination*): *a U-bolt; a U-turn.*

U[1] *symbol for:* **1** united. **2** unionist. **3** university. **4** (in Britain) **4a** universal (used to describe a category of film certified as suitable for viewing by anyone). **4b** (*as modifier*): *a U film.* **5** *Chem.* uranium. **6** *Biochem.* uracil. ◆ *adj* **7** *Brit. informal.* (esp. of language habits) characteristic of or appropriate to the upper class. Compare **non-U.**

U[2] (uː) *n* a Burmese title of respect for men, equivalent to *Mr.*

U. *abbrev. for:* **1** *Maths.* union. **2** unit. **3** united. **4** university. **5** upper.

U2 (ˈjuː ˈtuː) *n* Irish rock band (formed 1978), comprising Bono Vox (real name Paul Hewson, born 1960, vocals), the Edge (real name Dave Evans, born 1961, guitar), Adam Clayton (born 1960, bass), and Larry Mullen (born 1961, drums). Their albums include *The Unforgettable Fire* (1984), *The Joshua Tree* (1987), and *Pop* (1997).

UAE *abbrev. for* United Arab Emirates.

UAM *abbrev. for* underwater-to-air missile.

UAR *abbrev. for* United Arab Republic.

UART (ˈjuːˌɑːt) *n Electronics. acronym for* Universal Asynchronous Receiver Transmitter.

UB40 *n* (in Britain) **1** a registration card issued by the Department of Employment to a person registering as unemployed. **2** *Informal.* a person registered as unemployed.

Ubangi (juːˈbæŋgɪ) *n* a river in central Africa, flowing west and south, forming the border between the Democratic Republic of the Congo (formerly Zaïre) and the Central African Republic and the Republic of the Congo, into the River Congo. Length: (with the Uele) 2250 km (1400 miles). French name: **Oubangui.**

Ubangi-Shari *n* a former name (until 1958) of the **Central African Republic.**

U-bend *n* a U-shaped bend in a pipe or drain that traps water in the lower part of the U and prevents the escape of noxious fumes or vapours; trap.

Übermensch *German.* (ˈyːbərˌmɛnʃ) *n, pl* **-menschen** (-mɛnʃən). (esp. in the writings of Nietzsche) the German word for **superman.** [literally: over-man]

uberrima fides (ˈjuːbəˌriːmə ˈfaɪdiːz, juːˈbɛrɪmə) *n* another name for **utmost good faith.** [Latin: utmost good faith]

ubiety (juːˈbaɪɪtɪ) *n* the condition of being in a particular place. [C17: from Latin *ubī* where + *-ety,* on the model of *society*]

ubiquinone (juːˈbɪkwɪˌnəʊn) *n* another name for **coenzyme Q.**

ubiquitarian (juːˌbɪkwɪˈtɛərɪən) *n* **1** a member of the Lutheran church who holds that Christ is no more present in the elements of the Eucharist than elsewhere, as he is present in all places at all times. ◆ *adj* **2** denoting, relating to, or holding this belief. [C17: from Latin *ubīque* everywhere; see UBIQUITOUS] ▸ **uˌbiquiˈtarianˌism** *n*

ubiquitous (juːˈbɪkwɪtəs) *adj* having or seeming to have the ability to be everywhere at once; omnipresent. [C14: from Latin *ubīque* everywhere, from *ubī* where] ▸ **uˈbiquitously** *adv* ▸ **uˈbiquity** *or* **uˈbiquitousness** *n*

ubi supra *Latin.* (ˈuːbɪ ˈsuːprɑː) where (mentioned or cited) above.

U-boat *n* a German submarine, esp. in World Wars I and II. [from German *U-Boot,* abbreviation for *Unterseeboot,* literally: undersea boat]

U bolt *n* a metal bar bent into the shape of a *U* and threaded at both ends to receive securing nuts: used to secure leaf springs, ring bolts, shackles, etc.

UBR *abbrev. for* Uniform Business Rate.

Ubuntu (ʊˈbuːntʊ) *n S. African.* humanity or fellow feeling; kindness. [Nguni]

UC *abbrev. for* University College.

u.c. *Printing. abbrev. for* upper case.

UCAS (ˈjuːkæs) *n* (in Britain) *acronym for* Universities and Colleges Admissions Service.

UCATT (ˈʌkət) *n acronym for* Union of Construction, Allied Trades and Technicians.

Ucayali (*Spanish* ukaˈjali) *n* a river in E Peru, flowing north into the Marañón above Iquitos. Length: 1600 km (1000 miles).

UCCA (ˈʌkə) *n* (formerly, in Britain) *acronym for* Universities Central Council on Admissions.

Uccello (*Italian* utˈtʃɛllo) *n* **Paolo** (ˈpaːolo). 1397–1475, Florentine painter noted esp. for three paintings of *The Battle of San Romano, 1432* (1456–60).

UCL *abbrev. for* University College London.

UDA *abbrev. for* Ulster Defence Association.

Udaipur (uːˈdaɪpʊə, ˈuːdaɪˌpʊə) *n* **1** Also called: **Mewar.** a former state of NW India: became part of Rajasthan in 1947. **2** a city in NW India, in S Rajasthan. Pop.: 308 571 (1991).

udal (ˈjuːdᵊl) *n Law.* a form of freehold possession of land existing in northern Europe before the introduction of the feudal system and still used in Orkney and Shetland. [C16: Orkney and Shetland dialect, from Old Norse *othal;* related to Old English *ēthel, ōethel,* Old High German *wodal*]

Udall (ˈjuːdᵊl) *or* **Uvedale** (ˈjuːdᵊl, ˈjuːvˌdeɪl) *n* **Nicholas.** ?1505–56, English dramatist, whose comedy *Ralph Roister Doister* (?1553), modelled on Terence and Plautus, is the earliest known English comedy.

UDC (in Britain) *abbrev. for* Urban District Council.

udder (ˈʌdə) *n* the large baglike mammary gland of cows, sheep, etc., having two or more teats. [Old English *ūder;* related to Old High German *ūtar,* Old Norse *jūr,* Latin *über,* Sanskrit *ūdhar*] ▸ **ˈudder-ˌlike** *adj*

UDI *abbrev. for* Unilateral Declaration of Independence.

Udine (*Italian* ˈuːdine) *n* a city in NE Italy, in Friuli-Venezia Giulia region: partially damaged in an earthquake in 1976. Pop.: 98 872 (1990).

Udmurt Republic (ˈʊdmʊət) *n* a constituent republic of W central Russia, in the basin of the middle Kama. Capital: Izhevsk. Pop.: 1 641 000 (1995 est.). Area: 42 100 sq. km (16 250 sq. miles).

udo (ˈuːdəʊ) *n, pl* **udos.** a stout araliaceous perennial plant, *Aralia cordata,* of Japan and China, having berry-like black fruits and young shoots that are edible when blanched. [from Japanese]

udometer (juːˈdɒmɪtə) *n* another term for **rain gauge.** [C19: from French, from Latin *ūdus* damp]

UDR *abbrev. for* Ulster Defence Regiment.

UE (in New Zealand) *abbrev. for* university entrance (examination).

UEFA (juːˈeɪfə) *n acronym for* Union of European Football Associations.

Uele (ˈweɪlə) *n* a river in central Africa, rising near the border between the Democratic Republic of the Congo (formerly Zaïre) and Uganda and flowing west to join the Bomu River and form the Ubangi River. Length: about 1100 km (700 miles).

Ufa (*Russian* uˈfa) *n* a city in W central Russia, capital of the Bashkir Republic: university (1957). Pop.: 1 094 000 (1995 est.).

Uffizi (juːˈfɪtsɪ) *n* an art gallery in Florence; built by Giorgio Vasari in the 16th century and opened as a museum in 1765: contains chiefly Italian Renaissance paintings.

UFO (*sometimes* ˈjuːfəʊ) *abbrev. for* unidentified flying object.

ufology (ˌjuːˈfɒlədʒɪ) *n* the study of UFOs. ▸ **uˈfologist** *n*

ugali (uːˈgaliː) *n E African.* a type of stiff porridge made by mixing corn meal with boiling water: the basic starch constituent of a meal. [from Swahili]

Uganda (juːˈgændə) *n* a republic in E Africa: British protectorate established in 1894–96; gained independence in 1962 and became a republic in 1963; a member of the Commonwealth. It consists mostly of a savanna plateau with part of Lake Victoria in the southeast and mountains in the southwest, reaching 5109 m (16 763 ft.) in the Ruwenzori Range. Official language: English; Swahili, Luganda, and Luo are also widely spoken. Religion: Christian majority. Currency: Ugandan shilling. Capital: Kampala. Pop.: 22 167 000 (1998 est.). Area: 235 886 sq. km (91 076 sq. miles). ▸ **Uˈgandan** *adj, n*

Ugaritic (ˌuːgəˈrɪtɪk) *n* **1** an extinct Semitic language of N Syria. ◆ *adj* **2** of or relating to this language. [C19: after *Ugarit* (modern name: Ras Shamra), an ancient Syrian city-state]

UGC (in Britain) *abbrev. for* University Grants Committee.

ugh (ʊx, ʊh, ʌh) *interj* an exclamation of disgust, annoyance, or dislike.

UGLI (ˈʌglɪ) *n, pl* **-LIS** *or* **-LIES.** *Trademark.* a large juicy yellow-skinned citrus fruit of the Caribbean: a cross between a tangerine, grapefruit, and orange. Also called: **UGLI fruit.** [C20: probably an alteration of UGLY, referring to its wrinkled skin]

uglify (ˈʌglɪˌfaɪ) *vb* **-fies, -fying, -fied.** to make or become ugly or more ugly. ▸ **ˌuglifiˈcation** *n* ▸ **ˈugliˌfier** *n*

ugly (ˈʌglɪ) *adj* **-lier, -liest. 1** of unpleasant or unsightly appearance. **2** repulsive, objectionable, or displeasing in any way: *war is ugly.* **3** ominous or menacing: *an ugly situation.* **4** bad-tempered, angry, or sullen: *an ugly mood.* [C13: from Old Norse *uggligr* dreadful, from *ugga* fear] ▸ **ˈuglily** *adv* ▸ **ˈugliness** *n*

ugly duckling *n* a person or thing, initially ugly or unpromising, that changes into something beautiful or admirable. [an allusion to *The Ugly Duckling,* a story by Hans Christian Andersen]

Ugrian (ˈuːgrɪən, ˈjuː-) *adj* **1** of or relating to a light-haired subdivision of the Turanian people, who include the Samoyeds, Voguls, Ostyaks, and Magyars. ◆ *n* **2** a member of this group of peoples. **3** another word for **Ugric.** [C19: from Old Russian *Ugre* Hungarians]

Ugric (ˈuːgrɪk, ˈjuː-) *n* **1** one of the two branches of the Finno-Ugric family of languages, including Hungarian and some languages of NW Siberia. Compare **Finnic.** ◆ *adj* **2** of or relating to this group of languages or their speakers.

UHF *Radio. abbrev. for* ultrahigh frequency.

uh-huh (əˈhə) *sentence substitute. Informal.* a less emphatic variant of **yes.**

uhlan *or* **ulan** (ˈuːlɑːn, ˈjuːlən) *n History.* a member of a body of lancers first employed in the Polish army and later in W European armies. [C18: via German from Polish *ulan,* from Turkish *ōlan* young man]

Uhland (*German* ˈuːlant) *n* **Johann Ludwig** (joˈhan ˈluːtvɪç). 1787–1862, German romantic poet, esp. of lyrics and ballads.

UHT *abbrev. for* ultra heat treated.

uh-uh (ˈʌˈʌ) *sentence substitute. Informal, chiefly U.S.* a less emphatic variant of **no**[1].

uhuru (uːˈhuːruː) *n* (esp. in E Africa) **1** national independence. **2** freedom. [C20: from Swahili]

Uigur *or* **Uighur** (ˈwiːgʊə) *n* **1** (*pl* **-gur** *or* **-gurs**) a member of a Mongoloid people of NW China, Uzbekistan, Kyrgyzstan, and Kazakhstan. **2** the language of this people, belonging to the Turkic branch of the Altaic family. ▸ **Ui'gurian, Ui'ghurian** *or* **Ui'guric, Ui'ghuric** *adj*

uillean pipes ('uːlɪən) *pl n* bagpipes developed in Ireland and operated by squeezing bellows under the arm. Also called: **Irish pipes, union pipes.** [C19: Irish *píob uilleann,* from *píob* pipe + *uilleann* genitive sing of *uille* elbow]

Uinta Mountains (juˈɪntə) *pl n* a mountain range in NE Utah: part of the Rocky Mountains. Highest peak: Kings Peak, 4123 m (13 528 ft.).

uintathere (juːˈɪntəˌθɪə) *n* any of various extinct Tertiary rhinoceros-like mammals of North America, having six horny processes on the head. Also called: **dinoceras.** [from *Uinta,* a county in Wyoming + Greek *thērion* wild animal]

uitlander (ˈeɪtˌlandə, -ˌlæn-, ˈɔɪt-) *n* (*sometimes cap.*) *S. African.* a foreigner; alien. [C19: Afrikaans: outlander]

ujamaa village (uːdʒaˈma) *n* (*sometimes caps.*) a communally organized village in Tanzania. [C20: *ujamaa* socialism, from Swahili: brotherhood]

Ujiji (uːˈdʒiːdʒɪ) *n* a town in W Tanzania, on Lake Tanganyika: a former slave and ivory centre; the place where Stanley found Livingstone in 1871. It merged with the neighbouring town of Kigoma to form Kigoma-Ujiji in the 1960s.

Ujjain (uːˈdʒeɪn) *n* a city in W central India, in Madhya Pradesh: one of the seven sacred cities of the Hindus; a major agricultural trade centre. Pop.: 362 266 (1991).

Ujung Pandang (ˈuːdʒuŋ pænˈdæŋ) *n* a port in central Indonesia, on SW Sulawesi: an important native port before Portuguese (16th century) and Dutch (17th century) control; capital of Dutch East Indonesia (1946–49); a major Indonesian distribution and transshipment port. Pop.: 1 091 800 (1995 est.). Also called: **Makasar, Makassar, Macassar.**

UK *abbrev. for* United Kingdom.

UKAEA *abbrev. for* United Kingdom Atomic Energy Authority.

ukase (juːˈkeɪz) *n* **1** (in imperial Russia) an edict of the tsar. **2** a rare word for **edict.** [C18: from Russian *ukaz,* from *ukazat* to command]

UKCC *abbrev. for* United Kingdom Central Council for Nursing, Midwifery, and Health Visiting.

ukiyo-e (ˌuːkiːjəʊˈjeɪ) *n* a school of Japanese painting depicting subjects from everyday life. [Japanese: pictures of the floating world]

UK Overseas Territory *n* any of the territories that are governed by the UK but lie outside the British Isles; many were formerly British **crown colonies:** includes Bermuda, Falkland Islands, and Montserrat.

Ukr. *abbrev. for* Ukraine.

Ukraine (juːˈkreɪn) *n* **the.** a republic in SE Europe, on the Black Sea and the Sea of Azov: ruled by the Khazars (7th–9th centuries), by Rurik princes until the Mongol conquest in the 13th century, then by Lithuania, by Poland, and by Russia; one of the four original republics that formed the Soviet Union in 1922; unilaterally declared independence in 1990 which was recognized in 1991: consists chiefly of lowlands; economy based on rich agriculture and mineral resources and on the major heavy industries of the Donets Basin. Official language: Ukrainian. Religion: believers are mainly Christian. Currency: hryvna. Capital: Kiev. Pop.: 50 302 000 (1998 est.). Area: 603 700 sq. km (231 990 sq. miles).

Ukrainian (juːˈkreɪnɪən) *adj* **1** of or relating to the Ukraine, its people, or their language. ◆ *n* **2** the official language of the Ukraine: an East Slavonic language closely related to Russian. **3** a native or inhabitant of the Ukraine. ◆ Formerly called: **Little Russian.**

ukulele *or* **ukelele** (ˌjuːkəˈleɪlɪ) *n* a small four-stringed guitar, esp. of Hawaii. [C19: from Hawaiian, literally: jumping flea, from *'uku* flea + *lele* jumping]

ulan (ˈuːlɑːn, ˈjuːlən) *n* a less common variant of **uhlan.**

Ulan Bator (uˈlɑːn ˈbɑːtɔː) *n* the capital of Mongolia, in the N central part: developed in the mid-17th century around the Da Khure monastery, residence until 1924 of successive "living Buddhas" (third in rank of Buddhist-Lamaist leaders), and main junction of caravan routes across Mongolia; university (1942); industrial and commercial centre. Pop.: 627 300 (1997 est.). Former name (until 1924): **Urga.** Chinese name: **Kulun.**

Ulanova (uˈlaːnəvə) *n* **Galina** (**Sergeyevna**) (gəˈliːnə) 1910–98, Russian ballet dancer, who performed with the Leningrad Kirov ballet (1928–44) and the Moscow Bolshoi Ballet (1944–62).

Ulan-Ude (uˈlɑːnuˈdeɪ) *n* an industrial city in SE Russia, capital of the Buryat Republic: an important rail junction. Pop.: 366 000 (1995 est.). Former name (until 1934): **Verkhne-Udinsk.**

Ulbricht (*German* ˈulbrɪçt) *n* **Walter** (ˈvaltər). 1893-1973, East German statesman; largely responsible for the establishment and development of East German communism.

ULCC *abbrev. for* ultralarge crude carrier.

ulcer (ˈʌlsə) *n* **1** a disintegration of the surface of the skin or a mucous membrane resulting in an open sore that heals very slowly. See also **peptic ulcer. 2** a source or element of corruption or evil. [C14: from Latin *ulcus;* related to Greek *helkos* a sore]

ulcerate (ˈʌlsəˌreɪt) *vb* to make or become ulcerous.

ulceration (ˌʌlsəˈreɪʃən) *n* **1** the development or formation of an ulcer. **2** an ulcer or an ulcerous condition.

ulcerative (ˈʌlsərətɪv) *adj* of, relating to, or characterized by ulceration: *ulcerative colitis.*

ulcerous (ˈʌlsərəs) *adj* **1** relating to, characteristic of, or characterized by an ulcer or ulcers. **2** being or having a corrupting influence. ▸ **'ulcerously** *adv* ▸ **'ulcerousness** *n*

-ule *suffix forming nouns.* indicating smallness: *globule.* [from Latin *-ulus,* diminutive suffix]

Uleåborg (ˈuːlioˌbɔrjə) *n* the Swedish name for **Oulu.**

ulema (ˈuːlɪmə) *n* **1** a body of Muslim scholars or religious leaders. **2** a member of this body. [C17: from Arabic *'ulamā* scholars, from *'alama* to know]

-ulent *suffix forming adjectives.* abundant or full of: *fraudulent.* [from Latin *-ulentus*]

Ulfilas (ˈulfɪˌlæs), **Ulfila** (ˈulfɪlə), *or* **Wulfila** *n* ?311–?382 A.D., Christian bishop of the Goths who translated the Bible from Greek into Gothic.

ullage (ˈʌlɪdʒ) *n* **1** the volume by which a liquid container falls short of being full. **2a** the quantity of liquid lost from a container due to leakage or evaporation. **2b** (in customs terminology) the amount of liquid remaining in a container after such loss. ◆ *vb* (*tr*) **3** to create ullage in. **4** to determine the amount of ullage in. **5** to fill up ullage in. [C15: from Old French *ouillage* filling of a cask, from *ouiller* to fill a cask, from *ouil* eye, from Latin *oculus* eye] ▸ **'ullaged** *adj*

ullage rocket *n* a small hydrogen peroxide rocket engine that produces sufficient acceleration to keep propellants in their places when the main rocket is shut off.

Ullswater (ˈʌlzˌwɔːtə) *n* a lake in NW England, in Cumbria in the Lake District. Length: 12 km (7.5 miles).

Ulm (*German* ulm) *n* an industrial city in S Germany, in Baden-Württemberg on the Danube: a free imperial city (1155–1802). Pop.: 115 721 (1996 est.).

ulmaceous (ʌlˈmeɪʃəs) *adj* of, relating to, or belonging to the *Ulmaceae,* a temperate and tropical family of deciduous trees and shrubs having scaly buds, simple serrated leaves, and typically winged fruits: includes the elms. [C19: via New Latin *Ulmāceae,* from Latin *ulmus* elm tree]

ulna (ˈʌlnə) *n, pl* **-nae** (-niː) *or* **-nas. 1** the inner and longer of the two bones of the human forearm. **2** the corresponding bone in other vertebrates. [C16: from Latin: elbow, ELL[1]] ▸ **'ulnar** *adj*

ulnar nerve *n* a nerve situated along the inner side of the arm and passing close to the surface of the skin near the elbow. See **funny bone.**

ulotrichous (juːˈlɒtrɪkəs) *adj* having woolly or curly hair. [C19: from New Latin *Ulotrichī* (classification applied to humans having this type of hair), from Greek *oulothrix,* from *oulos* curly + *thrix* hair] ▸ **u'lotrichy** *n*

Ulpian (ˈʌlpɪən) *n* Latin name *Domitius Ulpianus.* died ?228 A.D., Roman jurist, born in Phoenicia.

ulster (ˈʌlstə) *n* a man's heavy double-breasted overcoat with a belt or half-belt at the back. [C19: so called because it was first produced in Northern Ireland]

Ulster (ˈʌlstə) *n* **1** a province and former kingdom of N Ireland: passed to the English Crown in 1461; confiscated land given to English and Scottish Protestant settlers in the 17th century, giving rise to serious long-term conflict; partitioned in 1921, six counties forming Northern Ireland and three counties joining the Republic of Ireland. Pop. (three Ulster counties of the Republic of Ireland): 232 206 (1991); (six Ulster counties of Northern Ireland): 1 631 800 (1993 est.). Area (Republic of Ireland): 8013 sq. km (3094 sq. miles); (Northern Ireland): 14 121 sq. km (5452 sq. miles). **2** an informal name for **Northern Ireland.**

Ulster Defence Association *n* (in Northern Ireland) a Loyalist paramilitary organization. Abbrev.: **UDA.**

Ulster Democratic Unionist Party *n* a Northern Irish political party advocating the maintenance of union with the UK.

Ulsterman (ˈʌlstəmən) *n, pl* **-men.** a native or inhabitant of Ulster. ▸ **'Ulsterˌwoman** *fem n*

Ulster Unionist Council *n* a Northern Irish political party advocating the maintenance of union with the UK.

ult. *abbrev. for:* **1** ultimate(ly). **2** Also: **ulto.** ultimo.

ulterior (ʌlˈtɪərɪə) *adj* **1** lying beneath or beyond what is revealed, evident, or supposed: *ulterior motives.* **2** succeeding, subsequent, or later. **3** lying beyond a certain line or point. [C17: from Latin: further, from *ulter* beyond] ▸ **ul'teriorly** *adv*

ultima (ˈʌltɪmə) *n* the final syllable of a word. [from Latin: the last, feminine of *ultimus* last; see ULTIMATE]

ultimate (ˈʌltɪmɪt) *adj* **1** conclusive in a series or process; last; final: *an ultimate question.* **2** the highest or most significant: *the ultimate goal.* **3** elemental, fundamental, basic, or essential. **4** most extreme: *genocide is the ultimate abuse of human rights.* **5** final or total: *an ultimate cost of twenty million pounds.* ◆ *n* **6** the most significant, highest, furthest, or greatest thing. [C17: from Late Latin *ultimāre* to come to an end, from Latin *ultimus* last, from *ulter* distant] ▸ **'ultimateness** *n*

ultimate constituent *n* a constituent of something, such as a linguistic construction, that cannot be further subdivided in the terms of the analysis being undertaken. Compare **immediate constituent.**

ultimately (ˈʌltɪmɪtlɪ) *adv* in the end; at last; finally.

ultimate strength *n* the maximum tensile stress that a material can withstand before rupture.

ultima Thule (ˈθjuːlɪ) *n* **1** another name for **Thule. 2** any distant or unknown region. **3** a remote goal or aim. [Latin: the most distant Thule]

ultimatum (ˌʌltɪˈmeɪtəm) *n, pl* **-tums** *or* **-ta** (-tə). **1** a final communication by a party, esp. a government, setting forth conditions on which it insists, as during negotiations on some topic. **2** any final or peremptory demand, offer, or proposal. [C18: from New Latin, neuter of *ultimatus* ULTIMATE]

ultimo (ˈʌltɪˌməʊ) *adv Now rare except when abbreviated in formal correspondence.* in or during the previous month: *a letter of the 7th ultimo.* Abbrev.: **ult.** Compare **instant, proximo.** [C16: from Latin *ultimō* on the last]

ultimogeniture (ˌʌltɪməʊˈdʒɛnɪtʃə) *n Law.* **1** a principle of inheritance whereby the youngest son succeeds to the estate of his ancestor. Compare **primogeniture. 2** another name for **borough-English.** [C19: *ultimo-* from Latin *ultimus* last + Late Latin *genitura* a birth; compare PRIMOGENITURE]

ultra (ˈʌltrə) *adj* **1** extreme or immoderate, esp. in beliefs or opinions. ◆ *n* **2** an extremist. [C19: from Latin: beyond, from *ulter* distant]

ultra- *prefix* **1** beyond or surpassing a specified extent, range, or limit: *ultra-*

microscopic. **2** extreme or extremely: *ultramodern*. [from Latin *ultrā* beyond; see ULTRA]

ultrabasic (ˌʌltrəˈbeɪsɪk) *adj* (of such igneous rocks as peridotite) containing less than 45 per cent silica.

ultracentrifuge (ˌʌltrəˈsɛntrɪˌfjuːdʒ) *Chem.* ♦ *n* **1** a high-speed centrifuge used to separate colloidal solutions. ♦ *vb* **2** (*tr*) to subject to the action of an ultracentrifuge. ▸ **ultracentrifugal** (ˌʌltrəsɛnˈtrɪfjʊgᵊl, -ˌsɛntrɪˈfjuːgᵊl) *adj* ▸ **ˌultracenˈtrifugally** *adv* ▸ **ultracentrifugation** (ˌʌltrəˌsɛntrɪfjʊˈgeɪʃən) *n*

ultraconservative (ˌʌltrəkənˈsɜːvətɪv) *adj* **1** highly reactionary. ♦ *n* **2** a reactionary person.

ultra-distance *n* (*modifier*) *Athletics.* covering a distance in excess of 30 miles, often as part of a longer race or competition: *an ultra-distance runner*.

ultrafiche (ˈʌltrəˌfiːʃ) *n* a sheet of film, usually the size of a filing card, that is similar to a microfiche but has a much larger number of microcopies. [C20: from ULTRA- + French *fiche* small card. See MICROFICHE]

ultrafilter (ˌʌltrəˈfɪltə) *n* a filter with small pores used to separate very small particles from a suspension or colloidal solution. ▸ **ultrafiltration** (ˌʌltrəfɪlˈtreɪʃən) *n*

ultra filtration *n Engineering.* filtration that removes particles less than 10 microns (10^{-6}m) in diameter.

ultrahigh frequency (ˈʌltrəˌhaɪ) *n* a radio-frequency band or radio frequency lying between 3000 and 300 megahertz. Abbrev.: **UHF**.

ultraism (ˈʌltrəˌɪzəm) *n* extreme philosophy, belief, or action. ▸ **ˈultraist** *n, adj* ▸ **ˌultraˈistic** *adj*

ultralarge crude carrier (ˌʌltrəˈlɑːdʒ) *n Oil industry.* an oil tanker with a capacity of over 400 000 tons.

ultramarine (ˌʌltrəməˈriːn) *n* **1** a blue pigment consisting of sodium and aluminium silicates and some sodium sulphide, obtained by powdering natural lapis lazuli or made synthetically: used in paints, printing ink, plastics, etc. **2** a vivid blue colour. ♦ *adj* **3** of the colour ultramarine. **4** from across the seas. [C17: from Medieval Latin *ultramarinus,* from *ultrā* beyond (see ULTRA-) + *mare* sea; so called because the lapis lazuli from which the pigment was made was imported from Asia]

ultramicrometer (ˌʌltrəmaɪˈkrɒmɪtə) *n* a micrometer for measuring extremely small distances.

ultramicroscope (ˌʌltrəˈmaɪkrəˌskəʊp) *n* a microscope used for studying colloids, in which the sample is illuminated from the side and colloidal particles are seen as bright points on a dark background. Also called: **dark-field microscope.**

ultramicroscopic (ˌʌltrəˌmaɪkrəˈskɒpɪk) *adj* **1** too small to be seen with an optical microscope. **2** of or relating to an ultramicroscope. ▸ **ultramicroscopy** (ˌʌltrəmaɪˈkrɒskəpɪ) *n*

ultramodern (ˌʌltrəˈmɒdən) *adj* extremely modern. ▸ **ˌultraˈmodernism** *n* ▸ **ˌultraˈmodernist** *n* ▸ **ˌultraˌmodernˈistic** *adj*

ultramontane (ˌʌltrəmɒnˈteɪn) *adj* **1** on the other side of the mountains, esp. the Alps, from the speaker or writer. Compare **cismontane. 2** of or relating to a movement in the Roman Catholic Church which favours the centralized authority and influence of the pope as opposed to local independence. Compare **cisalpine** (sense 2). ♦ *n* **3** a resident or native from beyond the mountains, esp. the Alps. **4** a member of the ultramontane party of the Roman Catholic Church.

ultramontanism (ˌʌltrəˈmɒntɪˌnɪzəm) *n R.C. Church.* the doctrine of central papal supremacy. Compare **Gallicanism.** ▸ **ˌultraˈmontanist** *n*

ultramundane (ˌʌltrəˈmʌndeɪn) *adj* extending beyond the world, this life, or the universe.

ultranationalism (ˌʌltrəˈnæʃnəˌlɪzəm) *n* extreme devotion to one's own nation. ▸ **ˌultraˈnational** *adj* ▸ **ˌultraˈnationalist** *adj, n* ▸ **ˌultraˌnationalˈistic** *adj*

ultrared (ˌʌltrəˈrɛd) *adj* an obsolete word for **infrared.**

ultrashort (ˌʌltrəˈʃɔːt) *adj* (of a radio wave) having a wavelength shorter than 10 metres.

ultrasonic (ˌʌltrəˈsɒnɪk) *adj* of, concerned with, or producing waves with the same nature as sound waves but frequencies above audio frequencies. See also **ultrasound.** ▸ **ˌultraˈsonically** *adv*

ultrasonic cleaning *n* the use of ultrasound to vibrate a piece to be cleaned while the piece is immersed in a cleaning fluid. The process produces a very high degree of cleanliness, and is used for jewellery and ornately shaped items.

ultrasonics (ˌʌltrəˈsɒnɪks) *n* (*functioning as sing*) the branch of physics concerned with ultrasonic waves. Also called: **supersonics.**

ultrasonic testing *n Engineering.* the scanning of material with an ultrasonic beam, during which reflections from faults in the material can be detected: a powerful nondestructive test method.

ultrasonic welding *n* the use of high-energy vibration of ultrasonic frequency to produce a weld between two components which are held in close contact.

ultrasonography (ˌʌltrəsəˈnɒgrəfɪ) *n* the technique of using ultrasound to produce pictures of structures within the body, as for example of a fetus.

ultrasound (ˌʌltrəˈsaʊnd) *n* ultrasonic waves at frequencies above the audible range (above about 20 kHz), used in cleaning metallic parts, echo sounding, medical diagnosis and therapy, etc.

ultrasound scanner *n* a device used to examine an internal bodily structure by the use of ultrasonic waves, esp. for the diagnosis of abnormality in a fetus.

ultrastructure (ˈʌltrəˌstrʌktʃə) *n* the minute structure of an organ, tissue, or cell, as revealed by microscopy, esp. electron microscopy. ▸ **ˌultraˈstructural** *adj*

ultraviolet (ˌʌltrəˈvaɪəlɪt) *n* **1** the part of the electromagnetic spectrum with wavelengths shorter than light but longer than X-rays; in the range 0.4×10^{-6} and 1×10^{-8} metres. ♦ *adj* **2** of, relating to, or consisting of radiation lying in the ultraviolet: *ultraviolet radiation*. Abbrev.: **UV.**

ultraviolet astronomy *n* the study of radiation from celestial sources in the wavelength range 91.2 to 320 nanometres, 12 to 91.2 nanometres being the extreme ultraviolet range.

ultra vires (ˈvaɪriːz) *adv, adj* (*predicative*) *Law.* beyond the legal power or authority of a person, corporation, agent, etc. [Latin, literally: beyond strength]

ultravirus (ˌʌltrəˈvaɪrəs) *n* a virus small enough to pass through the finest filter.

ululate (ˈjuːljʊˌleɪt) *vb* (*intr*) to howl or wail, as with grief. [C17: from Latin *ululāre* to howl, from *ulula* screech owl] ▸ **ˈululant** *adj* ▸ **ˌuluˈlation** *n*

Uluru (ˌuːləˈruː) *n* the world's largest monolith, in the Northern Territory of Australia: sacred to local Aboriginal people. Height: 330m (1100 ft.). Base circumference: 9 km (5.6 miles). Former name: **Ayers Rock.**

Ulyanovsk (*Russian* ulʲˈjanəfsk) *n* the former name (1924–91) of **Simbirsk.**

Ulysses (ˈjuːlɪˌsiːz, juːˈlɪsiːz) *n* the Latin name of **Odysseus.**

um (ʌm, ᵊm) *interj* a representation of a common sound made when hesitating in speech.

Umar (ˈuːmɑː) *n* a variant transliteration of the Arabic name for **Omar.**

Umar Tal (ˈuːmɑː tæl) *n* ?1797–1864, African religious and military leader, who created a Muslim empire in W Africa.

Umayyad (uːˈmaɪjæd) *n* a variant spelling of **Omayyad.**

umbel (ˈʌmbᵊl) *n* a racemose inflorescence, characteristic of umbelliferous plants, in which the flowers arise from the same point in the main stem and have stalks of the same length, to give a cluster with the youngest flowers at the centre. [C16: from Latin *umbella* a sunshade, from *umbra* shade] ▸ **umbellate** (ˈʌmbɪlɪt, -ˌleɪt), **umbellar** (ʌmˈbɛlə), *or* **ˈumbelˌlated** *adj* ▸ **ˈumbellately** *adv*

umbelliferous (ˌʌmbɪˈlɪfərəs) *adj* **1** of, relating to, or belonging to the *Umbelliferae,* a family of herbaceous plants and shrubs, typically having hollow stems, divided or compound leaves, and flowers in umbels: includes fennel, dill, parsley, carrot, celery, and parsnip. **2** designating any other plant bearing umbels. [C17: from New Latin *umbellifer,* from Latin *umbella* sunshade + *ferre* to bear] ▸ **umˈbellifer** *n*

umbellule (ʌmˈbɛljuːl, ˈʌmbɪˌljuːl) *n* any of the small secondary umbels that make up a compound umbel. [C18: from New Latin *umbellula,* diminutive of Latin *umbella;* see UMBEL] ▸ **umbellulate** (ʌmˈbɛljʊlɪt, -ˌleɪt) *adj*

umber (ˈʌmbə) *n* **1** any of various natural brown earths containing ferric oxide together with lime and oxides of aluminium, manganese, and silicon. See also **burnt umber. 2** any of the dark brown to greenish-brown colours produced by this pigment. **3** short for **umber moth. 4** *Obsolete.* **4a** shade or shadow. **4b** any dark, dusky, or indefinite colour. ♦ *adj* **5** of, relating to, or stained with umber. [C16: from French (*terre d'*) *ombre* or Italian (*terra di*) *ombra* shadow (earth), from Latin *umbra* shade]

umber moth *n* any of various brownish geometrid moths, esp. the **waved umber** (*Menophra abruptaria*) and **small waved umber** (*Horisme vitalbata*), that are cryptically marked to merge with tree bark, and the **mottled umber** (*Erannis defoliaria*) whose looper larvae can strip branches and even trees. Often shortened to **umber.**

Umberto I (*Italian* umˈbɛrto) *n* 1844–1900, king of Italy (1878–1900); son of Victor Emmanuel II: assassinated at Monza.

Umberto II *n* 1904–83, the last king of Italy (1946), following the abdication of his father Victor Emmanuel III: abdicated when a referendum supported the abolition of the monarchy.

umbilical (ʌmˈbɪlɪkᵊl, ˌʌmbɪˈlaɪkᵊl) *adj* **1** of, relating to, or resembling the umbilicus or the umbilical cord. **2** in the region of the umbilicus: *an umbilical hernia*. ♦ *n* **3** short for **umbilical cord.** ▸ **umˈbilically** *adv*

umbilical cord *n* **1** the long flexible tubelike structure connecting a fetus with the placenta: it provides a means of metabolic interchange with the mother. **2** any flexible cord, tube, or cable used to transfer information, power, oxygen, etc., as between an astronaut walking in space and his spacecraft or a deep-sea diver and his craft.

umbilicate (ʌmˈbɪlɪkɪt, -ˌkeɪt) *adj* **1** having an umbilicus or navel. **2** having a central depression: *an umbilicate leaf*. **3** shaped like a navel, as some bacterial colonies.

umbilication (ʌmˌbɪlɪˈkeɪʃən) *n* **1** *Biology, anatomy.* a navel-like notch or depression, as in the centre of a vesicle. **2** the condition of being umbilicated.

umbilicus (ʌmˈbɪlɪkəs, ˌʌmbɪˈlaɪkəs) *n, pl* **-bilici** (-ˈbɪlɪˌsaɪ, -bəˈlaɪsaɪ). **1** *Biology.* a hollow or navel-like structure, such as the cavity at the base of a gastropod shell. **2** *Anatomy.* a technical name for the **navel.** [C18: from Latin: navel, centre; compare Latin *umbō* shield boss, Greek *omphalos* navel] ▸ **umbiliform** (ʌmˈbɪlɪˌfɔːm) *adj*

umble pie (ˈʌmbᵊl) *n* See **humble pie** (sense 1).

umbles (ˈʌmbᵊlz) *pl n* another term for **numbles.**

umbo (ˈʌmbəʊ) *n, pl* **umbones** (ʌmˈbəʊniːz) *or* **umbos. 1** a small hump projecting from the centre of the cap in certain mushrooms. **2** a hooked prominence occurring at the apex of each half of the shell of a bivalve mollusc. **3** *Anatomy.* the slightly convex area at the centre of the outer surface of the eardrum, where the malleus is attached on the internal surface. **4** a large projecting central boss on a shield, esp. on a Saxon shield. [C18: from Latin: boss of a shield, projecting piece] ▸ **umbonate** (ˈʌmbənɪt, -ˌneɪt), **umbonal** (ˈʌmbənᵊl), *or* **umbonic** (ʌmˈbɒnɪk) *adj*

umbra (ˈʌmbrə) *n, pl* **-brae** (-briː) *or* **-bras. 1** a region of complete shadow resulting from the total obstruction of light by an opaque object, esp. the shadow cast by the moon onto the earth during a solar eclipse. **2** the darker inner region of a sunspot. ♦ Compare **penumbra.** [C16: from Latin: shade, shadow] ▸ **ˈumbral** *adj*

umbrage (ˈʌmbrɪdʒ) *n* **1** displeasure or resentment; offence (in the phrase **give**

or **take umbrage**). **2** the foliage of trees, considered as providing shade. **3** *Rare.* shadow or shade. **4** *Archaic.* a shadow or semblance. **[C15:** from Old French *umbrage,* from Latin *umbrāticus* relating to shade, from *umbra* shade, shadow**]**

umbrageous (ʌm'breɪdʒəs) *adj* shady or shading. ▸ **um'brageously** *adv* ▸ **um'brageousness** *n*

umbrella (ʌm'brɛlə) *n* **1** a portable device used for protection against rain, snow, etc., and consisting of a light canopy supported on a collapsible metal frame mounted on a central rod. **2** the flattened cone-shaped contractile body of a jellyfish or other medusa. **3** a protective shield or screen, esp. of aircraft or gunfire. **4** anything that has the effect of a protective screen or cover. **5a** any system or agency that provides centralized organization or general cover for a group of related companies, organizations, etc.: *dance umbrella.* **5b** (*as modifier*): *an umbrella fund; umbrella group.* **[C17:** from Italian *ombrella,* diminutive of *ombra* shade; see UMBRA**]** ▸ **um'brella-,like** *adj*

umbrella bird *n* a black tropical American passerine bird, *Cephalopterus ornatus,* having a large overhanging crest and a long feathered wattle: family *Cotingidae* (cotingas).

umbrella pine *n* another name for **stone pine.**

umbrella plant *n* an African sedge, *Cyperus alternifolius,* having large umbrella-like whorls of slender leaves: widely grown as an ornamental water plant.

umbrella stand *n* an upright rack or stand for umbrellas.

umbrella tree *n* **1** a North American magnolia, *Magnolia tripetala,* having long leaves clustered into an umbrella formation at the ends of the branches and unpleasant-smelling white flowers. **2** Also called: **umbrella bush.** any of various other trees or shrubs having leaves shaped like an umbrella or growing in an umbrella-like cluster.

Umbria ('ʌmbrɪə; *Italian* 'umbrja) *n* a mountainous region of central Italy, in the valley of the Tiber. Pop.: 825 910 (1996 est.). Area: 8456 sq. km (3265 sq. miles).

Umbrian ('ʌmbrɪən) *adj* **1** of or relating to Umbria, its inhabitants, their dialect of Italian, or the ancient language once spoken there. **2** of or relating to a Renaissance school of painting that included Raphael. ◆ *n* **3** a native or inhabitant of Umbria. **4** an extinct language of ancient S Italy, belonging to the Italic branch of the Indo-European family. See also **Osco-Umbrian.**

Umbriel ('ʌmbrɪəl) *n* one of the main satellites of Uranus.

umfazi (ʊm'fɑːzɪ) *n S. African.* an African married woman. **[**Nguni**]**

umiak *or* **oomiak** ('uːmɪ,æk) *n* a large open boat made of stretched skins, used by Eskimos. Compare **kayak. [C18:** from Greenland Eskimo: boat for the use of women**]**

UMIST ('juː,mɪst) *n acronym for* University of Manchester Institute of Science and Technology.

umlaut ('ʊmlaʊt) *n* **1** the mark (¨) placed over a vowel in some languages, such as German, indicating modification in the quality of the vowel. Compare **diaeresis. 2** (esp. in Germanic languages) the change of a vowel within a word brought about by the assimilating influence of a vowel or semivowel in a preceding or following syllable. **[C19:** German, from *um* around (in the sense of changing places) + *Laut* sound**]**

umlungu (ʊm'lʊŋgʊ) *n S. African.* a white man. **[**Nguni: a white man**]**

Ummah ('ʊmə) *n* the Muslim community throughout the world. **[**from Arabic: community**]**

umpire ('ʌmpaɪə) *n* **1** an official who rules on the playing of a game, as in cricket or baseball. **2** a person who rules on or judges disputes between contesting parties. ◆ *vb* **3** to act as umpire in (a game, dispute, or controversy). **[C15:** by mistaken division from *a noumpere,* from Old French *nomper* not one of a pair, from *nom-, non-* not + *per* equal, PEER[1]**]** ▸ **'umpireship** *or* **'umpirage** *n*

umpteen (,ʌmp'tiːn) *determiner Informal.* **a** very many: *umpteen things to do.* **b** (*as pronoun*): *umpteen of them came.* **[C20:** from *umpty* a great deal (perhaps from *-enty* as in *twenty*) + *-teen* ten**]** ▸ **,ump'teenth** *n, adj*

Umtali (ʊm'tɑːlɪ) *n* the former name (until 1982) of **Mutare.**

Umtata (ʌm'tɑːtə) *n* a city in South Africa, in Eastern Cape province; the capital of the former Transkei Bantu homeland. Pop.: 80 000 (1984 est.).

umwelt ('ʊmvɛlt) *n Biology, psychol.* the environmental factors, collectively, that are capable of affecting the behaviour of an animal or individual. **[C20:** from German *Umwelt* environment**]**

UN *abbrev. for* United Nations.

un-[1] *prefix* (*freely used with adjectives, participles, and their derivative adverbs and nouns: less frequently used with certain other nouns*) not; contrary to; opposite of: *uncertain; uncomplaining; unemotionally; untidiness; unbelief; unrest; untruth.* **[**from Old English *on-, un-;* related to Gothic *on-,* German *un-,* Latin *in-***]**

un-[2] *prefix forming verbs.* **1** denoting reversal of an action or state: *uncover; untangle.* **2** denoting removal from, release, or deprivation: *unharness; unman; unthrone.* **3** (intensifier): *unloose.* **[**from Old English *un-, on-;* related to Gothic *and-,* German *ent-,* Latin *ante***]**

'un *or* **un** (ən) *pron* a spelling of **one** intended to reflect a dialectal or informal pronunciation: *that's a big 'un.*

UNA (in Britain) *abbrev. for* United Nations Association.

unabated (,ʌnə'beɪtɪd) *adj* without losing any original force or violence; undiminished. ▸ **,una'batedly** *adv*

unable (ʌn'eɪbᵊl) *adj* **1** (*postpositive;* foll. by *to*) lacking the necessary power, ability, or authority (to do something); not able. **2** *Archaic.* incompetent.

unaccommodated (,ʌnə'kɒmə,deɪtɪd) *adj* **1** not suitable or apt; not adapted. **2** unprovided for.

unaccompanied (,ʌnə'kʌmpənɪd) *adj* **1** not accompanied. **2** *Music.* **2a** (of an instrument) playing alone. **2b** (of music for a group of singers) without instrumental accompaniment.

unaccomplished (,ʌnə'kɒmplɪʃt) *adj* **1** not accomplished or finished. **2** lacking accomplishments.

unaccountable (,ʌnə'kaʊntəbᵊl) *adj* **1** allowing of no explanation; inexplicable. **2** puzzling; extraordinary: *an unaccountable fear of hamburgers.* **3** not accountable or answerable to. ▸ **,unac'countableness** *or* **,unac,counta'bility** *n* ▸ **,unac'countably** *adv*

unaccounted-for (,ʌnə'kaʊntɪdfɔː) *adj* (*usually predicative*) not understood, explained, or taken into consideration.

unaccustomed (,ʌnə'kʌstəmd) *adj* **1** (foll. by *to*) not used (to): *unaccustomed to pain.* **2** not familiar; strange or unusual. ▸ **,unac'customedness** *n*

una corda ('uːnə 'kɔːdə) *adj, adv Music.* (of the piano) to be played with the soft pedal depressed. **[**Italian, literally: one string; the pedal moves the mechanism so that only one string of the three tuned to each note is struck by the hammer**]**

unadopted (,ʌnə'dɒptɪd) *adj* **1** (of a child) not adopted. **2** *Brit.* (of a road, etc.) not maintained by a local authority.

unadvised (,ʌnəd'vaɪzd) *adj* **1** rash or unwise. **2** not having received advice. ▸ **unadvisedly** (,ʌnəd'vaɪzɪdlɪ) *adv* ▸ **,unad'visedness** *n*

unaffected[1] (,ʌnə'fɛktɪd) *adj* unpretentious, natural, or sincere. ▸ **,unaf'fectedly** *adv* ▸ **,unaf'fectedness** *n*

unaffected[2] (,ʌnə'fɛktɪd) *adj* not affected.

Unalaska Island (,uːnə'læskə) *n* a large volcanic island in SW Alaska, in the Aleutian Islands. Length: 120 km (75 miles). Greatest width: about 40 km (25 miles).

unalienable (ʌn'eɪljənəbᵊl) *adj Law.* a variant of **inalienable.**

unalloyed (,ʌnə'lɔɪd) *adj* not mixed or intermingled with any other thing; pure: *unalloyed metal; unalloyed pleasure.*

un-American *adj* **1** not in accordance with the aims, ideals, customs, etc., of the U.S. **2** against the interests of the U.S. ▸ **,un-A'mericanism** *n*

Unamuno (*Spanish* una'muno) *n* **Miguel de** (mi'ɣel de). 1864–1936, Spanish philosopher and writer.

unaneled (,ʌnə'niːld) *adj Archaic.* not having received extreme unction. **[C17:** from UN-[1] + ANELE**]**

unanimous (juː'nænɪməs) *adj* **1** in complete or absolute agreement. **2** characterized by complete agreement: *a unanimous decision.* **[C17:** from Latin *ūnanimus* from *ūnus* one + *animus* mind**]** ▸ **u'nanimously** *adv* ▸ **unanimity** (,juːnə'nɪmɪtɪ) *or* **u'nanimousness** *n*

unanswerable (ʌn'ɑːnsərəbᵊl) *adj* **1** incapable of being refuted. **2** (of a question) not admitting of any answer. ▸ **un'answerableness** *n* ▸ **un'answerably** *adv*

unappealable (,ʌnə'piːləbᵊl) *adj Law.* (of a judgment, etc.) not capable of being appealed against. ▸ **,unap'pealableness** *n* ▸ **,unap'pealably** *adv*

unapproachable (,ʌnə'prəʊtʃəbᵊl) *adj* **1** discouraging intimacy, friendliness, etc.; aloof. **2** inaccessible. **3** not to be rivalled. ▸ **,unap'proachableness** *n* ▸ **,unap'proachably** *adv*

unappropriated (,ʌnə'prəʊprɪ,eɪtɪd) *adj* **1** not set aside for specific use. **2** *Accounting.* designating that portion of the profits of a business enterprise that is retained in the business and not withdrawn by the proprietor. **3** (of property) not having been taken into any person's possession or control.

unapt (ʌn'æpt) *adj* **1** (*usually postpositive;* often foll. by *for*) not suitable or qualified; unfitted. **2** mentally slow. **3** (*postpositive; may take an infinitive*) not disposed or likely (to). ▸ **un'aptly** *adv* ▸ **un'aptness** *n*

unarguable (ʌn'ɑːgjʊəbᵊl) *adj* **1** incapable of being argued. **2** incontestable; indisputable. ▸ **un'arguably** *adv*

unarm (ʌn'ɑːm) *vb* a less common word for **disarm.**

unarmed (ʌn'ɑːmd) *adj* **1** without weapons. **2** (of animals and plants) having no claws, prickles, spines, thorns, or similar structures. **3** of or relating to a projectile that does not use a detonator to initiate explosive action.

unary ('juːnərɪ) *adj* consisting of, or affecting, a single element or component; monadic. **[C16** (in the obsolete sense: a unit): from Latin *unus* one + -ARY**]**

unashamed (,ʌnə'ʃeɪmd) *adj* **1** lacking moral restraints. **2** not embarrassed,

,una'bashed *adj*
,unab'brevi,ated *adj*
,una'bridged *adj*
,unab'sorbed *adj*
,unaca'demic *adj*
,unac'cented *adj*
,unac'ceptable *adj*
,unac'counted *adj*
,unac'credited *adj*
,unac'knowledged *adj*
,unac'quainted *adj*
,unad'dressed *adj*
,una'dorned *adj*
,una'dulter,ated *adj*
,unad'venturous *adj*
,un'adver,tised *adj*
,unaf'fili,ated *adj*
,una'fraid *adj*
,unag'gressive *adj*
un'aided *adj*
,una'ligned *adj*
,una'like *adj*
un'alterable *adj*
un'altered *adj*
,unam'biguous *adj*
,unam'bitious *adj*
,una'mused *adj*
,unan'nounced *adj*
un'answered *adj*
,unan'tici,pated *adj*
,una,polo'getic *adj*
,unap'pealing *adj*
,unap'peasable *adj*
un'appe,tizing *or* **un'appe,tising** *adj*
,unap'preci,ated *adj*
,unap'preciative *adj*
,unap'proved *adj*
,unar'ticu,lated *adj*

contrite, or apologetic. ▸ **unashamedly** (ˌʌnəˈʃeɪmɪdlɪ) *adv* ▸ ˌ**unaˈshamedness** *n*
unasked (ʌnˈɑːskt) *adj* **1** not requested or demanded. **2** not invited.
unassailable (ˌʌnəˈseɪləbᵊl) *adj* **1** not able to be attacked. **2** undeniable or irrefutable. ▸ ˌ**unasˈsailableness** *n* ▸ ˌ**unasˈsailably** *adv*
unassuming (ˌʌnəˈsjuːmɪŋ) *adj* modest or unpretentious. ▸ ˌ**unasˈsumingly** *adv* ▸ ˌ**unasˈsumingness** *n*
unattached (ˌʌnəˈtætʃt) *adj* **1** not connected with any specific thing, body, group, etc.; independent. **2** not engaged or married. **3** (of property) not seized or held as security or in satisfaction of a judgment.
unattended (ˌʌnəˈtɛndɪd) *adj* **1** not looked after or cared for. **2** unaccompanied or alone. **3** not listened to.
unau (ˈjuːnaʊ) *n* another name for the **two-toed sloth** (see **sloth** (sense 1)). [C18: via French from Tupi]
unavailing (ˌʌnəˈveɪlɪŋ) *adj* useless or futile. ▸ ˌ**unaˈvailingly** *adv*
unavoidable (ˌʌnəˈvɔɪdəbᵊl) *adj* **1** unable to be avoided; inevitable. **2** *Law.* not capable of being declared null and void. ▸ ˌ**unaˌvoidaˈbility** *or* ˌ**unaˈvoidableness** *n* ▸ ˌ**unaˈvoidably** *adv*
unaware (ˌʌnəˈwɛə) *adj* **1** (*postpositive*) not aware or conscious (of): *unaware of the danger he ran across the road.* **2** not fully cognizant of what is going on in the world: *he's the most unaware person I've ever met.* ◆ *adv* **3** a variant of **unawares**. ▸ ˌ**unaˈwarely** *adv* ▸ ˌ**unaˈwareness** *n*
unawares (ˌʌnəˈwɛəz) *adv* **1** without prior warning or plan; unexpectedly: *she caught him unawares.* **2** without being aware of or knowing: *he lost it unawares.*
unbacked (ʌnˈbækt) *adj* **1** (of a book, chair, etc.) not having a back. **2** bereft of support, esp. on a financial basis. **3** (of a horse) **3a** not supported by bets. **3b** never having been ridden.
unbalance (ʌnˈbæləns) *vb* (*tr*) **1** to upset the equilibrium or balance of. **2** to disturb the mental stability of (a person or his mind). ◆ *n* **3** imbalance or instability.
unbalanced (ʌnˈbælənst) *adj* **1** lacking balance. **2** irrational or unsound; erratic. **3** mentally disordered or deranged. **4** biased; one-sided: *unbalanced reporting.* **5** (in double-entry book-keeping) not having total debit balances equal to total credit balances. **6** *Electronics.* (of signals or circuitry) not symmetrically disposed about earth or zero reference potential.
unbar (ʌnˈbɑː) *vb* **-bars, -barring, -barred.** (*tr*) **1** to take away a bar or bars from. **2** to unfasten bars, locks, etc., from (a door); open.
unbated (ʌnˈbeɪtɪd) *adj* **1** a less common spelling of **unabated**. **2** *Archaic.* (of a sword, lance, etc.) not covered with a protective button.
unbearable (ʌnˈbɛərəbᵊl) *adj* not able to be borne or endured. ▸ **unˈbearableness** *n* ▸ **unˈbearably** *adv*
unbeatable (ʌnˈbiːtəbᵊl) *adj* unable to be defeated or outclassed; surpassingly excellent.
unbeaten (ʌnˈbiːtᵊn) *adj* **1** having suffered no defeat. **2** not worn down; untrodden. **3** not mixed or stirred by beating: *unbeaten eggs.* **4** not beaten or struck.
unbecoming (ˌʌnbɪˈkʌmɪŋ) *adj* **1** unsuitable or inappropriate, esp. through being unattractive: *an unbecoming hat.* **2** (when *postpositive,* usually foll. by *of* or an object) not proper or seemly (for): *manners unbecoming a lady.* ▸ ˌ**unbeˈcomingly** *adv* ▸ ˌ**unbeˈcomingness** *n*
unbeknown (ˌʌnbɪˈnəʊn) *adv* **1** (*sentence modifier;* foll. by *to*) Also (esp. Brit.): ˌ**unbeˈknownst.** without the knowledge (of a person): *unbeknown to him she had left the country.* ◆ *adj* **2** (*postpositive;* usually foll. by *to*) *Rare.* not known (to). [C17: from the archaic *beknown* known; see BE-, KNOW]
unbelief (ˌʌnbɪˈliːf) *n* disbelief or rejection of belief.
unbelievable (ˌʌnbɪˈliːvəbᵊl) *adj* unable to be believed; incredible or astonishing. ▸ ˌ**unbeˌlievaˈbility** *or* ˌ**unbeˈlievableness** *n* ▸ ˌ**unbeˈlievably** *adv*
unbeliever (ˌʌnbɪˈliːvə) *n* a person who does not believe or withholds belief, esp. in religious matters.
unbelieving (ˌʌnbɪˈliːvɪŋ) *adj* **1** not believing; sceptical. **2** proceeding from or characterized by scepticism. ▸ ˌ**unbeˈlievingly** *adv* ▸ ˌ**unbeˈlievingness** *n*
unbelt (ʌnˈbɛlt) *vb* (*tr*) **1** to unbuckle the belt of (a garment). **2** to remove (something) from a belt.
unbend (ʌnˈbɛnd) *vb* **-bends, -bending, -bent. 1** to release or be released from the restraints of formality and ceremony. **2** *Informal.* to relax (the mind) or (of the mind) to become relaxed. **3** to become or be made straightened out from an originally bent shape or position. **4** (*tr*) *Nautical.* **4a** to remove (a sail) from a stay, mast, yard, etc. **4b** to untie (a rope, etc.) or cast (a cable) loose. ▸ **unˈbendable** *adj*
unbending (ʌnˈbɛndɪŋ) *adj* **1** rigid or inflexible. **2** characterized by sternness or severity: *an unbending rule.* ▸ **unˈbendingly** *adv* ▸ **unˈbendingness** *n*
unbent (ʌnˈbɛnt) *vb* **1** the past tense and past participle of **unbend**. ◆ *adj* **2** not bent or bowed. **3** not compelled to yield or give way by force.
unbiased *or* **unbiassed** (ʌnˈbaɪəst) *adj* **1** having no bias or prejudice; fair or impartial. **2** *Statistics.* **2a** (of a sample) not affected by any extraneous factors, conflated variables, or selectivity which influence its distribution; random. **2b** (of an estimator) having an expected value equal to the parameter being estimated; having zero bias. **2c** Also called: **discriminatory.** (of a significance test). having a power greater than the predetermined significance level. ▸ **unˈbiasedly** *or* **unˈbiassedly** *adv* ▸ **unˈbiasedness** *or* **unˈbiassedness** *n*
unbidden (ʌnˈbɪdᵊn) *adj* **1** not ordered or commanded; voluntary or spontaneous. **2** not invited or asked.
unbind (ʌnˈbaɪnd) *vb* **binds, binding, bound.** (*tr*) **1** to set free from restraining bonds or chains; release. **2** to unfasten or make loose (a bond, tie, etc.).
unbirthday (ˌʌnˈbɜːθdeɪ) *n Brit., jocular.* **a** any day other than one's birthday. **b** (*as modifier*): *an unbirthday present.* [C19: coined by Lewis Carroll in *Through the Looking-Glass*]
unblenched (ʌnˈblɛntʃt) *adj Obsolete.* undismayed. [C17: from UN-[1] + BLENCH[1]]
unblessed (ʌnˈblɛst) *adj* **1** deprived of blessing. **2** unhallowed, cursed, or evil. **3** unhappy or wretched. ▸ **unblessedness** (ʌnˈblɛsɪdnɪs) *n*
unblinking (ʌnˈblɪŋkɪŋ) *adj* **1** without blinking. **2** showing no visible response or emotion. **3** not wavering through trepidation or fear. ▸ **unˈblinkingly** *adv*
unblown (ʌnˈbləʊn) *adj* **1** *Archaic.* (of a flower) still in the bud. **2** not blown.
unblushing (ʌnˈblʌʃɪŋ) *adj* immodest or shameless. ▸ **unˈblushingly** *adv* ▸ **unˈblushingness** *n*
unbolt (ʌnˈbəʊlt) *vb* (*tr*) **1** to unfasten a bolt of (a door). **2** to undo (the nut) on a bolt.
unbolted (ʌnˈbəʊltɪd) *adj* (of grain, meal, or flour) not sifted.
unboned (ʌnˈbəʊnd) *adj* **1** (of meat, fish, etc.) not having had the bones removed. **2** (of animals) having no bones.
unborn (ʌnˈbɔːn) *adj* **1** not yet born or brought to birth. **2** still to come in the future: *the unborn world.*
unbosom (ʌnˈbʊzəm) *vb* (*tr*) to relieve (oneself) of (secrets, etc.) by telling someone. [C16: from UN-[2] + BOSOM (in the sense: seat of the emotions); compare Dutch *ontboezemen*] ▸ **unˈbosomer** *n*
unbound (ʌnˈbaʊnd) *vb* **1** the past tense and past participle of **unbind**. ◆ *adj* **2** (of a book) not bound within a cover. **3** not restrained or tied down by bonds. **4** (of a morpheme) able to form a word by itself; free.
unbounded (ʌnˈbaʊndɪd) *adj* having no boundaries or limits. ▸ **unˈboundedly** *adv* ▸ **unˈboundedness** *n*
unbowed (ʌnˈbaʊd) *adj* **1** not bowed or bent. **2** free or unconquered.
unbrace (ʌnˈbreɪs) *vb* (*tr*) **1** to remove tension or strain from; relax. **2** to remove a brace or braces from.
unbred (ʌnˈbrɛd) *adj* **1** a less common word for **ill-bred**. **2** not taught or instructed. **3** *Obsolete.* not born.
unbridle (ʌnˈbraɪdᵊl) *vb* (*tr*) **1** to remove the bridle from (a horse). **2** to remove all controls or restraints from.
unbridled (ʌnˈbraɪdᵊld) *adj* **1** with all restraints removed. **2** (of a horse, etc.) wearing no bridle. ▸ **unˈbridledly** *adv* ▸ **unˈbridledness** *n*
unbroken (ʌnˈbrəʊkən) *adj* **1** complete or whole. **2** continuous or incessant. **3** undaunted in spirit. **4** (of animals, esp. horses) not tamed; wild. **5** not disturbed or upset: *the unbroken silence of the afternoon.* **6** (of a record, esp. at sport) not improved upon. **7** (of a contract, law, etc.) not broken or infringed. ▸ **unˈbrokenly** *adv* ▸ **unˈbrokenness** *n*
unbundle (ʌnˈbʌndᵊl) *vb* (*tr*) *Computing.* to separate (hardware from software) for sales purposes.
unbundling (ʌnˈbʌndlɪŋ) *n Commerce.* the takeover of a large conglomerate with a view to retaining the core business and selling off some of the subsidiaries to help finance the takeover.
unburden (ʌnˈbɜːdᵊn) *vb* (*tr*) **1** to remove a load or burden from. **2** to relieve or make free (one's mind, oneself, etc.) of a worry, trouble, etc., by revelation or confession. ◆ Archaic spelling: **unburthen** (ʌnˈbɜːðən).
unbutton (ʌnˈbʌtᵊn) *vb* **1** to undo by unfastening (the buttons) of (a garment). **2** *Informal.* to release or relax (oneself, tension, etc.).
unbuttoned (ʌnˈbʌtᵊnd) *adj* **1** with buttons not fastened. **2** *Informal.* uninhibited; unrestrained: *hours of unbuttoned self-revelation.*
uncaged (ʌnˈkeɪdʒd) *adj* at liberty.
uncalled-for (ˌʌnˈkɔːldfɔː) *adj* unnecessary or unwarranted.
uncanny (ʌnˈkænɪ) *adj* **1** characterized by apparently supernatural wonder, horror, etc. **2** beyond what is normal or expected: *an uncanny accuracy.* ▸ **unˈcannily** *adv* ▸ **unˈcanniness** *n*
uncap (ʌnˈkæp) *vb* **-caps, -capping, -capped. 1** (*tr*) to remove a cap or top from (a container): *to uncap a bottle.* **2** to remove a cap from (the head).
uncared-for (ˌʌnˈkɛədfɔː) *adj* not cared for; neglected.
uncaused (ʌnˈkɔːzd) *adj Now rare.* not brought into existence by any cause; spontaneous or natural.
unceasing (ʌnˈsiːsɪŋ) *adj* not ceasing or ending. ▸ **unˈceasingly** *adv* ▸ **unˈceasingness** *n*
unceremonious (ˌʌnsɛrɪˈməʊnɪəs) *adj* without ceremony; informal, abrupt, rude, or undignified. ▸ ˌ**uncereˈmoniously** *adv* ▸ ˌ**uncereˈmoniousness** *n*
uncertain (ʌnˈsɜːtᵊn) *adj* **1** not able to be accurately known or predicted: *the*

unˈaspiˌrated *adj*
ˌ**unasˈsertive** *adj*
ˌ**unasˈsimiˌlated** *adj*
ˌ**unasˈsisted** *adj*
ˌ**unatˈtainable** *adj*
ˌ**unatˈtested** *adj*
ˌ**unatˈtractive** *adj*
ˌ**unatˈtributable** *adj*
ˌ**unatˈtributed** *adj*
ˌ**unauˈthentic** *adj*
unˈauthorˌized *or* **unˈauthorˌised** *adj*
ˌ**unaˈvailable** *adj*
ˌ**unaˈvenged** *adj*
unˈban *vb,* **-bans, -banning, -banned.**
ˌ**unbapˈtized** *or* ˌ**unbapˈtised** *adj*
unˈbleached *adj*
unˈblemished *adj*
unˈblock *vb*
unˈbreakable *adj*
unˈbruised *adj*
unˈbrushed *adj*
unˈbuckle *vb,* **-les, -ling, -led.**
unˈbudgeted *adj*
unˈbuilt *adj*
unˈburied *adj*
unˈcensored *adj*
unˈcensured *adj*

issue is uncertain. **2** (when *postpositive,* often foll. by *of*) not sure or confident (about): *a man of uncertain opinion.* **3** not precisely determined, established, or decided: *uncertain plans.* **4** not to be depended upon; unreliable: *an uncertain vote.* **5** liable to variation; changeable: *the weather is uncertain.* **6 in no uncertain terms. 6a** unambiguously. **6b** forcefully. ► **un'certainly** *adv* ► **un'certainness** *n*

uncertainty (ʌn'sɜːtᵊntɪ) *n, pl* **-ties. 1** Also called: **uncertainness.** the state or condition of being uncertain. **2** an uncertain matter, contingency, etc.

uncertainty principle *n* **the.** the principle that energy and time or position and momentum, cannot both be accurately measured simultaneously. The product of their uncertainties is always greater than or equal to $h/4\pi$, where h is the Planck constant. Also called: **Heisenberg uncertainty principle, indeterminacy principle.**

unchain (ʌn'tʃeɪn) *vb (tr)* **1** to remove a chain or chains from. **2** to set at liberty; make free.

unchancy (ʌn'tʃɑːnsɪ) *adj Scot.* unlucky, ill-omened, or dangerous. Compare **wanchancy.**

uncharged (ʌn'tʃɑːdʒd) *adj* **1** (of land or other property) not subject to a charge. **2** having no electric charge; neutral. **3** *Archaic.* (of a firearm) not loaded.

uncharted (ʌn'tʃɑːtɪd) *adj* (of a physical or nonphysical region or area) not yet mapped, surveyed, or investigated: *uncharted waters; the uncharted depths of the mind.*

unchartered (ʌn'tʃɑːtəd) *adj* **1** not authorized by charter; unregulated. **2** unauthorized, lawless, or irregular.

USAGE Care should be taken not to use *unchartered* where *uncharted* is meant: *uncharted* (not *unchartered*) *territory.*

unchecked (ʌn'tʃɛkt) *adj* **1** not prevented from continuing or growing: *unchecked population growth.* **2** not examined or inspected. ♦ *adv* **3** without being stopped or hindered: *the virus could spread unchecked.* **4** without being examined or inspected: *our luggage passed unchecked through customs.*

unchristian (ʌn'krɪstʃən) *adj* **1** not in accordance with the principles or ethics of Christianity. **2** non-Christian or pagan. ► **un'christianly** *adv*

unchurch (ʌn'tʃɜːtʃ) *vb (tr)* **1** to excommunicate. **2** to remove church status from (a building).

uncial ('ʌnsɪəl) *adj* **1** of, relating to, or written in majuscule letters, as used in Greek and Latin manuscripts of the third to ninth centuries, that resemble modern capitals, but are characterized by much greater curvature and inclination and general inequality of height. **2** pertaining to an inch or an ounce. **3** pertaining to the duodecimal system. ♦ *n* **4** an uncial letter or manuscript. **[C17:** from Late Latin *unciālēs litterae* letters an inch long, from Latin *unciālis,* from *uncia* one twelfth, inch, OUNCE[1]**]** ► **'uncially** *adv*

unciform ('ʌnsɪˌfɔːm) *adj* **1** *Anatomy, zoology, etc.* having the shape of a hook. ♦ *n* **2** Also called: **hamate bone.** *Anatomy.* any hook-shaped structure or part, esp. a small bone of the wrist (**unciform bone**). **[C18:** from New Latin *unciformis,* from Latin *uncus* a hook**]**

uncinariasis (ˌʌnsɪnə'raɪəsɪs) *n* the condition of being infested with hookworms; hookworm disease. **[C20:** via New Latin *Uncināria,* from Late Latin *uncīnus* a hook, from Latin *uncus***]**

uncinate ('ʌnsɪnɪt, -ˌneɪt) *adj Biology.* **1** shaped like a hook: *the uncinate process of the ribs of certain vertebrates.* **2** of, relating to, or possessing uncini. **[C18:** from Latin *uncīnātus,* from *uncīnus* a hook, from *uncus***]**

uncinus (ʌn'saɪnəs) *n, pl* **-cini** (-'saɪnaɪ). *Zoology.* a small hooked structure, such as any of the hooked chaetae of certain polychaete worms. **[C19:** from Late Latin: hook, from Latin *uncus***]**

uncircumcised (ʌn'sɜːkəmˌsaɪzd) *adj* **1** not circumcised. **2** not Jewish; gentile. **3** *Theol.* not purified.

uncircumcision (ˌʌnsɜːkəm'sɪʒən) *n Chiefly New Testament.* the state of being uncircumcised.

uncivil (ʌn'sɪvəl) *adj* **1** lacking civility or good manners. **2** an obsolete word for **uncivilized.** ► **uncivility** (ˌʌnsɪ'vɪlɪtɪ) *or* **un'civilness** *n* ► **un'civilly** *adv*

uncivilized *or* **uncivilised** (ʌn'sɪvɪˌlaɪzd) *adj* **1** (of a tribe or people) not yet civilized, esp. preliterate. **2** lacking culture or sophistication. ► **uncivilizedly** *or* **uncivilisedly** (ʌn'sɪvɪˌlaɪzɪdlɪ) *adv* ► **un'civiˌlizedness** *or* **un'civiˌlisedness** *n*

unclad (ʌn'klæd) *adj* having no clothes on; naked.

unclasp (ʌn'klɑːsp) *vb* **1** *(tr)* to unfasten the clasp of (something). **2** to release one's grip (upon an object).

unclassified (ʌn'klæsɪˌfaɪd) *adj* **1** not arranged in any specific order or grouping. **2** (of information) not possessing a security classification. **3** (of football results) not arranged in any special order or in divisions.

uncle ('ʌŋkᵊl) *n* **1** a brother of one's father or mother. **2** the husband of one's aunt. **3** a term of address sometimes used by children for a male friend of their parents. **4** *Slang.* a pawnbroker. ♦ Related adj: **avuncular. [C13:** from Old French *oncle,* from Latin *avunculus;* related to Latin *avus* grandfather**]**

unclean (ʌn'kliːn) *adj* lacking moral, spiritual, ritual, or physical cleanliness. ► **un'cleanness** *n*

uncleanly[1] (ʌn'kliːnlɪ) *adv* in an unclean manner.

uncleanly[2] (ʌn'klɛnlɪ) *adj* characterized by an absence of cleanliness; unclean. ► **un'cleanliness** *n*

unclear (ʌn'klɪə) *adj* not clear or definite; ambiguous. ► **un'clearly** *adv* ► **un'clearness** *n*

Uncle Sam *n* a personification of the government of the United States. **[C19:** apparently a humorous interpretation of the letters stamped on army supply boxes during the War of 1812: *U.S.***]**

Uncle Tom *n Informal, derogatory.* a Black whose behaviour towards Whites is regarded as obsequious and servile. **[C20:** after the slave who is the main character of H. B. Stowe's novel *Uncle Tom's Cabin* (1852)**]** ► **'Uncle 'Tomism** *n*

unclog (ʌn'klɒg) *vb* **-clogs, -clogging, -clogged.** *(tr)* to remove an obstruction from (a drain, etc.).

unclose (ʌn'kləʊz) *vb* **1** to open or cause to open. **2** to come or bring to light; reveal or be revealed.

unclothe (ʌn'kləʊð) *vb* **-clothes, -clothing, -clothed** *or* **-clad.** *(tr)* **1** to take off garments from; strip. **2** to uncover or lay bare.

unco ('ʌŋkəʊ) *Scot.* ♦ *adj* **uncoer, uncoest. 1** unfamiliar, strange, or odd. **2** remarkable or striking. ♦ *adv* **3** very; extremely. **4 the unco guid.** narrow-minded, excessively religious, or self-righteous people. ♦ *n, pl* **uncos** *or* **uncoes. 5** a novel or remarkable person or thing. **6** *Obsolete.* a stranger. **7** *(pl)* news. **[C15:** variant of UNCOUTH**]**

uncoil (ʌn'kɔɪl) *vb* to unwind or become unwound; untwist.

uncoined (ʌn'kɔɪnd) *adj* (of a metal) not made into coin.

uncomfortable (ʌn'kʌmftəbᵊl) *adj* **1** not comfortable. **2** feeling or causing discomfort or unease; disquieting. ► **un'comfortableness** *n* ► **un'comfortably** *adv*

uncommercial (ˌʌnkə'mɜːʃəl) *adj* **1** not concerned with commerce or trade. **2** not in accordance with the aims or principles of business or trade.

uncommitted (ˌʌnkə'mɪtɪd) *adj* not bound or pledged to a specific opinion, course of action, or cause.

uncommon (ʌn'kɒmən) *adj* **1** outside or beyond normal experience, conditions, etc.; unusual. **2** in excess of what is normal: *an uncommon liking for honey.* ♦ *adv* **3** an archaic word for **uncommonly** (sense 2). ► **un'commonness** *n*

uncommonly (ʌn'kɒmənlɪ) *adv* **1** in an uncommon or unusual manner or degree; rarely. **2** (intensifier): *you're uncommonly friendly.*

uncommunicative (ˌʌnkə'mjuːnɪkətɪv) *adj* disinclined to talk or give information or opinions. ► **ˌuncom'municatively** *adv* ► **ˌuncom'municativeness** *n*

uncompromising (ʌn'kɒmprəˌmaɪzɪŋ) *adj* not prepared to give ground or to compromise. ► **un'comproˌmisingly** *adv* ► **un'comproˌmisingness** *n*

unconcern (ˌʌnkən'sɜːn) *n* apathy or indifference.

unconcerned (ˌʌnkən'sɜːnd) *adj* **1** lacking in concern or involvement. **2** not worried; untroubled. ► **unconcernedly** (ˌʌnkən'sɜːnɪdlɪ) *adv* ► **ˌuncon'cernedness** *n*

unconditional (ˌʌnkən'dɪʃənᵊl) *adj* **1** without conditions or limitations; total: *unconditional surrender.* **2** *Maths.* (of an equality) true for all values of the variable: $(x+1)>x$ *is an unconditional equality.* ► **ˌuncon'ditionally** *adv* ► **ˌuncon'ditionalness** *or* **ˌunconˌdition'ality** *n*

unconditioned (ˌʌnkən'dɪʃənd) *adj* **1** *Psychol.* characterizing an innate reflex and the stimulus and response that form parts of it. Compare **conditioned** (sense 1). **2** *Metaphysics.* unrestricted by conditions; infinite; absolute. **3** without limitations; unconditional. ► **ˌuncon'ditionedness** *n*

unconditioned response *n* a reflex action innately elicited by a stimulus without the intervention of any learning process. Also called (esp. formerly): **unconditioned reflex.** Compare **conditioned response.**

unconditioned stimulus *n Psychol.* any stimulus evoking an unlearnt response, esp. in the context of classical conditioning, in which the conditioned stimulus is followed by the unconditioned one.

unconformable (ˌʌnkən'fɔːməbᵊl) *adj* **1** not conformable or conforming. **2** (of rock strata) consisting of a series of recent strata resting on different, much older rocks. ► **ˌunconˌforma'bility** *or* **ˌuncon'formableness** *n* ► **ˌuncon'formably** *adv*

unconformity (ˌʌnkən'fɔːmɪtɪ) *n, pl* **-ties. 1** lack of conformity. **2** the junction between recently deposited stratified rocks and much older or folded rocks.

unconnected (ˌʌnkə'nɛktɪd) *adj* **1** not linked; separate or independent. **2** disconnected or incoherent. ► **ˌuncon'nectedly** *adv* ► **ˌuncon'nectedness** *n*

unconscionable (ʌn'kɒnʃənəbᵊl) *adj* **1** unscrupulous or unprincipled: *an unconscionable liar.* **2** immoderate or excessive: *unconscionable demands.* ► **un'conscionableness** *n* ► **un'conscionably** *adv*

unconscious (ʌn'kɒnʃəs) *adj* **1** lacking normal sensory awareness of the environment; insensible. **2** not aware of one's actions, behaviour, etc.: *unconscious of his bad manners.* **3** characterized by lack of awareness or intention: *an unconscious blunder.* **4** coming from or produced by the unconscious: *unconscious resentment.* ♦ *n* **5** *Psychoanal.* the part of the mind containing instincts, impulses, images, and ideas that are not available for direct examina-

un'challengeable *adj*
un'challenged *adj*
un'changeable *adj*
un'changed *adj*
un'changing *adj*
un'chaperˌoned *adj*
ˌuncharacter'istic *adj*
un'charitable *adj*
un'chaste *adj*
un'claimed *adj*
un'clariˌfied *adj*
un'cleaned *adj*
un'clouded *adj*
un'cluttered *adj*
ˌuncol'lected *adj*
un'coloured *adj*
un'combed *adj*
ˌuncom'bined *adj*
ˌuncom'petitive *adj*
ˌuncom'plaining *adj*
ˌuncom'pleted *adj*
un'compliˌcated *adj*
ˌuncompli'mentary *adj*
ˌuncompre'hending *adj*
ˌuncon'cealed *adj*
un'confident *adj*
ˌuncon'fined *adj*
ˌuncon'firmed *adj*
ˌuncon'genial *adj*
un'conquered *adj*

tion. See also **collective unconscious.** Compare **subconscious, preconscious.** ► **un'consciously** *adv*

unconsciousness (ʌn'kɒnʃəsnɪs) *n* the state of being without normal sensory awareness; insensibility.

unconsidered (ˌʌnkən'sɪdəd) *adj* **1** not considered; disregarded. **2** done without consideration.

unconstitutional (ˌʌnkɒnstɪ'tjuːʃənᵊl) *adj* at variance with or not permitted by a constitution. ► **ˌunconstiˌtution'ality** *n*

unconstitutional strike *n* a stoppage of work which violates the dispute procedure agreed between the employer and the trade union or trade unions concerned.

uncontrollable (ˌʌnkən'trəʊləbᵊl) *adj* incapable of being controlled or managed. ► **ˌunconˌtrolla'bility** *or* **ˌuncon'trollableness** *n* ► **ˌuncon'trollably** *adv*

unconventional (ˌʌnkən'vɛnʃənᵊl) *adj* not conforming to accepted rules or standards. ► **ˌunconˌvention'ality** *n* ► **ˌuncon'ventionally** *adv*

uncool (ʌn'kuːl) *adj Slang.* **1** unsophisticated; unfashionable. **2** excitable; tense; not cool.

uncoordinated (ˌʌnkəʊ'ɔːdɪˌneɪtɪd) *adj* **1** lacking order, system, or organization. **2** (of a person, action, etc.) lacking muscular or emotional coordination.

uncork (ʌn'kɔːk) *vb* (*tr*) **1** to draw the cork from (a bottle, etc.). **2** to release or unleash (emotions, etc.).

uncountable (ʌn'kaʊntəbᵊl) *adj* **1** too many to be counted; innumerable. **2** *Linguistics.* denoting a noun that does not refer to an isolable object. See **mass noun.**

uncounted (ʌn'kaʊntɪd) *adj* **1** unable to be counted; innumerable. **2** not counted.

uncouple (ʌn'kʌpᵊl) *vb* **1** to disconnect or unfasten or become disconnected or unfastened. **2** (*tr*) to set loose; release.

uncouth (ʌn'kuːθ) *adj* lacking in good manners, refinement, or grace. [Old English *uncūth*, from UN-[1] + *cūth* familiar; related to Old High German *kund* known, Old Norse *kunnr*] ► **un'couthly** *adv* ► **un'couthness** *n*

uncovenanted (ʌn'kʌvɪnəntɪd) *adj Law.* **1** not guaranteed or promised by a covenant. **2** not in accordance with or sanctioned by a covenant.

uncover (ʌn'kʌvə) *vb* **1** (*tr*) to remove the cover, cap, top, etc., from. **2** (*tr*) to reveal or disclose: *to uncover a plot.* **3** to take off (one's head covering), esp. as a mark of respect.

uncovered (ʌn'kʌvəd) *adj* **1** not covered; revealed or bare. **2** not protected by insurance, security, etc. **3** with hat removed as a mark of respect.

uncrowned (ʌn'kraʊnd) *adj* **1** having the power of royalty without the title. **2** not having yet assumed the crown. **3 uncrowned king** *or* **queen.** a man or woman of high status among a certain group.

UNCTAD *abbrev. for* United Nations Conference on Trade and Development.

unction ('ʌŋkʃən) *n* **1** *Chiefly R.C. and Eastern Churches.* the act of anointing with oil in sacramental ceremonies, in the conferring of holy orders. **2** excessive suavity or affected charm. **3** an ointment or unguent. **4** anything soothing or comforting. [C14: from Latin *unctiō* an anointing, from *ungere* to anoint; see UNGUENT] ► **'unctionless** *adj*

unctuous ('ʌŋktjuəs) *adj* **1** slippery or greasy. **2** affecting an oily charm. [C14: from Medieval Latin *unctuōsus*, from Latin *unctum* ointment, from *ungere* to anoint] ► **unctuosity** (ˌʌŋktju'ɒsɪtɪ) *or* **'unctuousness** *n* ► **'unctuously** *adv*

uncurl (ʌn'kɜːl) *vb* to move or cause to move out of a curled or rolled up position.

uncus ('ʌŋkəs) *n, pl* **unci** ('ʌnsaɪ). *Zoology, anatomy.* a hooked part or process, as in the human cerebrum. [C19: from Latin: hook]

uncut (ʌn'kʌt) *adj* **1** (of a book) not having the edges of its pages trimmed or slit. **2** (of a gemstone) not cut and faceted. **3** not abridged or shortened.

undamped (ʌn'dæmpt) *adj* **1** (of an oscillating system) having unrestricted motion; not damped. **2** not repressed, discouraged, or subdued; undiminished.

undaunted (ʌn'dɔːntɪd) *adj* not put off, discouraged, or beaten. ► **un'dauntedly** *adv* ► **un'dauntedness** *n*

undecagon (ʌn'dɛkəˌgɒn) *n* a polygon having eleven sides. [C18: from Latin *undecim* eleven (from *unus* one + *decem* ten) + -GON]

undeceive (ˌʌndɪ'siːv) *vb* (*tr*) to reveal the truth to (someone previously misled or deceived); enlighten. ► **ˌunde'ceivable** *adj* ► **ˌunde'ceiver** *n*

undecided (ˌʌndɪ'saɪdɪd) *adj* **1** not having made up one's mind. **2** (of an issue, problem, etc.) not agreed or decided upon. ► **ˌunde'cidedly** *adv* ► **ˌunde'cidedness** *n*

undemonstrative (ˌʌndɪ'mɒnstrətɪv) *adj* tending not to show the feelings; of a reserved nature. ► **ˌunde'monstratively** *adv* ► **ˌunde'monstrativeness** *n*

undeniable (ˌʌndɪ'naɪəbᵊl) *adj* **1** unquestionably or obviously true. **2** of unquestionable excellence: *a man of undeniable character.* **3** unable to be resisted or denied. ► **ˌunde'niableness** *n* ► **ˌunde'niably** *adv*

under ('ʌndə) *prep* **1** directly below; on, to, or beneath the underside or base of: *under one's feet.* **2** less than: *under forty years.* **3** lower in rank than: *under a corporal.* **4** subject to the supervision, jurisdiction, control, or influence of. **5** subject to (conditions); in (certain circumstances). **6** within a classification of: *a book under theology.* **7** known by: *under an assumed name.* **8** planted with: *a field under corn.* **9** powered by: *under sail.* **10** *Astrology.* during the period that the sun is in (a sign of the zodiac): *born under Aries.* ◆ *adv* **11** below; to a position underneath something. [Old English; related to Old Saxon, Gothic *undar*, Old High German *untar*, Old Norse *undir*, Latin *infra*]

under- *prefix* **1** below or beneath: *underarm; underground.* **2** of lesser importance or lower rank: *undersecretary.* **3** to a lesser degree than is proper; insufficient or insufficiently: *undercharge; underemployed.* **4** indicating secrecy or deception: *underhand.*

underachieve (ˌʌndərə'tʃiːv) *vb* (*intr*) to fail to achieve a performance appropriate to one's age or talents. ► **ˌundera'chiever** *n* ► **ˌundera'chievement** *n*

underact (ˌʌndər'ækt) *vb Theatre.* to play (a role) without adequate emphasis. Compare **overact.**

underage (ˌʌndər'eɪdʒ) *adj* below the required or standard age, esp. below the legal age for voting or drinking.

underarm ('ʌndərˌɑːm) *adj* **1** (of a measurement) extending along the arm from wrist to armpit. **2** *Cricket, tennis, etc.* of or denoting a style of throwing, bowling, or serving in which the hand is swung below shoulder level. **3** below the arm. ◆ *adv* **4** in an underarm style.

underbelly ('ʌndəˌbelɪ) *n, pl* **-lies. 1** the part of an animal's belly nearest to the ground. **2** a vulnerable or unprotected part, aspect, or region.

underbid (ˌʌndə'bɪd) *vb* **-bids, -bidding, -bid.** (*tr*) **1** to submit a bid lower than that of (others): *Irena underbid the other dealers.* **2** to submit an excessively low bid for. **3** *Bridge.* to make a bid that will win fewer tricks than is justified by the strength of the hand: *he underbid his hand.* ► **'underˌbidder** *n*

underbody ('ʌndəˌbɒdɪ) *n, pl* **-bodies.** the underpart of a body, as of an animal or motor vehicle.

underbred (ˌʌndə'brɛd) *adj* **1** of impure stock; not thoroughbred. **2** a less common word for **ill-bred.** ► **ˌunder'breeding** *n*

underbrush ('ʌndəˌbrʌʃ) *or* **underbush** *n Chiefly U.S. and Canadian.* undergrowth.

underbuy (ˌʌndə'baɪ) *vb* **-buys, -buying, -bought. 1** to buy (stock in trade) in amounts lower than required. **2** (*tr*) to buy at a price below that paid by (others). **3** (*tr*) to pay a price less than the true value for.

undercapitalize *or* **undercapitalise** (ˌʌndə'kæpɪtəˌlaɪz) *vb* to provide or issue capital for (a commercial enterprise) in an amount insufficient for efficient operation.

undercarriage ('ʌndəˌkærɪdʒ) *n* **1** Also called: **landing gear.** the assembly of wheels, shock absorbers, struts, etc., that supports an aircraft on the ground and enables it to take off and land. **2** the framework that supports the body of a vehicle, carriage, etc.

undercart ('ʌndəˌkɑːt) *n Brit. informal.* another name for **undercarriage** (sense 1).

undercharge (ˌʌndə'tʃɑːdʒ) *vb* **1** to charge too little (for). **2** (*tr*) to load (a gun, cannon, etc.,) with an inadequate charge. ◆ *n* **3** an insufficient charge.

underclass ('ʌndəˌklɑːs) *n* a class beneath the usual social scale consisting of the most disadvantaged people, such as the unemployed in inner cities.

underclay ('ʌndəˌkleɪ) *n* a grey or whitish clay rock containing fossilized plant roots and occurring beneath coal seams. When used as a refractory, it is known as fireclay.

underclothes ('ʌndəˌkləʊðz) *pl n* a variant of **underwear.** Also called: **underclothing.**

undercoat ('ʌndəˌkəʊt) *n* **1** a coat of paint or other substance applied before the top coat. **2** a coat worn under an overcoat. **3** *Zoology.* another name for **underfur. 4** the U.S. name for **underseal.** ◆ *vb* **5** (*tr*) to apply an undercoat to (a surface).

undercool (ˌʌndə'kuːl) *vb* a less common word for **supercool.**

undercover (ˌʌndə'kʌvə) *adj* done or acting in secret: *undercover operations.*

undercroft ('ʌndəˌkrɒft) *n* an underground chamber, such as a church crypt, often with a vaulted ceiling. [C14: from *croft* a vault, cavern, from earlier *crofte*, ultimately from Latin *crypta* CRYPT]

undercurrent ('ʌndəˌkʌrənt) *n* **1** a current that is not apparent at the surface or lies beneath another current. **2** an opinion, emotion, etc., lying beneath apparent feeling or meaning. ◆ Also called: **underflow.**

undercut *vb* (ˌʌndə'kʌt, 'ʌndəˌkʌt) **-cuts, -cutting, -cut. 1** to charge less than (a competitor) in order to obtain trade. **2** to cut away the under part of (something). **3** *Tennis, etc.* to hit (a ball) in such a way as to impart backspin. ◆ *n* ('ʌndəˌkʌt). **4** the act or an instance of cutting underneath. **5** a part that is cut away underneath. **6** a tenderloin of beef, including the fillet. **7** *Forestry, chiefly*

un'conseˌcrated *adj*
ˌuncon'strained *adj*
un'consumˌmated *adj*
ˌuncon'tamiˌnated *adj*
ˌuncon'tested *adj*
ˌuncon'trived *adj*
ˌuncon'trolled *adj*
ˌuncontro'versial *adj*
ˌuncon'verted *adj*
ˌuncon'vinced *adj*
ˌuncon'vincing *adj*
un'cooked *adj*
ˌuncor'rectable *adj*
ˌuncor'rected *adj*
ˌuncor'roboˌrated *adj*
ˌuncor'rupted *adj*
ˌuncre'ative *adj*
un'critical *adj*
un'cross *vb*
un'crowded *adj*
un'cultiˌvated *adj*
un'cultured *adj*
un'cured *adj*
un'customary *adj*
un'damaged *adj*
un'dated *adj*
ˌunde'clared *adj*
un'decoˌrated *adj*
ˌunde'feated *adj*
ˌunde'fended *adj*
ˌunde'filed *adj*
ˌunde'finable *adj*
ˌunde'fined *adj*
'unde'manding *adj*
ˌundemo'cratic *adj*
ˌunde'pendable *adj*
ˌunder'active *adj*
ˌunder'cook *vb*

U.S. and Canadian. a notch cut in a tree trunk, to ensure a clean break in felling. **8** *Tennis, golf, etc.* a stroke that imparts backspin to the ball.

underdevelop (ˌʌndədɪˈvɛləp) *vb (tr) Photog.* to process (a film, plate, or paper) in developer for less than the required time, or at too low a temperature, or in an exhausted solution. ► ˌ**underdeˈvelopment** *n*

underdeveloped (ˌʌndədɪˈvɛləpt) *adj* **1** immature or undersized. **2** relating to societies in which both the surplus capital and the social organization necessary to advance are lacking. **3** *Photog.* (of a film, plate, or print) processed in developer for less than the required time, thus lacking in contrast.

underdog (ˈʌndəˌdɒg) *n* **1** the losing competitor in a fight or contest. **2** a person in adversity or a position of inferiority.

underdone (ˌʌndəˈdʌn) *adj* insufficiently or lightly cooked.

underdrain *n* (ˈʌndəˌdreɪn). **1** a drain buried below agricultural land. ◆ *vb* (ˌʌndəˈdreɪn). **2** to bury such drains below (agricultural land). ► ˈ**underˌdrainage** *n*

underdressed (ˌʌndəˈdrest) *adj* wearing clothes that are not elaborate or formal enough for a particular occasion.

underemployed (ˌʌndərɪmˈplɔɪd) *adj* not fully or adequately employed. ► ˌ**underemˈployment** *n*

underestimate *vb* (ˌʌndərˈɛstɪˌmeɪt). *(tr)* **1** to make too low an estimate of: *he underestimated the cost.* **2** to think insufficiently highly of: *to underestimate a person.* ◆ *n* (ˌʌndərˈɛstɪmɪt). **3** too low an estimate. ► ˌ**underˌestiˈmation** *n*

USAGE *Underestimate* is sometimes wrongly used where *overestimate* is meant: *the importance of his work cannot be overestimated* (not *cannot be underestimated*).

underexpose (ˌʌndərɪkˈspəʊz) *vb (tr)* **1** *Photog.* to expose (a film, plate, or paper) for too short a period or with insufficient light so as not to produce the required effect. **2** *(often passive)* to fail to subject to appropriate or expected publicity.

underexposure (ˌʌndərɪkˈspəʊʒə) *n* **1** *Photog.* **1a** inadequate exposure to light. **1b** an underexposed negative, print, or transparency. **2** insufficient attention or publicity.

underfeed *vb* (ˌʌndəˈfiːd), **-feeds, -feeding, -fed.** *(tr)* **1** to give too little food to. **2** to supply (a furnace, engine, etc.) with fuel from beneath. ◆ *n* (ˈʌndəˌfiːd). **3** an apparatus by which fuel, etc., is supplied from below.

underfelt (ˈʌndəˌfɛlt) *n* thick felt laid between floorboards and carpet to increase insulation and resilience.

underfloor (ˈʌndəˌflɔː) *adj* situated beneath the floor: *underfloor heating.*

underflow (ˈʌndəˌfləʊ) *n* **1** another word for **undercurrent. 2** *Computing.* a condition that occurs when arithmetic operations produce results too small to store in the available register.

underfoot (ˌʌndəˈfʊt) *adv* **1** underneath the feet; on the ground. **2** in a position of subjugation or subservience. **3** in the way.

underfur (ˈʌndəˌfɜː) *n* the layer of dense soft fur occurring beneath the outer coarser fur in certain mammals, such as the otter and seal. Also called: **undercoat.**

undergarment (ˈʌndəˌgɑːmənt) *n* any garment worn under the visible outer clothes, usually next to the skin.

undergird (ˌʌndəˈgɜːd) *vb* **-girds, -girding, -girded** *or* **-girt.** *(tr)* to strengthen or reinforce by passing a rope, cable, or chain around the underside of (an object, load, etc.). [C16: from UNDER- + GIRD[1]]

underglaze (ˈʌndəˌgleɪz) *adj* **1** *Ceramics.* applied to pottery or porcelain before the application of glaze. ◆ *n* **2** a pigment, etc., applied in this way.

undergo (ˌʌndəˈgəʊ) *vb* **-goes, -going, -went, -gone.** *(tr)* to experience, endure, or sustain: *to undergo a dramatic change of feelings.* [Old English: earlier meanings were more closely linked with the senses of *under* and *go*] ► ˈ**underˌgoer** *n*

undergraduate (ˌʌndəˈgrædjʊɪt) *n* a person studying in a university for a first degree. Sometimes shortened to **undergrad.** ► ˌ**underˈgraduateship** *n*

underground *adj* (ˈʌndəˌgraʊnd), *adv* (ˌʌndəˈgraʊnd). **1** occurring, situated, used, or going below ground level: *an underground tunnel; an underground explosion.* **2** secret; hidden: *underground activities.* ◆ *n* (ˈʌndəˌgraʊnd). **3** a space or region below ground level. **4a** a movement dedicated to overthrowing a government or occupation forces, as in the European countries occupied by the German army in World War II. **4b** *(as modifier): an underground group.* **5** (often preceded by *the*) an electric passenger railway operated in underground tunnels. U.S. and Canadian equivalent: **subway. 6** (usually preceded by *the*) **6a** any avant-garde, experimental, or subversive movement in popular art, films, music, etc. **6b** *(as modifier): the underground press; underground music.*

underground railroad *n (often caps.)* (in the pre-Civil War U.S.) the system established by abolitionists to aid escaping slaves.

undergrown (ˈʌndəˌgrəʊn, ˌʌndəˈgrəʊn) *adj* **1** not having the expected height. **2** having undergrowth.

undergrowth (ˈʌndəˌgrəʊθ) *n* **1** small trees, bushes, ferns, etc., growing beneath taller trees in a wood or forest. **2** the condition of being undergrown. **3** a growth of short fine hairs beneath longer ones; underfur.

underhand (ˈʌndəˌhænd) *adj also* **underhanded. 1** clandestine, deceptive, or secretive. **2** *Sport.* another word for **underarm.** ◆ *adv* **3** in an underhand manner or style.

underhand chop *n N.Z.* (in an axemen's competition) a chop where the axeman stands on the log, which is placed on the ground. Compare **standing chop.**

underhanded (ˌʌndəˈhændɪd) *adj* another word for **underhand** or **shorthanded.** ► ˌ**underˈhandedly** *adv* ► ˌ**underˈhandedness** *n*

underhung (ˌʌndəˈhʌŋ) *adj* **1** (of the lower jaw) projecting beyond the upper jaw; undershot. **2** (of a sliding door, etc.) supported at its lower edge by a track or rail.

underlaid (ˌʌndəˈleɪd) *adj* **1** laid underneath. **2** having an underlay or supporting layer underneath. ◆ *vb* **3** the past tense and past participle of **underlay.**

underlay *vb* (ˌʌndəˈleɪ), **-lays, -laying, -laid.** *(tr)* **1** to place (something) under or beneath. **2** to support by something laid beneath. **3** to achieve the correct printing pressure all over (a forme block) or to bring (a block) up to type height by adding material, such as paper, to the appropriate areas beneath it. ◆ *n* (ˈʌndəˌleɪ). **4** a layer, lining, support, etc., laid underneath something else. **5** *Printing.* material, such as paper, used to underlay a forme or block. **6** felt, rubber, etc., laid beneath a carpet to increase insulation and resilience.

underlet (ˌʌndəˈlɛt) *vb* **-lets, -letting, -let.** *(tr)* **1** to let for a price lower than expected or justified. **2** a less common word for **sublet.** ► ˈ**underˌletter** *n*

underlie (ˌʌndəˈlaɪ) *vb* **-lies, -lying, -lay, -lain.** *(tr)* **1** to lie or be placed under or beneath. **2** to be the foundation, cause, or basis of: *careful planning underlies all our decisions.* **3** *Finance.* to take priority over (another claim, liability, mortgage, etc.): *a first mortgage underlies a second.* **4** to be the root or stem from which (a word) is derived: *"happy" underlies "happiest".* ► ˈ**underˌlier** *n*

underline *vb* (ˌʌndəˈlaɪn). *(tr)* **1** to put a line under. **2** to state forcibly; emphasize or reinforce. ◆ *n* (ˈʌndəˌlaɪn). **3** a line underneath, esp. under written matter.

underlinen (ˈʌndəˌlɪnən) *n* underclothes, esp. when made of linen.

underling (ˈʌndəlɪŋ) *n* a subordinate or lackey.

underlying (ˌʌndəˈlaɪɪŋ) *adj* **1** concealed but detectable: *underlying guilt.* **2** fundamental; basic. **3** lying under. **4** *Finance.* (of a claim, liability, etc.) taking precedence; prior.

undermentioned (ˈʌndəˌmɛnʃənd) *adj* mentioned below or subsequently.

undermine (ˌʌndəˈmaɪn) *vb (tr)* **1** (of the sea, wind, etc.) to wear away the bottom or base of (land, cliffs, etc.). **2** to weaken gradually or insidiously: *their insults undermined her confidence.* **3** to tunnel or dig beneath. ► ˌ**underˈminer** *n*

undermost (ˈʌndəˌməʊst) *adj* **1** being the furthest under; lowest. ◆ *adv* **2** in the lowest place.

underneath (ˌʌndəˈniːθ) *prep, adv* **1** under; beneath. ◆ *adj* **2** lower. ◆ *n* **3** a lower part, surface, etc. [Old English *underneothan,* from UNDER + *neothan* below; related to Old Danish *underneden;* see BENEATH]

undernourish (ˌʌndəˈnʌrɪʃ) *vb (tr; usually passive)* to deprive of or fail to provide with nutrients essential for health and growth. ► ˌ**underˈnourishment** *n*

underpainting (ˈʌndəˌpeɪntɪŋ) *n* the first layer in a painting, indicating the design and main areas of light and shade.

underpants (ˈʌndəˌpænts) *pl n* a man's undergarment covering the body from the waist or hips to the top of the thighs or knees. Often shortened to **pants.**

underpass (ˈʌndəˌpɑːs) *n* **1** a section of a road that passes under another road, railway line, etc. **2** another word for **subway** (sense 1).

underpay (ˌʌndəˈpeɪ) *vb* **-pays, -paying, -paid.** to pay (someone) insufficiently. ► ˌ**underˈpayment** *n*

underpin (ˌʌndəˈpɪn) *vb* **-pins, -pinning, -pinned.** *(tr)* **1** to support from beneath, esp. by a prop, while avoiding damaging or weakening the superstructure: *to underpin a wall.* **2** to give corroboration, strength, or support to.

underpinning (ˈʌndəˌpɪnɪŋ) *n* a structure of masonry, concrete, etc., placed beneath a wall to provide support.

underpinnings (ˈʌndəˌpɪnɪŋz) *pl n* any supporting structure or system.

underpitch vault (ˈʌndəˌpɪtʃ) *n Architect.* a vault that is intersected by one or more vaults of lower pitch.

underplay (ˌʌndəˈpleɪ) *vb* **1** to play (a role) with restraint or subtlety. **2** to achieve (an effect) by deliberate lack of emphasis. **3** *(intr) Cards.* to lead or follow suit with a lower card when holding a higher one.

underplot (ˈʌndəˌplɒt) *n* **1** a subsidiary plot in a literary or dramatic work. **2** an undercover plot.

underprice (ˌʌndəˈpraɪs) *vb (tr)* to price (an article for sale) at too low a level or amount.

underprivileged (ˌʌndəˈprɪvɪlɪdʒd) *adj* lacking the rights and advantages of other members of society; deprived.

underproduction (ˌʌndəprəˈdʌkʃən) *n Commerce.* production below full capacity or below demand.

underproof (ˌʌndəˈpruːf) *adj* (of a spirit) containing less than 57.1 per cent alcohol by volume.

underprop (ˌʌndəˈprɒp) *vb* **-props, -propping, -propped.** *(tr)* to prop up from beneath. ► ˈ**underˌpropper** *n*

underquote (ˌʌndəˈkwəʊt) *vb* **1** to offer for sale (securities, goods, or services) at a price lower than the market price. **2** *(tr)* to quote a price lower than that quoted by (another).

underrate (ˌʌndəˈreɪt) *vb (tr)* to underestimate.

undersaturated (ˌʌndəˈsætʃəˌreɪtɪd) *adj* (of an igneous rock) having a low silica content.

underscore *vb* (ˌʌndəˈskɔː). *(tr)* **1** to draw or score a line or mark under. **2** to stress or reinforce. ◆ *n* (ˈʌndəˌskɔː). **3** a line drawn under written matter.

ˌ**underˈfunded** *adj*
ˌ**underinˈsured** *adj*
ˌ**under-manned** *adj*
ˌ**underˈpaid** *adj*
ˈ**underˌpart** *n*
ˌ**underˈpopuˌlated** *adj*
ˌ**underˈpowered** *adj*

undersea ('ʌndəˌsiː) *adj, adv also* **underseas** (ˌʌndə'siːz). below the surface of the sea.
underseal ('ʌndəˌsiːl) *Brit.* ◆ *n* **1** a coating of a tar or rubber-based material applied to the underside of a motor vehicle to retard corrosion. U.S. name: **undercoat.** ◆ *vb* **2** (*tr*) to apply a coating of underseal to (a motor vehicle).
undersecretary (ˌʌndə'sɛkrətrɪ) *n, pl* **-taries. 1** (in Britain) **1a** any of various senior civil servants in certain government departments. **1b** short for **undersecretary of state:** any of various high officials subordinate only to the minister in charge of a department. **2** (in the U.S.) a high government official subordinate only to the secretary in charge of a department. ► **ˌunder'secretaryˌship** *n*
undersell (ˌʌndə'sɛl) *vb* **-sells, -selling, -sold. 1** to sell for less than the usual or expected price. **2** (*tr*) to sell at a price lower than that of (another seller). **3** (*tr*) to advertise (merchandise) with moderation or restraint. ► **ˌunder'seller** *n*
underset ('ʌndəˌsɛt) *n* **1** an ocean undercurrent. **2** an underlying vein of ore. ◆ *vb* **-sets, -setting, -set. 3** (*tr*) to support from underneath.
undersexed (ˌʌndə'sɛkst) *adj* having weaker sex urges or responses than is considered normal.
undersheriff ('ʌndəˌʃɛrɪf) *n* a deputy sheriff.
undershirt ('ʌndəˌʃɜːt) *n Chiefly U.S. and Canadian.* an undergarment worn under a blouse or shirt. Brit. name: **vest.**
undershoot (ˌʌndə'ʃuːt) *vb* **-shoots, -shooting, -shot. 1** (of a pilot) to cause (an aircraft) to land short of (a runway) or (of an aircraft) to land in this way. **2** to shoot a projectile so that it falls short of (a target).
undershorts ('ʌndəˌʃɔːts) *pl n* another word for **shorts** (sense 2).
undershot ('ʌndəˌʃɒt) *adj* **1** (of the lower jaw) projecting beyond the upper jaw; underhung. **2** (of a water wheel) driven by a flow of water that passes under the wheel rather than over it. ◆ Compare **overshot.**
undershrub ('ʌndəˌʃrʌb) *n* another name for **subshrub.**
underside ('ʌndəˌsaɪd) *n* the bottom or lower surface.
undersigned ('ʌndəˌsaɪnd) *n* **1 the.** the person or persons who have signed at the foot of a document, statement, etc. ◆ *adj* **2** having signed one's name at the foot of a document, statement, etc. **3** (of a document) signed at the foot. **4** signed at the foot of a document.
undersized (ˌʌndə'saɪzd) *adj* of less than usual size.
underskirt ('ʌndəˌskɜːt) *n* any skirtlike garment worn under a skirt.
underslung (ˌʌndə'slʌŋ) *adj* **1** suspended below a supporting member, esp. (of a motor vehicle chassis) suspended below the axles. **2** having a low centre of gravity.
undersoil ('ʌndəˌsɔɪl) *n* another word for **subsoil** (sense 1a).
understand (ˌʌndə'stænd) *vb* **-stands, -standing, -stood. 1** (*may take a clause as object*) to know and comprehend the nature or meaning of: *I understand you; I understand what you mean.* **2** (*may take a clause as object*) to realize or grasp (something): *he understands your position.* **3** (*tr; may take a clause as object*) to assume, infer, or believe: *I understand you are thinking of marrying.* **4** (*tr*) to know how to translate or read: *can you understand Spanish?* **5** (*tr; may take a clause as object; often passive*) to accept as a condition or proviso: *it is understood that children must be kept quiet.* **6** (*tr*) to be sympathetic to or compatible with: *we understand each other.* [Old English *understandan;* related to Old Frisian *understonda,* Middle High German *understān* step under; see UNDER, STAND] ► **ˌunder'standable** *adj* ► **ˌunder'standably** *adv*
understanding (ˌʌndə'stændɪŋ) *n* **1** the ability to learn, judge, make decisions, etc.; intelligence or sense. **2** personal opinion or interpretation of a subject: *my understanding of your predicament.* **3** a mutual agreement or compact, esp. an informal or private one. **4** *Chiefly Brit.* an unofficial engagement to be married. **5** *Philosophy, archaic.* the mind, esp. the faculty of reason. **6 on the understanding that.** with the condition that; providing. ◆ *adj* **7** sympathetic, tolerant, or wise towards people. **8** possessing judgment and intelligence. ► **ˌunder'standingly** *adv*
understate (ˌʌndə'steɪt) *vb* **1** to state (something) in restrained terms, often to obtain an ironic effect. **2** to state that (something, such as a number) is less than it is. ► **ˌunder'statement** *n*
understeer ('ʌndəˌstɪə) *vb* (*intr*) (of a vehicle) to turn less sharply, for a particular movement of the steering wheel, than anticipated.
understood (ˌʌndə'stʊd) *vb* **1** the past tense and past participle of **understand.** ◆ *adj* **2** implied or inferred. **3** taken for granted; assumed.
understorey ('ʌndəˌstɔːrɪ) *n* a lower tier of shrubs and small trees under the main canopy of forest trees.
understrapper ('ʌndəˌstræpə) *n* a less common word for **underling.** [C18: from STRAP (in the archaic sense: to work hard)]
understudy ('ʌndəˌstʌdɪ) *vb* **-studies, -studying, -studied. 1** (*tr*) to study (a role or part) so as to be able to replace the usual actor or actress if necessary. **2** to act as understudy to (an actor or actress). ◆ *n, pl* **-studies. 3** an actor or actress who studies a part so as to be able to replace the usual actor or actress if necessary. **4** anyone who is trained to take the place of another in case of need.
undertake (ˌʌndə'teɪk) *vb* **-takes, -taking, -took, -taken. 1** (*tr*) to contract to or commit oneself to (something) or (to do something): *to undertake a job; to undertake to deliver the goods.* **2** (*tr*) to attempt to; agree to start. **3** (*tr*) to take (someone) in charge. **4** (*intr;* foll. by *for*) *Archaic.* to make oneself responsible (for). **5** (*tr*) to promise.
undertaker ('ʌndəˌteɪkə) *n* a person whose profession is the preparation of the dead for burial or cremation and the management of funerals; funeral director.
undertaking ('ʌndəˌteɪkɪŋ) *n* **1** something undertaken; task, venture, or enterprise. **2** an agreement to do something. **3** the business of an undertaker. **4** *Informal.* the practice of overtaking on an inner lane a vehicle which is travelling in an outer lane.
under the table *adj* **1** (**under-the-table** *when prenominal*) done illicitly and secretly. **2** *Slang.* drunk.
underthings ('ʌndəˌθɪŋz) *pl n* girls' or women's underwear.
underthrust ('ʌndəˌθrʌst) *n Geology.* a reverse fault in which the rocks on the lower surface of a fault plane have moved under the relatively static rocks on the upper surface. Compare **overthrust.**
undertint ('ʌndəˌtɪnt) *n* a slight, subdued, or delicate tint.
undertone ('ʌndəˌtəʊn) *n* **1** a quiet or hushed tone of voice. **2** an underlying tone or suggestion in words or actions: *his offer has undertones of dishonesty.* **3** a pale or subdued colour.
undertook (ˌʌndə'tʊk) *vb* the past tense of **undertake.**
undertow ('ʌndəˌtəʊ) *n* **1** the seaward undercurrent following the breaking of a wave on the beach. **2** any strong undercurrent flowing in a different direction from the surface current.
undertrick ('ʌndəˌtrɪk) *n Bridge.* a trick by which a declarer falls short of making his contract.
undertrump (ˌʌndə'trʌmp) *vb* (*intr*) *Cards.* to play a lower trump on a trick to which a higher trump has already been played.
undervalue (ˌʌndə'væljuː) *vb* **-values, -valuing, -valued.** (*tr*) to value at too low a level or price. ► **ˌunderˌvalu'ation** *n* ► **ˌunder'valuer** *n*
undervest ('ʌndəˌvɛst) *n Brit.* another name for **vest** (sense 1).
underwater ('ʌndə'wɔːtə) *adj* **1** being, occurring, or going under the surface of the water, esp. the sea: *underwater exploration.* **2** *Nautical.* below the water line of a vessel. ◆ *adv* **3** beneath the surface of the water.
under way *adj* (*postpositive*) **1** in progress; in operation: *the show was under way.* **2** *Nautical.* in motion.
underwear ('ʌndəˌwɛə) *n* clothing worn under the outer garments, usually next to the skin. Also called: **underclothes.**
underweight (ˌʌndə'weɪt) *adj* weighing less than is average, expected, or healthy.
underwent (ˌʌndə'wɛnt) *vb* the past tense of **undergo.**
underwhelm (ˌʌndə'wɛlm) *vb* (*tr*) to make no positive impact or impression on; disappoint. [C20: originally a humorous coinage based on *overwhelm*] ► **ˌunder'whelming** *adj*
underwing ('ʌndəˌwɪŋ) *n* **1** the hind wing of an insect, esp. when covered by the forewing. **2** See **red underwing, yellow underwing.**
underwood ('ʌndəˌwʊd) *n* a less common word for **undergrowth.**
underworld ('ʌndəˌwɜːld) *n* **1a** criminals and their associates considered collectively. **1b** (*as modifier*): *underworld connections.* **2** *Greek and Roman myth.* the regions below the earth's surface regarded as the abode of the dead; Hades. Related adjs.: **chtonian, chthonic. 3** the antipodes.
underwrite ('ʌndəˌraɪt, ˌʌndə'raɪt) *vb* **-writes, -writing, -wrote, -written.** (*tr*) **1** *Finance.* to undertake to purchase at an agreed price any unsold portion of (a public issue of shares, etc.). **2** to accept financial responsibility for (a commercial project or enterprise). **3** *Insurance.* **3a** to sign and issue (an insurance policy) thus accepting liability if specified losses occur. **3b** to insure (a property or risk). **3c** to accept liability up to (a specified amount) in an insurance policy. **4** to write (words, a signature, etc.) beneath (other written matter); subscribe. **5** to support or concur with (a decision, statement, etc.) by or as if by signature.
underwriter ('ʌndəˌraɪtə) *n* **1** a person or enterprise that underwrites public issues of shares, bonds, etc. **2a** a person or enterprise that underwrites insurance policies. **2b** an employee or agent of an insurance company who assesses risks and determines the premiums payable.
undescended (ˌʌndɪ'sɛndɪd) *adj* (of the testes) remaining in the abdominal cavity rather than descending to lie in the scrotum.
undesigned (ˌʌndɪ'zaɪnd) *adj* **1** (of an action) unintentional. **2** not yet designed.
undesigning (ˌʌndɪ'zaɪnɪŋ) *adj* (of a person) frank; straightforward.
undesirable (ˌʌndɪ'zaɪərəbᵊl) *adj* **1** not desirable or pleasant; objectionable. ◆ *n* **2** a person or thing that is considered undesirable. ► **ˌundeˌsira'bility** *or* **ˌunde'sirableness** *n* ► **ˌunde'sirably** *adv*
undetermined (ˌʌndɪ'tɜːmɪnd) *adj* **1** not yet resolved; undecided. **2** not known or discovered.
undid (ʌn'dɪd) *vb* the past tense of **undo.**
undies ('ʌndɪz) *pl n Informal.* women's underwear.
undine ('ʌndiːn) *n* any of various female water spirits. [C17: from New Latin *undina,* from Latin *unda* a wave]
undirected (ˌʌndɪ'rɛktɪd, -daɪ-) *adj* **1** lacking a clear purpose or objective. **2** (of a letter, parcel, etc.) having no address.
undisputed world champion *n Boxing.* a boxer who holds the World Box-

ˌunder'spend *vb,* **-'spends, -'spending, -'spent.**
ˌunder'staffed *adj*
'underˌsurface *n*
ˌunde'served *adj*
ˌunde'serving *adj*
ˌunde'sired *adj*
ˌunde'tected *adj*
ˌunde'terred *adj*
ˌunde'veloped *adj*
un'diagˌnosed *adj*
ˌundiffer'entiˌated *adj*
ˌundi'gested *adj*
un'digniˌfied *adj*
ˌundi'luted *adj*
ˌundi'minished *adj*
un'dimmed *adj*
ˌundiplo'matic *adj*
ˌundis'cerning *adj*
ˌundis'charged *adj*
un'disciplined *adj*
ˌundis'closed *adj*
ˌundis'covered *adj*
ˌundis'crimiˌnating *adj*
ˌundis'guised *adj*
ˌundis'mayed *adj*
ˌundis'posed *adj*
ˌundis'puted *adj*

ing Association, the World Boxing Council, the World Boxing Organization, and the International Boxing Federation world championship titles simultaneously.

undistinguished (ˌʌndɪˈstɪŋgwɪʃt) *adj* **1** not particularly good or bad. **2** without distinction: *undistinguished features.*

undistributed (ˌʌndɪsˈtrɪbjʊtɪd) *adj* **1** *Logic.* (of a term) referring only to some members of the class designated by the term, as *doctors* in *some doctors are overworked.* **2** *Business.* (of a profit) not paid in dividends to the shareholders of a company but retained to help finance its trading.

undo (ʌnˈduː) *vb* **-does, -doing, -did, -done.** (*mainly tr*) **1** (*also intr*) to untie, unwrap, or open or become untied, unwrapped, etc. **2** to reverse the effects of. **3** to cause the downfall of. **4** *Obsolete.* to explain or solve. ▸ **unˈdoer** *n*

undoing (ʌnˈduːɪŋ) *n* **1** ruin; downfall. **2** the cause of downfall: *drink was his undoing.*

undone[1] (ʌnˈdʌn) *adj* not done or completed; unfinished.

undone[2] (ʌnˈdʌn) *adj* **1** ruined; destroyed. **2** unfastened; untied.

undoubted (ʌnˈdaʊtɪd) *adj* beyond doubt; certain or indisputable. ▸ **unˈdoubtedly** *adv*

undreamed (ʌnˈdriːmd) *or* **undreamt** (ʌnˈdrɛmt) *adj* (often foll. by *of*) not thought of, conceived, or imagined.

undress *vb* (ʌnˈdrɛs). **1** to take off clothes from (oneself or another). **2** (*tr*) to strip of ornamentation. **3** (*tr*) to remove the dressing from (a wound). ◆ *n* (ʌnˈdrɛs). **4** partial or complete nakedness. **5** informal or normal working clothes or uniform. ◆ *adj* (ˈʌndrɛs). **6** characterized by or requiring informal or normal working dress or uniform.

undressed (ʌnˈdrɛst) *adj* **1** partially or completely naked. **2** (of an animal hide) not fully processed. **3** (of food, esp. salad) not prepared with sauce or dressing.

UNDRO (ˈʌnˌdrəʊ) *n acronym for* United Nations Disaster Relief Organization.

Undset (*Norwegian* ˈunsɛt) *n* **Sigrid** (ˈsigri). 1882–1949, Norwegian novelist, best known for her trilogy *Kristin Lavransdatter* (1920–22): Nobel prize for literature 1928.

undue (ʌnˈdjuː) *adj* **1** excessive or unwarranted. **2** unjust, improper, or illegal. **3** (of a debt, bond, etc.) not yet payable.

USAGE The use of *undue* in sentences such as *there is no cause for undue alarm* is redundant and should be avoided.

undulant (ˈʌndjʊlənt) *adj Rare.* resembling waves; undulating. ▸ **ˈundulance** *n*

undulant fever *n* another name for **brucellosis.** **[C19: so called because the fever symptoms are intermittent]**

undulate *vb* (ˈʌndjʊˌleɪt). **1** to move or cause to move in waves or as if in waves. **2** to have or provide with a wavy form or appearance. ◆ *adj* (ˈʌndjʊlɪt, -ˌleɪt), *also* **undulated. 3** having a wavy or rippled appearance, margin, or form: *an undulate leaf.* **[C17:** from Latin *undulātus,* from *unda* a wave**]** ▸ **ˈunduˌlator** *n*

undulation (ˌʌndjʊˈleɪʃən) *n* **1** the act or an instance of undulating. **2** any wave or wavelike form, line, etc.

undulatory (ˈʌndjʊlətərɪ, -trɪ) *adj* **1** caused by or characterized by waves or undulations. **2** having a wavelike motion or form.

unduly (ʌnˈdjuːlɪ) *adv* **1** immoderately; excessively. **2** in contradiction of moral or legal standards.

undying (ʌnˈdaɪɪŋ) *adj* unending; eternal. ▸ **unˈdyingly** *adv*

unearned (ʌnˈɜːnd) *adj* **1** not deserved. **2** not yet earned.

unearned income *n* income from property, investment, etc., comprising rent, interest, and dividends.

unearned increment *n* a rise in the market value of landed property resulting from general economic factors.

unearth (ʌnˈɜːθ) *vb* (*tr*) **1** to dig up out of the earth. **2** to reveal or discover, esp. by exhaustive searching.

unearthly (ʌnˈɜːθlɪ) *adj* **1** ghostly; eerie; weird: *unearthly screams.* **2** heavenly; sublime: *unearthly music.* **3** ridiculous or unreasonable (esp. in the phrase **unearthly hour**). ▸ **unˈearthliness** *n*

uneasy (ʌnˈiːzɪ) *adj* **1** (of a person) anxious; apprehensive. **2** (of a condition) precarious; uncomfortable: *an uneasy truce.* **3** (of a thought, etc.) disturbing; disquieting. ▸ **unˈease** *n* ▸ **unˈeasily** *adv* ▸ **unˈeasiness** *n*

uneconomic (ˌʌniːkəˈnɒmɪk, ˌʌnɛkə-) *adj* not economic; not profitable.

uneconomical (ˌʌniːkəˈnɒmɪkᵊl, -ɛkə-) *adj* not economical; wasteful.

UNEF (ˈjuːˌnɛf) *n acronym for* United Nations Emergency Force.

unemployable (ˌʌnɪmˈplɔɪəbᵊl) *adj* unable or unfit to keep a job. ▸ **ˌunemˌployaˈbility** *n*

unemployed (ˌʌnɪmˈplɔɪd) *adj* **1a** without remunerative employment; out of work. **1b** (*as collective n;* preceded by *the*): *the unemployed.* **2** not being used; idle.

unemployment (ˌʌnɪmˈplɔɪmənt) *n* **1** the condition of being unemployed. **2** the number of unemployed workers, often as a percentage of the total labour force.

unemployment benefit *n* **1** (in Britain, formerly) a regular payment to a person who is out of work: replaced by jobseeker's allowance in 1996. Informal term: **dole. 2** (in New Zealand) a means-tested monetary benefit paid weekly by the Social Security Department to the unemployed.

unemployment compensation *n* (in the U.S.) payment by a governmental agency to unemployed people.

unequal (ʌnˈiːkwəl) *adj* **1** not equal in quantity, size, rank, value, etc. **2** (foll. by *to*) inadequate; insufficient. **3** not evenly balanced. **4** (of character, quality, etc.) irregular; varying; inconsistent. **5** (of a contest, etc.) having competitors of different ability. **6** *Obsolete.* unjust. ▸ **unˈequally** *adv*

unequalled *or U.S.* **unequaled** (ʌnˈiːkwəld) *adj* not equalled; unparalleled or unrivalled; supreme.

unequivocal (ˌʌnɪˈkwɪvəkᵊl) *adj* not ambiguous; plain. ▸ **ˌuneˈquivocally** *adv* ▸ **ˌuneˈquivocalness** *n*

unerring (ʌnˈɜːrɪŋ) *adj* **1** not missing the mark or target. **2** consistently accurate; certain. ▸ **unˈerringly** *adv* ▸ **unˈerringness** *n*

UNESCO (juːˈnɛskəʊ) *n acronym for* United Nations Educational, Scientific, and Cultural Organization: an agency of the United Nations that sponsors programmes to promote education, communication, the arts, etc.

unessential (ˌʌnɪˈsɛnʃəl) *adj* **1** a less common word for **inessential.** ◆ *n* **2** something that is not essential. ▸ **ˌunesˈsentially** *adv*

uneven (ʌnˈiːvən) *adj* **1** (of a surface, etc.) not level or flat. **2** spasmodic or variable. **3** not parallel, straight, or horizontal. **4** not fairly matched: *an uneven race.* **5** *Archaic.* not equal. **6** *Obsolete.* unjust. ▸ **unˈevenly** *adv* ▸ **unˈevenness** *n*

uneventful (ˌʌnɪˈvɛntfʊl) *adj* ordinary, routine, or quiet. ▸ **ˌuneˈventfully** *adv* ▸ **ˌuneˈventfulness** *n*

unexampled (ˌʌnɪgˈzɑːmpᵊld) *adj* without precedent or parallel.

unexceptionable (ˌʌnɪkˈsɛpʃənəbᵊl) *adj* beyond criticism or objection. ▸ **ˌunexˈceptionableness** *or* **ˌunexˌceptionaˈbility** *n* ▸ **ˌunexˈceptionably** *adv*

unexceptional (ˌʌnɪkˈsɛpʃənᵊl) *adj* **1** usual, ordinary, or normal. **2** subject to or allowing no exceptions. **3** *Not standard.* another word for **unexceptionable.** ▸ **ˌunexˈceptionally** *adv*

unexcited (ˌʌnɪkˈsaɪtɪd) *adj* **1** not aroused to pleasure, interest, agitation, etc. **2** (of an atom, molecule, etc.) remaining in its ground state.

unexpected (ˌʌnɪkˈspɛktɪd) *adj* surprising or unforeseen. ▸ **ˌunexˈpectedly** *adv* ▸ **ˌunexˈpectedness** *n*

unexperienced (ˌʌnɪkˈspɪərɪənst) *adj* **1** (of a situation, sensation, fact, etc.) not having been undergone or known by experience. **2** inexperienced.

unexpressed (ˌʌnɪkˈsprɛst) *adj* **1** not expressed or said. **2** understood without being expressed.

unfailing (ʌnˈfeɪlɪŋ) *adj* **1** not failing; unflagging. **2** continuous or unceasing. **3** sure; certain. ▸ **unˈfailingly** *adv* ▸ **unˈfailingness** *n*

unfair (ʌnˈfɛə) *adj* **1** characterized by inequality or injustice. **2** dishonest or unethical. ▸ **unˈfairly** *adv* ▸ **unˈfairness** *n*

unfaithful (ʌnˈfeɪθfʊl) *adj* **1** not true to a promise, vow, etc. **2** not true to a wife, husband, lover, etc., esp. in having sexual intercourse with someone else. **3** inaccurate; inexact; unreliable; untrustworthy: *unfaithful copy.* **4** *Obsolete.* not having religious faith; infidel. **5** *Obsolete.* not upright; dishonest. ▸ **unˈfaithfully** *adv* ▸ **unˈfaithfulness** *n*

unfamiliar (ˌʌnfəˈmɪljə) *adj* **1** not known or experienced; strange. **2** (*postpositive;* foll. by *with*) not familiar. ▸ **unfamiliarity** (ˌʌnfəˌmɪlɪˈærɪtɪ) *n* ▸ **ˌunfaˈmiliarly** *adv*

unfasten (ʌnˈfɑːsᵊn) *vb* to undo, untie, or open or become undone, untied, or opened.

unfathered (ʌnˈfɑːðəd) *adj* **1** having no known father. **2** of unknown or uncertain origin. **3** *Archaic.* fatherless.

unfathomable (ʌnˈfæðəməbᵊl) *adj* **1** incapable of being fathomed; immeasurable. **2** incomprehensible. ▸ **unˈfathomableness** *n* ▸ **unˈfathomably** *adv*

unfavourable *or U.S.* **unfavorable** (ʌnˈfeɪvərəbᵊl, -ˈfeɪvrə-) *adj* not favourable; adverse or inauspicious. ▸ **unˈfavourableness** *or U.S.* **unˈfavorableness** *n* ▸ **unˈfavourably** *or U.S.* **unˈfavorably** *adv*

unfazed (ʌnˈfeɪzd) *adj Informal.* not disconcerted; unperturbed.

Unfederated Malay States (ʌnˈfɛdəˌreɪtɪd) *pl n* a former group of native states in the Malay Peninsula that became British protectorates between 1885 and 1909. All except Brunei joined the Malayan Union (later Federation of Malaya) in 1946. Brunei joined the Federation of Malaysia in 1963.

unfeeling (ʌnˈfiːlɪŋ) *adj* **1** without sympathy; callous. **2** without physical feeling or sensation. ▸ **unˈfeelingly** *adv* ▸ **unˈfeelingness** *n*

ˌundisˈsolved *adj*
ˌundisˈturbed *adj*
ˌundiˈvided *adj*
unˈdocuˌmented *adj*
ˌundoˈmestiˌcated *adj*
unˈdrained *adj*
ˌundraˈmatic *adj*
unˈdraped *adj*
unˈdrinkable *adj*
unˈdutiful *adj*
unˈdyed *adj*
unˈeatable *adj*
unˈeaten *adj*
unˈediˌfying *adj*
unˈedited *adj*
unˈeduˌcated *adj*
ˌuneˈlectable *adj*
ˌunemˈbarrassed *adj*
ˌunemˈbellished *adj*
ˌuneˈmotional *adj*
ˌunemˈphatic *adj*
ˌunenˈclosed *or* **ˌuninˈclosed** *adj*
ˌunenˈcumbered *or* **ˌuninˈcumbered** *adj*
unˈending *adj*
ˌunenˈdurable *adj*
ˌunenˈforced *adj*
ˌunenˈjoyable *adj*
ˌunenˈlightened *adj*
unˈentered *adj*
unˈenterˌprising *adj*
ˌunenˌthusiˈastic *adj*
unˈenviable *adj*
ˌuneˈquipped *adj*
ˌunesˈcorted *adj*
unˈethical *adj*
ˌunexˈcelled *adj*
ˌunexˈciting *adj*
ˌunexˈpired *adj*
ˌunexˈplainable *adj*
ˌunexˈplained *adj*
ˌunexˈploited *adj*
ˌunexˈplored *adj*
ˌunexˈposed *adj*
ˌunexˈpressive *adj*
unˈexpurˌgated *adj*
unˈfading *adj*
unˈfashionable *adj*
unˈfavoured *adj*
unˈfeasible *adj*
unˈfed *adj*

unfetter (ʌn'fetə) *vb (tr)* **1** to release from fetters, bonds, etc. **2** to release from restraint or inhibition. ▸ **un'fettered** *adj*

unfinished (ʌn'fɪnɪʃt) *adj* **1** incomplete or imperfect. **2** (of paint, polish, varnish, etc.) without an applied finish; rough. **3** (of fabric) unbleached or not processed. **4** (of fabric) with a short nap.

unfit (ʌn'fɪt) *adj* **1** (*postpositive;* often foll. by *for*) unqualified, incapable, or incompetent: *unfit for military service.* **2** (*postpositive;* often foll. by *for*) unsuitable or inappropriate: *the ground was unfit for football.* **3** in poor physical condition. ▸ **un'fitness** *n*

unfitted (ʌn'fɪtɪd) *adj* unsuitable: *unused to and unfitted for any form of manual labour.*

unfix (ʌn'fɪks) *vb (tr)* **1** to unfasten, detach, or loosen. **2** to unsettle or disturb.

unflappable (ʌn'flæpəbəl) *adj Informal.* hard to upset; imperturbable; calm; composed. ▸ **un,flappa'bility** *or* **un'flappableness** *n* ▸ **un'flappably** *adv*

unfledged (ʌn'flɛdʒd) *adj* **1** (of a young bird) not having developed adult feathers. **2** immature and undeveloped.

unflinching (ʌn'flɪntʃɪŋ) *adj* not shrinking from danger, difficulty, etc. ▸ **un'flinchingly** *adv*

unfold (ʌn'fəʊld) *vb* **1** to open or spread out or be opened or spread out from a folded state. **2** to reveal or be revealed: *the truth unfolds.* **3** to develop or expand or be developed or expanded. ▸ **un'folder** *n*

unforgettable (ˌʌnfə'gɛtəbəl) *adj* impossible to forget; highly memorable. ▸ **,unfor'gettably** *adv*

unforgiving (ˌʌnfə'gɪvɪŋ) *adj* **1** not willing to forgive; unmerciful. **2** (of a machine, system, etc.) allowing little or no opportunity for mistakes to be corrected. **3** harsh and unremitting: *an unforgiving and desolate landscape.*

unformed (ʌn'fɔːmd) *adj* **1** shapeless. **2** immature.

unfortunate (ʌn'fɔːtʃənɪt) *adj* **1** causing or attended by misfortune. **2** unlucky, unsuccessful, or unhappy: *an unfortunate character.* **3** regrettable or unsuitable: *an unfortunate speech.* ◆ *n* **4** an unlucky person. ▸ **un'fortunately** *adv* ▸ **un'fortunateness** *n*

unfounded (ʌn'faʊndɪd) *adj* **1** (of ideas, allegations, etc.) baseless; groundless. **2** not yet founded or established. ▸ **un'foundedly** *adv* ▸ **un'foundedness** *n*

unfranked income (ʌn'fræŋkt) *n* any income from an investment that does not qualify as franked investment income.

unfreeze (ʌn'friːz) *vb* **-freezes, -freezing, -froze, -frozen. 1** to thaw or cause to thaw. **2** (*tr*) to relax governmental restrictions on (wages, prices, credit, etc.) or on the manufacture or sale of (goods, etc.).

unfriended (ʌn'frɛndɪd) *adj Now rare.* without a friend or friends; friendless.

unfriendly (ʌn'frɛndlɪ) *adj* **-lier, -liest. 1** not friendly; hostile. **2** unfavourable or disagreeable. ◆ *adv* **3** *Rare.* in an unfriendly manner. ▸ **un'friendliness** *n*

unfrock (ʌn'frɒk) *vb (tr)* to deprive (a person in holy orders) of ecclesiastical status.

unfruitful (ʌn'fruːtfʊl) *adj* **1** barren, unproductive, or unprofitable. **2** failing to produce or develop into fruit. ▸ **un'fruitfully** *adv* ▸ **un'fruitfulness** *n*

unfunded debt (ʌn'fʌndɪd) *n* a short-term floating debt not represented by bonds.

unfurl (ʌn'fɜːl) *vb* to unroll, unfold, or spread out or be unrolled, unfolded, or spread out from a furled state.

ungainly (ʌn'geɪnlɪ) *adj* **-lier, -liest. 1** lacking grace when moving. **2** difficult to move or use; unwieldy. **3** *Rare.* crude or coarse. ◆ *adv* **4** *Rare.* clumsily. [C17: from UN-[1] + obsolete or dialect GAINLY graceful] ▸ **un'gainliness** *n*

Ungaretti (*Italian* unga'retti) *n* **Giuseppe** (dʒu'zeppe). 1888–1970, Italian poet, best known for his collection of war poems *Allegria di naufragi* (1919).

Ungava (ʌŋ'geɪvə, -'gɑː-) *n* a sparsely inhabited region of NE Canada, in N Quebec east of Hudson Bay: part of the Labrador peninsula: rich mineral resources. Area: 911 110 sq. km (351 780 sq. miles).

ungodly (ʌn'gɒdlɪ) *adj* **-lier, -liest. 1a** wicked; sinful. **1b** (*as collective n;* preceded by *the*)*: the ungodly.* **2** *Informal.* unseemly; outrageous (esp. in the phrase **an ungodly hour**). ▸ **un'godliness** *n*

ungotten (ʌn'gɒtən) *adj Archaic.* not obtained or won.

ungovernable (ʌn'gʌvənəbəl) *adj* not able to be disciplined, restrained, etc.: *an ungovernable temper.* ▸ **un'governableness** *n* ▸ **un'governably** *adv*

ungrateful (ʌn'greɪtfʊl) *adj* **1** not grateful or thankful. **2** unrewarding or unpleasant; thankless. **3** (of land) failing to increase fertility in response to cultivation. ▸ **un'gratefully** *adv* ▸ **un'gratefulness** *n*

ungrudging (ʌn'grʌdʒɪŋ) *adj* liberal; unstinted; willing: *ungrudging support.* ▸ **un'grudgingly** *adv*

ungual ('ʌŋgwəl) *or* **ungular** ('ʌŋgjʊlə) *adj* **1** of, relating to, or affecting the fingernails or toenails. **2** of or relating to an unguis. [C19: from Latin *unguis* nail, claw]

unguarded (ʌn'gɑːdɪd) *adj* **1** unprotected; vulnerable. **2** guileless; open; frank. **3** incautious or careless. ▸ **un'guardedly** *adv* ▸ **un'guardedness** *n*

unguent ('ʌŋgwənt) *n* a less common name for an **ointment.** [C15: from Latin *unguentum,* from *unguere* to anoint] ▸ **'unguentary** *adj*

unguiculate (ʌŋ'gwɪkjʊlɪt, -ˌleɪt) *adj* **1** (of mammals) having claws or nails. **2** (of petals) having a clawlike base. ◆ *n* **3** an unguiculate mammal. [C19: from New Latin *unguiculātus,* from Latin *unguiculus,* diminutive of *unguis* nail, claw]

unguinous ('ʌŋgwɪnəs) *adj Obsolete.* fatty; greasy; oily. [C17: from Latin *unguinōsus* oily, from *unguin-, unguen* a fatty substance, from *unguere* to anoint, besmear]

unguis ('ʌŋgwɪs) *n, pl* **-gues** (-gwiːz). **1** a nail, claw, or hoof, or the part of the digit giving rise to it. **2** the clawlike base of certain petals. [C18: from Latin]

ungula ('ʌŋgjʊlə) *n, pl* **-lae** (-ˌliː). **1** *Maths.* a truncated cone, cylinder, etc. **2** a rare word for **hoof.** [C18: from Latin: hoof, from *unguis* nail] ▸ **'ungular** *adj*

ungulate ('ʌŋgjʊlɪt, -ˌleɪt) *n* any of a large group of mammals all of which have hooves: divided into odd-toed ungulates (see **perissodactyl**) and even-toed ungulates (see **artiodactyl**). [C19: from Late Latin *ungulātus* having hooves, from UNGULA]

unguligrade ('ʌŋgjʊlɪˌgreɪd) *adj* (of horses, etc.) walking on hooves. [C19: from Latin *ungula* hoof + -GRADE]

unhair (ʌn'hɛə) *vb* to remove the hair from (a hide).

unhallow (ʌn'hæləʊ) *vb (tr) Archaic.* to desecrate.

unhallowed (ʌn'hæləʊd) *adj* **1** not consecrated or holy: *unhallowed ground.* **2** sinful or profane.

unhand (ʌn'hænd) *vb (tr) Archaic or literary.* to release from the grasp.

unhandy (ʌn'hændɪ) *adj* **1** not skilful with one's hands; clumsy; awkward. **2** inconvenient.

unhappy (ʌn'hæpɪ) *adj* **-pier, -piest. 1** not joyful; sad or depressed. **2** unfortunate or wretched: *an unhappy fellow.* **3** tactless or inappropriate: *an unhappy remark.* **4** *Archaic.* unfavourable. ▸ **un'happily** *adv* ▸ **un'happiness** *n*

unharness (ʌn'hɑːnɪs) *vb (tr)* **1** to remove the harness from (a horse, etc.). **2** *Archaic.* to remove the armour from.

UNHCR *abbrev. for* United Nations High Commissioner for Refugees.

unhealthy (ʌn'hɛlθɪ) *adj* **-healthier, -healthiest. 1** characterized by ill-health; sick; unwell. **2** characteristic of, conducive to, or resulting from ill-health: *an unhealthy complexion; an unhealthy atmosphere.* **3** morbid or unwholesome. **4** *Informal.* dangerous; risky. ▸ **un'healthily** *adv* ▸ **un'healthiness** *n*

unheard (ʌn'hɜːd) *adj* **1** not heard; not perceived by the ear. **2** not listened to or granted a hearing: *his warning went unheard.* **3** *Archaic.* unheard-of.

unheard-of *adj* **1** previously unknown: *an unheard-of actress.* **2** without precedent: *an unheard-of treatment.* **3** highly offensive: *unheard-of behaviour.*

unhelm (ʌn'hɛlm) *vb* to remove the helmet of (oneself or another). [C15: from UN-[2] + HELM[2]]

unhesitating (ʌn'hɛzɪˌteɪtɪŋ) *adj* **1** steadfast; unwavering: *unhesitating loyalty.* **2** without hesitation; prompt. ▸ **un'hesi,tatingly** *adv*

unhinge (ʌn'hɪndʒ) *vb (tr)* **1** to remove (a door, gate, etc.) from its hinges. **2** to derange or unbalance (a person, his mind, etc.). **3** to disrupt or unsettle (a process or state of affairs). **4** (usually foll. by *from*) to detach or dislodge.

unholy (ʌn'həʊlɪ) *adj* **-lier, -liest. 1** not holy or sacred. **2** immoral or depraved. **3** *Informal.* outrageous or unnatural: *an unholy alliance.* ▸ **un'holiness** *n*

unhook (ʌn'hʊk) *vb* **1** (*tr*) to remove (something) from a hook. **2** (*tr*) to unfasten the hook of (a dress, etc.). **3** (*intr*) to become unfastened or be capable of unfastening: *the dress wouldn't unhook.*

unhoped-for (ˌʌn'həʊptfɔː) *adj* (esp. of something pleasant) not anticipated; unexpected.

unhorse (ʌn'hɔːs) *vb (tr)* **1** (*usually passive*) to knock or throw from a horse. **2** to overthrow or dislodge, as from a powerful position. **3** *Now rare.* to unharness horses from (a carriage, etc.).

unhouseled (ʌn'haʊzəld) *adj Archaic.* not having received the Eucharist. [C16: from *un-* + obsolete *housel* to administer the sacrament, from Old English *hūsl* (n), *hūslian* (vb), of unknown origin]

unhurried (ʌn'hʌrɪd) *adj* leisurely or deliberate: *an unhurried walk.* ▸ **un'hurriedly** *adv*

uni ('juːnɪ) *n Informal.* short for **university.**

uni- *combining form.* consisting of, relating to, or having only one: *unilateral; unisexual.* [from Latin *ūnus* one]

un'feigned *adj*
un'feminine *adj*
,unfer'mented *adj*
un'ferti,lized *or* **un'ferti,lised** *adj*
un'filled *adj*
un'filtered *adj*
un'fired *adj*
un'flagging *adj*
un'flattering *adj*
un'flavoured *adj*
un'forced *adj*
,unfore'seeable *adj*
,unfore'seen *adj*
,unfor'givable *adj*
,unfor'given *adj*
,unfor'gotten *adj*
un'formu,lated *adj*
,unforth'coming *adj*
un'forti,fied *adj*
un'found *adj*
un'framed *adj*
,unfre'quented *adj*
,unful'filled *adj*
un'funny *adj*
un'furnished *adj*
un'fussy *adj*
un'gallant *adj*
un'generous *adj*
un'gentlemanly *adj*
un'glazed *adj*
un'graceful *adj*
un'gracious *adj*
,ungram'matical *adj*
un'guided *adj*
un'hampered *adj*
un'harmed *adj*
,unhar'monious *adj*
un'hatched *adj*
un'healed *adj*
un'heated *adj*
un'heeded *adj*
un'heeding *adj*
un'helpful *adj*
un'heralded *adj*
,unhe'roic *adj*
un'hindered *adj*
un'human *adj*
un'hurt *adj*
,unhy'gienic *adj*
un'hyphen,ated *adj*

Uniat ('juːnɪˌæt) *or* **Uniate** ('juːnɪɪt, -ˌeɪt) *adj* **1** designating any of the Eastern Churches that retain their own liturgy but submit to papal authority. ◆ *n* **2** a member of one of these Churches. [**C19**: from Russian *uniyat*, from Polish *unja* union, from Late Latin *ūniō*; see UNION] ▸ **'Uniˌatism** *n*

uniaxial (ˌjuːnɪ'æksɪəl) *adj* **1** (esp. of plants) having an unbranched main axis. **2** (of a crystal) having only one direction along which double refraction of light does not occur. ▸ **ˌuni'axially** *adv*

unicameral (ˌjuːnɪ'kæmərəl) *adj* of or characterized by a single legislative chamber. ▸ **ˌuni'cameralism** *n* ▸ **ˌuni'cameralist** *n* ▸ **ˌuni'camerally** *adv*

UNICEF ('juːnɪˌsɛf) *n acronym for* United Nations Children's Fund (formerly, United Nations International Children's Emergency Fund): an agency of the United Nations that administers programmes to aid education and child and maternal health in developing countries.

unicellular (ˌjuːnɪ'sɛljʊlə) *adj* (of organisms, such as protozoans and certain algae) consisting of a single cell. ▸ **ˌuniˌcellu'larity** *n*

unicolour *or U.S.* **unicolor** (ˌjuːnɪ'kʌlə) *adj* of one colour; monochromatic.

unicorn ('juːnɪˌkɔːn) *n* **1** an imaginary creature usually depicted as a white horse with one long spiralled horn growing from its forehead. **2** *Old Testament.* a two-horned animal, thought to be either the rhinoceros or the aurochs: (Deuteronomy 33:17): mistranslation in the Authorized Version of the original Hebrew. [**C13**: from Old French *unicorne*, from Latin *ūnicornis* one-horned, from *ūnus* one + *cornu* a horn]

unicostate (ˌjuːnɪ'kɒsteɪt) *adj Biology.* having only one rib or riblike part: *unicostate leaves.*

unicycle ('juːnɪˌsaɪkᵊl) *n* a one-wheeled vehicle driven by pedals, esp. one used in a circus, etc. Also called: **monocycle.** [from UNI- + CYCLE, on the model of TRICYCLE] ▸ **'uniˌcyclist** *n*

unidirectional (ˌjuːnɪdɪ'rɛkʃənᵊl, -daɪ-) *adj* having, moving in, or operating in only one direction.

UNIDO (juː'niːdəʊ) *n acronym for* United Nations Industrial Development Organization.

unific (juː'nɪfɪk) *adj Rare.* unifying; uniting.

unification (ˌjuːnɪfɪ'keɪʃən) *n* **1** an act, instance, or process of uniting. **2** the state of being united.

Unification Church *n* a religious sect founded in 1954 by Sun Myung Moon (born 1920), S Korean industrialist and religious leader. See also **Moonie.**

unified atomic mass unit *n* another name for **atomic mass unit.**

unified field theory *n* any theory capable of describing in one set of equations the properties of gravitational fields, electromagnetic fields, and strong and weak nuclear interactions. No satisfactory theory has yet been found.

unified screw thread *n* a screw thread system introduced for defence equipment (1939–44), in which the thread form and pitch were a compromise between British Standard Whitworth and American Standard Sellers: adopted by the International Standards Organization.

unifilar (ˌjuːnɪ'faɪlə) *adj Rare.* composed of, having, or using only one wire, thread, filament, etc. [from UNI- + Latin *fīlum* thread; see FILAMENT, FILAR]

unifoliate (ˌjuːnɪ'fəʊlɪɪt, -ˌeɪt) *adj* having a single leaf or leaflike part.

unifoliolate (ˌjuːnɪ'fəʊlɪəˌleɪt) *adj* (of a compound leaf) having only one leaflet.

uniform ('juːnɪˌfɔːm) *n* **1** a prescribed identifying set of clothes for the members of an organization, such as soldiers or schoolchildren. **2** a single set of such clothes. **3** a characteristic feature or fashion of some class or group. ◆ *adj* **4** unchanging in form, quality, quantity, etc.; regular: *a uniform surface.* **5** identical; alike or like: *a line of uniform toys.* ◆ *vb (tr)* **6** to fit out (a body of soldiers, etc.) with uniforms. **7** to make uniform. [**C16**: from Latin *ūniformis*, from *ūnus* one + *forma* shape] ▸ **'uniˌformly** *adv* ▸ **'uniˌformness** *n*

Uniform ('juːnɪˌfɔːm) *n Communications.* a code word for the letter *u.*

Uniform Business Rate *n* a local tax in the UK paid by businesses, based on a local valuation of their premises and a rate fixed by central government that applies throughout the country. Abbrev.: **UBR.**

uniformitarian (ˌjuːnɪˌfɔːmɪ'tɛərɪən) *adj* **1** of or relating to uniformitarianism. **2** of, characterized by, or conforming to uniformity. ◆ *n* **3** a supporter of a theory of uniformity or of uniformitarianism.

uniformitarianism (ˌjuːnɪˌfɔːmɪ'tɛərɪəˌnɪzəm) *n* the concept that the earth's surface was shaped in the past by gradual processes, such as erosion, and by small sudden changes, such as earthquakes, of the type acting today rather than by the sudden divine acts, such as Noah's flood, demanded by the doctrine of catastrophism.

uniformity (ˌjuːnɪ'fɔːmɪtɪ) *n, pl* **-ties.** **1** a state or condition in which everything is regular, homogeneous, or unvarying. **2** lack of diversity or variation, esp. to the point of boredom or monotony; sameness.

unify ('juːnɪˌfaɪ) *vb* **-fies, -fying, -fied.** to make or become one; unite. [**C16**: from Medieval Latin *ūnificāre*, from Latin *ūnus* one + *facere* to make] ▸ **'uniˌfiable** *adj* ▸ **'uniˌfier** *n*

unijugate (ˌjuːnɪ'dʒuːgɪt, -ˌgeɪt) *adj* (of a compound leaf) having only one pair of leaflets.

unilateral (ˌjuːnɪ'lætərəl) *adj* **1** of, having, affecting, or occurring on only one side. **2** involving or performed by only one party of several: *unilateral disarmament.* **3** *Law.* (of contracts, obligations, etc.) made by, affecting, or binding one party only and not involving the other party in reciprocal obligations. **4** *Botany.* having or designating parts situated or turned to one side of an axis. **5** *Sociol.* relating to or tracing the line of descent through ancestors of one sex only. Compare **bilateral** (sense 5). **6** *Phonetics.* denoting an (l) sound produced on one side of the tongue only. ▸ **ˌuni'lateralism** *or* **ˌuniˌlater'ality** *n* ▸ **ˌuni'laterally** *adv*

Unilateral Declaration of Independence *n* a declaration of independence made by a dependent state without the assent of the protecting state. Abbrev.: **UDI.**

unilateral neglect *n* a symptom of brain damage in which a person is unaware of one side of his body and of anything in the external world on the same side.

unilingual (ˌjuːnɪ'lɪŋgwəl) *adj* of or having only one language.

uniliteral (ˌjuːnɪ'lɪtərəl) *adj* consisting of one letter.

unilocular (ˌjuːnɪ'lɒkjʊlə) *adj* (esp. of a plant ovary or anther) having or consisting of a single chamber or cavity.

Unimak Island ('juːnɪˌmæk) *n* an island in SW Alaska, in the Aleutian Islands. Length: 113 km (70 miles).

unimpeachable (ˌʌnɪm'piːtʃəbᵊl) *adj* unquestionable as to honesty, truth, etc. ▸ **ˌunimˌpeacha'bility** *or* **ˌunim'peachableness** *n* ▸ **ˌunim'peachably** *adv*

unimproved (ˌʌnɪm'pruːvd) *adj* **1** not improved or made better. **2** (of land) not cleared, drained, cultivated, etc. **3** neglected; unused: *unimproved resources.*

unimproved value *n N.Z.* the valuation of land for rating purposes, disregarding the value of buildings or other development.

unincorporated (ˌʌnɪn'kɔːpəˌreɪtɪd) *adj* **1** *Law.* lacking corporate status. **2** not unified or included.

unincorporated business *n* a privately owned business, often owned by one person who has unlimited liability as the business is not legally registered as a company.

uninspired (ˌʌnɪn'spaɪəd) *adj* dull or ordinary; unimaginative: *an uninspired painting.*

unintelligent (ˌʌnɪn'tɛlɪdʒənt) *adj* **1** lacking intelligence; stupid; foolish. **2** not endowed with a mind or intelligence. ▸ **ˌunin'telligence** *n* ▸ **ˌunin'telligently** *adv*

uninterested (ʌn'ɪntrɪstɪd, -tərɪs-) *adj* indifferent; unconcerned. ▸ **un'interestedly** *adv* ▸ **un'interestedness** *n*

USAGE See at **disinterested.**

union ('juːnjən) *n* **1** the condition of being united, the act of uniting, or a conjunction formed by such an act. **2** an association, alliance, or confederation of individuals or groups for a common purpose, esp. political. **3** agreement or harmony. **4** short for **trade union.** **5** the act or state of marriage or sexual intercourse. **6** a device on a flag representing union, such as another flag depicted in the top left corner. **7** a device for coupling or linking parts, such as pipes. **8** *(often cap.)* **8a** an association of students at a university or college formed to look after the students' interests, provide facilities for recreation, etc. **8b** the building or buildings housing the facilities of such an organization. **9** Also called: **join.** *Maths.* a set containing all members of two given sets. Symbol: ∪, as in $A \cup B$. **10** (in 19th-century England) **10a** a number of parishes united for the administration of poor relief. **10b** a workhouse supported by such a combination. **11** *Textiles.* a piece of cloth or fabric consisting of two different kinds of yarn. **12** *(modifier)* of or related to a union, esp. a trade union. [**C15**: from Church Latin *ūniō* oneness, from Latin *ūnus* one]

Union ('juːnjən) *n* **the.** **1** *Brit.* **1a** the union of England and Wales from 1543. **1b** the union of the English and Scottish crowns (1603–1707). **1c** the union of England and Scotland from 1707. **1d** the political union of Great Britain and Ireland (1801–1920). **1e** the union of Great Britain and Northern Ireland from 1920. **2** *U.S.* **2a** the United States of America. **2b** the northern states of the U.S. during the Civil War. **2c** *(as modifier): Union supporters.* **3** short for the **Union of South Africa.**

union card *n* a membership card for a trade union.

union catalogue *n* a catalogue listing every publication held at cooperating libraries.

Union flag *n* the national flag of the United Kingdom, being a composite design composed of St George's Cross (England), Saint Andrew's Cross (Scotland), and Saint Patrick's Cross (Ireland). Often called: **Union Jack.**

unionism ('juːnjəˌnɪzəm) *n* **1** the principles of trade unions. **2** adherence to the principles of trade unions. **3** the principle or theory of any union.

Unionism ('juːnjəˌnɪzəm) *n (sometimes not cap.)* the principles or adherence to the principles of Unionists.

ˌuni'dentiˌfiable *adj*
ˌuni'dentiˌfied *adj*
ˌunim'aginable *adj*
ˌunim'aginably *adv*
ˌunim'aginative *adj*
ˌunim'aginatively *adv*
ˌunim'agined *adj*
ˌunim'paired *adj*
ˌunim'peded *adj*
ˌunim'portant *adj*
ˌunim'posing *adj*
ˌunim'pressed *adj*
ˌunim'pressive *adj*
ˌunin'fected *adj*
ˌunin'flected *adj*
un'influenced *adj*
ˌunin'formative *adj*
ˌunin'formed *adj*
ˌunin'habitable *adj*
ˌunin'habited *adj*
ˌunin'hibited *adj*
'unin'itiˌated *adj*
un'injured *adj*
ˌunin'spiring *adj*
ˌunin'surable *adj*
ˌunin'sured *adj*
ˌunintel'lectual *adj*
ˌunin'telligible *adj*
ˌunin'tended *adj*
ˌunin'tentional *adj*
ˌunin'tentionally *adv*
un'interesting *adj*
ˌuninter'rupted *adj*
ˌunin'ventive *adj*
ˌunin'vestiˌgated *adj*
ˌunin'vited *adj*
ˌunin'viting *adj*
ˌunin'volved *adj*

unionist (ˈjuːnjənɪst) *n* **1** a supporter or advocate of unionism or union. **2** a member of a trade union. ◆ *adj* **3** *Chiefly Brit.* of or relating to union or unionism, esp. trade unionism. ▸ ˌ**unionˈistic** *adj*

Unionist (ˈjuːnjənɪst) *n* **1** (*sometimes not cap.*) **1a** (before 1920) a supporter of the union of all Ireland and Great Britain. **1b** (since 1920) a supporter of union between Britain and Northern Ireland. ◆ *adj* **2** a supporter of the U.S. federal Union, esp. during the Civil War. **3** of, resembling, or relating to Unionists.

Unionist Party *n* (formerly, in Northern Ireland) the major Protestant political party, closely identified with union with Britain. It formed the Northern Ireland Government from 1920 to 1972. See also: **Ulster Democratic Unionist Party, Ulster Unionist Council.**

unionize *or* **unionise** (ˈjuːnjəˌnaɪz) *vb* **1** to organize (workers) into a trade union. **2** to join or cause to join a trade union. **3** (*tr*) to subject to the rules or codes of a trade union. ▸ ˌ**unioniˈzation** *or* ˌ**unioniˈsation** *n*

Union Jack *n* **1** a common name for **Union flag. 2** (*often not caps.*) a national flag flown at the jackstaff of a vessel.

Union of South Africa *n* the former name (1910–61) of the (Republic of) **South Africa.**

Union of Soviet Socialist Republics *n* the official name of the former **Soviet Union.**

union pipes *pl n* another name for **uillean pipes.**

union shop *n* (formerly) an establishment whose employment policy is governed by a contract between employer and a trade union permitting the employment of nonunion labour only on the condition that such labour joins the union within a specified time period. Compare **open shop, closed shop.**

union territory *n* one of the 9 administrative territories that, with 21 states, make up the Indian Republic.

uniparous (juːˈnɪpərəs) *adj* **1** (of certain animals) producing a single offspring at each birth. **2** (of a woman) having borne only one child. **3** *Botany.* (of a cyme) giving rise to only one branch from each flowering stem.

unipersonal (ˌjuːnɪˈpɜːsənᵊl) *adj* **1** existing in the form of only one person or being. Compare **tripersonal. 2** (of a verb) existing or used in only one person; for example, *rain* is used only in the third person. ▸ ˌ**uniˌpersonˈality** *n*

uniplanar (ˌjuːnɪˈpleɪnə) *adj* situated in one plane.

unipod (ˈjuːnɪˌpɒd) *n* a one-legged support, as for a camera.

unipolar (ˌjuːnɪˈpəʊlə) *adj* **1** of, concerned with, or having a single magnetic or electric pole. **2** (of a nerve cell) having a single process. **3** (of a transistor) utilizing charge carriers of one polarity only, as in a field-effect transistor. ◆ Compare **bipolar.** ▸ **unipolarity** (ˌjuːnɪpəʊˈlærɪtɪ) *n*

unique (juːˈniːk) *adj* **1** being the only one of a particular type; single; sole. **2** without equal or like; unparalleled. **3** *Informal.* very remarkable or unusual. **4** *Maths.* **4a** leading to only one result: *the sum of two integers is unique.* **4b** having precisely one value: *the unique positive square root of 4 is 2.* **[C17:** via French from Latin *ūnicus* unparalleled, from *ūnus* one**]** ▸ **uˈniquely** *adv* ▸ **uˈniqueness** *n*

USAGE *Unique* is normally taken to describe an absolute state, i.e. one that cannot be qualified; thus something is either *unique* or *not unique;* it cannot be *rather unique* or *very unique.* However *unique* is sometimes used informally to mean very remarkable or unusual and this makes it possible to use comparatives or intensifiers with it, although many people object to this use.

uniramous (ˌjuːnɪˈreɪməs) *adj* (esp. of the appendages of crustaceans) consisting of a single branch; undivided. Also: **uniramose** (ˌjuːnɪˈreɪməʊs, -ræˈməʊs)

uniseptate (ˌjuːnɪˈsɛpteɪt) *adj Biology.* having only one partition or septum: *a uniseptate fruit.*

uniserial (ˌjuːnɪˈsɪərɪəl) *adj* in or relating to a single series.

uniseriate (ˌjuːnɪˈsɪərɪˌeɪt) *adj Botany.* (of parts, cells, etc.) arranged in a single row, layer, or series.

unisex (ˈjuːnɪˌsɛks) *adj* of or relating to clothing, a hairstyle, etc., that can be worn by either sex. **[C20:** from UNI- + SEX**]**

unisexual (ˌjuːnɪˈsɛksjʊəl) *adj* **1** of or relating to one sex only. **2** (of some organisms) having either male or female reproductive organs but not both. ▸ ˌ**uniˌsexuˈality** *n* ▸ ˌ**uniˈsexually** *adv*

unison (ˈjuːnɪsᵊn, -zᵊn) *n* **1** *Music.* **1a** the interval between two sounds of identical pitch. **1b** (*modifier*) played or sung at the same pitch: *unison singing.* **2** complete agreement; harmony (esp. in the phrase **in unison**). **[C16:** from Late Latin *ūnisonus,* from UNI- + *sonus* sound**]** ▸ **uˈnisonous, uˈnisonal,** *or* **uˈnisonant** *adj*

UNISON (ˈjuːnɪsᵊn) *n* (in Britain) a trade union representing local government, health care, and other workers: formed in 1993 by the amalgamation of COHSE, NALGO, and NUPE.

unit (ˈjuːnɪt) *n* **1** a single undivided entity or whole. **2** any group or individual, esp. when regarded as a basic element of a larger whole. **3** a mechanical part or integrated assembly of parts that performs a subsidiary function: *a filter unit.* **4** a complete system, apparatus, or establishment that performs a specific function: *a production unit.* **5** a subdivision of a larger military formation. **6** Also called: **unit of measurement.** a standard amount of a physical quantity, such as length, mass, energy, etc., specified multiples of which are used to express magnitudes of that physical quantity: *the second is a unit of time.* **7** the amount of a drug, vaccine, etc., needed to produce a particular effect. **8** a standard measure used in calculating alcohol intake and its effect. **9** *Maths.* **9a** (*usually pl*) the first position in a place-value counting system, representing a single-digit number: *in the decimal system the number 27 has 7 units and 2 tens.* **9b** (*modifier*) having a value defined as one for the system: *unit vector.* **10** Also called: **unit set.** *Maths, logic.* a set having a single member. **11** short for **home unit. 12** short for **stock unit. 13** *N.Z.* a self-propelled railcar. **[C16:** back formation from UNITY, perhaps on the model of *digit***]**

Unit. *abbrev. for* Unitarian.

UNITA (juːˈniːtə) *n acronym for* União Nacional para a Independencia Total de Angola. **[**Portuguese: National Union for the Total Independence of Angola**]**

unitarian (ˌjuːnɪˈtɛərɪən) *n* **1** a supporter of unity or centralization. ◆ *adj* **2** of or relating to unity or centralization. **3** another word for **unitary.**

Unitarian (ˌjuːnɪˈtɛərɪən) *n* **1** *Theol.* a person who believes that God is one being and rejects the doctrine of the Trinity. **2** *Ecclesiast.* an upholder of Unitarianism, esp. a member of the Church (**Unitarian Church**) that embodies this system of belief. ◆ *adj* **3** of or relating to Unitarians or Unitarianism.

unitarianism (ˌjuːnɪˈtɛərɪəˌnɪzəm) *n* any unitary system, esp. of government.

Unitarianism (ˌjuːnɪˈtɛərɪəˌnɪzəm) *n* a system of Christian belief that maintains the unipersonality of God, rejects the Trinity and the divinity of Christ, and takes reason, conscience, and character as the criteria of belief and practice.

unitary (ˈjuːnɪtərɪ, -trɪ) *adj* **1** of a unit or units. **2** based on or characterized by unity. **3** individual; whole. **4** of or relating to a system of government in which all governing authority is held by the central government. Compare **federal.**

unitary authority *n* (in the UK) a district administered by a single tier of local government, esp. those districts of England that became administratively independent of the county councils in 1996–98.

unitary matrix *n Maths.* a square matrix that is the inverse of its Hermitian conjugate.

unit cell *n Crystallog.* the smallest group of atoms, ions, or molecules that is characteristic of a particular crystal lattice.

unit character *n Genetics.* a character inherited as a single unit and dependent on a single gene.

unit cost *n* the actual cost of producing one article.

unite[1] (juːˈnaɪt) *vb* **1** to make or become an integrated whole or a unity; combine. **2** to join, unify or be unified in purpose, action, beliefs, etc. **3** to enter or cause to enter into an association or alliance. **4** to adhere or cause to adhere; fuse. **5** (*tr*) to possess or display (qualities) in combination or at the same time: *he united charm with severity.* **6** *Archaic.* to join or become joined in marriage. **[C15:** from Late Latin *ūnīre,* from *ūnus* one**]** ▸ **uˈniter** *n*

unite[2] (ˈjuːnaɪt, juːˈnaɪt) *n* an English gold coin minted in the Stuart period, originally worth 20 shillings. **[C17:** from obsolete *unite* joined, alluding to the union of England and Scotland (1603)**]**

united (juːˈnaɪtɪd) *adj* **1** produced by two or more persons or things in combination or from their union or amalgamation: *a united effort.* **2** in agreement. **3** in association or alliance. ▸ **uˈnitedly** *adv* ▸ **uˈnitedness** *n*

United Arab Emirates *pl n* a group of seven emirates in SW Asia, on the Persian Gulf: consists of Abu Dhabi, Dubai, Sharjah, Ajman, Umm al Qaiwain, Ras el Khaimah, and Fujairah; a former British protectorate; became fully independent in 1971; consists mostly of flat desert, with mountains in the east; rich petroleum resources. Official language: Arabic. Official religion: Muslim. Currency: dirham. Capital: Abu Dhabi. Pop.: 2 744 000 (1998 est.). Area: 83 600 sq. km (32 300 sq. miles). Former name (until 1971): **Trucial States.** Abbrev.: **UAE.**

United Arab Republic *n* the official name (1958–71) of **Egypt.**

United Arab States *pl n* a federation (1958–61) between the United Arab Republic and Yemen.

United Church of Christ *n* a U.S. Protestant denomination formed in 1957 from the Evangelical and Reformed Church and the Congregational Christian Church.

United Empire Loyalist *n Canadian history.* any of the American colonists who settled in Canada during or after the War of American Independence because of loyalty to the British Crown.

United Kingdom *n* a kingdom of NW Europe, consisting chiefly of the island of Great Britain together with Northern Ireland: became the world's leading colonial power in the 18th century: the first country to undergo the Industrial Revolution. It became the **United Kingdom of Great Britain and Northern Ireland** in 1921, after the rest of Ireland became autonomous as the Irish Free State. Primarily it is a trading nation, the chief exports being manufactured goods; joined the Common Market (now the European Union) in January 1973. Official language: English; Gaelic, Welsh, and other minority languages. Religion: Christian majority. Currency: pound sterling. Capital: London. Pop.: 59 126 000 (1998 est.). Area: 244 110 sq. km (94 251 sq. miles). Abbrev.: **UK.** See also **Great Britain.**

United Kingdom Overseas Territory *n* See **UK Overseas Territory.**

United Kingdom Unionists *n* (in Britain) a political party, based in Northern Ireland: non-sectarian but opposed to a united Ireland.

United Nations *n* (*functioning as sing or pl*) **1** an international organization of independent states, with its headquarters in New York City, that was formed in 1945 to promote peace and international cooperation and security. Abbrev.: **UN. 2** (in World War II) a coalition of 26 nations that signed a joint declaration in Jan. 1942, pledging their full resources to defeating the Axis powers.

United Party *n* (formerly, in South Africa) the major opposition party, founded by General Smuts in 1934: the official Opposition in Parliament from 1948, the party was disbanded in 1977. See also **National Party, Progressive Federal Party.**

United Provinces *pl n* **1** a Dutch republic (1581–1795) formed by the union of the seven northern provinces of the Netherlands, which were in revolt against their suzerain, Philip II of Spain. **2** short for **United Provinces of Agra and Oudh:** the former name of **Uttar Pradesh.**

unˈironed *adj*

United Reformed Church *n* (in England and Wales) a Protestant denomination formed from the union of the Presbyterian and Congregational churches in 1972.

United States of America *n* (*functioning as sing or pl*) a federal republic mainly in North America consisting of 50 states and the District of Columbia: colonized principally by the English and French in the 17th century, the native Indians being gradually defeated and displaced; 13 colonies under British rule made the Declaration of Independence in 1776 and became the United States after the War of American Independence. The northern states defeated the South in the Civil War (1861–65). It is the world's most productive industrial nation and also exports agricultural products. It participated reluctantly in World Wars I and II but since the establishment of the United Nations in 1945 has played a major role in international affairs. It consists generally of the Rocky Mountains in the west, the Great Plains in the centre, the Appalachians in the east, deserts in the southwest, and coastal lowlands and swamps in the southeast. Language: predominantly English; Spanish is also widely spoken. Religion: Christian majority. Currency: dollar. Capital: Washington, D.C. Pop.: 270 262 000 (1998 est.). Area: 9 518 323 sq. km (3 675 031 sq. miles). Often shortened to: **United States.** Abbrevs.: **U.S., U.S.A.**

unit factor *n Genetics.* the gene responsible for the inheritance of a unit character.

unitive (ˈjuːnɪtɪv) *adj* **1** tending to unite or capable of uniting. **2** characterized by unity. ▸ **ˈunitively** *adv*

unitize *or* **unitise** (ˈjuːnɪˌtaɪz) *vb* (*tr*) *Finance.* to convert (an investment trust) into a unit trust. ▸ **ˌunitiˈzation** *or* **ˌunitiˈsation** *n*

unit-linked policy *n* a life-assurance policy the investment benefits of which are directly in proportion to the number of units in a unit trust purchased on the policyholder's behalf. Compare **traditional policy.**

unit magnetic pole *n* the strength of a magnetic pole that will repel a similar pole 1 centimetre distant from it, in a vacuum, with a force of 1 dyne.

unit of account *n* **1** *Economics.* the function of money that enables the user to keep accounts, value transactions, etc. **2** a monetary denomination used for accounting purposes, etc., but not necessarily corresponding to any real currency: *the ECU is the unit of account of the European Monetary Fund.* Also called (esp. U.S. and Canada): **money of account. 3** the unit of currency of a country.

unit price *n* a price for foodstuffs, etc., stated or shown as the cost per unit, as per pound, per kilogram, per dozen, etc.

unit pricing *n* a system of pricing foodstuffs, etc., in which the cost of a single unit is shown to enable shoppers to see the advantage of buying multipacks.

unit process *n Chemical engineering.* any of a number of standard operations, such as filtration or distillation, that are widely used in various chemical industries.

unit trust *n Brit.* an investment trust that issues units for public sale, the holders of which are creditors and not shareholders with their interests represented by a trust company independent of the issuing agency.

unity (ˈjuːnɪtɪ) *n, pl* **-ties. 1** the state or quality of being one; oneness. **2** the act, state, or quality of forming a whole from separate parts. **3** something whole or complete that is composed of separate parts. **4** mutual agreement; harmony or concord: *the participants were no longer in unity.* **5** uniformity or constancy: *unity of purpose.* **6** *Maths.* **6a** the number or numeral one. **6b** a quantity assuming the value of one: *the area of the triangle was regarded as unity.* **6c** the element of a set producing no change in a number following multiplication. **7** the arrangement of the elements in a work of art in accordance with a single overall design or purpose. **8** any one of the three principles of dramatic structure deriving from Aristotle's *Poetics* by which the action of a play should be limited to a single plot (unity of action), a single location (unity of place), and the events of a single day (unity of time). **[**C13: from Old French *unité,* from Latin *ūnitās,* from *ūnus* one**]**

unity of interest *n Property law.* the equal interest in property held by joint tenants.

unity ticket *n Austral.* a how-to-vote card in a union election associating Labor and Communist candidates.

univ. *abbrev. for:* **1** universal(ly). **2** university.

Univ. *abbrev. for:* **1** Universalist. **2** University.

univalent (ˌjuːnɪˈveɪlənt, juːˈnɪvələnt) *adj* **1** (of a chromosome during meiosis) not paired with its homologue. **2** *Chem.* another word for **monovalent.** ▸ **ˌuniˈvalency** *n*

univalve (ˈjuːnɪˌvælv) *Zoology.* ◆ *adj* **1** relating to, designating, or possessing a mollusc shell that consists of a single piece (valve). ◆ *n* **2** a gastropod mollusc or its shell.

universal (ˌjuːnɪˈvɜːsᵊl) *adj* **1** of, relating to, or typical of the whole of mankind or of nature. **2** common to, involving, or proceeding from all in a particular group. **3** applicable to or affecting many individuals, conditions, or cases; general. **4** existing or prevailing everywhere. **5** applicable or occurring throughout or relating to the universe; cosmic: *a universal constant.* **6** (esp. of a language) capable of being used and understood by all. **7** embracing or versed in many fields of knowledge, activity, interest, etc. **8** *Machinery.* designed or adapted for a range of sizes, fittings, or uses. **9** *Linguistics.* (of a constraint in a formal grammar) common to the grammatical description of all human languages, actual or possible. **10** *Logic.* (of a statement or proposition) affirming or denying something about every member of a class, as in *all men are wicked.* Compare **particular** (sense 6). ◆ *n* **11** *Philosophy.* **11a** a general term or concept or the type such a term signifies. **11b** a metaphysical entity taken to be the reference of a general term, as distinct from the class of individuals it describes. **11c** a Platonic Idea or Aristotelian form. **12** *Logic.* **12a** a universal proposition, statement, or formula. **12b** a universal quantifier. **13** a characteristic common to every member of a particular culture or to every human being. **14** short for **universal joint.** ▸ **ˌuniˈversalness** *n*

USAGE The use of *more universal* as in *his writings have long been admired by fellow scientists, but his latest book should have more universal appeal* is acceptable in modern English usage.

universal beam *n* a broad-flanged rolled steel joist suitable for a stanchion (axial load) or beam (bending load).

universal class *or* **set** *n* (in Boolean algebra) the class containing all points and including all other classes.

universal donor *n* a person who has blood of group O and whose blood may be safely transfused to persons with most other blood types.

universal gas constant *n* another name for **gas constant.**

universal grammar *n Linguistics.* (in Chomskyan transformation linguistics) the abstract limitations on the formal grammatical description of all human languages, actual or possible, that make them human languages.

universalism (ˌjuːnɪˈvɜːsəˌlɪzəm) *n* **1** a universal feature or characteristic. **2** another word for **universality. 3** *Social welfare.* the principle that welfare services should be available to all by right, according to need, and not restricted by individual ability to pay, but funded by general contributions through taxes, rates, or national insurance payments.

Universalism (ˌjuːnɪˈvɜːsəˌlɪzəm) *n* a system of religious beliefs maintaining that all men are predestined for salvation. ▸ **ˌUniˈversalist** *n, adj*

universalist (ˌjuːnɪˈvɜːsəlɪst) *n* **1** a person who has a wide range of interests, knowledge, activities, etc. ◆ *adj* **2** characterized by universality. ▸ **ˌuniˌverˈsalˈistic** *adj*

universality (ˌjuːnɪvɜːˈsælɪtɪ) *n* the state or quality of being universal.

universalizability *or* **universalisability** (ˌjuːnɪˌvɜːsəlaɪzəˈbɪlɪtɪ) *n Ethics.* **1** the thesis that any moral judgment must be equally applicable to every relevantly identical situation. **2** the Kantian principle that if a course of action cannot be universally adopted it must be morally impermissible.

universalize *or* **universalise** (ˌjuːnɪˈvɜːsəˌlaɪz) *vb* (*tr*) to make universal. ▸ **ˌuniˌversaliˈzation** *or* **ˌuniˌversaliˈsation** *n*

universal joint *or* **coupling** *n* a form of coupling between two rotating shafts allowing freedom of movement in all directions.

universally (ˌjuːnɪˈvɜːsəlɪ) *adv* everywhere or in every case; without exception: *this principle applies universally.*

universal motor *n* an electric motor capable of working on either direct current or single-phase alternating current at approximately the same speed and output.

universal quantifier *n Logic.* a formal device indicating that the open sentence that follows is true of every member of the relevant universe of interpretation, as $(\forall x)(Fx \rightarrow Gx)$ or $(x)(Fx \rightarrow Gx)$, literally, for everything, if it is an F it is a G, that is, all Fs are Gs. Usual symbol: ∀

Universal Soul *or* **Spirit** *n Hinduism.* Brahman in its aspect as the sacred syllable Om, the eternal and spiritual principle that permeates the universe.

universal time *n* **1** (from 1928) name adopted internationally for Greenwich Mean Time (measured from Greenwich midnight), now split into several slightly different scales, one of which (UT1) is used by astronomers. Abbrev.: **UT. 2** Also called: **universal coordinated time.** an internationally agreed system for civil timekeeping introduced in 1960 and redefined in 1972 as an atomic timescale. Available from broadcast signals, it has a second equal to the International Atomic Time (TAI) second, the difference between UTC and TAI being an integral number of seconds with leap seconds inserted when necessary to keep it within 0.9 seconds of UT1. Abbrev.: **UTC.**

universe (ˈjuːnɪˌvɜːs) *n* **1** *Astronomy.* the aggregate of all existing matter, energy, and space. **2** human beings collectively. **3** a province or sphere of thought or activity. **4** *Statistics.* another word for **population** (sense 7). **[**C16: from French *univers,* from Latin *ūniversum* the whole world, from *ūniversus* all together, from UNI- + *vertere* to turn**]**

universe of discourse *n Logic.* the complete range of objects, events, attributes, relations, ideas, etc., that are expressed, assumed, or implied in a discussion.

university (ˌjuːnɪˈvɜːsɪtɪ) *n, pl* **-ties. 1** an institution of higher education having authority to award bachelors' and higher degrees, usually having research facilities. **2** the buildings, members, staff, or campus of a university. **[**C14: from Old French *universite,* from Medieval Latin *universitās* group of scholars, from Late Latin: guild, society, body of men, from Latin: whole, totality, universe**]**

university entrance *n* (in New Zealand) **a** an examination taken by pupils of postprimary schools. **b** the certificate issued to a successful candidate. ◆ Abbrev.: **UE.**

univocal (ˌjuːnɪˈvəʊkᵊl) *adj* **1** unambiguous or unmistakable. ◆ *n* **2** a word or term that has only one meaning. ▸ **ˌuniˈvocally** *adv*

UNIX (ˈjuːnɪks) *n Trademark.* a multi-user multitasking operating system found on many types of computer.

unjust (ʌnˈdʒʌst) *adj* not in accordance with accepted standards of fairness or justice; unfair. ▸ **unˈjustly** *adv* ▸ **unˈjustness** *n*

unkempt (ʌnˈkɛmpt) *adj* **1** (of the hair) uncombed; dishevelled. **2** ungroomed; slovenly: *unkempt appearance.* **3** *Archaic.* crude or coarse. **[**Old English *uncembed;* from UN-[1] + *cembed,* past participle of *cemban* to COMB; related to Old Saxon *kembian,* Old High German *kemben* to comb**]** ▸ **unˈkemptly** *adv* ▸ **unˈkemptness** *n*

unˈjointed *adj*	**unˈjustiˌfiable** *adj*	**unˈjustiˌfiably** *adv*	**unˈjustiˌfied** *adj*

unkenned (ʌn'kɛnd) *or* **unkent** (ʌn'kɛnt) *adj Scot. and northern English dialect.* unknown. [C14: from UN-[1] + KEN]

unkennel (ʌn'kɛn^{ə}l) *vb* **-nels, -nelling, -nelled** *or U.S.* **-nels, -neling, -neled.** (*tr*) **1** to release from a kennel. **2** to drive from a hole or lair. **3** *Rare.* to bring to light.

unkind (ʌn'kaɪnd) *adj* **1** lacking kindness; unsympathetic or cruel. **2** *Archaic or dialect.* **2a** (of weather) unpleasant. **2b** (of soil) hard to cultivate. ▸ **un'kindly** *adv* ▸ **un'kindness** *n*

unknit (ʌn'nɪt) *vb* **-knits, -knitting, -knitted** *or* **-knit. 1** to make or become undone, untied, or unravelled. **2** (*tr*) to loosen, weaken, or destroy: *to unknit an alliance.* **3** (*tr*) *Rare.* to smooth out (a wrinkled brow).

unknowable (ʌn'nəʊəb^{ə}l) *adj* **1** incapable of being known or understood. **2a** beyond human understanding. **2b** (*as n*): *the unknowable.* ▸ **un'knowableness** *or* **un,knowa'bility** *n* ▸ **un'knowably** *adv*

Unknowable (ʌn'nəʊəb^{ə}l) *n* **the.** *Philosophy.* the ultimate reality that underlies all phenomena but cannot be known.

unknowing (ʌn'nəʊɪŋ) *adj* **1** not knowing; ignorant. **2** (*postpositive;* often foll. by *of*) without knowledge or unaware (of). ▸ **un'knowingly** *adv*

unknown (ʌn'nəʊn) *adj* **1** not known, understood, or recognized. **2** not established, identified, or discovered: *an unknown island.* **3** not famous; undistinguished: *some unknown artist.* ◆ *n* **4** an unknown person, quantity, or thing. **5** *Maths.* a variable, or the quantity it represents, the value of which is to be discovered by solving an equation; a variable in a conditional equation: *3y = 4x + 5 is an equation in two unknowns.* **6 unknown quantity.** a person or thing whose action, effect, etc., is unknown or unpredictable. ▸ **un'knownness** *n*

Unknown Soldier *or* **Warrior** *n* (in various countries) an unidentified soldier who has died in battle and for whom a tomb is established as a memorial to other unidentified dead of the nation's armed forces.

unlace (ʌn'leɪs) *vb* (*tr*) **1** to loosen or undo the lacing of (shoes, garments, etc.). **2** to unfasten or remove garments of (oneself or another) by or as if by undoing lacing.

unlade (ʌn'leɪd) *vb* a less common word for **unload.**

unlash (ʌn'læʃ) *vb* (*tr*) to untie or unfasten.

unlatch (ʌn'lætʃ) *vb* to open or unfasten or come open or unfastened by the lifting or release of a latch.

unlawful (ʌn'lɔːfʊl) *adj* **1** illegal. **2** illicit; immoral: *unlawful love.* **3** an archaic word for **illegitimate.** ▸ **un'lawfully** *adv* ▸ **un'lawfulness** *n*

unlawful assembly *n Law.* a meeting of three or more people with the intent of carrying out any unlawful purpose.

unlay (ʌn'leɪ) *vb* **-lays, -laying, -laid.** (*tr*) to untwist (a rope or cable) to separate its strands.

unlead (ʌn'lɛd) *vb* (*tr*) **1** to strip off lead. **2** *Printing.* to remove the leads or spaces from between (lines of type).

unleaded (ʌn'lɛdɪd) *adj* **1** (of petrol) containing a reduced amount of tetraethyl lead, in order to reduce environmental pollution. **2** not covered or weighted with lead. **3** *Printing.* (of lines of type, etc.) not spaced or separated with leads; solid. ◆ *n* **4** petrol containing a reduced amount of tetraethyl lead.

unlearn (ʌn'lɜːn) *vb* **-learns, -learning, -learned** (-'lɜːnd) *or* **-learnt.** to try to forget (something learnt) or to discard (accumulated knowledge).

unlearned (ʌn'lɜːnɪd) *adj* ignorant or untaught. ▸ **un'learnedly** *adv*

unlearnt (ʌn'lɜːnt) *or* **unlearned** (ʌn'lɜːnd) *adj* **1** denoting knowledge or skills innately present and therefore not learnt. **2** not learnt or taken notice of: *unlearnt lessons.*

unleash (ʌn'liːʃ) *vb* (*tr*) **1** to release from or as if from a leash. **2** to free from restraint or control.

unleavened (ʌn'lɛvənd) *adj* (of bread, biscuits, etc.) made from a dough containing no yeast or leavening.

unless (ʌn'lɛs) *conj* **1** (*subordinating*) except under the circumstances that; except on the condition that: *they'll sell it unless he hears otherwise.* ◆ *prep* **2** *Rare.* except. [C14: *onlesse,* from *on* ON + *lesse* LESS; compare French *à moins que,* literally: at less than]

unlettered (ʌn'lɛtəd) *adj* **1** uneducated; illiterate. **2** not marked with letters: *an unlettered tombstone.*

unlicensed (ʌn'laɪsənst) *adj* **1** having no licence: *an unlicensed restaurant.* **2** without permission; unauthorized. **3** unrestrained or lawless.

unlike (ʌn'laɪk) *adj* **1** not alike; dissimilar or unequal; different. **2** *Archaic or northern English dialect.* unlikely. ◆ *prep* **3** not like; not typical of: *unlike his father he lacks intelligence.* ▸ **un'likeness** *n*

unlikely (ʌn'laɪklɪ) *adj* not likely; improbable. ▸ **un'likeliness** *or* **un'likelihood** *n*

unlimber (ʌn'lɪmbə) *vb* **1** (*tr*) to disengage (a gun) from its limber. **2** to prepare (something) for use.

unlimited (ʌn'lɪmɪtɪd) *adj* **1** without limits or bounds: *unlimited knowledge.* **2** not restricted, limited, or qualified: *unlimited power.* **3** *Finance, Brit.* **3a** (of liability) not restricted to any unpaid portion of nominal capital invested in a business. **3b** (of a business enterprise) having owners with such unlimited liability. ▸ **un'limitedly** *adv* ▸ **un'limitedness** *n*

unlisted (ʌn'lɪstɪd) *adj* **1** not entered on a list. **2** *U.S. and Canadian.* (of a telephone number or telephone subscriber) not listed in a telephone directory. Brit. term: **ex-directory.**

unlisted securities market *n* a market on the London Stock Exchange, established in 1981, for trading in shares of smaller companies, who do not wish to comply with the requirements for a full listing. Abbrev.: **USM.**

unlive (ʌn'lɪv) *vb* (*tr*) to live so as to nullify, undo, or live down (past events or times).

unload (ʌn'ləʊd) *vb* **1** to remove a load or cargo from (a ship, lorry, etc.). **2** to discharge (cargo, freight, etc.). **3** (*tr*) to relieve of a burden or troubles. **4** (*tr*) to give vent to (anxiety, troubles, etc.). **5** (*tr*) to get rid of or dispose of (esp. surplus goods). **6** (*tr*) to remove the charge of ammunition from (a firearm). ▸ **un'loader** *n*

unlock (ʌn'lɒk) *vb* **1** (*tr*) to unfasten (a lock, door, etc.). **2** (*tr*) to open, release, or let loose. **3** (*tr*) to disclose or provide the key to: *unlock a puzzle.* **4** (*intr*) to become unlocked. ▸ **un'lockable** *adj*

unlooked-for (,ʌn'lʊktfɔː) *adj* unexpected; unforeseen.

unloose (ʌn'luːs) *or* **unloosen** *vb* (*tr*) **1** to set free; release. **2** to loosen or relax (a hold, grip, etc.). **3** to unfasten or untie.

unlovely (ʌn'lʌvlɪ) *adj* **1** unpleasant in appearance. **2** unpleasant in character. ▸ **un'loveliness** *n*

unlucky (ʌn'lʌkɪ) *adj* **1** characterized by misfortune or failure: *an unlucky person; an unlucky chance.* **2** ill-omened; inauspicious: *an unlucky date.* **3** regrettable; disappointing. **4** *Brit. dialect.* causing trouble; mischievous. ▸ **un'luckily** *adv* ▸ **un'luckiness** *n*

unmade (ʌn'meɪd) *vb* **1** the past tense and past participle of **unmake.** ◆ *adj* **2** not yet made. **3** existing without having been made or created. **4** *Falconry.* another word for **unmanned** (sense 4).

unmake (ʌn'meɪk) *vb* **-makes, -making, -made.** (*tr*) **1** to undo or destroy. **2** to depose from office, rank, or authority. **3** to alter the nature of. ▸ **un'maker** *n*

unman (ʌn'mæn) *vb* **-mans, -manning, -manned.** (*tr*) **1** to cause to lose courage or nerve. **2** to make effeminate. **3** to remove the men from. **4** *Archaic.* to deprive of human qualities.

unmanly (ʌn'mænlɪ) *adj* **1** not masculine or virile. **2** ignoble, cowardly, or dishonourable. ◆ *adv* ▸ **un'manliness** *n*

unmanned (ʌn'mænd) *adj* **1** lacking personnel or crew: *an unmanned ship.* **2** (of aircraft, spacecraft, etc.) operated by automatic or remote control. **3** uninhabited. **4** *Falconry.* (of a hawk or falcon) not yet trained to accept humans.

unmannered (ʌn'mænəd) *adj* **1** without good manners; coarse; rude. **2** not affected; without mannerisms.

unmannerly (ʌn'mænəlɪ) *adj* **1** lacking manners; discourteous. ◆ *adv* **2** *Archaic.* rudely; discourteously. ▸ **un'mannerliness** *n*

unmarked (ʌn'mɑːkt) *adj* **1** not carrying a mark or marks. **2** not noticed or observed.

unmarried (ʌn'mærɪd) *adj* **1** not married: *an unmarried mother.* **2** *Films.* denoting a print of a cinematograph film in which the picture and sound recordings are on separate reels.

unmask (ʌn'mɑːsk) *vb* **1** to remove (the mask or disguise) from (someone or oneself). **2** to appear or cause to appear in true character. **3** (*tr*) *Military.* to make evident the presence of (weapons), either by firing or by the removal of camouflage, etc. ▸ **un'masker** *n*

unmeaning (ʌn'miːnɪŋ) *adj* **1** having no meaning. **2** showing no intelligence; vacant: *an unmeaning face.* ▸ **un'meaningly** *adv* ▸ **un'meaningness** *n*

unmeant (ʌn'mɛnt) *adj* unintentional; accidental.

unmeasured (ʌn'mɛʒəd) *adj* **1** measureless; limitless. **2** unrestrained; unlimited or lavish. **3** *Music.* without bar lines and hence without a fixed pulse. ▸ **un'measurable** *adj* ▸ **un'measurableness** *n* ▸ **un'measurably** *adv* ▸ **un'measuredly** *adv*

unmeet (ʌn'miːt) *adj Literary or archaic.* not meet; unsuitable. ▸ **un'meetly** *adv* ▸ **un'meetness** *n*

unmentionable (ʌn'mɛnʃənəb^{ə}l) *adj* **a** unsuitable or forbidden as a topic of conversation. **b** (*as n*): *the unmentionable.* ▸ **un'mentionableness** *n* ▸ **un'mentionably** *adv*

unmentionables (ʌn'mɛnʃənəb^{ə}lz) *pl n Chiefly humorous.* underwear.

unmerciful (ʌn'mɜːsɪfʊl) *adj* **1** showing no mercy; relentless. **2** extreme or excessive. ▸ **un'mercifully** *adv* ▸ **un'mercifulness** *n*

unmindful (ʌn'maɪndfʊl) *adj* (*usually postpositive* and foll. by *of*) careless, heedless, or forgetful. ▸ **un'mindfully** *adv* ▸ **un'mindfulness** *n*

unmissable (ʌn'mɪsəb^{ə}l) *adj* (of a film, television programme, etc.) so good that it should not be missed.

unmistakable *or* **unmistakeable** (,ʌnmɪs'teɪkəb^{ə}l) *adj* not mistakable; clear, obvious, or unambiguous. ▸ **,unmis'takableness** *or* **,unmis'takeableness** *n* ▸ **,unmis'takably** *or* **,unmis'takeably** *adv*

unmitigated (ʌn'mɪtɪ,geɪtɪd) *adj* **1** not diminished in intensity, severity, etc. **2** (*prenominal*) (intensifier): *an unmitigated disaster.* ▸ **un'miti,gatedly** *adv*

unmoor (ʌn'mʊə, -'mɔː) *vb Nautical.* **1** to weigh the anchor or drop the mooring of (a vessel). **2** (*tr*) to reduce the mooring of (a vessel) to one anchor.

un'kept *adj*
un'labelled *adj*
un'laden *adj*
un'lady,like *adj*
un'laid *adj*
,unla'mented *adj*
un'leased *adj*
un'liber,ated *adj*
un'lighted *adj*
un'lined *adj*
un'lit *adj*
un'locked *adj*
un'lovable *or* **un'loveable** *adj*
un'loved *adj*
un'loving *adj*
un'manageable *adj*
un'marketable *adj*
un'matched *adj*
,unma'tured *adj*
un'melted *adj*
un'memorable *adj*
un'mentioned *adj*
un'merited *adj*
,unme'thodical *adj*
un'military *adj*
un'mixed *adj*
un'modi,fied *adj*
,unmo'lested *adj*

unmoral (ʌnˈmɒrəl) *adj* outside morality; amoral. ► **unmorality** (ˌʌnməˈrælɪtɪ) *n* ► **unˈmorally** *adv*
unmurmuring (ʌnˈmɜːmərɪŋ) *adj* not complaining.
unmusical (ʌnˈmjuːzɪkᵊl) *adj* **1** not musical or harmonious. **2** not talented in or appreciative of music. ► **unˈmusically** *adv* ► **unˈmusicalness** *n*
unmuzzle (ʌnˈmʌzᵊl) *vb (tr)* **1** to take the muzzle off (a dog, etc.). **2** to free from control or censorship.
unnamed (ʌnˈneɪmd) *adj* **1** having no name. **2** not mentioned by name: *the culprit shall remain unnamed.*
unnatural (ʌnˈnætʃərəl, -ˈnætʃrəl) *adj* **1** contrary to nature; abnormal. **2** not in accordance with accepted standards of behaviour or right and wrong: *unnatural love.* **3** uncanny; supernatural: *unnatural phenomena.* **4** affected or forced: *an unnatural manner.* **5** inhuman or monstrous; wicked: *an unnatural crime.* **6** *Obsolete.* illegitimate. ► **unˈnaturally** *adv* ► **unˈnaturalness** *n*
unnecessary (ʌnˈnɛsɪsərɪ, -ɪsrɪ) *adj* not necessary. ► **unˈnecessarily** *adv* ► **unˈnecessariness** *n*
unnerve (ʌnˈnɜːv) *vb (tr)* to cause to lose courage, strength, confidence, self-control, etc.
unnumbered (ʌnˈnʌmbəd) *adj* **1** countless; innumerable. **2** not counted or assigned a number.
UNO *abbrev. for* United Nations Organization.
unoccupied (ʌnˈɒkjʊˌpaɪd) *adj* **1** (of a building) without occupants. **2** unemployed or idle. **3** (of an area or country) not overrun by foreign troops.
unofficial (ˌʌnəˈfɪʃəl) *adj* **1** not official or formal: *an unofficial engagement.* **2** not confirmed officially: *an unofficial report.* **3** (of a strike) not approved by the strikers' trade union. **4** (of a medicinal drug) not listed in a pharmacopoeia. ► **ˌunofˈficially** *adv*
unorganized *or* **unorganised** (ʌnˈɔːgəˌnaɪzd) *adj* **1** not arranged into an organized system, structure, or unity. **2** (of workers) not unionized. **3** nonliving; inorganic.
unorthodox (ʌnˈɔːθəˌdɒks) *adj* not conventional in belief, behaviour, custom, etc. ► **unˈorthoˌdoxly** *adv*
unpack (ʌnˈpæk) *vb* **1** to remove the packed contents of (a case, trunk, etc.). **2** *(tr)* to take (something) out of a packed container. **3** *(tr)* to remove a pack from; unload: *to unpack a mule.* ► **unˈpacker** *n*
unpaged (ʌnˈpeɪdʒd) *adj* (of a book) having no page numbers.
unpaid (ʌnˈpeɪd) *adj* **1** (of a bill, debt, etc.) not yet paid. **2** working without pay. **3** having wages outstanding.
unparalleled (ʌnˈpærəˌlɛld) *adj* unmatched; unequalled.
unparliamentary (ˌʌnpɑːləˈmɛntərɪ, -trɪ) *adj* not consistent with parliamentary procedure or practice. ► **ˌunparliaˈmentarily** *adv* ► **ˌunparliaˈmentariness** *n*
unpeg (ʌnˈpɛg) *vb* **-pegs, -pegging, -pegged.** *(tr)* **1** to remove the peg or pegs from, esp. to unfasten. **2** to allow (prices, wages, etc.) to rise and fall freely.
unpeople (ʌnˈpiːpᵊl) *vb (tr)* to empty of people.
unperforated (ʌnˈpɜːfəˌreɪtɪd) *adj* (of a stamp) not provided with perforations.
unperson (ˈʌnpɜːsᵊn) *n* a person whose existence is officially denied or ignored.
unpick (ʌnˈpɪk) *vb (tr)* **1** to undo (the stitches) of (a piece of sewing). **2** to unravel or undo (a garment, etc.). **3** *Obsolete.* to open (a door, lock, etc.) by picking.
unpin (ʌnˈpɪn) *vb* **-pins, -pinning, -pinned.** *(tr)* **1** to remove a pin or pins from. **2** to unfasten by removing pins.
unplaced (ʌnˈpleɪst) *adj* **1** not given or put in a particular place. **2** *Horse racing.* not in the first three (sometimes four) runners in a race.
unpleasant (ʌnˈplɛzᵊnt) *adj* not pleasant or agreeable. ► **unˈpleasantly** *adv*
unpleasantness (ʌnˈplɛzəntnɪs) *n* **1** the state or quality of being unpleasant. **2** an unpleasant event, situation, etc. **3** a disagreement or quarrel.
unplug (ʌnˈplʌg) *vb* **-plugs, -plugging, -plugged.** *(tr)* **1** to disconnect (an electrical appliance) by taking the plug out of the socket. **2** to remove a plug or obstruction from.
unplugged (ʌnˈplʌgd) *adj* (of a performer or performance of popular music) using acoustic rather than electric instruments: *Eric Clapton unplugged; an unplugged version of the song.*
unplumbed (ʌnˈplʌmd) *adj* **1** unfathomed; unsounded. **2** not understood in depth. **3** (of a building) having no plumbing.
unpolitic (ʌnˈpɒlɪtɪk) *adj* another word for **impolitic.**
unpolled (ʌnˈpəʊld) *adj* **1** not included in an opinion poll. **2** not having voted. **3** *U.S.* not registered for an election: *unpolled votes.*
unpopular (ʌnˈpɒpjʊlə) *adj* not popular with an individual or group of people. ► **unpopularity** (ˌʌnpɒpjʊˈlærɪtɪ) *n* ► **unˈpopularly** *adv*
unpractical (ʌnˈpræktɪkᵊl) *adj* another word for **impractical.** ► **ˌunpractiˈcality** *or* **unˈpracticalness** *n* ► **unˈpractically** *adv*
unpractised *or U.S.* **unpracticed** (ʌnˈpræktɪst) *adj* **1** without skill, training, or experience. **2** not used or done often or repeatedly. **3** not yet tested.
unprecedented (ʌnˈprɛsɪˌdɛntɪd) *adj* having no precedent; unparalleled. ► **unˈpreceˌdentedly** *adv*
unpredictable (ˌʌnprɪˈdɪktəbᵊl) *adj* not capable of being predicted; changeable. ► **ˌunpreˌdictaˈbility** *or* **ˌunpreˈdictableness** *n* ► **ˌunpreˈdictably** *adv*
unprejudiced (ʌnˈprɛdʒʊdɪst) *adj* not prejudiced or biased; impartial. ► **unˈprejudicedly** *adv*
unpremeditated (ˌʌnprɪˈmɛdɪˌteɪtɪd) *adj* not planned beforehand; spontaneous. ► **ˌunpreˈmediˌtatedly** *adv* ► **ˌunpreˌmediˈtation** *n*
unprepared (ˌʌnprɪˈpɛəd) *adj* **1** having made inadequate preparations. **2** not made ready or prepared. **3** done without preparation; extemporaneous. ► **ˌunpreˈparedly** *adv* ► **ˌunpreˈparedness** *n*
unpriced (ʌnˈpraɪst) *adj* **1** having no fixed or marked price. **2** *Poetic.* beyond price; priceless.
unprincipled (ʌnˈprɪnsɪpᵊld) *adj* **1** lacking moral principles; unscrupulous. **2** (foll. by *in*) *Archaic.* not versed in the principles of (a subject). ► **unˈprincipledness** *n*
unprintable (ʌnˈprɪntəbᵊl) *adj* unsuitable for printing for reasons of obscenity, libel, bad taste, etc. ► **unˈprintableness** *n* ► **unˈprintably** *adv*
unproductive (ˌʌnprəˈdʌktɪv) *adj* **1** (often foll. by *of*) not productive of (anything). **2** not producing goods and services with exchange value. ► **ˌunproˈductively** *adv* ► **ˌunproˈductiveness** *n*
unprofessional (ˌʌnprəˈfɛʃənᵊl) *adj* **1** contrary to the accepted code of conduct of a profession. **2** amateur. **3** not belonging to or having the required qualifications for a profession. ► **ˌunproˈfessionally** *adv*
unprofitable (ʌnˈprɒfɪtəbᵊl) *adj* **1** not making a profit. **2** not fruitful or beneficial. ► **unˌprofitaˈbility** *or* **unˈprofitableness** *n* ► **unˈprofitably** *adv*
unprotected sex *n* an act of sexual intercourse or sodomy performed without the use of a condom thus involving the risk of sexually transmitted diseases.
unprovided (ˌʌnprəˈvaɪdɪd) *adj (postpositive)* **1** (foll. by *with*) not provided or supplied. **2** (often foll. by *for*) not prepared or ready. **3 unprovided for.** without income or means. ► **ˌunproˈvidedly** *adv*
unputdownable (ˌʌnpʊtˈdaʊnəbᵊl) *adj* (of a book, esp. a novel) so gripping as to be read right through at one sitting.
unqualified (ʌnˈkwɒlɪˌfaɪd) *adj* **1** lacking the necessary qualifications. **2** not restricted or modified: *an unqualified criticism.* **3** *(usually prenominal)* (intensifier): *an unqualified success.* ► **unˈqualiˌfiable** *adj* ► **unˈqualiˌfiedly** *adv* ► **unˈqualiˌfiedness** *n*
unquestionable (ʌnˈkwɛstʃənəbᵊl) *adj* **1** indubitable or indisputable. **2** not admitting of exception or qualification: *an unquestionable decision.* ► **unˌquestionaˈbility** *or* **unˈquestionableness** *n* ► **unˈquestionably** *adv*
unquestioned (ʌnˈkwɛstʃənd) *adj* **1** accepted without question. **2** not admitting of doubt or question: *unquestioned power.* **3** not questioned or interrogated. **4** *Rare.* not examined or investigated.
unquiet (ʌnˈkwaɪət) *Chiefly literary.* ◆ *adj* **1** characterized by disorder, unrest, or tumult: *unquiet times.* **2** anxious; uneasy. ◆ *n* **3** a state of unrest. ► **unˈquietly** *adv* ► **unˈquietness** *n*
unquote (ʌnˈkwəʊt) *interj* **1** an expression used parenthetically to indicate that the preceding quotation is finished. ◆ *vb* **2** to close (a quotation), esp. in printing.
unravel (ʌnˈrævᵊl) *vb* **-els, -elling, -elled** *or U.S.* **-els, -eling, -eled. 1** *(tr)* to reduce (something knitted or woven) to separate strands. **2** *(tr)* to undo or untangle (something tangled or knotted). **3** *(tr)* to explain or solve: *the mystery was unravelled.* **4** *(intr)* to become unravelled. ► **unˈraveller** *n* ► **unˈravelment** *n*
unreactive (ˌʌnrɪˈæktɪv) *adj* (of a substance) not readily partaking in chemical reactions.

unˈmotiˌvated *adj*
unˈmoulded *adj*
unˈmounted *adj*
unˈmourned *adj*
unˈmoved *adj*
unˈmoving *adj*
unˈnavigable *adj*
unˈneeded *adj*
unˈneighbourly *adj*
unˈnoticeable *adj*
unˈnoticeably *adv*
unˈnoticed *adj*
ˌunobˈjectionable *adj*
ˌunobˈscured *adj*
ˌunobˈservant *adj*
ˌunobˈserved *adj*
ˌunobˈstructed *adj*
ˌunobˈtainable *adj*
ˌunobˈtrusive *adj*
ˌunobˈtrusively *adv*
unˈopen *adj*
unˈopened *adj*
ˌunopˈposed *adj*
ˌunoˈriginal *adj*
ˌunostenˈtatious *adj*
ˌunostenˈtatiously *adv*
unˈowned *adj*
unˈpaired *adj*
unˈpalatable *adj*
unˈpardonable *adj*
unˈpasteurˌized *or* **unˈpasteurˌised** *adj*
ˌunpatriˈotic *adj*
unˈpaved *adj*
ˌunperˈceived *adj*
ˌunperˈceptive *adj*
ˌunperˈformed *adj*
ˌunperˈsuaded *adj*
ˌunperˈturbed *adj*
unˈpicked *adj*
unˈplanned *adj*
unˈplanted *adj*
unˈplayable *adj*
unˈplayed *adj*
unˈpleasing *adj*
unˈploughed *adj*
unˈpointed *adj*
unˈpolarˌized *or* **unˈpolarˌised** *adj*
unˈpolished *adj*
ˌunpolˈluted *adj*
unˈpopuˌlated *adj*
unˈposed *adj*
ˌunpreˈdicted *adj*
ˌunpreposˈsessing *adj*
unˈpressed *adj*
ˌunpreˈtentious *adj*
unˈprocessed *adj*
unˈpromising *adj*
unˈprompted *adj*
ˌunproˈnounceable *adj*
ˌunproˈpitious *adj*
ˌunproˈtected *adj*
ˌunproˈtesting *adj*
unˈproved *adj*
unˈproven *adj*
ˌunproˈvoked *adj*
unˈpublished *adj*
unˈpunctual *adj*
unˈpunished *adj*
unˈquantiˌfiable *adj*
unˈquelled *adj*
unˈquenched *adj*
unˈquestioning *adj*
unˈraised *adj*

unread (ʌnˈrɛd) *adj* **1** (of a book, newspaper, etc.) not yet read. **2** (of a person) having read little. **3** (*postpositive; foll. by in*) not versed (in a specified field).
unreadable (ʌnˈriːdəbᵊl) *adj* **1** illegible; undecipherable. **2** difficult or tedious to read. ▸ **unˌreadaˈbility** *or* **unˈreadableness** *n* ▸ **unˈreadably** *adv*
unready (ʌnˈrɛdɪ) *adj* **1** not ready or prepared. **2** slow or hesitant to see or act. **3** *Archaic or Brit. dialect.* not dressed. ▸ **unˈreadily** *adv* ▸ **unˈreadiness** *n*
unreal (ʌnˈrɪəl) *adj* **1** imaginary or fanciful or seemingly so: *an unreal situation.* **2** having no actual existence or substance. **3** insincere or artificial. ▸ **unˈreally** *adv*
unreality (ˌʌnrɪˈælɪtɪ) *n* **1** the quality or state of being unreal, fanciful, or impractical. **2** something that is unreal.
unreason (ʌnˈriːzᵊn) *n* **1** irrationality or madness. **2** something that lacks or is contrary to reason. **3** lack of order; chaos. ◆ *vb* **4** (*tr*) to deprive of reason.
unreasonable (ʌnˈriːznəbᵊl) *adj* **1** immoderate; excessive: *unreasonable demands.* **2** refusing to listen to reason. **3** lacking reason or judgment. ▸ **unˈreasonableness** *n* ▸ **unˈreasonably** *adv*
unreasonable behaviour *n Law.* conduct by a spouse sufficient to cause the irretrievable breakdown of a marriage.
unreasoning (ʌnˈriːzənɪŋ) *adj* not controlled by reason; irrational. ▸ **unˈreasoningly** *adv*
unreckonable (ʌnˈrɛkənəbᵊl) *adj* incalculable; unlimited.
unreconstructed (ˌʌnriːkənsˈtrʌktɪd) *adj Chiefly U.S.* unwilling to accept social and economic change, as exemplified by those White Southerners who refused to accept the Reconstruction after the Civil War.
unreeve (ʌnˈriːv) *vb* **-reeves, -reeving, -rove** *or* **-reeved.** *Nautical.* to withdraw (a rope) from a block, thimble, etc. [C17: from UN-[2] + REEVE[2]]
unrefined (ˌʌnrɪˈfaɪnd) *adj* **1** (of substances such as petroleum, ores, and sugar) not processed into a pure or usable form. **2** coarse in manners or language.
unreflected (ˌʌnrɪˈflɛktɪd) *adj* **1** (foll. by *on* or *upon*) not considered. **2** (of light, particles, etc., incident on a surface) not reflected; absorbed or transmitted.
unreflective (ˌʌnrɪˈflɛktɪv) *adj* not reflective or thoughtful; rash; unthinking. ▸ **ˌunreˈflectively** *adv*
unregenerate (ˌʌnrɪˈdʒɛnərɪt) *adj also* **unregenerated. 1** unrepentant; unreformed. **2** obstinately adhering to one's own views. ◆ *n* **3** an unregenerate person. ▸ **ˌunreˈgeneracy** *n* ▸ **ˌunreˈgenerately** *adv*
unrelenting (ˌʌnrɪˈlɛntɪŋ) *adj* **1** refusing to relent or take pity; relentless; merciless. **2** not diminishing in determination, speed, effort, force, etc. ▸ **ˌunreˈlentingly** *adv* ▸ **ˌunreˈlentingness** *n*
unreligious (ˌʌnrɪˈlɪdʒəs) *adj* **1** another word for **irreligious. 2** secular. ▸ **ˌunreˈligiously** *adv*
unremitting (ˌʌnrɪˈmɪtɪŋ) *adj* never slackening or stopping; unceasing; constant. ▸ **ˌunreˈmittingly** *adv* ▸ **ˌunreˈmittingness** *n*
unrepair (ˌʌnrɪˈpɛə) *n* a less common word for **disrepair.** ▸ **ˌunreˈpaired** *adj*
unrequited (ˌʌnrɪˈkwaɪtɪd) *adj* (of love, affection, etc.) not reciprocated or returned.
unreserved (ˌʌnrɪˈzɜːvd) *adj* **1** without reserve; having an open manner. **2** without reservation. **3** not booked or bookable. ▸ **unreservedly** (ˌʌnrɪˈzɜːvɪdlɪ) *adv* ▸ **ˌunreˈservedness** *n*
unrest (ʌnˈrɛst) *n* **1** a troubled or rebellious state of discontent. **2** an uneasy or troubled state.
unrestrained (ˌʌnrɪˈstreɪnd) *adj* not restrained or checked; free or natural. ▸ **unrestrainedly** (ˌʌnrɪˈstreɪnɪdlɪ) *adv*
unriddle (ʌnˈrɪdᵊl) *vb* (*tr*) to solve or puzzle out. [C16: from UN-[2] + RIDDLE[1]] ▸ **unˈriddler** *n*
unrifled (ʌnˈraɪfᵊld) *adj* (of a firearm or its bore) not rifled; smoothbore.
unrig (ʌnˈrɪg) *vb* **-rigs, -rigging, -rigged. 1** (*tr*) to strip (a vessel) of standing and running rigging. **2** *Archaic or dialect.* to undress (someone or oneself).
unrighteous (ʌnˈraɪtʃəs) *adj* **1a** sinful; wicked. **1b** (*as collective n; preceded by the*): *the unrighteous.* **2** not fair or right; unjust. ▸ **unˈrighteously** *adv* ▸ **unˈrighteousness** *n*
unrip (ʌnˈrɪp) *vb* **-rips, -ripping, -ripped.** (*tr*) **1** to rip open. **2** *Obsolete.* to reveal; disclose.
unripe (ʌnˈraɪp) *or* **unripened** *adj* **1** not fully matured. **2** not fully prepared or developed; not ready. **3** *Obsolete.* premature or untimely. ▸ **unˈripeness** *n*
unrivalled (ʌnˈraɪvᵊld) *adj* having no equal; matchless.
unroll (ʌnˈrəʊl) *vb* **1** to open out or unwind (something rolled, folded, or coiled) or (of something rolled, etc.) to become opened out or unwound. **2** to make or become visible or apparent, esp. gradually; unfold.
unroot (ʌnˈruːt) *vb* (*tr*) *Chiefly U.S.* a less common word for **uproot.**
unrounded (ʌnˈraʊndɪd) *adj Phonetics.* articulated with the lips spread; not rounded.
unruffled (ʌnˈrʌfᵊld) *adj* **1** unmoved; calm. **2** still: *the unruffled seas.* ▸ **unˈruffledness** *n*
unruly (ʌnˈruːlɪ) *adj* **-lier, -liest.** disposed to disobedience or indiscipline. ▸ **unˈruliness** *n*
unruly certificate *n* an informal name for **certificate of unruliness.**
UNRWA (ˈʌnrə) *n acronym for* United Nations Relief and Works Agency.
unsaddle (ʌnˈsædᵊl) *vb* **1** to remove the saddle from (a horse, mule, etc.). **2** (*tr*) to unhorse.
unsaddling enclosure *n* the area at a racecourse where horses are unsaddled after a race and often where awards are given to owners, trainers, and jockeys.
unsafe (ʌnˈseɪf) *adj* **1** not safe; perilous. **2** (of a criminal conviction) based on inadequate or false evidence.
unsaid (ʌnˈsɛd) *adj* not said or expressed; unspoken.
unsaturated (ʌnˈsætʃəˌreɪtɪd) *adj* **1** not saturated. **2** (of a chemical compound, esp. an organic compound) containing one or more double or triple bonds and thus capable of undergoing addition reactions. **3** (of a fat, esp. a vegetable fat) containing a high proportion of fatty acids having double bonds. **4** (of a solution) containing less solute than a saturated solution. ▸ **ˌunsatuˈration** *n*
unsavoury *or U.S.* **unsavory** (ʌnˈseɪvərɪ) *adj* **1** objectionable or distasteful: *an unsavoury character.* **2** disagreeable in odour or taste. ▸ **unˈsavourily** *or U.S.* **unˈsavorily** *adv* ▸ **unˈsavouriness** *or U.S.* **unˈsavoriness** *n*
unsay (ʌnˈseɪ) *vb* **-says, -saying, -said.** (*tr*) to retract or withdraw (something said or written).
unscathed (ʌnˈskeɪðd) *adj* not harmed or injured.
unschooled (ʌnˈskuːld) *adj* **1** having received no training or schooling. **2** spontaneous; natural: *unschooled talent.*
unscientific (ˌʌnsaɪənˈtɪfɪk) *adj* **1** not consistent with the methods or principles of science, esp. lacking objectivity. **2** ignorant of science. ▸ **ˌunscienˈtifically** *adv*
unscramble (ʌnˈskræmbᵊl) *vb* (*tr*) **1** to resolve from confusion or disorderliness. **2** to restore (a scrambled message) to an intelligible form. ▸ **unˈscrambler** *n*
unscratched (ʌnˈskrætʃt) *adj* quite unharmed.
unscreened (ʌnˈskriːnd) *adj* **1** not sheltered or concealed by a screen. **2** not passed through a screen; unsifted. **3** (of a film) not yet on show to the public. **4** not put through a security check.
unscrew (ʌnˈskruː) *vb* **1** (*tr*) to draw or remove a screw from (an object). **2** (*tr*) to loosen (a screw, lid, etc.) by rotating continuously, usually in an anticlockwise direction. **3** (*intr*) (esp. of an engaged threaded part) to become loosened or separated: *the lid wouldn't unscrew.*
unscripted (ʌnˈskrɪptɪd) *adj* (of a speech, play, etc.) not using or based on a script.
unscrupulous (ʌnˈskruːpjʊləs) *adj* without scruples; unprincipled. ▸ **unˈscrupulously** *adv* ▸ **unˈscrupulousness** *or* **unscrupulosity** (ʌnˌskruːpjʊˈlɒsɪtɪ) *n*
unseal (ʌnˈsiːl) *vb* (*tr*) **1** to remove or break the seal of. **2** to reveal or free (something concealed or closed as if sealed): *to unseal one's lips.* ▸ **unˈsealable** *adj*
unseam (ʌnˈsiːm) *vb* (*tr*) to open or undo the seam of.
unseasonable (ʌnˈsiːzənəbᵊl) *adj* **1** (esp. of the weather) inappropriate for the season. **2** untimely; inopportune. ▸ **unˈseasonableness** *n* ▸ **unˈseasonably** *adv*
unseasoned (ʌnˈsiːzənd) *adj* **1** (of persons) not sufficiently experienced: *unseasoned troops.* **2** not matured or seasoned: *unseasoned timber.* **3** (of food) not flavoured with seasoning. ▸ **unˈseasonedness** *n*
unseat (ʌnˈsiːt) *vb* (*tr*) **1** to throw or displace from a seat, saddle, etc. **2** to depose from office or position.
unsecured (ˌʌnsɪˈkjʊəd) *adj* **1** *Finance.* **1a** (of a loan, etc.) secured only against general assets and not against a specific asset. **1b** (of a creditor) having no security against a specific asset and with a claim inferior to those of secure creditors. **2** not made secure; loose.
unseeded (ʌnˈsiːdɪd) *adj* (of players in various sports) not assigned to a preferential position in the preliminary rounds of a tournament. See **seed** (sense 18).
unseemly (ʌnˈsiːmlɪ) *adj* **1** not in good style or taste; unbecoming. **2** *Obsolete.* unattractive. ◆ *adv* **3** *Rare.* in an unseemly manner. ▸ **unˈseemliness** *n*
unseen (ʌnˈsiːn) *adj* **1** not observed or perceived; invisible. **2** (of passages of writing) not previously seen or prepared. ◆ *n* **3** *Chiefly Brit.* a passage, not previously seen, that is presented to students for translation.

ˌunrealˈistic *adj*
unˈrealˌized *or* **unˈrealˌised** *adj*
unˈreasoned *adj*
ˌunreˈceptive *adj*
unˈrecogˌnizable *or* **unˈrecogˌnisable** *adj*
unˈrecogˌnized *or* **unˈrecogˌnised** *adj*
unˈreconˌciled *adj*
ˌunreˈcorded *adj*
ˌunreˈdeemed *adj*
unˈregistered *adj*
unˈreguˌlated *adj*
ˌunreˈhearsed *adj*
ˌunreˈlated *adj*
ˌunreˈliable *adj*
ˌunreˈlieved *adj*
ˌunreˈmarkable *adj*
unˈremedied *adj*
ˌunreˈmembered *adj*
ˌunreˈpeatable *adj*
ˌunreˈpentant *adj*
ˌunreˈported *adj*
ˌunrepreˈsentative *adj*
ˌunrepreˈsented *adj*
ˌunreˈsisting *adj*
ˌunreˈsolved *adj*
ˌunreˈsponsive *adj*
ˌunreˈstricted *adj*
ˌunreˈturned *adj*
ˌunreˈvealed *adj*
ˌunreˈvealing *adj*
ˌunreˈvised *adj*
ˌunreˈwarded *adj*
ˌunreˈwarding *adj*
unˈrhymed *adj*
unˈrhythmic *adj*
ˌunroˈmantic *adj*
unˈsaleable *adj*
unˈsalted *adj*
unˈsanctioned *adj*
unˈsanitary *adj*
ˌunsatisˈfactory *adj*
unˈsatisˌfied *adj*
unˈsatisˌfying *adj*
unˈsayable *adj*
unˈscarred *adj*
unˈscented *adj*
unˈscheduled *adj*
unˈseaˌworthy *adj*
unˈseeing *adj*

unselfish (ʌnˈsɛlfɪʃ) *adj* not selfish or greedy; generous. ▸ **unˈselfishly** *adv* ▸ **unˈselfishness** *n*

unset (ʌnˈsɛt) *adj* **1** not yet solidified or firm. **2** (of a gem) not yet in a setting. **3** (of textual matter) not yet composed.

unsettle (ʌnˈsetᵊl) *vb* **1** (*usually tr*) to change or become changed from a fixed or settled condition. **2** (*tr*) to confuse or agitate (emotions, the mind, etc.). ▸ **unˈsettlement** *n*

unsettled (ʌnˈsetᵊld) *adj* **1** lacking order or stability: *an unsettled era.* **2** unpredictable; uncertain: *an unsettled climate.* **3** constantly changing or moving from place to place: *an unsettled life.* **4** (of controversy, etc.) not brought to an agreed conclusion. **5** (of debts, law cases, etc.) not disposed of. **6** (of regions, etc.) devoid of settlers. ▸ **unˈsettledness** *n*

unsex (ʌnˈsɛks) *vb* (*tr*) *Chiefly literary.* to deprive (a person) of the attributes of his or her sex, esp. to make a woman more callous.

unshakable *or* **unshakeable** (ʌnˈʃeɪkəbᵊl) *adj* (of beliefs, convictions, etc.) utterly firm and unwavering. ▸ **unˈshakableness** *or* **unˈshakeableness** *n* ▸ **unˈshakably** *or* **unˈshakeably** *adv*

unshapen (ʌnˈʃeɪpᵊn) *adj* **1** having no definite shape; shapeless. **2** deformed; misshapen.

unsheathe (ʌnˈʃiːð) *vb* (*tr*) to draw or pull out (something, esp. a weapon) from a sheath or other covering.

unship (ʌnˈʃɪp) *vb* **-ships, -shipping, -shipped.** **1** to be or cause to be unloaded, discharged, or disembarked from a ship. **2** (*tr*) *Nautical.* to remove from a regular place: *to unship oars.*

unsighted (ʌnˈsaɪtɪd) *adj* **1** not sighted. **2** not having a clear view. **3a** (of a gun) not equipped with a sight. **3b** (of a shot) not aimed by means of a sight. ▸ **unˈsightedly** *adv*

unsightly (ʌnˈsaɪtlɪ) *adj* unpleasant or unattractive to look at; ugly. ▸ **unˈsightliness** *n*

unsized[1] (ʌnˈsaɪzd) *adj* not made or sorted according to size.

unsized[2] (ʌnˈsaɪzd) *adj* (of a wall, etc.) not treated with size.

unskilful *or U.S.* **unskillful** (ʌnˈskɪlfʊl) *adj* **1** lacking dexterity or proficiency. **2** (often foll. by *in*) *Obsolete.* ignorant (of). ▸ **unˈskilfully** *or U.S.* **unˈskillfully** *adv* ▸ **unˈskilfulness** *or U.S.* **unˈskillfulness** *n*

unskilled (ʌnˈskɪld) *adj* **1** not having or requiring any special skill or training: *unskilled workers; an unskilled job.* **2** having or displaying no skill; inexpert: *he is quite unskilled at dancing.*

unslaked lime (ʌnˈsleɪkt) *n* another name for **calcium oxide.** Compare **slaked lime.**

unsling (ʌnˈslɪŋ) *vb* **-slings, -slinging, -slung.** (*tr*) **1** to remove or release from a slung position. **2** to remove slings from.

unsnap (ʌnˈsnæp) *vb* **-snaps, -snapping, -snapped.** (*tr*) to unfasten (the snap or catch) of (something).

unsnarl (ʌnˈsnɑːl) *vb* (*tr*) to free from a snarl or tangle.

unsociable (ʌnˈsəʊʃəbᵊl) *adj* **1** (of a person) disinclined to associate or fraternize with others. **2** unconducive to social intercourse: *an unsociable neighbourhood.* ▸ **unˌsociaˈbility** *or* **unˈsociableness** *n* ▸ **unˈsociably** *adv*

unsocial (ʌnˈsəʊʃəl) *adj* **1** not social; antisocial. **2** (of the hours of work of certain jobs) falling outside the normal working day.

unsophisticated (ˌʌnsəˈfɪstɪˌkeɪtɪd) *adj* **1** lacking experience or worldly wisdom. **2** marked by a lack of refinement or complexity: *an unsophisticated machine.* **3** unadulterated or genuine. ▸ **ˌunsoˈphistiˌcatedly** *adv* ▸ **ˌunsoˈphistiˌcatedness** *or* **ˌunsoˌphistiˈcation** *n*

unsound (ʌnˈsaʊnd) *adj* **1** diseased, weak, or unstable: *of unsound mind.* **2** unreliable or fallacious: *unsound advice.* **3** lacking solidity, strength, or firmness: *unsound foundations.* **4** of doubtful financial or commercial viability: *an unsound enterprise.* **5** (of fruit, timber, etc.) not in an edible or usable condition. ▸ **unˈsoundly** *adv* ▸ **unˈsoundness** *n*

unsparing (ʌnˈspeərɪŋ) *adj* **1** not sparing or frugal; lavish; profuse. **2** showing harshness or severity; unmerciful. ▸ **unˈsparingly** *adv* ▸ **unˈsparingness** *n*

unspeak (ʌnˈspiːk) *vb* **-speaks, -speaking, -spoke, -spoken.** an obsolete word for **unsay.**

unspeakable (ʌnˈspiːkəbᵊl) *adj* **1** incapable of expression in words: *unspeakable ecstasy.* **2** indescribably bad or evil. **3** not to be uttered: *unspeakable thoughts.* ▸ **unˈspeakableness** *n* ▸ **unˈspeakably** *adv*

unsphere (ʌnˈsfɪə) *vb* (*tr*) *Chiefly poetic.* to remove from its, one's, etc., sphere or place.

unspoiled (ʌnˈspɔɪld) *or* **unspoilt** (ʌnˈspɔɪlt) *adj* (of a village, town, etc.) having an unaltered character.

unspoken (ʌnˈspəʊkən) *adj* **1** understood without needing to be spoken; tacit. **2** not uttered aloud.

unspotted (ʌnˈspɒtɪd) *adj* **1** without spots or stains. **2** (esp. of reputations) free from moral stigma or blemish. ▸ **unˈspottedness** *n*

unstable (ʌnˈsteɪbᵊl) *adj* **1** lacking stability, fixity, or firmness. **2** disposed to temperamental, emotional, or psychological variability. **3** (of a chemical compound) readily decomposing. **4** *Physics.* **4a** (of an elementary particle) having a very short lifetime. **4b** spontaneously decomposing by nuclear decay; radioactive: *an unstable nuclide.* **5** *Electronics.* (of an electrical circuit, mechanical body, etc.) having a tendency to self-oscillation. ▸ **unˈstableness** *n* ▸ **unˈstably** *adv*

unsteady (ʌnˈstɛdɪ) *adj* **1** not securely fixed: *an unsteady foothold.* **2** (of behaviour, etc.) lacking constancy; erratic. **3** without regularity: *an unsteady rhythm.* **4** (of a manner of walking, etc.) precarious or staggering, as from intoxication. ◆ *vb* **-steadies, -steadying, -steadied.** **5** (*tr*) to make unsteady. ▸ **unˈsteadily** *adv* ▸ **unˈsteadiness** *n*

unsteel (ʌnˈstiːl) *vb* (*tr*) to make (the heart, feelings, etc.) more gentle or compassionate.

unstep (ʌnˈstɛp) *vb* **-steps, -stepping, -stepped.** (*tr*) *Nautical.* to remove (a mast) from its step.

unstick (ʌnˈstɪk) *vb* **-sticks, -sticking, -stuck.** (*tr*) to free or loosen (something stuck).

unstop (ʌnˈstɒp) *vb* **-stops, -stopping, -stopped.** (*tr*) **1** to remove the stop or stopper from. **2** to free from any stoppage or obstruction; open. **3** to draw out the stops on (an organ).

unstoppable (ʌnˈstɒpəbᵊl) *adj* not capable of being stopped; extremely forceful. ▸ **unˈstoppably** *adv*

unstopped (ʌnˈstɒpt) *adj* **1** not obstructed or stopped up. **2** *Phonetics.* denoting a speech sound for whose articulation the closure is not complete, as in the pronunciation of a vowel, fricative, or continuant. **3** *Prosody.* (of verse) having the sense of the line carried over into the next. **4** (of an organ pipe or a string on a musical instrument) not stopped.

unstrained (ʌnˈstreɪnd) *adj* **1** not under strain; relaxed. **2** not cleared or separated by passing through a strainer.

unstratified (ʌnˈstrætɪˌfaɪd) *adj* (esp. of igneous rocks and rock formations) not occurring in distinct layers or strata; not stratified.

unstreamed (ʌnˈstriːmd) *adj Brit. education.* (of children) not divided into groups or streams according to ability.

unstressed (ʌnˈstrɛst) *adj* **1** carrying relatively little stress; unemphasized. **2** *Phonetics.* of, relating to, or denoting the weakest accent in a word or breath group, which in some languages, such as English or German, is also associated with a reduction in vowel quality to a centralized (ɪ) or (ə). **3** *Prosody.* (of a syllable in verse) having no stress or accent.

unstriated (ʌnˈstraɪˌeɪtɪd) *adj* (of muscle) composed of elongated cells that do not have striations; smooth.

unstring (ʌnˈstrɪŋ) *vb* **-strings, -stringing, -strung.** (*tr*) **1** to remove the strings of. **2** (of beads, pearls, etc.) to remove or take from a string. **3** to weaken or enfeeble emotionally (a person or his nerves).

unstriped (ʌnˈstraɪpt) *adj* (esp. of smooth muscle) not having stripes; unstriated.

unstructured (ʌnˈstrʌktʃəd) *adj* **1** without formal structure or systematic organization. **2** without a preformed shape; (esp. of clothes) loose; untailored.

unstrung (ʌnˈstrʌŋ) *adj* **1** emotionally distressed; unnerved. **2** (of a stringed instrument) with the strings detached.

unstuck (ʌnˈstʌk) *adj* **1** freed from being stuck, glued, fastened, etc. **2** **come unstuck.** to suffer failure or disaster.

unstudied (ʌnˈstʌdɪd) *adj* **1** natural; unaffected. **2** (foll. by *in*) without knowledge or training.

unsubstantial (ˌʌnsəbˈstænʃəl) *adj* **1** lacking weight, strength, or firmness. **2** (esp. of an argument) of doubtful validity. **3** of no material existence or substance; unreal. ▸ **ˌunsubˌstantiˈality** *n* ▸ **ˌunsubˈstantially** *adv*

unsung (ʌnˈsʌŋ) *adj* **1** not acclaimed or honoured; *unsung deeds.* **2** not yet sung.

unsupportable (ˌʌnsəˈpɔːtəbᵊl) *adj* **1** not able to be supported. **2** not able to be defended: *unsupportable actions.*

unsure (ʌnˈʃʊə) *adj* **1** lacking assurance or self-confidence. **2** (*usually postpositive*) without sure knowledge; uncertain: *unsure of her agreement.* **3** precarious; insecure. **4** not certain or reliable.

unsuspected (ˌʌnsəˈspɛktɪd) *adj* **1** not under suspicion. **2** not known to exist. ▸ **ˌunsusˈpectedly** *adv* ▸ **ˌunsusˈpectedness** *n*

unsuspecting (ˌʌnsəˈspɛktɪŋ) *adj* disposed to trust; not suspicious; trusting. ▸ **ˌunsusˈpectingly** *adv*

unswear (ʌnˈswɛə) *vb* **-swears, -swearing, -swore, -sworn.** to retract or revoke (a sworn oath); abjure.

unˈsegmented *adj*
ˌunseˈlected *adj*
ˌunselfˈconscious *adj*
ˌunsentiˈmental *adj*
unˈsepaˌrated *adj*
unˈserviceable *adj*
unˈshaded *adj*
unˈshaken *adj*
unˈshared *adj*
unˈshaved *adj*
unˈshaven *adj*
unˈshed *adj*
unˈsheltered *adj*
unˈshockable *adj*
unˈshod *adj*
unˈsigned *adj*
unˈsinkable *adj*
unˈsmiling *adj*
unˈsoiled *adj*
unˈsold *adj*
ˌunsoˈlicited *adj*
unˈsolvable *adj*
unˈsolved *adj*
unˈsorted *adj*
unˈsought *adj*
unˈspecialˌized *or* **unˈspecialˌised** *adj*
ˌunspeˈcific *adj*
unˈspeciˌfied *adj*
ˌunspecˈtacular *adj*
unˈspiritual *adj*
unˈsporting *adj*
unˈsportsmanˌlike *adj*
unˈstained *adj*
unˈstated *adj*
unˈsterile *adj*
unˈstinted *adj*
unˈstinting *adj*
unˈstrap *vb,* **-ˈstraps, -ˈstrapping, -ˈstrapped.**
ˌunsubˈstantiˌated *adj*
unˈsubtle *adj*
ˌunsucˈcessful *adj*
ˌunsucˈcessfully *adv*
unˈsuitable *adj*
unˈsuited *adj*
unˈsullied *adj*
unˈsuperˌvised *adj*
ˌunsupˈported *adj*
ˌunsupˈpressed *adj*
ˌunsurˈmountable *adj*
ˌunsurˈpassable *adj*
ˌunsurˈpassed *adj*
ˌunsurˈprised *adj*
ˌunsusˈceptible *adj*

unswerving (ʌnˈswɜːvɪŋ) *adj* not turning aside; constant.
untangle (ʌnˈtæŋɡəl) *vb* (*tr*) **1** to free from a tangled condition. **2** to free from perplexity or confusion.
untaught (ʌnˈtɔːt) *adj* **1** without training or education. **2** attained or achieved without instruction.
unteach (ʌnˈtiːtʃ) *vb* **-teaches, -teaching, -taught.** (*tr*) *Rare.* to cause to disbelieve (teaching).
untenable (ʌnˈtɛnəbəl) *adj* **1** (of theories, propositions, etc.) incapable of being maintained, defended, or vindicated. **2** unable to be maintained against attack. **3** *Rare.* (of a house, etc.) unfit for occupation. ► **unˌtenaˈbility** *or* **unˈtenableness** *n* ► **unˈtenably** *adv*
Unter den Linden (*German* ˈʊntər deːn ˈlɪndən) *n* the main street of Berlin, formerly in East Berlin, extending to the Brandenburg Gate.
Unterwalden (*German* ˈʊntərˌvaldən) *n* a canton of central Switzerland, on Lake Lucerne: consists of the demicantons of **Nidwalden** (east) and **Obwalden** (west). Capitals: (Nidwalden) Stans; (Obwalden) Sarnen. Pop.: (Nidwalden) 35 983 (1995 est.); (Obwalden) 30 958 (1995 est.). Areas: (Nidwalden) 274 sq. km (107 sq. miles); (Obwalden) 492 sq. km (192 sq. miles).
unthink (ʌnˈθɪŋk) *vb* **-thinks, -thinking, -thought.** (*tr*) **1** to reverse one's opinion about. **2** to dispel from the mind.
unthinkable (ʌnˈθɪŋkəbəl) *adj* **1** not to be contemplated; out of the question. **2** unimaginable; inconceivable. **3** unreasonable; improbable. ► **unˌthinkaˈbility** *or* **unˈthinkableness** *n* ► **unˈthinkably** *adv*
unthinking (ʌnˈθɪŋkɪŋ) *adj* **1** lacking thoughtfulness; inconsiderate. **2** heedless; inadvertent: *it was done in an unthinking moment.* **3** not thinking or able to think. ► **unˈthinkingly** *adv* ► **unˈthinkingness** *n*
unthought-of (ˌʌnˈθɔːtɒv) *adj* unimaginable; inconceivable.
unthread (ʌnˈθrɛd) *vb* (*tr*) **1** to draw out the thread or threads from (a needle, etc.). **2** to disentangle.
unthrone (ʌnˈθrəʊn) *vb* (*tr*) a less common word for **dethrone.**
untidy (ʌnˈtaɪdɪ) *adj* **-dier, -diest. 1** not neat; slovenly. ♦ *vb* **-dies, -dying, -died. 2** (*tr*) to make untidy. ► **unˈtidily** *adv* ► **unˈtidiness** *n*
untie (ʌnˈtaɪ) *vb* **-ties, -tying, -tied. 1** to unfasten or free (a knot or something that is tied) or (of a knot or something that is tied) to become unfastened. **2** (*tr*) to free from constraint or restriction.
until (ʌnˈtɪl) *conj* (*subordinating*) **1** up to (a time) that: *he laughed until he cried.* **2** (*used with a negative*) before (a time or event): *until you change, you can't go out.* ♦ *prep* **3** (often preceded by *up*) in or throughout the period before: *he waited until six.* **4** (*used with a negative*) earlier than; before: *he won't come until tomorrow.* [C13 *untill;* related to Old High German *unt* unto, until, Old Norse *und;* see TILL[1]]

USAGE The use of *until such time as* (as in *industrial action will continue until such time as our demands are met*) is unnecessary and should be avoided: *industrial action will continue until our demands are met.* See also at **till**[1].

untimely (ʌnˈtaɪmlɪ) *adj* **1** occurring before the expected, normal, or proper time: *an untimely death.* **2** inappropriate to the occasion, time, or season: *his joking at the funeral was most untimely.* ♦ *adv* **3** prematurely or inopportunely. ► **unˈtimeliness** *n*
untitled (ʌnˈtaɪtəld) *adj* **1** without a title: *an untitled manuscript.* **2** having no claim or title: *an untitled usurper.*
unto (ˈʌntuː) *prep* an archaic word for **to.** [C13: of Scandinavian origin; see UNTIL]
untogether (ˌʌntəˈɡɛðə) *adj Slang.* incompetent or badly organized; mentally or emotionally unstable.
untold (ʌnˈtəʊld) *adj* **1** incapable of description or expression: *untold suffering.* **2** incalculably great in number or quantity: *untold thousands.* **3** not told.
untouchable (ʌnˈtʌtʃəbəl) *adj* **1** lying beyond reach. **2** above reproach, suspicion, or impeachment. **3** unable to be touched. ♦ *n* **4** a member of the lowest class in India, whom those of the four main castes were formerly forbidden to touch. ► **unˌtouchaˈbility** *n*
untouched (ʌnˈtʌtʃt) *adj* **1** not used, handled, touched, etc. **2** not injured or harmed. **3** (*postpositive*) emotionally unmoved. **4** not changed, modified, or affected. **5** (of food or drink) left without being consumed. **6** not mentioned or referred to: *he left the subject untouched.*
untoward (ˌʌntəˈwɔːd, ʌnˈtəʊəd) *adj* **1** characterized by misfortune, disaster, or annoyance. **2** not auspicious; adverse; unfavourable. **3** unseemly or improper. **4** out of the ordinary; out of the way. **5** *Archaic.* refractory; perverse. **6** *Obsolete.* awkward, ungainly, or uncouth. ► **ˌuntoˈwardly** *adv* ► **ˌuntoˈwardness** *n*
untravelled (ʌnˈtrævəld) *adj* **1** (of persons) not having travelled widely; narrow or provincial. **2** (of a road) never travelled over.
untread (ʌnˈtrɛd) *vb* **-treads, -treading, -trod, -trodden** *or* **-trod.** (*tr*) *Rare.* to retrace (a course, path, etc.).
untried (ʌnˈtraɪd) *adj* **1** not tried, attempted, or proved; untested. **2** not tried by a judge or court.
untrue (ʌnˈtruː) *adj* **1** incorrect or false. **2** disloyal. **3** diverging from a rule, standard, or measure; inaccurate. ► **unˈtrueness** *n* ► **unˈtruly** *adv*
untruss (ʌnˈtrʌs) *vb* **1** (*tr*) to release from or as if from a truss; unfasten. **2** *Obsolete.* to undress.
untruth (ʌnˈtruːθ) *n* **1** the state or quality of being untrue. **2** a statement, fact, etc., that is not true.
untruthful (ʌnˈtruːθfʊl) *adj* **1** (of a person) given to lying. **2** diverging from the truth; untrue. ► **unˈtruthfully** *adv* ► **unˈtruthfulness** *n*
untuck (ʌnˈtʌk) *vb* to become or cause to become loose or not tucked in: *to untuck the blankets.*
untutored (ʌnˈtjuːtəd) *adj* **1** without formal instruction or education. **2** lacking sophistication or refinement.
unused *adj* **1** (ʌnˈjuːzd). not being or never having been made use of. **2** (ʌnˈjuːst). (*postpositive;* foll. by *to*) not accustomed or used (to something).
unusual (ʌnˈjuːʒʊəl) *adj* out of the ordinary; uncommon; extraordinary: *an unusual design.* ► **unˈusually** *adv* ► **unˈusualness** *n*
unutterable (ʌnˈʌtərəbəl) *adj* incapable of being expressed in words. ► **unˈutterableness** *n* ► **unˈutterably** *adv*
unvalued (ʌnˈvæljuːd) *adj* **1** not appreciated or valued. **2** not assessed or estimated as to price or valuation. **3** *Obsolete.* of great value.
unvarnished (ʌnˈvɑːnɪʃt) *adj* not elaborated upon or glossed; plain and direct: *the unvarnished truth.*
unveil (ʌnˈveɪl) *vb* **1** (*tr*) to remove the cover or shroud from, esp. in the ceremonial unveiling of a monument, etc. **2** to remove the veil from (one's own or another person's face). **3** (*tr*) to make (something secret or concealed) known or public; divulge; reveal.
unveiling (ʌnˈveɪlɪŋ) *n* **1** a ceremony involving the removal of a veil at the formal presentation of a statue, monument, etc., for the first time. **2** the presentation of something, esp. for the first time.
unvoice (ʌnˈvɔɪs) *vb* (*tr*) **1** to pronounce without vibration of the vocal cords. **2** another word for **devoice.**
unvoiced (ʌnˈvɔɪst) *adj* **1** not expressed or spoken. **2** articulated without vibration of the vocal cords; voiceless.
unwaged (ʌnˈweɪdʒd) *adj* of, relating to, or denoting a person who is not receiving pay because of either being unemployed or working in the home.
unwarrantable (ʌnˈwɒrəntəbəl) *adj* incapable of vindication or justification. ► **unˈwarrantableness** *n* ► **unˈwarrantably** *adv*
unwarranted (ʌnˈwɒrəntɪd) *adj* **1** lacking justification or authorization. **2** another word for **unwarrantable.**
unwary (ʌnˈwɛərɪ) *adj* lacking caution or prudence; not vigilant or careful. ► **unˈwarily** *adv* ► **unˈwariness** *n*
unwashed (ʌnˈwɒʃt) *adj* **1** not washed. ♦ *n* **2 the great unwashed.** *Informal and derogatory.* the masses.
unwatched (ʌnˈwɒtʃt) *adj* (of an automatic device, such as a beacon) not manned.
unwaxed (ʌnˈwækst) *adj* not treated with wax, esp. of oranges or lemons, not sprayed with a protective coating of wax.
unwearied (ʌnˈwɪərɪd) *adj* **1** not abating or tiring. **2** not fatigued; fresh. ► **unˈweariedly** *adv* ► **unˈweariedness** *n*
unweighed (ʌnˈweɪd) *adj* **1** (of quantities purchased, etc.) not measured for weight. **2** (of statements, etc.) not carefully considered.
unwelcome (ʌnˈwɛlkəm) *adj* **1** (of persons) not welcome. **2** causing dissatisfaction or displeasure. ► **unˈwelcomely** *adv* ► **unˈwelcomeness** *n*
unwell (ʌnˈwɛl) *adj* (*postpositive*) not well; ill.
unwept (ʌnˈwɛpt) *adj* **1** not wept for or lamented. **2** *Rare.* (of tears) not shed.
unwholesome (ʌnˈhəʊlsəm) *adj* **1** detrimental to physical or mental health: *an unwholesome climate.* **2** morally harmful or depraved: *unwholesome practices.* **3** indicative of illness, esp. in appearance. **4** (esp. of food) of inferior quality. ► **unˈwholesomely** *adv* ► **unˈwholesomeness** *n*
unwieldy (ʌnˈwiːldɪ) *or* **unwieldly** *adj* **1** too heavy, large, or awkwardly shaped to be easily handled. **2** ungainly; clumsy. ► **unˈwieldily** *or* **unˈwieldlily** *adv* ► **unˈwieldiness** *or* **unˈwieldliness** *n*
unwilled (ʌnˈwɪld) *adj* not intentional; involuntary.
unwilling (ʌnˈwɪlɪŋ) *adj* **1** unfavourably inclined; reluctant. **2** performed, given, or said with reluctance. ► **unˈwillingly** *adv* ► **unˈwillingness** *n*
unwind (ʌnˈwaɪnd) *vb* **-winds, -winding, -wound. 1** to slacken, undo, or unravel or cause to slacken, undo, or unravel. **2** (*tr*) to disentangle. **3** to make or become relaxed: *he finds it hard to unwind after a busy day at work.* ► **unˈwindable** *adj* ► **unˈwinder** *n*
unwinking (ʌnˈwɪŋkɪŋ) *adj* vigilant; watchful.

unˈswayed *adj*
unˈsweetened *adj*
ˌunsymˈmetrical *adj*
ˌunsympaˈthetic *adj*
ˌunsystemˈatic *adj*
unˈtainted *adj*
unˈtalented *adj*
unˈtamable *or* **unˈtameable** *adj*
unˈtamed *adj*
unˈtapped *adj*
unˈtarnished *adj*
unˈtasted *adj*
unˈtaxed *adj*
unˈteachable *adj*
unˈtempered *adj*
unˈtenanted *adj*
unˈtended *adj*
unˈtested *adj*
unˈtethered *adj*
unˈtilled *adj*
unˈtinged *adj*
unˈtiring *adj*
unˈtraceable *adj*
unˈtraced *adj*
unˈtrained *adj*
unˈtrammelled *adj*
ˌuntransˈlatable *adj*
ˌuntransˈlated *adj*
unˈtreated *adj*
unˈtrodden *adj*
unˈtroubled *adj*
unˈtrustˌworthy *adj*
unˈturned *adj*
unˈtwine *vb*
unˈtwist *vb*
unˈtypical *adj*
unˈusable *adj*
unˈvacciˌnated *adj*
unˈvanquished *adj*
unˈvaried *adj*
unˈvarying *adj*
unˈveriˌfiable *adj*
unˈveriˌfied *adj*
unˈversed *adj*
unˈviable *adj*
unˈvisited *adj*
unˈwanted *adj*
unˈwavering *adj*
unˈweaned *adj*

unwise (ʌnˈwaɪz) *adj* lacking wisdom or prudence; foolish. ▸ **unˈwisely** *adv* ▸ **unˈwiseness** *n*
unwish (ʌnˈwɪʃ) *vb (tr)* **1** to retract or revoke (a wish). **2** to desire (something) not to be or take place.
unwished (ʌnˈwɪʃt) *adj* not desired; unwelcome.
unwitnessed (ʌnˈwɪtnɪst) *adj* **1** without the signature or attestation of a witness. **2** not seen or observed.
unwitting (ʌnˈwɪtɪŋ) *adj* (*usually prenominal*) **1** not knowing or conscious. **2** not intentional; inadvertent. [Old English *unwitende,* from UN-[1] + *witting,* present participle of *witan* to know; related to Old High German *wizzan* to know, Old Norse *vita*] ▸ **unˈwittingly** *adv* ▸ **unˈwittingness** *n*
unwonted (ʌnˈwəʊntɪd) *adj* **1** out of the ordinary; unusual. **2** (usually foll. by *to*) *Archaic.* unaccustomed; unused. ▸ **unˈwontedly** *adv* ▸ **unˈwontedness** *n*
unworldly (ʌnˈwɜːldlɪ) *adj* **1** not concerned with material values or pursuits. **2** lacking sophistication; naive. **3** not of this earth or world. ▸ **unˈworldliness** *n*
unworthy (ʌnˈwɜːðɪ) *adj* **1** (often foll. by *of*) not deserving or worthy. **2** (often foll. by *of*) beneath the level considered befitting (to): *that remark is unworthy of you.* **3** lacking merit or value. **4** (of treatment) not warranted or deserved. ▸ **unˈworthily** *adv* ▸ **unˈworthiness** *n*
unwound (ʌnˈwaʊnd) *vb* the past tense and past participle of **unwind.**
unwrap (ʌnˈræp) *vb* **-wraps, -wrapping, -wrapped.** to remove the covering or wrapping from (something) or (of something wrapped) to have the covering come off.
unwritten (ʌnˈrɪtᵊn) *adj* **1** not printed or in writing. **2** effective only through custom; traditional. **3** without writing upon it.
unwritten law *n* **1** the law based upon custom, usage, and judicial decisions, as distinguished from the enactments of a legislature, orders or decrees in writing, etc. **2 the.** the tradition that a person may avenge any insult to family integrity, as used to justify criminal acts of vengeance.
unyoke (ʌnˈjəʊk) *vb* **1** to release (an animal, etc.) from a yoke. **2** *(tr)* to set free; liberate. **3** *(tr)* to disconnect or separate. **4** *(intr) Archaic.* to cease working.
unzip (ʌnˈzɪp) *vb* **-zips, -zipping, -zipped.** to unfasten the zip of (a garment) or (of a zip or garment with a zip) to become unfastened: *her skirt unzipped as she sat down.*
up (ʌp) *prep* **1** indicating movement from a lower to a higher position: *climbing up a mountain.* **2** at a higher or further level or position in or on: *soot up the chimney; a shop up the road.* ◆ *adv* **3** (*often particle*) to an upward, higher, or erect position, esp. indicating readiness for an activity: *looking up at the stars; up and doing something.* **4** (*particle*) indicating intensity or completion of an action: *he tore up the cheque; drink up now!* **5** to the place referred to or where the speaker is: *the man came up and asked the way.* **6a** to a more important place: *up to London.* **6b** to a more northerly place: *up to Scotland.* **6c** (of a member of some British universities) to or at university. **6d** in a particular part of the country: *up north.* **7** appearing for trial: *up before the magistrate.* **8** having gained: *ten pounds up on the deal.* **9** higher in price: *coffee is up again.* **10** raised (for discussion, etc.): *the plan was up for consideration.* **11** taught: *well up in physics.* **12** (*functioning as imperative*) get, stand, etc., up: *up with you!* **13 all up with.** *Informal.* **13a** over; finished. **13b** doomed to die. **14 up with.** (*functioning as imperative*) wanting the beginning or continuation of: *up with the monarchy!* **15 something's up.** *Informal.* something strange is happening. **16 up against. 16a** touching. **16b** having to cope with: *look what we're up against now.* **17 up and running.** in operation; functioning properly. **18 up for.** as a candidate or applicant for: *he's up for re-election again.* **19 up for it.** *Informal.* keen or willing to try something out or make a good effort: *it's a big challenge and I'm up for it.* **20 up to. 20a** devising or scheming; occupied with: *she's up to no good.* **20b** dependent or incumbent upon: *the decision is up to you.* **20c** equal to (a challenge, etc.) or capable of (doing, etc.): *are you up to playing in the final?* **20d** aware of: *up to a person's tricks.* **20e** as far as: *up to his waist in mud.* **20f** as many as: *up to two years waiting time.* **20g** comparable with: *not up to your normal standard.* **21 up top.** *Informal.* in the head or mind. **22 up yours.** *Slang.* a vulgar expression of contempt or refusal. **23 what's up?** *Informal.* **23a** what is the matter? **23b** what is happening? ◆ *adj* **24** (*predicative*) of a high or higher position. **25** (*predicative*) out of bed; awake: *the children aren't up yet.* **26** (*prenominal*) of or relating to a train or trains to a more important place or one regarded as higher: *the up platform.* **27** (*predicative*) over or completed: *the examiner announced that their time was up.* **28** (*predicative*) beating one's opponent by a specified amount: *three goals up by half-time.* ◆ *vb* **ups, upping, upped. 29** *(tr)* to increase or raise. **30** *(intr;* foll. by *and* with a verb) *Informal.* to do (something) suddenly, unexpectedly, etc.: *she upped and married someone else.* ◆ *n* **31** high point; good or pleasant period (esp. in the phrase **ups and downs**). **32** *Slang.* another word (esp. U.S.) for **upper** (sense 9). **33 on the up and up. 33a** trustworthy or honest. **33b** *Brit.* on the upward trend or movement: *our firm's on the up and up.* [Old English *upp;* related to Old Saxon, Old Norse *up,* Old High German *ūf,* Gothic *iup*]

USAGE The use of *up* before *until* is redundant and should be avoided: *the talks will continue until* (not *up until*) *23rd March.*

UP *abbrev. for:* **1** United Press. **2** Uttar Pradesh.
up- *prefix* up, upper, or upwards: *uproot; upmost; upthrust; upgrade; uplift.*
up-anchor *vb (intr) Nautical.* to weigh anchor.
up-and-coming *adj* promising continued or future success; enterprising.
up-and-down *adj* **1** moving, executed, or formed alternately upwards and downwards. **2** *Chiefly U.S.* very steep; vertical. ◆ *adv, prep* **up and down. 3** backwards and forwards (along).
up-and-over *adj* (of a door, etc.) opened by being lifted and moved into a horizontal position.
up-and-under *n Rugby League.* a high kick forwards followed by a charge to the place where the ball lands.
Upanishad (uːˈpʌnɪʃəd, -ˌʃæd, juː-) *n Hinduism.* any of a class of the Sanskrit sacred books probably composed between 400 and 200 B.C. and embodying the mystical and esoteric doctrines of ancient Hindu philosophy. [C19: from Sanskrit *upanisad* a sitting down near something, from *upa* near to + *ni* down + *sīdati* he sits] ▸ **Uˌpaniˈshadic** *adj*
upas (ˈjuːpəs) *n* **1** a large moraceous tree of Java, *Antiaria toxicaria,* having whitish bark and poisonous milky sap. **2** the sap of this tree, used as an arrow poison. ◆ Also called: **antiar.** [C19: from Malay: poison]
upbeat (ˈʌpˌbiːt) *n* **1** *Music.* **1a** a usually unaccented beat, esp. the last in a bar. **1b** the upward gesture of a conductor's baton indicating this. Compare **downbeat. 2** an upward trend (in prosperity, etc.). ◆ *adj* **3** *Informal.* marked by cheerfulness or optimism.
up-bow (ˈʌpˌbəʊ) *n* a stroke of the bow from its tip to its nut on a stringed instrument. Compare **down-bow.**
upbraid (ʌpˈbreɪd) *vb (tr)* **1** to reprove or reproach angrily. **2** to find fault with. [Old English *upbregdan;* related to Danish *bebreide;* see UP, BRAID] ▸ **upˈbraider** *n* ▸ **upˈbraiding** *n* ▸ **upˈbraidingly** *adv*
upbringing (ˈʌpˌbrɪŋɪŋ) *n* the education of a person during his formative years. Also called: **bringing-up.**
upbuild (ʌpˈbɪld) *vb* **-builds, -building, -built.** *(tr)* to build up; enlarge, increase, etc. ▸ **upˈbuilder** *n*
upcast (ˈʌpˌkɑːst) *n* **1** material cast or thrown up. **2** a ventilation shaft through which air leaves a mine. Compare **downcast** (sense 3). **3** *Geology.* (in a fault) the section of strata that has been displaced upwards. ◆ *adj* **4** directed or thrown upwards. ◆ *vb* **-casts, -casting, -cast. 5** *(tr)* to throw or cast up.
upcoming (ˌʌpˈkʌmɪŋ) *adj* coming soon; forthcoming.
upcountry (ʌpˈkʌntrɪ) *adj* **1** of or coming from the interior of a country or region. **2** *Disparaging.* lacking the sophistication associated with city-dwellers; countrified. ◆ *n* **3** the interior part of a region or country. ◆ *adv* **4** towards, in, or into the interior part of a country or region.
update *vb* (ʌpˈdeɪt). *(tr)* **1** to bring up to date. ◆ *n* (ˈʌpˌdeɪt). **2** the act of updating or something that is updated. ▸ **upˈdateable** *adj* ▸ **upˈdater** *n*
Updike (ˈʌpˌdaɪk) *n* **John (Hoyer).** born 1932, U.S. writer. His novels include *Rabbit, Run* (1960), *Couples* (1968), *The Coup* (1979), *Brazil* (1993), *Toward the End of Time* (1998), and *Rabbit is Rich* (1982) and *Rabbit at Rest* (1990), both of which won Pulitzer prizes.
updraught (ˈʌpˌdrɑːft) *n* an upward movement of air or other gas.
upend (ʌpˈɛnd) *vb* **1** to turn or set or become turned or set on end. **2** *(tr)* to affect or upset drastically.
upfront (ˈʌpˈfrʌnt) *adj* **1** *Informal.* open, frank, honest. ◆ *adv, adj* **2** (of money) paid out at the beginning of a business arrangement.
upgrade *vb* (ʌpˈgreɪd). *(tr)* **1** to assign or promote (a person or job) to a higher professional rank or position. **2** to raise in value, importance, esteem, etc. **3** to improve (a breed of livestock) by crossing with a better strain. ◆ *n* (ˈʌpˌgreɪd). **4** *U.S. and Canadian.* an upward slope. **5 on the upgrade.** improving or progressing, as in importance, status, health, etc. ◆ *adj* **6** *U.S. and Canadian.* going or sloping upwards. ◆ *adv* (ˈʌpˈgreɪd). **7** *U.S. and Canadian.* up an incline, hill, or slope. ▸ **upˈgrader** *n*
upgrowth (ˈʌpˌgrəʊθ) *n* **1** the process of developing or growing upwards. **2** a result of evolution or growth.
upheaval (ʌpˈhiːvᵊl) *n* **1** a strong, sudden, or violent disturbance, as in politics, social conditions, etc. **2** *Geology.* another word for **uplift** (sense 7).
upheave (ʌpˈhiːv) *vb* **-heaves, -heaving, -heaved** *or* **-hove. 1** to heave or rise upwards. **2** *Geology.* to thrust (land) upwards or (of land) to be thrust upwards. **3** *(tr)* to disturb violently; throw into disorder.
upheld (ʌpˈhɛld) *vb* the past tense and past participle of **uphold.**
Up-Helly-Aa (ˌʌpˈhɛlɪɑː) *n* a midwinter festival held in January in Shetland, originally a fire festival, but now a celebration of Shetland's Norse heritage, involving the ceremonial burning of a newly built Viking ship. [from UP (in the sense: finished) + *haliday* a Scottish form of HOLIDAY]
uphill (ˈʌpˈhɪl) *adj* **1** inclining, sloping, or leading upwards. **2** requiring arduous and protracted effort: *an uphill task.* ◆ *adv* **3** up an incline or slope; upwards. **4** against difficulties. ◆ *n* **5** a rising incline; ascent.
uphold (ʌpˈhəʊld) *vb* **-holds, -holding, -held.** *(tr)* **1** to maintain, affirm, or defend against opposition or challenge. **2** to give moral support or inspiration to. **3** *Rare.* to support physically. **4** to lift up. ▸ **upˈholder** *n*
upholster (ʌpˈhəʊlstə) *vb (tr)* to fit (chairs, sofas, etc.) with padding, springs, webbing, and covering.
upholsterer (ʌpˈhəʊlstərə) *n* a person who upholsters furniture as a profession. [C17: from *upholster* small furniture dealer; see UPHOLD, -STER, -ER[1]]
upholstery (ʌpˈhəʊlstərɪ) *n, pl* **-steries. 1** the padding, covering, etc., of a piece of furniture. **2** the business, work, or craft of upholstering.
uphroe (ˈjuːfrəʊ) *n Nautical.* a variant spelling of **euphroe.**
UPI *abbrev. for* United Press International.
upkeep (ˈʌpˌkiːp) *n* **1** the act or process of keeping something in good repair, esp. over a long period; maintenance. **2** the cost of maintenance.

unˈworkable *adj*	**unˈworried** *adj*	**unˈyielding** *adj*
unˈworn *adj*	**unˈwounded** *adj*	

upland ('ʌplənd) *n* **1** an area of high or relatively high ground. ◆ *adj* **2** relating to or situated in an upland.

upland cotton *n* **1** a tropical American cotton plant, *Gossypium hirsutum,* widely cultivated for its fibre. **2** the fibre of this plant, or the fabric woven from it.

upland plover *or* **sandpiper** *n* an American sandpiper, *Bartramia longicauda,* with a short slender bill and long tail.

uplift *vb* (ʌp'lɪft). (*tr*) **1** to raise; elevate; lift up. **2** to raise morally, spiritually, culturally, etc. **3** *Scot. and N.Z.* to collect (a passenger, parcel, etc.); pick up. ◆ *n* ('ʌp,lɪft). **4** the act, process, or result of lifting up. **5** the act or process of bettering moral, social or cultural conditions, etc. **6a** a brassiere for lifting and supporting the breasts. **6b** (*as modifier*): *an uplift bra.* **7** the process or result of land being raised to a higher level, as during a period of mountain building. ▸ **up'lifter** *n* ▸ **up'lifting** *adj*

uplighter ('ʌp,laɪtə) *n* a lamp or wall light designed or positioned to cast its light upwards.

uplink ('ʌp,lɪŋk) *n* the transmitter on the ground that sends signals up to a communications satellite.

up-market *adj* relating to commercial products, services, etc., that are relatively expensive and of superior quality.

upmost ('ʌp,məʊst) *adj* another word for **uppermost.**

Upolu (uː'pəʊluː) *n* an island in the SW central Pacific, in Western Samoa. Chief town: Apia. Pop.: 116 248 (1991). Area: 1114 sq. km (430 sq. miles).

upon (ə'pɒn) *prep* **1** another word for **on. 2** indicating a position reached by going up: *climb upon my knee.* **3** imminent for: *the weekend was upon us again.* [C13: from UP + ON]

upper ('ʌpə) *adj* **1** higher or highest in relation to physical position, wealth, rank, status, etc. **2** (*cap. when part of a name*) lying farther upstream, inland, or farther north: *the upper valley of the Loire.* **3** (*cap. when part of a name*) *Geology, archaeol.* denoting the late part or division of a period, system, formation, etc.: *Upper Palaeolithic.* **4** *Maths.* (of a limit or bound) greater than or equal to one or more numbers or variables. ◆ *n* **5** the higher of two objects, people, etc. **6** the part of a shoe above the sole, covering the upper surface of the foot. **7 on one's uppers.** extremely poor; destitute. **8** *Informal.* any tooth of the upper jaw. **9** Also called (esp. U.S.): **up.** *Slang.* any of various drugs having a stimulant or euphoric effect. Compare **downer.**

upper atmosphere *n Meteorol.* that part of the atmosphere above the troposphere, esp. at heights that cannot be reached by balloon.

Upper Austria *n* a state of N Austria: first divided from Lower Austria in 1251. Capital: Linz. Pop.: 1 383 620 (1994 est.). Area: 11 978 sq. km (4625 sq. miles). German name: **Oberösterreich.**

Upper Canada *n* **1** *History.* (from 1791–1841) the official name of the region of Canada lying southwest of the Ottawa River and north of the lower Great Lakes. Compare **Lower Canada. 2** (esp. in E Canada) another name for **Ontario.**

upper case *Printing.* ◆ *n* **1** the top half of a compositor's type case in which capital letters, reference marks, and accents are kept. ◆ *adj* (**upper-case** *when prenominal*). **2** of or relating to capital letters kept in this case and used in the setting or production of printed or typed matter. ◆ *vb* **upper-case. 3** (*tr*) to print with upper-case letters; capitalize.

upper chamber *n* another name for an **upper house.**

upper class *n* **1** the class occupying the highest position in the social hierarchy, esp. the wealthy or the aristocracy. ◆ *adj* (**upper-class** *when prenominal*). **2** of or relating to the upper class. **3** *U.S. education.* of or relating to the junior or senior classes of a college or high school.

upper crust *n Informal.* the upper class.

uppercut ('ʌpə,kʌt) *n* **1** a short swinging upward blow with the fist delivered at an opponent's chin. ◆ *vb* **-cuts, -cutting, -cut. 2** to hit (an opponent) with an uppercut.

Upper Egypt *n* one of the four main administrative districts of Egypt: extends south from Cairo to the Sudan.

upper hand *n* **the.** the position of control; advantage (esp. in the phrases **have** *or* **get the upper hand**).

upper house *n* (*often caps.*) one of the two houses of a bicameral legislature. Also called: **upper chamber.** Compare **lower house.**

upper mordent *n* another name for **inverted mordent.**

uppermost ('ʌpə,məʊst) *adj also* **upmost. 1** highest in position, power, importance, etc. ◆ *adv* **2** in or into the highest position, etc.

Upper Palaeolithic *n* **1** the latest of the three periods of the Palaeolithic, beginning about 40 000 B.C. and ending, in Europe, about 12 000 B.C.: characterized by the emergence of modern man, *Homo sapiens.* ◆ *adj* **2** of or relating to this period.

Upper Palatinate *n* See **Palatinate.**

Upper Peninsula *n* a peninsula in the northern U.S. between Lakes Superior and Michigan, constituting the N part of the state of Michigan.

upper regions *pl n* **the.** *Chiefly literary.* the sky; heavens.

upper school *n* the senior pupils in a secondary school, usually those in the fourth and fifth years and above.

Upper Silesia *n* a region of SW Poland, formerly ruled by Germany: coal mining and other heavy industry.

Upper Tunguska *n* See **Tunguska.**

Upper Volta ('vɒltə) *n* the former name (until 1984) of **Burkina-Faso.**

upper works *pl n Nautical.* the parts of a vessel above the waterline when fully laden.

uppish ('ʌpɪʃ) *adj Brit. informal.* snobbish, arrogant, or presumptuous. [C18: from UP + -ISH] ▸ **'uppishly** *adv* ▸ **'uppishness** *n*

uppity ('ʌpɪtɪ) *adj Informal.* **1** not yielding easily to persuasion or control. **2** another word for **uppish.** [from UP + fanciful ending, perhaps influenced by -ITY]

Uppsala *or* **Upsala** ('ʌpsɑːlə) *n* a city in E central Sweden: the royal headquarters in the 13th century; Gothic cathedral (the largest in Sweden) and Sweden's oldest university (1477). Pop.: 184 507 (1997 est.).

upraise (ʌp'reɪz) *vb* (*tr*) **1** *Chiefly literary.* to lift up; elevate. **2** *Archaic.* to praise; exalt. ▸ **up'raiser** *n*

uprate (ʌp'reɪt) *vb* **1** raise the value, rate, or size of, upgrade. **2** *Photog.* to increase the effective speed of (a film) by underexposing, usually up to two stops, and subsequently overdeveloping (pushing the processing).

uprear (ʌp'rɪə) *vb* (*tr*) to lift up; raise.

upright ('ʌp,raɪt) *adj* **1** vertical or erect. **2** honest, honourable, or just. ◆ *adv* **3** vertically. ◆ *n* **4** a vertical support, such as a stake or post. **5** short for **upright piano. 6** the state of being vertical. ◆ *vb* **7** (*tr*) to make upright. ▸ **'up,rightly** *adv* ▸ **'up,rightness** *n*

upright piano *n* a piano which has a rectangular vertical case. Compare **grand piano.**

uprise *vb* (ʌp'raɪz), **-rises, -rising, -rose, -risen. 1** (*tr*) to rise up. ◆ *n* ('ʌp,raɪz). **2** another word for **rise** (senses 24, 25, 30). ▸ **up'riser** *n*

uprising ('ʌp,raɪzɪŋ, ʌp'raɪzɪŋ) *n* **1** a revolt or rebellion. **2** *Archaic.* an ascent.

upriver ('ʌp'rɪvə) *adj, adv* **1** towards or near the source of a river. ◆ *n* **2** an area located upstream.

uproar ('ʌp,rɔː) *n* a commotion or disturbance characterized by loud noise and confusion; turmoil.

uproarious (ʌp'rɔːrɪəs) *adj* **1** causing or characterized by an uproar; tumultuous. **2** extremely funny; hilarious. **3** (of laughter) loud and boisterous. ▸ **up'roariously** *adv* ▸ **up'roariousness** *n*

uproot (ʌp'ruːt) *vb* (*tr*) **1** to pull up by or as if by the roots. **2** to displace (a person or persons) from native or habitual surroundings. **3** to remove or destroy utterly. ▸ **up'rootedness** *n* ▸ **up'rooter** *n*

uprouse (ʌp'raʊz) *vb* (*tr*) *Rare.* to rouse or stir up; arouse.

uprush ('ʌp,rʌʃ) *n* an upward rush, as of consciousness.

upsadaisy ('ʌpsə'deɪzɪ) *interj* a variant of **upsy-daisy.**

Upsala ('ʌpsɑːlə) *n* a variant spelling of **Uppsala.**

ups and downs *pl n* alternating periods of good and bad fortune, high and low spirits, etc.

upscale ('ʌp'skeɪl) *adj Informal.* of or for the upper end of an economic or social scale; up-market.

upset *vb* (ʌp'sɛt), **-sets, -setting, -set.** (*mainly tr*) **1** (*also intr*) to tip or be tipped over; overturn, capsize, or spill. **2** to disturb the normal state, course, or stability of : *to upset the balance of nature.* **3** to disturb mentally or emotionally. **4** to defeat or overthrow, usually unexpectedly. **5** to make physically ill: *seafood always upsets my stomach.* **6** to thicken or spread (the end of a bar, rivet, etc.) by forging, hammering, or swagging. ◆ *n* ('ʌp,sɛt). **7** an unexpected defeat or reversal, as in a contest or plans. **8** a disturbance or disorder of the emotions, body, etc. **9** a tool used to upset a bar or rivet; swage. **10** a forging or bar that has been upset in preparation for further processing. ◆ *adj* (ʌp'sɛt). **11** overturned or capsized. **12** emotionally or physically disturbed or distressed. **13** disordered; confused. **14** defeated or overthrown. [C14 (in the sense: to set up, erect; C19 in the sense: to overthrow); related to Middle High German *ūfsetzen* to put on, Middle Dutch *opzetten*] ▸ **up'settable** *adj* ▸ **up'setter** *n* ▸ **up'setting** *adj* ▸ **up'settingly** *adv*

upset price ('ʌp,sɛt) *n* another name (esp. Scot., U.S., and Canadian) for **reserve price.**

upsetting (ʌp'sɛtɪŋ) *n Metallurgy.* the process of hammering the end of a heated bar of metal so that its width is increased locally, as in the manufacture of bolts.

upshot ('ʌp,ʃɒt) *n* **1** the final result; conclusion; outcome. **2** *Archery.* the final shot in a match. [C16: from UP + SHOT[1]]

upside ('ʌp,saɪd) *n* the upper surface or part.

upside down *adj* **1** (*usually postpositive;* **upside-down** *when prenominal*) turned over completely; inverted. **2** *Informal.* confused; muddled; topsy-turvy: *an upside-down world.* ◆ *adv* **3** in an inverted fashion. **4** in a chaotic or crazy manner. [C16: variant, by folk etymology, of earlier *upsodown*] ▸ **,upside-'downness** *n*

upside-down cake *n* a sponge cake baked with sliced fruit at the bottom, then inverted before serving.

upsides ('ʌp,saɪdz) *adv Informal, chiefly Brit.* (foll. by *with*) equal or level (with), as through revenge or retaliation.

upsilon ('ʌpsɪ,lɒn, juːp'saɪlən) *n* the 20th letter in the Greek alphabet (Υ or υ) a vowel, transliterated as *y* or *u.* [C17: from Medieval Greek *u psilon* simple *u,* name adopted for graphic *u* to avoid confusion with graphic *oi,* since pronunciation was the same for both in Late Greek]

upskill ('ʌp,skɪl) *vb* (*tr*) *N.Z.* to improve a person's aptitude for work by additional training.

upspring *Archaic or literary.* ◆ *vb* (ʌp'sprɪŋ). **-springs, -springing, -sprang** *or* **-sprung, -sprung. 1** (*intr*) to spring up or come into existence. ◆ *n* ('ʌp,sprɪŋ). **2** a leap forwards or upwards. **3** the act of coming into existence.

upstage ('ʌp'steɪdʒ) *adv* **1** on, at, or to the rear of the stage. ◆ *adj* **2** of or relating to the back half of the stage. **3** *Informal.* haughty; supercilious; aloof. ◆ *vb* (*tr*) **4** to move upstage of (another actor), thus forcing him to turn away from the audience. **5** *Informal.* to draw attention to oneself from (someone else); steal the show from (someone). **6** *Informal.* to treat haughtily. ◆ *n* **7** the back half of the stage.

upstairs ('ʌp'stɛəz) *adv* **1** up the stairs; to or on an upper floor or level. **2** *Informal.* to or into a higher rank or office. **3** *Informal.* in the mind: *a little weak upstairs.* **4 kick upstairs.** *Informal.* to promote to a higher rank or position, esp. one that carries less power. ◆ *n* (*functioning as sing or pl*) **5a** an upper floor or level. **5b** *(as modifier): an upstairs room.* **6** *Brit. informal, old-fashioned.* the masters and mistresses of a household collectively, esp. of a large house. Compare **downstairs** (sense 3).

upstanding (ʌp'stændɪŋ) *adj* **1** of good character. **2** upright and vigorous in build. **3 be upstanding. 3a** (in a court of law) a direction to all persons present to rise to their feet before the judge enters or leaves the court. **3b** (at a formal dinner) a direction to all persons present to rise to their feet for a toast. ▸ **up'standingness** *n*

upstart *n* ('ʌp,stɑːt). **1a** a person, group, etc., that has risen suddenly to a position of power or wealth. **1b** *(as modifier): an upstart tyrant; an upstart family.* **2a** an arrogant or presumptuous person. **2b** *(as modifier): his upstart ambition.* ◆ *vb* (ʌp'stɑːt). **3** *(intr) Archaic.* to start up, as in surprise, etc.

upstate ('ʌp'steɪt) *U.S.* ◆ *adj, adv* **1** towards, in, from, or relating to the outlying or northern sections of a state, esp. of New York State. ◆ *n* **2** the outlying, esp. northern, sections of a state. ▸ **'up'stater** *n*

upstream ('ʌp'striːm) *adv, adj* **1** in or towards the higher part of a stream; against the current. **2** (in the oil industry) of or for any of the stages prior to oil production, such as exploration or research. Compare **downstream** (sense 2).

upstretched (ʌp'strɛtʃt) *adj* (esp. of the arms) stretched or raised up.

upstroke ('ʌp,strəʊk) *n* **1a** an upward stroke or movement, as of a pen or brush. **1b** the mark produced by such a stroke. **2** the upward movement of a piston in a reciprocating engine.

upsurge *vb* (ʌp'sɜːdʒ). **1** *(intr) Chiefly literary.* to surge up. ◆ *n* ('ʌp,sɜːdʒ). **2** a rapid rise or swell.

upsweep *n* ('ʌp,swiːp). **1** a curve or sweep upwards. **2** *U.S. and Canadian.* an upswept hairstyle. ◆ *vb* (ʌp'swiːp), **-sweeps, -sweeping, -swept. 3** to sweep, curve, or brush or be swept, curved, or brushed upwards.

upswell (ʌp'swɛl) *vb* **-swells, -swelling, -swelled, -swelled** *or* **-swollen.** *Rare.* to swell up or cause to swell up.

upswing *n* ('ʌp,swɪŋ). **1** *Economics.* a recovery period in the trade cycle. **2** an upward swing or movement or any increase or improvement. ◆ *vb* (ʌp'swɪŋ), **-swings, -swinging, -swung. 3** *(intr)* to swing or move up.

upsy-daisy ('ʌpsɪ'deɪzɪ) *or* **upsadaisy** *interj* an expression, usually of reassurance, uttered as when someone, esp. a child, stumbles or is being lifted up. [C18 *up-a-daisy,* irregularly formed from UP (adv)]

uptake ('ʌp,teɪk) *n* **1** a pipe, shaft, etc., that is used to convey smoke or gases, esp. one that connects a furnace to a chimney. **2** *Mining.* another term for **upcast** (sense 2). **3** taking up or lifting up. **4** the act of accepting or taking up something on offer or available. **5 quick** *(or* **slow) on the uptake.** *Informal.* quick (or slow) to understand or learn.

upthrow ('ʌp,θrəʊ). *n* **1** *Geology.* the upward movement of rocks on one side of a fault plane relative to rocks on the other side. **2** *Rare.* an upward thrust or throw; upheaval.

upthrust ('ʌp,θrʌst) *n* **1** an upward push or thrust. **2** *Geology.* a violent upheaval of the earth's surface.

uptight (ʌp'taɪt) *adj Informal.* **1** displaying tense repressed nervousness, irritability, or anger. **2** unable to give expression to one's feelings, personality, etc.

uptilt (ʌp'tɪlt) *vb (tr)* to tilt up.

uptime ('ʌp,taɪm) *n Commerce.* time during which a machine, such as a computer, actually operates.

up-to-date *adj* **a** modern, current, or fashionable: *an up-to-date magazine.* **b** *(predicative): the magazine is up to date.* ▸ **'up-to-'dately** *adv* ▸ **'up-to-'dateness** *n*

uptown ('ʌp'taʊn) *U.S. and Canadian.* ◆ *adj, adv* **1** towards, in, or relating to some part of a town that is away from the centre. ◆ *n* **2** such a part of a town, esp. a residential part. ▸ **'up'towner** *n*

upturn *vb* (ʌp'tɜːn). **1** to turn or cause to turn up, over, or upside down. **2** *(tr)* to create disorder. **3** *(tr)* to direct upwards. ◆ *n* ('ʌp,tɜːn). **4** an upward turn, trend, or improvement. **5** an upheaval or commotion.UPVC

UPVC *abbrev. for* unplasticized polyvinyl chloride. See also **PVC.**

upward ('ʌpwəd) *adj* **1** directed or moving towards a higher point or level. ◆ *adv* **2** a variant of **upwards.** ▸ **'upwardly** *adv* ▸ **'upwardness** *n*

upwardly mobile *adj* (of a person or social group) moving or aspiring to move to a higher social class or to a position of increased status or power.

upward mobility *n Sociol.* the movement of an individual, social group, or class to a position of increased status or power. Compare **downward mobility.** See also **horizontal mobility, vertical mobility.**

upwards ('ʌpwədz) *or* **upward** *adv* **1** from a lower to a higher place, level, condition, etc. **2** towards a higher level, standing, etc.

upwind ('ʌp'wɪnd) *adv* **1** into or against the wind. **2** towards or on the side where the wind is blowing; windward. ◆ *adj* **3** going against the wind: *the upwind leg of the course.* **4** on the windward side: *the upwind side of the house has weathered.*

Ur (ɜː) *n* an ancient city of Sumer located on a former channel of the Euphrates.

ur- *combining form.* a variant of **uro-**[1] and **uro-**[2] before a vowel.

Ur- *combining form.* original, primitive: *Ursprache.* [German]

uracil ('jʊərəsɪl) *n Biochem.* a pyrimidine present in all living cells, usually in a combined form, as in RNA. Formula: $C_4H_4N_2O_2$. [C20: from URO-[1] + ACETIC + -ILE]

uraemia *or U.S.* **uremia** (jʊ'riːmɪə) *n Pathol.* the accumulation of waste products, normally excreted in the urine, in the blood: causes severe headaches, vomiting, etc. Also called: **azotaemia.** [C19: from New Latin, from Greek *ouron* urine + *haima* blood] ▸ **u'raemic** *or U.S.* **u'remic** *adj*

uraeus (jʊ'riːəs) *n, pl* **-uses.** the sacred serpent represented on the headdresses of ancient Egyptian kings and gods. [C19: from New Latin, from Greek *ouraios,* from Egyptian *uro* asp]

Ural ('jʊərəl; *Russian* u'ral) *n* a river in central Russia, rising in the S Ural Mountains and flowing south to the Caspian Sea. Length: 2534 km (1575 miles).

Ural-Altaic *n* **1** a postulated group of related languages consisting of the Uralic and Altaic families of languages. ◆ *adj* **2** of or relating to this group of languages, characterized by agglutination and vowel harmony.

Uralic (jʊ'rælɪk) *or* **Uralian** (jʊ'reɪlɪən) *n* **1** a superfamily of languages consisting of the Finno-Ugric family together with Samoyed. See also **Ural-Altaic.** ◆ *adj* **2** of or relating to these languages.

uralite ('jʊərə,laɪt) *n* an amphibole mineral, similar to hornblende, that replaces pyroxene in some igneous and metamorphic rocks. [C19: from the URAL MOUNTAINS where it was first found + -ITE[1]] ▸ **uralitic** (,jʊərə'lɪtɪk) *adj*

Ural Mountains *or* **Urals** *pl n* a mountain system in W central Russia, extending over 2000 km (1250 miles) from the Arctic Ocean towards the Aral Sea: forms part of the geographical boundary between Europe and Asia; one of the richest mineral areas in the world, with many associated major industrial centres. Highest peak: Mount Narodnaya, 1894 m (6214 ft.).

uranalysis (,jʊərə'nælɪsɪs) *n, pl* **-ses** (-,siːz). *Med.* a variant spelling of **urinalysis.**

Urania (jʊ'reɪnɪə) *n Greek myth.* **1** the Muse of astronomy. **2** another name of **Aphrodite.** [C17: from Latin, from Greek *Ourania,* from *ouranios* heavenly, from *ouranos* heaven]

Uranian (jʊ'reɪnɪən) *n* **1** a hypothetical inhabitant of the planet Uranus. ◆ *adj* **2** of, occurring on, or relating to the planet Uranus. **3** of the heavens; celestial. **4** relating to astronomy; astronomical. **5** (as an epithet of Aphrodite) heavenly; spiritual. **6** of or relating to the Muse Urania.

uranic[1] (jʊ'rænɪk) *adj* of or containing uranium, esp. in a high valence state.

uranic[2] (jʊ'rænɪk) *adj Obsolete.* astronomical or celestial. [C19: from Greek *ouranos* heaven]

uranide ('jʊərə,naɪd) *n* any element having an atomic number greater than that of protactinium.

uraninite (jʊ'rænɪ,naɪt) *n* a blackish heavy radioactive mineral consisting of uranium oxide in cubic crystalline form together with radium, lead, helium, etc.: occurs in coarse granite. Formula: UO_2. [C19: see URANIUM, -IN, -ITE[1]]

uranism ('jʊərænɪzəm) *n* a rare word for **homosexuality** (esp. male homosexuality). [C20: from German *Uranismus,* from Greek *ouranios* heavenly, i.e. spiritual; compare URANIAN (sense 5)]

uranite ('jʊərə,naɪt) *n* any of various minerals containing uranium, esp. torbernite or autunite. ▸ **uranitic** (,jʊərə'nɪtɪk) *adj*

uranium (jʊ'reɪnɪəm) *n* a radioactive silvery-white metallic element of the actinide series. It occurs in several minerals including pitchblende, carnotite, and autunite and is used chiefly as a source of nuclear energy by fission of the radioisotope **uranium-235.** Symbol: U; atomic no.: 92; atomic wt.: 238.0289; half-life of most stable isotope, ^{238}U: 4.51×10^9 years; valency: 2-6; relative density: 18.95 (approx.); melting pt.: 1135°C; boiling pt.: 4134°C. [C18: from New Latin, from URANUS[2]; from the fact that the element was discovered soon after the planet]

uranium series *n Physics.* a radioactive series that starts with uranium-238 and proceeds by radioactive decay to lead-206.

urano- *combining form.* denoting the heavens: *uranography.* [from Greek *ouranos*]

uranography (,jʊərə'nɒgrəfɪ) *n* the branch of astronomy concerned with the description and mapping of the stars, galaxies, etc. ▸ **,ura'nographer** *or* **,ura'nographist** *n* ▸ **uranographic** (,jʊərənə'græfɪk) *or* **,urano'graphical** *adj*

uranous ('jʊərənəs) *adj* of or containing uranium, esp. in a low valence state.

Uranus[1] (jʊ'reɪnəs, 'jʊrənəs) *n Greek myth.* the personification of the sky, who, as a god, ruled the universe and fathered the Titans and Cyclopes on his wife and mother Gaea (earth). He was overthrown by his son Cronus.

Uranus[2] (jʊ'reɪnəs, 'jʊrənəs) *n* one of the giant planets, the seventh planet from the sun, sometimes visible to the naked eye. It has about 15 satellites, a ring system, and an axis of rotation almost lying in the plane of the orbit. Mean distance from sun: 2870 million km; period of revolution around sun: 84 years; period of axial rotation: 17.23 hours; diameter and mass: 4 and 14.5 times that of earth respectively. [C19: from Latin *Ūranus,* from Greek *Ouranos* heaven]

uranyl ('jʊərənɪl) *n (modifier)* of, consisting of, or containing the divalent ion UO_2^{2+} or the group $-UO_2$. [C19: from URANIUM + -YL] ▸ **,ura'nylic** *adj*

urate ('jʊəreɪt) *n* any salt or ester of uric acid. ▸ **uratic** (jʊ'rætɪk) *adj*

urban ('ɜːbᵊn) *adj* **1** of, relating to, or constituting a city or town. **2** living in a city or town. ◆ Compare **rural.** [C17: from Latin *urbānus,* from *urbs* city]

Urban II ('ɜːbᵊn) *n* original name *Odo* or *Udo.* ?1042–99, French ecclesiastic; pope (1088–99). He inaugurated the First Crusade at the Council of Clermont (1095).

Urban VI *n* original name *Bartolomeo Prignano.* ?1318–89, Italian ecclesiastic; pope (1378–89). His policies led to the election of an antipope by the French cardinals, thus beginning the Great Schism in the West.

Urban VIII *n* original name *Maffeo Barberini.* 1568–1644, Italian ecclesiastic; pope (1623–44) during the Thirty Years' War, in which he supported Richelieu against the Hapsburgs.

urban area *n* (in population censuses) a city area considered as the inner city plus built-up environs, irrespective of local body administrative boundaries.

urban blues *n (sometimes functioning as sing)* an extrovert and rhythmic style of blues, usually accompanied by a band. Compare **country blues.**

urban district *n* **1** (in England and Wales from 1888 to 1974 and Northern Ireland from 1898 to 1973) an urban division of an administrative county with an elected council in charge of housing and environmental services: usually made up of one or more thickly populated areas but lacking a borough charter. **2** (in the Republic of Ireland) any of 49 medium-sized towns with their own elected councils.

urbane (ɜː'beɪn) *adj* characterized by elegance or sophistication. [C16: from

Latin *urbānus* belonging to the town; see URBAN] ▸ **ur'banely** *adv* ▸ **ur'baneness** *n*

urban guerrilla *n* a guerrilla who operates in a town or city, engaging in terrorism, kidnapping, etc.

urbanism ('ɜːbəˌnɪzəm) *n Chiefly U.S.* **1a** the character of city life. **1b** the study of this. **2** a less common term for **urbanization.**

urbanite ('ɜːbəˌnaɪt) *n* a resident of an urban community; city dweller.

urbanity (ɜː'bænɪtɪ) *n, pl* **-ties. 1** the quality of being urbane. **2** (*usually pl*) civilities or courtesies.

urbanize *or* **urbanise** ('ɜːbəˌnaɪz) *vb* (*tr*) (*usually passive*) **a** to make (esp. a predominantly rural area or country) more industrialized and urban. **b** to cause the migration of an increasing proportion of (rural dwellers) into cities. ▸ **ˌurbani'zation** *or* **ˌurbani'sation** *n*

urban myth *or* **legend** *n* a story, esp. one with a shocking or amusing ending, related as having actually happened, usu. to someone vaguely connected with the teller.

urban renewal *n* the process of redeveloping dilapidated or no longer functional urban areas.

urbi et orbi *Latin.* ('ɜːbɪ ɛt 'ɔːbɪ) *adv R.C. Church.* to the city and the world: a phrase qualifying the solemn papal blessing.

URC *abbrev. for* United Reformed Church.

urceolate ('ɜːsɪəlɪt, -ˌleɪt) *adj Biology.* shaped like an urn or pitcher: *an urceolate corolla.* [**C18:** via New Latin *urceolātus,* from Latin *urceolus* diminutive of *urceus* a pitcher]

urchin ('ɜːtʃɪn) *n* **1** a mischievous roguish child, esp. one who is young, small, or raggedly dressed. **2** See **sea urchin, heart urchin. 3** an archaic or dialect name for a **hedgehog. 4** either of the two cylinders in a carding machine that are covered with carding cloth. **5** *Obsolete.* an elf or sprite. [**C13:** *urchon,* from Old French *heriçon,* from Latin *ēricius* hedgehog, from *ēr,* related to Greek *khēr* hedgehog]

urd (ɜːd) *n* another name for **black gram** (see **gram**[2] (sense 1)). [Hindi]

urdé *or* **urdée** ('ɜːdeɪ, -diː, -dɪ) *adj Heraldry.* having points; pointed. [**C16** *urdee:* probably a misreading and misunderstanding of French *vidée* in the phrase *croix aiquissée et vidée* cross sharply pointed and reduced]

Urdu ('ʊəduː, 'ɜː-) *n* an official language of Pakistan, also spoken in India. The script derives primarily from Persia. It belongs to the Indic branch of the Indo-European family of languages, being closely related to Hindi but containing many Arabic and Persian loan words. [**C18:** from Hindustani (*zabāni*) *urdū* (language of the) camp, from Persian *urdū* camp, from Turkish *ordū*]

-ure *suffix forming nouns.* **1** indicating act, process, or result: *seizure.* **2** indicating function or office: *legislature; prefecture.* [from French, from Latin *-ūra*]

urea ('jʊərɪə) *n* a white water-soluble crystalline compound with a saline taste and often an odour of ammonia, produced by protein metabolism and excreted in urine. A synthetic form is used as a fertilizer, animal feed, and in the manufacture of synthetic resins. Formula: $CO(NH_2)_2$. Also called: **carbamide.** [**C19:** from New Latin, from French *urée,* from Greek *ouron* URINE] ▸ **u'real** *or* **u'reic** *adj*

urea cycle *n* the sequence of metabolic reactions leading in vertebrates to the synthesis of urea.

urea-formaldehyde resin *n* any one of a class of rigid odourless synthetic materials that are made from urea and formaldehyde and are used in electrical fittings, adhesives, laminates, and finishes for textiles.

urease ('jʊərɪˌeɪs, -ˌeɪz) *n* an enzyme occurring in many plants, esp. fungi, that converts urea to ammonium carbonate.

uredium (jʊ'riːdɪəm) *or* **uredinium** (ˌjʊərɪ'dɪnɪəm) *n, pl* **-dia** (-dɪə) *or* **-dinia** (-'dɪnɪə). a spore-producing body of some rust fungi in which uredospores are formed. Also called: **uredosorus.** [**C20:** from New Latin, from UREDO] ▸ **u'redial** *adj*

uredo (jʊ'riːdəʊ) *n, pl* **uredines** (jʊ'riːdɪˌniːz). a less common name for **urticaria.** [**C18:** from Latin: burning itch, from *ūrere* to burn]

uredosorus (jʊˌriːdəʊ'sɔːrəs) *n, pl* **-sori** (-'sɔːraɪ). another word for **uredium.** [from UREDO + SORUS]

uredospore (jʊ'riːdəʊˌspɔː) *n* any of the brownish spores that are produced in each uredium of the rust fungi and spread the infection between hosts.

ureide ('jʊərɪˌaɪd) *n Chem.* **1** any of a class of organic compounds derived from urea by replacing one or more of its hydrogen atoms by organic groups. **2** any of a class of derivatives of urea and carboxylic acids, in which one or more of the hydrogen atoms have been replaced by acyl groups: includes the cyclic ureides, such as alloxan.

uremia (jʊ'riːmɪə) *n* the usual U.S. spelling of **uraemia.** ▸ **u'remic** *adj*

-uret *suffix.* formerly used to form the names of binary chemical compounds. [from New Latin *-uretum*]

ureter (jʊ'riːtə) *n* the tube that conveys urine from the kidney to the urinary bladder or cloaca. [**C16:** via New Latin from Greek *ourētēr,* from *ourein* to URINATE] ▸ **u'reteral** *or* **ureteric** (ˌjʊərɪ'tɛrɪk) *adj*

urethane ('jʊərɪˌθeɪn) *or* **urethan** ('jʊərɪˌθæn) *n* **1** short for **polyurethane. 2** another name for **ethyl carbamate.** [**C19:** from URO-[1] + ETHYL + -ANE]

urethra (jʊ'riːθrə) *n, pl* **-thrae** (-θriː) *or* **-thras.** the canal that in most mammals conveys urine from the bladder out of the body. In human males it also conveys semen. [**C17:** via Late Latin from Greek *ourēthra,* from *ourein* to URINATE] ▸ **u'rethral** *adj*

urethritis (ˌjʊərɪ'θraɪtɪs) *n* inflammation of the urethra. [**C19:** from New Latin, from Late Latin URETHRA] ▸ **urethritic** (ˌjʊərɪ'θrɪtɪk) *adj*

urethroscope (jʊ'riːθrəˌskəʊp) *n* a medical instrument for examining the urethra. [**C20:** see URETHRA, -SCOPE] ▸ **urethroscopic** (jʊˌriːθrə'skɒpɪk) *adj* ▸ **urethroscopy** (ˌjʊərɪ'θrɒskəpɪ) *n*

uretic (jʊ'rɛtɪk) *adj* of or relating to the urine. [**C19:** via Late Latin from Greek *ourētikos,* from *ouron* URINE]

Urey ('jʊərɪ) *n* **Harold Clayton.** 1893–1981, U.S. chemist, who discovered the heavy isotope of hydrogen, deuterium (1932), and worked on methods of separating uranium isotopes: Nobel prize for chemistry 1934.

Urfa ('ɜːfə) *n* a city in SE Turkey: market centre. Pop.: 362 598 (1996 est.). Ancient name: **Edessa.**

Urfé (*French* urfe) *n* **Honoré d'** (ɔnɔre d). 1568–1625, French writer, whose pastoral *L'Astrée* (1607–27) is considered the first French novel.

Urga ('ɜːgə) *n* the former name (until 1924) of **Ulan Bator.**

urge (ɜːdʒ) *vb* **1** (*tr*) to plead, press, or move (someone to do something): *we urged him to surrender.* **2** (*tr; may take a clause as object*) to advocate or recommend earnestly and persistently; plead or insist on: *to urge the need for safety.* **3** (*tr*) to impel, drive, or hasten onwards: *he urged the horses on.* **4** (*tr*) *Archaic or literary.* to stimulate, excite, or incite. ◆ *n* **5** a strong impulse, inner drive, or yearning. [**C16:** from Latin *urgēre*]

urgent ('ɜːdʒənt) *adj* **1** requiring or compelling speedy action or attention: *the matter is urgent; an urgent message.* **2** earnest and persistent. [**C15:** via French from Latin *urgent-, urgens,* present participle of *urgēre* to URGE] ▸ **urgency** ('ɜːdʒənsɪ) *n* ▸ **'urgently** *adv*

-urgy *n combining form.* indicating technology concerned with a specified material: *metallurgy.* [from Greek *-urgia,* from *ergon* WORK]

Uri (*German* 'uːri) *n* one of the original three cantons of Switzerland, in the centre of the country: mainly German-speaking and Roman Catholic. Capital: Altdorf. Pop.: 35 876 (1996 est.). Area: 1075 sq. km (415 sq. miles).

-uria *n combining form.* indicating a diseased or abnormal condition of the urine: *dysuria; pyuria.* [from Greek *-ouria,* from *ouron* urine] ▸ **-uric** *adj combining form.*

Uriah (jʊ'raɪə) *n Old Testament.* a Hittite officer, who was killed in battle on instructions from David so that he could marry Uriah's wife Bathsheba (II Samuel 11).

uric ('jʊərɪk) *adj* of, concerning, or derived from urine. [**C18:** from URO-[1] + -IC]

uric acid *n* a white odourless tasteless crystalline product of protein metabolism, present in the blood and urine; 2,6,8-trihydroxypurine. Formula: $C_5H_4N_4O_3$.

uridine ('jʊərɪˌdiːn) *n Biochem.* a nucleoside present in all living cells in a combined form, esp. in RNA. [**C20:** from URO-[1] + -IDE + -INE[2]]

uridylic acid (ˌjuːrɪ'dɪlɪk) *n* a nucleotide consisting of uracil, ribose, and a phosphate group. It is a constituent of RNA. Also called: **uridine monophosphate.**

Uriel ('jʊərɪəl) *n* one of the four chief angels in Jewish apocryphal writings.

Urim and Thummim ('jʊərɪm; 'θʌmɪm) *n Old Testament.* two objects probably used as oracles and carried in the breastplate of the high priest (Exodus 28:30). [**C16:** from Hebrew]

urinal (jʊ'raɪnᵊl, 'jʊərɪ-) *n* **1** a sanitary fitting, esp. one fixed to a wall, used by men for urination. **2** a room containing urinals. **3** any vessel for holding urine prior to its disposal.

urinalysis (ˌjʊərɪ'nælɪsɪs) *or* **uranalysis** *n, pl* **-ses** (-ˌsiːz). *Med.* chemical analysis of the urine to test for the presence of disease.

urinant ('jʊərɪnənt) *adj Heraldry.* having the head downwards. [**C17:** from Latin *ūrīnāri* to dive]

urinary ('jʊərɪnərɪ) *adj* **1** *Anatomy.* of or relating to urine or to the organs and structures that secrete and pass urine. ◆ *n, pl* **-naries. 2** a reservoir for urine. **3** another word for **urinal.**

urinary bladder *n* a distensible membranous sac in which the urine excreted from the kidneys is stored.

urinate ('jʊərɪˌneɪt) *vb* (*intr*) to excrete or void urine; micturate. ▸ **ˌuri'nation** *n* ▸ **'urinative** *adj*

urine ('jʊərɪn) *n* the pale yellow slightly acid fluid excreted by the kidneys, containing waste products removed from the blood. It is stored in the urinary bladder and discharged through the urethra. Related adj: **uretic.** [**C14:** via Old French from Latin *ūrīna;* related to Greek *ouron,* Latin *ūrīnāre* to plunge under water]

uriniferous (ˌjʊərɪ'nɪfərəs) *adj* conveying urine.

urinogenital (ˌjʊərɪnəʊ'dʒɛnɪtᵊl) *adj* another word for **urogenital** or **genitourinary.**

urinometer (ˌjʊərɪ'nɒmɪtə) *n Med.* an instrument for determining the specific gravity of urine.

urinous ('jʊərɪnəs) *or* **urinose** *adj* of, resembling, or containing urine.

URL *abbrev. for* uniform resource locator; a standardized address of a location on the Internet, esp. on the World Wide Web.

Urmia ('ɜːmɪə) *n* **Lake.** a shallow lake in NW Iran, at an altitude of 1300 m (4250 ft.): the largest lake in Iran, varying in area from 4000–6000 sq. km (1500–2300 sq. miles) between autumn and spring.

Urmston ('ɜːmstən) *n* a town in NW England, in Salford unitary authority, Greater Manchester. Pop.: 41 804 (1991).

urn (ɜːn) *n* **1** a vaselike receptacle or vessel, esp. a large bulbous one with a foot. **2** a vase used as a receptacle for the ashes of the dead. **3** a large vessel, usually of metal, with a tap, used for making and holding tea, coffee, etc. **4** *Botany.* the spore-producing capsule of a moss. [**C14:** from Latin *ūrna;* related to Latin *ūrere* to burn, *urceus* pitcher, Greek *hurkhē* jar] ▸ **'urnˌlike** *adj*

urnfield ('ɜːnˌfiːld) *n* **1** a cemetery full of individual cremation urns. ◆ *adj* **2** (of a number of Bronze Age cultures) characterized by cremation in urns, which began in E Europe about the second millennium B.C. and by the seventh century B.C. had covered almost all of mainland Europe.

urning ('ɜːnɪŋ) *n* a rare word for **homosexual** (esp. a male homosexual). [**C20:** from German, from URANIA (Aphrodite); compare URANISM]

uro-[1] *or before a vowel* **ur-** *combining form.* indicating urine or the urinary tract: *urochrome; urogenital; urolith; urology.* [from Greek *ouron* urine]

uro-[2] *or before a vowel* **ur-** *combining form.* indicating a tail: *urochord; uropod; urostyle.* [from Greek *oura*]

urobilin (ˌjʊərəʊˈbaɪlɪn) *n* a brownish pigment found in faeces and sometimes in urine. It is formed by oxidation of **urobilinogen**, a colourless substance produced by bacterial degradation of the bile pigment bilirubin in the intestine.

urochord (ˈjʊərəʊˌkɔːd) *n* **1** the notochord of a larval tunicate, typically confined to the tail region. ◆ *n, adj* **2** Also: **urochordate** (ˌjʊərəʊˈkɔːdeɪt). another word for **tunicate.** [C19: from URO-[2] + *chord,* a variant of CORD] ▸ ˌuroˈ**chordal** *adj*

urochrome (ˈjʊərəʊˌkrəʊm) *n* the yellowish pigment that colours urine. [C19: from URO-[1] + -CHROME]

urodele (ˈjʊərəʊˌdiːl) *n* **1** any amphibian of the order *Urodela,* having a long body and tail and four short limbs: includes the salamanders and newts. ◆ *adj* **2** of, relating to, or belonging to the *Urodela.* [C19: from French *urodèle,* from URO-[2] + *-dèle,* from Greek *dēlos* evident]

urodynamics (ˌjʊərəʊdaɪˈnæmɪks) *n* (*functioning as sing*) the study and measurement of the flow of urine in the urinary tract.

urogenital (ˌjʊərəʊˈdʒɛnɪtᵊl) *or* **urinogenital** *adj* of or relating to the urinary and genital organs and their functions. Also: **genitourinary.**

urogenital system *or* **tract** *n Anatomy.* the urinary tract and reproductive organs.

urogenous (jʊˈrɒdʒɪnəs) *adj* **1** producing or derived from urine. **2** involved in the secretion and excretion of urine.

urography (ˌjʊərˈɒgrəfɪ) *n* another name for **pyelography.**

urolith (ˈjʊərəʊlɪθ) *n Pathol.* a calculus in the urinary tract. [from URO-[1] + Greek *lithos* stone] ▸ ˌuroˈ**lithic** *adj*

urology (jʊˈrɒlədʒɪ) *n* the branch of medicine concerned with the study and treatment of diseases of the urogenital tract. ▸ **urologic** (ˌjʊərəˈlɒdʒɪk) *or* ˌuroˈ**logical** *adj* ▸ **u**ˈ**rologist** *n*

uropod (ˈjʊərəʊˌpɒd) *n* the paired appendage that arises from the last segment of the body in lobsters and related crustaceans and forms part of the tail fan. [C19: from URO-[2] + -POD] ▸ **uropodal** (jʊˈrɒpədᵊl) *or* **u**ˈ**ropodous** *adj*

uropygial gland *n* a gland, situated at the base of the tail in most birds, that secretes oil used in preening.

uropygium (ˌjʊərəˈpɪdʒɪəm) *n* the hindmost part of a bird's body, from which the tail feathers grow. [C19: via New Latin from Greek *ouropugion,* from URO-[2] + *pugē* rump] ▸ ˌuroˈ**pygial** *adj*

uroscopy (jʊˈrɒskəpɪ) *n Med.* examination of the urine. See also **urinalysis.** ▸ **uroscopic** (ˌjʊərəˈskɒpɪk) *adj* ▸ **u**ˈ**roscopist** *n*

urostyle (ˈjʊərəʊˌstaɪl) *n* the bony rod forming the last segment of the vertebral column of frogs, toads, and related amphibians. [C19: from URO-[2] + Greek *stulos* pillar]

Urquhart (ˈɜːkət) *n* Sir **Thomas.** 1611–60, Scottish author and translator of Rabelais' *Gargantua* and *Pantagruel* (1653; 1693).

Urquhart Castle *n* a castle near Drumnadrochit in Highland, Scotland: situated on Loch Ness.

Ursa Major (ˈɜːsə ˈmeɪdʒə) *n, Latin genitive* **Ursae Majoris** (ˈɜːsiː məˈdʒɔːrɪs). an extensive conspicuous constellation in the N hemisphere, visible north of latitude 40°. The seven brightest stars form the **Plough.** A line through the two brightest stars points to the Pole Star lying in **Ursa Minor.** Also called: the **Great Bear,** the **Bear.** [Latin: greater bear]

Ursa Minor (ˈɜːsə ˈmaɪnə) *n, Latin genitive* **Ursae Minoris** (ˈɜːsiː mɪˈnɔːrɪs). a small faint constellation, the brightest star of which is the Pole Star, lying 1° from the true celestial pole. Also called: the **Little Bear,** the **Bear,** (U.S. and Canadian) the **Little Dipper.** [Latin: lesser bear]

ursine (ˈɜːsaɪn) *adj* of, relating to, or resembling a bear or bears. [C16: from Latin *ursus* a bear]

Ursprache *German.* (ˈuːrʃpraːxə) *n* any hypothetical extinct and unrecorded language reconstructed from groups of related recorded languages. For example, Germanic is an Ursprache reconstructed by comparison of English, Dutch, German, the Scandinavian languages, and Gothic; Indo-European is an Ursprache reconstructed by comparison of the Germanic group, Latin, Sanskrit, etc. [from *ur-* primeval, original + *Sprache* language]

Ursula (ˈɜːsjʊlə) *n* **Saint.** a legendary British princess of the fourth or fifth century A.D., said to have been martyred together with 11 000 virgins by the Huns at Cologne. Feast day: Oct. 21.

Ursuline (ˈɜːsjʊˌlaɪn) *n* a member of an order of nuns devoted to teaching in the Roman Catholic Church: founded in 1537 at Brescia. [C16: named after St URSULA, patron saint of St Angela Merici, who founded the order]

Urtext *German.* (ˈuːrtɛkst) *n* **1** the earliest form of a text as established by linguistic scholars as a basis for variants in later texts still in existence. **2** an edition of a musical score showing the composer's intentions without later editorial interpolation. [from *ur-* original + TEXT]

urticaceous (ˌɜːtɪˈkeɪʃəs) *adj* of, relating to, or belonging to the *Urticaceae,* a family of plants, having small flowers and, in many species, stinging hairs: includes the nettles and pellitory. [C18: via New Latin from Latin *urtīca* nettle, from *ūrere* to burn]

urticaria (ˌɜːtɪˈkɛərɪə) *n* a skin condition characterized by the formation of itchy red or whitish raised patches, usually caused by an allergy. Nontechnical names: **hives, nettle rash.** [C18: from New Latin, from Latin *urtīca* nettle] ▸ ˌurtiˈ**carial** *or* ˌurtiˈ**carious** *adj*

urticate (ˈɜːtɪˌkeɪt) *adj* **1** Also: **urticant** (ˈɜːtɪkənt). characterized by the presence of weals. ◆ *vb* **2** to perform urtication. [C19: from Medieval Latin *urticāre* to sting, from Latin *urtīca* a nettle]

urtication (ˌɜːtɪˈkeɪʃən) *n* **1** a burning or itching sensation. **2** another name for **urticaria. 3** a former method of producing counterirritation of the skin by beating the area with nettles.

Uru. *abbrev. for* Uruguay.

Uruapan (*Spanish* uˈrwapan) *n* a city in SW Mexico, in Michoacán state: agricultural trading centre. Pop.: 187 623 (1990).

Uruguay (ˈjʊərəˌgwaɪ) *n* a republic in South America, on the Atlantic: Spanish colonization began in 1624, followed by Portuguese settlement in 1680; revolted against Spanish rule in 1820 but was annexed by the Portuguese to Brazil; gained independence in 1825. It consists mainly of rolling grassy plains, low hills, and plateaus. Official language: Spanish. Religion: Roman Catholic majority. Currency: peso. Capital: Montevideo. Pop.: 3 216 000 (1998 est.). Area: 176 215 sq. km (68 037 sq. miles). ▸ ˌUruˈ**guayan** *adj, n*

Urumchi (uːˈruːmtʃɪ), **Urumqi,** *or* **Wu-lu-mu-ch'i** *n* a city in NW China, capital of Xinjiang Uygur Autonomous Region: trading centre on a N route between China and central Asia. Pop.: 1 160 000 (1991 est.). Former name: **Tihwa.**

Urundi (uˈrʊndɪ) *n* the former name (until 1962) of **Burundi.**

urus (ˈjʊərəs) *n, pl* **uruses.** another name for the **aurochs.** [C17: from *ūrus,* of Germanic origin; compare Old High German *ūr,* Old Norse *urr,* Greek *ouros* aurochs]

urushiol (ˈuːrʊʃɪˌɒl, uːˈruː-) *n* a poisonous pale yellow liquid occurring in poison ivy and the lacquer tree. [from Japanese *urushi* lacquer + -OL[2]]

us (ʌs) *pron* (*objective*) **1** refers to the speaker or writer and another person or other people: *don't hurt us; to decide among us.* **2** refers to all people or people in general: *this table shows us the tides.* **3** an informal word for **me**[1]: *give us a kiss!* **4** a formal word for **me**[1] used by editors, monarchs, etc. **5** *Chiefly U.S.* a dialect word for **ourselves** when used as an indirect object: *we ought to get us a car.* [Old English *ūs;* related to Old High German *uns,* Old Norse *oss,* Latin *nōs,* Sanskrit *nas* we]

USAGE See at **me**[1].

u.s. *abbrev. for:* **1** ubi supra. **2** ut supra.

U.S. *or* **US** *abbrev. for* United States.

U/S *Informal. abbrev. for:* **1** unserviceable. **2** useless.

USA 1 *abbrev. for* United States Army. ◆ **2** *international car registration for* United States of America.

U.S.A. *or* **USA** *abbrev. for* United States of America.

usable *or* **useable** (ˈjuːzəbᵊl) *adj* able to be used. ▸ ˌusaˈ**bility,** ˌuseaˈ**bility** *or* ˈ**usableness,** ˈ**useableness** *n* ▸ ˈ**usably** *or* ˈ**useably** *adv*

USAF *abbrev. for* United States Air Force.

usage (ˈjuːsɪdʒ, -zɪdʒ) *n* **1** the act or a manner of using; use; employment. **2** constant use, custom, or habit. **3** something permitted or established by custom or practice. **4** what is actually said in a language, esp. as contrasted with what is prescribed. [C14: via Old French, from Latin *ūsus* USE (n)]

usance (ˈjuːzəns) *n* **1** *Commerce.* the period of time permitted by commercial usage for the redemption of foreign bills of exchange. **2** *Rare.* unearned income. **3** an obsolete word for **usage, usury,** or **use.** [C14: from Old French, from Medieval Latin *ūsantia,* from *ūsāre* to USE]

USDAW (ˈʌzˌdɔː) *n acronym for* Union of Shop, Distributive, and Allied Workers.

use *vb* (juːz). (*tr*) **1** to put into service or action; employ for a given purpose: *to use a spoon to stir with.* **2** to make a practice or habit of employing; exercise: *he uses his brain.* **3** to behave towards: *to use a friend well.* **4** to behave towards in a particular way for one's own ends: *he uses people.* **5** to consume, expend, or exhaust: *the engine uses very little oil.* **6** *Chiefly U.S. and Canadian.* to partake of (alcoholic drink, drugs, etc.) or smoke (tobacco, marijuana, etc.). ◆ *n* (juːs). **7** the act of using or the state of being used: *the carpet wore out through constant use.* **8** the ability, right, or permission to use. **9** the occasion to use; need: *I have no use for this paper.* **10** an instance or manner of using. **11** usefulness; advantage: *it is of no use to complain.* **12** custom; practice; habit: *long use has inured him to it.* **13** the purpose for which something is used; end. **14** *Christianity.* a distinctive form of liturgical or ritual observance, esp. one that is traditional in a Church or group of Churches. **15** the enjoyment of property, land, etc., by occupation or by deriving revenue or other benefit from it. **16** *Law.* the beneficial enjoyment of property the legal title to which is held by another person as trustee. **17** *Law.* an archaic word for **trust** (sense 7). **18** *Philosophy, logic, linguistics.* the occurrence of an expression in such a context that it performs its own linguistic function rather than being itself referred to. In *"Fido" refers to Fido,* the name *Fido* is used only on the second occurrence, first being mentioned. Compare **mention** (sense 7). See also **material mode. 19 have no use for. 19a** to have no need of. **19b** to have a contemptuous dislike for. **20 make use of. 20a** to employ; use. **20b** to exploit (a person). ◆ See also **used to, use up.** [C13: from Old French *user* to use, from Latin *ūsus* having used, from *ūtī* to use]

used (juːzd) *adj* bought or sold second-hand: *used cars.*

used to (juːst) *adj* **1** made familiar with; accustomed to: *I am used to hitchhiking.* ◆ *vb* (*tr*) **2** (*takes an infinitive or implied infinitive*) used as an auxiliary to express habitual or accustomed actions, states, etc., taking place in the past but not continuing into the present: *I don't drink these days, but I used to; I used to fish here every day.*

USAGE The most common negative form of *used to* is *didn't used to* (or *didn't use to*), but in formal contexts *used not to* is preferred.

useful (ˈjuːsfʊl) *adj* **1** able to be used advantageously, beneficially, or for several purposes; helpful or serviceable. **2** *Informal.* commendable or capable: *a useful term's work.* ◆ *n* **3** *Austral. informal.* an odd-jobman or general factotum. ▸ ˈ**usefully** *adv* ▸ ˈ**usefulness** *n*

useless (ˈjuːslɪs) *adj* **1** having no practical use or advantage. **2** *Informal.* ineffectual, weak, or stupid: *he's useless at history.* ▸ ˈ**uselessly** *adv* ▸ ˈ**uselessness** *n*

user (ˈjuːzə) *n* **1** *Law.* **1a** the continued exercise, use, or enjoyment of a right, esp. in property. **1b** a presumptive right based on long-continued use: *right of* *user.* **2** (*often in combination*) a person or thing that uses: *a road-user.* **3** *Informal.* a drug addict.

user-defined key *n* a key on the keyboard of a computer that can be used to carry out any of a limited number of predefined actions as selected by the user.

user-friendly *adj* **1** easy to use or understand: *a user-friendly dictionary.* **2** (of a computer system) easily operated and understood by means of a straightforward guide in jargon-free language. ▸ **user-friendliness** *n*

use up *vb* (*tr, adv*) **1** to finish (a supply); consume completely. **2** to exhaust; wear out.

Ushant ('ʌʃənt) *n* an island off the NW coast of France, at the tip of Brittany: scene of naval battles in 1778 and 1794 between France and Britain. Area: about 16 sq. km (6 sq. miles). French name: **Ouessant.**

U-shaped valley *n Geology.* a steep-sided valley caused by glacial erosion.

Ushas ('u:ʃəs) *n* the Hindu goddess of the dawn.

usher ('ʌʃə) *n* **1** an official who shows people to their seats, as in a church or theatre. **2** a person who acts as doorkeeper, esp. in a court of law. **3** (in England) a minor official charged with maintaining order in a court of law. **4** an officer responsible for preceding persons of rank in a procession or introducing strangers at formal functions. **5** *Brit., obsolete.* a teacher. ◆ *vb* (*tr*) **6** to conduct or escort, esp. in a courteous or obsequious way. **7** (usually foll. by *in*) to be a precursor or herald (of). [C14: from Old French *huissier* doorkeeper, from Vulgar Latin *ustiārius* (unattested), from Latin *ostium* door]

Usher ('ʌʃə) *n* a variant spelling of (James) **Ussher.**

usherette (ˌʌʃə'rɛt) *n* a woman assistant in a cinema, theatre, etc., who shows people to their seats.

Usk (ʌsk) *n* a river in SE Wales, flowing southeast and south to the Bristol Channel. Length: 113 km (70 miles).

Üsküb ('ʊsku:b) *n* the Turkish name (1392–1913) for **Skopje.**

Üsküdar (ˌu:sku:'dɑ:) *n* a town in NW Turkey, across the Bosporus from Istanbul: formerly a terminus of caravan routes from Syria and Asia; base of the British army in the Crimean War. Pop.: 261 141 (1980). Former name: **Scutari.**

USM *abbrev. for:* **1** *Stock Exchange.* unlisted securities market. **2** underwater-to-surface missile.

Usman dan Fodio ('u:smɑ:n dæn 'fəʊdɪəʊ) *n* 1754–1817, African mystic and revolutionary leader, who created a Muslim state in Nigeria.

USN *abbrev. for* United States Navy.

Usnach *or* **Usnech** ('ʊʃnəx) *n* (in Irish legend) the father of Naoise.

USO (in the U.S.) *abbrev. for* United Service Organization.

USP *abbrev. for* unique selling proposition: a characteristic of a product that can be used in advertising to differentiate it from its competitors.

Uspallata Pass (ˌu:spə'lɑ:tə; *Spanish* uspa'ʎata) *n* a pass over the Andes in S South America, between Mendoza (Argentina) and Santiago (Chile). Height: 3840 m (12 600 ft.). Also called: **La Cumbre.**

usquebaugh ('ʌskwɪˌbɔ:) *n* **1** *Irish.* the former name for **whiskey. 2** *Scot.* the former name for **whisky. 3** an Irish liqueur flavoured with coriander. [C16: from Irish Gaelic *uisce beathadh* or Scot. Gaelic *uisge beatha* water of life]

USS *abbrev. for:* **1** United States Senate. **2** United States Ship.

Ussher *or* **Usher** ('ʌʃə) *n* **James.** 1581–1656, Irish prelate and scholar. His system of biblical chronology, which dated the creation at 4004 B.C., was for long accepted.

USSR *abbrev. for* (formerly) Union of Soviet Socialist Republics.

Ussuri (*Russian* ussu'ri) *n* a river in E central Asia, flowing north, forming part of the Chinese border with Russia, to the Amur River. Length: about 800 km (500 miles).

Ustashi (ʊ'stɑ:ʃɪ) *n* (formerly) a terrorist organization of right-wing Yugoslav exiles dedicated to the overthrow of Communism in their homeland. [from Serbo-Croat]

Ústí nad Labem (*Czech* 'u:stji: nad 'labɛm) *n* a port in the Czech Republic, on the Elbe River: textile and chemical industries. Pop.: 118 000 (1993).

Ustinov ('ju:stɪnɒf) *n* Sir **Peter** (**Alexander**). born 1921, British stage and film actor, director, dramatist, and raconteur.

Ust-Kamenogorsk (*Russian* ustjkəmɪna'gɔrsk) *n* a city in E Kazakhstan: centre of a zinc-, lead-, and copper-mining area. Pop.: 326 300 (1995 est.).

ustulation (ˌʌstjʊ'leɪʃən) *n* the act or process of searing or burning. [C17: from Late Latin *ustulāre,* from Latin *ūrere* to burn]

Ustyurt *or* **Ust Urt** (*Russian* us'tjurt) *n* an arid plateau in central Asia, between the Caspian and Aral seas in Kazakhstan and Uzbekistan. Area: about 238 000 sq. km (92 000 sq. miles).

usual ('ju:ʒʊəl) *adj* **1** of the most normal, frequent, or regular type; customary: *that's the usual sort of application to send.* ◆ *n* **2** ordinary or commonplace events (esp. in the phrase **out of the usual**). **3 the usual.** *Informal.* the habitual or usual drink, meal, etc. [C14: from Late Latin *ūsuālis* ordinary, from Latin *ūsus* USE] ▸ **'usually** *adv* ▸ **'usualness** *n*

usufruct ('ju:sjʊˌfrʌkt) *n* the right to use and derive profit from a piece of property belonging to another, provided the property itself remains undiminished and uninjured in any way. [C17: from Late Latin *ūsūfrūctus,* from Latin *ūsus* use + *frūctus* enjoyment] ▸ ˌ**usu'fructuary** *n, adj*

Usumbura (ˌu:zəm'bʊərə) *n* the former name of **Bujumbura.**

usurer ('ju:ʒərə) *n* **1** a person who lends funds at an exorbitant rate of interest. **2** *Obsolete.* a moneylender.

usurp (ju:'zɜ:p) *vb* to seize, take over, or appropriate (land, a throne, etc.) without authority. [C14: from Old French *usurper,* from Latin *ūsūrpāre* to take into use, probably from *ūsus* use + *rapere* to seize] ▸ ˌ**usur'pation** *n* ▸ **u'surpative** *or* **u'surpatory** *adj* ▸ **u'surper** *n*

usury ('ju:ʒərɪ) *n, pl* **-ries. 1** the act or practice of loaning money at an exorbitant rate of interest. **2** an exorbitant or unlawfully high amount or rate of interest. **3** *Obsolete.* moneylending. [C14: from Medieval Latin *ūsūria,* from Latin *ūsūra* usage, from *ūsus* USE] ▸ **usurious** (ju:'ʒʊərɪəs) *adj*

USW *Radio. abbrev. for* ultrashort wave.

ut (ʌt, u:t) *n Music.* **1** the syllable used in the fixed system of solmization for the note C. **2** the first note of a hexachord in medieval music. [C14: from Latin *ut;* see GAMUT]

UT *abbrev. for:* **1** universal time. **2** Utah.

Utagawa Kuniyoshi (ˌu:tə'gɑ:wə ˌku:nɪ'jəʊʃɪ) *n* original name *Igusa Magosabwo.* 1797–1861, Japanese painter and printmaker of the ukiyo-e school, best known for his prints of warriors and landscapes.

Utah ('ju:tɔ:, 'ju:tɑ:) *n* a state of the western U.S.: settled by Mormons in 1847; situated in the Great Basin and the Rockies, with the Great Salt Lake in the northwest; mainly arid and mountainous. Capital: Salt Lake City. Pop.: 2 059 148 (1997 est.). Area: 212 628 sq. km (82 096 sq. miles). Abbrevs.: **Ut.** or (with zip code) **UT** ▸ **Utahan** (ju:'tɔ:ən, -'tɑ:ən) *adj, n*

Utamaro (ˌu:tə'mɑ:rəʊ) *n* **Kitagawa** (ˌki:tə'gɑ:wə), original name *Kitagawa Nebsuyoshi.* 1753–1806, Japanese master of wood-block prints, of the ukiyo-e school; noted esp. for his portraits of women.

UTC *abbrev. for* universal time coordinated. See **universal time.**

ut dict. (in prescriptions) *abbrev. for* as directed. [from Latin *ut dictum*]

ute (ju:t) *n Austral. and N.Z. informal.* short for **utility** (sense 6).

Ute (ju:t, 'ju:tɪ) *n* **1** (*pl* **Utes** *or* **Ute**) a member of a North American Indian people of Utah, Colorado, and New Mexico, related to the Aztecs. **2** the language of this people, belonging to the Shoshonean subfamily of the Uto-Aztecan family.

utensil (ju:'tɛnsəl) *n* an implement, tool, or container for practical use: *writing utensils.* [C14 *utensele,* via Old French from Latin *ūtēnsilia* necessaries, from *ūtēnsilis* available for use, from *ūtī* to use]

uterine ('ju:təˌraɪn) *adj* **1** of, relating to, or affecting the uterus. **2** (of offspring) born of the same mother but not the same father: *uterine brothers.*

uterus ('ju:tərəs) *n, pl* **uteri** ('ju:təˌraɪ). **1** *Anatomy.* a hollow muscular organ lying within the pelvic cavity of female mammals. It houses the developing fetus and by contractions aids in its expulsion at parturition. Nontechnical name: **womb. 2** the corresponding organ in other animals. [C17: from Latin; compare Greek *hustera* womb, *hoderos* belly, Sanskrit *udara* belly]

Utgard ('ʊtgɑ:d, 'u:t-) *n Norse myth.* one of the divisions of Jotunheim, land of the giants, ruled by Utgard-Loki.

Utgard-Loki *n Norse myth.* the giant king of Utgard.

U Thant ('u: 'θænt) *n* See (U) **Thant.**

Uther ('ju:θə) *or* **Uther Pendragon** *n* (in Arthurian legend) a king of Britain and father of Arthur.

Uthman ('u:θmɑ:n) *n* died 656 A.D., third caliph of Islam, who established an authoritative version of the Koran.

Utica ('ju:tɪkə) *n* an ancient city on the N coast of Africa, northwest of Carthage.

utile ('ju:taɪl, -tɪl) *adj* an obsolete word for **useful.** [C15: via Old French from Latin *ūtilis,* from *ūtī* to use]

utilitarian (ju:ˌtɪlɪ'tɛərɪən) *adj* **1** of or relating to utilitarianism. **2** designed for use rather than beauty. ◆ *n* **3** a person who believes in utilitarianism.

utilitarianism (ju:ˌtɪlɪ'tɛərɪəˌnɪzəm) *n Ethics.* **1** the doctrine that the morally correct course of action consists in the greatest good for the greatest number, that is, in maximizing the total benefit resulting, without regard to the distribution of benefits and burdens. **2** the theory that the criterion of virtue is utility. ◆ See also (John Stuart) **Mill.**

utility (ju:'tɪlɪtɪ) *n, pl* **-ties. 1a** the quality of practical use; usefulness; serviceability. **1b** (*as modifier*): *a utility fabric.* **2** something useful. **3a** a public service, such as the bus system; public utility. **3b** (*as modifier*): *utility vehicle.* **4** *Economics.* **4a** the ability of a commodity to satisfy human wants. **4b** the amount of such satisfaction. ◆ Compare **disutility. 5** *Statistics.* **5a** a measure of the total benefit or disadvantage attaching to each of a set of alternative courses of action. **5b** (*as modifier*): *utility function.* ◆ See also **expected utility, decision theory. 6** Also called: **utility truck,** (Informal) **ute.** *Austral. and N.Z.* a small truck with an open body and low sides, often with a removable tarpaulin cover; pick-up. **7** a piece of computer software designed for a routine task, such as examining or copying files. [C14: from Old French *utelite,* from Latin *ūtilitās* usefulness, from *ūtī* to use]

utility function *n Economics.* a function relating specific goods and services in an economy to individual preferences.

utility man *n Chiefly U.S.* **1** a worker who is expected to serve in any of several capacities. **2** an actor who plays any of numerous small parts.

utility player *n Sport.* a player who is capable of playing competently in any of several positions.

utility room *n* a room with equipment for domestic work like washing and ironing.

utility truck *n* another name for **utility** (sense 6).

utilize *or* **utilise** ('ju:tɪˌlaɪz) *vb* (*tr*) to make practical or worthwhile use of. ▸ **'utiˌlizable** *or* **'utiˌlisable** *adj* ▸ ˌ**utili'zation** *or* ˌ**utili'sation** *n* ▸ **'utiˌlizer** *or* **'utiˌliser** *n*

ut infra *Latin.* (ut 'ɪnfrɑ:) as below.

uti possidetis ('ju:taɪ ˌpɒsɪ'di:tɪs) *n International law.* the rule that territory and other property remains in the hands of the belligerent state actually in possession at the end of a war unless otherwise provided for by treaty. [from Latin, literally: as you possess]

utmost ('ʌtˌməʊst) *or* **uttermost** *adj* (*prenominal*) **1** of the greatest possible degree or amount: *the utmost degree.* **2** at the furthest limit: *the utmost town on the peninsula.* ◆ *n* **3** the greatest possible degree, extent, or amount: *he tried his utmost.* [Old English *ūtemest,* from *ūte* out + *-mest* MOST]

utmost good faith *n* a principle used in insurance contracts, legally obliging all parties to reveal to the others any information that might influence the others' decision to enter into the contract. Also called: ***uberrima fides.***

Uto-Aztecan ('ju:təʊ'æztɛkən) *n* **1** a family of North and Central American Indian languages including Nahuatl, Shoshone, Pima, and Ute. ◆ *adj* **2** of or relating to this family of languages or the peoples speaking them.

Utopia (juːˈtəʊpɪə) *n* (*sometimes not cap.*) any real or imaginary society, place, state, etc., considered to be perfect or ideal. [**C16**: from New Latin *Utopia* (coined by Sir Thomas More in 1516 as the title of his book that described an imaginary island representing the perfect society), literally: no place, from Greek *ou* not + *topos* a place]

Utopian (juːˈtəʊpɪən) (*sometimes not cap.*) ◆ *adj* **1** of or relating to a perfect or ideal existence. ◆ *n* **2** an idealistic social reformer. ► **Uˈtopianism** *n*

utopian socialism *n* (*sometimes caps.*) socialism established by the peaceful surrender of the means of production by capitalists moved by moral persuasion, example, etc.: the form of socialism advocated by Robert Owen, Fichte, and others. Compare **scientific socialism.**

Utrecht (*Dutch* ˈyːtrɛxt; *English* ˈjuːtrɛkt) *n* **1** a province of the W central Netherlands. Capital: Utrecht. Pop.: 1 070 600 (1996). Area: 1362 sq. km (526 sq. miles). **2** a city in the central Netherlands, capital of Utrecht province: scene of the signing (1579) of the **Union of Utrecht** (the foundation of the later kingdom of the Netherlands) and of the **Treaty of Utrecht** (1713), ending the War of the Spanish Succession. Pop.: 234 254 (1996 est.).

utricle (ˈjuːtrɪkᵊl) *or* **utriculus** (juːˈtrɪkjʊləs) *n, pl* **utricles** *or* **utriculi** (juːˈtrɪkjʊˌlaɪ). **1** *Anatomy.* the larger of the two parts of the membranous labyrinth of the internal ear. Compare **saccule. 2** *Botany.* the bladder-like one-seeded indehiscent fruit of certain plants. [**C18**: from Latin *ūtriculus* diminutive of *ūter* bag] ► **uˈtricular** *or* **uˈtriculate** *adj*

utriculitis (juːˌtrɪkjʊˈlaɪtɪs) *n* inflammation of the inner ear.

Utrillo (*French* ytrijo) *n* **Maurice** (mɔris). 1883–1955, French painter, noted for his Parisian street scenes.

ut supra *Latin.* (ut ˈsuːprɑː) as above.

Uttarakhand (ˈʊtərəkænd) *n* a planned new state of India, to be formed from part of Uttar Pradesh.

Uttar Pradesh (ˈʊtə ˈprɑːdɛʃ) *n* a state of N India: the most populous state; originated in 1877 with the merging of Agra and Oudh as the United Provinces; augmented by the states of Rampur, Benares, and Tehri-Garhwal in 1949; lies mostly on the Upper Ganges plain but rises over 7500 m (25 000 ft.) in the Himalayas in the northwest; agricultural. Capital: Lucknow. Pop.: 150 695 000 (1994 est.). Area: 294 413 sq. km (113 673 sq. miles).

utter[1] (ˈʌtə) *vb* **1** to give audible expression to (something): *to utter a growl.* **2** *Criminal law.* to put into circulation (counterfeit coin, forged banknotes, etc.). **3** (*tr*) to make publicly known; publish: *to utter slander.* **4** *Obsolete.* to give forth, issue, or emit. [**C14**: probably originally a commercial term, from Middle Dutch *ūteren* (modern Dutch *uiteren*) to make known; related to Middle Low German *ūtern* to sell, show] ► **ˈutterable** *adj* ► **ˈutterableness** *n* ► **ˈutterer** *n* ► **ˈutterless** *adj*

utter[2] (ˈʌtə) *adj* (*prenominal*) (intensifier): *an utter fool; utter bliss; the utter limit.* [**C15**: from Old English *utera* outer, comparative of *ūte* OUT (adv); related to Old High German *ūzaro,* Old Norse *ūtri*]

utterance[1] (ˈʌtərəns) *n* **1** something uttered, such as a statement. **2** the act or power of uttering or the ability to utter. **3** *Logic, philosophy.* an element of spoken language, esp. a sentence. Compare **inscription** (sense 4).

utterance[2] (ˈʌtərəns) *n Archaic or literary.* the bitter end (esp. in the phrase **to the utterance**). [**C13**: from Old French *oultrance,* from *oultrer* to carry to excess, from Latin *ultrā* beyond]

utter barrister *n Law.* the full title of a barrister who is not a Queen's Counsel. See also **junior** (sense 6).

utterly (ˈʌtəlɪ) *adv* (intensifier): *I'm utterly miserable.*

uttermost (ˈʌtəˌməʊst) *adj, n* a variant of **utmost.**

U-turn *n* **1** a turn made by a vehicle in the shape of a U, resulting in a reversal of direction. **2** a complete change in direction of political or other policy.

UU *abbrev. for* Ulster Unionist.

UV *abbrev. for* ultraviolet.

UV-A *or* **UVA** *abbrev. for* ultraviolet radiation with a range of 320–380 nanometres.

uvarovite (uːˈvɑːrəˌvaɪt) *n* an emerald-green garnet found in chromium deposits: consists of calcium chromium silicate. Formula: $Ca_3Cr_2(SiO_4)_3$. [**C19**: from German *Uvarovit;* named after Count Sergei S. *Uvarov* (1785–1855), Russian author and statesman]

UV-B *or* **UVB** *abbrev. for* ultraviolet radiation with a range of 280–320 nanometres.

uvea (ˈjuːvɪə) *n* the part of the eyeball consisting of the iris, ciliary body, and choroid. [**C16**: from Medieval Latin *ūvea,* from Latin *ūva* grape] ► **ˈuveal** *or* **ˈuveous** *adj*

Uvedale (ˈjuːdᵊl, ˈjuːvˌdeɪl) *n* a variant of (Nicholas) **Udall.**

uveitis (ˌjuːvɪˈaɪtɪs) *n* inflammation of the uvea. ► **uveitic** (ˌjuːvɪˈɪtɪk) *adj*

UVF *abbrev. for* Ulster Volunteer Force.

uvula (ˈjuːvjʊlə) *n, pl* **-las** *or* **-lae** (-ˌliː). a small fleshy finger-like flap of tissue that hangs in the back of the throat and is an extension of the soft palate. [**C14**: from Medieval Latin, literally: a little grape, from Latin *ūva* a grape]

uvular (ˈjuːvjʊlə) *adj* **1** of or relating to the uvula. **2** *Phonetics.* articulated with the uvula and the back of the tongue, such as the (r) sound of Parisian French. ◆ *n* **3** a uvular consonant. ► **ˈuvularly** *adv*

uvulitis (ˌjuːvjʊˈlaɪtɪs) *n* inflammation of the uvula.

UWIST (ˈjuːˌwɪst) *n acronym for* University of Wales Institute of Science and Technology.

ux. *abbrev. for* uxor. [Latin: wife]

Uxbridge (ˈʌksˌbrɪdʒ) *n* a town in SE England, part of the Greater London borough of Hillingdon since 1965; chiefly residential.

Uxmal (*Spanish* uzˈmal) *n* an ancient ruined city in SE Mexico, in Yucatán: capital of the later Maya empire.

uxorial (ʌkˈsɔːrɪəl) *adj* of or relating to a wife: *uxorial influence.* [**C19**: from Latin *uxor* wife] ► **uxˈorially** *adv*

uxoricide (ʌkˈsɔːrɪˌsaɪd) *n* **1** the act of killing one's wife. **2** a man who kills his wife. [**C19**: from Latin *uxor* wife + -CIDE] ► **uxˌoriˈcidal** *adj*

uxorious (ʌkˈsɔːrɪəs) *adj* excessively attached to or dependent on one's wife. [**C16**: from Latin *uxōrius* concerning a wife, from *uxor* wife] ► **uxˈoriously** *adv* ► **uxˈoriousness** *n*

Uzbek (ˈʊzbɛk, ˈʌz-) *n* **1** (*pl* **-beks** *or* **-bek**) a member of a Mongoloid people of Uzbekistan. **2** the language of this people, belonging to the Turkic branch of the Altaic family.

Uzbekistan (ˌʌzbɛkɪˈstɑːn) *n* a republic in central Asia: annexed by Russia in the 19th century, it became a separate Soviet Socialist republic in 1924 and gained independence in 1991; mining, textile, and chemical industries are important. Official language: Uzbek. Religion: believers are mainly Muslim. Currency: sum. Capital: Tashkent. Pop.: 24 091 000 (1998 est.). Area: 449 600 sq. km (173 546 sq. miles).

Uzi (ˈuːzɪ) *n* a sub-machine gun of Israeli design. [**C20**: after *Uziel Gal,* the Israeli army officer who designed it]

v *or* **V** (viː) *n, pl* **v's, V's,** *or* **Vs. 1** the 22nd letter and 17th consonant of the modern English alphabet. **2** a speech sound represented by this letter, in English usually a voiced labio-dental fricative, as in *vote.* **3a** something shaped like a V. **3b** (*in combination*): *a V neck.* See also **V-sign.**

v *symbol. for:* **1** *Physics.* velocity. **2** specific volume (of a gas).

V *symbol for:* **1** (in transformational grammar) verb. **2** volume (capacity). **3** volt. **4** *Chem.* vanadium. **5** luminous efficiency. **6** victory. ◆ **7** *the Roman numeral for* five. See **Roman numerals.** ◆ **8** *international car registration for* Vatican City.

v. *abbrev. for:* **1** ventral. **2** verb. **3** verse. **4** version. **5** verso. **6** (*usually italic*) versus. **7** very. **8** vide [Latin: see] **9** violin. **10** vocative. **11** voice. **12** volume. **13** von.

V. *abbrev. for:* **1** Venerable. **2** (in titles) Very. **3** (in titles) Vice. **4** Viscount.

V-1 *n* a robot bomb invented by the Germans in World War II: used esp. to bombard London. It was propelled by a pulsejet. Also called: **doodlebug, buzz bomb, flying bomb.** [from German *Vergeltungswaffe* revenge weapon]

V-2 *n* a rocket-powered ballistic missile invented by the Germans in World War II: used esp. to bombard London. It used ethanol as fuel and liquid oxygen as the oxidizer. [see V-1]

V6 *n* a car or internal-combustion engine having six cylinders arranged in the form of a V.

V8 *n* a car or internal-combustion engine having eight cylinders arranged in the form of a V.

VA *abbrev. for:* **1** (in the U.S.) Veterans' Administration. **2** Vicar Apostolic. **3** Vice Admiral. **4** (Order of) Victoria and Albert. **5** Virginia. **6** volt-ampere.

Va. *abbrev. for* Virginia.

v.a. *abbrev. for* verb active.

Vaal (vɑːl) *n* a river in South Africa, rising in the Drakensberg and flowing west to join the Orange River. Length: 1160 km (720 miles).

Vaasa (*Finnish* 'vɑːsɑ) *n* a port in W Finland, on the Gulf of Bothnia: the provisional capital of Finland (1918); textile industries. Pop.: 55 089 (1994). Former name: **Nikolainkaupunki.**

vac (væk) *n Brit. informal.* short for **vacation.**

vacancy ('veɪkənsɪ) *n, pl* **-cies. 1** the state or condition of being vacant or unoccupied; emptiness. **2** an unoccupied post or office: *we have a vacancy in the accounts department.* **3** an unoccupied room in a boarding house, hotel, etc.: *put the "No Vacancies" sign in the window.* **4** lack of thought or intelligent awareness; inanity: *an expression of vacancy on one's face.* **5** *Physics.* a defect in a crystalline solid caused by the absence of an atom, ion, or molecule from its position in the crystal lattice. **6** *Obsolete.* idleness or a period spent in idleness.

vacant ('veɪkənt) *adj* **1** without any contents; empty. **2** (*postpositive; foll. by of*) devoid (of something specified). **3** having no incumbent; unoccupied: *a vacant post.* **4** having no tenant or occupant: *a vacant house.* **5** characterized by or resulting from lack of thought or intelligent awareness: *a vacant stare.* **6** (of time, etc.) not allocated to any activity: *a vacant hour in one's day.* **7** spent in idleness or inactivity: *a vacant life.* **8** *Law.* (of an estate, etc.) having no heir or claimant. [C13: from Latin *vacāre* to be empty] ▸ **'vacantly** *adv* ▸ **'vacantness** *n*

vacant possession *n* ownership of an unoccupied house or property, any previous owner or tenant having departed.

vacate (və'keɪt) *vb* (*mainly tr*) **1** to cause (something) to be empty, esp. by departing from or abandoning it: *to vacate a room.* **2** (*also intr*) to give up the tenure, possession, or occupancy of (a place, post, etc.); leave or quit. **3** *Law.* **3a** to cancel or rescind. **3b** to make void or of no effect; annul. ▸ **va'catable** *adj*

vacation (və'keɪʃən) *n* **1** *Chiefly Brit.* a period of the year when the law courts or universities are closed. **2** another word (esp. U.S. and Canadian) for **holiday. 3** the act of departing from or abandoning property, etc. ◆ *vb* **4** (*intr*) *U.S. and Canadian.* to take a vacation; holiday. [C14: from Latin *vacātiō* freedom, from *vacāre* to be empty] ▸ **va'cationless** *adj*

vacationer (və'keɪʃənə) *or* **vacationist** (və'keɪʃənɪst) *n* U.S. and Canadian words for **holiday-maker.**

vaccinal ('væksɪnəl) *adj* of or relating to vaccine or vaccination.

vaccinate ('væksɪˌneɪt) *vb* to inoculate (a person) with vaccine so as to produce immunity against a specific disease. ▸ **'vacciˌnator** *n*

vaccination (ˌvæksɪ'neɪʃən) *n* **1** the act of vaccinating. **2** the scar left following inoculation with a vaccine.

vaccine ('væksiːn) *n Med.* **1** a suspension of dead, attenuated, or otherwise modified microorganisms (viruses, bacteria, or rickettsiae) for inoculation to produce immunity to a disease by stimulating the production of antibodies. **2** a preparation of the virus of cowpox taken from infected cows and inoculated in humans to produce immunity to smallpox. **3** (*modifier*) of or relating to vaccination or vaccinia. **4** *Computing.* a piece of software designed to detect and remove computer viruses from a system. [C18: from New Latin *variolae vaccīnae* cowpox, title of medical treatise (1798) by Edward Jenner, from Latin *vacca* a cow]

vaccinia (væk'sɪnɪə) *n* a technical name for **cowpox.** [C19: New Latin, from Latin *vaccīnus* of cows] ▸ **vac'cinial** *adj*

vacherin *French.* (vaʃrɛ̃) *n* a dessert consisting of a meringue shell filled with whipped cream, ice cream, fruit, etc. [also in France a type of cheese, from French *vache* cow, from Latin *vacca*]

vacillate ('væsɪˌleɪt) *vb* (*intr*) **1** to fluctuate in one's opinions; be indecisive. **2** to sway from side to side physically; totter or waver. [C16: from Latin *vacillāre* to sway, of obscure origin] ▸ **ˌvacil'lation** *n* ▸ **'vacilˌlator** *n*

vacillating ('væsɪˌleɪtɪŋ) *or* (*rarely*) **vacillant** ('væsɪlənt) *adj* inclined to waver; indecisive. ▸ **'vacilˌlatingly** *adv*

vacua ('vækjʊə) *n* a plural of **vacuum.**

vacuity (væ'kjuːɪtɪ) *n, pl* **-ties. 1** the state or quality of being vacuous; emptiness. **2** an empty space or void; vacuum. **3** a lack or absence of something specified: *a vacuity of wind.* **4** lack of normal intelligence or awareness; vacancy: *his stare gave an impression of complete vacuity.* **5** something, such as a statement, saying, etc., that is inane or pointless. **6** (in customs terminology) the difference in volume between the actual contents of a container and its full capacity. [C16: from Latin *vacuitās* empty space, from *vacuus* empty]

vacuole ('vækjʊˌəʊl) *n Biology.* a fluid-filled cavity in the cytoplasm of a cell. [C19: from French, literally: little vacuum, from Latin VACUUM] ▸ **vacuolar** (ˌvækjʊ'əʊlə) *adj* ▸ **vacuolate** ('vækjʊəlɪt, -ˌleɪt) *adj* ▸ **vacuolation** (ˌvækjʊə'leɪʃən) *n*

vacuous ('vækjʊəs) *adj* **1** containing nothing; empty. **2** bereft of ideas or intelligence; mindless. **3** characterized by or resulting from vacancy of mind: *a vacuous gaze.* **4** indulging in no useful mental or physical activity; idle. **5** *Logic, maths.* (of an operator or expression) having no import; idle: in (*x*) (*John is tall*) the quantifier (*x*) is vacuous. [C17: from Latin *vacuus* empty, from *vacāre* to be empty] ▸ **'vacuously** *adv* ▸ **'vacuousness** *n*

vacuum ('vækjʊəm) *n, pl* **vacuums** *or* **vacua** ('vækjʊə). **1** a region containing no matter; free space. Compare **plenum** (sense 3). **2** a region in which gas is present at a low pressure. **3** the degree of exhaustion of gas within an enclosed space: *a high vacuum; a perfect vacuum.* **4** a sense or feeling of emptiness: *his death left a vacuum in her life.* **5** short for **vacuum cleaner. 6** (*modifier*) of, containing, measuring, producing, or operated by a low gas pressure: *a vacuum tube; a vacuum brake.* ◆ *vb* **7** to clean (something) with a vacuum cleaner: *to vacuum a carpet.* [C16: from Latin: an empty space, from *vacuus* empty]

vacuum activity *n Ethology.* instinctive behaviour occurring in the absence of the appropriate stimulus.

vacuum brake *n* a brake system, used on British and many overseas railways, in which the brake is held off by a vacuum on one side of the brake-operating cylinder. If the vacuum is destroyed by controlled leakage of air or a disruptive emergency the brake is applied. It is now largely superseded by the Westinghouse brake system.

vacuum cleaner *n* an electrical household appliance used for cleaning floors, carpets, furniture, etc., by suction. ▸ **vacuum cleaning** *n*

vacuum distillation *n* distillation in which the liquid distilled is enclosed at a low pressure in order to reduce its boiling point.

vacuum flask *n* an insulating flask that has double walls, usually of silvered glass, with an evacuated space between them. It is used for maintaining substances at high or low temperatures. Also called: **Thermos, Dewar flask.**

vacuum forming *n* a process in which a sheet of warmed thermoplastic is shaped by placing it in a mould and applying suction.

vacuum frame *n Printing.* a machine from which the air is extracted in order to obtain close contact between the surfaces of two materials, e.g. the film and plate during platemaking.

vacuum gauge *n* any of a number of instruments for measuring pressures below atmospheric pressure.

vacuum-packed *adj* packed in an airtight container or packet under low pressure in order to maintain freshness, prevent corrosion, etc.

vacuum pump *n* a pump for producing a low gas pressure.

vacuum servo *n* a servomechanism that is operated by the lowering of pressure in the intake duct of an internal-combustion engine.

vacuum tube *or* **valve** *n* another name for **valve** (sense 3).

VAD 1 *abbrev. for* Voluntary Aid Detachment. ◆ *n* **2** a nurse serving in the Voluntary Aid Detachment.

vade mecum ('vɑːdɪ 'meɪkʊm) *n* a handbook or other aid carried on the person for immediate use when needed. [C17: from Latin, literally: go with me]

Vadodara (wə'dəʊdərə) *n* a city in W India, in SE Gujurat: textile manufacturing. Pop.: 1 031 346 (1991). Former name (until 1976): **Baroda.**

vadose ('veɪdəʊs) *adj* of, relating to, designating, or derived from water occurring above the water table: *vadose water; vadose deposits.* [C19: from Latin *vadōsus* full of shallows, from *vadum* a ford]

Vaduz (*German* fa'dʊts) *n* the capital of Liechtenstein, in the Rhine valley: an old market town, dominated by a medieval castle, residence of the prince of Liechtenstein. Pop.: 5017 (1997 est.).

vag (væg) *Austral. informal.* ◆ *n* **1** a vagrant. **2 the vag.** the Vagrancy Act: *the police finally got him on the vag.* ◆ *vb* **vags, vagging, vagged. 3** (*tr*) to arrest (someone) for vagrancy.

vagabond ('vægəˌbɒnd) *n* **1** a person with no fixed home. **2** an idle wandering beggar or thief. **3** (*modifier*) of or like a vagabond; shiftless or idle. [C15: from

Latin *vagābundus* wandering, from *vagārī* to roam, from *vagus* VAGUE] ► **'vaga,bondage** *n* ► **'vaga,bondish** *adj* ► **'vaga,bondism** *n*

vagal ('veɪgᵊl) *adj Anatomy.* of, relating to, or affecting the vagus nerve: *vagal inhibition.*

vagarious (və'gɛərɪəs) *adj Rare.* characterized or caused by vagaries; irregular or erratic. ► **va'gariously** *adv*

vagary ('veɪgərɪ, və'gɛərɪ) *n, pl* **-garies.** an erratic or outlandish notion or action; whim. [C16: probably from Latin *vagārī* to roam; compare Latin *vagus* VAGUE]

vagina (və'dʒaɪnə) *n, pl* **-nas** *or* **-nae** (-niː). **1** the moist canal in most female mammals, including humans, that extends from the cervix of the uterus to an external opening between the labia minora. **2** *Anatomy, biology.* any sheath or sheathlike structure, such as a leaf base that encloses a stem. [C17: from Latin: sheath] ► **vag'inal** *adj*

vaginate ('vædʒɪnɪt, -,neɪt) *adj* (esp. of plant parts) having a vagina or sheath; sheathed: *a vaginate leaf.*

vaginectomy (,vædʒɪ'nɛktəmɪ) *n* **1** surgical removal of all or part of the vagina. **2** surgical removal of part of the serous sheath surrounding the testis and epididymis.

vaginismus (,vædʒɪ'nɪzməs, -'nɪsməs) *n* painful spasm of the vagina. [C19: from New Latin, from VAGINA + *-ismus;* see -ISM]

vaginitis (,vædʒɪ'naɪtɪs) *n* inflammation of the vagina.

vagotomy (væ'gɒtəmɪ) *n, pl* **-mies.** surgical division of the vagus nerve, performed to limit gastric secretion in patients with severe peptic ulcers. [C19: from VAG(US) + -TOMY]

vagotonia (,veɪgə'təʊnɪə) *n* pathological overactivity of the vagus nerve, affecting various bodily functions controlled by this nerve. [C19: from VAG(US) + *-tonia,* from Latin *tonus* tension, TONE]

vagotropic (,veɪgə'trɒpɪk) *adj Physiol.* (of a drug) affecting the activity of the vagus nerve. [C20: from VAG(US) + -TROPIC]

vagrancy ('veɪgrənsɪ) *n, pl* **-cies. 1** the state or condition of being a vagrant. **2** the conduct or mode of living of a vagrant.

vagrant ('veɪgrənt) *n* **1** a person of no settled abode, income, or job; tramp. **2** a migratory bird or insect that is off course. ◆ *adj* **3** wandering about; nomadic. **4** of, relating to, or characteristic of a vagrant or vagabond. **5** moving in an erratic fashion, without aim or purpose; wayward. **6** (of plants) showing uncontrolled or straggling growth. ◆ Archaic equivalent: **vagrom** ('veɪgrəm). [C15: probably from Old French *waucrant* (from *wancrer* to roam, of Germanic origin), but also influenced by Old French *vagant* vagabond, from Latin *vagārī* to wander] ► **'vagrantly** *adv* ► **'vagrantness** *n*

vague (veɪg) *adj* **1** (of statements, meaning, etc.) not explicit; imprecise: *vague promises.* **2** not clearly perceptible or discernible; indistinct: *a vague idea; a vague shape.* **3** not clearly or definitely established or known: *a vague rumour.* **4** (of a person or his expression) demonstrating lack of precision or clear thinking; absent-minded. [C16: via French from Latin *vagus* wandering, of obscure origin] ► **'vaguely** *adv* ► **'vagueness** *n*

vagus *or* **vagus nerve** ('veɪgəs) *n, pl* **-gi** (-dʒaɪ). the tenth cranial nerve, which supplies the heart, lungs, and viscera. [C19: from Latin *vagus* wandering]

vahana ('vɑːhənə) *n Indian myth.* a vehicle. [Hindi, from Sanskrit, from *vaha* to carry]

vail[1] (veɪl) *vb (tr) Obsolete.* **1** to lower (something, such as a weapon), esp. as a sign of deference or submission. **2** to remove (the hat, cap, etc.) as a mark of respect or meekness. [C14 *valen,* from obsolete *avalen,* from Old French *avaler* to let fall, from Latin *ad vallem,* literally: to the valley, that is, down, from *ad* to + *vallis* VALLEY]

vail[2] (veɪl) *n, vb* an archaic word for **avail.**

vail[3] (veɪl) *n, vb* an archaic spelling of **veil.**

vain (veɪn) *adj* **1** inordinately proud of one's appearance, possessions, or achievements. **2** given to ostentatious display, esp. of one's beauty. **3** worthless. **4** senseless or futile. ◆ *n* **5 in vain.** to no avail; fruitlessly. **6 take someone's name in vain. 6a** to use the name of someone, esp. God, without due respect or reverence. **6b** *Jocular.* to mention someone's name. [C13: via Old French from Latin *vānus*] ► **'vainly** *adv* ► **'vainness** *n*

vainglory (,veɪn'glɔːrɪ) *n* **1** boastfulness or vanity. **2** ostentation. ► **,vain'glorious** *adj*

vair (vɛə) *n* **1** a fur, probably Russian squirrel, used to trim robes in the Middle Ages. **2** one of the two principal furs used on heraldic shields, conventionally represented by white and blue skins in alternate lines. Compare **ermine** (sense 3). [C13: from Old French: of more than one colour, from Latin *varius* variegated, VARIOUS]

Vaishnava ('vɪʃnəvə) *n Hinduism.* a member of a sect devoted to the cult of Vishnu, strongly anti-Brahminic and antipriestly in outlook and stressing devotion through image worship and simple ritual. [from Sanskrit *vaisnava* of VISHNU] ► **'Vaishnavism** *n*

Vaisya ('vaɪsjə, 'vaɪʃjə) *n* the third of the four main Hindu castes, the traders. [C18: from Sanskrit, literally: settler, from *viś* settlement]

Vajrayana (vʌdʒrʌ'jɑːnə) *n* a school of Tantric Buddhism of India and Tibet. [from Sanskrit: vehicle of the diamond or thunderbolt]

val. *abbrev. for:* **1** valuation. **2** value.

Valais (*French* valɛ) *n* a canton of S Switzerland: includes the entire valley of the upper Rhône and the highest peaks in Switzerland; produces a quarter of Switzerland's hydroelectricity. Capital: Sion. Pop.: 271 291 (1996 est.). Area: 5231 sq. km (2020 sq. miles). German name: **Wallis.**

valance ('væləns) *n* a short piece of drapery hung along a shelf, canopy, or bed, or across a window, to hide structural detail. [C15: perhaps named after VALENCE, France, town noted for its textiles] ► **'valanced** *adj*

Valdai Hills (vɑːl'daɪ) *pl n* a region of hills and plateaus in NW Russia, between Moscow and St Petersburg. Greatest height: 346 m (1135 ft.).

Valdemar I, II, *or* **IV** (*Danish* 'valdəmar) *n* a variant spelling of **Waldemar I, II,** *or* **IV.**

Val-de-Marne (*French* valdəmarn) *n* a department of N France, in Île-de-France region. Capital: Créteil. Pop.: 1 234 700 (1995). Area: 244 sq. km (95 sq. miles).

Valdivia[1] (*Spanish* bal'diβja) *n* a port in S Chile, on the **Valdivia River** about 19 km (12 miles) from the Pacific: developed chiefly by German settlers in the 1850s; university (1954). Pop.: 119 431 (1995 est.).

Valdivia[2] (*Spanish* bal'diβja) *n* **Pedro de** ('peðro de). ?1500–54, Spanish soldier; conqueror of Chile.

Val-d'Oise (*French* valdwaz) *n* a department of N France, in Île-de-France region. Capital: Pontoise. Pop.: 1 108 400 (1995). Area: 1249 sq. km (487 sq. miles).

vale[1] (veɪl) *n* a literary word for **valley.** [C13: from Old French *val,* from Latin *vallis* valley]

vale[2] *Latin.* ('vɑːleɪ) *sentence substitute.* farewell; goodbye.

valediction (,vælɪ'dɪkʃən) *n* **1** the act or an instance of saying goodbye. **2** any valedictory statement, speech, etc. [C17: from Latin *valedīcere,* from *valē* farewell + *dīcere* to say]

valedictorian (,vælɪdɪk'tɔːrɪən) *adj* also **valedictory. 1** saying goodbye. **2** of or relating to a farewell or an occasion of farewell. ◆ *n* **3** *U.S. and Canadian.* a person, usually the most outstanding graduate, who delivers a farewell speech at a graduation ceremony.

valedictory (,vælɪ'dɪktərɪ, -trɪ) *n, pl* **-ries. 1** a farewell address or speech. **2** *U.S. and Canadian.* a farewell speech delivered at a graduation ceremony, usually by the most outstanding graduate.

valence ('veɪləns) *n Chem.* **1** another name (esp. U.S. and Canadian) for **valency. 2** the phenomenon of forming chemical bonds.

Valence (*French* valɑ̃s) *n* a town in SE France, on the River Rhône. Pop.: 63 437 (1990).

valence band *n* See **energy band.**

valence-conduction band *n* See **energy band.**

Valencia (*Spanish* ba'lenθja) *n* **1** a port in E Spain, capital of Valencia province, on the Mediterranean: the third largest city in Spain; capital of the Moorish kingdom of Valencia (1021–1238); university (1501). Pop.: 763 299 (1995 est.). Latin name: **Valentia** (və'lɛntɪə). **2** a region and former kingdom of E Spain, on the Mediterranean. **3** a city in N Venezuela: one of the two main industrial centres in Venezuela. Pop.: 903 621 (1990).

Valenciennes[1] (,vælənsɪ'ɛn) *n* a flat bobbin lace typically having scroll and floral designs and originally made of linen, now often cotton. [named after VALENCIENNES[2], where it was originally made]

Valenciennes[2] (*French* valɑ̃sjɛn) *n* a town in N France, on the River Escaut: a coal-mining and heavy industrial centre. Pop.: 39 276 (1990).

valency ('veɪlənsɪ) *or esp. U.S. and Canadian* **valence** *n, pl* **-cies** *or* **-ces. 1** *Chem.* a property of atoms or groups, equal to the number of atoms of hydrogen that the atom or group could combine with or displace in forming compounds. **2** *Linguistics.* the number of satellite noun phrases with which a verb combines: *the English verb "give" takes a subject and two objects, so it has a valency of three.* **3** *Immunol.* **3a** the number of antigen-binding sites on an antibody molecule. **3b** the number of antigen-binding sites with which an antigen can combine. [C19: from Latin *valentia* strength, from *valēre* to be strong]

valency electron *n Chem.* an electron in the outer shell of an atom, responsible for forming chemical bonds.

valency grammar *n* a system of linguistic syntax, conceived by analogy with chemical valency, according to which verbs have valencies dependent on the number of noun phrases with which they combine. See **valency** (sense 2).

Valens ('veɪlɛnz) *n* ?328–378 A.D., emperor of the Eastern Roman Empire (364–378); appointed by his elder brother Valentinian I, emperor of the Western Empire.

-valent ('veɪlənt) *adj combining form. Chem.* having a specified valency: *bivalent; trivalent.* [C19: from Latin *valentia;* see VALENCY]

valentine ('vælən,taɪn) *n* **1** a card or gift expressing love or affection, sent, often anonymously, to one's sweetheart or satirically to a friend, on Saint Valentine's Day. **2** a sweetheart selected for such a greeting.

Valentine ('vælən,taɪn) *n* **Saint.** 3rd century A.D., Christian martyr, associated by historical accident with the custom of sending valentines; bishop of Terni. Feast day: Feb. 14.

Valentinian I (,vælən'tɪnɪən) *or* **Valentinianus I** (,vælən,tɪnɪ'eɪnəs) *n* 321–375 A.D., emperor of the Western Roman Empire (364–375); appointed his brother Valens to rule the Eastern Empire.

Valentinian II *or* **Valentinianus II** *n* 371–392 A.D., emperor of the Western Roman Empire (375–392), reigning jointly with his half brother Gratian until 383.

Valentinian III *or* **Valentinianus III** *n* ?419–455 A.D., emperor of the Western Roman Empire (425–455). His government lost Africa to the Vandals. With Pope Leo I he issued (444) an edict giving the bishop of Rome supremacy over the provincial churches.

Valentino (,vælən'tiːnəʊ) *n* **Rudolph,** original name *Rodolpho Guglielmi di Valentina d'Antonguolla.* 1895–1926, U.S. silent-film actor, born in Italy. He is famous for his romantic roles in such films as *The Sheik* (1921).

Vale of Glamorgan (,glə'mɔːgᵊn) *n* a county borough of S Wales, created in 1996 from parts of South Glamorgan and Mid Glamorgan. Administrative centre: Barry. Pop.: 119 200 (1996 est.). Area: 295 sq. km (114 sq. miles).

Valera (və'lɛərə, -'lɪərə) *n* See (Eamon) **de Valera.**

valerian (və'lɛərɪən) *n* **1** Also called: **allheal.** any of various Eurasian valerianaceous plants of the genus *Valeriana,* esp. *V. officinalis,* having small white or pinkish flowers and a medicinal root. **2** a sedative drug made from the dried roots of *V. officinalis.* [**C14**: via Old French from Medieval Latin *valeriana (herba)* (herb) of *Valerius,* unexplained Latin personal name]

Valerian (vəˈlɪərɪən) *n* Latin name *Publius Licinius Valerianus.* died 260 A.D., Roman emperor (253–260): renewed persecution of the Christians; defeated by the Persians.

valerianaceous (vəˌlɪərɪəˈneɪʃəs) *adj* of, relating to, or belonging to the *Valerianaceae,* a family of herbaceous plants having the calyx of the flower reduced to a ring of hairs: includes valerian, spikenard, and corn salad. [**C19**: from New Latin; see VALERIAN]

valeric (vəˈlɛrɪk, -ˈlɪərɪk) *adj* of, relating to, or derived from valerian.

valeric acid *n* another name for **pentanoic acid.**

Valéry (*French* valeri) *n* **Paul** (pɔl). 1871–1945, French poet and essayist, influenced by the symbolists, esp. Mallarmé. He wrote lyric poetry, rich in imagery, as in *La Jeune Parque* (1917) and *Album de vers anciens 1890–1900* (1920).

valet (ˈvælɪt, ˈvæleɪ) *n* **1** a manservant who acts as personal attendant to his employer, looking after his clothing, serving his meals, etc. French name: **valet de chambre. 2** a manservant who attends to the requirements of patrons in a hotel, passengers on board ship, etc.; steward. ◆ *vb* **-ets, -eting, -eted. 3** to act as a valet for (a person). **4** (*tr*) to clean the bodywork and interior of (a car) as a professional service. [**C16**: from Old French *vaslet* page, from Medieval Latin *vassus* servant; see VASSAL]

valeta *or* **veleta** (vəˈliːtə) *n* a ballroom dance in triple time. [from Spanish *veleta* weather vane]

valet de chambre *French.* (valɛ də ʃɑ̃brə) *n, pl* ***valets de chambre*** (valɛ də ʃɑ̃brə). the full French term for **valet** (sense 1).

valet parking *n* a system at hotels, airports, etc., in which patrons' cars are parked by a steward.

Valetta (vəˈlɛtə) *n* a variant spelling of **Valletta.**

valetudinarian (ˌvælɪˌtjuːdɪˈnɛərɪən) *or* **valetudinary** (ˌvælɪˈtjuːdɪnərɪ) *n, pl* **-narians** *or* **-naries. 1** a person who is chronically sick; invalid. **2** a person excessively worried about the state of his health; hypochondriac. ◆ *adj* **3** relating to, marked by, or resulting from poor health. **4** being a valetudinarian. **5** trying to return to a healthy state. [**C18**: from Latin *valētūdō* state of health, from *valēre* to be well] ▸ **ˌvaleˌtudiˈnarianism** *n*

valgus (ˈvælgəs) *adj Pathol.* displaced or twisted away from the midline of the body. See **hallux valgus.** [**C19**: from Latin: bow-legged]

Valhalla (vælˈhælə), **Walhalla, Valhall** (vælˈhæl, ˈvælhæl), *or* **Walhall** *n Norse myth.* the great hall of Odin where warriors who die as heroes in battle dwell eternally. [**C18**: from Old Norse, from *valr* slain warriors + *höll* HALL]

valiant (ˈvæljənt) *adj* **1** courageous, intrepid, or stout-hearted; brave. **2** marked by bravery or courage: *a valiant deed.* [**C14**: from Old French *vaillant,* from *valoir* to be of value, from Latin *valēre* to be strong] ▸ **ˈvaliance** *or* **ˈvaliancy** *n* ▸ **ˈvaliantly** *adv*

valid (ˈvælɪd) *adj* **1** having some foundation; based on truth. **2** legally acceptable: *a valid licence.* **3a** having legal force; effective. **3b** having legal authority; binding. **4** having some force or cogency: *a valid point in a debate.* **5** *Logic.* (of an inference or argument) having premises and conclusion so related that whenever the former are true the latter must also be true, esp. (**formally valid**) when the inference is justified by the form of the premises and conclusion alone. Thus *Tom is a bachelor; therefore Tom is unmarried* is valid but not formally so, while *today is hot and dry; therefore today is hot* is formally valid. Compare **invalid**[2] (sense 2). **6** *Archaic.* healthy or strong. [**C16**: from Latin *validus* robust, from *valēre* to be strong] ▸ **ˈvalidly** *adv* ▸ **validity** (vəˈlɪdɪtɪ) *or* **ˈvalidness** *n*

validate (ˈvælɪˌdeɪt) *vb* (*tr*) **1** to confirm or corroborate. **2** to give legal force or official confirmation to; declare legally valid. ▸ **ˌvaliˈdation** *n* ▸ **ˈvalidatory** *adj*

valine (ˈveɪliːn, ˈvæl-) *n* an essential amino acid; a component of proteins. [**C19**: from VAL(ERIC ACID) + -INE[2]]

valise (vəˈliːz) *n* a small overnight travelling case. [**C17**: via French from Italian *valigia,* of unknown origin]

Valium (ˈvælɪəm) *n Trademark.* a preparation of the drug diazepam used as a tranquillizer. See also **benzodiazepine.**

Valkyrie, Walkyrie (vælˈkɪərɪ, ˈvælkɪərɪ), *or* **Valkyr** (ˈvælkɪə) *n Norse myth.* any of the beautiful maidens who serve Odin and ride over battlefields to claim the dead heroes and take them to Valhalla. [**C18**: from Old Norse *Valkyrja,* from *valr* slain warriors + *köri* to CHOOSE] ▸ **ValˈKyrian** *adj*

Valla (*Italian* ˈvalla) *n* **Lorenzo** (loˈrɛntso). 1405–57, Italian humanist scholar. His writings include *De voluptate* (1431), a philosophical dialogue on pleasure.

Valladolid (*Spanish* baʎaðoˈlið) *n* **1** a city in NW Spain: residence of the Spanish court in the 16th century; university (1346). Pop.: 334 820 (1995 est.). **2** the former name (until 1828) of **Morelia.**

vallation (vəˈleɪʃən) *n* **1** the act or process of building fortifications. **2** a wall or rampart. [**C17**: from Late Latin *vallātiō,* from *vallum* rampart]

vallecula (vəˈlɛkjʊlə) *n, pl* **-lae** (-ˌliː). **1** *Anatomy.* any of various natural depressions or crevices, such as certain fissures of the brain. **2** *Botany.* a groove or furrow. [**C19**: from Late Latin: little valley, from Latin *vallis* valley] ▸ **valˈlecular** *or* **valˈlecuˌlate** *adj*

Valle d'Aosta (*Italian* ˈvalle daˈɔsta) *n* an autonomous region of NW Italy: under many different rulers until passing to the house of Savoy in the 11th century; established as an autonomous region in 1944. Capital: Aosta. Pop.: 118 723 (1996 est.). Area: 3263 sq. km (1260 sq. miles).

Valle-Inclán (*Spanish* ˈbaʎeiŋˈklan) *n* **Rámon María del.** 1866–1936, Spanish novelist and dramatist. His works include the novel *Tirano Banderas* (1926) and the satirical play *Don Friolera's Horns* (1925).

Vallejo (vəˈleɪəʊ, -ˈleɪhəʊ; *Spanish* baˈʎexo) *n* **César (Abraham)** (ˈsesar). 1892–1938, Peruvian poet, living in France and Spain from 1923: noted for his experimental style in such works as *Trilce* (1922).

Valletta *or* **Valetta** (vəˈlɛtə) *n* the capital of Malta, on the NE coast: founded by the Knights Hospitallers, after the victory over the Turks in 1565; became a major naval base after Malta's annexation by Britain (1814). Pop.: 9128 (1996 est.).

valley (ˈvælɪ) *n* **1** a long depression in the land surface, usually containing a river, formed by erosion or by movements in the earth's crust. **2** the broad area drained by a single river system: *the Thames valley.* **3** any elongated depression resembling a valley. **4** the junction of a roof slope with another or with a wall. **5** (*modifier*) relating to or proceeding by way of a valley: *a valley railway.* [**C13**: from Old French *valee,* from Latin *vallis*]

Valley Forge *n* an area in SE Pennsylvania, northwest of Philadelphia: winter camp (1777–78) of Washington and the American Revolutionary Army.

Valley of Ten Thousand Smokes *n* a volcanic region of SW Alaska, formed by the massive eruption of Mount Katmai in 1912; jets of steam issue from vents up to 45 m (150 ft.) across.

Vallombrosa (*Italian* vallomˈbroːsa) *n* a village and resort in central Italy, in Tuscany region: 11th-century Benedictine monastery.

vallum (ˈvæləm) *n Archaeol.* a Roman rampart or earthwork.

Valois[1] (*French* valwa) *n* a historic region and former duchy of N France.

Valois[2] (*French* valwa) *n* a royal house of France, ruling from 1328 to 1589.

Valois[3] (ˈvælwɑː) *n* Dame **Ninette de** (niːˈnɛt də). original name *Edris Stannus.* born 1898, British ballet dancer and choreographer, born in Ireland: a founder of the Vic-Wells Ballet Company (1931), which under her direction became the Royal Ballet (1956).

Valona (vəˈləʊnə) *n* another name for **Vlorë.**

valonia (vəˈləʊnɪə) *n* the acorn cups and unripe acorns of the Eurasian oak *Quercus aegilops,* used in tanning, dyeing, and making ink. [**C18**: from Italian *vallonia,* ultimately from Greek *balanos* acorn]

valorize *or* **valorise** (ˈvæləˌraɪz) *vb* (*tr*) to fix and maintain an artificial price for (a commodity) by governmental action. [**C20**: back formation from *valorization;* see VALOUR] ▸ **ˌvaloriˈzation** *or* **ˌvaloriˈsation** *n*

valour *or U.S.* **valor** (ˈvælə) *n* courage or bravery, esp. in battle. [**C15**: from Late Latin *valor,* from *valēre* to be strong] ▸ **ˈvalorous** *adj* ▸ **ˈvalorously** *adv*

Valparaíso (*Spanish* balparaˈiso) *n* a port in central Chile, on a wide bay of the Pacific: the third largest city and chief port of Chile; two universities. Pop.: 282 168 (1995 est.).

Valpolicella (ˌvælpɒlɪˈtʃɛlə; *Italian* valpoliˈtʃɛlla) *n* a dry red table wine from the Veneto region of NE Italy. [**C20**: named after a valley where it is produced]

valse *French.* (vals) *n* another word, esp. used in the titles of some pieces of music, for **waltz.**

valuable (ˈvæljʊəbᵊl) *adj* **1** having considerable monetary worth. **2** of considerable importance or quality: *a valuable friend; valuable information.* **3** able to be valued. ◆ *n* **4** (*usually pl*) a valuable article of personal property, esp. jewellery. ▸ **ˈvaluableness** *n* ▸ **ˈvaluably** *adv*

valuate (ˈvæljʊˌeɪt) *vb U.S.* another word for **value** (senses 10, 12) or **evaluate.**

valuation (ˌvæljʊˈeɪʃən) *n* **1** the act of valuing, esp. a formal assessment of the worth of property, jewellery, etc. **2** the price arrived at by the process of valuing: *the valuation of this property is considerable; I set a high valuation on technical ability.* ▸ **ˌvaluˈational** *adj* ▸ **ˌvaluˈationally** *adv*

valuator (ˈvæljʊˌeɪtə) *n* a person who estimates the value of objects, paintings, etc.; appraiser.

value (ˈvæljuː) *n* **1** the desirability of a thing, often in respect of some property such as usefulness or exchangeability: worth, merit, or importance. **2** an amount, esp. a material or monetary one, considered to be a fair exchange in return for a thing; assigned valuation: *the value of the picture is £10 000.* **3** reasonable or equivalent return; satisfaction: *value for money.* **4** precise meaning or significance. **5** (*pl*) the moral principles and beliefs or accepted standards of a person or social group: *a person with old-fashioned values.* **6** *Maths.* **6a** a particular magnitude, number, or amount: *the value of the variable was 7.* **6b** the particular quantity that is the result of applying a function or operation for some given argument: *the value of the function for x=3 was 9.* **7** *Music.* short for **time value. 8** (in painting, drawing, etc.) **8a** a gradation of tone from light to dark or of colour luminosity. **8b** the relation of one of these elements to another or to the whole picture. **9** *Phonetics.* the quality or tone of the speech sound associated with a written character representing it: *"g" has the value* (dʒ) *in English "gem."* ◆ *vb* **-ues, -uing, -ued.** (*tr*) **10** to assess or estimate the worth, merit, or desirability of; appraise. **11** to have a high regard for, esp. in respect of worth, usefulness, merit, etc.; esteem or prize: *to value freedom.* **12** (foll. by *at*) to fix the financial or material worth of (a unit of currency, work of art, etc.): *jewels valued at £40 000.* [**C14**: from Old French, from *valoir,* from Latin *valēre* to be worth, be strong] ▸ **ˈvaluer** *n*

value added *n* the difference between the total revenues of a firm, industry, etc., and its total purchases from other firms, industries, etc. The aggregate of values added throughout an economy (**gross value added**) represents that economy's gross domestic product.

value-added tax *n* (in Britain) the full name for **VAT.**

value date *n* the exact date on which a financial transaction, esp. in buying and selling foreign exchange, is deemed to take place: used for calculating exchange rates.

valued policy *n* an insurance policy in which the amount payable in the event of a valid claim is agreed upon between the company and policyholder when the policy is issued and is not related to the actual value of a loss. Compare **open policy.**

value judgment *n* a subjective assessment based on one's own code of values or that of one's class.

valueless ('væljʊlɪs) *adj* having or possessing no value; worthless. ► **'valuelessness** *n*

valuer ('væljʊə) *n* a person who assesses the monetary worth of a work of art, jewel, house, etc.; appraiser.

Valuer General *n Austral.* a state official who values properties for rating purposes.

valuta (vəˈluːtə) *n Rare.* the value of one currency in terms of its exchange rate with another. **[C20:** from Italian, literally: VALUE**]**

valvate ('vælveɪt) *adj* **1** furnished with a valve or valves. **2** functioning as or resembling a valve. **3** *Botany.* **3a** having or taking place by means of valves: *valvate dehiscence.* **3b** (of petals or sepals in the bud) having the margins touching but not overlapping.

valve (vælv) *n* **1** any device that shuts off, starts, regulates, or controls the flow of a fluid. **2** *Anatomy.* a flaplike structure in a hollow organ, such as the heart, that controls the one-way passage of fluid through that organ. **3** Also called: **tube, vacuum tube.** an evacuated electron tube containing a cathode, anode, and, usually, one or more additional control electrodes. When a positive potential is applied to the anode, electrons emitted from the cathode are attracted to the anode, constituting a flow of current which can be controlled by a voltage applied to the grid to produce amplification, oscillation, etc. See also **diode** (sense 2), **triode** (sense 1), **tetrode, pentode. 4** *Zoology.* any of the separable pieces that make up the shell of a mollusc. **5** *Music.* a device on some brass instruments by which the effective length of the tube may be varied to enable a chromatic scale to be produced. **6** *Botany.* **6a** any of the several parts that make up a dry dehiscent fruit, esp. a capsule. **6b** either of the two halves of a diatom cell wall. **7** *Archaic.* a leaf of a double door or of a folding door. **[C14:** from Latin *valva* a folding door**]** ► **'valveless** *adj* ► **'valve,like** *adj*

valve gear *n* a mechanism that operates the valves of a reciprocating engine, usually involving the use of cams, pushrods, rocker arms, etc.

valve-in-head engine *n* the U.S. name for **overhead-valve engine.**

valve spring *n* **1** a helical spring used to hold closed a valve in the cylinder head of an internal-combustion engine. **2** any spring that closes a valve after it has been opened mechanically or by flow pressure.

valvular ('vælvjʊlə) *adj* **1** of, relating to, operated by, or having a valve or valves. **2** having the shape or function of a valve.

valvule ('vælvjuːl) *or* **valvelet** ('vælvlɪt) *n* a small valve or a part resembling one. **[C18:** from New Latin *valvula,* diminutive of VALVE**]**

valvulitis (ˌvælvjʊˈlaɪtɪs) *n* inflammation of a bodily valve, esp. a heart valve. **[C19:** from VALVULE + -ITIS**]**

vambrace ('væmbreɪs) *n* a piece of armour used to protect the arm. **[C14:** from Anglo-French *vauntbras,* from *vaunt-* (from Old French *avant-* fore-) + *bras* arm**]** ► **'vambraced** *adj*

vamoose (vəˈmuːs) *vb (intr) Slang, chiefly U.S.* to leave a place hurriedly; decamp. **[C19:** from Spanish *vamos* let us go, from Latin *vādere* to go, walk rapidly**]**

vamp[1] (væmp) *Informal.* ◆ *n* **1** a seductive woman who exploits men by use of her sexual charms. ◆ *vb* **2** to exploit (a man) in the fashion of a vamp. **[C20:** short for VAMPIRE**]** ► **'vamper** *n* ► **'vampish** *adj*

vamp[2] (væmp) *n* **1** something patched up to make it look new. **2** the reworking of a theme, story, etc. **3** an improvised accompaniment, consisting largely of chords. **4** the front part of the upper of a shoe. ◆ *vb* **5** *(tr;* often foll. by *up)* to give a vamp to; make a renovation of. **6** to improvise (an accompaniment) to (a tune). **[C13:** from Old French *avantpié* the front part of a shoe (hence, something patched), from *avant-* fore- + *pié* foot, from Latin *pēs***]** ► **'vamper** *n*

vampire ('væmpaɪə) *n* **1** (in European folklore) a corpse that rises nightly from its grave to drink the blood of the living. **2** See **vampire bat. 3** a person who preys mercilessly upon others, such as a blackmailer. **4** See **vamp**[1] (sense 1). **5** *Theatre.* a trapdoor on a stage. **[C18:** from French, from German *Vampir,* from Magyar; perhaps related to Turkish *uber* witch, Russian *upyr* vampire**]** ► **vampiric** (væmˈpɪrɪk) *or* **vampirish** ('væmpaɪərɪʃ) *adj*

vampire bat *n* any bat, esp. *Desmodus rotundus,* of the family *Desmodontidae* of tropical regions of Central and South America, having sharp incisor and canine teeth and feeding on the blood of birds and mammals. Compare **false vampire.**

vampirism ('væmpaɪəˌrɪzəm) *n* **1** belief in the existence of vampires. **2** the actions of vampires; bloodsucking. **3** the act of preying upon or exploiting others.

van[1] (væn) *n* **1** short for **caravan** (sense 1). **2** a covered motor vehicle for transporting goods, etc., by road. **3** *Brit.* a closed railway wagon in which the guard travels, for transporting goods, mail, etc. **4** *Brit.* See **delivery van.**

van[2] (væn) *n* short for **vanguard.**

van[3] (væn) *n Tennis, chiefly Brit.* short for **advantage** (sense 3). Usual U.S. and Canadian word: **ad.**

van[4] (væn) *n* **1** any device for winnowing corn. **2** an archaic or poetic word for **wing. [C17:** variant of FAN[1]**]**

Van (vɑːn) *n* **1** a city in E Turkey, on Lake Van. Pop.: 197 679 (1995 est.). **2 Lake.** a salt lake in E Turkey, at an altitude of 1650 m (5400 ft.): fed by melting snow and glaciers. Area: 3737 sq. km (1433 sq. miles).

vanadate ('vænəˌdeɪt) *n* any salt or ester of a vanadic acid.

vanadic (vəˈnædɪk, -ˈneɪdɪk) *adj* of or containing vanadium, esp. in a trivalent or pentavalent state.

vanadic acid *n* any one of various oxyacids of vanadium, such as H_3VO_4 (**orthovanadic acid**), HVO_4 (**metavanadic acid**), and $H_4V_2O_7$ (**pyrovanadic acid**), known chiefly in the form of their vanadate salts.

vanadinite (vəˈnædɪˌnaɪt) *n* a red, yellow, or brownish mineral consisting of a chloride and vanadate of lead in hexagonal crystalline form. It results from weathering of lead ores in desert regions and is a source of vanadium. Formula: $Pb_5(VO_4)_3Cl$.

vanadium (vəˈneɪdɪəm) *n* a toxic silvery-white metallic element occurring chiefly in carnotite and vanadinite and used in steel alloys, high-speed tools, and as a catalyst. Symbol: V; atomic no.: 23; atomic wt.: 50.9415; valency: 2–5; relative density: 6.11; melting pt.: 1910±10°C; boiling pt.: 3409°C. **[C19:** New Latin, from Old Norse *Vanadis,* epithet of the goddess Freya + -IUM**]**

vanadium steel *n Engineering.* steel containing up to 0.5 per cent vanadium, usually with 1.1–1.5 per cent chromium and 0.4–0.5 per cent carbon to increase its tensile strength and elasticity.

vanadous ('vænədəs) *adj* of or containing vanadium, esp. in a divalent or trivalent state.

Van Allen (væn 'ælən) *n* **James Alfred.** born 1914, U.S. physicist, noted for his use of satellites to investigate cosmic radiation in the upper atmosphere.

Van Allen belt *n* either of two regions of charged particles above the earth, the inner one extending from 2400 to 5600 kilometres above the earth and the outer one from 13 000 to 19 000 kilometres. The charged particles result from cosmic rays and are trapped by the earth's magnetic field. **[C20:** named after its discoverer, J. A. VAN ALLEN**]**

vanaspati (vəˈnæspətɪ) *n* a hydrogenated vegetable fat commonly used in India as a substitute for butter. **[C20:** the Sanskrit name of a forest plant, from *vana* forest + *pati* lord**]**

Vanbrugh ('vænbrə) *n* Sir **John.** 1664–1726, English dramatist and baroque architect. His best-known plays are the Restoration comedies *The Relapse* (1697) and *The Provok'd Wife* (1697). As an architect, he is noted esp. for Blenheim Palace.

Van Buren (væn 'bjʊərən) *n* **Martin.** 1782–1862, U.S. Democratic statesman; 8th president of the U.S. (1837–41).

Vancouver[1] (vænˈkuːvə) *n* **1** an island of SW Canada, off the SW coast of British Columbia: separated from the Canadian mainland by the Strait of Georgia and Queen Charlotte Sound, and from the U.S. mainland by Juan de Fuca Strait; the largest island off the W coast of North America. Chief town: Victoria. Pop.: 461 573 (1981). Area: 32 137 sq. km (12 408 sq. miles). **2** a city in SW Canada, in SW British Columbia: Canada's chief Pacific port, named after Captain George Vancouver: university (1908). Pop.: 471 884 (1991), with a conurbation of 1 826 800 (1995). **3 Mount.** a mountain on the border between Canada and Alaska, in the St Elias Mountains. Height: 4785 m (15 700 ft.).

Vancouver[2] (vænˈkuːvə) *n* Captain **George.** 1757–98, English navigator, noted for his exploration of the Pacific coast of North America (1792–94).

vanda ('vændə) *n* any epiphytic orchid of the E hemisphere genus *Vanda,* having white, mauve, blue, or greenish fragrant flowers. **[C19:** New Latin, from Hindi *vandā* mistletoe, from Sanskrit**]**

V and A (in Britain) *abbrev. for* Victoria and Albert Museum.

vandal ('vændᵊl) *n* **a** a person who deliberately causes damage or destruction to personal or public property. **b** (*as modifier*): *vandal instincts.* **[C17:** from VANDAL, from Latin *Vandallus,* of Germanic origin**]**

Vandal ('vændᵊl) *n* a member of a Germanic people that raided Roman provinces in the 3rd and 4th centuries A.D. before devastating Gaul (406–409), conquering Spain and N Africa, and sacking Rome (455): crushed by Belisarius at Carthage (533). ► **Vandalic** (vænˈdælɪk) *adj* ► **'Vandal,ism** *n*

vandalism ('vændəˌlɪzəm) *n* the wanton or deliberate destruction caused by a vandal or an instance of such destruction. ► **,vandal'istic** *or* **'vandalish** *adj*

vandalize *or* **vandalise** ('vændəˌlaɪz) *vb (tr)* to destroy or damage (something) by an act of vandalism.

Van de Graaff generator ('væn də ˌgrɑːf) *n* a device for producing high electrostatic potentials (up to 15 million volts), consisting of a hollow metal sphere on which a charge is accumulated from a continuous moving belt of insulating material: used in particle accelerators. **[C20:** named after R. J. *Van de Graaff* (1901–67), U.S. physicist**]**

Vanderbilt ('vændəbɪlt) *n* **Cornelius,** known as *Commodore Vanderbilt.* 1794–1877, U.S. steamship and railway magnate and philanthropist.

Van der Hum (væn də hʌm) *n S. African.* a liqueur with tangerine flavouring. **[**of uncertain origin, but possibly derived from the humorous uncertainty of the name, equivalent of WHATSHISNAME**]**

Van der Merwe (væn də mɜːvə) *n S. African.* a stereotypical figure humorously representating Boer stupidity and prejudice. **[C20:** from a common Afrikaner surname**]**

Van der Post ('væn də ˌpəʊst) *n* Sir **Laurens (Jan).** 1906–96, South African writer and traveller. His works include the travel books *Venture to the Interior* (1952), *The Lost World of the Kalahari* (1958), and *Testament to the Bushmen* (1984) and the novels *The Hunter and the Whale* (1967) and *The Admiral's Baby* (1996).

van der Waals (*Dutch.* vɑn dər 'waːls) *n* **Johannes Diderik** (joːˈhɑnəs ˈdiːdərik). 1837–1923, Dutch physicist, noted for his research on the equations of state of gases and liquids: Nobel prize for physics in 1910.

van der Waals equation ('væn də ˌwɑːlz) *n* an equation of state for a fluid substance which is applicable approximately to both the liquid and the gaseous conditions.

van der Waals forces ('væn də ˌwɑːlz) *pl n* weak electrostatic forces between atoms and molecules caused by transient dissymmetries in the distribution of electrons in the interacting atoms or molecules.

van der Weyden (*Dutch* vɑn də 'wɛjdə) *n* **Rogier** (roːˈxiːr). ?1400–64, Flemish painter, esp. of religious works and portraits.

van de Velde (ˌvæn də 'veldə) *n* **1 Adriaen.** 1636–72, Dutch painter of landscapes with animals and figures. **2** his uncle, **Esaias.** ?1591–1630, Dutch landscape and genre painter, noted for such works as *The Winter Scene* (1623). **3 Henry.** 1863–1957, Belgian architect and designer, who introduced the British Arts and Crafts movement to the Continent and helped to develop the Art Nouveau style. **4 Willem,** known as *the Elder*: father of Adriaen van de Velde. 1611–93, Dutch marine painter, working in England as court painter to Charles II. **5** his son, **Willem,** known as *the Younger*. 1633–1707, Dutch marine painter, working in England as court painter to Charles II.

Van Diemen Gulf (væn 'diːmən) *n* an inlet of the Timor Sea in N Australia, in the Northern Territory.

Van Diemen's Land (væn 'diːmənz) *n* the former name (1642–1855) of **Tasmania.** ▸ **ˌVandeˈmonian** *n, adj*

Van Dyck *or* **Vandyke** (væn 'daɪk) *n* Sir **Anthony.** 1599–1641, Flemish painter; court painter to Charles I of England (1632–41). He is best known for his portraits of the aristocracy.

Vandyke beard ('vændaɪk) *n* a short pointed beard. Often shortened to **Vandyke.**

Vandyke brown *n* **1a** a moderate brown colour. **1b** (*as adj*): *a Vandyke-brown suit*. **2** any of various brown pigments, usually consisting of a mixture of ferric oxide and lampblack.

Vandyke collar *or* **cape** *n* a large white collar with several very deep points. Often shortened to **Vandyke.**

vane (veɪn) *n* **1** Also called: **weather vane, wind vane.** a flat plate or blade of metal mounted on a vertical axis in an exposed position to indicate wind direction. **2** any one of the flat blades or sails forming part of the wheel of a windmill. **3** any flat or shaped plate used to direct fluid flow, esp. a stator blade in a turbine, etc. **4** a fin or plate fitted to a projectile or missile to provide stabilization or guidance. **5** *Ornithol.* the flat part of a feather, consisting of two rows of barbs on either side of the shaft. **6** *Surveying.* **6a** a sight on a quadrant or compass. **6b** the movable marker on a levelling staff. [Old English *fana*; related to Old Saxon, Old High German *fano*, Old Norse *fani*, Latin *pannus* cloth] ▸ **vaned** *adj* ▸ **'vaneless** *adj*

Vane (veɪn) *n* Sir **Henry,** known as *Sir Harry Vane*. 1613–62, English Puritan statesman and colonial administrator; governor of Massachusetts (1636–37). He was executed for high treason after the Restoration.

Vänern (*Swedish* 'vɛːnərn) *n* **Lake.** a lake in SW Sweden: the largest lake in Sweden and W Europe; drains into the Kattegat. Area: 5585 sq. km (2156 sq. miles).

vanessid (və'nɛsɪd) *n* **1** a butterfly belonging to any of several brightly coloured species, including admirals, tortoiseshells, and the Camberwell beauty, which with the fritillaries comprise the *Nymphalidae*. ◆ *adj* **2** of, relating to, or belonging to this group. [C20: from New Latin *vanessa*]

van Eyck (væn 'aɪk) *n* **Jan** (jɑn). died 1441, Flemish painter; founder of the Flemish school of painting. His most famous work is the altarpiece *The Adoration of the Lamb*, in Ghent, in which he may have been assisted by his brother **Hubert** ('hyːbərt), died ?1426.

vang (væŋ) *n Nautical.* **1** a rope or tackle extended from the boom of a fore-and-aft mainsail to a deck fitting of a vessel when running, in order to keep the boom from riding up. **2** a guy extending from the end of a gaff to the vessel's rail on each side, used for steadying the gaff. [C18: from Dutch, from *vangen* to catch]

Van Gogh (væn 'gɒx; *Dutch* vɑn 'xɔx) *n* **Vincent** (vɪn'sɛnt). 1853–90, Dutch postimpressionist painter, noted for his landscapes and portraits, in which colour is used essentially for its expressive and emotive value.

vanguard ('vænˌgɑːd) *n* **1** the leading division or units of a military force. **2** the leading position in any movement or field, or the people who occupy such a position: *the vanguard of modern literature*. [C15: from Old French *avant-garde*, from *avant-* fore- + *garde* GUARD]

vanilla (və'nɪlə) *n* **1** any tropical climbing orchid of the genus *Vanilla*, esp. *V. planifolia*, having spikes of large fragrant greenish-yellow flowers and long fleshy pods containing the seeds (beans). **2** the pod or bean of certain of these plants, used to flavour food, etc. **3** a flavouring extract prepared from vanilla beans and used in cooking. ◆ *adj* **4** flavoured with or as if with vanilla: *vanilla ice cream*. **5** *Slang.* ordinary or conventional: *a vanilla kind of guy*. [C17: from New Latin, from Spanish *vainilla* pod, from *vaina* a sheath, from Latin *vāgīna* sheath]

vanillic (və'nɪlɪk) *adj* of, resembling, containing, or derived from vanilla or vanillin.

vanillin ('vænɪlɪn, və'nɪlɪn) *n* a white crystalline aldehyde found in vanilla and many natural balsams and resins; 3-methoxy-4-hydroxybenzaldehyde. It is a by-product of paper manufacture and is used as a flavouring and in perfumes and pharmaceuticals. Formula: $(CH_3O)(OH)C_6H_3CHO$.

Vanir ('vɑːnɪə) *n Norse myth.* a race of ancient gods often locked in struggle with the Aesir. The most notable of them are Njord and his children Frey and Freya. [from Old Norse *Vanr*, a fertility god]

vanish ('vænɪʃ) *vb* (*intr*) **1** to disappear, esp. suddenly or mysteriously. **2** to cease to exist; fade away. **3** *Maths.* to become zero. ◆ *n* **4** *Phonetics, rare.* the second and weaker of the two vowels in a falling diphthong. [C14 *vanissen*, from Old French *esvanir*, from Latin *ēvānēscere* to evaporate, from *ē-* EX-[1] + *vānēscere* to pass away, from *vānus* empty] ▸ **'vanisher** *n*

vanishing cream *n* a cosmetic cream that is colourless once applied, used as a foundation for powder or as a cleansing or moisturizing cream.

vanishing point *n* **1** the point to which parallel lines appear to converge in the rendering of perspective, usually on the horizon. **2** a point in space or time at or beyond which something disappears or ceases to exist.

vanity ('vænɪtɪ) *n, pl* **-ties. 1** the state or quality of being vain; excessive pride or conceit. **2** ostentation occasioned by ambition or pride. **3** an instance of being vain or something about which one is vain. **4** the state or quality of being valueless, futile, or unreal. **5** something that is worthless or useless. **6** *N.Z.* short for **vanity unit.** [C13: from Old French *vanité*, from Latin *vānitās* emptiness, from *vānus* empty]

vanity bag, case, *or* **box** *n* a woman's small bag or hand case used to carry cosmetics, etc.

Vanity Fair *n* (*often not caps.*) *Literary.* the social life of a community, esp. of a great city, or the world in general, considered as symbolizing worldly frivolity. [from Bunyan's *The Pilgrim's Progress*]

vanity publishing *n* the practice of the author of a book paying all or most of the costs of its publication.

vanity unit *n* a hand basin built into a wooden Formica-covered or tiled top, usually with a built-in cupboard below it. Also called (trademark): **Vanitory unit** ('vænɪtərɪ).

vanquish ('væŋkwɪʃ) *vb* (*tr*) **1** to defeat or overcome in a battle, contest, etc.; conquer. **2** to defeat or overcome in argument or debate. **3** to conquer (an emotion). [C14 *vanquisshen*, from Old French *venquis* vanquished, from *veintre* to overcome, from Latin *vincere*] ▸ **'vanquishable** *adj* ▸ **'vanquisher** *n* ▸ **'vanquishment** *n*

Vansittart (væn'sɪtət) *n* **Robert Gilbert,** 1st Baron Vansittart of Denham. 1881–1957, British diplomat and writer; a fierce opponent of Nazi Germany and of Communism.

vantage ('vɑːntɪdʒ) *n* **1** a state, position, or opportunity affording superiority or advantage. **2** superiority or benefit accruing from such a position, state, etc. **3** *Tennis.* short for **advantage.** [C13: from Old French *avantage* ADVANTAGE] ▸ **'vantageless** *adj*

vantage ground *n* a position or condition affording superiority or advantage over or as if over an opponent.

vantage point *n* a position or place that allows one a wide or favourable overall view of a scene or situation.

van't Hoff (*Dutch* vɑnt 'hɔf) *n* **Jacobus Hendricus** (jaː'koːbys hɛn'driːkœs). 1852–1911, Dutch physical chemist: founded stereochemistry with his theory of the asymmetric carbon atom; the first to apply thermodynamics to chemical reactions: Nobel prize for chemistry 1901.

Vanua Levu (vɑː'nuːə 'lɛvuː) *n* the second largest island of Fiji: mountainous. Area: 5535 sq. km (2137 sq. miles).

Vanuatu ('vænuːˌætuː) *n* a republic comprising a group of islands in the W Pacific, W of Fiji: a condominium under Anglo-French joint rule from 1906; attained partial autonomy in 1978 and full independence in 1980 as a member of the Commonwealth. Its economy is based chiefly on copra. Official languages: Bislama; French; English. Religion: Christian majority. Currency: vatu. Capital: Vila (on Efate). Pop.: 182 000 (1998 est.). Area: about 14 760 sq. km (5700 sq. miles). Official name: **Republic of Vanuatu.** Former name (until 1980): **New Hebrides.**

vanward ('vænwəd) *adj, adv* in or towards the front.

Vanzetti (væn'zɛtɪ) *n* **Bartolomeo** (bartolo'mɛːo). 1888–1927, U.S. radical agitator, born in Italy: executed with Sacco in a case that had worldwide political repercussions.

vapid ('væpɪd) *adj* **1** bereft of strength, sharpness, flavour, etc.; flat. **2** boring or dull; lifeless: *vapid talk*. [C17: from Latin *vapidus*; related to *vappa* tasteless or flat wine, and perhaps to *vapor* warmth] ▸ **va'pidity** *n* ▸ **'vapidly** *adv* ▸ **'vapidness** *n*

vapor ('veɪpə) *n* the U.S. spelling of **vapour.**

vaporescence (ˌveɪpə'rɛsəns) *n* the production or formation of vapour. ▸ **ˌvapor'escent** *adj*

vaporetto (ˌveɪpə'rɛtəʊ; *Italian* vapo'retto) *n, pl* **-ti** (-tɪ; *Italian* -ti) *or* **-tos.** a steam-powered passenger boat, as used on the canals in Venice. [Italian, from *vapore* a steamboat]

vaporific (ˌveɪpə'rɪfɪk) *adj* **1** producing, causing, or tending to produce vapour. **2** of, concerned with, or having the nature of vapour. **3** tending to become vapour; volatile. ◆ Also: **vaporous.** [C18: from New Latin *vaporificus*, from Latin *vapor* steam + *facere* to make]

vaporimeter (ˌveɪpə'rɪmɪtə) *n* an instrument for measuring vapour pressure, used to determine the volatility of oils or the amount of alcohol in alcoholic liquids.

vaporize *or* **vaporise** ('veɪpəˌraɪz) *vb* **1** to change or cause to change into vapour or into the gaseous state. **2** to evaporate or disappear or cause to evaporate or disappear, esp. suddenly. **3** to destroy or be destroyed by being turned into a gas as a result of the extreme heat generated by a nuclear explosion. ▸ **'vaporˌizable** *or* **'vaporˌisable** *adj* ▸ **ˌvapori'zation** *or* **ˌvapori'sation** *n*

vaporizer *or* **vaporiser** ('veɪpəˌraɪzə) *n* **1** a substance that vaporizes or a device that causes vaporization. **2** *Med.* a device that produces steam or atomizes medication for inhalation.

vaporous ('veɪpərəs) *adj* **1** resembling or full of vapour. **2** another word for **vaporific. 3** lacking permanence or substance; ephemeral or fanciful. **4** given to foolish imaginings. **5** dulled or obscured by an atmosphere of vapour. ▸ **'vaporously** *adv* ▸ **'vaporousness** *or* **vaporosity** (ˌveɪpə'rɒsɪtɪ) *n*

vapour *or* *U.S.* **vapor** ('veɪpə) *n* **1** particles of moisture or other substance suspended in air and visible as clouds, smoke, etc. **2** a gaseous substance at a temperature below its critical temperature. Compare **gas** (sense 3). **3** a substance that is in a gaseous state at a temperature below its boiling point. **4** *Rare.* something fanciful that lacks substance or permanence. **5 the vapours.** *Archaic.* a depressed mental condition believed originally to be the result of vaporous exhalations from the stomach. ◆ *vb* **6** to evaporate or cause to evaporate; vaporize. **7** (*intr*) to make vain empty boasts; brag. [C14: from Latin *vapor*] ▸ **'vapourable** *or U.S.* **'vaporable** *adj* ▸ **ˌvapoura'bility** *or U.S.* **ˌvapora'bility** *n* ▸ **'vapourer** *or U.S.* **'vaporer** *n* ▸ **'vapourish** *or U.S.* **'vaporish** *adj* ▸ **'vapourless** *or U.S.* **'vaporless** *adj* ▸ **'vapour-ˌlike** *or U.S.* **'vapor-ˌlike** *adj* ▸ **'vapoury** *or U.S.* **'vapory** *adj*

vapour density *n* the ratio of the density of a gas or vapour to that of hydrogen at the same temperature and pressure. See also **relative density.**

vapourer moth *n* a tussock moth, *Orgyia antiqua*, of hedgerows and trees, the female of which is wingless and lays her eggs on her former cocoon.

vapour lock *n* a stoppage in a pipe carrying a liquid caused by a bubble of gas, esp. such a stoppage caused by vaporization of the petrol in the pipe feeding the carburettor of an internal-combustion engine.

vapour pressure *n Physics.* the pressure exerted by a vapour, esp. that exerted by a vapour in equilibrium with its solid or liquid phase at a particular temperature.

vapour trail *n* a visible trail left by an aircraft flying at high altitude or through supercold air, caused by the deposition of water vapour in the engine exhaust as minute ice crystals. Also called: **condensation trail, contrail.**

var (vɑː) *n* a unit of reactive power of an alternating current, equal to the product of the current measured in amperes and the voltage measured in volts. **[**from *v(olt-)a(mperes) r(eactive)***]**

Var (*French* var) *n* **1** a department of SE France, in Provence-Alpes-Côte-d'Azur region. Capital: Toulon. Pop.: 872 900 (1995). Area: 6023 sq. km (2349 sq. miles). **2** a river in SE France, flowing southeast and south to the Mediterranean near Nice. Length: about 130 km (80 miles).

VAR *abbrev. for* visual aural range.

var. *abbrev. for:* **1** variable. **2** variant. **3** variation. **4** variety. **5** various.

vara ('vɑːrə) *n* a unit of length used in Spain, Portugal, and South America and having different values in different localities, usually between 32 and 43 inches (about 80 to 108 centimetres). **[C17:** via Spanish from Latin: wooden trestle, from *vārus* crooked**]**

varactor ('vɛəˌræktə) *n* a semiconductor diode that acts as a voltage-dependent capacitor, being operated with a reverse bias. Compare **varistor. [C20:** probably a blend of *variable reactor***]**

Varah ('værə) *n* **(Edward) Chad.** born 1911, British Anglican clergyman, who founded (1953) the Samaritans counselling service.

Varanasi (və'rɑːnəsɪ) *n* a city in NE India, in SE Uttar Pradesh on the River Ganges: probably dates from the 13th century B.C.; an early centre of Aryan philosophy and religion; a major place of pilgrimage for Hindus, Jains, Sikhs, and Buddhists, with many ghats along the Ganges; seat of the Banaras Hindu University (1916), India's leading university, and the Sanskrit University (1957). Pop.: 929 270 (1991). Former names: **Benares, Banaras.**

Varangian (və'rændʒɪən) *n* **1** one of the Scandinavians who invaded and settled parts of Russia and the Ukraine from the 8th to the 11th centuries, and who formed the bodyguard of the Byzantine emperor (**Varangian Guard**) in the late 10th and 11th centuries. ◆ *adj* **2** of or relating to the Varangians. **[C18:** from Medieval Latin *Varangus,* from Medieval Greek *Barangos,* from Old Norse *Væringi,* probably from *vār* pledge**]**

Vardar (*Serbo-Croat* 'vardar) *n* a river in S Europe, rising in W Macedonia and flowing northeast, then south past Skopje into Greece, where it is called the Axios and enters the Aegean at Thessaloníki. Length: about 320 km (200 miles).

Vardhamana (ˌvɑːdə'mɑːnə) *n* See **Mahavira.**

Vardon ('vɑːdᵊn) *n* **Harry.** 1870–1937, British golfer.

varec ('værɛk) *n* **1** another name for **kelp. 2** the ash obtained from kelp. **[C17:** from French, from Old Norse *wrek* (unattested); see WRECK**]**

Varese (*Italian* va'reːse) *n* a historic city in N Italy, in Lombardy near Lake Varese: manufacturing centre, esp. for leather goods. Pop.: 88 018 (1990).

Varèse (væ'rɛz) *n* **Edgar(d)** (ɛdgar). 1883–1965, U.S. composer, born in France. His works, which combine extreme dissonance with complex rhythms and the use of electronic techniques, include *Ionisation* (1931) and *Poème électronique* (1958).

Vargas (*Portuguese* 'vargas) *n* **Getúlio Dornelles** (ʒe'tulju dur'nɛləʃ). 1883–1954, Brazilian statesman; president (1930–45; 1951–54).

Vargas Llosa (*Spanish* 'barɣas 'ʎosa) *n* **(Jorge) Mario (Pedro)** born 1936, Peruvian novelist, writer, and political figure. His novels include *The City and the Dogs* (1963), *Conversation in the Cathedral* (1969), *The Storyteller* (1990), and *The Notebooks of Don Rigoberto* (1998). In 1990 he stood unsuccessfully for the presidency of Peru.

varia ('vɛərɪə) *pl n* a collection or miscellany, esp. of literary works. **[**Latin, neuter plural of *varius* VARIOUS**]**

variable ('vɛərɪəbᵊl) *adj* **1** liable to or capable of change: *variable weather.* **2** (of behaviour, opinions, emotions, etc.) lacking constancy; fickle. **3** *Maths.* having a range of possible values. **4** (of a species, characteristic, etc.) liable to deviate from the established type. **5** (of a wind) varying its direction and intensity. **6** (of an electrical component or device) designed so that a characteristic property, such as resistance, can be varied: *variable capacitor.* ◆ *n* **7** something that is subject to variation. **8** *Maths.* **8a** an expression that can be assigned any of a set of values. **8b** a symbol, esp. *x, y,* or *z,* representing an unspecified member of a class of objects, numbers, etc. See also **dependent variable, independent variable. 9** *Logic.* a symbol, esp. *x, y, z,* representing any member of a class of entities. **10** *Computing.* a named unit of storage that can be changed to any of a set of specified values during execution of a program. **11** *Astronomy.* See **variable star. 12** a variable wind. **13** (*pl*) a region where variable winds occur. **[C14:** from Latin *variābilis* changeable, from *variāre* to diversify**]** ▸ **ˌvaria'bility** *or* **'variableness** *n* ▸ **'variably** *adv*

variable cost *n* a cost that varies directly with output.

variable-density wind tunnel *n* a closed-circuit wind tunnel entirely contained in a casing in which the pressure and therefore the density of the working fluid can be maintained at a preselected value.

variable-geometry *or* **variable-sweep** *adj* denoting an aircraft in which the wings are hinged to give the variable aspect ratio colloquially known as a **swing-wing.**

variable star *n* any star that varies considerably in brightness, either irregularly or in regular periods. **Intrinsic variables,** in which the variation is a result of internal changes, include novae, supernovae, and pulsating stars. See also **eclipsing binary.**

variance ('vɛərɪəns) *n* **1** the act of varying or the quality, state, or degree of being divergent; discrepancy. **2** an instance of diverging; dissension: *our variance on this matter should not affect our friendship.* **3 at variance. 3a** (often foll. by *with*) (of facts, etc.) not in accord; conflicting. **3b** (of persons) in a state of dissension. **4** *Statistics.* a measure of dispersion obtained by taking the mean of the squared deviations of the observed values from their mean in a frequency distribution. **5** a difference or discrepancy between two steps in a legal proceeding, esp. between a statement in a pleading and the evidence given to support it. **6** (in the U.S. and Canada) a licence or authority issued by the board of variance to contravene the usual rule, esp. to build contrary to the provision of a zoning code. **7** *Chem.* the number of degrees of freedom of a system, used in the phase rule. **8** *Accounting.* the difference between actual and standard costs of production.

variant ('vɛərɪənt) *adj* **1** liable to or displaying variation. **2** differing from a standard or type: *a variant spelling.* **3** *Obsolete.* not constant; fickle. ◆ *n* **4** something that differs from a standard or type. **5** *Statistics.* another word for **variate** (sense 1). **[C14:** via Old French from Latin *variāns,* from *variāre* to diversify, from *varius* VARIOUS**]**

variate ('vɛərɪɪt) *n* **1** *Statistics.* a random variable or a numerical value taken by it. **2** a less common word for **variant** (sense 4). **[C16:** from Latin *variāre* to VARY**]**

variation (ˌvɛərɪ'eɪʃən) *n* **1** the act, process, condition, or result of changing or varying; diversity. **2** an instance of varying or the amount, rate, or degree of such change. **3** something that differs from a standard or convention. **4** *Music.* **4a** a repetition of a musical theme in which the rhythm, harmony, or melody is altered or embellished. **4b** (*as modifier*): *variation form.* **5** *Biology.* **5a** a marked deviation from the typical form or function. **5b** a characteristic or an organism showing this deviation. **6** *Astronomy.* any change in or deviation from the mean motion or orbit of a planet, satellite, etc., esp. a perturbation of the moon. **7** another word for **magnetic declination. 8** *Ballet.* a solo dance. **9** *Linguistics.* any form of morphophonemic change, such as one involved in inflection, conjugation, or vowel mutation. ▸ **ˌvari'ational** *adj* ▸ **ˌvari'ationally** *adv*

varicella (ˌværɪ'sɛlə) *n* the technical name for **chickenpox. [C18:** New Latin, irregular diminutive of VARIOLA**]** ▸ **ˌvari'cellar** *adj*

varicellate (ˌværɪ'sɛlɪt, -eɪt) *adj* (of certain shells) marked on the surface with small ridges. **[C19:** from New Latin *varicella,* diminutive of Latin *varix* dilated vein, VARIX**]**

varicelloid (ˌværɪ'sɛlɔɪd) *adj* resembling chickenpox.

varices ('værɪˌsiːz) *n* the plural of **varix.**

varico- *or before a vowel* **varic-** *combining form.* indicating a varix or varicose veins: *varicotomy.* **[**from Latin *varix, varic-* distended vein**]**

varicocele ('værɪkəʊˌsiːl) *n Pathol.* an abnormal distension of the veins of the spermatic cord in the scrotum.

varicoloured *or U.S.* **varicolored** ('vɛərɪˌkʌləd) *adj* having many colours; variegated; motley.

varicose ('værɪˌkəʊs) *adj* of or resulting from varicose veins: *a varicose ulcer.* **[C18:** from Latin *varicōsus,* from VARIX**]**

varicose veins *pl n* a condition in which the superficial veins, esp. of the legs, become tortuous, knotted, and swollen: caused by a defect in the venous valves or in the venous pump that normally moves the blood out of the legs when standing for long periods.

varicosis (ˌværɪ'kəʊsɪs) *n Pathol.* any condition characterized by distension of the veins. **[C18:** from New Latin, from Latin: VARIX**]**

varicosity (ˌværɪ'kɒsɪtɪ) *n, pl* **-ties.** *Pathol.* **1** the state, condition, or quality of being varicose. **2** an abnormally distended vein.

varicotomy (ˌværɪ'kɒtəmɪ) *n, pl* **-mies.** surgical excision of a varicose vein.

varied ('vɛərɪd) *adj* **1** displaying or characterized by variety; diverse. **2** modified or altered: *the amount may be varied without notice.* **3** varicoloured; variegated. ▸ **'variedly** *adv* ▸ **'variedness** *n*

variegate ('vɛərɪˌgeɪt) *vb* (*tr*) **1** to alter the appearance of, esp. by adding different colours. **2** to impart variety to. **[C17:** from Late Latin *variegāre,* from Latin *varius* diverse, VARIOUS + *agere* to make**]** ▸ **ˌvarie'gation** *n*

variegated ('vɛərɪˌgeɪtɪd) *adj* **1** displaying differently coloured spots, patches, streaks, etc. **2** (of foliage or flowers) having pale patches as a result of mutation, infection, etc.

varietal (və'raɪɪtᵊl) *adj* **1** of, relating to, characteristic of, designating, or forming a variety, esp. a biological variety. ◆ *n* **2** a wine labelled with the name of the grape from which it is pressed. ▸ **va'rietally** *adv*

variety (və'raɪɪtɪ) *n, pl* **-ties. 1** the quality or condition of being diversified or various. **2** a collection of unlike things, esp. of the same general group; assortment. **3** a different form or kind within a general category; sort: *varieties of behaviour.* **4a** *Taxonomy.* a race whose distinct characters are insufficient to justify classification as a separate species; a subspecies. **4b** *Horticulture, stockbreeding.* a strain of animal or plant produced by artificial breeding. **5a** entertainment consisting of a series of short unrelated performances or acts, such as comedy turns, songs, dances, sketches, etc. **5b** (*as modifier*): *a variety show.* **[C16:** from Latin *varietās,* from VARIOUS**]**

variety meat *n Chiefly U.S.* processed meat, such as sausage, or offal.

varifocal (ˌvɛərɪ'fəʊkᵊl) *adj* **1** *Optics.* having a focus that can vary. **2** relating to a lens that is graduated to permit any length of vision between near and distant.

varifocals (ˌvɛərɪ'fəʊkᵊlz) *pl n* a pair of spectacles with varifocal lenses.

variform ('vɛərɪˌfɔːm) *adj* varying in form or shape. ▸ **'variˌformly** *adv*

vario- *combining form.* indicating variety or difference: *variometer.* **[**from Latin *varius* VARIOUS**]**

variola (və'raɪələ) *n* the technical name for **smallpox. [C18:** from Medieval Latin: disease marked by little spots, from Latin *varius* spotted**]** ▸ **va'riolar** *adj*

variolate ('vɛərɪəˌleɪt) *vb* **1** (*tr*) to inoculate with the smallpox virus. ◆ *adj* **2**

marked or pitted with or as if with the scars of smallpox. [C18: from VARIOLA] ▸ ˌvario'lation, ˌvarioli'zation, *or* ˌvarioli'sation *n*

variole ('vɛərɪˌəʊl) *n* any of the rounded masses that make up the rock variolite. [C19: from French, from Medieval Latin; see VARIOLA]

variolite ('vɛərɪəˌlaɪt) *n* any basic igneous rock containing rounded bodies (varioles) consisting of radiating crystal fibres. [C18: from VARIOLA, referring to the pockmarked appearance of the rock] ▸ **variolitic** (ˌvɛərɪə'lɪtɪk) *adj*

varioloid ('vɛərɪəˌlɔɪd) *adj* **1** resembling smallpox. ◆ *n* **2** a mild form of smallpox occurring in persons with partial immunity.

variolous (və'raɪələs) *adj* relating to or resembling smallpox; variolar.

variometer (ˌvɛərɪ'ɒmɪtə) *n* **1** an instrument for measuring variations in a magnetic field, used esp. for studying the magnetic field of the earth. **2** *Electronics.* a variable inductor consisting of a movable coil mounted inside and connected in series with a fixed coil. **3** a sensitive rate-of-climb indicator, used mainly in gliders.

variorum (ˌvɛərɪ'ɔːrəm) *adj* **1** containing notes by various scholars or critics or various versions of the text: *a variorum edition.* ◆ *n* **2** an edition or text of this kind. [C18: from Latin phrase *ēditiō cum notīs variōrum* edition with the notes of various commentators]

various ('vɛərɪəs) *determiner* **1a** several different: *he is an authority on various subjects.* **1b** (*as pronoun;* foll. by *of*) *Not standard: various of them came.* ◆ *adj* **2** of different kinds, though often within the same general category; diverse: *various occurrences; his disguises are many and various.* **3** (*prenominal*) relating to a collection of separate persons or things: *the various members of the club.* **4** displaying variety; many-sided: *his various achievements are most impressive.* **5** *Poetic.* variegated. **6** *Obsolete.* inconstant. [C16: from Latin *varius* changing; perhaps related to Latin *vārus* crooked] ▸ **'variously** *adv* ▸ **'variousness** *n*

USAGE The use of *different* after *various* should be avoided: *the disease exists in various forms* (not *in various different forms*).

variscite ('værɪˌsaɪt) *n* a green secondary mineral consisting of hydrated aluminium. [from Medieval Latin *Variscia,* the district of Vogtland in Saxony]

varistor (və'rɪstə) *n* a two-electrode semiconductor device having a voltage-dependent nonlinear resistance. Compare **varactor.** [C20: a blend of *variable resistor*]

varitype ('vɛərɪˌtaɪp) *vb* **1** to produce (copy) on a Varityper. ◆ *n* **2** copy produced on a Varityper. ▸ **'variˌtypist** *n*

Varityper ('vɛərɪˌtaɪpə) *n Trademark.* a justifying typewriter used to produce copy in various type styles.

varix ('vɛərɪks) *n, pl* **varices** ('værɪˌsiːz). *Pathol.* **a** a tortuous dilated vein. See **varicose veins. b** Also called: **arterial varix, varix lymphaticus.** a similar condition affecting an artery or lymphatic vessel. [C15: from Latin]

varlet ('vɑːlɪt) *n Archaic.* **1** a menial servant. **2** a knight's page. **3** a rascal. [C15: from Old French, variant of *vallet* VALET]

varletry ('vɑːlɪtrɪ) *n Archaic.* **1 the.** rabble; mob. **2** varlets collectively.

varmint ('vɑːmɪnt) *n Informal.* an irritating or obnoxious person or animal. [C16: dialect variant of *varmin* VERMIN]

varna ('vɑːnə) *n* any of the four Hindu castes; Brahman, Kshatriya, Vaisya, or Sudra. [from Sanskrit: class]

Varna (*Bulgarian* 'varna) *n* a port in NE Bulgaria, on the Black Sea: founded by Greeks in the 6th century B.C.; under the Ottoman Turks (1391–1878). Pop.: 301 421 (1996 est.). Former name (1949–56): **Stalin.**

varnish ('vɑːnɪʃ) *n* **1** Also called: **oil varnish.** a preparation consisting of a solvent, a drying oil, and usually resin, rubber, bitumen, etc., for application to a surface where it polymerizes to yield a hard glossy, usually transparent, coating. **2** a similar preparation consisting of a substance, such as shellac or cellulose ester, dissolved in a volatile solvent, such as alcohol. It hardens to a film on evaporation of the solvent. See also **spirit varnish. 3** Also called: **natural varnish.** the sap of certain trees used to produce such a coating. **4** a smooth surface, coated with or as with varnish. **5** an artificial, superficial, or deceptively pleasing manner, covering, etc.; veneer. **6** *Chiefly Brit.* another word for **nail polish.** ◆ *vb* (*tr*) **7** to cover with varnish. **8** to give a smooth surface to, as if by painting with varnish. **9** to impart a more attractive appearance to. **10** to make superficially attractive. [C14: from Old French *vernis,* from Medieval Latin *veronix* sandarac, resin, from Medieval Greek *berenikē,* perhaps from Greek *Berenikē,* city in Cyrenaica, Libya where varnishes were used] ▸ **'varnisher** *n*

varnishing day *n* (at an exhibition of paintings) the day before the opening when artists may varnish or retouch their pictures after they have been hung.

varnish tree *n* any of various trees, such as the lacquer tree, yielding substances used to make varnish or lacquer.

Varro ('værəʊ) *n* **Marcus Terentius** ('mɑːkəs tə'rɛntɪəs). 116–27 B.C., Roman scholar and satirist.

varsity ('vɑːsɪtɪ) *n, pl* **-ties.** *Brit., N.Z., and S. African informal.* short for **university:** formerly used esp. at the universities of Oxford and Cambridge.

Varuna ('værʊnə, 'vʌ-) *n Hinduism.* the ancient sky god, later the god of the waters and rain-giver. In earlier traditions he was also the all-seeing divine judge.

varus ('vɛərəs) *adj Pathol.* turned inwards towards the midline of the body. [C19: from Latin: crooked, bent]

varve (vɑːv) *n Geology.* **1** a band of sediment deposited in glacial lakes, consisting of a light layer and a dark layer deposited at different seasons. **2** either of the layers of sediment making up this band. [C20: from Swedish *varv* layer, from *varva,* from Old Norse *hverfa* to turn]

vary ('vɛərɪ) *vb* **varies, varying, varied. 1** to undergo or cause to undergo change, alteration, or modification in appearance, character, form, attribute, etc. **2** to be different or cause to be different; be subject to change. **3** (*tr*) to give variety to. **4** (*intr;* foll. by *from*) to differ, as from a convention, standard, etc. **5** (*intr*) to change in accordance with another variable: *her mood varies with the weather; pressure varies directly with temperature and inversely with volume.* **6** (*tr*) *Music.* to modify (a theme) by the use of variation. [C14: from Latin *variāre,* from *varius* VARIOUS] ▸ **'varying** *adj* ▸ **'varyingly** *adv*

vas (væs) *n, pl* **vasa** ('veɪsə). *Anatomy, zoology.* a vessel, duct, or tube that carries a fluid. [C17: from Latin: vessel]

vas- *combining form.* a variant of **vaso-** before a vowel.

Vasarely (ˌvæsər'ɛlɪ) *n* **Victor.** 1908–97, French painter, born in Hungary; a leading exponent of op art.

Vasari (və'sɑːrɪ; *Italian* va'zaːri) *n* **Giorgio** ('dʒordʒo). 1511–74, Italian architect, painter, and art historian, noted for his *Lives of the Most Excellent Italian Architects, Painters, and Sculptors* (1550; 1568), a principal source for the history of Italian Renaissance art.

Vasco da Gama ('væskəʊ də 'gɑːmə) *n* See (Vasco da) **Gama.**

vascular ('væskjʊlə) *adj Biology, anatomy.* of, relating to, or having vessels that conduct and circulate liquids: *a vascular bundle; the blood vascular system.* [C17: from New Latin *vāsculāris,* from Latin: VASCULUM] ▸ **vascularity** (ˌvæskjʊ'lærɪtɪ) *n* ▸ **'vascularly** *adv*

vascular bundle *n* a longitudinal strand of vascular tissue in the stems and leaves of higher plants.

vascularization *or* **vascularisation** (ˌvæskjʊləraɪ'zeɪʃən) *n* the development of blood vessels in an organ or part.

vascular ray *n* another name for **medullary ray.**

vascular tissue *n* tissue of higher plants consisting mainly of xylem and phloem and occurring as a continuous system throughout the plant: it conducts water, mineral salts, and synthesized food substances and provides mechanical support. Also called: **conducting tissue.**

vasculum ('væskjʊləm) *n, pl* **-la** (-lə) *or* **-lums.** a metal box used by botanists in the field for carrying botanical specimens. [C19: from Latin: little vessel, from VAS]

vas deferens ('væs 'dɛfəˌrɛnz) *n, pl* **vasa deferentia** ('veɪsə ˌdɛfə'rɛnʃɪə). *Anatomy.* the duct that conveys spermatozoa from the epididymis to the urethra. [C16: from New Latin, from Latin *vās* vessel + *deferēns,* present participle of *deferre* to bear away]

vase (vɑːz) *n* a vessel used as an ornament or for holding cut flowers. [C17: via French from Latin *vās* vessel]

vasectomy (væ'sɛktəmɪ) *n, pl* **-mies.** surgical removal of all or part of the vas deferens, esp. as a method of contraception.

Vaseline ('væsɪˌliːn) *n* a trademark for **petrolatum.**

Vashti ('væʃtaɪ) *n Old Testament.* the wife of the Persian king Ahasuerus: deposed for refusing to display her beauty before his guests (Esther 1–2). Douay spelling: **Vasthi.**

vaso- *or before a vowel* **vas-** *combining form.* **1** indicating a blood vessel: *vasodilator.* **2** indicating the vas deferens: *vasectomy.* [from Latin *vās* vessel]

vasoactive (ˌveɪzəʊ'æktɪv) *adj* affecting the diameter of blood vessels: *vasoactive peptides.*

vasoconstrictor (ˌveɪzəʊkən'strɪktə) *n* **1** a drug, agent, or nerve that causes narrowing (**vasoconstriction**) of the walls of blood vessels. ◆ *adj* **2** causing vasoconstriction. ▸ ˌ**vasocon'strictive** *adj*

vasodilator (ˌveɪzəʊdaɪ'leɪtə) *n* **1** a drug, agent, or nerve that can cause dilation (**vasodilation**) of the walls of blood vessels. ◆ *adj* **2** causing vasodilation.

vasoinhibitor (ˌveɪzəʊɪn'hɪbɪtə) *n* any of a group of drugs that reduce or inhibit the action of the vasomotor nerves. ▸ **vasoinhibitory** (ˌveɪzəʊɪn'hɪbɪtərɪ, -trɪ) *adj*

vasomotor (ˌveɪzəʊ'məʊtə) *adj* (of a drug, agent, nerve, etc.) relating to or affecting the diameter of blood vessels.

vasopressin (ˌveɪzəʊ'prɛsɪn) *n* a polypeptide hormone secreted by the posterior lobe of the pituitary gland. It increases the reabsorption of water by the kidney tubules and increases blood pressure by constricting the arteries. Also called: **antidiuretic hormone.** Chemical name: **beta-hypophamine.** Compare **oxytocin.** [from *Vasopressin,* a trademark]

vasopressor (ˌveɪzəʊ'prɛsə) *Med.* ◆ adj. **1** causing an increase in blood pressure by constricting the arteries. ◆ *n* **2** a substance that has such an effect.

vassal ('væsᵊl) *n* **1** (in feudal society) a man who entered into a personal relationship with a lord to whom he paid homage and fealty in return for protection and often a fief. A **great vassal** was in vassalage to a king and a **rear vassal** to a great vassal. **2a** a person, nation, etc., in a subordinate, suppliant, or dependent position relative to another. **2b** (*as modifier*): *vassal status.* ◆ *adj* **3** of or relating to a vassal. [C14: via Old French from Medieval Latin *vassallus,* from *vassus* servant, of Celtic origin; compare Welsh *gwas* boy, Old Irish *foss* servant] ▸ **'vassal-less** *adj*

vassalage ('væsəlɪdʒ) *n* **1** (esp. in feudal society) **1a** the condition of being a vassal or the obligations to which a vassal was liable. **1b** the relationship between a vassal and his lord. **2** subjection, servitude, or dependence in general. **3** *Rare.* vassals collectively.

vassalize *or* **vassalise** ('væsəˌlaɪz) *vb* (*tr*) to make a vassal of.

vast (vɑːst) *adj* **1** unusually large in size, extent, degree, or number; immense. **2** (*prenominal*) (intensifier): *in vast haste.* ◆ *n* **3 the vast.** *Chiefly poetic.* immense or boundless space. **4** *Brit. dialect.* a very great amount or number. [C16: from Latin *vastus* deserted] ▸ **'vastity** *n* ▸ **'vastly** *adv* ▸ **'vastness** *n*

Västerås (*Swedish* vɛstər'oːs) *n* a city in central Sweden, on Lake Mälar: Sweden's largest inland port; site of several national parliaments in the 16th century. Pop.: 124 084 (1997 est.).

vastitude ('vɑːstɪˌtjuːd) *n Rare.* **1** the condition or quality of being vast. **2** a vast space, expanse, extent, etc.

vasty ('vɑːstɪ) *adj* **vastier, vastiest.** an archaic or poetic word for **vast.**

vat (væt) *n* **1** a large container for holding or storing liquids. **2** *Chem.* a preparation of reduced vat dye. ◆ *vb* **vats, vatting, vatted. 3** (*tr*) to place, store, or treat in a vat. [Old English *fæt;* related to Old Frisian *fet,* Old Saxon, Old Norse *fat,* Old High German *faz*]

VAT (*sometimes* væt) (in Britain) *abbrev. for* value-added tax: a tax levied on the difference between the cost of materials and the selling price of a commodity or service.

Vat. *abbrev. for* Vatican.

vat dye *n* a dye, such as indigo, that is applied by first reducing it to its leuco base, which is soluble in alkali, and then regenerating the insoluble dye by oxidation in the fibres of the material. ▸ **'vat-,dyed** *adj*

vatic ('vætɪk) *adj Rare.* of, relating to, or characteristic of a prophet; oracular. [C16: from Latin *vātēs* prophet]

Vatican ('vætɪkən) *n* **1a** the palace of the popes in Rome and their principal residence there since 1377, which includes administrative offices, a library, museum, etc., and is attached to the basilica of St Peter's. **1b** (*as modifier*): *the Vatican Council.* **2a** the authority of the Pope and the papal curia. **2b** (*as modifier*): *a Vatican edict.* [C16: from Latin *Vāticānus mons* Vatican hill, on the western bank of the Tiber, of Etruscan origin]

Vatican City *n* an independent state forming an enclave in Rome, with extraterritoriality over 12 churches and palaces in Rome: the only remaining Papal State; independence recognized by the Italian government in 1929; contains St Peter's Basilica and Square and the Vatican; the spiritual and administrative centre of the Roman Catholic Church. Languages: Italian and Latin. Currency: lira. Pop.: 1000 (1997 est.). Area: 44 hectares (109 acres). Italian name: **Città del Vaticano.** Also called: the **Holy See.**

Vaticanism ('vætɪkə,nɪzəm) *n Often derogatory.* the authority and policies of the Pope and the papal curia, esp. with regard to papal infallibility.

vaticide ('vætɪ,saɪd) *n Rare.* **a** the murder of a prophet. **b** a person guilty of this. [C18: from Latin *vātēs* prophet + -CIDE]

vaticinate (və'tɪsɪ,neɪt) *vb Rare.* to foretell; prophesy. [C17: from Latin *vāticinārī* from *vātēs* prophet + *canere* to foretell] ▸ **vaticination** (,vætɪsɪ'neɪʃən) *n* ▸ **va'tici,nator** *n* ▸ **vaticinal** (və'tɪsɪnᵊl) *or* **va'ticinatory** *adj*

Vättern (*Swedish* 'vɛtərn) *n* **Lake.** a lake in S central Sweden: the second largest lake in Sweden; linked to Lake Vänern by the Göta Canal; drains into the Baltic. Area: 1912 sq. km (738 sq. miles).

vatu ('vætu:) *n* the standard monetary unit of Vanuatu.

Vauban (*French* vobɑ̃) *n* **Sébastien Le Prestre de** (sebastjɛ̃ lə prɛtrə də). 1633–1707, French military engineer and marshal, who greatly developed the science of fortification and devised novel siege tactics using a series of parallel trenches.

Vaucluse (*French* voklyz) *n* a department of SE France, in Provence-Alpes-Côte-d'Azur region. Capital: Avignon. Pop.: 489 600 (1995). Area: 3578 sq. km (1395 sq. miles).

Vaud (*French* vo) *n* a canton of SW Switzerland: mountainous in the southeast; chief Swiss producer of wine. Capital: Lausanne. Pop.: 605 677 (1996 est.). Area: 3209 sq. km (1240 sq. miles). German name: **Waadt.**

vaudeville ('vəudəvɪl, 'vɔ:-) *n* **1** *Chiefly U.S. and Canadian.* variety entertainment consisting of short acts such as acrobatic turns, song-and-dance routines, animal acts, etc., popular esp. in the early 20th century. Brit. name: **music hall.** **2** a light or comic theatrical piece interspersed with songs and dances. [C18: from French, from *vaudevire* satirical folk song, shortened from *chanson du vau de Vire* song of the valley of Vire, a district in Normandy where this type of song flourished]

vaudevillian (,vəudə'vɪlɪən, ,vɔ:-) *n also* **vaudevillist.** **1** a person who writes for or performs in vaudeville. ◆ *adj* **2** of, characteristic of, or relating to vaudeville.

Vaudois ('vəudwɑ:) *pl n, sing* **-dois.** **1** another name for the **Waldenses.** **2** the inhabitants of Vaud.

Vaughan (vɔ:n) *n* **1 Henry.** 1622–95, Welsh mystic poet, best known for his *Silex Scintillans* (1650; 1655). **2** Dame **Janet (Maria).** 1899–1993, British physician and university official: helped set up Britain's first National Blood Transfusion Service (1939): after World War II, became Britain's expert on the effects of radiation on humans; Principal of Somerville College, Oxford (1945–67). **3 Sarah (Lois).** 1924–90, U.S. jazz vocalist and pianist, noted esp. for her skill in vocal improvisation.

Vaughan Williams ('wɪljəmz) *n* **Ralph.** 1872–1958, English composer, inspired by British folk songs and music of the Tudor period. He wrote operas, symphonies, hymns, and choral music.

vault[1] (vɔ:lt) *n* **1** an arched structure that forms a roof or ceiling. **2** a room, esp. a cellar, having an arched roof down to floor level. **3** a burial chamber, esp. when underground. **4** a strongroom for the safe-deposit and storage of valuables. **5** an underground room or part of such a room, used for the storage of wine, food, etc. **6** *Anatomy.* any arched or domed bodily cavity or space: *the cranial vault.* **7** something suggestive of an arched structure, as the sky. ◆ *vb* **8** (*tr*) to furnish with or as if with an arched roof. **9** (*tr*) to construct in the shape of a vault. **10** (*intr*) to curve, arch, or bend in the shape of a vault. [C14 *vaute,* from Old French, from Vulgar Latin *volvita* (unattested) a turn, probably from Latin *volvere* to roll] ▸ **'vault,like** *adj*

vault[2] (vɔ:lt) *vb* **1** to spring over (an object), esp. with the aid of a long pole or with the hands resting on the object. **2** (*intr*) to do, achieve, or attain something as if by a leap: *he vaulted to fame on the strength of his discovery.* **3** *Dressage.* to perform or cause to perform a curvet. ◆ *n* **4** the act of vaulting. **5** *Dressage.* a low leap; curvet. [C16: from Old French *voulter* to turn, from Italian *voltare* to turn, from Vulgar Latin *volvitāre* (unattested) to turn, leap; see VAULT[1]] ▸ **'vaulter** *n*

vaulting[1] ('vɔ:ltɪŋ) *n* one or more vaults in a building or such structures considered collectively.

vaulting[2] ('vɔ:ltɪŋ) *adj* (*prenominal*) **1** excessively confident; overreaching; exaggerated: *vaulting arrogance.* **2** used to vault: *a vaulting pole.*

vaunt (vɔ:nt) *vb* **1** (*tr*) to describe, praise, or display (one's success, possessions, etc.) boastfully. **2** (*intr*) *Rare or literary.* to use boastful language; brag. ◆ *n* **3** a boast. **4** *Archaic.* ostentatious display. [C14: from Old French *vanter,* from Late Latin *vānitāre* to brag, from Latin *vānus* VAIN] ▸ **'vaunter** *n*

vaunt-courier *n Archaic or poetic.* a person or thing that goes in advance; forerunner; herald. [C16: from French *avant-courrier;* see AVAUNT, COURIER]

v. aux. *abbrev. for* auxiliary verb.

Vauxhall ('vɒks,hɔ:l) *n* **1** a district in London, on the south bank of the Thames. **2** Also called: **Vauxhall Gardens.** a public garden at Vauxhall, laid out in 1661; a fashionable meeting place and site of lavish entertainments. Closed in 1859.

vav (vɔ:v) *n* the sixth letter of the Hebrew alphabet (ו) transliterated as *v* or *w.* Also called: **waw.** [from Hebrew *wāw* a hook]

vavasor ('vævə,sɔ:) *or* **vavasour** ('vævə,sυə) *n* (in feudal society) the noble or knightly vassal of a baron or great lord who also has vassals himself. Also: **vavassor.** [C13: from Old French *vavasour,* perhaps contraction of Medieval Latin *vassus vassōrum* vassal of vassals; see VASSAL]

Vavilov ('vævɪ,lɒf) *n* **Nikolai Ivanovich.** 1887–?1943, Soviet plant geneticist, noted for his research into the origins of cultivated plants. His findings were regarded as contrary to official ideology and he was arrested (1940), dying in a labour camp.

vb *abbrev. for* verb.

VB (in transformational grammar) *abbrev. for* verbal constituent.

VC *abbrev. for:* **1** Vice-chairman. **2** Vice Chancellor. **3** Vice Consul. **4** Victoria Cross. **5** Vietcong.

V-chip *n* a device within a television set that allows the set to be programmed not to receive transmissions that have been classified as containing sex, violence, or obscene language.

VCR *abbrev. for:* **1** video cassette recorder. **2** visual control room (at an airfield).

vd *abbrev. for* various dates.

VD *abbrev. for* venereal disease.

V-Day *n* a day nominated to celebrate victory, as in V-E Day or V-J Day in World War II.

VDC *abbrev. for* Volunteer Defence Corps.

VDQS *abbrev. for* vins délimités de qualité supérieure: on a bottle of French wine, indicates that it contains high-quality wine from an approved regional vineyard: the second highest French wine classification. Compare **AC,** ***vin de pays, vin de table.***

VDT *Computing. abbrev. for* visual display terminal.

VDU *Computing. abbrev. for* visual display unit.

've *contraction of* have: *I've; you've.*

Veadar *Hebrew.* ('vi:ə,dɑ:, 'veɪ-) *n Judaism.* another term for **Adar Sheni:** see **Adar.** [from Hebrew *va'adhar,* literally: and Adar, that is, the extra Adar]

veal (vi:l) *n* **1** the flesh of the calf used as food. **2** Also called: **veal calf.** a calf, esp. one bred for eating. Related adj: **vituline.** [C14: from Old French *veel,* from Latin *vitellus* a little calf, from *vitulus* calf]

vealer ('vi:lə) *n* **1** *U.S., Canadian and Austral.* another name for **veal** (sense 2). **2** *N.Z.* a young bovine animal of up to 14 months old grown for veal.

Veblen ('vɛblən) *n* **Thorstein** ('θɔ:stɪn). 1857–1929, U.S. economist and social scientist, noted for his analysis of social and economic institutions. His works include *The Theory of the Leisure Class* (1899) and *The Theory of Business Enterprise* (1904).

vector ('vɛktə) *n* **1** Also called: **polar vector.** *Maths.* a variable quantity, such as force, that has magnitude and direction and can be resolved into components that are odd functions of the coordinates. It is represented in print by a bold italic symbol: ***F*** or $\bar{F}$. Compare **pseudoscalar, pseudovector, scalar** (sense 1), **tensor** (sense 2). **2** *Maths.* an element of a vector space. **3** Also called: **carrier.** *Pathol.* an organism, esp. an insect, that carries a disease-producing microorganism from one host to another, either within or on the surface of its body. **4** Also called: **cloning vector.** *Genetics.* an agent, such as a bacteriophage or a plasmid, by means of which a fragment of foreign DNA is inserted into a host cell to produce a gene clone in genetic engineering. **5** the course or compass direction of an aircraft. **6** any behavioural influence, force, or drive. ◆ *vb* (*tr*) **7** to direct or guide (a pilot, aircraft, etc.) by directions transmitted by radio. **8** to alter the direction of (the thrust of a jet engine) as a means of steering an aircraft. [C18: from Latin: carrier, from *vehere* to convey] ▸ **vectorial** (vɛk'tɔ:rɪəl) *adj* ▸ **vec'torially** *adv*

vector field *n* a region of space under the influence of some vector quantity, such as magnetic field strength, in which each point can be described by a vector.

vector product *n* the product of two vectors that is a pseudovector, whose magnitude is the product of the magnitudes of the given vectors and the sine of the angle between them. Its axis is perpendicular to the plane of the given vectors. Written: $\boldsymbol{A}\times\boldsymbol{B}$ or $\boldsymbol{A}\wedge\boldsymbol{B}$. Compare **scalar product.** Also called: **cross product.**

vector space *n Maths.* a mathematical structure consisting of a set of objects (**vectors**) associated with a field of objects (**scalars**), such that the set constitutes an Abelian group and a further operation, scalar multiplication, is defined in which the product of a scalar and a vector is a vector. See also **scalar multiplication.**

vector sum *n* a vector whose length and direction are represented by the diagonal of a parallelogram whose sides represent the given vectors. See also **resultant.**

Veda ('veɪdə) *n* any or all of the most ancient sacred writings of Hinduism, esp. the Rig-Veda, Yajur-Veda, Sama-Veda, and Atharva-Veda. [C18: from Sanskrit: knowledge; related to *veda* I know] ▸ **Vedaic** (vɪ'deɪɪk) *adj* ▸ **Vedaism** ('veɪdə,ɪzəm) *n*

vedalia (vɪˈdeɪlɪə) *n* an Australian ladybird, *Rodolia cardinalis,* introduced elsewhere to control the scale insect *Icerya purchasi,* which is a pest of citrus fruits. [C20: from New Latin]

Vedanta (vɪˈdɑːntə, -ˈdæn-) *n* one of the six main philosophical schools of Hinduism, expounding the monism regarded as implicit in the Veda in accordance with the doctrines of the Upanishads. It teaches that only Brahman has reality, while the whole phenomenal world is the outcome of illusion (maya). [C19: from Sanskrit, from VEDA +*ánta* end] ▸ **Ve'dantic** *adj* ▸ **Ve'dantism** *n* ▸ **Ve'dantist** *n*

V-E Day *n* the day marking the Allied victory in Europe in World War II (May 8, 1945).

Vedda *or* **Veddah** (ˈvɛdə) *n, pl* **-da, -das** *or* **-dah, -dahs.** a member of an aboriginal people of Sri Lanka, characterized by slender build, dark complexion, and wavy hair, noted for their Stone Age technology. [C17: from Sinhalese: hunter, of Dravidian origin]

Veddoid (ˈvɛdɔɪd) *adj* **1** of, relating to, or resembling the Vedda. ◆ *n* **2** a Vedda. **3** a member of a postulated prehistoric race of S Asia, having slender build, dark complexion, and wavy hair: thought to be ancestors of the Vedda.

vedette (vɪˈdɛt) *n* **1** Also called: **vedette boat.** *Naval.* a small patrol vessel. **2** Also called: **vidette.** *Military.* a mounted sentry posted forward of a formation's position. [C17: from French, from Italian *vedetta* (influenced by *vedere* to see), from earlier *veletta,* perhaps from Spanish *vela* watch, from *velar* to keep vigil, from Latin *vigilāre*]

Vedic (ˈveɪdɪk) *adj* **1** of or relating to the Vedas or the ancient form of Sanskrit in which they are written. **2** of or relating to the ancient Indo-European settlers in India, regarded as the originators of many of the traditions preserved in the Vedas. ◆ *n* **3** the classical form of Sanskrit; the language of the Vedas.

veer[1] (vɪə) *vb* **1** to alter direction (of); swing around. **2** (*intr*) to change from one position, opinion, etc., to another. **3** (*intr*) (of the wind) **3a** to change direction clockwise in the northern hemisphere and anticlockwise in the southern. **3b** *Nautical.* to blow from a direction nearer the stern. Compare **haul** (sense 5). **4** *Nautical.* to steer (a vessel) off the wind. ◆ *n* **5** a change of course or direction. [C16: from Old French *virer,* probably of Celtic origin; compare Welsh *gwyro* to diverge]

veer[2] (vɪə) *vb* (*tr;* often foll. by *out* or *away*) *Nautical.* to slacken or pay out (cable or chain). [C16: from Dutch *vieren,* from Old High German *fieren* to give direction]

veery (ˈvɪərɪ) *n, pl* **veeries.** a tawny brown North American thrush, *Hylocichla fuscescens,* with a slightly spotted grey breast. [C19: probably imitative of its note]

veg (vɛdʒ) *n Informal.* a vegetable or vegetables.

Vega[1] (ˈviːgə) *n* the brightest star in the constellation Lyra and one of the most conspicuous in the N hemisphere. It is part of an optical double star having a faint companion. Distance: 26 light years. [C17: from Medieval Latin, from Arabic (*al nasr*) *al wāqi,* literally: the falling (vulture), that is, the constellation Lyra]

Vega[2] (ˈveɪgə; *Spanish* ˈbeɣa) *n* See **Lope de Vega.**

vegan (ˈviːgən) *n* a person who refrains from using any animal product whatever for food, clothing, or any other purpose.

vegeburger *or* **veggieburger** (ˈvɛdʒɪˌbɜːgə) *n* a flat cake of chopped seasoned vegetables and pulses that is grilled or fried and often served in a bread roll.

Vegemite (ˈvɛdʒɪˌmaɪt) *n Austral. trademark.* a vegetable extract used as a spread, flavouring, etc.

vegetable (ˈvɛdʒtəbᵊl) *n* **1** any of various herbaceous plants having parts that are used as food, such as peas, beans, cabbage, potatoes, cauliflower, and onions. **2** *Informal.* a person who has lost control of his mental faculties, limbs, etc., as from an injury, mental disease, etc. **3a** a dull inactive person. **3b** (*as modifier*): *a vegetable life.* **4** (*modifier*) consisting of or made from edible vegetables: *a vegetable diet.* **5** (*modifier*) of, relating to, characteristic of, derived from, or consisting of plants or plant material: *vegetable oils; the vegetable kingdom.* **6** *Rare.* any member of the plant kingdom. [C14 (adj): from Late Latin *vegetābilis* animating, from *vegetāre* to enliven, from Latin *vegēre* to excite]

vegetable butter *n* any of a group of vegetable fats having the consistency of butter.

vegetable ivory *n* **1** the hard whitish material obtained from the endosperm of the ivory nut: used to make buttons, ornaments, etc. **2** another name for the **ivory nut.**

vegetable kingdom *n* another name for **plant kingdom.**

vegetable marrow *n* **1** a cucurbitaceous plant, *Cucurbita pepo,* probably native to America but widely cultivated for its oblong green striped fruit, which is eaten as a vegetable. **2** Also called (in the U.S.): **marrow squash.** the fruit of this plant. Often shortened to **marrow.**

vegetable oil *n* any of a group of oils that are esters of fatty acids and glycerol and are obtained from plants.

vegetable oyster *n* another name for **salsify** (sense 1).

vegetable sheep *n N.Z.* any of various species of the genus *Raoulia,* esp. *R. mammillaris* or *R. eximia,* of New Zealand rocky mountains: a small low bush having white flowers and hairy leaves which, from a distance, make it look like a sheep.

vegetable silk *n* any of various silky fibres obtained from the seed pods of certain plants. See also **kapok.**

vegetable sponge *n* another name for **dishcloth gourd.**

vegetable tallow *n* any of various types of tallow that are obtained from plants.

vegetable wax *n* any of various waxes that occur on parts of certain plants, esp. the trunks of certain palms, and prevent loss of water from the plant.

vegetal (ˈvɛdʒɪtᵊl) *adj* **1** of, relating to, or characteristic of vegetables or plant life. **2** of or relating to processes in plants and animals that do not involve sexual reproduction; vegetative. [C15: from Late Latin *vegetāre* to quicken; see VEGETABLE]

vegetarian (ˌvɛdʒɪˈtɛərɪən) *n* **1** a person who advocates or practises vegetarianism. ◆ *adj* **2** relating to, advocating, or practising vegetarianism. **3** *Cookery.* strictly, consisting of vegetables and fruit only, but usually including milk, cheese, eggs, etc.

vegetarianism (ˌvɛdʒɪˈtɛərɪəˌnɪzəm) *n* the principle or practice of excluding all meat and fish, and sometimes, in the case of vegans, all animal products (such as eggs, cheese, etc.) from one's diet.

vegetate (ˈvɛdʒɪˌteɪt) *vb* (*intr*) **1** to grow like a plant; sprout. **2** to lead a life characterized by monotony, passivity, or mental inactivity. **3** *Pathol.* (of a wart, polyp, etc.) to develop fleshy outgrowths. [C17: from Late Latin *vegetāre* to invigorate]

vegetation (ˌvɛdʒɪˈteɪʃən) *n* **1** plant life as a whole, esp. the plant life of a particular region. **2** the process of vegetating. **3** *Pathol.* any abnormal growth, excrescence, etc. **4** a vegetative existence. ▸ **ˌvege'tational** *adj* ▸ **ˌvege'tatious** *adj*

vegetative (ˈvɛdʒɪtətɪv) *adj* **1** of, relating to, or concerned with vegetation, plant life, or plant growth. **2** (of reproduction) characterized by asexual processes. **3** of or relating to functions such as digestion, growth, and circulation rather than sexual reproduction. **4** (of a style of living) dull, stagnant, unthinking, or passive. ▸ **'vegetatively** *adv* ▸ **'vegetativeness** *n*

veggie (ˈvɛdʒɪ) *n, adj* an informal word for **vegetarian.**

veg out *vb* **vegges, vegging, vegged.** (*intr, adv*) *Slang, chiefly U.S.* to relax in an inert passive way; vegetate: *vegging out in front of the television set.*

vehement (ˈviːɪmənt) *adj* **1** marked by intensity of feeling or conviction; emphatic. **2** (of actions, gestures, etc.) characterized by great energy, vigour, or force; furious. [C15: from Latin *vehemēns* ardent; related to *vehere* to carry] ▸ **'vehemence** *n* ▸ **'vehemently** *adv*

vehicle (ˈviːɪkᵊl) *n* **1** any conveyance in or by which people or objects are transported, esp. one fitted with wheels. **2** a medium for the expression, communication, or achievement of ideas, information, power, etc. **3** *Pharmacol.* a therapeutically inactive substance mixed with the active ingredient to give bulk to a medicine. **4** Also called: **base.** a painting medium, such as oil, in which pigments are suspended. **5** (in the performing arts) a play, musical composition, etc., that enables a particular performer to display his talents. **6** a rocket excluding its payload. [C17: from Latin *vehiculum,* from *vehere* to carry] ▸ **vehicular** (vɪˈhɪkjʊlə) *adj*

Veii (ˈviːjaɪ) *n* an ancient Etruscan city, northwest of Rome: destroyed by the Romans in 396 B.C.

veil (veɪl) *n* **1** a piece of more or less transparent material, usually attached to a hat or headdress, used to conceal or protect a woman's face and head. **2** part of a nun's headdress falling round the face onto the shoulders. **3** something that covers, conceals, or separates; mask: *a veil of reticence.* **4 the veil.** the life of a nun in a religious order and the obligations entailed by it. **5 take the veil.** to become a nun. **6** Also called: **velum.** *Botany.* a membranous structure, esp. the thin layer of cells covering a young mushroom. **7** *Anatomy.* another word for **caul. 8** See **humeral veil.** ◆ *vb* **9** (*tr*) to cover, conceal, or separate with or as if with a veil. **10** (*intr*) to wear or put on a veil. [C13: from Norman French *veile,* from Latin *vēla* sails, pl of *vēlum* a covering] ▸ **'veiler** *n* ▸ **'veilless** *adj* ▸ **'veil-ˌlike** *adj*

Veil (*French* vaɪl) *n* **Simone (Annie)** (simɔn). born 1927, French stateswoman; president of the European Parliament (1979–82): a survivor of Nazi concentration camps.

veiled (veɪld) *adj* **1** disguised: *a veiled insult.* **2** (of sound, tone, the voice, etc.) not distinct; muffled. ▸ **veiledly** (ˈveɪlɪdlɪ) *adv*

veiling (ˈveɪlɪŋ) *n* a veil or the fabric used for veils.

vein (veɪn) *n* **1** any of the tubular vessels that convey oxygen-depleted blood to the heart. Compare **pulmonary vein, artery.** Related adj: **venous. 2** any of the hollow branching tubes that form the supporting framework of an insect's wing. **3** any of the vascular bundles of a leaf. **4** a clearly defined mass of ore, mineral, etc., typically occurring as a thin layer in a rock fissure or between rock strata. **5** an irregular streak of colour or alien substance in marble, wood, or other material. **6** a natural underground watercourse. **7** a crack or fissure. **8** a distinctive trait or quality in speech, writing, character, etc.; strain: *a vein of humour.* **9** a temporary disposition, attitude, or temper; mood: *the debate entered a frivolous vein.* **10** *Irish.* a parting in hair. ◆ *vb* (*tr*) **11** to diffuse over or cause to diffuse over in streaked patterns. **12** to fill, furnish, or mark with or as if with veins. [C13: from Old French *veine,* from Latin *vēna*] ▸ **'veinal** *adj* ▸ **'veinless** *adj* ▸ **'vein,like** *adj* ▸ **'veiny** *adj*

veining (ˈveɪnɪŋ) *n* a pattern or network of veins or streaks.

veinlet (ˈveɪnlɪt) *n* any small vein or venule.

veinstone (ˈveɪnˌstəʊn) *n* another word for **gangue.**

veinule (ˈveɪnjuːl) *n* a less common spelling of **venule.**

Vela (ˈviːlə) *n, Latin genitive* **Velorum** (viːˈlɔːrəm). a constellation in the S hemisphere, close to Puppis and Carina and crossed by the Milky Way, that has four second-magnitude stars.

velamen (vəˈleɪmɛn) *n, pl* **-lamina** (-ˈlæmɪnə). **1** the thick layer of dead cells that covers the aerial roots of certain orchids and aroids and absorbs moisture from the surroundings. **2** *Anatomy.* another word for **velum.** [C19: from Latin: a veil, from *vēlāre* to cover]

velar (ˈviːlə) *adj* **1** of, relating to, or attached to a velum: *velar tentacles.* **2** *Phonetics.* articulated with the soft palate and the back of the tongue, as in the sounds (k), (g), or (ŋ). [C18: from Latin *vēlāris,* from *vēlum* VEIL]

velarium (vɪˈlɛərɪəm) *n, pl* **-laria** (-ˈlɛərɪə). an awning used to protect the audience in ancient Roman theatres and amphitheatres. [C19: from Latin, from *vēlāre* to cover]

velarize *or* **velarise** ('viːləˌraɪz) *vb* (*tr*) *Phonetics.* to pronounce or supplement the pronunciation of (a speech sound) with articulation at the soft palate, as in dark (l) in English *tall.* ▸ **ˌvelariˈzation** *or* **ˌvelariˈsation** *n*

velate ('viːlɪt, -leɪt) *adj* having or covered with velum.

Velázquez (*Spanish* beˈlaθkeθ) *or* **Velásquez** (*Spanish* beˈlaskeθ) *n* **Diego Rodríguez de Silva y** ('djeyo rɔˈðriyeθ de ˈsilβa i). 1599–1660, Spanish painter, remarkable for the realism of his portraits, esp. those of Philip IV of Spain and the royal household.

Velcro ('velkrəʊ) *n Trademark.* a fastening consisting of two strips of nylon fabric, one having tiny hooked threads and the other a coarse surface, that form a strong bond when pressed together.

veld *or* **veldt** (fɛlt, vɛlt) *n* elevated open grassland in Southern Africa. See also **bushveld, highveld.** Compare **pampas, prairie, steppe.** [C19: from Afrikaans, from earlier Dutch *veldt* FIELD]

Velde ('vɛldə) *n* See **van de Velde.**

veldskoen ('fɛltˌskun, ˈvɛlt-) *n* an ankle-length boot of soft but strong rawhide. [from Afrikaans, literally: field shoe]

veleta (vəˈliːtə) *n* a variant spelling of **valeta.**

veliger ('vɛlɪdʒə) *n* the free-swimming larva of many molluscs, having a rudimentary shell and a ciliated velum used for feeding and locomotion. [C19: from New Latin, from VELUM + -GER(OUS)]

velites ('viːlɪˌtiːz) *pl n* light-armed troops in ancient Rome, drawn from the poorer classes. [C17: from Latin, pl of *vēles* light-armed foot soldier; related to *volāre* to fly]

velleity (vɛˈliːɪtɪ) *n, pl* **-ties.** *Rare.* **1** the weakest level of desire or volition. **2** a mere wish. [C17: from New Latin *velleitās,* from Latin *velle* to wish]

vellicate ('vɛlɪˌkeɪt) *vb Rare.* to twitch, pluck, or pinch. [C17: from Latin *vellicāre,* from *vellere* to tear off] ▸ **ˌvelliˈcation** *n* ▸ **ˈvellicative** *adj*

Vellore (vəˈlɔː) *n* a town in SE India, in NE Tamil Nadu: medical centre. Pop.: 175 061 (1991).

vellum ('vɛləm) *n* **1** a fine parchment prepared from the skin of a calf, kid, or lamb. **2** a work printed or written on vellum. **3** a creamy coloured heavy paper resembling vellum. ◆ *adj* **4** made of or resembling vellum. **5** (of a book) bound in vellum. [C15: from Old French *velin,* from *velin* of a calf, from *veel* VEAL]

veloce (vɪˈləʊtʃɪ) *adj, adv Music.* to be played rapidly. [from Italian, from Latin *vēlōx* quick]

velocipede (vɪˈlɒsɪˌpiːd) *n* **1** an early form of bicycle propelled by pushing along the ground with the feet. **2** any early form of bicycle or tricycle. [C19: from French *vélocipède,* from Latin *vēlōx* swift + *pēs* foot] ▸ **veˈlociˌpedist** *n*

velocity (vɪˈlɒsɪtɪ) *n, pl* **-ties. 1** speed of motion, action, or operation; rapidity; swiftness. **2** *Physics.* a measure of the rate of motion of a body expressed as the rate of change of its position in a particular direction with time. It is measured in metres per second, miles per hour, etc. Symbol: *u, v, w* **3** *Physics.* (not in technical usage) another word for **speed** (sense 3). [C16: from Latin *vēlōcitās,* from *vēlōx* swift; related to *volāre* to fly]

velocity head *n* the velocity of a fluid expressed in terms of the head or static pressure required to produce that velocity. It equals ρv/2 where ρ is the density of the fluid and v is the velocity. In hydrology the density of water can be written 1/G where G is the gravitational constant.

velocity modulation *n* the modulation in velocity of a beam of electrons or ions caused by passing the beam through a high-frequency electric field, as in a cavity resonator.

velocity of circulation *n Economics.* the average number of times a unit of money is used in a given time, esp. calculated as the ratio of the total money spent in that time to the total amount of money in circulation.

velodrome ('viːləˌdrəʊm, ˈvɛl-) *n* an arena with a banked track for cycle racing. [C20: from French *vélodrome,* from *vélo-* (from Latin *vēlōx* swift) + -DROME]

velour *or* **velours** (vɛˈlʊə) *n* any of various fabrics with a velvet-like finish, used for upholstery, coats, hats, etc. [C18: from Old French *velous,* from Old Provençal *velos* velvet, from Latin *villosus* shaggy, from *villus* shaggy hair; compare Latin *vellus* a fleece]

velouté (vəˈluːteɪ) *n* a rich white sauce or soup made from stock, egg yolks, and cream. [from French, literally: velvety, from Old French *velous;* see VELOUR]

Velsen (*Dutch* ˈvɛlsə) *n* a port in the W Netherlands, in North Holland at the mouth of the canal connecting Amsterdam with the North Sea: fishing and heavy industrial centre. Pop.: 63 617 (1994).

velum ('viːləm) *n, pl* **-la** (-lə). **1** *Zoology.* any of various membranous structures, such as the ciliated oral membrane of certain mollusc larvae or the veil-like membrane running around the rim of a jellyfish. **2** *Anatomy.* any of various veil-like bodily structures, esp. the soft palate. **3** *Botany.* another word for **veil** (sense 6). [C18: from Latin: veil]

velure (vəˈlʊə) *n* **1** velvet or a similar fabric. **2** a hatter's pad, used for smoothing silk hats. [C16: from Old French *velour,* from Old French *velous;* see VELOUR]

velutinous (vəˈluːtɪnəs) *adj* covered with short dense soft hairs: *velutinous leaves.* [C19: from New Latin *velūtīnus* like velvet]

velvet ('vɛlvɪt) *n* **1a** a fabric of silk, cotton, nylon, etc., with a thick close soft usually lustrous pile. **1b** (*as modifier*): *velvet curtains.* **2** anything with a smooth soft surface. **3a** smoothness; softness. **3b** (*as modifier*): *velvet skin; a velvet night.* **4** the furry covering of the newly formed antlers of a deer. **5** *Slang, chiefly U.S.* **5a** gambling or speculative winnings. **5b** a gain, esp. when unexpectedly high. **6 velvet glove.** gentleness or caution, often concealing strength or determination (esp. in the phrase **an iron fist** *or* **hand in a velvet glove**). [C14 *veluet,* from Old French *veluotte,* from *velu* hairy, from Vulgar Latin *villutus* (unattested), from Latin *villus* shaggy hair] ▸ **ˈvelvet-ˌlike** *adj* ▸ **ˈvelvety** *adj*

velvet ant *n* a solitary digger wasp of the family *Mutillidae.* [C19: so named from the wingless female]

velveteen (ˌvɛlvɪˈtiːn) *n* **1a** a cotton fabric resembling velvet with a short thick pile, used for clothing, etc. **1b** (*as modifier*): *velveteen trousers.* **2** (*pl*) trousers made of velveteen. ▸ **ˌvelvetˈeened** *adj*

velvet revolution *n* the peaceful overthrow of a government, esp. a communist government, as occurred in Czechoslovakia in late 1989.

velvet scoter *n* a European sea duck, *Melanitta fusca,* the male of which has a black plumage with white patches below the eyes and on the wings.

velvet shank *n* a bright yellow edible basidiomycetous fungus, *Flammulina velutipes,* common on trunks, stumps, or branches of broad-leaved trees in winter.

velvet stout *n* a less common name for **black velvet.**

Velvet Underground *n* **the.** U.S. avant-garde rock group (1965–70): originally comprised Lou Reed, John Cale (born 1940; bass guitar and viola), Sterling Morrison (1942–95; guitar), and Maureen Tucker (born 1945; drums). Their albums include *The Velvet Underground and Nico* (1967), *White Light/White Heat* (1967), and *Loaded* (1970). See also (Lou) **Reed.**

Ven. *abbrev. for* Venerable.

vena ('viːnə) *n, pl* **-nae** (-niː). *Anatomy.* a technical word for **vein.** [C15: from Latin *vēna* VEIN]

vena cava ('keɪvə) *n, pl* **venae cavae** ('keɪviː). either one of the two large veins that convey oxygen-depleted blood to the heart. [Latin: hollow vein]

venal ('viːnᵊl) *adj* **1** easily bribed or corrupted; mercenary: *a venal magistrate.* **2** characterized by corruption: *a venal civilization.* **3** open to purchase, esp. by bribery: *a venal contract.* [C17: from Latin *vēnālis,* from *vēnum* sale] ▸ **veˈnality** *n* ▸ **ˈvenally** *adv*

venatic (viːˈnætɪk) *or* **venatical** *adj* **1** of, relating to, or used in hunting. **2** (of people) engaged in or given to hunting. [C17: from Latin *vēnāticus,* from *vēnārī* to hunt] ▸ **veˈnatically** *adv*

venation (viːˈneɪʃən) *n* **1** the arrangement of the veins in a leaf or in the wing of an insect. **2** such veins collectively. ▸ **veˈnational** *adj*

vend (vɛnd) *vb* **1** to sell or be sold. **2** to sell (goods) for a living. **3** (*tr*) *Rare.* to utter or publish (an opinion, etc.). [C17: from Latin *vendere,* contraction of *vēnum dare* to offer for sale] ▸ **vendition** (vɛnˈdɪʃən) *n*

Venda[1] ('vɛndə) *n* **1** (*pl* **-da** *or* **-das**) a member of a Negroid people of southern Africa, living chiefly in NE South Africa. **2** the language of this people, belonging to the Bantu group of the Niger-Congo family but not easily related to any other members of the group.

Venda[2] ('vɛndə) *n* a former Bantu homeland in South Africa, near the Zimbabwe border; abolished in 1993. Capital: Thohoyandou.

vendace ('vɛndeɪs) *n, pl* **-daces** *or* **-dace.** either of two small whitefish, *Coregonus vandesius* (**Lochmaben vendace**) or *C. gracilior* (**Cumberland vendace**), occurring in lakes in Scotland and NW England respectively. See also **powan.** [C18: from New Latin *vandēsius,* from Old French *vandoise,* probably of Celtic origin]

vendee (vɛnˈdiː) *n Chiefly law.* a person to whom something, esp. real property, is sold; buyer.

Vendée (*French* vɑ̃de) *n* a department of W France, in Pays-de-la-Loire region: scene of the **Wars of the Vendée,** a series of peasant-royalist insurrections (1793–95) against the Revolutionary government. Capital: La Roche-sur-Yon. Pop.: 525 700 (1995). Area: 7016 sq. km (2709 sq. miles).

Vendémiaire *French.* (vɑ̃demjɛr) *n* the month of the grape harvest: the first month of the French Revolutionary calendar, extending from Sept. 23 to Oct. 22. [C18: from French, from Latin *vindēmia* vintage, from *vīnum* wine + *dēmere* to take away]

vendetta (vɛnˈdɛtə) *n* **1** a private feud, originally between Corsican or Sicilian families, in which the relatives of a murdered person seek vengeance by killing the murderer or some member of his family. **2** any prolonged feud, quarrel, etc. [C19: from Italian, from Latin *vindicta,* from *vindicāre* to avenge; see VINDICATE] ▸ **venˈdettist** *n*

vendible ('vɛndəbᵊl) *adj* **1** saleable or marketable. **2** *Obsolete.* venal. ◆ *n* **3** (*usually pl*) *Rare.* a saleable object. ▸ **ˌvendiˈbility** *or* **ˈvendibleness** *n*

vending machine *n* a machine that automatically dispenses consumer goods such as cigarettes, food, or petrol, when money is inserted. Also called: **automat.**

Vendôme (*French* vɑ̃dom) *n* **Louis Joseph de** (lwi ʒozɛf də). 1654–1712, French marshal, noted for his command during the War of the Spanish Succession (1701–14).

vendor ('vɛndɔː) *or* **vender** ('vɛndə) *n* **1** *Chiefly law.* a person who sells something, esp. real property. **2** another name for **vending machine.**

vendor placing *n Finance.* a method of financing the purchase of one company by another in which the purchasing company pays for the target company in its own shares, on condition that the vendor places these shares with investors for cash payment.

vendue ('vɛndjuː) *n U.S.* a public sale; auction. [C17: from Dutch *vendu,* from Old French *vendue* a sale, from *vendre* to sell, from Latin *vendere*]

veneer (vɪˈnɪə) *n* **1** a thin layer of wood, plastic, etc., with a decorative or fine finish that is bonded to the surface of a less expensive material, usually wood. **2** a superficial appearance, esp. one that is pleasing: *a veneer of gentility.* **3** any facing material that is applied to a different backing material. **4** any one of the layers of wood that is used to form plywood. ◆ *vb* (*tr*) **5** to cover (a surface) with a veneer. **6** to bond together (thin layers of wood) to make plywood. **7** to conceal (something) under a superficially pleasant surface. [C17: from German *furnieren* to veneer, from Old French *fournir* to FURNISH] ▸ **veˈneerer** *n*

veneering (vɪˈnɪərɪŋ) *n* **1** material used as veneer or a veneered surface. **2** *Rare.* a superficial show.

venepuncture ('vɛnɪˌpʌŋktʃə) *n* a variant spelling of **venipuncture.**

venerable ('vɛnərəbᵊl) *adj* **1** (esp. of a person) worthy of reverence on account of great age, religious associations, character, position, etc. **2** (of inanimate objects) hallowed or impressive on account of historical or religious association. **3** ancient: *venerable tomes.* **4** *R.C. Church.* a title bestowed on a deceased person when the first stage of his canonization has been accomplished and his holiness has been recognized in a decree of the official Church. **5** *Church of England.* a title given to an archdeacon. [C15: from Latin *venerābilis,* from *venerārī* to venerate] ▸ ˌ**venera'bility** *or* '**venerableness** *n* ▸ '**venerably** *adv*

venerate ('vɛnəˌreɪt) *vb* (*tr*) **1** to hold in deep respect; revere. **2** to honour in recognition of qualities of holiness, excellence, wisdom, etc. [C17: from Latin *venerārī,* from *venus* love] ▸ '**venerˌator** *n*

veneration (ˌvɛnə'reɪʃən) *n* **1** a feeling or expression of awe or reverence. **2** the act of venerating or the state of being venerated. ▸ ˌ**vener'ational** *adj* ▸ '**venerativeness** *n*

venereal (vɪ'nɪərɪəl) *adj* **1** of, relating to, or infected with venereal disease. **2** (of a disease) transmitted by sexual intercourse. **3** of, relating to, or involving the genitals. **4** of or relating to sexual intercourse or erotic desire; aphrodisiac. [C15: from Latin *venereus* concerning sexual love, from *venus* sexual love, from VENUS[1]]

venereal disease *n* any of various diseases, such as syphilis or gonorrhoea, transmitted by sexual intercourse. Abbrev.: **VD.**

venereology (vɪˌnɪərɪ'ɒlədʒɪ) *n* the branch of medicine concerned with the study and treatment of venereal disease. ▸ **veˌnere'ologist** *n*

venery[1] ('vɛnərɪ, 'viː-) *n Archaic.* the pursuit of sexual gratification. [C15: from Medieval Latin *veneria,* from Latin *venus* love, VENUS[1]]

venery[2] ('vɛnərɪ, 'viː-) *n* the art, sport, lore, or practice of hunting, esp. with hounds; the chase. [C14: from Old French *venerie,* from *vener* to hunt, from Latin *vēnārī*]

venesection ('vɛnɪˌsɛkʃən) *n* surgical incision into a vein. [C17: from New Latin *vēnae sectiō;* see VEIN, SECTION]

Veneti (vɛ'nɛtɪ, -taɪ) *n* **the.** (*functioning as pl*) an ancient people who established themselves at the head of the Adriatic around 950 B.C., later becoming Roman subjects.

Venetia (vɪ'niːʃə) *n* **1** the area of ancient Italy between the lower Po valley and the Alps: later a Roman province. **2** the territorial possessions of the medieval Venetian republic that were at the head of the Adriatic and correspond to the present-day region of Veneto and a large part of Friuli-Venezia Giulia.

Venetian (vɪ'niːʃən) *adj* **1** of, relating to, or characteristic of Venice or its inhabitants. ◆ *n* **2** a native or inhabitant of Venice. **3** See **Venetian blind. 4** (*sometimes not cap.*) one of the tapes that join the slats of a Venetian blind. **5** a cotton or woollen cloth used for linings.

Venetian blind *n* a window blind consisting of a number of horizontal slats whose angle may be altered to let in more or less light.

Venetian glass *n* fine ornamental glassware made in or near Venice, esp. at Murano.

Venetian red *n* **1** natural or synthetic ferric oxide used as a red pigment. **2a** a moderate to strong reddish-brown colour. **2b** (*as adj*): *a Venetian-red coat.*

Venetic (vɪ'nɛtɪk) *n* an ancient language of NE Italy, usually regarded as belonging to the Italic branch of the Indo-European family. It is recorded in about 200 inscriptions and was extinct by the 2nd century A.D.

Veneto (*Italian* 'veːneto) *n* a region of NE Italy, on the Adriatic: mountainous in the north with a fertile plain in the south, crossed by the Rivers Po, Adige, and Piave. Capital: Venice. Pop.: 4 433 060 (1996 est.). Area: 18 377 sq. km (7095 sq. miles). Also called: **Venezia-Euganea** (ve'nɛttsja eu'gaːnea).

Venez. *abbrev. for* Venezuela.

Venezia (ve'nɛttsja) *n* the Italian name for **Venice.**

Venezia Giulia (*Italian* 'dʒuːlja) *n* a former region of NE Italy at the N end of the Adriatic: divided between Yugoslavia and Italy after World War II; now divided between Italy and Slovenia.

Venezia Tridentina (*Italian* triden'tiːna) *n* the former name (until 1947) of **Trentino-Alto Adige.**

Venezuela (ˌvɛnɪ'zweɪlə) *n* **1** a republic in South America, on the Caribbean: colonized by the Spanish in the 16th century; independence from Spain declared in 1811 and won in 1819 after a war led by Simón Bolívar. It contains Lake Maracaibo and the northernmost chains of the Andes in the northwest, the Orinoco basin in the central part, and the Guiana Highlands in the south. Exports petroleum, iron ore, and coffee. Official language: Spanish. Religion: Roman Catholic majority. Currency: bolívar. Capital: Caracas. Pop.: 23 242 000 (1998 est.). Area: 912 050 sq. km (352 142 sq. miles). Official name: **Bolivarian Republic of Venezuela. 2 Gulf of.** an inlet of the Caribbean in NW Venezuela: continues south as Lake Maracaibo. ▸ ˌ**Vene'zuelan** *adj, n*

venge (vɛndʒ) *vb* (*tr*) an archaic word for **avenge.** [C13: from Old French *venger,* from Latin *vindicāre;* see VINDICATE]

vengeance ('vɛndʒəns) *n* **1** the act of or desire for taking revenge; retributive punishment. **2 with a vengeance.** (intensifier): *the 70's have returned with a vengeance.* [C13: from Old French, from *venger* to avenge, from Latin *vindicāre* to punish; see VINDICATE]

vengeful ('vɛndʒfʊl) *adj* **1** desiring revenge; vindictive. **2** characterized by or indicating a desire for revenge: *a vengeful glance.* **3** inflicting or taking revenge: *with vengeful blows.* ▸ '**vengefully** *adv* ▸ '**vengefulness** *n*

venial ('viːnɪəl) *adj* easily excused or forgiven: *a venial error.* [C13: via Old French from Late Latin *veniālis,* from Latin *venia* forgiveness; related to Latin *venus* love] ▸ ˌ**veni'ality** *n* ▸ '**venially** *adv*

venial sin *n Christianity.* a sin regarded as involving only a partial loss of grace. Compare **mortal sin.**

Venice ('vɛnɪs) *n* a port in NE Italy, capital of Veneto region, built on over 100 islands and mud flats in the **Lagoon of Venice** (an inlet of the **Gulf of Venice** at the head of the Adriatic): united under the first doge in 697 A.D.; became an independent republic and a great commercial and maritime power, defeating Genoa, the greatest rival, in 1380; contains the Grand Canal and about 170 smaller canals, providing waterways for city transport. Pop.: 298 915 (1996 est.). Italian name: **Venezia.** Related adj: **Venetian.**

venin ('vɛnɪn, 'viː-) *n* any of the poisonous constituents of animal venoms. [C20: from French *ven(in)* poison + -IN]

venipuncture *or* **venepuncture** ('vɛnɪˌpʌŋktʃə) *n Med.* the puncturing of a vein, esp. to take a sample of venous blood or inject a drug.

venire facias (vɪ'naɪrɪ 'feɪʃɪˌæs) *n Law.* (formerly) a writ directing a sheriff to summon suitable persons to form a jury. [C15: Latin, literally: you must make come]

venireman (vɪ'naɪərɪmən) *n, pl* **-men.** (in the U.S. and formerly in England) a person summoned for jury service under a venire facias.

venison ('vɛnzən; 'vɛnɪzᵊn, -sᵊn) *n* **1** the flesh of a deer, used as food. **2** *Archaic.* the flesh of any game animal used for food. [C13: from Old French *venaison,* from Latin *vēnātiō* hunting, from *vēnārī* to hunt]

Venite (vɪ'naɪtɪ) *n* **1** *Ecclesiast.* the opening word of the 95th psalm, an invitatory prayer at matins. **2** a musical setting of this. [Latin: come ye]

Venizélos (*Greek* veni'zɛlɔs) *n* **Eleuthérios** (ɛˌlefθe'riɔs). 1864–1936, Greek statesman, who greatly extended Greek territory: prime minister (1910–15; 1917–20; 1924; 1928–32; 1933).

Venlo *or* **Venloo** (*Dutch* 'vɛnloː) *n* a city in the SE Netherlands, in Limburg on the Maas River. Pop.: 63 820 (1988 est.).

Venn diagram (vɛn) *n Maths, logic.* a diagram in which mathematical sets or terms of a categorial statement are represented by overlapping circles within a boundary representing the universal set, so that all possible combinations of the relevant properties are represented by the various distinct areas in the diagram. [C19: named after John *Venn* (1834–1923), English logician]

vennel ('vɛnᵊl) *n Scot.* a lane; alley. [C15: from Old French *venelle,* from Latin *vēna* vein]

venography (vɪ'nɒgrəfɪ) *n Med.* radiography of veins after injection of a contrast medium. Also called: **phlebography.**

venom ('vɛnəm) *n* **1** a poisonous fluid secreted by such animals as certain snakes and scorpions and usually transmitted by a bite or sting. **2** malice; spite. [C13: from Old French *venim,* from Latin *venēnum* poison, love potion; related to *venus* sexual love] ▸ '**venomless** *adj* ▸ '**venomous** *adj* ▸ '**venomously** *adv* ▸ '**venomousness** *n*

venosclerosis (ˌviːnəʊsklɪ'rəʊsɪs) *n* another name for **phlebosclerosis.**

venose ('viːnəʊs) *adj* **1** having veins; venous. **2** (of a plant) covered with veins or similar ridges. [C17: via Latin *vēnōsus,* from *vēna* a VEIN]

venosity (vɪ'nɒsɪtɪ) *n* **1** an excessive quantity of blood in the venous system or in an organ or part. **2** an unusually large number of blood vessels in an organ or part.

venous ('viːnəs) *adj* **1** *Physiol.* of or relating to the blood circulating in the veins. **2** of or relating to the veins. [C17: see VENOSE] ▸ '**venously** *adv* ▸ '**venousness** *n*

vent[1] (vɛnt) *n* **1** a small opening for the passage or escape of fumes, liquids, etc. **2** the shaft of a volcano or an aperture in the earth's crust through which lava and gases erupt. **3** the external opening of the urinary or genital systems of lower vertebrates. **4** a small aperture at the breech of old guns through which the charge was ignited. **5** an exit, escape, or passage. **6 give vent to.** to release (an emotion, passion, idea, etc.) in an utterance or outburst. ◆ *vb* (*mainly tr*) **7** to release or give expression or utterance to (an emotion, idea, etc.): *he vents his anger on his wife.* **8** to provide a vent for or make vents in. **9** to let out (steam, liquid, etc.) through a vent. [C14: from Old French *esventer* to blow out, from EX-[1] + *venter,* from Vulgar Latin *ventāre* (unattested) to be windy, from Latin *ventus* wind] ▸ '**venter** *n* ▸ '**ventless** *adj*

vent[2] (vɛnt) *n* **1** a vertical slit at the back or both sides of a jacket. ◆ *vb* **2** (*tr*) to make a vent or vents in (a jacket). [C15: from Old French *fente* slit, from *fendre* to split, from Latin *findere* to cleave]

ventage ('vɛntɪdʒ) *n* **1** a small opening; vent. **2** a finger hole in a musical instrument such as a recorder.

ventail ('vɛnteɪl) *n* (in medieval armour) a covering for the lower part of the face. [C14: from Old French *ventaille* sluice, from *vent* wind, from Latin *ventus*]

venter ('vɛntə) *n* **1** *Anatomy, zoology.* **1a** the belly or abdomen of vertebrates. **1b** a protuberant structure or part, such as the belly of a muscle. **2** *Botany.* the swollen basal region of an archegonium, containing the developing ovum. **3** *Law.* the womb. **4 in venter.** *Law.* conceived but not yet born. [C16: from Latin]

ventifact ('vɛntɪˌfækt) *n Geology.* a pebble that has been shaped by wind-blown sand.

ventilate ('vɛntɪˌleɪt) *vb* (*tr*) **1** to drive foul air out of (an enclosed area). **2** to provide with a means of airing. **3** to expose (a question, grievance, etc.) to public examination or discussion. **4** *Physiol.* to oxygenate (the blood) in the capillaries of the lungs. **5** to winnow (grain). [C15: from Latin *ventilāre* to fan, from *ventulus* diminutive of *ventus* wind] ▸ '**ventilable** *adj*

ventilation (ˌvɛntɪ'leɪʃən) *n* **1** the act or process of ventilating or the state of being ventilated. **2** an installation in a building that provides a supply of fresh air. ▸ '**ventiˌlative** *adj* ▸ '**ventiˌlatory** *adj*

ventilator ('vɛntɪˌleɪtə) *n* **1** an opening or device, such as a fan, used to ventilate a room, building, etc. **2** *Med.* a machine that maintains a flow of air into and out of the lungs of a patient who is unable to breathe normally.

Ventôse *French.* (vãtoz) *n* the windy month: the sixth month of the French Revolutionary calendar, extending from Feb. 20 to March 21. [C18: from Latin *ventōsus* full of wind, from *ventus* wind]

ventouse (vɛn'tuːs) *n* an apparatus sometimes used to assist the delivery of a baby, consisting of a cup which is attached to the fetal head by suction, and a chain by which traction can be exerted in order to draw out the baby. [C16: from Old French *ventose* a cupping glass]

ventral ('vɛntrəl) *adj* **1** relating to the front part of the body; towards the belly. Compare **dorsal. 2** of, relating to, or situated on the upper or inner side of a plant organ, esp. a leaf, that is facing the axis. [C18: from Latin *ventrālis,* from *venter* abdomen] ▸ **'ventrally** *adv*

ventral fin *n* **1** another name for **pelvic fin. 2** any unpaired median fin situated on the undersurface of fishes and some other aquatic vertebrates.

ventricle ('vɛntrɪkᵊl) *n Anatomy.* **1** a chamber of the heart, having thick muscular walls, that receives blood from the atrium and pumps it to the arteries. **2** any one of the four main cavities of the vertebrate brain, which contain cerebrospinal fluid. **3** any of various other small cavities in the body. [C14: from Latin *ventriculus,* diminutive of *venter* belly]

ventricose ('vɛntrɪˌkəʊs) *adj* **1** *Botany, zoology, anatomy.* having a swelling on one side; unequally inflated: *the ventricose corolla of many labiate plants.* **2** another word for **corpulent.** [C18: from New Latin *ventricōsus,* from Latin *venter* belly] ▸ **ventricosity** (ˌvɛntrɪ'kɒsɪtɪ) *n*

ventricular (vɛn'trɪkjʊlə) *adj* **1** of, relating to, involving, or constituting a ventricle. **2** having a belly. **3** swollen or distended; ventricose.

ventriculography (vɛnˌtrɪkjʊ'lɒgrəfɪ) *n Med.* **1** radiography of the ventricles of the heart after injection of a contrast medium. **2** radiography of the ventricles of the brain after injection of air or a radiopaque material.

ventriculus (vɛn'trɪkjʊləs) *n, pl* **-li** (-ˌlaɪ). **1** *Zoology.* **1a** the midgut of an insect, where digestion takes place. **1b** the gizzard of a bird. **2** another word for **ventricle.** [C18: from Latin, diminutive of *venter* belly]

ventriloquism (vɛn'trɪləˌkwɪzəm) *or* **ventriloquy** *n* the art of producing vocal sounds that appear to come from another source. [C18: from Latin *venter* belly + *loquī* to speak] ▸ **ventriloquial** (ˌvɛntrɪ'ləʊkwɪəl) *or* **ventriloqual** (vɛn'trɪləkwəl) *adj* ▸ **ˌventri'loquially** *adv* ▸ **ven'triloquist** *n* ▸ **venˌtrilo'quistic** *adj*

ventriloquize *or* **ventriloquise** (vɛn'trɪləˌkwaɪz) *vb* to produce (sounds) in the manner of a ventriloquist.

Ventris ('vɛntrɪs) *n* **Michael George Francis.** 1922–56, English cryptographer, who deciphered the Linear B script, identifying it as an early form of Mycenaean Greek.

venture ('vɛntʃə) *vb* **1** (*tr*) to expose to danger; hazard: *he ventured his life.* **2** (*tr*) to brave the dangers of (something): *I'll venture the seas.* **3** (*tr*) to dare (to do something): *does he venture to object?* **4** (*tr; may take a clause as object*) to express in spite of possible refutation or criticism: *I venture that he is not that honest.* **5** (*intr;* often foll. by *out, forth,* etc.) to embark on a possibly hazardous journey, undertaking, etc.: *to venture forth upon the high seas.* ◆ *n* **6** an undertaking that is risky or of uncertain outcome. **7a** a commercial undertaking characterized by risk of loss as well as opportunity for profit. **7b** the merchandise, money, or other property placed at risk in such an undertaking. **8** something hazarded or risked in an adventure; stake. **9** *Archaic.* chance or fortune. **10 at a venture.** at random; by chance. [C15: variant of *aventure* ADVENTURE] ▸ **'venturer** *n*

venture capital *n* **1** capital that is provided for a new commercial enterprise by individuals or organizations other than those who own the new enterprise. **2** another name for **risk capital.**

Venture Scout *or* **Venturer** *n Brit.* a young man or woman, aged 16–20, who is a member of the senior branch of the Scouts. Former name: **Rover.** U.S. equivalent: **Explorer.**

venturesome ('vɛntʃəsəm) *or* **venturous** ('vɛntʃərəs) *adj* **1** willing to take risks; daring. **2** hazardous.

Venturi (vɛn'tjʊərɪ) *n* **Robert.** born 1925, U.S. architect, a pioneer of the postmodernist style. His writings include *Complexity and Contradiction in Architecture* (1966).

Venturi tube *n* **1** *Physics.* a device for measuring fluid flow, consisting of a tube so constricted that the pressure differential produced by fluid flowing through the constriction gives a measure of the rate of flow. **2** Also called: **venturi.** a tube with a constriction used to reduce or control fluid flow, as one in the air inlet of a carburettor. [C19: named after G. B. *Venturi* (1746–1822), Italian physicist]

venue ('vɛnjuː) *n* **1** *Law.* **1a** the place in which a cause of action arises. **1b** the place fixed for the trial of a cause. **1c** the locality from which the jurors must be summoned to try a particular cause. **2** a meeting place. **3** any place where an organized gathering, such as a rock concert or public meeting, is held. **4** *Chiefly U.S.* a position in an argument. [C14: from Old French, from *venir* to come, from Latin *venīre*]

venule ('vɛnjuːl) *n* **1** *Anatomy.* any of the small branches of a vein that receives oxygen-depleted blood from the capillaries and returns it to the heart via the venous system. **2** any of the branches of a vein in an insect's wing. [C19: from Latin *vēnula* diminutive of *vēna* VEIN] ▸ **venular** ('vɛnjʊlə) *adj*

Venus[1] ('viːnəs) *n* **1** the Roman goddess of love. Greek counterpart: **Aphrodite. 2 mount of Venus.** See **mons veneris.**

Venus[2] ('viːnəs) *n* **1** one of the inferior planets and the second nearest to the sun, visible as a bright morning or evening star. Its surface is extremely hot (over 400°C) and is completely shrouded by dense cloud. The atmosphere is principally carbon dioxide. Mean distance from sun: 108 million km; period of revolution around sun: 225 days; period of axial rotation: 244.3 days (retrograde motion); diameter and mass: 96.5 and 81.5 per cent that of earth respectively. **2** the alchemical name for **copper**[1].

Venusberg ('viːnəsˌbɜːg; *German* 'veːnusbɛrk) *n* a mountain in central Germany: contains caverns that, according to medieval legend, housed the palace of the goddess Venus.

Venusian (vɪ'njuːzɪən) *adj* **1** of, occurring on, or relating to the planet Venus. ◆ *n* **2** (in science fiction) an inhabitant of Venus.

Venus's flower basket *n* any of several deep-sea sponges of the genus *Euplectella,* esp. *E. aspergillum,* having a skeleton composed of interwoven glassy six-rayed spicules.

Venus's-flytrap *or* **Venus flytrap** *n* an insectivorous plant, *Dionaea muscipula,* of Carolina, having hinged two-lobed leaves that snap closed when the sensitive hairs on the surface are touched: family *Droseraceae.* See also **sundew, pitcher plant, butterwort.**

Venus's-girdle *n* a ctenophore, *Cestum veneris,* of warm seas, having an elongated ribbon-like body.

Venus's-hair *n* a fragile maidenhair fern, *Adiantum capillus-veneris,* of tropical and subtropical America, having fan-shaped leaves and a black stem.

Venus shell *n* a marine bivalve mollusc of the family Veneridae, typified by the intertidal *Venus gallina,* with somewhat rounded ribbed valves.

Venus's looking glass *n* a purple-flowered campanulaceous plant, *Legousia hybrida,* of Europe, W Asia, and N Africa.

ver. *abbrev. for:* **1** verse. **2** version.

veracious (vɛ'reɪʃəs) *adj* **1** habitually truthful or honest. **2** accurate; precise. [C17: from Latin *vērax,* from *vērus* true] ▸ **ve'raciously** *adv* ▸ **ve'raciousness** *n*

veracity (vɛ'ræsɪtɪ) *n, pl* **-ties. 1** truthfulness or honesty, esp. when consistent or habitual. **2** precision; accuracy. **3** something true; a truth. [C17: from Medieval Latin *vērācitās,* from Latin *vērax;* see VERACIOUS]

Veracruz (ˌvɛrə'kruːz; *Spanish* bera'kruθ) *n* **1** a state of E Mexico, on the Gulf of Mexico: consists of a hot humid coastal strip with lagoons, rising rapidly inland to the central plateau and Sierra Madre Oriental. Capital: Jalapa. Pop.: 6 734 545 (1995 est.). Area: 72 815 sq. km (28 114 sq. miles). **2** the chief port of Mexico, in Veracruz state on the Gulf of Mexico. Pop.: 438 821 (1990).

veranda *or* **verandah** (və'rændə) *n* **1** a porch or portico, sometimes partly enclosed, along the outside of a building. **2** *N.Z.* a canopy sheltering pedestrians in a shopping street. [C18: from Portuguese *varanda* railing; related to Hindi *varandā* railing] ▸ **ve'randaed** *or* **ve'randahed** *adj*

verapamil (vɪ'ræpəˌmɪl) *n Med.* a calcium antagonist used in the treatment of angina pectoris, hypertension, and irregular heart rhythm.

veratridine (vɪ'rætrɪˌdiːn) *n* a yellowish-white amorphous alkaloid obtained from the seeds of sabadilla. Formula: $C_{36}H_{51}NO_{11}$. [C20: from VERATR(INE) + -ID[3] + -INE[2]]

veratrine ('vɛrəˌtriːn) *or* **veratrin** ('vɛrətrɪn) *n* a white poisonous mixture obtained from the seeds of sabadilla, consisting of veratridine and several other alkaloids: formerly used in medicine as a counterirritant. [C19: from Latin *vērātrum* hellebore + -INE[2]]

verb (vɜːb) *n* **1** (in traditional grammar) any of a large class of words in a language that serve to indicate the occurrence or performance of an action, the existence of a state or condition, etc. In English, such words as *run, make, do,* and the like are verbs. **2** (in modern descriptive linguistic analysis) **2a** a word or group of words that functions as the predicate of a sentence or introduces the predicate. **2b** (*as modifier*): *a verb phrase.* ◆ Abbrevs.: **vb, v.** [C14: from Latin *verbum* a word] ▸ **'verbless** *adj*

verbal ('vɜːbᵊl) *adj* **1** of, relating to, or using words, esp. as opposed to ideas, etc.: *merely verbal concessions.* **2** oral rather than written: *a verbal agreement.* **3** verbatim; literal: *an almost verbal copy.* **4** *Grammar.* of or relating to verbs or a verb. ◆ *n* **5** *Grammar.* another word for **verbid. 6** (*pl*) *Slang.* a criminal's admission of guilt on arrest. ◆ *vb* **-bals, -balling, -balled.** (*tr*) **7** *Slang.* (of the police) to implicate (someone) in a crime by quoting alleged admission of guilt in court. ▸ **'verbally** *adv*

verbalism ('vɜːbəˌlɪzəm) *n* **1** a verbal expression; phrase or word. **2** an exaggerated emphasis on the importance of words by the uncritical acceptance of assertions in place of explanations, the use of rhetorical style, etc. **3** a statement lacking real content, esp. a cliché.

verbalist ('vɜːbəlɪst) *n* **1** a person who deals with words alone, rather than facts, ideas, feeling, etc. **2** a person skilled in the use of words.

verbalize *or* **verbalise** ('vɜːbəˌlaɪz) *vb* **1** to express (an idea, feeling, etc.) in words. **2** to change (any word that is not a verb) into a verb or derive a verb from (any word that is not a verb). **3** (*intr*) to be verbose. ▸ **ˌverbali'zation** *or* **ˌverbali'sation** *n* ▸ **'verbalˌizer** *or* **'verbalˌiser** *n*

verbal noun *n* a noun derived from a verb, such as *smoking* in the sentence *smoking is bad for you.* See also **gerund.**

verbascum (vɜː'bæskəm) *n* See **mullein.** [Latin: mullein]

verbatim (vɜː'beɪtɪm) *adv, adj* using exactly the same words; word for word. [C15: from Medieval Latin: word by word, from Latin *verbum* word]

verbena (vɜː'biːnə) *n* **1** any plant of the verbenaceous genus *Verbena,* chiefly of tropical and temperate America, having red, white, or purple fragrant flowers: much cultivated as garden plants. See also **vervain. 2** any of various similar or related plants, esp. the lemon verbena. [C16: via Medieval Latin, from Latin: sacred bough used by the priest in religious acts, VERVAIN]

verbenaceous (ˌvɜːbɪ'neɪʃəs) *adj* of, relating to, or belonging to the *Verbenaceae,* a family of herbaceous and climbing plants, shrubs, and trees, mostly of warm and tropical regions, having tubular typically two-lipped flowers: includes teak, lantana, vervain, and verbena. [C19: from New Latin *Verbēnāceae,* from Medieval Latin: VERBENA]

verbiage ('vɜːbɪɪdʒ) *n* **1** the excessive and often meaningless use of words; verbosity. **2** *Rare.* diction; wording. [C18: from French, from Old French *verbier* to chatter, from *verbe* word, from Latin *verbum*]

verbid ('vɜːbɪd) *n Grammar.* any nonfinite form of a verb or any nonverbal word derived from a verb: *participles, infinitives, and gerunds are all verbids.*

verbify ('vɜːbɪˌfaɪ) *vb* **-fies, -fying, -fied.** another word for **verbalize** (senses 2, 3). ▸ **ˌverbifi'cation** *n*

verbose (vɜːˈbəʊs) *adj* using or containing an excess of words, so as to be pedantic or boring; prolix. [C17: from Latin *verbōsus* from *verbum* word] ▸ **verˈbosely** *adv* ▸ **verbosity** (vɜːˈbɒsɪtɪ) *or* **verˈboseness** *n*

verboten *German.* (ferˈboːtən) *adj* forbidden; prohibited.

verb phrase *n Grammar.* a constituent of a sentence that contains the verb and any direct and indirect objects but not the subject. It is a controversial question in grammatical theory whether or not this constituent is to be identified with the predicate of the sentence. Abbrev.: **VP.**

verb. sap. *or* **sat.** *abbrev. for* verbum sapienti sat est. [Latin: a word is enough to the wise]

Vercelli (*Italian* verˈtʃɛlli) *n* a city in NW Italy, in Piedmont: an ancient Ligurian and later Roman city; has an outstanding library of manuscripts (notably the *Codex Vercellensis,* dating from the 10th century). Pop.: 50 313 (1990).

Vercingetorix (ˌvɜːsɪnˈdʒɛtərɪks) *n* died ?45 B.C., Gallic chieftain and hero, executed for leading a revolt against the Romans under Julius Caesar (52 B.C.).

verdant (ˈvɜːdᵊnt) *adj* **1** covered with green vegetation. **2** (of plants, etc.) green in colour. **3** immature or unsophisticated; green. [C16: from Old French *verdoyant,* from *verdoyer* to become green, from Old French *verd* green, from Latin *viridis,* from *virēre* to be green] ▸ **ˈverdancy** *n* ▸ **ˈverdantly** *adv*

verd antique (vɜːd) *n* **1** a dark green mottled impure variety of serpentine marble. **2** any of various similar marbles or stones. **3** another name for **verdigris.** [C18: from French, from Italian *verde antico* ancient green]

Verde (vɜːd) *n* **Cape.** a cape in Senegal, near Dakar: the westernmost point of Africa. See also **Cape Verde.**

verderer (ˈvɜːdərə) *n English legal history.* a judicial officer responsible for the maintenance of law and order in the royal forests. [C16: from Anglo-French, from Old French *verdier,* from *verd* green, from Latin *viridis;* compare Latin *viridārium* plantation of trees]

Verdi (ˈvɛədɪ; *Italian* ˈverdi) *n* **Giuseppe** (dʒuˈzɛppe). 1813–1901, Italian composer of operas, esp. *Rigoletto* (1851), *Il Trovatore* (1853), *La Traviata* (1853), and *Aïda* (1871).

verdict (ˈvɜːdɪkt) *n* **1** the findings of a jury on the issues of fact submitted to it for examination and trial; judgment. **2** any decision, judgment, or conclusion. [C13: from Medieval Latin *vērdictum,* from Latin *vērē dictum* truly spoken, from *vērus* true + *dīcere* to say]

verdigris (ˈvɜːdɪgrɪs) *n* **1** a green or bluish patina formed on copper, brass, or bronze and consisting of a basic salt of copper containing both copper oxide and a copper salt. **2** a green or blue crystalline substance obtained by the action of acetic acid on copper and used as a fungicide and pigment; basic copper acetate. [C14: from Old French *vert de Grice* green of Greece]

verdigris toadstool *n* a basidiomycetous fungus, *Stropharia aeruginosa,* having a distinctive and unusual blue-green cap and paler shaggy stem.

verdin (ˈvɜːdɪn) *n* a small W North American tit, *Auriparus flaviceps,* having a grey plumage with a yellow head. [French: yellowhammer]

Verdun (*French* vɛrdœ̃; *English* ˈvɛədʌn) *n* **1** a fortified town in NE France, on the Meuse: scene of the longest and most severe battle (1916) of World War I, in which the French repelled a powerful German offensive. Pop.: 23 430 (1990). Ancient name: **Verodunum** (ˌvɛrəˈdjuːnəm). **2 Treaty of.** an agreement reached in 843 A.D. by three grandsons of Charlemagne, dividing his empire into an E kingdom (later Germany), a W kingdom (later France), and a middle kingdom (containing what became the Low Countries, Lorraine, Burgundy, and N Italy).

verdure (ˈvɜːdʒə) *n* **1** flourishing green vegetation or its colour. **2** a condition of freshness or healthy growth. [C14: from Old French *verd* green, from Latin *viridis*] ▸ **ˈverdured** *adj* ▸ **ˈverdurous** *adj*

verecund (ˈvɛrɪˌkʌnd) *adj Rare.* shy or modest. [C16: from Latin *verēcundus* diffident, from *verērī* to fear]

Vereeniging (fəˈriːnɪkɪŋ, və-) *n* a city in E South Africa: scene of the signing (1902) of the treaty ending the Boer War. Pop.: 60 584 (1985).

verge[1] (vɜːdʒ) *n* **1** an edge or rim; margin. **2** a limit beyond which something occurs; brink: *on the verge of ecstasy.* **3** *Brit.* a grass border along a road. **4** an enclosing line, belt, or strip. **5** *Architect.* the edge of the roof tiles projecting over a gable. **6** *Architect.* the shaft of a classical column. **7** an enclosed space. **8** *Horology.* the spindle of a balance wheel in a vertical escapement, found only in very early clocks. **9** *English legal history.* **9a** the area encompassing the royal court that is subject to the jurisdiction of the Lord High Steward. **9b** a rod or wand carried as a symbol of office or emblem of authority, as in the Church. **9c** a rod held by a person swearing fealty to his lord on becoming a tenant, esp. of copyhold land. ◆ *vb* **10** (*intr;* foll. by *on*) to be near (to): *to verge on chaos.* **11** (when *intr,* sometimes foll. by *on*) to serve as the edge of (something): *this narrow strip verges the road.* [C15: from Old French, from Latin *virga* rod]

verge[2] (vɜːdʒ) *vb* (*intr;* foll. by *to* or *towards*) to move or incline in a certain direction. [C17: from Latin *vergere*]

vergeboard (ˈvɜːdʒˌbɔːd) *n* another name for **bargeboard.**

vergence (ˈvɜːdʒəns) *n* the inward or outward turning movement of the eyes in convergence or divergence. [C19: from VERGE[2] + -ENCE]

verger (ˈvɜːdʒə) *n Chiefly Church of England.* **1** a church official who acts as caretaker and attendant, looking after the interior of a church and often the vestments and church furnishings. **2** an official who carries the verge or rod of office before a bishop, dean, or other dignitary in ceremonies and processions. [C15: from Old French, from *verge,* from Latin *virga* rod, twig]

Vergil (ˈvɜːdʒɪl) *n* a variant spelling of **Virgil.**

verglas (ˈvɛəglɑː) *n, pl* **-glases** (-glɑː, -glɑːz). a thin film of ice on rock. [from Old French *verre-glaz* glass-ice, from *verre* glass (from Latin *vitrum*) + *glaz* ice (from Late Latin *glacia,* from Latin *glaciēs*)]

Verhaeren (vɜːˈhɑːrən) *n* **Émile.** 1855–1916, Belgian poet, writing in French. His works include the collections *Les Flamandes* (1883), *Les Soirs* (1887), and *Les Visages de la Vie* (1899).

veridical (vɪˈrɪdɪkᵊl) *adj* **1** truthful. **2** *Psychol.* of or relating to revelations in dreams, hallucinations, etc., that appear to be confirmed by subsequent events. [C17: from Latin *vēridicus,* from *vērus* true + *dīcere* to say] ▸ **veˌridiˈcality** *n* ▸ **veˈridically** *adv*

veriest (ˈvɛrɪɪst) *adj Archaic.* (intensifier): *the veriest coward.*

verification (ˌvɛrɪfɪˈkeɪʃən) *n* **1** establishment of the correctness of a theory, fact, etc. **2** evidence that provides proof of an assertion, theory, etc. **3** *Law.* **3a** (formerly) a short affidavit at the end of a pleading stating the pleader's readiness to prove his assertions. **3b** confirmatory evidence. ▸ **ˈverifiˌcative** *or* **ˈverifiˌcatory** *adj*

verification principle *n* (in the philosophy of the logical positivists) the doctrine that nontautologous statements are meaningful only if it is in principle possible to establish empirically whether they are true or false.

verify (ˈvɛrɪˌfaɪ) *vb* **-fies, -fying, -fied.** (*tr*) **1** to prove to be true; confirm; substantiate. **2** to check or determine the correctness or truth of by investigation, reference, etc. **3** *Law.* to add a verification to (a pleading); substantiate or confirm (an oath). [C14: from Old French *verifier,* from Medieval Latin *vērificāre,* from Latin *vērus* true + *facere* to make] ▸ **ˈveriˌfiable** *adj* ▸ **ˈveriˌfiableness** *n* ▸ **ˈveriˌfiably** *adv* ▸ **ˈveriˌfier** *n*

verily (ˈvɛrɪlɪ) *adv* (*sentence modifier*) *Archaic.* in truth; truly: *verily, thou art a man of God.* [C13: from VERY + -LY[2]]

verisimilar (ˌvɛrɪˈsɪmɪlə) *adj* appearing to be true; probable; likely. [C17: from Latin *vērīsimilis,* from *vērus* true + *similis* like] ▸ **ˌveriˈsimilarly** *adv*

verisimilitude (ˌvɛrɪsɪˈmɪlɪˌtjuːd) *n* **1** the appearance or semblance of truth or reality; quality of seeming true. **2** something that merely seems to be true or real, such as a doubtful statement. [C17: from Latin *vērisimilitūdō,* from *vērus* true + *similitūdō* SIMILITUDE]

verism (ˈvɪərɪzəm) *n* extreme naturalism in art or literature. [C19: from Italian *verismo,* from *vero* true, from Latin *vērus*] ▸ **ˈverist** *n, adj* ▸ **veˈristic** *adj*

verismo (vɛˈrɪzməʊ; *Italian* veˈrizmo) *n Music.* a school of composition that originated in Italian opera towards the end of the 19th century, drawing its themes from real life and emphasizing naturalistic elements. Its chief exponent was Puccini. [C19: from Italian; see VERISM]

veritable (ˈvɛrɪtəbᵊl) *adj* (*prenominal*) **1** (intensifier; *usually qualifying a word used metaphorically*): *he's a veritable swine!* **2** *Rare.* genuine or true; proper: *I require veritable proof.* [C15: from Old French, from *vérité* truth; see VERITY] ▸ **ˈveritableness** *n* ▸ **ˈveritably** *adv*

vérité (ˈvɛrɪːˌteɪ; *French* verite) *adj* involving a high degree of realism or naturalism: *a vérité look at David Bowie.* See also **cinéma vérité.** [French, literally: truth]

verity (ˈvɛrɪtɪ) *n, pl* **-ties. 1** the quality or state of being true, real, or correct. **2** a true principle, statement, idea, etc.; a truth or fact. [C14: from Old French *vérité,* from Latin *vēritās,* from *vērus* true]

verjuice (ˈvɜːˌdʒuːs) *n* **1a** the acid juice of unripe grapes, apples, or crab apples, formerly much used in making sauces, etc. **1b** (*as modifier*): *verjuice sauce.* **2** *Rare.* **2a** sourness or sharpness of temper, looks, etc. **2b** (*as modifier*): *a verjuice old wife.* ◆ *vb* **3** (*tr*) *Rare.* to make sour; embitter. [C14: from Old French *vert jus* green (unripe) juice, from Old French *vert* green (from Latin *viridis*) + *jus* juice (from Latin *jūs*)]

Verkhne-Udinsk (*Russian* ˈvjerxnɪuˈdjinsk) *n* the former name (until 1934) of **Ulan-Ude.**

verkrampte (fəˈkrɑmtə) *n* (in South Africa) **a** (during apartheid) an Afrikaner Nationalist who opposed any changes toward liberal trends in government policy, esp. relating to racial questions. **b** (*as modifier*): *verkrampte politics.* ◆ Compare **verligte.** [C20: from Afrikaans (adj), literally: restricted]

Verlaine (*French* vɛrlɛn) *n* **Paul** (pɔl). 1844–96, French poet. His verse includes *Poèmes saturniens* (1866), *Fêtes galantes* (1869) and *Romances sans paroles* (1874). He was closely associated with Rimbaud and was a precursor of the symbolists.

verligte (fəˈləxtə) *n* (in South Africa) **a** (during apartheid) a person of any of the White political parties who supported liberal trends in government policy. **b** (*as modifier*): *verligte politics.* ◆ Compare **verkrampte.** [C20: from Afrikaans (adj), literally: enlightened]

Vermeer (vɛəˈmɪə; *Dutch* vərˈmeːr) *n* **Jan** (jɑn). full name *Jan van der Meer van Delft.* 1632–75, Dutch genre painter, noted esp. for his masterly treatment of light.

vermeil (ˈvɜːmeɪl) *n* **1** gilded silver, bronze, or other metal, used esp. in the 19th century. **2a** vermilion. **2b** (*as adj*): *vermeil shoes.* [C15: from Old French, from Late Latin *vermiculus* insect (of the genus *Kermes*) or the red dye prepared from it, from Latin: little worm]

vermi- *combining form.* worm: *vermicide; vermiform; vermifuge.* [from Latin *vermis* worm]

vermicelli (ˌvɜːmɪˈsɛlɪ; *Italian* vermiˈtʃɛlli) *n* **1** very fine strands of pasta, used in soups. **2** tiny chocolate strands used to coat cakes, etc. [C17: from Italian: little worms, from *verme* a worm, from Latin *vermis*]

vermicide (ˈvɜːmɪˌsaɪd) *n* any substance used to kill worms. ▸ **ˌvermiˈcidal** *adj*

vermicular (vɜːˈmɪkjʊlə) *adj* **1** resembling the form, markings, motion, or tracks of worms. **2** of or relating to worms or wormlike animals. [C17: from Medieval Latin *vermiculāris,* from Latin *vermiculus,* diminutive of *vermis* worm] ▸ **verˈmicularly** *adv*

vermiculate *vb* (vɜːˈmɪkjʊˌleɪt). **1** (*tr*) to decorate with wavy or wormlike tracery or markings. ◆ *adj* (vɜːˈmɪkjʊlɪt, -ˌleɪt). **2** vermicular; sinuous. **3** worm-eaten or appearing as if worm-eaten. **4** (of thoughts, etc.) insinuating; subtly tortuous. [C17: from Latin *vermiculātus* in the form of worms, from *vermis* worm]

vermiculation (vɜːˌmɪkjʊˈleɪʃən) *n* **1** *Physiol.* any wormlike movement, esp. of the intestines; peristalsis. **2** decoration consisting of wormlike carving or marks. **3** the state of being worm-eaten.

vermiculite (vɜːˈmɪkjʊˌlaɪt) *n* any of a group of micaceous minerals consisting mainly of hydrated silicate of magnesium, aluminium, and iron: on heating they expand and exfoliate and in this form are used in heat and sound insulation, fireproofing, and as a bedding medium for young plants. **[C19:** from VERMICUL(AR) + -ITE[1]**]**

vermiform (ˈvɜːmɪˌfɔːm) *adj* resembling a worm.

vermiform appendix *or* **process** *n* a wormlike pouch extending from the lower end of the caecum in some mammals. In man it is vestigial. Also called: **appendix.**

vermifuge (ˈvɜːmɪˌfjuːdʒ) *n* any drug or agent able to destroy or expel intestinal worms. Also called: **anthelminthic, anthelmintic, helminthic.** ► **vermifugal** (ˌvɜːmɪˈfjuːgᵊl) *adj*

vermilion *or* **vermillion** (vəˈmɪljən) *n* **1a** a bright red to reddish-orange colour. **1b** (*as adj*): *a vermilion car.* **2** mercuric sulphide, esp. when used as a bright red pigment; cinnabar. **[C13:** from Old French *vermeillon,* from VERMEIL**]**

vermin (ˈvɜːmɪn) *n* **1** (*functioning as pl*) small animals collectively, esp. insects and rodents, that are troublesome to man, domestic animals, etc. **2** (*pl* **-min**) an unpleasant, obnoxious, or dangerous person. **[C13:** from Old French *vermine,* from Latin *vermis* a worm**]**

vermination (ˌvɜːmɪˈneɪʃən) *n* the spreading of or infestation with vermin.

verminous (ˈvɜːmɪnəs) *adj* relating to, infested with, or suggestive of vermin. ► **ˈverminously** *adv* ► **ˈverminousness** *n*

vermis (ˈvɜːmɪs) *n, pl* **-mes** (-miːz). *Anatomy.* the middle lobe connecting the two halves of the cerebellum. **[C19:** via New Latin from Latin: worm**]**

vermivorous (vɜːˈmɪvərəs) *adj* (of certain animals) feeding on worms.

Vermont (vɜːˈmɒnt) *n* a state in the northeastern U.S.: crossed from north to south by the Green Mountains; bounded on the east by the Connecticut River and by Lake Champlain in the northwest. Capital: Montpelier. Pop.: 588 978 (1997 est.). Area: 24 887 sq. km (9609 sq. miles). Abbrevs.: **Vt.** or (with zip code) **VT** ► **Verˈmonter** *n*

vermouth (ˈvɜːməθ, vəˈmuːθ) *n* any of several wines containing aromatic herbs and some other flavourings. **[C19:** from French, from German *Wermut* WORMWOOD (absinthe)**]**

vernacular (vəˈnækjʊlə) *n* **1 the.** the commonly spoken language or dialect of a particular people or place. **2** a local style of architecture, in which ordinary houses are built: *this group of architects have re-created a true English vernacular.* ◆ *adj* **3** relating to, using, or in the vernacular. **4** designating or relating to the common name of an animal or plant. **5** built in the local style of ordinary houses, rather than a grand architectural style. **[C17:** from Latin *vernāculus* belonging to a household slave, from *verna* household slave**]** ► **verˈnacularly** *adv*

vernacularism (vəˈnækjʊləˌrɪzəm) *n* the use of the vernacular or a term in the vernacular.

vernal (ˈvɜːnᵊl) *adj* **1** of or occurring in spring. **2** *Poetic.* of or characteristic of youth; fresh. **[C16:** from Latin *vernālis,* from *vēr* spring**]** ► **ˈvernally** *adv*

vernal equinox *n* **1** the time at which the sun crosses the plane of the equator towards the relevant hemisphere, making day and night of equal length. It occurs about March 21 in the N hemisphere (Sept. 23 in the S hemisphere). **2** *Astronomy.* the point on the celestial sphere, lying in the constellation of Pisces, at which the celestial equator intersects the ecliptic.

vernal grass *n* any of various Eurasian grasses of the genus *Anthoxanthum,* such as *A. odoratum* (**sweet vernal grass**), having the fragrant scent of coumarin.

vernalize *or* **vernalise** (ˈvɜːnəˌlaɪz) *vb* to shorten the period between sowing and flowering in (plants), esp. by subjection of the seeds to low temperatures before planting. ► **ˌvernaliˈzation** *or* **ˌvernaliˈsation** *n*

vernation (vɜːˈneɪʃən) *n* the way in which leaves are arranged in the bud. **[C18:** from New Latin *vernātiō,* from Latin *vernāre* to be springlike, from *vēr* spring**]**

Verne (vɜːn; *French* vɛrn) *n* **Jules** (ʒyl). 1828–1905, French writer, esp. of science fiction, such as *Twenty Thousand Leagues under the Sea* (1870) and *Around the World in Eighty Days* (1873).

Verner's law (ˈvɜːnəz) *n Linguistics.* a modification of Grimm's Law accommodating some of its exceptions. It states that noninitial voiceless fricatives in Proto-Germanic occurring as a result of Grimm's law became voiced fricatives if the previous syllable had been unstressed in Proto-Indo-European. **[C19:** named after Karl Adolph *Verner* (1846–96), Danish philologist, who formulated it**]** ► **Vernerian** (vɜːˈnɛərɪən) *adj*

vernier (ˈvɜːnɪə) *n* **1** a small movable scale running parallel to the main graduated scale in certain measuring instruments, such as theodolites, used to obtain a fractional reading of one of the divisions on the main scale. **2** an auxiliary device for making a fine adjustment to an instrument, usually by means of a fine screw thread. **3** (*modifier*) relating to or fitted with a vernier: *a vernier scale; a vernier barometer.* **[C18:** named after Paul *Vernier* (1580–1637), French mathematician, who described the scale**]**

vernier rocket *n* another name for **thruster** (sense 2).

vernissage (ˌvɜːnɪˈsɑːʒ) *n* **1** a preview or the opening or first day of an exhibition of paintings. **2** another term for **varnishing day.** **[**French, from *vernis* VARNISH**]**

Vernoleninsk (*Russian* vɪrnəlɪˈnjiːnsk) *n* the former name of **Nikolayev.**

Verny (*Russian* ˈvjɛrnɪj) *n* a former name (until 1927) of **Alma-Ata.**

Verona (vəˈrəʊnə; *Italian* veˈroːna) *n* a city in N Italy, in Veneto on the Adige River: strategically situated at the junction of major routes between Italy and N Europe; became a Roman colony (89 B.C.); under Austrian rule (1797–1866); many Roman remains. Pop.: 254 145 (1996 est.). ► **Veronese** (ˌvɛrəˈniːz) *adj, n*

Veronal (ˈvɛrənᵊl) *n* a trademark for **barbitone.**

Veronese (*Italian* veroˈneːse) *n* **Paolo** (ˈpaːolo), original name *Paolo Cagliari* or *Caliari.* 1528–88, Italian painter of the Venetian school. His works include *The Marriage at Cana* (1563) and *The Feast of the Levi* (1573).

veronica[1] (vəˈrɒnɪkə) *n* any scrophulariaceous plant of the genus *Veronica,* esp. the speedwells, of temperate and cold regions, having small blue, pink, or white flowers and flattened notched fruits. **[C16:** from Medieval Latin, perhaps from the name *Veronica***]**

veronica[2] (vəˈrɒnɪkə) *n R.C. Church.* **1** the representation of the face of Christ that, according to legend, was miraculously imprinted upon the headcloth that Saint Veronica offered him on his way to his crucifixion. **2** the cloth itself. **3** any similar representation of Christ's face.

veronica[3] (vəˈrɒnɪkə) *n Bullfighting.* a pass in which the matador slowly swings the cape away from the charging bull. **[**from Spanish, from the name *Veronica***]**

verra (ˈvɛrə) *adj, adv* a Scot. word for **very.**

Verrazano *or* **Verrazzano** (*Italian* verraˈtsaːno) *n* **Giovanni da** (dʒoˈvanni da). ?1485–?1528, Florentine navigator; the first European to sight what was to become New York (1524).

Verrocchio (vəˈrəʊkɪˌəʊ; *Italian* verˈrɔkkjo) *n* **Andrea del** (anˈdrɛːa del). 1435–88, Italian sculptor, painter, and goldsmith of the Florentine school: noted esp. for the equestrian statue of Bartolommeo Colleoni in Venice.

verruca (vɛˈruːkə) *n, pl* **-cae** (-siː) *or* **-cas. 1** *Pathol.* a wart, esp. one growing on the hand or foot. **2** *Biology.* a wartlike outgrowth, as in certain plants or on the skin of some animals. **[C16:** from Latin: wart**]**

verrucose (ˈvɛrʊˌkəʊs) *or* **verrucous** (ˈvɛrʊkəs, vɛˈruːkəs) *adj Botany.* covered with warty processes. **[C17:** from Latin *verrūcōsus* full of warts, from *verrūca* a wart**]** ► **verrucosity** (ˌvɛrʊˈkɒsɪtɪ) *n*

vers *abbrev. for* versed sine.

Versace (*Italian* verˈsatʃe) *n* **Gianni** (ˈdʒiani). 1946–97, Italian fashion designer.

Versailles (vɛəˈsaɪ, -ˈseɪlz; *French* vɛrsaj) *n* **1** a city in N central France, near Paris: site of an elaborate royal residence built for Louis XIV; seat of the French kings (1682–1789). Pop.: 87 789 (1990). **2 Treaty of. 2a** the treaty of 1919 imposed upon Germany by the Allies (except for the U.S. and the Soviet Union): the most important of the five peace treaties that concluded World War I. **2b** another name for the (Treaty of) **Paris** of 1783.

versant (ˈvɜːsᵊnt) *n* **1** the side or slope of a mountain or mountain range. **2** the slope of a region. **[C19:** from French, from *verser* to turn, from Latin *versāre***]**

versatile (ˈvɜːsəˌtaɪl) *adj* **1** capable of or adapted for many different uses, skills, etc. **2** variable or changeable. **3** *Botany.* (of an anther) attached to the filament by a small area so that it moves freely in the wind. **4** *Zoology.* able to turn forwards and backwards: *versatile antennae.* **[C17:** from Latin *versātilis* moving around, from *versāre* to turn**]** ► **ˈversaˌtilely** *adv* ► **versatility** (ˌvɜːsəˈtɪlɪtɪ) *n*

vers de société *French.* (vɛr də sɔsjete) *n* light, witty, and polished verse. **[**literally: society verse**]**

verse (vɜːs) *n* **1** (not in technical usage) a stanza or other short subdivision of a poem. **2** poetry as distinct from prose. **3a** a series of metrical feet forming a rhythmic unit of one line. **3b** (*as modifier*): *verse line.* **4** a specified type of metre or metrical structure: *iambic verse.* **5** one of the series of short subsections into which most of the writings in the Bible are divided. **6** a metrical composition; poem. ◆ *vb* **7** a rare word for **versify.** **[**Old English *vers,* from Latin *versus* a furrow, literally: a turning (of the plough), from *vertere* to turn**]**

versed (vɜːst) *adj* (*postpositive;* foll. by *in*) thoroughly knowledgeable (about), acquainted (with), or skilled (in).

versed sine *n* a trigonometric function equal to one minus the cosine of the specified angle. Abbrev.: **vers.** **[C16:** from New Latin *sinus versus,* from SINE[1] + *versus* turned, from *vertere* to turn**]**

versicle (ˈvɜːsɪkᵊl) *n* **1** a short verse. **2** a short sentence recited or sung by the minister at a liturgical ceremony and responded to by the choir or congregation. **[C14:** from Latin *versiculus* a little line, from *versus* VERSE**]**

versicolour *or U.S.* **versicolor** (ˈvɜːsɪˌkʌlə) *adj* of variable or various colours. **[C18:** from Latin *versicolor,* from *versāre* to turn + *color* COLOUR**]**

versicular (vɜːˈsɪkjʊlə) *adj Rare.* of, relating to, or consisting of verses or versicles.

versification (ˌvɜːsɪfɪˈkeɪʃən) *n* **1** the technique or art of versifying. **2** the form or metrical composition of a poem. **3** a metrical version of a prose text.

versify (ˈvɜːsɪˌfaɪ) *vb* **-fies, -fying, -fied. 1** (*tr*) to render (something) into metrical form or verse. **2** (*intr*) to write in verse. **[C14:** from Old French *versifier,* from Latin *versificāre,* from *versus* VERSE + *facere* to make**]** ► **ˈversiˌfier** *n*

version (ˈvɜːʃən, -ʒən) *n* **1** an account of a matter from a certain point of view, as contrasted with others: *his version of the accident is different from the policeman's.* **2** a translation, esp. of the Bible, from one language into another. **3** a variant form of something; type. **4** an adaptation, as of a book or play into a film. **5** *Med.* manual turning of a fetus to correct an irregular position within the uterus. **6** *Pathol.* an abnormal displacement of the uterus characterized by a tilting forwards (**anteversion**), backwards (**retroversion**), or to either side (**lateroversion**). **[C16:** from Medieval Latin *versiō* a turning, from Latin *vertere* to turn**]** ► **ˈversional** *adj*

vers libre *French.* (vɛr librə) *n* (in French poetry) another term for **free verse.**

verso (ˈvɜːsəʊ) *n, pl* **-sos. 1a** the back of a sheet of printed paper. **1b** Also called: **reverso.** the left-hand pages of a book, bearing the even numbers. Compare **recto. 2** the side of a coin opposite to the obverse; reverse. **[C19:** from the New Latin phrase *versō foliō* the leaf having been turned, from Latin *vertere* to turn + *folium* a leaf**]**

verst (vɛəst, vɜ:st) *n* a unit of length, used in Russia, equal to 1.067 kilometres (0.6629 miles). [C16: from French *verste* or German *Werst,* from Russian *versta* line]

versus ('vɜ:səs) *prep* **1** (esp. in a competition or lawsuit) against; in opposition to. Abbrev.: **v.**, (esp. U.S.) **vs. 2** as opposed to; in contrast with. [C15: from Latin: turned (in the direction of), opposite, from *vertere* to turn]

vert (vɜ:t) *n* **1** *English legal history.* **1a** the right to cut green wood in a forest. **1b** the wood itself. **2** *Heraldry.* **2a** the colour green. **2b** (*as adj, usually postpositive*): *a table vert.* [C15: from Old French *verd,* from Latin *viridis* green, from *virēre* to grow green]

vert. *abbrev. for* vertical.

vertebra ('vɜ:tɪbrə) *n, pl* **-brae** (-bri:) *or* **-bras.** one of the bony segments of the spinal column. [C17: from Latin: joint of the spine, from *vertere* to turn] ▸ **'vertebral** *adj* ▸ **'vertebrally** *adv*

vertebral column *n* another name for **spinal column.**

vertebrate ('vɜ:tɪˌbreɪt, -brɪt) *n* **1** any chordate animal of the subphylum *Vertebrata,* characterized by a bony or cartilaginous skeleton and a well-developed brain: the group contains fishes, amphibians, reptiles, birds, and mammals. ◆ *adj* **2** of, relating to, or belonging to the subphylum *Vertebrata.*

vertebration (ˌvɜ:tɪ'breɪʃən) *n* the formation of vertebrae or segmentation resembling vertebrae.

vertex ('vɜ:tɛks) *n, pl* **-texes** *or* **-tices** (-tɪˌsi:z). **1** the highest point. **2** *Maths.* **2a** the point opposite the base of a figure. **2b** the point of intersection of two sides of a plane figure or angle. **2c** the point of intersection of a pencil of lines or three or more planes of a solid figure. **3** *Astronomy.* a point in the sky towards which a star stream appears to move. **4** *Anatomy.* the crown of the head. [C16: from Latin: highest point, from *vertere* to turn]

vertical ('vɜ:tɪkᵊl) *adj* **1** at right angles to the horizon; perpendicular; upright: *a vertical wall.* Compare **horizontal** (sense 1). **2** extending in a perpendicular direction. **3** at or in the vertex or zenith; directly overhead. **4** *Economics.* of or relating to associated or consecutive, though not identical, stages of industrial activity: *vertical integration; vertical amalgamation.* **5** of or relating to the vertex. **6** *Anatomy.* of, relating to, or situated at the top of the head (vertex). ◆ *n* **7** a vertical plane, position, or line. **8** a vertical post, pillar, or other structural member. [C16: from Late Latin *verticālis,* from Latin VERTEX] ▸ **ˌverti'cality** *n* ▸ **'vertically** *adv*

vertical angles *pl n Geometry.* the pair of equal angles between a pair of intersecting lines; opposite angles. Also called: **vertically opposite angles.**

vertical circle *n Astronomy.* a great circle on the celestial sphere passing through the zenith and perpendicular to the horizon.

vertical grouping *n* another term for **family grouping.**

vertical mobility *n Sociol.* the movement of individuals or groups to positions in society that involve a change in class, status, and power. Compare **horizontal mobility.** See also **upward mobility, downward mobility.**

vertical stabilizer *n* the U.S. name for **fin**[1] (sense 3a).

vertical union *n* another name (esp. U.S.) for **industrial union.**

vertices ('vɜ:tɪˌsi:z) *n* a plural of **vertex** (in technical and scientific senses only).

verticil ('vɜ:tɪsɪl) *n Biology.* a circular arrangement of parts about an axis, esp. leaves around a stem. [C18: from Latin *verticillus* whorl (of a spindle), from VERTEX]

verticillaster (ˌvɜ:tɪsɪ'læstə) *n Botany.* an inflorescence, such as that of the dead-nettle, that resembles a whorl but consists of two crowded cymes on either side of the stem. [C19: from New Latin; see VERTICIL, -ASTER] ▸ **verticillastrate** (ˌvɜ:tɪsɪ'læsˌtreɪt, -trɪt) *adj*

verticillate (vɜ:'tɪsɪlɪt, -ˌleɪt; ˌvɜ:tɪ'sɪleɪt) *adj Biology.* having or arranged in whorls or verticils. ▸ **ver'ticillately** *adv* ▸ **verˌticil'lation** *n*

vertiginous (vɜ:'tɪdʒɪnəs) *adj* **1** of, relating to, or having vertigo. **2** producing dizziness. **3** whirling. **4** changeable; unstable. [C17: from Latin *vertīginōsus,* from VERTIGO] ▸ **ver'tiginously** *adv* ▸ **ver'tiginousness** *n*

vertigo ('vɜ:tɪˌgəʊ) *n, pl* **vertigoes** *or* **vertigines** (vɜ:'tɪdʒɪˌni:z). *Pathol.* a sensation of dizziness or abnormal motion resulting from a disorder of the sense of balance. [C16: from Latin: a whirling round, from *vertere* to turn]

vertu (vɜ:'tu:) *n* a variant spelling of **virtu.**

Vertumnus (vɜ:'tʌmnəs) *or* **Vortumnus** *n* a Roman god of gardens, orchards, and seasonal change. [from Latin, from *vertere* to turn, change]

Verulamium (ˌvɛrʊ'leɪmɪəm) *n* the Latin name of **Saint Albans.**

vervain ('vɜ:veɪn) *n* any of several verbenaceous plants of the genus *Verbena,* having square stems and long slender spikes of purple, blue, or white flowers. [C14: from Old French *verveine,* from Latin *verbēna* sacred bough; see VERBENA]

verve (vɜ:v) *n* **1** great vitality, enthusiasm, and liveliness; sparkle. **2** a rare word for **talent.** [C17: from Old French: garrulity, from Latin *verba* words, chatter]

vervet ('vɜ:vɪt) *n* a variety of a South African guenon monkey, *Cercopithecus aethiops,* having dark hair on the hands and feet and a reddish patch beneath the tail. Compare **green monkey, grivet.** [C19: from French, from *vert* green, but influenced by GRIVET]

Verwoerd (fə'vʊt, fɛə'vʊət) *n* **Hendrik Frensch** ('hɛndrɪk frɛns). 1901–66, South African statesman, born in the Netherlands: prime minister of South Africa (1958–66) and the principal architect of the apartheid system: assassinated.

very ('vɛrɪ) *adv* **1** (intensifier) used to add emphasis to adjectives that are able to be graded: *very good; very tall.* ◆ *adj* (*prenominal*) **2** (intensifier) used with nouns preceded by a definite article or possessive determiner, in order to give emphasis to the significance, appropriateness or relevance of a noun in a particular context, or to give exaggerated intensity to certain nouns: *the very man I want to see; his very name struck terror; the very back of the room.* **3** (intensifier) used in metaphors to emphasize the applicability of the image to the situation described: *he was a very lion in the fight.* **4** *Archaic.* **4a** real or true; genuine: *the very living God.* **4b** lawful: *the very vengeance of the gods.* [C13: from Old French *verai* true, from Latin *vērax* true, from *vērus* true]

USAGE In strict usage adverbs of degree such as *very, too, quite, really,* and *extremely* are used only to qualify adjectives: *he is very happy; she is too sad.* By this rule, these words should not be used to qualify past participles that follow the verb *to be,* since they would then be technically qualifying verbs. With the exception of certain participles, such as *tired* or *disappointed,* that have come to be regarded as adjectives, all other past participles are qualified by adverbs such as *much, greatly, seriously,* or *excessively: he has been much* (not *very*) *inconvenienced; she has been excessively* (not *too*) *criticized.*

very high frequency *n* a radio-frequency band or radio frequency lying between 30 and 300 megahertz. Abbrev.: **VHF.**

very large-scale integration *n Computing.* the process of fabricating a few thousand logic gates or more in a single integrated circuit. Abbrev.: **VLSI.**

Very light ('vɛrɪ) *n* a coloured flare fired from a special pistol (**Very pistol**) for signalling at night, esp. at sea. [C19: named after Edward W. *Very* (1852–1910), U.S. naval ordnance officer]

very low frequency *n* a radio-frequency band or radio frequency lying between 3 and 30 kilohertz. Abbrev.: **VLF.**

Very Reverend *n* a title of respect for a variety of ecclesiastical officials, such as deans and the superiors of some religious houses.

Vesalius (vɪ'seɪlɪəs) *n* **Andreas** (an'dre:as). 1514–64, Flemish anatomist, whose *De Humani Corporis fabrica* (1543) formed the basis of modern anatomical research and medicine.

vesica ('vɛsɪkə) *n, pl* **-cae** (-ˌsi:). **1** *Anatomy.* a technical name for **bladder** (sense 1). **2** (in medieval sculpture and painting) an aureole in the shape of a pointed oval. [C17: from Latin: bladder, sac, blister]

vesical ('vɛsɪkᵊl) *adj* of or relating to a vesica, esp. the urinary bladder.

vesicant ('vɛsɪkənt) *or* **vesicatory** ('vɛsɪˌkeɪtərɪ) *n, pl* **-cants** *or* **-catories. 1** any substance that causes blisters, used in medicine and in chemical warfare. ◆ *adj* **2** acting as a vesicant. [C19: see VESICA]

vesicate ('vɛsɪˌkeɪt) *vb* to blister. [C17: from New Latin *vēsīcāre* to blister; see VESICA] ▸ **ˌvesi'cation** *n*

vesicle ('vɛsɪkᵊl) *n* **1** *Pathol.* **1a** any small sac or cavity, esp. one containing serous fluid. **1b** a blister. **2** *Geology.* a rounded cavity within a rock formed during solidification by expansion of the gases present in the magma. **3** *Botany.* a small bladder-like cavity occurring in certain seaweeds and aquatic plants. **4** any small cavity or cell. [C16: from Latin *vēsīcula,* diminutive of VESICA] ▸ **vesicular** (vɛ'sɪkjʊlə) *adj* ▸ **ve'sicularly** *adv*

vesiculate *vb* (vɛ'sɪkjʊˌleɪt). **1** to make (an organ or part) vesicular or (of an organ or part) to become vesicular. ◆ *adj* (vɛ'sɪkjʊlɪt, -ˌleɪt). **2** containing, resembling, or characterized by a vesicle or vesicles. ▸ **veˌsicu'lation** *n*

Vespasian (vɛs'peɪʒɪən) *n* Latin name *Titus Flavius Sabinus Vespasianus.* 9–79 A.D., Roman emperor (69–79), who consolidated Roman rule, esp. in Britain and Germany. He began the building of the Colosseum.

vesper ('vɛspə) *n* **1** an evening prayer, service, or hymn. **2** an archaic word for **evening. 3** (*modifier*) of or relating to vespers. ◆ See also **vespers.** [C14: from Latin: evening, the evening star; compare Greek *hesperos* evening; see WEST]

Vesper ('vɛspə) *n* the planet Venus, when appearing as the evening star.

vesperal ('vɛspərəl) *n Christianity.* **1** a liturgical book containing the prayers, psalms, and hymns used at vespers. **2** the part of the antiphonary containing these. **3** a cloth laid over the altar cloth between offices or services.

vespers ('vɛspəz) *n* (*functioning as sing or pl*) **1** *Chiefly R.C. Church.* the sixth of the seven canonical hours of the divine office, originally fixed for the early evening and now often made a public service on Sundays and major feast days. **2** another word for **evensong** (sense 1).

vespertilionine (ˌvɛspə'tɪlɪəˌnaɪn, -nɪn) *adj* of, relating to, or belonging to the *Vespertilionidae,* a family of common and widespread bats. [C17: from Latin *vespertīliō* a bat, from *vesper* evening] ▸ **vespertilionid** (ˌvɛspə'tɪlɪənɪd) *adj, n*

vespertine ('vɛspəˌtaɪn) *adj* **1** *Botany, zoology.* appearing, opening, or active in the evening: *vespertine flowers.* **2** occurring in the evening or (esp. of stars) appearing or setting in the evening.

vespiary ('vɛspɪərɪ) *n, pl* **-aries.** a nest or colony of social wasps or hornets. [C19: from Latin *vespa* a wasp, on the model of *apiary*]

vespid ('vɛspɪd) *n* **1** any hymenopterous insect of the family *Vespidae,* including the common wasps and hornets. ◆ *adj* **2** of, relating to, or belonging to the family *Vespidae.* [C19: from New Latin *Vespidae,* from Latin *vespa* a wasp]

vespine ('vɛspaɪn) *adj* of, relating to, or resembling a wasp or wasps. [C19: from Latin *vespa* a wasp]

Vespucci (vɛ'spu:tʃɪ) *n* **Amerigo** (ame'ri:go), Latin name *Americus Vespucius.* ?1454–1512, Florentine navigator in the New World (1499–1500; 1501–02), after whom the continent of America was named.

vessel ('vɛsᵊl) *n* **1** any object used as a container, esp. for a liquid. **2** a passenger or freight-carrying ship, boat, etc. **3** an aircraft, esp. an airship. **4** *Anatomy.* a tubular structure that transports such body fluids as blood and lymph. **5** *Botany.* a tubular element of xylem tissue consisting of a row of cells in which the connecting cell walls have broken down. **6** *Rare.* a person regarded as an agent or vehicle for some purpose or quality: *she was the vessel of the Lord.* [C13: from Old French *vaissel,* from Late Latin *vascellum* urn, from Latin *vās* vessel]

vest (vɛst) *n* **1** an undergarment covering the body from the shoulders to the hips, made of cotton, nylon, etc. U.S. and Canadian equivalent: **T-shirt, undershirt.** Austral. equivalent: **singlet. 2** a similar sleeveless garment worn as outerwear. Austral. equivalent: **singlet. 3** the usual U.S., Canadian, and Austral. word for **waistcoat. 4** *Obsolete.* any form of dress, esp. a long robe. ◆ *vb* **5** (*tr;* foll. by *in*) to place or settle (power, rights, etc., in): *power was vested in the committee.* **6** (*tr;* foll. by *with*) to bestow or confer (on): *the company was* *vested with authority.* **7** (usually foll. by *in*) to confer (a right, title, property, etc., upon) or (of a right, title, etc.) to pass (to) or devolve (upon). **8** (*tr*) to clothe or array. **9** (*intr*) to put on clothes, ecclesiastical vestments, etc. **[C15:** from Old French *vestir* to clothe, from Latin *vestīre,* from *vestis* clothing**]** ▸ **'vestless** *adj* ▸ **'vest,like** *adj*

vesta ('vɛstə) *n* a short friction match, usually of wood. **[C19:** named after the goddess; see VESTA[1]**]**

Vesta[1] ('vɛstə) *n* the Roman goddess of the hearth and its fire. In her temple a perpetual flame was tended by the vestal virgins. Greek counterpart: **Hestia.**

Vesta[2] ('vɛstə) *n* the brightest of the four largest asteroids. Diameter: about 530 km (240 miles). **[C19:** named after the goddess; see VESTA[1]**]**

vestal ('vɛstᵊl) *adj* **1** chaste or pure; virginal. **2** of or relating to the Roman goddess Vesta. ◆ *n* **3** a chaste woman; virgin. **4** a rare word for **nun**[1] (sense 1).

vestal virgin *n* (in ancient Rome) one of the four, later six, virgin priestesses whose lives were dedicated to Vesta and to maintaining the sacred fire in her temple.

vested ('vɛstɪd) *adj Property law.* having a present right to the immediate or future possession and enjoyment of property. Compare **contingent.**

vested interest *n* **1** *Property law.* an existing and disposable right to the immediate or future possession and enjoyment of property. **2** a strong personal concern in a state of affairs, system, etc., usually resulting in private gain. **3** a person or group that has such an interest.

vestiary ('vɛstɪərɪ) *n, pl* **-aries. 1** *Obsolete.* a room for storing clothes or dressing in, such as a vestry. ◆ *adj* **2** *Rare.* of or relating to clothes. **[C17:** from Late Latin *vestiārius,* from *vestis* clothing**]**

vestibular system *n* the sensory mechanism in the inner ear that detects movement of the head and helps to control balance.

vestibule ('vɛstɪ,bjuːl) *n* **1** a small entrance hall or anteroom; lobby. **2** any small bodily cavity or space at the entrance to a passage or canal. **[C17:** from Latin *vestibulum***]** ▸ **vestibular** (vɛ'stɪbjulə) *adj*

vestige ('vɛstɪdʒ) *n* **1** a small trace, mark, or amount; hint: *a vestige of truth; no vestige of the meal.* **2** *Biology.* an organ or part of an organism that is a small nonfunctioning remnant of a functional organ in an ancestor. **[C17:** via French from Latin *vestīgium* track**]**

vestigial (vɛ'stɪdʒɪəl) *adj* **1** of, relating to, or being a vestige. **2** (of certain organs or parts of organisms) having attained a simple structure and reduced size and function during the evolution of the species: *the vestigial pelvic girdle of a snake.* ▸ **ves'tigially** *adv*

Vestmannaeyjar (,vestmæn'erjɑː) *n* a group of islands off the S coast of Iceland: they include the island of Surtsey (emerged 1963) and the volcano Helgafell (erupted 1974). Pop.: 4888 (1994). English name: **Vestmann Islands.**

vestment ('vɛstmənt) *n* **1** a garment or robe, esp. one denoting office, authority, or rank. **2** any of various ceremonial garments worn by the clergy at religious services. **[C13:** from Old French *vestiment,* from Latin *vestīmentum* clothing, from *vestīre* to clothe**]** ▸ **vestmental** (vɛst'mɛntᵊl) *adj*

vest-pocket *n* (*modifier*) *Chiefly U.S.* small enough to fit into a waistcoat pocket.

vestry ('vɛstrɪ) *n, pl* **-tries. 1** a room in or attached to a church in which vestments, sacred vessels, etc., are kept. **2** a room in or attached to some churches, used for Sunday school, meetings, etc. **3a** *Church of England.* a meeting of all the members of a parish or their representatives, to transact the official business of the parish. **3b** the body of members meeting for this; the parish council. **4** *Episcopalian* (*U.S.*) *and Anglican* (*Canadian*) *Churches.* a committee of vestrymen chosen by the congregation to manage the temporal affairs of their church. **[C14:** probably from Old French *vestiarie;* see VEST**]** ▸ **'vestral** *adj*

vestryman ('vɛstrɪmən) *n, pl* **-men.** a member of a church vestry.

vesture ('vɛstʃə) *n* **1** *Archaic.* a garment or something that seems like a garment: *a vesture of cloud.* **2** *Law.* **2a** everything except trees that grows on the land. **2b** a product of the land, such as grass, wheat, etc. ◆ *vb* **3** (*tr*) *Archaic.* to clothe. **[C14:** from Old French, from *vestir,* from Latin *vestīre,* from *vestis* clothing**]** ▸ **'vestural** *adj*

vesuvian (vɪ'suːvɪən) *n* **1** (esp. formerly) a match for lighting cigars; fusee. **2** another name for **vesuvianite. [C18** (the mineral), **C19** (the match): both named after VESUVIUS**]**

vesuvianite (vɪ'suːvɪə,naɪt) *n* a green, brown, or yellow mineral consisting of a hydrated silicate of calcium, magnesium, iron, and aluminium: it occurs as tetragonal crystals in limestones and is used as a gemstone. Formula: $Ca_{10}Al_4(MgFe)_2Si_9O_{34}(OH)_4$. Also called: **idocrase, vesuvian. [C19:** first found in the lava of VESUVIUS**]**

Vesuvius (vɪ'suːvɪəs) *n* a volcano in SW Italy, on the Bay of Naples: first recorded eruption in 79 A.D., which destroyed Pompeii, Herculaneum, and Stabiae; numerous eruptions since then. Average height: 1220 m (4003 ft.). Italian name: **Vesuvio** (ve'zuːvjo).

vet[1] (vɛt) *n* **1** short for **veterinary surgeon.** ◆ *vb* **vets, vetting, vetted. 2** (*tr*) *Chiefly Brit.* to make a prior examination and critical appraisal of (a person, document, scheme, etc.): *the candidates were well vetted.* See also **positive vetting. 3** to examine, treat, or cure (an animal).

vet[2] (vɛt) *n U.S. and Canadian.* short for **veteran** (senses 2, 3).

vet. *abbrev. for:* **1** veteran. **2** veterinarian. **3** veterinary. ◆ Also (for senses 2, 3): **veter.**

vetch (vɛtʃ) *n* **1** any of various climbing papilionaceous plants of the temperate genus *Vicia,* esp. *V. sativa,* having pinnate leaves, typically blue or purple flowers, and tendrils on the stems. **2** any of various similar and related plants, such as *Lathyrus sativus,* cultivated in parts of Europe, and the kidney vetch. **3** the beanlike fruit of any of these plants. **[C14** *fecche,* from Old French *veche,* from Latin *vicia***]**

vetchling ('vɛtʃlɪŋ) *n* any of various papilionaceous tendril-climbing plants of the genus *Lathyrus,* esp. *L. pratensis* (**meadow vetchling**), mainly of N temperate regions, having winged or angled stems and showy flowers. See also **sweet pea.**

veteran ('vɛtərən, 'vɛtrən) *n* **1a** a person or thing that has given long service in some capacity. **1b** (*as modifier*): *veteran firemen.* **2a** a soldier who has seen considerable active service. **2b** (*as modifier*): *veteran soldier.* **3** *U.S. and Canadian.* a person who has served in the military forces. **4** See **veteran car. [C16:** from Latin *veterānus,* from *vetus* old**]**

veteran car *n Brit.* a car constructed before 1919, esp. one constructed before 1905. Compare **vintage car.**

Veterans Day *n* the U.S. equivalent of **Armistice Day.**

veterinarian (,vɛtərɪ'nɛərɪən, ,vɛtrɪ-) *n* the U.S. and Canadian term for **veterinary surgeon.**

veterinary ('vɛtərɪnərɪ, 'vɛtrɪnrɪ) *adj* of or relating to veterinary medicine. **[C18:** from Latin *veterīnārius* concerning draught animals, from *veterīnae* draught animals; related to *vetus* mature (hence able to bear a burden)**]**

veterinary medicine *or* **science** *n* the branch of medicine concerned with the health of animals and the treatment of injuries or diseases that affect them.

veterinary surgeon *n Brit.* a person skilled in the practice of veterinary medicine. U.S. and Canadian term: **veterinarian.**

vetiver ('vɛtɪvə) *n* **1** a tall hairless grass, *Vetiveria zizanioides,* of tropical and subtropical Asia, having aromatic roots and stiff long narrow ornamental leaves. **2** the root of this plant used for making screens, mats, etc., and yielding a fragrant oil used in perfumery, medicine, etc. **[C19:** from French *vétiver,* from Tamil *vettivēru***]**

veto ('viːtəʊ) *n, pl* **-toes. 1** the power to prevent legislation or action proposed by others; prohibition: *the presidential veto.* **2** the exercise of this power. **3** Also called: **veto message.** *U.S. government.* a document containing the reasons why a chief executive has vetoed a measure. ◆ *vb* **-toes, -toing, -toed.** (*tr*) **4** to refuse consent to (a proposal, esp. a government bill). **5** to prohibit, ban, or forbid: *her parents vetoed her trip.* **[C17:** from Latin: I forbid, from *vetāre* to forbid**]** ▸ **'vetoer** *n* ▸ **'vetoless** *adj*

vex (vɛks) *vb* (*tr*) **1** to anger or annoy. **2** to confuse; worry. **3** *Archaic.* to agitate. **[C15:** from Old French *vexer,* from Latin *vexāre* to jolt (in carrying), from *vehere* to convey**]** ▸ **'vexer** *n* ▸ **'vexing** *adj* ▸ **'vexingly** *adv*

vexation (vɛk'seɪʃən) *n* **1** the act of vexing or the state of being vexed. **2** something that vexes.

vexatious (vɛk'seɪʃəs) *adj* **1** vexing or tending to vex. **2** vexed. **3** *Law.* (of a legal action or proceeding) instituted without sufficient grounds, esp. so as to cause annoyance or embarrassment to the defendant: *vexatious litigation.* ▸ **vex'atiously** *adv* ▸ **vex'atiousness** *n*

vexed (vɛkst) *adj* **1** annoyed, confused, or agitated. **2** much debated and discussed (esp. in the phrase **a vexed question**). ▸ **vexedly** ('vɛksɪdlɪ) *adv* ▸ **'vexedness** *n*

vexillology (,vɛksɪ'lɒlədʒɪ) *n* the study and collection of information about flags. **[C20:** from Latin *vexillum* flag + -LOGY**]** ▸ **,vexil'lologist** *n*

vexillum (vɛk'sɪləm) *n, pl* **-la** (-lə). **1** *Ornithol.* the vane of a feather. **2** *Botany.* another name for **standard** (sense 16). **[C18:** from Latin: banner, perhaps from *vēlum* sail**]** ▸ **'vexillary** *or* **vex'illar** *adj* ▸ **'vexillate** *adj*

VF *abbrev. for* video frequency.

VFA (in Australia) *abbrev. for* Victorian Football Association.

VFL (in Australia) *abbrev. for* Victorian Football League.

vg *abbrev. for* very good.

VG *abbrev. for* Vicar General.

VGA *abbrev. for* video graphics display; a computing standard that has a resolution of 640 × 480 pixels with 16 colours or of 320 × 200 pixels with 256 colours. **SVGA** (**super VGA**) is a later version with higher spatial and colour resolution, esp. 800 × 600 pixels with 256 colours.

VHF *or* **vhf** *Radio. abbrev. for* very high frequency.

VHS *Trademark. abbrev. for* video home system: a video cassette recording system using ½″ magnetic tape.

vi *abbrev. for* vide infra.

VI *abbrev. for:* **1** Vancouver Island. **2** Virgin Islands.

via ('vaɪə) *prep* by way of; by means of; through: *to London via Paris.* **[C18:** from Latin *viā,* from *via* way**]**

viable ('vaɪəbᵊl) *adj* **1** capable of becoming actual, useful, etc.; practicable: *a viable proposition.* **2** (of seeds, eggs, etc.) capable of normal growth and development. **3** (of a fetus) having reached a stage of development at which further development can occur independently of the mother. **[C19:** from French, from *vie* life, from Latin *vīta***]** ▸ **,via'bility** *n*

Via Dolorosa ('viːə ,dɒlə'rəʊsə) *n* **1** the route followed by Christ from the place of his condemnation to Calvary for his crucifixion. **2** an arduous or distressing course or experience. **[**Latin, literally: sorrowful road**]**

viaduct ('vaɪə,dʌkt) *n* a bridge, esp. for carrying a road or railway across a valley, etc., consisting of a set of arches supported by a row of piers or towers. **[C19:** from Latin *via* way + *dūcere* to bring, on the model of *aqueduct***]**

Viagra (vaɪ'ægrə, viː-) *n Trademark.* a drug that allows increased blood flow into the penis; used to treat impotence in men.

vial ('vaɪəl, vaɪl) *n* a less common variant of **phial. [C14** *fiole,* from Old French, from Old Provençal *fiola,* from Latin *phiala,* from Greek *phialē;* see PHIAL**]**

via media *Latin.* ('vaɪə 'miːdɪə) *n* a compromise between two extremes; middle course.

viand ('viːənd, 'vaɪ-) *n* **1** a type of food, esp. a delicacy. **2** (*pl*) provisions. **[C14:** from Old French *viande,* ultimately from Latin *vīvenda* things to be lived on, from *vīvere* to live**]**

Viareggio (*Italian* via'reddʒo) *n* a town and resort in W Italy, in Tuscany on the Ligurian Sea. Pop.: 50 310 (1987 est.).

viatical (vaɪ'ætɪkᵊl) *adj* **1** of or denoting a road or a journey. **2** *Botany.* (of a plant) growing by the side of a road. [C19: from Latin *viāticus* belonging to a journey + -AL[1]]

viatical settlement *n* the purchase by a charity of a life assurance policy owned by a person with only a short time to live, to enable that person to use the proceeds during his or her lifetime. See also **death futures**.

viaticum (vaɪˈætɪkəm) *n, pl* **-ca** (-kə) *or* **-cums. 1** *Christianity.* Holy Communion as administered to a person dying or in danger of death. **2** *Rare.* provisions or a travel allowance for a journey. [C16: from Latin, from *viāticus* belonging to a journey, from *viāre* to travel, from *via* way]

viator (vaɪˈeɪtɔː) *n, pl* **viatores** (ˌvaɪəˈtɔːriːz). *Rare.* a traveller. [C16: from Latin, from *viāre* to travel]

vibes (vaɪbz) *pl n* **1** *Informal.* (esp. in jazz) short for **vibraphone. 2** *Slang.* short for **vibrations.**

vibist (ˈvaɪbɪst) *n Informal.* a person who plays a vibraphone in a jazz band or group.

Viborg *n* **1** (ˈviːbɔrj). the Swedish name for **Vyborg. 2** (*Danish* ˈvibɔr). a town in N central Denmark, in Jutland: formerly a royal town and capital of Jutland. Pop.: 29 455 (1990).

vibraculum (vaɪˈbrækjʊləm) *n, pl* **-la** (-lə). *Zoology.* any of the specialized bristle-like polyps in certain bryozoans, the actions of which prevent parasites from settling on the colony. [C19: from New Latin, from Latin *vibrāre* to brandish] ▸ **viˈbracular** *adj* ▸ **viˈbracuˌloid** *adj*

Vibram (ˈvaɪbrəm) *n Trademark.* a special type of moulded rubber sole, widely used for climbing and walking boots. [C20: from *Vi(tale) Bram(ini)*, Italian climber who devised the product]

vibrant (ˈvaɪbrənt) *adj* **1** characterized by or exhibiting vibration; pulsating or trembling. **2** giving an impression of vigour and activity. **3** caused by vibration; resonant. **4** *Phonetics.* trilled or rolled. ◆ *n* **5** a vibrant speech sound, such as a trilled (r). [C16: from Latin *vibrāre* to agitate] ▸ **ˈvibrancy** *n* ▸ **ˈvibrantly** *adv*

vibraphone (ˈvaɪbrəˌfəʊn) *or esp. U.S.* **vibraharp** (ˈvaɪbrəˌhɑːp) *n* a percussion instrument, used esp. in jazz, consisting of a set of metal bars placed over tubular metal resonators, which are made to vibrate electronically. ▸ **ˈvibraˌphonist** *n*

vibrate (vaɪˈbreɪt) *vb* **1** to move or cause to move back and forth rapidly; shake, quiver, or throb. **2** (*intr*) to oscillate. **3** to send out (a sound) by vibration; resonate or cause to resonate. **4** (*intr*) to waver. **5** *Physics.* to undergo or cause to undergo an oscillatory or periodic process, as of an alternating current; oscillate. **6** (*intr*) *Rare.* to respond emotionally; thrill. [C17: from Latin *vibrāre*] ▸ **vibratile** (ˈvaɪbrəˌtaɪl) *adj* ▸ **viˈbrating** *adj* ▸ **viˈbratingly** *adv* ▸ **ˈvibratory** *adj*

vibration (vaɪˈbreɪʃən) *n* **1** the act or an instance of vibrating. **2** *Physics.* **2a** a periodic motion about an equilibrium position, such as the regular displacement of air in the propagation of sound. **2b** a single cycle of such a motion. **3** the process or state of vibrating or being vibrated. ▸ **viˈbrational** *adj* ▸ **viˈbrationless** *adj*

vibrations (vaɪˈbreɪʃənz) *pl n Slang.* **1** instinctive feelings supposedly influencing human communication. **2** a characteristic atmosphere felt to be emanating from places or objects. ◆ Often shortened to **vibes.**

vibrato (vɪˈbrɑːtəʊ) *n, pl* **-tos.** *Music.* **1** a slight, rapid, and regular fluctuation in the pitch of a note produced on a stringed instrument by a shaking movement of the hand stopping the strings. **2** an oscillatory effect produced in singing by fluctuation in breath pressure or pitch. ◆ Compare **tremolo.** [C19: from Italian, from Latin *vibrāre* to VIBRATE]

vibrator (vaɪˈbreɪtə) *n* **1a** a device for producing a vibratory motion, such as one used in massage. **1b** such a device with a vibrating part or tip, used as a dildo. **2** a device in which a vibrating conductor interrupts a circuit to produce a pulsating current from a steady current, usually so that the current can then be amplified or the voltage transformed. See also **chopper** (sense 6).

vibrio (ˈvɪbrɪˌəʊ) *n, pl* **-os.** any curved or spiral rodlike Gram-negative bacterium of the genus *Vibrio,* esp. the comma bacillus: family *Spirillaceae.* [C19: from New Latin, from Latin *vibrāre* to VIBRATE] ▸ **ˈvibriˌoid** *adj*

vibrissa (vaɪˈbrɪsə) *n, pl* **-sae** (-siː). (*usually pl*) **1** any of the bristle-like sensitive hairs on the face of many mammals; a whisker. **2** any of the specialized bristle-like feathers around the beak in certain insectivorous birds. [C17: from Latin, probably from *vibrāre* to shake] ▸ **viˈbrissal** *adj*

vibronic (vaɪˈbrɒnɪk) *adj Physics.* of, concerned with, or involving both electronic and vibrational energy levels: *a vibronic spectrum; a vibronic transition.* [C20: from *vibr(atory + electr)onic*]

Vibropac block (ˈvaɪbrəʊˌpæk) *n N.Z. trademark.* a precast concrete building block.

viburnum (vaɪˈbɜːnəm) *n* **1** any of various temperate and subtropical caprifoliaceous shrubs or trees of the genus *Viburnum,* such as the wayfaring tree, having small white flowers and berry-like red or black fruits. **2** the dried bark of several species of this tree, sometimes used in medicine. [C18: from Latin: wayfaring tree]

Vic. *Austral. abbrev. for* Victoria (the state).

vicar (ˈvɪkə) *n* **1** *Church of England.* **1a** (in Britain) a clergyman appointed to act as priest of a parish from which, formerly, he did not receive tithes but a stipend. **1b** a clergyman who acts as assistant to or substitute for the rector of a parish at Communion. **1c** (in the U.S.) a clergyman in charge of a chapel. **2** *R.C. Church.* a bishop or priest representing the pope or the ordinary of a diocese and exercising a limited jurisdiction. **3** Also called: **lay vicar, vicar choral.** *Church of England.* a member of a cathedral choir appointed to sing certain parts of the services. **4** a person appointed to do the work of another. [C13: from Old French *vicaire,* from Latin *vicārius* (n) a deputy, from *vicārius* (adj) VICARIOUS] ▸ **ˈvicarly** *adj*

vicarage (ˈvɪkərɪdʒ) *n* **1** the residence or benefice of a vicar. **2** a rare word for **vicariate** (sense 1).

vicar apostolic *n R.C. Church.* a titular bishop having jurisdiction in non-Catholic or missionary countries where the normal hierarchy has not yet been established.

vicar forane (fɒˈreɪn) *n, pl* **vicars forane.** *R.C. Church.* a priest or bishop appointed by the ordinary of the diocese to exercise a limited jurisdiction in a locality at some distance from the ordinary's official see. [*forane,* from Late Latin *forāneus* in a foreign land, from Latin *forās* outside]

vicar general *n, pl* **vicars general.** an official, usually a layman, appointed to assist the bishop of a diocese in discharging his administrative or judicial duties.

vicarial (vɪˈkeərɪəl, vaɪ-) *adj* **1** of or relating to a vicar, vicars, or a vicariate. **2** holding the office of a vicar. **3** vicarious: used esp. of certain ecclesiastical powers.

vicariate (vɪˈkeərɪɪt, vaɪ-) *n* **1** Also called: **vicarship** (ˈvɪkəʃɪp). the office, rank, or authority of a vicar. **2** the district that a vicar holds as his pastoral charge.

vicarious (vɪˈkeərɪəs, vaɪ-) *adj* **1** obtained or undergone at second hand through sympathetic participation in another's experiences. **2** suffered, undergone, or done as the substitute for another: *vicarious punishment.* **3** delegated: *vicarious authority.* **4** taking the place of another. **5** *Pathol.* (of menstrual bleeding) occurring at an abnormal site. See **endometriosis.** [C17: from Latin *vicārius* substituted, from *vicis* interchange; see VICE[3], VICISSITUDE] ▸ **viˈcariously** *adv* ▸ **viˈcariousness** *n*

Vicar of Bray (breɪ) *n* **1** a vicar (Simon Aleyn) appointed to the parish of Bray in Berkshire during Henry VIII's reign who changed his faith to Catholic when Mary I was on the throne and back to Protestant when Elizabeth I succeeded and so retained his living. **2** Also called: **In Good King Charles's Golden Days.** a ballad in which the vicar's changes of faith are transposed to the Stuart period. **3** a person who changes his or her views or allegiances in accordance with what is suitable at the time.

Vicar of Christ *n R.C. Church.* the pope when regarded as Christ's earthly representative.

vice[1] (vaɪs) *n* **1** an immoral, wicked, or evil habit, action, or trait. **2** habitual or frequent indulgence in pernicious, immoral, or degrading practices. **3** a specific form of pernicious conduct, esp. prostitution or sexual perversion. **4** a failing or imperfection in character, conduct, etc.: *smoking is his only vice.* **5** *Pathol., obsolete.* any physical defect or imperfection. **6** a bad trick or disposition, as of horses, dogs, etc. [C13: via Old French from Latin *vitium* a defect] ▸ **ˈviceless** *adj*

vice[2] *or U.S.* (*often*) **vise** (vaɪs) *n* **1** an appliance for holding an object while work is done upon it, usually having a pair of jaws. ◆ *vb* **2** (*tr*) to grip (something) with or as if with a vice. [C15: from Old French *vis* a screw, from Latin *vītis* vine, plant with spiralling tendrils (hence the later meaning)] ▸ **ˈviceˌlike** *or U.S.* (*often*) **ˈviseˌlike** *adj*

vice[3] (vaɪs) *adj* **1a** (*prenominal*) serving in the place of or as a deputy for. **1b** (*in combination*): *viceroy.* ◆ *n* **2** *Informal.* a person who serves as a deputy to another. [C18: from Latin *vice,* from *vicis* interchange]

vice[4] (ˈvaɪsɪ) *prep* instead of; as a substitute for. [C16: from Latin, ablative of *vicis* change]

Vice (vaɪs) *n* (in English morality plays) a character personifying a particular vice or vice in general.

vice admiral *n* a commissioned officer of flag rank in certain navies, junior to an admiral and senior to a rear admiral. ▸ **ˌvice-ˈadmiralty** *n*

vice-chairman *n, pl* **-men.** a person who deputizes for a chairman and serves in his place during his absence or indisposition. ▸ **ˌvice-ˈchairmanship** *n*

vice chancellor *n* **1** the chief executive or administrator at some British universities. Compare **chancellor** (sense 3). **2** (in the U.S.) a judge in courts of equity subordinate to the chancellor. **3** (formerly in England) a senior judge of the court of chancery who acted as assistant to the Lord Chancellor. **4** a person serving as the deputy of a chancellor. ▸ **ˌvice-ˈchancellorship** *n*

vicegerent (ˌvaɪsˈdʒɛrənt) *n* **1** a person appointed to exercise all or some of the authority of another, esp. the administrative powers of a ruler; deputy. **2** *R.C. Church.* the pope or any other representative of God or Christ on earth, such as a bishop. ◆ *adj* **3** invested with or characterized by delegated authority. [C16: from New Latin *vicegerēns,* from VICE[3] + Latin *gerere* to manage] ▸ **ˌviceˈgeral** *adj* ▸ **ˌviceˈgerency** *n*

vicenary (ˈvɪsɪnərɪ) *adj* **1** relating to or consisting of 20. **2** *Maths.* having or using a base 20. [C17 (in the sense: one who has charge over twenty persons): from Latin *vīcēnārius,*from *vīcēnī* twenty each, from *vīgintī* twenty]

vicennial (vɪˈsɛnɪəl) *adj* **1** occurring every 20 years. **2** relating to or lasting for a period of 20 years. [C18: from Late Latin *vīcennium* period of twenty years, from Latin *vīciēs* twenty times + *-ennium,* from *annus* year]

Vicente (*Portuguese* viˈsetə) *n* **Gil.** ?1465–?1536, Portuguese dramatist, noted for his court entertainments, religious dramas, and comedies.

Vicenza (*Italian* viˈtʃɛntsa) *n* a city in NE Italy, in Veneto: home of the 16th-century architect Andrea Palladio and site of some of his finest works. Pop.: 107 786 (1996 est.).

vice president *n* an officer ranking immediately below a president and serving as his deputy. A vice president takes the president's place during his absence or incapacity, after his death, and in certain other circumstances. Abbrevs.: **VP, V. Pres.** ▸ **ˌvice-ˈpresidency** *n* ▸ **ˌvice-ˌpresiˈdential** *adj*

viceregal (ˌvaɪsˈriːgᵊl) *adj* **1** of or relating to a viceroy or his viceroyalty. **2** *Chiefly Austral. and N.Z.* of or relating to a governor or governor general. ▸ **ˌviceˈregally** *adv*

viceregal assent *n Austral.* the formal signing of an act of parliament by a governor general, by which it becomes law.

vicereine (ˌvaɪsˈreɪn) *n* **1** the wife of a viceroy. **2** a female viceroy. [C19: from French, from VICE[3] + *reine* queen, from Latin *rēgīna*]

viceroy (ˈvaɪsrɔɪ) *n* a governor of a colony, country, or province who acts for and rules in the name of his sovereign or government. Related adj: **viceregal.** [C16: from French, from VICE[3] + *roy* king, from Latin *rex*] ▸ **ˈviceroyˌship** *n*

viceroyalty (ˌvaɪsˈrɔɪəltɪ) *n, pl* **-ties. 1** the office, authority, or dignity of a viceroy. **2** the domain governed by a viceroy. **3** the term of office of a viceroy.

vice squad *n* a police division to which is assigned the enforcement of gaming and prostitution laws.

vice versa (ˈvaɪsɪ ˈvɜːsə) *adv* with the order reversed; the other way around. [C17: from Latin: relations being reversed, from *vicis* change + *vertere* to turn]

Vichy (*French* viʃi; *English* ˈviːʃiː) *n* a town and spa in central France, on the River Allier: seat of the collaborationist government under Marshal Pétain (1940–44); mineral waters bottled for export. Pop.: 28 048 (1990). Latin name: **Vicus Calidus** (ˈviːkəs ˈkælɪdəs).

vichyssoise (*French* viʃiswaz) *n* a thick soup made from leeks, potatoes, chicken stock, and cream, usually served chilled. [French, from (*crème*) *Vichyssoise* (*glacée*) (ice-cold cream) from Vichy]

vichy water *n* **1** (*sometimes cap.*) a natural mineral water from springs at Vichy in France, reputed to be beneficial to the health. **2** any sparkling mineral water resembling this. ◆ Often shortened to **vichy.**

vicinage (ˈvɪsənɪdʒ) *n Now rare.* **1** the residents of a particular neighbourhood. **2** a less common word for **vicinity.** [C14: from Old French *vicenage*, from *vicin* neighbouring, from Latin *vīcīnus*; see VICINITY]

vicinal (ˈvɪsɪnᵊl) *adj* **1** neighbouring. **2** (esp. of roads) of or relating to a locality or neighbourhood. **3** *Chem.* relating to or designating two adjacent atoms to which groups are attached in a chain. [C17: from Latin *vīcīnālis* nearby, from *vīcīnus*, from *vīcus* a neighbourhood]

vicinity (vɪˈsɪnɪtɪ) *n, pl* **-ties. 1** a surrounding, adjacent, or nearby area; neighbourhood. **2** the fact or condition of being close in space or relationship. [C16: from Latin *vīcīnitās*, from *vīcīnus* neighbouring, from *vīcus* village]

vicious (ˈvɪʃəs) *adj* **1** wicked or cruel; villainous: *a vicious thug.* **2** characterized by violence or ferocity: *a vicious blow.* **3** *Informal.* unpleasantly severe; harsh: *a vicious wind.* **4** characterized by malice: *vicious lies.* **5** (esp. of dogs, horses, etc.) ferocious or hostile; dangerous. **6** characterized by or leading to vice. **7** invalidated by defects; unsound: *a vicious inference.* **8** *Obsolete.* noxious or morbid: *a vicious exhalation.* [C14: from Old French *vicieus*, from Latin *vitiōsus* full of faults, from *vitium* a defect] ▸ **ˈviciously** *adv* ▸ **ˈviciousness** *n*

vicious circle *n* **1** Also: **vicious cycle.** a situation in which an attempt to resolve one problem creates new problems that lead back to the original situation. **2** *Logic.* **2a** a form of reasoning in which a conclusion is inferred from premises the truth of which cannot be established independently of that conclusion. **2b** an explanation given in terms that cannot be understood independently of that which was to be explained. **2c** a situation in which some statement is shown to entail its negation and vice versa, as *this statement is false* is true only if false and false only if true. **3** *Med.* a condition in which one disease or disorder causes another, which in turn aggravates the first condition.

vicissitude (vɪˈsɪsɪˌtjuːd) *n* **1** variation or mutability in nature or life, esp. successive alternation from one condition or thing to another. **2** a variation in circumstance, fortune, character, etc. [C16: from Latin *vicissitūdō*, from *vicis* change, alternation] ▸ **viˌcissiˈtudinary** *or* **viˌcissiˈtudinous** *adj*

Vicksburg (ˈvɪksˌbɜːg) *n* a city in W Mississippi, on the Mississippi River: site of one of the most decisive campaigns (1863) of the American Civil War, in which the Confederates were besieged for nearly seven weeks before capitulating. Pop.: 20 908 (1990).

Vicky (ˈvɪkɪ) *n* professional name of *Victor Weisz.* 1913–66, British left-wing political cartoonist, born in Germany.

Vico (ˈvɪkəʊ; *Italian* ˈviːko) *n* **Giovanni Battista** (dʒoˈvanni batˈtista). 1668–1744, Italian philosopher. In *Scienza Nuova* (1721) he postulated that civilizations rise and fall in evolutionary cycles, making use of myths, poetry, and linguistics as historical evidence.

vicomte (*French* vikɔ̃t) *or* (*fem*) **vicomtesse** (*French* vikɔ̃tɛs) *n* a French noble holding a rank corresponding to that of a British viscount or viscountess.

Victa (ˈvɪktə) *n Austral. trademark.* a type of rotary lawnmower first manufactured in 1952. [C20: named after Mervyn *Victor* Richardson, who invented it]

victim (ˈvɪktɪm) *n* **1** a person or thing that suffers harm, death, etc., from another or from some adverse act, circumstance, etc.: *victims of tyranny.* **2** a person who is tricked or swindled; dupe. **3** a living person or animal sacrificed in a religious rite. [C15: from Latin *victima*]

victimize *or* **victimise** (ˈvɪktɪˌmaɪz) *vb* (*tr*) **1** to punish or discriminate against selectively or unfairly. **2** to make a victim of. **3** to kill as or in a manner resembling a sacrificial victim. ▸ **ˌvictimiˈzation** *or* **ˌvictimiˈsation** *n* ▸ **ˈvicˌtimˌizer** *or* **ˈvictimˌiser** *n*

victimology (ˌvɪktɪˈmɒlədʒɪ) *n* the study of the psychological effects experienced by the victims of crime. ▸ **ˌvictiˈmologist** *n*

victor (ˈvɪktə) *n* **1a** a person, nation, etc., that has defeated an adversary in war, etc. **1b** (*as modifier*): *the victor army.* **2** the winner of any contest, conflict, or struggle. [C14: from Latin, from *vincere* to conquer]

Victor (ˈvɪktə) *n Communications.* a code word for the letter *v.*

Victor Emmanuel II *n* 1820–78, king of Sardinia-Piedmont (1849–78) and first king of Italy from 1861.

Victor Emmanuel III *n* 1869–1947, last king of Italy (1900–46): dominated after 1922 by Mussolini, whom he appointed as premier; abdicated.

victoria (vɪkˈtɔːrɪə) *n* **1** a light four-wheeled horse-drawn carriage with a folding hood, two passenger seats, and a seat in front for the driver. **2** Also called: **victoria plum.** *Brit.* a large sweet variety of plum, red and yellow in colour. **3** any South American giant water lily of the genus *Victoria*, having very large floating leaves and large white, red, or pink fragrant flowers: family *Euryalaceae.* [C19: all named after Queen VICTORIA]

Victoria[1] (vɪkˈtɔːrɪə) *n* **1** a state of SE Australia: part of New South Wales colony until 1851; semiarid in the northwest, with the Great Dividing Range in the centre and east and the Murray River along the N border. Capital: Melbourne. Pop.: 4 533 300 (1996 est.). Area: 227 620 sq. km (87 884 sq. miles). **2 Lake.** Also called: **Victoria Nyanza.** a lake in East Africa, in Tanzania, Uganda, and Kenya, at an altitude of 1134 m (3720 ft.): the largest lake in Africa and second largest in the world; drained by the Victoria Nile. Area: 69 485 sq. km (26 828 sq. miles). **3** a port in SW Canada, capital of British Columbia, on Vancouver Island: founded in 1843 by the Hudson's Bay Company; made capital of British Columbia in 1868; university (1963). Pop.: 287 897 (1991). **4** the capital of the Seychelles, a port on NE Mahé. Pop.: 25 000 (1993 est.). **5** a region in S China, part of Hong Kong, on N Hong Kong Island: financial and administrative district; university (1911). Pop.: 595 000 (latest est.). **6 Mount.** a mountain in SE Papua New Guinea: the highest peak of the Owen Stanley Range. Height: 4073 m (13 363 ft.).

Victoria[2] (vɪkˈtɔːrɪə) *n* **1** 1819–1901, queen of the United Kingdom (1837–1901) and empress of India (1876–1901). She married Prince Albert of Saxe-Coburg-Gotha (1840). Her sense of vocation did much to restore the prestige of the British monarchy. **2** (*Spanish* bikˈtorja). **Tomás Luis de.** ?1548–1611, Spanish composer of motets and masses in the polyphonic style.

Victoria[3] (vɪkˈtɔːrɪə) *n* the Roman goddess of victory. Greek counterpart: **Nike.**

Victoria and Albert Museum *n* a museum of the fine and applied arts in London, originating from 1856 and given its present name and site in 1899. Abbrev.: **V and A.**

Victoria Cross *n* the highest decoration for gallantry in the face of the enemy awarded to the British and Commonwealth armed forces: instituted in 1856 by Queen Victoria.

Victoria Day *n* the Monday preceding May 24: observed in Canada as a national holiday in commemoration of the birthday of Queen Victoria.

Victoria Desert *n* See **Great Victoria Desert.**

Victoria Falls *pl n* a waterfall on the border between Zimbabwe and Zambia, on the Zambezi River. Height: about 108 m (355 ft.). Width: about 1400 m (4500 ft.).

Victoria Island *n* a large island in the Canadian Arctic: part of the Northwest Territories. Area: about 212 000 sq. km (82 000 sq. miles).

Victoria Land *n* a section of Antarctica, largely in the Ross Dependency on the Ross Sea.

Victorian (vɪkˈtɔːrɪən) *adj* **1** of, relating to, or characteristic of Queen Victoria or the period of her reign. **2** exhibiting the characteristics popularly attributed to the Victorians, esp. prudery, bigotry, or hypocrisy. Compare **Victorian values. 3** denoting, relating to, or having the style of architecture used in England during the reign of Queen Victoria, characterized by massive construction and elaborate ornamentation. **4** of or relating to Victoria (the state or any of the cities). ◆ *n* **5** a person who lived during the reign of Queen Victoria. **6** an inhabitant of Victoria (the state or any of the cities). ▸ **Vicˈtorianˌism** *n*

Victoriana (vɪkˌtɔːrɪˈɑːnə) *pl n* objects, ornaments, etc., of the Victorian period.

Victoria Nile *n* See **Nile.**

Victorian values *pl n* qualities considered to characterize the Victorian period, including enterprise and initiative and the importance of the family. Compare **Victorian** (sense 2).

victorious (vɪkˈtɔːrɪəs) *adj* **1** having defeated an adversary: *the victorious nations.* **2** of, relating to, indicative of, or characterized by victory: *a victorious conclusion.* ▸ **vicˈtoriously** *adv* ▸ **vicˈtoriousness** *n*

victory (ˈvɪktərɪ) *n, pl* **-ries. 1** final and complete superiority in a war. **2** a successful military engagement. **3** a success attained in a contest or struggle or over an opponent, obstacle, or problem. **4** the act of triumphing or state of having triumphed. [C14: from Old French *victorie*, from Latin *victōria*, from *vincere* to subdue]

Victory (ˈvɪktərɪ) *n* another name (in English) for the Roman goddess **Victoria** or the Greek **Nike.**

victory roll *n* a roll of an aircraft made by a pilot to announce or celebrate the shooting down of an enemy plane or other cause for celebration.

victual (ˈvɪtᵊl) *vb* **-uals, -ualling, -ualled** *or U.S.* **-uals, -ualing, -ualed. 1** to supply with or obtain victuals. **2** (*intr*) *Rare.* (esp. of animals) to partake of victuals. ◆ See also **victuals.** [C14: from Old French *vitaille*, from Late Latin *victuālia* provisions, from Latin *victuālis* concerning food, from *victus* sustenance, from *vīvere* to live] ▸ **ˈvictual-less** *adj*

victualage (ˈvɪtəlɪdʒ) *n* a rare word for **victuals.**

victualler (ˈvɪtələ, ˈvɪtlə) *n* **1** a supplier of victuals, as to an army; sutler. **2** *Brit.* a licensed purveyor of spirits; innkeeper. **3** a supply ship, esp. one carrying foodstuffs.

victuals (ˈvɪtᵊlz) *pl n* (*sometimes sing*) food or provisions.

vicuña (vɪˈkuːnjə) *or* **vicuna** (vɪˈkjuːnə) *n* **1** a tawny-coloured cud-chewing Andean artiodactyl mammal, *Vicugna vicugna*, similar to the llama: family *Camelidae.* **2** the fine light cloth made from the wool obtained from this animal. [C17: from Spanish *vicuña*, from Quechuan *wikúña*]

vid (vɪd) *n Informal.* short for **video** (sense 4).

Vidal (viːˈdæl) *n* **Gore.** born 1925, U.S. novelist and critic. His novels include *Burr* (1974), *Lincoln* (1984), and *The Season of Conflict* (1996).

vide (ˈvaɪdɪ) (used to direct a reader to a specified place in a text, another book, etc.) refer to, see (often in the phrases **vide ante** (see before), **vide infra** (see below), **vide post** (see after), **vide supra** (see above), **vide ut supra** (see as above), etc.). Abbrev.: **v., vid.** [C16: from Latin]

videlicet (vɪˈdiːlɪˌsɛt) *adv* namely: used to specify items, examples, etc. Abbrev.: **viz.** [C15: from Latin]

video (ˈvɪdɪˌəʊ) *adj* **1** relating to or employed in the transmission or reception of a televised image. **2** of, concerned with, or operating at video frequencies. ◆ *n, pl* **-os. 3** the visual elements of a television broadcast. **4** a film recorded on a video cassette. **5** short for **video cassette, video cassette recorder. 6** *Informal.* the quality of the visual image in a television. **7** *U.S.* an informal name for **television.** ◆ *vb* **videos, videoing, videoed. 8** to record (a television programme, etc.) on a video cassette recorder. ◆ Compare **audio.** [C20: from Latin *vidēre* to see, on the model of AUDIO]

video cassette *n* a cassette containing video tape.

video cassette recorder *n* a tape recorder for vision and sound signals using magnetic tape in closed plastic cassettes: used for recording and playing back television programmes and films. Often shortened to **video.** Abbrev.: **VCR.**

video conferencing *n* a facility enabling participants in distant locations to take part in a conference by means of electronic sound and video communication.

videodisk ('vɪdɪəʊˌdɪsk) *n* another name for **optical disc.**

video frequency *n* the frequency of a signal conveying the image and synchronizing pulses in a television broadcasting system. It lies in the range from about 50 hertz to 8 megahertz.

video game *n* any of various games that can be played by using an electronic control to move points of light or graphical symbols on the screen of a visual display unit.

video jockey *n* a person who introduces and plays videos, esp. of pop songs, on a television programme.

video nasty *n* a film, usually specially made for video, that is explicitly horrific, brutal, and pornographic.

videophone ('vɪdɪəˌfəʊn) *n* a telephonic device in which there is both verbal and visual communication between parties. ▸ **videophonic** (ˌvɪdɪə'fɒnɪk) *adj*

video tape *n* **1** magnetic tape used mainly for recording the vision and sound signals of a television programme or film for subsequent transmission. ◆ *vb* **video-tape. 2** to record (a programme, film, etc.) on video tape.

video tape recorder *n* a tape recorder for vision signals and sometimes accompanying sound, using magnetic tape on open spools: used in television broadcasting. Abbrev.: **VTR.**

Videotex ('vɪdɪəʊˌtɛks) *n Trademark.* an information system that displays information from a distant computer on a television screen. See also **Teletext, Viewdata.**

videotext ('vɪdɪəʊˌtɛkst) *n* a means of providing a written or graphical representation of computerized information on a television screen.

vidette (vɪ'dɛt) *n* a variant spelling of **vedette.**

Vidhan Sabha (vɪ'dɑːn 'sʌbə) *n* the legislative assembly of any of the states of India. [Hindi, from *vidhan* law + *sabha* assembly]

vidicon ('vɪdɪˌkɒn) *n* a small television camera tube, used in closed-circuit television and outside broadcasts, in which incident light forms an electric charge pattern on a photoconductive surface. Scanning by a low-velocity electron beam discharges the surface, producing a current in an adjacent conducting layer. See also **Plumbicon.** [C20: from VID(EO) + ICON(OSCOPE)]

vie (vaɪ) *vb* **vies, vying, vied. 1** (*intr;* foll. by *with* or *for*) to contend for superiority or victory (with) or strive in competition (for). **2** (*tr*) *Archaic.* to offer, exchange, or display in rivalry. [C15: probably from Old French *envier* to challenge, from Latin *invītāre* to INVITE] ▸ **'vier** *n* ▸ **'vying** *adj, n*

Vienna (vɪ'ɛnə) *n* the capital and the smallest state of Austria, in the northeast on the River Danube: seat of the Hapsburgs (1278-1918); residence of the Holy Roman Emperor (1558–1806); withstood sieges by Turks in 1529 and 1683; political and cultural centre in the 18th and 19th centuries, having associations with many composers; university (1365). Pop.: 1 593 000 (1995 est.). Area: 1075 sq. km (415 sq. miles). German name: **Wien.**

Vienna Union *or* **International** *n* **the.** an international conference of socialists who came together in Vienna in 1921 in an attempt to reconstruct a united International by offering an alternative to the right-wing remnant of the Second International and to the Comintern: merged into the Labour and Socialist International in 1923. Also called: **Two-and-a-half International.**

Vienne (*French* vjɛn) *n* **1** a department of W central France, in Poitou-Charentes region. Capital: Poitiers. Pop.: 390 400 (1995). Area: 7044 sq. km (2747 sq. miles). **2** a town in SE France, on the River Rhône: extensive Roman remains. Ancient name: **Vienna. 3** a river in SW central France, flowing west and north to the Loire below Chinon. Length: over 350 km (200 miles).

Viennese (ˌvɪə'niːz) *adj* **1** of, relating to, or characteristic of Vienna. ◆ *n, pl* **-nese. 2** a native or inhabitant of Vienna.

Vientiane (ˌvjɛntɪ'ɑːn) *n* the administrative capital of Laos, in the south near the border with Thailand: capital of the kingdom of Vientiane from 1707 until taken by the Thais in 1827. Pop.: 531 800 (1996 est.).

Vierwaldstättersee (fiːr'valtʃtɛtərˌzeː) *n* the German name for (Lake) **Lucerne.**

vies (fiːs) *adj S. African slang.* angry, furious, or disgusted. [Afrikaans]

vi et armis *Latin.* ('vaɪ ɛt 'ɑːmɪs) *n Legal history.* a kind of trespass accompanied by force and violence. [literally: by force and arms]

Vietcong (ˌvjɛt'kɒŋ) *or* **Viet Cong** *n* (in the Vietnam War) **1** the Communist-led guerrilla force and revolutionary army of South Vietnam; the armed forces of the National Liberation Front of South Vietnam. **2** a member of these armed forces. **3** (*modifier*) of or relating to the Vietcong or a Vietcong. [from Vietnamese *Viet Nam Cong San* Vietnamese Communist]

Vietminh (ˌvjɛt'mɪn) *or* **Viet Minh** *n* **1** a Vietnamese organization led by Ho Chi Minh that first fought the Japanese and then the French (1941–54) in their attempt to achieve national independence. **2** a member or group of members of this organization, esp. in the armed forces. **3** (*modifier*) of or relating to this organization or to its members. [from Vietnamese *Viet Nam Doc Lap Dong Minh Hoi* Vietnam League of Independence]

Vietnam (ˌvjɛt'næm) *or* **Viet Nam** *n* a republic in SE Asia: an ancient empire, conquered by France in the 19th century; occupied by Japan (1940–45) when the Communist-led Vietminh began resistance operations that were continued against restored French rule after 1945. In 1954 the country was divided along the 17th parallel, establishing North Vietnam (under the Vietminh) and South Vietnam (under French control), the latter becoming the independent **Republic of Vietnam** in 1955. From 1959 the country was dominated by war between the Communist Vietcong, supported by North Vietnam, and the South Vietnamese government; increasing numbers of U.S. forces were brought to the aid of the South Vietnamese army until a peace agreement (1973) led to the withdrawal of U.S. troops; further fighting led to the eventual defeat of the South Vietnamese government in March 1975 and in 1976 an elected National Assembly proclaimed the reunification of the country. Official language: Vietnamese. Religion: Buddhist majority. Currency: dong. Capital: Hanoi. Pop.: 76 236 000 (1998 est.). Area: 331 041 sq. km (127 816 sq. miles). Official name: **Socialist Republic of Vietnam.**

Vietnamese (ˌvjɛtnə'miːz) *adj* **1** of, relating to, or characteristic of Vietnam, its people, or their language. ◆ *n* **2** (*pl* **-ese**) a native or inhabitant of Vietnam. **3** the language of Vietnam, probably related to the Mon-Khmer languages.

Vietnamization *or* **Vietnamisation** (ˌvjɛtnəmaɪ'zeɪʃən) *n* (in the Vietnam War) a U.S. government policy of transferring the tasks of fighting and directing the war to the government and forces of South Vietnam.

vieux jeu *French.* (vjø ʒø) *adj* old-fashioned. [literally: old game]

view (vjuː) *n* **1** the act of seeing or observing; an inspection. **2** vision or sight, esp. range of vision: *the church is out of view.* **3** a scene, esp. of a fine tract of countryside: *the view from the top was superb.* **4** a pictorial representation of a scene, such as a photograph. **5** (*sometimes pl*) opinion; thought: *my own view on the matter differs from yours.* **6** chance or expectation: *the policy has little view of success.* **7** (foll. by *to*) a desired end or intention: *he has a view to securing further qualifications.* **8** a general survey of a topic, subject, etc.: *a comprehensive view of Shakespearean literature.* **9** visual aspect or appearance: *they look the same in outward view.* **10** *Law.* **10a** a formal inspection by a jury of the place where an alleged crime was committed. **10b** a formal inspection of property in dispute. **11** a sight of a hunted animal before or during the chase. **12 in view of.** taking into consideration. **13 on view.** exhibited to the public gaze. **14 take a dim** *or* **poor view of.** to regard (something) with disfavour or disapproval. **15 with a view to. 15a** with the intention of. **15b** in anticipation or hope of. ◆ *vb* **16** (*tr*) to look at. **17** (*tr*) to consider in a specified manner: *they view the growth of Communism with horror.* **18** (*tr*) to examine or inspect carefully: *to view the accounts.* **19** (*tr*) to survey mentally; contemplate: *to view the difficulties.* **20** to watch (television). **21** (*tr*) to sight (a hunted animal) before or during the chase. [C15: from Old French *veue,* from *veoir* to see, from Latin *vidēre*] ▸ **'viewable** *adj*

Viewdata ('vjuːˌdeɪtə) *n Trademark.* an interactive form of Videotext that sends information from a distant computer along telephone lines, enabling shopping, booking theatre and airline tickets, and banking transactions to be conducted from the home.

viewer ('vjuːə) *n* **1** a person who views something, esp. television. **2** any optical device by means of which something is viewed, esp. one used for viewing photographic transparencies. **3** *Law.* a person appointed by a court to inspect and report upon property, etc. ▸ **'viewership** *n*

viewfinder ('vjuːˌfaɪndə) *n* a device on a camera, consisting of a lens system and sometimes a ground-glass screen, enabling the user to see what will be included in his photograph. Sometimes shortened to **finder.**

view halloo *interj* **1** a huntsman's cry uttered when the quarry is seen breaking cover or shortly afterwards. ◆ *n* **2** a shout indicating an abrupt appearance.

viewing ('vjuːɪŋ) *n* **1** the act of watching television. **2** television programmes collectively: *late-night viewing.*

viewless ('vjuːlɪs) *adj* **1** (of windows, etc.) not affording a view. **2** having no opinions. **3** *Poetic.* invisible.

viewpoint ('vjuːˌpɔɪnt) *n* **1** the mental attitude that determines a person's opinions or judgments; point of view. **2** a place from which something can be viewed.

viewy ('vjuːɪ) *adj* **viewier, viewiest.** *Informal, rare.* **1** having fanciful opinions or ideas; visionary. **2** characterized by ostentation; showy. ▸ **'viewiness** *n*

VIFF (vɪf) *n* a technique used in flying VTOL aircraft to change direction suddenly by swivelling the jet engine nozzles. [C20: *v(ectoring) i(n) f(orward) f(light)*]

Vigée-Lebrun (*French* viʒeləbrœ̃) *n* (**Marie Louise**) **Élisabeth.** 1755–1842, French painter, noted for her portraits of women.

vigesimal (vaɪ'dʒɛsɪməl) *adj* **1** relating to or based on the number 20. **2** taking place or proceeding in intervals of 20. **3** twentieth. [C17: from Latin *vīgēsimus,* variant (influenced by *vīgintī* twenty) of *vīcēsimus* twentieth]

vigia ('vɪdʒɪə) *n Nautical.* a navigational hazard marked on a chart although its existence and nature has not been confirmed. [C19: from Spanish *vigía* reef, from Latin *vigilāre* to keep watch]

vigil ('vɪdʒɪl) *n* **1** a purposeful watch maintained, esp. at night, to guard, observe, pray, etc. **2** the period of such a watch. **3** *R.C. Church, Church of England.* the eve of certain major festivals, formerly observed as a night spent in prayer: often marked by fasting and abstinence and a special Mass and divine office. **4** a period of sleeplessness; insomnia. [C13: from Old French *vigile,* from Medieval Latin *vigilia* watch preceding a religious festival, from Latin: vigilance, from *vigil* alert, from *vigēre* to be lively]

vigilance ('vɪdʒɪləns) *n* **1** the fact, quality, or condition of being vigilant. **2** the abnormal state or condition of being unable to sleep.

vigilance committee *n* (in the U.S.) a self-appointed body of citizens organized to maintain order, punish crime, etc., where an efficient system of courts does not exist.

vigilant ('vɪdʒɪlənt) *adj* keenly alert to or heedful of trouble or danger, as while others are sleeping or unsuspicious. [C15: from Latin *vigilāns* keeping awake, from *vigilāre* to be watchful; see VIGIL] ▸ **'vigilantly** *adv* ▸ **'vigilantness** *n*

vigilante (ˌvɪdʒɪ'læntɪ) *n* **1** one of an organized group of citizens who take upon themselves the protection of their district, properties, etc. **2** Also called: **vigilance man.** *U.S.* a member of a vigilance committee. [C19: from Spanish, from Latin *vigilāre* to keep watch]

vigilantism (ˌvɪdʒɪ'læntɪzəm) *n U.S.* the methods, conduct, attitudes, etc., associated with vigilantes, esp. militancy, bigotry, or suspiciousness.

vigil light *n Chiefly R.C. Church.* **1** a small candle lit as an act of personal devotion before a shrine or statue, usually in a church. **2** a small lamp kept permanently burning before such a shrine or statue.

Vigil Mass *n R.C. Church.* a Mass held on Saturday evening, attendance at which fulfils one's obligation to attend Mass on Sunday.

vigneron ('viːnjərɒn; *French* viɲrɔ̃) *n* a person who grows grapes for winemaking. [French, from *vigne* vine]

vignette (vɪ'njɛt) *n* **1** a small illustration placed at the beginning or end of a book or chapter. **2** a short graceful literary essay or sketch. **3** a photograph, drawing, etc., with edges that are shaded off. **4** *Architect.* a carved ornamentation that has a design based upon tendrils, leaves, etc. **5** any small endearing scene, view, picture, etc. ◆ *vb* (*tr*) **6** to finish (a photograph, picture, etc.) with a fading border in the form of a vignette. **7a** to decorate with vignettes. **7b** to portray in or as in a vignette. [C18: from French, literally: little vine, from *vigne* VINE; with reference to the vine motif frequently used in embellishments to a text] ▸ **vi'gnettist** *n*

vignetting (vɪ'njɛtɪŋ) *n* **1** the technique of producing a photographic vignette, esp. a portrait, by progressively reducing the amount of light falling on the photographic surface towards the edges. **2** the reduction in area of a light beam passing through a camera lens as the obliquity of the beam is increased.

Vignola (*Italian* viɲ'ɲɔːla) *n* **Giacomo Barozzi da** ('dʒaːkomo ba'rɔttsi da). 1507–73, Italian architect, whose cruciform design for Il Gesù, Rome, greatly influenced later Church architecture.

Vigny (*French* viɲi) *n* **Alfred Victor de** (alfrɛd viktɔr də). 1797–1863, French romantic poet, novelist, and dramatist, noted for his pessimistic lyric verse *Poèmes antiques et modernes* (1826) and *Les Destinées* (1864), the novel *Cinq-Mars* (1826), and the play *Chatterton* (1835).

Vigo ('viːgəʊ; *Spanish* 'bigo) *n* a port in NW Spain, in Galicia on **Vigo Bay** (an inlet of the Atlantic): site of a British and Dutch naval victory (1702) over the French and Spanish. Pop.: 290 582 (1995 est.).

vigoro ('vɪgəˌrəʊ) *n Austral. sport.* a women's game similar to cricket with paddle-shaped bats, introduced into Australia in 1919 by its British inventor J. J. Grant. [C20: from VIGOUR]

vigorous ('vɪgərəs) *adj* **1** endowed with bodily or mental strength or vitality; robust. **2** displaying, involving, characterized by, or performed with vigour: *vigorous growth.* ▸ **'vigorously** *adv* ▸ **'vigorousness** *n*

vigour *or U.S.* **vigor** ('vɪgə) *n* **1** exuberant and resilient strength of body or mind; vitality. **2** substantial effective energy or force: *the vigour of the tempest.* **3** forcefulness; intensity: *I was surprised by the vigour of her complaints.* **4** the capacity for survival or strong healthy growth in a plant or animal: *hybrid vigour.* **5** the most active period or stage of life, manhood, etc.; prime. **6** *Chiefly U.S.* legal force or effectiveness; validity (esp. in the phrase **in vigour**). [C14: from Old French *vigeur,* from Latin *vigor* activity, from *vigēre* to be lively]

vihuela (*Spanish* bi'wela) *n* an obsolete plucked stringed instrument of Spain, related to the guitar. [from Spanish]

Viipuri ('viːpuri) *n* the Finnish name for **Vyborg.**

Vijayawada (ˌviːdʒaɪə'wɑːdə) *n* a town in SE India, in E central Andra Pradesh on the Krishna River: Hindu pilgrimage centre. Pop.: 701 827 (1991). Former name: **Bezwada.**

Viking ('vaɪkɪŋ) *n* (*sometimes not cap.*) **1** Also called: **Norseman, Northman.** any of the Danes, Norwegians, and Swedes who raided by sea most of N and W Europe from the 8th to the 11th centuries, later often settling, as in parts of Britain. **2** any sea rover, plunderer, or pirate. **3** either of two unmanned American spacecraft that reached Mars in 1976. **4** (*modifier*) of, relating to, or characteristic of a Viking or Vikings: *a Viking ship.* [C19: from Old Norse *víkingr,* probably from *vík* creek, sea inlet + *-ingr* (see -ING[3]); perhaps related to Old English *wīc* camp]

vil. *abbrev. for* village.

vilayet (vɪ'lɑːjɛt) *n* a major administrative division of Turkey. [C19: from Turkish, from Arabic *wilāyat,* from *walīy* governor]

vile (vaɪl) *adj* **1** abominably wicked; shameful or evil: *the vile development of slavery appalled them.* **2** morally despicable; ignoble: *vile accusations.* **3** disgusting to the senses or emotions; foul: *a vile smell; vile epithets.* **4** tending to humiliate or degrade: *only slaves would perform such vile tasks.* **5** unpleasant or bad: *vile weather.* **6** paltry: *a vile reward.* [C13: from Old French *vil,* from Latin *vīlis* cheap] ▸ **'vilely** *adv* ▸ **'vileness** *n*

vilify ('vɪlɪˌfaɪ) *vb* **-fies, -fying, -fied.** (*tr*) **1** to revile with abusive or defamatory language; malign. **2** *Rare.* to make vile; debase; degrade. [C15: from Late Latin *vīlificāre,* from Latin *vīlis* worthless + *facere* to make] ▸ **vilification** (ˌvɪlɪfɪ'keɪʃən) *n* ▸ **'viliˌfier** *n*

vilipend ('vɪlɪˌpɛnd) *vb* (*tr*) *Rare.* **1** to treat or regard with contempt. **2** to speak slanderously or slightingly of. [C15: from Late Latin *vīlipendere,* from Latin *vīlis* worthless + *pendere* to esteem] ▸ **'viliˌpender** *n*

villa ('vɪlə) *n* **1** (in ancient Rome) a country house, usually consisting of farm buildings and residential quarters around a courtyard. **2** a large and usually luxurious country residence. **3** *Brit.* a detached or semidetached suburban house. **4** *N.Z.* a medium-sized suburban house standing in its own grounds. [C17: via Italian from Latin; related to Latin *vīcus* a village] ▸ **'villa-ˌlike** *adj*

Villa ('viːə; *Spanish* 'biʎa) *n* **Francisco** (fran'sisko), called *Pancho Villa,* original name *Doroteo Arango.* ?1877–1923, Mexican revolutionary leader.

Villach (*German* 'fɪlax) *n* a city in S central Austria, on the Drava River: nearby hot mineral springs. Pop.: 54 640 (1991).

village ('vɪlɪdʒ) *n* **1** a small group of houses in a country area, larger than a hamlet. **2** the inhabitants of such a community collectively. **3** an incorporated municipality smaller than a town in various parts of the U.S. and Canada. **4** a group of habitats of certain animals. **5** *N.Z.* a self-contained city area having its own shops, etc. **6** (*modifier*) of, relating to, or characteristic of a village: *a village green.* [C15: from Old French, from *ville* farm, from Latin: VILLA] ▸ **'village-ˌlike** *adj*

village college *n Brit.* a centre, often for a group of villages, with educational and recreational facilities for the whole neighbourhood. Also called: **community college.**

villager ('vɪlɪdʒə) *n* **1** an inhabitant of a village. ◆ *adj* **2** *E African.* backward, unsophisticated, or illiterate.

Villahermosa (*Spanish* biʎaɛr'mosa) *n* a town in E Mexico, capital of Tabasco state: university (1959). Pop.: 261 231 (1990). Former name: **San Juan Bautista.**

villa home *n Austral.* one of a set of suburban bungalows built compactly on the one allotment, esp. on the former site of a single bungalow.

villain ('vɪlən) *n* **1** a wicked or malevolent person. **2** (in a novel, play, film, etc.) the main evil character and antagonist to the hero. **3** *Often jocular.* a mischievous person; rogue. **4** *Brit. police slang.* a criminal. **5** *History.* a variant spelling of **villein. 6** *Obsolete.* an uncouth person; boor. [C14: from Old French *vilein* serf, from Late Latin *vīllānus* worker on a country estate, from Latin: VILLA] ▸ **'villainess** *fem n*

villainage ('vɪlənɪdʒ) *n* a variant spelling of **villeinage.**

villainous ('vɪlənəs) *adj* **1** of, like, or appropriate to a villain. **2** very bad or disagreeable: *a villainous climate.* ▸ **'villainously** *adv* ▸ **'villainousness** *n*

villainy ('vɪlənɪ) *n, pl* **-lainies. 1** conduct befitting a villain; vicious behaviour or action. **2** an evil, abhorrent, or criminal act or deed. **3** the fact or condition of being villainous. **4** *English history.* a rare word for **villeinage.**

Villa-Lobos ('viːlɑː'ləʊbɒs, 'vɪlə-; *Portuguese* 'vila'lobus) *n* **Heitor** (ej'tor). 1887–1959, Brazilian composer, much of whose work is based on Brazilian folk tunes.

villanella (ˌvɪlə'nɛlə) *n, pl* **-las.** a type of part song originating in Naples during the 16th century. [C16: from Italian, from *villano* rustic, from Late Latin *vīllānus;* see VILLAIN]

villanelle (ˌvɪlə'nɛl) *n* a verse form of French origin consisting of 19 lines arranged in five tercets and a quatrain. The first and third lines of the first tercet recur alternately at the end of each subsequent tercet and both together at the end of the quatrain. [C16: from French, from Italian VILLANELLA]

Villanovan (ˌvɪlə'nəʊvən) *adj* **1** of or relating to an early Iron Age culture near Bologna, Italy, characterized by the use of bronze and the primitive use of iron. ◆ *n* **2** a member of this culture. [C19: named after the NE Italian town of *Villanova,* where the first remains of the culture were excavated in 1853]

Villars (*French* vilar) *n* **Claude Louis Hector de** (klod lwi ɛktɔr də). 1653–1734, French marshal, distinguished for his command in the War of the Spanish Succession (1701–14).

villatic (vɪ'lætɪk) *adj Literary.* of or relating to a villa, village, or farm; rustic; rural. [C17: from Latin *vīllatīcus,* from *villa* a farm]

-ville *n and adj combining form. Slang, chiefly U.S.* (denoting) a place, condition, or quality with a character as specified: *dragsville; squaresville.*

villein *or* **villain** ('vɪlən) *n* (in medieval Europe) a peasant personally bound to his lord, to whom he paid dues and services, sometimes commuted to rents, in return for his land. [C14: from Old French *vilein* serf; see VILLAIN]

villeinage *or* **villainage** ('vɪlənɪdʒ) *n* (in medieval Europe) **1** the status and condition of a villein. **2** the tenure by which a villein held his land.

Villeneuve (*French* vilnœv) *n* **Pierre Charles Jean Baptiste Silvestre de** (pjɛr ʃarl ʒɑ̃ batist silvɛstrə də). 1763–1806, French admiral, defeated by Nelson at the Battle of Trafalgar (1805).

Villeurbanne (*French* vijœrban) *n* a town in E France: an industrial suburb of E Lyons. Pop.: 119 848 (1990).

villi ('vɪlaɪ) *n* the plural of **villus.**

Villiers ('vɪləz, 'vɪljəz) *n* **George.** See (Dukes of) **Buckingham.**

Villiers de l'Isle Adam (*French* vilje də lil adɑ̃) *n* **August, Comte de** (ogyst, kɔ̃t də). 1838–89, French poet and dramatist; pioneer of the symbolist movement. His works include *Contes cruels* (1883) and the play *Axel* (1885).

villiform ('vɪlɪˌfɔːm) *adj* having the form of a villus or a series of villi. [C19: from New Latin *villiformis,* from Latin *villus* shaggy hair + -FORM]

Villon (*French* vijɔ̃) *n* **1 François** (frɑ̃swa). born 1431, French poet. His poems, such as those in *Le Petit testament* (?1456) and *Le Grand testament* (1461), are mostly ballades and rondeaux, verse forms that he revitalized. He was banished in 1463, after which nothing more was heard of him. **2 Jacques** (ʒak), real name *Gaston Duchamp.* 1875–1963, French cubist painter and engraver.

villosity (vɪ'lɒsɪtɪ) *n, pl* **-ties. 1** the state of being villous. **2** a villous coating or surface. **3** a villus or a collection of villi.

villous ('vɪləs) *adj* **1** (of plant parts) covered with long hairs. **2** of, relating to, or having villi. [C14: from Latin *villōsus,* from *villus* tuft of hair] ▸ **'villously** *adv*

villus ('vɪləs) *n, pl* **villi** ('vɪlaɪ). (*usually pl*) **1** *Zoology, anatomy.* any of the numerous finger-like projections of the mucous membrane lining the small intestine of many vertebrates. **2** any similar membranous process, such as any of those in the mammalian placenta. **3** *Botany.* any of various hairlike outgrowths, as from the stem of a moss. [C18: from Latin: shaggy hair]

Vilnius *or* **Vilnyus** ('vɪlnɪʊs) *n* the capital of Lithuania: passed to Russia in 1795; under Polish rule (1920–39); university (1578); an industrial and commercial centre. Pop.: 573 200 (1996 est.). Russian name: **Vilna** ('vilna). Polish name: **Wilno.**

vim (vɪm) *n Slang.* exuberant vigour and energy. [C19: from Latin, from *vīs;* related to Greek *is* strength]

vimen ('vaɪmen) *n, pl* **vimina** ('vɪmɪnə). a long flexible shoot that occurs in certain plants. [C19: from Latin: a pliant twig, osier]

Viminal ('vɪmɪnᵊl) *n* one of the seven hills on which ancient Rome was built. [from Latin *Vīminālis Collis* the Viminal Hill, from *vīminālis* of osiers, from *vīmen* an osier, referring to the willow grove on the hill]

vimineous (vɪ'mɪnɪəs) *adj Botany.* having, producing, or resembling long flexible shoots. [C17: from Latin *vīmineus* made of osiers, from *vīmen* flexible shoot]

vin- *combining form.* a variant of **vini-** before a vowel.

vina ('viːnə) *n* a stringed musical instrument, esp. of India, related to the sitar. [C18: from Hindi *bīnā,* from Sanskrit *vīnā*]

vinaceous (vaɪ'neɪʃəs) *adj* **1** of, relating to, or containing wine. **2** having a colour suggestive of red wine. [C17: from Late Latin *vīnāceus,* from Latin *vīnum* wine]

Viña del Mar (*Spanish* 'biɲa ðel 'mar) *n* a city and resort in central Chile, just north of Valparaíso on the Pacific: the second largest city of Chile. Pop.: 322 220 (1995 est.).

vinaigrette (ˌvɪneɪ'gret) *n* **1** Also called: **vinegarette.** a small decorative bottle or box with a perforated top, used for holding smelling salts, etc. **2** Also called: **vinaigrette sauce.** a salad dressing made from oil and vinegar with seasonings; French dressing. ◆ *adj* **3** served with vinaigrette. [C17: from French, from *vinaigre* VINEGAR]

vinasse (vɪ'næs) *n* the residue left in a still after distilling spirits, esp. brandy. [C20: from French]

vinblastine (vɪn'blæstiːn) *n* a cytotoxic drug used in the treatment of lymphomas, derived as an alkaloid from the tropical shrub Madagascar periwinkle (*Vinca rosea*). [C20: shortened from *vincaleukoblastine,* from VINCA + *leukoblast,* from *leukocyte* + -BLAST + -INE[2]]

vinca ('vɪŋkə) *n* See **periwinkle**[2]. [New Latin, from Latin *pervinca* periwinkle]

vinca alkaloid *n Med.* any of a group of alkaloids obtained from the periwinkle *Vinca rosea,* such as vinblastine and vincristine, that interfere with cell division and are used in the treatment of cancer.

Vincennes (*French* vɛ̃sɛn; *English* vɪn'sɛnz) *n* a suburb of E Paris: 14th-century castle. Pop.: 45 000 (latest est.).

Vincent de Paul ('vɪnsənt də 'pɔːl; *French* vɛ̃sɑ̃ də pɔl) *n* **Saint.** ?1581–1660, French Roman Catholic priest, who founded two charitable orders, the Lazarists (1625) and the Sisters of Charity (1634). Feast day: Sept. 27.

Vincent's angina *or* **disease** *n* an ulcerative bacterial infection of the mouth, esp. involving the throat and tonsils. [C20: named after J. H. *Vincent* (died 1950), French bacteriologist]

Vinci ('vɪntʃɪ) *n* See **Leonardo da Vinci.**

vincible ('vɪnsɪbᵊl) *adj Rare.* capable of being defeated or overcome. [C16: from Latin *vincibilis,* from *vincere* to conquer] ▸ ˌ**vinci'bility** *or* '**vincibleness** *n*

vincristine (vɪn'krɪstiːn) *n* a cytotoxic drug used in the treatment of leukaemia, derived as an alkaloid from the tropical shrub Madagascar periwinkle (*Vinca rosea*). [C20: from New Latin VINCA + Latin *crista* crest + -INE[2]]

vinculum ('vɪŋkjʊləm) *n, pl* **-la** (-lə). **1** a horizontal line drawn above a group of mathematical terms, used as an alternative to parentheses in mathematical expressions, as in $x + \overline{y - z}$ which is equivalent to $x + (y - z)$. **2** *Anatomy.* **2a** any bandlike structure, esp. one uniting two or more parts. **2b** another name for **ligament. 3** *Rare.* a unifying bond; tie. [C17: from Latin: bond, from *vincīre* to bind]

vindaloo (ˌvɪndə'luː) *n, pl* **-loos.** a type of very hot Indian curry. [C20: perhaps from Portuguese *vin d'alho* wine and garlic sauce]

vin de pays *French.* (vɛ̃ də pei) *n, pl* ***vins de pays*** (vɛ̃ də pei). the third highest French wine classification: indicates that the wine meets certain requirements concerning area of production, strength, etc. Also called: **vin du pays.** Abbrev.: **VDP.** Compare **AC, VDQS, *vin de table.*** [literally: local wine]

vin de table *French* (vɛ̃ də tabla) *n, pl* ***vins de table*** (vɛ̃ də tabla). the classification given to a French wine that does not meet the requirements of any of the three higher classifications. Compare **AC, VDQS, *vin de pays.*** [literally: table wine]

Vindhya Pradesh ('vɪndjə) *n* a former state of central India: merged with the reorganized Madhya Pradesh in 1956.

Vindhya Range *or* **Mountains** *n* a mountain range in central India: separates the Ganges basin from the Deccan, marking the limits of northern and peninsular India. Greatest height: 1113 m (3651 ft.).

vindicable ('vɪndɪkəbᵊl) *adj* capable of being vindicated; justifiable. ▸ ˌ**vindica'bility** *n*

vindicate ('vɪndɪˌkeɪt) *vb (tr)* **1** to clear from guilt, accusation, blame, etc., as by evidence or argument. **2** to provide justification for: *his promotion vindicated his unconventional attitude.* **3** to uphold, maintain, or defend (a cause, etc.): *to vindicate a claim.* **4** *Roman law.* to bring an action to regain possession of (property) under claim of legal title. **5** *Rare.* to claim, as for oneself or another. **6** *Obsolete.* to take revenge on or for; punish. **7** *Obsolete.* to set free. [C17: from Latin *vindicāre,* from *vindex* claimant] ▸ '**vindiˌcator** *n* ▸ '**vindiˌcatory** *adj*

vindication (ˌvɪndɪ'keɪʃən) *n* **1** the act of vindicating or the condition of being vindicated. **2** a means of exoneration from an accusation. **3** a fact, evidence, circumstance, etc., that serves to vindicate a theory or claim.

vindictive (vɪn'dɪktɪv) *adj* **1** disposed to seek vengeance. **2** characterized by spite or rancour. **3** *English law.* (of damages) in excess of the compensation due to the plaintiff and imposed in punishment of the defendant. [C17: from Latin *vindicta* revenge, from *vindicāre* to VINDICATE] ▸ **vin'dictively** *adv* ▸ **vin'dictiveness** *n*

vin du pays *French.* (vɛ̃ du pei) *n, pl* ***vins du pays.*** a variant spelling of ***vin de pays.***

vine (vaɪn) *n* **1** any of various plants, esp. the grapevine, having long flexible stems that creep along the ground or climb by clinging to a support by means of tendrils, leafstalks, etc. **2** the stem of such a plant. [C13: from Old French *vine,* from Latin *vīnea* vineyard, from *vīneus* belonging to wine, from *vīnum* wine] ▸ **vined** *adj* ▸ '**vineless** *adj* ▸ '**vineˌlike** *adj* ▸ '**viny** *adj*

Vine (vaɪn) *n* **Barbara.** See (Ruth) **Rendell.**

vinedresser ('vaɪnˌdrɛsə) *n* a person who prunes, tends, or cultivates grapevines.

vinegar ('vɪnɪgə) *n* **1** a sour-tasting liquid consisting of impure dilute acetic acid, made by oxidation of the ethyl alcohol in beer, wine, or cider. It is used as a condiment or preservative. **2** sourness or peevishness of temper, countenance, speech, etc. **3** *Pharmacol.* a medicinal solution in dilute acetic acid. **4** *U.S. and Canadian informal.* vitality. ◆ *vb* **5** *(tr)* to apply vinegar to. [C13: from Old French *vinaigre,* from *vin* WINE + *aigre* sour, from Latin *acer* sharp] ▸ '**vinegarish** *adj* ▸ '**vinegar-ˌlike** *adj* ▸ '**vinegary** *adj*

vinegar eel *n* a nematode worm, *Anguillula aceti,* that feeds on the organisms that cause fermentation in vinegar and other liquids. Also called: **vinegar worm, eelworm.**

vinegarette (ˌvɪnɪgə'rɛt) *n* a variant spelling of **vinaigrette** (sense 1).

vinegar fly *n* any of various dipterous flies of the genus *Drosophila.* See **drosophila.**

vinegarroon (ˌvɪnɪgə'ruːn) *n* a large whip scorpion, *Mastigoproctus giganteus,* of the southwestern U.S. and Mexico that emits a vinegary odour when alarmed. [from Mexican Spanish *vinagrón,* from Spanish *vinagre* VINEGAR]

Vineland ('vaɪnlənd) *n* a variant spelling of **Vinland.**

vinery ('vaɪnərɪ) *n, pl* **-eries. 1** a hothouse for growing grapes. **2** another name for a **vineyard. 3** vines collectively.

vineyard ('vɪnjəd) *n* a plantation of grapevines, esp. where wine grapes are produced. [Old English *wīngeard;* see VINE, YARD[2]; related to Old High German *wīngart,* Old Norse *vingarthr*] ▸ '**vineyardist** *n*

vingt-et-un *French.* (vɛ̃teœ̃) *n* another name for **pontoon**[2]. [literally: twenty-one]

vinho verde (ˌviːnjəʊ 'vɜːdɪ) *n* any of a variety of light, slightly sharp-tasting wines made from early-picked grapes in the Minho region of NW Portugal. [Portuguese, literally: green (or young) wine]

vini- *or before a vowel* **vin-** *combining form.* indicating wine: *viniculture.* [from Latin *vīnum*]

vinic ('vaɪnɪk, 'vɪnɪk) *adj* of, relating to, or contained in wine. [C19: from Latin *vīnum* wine]

viniculture ('vɪnɪˌkʌltʃə) *n* the process or business of growing grapes and making wine. ▸ ˌ**vini'cultural** *adj* ▸ ˌ**vini'culturist** *n*

viniferous (vɪ'nɪfərəs) *adj* wine-producing.

vinificator ('vɪnɪfɪˌkeɪtə) *n* a condenser that collects the alcohol vapour escaping from fermenting wine. [C19: from Latin *vīnum* wine + *facere* to make]

Vinland ('vɪnlənd) *or* **Vineland** *n* the stretch of the E coast of North America visited by Leif Ericson and other Vikings from about 1000.

Vinnitsa (*Russian* 'vinnitsə) *n* a city in central Ukraine: passed from Polish to Russian rule in 1793. Pop.: 388 000 (1996 est.).

vino ('viːnəʊ) *n, pl* **-nos.** an informal word for **wine.** [jocular use of Italian or Spanish *vino*]

vin ordinaire *French.* (vɛ̃n ɔrdinɛr) *n, pl* ***vins ordinaires*** (vɛ̃z ɔrdinɛr). cheap table wine, esp. French.

vinosity (vɪ'nɒsɪtɪ) *n* the distinctive and essential quality and flavour of wine. [C17: from Late Latin *vīnōsitas,* from Latin *vīnōsus* VINOUS]

vinous ('vaɪnəs) *adj* **1** of, relating to, or characteristic of wine. **2** indulging in or indicative of indulgence in wine: *a vinous complexion.* [C17: from Latin *vīnōsus,* from *vīnum* WINE]

vintage ('vɪntɪdʒ) *n* **1** the wine obtained from a harvest of grapes, esp. in an outstandingly good year, referred to by the year involved, the district, or the vineyard. **2** the harvest from which such a wine is obtained. **3a** the harvesting of wine grapes. **3b** the season of harvesting these grapes or for making wine. **4** a time of origin: *a car of Edwardian vintage.* **5** *Informal.* a group of people or objects of the same period: *a fashion of last season's vintage.* ◆ *adj* **6** (of wine) of an outstandingly good year. **7** representative of the best and most typical: *vintage Shakespeare.* **8** of lasting interest and importance; venerable; classic: *vintage films.* **9** old-fashioned; dated. ◆ *vb* **10** *(tr)* to gather (grapes) or make (wine). [C15: from Old French *vendage* (influenced by *vintener* VINTNER), from Latin *vindēmia,* from *vīnum* WINE, grape + *dēmere* to take away (from *dē-* away + *emere* to take)]

vintage car *n Chiefly Brit.* an old car, esp. one constructed between 1919 and 1930. Compare **veteran car.**

vintager ('vɪntɪdʒə) *n* a grape harvester.

vintner ('vɪntnə) *n* a wine merchant. [C15: from Old French *vinetier,* from Medieval Latin *vīnētārius,* from Latin *vīnētum* vineyard, from *vīnum* WINE]

vinyl ('vaɪnɪl) *n* **1** *(modifier)* of, consisting of, or containing the monovalent group of atoms CH_2CH-: *a vinyl polymer; vinyl chloride.* **2** *(modifier)* of, consisting of, or made of a vinyl resin: *a vinyl raincoat.* **3** any vinyl polymer, resin, or plastic, esp. PVC. **4** (collectively) conventional records made of vinyl as opposed to compact discs. [C19: from VINI- + -YL]

vinyl acetate *n* a colourless volatile liquid unsaturated ester that polymerizes readily in light and is used for making polyvinyl acetate. Formula: CH_2:$CHOOCCH_3$.

vinyl chloride *n* a colourless flammable gaseous unsaturated compound made by the chlorination of ethylene and used as a refrigerant and in the manufacture of PVC; chloroethylene; chloroethene. Formula: CH:CHCl.

vinylidene (vaɪ'nɪlɪˌdiːn) *n* (*modifier*) of, consisting of, or containing the group CH_2:C: *a vinylidene group or radical; vinylidene chloride; a vinylidene resin.* [C20: from VINYL + -IDE + -ENE]

vinyl resin *or* **polymer** *n* any one of a class of thermoplastic materials, esp. PVC and polyvinyl acetate, made by polymerizing vinyl compounds.

viol ('vaɪəl) *n* any of a family of stringed musical instruments that preceded the violin family, consisting of a fretted fingerboard, a body rather like that of a violin but having a flat back and six strings, played with a curved bow. They are held between the knees when played and have a quiet yet penetrating tone; they were much played, esp. in consorts, in the 16th and 17th centuries. [C15: from Old French *viole,* from Old Provençal *viola;* see VIOLA[1]]

viola[1] (vɪ'əʊlə) *n* **1** a bowed stringed instrument, the alto of the violin family; held beneath the chin when played. It is pitched and tuned an octave above the cello. **2** any of various instruments of the viol family, such as the viola da gamba. [C18: from Italian *viola,* probably from Old Provençal *viola,* of uncertain origin; perhaps related to Latin *vītulārī* to rejoice]

viola[2] ('vaɪələ, vaɪ'əʊ-) *n* any temperate perennial herbaceous plant of the violaceous genus *Viola,* the flowers of which have showy irregular petals, white, yellow, blue, or mauve in colour. See also **violet** (sense 1), **pansy** (sense 1). [C15: from Latin: violet]

violaceous (ˌvaɪə'leɪʃəs) *adj* **1** of, relating to, or belonging to the *Violaceae,* a family of herbaceous plants and shrubs including the violets and pansies. **2** of the colour violet. [C17: from Latin *violāceus,* from *viola* VIOLET]

viola clef *n* another term for **alto clef.**

viola da braccio (vɪ'əʊlə də 'brætʃɪˌəʊ) *n* **1** an old name for **viola**[1] (sense 1). **2** a type of viol held on the shoulder, from which the modern viola was developed. [from Italian, literally: viol for the arm]

viola da gamba (vɪ'əʊlə də 'gæmbə) *n* the second largest and lowest member of the viol family. See **viol.** [C18: from Italian, literally: viol for the leg]

viola d'amore (vɪ'əʊlə dæ'mɔːrɪ) *n* an instrument of the viol family having no frets, seven strings, and a set of sympathetic strings. It was held under the chin when played. [C18: from Italian, literally: viol of love]

violate ('vaɪəˌleɪt) *vb* (*tr*) **1** to break, disregard, or infringe (a law, agreement, etc.). **2** to rape or otherwise sexually assault. **3** to disturb rudely or improperly; break in upon. **4** to treat irreverently or disrespectfully; outrage: *he violated a sanctuary.* **5** *Obsolete.* to mistreat physically. ◆ *adj* **6** *Archaic.* violated or dishonoured. [C15: from Latin *violāre* to do violence to, from *vīs* strength] ▸ **'violable** *adj* ▸ **ˌviola'bility** *or* **'violableness** *n* ▸ **'violably** *adv* ▸ **ˌvio'lation** *n* ▸ **'violative** *adj* ▸ **'vioˌlator** *or* **'vioˌlater** *n*

violence ('vaɪələns) *n* **1** the exercise or an instance of physical force, usually effecting or intended to effect injuries, destruction, etc. **2** powerful, untamed, or devastating force: *the violence of the sea.* **3** great strength of feeling, as in language, etc.; fervour. **4** an unjust, unwarranted, or unlawful display of force, esp. such as tends to overawe or intimidate. **5 do violence to. 5a** to inflict harm upon; damage or violate: *they did violence to the prisoners.* **5b** to distort or twist the sense or intention of: *the reporters did violence to my speech.* [C13: via Old French from Latin *violentia* impetuosity, from *violentus* VIOLENT]

violent ('vaɪələnt) *adj* **1** marked or caused by great physical force or violence: *a violent stab.* **2** (of a person) tending to the use of violence, esp. in order to injure or intimidate others. **3** marked by intensity of any kind: *a violent clash of colours.* **4** characterized by an undue use of force; severe; harsh. **5** caused by or displaying strong or undue mental or emotional force: *a violent tongue.* **6** tending to distort the meaning or intent: *a violent interpretation of the text.* [C14: from Latin *violentus,* probably from *vīs* strength] ▸ **'violently** *adv*

violent storm *n* a wind of force 11 on the Beaufort scale, reaching speeds of 64–72 mph.

violet ('vaɪəlɪt) *n* **1** any of various temperate perennial herbaceous plants of the violaceous genus *Viola,* such as *V. odorata* (**sweet** (or **garden**) **violet**), typically having mauve or bluish flowers with irregular showy petals. **2** any other plant of the genus *Viola,* such as the wild pansy. **3** any of various similar but unrelated plants, such as the African violet. **4a** any of a group of colours that vary in saturation but have the same purplish-blue hue. They lie at one end of the visible spectrum, next to blue; approximate wavelength range 445–390 nanometres. **4b** (*as adj*)*: a violet dress.* **5** a dye or pigment of or producing these colours. **6** violet clothing: *dressed in violet.* **7 shrinking violet.** *Informal.* a shy person. [C14: from Old French *violete* a little violet, from *viole,* from Latin *viola* violet] ▸ **'violet-ˌlike** *adj*

violin (ˌvaɪə'lɪn) *n* a bowed stringed instrument, the highest member of the violin family, consisting of a fingerboard, a hollow wooden body with waisted sides, and a sounding board connected to the back by means of a soundpost that also supports the bridge. It has two f-shaped sound holes cut in the belly. The instrument, noted for its fine and flexible tone, is the most important of the stringed instruments. It is held under the chin when played. Range: roughly three and a half octaves upwards from G below middle C. [C16: from Italian *violino* a little viola, from VIOLA[1]]

violinist (ˌvaɪə'lɪnɪst) *n* a person who plays the violin.

violist[1] (vɪ'əʊlɪst) *n U.S.* a person who plays the viola.

violist[2] ('vaɪəlɪst) *n* a person who plays the viol.

Viollet-le-Duc (*French* vjɔlɛlədyk) *n* **Eugène Emmanuel** (øʒɛn ɛmanɥɛl). 1814–79, French architect and leader of the Gothic Revival in France, noted for his dictionary of French architecture (1854–68) and for his restoration of medieval buildings.

violoncello (ˌvaɪələn'tʃɛləʊ) *n, pl* **-los.** the full name for **cello.** [C18: from Italian, from VIOLONE + *-cello,* diminutive suffix] ▸ **ˌviolon'cellist** *n*

violone ('vaɪəˌləʊn) *n* the double-bass member of the viol family lying an octave below the viola da gamba. It corresponds to the double bass in the violin family. [C18: from Italian, from VIOLA[1] + *-one,* augmentative suffix]

VIP *abbrev. for:* **1** very important person. **2** vasoactive intestinal peptide: a polypeptide secreted by the small intestine during digestion and also found in the brain as a neurotransmitter: large amounts in the blood cause diarrhoea.

viper ('vaɪpə) *n* **1** any venomous Old World snake of the family *Viperidae,* esp. any of the genus *Vipera* (the adder and related forms), having hollow fangs in the upper jaw that are used to inject venom. **2** any of various other snakes, such as the horned viper. **3** See **pit viper. 4** a malicious or treacherous person. [C16: from Latin *vīpera,* perhaps from *vīvus* living + *parere* to bear, referring to a tradition that the viper was viviparous] ▸ **'viper-ˌlike** *adj*

viperous ('vaɪpərəs) *or* **viperish** *adj* **1** Also: **viperine** ('vaɪpəˌraɪn). of, relating to, or resembling a viper. **2** malicious. ▸ **'viperously** *or* **'viperishly** *adv*

viper's bugloss *n* **1** Also called (U.S.): **blueweed.** a Eurasian boraginaceous weed, *Echium vulgare,* having blue flowers and pink buds. **2** Also called: (Austral.) **Paterson's curse,** (South Australia) **Salvation Jane.** a related plant, *E. plantagineum,* that has purple flowers and is naturalized in Australia and New Zealand. See also **echium.**

VIR *abbrev. for* Victoria Imperatrix Regina. [Latin: Victoria, Empress and Queen]

virago (vɪ'rɑːgəʊ) *n, pl* **-goes** *or* **-gos. 1** a loud, violent, and ill-tempered woman; scold; shrew. **2** *Archaic.* a strong, brave, or warlike woman; amazon. [Old English, from Latin: a manlike maiden, from *vir* a man] ▸ **viraginous** (vɪ'rædʒɪnəs) *adj* ▸ **vi'rago-ˌlike** *adj*

viral ('vaɪrəl) *adj* of, relating to, or caused by a virus.

Vir Chakra ('viːr 'tʃʌkrə) *n* an award made to distinguished soldiers by the Government of India. [Hindi: *vir* brave man + *chakra* wheel]

Virchow (*German* 'fɪrço) *n* **Rudolf Ludwig Karl** ('ruːdɔlf 'luːtvɪç karl). 1821–1902, German pathologist, who is considered the founder of modern (cellular) pathology.

virelay ('vɪrɪˌleɪ) *n* **1** an old French verse form, rarely used in English, consisting of short lines arranged in stanzas having only two rhymes, and two opening lines recurring at intervals. **2** any of various similar forms. [C14: from Old French *virelai,* probably from *vireli* (associated with *lai* LAY[4]), meaningless word used as a refrain]

virement ('vɪəmɑ̃) *n* an administrative transfer of funds from one part of a budget to another. [from French, from Middle French: act of turning, from *virer* to turn]

Viren ('vɪərən) *n* **Lasse** ('læsɪ). born 1949, Finnish distance runner: winner of the 5000 metres and the 10 000 metres in the 1972 and 1976 Olympic Games.

vireo ('vɪrɪəʊ) *n, pl* **vireos.** any insectivorous American songbird of the family *Vireonidae,* esp. those of the genus *Vireo,* having an olive-grey back with pale underparts. [C19: from Latin: a bird, probably a greenfinch; compare *virēre* to be green]

virescence (vɪ'rɛsəns) *n* **1** (in plants) the state of becoming green, esp. by the action of disease, etc., in parts not normally green. **2** the condition of being or the process of becoming fgreen. [C19: see VIRESCENT]

virescent (vɪ'rɛsᵊnt) *adj* greenish or becoming green. [C19: from Latin *virescere* to grow green, from *virēre* to be green]

virga ('vɜːgə) *n* (*sometimes functioning as pl*) *Meteorol.* wisps of rain or snow, seen trailing from clouds, that evaporate before reaching the earth. [C20: from Latin: streak]

virgate[1] ('vɜːgɪt, -geɪt) *adj* long, straight, and thin; rod-shaped: *virgate stems.* [C19: from Latin *virgātus* made of twigs, from *virga* a rod]

virgate[2] ('vɜːgɪt, -geɪt) *n Brit.* an obsolete measure of land area, usually taken as equivalent to 30 acres. [C17: from Medieval Latin *virgāta* (*terrae*) a rod's measurement (of land), from Latin *virga* rod; the phrase is a translation of Old English *gierd landes* a yard of land]

Virgil *or* **Vergil** ('vɜːdʒɪl) *n* Latin name *Publius Vergilius Maro.* 70–19 B.C., Roman poet, patronized by Maecenas. The *Eclogues* (42–37), ten pastoral poems, and the *Georgics* (37–30), four books on the art of farming, established Virgil as the foremost poet of his age. His masterpiece is the *Aeneid* (30–19). ▸ **Vir'gilian** *or* **Ver'gilian** *adj*

virgin ('vɜːdʒɪn) *n* **1** a person, esp. a woman, who has never had sexual intercourse. **2** an unmarried woman who has taken a religious vow of chastity in order to dedicate herself totally to God. **3** any female animal that has never mated. **4** a female insect that produces offspring by parthenogenesis. **5** a person who is new to or inexperienced in a specified field: *a political virgin.* ◆ *adj* (*usually prenominal*) **6** of, relating to, resembling, suitable for, or characteristic of a virgin or virgins; chaste. **7** pure and natural, uncorrupted, unsullied, or untouched: *virgin purity.* **8** not yet cultivated, explored, exploited, etc., by man: *virgin territories.* **9** being the first or happening for the first time. **10** (of vegetable oils) obtained directly by the first pressing of fruits, leaves, or seeds of plants without applying heat. **11** (of a metal) made from an ore rather than from scrap. **12** occurring naturally in a pure and uncombined form: *virgin silver.* **13** *Physics.* (of a neutron) not having experienced a collision. [C13: from Old French *virgine,* from Latin *virgō* virgin]

Virgin[1] ('vɜːdʒɪn) *n* **1 the.** See **Virgin Mary. 2** a statue or other artistic representation of the Virgin Mary.

Virgin[2] ('vɜːdʒɪn) *n* **the.** the constellation Virgo, the sixth sign of the zodiac.

virginal[1] ('vɜːdʒɪnᵊl) *adj* **1** of, relating to, characterized by, proper to, or maintaining a state of virginity; chaste. **2** extremely pure or fresh; untouched; undefiled. [C15: from Latin *virginālis* maidenly, from *virgō* virgin] ▸ **'virginally** *adv*

virginal[2] ('vɜːdʒɪnᵊl) *n* (*often pl*) a smaller version of the harpsichord, but oblong in shape, having one manual and no pedals. [C16: probably from Latin *virginālis* VIRGINAL[1], perhaps because it was played largely by young ladies] ▸ **'virginalist** *n*

virgin birth *n* another name for **parthenogenesis** (sense 2).

Virgin Birth *n* the doctrine that Jesus Christ had no human father but was conceived solely by the direct intervention of the Holy Spirit so that Mary remained miraculously a virgin during and after his birth.

virgin forest *n* a forest in its natural state, before it has been explored or exploited by man.

Virginia[1] (və'dʒɪnɪə) *n* (*sometimes not cap.*) a type of flue-cured tobacco grown originally in Virginia.

Virginia[2] (və'dʒɪnɪə) *n* a state of the eastern U.S., on the Atlantic: site of the first permanent English settlement in North America; consists of a low-lying deeply indented coast rising inland to the Piedmont plateau and the Blue Ridge Mountains. Capital: Richmond. Pop.: 6 733 996 (1997 est.). Area: 103 030 sq. km (39 780 sq. miles). Abbrevs.: **Va.** or (with zip code) **VA** ► **Vir'ginian** *adj, n*

Virginia Beach *n* a city and resort in SE Virginia, on the Atlantic. Pop.: 430 385 (1996 est.).

Virginia creeper *n* **1** Also called (U.S.): **American ivy, woodbine.** a vitaceous woody vine, *Parthenocissus quinquefolia,* of North America, having tendrils with adhesive tips, bluish-black berry-like fruits, and compound leaves that turn red in autumn: widely planted for ornament. **2** Also called: **Japanese ivy.** a similar related plant, *Parthenocissus tricuspidata,* of SE Asia, having trilobed leaves and purple berries. U.S. name: **Boston ivy.**

Virginia deer *n* another name for **white-tailed deer.**

Virginia reel *n* **1** an American country dance. **2** music written for or in the manner of this dance.

Virginia stock *n* a Mediterranean cruciferous plant, *Malcomia maritima,* cultivated for its white and pink flowers.

Virgin Islands *pl n* a group of about 100 small islands (14 inhabited) in the Caribbean, east of Puerto Rico: discovered by Columbus (1493); consists of the British Virgin Islands in the east and the Virgin Islands of the United States in the west and south. Pop.: 17 000 (1993 est.). Area: 497 sq. km (192 sq. miles).

Virgin Islands of the United States *pl n* a territory of the U.S. in the Caribbean, consisting of islands west and south of the British Virgin Islands: purchased from Denmark in 1917 for their strategic importance. Capital: Charlotte Amalie. Pop.: 118 000 (1998 est.). Area: 344 sq. km (133 sq. miles). Former name: **Danish West Indies.**

virginity (və'dʒɪnɪtɪ) *n* **1** the condition or fact of being a virgin; maidenhood; chastity. **2** the condition of being untouched, unsullied, etc.

virginium (və'dʒɪnɪəm) *n Chem.* a former name for **francium.**

Virgin Mary *n* Mary, the mother of Christ. Also called: the **Virgin.**

Virgin Queen *n* **the.** another name for (Queen) **Elizabeth I** of England.

virgin's-bower *n* any of several American clematis plants, esp. *Clematis virginiana,* of E North America, which has clusters of small white flowers.

virgin soil *n* **1** soil that has not been cultivated before. **2** a person or thing that is as yet undeveloped.

virgin wool *n* wool that is being processed or woven for the first time.

Virgo ('vɜːgəʊ) *n, Latin genitive* **Virginis** ('vɜːdʒɪnɪs). **1** *Astronomy.* a large zodiacal constellation on the celestial equator, lying between Leo and Libra. It contains the star Spica and a cluster of several thousand galaxies, the **Virgo cluster**, lying 50 million light years away. **2** *Astrology.* **2a** Also called: the **Virgin.** the sixth sign of the zodiac, symbol ♍, having a mutable earth classification and ruled by the planet Mercury. The sun is in this sign between about Aug. 23 and Sept. 22. **2b** Also called: **Virgoan** (vɜː'gəʊən). a person born when the sun is in this sign. ◆ *adj* **3** Also: **Virgoan.** *Astrology.* born under or characteristic of Virgo. [C14: from Latin]

virgo intacta ('vɜːgəʊ ɪn'tæktə) *n* a girl or woman whose hymen has not been broken. [Latin, literally: untouched virgin]

virgulate ('vɜːgjʊlɪt, -ˌleɪt) *adj* rod-shaped or rodlike. [C19: from Latin *virgula* a little rod, from *virga* rod]

virgule ('vɜːgjuːl) *n Printing.* another name for **solidus.** [C19: from French: comma, from Latin *virgula* a little rod, from *virga* rod]

viridescent (ˌvɪrɪ'desᵊnt) *adj* greenish or tending to become green. [C19: from Late Latin *viridescere* to grow green, from Latin *viridis* green] ► ˌ**viri'descence** *n*

viridian (vɪ'rɪdɪən) *n* a green pigment consisting of a hydrated form of chromic oxide. [C19: from Latin *viridis* green]

viridity (vɪ'rɪdɪtɪ) *n* **1** the quality or state of being green; greenness; verdancy. **2** innocence, youth, or freshness. [C15: from Latin *viriditās,* from *viridis* green]

virile ('vɪraɪl) *adj* **1** of, relating to, or having the characteristics of an adult male. **2** (of a male) possessing high sexual drive and capacity for sexual intercourse. **3** of or capable of copulation or procreation. **4** strong, forceful, or vigorous. [C15: from Latin *virīlis* manly, from *vir* a man; related to Old English *wer* man and probably to Latin *vis* strength] ► **virility** (vɪ'rɪlɪtɪ) *n*

virilism ('vɪrɪˌlɪzəm) *n Med.* the abnormal development in a woman of male secondary sex characteristics.

virino (vɪ'riːnəʊ) *n* an entity postulated to be the causative agent of BSE and related diseases, said to consist of a fragment of nucleic acid surrounded by a protein coat derived from the host cell. [C20: from VIRUS + *-ino* diminutive form]

virion ('vaɪrɪən) *n* a virus in infective form, consisting of an RNA particle within a protein covering. [C20: from VIR(US) + ION]

viroid ('vaɪrɔɪd) *n* any of various infective RNA particles, smaller than a virus and known to cause some plant diseases. [C20: from VIR(US) + -OID]

virology (vaɪ'rɒlədʒɪ) *n* the branch of medicine concerned with the study of viruses and the diseases they cause. ► **virological** (ˌvaɪrə'lɒdʒɪkᵊl) *adj* ► **vi'rologist** *n*

virtu *or* **vertu** (vɜː'tuː) *n* **1** a taste or love for curios or works of fine art; connoisseurship. **2** such objects collectively. **3** the quality of being rare, beautiful, or otherwise appealing to a connoisseur (esp. in the phrases **articles of virtu; objects of virtu**). [C18: from Italian *virtù;* see VIRTUE]

virtual ('vɜːtʃʊəl) *adj* **1** having the essence or effect but not the appearance or form of: *a virtual revolution.* **2** *Physics.* being, relating to, or involving a virtual image: *a virtual focus.* **3** *Computing.* of or relating to virtual storage: *virtual memory.* **4** of or relating to a computer technique by which a person, wearing a headset or mask, has the experience of being in an environment created by the computer, and of interacting with and causing changes in it. **5** *Rare.* capable of producing an effect through inherent power or virtue. **6** *Physics.* designating or relating to a particle exchanged between other particles that are interacting by a field of force: *a virtual photon.* See also **exchange force.** [C14: from Medieval Latin *virtuālis* effective, from Latin *virtūs* VIRTUE] ► ˌ**virtu'ality** *n*

virtual image *n* an optical image formed by the apparent divergence of rays from a point, rather than their actual divergence from a point.

virtually ('vɜːtʃʊəlɪ) *adv* in effect though not in fact; practically; nearly.

virtual reality *n* a computer-generated environment that, to the person experiencing it, closely resembles reality. Abbrev.: **VR.** See also **virtual** (sense 4).

virtual storage *or* **memory** *n* a computer system in which the size of the memory is effectively increased by automatically transferring sections of a program from a large capacity backing store, such as a disk, into the smaller core memory as they are required.

virtue ('vɜːtjuː, -tʃuː) *n* **1** the quality or practice of moral excellence or righteousness. **2** a particular moral excellence: *the virtue of tolerance.* **3** any of the cardinal virtues (prudence, justice, fortitude, and temperance) or theological virtues (faith, hope, and charity). **4** any admirable quality, feature, or trait. **5** chastity, esp. in women. **6** *Archaic.* an effective, active, or inherent power or force. **7 by** *or* **in virtue of.** on account of or by reason of. **8 make a virtue of necessity.** to acquiesce in doing something unpleasant with a show of grace because one must do it in any case. [C13 *vertu,* from Old French, from Latin *virtūs* manliness, courage, from *vir* man] ► '**virtueless** *adj*

virtues ('vɜːtjuːz, -tʃuːz) *pl n* (*often cap.*) the fifth of the nine orders into which the angels are traditionally divided in medieval angelology.

virtuoso (ˌvɜːtjʊ'əʊzəʊ, -səʊ) *n, pl* **-sos** *or* **-si** (-siː). **1** a consummate master of musical technique and artistry. **2** a person who has a masterly or dazzling skill or technique in any field of activity. **3** a connoisseur, dilettante, or collector of art objects. **4** *Obsolete.* a scholar or savant. **5** (*modifier*) showing masterly skill or brilliance: *a virtuoso performance.* [C17: from Italian: skilled, from Late Latin *virtuōsus* good, virtuous; see VIRTUE] ► **virtuosic** (ˌvɜːtjʊ'ɒsɪk) *adj* ► ˌ**virtu'osity** *n*

virtuous ('vɜːtʃʊəs) *adj* **1** characterized by or possessing virtue or moral excellence; righteous; upright. **2** (of women) chaste or virginal. ► '**virtuously** *adv* ► '**virtuousness** *n*

virulence ('vɪrʊləns) *or* **virulency** *n* **1** the quality of being virulent. **2** the capacity of a microorganism for causing disease.

virulent ('vɪrʊlənt) *adj* **1a** (of a microorganism) extremely infective. **1b** (of a disease) having a rapid course and violent effect. **2** extremely poisonous, injurious, etc. **3** extremely bitter, hostile, etc. [C14: from Latin *vīrulentus* full of poison, from *vīrus* poison; see VIRUS] ► '**virulently** *adv*

virus ('vaɪrəs) *n, pl* **-ruses. 1** any of a group of submicroscopic entities consisting of a single nucleic acid surrounded by a protein coat and capable of replication only within the cells of animals and plants: many are pathogenic. **2** *Informal.* a disease caused by a virus. **3** any corrupting or infecting influence. **4** *Computing.* an unauthorized program that inserts itself into a computer system and then propagates itself to other computers via networks or disks; when activated it interferes with the operation of the computer. [C16: from Latin: slime, poisonous liquid; related to Old English *wāse* marsh, Greek *ios* poison] ► '**virus-**ˌ**like** *adj*

vis *Latin.* (vɪs) *n, pl* ***vires*** ('vaɪriːz). power, force, or strength.

Vis. *abbrev. for* Viscount *or* Viscountess.

visa ('viːzə) *n, pl* **-sas. 1** an endorsement in a passport or similar document, signifying that the document is in order and permitting its bearer to travel into or through the country of the government issuing it. **2** any sign or signature of approval. ◆ *vb* **-sas, -saing, -saed.** (*tr*) **3** to enter a visa into (a passport). **4** to endorse or ratify. [C19: via French from Latin *vīsa* things seen, from *vīsus,* past participle of *vidēre* to see]

visage ('vɪzɪdʒ) *n Chiefly literary.* **1** face or countenance. **2** appearance; aspect. [C13: from Old French: aspect, from *vis* face, from Latin *vīsus* appearance, from *vidēre* to see]

-visaged *adj* (*in combination*) having a visage as specified: *flat-visaged.*

visagiste (ˌviːzɑː'ʒiːst) *n* a person who designs and applies face make-up; make-up artist. [C20: from French, from *visage* face + *-iste* -ist]

Visakhapatnam (vɪˌsɑːkə'pʌtnəm) *n* a variant spelling of **Vishakhapatnam.**

vis-à-vis (ˌviːzɑː'viː) *prep* **1** in relation to; regarding. **2** face to face with; opposite. ◆ *adv, adj* **3** face to face; opposite. ◆ *n, pl* **vis-à-vis. 4** a person or thing that is situated opposite to another. **5** a person who corresponds to another in office, capacity, etc.; counterpart. **6** an upholstered sofa; tête-à-tête. **7** a type of horse-drawn carriage in which the passengers sit opposite one another. **8** a coin having an obverse upon which two portraits appear facing each other. [C18: French, from *vis* face]

Visayan (vɪ'sɑːjən) *or* **Bisayan** *n, pl* **-yans** *or* **-yan. 1** a member of the most numerous indigenous people of the Philippines. ◆ *adj* **2** of or relating to this people.

Visayan Islands *pl n* a group of seven large and several hundred small islands in the central Philippines. Chief islands: Negros and Panay. Pop.: 13 041 000 (1990). Area: about 61 000 sq. km (23 535 sq. miles). Spanish name: **Bisayas.**

Visby (*Swedish* 'viːsbyː) *n* a port in SE Sweden, on NW Gotland Island in the Baltic: an early member of the Hanseatic League and major N European commercial centre in the Middle Ages. Pop.: 57 110 (1990).

Visc. *abbrev. for* Viscount *or* Viscountess.

viscacha *or* **vizcacha** (vɪsˈkætʃə) *n* **1** a gregarious burrowing hystricomorph rodent, *Lagostomus maximus,* of southern South America, similar to but larger than the chinchillas: family *Chinchillidae.* **2 mountain viscacha.** another name for **mountain chinchilla** (see **chinchilla** (sense 3)). [C17: from Spanish, from Quechuan *wiskácha*]

viscaria (vɪsˈkɛərɪə) *n* any plant of the Eurasian perennial genus *Viscaria,* closely related to genus *Lychnis,* in which it is sometimes included: low-growing, with pink, white, or purple flowers: family *Carophyllaceae.* [New Latin, from *viscum* birdlime (from the viscid stems)]

viscera (ˈvɪsərə) *pl n, sing* **viscus** (ˈvɪskəs). **1** *Anatomy.* the large internal organs of the body collectively, esp. those in the abdominal cavity. Related adj: **splanchnic. 2** (less formally) the intestines; guts. [C17: from Latin: entrails, pl of *viscus* internal organ]

visceral (ˈvɪsərəl) *adj* **1** of, relating to, or affecting the viscera. **2** characterized by intuition or instinct rather than intellect. ▸ ˈ**viscerally** *adv*

visceromotor (ˈvɪsərəʊˌməʊtə) *adj Physiol.* relating to or controlling movements of the viscera.

viscerotonia (ˌvɪsərəʊˈtəʊnɪə) *n* a personality type characterized by hedonism and conviviality: said to be correlated with an endomorph body type. Compare **cerebrotonia, somatotonia.**

viscid (ˈvɪsɪd) *adj* **1** cohesive and sticky; glutinous; viscous. **2** (esp. of a leaf) covered with a sticky substance. [C17: from Late Latin *viscidus* sticky, from Latin *viscum* mistletoe or birdlime] ▸ **visˈcidity** *or* ˈ**viscidness** *n* ▸ ˈ**viscidly** *adv*

viscoelastic (ˌvɪskəʊɪˈlæstɪk) *adj Physics.* (of a solid or liquid) exhibiting both viscous and elastic behaviour when deformed. ▸ ˌ**viscoelasˈticity** *n*

viscoid (ˈvɪskɔɪd) *or* **viscoidal** (vɪsˈkɔɪdᵊl) *adj* (of a fluid) somewhat viscous.

viscometer (vɪsˈkɒmɪtə) *or* **viscosimeter** (ˌvɪskəʊˈsɪmɪtə) *n* any device for measuring viscosity. ▸ **viscometric** (ˌvɪskəˈmɛtrɪk) *or* ˌ**viscoˈmetrical** *adj* ▸ **visˈcometry** *n*

Visconti (*Italian* visˈkonti) *n* **1** the ruling family of Milan from 1277 to 1447. **2 Luchino,** real name *Luchino Visconti de Modrone.* 1906–76, Italian stage and film director, whose neorealist films include *Ossessione* (1942). His other films include *The Leopard* (1963), *Death in Venice* (1970), and *The Innocents* (1976).

viscose (ˈvɪskəʊs) *n* **1a** a viscous orange-brown solution obtained by dissolving cellulose in sodium hydroxide and carbon disulphide. It can be converted back to cellulose by an acid, as in the manufacture of rayon and cellophane. **1b** (*as modifier): viscose rayon.* **2** rayon made from this material. ◆ *adj* **3** another word for **viscous.** [C19: from Late Latin *viscōsus* full of birdlime, sticky, from *viscum* birdlime; see VISCID]

viscosity (vɪsˈkɒsɪtɪ) *n, pl* **-ties. 1** the state or property of being viscous. **2** *Physics.* **2a** the extent to which a fluid resists a tendency to flow. **2b** Also called: **absolute viscosity.** a measure of this resistance, equal to the tangential stress on a liquid undergoing streamline flow divided by its velocity gradient. It is measured in newton seconds per metre squared. Symbol: η See also **kinematic viscosity, specific viscosity.**

viscount (ˈvaɪkaʊnt) *n* **1** (in the British Isles) a nobleman ranking below an earl and above a baron. **2** (in various countries) a son or younger brother of a count. See also **vicomte. 3** (in medieval Europe) the deputy of a count. [C14: from Old French *visconte,* from Medieval Latin *vicecomes,* from Late Latin *vice-* VICE³ + *comes* COUNT²]

viscountcy (ˈvaɪkaʊntsɪ) *or* **viscounty** *n* the rank or position of a viscount.

viscountess (ˈvaɪkaʊntɪs) *n* **1** the wife or widow of a viscount. **2** a woman who holds the rank of viscount in her own right.

viscous (ˈvɪskəs) *or* **viscose** *adj* **1** (of liquids) thick and sticky; viscid. **2** having or involving viscosity. [C14: from Late Latin *viscōsus;* see VISCOSE] ▸ ˈ**viscously** *adv* ▸ ˈ**viscousness** *n*

viscous flow *n* another name for **streamline flow.**

Visct *abbrev. for* Viscount *or* Viscountess.

viscus (ˈvɪskəs) *n* the singular of **viscera.**

vise (vaɪs) *n, vb U.S.* a variant spelling of **vice².**

Viseu (*Portuguese* viˈzeu) *n* a city in N central Portugal: 12th-century cathedral. Pop.: 20 590 (1991).

Vishakhapatnam (vɪˌʃɑːkəˈpʌtnəm), **Visakhapatnam,** *or* **Vizagapatam** *n* a port in E India, in NE Andhra Pradesh on the Bay of Bengal: shipbuilding and oil-refining industries. Pop.: 752 037 (1991).

Vishinsky (*Russian* viˈʃinskij) *n* a variant spelling of (Andrei Yanuaryevich) **Vyshinsky.**

Vishnu (ˈvɪʃnuː) *n Hinduism.* the Pervader or Sustainer, originally a solar deity occupying a secondary place in the Hindu pantheon, later one of the three chief gods, the second member of the Trimurti, and, later still, the saviour appearing in many incarnations. [C17: from Sanskrit *Viṣṇu,* literally: the one who works everywhere] ▸ ˈ**Vishnuism** *n*

visibility (ˌvɪzɪˈbɪlɪtɪ) *n* **1** the condition or fact of being visible. **2** clarity of vision or relative possibility of seeing. **3** the range of vision: *visibility is 500 yards.*

visible (ˈvɪzɪbᵊl) *adj* **1** capable of being perceived by the eye. **2** capable of being perceived by the mind; evident: *no visible dangers.* **3** available: *the visible resources.* **4** (of an index or file) using a flexible display system for the contents. **5** of or relating to the balance of trade: *visible transactions.* **6** represented by visible symbols. ◆ *n* **7** a visible item of trade; product. [C14: from Latin *vīsibilis,* from *vidēre* to see] ▸ ˈ**visibleness** *n* ▸ ˈ**visibly** *adv*

visible balance *n* another name for **balance of trade.**

visible radiation *n* electromagnetic radiation that causes the sensation of sight; light. It has wavelengths between about 380 and 780 nanometres.

visible speech *n* a system of phonetic notation invented by Alexander Melville Bell (1819–1905) that utilized symbols based on the schematic representation of the articulations used for each speech sound.

Visigoth (ˈvɪzɪˌgɒθ) *n* a member of the western group of the Goths, who were driven into the Balkans in the late 4th century A.D. Moving on, they sacked Rome (410) and established a kingdom in present-day Spain and S France that lasted until 711. [C17: from Late Latin *Visigothī* (pl), of Germanic origin, *visi-* perhaps meaning: west] ▸ ˌ**Visiˈgothic** *adj*

vision (ˈvɪʒən) *n* **1** the act, faculty, or manner of perceiving with the eye; sight. **2a** the image on a television screen. **2b** (*as modifier*): *vision control.* **3** the ability or an instance of great perception, esp. of future developments: *a man of vision.* **4** mystical or religious experience of seeing some supernatural event, person, etc.: *the vision of St John of the Cross.* **5** that which is seen, esp. in such a mystical experience. **6** (*sometimes pl*) a vivid mental image produced by the imagination: *he had visions of becoming famous.* **7** a person or thing of extraordinary beauty. ◆ *vb* **8** (*tr*) to see or show in or as if in a vision. [C13: from Latin *vīsiō* sight, from *vidēre* to see] ▸ ˈ**visionless** *adj*

visional (ˈvɪʒənᵊl) *adj* of, relating to, or seen in a vision, apparition, etc. ▸ ˈ**visionally** *adv*

visionary (ˈvɪʒənərɪ) *adj* **1** marked by vision or foresight: *a visionary leader.* **2** incapable of being realized or effected; unrealistic. **3** (of people) characterized by idealistic or radical ideas, esp. impractical ones. **4** given to having visions. **5** of, of the nature of, or seen in visions. ◆ *n, pl* **-aries. 6** a visionary person. ▸ ˈ**visionariness** *n*

vision mixer *n Television.* **1** the person who selects and manipulates the television signals from cameras, film, and other sources, to make the composite programme. **2** the equipment used for vision mixing.

visit (ˈvɪzɪt) *vb* **-its, -iting, -ited. 1** to go or come to see (a person, place, etc.). **2** to stay with (someone) as a guest. **3** to go or come to (an institution, place, etc.) for the purpose of inspecting or examining. **4** (*tr*) (of a disease, disaster, etc.) to assail; afflict. **5** (*tr;* foll. by *upon* or *on*) to inflict (punishment, etc.): *the judge visited his full anger upon the defendant.* **6** (*tr;* usually foll. by *with*) *Archaic.* to afflict or plague (with punishment, etc.). **7** (often foll. by *with*) *U.S. and Canadian informal.* to chat or converse (with someone). ◆ *n* **8** the act or an instance of visiting. **9** a stay as a guest. **10** a professional or official call. **11** a formal call for the purpose of inspection or examination. **12** *International law.* the right of an officer of a belligerent state to stop and search neutral ships in war to verify their nationality and ascertain whether they carry contraband: *the right of visit and search.* **13** *U.S. and Canadian informal.* a friendly talk or chat. [C13: from Latin *vīsitāre* to go to see, from *vīsere* to examine, from *vidēre* to see] ▸ ˈ**visitable** *adj*

visitant (ˈvɪzɪtənt) *n* **1** a supernatural being; ghost; apparition. **2** a visitor or guest, usually from far away. **3** a pilgrim or tourist. **4** Also called: **visitor.** a migratory bird that is present in a particular region only at certain times: *a summer visitant.* ◆ *adj* **5** *Archaic.* paying a visit; visiting. [C16: from Latin *vīsitāns* going to see, from *vīsitāre;* see VISIT]

visitation (ˌvɪzɪˈteɪʃən) *n* **1** an official call or visit for the purpose of inspecting or examining an institution, esp. such a visit made by a bishop to his diocese. **2** a visiting of punishment or reward from heaven. **3** any disaster or catastrophe: *a visitation of the plague.* **4** an appearance or arrival of a supernatural being. **5** any call or visit. **6** *Informal.* an unduly prolonged social call. ▸ ˌ**visitˈational** *adj*

Visitation (ˌvɪzɪˈteɪʃən) *n* **1a** the visit made by the Virgin Mary to her cousin Elizabeth (Luke 1:39–56). **1b** the Church festival commemorating this, held on July 2. **2** a religious order of nuns, the **Order of the Visitation,** founded in 1610 by St Francis of Sales and dedicated to contemplation and the cultivation of humility, gentleness, and sisterly love.

visitatorial (ˌvɪzɪtəˈtɔːrɪəl) *or* **visitorial** *adj* **1** of, relating to, or for an official visitation or visitor. **2** empowered to make official visitations.

visiting card *n* another term for **calling card.**

visiting fireman *n U.S. informal.* a visitor whose presence is noticed because he is an important figure, a lavish spender, etc.

visiting nurse *n* (in the U.S.) a registered nurse employed by a community, hospital, etc., to visit and nurse the sick in their homes or to promote public health.

visiting professor *n* a professor invited to teach in a college or university other than his own, often in another country, for a certain period, such as a term or year.

visitor (ˈvɪzɪtə) *n* **1** a person who pays a visit; caller, guest, tourist, etc. **2** another name for **visitant** (sense 4). ▸ ˌ**visiˈtorial** *adj*

visitor centre *n* another term for **interpretive centre.**

visitor's passport *n* (formerly, in Britain) a passport, valid for one year and for certain countries only, that could be purchased from post offices. Also called: **British Visitor's Passport.**

Vislinsky Zaliv (*Russian* visˈlinski ˈzaːlɪf) *n* a transliteration of the Russian name for **Vistula** (sense 2).

vis major (ˈvɪs ˈmeɪdʒə) *n* See **force majeure.** [from Latin, literally: greater force]

visor *or* **vizor** (ˈvaɪzə) *n* **1** a transparent flap on a helmet that can be pulled down to protect the face. **2** a piece of armour fixed or hinged to the helmet to protect the face and with slits for the eyes. **3** another name for **peak** (on a cap). **4** a small movable screen used as protection against glare from the sun, esp. one attached above the windscreen of a motor vehicle. **5** *Archaic or literary.* a mask or any other means of disguise or concealment. ◆ *vb* **6** (*tr*) to cover, provide, or protect with a visor; shield. [C14: from Anglo-French *viser,* from Old French *visiere,* from *vis* face; see VISAGE] ▸ ˈ**visored** *or* ˈ**vizored** *adj* ▸ ˈ**visorless** *or* ˈ**vizorless** *adj*

vista (ˈvɪstə) *n* **1** a view, esp. through a long narrow avenue of trees, buildings, etc., or such a passage or avenue itself; prospect: *a vista of arches.* **2** a comprehensive mental view of a distant time or a lengthy series of events: *the vista of the future*. [C17: from Italian: a view, from *vedere* to see, from Latin *vidēre*] ▸ 'vistaed *adj* ▸ 'vistaless *adj*

VISTA ('vɪstə) *n* (in the U.S.) *acronym for* Volunteers in Service to America; an organization of volunteers established by the Federal government to assist the poor.

Vistula ('vɪstjʊlə) *n* **1** a river in central and N Poland, rising in the Carpathian Mountains and flowing generally north and northwest past Warsaw and Torun, then northeast to enter the Baltic via an extensive delta region. Length: 1090 km (677 miles). Polish name: **Wisla.** German name: **Weichsel. 2 Lagoon.** a shallow lagoon on the SW coast of the Baltic Sea, between Danzig and Kaliningrad, crossed by the border between Poland and Russia. German name: **Frisches Haff.** Polish name: **Wislany Zalew.** Russian name: **Vislinsky Zaliv.**

visual ('vɪʒʊəl, -zjʊ-) *adj* **1** of, relating to, done by, or used in seeing: *visual powers; visual steering*. **2** another word for **optical. 3** capable of being seen; visible. **4** of, occurring as, or induced by a mental image. ♦ *n* **5** a sketch to show the proposed layout of an advertisement, as in a newspaper. **6** (*often pl*) a photograph, film, or other display material. [C15: from Late Latin *vīsuālis*, from Latin *vīsus* sight, from *vidēre* to see] ▸ **'visually** *adv*

visual aids *pl n* devices, such as films, slides, models, and blackboards, that display in visual form material to be understood or remembered.

visual angle *n* the angle subtended by an object at the lens of the eye.

visual arts *pl n* the arts of painting, sculpting, photography, etc., as opposed to music, drama, and literature.

visual display unit *n Computing*. a device with a screen that displays characters or graphics representing data in a computer memory. It usually has a keyboard or light pen for the input of information or inquiries. Abbrev.: **VDU.**

visual field *n* the whole extent of the image falling on the retina when the eye is fixating a given point in space.

visualize *or* **visualise** ('vɪʒʊəˌlaɪz, -zjʊ-) *vb* **1** to form a mental image of (something incapable of being viewed or not at that moment visible). **2** *Med.* to view by means of an X-ray the outline of (a bodily organ, structure, or part). ▸ **ˌvisualiˈzation** *or* **ˌvisualiˈsation** *n* ▸ **'visualˌizer** *or* **'visualˌiser** *n*

visually handicapped *adj* **a** unable to carry out normal activities because of defects of vision, including blindness. **b** (*as collective n;* preceded by *the*): *the visually handicapped*. ▸ **visual handicap** *n*

visually impaired *adj* **a** having any defect of vision, whether disabling or not. **b** (*as collective n;* preceded by *the*): *the visually impaired*. ♦ Compare **partially sighted.** ▸ **visual impairment** *n*

visual magnitude *n Astronomy*. the magnitude of a star as determined by visual observation. Compare **photoelectric magnitude.**

visual purple *n* another name for **rhodopsin.**

visual violet *n* another name for **iodopsin.**

vita ('viːtə, 'vaɪ-) *n, pl* **vitae** ('viːtaɪ, 'vaɪtiː). *U.S. and Canadian*. a less common term for **curriculum vitae.** [from Latin: life]

vitaceous (vaɪ'teɪʃəs) *adj* of, relating to, or belonging to the *Vitaceae*, a family of tropical and subtropical flowering plants having a climbing habit and berry-like fruits: includes the grapevine and Virginia creeper. [C19: via New Latin *Vītāceae*, from Latin: vine]

vital ('vaɪtᵊl) *adj* **1** essential to maintain life: *the lungs perform a vital function*. **2** forceful, energetic, or lively: *a vital person*. **3** of, relating to, having, or displaying life: *a vital organism*. **4** indispensable or essential: *books vital to this study*. **5** of great importance; decisive: *a vital game*. **6** *Archaic*. influencing the course of life, esp. negatively: *a vital treachery*. ♦ *n* **7** (*pl*) **7a** the bodily organs, such as the brain, liver, heart, lungs, etc., that are necessary to maintain life. **7b** the organs of reproduction, esp. the male genitals. **8** (*pl*) the essential elements of anything. [C14: via Old French from Latin *vītālis* belonging to life, from *vīta* life] ▸ **'vitally** *adv*

vital capacity *n Physiol*. the volume of air that can be exhaled from the lungs after the deepest possible breath has been taken: a measure of lung function.

vital force *n* (esp. in early biological theory) a hypothetical force, independent of physical and chemical forces, regarded as being the causative factor of the evolution and development of living organisms.

vitalism ('vaɪtəˌlɪzəm) *n* the philosophical doctrine that the phenomena of life cannot be explained in purely mechanical terms because there is something immaterial which distinguishes living from inanimate matter. Compare **dynamism, mechanism.** ▸ **'vitalist** *n, adj* ▸ **ˌvital'istic** *adj*

vitality (vaɪ'tælɪtɪ) *n, pl* **-ties. 1** physical or mental vigour, energy, etc. **2** the power or ability to continue in existence, live, or grow: *the vitality of a movement*. **3** a less common name for **vital force.**

vitalize *or* **vitalise** ('vaɪtəˌlaɪz) *vb* (*tr*) to make vital, living, or alive; endow with life or vigour. ▸ **ˌvitali'zation** *or* **ˌvitali'sation** *n* ▸ **'vitalˌizer** *or* **'vitalˌiser** *n*

vital signs *pl n Med.* indications that a person is still alive. Vital signs include a heartbeat, a pulse that can be felt, breathing, and body temperature.

vital staining *n* the technique of treating living cells and tissues with dyes that do not immediately kill them, facilitating observation under a microscope.

vital statistics *pl n* **1** quantitative data concerning human life or the conditions and aspects affecting it, such as the death rate. **2** *Informal*. the measurements of a woman's bust, waist, and hips.

vitamin ('vɪtəmɪn, 'vaɪ-) *n* any of a group of substances that are essential, in small quantities, for the normal functioning of metabolism in the body. They cannot usually be synthesized in the body but they occur naturally in certain foods: insufficient supply of any particular vitamin results in a deficiency disease. [C20 *vit-* from Latin *vīta* life + *-amin* from AMINE; so named by Casimir FUNK, who believed the substances to be amines] ▸ **ˌvita'minic** *adj*

vitamin A *n* a fat-soluble yellow unsaturated alcohol occurring in green and yellow vegetables (esp. carrots), butter, egg yolk, and fish-liver oil (esp. halibut oil). It is essential for the prevention of night blindness and the protection of epithelial tissue. Formula: $C_{20}H_{30}O$. Also called: **vitamin A_1, retinol.**

vitamin A_2 *n* a vitamin that occurs in the tissues of freshwater fish and has a function similar to that of vitamin A. Formula: $C_{20}H_{28}O$. Also called: **dehydroretinol.**

vitamin B *n, pl* **B vitamins.** any of the vitamins in the vitamin B complex.

vitamin B_1 *n* another name for **thiamine.**

vitamin B_2 *n* another name for **riboflavin.**

vitamin B_6 *n* another name for **pyridoxine.**

vitamin B_{12} *n* another name for **cyanocobalamin.**

vitamin B complex *n* a large group of water-soluble vitamins occurring esp. in liver and yeast: includes thiamine, riboflavin, nicotinic acid, pyridoxine, pantothenic acid, biotin, choline, folic acid, and cyanocobalamin. Sometimes shortened to **B complex.**

vitamin C *n* another name for **ascorbic acid.**

vitamin D *n, pl* **D vitamins.** any of the fat-soluble vitamins, including calciferol and cholecalciferol, occurring in fish-liver oils (esp. cod-liver oil), milk, butter, and eggs: used in the treatment of rickets and osteomalacia.

vitamin D_1 *n* the first isolated form of vitamin D, consisting of calciferol and its precursor, lumisterol.

vitamin D_2 *n* another name for **calciferol.**

vitamin D_3 *n* another name for **cholecalciferol.**

vitamin E *n* another name for **tocopherol.**

vitamin G *n* another name (esp. U.S. and Canadian) for **riboflavin.**

vitamin H *n* another name (esp. U.S. and Canadian) for **biotin.**

vitamin K *n, pl* **K vitamins.** any of the fat-soluble vitamins, including phylloquinone and the menaquinones, which are essential for the normal clotting of blood.

vitamin K_1 *n* another name for **phylloquinone.**

vitamin K_2 *n* another name for **menaquinone.**

vitamin K_3 *n* a former name for **menadione.**

vitamin P *n, pl* **P vitamins.** any of a group of water-soluble crystalline substances occurring mainly in citrus fruits, blackcurrants, and rosehips: they regulate the permeability of the blood capillaries. Also called: **citrin, bioflavonoid.**

Vitaphone ('vaɪtəˌfəʊn) *n Trademark*. an early technique in commercial film-making in which the accompanying sound was produced by discs.

vitascope ('vaɪtəˌskəʊp) *n* an early type of film projector. [C19: from Latin *vīta* life + -SCOPE]

Vitebsk (*Russian* 'vitɪpsk) *n* a city in E Belarus, a port on the Dvina river: taken by Russia in 1772. Pop.: 365 000 (1996 est.).

vitellin (vɪ'tɛlɪn) *n Biochem*. a phosphoprotein that is the major protein in egg yolk. [C19: from VITELLUS + -IN]

vitelline (vɪ'tɛlɪn, -aɪn) *adj Zoology*. **1** of or relating to the yolk of an egg: *the vitelline gland*. **2** having the yellow colour of an egg yolk. [C15: from Medieval Latin *vitellīnus*, from Latin *vitellus* the yolk of an egg; see VITELLUS]

vitelline membrane *n Zoology*. a membrane that surrounds a fertilized ovum and prevents the entry of other spermatozoa.

vitellogenic (ˌvɪtələʊ'dʒɛnɪk) *or* **vitelligenous** (ˌvɪtə'lɪdʒɪnəs) *adj Zoology*. producing or stimulating the formation of yolk. [C20: from VITELLUS + -GENIC] ▸ **ˌvitello'genesis** *n*

vitellus (vɪ'tɛləs) *n, pl* **-luses** *or* **-li** (-laɪ). *Zoology, rare*. the yolk of an egg. [C18: from Latin, literally: little calf, later: yolk of an egg, from *vitulus* calf]

vitiate ('vɪʃɪˌeɪt) *vb* (*tr*) **1** to make faulty or imperfect. **2** to debase, pervert, or corrupt. **3** to destroy the force or legal effect of (a deed, etc.): *to vitiate a contract*. [C16: from Latin *vitiāre* to injure, from *vitium* a fault] ▸ **'vitiable** *adj* ▸ **ˌviti'ation** *n* ▸ **'vitiˌator** *n*

viticulture ('vɪtɪˌkʌltʃə) *n* **1** the science, art, or process of cultivating grapevines. **2** the study of grapes and the growing of grapes. [C19: *viti-*, from Latin *vītis* vine] ▸ **ˌviti'cultural** *adj* ▸ **ˌviti'culturer** *or* **ˌviti'culturist** *n*

Viti Levu ('viːtɪ 'lɛvuː) *n* the largest island of Fiji: mountainous. Chief town (and capital of the state): Suva. Pop.: 340 561 (1986). Area: 10 386 sq. km (4010 sq. miles).

vitiligo (ˌvɪtɪ'laɪgəʊ) *n* another name for **leucoderma.** [C17: from Latin: a skin disease, probably from *vitium* a blemish]

Vitoria[1] (*Spanish* bi'torja) *n* a city in NE Spain: scene of Wellington's decisive victory (1813) over Napoleon's forces in the Peninsular War. Pop.: 215 049 (1995 est.).

Vitoria[2] (*Spanish* bi'torja) *n* **Francisco de.** ?1486–1546, Spanish theologian, sometimes considered the father of international law. He criticized Spanish colonial policy in the New World and argued that war was only defensible in certain strictly defined circumstances.

Vitória (vɪ'tɔːrɪə; *Portuguese* vi'tɔrja) *n* a port in E Brazil, capital of Espírito Santo state, on an island in the Bay of Espírito Santo. Pop.: 258 243 (1991).

vitrain ('vɪtreɪn) *n* a type of coal occurring as horizontal glassy bands of a non-soiling friable material. [C20: from Latin *vitrum* glass + *-ain*, as in FUSAIN]

vitreous ('vɪtrɪəs) *adj* **1** of, relating to, or resembling glass. **2** made of, derived from, or containing glass. **3** of or relating to the vitreous humour or vitreous body. [C17: from Latin *vitreus* made of glass, from *vitrum* glass; probably related to *vidēre* to see] ▸ **'vitreously** *adv*

vitreous body *n* a transparent gelatinous substance, permeated by fine fibrils, that fills the interior of the eyeball between the lens and the retina.

vitreous humour *n* the aqueous fluid contained within the interstices of the vitreous body.

vitreous silica *n* another name for **silica glass.**

vitrescence (vɪ'trɛsəns) *n* **1** the quality or condition of being or becoming vitreous. **2** the process of producing a glass or turning a crystalline material into glass.

vitrescent (vɪ'tresᵊnt) *adj* **1** tending to turn into glass. **2** capable of being transformed into glass.
vitric ('vɪtrɪk) *adj* of, relating to, resembling, or having the nature of glass; vitreous.
vitrification (ˌvɪtrɪfɪ'keɪʃən) *n* **1** the process or act of vitrifying or the state of being vitrified. **2** something that is or has been vitrified.
vitriform ('vɪtrɪˌfɔːm) *adj* having the form or appearance of glass.
vitrify ('vɪtrɪˌfaɪ) *vb* **-fies, -fying, -fied.** to convert or be converted into glass or a glassy substance. [C16: from French *vitrifier,* from Latin *vitrum* glass] ► **'vitriˌfiable** *adj* ► **ˌvitriˌfia'bility** *n*
vitrine ('vɪtriːn) *n* a glass display case or cabinet for works of art, curios, etc. [C19: from French, from *vitre* pane of glass, from Latin *vitrum* glass]
vitriol ('vɪtrɪˌɒl) *n* **1** another name for **sulphuric acid. 2** any one of a number of sulphate salts, such as ferrous sulphate (**green vitriol**), copper sulphate (**blue vitriol**), or zinc sulphate (**white vitriol**). **3** speech, writing, etc., displaying rancour, vituperation, or bitterness. ◆ *vb* **-ols, -oling, -oled** *or* **-olling, -olled.** (*tr*) **4** to attack or injure with or as if with vitriol. **5** to treat with vitriol. [C14: from Medieval Latin *vitriolum,* from Late Latin *vitriolus* glassy, from Latin *vitrum* glass, referring to the glossy appearance of the sulphates]
vitriolic (ˌvɪtrɪ'ɒlɪk) *adj* **1** (of a substance, esp. a strong acid) highly corrosive. **2** severely bitter or caustic; virulent: *vitriolic criticism.*
vitriolize *or* **vitriolise** ('vɪtrɪəˌlaɪz) *vb* (*tr*) **1** to convert into or treat with vitriol. **2** to burn or injure with vitriol. ► **ˌvitrioli'zation** *or* **ˌvitrioli'sation** *n*
Vitruvius Pollio (vɪ'truːvɪəs 'pɒlɪˌəʊ) *n* **Marcus** ('mɑːkəs). 1st century B.C., Roman architect, noted for his treatise *De architectura,* the only surviving Roman work on architectural theory and a major influence on Renaissance architects. ► **Vi'truvian** *adj*
vitta ('vɪtə) *n, pl* **-tae** (-tiː). **1** any of numerous tubelike cavities containing oil or resin that occur in the fruits of certain plants, esp. of parsley and related plants. **2** *Biology.* a band or stripe of colour. [C17: from Latin: headband; related to *viēre* to plait] ► **'vittate** *adj*
vittle ('vɪtᵊl) *n, vb* an obsolete or dialect spelling of **victual.**
vituline ('vɪtjʊˌlaɪn, -lɪn) *adj* of or resembling a calf or veal. [C17: from Latin *vitulīnus,* from *vitulus* a calf]
vituperate (vɪ'tjuːpəˌreɪt) *vb* to berate or rail (against) abusively; revile. [C16: from Latin *vituperāre* to blame, from *vitium* a defect + *parāre* to make] ► **vi'tuperˌator** *n*
vituperation (vɪˌtjuːpə'reɪʃən) *n* **1** abusive language or venomous censure. **2** the act of vituperating. ► **vituperative** (vɪ'tjuːpərətɪv, -prətɪv) *adj* ► **vi'tuperatively** *adv*
viva[1] ('viːvə) *interj* long live; up with (a specified person or thing). [C17: from Italian, literally: may (he) live! from *vivere* to live, from Latin *vīvere*]
viva[2] ('vaɪvə) *Brit.* ◆ *n* **1** an oral examination. ◆ *vb* **-vas, -vaing, -vaed.** (*tr*) **2** to examine orally. [shortened from VIVA VOCE]
vivace (vɪ'vɑːtʃɪ) *adj, adv Music.* to be performed in a brisk lively manner. [C17: from Italian, from Latin *vīvax* long-lived, vigorous, from *vīvere* to live]
vivacious (vɪ'veɪʃəs) *adj* **1** full of high spirits and animation; lively or vital. **2** *Obsolete.* having or displaying tenacity of life. [C17: from Latin *vīvax* lively; see VIVACE] ► **vi'vaciously** *adv* ► **vi'vaciousness** *n*
vivacity (vɪ'væsɪtɪ) *n, pl* **-ties. 1** the quality or condition of being vivacious. **2** (*often pl*) *Rare.* a vivacious act or expression.
Vivaldi (vɪ'vældɪ) *n* **Antonio** (an'tɔːnjo). ?1675–1741, Italian composer and violinist, noted esp. for his development of the solo concerto. His best-known work is *The Four Seasons* (1725).
vivandière *French.* (vivɑ̃djɛr) *n* (formerly) a female sutler or victualler offering extra provisions and spirits to soldiers, esp. those of the French and British armies. [C16: see VIAND]
vivarium (vaɪ'vɛərɪəm) *n, pl* **-iums** *or* **-ia** (-ɪə). a place where live animals are kept under natural conditions for study, research, etc. [C16: from Latin: enclosure where live fish or game are kept, from *vīvus* alive]
viva voce ('vaɪvə 'vəʊtʃɪ) *adv, adj* **1** by word of mouth. ◆ *n, vb* **2** the full form of **viva**[2]. [C16: from Medieval Latin, literally: with living voice]
vive (viːv) *interj* long live; up with (a specified person or thing). [from French]
Vivekananda (ˌviːvɪkə'nʌndə) *n* original name *Narendranath Datta.* 1862–1902, Indian Hindu religious teacher. A disciple of Ramakrishna, he introduced Vedantism to the West.
viverrine (vaɪ'vɛraɪn) *adj* **1** of, relating to, or belonging to the *Viverridae,* a family of small to medium-sized predatory mammals of Eurasia and Africa, including genets, civets and mongooses: order *Carnivora* (carnivores). ◆ *n* **2** any animal belonging to the family *Viverridae.* [C19: from New Latin *viverrīnus,* from Latin *viverra* a ferret]
Vivian ('vɪvɪən) *n* (in Arthurian legend) the mistress of Merlin, sometimes identified with the **Lady of the Lake.**
vivid ('vɪvɪd) *adj* **1** (of a colour) very bright; having a very high saturation or purity; produced by a pure or almost pure colouring agent. **2** brilliantly coloured: *vivid plumage.* **3** conveying to the mind striking realism, freshness, or trueness to life; graphic: *a vivid account.* **4** (of a recollection, memory, etc.) remaining distinct in the mind. **5** (of the imagination, etc.) prolific in the formation of lifelike images. **6** making a powerful impact on the emotions or senses: *a vivid feeling of shame.* **7** uttered, operating, or acting with vigour: *vivid expostulations.* **8** full of life or vitality: *a vivid personality.* [C17: from Latin *vīvidus* animated, from *vīvere* to live] ► **'vividly** *adv* ► **'vividness** *n*
vivify ('vɪvɪˌfaɪ) *vb* **-fies, -fying, -fied.** (*tr*) **1** to bring to life; animate. **2** to make more vivid or striking. [C16: from Late Latin *vīvificāre,* from Latin *vīvus* alive + *facere* to make] ► **ˌvivifi'cation** *n* ► **'viviˌfier** *n*
viviparous (vɪ'vɪpərəs) *adj* **1** (of most mammals) giving birth to living offspring that develop within the uterus of the mother. Compare **oviparous, ovoviviparous. 2** (of seeds) germinating before separating from the parent plant. **3** (of plants) producing bulbils or young plants instead of flowers. [C17: from Latin *vīviparus,* from *vīvus* alive + *parere* to bring forth] ► **viviparity** (ˌvɪvɪ'pærɪtɪ), **vi'vipary, vi'viparism,** *or* **vi'viparousness** *n* ► **vi'viparously** *adv*
vivisect ('vɪvɪˌsɛkt, ˌvɪvɪ'sɛkt) *vb* to subject (an animal) to vivisection. [C19: back formation from VIVISECTION] ► **'viviˌsector** *n*
vivisection (ˌvɪvɪ'sɛkʃən) *n* the act or practice of performing experiments on living animals, involving cutting into or dissecting the body. [C18: from *vivi-,* from Latin *vīvus* living + SECTION, as in DISSECTION] ► **ˌvivi'sectional** *adj* ► **ˌvivi'sectionally** *adv*
vivisectionist (ˌvɪvɪ'sɛkʃənɪst) *n* **1** a person who practises vivisection. **2** a person who advocates the practice of vivisection as being useful or necessary to science.
vivo ('viːvəʊ) *adj, adv Music.* (*in combination*) with life and vigour: *allegro vivo.* [Italian: lively]
vixen ('vɪksən) *n* **1** a female fox. **2** a quarrelsome or spiteful woman. [C15 *fixen;* related to Old English *fyxe,* feminine of FOX; compare Old High German *fuhsīn*] ► **'vixenish** *adj* ► **'vixenishly** *adv* ► **'vixenishness** *n* ► **'vixenly** *adv, adj*
Viyella (vaɪ'ɛlə) *n Trademark.* a soft fabric made of wool and cotton, used esp. for blouses and shirts.
viz *abbrev. for* videlicet.
Vizagapatam (vɪˌzægə'pʌtəm) *n* a variant spelling of **Vishakhapatnam.**
vizard ('vɪzəd) *n Archaic or literary.* a means of disguise; mask; visor. [C16: variant of VISOR] ► **'vizarded** *adj*
vizcacha (vɪs'kætʃə) *n* a variant spelling of **viscacha.**
vizier (vɪ'zɪə) *n* a high official in certain Muslim countries, esp. in the former Ottoman Empire. Viziers served in various capacities, such as that of provincial governor or chief minister to the sultan. [C16: from Turkish *vezīr,* from Arabic *wazīr* porter, from *wazara* to bear a burden] ► **vi'zierial** *or* **vi'zirial** *adj* ► **vi'ziership** *n*
vizierate (vɪ'zɪərɪt, -eɪt) *n* **1** the position, rank, or authority of a vizier. **2** the term of office of a vizier.
vizor ('vaɪzə) *n, vb* a variant spelling of **visor.**
vizsla ('vɪʒlə) *n* a breed of Hungarian hunting dog with a smooth rusty-gold coat. [C20: named after *Vizsla,* Hungary]
VJ *abbrev. for:* **1** video jockey. **2** *Austral.* Vaucluse Junior: a type of small yacht.
V-J Day *n* the day marking the Allied victory over Japan in World War II (Aug. 15, 1945).
vl *abbrev. for* variant reading. [from Latin *varia lectio*]
VL *abbrev. for* Vulgar Latin.
Vlaardingen (*Dutch* 'vlaːrdɪŋə) *n* a port in the W Netherlands, in South Holland west of Rotterdam: the third largest port in the Netherlands. Pop.: 73 820 (1994).
Vlach (vlɑːk) or **Walach** ('wɑːlɒk) *n* **1** a member of a people scattered throughout SE Europe in the early Middle Ages, speaking a Romanic dialect. ◆ *adj* **2** of or relating to Vlachs or their dialect.
Vladikavkaz (*Russian* vlədikaf'kas) *n* a city in S Russia, capital of the North Ossetian Republic on the N slopes of the Caucasus. Pop.: 312 000 (1995 est.). Former names: **Dzaudzhikau** (1944–54); **Ordzhonikidze** (1954–91).
Vladimir[1] (*Russian* vla'dimir) *n* a city in W central Russia: capital of the principality of Vladimir until the court transferred to Moscow in 1328. Pop.: 339 000 (1995 est.).
Vladimir[2] ('vlædɪˌmɪə; *Russian* vla'dimir) *n* **Saint,** called *the Great.* ?956–1015, grand prince of Kiev (980–1015); first Christian ruler of Russia. Feast day: July 15.
Vladivostok (ˌvlædɪ'vɒstɒk; *Russian* vlədivas'tɔk) *n* a port in SE Russia, on the Sea of Japan: terminus of the Trans-Siberian Railway; the main Russian Pacific naval base since 1872 and chief commercial and civilian Russian port in the Far East; university (1956). Pop.: 632 000 (1995 est.).
Vlaminck (*French* vlamɛ̃k) *n* **Maurice de** (mɔris də). 1876–1958, French painter of the Fauve school.
VLCC *Oil industry. abbrev. for* very large crude carrier: an oil tanker with a capacity between 200 000 and 400 000 tons.
vlei (fleɪ, vleɪ) *n* **1** *S. African.* an area of low marshy ground, esp. one that feeds a stream. **2** *Northern U.S. dialect.* a marsh. [C19: from Afrikaans (for sense 1); from obsolete N American Dutch dialect (for sense 2): VALLEY]
VLF *or* **vlf** *Radio. abbrev. for* very low frequency.
Vlissingen ('vlɪsɪŋə) *n* the Dutch name for **Flushing.**
Vlorë (*Albanian* 'vlorə) *or* **Vlonë** (*Albanian* 'vlonə) *n* a port in SW Albania, on the **Bay of Vlorë:** under Turkish rule from 1462 until Albanian independence was declared here in 1912. Pop.: 76 000 (1991 est.). Ancient name: **Avlona.** Also called: **Valona.**
VLSI *Computing. abbrev. for* very large-scale integration.
Vltava (*Czech* 'vltava) *n* a river in the Czech Republic, rising in the Bohemian Forest and flowing generally southeast and then north to the River Elbe near Melnik. Length: 434 km (270 miles). German name: **Moldau.**
VMD *abbrev. for* Doctor of Veterinary Medicine. [Latin *veterinariae medicinae doctor*]
VMI *abbrev. for* vendor managed inventory: an inventory management system in which a supplier assumes responsibility for the timely replenishment of a customer's stock.
VN *international car registration for* Vietnam.
V neck *n* a neck on a garment that comes down to a point on the throat or chest, resembling the shape of the letter "V". ► **'V-ˌneck** *or* **'V-ˌnecked** *adj*
VO *abbrev. for:* **1** very old: used to imply that a brandy or whisky is old, now often extended to port and other dessert wines. **2** Royal Victorian Order.
vo. *abbrev. for* verso.

voc. *or* **vocat.** *abbrev. for* vocative.

vocab ('vəʊkæb) *n* short for **vocabulary.**

vocable ('vəʊkəbᵊl) *n* **1** any word, either written or spoken, regarded simply as a sequence of letters or spoken sounds, irrespective of its meaning. **2** a vocal sound; vowel. ◆ *adj* **3** capable of being uttered. [C16: from Latin *vocābulum* a designation, from *vocāre* to call] ▸ 'vocably *adv*

vocabulary (və'kæbjʊlərɪ) *n, pl* **-laries. 1** a listing, either selective or exhaustive, containing the words and phrases of a language, with meanings or translations into another language; glossary. **2** the aggregate of words in the use or comprehension of a specified person, class, profession, etc. **3** all the words contained in a language. **4** a range or system of symbols, qualities, or techniques constituting a means of communication or expression, as any of the arts or crafts: *a wide vocabulary of textures and colours.* [C16: from Medieval Latin *vocābulārium,* from *vocābulārius* concerning words, from Latin *vocābulum* VOCABLE]

vocal ('vəʊkᵊl) *adj* **1** of, relating to, or designed for the voice: *vocal music.* **2** produced or delivered by the voice: *vocal noises.* **3** connected with an attribute or the production of the voice: *vocal organs.* **4** frequently disposed to outspoken speech, criticism, etc.: *a vocal minority.* **5** full of sound or voices: *a vocal assembly.* **6** endowed with a voice. **7** eloquent or meaningful. **8** *Phonetics.* **8a** of or relating to a speech sound. **8b** of or relating to a voiced speech sound, esp. a vowel. ◆ *n* **9** a piece of jazz or pop music that is sung. **10** a performance of such a piece of music. [C14: from Latin *vōcālis* possessed of a voice, from *vōx* voice] ▸ **vocality** (vəʊ'kælɪtɪ) *n* ▸ **'vocally** *adv*

vocal cords *pl n* either of two pairs of mucomembranous folds in the larynx. The upper pair (**false vocal cords**) are not concerned with vocal production; the lower pair (**true vocal cords** or **vocal folds**) can be made to vibrate and produce sound when air from the lungs is forced over them. See also **glottis.** Related adj: **glottal.**

vocal folds *pl n* See **vocal cords.**

vocalic (vəʊ'kælɪk) *adj Phonetics.* of, relating to, or containing a vowel or vowels.

vocalise (ˌvəʊkə'li:z) *n* a musical passage sung upon one vowel as an exercise to develop flexibility and control of pitch and tone; solfeggio.

vocalism ('vəʊkəˌlɪzəm) *n* **1** the exercise of the voice, as in singing or speaking. **2** singing, esp. in respect to technique or skill. **3** *Phonetics.* **3a** a voiced speech sound, esp. a vowel. **3b** a system of vowels as used in a language.

vocalist ('vəʊkəlɪst) *n* a singer, esp. one who regularly appears with a jazz band or pop group.

vocalize *or* **vocalise** ('vəʊkəˌlaɪz) *vb* **1** to express with or use the voice; articulate (a speech, song, etc.). **2** (*tr*) to make vocal or articulate. **3** (*tr*) *Phonetics.* **3a** to articulate (a speech sound) with voice. **3b** to change (a consonant) into a vowel. **4** another word for **vowelize. 5** (*intr*) to sing a melody on a vowel, etc. ▸ **ˌvocali'zation** *or* **ˌvocali'sation** *n* ▸ **'vocalˌizer** *or* **'vocalˌiser** *n*

vocal sac *n Zoology.* either of the loose folds of skin on each side of the mouth in many male frogs that can be inflated and act as resonators.

vocal score *n* a musical score that shows voice parts in full and orchestral parts in the form of a piano transcription.

vocation (vəʊ'keɪʃən) *n* **1** a specified occupation, profession, or trade. **2a** a special urge, inclination, or predisposition to a particular calling or career, esp. a religious one. **2b** such a calling or career. [C15: from Latin *vocātiō* a calling, from *vocāre* to call]

vocational (vəʊ'keɪʃənᵊl) *adj* **1** of or relating to a vocation or vocations. **2** of or relating to applied educational courses concerned with skills needed for an occupation, trade, or profession: *vocational training.* ▸ **vo'cationally** *adv*

vocational guidance *n* a guidance service based on psychological tests and interviews to find out what career or occupation may best suit a person.

vocative ('vɒkətɪv) *adj* **1** relating to, used in, or characterized by calling. **2** *Grammar.* denoting a case of nouns, in some inflected languages, used when the referent of the noun is being addressed. ◆ *n* **3** *Grammar.* **3a** the vocative case. **3b** a vocative noun or speech element. [C15: from Latin phrase *vocātīvus cāsus* the calling case, from *vocāre* to call] ▸ **'vocatively** *adv*

voces ('vəʊsi:z) *n* the plural of **vox.**

vociferant (vəʊ'sɪfərənt) *adj* **1** a less common word for **vociferous.** ◆ *n* **2** *Rare.* a vociferous person. [C17: from Latin *vōciferārī* to bawl; see VOCIFERATE] ▸ **vo'ciferance** *n*

vociferate (vəʊ'sɪfəˌreɪt) *vb* to exclaim or cry out about (something) clamorously, vehemently, or insistently. [C17: from Latin *vōciferārī* to clamour, from *vōx* voice + *ferre* to bear] ▸ **voˌcifer'ation** *n* ▸ **vo'ciferˌator** *n*

vociferous (vəʊ'sɪfərəs) *adj* **1** characterized by vehemence, clamour, or noisiness: *vociferous protests.* **2** making an outcry or loud noises; clamorous: *a vociferous mob.* ▸ **vo'ciferously** *adv* ▸ **vo'ciferousness** *n*

vocoder ('vəʊ'kəʊdə) *n Music.* a type of synthesizer that uses the human voice as an oscillator.

vodka ('vɒdkə) *n* an alcoholic drink originating in Russia, made from grain, potatoes, etc., usually consisting only of rectified spirit and water. [C19: from Russian, diminutive of *voda* water; related to Sanskrit *udan* water, Greek *hudōr*]

voe (vəʊ; *Scot.* vo) *n* (in Orkney and Shetland) a small bay or narrow creek. [C17: from Old Norse *vagr*]

voetsek *or* **voetsak** ('fʊtsʌk, 'vʊt-) *interj S. African offensive, informal.* an expression of dismissal or rejection. [C19: Afrikaans, from Dutch *voort se ek* forward, I say, commonly applied to animals]

voetstoots *or* **voetstoets** ('fʊtstʊts, 'vʊt-) *S. African.* ◆ *adj* **1** denoting a sale in which the vendor is freed from all responsibility for the condition of the goods being sold. ◆ *adv* **2** without responsibility for the condition of the goods sold. [from Afrikaans *voetstoots* as it is]

Vogel ('vəʊgᵊl) *n* Sir **Julius.** 1835–99, New Zealand statesman; prime minister of New Zealand (1873–75; 1876).

Vogelweide (*German* 'fo:gəlvaidə) *n* See **Walther von der Vogelweide.**

vogue (vəʊg) *n* **1** the popular style at a specified time (esp. in the phrase **in vogue**). **2** a period of general or popular usage or favour: *the vogue for such dances is now over.* ◆ *adj* **3** (*usually prenominal*) popular or fashionable: *a vogue word.* [C16: from French: a rowing, fashion, from Old Italian *voga,* from *vogare* to row, of unknown origin] ▸ **'voguish** *adj*

vogueing ('vəʊgɪŋ) *n* a dance style of the late 1980s, in which a fashion model's movements and postures are imitated in a highly stylized manner. [C20: from *Vogue* magazine]

Vogul ('vəʊgᵊl) *n* **1** (*pl* **-gul** *or* **-guls**) a member of a people living in W Siberia and NE Europe. **2** the language of this people, belonging to the Finno-Ugric family: related to Hungarian.

voice (vɔɪs) *n* **1** the sound made by the vibration of the vocal cords, esp. when modified by the resonant effect of the tongue and mouth. See also **speech.** Related adj: **vocal. 2** the natural and distinctive tone of the speech sounds characteristic of a particular person: *nobody could mistake his voice.* **3** the condition, quality, effectiveness, or tone of such sounds: *a hysterical voice.* **4** the musical sound of a singing voice, with respect to its quality or tone: *she has a lovely voice.* **5** the ability to speak, sing, etc.: *he has lost his voice.* **6** a sound resembling or suggestive of vocal utterance: *the voice of the sea; the voice of hard experience.* **7** written or spoken expression, as of feeling, opinion, etc. (esp. in the phrase **give voice to**). **8** a stated choice, wish, or opinion or the power or right to have an opinion heard and considered: *to give someone a voice in a decision.* **9** an agency through which is communicated another's purpose, policy, etc.: *such groups are the voice of our enemies.* **10** *Music.* **10a** musical notes produced by vibrations of the vocal cords at various frequencies and in certain registers: *a tenor voice.* **10b** (in harmony) an independent melodic line or part: *a fugue in five voices.* **11** *Phonetics.* the sound characterizing the articulation of several speech sounds, including all vowels or sonants, that is produced when the vocal cords make loose contact with each other and are set in vibration by the breath as it forces its way through the glottis. **12** *Grammar.* a category of the verb or verbal inflections that expresses whether the relation between the subject and the verb is that of agent and action, action and recipient, or some other relation. See **active** (sense 5), **passive** (sense 5), **middle** (sense 5). **13** *Obsolete.* rumour. **14** (foll. by *of*) *Obsolete.* fame; renown. **15 in voice.** in a condition to sing or speak well. **16 out of voice.** with the voice temporarily in a poor condition, esp. for singing. **17 with one voice.** unanimously. ◆ *vb* (*tr*) **18** to utter in words; give expression to: *to voice a complaint.* **19** to articulate (a speech sound) with voice. **20** *Music.* to adjust (a wind instrument or organ pipe) so that it conforms to the correct standards of tone colour, pitch, etc. [C13: from Old French *voiz,* from Latin *vōx*] ▸ **'voicer** *n*

voice box *n* **1** another word for the **larynx.** Related adj: **laryngeal. 2** Also called: **talkbox.** an electronic guitar attachment with a tube into the player's mouth to modulate the sound vocally.

voiced (vɔɪst) *adj* **1** declared or expressed by the voice. **2** (*in combination*) having a voice as specified: *loud-voiced.* **3** *Phonetics.* articulated with accompanying vibration of the vocal cords: *in English* (b) *is a voiced consonant.* Compare **voiceless.**

voiceful ('vɔɪsfʊl) *adj Poetic.* **1** endowed with a voice, esp. of loud quality. **2** full of voices. ▸ **'voicefulness** *n*

voice input *n* the control and operation of computer systems by spoken commands.

voice-leading ('vɔɪsˌli:dɪŋ) *n U.S.* another term for **part-writing.**

voiceless ('vɔɪslɪs) *adj* **1** without a voice; mute. **2** not articulated: *voiceless misery.* **3** lacking a musical voice. **4** silent. **5** without the power or right to express an opinion. **6** *Phonetics.* articulated without accompanying vibration of the vocal cords: *In English* (p) *is a voiceless consonant.* ▸ **'voicelessly** *adv* ▸ **'voicelessness** *n*

voice mail *n* an electronic system for the transfer and storage of telephone messages, which can then be dealt with by the user at his or her convenience.

voice-over *n* the voice of an unseen commentator heard during a film, television programme, etc.

voice part *n* a melodic line written for the voice.

voiceprint ('vɔɪsˌprɪnt) *n* a graphic representation of a person's voice recorded electronically, usually having time plotted along the horizontal axis and the frequency of the speech on the vertical axis.

voice recognition *n* the control of a computer system by a voice or voices that the computer has been instructed to accept.

voice response *n* output of information from a computer system in the form of speech rather than displayed text.

voice vote *n* a vote taken in a legislative body by calling for the ayes and the noes and estimating which faction is more numerous from the volume of the noise.

void (vɔɪd) *adj* **1** without contents; empty. **2** not legally binding: *null and void.* **3** (of an office, house, position, etc.) without an incumbent; unoccupied. **4** (*postpositive;* foll. by *of*) destitute or devoid: *void of resources.* **5** having no effect; useless: *all his efforts were rendered void.* **6** (of a card suit or player) having no cards in a particular suit: *his spades were void.* ◆ *n* **7** an empty space or area: *the huge desert voids of Asia.* **8** a feeling or condition of loneliness or deprivation: *his divorce left him in a void.* **9** a lack of any cards in one suit: *to have a void in spades.* **10** Also called: **counter.** the inside area of a character of type, such as the inside of an *o.* ◆ *vb* (*mainly tr*) **11** to make ineffective or invalid. **12** to empty (contents, etc.) or make empty of contents. **13** (*also intr*) to discharge the contents of (the bowels or urinary bladder). **14** *Archaic.* to vacate (a place, room, etc.). **15** *Obsolete.* to expel. [C13: from Old French *vuide,* from Vulgar

Latin *vocītus* (unattested), from Latin *vacuus* empty, from *vacāre* to be empty] ▸ **'voider** *n* ▸ **'voidness** *n*

voidable ('vɔɪdəbᵊl) *adj* **1** capable of being voided. **2** capable of being legally annulled or made void. ▸ **'voidableness** *n*

voidance ('vɔɪdᵊns) *n* **1** an annulment, as of a contract. **2** the condition of being vacant, as an office, benefice, etc. **3** the act of voiding, ejecting, or evacuating. [C14: variant of AVOIDANCE]

voided ('vɔɪdɪd) *adj* **1** *Heraldry.* (of a design) with a hole in the centre of the same shape as the design: *a voided lozenge.* **2** *Rare.* having a void or made void.

voile (vɔɪl; *French* vwal) *n* a light semitransparent fabric of silk, rayon, cotton, etc., used for dresses, scarves, shirts, etc. [C19: from French: VEIL]

Voiotia (*Greek* vjɔ'ti:a) *n* a department of E central Greece: corresponds to ancient Boeotia and part of ancient Phocis. Pop.: 134 108 (1991). Area: 3173 sq. km (1225 sq. miles). Modern Greek name: **Boeotia.**

voir dire (vwɑ: 'dɪə) *n Law.* **1** the preliminary examination on oath of a proposed witness by the judge. **2** the oath administered to such a witness. [C17: from Old French: to speak the truth]

voix céleste (vwɑ: se'lɛst) *n* an organ stop which produces a tremolo effect through the acoustic phenomenon of beats. [from French: heavenly voice]

Vojvodina *or* **Voivodina** (*Serbo-Croat* 'vɔjvɔdina) *n* a region of NE Yugoslavia, in N Serbia: stripped of its previous autonomous status in 1990 after ethnic unrest. Capital: Novi Sad. Pop.: 2 114 000 (1995 est.). Area: 22 489 sq. km (8683 sq. miles).

vol. *abbrev. for:* **1** volcano. **2** volume. **3** volunteer.

Volans ('vəulænz) *n, Latin genitive* **Volantis** (vəu'læntɪs). a small constellation in the S hemisphere lying between Carina and Hydrus. [C19: from Latin, literally: flying, from *volāre* to fly]

volant ('vəulənt) *adj* **1** (*usually postpositive*) *Heraldry.* in a flying position. **2** *Rare.* flying or capable of flight. **3** *Poetic.* moving lightly or agilely; nimble. [C16: from French: flying, from *voler* to fly, from Latin *volāre*]

Volapuk *or* **Volapük** ('vɒlə,pʊk) *n* an artificial language based on English, French, German, Latin, etc., invented by Johann Schleyer (1831–1912) in 1880. [C19: from *vol,* based on WORLD + euphonic *-a-* + *pük* speech, based on SPEAK]

volar ('vəulə) *adj Anatomy.* of or relating to the palm of the hand or the sole of the foot. [C19: from Latin *vola* hollow of the hand, palm, sole of the foot]

volatile ('vɒlə,taɪl) *adj* **1** (of a substance) capable of readily changing from a solid or liquid form to a vapour; having a high vapour pressure and a low boiling point. **2** (of persons) disposed to caprice or inconstancy; fickle; mercurial. **3** (of circumstances) liable to sudden, unpredictable, or explosive change. **4** lasting only a short time: *volatile business interests.* **5** *Computing.* (of a memory) not retaining stored information when the power supply is cut off. **6** *Obsolete.* flying or capable of flight; volant. ◆ *n* **7** a volatile substance. **8** *Rare.* a winged creature. [C17: from Latin *volātilis* flying, from *volāre* to fly] ▸ **'volatileness** *or* **volatility** (,vɒlə'tɪlɪtɪ) *n*

volatile oil *n* another name for **essential oil.**

volatile salt *n* another name for **sal volatile.**

volatilize *or* **volatilise** (vɒ'lætɪ,laɪz) *vb* to change or cause to change from a solid or liquid to a vapour. ▸ **vo'lati,lizable** *or* **vo'lati,lisable** *adj* ▸ **vo,latiliz'ation** *or* **vo,latilis'ation** *n*

vol-au-vent (*French* vɔlovɑ̃) *n* a very light puff pastry case filled either with a savoury mixture in a richly flavoured sauce or sometimes with fruit. [C19: from French, literally: flight in the wind]

volcanic (vɒl'kænɪk) *adj* **1** of, relating to, produced by, or characterized by the presence of volcanoes: *a volcanic region.* **2** suggestive of or resembling an erupting volcano: *a volcanic era.* **3** another word for **extrusive** (sense 2). ▸ **vol'canically** *adv* ▸ **volcanicity** (,vɒlkə'nɪsɪtɪ) *n*

volcanic bomb *n* See **bomb** (sense 4).

volcanic glass *n* any of several glassy volcanic igneous rocks, such as obsidian and pitchstone.

volcanism ('vɒlkə,nɪzəm) *or* **vulcanism** *n* those processes collectively that result in the formation of volcanoes and their products.

volcanize *or* **volcanise** ('vɒlkə,naɪz) *vb* (*tr*) to subject to the effects of or change by volcanic heat. ▸ **,volcani'zation** *or* **,volcani'sation** *n*

volcano (vɒl'keɪnəu) *n, pl* **-noes** *or* **-nos. 1** an opening in the earth's crust from which molten lava, rock fragments, ashes, dust, and gases are ejected from below the earth's surface. **2** a mountain formed from volcanic material ejected from a vent in a central crater. [C17: from Italian, from Latin *Volcānus* VULCAN[1], whose forges were believed to be responsible for volcanic rumblings]

Volcano Islands *pl n* a group of three volcanic islands in the W Pacific, about 1100 km (700 miles) south of Japan: the largest is Iwo Jima, taken by U.S. forces in 1945 and returned to Japan in 1968. Area: about 28 sq. km (11 sq. miles). Japanese name: **Kazan Retto.**

volcanology (,vɒlkə'nɒlədʒɪ) *or* **vulcanology** *n* the study of volcanoes and volcanic phenomena. ▸ **volcanological** (,vɒlkənə'lɒdʒɪkᵊl) *or* **,vulcano'logical** *adj* ▸ **,volcan'ologist** *or* **,vulcan'ologist** *n*

vole[1] (vəul) *n* any of numerous small rodents of the genus *Microtus* and related genera, mostly of Eurasia and North America and having a stocky body, short tail, and inconspicuous ears: family *Cricetidae.* See also **water vole.** [C19: short for *volemouse,* from Old Norse *vollr* field + *mus* MOUSE; related to Icelandic *vollarmus*]

vole[2] (vəul) *n* (in some card games, such as écarté) the taking of all the tricks in a deal, thus scoring extra points. [C17: from French, from *voler* to fly, from Latin *volāre*]

Volga ('vɒlgə) *n* a river in W Russia, rising in the Valdai Range and flowing through a chain of small lakes to the Rybinsk Reservoir and south to the Caspian Sea through Volgograd: the longest river in Europe. Length: 3690 km (2293 miles).

Volgograd (*Russian* vəlga'grat; *English* 'vɒlgə,græd) *n* a port in SW Russia, on the River Volga: scene of a major engagement (1918) during the civil war and again in World War II (1942–43), in which the German forces were defeated; major industrial centre. Pop.: 1 003 000 (1995 est.). Former names: **Tsaritsyn** (until 1925), **Stalingrad** (1925–61).

volitant ('vɒlɪtənt) *adj* **1** flying or moving about rapidly. **2** capable of flying. [C19: from Latin *volitāre* to flit, from *volāre* to fly]

volition (və'lɪʃən) *n* **1** the act of exercising the will: *of one's own volition.* **2** the faculty or capability of conscious choice, decision, and intention; the will. **3** the resulting choice or resolution. **4** *Philosophy.* an act of will as distinguished from the physical movement it intends to bring about. [C17: from Medieval Latin *volitiō,* from Latin *vol-* as in *volō* I will, present stem of *velle* to wish] ▸ **vo'litional** *or* **vo'litionary** *adj* ▸ **vo'litionally** *adv*

volitive ('vɒlɪtɪv) *adj* **1** of, relating to, or emanating from the will. **2** *Grammar.* another word for **desiderative.**

volk (fɔlk) *n S. African.* the people or nation, esp. the nation of Afrikaners. [Afrikaans]

Völkerwanderung *German.* ('fœlkərvandəruŋ) *n* the migration of peoples, esp. of Germanic and Slavic peoples into S and W Europe from 2nd to 11th centuries. [literally: nations wandering, German translation of Latin *migrātiō gentium*]

Volkslied *German.* ('fɔlksli:t) *n, pl* ***-lieder*** (-li:dər). a type of popular German folk song. [literally: folk song]

Volksraad ('fɔlks,rɑ:t) *n S. African.* the legislative assembly of the Boer republics in South Africa during the latter half of the 19th century. [Afrikaans *volk* people + *raad* council]

volley ('vɒlɪ) *n* **1** the simultaneous discharge of several weapons, esp. firearms. **2** the projectiles or missiles so discharged. **3** a burst of oaths, protests, etc., occurring simultaneously or in rapid succession. **4** *Sport.* a stroke, shot, or kick at a moving ball before it hits the ground. Compare **half volley. 5** *Cricket.* the flight of such a ball or the ball itself. **6** the simultaneous explosion of several blastings of rock. ◆ *vb* **7** to discharge (weapons, etc.) in or as if in a volley or (of weapons, etc.) to be discharged. **8** (*tr*) to utter vehemently or sound loudly and continuously. **9** (*tr*) *Sport.* to strike or kick (a moving ball) before it hits the ground. **10** (*intr*) to issue or move rapidly or indiscriminately. [C16: from French *volée* a flight, from *voler* to fly, from Latin *volāre*] ▸ **'volleyer** *n*

volleyball ('vɒlɪ,bɔ:l) *n* **1** a game in which two teams hit a large ball back and forth over a high net with their hands. **2** the ball used in this game.

Vologda (*Russian* 'vɔləgdə) *n* an industrial city in W central Russia. Pop.: 299 000 (1995 est.).

Vólos (*Greek* 'vɔlɔs) *n* a port in E Greece, in Thessaly on the **Gulf of Volos** (an inlet of the Aegean): the third largest port in Greece. Pop.: 70 000 (latest est.).

volost ('vəulɒst) *n* **1** (in the former Soviet Union) a rural soviet. **2** (in tsarist Russia) a peasant community consisting of several villages or hamlets. [from Russian]

vols. *abbrev. for* volumes.

Volsci ('vɒlski:) *pl n* a warlike people of ancient Latium, subdued by Rome in the fifth and fourth centuries B.C.

Volscian ('vɒlskɪən) *n* **1** a member of the Volsci. **2** the extinct language of the Volsci, closely related to Umbrian. ◆ *adj* **3** of or relating to the Volsci or their language.

Volsung ('vɒlsuŋ) *n* **1** a great hero of Norse and Germanic legend and poetry who gave his name to a race of warriors; father of Sigmund and Signy. **2** any member of his family.

Volsunga Saga ('vɒlsuŋgə) *n* a 13th-century Icelandic saga about the family of the Volsungs and the deeds of Sigurd, related in theme and story to the Nibelungenlied.

volt[1] (vəult) *n* the derived SI unit of electric potential; the potential difference between two points on a conductor carrying a current of 1 ampere, when the power dissipated between these points is 1 watt. Symbol: V [C19: named after Count Alessandro Volta; see VOLTA[2]]

volt[2] *or* **volte** (vɒlt) *n* **1** a small circle of determined size executed in dressage. **2** a leap made in fencing to avoid an opponent's thrust. [C17: from French *volte,* from Italian *volta* a turn, ultimately from Latin *volvere* to turn]

volta ('vɒltə; *Italian* 'vɔlta) *n, pl* **-te** (*Italian* -te). **1** a quick-moving Italian dance popular during the 16th and 17th centuries. **2** a piece of music written for or in the rhythm of this dance, in triple time. [C17: from Italian: turn; see VOLT[2]]

Volta[1] ('vɒltə) *n* **1** a river in W Africa, formed by the confluence of the **Black Volta** and the **White Volta** in N central Ghana: flows south to the Bight of Benin: the chief river of Ghana. Length: 480 km (300 miles); (including the Black Volta) 1600 km (1000 miles). **2 Lake.** an artificial lake in Ghana, extending 408 km (250 miles) upstream from the **Volta River Dam** on the Volta River: completed in 1966. Area: 8482 sq. km (3275 sq. miles).

Volta[2] ('vəultə; *Italian* 'vɔlta) *n* Count **Alessandro** (ales'sandro). 1745–1827, Italian physicist after whom the volt is named. He made important contributions to the theory of current electricity and invented the voltaic pile (1800), the electrophorus (1775), and an electroscope.

voltage ('vəultɪdʒ) *n* an electromotive force or potential difference expressed in volts.

voltage divider *n* another name for a **potential divider.**

voltaic (vɒl'teɪɪk) *adj* another word for **galvanic** (sense 1).

Voltaic (vɒl'teɪɪk) *adj* **1** of or relating to Burkina-Faso, formerly known as Upper Volta. **2** denoting, belonging to, or relating to the Gur group of African languages. ◆ *n* **3** this group of languages. See also **Gur.**

voltaic cell *n* another name for **primary cell.**

voltaic couple *n Physics.* a pair of dissimilar metals in an electrolyte with a potential difference between the metals resulting from chemical action.

voltaic pile *n* an early form of battery consisting of a pile of paired plates of dissimilar metals, such as zinc and copper, each pair being separated from the next by a pad moistened with an electrolyte. Also called: **pile, galvanic pile, Volta's pile.**

Voltaire (vɒl'tɛə, vəʊl-; *French* vɔltɛr) *n* pseudonym of *François Marie Arouet.* 1694–1778, French writer, whose outspoken belief in religious, political, and social liberty made him the embodiment of the 18th-century Enlightenment. His major works include *Lettres philosophiques* (1734) and the satire *Candide* (1759). He also wrote plays, such as *Zaïre* (1732), poems, and scientific studies. He suffered several periods of banishment for his radical views. ► **Vol'tairean** *or* **Vol'tairian** *adj, n*

voltaism ('vɒltəˌɪzəm) *n* another name for **galvanism.**

voltameter (vɒl'tæmɪtə) *n* another name for **coulometer.** ► **voltametric** (ˌvɒltə'mɛtrɪk) *adj*

voltammeter (ˌvəʊlt'æmˌmiːtə) *n* a dual-purpose instrument that can measure both potential difference and electric current, usually in volts and amperes respectively.

volt-ampere ('vəʊlt'æmpɛə) *n* the product of the potential in volts across an electrical circuit and the resultant current in amperes. Abbrev.: **VA.**

Volta Redonda (*Portuguese* 'voltə rə'dõdə) *n* a city in SE Brazil, in Rio de Janeiro state on the Paraíba River: founded in 1941; site of South America's largest steelworks. Pop.: 219 988 (1991).

volte (vɒlt) *n* a variant spelling of **volt**[2].

volte-face ('vɒlt'fɑːs) *n, pl* **volte-face. 1** a reversal, as in opinion or policy. **2** a change of position so as to look, lie, etc., in the opposite direction. [C19: from French, from Italian *volta-faccia,* from *volta* a turn + *faccia* face]

voltmeter ('vəʊltˌmiːtə) *n* an instrument for measuring potential difference or electromotive force.

Volturno (*Italian* vol'turno) *n* a river in S central Italy, flowing southeast and southwest to the Tyrrhenian Sea: scene of a battle (1860) during the wars for Italian unity, in which Garibaldi defeated the Neapolitans; German line of defence during World War II. Length: 175 km (109 miles).

voluble ('vɒljʊbᵊl) *adj* **1** talking easily, readily, and at length; fluent. **2** *Archaic.* easily turning or rotating, as on an axis. **3** *Rare.* (of a plant) twining or twisting. [C16: from Latin *volūbilis* turning readily, fluent, from *volvere* to turn] ► ˌ**volu'bility** *or* '**volubleness** *n* ► '**volubly** *adv*

volume ('vɒljuːm) *n* **1** the magnitude of the three-dimensional space enclosed within or occupied by an object, geometric solid, etc. Symbol: *V* **2** a large mass or quantity: *the volume of protest.* **3** an amount or total: *the volume of exports.* **4** fullness or intensity of tone or sound. **5** the control on a radio, etc., for adjusting the intensity of sound. **6** a bound collection of printed or written pages; book. **7** any of several books either bound in an identical format or part of a series. **8** the complete set of issues of a periodical over a specified period, esp. one year. **9** *History.* a roll or scroll of parchment, papyrus, etc. **10 speak volumes.** to convey much significant information. ◆ Abbrevs. (for senses 6–8): **v., vol.** [C14: from Old French *volum,* from Latin *volūmen* a roll, book, from *volvere* to roll up]

volumed ('vɒljuːmd) *adj* **1** (of literary works) **1a** consisting of or being in volumes. **1b** (*in combination*): *a three-volumed history.* **2** *Rare.* having bulk or volume. **3** *Poetic.* forming a rounded mass.

volumeter (vɒ'ljuːmɪtə) *n* any instrument for measuring the volume of a solid, liquid, or gas.

volumetric (ˌvɒljʊ'mɛtrɪk) *adj* of, concerning, or using measurement by volume: *volumetric analysis.* Compare **gravimetric.** ► ˌ**volu'metrically** *adv* ► **volumetry** (vɒ'ljuːmɪtrɪ) *n*

volumetric analysis *n Chem.* **1** quantitative analysis of liquids or solutions by comparing the volumes that react with known volumes of standard reagents, usually by titration. Compare **gravimetric analysis. 2** quantitative analysis of gases by volume.

volumetric displacement *n* the volume of air per revolution that passes through a mechanical pump when the pressure at the intake and the exhaust is the same as that of the atmosphere. Also called: **swept volume.**

volumetric efficiency *n* **1** the ratio of fluid delivered by a piston or ram pump per stroke to the displacement volume of the piston or ram. **2** the ratio of air or gas-air mixture drawn into the cylinder of an internal-combustion engine to the volumetric displacement of the piston.

voluminous (və'luːmɪnəs) *adj* **1** of great size, quantity, volume, or extent. **2** (of writing) consisting of or sufficient to fill volumes. **3** prolific in writing or speech. **4** *Obsolete.* winding. [C17: from Late Latin *volūminōsus* full of windings, from *volūmen* VOLUME] ► **voluminosity** (vəˌluːmɪ'nɒsɪtɪ) *or* **vo'luminousness** *n* ► **vo'luminously** *adv*

Völund ('vølʊnd) *n* the Scandinavian name of **Wayland.**

voluntarism ('vɒləntəˌrɪzəm) *n* **1** *Philosophy.* the theory that the will rather than the intellect is the ultimate principle of reality. **2** a doctrine or system based on voluntary participation in a course of action. **3** the belief that the state, government, and the law should not interfere with the procedures of collective bargaining and of trade union organization. **4** another name for **voluntaryism.** ► '**voluntarist** *n, adj* ► ˌ**volunta'ristic** *adj*

voluntary ('vɒləntərɪ, -trɪ) *adj* **1** performed, undertaken, or brought about by free choice, willingly, or without being asked: *a voluntary donation.* **2** (of persons) serving or acting in a specified function of one's own accord and without compulsion or promise of remuneration: *a voluntary social worker.* **3** done by, composed of, or functioning with the aid of volunteers: *a voluntary association.* **4** endowed with, exercising, or having the faculty of willing: *a voluntary agent.* **5** arising from natural impulse; spontaneous: *voluntary laughter.* **6** *Law.* **6a** acting or done without legal obligation, compulsion, or persuasion. **6b** made without payment or recompense in any form: *a voluntary conveyance.* **7** (of the muscles of the limbs, neck, etc.) having their action controlled by the will. **8** maintained or provided by the voluntary actions or contributions of individuals and not by the state: *voluntary schools, the voluntary system.* ◆ *n, pl* **-taries. 9** *Music.* a composition or improvisation, usually for organ, played at the beginning or end of a church service. **10** work done without compulsion. **11** *Obsolete.* a volunteer, esp. in an army. [C14: from Latin *voluntārius,* from *voluntās* will, from *velle* to wish] ► **volun'tarily** *adv* ► '**voluntariness** *n*

Voluntary Aid Detachment *n* (in World War I) an organization of British women volunteers who assisted in military hospitals and ambulance duties. Abbrev.: **VAD.**

voluntary arrangement *n Law.* a procedure enabling an insolvent company to come to an arrangement with its creditors and resolve its financial problems, often in compliance with a court order.

voluntaryism ('vɒləntərɪˌɪzəm, -trɪ-) *or* **voluntarism** *n* **1** the principle of supporting churches, schools, and various other institutions by voluntary contributions rather than with state funds. **2** any system based on this principle. ► '**voluntaryist** *or* '**voluntarist** *n*

voluntary retailer *n* another name for **symbol retailer.**

volunteer (ˌvɒlən'tɪə) *n* **1a** a person who performs or offers to perform voluntary service. **1b** (*as modifier*): *a volunteer system; volunteer advice.* **2** a person who freely undertakes military service, esp. temporary or special service. **3** *Law.* **3a** a person who does some act or enters into a transaction without being under any legal obligation to do so and without being promised any remuneration for his services. **3b** *Property law.* a person to whom property is transferred without his giving any valuable consideration in return, as a legatee under a will. **4a** a plant that grows from seed that has not been deliberately sown. **4b** (*as modifier*): *a volunteer plant.* ◆ *vb* **5** to offer (oneself or one's services) for an undertaking by choice and without request or obligation. **6** (*tr*) to perform, give, or communicate voluntarily: *to volunteer help; to volunteer a speech.* **7** (*intr*) to enlist voluntarily for military service. [C17: from French *volontaire,* from Latin *voluntārius* willing; see VOLUNTARY]

volunteer bureau *n* (*often caps.*) (in Britain) *Social welfare.* an agency that matches up people wishing to do voluntary work with appropriate voluntary organizations.

Volunteers of America *pl n* a religious body aimed at reform and relief of human need and resembling the Salvation Army in organization and tenets, founded in New York City in 1896 by Ballington Booth.

voluptuary (və'lʌptjʊərɪ) *n, pl* **-aries. 1** a person devoted or addicted to luxury and sensual pleasures. ◆ *adj* **2** of, relating to, characterized by, or furthering sensual gratification or luxury. [C17: from Late Latin *voluptuārius* delightful, from Latin *voluptās* pleasure]

voluptuous (və'lʌptjʊəs) *adj* **1** relating to, characterized by, or consisting of pleasures of the body or senses; sensual. **2** disposed, devoted, or addicted to sensual indulgence or luxurious pleasures. **3** provocative and sexually alluring, esp. through shapeliness or fullness: *a voluptuous woman.* [C14: from Latin *voluptuōsus* full of gratification, from *voluptās* pleasure] ► **vo'luptuously** *adv* ► **vo'luptuousness** *n*

volute ('vɒljuːt, və'luːt) *n* **1** a spiral or twisting turn, form, or object; spiral; whorl. **2** Also called: **helix.** a carved ornament, esp. as used on an Ionic capital, that has the form of a spiral scroll. **3** any of the whorls of the spirally coiled shell of a snail or similar gastropod mollusc. **4** any tropical marine gastropod mollusc of the family *Volutidae,* typically having a spiral shell with beautiful markings. **5** a tangential part, resembling the volute of a snail's shell, that collects the fluids emerging from the periphery of a turbine, impeller pump, etc. ◆ *adj also* **voluted** (və'luːtɪd). **6** having the form of a volute; spiral. **7** *Machinery.* moving in a spiral path. [C17: from Latin *volūta* a spiral decoration, from *volūtus* rolled, from *volvere* to roll up]

volution (və'luːʃən) *n* **1** a rolling, revolving, or spiral form or motion. **2** a whorl of a spiral gastropod shell.

volva ('vɒlvə) *n, pl* **-vae** (-viː) *or* **-vas.** *Botany.* a cup-shaped structure that sheathes the base of the stalk of certain mushrooms. [C18: from Latin: a covering, from *volvere* to wrap] ► **volvate** ('vɒlvɪt, -veɪt) *adj*

volvox ('vɒlvɒks) *n* any freshwater flagellate protozoan of the genus *Volvox,* occurring in colonies in the form of hollow multicellular spheres. [C18: from New Latin, from Latin *volvere* to roll]

volvulus ('vɒlvjʊləs) *n, pl* **-luses.** *Pathol.* an abnormal twisting of the intestines causing obstruction. [C17: from New Latin, from Latin *volvere* to twist]

vomer ('vəʊmə) *n* the thin flat bone forming part of the separation between the nasal passages in mammals. [C18: from Latin: ploughshare] ► **vomerine** ('vəʊməˌraɪn, -rɪn, 'vɒm-) *adj*

vomit ('vɒmɪt) *vb* **-its, -iting, -ited. 1** to eject (the contents of the stomach) through the mouth as the result of involuntary muscular spasms of the stomach and oesophagus. **2** to eject or be ejected forcefully; spew forth. ◆ *n* **3** the matter ejected in vomiting. **4** the act of vomiting. **5** a drug or agent that induces vomiting; emetic. [C14: from Latin *vomitāre* to vomit repeatedly, from *vomere* to vomit] ► '**vomiter** *n*

vomitory ('vɒmɪtərɪ, -trɪ) *adj* **1** Also: **vomitive** ('vɒmɪtɪv). causing vomiting; emetic. ◆ *n, pl* **-ries. 2** Also called: **vomitive.** a vomitory agent. **3** *Rare.* a container for receiving vomitus. **4** Also called: **vomitorium** (ˌvɒmɪ'tɔːrɪəm). a passageway in an ancient Roman amphitheatre that connects an outside entrance to a tier of seats. **5** an opening through which matter is ejected.

vomiturition (ˌvɒmɪtjʊ'rɪʃən) *n* the act of retching.

vomitus ('vɒmɪtəs) *n, pl* **-tuses. 1** matter that has been vomited. **2** the act of vomiting. [Latin: a vomiting]

von Braun (vɒn 'braʊn, fɒn) *n* **Wernher** ('vɛrnər). 1912–77, U.S. rocket engineer, born in Germany, where he designed the V-2 missile used in World War II. In the U.S. he worked on the Apollo project.

Vondel (*Dutch* 'vɔndəl) *n* **Joost van den** ('joːst vɑn dən). 1587–1679, Dutch poet and dramatist, author of the Biblical plays *Lucifer* (1654), *Adam in Exile* (1664), and *Noah* (1667).

von Euler (*German* fɔn 'ɔɪlər) *n* See (Ulf von) **Euler.**

von Laue (*German* (fɔn 'lauə) *n* See (Max Theodor Felix von) **Laue.**

Vonnegut ('vɒnɪgʌt) *n* **Kurt.** born 1922, U.S. novelist. His works include *Cat's Cradle* (1963), *Slaughterhouse Five* (1969), *Galapagos* (1985), *Hocus Pocus* (1990), and *Timequake* (1997).

von Neumann (vɒn 'njuːmən, fɒn) *n* **John.** 1903–57, U.S. mathematician, born in Hungary. He formulated game theory and contributed to the development of the atomic bomb and to the development of the stored-program computer (**von Neumann machine**).

von Rundstedt (*German* fɔn 'rʊntʃtɛt) *n* See (Karl Rudolf Gerd von) **Rundstedt.**

von Sternberg (vɒn 'stɜːn,bɜːg; *German* fɔn 'ʃtɛrnbɛrk) *n* **Joseph** ('joːzɛf), real name *Jonas Sternberg*. 1894–1969, U.S. film director, born in Austria, whose films include *The Blue Angel* (1930), *Blonde Venus* (1932), *The Scarlet Empress* (1934), and the unfinished *I, Claudius* (1937).

von Stroheim (vɒn 'strəʊ,haɪm, 'ʃtrəʊ-; fɒn) *n* **Erich** ('eːrɪç), real name *Hans Erich Maria Stroheim von Nordenwall*. 1885–1957, U.S. film director and actor, born in Austria, whose films include *Foolish Wives* (1921) and *Greed* (1923).

voodoo ('vuːduː) *n, pl* **-doos. 1** Also called: **voodooism.** a religious cult involving witchcraft and communication by trance with ancestors and animistic deities, common in Haiti and other Caribbean islands. **2** a person who practises voodoo. **3** a charm, spell, or fetish involved in voodoo worship and ritual. ◆ *adj* **4** relating to or associated with voodoo. ◆ *vb* **-doos, -dooing, -dooed. 5** (*tr*) to affect by or as if by the power of voodoo. [C19: from Louisiana French *voudou*, ultimately of West African origin; compare Ewe *vodu* guardian spirit] ▸ **'voodooist** *n* ▸ **,voodoo'istic** *adj*

voorkamer ('fʊə,kɑːmə) *n S. African.* the front room, esp. of a Cape Dutch house or farmhouse. [from Afrikaans *voor* front + *kamer* room]

voorskot ('fʊə,skɒt) *n S. African.* advance payment made to a farmer for crops. Compare **agterskot.** [C20: Afrikaans, from *voor* before + *skot* shot, payment]

Voortrekker ('fʊə,trɛkə, 'vʊə-) *n* (in South Africa) **1** one of the original Afrikaner settlers of the Transvaal and the Orange Free State who migrated from the Cape Colony in the 1830s. **2** a member of the Afrikaner youth movement founded in 1931. [C19: from Dutch, from *voor-* FORE- + *trekken* to TREK]

voracious (vɒ'reɪʃəs) *adj* **1** devouring or craving food in great quantities. **2** very eager or unremitting in some activity: *voracious reading.* [C17: from Latin *vorāx* swallowing greedily, from *vorāre* to devour] ▸ **vo'raciously** *adv* ▸ **voracity** (vɒ'ræsɪtɪ) *or* **vo'raciousness** *n*

Vorarlberg (*German* 'foːrarlbɛrk) *n* a mountainous state of W Austria. Capital: Bregenz. Pop.: 343 000 (1995 est.). Area: 2601 sq. km (1004 sq. miles).

Vorlage *German.* ('fɔːrlaːgə) *n Skiing.* a position in which a skier leans forward but keeps his heels on the skis. [from *vor* before, in front of + *Lage* position, stance]

Voronezh (*Russian* va'rɔnɪʃ) *n* a city in W Russia: engineering, chemical, and food-processing industries; university (1918). Pop.: 908 000 (1995 est.).

Voroshilov (*Russian* vərə'ʃiləf) *n* **Kliment Yefremovich** ('klimɪnt jɪ'frjɛməvitʃ). 1881–1969, Soviet military leader; president of the Soviet Union (1953–60).

Voroshilovgrad (*Russian* vərəʃilaw'grat) *n* the former name (1935–91) of **Lugansk.**

Voroshilovsk (*Russian* vəra'ʃiləfsk) *n* the former name (1940–44) of **Stavropol.**

-vorous *adj combining form.* feeding on or devouring: *carnivorous.* [from Latin *-vorus*; related to *vorāre* to swallow up, DEVOUR] ▸ **-vore** *n combining form.*

Vorster ('fɔːstə, 'vɔː-) *n* **Balthazar Johannes,** known as *John*. 1915–83, South African statesman; Nationalist prime minister (1966–78); president (1978).

vortex ('vɔːtɛks) *n, pl* **-texes** *or* **-tices** (-tɪ,siːz). **1** a whirling mass or rotary motion in a liquid, gas, flame, etc., such as the spiralling movement of water around a whirlpool. **2** any activity, situation, or way of life regarded as irresistibly engulfing. [C17: from Latin: a whirlpool; variant of VERTEX] ▸ **vortical** ('vɔːtɪk°l) *adj* ▸ **'vortically** *adv*

vortex drag *n* See **trailing vortex drag.**

vortex ring *n* a stable perturbation in a fluid that takes the form of a torus in which the flow rotates in the section of the torus so that the pressure difference between the inside and outside of the torus balances body forces. The best-known vortex ring is a smoke ring.

vortex shedding *n* the process by which vortices formed continuously by the aerodynamic conditions associated with a solid body in a gas or air stream are carried downstream by the flow in the form of a vortex street. See also **vortex street.**

vortex street *n* a regular stream of vortices or parallel streams of vortices carried downstream by the flow of a fluid over a body. These are sometimes made visible by vapour condensation as in the vortex trails from the wing tips of an aeroplane. See also **Kármán vortex street, vortex shedding.**

vorticella (,vɔːtɪ'sɛlə) *n, pl* **-lae** (-liː). any protozoan of the genus *Vorticella*, consisting of a goblet-shaped ciliated cell attached to the substratum by a long contractile stalk. [C18: from New Latin, literally: a little eddy, from VORTEX]

vorticism ('vɔːtɪ,sɪzəm) *n* an art movement in England initiated in 1913 by Wyndham Lewis combining the techniques of cubism with the concern for the problems of the machine age evinced in futurism. [C20: referring to the "vortices" of modern life on which the movement was based] ▸ **'vorticist** *n*

vorticose ('vɔːtɪ,kəʊs) *adj Rare.* rotating quickly; whirling. [C18: from Latin *vorticōsus*, variant of *verticōsus* full of whirlpools; see VERTEX]

vortiginous (vɔː'tɪdʒɪnəs) *adj* like a vortex; vortical; whirling. [C17: variant of VERTIGINOUS]

Vortumnus (vɔː'tʌmnəs) *n* a variant spelling of **Vertumnus.**

Vosges (*French* voʒ) *n* **1** a mountain range in E France, west of the Rhine valley. Highest peak: 1423 m (4672 ft.). **2** a department of NE France, in Lorraine region. Capital: Épinal. Pop.: 385 400 (1995). Area: 5903 sq. km (2302 sq. miles).

Vostok ('vɒstɒk) *n* any of six manned Soviet spacecraft made to orbit the earth. **Vostok 1,** launched in April 1961, carried Yuri Gagarin, the first man in space; **Vostok 6** carried Valentina Tereshkova, the first woman in space.

vostro account ('vɒstrəʊ) *n* a bank account held by a foreign bank with a British bank, usually in sterling. Compare **nostro account.**

votary ('vəʊtərɪ) *n, pl* **-ries,** *also* **votarist. 1** *R.C. Church, Eastern Churches.* a person, such as a monk or nun, who has dedicated himself or herself to religion by taking vows. **2** a devoted adherent of a religion, cause, leader, pursuit, etc. ◆ *adj* **3** ardently devoted to the services or worship of God, a deity, or a saint. [C16: from Latin *vōtum* a vow, from *vovēre* to vow] ▸ **'votaress** *or* **'votress** *fem n*

vote (vəʊt) *n* **1** an indication of choice, opinion, or will on a question, such as the choosing of a candidate, by or as if by some recognized means, such as a ballot: *10 votes for Jones.* **2** the opinion of a group of persons as determined by voting: *it was put to the vote; do not take a vote; it came to a vote.* **3** a body of votes or voters collectively: *the Jewish vote.* **4** the total number of votes cast: *the vote decreased at the last election.* **5** the ticket, ballot, etc., by which a vote is expressed. **6a** the right to vote; franchise; suffrage. **6b** a person regarded as the embodiment of this right. **7** a means of voting, such as a ballot. **8** *Chiefly Brit.* a grant or other proposition to be voted upon. ◆ *vb* **9** (when *tr, takes a clause as object or an infinitive*) to express or signify (one's preference, opinion, or will) (for or against some question, etc.): *to vote by ballot; we voted that it was time to adjourn; vote for me!* **10** (*intr*) to declare oneself as being (something or in favour of something) by exercising one's vote: *to vote socialist.* **11** (*tr; foll. by into or out of, etc.*) to appoint or elect (a person to or from a particular post): *they voted him into the presidency; he was voted out of office.* **12** (*tr*) to determine the condition of in a specified way by voting: *the court voted itself out of existence.* **13** (*tr*) to authorize, confer, or allow by voting: *vote us a rise.* **14** (*tr*) *Informal.* to declare by common opinion: *the party was voted a failure.* **15** (*tr*) to influence or control the voting of: *do not try to vote us!* [C15: from Latin *vōtum* a solemn promise, from *vovēre* to vow] ▸ **'votable** *or* **'voteable** *adj* ▸ **'voteless** *adj*

vote down *vb* (*tr, adv*) to decide against or defeat in a vote: *the bill was voted down.*

vote of no confidence *n Parliament.* a vote on a motion put by the Opposition censuring an aspect of the Government's policy; if the motion is carried the Government is obliged to resign. Also called: **vote of censure.**

voter ('vəʊtə) *n* a person who can or does vote.

voting machine *n* (esp. in the U.S.) a machine at a polling station that voters operate to register their votes and that mechanically or electronically counts all votes cast.

votive ('vəʊtɪv) *adj* **1** offered, given, undertaken, performed or dedicated in fulfilment of or in accordance with a vow. **2** *R.C. Church.* optional; not prescribed; having the nature of a voluntary offering: *a votive Mass; a votive candle.* [C16: from Latin *vōtīvus* promised by a vow, from *vōtum* a vow] ▸ **'votively** *adv* ▸ **'votiveness** *n*

Votyak ('vəʊtɪ,æk) *n* **1** (*pl* **-aks** *or* **-ak**) a member of a Finnish people living chiefly in the Udmurt Autonomous Republic, between the Volga and the Urals. **2** Also called: **Udmurt.** the language of this people, belonging to the Finno-Ugric family.

vouch (vaʊtʃ) *vb* **1** (*intr*; usually foll. by *for*) to give personal assurance; guarantee: *I'll vouch for his safety.* **2** (when *tr, usually takes a clause as object*; when *intr,* usually foll. by *for*) to furnish supporting evidence (for) or function as proof (of). **3** (*tr*) *English legal history.* to summon (a person who had warranted title to land) to defend that title or give up land of equal value. **4** (*tr*) *Archaic.* to cite (authors, principles, etc.) in support of something. **5** (*tr*) *Obsolete.* to assert. ◆ *n* **6** *Obsolete.* the act of vouching; assertion or allegation. [C14: from Old French *vocher* to summon, ultimately from Latin *vocāre* to call]

voucher ('vaʊtʃə) *n* **1** a document serving as evidence for some claimed transaction, as the receipt or expenditure of money. **2** *Brit.* a ticket or card serving as a substitute for cash: *a gift voucher.* **3** a person or thing that vouches for the truth of some statement, etc. **4** any of certain documents that various groups of British nationals born outside Britain must obtain in order to settle in Britain. **5** *English law, obsolete.* **5a** the summoning into court of a person to warrant a title to property. **5b** the person so summoned. [C16: from Anglo-French, noun use of Old French *voucher* to summon; see VOUCH]

vouchsafe (,vaʊtʃ'seɪf) *vb* (*tr*) **1** to give or grant or condescend to give or grant: *she vouchsafed no reply; he vouchsafed me no encouragement.* **2** (*may take a clause as object or an infinitive*) to agree, promise, or permit, often graciously or condescendingly: *he vouchsafed to come yesterday.* **3** *Obsolete.* **3a** to warrant as being safe. **3b** to bestow as a favour (upon). [C14 *vouchen sauf*; see VOUCH, SAFE] ▸ **,vouch'safement** *n*

vouge (vuːʒ) *n* a form of pike or halberd used by foot soldiers in the 14th century and later. [from Old French *voulge, vouge* (Medieval Latin *vanga*), of obscure origin]

voussoir (vuː'swɑː) *n* a wedge-shaped stone or brick that is used with others to construct an arch or vault. [C18: from French, from Vulgar Latin *volsōrium* (unattested), ultimately from Latin *volvere* to turn, roll]

Vouvray ('vuːvreɪ; *French* vuvrɛ) *n* a dry white wine, which can be still, sparkling, or semisparkling, produced around Touraine in the Loire Valley.

vow (vaʊ) *n* **1** a solemn or earnest pledge or promise binding the person making it to perform a specified act or behave in a certain way. **2** a solemn promise made to a deity or saint, by which the promiser pledges himself to some future act, course of action, or way of life. **3 take vows.** to enter a religious order and commit oneself to its rule of life by the vows of poverty, chastity, and obedience, which may be taken for a limited period as **simple vows** or as a perpetual and still more solemn commitment as **solemn vows.** ◆ *vb* **4** (*tr; may take a clause as object or an infinitive*) to pledge, promise, or undertake solemnly: *he vowed that he would continue; he vowed to return.* **5** (*tr*) to dedicate or consecrate to God, a deity, or a saint. **6** (*tr; usually takes a clause as object*) to assert or swear emphatically. **7** (*intr*) *Archaic.* to declare solemnly. [C13: from Old French *vou,* from Latin *vōtum* a solemn promise, from *vovēre* to vow] ▸ **'vower** *n* ▸ **'vowless** *adj*

vowel ('vaʊəl) *n* **1** *Phonetics.* a voiced speech sound whose articulation is characterized by the absence of friction-causing obstruction in the vocal tract, allowing the breath stream free passage. The timbre of a vowel is chiefly determined by the position of the tongue and the lips. **2** a letter or character representing a vowel. [C14: from Old French *vouel,* from Latin *vocālis littera* a vowel, from *vocālis* sonorous, from *vox* a voice] ▸ **'vowel-less** *adj* ▸ **'vowel-ˌlike** *adj*

vowel gradation *n* another name for **ablaut.** See **gradation** (sense 5).

vowelize *or* **vowelise** ('vaʊəˌlaɪz) *vb* (*tr*) to mark the vowel points in (a Hebrew word or text). Also: **vocalize.** ▸ **ˌvoweli'zation** *or* **ˌvoweli'sation** *n*

vowel mutation *n* another name for **umlaut.**

vowel point *n* any of several marks or points placed above or below consonants, esp. those evolved for Hebrew or Arabic, in order to indicate vowel sounds.

vox (vɒks) *n, pl* **voces** ('vəʊsiːz). a voice or sound. [Latin: voice]

vox angelica (æn'dʒelɪkə) *n* an organ stop with a soft tone, often similar to the voix céleste. [C18: from Latin: angelic voice]

vox humana (hjuː'mɑːnə) *n* a reed stop on an organ supposedly imitative of the human voice. [C18: from Latin: human voice]

vox pop *n* interviews with members of the public on a radio or television programme. [C20: shortened from VOX POPULI]

vox populi ('pɒpjʊˌlaɪ) *n* the voice of the people; popular or public opinion. [Latin]

voyage ('vɔɪɪdʒ) *n* **1** a journey, travel, or passage, esp. one to a distant land or by sea or air. **2** *Obsolete.* an ambitious project. ◆ *vb* **3** to travel over or traverse (something): *we will voyage to Africa.* [C13: from Old French *veiage,* from Latin *viāticum* provision for travelling, from *viāticus* concerning a journey, from *via* a way] ▸ **'voyager** *n*

voyage charter *n* the hire of a ship or aircraft for a specified number of voyages. Compare **time charter.**

Voyager ('vɔɪədʒər) *n* either of two US spacecraft that studied the outer solar system; **Voyager 1** visited Jupiter (1979) and Saturn (1980), **Voyager 2** visited Jupiter (1979), Saturn (1981), and made the first flyby of Uranus (1986) and Neptune (1989).

voyageur (ˌvɔɪə'dʒɜː) *n Canadian.* **1** *History.* a boatman employed by one of the early fur-trading companies, esp. in the interior. **2** a woodsman, guide, trapper, boatman, or explorer, esp. in the North. [C19: from French: traveller, from *voyager* to VOYAGE]

voyeur (vwaɪ'ɜː; *French* vwajœr) *n* a person who obtains sexual pleasure or excitement from the observation of someone undressing, having intercourse, etc. [C20: French, literally: one who sees, from *voir* to see, from Latin *vidēre*] ▸ **vo'yeurism** *n* ▸ **ˌvoyeur'istic** *adj* ▸ **ˌvoyeur'istically** *adv*

Voysey ('vɔɪzɪ) *n* **Charles (Francis Annesley).** 1857–1941, British architect and designer of furniture, fittings, and decor.

Voznesensky (*Russian* vəznɪ'sjenskij) *n* **Andrei (Andreievich)** (an'drjej). born 1933, Russian poet, noted for his experimental style.

VP *abbrev. for* **1** Vice President. **2** verb phrase.

VPL *Jocular abbrev. for* visible panty line.

VR *abbrev. for:* **1** variant reading. **2** Victoria Regina. [Latin: Queen Victoria] **3** virtual reality. **4** Volunteer Reserve.

vraisemblance (ˌvreɪsɒm'blɒns; *French* vrɛsɑ̃blɑ̃s) *n* verisimilitude; appearance of truth. [French, from *vrai* true + SEMBLANCE]

V. Rev. *abbrev. for* Very Reverend.

VRI *abbrev. for* Victoria Regina et Imperatrix. [Latin: Victoria, Queen and Empress]

Vries (vriːs) *n* See (Hugo) **De Vries.**

vrou (fraʊ) *n S. African.* a woman or wife. [Afrikaans]

vroom (vruːm, vrʊm) *interj* an exclamation imitative of a car engine revving up, as for high-speed motor racing.

vs *abbrev. for* versus.

VS *abbrev. for* Veterinary Surgeon.

v.s. *abbrev. for* vide supra. See **vide.**

vsb *abbrev. for* vestigial sideband: a transmission in an amplitude-modulated signal in which one complete sideband is transmitted, but only part of the other.

V-sign *n* **1** (in Britain) an offensive gesture made by sticking up the index and middle fingers with the palm of the hand inwards as an indication of contempt, defiance, etc. **2** a similar gesture with the palm outwards meaning victory or peace.

VSO *abbrev. for:* **1** very superior old: used to indicate that a brandy, port, etc., is between 12 and 17 years old. **2** (in Britain) Voluntary Service Overseas: an organization that sends young volunteers to use and teach their skills in developing countries.

VSOP *abbrev. for* very special (or superior) old pale: used to indicate that a brandy, port, etc., is between 20 and 25 years old.

Vt. *or* **VT** *abbrev. for* Vermont.

VTOL ('viːtɒl) *n* **1** vertical takeoff and landing; a system in which an aircraft can take off and land vertically. **2** an aircraft that uses this system. Compare **STOL.**

VTR *abbrev. for* video tape recorder.

V-type engine *n* a type of internal-combustion engine having two cylinder blocks attached to a single crankcase, the angle between the two blocks forming a V.

Vuelta Abajo (*Spanish* 'bwelta a'βaxo) *n* a region of W Cuba: famous for its tobacco.

vug, vugg, *or* **vugh** (vʌg) *n Mining.* a small cavity in a rock or vein, usually lined with crystals. [C19: from Cornish *vooga* cave] ▸ **'vuggy** *or* **'vughy** *adj*

Vuillard (*French* vɥijar) *n* **Jean Édouard** (ʒɑ̃ edwar). 1868–1940, French painter and lithographer.

Vul. *abbrev. for* Vulgate.

Vulcan[1] ('vʌlkən) *n* the Roman god of fire and metalworking. Greek counterpart: **Hephaestus.** ▸ **Vulcanian** (vʌl'keɪnɪən) *adj*

Vulcan[2] ('vʌlkən) *n* a hypothetical planet once thought to lie within the orbit of Mercury. ▸ **Vulcanian** (vʌl'keɪnɪən) *adj*

vulcanian (vʌl'keɪnɪən) *adj Geology.* **a** of or relating to a volcanic eruption characterized by the explosive discharge of gases, fine ash, and viscous lava that hardens in the crater. **b** a less common word for **volcanic.**

vulcanism ('vʌlkəˌnɪzəm) *n* a variant spelling of **volcanism.**

vulcanite ('vʌlkəˌnaɪt) *n* a hard usually black rubber produced by vulcanizing natural rubber with large amounts of sulphur. It is resistant to chemical attack: used for chemical containers, electrical insulators, etc. Also called: **ebonite.**

vulcanize *or* **vulcanise** ('vʌlkəˌnaɪz) *vb* (*tr*) **1** to treat (rubber) with sulphur or sulphur compounds under heat and pressure to improve elasticity and strength or to produce a hard substance such as vulcanite. **2** to treat (substances other than rubber) by a similar process in order to improve their properties. ▸ **'vulcanˌizable** *or* **'vulcanˌisable** *adj* ▸ **ˌvulcani'zation** *or* **ˌvulcani'sation** *n* ▸ **'vulcanˌizer** *or* **'vulcanˌiser** *n*

vulcanology (ˌvʌlkə'nɒlədʒɪ) *n* a variant spelling of **volcanology.** ▸ **vulcanological** (ˌvʌlkənə'lɒdʒɪkəl) *adj* ▸ **ˌvulcan'ologist** *n*

vulg. *abbrev. for* vulgar(ly).

Vulg. *abbrev. for* Vulgate.

vulgar ('vʌlgə) *adj* **1** marked by lack of taste, culture, delicacy, manners, etc.: *vulgar behaviour; vulgar language.* **2** (*often cap.; usually prenominal*) denoting a form of a language, esp. of Latin, current among common people, esp. at a period when the formal language is archaic and not in general spoken use. **3** *Archaic.* **3a** of, relating to, or current among the great mass of common people, in contrast to the educated, cultured, or privileged; ordinary. **3b** (*as collective n; preceded by the*): *the vulgar.* [C14: from Latin *vulgāris* belonging to the multitude, from *vulgus* the common people] ▸ **'vulgarly** *adv*

vulgar fraction *n* another name for **simple fraction.**

vulgarian (vʌl'gɛərɪən) *n* a vulgar person, esp. one who is rich or has pretensions to good taste.

vulgarism ('vʌlgəˌrɪzəm) *n* **1** a coarse, crude, or obscene expression. **2** a word or phrase found only in the vulgar form of a language. **3** another word for **vulgarity.**

vulgarity (vʌl'gærɪtɪ) *n, pl* **-ties. 1** the condition of being vulgar; lack of good manners. **2** a vulgar action, phrase, etc.

vulgarize *or* **vulgarise** ('vʌlgəˌraɪz) *vb* (*tr*) **1** to make commonplace or vulgar; debase. **2** to make (something little known or difficult to understand) widely known or popular among the public; popularize. ▸ **ˌvulgari'zation** *or* **ˌvulgari'sation** *n* ▸ **'vulgarˌizer** *or* **'vulgarˌiser** *n*

Vulgar Latin *n* any of the dialects of Latin spoken in the Roman Empire other than classical Latin. The Romance languages developed from them.

vulgate ('vʌlgeɪt, -gɪt) *Rare.* ◆ *n* **1** a commonly recognized text or version. **2** everyday or informal speech; the vernacular. ◆ *adj* **3** generally accepted; common.

Vulgate ('vʌlgeɪt, -gɪt) *n* **a** (from the 13th century onwards) the fourth-century version of the Bible produced by Jerome, partly by translating the original languages, and partly by revising the earlier Latin text based on the Greek versions. **b** (*as modifier*): *the Vulgate version.* [C17: from Medieval Latin *Vulgāta,* from Late Latin *vulgāta editiō* popular version (of the Bible), from Latin *vulgāre* to make common, from *vulgus* the common people]

vulnerable ('vʌlnərəbəl) *adj* **1** capable of being physically or emotionally wounded or hurt. **2** open to temptation, persuasion, censure, etc. **3** liable or exposed to disease, disaster, etc. **4** *Military.* liable or exposed to attack. **5** *Bridge.* (of a side who have won one game towards rubber) subject to increased bonuses or penalties. [C17: from Late Latin *vulnerābilis,* from Latin *vulnerāre* to wound, from *vulnus* a wound] ▸ **ˌvulnera'bility** *or* **'vulnerableness** *n* ▸ **'vulnerably** *adv*

vulnerary ('vʌlnərərɪ) *Med.* ◆ *adj* **1** of, relating to, or used to heal a wound. ◆ *n, pl* **-aries. 2** a vulnerary drug or agent. [C16: from Latin *vulnerārius* belonging to wounds, from *vulnus* a wound]

Vulpecula (vʌl'pɛkjʊlə) *n, Latin genitive* **Vulpeculae** (vʌl'pɛkjʊˌliː). a faint constellation in the N hemisphere lying between Cygnus and Aquila. [C19: from Latin: a little fox, from *vulpēs* a fox]

vulpine ('vʌlpaɪn) *adj* **1** Also: **vulpecular** (vʌl'pɛkjʊlə). of, relating to, or resembling a fox. **2** possessing the characteristics often attributed to foxes; crafty, clever, etc. [C17: from Latin *vulpīnus* foxlike, from *vulpēs* a fox]

vulture ('vʌltʃə) *n* **1** any of various very large diurnal birds of prey of the genera *Neophron, Gyps, Gypaetus,* etc., of Africa, Asia, and warm parts of Europe, typically having broad wings and soaring flight and feeding on carrion: family *Accipitridae* (hawks). See also **griffon**[1] (sense 2), **lammergeier. 2** any similar bird of the family *Cathartidae* of North, Central, and South America. See also **condor, turkey buzzard. 3** a person or thing that preys greedily and ruthlessly on others, esp. the helpless. **[C14**: from Old French *voltour,* from Latin *vultur;* perhaps related to Latin *vellere* to pluck, tear**]** ▸ **'vulture-ˌlike** *adj*

vulturine ('vʌltʃəˌraɪn) *adj* **1** of, relating to, or resembling a vulture. **2** Also: **'vulturous.** rapacious, predatory, or greedy.

vulva ('vʌlvə) *n, pl* **-vae** (-viː) *or* **-vas.** the external genitals of human females, including the labia, mons veneris, clitoris, and the vaginal orifice. **[C16**: from Latin: covering, womb, matrix**]** ▸ **'vulval, 'vulvar,** *or* **vulvate** ('vʌlveɪt) *adj* ▸ **vulviform** ('vʌlvɪˌfɔːm) *adj*

vulvitis (vʌl'vaɪtɪs) *n* inflammation of the vulva.

vulvovaginitis (ˌvʌlvəʊˌvædʒɪ'naɪtɪs) *n* inflammation of the vulva and vagina or of the small glands (**vulvovaginal glands**) on either side of the lower part of the vagina.

vv *abbrev. for* vice versa.

vv. *abbrev. for:* **1** versus. **2** *Music.* volumes.

VW *abbrev. for* **1** Very Worshipful. **2** Volkswagen.

VX *n* a U.S. lethal nerve gas.

Vyatka (*Russian* 'vjatkə) *n* the former name (1780–1934) of **Kirov**[1].

Vyborg (*Russian* 'vibərk) *n* a port in NW Russia, at the head of **Vyborg Bay** (an inlet of the Gulf of Finland): belonged to Finland (1918–40). Pop.: 80 000 (1988 est.). Finnish name: **Viipuri.** Swedish name: **Viborg.**

vying ('vaɪɪŋ) *vb* **1** the present participle of **vie.** ◆ *adj* **2** competing: *two vying patriarchs.*

Vyshinsky *or* **Vishinsky** (*Russian* vi'ʃinskij) *n* **Andrei Yanuaryevich** (an'drjej jənu'arjɪvitʃ). 1883–1954, Soviet jurist, statesman, and diplomat; foreign minister (1949–53). He was public prosecutor (1935–38) at the trials held to purge Stalin's rivals and was the Soviet representative at the United Nations (1945–49; 1953–54).

w *or* **W** ('dʌbᵊl,juː) *n, pl* **w's, W's,** *or* **Ws. 1** the 23rd letter and 18th consonant of the modern English alphabet. **2** a speech sound represented by this letter, in English usually a bilabial semivowel, as in *web.*

W *symbol for:* **1** watt. **2** West. **3** *Physics.* work. **4** *Chem.* tungsten [from New Latin *wolframium,* from German *Wolfram*] **5** women's (size).

w. *abbrev. for:* **1** week. **2** weight. **3** width. **4** wife. **5** with. **6** *Cricket.* **6a** wide. **6b** wicket.

W. *abbrev. for:* **1** Wales. **2** Warden. **3** Welsh.

WA *abbrev. for* **1** Washington (state). **2** Western Australia.

WAAAF (formerly) *abbrev. for* Women's Auxiliary Australian Air Force.

WAAC (wæk) *n* (formerly) **1** *acronym for* Women's Army Auxiliary Corps. **2** Also called: **waac.** a member of this corps.

Waadt (vat) *n* the German name for **Vaud.**

WAAF (wæf) *n* (formerly) **1** *acronym for:* **1a** Women's Auxiliary Air Force. **1b** Women's Auxiliary Australian Air Force. **2** Also called: **Waaf.** a member of either of these forces.

Waal (*Dutch* waːl) *n* a river in the central Netherlands: the S branch of the Lower Rhine. Length: 84 km (52 miles).

Wabash ('wɔːbæʃ) *n* a river in the E central U.S., rising in W Ohio and flowing west and southwest to join the Ohio River in Indiana. Length: 764 km (475 miles).

wabbit ('wæbɪt) *adj Scot.* weary; exhausted. [C19: from earlier *wobart* withered, feeble]

wabble ('wɒbᵊl) *vb, n* a variant spelling of **wobble.** ▸ **'wabbler** *n* ▸ **'wabbly** *adj*

Wace (weɪs) *n* **Robert.** born ?1100, Anglo-Norman poet; author of the *Roman de Brut* and *Roman de Rou.*

wack (wæk) *or* **wacker** ('wækə) *n Liverpool and Midlands dialect.* friend; pal: used chiefly as a term of address. [perhaps from dialect *wack* or *whack* to share out, hence one who shares, a friend]

wacke ('wækə) *n Obsolete.* any of various soft earthy rocks that resemble or are derived from basaltic rocks. [C18: from German: rock, gravel, basalt]

wacko ('wækəʊ) *Informal.* ◆ *adj* **1** mad or eccentric. ◆ *n, pl* **wackos 2** a mad or eccentric person. [C20: back formation from WACKY]

wacky ('wækɪ) *adj* **wackier, wackiest.** *Slang.* eccentric, erratic, or unpredictable. [C19 (in dialect sense: a fool, an eccentric): from WHACK (hence, a *whacky,* a person who behaves as if he had been whacked on the head)] ▸ **'wackily** *adv* ▸ **'wackiness** *n*

wad[1] (wɒd) *n* **1** a small mass or ball of fibrous or soft material, such as cotton wool, used esp. for packing or stuffing. **2a** a plug of paper, cloth, leather, etc., pressed against a charge to hold it in place in a muzzle-loading cannon. **2b** a disc of paper, felt, pasteboard, etc., used to hold in place the powder and shot in a shotgun cartridge. **3** a roll or bundle of something, esp. of banknotes. **4** *U.S. and Canadian slang.* a large quantity, esp. of money. **5** *Brit. dialect.* a bundle of hay or straw. **6** *Brit. military slang.* a bun: *char and a wad.* ◆ *vb* **wads, wadding, wadded. 7** to form (something) into a wad. **8** (*tr*) to roll into a wad or bundle. **9** (*tr*) **9a** to hold (a charge) in place with a wad. **9b** to insert a wad into (a gun). **10** (*tr*) to pack or stuff with wadding; pad. [C14: from Late Latin *wadda;* related to German *Watte* cotton wool] ▸ **'wadder** *n*

wad[2] (wɒd) *n* a soft dark earthy amorphous material consisting of decomposed manganese minerals: occurs in damp marshy areas. [C17: of unknown origin]

Wadai (wɑː'daɪ) *n* a former independent sultanate of NE central Africa: now the E part of Chad.

Waddenzee (*Dutch* 'wɑdənzeː) *n* the part of the North Sea between the Dutch mainland and the West Frisian Islands.

Waddesdon Manor ('wɒdzdən) *n* a mansion near Aylesbury in Buckinghamshire: built (1880–89) in the French style for the Rothschild family: noted for its furnishings and collections of porcelain and paintings.

wadding ('wɒdɪŋ) *n* **1a** any fibrous or soft substance used as padding, stuffing, etc., esp. sheets of carded cotton prepared for the purpose. **1b** a piece of this. **2** material for wads used in cartridges or guns.

Waddington ('wɒdɪŋtən) *n* **C(onrad) H(all).** 1905–75, British embryologist and geneticist: author of *Principles of Embryology* (1956) and *The Ethical Animal* (1960).

waddle ('wɒdᵊl) *vb* (*intr*) **1** to walk with short steps, rocking slightly from side to side. ◆ *n* **2** a swaying gait or motion. [C16: probably frequentative of WADE] ▸ **'waddler** *n* ▸ **'waddling** *adj* ▸ **'waddly** *adj*

waddy ('wɒdɪ) *n, pl* **-dies. 1** a heavy wooden club used as a weapon by native Australians. ◆ *vb* **-dies, -dying, -died. 2** (*tr*) to hit with a waddy. [C19: from a native Australian language, perhaps based on English WOOD[1]]

wade (weɪd) *vb* **1** to walk with the feet immersed in (water, a stream, etc.): *the girls waded the river at the ford.* **2** (*intr;* often foll. by *through*) to proceed with difficulty: *to wade through a book.* **3** (*intr;* foll. by *in* or *into*) to attack energetically. ◆ *n* **4** the act or an instance of wading. [Old English *wadan;* related to Old Frisian *wada,* Old High German *watan,* Old Norse *vatha,* Latin *vadum* FORD] ▸ **'wadable** *or* **'wadeable** *adj*

Wade (weɪd) *n* **(Sarah) Virginia.** born 1945, British tennis player: Wimbledon champion 1977.

wader ('weɪdə) *n* **1** a person or thing that wades. **2** Also called: **wading bird.** any of various long-legged birds, esp. those of the order *Ciconiiformes* (herons, storks, etc.), that live near water and feed on fish, etc. **3** a Brit. name for **shore bird.**

waders ('weɪdəz) *pl n* long waterproof boots, sometimes extending to the chest like trousers, worn by anglers.

wadi *or* **wady** ('wɒdɪ) *n, pl* **-dies.** a watercourse in N Africa and Arabia, dry except in the rainy season. [C19: from Arabic]

Wadi Halfa ('wɒdɪ 'hælfə) *n* a town in the N Sudan that was partly submerged by Lake Nasser: an important archaeological site.

wadmal ('wɒdməl) *n* a coarse thick woollen fabric, formerly woven esp. in Orkney and Shetland, for outer garments. [C14: from Old Norse *vathmal,* from *vath* cloth + *mal* measure]

Wad Medani (wɑːd mɪ'dɑːniː) *n* a town in the E Sudan, on the Blue Nile: headquarters of the Gezira irrigation scheme; agricultural research centre. Pop.: 218 714 (1993).

wadset ('wɒd,sɛt) *Scots Law.* ◆ *n* **1** another name for **mortgage.** ◆ *vb* **-sets, -setting, -setted. 2** (*tr*) to pledge or mortgage. [C14: *wad,* a Scottish variant of WED + SET[1]; compare Old English *wedd settan* to deposit a pledge]

Wafd (wɒft) *n* a nationalist Egyptian political party: founded in 1924 and dissolved in 1952. [Arabic: deputation] ▸ **'Wafdist** *n, adj*

wafer ('weɪfə) *n* **1** a thin crisp sweetened biscuit with different flavourings, served with ice cream, etc. **2** *Christianity.* a thin disc of unleavened bread used in the Eucharist as celebrated by the Western Church. **3** *Pharmacol.* an envelope of rice paper enclosing a medicament. **4** *Electronics.* a large single crystal of semiconductor material, such as silicon, on which numerous integrated circuits are manufactured and then separated. **5** a small thin disc of adhesive material used to seal letters, documents, etc. ◆ *vb* **6** (*tr*) to seal, fasten, or attach with a wafer. [C14: from Old Northern French *waufre,* from Middle Low German *wāfel;* related to WAFFLE[1]] ▸ **'wafer-,like** *or* **'wafery** *adj*

waff (wæf, wɑːf) *n Scot. and northern English dialect.* **1** a gust or puff of air. **2** a glance; glimpse. ◆ *vb* **3** to flutter or cause to flutter. [C16: Scottish and northern English variant of WAVE]

waffle[1] ('wɒfᵊl) *n* **a** a crisp golden-brown pancake with deep indentations on both sides. **b** (*as modifier*): *waffle iron.* [C19: from Dutch *wafel* (earlier *wæfel*), of Germanic origin; related to Old High German *wabo* honeycomb]

waffle[2] ('wɒfᵊl) *Informal, chiefly Brit.* ◆ *vb* **1** (*intr;* often foll. by *on*) to speak or write in a vague and wordy manner: *he waffled on for hours.* ◆ *n* **2** vague and wordy speech or writing. [C19: of unknown origin] ▸ **'waffler** *n* ▸ **'waffling** *adj, n* ▸ **'waffly** *adj*

waft (wɑːft, wɒft) *vb* **1** to carry or be carried gently on or as if on the air or water. ◆ *n* **2** the act or an instance of wafting. **3** something, such as a scent, carried on the air. **4** a wafting motion. **5** Also called: **waif.** *Nautical.* (formerly) a signal flag hoisted furled to signify various messages depending on where it was flown. [C16 (in obsolete sense: to convey by ship): back formation from C15 *wafter* a convoy vessel, from Middle Dutch *wachter* guard, from *wachten* to guard; influenced by WAFF] ▸ **'waftage** *n*

wafter ('wɑːftə, 'wɒf-) *n* a device that causes a draught.

wafture ('wɑːftʃə, 'wɒf-) *n Archaic.* **1** the act of wafting or waving. **2** anything that is wafted.

wag[1] (wæg) *vb* **wags, wagging, wagged. 1** to move or cause to move rapidly and repeatedly from side to side or up and down. **2** to move (the tongue) or (of the tongue) to be moved rapidly in talking, esp. in idle gossip. **3** to move (the finger) or (of the finger) to be moved from side to side, in or as in admonition. **4** *Slang.* to play truant (esp. in the phrase **wag it**). ◆ *n* **5** the act or an instance of wagging. [C13: from Old English *wagian* to shake; compare Old Norse *vagga* cradle]

wag[2] (wæg) *n* a humorous or jocular person; wit. [C16: of uncertain origin] ▸ **'waggery** *n* ▸ **'waggish** *adj* ▸ **'waggishly** *adv* ▸ **'waggishness** *n*

WAG *international car registration for* (West Africa) Gambia.

wage (weɪdʒ) *n* **1a** (*often pl*) payment in return for work or services, esp. that made to workmen on a daily, hourly, weekly, or piece-work basis. Compare **salary. 1b** (*as modifier*): *wage freeze.* **2** (*pl*) *Economics.* the portion of the national income accruing to labour as earned income, as contrasted with the unearned income accruing to capital in the form of rent, interest, and dividends. **3** (*often pl*) recompense, return, or yield. **4** an obsolete word for **pledge.** ◆ *vb* (*tr*) **5** to engage in. **6** *Obsolete.* to pledge or wager. **7** *Obsolete or Brit. dialect.* another word for **hire** (senses 1, 2). [C14: from Old Northern French *wagier* to pledge, from *wage,* of Germanic origin; compare Old English *weddian* to pledge, WED] ▸ **'wageless** *adj* ▸ **'wagelessness** *n*

wage determination *n* the process of setting wage rates or establishing wage structures in particular situations.

wage differential *n* the difference in wages between workers with different skills in the same industry or between those with comparable skills in different industries or localities.

wage earner *or U.S.* **wage worker** *n* **1** a person who works for wages, esp. as distinguished from one paid a salary. **2** the person who earns money to support a household by working.

wage incentive *n* additional wage payments intended to stimulate improved work performance.

wager ('weɪdʒə) *n* **1** an agreement or pledge to pay an amount of money as a result of the outcome of an unsettled matter. **2** an amount staked on the outcome of such a matter or event. **3 wager of battle**. (in medieval Britain) a pledge to do battle for a cause, esp. to decide guilt or innocence by single combat. **4 wager of law.** *English legal history*. a form of trial in which the accused offered to make oath of his innocence, supported by the oaths of 11 of his neighbours declaring their belief in his statements. ◆ *vb* **5** (when *tr, may take a clause as object*) to risk or bet (something) on the outcome of an unsettled matter. **6** (*tr*) *History*. to pledge oneself to (battle). **[C14:** from Anglo-French *wageure* a pledge, from Old Northern French *wagier* to pledge; see WAGE**]** ▸ **'wagerer** *n*

wage scale *n* **1** a schedule of wages paid to workers for various jobs in an industry, company, etc. **2** an employer's schedule of wages.

wages council *n* (formerly, in Britain) a statutory body empowered to fix minimum wages in an industry; abolished in 1994.

wage slave *n Ironical*. a person dependent on a wage or salary.

wagga ('wɒgə) *n Austral*. a blanket or bed covering made out of sacks stitched together. **[C19:** named after WAGGA WAGGA**]**

Wagga Wagga ('wɒgə 'wɒgə) *n* a city in SE Australia, in New South Wales on the Murrumbidgee River: agricultural trading centre. Pop.: 50 380 (1986).

waggle ('wæg^{ə}l) *vb* **1** to move or cause to move with a rapid shaking or wobbling motion. ◆ *n* **2** a rapid shaking or wobbling motion. **[C16:** frequentative of WAG[1]**]** ▸ **'wagglingly** *adv* ▸ **'waggly** *adj*

waggler ('wæglə) *n Angling*. a float only the bottom of which is attached to the line.

waggon ('wægən) *n, vb* a variant spelling (esp. Brit.) of **wagon.**

Wagner ('vɑːgnə) *n* **1 Otto.** 1841–1918, Austrian architect, whose emphasis on function and structure in such buildings as the Post Office Savings Bank, Vienna (1904–06), influenced the development of modern architecture. **2 (Wilhelm) Richard** ('rɪçart). 1813–83, German romantic composer noted chiefly for his invention of the music drama. His cycle of four such dramas *The Ring of the Nibelung* was produced at his own theatre in Bayreuth in 1876. His other operas include *Tannhäuser* (1845; revised 1861), *Tristan and Isolde* (1865), and *Parsifal* (1882).

Wagnerian (vɑːg'nɪərɪən) *adj* **1** of or suggestive of the dramatic musical compositions of Richard Wagner, their massive scale, dramatic and emotional intensity, etc. **2** denoting or relating to a singer who has a voice suitable for singing Wagner. **3** of or relating to a big, powerful, or domineering woman: *a Wagnerian maiden*. ◆ *n also* **Wagnerite. 4** a follower or disciple of the music or theories of Richard Wagner.

Wagner-Jauregg (*German* 'vagnər'jaurɛk) *n* **Julius.** 1857–1940, Austrian psychiatrist and neurologist; a pioneer of the use of fever therapy in the treatment of mental disorders. Nobel prize for physiology or medicine 1927.

wagon *or* **waggon** ('wægən) *n* **1** any of various types of wheeled vehicles, ranging from carts to lorries, esp. a vehicle with four wheels drawn by a horse, tractor, etc., and used for carrying crops, heavy loads, etc. **2** *Brit*. a railway freight truck, esp. an open one. **3** *U.S. and Canadian*. a child's four-wheeled cart. **4** *U.S. and Canadian*. a police van for transporting prisoners and those arrested. **5** *Chiefly U.S. and Canadian*. See **station wagon. 6** an obsolete word for **chariot. 7 on** (*or* **off**) **the wagon.** *Informal*. abstaining (or no longer abstaining) from alcoholic drinks. ◆ *vb* **8** (*tr*) to transport by wagon. **[C16:** from Dutch *wagen* WAIN**]** ▸ **'wagonless** *or* **'waggonless** *adj*

Wagon *or* **Waggon** ('wægən) *n* **the.** another name for the **Plough.**

wagoner *or* **waggoner** ('wægənə) *n* a person who drives a wagon.

wagonette *or* **waggonette** (ˌwægə'nɛt) *n* a light four-wheeled horse-drawn vehicle with two lengthwise seats facing each other behind a crosswise driver's seat.

wagon-lit (*French* vagɔ̃li) *n, pl* **wagons-lits** (vagɔ̃li). **1** a sleeping car on a European railway. **2** a compartment on such a car. **[C19:** from French, from *wagon* railway coach + *lit* bed**]**

wagonload *or* **waggonload** ('wægənˌləʊd) *n* the load that is or can be carried by a wagon.

wagon soldier *n U.S. slang*. a soldier belonging to the field artillery.

wagon train *n* a supply train of horses and wagons, esp. one going over rough terrain.

wagon vault *n* another name for **barrel vault.**

Wagram (*German* 'vaːgram) *n* a village in NE Austria: scene of the defeat of the Austrians by Napoleon in 1809.

wagtail ('wægˌteɪl) *n* any of various passerine songbirds of the genera *Motacilla* and *Dendronanthus*, of Eurasia and Africa, having a very long tail that wags when the bird walks: family *Motacillidae*.

Wahhabi *or* **Wahabi** (wə'hɑːbɪ) *n, pl* **-bis.** a member of a strictly conservative Muslim sect founded in the 18th century with the aim of eliminating all innovations later than the 3rd century of Islam. ▸ **Wah'habism** *or* **Wa'habism** *n*

wahine (wɑː'hiːnɪ) *n* (esp. in the Pacific islands) a Polynesian or Maori woman, esp. a girlfriend or wife. **[C19:** from Maori and Hawaiian**]**

wahoo[1] (wɑː'huː, 'wɑːhuː) *n, pl* **-hoos.** an elm, *Ulmus alata*, of SE North America having twigs with winged corky edges. Also called: **winged elm. [**from Creek *ŭhawhu* cork elm**]**

wahoo[2] (wɑː'huː, 'wɑːhuː) *n, pl* **-hoos.** an E North American shrub or small tree, *Euonymus atropurpureus*, with scarlet capsules and seeds. Also called: **burning bush. [C19:** from Dakota *wāhu* arrowwood**]**

wahoo[3] (wɑː'huː, 'wɑːhuː) *n, pl* **-hoos.** a large fast-moving food and game fish, *Acanthocybium solandri*, of tropical seas: family *Scombridae* (mackerels and tunnies). **[**of unknown origin**]**

wah-wah ('wɑːˌwɑː) *n* **1** the sound made by a trumpet, cornet, etc., when the bell is alternately covered and uncovered: much used in jazz. **2** an electronic attachment for an electric guitar, etc., that simulates this effect. **[C20:** of imitative origin**]**

waif (weɪf) *n* **1** a person, esp. a child, who is homeless, friendless, or neglected. **2** anything found and not claimed, the owner being unknown. **3** *Nautical*. another name for **waft** (sense 5). **4** *Law, obsolete*. a stolen article thrown away by a thief in his flight and forfeited to the Crown or to the lord of the manor. **[C14:** from Anglo-Norman, variant of Old Northern French *gaif*, of Scandinavian origin; related to Old Norse *veif* a flapping thing**]** ▸ **'waifˌlike** *adj*

Waikaremoana (waɪ'kɒrəməʊˌɑːnə) *n* **Lake.** a lake in the North Island of New Zealand in a dense bush setting. Area: about 55 sq. km (21 sq. miles).

Waikato ('waɪˌkɑːtəʊ) *n* the longest river in New Zealand, flowing northwest across North Island to the Tasman Sea. Length: 350 km (220 miles).

Waikiki ('waɪkɪˌkiː, ˌwaɪkɪ'kiː) *n* a resort area in Hawaii, on SE Oahu: a suburb of Honolulu.

wail (weɪl) *vb* **1** (*intr*) to utter a prolonged high-pitched cry, as of grief or misery. **2** (*intr*) to make a sound resembling such a cry: *the wind wailed in the trees*. **3** (*tr*) to lament, esp. with mournful sounds. ◆ *n* **4** a prolonged high-pitched mournful cry or sound. **[C14:** of Scandinavian origin; related to Old Norse *vǣla* to wail, Old English *wā* WOE**]** ▸ **'wailer** *n* ▸ **'wailful** *adj* ▸ **'wailfully** *adv*

Wailing Wall *n* another name for **Western Wall.**

wain (weɪn) *n Chiefly poetic*. a farm wagon or cart. **[**Old English *wægn*; related to Old Frisian *wein*, Old Norse *vagn***]**

Wain (weɪn) *n* **John (Barrington).** 1925–94, British novelist, poet, and critic. His novels include *Hurry on Down* (1953), *Strike the Father Dead* (1962), and *Young Shoulders* (1982).

wainscot ('weɪnskət) *n* **1** Also called: **wainscoting** *or* **wainscotting.** a lining applied to the walls of a room, esp. one of wood panelling. **2** the lower part of the walls of a room, esp. when finished in a material different from the upper part. **3** fine quality oak used as wainscot. ◆ *vb* **4** (*tr*) to line (a wall of a room) with a wainscot. **[C14:** from Middle Low German *wagenschot*, perhaps from *wagen* WAGON + *schot* planking, related to German *Scheit* piece of wood**]**

wainwright ('weɪnˌraɪt) *n* a person who makes wagons.

wairsh (weɪʃ) *adj Scot*. a variant spelling of **wersh.**

waist (weɪst) *n* **1** *Anatomy*. the constricted part of the trunk between the ribs and hips. **2** the part of a garment covering the waist. **3** the middle part of an object that resembles the waist in narrowness or position. **4** the middle part of a ship. **5** Also called: **centre section.** the middle section of an aircraft fuselage. **6** the constriction between the thorax and abdomen in wasps and similar insects. **[C14:** origin uncertain; related to Old English *wæstm* WAX[2]**]** ▸ **'waistless** *adj*

waistband ('weɪstˌbænd) *n* an encircling band of material to finish and strengthen a skirt or trousers at the waist.

waistcloth ('weɪstˌklɒθ) *n Obsolete*. another word for **loincloth.**

waistcoat ('weɪsˌkəʊt) *n* **1** a man's sleeveless waistlength garment worn under a suit jacket, usually buttoning up the front. U.S. and Canadian name: **vest. 2** a man's garment worn under a doublet in the 16th century. ▸ **'waistˌcoated** *adj*

waisted ('weɪstɪd) *adj* **a** having a waist or waistlike part: *a waisted air-gun pellet*. **b** (*in combination*): *high-waisted*.

waistline ('weɪstˌlaɪn) *n* **1** a line or indentation around the body at the narrowest part of the waist. **2** the intersection of the bodice and the skirt of a dress, etc., or the level of this: *a low waistline*.

wait (weɪt) *vb* **1** (when *intr*, often foll. by *for*, *until*, or *to*) to stay in one place or remain inactive in expectation (of something); hold oneself in readiness (for something). **2** to delay temporarily or be temporarily delayed: *that work can wait*. **3** (when *intr*, usually foll. by *for*) (of things) to be in store (for a person): *success waits for you in your new job*. **4** (*intr*) to act as a waiter or waitress. ◆ *n* **5** the act or an instance of waiting. **6** a period of waiting. **7** (*pl*) *Rare*. a band of musicians who go around the streets, esp. at Christmas, singing and playing carols. **8** an interlude or interval between two acts or scenes in a play, etc. **9 lie in wait.** to prepare an ambush (for someone). ◆ See also **wait on, wait up. [C12:** from Old French *waitier*; related to Old High German *wahtēn* to WAKE[1]**]**

wait-a-bit *n* any of various plants having sharp hooked thorns or similar appendages, esp. the greenbrier and the grapple plant.

Waitangi Day (waɪ'tʌŋiː) *n* the national day of New Zealand (Feb. 6), commemorating the signing of the **Treaty of Waitangi** (1840) by Maori chiefs and a representative of the British Government. The treaty provided the basis for the British annexation of New Zealand.

Waitangi Tribunal *n* (in New Zealand) a government tribunal empowered to examine and make recommendations on Maori claims under the Treaty of Waitangi.

Waite (weɪt) *n* **Terry**, full name *Terence Hardy Waite*. born 1939, British special envoy to the Archbishop of Canterbury, who negotiated the release of Western hostages held in the Middle East before being taken hostage himself (1987–91) in Lebanon.

waiter ('weɪtə) *n* **1** a man whose occupation is to serve at table, as in a restaurant. **2** an attendant at the London Stock Exchange or Lloyd's who carries messages: the modern equivalent of waiters who performed these duties in the 17th-century London coffee houses in which these institutions originated. **3** a person who waits. **4** a tray or salver on which dishes, etc., are carried.

waiting game *n* the postponement of action or decision in order to gain the advantage.

waiting list *n* a list of people waiting to obtain some object, treatment, status, etc.

waiting room *n* a room in which people may wait, as at a railway station, doctor's or dentist's office, etc.

wait on *vb* (*intr, prep*) **1** to serve at the table of. **2** to act as an attendant or servant to. 3 *Archaic.* to visit. ◆ *interj* 4 *Austral. and N.Z.* stop! hold on! ◆ Also (for senses 1, 2, 3) **wait upon.**

waitress ('weɪtrɪs) *n* **1** a woman who serves at table, as in a restaurant. ◆ *vb* **2** (*intr*) to act as a waitress.

wait up *vb* (*intr, adv*) **1** to delay going to bed in order to await some event. **2** *Informal, chiefly U.S. and Canadian.* to halt and pause in order that another person may catch up.

Waitz (vaɪts) *n* **Greta.** born 1953, Norwegian long-distance runner and former marathon world champion.

waive (weɪv) *vb* (*tr*) **1** to set aside or relinquish: *to waive one's right to something.* **2** to refrain from enforcing or applying (a law, penalty, etc.). **3** to defer. [C13: from Old Northern French *weyver,* from *waif* abandoned; see WAIF]

waiver ('weɪvə) *n* **1** the voluntary relinquishment, expressly or by implication, of some claim or right. **2** the act or an instance of relinquishing a claim or right. **3** a formal statement in writing of such relinquishment. [C17: from Old Northern French *weyver* to relinquish, WAIVE]

Wajda (*Polish* 'vajda) *n* **Andrei** or **Andrzej** ('andʒej). born 1926, Polish film director. His films include *Ashes and Diamonds* (1958), *The Wedding* (1972), *Man of Iron* (1980), *Danton* (1982), and *Ring of the Crowned Eagle* (1993).

waka ('wɔːkə) *n N.Z.* **1** a Maori canoe, usually made from a tree trunk. **2** a tribal group claiming descent from the first Maori settlers in New Zealand. [Maori]

Wakashan (wɑː'kæʃən, 'wɔːkə,ʃɑːn) *n* **1** a family of North American Indian languages of British Columbia and Washington, including Kwakiutl and Nootka. **2** a speaker of any of these languages.

Wakayama (,wækə'jɑːmə) *n* an industrial city in S Japan, on S Honshu. Pop.: 393 951 (1995).

wake[1] (weɪk) *vb* **wakes, waking, woke, woken. 1** (often foll. by *up*) to rouse or become roused from sleep. **2** (often foll. by *up*) to rouse or become roused from inactivity. **3** (*intr;* often foll. by *to* or *up to*) to become conscious or aware: *at last he woke to the situation.* **4** (*intr*) to be or remain awake. **5** *Dialect.* to hold a wake over (a corpse). **6** *Archaic or dialect.* to keep watch over. ◆ *n* **7** a watch or vigil held over the body of a dead person during the night before burial. **8** (in Ireland) festivities held after a funeral. **9** the patronal or dedication festival of English parish churches. **10** a solemn or ceremonial vigil. **11** (*usually pl*) an annual holiday in any of various towns in northern England, when the local factory or factories close, usually for a week or two weeks. **12** *Rare.* the state of being awake. [Old English *wacian;* related to Old Frisian *wakia,* Old High German *wahtēn*] ▸ **'waker** *n*

USAGE Where there is an object and the sense is the literal one *wake* (*up*) and *waken* are the commonest forms: *I wakened him; I woke him* (*up*). Both verbs are also commonly used without an object: *I woke up. Awake* and *awaken* are preferred to other forms of *wake* where the sense is a figurative one: *he awoke to the danger.*

wake[2] (weɪk) *n* **1** the waves or track left by a vessel or other object moving through water. **2** the track or path left by anything that has passed: *wrecked houses in the wake of the hurricane.* [C16: of Scandinavian origin; compare Old Norse *vaka, vök* hole cut in ice, Swedish *vak,* Danish *vaage;* perhaps related to Old Norse *vökr,* Middle Dutch *wak* wet]

Wakefield ('weɪk,fiːld) *n* **1** a city in N England, in Wakefield unitary authority, West Yorkshire: important since medieval times as an agricultural and textile centre. Pop.: 73 955 (1991). **2** a unitary authority in N England, in West Yorkshire. Pop.: 317 100 (1995 est.). Area: 333 sq. km (129 sq. miles).

wakeful ('weɪkfʊl) *adj* **1** unable or unwilling to sleep. **2** sleepless. **3** alert. ▸ **'wakefully** *adv* ▸ **'wakefulness** *n*

Wake Island *n* an atoll in the N central Pacific: claimed by the U.S. in 1899; developed as a civil and naval air station in the late 1930s. Area: 8 sq. km (3 sq. miles).

wakeless ('weɪklɪs) *adj* (of sleep) deep or unbroken.

waken ('weɪkən) *vb* to rouse or be roused from sleep or some other inactive state. ▸ **'wakener** *n*

USAGE See at **wake**[1].

wake-robin *n* **1** any of various North American herbaceous plants of the genus *Trillium,* such as *T. grandiflorum,* having a whorl of three leaves and three-petalled solitary flowers: family *Trilliaceae.* **2** *U.S.* any of various aroid plants, esp. the cuckoopint.

wake-up *n* **1** *Austral. informal.* an alert or intelligent person. **2 a wake-up to.** *Austral. informal.* fully alert to (a person, thing, action, etc.). **3 wake-up call.** *U.S.* **3a** a telephone call that wakes a person from sleep. **3b** an event that alerts people to a danger or difficulty.

Waksman ('wæksmən) *n* **Selman Abraham.** 1888–1973, U.S. microbiologist, born in Russia. He discovered streptomycin: Nobel prize for physiology or medicine 1952.

WAL *international car registration for* Sierra Leone. [from *W(est) A(frica) L(eone)*]

Wal. *abbrev. for* Walloon.

Walach ('wɑːlɒk) *n, adj* a variant spelling of **Vlach.**

Walachia *or* **Wallachia** (wɒ'leɪkɪə) *n* a former principality of SE Europe: a vassal state of the Ottoman Empire from the 15th century until its union with Moldavia in 1859, subsequently forming present-day Romania. ▸ **Wa'lachian** *or* **Wal'lachian** *n, adj*

Wałbrzych (*Polish* 'vaubʒix) *n* an industrial city in SW Poland. Pop.: 139 600 (1996 est.). German name: **Waldenburg.**

Walcheren (*Dutch* 'walxərə) *n* an island in the SW Netherlands, in the Scheldt estuary: administratively part of Zeeland province; suffered severely in World War II, when the dykes were breached, and again in the floods of 1953. Area: 212 sq. km (82 sq. miles).

Walcott ('wɔːlkət) *n* **1 Derek (Alton).** born 1930, St Lucian poet and playwright, whose works include the poetry collections *In a Green Night* (1962) and *The Bounty* (1997), the play *The Dream on Monkey Mountain* (1967), and the long poem *Omeros* (1990): awarded the Nobel prize for literature 1992. **2 Jersey Joe,** real name *Arnold Raymond Cream.* 1914–94, U.S. boxer: world heavyweight champion 1951–52.

Waldemar I *or* **Valdemar I** ('vældɪ,mɑː) *n* known as *Waldemar the Great.* 1131–82, king of Denmark (1157–82). He conquered the Wends (1169), increased the territory of Denmark, and established the hereditary rule of his line.

Waldemar II *or* **Valdemar II** *n* known as *Waldemar the Victorious.* 1170–1241, king of Denmark (1202–41); son of Waldemar I. He extended the Danish empire, conquering much of Estonia (1219).

Waldemar IV *or* **Valdemar IV** *n* surnamed *Atterdag.* ?1320–75, king of Denmark (1340–75), who reunited the Danish territories but was defeated (1368) by a coalition of his Baltic neighbours.

Waldenburg ('valdənbʊrk) *n* the German name for **Wałbrzych.**

Waldenses (wɒl'dɛnsiːz) *pl n* the members of a small sect founded as a reform movement within the Roman Catholic Church by Peter Waldo, a merchant of Lyons in the late 12th century, which in the 16th century joined the Reformation movement. Also called: **Vaudois.** ▸ **Waldensian** (wɒl'dɛnsɪən) *n, adj*

waldgrave ('wɔːld,greɪv) *n* (in medieval Germany) an officer with jurisdiction over a royal forest. [from German *Waldgraf,* from *Wald* forest + *Graf* count]

Waldheim (*German* 'valthaim) *n* **Kurt** (kʊrt). born 1918, Austrian diplomat; secretary-general of the United Nations (1972–81); president of Austria (1986–92).

waldo ('wɔːldəʊ) *n, pl* **-dos** *or* **-does.** a gadget for manipulating objects by remote control. [C20: named after *Waldo* F. Jones, inventor in a science-fiction story by Robert Heinlein]

Waldorf salad ('wɔːldɔːf) *n* a salad of diced apples, celery, and walnuts mixed with mayonnaise. [C20: named after the *Waldorf-Astoria Hotel* in New York City]

Waldstein (*German* 'valtʃtaɪn) *n* a variant of (Albrecht Wenzel Eusebius von) **Wallenstein.**

waldsterben ('wɔːld,stɜːbən) *n Ecology.* the symptoms of tree decline in central Europe from the 1970s, considered to be caused by atmospheric pollution. [C20: from German *Wald* forest + *sterben* to die]

wale[1] (weɪl) *n* **1** the raised mark left on the skin after the stroke of a rod or whip. **2a** the weave or texture of a fabric, such as the ribs in corduroy. **2b** a vertical row of stitches in knitting. Compare **course** (sense 14). **3** *Nautical.* **3a** a ridge of planking along the rail of a ship. **3b** See **gunwale.** ◆ *vb* (*tr*) **4** to raise a wale or wales on by striking. **5** to weave with a wale. [Old English *walu* WEAL[1]; related to Old Norse *vala* knuckle, Dutch *wäle*]

wale[2] (weɪl) *Scot. and northern English dialect.* ◆ *n* **1** a choice. **2** anything chosen as the best. ◆ *adj* **3** choice. ◆ *vb* **4** (*tr*) to choose. [C14: from Old Norse *val* choice, related to German *Wahl*]

Waler ('weɪlə) *n Chiefly Austral.* a saddle horse originating in New South Wales. [C19: from *Wales,* in *New South Wales*]

Wales (weɪlz) *n* a principality that is part of the United Kingdom, in the west of Great Britain; conquered by the English in 1282; parliamentary union with England took place in 1536: a separate Welsh Assembly with limited powers was established in 1999. Wales consists mainly of moorlands and mountains and has an economy that is chiefly agricultural, with an industrial and former coal-mining area in the south. Capital: Cardiff. Pop.: 2 811 865 (1991). Area: 20 768 sq. km (8017 sq. miles). Welsh name: **Cymru.** Medieval Latin name: **Cambria.**

Wałęsa (væ'wɛnsə) *n* **Lech** (lɛç). born 1943, Polish statesman: president of Poland (1990–95); leader of the independent trade union Solidarity 1980–90; Nobel peace prize 1983.

Waley ('weɪlɪ) *n* **Arthur.** real name *Arthur Schloss.* 1889–1966, English orientalist, best known for his translations of Chinese poetry.

Walfish Bay ('wɔːlfɪʃ) *n* a variant spelling of **Walvis Bay.**

Walhalla (wæl'hælə, væl-) *or* **Walhall** (wæl'hæl, væl-) *n* variants of **Valhalla.**

walk (wɔːk) *vb* **1** (*intr*) to move along or travel on foot at a moderate rate; advance in such a manner that at least one foot is always on the ground. **2** (*tr*) to pass through, on, or over on foot, esp. habitually. **3** (*tr*) to cause, assist, or force to move along at a moderate rate: *to walk a dog.* **4** (*tr*) to escort or conduct by walking: *to walk someone home.* **5** (*intr*) (of ghosts, spirits, etc.) to appear or move about in visible form. **6** (of inanimate objects) to move or cause to move in a manner that resembles walking. **7** (*intr*) to follow a certain course or way of life: *to walk in misery.* **8** (*tr*) to bring into a certain condition by walking: *I walked my shoes to shreds.* **9** (*tr*) to measure, survey, or examine by walking. **10** (*intr*) *Basketball.* to take more than two steps without passing or dribbling the ball. **11** to disappear or be stolen: *where's my pencil? It seems to have walked.* **12** (*intr*) *Slang, chiefly U.S.* (in a court of law) to be acquitted or given a noncustodial sentence. **13 walk it.** to win easily. **14 walk the plank.** See **plank** (sense 4). **15 walk on air.** to be delighted or exhilarated. **16 walk tall.** *Informal.* to have self-respect or pride. **17 walk the streets. 17a** to be a prostitute. **17b** to wander round a town or city, esp. when looking for work or having nowhere to stay. ◆ *n* **18** the act or an instance of walking. **19** the distance or extent walked. **20** a manner of walking; gait. **21** a place set aside for walking; promenade. **22** a chosen profession or sphere of activity (esp. in the phrase **walk of life**). **23** a foot race in which competitors walk. **24a** an arrangement of trees or shrubs in widely separated rows. **24b** the space between such rows. **25** an enclosed ground for the exercise or feeding of domestic animals, esp. horses. **26** *Chiefly Brit.* the route covered in the course of work, as by a tradesman or postman. **27** a procession; march: *Orange walk.* **28** *Obsolete.* the section of a forest controlled by a keeper. ◆ See also **walk away, walk into, walk off, walk out, walkover, walk through.** [Old English *wealcan;* related to Old High German *walchan,* Sanskrit *valgati* he moves] ▸ **'walkable** *adj*

walkabout ('wɔːkə,baʊt) *n* **1** a periodic nomadic excursion into the Australian bush made by a native Australian. **2** a walking tour. **3** *Chiefly journalistic.* an occasion when celebrities, royalty, etc., walk among and meet the public. **4 go walkabout.** *Austral.* **4a** to wander through the bush. **4b** *Informal.* to be lost or misplaced. **4c** *Informal.* to lose one's concentration.

walk away *vb (intr, adv)* **1** to leave, esp. callously and disregarding someone else's distress. **2 walk away with.** to achieve or win easily.

walker ('wɔːkə) *n* **1** a person who walks. **2** Also called: **baby walker.** a tubular frame on wheels or castors to support a baby learning to walk. **3** a similar support for walking, often with rubber feet, for use by disabled or infirm people.

Walker ('wɔːkə) *n* **1 Alice (Malsenior).** born 1944, U.S. writer: her works include *In Love and Trouble: Stories of Black Women* (1973) and the novels *Meridian* (1976), *The Color Purple* (1982), and *Possessing the Secret of Joy* (1992). **2 John.** born 1952, New Zealand middle-distance runner, the first athlete to run one hundred sub-four-minute miles.

walkie-talkie *or* **walky-talky** (ˌwɔːkɪ'tɔːkɪ) *n, pl* **-talkies.** a small combined radio transmitter and receiver, usually operating on shortwave, that can be carried around by one person: widely used by the police, medical services, etc.

walk-in *adj* **1** (of a cupboard) large enough to allow a person to enter and move about in. **2** *U.S.* (of a building or apartment) located so as to admit of direct access from the street. **3** (of a flat or house) in a suitable condition for immediate occupation.

walking ('wɔːkɪŋ) *adj* (of a person) considered to possess the qualities of something inanimate as specified: *he is a walking encyclopedia.*

walking bass (beɪs) *n Jazz.* a simple accompaniment played by the double bass at medium tempo, usually consisting of ascending and descending tones or semitones, one to each beat.

walking delegate *n* **1** (in the U.S.) an agent appointed by a trade union to visit branches, check whether agreements are observed, and negotiate with employers. **2** (in N.Z.) a trade union official who visits dispersed working areas on a wharf.

walking dragline *n* a very large-capacity dragline mounted on feet or pads instead of tracks. See **dragline** (sense 2).

walking fern *or* **leaf** *n* a North American fern, *Camptosorus rhizophyllus,* having sword-shaped fronds, the tips of which take root when in contact with the ground: family *Aspleniaceae.*

walking papers *pl n Slang, chiefly U.S. and Canadian.* notice of dismissal.

walking stick *n* **1** a stick or cane carried in the hand to assist walking. **2** the usual U.S. name for **stick insect.**

walk into *vb (intr, prep)* to meet with unwittingly: *to walk into a trap.*

Walkman ('wɔːkmən) *n Trademark.* a small portable cassette player with light headphones.

walk off *vb* **1** *(intr)* to depart suddenly. **2** *(tr, adv)* to get rid of by walking: *to walk off an attack of depression.* **3 walk (a person) off his feet.** to make (someone) walk so fast or far that he or she is exhausted. **4 walk off with. 4a** to steal. **4b** to win, esp. easily.

walk-on *n* **1a** a small part in a play or theatrical entertainment, esp. one without any lines. **1b** *(as modifier): a walk-on part.* ◆ *adj* **2** (of an aircraft or air service) having seats to be booked immediately before departure rather than in advance.

walk out *vb (intr, adv)* **1** to leave without explanation, esp. in anger. **2** to go on strike. **3 walk out on.** *Informal.* to abandon or desert. **4 walk out with.** *Brit., obsolete or dialect.* to court or be courted by. ◆ *n* **walkout. 5** a strike by workers. **6** the act of leaving a meeting, conference, etc., as a protest.

walkover ('wɔːkˌəʊvə) *n* **1** *Informal.* an easy or unopposed victory. **2** *Horse racing.* **2a** the running or walking over the course by the only contestant entered in a race at the time of starting. **2b** a race won in this way. ◆ *vb* **walk over.** *(intr, mainly prep)* **3** *(also adv)* to win a race by a walkover. **4** *Informal.* to beat (an opponent) conclusively or easily. **5** *Informal.* to take advantage of (someone).

walk socks *pl n N.Z.* men's knee-length stockings.

walk through *Theatre.* ◆ *vb* **1** *(tr)* to act or recite (a part) in a perfunctory manner, as at a first rehearsal. ◆ *n* **walk-through. 2** a rehearsal of a part.

walk-up *n U.S. and Canadian informal.* **a** a block of flats having no lift. **b** *(as modifier): a walk-up block.*

walkway ('wɔːkˌweɪ) *n* **1** a path designed, and sometimes landscaped, for pedestrian use. **2** a passage or path connecting buildings. **3** a passage or path, esp. one for walking over machinery, etc.

Walkyrie (væl'kɪərɪ, 'vælkɪərɪ) *n* a variant spelling of **Valkyrie.**

wall (wɔːl) *n* **1a** a vertical construction made of stone, brick, wood, etc., with a length and height much greater than its thickness, used to enclose, divide, or support. **1b** *(as modifier): wall hangings.* Related adj: **mural. 2** *(often pl)* a structure or rampart built to protect and surround a position or place for defensive purposes. **3** *Anatomy.* any lining, membrane, or investing part that encloses or bounds a bodily cavity or structure: *abdominal wall.* Technical name: **paries.** Related adj: **parietal. 4** *Mountaineering.* a vertical or almost vertical smooth rock face. **5** anything that suggests a wall in function or effect: *a wall of fire; a wall of prejudice.* **6 bang one's head against a brick wall.** to try to achieve something impossible. **7 drive** *(or* **push) to the wall.** to force into an awkward situation. **8 go to the wall.** to be ruined; collapse financially. **9 go** *(or* **drive) up the wall.** *Slang.* to become (or cause to become) crazy or furious. **10 have one's back to the wall.** to be in a very difficult situation. **11** See **off-the-wall. 12** See **wall-to-wall.** ◆ *vb (tr)* **13** to protect, provide, or confine with or as if with a wall. **14** (often foll. by *up*) to block (an opening) with a wall. **15** (often foll. by *in* or *up*) to seal by or within a wall or walls. [Old English *weall,* from Latin *vallum* palisade, from *vallus* stake] ▸ **walled** *adj* ▸ **'wall-less** *adj* ▸ **'wall-ˌlike** *adj*

wallaby ('wɒləbɪ) *n, pl* **-bies** *or* **-by. 1** any of various herbivorous marsupials of the genera *Lagorchestes* (**hare wallabies**), *Petrogale* (**rock wallabies**), *Protemnodon,* etc., of Australia and New Guinea, similar to but smaller than kangaroos: family *Macropodidae.* **2 on the wallaby (track).** *Austral. slang.* (of a person) wandering about looking for work. [C19: from native Australian *wolabā*]

Wallaby ('wɒləbɪ) *n, pl* **-bies.** a member of the international Rugby Union football team of Australia.

Wallace ('wɒlɪs) *n* **1 Alfred Russel.** 1823–1913, British naturalist, whose work on the theory of natural selection influenced Charles Darwin. **2 Edgar.** 1875–1932, English crime novelist. **3** Sir **Richard.** 1818–90, English art collector and philanthropist. His bequest to the nation forms the Wallace Collection, London. **4** Sir **William.** ?1272–1305, Scottish patriot, who defeated the army of Edward I of England at Stirling (1297) but was routed at Falkirk (1298) and later executed.

Wallace's line *n* the hypothetical boundary between the Oriental and Australasian zoogeographical regions, which runs between the Indonesian islands of Bali and Lombok, through the Macassar Strait, and SE of the Philippines. [C20: named after A. R. WALLACE]

Wallachia (wɒ'leɪkɪə) *n* a variant spelling of **Walachia.**

wallah *or* **walla** ('wɒlə) *n (usually in combination) Informal.* a person involved with or in charge of (a specified thing): *the book wallah.* [C18: from Hindi *-wālā* from Sanskrit *pāla* protector]

wallaroo (ˌwɒlə'ruː) *n, pl* **-roos** *or* **-roo.** a large stocky Australian kangaroo, *Macropus* (or *Osphranter*) *robustus,* of rocky regions. [C19: from native Australian *wolarū*]

Wallasey ('wɒləsɪ) *n* a town in NW England, in Wirral unitary authority, Merseyside; near the mouth of the River Mersey, opposite Liverpool. Pop.: 60 895 (1991).

wall bars *pl n* a series of horizontal bars attached to a wall and used in gymnastics.

wallboard ('wɔːlˌbɔːd) *n* a thin board made of materials, such as compressed wood fibres or gypsum plaster, between stiff paper, and used to cover walls, partitions, etc.

wall brown *n* any of three species of brown butterfly, esp. the common *Lasiommata megera,* that habitually sun themselves on rocks and walls.

wall creeper *n* a pink-and-grey woodpecker-like songbird, *Tichodroma muraria,* of Eurasian mountain regions: family *Sittidae* (nuthatches).

walled plain *n* any of the largest of the lunar craters, having diameters between 50 and 300 kilometres.

Wallenberg ('vaːlənbɜːg) *n* **Raoul** (raʊᵊl). 1912–? Swedish diplomat, who helped (1944–45) thousands of Hungarian Jews to escape from the Nazis. After his arrest (1945) by the Soviets nothing is certainly known of him: despite claims that he is still alive he is presumed to have died in prison.

Wallenstein (*German* 'valənʃtain) *or* **Waldstein** *n* **Albrecht Wenzel Eusebius von** ('albreçt 'ventsəl ɔy'zeːbius fɔn), duke of Friedland and Mecklenburg, prince of Sagan. 1583–1634, German general and statesman, born in Bohemia. As leader of the Hapsburg forces in the Thirty Years' War he won many successes until his defeat at Lützen (1632) by Gustavus Adolphus.

Waller ('wɒlə) *n* **1 Edmund.** 1606–87, English poet and politician, famous for his poem *Go, Lovely Rose.* **2 Fats,** real name *Thomas Waller.* 1904–43, U.S. jazz pianist and singer.

wallet ('wɒlɪt) *n* **1** a small folding case, usually of leather, for holding paper money, documents, etc. **2** a bag used to carry tools. **3** *Archaic, chiefly Brit.* a rucksack or knapsack. [C14: of Germanic origin; compare Old English *weallian,* Old High German *wallōn* to roam, German *wallen* to go on a pilgrimage]

walleye ('wɔːlˌaɪ) *n, pl* **-eyes** *or* **-eye. 1** a divergent squint. **2** opacity of the cornea. **3** an eye having a white or light-coloured iris. **4** (in some collies) an eye that is particoloured white and blue. **5** Also called: **walleyed pike.** a North American pikeperch, *Stizostedion vitreum,* valued as a food and game fish. **6** any of various other fishes having large staring eyes. [back formation from earlier *walleyed,* from Old Norse *vagleygr,* from *vage,* perhaps: a film over the eye (compare Swedish *vagel* sty in the eye) + *-eygr* -eyed, from *auga* eye; modern form influenced by WALL] ▸ **'wallˌeyed** *adj*

wallflower ('wɔːlˌflaʊə) *n* **1** Also called: **gillyflower.** a cruciferous plant, *Cheiranthus cheiri,* of S Europe, grown for its clusters of yellow, orange, brown, red, or purple fragrant flowers and naturalized on old walls, cliffs, etc. **2** any of numerous other cruciferous plants of the genera *Cheiranthus* and *Erysimum,* having orange or yellow flowers. **3** *Informal.* a person who stays on the fringes of a dance or party on account of lacking a partner or being shy.

wall fruit *n* fruit grown on trees trained against a wall for the shelter and warmth it provides.

wall game *n* a type of football played at Eton against a wall.

wallies ('wælɪz) *pl n Central Scot. dialect.* false teeth; dentures. [see WALLY²]

Wallis¹ ('valɪs) *n* the German name for **Valais.**

Wallis² ('wɒlɪs) *n* Sir **Barnes (Neville).** 1887–1979, English aeronautical engineer. He designed the airship R100, the Wellesley and Wellington bombers, and the bouncing bomb (1943), which was used to destroy the Ruhr dams during World War II.

Wallis and Futuna Islands ('wɒlɪs; fuː'tjuːnə) *pl n* a French overseas territory in the SW Pacific, west of Samoa. Capital: Mata-Utu. Pop.: 14 400 (1993 est.). Area: 367 sq. km (143 sq. miles).

wall knot *n* a knot forming a knob at the end of a rope, made by unwinding the strands and weaving them together.

wall lizard *n* a small mottled grey lizard, *Lacerta muralis,* of Europe, N Africa, and SW Asia: family *Lacertidae.*

wall mustard *n* another name for **stinkweed** (sense 1).

wall of death *n* (at a fairground) a giant cylinder round the inside walls of which a motorcyclist rides.

Walloon (wɒ'luːn) *n* **1** a member of a French-speaking people living chiefly in S Belgium and adjacent parts of France. Compare **Fleming¹. 2** the French dialect of Belgium. ◆ *adj* **3** of, relating to, or characteristic of the Walloons or their dialect. [C16: from Old French *Wallon*, from Medieval Latin: foreigner, of Germanic origin, compare Old English *wealh* foreign, WELSH[1]]

Walloon Brabant *n* a province of central Belgium, formed in 1995 from the S part of Brabant province: densely populated and intensively farmed, with large industrial centres. Pop.: 339 062 (1996 est.). Area: 1091 sq. km (421 sq. miles).

wallop ('wɒləp) *vb* **-lops, -loping, -loped. 1** (*tr*) *Informal.* to beat soundly; strike hard. **2** (*tr*) *Informal.* to defeat utterly. **3** (*intr*) *Dialect.* to move in a clumsy manner. **4** (*intr*) (of liquids) to boil violently. ◆ *n* **5** *Informal.* a hard blow. **6** *Informal.* the ability to hit powerfully, as of a boxer. **7** *Informal.* a forceful impression. **8** *Brit.* a slang word for **beer.** ◆ *vb, n* **9** an obsolete word for **gallop.** [C14: from Old Northern French *waloper* to gallop, from Old French *galoper*, of unknown origin]

walloper ('wɒləpə) *n* **1** a person or thing that wallops. **2** *Austral. slang.* a policeman.

walloping ('wɒləpɪŋ) *Informal.* ◆ *n* **1** a thrashing. ◆ *adj* **2** (intensifier): *a walloping drop in sales.*

wallow ('wɒləʊ) *vb* (*intr*) **1** (esp. of certain animals) to roll about in mud, water, etc., for pleasure. **2** to move about with difficulty. **3** to indulge oneself in possessions, emotion, etc.: *to wallow in self-pity.* **4** (of smoke, waves, etc.) to billow. ◆ *n* **5** the act or an instance of wallowing. **6** a muddy place or depression where animals wallow. [Old English *wealwian* to roll (in mud); related to Latin *volvere* to turn, Greek *oulos* curly, Russian *valun* round pebble] ▸ **'wallower** *n*

wallpaper ('wɔːlˌpeɪpə) *n* **1** paper usually printed or embossed with designs for pasting onto walls and ceilings. **2a** something pleasant but bland which serves as an unobtrusive background. **2b** (*as modifier*): *wallpaper music.* **3** *Computing.* a graphics file that can be displayed in certain applications behind or around the main dialogue boxes, working display areas, etc., for decoration. ◆ *vb* **4** to cover (a surface) with wallpaper.

wall pass *n Soccer.* a movement in which one player passes the ball to another and sprints forward to receive the quickly played return. Also called: **one-two.**

wall pellitory *n* See **pellitory** (sense 1).

wall pepper *n* a small Eurasian crassulaceous plant, *Sedum acre,* having creeping stems, yellow flowers, and acrid-tasting leaves.

wall plate *n* a horizontal timber member placed along the top of a wall to support the ends of joists, rafters, etc., and distribute the load.

wallposter ('wɔːlˌpəʊstə) *n* (in China) a bulletin or political message painted in large characters on walls.

wall rock *n* rock that is immediately adjacent to a mineral vein, fault, or igneous intrusion.

wall rocket *n* any of several yellow-flowered European cruciferous plants of the genus *Diplotaxis,* such as *D. muralis,* that grow on old walls and in waste places.

wall rue *n* a delicate fern, *Asplenium ruta-muraria,* that grows in rocky crevices and walls in North America and Eurasia.

Wallsend ('wɔːlzˌɛnd) *n* a town in NE England, in North Tyneside unitary authority, Tyne and Wear: situated on the River Tyne at the E end of Hadrian's Wall. Pop.: 45 280 (1991).

Wall Street *n* a street in lower Manhattan, New York, where the Stock Exchange and major banks are situated, regarded as the embodiment of American finance.

wall-to-wall *adj* **1** (of carpeting) completely covering a floor. **2** *Informal.* as far as the eye can see; widespread: *wall-to-wall sales in the high street shops.*

wally[1] ('weɪlɪ) *adj Scot. archaic.* **1** fine, pleasing, or splendid. **2** robust or strong. [C16: of obscure origin]

wally[2] ('wælɪ) *adj Central Scot. dialect.* **1** made of china: *a wally dug; a wally vase.* **2** lined with ceramic tiles: *a wally close.* ◆ See also **wallies.** [from obsolete dialect *wallow* faded, adjectival use of *wallow* to fade, from Old English *wealwian*]

wally[3] ('wɒlɪ) *n, pl* **-lies.** *Slang.* a stupid person. [C20: shortened form of the given name *Walter*]

walnut ('wɔːlˌnʌt) *n* **1** any juglandaceous deciduous tree of the genus *Juglans,* of America, SE Europe, and Asia, esp. *J. regia,* which is native to W Asia but introduced elsewhere. They have aromatic leaves and flowers in catkins and are grown for their edible nuts and for their wood. **2** the nut of any of these trees, having a wrinkled two-lobed seed and a hard wrinkled shell. **3** the wood of any of these trees, used in making furniture, panelling, etc. **4** a light yellowish-brown colour. ◆ *adj* **5** made from the wood of a walnut tree: *a walnut table.* **6** of the colour walnut. [Old English *walh-hnutu,* literally: foreign nut; compare Old French *noux gauge* walnut, probably translation of Vulgar Latin phrase *nux gallica* (unattested) Gaulish (hence, foreign) nut]

Walpole ('wɔːlˌpəʊl) *n* **1 Horace,** 4th Earl of Orford. 1717–97, British writer, noted for his letters and for his delight in the Gothic, as seen in his house Strawberry Hill and his novel *The Castle of Otranto* (1764). **2** Sir **Hugh** (**Seymour**). 1884–1941, British novelist, born in New Zealand: best known for *The Herries Chronicle* (1930–33), a sequence of historical novels set in the Lake District. **3** Sir **Robert,** 1st Earl of Orford, father of Horace Walpole. 1676–1745, English Whig statesman. As first lord of the Treasury and Chancellor of the Exchequer (1721–42) he was effectively Britain's first prime minister.

Walpurgis Night (væl'pʊəgɪs) *n* the eve of May 1, believed in German folklore to be the night of a witches' sabbath on the Brocken, in the Harz Mountains. [C19: translation of German *Walpurgisnacht,* the eve of the feast day of St Walpurga, 8th-century abbess in Germany]

walrus ('wɔːlrəs, 'wɒl-) *n, pl* **-ruses** *or* **-rus.** a pinniped mammal, *Odobenus rosmarus,* of northern seas, having a tough thick skin, upper canine teeth enlarged as tusks, and coarse whiskers and feeding mainly on shellfish: family *Odobenidae.* [C17: probably from Dutch, from Scandinavian; compare Old Norse *hrosshvalr* (literally: horse whale) and Old English *horschwæl;* see HORSE, WHALE]

walrus moustache *n* a long thick moustache drooping at the ends.

Walsall ('wɔːlsɔːl) *n* **1** an industrial town in central England, in Walsall unitary authority, West Midlands. Pop.: 174 739 (1991). **2** a unitary authority in central England, in the West Midlands. Pop.: 262 800 (1995 est.). Area: 106 sq. km (41 sq. miles).

Walsingham[1] ('wɔːlsɪŋəm) *n* a village in E England, in Norfolk: remains of a medieval priory; site of the shrine of Our Lady of Walsingham.

Walsingham[2] ('wɔːlsɪŋəm) *n* Sir **Francis.** ?1530–90, English statesman. As secretary of state (1573–90) to Elizabeth I he developed a system of domestic and foreign espionage and uncovered several plots against the Queen.

Walter *n* **1** (*German* 'valtər). **Bruno** ('bruːno), real name *Bruno Walter Schlesinger.* 1876–1962, U.S. conductor, born in Germany: famous for his performances of Haydn, Mozart, and Mahler. **2** ('wɔːltə). **John.** 1739–1812, English publisher; founded *The Daily Universal Register* (1785), which in 1788 became *The Times.*

Waltham Forest ('wɔːlθəm) *n* a borough of NE Greater London. Pop.: 221 800 (1994 est.). Area: 40 sq. km (15 sq. miles).

Walther von der Vogelweide (*German* 'valtər fɔn der 'foːgəlvaidə) *n* ?1170–?1230, German minnesinger, noted for his lyric verse on political and moral themes.

Walton ('wɔːltᵊn) *n* **1 Ernest Thomas Sinton.** 1903–95, Irish physicist. He succeeded in producing the first artificial transmutation of an atomic nucleus (1932) with Sir John Cockcroft, with whom he shared the Nobel prize for physics 1951. **2 Izaak** ('aɪzək). 1593–1683, English writer, best known for *The Compleat Angler* (1653; enlarged 1676). **3** Sir **William** (**Turner**). 1902–83, English composer. His works include *Façade* (1923), a setting of satirical verses by Edith Sitwell, the *Viola Concerto* (1929), and the oratorio *Belshazzar's Feast* (1931).

waltz (wɔːls) *n* **1** a ballroom dance in triple time in which couples spin around as they progress round the room. **2** a piece of music composed for or in the rhythm of this dance. ◆ *vb* **3** to dance or lead (someone) in or as in a waltz: *he waltzed her off her feet.* **4** (*intr*) to move in a sprightly and self-assured manner. **5** (*intr*) *Informal.* to succeed easily. [C18: from German *Walzer,* from Middle High German *walzen* to roll; compare WELTER] ▸ **'waltzˌlike** *adj*

waltzer ('wɔːlsə) *n* **1** a person who waltzes. **2** a fairground roundabout on which people are spun round and moved up and down as it revolves.

waltz Matilda *vb Austral.* See **Matilda**[1].

Walvis Bay ('wɔːlvɪs) *or* **Walfish Bay** *n* a port in Namibia, on the Atlantic: formed an exclave of South Africa, covering an area of 1124 sq. km (434 sq. miles) with its hinterland, but has been administered by Namibia since 1992; formally returned to Namibia in 1994; chief port of Namibia and rich fishing centre. Pop.: 23 000 (1992 est.).

wambenger (wɒm'bɛŋə) *n Austral.* another name for **tuan**[2]. [from a native Australian language]

wamble ('wɒmbəl) *Dialect, chiefly Brit.* ◆ *vb* (*intr*) **1** to move unsteadily. **2** to twist the body. **3** to feel nausea. ◆ *n* **4** an unsteady movement. **5** a sensation of nausea. [C14 *wamelen* to feel ill, perhaps of Scandinavian origin; compare Norwegian *vamla* to stagger] ▸ **'wambliness** *n* ▸ **'wambly** *adj*

wame (weɪm) *n Scot. and northern English dialect.* the belly, abdomen, or womb. [C14: northern variant of WOMB]

wampum ('wɒmpəm) *n* **1** (formerly) money used by North American Indians, made of cylindrical shells strung or woven together, esp. white shells rather than the more valuable black or purple ones. **2** *U.S. and Canadian informal.* money or wealth. ◆ Also called: **peag, peage.** [C17: short for *wampumpeag,* from Narraganset *wampompeag,* from *wampan* light + *api* string + *-ag* plural suffix]

wan (wɒn) *adj* **wanner, wannest. 1** unnaturally pale esp. from sickness, grief, etc. **2** characteristic or suggestive of ill health, unhappiness, etc. **3** (of light, stars, etc.) faint or dim. ◆ *vb* **wans, wanning, wanned. 4** to make or become wan. [Old English *wann* dark; related to *wanian* to WANE] ▸ **'wanly** *adv* ▸ **'wanness** *n*

WAN *abbrev. for:* **1** wide area network. ◆ **2** *international car registration for* (West Africa) Nigeria.

wanchancy (wɒn'tʃænsɪ) *adj Scot.* **1** unlucky. **2** dangerous; risky. **3** uncanny; eerie. ◆ Compare **unchancy.** [C18: from *wanchance* ill luck, from *wan-* prefix expressing negation or privation + CHANCE]

Wanchüan *or* **Wan-ch'uan** (ˌwæntʃu'ɑːn) *n* a former name of **Zhangjiakou.**

wand (wɒnd) *n* **1** a slender supple stick or twig. **2** a thin rod carried as a symbol of authority. **3** a rod used by a magician, water diviner, etc. **4** *Informal.* a conductor's baton. **5** *Archery.* a marker used to show the distance at which the archer stands from the target. **6** a hand-held electronic device, such as a light pen or bar-code reader, which is pointed at or passed over an item to read the data stored there. [C12: from Old Norse *vǫndr;* related to Gothic *wandus* and English WEND] ▸ **'wandˌlike** *adj*

wander ('wɒndə) *vb* (*mainly intr*) **1** (*also tr*) to move or travel about, in, or through (a place) without any definite purpose or destination. **2** to proceed in an irregular course; meander. **3** to go astray, as from a path or course. **4** (of the mind, thoughts, etc.) to lose concentration or direction. **5** to think or speak incoherently or illogically. ◆ *n* **6** the act or an instance of wandering. [Old English *wandrian;* related to Old Frisian *wandria,* Middle Dutch, Middle High German *wanderen*] ▸ **'wanderer** *n* ▸ **'wandering** *adj, n* ▸ **'wanderingly** *adv*

wandering albatross *n* a large albatross, *Diomedea exulans,* having a very wide wingspan and a white plumage with black wings.

wandering Jew *n* **1** any of several related creeping or trailing plants of tropical

America, esp. *Tradescantia fluminensis* and *Zebrina pendula:* family *Commelinaceae.* **2** *Austral.* a similar creeping plant of the genus *Commelina.*

Wandering Jew *n* (in medieval legend) a character condemned to roam the world eternally because he mocked Christ on the day of the Crucifixion.

Wanderjahr *German.* ('vandərja:r) *n, pl* ***-jahre*** (-ja:rə). (formerly) a year in which an apprentice travelled to improve his skills. [German, literally: wander year]

wanderlust ('wɒndə,lʌst) *n* a great desire to travel and rove about. [German, literally: wander desire]

wanderoo (,wɒndə'ru:) *n, pl* **-deroos.** a macaque monkey, *Macaca silenus,* of India and Sri Lanka, having black fur with a ruff of long greyish fur on each side of the face. [C17: from Sinhalese *vanduru* monkeys, literally: forest-dwellers, from Sanskrit *vānara* monkey, from *vana* forest]

wander plug *n* an electrical plug on the end of a flexible wire, for insertion into any of a number of sockets.

wandoo ('wɒndu:) *n* a eucalyptus tree, *Eucalyptus redunca,* of W Australia, having white bark and durable wood. [from a native Australian language]

Wandsworth ('wɒnzwəθ) *n* a borough of S Greater London, on the River Thames. Pop.: 266 600 (1994 est.). Area: 35 sq. km (13 sq. miles).

wane (weɪn) *vb* (*intr*) **1** (of the moon) to show a gradually decreasing portion of illuminated surface, between full moon and new moon. Compare **wax**[2] (sense 2). **2** to decrease gradually in size, strength, power, etc. **3** to draw to a close. ◆ *n* **4** a decrease, as in size, strength, power, etc. **5** the period during which the moon wanes. **6** the act or an instance of drawing to a close. **7** a rounded surface or defective edge of a plank, where the bark was. **8 on the wane.** in a state of decline. [Old English *wanian* (vb); related to *wan-,* prefix indicating privation, *wana* defect, Old Norse *vana*] ▸ **'waney** *or* **'wany** *adj*

Wang An Shi *or* **Wang An-shih** ('wæŋ ɑ:n 'ʃɪ) *n* 1021–86, Chinese statesman and writer: remembered for his economic reforms, known as the New Policies (1069–76).

Wanganui (,wɒŋə'nu:ɪ) *n* a port in New Zealand, on SW North Island: centre for a dairy-farming and sheep-rearing district. Pop.: 42 200 (1995 est.).

Wang Jing Wei *or* **Wang Ching-wei** ('wæŋ dʒɪŋ 'weɪ) *n* 1883–1944, Chinese politician. A leading revolutionary, he struggled (1927–32) with Chiang Kai-shek for control of the Kuomintang. During World War II he was head of a Japanese puppet government in Nanjing.

wangle ('wæŋg[ə]l) *Informal.* ◆ *vb* **1** (*tr*) to use devious or illicit methods to get or achieve (something) for (oneself or another): *he wangled himself a salary increase.* **2** to manipulate or falsify (a situation, action, etc.). ◆ *n* **3** the act or an instance of wangling. [C19: originally printers' slang, perhaps a blend of WAGGLE and dialect *wankle* wavering, from Old English *wancol;* compare Old High German *wankōn* to waver] ▸ **'wangler** *n*

Wanhsien *or* **Wan-Hsien** ('wæn'ʃjɛn) *n* a variant transliteration of the Chinese name for **Wanxian.**

wank (wæŋk) *Taboo slang.* ◆ *vb* **1** (*intr*) to masturbate. ◆ *n* **2** an instance of wanking. [of uncertain origin]

Wankel engine ('wæŋk[ə]l) *n* a type of four-stroke internal-combustion engine without reciprocating parts. It consists of one or more approximately elliptical combustion chambers within which a curved triangular-shaped piston rotates, by the explosion of compressed gas, dividing the combustion chamber into three gastight sections. [C20: named after Felix *Wankel* (1902–88), German engineer who invented it]

wanker ('wæŋkə) *n* **1** *Taboo slang.* a person who wanks; masturbator. **2** *Derogatory slang.* a worthless fellow.

Wankie ('wɑ:ŋkɪ) *n* the former name (until 1982) of **Hwange.**

wanna ('wɒnə) *vb* a spelling of **want to** intended to reflect a dialectal or informal pronunciation: *I wanna go home.*

wannabe *or* **wannabee** ('wɒnə,bi:) *n Informal.* **a** a person who desires to be, or be like, someone or something else. **b** (*as modifier*): *a wannabe film star.* [C20: phonetic shortening of *want to be*]

Wanne-Eickel (*German* 'vanə'aikəl) *n* an industrial town in W Germany, in North Rhine-Westphalia on the Rhine-Herne Canal: formed in 1926 by the merging of two townships. Pop.: 98 800 (latest est.).

want (wɒnt) *vb* **1** (*tr*) to feel a need or longing for: *I want a new hat.* **2** (when *tr, may take a clause as object or an infinitive*) to wish, need, or desire (something or to do something): *he wants to go home.* **3** (*intr;* usually used with a negative and often foll. by *for*) to be lacking or deficient (in something necessary or desirable): *the child wants for nothing.* **4** (*tr*) to feel the absence of: *lying on the ground makes me want my bed.* **5** (*tr*) to fall short by (a specified amount). **6** (*tr*) *Chiefly Brit.* to have need of or require (doing or being something): *your shoes want cleaning.* **7** (*intr*) to be destitute. **8** (*tr; often passive*) to seek or request the presence of: *you're wanted upstairs.* **9** (*intr*) to be absent. **10** (*tr; takes an infinitive*) *Informal.* should or ought (to do something): *you don't want to go out so late.* **11 want in** (*or* **out**). *Informal.* to wish to be included in (or excluded from) a venture. ◆ *n* **12** the act or an instance of wanting. **13** anything that is needed, desired, or lacked: *to supply someone's wants.* **14** a lack, shortage, or absence: *for want of common sense.* **15** the state of being in need; destitution: *the state should help those in want.* **16** a sense of lack; craving. [C12 (vb, in the sense: it is lacking), C13 (n): from Old Norse *vanta* to be deficient; related to Old English *wanian* to WANE] ▸ **'wanter** *n*

want ad *n Informal.* a classified advertisement in a newspaper, magazine, etc., for something wanted, such as property or employment.

wanted ('wɒntɪd) *adj* being searched for by the police in connection with a crime that has been committed.

wanting ('wɒntɪŋ) *adj* (*postpositive*) **1** lacking or absent; missing. **2** not meeting requirements or expectations: *you have been found wanting.* ◆ *prep* **3** without. **4** *Archaic.* minus.

wanton ('wɒntən) *adj* **1** dissolute, licentious, or immoral. **2** without motive, provocation, or justification: *wanton destruction.* **3** maliciously and unnecessarily cruel or destructive. **4** unrestrained: *wanton spending.* **5** *Archaic or poetic.* playful or capricious. **6** *Archaic.* (of vegetation, etc.) luxuriant or superabundant. ◆ *n* **7** a licentious person, esp. a woman. **8** a playful or capricious person. ◆ *vb* **9** (*intr*) to behave in a wanton manner. **10** (*tr*) to squander or waste. [C13 *wantowen* (in the obsolete sense: unmanageable, unruly): from *wan-* (prefix equivalent to UN-[1]; related to Old English *wanian* to WANE) + *-towen,* from Old English *togen* brought up, from *tēonto* bring up] ▸ **'wantonly** *adv* ▸ **'wantonness** *n*

Wanxian, Wanhsien, *or* **Wan-Hsien** ('wæn'ʃjɛn) *n* an inland port in central China, in E Sichuan province, on the Yangtze River. Pop.: 156 823 (1990 est.).

wapentake ('wɒpən,teɪk, 'wæp-) *n English legal history.* a subdivision of certain shires or counties, esp. in the Midlands and North of England, corresponding to the hundred in other shires. [Old English *wǣpen(ge)tæc,* from Old Norse *vāpnatak,* from *vápn* WEAPON + *tak* TAKE]

wapiti ('wɒpɪtɪ) *n, pl* **-tis.** a large deer, *Cervus canadensis,* with large much-branched antlers, native to North America and now also common in the South Island of New Zealand. Also called: **American elk.** [C19: from Shawnee, literally: white deer, from *wap* (unattested) white; from the animal's white tail and rump]

wappenshaw ('wæpənʃɔ:, 'wɒp-) *n* (formerly) a muster of men in a particular area in Scotland to show that they were properly armed. [C16: from Northern English *wapen,* from Old Norse *vápn* WEAPON + *schaw* SHOW]

war (wɔ:) *n* **1** open armed conflict between two or more parties, nations, or states. Related adjs: **belligerent, martial. 2** a particular armed conflict: *the 1973 war in the Middle East.* **3** the techniques of armed conflict as a study, science, or profession. **4** any conflict or contest: *a war of wits; the war against crime.* **5** (*modifier*) of, relating to, resulting from, or characteristic of war: *a war hero; war damage; a war story.* **6 to have had a good war.** to have made the most of the opportunities presented to one during wartime. **7 in the wars.** *Informal.* (esp. of a child) hurt or knocked about, esp. as a result of quarrelling and fighting. ◆ *vb* **wars, warring, warred. 8** (*intr*) to conduct a war. [C12: from Old Northern French *werre* (variant of Old French *guerre*), of Germanic origin; related to Old High German *werra*]

War. *abbrev. for* Warwickshire.

waragi ('waragɪ, -dʒɪ) *n* a Ugandan alcoholic drink made from bananas. [from Luganda]

Warangal ('wʌrəŋgəl) *n* a city in S central India, in N Andhra Pradesh: capital of a 12th-century Hindu kingdom. Pop.: 447 657 (1991).

waratah (,wɒrə'tɑ:) *n Austral.* a proteaceous shrub, *Telopea speciosissima,* the floral emblem of New South Wales, having dark green leaves and large clusters of crimson flowers. [from a native Australian language]

warb (wɔ:b) *n Austral. slang.* a dirty or insignificant person. [C20: of unknown origin] ▸ **'warby** *adj*

war baby *n* a child born in wartime, esp. the illegitimate child of a soldier.

Warbeck ('wɔ:bɛk) *n* **Perkin** ('pɜ:kɪn). ?1474–99, Flemish impostor, pretender to the English throne. Professing to be Richard, Duke of York, he led an unsuccessful rising against Henry VII (1497) and was later executed.

War Between the States *n* the American Civil War.

warble[1] ('wɔ:b[ə]l) *vb* **1** to sing (words, songs, etc.) with trills, runs, and other embellishments. **2** (*tr*) to utter in a song. **3** *U.S.* another word for **yodel.** ◆ *n* **4** the act or an instance of warbling. [C14: via Old French *werbler* from Germanic; compare Frankish *hwirbilōn* (unattested), Old High German *wirbil* whirlwind; see WHIRL]

warble[2] ('wɔ:b[ə]l) *n Vet. science.* **1** a small lumpy abscess under the skin of cattle caused by infestation with larvae of the warble fly. **2** a hard tumorous lump of tissue on a horse's back, caused by prolonged friction of a saddle. [C16: of uncertain origin] ▸ **'warbled** *adj*

warble fly *n* any of various hairy beelike dipterous flies of the genus *Hypoderma* and related genera, the larvae of which produce warbles in cattle: family *Oestridae.*

warbler ('wɔ:blə) *n* **1** a person or thing that warbles. **2** any small active passerine songbird of the Old World subfamily *Sylviinae:* family *Muscicapidae.* They have a cryptic plumage and slender bill and are arboreal insectivores. **3** Also called: **wood warbler.** any small bird of the American family *Parulidae,* similar to the Old World forms but often brightly coloured.

war bonnet *n* a headband with trailing feathers, worn by certain North American Indian warriors as a headdress.

war bride *n* a soldier's bride met as a result of troop movements in wartime, esp. a foreign national.

Warburg (*German* 'varburk) *n* **Otto** (**Heinrich**) ('oto). 1883–1970, German biochemist and physiologist: Nobel prize for physiology or medicine (1931) for his work on respiratory enzymes.

war chest *n U.S.* a fund collected for a specific purpose, such as an election campaign.

war correspondent *n* a journalist who reports on a war from the scene of action.

war crime *n* a crime committed in wartime in violation of the accepted rules and customs of war, such as genocide, ill-treatment of prisoners of war, etc. ▸ **war criminal** *n*

war cry *n* **1** a rallying cry used by combatants in battle. **2** a cry, slogan, etc., used to rally support for a cause.

ward (wɔ:d) *n* **1** (in many countries) a district into which a city, town, parish, or other area is divided for administration, election of representatives, etc. **2** a room in a hospital, esp. one for patients requiring similar kinds of care: *a maternity ward.* **3** one of the divisions of a prison. **4** an open space enclosed within the walls of a castle. **5** *Law.* **5a** Also called: **ward of court.** a person, esp. a minor or one legally incapable of managing his own affairs, placed under the control or protection of a guardian or of a court. **5b** guardianship, as of a minor or legally incompetent person. **6** the state of being under guard or in custody. **7** a person who is under the protection or in the custody of another. **8** a means of protection. **9a** an internal ridge or bar in a lock that prevents an incorrectly cut key from turning. **9b** a corresponding groove cut in a key. **10** a less common word for **warden**[1]. ◆ *vb* **11** *(tr) Archaic.* to guard or protect. ◆ See also **ward off.** [Old English *weard* protector; related to Old High German *wart,* Old Saxon *ward,* Old Norse *vorthr.* See GUARD] ▸ **'wardless** *adj*

Ward (wɔːd) *n* **1** Dame **Barbara (Mary),** Baroness Jackson. 1914–81, British economist, environmentalist, and writer. Her books include *Spaceship Earth* (1966). **2** Mrs **Humphry,** married name of *Mary Augusta Arnold.* 1851–1920, English novelist. Her novels include *Robert Elsmere* (1888) and *The Case of Richard Meynell* (1911). **3** Sir **Joseph George.** 1856–1930, New Zealand statesman; prime minister of New Zealand (1906–12; 1928–30).

-ward *suffix.* **1** *(forming adjectives)* indicating direction towards: *a backward step; heavenward progress.* **2** *(forming adverbs)* a variant and the usual U.S. and Canadian form of **-wards.** [Old English *-weard* towards]

war dance *n* **1** a ceremonial dance performed before going to battle or after victory, esp. by certain North American Indian peoples. **2** a dance representing warlike action.

warded ('wɔːdɪd) *adj* (of locks, keys, etc.) having wards.

warden[1] ('wɔːdᵊn) *n* **1** a person who has the charge or care of something, esp. a building, or someone. **2** *Archaic.* any of various public officials, esp. one responsible for the enforcement of certain regulations. **3** *Chiefly U.S. and Canadian.* the chief officer in charge of a prison. **4** *Brit.* the principal or president of any of various universities or colleges. **5** See **churchwarden** (sense 1). [C13: from Old Northern French *wardein,* from *warder* to guard, of Germanic origin; see GUARD] ▸ **'wardenry** *n*

warden[2] ('wɔːdᵊn) *n* a variety of pear that has crisp firm flesh and is used for cooking. [C15: of obscure origin]

warder[1] ('wɔːdə) *or (fem)* **wardress** *n* **1** *Chiefly Brit.* an officer in charge of prisoners in a jail. **2** a person who guards or has charge of something. [C14: from Anglo-French *wardere,* from Old French *warder* to GUARD, of Germanic origin] ▸ **'wardership** *n*

warder[2] ('wɔːdə) *n* (formerly) a staff or truncheon carried by a ruler as an emblem of authority and used to signal his wishes or intentions. [C15: perhaps from Middle English *warden* to WARD]

ward heeler *n U.S. politics, disparaging.* a party worker who canvasses votes and performs chores for a political boss. Also called: **heeler.**

wardian case ('wɔːdɪən) *n* a type of glass container used for housing delicate ferns and similar plants. [C19: named after N. B. *Ward* (died 1868), English botanist]

wardmote ('wɔːdməʊt) *n Brit.* an assembly of the citizens or liverymen of a ward. [C14: see WARD, MOOT]

ward off *vb (tr, adv)* to turn aside or repel; avert.

Wardour Street ('wɔːdə) *n* **1** a street in Soho where many film companies have their London offices: formerly noted for shops selling antiques and mock antiques. **2 Wardour Street English.** affectedly archaic speech or writing.

wardrobe ('wɔːdrəʊb) *n* **1** a tall closet or cupboard, with a rail or hooks on which to hang clothes. **2** the total collection of articles of clothing belonging to one person. **3** the collection of costumes belonging to a theatre or theatrical company. [C14: from Old Northern French *warderobe,* from *warder* to GUARD + *robe* ROBE]

wardrobe mistress *n* a person responsible for maintaining and sometimes making the costumes in a theatre.

wardrobe trunk *n* a large upright rectangular travelling case, usually opening longitudinally, with one side having a hanging rail, the other having drawers or compartments.

wardroom ('wɔːd,ruːm, -,rʊm) *n* **1** the quarters assigned to the officers (except the captain) of a warship. **2** the officers of a warship collectively, excepting the captain.

-wards *or* **-ward** *suffix forming adverbs.* indicating direction towards: *a step backwards; to sail shorewards.* Compare **-ward.** [Old English *-weardes* towards]

wardship ('wɔːdʃɪp) *n* the state of being a ward.

ware[1] (wɛə) *n (often in combination)* **1** *(functioning as sing)* articles of the same kind or material: *glassware; silverware.* **2** porcelain or pottery of a specified type: *agateware; jasper ware.* ◆ See also **wares.** [Old English *waru;* related to Old Frisian *were,* Old Norse *vara,* Middle Dutch *Ware*]

ware[2] (wɛə) *Archaic.* ◆ *vb* **1** another word for **beware.** ◆ *adj* **2** another word for **wary** or **wise**[1]. [Old English *wær;* related to Old Saxon, Old High German *giwar,* Old Norse *varr,* Gothic *war,* Latin *vereor.* See AWARE, BEWARE]

ware[3] (wɛə) *vb (tr) Northern Brit. dialect.* to spend or squander. [C15: of Scandinavian origin; related to Icelandic *verja*]

warehouse *n* ('wɛə,haʊs). **1** a place where goods are stored prior to their use, distribution, or sale. **2** See **bonded warehouse. 3** *Chiefly Brit.* a large commercial, esp. wholesale, establishment. ◆ *vb* ('wɛə,haʊz, -,haʊs). **4** *(tr)* to store or place in a warehouse, esp. a bonded warehouse.

warehouseman ('wɛə,haʊsmən) *n, pl* **-men.** a person who manages, is employed in, or owns a warehouse.

warehousing ('wɛə,haʊzɪŋ) *n Stock Exchange.* an attempt to maintain the price of a company's shares or to gain a significant stake in a company without revealing the true identity of the purchaser. Shares are purchased through an insurance company, a unit trust, or nominees.

wares (wɛəz) *pl n* **1** articles of manufacture considered as being for sale. **2** any talent or asset regarded as a commercial or saleable commodity. **3** *Caribbean.* earthenware.

war establishment *n* the full wartime complement of men, equipment, and vehicles of a military unit.

warfare ('wɔː,fɛə) *n* **1** the act, process, or an instance of waging war. **2** conflict, struggle, or strife.

warfarin ('wɔːfərɪn) *n* a crystalline insoluble optically active compound, used as a rodenticide and, in the form of its sodium salt, as a medical anticoagulant. Formula: $C_{19}H_{16}O_4$. [C20: from the patent owners *W(isconsin) A(lumni) R(esearch) F(oundation)* + (COUM)ARIN]

war game *n* **1** a notional tactical exercise for training military commanders, in which no military units are actually deployed. **2** a game in which model soldiers are used to create battles, esp. past battles, in order to study tactics.

warhead ('wɔː,hɛd) *n* the part of the fore end of a missile or projectile that contains explosives.

Warhol ('wɔːhəʊl) *n* **Andy,** real name *Andrew Warhola.* ?1926–87, U.S. artist and film maker; one of the foremost exponents of pop art.

warhorse ('wɔː,hɔːs) *n* **1** a horse used in battle. **2** *Informal.* a veteran soldier, politician, or elderly person, esp. one who is aggressive.

warison ('wærɪsən) *n* (esp. formerly) a bugle note used as an order to a military force to attack. [C13: from Old Northern French, from *warir* to protect, of Germanic origin; compare Old English *warian* to defend]

wark (waːrk, wɔːrk) *n* a Scot. word for **work.**

Warks *abbrev. for* Warwickshire.

Warley ('wɔːlɪ) *n* an industrial town in W central England, in Sandwell unitary authority, West Midlands: formed in 1966 by the amalgamation of Smethwick, Oldbury, and Rowley Regis. Pop.: 145 542 (1991).

warlike ('wɔː,laɪk) *adj* **1** of, relating to, or used in war. **2** hostile or belligerent. **3** fit or ready for war.

warlock ('wɔː,lɒk) *n* **1** a man who practises black magic; sorcerer. **2** a fortune-teller, conjuror, or magician. [Old English *wǣrloga* oath breaker, from *wǣr* oath + *-loga* liar, from *lēogan* to LIE[1]]

Warlock ('wɔː,lɒk) *n* **Peter,** real name *Philip Arnold Heseltine.* 1894–1930, British composer and scholar of early English music. His works include song cycles, such as *The Curlew* (1920–22), and the *Capriol Suite* (1926) for strings.

warlord ('wɔː,lɔːd) *n* a military leader of a nation or part of a nation, esp. one who is accountable to nobody when the central government is weak: *the Chinese warlords.*

Warlpiri ('walpri) *n* an Aboriginal language of central Australia.

warm (wɔːm) *adj* **1** characterized by or having a moderate degree of heat; moderately hot. **2** maintaining or imparting heat: *a warm coat.* **3** having or showing ready affection, kindliness, etc. *a warm personality.* **4** lively, vigorous, or passionate: *a warm debate.* **5** cordial or enthusiastic; ardent: *warm support.* **6** quickly or easily aroused: *a warm temper.* **7** (of colours) predominantly red or yellow in tone. **8** (of a scent, trail, etc.) recently made; strong. **9** near to finding a hidden object or discovering or guessing facts, as in children's games. **10** *Informal.* uncomfortable or disagreeable, esp. because of the proximity of danger. ◆ *vb* **11** (sometimes foll. by *up*) to raise or be raised in temperature; make or become warm or warmer. **12** (when *intr,* often foll. by *to*) to make or become excited, enthusiastic, etc. (about): *he warmed to the idea of buying a new car.* **13** *(intr;* often foll. by *to)* to feel affection, kindness, etc. (for someone): *I warmed to her mother from the start.* **14** *(tr) Brit.* to give a caning to: *I'll warm you in a minute.* ◆ *n* **15** *Informal.* a warm place or area: *come into the warm.* **16** *Informal.* the act or an instance of warming or being warmed. ◆ See also **warm over, warm up.** [Old English *wearm;* related to Old Frisian, Old Saxon *warm,* Old Norse *varmr*] ▸ **'warmer** *n* ▸ **'warmish** *adj* ▸ **'warmly** *adv* ▸ **'warmness** *n*

warm-blooded *adj* **1** ardent, impetuous, or passionate. **2** (of birds and mammals) having a constant body temperature, usually higher than the temperature of the surroundings. Technical name: **homoiothermic.** ▸ **,warm-'bloodedness** *n*

warm-down *n* light exercises performed to aid recovery from strenuous physical activity.

war memorial *n* a monument, usually an obelisk or cross, to those who die in a war, esp. those from a particular locality.

warm front *n Meteorol.* the boundary between a warm air mass and the cold air above which it is rising, at a less steep angle than at the cold front. Compare **cold front, occluded front.**

warm-hearted *adj* kindly, generous, or readily sympathetic. ▸ **,warm-'heartedly** *adv* ▸ **,warm-'heartedness** *n*

warming pan *n* a pan, often of copper and having a long handle, filled with hot coals or hot water and formerly drawn over the sheets to warm a bed.

warmonger ('wɔː,mʌŋgə) *n* a person who fosters warlike ideas or advocates war. ▸ **'war,mongering** *n*

warm over *vb (tr, adv)* **1** *U.S. and Canadian.* to reheat (food). **2** *Informal.* to present (an idea, etc.) again, esp. without freshness or originality.

warm sector *n Meteorol.* a wedge of warm air between the warm and cold fronts of a depression, which is eventually occluded. See also **cold front, warm front.**

warmth (wɔːmθ) *n* **1** the state, quality, or sensation of being warm. **2** intensity of emotion: *he denied the accusation with some warmth.* **3** affection or cordiality.

warm up *vb (adv)* **1** to make or become warm or warmer. **2** *(intr)* to exercise in preparation for and immediately before a game, contest, or more vigorous exercise. **3** to get ready for something important; prepare. **4** to run or operate (an engine, etc.) until the normal working temperature or condition is attained, or (of an engine, etc.) to undergo this process. **5** to make or become more animated or enthusiastic: *the party warmed up when Tom came.* **6** to reheat (already cooked food) or (of such food) to be reheated. **7** *(tr)* to make (an audience) relaxed and receptive before a show, esp. a television comedy show. ◆ *n*

warm-up. 8 the act or an instance of warming up. 9 a preparatory exercise routine.

warn (wɔːn) *vb* 1 to notify or make (someone) aware of danger, harm, etc. 2 (*tr; often takes a negative and an infinitive*) to advise or admonish (someone) as to action, conduct, etc.: *I warn you not to do that again.* 3 (*takes a clause as object or an infinitive*) to inform (someone) in advance: *he warned them that he would arrive late.* 4 (*tr;* usually foll. by *away, off,* etc.) to give notice to go away, be off, etc.: *he warned the trespassers off his ground.* [Old English *wearnian;* related to Old High German *warnēn,* Old Norse *varna* to refuse] ▸ **'warner** *n*

warning ('wɔːnɪŋ) *n* 1 a hint, intimation, threat, etc., of harm or danger. 2 advice to beware or desist. 3 an archaic word for **notice** (sense 6). ◆ *adj* 4 (*prenominal*) intended or serving to warn: *a warning look.* 5 (of the coloration of certain distasteful or poisonous animals) having conspicuous markings, which predators recognize and learn to avoid; aposematic. ▸ **'warningly** *adv*

War of American Independence *n* the conflict following the revolt of the North American colonies against British rule, particularly on the issue of taxation. Hostilities began in 1775 when British and American forces clashed at Lexington and Concord. Articles of Confederation agreed in the Continental Congress in 1777 provided for a confederacy to be known as the United States of America. The war was effectively ended with the surrender of the British at Yorktown in 1781 and peace was signed at Paris in Sept. 1783. Also called: **American Revolution** or **Revolutionary War.**

War of 1812 *n* a war between Great Britain and the U.S., fought chiefly along the Canadian border (1812–14).

War Office *n Brit.* (formerly) **a** the department of state responsible for the British Army. **b** the premises of this department in Whitehall, London.

war of nerves *n* the use of psychological tactics against an opponent, such as shattering his morale by the use of propaganda.

War of Secession *n* another name for the (American) **Civil War.**

War of the Austrian Succession *n* the war (1740–48) fought by Austria, Britain, and the Netherlands against Prussia, France, and Spain in support of the right of succession of Maria Theresa to the Austrian throne and against the territorial aims of Prussia.

War of the Grand Alliance *n* the war (1689–97) waged by the Grand Alliance, led by Britain, the Netherlands, and Austria, against Louis XIV of France, following his invasion (1688) of the Palatinate.

War of the Spanish Succession *n* the war (1701–14) between Austria, Britain, Prussia, and the Netherlands on the one side and France, Spain, and Bavaria on the other over the disputed succession to the Spanish throne.

warp (wɔːp) *vb* 1 to twist or cause to twist out of shape, as from heat, damp, etc. 2 to turn or cause to turn from a true, correct, or proper course. 3 to pervert or be perverted. 4 (*tr*) to prepare (yarn) as a warp. 5 *Nautical.* to move (a vessel) by hauling on a rope fixed to a stationary object ashore or (of a vessel) to be moved thus. 6 (*tr*) (formerly) to curve or twist (an aircraft wing) in order to assist control in flight. 7 (*tr*) to flood (land) with water from which alluvial matter is deposited. ◆ *n* 8 the state or condition of being twisted out of shape. 9 a twist, distortion, or bias. 10 a mental or moral deviation. 11 the yarns arranged lengthways on a loom, forming the threads through which the weft yarns are woven. 12 the heavy threads used to reinforce the rubber in the casing of a pneumatic tyre. 13 *Nautical.* a rope used for warping a vessel. 14 alluvial sediment deposited by water. [Old English *wearp* a throw; related to Old High German *warf,* Old Norse *varp* throw of a dragging net, Old English *weorpan* to throw] ▸ **'warpage** *n* ▸ **warped** *adj* ▸ **'warper** *n*

war paint *n* 1 painted decoration of the face and body applied by certain North American Indians before battle. 2 *Informal.* finery or regalia. 3 *Informal.* cosmetics.

warpath ('wɔːˌpɑːθ) *n* 1 the route taken by North American Indians on a warlike expedition. 2 **on the warpath.** 2a preparing to engage in battle. 2b *Informal.* in a state of anger.

warplane ('wɔːˌpleɪn) *n* any aircraft designed for and used in warfare. Also called (U.S.): **battle plane.**

warrant ('wɒrənt) *n* 1 anything that gives authority for an action or decision; authorization; sanction. 2 a document that certifies or guarantees, such as a receipt for goods stored in a warehouse, a licence, or a commission. 3 *Law.* an authorization issued by a magistrate or other official allowing a constable or other officer to search or seize property, arrest a person, or perform some other specified act. 4 (in certain armed services) the official authority for the appointment of warrant officers. 5 a security that functions as a stock option by giving the owner the right to buy ordinary shares in a company at a specified date, often at a specified price. ◆ *vb* (*tr*) 6 to guarantee the quality, condition, etc., of (something). 7 to give authority or power to. 8 to attest to or assure the character, worthiness, etc., of. 9 to guarantee (a purchaser of merchandise) against loss of, damage to, or misrepresentation concerning the merchandise. 10 *Law.* to guarantee (the title to an estate or other property). 11 to declare confidently. [C13: from Anglo-French *warrant,* variant of Old French *guarant,* from *guarantir* to guarantee, of Germanic origin; compare GUARANTY] ▸ **'warrantable** *adj* ▸ **ˌwarranta'bility** *n* ▸ **'warrantably** *adv* ▸ **'warranter** *n* ▸ **'warrantless** *adj*

warrantee (ˌwɒrən'tiː) *n* a person to whom a warranty is given.

warrant officer *n* an officer in certain armed services who holds a rank between those of commissioned and noncommissioned officers. In the British army, the rank has two classes: see **regimental sergeant major, company sergeant major.**

Warrant of Fitness *n N.Z.* a six-monthly certificate required for motor vehicles certifying mechanical soundness.

warrantor ('wɒrənˌtɔː) *n* an individual or company that provides a warranty.

warrant sale *n Scots Law.* a sale of someone's personal belongings or household effects that have been seized to meet unpaid debts.

warranty ('wɒrəntɪ) *n, pl* **-ties.** 1 *Property law.* a covenant, express or implied, by which the vendor of real property vouches for the security of the title conveyed. 2 *Contract law.* an express or implied term in a contract collateral to the main purpose, such as an undertaking that goods contracted to be sold shall meet specified requirements as to quality, etc. 3 *Insurance law.* an undertaking by the party insured that the facts given regarding the risk are as stated. 4 the act of warranting. [C14: from Anglo-French *warantie,* from *warantir* to warrant, variant of Old French *guarantir;* see WARRANT]

warren ('wɒrən) *n* 1 a series of interconnected underground tunnels in which rabbits live. 2 a colony of rabbits. 3 an overcrowded area or dwelling. 4a *Chiefly Brit.* an enclosed place where small game animals or birds are kept, esp. for breeding, or a part of a river or lake enclosed by nets in which fish are kept (esp. in the phrase **beasts** or **fowls of warren**). 4b *English legal history.* a franchise permitting one to keep animals, birds, or fish in this way. [C14: from Anglo-French *warenne,* of Germanic origin; compare Old High German *werien* to preserve]

Warren[1] ('wɒrən) *n* a city in the U.S., in SE Michigan, northeast of Detroit. Pop.: 138 078 (1996 est.).

Warren[2] ('wɒrən) *n* **Earl.** 1891–1974, U.S. lawyer; chief justice of the U.S. (1953–69). He chaired the commission that investigated the murder of President Kennedy.

warrener ('wɒrənə) *n Obsolete.* a gamekeeper or keeper of a warren (sense 4).

warrigal ('wɒrɪgæl) *Austral.* ◆ *n* 1 a dingo. ◆ *adj* 2 untamed or wild. [C19: from a native Australian language]

Warrington ('wɒrɪŋtən) *n* an industrial town and from 1998 a unitary authority in NW England, in N Cheshire on the River Mersey: dates from Roman times. Pop.: 188 000 (1995 est.). Area: 176 sq. km (68 sq. miles).

warrior ('wɒrɪə) *n* **a** a person engaged in, experienced in, or devoted to war. **b** (*as modifier*): *a warrior nation.* [C13: from Old Northern French *werreieor,* from *werre* WAR]

Warsaw ('wɔːsɔː) *n* the capital of Poland, in the E central part on the River Vistula: became capital at the end of the 16th century; almost completely destroyed in World War II as the main centre of the Polish resistance movement; rebuilt within about six years; university (1818); situated at the junction of important trans-European routes. Pop.: 1 638 300 (1996 est.). Polish name: **Warszawa** (var'ʃava).

Warsaw Pact *n* a military treaty and association of E European countries, formed in 1955 by the Soviet Union, Bulgaria, Czechoslovakia, East Germany, Hungary, Poland, and Romania: East Germany left in 1990; the remaining members dissolved the Pact in 1991.

warship ('wɔːˌʃɪp) *n* a vessel armed, armoured, and otherwise equipped for naval warfare.

Wars of the Roses *pl n* the conflicts in England (1455–85) centred on the struggle for the throne between the house of York (symbolized by the white rose) and the house of Lancaster (of which one badge was the red rose).

wart (wɔːt) *n* 1 Also called: **verruca.** *Pathol.* any firm abnormal elevation of the skin caused by a virus. 2 *Botany.* a small rounded outgrowth. 3 **warts and all.** with all blemishes evident. [Old English *weart(e);* related to Old High German *warza,* Old Norse *varta*] ▸ **'warted** *adj* ▸ **'wartˌlike** *adj* ▸ **'warty** *adj*

Warta (*Polish* 'varta) *n* a river in Poland, flowing generally north and west across the whole W Polish Plain to the River Oder. Length: 808 km (502 miles).

Wartburg (*German* 'vartburk) *n* a medieval castle in central Germany, in Thuringia southwest of Eisenach: residence of Luther (1521–22) when he began his German translation of the New Testament.

wart cress *n* either of two prostrate cruciferous annuals, *Coronopus squamatus* and *C. didymus,* having small white flowers. Also called: **swine's cress.**

warthog ('wɔːthɒg) *n* a wild pig, *Phacochoerus aethiopicus,* of southern and E Africa, having heavy tusks, wartlike protuberances on the face, and a mane of coarse hair.

wartime ('wɔːˌtaɪm) *n* **a** a period or time of war. **b** (*as modifier*): *wartime conditions.*

Warton ('wɔːtᵊn) *n* 1 **Joseph.** 1722–1800, British poet and critic, noted for his poem *The Enthusiast* (1744) and his *Essay on the Writings and Genius of Pope* (1756). 2 his brother **Thomas.** 1728–90, poet laureate (1785–90); author of the poem *The Pleasures of Melancholy* (1747) and the first *History of English Poetry* (1774–81).

war whoop *n* the yell or howl uttered, esp. by North American Indians, while making an attack.

Warwick[1] ('wɒrɪk) *n* a town in central England, administrative centre of Warwickshire, on the River Avon: 14th-century castle, with collections of armour and waxworks: the university of Warwick (1965) is in Coventry. Pop.: 22 476 (1991).

Warwick[2] ('wɒrɪk) *n* **Earl of,** title of *Richard Neville,* known as *the Kingmaker.* 1428–71, English statesman. During the Wars of the Roses, he fought first for the Yorkists, securing the throne (1461) for Edward IV, and then for the Lancastrians, restoring Henry VI (1470). He was killed at Barnet by Edward IV.

Warwickshire ('wɒrɪkˌʃɪə, -ʃə) *n* a county of central England: until 1974, when the West Midlands metropolitan county was created, it contained one of the most highly industrialized regions in the world, centred on Birmingham. Administrative centre: Warwick. Pop.: 496 300 (1994 est.). Area: 1981 sq. km (765 sq. miles).

wary ('wɛərɪ) *adj* **warier, wariest.** 1 watchful, cautious, or alert. 2 characterized by caution or watchfulness. [C16: from WARE[2] + -Y[1]] ▸ **'warily** *adv* ▸ **'wariness** *n*

was (wɒz; *unstressed* wəz) *vb* (used with *I, he, she, it,* and with singular nouns) 1 the past tense (indicative mood) of **be.** 2 *Not standard.* a form of the subjunctive mood used in place of *were*, esp. in conditional sentences: *if the film was to be with you, would you be able to process it?* [Old English *wæs*, from *wesan* to be; related to Old Frisian, Old High German *was*, Old Norse *var*]

Wasatch Range ('wɔːsætʃ) *n* a mountain range in the W central U.S., in N Utah and SE Idaho. Highest peak: Mount Timpanogos, 3581 m (11 750 ft.).

wash (wɒʃ) *vb* **1** to apply water or other liquid, usually with soap, to (oneself, clothes, etc.) in order to cleanse. **2** (*tr*; often foll. by *away, from, off*, etc.) to remove by the application of water or other liquid and usually soap: *she washed the dirt from her clothes.* **3** (*intr*) to be capable of being washed without damage or loss of colour. **4** (of an animal such as a cat) to cleanse (itself or another animal) by licking. **5** (*tr*) to cleanse from pollution or defilement. **6** (*tr*) to make wet or moist. **7** (often foll. by *away*, etc.) to move or be moved by water: *the flood washed away the bridge.* **8** (esp. of waves) to flow or sweep against or over (a surface or object), often with a lapping sound. **9** to form by erosion or be eroded: *the stream washed a ravine in the hill.* **10** (*tr*) to apply a thin coating of paint, metal, etc., to. **11** (*tr*) to separate (ore, precious stones, etc.) from (gravel, earth, or sand) by immersion in water. **12** (*intr; usually used with a negative*) *Informal, chiefly Brit.* to admit of testing or proof: *your excuses won't wash.* **13 wash one's hands. 13a** *Euphemistic.* to go to the lavatory. **13b** (usually foll. by *of*) to refuse to have anything more to do (with). ◆ *n* **14** the act or process of washing; ablution. **15** a quantity of articles washed together. **16** a preparation or thin liquid used as a coating or in washing: *a thin wash of paint; a hair wash.* **17** *Med.* **17a** any medicinal or soothing lotion for application to a part of the body. **17b** (*in combination*): *an eyewash.* **18** the flow of water, esp. waves, against a surface, or the sound made by such a flow. **19a** the technique of making wash drawings. **19b** See **wash drawing. 20** the erosion of soil by the action of flowing water. **21** a mass of alluvial material transported and deposited by flowing water. **22** land that is habitually washed by tidal or river waters. **23** the disturbance in the air or water produced at the rear of an aircraft, boat, or other moving object. **24** gravel, earth, etc., from which valuable minerals may be washed. **25** waste liquid matter or liquid refuse, esp. as fed to pigs; swill. **26** an alcoholic liquid resembling strong beer, resulting from the fermentation of wort in the production of whisky. **27 come out in the wash.** *Informal.* to become known or apparent in the course of time. ◆ See also **wash down, wash out, wash up.** [Old English *wæscan, waxan*; related to Old High German *wascan*; see WATER]

Wash (wɒʃ) *n* **the.** a shallow inlet of the North Sea on the E coast of England, between Lincolnshire and Norfolk.

Wash. *abbrev. for* Washington.

washable ('wɒʃəbᵊl) *adj* (esp. of fabrics or clothes) capable of being washed without deteriorating. ► ˌ**washa'bility** *n*

wash-and-wear *adj* (of fabrics, garments, etc.) requiring only light washing, short drying time, and little or no ironing.

washaway ('wɒʃəˌweɪ) *n Austral.* another word for **washout** (sense 4).

washbasin ('wɒʃˌbeɪsᵊn) *n* a basin or bowl for washing the face and hands. Also called: **washbowl.**

washboard ('wɒʃˌbɔːd) *n* **1** a board having a surface, usually of corrugated metal, on which esp. formerly, clothes were scrubbed. **2** such a board used as a rhythm instrument played with the fingers in skiffle, Country and Western music, etc. **3** a less common U.S. word for **skirting board. 4** *Nautical.* **4a** a vertical planklike shield fastened to the gunwales of a boat to prevent water from splashing over the side. **4b** Also called: **splashboard.** a shield under a port for the same purpose.

washcloth ('wɒʃˌklɒθ) *n* **1** another name for **dishcloth. 2** the U.S. and Canadian word for **face cloth.**

washday ('wɒʃˌdeɪ) *n* a day on which clothes and linen are washed, often the same day each week.

wash down *vb* (*tr, adv*) **1** to wash completely, esp. from top to bottom. **2** to take drink with or after (food or another drink).

wash drawing *n* a pen-and-ink drawing that has been lightly brushed over with water to soften the lines.

washed out *adj* (**washed-out** *when prenominal*). **1** faded or colourless. **2** exhausted, esp. when being pale in appearance.

washed up *adj* (**washed-up** *when prenominal*). *Informal, chiefly U.S., Canadian, and N.Z.* **1** no longer useful, successful, hopeful, etc.: *our hopes for the new deal are all washed up.* **2** exhausted.

washer ('wɒʃə) *n* **1** a person or thing that washes. **2** a flat ring or drilled disc of metal used under the head of a bolt or nut to spread the load when tightened. **3** any flat ring of rubber, felt, metal, etc., used to provide a seal under a nut or in a tap or valve seat. **4** See **washing machine. 5** *Chemical engineering.* a device for cleaning or washing gases or vapours; scrubber. **6** *Austral.* a face cloth; flannel.

washerwoman ('wɒʃəˌwʊmən), **washwoman,** *or* (*masc*) **washerman** *n, pl* **-women** *or* **-men.** a person who washes clothes for a living.

washery ('wɒʃərɪ) *n* a plant at a mine where water or other liquid is used to remove dirt from a mineral, esp. coal.

wash house *n* (formerly) a building or outbuilding in which laundry was done.

washin ('wɒʃɪn) *n Aeronautics.* an increase in the angle of attack of an aircraft wing towards the wing tip. [C20: from WASH (flow) + IN]

washing ('wɒʃɪŋ) *n* **1** articles that have been or are to be washed together on a single occasion. **2** liquid in which an article has been washed. **3** something, such as gold dust or metal ore, that has been obtained by washing. **4** a thin coat of something applied in liquid form.

washing machine *n* a mechanical apparatus, usually powered by electricity, for washing clothing, linens, etc.

washing powder *n* powdered detergent for washing fabrics.

washing soda *n* the crystalline decahydrate of sodium carbonate, esp. when used as a cleansing agent.

Washington[1] ('wɒʃɪŋtən) *n* **1** a state of the northwestern U.S., on the Pacific: consists of the Coast Range and the Olympic Mountains in the west and the Columbia Plateau in the east. Capital: Olympia. Pop.: 5 610 362 (1997 est.). Area: 172 416 sq. km (66 570 sq. miles). Abbrevs.: **Wash.** or (with zip code) **WA 2** the capital of the U.S., coextensive with the District of Columbia and situated near the E coast on the Potomac River: site chosen by President Washington in 1790; contains the White House and the Capitol; a major educational and administrative centre. Pop.: 543 213 (1996 est.). Also called: **Washington, DC. 3** a town in Tyne and Wear: designated a new town in 1964. Pop.: 56 848 (1991). **4 Mount.** a mountain in N New Hampshire, in the White Mountains: the highest peak in the northeast U.S.; noted for extreme weather conditions. Height: 1917 m (6288 ft.). **5 Lake.** a lake in W Washington, forming the E boundary of the city of Seattle: linked by canal with Puget Sound. Length: about 32 km (20 miles). Width: 6 km (4 miles). ► **Washingtonian** (ˌwɒʃɪŋ'təʊnɪən) *adj, n*

Washington[2] ('wɒʃɪŋtən) *n* **1 Booker T(aliaferro).** 1856–1915, U.S. Black educationalist and writer. **2 George.** 1732–99, U.S. general and statesman; first president of the U.S. (1789–97). He was appointed commander in chief of the Continental Army (1775) at the outbreak of the War of American Independence, which ended with his defeat of Cornwallis at Yorktown (1781). He presided over the convention at Philadelphia (1787) that formulated the constitution of the U.S. and elected him president.

Washington palm *n* a palm tree, *Washingtonia filifera*, of California and Florida, having large fan-shaped leaves and small black fruits. Also called: **desert palm.**

washing-up *n Brit.* **1** the washing of dishes, cutlery, etc., after a meal. **2** dishes and cutlery waiting to be washed up. **3** (*as modifier*): *a washing-up machine.*

wash out *vb* (*adv*) **1** (*tr*) to wash (the inside of something) so as to remove (dirt). **2** Also: **wash off.** to remove or be removed by washing: *grass stains don't wash out easily.* **3** (*tr*) to cancel or abandon (a sporting event). ◆ *n* **washout. 4** *Geology.* **4a** erosion of the earth's surface by the action of running water. **4b** a narrow channel produced by this erosion. **5** *Informal.* **5a** a total failure or disaster. **5b** an incompetent person. **6** a sporting or social event that is cancelled due to rain. **7** *Aeronautics.* a decrease in the angle of attack of an aircraft wing towards the wing tip.

washrag ('wɒʃˌræg) *n U.S.* another word for **flannel** (sense 4).

washroom ('wɒʃˌruːm, -ˌrʊm) *n* **1** a room, esp. in a factory or office block, in which lavatories, washbasins, etc., are situated. **2** *U.S. and Canadian.* a euphemism for **lavatory.**

wash sale *n U.S.* the illegal stock-exchange practice of buying and selling the same securities at an inflated price through a colluding broker to give the impression that the security has a strong market.

washstand ('wɒʃˌstænd) *n* a piece of furniture designed to hold a basin, etc., for washing the face and hands.

washtub ('wɒʃˌtʌb) *n* a tub or large container used for washing anything, esp. clothes.

wash up *vb* (*adv*) **1** *Chiefly Brit.* to wash (dishes, cutlery, etc.) after a meal. **2** (*intr*) *U.S.* to wash one's face and hands. ◆ *n* **washup. 3** *Austral.* the end, outcome of a process: *in the washup, three candidates were elected.*

washwoman ('wɒʃˌwʊmən) *n, pl* **-women.** a less common word for **washerwoman.**

washy ('wɒʃɪ) *adj* **washier, washiest. 1** overdiluted, watery, or weak. **2** lacking intensity or strength. ► '**washily** *adv* ► '**washiness** *n*

wasn't ('wɒzᵊnt) *vb contraction of* was not.

wasp (wɒsp) *n* **1** any social hymenopterous insect of the family *Vespidae*, esp. *Vespula vulgaris* (**common wasp**), typically having a black-and-yellow body and an ovipositor specialized for stinging. See also **potter wasp, hornet.** Related adj: **vespine. 2** any of various solitary hymenopterans, such as the digger wasp and gall wasp. [Old English *wæsp*; related to Old Saxon *waspa*, Old High German *wefsa*, Latin *vespa*] ► '**wasp**ˌ**like** *adj* ► '**waspy** *adj* ► '**waspily** *adv* ► '**waspiness** *n*

Wasp *or* **WASP** (wɒsp) *n* (in the U.S.) acronym for White Anglo-Saxon Protestant: a person descended from N European, usually Protestant stock, forming a group often considered the most dominant, privileged, and influential in American society.

waspish ('wɒspɪʃ) *adj* **1** relating to or suggestive of a wasp. **2** easily annoyed or angered. ► '**waspishly** *adv* ► '**waspishness** *n*

wasp waist *n* a very slender waist, esp. one that is tightly corseted. ► '**wasp-**ˌ**waisted** *adj*

wassail ('wɒseɪl) *n* **1** (formerly) a toast or salutation made to a person at festivities. **2** a festivity when much drinking takes place. **3** alcoholic drink drunk at such a festivity, esp. spiced beer or mulled wine. **4** the singing of Christmas carols, going from house to house. **5** *Archaic.* a drinking song. ◆ *vb* **6** to drink the health of (a person) at a wassail. **7** (*intr*) to go from house to house singing carols at Christmas. [C13: from Old Norse *ves heill* be in good health; related to Old English *wes hāl*; see HALE[1]] ► '**wassailer** *n*

Wassermann test *or* **reaction** ('wæsəmən; *German* 'vasərman) *n Med.* a diagnostic test for syphilis. See **complement fixation test.** [C20: named after August von *Wassermann* (1866–1925), German bacteriologist]

wast (wɒst; *unstressed* wəst) *vb Archaic or dialect.* (used with the pronoun *thou* or its relative equivalent) a singular form of the past tense (indicative mood) of **be.**

wastage ('weɪstɪdʒ) *n* **1** anything lost by wear or waste. **2** the process of wasting. **3** reduction in size of a workforce by retirement, voluntary resignation, etc. (esp. in the phrase **natural wastage**).

USAGE *Waste* and *wastage* are to some extent interchangeable, but many people think that *wastage* should not be used to refer to loss resulting from human carelessness, inefficiency, etc.: *a waste* (not *a wastage*) *of time/money/effort* etc.

waste (weɪst) *vb* **1** (*tr*) to use, consume, or expend thoughtlessly, carelessly, or to no avail. **2** (*tr*) to fail to take advantage of: *to waste an opportunity.* **3** (when *intr,* often foll. by *away*) to lose or cause to lose bodily strength, health, etc. **4** to exhaust or become exhausted. **5** (*tr*) to ravage. **6** (*tr*) *Informal.* to murder or kill: *I want that guy wasted by tomorrow.* ◆ *n* **7** the act of wasting or state of being wasted. **8** a failure to take advantage of something. **9** anything unused or not used to full advantage. **10** anything or anyone rejected as useless, worthless, or in excess of what is required. **11** garbage, rubbish, or trash. **12** a land or region that is devastated or ruined. **13** a land or region that is wild or uncultivated. **14** *Physiol.* **14a** the useless products of metabolism. **14b** indigestible food residue. **15** disintegrated rock material resulting from erosion. **16** *Law.* reduction in the value of an estate caused by act or neglect, esp. by a life-tenant. ◆ *adj* **17** rejected as useless, unwanted, or worthless. **18** produced in excess of what is required. **19** not cultivated, inhabited, or productive: *waste land.* **20a** of or denoting the useless products of metabolism. **20b** of or denoting indigestible food residue. **21** destroyed, devastated, or ruined. **22** designed to contain or convey waste products. **23 lay waste.** to devastate or destroy. [C13: from Anglo-French *waster,* from Latin *vastāre* to lay waste, from *vastus* empty] ▶ **'wastable** *adj*

wastebasket ('weɪstˌbɑːskɪt) *n* another term (esp. U.S. and Canadian) for **wastepaper basket.**

wasted ('weɪstɪd) *adj* **1** not exploited or taken advantage of: *a wasted opportunity.* **2** useless or unprofitable: *wasted effort.* **3** physically enfeebled and emaciated: *a thin wasted figure.* **4** *Slang.* showing signs of habitual drug abuse.

waste disposal unit *n* an electrically operated fitment in the plughole of a kitchen sink that breaks up food refuse so that it goes down the waste pipe.

wasteful ('weɪstfʊl) *adj* **1** tending to waste or squander; extravagant. **2** causing waste, destruction, or devastation. ▶ **'wastefully** *adv* ▶ **'wastefulness** *n*

waste heat recovery *n* the use of heat that is produced in a thermodynamic cycle, as in a furnace, combustion engine, etc., in another process, such as heating feedwater or air.

wasteland ('weɪstˌlænd) *n* **1** a barren or desolate area of land, not or no longer used for cultivation or building. **2** a region, period in history, etc., that is considered spiritually, intellectually, or aesthetically barren or desolate: *American television is a cultural wasteland.*

wastelot ('weɪstˌlɒt) *n Chiefly Canadian.* a piece of waste ground in a city.

wastepaper ('weɪstˌpeɪpə) *n* paper discarded after use.

wastepaper basket *or* **bin** *n* an open receptacle for paper and other dry litter. Usual U.S. and Canadian word: **wastebasket.**

waste pipe *n* a pipe to take excess or used water away, as from a sink to a drain.

waster ('weɪstə) *n* **1** a person or thing that wastes. **2** a ne'er-do-well; wastrel. **3** an article spoiled in manufacture.

wasteweir ('weɪstˌwɪə) *n* another name for **spillway.**

wasting ('weɪstɪŋ) *adj* (*prenominal*) reducing the vitality, strength, or robustness of the body: *a wasting disease.* ▶ **'wastingly** *adv*

wasting asset *n* an unreplaceable business asset of limited life, such as a coal mine or an oil well.

wastrel ('weɪstrəl) *n* **1** a wasteful person; spendthrift; prodigal. **2** an idler or vagabond.

Wast Water (wɒst) *n* a lake in NW England, in Cumbria in the Lake District. Length: 5 km (3 miles).

wat (wɑːt) *n* a Thai Buddhist monastery or temple. [Thai, from Sanskrit *vāta* enclosure]

watap (wæ'tɑːp, wɑː-) *n* a stringy thread made by North American Indians from the roots of various conifers and used for weaving and sewing. [C18: from Canadian French, from Cree *watapiy*]

watch (wɒtʃ) *vb* **1** to look at or observe closely or attentively. **2** (*intr;* foll. by *for*) to wait attentively or expectantly. **3** to guard or tend (something) closely or carefully. **4** (*intr*) to keep vigil. **5** (*tr*) to maintain an interest in: *to watch the progress of a child at school.* **6 watch it!** be careful! look out! ◆ *n* **7a** a small portable timepiece, usually worn strapped to the wrist (a **wristwatch**) or in a waistcoat pocket. **7b** (*as modifier*): *a watch spring.* **8** the act or an instance of watching. **9** a period of vigil, esp. during the night. **10** (formerly) one of a set of periods of any of various lengths into which the night was divided. **11** *Nautical.* **11a** any of the usually four-hour periods beginning at midnight and again at noon during which part of a ship's crew are on duty. **11b** those officers and crew on duty during a specified watch. **12** the period during which a guard is on duty. **13** (formerly) a watchman or band of watchmen. **14 on the watch.** on the lookout; alert. ◆ See also **watch out.** [Old English *wæccan* (vb), *wæcce* (n); related to WAKE[1]]

-watch *suffix of nouns.* indicating a regular television programme or newspaper feature on the topic specified: *Crimewatch.*

watchable ('wɒtʃəbᵊl) *adj* **1** capable of being watched. **2** interesting, enjoyable, or entertaining: *a watchable television documentary.*

watchband ('wɒtʃˌbænd) *n* a U.S., Canadian, and Australian word for **watchstrap.**

watch cap *n* a knitted navy-blue woollen cap worn by seamen in cold weather.

watchcase ('wɒtʃˌkeɪs) *n* a protective case for a watch, generally of metal such as gold, silver, brass, or gunmetal.

watch chain *n* a chain used for fastening a pocket watch to the clothing. See also **fob**[1].

Watch Committee *n Brit. history.* a local government committee composed of magistrates and representatives of the county borough council responsible for the efficiency of the local police force.

watchdog ('wɒtʃˌdɒg) *n* **1** a dog kept to guard property. **2a** a person or group of persons that acts as a protector or guardian against inefficiency, illegal practices, etc. **2b** (*as modifier*): *a watchdog committee.*

watcher ('wɒtʃə) *n* **1** a person who watches. **2** a person who maintains a vigil at the bedside of an invalid. **3** *U.S.* a representative of a candidate or party stationed at a poll on election day to watch out for fraud.

watch fire *n* a fire kept burning at night as a signal or for warmth and light by a person keeping watch.

watchful ('wɒtʃfʊl) *adj* **1** vigilant or alert. **2** *Archaic.* not sleeping. ▶ **'watchfully** *adv* ▶ **'watchfulness** *n*

watch-glass *n* **1** a curved glass disc that covers the dial of a watch. **2** a similarly shaped piece of glass used in laboratories for evaporating small samples of a solution, etc.

watchmaker ('wɒtʃˌmeɪkə) *n* a person who makes or mends watches. ▶ **'watchˌmaking** *n*

watchman ('wɒtʃmən) *n, pl* **-men.** **1** a person employed to guard buildings or property. **2** (formerly) a man employed to patrol or guard the streets at night.

watch night *n* (in Protestant churches) **1a** the night of December 24, during which a service is held to mark the arrival of Christmas Day. **1b** the night of December 31, during which a service is held to mark the passing of the old year and the beginning of the new. **2** the service held on either of these nights.

watch out *vb* **1** (*intr, adv*) to be careful or on one's guard. ◆ *n* **watchout.** **2** a less common word for **lookout** (sense 1).

watchstrap ('wɒtʃˌstræp) *n* a strap of leather, cloth, etc., attached to a watch for fastening it around the wrist. Also called (U.S. and Canadian): **watchband.**

watchtower ('wɒtʃˌtaʊə) *n* a tower on which a sentry keeps watch.

watchword ('wɒtʃˌwɜːd) *n* **1** another word for **password.** **2** a rallying cry or slogan.

water ('wɔːtə) *n* **1** a clear colourless tasteless odourless liquid that is essential for plant and animal life and constitutes, in impure form, rain, oceans, rivers, lakes, etc. It is a neutral substance, an effective solvent for many compounds, and is used as a standard for many physical properties. Formula: H_2O. Related adj: **aqueous.** Related combining forms: **hydro-, aqua-.** **2a** any body or area of this liquid, such as a sea, lake, river, etc. **2b** (*as modifier*): *water sports; water transport; a water plant.* Related adj: **aquatic.** **3** the surface of such a body or area: *fish swam below the water.* **4** any form or variety of this liquid, such as rain. **5** See **high water, low water.** **6** any of various solutions of chemical substances in water: *lithia water; ammonia water.* **7** *Physiol.* **7a** any fluid secreted from the body, such as sweat, urine, or tears. **7b** (*usually pl*) the amniotic fluid surrounding a fetus in the womb. **8** a wavy lustrous finish on some fabrics, esp. silk. **9** *Archaic.* the degree of brilliance in a diamond. See also **first water.** **10** excellence, quality, or degree (in the phrase **of the first water**). **11** *Finance.* **11a** capital stock issued without a corresponding increase in paid-up capital, so that the book value of the company's capital is not fully represented by assets or earning power. **11b** the fictitious or unrealistic asset entries that reflect such inflated book value of capital. **12** (*modifier*) *Astrology.* of or relating to the three signs of the zodiac Cancer, Scorpio, and Pisces. Compare **air** (sense 19), **earth** (sense 10), **fire** (sense 24). **13 above the water.** *Informal.* out of trouble or difficulty, esp. financial trouble. **14 hold water.** to prove credible, logical, or consistent: *the alibi did not hold water.* **15 in deep water.** in trouble or difficulty. **16 make water.** **16a** to urinate. **16b** (of a boat, hull, etc.) to let in water. **17 pass water.** to urinate. **18 test the water.** See **test**[1] (sense 5). **19 throw** (*or* **pour**) **cold water on.** *Informal.* to be unenthusiastic about or discourage. **20 water under the bridge.** events that are past and done with. ◆ *vb* **21** (*tr*) to sprinkle, moisten, or soak with water. **22** (*tr;* often foll. by *down*) to weaken by the addition of water. **23** (*intr*) (of the eyes) to fill with tears. **24** (*intr*) (of the mouth) to salivate, esp. in anticipation of food (esp. in the phrase **make one's mouth water**). **25** (*tr*) to irrigate or provide with water: *to water the land; he watered the cattle.* **26** (*intr*) to drink water. **27** (*intr*) (of a ship, etc.) to take in a supply of water. **28** (*tr*) *Finance.* to raise the par value of (issued capital stock) without a corresponding increase in the real value of assets. **29** (*tr*) to produce a wavy lustrous finish on (fabrics, esp. silk). ◆ See also **water down.** [Old English *wæter,* of Germanic origin; compare Old Saxon *watar,* Old High German *wazzar,* Gothic *watō,* Old Slavonic *voda;* related to Greek *hudor*] ▶ **'waterer** *n* ▶ **'waterish** *adj* ▶ **'waterless** *adj* ▶ **'water-ˌlike** *adj*

waterage ('wɔːtərɪdʒ) *n Brit.* the transportation of cargo by means of ships, or the charges for such transportation.

water back *n* the U.S. name for **back boiler.**

water bag *n* a bag, sometimes made of skin, leather, etc., but in Australia usually canvas, for holding, carrying, and keeping water cool.

water bailiff *n* an official responsible for enforcing laws on river management and fishing.

water-bath *n Chem.* a vessel containing heated water, used for heating substances.

water bear *n* another name for a **tardigrade.**

water bed *n* a waterproof mattress filled with water.

water beetle *n* any of various beetles of the families *Dysticidae, Hydrophilidae,* etc., that live most of the time in freshwater ponds, rivers, etc. See **whirligig beetle.**

water bird *n* any aquatic bird, including the wading and swimming birds.

water biscuit *n* a thin crisp plain biscuit, usually served with butter or cheese.

water blister *n* a blister containing watery or serous fluid, without any blood or pus.

water boatman *n* any of various aquatic bugs of the families *Notonectidae* and *Corixidae,* having a flattened body and oarlike hind legs, adapted for swimming.

waterborne ('wɔːtəˌbɔːn) *adj* **1** floating or travelling on water. **2** (of a disease, etc.) transported or transmitted by water.

water bottle *n* any of various types of container for drinking water, such as a skin or leather bag used in some countries, a glass bottle for table use, or a flask used by soldiers or travellers.
waterbrain ('wɔːtəˌbreɪn) *n Vet. science.* another name for **gid.**
water brash *n Pathol.* another term for **heartburn.**
waterbuck ('wɔːtəˌbʌk) *n* any of various antelopes of the genus *Kobus,* esp. *K. ellipsiprymnus,* of swampy areas of Africa, having long curved ridged horns.
water buffalo *or* **ox** *n* a member of the cattle tribe, *Bubalus bubalis,* of swampy regions of S Asia, having widely spreading back-curving horns. Domesticated forms are used as draught animals. Also called: **Asiatic buffalo, Indian buffalo, carabao.**
water bug *n* any of various heteropterous insects adapted to living in the water or on its surface, esp. any of the family *Belostomatidae* (**giant water bugs**), of North America, India, and southern Africa, which have flattened hairy legs.
water butt *n* a barrel for collecting rainwater, esp. from a drainpipe.
water cannon *n* an apparatus for pumping water through a nozzle at high pressure, used in quelling riots.
Water Carrier *or* **Bearer** *n* **the.** the constellation Aquarius, the 11th sign of the zodiac.
water chestnut *n* **1** Also called: **water caltrop.** a floating aquatic onagraceous plant, *Trapa natans,* of Asia, having four-pronged edible nutlike fruits. **2 Chinese water chestnut.** a Chinese cyperaceous plant, *Eleocharis tuberosa,* with an edible succulent corm. **3** the corm of the Chinese water chestnut, used in Oriental cookery.
water chinquapin *n* a North American aquatic plant, *Nelumbo lutea,* having large umbrella-shaped leaves, pale yellow flowers, and edible nutlike seeds: family *Nelumbonaceae.* Compare **chinquapin.**
water clock *or* **glass** *n* any of various devices for measuring time that use the escape of water as the motive force.
water closet *n* **1** a lavatory flushed by water. **2** a small room that has a lavatory. ♦ Usually abbreviated to **WC.**
watercolour *or U.S.* **watercolor** ('wɔːtəˌkʌlə) *n* **1a** Also called: **pure watercolour.** water-soluble pigment, applied in transparent washes and without the admixture of white pigment in the lighter tones. **1b** any water-soluble pigment, including opaque kinds such as gouache and tempera. **2a** a painting done in watercolours. **2b** *(as modifier): a watercolour masterpiece.* **3** the art or technique of painting with such pigments. ▸ **'waterˌcolourist** *or U.S.* **'waterˌcolorist** *n*
water-cool *vb (tr)* to cool (an engine, etc.) by a flow of water circulating in an enclosed jacket. Compare **air-cool.** ▸ **'water-ˌcooled** *adj* ▸ **'water-ˌcooling** *adj*
water cooler *n* a device for cooling and dispensing drinking water.
watercourse ('wɔːtəˌkɔːs) *n* **1** a stream, river, or canal. **2** the channel, bed, or route along which this flows.
watercraft ('wɔːtəˌkrɑːft) *n* **1** a boat or ship or such vessels collectively. **2** skill in handling boats or in water sports.
water crake *n* another name for **spotted crake** and **dipper** (the bird).
watercress ('wɔːtəˌkres) *n* **1** an Old World cruciferous plant, *Rorippa nasturtium-aquaticum* (or *Nasturtium officinale*), of clear ponds and streams, having pungent leaves that are used in salads and as a garnish. **2** any of several similar or related plants.
water cure *n* **1** *Med.* a nontechnical name for **hydropathy** or **hydrotherapy.** **2** *Informal.* a form of torture in which the victim is forced to drink very large amounts of water.
water cycle *n* the circulation of the earth's water, in which water evaporates from the sea into the atmosphere, where it condenses and falls as rain or snow, returning to the sea by rivers or returning to the atmosphere by evapotranspiration. Also called: **hydrologic cycle.**
water diviner *n Brit.* a person able to locate the presence of water, esp. underground, with a divining rod. U.S. name: **waterfinder.**
water dog *n* **1** a dog trained to hunt in water. **2** *Informal.* a dog or person who enjoys going in or on the water.
water down *vb (tr, adv)* **1** to dilute or weaken with water. **2** to modify or adulterate, esp. so as to omit anything harsh, unpleasant, or offensive: *to water down the truth.* ▸ **ˌwatered-'down** *adj*
water dropwort *n* See **dropwort** (sense 2).
waterfall ('wɔːtəˌfɔːl) *n* a cascade of falling water where there is a vertical or almost vertical step in a river.
water flea *n* any of numerous minute freshwater branchiopod crustaceans of the order *Cladocera,* which swim by means of hairy branched antennae. See also **daphnia.**
Waterford ('wɔːtəfəd) *n* **1** a county of S Republic of Ireland, in Munster province on the Atlantic: mountainous in the centre and in the northwest. County town: Waterford. Pop.: 95 000 (1996). Area: 1838 sq. km (710 sq. miles). **2** a port in S Republic of Ireland, county town of Co. Waterford: famous glass industry; fishing. Pop.: 40 345 (1991).
waterfowl ('wɔːtəˌfaʊl) *n* **1** any aquatic freshwater bird, esp. any species of the family *Anatidae* (ducks, geese, and swans). **2** such birds collectively.
waterfront ('wɔːtəˌfrʌnt) *n* the area of a town or city alongside a body of water, such as a harbour or dockyard.
water gap *n* a deep valley in a ridge, containing a stream.
water gas *n* a mixture of hydrogen and carbon monoxide produced by passing steam over hot carbon, used as a fuel and raw material. See also **producer gas.**
water gate *n* **1** a gate in a canal, leat, etc. that can be opened or closed to control the flow of water. **2** a gate through which access may be gained to a body of water.
Watergate ('wɔːtəˌgeɪt) *n* **1** an incident during the 1972 U.S. presidential campaign, when a group of agents employed by the re-election organization of President Richard Nixon were caught breaking into the Democratic Party headquarters in the Watergate building, Washington, DC. The consequent political scandal was exacerbated by attempts to conceal the fact that senior White House officials had approved the burglary, and eventually forced the resignation of President Nixon. **2** any similar public scandal, esp. involving politicians or a possible cover-up. See also **-gate.**
water gauge *n* an instrument that indicates the presence or the quantity of water in a tank, reservoir, or boiler feed. Also called: **water glass.**
water glass *n* **1** a viscous syrupy solution of sodium silicate in water: used as a protective coating for cement and a preservative, esp. for eggs. **2** another name for **water clock** or **water gauge.**
water gum *n* **1** any of several gum trees, esp. *Nyssa biflora* (or *tupelo*), of swampy areas of North America: family *Nyssaceae.* **2** any of several Australian myrtaceous trees, esp. *Tristania laurina,* of swampy ground.
water gun *n* another term (esp. U.S.) for **water pistol.**
water hammer *n* a sharp concussion produced when the flow of water in a pipe is suddenly blocked.
water hemlock *n* another name for **cowbane** (sense 1).
water hen *n* another name for **gallinule.**
water hole *n* **1** a depression, such as a pond or pool, containing water, esp. one used by animals as a drinking place. **2** a source of drinking water in a desert.
Waterhouse ('wɔːtəˌhaʊs) *n* **1 Alfred.** 1830–1905, British architect; a leader of the Gothic Revival. His buildings include Manchester Town Hall (1868) and the Natural History Museum, London (1881). **2 George Marsden.** 1824–1906, New Zealand statesman, born in England: prime minister of New Zealand (1872–73). **3 Keith (Spencer).** born 1929, British novelist, dramatist, and journalist: best known for the novel *Billy Liar* (1959) and his collaborations with the dramatist Willis Hall (born 1929).
water hyacinth *n* a floating aquatic plant, *Eichhornia crassipes,* of tropical America, having showy bluish-purple flowers and swollen leafstalks: family *Pontederiaceae.* It forms dense masses in rivers, ponds, etc., and is a serious problem in the southern U.S., Australia, and parts of Africa.
water ice *n* an ice cream made from a frozen sugar syrup flavoured with fruit juice or purée; sorbet.
watering can *n* a container with a handle and a spout with a perforated nozzle used to sprinkle water over plants.
watering hole *n* **1** a pool where animals drink; water hole. **2** *Facetious slang.* a pub.
watering place *n* **1** a place where drinking water for men or animals may be obtained. **2** *Brit.* a spa. **3** *Brit.* a seaside resort.
watering pot *n* another name (U.S.) for **watering can.**
water jacket *n* a water-filled envelope or container surrounding a machine, engine, or part for cooling purposes, esp. the casing around the cylinder block of a pump or internal-combustion engine. Compare **air jacket.**
water jump *n* a ditch, brook, or pond over which athletes or horses must jump in a steeplechase or similar contest.
water level *n* **1** the level reached by the surface of a body of water. **2** the water line of a boat or ship.
water lily *n* **1** any of various aquatic plants of the genus *Nymphaea* and related genera, of temperate and tropical regions, having large leaves and showy flowers that float on the surface of the water: family *Nymphaeaceae.* **2** any of various similar and related plants, such as the yellow water lily.
water line *n* **1** a line marked at the level around a vessel's hull to which the vessel will be immersed when afloat. **2** a line marking the level reached by a body of water.
waterlogged ('wɔːtəˌlɒgd) *adj* **1** saturated with water. **2** (of a vessel still afloat) having taken in so much water as to be unmanageable.
Waterloo (ˌwɔːtə'luː) *n* **1** a small town in central Belgium, in Walloon Brabant province south of Brussels: battle (1815) fought nearby in which British and Prussian forces under the Duke of Wellington and Blücher routed the French under Napoleon. Pop.: 17 800 (latest est.). **2** a total or crushing defeat (esp. in **meet one's Waterloo**).
water louse *n* an aquatic isopod of the genus *Asellus,* common in weedy water. Also called: **water slater.**
water main *n* a principal supply pipe in an arrangement of pipes for distributing water.
waterman ('wɔːtəmən) *n, pl* **-men.** a skilled boatman. ▸ **'watermanˌship** *n*
watermark ('wɔːtəˌmɑːk) *n* **1** a distinguishing mark impressed on paper during manufacture, visible when the paper is held up to the light. **2** another word for **water line** (senses 1, 2). ♦ *vb (tr)* **3** to mark (paper) with a watermark.
water meadow *n* a meadow that remains fertile by being periodically flooded by a stream.
water measurer *n* a slender heteropterous bug, *Hydrometra stagnorum,* that has a greatly elongated head and is found on still or sluggish water where it preys on water fleas, mosquito larvae, etc.
watermelon ('wɔːtəˌmɛlən) *n* **1** an African melon, *Citrullus vulgaris,* widely cultivated for its large edible fruit. **2** the fruit of this plant, which has a hard green rind and sweet watery reddish flesh.
water meter *n* a device for measuring the quantity or rate of water flowing through a pipe.
water milfoil *n* any of various pond plants of the genus *Myriophyllum,* having feathery underwater leaves and small inconspicuous flowers: family *Haloragidaceae.*
water mill *n* a mill operated by a water wheel.
water mint *n* a Eurasian mint plant, *Mentha aquatica,* of marshy places, having scented leaves and whorls of small flowers.
water moccasin *n* a large dark grey venomous snake, *Agkistrodon piscivorus,*

of swamps in the southern U.S.: family *Crotalidae* (pit vipers). Also called: **cottonmouth.**

water nymph *n* **1** any fabled nymph of the water, such as the Naiad, Nereid, or Oceanid of Greek mythology. **2** any of various aquatic plants, esp. a water lily or a naiad.

water of crystallization *n* water present in the crystals of certain compounds. It is chemically combined in stoichiometric amounts, usually by coordinate or hydrogen bonds, but can often be easily expelled.

water ouzel *n* another name for **dipper** (the bird).

water ox *n* another term for **water buffalo.**

water paint *n* any water-based paint, such as an emulsion or an acrylic paint.

water parting *n* another term (esp. U.S.) for **watershed** (sense 1).

water pepper *n* any of several polygonaceous plants of the genus *Polygonum,* esp. *P. hydropiper,* of marshy regions, having reddish stems, clusters of small greenish flowers, and acrid-tasting leaves.

water pimpernel *n* another name for **brookweed.**

water pipe *n* **1** a pipe for water. **2** another name for **hookah.**

water pistol *n* a toy pistol that squirts a stream of water or other liquid. Also called (U.S.): **water gun.**

water plantain *n* any of several marsh plants of the genus *Alisma,* esp. *A. plantago-aquatica,* of N temperate regions and Australia, having clusters of small white or pinkish flowers and broad pointed leaves: family *Alismataceae.*

water polo *n* a game played in water by two teams of seven swimmers in which each side tries to throw or propel an inflated ball into the opponents' goal.

water power *n* **1** the power latent in a dynamic or static head of water as used to drive machinery, esp. for generating electricity. **2** a source of such power, such as a drop in the level of a river, etc. **3** the right to the use of water for such a purpose, as possessed by a water mill.

waterproof ('wɔːtəˌpruːf) *adj* **1** not penetrable by water. Compare **water-repellent, water-resistant.** ♦ *n* **2** *Chiefly Brit.* a waterproof garment, esp. a raincoat. ♦ *vb (tr)* **3** to make (a fabric, item of clothing, etc.) waterproof.

water purslane *n* **1** an onagraceous marsh plant, *Ludwigia palustris,* of temperate and warm regions, having reddish stems and small reddish flowers. **2** any of several lythraceous plants of wet places that resemble purslane, such as *Peplis portular* of Europe, which has small pinkish flowers, and *Didiplis diandris* of North America, which has small greenish flowers.

water rail *n* a large Eurasian rail, *Rallus aquaticus,* of swamps, ponds, etc., having a long red bill.

water rat *n* **1** any of several small amphibious rodents, esp. the water vole or the muskrat. **2** any of various amphibious rats of the subfamily *Hydromyinae,* of New Guinea, the Philippines, and Australia. **3** *Informal.* a person who is very fond of water sports.

water-repellent *adj* (of fabrics, garments, etc.) having a finish that resists the absorption of water.

water-resistant *adj* (esp. of fabrics) designed to resist but not entirely prevent the penetration of water.

water right *n* the right to make use of a water supply, as for irrigation.

Waters ('wɔːtəz) *n* **Muddy,** real name *McKinley Morganfield.* 1915–83, U.S. blues guitarist, singer, and songwriter. His songs include "Rollin' Stone" (1948) and "Got my Mojo Working" (1954).

water sapphire *n* a deep blue variety of the mineral cordierite that occurs in Sri Lanka: used as a gemstone.

waterscape ('wɔːtəˌskeɪp) *n* a picture, view, or representation of a body of water.

water scorpion *n* any of various long-legged aquatic insects of the heteropterous family *Nepidae,* which breathe by means of a long spinelike tube that projects from the rear of the body and penetrates the surface of the water.

water seal *n* a small amount of water contained in the trap of a drain to prevent the passage of foul smells.

watershed ('wɔːtəˌʃɛd) *n* **1** the dividing line between two adjacent river systems, such as a ridge. **2** an important period or factor that serves as a dividing line.

water shield *n* **1** a North American nymphaeaceous plant, *Brasenia schreberi,* with floating oval leaves and purple flowers. **2** any of several similar and related plants of the genus *Cabomba.*

water shrew *n* either of two small amphibious shrews, *Neomys fodiens* (**European water shrew**) or *N. anomalus* (**Mediterranean water shrew**), having a dark pelage with paler underparts.

water-sick *adj* (of land) made infertile or uncultivable by excessive irrigation.

waterside ('wɔːtəˌsaɪd) *n* **a** the area of land beside a body of water. **b** (*as modifier*): *waterside houses.*

watersider ('wɔːtəˌsaɪdə) *n Austral. and N.Z.* a wharf labourer.

water-ski *n also* **water ski. 1** a type of ski used for planing or gliding over water. ♦ *vb* **-skis, -skiing, -skied** *or* **-ski'd. 2** *(intr)* to ride over water on a water-ski or water-skis while holding a rope towed by a speedboat. ▸ **'water-ˌskier** *n* ▸ **'water-ˌskiing** *n*

water snake *n* any of various colubrid snakes that live in or near water, esp. any of numerous harmless North American snakes of the genus *Natrix,* such as *N. sipedon.*

water-soak *vb (tr)* to soak or drench with or in water.

water softener *n* **1** any substance that lessens the hardness of water, usually by precipitating or absorbing calcium and magnesium ions. **2** a tank, apparatus, or chemical plant that is used to filter or treat water to remove chemicals that cause hardness.

water soldier *n* an aquatic plant, *Stratiotes aloides,* of Europe and NW Asia, having rosettes of large leaves and large three-petalled white flowers: family *Hydrocharitaceae.*

water spaniel *n* either of two large curly-coated breeds of spaniel (the Irish and the American), which are used for hunting waterfowl. See also **Irish water spaniel.**

water spider *n* a Eurasian spider, *Argyroneta aquatica,* that spins a web in the form of an air-filled chamber in which it lives submerged in streams and ponds.

water splash *n* a place where a stream runs over a road.

water sports *pl n* **1** various sports, such as swimming, water-skiing, or windsurfing, that take place in or on water. **2** *Slang.* sexual practices that involve urination.

waterspout ('wɔːtəˌspaʊt) *n* **1** *Meteorol.* **1a** a tornado occurring over water that forms a column of water and mist extending between the surface and the clouds above. **1b** a sudden downpour of heavy rain. **2** a pipe or channel through which water is discharged, esp. one used for drainage from the gutters of a roof.

water starwort *n* See **starwort** (sense 2).

water stick insect *n* a slender sticklike flightless water bug, *Ranatra linearis,* that is predatory on small creatures such as water fleas.

water strider *or* **skater** *n* another name for a **pond-skater.**

water supply *n* **1** an arrangement of reservoirs, purification plant, distribution pipes, etc., for providing water to a community. **2** the supply of treated and purified water for a community.

water system *n* **1** a river and all its tributaries. **2** a system for supplying water to a community.

water table *n* **1** the surface of the water-saturated part of the ground, usually following approximately the contours of the overlying land surface. **2** an offset or string course that has a moulding designed to throw rainwater clear of the wall below.

water thrush *n* either of two North American warblers, *Seiurus motacilla* or *S. noveboracensis,* having a brownish back and striped underparts and occurring near water.

watertight ('wɔːtəˌtaɪt) *adj* **1** not permitting the passage of water either in or out: *a watertight boat.* **2** without loopholes: *a watertight argument.* **3** kept separate from other subjects or influences: *different disciplines are often thought of in watertight compartments.* ▸ **'waterˌtightness** *n*

water torture *n* any of various forms of torture using water, esp. one in which water drips or is slowly poured onto the victim's forehead.

water tower *n* a reservoir or storage tank mounted on a tower-like structure at the summit of an area of high ground in a place where the water pressure would otherwise be inadequate for distribution at a uniform pressure.

water tube boiler *n* a steam generator consisting of water drums and steam drums connected by banks of tubes through which the water is circulated. The tubes are exposed to the hot gases of the furnace and the heat transfer rate is high.

water vapour *n* water in the gaseous state, esp. when due to evaporation at a temperature below the boiling point. Compare **steam.**

water vole *n* a large amphibious vole, *Arvicola terrestris,* of Eurasian river banks: family *Cricetidae.* Also called: **water rat.**

water wagtail *n* another name for **pied wagtail.**

waterway ('wɔːtəˌweɪ) *n* a river, canal, or other navigable channel used as a means of travel or transport.

waterweed ('wɔːtəˌwiːd) *n* **1** any of various weedy aquatic plants. **2** another name for **pondweed** (sense 2).

water wheel *n* **1** a simple water-driven turbine consisting of a wheel having vanes set axially across its rim, used to drive machinery. **2** a wheel with buckets attached to its rim for raising water from a stream, pond, etc.

water wings *pl n* an inflatable rubber device shaped like a pair of wings, which is placed round the front of the body and under the arms of a person learning to swim.

water witch *n* a person who claims the ability to detect water underground by means of a divining rod.

waterworks ('wɔːtəˌwɜːks) *n* **1** *(functioning as sing)* an establishment for storing, purifying, and distributing water for community supply. **2** *(functioning as pl)* a display of water in movement, as in fountains. **3** *(functioning as pl) Brit. informal euphemism.* the urinary system, esp. with reference to its normal functioning: *he has trouble with his waterworks.* **4** *(functioning as pl) Informal.* crying; tears.

waterworn ('wɔːtəˌwɔːn) *adj* worn smooth by the action or passage of water.

watery ('wɔːtərɪ) *adj* **1** relating to, consisting of, containing, or resembling water. **2** discharging or secreting water or a water-like fluid: *a watery wound.* **3** tearful; weepy. **4** insipid, thin, or weak. ▸ **'wateriness** *n*

Watford ('wɒtfəd) *n* a town in SE England, in SW Hertfordshire: printing. Pop.: 113 080 (1991).

Watling Island ('wɒtlɪŋ) *n* another name for **San Salvador Island.**

Watson ('wɒtsən) *n* **1 James Dewey.** born 1928, U.S. biologist, whose contribution to the discovery of the helical structure of DNA won him a Nobel prize for physiology or medicine shared with Francis Crick and Maurice Wilkins in 1962. **2 John B(roadus).** 1878–1958, U.S. psychologist; a leading exponent of behaviourism. **3 John Christian.** 1867–1941, Australian statesman, born in Chile: prime minister of Australia (1904). **4 Tom,** full name *Thomas Sturges Watson.* born 1949, U.S. golfer: won the U.S. Open Championship (1982), the British Open Championship (1975, 1977, 1980, 1982, 1983), and the World Series (1975, 1977, 1980).

Watson-Watt ('wɒtsən'wɒt) *n* Sir **Robert Alexander.** 1892–1973, Scottish physicist, who played a leading role in the development of radar.

watt (wɒt) *n* the derived SI unit of power, equal to 1 joule per second; the power dissipated by a current of 1 ampere flowing across a potential difference of 1 volt. 1 watt is equivalent to 1.341×10^{-3} horsepower. Symbol: W **[C19:** named after J. WATT**]**

Watt (wɒt) *n* **James.** 1736–1819, Scottish engineer and inventor. His fundamental improvements to the steam engine led to the widespread use of steam power in industry.

wattage ('wɒtɪdʒ) *n* **1** power, esp. electric power, measured in watts. **2** the power rating, measured in watts, of an electrical appliance.

Watteau ('wɒtəʊ; *French* vato) *n* **Jean-Antoine** (ʒɑ̃ ɑ̃twan). 1684–1721, French painter, esp. of *fêtes champêtres.*

Watteau back *n* a section at the back of a woman's dress that is caught in pleats or gathers at the neck and falls unbelted to the floor.

Wattenscheid (*German* 'vatənʃait) *n* an industrial town in NW Germany, in North Rhine-Westphalia east of Essen. Pop.: 81 200 (latest est.).

watt-hour *n* a unit of energy equal to a power of one watt operating for one hour. 1 watt-hour equals 3600 joules.

wattle ('wɒtᵊl) *n* **1** a frame of rods or stakes interwoven with twigs, branches, etc., esp. when used to make fences. **2** the material used in such a construction. **3** a loose fold of skin, often brightly coloured, hanging from the neck or throat of certain birds, lizards, etc. **4** any of various chiefly Australian acacia trees having spikes of small brightly coloured flowers and flexible branches, which were used by early settlers for making fences. See also **golden wattle. 5** a southern African caesalpinaceous tree, *Peltophorum africanum,* with yellow flowers. ◆ *vb* (*tr*) **6** to construct from wattle. **7** to bind or frame with wattle. **8** to weave or twist (branches, twigs, etc.) into a frame. ◆ *adj* **9** made of, formed by, or covered with wattle. [Old English *watol;* related to *wethel* wrap, Old High German *wadal,* German *Wedel*] ▸ **'wattled** *adj*

wattle and daub *n* **a** a form of wall construction consisting of interwoven twigs plastered with a mixture of clay, lime, water, and sometimes dung and chopped straw. **b** (*as modifier*): *a wattle-and-daub hut.*

wattlebird ('wɒtᵊl,bɜːd) *n* **1** any of various Australian honeyeaters of the genus *Anthochaera,* such as *A. paradoxa* (**yellow wattlebird**), that have red or yellow wattles on both sides of the head. **2** any arboreal New Zealand songbird of the family *Callaeidae,* having wattles on both sides of the bill.

wattmeter ('wɒt,miːtə) *n* a meter for measuring electric power in watts.

Watts (wɒts) *n* **1 George Frederick.** 1817–1904, English painter and sculptor, noted esp. for his painting *Hope* (1886) and his sculpture *Physical Energy* (1904) in Kensington Gardens, London. **2 Isaac.** 1674–1748, English hymn-writer.

Watusi (wə'tuːzɪ) *or* **Watutsi** (wə'tʊtsɪ) *n, pl* **-sis** *or* **-si.** a member of a cattle-owning Negroid people of Rwanda and Burundi in Africa.

Waugh (wɔː) *n* **Evelyn** (**Arthur St. John**) ('iːvlɪn). 1903–66, English novelist. His early satirical novels include *Decline and Fall* (1928), *Vile Bodies* (1930), *A Handful of Dust* (1934), and *Scoop* (1938). His later novels include the more sombre *Brideshead Revisited* (1945) and the trilogy of World War II *Men at Arms* (1952), *Officers and Gentlemen* (1955), and *Unconditional Surrender* (1961).

wauk[1] (wɔːk) *vb* a Scot. word for **wake**[1].

wauk[2] *or* **waulk** (wɔːk) *vb* (*tr*) *Scot.* to full (cloth). [C15: variant of WALK]

waul *or* **wawl** (wɔːl) *vb* (*intr*) to cry or wail plaintively like a cat. [C16: of imitative origin]

waur[1] (wɔːr) *adj, n, adv* a Scot. word for **worse.**

waur[2] (wɔːr) *adj* a Scot. word for **wary.**

wave (weɪv) *vb* **1** to move or cause to move freely to and fro: *the banner waved in the wind.* **2** (*intr*) to move the hand to and fro as a greeting. **3** to signal or signify by or as if by waving something. **4** (*tr*) to direct to move by or as if by waving something: *he waved me on.* **5** to form or be formed into curves, undulations, etc. **6** (*tr*) to give a wavy or watered appearance to (silk, etc.). **7** (*tr*) to set waves in (the hair). ◆ *n* **8** one of a sequence of ridges or undulations that moves across the surface of a body of a liquid, esp. the sea: created by the wind or a moving object and gravity. **9** any undulation on or at the edge of a surface reminiscent of such a wave: *a wave across the field of corn.* **10 the waves.** the sea. **11** anything that suggests the movement of a wave, as by a sudden rise: *a crime wave.* **12** a widespread movement that advances in a body: *a wave of settlers swept into the country.* **13** the act or an instance of waving. **14** *Physics.* an oscillation propagated through a medium or space such that energy is periodically interchanged between two kinds of disturbance. For example, an oscillating electric field generates a magnetic oscillation and vice versa, hence an electromagnetic wave is produced. Similarly a wave on a liquid comprises vertical and horizontal displacements. See also **antinode, longitudinal wave, node, standing wave, transverse wave. 15** *Physics.* a graphical representation of a wave obtained by plotting the magnitude of the disturbance against time at a particular point in the medium or space; waveform. **16** a prolonged spell of some weather condition: *a heat wave.* **17** an undulating curve or series of curves or loose curls in the hair. **18** an undulating pattern or finish on a fabric. **19** short for **wave moth. 20 make waves.** to cause trouble; disturb the status quo. [Old English *wafian* (vb); related to Old High German *weban* to WEAVE, Old Norse *vafra;* see WAVER; C16 (n) changed from earlier *wāwe,* probably from Old English *wǣg* motion; compare WAG[1]] ▸ **'waveless** *adj* ▸ **'wave,like** *adj*

waveband ('weɪv,bænd) *n* a range of wavelengths or frequencies used for a particular type of radio transmission.

wave-cut platform *n* a flat surface at the base of a cliff formed by erosion by waves.

wave down *vb* (*tr, adv*) to signal with a wave to (a driver or vehicle) to stop.

wave energy *n* energy obtained by harnessing wave power.

wave equation *n Physics.* a partial differential equation describing wave motion. It has the form $\nabla^2\phi = (1/c^2) \times (\partial^2\phi/\partial t^2)$, where ∇^2 is the Laplace operator, *t* the time, *c* the velocity of propagation, and ϕ is a function characterizing the displacement of the wave.

waveform ('weɪv,fɔːm) *n Physics.* the shape of the graph of a wave or oscillation obtained by plotting the value of some changing quantity against time.

wavefront ('weɪv,frʌnt) *n Physics.* a surface associated with a propagating wave and passing through all points in the wave that have the same phase. It is usually perpendicular to the direction of propagation.

wave function *n Physics.* a mathematical function of position and sometimes time, used in wave mechanics to describe the state of a physical system. Symbol: ψ

waveguide ('weɪv,gaɪd) *n Electronics.* a solid rod of dielectric or a hollow metal tube, usually of rectangular cross section, used as a path to guide microwaves.

wavelength ('weɪv,leŋθ) *n* **1** the distance, measured in the direction of propagation, between two points of the same phase in consecutive cycles of a wave. Symbol: λ **2** the wavelength of the carrier wave used by a particular broadcasting station. **3 on someone's** (*or* **the same**) **wavelength.** *Informal.* having similar views, feelings, or thoughts (as someone else).

wavelet ('weɪvlɪt) *n* a small wave.

Wavell ('weɪvᵊl) *n* **Archibald** (**Percival**), 1st Earl. 1883–1950, British field marshal. During World War II he was commander in chief in the Middle East (1939–41), defeating the Italians in N Africa. He was commander in chief in India (1941–43) and viceroy of India (1943–47).

wavellite ('weɪvə,laɪt) *n* a greyish-white, yellow, or brown mineral consisting of hydrated basic aluminium phosphate in radiating clusters of small orthorhombic crystals. Formula: $Al_3(OH)_3(PO_4)_2.5H_2O$. [C19: named after William *Wavell* (died 1829), English physician]

wave mechanics *n* (*functioning as sing*) *Physics.* the formulation of quantum mechanics in which the behaviour of systems, such as atoms, is described in terms of their wave functions.

wavemeter ('weɪv,miːtə) *n* an instrument for measuring the frequency or wavelength of radio waves.

wave moth *n* any of several small geometrid moths with wavy markings, such as the **common wave** (*Deilinia exanthemata*), with grey-marked wings, and the lighter **common white wave** (*D. pusaria*). Often shortened to **wave.**

wave number *n Physics.* the reciprocal of the wavelength of a wave. Symbol: ν, σ

waveoff ('weɪv,ɒf) *n* a signal or instruction to an aircraft not to land.

wave power *n* power extracted from the motion of sea waves at the coast.

waver ('weɪvə) *vb* (*intr*) **1** to be irresolute; hesitate between two possibilities. **2** to become unsteady. **3** to fluctuate or vary. **4** to move back and forth or one way and another. **5** (of light) to flicker or flash. ◆ *n* **6** the act or an instance of wavering. [C14: from Old Norse *vafra* to flicker; related to German *wabern* to move about] ▸ **'waverer** *n* ▸ **'wavering** *adj* ▸ **'waveringly** *adv*

WAVES *or* **Waves** (weɪvz) *n* (in the U.S.) *acronym for* Women Accepted for Volunteer Emergency Service; the women's reserve of the U.S. navy.

wave speed *or* **velocity** *n* other names for **phase speed.**

wave theory *n* **1** the theory proposed by Huygens that light is transmitted by waves. **2** any theory that light or other radiation is transmitted as waves. See **electromagnetic wave.** ◆ Compare **corpuscular theory.**

wave train *n Physics.* a series of waves travelling in the same direction and spaced at regular intervals.

wavey ('weɪvɪ) *n Canadian.* a snow goose or other wild goose. Also called: **wawa.** [via Canadian French from Algonquian (Cree *wehwew*)]

wavy ('weɪvɪ) *adj* **wavier, waviest. 1** abounding in or full of waves. **2** moving or proceeding in waves or undulations. **3** (of hair) set in or having waves and curls. **4** unstable or wavering. ▸ **'wavily** *adv* ▸ **'waviness** *n*

waw (wɔː) *n* another name for **vav.**

wawa[1] ('wɑː,wɑː) *Canadian W coast slang.* ◆ *n* **1** speech; language. ◆ *vb* **2** (*intr*) to speak. [C19: from Chinook Jargon; probably of imitative origin]

wawa[2] ('wɑː,wɑː, 'wɑːwə) *n Canadian.* a variant of **wavey.**

wawl (wɔːl) *vb* a variant spelling of **waul.**

wax[1] (wæks) *n* **1** any of various viscous or solid materials of natural origin: characteristically lustrous, insoluble in water, and having a low softening temperature, they consist largely of esters of fatty acids. **2** any of various similar substances, such as paraffin wax or ozocerite, that have a mineral origin and consist largely of hydrocarbons. **3** short for **beeswax** or **sealing wax. 4** *Physiol.* another name for **cerumen. 5** a resinous preparation used by shoemakers to rub on thread. **6 bone wax.** a mixture of wax, oil, and carbolic acid applied to the cut surface of a bone to prevent bleeding. **7** any substance or object that is pliable or easily moulded: *he was wax in the hands of the political bosses.* **8** (*modifier*) made of or resembling wax: *a wax figure.* ◆ *vb* **9** (*tr*) to coat, polish, etc., with wax. [Old English *weax,* related to Old Saxon, Old High German *wahs,* Old Norse *vax*] ▸ **'waxer** *n* ▸ **'wax,like** *adj*

wax[2] (wæks) *vb* (*intr*) **1** to become larger, more powerful, etc. **2** (of the moon) to show a gradually increasing portion of illuminated surface, between new moon and full moon. Compare **wane** (sense 1). **3** *Archaic.* to become as specified: *the time waxed late.* [Old English *weaxan;* related to Old Frisian *waxa,* Old Saxon, Old High German *wahsan,* Gothic *wahsjan*]

wax[3] (wæks) *n Brit. informal, old-fashioned.* a fit of rage or temper: *he's in a wax today.* [of obscure origin; perhaps from the phrase *to wax angry*]

wax bean *n U.S.* any of certain string beans that have yellow waxy pods and are grown in the U.S.

waxberry ('wæksbərɪ, -brɪ) *n, pl* **-ries.** the waxy fruit of the wax myrtle or the snowberry.

waxbill ('wæks,bɪl) *n* any of various chiefly African finchlike weaverbirds of the genus *Estrilda* and related genera, having a brightly coloured bill and plumage.

wax cap *n* any fungus of the basidiomycetous family Hygrophoraceae, having thick waxy gills. Many are brightly coloured, like the **parrot toadstool** (*Hygrophorus psittacinus*), which is yellow with a covering of green slime, and the orange-red *H. conicus.*

waxcloth ('wæks,klɒθ) *n* **1** another name for **oilcloth. 2** another name for **linoleum.**

waxen[1] ('wæksən) *adj* **1** made of, treated with, or covered with wax. **2** resembling wax in colour or texture.

waxen[2] ('wæksən) *vb Archaic.* a past participle of **wax**[2].

waxeye ('wæks,aɪ) *n Austral. and N.Z.* another name for **white-eye.**

wax flower *n Austral.* any of several rutaceous shrubs of the genus *Eriostemon,* having waxy pink-white five-petalled flowers.

wax insect *n* any of various scale insects that secrete wax or a waxy substance, esp. the oriental species *Ceroplastes ceriferus,* which produces Chinese wax.

wax light *n* a candle or taper of wax.

wax moth *n* a brown pyralid moth, *Galleria mellonella,* the larvae of which feed on the combs of beehives. Also called: **honeycomb moth, bee moth.**

wax myrtle *n* a shrub, *Myrica cerifera,* of SE North America, having evergreen leaves and a small berry-like fruit with a waxy coating: family *Myricaceae.* Also called: **bayberry, candleberry, waxberry.**

wax palm *n* **1** a tall Andean palm tree, *Ceroxylon andicola,* having pinnate leaves that yield a resinous wax used in making candles. **2** another name for **carnauba** (sense 1).

wax paper *n* paper treated or coated with wax or paraffin to make it waterproof.

waxplant ('wæks,plɑːnt) *n* **1** a climbing asclepiadaceous shrub, *Hoya carnosa,* of E Asia and Australia, having fleshy leaves and clusters of small waxy white pink-centred flowers. **2** any of various similar plants of the genus *Hoya.*

wax tree *n* a Japanese anacardiaceous tree, *Rhus succedanea,* having white berries that yield wax.

waxwing ('wæks,wɪŋ) *n* any of several gregarious passerine songbirds of the genus *Bombycilla,* esp. *B. garrulus,* having red waxy wing tips and crested heads: family *Bombycillidae.*

waxwork ('wæks,wɜːk) *n* **1** an object reproduced in wax, esp. as an ornament. **2** a life-size lifelike figure, esp. of a famous person, reproduced in wax. **3** (*pl; functioning as sing or pl*) a museum or exhibition of wax figures or objects. ▸ **'wax,worker** *n*

waxy[1] ('wæksɪ) *adj* **waxier, waxiest. 1** resembling wax in colour, appearance, or texture. **2** made of, covered with, or abounding in wax. ▸ **'waxily** *adv* ▸ **'waxiness** *n*

waxy[2] ('wæksɪ) *adj* **waxier, waxiest.** *Brit. informal, old-fashioned.* bad-tempered or irritable; angry.

way (weɪ) *n* **1** a manner, method, or means: *a way of life; a way of knowing.* **2** a route or direction: *the way home.* **3a** a means or line of passage, such as a path or track. **3b** (*in combination*): *waterway.* **4** space or room for movement or activity (esp. in the phrases **make way, in the way, out of the way**). **5** distance, usually distance in general: *you've come a long way.* **6** a passage or journey: *on the way.* **7** characteristic style or manner: *I did it in my own way.* **8** (*often pl*) habits; idiosyncrasies: *he has some offensive ways.* **9** an aspect of something; particular: *in many ways he was right.* **10a** a street in or leading out of a town. **10b** (*cap. when part of a street name*): *Icknield Way.* **11** something that one wants in a determined manner (esp. in the phrases **get** *or* **have one's** (**own**) **way**). **12** the experience or sphere in which one comes into contact with things (esp. in the phrase **come one's way**). **13** *Informal.* a state or condition, usually financial or concerning health (esp. in the phrases **in a good** (*or* **bad**) **way**). **14** *Informal.* the area or direction of one's home: *drop in if you're ever over my way.* **15** movement of a ship or other vessel. **16** a right of way in law. **17** a guide along which something can be moved, such as the surface of a lathe along which the tailstock slides. **18** (*pl*) the wooden or metal tracks down which a ship slides to be launched. **19** a course of life including experiences, conduct, etc.: *the way of sin.* **20** *Archaic.* calling or trade. **21 by the way.** (*sentence modifier*) in passing or incidentally. **22 by way of. 22a** via. **22b** serving as: *by way of introduction.* **22c** in the state or condition of: *by way of being an artist.* **23 each way.** (of a bet) laid on a horse, dog, etc., to win or gain a place. **24 give way. 24a** to collapse or break down. **24b** to withdraw or yield. **25 give way to. 25a** to step aside for or stop for. **25b** to give full rein to (emotions, etc.). **26 go out of one's way.** to take considerable trouble or inconvenience oneself. **27 have a way with.** to have such a manner or skill as to handle successfully. **28 have it both ways.** to enjoy two things that would normally contradict each other or be mutually exclusive. **29 in a way.** in some respects. **30 in no way.** not at all. **31 lead the way. 31a** to go first. **31b** to set an example or precedent. **32 make one's way. 32a** to proceed or advance. **32b** to achieve success in life. **33 no way.** *Informal.* that is impossible. **34 on the way out.** *Informal.* **34a** becoming unfashionable, obsolete, etc. **34b** dying. **35 out of the way. 35a** removed or dealt with so as to be no longer a hindrance. **35b** remote. **35c** unusual and sometimes improper. **36 pay one's way.** See **pay** (sense 11). **37 see one's way** (**clear**). to find it possible and be willing (to do something). **38 the way.** *Irish.* so that: *I left early the way I would avoid the traffic.* **39 under way.** having started moving or making progress. ◆ *adv* **40** *Informal.* **40a** at a considerable distance or extent: *way over yonder.* **40b** very far: *they're way up the mountain.* **41** *Informal.* by far; considerably: *way better.* [Old English *weg;* related to Old Frisian *wei,* Old Norse *vegr,* Gothic *wigs*]

waybill ('weɪ,bɪl) *n* a document attached to goods in transit specifying their nature, point of origin, and destination as well as the route to be taken and the rate to be charged.

wayfarer ('weɪ,fɛərə) *n* a person who goes on a journey. ▸ **'way,faring** *n, adj*

wayfaring tree *n* a caprifoliaceous shrub, *Viburnum lantana,* of Europe and W Asia, having white flowers and berries that turn from red to black.

Wayland *or* **Wayland Smith** ('weɪlənd) *n* a smith, artificer, and king of the elves in European folklore. Scandinavian name: **Völund.** German name: **Wieland.**

waylay (weɪ'leɪ) *vb* **-lays, -laying, -laid.** (*tr*) **1** to lie in wait for and attack. **2** to await and intercept unexpectedly. [C16: from WAY + LAY[1]] ▸ **way'layer** *n*

wayleave ('weɪ,liːv) *n* access to property granted by a landowner for payment, for example to allow a contractor access to a building site.

wayleggo (,weɪlɛ'gəʊ) *interj N.Z.* away here! let go!; a shepherd's call to a dog on completion of a task.

waymark ('weɪ,mɑːk) *n* a symbol or signpost marking the route of a footpath. ▸ **'way,marked** *adj*

Wayne (weɪn) *n* **John,** real name *Marion Michael Morrison.* 1907–79, U.S. film actor, noted esp. for his many Westerns, which include *Stagecoach* (1939), *The Alamo* (1960), and *True Grit* (1969), for which he won an Oscar.

way-out *adj Informal.* **1** extremely unconventional or experimental; avant-garde. **2** excellent or amazing.

-ways *suffix forming adverbs.* indicating direction or manner: *sideways.* [Old English *weges,* literally: of the way, from *weg* WAY]

ways and means *pl n* **1** the revenues and methods of raising the revenues needed for the functioning of a state or other political unit. **2** (*usually cap.*) a standing committee of the U.S. House of Representatives that supervises all financial legislation. **3** the methods and resources for accomplishing some purpose.

wayside ('weɪ,saɪd) *n* **1a** the side or edge of a road. **1b** (*modifier*) situated by the wayside: *a wayside inn.* **2 fall by the wayside.** to cease or fail to continue doing something: *of the nine starters, three fell by the wayside.* **3 go by the wayside.** to be put aside on account of something more urgent.

wayward ('weɪwəd) *adj* **1** wanting to have one's own way regardless of the wishes or good of others. **2** capricious, erratic, or unpredictable. [C14: changed from *awayward* turned or turning away] ▸ **'waywardly** *adv* ▸ **'waywardness** *n*

wayworn ('weɪ,wɔːn) *adj Rare.* worn or tired by travel.

wayzgoose ('weɪz,guːs) *n* a works outing made annually by a printing house. [C18: from earlier *waygoose,* of unknown origin]

Waziristan (wə,zɪərɪ'stɑːn) *n* a mountainous region of N Pakistan, on the border with Afghanistan.

wb *abbrev. for:* **1** water ballast. **2** Also: **W/B, WB** waybill. **3** westbound.

Wb *Physics. symbol for* weber.

WBA *abbrev. for* World Boxing Association.

WBC *abbrev. for* World Boxing Council.

W boson *n Physics.* another name for **W particle.**

WBU *abbrev. for* World Boxing Union.

wc *abbrev. for:* **1** water closet. **2** without charge.

WC *abbrev. for:* **1** water closet. **2** (in London postal code) West Central.

WCC *abbrev. for* World Council of Churches.

wd *abbrev. for:* **1** ward. **2** wood. **3** word.

WD *abbrev. for:* **1** War Department. **2** Works Department. **3** *international car registration for* (Windward Islands) Dominica.

WDA *abbrev. for* Welsh Development Agency.

WDM *or* **wdm** *abbrev. for* wavelength division multiplex: a system in which several independent signals may be sent down an optical fibre link by monitoring them on light-carriers of different wavelengths.

we (wiː) *pron* (*subjective*) **1** refers to the speaker or writer and another person or other people: *we should go now.* **2** refers to all people or people in general: *the planet on which we live.* **3a** a formal word for **I**[1] used by editors or other writers, and formerly by monarchs. **3b** (*as n*): *he uses the royal we in his pompous moods.* **4** *Informal.* used instead of *you* with a tone of persuasiveness, condescension, or sarcasm: *how are we today?* [Old English *wē,* related to Old Saxon *wī,* Old High German *wir,* Old Norse *vēr,* Danish, Swedish *vi,* Sanskrit *vayam*]

WEA (in Britain) *abbrev. for* Workers' Educational Association.

weak (wiːk) *adj* **1** lacking in physical or mental strength or force; frail or feeble. **2** liable to yield, break, or give way: *a weak link in a chain.* **3** lacking in resolution or firmness of character. **4** lacking strength, power, or intensity: *a weak voice.* **5** lacking strength in a particular part: *a team weak in defence.* **6a** not functioning as well as normal: *weak eyes.* **6b** easily upset: *a weak stomach.* **7** lacking in conviction, persuasiveness, etc.: *a weak argument.* **8** lacking in political or strategic strength: *a weak state.* **9** lacking the usual, full, or desirable strength of flavour: *weak tea.* **10** *Grammar.* **10a** denoting or belonging to a class of verbs, in certain languages including the Germanic languages, whose conjugation relies on inflectional endings rather than internal vowel gradation, as *look, looks, looking, looked.* **10b** belonging to any part-of-speech class, in any of various languages, whose inflections follow the more regular of two possible patterns. Compare **strong** (sense 13). **11** (of a syllable) not accented or stressed. **12** (of a fuel-air mixture) containing a relatively low proportion of fuel. Compare **rich** (sense 13). **13** *Photog.* having low density or contrast; thin. **14** (of an industry, market, currency, securities, etc.) falling in price or characterized by falling prices. [Old English *wāc* soft, miserable; related to Old Saxon *wēk,* Old High German *weih,* Old Norse *veikr*] ▸ **'weakish** *adj* ▸ **'weakishly** *adv* ▸ **'weakishness** *n*

weaken ('wiːkən) *vb* to become or cause to become weak or weaker. ▸ **'weakener** *n*

weaker sex ('wiːkə) *n* the female sex.

weakfish ('wiːk,fɪʃ) *n, pl* **-fish** *or* **-fishes.** any of several sciaenid sea trouts, esp. *Cynoscion regalis,* a food and game fish of American Atlantic coastal waters.

weak interaction *or* **force** *n Physics.* an interaction between elementary particles that is responsible for certain decay processes, operates at distances less than about 10^{-15} metres, and is 10^{12} times weaker than the strong interaction. Also called: **weak nuclear interaction** *or* **force.** See **interaction** (sense 2), **electroweak interaction.**

weak-kneed *adj Informal.* yielding readily to force, persuasion, intimidation, etc. ▸ ˌ**weak-'kneedly** *adv* ▸ ˌ**weak-'kneedness** *n*

weakling ('wiːklɪŋ) *n* a person or animal that is lacking in strength or weak in constitution or character.

weakly ('wiːklɪ) *adj* **-lier, -liest. 1** sickly; feeble. ♦ *adv* **2** in a weak or feeble manner. ▸ '**weakliness** *n*

weak-minded *adj* **1** lacking in stability of mind or character. **2** another word for **feeble-minded.** ▸ ˌ**weak-'mindedly** *adv* ▸ ˌ**weak-'mindedness** *n*

weakness ('wiːknɪs) *n* **1** the state or quality of being weak. **2** a deficiency or failing, as in a person's character. **3** a self-indulgent fondness or liking: *a weakness for chocolates.*

weak sister *n U.S. informal.* a person in a group who is regarded as weak or unreliable.

weak-willed *adj* lacking strength of will.

weal[1] (wiːl) *n* a raised mark on the surface of the body produced by a blow. Also called: **wale, welt, wheal.** [C19: variant of WALE[1], influenced in form by WHEAL]

weal[2] (wiːl) *n* **1** *Archaic.* prosperity or wellbeing (now esp. in the phrases **the public weal, the common weal**). **2** *Obsolete.* the state. **3** *Obsolete.* wealth. [Old English *wela;* related to Old Saxon *welo,* Old High German *wolo*]

weald (wiːld) *n Brit. archaic.* open or forested country. [Old English; related to Old Saxon, Old High German *wald,* Old Norse *vollr,* probably related to WILD]

Weald (wiːld) *n* **the.** a region of SE England, in Kent, Surrey, and East and West Sussex between the North Downs and the South Downs: formerly forested.

wealth (wɛlθ) *n* **1** a large amount of money and valuable material possessions. **2** the state of being rich. **3** a great profusion: *a wealth of gifts.* **4** *Economics.* all goods and services with monetary, exchangeable, or productive value. [C13 *welthe,* from WEAL[2]; related to WELL[1]] ▸ '**wealthless** *adj*

wealth tax *n* a tax on personal property; capital levy.

wealthy ('wɛlθɪ) *adj* **wealthier, wealthiest. 1** possessing wealth; affluent; rich. **2** of, characterized by, or relating to wealth. **3** abounding: *wealthy in friends.* ▸ '**wealthily** *adv* ▸ '**wealthiness** *n*

wean[1] (wiːn) *vb (tr)* **1** to cause (a child or young mammal) to replace mother's milk by other nourishment. **2** (usually foll. by *from*) to cause to desert former habits, pursuits, etc. [Old English *wenian* to accustom; related to German *gewöhnen* to get used to] ▸ '**weaning** *n*

wean[2] (weɪn; wiːn) *n Scot. and northern English dialect.* a child; infant. [a contraction of *wee ane* or perhaps a shortened form of WEANLING]

weaner ('wiːnə) *n* **1** a person or thing that weans. **2** a pig that has just been weaned and weighs less than 40 kg. **3** *Austral. and N.Z.* a lamb, pig, or calf in the year in which it is weaned.

weanling ('wiːnlɪŋ) *n* **a** a child or young animal recently weaned. **b** (*as modifier*): *a weanling calf.* [C16: from WEAN[1] + -LING[1]]

weapon ('wɛpən) *n* **1** an object or instrument used in fighting. **2** anything that serves to outwit or get the better of an opponent: *his power of speech was his best weapon.* **3** any part of an animal that is used to defend itself, to attack prey, etc., such as claws, teeth, horns, or a sting. **4** a slang word for **penis.** [Old English *wǣpen;* related to Old Norse *vápn,* Old Frisian *wēpen,* Old High German *wāffan*] ▸ '**weaponed** *adj* ▸ '**weaponless** *adj*

weaponeer (ˌwɛpə'nɪə) *n* a person associated with the use or maintenance of weapons, esp. nuclear weapons.

weaponry ('wɛpənrɪ) *n* weapons regarded collectively.

weapon system *n Military.* a weapon and the components necessary to its proper function, such as targeting and guidance devices.

wear[1] (wɛə) *vb* **wears, wearing, wore, worn. 1** *(tr)* to carry or have (a garment, etc.) on one's person as clothing, ornament, etc. **2** *(tr)* to carry or have on one's person habitually: *she wears a lot of red.* **3** *(tr)* to have in one's aspect: *to wear a smile.* **4** *(tr)* to display, show, or fly: *a ship wears its colours.* **5** to deteriorate or cause to deteriorate by constant use or action. **6** to produce or be produced by constant rubbing, scraping, etc.: *to wear a hole in one's trousers.* **7** to bring or be brought to a specified condition by constant use or action: *to wear a tyre to shreds.* **8** *(intr)* to submit to constant use or action in a specified way: *his suit wears well.* **9** *(tr)* to harass or weaken. **10** (when *intr,* often foll. by *on*) (of time) to pass or be passed slowly. **11** *(tr) Brit. slang.* to accept: *Larry won't wear that argument.* **12 wear ship.** to change the tack of a sailing vessel, esp. a square-rigger, by coming about so that the wind passes astern. ♦ *n* **13** the act of wearing or state of being worn. **14a** anything designed to be worn: *leisure wear.* **14b** (*in combination*): *nightwear.* **15** deterioration from constant or normal use or action. **16** the quality of resisting the effects of constant use. ♦ See also **wear down, wear off, wear out.** [Old English *werian;* related to Old High German *werien,* Old Norse *verja,* Gothic *vasjan*] ▸ '**wearer** *n*

wear[2] (wɛə) *vb* **wears, wearing, wore, worn.** *Nautical.* to tack by gybing instead of by going through stays. [C17: from earlier *weare,* of unknown origin]

Wear (wɪə) *n* a river in NE England, rising in NW Durham and flowing southeast then northeast to the North Sea at Sunderland. Length: 105 km (65 miles).

wearable ('wɛərəb^əl) *adj* **1** suitable for wear or able to be worn. ♦ *n* **2** (*often pl*) any garment that can be worn. ▸ ˌ**weara'bility** *n*

wear and tear *n* damage, depreciation, or loss resulting from ordinary use.

wear down *vb (adv)* **1** to consume or be consumed by long or constant wearing, rubbing, etc. **2** to overcome or be overcome gradually by persistent effort.

weariless ('wɪərɪlɪs) *adj* not wearied or able to be wearied. ▸ '**wearilessly** *adv*

wearing ('wɛərɪŋ) *adj* causing fatigue or exhaustion; tiring. ▸ '**wearingly** *adv*

wearing course *n* the top layer of a road that carries the traffic; road surface.

wearisome ('wɪərɪsəm) *or* **weariful** *adj* causing fatigue or annoyance; tedious. ▸ '**wearisomely** *or* '**wearifully** *adv* ▸ '**wearisomeness** *or* '**wearifulness** *n*

wear off *vb (adv)* **1** *(intr)* to decrease in intensity gradually: *the pain will wear off in an hour.* **2** to disappear or cause to disappear gradually through exposure, use, etc.: *the pattern on the ring had been worn off.*

wear out *vb (adv)* **1** to make or become unfit or useless through wear. **2** *(tr)* to exhaust or tire.

wearproof ('wɛəˌpruːf) *adj* resistant to damage from normal wear or usage.

weary ('wɪərɪ) *adj* **-rier, -riest. 1** tired or exhausted. **2** causing fatigue or exhaustion. **3** caused by or suggestive of weariness: *a weary laugh.* **4** (*postpositive;* often foll. by *of* or *with*) discontented or bored, esp. by the long continuance of something. ♦ *vb* **-ries, -rying, -ried. 5** to make or become weary. **6** to make or become discontented or impatient, esp. by the long continuance of something. [Old English *wērig;* related to Old Saxon *wōrig,* Old High German *wuorag* drunk, Greek *hōrakian* to faint] ▸ '**wearily** *adv* ▸ '**weariness** *n* ▸ '**wearying** *adj* ▸ '**wearyingly** *adv*

weasand ('wiːzənd) *n* a former name for the **trachea.** [Old English *wǣsend, wāsend;* related to Old Frisian *wāsenda,* Old High German *weisont* vein, Danish *vissen*]

weasel ('wiːz^əl) *n, pl* **-sels** *or* **-sel. 1** any of various small predatory musteline mammals of the genus *Mustela* and related genera, esp. *M. nivalis* (**European weasel**), having reddish-brown fur, an elongated body and neck, and short legs. **2** *Informal.* a sly or treacherous person. **3** *Chiefly U.S.* a motor vehicle for use in snow, esp. one with caterpillar tracks. [Old English *weosule, wesle;* related to Old Norse *visla,* Old High German *wisula,* Middle Dutch *wesel*] ▸ '**weaselly** *adj*

weasel out *vb (intr, adv) Informal.* **1** to go back on a commitment. **2** to evade a responsibility, esp. in a despicable manner.

weasel words *pl n Informal.* intentionally evasive or misleading speech; equivocation. [C20: alluding to the weasel's supposed ability to suck an egg out of its shell without seeming to break the shell] ▸ '**weasel-ˌworded** *adj*

weather ('wɛðə) *n* **1a** the day-to-day meteorological conditions, esp. temperature, cloudiness, and rainfall, affecting a specific place. Compare **climate** (sense 1). **1b** (*modifier*): relating to the forecasting of weather: *a weather ship.* **2** a prevailing state or condition. **3 make heavy weather. 3a** (of a vessel) to roll and pitch in heavy seas. **3b** (foll. by *of*) to carry out with great difficulty or unnecessarily great effort. **4 under the weather.** *Informal.* **4a** not in good health. **4b** intoxicated. ♦ *adj* **5** (*prenominal*) on or at the side or part towards the wind; windward: *the weather anchor.* Compare **lee** (sense 4). ♦ *vb* **6** to expose or be exposed to the action of the weather. **7** to undergo or cause to undergo changes, such as discoloration, due to the action of the weather. **8** *(intr)* to withstand the action of the weather. **9** (when *intr,* foll. by *through*) to endure (a crisis, danger, etc.). **10** *(tr)* to slope (a surface, such as a roof, sill, etc.) so as to throw rainwater clear. **11** *(tr)* to sail to the windward of: *to weather a point.* [Old English *weder;* related to Old Saxon *wedar,* Old High German *wetar,* Old Norse *vethr*] ▸ ˌ**weathera'bility** *n* ▸ '**weatherer** *n*

weather-beaten *adj* **1** showing signs of exposure to the weather. **2** tanned or hardened by exposure to the weather.

weatherboard ('wɛðəˌbɔːd) *n* **1** a timber board, with a groove (rabbet) along the front of its top edge and along the back of its lower edge, that is fixed horizontally with others to form an exterior cladding on a wall or roof. Compare **clapboard. 2** a sloping timber board fixed at the bottom of a door to deflect rain. **3** the windward side of a vessel. **4** Also called: **weatherboard house.** *Chiefly Austral. and N.Z.* a house having walls made entirely of weatherboarding.

weatherboarding ('wɛðəˌbɔːdɪŋ) *n* **1** an area or covering of weatherboards. **2** weatherboards collectively.

weather-bound *adj* (of a vessel, aircraft, etc.) delayed by bad weather.

weathercock ('wɛðəˌkɒk) *n* **1** a weather vane in the form of a cock. **2** a person who is fickle or changeable. ♦ *vb* **3** *(intr)* (of an aircraft) to turn or tend to turn into the wind.

weathered ('wɛðəd) *adj* **1** affected by exposure to the action of the weather. **2** (of rocks and rock formations) eroded, decomposed, or otherwise altered by the action of wind, frost, heat, etc. **3** (of a sill, roof, etc.) having a sloped surface so as to allow rainwater to run off. **4** (of wood) artificially stained so as to appear weather-beaten.

weather eye *n* **1** the vision of a person trained to observe changes in the weather. **2** *Informal.* an alert or observant gaze. **3 keep one's weather eye open.** to stay on the alert.

weatherglass ('wɛðəˌglɑːs) *n* any of various instruments, esp. a barometer, that measure atmospheric conditions.

weather house *n* a model house with two human figures, one that comes out to foretell bad weather and the other to foretell good weather.

weathering ('wɛðərɪŋ) *n* the mechanical and chemical breakdown of rocks by the action of rain, snow, cold, etc.

weatherly ('wɛðəlɪ) *adj* (of a sailing vessel) making very little leeway when close-hauled, even in a stiff breeze. ▸ '**weatherliness** *n*

weatherman ('wɛðəˌmæn) *n, pl* **-men.** a person who forecasts the weather, esp. one who works in a meteorological office.

Weatherman ('wɛðəˌmæn) *n, pl* **-men.** *U.S.* a member of a militant revolutionary group active in the U.S. during the 1970s. [C20: name adopted from a line in Bob Dylan's song "Subterranean Homesick Blues": "You don't need a weatherman To know which way the wind blows."]

weather map *or* **chart** *n* a synoptic chart showing weather conditions, compiled from simultaneous observations taken at various weather stations.

weatherproof ('wɛðəˌpruːf) *adj* **1** designed or able to withstand exposure to weather without deterioration. ♦ *vb* **2** *(tr)* to render (something) weatherproof. ▸ '**weatherˌproofness** *n*

weather station *n* one of a network of meteorological observation posts where weather data is recorded.

weather strip *n* a thin strip of compressible material, such as spring metal, felt, etc., that is fitted between the frame of a door or window and the opening part to exclude wind and rain. Also called: **weatherstripping.**

weather vane *n* a vane designed to indicate the direction in which the wind is blowing.

weather window *n* a limited interval when weather conditions can be expected to be suitable for a particular project, such as laying offshore pipelines, reaching a high mountain summit, launching a satellite, etc.

weather-wise *adj* **1** skilful or experienced in predicting weather conditions. **2** skilful or experienced in predicting trends in public opinion, reactions, etc.

weatherworn ('wɛðə,wɔːn) *adj* another word for **weather-beaten.**

weave (wiːv) *vb* **weaves, weaving, wove** *or* **weaved; woven** *or* **weaved. 1** to form (a fabric) by interlacing (yarn, etc.), esp. on a loom. **2** (*tr*) to make or construct by such a process: *to weave a shawl.* **3** (*tr*) to make or construct (an artefact, such as a basket) by interlacing (a pliable material, such as cane). **4** (of a spider) to make (a web). **5** (*tr*) to construct by combining separate elements into a whole. **6** (*tr; often foll. by in, into, through,* etc.) to introduce: *to weave factual details into a fiction.* **7** to create (a way, etc.) by moving from side to side: *to weave through a crowd.* **8 get weaving.** *Informal.* to hurry; start to do something. ◆ *n* **9** the method or pattern of weaving or the structure of a woven fabric: *a twill weave; an open weave.* [Old English *wefan;* related to Old High German *weban,* Old Norse *vefa,* Greek *hyphos,* Sanskrit *vābhis;* compare WEB, WEEVIL, WASP] ▸ **'weaving** *n*

weaver ('wiːvə) *n* **1** a person who weaves, esp. as a means of livelihood. **2** short for **weaverbird.**

weaverbird ('wiːvə,bɜːd) *or* **weaver** *n* **1** any small Old World passerine songbird of the chiefly African family *Ploceidae,* having a short thick bill and a dull plumage and building covered nests: includes the house sparrow and whydahs. **2** any similar bird of the family *Estrilidae,* of warm regions of the Old World: includes the waxbills, grassfinches, and Java sparrow. Also called: **weaver finch.**

weaver's hitch *or* **knot** *n* another name for **sheet bend.**

web (wɛb) *n* **1** any structure, construction, fabric, etc., formed by or as if by weaving or interweaving. Related adj: **retiary. 2** a mesh of fine tough scleroprotein threads built by a spider from a liquid secreted from its spinnerets and used to trap insects. See also **cobweb** (sense 1). **3** a similar network of threads spun by certain insect larvae, such as the silkworm. **4** a fabric, esp. one in the process of being woven. **5** a membrane connecting the toes of some aquatic birds or the digits of such aquatic mammals as the otter. **6** the vane of a bird's feather. **7** *Architect.* the surface of a ribbed vault that lies between the ribs. **8** the central section of an I-beam or H-beam that joins the two flanges of the beam. **9** the radial portion of a crank that connects the crankpin to the crankshaft. **10** a thin piece of superfluous material left attached to a forging; fin. **11a** a continuous strip of paper as formed on a paper machine or fed from a reel into some printing presses. **11b** (*as modifier*): *web offset; a web press.* **12** the woven edge, without pile, of some carpets. **13a** (*often cap.;* preceded by *the*) short for **World Wide Web. 13b** (*as modifier*): *a web site; web pages.* **14** any structure, construction, etc., that is intricately formed or complex: *a web of intrigue.* ◆ *vb* **webs, webbing, webbed. 15** (*tr*) to cover with or as if with a web. **16** (*tr*) to entangle or ensnare. **17** (*intr*) to construct a web. [Old English *webb;* related to Old Saxon, Old High German *webbi,* Old Norse *vefr*] ▸ **'webless** *adj* ▸ **'web,like** *adj*

Webb (wɛb) *n* **1** Sir **Aston.** 1849–1930, British architect. His work includes the Victoria and Albert Museum (1909), the Victoria Memorial (1911), and Admiralty Arch (1911). **2 Mary (Gladys).** 1881–1927, British novelist, remembered for her novels of rustic life, notably *Precious Bane* (1924). **3 Sidney (James),** Baron Passfield. 1859–1947, British economist, social historian, and Fabian socialist. He and his wife **(Martha) Beatrice** (née *Potter*), 1858–1943, British writer on social and economic problems, collaborated in *The History of Trade Unionism* (1894) and *English Local Government* (1906–29), helped found the London School of Economics (1895), and started the *New Statesman* (1913).

webbed (wɛbd) *adj* **1** (of the feet of certain animals) having the digits connected by a thin fold of skin; palmate. **2** having, consisting of, or resembling a web.

webbing ('wɛbɪŋ) *n* **1** a strong fabric of hemp, cotton, jute, etc., woven in strips and used under springs in upholstery or for straps, etc. **2** the skin that unites the digits of a webbed foot. **3** anything that forms a web.

webby ('wɛbɪ) *adj* **-bier, -biest.** of, relating to, resembling, or consisting of a web.

weber ('veɪbə) *n* the derived SI unit of magnetic flux; the flux that, when linking a circuit of one turn, produces in it an emf of 1 volt as it is reduced to zero at a uniform rate in one second. 1 weber is equivalent to 10^8 maxwells. Symbol: Wb [C20: named after W. E. WEBER]

Weber (*German* 'veːbər) *n* **1** Baron **Carl Maria Friedrich Ernst von** (karl maˈriːa ˈfriːdrɪç ɛrnst fɔn). 1786–1826, German composer and conductor. His three romantic operas are *Der Freischütz* (1821), *Euryanthe* (1823), and *Oberon* (1826). **2 Ernst Heinrich** (ɛrnst ˈhainrɪç). 1795–1878, German physiologist and anatomist. He introduced the psychological concept of the just noticeable difference between stimuli. **3 Max** (maks). 1864–1920, German economist and sociologist, best known for *The Protestant Ethic and the Spirit of Capitalism* (1904–05). **4 Wilhelm Eduard** ('vɪlhɛlm 'eːduart), brother of Ernst Heinrich Weber. 1804–91, German physicist, who conducted research into electricity and magnetism.

Webern (*German* 'veːbərn) *n* **Anton von** ('antoːn fɔn). 1883–1945, Austrian composer; pupil of Schoenberg, whose twelve-tone technique he adopted. His works include those for chamber ensemble, such as *Five Pieces for Orchestra* (1911–13).

webfoot ('wɛb,fʊt) *n* **1** *Zoology.* a foot having the toes connected by folds of skin. **2** *Anatomy.* a foot having an abnormal membrane connecting adjacent toes.

web-footed *or* **web-toed** *adj* (of certain animals) having webbed feet that facilitate swimming.

website ('wɛb,saɪt) *n* a group of connected pages on the World Wide Web containing information on a particular subject.

web spinner *n* any small fragile dull-coloured typically tropical insect of the order *Embioptera,* which has biting mouthparts and constructs silken tunnels in which to live.

webster ('wɛbstə) *n* an archaic word for **weaver** (sense 1). [Old English *webbestre,* from *webba* a weaver, from *webb* WEB]

Webster ('wɛbstə) *n* **1 Daniel.** 1782–1852, U.S. politician and orator. **2 John.** ?1580–?1625, English dramatist, noted for his revenge tragedies *The White Devil* (?1612) and *The Duchess of Malfi* (?1613). **3 Noah.** 1758–1843, U.S. lexicographer, famous for his *American Dictionary of the English Language* (1828).

webwheel ('wɛb,wiːl) *n* **1** a wheel containing a plate or web instead of spokes. **2** a wheel of which the rim, spokes, and centre are in one piece.

wed (wɛd) *vb* **weds, wedding, wedded** *or* **wed. 1** to take (a person of the opposite sex) as a husband or wife; marry. **2** (*tr*) to join (two people) in matrimony. **3** (*tr*) to unite closely. [Old English *weddian;* related to Old Frisian *weddia,* Old Norse *vethja,* Gothic *wadi* pledge]

we'd (wiːd; *unstressed* wɪd) *contraction of* we had *or* we would.

Wed. *abbrev. for* Wednesday.

wedded ('wɛdɪd) *adj* **1** of marriage: *wedded bliss.* **2** firmly in support of an idea or institution: *wedded to the virtues of capitalism.*

Weddell Sea ('wɛdᵊl) *n* an arm of the S Atlantic in Antarctica.

wedding ('wɛdɪŋ) *n* **1a** the act of marrying or the celebration of a marriage. **1b** (*as modifier*): *wedding day.* **2** the anniversary of a marriage (in such combinations as **silver wedding** or **diamond wedding**). **3** the combination or blending of two separate elements.

wedding breakfast *n* the meal usually served after a wedding ceremony or just before the bride and bridegroom leave for their honeymoon.

wedding cake *n* a rich fruit cake, with one, two, or more tiers, covered with almond paste and decorated with royal icing, which is served at a wedding reception.

wedding ring *n* a band ring with parallel sides, typically of precious metal, worn to indicate married status.

Wedekind (*German* 'veːdəkɪnt) *n* **Frank.** 1864–1918, German dramatist, whose plays, such as *The Awakening of Spring* (1891) and *Pandora's Box* (1904), bitterly satirize the sexual repressiveness of society.

wedeln ('veɪdəln) *n* a succession of high-speed turns performed in skiing. [from German, literally: to wag]

wedge (wɛdʒ) *n* **1** a block of solid material, esp. wood or metal, that is shaped like a narrow V in cross section and can be pushed or driven between two objects or parts of an object in order to split or secure them. **2** any formation, structure, or substance in the shape of a wedge: *a wedge of cheese.* **3** something such as an idea, action, etc., that tends to cause division. **4** a shoe with a wedge heel. **5** *Golf.* a club with a face angle of more than 50°, used for bunker shots (**sand wedge**) or pitch shots (**pitching wedge**). **6** a wedge-shaped extension of the high pressure area of an anticyclone, narrower than a ridge. **7** *Mountaineering.* a wedge-shaped device, formerly of wood, now usually of hollow steel, for hammering into a crack to provide an anchor point. **8** any of the triangular characters used in cuneiform writing. **9** (formerly) a body of troops formed in a V-shape. **10** *Photog.* a strip of glass coated in such a way that it is clear at one end but becomes progressively more opaque towards the other end: used in making measurements of transmission density. **11 thin end of the wedge.** anything unimportant in itself that implies the start of something much larger. ◆ *vb* **12** (*tr*) to secure with or as if with a wedge. **13** to squeeze or be squeezed like a wedge into a narrow space. **14** (*tr*) to force apart or divide with or as if with a wedge. [Old English *wecg;* related to Old Saxon *weggi,* Old High German *wecki,* Old Norse *veggr* wall] ▸ **'wedge,like** *adj* ▸ **'wedgy** *adj*

wedge heel *n* **1** a raised shoe heel with the heel and sole forming a solid block. **2** a shoe with such a heel.

wedge-tailed eagle *n* a large brown Australian eagle, *Aquila audax,* having a wedge-shaped tail and a wingspan of 3 m. Also called: **eaglehawk.**

Wedgwood[1] ('wɛdʒwʊd) **1** *Trademark.* **1a** pottery produced, esp. during the late 18th and early 19th centuries, at the Wedgwood factories. **1b** such pottery having applied classical decoration in white on a blue or other coloured ground. ◆ *adj* **2** relating to or characteristic of such pottery: *Wedgwood blue.*

Wedgewood[2] *n* **Josiah.** 1730–95, British potter and industrialist, who founded several pottery works near Stoke-on-Trent in Staffordshire.

Wedgwood blue *n* **a** a pale blue or greyish-blue colour. **b** (*as adj*): *a Wedgwood-blue door.*

wedlock ('wɛdlɒk) *n* **1** the state of being married. **2 born out of wedlock.** born when one's parents are not legally married. [Old English *wedlāc,* from *wedd* pledge + *-lāc,* suffix denoting activity, perhaps from *lāc* game, battle (related to Gothic *laiks* dance, Old Norse *leikr*)]

Wednesday ('wɛnzdɪ) *n* the fourth day of the week; third day of the working week. [Old English *Wōdnes dæg* Woden's day, translation of Latin *mercurii dies* Mercury's day; related to Old Frisian *wōnsdei,* Middle Dutch *wōdensdach* (Dutch *woensdag*)]

wee[1] (wiː) *adj* **1** very small; tiny; minute. ◆ *n* **2** *Chiefly Scot.* a short time (esp. in the phrase **bide a wee.**). [C13: from Old English *wǣg* WEIGHT]

wee[2] (wiː) *Brit., Austral., and N.Z. informal.* ◆ *n* **1a** the act or an instance of urinating. **1b** urine. ◆ *vb* **2** (*intr*) to urinate. ◆ Also: **wee-wee.** [of unknown origin]

weed[1] (wiːd) *n* **1** any plant that grows wild and profusely, esp. one that grows among cultivated plants, depriving them of space, food, etc. **2** *Slang.* **2a the weed.** tobacco. **2b** marijuana. **3** *Informal.* a thin or unprepossessing person. **4** an inferior horse, esp. one showing signs of weakness of constitution. ◆ *vb* **5** to remove (useless or troublesome plants) from (a garden, etc.). [Old English *weod;* related to Old Saxon *wiod,* Old High German *wiota* fern] ► ˈ**weeder** *n* ► ˈ**weedless** *adj* ► ˈ**weed,like** *adj*

weed[2] (wiːd) *n Rare.* a black crepe band worn to indicate mourning. See also **weeds.** [Old English *wǣd, wēd;* related to Old Saxon *wād,* Old High German *wāt,* Old Norse *vāth*]

weedkiller (ˈwiːd,kɪlə) *n* a substance, usually a chemical or hormone, used for killing weeds.

weed out *vb* (*tr, adv*) to separate out, remove, or eliminate (anything unwanted): *to weed out troublesome students.*

weeds (wiːdz) *pl n* **1** Also called: **widow's weeds.** a widow's black mourning clothes. **2** *Obsolete.* any clothing. [pl. of WEED[2]]

weedy (ˈwiːdɪ) *adj* **weedier, weediest. 1** full of or containing weeds: *weedy land.* **2** (of a plant) resembling a weed in rapid or straggling growth. **3** *Informal.* thin or weakly in appearance. ► ˈ**weedily** *adv* ► ˈ**weediness** *n*

Wee Free *n Informal, often derogatory.* a member of the minority of the Free Church of Scotland that refused to be joined with the United Free Church in 1900.

week (wiːk) *n* **1** a period of seven consecutive days, esp., one beginning with Sunday. Related adj: **hebdomadal. 2** a period of seven consecutive days beginning from or including a specified day: *Easter week; a week from Wednesday.* **3** the period of time within a week devoted to work. **4** a week devoted to the celebration of a cause. ◆ *adv* **5** *Chiefly Brit.* seven days before or after a specified day: *I'll visit you Wednesday week.* [Old English *wice, wicu, wucu;* related to Old Norse *vika,* Gothic *wikō* order]

weekday (ˈwiːk,deɪ) *n* any day of the week other than Sunday and, often, Saturday.

weekend *n* (,wiːkˈɛnd). **1a** the end of the week, esp. the period from Friday night until the end of Sunday. **1b** (*as modifier*): *a weekend party.* ◆ *vb* (ˈwiːk,ɛnd). **2** (*intr*) *Informal.* to spend or pass a weekend. ◆ See also **weekends.**

weekender (,wiːkˈɛndə) *n* **1** a person spending a weekend holiday in a place, esp. habitually. **2** *Austral.* a house, shack, etc., occupied only at weekends, for holidays, etc.

weekends (,wiːkˈɛndz) *adv Informal.* at the weekend, esp. regularly or during every weekend.

weekly (ˈwiːklɪ) *adj* **1** happening or taking place once a week or every week. **2** determined or calculated by the week. ◆ *adv* **3** once a week or every week. ◆ *n, pl* **-lies. 4** a newspaper or magazine issued every week.

weeknight (ˈwiːk,naɪt) *n* the evening or night of a weekday.

weel (wiːl) *adv, adj, interj, sentence connector.* a Scot. word for **well**[1].

Weelkes (wiːlks) *n* **Thomas.** ?1575–1623, English composer of madrigals.

ween (wiːn) *vb Archaic.* to think or imagine (something). [Old English *wēnan;* related to Old Saxon *wānian,* Gothic *wēnjan,* German *wähnen* to assume wrongly]

weeny (ˈwiːnɪ) *or* **weensy** (ˈwiːnzɪ) *adj* **-nier, -niest** *or* **-sier, -siest.** *Informal.* very small; tiny. [C18: from WEE[1] with the ending *-ny* as in TINY]

weeny-bopper *n Informal.* a child of 8 to 12 years, esp. a girl, who is a keen follower of pop music. [C20: formed on the model of TEENYBOPPER, from *weeny,* as in *teeny-weeny* very small]

weep (wiːp) *vb* **weeps, weeping, wept. 1** to shed (tears) as an expression of grief or unhappiness. **2** (*tr;* foll. by *out*) to utter, shedding tears. **3** (when *intr,* foll. by *for*) to mourn or lament (for something). **4** to exude (drops of liquid). **5** (*intr*) (of a wound, etc.) to exude a watery or serous fluid. ◆ *n* **6** a spell of weeping. [Old English *wēpan;* related to Gothic *wōpjan,* Old High German *wuofan,* Old Slavonic *vabiti* to call]

weeper (ˈwiːpə) *n* **1** a person who weeps, esp. a hired mourner. **2** something worn as a sign of mourning. **3** a hole through a wall, to allow water to drain away.

weeping (ˈwiːpɪŋ) *adj* (of plants) having slender hanging branches. ► ˈ**weepingly** *adv*

weeping ivy *n* a climbing plant, *Ficus benjamina,* of the fig family, grown as a greenhouse or house plant for its graceful glossy leaves on slender drooping branches.

weeping willow *n* a Chinese willow tree, *Salix babylonica,* having long hanging branches: widely planted for ornament.

weepy (ˈwiːpɪ) *Informal.* ◆ *adj* **weepier, weepiest. 1** liable or tending to weep. ◆ *n, pl* **weepies. 2** a romantic and sentimental film or book. ► ˈ**weepily** *adv* ► ˈ**weepiness** *n*

weever (ˈwiːvə) *n* any small marine percoid fish of the family *Trachinidae,* such as *Trachinus vipera* of European waters, having venomous spines around the gills and the dorsal fin. [C17: from Old Northern French *wivre* viper, ultimately from Latin *vīpera* VIPER]

weevil (ˈwiːvɪl) *n* **1** Also called: **snout beetle.** any beetle of the family *Curculionidae,* having an elongated snout (rostrum): they are pests, feeding on plants and plant products. See also **boll weevil. 2** Also called: **pea** or **bean weevil.** any of various beetles of the family *Bruchidae* (or *Lariidae*), the larvae of which live in the seeds of leguminous plants. **3** any of various similar or related beetles. [Old English *wifel;* related to Old High German *wibil;* compare Old Norse *tordȳfill* dungbeetle] ► ˈ**weevily** *adj*

wee-wee *n, vb* a variant of **wee**[2].

w.e.f. *abbrev. for* with effect from.

weft (wɛft) *n* the yarn woven across the width of the fabric through the lengthwise warp yarn. Also called: **filling, woof.** [Old English, related to Old Norse *veptr;* see WEAVE]

Wegener (*German* ˈveːgənər) *n* **Alfred** (ˈalfreːt). 1880–1930, German meteorologist: regarded as the originator of the theory of continental drift.

Wehrmacht *German.* (ˈveːr,maxt) *n* the armed services of the German Third Reich from 1935 to 1945. [from *Wehr* defence + *Macht* force]

Weichsel (ˈvaiksəl) *n* the German name for the **Vistula** (sense 1).

weigela (waɪˈgiːlə, -ˈdʒiː-; ˈwaɪgɪlə) *n* any caprifoliaceous shrub of the Asian genus *Weigela,* having clusters of pink, purple, red, or white showy bell-shaped flowers. [C19: from New Latin, named after C. E. *Weigel* (1748–1831), German physician]

weigh[1] (weɪ) *vb* **1** (*tr*) to measure the weight of. **2** (*intr*) to have weight or be heavy: *she weighs more than her sister.* **3** (*tr;* often foll. by *out*) to apportion according to weight. **4** (*tr*) to consider carefully: *to weigh the facts of a case.* **5** (*intr*) to be influential: *his words weighed little with the jury.* **6** (*intr;* often foll. by *on*) to be oppressive or burdensome (to). **7** *Obsolete.* to regard or esteem. **8** **weigh anchor.** to raise a vessel's anchor or (of a vessel) to have its anchor raised preparatory to departure. ◆ See also **weigh down, weigh in, weigh up.** [Old English *wegan;* related to Old Frisian *wega,* Old Norse *vega,* Gothic *gawigan,* German *wiegen*] ► ˈ**weighable** *adj* ► ˈ**weigher** *n*

weigh[2] (weɪ) *n* **under weigh.** a variant spelling of **under way.** [C18: variation due to the influence of phrases such as *to weigh anchor*]

weighbridge (ˈweɪ,brɪdʒ) *n* a machine for weighing vehicles, etc., by means of a metal plate set into a road.

weigh down *vb* (*adv*) to press (a person) down by or as if by weight: *his troubles weighed him down.*

weigh in *vb* (*intr, adv*) **1a** (of a boxer or wrestler) to be weighed before a bout. **1b** (of a jockey) to be weighed after, or sometimes before, a race. **2** *Informal.* to contribute, as in a discussion, etc.: *he weighed in with a few sharp comments.* ◆ *n* **weigh-in. 3** the act of checking a competitor's weight, as in boxing, horse racing, etc.

weight (weɪt) *n* **1** a measure of the heaviness of an object; the amount anything weighs. **2** *Physics.* the vertical force experienced by a mass as a result of gravitation. It equals the mass of the body multiplied by the acceleration of free fall. Its units are units of force (such as newtons or poundals) but is often given as a mass unit (kilogram or pound). Symbol: *W* **3** a system of units used to express the weight of a substance: *troy weight.* **4** a unit used to measure weight: *the kilogram is the weight used in the metric system.* **5** any mass or heavy object used to exert pressure or weigh down. **6** an oppressive force: *the weight of cares.* **7** any heavy load: *the bag was such a weight.* **8** the main or greatest force: preponderance: *the weight of evidence.* **9** importance, influence, or consequence: *his opinion carries weight.* **10** *Statistics.* one of a set of coefficients assigned to items of a frequency distribution that are analysed in order to represent the relative importance of the different items. **11** *Printing.* the apparent blackness of a printed typeface. **12** *Slang.* a pound of a drug, esp. cannabis. **13 pull one's weight.** *Informal.* to do one's full or proper share of a task. **14 throw one's weight around.** *Informal.* to act in an overauthoritarian or aggressive manner. ◆ *vb* (*tr*) **15** to add weight to. **16** to burden or oppress. **17** to add importance, value, etc., to one side rather than another; bias; favour: *a law weighted towards landlords.* **18** *Statistics.* to attach a weight or weights to. **19** to make (fabric, threads, etc.) heavier by treating with mineral substances, etc. [Old English *wiht;* related to Old Frisian, Middle Dutch *wicht,* Old Norse *vētt,* German *Gewicht*] ► ˈ**weighter** *n*

weighted average *n* an average calculated by taking into account not only the frequencies of the values of a variable but also some other factor such as their variance. The weighted average of observed data is the result of dividing the sum of the products of each observed value, the number of times it occurs, and this other factor by the total number of observations.

weighting (ˈweɪtɪŋ) *n* **1** a factor by which some quantity is multiplied in order to make it comparable with others. See also **weighted average. 2** an increase in some quantity, esp. an additional allowance paid to compensate for higher living costs: *a London weighting.*

weightlessness (ˈweɪtlɪsnɪs) *n* a state in which an object has no actual weight (because it is in space and unaffected by gravitational attraction) or no apparent weight (because the gravitational attraction equals the centripetal force and the object is in free fall). ► ˈ**weightless** *adj*

weightlifting (ˈweɪt,lɪftɪŋ) *n* the sport of lifting barbells of specified weights in a prescribed manner for competition or exercise. ► ˈ**weight,lifter** *n*

weight training *n* physical exercise involving lifting weights to improve muscle performance.

weight watcher *n* a person who tries to lose weight, esp. by dieting.

Weightwatchers (ˈweɪt,wɒtʃəz) *n* (*functioning as sing*) *Trademark.* an organization that assists people wishing to lose weight.

weighty (ˈweɪtɪ) *adj* **weightier, weightiest. 1** having great weight. **2** important or momentous. **3** causing anxiety or worry. ► ˈ**weightily** *adv* ► ˈ**weightiness** *n*

weigh up *vb* (*tr, adv*) to make an assessment of (a person, situation, etc.); judge.

Weihai *or* **Wei-hai** (ˈweɪˈhaɪ) *n* a port in NE China, in NE Shandong on the Yellow Sea: leased to Britain as a naval base (1898–1930). Pop.: 128 888 (1990 est.). Also called: **Weihaiwei** (,weɪˈhaɪ,weɪ).

Weil (*French* vail) *n* **Simone** (simɔn). 1909–43, French philosopher and mystic, whose works include *Waiting for God* (1951), *The Need for Roots* (1952), and *Notebooks* (1956).

Weill (vaɪl) *n* **Kurt** (kʊrt). 1900–50, German composer, in the U.S. from 1935. He wrote the music for Brecht's *The Rise and Fall of the City of Mahagonny* (1927) and *The Threepenny Opera* (1928).

Weil's disease (vaɪlz) *n* another name for **leptospirosis.** [named after Adolf *Weil* (1848–1916), German physician]

Weimar (*German* ˈvaimar) *n* a city in E central Germany, in Thuringia: a cultural centre in the 18th and early 19th century; scene of the adoption (1919) of the constitution of the Weimar Republic. Pop.: 59 100 (1991).

Weimaraner (ˈvaɪmə,rɑːnə, ˈwaɪmə,rɑː-) *n* a breed of hunting dog, having a very short sleek grey coat and short tail. [C20: named after WEIMAR, where the breed was developed]

Weimar Republic *n* the German republic that existed from 1919 to Hitler's accession to power in 1933.

Weinberg ('waɪnbɜːg) *n* **Steven.** born 1933, U.S. physicist, who shared the Nobel prize for physics (1979) with Sheldon Glashow and Abdus Salam for his role in formulating the electroweak theory.

weir (wɪə) *n* **1** a low dam that is built across a river to raise the water level, divert the water, or control its flow. **2** a series of traps or enclosures placed in a stream to catch fish. [Old English *wer;* related to Old Norse *ver,* Old Frisian *were,* German *Wehr*]

Weir (wɪə) *n* **1 Judith.** born 1954, Scottish composer, noted esp. for her opera *A Night at the Chinese Opera* (1987). **2 Peter.** born 1944, Australian film director; his films include *Dead Poets Society* (1989) and *The Truman Show* (1998).

weird (wɪəd) *adj* **1** suggestive of or relating to the supernatural; eerie. **2** strange or bizarre. **3** *Archaic.* of or relating to fate or the Fates. ◆ *n* **4** *Archaic, chiefly Scot.* **4a** fate or destiny. **4b** one of the Fates. **5 dree one's weird.** *Scot.* see **dree.** ◆ *vb* **6** *(tr) Scot.* to destine or ordain by fate; predict. [Old English *(ge)wyrd* destiny; related to *weorthan* to become, Old Norse *urthr* bane, Old Saxon *wurd;* see WORTH[2]] ▸ **'weirdly** *adv* ▸ **'weirdness** *n*

weirdo ('wɪədəʊ) *or* **weirdie** ('wɪədɪ) *n, pl* **-dos** *or* **-dies.** *Informal.* a person who behaves in a bizarre or eccentric manner.

weird sisters *pl n* **1** another name for the **Fates. 2** *Norse myth.* another name for the **Norns** (see **Norn**[1]).

Weismannism ('vaɪsmən,ɪzəm) *n* the doctrine of the continuity of the germ plasm. This theory of heredity states that all inheritable characteristics are transmitted by the reproductive cells and that characteristics acquired during the lifetime of the organism are not inherited. [C19: named after August *Weismann* (1834–1914), German biologist]

Weisshorn ('vaɪs,hɔːn) *n* a mountain in S Switzerland, in the Pennine Alps. Height: 4505 m (14 781 ft.).

Weissmuller ('waɪs,mʌlə) *n* **John Peter** known as *Johnny.* 1904–84, U.S. swimmer and film actor, who won Olympic gold medals in 1924 and 1928 and played the title role in the early Tarzan films.

Weizmann ('waɪtsmən, 'waɪz-) *n* **Chaim** ('xaɪɪm). 1874–1952, Israeli statesman, born in Russia. As a leading Zionist, he was largely responsible for securing the Balfour Declaration (1917); first president of Israel (1949–52).

weka ('weɪkə, 'wiːkə) *n* any flightless New Zealand rail of the genus *Gallirallus,* having a mottled brown plumage and rudimentary wings. Also called: **Maori hen, wood hen.** [C19: from Maori, of imitative origin]

welch (wɛlʃ) *vb* a variant spelling of **welsh.** ▸ **'welcher** *n*

Welch (wɛlʃ) *adj* an archaic spelling of **Welsh**[1].

welcome ('wɛlkəm) *adj* **1** gladly and cordially received or admitted: *a welcome guest.* **2** bringing pleasure or gratitude: *a welcome gift.* **3** freely permitted or invited: *you are welcome to call.* **4** under no obligation (only in such phrases as **you're welcome** or **he's welcome,** as conventional responses to thanks). ◆ *sentence substitute.* **5** an expression of cordial greeting, esp. to a person whose arrival is desired or pleasing. ◆ *n* **6** the act of greeting or receiving a person or thing; reception: *the new theory had a cool welcome.* **7 wear out one's welcome.** to come more often or stay longer than is acceptable or pleasing. ◆ *vb (tr)* **8** to greet the arrival of (visitors, guests, etc.) cordially or gladly. **9** to receive or accept, esp. gladly. [C12: changed (through influence of WELL[1]) from Old English *wilcuma* (agent noun referring to a welcome guest), *wilcume* (a greeting of welcome), from *wil* WILL[2] + *cuman* to COME] ▸ **'welcomely** *adv* ▸ **'welcomeness** *n* ▸ **'welcomer** *n*

weld[1] (wɛld) *vb* **1** *(tr)* to unite (pieces of metal or plastic) together, as by softening with heat and hammering or by fusion. **2** to bring or admit of being brought into close association or union. ◆ *n* **3** a joint formed by welding. [C16: variant probably based on past participle of WELL[2] in obsolete sense to boil, heat] ▸ **'weldable** *adj* ▸ **,welda'bility** *n* ▸ **'welder** *or* **'weldor** *n* ▸ **'weldless** *adj*

weld[2] (wɛld), **wold,** *or* **woald** (wəʊld) *n* **1** a yellow dye obtained from the plant dyer's rocket. **2** another name for **dyer's rocket.** [C14: from Low German; compare Middle Low German *walde, waude,* Dutch *wouw*]

Weld (wɛld) *n* Sir **Frederick Aloysius.** 1823–91, New Zealand statesman, born in England: prime minister of New Zealand (1864–65).

welding rod *n Electrical engineering.* filler metal supplied in the form of a rod, usually coated with flux.

Weldon ('wɛldən) *n* **Fay.** born 1931, British novelist and writer. Her novels include *Praxis* (1978), *Life and Loves of a She-Devil* (1984), *Worst Fears* (1996), and *Nobody Likes Me!* (1997).

welfare ('wɛl,fɛə) *n* **1** health, happiness, prosperity, and well-being in general. **2a** financial and other assistance given to people in need. **2b** *(as modifier): welfare services.* **3** Also called: **welfare work.** plans or work to better the social or economic conditions of various underprivileged groups. **4 the welfare.** *Informal, chiefly Brit.* the public agencies involved with giving such assistance. **5 on welfare.** *Chiefly U.S. and Canadian.* in receipt of financial aid from a government agency or other source. [C14: from the phrase *wel fare;* related to Old Norse *velferth,* German *Wohlfahrt;* see WELL[1], FARE]

welfare economics *n (functioning as sing)* the aspects of economic theory concerned with the welfare of society and priorities to be observed in the allocation of resources.

welfare state *n* **1** a system in which the government undertakes the chief responsibility for providing for the social and economic security of its population, usually through unemployment insurance, old-age pensions, and other social-security measures. **2** a social system characterized by such policies.

welfarism ('wɛl,fɛərɪzəm) *n* policies or attitudes associated with a welfare state. ▸ **'wel,farist** *n*

welkin ('wɛlkɪn) *n Archaic.* the sky, heavens, or upper air. [Old English *wolcen, welcen;* related to Old Frisian *wolken,* Old Saxon, Old High German *wolcan*]

Welkom ('wɛlkəm, 'vɛl-) *n* a town in central South Africa; developed rapidly following the discovery of gold. Pop.: 228 000 (latest est.).

well[1] (wɛl) *adv* **better, best. 1** *(often used in combination)* in a satisfactory manner: *the party went very well.* **2** *(often used in combination)* in a good, skilful, or pleasing manner: *she plays the violin well.* **3** in a correct or careful manner: *listen well to my words.* **4** in a comfortable or prosperous manner: *to live well.* **5** *(usually used with auxiliaries)* suitably; fittingly: *you can't very well say that.* **6** intimately: *I knew him well.* **7** in a kind or favourable manner: *she speaks well of you.* **8** to a great or considerable extent; fully: *to be well informed.* **9** by a considerable margin: *let me know well in advance.* **10** (preceded by *could, might,* or *may*) indeed: *you may well have to do it yourself.* **11** *Informal.* (intensifier): *well safe.* **12 all very well.** used ironically to express discontent, dissent, etc. **13 as well. 13a** in addition; too. **13b** (preceded by *may* or *might*) with equal effect: *you might as well come.* **14 as well as.** in addition to. **15 (just) as well.** preferable or advisable: *it would be just as well if you paid me now.* **16 leave well (enough) alone.** to refrain from interfering with something that is satisfactory. **17 well and good.** used to indicate calm acceptance, as of a decision: *if you accept my offer, well and good.* **18 well up in.** well acquainted with (a particular subject); knowledgeable about. ◆ *adj (usually postpositive)* **19** (when *prenominal, usually used with a negative*) in good health: *I'm very well, thank you; he's not a well man.* **20** satisfactory, agreeable, or pleasing. **21** prudent; advisable: *it would be well to make no comment.* **22** prosperous or comfortable. **23** fortunate or happy: *it is well that you agreed to go.* ◆ *interj* **24a** an expression of surprise, indignation, or reproof. **24b** an expression of anticipation in waiting for an answer or remark. ◆ *sentence connector.* **25** an expression used to preface a remark, gain time, etc.: *well, I don't think I will come.* [Old English *wel;* related to Old High German *wala, wola* (German *wohl*), Old Norse *val,* Gothic *waila*]

well[2] (wɛl) *n* **1** a hole or shaft that is excavated, drilled, bored, or cut into the earth so as to tap a supply of water, oil, gas, etc. **2** a natural pool where ground water comes to the surface. **3a** a cavity, space, or vessel used to contain a liquid. **3b** *(in combination): an inkwell.* **4** an open shaft through the floors of a building, such as one used for a staircase. **5** a deep enclosed space in a building or between buildings that is open to the sky to permit light and air to enter. **6a** a bulkheaded compartment built around a ship's pumps for protection and ease of access. **6b** another word for **cockpit. 7** a perforated tank in the hold of a fishing boat for keeping caught fish alive. **8** (in England) the open space in the centre of a law court. **9** a source, esp. one that provides a continuous supply: *he is a well of knowledge.* ◆ *vb* **10** to flow or cause to flow upwards or outwards: *tears welled from her eyes.* [Old English *wella;* related to Old High German *wella* (German *Welle* wave), Old Norse *vella* boiling heat]

we'll (wiːl) *contraction of* we will *or* we shall.

well-advised *adj* (**well advised** *when postpositive*). **1** acting with deliberation or reason. **2** well thought out; considered: *a well-advised plan.*

well-affected *adj* (**well affected** *when postpositive*). favourably disposed (towards); steadfast or loyal.

Welland Canal ('wɛlənd) *n* a canal in S Canada, in Ontario, linking Lake Erie to Lake Ontario: part of the St Lawrence Seaway, with eight locks. Length: 44 km (28 miles). Also called: **Welland Ship Canal.**

well-appointed *adj* (**well appointed** *when postpositive*). well equipped or furnished; properly supplied.

wellaway ('wɛlə'weɪ) *interj Archaic.* woe! alas! [Old English, from *wei lā wei,* variant of *wā lā wā,* literally: woe! lo woe]

well-balanced *adj* (**well balanced** *when postpositive*). **1** having good balance or proportions. **2** of balanced mind; sane or sensible.

wellbeing ('wɛl'biːɪŋ) *n* the condition of being contented, healthy, or successful; welfare.

well-bred *adj* (**well bred** *when postpositive*). **1** Also: **well-born.** of respected or noble lineage. **2** indicating good breeding: well-bred manners. **3** of good thoroughbred stock: a well-bred spaniel.

well-chosen *adj* (**well chosen** *when postpositive*). carefully selected to produce a desired effect; apt: *a few well-chosen words may be more effective than a long speech.*

'well-ac'cepted *adj*
'well-ac'customed *adj*
'well-ac'quainted *adj*
'well-'acted *adj*
'well-a'dapted *adj*
'well-ad'justed *adj*
'well-ad'ministered *adj*
'well-'adver,tised *adj*
'well-'aimed *adj*
'well-'aired *adj*
'well-'argued *adj*
'well-'armed *adj*
'well-ar'ranged *adj*
'well-as'sorted *adj*
'well-at'tended *adj*
'well-at'tested *adj*
'well-au'thenti,cated *adj*
'well-a'ware *adj*
'well-be'haved *adj*
'well-be'loved *adj, n*
'well-'blessed *adj*
'well-'born *adj*
'well-'built *adj*
'well-'calcu,lated *adj*

well-connected *adj* (**well connected** *when postpositive*). having influential or important relatives or friends.

well-disposed *adj* (**well disposed** *when postpositive*). inclined to be sympathetic, kindly, or friendly: *he was never well disposed towards her relatives.*

well-done *adj* (**well done** *when postpositive*). **1** (of food, esp. meat) cooked thoroughly. **2** made or accomplished satisfactorily.

well dressing *n* the decoration of wells with flowers, etc.: a traditional annual ceremony of great antiquity in some parts of Britain, originally associated with the cult of water deities.

Welles (wɛlz) *n* **(George) Orson** ('ɔːsᵊn). 1915–85, U.S. film director, actor, producer, and screenwriter. His *Citizen Kane* (1941) and *The Magnificent Ambersons* (1942) are regarded as film classics.

Wellesley ('wɛlzlɪ) *n* **1 Arthur.** See (1st Duke of) **Wellington. 2** his brother, **Richard Colley,** Marquis Wellesley. 1760–1842, British administrator. As governor general of Bengal (1797–1805) he consolidated British power in India.

Wellesz (*German* 'vɛlɛs) *n* **Egon** ('eːgɔn). 1885–1974, British composer, born in Austria.

well-favoured *adj* (**well favoured** *when postpositive*). having good features; good-looking.

well-fed *adj* (**well fed** *when postpositive*). **1** having a nutritious diet; well nourished. **2** plump; fat.

well-formed *adj Logic, linguistics.* (of a formula, expression, etc.) constructed in accordance with the syntactic rules of a particular system; grammatically correct. ► **well-formedness** *n*

well-found *adj* (**well found** *when postpositive*). furnished or supplied with all or most necessary things.

well-founded *adj* (**well founded** *when postpositive*). having good grounds: *well-founded rumours.*

well-groomed *adj* (**well groomed** *when postpositive*). **1** (of a person) having a tidy pleasing appearance. **2** kept tidy and neat: *a well-groomed garden.* **3** well turned out and tended: *a well-groomed horse.*

well-grounded *adj* (**well grounded** *when postpositive*). **1** well instructed in the basic elements of a subject. **2** another term for **well-founded.**

wellhead ('wɛl,hɛd) *n* **1** the source of a well or stream. **2** a source, fountainhead, or origin.

well-heeled *adj* (**well heeled** *when postpositive*). *Informal.* rich; prosperous; wealthy.

well-hung *adj* (**well hung** *when postpositive*). **1** (of game) hung for a sufficient length of time. **2** *Taboo slang.* (of a man) having large genitals.

wellies ('wɛlɪz) *pl n Brit. informal.* Wellington boots.

well in *adj* (*postpositive*; often foll. by *with*) *Informal.* on good terms or favourably placed (with): *the foreman was well in with the management.*

well-informed *adj* (**well informed** *when postpositive*). **1** having knowledge about a great variety of subjects: *he seems to be a well-informed person.* **2** possessing reliable information on a particular subject.

Wellingborough ('wɛlɪŋbərə, -brə) *n* a town in central England, in Northamptonshire. Pop.: 41 602 (1991).

Wellington[1] ('wɛlɪŋtən) *n* **1** an administrative district, formerly a province, of New Zealand, on SW North Island: major livestock producer in New Zealand. Capital: Wellington. Pop.: 413 100 (1995 est.). Area: 28 153 sq. km (10 870 sq. miles). **2** the capital city of New Zealand. Its port, historically Port Nicholson, on **Wellington Harbour** has a car and rail ferry link between the North and South Islands; university (1899). Pop.: 331 100 (1995 est.).

Wellington[2] ('wɛlɪŋtən) *n* **1st Duke of,** title of *Arthur Wellesley.* 1769–1852, British soldier and statesman; prime minister (1828–30). He was given command of the British forces against the French in the Peninsular War (1808–14) and routed Napoleon at Waterloo (1815).

Wellington boots *pl n* **1** Also called: **gumboots, wellingtons.** *Brit.* knee-length or calf-length rubber or rubberized boots, worn esp. in wet conditions. Often shortened to **wellies. 2** military leather boots covering the front of the knee but cut away at the back to allow easier bending of the knee. **[C19:** named after the 1st Duke of *Wellington***]**

wellingtonia (,wɛlɪŋ'təʊnɪə) *n* another name for **big tree. [C19:** named after the 1st Duke of *Wellington***]**

well-intentioned *adj* (**well intentioned** *when postpositive*). having or indicating benevolent intentions, usually with unfortunate results.

well-knit *adj* (**well knit** *when postpositive*). strong, firm, or sturdy.

well-known *adj* (**well known** *when postpositive*). **1** widely known; famous; celebrated. **2** known fully or clearly.

well-mannered *adj* (**well mannered** *when postpositive*). having good manners; courteous; polite.

well-meaning *adj* (**well meaning** *when postpositive*). having or indicating good or benevolent intentions, usually with unfortunate results.

well-nigh *adv* nearly; almost: *it's well-nigh three o'clock.*

well-off *adj* (**well off** *when postpositive*). **1** in a comfortable or favourable position or state. **2** financially well provided for; moderately rich.

well-oiled *adj* (**well oiled** *when postpositive*). *Informal.* drunk.

well-ordered *adj Logic, maths.* (of a relation) having the property that every nonempty subset of its field has a least member under the relation: *less than* is well-ordered on the natural numbers but not on the reals, since an open set has no least member.

well-padded *adj* (**well padded** *when postpositive*). (of a person) corpulent; portly; fat.

well-preserved *adj* (**well preserved** *when postpositive*). **1** kept in a good condition. **2** continuing to appear youthful: *she was a well-preserved old lady.*

well-read ('wɛl'rɛd) *adj* (**well read** *when postpositive*). having read widely and intelligently; erudite.

well-rounded *adj* (**well rounded** *when postpositive*). **1** rounded in shape or well developed: *a well-rounded figure.* **2** full, varied, and satisfying: *a well-rounded life.* **3** well planned and balanced: *a well-rounded programme.*

Wells[1] (wɛlz) *n* a city in SW England, in Somerset: 12th-century cathedral. Pop.: 9763 (1991).

Wells[2] (wɛlz) *n* **1 Henry.** 1805–78, U.S. businessman, who founded (1852) with William Fargo the express mail service Wells, Fargo and Company. **2 H(erbert) G(eorge).** 1866–1946, British writer. His science-fiction stories include *The Time Machine* (1895), *War of the Worlds* (1898), and *The Shape of Things to Come* (1933). His novels on contemporary social questions, such as *Kipps* (1905), *Tono-Bungay* (1909), and *Ann Veronica* (1909), affected the opinions of his day. His nonfiction works include *The Outline of History* (1920).

well-set *adj* (**well set** *when postpositive*). **1** firmly established. **2** (of a person) strongly built.

well-spoken *adj* (**well spoken** *when postpositive*). **1** having a clear, articulate, and socially acceptable accent and way of speaking. **2** spoken satisfactorily or pleasingly.

wellspring ('wɛl,sprɪŋ) *n* **1** the source of a spring or stream; fountainhead. **2** a source of continual or abundant supply. **[**Old English *welspryng, wylspring;* see WELL[2], SPRING**]**

well-stacked *adj* (**well stacked** *when postpositive*). *Brit. slang.* (of a woman) of voluptuous proportions.

well sweep *n* a device for raising buckets from and lowering them into a well, consisting of a long pivoted pole, the bucket being attached to one end by a long rope.

well-tempered *adj* (**well tempered** *when postpositive*). (of a musical scale or instrument) conforming to the system of equal temperament. See **temperament** (sense 4).

well-thought-of *adj* having a good reputation; respected.

well-thought-out *adj* (**well thought out** *when postpositive*). carefully planned.

well-thumbed *adj* (**well thumbed** *when postpositive*). (of a copy of a book) having the pages marked from frequent turning.

well-to-do *adj* moderately wealthy.

well-turned *adj* (**well turned** *when postpositive*). **1** (of a phrase, speech, etc.) apt and pleasingly sonorous. **2** having a pleasing shape: *a well-turned leg.*

well-upholstered *adj* (**well upholstered** *when postpositive*) *Informal.* (of a person) fat.

'well-'clothed *adj*
'well-con'cealed *adj*
'well-con'ditioned *adj*
'well-con'ducted *adj*
'well-con'sidered *adj*
'well-con'structed *adj*
'well-con'trolled *adj*
'well-'cooked *adj*
'well-'covered *adj*
'well-'culti,vated *adj*
'well-de'fended *adj*
'well-de'fined *adj*
'well-'demon,strated *adj*
'well-de'scribed *adj*
'well-de'served *adj*
'well-de'veloped *adj*
'well-'disciplined *adj*
'well-'docu,mented *adj*
'well-'dressed *adj*
'well-'earned *adj*
'well-'edu,cated *adj*
'well-en'dowed *adj*
'well-e'quipped *adj*
'well-es'tablished *adj*
'well-fi'nanced *adj*
'well-'finished *adj*
'well-'fitted *adj*
'well-'forti,fied *adj*
'well-'fought *adj*
'well-'furnished *adj*
'well-'governed *adj*
'well-'guarded *adj*
'well-'handled *adj*
'well-'hidden *adj*
'well-'illus,trated *adj*
'well-'judged *adj*
'well-'justi,fied *adj*
'well-'kept *adj*
'well-'liked *adj*
'well-'loved *adj*
'well-'made *adj*
'well-'managed *adj*
'well-'marked *adj*
'well-'matched *adj*
'well-'merited *adj*
'well-'mixed *adj*
'well-'moti,vated *adj*
'well-'organ,ized *or* **'well-'organ,ised** *adj*
'well-'paid *adj*
'well-'placed *adj*
'well-'planned *adj*
'well-'played *adj*
'well-'pleased *adj*
'well-'practised *adj*
'well-pre'pared *adj*
'well-pro'portioned *adj*
'well-pro'tected *adj*
'well-pro'vided *adj*
'well-'quali,fied *adj*
'well-'reasoned *adj*
'well-re'ceived *adj*
'well-recom'mended *adj*
'well-re'garded *adj*
'well-'regu,lated *adj*
'well-re'hearsed *adj*
'well-re'membered *adj*
'well-repre'sented *adj*
'well-re'spected *adj*
'well-'ripened *adj*
'well-'satis,fied *adj*
'well-'schooled *adj*
'well-'seasoned *adj*
'well-se'cured *adj*
'well-'shaped *adj*
'well-'situ,ated *adj*
'well-'spent *adj*
'well-'stocked *adj*
'well-'suited *adj*
'well-sup'plied *adj*
'well-sup'ported *adj*
'well-'taught *adj*
'well-'timed *adj*
'well-'trained *adj*
'well-'travelled *adj*
'well-'treated *adj*
'well-'tried *adj*
'well-'trodden *adj*
'well-under'stood *adj*

well-wisher *n* a person who shows benevolence or sympathy towards a person, cause, etc. ▸ **'well-,wishing** *adj, n*

well-woman *n, pl* **-women.** *Social welfare.* **a** a woman who, although not ill, attends a health-service clinic for preventive monitoring, health education, and advice. **b** (*as modifier*): *well-woman clinic.*

well-worn *adj* (**well worn** *when postpositive*). **1** so much used as to be affected by wear: *a well-worn coat.* **2** used too often; hackneyed: *a well-worn phrase.*

welly ('wɛlɪ) *n* **1** (*pl* **-lies.**) *Informal.* Also called: **welly boot.** a Wellington boot. **2** *Slang.* energy, concentration, or commitment (esp. in the phrase **give it some welly**).

Wels (*German* vɛls) *n* an industrial city in N central Austria, in Upper Austria. Pop.: 52 594 (1991).

Welsbach burner ('wɛlzbæk; *German* 'vɛlsbax) *n Trademark.* a type of gaslight in which a mantle containing thorium and cerium compounds becomes incandescent when heated by a gas flame. [**C19**: named after Carl Auer, Baron von *Welsbach* (1858–1929), Austrian chemist, who invented it]

welsh *or* **welch** (wɛlʃ) *vb* (*intr;* often foll. by *on*) *Slang.* **1** to fail to pay a gambling debt. **2** to fail to fulfil an obligation. [**C19**: of unknown origin] ▸ **'welsher** *or* **'welcher** *n*

Welsh[1] (wɛlʃ) *adj* **1** of, relating to, or characteristic of Wales, its people, their Celtic language, or their dialect of English. ◆ *n* **2** a language of Wales, belonging to the S Celtic branch of the Indo-European family. Welsh shows considerable diversity between dialects. **3 the Welsh.** (*functioning as pl*) the natives or inhabitants of Wales collectively. ◆ Also (rare): **Welch.** [Old English *Wēlisc, Wǣlisc;* related to *wealh* foreigner, Old High German *walahisc* (German *welsch*), Old Norse *valskr,* Latin *Volcae*]

Welsh[2] (wɛlʃ) *n* a white long-bodied lop-eared breed of pig, kept chiefly for bacon.

Welsh corgi *n* another name for **corgi.**

Welsh dresser *n* a sideboard with drawers and cupboards below and open shelves above.

Welsh harp *n* a type of harp in which the strings are arranged in three rows, used esp. for the accompaniment of singing, improvisation on folk tunes, etc.

Welshman ('wɛlʃmən) *or* (*fem*) **Welshwoman** *n, pl* **-men** *or* **-women.** a native or inhabitant of Wales.

Welshman's button *n* an angler's name for a species of caddis fly, *Sericostoma personatum.*

Welsh Mountain *n* a common breed of small hardy sheep kept mainly in the mountains of Wales.

Welsh mountain pony *n* a small sturdy but graceful breed of pony used mostly for riding, originally from Wales.

Welsh poppy *n* a perennial W European papaveraceous plant, *Meconopsis cambrica,* with large yellow flowers.

Welsh rabbit *n* a savoury dish consisting of melted cheese sometimes mixed with milk, seasonings, etc., on hot buttered toast. Also called: **Welsh rarebit, rarebit.** [**C18**: a fanciful coinage; *rarebit* is a later folk-etymological variant]

Welsh springer spaniel *n* See **springer spaniel.**

Welsh terrier *n* a wire-haired breed of terrier with a black-and-tan coat.

welt (wɛlt) *n* **1** a raised or strengthened seam or edge, sewn in or on a knitted garment. **2** another word for **weal**[1]. **3** (in shoemaking) a strip of leather, etc., put in between the outer sole and the inner sole and upper. ◆ *vb* (*tr*) **4** to put a welt in (a garment, etc.). **5** to beat or flog soundly. [**C15**: origin unknown]

Weltanschauung *German.* ('vɛltanʃauuŋ) *n* a comprehensive view or personal philosophy of human life and the universe. [from *Welt* world + *Anschauung* view]

welter ('wɛltə) *vb* (*intr*) **1** to roll about, writhe, or wallow. **2** (esp. of the sea) to surge, heave, or toss. **3** to lie drenched in a liquid, esp. blood. ◆ *n* **4** a rolling motion, as of the sea. **5** a confused mass; jumble. [**C13**: from Middle Low German, Middle Dutch *weltern;* related to Old High German *walzan, welzen* to roll]

welterweight ('wɛltə,weɪt) *n* **1a** a professional boxer weighing 140–147 pounds (63.5–66.5 kg). **1b** an amateur boxer weighing 63.5–67 kg (140–148 pounds). **1c** (*as modifier*): *a great welterweight era.* **2** a wrestler in a similar weight category (usually 154–172 pounds (70–78 kg)).

Weltpolitik *German.* ('vɛltpoliti:k) *n* the policy of participation in world affairs. [literally: world politics]

Weltschmerz *German.* ('vɛltʃmɛrts) *n* sadness or melancholy at the evils of the world; world-weariness. [literally: world pain]

Welty ('wɛltɪ) *n* **Eudora.** born 1909, U.S. novelist and short-story writer, noted for her depiction of life in the Mississippi delta. Her novels include *Delta Wedding* (1946) and *The Optimist's Daughter* (1972).

welwitschia (wel'wɪtʃɪə) *n* a gymnosperm plant, *Welwitschia mirabilis,* of arid regions of tropical and southern Africa, consisting of two large woody leaves lying on the ground with a conelike structure arising between them: phylum *Gnetophyta.* [**C19**: named after F. M. J. *Welwitsch* (1807–72), Portuguese botanist, born in Austria]

Welwyn Garden City ('wɛlɪn) *n* a town in SE England, in Hertfordshire: established (1920) as a planned industrial and residential community. Pop.: 42 087 (1991).

Wembley ('wɛmblɪ) *n* part of the Greater London borough of Brent: site of the English national soccer stadium.

wen[1] (wɛn) *n* **1** *Pathol.* a sebaceous cyst, esp. one occurring on the scalp. **2** a large overcrowded city (esp. London in the phrase **the great wen**). [Old English *wenn;* related to Danish dialect *van, væne,* Dutch *wenn*]

wen[2] (wɛn) *n* a rune having the sound of Modern English *w.* [Old English *wen, wyn*]

Wenceslaus *or* **Wenceslas** ('wɛnsɪsləs) *n* **1** 1361–1419, Holy Roman Emperor (1378–1400) and, as **Wenceslaus IV,** king of Bohemia (1378–1419). **2 Saint,** known as *Good King Wenceslaus.* ?907–929, duke of Bohemia (?925–29); patron saint of Bohemia. Feast day: Sept. 28.

wench (wɛntʃ) *n* **1** a girl or young woman, esp. a buxom or lively one: now used facetiously. **2** *Archaic.* a female servant. **3** *Archaic.* a prostitute. ◆ *vb* (*intr*) **4** *Archaic.* to frequent the company of prostitutes. [Old English *wencel* child, from *wancol* weak; related to Old High German *wanchal, wankōn*] ▸ **'wencher** *n*

wend (wɛnd) *vb* to direct (one's course or way); travel. [Old English *wendan;* related to Old High German *wenten,* Gothic *wandjan;* see WIND[2]]

Wend (wɛnd) *n* (esp. in medieval European history) a Sorb; a member of the Slavonic people who inhabited the area between the Rivers Saale and Oder in the early Middle Ages and were conquered by Germanic invaders by the 12th century. See also **Lusatia.**

wendigo ('wɛndɪ,gəʊ) *n Canadian.* **1** (*pl* **-gos**) (among Algonquian Indians) an evil spirit or cannibal. **2** (*pl* **-go** *or* **-gos**) another name for **splake.** [from Algonquian: evil spirit or cannibal]

Wendish ('wɛndɪʃ) *adj* **1** of or relating to the Wends. ◆ *n* **2** the West Slavonic language of the Wends. See also **Sorbian.**

Wendy house ('wɛndɪ) *n* a small model house that children can enter and play in. [**C20**: named after the house built for *Wendy,* the girl in J. M. Barrie's play *Peter Pan* (1904)]

wensleydale ('wɛnzlɪ,deɪl) *n* **1** a type of white cheese with a flaky texture. **2** a breed of sheep with long woolly fleece. [named after *Wensleydale,* North Yorkshire]

went (wɛnt) *vb* the past tense of **go.**

wentletrap ('wɛnt[ə]l,træp) *n* any marine gastropod mollusc of the family *Epitoniidae,* having a long pointed pale-coloured longitudinally ridged shell. [**C18**: from Dutch *winteltrap* spiral shell, from *wintel,* earlier *windel,* from *wenden* to wind + *trap* a step, stairs]

Wentworth ('wɛntwəθ) *n* **1 Thomas.** See (Earl of) **Strafford. 2 William Charles.** 1790–1872, Australian explorer and statesman who was a member of the exploring party that first crossed the Blue Mountains in 1813 and was later a leader in the movement for self-government in New South Wales.

Wentworth scale *n Geology.* a scale for specifying the sizes (diameters) of sedimentary particles, ranging from clay particles (less than 1/256 mm) to boulders (over 256 mm). [after C. K. *Wentworth* (1891–1969), U.S. geologist]

Wenzhou, Wen-chou, *or* **Wenchow** ('wɛn'tʃu:) *n* a port in SE China, in Zhejiang province: noted for its historic buildings. Pop.: 401 871 (1990 est.).

wept (wɛpt) *vb* the past tense and past participle of **weep.**

were (wɜ:; *unstressed* wə) *vb* the plural form of the past tense (indicative mood) of **be** and the singular form used with *you.* It is also used as a subjunctive, esp. in conditional sentences. [Old English *wērun, wæron* past tense plural of *wesan* to be; related to Old Norse *vera,* Old Frisian *weria,* Old High German *werōn* to last]

USAGE *Were,* as a remnant of the past subjunctive in English, is used in formal contexts in clauses expressing hypotheses (*if he were to die, she would inherit everything*), suppositions contrary to fact (*if I were you, I would be careful*), and desire (*I wish he were there now*). In informal speech, however, *was* is often used instead.

we're (wɪə) *contraction of* we are.

weren't (wɜ:nt) *vb contraction of* were not.

werewolf ('wɪə,wʊlf, 'wɛə-) *n, pl* **-wolves.** a person fabled in folklore and superstition to have been changed into a wolf by being bewitched or said to be able to assume wolf form at will. [Old English *werewulf,* from *wer* man + *wulf* WOLF; related to Old High German *werwolf,* Middle Dutch *weerwolf*]

Werfel (*German* 'vɛrfəl) *n* **Franz** (frants). 1890–1945, Austro-Hungarian poet, novelist, and dramatist of the German expressionist movement. His novels include *The Forty Days of Musa Dagh* (1933) and *The Song of Bernadette* (1941).

Wergeland (*Norwegian* 'værgəlan) *n* **Henrik Arnold.** 1808–45, Norwegian poet and nationalist, remembered for his lyric and narrative verse.

wergild, weregild ('wɜ:,gɪld, 'wɛə-), *or* **wergeld** ('wɜ:,gɛld, 'wɛə-) *n* the price set on a man's life in successive Anglo-Saxon and Germanic law codes, to be paid as compensation by his slayer. [Old English *wergeld,* from *wer* man (related to Old Norse *ver,* Latin *vir*) + *gield* tribute (related to Gothic *gild,* Old High German *gelt* payment); see YIELD]

Werner (*German* 'vɛrnər) *n* **1 Abraham Gottlob** ('a:brəham 'gɔtlo:p). 1749–1817, German geologist. He emphasized the importance of field and laboratory observation for understanding the earth. **2 Alfred** ('alfre:t). 1866–1919, Swiss chemist, born in Germany. He developed a coordination theory of the valency of inorganic complexes: Nobel prize for chemistry 1913.

wernerite ('wɜ:nə,raɪt) *n* another name for **scapolite.** [**C19**: named after A.G. WERNER]

wersh (wɜ:ʃ; *Scot.* wɛrʃ) *adj Scot.* **1** tasteless; insipid. **2** sour; bitter. [**C16**: perhaps alteration of dialect *wearish,* probably of Germanic origin]

wert (wɜ:t; *unstressed* wət) *vb Archaic or dialect.* (used with the pronoun *thou* or its relative equivalent) a singular form of the past tense (indicative mood) of **be.**

'well-'used *adj*
'well-'versed *adj*
'well-'wooded *adj*
'well-'written *adj*
'well-'wrought *adj*

Wesak (wɛsʌk) *n Buddhism.* a festival in May celebrating the birth, enlightenment, and death of the Buddha. [Sinhalese]

Weser (*German* 'veːzər) *n* a river in NW Germany: flows northwest to the North Sea at Bremerhaven and is linked by the Mittelland Canal to the Ems, Rhine, and Elbe waterways. Length: 477 km (196 miles).

Wesermünde (*German* veːzər'myndə) *n* the former name (until 1947) of **Bremerhaven.**

Wesker ('wɛskə) *n* **Arnold.** born 1932, British dramatist, whose plays include *Roots* (1959), *Chips With Everything* (1962), *The Merchant* (1976), *Shoeshine* (1988), and *Break My Heart* (1997).

weskit ('wɛskɪt) *n* an informal word for **waistcoat.**

Wesley ('wɛzlɪ) *n* **1 Charles.** 1707–88, English Methodist preacher and writer of hymns. **2** his brother, **John.** 1703–91, English preacher, who founded Methodism. **3 Mary,** pseudonym of *Mary Aline Siepmann.* born 1912, British writer: her novels include *The Camomile Lawn* (1984) and *An Imaginative Experience* (1994).

Wesleyan ('wɛzlɪən) *adj* **1** of, relating to, or deriving from John Wesley. **2** of, relating to, or characterizing Methodism, esp. in its original form or as upheld by the branch of the Methodist Church known as the **Wesleyan Methodists.** ◆ *n* **3** a follower of John Wesley. **4** a member of the Methodist Church or (formerly) of the Wesleyan Methodists. ▸ **'Wesleyanism** *n*

Wessex[1] ('wɛsɪks) *n* **1** an Anglo-Saxon kingdom in S and SW England that became the most powerful English kingdom by the 10th century A.D. **2a** (in Thomas Hardy's works) the southwestern counties of England, esp. Dorset. **2b** (*as modifier*): *Wessex Poems.*

Wessex[2] *n* **Earl of.** See **Edward**[2] (sense 2).

Wessi ('vɛsɪ; *German* 'vɛsi) *n Informal.* a native, inhabitant, or citizen of that part of Germany that was formerly West Germany. [C20: from German *westdeutsch* West German]

west (wɛst) *n* **1** one of the four cardinal points of the compass, 270° clockwise from north and 180° from east. **2** the direction along a parallel towards the sunset, at 270° clockwise from north. **3 the west.** (*often cap.*) any area lying in or towards the west. Related adjs: **Hesperian, Occidental. 4** *Cards.* (*usually cap.*) the player or position at the table corresponding to west on the compass. ◆ *adj* **5** situated in, moving towards, or facing the west. **6** (esp. of the wind) from the west. ◆ *adv* **7** in, to, or towards the west. **8** *Archaic.* (of the wind) from the west. **9 go west.** *Informal.* **9a** to be lost or destroyed irrevocably. **9b** to die. ◆ Symbol: W [Old English; related to Old Norse *vestr,* Sanskrit *avāstāt,* Latin *vesper* evening, Greek *hésperos*]

West[1] (wɛst) *n* **the. 1** the western part of the world contrasted historically and culturally with the East or Orient; the Occident. **2** (formerly) the non-Communist countries of Europe and America contrasted with the Communist states of the East. Compare **East** (sense 2). **3** (in the U.S.) **3a** that part of the U.S. lying approximately to the west of the Mississippi. **3b** (during the Colonial period) the region outside the 13 colonies, lying mainly to the west of the Alleghenies. **4** (in the ancient and medieval world) the Western Roman Empire and, later, the Holy Roman Empire. ◆ *adj* **5a** of or denoting the western part of a specified country, area, etc. **5b** (*as part of a name*): *the West Coast.*

West[2] (wɛst) *n* **1 Benjamin.** 1738–1820, U.S. painter, in England from 1763. **2 Mae.** 1892–1980, U.S. film actress. **3 Nathanael,** real name *Nathan Weinstein.* 1903–40, U.S. novelist: author of *Miss Lonely-Hearts* (1933) and *The Day of the Locust* (1939). **4** Dame **Rebecca,** real name *Cicily Isabel Andrews* (née *Fairfield*). 1892–1983, British journalist, novelist, and critic.

West Atlantic *n* **1** the W part of the Atlantic Ocean, esp. the N Atlantic around North America. **2** a branch of the Niger-Congo family of African languages, spoken in Senegal and in scattered areas eastwards, including Fulani and Wolof. ◆ *adj* **3** relating to or belonging to this group of languages.

West Bank *n* **the.** an autonomous Palestinian region in the Middle East on the W bank of the River Jordan, comprising the hills of Judaea and Samaria and part of Jerusalem: formerly part of Palestine: became part of Jordan after the ceasefire of 1949: occupied by Israel since the 1967 Arab-Israeli War. The provision of the Camp David Agreement that the West Bank should be granted a degree of Palestinian autonomy was re-established in 1993 by a peace treaty between Israel and the Palestinian Liberation Organization. Negotiations to determine the final status of the region have continued. Pop.: 1 881 000 (1998 est.). Area: 5879 sq. km (2270 sq. miles).

West Bengal *n* a state of E India, on the Bay of Bengal: formed in 1947 from the Hindu area of Bengal; additional territories added in 1950 (Cooch Behar), 1954 (Chandernagor), and 1956 (part of Bihar); mostly low-lying and crossed by the Hooghly River. Capital: Calcutta. Pop.: 73 600 000 (1994 est.). Area: 88 752 sq. km (34 260 sq. miles).

West Berkshire *n* a unitary authority in S England. Pop.: 143 700 (1996 est.). Area: 705 sq. km (272 sq. miles).

West Berlin *n* (formerly) the part of Berlin under U.S., British, and French control. ▸ **West Berliner** *n, adj*

westbound ('wɛst,baʊnd) *adj* going or leading towards the west.

West Bromwich ('brɒmɪdʒ, -ɪtʃ) *n* a town in central England, in Sandwell unitary authority, West Midlands: industrial centre. Pop.: 146 386 (1991).

west by north *n* **1** one point on the compass north of west, 281° 15′ clockwise from north. ◆ *adj, adv* **2** in, from, or towards this direction.

west by south *n* **1** one point on the compass south of west, 258° 45′ clockwise from north. ◆ *adj, adv* **2** in, from, or towards this direction.

West Coast jazz *n* a type of cool jazz displaying a soft intimate sound, regular rhythms, and a tendency to incorporate academic classical devices into jazz, such as fugue.

West Country *n* **the.** the southwest of England, esp. Cornwall, Devon, and Somerset.

West Dunbartonshire *n* a council area of W central Scotland, on Loch Lomond and the Clyde estuary: corresponds to part of the historical county of Dunbartonshire; part of Strathclyde Region from 1975 to 1996: engineering industries. Administrative centre: Dumbarton. Pop.: 95 760 (1996 est.). Area: 162 sq. km (63 sq. miles).

West End *n* **the.** a part of W central London containing the main shopping and entertainment areas.

wester ('wɛstə) *vb* **1** (*intr*) (of the sun, moon, or a star) to move or appear to move towards the west. ◆ *n* **2** a strong wind or storm from the west.

westering ('wɛstərɪŋ) *adj Poetic.* moving towards the west: *the westering star.*

Westerlies ('wɛstəlɪz) *pl n Meteorol.* the prevailing winds blowing from the west on the poleward sides of the horse latitudes, often bringing depressions and anticyclones.

westerly ('wɛstəlɪ) *adj* **1** of, relating to, or situated in the west. ◆ *adv, adj* **2** towards or in the direction of the west. **3** (esp. of the wind) from the west. ◆ *n, pl* **-lies. 4** a wind blowing from the west. ▸ **'westerliness** *n*

western ('wɛstən) *adj* **1** situated in or towards or facing the west. **2** going or directed to or towards the west. **3** (of a wind, etc.) coming or originating from the west. **4** native to, inhabiting, or growing in the west. **5** *Music.* See **country and western.**

Western ('wɛstən) *adj* **1** of, relating to, or characteristic of the West as opposed to the Orient. **2** (formerly) of, relating to, or characteristic of the Americas and the parts of Europe not under Communist rule. **3** of, relating to, or characteristic of the western states of the U.S. ◆ *n* **4** a film, book, etc., concerned with life in the western states of the U.S., esp. during the era of exploration and early development.

Western Australia *n* a state of W Australia: mostly an arid undulating plateau, with the Great Sandy Desert, Gibson Desert, and Great Victoria Desert in the interior; settlement concentrated in the southwest; rich mineral resources. Capital: Perth. Pop.: 1 755 500 (1996 est.). Area: 2 527 636 sq. km (975 920 sq. miles).

Western Church *n* **1** the part of Christendom that derives its liturgy, discipline, and traditions principally from the patriarchate of Rome, as contrasted with the part that derives these from the other ancient patriarchates, esp. that of Constantinople. **2** the Roman Catholic Church, sometimes together with the Anglican Communion of Churches.

westerner ('wɛstənə) *n* (*sometimes cap.*) a native or inhabitant of the west of any specific region, esp. of the western states of the U.S. or of the western hemisphere.

Western Ghats *pl n* a mountain range in W peninsular India, parallel to the Malabar coast of the Arabian Sea. Highest peak: Anai Mudi, 2695 m (8841 ft.).

western hemisphere *n* (*often caps.*) **1** that half of the globe containing the Americas, lying to the west of the Greenwich or another meridian. **2** the lands contained in this, esp. the Americas.

western hemlock *n* a North American coniferous evergreen tree, *Tsuga heterophylla,* having hanging branches and oblong cones: family *Pinaceae.*

Western Isles *n* (*functioning as sing or pl*) **1** an island authority in W Scotland, consisting of the Outer Hebrides; created in 1975. Administrative centre: Stornoway. Pop.: 31 834 (1996 est.). Area: 2900 sq. km (1120 sq. miles). **2** Also called: **Western Islands.** another name for the **Hebrides.**

westernism ('wɛstə,nɪzəm) *n* a word, habit, practice, etc., characteristic of western people or of the American West.

westernize *or* **westernise** ('wɛstə,naɪz) *vb* (*tr*) to influence or make familiar with the customs, practices, etc., of the West. ▸ **,westerni'zation** *or* **,westerni'sation** *n*

western larch *n* a North American larch, *Larix occidentalis,* having oval cones and found mainly in S British Columbia.

westernmost ('wɛstən,məʊst) *adj* situated or occurring farthest west.

Western Ocean *n* (formerly) another name for the **Atlantic Ocean.**

western red cedar *n* **1** a large North American arbor vitae, *Thuja plicata,* found along and near the Pacific coast. **2** the wood of this tree, used by North American Indians for building and for carving totem poles.

western roll *n* a technique in high-jumping in which the jumper executes a half-turn of the body to clear the bar.

Western Roman Empire *n* the westernmost of the two empires created by the division of the later Roman Empire, esp. after its final severance from the Eastern Roman Empire (395 A.D.). Also called: **Western Empire.**

Western Sahara *n* a disputed region of NW Africa, on the Atlantic: mainly desert; rich phosphate deposits; a Spanish overseas province from 1958 to 1975; partitioned in 1976 between Morocco and Mauritania who faced growing resistance from the Polisario Front, an organization aiming for the independence of the region as the Democratic Saharan Arab Republic. Mauritania renounced its claim in 1979 and it was taken over by Morocco. Polisario agreed to a UN-brokered cease-fire in 1991 but attempts to settle the status of the region have failed. Pop.: 288 000 (1998 est.). Area: 266 000 sq. km (102 680 sq. miles). Former name (until 1975): **Spanish Sahara.**

Western Samoa *n* See **Samoa** (sense 1).

western swing *n* a 1930s jazz-influenced style of country music.

Western Wall *n Judaism.* a wall in Jerusalem, the last extant part of the Temple of Herod, held sacred by Jews as a place of prayer and pilgrimage. Also called: **Wailing Wall.**

Westfalen (vɛst'faːlən) *n* the German name for **Westphalia.**

West Flanders *n* a province of W Belgium: the country's chief agricultural province. Capital: Bruges. Pop.: 1 122 849 (1996 est.). Area: 3132 sq. km (1209 sq. miles).

West Germanic *n* a subbranch of the Germanic languages that consists of English, Frisian, Dutch, Flemish, Afrikaans, Low German, German, Yiddish, and their associated dialects.

West Germany *n* a former republic in N central Europe, on the North Sea: established in 1949 from the zones of Germany occupied by the British, Americans, and French after the defeat of Nazi Germany; a member of the European Community; reunited with East Germany in 1990. Official name: **Federal Republic of Germany.** See also **Germany.** ▸ **West German** *adj, n*

West Glamorgan *n* a former county in S Wales, formed in 1974 from part of Glamorgan and the county borough of Swansea: replaced in 1996 by the county of Swansea and the county borough of Neath Port Talbot.

West Hartlepool ('hɑːtlɪ,puːl) *n* a former town in NE England, in Co. Durham: part of Hartlepool since 1967.

West Highland white terrier *n* a small pure white terrier having a hard straight coat and erect ears and tail.

West Indian *adj* **1** of or relating to the West Indies, its inhabitants, or their language or culture. **2** native to or derived from the West Indies. ◆ *n* **3** a native or inhabitant of the West Indies. **4** a person of West Indian descent.

West Indies ('ɪndɪz) *pl n* an archipelago off Central America, extending over 2400 km (1500 miles) in an arc from the peninsula of Florida to Venezuela, separating the Caribbean Sea from the Atlantic Ocean: consists of the Greater Antilles, the Lesser Antilles, and the Bahamas; largest island is Cuba. Area: over 235 000 sq. km (91 000 sq. miles). Also called: **the Caribbean.**

westing ('wɛstɪŋ) *n Navigation.* movement, deviation, or distance covered in a westerly direction, esp. as expressed in the resulting difference in longitude.

Westinghouse brake ('wɛstɪŋ,haʊs) *n* a braking system, invented by Westinghouse in 1872 and adopted by U.S. railways, in which the brakes are held off by compressed air in the operating cylinder: controlled leakage of the air or a disruptive emergency causes the brakes to be applied. The system is used on most heavy vehicles and is replacing the vacuum system on many railways. [named after George *Westinghouse* (1846–1914), U.S. inventor and manufacturer]

West Irian *n* the English name for **Irian Jaya.**

West Lothian *n* a council area and historical county of central Scotland, on the Firth of Forth: became part of Lothian region in 1975: reinstated as an independent authority (with revised boundaries) in 1996: agriculture, oil-refining. Administrative centre: Livingston. Pop.: 150 770 (1996 est.). Area: 425 sq. km (164 sq. miles).

Westm. *abbrev. for* Westminster.

Westmeath (,wɛst'miːð) *n* a county of N central Republic of Ireland, in Leinster province: mostly low-lying, with many lakes and bogs. County town: Mullingar. Pop.: 63 000 (1996). Area: 1764 sq. km (681 sq. miles).

West Midlands *n (functioning as sing or pl)* a metropolitan county of central England, administered since 1986 by the unitary authorities of Wolverhampton, Walsall, Dudley, Sandwell, Birmingham, Solihull, and Coventry. Area: 899 sq. km (347 sq. miles).

Westminster ('wɛst,mɪnstə) *n* **1** Also called: **City of Westminster.** a borough of Greater London, on the River Thames: contains the Houses of Parliament, Westminster Abbey, and Buckingham Palace. Pop.: 190 100 (1991 est.). Area: 22 sq. km (8 sq. miles). **2** the Houses of Parliament at Westminster.

Westminster Abbey *n* a Gothic church in London: site of a Benedictine monastery (1050–65); scene of the coronations of almost all English monarchs since William I.

Westmorland ('wɛstmələnd, 'wɛsmə-) *n* (until 1974) a county of NW England, now part of Cumbria.

west-northwest *n* **1** the point on the compass or the direction midway between west and northwest, 292° 30′ clockwise from north. ◆ *adj, adv* **2** in, from, or towards this direction. ◆ *Symbol:* WNW

Weston standard cell ('wɛstən) *n* a primary cell used as a standard of emf, producing 1.018636 volts: consists of a mercury anode and a cadmium amalgam cathode in an electrolyte of saturated cadmium sulphate. Former name: **cadmium cell.** [C20: from a trademark]

Weston-super-Mare ('wɛstən,suːpə'mɛə, -,sjuː-) *n* a town and resort in SW England, in North Somerset unitary authority, Somerset, on the Bristol Channel. Pop.: 69 372 (1991).

West Pakistan *n* the former name (until the end of 1971) of **Pakistan.**

Westphalia (wɛst'feɪlɪə) *n* a historic region of NW Germany, now mostly in the state of North Rhine-Westphalia. German name: **Westfalen.** ▸ **West'phalian** *adj, n*

West Point *n* the U.S. Army installation in New York State that houses the U.S. Military Academy.

West Prussia *n* a former province of NE Prussia, on the Baltic: assigned to Poland in 1945. German name: **Westpreussen** ('vɛstprɔysən).

West Riding *n* (until 1974) an administrative division of Yorkshire, now part of West Yorkshire, North Yorkshire, Cumbria, and Lancashire.

West Saxon (in Anglo-Saxon England) ◆ *adj* **1** of or relating to Wessex, its inhabitants, or their dialect. ◆ *n* **2** the dialect of Old English spoken in Wessex: the chief literary dialect of Old English. See also **Anglian, Kentish. 3** an inhabitant of Wessex.

west-southwest *n* **1** the point on the compass or the direction midway between southwest and west, 247° 30′ clockwise from north. ◆ *adj, adv* **2** in, from, or towards this direction. ◆ *Symbol:* WSW

West Sussex *n* a county of SE England, comprising part of the former county of Sussex. Administrative centre: Chichester. Pop.: 714 100 (1989 est.). Area: 1989 sq. km (768 sq. miles).

West Virginia *n* a state of the eastern U.S.: part of Virginia until the outbreak of the American Civil War (1861); consists chiefly of the Allegheny Plateau; bounded on the west by the Ohio River; coal-mining. Capital: Charleston. Pop.: 1 815 787 (1997 est.). Area: 62 341 sq. km (24 070 sq. miles). Abbrevs.: **W. Va.** or (with zip code) **WV** ▸ **West Virginian** *adj, n*

westward ('wɛstwəd) *adj* **1** moving, facing, or situated in the west. ◆ *adv* **2** Also: **westwards.** towards the west. ◆ *n* **3** the westward part, direction, etc.; the west. ▸ **'westwardly** *adj, adv*

Westwood ('wɛst,wʊd) *n* **Vivienne** (**Isabel**). born 1941, British fashion designer: noted for her punk designs of the late 1970s.

West Yorkshire *n* a metropolitan county of N England, administered since 1986 by the unitary authorities of Bradford, Leeds, Calderdale, Kirklees, and Wakefield. Area: 2039 sq. km (787 sq. miles).

wet (wɛt) *adj* **wetter, wettest. 1** moistened, covered, saturated, etc., with water or some other liquid. **2** not yet dry or solid: *wet varnish.* **3** rainy, foggy, misty, or humid: *wet weather.* **4** employing a liquid, usually water: *a wet method of chemical analysis.* **5** *Chiefly U.S. and Canadian.* characterized by or permitting the free sale of alcoholic beverages: *a wet state.* **6** *Brit. informal.* feeble or foolish. **7 wet behind the ears.** *Informal.* immature or inexperienced; naive. ◆ *n* **8** wetness or moisture. **9** damp or rainy weather. **10** *Brit. informal.* a Conservative politician who is considered not to be a hard-liner. Compare **dry** (sense 21). **11** *Brit. informal.* a feeble or foolish person. **12** *Chiefly U.S. and Canadian.* a person who advocates free sale of alcoholic beverages. **13 the wet.** *Austral.* (in northern and central Australia) the rainy season. ◆ *vb* **wets, wetting, wet** *or* **wetted. 14** to make or become wet. **15** to urinate on (something). **16** *(tr) Dialect.* to prepare (tea) by boiling or infusing. **17 wet one's whistle.** *Informal.* to take an alcoholic drink. [Old English *wǣt;* related to Old Frisian *wēt,* Old Norse *vātr,* Old Slavonic *vedro* bucket] ▸ **'wetly** *adv* ▸ **'wetness** *n* ▸ **,wetta'bility** *n* ▸ **'wettable** *adj* ▸ **'wetter** *n* ▸ **'wettish** *adj*

weta ('wɛtə) *n* any of various wingless insects of the family *Stenopelmatidae* of New Zealand, with long spiny legs. [Maori]

wet-and-dry-bulb thermometer *n* another name for **psychrometer.**

wetback ('wɛt,bæk) *n U.S. informal.* a Mexican labourer who enters the U.S. illegally.

wet blanket *n Informal.* a person whose low spirits or lack of enthusiasm have a depressing effect on others.

wet-bulb thermometer *n* a thermometer the bulb of which is covered by a moist muslin bag, used together with a dry-bulb thermometer to measure humidity.

wet cell *n* a primary cell in which the electrolyte is a liquid. Compare **dry cell.**

wet dream *n* an erotic dream accompanied by an emission of semen during or just after sleep.

wet fish *n* **a** fresh fish as opposed to frozen or cooked fish. **b** *(as modifier)*: *a wet-fish shop.*

wet fly *n Angling.* **a** an artificial fly designed to float or ride below the water surface. **b** *(as modifier)*: *wet-fly fishing.* ◆ Compare **dry fly.**

wether ('wɛðə) *n* a male sheep, esp. a castrated one. [Old English *hwæther;* related to Old Frisian *hweder,* Old High German *hwedar,* Old Norse *hvatharr*]

wetland ('wɛtlənd) *n (sometimes pl)* **a** an area of swampy or marshy land, esp. considered as part of an ecological system. **b** *(as modifier)*: *wetland species.*

wet look *n* a shiny finish given to certain clothing and footwear materials, esp. plastic and leather.

wet nurse *n* **1** a woman hired to suckle the child of another. ◆ *vb* **wet-nurse.** *(tr)* **2** to act as a wet nurse to (a child). **3** *Informal.* to attend with great devotion.

wet pack *n Med.* a hot or cold damp sheet or blanket for wrapping around a patient.

wet rot *n* **1** a state of decay in timber caused by various fungi, esp. *Coniophora puteana.* The hyphal strands of the fungus are seldom visible and affected timber turns dark brown. **2** any of the fungi causing this decay.

wet steam *n* steam, usually low-pressure, that contains water droplets in suspension.

wet suit *n* a close-fitting rubber suit used by skin divers, yachtsmen, etc., to retain body heat when they are immersed in water or sailing in cold weather.

Wetterhorn (*German* 'vɛtər,hɔrn) *n* a mountain in S Switzerland, in the Bernese Alps. Height: 3701 m (12 143 ft.).

wetting agent *n Chem.* any substance added to a liquid to lower its surface tension and thus increase its ability to spread across or penetrate into a solid.

WEU *abbrev. for* Western European Union.

we've (wiːv) *contraction of* we have.

Wexford ('wɛksfəd) *n* **1** a county of SE Republic of Ireland, in Leinster province on the Irish Sea: the first Irish county to be colonized from England; mostly low-lying and fertile. County town: Wexford. Pop.: 104 000 (1996). Area: 2352 sq. km (908 sq. miles). **2** a port in SE Republic of Ireland, county town of Co. Wexford: sacked by Oliver Cromwell in 1649. Pop.: 9540 (1991).

Weygand (*French* vegɑ̃) *n* **Maxime** (maksim). 1867–1965, French general; as commander in chief of the Allied armies in France (1940) he advised the French Government to surrender to Germany.

Weyl (vaɪl) *n* **Hermann.** 1885–1955, U.S. mathematician, born in Germany; noted for his work on group theory and the mathematics of relativity.

Weymouth ('weɪməθ) *n* a port and resort in S England, in Dorset on the English Channel: administratively part of the borough of **Weymouth and Melcombe Regis.** Pop. (with Melcombe Regis): 53 235 (1991).

WFF *Logic. abbrev. for* well-formed formula.

WFTU *abbrev. for* World Federation of Trade Unions.

wg *or* **WG** *abbrev. for:* **1** water gauge. **2** wire gauge.

WG *international car registration for* (Windward Islands) Grenada.

W. Glam *abbrev. for* West Glamorgan.

wh. *abbrev. for* white.

wha (hwɔː) *or* **whae** (hwe) *pron* a Scot. word for **who.**

whack (wæk) *vb (tr)* **1** to strike with a sharp resounding blow. **2** *(usually passive) Brit. informal.* to exhaust completely. ◆ *n* **3** a sharp resounding blow or the noise made by such a blow. **4** *Informal.* a share or portion. **5** *Informal.* a try or attempt (esp. in the phrase **have a whack at**). **6 out of whack.** *Informal.* out of order; unbalanced: *the whole system is out of whack.* ◆ *interj* **7** an exclamation imitating the noise of a sharp resounding blow. [C18: perhaps a variant of THWACK, ultimately of imitative origin] ▸ **'whacker** *n*

whacking ('wækɪŋ) *Informal, chiefly Brit.* ◆ *adj* **1** enormous. ◆ *adv* **2** (intensifier): *a whacking big lie.*

whack off *vb* (*intr, adv*) *Taboo slang.* to masturbate.

whacky ('wækɪ) *adj* **whackier, whackiest.** *U.S. slang.* a variant spelling of **wacky.**

whakapapa ('hwækəpæpə, 'fæk-) *n N.Z.* genealogy; family tree. [Maori]

whale[1] (weɪl) *n, pl* **whales** *or* **whale. 1** any of the larger cetacean mammals, excluding dolphins, porpoises, and narwhals. They have flippers, a streamlined body, and a horizontally flattened tail and breathe through a blowhole on the top of the head. Related adj: **cetacean. 2** any cetacean mammal. See also **toothed whale, whalebone whale. 3 a whale of a.** *Informal.* an exceptionally large, fine, etc., example of a (person or thing): *we had a whale of a time on holiday.* [Old English *hwæl;* related to Old Saxon, Old High German *hwal,* Old Norse *hvalr,* Latin *squalus* seapig]

whale[2] (weɪl) *vb* (*tr*) to beat or thrash soundly. [C18: variant of WALE[1]]

whaleback ('weɪl,bæk) *n* **1** something shaped like the back of a whale. **2** a steamboat having a curved upper deck.

whaleboat ('weɪl,bəʊt) *n* a narrow boat from 20 to 30 feet long having a sharp prow and stern, formerly used in whaling. Also called: **whaler.**

whalebone ('weɪl,bəʊn) *n* **1** Also called: **baleen.** a horny elastic material forming a series of numerous thin plates that hang from the upper jaw on either side of the palate in the toothless (whalebone) whales and strain plankton from water entering the mouth. **2** a thin strip of this substance, used in stiffening corsets, bodices, etc.

whalebone whale *n* any whale belonging to the cetacean suborder *Mysticeti,* having a double blowhole and strips of whalebone between the jaws instead of teeth: includes the rorquals, right whales, and the blue whale. Compare **toothed whale.**

whale catcher *n* a vessel engaged in the actual harpooning of whales.

whale oil *n* oil obtained either from the blubber of whales (train oil) or the head of the sperm whale (sperm oil).

whaler ('weɪlə) *n* **1** Also called (U.S.): **whaleman.** a person employed in whaling. **2** a vessel engaged in whaling. See **factory ship, whale catcher. 3** another word for **whaleboat. 4** *Austral.* a nomad surviving in the bush without working.

whale shark *n* a large spotted whalelike shark, *Rhincodon typus,* of warm seas, that feeds on plankton and small animals: family *Rhincodontidae.*

whaling ('weɪlɪŋ) *n* **1** the work or industry of hunting and processing whales for food, oil, etc. ◆ *adv* **2** *Informal.* (intensifier): *a whaling good time.*

wham (wæm) *n* **1** a forceful blow or impact or the sound produced by such a blow or impact. ◆ *interj* **2** an exclamation imitative of this sound. ◆ *vb* **whams, whamming, whammed. 3** to strike or cause to strike with great force. [C20: of imitative origin]

whammy ('wæmɪ) *n, pl* **-mies.** *Informal.* **1** a devastating setback: *the double whammy of high interest rates and low wage increases.* **2** an evil spell or curse: *she was convinced he had put the whammy on her.* [C20: WHAM + -Y[2]]

whanau ('fɑːnaʊ) *n N.Z.* (in Maori societies) a family, esp. an extended family. [Maori]

whang[1] (wæŋ) *vb* **1** to strike or be struck so as to cause a resounding noise. ◆ *n* **2** the resounding noise produced by a heavy blow. **3** a heavy blow. [C19: of imitative origin]

whang[2] (wæŋ) *n Scot.* **1** a leather thong. ◆ *vb* **2** (*tr*) to strike with or as if with a thong. [C17: variant of THONG]

Whangarei (,wɑːŋɑː'reɪ) *n* a port in New Zealand, the northernmost city of North Island: oil refinery. Pop.: 44 800 (1994).

whangee (wæŋ'iː) *n* **1** any tall woody grass of the S and SE Asian genus *Phyllostachys,* grown for its stems, which are used for bamboo canes and as a source of paper pulp. **2** a cane or walking stick made from the stem of any of these plants. [C19: probably from Chinese (Mandarin) *huangli,* from *huang* yellow + *li* bamboo cane]

whap (wɒp) *vb* **whaps, whapping, whapped,** *n* a less common spelling of **whop.**

whare ('wɔːrɪ; *Maori* 'fɒre) *n N.Z.* **1** a Maori hut or dwelling place. **2** any simple dwelling place, esp. at a beach or in the bush. [from Maori]

wharepuni ('fɒrɛ,pʊnɪ) *n N.Z.* another name for **meeting house** (sense 2).

wharf (wɔːf) *n, pl* **wharves** (wɔːvz) *or* **wharfs. 1** a platform of timber, stone, concrete, etc., built parallel to the waterfront at a harbour or navigable river for the docking, loading, and unloading of ships. **2 the wharves.** *N.Z.* the working area of a dock. **3** an obsolete word for **shore**[1]. ◆ *vb* (*tr*) **4** to moor or dock at a wharf. **5** to provide or equip with a wharf or wharves. **6** to store or unload on a wharf. [Old English *hwearf* heap; related to Old Saxon *hwarf,* Old High German *hwarb* a turn, Old Norse *hvarf* circle]

wharfage ('wɔːfɪdʒ) *n* **1** accommodation for ships at wharves. **2** a charge for use of a wharf. **3** wharves collectively.

wharfie ('wɔːfɪ) *n Austral. and N.Z.* a wharf labourer; docker.

wharfinger ('wɔːfɪndʒə) *n* an owner or manager of a wharf. [C16: probably alteration of *wharfager* (see WHARFAGE, -ER[1]); compare HARBINGER]

wharf rat *n* **1** any rat, usually a brown rat, that infests wharves. **2** *Informal.* a person who haunts wharves, usually for dishonest purposes.

Wharton ('wɔːtᵊn) *n* **Edith (Newbold).** 1862–1937, U.S. novelist; author of *The House of Mirth* (1905) and *Ethan Frome* (1911).

wharve (wɔːv) *n* a wooden disc or wheel on a shaft serving as a flywheel or pulley. [Old English *hweorfa,* from *hweorfan* to revolve; related to Old Saxon *hwervo* axis, Old High German *hwerbo* a turn]

what (wɒt; *unstressed* wət) *determiner* **1a** used with a noun in requesting further information about the identity or categorization of something: *what job does he do?* **1b** (*as pronoun*): *what is her address?* **1c** (*used in indirect questions*): *does he know what man did this? tell me what he said.* **2a** the (person, thing, persons, or things) that: *we photographed what animals we could see.* **2b** (*as pronoun*): *bring me what you've written; come what may.* **3** (intensifier; used in exclamations): *what a good book!* ◆ *adv* **4** in what respect? to what degree?: *what do you care?* ◆ *pron* **5** *Not standard.* which, who, or that, when used as relative pronouns: *this is the man what I saw in the park yesterday.* **6 what about.** what do you think, know, feel, etc., concerning? **7 what for. 7a** for what purpose? why? **7b** *Informal.* a punishment or reprimand (esp. in the phrase **give (a person) what for**). **8 what have you.** someone, something, or somewhere unknown or unspecified: *cars, motorcycles, or what have you.* **9 what if. 9a** what would happen if? **9b** what difference would it make if? **10 what matter.** what does it matter? **11 what's what.** *Informal.* the true or real state of affairs. ◆ *interj* **12** *Informal.* don't you think? don't you agree?: *splendid party, what?* [Old English *hwæt;* related to Old Frisian *whet,* Old High German *hwaz* (German *was*), Old Norse *hvatr*]

USAGE The use of *are* in sentences such as *what we need are more doctors* is common, although many people think *is* should be used: *what we need is more doctors.*

whatever (wɒt'ɛvə, wət-) *pron* **1** everything or anything that: *do whatever he asks you to.* **2** no matter what: *whatever he does, he is forgiven.* **3** *Informal.* an unknown or unspecified thing or things: *take a hammer, chisel, or whatever.* **4** an intensive form of *what,* used in questions: *whatever can he have said to upset her so much?* ◆ *determiner* **5** an intensive form of *what: use whatever tools you can get hold of.* ◆ *adj* **6** (*postpositive*) absolutely; whatsoever: *I saw no point whatever in continuing.*

whatnot ('wɒt,nɒt) *n* **1** Also called: **what-d'you-call-it.** *Informal.* a person or thing the name of which is unknown, temporarily forgotten, or deliberately overlooked. **2** *Informal.* unspecified assorted material. **3** a portable stand with shelves, used for displaying ornaments, etc.

whatsit ('wɒtsɪt), **whatsitsname,** (*masc*) **whatshisname,** *or* (*fem*) **whatshername** *n Informal.* a person or thing the name of which is unknown, temporarily forgotten, or deliberately overlooked.

whatsoever (,wɒtsəʊ'ɛvə) *adj* **1** (*postpositive*) at all: used as an intensifier with indefinite pronouns and determiners such as *none, any, no one, anybody,* etc. ◆ *pron* **2** an archaic word for **whatever.**

whaup (wɔːp; *Scot.* hwɔːp) *n Chiefly Scot.* a popular name for the **curlew.** [C16: related to Old English *huilpe,* ultimately imitative of the bird's cry; compare Low German *regenwilp* sandpiper]

whaur (hwɔːr) *adv, pron, conj, n* a Scot. word for **where.**

wheal (wiːl) *n* a variant spelling of **weal**[1].

wheat (wiːt) *n* **1** any annual or biennial grass of the genus *Triticum,* native to the Mediterranean region and W Asia but widely cultivated, having erect flower spikes and light brown grains. **2** the grain of any of these grasses, used in making flour, pasta, etc. ◆ See also **emmer, durum.** [Old English *hwǣte,* related to Old Frisian, Old Saxon *hwēti,* Old High German *hweizi,* Old Norse *hveiti;* see WHITE]

wheat beer *n* any of various beers brewed using a mixture of wheat malt and barley malt.

wheatear ('wiːt,ɪə) *n* any small northern songbird of the genus *Oenanthe,* esp. *O. oenanthe,* a species having a pale grey back, black wings and tail, white rump, and pale brown underparts: subfamily *Turdinae* (thrushes). [C16: back formation from *wheatears* (wrongly taken as plural), probably from WHITE + ARSE; compare Dutch *witstaart,* French *culblanc* white tail]

wheaten ('wiːtᵊn) *adj* **1** made of the grain or flour of wheat: *wheaten bread.* **2** of a pale yellow colour.

wheat germ *n* the vitamin-rich embryo of the wheat kernel, which is largely removed before milling and is used in cereals, as a food supplement, etc.

wheatmeal ('wiːt,miːl) *n* **a** a brown flour intermediate between white flour and wholemeal flour. **b** (*as modifier*): *a wheatmeal loaf.*

wheat rust *n* **1** a rust fungus, *Puccinia graminis,* that attacks cereals, esp. wheat, and the barberry. **2** the disease caused by this fungus.

Wheatstone bridge ('wiːtstən) *n* a device for determining the value of an unknown resistance by comparison with a known standard resistance. [C19: named after Sir Charles *Wheatstone* (1802–75), British physicist and inventor]

wheatworm ('wiːt,wɜːm) *n* a parasitic nematode worm, *Anguina tritici,* that forms galls in the seeds of wheat.

whee (wiː) *interj* an exclamation of joy, thrill, etc.

wheedle ('wiːdᵊl) *vb* **1** to persuade or try to persuade (someone) by coaxing words, flattery, etc. **2** (*tr*) to obtain by coaxing and flattery: *she wheedled some money out of her father.* [C17: perhaps from German *wedeln* to wag one's tail, from Old High German *wedil, wadil* tail] ▸ **'wheedler** *n* ▸ **'wheedling** *adj* ▸ **'wheedlingly** *adv*

wheel (wiːl) *n* **1** a solid disc, or a circular rim joined to a hub by radial or tangential spokes, that is mounted on a shaft about which it can turn, as in vehicles and machines. **2** anything like a wheel in shape or function. **3** a device consisting of or resembling a wheel or having a wheel as its principal component: *a steering wheel; a water wheel.* **4** (usually preceded by *the*) a medieval torture consisting of a wheel to which the victim was tied and then had his limbs struck and broken by an iron bar. **5** short for **wheel of fortune** or **potter's wheel. 6** the act of turning. **7** a pivoting movement of troops, ships, etc. **8** a type of firework coiled to make it rotate when let off. **9** a set of short rhyming lines, usually four or five in number, forming the concluding part of a stanza. Compare **bob**[2] (sense 7). **10** the disc in which the ball is spun in roulette. **11** *U.S. and Canadian.* an informal word for **bicycle. 12** *Archaic.* a refrain. **13** *Informal, chiefly U.S. and Canadian.* a person of great influence (esp. in the phrase **big**

wheel). **14 at the wheel. 14a** driving or steering a vehicle or vessel. **14b** in charge. ◆ *vb* **15** (when *intr* sometimes foll. by *about* or *round*) to turn or cause to turn on or as if on an axis. **16** to move or cause to move on or as if on wheels; roll. **17** (*tr*) to perform with or in a circular movement. **18** (*tr*) to provide with a wheel or wheels. **19** (*intr;* often foll. by *about*) to change one's mind or opinion. **20 wheel and deal.** *Informal.* to be a free agent, esp. to advance one's own interests. ◆ See also **wheels.** [Old English *hweol, hweowol;* related to Old Norse *hvēl,* Greek *kuklos,* Middle Low German *wēl,* Dutch *wiel*] ▸ **'wheel-less** *adj*

wheel and axle *n* a simple machine for raising weights in which a rope unwinding from a wheel is wound onto a cylindrical drum or shaft coaxial with or joined to the wheel to provide mechanical advantage.

wheel animalcule *n* another name for **rotifer.**

wheelbarrow ('wiːlˌbærəʊ) *n* **1** a simple vehicle for carrying small loads, typically being an open container supported by a wheel at the front and two legs behind. ◆ *vb* **2** (*tr*) to convey in a wheelbarrow.

wheelbase ('wiːlˌbeɪs) *n* the distance between the front and back axles of a motor vehicle.

wheel bug *n* a large predatory North American heteropterous insect, *Arilus cristatus,* having a semicircular thoracic projection: family *Reduviidae* (assassin bugs).

wheelchair ('wiːlˌtʃɛə) *n Med.* a special chair mounted on large wheels, for use by invalids or others for whom walking is impossible or temporarily inadvisable.

wheelchair housing *n Social welfare.* housing designed or adapted for a chairbound person. See also **mobility housing.**

wheel clamp *n* a device fixed onto one wheel of an illegally parked car in order to immobilize it. The driver has to pay to have it removed.

wheeled (wiːld) *adj* **a** having or equipped with a wheel or wheels. **b** (*in combination*): *four-wheeled.*

wheeler ('wiːlə) *n* **1** Also called: **wheel horse.** a horse or other draught animal nearest the wheel. **2** (*in combination*) something equipped with a specified sort or number of wheels: *a three-wheeler.* **3** a person or thing that wheels.

Wheeler ('wiːlə) *n* **1 John Archibald.** born 1911, U.S. physicist, noted for his work on nuclear fission and the development (1949–51) of the hydrogen bomb, also for his work on unified field theory. **2** Sir (**Robert Eric**) **Mortimer.** 1890–1976, Scottish archaeologist, who did much to increase public interest in archaeology. He is noted esp. for his excavations at Mohenjo-Daro and Harappa in the Indus Valley and at Maiden Castle in Dorset.

wheeler-dealer *n Informal.* a person who wheels and deals.

wheel horse *n* **1** another word for **wheeler** (sense 1). **2** *U.S. and Canadian.* a person who works steadily or hard.

wheelhouse ('wiːlˌhaʊs) *n* another term for **pilot house.**

wheelie ('wiːlɪ) *n, pl* **-ies.** a manoeuvre on a bicycle or motorbike in which the front wheel is raised off the ground.

wheelie bin *or* **wheely bin** *n* a large container for rubbish, esp. one used by a household, mounted on wheels so that it can be moved more easily.

wheel lock *n* **1** a gunlock formerly in use in which the firing mechanism was activated by sparks produced by friction between a small steel wheel and a flint. **2** a gun having such a lock.

wheel man *n* **1** a cyclist. **2** Also called: **wheelsman.** *U.S.* a helmsman.

wheel of fortune *n* (in mythology and literature) a revolving device spun by a deity of fate selecting random changes in the affairs of man. Often shortened to **wheel.**

wheels (wiːlz) *pl n* **1** the main directing force behind an organization, movement, etc.: *the wheels of government.* **2** an informal word for **car. 3 wheels within wheels.** a series of intricately connected events, plots, etc.

wheel window *n* another name for **rose window.**

wheel wobble *n* an oscillation of the front wheels of a vehicle caused by a defect in the steering gear, unbalanced wheels, etc.

wheelwork ('wiːlˌwɜːk) *n* an arrangement of wheels in a machine, esp. a train of gears.

wheelwright ('wiːlˌraɪt) *n* a person who makes or mends wheels as a trade.

ween (wiːn; *Scot.* hwiːn) *determiner Scot. and northern English dialect.* **1** few; some. **2** (preceded by *a*) **2a** a small number of. **2b** a good number of. **2c** (*as pronoun; functioning as pl*): *a ween of years.* [Old English *hwēne,* instrumental of *hwōn* few, a few]

wheesh (hwiːʃ) *or* **wheesht** (hwiːʃt) *Scot.* ◆ *interj* **1** a plea or demand for silence; hush. ◆ *vb* **2** to silence (a person, noise, etc.) or to be silent. ◆ *n* **3** silence; hush. **4 haud your wheesht!** be silent! hush! [of imitative origin; compare HUSH[1]]

wheeze (wiːz) *vb* **1** to breathe or utter (something) with a rasping or whistling sound. **2** (*intr*) to make or move with a noise suggestive of wheezy breathing. ◆ *n* **3** a husky, rasping, or whistling sound or breathing. **4** *Brit. slang.* a trick, idea, or plan (esp. in the phrase **good wheeze**). **5** *Informal.* a hackneyed joke or anecdote. [C15: probably from Old Norse *hvæsa* to hiss] ▸ **'wheezer** *n* ▸ **'wheezy** *adj* ▸ **'wheezily** *adv* ▸ **'wheeziness** *n*

whelk[1] (wɛlk) *n* any carnivorous marine gastropod mollusc of the family *Buccinidae,* of coastal waters and intertidal regions, having a strong snail-like shell. [Old English *weoloc;* related to Middle Dutch *willok,* Old Norse *vil* entrails]

whelk[2] (wɛlk) *n* a raised lesion on the skin; wheal. [Old English *hwylca,* of obscure origin] ▸ **'whelky** *adj*

whelm (wɛlm) *vb* (*tr*) *Archaic.* **1** to engulf entirely with or as if with water. **2** another word for **overwhelm.** [C13: *whelmen* to turn over, of uncertain origin]

whelp (wɛlp) *n* **1** a young offspring of certain animals, esp. of a wolf or dog. **2** *Disparaging.* a young man or youth. **3** *Jocular.* a young child. **4** *Nautical.* any of the ridges, parallel to the axis, on the drum of a capstan to keep a rope, cable, or chain from slipping. ◆ *vb* **5** (of an animal or, disparagingly, a woman) to give birth to (young). [Old English *hwelp(a);* related to Old High German *hwelf,* Old Norse *hvelpr,* Danish *hvalp*]

when (wɛn) *adv* **1a** at what time? over what period?: *when is he due?* **1b** (*used in indirect questions*): *ask him when he's due.* **2 say when.** to state when an action is to be stopped or begun, as when someone is pouring a drink. ◆ *conj* **3** (*subordinating*) at a time at which; at the time at which; just as; after: *I found it easily when I started to look seriously.* **4** although: *he drives when he might walk.* **5** considering the fact that: *how did you pass the exam when you'd not worked for it?* ◆ *pron* **6** at which (time); over which (period): *an age when men were men.* ◆ *n* **7** (*usually pl*) a question as to the time of some occurrence. [Old English *hwanne, hwænne;* related to Old High German *hwanne, hwenne,* Latin *cum*]

USAGE *When* should not be used loosely as a substitute for *in which* after a noun which does not refer to a period of time: *paralysis is a condition in which* (not *when*) *parts of the body cannot be moved.*

whenas (wɛn'æz) *conj* **1** *Archaic.* **1a** when; whenever. **1b** inasmuch as; while. **2** *Obsolete.* whereas; although.

whence (wɛns) *Archaic or formal.* ◆ *adv* **1** from what place, cause, or origin? ◆ *pron* **2** (*subordinating*) from what place, cause, or origin. [C13 *whannes,* adverbial genitive of Old English *hwanon;* related to Old Frisian *hwana,* Old High German *hwanan*]

USAGE The expression *from whence* should be avoided, since *whence* already means from which place: *the tradition whence* (not *from whence*) *such ideas flowed.*

whencesoever (ˌwɛnssəʊ'ɛvə) *conj* (*subordinating*), *adv Archaic.* out of whatsoever place, cause, or origin.

whene'er (wɛn'ɛə) *adv, conj* a poetic contraction of **whenever.**

whenever (wɛn'ɛvə) *conj* **1** (*subordinating*) at every or any time that; when: *I laugh whenever I see that.* ◆ *adv also* **when ever. 2** no matter when: *it'll be here, whenever you decide to come for it.* **3** *Informal.* at an unknown or unspecified time: *I'll take it if it comes today, tomorrow, or whenever.* **4** an intensive form of *when,* used in questions: *whenever did he escape?*

whensoever (ˌwɛnsəʊ'ɛvə) *conj, adv Rare.* an intensive form of **whenever.**

whenua (fɛn'uə) *n N.Z.* land. [Maori]

where (wɛə) *adv* **1a** in, at, or to what place, point, or position?: *where are you going?* **1b** (*used in indirect questions*): *I don't know where they are.* ◆ *pron* **2** in, at, or to which (place): *the hotel where we spent our honeymoon.* ◆ *conj* **3** (*subordinating*) in the place at which: *where we live it's always raining.* ◆ *n* **4** (*usually pl*) a question as to the position, direction, or destination of something. [Old English *hwǣr, hwār(a);* related to Old Frisian *hwēr,* Old Saxon, Old High German *hwār,* Old Norse, Gothic *hvar*]

USAGE It was formerly considered incorrect to use *where* as a substitute for *in which* after a noun which did not refer to a place or position, but this use has now become acceptable: *we now have a situation where/in which no further action is needed.*

whereabouts ('wɛərəˌbaʊts) *adv* **1** Also: **whereabout.** at what approximate location or place; where: *whereabouts are you?* **2** *Obsolete.* about or concerning which. ◆ *n* **3** (*functioning as sing or pl*) the place, esp. the approximate place, where a person or thing is.

whereafter (ˌwɛər'ɑːftə) *sentence connector. Archaic or formal.* after which.

whereas (wɛər'æz) *conj* **1** (*coordinating*) but on the other hand: *I like to go swimming whereas Sheila likes to sail.* ◆ *sentence connector.* **2** (in formal documents to begin sentences) it being the case that; since.

whereat (wɛər'æt) *Archaic.* ◆ *adv* **1** at or to which place. ◆ *sentence connector.* **2** upon which occasion.

whereby (wɛə'baɪ) *pron* **1** by or because of which: *the means whereby he took his life.* ◆ *adv* **2** *Archaic.* how? by what means?: *whereby does he recognize me?*

where'er (wɛər'ɛə) *adv, conj* a poetic contraction of **wherever.**

wherefore ('wɛəˌfɔː) *n* **1** (*usually pl*) an explanation or reason (esp. in the phrase **the whys and wherefores**). ◆ *adv* **2** *Archaic.* for what reason? why? ◆ *sentence connector.* **3** *Archaic or formal.* for which reason: used as an introductory word in legal preambles.

wherefrom (wɛə'frɒm) *Archaic.* ◆ *adv* **1** from what or where? whence? ◆ *pron* **2** from which place; whence.

wherein (wɛər'ɪn) *Archaic or formal.* ◆ *adv* **1** in what place or respect? ◆ *pron* **2** in which place, thing, etc.

whereinto (wɛər'ɪntuː) *Archaic.* ◆ *adv* **1** into what place? ◆ *pron* **2** into which place.

whereof (wɛər'ɒv) *Archaic or formal.* ◆ *adv* **1** of what or which person or thing? ◆ *pron* **2** of which (person or thing): *the man whereof I speak is no longer alive.*

whereon (wɛər'ɒn) *Archaic.* ◆ *adv* **1** on what thing or place? ◆ *pron* **2** on which thing, place, etc.

wheresoever (ˌwɛəsəʊ'ɛvə) *conj* (*subordinating*), *adv, pron Rare.* an intensive form of **wherever.**

whereto (wɛə'tuː) *Archaic or formal.* ◆ *adv* **1** towards what (place, end, etc.)? ◆ *pron* **2** to which. ◆ Also (archaic): **whereunto.**

whereupon (ˌwɛərə'pɒn) *sentence connector.* **1** at which; at which point; upon which. ◆ *adv* **2** *Archaic.* upon what?

wherever (wɛər'ɛvə) *pron* **1** at, in, or to every place or point which; where: *wherever she went, he would be there.* ◆ *conj* **2** (*subordinating*) in, to, or at whatever place: *wherever we go the weather is always bad.* ◆ *adv also* **where ever. 3** no matter where: *I'll find you, wherever you are.* **4** *Informal.* at, in, or to an unknown or unspecified place: *I'll go anywhere to escape: London, Paris, or wherever.* **5** an intensive form of *where,* used in questions: *wherever can they be?*

wherewith (wɛəˈwɪθ, -ˈwɪð) *Archaic or formal.* ◆ *pron* **1** (*often foll. by an infinitive*) with or by which: *the pen wherewith I am wont to write.* **2** something with which: *I have not wherewith to buy my bread.* ◆ *adv* **3** with what? ◆ *sentence connector* **4** with or after that; whereupon.

wherewithal *n* (ˈwɛəwɪðˌɔːl). **1 the wherewithal.** necessary funds, resources, or equipment (for something or to do something): *these people lack the wherewithal for a decent existence.* ◆ *pron* (ˌwɛəwɪðˈɔːl). **2** a less common word for **wherewith** (senses 1, 2).

wherret (ˈwɛrət) *Dialect.* ◆ *vb* **1** (*tr*) to strike (someone) a blow. ◆ *n* **2** a blow, esp. a slap on the face; stroke. [probably of imitative origin]

wherrit (ˈwɛrɪt) *vb* **1** to worry or cause to worry. **2** (*intr*) to complain or moan. [perhaps from *thwert,* obsolete variant of THWART; compare WORRIT]

wherry (ˈwɛrɪ) *n, pl* **-ries. 1** any of certain kinds of half-decked commercial boats, such as barges, used in Britain. **2** a light rowing boat used in inland waters and harbours. [C15: origin unknown] ▸ **ˈwherryman** *n*

whet (wɛt) *vb* **whets, whetting, whetted.** (*tr*) **1** to sharpen, as by grinding or friction. **2** to increase or enhance (the appetite, desire, etc.); stimulate. ◆ *n* **3** the act of whetting. **4** a person or thing that whets. [Old English *hwettan;* related to *hvæt* sharp, Old High German *hwezzen,* Old Norse *hvetja,* Gothic *hvatjan*] ▸ **ˈwhetter** *n*

whether (ˈwɛðə) *conj* **1** (*subordinating*) used to introduce an indirect question or a clause after a verb expressing or implying doubt or choice in order to indicate two or more alternatives, the second or last of which is introduced by *or* or *or whether: he doesn't know whether she's in Britain or whether she's gone to France.* **2** (*subordinating;* often foll. by *or not*) used to introduce any indirect question: *he was not certain whether his friend was there or not.* **3** (*coordinating*) another word for **either** (sense 3): *any man, whether liberal or conservative, would agree with me.* **4** (*coordinating*) *Archaic.* used to introduce a direct question consisting of two alternatives, the second of which is introduced by *or* or *or whether: whether does he live at home or abroad.* **5 whether or no. 5a** used as a conjunction as a variant of **whether** (sense 1). **5b** under any circumstances: *he will be here tomorrow, whether or no.* **6 whether...or (whether).** if on the one hand...or even if on the other hand: *you'll eat that, whether you like it or not.* ◆ *determiner, pron* **7** *Obsolete.* which (of two): used in direct or indirect questions. [Old English *hwæther, hwether;* related to Old Frisian *hweder, hoder,* Old High German *hwedar,* Old Norse *hvatharr, hvarr,* Gothic *hwathar*]

whetstone (ˈwɛtˌstəʊn) *n* **1** a stone used for sharpening edged tools, knives, etc. **2** something that sharpens.

whew (hwjuː) *interj* an exclamation or sharply exhaled breath expressing relief, surprise, delight, etc.

whey (weɪ) *n* the watery liquid that separates from the curd when the milk is clotted, as in making cheese. [Old English *hwǣg;* related to Middle Low German *wei, heie,* Dutch *hui*] ▸ **ˈwheyey, ˈwheyish,** *or* **ˈwheyˌlike** *adj*

wheyface (ˈweɪˌfeɪs) *n* **1** a pale bloodless face. **2** a person with such a face. ▸ **ˈwheyˌfaced** *adj*

whf *abbrev. for* wharf.

which (wɪtʃ) *determiner* **1a** used with a noun in requesting that its referent be further specified, identified, or distinguished from the other members of a class: *which house did you want to buy?* **1b** (*as pronoun*): *which did you find?* **1c** (*used in indirect questions*): *I wondered which apples were cheaper.* **2a** whatever of a class; whichever: *bring which car you want.* **2b** (*as pronoun*): *choose which of the cars suits you.* ◆ *pron* **3** used in relative clauses with inanimate antecedents: *the house, which is old, is in poor repair.* **4** as; and that: used in relative clauses with verb phrases or sentences as their antecedents: *he died of cancer, which is what I predicted.* **5 the which.** *Archaic.* a longer form of **which,** often used as a sentence connector. [Old English *hwelc, hwilc;* related to Old High German *hwelīh* (German *welch*), Old Norse *hvelīkr,* Gothic *hvileiks,* Latin *quis, quid*]

USAGE See at **that.**

whichever (wɪtʃˈɛvə) *determiner* **1a** any (one, two, etc., out of several): *take whichever car you like.* **1b** (*as pronoun*): *choose whichever appeals to you.* **2a** no matter which (one or ones): *whichever card you pick you'll still be making a mistake.* **2b** (*as pronoun*): *it won't make any difference, whichever comes first.*

whichsoever (ˌwɪtʃsəʊˈɛvə) *pron* an archaic or formal word for **whichever.**

whicker (ˈwɪkə) *vb* (*intr*) (of a horse) to whinny or neigh; nicker. [C17: of imitative origin]

whidah (ˈwɪdə) *n* a variant spelling of **whydah.**

whiff[1] (wɪf) *n* **1** a passing odour. **2** a brief gentle gust of air. **3** a single inhalation or exhalation from the mouth or nose. ◆ *vb* **4** to come, convey, or go in whiffs; puff or waft. **5** to take in or breathe out (tobacco smoke, air, etc.). **6** (*tr*) to sniff or smell. **7** (*intr*) *Brit. slang.* to have an unpleasant smell; stink. [C16: of imitative origin] ▸ **ˈwhiffer** *n*

whiff[2] (wɪf) *n Chiefly Brit.* a narrow clinker-built skiff having outriggers, for one oarsman. [C19: special use of WHIFF[1]]

whiffle (ˈwɪfᵊl) *vb* **1** (*intr*) to think or behave in an erratic or unpredictable way. **2** to blow or be blown fitfully or in gusts. **3** (*intr*) to whistle softly. [C16: frequentative of WHIFF[1]]

whiffler[1] (ˈwɪflə) *n* a person who whiffles.

whiffler[2] (ˈwɪflə) *n Archaic.* an attendant who cleared the way for a procession. [C16: from *wifle* battle-axe, from Old English *wifel,* of Germanic origin; the attendants originally carried weapons to clear the way]

whiffletree (ˈwɪfᵊlˌtriː) *n* another name (esp. U.S.) for **swingletree.** [C19: variant of WHIPPLETREE]

whiffy (ˈwɪfɪ) *adj* **-fier, -fiest.** *Slang.* smelly.

Whig (wɪg) *n* **1** a member of the English political party or grouping that opposed the succession to the throne of James, Duke of York (1679–80), on the grounds that he was a Catholic. Standing for a limited monarchy, the Whigs represented the great aristocracy and the moneyed middle class for the next 80 years. In the late 18th and early 19th centuries the Whigs represented the desires of industrialists and Dissenters for political and social reform. The Whigs provided the core of the Liberal Party. **2** (in the U.S.) a supporter of the War of American Independence. Compare **Tory. 3** a member of the American political party that opposed the Democrats from about 1834 to 1855 and represented propertied and professional interests. **4** a conservative member of the Liberal Party in Great Britain. **5** a person who advocates and believes in an unrestricted laissez-faire economy. **6** *History.* a 17th-century Scottish Presbyterian, esp. one in rebellion against the Crown. ◆ *adj* **7** of, characteristic of, or relating to Whigs. [C17: probably shortened from *whiggamore,* one of a group of 17th-century Scottish rebels who joined in an attack on Edinburgh known as *the whiggamore raid;* probably from Scottish *whig* to drive (of obscure origin) + *more, mer, maire* horse, MARE[1]] ▸ **ˈWhiggery** *or* **ˈWhiggism** *n* ▸ **ˈWhiggish** *adj* ▸ **ˈWhiggishly** *adv* ▸ **ˈWhiggishness** *n*

whigmaleerie (ˌhwɪgməˈliːrɪ) *n Scot.* **1** a trinket, whimsical ornament, or trifle. **2** a whim or caprice. [C18: of unknown origin]

while (waɪl) *conj also* **whilst** (waɪlst). **1** (*subordinating*) at the same time that: *please light the fire while I'm cooking.* **2** (*subordinating*) all the time that: *I stay inside while it's raining.* **3** (*subordinating*) in spite of the fact that: *while I agree about his brilliance I still think he's rude.* **4** (*coordinating*) whereas; and in contrast: *flats are expensive, while houses are cheap.* **5** (*subordinating; used with a gerund*) during the activity of: *while walking I often whistle.* ◆ *prep, conj* **6** *Scot. and northern English dialect.* another word for **until:** *you'll have to wait while Monday for these sheets; you'll never make any progress while you listen to me.* ◆ *n* **7** (*usually used in adverbial phrases*) a period or interval of time: *once in a long while.* **8** trouble or time (esp. in the phrase **worth one's while**): *it's hardly worth your while to begin work today.* **9 the while.** at that time: *he was working the while.* ◆ See also **whiles.** [Old English *hwīl;* related to Old High German *hwīla* (German *Weile*), Gothic *hveila,* Latin *quiēs* peace, *tranquīlus* TRANQUIL]

USAGE It was formerly considered incorrect to use *while* to mean *in spite of the fact that* or *whereas,* but these uses have now become acceptable.

while away *vb* (*tr, adv*) to pass (time) idly and usually pleasantly.

whiles (waɪlz; *Scot.* hwaɪlz) *Archaic or dialect.* ◆ *adv* **1** at times; occasionally. ◆ *conj* **2** while; whilst.

whilk (hwɪlk) *pron* an archaic and dialect word for **which.**

whilom (ˈwaɪləm) *Archaic.* ◆ *adv* **1** formerly; once. ◆ *adj* **2** (*prenominal*) onetime; former. [Old English *hwīlum,* dative plural of *hwīl* WHILE; related to Old High German *hwīlōm,* German *weiland* of old]

whilst (waɪlst) *conj Chiefly Brit.* another word for **while** (senses 1–5). [C13: from WHILES + *-t* as in *amidst*]

whim (wɪm) *n* **1** a sudden, passing, and often fanciful idea; impulsive or irrational thought. **2** a horse-drawn winch formerly used in mining to lift ore or water. [C17: from WHIM-WHAM]

whimbrel (ˈwɪmbrəl) *n* a small European curlew, *Numenius phaeopus,* with a striped head. [C16: from dialect *whimp* or from WHIMPER, alluding to its cry]

whimper (ˈwɪmpə) *vb* **1** (*intr*) to cry, sob, or whine softly or intermittently. **2** to complain or say (something) in a whining plaintive way. ◆ *n* **3** a soft plaintive whine. [C16: from dialect *whimp,* of imitative origin] ▸ **ˈwhimperer** *n* ▸ **ˈwhimpering** *n* ▸ **ˈwhimperingly** *adv*

whimsical (ˈwɪmzɪkᵊl) *adj* **1** spontaneously fanciful or playful. **2** given to whims; capricious. **3** quaint, unusual, or fantastic. ▸ **whimsicality** (ˌwɪmzɪˈkælɪtɪ) *n* ▸ **ˈwhimsically** *adv* ▸ **ˈwhimsicalness** *n*

whimsy *or* **whimsey** (ˈwɪmzɪ) *n, pl* **-sies** *or* **-seys. 1** a capricious idea or notion. **2** light or fanciful humour. **3** something quaint or unusual. ◆ *adj* **-sier, -siest. 4** quaint, comical, or unusual, often in a tasteless way. [C17: from WHIM; compare FLIMSY]

whim-wham *n Archaic.* something fanciful; a trifle. [C16: of unknown origin; compare FLIMFLAM]

whin[1] (wɪn) *n* another name for **gorse.** [C11: from Scandinavian; compare Old Danish *hvine* (*græs*), Norwegian *hvine,* Swedish *hven*]

whin[2] (wɪn) *n* short for **whinstone.** [C14 *quin,* of obscure origin]

whinchat (ˈwɪnˌtʃæt) *n* an Old World songbird, *Saxicola rubetra,* having a mottled brown-and-white plumage with pale cream underparts: subfamily *Turdinae* (thrushes). [C17: from WHIN[1] + CHAT[1]]

whine (waɪn) *n* **1** a long high-pitched plaintive cry or moan. **2** a continuous high-pitched sound. **3** a peevish complaint, esp. one repeated. ◆ *vb* **4** to make a whine or utter in a whine. [Old English *hwīnan;* related to Old Norse *hvīna,* Swedish *hvija* to scream] ▸ **ˈwhiner** *n* ▸ **ˈwhining** *adj* ▸ **ˈwhiningly** *adv* ▸ **ˈwhiny** *adj*

whinge (wɪndʒ) *Informal.* ◆ *vb* **whinges, whingeing, whinged.** (*intr*) **1** to cry in a fretful way. **2** to complain. ◆ *n* **3** a complaint. [from a Northern variant of Old English *hwinsian* to whine; related to Old High German *winsan, winisan,* whence Middle High German *winsen*] ▸ **ˈwhingeing** *n, adj* ▸ **ˈwhinger** *n*

whinny (ˈwɪnɪ) *vb* **-nies, -nying, -nied.** (*intr*) **1** (of a horse) to neigh softly or gently. **2** to make a sound resembling a neigh, such as a laugh. ◆ *n, pl* **-nies. 3** a gentle or low-pitched neigh. [C16: of imitative origin]

whinstone (ˈwɪnˌstəʊn) *n* any dark hard fine-grained rock, such as basalt. [C16: from WHIN[2] + STONE]

whip (wɪp) *vb* **whips, whipping, whipped. 1** to strike (a person or thing) with several strokes of a strap, rod, etc. **2** (*tr*) to punish by striking in this manner. **3** (*tr;* foll. by *out, away,* etc.) to pull, remove, etc., with sudden rapid motion: *to whip out a gun.* **4** (*intr;* foll. by *down, into, out of,* etc.) *Informal.* to come, go, etc., in a rapid sudden manner: *they whipped into the bar for a drink.* **5** to strike or be struck as if by whipping: *the tempest whipped the surface of the sea.* **6** (*tr*) to criticize virulently. **7** (*tr*) to bring, train, etc., forcefully into a desired condition (esp. in the phrases **whip into line** and **whip into shape**). **8** (*tr*) *Informal.* to overcome or outdo: *I know when I've been whipped.* **9** (*tr;* often foll. by *on, out,* or *off*) to drive, urge, compel, etc., by or as if by whipping. **10** (*tr*) to wrap or wind (a cord, thread, etc.) around (a rope, cable, etc.) to prevent chafing or fraying. **11** (*tr*) *Nautical.* to hoist by means of a rope through a single pulley. **12** (*tr*) (in fly-fishing) to cast the fly repeatedly onto (the water) in a whipping motion. **13** (*tr*) (in sewing) to join, finish, or gather with whipstitch. **14** to beat (eggs, cream, etc.) with a whisk or similar utensil to incorporate air and produce expansion. **15** (*tr*) to spin (a top). **16** (*tr*) *Informal.* to steal: *he whipped her purse.* ◆ *n* **17** a device consisting of a lash or flexible rod attached at one end to a stiff handle and used for driving animals, inflicting corporal punishment, etc. **18** a whipping stroke or motion. **19** a person adept at handling a whip, as a coachman, etc. **20** (in a legislative body) **20a** a member of a party chosen to organize and discipline the members of his faction, esp. in voting and to assist in the arrangement of the business. **20b** a call issued to members of a party, insisting with varying degrees of urgency upon their presence or loyal voting behaviour. **20c** (in the Brit. Parliament) a schedule of business sent to members of a party each week. Each item on it is underlined to indicate its importance: one line means that no division is expected, two lines means that the item is fairly important, and three lines means that the item is very important and every member must attend and vote according to the party line. **21** an apparatus for hoisting, consisting of a rope, pulley, and snatch block. **22** any of a variety of desserts made from egg whites or cream beaten stiff, sweetened, and flavoured with fruit, fruit juice, etc. **23** See **whipper-in**. **24** a windmill vane. **25** transient elastic movement of a structure or part, such as a shaft, when subjected to sudden loads or dynamic excitation. **26** a percussion instrument consisting of two strips of wood, joined forming the shape of a V, and clapped loudly together. **27** flexibility, as in the shaft of a golf club, etc. **28** a ride in a funfair involving bumper cars that move with sudden jerks. **29** a wrestling throw in which a wrestler seizes his opponent's arm and spins him to the floor. **30 a fair crack of the whip.** *Informal.* a fair chance or opportunity. ◆ See also **whip in, whip-round, whips, whip up.** [C13: perhaps from Middle Dutch *wippen* to swing; related to Middle Dutch *wipfen* to dance, German *Wipfel* tree top] ▸ **'whip,like** *adj* ▸ **'whipper** *n*

whip bird *n Austral.* **1** any of several birds of the genus *Psophodes,* esp. *P. olivaceus* (**eastern whip bird**) and *P. nigrogularis* (**black-throated whip bird**), having a whistle ending in a whipcrack note. **2** any of various other birds, such as *Pachycephala pectoralis* and *P. rufiventris* (**mock whip bird**).

whipcord ('wɪp,kɔːd) *n* **1** a strong worsted or cotton fabric with a diagonally ribbed surface. **2** a closely twisted hard cord used for the lashes of whips, etc.

whip graft *n Horticulture.* a graft made by inserting a tongue cut on the sloping base of the scion into a slit on the sloping top of the stock.

whip hand *n* (usually preceded by *the*) **1** (in driving horses) the hand holding the whip. **2** advantage or dominating position.

whip in *vb* (*adv*) **1** (*intr*) to perform the duties of a whipper-in to a pack of hounds. **2** (*tr*) *Chiefly U.S.* to keep (members of a political party, etc.) together.

whiplash ('wɪp,læʃ) *n* **1** a quick lash or stroke of a whip or like that of a whip. **2** *Med.* See **whiplash injury.**

whiplash injury *n Med. informal.* any injury to the neck resulting from a sudden thrusting forwards and snapping back of the unsupported head. Technical name: **hyperextension-hyperflexion injury.**

whipper-in *n, pl* **whippers-in.** a person employed to assist the huntsman managing the hounds.

whippersnapper ('wɪpə,snæpə) *n* an insignificant but pretentious or cheeky person, often a young one. Also called: **whipster.** [C17: probably from *whipsnapper* a person who snaps whips, influenced by earlier *snippersnapper,* of obscure origin]

whippet ('wɪpɪt) *n* a small slender breed of dog similar to a greyhound in appearance. [C16: of uncertain origin; perhaps based on the phrase *whip it!* move quickly!]

whipping ('wɪpɪŋ) *n* **1** a thrashing or beating with a whip or similar implement. **2** cord or twine used for binding or lashing.

whipping boy *n* a person of little importance who is blamed for the errors, incompetence, etc., of others, esp. his superiors; scapegoat. [C17: originally referring to a boy who was educated with a prince and who received punishment for any faults committed by the prince]

whipping cream *n* cream that contains just enough butterfat to allow it to be whipped until stiff.

whippletree ('wɪpᵊl,triː) *n* another name for **swingletree.** [C18: apparently from WHIP]

whippoorwill ('wɪpʊ,wɪl) *n* a nightjar, *Caprimulgus vociferus,* of North and Central America, having a dark plumage with white patches on the tail. [C18: imitative of its cry]

whip-round *Informal, chiefly Brit.* ◆ *n* **1** an impromptu collection of money. ◆ *vb* **whip round. 2** (*intr, adv*) to make such a collection of money.

whips (wɪps) *pl n* (often foll. by *of*) *Austral. informal.* a large quantity: *I've got whips of cash at the moment.*

whipsaw ('wɪp,sɔː) *n* **1** any saw with a flexible blade, such as a bandsaw. ◆ *vb* **-saws, -sawing, -sawed, -sawed** *or* **-sawn.** (*tr*) **2** to saw with a whipsaw. **3** *U.S.* to defeat in two ways at once.

whip scorpion *n* any nonvenomous arachnid of the order *Uropygi* (or *Pedipalpi*), typically resembling a scorpion but lacking a sting. See also **vinegarroon.**

whip snake *n* **1** any of several long slender fast-moving nonvenomous snakes of the colubrid genus *Coluber,* such as *C. hippocrepis* (**horseshoe whipsnake**) of Eurasia. **2** any of various other slender nonvenomous snakes, such as *Masticophis flagellum* (**coachwhip snake**) of the U.S.

whipstall ('wɪp,stɔːl) *n* a stall in which an aircraft goes into a nearly vertical climb, pauses, slips backwards momentarily, and drops suddenly with its nose down.

whipstitch ('wɪp,stɪtʃ) *n* **1** a sewing stitch passing over an edge. **2** *U.S. slang.* an instant; moment. ◆ *vb* **3** (*tr*) to sew (an edge) using whipstitch; overcast.

whipstock ('wɪp,stɒk) *n* a whip handle.

whip up *vb* (*tr, adv*) **1** to excite; arouse: *to whip up a mob; to whip up discontent.* **2** *Informal.* to prepare quickly: *to whip up a meal.*

whipworm ('wɪp,wɜːm) *n* any of several parasitic nematode worms of the genus *Trichuris,* esp. *T. trichiura,* having a whiplike body and living in the intestines of mammals.

whir *or* **whirr** (wɜː) *n* **1** a prolonged soft swish or buzz, as of a motor working or wings flapping. **2** a bustle or rush. ◆ *vb* **whirs** or **whirrs, whirring, whirred. 3** to make or cause to make a whir. [C14: probably from Scandinavian; compare Norwegian *kvirra,* Danish *hvirre;* see WHIRL]

whirl (wɜːl) *vb* **1** to spin, turn, or revolve or cause to spin, turn, or revolve. **2** (*intr*) to turn around or away rapidly. **3** (*intr*) to have a spinning sensation, as from dizziness, etc. **4** to move or drive or be moved or driven at high speed. ◆ *n* **5** the act or an instance of whirling; swift rotation or a rapid whirling movement. **6** a condition of confusion or giddiness: *her accident left me in a whirl.* **7** a swift round, as of events, meetings, etc. **8** a tumult; stir. **9** *Informal.* a brief trip, dance, etc. **10 give (something) a whirl.** *Informal.* to attempt or give a trial to (something). [C13: from Old Norse *hvirfla* to turn about; related to Old High German *wirbil* whirlwind] ▸ **'whirler** *n* ▸ **'whirling** *adj* ▸ **'whirlingly** *adv*

whirlabout ('wɜːlə,baʊt) *n* **1** anything that whirls around; whirligig. **2** the act or an instance of whirling around.

whirligig ('wɜːlɪ,gɪg) *n* **1** any spinning toy, such as a top. **2** another name for **merry-go-round. 3** anything that whirls about, spins, or moves in a circular or giddy way: *the whirligig of social life.* **4** another name for **windmill** (the toy). [C15 *whirlegigge,* from WHIRL + GIG[1]]

whirligig beetle *n* any flat-bodied water beetle of the family *Gyrinidae,* which circles rapidly on the surface of the water.

whirlpool ('wɜːl,puːl) *n* **1** a powerful circular current or vortex of water, usually produced by conflicting tidal currents or by eddying at the foot of a waterfall. **2** something resembling a whirlpool in motion or the power to attract into its vortex. **3** short for **whirlpool bath.**

whirlpool bath *n* a bath having a device for maintaining the water in a swirling motion.

whirlwind ('wɜːl,wɪnd) *n* **1** a column of air whirling around and towards a more or less vertical axis of low pressure, which moves along the land or ocean surface. **2a** a motion or course resembling this, esp. in rapidity. **2b** (*as modifier*): *a whirlwind romance.* **3** an impetuously active person.

whirlybird ('wɜːlɪ,bɜːd) *n* an informal word for **helicopter.**

whish (wɪʃ) *n, vb* a less common word for **swish.**

whisht (hwɪʃt) *or* **whist** (hwɪst) *Scot., or archaic, or dialect.* ◆ *interj* **1** hush! be quiet! ◆ *adj* **2** silent or still. ◆ *vb* **3** to make or become silent. ◆ See also **wheesh.** [C14: compare HIST; also obsolete v. *whist* to become silent]

whisk (wɪsk) *vb* **1** (*tr;* often foll. by *away* or *off*) to brush, sweep, or wipe off lightly. **2** (*tr*) to move, carry, etc., with a light or rapid sweeping motion: *the taxi whisked us to the airport.* **3** (*intr*) to move, go, etc., quickly and nimbly: *to whisk downstairs for a drink.* **4** (*tr*) to whip (eggs, cream, etc.) to a froth. ◆ *n* **5** the act of whisking. **6** a light rapid sweeping movement or stroke. **7** a utensil, often incorporating a coil of wires, for whipping eggs, etc. **8** a small brush or broom. **9** a small bunch or bundle, as of grass, straw, etc. [C14: from Old Norse *visk* wisp; related to Middle Dutch *wisch,* Old High German *wisc*]

whisker ('wɪskə) *n* **1** any of the stiff sensory hairs growing on the face of a cat, rat, or other mammal. Technical name: **vibrissa. 2** any of the hairs growing on a person's face, esp. on the cheeks or chin. **3** (*pl*) a beard or that part of it growing on the sides of the face. **4** (*pl*) *Informal.* a moustache. **5** Also called: **whisker boom, whisker pole.** any light spar used for extending the clews of a sail, esp. in light airs. **6** *Chem.* a very fine filamentary crystal having greater strength than the bulk material since it is a single crystal. Such crystals often show unusual electrical properties. **7** a person or thing that whisks. **8** a narrow margin; a small distance: *he escaped death by a whisker.* ▸ **'whiskered** *or* **'whiskery** *adj*

whiskey ('wɪskɪ) *n* the usual Irish and U.S. spelling of **whisky.**

Whiskey ('wɪskɪ) *n Communications.* a code word for the letter *w.*

whiskey sour *n U.S.* a mixed drink of whisky and lime or lemon juice, sometimes sweetened.

whisky ('wɪskɪ) *n, pl* **-kies.** a spirit made by distilling fermented cereals, which is matured and often blended. [C18: shortened from *whiskybae,* from Scottish Gaelic *uisge beatha,* literally: water of life; see USQUEBAUGH]

whisky mac *n Brit.* a drink consisting of whisky and ginger wine.

whisper ('wɪspə) *vb* **1** to speak or utter (something) in a soft hushed tone, esp. without vibration of the vocal cords. **2** (*intr*) to speak secretly or furtively, as in promoting intrigue, gossip, etc. **3** (*intr*) (of leaves, trees, etc.) to make a low soft rustling sound. **4** (*tr*) to utter or suggest secretly or privately: *to whisper treason.* ◆ *n* **5** a low soft voice: *to speak in a whisper.* **6** something uttered in such a voice. **7** a low soft rustling sound. **8** a trace or suspicion. **9** *Informal.* a rumour or secret. [Old English *hwisprian;* related to Old Norse *hvīskra,* Old High German *hwispalōn,* Dutch *wispern*] ▸ **'whisperer** *n*

whispering campaign *n* the organized diffusion by word of mouth of defamatory rumours designed to discredit a person, group, etc.

whispering gallery *n* a gallery or dome with acoustic characteristics such that a sound made at one point is audible at distant points.

whist[1] (wɪst) *n* a card game for four in which the two sides try to win the balance of the 13 tricks: forerunner of bridge. [C17: perhaps changed from WHISK, referring to the sweeping up or whisking up of the tricks]

whist[2] (hwɪst) *interj, adj, vb* a variant of **whisht.**

whist drive *n* a social gathering where whist is played; the winners of each hand move to different tables to play the losers of the previous hand.

whistle ('wɪsəl) *vb* **1** to produce (shrill or flutelike musical sounds), as by passing breath through a narrow constriction most easily formed by the pursed lips: *he whistled a melody.* **2** (*tr*) to signal, summon, or command by whistling or blowing a whistle: *the referee whistled the end of the game.* **3** (of a kettle, train, etc.) to produce (a shrill sound) caused by the emission of steam through a small aperture. **4** (*intr*) to move with a whistling sound caused by rapid passage through the air. **5** (of animals, esp. birds) to emit (a shrill sound) resembling human whistling. ◆ *n* **6** a device for making a shrill high-pitched sound by means of air or steam under pressure. **7** a shrill sound effected by whistling. **8** a whistling sound, as of a bird, bullet, the wind, etc. **9** a signal, warning, command, etc., transmitted by or as if by a whistle. **10** the act of whistling. **11** *Music.* any pipe that is blown down its end and produces sounds on the principle of a flue pipe, usually having as a mouthpiece a fipple cut in the side. **12** **wet one's whistle.** *Informal.* to take an alcoholic drink. **13** **blow the whistle.** (usually foll. by *on*) *Informal.* **13a** to inform (on). **13b** to bring a stop (to). **14** **whistle in the dark.** to try to keep up one's confidence in spite of fear. ◆ See also **whistle for, whistle up.** [Old English *hwistlian;* related to Old Norse *hvīsla*]

whistle-blower *n Informal.* a person who informs on someone or puts a stop to something.

whistle for *vb* (*intr, prep*) *Informal.* to seek or expect in vain.

whistler ('wɪslə) *n* **1** a person or thing that whistles. **2** *Radio.* an atmospheric disturbance picked up by radio receivers, characterized by a whistling sound of decreasing pitch. It is caused by the electromagnetic radiation produced by lightning. **3** any of various birds having a whistling call, such as certain Australian flycatchers (see **thickhead** (sense 2)) and the goldeneye. **4** any of various North American marmots of the genus *Marmota,* esp. *M. caligata* (**hoary marmot**). **5** *Vet. science.* a horse affected with whistling.

Whistler ('wɪslə) *n* **James Abbott McNeill.** 1834–1903, U.S. painter and etcher, living in Europe. He is best known for his sequence of nocturnes and his portraits.

whistle stop *n* **1** *U.S. and Canadian.* **1a** a minor railway station where trains stop only on signal. **1b** a small town having such a station. **2a** a brief appearance in a town, esp. by a political candidate to make a speech, shake hands, etc. **2b** (*as modifier*): *a whistle-stop tour.* ◆ *vb* **whistle-stop, -stops, -stopping, -stopped.** **3** (*intr*) to campaign for office by visiting many small towns to give short speeches.

whistle up *vb* (*tr, adv*) to call or summon (a person or animal) by whistling.

whistling ('wɪslɪŋ) *n Vet. science.* a breathing defect of horses characterized by a high-pitched sound with each intake of air. Compare **roaring** (sense 6).

whistling swan *n* a white North American swan, *Cygnus columbianus,* with a black bill and straight neck. Compare **mute swan.**

whit (wɪt) *n* (*usually used with a negative*) the smallest particle; iota; jot: *he has changed not a whit.* [C15: probably variant of WIGHT[1]]

Whit (wɪt) *n* **1** See **Whitsuntide.** ◆ *adj* **2** of or relating to Whitsuntide.

Whitaker ('wɪtəkə) *n* Sir **Frederick.** 1812–91, New Zealand statesman, born in England: prime minister of New Zealand (1863–64; 1882–83).

Whitbread ('wɪt,brɛd) *n* **Fatima.** born 1961, British javelin thrower.

Whitby ('wɪtbɪ) *n* a fishing port and resort in NE England, in E North Yorkshire at the mouth of the River Esk: an important ecclesiastical centre in Anglo-Saxon times; site of an abbey founded in 656. See also **Synod of Whitby.** Pop.: 13 640 (1991).

white (waɪt) *adj* **1** having no hue due to the reflection of all or almost all incident light. Compare **black** (sense 1). **2** (of light, such as sunlight) consisting of all the colours of the spectrum or produced by certain mixtures of three additive primary colours, such as red, green, and blue. **3** comparatively white or whitish-grey in colour or having parts of this colour: *white clover.* **4** (of an animal) having pale-coloured or white skin, fur, or feathers. **5** bloodless or pale, as from pain, emotion, etc. **6** (of hair, a beard, etc.) silvery or grey, usually from age. **7** benevolent or without malicious intent: *white magic.* **8** colourless or transparent: *white glass.* **9** capped with or accompanied by snow: *a white Christmas.* **10** (*sometimes cap.*) counterrevolutionary, very conservative, or royalist. Compare **Red** (sense 2). **11** blank, as an unprinted area of a page. **12** (of wine) made from pale grapes or from black grapes separated from their skins. **13a** (of coffee or tea) with milk or cream. **13b** (of bread) made with white flour. **14** *Physics.* having or characterized by a continuous distribution of energy, wavelength, or frequency: *white noise.* **15** *Informal.* honourable or generous. **16** (of armour) made completely of iron or steel (esp. in the phrase **white harness**). **17** *Rare.* morally unblemished. **18** *Rare.* (of times, seasons, etc.) auspicious; favourable. **19** *Poetic or archaic.* having a fair complexion; blond. **20** **bleed white.** to deprive slowly of resources. **21** **whiter than white.** **21a** extremely clean and white. **21b** *Informal.* very pure, honest, and moral. ◆ *n* **22** a white colour. **23** the condition or quality of being white; whiteness. **24** the white or lightly coloured part or area of something. **25** (usually preceded by *the*) the viscous fluid that surrounds the yolk of a bird's egg, esp. a hen's egg; albumen. **26** *Anatomy.* the white part (sclera) of the eyeball. **27** any of various butterflies of the family *Pieridae.* See **large white, small white,** and also **cabbage white.** **28** *Chess, draughts.* **28a** a white or light-coloured piece or square. **28b** (*usually cap.*) the player playing with such pieces. **29** anything that has or is characterized by a white colour, such as a white paint or pigment, a white cloth, a white ball in billiards. **30** an unprinted area of a page. **31** *Archery.* **31a** the outer ring of the target, having the lowest score. **31b** a shot or arrow hitting this ring. **32** *Poetic.* fairness of complexion. **33** **in the white.** (of wood or furniture) left unpainted or unvarnished. ◆ *vb* **34** (usually foll. by *out*) to create or leave white spaces in (printed or other matter). **35** *Obsolete.* to make or become white. ◆ See also **white out, whites.** [Old English *hwīt;* related to Old Frisian *hwīt,* Old Saxon *hwīt,* Old Norse *hvītr,* Gothic *hveits,* Old High German *hwīz* (German *weiss*)] ▸ **'whitely** *adv* ▸ **'whiteness** *n* ▸ **'whitish** *adj*

White[1] (waɪt) *n* **1** a member of the Caucasoid race. **2** a person of European ancestry. ◆ *adj* **3** denoting or relating to a White or Whites.

White[2] (waɪt) *n* **1** **Gilbert.** 1720–93, English clergyman and naturalist, noted for his *Natural History and Antiquities of Selborne* (1789). **2** **Jimmy.** born 1962, British snooker player. **3** **Patrick** (**Victor Martindale**). 1912–90, Australian novelist: his works include *Voss* (1957), *The Eye of the Storm* (1973), and *A Fringe of Leaves* (1976): Nobel prize for literature 1973. **4** **T**(**erence**) **H**(**anbury**). 1906–64, British novelist: author of the Arthurian sequence *The Once and Future King* (1939–58).

white admiral *n* a nymphalid butterfly, *Limenitis camilla,* of Eurasia, having brown wings with white markings. See also **red admiral.**

white alkali *n* **1** refined sodium carbonate. **2** any of several mineral salts, esp. sodium sulphate, sodium chloride, and magnesium sulphate, that often appear on the surface of soils as a whitish layer in dry conditions.

white ant *n* another name for **termite.**

white area *n* an area of land for which no specific planning proposal has been adopted.

White Australia policy *n History.* an unofficial term for an immigration policy designed to restrict the entry of coloured people into Australia.

whitebait ('waɪt,beɪt) *n* **1** the young of herrings, sprats, etc., cooked and eaten whole as a delicacy. **2** any of various small silvery fishes, such as *Galaxias attenuatus* of Australia and New Zealand and *Allosmerus elongatus* of North American coastal regions of the Pacific. [C18: from its formerly having been used as bait]

whitebeam ('waɪt,biːm) *n* a N temperate rosaceous tree, *Sorbus aria,* having leaves that are densely hairy on the undersurface and hard timber.

white bear *n* another name for **polar bear.**

white birch *n* any of several birch trees with white bark, such as the silver birch of Europe and the paper birch of North America. See also **birch** (sense 1).

white blood cell *n* a nontechnical name for **leucocyte.**

white book *n* an official government publication in some countries.

Whiteboy ('waɪtbɔɪ) *n Irish history.* a member of a secret society of violent agrarian protest, formed around 1760. [C18: adopted from the earlier use of the phrase as a term of endearment for a boy or man]

white bryony *n* a climbing herbaceous cucurbitaceous plant, *Bryonia dioica,* of Europe and North Africa, having greenish flowers and red berries. Also called: **red bryony.** See also **black bryony, bryony.**

whitecap ('waɪt,kæp) *n* **1** a wave with a white broken crest. **2** *U.S.* a member of a vigilante organization that attempts to control a community.

white cedar *n* **1** a coniferous tree, *Chamaecyparis thyoides,* of swampy regions in North America, having scalelike leaves and boxlike cones: family *Cupressaceae.* See also **cypress**[1] (sense 2). **2** the wood of this tree, which is used for building boats, etc. **3** a coniferous tree, *Thuja occidentalis,* of NE North America, having scalelike leaves: family *Cupressaceae.* See also **arbor vitae.** **4** the wood of this tree, much used for telegraph poles.

Whitechapel ('waɪt,tʃæpəl) *n Billiards.* the act of potting one's opponent's white ball. [C19: slang use of *Whitechapel,* a district of London]

white clover *n* a Eurasian clover plant, *Trifolium repens,* with rounded white flower heads: cultivated as a forage plant.

white coal *n* water, esp. when flowing and providing a potential source of usable power.

white-collar *adj* of, relating to, or designating nonmanual and usually salaried workers employed in professional and clerical occupations: *white-collar union.* Compare **blue-collar, pink-collar.**

white currant *n* a cultivated N temperate shrub, *Ribes sativum,* having small rounded white edible berries: family *Grossulariaceae.*

whitedamp ('waɪt,dæmp) *n* a mixture of poisonous gases, mainly carbon monoxide, occurring in coal mines. See also **afterdamp.**

whited sepulchre ('waɪtɪd) *n* a hypocrite. [from Matthew 23:27]

white dwarf *n* one of a large class of small faint stars of enormous density (on average 10^8 kg/m^3) known to cause an Einstein shift of spectral lines. It is thought to mark the final stage in the evolution of a sun-like star.

white elephant *n* **1** a rare albino or pale grey variety of the Indian elephant, regarded as sacred in parts of S Asia. **2** a possession that is unwanted by its owner. **3** an elaborate venture, construction, etc., that proves useless. **4** a rare or valuable possession the upkeep of which is very expensive.

White Ensign *n* the ensign of the Royal Navy and the Royal Yacht Squadron, having a red cross on a white background with the Union Jack at the upper corner of the vertical edge alongside the hoist. Compare **Red Ensign, Blue Ensign.**

white-eye *n* **1** Also called (N.Z.): **blighty, silvereye, waxeye.** any songbird of the family *Zosteropidae* of Africa, Australia, New Zealand, and Asia, having a greenish plumage with a white ring around each eye. **2** any of certain other birds having a white ring or patch around the eye.

white feather *n* **1** a symbol or mark of cowardice. **2** **show the white feather.** to act in a cowardly manner. [from the belief that a white feather in a gamecock's tail was a sign of a poor fighter]

Whitefield ('wɪt,fiːld) *n* **George.** 1714–70, English Methodist preacher, who separated from the Wesleys (?1741) because of his Calvinistic views.

whitefish ('waɪt,fɪʃ) *n, pl* **-fish** *or* **-fishes.** any herring-like salmonoid food fish of the genus *Coregonus* and family *Coregonidae,* typically of deep cold lakes of the N hemisphere, having large silvery scales and a small head.

white fish *n* (in the British fishing industry) any edible marine fish or invertebrate in which the main reserves of fat are in the liver, excluding herring, trout, sprat, mackerel, salmon, and shellfish.

white flag *n* a white flag or a piece of white cloth hoisted to signify surrender or request a truce.

white flint *n* another name for **flint** (sense 4).

white flour *n* flour that consists substantially of the starchy endosperm of wheat, most of the bran and the germ having been removed by the milling process.

whitefly ('waɪtˌflaɪ) *n, pl* **-flies.** any hemipterous insect of the family *Aleyrodidae,* typically having a body covered with powdery wax. Many are pests of greenhouse crops.

white-footed mouse *n* any of various mice of the genus *Peromyscus,* esp. *P. leucopus,* of North and Central America, having brownish fur with white underparts: family *Cricetidae.* See also **deer mouse.**

white fox *n* another name for **arctic fox.**

white friar *n* a Carmelite friar, so called because of the white cloak that forms part of the habit of this order.

white frost *n* another term for **hoarfrost.**

white gold *n* any of various white lustrous hard-wearing alloys containing gold together with platinum and palladium and sometimes smaller amounts of silver, nickel, or copper: used in jewellery.

white goods *pl n* **1** *Marketing.* large household appliances, such as refrigerators, cookers. Compare **brown goods. 2** household linen such as sheets, towels, tablecloths, etc.

white gum *n* any of various Australian eucalyptus trees with whitish bark.

white-haired boy *or* **white-headed boy** *n* a favourite; darling.

Whitehall (ˌwaɪt'hɔːl) *n* **1** a street in London stretching from Trafalgar Square to the Houses of Parliament: site of the main government offices. **2** the British Government or its central administration.

Whitehead ('waɪtˌhɛd) *n* **Alfred North.** 1861–1947, English mathematician and philosopher, who collaborated with Bertrand Russell in writing *Principia Mathematica* (1910–13), and developed a holistic philosophy of science, chiefly in *Process and Reality* (1929).

white heat *n* **1** intense heat or a very high temperature, characterized by emission of white light. **2** *Informal.* a state of intense excitement or activity.

white hope *n Informal.* a person who is expected to bring honour or glory to his group, team, etc.

white horse *n* **1** the outline of a horse carved into the side of a chalk hill, usually dating to the Neolithic, Bronze, or Iron Ages, such as that at Uffington, Berkshire. **2** (*usually pl*) a wave with a white broken crest.

Whitehorse ('waɪtˌhɔːs) *n* a town in NW Canada: capital of the Yukon Territory. Pop.: 22 884 (1995 est.).

white-hot *adj* **1** at such a high temperature that white light is emitted. **2** *Informal.* in a state of intense emotion.

White House *n* **the. 1** the official Washington residence of the president of the U.S. **2** the U.S. presidency.

white knight *n* a champion or rescuer, esp. a person or organization that rescues a company from financial difficulties, an unwelcome takeover bid, etc.

white-knuckle *adj* causing or experiencing fear or anxiety: *a white-knuckle ride.*

white lady *n* **1** a cocktail consisting of gin, Cointreau, and lemon juice. **2** *Austral. informal.* methylated spirits as a drink, sometimes mixed with shoe polish or other additives.

Whitelaw ('waɪtˌlɔː) *n* **William** (**Stephen Ian**), 1st Viscount Whitelaw of Penrith. 1918–99, British Conservative politician; Home Secretary (1979–83); leader of the House of Lords (1983–88).

white lead (lɛd) *n* **1** Also called: **ceruse.** a white solid usually regarded as a mixture of lead carbonate and lead hydroxide; basic lead carbonate: used in paint and in making putty and ointments for the treatment of burns. Formula: $2PbCO_3.Pb(OH)_2$. **2** either of two similar white pigments based on lead sulphate or lead silicate. **3** a type of putty made by mixing white lead with boiled linseed oil.

white lead ore (lɛd) *n* another name for **cerussite.**

white leather *n* leather that has been treated with a chemical, such as alum or salt, to make it white. Also called: **whitleather** ('wɪtˈlɛðə).

white leg *n* another name for **milk leg.**

white lias *n* a type of rock composed of pale-coloured limestones and marls. See also **Lias.**

white lie *n* a minor or unimportant lie, esp. one uttered in the interests of tact or politeness.

white light *n* light that contains all the wavelengths of visible light at approximately equal intensities, as in sunlight or the light from white-hot solids.

white line *n* **1** a line or strip of white in the centre of a road to separate traffic going in different directions. **2** a white lamination in the hoof of a horse.

white list *n* a list of countries considered to pose an insignificant threat to human rights, from which applications for political asylum are presumed to be unfounded.

white-livered *adj* **1** lacking in spirit or courage. **2** pallid and unhealthy in appearance.

White man's burden *n* the supposed duty of the White race to bring education and Western culture to the non-White inhabitants of their colonies.

white matter *n* the whitish tissue of the brain and spinal cord, consisting mainly of myelinated nerve fibres. Technical name: **substantia alba.** Compare **grey matter.**

white meat *n* any meat that is light in colour, such as veal or the breast of turkey. Compare **red meat.**

white metal *n* any of various alloys, such as Babbitt metal, used for bearings. Also called: **antifriction metal.**

white meter *n Brit.* an electricity meter used to record the consumption of off-peak electricity.

White Mountains *pl n* **1** a mountain range in the U.S., chiefly in N New Hampshire: part of the Appalachians. Highest peak: Mount Washington, 1917 m (6288 ft.). **2** a mountain range in the U.S., in E California and SW Nevada. Highest peak: White Mountain, 4342 m (14 246 ft.).

white mustard *n* a Eurasian cruciferous plant, *Brassica hirta* (or *Sinapis alba*), having clusters of yellow flowers and pungent seeds from which the condiment mustard is made.

whiten ('waɪtᵊn) *vb* to make or become white or whiter; bleach. ▸ **'whitener** *n* ▸ **'whitening** *n*

White Nile *n* See **Nile.**

white noise *n* **a** sound or electrical noise that has a relatively wide continuous range of frequencies of uniform intensity. **b** noise containing all frequencies rising in level by six decibels every octave.

white oak *n* **1** a large oak tree, *Quercus alba,* of E North America, having pale bark, leaves with rounded lobes, and heavy light-coloured wood. **2** any of several other oaks, such as the roble.

white out *vb* (*adv*) **1** (*intr*) to lose or lack daylight visibility owing to snow or fog. **2** (*tr*) to create or leave white spaces in (printed or other matter). **3** (*tr*) to delete (typewritten words or characters) with a white correcting fluid. ◆ *n* **whiteout. 4** an atmospheric condition consisting of loss of visibility and sense of distance and direction due to a uniform whiteness of a heavy cloud cover and snow-covered ground, which reflects almost all the light it receives.

white paper *n* (*often caps.*) an official government report in any of a number of countries, including Britain, Australia, New Zealand, and Canada, which sets out the government's policy on a matter that is or will come before Parliament.

white pepper *n* a condiment, less pungent than black pepper, made from the husked dried beans of the pepper plant *Piper nigrum,* used either whole or ground.

white pine *n* **1** a North American coniferous tree, *Pinus strobus,* having blue-green needle-like leaves, hanging brown cones, and rough bark: family *Pinaceae.* **2** the light-coloured wood of this tree, much used commercially. **3** another name for **kahikatea.**

white plague *n Informal.* tuberculosis of the lungs.

white poplar *n* **1** Also called: **abele.** a Eurasian salicaceous tree, *Populus alba,* having leaves covered with dense silvery-white hairs. **2** another name for **tulipwood** (sense 1).

white potato *n* another name for **potato** (sense 1).

white pudding *n* (in Britain) a kind of sausage made like black pudding but without pigs' blood.

white rainbow *n* another name for **fogbow.**

white rat *n* a white variety of the brown rat (*Rattus norvegicus*), used extensively in scientific research.

white rose *n English history.* a widely used emblem or badge of the House of York. See also **Wars of the Roses, red rose.**

White Russia *n* another name for **Belarus.**

White Russian *adj, n* another term for **Belarussian.**

whites (waɪts) *pl n* **1** household linen or cotton goods, such as sheets. **2** white or off-white clothing, such as that worn for playing cricket. **3** an informal name for **leucorrhoea.**

white sale *n* a sale of household linens at reduced prices.

white sapphire *n* a white pure variety of corundum, used as a gemstone.

white sauce *n* a thick sauce made from flour, butter, seasonings, and milk or stock.

White Sea *n* an almost landlocked inlet of the Barents Sea on the coast of NW Russia. Area: 90 000 sq. km (34 700 sq. miles).

white settler *n* a well-off incomer to a district who takes advantage of what it has to offer without regard to the local inhabitants. [**C20:** from earlier colonial sense]

white slave *n* a girl or woman forced or sold into prostitution. ▸ **white slavery** *n*

white-slaver *n* a person who procures or forces women to become prostitutes.

whitesmith ('waɪtˌsmɪθ) *n* a person who finishes and polishes metals, particularly tin plate and galvanized iron.

white spirit *n* a colourless liquid obtained from petroleum and used as a substitute for turpentine.

white spruce *n* a N North American spruce tree, *Picea glauca,* having grey bark, pale brown oblong cones, and bluish-green needle-like leaves.

white squall *n* a violent highly localized weather disturbance at sea, in which the surface of the water is whipped to a white spray by the winds.

white stick *n* a walking stick used by a blind person for feeling the way: painted white as a sign to others that the person is blind.

White supremacy *n* the theory or belief that White people are innately superior to people of other races. ▸ **White supremacist** *n, adj*

white-tailed deer *n* a deer, *Odocoileus virginianus,* of North America and N South America: the coat varies in colour, being typically reddish-brown in the summer, and the tail is white. Also called: **Virginia deer.**

whitethorn ('waɪtˌθɔːn) *n* another name for **hawthorn.**

whitethroat ('waɪtˌθrəʊt) *n* either of two Old World warblers, *Sylvia communis* or *S. curruca* (**lesser whitethroat**), having a greyish-brown plumage with a white throat and underparts.

white tie *n* **1** a white bow tie worn as part of a man's formal evening dress. **2a** formal evening dress for men. **2b** (*as modifier*)*: a white-tie occasion.*

white trash *n Disparaging.* **a** poor White people living in the U.S., esp. the South. **b** (*as modifier*)*: white-trash culture.*

white vitriol *n* another name for **zinc sulphate.**

White Volta *n* a river in W Africa, rising in N Burkina-Faso flowing southwest and south to join the Black Volta in central Ghana and form the Volta River. Length: about 885 km (550 miles).

whitewall ('waɪt,wɔːl) *n* a pneumatic tyre having white sidewalls.

white walnut *n* another name for **butternut** (senses 1–4).

whitewash ('waɪt,wɒʃ) *n* **1** a substance used for whitening walls and other surfaces, consisting of a suspension of lime or whiting in water, often with other substances, such as size, added. **2** *Informal.* deceptive or specious words or actions intended to conceal defects, gloss over failings, etc. **3** *Informal.* a defeat in a sporting contest in which the loser is beaten in every match, game, etc. in a series: *they face the prospect of a whitewash in the five-test series.* ♦ *vb (tr)* **4** to cover or whiten with whitewash. **5** *Informal.* to conceal, gloss over, or suppress. **6** *Informal.* to defeat (an opponent or opposing team) by winning every match in a series. ► **'white,washer** *n*

white water *n* **1** a stretch of water with a broken foamy surface, as in rapids. **2** light-coloured sea water, esp. over shoals or shallows.

white whale *n* a small white toothed whale, *Delphinapterus leucas,* of northern waters: family *Monodontidae.* Also called: **beluga.**

whitewood ('waɪt,wʊd) *n* **1** any of various trees with light-coloured wood, such as the tulip tree, basswood, and cottonwood. **2** the wood of any of these trees.

whitey *or* **whity** ('waɪtɪ) *n Chiefly U.S.* (used contemptuously by Blacks) a White man.

Whitgift ('wɪt,gɪft) *n* **John.** ?1530–1604, English churchman; as archbishop of Canterbury (1583–1604) he tried to curb the influence of Puritanism.

whither ('wɪðə) *Archaic or poetic.* ♦ *adv* **1** to what place? **2** to what end or purpose? ♦ *conj* **3** to whatever place, purpose, etc. [Old English *hwider, hwæder;* related to Gothic *hvadrē;* modern English form influenced by HITHER]

whithersoever (,wɪðəsəʊ'ɛvə) *adv, conj Archaic or poetic.* to whichever place.

whitherward ('wɪðəwəd) *adv Archaic or poetic.* in which direction.

whiting[1] ('waɪtɪŋ) *n* **1** an important gadoid food fish, *Merlangius* (or *Gadus*) *merlangus,* of European seas, having a dark back with silvery sides and underparts. **2** any of various similar fishes, such as *Merluccius bilinearis,* a hake of American Atlantic waters, and any of several Atlantic sciaenid fishes of the genus *Menticirrhus.* **3** *Austral.* any of several marine food fishes of the genus *Sillago.* **4 whiting pout.** another name for **bib** (the fish). [C15: perhaps from Old English *hwītling;* related to Middle Dutch *wijting.* See WHITE, -ING[3]]

whiting[2] ('waɪtɪŋ) *n* white chalk that has been ground and washed, used in making whitewash, metal polish, etc. Also called: **whitening.**

Whitlam ('wɪtləm) *n* (**Edward**) **Gough** (gɒf). born 1916, Australian Labor statesman: prime minister (1972–75).

Whitley Bay ('wɪtlɪ) *n* a resort in NE England, in North Tyneside unitary authority, Tyne and Wear, on the North Sea. Pop.: 33 335 (1991).

Whitley Council *n* any of a number of organizations made up of representatives of employees and employers for joint consultation on and settlement of industrial relations and conditions for a particular industry or service. [C20: named after J. H. *Whitley* (1866–1935), chairman of the committee that recommended setting up such councils (1917)]

whitlow ('wɪtləʊ) *n* any pussy inflammation of the end of a finger or toe. [C14: changed from *whitflaw,* from WHITE + FLAW[1]]

whitlow grass *n* any of various grasses of the genera *Draba* and *Erophila,* once thought to cure whitlows.

Whitman ('wɪtmən) *n* **Walt(er).** 1819–92, U.S. poet, whose life's work is collected in *Leaves of Grass* (1855 and subsequent enlarged editions). His poems celebrate existence and the multiple elements that make up a democratic society.

Whit Monday *n* the Monday following Whit Sunday.

Whitney[1] ('wɪtnɪ) *n* **Mount.** a mountain in E California: the highest peak in the Sierra Nevada Mountains and in continental U.S. (excluding Alaska). Height: 4418 m (14 495 ft.).

Whitney[2] ('wɪtnɪ) *n* **1 Eli.** 1765–1825, U.S. inventor of a mechanical cotton gin (1793) and pioneer manufacturer of interchangeable parts. **2 William Dwight.** 1827–94, U.S. philologist, noted esp. for his *Sanskrit Grammar* (1879).

Whitsun ('wɪtsᵊn) *n* **1** short for **Whitsuntide.** ♦ *adj* **2** of or relating to Whit Sunday or Whitsuntide.

Whitsunday (,hwɪt'sʌndɪ, ,wɪt-) *n* (in Scotland) May 15, one of the four quarter days.

Whit Sunday *n* the seventh Sunday after Easter, observed as a feast in commemoration of the descent of the Holy Spirit on the apostles 50 days after Easter. Also called: **Pentecost.** [Old English *hwīta sunnandæg* white Sunday, probably named after the ancient custom of wearing white robes at or after baptism]

Whitsuntide ('wɪtsᵊn,taɪd) *n* the week that begins with Whit Sunday, esp. the first three days.

whitter ('wɪtə) *vb, n* a variant spelling of **witter.**

Whittier ('wɪtɪə) *n* **John Greenleaf.** 1807–92, U.S. poet and humanitarian: a leading campaigner in the antislavery movement. His poems include *Snow-Bound* (1866).

Whittington ('wɪtɪŋtən) *n* **Richard,** known as *Dick.* died 1423, English merchant, three times mayor of London. According to legend, he walked to London at the age of 13 with his cat and was prevented from leaving again only by the call of the church bells.

whittle ('wɪtᵊl) *vb* **1** to cut or shave strips or pieces from (wood, a stick, etc.), esp. with a knife. **2** *(tr)* to make or shape by paring or shaving. **3** *(tr;* often foll. by *away, down, off,* etc.) to reduce, destroy, or wear away gradually: ♦ *n* **4** *Brit. dialect.* a knife, esp. a large one. [C16: variant of C15 *thwittle* large knife, from Old English *thwitel,* from *thwītan* to cut; related to Old Norse *thveitr* cut, *thveita* to beat] ► **'whittler** *n*

Whittle ('wɪtᵊl) *n* Sir **Frank.** 1907–96, English engineer, who invented the jet engine for aircraft; flew first British jet aircraft (1941).

whittlings ('wɪtlɪŋz) *pl n* chips or shavings whittled off from an object.

whittret ('wɪtrət) *or* **whitrick** ('wɪtrɪk) *n Dialect.* a male weasel. [Old English *whytrate, whittratt;* perhaps from *hwīt* WHITE + *rætt* RAT]

Whitworth screw thread ('wɪtwəθ) *n* a thread form and system of standard sizes, proposed by Whitworth in 1841 and adopted as standard in the U.K., having a flank angle of 55° and a rounded top and foot. [named after Sir Joseph *Whitworth* (1803–87), English engineer]

whity ('waɪtɪ) *n, pl* **whities 1** *Informal.* a variant spelling of **whitey.** ♦ *adj* **2a** whitish in colour. **2b** *(in combination): whity-brown.*

whizz *or* **whiz** (wɪz) *vb* **whizzes, whizzing, whizzed. 1** to make or cause to make a loud humming or buzzing sound. **2** to move or cause to move with such a sound. **3** *(intr) Informal.* to move or go rapidly. ♦ *n* **4** a loud humming or buzzing sound. **5** *Informal.* a person who is extremely skilful at some activity. **6** a slang word for **amphetamine.** [C16: of imitative origin]

whizz-bang *or* **whiz-bang** *n* **1** a small-calibre World War I shell that, when discharged, travelled at such a high velocity that the sound of its flight was heard only an instant, if at all, before the sound of its explosion. ♦ *adj* **2** *Informal.* excellent or first-rate.

whizz kid, whiz kid, *or* **wiz kid** *n Informal.* a person who is pushing, enthusiastic, and outstandingly successful for his or her age. [C20: from WHIZZ, perhaps influenced by WIZARD]

who (huː) *pron* **1** which person? what person? used in direct and indirect questions: *he can't remember who did it; who met you?* **2** used to introduce relative clauses with antecedents referring to human beings: *the people who lived here have left.* **3** the one or ones who; whoever: *bring who you want.* [Old English *hwā;* related to Old Saxon *hwē,* Old High German *hwer,* Gothic *hvas,* Lithuanian *kàs,* Danish *hvo*]

USAGE See at **whom.**

Who (huː) *n* **the.** English rock group formed in 1964, originally comprising Roger Daltrey (born 1944; vocals), Pete Townshend (born 1945; guitar), John Entwistle (born 1944; bass guitar), and Keith Moon (1947–78; drums). Their recordings include "My Generation" (1965), "Substitute" (1966), *Tommy* (1969), and *Quadrophenia* (1974).

WHO *abbrev. for* World Health Organization.

whoa (wəʊ) *interj* a command used esp. to horses to stop or slow down. [C19: variant of HO[1]]

who'd (huːd) *contraction of* who had *or* who would.

who-does-what *adj* (of a dispute, strike, etc.) relating to the separation of kinds of work performed by different trade unions.

whodunnit *or* **whodunit** (huː'dʌnɪt) *n Informal.* a novel, play, etc., concerned with a crime, usually murder.

whoever (huː'ɛvə) *pron* **1** any person who; anyone that: *whoever wants it can have it.* **2** no matter who: *I'll come round tomorrow, whoever may be here.* **3** an intensive form of *who,* used in questions: *whoever could have thought that?* **4** *Informal.* an unknown or unspecified person: *give those to John, or Cathy, or whoever.*

whole (həʊl) *adj* **1** containing all the component parts necessary to form a total; complete: *a whole apple.* **2** constituting the full quantity, extent, etc. **3** uninjured or undamaged. **4** healthy. **5** having no fractional or decimal part; integral: *a whole number.* **6** of, relating to, or designating a relationship established by descent from the same parents; full: *whole brothers.* **7 out of whole cloth.** *U.S. and Canadian informal.* entirely without a factual basis. ♦ *adv* **8** in an undivided or unbroken piece: *to swallow a plum whole.* ♦ *n* **9** all the parts, elements, etc., of a thing. **10** an assemblage of parts viewed together as a unit. **11** a thing complete in itself. **12 as a whole.** considered altogether; completely. **13 on the whole. 13a** taking all things into consideration. **13b** in general. [Old English *hāl, hæl;* related to Old Frisian *hāl, hēl,* Old High German *heil,* Gothic *hails;* compare HALE[1]] ► **'wholeness** *n*

whole blood *n* blood obtained from a donor for transfusion from which none of the elements has been removed.

wholefood ('həʊl,fuːd) *n (sometimes pl)* **a** food that has been refined or processed as little as possible and is eaten in its natural state, such as brown rice, wholemeal flour, etc. **b** *(as modifier): a wholefood restaurant.*

whole gale *n* a wind of force ten on the Beaufort scale, seldom experienced inland.

wholehearted (,həʊl'hɑːtɪd) *adj* done, acted, given, etc., with total sincerity, enthusiasm, or commitment. ► **,whole'heartedly** *adv* ► **,whole'heartedness** *n*

whole hog *n Slang.* the whole or total extent (esp. in the phrase **go the whole hog**).

wholemeal ('həʊl,miːl) *adj Brit.* (of flour, bread, etc.) made from the entire wheat kernel. U.S. and Canadian term: **whole-wheat.**

whole milk *n* milk from which no constituent has been removed. Compare **skimmed milk.**

whole note *n* the usual U.S. and Canadian name for **semibreve.**

whole number *n* **1** an integer. **2** a natural number.

wholesale ('həʊl,seɪl) *n* **1** the business of selling goods to retailers in larger quantities than they are sold to final consumers but in smaller quantities than they are purchased from manufacturers. Compare **retail** (sense 1). **2 at wholesale. 2a** in large quantities. **2b** at wholesale prices. ♦ *adj* **3** of, relating to, or engaged in such business. **4** made, done, etc., on a large scale or without discrimination. ♦ *adv* **5** on a large scale or without discrimination. ♦ *vb* **6** to sell (goods) at wholesale. ► **'whole,saler** *n*

wholesale price index *n* an indicator of price changes in the wholesale market.

wholesome ('həʊlsəm) *adj* **1** conducive to health or physical wellbeing. **2** conducive to moral wellbeing. **3** characteristic or suggestive of health or wellbeing, esp. in appearance. [C12: from WHOLE (healthy) + -SOME[1]; related to German *heilsam* healing] ▸ **'wholesomely** *adv* ▸ **'wholesomeness** *n*

whole tone *or U.S. and Canadian* **whole step** *n* an interval of two semitones; a frequency difference of 200 cents in the system of equal temperament. Often shortened to **tone.**

whole-tone scale *n* either of two scales produced by commencing on one of any two notes a chromatic semitone apart and proceeding upwards or downwards in whole tones for an octave. Such a scale, consisting of six degrees to the octave, is used by Debussy and subsequent composers.

whole-wheat *adj* another term (esp. U.S. and Canadian) for **wholemeal.**

who'll (hu:l) *contraction of* who will *or* who shall.

wholly ('həʊllɪ) *adv* **1** completely, totally, or entirely. **2** without exception; exclusively.

whom (hu:m) *pron* the objective form of *who,* used when *who* is not the subject of its own clause: *whom did you say you had seen? he can't remember whom he saw.* [Old English *hwām,* dative of *hwā* WHO]

USAGE It was formerly considered correct to use *whom* whenever the objective form of *who* was required. This is no longer thought to be necessary and the objective form *who* is now commonly used, even in formal writing: *there were several people there who he had met before. Who* cannot be used directly after a preposition – the preposition is usually displaced, as in *the man (who) he sold his car to.* In formal writing *whom* is preferred in sentences like these: *the man to whom he sold his car.* There are some types of sentence in which *who* cannot be used: *the refugees, many of whom were old and ill, were allowed across the border.*

whomever (hu:m'ɛvə) *pron* the objective form of *whoever: I'll hire whomever I can find.*

whomsoever (ˌhu:msəʊ'ɛvə) *pron Archaic or formal.* the objective form of *whosoever: to whomsoever it may concern.*

whoop (wu:p) *vb* **1** to utter (speech) with loud cries, as of enthusiasm or excitement. **2** *Med.* to cough convulsively with a crowing sound made at each inspiration. **3** (of certain birds) to utter (a hooting cry). **4** (*tr*) to urge on or call with or as if with whoops. **5** (wʊp, wu:p). **whoop it up.** *Informal.* **5a** to indulge in a noisy celebration. **5b** *U.S.* to arouse enthusiasm. ◆ *n* **6** a loud cry, esp. one expressing enthusiasm or excitement. **7** *Med.* the convulsive crowing sound made during a paroxysm of whooping cough. **8 not worth a whoop.** *Informal.* worthless. ◆ See also **whoops.** [C14: of imitative origin]

whoopee *Informal.* ◆ *interj* (wʊ'pi:). **1** an exclamation of joy, excitement, etc. ◆ *n* ('wʊpi:). **2 make whoopee. 2a** to engage in noisy merrymaking. **2b** to make love.

whoopee cushion *n* a joke cushion that emits a sound like the breaking of wind when someone sits on it.

whooper *or* **whooper swan** ('wu:pə) *n* a large white Old World swan, *Cygnus cygnus,* having a black bill with a yellow base and a noisy whooping cry.

whooping cough ('hu:pɪŋ) *n* an acute infectious disease characterized by coughing spasms that end with a shrill crowing sound on inspiration: caused by infection with the bacillus *Bordetella pertussis.* Technical name: **pertussis.**

whooping crane *n* a rare North American crane, *Grus americana,* having a white plumage with black wings and a red naked face.

whoops (wʊps) *interj* an exclamation of surprise, as when a person falls over, or of apology.

whoosh *or* **woosh** (wʊʃ) *n* **1** a hissing or rushing sound. ◆ *vb* **2** (*intr*) to make or move with such a sound.

whop, wop, *or (less commonly)* **whap** (wɒp) *Informal.* ◆ *vb* **whops, whopping, whopped. 1** (*tr*) to strike, beat, or thrash. **2** (*tr*) to defeat utterly. **3** (*intr*) to drop or fall. ◆ *n* **4** a heavy blow or the sound made by such a blow. [C14: variant of *wap,* perhaps of imitative origin]

whopper ('wɒpə) *n Informal.* **1** anything uncommonly large of its kind. **2** a big lie. [C18: from WHOP]

whopping ('wɒpɪŋ) *adj Informal.* uncommonly large.

whore (hɔ:) *n* **1** a prostitute or promiscuous woman: often a term of abuse. ◆ *vb* (*intr*) **2** to be or act as a prostitute. **3** (of a man) to have promiscuous sexual relations, esp. with prostitutes. **4** (often foll. by *after*) to seek that which is immoral, idolatrous, etc. [Old English *hōre;* related to Old Norse *hōra,* Old High German *hvora,* Latin *carus* dear] ▸ **'whorish** *adj* ▸ **'whorishly** *adv* ▸ **'whorishness** *n*

whoredom ('hɔ:dəm) *n* **1** the activity of whoring or state of being a whore. **2** a biblical word for **idolatry.**

whorehouse ('hɔ:ˌhaʊs) *n* another word for **brothel.**

whoremaster ('hɔ:ˌmɑ:stə) *n Archaic.* a person who consorts with or procures whores. ▸ **'whoreˌmastery** *n*

whoremonger ('hɔ:ˌmʌŋgə) *n* a person who consorts with whores; lecher. ▸ **'whoreˌmongery** *n*

whoreson ('hɔ:sən) *Archaic.* ◆ *n* **1** a bastard. **2** a scoundrel; wretch. ◆ *adj* **3** vile or hateful.

Whorf (wɔ:f) *n* **Benjamin Lee.** (1897–1943), U.S. linguist, who argued that human language determines perception. See also **Sapir-Whorf hypothesis.**

whorl (wɜ:l) *n* **1** *Botany.* a radial arrangement of three or more petals, stamens, leaves, etc., around a stem. **2** *Zoology.* a single turn in a spiral shell. **3** one of the basic patterns of the human fingerprint, formed by several complete circular ridges one inside another. Compare **arch**[1] (sense 4b), **loop**[1] (sense 10a). **4** anything shaped like a coil. [C15: probably variant of *wherville* WHIRL, influenced by Dutch *worvel*] ▸ **whorled** *adj*

whortleberry ('wɜ:tᵊlˌberɪ) *n, pl* **-ries. 1** Also called: **bilberry, blaeberry, huckleberry** and (dialect) **hurt, whort.** a small Eurasian ericaceous shrub, *Vaccinium myrtillus,* greenish-pink flowers and edible sweet blackish berries. **2** the fruit of this shrub. **3 bog whortleberry.** a related plant, *V. uliginosum,* of mountain regions, having pink flowers and black fruits. [C16: south-western English dialect form of *hurtleberry;* of unknown origin]

who's (hu:z) *contraction of* who is.

whose (hu:z) *determiner* **1a** of whom? belonging to whom? used in direct and indirect questions: *I told him whose fault it was; whose car is this?* **1b** (*as pronoun*): *whose is that?* **2** of whom; belonging to whom; of which; belonging to which: used as a relative pronoun: *a house whose windows are broken; a man whose reputation has suffered.* [Old English *hwæs,* genitive of *hwā* WHO and *hwæt* WHAT]

whoso ('hu:səʊ) *pron* an archaic word for **whoever.**

whosoever (ˌhu:səʊ'ɛvə) *pron* an archaic or formal word for **whoever.**

who's who *n* a book or list containing the names and short biographies of famous people.

WH question *n* a question in English to which an appropriate answer is to give information rather than to answer "yes" or "no": typically introduced by the word *who, which, what, where, when,* or *how.* Also called: **information question.**

Whr *abbrev. for* watt-hour.

whsle *abbrev. for* wholesale.

why (waɪ) *adv* **1a** for what reason, purpose, or cause?: *why are you here?* **1b** (*used in indirect questions*): *tell me why you're here.* ◆ *pron* **2** for or because of which: *there is no reason why he shouldn't come.* ◆ *n, pl* **whys. 3** (*usually pl*) the reason, purpose, or cause of something (esp. in the phrase **the whys and wherefores**). ◆ *interj* **4** an introductory expression of surprise, disagreement, indignation, etc.: *why, don't be silly!* [Old English *hwī;* related to Old Norse *hvī,* Gothic *hveileiks* what kind of, Latin *quī*]

Whyalla (waɪ'ælə) *n* a port in S South Australia, on Spencer Gulf: iron and steel and shipbuilding industries. Pop.: 25 526 (1991).

whydah *or* **whidah** ('wɪdə) *n* any of various predominantly black African weaverbirds of the genus *Vidua* and related genera, the males of which grow very long tail feathers in the breeding season. Also called: **whydah bird, whidah bird, widow bird.** [C18: after the name of a town in Benin]

WI *abbrev. for:* **1** West Indian. **2** West Indies. **3** Wisconsin. **4** (in Britain) Women's Institute.

Wicca ('wɪkə) *n* (*sometimes not cap.*) the cult or practice of witchcraft. [C20: revival of Old English *wicca* witch]

Wichita ('wɪtʃɪˌtɔ:) *n* a city in S Kansas, on the Arkansas River: the largest city in the state; two universities. Pop.: 320 395 (1996 est.).

wick[1] (wɪk) *n* **1** a cord or band of loosely twisted or woven fibres, as in a candle, cigarette lighter, etc., that supplies fuel to a flame by capillary action. **2 get on (someone's) wick.** *Brit. slang.* to cause irritation to (a person). [Old English *weoce;* related to Old High German *wioh,* Middle Dutch *wēke* (Dutch *wiek*)] ▸ **'wicking** *n*

wick[2] (wɪk) *n Archaic.* a village or hamlet. [Old English *wīc;* related to *-wich* in place names, Latin *vīcus,* Greek *oîkos*]

wick[3] (wɪk) *adj Northern English dialect.* **1** lively or active. **2** alive or crawling: *wick with fleas.* [dialect variant of QUICK alive]

Wick (wɪk) *n* a town in N Scotland, in Highland, at the head of **Wick Bay** (an inlet of the North Sea). Pop.: 7681 (1991).

wicked ('wɪkɪd) *adj* **1a** morally bad in principle or practice. **1b** (*as collective n* preceded by *the*): *the wicked.* **2** mischievous or roguish, esp. in a playful way: *a wicked grin.* **3** causing injury or harm. **4** troublesome, unpleasant, or offensive. **5** *Slang.* very good. [C13: from dialect *wick,* from Old English *wicca* sorcerer, *wicce* WITCH[1]] ▸ **'wickedly** *adv* ▸ **'wickedness** *n*

wicker ('wɪkə) *n* **1** a slender flexible twig or shoot, esp. of willow. **2** short for **wickerwork.** ◆ *adj* **3** made, consisting of, or constructed from wicker. [C14: from Scandinavian; compare Swedish *viker,* Danish *viger* willow, Swedish *vika* to bend]

wickerwork ('wɪkəˌwɜ:k) *n* **a** a material consisting of wicker. **b** (*as modifier*): *a wickerwork chair.*

wicket ('wɪkɪt) *n* **1** a small door or gate, esp. one that is near to or part of a larger one. **2** *U.S.* a small window or opening in a door, esp. one fitted with a grating or glass pane, used as a means of communication in a ticket office, bank, etc. **3** a small sluicegate, esp. one in a canal lock gate or by a water wheel. **4** *U.S.* a croquet hoop. **5a** *Cricket.* either of two constructions, placed 22 yards apart, consisting of three pointed stumps stuck parallel in the ground with two wooden bails resting on top, at which the batsman stands. **5b** the strip of ground between these. **5c** a batsman's turn at batting or the period during which two batsmen bat: *a third-wicket partnership.* **5d** the act or instance of a batsman being got out: *the bowler took six wickets.* **6 keep wicket.** to act as a wicket-keeper. **7 on a good, sticky,** *etc.,* **wicket.** *Informal.* in an advantageous, awkward, etc., situation. [C18: from Old Northern French *wiket;* related to Old Norse *vikja* to move]

wicketkeeper ('wɪkɪtˌki:pə) *n Cricket.* the player on the fielding side positioned directly behind the wicket.

wicket maiden *n Cricket.* an over in which no runs are scored with the bat and at least one wicket is taken by the bowler. See also **maiden over.**

wickiup, wikiup, *or* **wickyup** ('wɪkɪˌʌp) *n U.S. and Canadian.* a crude shelter made of brushwood, mats, or grass and having an oval frame, esp. of a kind used by nomadic Indians now in Oklahoma and neighbouring states of the U.S. [C19: from Sac, Fox, and Kickapoo *wikiyap;* compare WIGWAM]

Wickliffe *or* **Wiclif** ('wɪklɪf) *n* variant spellings of (John) **Wycliffe.**

Wicklow ('wɪkləʊ) *n* **1** a county of E Republic of Ireland, in Leinster province on the Irish Sea: consists of a coastal strip rising inland to the **Wicklow Mountains;** mainly agricultural, with several resorts. County town: Wicklow. Pop.: 102 000 (1996). Area: 2025 sq. km (782 sq. miles). **2** a port in E Republic of Ireland, county town of Co. Wicklow. Pop.: 5850 (1991).

wickthing ('wɪk,θɪŋ) *n Lancashire dialect.* a creeping animal, such as a woodlouse. [from WICK[3] + THING[1]]

wicopy ('wɪkəpɪ) *n, pl* **-pies.** *U.S.* any of various North American trees, shrubs, or herbaceous plants, esp. the leatherwood, various willowherbs, and the basswood. [C18: from Cree *wikupiy* inner bark, willow bark]

widdershins ('wɪdə,ʃɪnz; *Scot.* 'wɪdər-) *adv Chiefly Scot.* a variant spelling of **withershins.**

wide (waɪd) *adj* **1** having a great extent from side to side. **2** of vast size or scope; spacious or extensive. **3a** (*postpositive*) having a specified extent, esp. from side to side: *two yards wide.* **3b** (*in combination*): covering or extending throughout: *nationwide.* **4** distant or remote from the desired point, mark, etc.: *your guess is wide of the mark.* **5** (of eyes) opened fully. **6** loose, full, or roomy: *wide trousers.* **7** exhibiting a considerable spread, as between certain limits: *a wide variation.* **8** *Phonetics.* another word for **lax** (sense 4) or **open** (sense 34). **9** *Brit. slang.* unscrupulous and astute: *a wide boy.* ◆ *adv* **10** over an extensive area: *to travel far and wide.* **11** to the full extent: *he opened the door wide.* **12** far from the desired point, mark, etc. ◆ *n* **13** (in cricket) a bowled ball that is outside the batsman's reach and scores a run for the batting side. **14** *Archaic or poetic.* a wide space or extent. **15 to the wide.** completely. [Old English *wīd;* related to Old Norse *vīthr,* Old High German *wīt*] ▸ **'widely** *adv* ▸ **'wideness** *n* ▸ **'widish** *adj*

wide-angle lens *n* a lens system on a camera that can cover an angle of view of 60° or more and therefore has a fairly small focal length. See also **fisheye lens.**

wide area network *n Computing.* a network of computers interconnected over large distances, often by optical fibres or microwave communications. Abbrev.: **WAN.**

wide-awake *adj* (**wide awake** *when postpositive*). **1** fully awake. **2** keen, alert, or observant. ◆ *n* **3** Also called: **wide-awake hat.** a hat with a low crown and very wide brim. ▸ **'wide-a'wakeness** *n*

wide-body *adj* (of an aircraft) having a wide fuselage, esp. wide enough to contain three rows of seats abreast.

wide-eyed *adj* innocent or credulous.

widen ('waɪd^ə^n) *vb* to make or become wide or wider. ▸ **'widener** *n*

wide-open *adj* (**wide open** *when postpositive*). **1** open to the full extent. **2** (*postpositive*) exposed to attack; vulnerable. **3** uncertain as to outcome. **4** *U.S. informal.* (of a town or city) lax in the enforcement of certain laws, esp. those relating to the sale and consumption of alcohol, gambling, the control of vice, etc.

wide receiver *n American football.* a player whose function is to catch long passes from the quarterback.

wide-screen *adj* of or relating to a form of film projection in which the screen has much greater width than height.

widespread ('waɪd,sprɛd) *adj* **1** extending over a wide area. **2** accepted by or occurring among many people.

widgeon ('wɪdʒən) *n* a variant spelling of **wigeon.**

widget ('wɪdʒɪt) *n* **1** *Informal.* any small mechanism or device, the name of which is unknown or temporarily forgotten. **2** a small device in a beer can which, when the can is opened, releases nitrogen gas into the beer, giving it a head. [C20: changed from GADGET]

widgie ('wɪdʒɪ) *n Austral. slang.* a female larrikin or bodgie. [C20: alteration of BODGIE]

Widnes ('wɪdnɪs) *n* a town in NW England, in N Cheshire on the River Mersey: chemical industry. Pop.: 57 162 (1991).

widow ('wɪdəʊ) *n* **1** a woman who has survived her husband, esp. one who has not remarried. **2** (*usually with a modifier*) *Informal.* a woman whose husband frequently leaves her alone while he indulges in a sport, etc.: *a golf widow.* **3** *Printing.* a short line at the end of a paragraph, esp. one that occurs as the top line of a page or column. Compare **orphan** (sense 3). **4** (in some card games) an additional hand or set of cards exposed on the table. ◆ *vb* (*tr; usually passive*) **5** to cause to become a widow. **6** to deprive of something valued or desirable. [Old English *widuwe;* related to German *Witwe,* Latin *vidua* (feminine of *viduus* deprived), Sanskrit *vidhavā*] ▸ **'widowhood** *n*

widow bird *n* another name for **whydah.**

widower ('wɪdəʊə) *n* a man whose wife has died and who has not remarried.

widow's benefit *n* (in the British National Insurance scheme) a weekly payment made to a widow.

widow's cruse *n* an endless or unfailing source of supply. [allusion to I Kings 17:16]

widow's mite *n* a small contribution given by a person who has very little. [allusion to Mark 12:43]

widow's peak *n* a V-shaped point in the hairline in the middle of the forehead. [from the belief that it presaged early widowhood]

widow woman *n Archaic or dialect.* another term for **widow** (sense 1).

width (wɪdθ) *n* **1** the linear extent or measurement of something from side to side, usually being the shortest dimension or (for something fixed) the shortest horizontal dimension. **2** the state or fact of being wide. **3** a piece or section of something at its full extent from side to side: *a width of cloth.* **4** the distance across a rectangular swimming bath, as opposed to its length. [C17: from WIDE + -TH[1], analogous to BREADTH]

widthwise ('wɪdθ,waɪz) *or* **widthways** ('wɪdθ,weɪz) *adv* in the direction of the width; from side to side.

Wieland[1] ('viːlant) *n* the German name for **Wayland.**

Wieland[2] (*German* 'viːlant) *n* **Christoph Martin** ('krɪstɔf 'martiːn). 1733–1813, German writer, noted esp. for his verse epic *Oberon* (1780).

wield (wiːld) *vb* (*tr*) **1** to handle or use (a weapon, tool, etc.). **2** to exert or maintain (power or authority). **3** *Obsolete.* to rule. [Old English *wieldan, wealdan;* related to Old Norse *valda,* Old Saxon *waldan,* German *walten,* Latin *valēre* to be strong] ▸ **'wieldable** *adj* ▸ **'wielder** *n*

wieldy ('wiːldɪ) *adj* **wieldier, wieldiest.** easily handled, used, or managed.

Wien[1] (viːn) *n* the German name for **Vienna.**

Wien[2] (*German* viːn) *n* **Wilhelm** ('vɪlhɛlm). 1864–1928, German physicist, who studied black-body radiation: Nobel prize for physics 1911.

wiener ('wiːnə) *or* **wienerwurst** ('wiːnə,wɜːst) *n U.S. and Canadian.* a kind of smoked beef or pork sausage, similar to a frankfurter. Also called: **wienie, weenie** ('wiːnɪ). [C20: shortened from German *Wiener Wurst* Viennese sausage]

Wiener ('wiːnə) *n* **Norbert** ('nɔːbət). 1894–1964, U.S. mathematician, who developed the concept of cybernetics.

Wiener Neustadt (*German* 'viːnər 'nɔyʃtat) *n* a city in E Austria, in Lower Austria. Pop.: 35 268 (1991).

Wiener schnitzel ('viːnə 'ʃnɪtsəl) *n* a large thin escalope of veal, coated in egg and crumbs, fried, and traditionally served with a garnish. [German: Viennese cutlet]

Wiesbaden (*German* 'viːsbaːdən) *n* a city in W Germany, capital of Hesse state: a spa resort since Roman times. Pop.: 267 122 (1996 est.). Latin name: **Aquae Mattiacorum** ('ækwiː ,mætjə'kəʊrəm).

Wiesel ('viːzəl) *n* **Elie.** born 1928, U.S. human rights campaigner: noted esp. for his documentaries of wartime atrocities against the Jews; Nobel peace prize 1986.

Wiesenthal ('viːzən,tɑːl) *n* **Simon.** born 1908, Austrian investigator of Nazi war crimes. A survivor of the concentration camps, he has been active since 1945 in documenting Nazi crimes against the Jews, tracking down their perpetrators, and assisting surviving victims.

wife (waɪf) *n, pl* **wives** (waɪvz). **1** a man's partner in marriage; a married woman. Related adj: **uxorial. 2** an archaic or dialect word for **woman. 3 take to wife.** to marry (a woman). [Old English *wīf;* related to Old Norse *vīf* (perhaps from *vīfathr* veiled), Old High German *wīb* (German *Weib*)] ▸ **'wifehood** *n* ▸ **'wifeless** *adj* ▸ **'wife,like** *adj* ▸ **'wifeliness** *n* ▸ **'wifely** *adj*

wife swapping *n* **a** the temporary exchange of wives between married couples for sexual relations. **b** (*as modifier*): *a wife-swapping party.*

wig (wɪg) *n* **1** an artificial head of hair, either human or synthetic, worn to disguise baldness, as part of a theatrical or ceremonial dress, as a disguise, or for adornment. ◆ *vb* **wigs, wigging, wigged.** (*tr*) **2** *Obsolete.* to furnish with a wig. **3** *Brit. slang.* to berate severely. [C17: shortened from PERIWIG] ▸ **wigged** *adj* ▸ **'wigless** *adj* ▸ **'wig,like** *adj*

Wig. *abbrev. for* Wigtownshire.

Wigan ('wɪgən) *n* **1** an industrial town in NW England, in Wigan unitary authority, Greater Manchester: former coal-mining centre. Pop.: 85 819 (1991). **2** a unitary authority in NW England, in Greater Manchester. Pop.: 309 800 (1995 est.). Area: 199 sq. km (77 sq. miles).

wigeon *or* **widgeon** ('wɪdʒən) *n* **1** a Eurasian duck, *Anas penelope,* of marshes, swamps, etc., the male of which has a reddish-brown head and chest and grey and white back and wings. **2 American wigeon.** Also called: **baldpate.** a similar bird, *Anas americana,* of North America, the male of which has a white crown. [C16: of uncertain origin]

wigging ('wɪgɪŋ) *n* **1** *Brit. slang.* a rebuke or reprimand. **2** *N.Z.* the shearing of wool from the head of a sheep.

wiggle ('wɪg^ə^l) *vb* **1** to move or cause to move with jerky movements, esp. from side to side. ◆ *n* **2** the act or an instance of wiggling. **3 get a wiggle on.** *Slang, chiefly U.S.* to hurry up. [C13: from Middle Low German, Middle Dutch *wiggelen*] ▸ **'wiggler** *n* ▸ **'wiggly** *adj*

wight[1] (waɪt) *n Archaic.* a human being. [Old English *wiht;* related to Old Frisian *āwet* something, Old Norse *vættr* being, Gothic *waihts* thing, German *Wicht* small person]

wight[2] (waɪt) *adj Archaic.* strong and brave; valiant. [C13: from Old Norse *vīgt;* related to Old English *wīg* battle, Latin *vincere* to conquer]

Wight (waɪt) *n* **Isle of.** an island and county of S England in the English Channel. Administrative centre: Newport. Pop.: 124 600 (1994 est.). Area: 380 sq. km (147 sq. miles).

Wigner ('wɪgnə) *n* **Eugene Paul.** 1902–95, U.S. physicist, born in Hungary. He is noted for his contributions to nuclear physics: shared the Nobel prize for physics 1963.

Wigtownshire ('wɪgtən,ʃɪə, -ʃə) *n* (until 1975) a county of SW Scotland, now part of Dumfries and Galloway.

wigwag ('wɪg,wæg) *vb* **-wags, -wagging, -wagged. 1** to move (something) back and forth. **2** to communicate with (someone) by means of a flag semaphore. ◆ *n* **3a** a system of communication by flag semaphore. **3b** the message signalled. [C16: from obsolete *wig,* probably short for WIGGLE + WAG[1]] ▸ **'wig,wagger** *n*

wigwam ('wɪg,wæm) *n* **1** any dwelling of the North American Indians, esp. one made of bark, rushes, or skins spread over or enclosed by a set of arched poles lashed together. Compare **tepee. 2** a similar structure for children. [from Abnaki and Massachuset *wīkwām,* literally: their abode]

wikiup ('wɪkɪ,ʌp) *n* a variant spelling of **wickiup.**

Wilberforce ('wɪlbə,fɔːs) *n* **1 Samuel.** 1805–73, British Anglican churchman; bishop of Oxford (1845–69) and Winchester (1869–73). **2** his father, **William.** 1759–1833, British politician and philanthropist, whose efforts secured the abolition of the slave trade (1807) and of slavery (1833) in the British Empire.

wilco (,wɪl'kəʊ) *interj* an expression in signalling, telecommunications, etc., indicating that a message just received will be complied with. Compare **roger.** [C20: abbreviation for *I will comply*]

Wilcoxon test (wɪl'kɒks^ə^n) *n* **a** Also called: **Wilcoxon matched-pairs signed-ranks test.** a statistical test for the relative size of the scores of the same or matched subjects under two experimental conditions by comparing the distributions for positive and negative differences of the ranks of their absolute values. b **Wilcoxon Mann-Whitney test.** See **Mann-Whitney test.** [named after Frank *Wilcoxon* (1892–1965), Irish mathematician and statistician]

wild (waɪld) *adj* **1** (of animals) living independently of man; not domesticated or tame. **2** (of plants) growing in a natural state; not cultivated. **3** uninhabited or uncultivated; desolate: *a wild stretch of land.* **4** living in a savage or uncivilized way: *wild tribes.* **5** lacking restraint: *wild merriment.* **6** of great violence or intensity: *a wild storm.* **7** disorderly or chaotic: *wild thoughts; wild talk.* **8** dishevelled; untidy: *wild hair.* **9** in a state of extreme emotional intensity: *wild with anger.* **10** reckless: *wild speculations.* **11** not calculated; random: *a wild guess.* **12** unconventional; fantastic; crazy: *wild friends.* **13** (*postpositive;* foll. by *about*) *Informal.* intensely enthusiastic or excited: *I'm wild about my new boyfriend.* **14** (of a card, such as a joker or deuce in some games) able to be given any value the holder pleases: *jacks are wild.* **15 wild and woolly. 15a** rough; untamed; barbarous. **15b** (of theories, plans, etc.) not fully thought out. ◆ *adv* **16** in a wild manner. **17 run wild. 17a** to grow without cultivation or care: *the garden has run wild.* **17b** to behave without restraint: *he has let his children run wild.* ◆ *n* **18** (*often pl*) a desolate, uncultivated, or uninhabited region. **19 the wild. 19a** a free natural state of living. **19b** the wilderness. [Old English *wilde;* related to Old Saxon, Old High German *wildi,* Old Norse *villr,* Gothic *wiltheis*] ▸ **'wildish** *adj* ▸ **'wildly** *adv* ▸ **'wildness** *n*

Wild (waɪld) *n* **Jonathan.** ?1682–1725, British criminal, who organized a network of thieves, highwaymen, etc., while also working as an informer: said to have sent over a hundred men to the gallows before being hanged himself.

wild boar *n* a wild pig, *Sus scrofa,* of parts of Europe and central Asia, having a pale grey to black coat, thin legs, a narrow body, and prominent tusks.

wild brier *n* another name for **wild rose.**

wild card *n* **1** See **wild** (sense 14). **2** *Sport.* a player or team that has not qualified for a competition but is allowed to take part, at the organizers' discretion, after all the regular places have been taken. **3** an unpredictable element in a situation. **4** *Computing.* a symbol that can represent any character or group of characters, as in a filename.

wild carrot *n* an umbelliferous plant, *Daucus carota,* of temperate regions, having clusters of white flowers and hooked fruits. Also called: **Queen Anne's lace.**

wildcat ('waɪldˌkæt) *n, pl* **-cats** *or* **-cat. 1** a wild European cat, *Felis silvestris,* that resembles the domestic tabby but is larger and has a bushy tail. **2** any of various other felines, esp. of the genus *Lynx,* such as the lynx and the caracal. **3** *U.S. and Canadian.* another name for **bobcat. 4** *Informal.* a savage or aggressive person. **5** an exploratory drilling for petroleum or natural gas. **6** *U.S. and Canadian.* an unsound commercial enterprise. **7** the U.S. and Canadian name for **light engine. 8** (*modifier*) *U.S. and Canadian.* **8a** of or relating to an unsound business enterprise: *wildcat stock.* **8b** financially or commercially unsound: *a wildcat project.* **9** (*modifier*) *U.S. and Canadian.* (of a train) running without permission or outside the timetable. ◆ *vb* **-cats, -catting, -catted. 10** (*intr*) to drill for petroleum or natural gas in an area having no known reserves. ▸ **'wildˌcatting** *n, adj*

wildcat strike *n* a strike begun by workers spontaneously or without union approval.

wildcatter ('waɪldˌkætə) *n U.S. and Canadian informal.* a prospector for oil or ores in areas having no proved resources.

wild celery *n* a strongly scented umbelliferous plant, *Apium graveolens,* of temperate regions: the ancestor of cultivated celery. Archaic name: **smallage.**

wild cherry *n* another name for **gean** (sense 1).

wild dog *n* another name for **dingo.**

Wilde (waɪld) *n* **Oscar (Fingal O'Flahertie Wills).** 1854–1900, Irish writer and wit, famous for such plays as *Lady Windermere's Fan* (1892) and *The Importance of being Earnest* (1895). *The Picture of Dorian Gray* (1891) is a macabre novel about a hedonist and *The Ballad of Reading Gaol* (1898) relates to his experiences in prison while serving a two-year sentence for homosexuality.

wildebeest ('wɪldɪˌbiːst, 'vɪl-) *n, pl* **-beests** *or* **-beest.** another name for **gnu.** [C19: from Afrikaans, literally: wild beast]

wilder ('wɪldə) *vb Archaic.* **1** to lead or be led astray. **2** to bewilder or become bewildered. [C17: of uncertain origin] ▸ **'wilderment** *n*

Wilder ('waɪldə) *n* **1 Billy,** real name *Samuel Wilder.* born 1906, U.S. film director and screenwriter, born in Austria. His films include *Double Indemnity* (1944), *The Lost Weekend* (1945), *Sunset Boulevard* (1950), *The Seven Year Itch* (1955), *Some Like it Hot* (1959), *The Apartment* (1960), and *Buddy Buddy* (1981). **2 Thornton.** 1897–1975 U.S. novelist and dramatist. His works include the novel *The Bridge of San Luis Rey* (1927) and the play *The Skin of Our Teeth* (1942).

wilderness ('wɪldənɪs) *n* **1** a wild, uninhabited, and uncultivated region. **2** any desolate tract or area. **3** a confused mass or collection. **4 a voice (crying) in the wilderness.** a person, group, etc., making a suggestion or plea that is ignored. **5 in the wilderness.** no longer having influence, recognition, or publicity. [Old English *wildēornes,* from *wildēor* wild beast (from WILD + *dēor* beast, DEER) + -NESS; related to Middle Dutch *wildernisse,* German *Wildernis*]

Wilderness ('wɪldənɪs) *n* **the.** the barren regions to the south and east of Palestine, esp. those in which the Israelites wandered before entering the Promised Land and in which Christ fasted for 40 days and nights.

wild-eyed *adj* **1** glaring in an angry, distracted, or wild manner. **2** ill-conceived or totally impracticable.

wildfire ('waɪldˌfaɪə) *n* **1** a highly flammable material, such as Greek fire, formerly used in warfare. **2a** a raging and uncontrollable fire. **2b** anything that is disseminated quickly (esp. in the phrase **spread like wildfire**). **3** lightning without audible thunder. **4** another name for **will-o'-the-wisp.**

wild flower *n* **1** any flowering plant that grows in an uncultivated state. **2** the flower of such a plant.

wildfowl ('waɪldˌfaʊl) *n* **1** any bird that is hunted by man, esp. any duck or similar aquatic bird. **2** such birds collectively. ▸ **'wildˌfowler** *n* ▸ **'wildˌfowling** *adj, n*

Wild Geese *n* **the.** the Irish expatriates who served as professional soldiers with the Catholic powers of Europe, esp. France, from the late 17th to the early 20th centuries.

wild ginger *n* a North American plant, *Asarum canadense,* having a solitary brownish flower and an aromatic root: family *Aristolochiaceae.* See also **asarabacca, asarum.**

wild-goose chase *n* an absurd or hopeless pursuit, as of something unattainable.

wild hyacinth *n* another name for **bluebell** (sense 1).

wild indigo *n* any of several North American leguminous plants of the genus *Baptisia,* esp. *B. tinctoria,* which has yellow flowers and three-lobed leaves.

wilding ('waɪldɪŋ) *n* **1** an uncultivated plant, esp. the crab apple, or a cultivated plant that has become wild. **2** a wild animal. ◆ Also called: **'wildling.**

wild Irishman *n N.Z.* another name for **matagouri.**

wild lettuce *n* any of several uncultivated lettuce plants, such as *Lactuca serriola* (or *L. scariola*) of Eurasia and *L. canadensis* (**horseweed**) of North America, which grow as weeds and have yellow or blue flowers, milky juice in the stem, and prickly leaves: family *Compositae* (composites).

wildlife ('waɪldˌlaɪf) *n* wild animals and plants collectively.

wild liquorice *n* **1** another name for *Astragalus glycyphyllos:* see **milk vetch. 2** another name for **liquorice** (sense 1). **3** a North American plant, *Glycyrrhiza lepidota,* that is related to true liquorice and has similar properties.

wild man *n* **1** a savage. **2** an extremist in politics.

wild mustard *n* another name for **charlock** (sense 1).

wild oat *n* any of several temperate annual grasses of the genus *Avena,* esp. *A. fatua,* that grow as weeds and have long bristles on their flower spikes.

wild oats *pl n Slang.* the indiscretions of youth, esp. dissoluteness before settling down (esp. in the phrase **sow one's wild oats**).

wild olive *n* any of various trees or shrubs that resemble the olive tree or bear olive-like fruits, esp. the oleaster.

wild pansy *n* **1** Also called: **heartsease, love-in-idleness,** and (in the U.S.) **Johnny-jump-up.** a Eurasian violaceous plant, *Viola tricolor,* having purple, yellow, and pale mauve spurred flowers. **2** any of various similar plants of the genus *Viola.*

wild parsley *n* any of various uncultivated umbelliferous plants that resemble parsley.

wild parsnip *n* a strong-smelling umbelliferous plant, *Pastinaca sativa,* that has an inedible root: the ancestor of the cultivated parsnip.

wild rice *n* another name for **Indian rice.**

wild rose *n* any of numerous roses, such as the dogrose and sweetbrier, that grow wild and have flowers with only one whorl of petals.

wild rubber *n* rubber obtained from uncultivated rubber trees.

wild rye *n* any of various perennial grasses of the N temperate genus *Elymus,* resembling cultivated rye in having paired bristly ears or spikes and flat leaves.

wild silk *n* **1** silk produced by wild silkworms. **2** a fabric made from this, or from short fibres of silk designed to imitate it.

wild Spaniard *n* any of various subalpine perennials of the genus *Aciphylla* of New Zealand, with sharp leaves. Often shortened to **Spaniard.**

wild track *n* a soundtrack recorded other than with a synchronized picture, usually carrying sound effects, random dialogue, etc.

wild type *n Biology.* the typical form of a species of organism resulting from breeding under natural conditions.

wild water *n* **a** turbulent water in a river, esp. as an area for navigating in a canoe as a sport. **b** (*as modifier*): *wild-water racing.*

Wild West *n* the western U.S. during its settlement, esp. with reference to its frontier lawlessness.

Wild West show *n U.S.* a show or circus act presenting feats of horsemanship, shooting, etc.

wildwood ('waɪldˌwʊd) *n Archaic.* a wood or forest growing in a natural uncultivated state.

wile (waɪl) *n* **1** trickery, cunning, or craftiness. **2** (*usually pl*) an artful or seductive trick or ploy. ◆ *vb* **3** (*tr*) to lure, beguile, or entice. [C12: from Old Norse *vel* craft; probably related to Old French *wīle,* Old English *wīgle* magic. See GUILE]

Wilfrid ('wɪlfrɪd) *n* **Saint.** 634–709 A.D., English churchman; bishop of York (?663–?703). At the Synod of Whitby (664) he argued successfully that Celtic practices should be replaced by Roman ones in the English Church. Feast day: Oct. 12.

wilful *or U.S.* **willful** ('wɪlfʊl) *adj* **1** intent on having one's own way; headstrong or obstinate. **2** intentional: *wilful murder.* ▸ **'wilfully** *or U.S.* **'willfully** *adv* ▸ **'wilfulness** *or U.S.* **'willfulness** *n*

wilga ('wɪlgə) *n* a small drought-resistant tree, *Geijera parviflora,* of Australia, having hard aromatic wood and foliage that resembles that of the willow. [C19: from a native Australian language]

Wilhelm I ('vɪlhelm) *n* the German name of **William I** (sense 5).

Wilhelm II *n* the German name of **William II** (sense 4).

Wilhelmina I (ˌwɪlə'miːnə; *Dutch* wɪlhɛl'miːnaː) *n* 1880–1962, queen of the Netherlands from 1890 until her abdication (1948) in favour of her daughter Juliana.

Wilhelmshaven (*German* vɪlhɛlms'haːfən) *n* a port and resort in NW Germany, in Lower Saxony: founded in 1853; was the chief German North Sea naval base until 1945; a major oil port. Pop.: 91 150 (1991).

Wilhelmstrasse (*German* 'vɪlhɛlmʃtraːsə) *n* **1** a street in the centre of Berlin, where the German foreign office and other government buildings were situated until 1945. **2** Germany's ministry of foreign affairs until 1945.

Wilkes (wɪlks) *n* **1 Charles.** 1798–1877, U.S. explorer of Antarctica. **2 John.** 1727–97, English politician, who was expelled from the House of Commons and outlawed for writing scurrilous articles about the government. He became a champion of parliamentary reform.

Wilkes Land *n* a region in Antarctica south of Australia, on the Indian Ocean.

Wilkins ('wɪlkɪnz) *n* **1** Sir **George Hubert.** 1888–1958, Australian polar explorer and aviator. **2 Maurice Hugh Frederick.** born 1916, British biochemist, born in New Zealand. With Crick and Watson, he shared the Nobel prize 1962 for his work on the structure of DNA.

will[1] (wɪl) *vb past* **would.** (takes an infinitive without *to* or an implied infinitive) used as an auxiliary. **1** (esp. with *you, he, she, it, they,* or a noun as subject) to make the future tense. Compare **shall** (sense 1). **2** to express resolution on the part of the speaker: *I will buy that radio if it's the last thing I do.* **3** to indicate willingness or desire: *will you help me with this problem?* **4** to express compulsion, as in commands: *you will report your findings to me tomorrow.* **5** to express capacity or ability: *this rope will support a load.* **6** to express probability or expectation on the part of the speaker: *that will be Jim telephoning.* **7** to express customary practice or inevitability: *boys will be boys.* **8** (*with the infinitive always implied*) to express desire: usually in polite requests: *stay if you will.* **9 what you will.** whatever you like. **10 will do.** *Informal.* a declaration of willingness to do what is requested. [Old English *willan;* related to Old Saxon *willian,* Old Norse *vilja,* Old High German *wollen,* Latin *velle* to wish, will]

USAGE See at **shall.**

will[2] (wɪl) *n* **1** the faculty of conscious and deliberate choice of action; volition. Related adjs: **voluntary, volitive. 2** the act or an instance of asserting a choice. **3a** the declaration of a person's wishes regarding the disposal of his property after his death. Related adj: **testamentary. 3b** a revocable instrument by which such wishes are expressed. **4** anything decided upon or chosen, esp. by a person in authority; desire; wish. **5** determined intention: *where there's a will there's a way.* **6** disposition or attitude towards others: *he bears you no ill will.* **7 at will.** at one's own desire, inclination, or choice. **8 with a will.** heartily; energetically. **9 with the best will in the world.** even with the best of intentions. ◆ *vb* (*mainly tr; often takes a clause as object or an infinitive*) **10** (*also intr*) to exercise the faculty of volition in an attempt to accomplish (something): *he willed his wife's recovery from her illness.* **11** to give (property) by will to a person, society, etc.: *he willed his art collection to the nation.* **12** (*also intr*) to order or decree: *the king wills that you shall die.* **13** to choose or prefer: *wander where you will.* **14** to yearn for or desire: *to will that one's friends be happy.* [Old English *willa;* related to Old Norse *vili,* Old High German *willeo* (German *Wille*), Gothic *wilja,* Old Slavonic *volja*] ► **'willer** *n*

willable ('wɪləbᵊl) *adj* able to be wished or determined by the will.

willed (wɪld) *adj* (*in combination*) having a will as specified: *weak-willed.*

willemite ('wɪləˌmaɪt) *n* a secondary mineral consisting of zinc silicate in hexagonal crystalline form. It is white, colourless, or coloured by impurities and is found in veins of zinc ore. Formula: Zn_2SiO_4. [C19: from Dutch *willemit,* named after *Willem* I of the Netherlands (1772–1834)]

Willemstad (*Dutch* 'wɪləmstɑt) *n* the capital of the Netherlands Antilles, a port on the SW coast of Curaçao: important for refining Venezuelan oil. Pop.: 197 019 (1993 est.).

willet ('wɪlɪt) *n* a large American shore bird, *Catoptrophorus semipalmatus,* having a long stout bill, long legs, and a grey plumage with black-and-white wings: family *Scolopacidae* (sandpipers, etc.), order *Charadriiformes.* [short for *pill-will-willet* imitation of its cry]

willful ('wɪlfʊl) *adj* the U.S. spelling of **wilful.**

William ('wɪljəm) *n* **1** known as *William the Lion.* ?1143–1214, king of Scotland (1165–1214). **2 Prince.** born 1982, son of Prince Charles, and Diana, Princess of Wales.

William I *n* **1** known as *William the Conqueror.* ?1027–1087, duke of Normandy (1035–87) and king of England (1066–87). He claimed to have been promised the English crown by Edward the Confessor, after whose death he disputed the succession of Harold II, invading England in 1066 and defeating Harold at Hastings. The conquest of England resulted in the introduction to England of many Norman customs, esp. feudalism. In 1085 he ordered the Domesday Book to be compiled. **2** known as *William the Bad.* 1120–66, Norman king of Sicily (1154–66). **3** known as *William the Silent.* 1533–84, prince of Orange and count of Nassau: led the revolt of the Netherlands against Spain (1568–76) and became first stadholder of the United Provinces of the Netherlands (1579–84); assassinated. **4** 1772–1843, king of the Netherlands (1815–40): abdicated in favour of his son William II. **5** German name *Wilhelm I.* 1797–1888, king of Prussia (1861–88) and first emperor of Germany (1871–88).

William II *n* **1** known as *William Rufus.* ?1056–1100, king of England (1087–1100); the son of William the Conqueror. He was killed by an arrow while hunting in the New Forest. **2** known as *William the Good.* 1154–89, last Norman king of Sicily (1166–89). **3** 1792–1849, king of the Netherlands (1840–49); son of William I. **4** German name *Kaiser Wilhelm.* 1859–1941, German emperor and king of Prussia (1888–1918): asserted Germany's claim to world leadership; forced to abdicate at the end of World War I.

William III *n* known as *William of Orange.* 1650–1702, stadholder of the Netherlands (1672–1702) and king of Great Britain and Ireland (1689–1702). He was invited by opponents of James II to accept the British throne (1688) and ruled jointly with his wife Mary II (James' daughter) until her death in 1694.

William IV *n* known as the *Sailor King.* 1765–1837, king of the United Kingdom and of Hanover (1830–37), succeeding his brother George IV; the third son of George III.

William of Malmesbury ('mɑːmzbərɪ, -brɪ) *n* ?1090–?1143, English monk and chronicler, whose *Gesta regum Anglorum* and *Historia novella* are valuable sources for English history to 1142.

Williams ('wɪljəmz) *n* **1 Hank,** real name *Hiram Williams.* 1923–53, U.S. country singer and songwriter. His songs (all 1948–52) include "Jambalaya", "Your Cheatin' Heart", and "Why Don't you Love me (like you Used to Do?)". **2 John.** born 1941, Australian classical guitarist, living in Britain. **3 Ralph Vaughan.** See (Ralph) **Vaughan Williams. 4 Raymond** (**Henry**). 1921–88, British literary critic and novelist, noted esp. for such works as *Culture and Society* (1958) and *The Long Revolution* (1961), which offer a socialist analysis of the relationship between society and culture. **5 Tennessee.** real name *Thomas Lanier Williams.* 1911–83, U.S. dramatist. His plays include *The Glass Menagerie* (1944), *A Streetcar Named Desire* (1947), *Cat on a Hot Tin Roof* (1955), and *Night of the Iguana* (1961). **6 William Carlos** ('kɑːləs). 1883–1963, U.S. poet, who formulated the poetic concept "no ideas but in things". His works include *Paterson* (1946–58), which explores the daily life of a man living in a modern city, and the prose work *In the American Grain* (1925).

Williamsburg ('wɪljəmzˌbɜːg) *n* a city in SE Virginia: the capital of Virginia (1693–1779); the restoration of large sections of the colonial city was begun in 1926. Pop.: 11 530 (1990).

Williamson ('wɪljəmsən) *n* **1 Henry.** 1895–1977, British novelist, best known for *Tarka the Otter* (1927) and other animal stories. **2 Malcolm.** born 1931, Australian composer, living in Britain: Master of the Queen's Music since 1975. His works include operas and music for children.

Williams pear *n* a variety of pear that has large yellow juicy sweet fruit. Also called: **William's Bon Chrétien.**

William the Conqueror *n* See **William I** (sense 1).

willies ('wɪlɪz) *pl n* **the.** *Slang.* nervousness, jitters, or fright (esp. in the phrase **give** (*or* **get**) **the willies**). [C20: of unknown origin]

willing ('wɪlɪŋ) *adj* **1** favourably disposed or inclined; ready. **2** cheerfully or eagerly compliant. **3** done, given, accepted, etc., freely or voluntarily. ► **'willingly** *adv* ► **'willingness** *n*

willing horse *n* a person prepared to work hard.

Willis ('wɪlɪs) *n* **1 Norman** (**David**). born 1933, British trade union leader; general secretary of the Trades Union Congress (1984–93). **2 Ted.** Baron Willis of Chislehurst. 1918–92, British author. His works include the play *Hot Summer Night* (1959) and the novel *Death May Surprise Us* (1974).

williwaw ('wɪlɪˌwɔː) *n U.S. and Canadian.* **1** a sudden strong gust of cold wind blowing offshore from a mountainous coast, as in the Strait of Magellan. **2** a state of great turmoil. [C19: of unknown origin]

will-o'-the-wisp (ˌwɪləðə'wɪsp) *n* **1** Also called: **friar's lantern, ignis fatuus, jack-o'-lantern.** a pale flame or phosphorescence sometimes seen over marshy ground at night. It is believed to be due to the spontaneous combustion of methane or other hydrocarbons originating from decomposing organic matter. **2** a person or thing that is elusive or allures and misleads. [C17: originally *Will with the wisp,* from *Will* short for *William* and *wisp* in former sense of a twist of hay or straw burning as a torch] ► ˌ**will-o'-the-'wispish** *or* ˌ**will-o'-the-'wispy** *adj*

willow ('wɪləʊ) *n* **1** any of numerous salicaceous trees and shrubs of the genus *Salix,* such as the weeping willow and osiers of N temperate regions, which have graceful flexible branches and flowers in catkins. **2** the whitish wood of certain of these trees. **3** something made of willow wood, such as a cricket or baseball bat. **4** a machine having a system of revolving spikes for opening and cleaning raw textile fibres. [Old English *welig;* related to *wilige* wicker basket, Old Saxon *wilgia,* Middle High German *wilge,* Greek *helikē* willow, *helix* twisted] ► **'willowish** *or* **'willow-ˌlike** *adj*

willow fly *n* a stonefly, *Leuctra geniculata,* of the English chalk streams, esteemed by trout and therefore by anglers.

willow grouse *n* a N European grouse, *Lagopus lagopus,* with a reddish-brown plumage and white wings: now regarded as the same species as the red grouse (*L. lagopus scoticus*) of Britain.

willowherb ('wɪləʊˌhɜːb) *n* **1** any of various temperate and arctic onagraceous plants of the genus *Epilobium,* having narrow leaves and terminal clusters of pink, purplish, or white flowers. **2** short for **rosebay willowherb** (see **rosebay**). **3** (not in botanical usage) another name for **purple loosestrife** (see **loosestrife**). **4 hairy willowherb.** See **codlins-and-cream.**

willow pattern *n* **a** a pattern incorporating a willow tree, river, bridge, and figures, typically in blue on a white ground, used on pottery and porcelain. **b** (*as modifier*): *a willow-pattern plate.*

Willow South *n* a city in S Alaska, about 113 km (70 miles) northwest of Anchorage: chosen as the site of the projected new state capital in 1976.

willow tit *n* a small tit, *Parus montanus,* of marshy woods in Europe, having a greyish-brown body and dull black crown.

willow warbler *n* an Old World warbler, *Phylloscopus trochilis,* of Eurasian woodlands.

willowy ('wɪləʊɪ) *adj* **1** slender and graceful. **2** flexible or pliant. **3** covered or shaded with willows.

willpower ('wɪlˌpaʊə) *n* **1** the ability to control oneself and determine one's actions. **2** firmness of will.

Wills (wɪlz) *n* **1 Helen Newington,** married name *Helen Wills Moody Roark.* 1905–98, U.S. tennis player. She was Wimbledon singles champion eight times between 1927 and 1938. She also won the U.S. title seven times and the French title four times. **2 William John.** 1834–61, English explorer: Robert Burke's deputy in an expedition on which both men died after crossing Australia from north to south for the first time.

willy ('wɪlɪ) *n Brit. informal.* a childish or jocular term for **penis.**

willy-nilly ('wɪlɪ'nɪlɪ) *adv* **1** whether desired or not. ◆ *adj* **2** occurring or taking place whether desired or not. [Old English *wile hē, nyle hē,* literally: will he or will he not; *nyle,* from *ne* not + *willan* to WILL[1]]

willy wagtail *n Austral.* a black-and-white flycatcher, *Rhipidura leucophrys,* having white feathers over the brows.

willy-willy ('wɪlɪ'wɪlɪ) *n Austral.* a tropical cyclone or duststorm. [from a native Australian language]

Wilmington ('wɪlmɪŋtən) *n* a port in N Delaware, on the Delaware River: industrial centre. Pop.: 71 529 (1990).

Wilno ('viːlnɔ) *n* the Polish name for **Vilnius.**

Wilson ('wɪlsən) *n* **1 Alexander.** 1766–1813, Scottish ornithologist in the U.S. **2** Sir **Angus** (**Frank Johnstone**). 1913–91, British writer, whose works include the collection of short stories *The Wrong Set* (1949) and the novels *Anglo-Saxon Attitudes* (1956) and *No Laughing Matter* (1967). **3 Charles Thomson Rees.** 1869–1959, Scottish physicist, who invented the cloud chamber: shared the Nobel prize for physics 1927. **4 Edmund.** 1895–1972, U.S. critic, noted esp. for *Axel's Castle* (1931), a study of the symbolist movement. **5** (**James**) **Harold,** Baron Wilson of Rievaulx. 1916–95, British Labour statesman; prime minister (1964–70; 1974–76). **6 Richard.** 1714–82, Welsh landscape painter. **7** (**Thomas**) **Woodrow** ('wʊdrəʊ). 1856–1924, U.S. Democratic statesman; 28th president of the U.S. (1913–21). He led the U.S. into World War I in 1917 and proposed the Fourteen Points (1918) as a basis for peace. Although he secured the formation of the League of Nations, the U.S. Senate refused to support it: Nobel peace prize 1919. ► **Wilsonian** (wɪl'səʊnɪən) *adj*

Wilson cloud chamber *n* the full name for **cloud chamber.**

Wilson's petrel *n* a common storm petrel, *Oceanites oceanicus,* that breeds around Antarctica but is often seen in the Atlantic. See **storm petrel.**

Wilson's snipe *n* another name for the **common snipe.** See **snipe** (sense 1).

wilt[1] (wɪlt) *vb* **1** to become or cause to become limp, flaccid, or drooping: *insufficient water makes plants wilt.* **2** to lose or cause to lose courage, strength, etc. ◆ *n* **3** the act of wilting or state of becoming wilted. **4** any of various plant diseases characterized by permanent wilting, usually caused by fungal parasites attacking the roots. [C17: perhaps variant of *wilk* to wither, from Middle Dutch *welken*]

wilt[2] (wɪlt) *vb Archaic or dialect.* (used with the pronoun *thou* or its relative equivalent) a singular form of the present tense (indicative mood) of **will**[1].

Wilton ('wɪltən) *n* a kind of carpet with a close velvet pile of cut loops. [C18: named after *Wilton,* Wiltshire, noted for carpet manufacture]

Wilton House *n* a mansion in Wilton in Wiltshire: built for the 1st Earl of Pembroke in the 16th century; rebuilt after a fire in 1647 by Inigo Jones and John Webb; altered in the 19th century by James Wyatt; landscaped grounds include a famous Palladian bridge.

Wilts (wɪlts) *abbrev. for* Wiltshire.

Wiltshire ('wɪltʃə, -ʃɪə) *n* a county of S England, consisting mainly of chalk uplands, with Salisbury Plain in the south and the Marlborough Downs in the north; prehistoric remains (at Stonehenge and Avebury): the geographical and ceremonial county includes Thamesdown unitary authority (established in 1997). Administrative centre: Trowbridge. Pop. (including Thamesdown): 586 300 (1994 est.). Area (including Thamesdown): 3481 sq. km (1344 sq. miles).

wily ('waɪlɪ) *adj* **wilier, wiliest.** characterized by or proceeding from wiles; sly or crafty. ► '**wiliness** *n*

wimble ('wɪmbᵊl) *n* **1** any of a number of hand tools, such as a brace and bit or a gimlet, used for boring holes. ◆ *vb* **2** to bore (a hole) with or as if with a wimble. [C13: from Middle Dutch *wimmel* auger]

Wimbledon ('wɪmbᵊldən) *n* part of the Greater London borough of Merton: headquarters of the All England Lawn Tennis Club since 1877 and the site of the annual international tennis championships.

wimp (wɪmp) *n Informal.* a feeble ineffective person. [C20: of unknown origin] ► '**wimpish** *or* '**wimpy** *adj*

WIMP (wɪmp) *acronym for:* **1** windows, icons, menus (*or* mice), pointers: denoting a type of user-friendly screen display used on small computers: *a WIMP system.* **2** *Physics.* weakly interacting massive particle.

wimple ('wɪmpᵊl) *n* **1** a piece of cloth draped around the head to frame the face, worn by women in the Middle Ages and still a part of the habit of some nuns. **2** *Scot.* a curve or bend, as in a river. ◆ *vb* **3** *Rare.* to ripple or cause to ripple or undulate. **4** (*tr*) *Archaic.* to cover with or put a wimple on. **5** *Archaic.* (esp. of a veil) to lie or cause to lie in folds or pleats. [Old English *wimpel;* related to Old Saxon *wimpal,* Middle Dutch *wumpel,* Middle High German *bewimpfen* to veil]

wimp out *vb* (*intr, adv*) *Slang.* to fail to do or complete something through fear or lack of conviction.

Wimshurst machine ('wɪmzhɜːst) *n* a type of electrostatic generator with two parallel insulating discs revolving in different directions, each being in contact with a thin metal wiper that produces a charge on the disc: usually used for demonstration purposes. [C19: named after J. *Wimshurst* (1832–1903), English engineer]

win[1] (wɪn) *vb* **wins, winning, won. 1** (*intr*) to achieve first place in a competition. **2** (*tr*) to gain or receive (a prize, first place, etc.) in a competition. **3** (*tr*) to succeed in or gain (something) with an effort: *we won recognition.* **4 win one's spurs. 4a** to achieve recognition in some field of endeavour. **4b** *History.* to be knighted. **5** to gain victory or triumph in (a battle, argument, etc.). **6** (*tr*) to earn or procure (a living, etc.) by work. **7** (*tr*) to take possession of, esp. violently; capture: *the Germans never won Leningrad.* **8** (when *intr,* foll. by *out, through,* etc.) to reach with difficulty (a desired condition or position) or become free, loose, etc., with effort: *the boat won the shore; the boat won through to the shore.* **9** (*tr*) to turn someone into (a supporter, enemy, etc.): *you have just won an ally.* **10** (*tr*) to gain (the sympathy, loyalty, etc.) of someone. **11** (*tr*) to obtain (a woman, etc.) in marriage. **12** (*tr*) **12a** to extract (ore, coal, etc.) from a mine. **12b** to extract (metal or other minerals) from ore. **12c** to discover and make (a mineral deposit) accessible for mining. **13 you can't win.** *Informal.* an expression of resignation after an unsuccessful attempt to overcome difficulties. ◆ *n* **14** *Informal.* a success, victory, or triumph. **15** profit; winnings. **16** the act or fact of reaching the finishing line or post first. ◆ See also **win out.** [Old English *winnan;* related to Old Norse *vinna,* German *gewinnen*] ► '**winnable** *adj*

win[2] (wɪn) *vb* **wins, winning, won** *or* **winned.** (*tr*) *Irish, Scot., and northern English dialect.* **1** to dry (grain, hay, peat, etc.) by exposure to sun and air. **2** a less common word for **winnow.** [Old English, perhaps a variant of WINNOW]

wince[1] (wɪns) *vb* **1** (*intr*) to start slightly, as with sudden pain; flinch. ◆ *n* **2** the act of wincing. [C18 (earlier (C13) meaning: to kick): via Old French *wencier, guenchir* to avoid, from Germanic; compare Old Saxon *wenkian,* Old High German *wenken*] ► '**wincer** *n*

wince[2] (wɪns) *n* a roller for transferring pieces of cloth between dyeing vats. [C17: variant of WINCH]

wincey ('wɪnsɪ) *n Brit.* a plain- or twill-weave cloth, usually having a cotton or linen warp and a wool filling. [C19: of Scottish origin, probably an alteration of *woolsey* as in LINSEY-WOOLSEY]

winceyette (ˌwɪnsɪ'ɛt) *n Brit.* a plain-weave cotton fabric with slightly raised two-sided nap.

winch[1] (wɪntʃ) *n* **1** a windlass driven by a hand- or power-operated crank. **2** a hand- or power-operated crank by which a machine is driven. ◆ *vb* **3** (*tr;* often foll. by *up* or *in*) to pull (in a rope) or lift (a weight) using a winch. [Old English *wince* pulley; related to WINK[1]] ► '**wincher** *n*

winch[2] (wɪntʃ) *vb* (*intr*) an obsolete word for **wince**[1].

winchester ('wɪntʃɪstə) *n* (*sometimes cap.*) a large cylindrical bottle with a narrow neck used for transporting chemicals. It contains about 2.5 litres. [after *Winchester,* Hampshire]

Winchester ('wɪntʃɪstə) *n* a city in S England, administrative centre of Hampshire: a Romano-British town; Saxon capital of Wessex; 11th-century cathedral; site of **Winchester College** (1382), English public school. Pop.: 36 121 (1991).

Winchester disk *n* a type of hard disk in which disks are permanently sealed, together with read-write heads, in an airtight container to keep dust out. [C20: named after the 3030 WINCHESTER RIFLE, as the original device would have had 3030 as its IBM number]

Winchester rifle *n Trademark.* a breech-loading lever-action repeating rifle with a tubular magazine under the barrel. Often shortened to **Winchester.** [C19: named after O. F. *Winchester* (1810–80), U.S. manufacturer]

Winckelmann (*German* 'vɪŋkəlman) *n* **Johann Joachim** (jo'han 'joːaxɪm). 1717–68, German archaeologist and art historian; one of the founders of neoclassicism.

wind[1] (wɪnd) *n* **1** a current of air, sometimes of considerable force, moving generally horizontally from areas of high pressure to areas of low pressure. See also **Beaufort scale.** Related adj: **aeolian. 2** *Chiefly poetic.* the direction from which a wind blows, usually a cardinal point of the compass. **3** air artificially moved, as by a fan, pump, etc. **4** any sweeping and destructive force. **5** a trend, tendency, or force: *the winds of revolution.* **6** *Informal.* a hint; suggestion: *we got wind that you were coming.* **7** something deemed insubstantial: *his talk was all wind.* **8** breath, as used in respiration or talk: *you're just wasting wind.* **9** (often used in sports) the power to breathe normally: *his wind is weak.* See also **second wind. 10** *Music.* **10a** a wind instrument or wind instruments considered collectively. **10b** (*often pl*) the musicians who play wind instruments in an orchestra. **10c** (*modifier*): of, relating to, or composed of wind instruments: *a wind ensemble.* **11** an informal name for **flatus. 12** the air on which the scent of an animal is carried to hounds or on which the scent of a hunter is carried to his quarry. **13 between wind and water. 13a** the part of a vessel's hull below the water line that is exposed by rolling or by wave action. **13b** any point particularly susceptible to attack or injury. **14 break wind.** to release intestinal gas through the anus. **15 get** *or* **have the wind up.** *Informal.* to become frightened. **16 have in the wind.** to be in the act of following (quarry) by scent. **17 how** *or* **which way the wind blows** *or* **lies.** what appears probable. **18 in the wind.** about to happen. **19 in the wind** *or* **three sheets in the wind.** *Informal.* intoxicated; drunk. **20 in the teeth** (*or* **eye**) **of the wind.** directly into the wind. **21 into the wind.** against the wind or upwind. **22 off the wind.** *Nautical.* away from the direction from which the wind is blowing. **23 on the wind.** *Nautical.* as near as possible to the direction from which the wind is blowing. **24 put the wind up.** *Informal.* to frighten or alarm. **25 raise the wind.** *Brit. informal.* to obtain the necessary funds. **26 sail close** *or* **near to the wind. 26a** to come near the limits of danger or indecency. **26b** to live frugally or manage one's affairs economically. **27 take the wind out of someone's sails.** to destroy someone's advantage; disconcert or deflate. ◆ *vb* (*tr*) **28** to cause (someone) to be short of breath: *the blow winded him.* **29a** to detect the scent of. **29b** to pursue (quarry) by following its scent. **30** to cause (a baby) to bring up wind after feeding by patting or rubbing on the back. **31** to expose to air, as in drying, ventilating, etc. [Old English *wind;* related to Old High German *wint,* Old Norse *vindr,* Gothic *winds,* Latin *ventus*] ► '**windless** *adj* ► '**windlessly** *adv* ► '**windlessness** *n*

wind[2] (waɪnd) *vb* **winds, winding, wound. 1** (often foll. by *around, about, or upon*) to turn or coil (string, cotton, etc.) around some object or point or (of string, etc.) to be turned etc., around some object or point: *he wound a scarf around his head.* **2** (*tr*) to twine, cover, or wreathe by or as if by coiling, wrapping, etc.; encircle: *we wound the body in a shroud.* **3** (*tr;* often foll. by *up*) to tighten the spring of (a clockwork mechanism). **4** (*tr;* foll. by *off*) to remove by uncoiling or unwinding. **5** (*usually intr*) to move or cause to move in a sinuous, spiral, or circular course: *the river winds through the hills.* **6** (*tr*) to introduce indirectly or deviously: *he is winding his own opinions into the report.* **7** (*tr*) to cause to twist or revolve: *he wound the handle.* **8** (*tr;* usually foll. by *up* or *down*) to move by cranking: *please wind up the window.* **9** (*tr*) to haul, lift, or hoist (a weight, etc.) by means of a wind or windlass. **10** (*intr*) (of a board, etc.) to be warped or twisted. **11** (*intr*) *Archaic.* to proceed deviously or indirectly. ◆ *n* **12** the act of winding or state of being wound. **13** a single turn, bend, etc.: *a wind in the river.* **14** Also called: **winding.** a twist in a board or plank. ◆ See also **wind down, wind up.** [Old English *windan;* related to Old Norse *vinda,* Old High German *wintan* (German *winden*)] ▸ **'windable** *adj*

wind[3] (waɪnd) *vb* **winds, winding, winded** *or* **wound.** (*tr*) *Poetic.* to blow (a note or signal) on (a horn, bugle, etc.). [C16: special use of WIND[1]]

windage ('wɪndɪdʒ) *n* **1a** a deflection of a projectile as a result of the effect of the wind. **1b** the degree of such deflection. **1c** the extent to which it is necessary to adjust the wind gauge of a gun sight in order to compensate for such deflection. **2** the difference between a firearm's bore and the diameter of its projectile. **3** *Nautical.* the exposed part of the hull of a vessel responsible for wind resistance. **4** the retarding force upon a rotating machine resulting from the drag of the air.

windbag ('wɪnd,bæg) *n* **1** *Slang.* a voluble person who has little of interest to communicate. **2** the bag in a set of bagpipes, which provides a continuous flow of air to the pipes.

windblown ('wɪnd,bləʊn) *adj* **1** blown by the wind. **2** (of a woman's hair style) cut short and combed to look as though it has been dishevelled by the wind. **3** (of trees, shrubs, etc.) growing in a shape determined by the prevailing winds. **4** *N.Z.* (of trees) felled by the wind.

wind-borne *adj* (esp. of plant seeds or pollen) transported by wind.

windbound ('wɪnd,baʊnd) *adj* (of a sailing vessel) prevented from sailing by an unfavourable wind.

windbreak ('wɪnd,breɪk) *n* a fence, line of trees, etc., serving as a protection from the wind by breaking its force.

wind-broken *adj* (of a horse) asthmatic or heaving.

windburn ('wɪnd,bɜːn) *n* irritation and redness of the skin caused by prolonged exposure to winds of high velocity. ▸ **'wind,burnt** *or* **'wind,burned** *adj*

windcheater ('wɪnd,tʃiːtə) *Trademark in Austral. n* a warm jacket, usually with a close-fitting knitted neck, cuffs, and waistband. Also called: **windjammer,** U.S. name (trademark): **Windbreaker** ('wɪnd,breɪkə).

wind chest (wɪnd) *n* a box in an organ in which air from the bellows is stored under pressure before being supplied to the pipes or reeds.

wind-chill (wɪnd-) *n* **a** the serious chilling effect of wind and low temperature: it is measured on a scale that runs from hot to fatal to life and allows for varying combinations of air temperature and wind speed. **b** (*as modifier*): *wind-chill factor.*

wind chimes (wɪnd) *pl n* a decorative arrangement of small discs of metal, shell, etc., hung near a window or door, that shake together with a tinkling sound in a draught.

wind cone (wɪnd) *n* another name for **windsock.**

wind down (waɪnd) *vb* (*adv*) **1** (*tr*) to lower or move down by cranking. **2** (*intr*) (of a clock spring) to become slack. **3** (*intr*) to diminish gradually in force or power; relax.

winded ('wɪndɪd) *adj* **1** out of breath, as from strenuous exercise. **2** (*in combination*) having breath or wind as specified: *broken-winded; short-winded.*

winder ('waɪndə) *n* **1** a person or device that winds, as an engine for hoisting the cages in a mine shaft or a device for winding the yarn in textile manufacture. **2** an object, such as a bobbin, around which something is wound. **3** a knob or key used to wind up a clock, watch, or similar mechanism. **4** any plant that twists itself around a support. **5** a step of a spiral staircase.

Windermere ('wɪndə,mɪə) *n* **Lake.** a lake in NW England, in Cumbria in the SE part of the Lake District: the largest lake in England. Length: 17 km (10.5 miles).

windfall ('wɪnd,fɔːl) *n* **1** a piece of unexpected good fortune, esp. financial gain. **2** something blown down by the wind, esp. a piece of fruit. **3** *Chiefly U.S. and Canadian.* a plot of land covered with trees blown down by the wind.

windfall tax *n* a tax levied on an organization considered to have made excessive profits, esp. a privatized utility company that has exploited a monopoly.

wind farm *n* a large group of wind-driven generators for electricity supply.

windflower ('wɪnd,flaʊə) *n* any of various anemone plants, such as the wood anemone.

windgall ('wɪnd,gɔːl) *n Vet. science.* a soft swelling in the area of the fetlock joint of a horse. [C16: from WIND[1] + GALL[2]] ▸ **'wind,galled** *adj*

wind gap (wɪnd) *n* a narrow dry valley on a mountain or ridge.

wind gauge (wɪnd) *n* **1** another name for **anemometer** (sense 1). **2** a scale on a gun sight indicating the amount of deflection necessary to allow for windage. **3** *Music.* a device for measuring the wind pressure in the bellows of an organ.

wind harp (wɪnd) *n* a less common name for **aeolian harp.**

Windhoek ('vɪnt,hʊk, 'vɪnt-) *n* the capital of Namibia, in the centre, at an altitude of 1654 m (5428 ft.): formerly the capital of German South West Africa. Pop.: 161 000 (1992 est.).

windhover ('wɪnd,hɒvə) *n Brit.* a dialect name for a **kestrel.**

winding ('waɪndɪŋ) *n* **1** a curving or sinuous course or movement. **2** anything that has been wound or wrapped around something. **3** a particular manner or style in which something has been wound. **4** a curve, bend, or complete turn in wound material, a road, etc. **5** (*often pl*) devious thoughts or behaviour: *the tortuous windings of political argumentation.* **6** one or more turns of wire forming a continuous coil through which an electric current can pass, as used in transformers, generators, etc. **7** another name for **wind**[2] (sense 14). **8** a coil of tubing in certain brass instruments, esp. the French horn. ◆ *adj* **9** curving; sinuous: *a winding road.* ▸ **'windingly** *adv*

winding drum ('waɪndɪŋ) *n* a rotating drum usually grooved to nest a wire rope which is wound onto it as part of the mechanism of a hoist.

winding sheet *n* a sheet in which a corpse is wrapped for burial; shroud.

winding staircase *n* another word for **spiral staircase.**

winding-up *n* the process of finishing or closing something, esp. the process of closing down a business.

wind instrument (wɪnd) *n* any musical instrument sounded by the breath, such as the woodwinds and brass instruments of an orchestra.

windjammer ('wɪnd,dʒæmə) *n* **1** a large merchant sailing ship. **2** another name for **windcheater.**

windlass ('wɪndləs) *n* **1** a machine for raising weights by winding a rope or chain upon a barrel or drum driven by a crank, motor, etc. ◆ *vb* **2** (*tr*) to raise or haul (a weight, etc.) by means of a windlass. [C14: from Old Norse *vindáss,* from *vinda* to WIND[2] + *ass* pole; related to Old French *guindas,* Middle Low German, Dutch *windas*]

windlestraw ('wɪndᵊl,strɔː) *n Irish, Scot., and English dialect.* **1** the dried stalk of any of various grasses. **2** anything weak or feeble, esp. a thin unhealthy person. [Old English *windelstrēaw,* from *windel* basket, from *windan* to WIND[2] + *strēaw* STRAW[1]]

wind machine (wɪnd) *n* a machine used, esp. in the theatre, to produce wind or the sound of wind.

windmill ('wɪnd,mɪl, 'wɪn,mɪl) *n* **1** a machine for grinding or pumping driven by a set of adjustable vanes or sails that are caused to turn by the force of the wind. **2** the set of vanes or sails that drives such a mill. **3** Also called: **whirligig.** *Brit.* a toy consisting of plastic or paper vanes attached to a stick in such a manner that they revolve like the sails of a windmill. U.S. and Canadian name: **pinwheel.** **4** an imaginary opponent or evil (esp. in the phrase **tilt at** *or* **fight windmills**). **5** a small air-driven propeller fitted to a light aircraft to drive auxiliary equipment. Compare **ram-air turbine.** **6** an informal name for **helicopter.** **7** an informal name for **propeller** (sense 1). ◆ *vb* **8** to move or cause to move like the arms of a windmill. **9** (*intr*) (of an aircraft propeller, rotor of a turbine, etc.) to rotate as a result of the force of a current of air rather than under power.

window ('wɪndəʊ) *n* **1** a light framework, made of timber, metal, or plastic, that contains glass or glazed opening frames and is placed in a wall or roof to let in light or air or to see through. Related adj: **fenestral.** **2** an opening in the wall or roof of a building that is provided to let in light or air or to see through. **3** See **windowpane.** **4** the display space in and directly behind a shop window: *the dress in the window.* **5** any opening or structure resembling a window in function or appearance, such as the transparent area of an envelope revealing an address within. **6** an opportunity to see or understand something usually unseen: *a window on the workings of Parliament.* **7** a period of unbooked time in a diary, schedule, etc. **8** short for **launch window** or **weather window.** **9** *Physics.* a region of the spectrum in which a medium transmits electromagnetic radiation. See also **radio window.** **10** *Computing.* an area of a VDU display that may be manipulated separately from the rest of the display area; typically different files can be displayed simultaneously in different overlapping windows. **11** (*modifier*): of or relating to a window or windows: *a window ledge.* **12 out of the window.** *Informal.* dispensed with; disregarded. ◆ *vb* **13** (*tr*) to furnish with or as if with windows. [C13: from Old Norse *vindauga,* from *vindr* WIND[1] + *auga* EYE[1]]

window box *n* **1** a long narrow box, placed on or outside a windowsill, in which plants are grown. **2** either of a pair of vertical boxes, attached to the sides of a sash window frame, that enclose a sash cord and counterbalancing weight.

window-dresser *n* a person employed to design and build up a display in a shop window.

window-dressing *n* **1** the ornamentation of shop windows, designed to attract customers. **2** the pleasant, showy, or false aspect of an idea, policy, etc., which is stressed to conceal the real or unpleasant nature; façade.

window envelope *n* a type of envelope, esp. for business use, having a transparent area that reveals the address within.

windowpane ('wɪndəʊ,peɪn) *n* a sheet of glass in a window.

window sash *n* a glazed window frame, esp. one that opens.

window seat *n* **1** a seat below a window, esp. in a bay window. **2** a seat beside a window in a bus, train, etc.

window-shop *vb* **-shops, -shopping, -shopped.** (*intr*) to look at goods in shop windows without buying them. ▸ **'window-,shopper** *n* ▸ **'window-,shopping** *n*

windowsill ('wɪndəʊ,sɪl) *n* a sill below a window.

window tax *n History.* a tax on windows in houses levied between 1696 and 1851.

windpipe ('wɪnd,paɪp) *n* a nontechnical name for **trachea** (sense 1). Related adj: **tracheal.**

wind-pollinated *adj* (of certain plants) pollinated by wind-borne pollen. ▸ **'wind-,polli'nation** *n*

wind power (wɪnd) *n* power produced from windmills and wind turbines.

Wind River Range (wɪnd) *n* a mountain range in W Wyoming: one of the highest ranges of the central Rockies. Highest peak: Gannet Peak, 4202 m (13 785 ft.).

wind rose (wɪnd) *n* a diagram with radiating lines showing the frequency and strength of winds from each direction affecting a specific place.

windrow ('wɪnd,rəʊ, 'wɪn,rəʊ) *n* **1** a long low ridge or line of hay or a similar crop, designed to achieve the best conditions for drying or curing. **2** a line of leaves, snow, dust, etc., swept together by the wind. ◆ *vb* **3** (*tr*) to put (hay or a similar crop) into windrows. ▸ **'wind,rower** *n*

windsail ('wɪnd,seɪl) *n* **1** a sail rigged as an air scoop over a hatch or companionway to catch breezes and divert them below. **2** any of the vanes or sails of a windmill.

wind scale (wɪnd) *n* a numerical scale of wind force, such as the Beaufort scale.

Windscale ('wɪnd,skeɪl) *n* the former name of **Sellafield.**

windscreen ('wɪnd,skriːn) *n Brit.* the sheet of flat or curved glass that forms a window of a motor vehicle, esp. the front window. U.S. and Canadian name: **windshield.**

windscreen wiper *n Brit.* an electrically operated blade with a rubber edge that wipes a windscreen clear of rain, snow, etc. U.S. and Canadian name: **windshield wiper.**

wind shake (wɪnd) *n* a crack between the annual rings in wood: caused by strong winds bending the tree trunk.

wind shear (wɪnd) *n* stress on an aircraft in an area in which winds of different speeds and directions are close together.

windshield (ˈwɪndˌʃiːld) *n* **1** the U.S. and Canadian name for **windscreen. 2** an object designed to shield something from the wind.

windsock (ˈwɪndˌsɒk) *n* a truncated cone of textile mounted on a mast so that it is free to rotate about a vertical axis: used, esp. at airports, to indicate the local wind direction. Also called: **air sock, drogue, wind sleeve, wind cone.**

Windsor[1] (ˈwɪnzə) *n* **1** a town in S England, in Windsor and Maidenhead unitary authority on the River Thames, linked by bridge with Eton: site of **Windsor Castle,** residence of English monarchs since its founding by William the Conqueror; **Old Windsor**, royal residence in the time of Edward the Confessor, is 3 km (2 miles) southeast. Pop.: 30 136 (1991). Official name: **New Windsor. 2** a city in SE Canada, in S Ontario on the Detroit River opposite Detroit: motor-vehicle manufacturing; university (1963). Pop.: 191 435 (1991).

Windsor[2] (ˈwɪnzə) *n* **1** the official name of the British royal family from 1917. **2 Duke of.** the title of **Edward VIII** from 1937.

Windsor and Maidenhead *n* a unitary authority in S England, in Berkshire. Pop.: 141 500 (1996 est.). Area: 197 sq. km (76 sq. miles).

Windsor chair *n* a simple wooden chair, popular in England and America from the 18th century, usually having a shaped seat, splayed legs, and a back of many spindles.

Windsor knot *n* a wide triangular knot, produced by making extra turns in tying a tie.

Windsor rocker *n U.S. and Canadian.* a Windsor chair on rockers.

Windsor tie *n* a wide silk tie worn in a floppy bow.

windstorm (ˈwɪndˌstɔːm) *n* a storm consisting of violent winds.

wind-sucking *n* a harmful habit of horses in which the animal arches its neck and swallows a gulp of air. ▸ **ˈwindˌsucker** *n*

windsurf (ˈwɪndˌsɜːf) *vb (intr)* to take part in the sport of windsurfing. ▸ **ˈwindˌsurfer** *n*

windsurfing (ˈwɪndˌsɜːfɪŋ) *n* the sport of sailing standing up on a sailboard that is equipped with a mast, sail, and wishbone boom. Also called: **boardsailing, sailboarding.**

wind surge (wɪnd) *n* a wind-induced rise in the water level at the coast or the shore of an inland expanse of water. It has a definite frequency and if this is close to the tidal frequency serious flooding can result.

windswept (ˈwɪndˌswɛpt) *adj* **1** open to or swept by the wind. **2** another word for **windblown** (sense 2).

wind tee (wɪnd) *n* a large weather vane shaped like a *T,* located at an airfield to indicate the wind direction.

wind tunnel (wɪnd) *n* a chamber for testing the aerodynamic properties of aircraft, aerofoils, etc., in which a current of air can be maintained at a constant velocity.

wind up (waɪnd) *vb (adv)* **1** to bring to or reach a conclusion: *he wound up the proceedings.* **2** *(tr)* to tighten the spring of (a clockwork mechanism). **3** *(tr; usually passive) Informal.* to make nervous, tense, etc.; excite: *he was all wound up before the big fight.* **4** *(tr)* to roll (thread, etc.) into a ball. **5** an informal word for **liquidate** (sense 2). **6** *(intr) Informal.* to end up (in a specified state): *you'll wind up without any teeth.* **7** *(tr; usually passive)* to involve; entangle: *they were wound up in three different scandals.* **8** *(tr)* to hoist or haul up. **9** *(tr) Brit. slang.* to tease (someone). ◆ *n* **wind-up. 10** the act of concluding. **11** the finish; end.

windward (ˈwɪndwəd) *Chiefly nautical.* ◆ *adj* **1** of, in, or moving to the quarter from which the wind blows. **2 to windward of.** advantageously situated with respect to. ◆ *n* **3** the windward point. **4** the side towards the wind. ◆ *adv* **5** towards the wind. ◆ Compare **leeward.**

Windward Islands *pl n* **1** a group of islands in the SE Caribbean, in the Lesser Antilles: consists of the French Overseas Department of Martinique and the independent states of Grenada, St Lucia, and St Vincent and the Grenadines. **2** a group of islands in the S Pacific, in French Polynesia in the W Society Archipelago: Moorea, Maio (Tubuai Manu), and Mehetia and Tetiaoro. Pop.: 140 341 (1988). French name: **Îles du Vent.**

Windward Passage *n* a strait in the Caribbean, between E Cuba and NW Haiti. Width: 80 km (50 miles).

windy (ˈwɪndɪ) *adj* **windier, windiest. 1** of, characterized by, resembling, or relating to wind; stormy. **2** swept by or open to powerful winds. **3** marked by or given to empty, prolonged, and often boastful speech; bombastic: *windy orations.* **4** void of substance. **5** an informal word for **flatulent. 6** *Slang.* afraid; frightened; nervous. ▸ **ˈwindily** *adv* ▸ **ˈwindiness** *n*

Windy City *n* **the.** *Informal.* Chicago, Illinois.

wine (waɪn) *n* **1a** an alcoholic drink produced by the fermenting of grapes with water and sugar. Related adjs: **vinaceous, vinous. 1b** an alcoholic drink produced in this way from other fruits, flowers, etc.: *elderberry wine.* **2a** a dark red colour, sometimes with a purplish tinge. **2b** *(as adj): wine-coloured.* **3** anything resembling wine in its intoxicating or invigorating effect. **4** *Pharmacol.* fermented grape juice containing medicaments. **5 Adam's wine.** *Brit.* a dialect word for **water. 6 new wine in old bottles.** something new added to or imposed upon an old or established order. ◆ *vb* **7** *(intr)* to drink wine. **8 wine and dine.** to entertain or be entertained with wine and fine food. [Old English *wīn,* from Latin *vīnum;* related to Greek *oinos,* of obscure origin] ▸ **ˈwineless** *adj*

wine bar *n* a bar in a restaurant, etc., or an establishment that specializes in serving wine and usually food.

wineberry (ˈwaɪnˌbɛrɪ) *n, pl* **-ries.** *N.Z.* another name for **mako**[2] (sense 1).

winebibber (ˈwaɪnˌbɪbə) *n* a person who drinks a great deal of wine. ▸ **ˈwineˌbibbing** *n*

wine box *n* wine sold in a cubic carton, usually of three-litre capacity, having a plastic lining and a tap for dispensing.

wine cellar *n* **1** a place, such as a dark cool cellar, where wine is stored. **2** the stock of wines stored there.

wine cooler *n* **1** a bucket-like vessel containing ice in which a bottle of wine is placed to be cooled. **2** the full name for **cooler** (sense 3).

wine gallon *n Brit.* a former unit of capacity equal to 231 cubic inches.

wineglass (ˈwaɪnˌglɑːs) *n* **1** a glass drinking vessel, typically having a small bowl on a stem, with a flared foot. **2** Also called: **wineglassful.** the amount that such a glass will hold.

wine grower *n* a person engaged in cultivating vines in order to make wine. ▸ **wine growing** *n*

wine palm *n* any of various palm trees, the sap of which is used, esp. when fermented, as a drink. See **toddy** (sense 2). Also called: **toddy palm.**

winepress (ˈwaɪnˌprɛs) *n* any equipment used for squeezing the juice from grapes in order to make wine.

winery (ˈwaɪnərɪ) *n, pl* **-eries.** *Chiefly U.S. and Canadian.* a place where wine is made.

wineskin (ˈwaɪnˌskɪn) *n* the skin of a sheep or goat sewn up and used as a holder for wine.

wine tasting *n* an occasion for sampling a number of wines. ▸ **wine taster** *n*

wing (wɪŋ) *n* **1** either of the modified forelimbs of a bird that are covered with large feathers and specialized for flight in most species. **2** one of the organs of flight of an insect, consisting of a membranous outgrowth from the thorax containing a network of veins. **3** either of the organs of flight in certain other animals, esp. the forelimb of a bat. **4a** a half of the main supporting surface on an aircraft, confined to one side of it. **4b** the full span of the main supporting surface on both sides of an aircraft. **4c** an aircraft designed as one complete wing. **4d** a position in flight formation, just to the rear and to one side of an aircraft. **5a** an organ or apparatus resembling a wing. **5b** *Anatomy.* any bodily structure resembling a wing: *the wings of a sphenoid bone.* Technical name: **ala. 6** anything suggesting a wing in form, function, or position, such as a sail of a windmill or a ship. **7** *Botany.* **7a** either of the lateral petals of a sweetpea or related flower. **7b** any of various outgrowths of a plant part, esp. the process on a wind-dispersed fruit or seed. **8** a means or cause of flight or rapid motion; flight: *fear gave wings to his feet.* **9** the act or manner of flying: *a bird of strong wing.* **10** *Brit.* the part of a car body that surrounds the wheels. U.S. and Canadian name: **fender. 11** any affiliate of or subsidiary to a parent organization. **12** *Soccer, hockey, etc.* **12a** either of the two sides of the pitch near the touchline. **12b** a player stationed in such a position; winger. **13** a faction or group within a political party or other organization. See also **left wing, right wing. 14** a part of a building that is subordinate to the main part. **15** *(pl)* the space offstage to the right or left of the acting area in a theatre. **16 in the wings.** ready to step in when needed. **17** *Fortifications.* a side connecting the main fort and an outwork. **18** a folding panel, as of a double door or a movable partition. **19** either of the two pieces that project forwards from the sides of some chairbacks. **20** the U.S. name for **quarterlight. 21** a surface fitted to a racing car to produce aerodynamic download to hold it on the road at high speed. **22** *(pl)* an insignia in the form of stylized wings worn by a qualified aircraft pilot. **23** a tactical formation in some air forces, consisting of two or more squadrons. **24** any of various flattened organs or extensions in lower animals, esp. when used in locomotion. **25** the side of a hold alongside a ship's hull. **26** the outside angle of the cutting edge on the share and mouldboard of a plough. **27** a jetty or dam for narrowing a channel of water. **28 on a wing and a prayer.** with only the slightest hope of succeeding. **29 on the wing. 29a** flying. **29b** travelling. **29c** about to leave. **30 take wing. 30a** to lift off or fly away. **30b** to depart in haste. **30c** to become joyful. **31 under one's wing.** in one's care or tutelage. **32 clip (someone's) wings. 32a** to restrict (someone's) freedom. **32b** to thwart (someone's) ambition. **33 on wings.** flying or as if flying. **34 spread** *or* **stretch one's wings.** to make full use of one's abilities. ◆ *vb (mainly tr)* **35** *(also intr)* to make (one's way) swiftly on or as if on wings. **36** to shoot or wound (a bird, person, etc.) superficially, in the wing or arm, etc. **37** to cause to fly or move swiftly: *to wing an arrow.* **38** to fit (an arrow) with a feather. **39** to provide with wings. **40** (of buildings, altars, etc.) to provide with lateral extensions. **41 wing it.** *Informal.* to accomplish or perform something without full preparation or knowledge; improvise. [C12: from Scandinavian; compare Old Norse *vængir* (plural), Norwegian *veng*] ▸ **ˈwingˌlike** *adj*

wing and wing *adv* with sails extended on both sides by booms.

Wingate (ˈwɪnˌgeɪt) *n* **Orde (Charles)** (ɔːd). 1903–44, British soldier. During World War II he organized the Chindits in Burma (Myanmar) to disrupt Japanese communications. He died in an air crash.

wing beat *n* a complete cycle of moving the wing by a bird when flying.

wing bow (bəʊ) *n* a distinctive band of colour marking the wing of a bird.

wing-case *n* the nontechnical name for **elytron.**

wing chair *n* an easy chair having wings on each side of the back.

wing collar *n* a stiff turned-up shirt collar worn with the points turned down over the tie.

wing commander *n* an officer holding commissioned rank in certain air forces, such as the Royal Air Force: junior to a group captain and senior to a squadron leader.

wing covert *n* any of the covert feathers of the wing of a bird, occurring in distinct rows.

wingding (ˈwɪŋˌdɪŋ) *n Slang, chiefly U.S. and Canadian.* **1a** a noisy lively party or festivity. **1b** (*as modifier*): *a real wingding party.* **2** a real or pretended fit or seizure. [C20: of unknown origin]

winged (wɪŋd) *adj* **1** furnished with wings: *winged god; winged horse.* **2** flying straight and true as if by wing: *winged words.*

winger ('wɪŋə) *n Soccer, hockey, etc.* a player stationed on the wing.

wing-footed *adj Archaic.* fleet; swift.

wingless ('wɪŋlɪs) *adj* **1** having no wings or vestigial wings. **2** designating primitive insects of the subclass *Apterygota,* characterized by small size, lack of wings, and larvae resembling the adults: includes the springtails and bristletails. ► **'winglessness** *n*

winglet ('wɪŋlɪt) *n* **1** a small wing, esp. the bastard wing of a bird. **2** a small wing placed at the tip of the main wing of an aircraft and perpendicular to it designed to reduce the aircraft's vortex drag.

wing loading *n* the total weight of an aircraft divided by its wing area.

wingman ('wɪŋmæn) *n, pl* **-men.** a player in the wing position in Australian Rules.

wing nut *n* a threaded nut tightened by hand by means of two flat lugs or wings projecting from the central body. Also called: **butterfly nut.**

wingover ('wɪŋ,əʊvə) *n* a manoeuvre in which the direction of flight of an aircraft is reversed by putting it into a climbing turn until nearly stalled, the nose then being allowed to fall while continuing the turn.

wing shot *n* **1** a shot taken at a bird in flight. **2** an expert at shooting birds in flight.

wingspan ('wɪŋ,spæn) *or* **wingspread** ('wɪŋ,spred) *n* the distance between the wing tips of an aircraft, bird, etc.

wing tip *n* the outermost edge of a wing.

wink[1] (wɪŋk) *vb* **1** (*intr*) to close and open one eye quickly, deliberately, or in an exaggerated fashion to convey friendliness, etc. **2** to close and open (an eye or the eyes) momentarily. **3** (*tr; foll. by away, back,* etc.) to force away (tears, etc.) by winking. **4** (*tr*) to signal with a wink. **5** (*intr*) (of a light) to gleam or flash intermittently. ◆ *n* **6** a winking movement, esp. one conveying a signal, etc., or such a signal. **7** an interrupted flashing of light. **8** a brief moment of time; instant. **9** *Informal.* the smallest amount, esp. of sleep. See also **forty winks. 10 tip the wink.** *Brit. informal.* to give a hint. [Old English *wincian;* related to Old Saxon *wincon,* Old High German *winchan,* German *winken* to wave. See WENCH, WINCH]

wink[2] (wɪŋk) *n* a disc used in the game of tiddlywinks. [C20: shortened from TIDDLYWINKS]

wink at *vb* (*intr, prep*) to connive at; disregard: *the authorities winked at corruption.*

Winkelried (*German* 'vɪŋkəlriːt) *n* **Arnold von** ('arnɔlt fɔn). died ?1386, Swiss hero of the battle of Sempach (1386) against the Austrians.

winker ('wɪŋkə) *n* **1** a person or thing that winks. **2** *U.S. and Canadian slang, English dialect.* an eye, eyelash, or eyelid. **3** another name for **blinker** (sense 1).

winkle ('wɪŋk°l) *n* **1** See **periwinkle**[1]. ◆ *vb* **2** (*tr;* usually foll. by *out, out of,* etc.) *Informal, chiefly Brit.* to extract or prise out. [C16: shortened from PERIWINKLE[1]]

winkle-pickers *pl n* shoes or boots with very pointed narrow toes, popular in the mid-20th century.

Winnebago (,wɪnɪ'beɪgəʊ) *n* **1 Lake.** a lake in E Wisconsin, fed and drained by the Fox river: the largest lake in the state. Area: 557 sq. km (215 sq. miles). **2** (*pl* **-gos** *or* **-go**) a member of a North American Indian people living in Wisconsin and Nebraska. **3** the language of this people, belonging to the Siouan family.

winner ('wɪnə) *n* **1** a person or thing that wins. **2** *Informal.* a person or thing that seems sure to win or succeed.

winner's enclosure *or* **circle** *n* See **unsaddling enclosure.**

winning ('wɪnɪŋ) *adj* **1** (of a person, character, etc.) charming, engaging, or attractive: *winning ways; a winning smile.* **2** gaining victory: *the winning stroke.* ◆ *n* **3a** a shaft or seam of coal. **3b** the extraction of coal or ore from the ground. **4** (*pl*) money, prizes, or valuables won, esp. in gambling. ► **'winningly** *adv* ► **'winningness** *n*

winning gallery *n Real Tennis.* the gallery farthest from the net on either side of the court, into which any shot played wins a point.

winning opening *n Real Tennis.* the grille, dedans, or winning gallery, into which any shot played wins a point.

winning post *n* the post marking the finishing line on a racecourse.

Winnipeg ('wɪnɪ,peg) *n* **1** a city in S Canada, capital of Manitoba at the confluence of the Assiniboine and Red Rivers: University of Manitoba (1877) and University of Winnipeg (1871). Pop.: 616 790 (1991). **2 Lake.** a lake in S Canada, in Manitoba: drains through the Nelson River into Hudson Bay. Area: 23 553 sq. km (9094 sq. miles). ► **'Winni,pegger** *n*

Winnipeg couch *n Canadian.* a couch with no arms or back, opening out into a double bed.

Winnipegosis (,wɪnɪpə'gəʊsɪs) *n* **Lake.** a lake in S Canada, in W Manitoba. Area: 5400 sq. km (2086 sq. miles).

winnow ('wɪnəʊ) *vb* **1** to separate (grain) from (chaff) by means of a wind or current of air. **2** (*tr*) to examine in order to select the desirable elements. **3** (*tr*) *Archaic.* to beat (the air) with wings. **4** (*tr*) *Rare.* to blow upon; fan. ◆ *n* **5a** a device for winnowing. **5b** the act or process of winnowing. [Old English *windwian;* related to Old High German *wintōn,* Gothic *diswinthjan,* Latin *ventilāre.* See WIND[1]] ► **'winnower** *n*

wino ('waɪnəʊ) *n, pl* **-os.** *Informal.* a person who habitually drinks wine as a means of getting drunk.

win out *vb* (*intr, adv*) *Informal.* to succeed or prevail as if in a contest: *sanity rarely wins out over prejudice.*

win over *vb* (*tr, adv*) to gain the support or consent of (someone). Also: **win round.**

winsome ('wɪnsəm) *adj* charming; winning; engaging: *a winsome smile.* [Old English *wynsum,* from *wynn* joy (related to Old High German *wunnia,* German *Wonne*) + *-sum* -SOME[1]] ► **'winsomely** *adv* ► **'winsomeness** *n*

Winstanley ('wɪnstənlɪ, wɪn'stænlɪ) *n* **Gerrard.** ?1609–60, English radical; leader of the Diggers (1649–50) and author of the pamphlet *The Law of Freedom in a Platform* (1652).

Winston-Salem ('wɪnstən'seɪləm) *n* a city in N central North Carolina: formed in 1913 by the uniting of Salem and Winston; a major tobacco manufacturing centre. Pop.: 153 541 (1996 est.).

winter ('wɪntə) *n* **1a** (*sometimes cap.*) the coldest season of the year, between autumn and spring, astronomically from the December solstice to the March equinox in the N hemisphere and at the opposite time of year in the S hemisphere. **1b** (*as modifier*): *winter pasture.* **2** the period of cold weather associated with the winter. **3** a time of decline, decay, etc. **4** *Chiefly poetic.* a year represented by this season: *a man of 72 winters.* Related adjs: **brumal, hibernal, hiemal.** ◆ *vb* **5** (*intr*) to spend the winter in a specified place. **6** to keep or feed (farm animals, etc.) during the winter or (of farm animals) to be kept or fed during the winter. [Old English; related to Old Saxon, Old High German *wintar,* Old Norse *vetr,* Gothic *wintrus*] ► **'winterer** *n* ► **'winterish** *or* **'winter-,like** *adj* ► **'winterless** *adj*

winter aconite *n* a small Old World ranunculaceous herbaceous plant, *Eranthis hyemalis,* cultivated for its yellow flowers, which appear early in spring.

winterbourne ('wɪntə,bɔːn) *n* a stream flowing only after heavy rainfall, esp. in winter. [Old English *winterburna;* see WINTER, BURN[2]]

winter cherry *n* **1** a Eurasian solanaceous plant, *Physalis alkekengi,* cultivated for its ornamental inflated papery orange-red calyx. **2** the calyx of this plant. ◆ See also **Chinese lantern, ground cherry.**

wintercress ('wɪntə,kres) *n* **1** a bitter-tasting yellow-flowered perennial, *Barbarea vulgaris,* somewhat resembling mustard. **2** a commercial hybrid, *Rorippa × sterilis,* between watercress and *R. microphylla.*

winterfeed ('wɪntə,fiːd) *vb* **-feeds, -feeding, -fed.** to feed (livestock) in winter when the grazing is not rich enough.

winter garden *n* **1** a garden of evergreen plants. **2** a conservatory in which flowers are grown in winter.

wintergreen ('wɪntə,griːn) *n* **1** Also called: **boxberry, checkerberry, teaberry, spiceberry, partridgeberry.** any of several evergreen ericaceous shrubs of the genus *Gaultheria,* esp. *G. procumbens,* of E North America, which has white bell-shaped flowers and edible red berries. **2 oil of wintergreen.** an aromatic compound, formerly made from this and various other plants but now synthesized: used medicinally and for flavouring. **3** any of various plants of the genus *Pyrola,* esp. *P. minor* (**common wintergreen**), of temperate and arctic regions, having rounded leaves and small pink globose flowers: family *Pyrolaceae.* Usual U.S. name: **shinleaf. 4** any of several plants of the genera *Orthilia* and *Moneses:* family *Pyrolaceae.* **5 chickweed wintergreen.** a primulaceous plant, *Trientalis europaea,* of N Europe and N Asia, having white flowers and leaves arranged in a whorl. [C16: from Dutch *wintergroen* or German *Wintergrün;* see WINTER, GREEN]

winter hedge *n West Yorkshire, south Lancashire, and Derbyshire dialect.* a clothes horse. [so called in contrast to a hedge on which clothes are dried in summer]

winter heliotrope *n* a creeping perennial, *Petasites fragrans,* related to the butterbur, having lilac to heliotrope coloured flowers smelling of vanilla: found chiefly on road verges.

winterize *or* **winterise** ('wɪntə,raɪz) *vb* (*tr*) *U.S. and Canadian.* to prepare (a house, car, etc.) to withstand winter conditions. ► **,winteri'zation** *or* **,winteri'sation** *n*

winter jasmine *n* a jasmine shrub, *Jasminum nudiflorum,* widely cultivated for its winter-blooming yellow flowers.

winterkill ('wɪntə,kɪl) *vb Chiefly U.S. and Canadian.* to kill (crops or other plants) by exposure to frost, cold, etc., or (of plants) to die by this means. ► **'winter,killing** *adj, n*

winter melon *n* a variety of muskmelon, *Cucumis melo inodorus,* that has sweet fruit with pale orange flesh and an unridged rind. Also called: **Persian melon.**

winter moth *n* a brown geometrid moth, *Operophtera brumata,* of which the male is often seen against lighted windows in winter, the female being wingless.

Winter Olympic Games *n* (*functioning as sing or pl*) an international contest of winter sports, esp. skiing, held every four years. Also called: **Winter Olympics.**

winter quarters *pl n* housing or accommodation for the winter, esp. for military personnel.

winter rose *n* another name for **Christmas rose.**

winter solstice *n* **1** the time at which the sun is at its southernmost point in the sky (northernmost point in the S hemisphere) appearing at noon at its lowest altitude above the horizon. It occurs about December 22 (June 21 in the S hemisphere). **2** *Astronomy.* the point on the celestial sphere, opposite the **summer solstice,** at which the ecliptic is furthest south from the celestial equator. Right ascension: 18 hours; declination: –23.5°.

winter sports *pl n* sports held in the open air on snow or ice, esp. skiing.

Winterthur (*German* 'vɪntərtuːr) *n* an industrial town in NE central Switzerland, in Zürich canton: has the largest technical college in the country. Pop.: 88 168 (1994).

wintertime ('wɪntə,taɪm) *n* the winter season. Also (archaic): **'winter,tide.**

Winter War *n* the war of the winter of 1939–40 between Finland and the USSR after which the Finns surrendered the Karelian Isthmus to the USSR.

winterweight ('wɪntə,weɪt) *adj* (of clothes) suitable in weight for wear in the winter; relatively heavy.

winter wheat *n* a type of wheat that is planted in the autumn and is harvested the following summer.

Winthrop ('wɪnˌθrɒp) *n* **1 John.** 1588–1649, English lawyer and colonist, first governor of the Massachusetts Bay colony: the leading figure among the Puritan settlers of New England. **2** his son, **John.** 1606–76, English lawyer and colonist; a founder of Agawan (now Ipswich), Massachusetts; governor of Connecticut.

wintry ('wɪntrɪ), **wintery** ('wɪntərɪ, -trɪ), *or (less commonly)* **winterly** *adj* **-trier, -triest. 1** (esp. of weather) of or characteristic of winter. **2** lacking cheer or warmth; bleak. ► **'wintrily** *adv* ► **'wintriness, 'winteriness,** *or (less commonly)* **'winterliness** *n*

winy ('waɪnɪ) *adj* **winier, winiest.** having the taste or qualities of wine, esp. in being intoxicating; heady.

winze (wɪnz) *n Mining.* a steeply inclined shaft, as for ventilation between levels. [C18: from earlier *winds,* probably from C14 *wynde* windlass, from Middle Dutch or Middle Low German *winde;* related to Danish *vinde* pulley]

wipe (waɪp) *vb (tr)* **1** to rub (a surface or object) lightly, esp. with (a cloth, hand, etc.), as in removing dust, water, grime, etc. **2** (usually foll. by *off, away, from, up,* etc.) to remove by or as if by rubbing lightly: *he wiped the dirt from his hands.* **3** to eradicate or cancel (a thought, memory, etc.). **4** to erase a recording from (an audio or video tape). **5** *Austral. informal.* to abandon or reject (a person). **6** to apply (oil, grease, etc.) by wiping. **7** to form (a joint between two lead pipes) with solder or soft lead. **8 wipe the floor with (someone).** *Informal.* to defeat decisively. ♦ *n* **9** the act or an instance of wiping. **10** (in film editing) an effect causing the transition from one scene to the next in which the image of the first scene appears to be wiped off the screen by that of the second. **11** *Dialect.* a sweeping blow or stroke. **12** *Brit. dialect.* a gibe or jeer. **13** *Obsolete.* a slang name for **handkerchief.** [Old English *wīpian,* related to Middle Low German *wīpen, wīp* bundle (of cloth), Old High German *wīffa, wīfan* to wind, Gothic *weipan* to wreathe]

wipe out *vb (adv)* **1** *(tr)* to destroy completely; eradicate. **2** *(tr) Informal.* to murder or kill. **3** *(intr)* to fall or jump off a surfboard or skateboard. ♦ *n* **wipe-out. 4** an act or instance of wiping out. **5** the interference of one radio signal by another so that reception is impossible.

wiper ('waɪpə) *n* **1** any piece of cloth, such as a handkerchief, towel, etc., used for wiping. **2** a cam rotated to ease a part and allow it to fall under its own weight, as used in stamping machines, etc. **3** See **windscreen wiper. 4** *Electrical engineering.* a movable conducting arm, esp. one in a switching or selecting device, that makes contact with a row or ring of contacts.

WIPO *or* **Wipo** ('waɪpəʊ) *n acronym for* World Intellectual Property Organization.

wire (waɪə) *n* **1** a slender flexible strand or rod of metal. **2** a cable consisting of several metal strands twisted together. **3** a flexible metallic conductor, esp. one made of copper, usually insulated, and used to carry electric current in a circuit. **4** *(modifier)* of, relating to, or made of wire: *a wire fence; a wire stripper.* **5** anything made of wire, such as wire netting, a barbed wire fence, etc. **6** a long continuous wire or cable connecting points in a telephone or telegraph system. **7** *Old-fashioned.* **7a** an informal name for **telegram** or **telegraph. 7b the wire.** an informal name for **telephone. 8** a metallic string on a guitar, piano, etc. **9** *Horse racing, chiefly U.S. and Canadian.* the finishing line on a racecourse. **10** a wire-gauze screen upon which pulp is spread to form paper during the manufacturing process. **11** anything resembling a wire, such as a hair. **12** a snare made of wire for rabbits and similar animals. **13 down** *or* **up to the wire.** *Informal.* right up to the last moment. **14 get in under the wire.** *Informal, chiefly U.S. and Canadian.* to accomplish something with little time to spare. **15 get one's wires crossed.** *Informal.* to misunderstand. **16 pull wires.** *Chiefly U.S. and Canadian.* to exert influence behind the scenes, esp. through personal connections; pull strings. ♦ *vb (mainly tr)* **17** *(also intr)* to send a telegram to (a person or place). **18** to send (news, a message, etc.) by telegraph. **19** to equip (an electrical system, circuit, or component) with wires. **20** to fasten or furnish with wire. **21** (often foll. by *up*) to provide (an area) with fibre optic cabling to receive cable television. **22** to string (beads, etc.) on wire. **23** *Croquet.* to leave (a player's ball) so that a hoop or peg lies between it and the other balls. **24** to snare with wire. **25 wire in.** *Informal.* to set about (something, esp. food) with enthusiasm. [Old English *wīr;* related to Old High German *wiara,* Old Norse *vīra,* Latin *viriae* bracelet] ► **'wire,like** *adj*

wire brush *n* a brush having wire bristles, used for cleaning metal, esp. for removing rust, or for brushing against a cymbal.

wire cloth *n* a mesh or netting woven from fine wire, used in window screens, strainers, etc.

wired (waɪəd) *adj Slang.* edgy from stimulant intake.

wiredraw ('waɪəˌdrɔː) *vb* **-draws, -drawing, -drew, -drawn.** to convert (metal) into wire by drawing through successively smaller dies.

wire entanglement *n* a barrier or obstruction of barbed wire used in warfare.

wire-gauge *n* **1** a flat plate with slots in which standard wire sizes can be measured. **2** a standard system of sizes for measuring the diameters of wires.

wire gauze *n* a stiff meshed fabric woven of fine wires.

wire glass *n* a sheet glass that contains a layer of reinforcing wire netting within it.

wire grass *n* any of various grasses, such as Bermuda grass, that have tough wiry roots or rhizomes.

wire-guided *adj* (of a missile) controlled by signals transmitted through fine wires uncoiled during the missile's flight.

wire-haired *adj* (of an animal) having a rough wiry coat.

wireless ('waɪəlɪs) *n, vb Chiefly Brit., old-fashioned.* another word for **radio.**

wireless telegraphy *n* another name for **radiotelegraphy.**

wireless telephone *n* another name for **radiotelephone.** ► **wireless telephony** *n*

wireman ('waɪəmən) *n, pl* **-men.** *Chiefly U.S.* a person who installs and maintains electric wiring, cables, etc.

wire netting *n* a net made of wire, often galvanized, that is used for fencing, as a light reinforcement, etc.

wirephoto ('waɪəˌfəʊtəʊ) *n, pl* **-tos.** a facsimile of a photograph transmitted electronically via a telephone system.

wirepuller ('waɪəˌpʊlə) *n Chiefly U.S. and Canadian.* a person who uses private or secret influence for his own ends. ► **'wire,pulling** *n*

wirer ('waɪərə) *n* a person who sets or uses wires to snare rabbits and similar animals.

wire recorder *n* an early type of magnetic recorder in which sounds were recorded on a thin steel wire magnetized by an electromagnet. Compare **tape recorder.** ► **wire recording** *n*

wire rope *n* rope made of strands of wire twisted together.

wire service *n Chiefly U.S. and Canadian.* an agency supplying news, etc., to newspapers, radio and television stations, etc.

wiretap ('waɪəˌtæp) *vb* **-taps, -tapping, -tapped.** to make a connection to a telegraph or telephone wire in order to obtain information secretly. ► **'wire,tapper** *n* ► **'wire,tapping** *n*

wirewalker ('waɪəˌwɔːkə) *n Chiefly U.S.* another name for **tightrope walker.**

wire wheel *n* **1** a wheel in which the rim is held to the hub by wire spokes, esp. one used on a sports car. Compare **disc wheel. 2** a power-driven rotary wire brush for scaling or burnishing.

wire wool *n* a mass of fine wire used for cleaning and scouring.

wirework ('waɪəˌwɜːk) *n* **1** functional or decorative work made of wire. **2** objects made of wire, esp. netting. **3** the work performed by acrobats on a tightrope.

wireworks ('waɪəˌwɜːks) *n (functioning as sing or pl)* a factory where wire or articles of wire are made.

wireworm ('waɪəˌwɜːm) *n* the wormlike larva of various elaterid beetles, which feeds on the roots of many crop plants and is a serious agricultural pest.

wire-wove *adj* **1** of, relating to, or comprising a high-grade glazed paper, usually for writing. **2** woven of wire.

wiring ('waɪərɪŋ) *n* **1** the network of wires used in an electrical system, device, or circuit. **2** the quality or condition of such a network. ♦ *adj* **3** used in wiring.

wirra ('wɪrə) *interj Irish.* an exclamation of sorrow or deep concern. [C19: shortened from Irish Gaelic *a Muire!* O Mary! as invocation to the Virgin Mary]

wirrah ('wɪrə) *n* a saltwater fish, *Acanthistius serratus,* of Australia, with bright blue spots. [from a native Australian language]

Wirral ('wɪrəl) *n* **1 the.** a peninsula in NW England between the estuaries of the Rivers Mersey and Dee. **2** a unitary authority in NW England, in Merseyside. Pop.: 331 500 (1995 est.). Area: 158 sq. km (61 sq. miles).

wiry ('waɪərɪ) *adj* **wirier, wiriest. 1** (of people or animals) slender but strong in constitution. **2** made of or resembling wire, esp. in stiffness: *wiry hair.* **3** (of a sound) produced by or as if by a vibrating wire. ► **'wirily** *adv* ► **'wiriness** *n*

wis (wɪs) *vb Archaic.* to know or suppose (something). [C17: a form derived from IWIS, mistakenly interpreted as *I wis* I know, as if from Old English *witan* to know]

Wis. *abbrev. for* Wisconsin.

Wisbech ('wɪzbiːtʃ) *n* a town in E England, in N Cambridgeshire: market-gardening. Pop.: 24 981 (1991).

Wisconsin (wɪs'kɒnsɪn) *n* **1** a state of the N central U.S., on Lake Superior and Lake Michigan: consists of an undulating plain, with uplands in the north and west; over 168 m (550 ft.) above sea level along the shore of Lake Michigan. Capital: Madison. Pop.: 5 169 677 (1997 est.). Area: 141 061 sq. km (54 464 sq. miles). Abbrevs.: **Wis.** or (with zip code) **WI 2** a river in central and SW Wisconsin, flowing south and west to the Mississippi. Length: 692 km (430 miles). ► **Wis'consin,ite** *n*

Wisd. *abbrev. for* Wisdom of Solomon.

Wisden ('wɪzdən) *n* **John.** 1826–84, English cricketer; publisher of *Wisden Cricketers' Almanack,* which first appeared in 1864.

wisdom ('wɪzdəm) *n* **1** the ability or result of an ability to think and act utilizing knowledge, experience, understanding, common sense, and insight. **2** accumulated knowledge, erudition, or enlightenment. **3** *Archaic.* a wise saying or wise sayings or teachings. **4** *Obsolete.* soundness of mind. ♦ Related adj: **sagacious.** [Old English *wīsdōm;* see WISE[1], -DOM]

Wisdom of Jesus, the Son of Sirach ('saɪræk) *n* **the.** another name for **Ecclesiasticus.**

Wisdom of Solomon *n* a book of the Apocrypha, probably written about 50 B.C., addressed primarily to Jews who were under the influence of Hellenistic learning.

wisdom tooth *n* **1** any of the four molar teeth, one at the back of each side of the jaw, that are the last of the permanent teeth to erupt. Technical name: **third molar. 2 cut one's wisdom teeth.** to arrive at the age of discretion.

wise[1] (waɪz) *adj* **1** possessing, showing, or prompted by wisdom or discernment. **2** prudent; sensible. **3** shrewd; crafty: *a wise plan.* **4** well-informed; erudite. **5** aware, informed, or knowing (esp. in the phrase **none the wiser**). **6** *Slang.* (*postpositive;* often foll. by *to*) in the know, esp. possessing inside information (about). **7** *Archaic or Brit. dialect.* possessing powers of magic. **8** *Slang, chiefly U.S. and Canadian.* cocksure or insolent. **9 be** *or* **get wise.** (often foll. by *to*) *Informal.* to be or become aware or informed (of something) or to face up (to facts). **10 put wise.** (often foll. by *to*) *Slang.* to inform or warn (of). ♦ *vb* **11** See **wise up.** [Old English *wīs;* related to Old Norse *vīss,* Gothic *weis,* German *weise*] ► **'wisely** *adv* ► **'wiseness** *n*

wise[2] (waɪz) *n Archaic.* way, manner, fashion, or respect (esp. in the phrases **any wise, in no wise**). [Old English *wīse* manner; related to Old Saxon *wīsa,* German *Weise,* Old Norse *vīsa* verse, Latin *vīsus* face]

-wise *adv combining form.* **1** Also: **-ways.** indicating direction or manner:

clockwise; likewise. **2** with reference to: *profitwise; businesswise.* [Old English *-wisan;* see WISE[2]]

wiseacre ('waɪz,eɪkə) *n* **1** a person who wishes to seem wise. **2** a wise person: often used facetiously or contemptuously. [C16: from Middle Dutch *wijsseggher* soothsayer; related to Old High German *wīssaga,* German *Weissager.* See WISE[1], SAY]

wisecrack ('waɪz,kræk) *Informal.* ◆ *n* **1** a flippant gibe or sardonic remark. ◆ *vb* **2** to make a wisecrack. ▸ **'wise,cracker** *n*

wise guy *n Informal.* a person who is given to making conceited, sardonic, or insolent comments.

Wiseman ('waɪzmən) *n* **Nicholas Patrick Stephen.** 1802–65, British cardinal; first Roman Catholic archbishop of Westminster (1850–65).

wisent ('wiːzᵊnt) *n* another name for **European bison.** See **bison** (sense 2). [German, from Old High German *wisunt* BISON]

wise up *vb* (*adv*) *Slang.* (often foll. by *to*) to become or cause to become aware or informed (of).

wish (wɪʃ) *vb* **1** (when *tr, takes a clause as object or an infinitive;* when *intr,* often foll. by *for*) to want or desire (something, often that which cannot be or is not the case): *I wish I lived in Italy; to wish for peace.* **2** (*tr*) to feel or express a desire or hope concerning the future or fortune of: *I wish you well.* **3** (*tr*) to desire or prefer to be as specified. **4** (*tr*) to greet as specified; bid: *he wished us good afternoon.* **5** (*tr*) *Formal.* to order politely: *I wish you to come at three o'clock.* ◆ *n* **6** the act of wishing; the expression of some desire or mental inclination: *to make a wish.* **7** something desired or wished for: *he got his wish.* **8** (*usually pl*) expressed hopes or desire, esp. for someone's welfare, health, etc. **9** (*often pl*) *Formal.* a polite order or request. ◆ See also **wish on.** [Old English *wȳscan;* related to Old Norse *óskja,* German *wünschen,* Dutch *wenschen*] ▸ **'wisher** *n* ▸ **'wishless** *adj*

wishbone ('wɪʃ,bəʊn) *n* the V-shaped bone above the breastbone in most birds consisting of the fused clavicles; furcula. [C17: from the custom of two people breaking apart the bone after eating: the person with the longer part makes a wish]

wishbone boom *n* a boom on a sailboard having two arms that are joined at the mast and at the foot of the sail. The windsurfer holds onto it for support and to steer the sailboard.

wishful ('wɪʃfʊl) *adj* having wishes or characterized by wishing. ▸ **'wishfully** *adv* ▸ **'wishfulness** *n*

wish fulfilment *n* (in Freudian psychology) any successful attempt to fulfil a wish stemming from the unconscious mind, whether in fact, in fantasy, or by such disguised means as sublimation. See also **pleasure principle.**

wishful thinking *n* the erroneous belief that one's wishes are in accordance with reality. ▸ **wishful thinker** *n*

wish on *vb* (*tr, prep*) to hope that (someone or something) should be imposed (on someone); foist: *I wouldn't wish my cold on anyone.*

wish-wash *n Informal.* **1** any thin weak drink. **2** rubbishy talk or writing.

wishy-washy ('wɪʃɪ,wɒʃɪ) *adj Informal.* **1** lacking in substance, force, colour, etc. **2** watery; thin. ▸ **'wishy-,washily** *adv* ▸ **'wishy-,washiness** *n*

Wisła ('viswa) *n* the Polish name for **Vistula** (sense 1).

Wislany Zalew (*Polish* viʃ'laːni 'zaːlɛf) *n* the Polish name for the **Vistula** (sense 2).

Wismar (*German* 'vɪsmar) *n* a port in NE Germany, on an inlet of the Baltic, in Mecklenburg-West Pomerania: shipbuilding industries. Pop.: 54 470 (1991).

wisp (wɪsp) *n* **1** a thin, light, delicate, or fibrous piece or strand, such as a streak of smoke or a lock of hair. **2** a small bundle, as of hay or straw. **3** anything slender and delicate: *a wisp of a girl.* **4** a mere suggestion or hint. **5** a flock of birds, esp. snipe. ◆ *vb* **6** (*intr;* often foll. by *away*) to move or act like a wisp. **7** (*tr*) *Chiefly Brit. dialect.* to twist into a wisp. **8** (*tr*) *Chiefly Brit.* to groom (a horse) with a wisp of straw, etc. [C14: variant of *wips,* of obscure origin; compare WIPE] ▸ **'wisp,like** *adj*

wispy ('wɪspɪ) *adj* **wispier, wispiest.** wisplike; delicate, faint, light, etc. ▸ **'wispily** *adv* ▸ **'wispiness** *n*

wist (wɪst) *vb Archaic.* the past tense and past participle of **wit**[2].

wisteria (wɪ'stɪərɪə) *n* any twining leguminous woody climbing plant of the genus *Wisteria,* of E Asia and North America, having blue, purple, or white flowers in large drooping clusters. [C19: from New Latin, named after Caspar *Wistar* (1761–1818), American anatomist]

wistful ('wɪstfʊl) *adj* sadly pensive, esp. about something yearned for. ▸ **'wistfully** *adv* ▸ **'wistfulness** *n*

wit[1] (wɪt) *n* **1** the talent or quality of using unexpected associations between contrasting or disparate words or ideas to make a clever humorous effect. **2** speech or writing showing this quality. **3** a person possessing, showing, or noted for such an ability, esp. in repartee. **4** practical intelligence (esp. in the phrase **have the wit to**). **5** *Scot. and northern English dialect.* information or knowledge (esp. in the phrase **get wit of**). **6** *Archaic.* mental capacity or a person possessing it. **7** *Obsolete.* the mind or memory. ◆ See also **wits.** [Old English *witt;* related to Old Saxon *giwitt,* Old High German *wizzi* (German *Witz*), Old Norse *vit,* Gothic *witi.* See WIT[2]]

wit[2] (wɪt) *vb* **1** *Archaic.* to be or become aware of (something). ◆ *adv* **2 to wit.** that is to say; namely (used to introduce statements, as in legal documents). [Old English *witan;* related to Old High German *wizzan* (German *wissen*), Old Norse *vita,* Latin *vidēre* to see]

witan ('wɪtᵊn) *n* (in Anglo-Saxon England) **1** an assembly of higher ecclesiastics and important laymen, including king's thegns, that met to counsel the king on matters such as judicial problems. **2** the members of this assembly. ◆ Also called: **witenagemot.** [Old English *witan,* plural of *wita* wise man; see WIT[2], WITNESS]

witblits ('vɪt,blɪts) *n S. African.* an extremely potent illegally distilled spirit. [from Afrikaans *wit* white + *blits* lightning]

witch[1] (wɪtʃ) *n* **1** a person, usually female, who practises or professes to practise magic or sorcery, esp. black magic, or is believed to have dealings with the devil. **2** an ugly or wicked old woman. **3** a fascinating or enchanting woman. **4** short for **water witch.** ◆ *vb* **5** (*tr*) to cause or change by or as if by witchcraft. **6** a less common word for **bewitch.** [Old English *wicca;* related to Middle Low German *wicken* to conjure, Swedish *vicka* to move to and fro] ▸ **'witch,like** *adj*

witch[2] (wɪtʃ) *n* a flatfish, *Pleuronectes* (or *Glyptocephalus*) *cynoglossus,* of N Atlantic coastal waters, having a narrow greyish-brown body marked with tiny black spots: family *Pleuronectidae* (plaice, flounders, etc.). [C19: perhaps from WITCH[1], alluding to the appearance of the fish]

witch- *or* **wych-** *prefix* having pliant branches: *witch-elm.* [Old English *wice* and *wic;* probably from Germanic *wik-* bend]

witchcraft ('wɪtʃ,krɑːft) *n* **1** the art or power of bringing magical or preternatural power to bear or the act or practice of attempting to do so. **2** the influence of magic or sorcery. **3** fascinating or bewitching influence or charm.

witch doctor *n* **1** Also called: **shaman, medicine man.** a man in certain societies, esp. preliterate ones, who appears to possess magical powers, used esp. to cure sickness but also to harm people. **2** a person who seeks out or hunts witches in some African tribal cultures.

witch-elm *n* a variant spelling of **wych-elm.**

witchery ('wɪtʃərɪ) *n, pl* **-eries. 1** the practice of witchcraft. **2** magical or bewitching influence or charm.

witches'-broom, witchbroom ('wɪtʃ,bruːm), *or* **witches'-besom** *n* a dense abnormal growth of shoots on a tree or other woody plant, usually caused by parasitic fungi of the genus *Taphrina.*

witches' butter *n* See **jelly fungus.**

witches' Sabbath *n* See **Sabbath** (sense 4).

witchetty grub ('wɪtʃɪtɪ) *n* the wood-boring edible caterpillar of an Australian moth, *Xyleutes leucomochla:* family *Cossidae.* [C19 *witchetty,* from a native Australian language]

witch hazel *or* **wych-hazel** *n* **1** any of several trees and shrubs of the genus *Hamamelis,* esp. *H. virginiana,* of North America, having ornamental yellow flowers and medicinal properties: family *Hamamelidaceae.* **2** an astringent medicinal solution containing an extract of the bark and leaves of *H. virginiana,* applied to treat bruises, inflammation, etc.

witch-hunt *n* a rigorous campaign to round up or expose dissenters on the pretext of safeguarding the welfare of the public. ▸ **'witch-,hunter** *n* ▸ **'witch-,hunting** *n, adj*

witching ('wɪtʃɪŋ) *adj* **1** relating to or appropriate for witchcraft. **2** *Now rare.* bewitching. ◆ *n* **3** witchcraft; magic. ▸ **'witchingly** *adv*

witching hour *n* **the.** the hour at which witches are supposed to appear, usually midnight.

witch of Agnesi (ɑːn'jeɪzɪ) *n Maths.* a plane curve, symmetrical about the *y*-axis, having the equation $x^2y = 4a^2(2a-y)$. Sometimes shortened to **witch.** [C19: named after M. G. AGNESI; probably so called from the resemblance of the curve to the outline of a witch's hat]

witenagemot (,wɪtɪnəgɪ'məʊt) *n* another word for **witan.** [Old English *witena,* genitive plural of *wita* councillor + *gemōt* meeting, MOOT]

with (wɪð, wɪθ) *prep* **1** using; by means of: *he killed her with an axe.* **2** accompanying; in the company of: *the lady you were with.* **3** possessing; having: *a man with a red moustache.* **4** concerning or regarding: *be patient with her.* **5** in spite of: *with all his talents, he was still humble.* **6** used to indicate a time or distance by which something is away from something else: *with three miles to go, he collapsed.* **7** in a manner characterized by: *writing with abandon.* **8** caused or prompted by: *shaking with rage.* **9** often used with a verb indicating a reciprocal action or relation between the subject and the preposition's object: *agreeing with me; chatting with the troops.* **10 not with you.** *Informal.* not able to grasp or follow what you are saying. **11 with it.** *Informal.* **11a** fashionable; in style. **11b** comprehending what is happening or being said. **12 with that.** after that; having said or done that. [Old English; related to Old Norse *vith,* Gothic *withra,* Latin *vitricus* stepfather, Sanskrit *vitarám* wider]

withal (wɪ'ðɔːl) *adv* **1** *Literary.* as well; likewise. **2** *Literary.* nevertheless. **3** *Archaic.* therewith. ◆ *prep* **4** (*postpositive*) an archaic word for **with.** [C12: from WITH + ALL]

withdraw (wɪð'drɔː) *vb* **-draws, -drawing, -drew, -drawn. 1** (*tr*) to take or draw back or away; remove. **2** (*tr*) to remove from deposit or investment in a bank, building society, etc. **3** (*tr*) to retract or recall (a statement, promise, etc.). **4** (*intr*) to retire or retreat: *the troops withdrew.* **5** (*intr;* often foll. by *from*) to back out (of) or depart (from): *he withdrew from public life.* **6** (*intr*) to detach oneself socially, emotionally, or mentally. [C13: from WITH (in the sense: away from) + DRAW] ▸ **with'drawable** *adj* ▸ **with'drawer** *n*

withdrawal (wɪð'drɔːəl) *n* **1** an act or process of withdrawing; retreat, removal, or detachment. **2** the period a drug addict goes through following abrupt termination in the use of narcotics, usually characterized by physical and mental symptoms (**withdrawal symptoms**).

withdrawing room *n* an archaic term for **drawing room.**

withdrawn (wɪð'drɔːn) *vb* **1** the past participle of **withdraw.** ◆ *adj* **2** unusually reserved, introverted, or shy. **3** secluded or remote. ▸ **with'drawnness** *n*

withdrew (wɪð'druː) *vb* the past tense of **withdraw.**

withe (wɪθ, wɪð, waɪð) *n* **1** a strong flexible twig, esp. of willow, suitable for binding things together; withy. **2** a band or rope of twisted twigs or stems. **3** a handle made of elastic material, fitted on some tools to reduce the shock during use. **4** a wall with a thickness of half a brick, such as a leaf of a cavity wall, or a division between two chimney flues. ◆ *vb* **5** (*tr*) to bind with withes. [Old English *withthe;* related to Old Norse *vithja,* Old High German *witta, widi,* Gothic *wida*]

wither ('wɪðə) *vb* **1** (*intr*) (esp. of a plant) to droop, wilt, or shrivel up. **2** (*intr;*

often foll. by *away*) to fade or waste: *all hope withered away.* **3** (*intr*) to decay, decline, or disintegrate. **4** (*tr*) to cause to wilt, fade, or lose vitality. **5** (*tr*) to abash, esp. with a scornful look. **6** (*tr*) to harm or damage. **[C14:** perhaps variant of WEATHER (vb); related to German *verwittern* to decay**]** ▸ **'withered** *adj* ▸ **'witherer** *n* ▸ **'withering** *adj* ▸ **'witheringly** *adv*

witherite ('wɪðəˌraɪt) *n* a white, grey, or yellowish mineral consisting of barium carbonate in orthorhombic crystalline form: occurs in veins of lead ore. Formula: $BaCO_3$. **[C18:** named after W. *Withering* (1741–99), English scientist, who first described it**]**

withers ('wɪðəz) *pl n* the highest part of the back of a horse, behind the neck between the shoulders. **[C16:** short for *widersones,* from *wider* WITH + *-sones,* perhaps variant of SINEW; related to German *Widerrist,* Old English *withre* resistance**]**

withershins ('wɪðəˌʃɪnz; *Scot.* 'wɪðər-) *or* **widdershins** *adv Chiefly Scot.* **1** in the direction contrary to the apparent course of the sun; anticlockwise. **2** in a direction contrary to the usual; in the wrong direction. Compare **deasil. [C16:** from Middle Low German *weddersinnes,* from Middle High German, literally: opposite course, from *wider* against + *sinnes,* genitive of *sin* course**]**

withhold (wɪð'həʊld) *vb* **-holds, -holding, -held. 1** (*tr*) to keep back; refrain from giving: *he withheld his permission.* **2** (*tr*) to hold back; restrain. **3** (*tr*) to deduct (taxes, etc.) from a salary or wages. **4** (*intr; usually foll. by from*) to refrain or forbear. ▸ **with'holder** *n*

withholding tax *n* **1** tax deducted at source from income, esp. from dividends, paid to nonresidents of a country, which may be reclaimed if a double-taxation agreement exists between the country in which the income is paid and the country of residence of the recipient. **2** *U.S.* a portion of an employee's tax liability paid directly to the government by the employer.

within (wɪ'ðɪn) *prep* **1** in; inside; enclosed or encased by. **2** before (a period of time) has elapsed: *within a week.* **3** not beyond the limits of; not differing by more than (a specified amount) from: *live within your means; within seconds of the world record.* ◆ *adv* **4** *Formal.* inside; internally.

withindoors ('wɪðɪn'dɔːz) *adv* an obsolete word for **indoors.**

within-subjects design *n* (*modifier*) *Statistics.* (of an experiment) concerned with measuring the value of the dependent variable for the same subjects under the various experimental conditions. Compare **between-subjects design, matched-pairs design.**

without (wɪ'ðaʊt) *prep* **1** not having: *a traveller without much money.* **2** not accompanied by: *he came without his wife.* **3** not making use of: *it is not easy to undo screws without a screwdriver.* **4** (*foll. by a verbal noun or noun phrase*) not, while not, or after not: *she can sing for two minutes without drawing breath.* **5** *Archaic.* on the outside of: *without the city walls.* ◆ *adv* **6** *Formal.* outside; outwardly. ◆ *conj* **7** *Not standard.* unless: *don't come without you have some money.*

withoutdoors ('wɪðaʊt'dɔːz) *adv* an obsolete word for **outdoors.**

withstand (wɪð'stænd) *vb* **-stands, -standing, -stood. 1** (*tr*) to stand up to forcefully; resist. **2** (*intr*) to remain firm in endurance or opposition. ▸ **with'stander** *n*

withy ('wɪðɪ) *n, pl* **withies. 1** a variant spelling of **withe** (senses 1, 2). **2** a willow tree, esp. an osier. ◆ *adj* **3** (of people) tough and agile. **4** *Rare.* resembling a withe in strength or flexibility. **[**Old English *wīdig(e);* related to Old Norse *vīthir,* Old High German *wīda,* Latin *vītis* vine, Sanskrit *vītika* fetter. See WITHE, WIRE**]**

witless ('wɪtlɪs) *adj* lacking wit, intelligence, or sense; stupid. ▸ **'witlessly** *adv* ▸ **'witlessness** *n*

witling ('wɪtlɪŋ) *n Archaic.* a person who thinks himself witty.

witness ('wɪtnɪs) *n* **1** a person who has seen or can give first-hand evidence of some event. **2** a person or thing giving or serving as evidence. **3** a person who testifies, esp. in a court of law, to events or facts within his own knowledge. **4** a person who attests to the genuineness of a document, signature, etc., by adding his own signature. **5 bear witness. 5a** to give written or oral testimony. **5b** to be evidence or proof of. ◆ Related adj: **testimonial.** ◆ *vb* **6** (*tr*) to see, be present at, or know at first hand. **7** to give or serve as evidence (of). **8** (*tr*) to be the scene or setting of: *this field has witnessed a battle.* **9** (*intr*) to testify, esp. in a court of law, to events within a person's own knowledge. **10** (*tr*) to attest to the genuineness of (a document, signature, etc.) by adding one's own signature. **[**Old English *witnes* (meaning both *testimony* and *witness*), from *witan* to know, WIT[2] + -NESS; related to Old Norse *vitni***]** ▸ **'witnessable** *adj* ▸ **'witnesser** *n*

witness box *or esp. U.S.* **witness stand** *n* the place in a court of law in which witnesses stand to give evidence.

wits (wɪts) *pl n* **1** (*sometimes sing*) the ability to reason and act, esp. quickly (esp. in the phrase **have one's wits about one**). **2** (*sometimes sing*) right mind, sanity (esp. in the phrase **out of one's wits**). **3 at one's wits' end.** at a loss to know how to proceed. **4 five wits.** *Obsolete.* the five senses or mental faculties. **5 live by one's wits.** to gain a livelihood by craftiness rather than by hard work.

Witt (wɪt) *n* **Johan de.** 1625–72, Dutch statesman; chief minister of the United Provinces of the Netherlands (1653–72).

Witte ('vɪtə; *Russian* 'vjitjə) *n* **Sergei Yulievich** (sjɪr'gjej ju'ljevitʃ). 1849–1915, Russian statesman; prime minister (1905–06). As minister of finance (1892–1903) he tried to modernize the Russian economy.

-witted *adj* (*in combination*) having wits or intelligence as specified: *slow-witted; dim-witted.*

Wittenberg (*German* 'vɪtənbɛrk; *English* 'wɪtᵊnˌbɜːg) *n* a city in E Germany, on the River Elbe, in Brandenburg: Martin Luther, as a philosophy teacher at Wittenberg university, began the Reformation here in 1517 by nailing his 95 theses to the doors of a church. Pop.: 87 000 (1991).

witter ('wɪtə) *Informal.* ◆ *vb* **1** (*intr, often foll. by on*) to chatter or babble pointlessly or at unnecessary length. ◆ *n* **2** pointless chat; chatter. **[C20:** from dialect; compare TWITTER**]**

Wittgenstein ('vɪtgənˌʃtaɪn, -ˌstaɪn) *n* **Ludwig Josef Johann** ('luːtvɪç 'joːzɛf jo'han). 1889–1951, British philosopher, born in Austria. After studying with Bertrand Russell, he wrote the *Tractatus Logico-Philosophicus* (1921), which explores the relationship of language to the world. He was a major influence on logical positivism but later repudiated this, and in *Philosophical Investigations* (1953) he argues that philosophical problems arise from insufficient attention to the variety of natural language use.

Wittgensteinian ('vɪtgənˌʃtaɪnɪən, -ˌstaɪnɪən) *adj* (of a philosophical position or argument) derived from or related to the work of Wittgenstein and esp. the later work in which he attacks essentialism and stresses the open texture and variety of use of ordinary language.

witticism ('wɪtɪˌsɪzəm) *n* a clever or witty remark. **[C17:** from WITTY; coined by Dryden (1677) by analogy with *criticism***]**

witting ('wɪtɪŋ) *adj Rare.* **1** deliberate; intentional: *a witting insult.* **2** aware; knowing. ▸ **'wittingly** *adv*

wittol ('wɪtᵊl) *n Obsolete.* a man who tolerates his wife's unfaithfulness. **[C15** *wetewold,* from *witen* to know (see WIT[2]) + *-wold,* perhaps from *cokewold* CUCKOLD**]**

witty ('wɪtɪ) *adj* **-tier, -tiest. 1** characterized by clever humour or wit. **2** *Archaic or dialect.* intelligent or sensible. ▸ **'wittily** *adv* ▸ **'wittiness** *n*

Witwatersrand (wɪt'wɔːtəzˌrænd; *Afrikaans* vət'vaːtərs'rant) *n* a rocky ridge in NE South Africa: contains the richest gold deposits in the world, also coal and manganese; chief industrial centre is Johannesburg. Height: 1500–1800 m (5000–6000 ft.). Also called: **the Rand, the Reef.**

wive (waɪv) *vb Archaic.* **1** to marry (a woman). **2** (*tr*) to supply with a wife. **[**Old English *gewīfian,* from *wīf* WIFE**]**

wivern ('waɪvən) *n* a less common spelling of **wyvern.**

wives (waɪvz) *n* the plural of **wife.**

wiz (wɪz) *n Informal.* a variant spelling of **whizz** (sense 5).

wizard ('wɪzəd) *n* **1** a male witch or a man who practises or professes to practise magic or sorcery. **2** a person who is outstandingly clever in some specified field; expert. **3** *Obsolete.* a wise man. **4** *Computing.* a computer program that guides a user through a complex task. ◆ *adj* **5** *Informal, chiefly Brit.* superb; outstanding. **6** of or relating to a wizard or wizardry. **[C15:** variant of *wissard,* from WISE[1] + -ARD**]** ▸ **'wizardly** *adj*

wizardry ('wɪzədrɪ) *n* the art, skills, and practices of a wizard, sorcerer, or magician.

wizen[1] ('wɪzᵊn) *vb* **1** to make or become shrivelled. ◆ *adj* **2** a variant of **wizened. [**Old English *wisnian;* related to Old Norse *visna,* Old High German *wesanēn***]**

wizen[2] ('wiːzᵊn) *n* an archaic word for **weasand** (the gullet).

wizened ('wɪzᵊnd) *or* **wizen** *adj* shrivelled, wrinkled, or dried up, esp. with age.

wk *abbrev. for:* **1** (*pl* **wks**) week. **2** work. **3** weak.

wkly *abbrev. for* weekly.

WL *international car registration for* (Windward Islands) St Lucia.

w.l. *or* **WL** *abbrev. for* water line.

Władysław II ('vlædɪslæf) *n* original name *Jogaila.* ?1351–1434, grand duke of Lithuania (1377–1401) and king of Poland (1386–1434). He united Lithuania and Poland and founded the Jagiellon dynasty.

Władysław IV *n* 1595–1648, king of Poland (1632–48).

WLM *abbrev. for* women's liberation movement.

wmk *abbrev. for* watermark.

WMO *abbrev. for* World Meteorological Organization.

WNW *symbol for* west-northwest.

wo (wəʊ) *n, pl* **wos.** an archaic spelling of **woe.**

WO *abbrev. for:* **1** War Office. **2** Warrant Officer. **3** wireless operator.

w/o *abbrev. for:* **1** without. **2** written off.

woad (wəʊd) *n* **1** a European cruciferous plant, *Isatis tinctoria,* formerly cultivated for its leaves, which yield a blue dye. See also **dyer's-weed, dyer's rocket. 2** the dye obtained from this plant, used esp. by the ancient Britons, as a body dye. **[**Old English *wād;* related to Old High German *weit;* Middle Dutch *wēd,* Latin *vitrum***]**

woaded ('wəʊdɪd) *adj* coloured blue with woad.

woadwaxen ('wəʊdˌwæksən) *n* another name for **dyer's-greenweed.**

woald (wəʊld) *n* another name for **weld**[2].

wobbegong ('wɒbɪˌgɒŋ) *n* any of various carpet sharks of the family *Orectolobidae,* of Australian waters, having a richly patterned brown-and-white skin. **[**from a native Australian language**]**

wobble ('wɒbᵊl) *vb* **1** (*intr*) to move, rock, or sway unsteadily. **2** (*intr*) to tremble or shake: *her voice wobbled with emotion.* **3** (*intr*) to vacillate with indecision. **4** (*tr*) to cause to wobble. ◆ *n* **5** a wobbling movement, motion, or sound. ◆ Also: **wabble. [C17:** variant of *wabble,* from Low German *wabbeln;* related to Middle High German *wabelen* to WAVER**]** ▸ **'wobbler** *n*

wobble board *n Austral.* a piece of fibreboard used as a musical instrument, producing a characteristic sound when flexed.

wobble plate *n* another name for **swash plate.**

wobbly ('wɒblɪ) *adj* **-blier, -bliest. 1** unsteady. **2** trembling, shaking. ◆ *n* **3 throw a wobbly.** *Slang.* to become suddenly very agitated or angry. ▸ **'wobbliness** *n*

Wobbly ('wɒblɪ) *n, pl* **-blies.** a member of the Industrial Workers of the World.

Woburn Abbey ('wəʊbən) *n* a mansion in Woburn in Bedfordshire: originally an abbey; rebuilt in the 17th century for the Dukes of Bedford, altered by Henry Holland in the 18th century; deer park landscaped by Humphrey Repton.

Wodehouse ('wʊdˌhaʊs) *n* Sir **P(elham) G(renville).** 1881–1975, U.S. author, born in England. His humorous novels of upper-class life in England include the *Psmith* and *Jeeves* series. ▸ **Wode'housian** *adj*

Woden *or* **Wodan** ('wəudən) *n* the foremost Anglo-Saxon god. Norse counterpart: **Odin.** [Old English *Wōden;* related to Old Norse *Ōthinn,* Old High German *Wuotan,* German *Wotan;* see WEDNESDAY]

wodge (wɒdʒ) *n Brit. informal.* a thick lump or chunk cut or broken off something. [C20: alteration of WEDGE]

woe (wəu) *n* **1** *Literary.* intense grief or misery. **2** (*often pl*) affliction or misfortune. **3 woe betide (someone).** misfortune will befall (someone): *woe betide you if you arrive late.* ◆ *interj* **4** Also: **woe is me.** *Archaic.* an exclamation of sorrow or distress. [Old English *wā, wǣ;* related to Old Saxon, Old High German *wē,* Old Norse *vei,* Gothic *wai,* Latin *vae,* Sanskrit *uvē;* see WAIL]

woebegone ('wəubɪ,gɒn) *adj* **1** sorrowful or sad in appearance. **2** *Archaic.* afflicted with woe. [C14: from a phrase such as *me is wo begon* woe has beset me]

woeful ('wəufᵊl) *adj* **1** expressing or characterized by sorrow. **2** bringing or causing woe. **3** pitiful; miserable: *a woeful standard of work.* ▸ **'woefully** *adv* ▸ **'woefulness** *n*

WOF (in New Zealand) *abbrev. for* Warrant of Fitness.

Woffington ('wɒfɪŋtən) *n* **Peg,** full name *Margaret Woffington.* ?1714–60, Irish actress.

wog[1] (wɒg) *n Brit. slang, derogatory.* a foreigner, esp. one who is not White. [probably from GOLLIWOG]

wog[2] (wɒg) *n Slang, chiefly Austral.* influenza or any similar illness. [C20: of unknown origin]

woggle ('wɒgᵊl) *n* the ring of leather through which a Scout neckerchief is threaded. [C20: of unknown origin]

Wöhler (*German* 'vøːlər) *n* **Friedrich** ('friːdrɪç). 1800–82, German chemist, who proved that organic compounds could be synthesized from inorganic compounds.

wok (wɒk) *n* a large metal Chinese cooking pot having a curved base like a bowl and traditionally with a wooden handle. [from Chinese (Cantonese)]

woke (wəuk) *vb* a past tense of **wake.**

woken ('wəukən) *vb* a past participle of **wake.**

Woking ('wəukɪŋ) *n* a town in S England, in central Surrey: mainly residential. Pop.: 98 138 (1991).

wokka board ('wɒkə) *n Austral.* another name for **wobble board.**

wold[1] (wəuld) *n Chiefly literary.* a tract of open rolling country, esp. upland. [Old English *weald* bush; related to Old Saxon *wald,* German *Wald* forest, Old Norse *vollr* ground; see WILD]

wold[2] (wəuld) *n* another name for **weld**[2].

Wolds (wəuldz) *pl n* **the.** a range of chalk hills in NE England: consists of the **Yorkshire Wolds** to the north, separated from the **Lincolnshire Wolds** by the Humber estuary.

wolf (wulf) *n, pl* **wolves** (wulvz). **1** a predatory canine mammal, *Canis lupus,* which hunts in packs and was formerly widespread in North America and Eurasia but is now less common. See also **timber wolf.** Related adj: **lupine. 2** any of several similar and related canines, such as the red wolf and the coyote (**prairie wolf**). **3** the fur of any such animal. **4 Tasmanian wolf.** another name for the **thylacine. 5** a voracious, grabbing, or fiercely cruel person or thing. **6** *Informal.* a man who habitually tries to seduce women. **7** *Informal.* the destructive larva of any of various moths and beetles. **8** Also called: **wolf note.** *Music.* **8a** an unpleasant sound produced in some notes played on the violin, cello, etc., owing to resonant vibrations of the belly. **8b** an out-of-tune effect produced on keyboard instruments accommodated esp. to the system of mean-tone temperament. See **temperament** (sense 4). **9 cry wolf.** to give a false alarm. **10 keep the wolf from the door.** to ward off starvation or privation. **11 lone wolf.** a person or animal who prefers to be alone. **12 throw to the wolves.** to abandon or deliver to destruction. **13 wolf in sheep's clothing.** a malicious person in a harmless or benevolent disguise. ◆ *vb* **14** (*tr;* often foll. by *down*) to gulp (down). **15** (*intr*) to hunt wolves. [Old English *wulf;* related to Old High German *wolf,* Old Norse *ulfr,* Gothic *wulfs,* Latin *lupus* and *vulpēs* fox] ▸ **'wolfish** *adj* ▸ **'wolf,like** *adj*

Wolf (*German* vɔlf) *n* **1 Friedrich August** ('friːdrɪç 'august). 1759–1824, German classical scholar, who suggested that the Homeric poems, esp. the *Iliad,* are products of an oral tradition. **2 Hugo** ('huːgo). 1860–1903, Austrian composer, esp. of songs, including the *Italienisches Liederbuch* and the *Spanisches Liederbuch.* **3** (wulf). **Howlin'.** See **Howlin' Wolf.**

Wolf Cub *n Brit.* the former name for **Cub Scout.**

Wolfe (wulf) *n* **1 James.** 1727–59, English soldier, who commanded the British capture of Quebec, in which he was killed. **2 Thomas** (**Clayton**). 1900–38, U.S. novelist, noted for his autobiographical fiction, esp. *Look Homeward, Angel* (1929).

Wolfenden Report ('wulfəndən) *n* a study produced in 1957 by the Committee on Homosexual Offences and Prostitution in Britain, which recommended that homosexual relations between consenting adults be legalized. [C20: named after Baron John Frederick *Wolfenden* (1906–85), who chaired the Committee]

wolfer ('wulfə) *n* a less common spelling of **wolver.**

Wolf-Ferrari (*Italian* 'vɔlffer'raːri) *n* **Ermanno** (er'manno). 1876–1948, Italian composer born of a German father, in Germany from 1909. His works, mainly in a lyrical style, include operas, such as *The Jewels of the Madonna* (1911) and *Susanna's Secret* (1909).

Wolffian body ('vɒlfɪən) *n Embryol.* another name for **mesonephros.** [C19: named after K. F. *Wolff* (1733–94), German embryologist]

wolffish ('wulf,fɪʃ) *n, pl* **-fish** *or* **-fishes.** any large northern deep-sea blennioid fish of the family *Anarhichadidae,* such as *Anarhichas lupus.* They have large sharp teeth and no pelvic fins and are used as food fishes. Also called: **catfish.**

wolfhound ('wulf,haund) *n* the largest breed of dog, used formerly to hunt wolves.

Wolfit ('wulfɪt) *n* Sir **Donald.** 1902–68, English stage actor and manager.

wolfram ('wulfrəm) *n* another name for **tungsten.** [C18: from German, originally perhaps from the proper name, *Wolfram,* used pejoratively of tungsten because it was thought inferior to tin]

wolframite ('wulfrə,maɪt) *n* a black to reddish-brown mineral consisting of tungstates of iron and manganese in monoclinic crystalline form: it occurs mainly in quartz veins and is the chief ore of tungsten. Formula: $(Fe,Mn)WO_4$.

Wolfram von Eschenbach (*German* 'vɔlfram fɔn 'ɛʃənbax) *n* died ?1220, German poet: author of the epic *Parzival,* incorporating the story of the Grail.

Wolf-Rayet star ('wulf'reɪət) *n* any of a small class of very hot intensely luminous stars surrounded by a rapidly expanding envelope of gas. [C19: named after Charles *Wolf* (1827–1918) and Georges *Rayet* (1839–1906), French astronomers]

wolfsbane *or* **wolf's-bane** ('wulfs,beɪn) *n* any of several poisonous N temperate plants of the ranunculaceous genus *Aconitum,* esp. *A. lycoctonum,* which has yellow hoodlike flowers.

Wolfsburg (*German* 'vɔlfsburk) *n* a city in N central Germany, in Lower Saxony: founded in 1938; motor-vehicle industry. Pop.: 126 331 (1996 est.).

wolf spider *n* any spider of the family *Lycosidae,* which chase their prey to catch it. Also called: **hunting spider.**

wolf whistle *n* **1** a whistle made by a man to express admiration of a woman's appearance. ◆ *vb* **wolf-whistle. 2** (when *intr,* sometimes foll. by *at*) to make such a whistle (at someone).

wollastonite ('wulәstә,naɪt) *n* a white or grey mineral consisting of calcium silicate in triclinic crystalline form: occurs in metamorphosed limestones. Formula: $CaSiO_3$. [C19: named after W. H. *Wollaston* (1766–1828), English physicist]

Wollongong ('wulәŋ,gɒŋ) *n* a city in E Australia, in E New South Wales on the Pacific: an early centre of dairy farming; now a coal-mining and heavy industrial centre. Pop.: 249 500 (1993).

Wollstonecraft ('wulstәn,krɑːft) *n* **Mary.** 1759–97, British feminist and writer, author of *A Vindication of the Rights of Women* (1792); wife of William Godwin and mother of Mary Shelley.

wolly ('wɒlɪ) *n, pl* **-lies.** *East London dialect.* a pickled cucumber or olive. [perhaps from OLIVE]

Wolof ('wɒlɒf) *n* **1** (*pl* **-of** *or* **-ofs**) a member of a Negroid people of W Africa living chiefly in Senegal. **2** the language of this people, belonging to the West Atlantic branch of the Niger-Congo family.

Wolseley ('wulzlɪ) *n* **Garnet Joseph,** 1st Viscount. 1833–1913, British field marshal, noted for his army reforms.

Wolsey ('wulzɪ) *n* **Thomas.** ?1475–1530, English cardinal and statesman; archbishop of York (1514–30); lord chancellor (1515–29). He dominated Henry VIII's foreign and domestic policies but his failure to obtain papal consent for the annulment of the king's marriage to Catherine of Aragon led to his arrest for high treason (1530); he died on the journey to face trial.

wolver ('wulvә) *or* **wolfer** *n* a person who hunts wolves.

Wolverhampton (,wulvә'hæmptәn) *n* **1** a town in W central England, in Wolverhampton unitary authority, West Midlands: iron and steel foundries. Pop.: 257 943 (1991). **2** a unitary authority in W central England, in the West Midlands. Pop.: 244 300 (1995 est.). Area: 69 sq. km (27 sq. miles).

wolverine ('wulvә,riːn) *n* a large musteline mammal, *Gulo gulo,* of northern forests of Eurasia and North America having dark very thick water-resistant fur. Also called: **glutton.** [C16 *wolvering,* from WOLF + -ING[3] (later altered to *-ine*)]

wolves (wulvz) *n* the plural of **wolf.**

woman ('wumәn) *n, pl* **women** ('wɪmɪn). **1** an adult female human being. **2** (*modifier*) female or feminine: *a woman politician; woman talk.* **3** women collectively; womankind. **4** (usually preceded by *the*) feminine nature or feelings: *babies bring out the woman in her.* **5** a female servant or domestic help. **6** a man considered as having supposed female characteristics, such as meekness or timidity. **7** *Informal.* a wife, mistress, or girlfriend. **8 the little woman.** *Informal.* one's wife. **9 woman of the streets.** a prostitute. ◆ *vb* (*tr*) **10** *Rare.* to provide with women. **11** *Obsolete.* to make effeminate. ◆ Related prefixes: **gyno-, gynaeco-.** [Old English *wīfmann, wimman;* from WIFE + MAN (human being)] ▸ **'womanless** *adj* ▸ **'woman-,like** *adj*

womanhood ('wumәn,hud) *n* **1** the state or quality of being a woman or being womanly. **2** women collectively.

womanish ('wumәnɪʃ) *adj* **1** having qualities or characteristics regarded as unsuitable to a strong character of either sex, esp. a man. **2** characteristic of or suitable for a woman. ▸ **'womanishly** *adv* ▸ **'womanishness** *n*

womanize *or* **womanise** ('wumә,naɪz) *vb* **1** (*intr*) (of a man) to indulge in many casual affairs with women; philander. **2** (*tr*) to make effeminate. ▸ **'woman,izer** *or* **'woman,iser** *n* ▸ **'woman,izing** *or* **'woman,ising** *n, adj*

womankind ('wumәn,kaɪnd) *n* the female members of the human race; women collectively.

womanly ('wumәnlɪ) *adj* **1** possessing qualities, such as warmth, attractiveness, etc., generally regarded as typical of a woman, esp. a mature woman. **2** characteristic of or belonging to a woman. ▸ **'womanliness** *n*

womb (wuːm) *n* **1** the nontechnical name for **uterus.** Related adj: **uterine. 2** a hollow space enclosing something, esp. when dark, warm, or sheltering. **3** a place where something is conceived: *the Near East is the womb of western civilization.* **4** *Obsolete.* the belly. [Old English *wamb;* related to Old Norse *vomb,* Gothic *wamba,* Middle Low German *wamme,* Swedish *våmm*] ▸ **wombed** *adj* ▸ **'womblike** *adj*

wombat ('wɒmbæt) *n* either of two burrowing herbivorous Australian marsupials, *Vombatus ursinus* or *Lasiorhinus latifrons,* constituting the family *Vom-*

batidae (or *Phascolomidae*) and having short limbs, a heavy body, and coarse dense fur. [C18: from a native Australian language]

women (ˈwɪmɪn) *n* the plural of **woman.**

womenfolk (ˈwɪmɪnˌfəʊk) *or U.S.* (*sometimes*) **womenfolks** *pl n* **1** women collectively. **2** a group of women, esp. the female members of one's family.

Women's Institute *n* (in Britain and Commonwealth countries) a society for women interested in the problems of the home and in engaging in social activities.

Women's Liberation *n* a movement directed towards the removal of attitudes and practices that preserve inequalities based upon the assumption that men are superior to women. Also called: **women's lib.**

Women's Movement *n* a grass-roots movement of women concerned with women's liberation. See **Women's Liberation.**

women's refuge *n Social welfare.* a house where battered women and their children can go for protection from their oppressors.

Women's Royal Voluntary Service *n* a British auxiliary service organized in 1938 as the Women's Voluntary Service for work in air raids and civil defence: active throughout World War II and since 1945 in providing support services for those in need: became the Women's Royal Voluntary Service in 1966. Abbrev.: **WRVS.**

women's studies *pl n* courses in history, literature, psychology, etc., that are particularly concerned with women's roles, experiences, and achievements.

women's suffrage *n* the right of women to vote. See also **suffragette.**

womera (ˈwʊmərə) *n* a variant spelling of **woomera.**

won[1] (wʌn) *vb* the past tense of **win**[1].

won[2] (wɒn) *n, pl* **won. 1** the standard monetary unit of North Korea, divided into 100 chon. **2** the standard monetary unit of South Korea, divided into 100 chon. ◆ Also called: **hwan.** [Korean *wăn*]

won[3] (wʌn, wʊn, wəʊn) *vb* **wons, wonning, wonned.** (*intr*) *Archaic.* to live or dwell. [Old English *wunian* to become accustomed to; related to WIN[1]]

wonder (ˈwʌndə) *n* **1** the feeling excited by something strange; a mixture of surprise, curiosity, and sometimes awe. **2** something that causes such a feeling, such as a miracle. **3** See **Seven Wonders of the World. 4** (*modifier*) exciting wonder by virtue of spectacular results achieved, feats performed, etc.: *a wonder drug; a wonder horse.* **5 do** *or* **work wonders.** to achieve spectacularly fine results. **6 for a wonder.** surprisingly or amazingly. **7 nine days' wonder.** a subject that arouses general surprise or public interest for a short time. **8 no wonder.** (*sentence connector*) (I am) not surprised at all (that): *no wonder he couldn't come.* **9 small wonder.** (*sentence connector*) (I am) hardly surprised (that): *small wonder he couldn't make it tonight.* ◆ *vb* (when *tr, may take a clause as object*) **10** (when *intr*, often foll. by *about*) to indulge in speculative inquiry, often accompanied by an element of doubt (concerning something): *I wondered about what she said; I wonder what happened.* **11** (when *intr*, often foll. by *at*) to be amazed (at something): *I wonder at your impudence.* [Old English *wundor;* related to Old Saxon *wundar,* Old Norse *undr,* German *Wunder*] ▸ ˈ**wonderer** *n* ▸ ˈ**wonderless** *adj*

Wonder (ˈwʌndə) *n* **Stevie.** real name *Steveland Judkins Morris.* born 1950, U.S. Motown singer, songwriter, and multi-instrumentalist. His recordings include *Up-Tight* (1966), "Superstition" (1972), *Innervisions* (1973), *Songs in the Key of Life* (1976), and "I Just Called to Say I Love You" (1985).

wonderful (ˈwʌndəfʊl) *adj* **1** exciting a feeling of wonder; marvellous or strange. **2** extremely fine; excellent. ▸ ˈ**wonderfully** *adv* ▸ ˈ**wonderfulness** *n*

wonderland (ˈwʌndəˌlænd) *n* **1** an imaginary land of marvels or wonders. **2** an actual place or scene of great or strange beauty or wonder.

wonderment (ˈwʌndəmənt) *n* **1** rapt surprise; awe. **2** puzzled interest. **3** something that excites wonder.

wonderwork (ˈwʌndəˌwɜːk) *n* something done or made that excites wonder; miracle or wonder. ▸ ˈ**wonder-ˌworker** *n* ▸ ˈ**wonder-ˌworking** *n, adj*

wondrous (ˈwʌndrəs) *Archaic or literary.* ◆ *adj* **1** exciting wonder; marvellous. ◆ *adv* **2** (intensifier): *it is wondrous cold.* ▸ ˈ**wondrously** *adv* ▸ ˈ**wondrousness** *n*

wonga-wonga (ˈwɒŋəˈwɒŋə) *n* **1** Also called: **wonga pigeon.** a large Australian pigeon, *Leucosarcia melanoleuca.* **2** an Australian evergreen vine of the genus *Pandorea* or *Tecoma,* esp. *T. australis.* [from a native Australian language]

wonk (wɒŋk) *n Informal.* a person who is obsessively interested in a specified subject: *a foreign policy wonk.* [C20: of uncertain origin]

wonky (ˈwɒŋkɪ) *adj* **-kier, -kiest.** *Brit. informal.* **1** shaky or unsteady. **2** not in correct alignment; askew. **3** liable to break down or develop a fault. [C20: variant of dialect *wanky,* from Old English *wancol*]

Wŏnsan (ˈwɒnˈsæn) *n* a port in SE North Korea, on the Sea of Japan: oil refineries. Pop.: 274 000 (1987).

wont (wəʊnt) *adj* **1** (*postpositive*) accustomed (to doing something): *he was wont to come early.* ◆ *n* **2** a manner or action habitually employed by or associated with someone (often in the phrases **as is my wont, as is his wont,** etc.). ◆ *vb* **3** (when *tr, usually passive*) to become or cause to become accustomed. [Old English *gewunod,* past participle of *wunian* to be accustomed to; related to Old High German *wunēn* (German *wohnen*), Old Norse *una* to be satisfied; see WEAN[1], WISH, WINSOME]

won't (wəʊnt) *vb contraction of* will not.

wonted (ˈwəʊntɪd) *adj* **1** (*postpositive*) accustomed or habituated (to doing something). **2** (*prenominal*) customary; usual: *she is in her wonted place.*

won ton (ˈwɒn ˈtɒn) *n Chinese cookery.* **1** a dumpling filled with spiced minced pork, usually served in soup. **2** soup containing such dumplings. [from Chinese (Cantonese) *wan t'an* pastry]

woo (wuː) *vb* **woos, wooing, wooed. 1** to seek the affection, favour, or love of (a woman) with a view to marriage. **2** (*tr*) to seek after zealously or hopefully: *to woo fame.* **3** (*tr*) to bring upon oneself (good or evil results) by one's own action. **4** (*tr*) to beg or importune (someone). [Old English *wōgian,* of obscure origin] ▸ ˈ**wooer** *n* ▸ ˈ**wooing** *n*

wood[1] (wʊd) *n* **1** the hard fibrous substance consisting of xylem tissue that occurs beneath the bark in trees, shrubs, and similar plants. Related adjs: **ligneous, xyloid. 2** the trunks of trees that have been cut and prepared for use as a building material. **3** a collection of trees, shrubs, herbs, grasses, etc., usually dominated by one or a few species of tree: usually smaller than a forest: *an oak wood.* Related adj: **sylvan. 4** fuel; firewood. **5** *Golf.* **5a** a long-shafted club with a broad wooden or metal head, used for driving: numbered from 1 to 7 according to size, angle of face, etc. **5b** (*as modifier*): *a wood shot.* **6** *Tennis, etc.* the frame of a racket: *he hit a winning shot off the wood.* **7** one of the biased wooden bowls used in the game of bowls. **8** *Music.* short for **woodwind.** See also **woods** (sense 3). **9a** casks, barrels, etc., made of wood. **9b from the wood.** (of a beverage) from a wooden container rather than a metal or glass one. **10 have (got) the wood on.** *Austral. and N.Z. informal.* to have an advantage over. **11 out of the wood** *or* **woods.** clear of or safe from dangers or doubts: *we're not out of the wood yet.* **12 see the wood for the trees.** (*used with a negative*) to obtain a general view of a situation, problem, etc., without allowing details to cloud one's analysis: *he can't see the wood for the trees.* **13** (*modifier*) made of, used for, employing, or handling wood: *a wood fire.* **14** (*modifier*) dwelling in, concerning, or situated in a wood: *a wood nymph.* ◆ *vb* **15** (*tr*) to plant a wood upon. **16** to supply or be supplied with fuel or firewood. ◆ See also **woods.** [Old English *widu, wudu;* related to Old High German *witu,* Old Norse *vithr*] ▸ ˈ**woodless** *adj*

wood[2] (wʊd) *adj Obsolete.* raging or raving like a maniac. [Old English *wōd;* related to Old High German *wuot* (German *Wut*), Old Norse *ōthr,* Gothic *wōths,* Latin *vātēs* seer]

Wood (wʊd) *n* **1** Mrs **Henry,** married name of *Ellen Price.* 1814–87, British novelist, noted esp. for the melodramatic novel *East Lynne* (1861). **2** Sir **Henry (Joseph).** 1869–1944, English conductor, who founded the Promenade Concerts in London. **3 John,** known as *the Elder.* 1707–54, British architect and town planner, working mainly in Bath, where he designed the North and South Parades (1728) and the Circus (1754). **4** his son, **John,** known as *the Younger.* 1727–82, British architect: designed the Royal Crescent (1767–71) and the Assembly Rooms (1769–71), Bath. **5 Ralph.** 1715–72, British potter, working in Staffordshire, who made the first toby jug (1762).

wood alcohol *n* another name for **methanol.**

wood-and-water joey *n Austral. informal.* a person employed to carry out menial tasks. [from the biblical phrase "hewers of wood and drawers of water" (Joshua 9:21) and JOEY]

wood anemone *n* any of several woodland anemone plants, esp. *Anemone quinquefolia* of E North America and *A. nemorosa* of Europe, having finely divided leaves and solitary white flowers. Also called: **windflower.**

wood ant *n* a reddish-brown European ant, *Formica rufa,* typically living in anthills in woodlands.

wood avens *n* another name for **herb bennet.**

woodbine (ˈwʊdˌbaɪn) *n* **1** a honeysuckle, *Lonicera periclymenum,* of Europe, SW Asia, and N Africa, having fragrant yellow flowers. **2 American woodbine.** a related North American plant, *L. caprifolium.* **3** *U.S.* another name for **Virginia creeper** (sense 1). **4** *Austral. obsolete slang.* an Englishman. [sense 4 from the English brand of cigarettes so named]

wood block *n* **1** a small rectangular flat block of wood that is laid with others as a floor surface. **2** *Music.* another word for **Chinese block.**

woodborer (ˈwʊdˌbɔːrə) *n* **1** any of various beetles of the families *Anobiidae, Buprestidae,* etc., the larvae of which bore into and damage wood. **2** any of various other unrelated invertebrates that bore into wood.

woodcarving (ˈwʊdˌkɑːvɪŋ) *n* **1** the act of carving wood, esp. as an art form. **2** a work of art produced by carving wood. ▸ ˈ**woodˌcarver** *n*

woodchat *or* **woodchat shrike** (ˈwʊdˌtʃæt) *n* a songbird, *Lanius senator,* of Europe and N Africa, having a black-and-white plumage with a reddish-brown crown and a hooked bill: family *Laniidae* (shrikes).

woodchop (ˈwʊdˌtʃɒp) *n Austral.* a wood-chopping competition, esp. at a show.

woodchuck (ˈwʊdˌtʃʌk) *n* a North American marmot, *Marmota monax,* having coarse reddish-brown fur. Also called: **groundhog.** [C17: by folk etymology from Cree *otcheck* fisher, marten]

wood coal *n* another name for **lignite** or **charcoal.**

woodcock (ˈwʊdˌkɒk) *n* **1** an Old World game bird, *Scolopax rusticola,* resembling the snipe but larger and having shorter legs and neck: family *Scolopacidae* (sandpipers, etc.), order *Charadriiformes.* **2** a related North American bird, *Philohela minor.* **3** *Obsolete.* a simpleton.

woodcraft (ˈwʊdˌkrɑːft) *n Chiefly U.S. and Canadian.* **1** ability and experience in matters concerned with living in a wood or forest. **2** ability or skill at woodwork, carving, etc. **3** skill in caring for trees. ▸ ˈ**woodˌcraftsman** *n*

woodcut (ˈwʊdˌkʌt) *n* **1** a block of wood cut along the grain and with a design, illustration, etc., incised with a knife, from which prints are made. **2** a print from a woodcut.

woodcutter (ˈwʊdˌkʌtə) *n* **1** a person who fells trees or chops wood. **2** a person who makes woodcuts. ▸ ˈ**woodˌcutting** *n*

wood duck *n* a duck, *Aix sponsa,* of wooded swamps, lakes, etc., in North America, having a very brightly coloured plumage in the male.

wooded (ˈwʊdɪd) *adj* **1** covered with or abounding in woods or trees. **2** (*in combination*) having wood of a specified character: *a soft-wooded tree.*

wooden (ˈwʊdᵊn) *adj* **1** made from or consisting of wood. **2** awkward or clumsy. **3** bereft of spirit or animation: *a wooden expression.* **4** obstinately unyielding: *a wooden attitude.* **5** mentally slow or dull. **6** not highly resonant: *a* *wooden thud.* ◆ *vb* **7** (*tr*) *Austral. slang.* to fell or kill (a person or animal). ▸ **ˈwoodenly** *adv* ▸ **ˈwoodenness** *n*

wood engraving *n* **1** the art of engraving pictures or designs on wood for printing by incising them with a burin on a block of wood cut across the grain. **2** a block of wood so engraved or a print taken from it. ▸ **wood engraver** *n*

woodenhead (ˈwʊdᵊnˌhɛd) *n Informal.* a dull, foolish, or unintelligent person. ▸ **ˌwoodenˈheaded** *adj* ▸ **ˌwoodenˈheadedness** *n*

Wooden Horse *n* another name for the **Trojan Horse** (sense 1).

wooden spoon *n* a booby prize, esp. in sporting contests.

woodfree (ˈwʊdˌfriː) *adj* (of high-quality paper) made from pulp that has been treated chemically, removing impurities.

woodgrouse (ˈwʊdˌgraʊs) *n* another name for **capercaillie.**

wood hedgehog *n* a pale buff basidiomycetous fungus, *Hydnum repandum,* found in broad-leaved woodlands having a spiny underside to the cap.

woodhen (ˈwʊdˌhɛn) *n N.Z.* another name for **weka.**

wood hyacinth *n* another name for **bluebell** (sense 1).

wood ibis *n* any of several storks having a downward-curved bill, esp. *Mycteria americana* of America and *Ibis ibis* of Africa.

woodland (ˈwʊdlənd) *n* **a** land that is mostly covered with woods or dense growths of trees and shrubs. **b** (*as modifier*): *woodland fauna.* ▸ **ˈwoodlander** *n*

woodlark (ˈwʊdˌlɑːk) *n* an Old World lark, *Lullula arborea,* similar to but slightly smaller than the skylark.

woodlot (ˈwʊdˌlɒt) *n* an area restricted to the growing of trees. Also called (esp. Canadian): **bush lot.**

woodlouse (ˈwʊdˌlaʊs) *n, pl* **-lice** (-ˌlaɪs). any of various small terrestrial isopod crustaceans of the genera *Oniscus, Porcellio,* etc., which have a flattened segmented body and occur in damp habitats. See also **pill bug.**

woodman (ˈwʊdmən) *n, pl* **-men. 1** a person who looks after and fells trees used for timber. **2** another word for **woodsman. 3** *Obsolete.* a hunter who is knowledgeable about woods and the animals living in them.

woodnote (ˈwʊdˌnəʊt) *n* a natural musical note or song, like that of a wild bird.

wood nymph *n* one of a class of nymphs fabled to inhabit the woods, such as a dryad.

wood opal *n* a form of petrified wood impregnated by common opal.

wood owl *n* another name for **tawny owl.**

woodpecker (ˈwʊdˌpɛkə) *n* any climbing bird of the family *Picidae,* typically having a brightly coloured plumage and strong chisel-like bill with which they bore into trees for insects: order *Piciformes.*

wood pigeon *n* a large Eurasian pigeon, *Columba palumbus,* having white patches on the wings and neck. Also called: **ringdove, cushat.**

woodpile (ˈwʊdˌpaɪl) *n* **1** a pile or heap of firewood. **2 nigger in the woodpile.** See **nigger** (sense 3).

wood pitch *n* the dark viscid residue left after the distillation of wood tar: used as a binder in briquettes.

wood preservative *n* a coating applied to timber as a protection against decay, insects, weather, etc.

woodprint (ˈwʊdˌprɪnt) *n* another name for **woodcut** (sense 2).

wood pulp *n* **1** wood that has been ground to a fine pulp for use in making newsprint and other cheap forms of paper, and in the production of hardboard. **2** finely pulped wood that has been digested by a chemical, such as caustic soda, and sometimes bleached: used in making paper.

wood rat *n* another name for **pack rat.**

woodruff (ˈwʊdrʌf) *n* any of several rubiaceous plants of the genus *Asperula,* esp. *A. odorata* (or *Galium odoratum*) (**sweet woodruff**), of Eurasia, which has small sweet-scented white flowers and whorls of narrow fragrant leaves used to flavour wine and liqueurs and in perfumery. [Old English *wudurofe,* from WOOD[1] + *rōfe,* related to Old High German *ruoba,* Middle Low German *rōve* (beet)root, Latin *rēpere* to creep]

Woodruff key (ˈwʊdrʌf) *n Engineering.* a semicircular key restrained in a curved keyway in a shaft. [C19: named after the *Woodruff Manufacturing Co.,* in Hartford, Connecticut, who first manufactured it in 1892]

woodrush (ˈwʊdˌrʌʃ) *n* any of various juncaceous plants of the genus *Luzula,* chiefly of cold and temperate regions of the N hemisphere, having grasslike leaves and small brown flowers.

woods (wʊdz) *pl n* **1** closely packed trees forming a forest or wood, esp. a specific one. **2** another word for **backwoods** (sense 2). **3** the woodwind instruments in an orchestra. See also **wood**[1] (sense 8). **4 neck of the woods.** *Informal.* an area or locality: *a quiet neck of the woods.*

Woods[1] *n* **Lake of the.** See **Lake of the Woods.**

Woods[2] (wʊdz) *n* **Tiger,** real name *Eldrick Woods.* born 1975, U.S. golfer: youngest U.S. Masters champion (1997) and first Black golfer to win a major championship; also won USPGA in 1999.

wood sage *n* a downy labiate perennial, *Teucrium scorodonia,* having spikes of green-yellow flowers: common on acid heath and scree.

woodscrew (ˈwʊdˌskruː) *n* a metal screw that tapers to a point so that it can be driven into wood by a screwdriver.

Woodser (ˈwʊdzə) *n* See **Jimmy Woodser.**

woodshed (ˈwʊdˌʃɛd) *n* a small outbuilding where firewood, garden tools, etc., are stored.

woodsia (ˈwʊdzɪə) *n* any small fern of the genus *Woodsia,* of temperate and cold regions, having tufted rhizomes and numerous wiry fronds: family *Polypodiaceae.*

woodsman (ˈwʊdzmən) *n, pl* **-men.** a person who lives in a wood or who is skilled in woodcraft. Also called: **woodman.**

wood sorrel *n* a Eurasian plant, *Oxalis acetosella,* having trifoliate leaves, an underground creeping stem, and white purple-veined flowers: family *Oxalidaceae.*

wood spirit *n Chem.* another name for **methanol.**

Woodstock (ˈwʊdstɒk) *n* a town in New York State, the site of a large rock festival in August 1969. Pop.: 1870 (1990).

wood sugar *n Chem.* another name for **xylose.**

woodswallow (ˈwʊdˌswɒləʊ) *n* any of several insectivorous birds of the genus *Artamus* of Australia.

woodsy (ˈwʊdzɪ) *adj* **woodsier, woodsiest.** *U.S. and Canadian informal.* of, reminiscent of, or connected with woods.

wood tar *n* any tar produced by the destructive distillation of wood: used in producing tarred cord and rope and formerly in medicine as disinfectants and antiseptics.

Woodville (ˈwʊdvɪl) *n* **Elizabeth.** ?1437–92, wife of Edward IV of England and mother of Edward V.

wood vinegar *n* another name for **pyroligneous acid.**

wood warbler *n* **1** a European woodland warbler, *Phylloscopus sibilatrix,* with a dull yellow plumage. **2** another name for the **American warbler.** See **warbler** (sense 3).

Woodward (ˈwʊdwəd) *n* **R(obert) B(urns).** 1917–79, U.S. chemist. For his work on the synthesis of quinine, strychnine, cholesterol, and other organic compounds he won the Nobel prize for chemistry 1965.

wood wasp *n* another name for the **horntail.**

woodwaxen (ˈwʊdˌwæksᵊn) *n* another name for **dyer's-greenweed.**

woodwind (ˈwʊdˌwɪnd) *Music.* ◆ *adj* **1** of, relating to, or denoting a type of wind instrument, excluding the brass instruments, formerly made of wood but now often made of metal, such as the flute or clarinet. ◆ *n* **2** (*functioning as pl*) woodwind instruments collectively.

wood woollyfoot (ˈwʊlɪˌfʊt) *n* a common yellowish basidiomycetous fungus, *Collybia peronata,* of broad-leaved woodland, having a hairy tuft at the foot of the stem.

woodwork (ˈwʊdˌwɜːk) *n* **1** the art, craft, or skill of making things in wood; carpentry. **2** components made of wood, such as doors, staircases, etc.

woodworker (ˈwʊdˌwɜːkə) *n* a person who works in wood, such as a carpenter, joiner, or cabinet-maker.

woodworking (ˈwʊdˌwɜːkɪŋ) *n* **1** the process of working wood. ◆ *adj* **2** of, relating to, or used in woodworking.

woodworm (ˈwʊdˌwɜːm) *n* **1** any of various insect larvae that bore into wooden furniture, beams, etc., esp. the larvae of the furniture beetle, *Anobium punctatum,* and the deathwatch beetle. **2** the condition caused in wood by any of these larvae.

woody (ˈwʊdɪ) *adj* **woodier, woodiest. 1** abounding in or covered with forest or woods. **2** connected with, belonging to, or situated in a wood. **3** consisting of or containing wood or lignin: *woody tissue; woody stems.* **4** resembling wood in hardness or texture. ▸ **ˈwoodiness** *n*

woodyard (ˈwʊdˌjɑːd) *n* a place where timber is cut and stored.

woody nightshade *n* a scrambling woody Eurasian solanaceous plant, *Solanum dulcamara,* having purple flowers with recurved petals and a protruding cone of yellow anthers and producing poisonous red berry-like fruits. Also called: **bittersweet.**

woof[1] (wuːf) *n* **1** the crosswise yarns that fill the warp yarns in weaving; weft. **2** a woven fabric or its texture. [Old English *ōwef,* from *ō-,* perhaps from ON, + *wef* WEB (see WEAVE); modern form influenced by WARP]

woof[2] (wʊf) *interj* **1** an imitation of the bark or growl of a dog. ◆ *vb* **2** (*intr*) (of dogs) to bark or growl.

woofer (ˈwuːfə) *n* a loudspeaker used in high-fidelity systems for the reproduction of low audio frequencies.

woofter (ˈwʊftə, ˈwuːftə) *n Derogatory slang.* a male homosexual.

Wookey Hole (ˈwʊkɪ həʊl) *n* a village in SW England, in Somerset, near Wells: noted for the nearby limestone cave in which prehistoric remains have been found. Pop.: 1000 (latest est.).

wool (wʊl) *n* **1** the outer coat of sheep, yaks, etc., which consists of short curly hairs. **2** yarn spun from the coat of sheep, etc., used in weaving, knitting, etc. **3a** cloth or a garment made from this yarn. **3b** (*as modifier*): *a wool dress.* **4** any of certain fibrous materials: *glass wool; steel wool.* **5** *Informal.* short thick curly hair. **6** a tangled mass of soft fine hairs that occurs in certain plants. **7 dyed in the wool.** confirmed in one's beliefs or opinions. **8 pull the wool over someone's eyes.** to deceive or delude someone. [Old English *wull;* related to Old Frisian, Middle Dutch *wulle,* Old High German *wolla* (German *Wolle*), Old Norse *ull,* Latin *lāna* and *vellus* fleece] ▸ **ˈwool-ˌlike** *adj*

wool bale *n Austral. and N.Z.* a standard-sized jute, flax, etc., cubical container of compressed wool weighing over 100 kg when containing fleece or lamb's wool and weighing 204 kg when containing oddments.

wool cheque *n N.Z.* the annual return for a sheep farmer.

wool classing *n Austral. and N.Z.* the grading and grouping together of similar types of wool.

wool clip *n* the total amount of wool shorn from a particular flock, or from flocks in a particular region or country, in one year.

Woolf (wʊlf) *n* **1 Leonard Sidney.** 1880–1969, English publisher and political writer. **2** his wife, **Virginia.** 1882–1941, English novelist and critic. Her novels, which include *Mrs Dalloway* (1925), *To the Lighthouse* (1927), *The Waves* (1931), and *Between the Acts* (1941), employ such techniques as the interior monologue and stream of consciousness.

wool fat *or* **grease** *n* another name for **lanolin.**

woolfell (ˈwʊlˌfɛl) *n Obsolete.* the skin of a sheep or similar animal with the fleece still attached.

woolgathering (ˈwʊlˌgæðərɪŋ) *n* idle or absent-minded indulgence in fantasy; daydreaming. ▸ **ˈwoolˌgatherer** *n*

woolgrower (ˈwʊlˌgrəʊə) *n* a person who keeps sheep for their wool. ▸ **ˈwoolˌgrowing** *n, adj*

Woollcott ('wʊlkɒt) *n* **Alexander.** 1887–1943, U.S. writer and critic. His collected essays include *Shouts and Murmurs* (1922).

woolled (wʊld) *adj* **1** (of animals) having wool. **2** having wool as specified: *coarse-woolled.*

woollen *or U.S.* **woolen** ('wʊlən) *adj* **1** relating to or consisting partly or wholly of wool. ◆ *n* **2** (*often pl*) a garment or piece of cloth made wholly or partly of wool, esp. a knitted one.

Woolley ('wʊlɪ) *n* Sir (**Charles**) **Leonard.** 1880–1960, British archaeologist, noted for his excavations at Ur in Mesopotamia (1922–34).

woolly *or U.S.* (*sometimes*) **wooly** ('wʊlɪ) *adj* **woollier, woolliest** *or U.S.* (*sometimes*) **woolier, wooliest. 1** consisting of, resembling, or having the nature of wool. **2** covered or clothed in wool or something resembling it. **3** lacking clarity or substance: *woolly thinking.* **4** *Botany.* covered with long soft whitish hairs: *woolly stems.* **5** *U.S.* recalling the rough and lawless period of the early West of America (esp. in the phrase **wild and woolly**). ◆ *n, pl* **woollies** *or U.S.* (*sometimes*) **woolies. 6** (*often pl*) a garment, such as a sweater, made of wool or something similar. **7** *Western U.S. and Austral.* (*usually pl*) an informal word for **sheep.** ▸ **'woollily** *adv* ▸ **'woolliness** *n*

woolly bear *n* the caterpillar of any of various tiger moths, esp. *Arctia caja* of Europe and *Isia isabella* of North America, having a dense covering of soft hairs.

woollybutt ('wʊlɪˌbʌt) *n Austral.* any of several eucalyptus trees, esp. *Eucalyptus longifolia,* having loose fibrous bark around the base of the trunk.

woolly-minded *adj* showing a vague or muddled way of thinking.

woolpack ('wʊlˌpæk) *n* **1** the cloth or canvas wrapping used to pack a bale of wool. **2** a bale of wool.

woolsack ('wʊlˌsæk) *n* **1** a sack containing or intended to contain wool. **2** (in Britain) the seat of the Lord Chancellor in the House of Lords, formerly made of a large square sack of wool.

woolshed ('wʊlˌʃɛd) *n Austral. and N.Z.* a shearing shed.

wool-sorter's disease *n* another name for **anthrax.**

wool stapler *n* a person who sorts wool into different grades or classifications. ▸ **'wool-ˌstapling** *n, adj*

wool store *n Austral. and N.Z.* a building where bales of wool are stored and made available to prospective buyers for inspection.

wool table *n N.Z.* a slatted wooden table in a shearing shed where fleeces are skirted and classed.

Woolworth ('wʊlwəθ) *n* **Frank Winfield** ('wɪnˌfiːld). 1852–1919, U.S. merchant; founder of an international chain of department stores selling inexpensive goods.

woomera *or* **womera** ('wʊmərə) *n Austral.* a type of notched stick used by native Australians to increase leverage and propulsion in the throwing of a spear. [from a native Australian language]

Woomera ('wʊmərə) *n* a town in South Australia: site of the Long Range Weapons Establishment. Pop.: 1660 (latest est.).

Woop Woop ('wuːp ˌwuːp) *n Austral. slang.* a jocular name for any backward or remote town or district.

woorali (wʊ'rɑːlɪ) *n* a less common name for **curare.** [C18: from the native S American name]

woosh (wʊʃ) *n, vb* a variant spelling of **whoosh.**

Wootton ('wʊtᵊn) *n* **Barbara** (**Frances**), Baroness of Abinger. 1897–1988, English economist, educationalist, social scientist, and criminologist.

woozy ('wuːzɪ) *adj* **woozier, wooziest.** *Informal.* **1** dazed or confused. **2** experiencing dizziness, nausea, etc. [C19: perhaps from a blend of *woolly* + *muzzy* or *dizzy*] ▸ **'woozily** *adv* ▸ **'wooziness** *n*

wop[1] (wɒp) *n Slang, derogatory.* a member of a Latin people, esp. an Italian. [C20: probably from southern Italian dialect *guappo* dandy, braggart, from Spanish *guapo*]

wop[2] (wɒp) *vb* **wops, wopping, wopped,** *n* a variant spelling of **whop.**

wop-wops ('wɒpˌwɒps) *n* (*functioning as pl or sing*) **the.** *N.Z. informal.* the backblocks, the back of beyond.

Worcester ('wʊstə) *n* **1** a cathedral city in W central England, the administrative centre of Worcestershire on the River Severn: scene of the battle (1651) in which Charles II was defeated by Cromwell. Pop.: 82 661 (1991). **2** an industrial city in the U.S., in central Massachusetts: Clark University (1887). Pop.: 166 350 (1996 est.). **3** a town in S South Africa; centre of a fruit-growing region. Pop.: 60 324 (1990).

Worcester china *or* **porcelain** *n* porcelain articles made in Worcester (England) from 1751 in a factory that became, in 1862, the Royal Worcester Porcelain Company. Sometimes shortened to **Worcester.**

Worcester sauce *or* **Worcestershire sauce** *n* a commercially prepared piquant sauce, made from a basis of soy sauce, with vinegar, spices, etc.

Worcestershire ('wʊstəˌʃɪə, -ʃə) *n* a county of W central England, formerly (1974–98) part of Hereford and Worcester. Administrative centre: Worcester. Pop.: 528 100 (1998 est.). Area: 1742 sq. km (674 sq. miles).

Worcs *abbrev. for* Worcestershire.

word (wɜːd) *n* **1** one of the units of speech or writing that native speakers of a language usually regard as the smallest isolable meaningful element of the language, although linguists would analyse these further into morphemes. Related adj: **lexical, verbal. 2** an instance of vocal intercourse; chat, talk, or discussion: *to have a word with someone.* **3** an utterance or expression, esp. a brief one: *a word of greeting.* **4** news or information: *he sent word that he would be late.* **5** a verbal signal for action; command: *when I give the word, fire!* **6** an undertaking or promise: *I give you my word; he kept his word.* **7** an autocratic decree or utterance; order: *his word must be obeyed.* **8** a watchword or slogan, as of a political party: *the word now is "freedom".* **9** *Computing.* a set of bits used to store, transmit, or operate upon an item of information in a computer, such as a program instruction. **10 as good as one's word.** doing what one has undertaken or promised to do. **11 at a word.** at once. **12 by word of mouth.** orally rather than by written means. **13 in a word.** briefly or in short. **14 my word! 14a** an exclamation of surprise, annoyance, etc. **14b** *Austral.* an exclamation of agreement. **15 of one's word.** given to or noted for keeping one's promises: *I am a man of my word.* **16 put in a word** *or* **good word for.** to make favourable mention of (someone); recommend. **17 take someone at his** *or* **her word.** to assume that someone means, or will do, what he or she says: *when he told her to go, she took him at his word and left.* **18 take someone's word for it.** to accept or believe what someone says. **19 the last word. 19a** the closing remark of a conversation or argument, esp. a remark that supposedly settles an issue. **19b** the latest or most fashionable design, make, or model: *the last word in bikinis.* **19c** the finest example (of some quality, condition, etc.); *the last word in luxury.* **20 the word.** the proper or most fitting expression: *cold is not the word for it, it's freezing!* **21 upon my word! 21a** *Archaic.* on my honour. **21b** an exclamation of surprise, annoyance, etc. **22 word for word. 22a** (of a report, transcription, etc.) using exactly the same words as those employed in the situation being reported; verbatim. **22b** translated by substituting each word in the new text for each corresponding word in the original rather than by general sense. **23 word of honour.** a promise; oath. **24** (*modifier*) of, relating to, or consisting of words: *a word list.* ◆ *vb* **25** (*tr*) to state in words, usually specially selected ones; phrase. **26** (*tr;* often foll. by *up*) *Austral. informal.* to inform or advise (a person). ◆ See also **words.** [Old English *word;* related to Old High German *wort,* Old Norse *orth,* Gothic *waurd,* Latin *verbum,* Sanskrit *vratá* command]

Word (wɜːd) *n* **the. 1** *Christianity.* the 2nd person of the Trinity. **2** Scripture, the Bible, or the Gospels as embodying or representing divine revelation. Often called: **the Word of God.** [translation of Greek *logos,* as in John 1:1]

-word *n combining form.* (*preceded by* **the** *and an initial letter*) a euphemistic way of referring to a word by its first letter because it is considered to be in some way unmentionable by the user: *the C-word, meaning cancer.*

wordage ('wɜːdɪdʒ) *n* words considered collectively, esp. a quantity of words.

word association *n* an early method of psychoanalysis in which the patient thinks of the first word that comes into consciousness on hearing a given word. In this way it was claimed that aspects of the unconscious could be revealed before defence mechanisms intervene.

word blindness *n* the nontechnical name for **alexia** and **dyslexia.** ▸ **'word-ˌblind** *adj*

wordbook ('wɜːdˌbʊk) *n* **1** a book containing words, usually with their meanings. **2** a libretto for an opera.

wordbreak ('wɜːdˌbreɪk) *n Printing.* the point at which a word is divided when it runs over from one line of print to the next.

word class *n Linguistics.* a form class in which the members are words. See **part of speech.**

word deafness *n* loss of ability to understand spoken words, esp. as the result of a cerebral lesion. Also called: **auditory aphasia.** ▸ **'word-ˌdeaf** *adj*

word game *n* any game involving the formation, discovery, or alteration of a word or words.

wording ('wɜːdɪŋ) *n* **1** the way in which words are used to express a statement, report, etc., esp. a written one. **2** the words themselves, as used in a written statement or a sign.

wordless ('wɜːdlɪs) *adj* **1** inarticulate or silent. **2** *Music.* of or relating to vocal music that is not provided with an articulated text: *a wordless chorus.* ▸ **'wordlessly** *adv* ▸ **'wordlessness** *n*

word order *n* the arrangement of words in a phrase, clause, or sentence. In many languages, including English, word order plays an important part in determining meanings expressed in other languages by inflections.

word-perfect *or U.S.* **letter-perfect** *adj* **1** correct in every detail. **2** (of a speech, part in a play, etc.) memorized perfectly. **3** (of a speaker, actor, etc.) knowing one's speech, role, etc., perfectly.

word picture *n* a verbal description, esp. a vivid one.

wordplay ('wɜːdˌpleɪ) *n* verbal wit based on the meanings and ambiguities of words; puns, clever repartee, etc.

word processing *n* the composition of documents using a computer system to input, edit, store, and print them.

word processor *n* **a** a computer program that performs word processing. **b** a computer system designed for word processing.

words (wɜːdz) *pl n* **1** the text of a part of an actor, etc. **2** the text or lyrics of a song, as opposed to the music. **3** angry speech (esp. in the phrase **have words with someone**). **4 eat one's words.** to retract a statement. **5 for words.** (preceded by *too* and an adj or adv) indescribably; extremely: *the play was too funny for words.* **6 have no words for.** to be incapable of describing. **7 in other words.** expressing the same idea but differently. **8 in so many words.** explicitly or precisely. **9 of many** (*or* **few**) **words.** (not) talkative. **10 put into words.** to express in speech or writing as well as thought. **11 say a few words.** to give a brief speech. **12 take the words out of one's** (*or* **someone's**) **mouth.** to say exactly what someone else was about to say. **13 words fail me.** I am too happy, sad, amazed, etc., to express my thoughts.

wordsmith ('wɜːdˌsmɪθ) *n* a person skilled in using words.

word square *n* a puzzle in which the player must fill a square grid with words that read the same across as down.

word stress *n* the stress accent on the syllables of individual words either in a sentence or in isolation.

Wordsworth ('wɜːdzˌwəθ) *n* **1 Dorothy.** 1771–1855, English writer, whose *Journals* are noted esp. for their descriptions of nature. **2** her brother, **William.** 1770–1850, English poet, whose work, celebrating nature, was greatly inspired by the Lake District, in which he spent most of his life. *Lyrical Ballads* (1798), to which Coleridge contributed, is often taken as the first example of English romantic poetry and includes his *Lines Written above Tintern Abbey.* Among his other works are *The Prelude* (completed in 1805; revised thereafter and published posthumously) and *Poems in Two Volumes* (1807), which includes *The Solitary Reaper* and *Intimations of Immortality*. ▸ **Wordsworthian** (ˌwɜːdzˈwɜːðɪən) *adj, n*

word wrapping *n Computing.* the automatic shifting of a word at the end of a line to a new line in order to keep within preset margins.

wordy (ˈwɜːdɪ) *adj* **wordier, wordiest. 1** using, inclined to use, or containing an excess of words: *a wordy writer; a wordy document.* **2** of the nature of or relating to words; verbal. ▸ ˈ**wordily** *adv* ▸ ˈ**wordiness** *n*

wore (wɔː) *vb* the past tense of **wear.**

work (wɜːk) *n* **1** physical or mental effort directed towards doing or making something. **2** paid employment at a job or a trade, occupation, or profession. **3** a duty, task, or undertaking. **4** something done, made, etc., as a result of effort or exertion: *a work of art.* **5** materials or tasks on which to expend effort or exertion. **6** another word for **workmanship** (sense 3). **7** the place, office, etc., where a person is employed. **8** any piece of material that is undergoing a manufacturing operation or process; workpiece. **9a** decoration or ornamentation, esp. of a specified kind. **9b** (in combination): *wirework; woolwork.* **10** an engineering structure such as a bridge, building, etc. **11** *Physics.* the transfer of energy expressed as the product of a force and the distance through which its point of application moves in the direction of the force. Abbrevs.: *W, w* **12** a structure, wall, etc., built or used as part of a fortification system. **13 at work. 13a** at one's job or place of employment. **13b** in action; operating. **14 make short work of.** *Informal.* to handle or dispose of very quickly. **15** (*modifier*) of, relating to, or used for work: *work clothes; a work permit.* ◆ *vb* **16** (*intr*) to exert effort in order to do, make, or perform something. **17** (*intr*) to be employed. **18** (*tr*) to carry on operations, activity, etc., in (a place or area): *that salesman works the southern region.* **19** (*tr*) to cause to labour or toil: *he works his men hard.* **20** to operate or cause to operate, esp. properly or effectively: *to work a lathe; that clock doesn't work.* **21** (*tr*) to till or cultivate (land). **22** to handle or manipulate or be handled or manipulated: *to work dough.* **23** to shape, form, or process or be shaped, formed, or processed: *to work copper.* **24** to reach or cause to reach a specific condition, esp. gradually: *the rope worked loose.* **25** (*tr*) *Chiefly U.S. and Canadian.* to solve (a mathematical problem). **26** (*intr*) to move in agitation: *his face worked with anger.* **27** (*tr;* often foll. by *up*) to provoke or arouse: *to work someone into a frenzy.* **28** (*tr*) to effect or accomplish: *to work one's revenge.* **29** to make (one's way) with effort: *he worked his way through the crowd.* **30** (*tr*) to make or decorate by hand in embroidery, tapestry, etc.: *she was working a sampler.* **31** (*intr*) (of a mechanism) to move in a loose or otherwise imperfect fashion. **32** (*intr*) (of liquids) to ferment, as in brewing. **33** (*tr*) *Informal.* to manipulate or exploit to one's own advantage. **34** (*tr*) *Slang.* to cheat or swindle. ◆ See also **work back, work in, work off, work on, work out, work over, works, work up.** [Old English *weorc* (n), *wircan, wyrcan* (vb); related to Old High German *wurchen,* German *wirken,* Old Norse *yrkja,* Gothic *waurkjan*] ▸ ˈ**workless** *adj* ▸ ˈ**worklessness** *n*

workable (ˈwɜːkəbᵊl) *adj* **1** practicable or feasible. **2** able to be worked. ▸ ˌ**workaˈbility** *or* ˈ**workableness** *n*

workaday (ˈwɜːkəˌdeɪ) *adj* (*usually prenominal*) **1** being a part of general human experience; ordinary. **2** suitable for working days; everyday or practical.

workaholic (ˌwɜːkəˈhɒlɪk) *n* **a** a person obsessively addicted to work. **b** (*as modifier*): *workaholic behaviour.* [C20: from WORK + -HOLIC, coined in 1971 by Wayne Oates, U.S. author]

work back *vb* (*intr, adv*) *Austral. informal.* to work overtime.

workbag (ˈwɜːkˌbæg) *n* a container for implements, tools, or materials, esp. sewing equipment. Also called: **work basket, workbox.**

workbench (ˈwɜːkˌbɛntʃ) *n* a heavy table at which work is done by a carpenter, mechanic, toolmaker, etc.

workbook (ˈwɜːkˌbʊk) *n* **1** an exercise book or textbook used for study, esp. a textbook with spaces for answers. **2** a book of instructions for some process. **3** a book in which is recorded all work done or planned.

work camp *n* a camp set up for young people who voluntarily do manual work on a worthwhile project.

workday (ˈwɜːkˌdeɪ) *n* **1** the usual U.S. term for **working day.** ◆ *adj* **2** another word for **workaday.**

worked (wɜːkt) *adj* made or decorated with evidence of workmanship; wrought, as with embroidery or tracery.

worked up *adj* agitated or excited.

worker (ˈwɜːkə) *n* **1** a person or thing that works, usually at a specific job: *a good worker; a research worker.* **2** an employee in an organization, as opposed to an employer or manager. **3** a manual labourer or other employee working in a manufacturing or other industry. **4** any other member of the working class. **5** a sterile female member of a colony of bees, ants, or wasps that forages for food, cares for the larvae, etc. ▸ ˈ**workerless** *adj*

worker director *n* a worker elected to the governing board of a business concern to represent the interests of the employees in decision making.

worker participation *n* a process by which subordinate employees, either individually or collectively, become involved in one or more aspects of organizational decision making within the enterprises in which they work.

worker-priest *n* a Roman Catholic priest who has full-time or part-time employment in a secular job to be more closely in touch with the problems of the laity.

workers' cooperative *n* See **cooperative** (sense 4).

work ethic *n* a belief in the moral value of work (often in the phrase **Protestant work ethic**).

workfare (ˈwɜːkˌfɛə) *n* a scheme under which the government of a country requires unemployed people to do community work or undergo job training in return for social-security payments. [C20: from WORK + (WEL)FARE]

workfolk (ˈwɜːkˌfəʊk) *or U.S.* (*informal*) **workfolks** *pl n* working people, esp. labourers on a farm.

workforce (ˈwɜːkˌfɔːs) *n* **1** the total number of workers employed by a company on a specific job, project, etc. **2** the total number of people who could be employed: *the country's workforce is growing rapidly.*

work function *n* **1** *Physics.* the minimum energy required to transfer an electron from a point within a solid to a point just outside its surface. Symbol: ϕ or Φ **2** *Thermodynamics.* another name (not now used because of confusion with sense 1) for **Helmholtz function.**

work-harden *vb* (*tr*) to increase the strength or hardness of (a metal) by a mechanical process, such as tension, compression, or torsion. ▸ ˈ**work-ˌhardening** *n*

workhorse (ˈwɜːkˌhɔːs) *n* **1** a horse used for nonrecreational activities. **2** *Informal.* a person who takes on the greatest amount of work in a project or job.

workhouse (ˈwɜːkˌhaʊs) *n* **1** (formerly in England) an institution maintained at public expense where able-bodied paupers did unpaid work in return for food and accommodation. **2** (in the U.S.) a prison for petty offenders serving short sentences at manual labour.

work in *vb* (*adv*) **1** to insert or become inserted: *she worked the patch in carefully.* **2** (*tr*) to find space for: *I'll work this job in during the day.* ◆ *n* **work-in. 3** a form of industrial action in which a factory that is to be closed down is occupied and run by its workers.

working (ˈwɜːkɪŋ) *n* **1** the operation or mode of operation of something. **2** the act or process of moulding something pliable. **3** a convulsive or jerking motion, as from excitement. **4** (*often pl*) a part of a mine or quarry that is being or has been worked. **5** (*pl*) the whole system of excavations in a mine. **6** a record of the steps by which the result of a calculation or the solution of a problem is obtained: *all working is to be submitted to the examiners.* **7** *Rare.* slow advance against or as if against resistance. ◆ *adj* (*prenominal*) **8** relating to or concerned with a person or thing that works: *a working man.* **9** concerned with, used in, or suitable for work: *working clothes.* **10** (of a meal or occasion) during which business discussions are carried on: *working lunch; working breakfast.* **11** capable of being operated or used: *a working model.* **12** sufficiently large or accurate to be useful or to accomplish a desired end: *a working majority; a working knowledge of German.* **13** (of a theory, etc.) providing a basis, usually a temporary one, on which operations or procedures may be carried out.

working bee *n N.Z.* a voluntary group doing a job for charity.

working capital *n* **1** *Accounting.* current assets minus current liabilities. **2** current or liquid assets. **3** that part of the capital of a business enterprise available for operations.

working class *n* **1** Also called: **proletariat.** the social stratum, usually of low status, that consists of those who earn wages, esp. as manual workers. Compare **lower class, middle class, upper class.** ◆ *adj* **working-class. 2** of, relating to, or characteristic of the working class.

working day *or esp. U.S.* **workday** *n* **1** a day on which work is done, esp. for an agreed or stipulated number of hours in return for a salary or wage. **2** the part of the day allocated to work: *a seven-hour working day.* **3** (*often pl*) *Commerce.* any day of the week except Sunday, public holidays, and, in some cases, Saturday.

working dog *n* a dog of suitable breed or training kept for its practical use, such as herding sheep, rather than as a pet or for showing.

working drawing *n* a scale drawing of a part or assembly that provides a guide for manufacture.

working memory *n Psychol.* the current contents of consciousness.

working papers *pl n* **1** papers or notes showing the intermediate stages of a proposal, solution, etc., arrived at or being worked on. **2** legal documents that certain people in some countries must possess to be allowed to work.

working party *n* **1** a committee established to investigate a problem, question, etc. **2** a group of soldiers or prisoners assigned to perform some manual task or duty.

working substance *or* **fluid** *n* the fluid, esp. water, steam, or compressed air, that operates an engine, etc.

working week *or esp. U.S. and Canadian* **workweek** (ˈwɜːkˌwiːk) *n* the number of hours or days in a week actually or officially allocated to work: *a four-day working week.*

work-in-progress *n Book-keeping.* the value of work begun but not completed, as shown in a profit-and-loss account.

workload (ˈwɜːkˌləʊd) *n* the amount of work to be done, esp. in a specified period by a person, machine, etc.

workman (ˈwɜːkmən) *n, pl* **-men. 1** a man who is employed in manual labour or who works an industrial machine. **2** a craftsman of skill as specified: *a bad workman.*

workmanlike (ˈwɜːkmənˌlaɪk) *or* (*less commonly*) **workmanly** (ˈwɜːkmənlɪ) *adj* appropriate to or befitting a good workman.

workmanship (ˈwɜːkmənʃɪp) *n* **1** the art or skill of a workman. **2** the art or skill with which something is made or executed. **3** the degree of art or skill exhibited in the finished product. **4** the piece of work so produced.

workmate (ˈwɜːkˌmeɪt) *n* a person who works with another; fellow worker.

workmen's *or* **worker's compensation** *n* compensation for death, injury, or accident suffered by a workman in the course of his employment and paid to him or his dependents.

work of art *n* **1** a piece of fine art, such as a painting or sculpture. **2** something that may be likened to a piece of fine art, esp. in beauty, intricacy, etc.

work off *vb* (*tr, adv*) **1** to get rid of or dissipate, as by effort: *he worked off some of his energy by digging the garden.* **2** to discharge (a debt) by labour rather than payment.

work on *vb* (*intr, prep*) to persuade or influence or attempt to persuade or influence.

work out *vb (adv)* **1** *(tr)* to achieve or accomplish by effort. **2** *(tr)* to solve or find out by reasoning or calculation: *to work out an answer; to work out a sum.* **3** *(tr)* to devise or formulate: *to work out a plan.* **4** *(intr)* to prove satisfactory or effective: *did your plan work out?* **5** *(intr)* to happen as specified: *it all worked out well.* **6** *(intr)* to take part in physical exercise, as in training. **7** *(tr)* to remove all the mineral in (a mine, body of ore, etc.) that can be profitably exploited. **8** *(intr; often foll. by to or at)* to reach a total: *your bill works out at a pound.* **9** *(tr) Informal.* to understand the real nature of: *I shall never work you out.* ◆ *n* **work-out. 10** a session of physical exercise, esp. for training or practice.

work over *vb* **1** *(tr, adv)* to do again; repeat. **2** *(intr, prep)* to examine closely and thoroughly. **3** *(tr, adv) Slang.* to assault or thrash.

workpeople ('wɜːk,piːpᵊl) *pl n* the working members of a population, esp. those employed in manual tasks.

workpiece ('wɜːk,piːs) *n* a piece of metal or other material that is in the process of being worked on or made or has actually been cut or shaped by a hand tool or machine.

workplace ('wɜːk,pleɪs) *n* a place, such as a factory or office, where people work.

workroom ('wɜːk,ruːm, -,rʊm) *n* **1** a room in which work, usually manual labour, is done. **2** a room in a house set aside for a hobby, such as sewing.

works (wɜːks) *pl n* **1** *(often functioning as sing)* a place where a number of people are employed, such as a factory. **2** the sum total of a writer's or artist's achievements, esp. when considered together: *the works of Shakespeare.* **3** the deeds of a person, esp. virtuous or moral deeds performed as religious acts: *works of charity.* **4** the interior parts of the mechanism of a machine, etc.: *the works of a clock.* **5 in the works.** *Informal.* in preparation. **6 spanner in the works.** See **spanner** (sense 2). **7 the works.** *Slang.* **7a** full or extreme treatment. **7b** a very violent physical beating: *to give someone the works.* **8** *Slang.* a syringe. **9** *(modifier)* of or denoting a racing car, etc., that is officially entered by a manufacturer in an event: *a works entry.*

works council *n Chiefly Brit.* **1** a council composed of both employer and employees convened to discuss matters of common interest concerning a factory, plant, business policy, etc., not covered by regular trade union agreements. **2** a body representing the workers of a plant, factory, etc., elected to negotiate with the management about working conditions, wages, etc. ◆ Also called: **works committee.**

work-sharing *n* an arrangement whereby one full-time job may be carried out by two people working part time. ▸ **'work-,sharer** *n*

worksheet ('wɜːk,ʃiːt) *n* **1** a sheet of paper used for the preliminary or rough draft of a problem, design, etc. **2** a piece of paper recording work being planned or already in progress. **3** a sheet of paper containing exercises to be completed by a pupil or student.

workshop ('wɜːk,ʃɒp) *n* **1** a room or building in which manufacturing or other forms of manual work are carried on. **2** a room in a private dwelling, school, etc., set aside for crafts. **3** a group of people engaged in study or work on a creative project or subject: *a music workshop.*

workshy ('wɜːk,ʃaɪ) *adj* not inclined to work.

Worksop ('wɜːksɒp) *n* a mining town in N central England, in N Nottinghamshire. Pop.: 37 247 (1991).

work station *n* **1** an area in an office where one person works. **2** *Computing.* a device or component of an electronic office system consisting of a display screen and keyboard used to handle electronic office work.

work-study *n* an examination of ways of finding the most efficient method of doing a job, esp. in terms of time and effort.

worktable ('wɜːk,teɪbᵊl) *n* **a** any table at which writing, sewing, or other work may be done. **b** (in English cabinetwork) a small elegant table fitted with sewing accessories.

work through *vb (tr, adv) Psychol.* to resolve (a problem, esp. an emotional one), by thinking about it repeatedly and hence lessening its intensity either by gaining insight or by becoming bored by it.

worktop ('wɜːk,tɒp) *n* a surface in a kitchen, often of heat-resistant laminated plastic, that is used for food preparation.

work-to-rule *n* **1** a form of industrial action in which employees adhere strictly to all the working rules laid down by their employers, with the deliberate intention of reducing the rate of working. ◆ *vb* **work to rule. 2** *(intr)* to decrease the rate of working by this means.

work up *vb (tr, mainly adv)* **1** to arouse the feelings of; excite. **2** to cause to grow or develop: *to work up a hunger.* **3** *(also prep)* to move or cause to move gradually upwards. **4** to manipulate or mix into a specified object or shape. **5** to gain knowledge of or skill at (a subject).

workwear ('wɜːk,wɛə) *n* clothes, such as overalls, as worn for work in a factory, shop, etc.; working clothes.

workweek ('wɜːk,wiːk) *n* the usual U.S. and Canadian term for **working week.**

world (wɜːld) *n* **1** the earth as a planet, esp. including its inhabitants. **2** mankind; the human race. **3** people generally; the public: *in the eyes of the world.* **4** social or public life: *to go out into the world.* **5** the universe or cosmos; everything in existence. **6** a complex united whole regarded as resembling the universe. **7** any star or planet, esp. one that might be inhabited. **8** *(often cap.)* a division or section of the earth, its history, or its inhabitants: *the Western World; the Ancient World; the Third World.* **9** an area, sphere, or realm considered as a complete environment: *the animal world.* **10** any field of human activity or way of life or those involved in it: *the world of television.* **11** a period or state of existence: *the next world.* **12** the total circumstances and experience of an individual that make up his life, esp. that part of it relating to happiness: *you have shattered my world.* **13** a large amount, number, or distance: *worlds apart.* **14** worldly or secular life, ways, or people. **15** *Logic.* See **possible world. 16 all the world and his wife.** a large group of people of various kinds. **17 bring into the world. 17a** (of a midwife, doctor, etc.) to deliver (a baby). **17b** to give birth to. **18 come into the world.** to be born. **19 dead to the world.** *Informal.* unaware of one's surroundings, esp. fast asleep or very drunk. **20 for the world.** *(used with a negative)* for any inducement, however great. **21 for all the world.** in every way; exactly. **22 give to the world.** to publish. **23 in the world.** (intensifier; *usually used with a negative*): *no-one in the world can change things.* **24 man** (*or* **woman**) **of the world.** a man (or woman) experienced in social or public life. **25 not long for this world.** nearing death. **26 on top of the world.** *Informal.* exultant, elated, or very happy. **27 out of this world.** *Informal.* wonderful; excellent. **28 set the world on fire.** to be exceptionally or sensationally successful. **29 the best of both worlds.** the benefits from two different or opposed ways of life, philosophies, etc. **30 think the world of.** to be extremely fond of or hold in very high esteem. **31 world of one's own.** a state of mental detachment from other people. **32 world without end.** for ever. **33** *(modifier)* of or concerning most or all countries; worldwide: *world politics; a world record.* **34** *(in combination)* throughout the world: *world-famous.* [Old English *w(e)orold,* from *wer* man + *ald* age, life; related to Old Frisian *warld, wrald,* Old Norse *verold,* Old High German *wealt* (German *Welt*)]

World Bank *n* an international cooperative organization established in 1945 under the Bretton Woods Agreement to assist economic development, esp. of backward nations, by the advance of loans guaranteed by member governments. Officially called: **International Bank for Reconstruction and Development.**

World Bank Group *n* the collective name for the International Bank for Reconstruction and Development, the International Finance Corporation, and the International Development Association, whose headquarters are all in Washington.

world-beater *n* a person or thing that surpasses all others in its category; champion. ▸ **'world-,beating** *n, adj*

world-class *adj* of or denoting someone with a skill or attribute that puts him or her in the highest class in the world: *a world-class swimmer.*

World Council of Churches *n* the ecumenical fellowship of Churches other than the Roman Catholic Church, formally constituted at Amsterdam in 1948 for coordinated action in theological, ecclesiastical, and secular matters.

World Court *n* another name for **International Court of Justice.**

World Cup *n* an international competition held between national teams in various sports, most notably association football.

World Health Organization *n* an agency of the United Nations, established in 1948 with headquarters in Geneva, responsible for coordinating international health activities, aiding governments in improving health services, etc. Abbrev.: **WHO.**

world language *n* **1** a language spoken and known in many countries, such as English. **2** an artificial language for international use, such as Esperanto.

world-line *n Physics.* a line on a space–time path that shows the path of a body.

worldling ('wɜːldlɪŋ) *n* a person who is primarily concerned with worldly matters or material things.

worldly ('wɜːldlɪ) *adj* **-lier, -liest. 1** not spiritual; mundane or temporal. **2** Also: **worldly-minded.** absorbed in or concerned with material things or matters that are immediately relevant. **3** Also: **worldly-wise.** versed in the ways of the world; sophisticated. **4** *Archaic.* existing on or relating to the earth. **5** *Obsolete.* secular; lay. ◆ *adv* **6** *Archaic.* in a worldly manner. ▸ **'worldliness** *n*

world music *n* popular music of various ethnic origins and styles outside the tradition of Western pop and rock music.

world power *n* a state that possesses sufficient power to influence events throughout the world.

World Series *or* **World's Series** *n Baseball.* (in the U.S.) a best-of-seven playoff for the world championship between the two winning teams in the major leagues at the end of the season.

world-shaking *adj* of enormous significance; momentous.

World Trade Organization *n* an international body concerned with promoting and regulating trade between its member states; established in 1995 as a successor to GATT.

world-view *n* another word for **Weltanschauung.**

World War I *n* the war (1914–18), fought mainly in Europe and the Middle East, in which the Allies (principally France, Russia, Britain, Italy after 1915, and the U.S. after 1917) defeated the Central Powers (principally Germany, Austria-Hungary, and Turkey). The war was precipitated by the assassination of Austria's crown prince (Archduke Franz Ferdinand) at Sarajevo on June 28, 1914 and swiftly developed its major front in E France, where millions died in static trench warfare. After the October Revolution (1917) the Bolsheviks ended Russian participation in the war (Dec. 15, 1917). The exhausted Central Powers agreed to an armistice on Nov. 11, 1918 and quickly succumbed to internal revolution, before being forced to sign the Treaty of Versailles (June 28, 1919) and other treaties. Also called: **First World War, Great War.**

World War II *n* the war (1939–45) in which the Allies (principally Britain, the Soviet Union, and the U.S.) defeated the Axis powers (principally Germany, Italy, and Japan). Britain and France declared war on Germany (Sept. 3, 1939) as a result of the German invasion of Poland (Sept. 1, 1939). Italy entered the war on June 10, 1940 shortly before the collapse of France (armistice signed June 22, 1940). On June 22, 1941 Germany attacked the Soviet Union and on Dec. 7, 1941 the Japanese attacked the U.S. at Pearl Harbor. On Sept. 8, 1943 Italy surrendered, the war in Europe ending on May 7, 1945 with the unconditional surrender of the Germans. The Japanese capitulated on Aug. 14, 1945 as a direct result of the atomic bombs dropped by the Americans on Hiroshima and Nagasaki. Also called: **Second World War.**

world-weary *adj* no longer finding pleasure in living; tired of the world. ▸ **'world-,weariness** *n*

worldwide (ˈwɜːldˈwaɪd) *adj* applying or extending throughout the world; universal.

World Wide Web *n Computing.* a vast network of linked hypertext files, stored on computers throughout the world, that can provide a computer user with information on a huge variety of subjects. Abbrev.: **WWW.**

worm (wɜːm) *n* **1** any of various invertebrates, esp. the annelids (earthworms, etc.), nematodes (roundworms), and flatworms, having a slender elongated body. Related adj: **vermicular. 2** any of various insect larvae having an elongated body, such as the silkworm and wireworm. **3** any of various unrelated animals that resemble annelids, nematodes, etc., such as the glow-worm and shipworm. **4** a gnawing or insinuating force or agent that torments or slowly eats away. **5** a wretched or spineless person. **6** anything that resembles a worm in appearance or movement. **7** a shaft on which a helical groove has been cut, as in a gear arrangement in which such a shaft meshes with a toothed wheel. **8** a spiral pipe cooled by air or flowing water, used as a condenser in a still. **9** a nontechnical name for **lytta. 10** *Anatomy.* any wormlike organ, structure, or part, such as the middle lobe of the cerebellum (*vermis cerebelli*). Technical name: **vermis. 11** *Computing.* a program that duplicates itself many times in a network and prevents its destruction. It often carries a logic bomb or virus. ◆ *vb* **12** to move, act, or cause to move or act with the slow sinuous movement of a worm. **13** (foll. by *in, into, out of,* etc.) to make (one's way) slowly and stealthily; insinuate (oneself). **14** (*tr;* often foll. by *out of* or *from*) to extract (information, a secret, etc.) from by persistent questioning. **15** (*tr*) to free from or purge of worms. **16** (*tr*) *Nautical.* to wind yarn around (a rope) so as to fill the spaces between the strands and render the surface smooth for parcelling and serving. ◆ See also **worms.** [Old English *wyrm;* related to Old Frisian *wirm,* Old High German *wurm,* Old Norse *ormr,* Gothic *waurms,* Latin *vermis,* Greek *romos* woodworm] ▸ **ˈwormer** *n* ▸ **ˈwormˌlike** *or* **ˈwormish** *adj*

WORM (wɜːm) *n Computers. acronym for* write once read many times: an optical disk that enables users to store data but not change it.

wormcast (ˈwɜːmˌkɑːst) *n* a coil of earth or sand that has been egested by a burrowing earthworm or lugworm.

worm conveyor *n* another name for **screw conveyor.**

worm-eaten *adj* **1** eaten into by worms: *a worm-eaten table.* **2** decayed; rotten. **3** old-fashioned; antiquated.

wormery (ˈwɜːmərɪ) *n, pl* **-eries. 1** a piece of apparatus, having a glass side or sides, in which worms are kept for study. **2** a container in which worms are kept and bred, esp. for fishing bait.

wormfly (ˈwɜːmˌflaɪ) *n Angling.* a type of lure dressed on a double hook, the barbs of which sit one above the other and back-to-back.

worm gear *n* **1** a device consisting of a threaded shaft (**worm**) that mates with a gearwheel (**worm wheel**) so that rotary motion can be transferred between two shafts at right angles to each other. **2** Also called: **worm wheel.** a gearwheel driven by a threaded shaft or worm.

wormhole (ˈwɜːmˌhəʊl) *n* **1** a hole made by a worm in timber, plants, etc. **2** *Physics.* a tunnel in the geometry of space–time postulated to connect different parts of the universe. ▸ **ˈwormˌholed** *adj*

worm lizard *n* any wormlike burrowing legless lizard of the family *Amphisbaenidae,* of Africa, South and Central America, and S Europe.

worms (wɜːmz) *n* (*functioning as sing*) any disease or disorder, usually of the intestine, characterized by infestation with parasitic worms.

Worms (wɜːmz; *German* vɔrms) *n* a city in SW Germany, in Rhineland-Palatinate on the Rhine: famous as the seat of imperial diets, notably that of 1521, before which Luther defended his doctrines in the presence of Charles V; river port and manufacturing centre with a large wine trade. Pop.: 77 430 (1991).

wormseed (ˈwɜːmˌsiːd) *n* **1** any of various plants having seeds or other parts used in medicine to treat worm infestation, esp. an American chenopodiaceous plant, *Chenopodium anthelminticum* (or *C. ambrosioides*) (**American wormseed**), and the santonica plant. **2** the part of any of these plants that is used as an anthelmintic.

worm's eye view *n* a view seen from below or from a more lowly or humble point.

wormwood (ˈwɜːmˌwʊd) *n* **1** Also called: **absinthe.** any of various plants of the chiefly N temperate genus *Artemisia,* esp. *A. absinthium,* a European plant yielding a bitter extract used in making absinthe: family *Compositae* (composites). **2** something that embitters, such as a painful experience. [C15: changed (through influence of WORM and WOOD[1]) from Old English *wormōd, wermōd;* related to Old High German *wermuata,* German *Wermut;* see VERMOUTH]

wormy (ˈwɜːmɪ) *adj* **wormier, wormiest. 1** worm-infested or worm-eaten. **2** resembling a worm in appearance, ways, or condition. **3** (of wood) having irregular small tunnels bored into it and tracked over its surface, made either by worms or artificially. **4** low or grovelling. ▸ **ˈworminess** *n*

worn (wɔːn) *vb* **1** the past participle of **wear.** ◆ *adj* **2** affected, esp. adversely, by long use or action: *a worn suit.* **3** haggard; drawn. **4** exhausted; spent. ▸ **ˈwornness** *n*

worn-out *adj* (**worn out** *when postpositive*). **1** worn or used until threadbare, valueless, or useless. **2** exhausted; very weary.

worriment (ˈwʌrɪmənt) *n Informal, chiefly U.S. and Canadian.* anxiety or the trouble that causes it; worry.

worrisome (ˈwʌrɪsəm) *adj* **1** causing worry; vexing. **2** tending to worry. ▸ **ˈworrisomely** *adv*

worrit (ˈwʌrɪt) *vb* (*tr*) *Dialect.* to tease or worry. [probably variant of WORRY, but compare WHERRIT]

worry (ˈwʌrɪ) *vb* **-ries, -rying, -ried. 1** to be or cause to be anxious or uneasy, esp. about something uncertain or potentially dangerous. **2** (*tr*) to disturb the peace of mind of; bother: *don't worry me with trivialities.* **3** (*intr;* often foll. by *along* or *through*) to proceed despite difficulties. **4** (*intr;* often foll. by *away*) to struggle or work: *to worry away at a problem.* **5** (*tr*) (of a dog, wolf, etc.) to lacerate or kill by biting, shaking, etc. **6** (when *intr,* foll. by *at*) to bite, tear, or gnaw (at) with the teeth: *a dog worrying a bone.* **7** (*tr*) to move as specified, esp. by repeated pushes: *they worried the log into the river.* **8** (*tr*) to touch or poke repeatedly and idly. **9** *Obsolete.* to choke or cause to choke. **10 not to worry.** *Informal.* you need not worry. ◆ *n, pl* **-ries. 11** a state or feeling of anxiety. **12** a person or thing that causes anxiety. **13** an act of worrying. [Old English *wyrgan;* related to Old Frisian *wergia* to kill, Old High German *wurgen* (German (*er*)*würgen* to strangle), Old Norse *virgill, urga* rope] ▸ **ˈworried** *adj* ▸ **ˈworriedly** *adv* ▸ **ˈworrying** *adj* ▸ **ˈworryingly** *adv*

worry beads *pl n* a string of beads that when fingered or played with supposedly relieves nervous tension.

worryguts (ˈwʌrɪˌgʌts) *or* **worrywart** (ˈwʌrɪˌwɔːt) *n Informal.* a person who tends to worry, esp. about insignificant matters.

worse (wɜːs) *adj* **1** the comparative of **bad. 2 none the worse for.** not harmed by (adverse events or circumstances). **3 the worse for wear. 3a** shabby or worn. **3b** a slang term for **drunk. 4 worse luck!** *Informal.* unhappily; unfortunately. **5** (*postpositive*) **worse off.** in a worse, esp. a worse financial, condition. ◆ *n* **6** something that is worse. **7 for the worse.** into a less desirable or inferior state or condition: *a change for the worse.* **8 go from bad to worse.** to deteriorate even more. ◆ *adv* **9** in a more severe or unpleasant manner. **10** in a less effective or successful manner. [Old English *wiersa;* related to Old Frisian *werra,* Old High German *wirsiro,* Old Norse *verri,* Gothic *wairsiza*]

worsen (ˈwɜːsᵊn) *vb* to grow or cause to grow worse.

worser (ˈwɜːsə) *adj* an archaic or nonstandard word for **worse.**

worship (ˈwɜːʃɪp) *vb* **-ships, -shipping, -shipped** *or U.S.* **-ships, -shiping, -shiped. 1** (*tr*) to show profound religious devotion and respect to; adore or venerate (God or any person or thing considered divine). **2** (*tr*) to be devoted to and full of admiration for. **3** (*intr*) to have or express feelings of profound adoration. **4** (*intr*) to attend services for worship. **5** (*tr*) *Obsolete.* to honour. ◆ *n* **6** religious adoration or devotion. **7** the formal expression of religious adoration; rites, prayers, etc. **8** admiring love or devotion. **9** *Archaic.* dignity or standing. [Old English *weorthscipe,* from WORTH[1] + -SHIP] ▸ **ˈworshipable** *adj* ▸ **ˈworshipper** *n*

Worship (ˈwɜːʃɪp) *n Chiefly Brit.* (preceded by *Your, His,* or *Her*) a title used to address or refer to a mayor, magistrate, or a person of similar high rank.

worshipful (ˈwɜːʃɪpfʊl) *adj* **1** feeling or showing reverence or adoration. **2** (*often cap.*) *Chiefly Brit.* a title used to address or refer to various people or bodies of distinguished rank, such as mayors and certain ancient companies of the City of London. ▸ **ˈworshipfully** *adv* ▸ **ˈworshipfulness** *n*

worst (wɜːst) *adj* **1** the superlative of **bad.** ◆ *adv* **2** in the most extreme or bad manner or degree. **3** least well, suitably, or acceptably. **4** (*in combination*) in or to the smallest degree or extent; least: *worst-loved.* ◆ *n* **5 the worst.** the least good or most inferior person, thing, or part in a group, narrative, etc. **6** (often preceded by *at*) the most poor, unpleasant, or unskilled quality or condition: *television is at its worst these days.* **7** the greatest amount of damage or wickedness of which a person or group is capable: *the invaders came and did their worst.* **8** the weakest effort or poorest achievement that a person or group is capable of making: *the applicant did his worst at the test because he did not want the job.* **9 at worst. 9a** in the least favourable interpretation or view. **9b** under the least favourable conditions. **10 if the worst comes to the worst.** if all the more desirable alternatives become impossible or if the worst possible thing happens. **11 come off worst** *or* **get the worst of it.** to enjoy the least benefit from an issue or be defeated in it. ◆ *vb* **12** (*tr*) to get the advantage over; defeat or beat. [Old English *wierrest;* related to Old Frisian *wersta,* Old Saxon, Old High German *wirsisto,* Old Norse *verstr*]

worst case *n* **a** a situation in which the most unfavourable conditions prevail. **b** (*as modifier*): *a worst-case projection of a massive accident.*

worsted (ˈwʊstɪd) *n* **1** a closely twisted yarn or thread made from combed long-staple wool. **2** a fabric made from this, with a hard smooth close-textured surface and no nap. **3** (*modifier*) made of this yarn or fabric: *a worsted suit.* [C13: named after *Worstead,* a district in Norfolk]

wort (wɜːt) *n* **1** (*in combination*) any of various unrelated plants, esp. ones formerly used to cure diseases: *liverwort; spleenwort.* **2** the sweet liquid obtained from the soaked mixture of warm water and ground malt, used to make a malt liquor. [Old English *wyrt* root, related to Old High German *warz,* Gothic *waurts* root]

worth[1] (wɜːθ) *adj* (governing a noun with prepositional force) **1** worthy of; meriting or justifying: *it's not worth discussing; an idea worth some thought.* **2** having a value of: *the book is worth 30 pounds.* **3 for all one is worth.** to the utmost; to the full extent of one's powers or ability. **4 worth one's weight in gold.** extremely helpful, kind, etc. ◆ *n* **5** high quality; excellence. **6** value, price. **7** the amount or quantity of something of a specified value: *five pounds worth of petrol.* [Old English *weorth;* related to Old Saxon, Old High German *werth* (German *Wert*), Old Norse *verthr,* Gothic *wairths*]

worth[2] (wɜːθ) *vb* (*intr*) *Archaic.* to happen or betide (esp. in the phrase **woe worth the day**). [Old English *weorthan;* related to Old Frisian *wertha,* Old Saxon, Old High German *werthan* (German *werden*), Old Norse *vertha,* Gothic *wairthan,* Latin *vertere* to turn]

Worth (wɜːθ; *French* vɔrt) *n* **Charles Frederick.** 1825–95, English couturier, who founded Parisian *haute couture.*

Worthing (ˈwɜːðɪŋ) *n* a resort in S England, in West Sussex on the English Channel. Pop.: 95 732 (1991).

worthless (ˈwɜːθlɪs) *adj* **1** without practical value or usefulness. **2** without merit; good-for-nothing. ▸ **ˈworthlessly** *adv* ▸ **ˈworthlessness** *n*

worthwhile (ˌwɜːθˈwaɪl) *adj* sufficiently important, rewarding, or valuable to justify time or effort spent.

worthy (ˈwɜːðɪ) *adj* **-thier, -thiest. 1** (*postpositive;* often foll. by *of* or an infinitive) having sufficient merit or value (for something or someone specified); deserving. **2** having worth, value, or merit. ◆ *n, pl* **-thies**. **3** *Often facetious*. a person of distinguished character, merit, or importance. ► '**worthily** *adv* ► '**worthiness** *n*

wot (wɒt) *vb Archaic or dialect*. (used with *I, she, he, it*, or a singular noun) a form of the present tense (indicative mood) of **wit**[2].

Wotan ('vəʊtɑːn, 'vɔː-) *n* the supreme god in Germanic mythology. Norse counterpart: **Odin**.

wotcher ('wɒtʃə) *sentence substitute*. a slang term of greeting (esp. in the phrase **wotcher cock!**). [C19: Cockney for *what cheer?*]

Wotton ('wɒtᵊn, 'wʊtᵊn) *n* **Henry**. 1568–1639, English poet and diplomat.

would (wʊd; *unstressed* wəd) *vb* (takes an infinitive without *to* or an implied infinitive) used as an auxiliary: **1** to form the past tense or subjunctive mood of **will**[1]. **2** (with *you, he, she, it, they*, or a noun as subject) to indicate willingness or desire in a polite manner: *would you help me, please?* **3** to describe a past action as being accustomed or habitual: *every day we would go for walks*. **4** I wish: *would that he were here*.

USAGE See at **should**.

would-be *adj* (*prenominal*) **1** *Usually derogatory*. wanting or professing to be: *a would-be politician*. **2** intended to be: *would-be generosity*. ◆ *n* **3** *Derogatory*. a person who wants or professes to be something that he is not.

wouldn't ('wʊdᵊnt) *vb contraction of* would not.

wouldst (wʊdst) *vb Archaic or dialect*. (used with the pronoun *thou* or its relative equivalent) a singular form of the past tense of **will**[1].

Woulfe bottle (wʊlf) *n Chem*. a bottle with more than one neck, used for passing gases through liquids. [C18: named after Peter *Woulfe* (?1727–1803), English chemist]

wound[1] (wuːnd) *n* **1** any break in the skin or an organ or part as the result of violence or a surgical incision. **2** an injury to plant tissue. **3** any injury or slight to the feelings or reputation. ◆ *vb* **4** to inflict a wound or wounds upon (someone or something). [Old English *wund;* related to Old Frisian *wunde*, Old High German *wunta* (German *Wunde*), Old Norse *und*, Gothic *wunds*] ► '**woundable** *adj* ► '**wounder** *n* ► '**wounding** *adj* ► '**woundingly** *adv* ► '**woundless** *adj*

wound[2] (waʊnd) *vb* the past tense and past participle of **wind**[2].

wounded ('wuːndɪd) *adj* **1a** suffering from wounds; injured, esp. in a battle or fight. **1b** (*as collective n;* preceded by *the*): *the wounded*. **2** (of feelings) damaged or hurt.

woundwort ('wuːnd,wɜːt) *n* **1** any of various plants of the genus *Stachys*, such as *S. arvensis* (**field woundwort**), having purple, scarlet, yellow, or white flowers and formerly used for dressing wounds: family *Labiatae* (labiates). **2** any of various other plants used in this way.

wove (wəʊv) *vb* a past tense of **weave**.

woven ('wəʊvᵊn) *vb* a past participle of **weave**.

wove paper *n* paper with a very faint mesh impressed on it by the dandy roller on the paper-making machine. Compare **laid paper**.

wow[1] (waʊ) *interj* **1** an exclamation of admiration, amazement, etc. ◆ *n* **2** *Slang*. a person or thing that is amazingly successful, attractive, etc. ◆ *vb* **3** (*tr*) *Slang*. to arouse great enthusiasm in. [C16: originally Scottish, expressive of surprise, amazement, etc.]

wow[2] (waʊ, wəʊ) *n* a slow variation or distortion in pitch that occurs at very low audio frequencies in sound-reproducing systems, such as a record player, usually due to variation in speed of the turntable, etc. See also **flutter** (sense 14). [C20: of imitative origin]

WOW *abbrev. for* waiting on weather: used esp. in the oil industry.

wowser ('waʊzə) *n Austral. and N.Z. slang*. **1** a fanatically puritanical person. **2** a teetotaller. [C20: from English dialect *wow* to whine, complain]

WP *abbrev. for:* **1** weather permitting. **2** word processing. **3** word processor.

WPA (in the U.S.) *abbrev. for* Work Projects Administration or Works Progress Administration.

W particle *n Physics*. a type of elementary particle with either a positive or negative charge considered to transmit the weak interaction between other elementary particles. W particles have a rest mass of about 10^{-25} kg. Also called: **W boson**. See also **Z particle**.

WPB *or* **wpb** *abbrev. for* waste paper basket.

WPC (in Britain) *abbrev. for* woman police constable.

wpm *abbrev. for* words per minute.

WR *abbrev. for* Western Region.

Wraac (ræk) *n* a member of the Women's Royal Australian Army Corps.

WRAAC *abbrev. for* Women's Royal Australian Army Corps.

WRAAF *abbrev. for* Women's Royal Australian Air Force.

WRAC (in Britain) *abbrev. for* Women's Royal Army Corps.

wrack[1] *or* **rack** (ræk) *n* **1** collapse or destruction (esp. in the phrase **wrack and ruin**). **2** something destroyed or a remnant of such. ◆ *vb* **3** a variant spelling of **rack**[1]. [Old English *wræc* persecution, misery; related to Gothic *wraka*, Old Norse *rāk*. Compare WRECK, WRETCH]

USAGE The use of the spelling *wrack* rather than *rack* in sentences such as *she was wracked by grief* or *the country was wracked by civil war* is very common but is thought by many people to be incorrect.

wrack[2] (ræk) *n* **1** seaweed or other marine vegetation that is floating in the sea or has been cast ashore. **2** any of various seaweeds of the genus *Fucus*, such as *F. serratus* (**serrated wrack**). **3** *Literary or dialect*. **3a** a wreck or piece of wreckage. **3b** a remnant or fragment of something destroyed. [C14 (in the sense: a wrecked ship, wreckage, hence later applied to marine vegetation washed ashore): perhaps from Middle Dutch *wrak* wreckage; the term corresponds to Old English *wræc* WRACK[1]]

WRAF (in Britain) *abbrev. for* Women's Royal Air Force.

wraith (reɪθ) *n* **1** the apparition of a person living or thought to be alive, supposed to appear around the time of his death. **2** a ghost or any apparition. **3** an insubstantial copy of something. **4** something pale, thin, and lacking in substance, such as a column of smoke. [C16: Scottish, of unknown origin] ► '**wraith,like** *adj*

Wran (ræn) *n* a member of the Women's Royal Australian Naval Service.

wrang (ræŋ) *adj, adv, n, vb* a Scot. word for **wrong**.

Wrangel Island ('ræŋgᵊl) *n* an island in the Arctic Ocean, off the coast of the extreme NE of Russia: administratively part of Russia; mountainous and mostly tundra. Area: about 7300 sq. km (2800 sq. miles).

Wrangell ('ræŋgᵊl) *n* **Mount**. a mountain in S Alaska, in the W Wrangell Mountains. Height: 4269 m (14 005 ft.).

Wrangell Mountains *pl n* a mountain range in SE Alaska, extending into the Yukon, Canada. Highest peak: Mount Blackburn, 5037 m (16 523 ft.).

wrangle ('ræŋgᵊl) *vb* **1** (*intr*) to argue, esp. noisily or angrily. **2** (*tr*) to encourage, persuade, or obtain by argument. **3** (*tr*) *Western U.S. and Canadian*. to herd (cattle or horses). ◆ *n* **4** a noisy or angry argument. [C14: from Low German *wrangeln;* related to Norwegian *vrangla*]

wrangler ('ræŋglə) *n* **1** one who wrangles. **2** *Western U.S. and Canadian*. a herder; cowboy. **3** a person who handles or controls animals involved in the making of a film or television programme: *a snake wrangler*. **4** *Brit*. (at Cambridge University) a candidate who has obtained first-class honours in Part II of the mathematics tripos. The wrangler with the highest marks is called the **senior wrangler**.

WRANS *abbrev. for* Women's Royal Australian Naval Service.

wrap (ræp) *vb* **wraps, wrapping, wrapped**. (*mainly tr*) **1** to fold or wind (paper, cloth, etc.) around (a person or thing) so as to cover. **2** (often foll. by *up*) to fold paper, etc., around to fasten securely. **3** to surround or conceal by surrounding. **4** to enclose, immerse, or absorb: *wrapped in sorrow*. **5** to fold, wind, or roll up. **6** (*intr;* often foll. by *about, around*, etc.) to be or become wound or extended. **7** to complete the filming of (a motion picture or television programme). **8** (often foll. by *up*) Also: **rap**. *Austral. informal*. to praise (someone). ◆ *n* **9** a garment worn wrapped around the body, esp. the shoulders, such as a shawl or cloak. **10** short for **wrapround** (sense 5). **11** *Chiefly U.S.* wrapping or a wrapper. **12** Also called: **rap**. *Austral. informal*. a commendation. **13a** the end of a working day during the filming of a motion picture or television programme. **13b** the completion of filming of a motion picture or television programme. **14 keep under wraps**. to keep secret. **15 take the wraps off**. to reveal. [C14: origin unknown]

wraparound ('ræpə,raʊnd) *n Computing*. another name for **word wrapping**.

wrapover ('ræp,əʊvə) *or* **wrapround** *adj* **1** (of a garment, esp. a skirt) not sewn up at one side, but worn wrapped round the body and fastened so that the open edges overlap. ◆ *n* **2** such a garment.

wrapped (ræpt) *vb* **1** the past tense and past participle of **wrap**. ◆ *adj* **2** *Austral. and N.Z. informal*. a variant spelling of **rapt**[2]. **3 wrapped up in**. *Informal*. **3a** completely absorbed or engrossed in. **3b** implicated or involved in.

wrapper ('ræpə) *n* **1** the cover, usually of paper or cellophane, in which something is wrapped. **2** a dust jacket of a book. **3** the ripe firm tobacco leaf forming the outermost portion of a cigar and wound around its body. **4** a loose negligee or dressing gown, esp. in the 19th century.

wrapping ('ræpɪŋ) *n* the material used to wrap something.

wrapround ('ræp,raʊnd) *or* **wraparound** ('ræpə,raʊnd) *adj* **1** made so as to be wrapped round something: *a wrapround skirt*. **2** surrounding, curving round, or overlapping. **3** curving round in one continuous piece: *a wrapround windscreen*. ◆ *n* **4** *Printing*. a flexible plate of plastic, metal, or rubber that is made flat but used wrapped round the plate cylinder of a rotary press. **5** Also called: **outsert**. *Printing*. a separately printed sheet folded around a section for binding. Sometimes shortened to **wrap**. **6** a slip of paper folded round the dust jacket of a book to announce a price reduction, special offer, etc. **7** another name for **wrapover**.

wrap up *vb* (*adv*) **1** (*tr*) to fold paper around. **2** to put warm clothes on. **3** (*usually imperative*) *Slang*. to be silent. **4** (*tr*) *Informal*. **4a** to settle the final details of. **4b** to make a summary of.

wrasse (ræs) *n* any marine percoid fish of the family *Labridae*, of tropical and temperate seas, having thick lips, strong teeth, and usually a bright coloration: many are used as food fishes. [C17: from Cornish *wrach;* related to Welsh *gwrach* old woman]

wrath (rɒθ) *n* **1** angry, violent, or stern indignation. **2** divine vengeance or retribution. **3** *Archaic*. a fit of anger or an act resulting from anger. ◆ *adj* **4** *Obsolete*. incensed; angry. [Old English *wrǣththu;* see WROTH] ► '**wrathless** *adj*

Wrath (rɒθ, rɔːθ) *n* **Cape**. a promontory at the NW extremity of the Scottish mainland.

wrathful ('rɒθfʊl) *adj* **1** full of wrath; raging or furious. **2** resulting from or expressing wrath. ◆ Also (informal): '**wrathy**. ► '**wrathfully** *adv* ► '**wrathfulness** *n*

wreak (riːk) *vb* (*tr*) **1** to inflict (vengeance, etc.) or to cause (chaos, etc.): *to wreak havoc on the enemy*. **2** to express, or gratify (anger, hatred, etc.). **3** *Archaic*. to take vengeance for. [Old English *wrecan;* related to Old Frisian *wreka*, Old High German *rehhan* (German *rächen*), Old Norse *reka*, Latin *urgēre* to push] ► '**wreaker** *n*

USAGE See at **wrought**.

wreath (riːθ) *n, pl* **wreaths** (riːðz, riːθs). **1** a band of flowers or foliage intertwined into a ring, usually placed on a grave as a memorial or worn on the head as a garland or a mark of honour. **2** any circular or spiral band or formation. **3** a spiral or circular defect appearing in porcelain and glassware. [Old English *wrǣth, wrǣd;* related to Middle Low German *wrēden* to twist. See WRITHE] ► '**wreathless** *adj* ► '**wreath,like** *adj*

wreathe (riːð) *vb* **1** to form into or take the form of a wreath by intertwining or twisting together. **2** (*tr*) to decorate, crown, or encircle with wreaths. **3** to move or cause to move in a twisting way: *smoke wreathed up to the ceiling.* [C16: perhaps back formation from *wrēthen,* from Old English *writhen,* past participle of *wrīthan* to WRITHE; see WREATH]

wreck (rɛk) *vb* **1** to involve in or suffer disaster or destruction. **2** (*tr*) to cause the wreck of (a ship). ◆ *n* **3a** the accidental destruction of a ship at sea. **3b** the ship so destroyed. **4** *Maritime law.* goods cast ashore from a wrecked vessel. **5** a person or thing that has suffered ruin or dilapidation. **6** Also called: '**wreckage.** the remains of something that has been destroyed. **7** Also called: '**wreckage.** the act of wrecking or the state of being wrecked; ruin or destruction. [C13: from Scandinavian; compare Icelandic *rek.* See WRACK², WREAK]

wrecked (rɛkt) *adj Slang.* in a state of intoxication, stupor, or euphoria, induced by drugs or alcohol.

wrecker ('rɛkə) *n* **1** a person or thing that ruins or destroys. **2** *Chiefly U.S. and Canadian.* a person whose job is to demolish buildings or dismantle cars. **3** (formerly) a person who lures ships to destruction to plunder the wreckage. **4** a U.S. and Canadian name for **breakdown van.**

wreckfish ('rɛk,fɪʃ) *n, pl* **-fish** *or* **-fishes.** another name for **stone bass.** [so called because it is often found near wrecked ships]

wreckful ('rɛkfʊl) *adj Poetic.* causing wreckage.

wrecking bar *n* a short crowbar, forked at one end and slightly angled at the other to make a fulcrum.

Wrekin ('riːkɪn) *n* **1 the.** an isolated hill in the English Midlands in Shropshire. Height: 400 m (1335 ft.). **2** **(all) round the Wrekin.** *Midland English dialect.* the long way round: *he went all round the Wrekin instead of explaining clearly.*

wren (rɛn) *n* **1** any small brown passerine songbird of the chiefly American family *Troglodytidae,* esp. *Troglodytes troglodytes* (**wren** in Britain, **winter wren** in the U.S. and Canada). They have a slender bill and feed on insects. **2** any of various similar birds of the families *Muscicapidae* (Australian warblers), *Xenicidae* (New Zealand wrens), etc. [Old English *wrenna, werna;* related to Old High German *wrendo, rentilo,* Old Norse *rindill*]

Wren¹ (rɛn) *n Informal.* (in Britain and certain other nations) a member of the Women's Royal Naval Service. [C20: from the abbreviation *WRNS*]

Wren² (rɛn) *n* Sir **Christopher.** 1632–1723, English architect. He designed St Paul's Cathedral and over 50 other London churches after the Great Fire as well as many secular buildings.

wrench (rɛntʃ) *vb* **1** to give (something) a sudden or violent twist or pull esp. so as to remove (something) from that to which it is attached: *to wrench a door off its hinges.* **2** (*tr*) to twist suddenly so as to sprain (a limb): *to wrench one's ankle.* **3** (*tr*) to give pain to. **4** (*tr*) to twist from the original meaning or purpose. **5** (*intr*) to make a sudden twisting motion. ◆ *n* **6** a forceful twist or pull. **7** an injury to a limb, caused by twisting. **8** sudden pain caused esp. by parting. **9** a parting that is difficult or painful to make. **10** a distorting of the original meaning or purpose. **11** a spanner, esp. one with adjustable jaws. See also **torque wrench.** [Old English *wrencan;* related to Old High German *renken,* Lithuanian *rangyti* to twist. See WRINKLE¹]

wrest (rɛst) *vb* (*tr*) **1** to take or force away by violent pulling or twisting. **2** to seize forcibly by violent or unlawful means. **3** to obtain by laborious effort. **4** to distort in meaning, purpose, etc. ◆ *n* **5** the act or an instance of wresting. **6** *Archaic.* a small key used to tune a piano or harp. [Old English *wrǣstan;* related to Old Norse *reista.* See WRITHE] ▸ '**wrester** *n*

wrestle ('rɛsᵊl) *vb* **1** to fight (another person) by holding, throwing, etc., without punching with the closed fist. **2** (*intr*) to participate in wrestling. **3** (when *intr,* foll. by *with* or *against*) to fight with (a person, problem, or thing): *wrestle with one's conscience.* **4** (*tr*) to move laboriously, as with wrestling movements. **5** (*tr*) *U.S. and Canadian.* to throw (an animal) for branding. ◆ *n* **6** the act of wrestling. **7** a struggle or tussle. [Old English *wrǣstlian;* related to Middle Dutch *wrastelen* (Dutch *worstelen*), Old Norse *rost* current, race] ▸ '**wrestler** *n*

wrestling ('rɛslɪŋ) *n* any of certain sports in which the contestants fight each other according to various rules governing holds and usually forbidding blows with the closed fist. The principal object is to overcome the opponent either by throwing or pinning him to the ground or by causing him to submit. See **freestyle, Graeco-Roman, sumo.**

wrest pin *n* (on a piano, harp, etc.) a pin around which one end of a string is wound: it may be turned by means of a tuning key to alter the tension of the string. In a piano the wrest pin is embedded in the **wrest plank.**

wretch (rɛtʃ) *n* **1** a despicable person. **2** a person pitied for his misfortune. [Old English *wrecca;* related to Old Saxon *wrekkeo,* Old High German *reccheo* (German *Recke* warrior), Old Norse *rek(n)ingr*]

wretched ('rɛtʃɪd) *adj* **1** in poor or pitiful circumstances. **2** characterized by or causing misery. **3** despicable; base. **4** poor, inferior, or paltry. **5** (*prenominal*) (intensifier qualifying something undesirable): *a wretched nuisance.* ▸ '**wretchedly** *adv* ▸ '**wretchedness** *n*

Wrexham ('rɛksəm) *n* **1** a town in N Wales, in Wrexham county borough: seat of the Roman Catholic bishopric of Wales (except the former Glamorganshire); formerly noted for coal-mining. Pop.: 40 614 (1991). **2** a county borough in NE Wales, created in 1996 from part of Clwyd. Pop.: 123 400 (1996 est.). Area: 500 sq. km (193 sq. miles).

wrick (rɪk) *vb* a variant spelling (chiefly Brit.) of **rick**². [C19: earlier *rick;* perhaps from Middle Low German *wricken* to move jerkily, sprain]

wrier *or* **wryer** ('raɪə) *adj* the comparative of **wry.**

wriest *or* **wryest** ('raɪɪst) *adj* the superlative of **wry.**

wriggle ('rɪgᵊl) *vb* **1** to make or cause to make twisting movements. **2** (*intr*) to progress by twisting and turning. **3** (*intr;* foll. by *into* or *out of*) to manoeuvre oneself by clever or devious means: *wriggle out of an embarrassing situation.* ◆ *n* **4** a wriggling movement or action. **5** a sinuous marking or course. [C15: from Middle Low German; compare Dutch *wriggelen*] ▸ '**wriggler** *n* ▸ '**wriggly** *adj*

wright (raɪt) *n* (*now chiefly in combination*) a person who creates, builds, or repairs something specified: *a playwright; a shipwright.* [Old English *wryhta, wyrhta;* related to Old Frisian *wrichta,* Old Saxon, Old High German *wurhtio.* See WORK]

Wright (raɪt) *n* **1 Frank Lloyd.** 1869–1959, U.S. architect, whose designs include the Imperial Hotel, Tokyo (1916), the Guggenheim Museum, New York (1943), and many private houses. His "organic architecture" sought a close relationship between buildings and their natural surroundings. **2 Joseph,** known as *Wright of Derby.* 1734–97, British painter, noted for his paintings of industrial and scientific subjects, esp. *The Orrery* (?1765) and *The Air Pump* (1768). **3 Joseph.** 1855–1930, British philologist; editor of *The English Dialect Dictionary* (1898–1905). **4 Judith (Arundel).** born 1915, Australian poet, critic, and conservationist. Her collections of poetry include *The Moving Image* (1946), *Woman to Man* (1949), and *A Human Pattern* (1990). **5 Richard.** 1908–60, U.S. Black novelist and short-story writer, best known for the novel *Native Son* (1940). **6 Wilbur** (1867–1912) and his brother, **Orville** (1871–1948), U.S. aviation pioneers, who designed and flew the first powered aircraft (1903). **7 William,** known as *Billy.* 1924–94, English footballer: winner of 105 caps.

wring (rɪŋ) *vb* **wrings, wringing, wrung. 1** (often foll. by *out*) to twist and compress to squeeze (a liquid) from (cloth, etc.). **2** (*tr*) to twist forcibly: *wring its neck.* **3** (*tr*) to clasp and twist (one's hands), esp. in anguish. **4** (*tr*) to distress: *wring one's heart.* **5** (*tr*) to grip (someone's hand) vigorously in greeting. **6** (*tr*) to obtain by or as if by forceful means: *wring information out of.* **7** (*intr*) to writhe with or as if with pain. **8 wringing wet.** soaking; drenched. ◆ *n* **9** an act or the process of wringing. [Old English *wringan;* related to Old High German *ringan* (German *wringen*), Gothic *wrungō* snare. See WRANGLE, WRONG]

wringer ('rɪŋə) *n* another name for **mangle**² (sense 1).

wring together *vb* (*tr, adv*) *Engineering.* to join (two smooth flat surfaces, esp. slip gauges) by hand pressure and a slight twisting movement.

wrinkle¹ ('rɪŋkᵊl) *n* **1** a slight ridge in the smoothness of a surface, such as a crease in the skin as a result of age. ◆ *vb* **2** to make or become wrinkled, as by crumpling, creasing, or puckering. [C15: back formation from *wrinkled,* from Old English *gewrinclod,* past participle of *wrinclian* to wind around; related to Swedish *vrinka* to sprain, Lithuanian *reñgti* to twist. See WRENCH] ▸ '**wrinkleless** *adj* ▸ '**wrinkly** *adj*

wrinkle² ('rɪŋkᵊl) *n Informal.* a clever or useful trick, hint, or dodge. [Old English *wrenc* trick; related to Middle Low German *wrank* struggle, Middle High German *ranc* sudden turn. See WRENCH]

wrinklies ('rɪŋklɪz) *pl n Informal, derogatory.* old people.

wrist (rɪst) *n* **1** *Anatomy.* the joint between the forearm and the hand. Technical name: **carpus. 2** the part of a sleeve or glove that covers the wrist. **3** *Machinery.* **3a** See **wrist pin. 3b** a joint in which a wrist pin forms the pivot. [Old English; related to Old High German, Old Norse *rist.* See WRIGGLE, WRY]

wristband ('rɪst,bænd) *n* **1** a band around the wrist, esp. one attached to a watch or forming part of a long sleeve. **2** a sweatband around the wrist.

wrist-drop *n* paralysis of the extensor muscles of the wrist and fingers.

wristlet ('rɪstlɪt) *n* a band or bracelet worn around the wrist.

wristlock ('rɪst,lɒk) *n* a wrestling hold in which a wrestler seizes his opponent's wrist and exerts pressure against the joints of his hand, arm, or shoulder.

wrist pin *n* **1** a cylindrical boss or pin attached to the side of a wheel parallel with the axis, esp. one forming a bearing for a crank. **2** the U.S. and Canadian name for **gudgeon pin.**

wristwatch ('rɪst,wɒtʃ) *n* a watch worn strapped around the wrist.

wristy ('rɪstɪ) *adj* (of a player's style of hitting the ball in cricket, tennis, etc.) characterized by considerable movement of the wrist.

writ¹ (rɪt) *n* **1** a document under seal, issued in the name of the Crown or a court, commanding the person to whom it is addressed to do or refrain from doing some specified act. **2** *Archaic.* a piece or body of writing: *Holy Writ.* [Old English; related to Old Norse *rit,* Gothic *writs* stroke, Old High German *riz* (German *Riss* a tear). See WRITE]

writ² (rɪt) *vb* **1** *Archaic or dialect.* a past tense and past participle of **write. 2 writ large.** plain to see; very obvious.

write (raɪt) *vb* **writes, writing, wrote, written. 1** to draw or mark (symbols, words, etc.) on a surface, usually paper, with a pen, pencil, or other instrument. **2** to describe or record (ideas, experiences, etc.) in writing. **3** to compose (a letter) to or correspond regularly with (a person, organization, etc.). **4** (*tr; may take a clause as object*) to say or communicate by letter: *he wrote that he was on his way.* **5** (*tr*) *Informal, chiefly U.S. and Canadian.* to send a letter to (a person, etc.). **6** to write (words) in cursive as opposed to printed style. **7** (*tr*) to be sufficiently familiar with (a specified style, language, etc.) to use it in writing. **8** to be the author or composer of (books, music, etc.). **9** (*tr*) to fill in the details for (a document, form, etc.). **10** (*tr*) to draw up or draft. **11** (*tr*) to produce by writing: *he wrote ten pages.* **12** (*tr*) to show clearly: *envy was written all over his face.* **13** (*tr*) to spell, inscribe, or entitle. **14** (*tr*) to ordain or prophesy: *it is written.* **15** (*intr*) to produce writing as specified. **16** *Computing.* to record (data) in a location in a storage device. Compare **read**¹ (sense 16). **17** (*tr*) See **underwrite** (sense 3a). ◆ See also **write down, write in, write off, write out, write up.** [Old English *wrītan* (originally: to scratch runes into bark); related to Old Frisian *wrīta,* Old Norse *rīta,* Old High German *rīzan* (German *reissen* to tear)] ▸ '**writable** *adj*

write down *vb* (*adv*) **1** (*tr*) to set down in writing. **2** (*tr*) to harm or belittle by writing about (a person) in derogatory terms. **3** (*intr;* foll. by *to* or *for*) to write in a simplified way (to a supposedly less cultured readership). **4** (*tr*) *Accounting.* to decrease the book value of (an asset). ◆ *n* **write-down. 5** *Accounting.* a reduction made in the book value of an asset.

write in *vb* (*tr*) **1** to insert in (a document, form, etc.) in writing. **2** (*adv*) *U.S.* **2a** to vote for (a person not on a ballot) by writing in his name. **2b** to cast (a vote) for such a person by writing in his name. ◆ *n* **write-in.** *U.S.* **3** the act of voting for a person by writing his name on a ballot. **4** a candidate or vote that has been written in. **5** (*as modifier*): *a write-in campaign.*

write off *vb* (*tr, adv*) **1** *Accounting.* **1a** to cancel (a bad debt or obsolete asset) from the accounts. **1b** to consider (a transaction, etc.) as a loss or set off (a loss) against revenues. **1c** to depreciate (an asset) by periodic charges. **1d** to charge (a specified amount) against gross profits as depreciation of an asset. **2** to cause or acknowledge the complete loss of. **3** to send a written order for (something): *she wrote off for a brochure.* **4** *Informal.* to damage (something, esp. a car) beyond repair. ◆ *n* **write-off.** **5** *Accounting.* **5a** the act of cancelling a bad debt or obsolete asset from the accounts. **5b** the bad debt or obsolete asset cancelled. **5c** the amount cancelled against gross profits, corresponding to the book value of the bad debt or obsolete asset. **6** *Informal.* something damaged beyond repair, esp. a car.

write out *vb* (*tr, adv*) **1** to put into writing or reproduce in full form in writing. **2** to exhaust (oneself or one's creativity) by excessive writing. **3** to remove (a character) from a television or radio series.

writer ('raɪtə) *n* **1** a person who writes books, articles, etc., esp. as an occupation. **2** the person who has written something specified. **3** a person who is able to write or write well. **4** a scribe or clerk. **5** a composer of music. **6** *Scot.* a legal practitioner, such as a notary or solicitor. **7** **Writer to the Signet.** (in Scotland) a member of an ancient society of solicitors, now having the exclusive privilege of preparing crown writs.

writerly ('raɪtəlɪ) *adj* of or characteristic of a writer; literary.

writer's cramp *n* a muscular spasm or temporary paralysis of the muscles of the thumb and first two fingers caused by prolonged writing.

write up *vb* (*tr, adv*) **1** to describe fully, complete, or bring up to date in writing: *write up a diary.* **2** to praise or bring to public notice in writing. **3** *Accounting, U.S.* **3a** to place an excessively high value on (an asset). **3b** to increase the book value of (an asset) in order to reflect more accurately its current worth in the market. ◆ *n* **write-up.** **4** a published account of something, such as a review in a newspaper or magazine. **5** *Accounting, U.S.* **5a** an excessive or illegally high valuation of corporate assets. **5b** a raising of the book value of an asset.

writhe (raɪð) *vb* **1** to twist or squirm in or as if in pain. **2** (*intr*) to move with such motions. **3** (*intr*) to suffer acutely from embarrassment, revulsion, etc. ◆ *n* **4** the act or an instance of writhing. [Old English *wrīthan;* related to Old High German *rīdan,* Old Norse *rītha.* See WRATH, WREATH, WRIST, WROTH] ► **'writher** *n*

writhen ('rɪðən) *Archaic or poetic.* ◆ *vb* **1** a past participle of **writhe.** ◆ *adj* **2** twisted; distorted.

writing ('raɪtɪŋ) *n* **1** a group of letters or symbols written or marked on a surface as a means of communicating ideas by making each symbol stand for an idea, concept, or thing (see **ideogram**), by using each symbol to represent a set of sounds grouped into syllables (**syllabic writing**), or by regarding each symbol as corresponding roughly or exactly to each of the sounds in the language (**alphabetic writing**). **2** short for **handwriting.** **3** anything expressed in letters, esp. a literary composition. **4** the work of a writer. **5** literary style, art, or practice. **6** written form: *give it to me in writing.* **7** (*modifier*): related to or used in writing: *writing ink.* **8** **writing on the wall.** a sign or signs of approaching disaster. [sense 8: allusion to Daniel 5:5]

writing case *n* a portable folder with compartments for holding writing materials.

writing desk *n* a piece of furniture with a writing surface and drawers and compartments for papers, writing materials, etc.

writing paper *n* paper sized to take writing ink and used for letters and other manuscripts.

Writings ('raɪtɪŋz) *pl n* **the.** another term for the **Hagiographa.**

writing table *n* a table designed or used for writing at.

writ of execution *n Law.* a writ ordering that a judgment be enforced.

written ('rɪtᵊn) *vb* **1** the past participle of **write.** ◆ *adj* **2** taken down in writing; transcribed: *written evidence; the written word.* Compare **spoken** (sense 2).

Written Law *n Judaism.* another name for the **Torah.**

WRNS *abbrev. for* Women's Royal Naval Service. See also **Wren**[1].

wrnt *abbrev. for* warrant.

Wrocław (*Polish* 'vrɔtswaf) *n* an industrial city in SW Poland, on the River Oder: passed to Austria (1527) and to Prussia (1741); returned to Poland in 1945. Pop.: 642 700 (1996 est.). German name: **Breslau.**

wrong (rɒŋ) *adj* **1** not correct or truthful: *the wrong answer.* **2** acting or judging in error: *you are wrong to think that.* **3** (*postpositive*) immoral; bad: *it is wrong to cheat.* **4** deviating from or unacceptable to correct or conventional laws, usage, etc. **5** not intended or wanted: *the wrong road.* **6** (*postpositive*) not working properly; amiss: *something is wrong with the engine.* **7** (of a side, esp. of a fabric) intended to face the inside so as not to be seen. **8** **get on the wrong side of** *or* (*U.S.*) **get in wrong with.** *Informal.* to come into disfavour with. **9** **go down the wrong way.** (of food) to pass into the windpipe instead of the gullet. ◆ *adv* **10** in the wrong direction or manner. **11** **go wrong.** **11a** to turn out other than intended. **11b** to make a mistake. **11c** (of a machine, etc.) to cease to function properly. **11d** to go astray morally. **12** **get wrong.** **12a** to fail to understand properly. **12b** to fail to provide the correct answer to. ◆ *n* **13** a bad, immoral, or unjust thing or action. **14** *Law.* **14a** an infringement of another person's rights, rendering the offender liable to a civil action, as for breach of contract or tort: *a private wrong.* **14b** a violation of public rights and duties, affecting the community as a whole and actionable at the instance of the Crown: *a public wrong.* **15** **in the wrong.** mistaken or guilty. ◆ *vb* (*tr*) **16** to treat unjustly. **17** to discredit, malign, or misrepresent. **18** to seduce or violate. [Old English *wrang* injustice, from Old Norse *vrang;* see WRING] ► **'wronger** *n* ► **'wrongly** *adv* ► **'wrongness** *n*

wrongdoer ('rɒŋˌduːə) *n* a person who acts immorally or illegally. ► **'wrongˌdoing** *n*

wrong-foot *vb* (*tr*) **1** *Tennis, etc.* to play a shot in such a way as to cause (one's opponent) to be off balance. **2** to take by surprise so as to place in an embarrassing or disadvantageous situation.

wrong fount *n Printing.* an error in composition in which a type of the wrong face or size is used. Abbrev.: **wf.**

wrongful ('rɒŋfʊl) *adj* immoral, unjust, or illegal. ► **'wrongfully** *adv* ► **'wrongfulness** *n*

wrong-headed *adj* **1** constantly wrong in judgment. **2** foolishly stubborn; obstinate. ► **ˌwrong-'headedly** *adv* ► **ˌwrong-'headedness** *n*

wrong number *n* a telephone number wrongly connected or dialled in error or the person so contacted.

wrote (rəʊt) *vb* the past tense of **write.**

wroth (rəʊθ, rɒθ) *adj Archaic or literary.* angry; irate. [Old English *wrāth;* related to Old Saxon *wrēth,* Old Norse *reithr,* Old High German *reid* curly haired]

wrought (rɔːt) *vb* **1** *Archaic.* a past tense and past participle of **work.** ◆ *adj* **2** *Metallurgy.* shaped by hammering or beating. **3** (*often in combination*) formed, fashioned, or worked as specified: *well-wrought.* **4** decorated or made with delicate care. [C16: variant of *worht,* from Old English *geworht,* past participle of (*ge*)*wyrcan* to WORK]

USAGE *Wrought* is sometimes used as if it were the past tense and past participle of *wreak* as in *the hurricane wrought havoc in coastal areas.* Many people think this use is incorrect.

wrought iron *n* **a** a pure form of iron having a low carbon content and a fibrous microstructure. It is made by various processes and is often used for decorative work. **b** (*as modifier*): *wrought-iron gates.*

wrought-up *adj* agitated or excited.

wrung (rʌŋ) *vb* the past tense and past participle of **wring.**

WRVS *abbrev. for* Women's Royal Voluntary Service.

wry (raɪ) *adj* **wrier, wriest** *or* **wryer, wryest.** **1** twisted, contorted, or askew. **2** (of a facial expression) produced or characterized by contorting of the features, usually indicating dislike. **3** drily humorous; sardonic. **4** warped, misdirected, or perverse. **5** (of words, thoughts, etc.) unsuitable or wrong. ◆ *vb* **wries, wrying, wried.** **6** (*tr*) to twist or contort. [C16: from dialect *wry* to twist, from Old English *wrīgian* to turn; related to Old Frisian *wrīgia* to bend, Old Norse *riga* to move, Middle Low German *wrīch* bent, stubborn] ► **'wryly** *adv* ► **'wryness** *n*

wrybill ('raɪˌbɪl) *n* a New Zealand plover, *Anarhynchus frontalis,* having its bill deflected to one side enabling it to search for food beneath stones.

wryneck ('raɪˌnɛk) *n* **1** either of two cryptically coloured Old World woodpeckers, *Jynx torquilla* or *J. ruficollis,* which do not drum on trees. **2** another name for **torticollis.** **3** *Informal.* a person who has a twisted neck.

WS **1** *abbrev. for* Writer to the Signet. ◆ **2** *international car registration for* Western Samoa.

WSW *symbol for* west-southwest.

wt. *abbrev. for* weight.

WTO *abbrev. for* World Trade Organization.

Wu (wuː) *n* a group of dialects of Chinese spoken around the Yangtze delta.

Wuchang *or* **Wu-ch'ang** ('wuː'tʃæŋ) *n* a former city of E central China: now a part of Wuhan.

Wu Di ('wuː 'diː) *or* **Wu Ti** *n* 156 B.C.–86 B.C., Chinese emperor (140–86) of the Han dynasty, who greatly extended the Chinese empire and made Confucianism the state religion.

wudu (wudu) *n Islam.* the practice of ritual washing before daily prayer. [from Arabic]

Wuhan ('wuː'hæn) *n* a city in SE China, in Hubei province, at the confluence of the Han and Yangtze Rivers: formed in 1950 by the union of the cities of Hanyang, Hankou, and Wuchang (the Han Cities); river port and industrial centre; university (1913). Pop.: 3 750 000 (1990 est.).

Wu Hou ('wuː 'haʊ) *n* 625–705 A.D. Chinese empress (655–705) of the Tang dynasty.

Wuhsien ('wuː'ʃjɛn) *n* another name for **Suzhou.**

Wuhu ('wuː'huː) *n* a port in E China, in E Anhui province on the Yangtze River. Pop.: 425 740 (1990 est.).

wulfenite ('wʊlfəˌnaɪt) *n* a yellow, orange, red, or grey lustrous secondary mineral consisting of lead molybdate in the form of platelike tetragonal crystals. It occurs with lead ores and is a source of molybdenum. Formula: $PbMoO_4$. [C19: from German *Wulfenit,* named after F. X. von *Wulfen* (1728–1805), Austrian mineralogist]

Wulfila ('wʊlfɪlə) *n* a variant of **Ulfilas.**

Wu-lu-mu-ch'i ('wuː'luː'muː'tʃiː) *n* a variant of **Urumchi.**

wunderkind ('wʌndəˌkɪnd; *German* 'vʊndərˌkɪnt) *n, pl* **-kinds** *or* **-kinder** (*German* -kɪndər). **1** a child prodigy. **2** a person who is exceptionally successful in his field while still young. [C20: German, literally: wonder child]

Wundt (*German* vʊnt) *n* **Wilhelm Max** ('vɪlhɛlm maks). 1832–1920, German experimental psychologist.

Wuppertal (*German* 'vʊpərtaːl) *n* a city in W Germany, in North Rhine-Westphalia state on the **Wupper River** (a Rhine tributary): formed in 1929 from the amalgamation of the towns of Barmen and Elberfeld and other smaller towns; textile centre. Pop.: 381 884 (1996 est.).

wurley *or* **wurlie** ('wɜːlɪ) *n Austral.* an Aboriginal hut. [from a native Australian language]

Würm (vʊəm, wɜːm) *n* the fourth and final Pleistocene glaciation in Alpine Europe. See also **Günz, Riss, Mindel.** [C20: named after the river *Würm* in Bavaria, Germany]

wurst (wɜːst, wʊəst, vʊəst) *n* a large sausage, esp. of a type made in Germany, Austria, etc. [from German, literally: something rolled; related to Latin *vertere* to turn]

Württemberg (ˈvɜːtəmˌbɜːɡ; *German* ˈvyrtəmbɛrk) *n* a historic region and former state of S Germany; since 1952 part of the state of Baden-Württemberg.

Würzburg (ˈvɜːtsˌbɜːɡ; *German* ˈvyrtsbʊrk) *n* a city in S central Germany, in NW Bavaria on the River Main: university (1582). Pop.: 127 295 (1996 est.).

wus (wʌs) *n South Wales dialect.* a casual term of address: *fancy a drink, wus?* [from Welsh *was,* variant of *gwas* servant]

wuss (wʊs) *or* **wussy** (ˈwʊsɪ) *n, pl* **wusses** *or* **wussies.** *Slang., chiefly U.S.* a feeble or effeminate person. [C20: perhaps from PUSSY[1] (cat)]

wuthering (ˈwʌðərɪŋ) *adj Northern English dialect.* **1** (of a wind) blowing strongly with a roaring sound. **2** (of a place) characterized by such a sound. [variant of *whitherin,* from *whither* blow, from Old Norse *hvithra;* related to *hvitha* squall of wind, Old English *hweothu* wind]

Wu Ti (ˈwuː ˈtiː) *n* See **Wu Di.**

Wutsin (ˈwuːˈtsɪn) *n* the former name (until 1949) of **Zangzhou** (sense 1).

Wuxi, Wusih, *or* **Wu-hsi** (ˈwuːˈʃiː, -ˈsiː) *n* a city in E China, in S Jiangsu province on the Grand Canal: textile industry. Pop.: 826 833 (1990 est.).

WV 1 *abbrev. for* West Virginia. ◆ **2** *international car registration for* (Windward Islands) St Vincent.

W. Va. *abbrev. for* West Virginia.

WVS (formerly, in Britain) *abbrev. for* Women's Voluntary Service, since 1966 **WRVS.**

WWI *abbrev. for* World War One.

WWII *abbrev. for* World War Two.

WWF *abbrev. for* Worldwide Fund for Nature.

WWW *abbrev. for* World Wide Web.

WY *or* **Wy.** *abbrev. for* Wyoming.

Wyandotte (ˈwaɪənˌdɒt) *n* a heavy American breed of domestic fowl with many different varieties. [C19: from *Wyandot,* a N American Indian people]

Wyatt (ˈwaɪət) *n* **1 James.** 1746–1813, British architect; a pioneer of the Gothic Revival. **2** Sir **Thomas.** ?1503–42, English poet at the court of Henry VIII.

wych- *prefix* a variant of **witch-.**

wych-elm *or* **witch-elm** (ˈwɪtʃˌɛlm) *n* **1** Eurasian elm tree, *Ulmus glabra,* having a rounded shape, longish pointed leaves, clusters of small flowers, and winged fruits. **2** the wood of this tree. [C17: from Old English *wice* wych-elm]

Wycherley (ˈwɪtʃəlɪ) *n* **William.** ?1640–1716, English dramatist. His Restoration comedies include *The Country Wife* (1675) and *The Plain Dealer* (1676).

wych-hazel *n* a variant spelling of **witch hazel.**

Wycliffe *or* **Wyclif** (ˈwɪklɪf) *n* **John.** ?1330–84, English religious reformer. A precursor of the Reformation, whose writings were condemned as heretical, he attacked the doctrines and abuses of the Church. He instigated the first complete translation of the Bible into English. His followers were called Lollards. Also: **ˈWiclif, ˈWickliffe.** ▸ **ˈWycliffism** *or* **ˈWyclifism** *n*

Wycliffite *or* **Wyclifite** (ˈwɪklɪˌfaɪt) *English history.* ◆ *n* **1** a follower of John Wycliffe or an adherent of his religious ideas; a Lollard. ◆ *adj* **2** of or relating to Wycliffe, his followers, or his religious ideas.

Wye (waɪ) *n* a river in E Wales and W England, rising in Powys and flowing southeast into England, then south to the Severn estuary. Length: 210 km (130 miles).

Wykeham (ˈwɪkəm) *n* **William of.** 1324–1404, English prelate and statesman, who founded New College, Oxford, and Winchester College: chancellor of England (1367–71; 1389–91); bishop of Winchester (1367–1404).

Wykehamist (ˈwɪkəmɪst) *n* a pupil or former pupil of Winchester College.

wynd (waɪnd) *n Scot.* a narrow lane or alley. [C15: from the stem of WIND[2]]

Wyndham (ˈwɪndəm) *n* **John,** pseudonym of *John Wyndham Parkes Lucas Beynon Harris.* 1903–69, British writer of science fiction novels and stories. His works include *The Day of the Triffids* (1951), *The Kraken Wakes* (1953), and *The Midwich Cuckoos* (1957).

Wyo. *abbrev. for* Wyoming.

Wyoming (waɪˈəʊmɪŋ) *n* a state of the western U.S.: consists largely of ranges of the Rockies in the west and north, with part of the Great Plains in the east and several regions of hot springs. Capital: Cheyenne. Pop.: 479 743 (1997 est.). Area: 253 597 sq. km (97 914 sq. miles). Abbrevs.: **Wyo., Wy.,** or (with zip code) **WY** ▸ **Wyˈomingˌite** *n*

WYSIWYG (ˈwɪzɪˌwɪɡ) *n, adj Computers. acronym for* what you see is what you get: referring to what is displayed on the screen being the same as what will be printed out.

wyvern *or* (*less commonly*) **wivern** (ˈwaɪvən) *n* a heraldic beast having a serpent's tail and a dragon's head and a body with wings and two legs. [C17: variant of earlier *wyver,* from Old French, from Latin *vīpera* VIPER]

x *or* **X** (ɛks) *n, pl* **x's, X's,** *or* **Xs. 1** the 24th letter and 19th consonant of the modern English alphabet. **2** a speech sound sequence represented by this letter, in English pronounced as *ks* or *gz* or, in initial position, *z*, as in *xylophone.*

x *symbol for:* **1** *Commerce, finance, etc.* ex. **2** *Maths.* the *x*-axis or a coordinate measured along the *x*-axis in a Cartesian coordinate system. **3** an algebraic variable.

X *symbol:* **1a** (in Britain, formerly) indicating a film that may not be publicly shown to anyone under 18. Since 1982 replaced by symbol 18. **1b** (*as modifier*): *an X film.* **2** denoting any unknown, unspecified, or variable factor, number, person, or thing. **3** (on letters, cards, etc.) denoting a kiss. **4** (on ballot papers, etc.) indicating choice. **5** (on examination papers, etc.) indicating error. **6** for Christ; Christian. **[**from the form of the Greek letter khi (X), first letter of *Khristos* Christ**]** ◆ **7** *the Roman numeral for* ten. See **Roman numerals.**

xanthate ('zænθeɪt) *n* any salt or ester of xanthic acid. ▸ **xan'thation** *n*

xanthein ('zænθiːɪn) *n* the soluble part of the yellow pigment that is found in the cell sap of some flowers.

xanthene ('zænθiːn) *n* a yellowish crystalline heterocyclic compound used as a fungicide; benzo-1,4-pyran. Its molecular structural unit is found in many dyes, such as rhodamine and fluorescein. Formula: $CH_2(C_6H_4)_2O$.

xanthic ('zænθɪk) *adj* **1** of, containing, or derived from xanthic acid. **2** *Botany, rare.* having a yellow colour.

xanthic acid *n* any of a class of organic sulphur-containing acids with the general formula ROC(S)SH, where R is an organic group. Their salts are the xanthates.

xanthin ('zænθɪn) *n* any of a group of yellow or orange carotene derivatives that occur in the fruit and flowers of certain plants.

xanthine ('zænθiːn, -θaɪn) *n* **1** a crystalline compound related in structure to uric acid and found in urine, blood, certain plants, and certain animal tissues. Formula: $C_5H_4N_4O_2$. **2** any substituted derivative of xanthine, esp. one of the three pharmacologically active methylated xanthines, caffeine, theophylline, or theobromine, which act as stimulants and diuretics.

Xanthippe (zæn'θɪpɪ) *or* **Xantippe** (zæn'tɪpɪ) *n* **1** the wife of Socrates, proverbial as a scolding and quarrelsome woman. **2** any nagging, peevish, or irritable woman.

xanthism ('zæn,θɪzəm) *n* a condition of skin, fur, or feathers in which yellow coloration predominates.

xantho- *or before a vowel* **xanth-** *combining form.* indicating yellow: *xanthophyll.* **[**from Greek *xanthos***]**

xanthochroid ('zænθəʊ,krɔɪd) *adj Rare.* of, relating to, or designating races having light-coloured hair and a pale complexion. **[C19:** New Latin *xanthochroi,* from XANTHO- + Greek *ōkhros* pale**]**

xanthochroism (zæn'θɒkrəʊ,ɪzəm) *n* a condition in certain animals, esp. aquarium goldfish, in which all skin pigments other than yellow and orange disappear. **[C19:** from Greek *xanthokhro(os)* yellow-skinned (from *xanthos* yellow + *khroia* skin) + -ISM**]**

xanthoma (zæn'θəʊmə) *n Pathol.* the presence in the skin of fatty yellow or brownish plaques or nodules, esp. on the eyelids, caused by a disorder of lipid metabolism.

xanthophyll *or esp. U.S.* **xanthophyl** ('zænθəʊfɪl) *n* any of a group of yellow carotenoid pigments occurring in plant and animal tissue. ▸ **,xantho'phyllous** *adj*

xanthous ('zænθəs) *adj* of, relating to, or designating races with yellowish hair and a light complexion.

Xanthus ('zænθəs) *n* the chief city of ancient Lycia in SW Asia Minor: source of some important antiquities. ▸ **'Xanthian** *adj*

Xavier ('zeɪvɪə, 'zæv-; *Spanish* xa'βjer) *n* **Saint Francis,** known as the *Apostle of the Indies.* 1506–52, Spanish missionary, who was a founding member of the Jesuit society (1534) and later preached in Goa, Ceylon, the East Indies, and Japan. Feast day: Dec. 3.

***x*-axis** *n* a reference axis, usually horizontal, of a graph or two- or three-dimensional Cartesian coordinate system along which the *x*-coordinate is measured.

X-chromosome *n* the sex chromosome that occurs in pairs in the diploid cells of the females of many animals, including humans, and as one of a pair with the Y-chromosome in those of males. Compare **Y-chromosome.**

Xe *the chemical symbol for* xenon.

xebec, zebec, *or* **zebeck** ('ziːbɛk) *n* a small three-masted Mediterranean vessel with both square and lateen sails, formerly used by Algerian pirates and later used for commerce. **[C18:** earlier *chebec* from French, ultimately from Arabic *shabbāk;* present spelling influenced by Catalan *xabec,* Spanish *xabeque* (now *jabeque*)**]**

Xenakis (zɛ'nɑːkɪs; *Greek* ksɛ'nakis) *n* **Yannis** ('janis). born 1922, Greek composer and musical theorist, born in Romania. He is noted for his use of electronic computers in composition: his works include *ST/10-1, 080262* (1962) and *Dox-orkh* (1991).

xenia ('ziːnɪə) *n Botany.* the influence of pollen upon the form of the fruit developing after pollination. **[C19:** from New Latin, from Greek: hospitality, from *xenos* guest**]** ▸ **'xenial** *adj*

xeno- *or before a vowel* **xen-** *combining form.* indicating something strange, different, or foreign: *xenogamy.* **[**from Greek *xenos* strange**]**

Xenocrates (zɛ'nɒkrə,tiːz) *n* ?396–314 B.C., Greek Platonic philosopher. ▸ **Xenocratic** (,zɛnə'krætɪk) *adj*

xenocryst ('zɛnə,krɪst) *n* a crystal included within an igneous rock as the magma cooled but not formed from it. **[C20:** from XENO- + CRYST(AL)**]**

xenogamy (zɛ'nɒgəmɪ) *n Botany.* another name for **cross-fertilization.** ▸ **xe'nogamous** *adj*

xenogeneic (,zɛnəʊdʒɪ'neɪɪk) *adj Med.* derived from an individual of a different species: *a xenogeneic tissue graft.*

xenogenesis (,zɛnə'dʒɛnɪsɪs) *n* **1** the supposed production of offspring completely unlike either parent. **2** another name for **abiogenesis** or **alternation of generations.** ▸ **xenogenetic** (,zɛnəʊdʒɪ'nɛtɪk) *or* **,xeno'genic** *adj*

xenoglossia (,zɛnə'glɒsɪə) *or* **xenoglossy** ('zɛnə,glɒsɪ) *n* an ability claimed by some mediums, clairvoyants, etc., to speak a language with which they are unfamiliar. **[C20:** from Greek, from XENO- + Attic Greek *glossa* tongue, language**]**

xenograft ('zɛnəʊ,grɑːft) *n* another word for **heterograft.**

xenolith ('zɛnəlɪθ) *n* a fragment of rock differing in origin, composition, structure, etc., from the igneous rock enclosing it. ▸ **,xeno'lithic** *adj*

xenomorphic (,zɛnə'mɔːfɪk) *adj* (of a mineral constituent of an igneous rock) not having its characteristic crystal shape because of deforming pressure from adjacent minerals. ▸ **,xeno'morphically** *adv*

xenon ('zɛnɒn) *n* a colourless odourless gaseous element occurring in trace amounts in air; formerly considered inert it is now known to form compounds and is used in radio valves, stroboscopic and bactericidal lamps, and bubble chambers. Symbol: Xe; atomic no.: 54; atomic wt.: 131.29; valency: 0; density: 5.887 kg/m^3; melting pt.: –111.76°C; boiling pt.: –108.0°C. **[C19:** from Greek: something strange**]**

Xenophanes (zɛ'nɒfə,niːz) *n* ?570–?480 B.C., Greek philosopher and poet, noted for his monotheism and regarded as a founder of the Eleatic school.

xenophile ('zɛnə,faɪl) *n* a person who likes foreigners or things foreign. **[C19:** from Greek, from XENO- + -PHILE**]**

xenophobe ('zɛnə,fəʊb) *n* a person who hates or fears foreigners or strangers. **[C20:** from Greek, from XENO- + -PHOBE**]**

xenophobia (,zɛnə'fəʊbɪə) *n* hatred or fear of foreigners or strangers or of their politics or culture. ▸ **,xeno'phobic** *adj*

Xenophon ('zɛnəfən) *n* 431–?355 B.C., Greek general and historian; a disciple of Socrates. He accompanied Cyrus the Younger against Artaxerxes II and, after Cyrus' death at Cunaxa (401), he led his army of 10 000 Greek soldiers to the Black Sea, an expedition described in his *Anabasis.* His other works include *Hellenica,* a history of Greece, and the *Memorabilia, Apology,* and *Symposium,* which contain recollections of Socrates.

xenotransplant ('zɛnəʊ,træns,plɑːnt) *n Surgery.* an operation in which an organ or tissue is transferred from one animal to another of a different species. ▸ **'xeno,transplan,tation** *n*

xeranthemum (zɪə'rænθəməm) *n* any of a Mediterranean genus of plants having flower heads that are dry and retain their colour and shape for years: family *Compositae* (composites). See also **immortelle. [C18:** New Latin, from Greek XERO- + *anthemon* flower**]**

xerarch ('zɪərɑːk) *adj Ecology.* (of a sere) having its origin in a dry habitat. **[**from XER(O)- + Greek *arkhē* a beginning, from *arkhein* to begin**]**

Xeres (*Spanish* 'xereθ) *n* the former name of **Jerez.**

xeric ('zɪərɪk) *adj Ecology.* of, relating to, or growing in dry conditions. ▸ **'xerically** *adv*

xero- *or before a vowel* **xer-** *combining form.* indicating dryness: *xeroderma.* **[**from Greek *xēros* dry**]**

xeroderma (,zɪərəʊ'dɜːmə) *or* **xerodermia** (,zɪərəʊ'dɜːmɪə) *n Pathol.* **1** any abnormal dryness of the skin as the result of diminished secretions from the sweat or sebaceous glands. **2** another name for **ichthyosis.** ▸ **xerodermatic** (,zɪərəʊdə'mætɪk) *or* **,xero'dermatous** *adj*

xerography (zɪ'rɒgrəfɪ) *n* a photocopying process in which an electrostatic image is formed on a selenium plate or cylinder. The plate or cylinder is dusted with a resinous powder, which adheres to the charged regions, and the image is then transferred to a sheet of paper on which it is fixed by heating. ▸ **xe'rographer** *n* ▸ **xerographic** (,zɪərə'græfɪk) *adj* ▸ **,xero'graphically** *adv*

xeromorphic (,zɪərə'mɔːfɪk) *adj* (of plants or plant parts) having characteristics that serve as protection against excessive loss of water.

xerophilous (zɪ'rɒfɪləs) *adj* (of plants or animals) adapted for growing or living in dry surroundings. ▸ **xerophile** ('zɪərəʊ,faɪl) *n* ▸ **xe'rophily** *n*

xerophthalmia (,zɪərɒf'θælmɪə) *n Pathol.* excessive dryness of the cornea and conjunctiva, caused by a deficiency of vitamin A. Also called: **xeroma** (zɪ'rəʊmə). ▸ **,xeroph'thalmic** *adj*

xerophyte ('zɪərə,faɪt) *n* a xerophilous plant, such as a cactus. ▸ **xerophytic** (,zɪərə'fɪtɪk) *adj* ▸ **,xero'phytically** *adv* ▸ **'xero,phytism** *n*

xerosere ('zɪərə,sɪə) *n Ecology.* a sere that originates in dry surroundings.

xerosis (zɪ'rəʊsɪs) *n Pathol.* abnormal dryness of bodily tissues, esp. the skin, eyes, or mucous membranes. ▸ **xerotic** (zɪ'rɒtɪk) *adj*

xerostomia (ˌziːrəˈstəʊmɪə) *n* abnormal lack of saliva; dryness of the mouth. [C19: from XERO- + -STOM(E) + -IA]

Xerox (ˈzɪərɒks) *n* **1** *Trademark.* **1a** a xerographic copying process. **1b** a machine employing this process. **1c** a copy produced by this process. ◆ *vb* **2** to produce a copy of (a document, illustration, etc.) by this process.

Xerxes I (ˈzɜːksiːz) *n* ?519–465 B.C., king of Persia (485–465), who led a vast army against Greece. His forces were victorious at Thermopylae but his fleet was defeated at Salamis (480) and his army at Plataea (479).

x-height *n Printing.* the height of lower case letters of a typeface, without ascenders or descenders.

Xhosa (ˈkɔːsə) *n* **1** (*pl* **-sa** *or* **-sas**) a member of a cattle-rearing Negroid people of southern Africa, living chiefly in South Africa. **2** the language of this people, belonging to the Bantu group of the Niger-Congo family: closely related to Swazi and Zulu and characterized by several clicks in its sound system. ▸ **ˈXhosan** *adj*

xi (zaɪ, saɪ, ksaɪ, ksiː) *n, pl* **xis.** the 14th letter in the Greek alphabet (Ξ, ξ), a composite consonant, transliterated as *x.*

Xi, Hsi, *or* **Si** (ʃiː) *n* a river in S China, rising in Yünnan province and flowing east to the Canton delta on the South China Sea: the main river system of S China. Length: about 1900 km (1200 miles).

Xia Gui (ˈʃjɑː ˈkweɪ) *or* **Hsia Kuei** *n* ?1180–1230, Chinese landscape painter of the Sung dynasty; noted for his misty mountain landscapes in ink monochrome.

Xiamen (ˈʃjɑːˈmɛn) *n* a variant transliteration of the Chinese name for **Amoy.**

Xi An, Hsian, *or* **Sian** (ʃjɑːn) *n* an industrial city in central China, capital of Shaanxi province: capital of China for 970 years at various times between the 3rd century B.C. and the 10th century A.D.; seat of the Northwestern University (1937). Pop.: 2 760 000 (1991 est.). Former name: **Siking.**

Xiang, Hsiang, *or* **Siang** (ʃjɑːŋ) *n* **1** a river in SE central China, rising in NE Guangxi Zhuang and flowing northeast and north to Dongting Lake. Length: about 1150 km (715 miles). **2** a river in S China, rising in SE Yünnan and flowing generally east to the Hongxiu (the upper course of the Xi River). Length: about 800 km (500 miles).

Xiangtan *or* **Siangtan** (ˈʃjɑːŋˈtɑːn) *n* a city in S central China, in NE Hunan on the Xiang River: centre of a region noted for tea production. Pop.: 441 968 (1990 est.).

Ximenes *or* **Ximenez** (*Spanish* xiˈmenes; *English* ˈzɪmɪˌniːz) *n* See (Francisco) **Jiménez de Cisneros.**

Xingú (*Portuguese* ʃiŋˈgu) *n* a river in central Brazil, rising on the Mato Grosso plateau and flowing north to the Amazon delta, with over 650 km (400 miles) of rapids in its middle course. Length: 1932 km (1200 miles).

Xining, Hsining, *or* **Sining** (ˈʃiːˈnɪŋ) *n* a city in W China, capital of Qinghai province, at an altitude of 2300 m (7500 ft.). Pop.: 551 776 (1990 est.).

Xinjiang Uygur (ˈʃɪnˈdʒjæŋ ˈwiːɡʊə) *or* **Sinkiang-Uighur Autonomous Region** *n* an administrative division of NW China: established in 1955 for the Uygur ethnic minority, with autonomous subdivisions for other small minorities; produces over half China's wool and contains valuable mineral resources. Capital: Urumqi. Pop.: 16 610 000 (1996 est.). Area: 1 646 799 sq. km (635 829 sq. miles).

xiphi- *or before a vowel* **xiph-** *combining form.* indicating a sword, esp. something shaped like or resembling a sword: *xiphisternum; xiphoid.* [from Greek *xiphos* sword]

xiphisternum (ˌzɪfɪˈstɜːnəm) *n, pl* **-na** (-nə). *Anatomy, zoology.* the cartilaginous process forming the lowermost part of the breastbone (sternum). Also called: **xiphoid, xiphoid process.**

xiphoid (ˈzɪfɔɪd) *adj* **1** *Biology.* shaped like a sword. **2** of or relating to the xiphisternum. ◆ *n* **3** Also called: **xiphoid process.** another name for **xiphisternum.**

xiphosuran (ˌzɪfəˈsjʊərən) *n* **1** any chelicerate arthropod of the subclass *Xiphosura,* including the horseshoe crabs and many extinct forms. ◆ *adj* **2** of, relating to, or belonging to the subclass *Xiphosura.* [C19: from New Latin *Xiphosura,* irregularly from Greek *xiphos* sword + *oura* tail]

Xizang Autonomous Region (ˈʃiːˈzæŋ) *n* the Pinyin transliteration of the Chinese name for **Tibet.**

XL *symbol for* extra large.

Xmas (ˈɛksməs, ˈkrɪsməs) *n Informal.* short for **Christmas.** [C16: from symbol X for Christ + -MAS]

Xn *or* **Xtian** *abbrev. for* Christian.

Xnty *or* **Xty** *abbrev. for* Christianity.

xoanon (ˈzəʊəˌnɒn) *n, pl* **-na** (-nə). a primitive image of a god, carved, esp. originally, in wood, and supposed to have fallen from heaven. [C18: from Greek, from *xuō* to scrape, smooth]

Xochimilco (ˌkɒtʃɪˈmɪlkəʊ) *n* a town in central Mexico, on Lake Xochimilco: noted for its floating gardens. Pop.: 271 020 (1990).

XP *n* the Christian monogram made up of the Greek letters *khi* and *rho,* the first two letters of *Khristos,* the Greek form of Christ's name.

x-radiation *n* another term for **X-ray.**

X-rated *adj* **1** (formerly, in Britain) (of a film) considered suitable for viewing by adults only. **2** *Informal.* involving bad language, violence, or sex: *an X-rated conversation.*

X-ray *or* **x-ray** *n* **1a** electromagnetic radiation emitted when matter is bombarded with fast electrons. X-rays have wavelengths shorter than that of ultraviolet radiation, that is less than about 1×10^{-8} metres. They extend to indefinitely short wavelengths, but below about 1×10^{-11} metres they are often called gamma radiation or bremsstrahlung. **1b** (*as modifier*): *X-ray astronomy.* **2** a picture produced by exposing photographic film to X-rays: used in medicine as a diagnostic aid as parts of the body, such as bones, absorb X-rays and so appear as opaque areas on the picture. **3** (*usually cap.*) *Communications.* a code word for the letter *x.* ◆ *vb* (*tr*) **4** to photograph (part of the body, etc.) using X-rays. **5** to treat or examine by means of X-rays. [C19: partial translation of German *X-Strahlen* (from *Strahl* ray), coined by W. K. RÖNTGEN in 1895]

X-ray astronomy *n* the branch of astronomy concerned with the detection and measurement of X-rays emitted by certain celestial bodies. As X-rays are absorbed by the atmosphere, satellites and rockets are used.

X-ray binary *n* a binary star that is an intense source of X-rays and is composed of a normal star in close orbit with a white dwarf, neutron star, or black hole.

X-ray crystallography *n* the study and practice of determining the structure of a crystal by passing a beam of X-rays through it and observing and analysing the diffraction pattern produced.

X-ray diffraction *n* the scattering of X-rays on contact with matter, resulting in changes in radiation intensity, which is used for studying atomic structure.

X-ray therapy *n Med.* the therapeutic use of X-rays.

X-ray tube *n* an evacuated tube containing a metal target onto which is directed a beam of electrons at high energy for the generation of X-rays.

Xt *abbrev. for* Christ. [representing the initial letter (chi) and the t (tau) of Greek *Khristos*]

Xuan-tong (ˈʃwɑːnˈtʊŋ) *n* the Pinyin transliteration of the title as emperor of China of (Henry) **Pu-yi.**

Xuan Zang (ˈʃwɑːn ˈtsæŋ) *or* **Hsüan-tsang** *n* 602–664 A.D., Chinese Buddhist monk, who travelled to India to study the Buddhist scriptures, many of which he translated into Chinese: noted also for his account of his travels.

Xuan Zong (ˈʃwɑːn ˈtsɒŋ) *or* **Hsüan-tsung** *n* 685–762 A.D., Chinese emperor (712–56) of the Tang dynasty.

x-unit *n* a unit of length equal to $0.100\,202 \times 10^{-12}$ metre, for expressing the wavelengths of X-rays and gamma rays.

Xun Zi (ˈʃʊn ˈdʒiː) *or* **Hsün-tzu** *n* original name *Hsun Kuang.* c. 300 B.C.–c. 230 B.C., Chinese philosopher, who systematized Confucian teaching.

Xuthus (ˈzuːθəs) *n Greek myth.* a son of Hellen, regarded as an ancestor of the Ionian Greeks through his son Ion.

XUV *abbrev. for* extreme ultraviolet: involving radiation bridging the gap between X-rays and ultraviolet radiation: *XUV astronomy; XUV waveband.* Also: **EUV.**

Xuzhou (ˈʃuːˈdʒəʊ), **Hsü-chou,** *or* **Süchow** *n* a city in N central China, in NW Jiangsu province: scene of a decisive battle (1949) in which the Communists defeated the Nationalists. Pop.: 805 695 (1990 est.).

xylan (ˈzaɪlæn) *n Biochem.* a yellow polysaccharide consisting of xylose units: occurs in straw husks and other woody tissue.

xylem (ˈzaɪləm, -lɛm) *n* a plant tissue that conducts water and mineral salts from the roots to all other parts, provides mechanical support, and forms the wood of trees and shrubs. It is of two types (see **protoxylem, metaxylem**), both of which are made up of vessels, tracheids, and other elements. [C19: from Greek *xulon* wood]

xylene (ˈzaɪliːn) *n* an aromatic hydrocarbon existing in three isomeric forms, all three being colourless flammable volatile liquids used as solvents and in the manufacture of synthetic resins, dyes, and insecticides; dimethylbenzene. Formula: $C_6H_4(CH_3)_2$. Also called: **xylol.**

xylidine (ˈzaɪlɪˌdiːn, -ˌdaɪn, ˈzɪlɪ-) *n* **1** a mixture of six isomeric amines derived from xylene and used in dyes. Formula: $(CH_3)_2C_6H_3NH_2$. **2** any one of these isomers.

xylo- *or before a vowel* **xyl-** *combining form.* **1** indicating wood: *xylophone.* **2** indicating xylene: *xylidine.* [from Greek *xulon* wood]

xylocarp (ˈzaɪləˌkɑːp) *n Botany.* a fruit, such as a coconut, having a hard woody pericarp. ▸ **ˌxyloˈcarpous** *adj*

xylogenous (zaɪˈlɒdʒɪnəs) *adj Biology.* living in or on wood. Also: **xylophilous** (zaɪˈlɒfɪləs).

xylograph (ˈzaɪləˌgrɑːf, -ˌgræf) *n* **1** an engraving in wood. **2** a print taken from a wood block. ◆ *vb* **3** (*tr*) to print (a design, illustration, etc.) from a wood engraving.

xylography (zaɪˈlɒgrəfɪ) *n* the art, craft, or process of printing from wooden blocks. ▸ **xyˈlographer** *n* ▸ **xylographic** (ˌzaɪləˈgræfɪk) *or* **ˌxyloˈgraphical** *adj*

xyloid (ˈzaɪlɔɪd) *adj Botany.* of, relating to, or resembling wood; woody.

xylol (ˈzaɪlɒl) *n* another name (not in technical usage) for **xylene.**

xylophagous (zaɪˈlɒfəgəs) *adj* (of certain insects, crustaceans, etc.) feeding on or living within wood.

xylophone (ˈzaɪləˌfəʊn) *n Music.* a percussion instrument consisting of a set of wooden bars of graduated length. It is played with hard-headed hammers. [C19: from XYLO- + -PHONE] ▸ **xylophonic** (ˌzaɪləˈfɒnɪk) *adj* ▸ **xylophonist** (zaɪˈlɒfənɪst) *n*

xylorimba (ˌzaɪləˈrɪmbə) *n* a large xylophone with an extended range of five octaves. [C20: XYLO(PHONE) + (MA)RIMBA]

xylose (ˈzaɪləʊz, -ləʊs) *n* a white crystalline dextrorotatory sugar found in the form of xylan in wood and straw. It is extracted by hydrolysis with acids and used in dyeing, tanning, and in foods for diabetics. Formula: $C_5H_{10}O_5$.

xylotomous (zaɪˈlɒtəməs) *adj* (of certain insects, insect larvae, etc.) cutting or boring into wood.

xylotomy (zaɪˈlɒtəmɪ) *n* the preparation of sections of wood for examination by microscope. ▸ **xyˈlotomist** *n*

xylyl (ˈzaɪlɪl) *n* (*modifier*) of, containing, or denoting the group of atoms $(CH_3)_2C_6H_3$-, derived from xylene.

xyst (zɪst), **xystus,** *or* **xystos** (ˈzɪstəs) *n* **1** a long portico, esp. one used in ancient Greece for athletics. **2** (in ancient Rome) a covered garden walk or one lined with trees. [C17: from Latin *xystus,* from Greek *xustos,* literally: smoothed, polished (area), from *xuein* to scrape, make smooth]

xyster (ˈzɪstə) *n* a surgical instrument for scraping bone; surgical rasp or file. [C17: via New Latin from Greek: tool for scraping, from *xuein* to scrape, make smooth]

Yy

y *or* **Y** (waɪ) *n, pl* **y's, Y's,** *or* **Ys. 1** the 25th letter of the modern English alphabet. **2** a speech sound represented by this letter, in English usually a semivowel, as in *yawn,* or a vowel, as in *symbol* or *shy.* **3a** something shaped like a Y. **3b** (*in combination*): *a Y-cross.*

y *Maths. symbol for:* **1** the *y*-axis or a coordinate measured along the *y*-axis in a Cartesian coordinate system. **2** an algebraic variable.

Y *symbol for:* **1** any unknown, unspecified, or variable factor, number, person, or thing. **2** *Chem.* yttrium. **3** *Currency.* **3a** yen. **3b** yuan.

y. *abbrev. for* year.

Y. *abbrev. for* YMCA or YWCA.

-y[1] *or* **-ey** *suffix forming adjectives.* **1** (*from nouns*) characterized by; consisting of; filled with; relating to; resembling: *sunny; sandy; smoky; classy.* **2** (*from verbs*) tending to; acting or existing as specified: *leaky; shiny.* [from Old English *-ig, -æg*]

-y[2], **-ie,** *or* **-ey** *suffix of nouns. Informal.* **1** denoting smallness and expressing affection and familiarity: *a doggy; a granny; Jamie.* **2** a person or thing concerned with or characterized by being: *a groupie; a fatty.* [C14: from Scottish *-ie, -y,* familiar suffix occurring originally in names, as in *Jamie* (*James*)]

-y[3] *suffix forming nouns.* **1** (*from verbs*) indicating the act of doing what is indicated by the verbal element: *inquiry.* **2** (*esp. with combining forms of Greek, Latin, or French origin*) indicating state, condition, or quality: *geography; jealousy.* [from Old French *-ie,* from Latin *-ia*]

Y2K *n Informal.* another name for the year 2000 A.D. (esp. referring to the millennium bug). [C20: Y(EAR) + 2 + K (in the sense: thousand)]

yabber (ˈjæbə) *Informal, chiefly Austral.* ◆ *vb* **1** (*intr*) to talk or jabber. ◆ *n* **2** talk or jabber. [C19: from a native Australian language *yabba* talk, probably influenced by JABBER]

yabby *or* **yabbie** (ˈjæbɪ) *Austral.* ◆ *n, pl* **-bies. 1** a small freshwater crayfish of the genus *Cherax.* **2** Also called: **nipper.** a marine prawn used as bait.◆ *vb* **-bies, -bying, -bied. 3** (*intr*) to go out to catch yabbies. [from a native Australian language]

Yablonovy Mountains (*Russian* ˈjabləneviј) *pl n* a mountain range in Siberia. Highest peak: 1680 m (5512 ft.). Also called: **Yablonoi Mountains** (ˈjɑːblə,nɔɪ).

yacht (jɒt) *n* **1** a vessel propelled by sail or power, used esp. for pleasure cruising, racing, etc. **2** short for **sand yacht** or **ice yacht.** ◆ *vb* **3** (*intr*) to sail or cruise in a yacht. [C16: from obsolete Dutch *jaghte,* short for *jahtschip,* from *jagen* to chase + *schip* SHIP]

yachtie (ˈjɒtɪ) *n Austral. and N.Z. informal.* a yachtsman; sailing enthusiast.

yachting (ˈjɒtɪŋ) *n* **a** the sport or practice of navigating a yacht. **b** (*as modifier*): *yachting clothes.*

yachtsman (ˈjɒtsmən) *or* (*fem*) **yachtswoman** *n, pl* **-men** *or* **-women.** a person who sails a yacht or yachts. ▸ **ˈyachtsman,ship** *n*

yack (jæk) *n, vb* a variant spelling of **yak**[2].

yackety-yak (ˌjækɪtɪˈjæk) *n Slang.* noisy, continuous, and trivial talk or conversation. Sometimes shortened to **yak.** [of imitative origin]

yad (jɑd) *n Judaism.* a hand-held pointer used for reading the sefer torah. [Hebrew]

yae (je) *adj Scot.* a variant of **ae.**

yaffle (ˈjæfᵊl) *n* another name for **green woodpecker.** [C18: imitative of its cry]

Yafo (ˈjɑːfɔː) *n* transliteration of the Hebrew name for **Jaffa** (sense 1).

Yagi aerial (ˈjɑːgɪ, ˈjægɪ) *n* a sharply directional aerial, used esp. in television and radio astronomy, consisting of three or more elements lying parallel to each other, the principal direction of radiation being along the line of the centres. [C20: named after Hidetsugu *Yagi* (1886–1976), Japanese engineer]

yah (jɑː, jɛə) *sentence substitute.* **1** an informal word for **yes,** often used to indicate derision or contempt. ◆ *interj* **2** an exclamation of derision or disgust.

Yahata (ˈjɑːhɑː,tɑː) *n* a variant of **Yawata.**

yahoo (jəˈhuː) *n, pl* **-hoos.** a crude, brutish, or obscenely coarse person. [C18: from the name of a race of brutish creatures resembling men in Jonathan Swift's *Gulliver's Travels* (1726)] ▸ **yaˈhooism** *n*

Yahrzeit (ˈjɔːtsaɪt) *n Judaism.* the anniversary of the death of a close relative, on which it is customary to kindle a light and recite the Kaddish and also, in some communities, to observe a fast. [Yiddish, from Middle High German *jārzīt* anniversary; see YEAR, TIDE[1]]

Yahweh, Jahweh (ˈjɑːweɪ) *or* **Yahveh, Jahveh** (ˈjɑːveɪ) *n Old Testament.* a vocalization of the Tetragrammaton, used esp. by Christian theologians. [from Hebrew, from YHVH, with conjectural vowels; perhaps related to *hāwāh* to be; see also JEHOVAH]

Yahwism, Jahwism (ˈjɑːwɪzəm) *or* **Yahvism, Jahvism** (ˈjɑːvɪzəm) *n* the use of the name Yahweh, esp. in parts of the Old Testament, as the personal name of God.

Yahwist, Jahwist (ˈjɑːwɪst) *or* **Yahvist, Jahvist** (ˈjɑːvɪst) *n Bible.* **the. a** the conjectured author or authors of the earliest of four main sources or strands of tradition of which the Pentateuch is composed and in which God is called *Yahweh* throughout. **b** (*as modifier*): *the Yahwist source.*

Yahwistic, Jahwistic (jɑːˈwɪstɪk) *or* **Yahvistic, Jahvistic** (jɑːˈvɪstɪk) *adj Bible.* of or relating to Yahwism, the Yahwist, or Yahweh.

Yajur-Veda (ˈjʌdʒʊəˈveɪdə) *n Hinduism.* the second Veda, consisting of prayers and sacrificial formulas primarily for use by the priests. [from Sanskrit, from *yajur* sacred, holy (compare Greek *hagios* holy) + VEDA]

yak[1] (jæk) *n* a wild and domesticated type of cattle, *Bos grunniens,* of Tibet, having long horns and long shaggy hair. [C19: from Tibetan *gyag*]

yak[2] (jæk) *Slang.* ◆ *n* **1** noisy, continuous, and trivial talk or conversation. ◆ *vb* **yaks, yakking, yakked. 2** (*intr*) to chatter or talk in this way; jabber. ◆ Also: **yakety-yak** (ˌjækɪtɪˈjæk). [C20: of imitative origin]

yakka, yakker, *or* **yacker** (ˈjækə) *n Austral. and N.Z. informal.* work. [C19: from a native Australian language]

Yakut (jæˈkut) *n* **1** (*pl* **-kuts** *or* **-kut**) a native or inhabitant of the Sakha Republic, in Russia. **2** the language of this people, belonging to the Turkic branch of the Altaic family.

Yakut Republic *n* the former name of the **Sakha Republic.**

Yakutsk (*Russian* jɪˈkutsk) *n* a port in E Russia, capital of the Sakha Republic, on the Lena River. Pop.: 192 000 (1995 est.).

yakuza (jəˈkuːzə) *n, pl* **-kuza. 1 the.** a Japanese criminal organization involved in illegal gambling, extortion, gun-running, etc. **2** a member of this organization. [C20: from Japanese *ya* eight + *ku* nine + *za* three, the worst hand in a game of cards]

Yale lock (jeɪl) *n Trademark.* a type of cylinder lock using a flat serrated key.

Yalta (*Russian* ˈjaltə) *n* a port and resort in the S Ukraine, in the Crimea on the Black Sea: scene of a conference (1945) between Churchill, Roosevelt, and Stalin, who met to plan the final defeat and occupation of Nazi Germany. Pop.: 89 000 (1988 est.).

Yalu (ˈjɑː,luː) *n* a river in E Asia, rising in N North Korea and flowing southwest to Korea Bay, forming a large part of the border between North Korea and NE China. Length: 806 km (501 miles).

yam (jæm) *n* **1** any of various twining plants of the genus *Dioscorea,* of tropical and subtropical regions, cultivated for their edible tubers: family *Dioscoreaceae.* **2** the starchy tuber of any of these plants, which is eaten as a vegetable. **3** *Southern U.S.* any of certain large varieties of sweet potato. **4** a former Scot. name for the (common) **potato.** [C17: from Portuguese *inhame,* ultimately of West African origin; compare Senegal *nyami* to eat]

Yamagata (ˌjæməˈgɑːtə) *n* Prince **Aritomo** (ˌærɪˈtəuməu). 1838–1922, Japanese soldier and politician. As war minister (1873) and chief of staff (1878), he modernized Japan's military system. He was premier of Japan (1889–93; 1898).

Yamani (jəˈmɑːnɪ) *n* Sheikh **Ahmed Zaki** (ˈɑːmɛdˈzɑːkɪ). born 1930, Saudi Arabian politician; minister of petroleum and mineral resources (1962–86).

Yamasaki (ˌjæməˈsɑːkɪ) *n* **Minoru.** 1912–86, U.S. architect. His buildings include St Louis Airport, Missouri (1953–55) and the World Trade Center, New York (1970–77).

Yamashita (ˌjæməˈʃiːtə) *n* **Tomoyuki** (ˌtəuməuˈjuːkɪ). 1885–1946, Japanese general. He commanded Japanese forces in the Malayan campaign in World War II and took Singapore (1942); captured (1945) and hanged.

yamen (ˈjɑːmɛn) *n* (in imperial China) the office or residence of a public official. [C19: from Chinese, from *ya* general's office + *měn* gate]

Yamim Nora'im (jɑˈmim nɔrɑˈim) *or* **Yomim Noro'im** (ˈjɔmim nəuˈroim) *pl n* another name for **High Holidays.** [Hebrew, literally: Days of Awe]

yammer (ˈjæmə) *Informal.* ◆ *vb* **1** to utter or whine in a complaining or peevish manner. **2** to make (a complaint) loudly or persistently. **3** (*intr*) (esp. of an animal) to howl or wail plaintively or distressingly; yelp or yowl. ◆ *n* **4** a yammering sound, wail, or utterance. **5** nonsense; jabber. [Old English *geōmrian* to grumble, complain; related to Old High German *iāmar* misery, lamentation, Old Norse *amra* to howl] ▸ **ˈyammerer** *n*

Yamoussoukro (ˌjæmuˈsuːkrəu) *n* the capital of the Côte d'Ivoire, situated in the S centre of the country. It replaced Abidjan as capital in 1983. Pop.: 110 000 (1995 est.).

Yanan (ˈjænˈæn) *or* **Yenan** *n* a city in NE China, in N Shaanxi province: political and military capital of the Chinese Communists (1935–49). Pop.: 113 277 (1990 est.). Also called: **Fushih.**

Yang[1] (jæŋ) *n* See **Yin and Yang.**

Yang[2] (jæŋ) *n* **Chen Ning** (ˈtʃɛn ˈnɪŋ). born 1922, US physicist, born in China: with Tsung-Dao Lee, he disproved the physical principle known as the conservation of parity and shared the Nobel prize for physics (1957).

Yangon (jæŋˈgɒn) *n* the capital and chief port of Myanmar (formerly Burma): an industrial city and transport centre; dominated by the gold-covered Shwe Dagon pagoda, 112 m (368 ft.) high. Pop.: 2 500 000 (latest est.). Former name (until 1989): **Rangoon.**

Yangtze (ˈjæŋtsɪ, ˈjæŋktsɪ) *n* the longest river in China, rising in SE Qinghai province and flowing east to the East China Sea near Shanghai: a major commercial waterway in one of the most densely populated areas of the world. Length: 5528 km (3434 miles). Also called: **Yangtze Jiang, Chang Jiang, Chang.**

Yanina (ˈjɑːnɪnə) *n* a variant spelling of **Ioánnina.**

yank (jæŋk) *vb* **1** to pull, jerk, or move with a sharp movement; tug. ◆ *n* **2** a sharp jerking movement; tug. [C19: of unknown origin]

Yank (jæŋk) *n* **1** a slang word for an American. **2** *U.S. informal.* short for **Yankee.**

Yankee ('jæŋkɪ) *or (informal)* **Yank** *n* **1** *Often disparaging.* a native or inhabitant of the U.S.; American. **2** a native or inhabitant of New England. **3** a native or inhabitant of the Northern U.S., esp. a Northern soldier in the Civil War. **4** *Communications.* a code word for the letter *y*. **5** *Finance.* a bond issued in the U.S. by a foreign borrower. ◆ *adj* **6** of, relating to, or characteristic of Yankees. [C18: perhaps from Dutch *Jan Kees* John Cheese, nickname used derisively by Dutch settlers in New York to designate English colonists in Connecticut]

Yankee Doodle *n* **1** an American song, popularly regarded as a characteristically national melody. **2** another name for **Yankee.**

Yankeeism ('jæŋkɪɪzəm) *n* **1** Yankee character, behaviour, or attitudes. **2** a typical Yankee word, expression, or trait.

Yantai ('jæn'taɪ), **Yentai,** *or* **Yen-t'ai** *n* a port in E China, in NE Shandong. Pop.: 452 127 (1990 est.). Also called: **Chefoo.**

Yaoundé *or* **Yaunde** (*French* jaunde) *n* the capital of Cameroon, in the southwest: University of Cameroon (1962). Pop.: 800 000 (1992 est.).

yap (jæp) *vb* **yaps, yapping, yapped.** (*intr*) **1** (of a dog) to bark in quick sharp bursts; yelp. **2** *Informal.* to talk at length in an annoying or stupid way; jabber. ◆ *n* **3** a high-pitched or sharp bark; yelp. **4** *Slang.* annoying or stupid speech; jabber. **5** *Slang.* a derogatory word for **mouth.** ◆ *interj* **6** (*usually reiterated*) an imitation or representation of the sound of a dog yapping or people jabbering. [C17: of imitative origin] ▸ **'yapper** *n* ▸ **'yappy** *adj*

Yap (jɑːp, jæp) *n* a group of four main islands in the W Pacific, in the W Caroline Islands: administratively a district of the U.S. Trust Territory of the Pacific Islands from 1947; became self-governing in 1979 as part of the Federated States of Micronesia; important Japanese naval base in World War II. Pop.: 11 128 (1994). Area: 101 sq. km (39 sq. miles).

yapok (jə'pɒk) *n* an amphibious nocturnal opossum, *Chironectes minimus*, of Central and South America, having dense fur and preying on shrimps, crayfish, etc. Also called: **water opossum.** [C19: named after *Oyapok*, a river flowing between French Guiana and Brazil]

yapon ('jɔːpᵊn) *n* a variant spelling of **yaupon.**

Yapurá (japu'ra) *n* the Spanish name for **Japurá.**

Yaqui (*Spanish* 'jaki) *n* a river in NW Mexico, rising near the border with the U.S. and flowing south to the Gulf of California. Length: about 676 km (420 miles).

yarborough ('jɑːbərə, -brə) *n Bridge, whist.* a hand of 13 cards in which no card is higher than nine. [C19: supposed to be named after the second Earl of *Yarborough* (1809–62), who is said to have bet a thousand to one against the occurrence of such a hand]

yard[1] (jɑːd) *n* **1** a unit of length equal to 3 feet and defined in 1963 as exactly 0.9144 metre. Abbrev.: **yd. 2** a cylindrical wooden or hollow metal spar, tapered at the ends, slung from a mast of a square-rigged or lateen-rigged vessel and used for suspending a sail. **3** short for **yardstick** (sense 2). [Old English *gierd* rod, twig; related to Old Frisian *jerde*, Old Saxon *gerdia*, Old High German *gertia*, Old Norse *gaddr*]

yard[2] (jɑːd) *n* **1** a piece of enclosed ground, usually either paved or laid with concrete and often adjoining or surrounded by a building or buildings. **2a** an enclosed or open area used for some commercial activity, for storage, etc.: *a railway yard.* **2b** (*in combination*): *a brickyard; a shipyard.* **3** a U.S. and Canadian word for **garden** (sense 1). **4** an area having a network of railway tracks and sidings, used for storing rolling stock, making up trains, etc. **5** *U.S. and Canadian.* the winter pasture of deer, moose, and similar animals. **6** *Austral. and N.Z.* an enclosed area used to draw off part of a herd, etc. **7** *N.Z.* short for **saleyard** or **stockyard.** ◆ *vb* (*tr*) **8** to draft (animals), esp. to a saleyard. [Old English *geard*; related to Old Saxon *gard*, Old High German *gart*, Old Norse *garthr* yard, Gothic *gards* house, Old Slavonic *gradu* town, castle, Albanian *garth* hedge]

Yard (jɑːd) *n* **the.** *Brit. informal.* short for **Scotland Yard.**

yardage[1] ('jɑːdɪdʒ) *n* a length measured in yards.

yardage[2] ('jɑːdɪdʒ) *n* **1** the use of a railway yard in the transportation of cattle. **2** the charge for this.

yardarm ('jɑːd,ɑːm) *n Nautical.* the two tapering outer ends of a ship's yard.

yardbird ('jɑːd,bɜːd) *n U.S. military.* an inexperienced, untrained, or clumsy soldier, esp. one employed on menial duties.

yard grass *n* an Old World perennial grass, *Eleusine indica*, with prostrate leaves, growing as a troublesome weed on open ground, yards, etc. Also called: **wire grass.**

Yardie ('jɑːdɪ) *n* a member of a Black criminal syndicate originally based in Jamaica. [origin unknown]

yarding ('jɑːdɪŋ) *n* a group of animals displayed for sale: *a good yarding.*

yard of ale *n* **1** the beer or ale contained in a narrow horn-shaped drinking glass, usually about one yard long and holding between two and three pints. **2** such a drinking glass itself.

yardstick ('jɑːd,stɪk) *n* **1** a measure or standard used for comparison: *on what kind of yardstick is he basing his criticism?* **2** a graduated stick, one yard long, used for measurement.

yare (jeə) *adj* **yarer, yarest. 1** *Archaic or dialect.* ready, brisk, or eager. **2** (of a vessel) answering swiftly to the helm; easily handled. ◆ *adv* **3** *Obsolete.* readily or eagerly. [Old English *gearu* ready; related to Old Saxon, Old High German *garo* ready, prepared, Old Norse *gorr*] ▸ **'yarely** *adv*

Yarkand (,jɑː'kænd) *n* another name for **Shache.**

Yarmouth ('jɑːməθ) *n* short for **Great Yarmouth.**

yarmulke ('jɑːməlkə) *n Judaism.* a skullcap worn by orthodox male Jews at all times, and by others during prayer. [from Yiddish, from Ukrainian and Polish *yarmulka* cap, probably from Turkish *yağmurluk* raincoat, from *yağmur* rain]

yarn (jɑːn) *n* **1** a continuous twisted strand of natural or synthetic fibres, used in weaving, knitting, etc. **2** *Informal.* a long and often involved story or account, usually telling of incredible or fantastic events. **3 spin a yarn.** *Informal.* **3a** to tell such a story. **3b** to make up or relate a series of excuses. ◆ *vb* **4** (*intr*) to tell such a story or stories. [Old English *gearn*; related to Old High German *garn* yarn, Old Norse *görn* gut, Greek *khordē* string, gut]

yarn-dyed *adj* (of fabric) dyed while still in yarn form, before being woven. Compare **piece-dyed.**

Yaroslavl (*Russian* jɪra'slavlj) *n* a city in W Russia, on the River Volga: a major trading centre since early times and one of the first industrial centres in Russia; textile industries were established in the 18th century. Pop.: 629 000 (1995 est.).

yarraman ('jærəmən) *n, pl* **-mans** *or* **-men.** *Austral.* a horse. [C19: from a native Australian language]

yarran ('jærən) *n* a small hardy tree, *Acacia homalophylla*, of inland Australia: useful as fodder and for firewood. [from a native Australian language]

Yarra River ('jærə) *n* a river in SE Australia, rising in the Great Dividing Range and flowing west and southwest through Melbourne to Port Phillip Bay. Length: 250 km (155 miles).

yarrow ('jærəʊ) *n* any of several plants of the genus *Achillea*, esp. *A. millefolium*, of Eurasia, having finely dissected leaves and flat clusters of white flower heads: family *Compositae* (composites). Also called: **milfoil.** See also **sneezewort.** [Old English *gearwe*; related to Old High German *garwa*, Dutch *gerwe*]

yashmak *or* **yashmac** ('jæʃmæk) *n* the face veil worn by Muslim women when in public. [C19: from Arabic]

yataghan ('jætəgən) *or* **ataghan** *n* a Turkish sword with a curved single-edged blade. [C19: from Turkish *yatağan*]

yate (jeɪt) *n Austral.* any of several small eucalyptus trees, esp. *Eucalyptus cornuta*, yielding a very hard timber. [from a native Australian language]

Yathrib ('jæθrɪb) *n* the ancient Arabic name for **Medina.**

yatter ('jætə; *Scot.* 'jɑtər) *Scot.* ◆ *vb* (*intr*) **1** to talk at length; chatter. ◆ *n* **2** continuous chatter. [of imitative origin]

Yaunde (*French* jaunde) *n* a variant spelling of **Yaoundé.**

yaup (jɔːp) *vb, n* a variant spelling of **yawp.** ▸ **'yauper** *n*

yaupon *or* **yapon** ('jɔːpᵊn) *n* a southern U.S. evergreen holly shrub, *Ilex vomitoria*, with spreading branches, scarlet fruits, and oval leaves: used as a substitute for tea. [from Catawba *yopun* shrub, diminutive of *yop* tree]

yautia ('jɔːtɪə) *n* **1** any of several Caribbean aroid plants of the genus *Xanthosoma*, such as *X. sagittifolium*, cultivated for their edible leaves and underground stems. **2** the leaves or underground stems of these plants, which can be eaten as vegetables. [C19: American Spanish, from Taino]

Yavarí (jaβa'ri) *n* the Spanish name for **Javari.**

yaw (jɔː) *vb* **1** (*intr*) (of an aircraft, missile, etc.) to turn about its vertical axis. Compare **pitch**[1] (sense 11), **roll** (sense 14). **2** (*intr*) (of a ship, etc.) to deviate temporarily from a straight course. **3** (*tr*) to cause (an aircraft, ship, etc.) to yaw. ◆ *n* **4** the angular movement of an aircraft, missile, etc., about its vertical axis. **5** the deviation of a vessel from a straight course. [C16: of unknown origin]

Yawata ('jɑːwɑː,tɑː) *or* **Yahata** *n* a former city in Japan, on N Kyushu: merged with Moji, Kokura, Tobata, and Wakamatsu in 1963 to form **Kitakyushu.**

yawl[1] (jɔːl) *n* **1** a two-masted sailing vessel, rigged fore-and-aft, with a large mainmast and a small mizzenmast stepped aft of the rudderpost. Compare **ketch, sloop. 2** a ship's small boat, usually rowed by four or six oars. [C17: from Dutch *jol* or Middle Low German *jolle*, of unknown origin]

yawl[2] (jɔːl) *vb* (*intr*) *Brit. dialect.* to howl, weep, or scream harshly; yowl. [C14: from Low German *jaulen*; see YOWL]

yawn (jɔːn) *vb* **1** (*intr*) to open the mouth wide and take in air deeply, often as in involuntary reaction to tiredness, sleepiness, or boredom. **2** (*tr*) to express or utter while yawning. **3** (*intr*) to be open wide as if threatening to engulf (someone or something): *the mine shaft yawned below.* ◆ *n* **4** the act or an instance of yawning. [Old English *gionian*; related to Old Saxon *ginōn*, Old High German *ginēn* to yawn, Old Norse *gjā* gap] ▸ **'yawner** *n* ▸ **'yawning** *adj* ▸ **'yawningly** *adv*

yawp (jɔːp) *Dialect and U.S. and Canadian informal.* ◆ *vb* (*intr*) **1** to gape or yawn, esp. audibly. **2** to shout, cry, or talk noisily; bawl. **3** to bark, yelp, or yowl. ◆ *n* **4** a shout, bark, yelp, or cry. **5** a noisy, foolish, or raucous utterance. [C15 *yolpen*, probably of imitative origin; see YAP, YELP] ▸ **'yawper** *n*

yaws (jɔːz) *n* (*usually functioning as sing*) an infectious nonvenereal disease of tropical climates with early symptoms resembling syphilis, characterized by red skin eruptions and, later, pain in the joints: it is caused by the spiral bacterium *Treponema pertenue*. Also called: **framboesia.** [C17: of Carib origin]

***y*-axis** *n* a reference axis, usually vertical, of a graph or two- or three-dimensional Cartesian coordinate system along which the *y*-coordinate is measured.

Yazd (jɑːzd) *or* **Yezd** *n* a city in central Iran: a major centre of silk weaving. Pop.: 306 268 (1994 est.).

Yb *the chemical symbol for* ytterbium.

YC (in Britain) *abbrev. for* Young Conservative.

Y-chromosome *n* the sex chromosome that occurs as one of a pair with the X-chromosome in the diploid cells of the males of many animals, including humans. Compare **X-chromosome.**

yclept (ɪ'klɛpt) *Obsolete.* ◆ *vb* **1** a past participle of **clepe.** ◆ *adj* **2** having the name of; called. [Old English *gecleopod*, past participle of *cleopian* to call]

Y connection *n Electrical engineering.* a three-phase star connection.

yd *or* **yd.** *abbrev. for* yard (measure).

ye[1] (jiː, *unstressed* jɪ) *pron* **1** *Archaic or dialect.* refers to more than one person including the person addressed but not including the speaker. **2** Also: **ee** (iː). *Dialect.* refers to one person addressed: *I tell ye.* [Old English *gē*; related to Dutch *gij*, Old Norse *ēr*, Gothic *jus*]

ye[2] (ðiː, *spelling pron* jiː) *determiner* a form of **the**[1], used as a supposed archaism, esp. in conjunction with other putative archaic spellings: *ye olde oake.* [from a misinterpretation of *the* as written in some Middle English texts. The runic letter thorn (Þ, representing *th*) was incorrectly transcribed as *y* because of a resemblance in their shapes]

yea (jeɪ) *sentence substitute.* **1** a less common word for **aye** (yes). ◆ *adv* **2** (*sentence modifier*) *Archaic or literary.* indeed; truly: *yea, though my enemies spurn me, I shall prevail.* [Old English *gēa;* related to Old Frisian *jē,* Old Saxon, Old Norse, Old High German *jā,* Gothic *jai*]

yeah (jɛə) *sentence substitute.* an informal word for **yes.**

yean (jiːn) *vb* (of a sheep or goat) to give birth to (offspring). [Old English *geēanian;* related to Dutch *oonen* to bring forth young, Latin *agnus* lamb; see EWE]

yeanling (ˈjiːnlɪŋ) *n* the young of a goat or sheep.

year (jɪə) *n* **1** Also called: **civil year.** the period of time, the **calendar year,** containing 365 days or in a **leap year** 366 days. It is based on the Gregorian calendar, being divided into 12 calendar months, and is reckoned from January 1 to December 31. **2** a period of twelve months from any specified date, such as one based on the four seasons. **3** a specific period of time, usually occupying a definite part or parts of a twelve-month period, used for some particular activity: *a school year.* **4** Also called: **astronomical year, tropical year,** the period of time, the **solar year,** during which the earth makes one revolution around the sun, measured between two successive vernal equinoxes: equal to 365.242 19 days. **5** the period of time, the **sidereal year,** during which the earth makes one revolution around the sun, measured between two successive conjunctions of a particular star: equal to 365.256 36 days. **6** the period of time, the **lunar year,** containing 12 lunar months and equal to 354.3671 days. **7** the period of time taken by a specified planet to complete one revolution around the sun: *the Martian year.* **8** (*pl*) age, esp. old age: *a man of his years should be more careful.* **9** (*pl*) time: *in years to come.* **10** a group of pupils or students, who are taught or study together, divided into classes at school: *they are the best year we've ever had for history.* **11 the year dot.** *Informal.* as long ago as can be remembered. **12 year and a day.** *English law.* a period fixed by law to ensure the completion of a full year. It is applied for certain purposes, such as to determine the time within which wrecks must be claimed. **13 year in, year out.** regularly or monotonously, over a long period. ◆ Related adj: **annual.** [Old English *gear;* related to Gothic *jēr,* Old Saxon, Old High German *jār,* Old Norse *ār* year, Polish *jar* springtime, Latin *hōrnus* of this year]

USAGE In writing spans of years, it is important to choose a style that avoids ambiguity. The practice adopted in this dictionary is, in four-figure dates, to specify the last two digits of the second date if it falls within the same century as the first: *1801–08; 1850–51; 1899–1901.* In writing three-figure B.C. dates, it is advisable to give both dates in full: *159–156* B.C., not *159–56* B.C. unless of course the span referred to consists of 103 years rather than three years. It is also advisable to specify B.C. or A.D. in years under 1000 unless the context makes this self-evident.

yearbook (ˈjɪəˌbʊk) *n* an almanac or reference book published annually and containing details of events of the previous year.

yearling (ˈjɪəlɪŋ) *n* **1** the young of any of various animals, including the antelope and buffalo, between one and two years of age. **2** a thoroughbred racehorse counted for racing purposes as being one year old until the second Jan. 1 following its birth. **3a** a bond that is intended to mature after one year. **3b** (*as modifier*): *yearling bonds.* ◆ *adj* **4** being a year old.

yearlong (ˈjɪəˈlɒŋ) *adj* throughout a whole year.

yearly (ˈjɪəlɪ) *adj* **1** occurring, done, appearing, etc., once a year or every year; annual. **2** lasting or valid for a year; annual: *a yearly subscription.* ◆ *adv* **3** once a year; annually. ◆ *n, pl* **-lies. 4** a publication, event, etc., that occurs once a year.

yearn (jɜːn) *vb* (*intr*) **1** (usually foll. by *for* or *after* or an infinitive) to have an intense desire or longing (for); pine (for). **2** to feel tenderness or affection. [Old English *giernan;* related to Old Saxon *girnian,* Old Norse *girna,* Gothic *gairnjan,* Old High German *gerōn* to long for, Sanskrit *haryati* he likes] ▸ **ˈyearner** *n*

yearning (ˈjɜːnɪŋ) *n* an intense or overpowering longing, desire, or need; craving. ▸ **ˈyearningly** *adv*

year of grace *n* any year of the Christian era, as dated from the presumed date of Christ's birth.

year-round *adj* open, in use, operating, etc., throughout the year.

yeast (jiːst) *n* **1** any of various single-celled ascomycetous fungi of the genus *Saccharomyces* and related genera, which reproduce by budding and are able to ferment sugars: a rich source of vitamins of the B complex. **2** a commercial preparation containing yeast cells and inert material such as meal, used in raising dough for bread or for fermenting beer, whisky, etc. See also **brewer's yeast. 3** a preparation containing yeast cells, used to treat diseases caused by vitamin B deficiency. **4** froth or foam, esp. on beer. ◆ *vb* **5** (*intr*) to froth or foam. [Old English *giest;* related to Old Norse *jostr,* Old High German *jesan,* Swedish *esa,* Norwegian *asa,* Sanskrit *yasati*] ▸ **ˈyeastless** *adj* ▸ **ˈyeastˌlike** *adj*

yeast cake *n Chiefly U.S. and Canadian.* living yeast cells compressed with starch into a cake, for use in baking or brewing.

yeasty (ˈjiːstɪ) *adj* **yeastier, yeastiest. 1** of, resembling, or containing yeast. **2** fermenting or causing fermentation. **3** tasting of or like yeast. **4** insubstantial or frivolous. **5** restless, agitated, or unsettled. **6** covered with or containing froth or foam. ▸ **ˈyeastily** *adv* ▸ **ˈyeastiness** *n*

Yeats (jeɪts) *n* **1 Jack Butler.** 1871–1957, Irish painter. **2** his brother **W(illiam) B(utler).** 1865–1939, Irish poet and dramatist. His collections of verse include *Responsibilities* (1914), *The Tower* (1928), and *The Winding Stair* (1929). Among his plays are *The Countess Cathleen* (1892; 1912) and *Cathleen ni Houlihan* (1902); he was a founder of the Irish National Theatre Company at the Abbey Theatre in Dublin. He was awarded the Nobel prize for literature 1923.

yebo (ˈjebaʊ) *sentence substitute. S. African informal.* an expression of affirmation. [Zulu *yebo* yes, I agree]

yegg (jeg) *n Slang, chiefly U.S.* a burglar or safe-breaker. [C20: perhaps from the surname of a burglar]

Yeisk, Yeysk, *or* **Eisk** (*Russian* jejsk) *n* a port and resort in SW Russia, on the Sea of Azov. Pop.: 86 300 (1991 est.).

Yekaterinburg *or* **Ekaterinburg** (*Russian* jɪkətɪrimˈburk) *n* a city in NW Russia, in the Ural Mountains: scene of the execution (1918) of Nicholas II and his family; university (1920); one of the largest centres of heavy engineering in Russia. Pop.: 1 280 000 (1995 est.). Former name (1924–91): **Sverdlovsk.**

Yekaterinodar *or* **Ekaterinodar** (*Russian* jɪkətɪrinaˈdar) *n* the former name (until 1920) of **Krasnodar.**

Yekaterinoslav *or* **Ekaterinoslav** (*Russian* jɪkətɪrinaˈslaf) *n* the former name (1787–96, 1802–1926) of **Dnepropetrovsk.**

yeld (jɛld) *adj Scot. and northern English dialect.* **1** (of an animal) barren or too young to bear young. **2** (of a cow) not yielding milk. [Old English *gelde* barren; related to GELD[1]]

Yelisavetgrad *or* **Elisavetgrad** (*Russian* jɪlizaˈvjɛtgrət) *n* the former name (until 1924) of **Kirovograd.**

Yelisavetpol *or* **Elisavetpol** (*Russian* jɪlizaˈvjɛtpəlj) *n* the former name (until 1920) of **Kirovabad.**

Yelizaveta Petrovna (*Russian* jɪlizaˈvjɛtə pɪˈtrɔvnə) *n* See **Elizabeth**[2] (sense 3).

yelk (jɛlk) *n* a dialect word for **yolk** (of an egg).

yell (jɛl) *vb* **1** to shout, scream, cheer, or utter in a loud or piercing way. ◆ *n* **2** a loud piercing inarticulate cry, as of pain, anger, or fear. **3** *U.S. and Canadian.* a rhythmic cry of words or syllables, used in cheering in unison. [Old English *giellan;* related to Old Saxon *gellon,* Old High German *gellan,* Old Norse *gjalla;* see NIGHTINGALE] ▸ **ˈyeller** *n*

yellow (ˈjɛləʊ) *n* **1** any of a group of colours that vary in saturation but have the same hue. They lie in the approximate wavelength range 585–575 nanometres. Yellow is the complementary colour of blue and with cyan and magenta forms a set of primary colours. Related adj: **xanthous. 2** a pigment or dye of or producing these colours. **3** yellow cloth or clothing: *dressed in yellow.* **4** the yolk of an egg. **5** a yellow ball in snooker, etc. **6** any of a group of pieridine butterflies the males of which have yellow or yellowish wings, esp. the clouded yellows (*Colias* spp.) and the brimstone. ◆ *adj* **7** of the colour yellow. **8** yellowish in colour or having parts or marks that are yellowish: *yellow jasmine.* **9** having a yellowish skin; Mongoloid. **10** *Informal.* cowardly or afraid. **11** offensively sensational, as a cheap newspaper (esp. in the phrase **yellow press**). ◆ *vb* **12** to make or become yellow. See also **yellows.** [Old English *geolu;* related to Old Saxon, Old High German *gelo,* Old Norse *gulr,* Latin *helvus*] ▸ **ˈyellowish** *adj* ▸ **ˈyellowly** *adv* ▸ **ˈyellowness** *n* ▸ **ˈyellowy** *adj*

yellow archangel *n* See **archangel** (sense 3).

yellowbark (ˈjɛləʊˌbɑːk) *n* another name for **calisaya.**

yellow belly *n* **1** *Dialect.* a native of Lincolnshire, esp. of the fens. **2** *Austral.* any of several freshwater food fishes with yellow underparts.

yellow-belly *n, pl* **-lies.** a slang word for **coward.** ▸ **ˈyellow-ˌbellied** *adj*

yellow bile *n Archaic.* one of the four bodily humours, choler.

yellowbird (ˈjɛləʊˌbɜːd) *n* any of various birds having a yellow plumage, such as the American goldfinch.

yellow brain fungus *n* See **jelly fungus.**

yellow cake *n Informal.* semirefined uranium ore.

yellow card *n Soccer.* a card of a yellow colour displayed by a referee to indicate that a player has been officially cautioned for some offence.

yellow cress *n* any of various species of cress (*Rorippa*) that are related to watercress and have yellow flowers. They are not confined to water margins and some are garden weeds.

yellow-dog contract *n U.S.* a contract with an employer, now illegal, in which an employee agreed not to join a trade union during his employment. [C20: from U.S. *yellow-dog* anti-trade union, from *yellow dog* mongrel, contemptible person]

yellow fever *n* an acute infectious disease of tropical and subtropical climates, characterized by fever, haemorrhages, vomiting of blood, and jaundice: caused by a virus transmitted by the bite of a female mosquito of the species *Aedes aegypti.* Also called: **yellow jack, black vomit.**

yellow flag *n* **1** another name for **quarantine flag. 2** See **flag**[2] (sense 1).

yellowhammer (ˈjɛləʊˌhæmə) *n* **1** a European bunting, *Emberiza citrinella,* having a yellowish head and body and brown streaked wings and tail. **2** *U.S. and Canadian.* an informal name for the **yellow-shafted flicker,** an American woodpecker (see **flicker**[2]). [C16: of uncertain origin]

yellowhead (ˈjɛləʊˌhɛd) *n* a small bush bird, *Mohoua ochrocephala,* of South Island, New Zealand, having a yellow head and breast.

yellow jack *n* **1** *Pathol.* another name for **yellow fever. 2** another name for **quarantine flag. 3** any of certain large yellowish carangid food fishes, esp. *Caranx bartholomaei,* of warm and tropical Atlantic waters.

yellow jacket *n U.S. and Canadian.* any of several social wasps of the genus *Vespa,* having yellow markings on the body.

yellow jasmine *n* a climbing shrub, *Gelsemium sempervirens,* of the south-eastern U.S., having fragrant funnel-shaped yellow flowers: family *Loganiaceae.* See also **gelsemium.**

yellow jersey *n* (in the Tour de France) a yellow jersey awarded as a trophy to the cyclist with the fastest time in each stage of the race.

yellow journalism *n* the type of journalism that relies on sensationalism and lurid exaggeration to attract readers. [C19: perhaps shortened from the phrase *Yellow Kid journalism,* referring to the *Yellow Kid,* a cartoon (1895) in the *New York World,* a newspaper having a reputation for sensationalism]

Yellowknife ('jɛləʊ,naɪf) *n* a city in N Canada, capital of the Northwest Territories on Great Slave Lake. Pop.: 15 179 (1991).

yellowlegs ('jɛləʊ,lɛgz) *n* (*functioning as sing*) either of two North American sandpipers, *Tringa melanoleuca* (or *Totanus melanoleucus*) (**greater yellowlegs**) or *T. flavipes* (**lesser yellowlegs**), having bright yellow legs.

yellow line *n Brit.* a yellow line painted along the edge of a road indicating waiting restrictions.

yellow metal *n* **1** a type of brass having about 60 per cent copper and 40 per cent zinc. **2** another name for **gold.**

Yellow Pages *pl n Trademark.* a classified telephone directory, often printed on yellow paper, that lists subscribers by the business or service provided.

yellow peril *n* the power or alleged power of Asiatic peoples, esp. the Chinese, to threaten or destroy the supremacy of White or Western civilization.

yellow poplar *n* another name for **tulip tree** (sense 1) or **tulipwood** (sense 1).

yellow rain *n* a type of yellow precipitation described in parts of SE Asia and alleged by some to be evidence of chemical warfare using mycotoxins.

yellow rattle *n* See **rattle**[1] (sense 10).

Yellow River *n* the second longest river in China, rising in SE Qinghai and flowing east, south, and east again to the Gulf of Bohai south of Tianjin; it has changed its course several times in recorded history. Length: about 4350 km (2700 miles). Chinese name: **Hwang Ho.**

yellows ('jɛləʊz) *n* (*functioning as sing*) **1** any of various fungal or viral diseases of plants, characterized by yellowish discoloration and stunting. **2** *Vet. science.* another name for **jaundice.**

yellow sally *n* an angler's name for either of two small yellow stoneflies: *Isoperla grammatica* of chalk streams and *Chloroperla torrentium* of upland streams.

Yellow Sea *n* a shallow arm of the Pacific between Korea and NE China. Area: about 466 200 sq. km (180 000 sq. miles). Chinese name: **Hwang Hai.**

yellow spot *n Anatomy.* another name for **macula lutea.**

Yellowstone ('jɛləʊ,stəʊn) *n* a river rising in N Wyoming and flowing north through Yellowstone National Park, then east to the Missouri. Length: 1080 km (671 miles).

Yellowstone Falls *pl n* a waterfall in NW Wyoming, in Yellowstone National Park on the Yellowstone River.

Yellowstone National Park *n* a national park in the NW central U.S., mostly in NW Wyoming: the oldest and largest national park in the U.S., containing unusual geological formations and geysers. Area: 8956 sq. km (3458 sq. miles).

yellow streak *n Informal.* a cowardly or weak trait, characteristic, or flaw in a person's nature.

yellowtail ('jɛləʊ,teɪl) *n, pl* **-tails** *or* **-tail. 1** a carangid game fish, *Seriola dorsalis,* of coastal waters of S California and Mexico, having a yellow tail fin. **2** any of various similar fishes. **3** Also called: **yellowtail moth.** another name for **goldtail moth.**

yellow underwing *n* any of several species of noctuid moths (*Noctua* and *Anarta* species), the hind wings of which are yellow with a black bar.

yellow water lily *n* an aquatic nymphaeaceous plant, *Nuphar lutea,* of Europe and N Asia, having floating heart-shaped leaves and yellow flowers. Also called: **brandy bottle.**

yellowweed ('jɛləʊ,wiːd) *n* any of various yellow-flowered plants, such as the ragwort in Europe and some species of goldenrod in the U.S.

yellowwood ('jɛləʊ,wʊd) *n* **1** Also called (U.S.): **gopherwood.** any of several leguminous trees of the genus *Cladrastis,* esp. *C. lutea,* of the southeastern U.S., having clusters of white flowers and yellow wood yielding a yellow dye. **2** Also called: **West Indian satinwood.** a rutaceous tree, *Zanthoxylum flavum,* of the Caribbean, with smooth hard wood. **3** any of several other trees with yellow wood, esp. *Podocarpus falcatus,* a conifer of southern Africa: family *Podocarpaceae.* **4** the wood of any of these trees.

yellowwort ('jɛləʊ,wɜːt) *n* a gentianaceous perennial, *Blackstonia perfoliata,* that is related to centaury and has waxy grey foliage and yellow flowers: characteristically found on chalk turf.

yellow-yite *n* a Scot. word for **yellowhammer** (sense 1). Also called: **yite, yitie.**

yelp (jɛlp) *vb* (*intr*) **1** (esp. of a dog) to utter a sharp or high-pitched cry or bark, often indicating pain. ◆ *n* **2** a sharp or high-pitched cry or bark. [Old English *gielpan* to boast; related to Low German *galpen* to croak, Danish *gylpe* to croak] ▸ **'yelper** *n*

Yeltsin ('jɛltsɪn; *Russian* jeltsin) *n* **Boris (Nicolayevich).** born 1931, Russian politician: president of the Russian Soviet Federative Socialist Republic (1990–91); president of Russia from 1991.

Yemen ('jɛmən) *n* a republic in SW Arabia, on the Red Sea and the Gulf of Aden: formed in 1990 from the union of North Yemen and South Yemen: consists of arid coastal lowlands, rising to fertile upland valleys and mountains in the west and to the Hadhramaut plateau in the SE: the north and east contains part of the Great Sandy Desert. Official language: Arabic. Official religion: Muslim. Currency: riyal. Capital: San'a. Pop.: 16 388 000 (1998 est.). Area (including territory claimed by Yemen along the undemarcated eastern border with Saudi Arabia): 472 099 sq. km (182 278 sq. miles). Official name: **Yemen Republic.** See also: **North Yemen, South Yemen.** ▸ **'Yemeni** *adj, n*

yen[1] (jɛn) *n, pl* **yen.** the standard monetary unit of Japan, (notionally) divided into 100 sen. [C19: from Japanese *en,* from Chinese *yüan* circular object, dollar]

yen[2] (jɛn) *Informal.* ◆ *n* **1** a passionate, ardent, or intense longing or desire. ◆ *vb* **yens, yenning, yenned. 2** (*intr*) to yearn. [perhaps from Chinese (Cantonese) *yǎn* a craving, addiction]

Yenan ('jɛn'æn) *n* a variant transliteration of the Chinese name for **Yanan.**

Yenisei *or* **Yenisey** (,jɛnɪ'seɪ; *Russian* jɪni'sjej) *n* a river in central Russia, in central Siberia, formed by the confluence of two headstreams in the Tuva Republic: flows west and north to the Arctic Ocean; the largest river in volume in Russia. Length: 4129 km (2566 miles).

Yentai *or* **Yen-t'ai** ('jɛn'taɪ) *n* a variant transliteration of the Chinese name for **Yantai.**

yeoman ('jəʊmən) *n, pl* **-men. 1** *History.* **1a** a member of a class of small freeholders of common birth who cultivated their own land. **1b** an assistant or other subordinate to an official, such as a sheriff, or to a craftsman or trader. **1c** an attendant or lesser official in a royal or noble household. **2** (in Britain) another name for **yeoman of the guard. 3** (*modifier*) characteristic of or relating to a yeoman. **4** a petty officer or noncommissioned officer in the Royal Navy or Marines in charge of signals. [C15: perhaps from *yongman* young man]

yeomanly ('jəʊmənlɪ) *adj* **1** of, relating to, or like a yeoman. **2** having the virtues attributed to yeomen, such as staunchness, loyalty, and courage. ◆ *adv* **3** in a yeomanly manner, as in being brave, staunch, or loyal.

yeoman of the guard *n* a member of the bodyguard (**Yeomen of the Guard**) of the English monarch. This unit was founded in 1485 and now retains ceremonial functions only.

yeomanry ('jəʊmənrɪ) *n* **1** yeomen collectively. **2** (in Britain) a volunteer cavalry force, organized in 1761 for home defence: merged into the Territorial Army in 1907.

yep (jɛp) *sentence substitute.* an informal word for **yes.**

yerba *or* **yerba maté** ('jɛəbə, 'jɜːbə) *n* another name for **maté.** [from Spanish *yerba maté* herb maté]

Yerevan (*Russian* jɪrɪ'van) *n* the capital of Armenia: founded in the 8th century B.C.; an industrial city and a main focus of trade routes since ancient times; university. Pop.: 1 226 000 (1994 est.). Also called: **Erevan** *or* **Erivan.**

Yerwa-Maiduguri ('jɜːwə,maɪdu'guːrɪ) *n* another name for **Maiduguri.**

yes (jɛs) *sentence substitute.* **1** used to express acknowledgment, affirmation, consent, agreement, or approval or to answer when one is addressed. **2** used, often with interrogative intonation, to signal someone to speak or keep speaking, enter a room, or do something. ◆ *n* **3** an answer or vote of *yes.* **4** (*often pl*) a person who votes in the affirmative. ◆ Compare **no**[1]. [Old English *gēse,* from *iā sīe* may it be; see YEA]

Yesenin (je'sɛnɪn) *n* **Sergey Aleksandrovich.** See (Sergey Aleksandrovich) **Esenin.**

yeshiva (jə'ʃiːvə; *Hebrew* jə'ʃiːva) *n, pl* **-vahs** *or* **-voth** (*Hebrew* -vɔt). **1** a traditional Jewish school devoted chiefly to the study of rabbinic literature and the Talmud. **2** a school run by Orthodox Jews for children of primary school age, providing both religious and secular instruction. [from Hebrew *yĕshībhāh* a sitting, seat, hence, an academy]

Yeşil Irmak (je'ʃiːl ɪə'mɑːk) *n* a river in N Turkey, flowing northwest to the Black Sea. Length: 418 km (260 miles). Ancient name: **Iris.**

Yeşilköy (je'ʃil,kœi) *n* the Turkish name for **San Stefano.**

yes man *n* a servile, submissive, or acquiescent subordinate, assistant, or associate; sycophant.

yes/no question *n Grammar.* a question inviting the answer "yes" or "no". Compare **WH question.**

yester ('jɛstə) *adj Archaic.* of or relating to yesterday: *yester sun.* Also: **yestern** ('jɛstən). [Old English *geostror;* related to Old High German *gestaron,* Gothic *gistra,* Old Norse *ī gær*]

yester- *prefix* **1** indicating the day before today: *yesterday.* **2** indicating a period of time before the present one: *yesteryear.* [Old English *geostran;* compare German *gestern,* Latin *hesternus* of yesterday]

yesterday ('jɛstədɪ, -,deɪ) *n* **1** the day immediately preceding today. **2** (*often pl*) the recent past. ◆ *adv* **3** on or during the day before today. **4** in the recent past.

yesteryear ('jɛstə,jɪə) *Formal or literary.* ◆ *n* **1** last year or the past in general. ◆ *adv* **2** during last year or the past in general.

yestreen (je'striːn) *adv Scot.* yesterday evening. [C14: from YEST(E)R- + E(V)EN[2]]

yet (jɛt) *sentence connector.* **1** nevertheless; still; in spite of that: *I want to and yet I haven't the courage; she is strange yet kind.* ◆ *adv* **2** (*usually used with a negative or interrogative*) so far; up until then or now: *they're not home yet; is it teatime yet?* **3** (often preceded by *just; usually used with a negative*) now (as contrasted with later): *we can't stop yet.* **4** (*often used with a comparative*) even; still: *yet more potatoes for sale; yet another problem family.* **5** eventually, in spite of everything: *we'll convince him yet.* **6 as yet.** so far; up until then or now. [Old English *gēta;* related to Old Frisian *jēta*]

yeti ('jɛtɪ) *n* another term for **abominable snowman.** [C20: from Tibetan]

yett (jɛt) *n Scot.* a gate or door. [Old English variant of GATE[1]]

Yevtushenko (,jɛvtuː'ʃɛŋkəʊ; *Russian* jɪftu'ʃenkə) *n* **Yevgeny Aleksandrovich** (jɪv'gjenij alɪk'sandrəvitʃ). born 1933, Russian poet. His often outspoken poetry includes *Babi Yar* (1962), *Bratsk Station* (1966), and *Farewell to Red Banner* (1992).

yew (juː) *n* **1** any coniferous tree of the genus *Taxus,* of the Old World and North America, esp. *T. baccata,* having flattened needle-like leaves, fine-grained elastic wood, and cuplike red waxy cones resembling berries: family *Taxaceae.* **2** the wood of any of these trees, used to make bows for archery. **3** *Archery.* a bow made of yew. [Old English *īw;* related to Old High German *īwa,* Old Norse *ȳr* yew, Latin *ūva* grape, Russian *iva* willow]

Yeysk (*Russian* jejsk) *n* a variant spelling of **Yeisk.**

Yezd (jɛzd) *n* a variant of **Yazd.**

Yezidis ('jɛzɪdɪz) *pl n* a religious sect based around Mosul, Iraq, that combines elements of Islam and Christianity and incorporates worship of the devil as an agent of God. [C19: perhaps from *Yazid,* native name for the devil]

Y-fronts *pl n Trademark.* boys' or men's underpants having a front opening within an inverted Y shape.

Ygerne (iː'gɛən) *n* a variant of **Igraine.**

Yggdrasil, Ygdrasil, *or* **Igdrasil** ('ɪgdrəsɪl) *n Norse myth.* the ash tree that was thought to overshadow the whole world, binding together earth, heaven, and hell with its roots and branches. [Old Norse (probably meaning: Uggr's horse), from *Uggr* a name of Odin, from *yggr, uggr* frightful + *drasill* horse, of obscure origin]

YHA *abbrev. for* Youth Hostels Association.

YHVH, YHWH, JHVH, *or* **JHWH** *Old Testament.* the letters of the **Tetragrammaton.** See also **Yahweh, Jehovah.**

Yibin ('ji:'bɪn) *or* **I-pin** *n* a port in S central China, in Sichuan province: a commercial centre. Pop.: 241 019 (1990 est.).

Yichang ('ji:'tʃæŋ), **Ichang,** *or* **I-ch'ang** *n* a port in S central China, in Hubei province on the Yangtze River 1600 km (1000 miles) from the East China Sea: head of navigation of the Yangtze. Pop.: 371 601 (1990 est.).

yid (jɪd) *n Slang.* a derogatory word for a Jew. [C20: probably from *Yiddish,* from Middle High German *Jude* JEW]

Yiddish ('jɪdɪʃ) *n* **1** a language spoken as a vernacular by Jews in Europe and elsewhere by Jewish emigrants, usually written in the Hebrew alphabet. Historically, it is a dialect of High German with an admixture of words of Hebrew, Romance, and Slavonic origin, developed in central and E Europe during the Middle Ages. ◆ *adj* **2** in or relating to this language. [C19: from German *jüdisch,* from *Jude* JEW]

Yiddisher ('jɪdɪʃə) *adj* **1** in or relating to Yiddish. **2** Jewish ◆ *n* **3** a speaker of Yiddish; Jew.

yield (ji:ld) *vb* **1** to give forth or supply (a product, result, etc.), esp. by cultivation, labour, etc.; produce or bear. **2** (*tr*) to furnish as a return: *the shares yielded three per cent.* **3** (*tr;* often foll. by *up*) to surrender or relinquish, esp. as a result of force, persuasion, etc. **4** (*intr;* sometimes foll. by *to*) to give way, submit, or surrender, as through force or persuasion: *she yielded to his superior knowledge.* **5** (*intr;* often foll. by *to*) to agree; comply; assent: *he eventually yielded to their request for money.* **6** (*tr*) to grant or allow; concede: *to yield right of way.* **7** (*tr*) *Obsolete.* to pay or repay: *God yield thee!* ◆ *n* **8** the result, product, or amount yielded. **9** the profit or return, as from an investment or tax. **10** the annual income provided by an investment, usually expressed as a percentage of its cost or of its current value: *the yield on these shares is 15 per cent at today's market value.* **11** the energy released by the explosion of a nuclear weapon expressed in terms of the amount of TNT necessary to produce the same energy. **12** *Chem.* the quantity of a specified product obtained in a reaction or series of reactions, usually expressed as a percentage of the quantity that is theoretically obtainable. [Old English *gieldan;* related to Old Frisian *jelda,* Old High German *geltan,* Old Norse *gjalda,* Gothic *gildan*] ▸ **'yieldable** *adj* ▸ **'yielder** *n*

yielding ('ji:ldɪŋ) *adj* **1** compliant, submissive, or flexible. **2** pliable or soft: *a yielding material.* ▸ **'yieldingly** *adv* ▸ **'yieldingness** *n*

yield point *n* the stress at which an elastic material under increasing stress ceases to behave elastically; under conditions of tensile strength the elongation is greater than the increase in stress. Also called: **yield stress, yield strength.**

yield stress *n* the stress level at which a metal or other material ceases to behave elastically. The stress divided by the strain is no longer constant. The point at which this occurs is known as the yield point. Compare **proof stress.**

yike (jaɪk) *Austral. informal, archaic.* ◆ *n* **1** an argument, squabble, or fight. ◆ *vb* (*intr*) **2** to argue, squabble, or fight. [origin unknown]

yin (jɪn) *determiner, pron, n* a Scot. word for **one.**

Yin and Yang (jɪn) *n* two complementary principles of Chinese philosophy: Yin is negative, dark, and feminine, Yang positive, bright, and masculine. Their interaction is thought to maintain the harmony of the universe and to influence everything within it. [from Chinese (Peking) *yin* dark + *yang* bright]

Yinchuan, Yin-ch'uan, *or* **Yinchwan** ('jɪn'tʃwɑ:n) *n* a city in N central China, capital of the Ningxia Hui AR, on the Yellow River. Pop.: 356 652 (1990 est.).

Yingkou *or* **Yingkow** ('jɪŋ'kaʊ) *n* a port in NE China, in SW Liaoning province: a major shipping centre for Manchuria. Pop.: 421 589 (1990 est.).

Yinglish ('jɪŋglɪʃ) *n* a dialect of English spoken esp. by Jewish immigrants to New York, and heavily influenced by Yiddish constructions and loan words. Also: **Yenglish.** [from YI(DDISH) + (E)NGLISH]

yippee (jɪ'pi:) *interj* an exclamation of joy, pleasure, anticipation, etc.

yips (jɪps) *pl n* **the.** *Informal.* (in sport, originally esp. golf) nervous twitching or tension that destroys concentration and spoils performance. [C20: of unknown origin]

yite (jaɪt) *or* **yitie** ('jaɪtɪ) *n* Scot. words for **yellowhammer** (sense 1). Also called: **yellow-yite.** [C19: of unknown origin]

Yizkor ('jizkor) *n Judaism.* a memorial prayer included in the liturgy for certain festivals. [from Hebrew, literally: let him remember]

-yl *suffix of nouns.* (in chemistry) indicating a group or radical: *methyl; carbonyl.* [from Greek *hulē* wood, matter]

ylang-ylang *or* **ilang-ilang** ('i:læŋ'i:læŋ) *n* **1** an aromatic Asian tree, *Cananga odorata* (or *Canangium odoratum*), with fragrant greenish-yellow flowers yielding a volatile oil: family *Annonaceae.* **2** the oil obtained from this tree, used in perfumery. [C19: from Tagalog *ilang-ilang*]

ylem ('aɪləm) *n* the original matter from which the basic elements are said to have been formed following the explosion postulated in the big bang theory of cosmology. [Middle English, from Old French *ilem,* from Latin *hȳlē* stuff, matter, from Greek *hulē* wood, matter]

Y-level *n Surveying.* a level mounted on a Y-shaped support that can be rotated.

YMCA *abbrev. for* Young Men's Christian Association.

YMHA *abbrev. for* Young Men's Hebrew Association.

Ymir ('i:mɪə) *or* **Ymer** ('i:mə) *n Norse myth.* the first being and forefather of the giants. He was slain by Odin and his brothers, who made the earth from his flesh, the water from his blood, and the sky from his skull.

-yne *suffix forming nouns.* denoting an organic chemical containing a triple bond: *alkyne.* [alteration of -INE[2]]

yo (jəʊ) *sentence substitute.* an expression used as a greeting, to attract someone's attention, etc. [C20: of unknown origin]

yob (jɒb) *or* **yobbo** ('jɒbəʊ) *n, pl* **yobs** *or* **yobbos.** *Brit. slang.* an aggressive and surly youth, esp. a teenager. [C19: perhaps back slang for BOY] ▸ **'yobbish** *adj* ▸ **'yobbery** *n*

yod *or* **yodh** (jʊd) *n* the tenth letter in the Hebrew alphabet (י), transliterated as *y.* [C18: from Hebrew, literally: hand]

yodel ('jəʊd^{ə}l) *n* **1** an effect produced in singing by an abrupt change of register from the chest voice to falsetto, esp. in popular folk songs of the Swiss Alps. ◆ *vb* **-dels, -delling, -delled** *or U.S.* **-dels, -deling, -deled. 2** to sing (a song) in which a yodel is used. [C19: from German *jodeln,* of imitative origin] ▸ **'yodeller** *n*

yodle ('jəʊd^{ə}l) *n* a variant spelling of **yodel.** ▸ **'yodler** *n*

yoga ('jəʊgə) *n* (*often cap.*) **1** a Hindu system of philosophy aiming at the mystical union of the self with the Supreme Being in a state of complete awareness and tranquillity through certain physical and mental exercises. **2** any method by which such awareness and tranquillity are attained, esp. a course of related exercises and postures designed to promote physical and spiritual wellbeing. See **hatha yoga, raja yoga.** [C19: from Sanskrit: a yoking, union, from *yunakti* he yokes] ▸ **yogic** ('jəʊgɪk) *adj*

yogh (jɒg) *n* **1** a character (ȝ) used in Old and Middle English to represent a palatal fricative very close to the semivowel sound of Modern English *y,* as in Old English *ȝeong* (young). **2** this same character as used in Middle English for both the voiced and voiceless palatal fricatives; when final or in a closed syllable in medial position the sound approached that of German *ch* in *ich,* as in *knyȝt* (knight). After the 14th century this symbol became the modern consonantal (semivocalic) *y* when initial or commencing a syllable, and though no longer pronounced in medial position it is preserved in many words by a modern *gh,* as in *thought.* [C14: perhaps from *yok* YOKE, referring to the letter's shape]

yogi ('jəʊgɪ) *n, pl* **-gis** *or* **-gin** (-gɪn). a person who is a master of yoga. ▸ **yogini** (jəʊ'gi:ni:) *fem n*

yogurt *or* **yoghurt** ('jəʊgət, 'jɒg-) *n* a thick custard-like food prepared from milk that has been curdled by bacteria, often sweetened and flavoured with fruit, chocolate, etc. [C19: from Turkish *yoğurt*]

Yogyakarta (ˌjəʊgjɑ:'kɑ:tɑ:, 'jɒg-), **Jogjakarta, Jokjakarta,** *or* **Djokjakarta** *n* a city in S Indonesia, in central Java: seat of government of Indonesia (1946–49); university (1949). Pop.: 419 500 (1995 est.).

yo-heave-ho (ˌjəʊhi:v'həʊ) *interj* a cry formerly used by sailors while pulling or lifting together in rhythm.

yohimbine (jəʊ'hɪmbi:n) *n* an alkaloid found in the bark of the tree *Corynanthe yohimbe.* It is used in medicine as an adrenergic blocking agent. Formula: $C_{21}H_{26}N_2O_3$. [C19: from Bantu *yohimbé* a tropical African tree + -INE[1]]

yo-ho-ho *interj* **1** an exclamation to call attention. **2** another word for **yo-heave-ho.**

yoicks (haɪk; *spelling pron* jɔɪks) *interj* a cry used by huntsmen to urge on the hounds to the fox.

yoke (jəʊk) *n, pl* **yokes** *or* **yoke. 1** a wooden frame, usually consisting of a bar with an oxbow or similar collar-like piece at either end, for attaching to the necks of a pair of draught animals, esp. oxen, so that they can be worked as a team. **2** something resembling a yoke in form or function, such as a frame fitting over a person's shoulders for carrying buckets suspended at either end. **3** a fitted part of a garment, esp. around the neck, shoulders, and chest or around the hips, to which a gathered, pleated, flared, or unfitted part is attached. **4** an immense oppressive force or burden: *under the yoke of a tyrant.* **5** a pair of oxen or other draught animals joined together by a yoke. **6** a part, esp. one of relatively thick cross section, that secures two or more components so that they move together. **7** a crosshead that transmits the drive of an opposed piston engine from the upper of a pair of linked pistons to the crankshaft through a connecting rod. **8** a steel framework around the formwork during the casting of concrete. **9** *Nautical.* a crossbar fixed athwartships to the head of a rudderpost in a small boat, to which are attached ropes or cables for steering. **10** a Y-shaped cable, rope, or chain, used for holding, towing, etc. **11** (in the ancient world) a symbolic reconstruction of a yoke, consisting of two upright spears with a third lashed across them, under which conquered enemies were compelled to march, esp. in Rome. **12** a mark, token, or symbol of slavery, subjection, or suffering. **13** *Now rare.* a link, tie, or bond: *the yoke of love.* **14** *Brit. dialect.* a period of steady work, esp. the time during which a ploughman and his team work at a stretch. **15** *Irish.* any device, unusual object, or gadget: *where's the yoke for opening tins?* ◆ *vb* **16** (*tr*) to secure or harness (a draught animal) to (a plough, vehicle, etc.) by means of a yoke. **17** to join or be joined by means of a yoke; couple, unite, or link. **18** (*tr*) *Obsolete.* to oppress, burden, or enslave. [Old English *geoc;* related to Old High German *ioh,* Old Norse *ok,* Gothic *juk,* Latin *iugum,* Sanskrit *yugam*] ▸ **'yokeless** *adj*

yokefellow ('jəʊkˌfeləʊ) *n Archaic.* a working companion.

yokel ('jəʊk^{ə}l) *n Disparaging.* (used chiefly by townspeople) a person who lives in the country, esp. one who appears to be simple and old-fashioned. [C19: perhaps from dialect *yokel* green woodpecker, yellowhammer] ▸ **'yokelish** *adj*

Yokohama (ˌjəʊkəʊ'hɑ:mə) *n* a port in central Japan, on SE Honshu on Tokyo Bay: a major port and the country's second largest city situated in the largest and most populous industrial region of Japan. Pop.: 3 307 408 (1995).

Yokosuka (ˌjəʊkəʊ'su:kə) *n* a port in Japan, in SE Honshu: a major naval base with shipbuilding industries. Pop.: 432 202 (1995).

Yokozuna (ˌjəʊkəʊ'zu:nə) *n, pl* **-na** *or* **-ni.** a grand champion sumo wrestler. [from Japanese *yoko* across + *zuna* rope, from the sacred straw rope presented to the grand champion]

yolk (jəʊk) *n* **1** the substance in an animal ovum consisting of protein and fat that nourishes the developing embryo. Related adj: **vitelline. 2** a greasy substance secreted by the skin of a sheep and present in the fleece. [Old English *geoloca,* from *geolu* YELLOW] ▸ **'yolkless** *adj* ▸ **'yolky** *adj*

yolk sac *n Zoology.* **1** the membranous sac that is attached to the ventral surface of the embryos of birds, reptiles, and some fishes and contains yolk. **2** the corresponding part in the embryo of mammals, which contains no yolk.

Yom Kippur (jɒm 'kɪpə; *Hebrew* jɔm ki'pur) *n* an annual Jewish holiday celebrated on Tishri 10 as a day of fasting, on which prayers of penitence are recited in the synagogue throughout the day. Also called: **Day of Atonement.** [from Hebrew, from *yōm* day + *kippūr* atonement]

Yom Kippur War *n* a war in which Egypt and Syria launched a joint surprise attack on Israel on the Jewish festival of Yom Kippur (Oct. 6, 1973). It ended with a ceasefire (Oct. 25, 1973), Syrian forces having been repulsed, Egypt having reoccupied a belt of the Sinai desert on the E bank of the Suez Canal, and Israel having established a salient on the W bank of the Suez Canal.

yomp (jɒmp) *vb* (*intr*) to walk or trek laboriously, esp. heavily laden and over difficult terrain. [C20: military slang, of uncertain origin]

yom tov ('jɔm 'tɔv, 'jɒmtəv) *n, pl* **yamin tovim** (jɑ'min tɔ'vim). *Judaism.* a festival, esp. that of Passover, Shabuoth, Sukkoth, or Rosh Hashana.

yon (jɒn) *or* **yond** (jɒnd) *determiner* **1** *Chiefly Scot. and northern English* **1a** an archaic or dialect word for **that:** *yon man.* **1b** (*as pronoun*): *yon's a fool.* **2** variants of **yonder.** [Old English *geon;* related to Old Frisian *jen,* Old High German *jenēr,* Old Norse *enn,* Gothic *jains*]

yonder ('jɒndə) *adv* **1** at, in, or to that relatively distant place; over there. ♦ *determiner* **2** being at a distance, either within view or as if within view: *yonder valleys.* [C13: from Old English *geond* yond; related to Old Saxon *jendra,* Old High German *jenēr,* Gothic *jaind*]

Yonge (jʌŋ) *n* **Charlotte M(ary).** 1823–1901, British novelist, whose works reflect the religious ideals of the Oxford Movement. Her best-known book is *The Heir of Redclyffe* (1853).

Yong Lo ('jɒŋ 'ləʊ) *or* **Yung-Lo** *n* 1360–1424, Chinese emperor (1404–24) of the Ming dynasty. He moved the capital from Nanjing to Peking (now Beijing), which he rebuilt. Also called: *Ch'eng Tsu.*

yoni ('jəʊnɪ) *n Hinduism.* **1** the female genitalia, regarded as a divine symbol of sexual pleasure and matrix of generation and the visible form of Sakti. **2** an image of these as an object of worship. [C18: from Sanskrit, literally: vulva, womb]

Yonkers ('jɒŋkəz) *n* a city in SE New York State, near New York City on the Hudson River. Pop.: 190 316 (1996 est.).

yonks (jɒŋks) *pl n Informal.* a very long time; ages: *I haven't seen him for yonks.* [C20: of unknown origin]

Yonne (*French* jɔn) *n* **1** a department of N central France, in Burgundy region. Capital: Auxerre. Pop.: 331 400 (1995). Area: 7461 sq. km (2910 sq. miles). **2** a river in N France, flowing generally northwest to the Seine at Montereau. Length: 290 km (180 miles).

yonnie ('jɒnɪ) *n Austral. children's slang.* a stone. [from a native Australian language]

yoo-hoo ('juː,huː) *interj* a call to attract a person's attention.

YOP (jɒp) *n* (formerly, in Britain) **1a** *acronym for* Youth Opportunities Programme. **1b** (*as modifier*): *a YOP scheme.* **2** Also called: **'yopper.** *Informal.* a young person employed through this government programme.

yore (jɔː) *n* **1** time long past (now only in the phrase **of yore**). ♦ *adv* **2** *Obsolete.* in the past; long ago. [Old English *geāra,* genitive plural of *gēar* YEAR; see HOUR]

york (jɔːk) *vb* (*tr*) *Cricket.* to bowl or try to bowl (a batsman) by pitching the ball under or just beyond the bat. [C19: back formation from YORKER]

York[1] (jɔːk) *n* **1** a walled city in NE England, in York unitary authority, North Yorkshire, on the River Ouse: the military capital of Roman Britain; capital of the N archiepiscopal province of Britain since 625, with a cathedral (the Minster) begun in 1154; noted for its cycle of medieval mystery plays; university (1963). Pop.: 104 100 (1994 est.). Latin name: **Eboracum. 2** a unitary authority in NE England, in North Yorkshire. Pop.: 124 100 (1996 est.). Area: 272 sq. km (105 sq. miles). **3 Cape.** a cape in NE Australia, in Queensland at the N tip of Cape York Peninsula, extending into Torres Strait: the northernmost point of Australia.

York[2] (jɔːk) *n* **1** the English royal house that reigned from 1461 to 1485 and was descended from Richard Plantagenet, **Duke of York** (1411–60), whose claim to the throne precipitated the Wars of the Roses. His sons reigned as Edward IV and Richard III. **2 Alvin C(ullum).** 1887–1964, U.S. soldier and hero of World War I. **3 Duke of,** full name *Prince Frederick Augustus, Duke of York and Albany.* 1763–1827, second son of George III of Great Britain and Ireland. An undistinguished commander-in-chief of the British army (1798–1809), he is the "grand old Duke of York" of the nursery rhyme. **4 Prince Andrew, Duke of.** born 1960, second son of Elizabeth II of Great Britain and Northern Ireland. He married (1986) Miss Sarah Ferguson; they divorced in 1996; their first daughter, Princess Beatrice of York, was born in 1988 and their second, Princess Eugenie of York, in 1990.

Yorke Peninsula (jɔːk) *n* a peninsula in South Australia, between Spencer Gulf and St Vincent Gulf: mainly agricultural with several coastal resorts.

yorker (jɔːkə) *n Cricket.* a ball bowled so as to pitch just under or just beyond the bat. [C19: probably named after the *Yorkshire* County Cricket Club]

yorkie ('jɔːkɪ) *n* another name for **Yorkshire terrier.**

Yorkist ('jɔːkɪst) *English history* ♦ *n* **1** a member or adherent of the royal house of York, esp. during the Wars of the Roses. ♦ *adj* **2** of, belonging to, or relating to the supporters or members of the house of York.

Yorks. (jɔːks) *abbrev. for* Yorkshire.

Yorkshire ('jɔːk,ʃɪə, -ʃə) *n* a former county of N England: it was the largest English county, divided administratively into East, West, and North Ridings. In 1974 it was much reduced in size and divided into the new counties of North, West, and South Yorkshire: in 1996 the East Riding of Yorkshire was reinstated as a county and parts of the NE were returned to North Yorkshire for geographical and ceremonial purposes.

Yorkshire Dales *pl n* the valleys of the rivers flowing from the Pennines in W Yorkshire: chiefly Airedale, Ribbledale, Teesdale, Swaledale, Nidderdale, Wharfedale, and Wensleydale; tourist area. Also called: **the Dales.**

Yorkshire fog *n* a common tufted grass, *Holcus lanatus,* having downy leaves and flower heads that are white or pink and branched, with spikelets carrying the flowers.

Yorkshire pudding *n Chiefly Brit.* a light puffy baked pudding made from a batter of flour, eggs, and milk, traditionally served with roast beef.

Yorkshire terrier *n* a very small breed of terrier with a long straight glossy coat of steel-blue and tan. Also called: **yorkie.**

Yorktown ('jɔːk,taʊn) *n* a village in SE Virginia: scene of the surrender (1781) of the British under Cornwallis to the Americans under Washington at the end of the War of American Independence.

Yoruba ('jɒrʊbə) *n* **1** (*pl* **-bas** *or* **-ba**) a member of a Negroid people of W Africa, living chiefly in the coastal regions of SW Nigeria: noted for their former city states and complex material culture, particularly as evidenced in their music, art, and sculpture. **2** the language of this people, belonging to the Kwa branch of the Niger-Congo family. ▸ **'Yoruban** *adj*

Yosemite Falls (jəʊ'sɛmɪtɪ) *pl n* a series of waterfalls in central California, in the Yosemite National Park, with a total drop of 770 m (2525 ft.): includes the **Upper Yosemite Falls,** 436 m (1430 ft.) high, and the **Lower Yosemite Falls,** 98 m (320 ft.) high.

Yosemite National Park *n* a national park in central California, in the Sierra Nevada Mountains: contains the **Yosemite Valley,** at an altitude of about 1200 m (4000 ft.), with sheer walls rising about another 1200 m (4000 ft.). Area: 3061 sq. km (1182 sq. miles).

Yoshihito (,jɒʃɪ'hiːtəʊ) *n* See **Taisho.**

Yoshkar-Ola (*Russian* jaʃ'kara'la) *n* a city in Russia, capital of the Mari El Republic. Pop.: 251 000 (1995 est.).

you (juː; *unstressed* jʊ) *pron* (*subjective or objective*) **1** refers to the person addressed or to more than one person including the person or persons addressed but not including the speaker: *you know better; the culprit is among you.* **2** Also: **one.** refers to an unspecified person or people in general: *you can't tell the boys from the girls.* **3** *Chiefly U.S.* a dialect word for **yourself** or **yourselves** when used as an indirect object: *you should get you a wife now.* ♦ *n* **4** *Informal.* the personality of the person being addressed or something that expresses it: *that hat isn't really you.* **5 you know what** *or* **who.** a thing or person that the speaker cannot or does not want to specify. [Old English *ēow,* dative and accusative of *gē* YE[1]; related to Old Saxon *eu,* Old High German *iu,* Gothic *izwis*]

USAGE See at **me**[1].

you-all *pron* a U.S., esp. Southern, word for **you,** esp. when addressing more than one person.

you'd (juːd; *unstressed* jʊd) *contraction of* you had *or* you would.

you'll (juːl; *unstressed* jʊl) *contraction of* you will *or* you shall.

young (jʌŋ) *adj* **younger** ('jʌŋgə), **youngest** ('jʌŋgɪst). **1a** having lived, existed, or been made or known for a relatively short time: *a young man; a young movement; a young country.* **1b** (*as collective n;* preceded by *the*): *the young.* **2** youthful or having qualities associated with youth; vigorous or lively: *she's very young for her age.* **3** of or relating to youth: *in my young days.* **4** having been established or introduced for a relatively short time: *a young member.* **5** in an early stage of progress or development; not far advanced: *the day was young.* **6** *Geography.* **6a** (of mountains) formed in the Alpine orogeny and still usually rugged in outline. **6b** another term for **youthful** (sense 4). **7** (*often cap.*) of or relating to a rejuvenated group or movement or one claiming to represent the younger members of the population, esp. one adhering to a political ideology: *Young England; Young Socialists.* ♦ *n* **8** (*functioning as pl*) offspring, esp. young animals: *a rabbit with her young.* **9 with young.** (of animals) pregnant. [Old English *geong;* related to Old Saxon, Old High German *iung,* Old Norse *ungr,* Latin *iuvenis,* Sanskrit *yuvan*] ▸ **'youngish** *adj*

Young (jʌŋ) *n* **1 Brigham** ('brɪgəm). 1801–77, U.S. Mormon leader, who led the Mormon migration to Utah and founded Salt Lake City (1847). **2 Edward.** 1683–1765, English poet and dramatist, noted for his *Night Thoughts on Life, Death, and Immortality* (1742–45). **3 Lester.** 1909–59, U.S. saxophonist and clarinetist. He was a leading early exponent of the tenor saxophone in jazz. **4 Neil (Percival).** born 1945, Canadian rock guitarist, singer, and songwriter. His albums include *Harvest* (1972), *Rust Never Sleeps* (1979), and *Sleeps with Angels* (1994). **5 Thomas.** 1773–1829, English physicist, physician, and Egyptologist. He helped to establish the wave theory of light by his experiments on optical interference and assisted in the decipherment of the Rosetta Stone.

youngberry ('jʌŋbərɪ, -brɪ) *n, pl* **-ries. 1** a trailing bramble of the southwestern U.S. that is a hybrid of a blackberry and dewberry with large sweet dark purple fruits. **2** the fruit of this plant. [C20: named after B. M. *Young,* U.S. fruit-grower who was first to cultivate it (circa 1900)]

young blood *n* young, fresh, or vigorous new people, ideas, attitudes, etc.

Young Fogey *n* a young or fairly young person who adopts the conservative values of an older generation.

Younghusband ('jʌŋ,hʌsbənd) *n* Sir **Francis Edward.** 1863–1942, British explorer, mainly of N India and Tibet. He used military force to compel the Dalai Lama to sign (1904) a trade agreement with Britain.

Young Ireland *n* a movement or party of Irish patriots in the 1840s who split with Daniel O'Connell because they favoured a more violent policy than that which he promoted.

young lady *n* a girlfriend; sweetheart.

youngling ('jʌŋlɪŋ) *n Literary.* **a** a young person, animal, or plant. **b** (*as modifier*): *a youngling brood.* [Old English *geongling*]

young man *n* a boyfriend; sweetheart.

young offender institution *n* (in Britain) a place where offenders aged 15 to 21 may be detained and given training, instruction, and work. Former names: **borstal, youth custody centre.**

Young Pretender *n* See (Charles Edward) **Stuart.**

Young's modulus *n* a modulus of elasticity, applicable to the stretching of a wire etc., equal to the ratio of the applied load per unit area of cross section to the increase in length per unit length. Symbol: *E* [C19: named after Thomas YOUNG]

youngster ('jʌŋstə) *n* **1** a young person; child or youth. **2** a young animal, esp. a horse.

Youngstown ('jʌŋz,taun) *n* a city in NE Ohio: a major centre of steel production: university (1908). Pop.: 87 405 (1996 est.).

Young Turk *n* **1** a progressive, revolutionary, or rebellious member of an organization, political party, etc., esp. one agitating for radical reform. **2** a member of an abortive reform movement in the Ottoman Empire, originally made up of exiles in W Europe who advocated liberal reforms. The movement fell under the domination of young Turkish army officers of a nationalist bent, who wielded great influence in the government between 1908 and 1918.

younker ('jʌŋkə) *n* **1** *Archaic or literary.* a young man; lad. **2** *Obsolete.* a young gentleman or knight. [C16: from Dutch *jonker,* from Middle Dutch *jonc* YOUNG]

your (jɔː, jʊə; *unstressed* jə) *determiner* **1** of, belonging to, or associated with you: *your nose; your house; your first taste of freedom.* **2** belonging to or associated with an unspecified person or people in general: *the path is on your left heading north; this lotion is for your head only.* **3** *Informal.* used to indicate all things or people of a certain type: *your part-time worker is a problem.* **4 your actual.** *Brit. informal.* (intensifier): *here is your actual automatic tin-opener.* [Old English *eower,* genitive of *gē* YE[1]; related to Old Frisian *jūwe,* Old Saxon *euwa,* Old High German *iuwēr*]

Yourcenar ('juːkənɑː) *n* **Marguerite**, original name *Marguerite de Crayencour.* 1903–87, French novelist and writer, in the U.S. from 1939; noted for her historical novels, esp. *Mémoires d'Hadrien* (1952).

you're (jʊə, jɔː; *unstressed* jə) *contraction of* you are.

yours (jɔːz, jʊəz) *pron* **1** something or someone belonging to or associated in some way with you: *I've eaten yours.* **2** your family: *greetings to you and yours.* **3** used in conventional closing phrases at the end of a letter: *yours sincerely, yours faithfully.* **4 of yours.** belonging to or associated with you. **5 what's yours?** *Jocular.* what would you like to drink?

yourself (jɔː'sɛlf, jʊə-) *pron, pl* **-selves. 1a** the reflexive form of *you.* **1b** (intensifier): *you yourself control your destiny.* **2** (*preceded by a copula*) your normal or usual self: *you're not yourself these days.*

yours truly *pron* an informal term for *I, myself,* or *me.* [from the conventional closing phrase used at the end of letters]

yous *or* **youse** (juːz) *pron Dialect or nonstandard.* refers to more than one person including the person or persons addressed but not including the speaker: *yous have all had it now; I'm fed up with yous.*

youth (juːθ) *n, pl* **youths** (juːðz). **1** the quality or condition of being young, immature, or inexperienced: *his youth told against him in the contest.* **2** the period between childhood and maturity, esp. adolescence and early adulthood. **3** the freshness, vigour, or vitality characteristic of young people: *youth shone out from her face.* **4** any period of early development: *the project was in its youth.* **5** a young person, esp. a young man or boy. **6** young people collectively: *youth everywhere is rising in revolt.* [Old English *geogoth;* related to Old Frisian *jogethe,* Old High German *iugund,* Gothic *junda,* Latin *juventus*] ► **'youthless** *adj*

Youth (juːθ) *n* **Isle of.** an island in the NW Caribbean, south of Cuba: administratively part of Cuba from 1925. Chief town: Nueva Gerona. Pop.: 73 319 (1990 est.). Area: 3061 sq. km (1182 sq. miles). Former name: **Isle of Pines.** Spanish name: **Isla de la Juventud** ('izla ðe la xuβen'tuð).

youth club *n* a centre providing leisure activities for young people, often associated with a church or community centre.

youth court *n* a court that deals with juvenile offenders and children beyond parental control or in need of care. Former name: **juvenile court.**

youth custody *n* (in Britain) a sentence of from four to eighteen months' detention passed on a person aged 15 to 21.

youth custody centre *n* the former name for **young offender institution.**

youthful ('juːθfʊl) *adj* **1** of, relating to, possessing, or characteristic of youth. **2** fresh, vigorous, or active: *he's surprisingly youthful for his age.* **3** in an early stage of development: *a youthful culture.* **4** Also: **young.** (of a river, valley, or land surface) in the early stage of the cycle of erosion, characterized by steep slopes, lack of flood plains, and V-shaped valleys. Compare **mature** (sense 6), **old** (sense 18). ► **'youthfully** *adv* ► **'youthfulness** *n*

youth hostel *n* one of a chain of inexpensive lodging places for young people travelling cheaply. Often shortened to **hostel.**

Youth Training Scheme *n* (formerly, in Britain) a scheme, run by the Training Agency, to provide vocational training for unemployed 16–17-year-olds. Abbrev.: **YTS.**

you've (juːv; *unstressed* jʊv) *contraction of* you have.

yowe (jau) *n* a Scot. word for **ewe.**

yowl (jaul) *vb* **1** to express with or produce a loud mournful wail or cry; howl. ◆ *n* **2** a loud mournful cry; wail or howl. [C13: from Old Norse *gaula;* related to German *jaulen;* see YAWL[2]] ► **'yowler** *n*

yo-yo ('jəujəu) *n, pl* **-yos. 1** a toy consisting of a spool attached to a string, the end of which is held while it is repeatedly spun out and reeled in. **2** *U.S. and Canadian slang.* a stupid person, esp. one who is easily manipulated. ◆ *vb* **yo-yos, yo-yoing, yo-yoed.** (*intr*) **3** *Informal.* to change repeatedly from one position to another; fluctuate. ◆ *adj* **4** *Informal.* changing repeatedly; fluctuating. [from Filipino *yo yo,* come come, a weapon consisting of a spindle attached to a thong]

Ypres (*French* iprə) *n* a town in W Belgium, in W Flanders province near the border with France: scene of many sieges and battles, esp. in World War I, when it was completely destroyed. Pop.: 21 400 (1991 est.). Flemish name: **Ieper.**

Ypsilanti (,ɪpsɪ'læntɪ), **Hypsilantis,** *or* **Hypsilantes** *n* **1 Alexander** (,alek'sander). 1792–1828, Greek patriot, who led an unsuccessful revolt against the Turks (1821). **2** his brother, **Demetrios** (ðimitri'ɔs). 1793–1832, Greek revolutionary leader; commander in chief of Greek forces (1828–30) during the war of independence.

Yquem (iː'kɛm) *n* a French vineyard of the Sauternes area of Bordeaux that produces a sweet white table wine. Also called: **Château d'Yquem.**

yr *abbrev. for:* **1** (*pl* **yrs**) year. **2** younger. **3** your.

yrs *abbrev. for:* **1** years. **2** yours.

Yser (*French* izɛr) *n* a river in NW central Europe, rising in N France and flowing through SW Belgium to the North Sea: scene of battles in World War I. Length: 77 km (48 miles).

Yseult (ɪ'suːlt) *n* a variant spelling of **Iseult.**

Yssel ('aɪsᵊl) *n* a variant spelling of **IJssel.**

Yt *the former chemical symbol for* yttrium (now **Y**).

YT *abbrev. for* Yukon Territory.

YTS (in Britain) *abbrev. for* Youth Training Scheme.

ytterbia (ɪ'tɜːbɪə) *n* another name for **ytterbium oxide.** [C19: New Latin, named after *Ytterby,* Swedish quarry where it was discovered]

ytterbite (ɪ'tɜːbaɪt) *n* another name for **gadolinite.**

ytterbium (ɪ'tɜːbɪəm) *n* a soft malleable silvery element of the lanthanide series of metals that occurs in monazite and is used to improve the mechanical properties of steel. Symbol: Yb; atomic no.: 70; atomic wt.: 173.04; valency: 2 or 3; relative density: 6.903 (alpha), 6.966 (beta); melting pt.: 819°C; boiling pt.: 1196°C. [C19: New Latin; see YTTERBIA]

ytterbium oxide *n* a colourless weakly basic hygroscopic substance used in certain alloys and ceramics. Formula: Yb_2O_3. Also called: **ytterbia.**

yttria ('ɪtrɪə) *n* another name for **yttrium oxide.** [C19: New Latin, named after *Ytterby;* see YTTERBIA]

yttriferous (ɪ'trɪfərəs) *adj* containing or yielding yttrium.

yttrium ('ɪtrɪəm) *n* a silvery metallic element occurring in monazite and gadolinite and used in various alloys, in lasers, and as a catalyst. Symbol: Y; atomic no.: 39; atomic wt.: 88.90585; valency: 3; relative density: 4.469; melting pt.: 1522°C; boiling pt.: 3338°C. [C19: New Latin; see YTTERBIA] ► **'yttric** *adj*

yttrium metal *n Chem.* any one of a group of elements including yttrium and the related lanthanides, holmium, erbium, thulium, ytterbium, and lutecium.

yttrium oxide *n* a colourless or white insoluble solid used mainly in incandescent mantles. Formula: Y_2O_3. Also called: **yttria.**

YU *international car registration for* Yugoslavia.

yuan ('juː'æn) *n, pl* **-an. 1** the standard monetary unit of China, divided into 10 jiao and 100 fen. **2** the former name for **dollar** (sense 2). [from Chinese *yüan* round object; see YEN[1]]

Yüan[1] ('juː'æn) *n* **1** the imperial dynasty of China from 1279 to 1368. ◆ *adj* **2** of or relating to the Chinese porcelain produced during the Yüan dynasty, characterized by the appearance of under-glaze blue-and-white ware.

Yüan[2] ('juː'æn) *or* **Yüen** ('juː'ɛn) *n* a river in SE central China, rising in central Guizhou province and flowing northeast to Lake Tungting. Length: about 800 km (500 miles).

Yuan Shi Kai ('juː'æn 'ʃiː 'kaɪ) *n* 1859–1916, Chinese general and statesman: first president (1912–16) of the Chinese republic.

Yuan Tan ('juː'æn 'tæn) *n* an annual Chinese festival marking the Chinese New Year. It can last over three days and includes the exchange of gifts, firework displays, and dancing.

Yucatán (,juːkə'tɑːn; *Spanish* juka'tan) *n* **1** a state of SE Mexico, occupying the N part of the Yucatán peninsula. Capital: Mérida. Pop.: 1 555 733 (1995 est.). Area: 39 340 sq. km (15 186 sq. miles). **2** a peninsula of Central America between the Gulf of Mexico and the Caribbean, including the Mexican states of Campeche, Yucatán, and Quintana Roo, and part of Belize: a centre of Mayan civilization from about 100 B.C. to the 18th century. Area: about 181 300 sq. km (70 000 sq. miles).

Yucatán Channel *n* a channel between W Cuba and the Yucatán peninsula.

yucca ('jʌkə) *n* any of several liliaceous plants of the genus *Yucca,* of tropical and subtropical America, having stiff lancelike leaves and spikes of white flowers. See also **Adam's-needle, Spanish bayonet.** [C16: from American Spanish *yuca,* ultimately from an American Indian word]

yuck *or* **yuk** (jʌk) *interj Slang.* an exclamation indicating contempt, dislike, or disgust.

yucky *or* **yukky** ('jʌkɪ) *adj* **yuckier, yuckiest** *or* **yukkier, yukkiest.** *Slang.* disgusting; sickening; nasty.

Yuga ('jugə) *n* (in Hindu cosmology) one of the four ages of mankind, together lasting over 4 million years and marked by a progressive decline in the vitality and morals of men. [C18: from Sanskrit: yoke, race of men, era; see YOKE]

yugarie ('juːgərɪ) *n* a variant spelling of **eugarie.**

Yugo. *abbrev. for* Yugoslavia.

Yugoslav *or* **Jugoslav** ('juːgəu,slɑːv) *n* **1** a native, inhabitant, or citizen of Yugoslavia. **2** (not in technical use) another name for **Serbo-Croat** (the language). ◆ *adj* **3** of, relating to, or characteristic of Yugoslavia or its people.

Yugoslavia *or* **Jugoslavia** (,juːgəu'slɑːvɪə) *n* **1 Federal Republic of Yugoslavia.** a country, comprising Serbia and Montenegro, that was formed in 1991 but has not been internationally recognized, mainly because of Serbia's imperialist policies and role in the civil war in Bosnia-Herzegovina. It is mainly mountainous and rugged with the fertile Danube-Sava Basin in the northeast. **2** a former country in SE Europe, on the Adriatic: established in 1918 from the independent states of Serbia and Montenegro, and regions that until World War I had belonged to Austria-Hungary (Croatia, Slovenia, and Bosnia-Herzegovina); the name was changed from Kingdom of Serbs, Croats, and Slovenes to Yugoslavia in 1929; German invasion of 1941–44 was resisted chiefly by a Communist group led by Tito, who declared a people's republic in 1945; it became the Socialist Federal Republic of Yugoslavia in 1963; in 1991 following political crises Slovenia, Croatia, and Bosnia-Herzegovina declared independence, followed by Macedonia in 1992. ▸ **ˌYugo'slavian** *or* **ˌJugo'slavian** *adj, n*

Yukawa (juː'kɑːwə) *n* **Hideki** ('hiːdekɪ). 1907–81, Japanese nuclear physicist, who predicted (1935) the existence of mesons: Nobel prize for physics 1949.

Yukon ('juːkɒn) *n* **the.** a territory of NW Canada, on the Beaufort Sea, between the Northwest Territories and Alaska: arctic and mountainous, reaching 6050 m (19 850 ft.) at Mount Logan, Canada's highest peak; mineral resources. Capital: Whitehorse. Pop.: 31 600 (1997 est.). Area: 536 327 sq. km (207 076 sq. miles). Abbrev.: **YT.** ▸ **'Yukoner** *n*

Yukon River *n* a river in NW North America, rising in NW Canada on the border between the Yukon Territory and British Columbia: flows northwest into Alaska, U.S., and then southwest to the Bering Sea; navigable for about 2850 km (1775 miles) to Whitehorse. Length: 3185 km (1979 miles).

yulan ('juːlæn) *n* a Chinese magnolia, *Magnolia denudata,* that is often cultivated for its showy white flowers. [C19: from Chinese, from *yu* a gem + *lan* plant]

yule (juːl) *n* (*sometimes cap.*) *Literary, archaic, or dialect.* **a** Christmas, the Christmas season, or Christmas festivities. **b** (*in combination*): *yuletide.* [Old English *geōla,* originally a name of a pagan feast lasting 12 days; related to Old Norse *jōl,* Swedish *jul,* Gothic *jiuleis*]

yule log *n* a large log of wood traditionally used as the foundation of a fire in the hearth at Christmas.

Yuman ('juːmən) *n* **1** a family of North American Indian languages spoken chiefly in Arizona, California, and Mexico. ◆ *adj* **2** relating to or belonging to this family of languages.

yummy ('jʌmɪ) *Slang.* ◆ *interj* **1** Also: **yum-yum.** an exclamation indicating pleasure or delight, as in anticipation of delicious food. ◆ *adj* **-mier, -miest. 2** delicious, delightful, or attractive. [C20: from *yum-yum,* of imitative origin]

Yung-lo ('jʊŋ'ləʊ) *n* a variant transliteration of the Chinese name for **Yong Lo.**

Yünnan (juː'næn) *n* a province of SW China: consists mainly of a plateau broken in the southeast by the Red and Black Rivers, with mountains in the west, rising over 5500 m (18 000 ft.); large deposits of tin, lead, zinc, and coal. Capital: Kunming. Pop.: 39 900 000 (1996 est.). Area: 436 200 sq. km (168 400 sq. miles).

yup (jʌp) *sentence substitute.* an informal word for **yes.**

Yupik ('juːpɪk) *n* a western Eskimo, of Alaska or Asia. Compare **Inuit.**

yuppie *or* **yuppy** ('jʌpɪ) (*sometimes cap.*) ◆ *n* **1** an affluent young professional person. ◆ *adj* **2** typical of or reflecting the values characteristic of yuppies. [C20: from *y*(*oung*) *u*(*rban*) or *up*(*wardly mobile*) *p*(*rofessional*) + -IE] ▸ **'yuppiedom** *n*

yuppie disease *or* **flu** *n Informal, sometimes considered offensive.* any of a number of debilitating long-lasting viral disorders associated with stress, such as chronic fatigue syndrome, whose symptoms include muscle weakness, chronic tiredness, and depression.

yuppify ('jʌpɪˌfaɪ) *vb* (*tr*) **-fies, -fying, -fied.** to make yuppie in nature. ▸ **ˌyuppifi'cation** *n*

Yurev (*Russian* 'jurjɪf) *n* the former name (11th century until 1918) of **Tartu.**

yurt (jʊət) *n* a circular tent consisting of a framework of poles covered with felt or skins, used by Mongolian and Turkic nomads of E and central Asia. [from Russian *yurta,* of Turkic origin; compare Turkish *yurt* abode, home]

Yuzovka (*Russian* 'juzəfkə) *n* a former name (1872 until after the Revolution) of **Donetsk.**

YV *international car registration for* Venezuela.

Yvelines (*French* ivlin) *n* a department of N France, in Île de France region. Capital: Versailles. Pop.: 1 367 700 (1995). Area: 2271 sq. km (886 sq. miles).

YWCA *abbrev. for* Young Women's Christian Association.

YWHA *abbrev. for* Young Women's Hebrew Association.

ywis (ɪ'wɪs) *adv* a variant spelling of **iwis.**

Zz

z *or* **Z** (zɛd; *U.S.* ziː) *n, pl* **z's, Z's,** *or* **Zs. 1** the 26th and last letter and the 20th consonant of the modern English alphabet. **2** a speech sound represented by this letter, in English usually a voiced alveolar fricative, as in *zip.* **3a** something shaped like a Z. **3b** (*in combination*): *a Z-bend in a road.*

z *Maths. symbol for:* **1** the *z*-axis or a coordinate measured along the *z*-axis in a Cartesian or cylindrical coordinate system. **2** an algebraic variable.

Z *symbol for:* **1** any unknown, variable, or unspecified factor, number, person, or thing. **2** *Chem.* atomic number. **3** *Physics.* impedance. **4** zone. **5** *Currency.* zaïre. ◆ **6** *international car registration for* Zambia.

z. *abbrev. for:* **1** zero. **2** zone.

ZA *international car registration for* South Africa. [from Afrikaans *Zuid Afrika*]

Zaandam (*Dutch* zaːnˈdɑm) *n* a former town in the W Netherlands, in North Holland: an important shipbuilding centre in the 17th century. It became part of Zaanstad in 1974.

Zaanstad (*Dutch* zaːnˈʃtat) *n* a port in the W Netherlands, in North Holland: formed (1974) from Zaandam, Koog a/d Zaan, Zaandijk, Wormerveer, Krommenie, Westzaan, and Assendelft; food and machinery industries. Pop.: 133 817 (1996 est.).

zabaglione (ˌzæbəˈljəʊnɪ) *n* a light foamy dessert made of egg yolks, sugar, and marsala, whipped together and served warm in a glass. [Italian; probably related to Late Latin *sabaia* Illyrian drink made from grain]

Zabrze (*Polish* ˈzabʒɛ) *n* a city in SW Poland: a Prussian and German town from 1742 until 1945, when it passed to Poland; industrial centre in a coal-mining region. Pop.: 201 600 (1996 est.). German name: **Hindenburg.**

Zacatecas (*Spanish* θakaˈtekas) *n* **1** a state of N central Mexico, on the central plateau: rich mineral resources. Capital: Zacatecas. Pop.: 1 336 348 (1995 est.). Area: 75 040 sq. km (28 973 sq. miles). **2** a city in N central Mexico, capital of Zacatecas state: silver mines. Pop.: 100 051 (1990).

Zacharias (ˌzækəˈraɪəs), **Zachariah** (ˌzækəˈraɪə), *or* **Zachary** (ˈzækərɪ) *n New Testament.* John the Baptist's father, who underwent a temporary period of dumbness for his lack of faith (Luke 1).

Zacynthus (zəˈsɪnθəs, -ˈkɪn-) *n* the Latin name for **Zante.**

zaffer *or* **zaffre** (ˈzæfə) *n* impure cobalt oxide, used to impart a blue colour to enamels. [C17: from Italian *zaffera;* perhaps related to Latin *sapphīrus* SAPPHIRE]

Zagazig (ˈzægəˌzɪg) *or* **Zaqaziq** *n* a city in NE Egypt, in the Nile Delta: major cotton market. Pop.: 287 000 (1992 est.).

Zaghlul (ˈzɑːgluːl) *n* **Saad** (sɑːd). 1857–1927, Egyptian nationalist politician; prime minister (1924).

Zagreb (ˈzɑːgrɛb) *n* the capital of Croatia, on the River Sava; gothic cathedral; university (1874); industrial centre. Pop.: 867 717 (1991). German name: **Agram.**

Zagreus (ˈzægrɪəs) *n Greek myth.* a young god whose cult came from Crete to Greece, where he was identified with Dionysus. The son of Zeus by either Demeter or Persephone, he was killed by the Titans at the behest of Hera.

Zagros Mountains (ˈzægrɒs) *pl n* a mountain range in S Iran: has Iran's main oilfields in its W central foothills. Highest peak: Zard Kuh, 4548 m (14 920 ft.).

Zahir-ud-din Muhammad *n* the original name of **Baber.**

zaibatsu (ˈzaɪbætˈsuː) *n* (*functioning as sing or pl*) the group or combine comprising a few wealthy families that controls industry, business, and finance in Japan. [from Japanese, from *zai* wealth, from Chinese *ts'ai* + *batsu* family, person of influence, from Chinese *fa*]

Zaïre (zɑːˈɪə) *n* **1** the former name (1971–97) of the (**Democratic Republic of the**) **Congo** (sense 2). **2** (formerly) the Zaïrian name (1971–97) for the (River) **Congo.** ▸ ˈ**Zaïrian** *or* ˈ**Zaïrean** *adj, n*

zakat (ˈzakat) *n Islam.* an annual tax on Muslims to aid the poor in the Muslim community. [from Arabic *zakāt* alms]

Zákinthos (ˈzakinˌθɔs) *n* transliteration of the Modern Greek name for **Zante.**

zakuski *or* **zakouski** (zæˈkuskɪ) *pl n, sing* **-ka** (-kə). *Russian cookery.* hors d'oeuvres, consisting of tiny open sandwiches spread with caviar, smoked sausage, etc., or a cold dish such as radishes in sour cream, all usually served with vodka. [Russian, from *zakusit'* to have a snack]

Zama (ˈzɑːmə) *n* the name of several ancient cities in N Africa, including the one near the site of Scipio's decisive defeat of Hannibal (202 B.C.).

Zambezi *or* **Zambese** (zæmˈbiːzɪ) *n* a river in S central and E Africa, rising in NW Zambia and flowing across E Angola back into Zambia, continuing south to the Caprivi Strip of Namibia, then east forming the Zambia–Zimbabwe border, and finally crossing Mozambique to the Indian Ocean: the fourth longest river in Africa. Length: 2740 km (1700 miles). ▸ **Zam**ˈ**bezian** *adj*

Zambia (ˈzæmbɪə) *n* a republic in southern Africa: an early site of human settlement; controlled by the British South Africa Company by 1900 and unified as Northern Rhodesia in 1911; made a British protectorate in 1924; part of the Federation of Rhodesia and Nyasaland (1953–63), gaining independence as a member of the Commonwealth in 1964; important mineral exports, esp. copper. Official language: English. Religion: Christian majority, animist minority. Currency: kwacha. Capital: Lusaka. Pop.: 9 461 000 (1998 est.). Area: 752 617 sq. km (290 587 sq. miles). Former name (until 1964): **Northern Rhodesia.** ▸ ˈ**Zambian** *adj, n*

Zamboanga (ˌzæmbəʊˈæŋgə) *n* a port in the Philippines, on SW Mindanao on Basilan Strait: founded by the Spanish in 1635; tourist centre, with fisheries. Pop.: 464 466 (1994 est.).

zambuck (ˈzæmbʌk) *n Austral. and N.Z. informal.* a St John ambulance attendant, esp. at a sports meeting. [C20: from *Zam-Buck,* the trade name of an ointment which comes in a black-and-white container, black and white being the colours of the St John uniform]

Zamenhof (*Polish* ˈzamɛnxɔf) *n* **Lazarus Ludwig** (laˈzarus ˈludvik). 1859–1917, Polish oculist; invented Esperanto.

zamia (ˈzeɪmɪə) *n* any cycadaceous plant of the genus *Zamia,* of tropical and subtropical America, having a short thick trunk, palmlike leaves, and short stout cones. [C19: from New Latin, from Latin *zamiae,* erroneous reading of phrase *nucēs azāniae* pine cones, probably from Greek *azainein* to dry up]

zamindar *or* **zemindar** (zəmiːnˈdɑː) *n* (in India) the owner of an agricultural estate. [via Hindi from Persian: landholder, from *zamīn* land + *-dār* holder]

zamindari *or* **zemindari** (zəmiːnˈdɑːrɪ) *n, pl* **-is.** (in India) a large agricultural estate.

Zamora (*Spanish* θaˈmora) *n* a city in NW central Spain, on the Douro River. Pop.: 58 560 (1980).

Zamyatin (*Russian* zaˈmjatjin) *n* **Yevgenii Ivanovich** (jɪvˈgjenij ɪˈvanəvitʃ). 1884–1937, Russian novelist and writer, in Paris from 1931, whose works include satirical studies of provincial life in Russia and England, where he worked during World War I, and the dystopian novel *We* (1924).

zander (ˈzændə) *n, pl* **zander** *or* **zanders.** a freshwater teleost pikeperch of Europe, *Stizostedion lucioperca,* valued as a food fish.

Zante (ˈzæntɪ) *n* an island in the Ionian Sea, off the W coast of Greece: southernmost of the Ionian Islands; traditionally belonged to Ulysses, king of Ithaca. Pop.: 32 557 (1991). Area: 402 sq. km (155 sq. miles). Latin name: **Zacynthus.** Ancient Greek name: **Zakynthos** (zəˈkuːnθɒs). Modern Greek name: **Zákinthos.**

zanthoxylum (zænˈθɒksɪləm) *n* any rutaceous shrub or tree of the genus *Zanthoxylum,* of temperate and subtropical E Asia and North America: includes the prickly ash and the West Indian yellowwood (or satinwood). [C19 *zantho-* variant of XANTHO- + Greek *xulon* wood]

Zanu(PF) (ˌzænuː (ˌpiːˈɛf)) *n acronym for* Zimbabwe African National Union (Patriotic Front).

zany (ˈzeɪnɪ) *adj* **-nier, -niest. 1** comical in an endearing way; imaginatively funny or comical, esp. in behaviour. ◆ *n, pl* **-nies. 2** a clown or buffoon, esp. one in old comedies who imitated other performers with ludicrous effect. **3** a ludicrous or foolish person. [C16: from Italian *zanni,* from dialect (Venice and Lombardy) *Zanni,* nickname for *Giovanni* John; one of the traditional names for a clown] ▸ ˈ**zanily** *adv* ▸ ˈ**zaniness** *n* ▸ ˈ**zanyism** *n*

Zanzibar (ˌzænzɪˈbɑː) *n* an island in the Indian Ocean, off the E coast of Africa: settled by Persians and Arabs from the 7th century onwards; became a flourishing trading centre for slaves, ivory, and cloves; made a British protectorate in 1890, becoming independent within the Commonwealth in 1963 and a republic in 1964; joined with Tanganyika in 1964 to form the United Republic of Tanzania. Pop.: 444 000 (1994 est.). ▸ ˌ**Zanzi**ˈ**bari** *adj, n*

zap (zæp) *Slang.* ◆ *vb* **zaps, zapping, zapped. 1** (*tr*) to attack, kill, or destroy, as with a sudden bombardment. **2** (*intr*) to move quickly; rush. **3** (*tr*) *Computing.* **3a** to clear from the screen. **3b** to erase. **4** (*intr*) *Television.* to change channels rapidly by remote control. ◆ *n* **5** energy, vigour, or pep. ◆ *interj* **6** an exclamation used to express sudden or swift action. [of imitative origin]

Zapata (zəˈpɑːtə; *Spanish* θaˈpata) *n* **Emiliano** (emiˈljano). ?1877–1919, Mexican guerrilla leader.

zapateado *Spanish.* (θapateˈaðo) *n, pl* ***-dos*** (-ðos). a Spanish dance with stamping and very fast footwork. [from *zapatear* to tap with the shoe, from *zapato* shoe]

Zaporozhye (*Russian* zəpaˈrɔʒjɛ) *n* a city in the E Ukraine on the Dnieper River: developed as a major industrial centre after the construction (1932) of the Dnieper hydroelectric station. Pop.: 882 000 (1996 est.). Former name (until 1921): **Aleksandrovsk.**

Zapotec (ˈzɑːpəˌtɛk) *n* **1** (*pl* **-tecs** *or* **-tec**) Also called: **Zapotecan** (ˌzæpəʊˈtɛkən, ˌzɑː-). any member of a large tribe of central American Indians inhabiting S Mexico, esp. the Mexican state of Oaxaca. **2** the group of languages spoken by this people. **3** Also: **Zapotecan.** of or relating to this people or their language. [from Spanish *Zapoteca,* from Nahuatl *Tzapoteca,* literally: people of the land of the sapodillas, from *tzapotl* sapodilla]

Zappa (ˈzæpə) *n* **Frank.** 1940–93, U.S. rock musician, songwriter, and producer: founder and only permanent member of the Mothers of Invention. His recordings include *Freak Out* (1966), *Hot Rats* (1969), and *Sheik Yerbouti* (1979).

zappy (ˈzæpɪ) *adj* **zappier, zappiest.** *Slang.* full of energy; snappy; zippy.

ZAPU (ˈzæpuː) *n acronym for* Zimbabwe African People's Union.

Zaqaziq (ˈzækəˌzɪk) *n* a variant of **Zagazig.**

Zaragoza (*Spanish* θaraˈɣoθa) *n* a city in NE Spain, on the River Ebro: Roman colony established 25 B.C.; under Moorish rule (714–1118); capital of Aragon (12th–15th centuries); twice besieged by the French during the Peninsular War and captured (1809); university (1474). Pop.: 607 899 (1995 est.). Pre-Roman name: **Salduba.** Latin name: **Caesaraugusta.** English name: **Saragossa.**

Zarathustra (ˌzærəˈθuːstrə) *n* the Avestan name of **Zoroaster.** ▸ ˌ**Zaraˈthustrian** *or* ˌ**Zaraˈthustric** *adj, n*

zaratite (ˈzærəˌtaɪt) *n* a green amorphous mineral consisting of hydrated nickel carbonate. Formula: $NiCO_3.2Ni(OH)_2.4H_2O$. **[C19:** from Spanish *zaratita,* named after G. *Zárate,* 19th-century Spaniard**]**

zareba *or* **zareeba** (zəˈriːbə) *n* (in northern E Africa, esp. formerly) **1** a stockade or enclosure of thorn bushes around a village or campsite. **2** the area so protected or enclosed. **[C19:** from Arabic *zarībah* cattlepen, from *zarb* sheepfold**]**

zarf (zɑːf) *n* (esp. in the Middle East) a holder, usually ornamental, for a hot coffee cup. **[**from Arabic: container, sheath**]**

Zaria (ˈzɑːrɪə) *n* a city in N central Nigeria: former capital of a Hausa state; agricultural trading centre; university (1962). Pop.: 379 200 (1997 est.).

Zarqa (ˈzɑːkə) *n* the second largest town in Jordan, northeast of Amman. Pop.: 344 524 (1994).

zarzuela (zɑːˈzweɪlə) *n* **1** a type of Spanish vaudeville or operetta, usually satirical in nature. **2** a seafood stew. **[**from Spanish, from *La Zarzuela,* name of the palace near Madrid where such vaudeville was first performed (1629)**]**

zastruga (zəˈstruːgə, zæ-) *n* a variant spelling of **sastruga.**

Zátopek (*Czech* ˈzaːtɔpɛk) *n* **Emil** (ˈemil). born 1922, Czech runner; winner of the 5000 and 10 000 metres and the marathon at the 1952 Olympic Games in Helsinki.

zax (zæks) *n* a variant of **sax**[1].

***z*-axis** *n* a reference axis of a three-dimensional Cartesian coordinate system along which the *z*-coordinate is measured.

zayin (ˈzɑːjɪn) *n* the seventh letter of the Hebrew alphabet (ז), transliterated as *z.* **[**from Hebrew, literally: weapon**]**

zazen (zʌzen) (in Zen Buddhism) deep meditation undertaken whilst sitting upright with legs crossed.

Z boson *n Physics.* another name for **Z particle.**

ZB station *n* (in New Zealand) a radio station of a commercial network.

Z chart *n Statistics.* a chart often used in industry and constructed by plotting on it three series: monthly, weekly, or daily data, the moving annual total, and the cumulative total dating from the beginning of the current year.

Zea (ˈtsɛːa) *n* the Italian name for **Keos.**

zeal (ziːl) *n* fervent or enthusiastic devotion, often extreme or fanatical in nature, as to a religious movement, political cause, ideal, or aspiration. **[C14:** from Late Latin *zēlus,* from Greek *zēlos***]**

Zealand (ˈziːlənd) *n* the largest island of Denmark, separated from the island of Fyn by the Great Belt and from S Sweden by the Sound. Chief town: Copenhagen. Pop.: 2 000 254 (1988 est.). Area: 7016 sq. km (2709 sq. miles). Danish name: **Sjælland.** German name: **Seeland.**

zealot (ˈzɛlət) *n* an immoderate, fanatical, or extremely zealous adherent to a cause, esp. a religious one. **[C16:** from Late Latin *zēlōtēs,* from Greek, from *zēloun* to be zealous, from *zēlos* ZEAL**]**

Zealot (ˈzɛlət) *n* any of the members of an extreme Jewish sect or political party that resisted all aspects of Roman rule in Palestine in the 1st century A.D.

zealotry (ˈzɛlətrɪ) *n* extreme or excessive zeal or devotion.

zealous (ˈzɛləs) *adj* filled with or inspired by intense enthusiasm or zeal; ardent; fervent. ▸ ˈ**zealously** *adv* ▸ ˈ**zealousness** *n*

Zeami *or* **Seami** (siːˈɑːmɪ) *n* **Motokiyo** (ˌməʊtəʊˈkiːəʊ). 1363–1443, Japanese dramatist, regarded as the greatest figure in the history of No drama.

zebec *or* **zebeck** (ˈziːbɛk) *n* variant spellings of **xebec.**

Zebedee (ˈzɛbɪˌdiː) *n New Testament.* the father of the apostles James and John (Matthew 4:21).

zebra (ˈziːbrə, ˈzɛbrə) *n, pl* **-ras** *or* **-ra.** any of several mammals of the horse family (*Equidae*), such as *Equus burchelli* (the **common zebra**), of southern and eastern Africa, having distinctive black-and-white striped hides. **[C16:** via Italian from Old Spanish: wild ass, probably from Vulgar Latin *eciferus* (unattested) wild horse, from Latin *equiferus,* from *equus* horse + *ferus* wild**]** ▸ ˈ**zebra-**ˌ**like** *or* **zebraic** (zɪˈbreɪɪk) *adj* ▸ **zebrine** (ˈziːbraɪn, ˈzɛb-) *or* ˈ**zebroid** *adj*

Zebra (ˈziːbrə, ˈzɛbrə) *n Finance.* a noninterest-paying bond in which the accrued income is taxed annually rather than on redemption. Compare **zero** (sense 12). **[C20:** from *zero-coupon bond***]**

zebra crossing *n Brit.* a pedestrian crossing marked on a road by broad alternate black and white stripes. Once on the crossing the pedestrian has right of way.

zebra finch *n* any of various Australasian songbirds with zebra-like markings, such as the grassfinch *Poephila castanotis.*

zebra plant *n* See **calathea.**

zebrawood (ˈzɛbrəˌwʊd, ˈziː-) *n* **1** a tree, *Connarus guianensis,* of tropical America, Asia, and Africa, yielding striped hardwood used in cabinetwork: family *Connaraceae.* **2** any of various other trees or shrubs having striped wood. **3** the wood of any of these trees.

zebu (ˈziːbuː) *n* a domesticated ox, *Bos indicus,* having a humped back, long horns, and a large dewlap: used in India and E Asia as a draught animal. **[C18:** from French *zébu,* perhaps of Tibetan origin**]**

Zebulun (ˈzɛbjʊlən, zəˈbjuː-) *n Old Testament.* **1** the sixth son whom Leah bore to Jacob: one of the 12 patriarchs of Israel (Genesis 30:20). **2** the tribe descended from him. **3** the territory of this tribe, lying in lower Galilee to the north of Mount Carmel and to the east of the coastal plain. Douay spelling: **Zabulon** (ˈzæbjʊlən, zəˈbjuː-).

zecchino (zɛˈkiːnəʊ) *n, pl* **-ni** (-nɪ). another word for **sequin** (the coin). **[C18:** from Italian; see SEQUIN**]**

Zech. *Bible. abbrev. for* Zechariah.

Zechariah (ˌzɛkəˈraɪə) *n* **1** *Old Testament.* **1a** a Hebrew prophet of the late 6th century B.C. **1b** the book containing his oracles, which are chiefly concerned with the renewal of Israel after the exile as a national, religious, and messianic community with the restored Temple and rebuilt Jerusalem as its centre. Douay spelling: **Zacharias. 2** a variant spelling of **Zachariah.** See **Zacharias.**

zed (zɛd) *n* the Brit. spoken form of the letter *z.* U.S. word: **zee. [C15:** from Old French *zede,* via Late Latin from Greek *zēta***]**

Zedekiah (ˌzɛdəˈkaɪə) *n Old Testament.* the last king of Judah, who died in captivity at Babylon. Douay spelling: **Sedecias** (ˌsɛdəˈkaɪəs).

zedoary (ˈzɛdəʊərɪ) *n* the dried rhizome of the tropical Asian plant *Curcuma zedoaria,* used as a stimulant and a condiment: family *Zingiberaceae.* **[C15:** from Medieval Latin *zedoaria,* from Arabic *zadwār,* of Persian origin**]**

zee (ziː) *n* the U.S. word for **zed** (letter *z*).

Zeebrugge (*Flemish* ˈzeːbryxə; *English* ˈziːˌbrʊgə) *n* a port in NW Belgium, in W Flanders on the North Sea: linked by canal with Bruges; German submarine base in World War I.

Zeeland (*Dutch* ˈzeːlɑnt; *English* ˈziːlənd) *n* a province of the SW Netherlands: consists of a small area on the mainland together with a number of islands in the Scheldt estuary; mostly below sea level. Capital: Middelburg. Pop.: 367 400 (1996 est.). Area: 1787 sq. km (690 sq. miles). ▸ ˈ**Zeelander** *n*

Zeeman effect (ˈziːmən) *n* the splitting of a spectral line of a substance into several closely spaced lines when the substance is placed in a magnetic field. **[C20:** named after Pieter *Zeeman* (1865–1943), Dutch physicist**]**

Zeffirelli (*Italian* dzeffiˈrelli) *n* **Franco** (ˈfraŋko). born 1923, Italian stage and film director and designer, noted esp. for his work in opera.

zein (ˈziːɪn) *n* a protein of the prolamine group occurring in maize and used in the manufacture of plastics, paper coatings, adhesives, etc. **[C19:** from New Latin *zēa* maize, from Latin: a kind of grain, from Greek *zeia* barley**]**

Zeist (zaɪst; *Dutch* zɛjst) *n* a city in the central Netherlands, near Utrecht. Pop.: 59 258 (1994).

Zeitgeist *German.* (ˈtsaitgaist) *n* the spirit, attitude, or general outlook of a specific time or period, esp. as it is reflected in literature, philosophy, etc. **[**German, literally: time spirit; see TIDE[1], GHOST**]**

zemindar (zəmiːnˈdɑː) *n* a variant spelling of **zamindar.** ▸ **zeminˈdari** *n*

Zemlinsky (zɛmˈlɪnskɪ) *n* **Alexander.** 1871–1942, Austrian composer, living in the U.S. from 1938. His works include the operas *Es war einmal* (1900) and *Eine florentische Tragödie* (1917) and the *Lyric Symphony* (1923).

zemstvo (ˈzɛmstvəʊ; *Russian* ˈzjɛmstvə) *n, pl* **-stvos.** (in tsarist Russia) an elective provincial or district council established in most provinces of Russia by Alexander II in 1864 as part of his reform policy. **[C19:** from Russian, from *zemlya* land; related to Latin *humus* earth, Greek *khamai* on the ground**]**

Zen (zɛn) *Buddhism.* ◆ *n* **1** a Japanese school, of 12th-century Chinese origin, teaching that contemplation of one's essential nature to the exclusion of all else is the only way of achieving pure enlightenment. **2** (*modifier*) of or relating to this school: *Zen Buddhism.* **[**from Japanese, from Chinese *ch'an* religious meditation, from Pali *jhāna,* from Sanskrit *dhyāna***]** ▸ ˈ**Zenic** *adj* ▸ ˈ**Zenist** *n*

zenana (zɛˈnɑːnə) *n* (in the East, esp. in Muslim and Hindu homes) part of a house reserved for the women and girls of a household. **[C18:** from Hindi *zanāna,* from Persian, from *zan* woman**]**

Zend (zɛnd) *n* **1** a former name for **Avestan. 2** short for **Zend-Avesta. 3** an exposition of the Avesta in the Middle Persian language (Pahlavi). **[C18:** from Persian *zand* commentary, exposition; used specifically of the Middle Persian commentary on the Avesta, hence of the language of the Avesta itself**]** ▸ ˈ**Zendic** *adj*

Zend-Avesta (ˌzɛndəˈvɛstə) *n* the Avesta together with the traditional interpretative commentary known as the Zend, esp. as preserved in the Avestan language among the Parsees. **[**from Avestan, representing *Avesta'-va-zend* Avesta with interpretation**]** ▸ **Zend-Avestaic** (ˌzɛndəvɛsˈteɪɪk) *adj*

Zener diode (ˈziːnə) *n* a semiconductor diode that exhibits a sharp increase in reverse current at a well-defined reverse voltage: used as a voltage regulator. **[C20:** named after C. M. *Zener* (1905–93), U.S. physicist**]**

zenith (ˈzɛnɪθ; *U.S.* ˈziːnɪθ) *n* **1** *Astronomy.* the point on the celestial sphere vertically above an observer. **2** the highest point; peak; acme: *the zenith of someone's achievements.* ◆ Compare **nadir. [C17:** from French *cenith,* from Medieval Latin *zenit,* from Old Spanish *zenit,* based on Arabic *samt,* as in *samt arrās* path over one's head, from *samt* way, path + *al* the + *rās* head**]** ▸ ˈ**zenithal** *adj*

zenithal projection *n* a type of map projection in which part of the earth's surface is projected onto a plane tangential to it, either at one of the poles (**polar zenithal**), at the equator (**equatorial zenithal**), or between (**oblique zenithal**).

zenith telescope *n* an instrument used to determine the latitude of stars, similar to the meridian circle but fitted with an extremely sensitive level and a declination micrometer.

Zenobia (zɪˈnəʊbɪə) *n* 3rd century A.D., queen of Palmyra (?267–272), who was captured by the Roman emperor Aurelian.

Zeno of Citium (ˈziːnəʊ əv ˈsɪtɪəm) *n* ?336–?264 B.C., Greek philosopher, who founded the Stoic school in Athens.

Zeno of Elea *n* ?490–?430 B.C., Greek Eleatic philosopher; disciple of Parmenides. He defended the belief that motion and change are illusions in a series of paradoxical arguments, of which the best known is that of Achilles and the tortoise.

zeolite (ˈziːəˌlaɪt) *n* **1** any of a large group of glassy secondary minerals consisting of hydrated aluminium silicates of calcium, sodium, or potassium: formed in cavities in lava flows and plutonic rocks. **2** any of a class of similar synthetic materials used in ion exchange and as selective absorbents. See **molecular sieve.** [C18 *zeo-*, from Greek *zein* to boil + -LITE; from the swelling up that occurs under the blowpipe] ▸ **zeolitic** (ˌziːəˈlɪtɪk) *adj*

Zeph. *Bible. abbrev. for* Zephaniah.

Zephaniah (ˌzɛfəˈnaɪə) *n Old Testament.* **1** a Hebrew prophet of the late 7th century B.C. **2** the book containing his oracles, which are chiefly concerned with the approaching judgment by God upon the sinners of Judah. Douay spelling: **Sophonias** (ˌsɒfəˈnaɪəs).

zephyr (ˈzɛfə) *n* **1** a soft or gentle breeze. **2** any of several delicate soft yarns, fabrics, or garments, usually of wool. [C16: from Latin *zephyrus*, from Greek *zephuros* the west wind; probably related to Greek *zophos* darkness, west]

Zephyrus (ˈzɛfərəs) *n Greek myth.* the god of the west wind.

zeppelin (ˈzɛpəlɪn) *n* (*sometimes cap.*) a large cylindrical rigid airship built from 1900 to carry passengers, and used in World War I for bombing and reconnaissance. [C20: named after Count von ZEPPELIN]

Zeppelin (*German* ˈtsɛpəliːn) *n* Count **Ferdinand von** (ˈfɛrdinant fɔn). 1838–1917, German aeronautical pioneer, who designed and manufactured airships (zeppelins).

Zermatt (*German* tsɛrˈmat) *n* a village and resort in S Switzerland, in Valais canton at the foot of the Matterhorn: cars are not allowed in the area. Pop.: 4200 (1989 est.).

zero (ˈzɪərəʊ) *n, pl* **-ros** *or* **-roes. 1** the symbol 0, indicating an absence of quantity or magnitude; nought. Former name: **cipher. 2** the integer denoted by the symbol 0; nought. **3** the cardinal number between +1 and −1. **4** nothing; nil. **5** a person or thing of no significance; nonentity. **6** the lowest point or degree: *his prospects were put at zero.* **7** the line or point on a scale of measurement from which the graduations commence. **8a** the temperature, pressure, etc., that registers a reading of zero on a scale. **8b** the value of a variable, such as temperature, obtained under specified conditions. **9** a gunsight setting in which accurate allowance has been made for both windage and elevation for a specified range. **10** *Maths.* **10a** the cardinal number of a set with no members. **10b** the identity element of addition. **11** *Linguistics.* **11a** an allomorph with no phonetic realization, as the plural marker of English *sheep.* **11b** (*as modifier*): *a zero form.* **12** *Finance.* Also called **zero-coupon bond.** a bond that pays no interest, the equivalent being paid in its redemption value. Compare **Zebra.** ◆ *adj* **13** having no measurable quantity, magnitude, etc. **14** *Meteorol.* **14a** (of a cloud ceiling) limiting visibility to 15 metres (50 feet) or less. **14b** (of horizontal visibility) limited to 50 metres (165 feet) or less. ◆ *vb* **-roes, -roing, -roed. 15** (*tr*) to adjust (an instrument, apparatus, etc.) so as to read zero or a position taken as zero. ◆ *determiner.* **16** *Informal, chiefly U.S.* no (thing) at all: *this job has zero interest.* [C17: from Italian, from Medieval Latin *zephirum*, from Arabic *sifr* empty, CIPHER]

zero defects *pl n* an aspect of total quality management that stresses the objective of error-free performance in providing goods or services.

zero gravity *n* the state or condition of weightlessness.

zero grazing *n* a type of dairy farming in which the cattle are fed with cut grass.

zero hour *n* **1** *Military.* the time set for the start of an attack or the initial stage of an operation. **2** *Informal.* a critical time, esp. at the commencement of an action.

zero in *vb* (*adv*) **1** (often foll. by *on*) to bring (a weapon) to bear (on a target), as while firing repeatedly. **2** (*intr;* foll. by *on*) *Informal.* to bring one's attention to bear (on a problem, etc.). **3** (*intr;* foll. by *on*) *Informal.* to converge (upon): *the police zeroed in on the site of the crime.*

zero option *n* (in international nuclear arms negotiations) an offer to remove all shorter-range nuclear missiles or, in the case of the **zero-zero option** all intermediate-range nuclear missiles, if the other side will do the same.

zero-rated *adj* denoting goods on which the buyer pays no value-added tax although the seller can claim back any tax he has paid.

zero stage *n* a solid-propellant rocket attached to a liquid-propellant rocket to provide greater thrust at liftoff.

zero-sum game *n* (in game theory) a contest in which one person's loss is equal to the other person's gain.

zeroth (ˈzɪərəʊθ) *adj* denoting a term in a series that precedes the term otherwise regarded as the first term. [C20: from ZERO + -TH[2]]

zero tolerance *n* the policy of applying laws or penalties to even minor infringements of a code in order to reinforce its overall importance.

zest (zɛst) *n* **1** invigorating or keen excitement or enjoyment: *a zest for living.* **2** added interest, flavour, or charm; piquancy: *her presence gave zest to the occasion.* **3** something added to give flavour or relish. **4** the peel or skin of an orange or lemon, used as flavouring in drinks, etc. ◆ *vb* **5** (*tr*) to give flavour, interest, or piquancy to. [C17: from French *zeste* peel of citrous fruits used as flavouring, of unknown origin] ▸ **ˈzestful** *adj* ▸ **ˈzestfully** *adv* ▸ **ˈzestfulness** *n* ▸ **ˈzestless** *adj* ▸ **ˈzesty** *adj*

zeta (ˈziːtə) *n* the sixth letter in the Greek alphabet (Z, ζ), a consonant, transliterated as *z.* [from Greek, of Semitic origin; compare Hebrew *sādhē*]

Zeta (ˈziːtə) *n* (*foll. by the genitive case of a specified constellation*) the sixth brightest star in a constellation: *Zeta Tauri.*

ZETA (ˈziːtə) *n* a torus-shaped apparatus used for research on controlled thermonuclear reactions and plasma physics. [C20: from *z(ero)-e(nergy) t(hermonuclear) a(pparatus)*]

zetetic (zəˈtɛtɪk) *adj* proceeding by inquiry; investigating. [C17: from New Latin, from Greek *zētētikos*, from *zēteō* to seek]

Zetland (ˈzɛtlənd) *n* the official name (until 1974) of **Shetland.**

zeugma (ˈzjuːgmə) *n* a figure of speech in which a word is used to modify or govern two or more words although appropriate to only one of them or making a different sense with each, as in the sentence *Mr. Pickwick took his hat and his leave* (Charles Dickens). [C16: via Latin from Greek: a yoking, from *zeugnunai* to yoke] ▸ **zeugmatic** (zjuːgˈmætɪk) *adj* ▸ **zeugˈmatically** *adv*

Zeus (zjuːs) *n* the supreme god of the ancient Greeks, who became ruler of gods and men after he dethroned his father Cronus and defeated the Titans. He was the husband of his sister Hera and father by her and others of many gods, demigods, and mortals. He wielded thunderbolts and ruled the heavens, while his brothers Poseidon and Hades ruled the sea and underworld respectively. Roman counterpart: **Jupiter.**

Zeuxis (ˈzjuːksɪs) *n* late 5th century B.C., Greek painter, noted for the verisimilitude of his works.

Zhangjiakou (ˈdʒæŋˈdʒjækəʊ), **Changchiakow,** *or* **Changchiak'ou** *n* a city in NE China, in NW Hebei province: a military centre, controlling the route to Mongolia, under the Ming and Manchu dynasties. Pop.: 529 136 (1990 est.). Former names: **Wanchüan, Kalgan.**

Zhangzhou (ˈdʒæŋˈdʒəʊ), **Changchow,** *or* **Ch'ang-chou** *n* **1** a city in E China, in S Jiangsu province, on the Grand Canal: also known as **Wutsin** until 1949, when the 7th-century name was officially readopted. Pop.: 531 470 (1990 est.). **2** a city in SE China, in S Fujian province on the Saikoe River. Pop.: 181 424 (1990 est.). Former name: **Lungki.**

Zhdanov (*Russian* ˈʒdanəf) *n* the former name (1948–91) of **Mariupol.**

Zhejiang (ˈdʒɜˈdʒjæŋ) *or* **Chekiang** *n* a province of E China: mountainous and densely populated; a cultural centre since the 12th century. Capital: Hangzhou. Pop.: 43 190 000 (1996 est.). Area: 102 000 sq. km (39 780 sq. miles).

Zhengzhou (ˈdʒʌŋˈdʒəʊ), **Chengchow,** *or* **Cheng-chou** *n* a city in E central China, capital of Henan province; an administrative centre. Pop.: 1 710 000 (1991 est.).

Zhitomir (*Russian* ʒiˈtɔmir) *n* a city in the central Ukraine; centre of an agricultural region. Pop.: 301 000 (1996 est.).

Zhivkov (*Bulgarian* ˈʒifkof) *n* **Todor** (ˈtɔdor). 1911–98, Bulgarian statesman and party leader; prime minister (1962–71); president (1971–89).

zho (zəʊ) *n, pl* **zhos** *or* **zho.** a variant spelling of **zo.**

Zhou (dʒəʊ) *n* the Pinyin transliteration of the Chinese name for **Chou.**

Zhou En Lai (ɛn laɪ) *n* the Pinyin transliteration of the Chinese name for **Chou En-lai.**

Zhuangzi (ˈʒwæŋˈziː) *or* **Chuang-tzu** *n* ?369–286 B.C., Chinese philosopher, who greatly influenced Chinese religion through the book of Taoist philosophy that bears his name.

Zhu De (ˈdʒuː ˈdeɪ) *n* the Pinyin transliteration of the Chinese name for **Chu Teh.**

Zhu Jiang (ˈdʒuː ˈdʒjæŋ), **Chu Chiang,** *or* **Chu Kiang** *n* a river in SE China, in S Guangdong province, flowing southeast from Canton to the South China Sea. Length: about 177 km (110 miles). Also called: **Canton River, Pearl River.**

Zhukov (*Russian* ˈʒukəf) *n* **Georgi Konstantinovich** (gɪˈɔrgij kənstanˈtinəvitʃ). 1896–1974, Soviet marshal. In World War II, he led the offensives that broke the sieges of Stalingrad and Leningrad (1942–43) and later captured Warsaw and Berlin; minister of defence (1955–57).

Zia ul Haq (ˈzɪə ʊl ˈhak) *n* **Mohammed** (məʊˈhæmɪd). 1924–88, Pakistani general: president of Pakistan (1978–88), following the overthrow (1977) of Z. A. Bhutto by a military coup. He was killed in an air crash, possibly through sabotage.

zibeline (ˈzɪbəˌlaɪn, -lɪn) *n* **1** a sable or the fur of this animal. **2** a thick cloth made of wool or other animal hair, having a long nap and a dull sheen. ◆ *adj* **3** of, relating to, or resembling a sable. [C16: from French, from Old Italian *zibellino*, ultimately of Slavonic origin; compare SABLE]

zibet (ˈzɪbɪt) *n* a large civet, *Viverra zibetha*, of S and SE Asia, having tawny fur marked with black spots and stripes. [C16: from Medieval Latin *zibethum*, from Arabic *zabād* CIVET]

Zibo (ˈziːˈbɔː), **Tzu-po,** *or* **Tzepo** *n* a city in NE China, in Shandong province. Pop.: 2 460 000 (1991 est.).

zidovudine (zaɪˈdɒvjʊˌdiːn) *n* a drug that prolongs life and alleviates symptoms among some AIDS sufferers. Also called: **AZT.**

Ziegfeld (ˈziːgˌfɛld) *n* **Florenz** (ˈflɒrənz). 1869–1932, U.S. theatrical producer, noted for his series of extravagant revues (1907–31), known as the Ziegfeld Follies.

Ziegler catalyst (ˈziːglə) *n* any of a group of catalysts, such as titanium trichloride ($TiCl_3$) and aluminium alkyl ($Al(CH_3)_3$), that produce stereospecific polymers. [C20: named after Carl *Ziegler* (1898–1973), German chemist]

ziff (zɪf) *n Austral. informal.* a beard. [C20: of unknown origin]

ziggurat (ˈzɪgʊˌræt), **zikkurat,** *or* **zikurat** (ˈzɪkʊˌræt) *n* a type of rectangular temple tower or tiered mound erected by the Sumerians, Akkadians, and Babylonians in Mesopotamia. The tower of Babel is thought to be one of these. [C19: from Assyrian *ziqqurati* summit, height]

Zigong (ˈziːˈgʊŋ), **Tzekung,** *or* **Tzu-kung** *n* an industrial city in W central China, in Sichuan. Pop.: 393 184 (1990 est.).

zigzag (ˈzɪgˌzæg) *n* **1** a line or course characterized by sharp turns in alternating directions. **2** one of the series of such turns. **3** something having the form of a zigzag. ◆ *adj* **4** (*usually prenominal*) formed in or proceeding in a zigzag. **5** (of sewing machine stitches) produced in a zigzag by a swing needle: used for joining stretch fabrics, neatening raw edges, etc. ◆ *adv* **6** in a zigzag manner. ◆ *vb* **-zags, -zagging, -zagged. 7** to proceed or cause to proceed in a zigzag. **8** (*tr*) to form into a zigzag. [C18: from French, from German *zickzack*, from *Zacke* point, jagged projection; see TACK[1]] ▸ **ˈzigˌzaggedness** *n*

zila, zilla, *or* **zillah** (ˈzɪlɑː) *n* an administrative district in India. [C19: from Hindi *dilah* division, from Arabic *dil'* part]

zila parishad (ˈpʌrɪʃəd) *n* a district council in India. [Hindi, from *zila'* district (from Arabic *dil'* part) + *parishad* assembly, council]

zilch (zɪltʃ) *n Slang.* **1** nothing. **2** *U.S. and Canadian sport.* nil. [C20: of uncertain origin]

zillion ('zɪljən) *Informal.* ◆ *n, pl* **-lions** *or* **-lion. 1** (*often pl*) an extremely large but unspecified number, quantity, or amount: *zillions of flies in this camp.* ◆ *determiner* **2a** amounting to a zillion: *a zillion different problems.* **2b** (*as pronoun*): *I found a zillion under the sink.* [on the model of *million*]

Zilpah ('zɪlpə) *n Old Testament.* Leah's maidservant, who bore Gad and Asher to Jacob (Genesis 30:10–13).

Zimbabwe (zɪm'bɑːbwɪ, -weɪ) *n* **1** a country in SE Africa, formerly a self-governing British colony founded in 1890 by the British South Africa Company, which administered the country until a self-governing colony was established in 1923; joined with Northern Rhodesia (now Zambia) and Nyasaland (now Malawi) as the Federation of Rhodesia and Nyasaland from 1953 to 1963; made a unilateral declaration of independence under the leadership of Ian Smith in 1965 on the basis of White minority rule; proclaimed a republic in 1970; in 1976 the principle of Black majority rule was accepted and in 1978 a transitional government was set up, strongly opposed by some Black nationalist organizations; gained independence in 1980 following the Lancaster House Conference (1979–80); a member of the Commonwealth. Official language: English. Religion: Christian majority. Currency: Zimbabwe dollar. Capital: Harare. Pop: 11 044 000 (1998 est.). Area: 390 624 sq. km (150 820 sq. miles). Former names: **Southern Rhodesia** (until 1964), **Rhodesia** (1964–79). **2** a ruined fortified settlement in Zimbabwe, which at its height, in the 15th century, was probably the capital of an empire covering SE Africa. ► **Zim'babwean** *n, adj*

Zimmer ('zɪmə) *n Trademark.* another name for **walker** (sense 3). Also called: **Zimmer frame.**

zinc (zɪŋk) *n* **1** a brittle bluish-white metallic element that becomes coated with a corrosion-resistant layer in moist air and occurs chiefly in sphalerite and smithsonite. It is a constituent of several alloys, esp. brass and nickel-silver, and is used in die-casting, galvanizing metals, and in battery electrodes. Symbol: Zn; atomic no.: 30; atomic wt.: 65.39; valency: 2; relative density: 7.133; melting pt.: 419.58°C; boiling pt.: 907°C. **2** *Informal.* corrugated galvanized iron. [C17: from German *Zink*, perhaps from *Zinke* prong, from its jagged appearance in the furnace] ► **'zincic, 'zincous,** *or* **'zincoid** *adj* ► **'zincky, 'zincy,** *or* **'zinky** *adj*

zincate ('zɪŋkeɪt) *n* any of a class of salts derived from the amphoteric hydroxide of zinc, $Zn(OH)_2$, often thought of as the acid H_2ZnO_2.

zinc blende *n* another name for **sphalerite.**

zinc chloride *n* a white odourless soluble poisonous granular solid used in manufacturing parchment paper and vulcanized fibre and in preserving wood. It is also a soldering flux, embalming agent, and a medical astringent and antiseptic. Formula: $ZnCl_2$ Also called: **butter of zinc.**

zinciferous (zɪŋ'kɪfərəs) *adj* containing or yielding zinc.

zincite ('zɪŋkaɪt) *n* a red or yellow mineral consisting of zinc oxide in hexagonal crystalline form. It occurs in metamorphosed limestone. Formula: ZnO.

zinckenite ('zɪŋkəˌnaɪt) *n* a variant spelling of **zinkenite.**

zinco ('zɪŋkəʊ) *n, pl* **-cos.** short for **zincograph** (sense 1).

zincograph ('zɪŋkəˌgrɑːf, -ˌgræf) *n* **1** a printing plate made by zincography. **2** a print taken from such a plate.

zincography (zɪŋ'kɒgrəfɪ) *n* the art or process of etching on zinc to form a printing plate. ► **zin'cographer** *n* ► **zincographic** (ˌzɪŋkə'græfɪk) *or* **ˌzinco'graphical** *adj*

zinc ointment *n* a medicinal ointment consisting of zinc oxide, petrolatum, and paraffin, used to treat certain skin diseases.

zinc oxide *n* a white insoluble powder used as a pigment in paints (**zinc white** or **Chinese white**), cosmetics, glass, and printing inks. It is an antiseptic and astringent and is used in making zinc ointment. Formula: ZnO. Also called: **flowers of zinc, philosopher's wool.**

zinc sulphate *n* a colourless soluble crystalline substance usually existing as the heptahydrate or monohydrate: used as a mordant, in preserving wood and skins, and in the electrodeposition of zinc. Formula: $ZnSO_4$. Also called: **white vitriol, zinc vitriol.**

zinc white *n* another name for **Chinese white.**

zindabad ('zɪndɑːˌbɑːd) *vb* (*tr*) *Indian.* long live: used as part of a slogan in India, Pakistan, etc. Compare **murdabad.** [Hindi, from Persian]

zine (ziːn) *n Informal.* a magazine or fanzine.

Zinfandel ('zɪnfənˌdɛl) *n* a Californian wine grape originally transplanted from Europe and producing a quick-maturing fruity red wine. [C19: of unknown origin]

zing (zɪŋ) *n Informal.* **1** a short high-pitched buzzing sound, as of a bullet or vibrating string. **2** vitality; zest. ◆ *vb* **3** (*intr*) to make or move with or as if with a high-pitched buzzing sound. [C20: of imitative origin] ► **'zingy** *adj*

zingaro ('dzingaro) *or* (*fem*) ***zingara*** ('dzingara) *Italian. n, pl* ***-ri*** (-ri) *or* ***-re*** (-re). an Italian Gypsy. [C16: ultimately from Greek *Athinganoi*, name of an oriental people]

zingiberaceous (ˌzɪndʒɪbə'reɪʃəs) *adj* of, relating to, or belonging to the *Zingiberaceae*, a family of tropical aromatic plants that typically have fleshy rhizomes and flowers in spikes or clusters: includes ginger and the plants yielding arrowroot and turmeric. [C19: via New Latin from *zingiber* GINGER]

zinjanthropus (zɪn'dʒænθrəpəs) *n* a type of australopithecine, *Australopithecus boisei* (formerly *Zinjanthropus boisei*), remains of which were discovered in the Olduvai Gorge in Tanzania in 1959. [C20: New Latin, from Arabic *Zinj* East Africa + Greek *anthrōpos* man]

zinkenite *or* **zinckenite** ('zɪŋkəˌnaɪt) *n* a steel-grey metallic mineral consisting of a sulphide of lead and antimony. Formula: $PbSb_2S_4$. [C19: named after J. K. L. *Zincken* (1790–1862), German mineralogist]

zinnia ('zɪnɪə) *n* any annual or perennial plant of the genus *Zinnia*, of tropical and subtropical America, having solitary heads of brightly coloured flowers: family *Compositae* (composites). [C18: named after J. G. *Zinn* (died 1759), German botanist]

Zinoviev (zɪ'nəʊvɪəf; *Russian* zi'nɔvjɪf) *n* **Grigori Yevseevich,** original name *Ovsel Gershon Aronov Radomyslsky.* 1883–1936, Soviet politician; chairman of the Comintern (1919–26): executed for supposed complicity in the murder of Kirov. He was the alleged author of the 'Zinoviev letter' urging British Communists to revolt, publication of which helped to defeat (1924) the first Labour Government.

Zinovievsk (*Russian* zi'nɔvjɪfsk) *n* a former name (1924–36) for **Kirovograd.**

Zinzendorf (*German* 'tsɪntsəndɔrf) *n* Count **Nikolaus Ludwig von** ('niːkolaus 'luːtvɪç fɔn). 1700–60, German religious reformer, who organized the Moravian Church.

Zion ('zaɪən) *or* **Sion** *n* **1** the hill on which the city of Jerusalem stands. **2** *Judaism.* **2a** the ancient Israelites of the Bible. **2b** the modern Jewish nation. **2c** Israel as the national home of the Jewish people. **3** *Christianity.* heaven regarded as the city of God and the final abode of his elect. **4** any form of social organization, way of life, or life after death regarded as an ultimate goal. **5a** a religious community or its site, regarded as chosen by God and under his special protection. **5b** an ideal theocratic community, esp. any of the Christian Churches regarded as such a community.

Zionism ('zaɪəˌnɪzəm) *n* **1** a political movement for the establishment and support of a national homeland for Jews in Palestine, now concerned chiefly with the development of the modern state of Israel. **2** a policy or movement for Jews to return to Palestine from the Diaspora. ► **'Zionist** *n, adj* ► **ˌZion'istic** *adj*

zip (zɪp) *n* **1a** Also called: **zip fastener.** a fastening device operating by means of two parallel rows of metal or plastic teeth on either side of a closure that are interlocked by a sliding tab. U.S. and Canadian term: **zipper. 1b** (*modifier*) having or equipped with such a device: *a zip bag.* **2** a short sharp whizzing sound, as of a passing bullet. **3** *Informal.* energy; vigour; vitality. **4** *U.S. slang.* nothing. **5** *Sport, U.S. and Canadian slang.* nil. **6** *N.Z. trademark.* an electric water heater. ◆ *vb* **zips, zipping, zipped. 7** (*tr;* often foll. by *up*) to fasten (clothing, a bag, etc.) with a zip. **8** (*intr*) to move with a zip: *the bullet zipped past.* **9** (*intr;* often foll. by *along, through,* etc.) to hurry; rush: *they zipped through town.* [C19: of imitative origin]

Zipangu (zɪ'pæŋguː) *n* Marco Polo's name for **Cipango.**

zip code *n* the U.S. equivalent of **postcode.** [C20: from *z(one) i(mprovement) p(lan)*]

zip gun *n U.S. and Canadian slang.* a crude homemade pistol, esp. one powered by a spring or rubber band.

zipper ('zɪpə) *n* the U.S. and Canadian word for **zip** (sense 1a).

zippy ('zɪpɪ) *adj* **-pier, -piest.** *Informal.* full of energy; lively.

zircalloy (zɜː'kælɔɪ) *n* an alloy of zirconium containing small amounts of tin, chromium, and nickel. It is used in pressurized-water reactors.

zircon ('zɜːkɒn) *n* a reddish-brown, grey, green, blue, or colourless hard mineral consisting of zirconium silicate in tetragonal crystalline form with hafnium and some rare earths as impurities. It occurs principally in igneous rocks and is an important source of zirconium, zirconia, and hafnia: it is used as a gemstone and a refractory. Formula: $ZrSiO_4$. [C18: from German *Zirkon*, from French *jargon*, via Italian and Arabic, from Persian *zargūn* golden]

zirconia (zɜː'kəʊnɪə) *n* another name (not in technical usage) for **zirconium oxide.**

zirconium (zɜː'kəʊnɪəm) *n* a greyish-white metallic element, occurring chiefly in zircon, that is exceptionally corrosion-resistant and has low neutron absorption. It is used as a coating in nuclear and chemical plants, as a deoxidizer in steel, and alloyed with niobium in superconductive magnets. Symbol: Zr; atomic no.: 40; atomic wt.: 91.224; valency: 2, 3, or 4; relative density: 6.506; melting pt.: 1855±2°C; boiling pt.: 4409°C. [C19: from New Latin; see ZIRCON] ► **zirconic** (zɜː'kɒnɪk) *adj*

zirconium oxide *n* a white amorphous powder that is insoluble in water and highly refractory, used as a pigment for paints, a catalyst, and an abrasive. Formula: ZrO_2. Also called: **zirconia.**

Ziska ('zɪskə) *or* **Žižka** (*Czech* 'ʒiʃka) *n* **Jan** (jan). ?1370–1424, Bohemian soldier, who successfully led the Hussite rebellion (1420–24) against emperor Sigismund.

zit (zɪt) *n Slang.* a pimple. [of unknown origin]

zither ('zɪðə) *n* a plucked musical instrument consisting of numerous strings stretched over a resonating box, a few of which may be stopped on a fretted fingerboard. [C19: from German, from Latin *cithara*, from Greek *kithara*] ► **'zitherist** *n*

Zi Xi ('tsiː 'ʃiː) *or* **Tz'u-hsi** *n* 1835–1908, Chinese empress dowager, who as regent for her son Tong Zhi and her nephew Guang Xu dominated Chinese politics from 1861 to 1908. Her reactionary policies were instrumental in the fall of imperial China.

zizith ('tsɪtsɪs, tsiː'tsiːt) *n* (*functioning as sing or pl*) *Judaism.* a variant spelling of **tsitsith.**

zizz (zɪz) *Brit. informal.* ◆ *n* **1** a short sleep; nap ◆ *vb* (*intr*). **2** to take a short sleep, snooze. [C20: of imitative origin]

Zl *symbol for* zloty.

Zlatoust (*Russian* zləta'ust) *n* a town in W Russia, on the Ay river: one of the chief metallurgical centres of the Urals since the 18th century. Pop.: 203 000 (1995 est.).

zloty ('zlɒtɪ) *n, pl* **-tys** *or* **-ty.** the standard monetary unit of Poland, divided into 100 groszy. [from Polish: golden, from *zlyoto* gold; related to Russian *zoloto* gold]

Zn *the chemical symbol for* zinc.

zo, zho, *or* **dzo** (zəʊ) *n, pl* **zos, zhos, dzos** *or* **zo, zho, dzo.** a Tibetan breed of cattle, developed by crossing the yak with common cattle. [C20: from Tibetan]

zo- *combining form.* a variant of **zoo-** before a vowel.
zoa ('zəʊə) *n* the plural of **zoon.**
-zoa *suffix forming plural proper nouns.* indicating groups of animal organisms: *Metazoa.* [from New Latin, from Greek *zōia,* plural of *zōion* animal, living being]
zoaea (zəʊ'iːə) *n, pl* **zoaeae** (zəʊ'iːiː) *or* **zoaeas.** a variant spelling of **zoea.**
Zoan ('zəʊæn) *n* the Biblical name for **Tanis.**
zod. *abbrev. for* zodiac.
zodiac ('zəʊdɪˌæk) *n* **1** an imaginary belt extending 8° either side of the ecliptic, which contains the 12 **zodiacal constellations** and within which the moon and planets appear to move. It is divided into 12 equal areas, called **signs of the zodiac,** each named after the constellation which once lay in it. **2** *Astrology.* a diagram, usually circular, representing this belt and showing the symbols, illustrations, etc., associated with each of the 12 signs of the zodiac, used to predict the future. **3** *Rare.* a complete circuit; circle. [C14: from Old French *zodiaque,* from Latin *zōdiacus,* from Greek *zōidiakos* (*kuklos*) (circle) of signs, from *zōidion* animal sign, carved figure, from *zōion* animal] ▸ **zodiacal** (zəʊ'daɪəkəl) *adj*
zodiacal constellation *n* any of the 12 constellations after which the signs of the zodiac are named: Aries, Taurus, Gemini, Cancer, Leo, Virgo, Libra, Scorpio, Sagittarius, Capricorn, Aquarius, or Pisces.
zodiacal light *n* a very faint cone of light in the sky, visible in the east just before sunrise and in the west just after sunset. It is probably due to the reflection of sunlight from cosmic dust in the plane of the ecliptic.
zoea *or* **zoaea** (zəʊ'iːə) *n, pl* **zoeae, zoaeae** (zəʊ'iːiː) *or* **zoeas, zoaeas.** the free-swimming larva of a crab or related crustacean, which has well-developed abdominal appendages and may bear one or more spines. [C20: New Latin, from Greek *zōē* life]
zoetrope ('zəʊɪˌtrəʊp) *n* a cylinder-shaped toy with a sequence of pictures on its inner surface which, when viewed through the vertical slits spaced regularly around it while the toy is rotated, produce an illusion of animation. [C19: Greek *zoe* life + *trope* turn]
Zoffany ('zɒfənɪ) *n* **John** or **Johann** ?1733–1810, British painter, esp. of portraits; born in Germany.
Zog I (zɒg) *n* 1895–1961, king of Albania (1928–39), formerly prime minister (1922–24) and president (1925–28). He allowed Albania to become dominated by Fascist Italy and fled into exile when Mussolini invaded (1939).
Zohar ('zəʊhɑː) *n Judaism.* a mystical work, consisting of a commentary on parts of the Pentateuch and the Hagiographa, probably composed in the 2nd century A.D.
zoic ('zəʊɪk) *adj* **1** relating to or having animal life. **2** *Geology.* (of rocks, strata, etc.) containing fossilized animals. [C19: from New Latin, from Greek *zōion* animal]
-zoic *adj and n combining form.* indicating a geological era: *Palaeozoic.* [from Greek *zōē* life + -IC]
zoisite ('zɔɪˌsaɪt) *n* a grey, brown, or pink mineral consisting of hydrated calcium aluminium silicate in orthorhombic crystalline form. Formula: $Ca_2Al_3(SiO_4)_3(OH)$. [C19: from German *Zoisit;* named after Baron Sigismund *Zois* von Edelstein (1747–1819), Slovenian nobleman; see -ITE[1]]
Zola ('zəʊlə; *French* zɔla) *n* **Émile** (emil). 1840–1902, French novelist and critic; chief exponent of naturalism. In *Les Rougon-Macquart* (1871–93), a cycle of 20 novels, he explains the behaviour of his characters in terms of their heredity: it includes *L'Assommoir* (1877), *Nana* (1880), *Germinal* (1885), and *La Terre* (1887). He is also noted for his defence of Dreyfus in his pamphlet *J'accuse* (1898).
Zola Budd (bʌd) *n S. African informal.* a black taxi or minibus. [C20: after *Zola Budd* maiden name of Zola Pieterse (born 1966), South African athlete]
Zollverein *German.* ('tsɔlfɛrˌain) *n* the customs union of German states organized in the early 1830s under Prussian auspices. [C19: from *Zoll* tax, TOLL[2] + *Verein* union]
Zomba ('zɒmbə) *n* a city in S Malawi: the capital of Malawi until 1971. Pop.: 62 700 (1994 est.).
zombie *or* **zombi** ('zɒmbɪ) *n, pl* **-bies** *or* **-bis. 1** a person who is or appears to be lifeless, apathetic, or totally lacking in independent judgment; automaton. **2** a supernatural spirit that reanimates a dead body. **3** a corpse brought to life in this manner. **4** the snake god of voodoo cults in the West Indies, esp. Haiti, and in scattered areas of the southern U.S. **5** the python god revered in parts of West Africa. [from Kongo *zumbi* good-luck fetish] ▸ **'zombiism** *n*
zonal ('zəʊnᵊl) *or* (*less commonly*) **zonary** ('zəʊnərɪ) *adj* of, relating to, or of the nature of a zone. ▸ **'zonally** *adv*
zonal soil *n* soil having a profile determined mainly by the local climate and vegetation. Compare **azonal soil, intrazonal soil.**
zonate ('zəʊneɪt) *or* **zonated** *adj* marked with, divided into, or arranged in zones.
zonation (zəʊ'neɪʃən) *n* arrangement in zones; zonate formation.
Zond (zɒnd) *n* any of a series of unmanned Soviet spacecraft, first launched in 1964 as interplanetary space probes, the most successful of which, **Zond 3,** sent back photographs of the hidden side of the moon in 1965.
zone (zəʊn) *n* **1** a region, area, or section characterized by some distinctive feature or quality. **2** a sphere of thought, disagreement, argument, etc. **3** an area subject to a particular political, military, or government function, use, or jurisdiction: *a demilitarized zone.* **4** (*often cap.*) *Geography.* one of the divisions of the earth's surface, esp. divided into latitudinal belts according to temperature. See **Torrid Zone, Frigid Zone, Temperate Zone. 5** *Geology.* a distinctive layer or region of rock, characterized by particular fossils (**zone fossils**), metamorphism, structural deformity, etc. **6** *Ecology.* an area, esp. a belt of land, having a particular flora and fauna determined by the prevailing environmental conditions. **7** *Maths.* a portion of a sphere between two parallel planes intersecting the sphere. **8** *Sport.* **8a** a period during which a competitor is performing particularly well: *Hingis is in the zone at the moment.* **8b** (*modifier*) of or relating to competitive performance that depends on the mood or state of mind of the participant: *a zone player.* **9** *Archaic or literary.* a girdle or belt. **10** *N.Z.* a section on a transport route; fare stage. **11** *N.Z.* a catchment area for pupils for a specific school. ◆ *vb* (*tr*) **12** to divide into zones, as for different use, jurisdiction, activities, etc. **13** to designate as a zone. **14** to mark with or divide into zones. **15** *N.Z.* to establish (an area) as a zone for a specific school. [C15: from Latin *zōna* girdle, climatic zone, from Greek *zōnē*] ▸ **'zoning** *n*
zone of saturation *n* the ground below the water table.
zone refining *n* a technique for producing solids of extreme purity, esp. for use in semiconductors. The material, in the form of a bar, is melted in one small region that is passed along the solid. Impurities concentrate in the melt and are moved to the end of the bar.
zonetime ('zəʊnˌtaɪm) *n* the standard time of the time zone in which a ship is located at sea, each zone extending 7½° to each side of a meridian.
zonked (zɒŋkt) *adj Slang.* **1** highly intoxicated from drugs or alcohol. **2** utterly exhausted. [C20: of imitative origin]
zonule ('zɒnjuːl) *n* a small zone, band, or area. [C19: from New Latin *zōnula* a little ZONE] ▸ **zonular** ('zɒnjʊlə) *adj*
zoo (zuː) *n, pl* **zoos.** a place where live animals are kept, studied, bred, and exhibited to the public. Formal term: **zoological garden.** [C19: shortened from *zoological gardens* (originally applied to those in London)]
zoo- *or before a vowel* **zo-** *combining form.* indicating animals: *zooplankton.* [from Greek *zōion* animal]
zoobiotic (ˌzəʊəbaɪ'ɒtɪk) *adj Biology.* parasitic on or living in association with an animal.
zoochemistry (ˌzəʊə'kɛmɪstrɪ) *n* the branch of biochemistry that is concerned with the constituents of an animal's body. ▸ **ˌzoo'chemical** *adj*
zoochore ('zəʊəˌkɔː) *n* a plant the spores or seeds of which are dispersed by animals. [from ZOO- + -CHORE] ▸ **ˌzoo'chorous** *adj*
zoogeography (ˌzəʊədʒɪ'ɒgrəfɪ) *n* the branch of zoology concerned with the geographical distribution of animals. ▸ **ˌzooge'ographer** *n* ▸ **zoogeographic** (ˌzəʊəˌdʒɪə'græfɪk) *or* **ˌzooˌgeo'graphical** *adj* ▸ **ˌzooˌgeo'graphically** *adv*
zoogloea (ˌzəʊə'gliːə) *n* a mass of bacteria adhering together by a jelly-like substance derived from their cell walls. [C19: ZOO- + New Latin *gloea* glue, from Greek *gloia*] ▸ **ˌzoo'gloeal** *adj*
zoography (zəʊ'ɒgrəfɪ) *n* the branch of zoology concerned with the description of animals. ▸ **zo'ographer** *n* ▸ **zoographic** (ˌzəʊə'græfɪk) *or* **ˌzoo'graphical** *adj*
zooid ('zəʊɔɪd) *n* **1** any independent animal body, such as an individual of a coelenterate colony. **2** a motile cell or body, such as a gamete, produced by an organism. ▸ **zo'oidal** *adj*
zool. *abbrev. for:* **1** zoological. **2** zoology.
zoolatry (zəʊ'ɒlətrɪ) *n* **1** (esp. in ancient or primitive religions) the worship of animals as the incarnations of certain deities, symbols of particular qualities or natural forces, etc. **2** extreme or excessive devotion to animals, particularly domestic pets. ▸ **zo'olater** *n* ▸ **zo'olatrous** *adj*
zoological garden *n* the formal term for **zoo.**
zoology (zəʊ'ɒlədʒɪ, zuː-) *n, pl* **-gies. 1** the study of animals, including their classification, structure, physiology, and history. **2** the biological characteristics of a particular animal or animal group. **3** the fauna characteristic of a particular region. **4** a book, treatise, etc., dealing with any aspect of the study of animals. ▸ **zoological** (ˌzəʊə'lɒdʒɪkᵊl, ˌzuːə-) *adj* ▸ **zo'ologist** *n*
zoom (zuːm) *vb* **1** to make or cause to make a continuous buzzing or humming sound. **2** to move or cause to move with such a sound. **3** (*intr*) to move very rapidly; rush: *we zoomed through town.* **4** to cause (an aircraft) to climb briefly at an unusually steep angle, or (of an aircraft) to climb in this way. **5** (*intr*) (of prices) to rise rapidly. ◆ *n* **6** the sound or act of zooming. **7** See **zoom lens.** [C20: of imitative origin]
zoometry (zəʊ'ɒmɪtrɪ) *n* the branch of zoology concerned with the relative length or size of the different parts of an animal or animals. ▸ **zoometric** (ˌzəʊə'mɛtrɪk) *or* **ˌzoo'metrical** *adj*
zoom in *or* **out** *vb* (*intr, adv*) *Photog., films, television.* to rapidly increase or decrease the magnification of the image of a distant object by means of a zoom lens.
zoom lens *n* a lens system that allows the focal length of a camera lens to be varied continuously without altering the sharpness of the image. See also **telephoto lens.**
zoomorphism (ˌzəʊə'mɔːfɪzəm) *n* **1** the conception or representation of deities in the form of animals. **2** the use of animal forms or symbols in art, literature, etc. ▸ **ˌzoo'morphic** *adj*
zoon ('zəʊɒn) *n, pl* **zoa** ('zəʊə) *or* **zoons.** a less common term for **zooid** (sense 1). [C19: from New Latin, from Greek *zōion* animal; related to Greek *zōē* life] ▸ **zo'onal** *adj*
-zoon *n combining form.* indicating an individual animal or an independently moving entity derived from an animal: *spermatozoon.* [from Greek *zōion* animal]
zoonosis (zəʊ'ɒnəsɪs, ˌzəʊə'nəʊsɪs) *n, pl* **-ses** (-siːz). *Pathol.* any infection or disease that is transmitted to man from lower vertebrates. [from ZOO- + Greek *nosos* disease]
zoophagous (zəʊ'ɒfəgəs) *adj* feeding on animals.
zoophile ('zəʊəˌfaɪl) *n* a person who is devoted to animals and their protection from practices such as vivisection. ▸ **zoophilic** (ˌzəʊə'fɪlɪk) *adj*
zoophilia (ˌzəʊə'fɪlɪə) *n* a morbid condition in which a person has a sexual attraction to animals; bestiality.

zoophilism (zəʊ'ɒfɪˌlɪzəm) *n* the tendency to be emotionally attached to animals.
zoophilous (zəʊ'ɒfɪləs) *adj* **1** (of plants) pollinated by animals. **2** of, characterized by, or relating to zoophilism.
zoophobia (ˌzəʊə'fəʊbɪə) *n* an unusual or morbid dread of animals. ▸ **zoophobous** (zəʊ'ɒfəbəs) *adj*
zoophyte ('zəʊəˌfaɪt) *n* any animal resembling a plant, such as a sea anemone. ▸ **zoophytic** (ˌzəʊə'fɪtɪk) *or* ˌ**zoo'phytical** *adj*
zooplankton (ˌzəʊə'plæŋktən) *n* the animal constituent of plankton, which consists mainly of small crustaceans and fish larvae. Compare **phytoplankton.**
zooplasty ('zəʊəˌplæstɪ) *n* the surgical transplantation to man of animal tissues. ▸ ˌ**zoo'plastic** *adj*
zoosperm ('zəʊəˌspɜːm) *n* another word for **spermatozoon.** ▸ **zoospermatic** (ˌzəʊəspɜː'mætɪk) *adj*
zoosporangium (ˌzəʊəspɔː'rændʒɪəm) *n, pl* **-gia** (-dʒɪə). *Botany.* a sporangium that produces zoospores. ▸ ˌ**zoospo'rangial** *adj*
zoospore ('zəʊəˌspɔː) *n* **1** an asexual spore of some algae and fungi that moves by means of flagella. **2** one of several spores produced in a saclike body (sporocyst) by some parasitic protozoans. ▸ ˌ**zoo'sporic** *or* **zoosporous** (zəʊ'ɒspərəs, ˌzəʊə'spɔːrəs) *adj*
zoosterol (zəʊ'ɒstəˌrɒl) *n* any of a group of animal sterols, such as cholesterol.
zootechnics (ˌzəʊə'teknɪks) *n* (*functioning as sing*) the science concerned with the domestication and breeding of animals.
zootomy (zəʊ'ɒtəmɪ) *n* the branch of zoology concerned with the dissection and anatomy of animals. ▸ **zootomic** (ˌzəʊə'tɒmɪk) *or* ˌ**zoo'tomical** *adj* ▸ ˌ**zoo'tomically** *adv* ▸ **zo'otomist** *n*
zootoxin (ˌzəʊə'tɒksɪn) *n* a toxin, such as snake venom, that is produced by an animal. Compare **phytotoxin.** ▸ ˌ**zoo'toxic** *adj*
zoot suit (zuːt) *n Slang.* a man's suit consisting of baggy trousers with very tapered bottoms and a long jacket with wide padded shoulders, popular esp. in the U.S. in the 1940s. [C20: of uncertain origin; perhaps an arbitrary rhyme on *suit*] ▸ **'zoot-ˌsuiter** *n*
zorilla (zə'rɪlə) *or* **zorille** (zə'rɪl) *n* a skunk-like African musteline mammal, *Ictonyx striatus,* having a long black-and-white coat. [C18: from French, from Spanish *zorrillo* a little fox, from *zorro* fox]
Zorn (*Swedish* soːrn) *n* **Anders Leonhard** ('andərs 'leːɔnard). 1860–1920, Swedish painter and etcher, esp. of impressionist portraits and landscapes.
Zoroaster (ˌzɒrəʊ'æstə) *n* Avestan name **Zarathustra.** ?628–?551 B.C., Persian prophet; founder of Zoroastrianism.
Zoroastrian (ˌzɒrəʊ'æstrɪən) *adj* **1** of or relating to Zoroastrianism or Zoroaster. ◆ *n* **2** a follower of Zoroaster or adherent of Zoroastrianism: in modern times a Gabar or a Parsee.
Zoroastrianism (ˌzɒrəʊ'æstrɪənˌɪzəm) *or* **Zoroastrism** *n* the dualistic religion founded by the Persian prophet Zoroaster in the late 7th or early 6th centuries B.C. and set forth in the sacred writings of the Zend-Avesta. It is based on the concept of a continuous struggle between Ormazd (or Ahura Mazda), the god of creation, light, and goodness, and his arch enemy, Ahriman, the spirit of evil and darkness, and it includes a highly developed ethical code. Also called: **Mazdaism.**
Zorrilla y Moral (*Spanish* θɔ'rriʎa i mo'ral) *n* **José** (xo'se). 1817–93, Spanish poet and dramatist, noted for his romantic plays based on national legends, esp. *Don Juan Tenorio* (1844).
zoster ('zɒstə) *n Pathol.* short for **herpes zoster.** [C18: from Latin: shingles, from Greek *zōster* girdle]
Zouave (zuː'ɑːv, zwɑːv) *n* **1** (formerly) a member of a body of French infantry composed of Algerian recruits noted for their dash, hardiness, and colourful uniforms. **2** a member of any body of soldiers wearing a similar uniform or otherwise modelled on the French Zouaves, esp. a volunteer in such a unit of the Union Army in the American Civil War. [C19: from French, from *Zwāwa,* tribal name in Algeria]
Zoug (zug) *n* the French name for **Zug.**
zouk (zuːk) *n* a style of dance music that combines African and Latin American rhythms and uses electronic instruments and modern studio technology. [C20: from West Indian Creole *zouk* to have a good time]
zounds (zaʊndz) *or* **swounds** (zwaʊndz, zaʊndz) *interj Archaic.* a mild oath indicating surprise, indignation, etc. [C16: euphemistic shortening of *God's wounds*]
zoysia ('zɔɪzɪə) *n* any creeping perennial grass of the genus *Zoysia,* of warm dry regions, having short stiffly pointed leaves: often used for lawns. [C19: from New Latin, named after Karl von *Zois* (died 1800), German botanist]
Z particle *n Physics.* a type of neutral elementary particle considered to transmit the weak interaction between other elementary particles. Z particles have a rest mass of about 10^{-24} kg. Also called: **Z boson.** See also **W particle.**
ZPG *abbrev. for* zero population growth.
Zr *the chemical symbol for* zirconium.
Zsigmondy (*German* 'ʃɪgmɔndi) *n* **Richard Adolf** ('rɪçart 'aːdɔlf). 1865–1929, German chemist, born in Austria, noted for his work on colloidal particles and, with H. Siedentopf, his introduction (1903) of the ultramicroscope: Nobel prize for chemistry 1925.
zucchetto (tsuː'ketəʊ, suː-, zuː-) *n, pl* **-tos.** *R.C. Church.* a small round skullcap worn by certain ecclesiastics and varying in colour according to the rank of the wearer, the Pope wearing white, cardinals red, bishops violet, and others black. [C19: from Italian, from *zucca* a gourd, head, from Late Latin *cucutia* gourd, probably from Latin *cucurbita*]
zucchini (tsuː'kiːnɪ, zuː-) *n, pl* **-ni** *or* **-nis.** the U.S. and Canadian name for **courgette.** [Italian, pl of *zucchino,* literally: a little gourd, from *zucca* gourd; see ZUCCHETTO]
Zuckerman ('zʊkəmən) *n* **Solly** ('sɒlɪ), Baron. 1904–93, British zoologist, born in South Africa; chief scientific adviser (1964–71) to the British Government. His books include *The Social Life of Monkeys* (1932) and the autobiography *From Apes to Warlords* (1978).
Zug (*German* tsuːk) *n* **1** a canton of N central Switzerland: the smallest Swiss canton; mainly German-speaking and Roman Catholic; joined the Swiss Confederation in 1352. Capital: Zug. Pop.: 92 392 (1996 est.). Area: 239 sq. km (92 sq. miles). **2** a town in N central Switzerland, the capital of Zug canton, on Lake Zug. Pop.: 21 467 (1990). **3 Lake.** a lake in N central Switzerland, in Zug and Schwyz cantons. Area: 39 sq. km (15 sq. miles). French name: **Zoug.**
Zugspitze ('tsʊgˌʃpɪtsə) *n* a mountain peak in S Germany in the Bavarian Alps, on the Austrian border: the highest peak in Germany. Height: 2963 m (9721 ft.).
zugzwang (*German* 'tsuːktsvaŋ) *Chess.* ◆ *n* **1** a position in which one player can move only with loss or severe disadvantage. ◆ *vb* **2** (*tr*) to manoeuvre (one's opponent) into a zugzwang. [from German, from *Zug* a pull, tug + *Zwang* force, compulsion]
Zuider Zee *or* **Zuyder Zee** ('zaɪdə 'ziː; *Dutch* 'zœidər 'zeː) *n* a former inlet of the North Sea in the N coast of the Netherlands: sealed off from the sea by a dam in 1932, dividing it into the Waddenzee and the freshwater IJsselmeer, with several large areas under reclamation.
Zuidholland (zœit'hɔlɑnt) *n* the Dutch name for **South Holland.**
Zukerman ('zʊkəmən) *n* **Pinchas.** born 1948, Israeli violinist.
Zulu ('zuːluː -luː) *n* **1** (*pl* **-lus** *or* **-lu**) a member of a tall Negroid people of SE Africa, living chiefly in South Africa, who became dominant during the 19th century due to a warrior-clan system organized by the powerful leader, Shaka. **2** the language of this people, belonging to the Bantu group of the Niger-Congo family, closely related to Swazi and Xhosa. **3** *Communications.* a code word for the letter z. [from Zulu *amaZulu* people of the sky]
Zululand ('zuːlʊˌlænd, 'zuːluː-) *n* a region of E South Africa, on the Indian Ocean; partly corresponds to KwaZulu/Natal. Chief town: Eshowe.
Zungaria (zʊŋ'geərɪə) *n* a variant transliteration of **Junggar Pendi.**
Zuñi ('zuːnjiː, 'suː-) *n* **1** (*pl* **-ñis** *or* **-ñi**) a member of a North American Indian people of W New Mexico. **2** the language of this people, a member of the Penutian phylum of languages. ▸ **'Zuñian** *adj, n*
Zurbarán (*Spanish* θurβa'ran) *n* **Francisco de** (fran'θisko de). 1598–1664, Spanish Baroque painter, esp. of religious subjects.
Zürich ('zjʊərɪk; *German* 'tsyːrɪç) *n* **1** a canton of NE Switzerland: mainly Protestant and German-speaking. Capital: Zürich. Pop.: 1 175 457 (1996 est.). Area: 1729 sq. km (668 sq. miles). **2** a city in NE Switzerland, the capital of Zürich canton, on Lake Zürich: the largest city and industrial centre in Switzerland; centre of the Swiss Reformation; financial centre. Pop.: 343 869 (1996 est.). **3 Lake.** a lake in N Switzerland, mostly in Zürich canton. Area: 89 sq. km (34 sq. miles).
Zuyder Zee ('zaɪdə 'ziː; *Dutch* 'zœidər 'zeː) *n* a variant spelling of **Zuider Zee.**
ZW *international car registration for* Zimbabwe.
Zweig (*German* tsvaik) *n* **1 Arnold** ('arnɔlt). 1887–1968, German novelist, famous for his realistic war novel *The Case of Sergeant Grischa* (1927). **2 Stefan** ('ʃtefan). 1881–1942, Austrian novelist, dramatist, essayist, and poet.
Zwickau (*German* 'tsvɪkau) *n* a city in E Germany, in Saxony: Anabaptist movement founded here (1521); coal-mining and industrial centre. Pop.: 102 563 (1996 est.).
Zwicky ('tsvɪkɪ) *n* **Fritz.** 1898–1974, Swiss astronomer and physicist, working in the U.S. from 1925; noted for his study of supernovae.
zwieback ('zwaɪˌbæk, 'zwiː-; *German* 'tsviːbak) *n* a small type of rusk, which has been baked first as a loaf, then sliced and toasted, usually bought ready-made. [German: twice-baked]
Zwingli (*German* 'tsvɪŋli) *n* **Ulrich** ('ʊlrɪç) *or* **Huldreich** ('hʊltraiç). 1484–1531, Swiss leader of the Reformation, based in Zurich. He denied the Eucharistic presence, holding that the Communion was merely a commemoration of Christ's death.
Zwinglian ('zwɪŋglɪən, 'swɪŋg-, 'tsvɪŋ-) *n* **1** an upholder of the religious doctrines or movement of Zwingli. ◆ *adj* **2** of or relating to Zwingli, his religious movement, or his doctrines, esp. his interpretation of the Eucharist. ▸ **'Zwinglianism** *n* ▸ **'Zwinglianist** *n*
zwischenzug ('zvɪʃənzuːg) *n Chess.* a tactical move interpolated into an exchange or series of exchanges to improve the outcome. [C20: German: in-between move]
zwitterion ('tsvɪtərˌaɪən) *n Chem.* an ion that carries both a positive and a negative charge. [C20: from German *Zwitter* hermaphrodite + ION] ▸ **zwitterionic** (ˌtsvɪtəraɪ'ɒnɪk) *adj*
Zwolle (*Dutch* 'zwɔlə) *n* a town in the central Netherlands, capital of Overijssel province. Pop.: 100 835 (1996 est.).
Zworykin ('zwɔːrɪkɪn) *n* **Vladimir Kosma** ('vlædɪmɪə 'kɒsmə). 1889–1982, U.S. physicist and television pioneer, born in Russia. He developed the first practical television camera.
zydeco ('zaɪdəˌkəʊ) *n* a type of Black Cajun music.
zygapophysis (ˌzɪgə'pɒfɪsɪs, ˌzaɪgə-) *n, pl* **-ses** (-ˌsiːz). *Anatomy, zoology.* one of several processes on a vertebra that articulates with the corresponding process on an adjacent vertebra. [C19: from ZYGO- + APOPHYSIS] ▸ **zygapophyseal** (ˌzɪgæpə'fɪzɪəl) *adj*
zygo- *or before a vowel* **zyg-** *combining form.* indicating a pair or a union: *zygodactyl; zygospore.* [from Greek *zugon* yoke]
zygodactyl (ˌzaɪgəʊ'dæktɪl, ˌzɪgə-) *adj also* **zygodactylous. 1** (of the feet of certain birds) having the first and fourth toes directed backwards and the second and third forwards. ◆ *n* **2** a zygodactyl bird. ◆ Compare **heterodactyl.** ▸ ˌ**zygo'dactylism** *n*
zygoma (zaɪ'gəʊmə, zɪ-) *n, pl* **-mata** (-mətə). another name for **zygomatic**

arch. [C17: via New Latin from Greek, from *zugon* yoke] ▸ **zygomatic** (ˌzaɪgəʊˈmætɪk, ˌzɪg-) *adj*

zygomatic arch *n* the slender arch of bone that forms a bridge between the cheekbone and the temporal bone on each side of the skull of mammals. Also called: **zygoma.**

zygomatic bone *n* either of two bones, one on each side of the skull, that form part of the side wall of the eye socket and part of the zygomatic arch; cheekbone. Also called: **malar, malar bone.**

zygomatic process *n* a slender bony process of the temporal bone that forms part of the zygomatic arch.

zygomorphic (ˌzaɪgəʊˈmɔːfɪk, ˌzɪg-) *or* **zygomorphous** *adj* (of a flower) capable of being cut in only one plane so that the two halves are mirror images. See also **actinomorphic.** ▸ **ˌzygoˈmorphism** *or* **ˈzygoˌmorphy** *n*

zygomycete (ˌzaɪgəʊˈmaɪsiːt) *n* any filamentous fungus of the phylum *Zygomycota* (or *Zygomycetes*), which reproduces sexually by means of zygospores: includes the bread mould. ▸ **ˌzygomyˈcetous** *adj*

zygophyllaceous (ˌzaɪgəʊfɪˈleɪʃəs, ˌzɪg-) *adj* of, relating to, or belonging to the *Zygophyllaceae,* an Old World family of flowering plants having pinnate leaves and capsules as fruits: includes the bean caper and guaiacum.

zygosis (zaɪˈgəʊsɪs, zɪ-) *n Biology.* another name for **conjugation.** ▸ **zygose** (ˈzaɪgəʊs, ˈzɪg-) *adj*

zygospore (ˈzaɪgəʊˌspɔː, ˈzɪg-) *n* a thick-walled sexual spore formed from the zygote of some fungi and algae. ▸ **ˌzygoˈsporic** *adj*

zygote (ˈzaɪgəʊt, ˈzɪg-) *n* **1** the cell resulting from the union of an ovum and a spermatozoon. **2** the organism that develops from such a cell. [C19: from Greek *zugōtos* yoked, from *zugoun* to yoke] ▸ **zygotic** (zaɪˈgɒtɪk, zɪ-) *adj* ▸ **zyˈgotically** *adv*

zygotene (ˈzaɪgəˌtiːn, ˈzɪg-) *n* the second stage of the prophase of meiosis, during which homologous chromosomes become associated in pairs (bivalents).

zymase (ˈzaɪmeɪs) *n* a mixture of enzymes that is obtained as an extract from yeast and ferments sugars.

zymo- *or before a vowel* **zym-** *combining form.* indicating fermentation: *zymology.* [from Greek *zumē* leaven]

zymogen (ˈzaɪməʊˌdʒɛn) *n Biochem.* any of a group of compounds that are inactive precursors of enzymes and are activated by a kinase.

zymogenesis (ˌzaɪməʊˈdʒɛnɪsɪs) *n* the conversion of a zymogen into an enzyme.

zymogenic (ˌzaɪməʊˈdʒɛnɪk) *adj* **1** of, or relating to a zymogen. **2** capable of causing zymogenesis.

zymology (zaɪˈmɒlədʒɪ) *n* the chemistry of fermentation. ▸ **zymologic** (ˌzaɪməʊˈlɒdʒɪk) *or* **ˌzymoˈlogical** *adj* ▸ **zyˈmologist** *n*

zymolysis (zaɪˈmɒlɪsɪs) *n* the process of fermentation. Also called: **zymosis.** ▸ **zymolytic** (ˌzaɪməʊˈlɪtɪk) *adj*

zymometer (zaɪˈmɒmɪtə) *n* an instrument for estimating the degree of fermentation.

zymosis (zaɪˈməʊsɪs) *n, pl* **-ses** (-siːz). **1** *Med.* **1a** any infectious disease. **1b** the development process or spread of such a disease. **2** another name for **zymolysis.**

zymotic (zaɪˈmɒtɪk) *adj* **1** of, relating to, or causing fermentation. **2** relating to or caused by infection; denoting or relating to an infectious disease. ▸ **zyˈmotically** *adv*

zymurgy (ˈzaɪmɜːdʒɪ) *n* the branch of chemistry concerned with fermentation processes in brewing, etc.

Zyrian (ˈzɪrɪən) *n* **1** the language of the people of the Komi Autonomous Republic, belonging to the Finno-Ugric family; Komi. ◆ *adj* **2** of or relating to this language or its speakers.

Tables of Weights and Measures

The Metric System

Linear Measure

		1 millimetre	= 0.039 37	inch
10 millimetres	=	1 centimetre	= 0.3937	inch
10 decimetres	=	1 metre	= 39.37	inches or 3.2808 feet
		1 kilometre	= 0.621	mile or 3280.8 feet

Square Measure

		1 square millimetre	=	0.001 55	square inch
100 square millimetres	=	1 square centimetre	=	0.154 99	square inch
100 square decimetres	=	1 square metre	=	1549.9	square inches or 1.196 square yards
100 square hectometres	=	1 square kilometre	=	0.386	square mile or 247.1 acres

Land Measure

100 centiares	=	1 are	=	119.6	square yards
100 ares	=	1 hectare	=	2.471	acres
100 hectares	=	1 square kilometre	=	0.386	square mile or 247.1 acres

Volume Measure

1000 cubic millimetres	=	1 cubic centimetre	=	0.061 02	cubic inch
1000 cubic centimetres	=	1 cubic decimetre (1 litre)	=	61.023	cubic inches or 0.0353 cubic foot
1000 cubic decimetres	=	1 cubic metre	=	35.314	cubic feet or 1.308 cubic yards

Weights

10 decigrammes	=	1 gram	=	15.432	grains or 0.035 274 ounce (avdp.)
10 hectogrammes	=	1 kilogram	=	2.2046	pounds
10 quintals	=	1 metric ton	=	2204.6	pounds

The Imperial System

Linear Measure

1 mil	=	0.001 inch	=	0.0254	millimetre
1 inch	=	1000 mils	=	2.54	centimetres
12 inches	=	1 foot	=	0.3048	metre
3 feet	=	1 yard	=	0.9144	metre
5½ yards or 16½ feet	=	1 rod (or pole or perch)	=	5.029	metres
40 rods	=	1 furlong	=	201.168	metres
8 furlongs or 1760 yards or 5280 feet	=	1 (statute) mile	=	1.6093	kilometres

Square Measure

		1 square inch	=	6.452	square centimetres
144 square inches	=	1 square foot	=	929.03	square centimetres
9 square feet	=	1 square yard	=	0.8361	square metre
30¼ square yards	=	1 square rod (or square pole or square perch)	=	25.292	square metres
160 square rods or 4840 square yards or 43 560 square feet	=	1 acre	=	0.4047	hectare
640 acres	=	1 square mile	=	259.00	hectares or 2.590 square kilometres

Cubic Measure

		1 cubic inch	=	16.387	cubic centimetres
1728 cubic inches	=	1 cubic foot	=	0.0283	cubic metre
27 cubic feet	=	1 cubic yard	=	0.7646	cubic metre

Nautical Measure

6 feet	=	1 fathom	=	1.829	metres
100 fathoms	=	1 cable's length			

(*in the Royal Navy, 608 feet, or 185.319 metres = 1 cable's length*)

10 cables' length	=	1 international nautical mile	=	1.852	kilometres (exactly)
1 international nautical mile	=	1.150 779 statute miles			

(*the length of a minute of latitude at the equator*)

60 nautical miles	=	*1 degree of a great circle of the earth*	=	69.047	statute miles

Liquid and Dry Measure

1 gill	=	5 fluid ounces	=	9.0235	cubic inches	=	0.1480	litre
4 gills	=	1 pint	=	34.68	cubic inches	=	0.568	litre
2 pints	=	1 quart	=	69.36	cubic inches	=	1.136	litres
4 quarts	=	1 gallon	=	277.4	cubic inches	=	4.546	litres
2 gallons	=	1 peck	=	554.8	cubic inches	=	9.092	litres
4 pecks	=	1 bushel	=	2219.2	cubic inches	=	36.37	litres

The U.S. gallon (4 U.S. quarts) = 231 cubic inches = 3.7854 litres.

Apothecaries' Fluid Measure

		1 minim	=	0.0038	cubic inch	=	0.0616	millilitre
60 minims	=	1 fluid dram	=	0.2256	cubic inch	=	3.6966	millilitres
8 fluid drams	=	1 fluid ounce	=	1.8047	cubic inches	=	0.0296	litre
20 fluid ounces	=	1 pint	=	34.68	cubic inches	=	0.568	litre

The U.S. pint = 16 fluid ounces.

Avoirdupois Weight

(The grain, equal to 0.0648 gram, is the same in all three tables of weight.)

1 dram or 27.34 grains			=	1.772	grams
16 drams or 437.5 grains	=	1 ounce	=	28.3495	grams
16 ounces or 7000 grains	=	1 pound	=	453.59	grams
14 pounds	=	1 stone	=	6.35	kilograms
112 pounds	=	1 hundredweight	=	50.80	kilograms
2240 pounds	=	1 (long) ton	=	1016.05	kilograms
2000 pounds	=	1 (short) ton	=	907.18	kilograms

Troy Weight

(The grain, equal to 0.0648 gram, is the same in all three tables of weight.)

3.086 grains	=	1 carat	=	200.00	milligrams
24 grains	=	1 pennyweight	=	1.5552	grams
20 pennyweights or 480 grains	=	1 ounce	=	31.1035	grams
12 ounces or 5760 grains	=	1 pound	=	373.24	grams

Apothecaries' Weight

(The grain, equal to 0.0648 gram, is the same in all three tables of weight.)

20 grains	=	1 scruple	=	1.296	grams
3 scruples	=	1 dram	=	3.888	grams
8 drams or 480 grains	=	1 ounce	=	31.1035	grams

SI Units

Prefixes used with SI Units

Factor	*Name of prefix*	*Symbol*
10^{-1}	deci-	d
10^{-2}	centi-	c
10^{-3}	milli-	m
10^{-6}	micro-	μ
10^{-9}	nano-	n
10^{-12}	pico-	p
10^{-15}	femto-	f
10^{-18}	atto-	a
10	deca-	da
10^{2}	hecto-	h
10^{3}	kilo-	k
10^{6}	mega-	M
10^{9}	giga-	G
10^{12}	tera-	T
10^{15}	peta-	P
10^{18}	exa-	E

Base SI Units

Physical quantity	*Name*	*Symbol*
length	metre	m
mass	kilogram	kg
time	second	s
electric current	ampere	A
thermodynamic temperature	kelvin	K
amount of substance	mole	mol
luminous intensity	candela	cd

Supplementary SI Units

Physical quantity	*Name*	*Symbol*
plane angle	radian	rad
solid angle	steradian	sr

Derived SI Units with Special Names

Physical quantity	*Name*	*Symbol*
frequency	hertz	Hz
energy	joule	J
force	newton	N
power	watt	W
pressure	pascal	Pa
electric charge	coulomb	C
electric potential difference	volt	V
electric resistance	ohm	Ω
electric conductance	siemens	S
electric capacitance	farad	F
magnetic flux	weber	Wb
inductance	henry	H
magnetic flux density	tesla	T

Chemical Elements

No.	Element	Symbol	No.	Element	Symbol
1	hydrogen	H	56	barium	Ba
2	helium	He	57	lanthanum	La
3	lithium	Li	58	cerium	Ce
4	beryllium	Be	59	praseodymium	Pr
5	boron	B	60	neodymium	Nd
6	carbon	C	61	promethium	Pm
7	nitrogen	N	62	samarium	Sm
8	oxygen	O	63	europium	Eu
9	fluorine	F	64	gadolinium	Gd
10	neon	Ne	65	terbium	Tb
11	sodium	Na	66	dysprosium	Dy
12	magnesium	Mg	67	holmium	Ho
13	aluminium	Al	68	erbium	Er
14	silicon	Si	69	thulium	Tm
15	phosphorus	P	70	ytterbium	Yb
16	sulphur	S	71	lutetium	Lu
17	chlorine	Cl	72	hafnium	Hf
18	argon	Ar	73	tantalum	Ta
19	potassium	K	74	tungsten	W
20	calcium	Ca	75	rhenium	Re
21	scandium	Sc	76	osmium	Os
22	titanium	Ti	77	iridium	Ir
23	vanadium	V	78	platinum	Pt
24	chromium	Cr	79	gold	Au
25	manganese	Mn	80	mercury	Hg
26	iron	Fe	81	thallium	Tl
27	cobalt	Co	82	lead	Pb
28	nickel	Ni	83	bismuth	Bi
29	copper	Cu	84	polonium	Po
30	zinc	Zn	85	astatine	At
31	gallium	Ga	86	radon	Rn
32	germanium	Ge	87	francium	Fr
33	arsenic	As	88	radium	Ra
34	selenium	Se	89	actinium	Ac
35	bromine	Br	90	thorium	Th
36	krypton	Kr	91	protactinium	Pa
37	rubidium	Rb	92	uranium	U
38	strontium	Sr	93	neptunium	Np
39	yttrium	Y	94	plutonium	Pu
40	zirconium	Zr	95	americium	Am
41	niobium	Nb	96	curium	Cm
42	molybdenum	Mo	97	berkelium	Bk
43	technetium	Tc	98	californium	Cf
44	ruthenium	Ru	99	einsteinium	Es
45	rhodium	Rh	100	fermium	Fm
46	palladium	Pd	101	mendelevium	Md
47	silver	Ag	102	nobelium	No
48	cadmium	Cd	103	lawrencium	Lr
49	indium	In	104	rutherfordium	Rf
50	tin	Sn	105	dubnium	Db
51	antimony	Sb	106	seaborgium	Sg
52	tellurium	Te	107	bohrium	Bh
53	iodine	I	108	hassium	Hs
54	xenon	Xe	109	meitnerium	Mt
55	caesium	Cs			

The Plant Kingdom

(Simplified classifications)

Traditional classifications

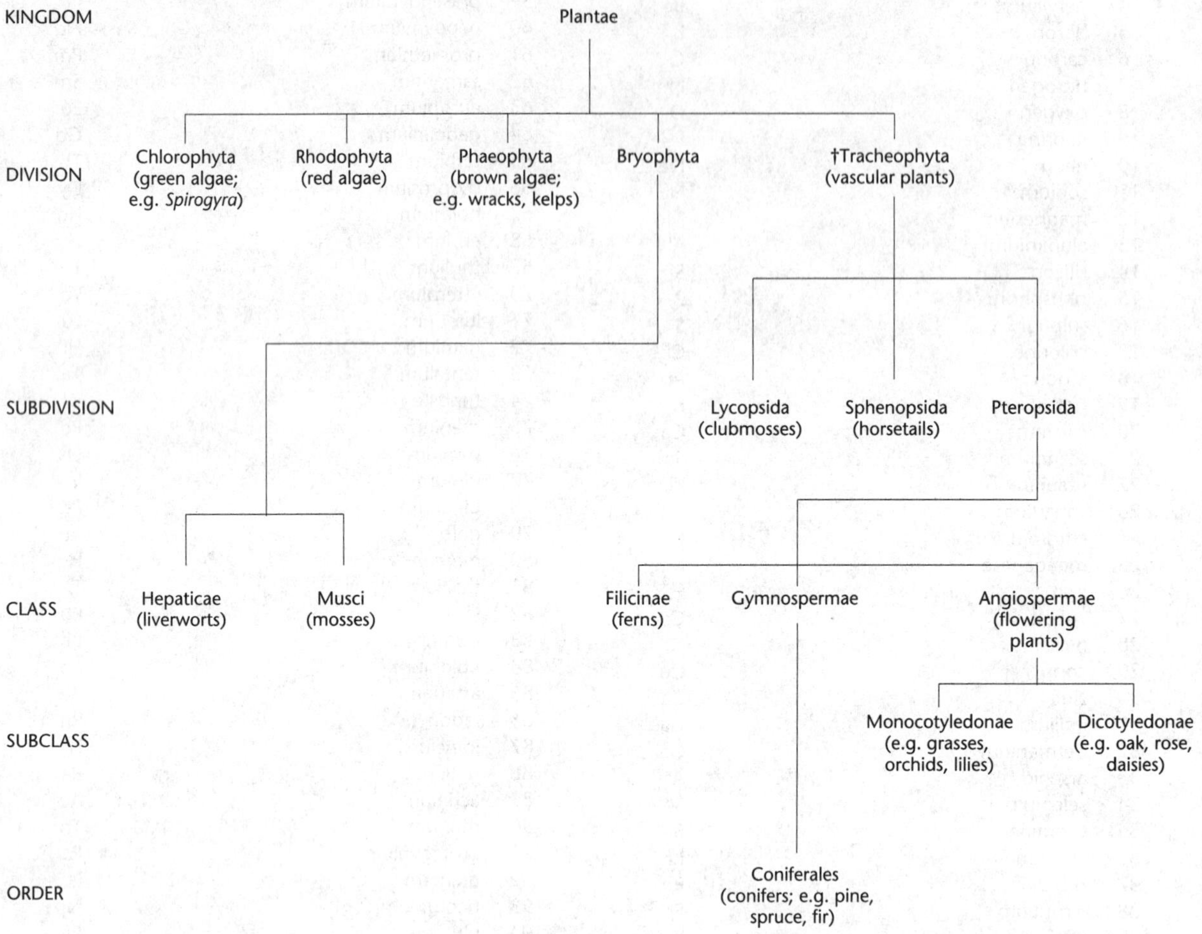

KINGDOM
Plantae
DIVISION
Chlorophyta (green algae; e.g. Spirogyra)
Rhodophyta (red algae)
Phaeophyta (brown algae; e.g. wracks, kelps)
Bryophyta
†Tracheophyta (vascular plants)
SUBDIVISION
Lycopsida (clubmosses)
Sphenopsida (horsetails)
Pteropsida
CLASS
Hepaticae (liverworts)
Musci (mosses)
Filicinae (ferns)
Gymnospermae
Angiospermae (flowering plants)
SUBCLASS
Monocotyledonae (e.g. grasses, orchids, lilies)
Dicotyledonae (e.g. oak, rose, daisies)
ORDER
Coniferales (conifers; e.g. pine, spruce, fir)

†In some classifications vascular plants are split into two divisions: Pteridophyta (clubmosses, horsetails, and ferns) and Spermatophyta (seed plants).

Five-kingdom classification

KINGDOM
Plantae
PHYLUM
algae classified in separate phyla in the kingdom Protoctista
Bryophyta
Lycopodophyta (clubmosses)
Sphenophyta (horsetails)
Filicinophyta (ferns)
Coniferophyta (conifers)
Angiospermophyta (flowering plants)
CLASS
Hepaticae
Musci
Monocotyledonae
Dicotyledonae

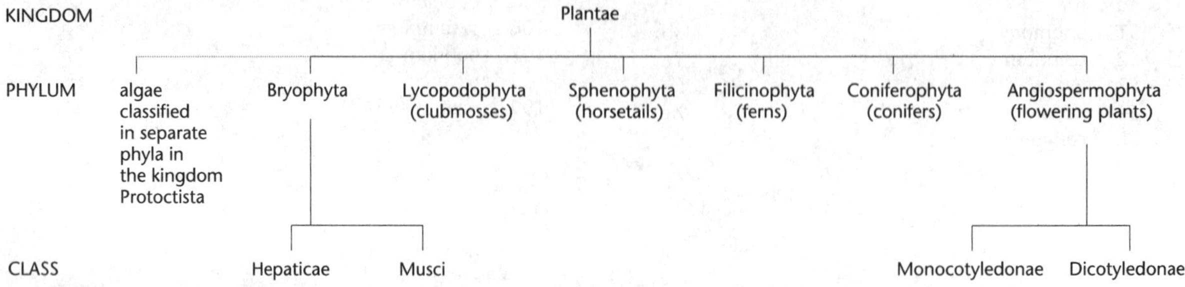

The Animal Kingdom

A simplified classification

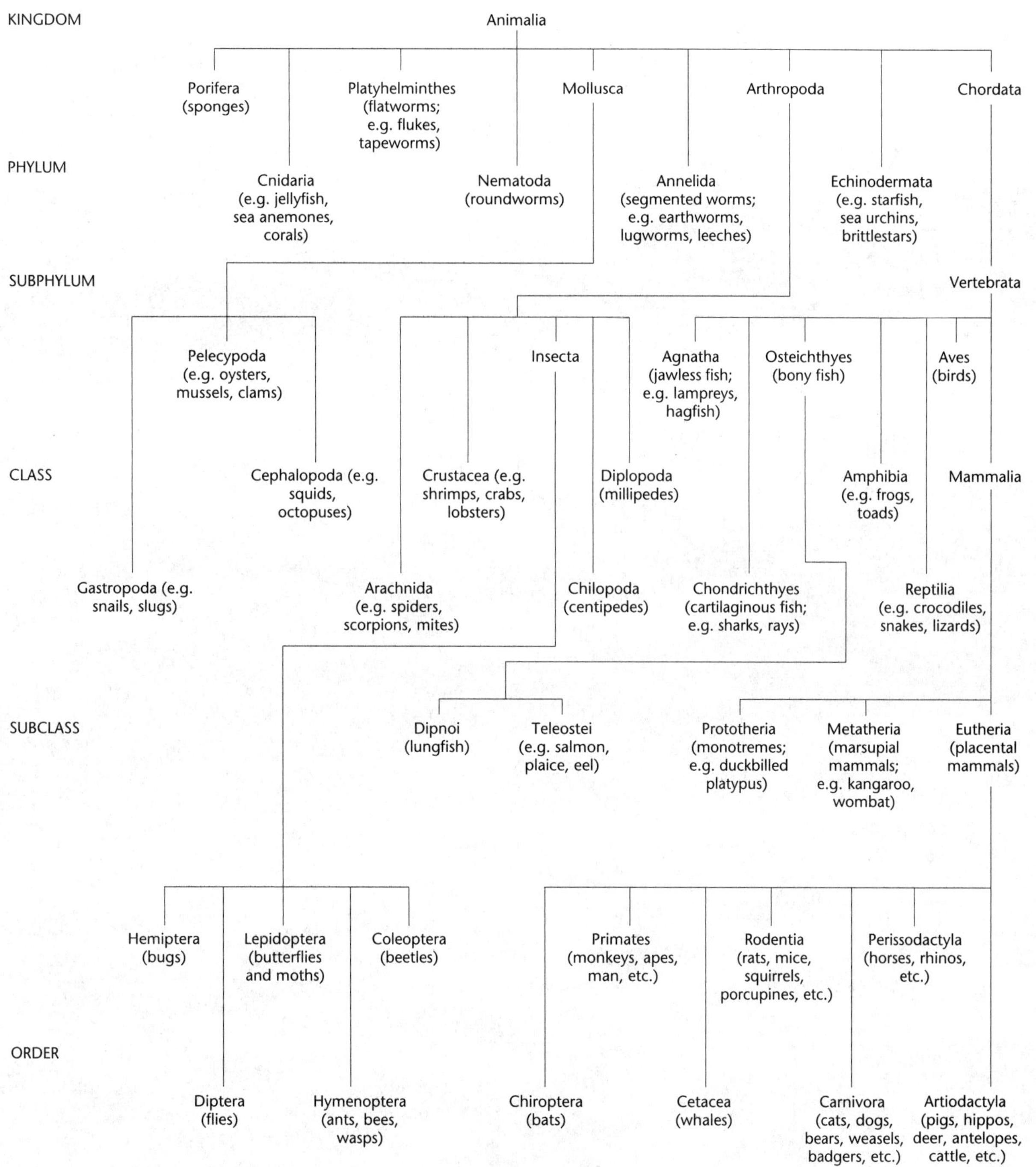

THE TIMES GUIDE TO ENGLISH STYLE AND USAGE

Introduction

This Style Guide was originally written to provide writers and sub-editors on *The Times* with a quick reference to contentious points of grammar and spelling, to proper names and to specialised usages which can cause confusion. It was meant as a guide and a means of ensuring overall consistency thus creating a coherent house style. In publishing this Guide for a wider audience, it is intended as a helpful reference tool.

However, it should be remembered that some spellings or constructions within this Guide are a matter of choice for *The Times* and that the rejected usages are not necessarily wrong. A full picture of the possible variations and alternatives available in the English language can be found in The Times English Dictionary.

Abbreviations used in the Style Guide:
cap(s) – capital letter(s)
l/c – lower case letter(s)

Aa

a, an use *a* before all words beginning with a vowel or diphthong with the sound of *u* (as in *unit*) – *a eulogy, a European* etc; but use *an* before unaspirated *h* – *an heir, an honest woman, an honour*; also, prefer *an hotel, an historic*, and *an heroic*

abattoir

Abbey National (bank, not building society); others with similarly changed status include the Halifax, the Woolwich, the Alliance & Leicester etc. See **building societies**

abbreviated negatives (can't, don't, shan't etc, plus similar abbreviations such as I'll, you're) should be discouraged in all text except in direct quotes, though they are permissible when the full form would sound pedantic

abbreviations prefer not to abbreviate Professor to Prof, Father to Fr etc; see **military ranks**

Abdication cap with specific reference to Edward VIII's; in general sense, use l/c. See **Royal Family**

Aboriginal (native Australian) singular noun and adjective; for plural use *Aborigines*; note l/c *aboriginal* for wider adjectival use

Acas the Advisory, Conciliation and Arbitration Service

accents give French, Spanish, Portuguese, German, Italian and Ancient Greek words their proper accents and diacritical marks; omit in other languages unless you are sure of them. Accents are not necessary in headlines. There is no need for accents in foreign words that have become Anglicised (*hotel, depot, debacle, elite, regime* etc), but keep the accent when it makes a crucial difference to pronunciation – *café, communiqué, fête, fiancée, mêlée, émigré, protégé*; also note *vis-à-vis, façade*. See **foreign words**

Achilles' heel

acknowledgement

acoustic(s) (not accoustic)

Act and **Bill** cap whether fully identified or not

actor, actress see **feminine designations**

Actuary the *Government Actuary* takes caps

AD, BC note that AD comes before the date, eg, *AD35*; BC comes after, eg, *350BC*. With century, both are used after, eg, *3rd century BC/AD*

adapter (person who adapts); *adaptor* (plug, device)

Addenbrooke's Hospital, Cambridge

addresses no commas in *1 Virginia Street* etc; and do not abbreviate *Street*. See **postal addresses**

adidas note l/c

adjectives avoid clichéd adjectives as in *long-felt* want, *serious* danger, *widespread* concern, *substantial* majority etc

Adjutant-General takes the hyphen

Administration (US)

Admiral do not abbreviate to *Adm Jones* etc except in lists; on subsequent mentions, use *the admiral*. See **Armed Forces** special section (page 1847)

admissible, inadmissible (not -able)

ad nauseam (not ad nauseum)

adrenalin prefer to adrenaline

adverbs when they are used to qualify adjectives, the joining hyphen is rarely needed, eg, heavily pregnant, classically carved, colourfully decorated. But in some cases, such as well-founded, ill-educated, a hyphen makes the sense clearer. The best guidance is to use the hyphen in these phrases as little as possible or when the phrase would otherwise be ambiguous

adviser (never advisor)

affect, effect as a verb, *to affect* means to produce an effect on, to touch the feelings of, or to pretend to have or feel (as in affectation); *to effect* is to bring about, to accomplish

Afghan (noun or adjective); an *afghani* (l/c) is a unit of currency, not a person

Afrikaans (language) note *Afrikaners* (the people)

after almost invariably to be used rather than *following*. Also, beware of careless use in sentences such as "The British player won a place in the final after beating the seeded German". Instead use "... by beating the seeded German". See **as, following**

afterlife one word

ageing note the middle *e* – as in *axeing, likeable, mileage, moveable, rateable, sizeable, unlikeable, unshakeable* etc. Common exceptions are listed separately, eg, see **unmistakable**

ages normal style is *Joe Brown, 33, a porter*; keep children's ages in this format as figure for the sake of consistency, eg, "Emma Watson, 7, who..."; but "the seven-year-old child said ..." (up to and including ten); occasional variations such as "Andrew Hunt, who is 74, said..." are also permissible. Note caps in *Ice Age, Stone Age*, the *Dark Ages* etc

aggravate means to make (an evil or complaint) worse. It does not mean to annoy or irritate

AGM caps, but prefer *annual meeting* in text

agoraphobia (not agaro-, agra- etc)

Aids short for acquired immune deficiency syndrome (not auto-immune etc); it is not a disease, but a medical condition. Diseases that affect people who are HIV-positive may be called Aids-related diseases; although prefer not to use the phrase "died of Aids", it is now permissible in standfirsts, headings etc. See **HIV**

AIM the Alternative Investment Market; keep caps in abbreviation

Air Accidents Investigation Branch caps; note *Accidents*

airbase, airstrip, airspace no hyphens; but see **air fares, air show, airstrikes**

air-conditioner, air-conditioning (hyphenate)

aircraft try to avoid *planes* in text, though *planes* would be acceptable in headlines. Even there, *jets* (where applicable – remember that some aircraft are still turbo-prop) or *aircraft* would be better. See **planes**

aircraft names are italicised, as with ships' or locomotive names, eg, the *Enola Gay* (Hiroshima bomber). See **locomotive names, ships**

aircraft types no hyphens between letter and numbers, eg, B52, F111 etc

aircraftman, aircraftwoman (not aircraftsman etc); see **Armed Forces** special section (page 1847)

air fares two words, as *rail fares, bus fares* etc

air force cap in full name such as Royal Air Force (thereafter the RAF), US Air Force (USAF), Brazilian Air Force (thereafter the air force, l/c); and l/c in adjectival use, eg, *an air force raid*. See **Armed Forces** special section (page 1847)

Air Miles take care when to cap: the Air Miles scheme is run by BA and should usually be capped; but use l/c in a general context

airports as a general rule for British airports, use the name of the city or town followed by l/c airport, eg, Manchester airport, Leeds/Bradford airport, East Midlands airport, Luton airport; but see **Heathrow, Gatwick, Stansted**

air raid two words, but see **airstrikes**

air show two words; cap when specific, eg, the Paris Air Show, the Farnborough Air Show

airstrikes one word in military sense, but see **air raid**

akimbo use only with reference to arms (never legs). It means hands on the hips with elbows turned outwards

al- as the prefix to Arabic nouns (including names), prefer *al-* to the *el-* form, except where *el-* has become widely accepted

Albert Hall generally omit Royal

A level, O level hyphenate only when adjectival, eg, A-level results etc. See **examinations**

Alfa Romeo

Al Fayed Mohamed Al Fayed is chairman of Harrods. His youngest brother Ali Fayed is deputy chairman of Harrods. Their brother Saleh Fayed is not a resident of the UK. The brothers should be spelt like this, with no variation. The late elder son was Dodi Fayed

alibi not a general alternative to *excuse*; it means being elsewhere at the material time

Allahu akbar (God is greatest)

allcomers one word

Allende, Isabel, the Chilean novelist (born in Lima, Peru) is the niece and goddaughter of the former Chilean President, Salvador Allende, NOT his daughter

allege avoid the suggestion that the writer is making the allegation, so specify its source. Do not use *alleged* as a synonym of *ostensible, apparent* or *reputed*

All England Club (home of the Wimbledon championships); no hyphen

Allies cap the Allies in the Second World War context; generally, l/c *alliance*, as in the *Atlantic alliance, Gulf War alliance* etc

Allitt, Beverly (child-killer convicted in May 1993)

all right (never alright)

All Souls College, Oxford no apostrophe; see **Oxford colleges**

all-time avoid as in *all-time high;* use *highest* instead

alsatian (German shepherd dog); l/c as for other breeds of dogs; but note exceptions such as Yorkshire terrier. See **dogs**

alternative of two things; of three or more, use *choice*

al-Yamamah (oil-for-arms defence project); note l/c and hyphen

Amateur Athletic Association (not Athletics)

Ambassador cap when specific, eg, the French Ambassador, thereafter *the ambassador*

America(n)/US in general, use American as in "American cities, American food" etc; but use US in headlines and in the context of government institutions, such as US Congress, US Navy, US military operation. Never use *America* when ambiguity could occur with Canada or Latin America. See **United States**

American spellings normally use the English spelling even with offices or institutions such as Secretary of Defense (change to *Defence*), American Federation of Labor (change to *Labour*), or with buildings, eg, the Lincoln Center (change to *Centre*); but *Labor Day* (which has no UK equivalent) is an exception; see also **Pearl Harbor**

America's Cup, the (yachting)

amid (not amidst); similarly *among,* not amongst

amok (not amock or amuck)

amphitheatres in classical context these are oval or circular (eg, the Colosseum in Rome); do not confuse with theatres which are semi-circular or horseshoe-shaped

Amsterdam treaty l/c *t*, but note caps for the Treaty of Amsterdam. See **Maastricht**

analog (in computer context); but use *analogue* as in an analogous or parallel thing. See **program**

ancestor strictly means a person from whom another is directly descended, especially someone more distant than a grandparent. Do not use in the looser sense of *predecessor*, eg, Queen Elizabeth I is not the *ancestor* of the present Queen

Ancient Briton/Britain note also Ancient Greek/Greece, Ancient Egyptian/Egypt, Ancient Roman/Rome

Andersen, Hans Christian (not Anderson)

aneurysm (not aneurism)

Anglicise, Anglophile caps, note l/c *anglophone*

Anglo-Irish agreement See **Ireland**

angst roman l/c

animals beware the solecism "birds and animals"; use *birds and mammals* instead

animal names call an animal "he" or "she" if the sex is definitely known or if called by a masculine or feminine name (eg, Felix the cat had only himself to blame). But use "it" if the sex is unspecified. On the racing pages, horses are always "he" or "she"

annexe (noun), but to *annex* (verb)

anoint (not annoint)

answerphone or use *answering machine*

Antarctic, Arctic (never Antartic etc)

antennae plural of *antenna* in zoological sense; use *antennas* in radio or aerial sense

Antichrist (initial cap)

anticipate do not use for *expect.* It means to deal with, or use, in advance of, or before, the due time. To anticipate marriage is different from expecting to marry

antidepressant noun or adjective, no hyphen

anti-Semitic, anti-Semitism

antisocial, anticlimax

Anti-Terrorist Branch, Special Branch note caps; but police squads in most cases l/c, except *Flying Squad* and *Royalty and Diplomatic Protection Squad*

any more always two words

Apennines, Italy (not Appenines)

apostrophes with proper names/nouns ending in *s* that are singular, follow the rule of writing what is voiced, eg, *Keats's poetry, Sobers's batting, The Times's style* (or *Times style*); and with names where the final *s* is soft, use *s'*, eg, *Rabelais' writings, Delors' presidency*; plurals follow normal form, eg, *Lehman Brothers' loss* etc. Note that with Greek names of more than one syllable that end in *s*, do not use the apostrophe *s*, eg, *Aristophanes' plays, Achilles' heel, Archimedes' principle.* Beware of organisations that have variations as their house style, eg, St Thomas' Hospital, where we must respect their whim.

Also, take care with apostrophes with plural nouns, eg, *women's*, not womens'; *children's*, not childrens'; *people's*, not peoples'

An apostrophe should be used to indicate the plural of single letters, eg, *p's and q's.* Use the apostrophe in expressions such as *two years' time, several hours' delay* etc.

apparatchik

appellations almost every person should be granted the courtesy of a title. The exceptions are convicted offenders, the dead (but not the recently dead, except in obituaries) and cases where common usage omits a title. Sportsmen, artists, authors etc should normally be given a title except where it sounds inappropriate.

General rules:

a First mention, Herbert Palfry, Juliette Worth, subsequently Mr Palfry, Mrs/Miss/Ms Worth

b Put the name first, then the age (if relevant), then the description; eg, Jane Fonda, 57, the American actress; avoid the journalese construction "actress Jane Fonda"

c Avoid initials and middle initials (as in American names) unless the person is best-known thereby (eg, W.G. Grace)

d Ms is nowadays fully acceptable when a woman wants to be called thus, or when it is not known for certain if she is Mrs or Miss

e Dr is no longer confined to medical doctors; if a person has a doctorate from a reputable university, Dr is acceptable

f Court proceedings: accused people should be accorded the appropriate title (Mr, Miss etc) after name and first name have been given at first mention; only convicted persons should be referred to by surname alone.

See also **foreign names**, **titles**, **Armed Forces** special section (page 1847), **Courts** special section (page 1851)

appendix plural *appendices*, but note *appendixes* in anatomy

appraise means *evaluate*; do not confuse with *apprise* meaning *inform*

April Fool's Day, April fool, but *All Fools' Day*

Aqaba, Gulf of (Red Sea)

aqueduct (not aquaduct)

Arab use with care

Arabic names use with care; but remember the basic rule of *al-X* (l/c *al* with hyphen, before name; rarely use the *el-* form); see **al-**

Arafat, Yassir (not Yasser)

arbitrate, arbitration do not confuse with *mediate, mediation*. An *arbitrator* hears evidence from different parties then hands down a decision; a *mediator* listens to the different arguments then tries to bring the parties to agreement

archaeologist, archaeology

archbishops

a *Anglican archbishops and diocesan bishops*: at first mention, the Archbishop of Barchester, the Most Rev John Smith; or the Bishop of Barchester, the Right Rev John Smith, but if a doctor, the Bishop of Barchester, Dr John Smith; subsequent references, *the archbishop* (*the bishop*), or Dr Smith (if so entitled) – never Mr Smith

b The Archbishop of Canterbury is Primate of All England, the Archbishop of York is Primate of England

c Anglican bishops are *consecrated*, Roman Catholic bishops *ordained*

d *Roman Catholic archbishops and bishops*: at first mention: the Roman Catholic Archbishop of Liverpool, the Most Rev John X; or the Roman Catholic Bishop of Plymouth, the Right Rev Christopher Y; subsequent mentions, Archbishop X (Bishop Y) or *the archbishop* (*the bishop*), or Dr Y (if so entitled). See **Churches** special section (page 1850)

Argentine adjective; note an *Argentinian* is a person from Argentina (never the Argentine)

armada be careful with use of this word: it means a fleet of armed ships, so strictly should not be applied to any collection of boats or ships

Armageddon cap

armchair, deckchair no hyphens

Armed Forces, the caps; see also **Services**

Armistice Day not the same as Remembrance Sunday (unless November 11 falls on a Sunday); see **two minutes' silence, Remembrance Sunday**

Army cap in context of the *British Army* (thereafter *the Army*, capped) and foreign armies, as in the *Belgian Army, Iraqi Army* (but thereafter *the army*, l/c); note always l/c when used adjectivally, eg, *an army helicopter*; see **Armed Forces** special section (page 1847)

Arran, Isle of (Firth of Clyde); note the *Aran Islands* (one *r*) off Co Galway in western Ireland, *Aran Island* (singular) off Co Donegal and an *Aran sweater* etc

artefact do not use *artifact*

artistic movements cap *Art Deco, Classical, Neo-Classical, Cubist, Gothic, Impressionist, Minimalist, Modernist, Post-Modern, Pre-Columbian, Pre-Raphaelite, Romantic, Surrealist* etc in cultural contexts; but in wider general use, l/c, eg, "He had a surrealist sense of humour but a romantic nature"

as beware of sloppy use in sentences such as "They were moved out as the blast tore open the building"; instead use simply "*after* the blast..."

Asean Association of South East Asian Nations: Indonesia, Singapore, Malaysia, Thailand, the Philippines, Brunei, Vietnam, Burma and Laos. Note that Cambodia is due to join at some unspecified date. See **South-East Asia, Far East**

ASH Action on Smoking and Health; use caps for abbreviation of the anti-smoking pressure group

Asia-Pacific Economic Co-operation forum use Apec as abbreviation

assassin, assassination only to be used in the murder of a statesman or politician from a political motive; not to be used for the killing of general celebrities or others. See **execution, killer**

Assisted Places Scheme caps, but *assisted places* (in schools)

assizes like quarter sessions, no longer function, having been replaced by Crown Courts. See **quarter sessions**

Association of First Division Civil Servants use *First Division Association* for short

assure you *assure* your life; *ensure* means to make certain; you *insure* against risk

asylum-seekers hyphenate

at the present time, at this time use *now;* but avoid the phrase *as of now*

Athenaeum, the see **London clubs**

Atlantic (Ocean), North Atlantic, South Atlantic see **transatlantic**

Atomic Energy Authority, UK (not Agency); abbreviated to AEA; but note *International Atomic Energy Agency*, abbreviated to IAEA

Attorney-General, Solicitor-General (law officers, not legal officers); hyphenate both; see **Courts** special section (page 1851)

Auditor-General hyphenate

Auntie (not aunty) as colloquialism for the BBC. See **BBC**

Autocue proprietary term, so cap

Autumn Statement (caps); see **Budget**

Awol (not AWOL) absent without leave

AXA League (Sunday cricket league); note also the *Benson and Hedges Cup*. See **Sports** special section (page 1854)

axeing note middle *e*; but try to avoid in sense of *cutting jobs, dismissal* etc

ay (yes), *aye* (ever), *Ayes* (debate)

Ayckbourn, Alan

Bb

BAA (airports operator); no longer British Airports Authority

Baath party (not Ba'ath)

baby-walker

baccalaureate use Anglicised spelling with l/c for general use, but cap in specific context of the *International Baccalaureate*; and note the specifically French examination or degree, the *Baccalauréat* (italic, cap, accent, no final "e")

Bacharach, Burt

B&B (abbreviation for bed and breakfast); use caps and close up around ampersand

back benches (parliamentary); two words, but note *backbenchers, backbench* (adjective, as in *backbench revolt*). See **Politics** special section (page 1853)

back burner (no hyphen), but be sparing of the cliché "on the back burner"

backlash overworked word; always try to avoid

backstreet(s) noun or adjective, no hyphen; similarly, *backyard*

"back to basics" use in quotes, no hyphen

bacteria note the term is not interchangeable with viruses. Note that antibiotics are used to treat bacterial but not viral infections. See **medical terms, meningitis**

bail out (as in to *bail someone out of trouble*); note also *to bail water from a boat*, but *to* **bale out** *of an aircraft* (to escape); and *bailout*

balk (not baulk)

ball plural in Court Page headlines is *dances*

ballets use italics for titles; see **Arts** special section (page 1849)

ballgown one word

balloted like *benefited, budgeted* etc, has only one *t*

Balpa British Air Line Pilots' Association

banister (not bannister)

Bank Holiday also *Bank Holiday Monday* etc

bankruptcy in Britain people *file a petition for bankruptcy*; they do not *file for bankruptcy*

Bar, the (legal); also cap for the *Bar of the House of Commons*. See **Courts** special section (page 1851) and **Politics** special section (page 1853)

barbecue, barbecuing

Barnardo's (no longer Dr Barnardo's Homes)

Bar school l/c *s*, as this is not its official title, and no longer Bar law school. Its full name is the *Inns of Court School of Law*

Bart's abbreviation of St Bartholomew's Hospital, London

basically greatly overworked word which rarely adds anything to a sentence. Always try to avoid

basis *on a ... basis* is a cliché and should be avoided; for *employment on a part-time basis* use *part-time employment*

Basle, Switzerland (not Basel); see **Berne**

battalion (not batallion). Write *1st Battalion, 7th Battalion* etc (not First, Seventh). See **Armed Forces** special section (page 1847)

Battersea Dogs' Home (formal title is *The Dogs' Home, Battersea*, but not usually necessary to spell it out)

battle avoid using as a transitive verb as in "The students battled the police..."; use *fought* or *battled against* instead

BBC no need to spell out as British Broadcasting Corporation, though *the corporation* is a useful alternative in text. Note BBC Television, BBC1, BBC2, and BBC Radio (caps). Note also *Chairman of the (Board of) Governors* takes caps (although chairman in most other cases is l/c). This is because we cap the *Director-General* and when both appear in the same story it is anomalous to cap the one and not the other. Cap *the BBC Board of Governors*, but l/c *the governors* at other mentions. See **radio, television**

BBC Charter cap when in full, l/c for *charter* on subsequent mentions

BC see **AD**

Beatles, the no need to cap *the* unless at the start of a sentence; similarly *the Rolling Stones* and *the Manic Street Preachers* etc, but prefer to keep cap *T* with *The Who* and *The The*

Becket note *à* with St Thomas à Becket

Beduin plural; the singular is *Bedu*

Beethoven, Ludwig van (not von); normally Beethoven will suffice; see **Van**

beg the question do not confuse with *ask the question*. To beg a question is to *evade* it

Beijing (no longer Peking); see **Chinese names**

Belarus (no longer Belorussia)

beleaguered rapidly becoming a cliché, especially in a political context, so best avoided

Belfast see **Ireland**

bellringer, bellringing, belltower no hyphens. See **peal**

benchmark (no hyphen)

benefited

benzene (substance obtained from coal-tar); note *benzine*, a spirit obtained from petroleum

-berg, -burg always check spelling of towns with these endings, and those ending in *-burgh, -borough, -brough*

Berkeley Square, West End of London; similarly, Berkeley, California

Bermudian (not Bermudan); but note a *Bermuda-rigged boat*

Berne, Switzerland (not Bern)

berserk (not beserk)

BEST Investment (no longer BESt)

bestseller, bestselling one word

bête noire note italics and final *e*

Betjeman, Sir John (not Betjamin)

Bevan, Aneurin, but **Ernest Bevin**

Beverly Hills

Bhutto, Benazir use Miss rather than Ms or Mrs on subsequent mentions

bi- take care with this difficult prefix. Its correct use is in Latin compounds, where it has the force of two, not half, such as *bicentenary/bicentennial* (a two-hundredth anniversary), or *biennial* (recurring every two years). *Biannual* means twice a year; to avoid confusion, use *twice a year*

biased

Bible cap and roman, not italic, but note l/c *biblical*; for biblical references: II Corinthians ii, 2; Luke iv, 5. Note *Bible Belt*. See **Churches** special section (page 1850)

bid do not use in text as synonym of *effort, attempt* or *try*, though it may be used sparingly in headlines in this context

bight (curve in a coastline or river); do not confuse with *bite* involving teeth. See **bite, German Bight**

Bill and **Act** caps whether fully identified or not

Bill of Rights cap even when non-specific, eg, "If the Government were to introduce a Bill of Rights..."

billion (one thousand million, not a million million). Write £5 billion, £15 billion (£5bn, £15bn in headlines), three billion, 15 billion etc. See **millions, trillion**

biological terms see **scientific names**

Biro trade name, so cap; alternative is *ballpoint pen*

birthday people and animals have *birthdays*; everything else has *anniversaries*. Better to write *33rd birthday, 65th birthday* etc (any number higher than tenth), despite the usual rules on spelling out ordinals. See **numbers**

birthrate, birthright, birthplace no hyphens, but note *birth control, birth certificate* etc

bisexual pronouns *he* and *his* can no longer refer to both sexes equally; *he or she* will sometimes do. Always be sensitive in this contentious area

bishops see **archbishops**

Bishopsgate, City of London (not Bishopgate)

Bishop's Stortford

bite (as with teeth) do not confuse with the computing term *byte* or the geographical *bight*. See **bight, byte, soundbite**

blacklist one word as noun or verb; see **shortlist**

blackout noun, one word

blacks (people), l/c; do not use *non-whites* and be sensitive to local usage, eg, *African-American* is now often used in the United States. See **Coloureds, race**

blackspot (accident, unemployment etc), one word; similarly, *troublespot*

blame take care with this word; blame is attached to causes, not effects. So write "Bad weather is blamed for my bronchitis", not "My bronchitis is blamed on bad weather"

bloc use in context such as the *former Soviet bloc*, a *power bloc* etc; but note *block vote*

blond (men), *blonde* (women)

bloodied as in *bloodied but unbowed*; but *red-blooded* etc

blood sports similarly field sports; see **foxhunt**

Bloomingdale's (New York store)

Blue cap both for an Oxbridge sportsman or woman and for the award itself. See **Sports** special section (page 1854)

blue-collar workers similarly *white-collar workers*

blueprint avoid this greatly overworked word when all you mean is *plan, scheme* or *proposal*

Boadicea (no longer Boudicca)

boat generally used of a small vessel, including fishing boats up to the size of a trawler; a *ship* is a large seagoing vessel big enough to carry smaller boats. In the Royal Navy, submarines are called boats. All take the pronoun *she* and the possessive *her*. See **ships**

Boat Race (annual Oxford-Cambridge race); use caps

boffin do not use as a synonym of *scientist*, except ironically or in direct quotes

Bogart, Humphrey but note (Sir) Dirk Bogarde

bogey (golf); note also *bogie* (wheels), *bogy* (ghost) and *bogeyman*

Bogotá (capital of Colombia)

Bohemian cap noun, but note l/c adjective *bohemian*

Bolshevik

bombshell avoid metaphorical use, as in cliché *drop a bombshell*

bonanza greatly overworked word that should be avoided wherever possible

Bonhams (auction house); no apostrophe

Boodle's (London club). See **London clubs**

Booth, Cherie Tony Blair's wife should be referred to as Cherie Booth wherever possible; refer to Cherie Blair only in contexts when she is clearly in the role of Prime Minister's wife, eg, at summit meetings or on the campaign trail. In legal contexts, write Cherie Booth, QC, at first mention. Subsequent mentions, Ms Booth

bored with (not *of*)

borscht (Russian or Polish soup)

borstals no longer exist; now known as *young offender institutions*

Bosphorus

Boutros Boutros Ghali (former UN Secretary-General); no hyphens and at subsequent mentions, Dr Boutros Ghali. His successor is the Ghanaian Kofi Annan

Bowes Lyon no hyphen for most of the family, but always important to check in *Who's Who* or *Debrett*

bow-tie

box office as noun, two words; hyphenate when adjectival, eg, *box-office success*

boyfriend, girlfriend

Boy Scouts now known as *Scouts* in the UK. *Cub Scouts* have replaced Wolf Cubs; *Scoutleaders* have replaced Scoutmasters. Also cap *Scouting* in the context of the movement. In the US they are still known as Boy Scouts. See also **Girl Guides**

braille l/c

brainchild try to avoid this cliché

branch note *Special Branch, Anti-Terrorist Branch* in police context

Brands Hatch

breakout, breakdown one word as noun; but note *to break out* etc, and hyphenated *break-up*

breathtaking no hyphen

Brent Spar is a storage buoy, not an oil platform or rig; note that *oil platforms* stand on the seabed; *oilrigs* are small mobile installations for oil exploration

Bretton Woods (as in world trade)

Breughel (artists)

bridges cap as in Severn Bridge, London Bridge, Southwark Bridge, Golden Gate Bridge

Bridgwater, Somerset (note no middle *e*)

Brink's-Mat

Britain/Great Britain = England, Wales and Scotland. *United Kingdom* = Britain and Northern Ireland. *British Isles* = United Kingdom and the Republic of Ireland, Isle of Man and Channel Islands. Take care with these distinctions

Britannia see **Royal Yacht**

British Athletic Federation (not Athletics)

British Home Stores note the abbreviation Bhs

British Standards Institution (not Institute); abbreviation is BSI. It awards companies, goods etc its *Kitemark* (cap)

Britpop (not Brit Pop)

Brittany Bretagne in French

Broadcasting Standards Commission formed from merged Broadcasting Standards Council and Broadcasting Complaints Commission

Broadmoor inmates are *patients*, not prisoners

broadsheet preferable to *quality* for describing the serious British press

Brookings Institution, Washington (not Institute)

Brooks's (London club). See **London clubs**

Brummie (not Brummy); cap people and dialect, eg, *Geordie, Scouse* etc. See **Cockney**

Brylcreem

BSE bovine spongiform encephalopathy, or "mad cow" disease

BSkyB News International, the subsidiary of The News Corporation that owns *The Times*, owns 40 per cent of BSkyB (British Sky Broadcasting Group Ltd). So BSkyB can be called an associate company of News International, or of News Corp. There is a choice of up to 40 channels available in the UK on the Astra satellite; BSkyB owns 11. See **News International, *The Times***

BT usual abbreviated form of British Telecommunications plc, but it is often convenient to use British Telecom at first mention, and BT subsequently

Budget cap the *British Budget*, otherwise l/c. Note l/c *d* for

Budget day and also note *Pre-Budget Report* and *Autumn Statement* (caps)

Buggins's turn (not Buggins')

builder's merchant(s)

building societies cap full name, eg, Skipton Building Society, thereafter *the Skipton*, or *the society* etc. Take care with societies that have become banks. See **Abbey National**

bullion (gold or silver in unminted form)

bull-mastiff, bull-terrier see **dogs**

bullring but the *Bull Ring* in Birmingham

bull's-eye (use hyphen)

bungee (as in jumping)

Bunsen burner

BUPA (no longer Bupa)

Burma (not Myanmar except in direct quotes); the inhabitants are *Burmese*, and note that *Burmans* are a Burmese people

Burnet, (Sir) Alastair

Burns Night (January 25); caps, no apostrophe

burnt (not burned)

Burton upon Trent no hyphens; note l/c for the colloquial *gone for a burton*

bus, buses noun; but in verbal use *busses, bussed, bussing*

Bush, George W. (do not use Jr)

Bushey, Hertfordshire but Bushy Park, near Hampton Court

Bussell, Darcey (ballerina)

buyout, buyback one word; but prefer hyphens for *buy-in, take-off, shake-out, shake-up, sell-off, sell-out* etc

by-election

bylaw

bypass noun or verb

by-product

bystander

byte (computer term for a small collection of bits – binary digits – roughly equivalent to one character); do not confuse with *bite* (as with teeth). But note *soundbite*

Byzantine cap in all contexts

BZW Barclays de Zoete Wedd

Cc

cabbie (not cabby) as colloquialism for taxi driver

Cabinet cap in both British and foreign use, whether used as a noun or adjectivally. The only exception is the informal *kitchen cabinet*. Note *Cabinet Office, Cabinet Secretary* (or *Secretary of the Cabinet*). Cabinet committees should be capped, eg, *the Cabinet Committee on Science and Technology*. See **Politics** special section (page 1853)

Caernarfon (town and parliamentary constituency, no longer Caernarvon); but note Lord Carnarvon

Caesarean section

café note accent

cagoule but note *kaftan*

call-up noun, but note *to call up*

camaraderie (not cameraderie)

Camborne, Cornwall (not Cambourne)

Cambridge University colleges and halls are: Christ's College; Churchill College; Clare College; Clare Hall; Corpus Christi College; Darwin College; Downing College; Emmanuel College; Fitzwilliam College; Girton College; Gonville and Caius College; Homerton College; Hughes Hall; Jesus College; King's College; Lucy Cavendish College; Magdalene College; New Hall; Newnham College; Pembroke College; Peterhouse; Queens' College; Robinson College; St Catharine's College; St Edmund's College; St John's College; Selwyn College; Sidney Sussex College; Trinity College; Trinity Hall; Wolfson College

camellia (not camelia)

Campbell, Alastair (not Alistair); Tony Blair's press secretary

Camra the Campaign for Real Ale; note l/c

cancer heart disease not cancer is "the biggest killer" in the UK

cannon (military), singular and plural; but note *canons* (both churchmen and church laws) and *canon* as a collection or list of an author

Canton now Guangzhou; see **Chinese names**

canvas (material, painting); note *canvass* (votes)

CAP common agricultural policy; l/c when spelt out in text

Cape Town

capitalisation in general, the proper names of people and places, formal titles or titles of important offices, and the names of well-known and substantial institutions, all require capitals. As a rule of thumb, cap specifics (eg, *the French Foreign Minister*), but l/c non-specifics (eg, *EU foreign ministers*). But some terms, eg, *Act, Bill, Cabinet, Civil Service*, always cap. See **initials**

capsize see **-ise, -isation**

captions when space is tight, just the surname is acceptable, even when the person is titled, eg, Sir Marcus Fox would be simply Fox, as in headlines. Where women are photographed, give the woman's first name and surname where possible.
Identify people in a photograph with *left* and *right* etc, using commas, not parentheses (eg, Fred Smith, left, and his wife leaving the court)

car boot sale no hyphen

carcass

cardholder

Carlos the Jackal no quotes, no commas; always mention his full name, Ilich Ramírez Sánchez

carmaker one word

car park two words, note *multistorey car park*

carpetbagger one word

Carrott, Jasper (not Carrot)

cashcard (in general sense); note also *cashflow, cashback*

Cashpoint Lloyds Bank's cash machine system, so cap and do not use generically; in the general sense, use *cash dispenser* or *cash machine*, or less formally, *hole in the wall*

Castro, President (Fidel) use *Señor* or *the President* after first mention, not Dr

Catch-22 avoid the grossly overworked cliché *Catch-22 situation*

cathedrals cap when giving the full name, eg, St Paul's Cathedral, Wells Cathedral; similarly the names of churches, eg, St Mary's Church, Ely, unless the church name specifically excludes it, eg, St Stephen's, Ely

Catherine always check the spelling; note a Catherine wheel (firework); St Catharine's College, Cambridge; St Katharine Docks, London

Catholic in church context, use *Roman Catholic* at first mention, then *Catholic*. See **Churches** special section (page 1850)

Catmark the new financial products version of the Kitemark; similarly *Cat standard* etc

cat's eyes should preferably be called reflecting roadstuds; *Catseye* is a trademark

caviare (not caviar)

CD-Rom compact disc, read only memory; note CD-i (interactive compact disc system)

ceasefire

Ceausescu, Nicolae (not Ceaucescu)

ceilidh Highland social gathering

Cellophane proprietary term, so cap

celsius, centigrade use either term. In news stories, use both centigrade and fahrenheit, eg, "The temperature rose to 16C (61F)"; do not use degree sign

centenarian see also **septuagenarian, octogenarian, nonagenarian**

centenaries use *centenary, bicentenary, tercentenary*; after that, use *four hundredth anniversary*, etc

Center Parcs

Central Europe note cap *C*

Central St Martins College of Art and Design no apostrophe in St Martins; use *St Martins* at subsequent mentions

Centre, the use cap in political context of *the Centre*, as with *Left* and *Right*. Similarly, *Centre Left, Centre Right* as nouns, but note l/c for adjectival use, eg, *a centre-left politician, a right-wing policy*. See **Left**, **Right**, **Politics** special section (page 1853)

Centre Court see **Wimbledon**

centrepiece no hyphen

centring but note *centering of arches* in bridge-building

centuries write *the 3rd century BC, the 9th century, the 18th century* etc; and hyphenate when used adjectivally, eg, *20th-century architecture*

CERN the European Organisation for Nuclear Research, based in Geneva; note all caps

Ceylon now Sri Lanka. The people are *Sri Lankan*, the majority group are the *Sinhalese*

cha-cha-cha (not cha-cha)

chainsaw one word

chairman still common usage referring to men and women, except in quotes, but *chairwoman* is acceptable. Avoid *chair* and *chairperson* (except in quotes and phrases such as *addressing remarks to the chair*). In most cases, keep *chairman* l/c, but occasionally cap, as with BBC, Bar Council, and US Federal Reserve Board

chamber (of the House of Commons); use l/c. See **Politics** special section (page 1853)

champagne note l/c; use only for the product of the Champagne region of France; otherwise use *sparkling wine*. The champagne producers protect their name rigorously. See **wines**

changeable

Changing the Guard (not ... of the Guard); see **Trooping the Colour**

Channel 4, Channel 5 (not Four, Five); see **television**

Channel Tunnel with cap *T*, but thereafter l/c *tunnel* if the context is clear; note also *Channel Tunnel rail link*. Note that *Le Shuttle* trains are no longer called thus; they are now *Eurotunnel trains*. See **Eurotunnel**

Chanukkah prefer this to variants such as Hanukkah etc, for the Jewish festival of lights

charge that do not use this Americanism as a synonym of *allege that*

charisma find an alternative such as *presence, inspiration* etc for this boring cliché

Charity Commission (not Charities)

Charollais (cattle or sheep)

charters (as in John Major's initiative) see **Citizen's Charter, Parent's Charter, Patient's Charter.** Note also *Charter Mark*

Château-Lafite (not Lafitte); note hyphen

chat show, game show, quiz show, talk show no hyphens; note also *chatline, sexline*

cheap goods are *cheap*, prices are *low*

Chechnya (not Chechenia); note adjective *Chechen*

check-in noun, but note *checklist, checkout counter*

cheerleader one word

Chekhov, Anton

chequebook one word, either as noun or adjective, eg, *chequebook journalism*

chess names note Garry Kasparov, Anatoly Karpov, Judit Polgar. Note also Fide, not FIDE, and l/c *grandmaster*. See **Russian names**

Chester-le-Street

chickenpox no hyphen; similarly *smallpox*

Chief Constable caps when referring to a specific, as in *Chief Constable of Lancashire*; thereafter, *the chief constable*. See **police ranks**

Chief Inspector of Prisons/... of Schools note also *Chief Medical Officer*

Chief Whip caps; see **whips**

childcare similarly *healthcare*

ChildLine (charity); note cap *L*

Children Act 1989 (not Children's); note also cap *T* for *The Children's Society*

chimpanzees are apes, not monkeys

Chinese names the Pinyin rather than the traditional Wade-Giles system is now used, so write Beijing, Mao Zedong (though Chairman Mao or just Mao are acceptable), Zhou Enlai etc. For Chinese place names, follow spellings in *The Times Atlas of the World*: eg, Guangzhou (formerly Canton), Sichuan (formerly Szechuan). See **Peking**

chopper, copter never use as substitutes for *helicopter*, even in headlines

Christ Church, Oxford (never Christ Church College). See **Peterhouse, Oxford University**

Christchurch, Dorset and New Zealand

christened people are *christened*, ships and trains etc are *named*

Christian, Christianity note also *unchristian, non-Christian, antichristian, Antichrist*

Christian Democrat noun and adjective, as in *Christian Democrat MP*

Christian names in context of non-Christians use *forename* or *first name*

Christian terms cap the Bible, the Commandments, the Cross, the Crucifixion, the Resurrection, the Gospels, Mass, Holy Communion (and simply Communion), Eucharist, Blessed Sacrament, Advent, Nativity (but note l/c when used adjectivally, eg, *a nativity play*); also use *He* and *His* when referring to God and Jesus Christ. Use l/c for *evensong, matins*. See **Churches** special section (page 1850)

Christie's note apostrophe also for Christie's, New York, and Christie's International

Christmas Day, Christmas Eve

Church cap in context of the institution (Anglican, Roman Catholic, Orthodox etc), but not when used adjectivally. See **archbishops, Churches** special section (page 1850)

churchwarden one word

cider (not cyder)

CIMA the Chartered Institute of Management Accountants; note caps for the abbreviation

Cincinnati, Ohio

cinemagoer similarly *concertgoer, theatregoer* etc

CinemaScope trade name, so cap; note also cap *S* in middle

cipher (not cypher)

cissy, cissies (not sissy)

Cites (not CITES); the Convention on International Trade in Endangered Species

Citizens Advice Bureau/Bureaux no apostrophe, and note final *x* as plural

Citizen's Charter

Citroën

City and Guilds of London Institute abbreviate to *City & Guilds*, with ampersand

City of London note also *the City, City prices*. See **London**

Civil List caps

Civil Service but note *civil servants*. Always cap *Civil Service*, even in adjectival use, eg, *a Civil Service memorandum*. Caps to be restored to the administrative grade, ie, *Permanent Secretary, Deputy Secretary* and *Assistant Secretary*. For executive grade (ie, below Assistant Secretary), use l/c. Note also *Secretary of the Cabinet and Head of the Home Civil Service*. See **Politics** special section (page 1853)

claim do not use when simply *said* or *declared* would do. The word carries a suspicion of incredulity. Also, avoid the loose construction in sentences such as "The firm launched a drink which is claimed to promote learning ability". This should read "... a drink which, it is claimed, promotes learning ability"

clamour, clamouring but note *clamorous*

clampdown not banned, but use as little as possible

Claridge's

Clause Four (as in Labour Party policy); but Clause 4 permissible in headlines

clichés some of the most common, to be resisted strongly in almost every context, are: *backlash, basically, beleaguered, blueprint, bombshell, bonanza, brainchild, chaos, charisma, clampdown, consensus, crackdown, crisis, crunch, drama/dramatic, escalate, facelift, gunned down, hopefully, ironically, legendary, major, massive, mega-, nightmare, prestigious, quantum leap, reportedly, shambles, shock, shoot-out, situation, trauma/traumatic, unique*

Clinton use simply President Clinton (not President Bill Clinton), thereafter the President or Mr Clinton. The First Lady is Hillary Rodham Clinton (usually write Hillary Clinton or Mrs Clinton)

closed-circuit television

clothing use *menswear, women's wear, children's wear, sportswear*. See **wear**

cloud-cuckoo-land note two hyphens

clubs see **London clubs**

co- the prefix does not normally require a hyphen even before an *e* or another *o* unless confusion might result. Thus *co-operate* (but *uncooperative*), *co-opt*, *co-ordinate* (but *uncoordinated*), *coeducation, coexist*. See **co-production**

coalface, coalfield, coalmine one word; prefer *miner* to *coalminer*. Note also *gasfield, oilfield*

coastguard l/c and one word, in the British context; but note the new *Coastguard Agency* (caps), though the *coastguard service* (generic) retains the l/c. Note also the *US Coast Guard*

coasts cap *South Coast, East Coast* and *West Coast* in British context (as in *West Coast main line*); note also *East Coast* and *West Coast* in US

coats of arms see **heraldry**

Coca-Cola note hyphen; similarly *Pepsi-Cola*

Cockney cap for the person and the dialect, but l/c for general adjectival use, eg, *a cockney welcome*

coeducation(al) but *co-ed* is acceptable in headlines

coexist

Coldstream Guards may be called *the Coldstream* and the men *Coldstreamers* or *Coldstream Guards*; neither should be called *Coldstreams*. See **Armed Forces** special section (page 1847)

Cold War

collarbone one word

collectibles (not -ables)

collective nouns usually use the singular verb, as with corporate bodies (the company, the Government, the council etc). But this rule is not inviolable; the key is to stick to the singular or plural throughout the story – sentences such as "The committee, which was elected recently, presented their report" are unacceptable

Colombia (country); Columbia is the Hollywood studio, university, river and Washington district. Note also British Columbia and Pre-Columbian

Colosseum, Rome but the Coliseum, London

Coloureds (South Africa); use cap

comedienne avoid wherever possible; use *comedian* for both sexes. See **feminine designations**

comeuppance no hyphen

Commander-in-Chief, Officer Commanding use caps

Commandments cap in biblical context, as *the Ten Commandments, the Fourth Commandment*. See **Christian terms**

commando note plural *commandos* (not -oes)

Commission, Commissioner see **European Commission**

Commissioner of the Metropolitan Police similarly, cap *City of London Police, British Transport Police* and all police forces when the full title is given. For full list, see **police forces**

committee note cap in *1922 Committee of Tory backbenchers*. Committees of inquiry etc should be capped only when the full title is given, eg, *the Neill Committee on Standards in Public Life*, but *the Neill committee*. Cabinet committees should be capped. See **Cabinet**, **select committees**, **royal commissions**, **Conservative**, **Tory**, and **Politics** special section (page 1853)

common agricultural policy l/c; see **CAP**

Common Market usually use EU or EC (see **European Union**); but Common Market is acceptable in historical context

common sense noun; but note adjective *commonsense, commonsensical*

Common Serjeant see **Courts** special section (page 1851)

Commonwealth Heads of Government Meeting use caps

communiqué

communism, communist as with *socialism* and *socialist*, the best rule is to cap only when in specific party context, eg, *a Communist candidate, a Communist rally, the Communist Mayor of Lille*; but *communist ideology, communist countries* etc. It will help to think of a parallel with Conservative/conservatism or Liberal/liberalism. But *Marxist, Stalinist, Nazi* and *Fascist* should be capped

companies abbreviate to *Co* in, eg, John Brown & Co. Company is singular. Do not confuse *company* and *firm*, even in headlines. A *firm* implies a business partnership, as in the legal or accountancy professions, estate agents etc. Full points in company titles usually unnecessary, as in WH Smith and J Sainsbury. Do not abbreviate Ford of Europe to Fords, Swan Hunter to Swans etc. See **Ltd**, **plc**

comparatively, relatively avoid using as synonyms of *fairly, middling*

compare with/to use *compare with* (the most common) when differences or contrasts are the point, eg, *compare the saints with the devils* or *compared with last year's figures*; use *compare to* for likenesses, eg, *compare this image to a damsel fair*

compass points in the UK, regional phrases, if well established and in common use, take caps as in the North, the South, the West, the South East, the North East, the South West, the West Country, the West Midlands, the East Midlands, East Anglia, North Wales, South Wales, West Wales, the East/West End of London. But when used adjectivally, use *southeast* England (though note the South East of England).

Overseas, cap the following: the Midwest (US), Central America, West Africa, North Africa, East Africa, Central Africa, South Africa but southern Africa, North and South Atlantic and Pacific, the Middle/Far East, but sub-Saharan Africa and south India etc

complement (completing something); but *compliment* (praise or tribute). Note also *complimentary*, as in free gifts etc

comprise means *to consist of, be composed of*; see **include**

Comptroller General

concertgoer similarly *partygoer, theatregoer*, but *concert hall*

confectionery (not -ary)

conference keep l/c in *Labour Party conference; Lib Dem conference* etc

Congo take care to distinguish between the Democratic Republic of Congo (formerly Zaire) and Congo-Brazzaville (formerly French Congo). See **Zaire**

Congress (US); note l/c *congressional* and *congressman* except when with a name, eg, Congressman John Waldorfburger; but generally try to avoid this construction and use John W, a congressman from Minnesota, etc. See **Senate**

Congress Party (India); now takes cap *P* and is no longer known as Congress (I)

connection

Connolly, Billy (comedian)

consensus (never concensus); avoid this cliché wherever possible

Conservative Party note *Conservative Central Office*, but *Conservative chairman, manifesto* etc; *Tory* is permissible as a less formal alternative, but note *Tory party* (l/c *p*). Abbreviate in lists etc to C (not Con). See **Tory**, **Politics** special section (page 1853)

considerable avoid its use as a lazy adjective implying emphasis

Consolidated Fund, the

consortium plural *consortiums* (not consortia); as a general rule, use the *-ums* plural. Similarly *memorandums*

constitution (of a country); cap only when an actual document, eg, *the American Constitution*, but *the British constitution*

consult (never *consult with)*

Consumers' Association

Contact Group UN group on former Yugoslavia: US, Russia, Britain, France, Germany and Italy

Continent, the refers to mainland Europe; note l/c *continental*

continuous means *without intermission*; *continual* means *frequently recurring*

contract out no hyphen

Contract with America (the Republicans' 1995 programme); note italics

Contras, the cap in Nicaragua context

Controller of Radio 1 etc note cap *C*. See **BBC**

controversial avoid where possible

convener (not convenor)

convertible (not -able); noun and adjective

conveyor belt; a *conveyer* is a person who conveys

Cooke, Alistair (not Alastair)

cooling towers these should not be used to illustrate air pollution stories, as they emit harmless water vapour

Co-op, the acceptable abbreviation of *Co-operative Society*

co-operate, co-ordinate etc but note *uncooperative, uncoordinated, non-cooperation*

co-production, co-producer etc use hyphen to avoid ambiguity with *copro-*, as in dung

copycat (no hyphen)

copyright (sole right in artistic work etc); note *copywriter* (advertising)

cornflake (generic), but note *Kellogg's Corn Flakes*

Coronation cap *Coronation Oath* and when referring to a specific event, such as Elizabeth II's Coronation in 1953; but l/c in most adjectival uses, eg, *coronation ceremony, coronation broadcast*

coroner's court at inquests, the *coroner* is l/c unless specific, as in the Westminster Coroner. Juries *return* the verdict, the coroner *records* it. There are no coroner's inquests in Scotland; violent deaths are reported to the *Procurator Fiscal*, who may hold an inquiry. See **Courts** special section (page 1851)

correspondents wherever possible, write the political correspondent of *The Times*, the Moscow correspondent of *The Times* etc; but the *Times* political correspondent, the *Times* Moscow correspondent etc, is permissible. See ***The Times***

coruscating (not corruscating)

Côte d'Azur note no final *e*

councils cap in full title, eg, Birmingham City Council, otherwise l/c

council tax replacement for *poll tax/community charge*, so use the latter only in historical context

counter-productive, counter-attack etc, but *countertenor* (one word)

counties spell out names except in lists. Do not add *-shire* to Devon (except in Devonshire cream or the Duke of Devonshire), Dorset, Somerset. Irish counties should be as Co Donegal (cap *C*, no full point); Co Durham takes the same style. Take great care with new, reorganised or abolished counties. See **Durham**, **unitary authorities**

Courchevel (Alpine ski resort; not Courcheval)

court martial note plural *courts martial*; also *Courts-Martial Appeal Court*; and verb *to court-martial*

Court of Appeal always use the full title at first mention and wherever possible thereafter, though l/c *appeal court* may be used sparingly. See **Courts** special section (page 1851)

Court of Arches (court of appeal of the Province of Canterbury in the Church of England); do not use *Arches Court*

Court of St James's

Court of Session, Edinburgh (not Sessions)

Court Service, the (not Courts); note caps

courts cap all courts when specific, eg, Birmingham Crown Court, Clerkenwell County Court, Dawlish Magistrates' Court, Ashford Youth Court etc; in a general, unspecific context, always cap the *Crown Court* (it sits in about 90 centres), but l/c *county court, magistrates' court* and *youth court* etc. See **coroner's court**, **Inns of Court**, **Courts** special section (page 1851)

Coutts Bank

Coward, Noël note the diaeresis

crackdown not banned, but use as little as possible

Cracow (not Krakow or variations); see **foreign places**

crèche (not crêche)

creditworthy, creditworthiness no hyphen

Creole person born in the West Indies or Latin America whose ancestry is wholly or partly European. It does not imply mixed race

crescendo means getting louder, growing in force. Nothing *rises to a crescendo*. Plural is *crescendos*

Creutzfeldt-Jakob disease abbreviation CJD

crisis always try to find an alternative for this greatly overworked word

criterion plural *criteria*

Croat (people and language); *Croatian* is the adjective; see **Slovak**

Cross, the note cap; see **Christian terms**

cross benches but note *crossbenchers*, and adjective *crossbench*

cross-Channel but note *transatlantic*

Crown (in constitutional sense); cap, as in *Crown property, the Crown representative*. See **Royal Family**

Crown Estate Commissioners (not Estates)

Crown Jewels note caps

Crown Prosecution Service abbreviate to CPS

Crufts Show or just Crufts; note no apostrophe

cruise missiles but *Pershing missiles* and the *Stealth bomber*

crunch avoid clichés such as *reaches crunch point, the situation came to a crunch*

CSCE no longer exists; see **OSCE**

Cup cap *Final* only in *FA Cup Final* (or *Cup Final* for short), but l/c all others, such as *European Cup final, World Cup final, Davis Cup final* etc. See **Sports** special section (page 1854)

cupfuls, spoonfuls etc (not cupsful or cupfulls)

currencies always convert to sterling on news, sport and features pages – usually at first mention of the foreign currency. But on Business pages, US dollars, French francs and German marks need not be converted, unless to help the flow of the story. See **deutschemark**, **dollar**, **franc** and **peseta**

current avoid wherever possible as synonym of *present*

curriculums plural *s* (not curricula); note *extracurricular activities*; abbreviate *curriculum vitae* to *CV*, note plural *curricula vitae*. See **national curriculum**

curtsy (not curtsey); note plural *curtsies*

Custom House (the headquarters building)

Customs and Excise cap for the organisation (or simply *Customs*), l/c for *customs officer, customs post, customs regulations* etc

cutthroat no hyphen

Cyprus, northern keep l/c in *northern*, as the "state" is recognised only by the Turkish Government; also l/c *government* in northern Cyprus, as with provincial or state governments in Australia or Canada etc

czar although usual style (in Russian context) is *tsar, czar* is permissible in the phrase *drugs czar*

Czech Republic use Czechoslovakia only in the historical sense. The two countries since their division are the Czech Republic and Slovakia

Dd

dad, mum cap when referring to specific parents, l/c in general context

Dail Eireann (lower house of the Irish parliament); usually just *the Dail*

Dagestan (not Daghestan)

Dales, the Yorkshire or Derbyshire or simply *the Dales*

dancefloor

Dar es Salaam, Tanzania (no hyphens). Note, capital is Dodoma

Dark Ages caps, but take care: the period after the fall of the Roman Empire is no longer considered wholly obscure and barbaric

data strictly plural, but can be singular through common usage

databank, database

dates Note *Monday, April 18, 1994* (never 18th April); but *April 1994*. When citing periods of years, write *1992–93* (not 1992–3) and for the millennium, *1999–2000*, then *2003–09* etc; *from 1939 to 1941* (not from 1939–41); *the Forties, Eighties, Nineties* (*or 1940s, 1980s, 1990s*). But note l/c for people's ages, eg, *she was in her forties, eighties, nineties* etc. Common usage says that the past decade ended on December 31, 1989, and that the century ends on December 31, 1999. See **millennium**

Day-Glo proprietary term, so cap

daytime but note *night-time*

daytrip but note *day-tripper*

D-Day, VE-Day, VJ-Day

deathbed no hyphen

death row (as in American prisons); l/c

debacle accents unnecessary

debatable

Debrett or full title, *Debrett's Peerage*

debut no accent

decades use either *the Sixties* or *the 1960s*; see **dates**

decimals do not mix decimals and fractions in the same story. See **millions, per cent**

decimate means to kill one in ten; custom has extended its use to indicate heavy casualties, but use sparingly

deckchair no hyphens; similarly *armchair*

decor no accent

decorations see **honours**

defuse means to remove the fuse from, or reduce tension in a crisis etc; never confuse with *diffuse*, which means to spread in all directions, scatter etc, or (as adjective) verbose, not concise, spread over a large area etc

Degas no accent

de Gaulle never cap *de* in this name unless at the start of a sentence or headline

de Havilland

de Klerk, F.W. see **full points**

de la Mare, Walter

De La Rue

DeLorean

De Niro, Robert

de Sancha, Antonia

de Valera, Eamon

degrees (educational) *a first, a second, an upper second* (*a 2:1*), *a lower second* (*a 2:2*), *a third* etc. D Lit, D Litt, LitD etc are abbreviations for doctorates of literature (or letters); Oxford and York have D Phil instead of the more usual PhD. Oxford has DM for the more usual MD. Cambridge has ScD for doctor of science. No full points in degrees

degrees (weather) omit degree sign in temperatures. See **celsius**

déjà vu use accents but not italic

demise strictly means the death of a person, or the failure of an enterprise or institution. Keep to these definitions. It is wrong to refer to the demise of Glenn Hoddle or Peter Mandelson

Democratic Party (US; not Democrat Party); the adjective is usually *Democrat* in other uses, such as *the Democrat spokesman* (but note *the Democratic convention*)

demonstrator but note *protester*

Deng, Wendi Rupert Murdoch's wife; see **Murdoch**

Denktas, Rauf (not Denktash), the president of northern Cyprus (l/c *p* because not an internationally recognised state); better to describe him as the *Turkish Cypriot leader*. See **Cyprus**

deny does not mean the same as *rebut* (which means argue to the contrary, producing evidence), or *refute* (which means to win such an argument). See **rebut, refute**

Department for Culture, Media and Sport (not of) replaced the Department of National Heritage in July 1997. *Culture Secretary* is an acceptable short form for the Secretary of State

Department for Education and Employment (not of); use *Education and Employment Department* or *the department* at subsequent mentions. Avoid the ugly abbreviations DfE or DfEE except in direct quotes

Department of the Environment, Transport and the Regions

dependant noun; note *dependent* (adj), and *dependency*

Deputy Prime Minister caps; similarly *Deputy Governor of the Bank of England*. Note these are the exceptions to the rule that deputy posts should take l/c, eg, *deputy editor*

desiccate

desktop (computer, publishing), no hyphen; similarly *laptop*

despite acceptable alternative for *in spite of*. But do not use *despite the fact that*; use *although* instead

despoiled (not despoilt)

despoliation, or **despoilment** (not despoilation)

Deutsche Bank German commercial bank not to be confused with *Deutsche Bundesbank*, or *Bundesbank*, the German central bank

deutschemark/deutschmark/D-mark never use these forms. Always use simply *the mark*, or with figures, *DM500*. See **currencies**

Devil, the cap; but note *devils* (l/c), *devilish*

dextrous prefer to dexterous

Dhaka (capital of Bangladesh; not Dacca)

Diaghilev

diagnose take great care: *illnesses* are diagnosed, not patients

Diana, Princess of Wales since her death, use the form *the late Princess* where appropriate. Never use Princess Di or Lady Di. Note also one comma only for *the Diana, Princess of Wales Memorial Fund*. See **Royal Family, Titles** special section (page 1855)

Diaspora cap in Jewish context, but l/c in general sense of a dispersal

Di Canio, Paulo (cap Di every time)

DiCaprio, Leonardo

Dickins & Jones (department store)

Dictaphone trade name, so cap

diehard

different from (never different to or than); similarly *differ from*

dignitaries

dilapidated (not delapidated)

dilate *dilation* means normal widening, as in pupils of the eye; *dilatation* is widening by force, as in child abuse cases. Take care

Dillons (bookshop)

dining room (no hyphen)

diphtheria note *ph*; similarly *diphthong*

Diplomatic Service caps; similarly *Civil Service*

directives (EU); l/c in general context, caps when specific, eg, *Working Time Directive*

Direct Line, Direct Line Insurance trademarks, so must not be used in generic sense even with l/c, as in direct line companies, direct line telephone insurers etc; in this wider sense, use *direct insurance, direct telephone insurance* etc

Director-General of the BBC, CBI, Institute of Directors, Fair Trading, and the regulatory bodies etc. See **regulators, Secretary-General**

Director of Public Prosecutions abbreviation DPP

Directory Enquiries (despite usual style, *inquiries*)

disc (musical recording, or shape, eg, *disc jockey, compact disc, disc brake*); but use *disk* in general computing context, eg, *disk drive, floppy disk*

discomfit take great care with this verb; it means primarily to thwart, defeat or rout, but by extension can mean thoroughly to embarrass or disconcert (noun *discomfiture*). It has no connection with discomfort, which means to deprive of comfort or make uneasy

discreet means tactful, circumspect (noun *discretion*); *discrete* means individually distinct (noun *discreteness*)

disinterested means impartial, unbiased (noun *disinterest*); never confuse with *uninterested*, which means having a lack of interest

Disney the theme parks are *Disneyland* (California); *Disney World* (Florida); *Disneyland Paris* (Euro Disney should strictly be confined to the name of the European company); and *Tokyo Disneyland* (owned by a Japanese company, but Disney earns royalties from it)

disorientate (not disorient). See **orientate**

dispatch (not despatch); also *dispatch box*

dissociate (not disassociate)

distil but note *distilled, distillation*

divorcé (man); note *divorcée* (woman), use *divorcees* (no accent) in reference to both men and women

DIY spell out *do-it-yourself* at first mention

D-notice, D-notice committee

Docklands note cap *D* for London, elsewhere *docklands*

doctor the title *Dr* should no longer be confined to medical practitioners. If a person has a doctorate from a reputable institution, and wishes to be known as Dr Smith, he or she should be so titled

docusoap, docudrama etc (no hyphens)

dogs l/c with most breeds, such as *alsatian, borzoi, labrador, rottweiler*, though there are obvious exceptions such as West Highland terrier, Yorkshire terrier etc

Dole, Bob (not Robert)

dollar with figures use $5 (when American), A$5 (Australian), C$5 (Canadian), S$5 (Singapore)

doll's house (not dolls')

Dome cap *D* in *Millennium Dome* and when used on its own. See **millennium**

Domesday Book roman, similarly Magna Carta; but note *doomsday* in general or biblical sense

Dominican Republic (neighbour to Haiti); note *Dominica*, one of the Windward Islands. Both are sovereign states. See **Haiti**

donate use *give* or *present* wherever possible

Dorchester, the (not Dorchester Hotel)

do's and don'ts

Dostoevsky

doveish (rather than dovish)

down avoid unnecessary use after verbs, as in close down, shut down. See **up**

Downing Street write *10 Downing Street* (or *11*...), or simply *No 10*; note *Downing Street policy unit*. See **Politics** special section (page 1853)

Downing Street declaration see **Ireland**

downmarket no hyphen; similarly *upmarket*

Down's syndrome (never mongol)

Down Under cap as a colloquialism for Australasia (especially Australia)

D'Oyly Carte

D-Rams note also *CD-Roms*

drachmas (not drachmae)

draconian note l/c

draftsman (legal); but note *draughtsman* (art, design)

drama, dramatic confine their use to the theatrical context wherever possible; *dramatic events* and the like are overworked clichés

Dr Dolittle (italics for the film, roman for the character)

dreamt (not dreamed)

drier (comparative of dry); note *dryer* (noun), as in *tumble dryer*

drink-drive, drink-driver, drink-driving note that the limits are 35 *micrograms* of alcohol per 100 millilitres of *breath*; and 80 *milligrams* of alcohol per 100 millilitres of *blood*

drivers no hyphens in *taxi driver, bus driver, car driver* etc

drop a bombshell avoid this cliché

dropout noun or adjective as in students; note *drop-out* (rugby); and *to drop out* (verb)

Drug Enforcement Administration (US); thereafter DEA

drugs do not confuse *narcotics* (which include cocaine and heroin) with other illicit drugs such as cannabis, LSD and amphetamines

Druid(s) cap

Druze (religious sect and militia group in Lebanon)

Dr Who roman for the character (subsequent mentions *the Doctor*), but italics for the programme

dry-clean, dry-cleaning etc

drystone wall

dual of two, eg, *dual carriageway*; note *duel* (fight)

du Cann, (Sir) Edward

Duchess of York no longer a member of the Royal Family since her divorce. After first mention as Duchess of York, refer to *the duchess* (l/c) subsequently – never Fergie or any such vulgarity. See **Titles** special section (page 1855)

due to must not be used as the equivalent of *because of* or *owing to*. The phrase must be attached to a noun or pronoun: "His absence was due to illness" is correct; "He was absent due to illness" is wrong

duffel bag, duffel coat

Duke of Edinburgh write the Duke (cap) or Prince Philip after first mention; but this cap rule applies only to the British Royal Family and overseas heads of state, so the Duke of Rutland would become *the duke* (l/c) after first mention. See **Royal Family, heads of state, Titles** special section (page 1855)

dump do not use as synonym of *dismiss* or *sack*

Durham use Co Durham for the county and (if any question of ambiguity) Durham city for the city; see **counties**

duty-free hyphenate noun and adjective

dwarf as plural, prefer *dwarfs* (not dwarves); avoid "politically correct" circumlocutions such as *person of restricted growth*

dyke (embankment; not dike)

dysentery (not dysentry or disentery)

dyspepsia

Ee

each, every although singular, they are acceptable now with plural pronouns, as the plural is increasingly a way of avoiding "he or she", or "his or her". Hence, "everyone has what they want", "each of us has our secrets", but "everyone has secrets"

Earhart, Amelia (1930s aviatrix)

Earls Court no apostrophe

early hours avoid the phrase *in the early hours of the morning*; write simply *the early hours* or, better, *early yesterday/today*

earned (never earnt)

earring no hyphen

Earth cap only in planetary or astronomical sense, not in phrases such as *down to earth*. The same rule applies to Moon and Sun. See **Universe**

earthquake can abbreviate to *quake* in headings. See **Richter scale**

east, eastern for when to cap, see **compass points**

East End also West End of London; and East, West, North, South, Central, Inner London. See **London**

EastEnders (TV soap opera)

Easter Day (not Easter Sunday)

Eastern Europe but note *eastern Germany*. See **Germany**

easygoing

easyJet

EBRD European Bank for Reconstruction and Development

EC must not be used as an abbreviation for the European Commission in text or headlines. EC remains the short form only of the European Community, although in almost all contexts now, EU is preferred. See **European Commission, European Union**

E.coli italics in text, but roman and no point in headlines

e-commerce (as *e-mail*)

ecosystem no hyphen, but note *eco-warrior*

Ecstasy (drug)

ecu (European currency unit)

Ecuadorean (not -ian)

ecumenical (not oecumenical, but respect titles). See **Churches** special section (page 1850)

editor cap first mention of editors of well-known leading publications, such as the Editor of *The Times*, Editor of *The Mirror*, Editor of the *Yorkshire Post*, Editor of *The Spectator;* subsequent mentions, revert to l/c. Similarly, Editor-in-Chief. Note that deputy editors and below retain l/c. See **job titles, newspapers**

education action zones (EAZs), l/c in general context but cap specifics, eg, Barnsley Education Action Zone. Similar style to *local education authorities* (LEAs)

educationist (not educationalist)

eg no points, but use a comma before and after. See **ie**

Eire do not use except in historical context. See **Ireland**

eisteddfod l/c except when naming a particular one in full, eg, the International Eisteddfod at Llangollen; note plural *eisteddfodau*

either takes a singular verb when both subjects are embraced, eg, *either is good enough*. See **neither**

elderly, aged, old be sensitive in the use of these words, and generally do not use for people under 65

electrocardiographs (machines for measuring heart function); note *electrocardiograms*, the tracings made by electrocardiographs

electrocute means to kill by electric shock

Elgin Marbles subsequently the *Marbles*

elicit means to evoke, bring to light, or draw out; never confuse with *illicit* (unlawful, forbidden)

elite roman, no accent

e-mail

embarkation (not embarcation). You *embark in* (not on) a ship. See **Armed Forces** special section (page 1847)

embarrass(ment) but note the French *embarras de choix, embarras de richesses*

Embassy same style as for *Ambassador*, eg, *the French Embassy in Rome*, thereafter *the embassy*

Emmies plural of the *Emmy awards*

emphasise prefer this to *stress* in phrases such as "he emphasised the importance", "she emphasised that the ruling was final". See **stress**

empire cap as in *British* or *Roman Empire*; similarly, cap *emperor* when specific, eg, Emperor Claudius

employment tribunals have replaced industrial tribunals. See **industrial tribunals**

EMS European Monetary System

EMU economic and monetary union (in Europe); see **ERM**

encyclopaedia (not encyclopedia)

England, English beware of these when the meaning is *Britain, British*

England and Wales Cricket Board has replaced the TCCB, and is abbreviated as ECB; do not shorten to England/English Cricket Board. See **Sports** special section (page 1854)

enormity does not mean great size; it means quality or character of being outrageous, or extreme wickedness or serious error. Do not misuse. For great size, use *immensity*

en route not italics

ensign the *White Ensign* is the ensign of the Royal Navy and the Royal Yacht Squadron; the *Red Ensign* is the British Merchant Navy's flag; the *Blue Ensign* is flown by Royal Fleet Auxiliary vessels and by certain yacht clubs. There is no such thing as the Royal Ensign; however, the *Royal Standard* will fly from one of the Queen's homes when she is there. See **Royal Standard**

ensure means to make certain; you *insure* against risk; you *assure* your life. The verb *ensure* usually needs *that* after it if accompanied by a following verb (eg, "he tried to ensure that the policy was adopted"); but omit *that* if followed by a noun (eg, "he tried to ensure its success")

enthral

Environment Agency note caps

Equator cap, but *equatorial* in general sense

ERM exchange-rate mechanism (in European contexts); a part of the wider concept of EMU

escalate, escalation avoid these clichés; use *rise, grow* or *soar* instead

escapers (never escapees)

Eskimo plural *Eskimos*; preferred to Inuit

Establishment, the cap in sense of the perceived leaders of society; but l/c as in the *medical establishment*, the *legal establishment*, when the sense is more restricted

Eucharist cap; see **Christian terms**

euro (European common currency); note l/c (as franc, pound, mark, peseta etc); also *eurozone* or *euroland* for the single currency area

eurocheques, eurobonds l/c, no hyphen

Europe note caps for Western, Eastern, Central. Europe includes the British Isles, so do not use the name as equivalent to the Continent. Britain does not export to Europe, but to the *rest* of Europe

European Commission, Commissioners cap *Commission* throughout as a noun, but l/c when adjectival, eg, a *commission ruling* (the same rule as for Government/government); cap *commissioner* only when referring to a specific person (eg, Mario Monti, the Competition Commissioner; thereafter, *the commissioner*). The President of the European Commission is capped throughout (as with all foreign Presidents)

European Economic Area (EEA) European tariff-free zone, comprising the 15 members of the EU plus Norway, Iceland and Liechtenstein

European Parliament Members of the European Parliament (MEPs), or Euro MPs

European Union (EU), European Community (EC) the first is now the preferred phrase except where the context is trade. If you must use *the Union*, cap it throughout, but wherever possible use EU. Use *Common Market* and *EEC* only in historical context

Eurosceptic no longer hyphenated; similarly *Europhobia, Europhiles*

Eurotunnel one word; note that *Le Shuttle* no longer exists – the shuttle trains are now also called Eurotunnel trains. *Eurostar* passenger trains continue as before; see **Channel Tunnel**

evensong l/c; see **matins, Christian terms**

eventuate avoid; use *happen* instead

ever rarely necessary; avoid phrases such as *best-ever, fastest-ever*, and use simply *best* and *fastest*, qualifying (where appropriate) with *yet*. See **first, superlatives, universal claims**

ex- prefer *former* in most contexts, as in *former Yugoslavia*, though *ex-serviceman* is unavoidable and *ex-* is fine for headlines

examinations *11-plus, 7-plus* etc; also *A levels*, but *A-level results* etc (hyphenate only when adjectival). Abbreviate to *exam* only in headlines. GCSE, the General Certificate of Secondary Education, need not normally be spelt out

excepting do not use when *except* or *except for* is possible

exclamation marks nearly always unnecessary

exclusive avoid with story or interview. The phrase "in an interview with *The Times*" is sufficient

execution take care: as with *assassination*, do not use as a synonym of any killing or murder. An execution is a judicial killing after due process of law

exhibitions titles of art exhibitions now in italics. See **Arts** special section (page 1849)

existing use *present* wherever possible as an alternative

Exocet note cap

expatriate (not ex-patriate and never expatriot); noun, verb or adjective

Export Credits Guarantee Department abbreviate to ECGD; note *Credits* plural

extramarital no hyphen; similarly *extramural, extracurricular, extrasensory* etc

exuberant (never exhuberant); but note *exhilarate, exhort*

eye of a storm do not refer to the *calm in the eye of the storm*; the eye, by definition, is the calm area at the centre of a storm or hurricane

eye to eye no hyphens

eyeing

eyewitness use *witness* instead wherever possible (except in direct quotes)

Ff

F111s no hyphen; see **aircraft types**

façade use the cedilla

facelift use sparingly in its metaphorical sense, where it has become overworked. In cosmetic context quite acceptable, however

fact sheet

fact that almost always an unnecessary circumlocution, so avoid, eg, "owing to the fact that" means *because*

Faeroe Isles or *the Faeroes*

fahrenheit see **celsius**

fairytale no hyphen

Faithfull, Marianne

falangist (Spain); note *phalangist* (Lebanon)

fallacy means a *faulty argument*, not an erroneous belief

fallout noun; no longer hyphenated

fan acceptable nowadays for football supporter or pop music enthusiast

Far East encompasses the following: China, Hong Kong, Japan, North and South Korea, Macau, Mongolia, Taiwan. See **Asean**, **South-East Asia**

farther is applied only to distance (literal or figurative), eg, "nothing could be farther from the truth". *Further* means *in addition to, another*, eg, "a further point"

fascia (not facia)

Fascist cap in the political sense, but as a term of abuse, l/c; but note *fascism* l/c except in specifically party context. See **communism**

Father (as in priest); avoid the ugly abbreviation Fr before a name

Father's Day (not Fathers'). See **Mother's Day**

fatwa (Muslim religious edict, not a sentence of punishment); not italic

fault-line (hyphenate)

Fayed, Dodi (the late elder son of Mohamed Al Fayed; not Dodi Al Fayed)

Fed, the (US); use *Federal Reserve* (Board not usually necessary) at first mention; cap the *Chairman* of the Fed, as with *Governor of the Bank of England, President of the Bundesbank* etc

Federal Aviation Administration (US); abbreviation FAA; (not Agency or Authority)

"feel-good" factor

Fellow cap in specific title such as Dr Arthur Brown, a Fellow of Magdalen, or in the more obvious Fellow of the Royal College of Surgeons (FRCS); but l/c in general sense, eg, *a group of fellows in the quadrangle*; keep *fellowship* l/c

female do not write, for example, *female councillors, female directors;* instead use (where gender is relevant) *women councillors, women directors* etc

feminine designations *authoress, poetess, wardress* etc should be avoided. But *actress* is such common usage that it is acceptable. See **comedienne**

Ferris wheel

Festival Hall generally omit *Royal*

festivals cap the Edinburgh Festival (cultural), Reading Festival (pop), Cheltenham Festival (racing) etc, thereafter *the festival* (l/c). See **Fringe**

fête with accent

fewer of numbers, eg, *fewer people, fewer goals*; use *less* with size, quantity, or singular nouns, eg, *less population, less meat.* See **less**

fiancé (man), note **fiancée** (woman); see **divorcé**

Fianna Fail, Fine Gael see **Ireland**

Fide (world chess body; not FIDE); see **chess names**

fifty write *50-50 chance*; note cap for the decade, eg, *Fifties*, but l/c for age, eg, *she was in her fifties*

fighting for his/her life avoid this meaningless phrase. Instead use *critically ill/injured*

figures see **numbers**

filibuster (not fillibuster)

Filipinos, Filipinas (women), **the Philippines** (country)

films titles in italics; see **Arts** special section (page 1849); note *film-maker*, see **movies**

film star two words

Financial Services Authority (FSA) has replaced the Securities and Investments Board (SIB)

fiord (not fjord)

firearms do not confuse bullets with shotgun cartridges (containing pellets); a gunshot wound is markedly different from a bullet wound

fire brigade l/c in general context, but cap specifics, eg, *Kent Fire Brigade*

firefight should not be used as a synonym of *military skirmish* or *exchange of fire*; *firefighters* try to extinguish flames

firm do not use as a synonym of *company*. See **companies**

first serves as an adverb, so avoid *firstly*. If a list of priorities is essential in a story, write *first, secondly, thirdly* etc. Never use *first-ever*. See **ever**, **superlatives**, **universal claims**

first aid noun, no hyphen; but hyphenate when adjectival, eg, *first-aid qualifications*

First World War (not World War One); similarly *Second World War*. See **wars**

Fitzgerald, Garret

Five Nations Championship (initial caps) becomes the *Six Nations Championship* in 2000 (England, Wales, Scotland, Ireland, France and Italy)

flair (as in talent); do not confuse with *flare* (as in fire, fashion etc)

flat-owners hyphen, but note *homeowners*

flaunt means to make an ostentatious or defiant display, eg, *she flaunted her finery*; to *flout* is to show contempt for, eg, *he flouted the law*

fledgeling

fleur-de-lys (not lis)

flight numbers cap in stories where the number of the flight is relevant, eg, *Flight 103* (Lockerbie disaster)

floodlighting but note *floodlit*

flotation (shares), but note *floatation* (tanks)

flout see **flaunt**

flowerbed one word; similarly *flowerpot*

flu no apostrophe; acceptable abbreviation for *influenza*

Flushing Meadows (New York home of the US Open tennis championships; not Meadow)

Flying Squad cap, as it is the only one in the UK. But l/c *fraud squads* as there are several; similarly *vice squads, drug squads, crime squads, regional crime squads*

focused

folk-song, folk-singer (use hyphen)

following do not use as synonym of *after*. Always use *after* instead

Food and Drug Administration (US)

foodstuffs where place names form part of the phrase, generally use the cap, eg, *Brussels sprouts, Cheddar cheese, chicken Kiev, Cornish pasties, potatoes Lyonnaise*; but keep l/c for *hamburger, frankfurter* etc. See **metric**

foolproof no hyphen

foot-and-mouth disease

football *soccer* is now an acceptable synonym of *association football.* See **Premiership**

for-, fore- the general rule is that *e* is added only when the prefix has the meaning of *before*. Thus *forbears* (refrains), *forebears* (ancestors); *forgo* (go without), *forego* (go before, as in *foregone conclusion*). Take particular care with *forswear* and *foresee(able)*, both frequently misspelt

Forces use the *Armed Forces* wherever possible, but if the word has to be used alone, cap *Forces* both as a noun and adjectivally (as *Service*). See **Armed Forces** special section (page 1847)

Foreign and Commonwealth Office usually shorten to *Foreign Office* or *FCO* (abbreviation permissible in headlines); no longer use *FO*

foreign appellations *The Times* uses local honorifics for:
France: M, Mme, Mlle and Me (for Maître, legal)
Germany and **Austria:** Herr, Frau, Fräulein
Spain and Spanish-speaking **Latin America:** Señor, Señora, Señorita
Italy: Signor, Signora, Signorina
Portugal and **Brazil:** Senhor, Senhora (but not Senhorina)

Note that with Belgium, Luxembourg, Switzerland and Canada, Mr, Mrs, Miss, Ms etc are used because of those countries' linguistic sensitivities, eg, Jacques Santer, former President of the European Commission, will subsequently be Mr Santer. Similarly the English forms with Francophone Africa, where French is more the language of the elite rather than the lingua franca.

For all other nationalities, use English except where it is possible to use a local title (eg, *Ayatollah, Begum, Chief, Pandit, Sheikh*), or a military one (eg, Colonel Gaddafi); occasionally, where titles are in general use (eg, Baron von X in Germany), we would respect such exceptions

Note in Burma, U means Mr, Daw means Mrs; in China, the first Chinese name is the surname, eg, Deng Xiaoping becomes Mr Deng

foreign places as a general rule, use the spellings in *The Times Atlas of the World,* including Chinese place names (see **Chinese names**). However, *The Times* retains the Anglicised or commonly accepted spellings of many familiar (and especially European) countries and cities, such as *Brussels, Cologne, Cracow, Dunkirk, Florence, Geneva, Gothenburg, The Hague, Lyons, Majorca, Marseilles, Mexico City, Minorca, Moscow, Munich, Naples, Prague, Rheims, Rome, Salonika, Venice.* See also **Spanish regions**

foreign words write in roman when foreign words and phrases have become essentially a part of the English language (eg, an elite, a debacle, a fête); otherwise, use italic (eg, a *bon mot,* a *bête noire,* the *raison d'être*). Avoid pretension by using an English phrase wherever one will serve. See **accents**

forensic means *pertaining to the courts.* A forensic expert could be a solicitor or a biochemist; make your meaning clear by writing *forensic scientist, forensic medicine* etc

for ever means *always*; note *forever* means *continuously*

forklift truck

Formica proprietary term, so cap

formula plural usually *formulas*, but use *formulae* in mathematical contexts

fortuitous does not mean *fortunate*. It means *by chance* or *accidental.* Do not confuse

forum plural *forums*; see **referendum**

four-letter words avoid where possible, but if there is no alternative (eg, in direct quotes, where they are essential to the story), soften them with asterisks, eg, f***, c*** etc. See **obscenities**

foxhunt, foxhunting without hyphens, similarly *foxhound, foxhole, master of foxhounds* (l/c *m*)

fractions do not mix fractions and decimals in the same story. Compounds such as *half-hour, half-dozen* etc take a hyphen; *half an hour, half a dozen* do not. Hyphenate when fractions are adjectival, eg, *two-thirds full,* but not as nouns, eg, *two thirds of the bus was empty.* See **two thirds**

framework document (Anglo-Irish proposals for Northern Ireland, February 1995) note l/c; full title of the document is *Frameworks for the Future.* See **Ireland**

franc l/c, and abbreviate as *Fr40*; specify if not French, eg, *BFr40 (Belgian), SwFr40 (Swiss)*

franchisor (no longer franchiser)

Frankenstein foods never use this pejorative phrase to describe genetically modified (GM) foods, except in direct quotations

fraud squad l/c; see **Flying Squad**

free avoid the modern cliché *for free* when the meaning is simply *free*

"freebie" just permissible as colloquialism for *handout, free trip* etc, but use inverted commas

Free Churches, Free Churchman caps

freefall no hyphen

Freemasonry, Mason, Masonic

French names prefer the more Anglicised style for street names etc, eg, *Rue Royale, Place de la Victoire, Boulevard des Montagnes.* No need to hyphenate place names such as St Malo, St Etienne etc

french windows l/c

frescoes (not frescos)

Freud, Lucian (not Lucien)

Fringe, the Edinburgh always cap, whether as noun or adjective

Frisbee proprietary term, so cap

front bench, the noun; but note *frontbencher, frontbench power* etc. See **Politics** special section (page 1853)

frontline adjective, as in the *frontline states*; but note the noun *front line*

front-runner

FTSE 100 index no longer hyphenate FT-SE; note also the *FTSE all-share index*

fuchsia

fuel greatly overworked verb, especially in headlines; always seek alternatives such as *raise, increase, add to, boost*

Fujiyama, or **Mount Fuji** (not Mount Fujiyama)

-ful, -fuls so *cupfuls* (not cupsful)

fulfil but note *fulfilled, fulfilling*

full points note thin space after initials and points, eg, F. W. de Klerk. But with companies, omit the full points, eg, WH Smith. See **companies, initials**

full-time adj, but note noun *full time* (as in football)

fulsome be very careful – and sparing – with the use of this word. It means *excessive* or *insincere* (the cliché *fulsome praise* actually means excessive praise, not generous or warm praise). Try to avoid it, especially the cliché

fundholders (NHS)

fundraising, fundraiser no hyphen

further see **farther**

fusillade

Gg

Gaddafi, Colonel Muammar (Libyan leader)

gaff (hook or spar); but *gaffe* (blunder or indiscretion). Note *to blow the gaff* (let out a secret)

Gambia, The always cap the definite article

gambit (technical term in chess, meaning an opening involving a sacrifice in return for general advantage); *opening gambit* is thus tautological. Take care with its use as a metaphor, and use sparingly

game show no hyphen; similarly *chat show, quiz show, talk show* etc

Gandhi, Mahatma, Indira etc (never Ghandi)

Garda see **Ireland**

Gardeners' Question Time (not Gardener's)

gas, gases noun; but *gassed, gassing* (verbal use); note also *gases* (not gasses) for present tense, eg, *doctor gases patient*

gasfield similarly *coalfield, oilfield*

Gatt the General Agreement on Tariffs and Trade. Its successor body is now the *World Trade Organisation* (WTO). See **Uruguay Round, World Trade Organisation**

Gatwick sufficiently well-known not to need airport in title. See **airports, Heathrow**

gauge (not guage)

Gaultier, Jean Paul no hyphen

gay where possible, use *homosexual* or *lesbian*, but *gay* has become such common currency that we should avoid looking or sounding pompous in this context. See **straight**

GCSE see **examinations**

GDP gross domestic product

GEC Alsthom became simply *Alstom* (note no "h") in mid-1998

gelatine rather than gelatin

Geldof, Bob do not write *Sir* Bob Geldof, as he is an honorary KBE

gender (term of grammar); do not use as synonym of a person's sex

general election always l/c

General Secretary of the TUC caps; but note l/c for *general secretary* of individual unions; see **TUC**

General Strike (of 1926); caps

General Synod (of the Church of England), thereafter *the synod.* See **Churches** special section (page 1850)

Gentile(s) cap

geriatric does not mean *elderly,* but is applied to medical treatment for the elderly, eg, *geriatric hospital.* Never use as a term of abuse

German Bight (as in shipping forecast; not Bite)

Germany full title is the *Federal Republic of Germany.* If referring to the area that was East Germany, say *eastern Germany* or the *former East Germany;* similarly *western Germany* or the *former West Germany. Ossis, Wessis* permissible vernacular for inhabitants of the two parts

gerrymander

get, got a lazy verb, so avoid where possible

Getty, Sir Paul do not use John or J. in his name any longer

Ghanaian (not Ghanian)

ghetto use only in the sense of an area of enforced or customary segregation, not as an ethnic neighbourhood, eg, middle-class *district,* not *ghetto.* Note plural *ghettos*

giant-killer, giant-killing

gibe means *taunt* or *sneer,* note also *gybe* meaning to *shift direction* or *change course,* particularly in sailing. For the sake of clarity, *jibe* (a variant of both) should no longer be used

Gibraltar (never Gibralter); note *Strait of Gibraltar* (not Straits)

gig acceptable for a musical event; similarly *rave*

gillie rather than ghillie

gipsy see **gypsy**

girl do not use as a synonym of *woman*

girlfriend one word; similarly *boyfriend.* Use *girlfriend* only for young people; otherwise *woman friend* or just *friend* (where the gender is obvious)

Girl Guides now simply *Guides;* see **Boy Scouts**

giro (l/c), as in benefit payments, cheques etc

Giscard d'Estaing, Valéry thereafter M Giscard

giveaway noun or adjective; one word, similarly *takeaway;* but note *to give away*

glamorise, glamorous but note *glamour*

glasnost not italic

glassmaker

Glen Coe (valley); but note *Glencoe* (battle, village and pass)

Glorious Twelfth, the caps

GMB write the GMB general union

gobbledegook

God cap when referring to just one, in any religion. *He, His, Him* are also capped. When non-specific, use l/c, eg, *Greek gods.* See **Christian terms, Churches** special section (page 1850)

godforsaken but note *God-fearing*

godparents, godfather, godmother, godson, goddaughter, godchild

Goebbels, Joseph (not Goebells etc)

-goer as a suffix, run on as one word, as in *churchgoer, partygoer, theatregoer* etc

Goldeneye (James Bond film; not GoldenEye)

Golders Green no apostrophe

goldmine, goldmining

Goldsmiths College, London no longer use apostrophe

goodbye

goodwill one word, whether used as a noun or adjective

Gorazde, Bosnia (not Goradze)

Gorbachev, Mikhail

gorilla

Gormley, Antony (the sculptor)

Gothenburg (not Göteborg)

Gothic cap; preferable to Gothick

Government cap all governments, British and overseas, when referring to a specific one, eg, "the Government resigned last night", "the Argentine Government sent troops", and specific past administrations such as "the Heath Government"; only l/c when unspecific or one that has yet to be formed, eg, "all the governments since the war", or "the next Tory government would raise pensions".

Also l/c government in all adjectival contexts, eg, *a government minister, a government decision, government expenditure.* A further instance of l/c use is in phrases such as *the Bosnian government troops* or *the British government-backed trade delegation,* when the use is again principally adjectival.

Also, note that provincial or state governments in Australia, Canada, India etc retain l/c. See **Politics** special section (page 1853)

government departments cap both when giving full title (eg, *Department of Trade and Industry*), and even when abbreviated, as in *Health Department, Education Department, Trade*

Department etc. The same applies to *ministries*, home and overseas

Governor (of the Bank of England); cap at every mention, also cap Deputy Governor of the Bank. Also, cap the Governor of Hong Kong at every mention; but cap prison governors at first mention only, eg, James X, Governor of Parkhurst, thereafter l/c, and l/c deputy governors

Graces *The Three Graces* (Canova's statue). See **Arts** special section (page 1849)

Grade II listed, **Grade II* listed** etc

gram (not gramme); similarly *kilogram*; see **metric**

grandad but note *granddaughter*

Grand Jury (caps) in US contexts

grandmaster (chess); l/c. See **chess names**

Grappelli, Stéphane

grassroots adjective; note the noun *grass roots*. Use this cliché sparingly

great and the good, the all l/c; quotes usually unnecessary

greater or lesser degree *lesser* is not correct but is common usage

Great Ormond Street Hospital for Children (no longer Sick Children)

Greco- (not Graeco-)

green belt l/c

Green Paper caps; see **White Paper**

Green Party, or **the Greens** but note *green issues* etc

grisly means *horrifying, repugnant*; note *grizzly* which means *greyish, grizzled*, or is a short form of *grizzly bear*

grottoes

ground(s) in the sense of *reason*, do not use plural unless more than one is given; eg, "he gave up his job on the ground of illness"; but "he gave up his job on the grounds of his failed marriage and illness"

Group 4 (security company)

G-string

guerrilla beware of loaded terms for advocates of political violence; see **terrorist**

guesthouse no hyphen

guidebook similarly *chequebook, stylebook, textbook, formbook* etc

Guildhall, London (never *the* Guildhall)

guinea-pig (hyphen)

Gulf, the avoid the term *Persian Gulf* as it angers Iraqis and many other Arabs

gunboat, gunfight, gunfire, gunman, gunpoint, gunshot, gunsmith but note *gun dog*

gunned down avoid this Americanism; instead say *shot dead*

gunwales (nautical, not gunwhales)

Gurkhas

guttural (not gutteral)

Guyana (formerly British Guiana, now independent); do not confuse with *French Guiana* (French overseas territory)

Gypsy/gypsy (not gipsy). Cap when referring to a specific group of this semi-nomadic people, but l/c in the more general sense of somebody constantly on the move, eg, "the Gypsies on Epsom Downs threatened to retaliate"; but "police said they would chase all gypsies from the county". The other wandering groups in Britain are the Irish tinkers, who prefer the name *Irish travellers*; the *Scottish tinkers* (or *tinklers*); and the hippies, whom we can call *New Age travellers*; *travellers* is a useful generic term

Hh

Häagen-Dazs (brand of ice-cream originating in America)

Haberdashers' Aske's School, Elstree

Habsburg no longer Hapsburg

haemorrhage means heavy and potentially dangerous bleeding, not simply bleeding. Beware of misuse in metaphor

Hague, Ffion follow Cherie Blair/Booth style for William's wife: *Ffion Hague* (or *Mrs Hague*) when with her husband, but *Ffion Jenkins* (subsequently *Ms Jenkins*) when at functions in her own right

Hague, The

hairdresser, hairbrush, haircut, hairdryer, hairpin, hairstyle

Haiti, Haitian note that Haiti must never be described as an island; it is joined to the Dominican Republic and together they constitute the island of Hispaniola

haj (pilgrimage to Mecca); l/c and roman

haka (Maori war-dance); l/c and roman

half-time (in football match etc); note the *half time* in business context, but hyphenate when used adjectivally, eg, *half-time results*

halfway no hyphen; but note *half-hearted*

Halley's comet see **heavenly bodies**

Hallowe'en

handmade, handbuilt (no hyphen)

handout as a noun, no hyphen

hangar (aircraft); note *hanger* (clothes)

hanged "The murderer was hanged at dawn" – note never *hung*. Clothes are hung on a washing line or a hanger

Hansard

harass, harassment

hardcore one word as adjective, eg, *hardcore pornography*; but note two words as noun, eg, *the hard core of the rebels*; similarly *hard core* (rubble)

hardline adjective; but note *to take a hard line*

Haringey (London borough and council); note also *Harringay* (London neighbourhood)

HarperCollins, or **HarperCollins Publishers** owned by The News Corporation; see **News International**

Harpers & Queen

Harrods no apostrophe; see **Al Fayed**

harvest festival l/c

Hattersley, Lord (not "of Sparkbrook")

Havisham, Miss (not Miss Haversham) in Dickens's *Great Expectations*

Hawaiian

hay fever no hyphen

headache avoid as a synonym of *difficulty*

head-butt noun or verb

headhunt, headhunting, headhunter no hyphens

headlines avoid the worst clichés and hyperboles such as *bash, crash, shock, slam* etc; but words such as *bid* (for attempt), *crisis, hit* (adversely affect), *row* (clash or dispute) and *phone* (telephone) – all of which should not normally appear in text – are permissible in headlines, provided they are not overworked.

Inverted commas must always be single in headlines, straps and display panels. See **quotation marks**

headmaster, headmistress one word and l/c except in the formal, official title (and then cap at first mention only). Some schools have variants on the usual style; Eton, Harrow, Rugby and Westminster have a *Head Master*, St Paul's School and Manchester Grammar School have a *High Master*, King Edward's School, Birmingham, has a *Chief Master*, Dulwich, Haileybury and Marlborough have a *Master*. The correct form is given in the *Independent Schools Year Book*. Use the colloquial *head* only in headlines; and note that *head teacher* is two words except when part of the designated title

heads of state when these are royals, such as King Abdullah of Jordan, after the first mention refer to them as *the King* (cap). The cap at subsequent mentions applies only to overseas heads of state and the British Royal Family, eg, Prince B. of Thailand (a minor royal) would become *the prince* thereafter. See **Royal Family**, **Titles** special section (page 1855)

healthcare one word

heartbroken, heartbreaking, heartfelt, heartstrings, but hyphenate *heart-rending, heart-throb*

Heathrow sufficiently well-known not to need airport in title. Note at Heathrow, *Terminal 1, 2, 3, 4, 5* etc. See **airports, Gatwick**

Heaven, Hell cap in religious context only; see **Devil**

heavenly bodies cap the proper names of planets, stars, constellations etc: *Venus, Arcturus, the Plough, Aries*; for comets, l/c the word comet in, for example, *Halley's comet*. The Sun, the Moon, the Earth, the Universe are capped in their planetary or astronomical sense (see **Earth**). Use l/c for the adjectives *lunar* and *solar*, but cap *Martian* both adjectivally and as a noun

Heep, Uriah (not Heap)

Hell's Angels

help to use *to* plus verb, eg, "he helped *to* make the cake" (not "he helped make the cake")

helping the police with their inquiries avoid this phrase – suspects rarely willingly help the police. Say *were being interviewed* instead

helpline one word; similarly *hotline*

hemisphere l/c northern, southern, eastern, western

heraldry do not confuse *crests* with *coats of arms*. Most arms consist of a shield and a crest; crests are the topmost part of the coat of arms (think of the crest of a bird or a wave)

Hereford and Worcester see **unitary authorities**

Heriot-Watt University, Edinburgh

Her Majesty's pleasure (as in *detained at ...*)

Herzegovina (as in Bosnia-Herzegovina)

Heyhoe Flint, Rachael (no hyphen, not Rachel)

Hezbollah (Party of God in Iran and Lebanon); soft-hyphenate (on a break) as Hezb-ollah

Hibernian means of or concerning Ireland, not Scotland, despite the Edinburgh football club of the same name

hiccup (not hiccough)

hi-fi acceptable abbreviation, noun or adjective, of *high fidelity*

high acceptable usage as a noun, eg, *she was on a high*. But avoid clichés such as *all-time high* and *hits new high*

highbrow, lowbrow

high command avoid clichéd use, as in *Tory high command*. See **Politics** special section (page 1853)

High Commissioner caps when specific, eg, *the Indian High Commissioner*, thereafter *the high commissioner*. Remember that Commonwealth countries and the UK have high commissioners serving in high commissions in each other's countries, not ambassadors serving in embassies. See **Ambassador**

High Court see **Courts** special section (page 1851)

highfalutin

high-flyer

High Sheriff caps when specific

high street l/c and no hyphen in general sense, as in *high street prices*. But cap when specific, eg, *Putney High Street*

high-tech adjective; spell out in text, but *hi-tech* is acceptable in headlines

hike never use in the American sense of a *rise* or *to raise* (rates etc); permissible only in direct quotes, or in context of walking (hitch-hike etc)

Hinckley, Leicestershire but note *Hinkley Point*, Somerset

Hindi for language contexts (the Hindi language); but use *Hindu* for religious and ethnic contexts (an adherent to Hinduism, or relating to Hinduism)

hippy, hippies nowadays as old-fashioned as *beatniks*; see **Gypsy**, **travellers**

Hirst, Damien (artist; not Damian)

historic, historical prefer *an historic event* rather than *a historic*; see **a**, **an**. Also, take care with use of *historical* and *historic*; the former can refer only to past history, while the latter can refer to a contemporary event likely to be of long-term significance. But *an historic building* is now in common usage as a synonym of an old building

hit avoid in text in sense of *affected*, eg, "Homeowners were hit last night by an interest rate rise", or in the sense of attack, eg, "The minister hit out at his critics". Sparing use of the verb in headlines is permissible

hitch-hiker, hitch-hiking etc

Hitchin, Hertfordshire (not Hitchen)

hitlist, hitman now no hyphens

HIV is a virus, not a disease. Do not write *HIV virus* (tautology), but use a phrase such as *HIV-infected*. See **Aids**

hoards (stocks or stores of treasure, for example); note *to hoard* (to amass and store food, money etc); never confuse with **hordes** (large groups or gangs of wild beasts etc)

Hogmanay cap

holidaymaker one word

Holland, now use **The Netherlands** for all contexts except sports teams or historical uses, or when referring to the provinces of North or South Holland. The adjective is *Dutch*

Holy Communion caps; see **Christian terms**

Holy Grail caps

Holyroodhouse see **Palace of Holyroodhouse**

homebuyers, homeowners no hyphens

home town (two words), but hyphenate in adjectival use, eg, *home-town memories*

Home Counties, the caps

homoeopathy (not the American homeopathy)

homogeneous means having parts all of the same kind; *homogenous* means similar owing to common descent

Homo sapiens see **scientific names**

homosexual see **gay**

Hon, the normally use this form of address (the Hon So-and-So) only on the Court Page

Hong Kong but note *Hongkong and Shanghai Banking Corporation (HSBC)*. Until July 1, 1997, when Britain handed the colony over to China, Hong Kong had a *Governor* (cap). See **Midland**

honours people are *appointed* Privy Counsellor, Baronet, KBE, CBE, OBE, MBE etc; never say they were made, received, were awarded, or got the OBE etc. *Peers* and above (viscounts etc) are *created*, not appointed etc. At investitures, those honoured receive the insignia of the award, not the award itself. Normally omit honours and decorations after names, but the following can be used where relevant: KG, KT, VC, GC, OM, CH, MP, QC, RA, FRS etc. See **Titles** special section (page 1855)

honours lists see **New Year Honours**

Hoover trade name, so cap; generally use *vacuum cleaner* and *to vacuum*

hopefully try to avoid in the sense of *it is hoped that*, even though this usage is widespread

Horse Guards Parade

horse race/racing two words, but *racing* alone is preferable. Note *Horserace Betting Levy Board*; see **racecourse**, **Sports** special section (page 1854)

horticulturist (not horticulturalist)

hospitalise, hospitalisation always avoid these Americanisms; use *taken to hospital* etc

host avoid using as a verb as in "Arsenal will host Aston Villa on Saturday"; use *play host to* instead. But note a *person* can *host* an event

hotline one word; similarly *helpline*

hotpants one word

hoummos see **taramasalata**

housebuilder, housebuilding but note *the House-Builders' Federation*

however when used in the sense of *nevertheless*, always place a comma after it (and before, when in the middle of a sentence, eg, "It was said, however, that the agent ...")

Hubble Space Telescope

Hudson Bay but note *Hudson's Bay Company*

human beings rather than just humans

human rights European Convention on Human Rights; European Court of Human Rights; the now-defunct European Commission of Human Rights; all established under the aegis of the Council of Europe, not the EU (or EC). See **Courts** special section (page 1851)

humorist (not humourist)

Humphrys, John (radio and TV); but note Barry Humphries (Dame Edna Everage etc)

Hussein, King the late King of Jordan, not *Husain*; similarly, President Saddam Hussein (Iraq)

Hutus, Tutsis note plural of the Rwandan tribes (not simply Hutu, Tutsi)

hyphens generally be sparing with hyphens and run together words where the sense suggests and where they look familiar; eg, *blacklist, businessman, goldmine, knockout, intercontinental, motorcycle, takeover*, and *walkover*. Unusual hyphenations are listed separately in this guide. However, a few guidelines can be specified:

a usually run together prefixes except where the last letter of the prefix is the same as the first letter of the word to which it attaches: *prearrange, postwar, prewar, nonconformist*; but *pre-empt, co-ordinate, co-operate, re-establish*

b hyphenate composites where the same two letters come together, eg, *film-makers*, but an exception should be made when double *r* occurs in the middle: *override, overrule* (not over-ride etc), and note *granddaughter* and *goddaughter*

c generally do not use dangling hyphens, eg, *full and part-time employment* etc; this does not apply to prefixes, eg, *pre- or post-match drinks*

d for hyphenation when qualifying adjectives, see **adverbs**

e always use a hyphen rather than a slash in dates etc, eg, 1982–83 (not 1982/83)

Ii

IATA International Air Transport Association; all caps

ice-cream hyphen, similarly *ice-lolly*; see also **Häagen-Dazs**

Identikit proprietary term, so cap; but note l/c *photofit*

ie use comma either side. See **eg**

ill-health hyphen; similarly *ill-feeling, ill-intentioned* etc

Immigration Service caps; similarly *Prison Service, Probation Service*

impacted on avoid this Americanism

imply see **infer**

impostor (not imposter)

impresario

Impressionist, Post-Impressionist see **artistic movements**

in addition to prefer *as well as* or *besides*

inadmissible (not -able)

include do not confuse with *comprise*: "breakfast includes toast and coffee", but "breakfast comprises cereals, toast, butter, marmalade and coffee" (ie, where the full list of elements is given)

incommunicado

indestructible (not -able)

index plural is *indices*, but note *indexes* for books

indispensable (not -ible)

Indo-China

Industrial Revolution, the use caps

industrial tribunals these no longer exist; they are now *employment tribunals*. They end with a *judgment* or a *decision*, not a verdict. Only juries in court hearings, or magistrates hearing cases summarily, deliver a verdict. Note that *immigration adjudicators* and *immigration appeal tribunals* deliver *determinations*. See **Courts** special section (page 1851)

inevitable do not use as a synonym of *customary, usual* or *predictable*

in fact can almost invariably be omitted

infer do not confuse with *imply*: to *infer* is to draw a conclusion from a suggestion, to imply is to make the suggestion. A useful mnemonic: we *imply* things when we speak, we *infer* things when we listen

infighting one word, but note hyphen with *in-house*

infra-red

initials where familiar, no need to spell out at first mention (eg, BBC, TUC, Nato etc). Otherwise, usually give name in full followed by initials in parentheses, and the abbreviated form thereafter (though sometimes a word such as *the organisation* or *the group* will be preferable to avoid a mass of initials in the same story). Also, with a body as well known as the UN, it would be absurd to write the United Nations (UN), so use discretion.

Where the initials can be spoken as a word, write them as upper and lower case, eg, Nato, Gatt, Unesco, Efta – but there are some important exceptions to this, eg, MORI, IATA, RADA, RIBA, SANE, MIND, BUPA and AXA

With people's names, put points between the initials (with thin space between), though omit points in names of firms such as WH Smith, J Sainsbury

injure, injury implies something more serious than *hurt*. Avoid writing "John *received* an injury" – instead use *suffered* or *sustained* an injury, or (simply) *was injured*. Injured or sick people should not be described as *satisfactory* or *critical* – it is their *condition* that is satisfactory etc

Inland Revenue subsequent mentions, *the Revenue* (cap). See **taxman**

innocent take great care with this word, and avoid phrases such as *the innocent victim of the attack* and clichés such as *innocent children*. Best to stick to its literal sense of *not guilty*

innocuous

Inns of Court the order of precedence among the Inns is Lincoln's Inn, Inner Temple, Middle Temple, Gray's Inn

inoculate

inpatients, outpatients no hyphen

inquests see **coroner's court**

inquire, inquiry (not enquire, enquiry). But note the exception, *Directory Enquiries*

insignia plural; see **honours**

install but note *instalment*

instil

Institute of Contemporary Arts ("of" not "for" and plural Arts)

Institute of Directors IoD acceptable for headings and occasionally in text, though prefer *the institute* after first mention in full

insure you *insure* against risk; you *assure* your life; *ensure* means to make certain

Intelligence cap as a noun in the context of the security services, eg, "he was in British Intelligence", but l/c adjectival uses, eg, "she was interviewed by intelligence officers"

intelligentsia

intensive do not confuse with *intense* or *extreme*. It means concentrated, as in *intensive care*

InterCity (rail); but note adjective *inter-city*

interdependence

interesting avoid as an adjective in text; let the reader decide

interest rate cuts/rises no hyphens; never use *hikes* for *rises*

inter-governmental conference (EU's continuing discussions on the single currency etc); IGC as abbreviation. See **Maastricht**

International Atomic Energy Agency (never Authority); abbreviate to IAEA

International Olympic Committee (not Olympics); IOC as abbreviation. See **Olympics**

Internazionale (Milan football club); must not be called Inter Milan. It can be shortened to *Inter*, the other big club in the city is *AC Milan* (shortened to *Milan*)

Internet, the cap; use *the Net* (cap) for short. See **World Wide Web**

interpretative (not interpretive)

interred (buried); do not confuse with *interned* (imprisoned)

intifada (religious struggle or uprising); l/c and roman

inverted commas should be used as sparingly as possible in text: eg, unnecessary in constructions such as *he described the book as "turgid"*. They are no longer used with works of art. See also **italics, quotation marks**

Iran use Persia only in historical context; note the language is *Farsi*, not Iranian or Persian

irascible (not irrascible)

Ireland the two parts should be called the *Republic of Ireland* or the *Irish Republic* (avoid Eire except in direct quotes or historical context), and *Northern Ireland* or *Ulster*. Do not use the phrase the Six Counties. Other important styles:

a *loyalist* with l/c *l* and no quotes – to balance *republican* and *nationalist*

b *Unionist, Unionism* (caps)

c *the North, the South* (caps in this specific Irish context)

d similarly *the Republic, the Province*

e *the Troubles*

f *the Garda* (the police force; but note *garda/gardai* for policeman/policemen); but the phrase *Irish police* is acceptable
g *Londonderry*, but Derry City Council; and Derry when in direct quotes or in a specifically republican context (this latter rarely)
h *West Belfast, East Belfast* (caps because of clearly defined sectarian areas); but north Belfast, south Belfast (unspecific, directional); note Shankill Road (not Shankhill)
i *Downing Street declaration*
j *Anglo-Irish agreement*
k *Frameworks for the Future*, or *the framework document* (l/c) for the Anglo-Irish proposals of February 1995
l *Northern Ireland Assembly*, with cap for *Assembly*
m avoid *Provos* as synonym of the Provisional IRA, except in quotes
n *Taoiseach* is an acceptable alternative for Irish Prime Minister
o Irish counties should be written as *Co Donegal, Co Down* etc
p *Orange Order, Orangemen* (caps)

iridescent (not irr-)

Iron Curtain

ironic beware of misuse. It means using or displaying irony, or in the nature of irony; it does not mean strange or paradoxical

irreconcilable

irresistible (not -able)

Isa(s) individual savings account(s), l/c; hyphenate *mini-Isas, maxi-Isas*. See also **Tessa(s), Pep(s)**

-ise, -isation avoid the *z* construction in almost all cases, eg, *apologise, organise, emphasise, televise*. But note *capsize, synthesizer*

ISIS Independent Schools Information Service (not Isis)

Islam (religion of the Muslims); *Islamic* is interchangeable with *Muslim* as the adjective, though normally use Islamic with religion and fundamentalism, Muslim with architecture, politics etc

Israeli (native of Israel); *Israelite* refers to Ancient Israel

italics avoid in headlines and use sparingly in text. However, there are certain guidelines for using italics:
a all works of art, even where quotation marks used to be used, including titles of books, long and short poems, short stories, newspapers (see separate list under **newspapers**), magazines, pamphlets, chapter headings, White Papers, Green Papers, official reports and studies, programmes on radio and television, films, plays, computer games, musical works including operas, songs, hymns, album titles etc (see **musical vocabulary**), paintings, drawings, sculptures, titles of exhibitions. See **Arts** special section (page 1849)
b less common, non-Anglicised foreign words go in italics, but err on the side of roman (eg, in extremis, hors d'oeuvre, angst); see **foreign words**
c names of ships, aircraft, locomotives etc
d a word may be italicised for emphasis, but again be sparing with this device

ITN never write ITN news; see **television**

ITV acceptable alternative for *independent television*; see **television**

Jj

Jacuzzi trade name, so cap; use *whirlpool bath* if in doubt

jail, jailer (not gaol, gaoler)

jargon like journalese and slang, to be strictly avoided

Jedda

Jeep proprietary term, so cap; use only if strictly applicable, otherwise *cross-country vehicle, small military truck* etc

Jehovah's Witness(es)

Jekyll and Hyde (*The Strange Case of Dr Jekyll and Mr Hyde,* by R.L.Stevenson)

Jerusalem l/c for east/west Jerusalem

jet lag two words

jetliner avoid; write *airliner* or simply *jet*

jet ski two words as noun; note hyphen with verb *to jet-ski*

jeweller, jewellery

jibe avoid this spelling; see **gibe**

jihad (holy war); roman, l/c

jobcentre takes l/c in general sense, but cap as in *Runcorn Jobcentre*

jobseeker's allowance

job titles the general rule is to cap the most senior high-profile jobs at first mention, and thereafter l/c. Thus cap at first mention Archbishop and church titles, senior civil servants, diplomatic and political leaders, civic leaders, Editor (of well-known leading publications), Director-General (of the BBC, CBI etc), Vice-Chancellor and academic titles, Chief Constable and police ranks, military titles, President of a small number of high-profile national institutions (eg, President of the Law Society, the TUC etc) and then – usually – l/c thereafter.

However, *chairman, director, managing director* (of a company), *general secretary* (of a union), *artistic director* (of a theatre) etc are l/c; as are most presidents and chairmen of societies and institutions. A certain amount of discretion is needed in this difficult area

jodhpurs

John le Carré

John o'Groat's

Johns Hopkins University, Baltimore

Joint Chiefs of Staff (US)

Jones, Vinnie (footballer; not Vinny)

Jonsson, Ulrika

joyrider no hyphen, but use as little as possible as the term can give offence; an alternative could be *young car thief*

JP (Justice of the Peace), acceptable alternative for *non-stipendiary magistrate*; see **magistrates' courts**

jubilee strictly a fiftieth anniversary, though Queen Victoria had a golden and a diamond one; so the word can be used as a periodic celebration, especially of royalty. Note *Jubilee Line* (caps) on the London Underground

Judaea (not Judea)

judges' names all circuit judges and below (ie, those in Crown Courts, in county courts, and district judges) must now always include their first name at first mention. Thus, write *Judge Fred Potts* at first mention, subsequently *Judge Potts* or simply *the judge.*

First names will not normally be necessary with High Court judges unless there are two or more with the same surname, where again it will be essential to differentiate.

The failure to identify a judge correctly can lead to complaints, corrections and even the payment of substantial damages.

In the High Court, Mr Justice X should be referred to this way throughout a story (or simply the judge) – never as Judge X. Be careful not to confuse a judge in the Court of Appeal (a Lord Justice of Appeal) with a law lord of the House of Lords, the most senior judges, who are Lords of Appeal in Ordinary (such as Lord Nolan and Lord Hoffmann).

Note designation of Lady Justice Butler-Sloss.

See **Courts** special section (page 1851)

judging by one of the most frequently misused unrelated (or disconnected) participle constructions. Remember, the phrase must have a related subject to follow (I, we, she etc). A convenient alternative is "to judge from …" (eg, "Judging by this film, the country is in a mess" is wrong; "To judge from this film, the country is in a mess" is correct; so is "Judging by this film, we conclude that the country is in a mess"). See **participles**

judgment (not judgement)

jukebox (no hyphen)

jump-jet hyphen; but note *jumbo jet* (no hyphen)

junior abbreviate to *Jr* (not Jnr) in the American context, eg, John Eisendorf Jr; see **senior**

Justices' Clerks' Society note two apostrophes

juvenile courts no longer exist; they are now called *youth courts.* See **Courts** special section (page 1851)

Kk

k avoid for 1,000 except in direct quotes
kaftan but note *cagoule*
Kant, Immanuel (not Emmanuel)
Karajan, Herbert von; thereafter just Karajan (not von Karajan)
Karpov, Anatoly note also Kasparov, Garry. See **chess names, Russian names**
Kathmandu
Kellogg's Corn Flakes but *cornflakes* (generic)
kerosene (American for paraffin)
Kevorkian, Dr Jack (the American euthanasia doctor; not Kervorkian)
Kfor, the Nato-led force in Kosovo (not KFOR)
Khan Imran Khan and Jemima Khan are happy to be known as Mr Khan and Mrs Khan respectively after first mention. Imran is permissible on its own in headlines. But in most cases, beware of Khan as the family name: it is usually a title given to officials or rulers in Central Asia
Khartoum
Khashoggi, Soraya, Adnan etc
Khmer Rouge (Cambodian faction); note a *Khmer* is a Cambodian
Khrushchev, Nikita
kick-off noun; but note *to kick off*
kick-start hyphenate, noun or verb
killer can be used for *murderer* but do not use *assassin* as a synonym
kilogram (not kilogramme); see **gram, metric**
kilometres per hour correct abbreviation is *km/h* rather than kph
kilowatt-hour correct abbreviation is *kWh*. The cost of generating electricity at a power station is usually expressed in pence per kilowatt-hour (*2.9p/kWh*). See **megawatts**
King's College London apostrophe, no commas
King's Cross, London
King's Lynn, Norfolk
Kings Road, Chelsea (do not use apostrophe)
Kingston upon Hull official name for Hull; normally just use Hull. Note that Humberside no longer exists as a local authority; see **unitary authorities**
Kingston upon Thames no hyphens; use *southwest London* rather than Surrey; but note that Surrey County Council is still based in Kingston. See **postal addresses**
kitchen cabinet l/c *cabinet* in this informal context. See **Cabinet**
Kitemark see **British Standards Institution**
kneejerk (reaction etc); no hyphen, but beware of overuse
knockout noun; but note *to knock out*
knowhow one word as noun
knowledgeable
Knox-Johnston, (Sir) Robin (yachtsman)
Kodak trade name, so cap
Koh-i-noor (diamond)
Koran, the cap and roman, like the Bible
Korean names note all initial caps and no hyphens, eg, Roh Tae Woo
Kosovo, Kosovan do not use Kosova, Kosovar
kowtow no hyphen
Ku Klux Klan no longer use hyphens
KwaZulu/Natal (not Natal/KwaZulu); see **South Africa**
Kyrgyzstan (no longer Kirghizia)

Ll

Labor Day (US); no equivalent in UK so retain US spelling; Anglicise the *Defence Department* etc

Labor Party (Australia)

Labour Party (UK); abbreviate in lists etc to *Lab.* See **Politics** special section (page 1853)

Ladbrokes (betting shop); but *Ladbroke plc*; note also *William Hill* and *Coral* (neither takes final *s*)

lady, ladies prefer *woman, women*

Lafite, Château- see **wines**

Lagos, Nigeria (note Abuja is the capital of Nigeria)

laissez faire no longer use *laisser* version

Lake District do not include *Lake* when the name contains its equivalent; thus Windermere, Derwent Water, but Lake Bassenthwaite

lambast (not lambaste)

lamé use accent to distinguish it from *lame*

lamppost no hyphen

landmine no hyphen

Land Rover no hyphen; similarly *Range Rover*

Land's End

landslide (political); but *landslip* (earth)

languor, languorous (not -our)

laptop (computer), no hyphen; note also *desktop*

largesse (not largess)

last, past *last* should not be used as a synonym of *latest;* "the last few days" means the *final* few days; "the past few days" means the *most recent* few days

Last Post like Reveille, is *sounded* (not played)

Latin be sparing in its use, apart from in the Law Report. When Latin phrases are in common usage, use roman rather than italics, eg, quid pro quo, QED, ex parte injunction, habeas corpus

Latin dancing cap Latin in this and all other contexts, eg, *the Latin language, Latin music, Latin temperament* etc

latitude, longitude write 45° 32'N, 40° 17'W etc

La traviata note l/c *t*

launderette (not laundrette)

Lautro Life Assurance and Unit Trust Regulatory Organisation

law lords, law officers l/c; see **judges**, **Courts** special section (page 1851)

lawnmower one word

Law Report in *The Times*, always initial caps and singular (not Reports); so the style for x-refs is bold, right, eg, **Law Report, page 42**

lay, lie a person *lays* a carpet (transitive verb), but *lies* on a carpet (intransitive). Do not confuse

lay-by but note *layout*

Leader use caps for Leader of the Commons/House of Lords/Opposition; but note l/c *Labour leader, Tory leader* etc

lean, leap past tenses *leant, leapt* (not leaned, leaped)

Lea River but *Lee Valley Regional Park Authority* etc

learnt past tense and past participle of *learn*; note adjective *learned* (as in scholarly)

Lebanon (not the Lebanon, except occasionally in historical context); see **Sudan**

Lebed, Aleksandr call him General Lebed, not Mr

le Carré, John

Lecs local enterprise councils; initial cap only. See **Tecs**

Lee Kuan Yew (of Singapore)

Left, the cap in the political context when referring to a group of like-minded individuals, eg, "The Left added to Tony Blair's worries"; but l/c in "the party swung to the left". When the Left is qualified, keep the adjective l/c, eg, *the hard Left, the far Left.* Also *the left wing, left-wing contenders, leftwingers.* See **Right**

legal aid l/c and never hyphenate, even adjectivally in phrases such as *legal aid cases.* But note *Legal Aid Board*

legal terms in general, use l/c for titles etc except when in full or specific: thus, the Recorder of Liverpool (thereafter *the recorder*), the West London Magistrate, Chelmsford Crown Court, Horseferry Road Magistrates' Court (caps on first mention), etc; but "the court was told", "the judge said", "the magistrate ordered" etc.

The *Bench* is capped only when referring to the judges as a group; a *bench of magistrates* is always l/c. See **magistrates' courts**.

Always cap the *Bar* and the *Inn* (even when used on its own). See **Courts** special section (page 1851)

legendary avoid its clichéd use

legionella, listeria, salmonella note all are bacteria, not viruses

legionnaires' disease

Legion of Honour or **Légion d'honneur** either form is acceptable, according to context

Le Manoir aux Quat' Saisons (restaurant)

Leonardo da Vinci at second mention always Leonardo (never da Vinci)

leper do not use as a metaphor or as an insult

lèse-majesté (treason, or insult to a monarch); note italic and accents

less use *less* for quantity, *fewer* for number; see **fewer**

lesser opposite to *greater* (eg, *the lesser evil*); not to be used as a synonym of *less*

letter bomb hyphenate only in adjectival use

letterbox, postbox no hyphens

leukaemia

Levi's (jeans) should take the apostrophe; but use *Levi Strauss* for the company

liaison, liaise the word *link* is often better. The verb *to liaise* has forced its way into the language; however, use sparingly and only in its correct sense – to establish co-operation, to act as a link with – not as a synonym of *meet* or *talk*

Liberal Democrats *Lib Dems* is an acceptable alternative in either headlines or text; do not shorten to Liberals. Abbreviate in lists etc to *LD.* See **Politics** special section (page 1853)

licence noun, note **license** (verb), *licensee* (noun), *licensed, licensing.* See **practice**

Liechtenstein

lifeguard (on a beach); note *Life Guardsman* (on a horse)

lifelong one word as adjective

liferaft one word; similarly *lifeboat, lifebelt* etc

lifesize(d) no hyphen

lift-off (spacecraft etc); similarly *take-off*

lightning (as in electrical storm); *lightening* (as in making lighter)

light-year

like do not use as a synonym of *such as* (eg, write "cities such as Manchester are ambitious", not "cities like Manchester ..."); nor as a synonym of *as if* (eg, write "he looks as if he is succeeding", not "he looks like he is succeeding")

likeable

lily of the valley

linchpin (not lynchpin)

liner take care with this word, which strictly no longer applies to passenger cruise ships. Liners nowadays are cargo vessels trading regularly between designated ports, eg, container ships. Confine use of *liner* for passenger ships to historical contexts, eg, the transatlantic liner *Queen Mary*

line-up noun; but note verb *to line up*

Lipizzaner horses (do not use Lippizaner)

liquefy (not liquify); but note *to liquidate*

liquorice (not the American licorice)

lira (Italian currency) singular; note the plural *lire*

literally avoid as expression of emphasis: "he literally exploded with anger" is absurd

livery halls (City of London) note no definite article (eg, Drapers' Hall, not the Drapers' Hall); see **London**

living room no hyphen as *dining room* etc

Livingstone, Ken, Dr David Livingstone (explorer), but *Livingston*, West Lothian

Livorno, rather than *Leghorn*, despite usual style of Anglicising foreign names

Lloyds TSB, the bank, but **Lloyd's of London** (insurance)

Lloyd's names (not Names)

Lloyd-Webber use hyphen for Lord L-W, but no hyphen for brother Julian

loan noun (ie, never say "I loaned him £20" etc); the verb is *lend/lent*

loathe (verb); note the adjective *loath* (not loth)

local government cap councils when full title, eg, Watford Borough Council, Newtown District Council (thereafter the council); but l/c when title is not in full, eg, Watford council; use l/c for all council committees; cap Mayor at first mention (eg, Albert Hobart, Mayor of Rochdale), l/c for council officials such as *borough surveyor, town clerk*; cap the seat of local government if we are sure of its title (eg, Leeds City Hall, Birmingham Council House – not to be confused with Birmingham Town Hall – Lambeth Town Hall)

lochs (Scotland); note *loughs* (Ireland)

Lockerbie suspects the two accused are Abdul Baset Ali al-Megrahi (after first mention, al-Megrahi); and Lamin Khalifa Fhimah (thereafter Fhimah)

lockout (in industrial disputes etc), one word; but *to lock out*

locomotive names italicise, as with ships' or aircraft names, eg, *Mallard.* Do not use *the* unless certain it is part of the name. See **aircraft names, ships**

London cap the *East End* and the *West End* of London, and now also *North London, South London, East London* and *West London, Central London, Inner London*; but l/c *southeast London, southwest London* etc. The local council for the City of London is the Court of Common Council, whose members are common councilmen; cap Borough in titles of particular boroughs, eg, London Borough of Bromley; see **livery halls**

London Clinic, The cap *T*

London clubs note particularly *the Athenaeum; Boodle's; Brooks's; Buck's Club; Pratt's Club; the Queen's Club; Royal Over-Seas League; Savile Club; Travellers Club; United Oxford and Cambridge University Club; White's Club.* It would be wrong to say, eg, Boodle's Club; on the other hand, it is permissible to refer to the Garrick Club, the Reform Club, the Savage Club etc simply as the Garrick, the Reform or the Savage

Londonderry see **Ireland**

London hotels, restaurants as with London clubs, it is essential to give the correct form of the following: *Berkeley Hotel; Brown's Hotel; Claridge's; the Dorchester; Four Seasons hotel; Grosvenor House; Hilton International Kensington; Hyatt Carlton Tower hotel; Hyde Park Hotel; The Lanesborough; Langham Hilton; Le Meridien Piccadilly; London Hilton on Park Lane; Marriott Hotel; New Connaught Rooms; Park Lane Hotel; Quaglino's; Ritz Hotel; Savoy Hotel; Simpson's-in-the-Strand; Waldorf Hotel; Westmoreland Hotel*

London Zoo cap *Zoo*

Longchamp (French racecourse; not Longchamps)

longstanding no longer use hyphen

lookout noun, no hyphen

Lord Advocate do not add *for Scotland*

Lord Chancellor's Department caps, and not Lord Chancellor's Office

lord-lieutenant should be hyphenated, according to the Association of Lord-Lieutenants (note this plural, not lords-lieutenant); use l/c in general use, but the Lord-Lieutenant of Gloucestershire etc (when specific)

Lord Mayor caps, as in Lord Mayor of London, Birmingham etc; thereafter *the lord mayor*; the same applies to Mayor of Guildford etc

Lord's (cricket ground)

lords justices both words take the plural

lorry prefer *lorry* to the American *truck*, but truck has become ubiquitous and cannot be banned, especially from foreign stories

loss-maker, loss-making

loveable note the middle *e*; similarly *likeable*

lowbrow similarly *highbrow*

Lower House, Upper House (of Parliament); see **Politics** special section (page 1853)

low-key

loyalist see **Ireland**

Ltd can usually be dropped from company names (as can plc)

lullaby (not -bye)

lumbar as in the lower back (eg, *lumbar puncture*); note *lumber* as in junk furniture, lumberjacks, or (verbally) moving clumsily about etc

Lusta (not Lusa), in Skye, often quoted as the wettest place in the UK

Luton airport note l/c airport; resist pressure to insert *international.* See **airports**

Luxembourg (not -burg); the inhabitants should be called Mr, Mrs etc, rather than M or Mme (see **foreign appellations**, and **Santer**); but note *Rosa Luxemburg* (leader of Berlin uprising in 1919)

Lycra proprietary term, so cap

Lyons (not Lyon); see **Marseilles, foreign places**

-lyse the style is *analyse, paralyse* etc (not -ize); see **-ise, -isation**

Lytham St Anne's, Lancashire (note apostrophe, but no hyphens)

Lyttelton Theatre (at the National); similarly, Humphrey Lyttelton (jazz musician)

Mm

M1 (do not write M1 motorway)

Maastricht treaty l/c *treaty*, but note *Treaty of Maastricht*; for an unofficial name for the updated version of the treaty, write *Maastricht II* (not 2 or Two). See **inter-governmental conference**

Mac, Mc always check spelling of these prefixes in *Who's Who;* in alphabetical lists, treat Mc as Mac

Macau (not Macao)

McCarthy, Senator Joseph note *McCarthyism*

McCartney, (Sir) Paul

MacDonald, Ramsay

McDonald, Trevor (newsreader)

McDonald's (hamburger chain)

McDonnell Douglas no hyphen

MacDowell, Andie

Macedonia the correct (and politically sensitive) title of the new republic is the Former Yugoslav Republic of Macedonia (caps as shown). See **Yugoslav**

Machiavelli(an)

machinegun but note *sub-machinegun*

mackintosh (raincoat)

Mackintosh, (Sir) Cameron

MacLaine, Shirley

MacLean, Donald

McLuhan, Marshall

Macmillan, Harold same spelling for the publishers

Macpherson, Elle

macroeconomic, microeconomic no hyphen

Macy's (New York store)

Madame Tussaud's

"mad cow" disease see **BSE**, **Creutzfeldt-Jakob disease**

Madejski Stadium, Reading (not Madjeski)

Madison Square Garden, New York (not Gardens)

maestros (not maestri); plural of *maestro*

Mafia cap only in Italian or US context; l/c *mafia* in countries such as Russia when used as a synonym of gangsters

Mafikeng, the new name (since 1980) of Mafeking. Spell according to historical context

Magdalen College, Oxford; but note *Magdalene College*, Cambridge. See **Oxford University**, **Cambridge University**

Maghreb see **Middle East**

magistrates' courts caps for *the Metropolitan Magistrate, West London Magistrate* etc, but usually magistrates take l/c. An acceptable alternative for a non-stipendiary (ie, lay) magistrate is JP (Justice of the Peace). When the accused is appearing before the bench, he appears before the magistrates (plural) unless a stipendiary magistrate, who usually sits on his own. The full name of the court is capped, as in *Bow Street Magistrates' Court.* See **courts**, **legal terms**, **Courts** special section (page 1851)

Magna Carta (not *the* Magna Carta)

MAID (not Maid); now renamed Dialog Corporation

mailshot

major do not use as a lazy alternative for *big, chief, important* or *main*

Majorca, Minorca use the Anglicised forms. See **Spanish regions**

majority of do not use as alternative for *most of*

makeover one word as noun; but try to avoid this cliché – use *remodelling* instead

make-up (cosmetics or typography; not makeup)

Malaysia Datuk Seri Dr Mahathir Mohamad, the Prime Minister; thereafter Dr Mahathir

Mall, The note cap *T*

management buyout spell out first time, though MBO is acceptable on Business pages

manifestos (not -oes)

Manila (capital of the Philippines)

manoeuvre, manoeuvring, manoeuvrable

mantelpiece (not mantlepiece)

manuscript(s) write out when part of a sentence, but abbreviate to MSS when quotation from catalogue, or in headline if context is clear

Mao Zedong (no longer Mao Tse-tung); see **Chinese names**

marathon avoid in clichéd sense of *a long time* as in "a marathon session"

march past noun; two words in military context

Mardi Gras, the Shrove Tuesday festival; but note the self-styled *Mardi Gra bomber*

Margrethe, Queen of Denmark (not Margarethe)

Marines cap in both *Royal Marines* and *US Marines*; note also *a Marine*

marketplace one word; but note *market-maker*

Marks & Spencer use the ampersand rather than *and* in text; can abbreviate to M&S in headlines; the formal legal title is *Marks and Spencer plc*, but this form is used only rarely

marquess (not marquis, except in foreign titles). See **Titles** special section (page 1855)

Marrakesh (not Marrakech)

married couple's allowance

Marseilles (not Marseille); call the football club *Marseilles* (not Olympique de Marseille)

Martini trade name, so cap

Marxist, Marxism derived from Karl Marx, so cap. Do not use as loose variant of communism; see **communism**

Mary Celeste (not *Marie Celeste*)

Mass cap in its religious context; note also *Holy Mass* and *Requiem Mass.* See **Churches** special section (page 1850)

Massachusetts

massive avoid as a synonym of *big*

MasterCard

masterclass (musical etc); no hyphen

master of foxhounds l/c; see **foxhunt**

Master of the Queen's Music

Master of the Rolls see **Courts** special section (page 1851)

Matabele singular and plural – *a Matabele, the Matabele*

materialise avoid as a synonym of *appear, come about* or *happen*

mathematics spell out in text, though maths acceptable in direct quotes and headlines

Mathews, Meg (married to Noel Gallagher)

matinee no accent; similarly *premiere, debut, decor* etc. See **Arts** special section (page 1849)

matins l/c; see **evensong**, **Christian terms**

Maupassant, Guy de

Mauretania (liner); note **Mauritania** (country)

may/might do not confuse; use *might* in sentences referring to past possibilities that did not happen, eg, "If that had happened ten days ago, my whole life might have been different". A clear distinction is evident in the following: "He might have been captured by the Iraqis – but he wasn't", compared with "He may have been captured by the Iraqis – it is possible but we don't know"

Maya, one of the Indian people of Central America; *Mayas*, plural; and *Mayan*, adjective

mayday (SOS call) l/c; but note *May Day* (holiday)

Mayfair but note *May Fair Hotel*

mayor for when to cap, see **local government**, **Lord Mayor**

Maze prison, Northern Ireland use Long Kesh only in historical context

MCC do not write *the MCC*. See **Sports** special section (page 1854)

mealtimes write *breakfast time, lunchtime, teatime, dinner time, supper time* (but use hyphens in compounds when adjectival)

means-test, means-tested etc (hyphenate whether as noun, verb or adjective)

means to an end singular; but note "his means *are* modest"

Médecins sans Frontières

media plural as in *mass media*; but note *mediums* (spiritualists)

medical officer of health MoH acceptable in headlines

medical terms never use these (*geriatric, paralytic, schizophrenic* etc) metaphorically or as terms of abuse.

In words ending in *-tomy* (*appendectomy, hysterectomy* etc), the word "operation" is tautologous and must not be used. See also **bacteria**, **X-ray**

medieval (not mediaeval)

Mediterranean

meet never use *meet with*

mega- be very sparing with this as a colloquial prefix meaning *big*

megawatts the capacity of a power station is measured in *megawatts*; the output is measured in *megawatt hours*. The correct abbreviation of megawatt is *MW* (not mW, which means milliwatt). See **kilowatt-hour**

mêlée

Member of Parliament cap *Member*, but MP almost always preferable

mementoes (not -os)

memoirs (not memoires)

memorandum plural *memorandums* (not -a)

meningitis distinguish whether bacterial or viral; the headline cases are usually bacterial

Mercedes-Benz hyphen

Merchant Navy caps

Merchant Taylors' School, Middlesex and Liverpool

Merthyr Tydfil (South Wales unitary authority) never shorten to Merthyr, which is a village in Carmarthenshire. See **unitary authorities**

Messerschmitt (not -schmidt)

mete out (in context of punishment; not meet out)

metres (as in distance, poetry etc); note *meters* (as in gas, electricity or parking etc)

metric in general non-scientific contexts continue to use the non-metric forms (miles rather than kilometres, pounds rather than kilograms, pints rather than litres). In sporting, foreign, engineering and scientific stories it will often be better to use the metric.

However, with petrol and fuel now sold in litres rather than gallons, it will be essential to give both measurements, eg, 55p a litre (£2.50 per gallon). For the foreseeable future, continue to give fuel consumption in miles per gallon, but also metric conversion in brackets at first mention.

With foodstuffs, such as cheese, prefer the metric first with the imperial conversion where practicable, though a conversion every time in a long list is unnecessary

Metropolitan Police see **Commissioner**; note also *Metropolitan Magistrate* (see **magistrates' courts**)

Michelangelo

microchip

microgram do not abbreviate, and certainly not to mcg, meaningless under international scientific standard abbreviations. The l/c *m* stands for *milli-* as a prefix. So *mg* is correct for *milligram*

mid-air hyphenate, noun or adjective

midday, midweek no hyphens

Middle Ages, the caps

Middle East comprises Bahrain, Cyprus, Egypt, Iran, Iraq, Israel, Jordan, Kuwait, Lebanon, Oman, Qatar, Saudi Arabia, Sudan, Syria, Turkey, United Arab Emirates, Yemen. In a general sense, it also takes in the countries of the Maghreb: Algeria, Libya, Mauritania, Morocco, Tunisia, Western Sahara. Never abbreviate to the Americanism Mideast

Middle England caps, in political context

Middlesbrough

Middlesex no longer a county. See **postal addresses**

Mideast unacceptable as abbreviation of Middle East

Mid Glamorgan no longer exists as a local government authority, but name persists in some organisations' titles, eg, Mid Glamorgan Tec. Note no hyphen. See **unitary authorities**

Midland Bank no longer exists as a trading entity. It is now part of *HSBC*, so use *Midland* only in historical contexts. See **Hong Kong**

midlife crisis but do not overuse this cliché

midnight (not 12 midnight); see **noon**

midsummer, midwinter

Midwest (US)

MiG (former Soviet aircraft)

migrant do not use in place of *emigrant* or *immigrant*. It means one who is in the process of migrating

mileage

military ranks use hyphens in compounds such as *Major-General, Lieutenant-Colonel* etc (where two ranks are joined), but not with *Second Lieutenant, Lance Corporal, Air Commodore* etc. Do not abbreviate ranks except in lists. See **Armed Forces** special section (page 1847)

militate (against or in favour of); do not confuse with *mitigate*

millennium common usage says that the millennium ends on December 31, 1999, though technically it should be December 31, 2000. We should accept the former. Note caps for *the Millennium Dome* (thereafter *the Dome*), *Millennium Fund, Millennium Commission, Millennium Exhibition*. Also *Millennium Eve* (as New Year's Eve). The plural of millennium is *millennia* (unlike *memorandums* etc; see **referendum**). Note also *millenarian* (only one middle *n*) meaning of, or related to, the millennium

millions write out millions from one to ten, thereafter 11 million etc. Abbreviate to *m* only for headlines. For currencies, spell out in text, eg, £15 million, but abbreviate to £15m in headlines. With decimal notations, best to restrict to two decimal points in text, rounded up or down (eg, £1.53 million), though in headlines try to avoid decimals altogether. In text, write 2.5 million rather than two and a half million; but "three million shares changed hands" (not 3 million shares) etc

MIND the mental health charity wishes to be known thus; see **SANE**, **initials**

mind-set prefer *mentality* to this cliché

minimal do not use as a synonym of *small;* it means smallest, or the least possible in size, duration etc

miniskirt no hyphen; note also *minicab*

ministers (political) cap all ministers, whether in the Cabinet or not. The same applies to ministers in overseas governments: give name and full title (capped) first time, thereafter name or just *the minister*. See **Politics** special section (page 1853)

Minnelli, Liza

minuscule (not miniscule). Originally, a medieval script. Use sparingly, as it is heavily overworked as a synonym of *very small* or *unimportant*

Mishcon de Reya (solicitors); note l/c *de*

mis-hit hyphen; similarly *mis-sell*; but note *misspell*

Miss, Ms Ms is nowadays fully acceptable when a woman (married or unmarried) wants to be called thus, or when it is not known for certain if she is Mrs or Miss. Ms is increasingly common in American contexts. See **appellations**

missing do not say *gone/went missing*, prefer *disappeared* or *vanished*

Mississippi

misspell no hyphen; see **spelt**

mitigate means to *make milder, moderating* (as in mitigating circumstances in a law case); do not confuse with *militate*

Mitterrand, François (late French President)

MoD acceptable abbreviation for *Ministry of Defence*, especially in headlines

Moët et Chandon

Mogul (not Mughal); as in empire and art

Mohammed see **Muhammad**

Moldova (no longer Moldavia)

Mona Lisa (not Monna Lisa)

monarch, the l/c for the British monarch; but note *the Sovereign, the Crown*. See **Royal Family**

Mönchengladbach (no hyphen)

Monetary Policy Committee (of the Bank of England); note caps; use MPC at subsequent mentions

moneys plural of money, but *money* will usually serve. Note also *moneyed* (not monied)

Mongol, Mongolian (race); never refer to a Down's syndrome sufferer as a mongol

Monopolies and Mergers Commission (MMC) is now renamed the *Competition Commission*. Refer to the *MMC* now only in historical context

Montagu of Beaulieu, Lord

Montenegrin is the adjective from Montenegro (not Montenegran)

months abbreviate (only in lists or listings) as follows: Jan, Feb, March, April, May, June, July, Aug, Sept, Oct, Nov, Dec

Moon cap in planetary context, otherwise l/c. See **Earth**, **Sun**, **Universe**

more than rather than *over* with numbers, eg, "more than 2,500 people attended the rally", not "over 2,500 ..."

Moreton-in-Marsh (not Morton, nor -in-the-)

MORI must cap

Morrell, Lady Ottoline (not Otteline)

morris dancing/dancers

Morse code

mortar do not use by itself when the meaning is *mortar bomb*; the mortar is the launcher from which the shell is fired. But *mortar attack* is perfectly correct

mosquitoes (not -os as plural)

most favoured nation status

MoT certificate, test; but note otherwise *the Department of Transport*, or *Transport Department* (not Ministry of ...)

Mother Teresa (not Theresa)

Mother's Day, or Mothering Sunday (not Mothers')

motocross (not motorcross)

motorcade acceptable for a procession of vehicles

motorcycle, motorcyclist, motorbike etc

motoring terms the following terms are appearing increasingly in the Saturday motoring pages and should be standardised: *carburettor, wheelspin, four-wheel drive* (shorten to *4WD*), but *a four-wheel-drive vehicle* (two hyphens when adjectival), *power steering, anti-lock brakes, 3-litre car, 1.9 diesel* (hyphenated when adjectival), *four-door, hatchback, four-star petrol, E-type Jaguar, Mercedes-Benz E-class* etc, *airbag, seatbelt, numberplate, sports car*.

For the foreseeable future, continue to give fuel consumption figures in miles per gallon, but also give the metric conversion in brackets at first mention. See **metric**

motor neurone disease (not neuron)

moveable keep middle *e*

movies although an Americanism, is now so common as to be an acceptable synonym of *films;* but use *films* whenever possible

MP, QC use commas each side after name. Note the plural MPs (never MP's). See **Member of Parliament**, **Politics** special section (page 1853), **Courts** special section (page 1851)

Mr, Mrs, Miss, Ms see **appellations**

mugging strictly means theft by violence in the open air. Take care not to overuse

Muhammad use this spelling for the Prophet, but respect the other spellings of the name according to individuals' preference; if in doubt, use Muhammad. Note also *Muhammad Ali*; but *King Mohammed VI* of Morocco; see **names**

Muhammad al-Masari (Saudi dissident); then Dr Masari

Mujahidin (fighters in a jihad or holy war); note cap

multi incline towards making *multi* compounds one word wherever possible, whether used as a noun or as an adjective, eg, *multimillionaire, multinational, multilateral, multimedia, multiracial, multispeed, multistorey, multitrack* (and note *multi-speed, multitrack Europe*). However, hyphenate when two vowels come together, eg, multi-ethnic

multimillion-pound, multimillion-dollar as in deal etc

mum see **dad**

Murdoch, Elisabeth refer to her as Ms Murdoch at subsequent mentions

Murdoch, Rupert at first mention he should be described as "chairman and chief executive of The News Corporation, parent company of *The Times*"

musical vocabulary

a *song titles* (classical or pop), *album titles, operas* (including arias) take italics

b *symphonies* take roman, caps, eg, Symphony No 3, but where symphonies have numbers and popular alternative titles, use italics, eg, *Eroica*

c *concertos* take roman, caps, eg, First Violin Concerto. For fuller list, see **Arts** special section (page 1849)

music-hall

Muslim (not Moslem or Mohamedan); see **Islam**, **Muhammad**

Muzak proprietary term, so cap

Myanmar continue to call the country Burma

mynah bird prefer to mina, myna

Nn

Naafi the Navy, Army and Air Force Institutes; commonly used to describe the canteen for Service personnel run by the Naafi

Nafta North American Free Trade Agreement (not Area or Association)

naive, naivety (no diaeresis)

names as a general rule, people are entitled to be known as they wish to be known, provided their identities are clear. Thus Cassius Clay became Muhammad Ali; but in such changes, give both names until the new one is widely known. Note *Lloyd's names* (l/c). See **appellations, Lloyd's**

names starting stories cap both names, eg, "GORDON BROWN said last night ..." Where the name is too long to contain in the first line, reconstruct the sentence to place the name away from the start

narcotics take care to use this word correctly; see **drugs**

Nasa National Aeronautics and Space Administration (US); rarely necessary to spell out

national avoid as a synonym of *citizen*, as in *a French national*

National Air Traffic Services (caps and note plural), or the air traffic control service (informal alternative, l/c)

national anthem l/c

National Association of Schoolmasters and Union of Women Teachers full title, then abbreviate to NASUWT (no slash)

national curriculum l/c

National Health Service abbreviate to the NHS, or the health service (NHS is acceptable in headlines)

national insurance l/c, like other taxes

National Lottery caps, but usually l/c the lottery at subsequent mentions unless context unclear. Note *National Lottery Charities Board*. See **rollover**

National Parks cap, in both specific names and in general (eg, *Snowdonia National Park*; and "the policy applies particularly to National Parks")

National Rivers Authority (not River)

National Service caps

National Theatre caps; generally omit Royal. See **Lyttelton**

nationalist l/c except when referring to name of a political party. Thus *Scottish National Party* (SNP), and *Scottish Nationalists*. In Irish contexts, again l/c. See **Ireland**

nationwide no hyphen, but use sparingly as it borders on being a cliché; prefer *national* or *nationally*. See **wide**

Native American cap the N when referring to American Indians

Nato (never NATO)

NatWest acceptable abbreviation for National Westminster Bank in text or headlines

naught as in *come to naught* (not nought)

nave (central space in a church); journalists who misspell the word are *knaves*

navy, naval the Royal Navy at first mention (thereafter *the Navy*, capped); the Merchant Navy, the US Navy, the Brazilian Navy etc (thereafter *the navy*, l/c); *naval* is l/c except in titles such as Royal Naval Volunteer Reserve (RNVR) etc. See **officers, ships, warships, Armed Forces** special section (page 1847)

Nazi, Nazism caps; see **communist**

Neanderthal (not -tal); note cap

nearby, near by the first is adjectival, eg, "the nearby school was convenient"; the second is adverbial, eg, "he sat on a bench near by"

nearly one in three ... is prefer singular to plural *are* in these constructions. See **one**

Neighbourhood Watch

Neill Committee on Standards in Public Life (headed by Lord Neill of Bladen); caps for full title

neither takes a singular verb, eg, "neither Bert nor Fred has any idea". Do not use "neither ... or" (must use nor). See **none**

nerve-racking (not -wracking); see **racked, wrack**

Nestlé

Netanyahu, Binyamin (Israeli politician; not Benjamin)

Net Book Agreement caps

Netherlands, The no longer interchangeable with Holland (see **Holland**)

Network SouthEast no longer exists

nevertheless one word; similarly *nonetheless*

new frequently redundant; always omit in "setting a *new* record"

New Age travellers no quotes; see **Gypsy**

newborn (as in babies); no hyphen

Newcastle upon Tyne, Newcastle-under-Lyme

New Deal caps for Labour's welfare programme; quotes at first mention if appropriate

newfound (no hyphen)

Newhaven, East Sussex but note *New Haven*, Connecticut

new Labour l/c *n*, quotes not usually necessary, except when the writer or speaker is making a particular, perhaps ironic, point. But keep caps in slogans such as *New Labour, New Danger*. See **Politics** special section (page 1853)

newscaster prefer *newsreader*

News International Rupert Murdoch is chairman and chief executive of The News Corporation (second mention, News Corp). News Corp can be described as "parent company of *The Times*".

A subsidiary of News Corp is News International, a British company that owns Times Newspapers Holdings. The operating subsidiary of Times Newspapers Holdings is Times Newspapers Ltd, publisher of *The Times* and *The Sunday Times*. Times Supplements Ltd publishes the supplements – *The Times Educational Supplement, The Times Higher Education Supplement, The Times Literary Supplement* and *Nursery World* – and is a subsidiary of News International plc.

Times Newspapers Holdings is chaired by Mr Murdoch (the vice-chairman is Sir Edward Pickering) and the board includes the independent national directors of *The Times* and *The Sunday Times*. It is thus the controlling company.

News Group Newspapers, another operating subsidiary of News International, is the publisher of *The Sun* and *News of the World*.

News Ltd is the Australian arm of News Corp.

Mr Murdoch does not "own" any of these companies, though his family is the largest single (though not majority) shareholder in News Corp. See **BSkyB, Murdoch, *The Times***

newspapers/journals use italics for titles and include *The* in the title whenever appropriate. The lists that follow (source, *Willings Press Guide 1994*), though not exhaustive, should cover the most usual:

a With *The* in the masthead: *The Times, The Sunday Times, The Sun, The Mirror* (formerly *Daily Mirror*), *The Guardian, The Independent, The Daily Telegraph, The Sunday Telegraph, The Express* (formerly *Daily Express*), *The Express on Saturday, The Observer, The Mail on Sunday, The European, The Scotsman, The Herald* (formerly *The Glasgow Herald*), *The Birmingham Post, The Journal* (Newcastle), *The Northern Echo, The Irish Times, The Spectator, The Economist, The Lancet, The Sporting Life, The Big Issue*

b Without *The* in the masthead: *News of the World, Financial*

Times, Daily Mail, Daily Star, Daily Sport, Sunday Sport, Sunday Mirror, Sunday Express, Sunday People, Evening Standard, Independent on Sunday, Scotland on Sunday, Yorkshire Post, Daily Post (Liverpool), *Manchester Evening News, Western Daily Press* (Bristol), *Western Mail* (Cardiff), *Western Morning News* (Plymouth), *Evening Argus* (Brighton), *Evening Mail* (Birmingham), *Sunday Herald* (Glasgow), *Express & Star* (Wolverhampton), *Telegraph & Argus* (Bradford), *Oxford Mail, Sunday Independent* (Dublin), *New Statesman & Society* (although just *New Statesman* is usually acceptable), *British Medical Journal* (the *BMJ*), *Jewish Chronicle, Which?, Which Car?* etc, *Racing Post*

c **Abroad** *The Boston Globe; Chicago Tribune; Los Angeles Times; The Miami Herald; The New York Times; New York Daily News; New York Post; The New Yorker; The Washington Post; USA Today; The Wall Street Journal; International Herald Tribune; The Globe and Mail* (Toronto); *Bild am Sonntag; Stern; Der Spiegel; Die Welt; Izvestia; The Times of India; El País; Le Monde; Le Figaro; L'Espresso* (Italy); *Corriere della Sera; Far Eastern Economic Review; South China Morning Post; The Straits Times* (Singapore); *New Straits Times* (Malaysia); *The Australian; The Sydney Morning Herald; The Jerusalem Post*

d When the journal's name is used adjectivally, omit *The*, eg, "the *Times* reporter was attacked ..."

e Always properly attribute material from another newspaper: never say "a report in another newspaper ..." but "a report in *The Guardian* ..." etc. However, the general phrases *media reports* or *press reports* are acceptable when material has been widely disseminated

New Year Honours or **New Year's Honours List** caps; note also caps for *the Queen's Birthday Honours.* See **honours**

New Year's Day, New Year's Eve but note **the new year** and **Chinese new year**

New York City, New York State caps, usually *New York* is sufficient for the city; *upstate New York* is permissible. Normally, l/c *state* in contexts such as *the state of Virginia,* but see **Washington**

New Zealand (never NZ, even in headlines)

Nicolson, (Sir) Harold but note *Jack Nicholson* (actor)

Nietzsche

nightclub

nightmare use only in its proper sense of an unpleasant dream, not as a lazy cliché for something that goes wrong

night-time hyphen; but note *daytime* (one word)

Nikkei average

Nissan (cars); but note *Nissen hut*

No 10, or **10 Downing Street** (not Number 10 or Downing St); see **Downing Street, Politics** special section (page 1853)

no-fly zone

no man's land

no one two words, no hyphen

"no" vote, "yes" vote

"no win, no fee" (legislation/agreement etc); see **Courts** special section (page 1851)

Nobel Prize for Literature, Medicine etc; or *Nobel Peace/Literature Prize*; but note l/c for *Nobel prize* (unspecific), *Nobel prizewinner* (but *Nobel Prize-winning author*), *Nobel laureate*

nonagenarian (not nono-)

nonconformist but note *the Nonconformist Church* and *Nonconformist churches* (buildings); see **Churches** special section (page 1850)

non-cooperation see **co-operate**

none almost always takes the singular verb, eg, "none is available at present". But occasionally a plural is permissible, eg, "None are better singers than the Welsh" or "none of them have done their best" (where the inelegant alternative would be "none of them has done his or her best"). See **neither**

nonetheless one word

non-existent

non-profitmaking

noon (not 12 noon, 12am or 12pm). See **midnight**

normalcy avoid; use *normality* instead

north, northeast, northern for when to cap, see **compass points**

Northern Ireland see **Ireland**

Northumberland (county); Northumbria is a health, police or tourist authority

North York Moors (not North Yorkshire Moors); see **Yorkshire**

notable (no middle *e*)

Note cap in the diplomatic sense

not only ... followed by *but* (and usually) *also*; often better to say simply *both ... and*

nuclear terms should be used with precision. Take special care not to confuse *fission* and *fusion*

numberplate (on vehicles etc); one word; see **motoring terms**

numbers write from one to ten in full, 11 upwards as numerals except when they are approximations, eg, "about thirty people turned up". Keep consistency within a sentence: write "the number injured rose from eight to fourteen", and do not mix fractions and decimals. At the start of a sentence, write all numbers in full.
ordinals: write out up to hundredth, then 101st, 122nd etc, except with names such as 42nd Street, 38th parallel etc. See **birthday, millions, currencies, fractions**

Nuremberg (not -burg)

Nursing, Royal College of (not Nurses)

NVQ national vocational qualification; note l/c when spelt out

Oo

oblivious of means *forgetful of, unaware of.* It does not mean ignorant or uncomprehending

O'Brien, Conor Cruise, likewise **Edna**

obscenities "four-letter words" and profanities should be avoided. However, in direct quotes and where they are essential to the story, style obscenities with asterisks: f***, c*** etc

occupied territories, the all l/c

occurred (not occured)

o'clock see **times**

octogenarian

octopuses plural of octopus (not octopi)

Oder-Neisse Line (boundary between Poland and Germany)

Odone, Cristina (not Christina), journalist

OECD Organisation for Economic Co-operation and Development

of avoid expressions such as "all of the people attending", "half of the children replied"; say simply "all the people", "half the children" etc

of all time do not use this phrase, as in "best golfer of all time", in any circumstances

offbeat no hyphen

Office for National Statistics (no longer the Central Statistical Office)

Office for Standards in Education, but *Ofsted* usually sufficient on its own. See **regulators**

officers (naval and military); do not describe ratings or NCOs as *officers,* especially in headlines and captions. See **Armed Forces** special section (page 1847)

oil-drilling, oil-fired, oil-slick, oil-tanker but note *oildrum, oilfield, oilrig* and *oil platform.* See **Brent Spar**

OK rather than *okay*

Old Etonian, Old Harrovian etc

Old Masters caps to avoid confusion

Olivier, Laurence (not Lawrence), the late Lord Olivier

Olympics can be used as a short form of *the Olympic Games.* Similarly, *the Games* (always capped) can be used. Always cap Olympics and Olympic even when used adjectivally, eg, *an Olympic athlete.* Note *International Olympic Committee* (no final *s* on Olympic)

ombudsman, ombudswoman keep l/c in general context, eg, "he referred the matter to the ombudsman"; but cap for specifics, as in *the Banking Ombudsman, the Legal Services Ombudsman,* and even the unofficial title of *Parliamentary Ombudsman* (the Parliamentary Commissioner for Administration). Do not confuse the Parliamentary Ombudsman with the Parliamentary Commissioner for Standards, an entirely separate post

on behalf of frequently misused phrase. It means *in the interest of* (a person etc) or *as representative of* (eg, "acting on behalf of his client" is correct). It must not be used as a verbose way of saying *by;* eg, "the book betrays a lack of understanding on behalf of the author" is wrong

ONdigital

one use the singular verb in structures such as "one in three says that ..." See **nearly**. In first-person pieces, try to avoid the use of *one* as a synonym of *I*

One Nation Tories, One Nation politicians etc note cap *O* and cap *N*

one-time do not use as synonym of *former* as in "one-time chairman" etc

One 2 One the mobile phone company (note spaces)

ongoing avoid this ugly adjective; use *continuing* if necessary

online one word in computer context

only take great care to place *only* before the word or phrase it qualifies; "she *only* touched the key, but did not press it; she touched *only* the key, not the switch; she touched the *only* key". Similarly, "he only played cricket" is wrong; "he played only cricket" is correct

on to unlike *into,* two words usually better than one, as in "she moved on to better things", though "he collapsed onto the floor" is acceptable. As a general rule, use *onto* as little as possible

Opec the Organisation of Petroleum Exporting Countries

opencast mining

open-heart surgery note also *open-door policy* (if this overworked phrase has to be used); *open-plan living room*

operations see **medical terms**

ophthalmologist, ophthalmic etc (not opthalmic)

Opposition the same cap or l/c rules apply as to Government – cap as a noun but generally l/c as adjective; eg, "He accused the Opposition of lying", but "He said it was an opposition lie". See **Politics** special section (page 1853)

or need not be preceded by *either,* though it is strengthened thereby if two options are mentioned. Usually avoid a comma before it

oral do not confuse with *verbal*; *oral* means pertaining to the mouth, often in the spoken context (eg, *the oral tradition, by word of mouth*); *verbal* means pertaining to words (contrasted with, eg, physical or choral). See **verbal**

Orders in Council are *approved,* not signed, by the Queen

ordinals see **numbers**

Ordnance Survey note *ordnance* in military contexts; but *ordinance* as in regulations

Orient, the wherever possible, use *the East.* The adjective is l/c *oriental.* The East London football club is *Leyton Orient*

orientate, orientation prefer to *orient, oriented* etc. See **disorientate**

Orkney, or **the Orkney Islands** (not the Orkneys); see **Shetland**

Oscar Award(s), or **the Oscars** registered trademarks, so cap

OSCE the Organisation for Security and Co-operation in Europe, has replaced the former CSCE (Conference on Security and Co-operation in Europe)

Ouija board proprietary term, so cap

-out suffixes in nouns, generally join up rather than hyphenate, as in *fallout, knockout, printout, callout, dropout, bailout* etc; but note *to fall out* etc

Outback, the (Australia)

outdoor adjective; but note *the outdoors*

outpatients, inpatients no hyphen

OutRage! (homosexual "outing" group)

outside (never *outside of*)

Outward Bound must be used only when specifically referring to the work or courses of the Outward Bound Trust Ltd, and never in general use in phrases such as *outward bound-style activities.* Use alternatives such as *outdoor pursuits, adventure training, outdoor adventure courses* etc. Outward Bound's lawyers pounce on every perceived infringement of its service mark. Take care

over do not use as a synonym of *more than* when followed by a number, eg, "she waited over four hours for the train" should be "... more than four hours ..."; "there were over 60 victims" should be "... more than 60 ...". See **more than**

over as prefix wherever the word does not look too ugly, dispense with the hyphen, even when this leads to a double *r* in the middle: *overcapacity, overestimate, overreact, override, overrule, overuse, overvalue*; an obvious exception where the hyphen is essential is *over-age*

overall one word as adjective, but use sparingly

overly do not use as an alternative for *over* or *too*

Overseas Development Administration (not Agency)

owing to see **due to**

Oxbridge be sparing in using the term as a "catch-all" for Oxford and Cambridge Universities

Oxford University colleges and halls are: All Souls College; Balliol College; Blackfriars; Brasenose College; Campion Hall; Christ Church; Corpus Christi College; Exeter College; Green College; Greyfriars; Harris Manchester College; Hertford College; Jesus College; Keble College; Kellogg College; Lady Margaret Hall; Linacre College; Lincoln College; Magdalen College; Mansfield College; Merton College; New College; Nuffield College; Oriel College; Pembroke College; The Queen's College; Regent's Park College; St Anne's College; St Antony's College; St Benet's Hall; St Catherine's College; St Cross College; St Edmund Hall; St Hilda's College; St Hugh's College; St John's College; St Peter's College; Somerville College; Templeton College; Trinity College; University College; Wadham College; Wolfson College; Worcester College

Pp

p's and q's see **apostrophes**

Pacific Rim, South Pacific, North Pacific etc

page 1, page 3, page 187 etc but note *a Page 3 Girl*

paintings titles in italic. See **Arts** special section (page 1849)

Pakistani use both for the people of Pakistan and adjectivally, eg, *Pakistani culture*

palace cap in full names, such as Blenheim Palace, thereafter *the palace*. However, note that *the Palace* is acceptable for Buckingham Palace in stories about royalty. See **Royal Family**

Palace of Holyroodhouse, Edinburgh

palaeo- (not paleo-); similarly *palaeography* etc

Palestinian National Authority (not Palestine) – usually *the Palestinian Authority* will suffice; but note *the Palestine Liberation Organisation* (PLO)

Palmer-Tomkinson, Tara and **Santa**

paparazzi

paperboy, papergirl

paraffin see **kerosene**

paraphernalia (not paraphanalia)

paratroops general term for troops dropped by parachute; a *parachutist* is a specialist in the activity. Note *The Parachute Regiment*

Pardo Palace (royal palace on the outskirts of Madrid); the Madrid art gallery is the *Prado*

Parent's Charter

Paris some of the more familiar place names prone to error are the *Champs Elysées*, the *Elysée Palace*, the *Quai d'Orsay*, the *Jardin du Luxembourg* (not de), the *Jardin des Tuileries* (not de) and the *Jeu de Paume* (not Pomme)

Parker Bowles, Camilla no hyphen

Parkinson's disease

Parliament cap always in British context, and in overseas contexts when the word forms part of the institution, eg, the European Parliament, Canadian Parliament. However, note l/c for the Spanish parliament (the Cortes), the Russian parliament (Duma), the Israeli parliament (Knesset), Polish parliament (Sejm) etc; and l/c when it is only a mooted body, such as the English parliament.

Also, l/c *parliamentary*, even in *parliamentary private secretary* (abbreviated to PPS) because there are many of them; but note *Parliamentary Labour Party* (PLP), of which there is one, and similarly *Parliamentary Ombudsman*. See **PLP**, **ombudsman**, and **Politics** special section (page 1853)

Parliamentary Commissioner for Standards caps for the new post created in the light of the Neill (formerly Nolan) Committee on Standards in Public Life. He must not be referred to as the *Parliamentary Ombudsman*, who is the *Parliamentary Commissioner for Administration*. See **ombudsman**

partially, partly *partially* is of *degree*, eg, *partially deaf*; *partly* is of *extension*, eg, *partly under water*

participles beware the grammar trap of the disconnected (or unrelated) participle; eg, "Judging by the lingering camera shots, X's luck was not about to change" is wrong – the present participle *judging* has to have a following noun or pronoun in agreement (in other words, X's luck is not doing the judging). So the sentence has to be rephrased, as "Judging by the lingering camera shots, I saw that X's luck ...", or "To judge from the lingering camera shots, X's luck ..."

parties (political) cap *Labour Party, Conservative Party*, or any other party; also overseas parties, such as *Republican Party, Democratic Party* (though usually *Republicans* and *Democrats* will suffice). See **Tory**, **Politics** special section (page 1853)

part-time, part-timer note hyphens

partygoer see **-goer**

Passchendaele

passer-by, passers-by

past use rather than *last* in such phrases as "the past two weeks". See **last**

pastime

past tense (of verbs); almost always prefer the shorter form using final *-t* where appropriate; eg, *spelt* (not spelled), *dreamt* (not dreamed); but never earnt for *earned*

Patient's Charter

PAYE pay as you earn; note caps

Paymaster General

payout, payoff no hyphens

Peace Implementation Council (in the former Yugoslavia, part of the Dayton agreement)

peacekeeping, peacemaking etc no hyphens

peal (of bells); but **peel** (of an orange etc)

Pearl Harbor (not Harbour)

pedal (as in bicycle); note *peddle* (as in selling drugs or advocating ideas). A *pedaller* is someone who pedals a bike; a *pedlar* is a small trader; and a drug-pusher is a *peddler*

peers a peer or a peeress has a seat in the House of Lords. A female life peer is a peeress usually referred to as Baroness X. After the first mention of the Marquess of Paddington, Earl of Euston, Viscount Pimlico or Lord Holborn, call them all Lord Paddington, Lord Euston etc. See **Titles** special section (page 1855)

pejorative (not perjorative)

Peking use only in phrases such as *Peking duck* or *Peking man*. The city is now *Beijing*. Note *pekinese dogs*. See **Chinese names**

Peloponnese

PEN (international association of writers)

peninsula never *peninsular* when used as a noun; peninsular is the adjective, as in the Peninsular War

pensioners take care with this word. Some readers take exception to "ambiguous" usage, so it should strictly be confined to people drawing their state pension (men at 65, women at 60). If in doubt, write *the elderly*, or as last resort, *senior citizen*. See **elderly**

pension funds (not pensions funds as plural)

people use rather than *persons* wherever appropriate; exceptions would be "the law is no respecter of persons" or the ubiquitous *missing persons*. Take care with the apostrophe: remember that people is a plural, so the normal use is apostrophe *s*, eg, "it is the people's wish"; very occasionally, *peoples* in the sense of *races* can take an *s* apostrophe, eg, "the African peoples' common heritage"

Pep(s) personal equity plan; spell out in general news, but not necessarily in Business stories

Pepsi-Cola hyphen; similarly *Coca-Cola*

per try to avoid in phrases such as "six times per year"; "six times a year" is better

per cent always takes figures rather than the word, eg, 3 per cent, not three per cent. Usually use decimals rather than fractions (3.25 per cent rather than 3¼ per cent). Use % sign in headlines, never pc, and spell out *per cent* in text

percentage, proportion do not use as a synonym of *part* or *many* if that is all they mean in a sentence: eg, instead of "a large percentage of parents objected" write "many parents objected"

percentage points take care. If the mortgage rate rises from 8 per cent to 10 per cent, it does not rise by 2 per cent, but by two percentage points. Similarly if a political party's support drops from 50 per cent to 40 per cent in an opinion poll, it has lost ten percentage points or 20 per cent of its support

perestroika not italics

performance-related pay

Performing Right Society (not Rights)

Pergau dam (Malaysia)

Persia use Iran for the modern state, and never Persian Gulf except in historical context. See **Gulf**

Personal Investment Authority (not Investments); abbreviate to PIA

personnel prefer *people* or *employees* or *workers* wherever possible

Perspex trade name, so cap

peseta do not abbreviate the Spanish currency in any context

Peterhouse (Cambridge college); never takes College after the name. Neither does Christ Church, Oxford; nor do any Oxford or Cambridge colleges ending with Hall, eg, Lady Margaret Hall. See **Cambridge University**, **Oxford University**

petfood no hyphen; similarly *catfood, dogfood*

phalangist (Lebanon); see **falangist**

Pharaoh (not -oah); note l/c adjective *pharaonic*

phenomenon plural *phenomena*; beware the use of *phenomenal* as a cliché meaning remarkable or big

Philips (Dutch electronics company); note no apostrophe for *Phillips* (auction house)

phone now so common that it is permissible in text as well as headlines

phoney (not phony)

phosphorus noun; but note *phosphorous, phosphoric* (adjectives); *phosphorescence*

photo call two words; similarly *photo opportunity*

photo-finish

photofit l/c; but note cap for *Identikit*

pidgin English (not pigeon)

piecemeal, piecework

pigeonholed

pigheaded

Pigott-Smith, Tim (not Piggott), actor, but **Lester Piggott**, jockey

pilgrims l/c; but note *the Pilgrim Fathers*; note also John Bunyan's *The Pilgrim's Progress*

Pill, the (contraceptive)

Pimm's (the drink)

PIN personal identification number (not Pin); note that *PIN number* is a tautology

pinstripes (-d)

pitbull (terrier)

pitstop (motor racing)

PKK, the Kurdish Workers' Party (not Kurdistan...)

place names refer to the *Bartholomew Gazetteer* for place names in England, Wales and Scotland, and *The Times Atlas of the World* for the rest of the world. But there are exceptions: beware the new Welsh county names, and see **unitary authorities**, **foreign places**, **Spanish regions**

place name constructions two ugly devices to avoid are, eg, a *Gosport, Hampshire, housewife*, and *Manchester's Piccadilly station;* say instead a *housewife from Gosport, Hampshire*, and *Piccadilly station, Manchester*

Plaid Cymru (Welsh Nationalist Party)

plane as in *on a higher plane* (not plain)

planes try to avoid in text as a synonym of aircraft, and be very sparing in headlines, where *jets* (where applicable) or *aircraft* are always better. See **aircraft**

play-off

plays titles in italics. See **Arts** special section (page 1849)

PlayStation

plc all l/c; can usually be dropped from company names; see **Ltd**

PLP Parliamentary Labour Party; see **Politics** special section (page 1853)

plurals make corporate bodies and institutions singular unless this looks odd. Thus "The National Trust is ...", but sports teams are plural, eg, "Arsenal were worth their 8-0 lead". Whether singular or plural, always maintain consistency within a story

plus, minus do not use as variants of *and* or *without*

poetess avoid, use *poet* instead; see **feminine designations**

Poet Laureate caps; note plural *Poets Laureate*

point-to-point

Polaroid trade name, so cap

Polgar, Judit see **chess names**

police forces cap the word Police when it is part of the full name of the force. This applies to the following forces: *Metropolitan Police, City of London Police, British Transport Police, Ministry of Defence Police, Bedfordshire Police, Dorset Police* (Force), *Essex Police, Greater Manchester Police, Humberside Police, Lincolnshire Police, Merseyside Police, Northamptonshire Police, Northumbria Police, North Yorkshire Police, South Yorkshire Police, Staffordshire Police, Surrey Police, Sussex Police, Thames Valley Police, West Midlands Police, West Yorkshire Police, Dyfed-Powys Police, North Wales Police, Central Scotland Police, Grampian Police, Lothian and Borders Police, Strathclyde Police, Tayside Police.*

Other forces use Constabulary instead of Police (eg, *Cleveland Constabulary, Kent Constabulary*), so either give that full title or, more commonly, write *Cleveland police, Kent police* etc. Do not cap when referring to a local division, eg, *Luton police*, or *police in Luton*. If in doubt, consult *Whitaker's Almanack* under "Police Authorities"

policemen take care with this word. Certain senior officers, men and women, regularly chide us for using *policemen* when we mean *police officers*. If in doubt, use the latter.

police ranks wherever possible outside lists, avoid the inelegant abbreviated forms such as *Det Con, Det Chief Insp*. Spell out, even if inconvenient sometimes. An exception is *PC*, or *WPC* (for Woman Police Constable). *PC* also acceptable in headlines. Compound titles do not take hyphens in the police force. Detective Sergeant X becomes Sergeant X after the first mention. Inspector and all ranks above are usually Mr after the first mention. See **Chief Constable**

Police Staff College at Bramshill, Hampshire; or simply *the police college* (l/c), Bramshill

policyholder, policymaker but note *policy document*

Politburo usually cap

Pope, the not usually necessary to give his full name, eg, Pope John Paul II (unless several Popes are mentioned in a story), but always cap. Note *papacy, pontiff* (l/c). See **Churches** special section (page 1850)

poppadum

populist should not be confused with, or used as a synonym of, *popular*, it means supporting the interest of ordinary people, or pandering to mass public taste

Porritt, Jonathon despite his baronetcy, prefers not to use Sir

Portakabin trade name, so cap

possibly like most qualifiers, this word can (usually) be omitted

postal addresses in news and features, prefer to say *Bromley, southeast London* (rather than Kent), and *Kingston upon Thames, southwest London* (rather than Surrey) etc. This leaves the old counties such as Middlesex to be used only in their historical or sporting contexts.

Also avoid the clumsy possessive form such as *Manchester's Moss Side, London's East End*; say *Moss Side, Manchester, the East End of London*. There is no need to use postcodes except when giving an address for information. See **addresses**

postcode (no hyphen)

postgraduate, undergraduate noun and adjective both one word

Post-Modern caps, hyphen; see **artistic movements**

post mortem wherever possible write *post-mortem examination* in reports, though *post mortem* is acceptable nowadays in headlines

Post Office caps for the corporation, but l/c *post office* for the branches. Note also *sub-post office, sub-postmaster, Post Office Counters, Royal Mail, ParcelForce*

postwar, prewar adjectives, commonly referring to Second World War. Do not use adverbially (as in "there were a million jobless prewar")

potatoes plural; similarly *tomatoes*

pothole (as in caving or road surfaces); similarly *potholer*

PoW (prisoner of war); note plural *PoWs*

PowerGen

PPE the university degree is philosophy, politics and economics (not politics, philosophy etc)

practical, practicable do not confuse. *Practical* means adapted to actual conditions or (of a person) able to make things function well; *practicable* means capable of being effected or accomplished

practice noun; but **practise** (verb). It is an inexcusable *practice* for sub-editors to confuse the two; writers should *practise* getting it right

Prado gallery, Madrid see **Pardo**

praesidium (not presidium)

praying mantis (not preying)

prearrange

predilection (not predeliction)

pre-empt

Premier do not use in text as a synonym of *Prime Minister,* though very occasionally its use in the headline of a foreign story (never British) may be permitted. Generally, confine the word to heads of government of the Canadian provinces or Australian states, when it should take a cap. *Premiership* is preferable to *prime-ministership*

premiere (of a play, ballet etc); no accent

Premiership (football); refer to the *FA Carling Premiership* at first mention, *the Premiership* thereafter, for the top division in English football; the organisation that runs it is the *FA Premier League.*

Similarly, the lower divisions form the *Nationwide* (no longer Endsleigh) *League, first division, second division* (note l/c) etc; this competition is run by the *Football League.* See **Sports** special section (page 1854)

premise (assumption in an argument); note the word *premises* (property) takes the plural verb, eg, "the premises are well positioned"

Premium Bonds caps

prepositional verbs avoid wherever possible. Examples such as *measure up to, get on with* are acceptable on the odd occasion. Others such as *consult with, meet with* (where the preposition is tautologous) must never be used

Pre-Raphaelite

Presbyterian beware, especially with the adjective *Scots.* See **Church, Churches** special section (page 1850)

present better than *current* but often redundant

President cap *the President* of any country, also *President of the European Commission* at first and all subsequent mentions; but l/c *presidency* (as in *the French presidency of the EU*). Also note that *presidents of companies* or *organisations* normally take l/c, though this rule should be relaxed for leading national organisations, such as *President of the Law Society* and *President of the TUC*

press always l/c except in titles such as *the Press Complaints Commission.* See **broadsheet**

prestigious try to avoid this much-overworked word and find an appropriate substitute such as *highly regarded, admired, eminent, esteemed, leading, noted, outstanding, powerful* etc

pretension but note *pretentious*

prevaricate (to speak or act evasively); do not confuse with **procrastinate** (to defer action, to be dilatory)

preventive (not preventative)

PricewaterhouseCoopers (*PwC* for short), the merged accountants

prime meridian l/c

Prime Minister cap for every country. But l/c when referring to an unspecific, eg, "he would make a good prime minister". Never say, eg, Prime Minister Tony Blair or even Tony Blair, the Prime Minister; write instead *Tony Blair* at first mention, then *the Prime Minister* at next mention. Never use Premier for the British Prime Minister, and never use PM even in headlines. See **Premier**

primeval

Prince avoid the familiar forms of Prince Charles and Prince Philip at least until they have been given their full designation of *Prince of Wales* and *Duke of Edinburgh*; even then, prefer *the Prince* and *the Duke* at subsequent mentions. Note *The Prince's Trust.* See **royal, Royal Family**

Princess of Wales see **Diana, Princess of Wales**

Princes Street, Edinburgh

principal noun or adjective; means chief, main, important, head etc; eg, *the principal of a college,* or *the team's principal objective.* Do not confuse with **principle**, which is a noun meaning concept, ideal, rule, moral etc; eg, *her Christian principles*

Principality, the cap in Welsh context

printout

prior to avoid wherever possible; use *before*

Prison Service note caps and *s* in *Prisons Board*; also caps for *Director-General of the Prison Service* and *Chief Inspector of Prisons*; see **Governor, Probation Service**

prison visitors be careful to differentiate clearly between two groups of prison visitors:
a members of the National Association of Prison Visitors, who visit prisoners in the "social" sense of visiting
b members of prison boards of visitors, who visit as watchdogs in an official role and sometimes make recommendations on matters such as discipline and security

Private Finance Initiative (PFI), sometimes now known as *Public Private Partnerships* (initial caps)

private sector, public sector do not use hyphens even when employed adjectivally, eg, *public sector pay* (as *high street shopping*)

privatised industries see **regulators**

Privileges, Committee of

Privy Council but note *Privy Counsellors* (not Councillors)

prizewinner one word

Probation Service caps; similarly *Prison Service*

probe use only in a scientific, medical or space context. Never to be used as *inquiry,* even in headlines

problem be sparing with this overworked word

procrastinate (to defer action, to be dilatory). See **prevaricate**

Procter & Gamble note *-er* and ampersand

Procurator Fiscal (Crown prosecutor in Scotland); see **Courts** special section (page 1851)

profanities see **obscenities**

Professor caps for *Professor of History* etc; thereafter *the professor* or *Professor X*; see **university posts**

proffer, proffered (not profer, proferred)

profits especially in Business stories, should always state the basis of the figure (pre-tax, operating etc)

program (computers); *programme* (the arts etc)

pro-life beware this contentious phrase for the anti-abortion lobby (especially in US context); use the phrase *anti-abortion* wherever possible, but when "pro-life" is unavoidable always quote it

Proms acceptable abbreviation of Promenade Concerts; note also *Promenaders* and *the Last Night of the Proms*

prone (lying face-down); note *supine* (face-up)

propeller (not -or)

prophecy noun; note verb **prophesy**

proportion see **percentage**

pros and cons

protagonist means a *supporter* (of either side) in a debate or quarrel; it does not mean *advocate* or *proponent*

protégé

Protestant beware of using for all Christians who are not Roman Catholic. See **Churches** special section (page 1850)

protester (never -or); but see **demonstrator**

proven *not proven* is the Scottish legal verdict. In general use, prefer *proved* to *proven;* but *proven* and *unproven* may be used as a colloquial alternative

provided that (not providing that)

Province, the see **Ireland**

provinces, provincial take great care of these words in the context of "outside London". Many regard them as patronising; use *the regions* or *regional* wherever possible

prurient means having an unhealthy obsession with sex; it does not mean puritanical

PSBR public sector borrowing requirement

public house *pub* is now fully acceptable in text or headlines

public interest immunity certificate abbreviate to PIIC, or simply *the certificate*

publicly (never publically)

Public Record Office (not Records)

public school independent school is now a preferable term; use *public schoolboys, public schoolgirls,* if necessary

public sector see **private sector**

Pulitzer prizes see **Nobel prize** for when to cap

pullout noun, one word; but note *to pull out*

punctuation some important reminders:

- **a Commas** keep commas inside quotes in the following type of "broken" sentence: "The trouble is," he said, "that this is a contentious issue." Omit the comma before *if, unless, before, since, when* unless the rhythm or sense of the sentence demands it. Avoid the so-called *Oxford comma*; say "he ate bread, butter and jam" rather than "he ate bread, butter, and jam".
- **b Dashes** do not use in place of commas. Too many dashes can be ugly and disruptive.
- **c Punctuation marks** place inside inverted commas if they relate to the words quoted, outside if they relate to the main sentence, eg, She is going to classes in "health and beauty". If the whole sentence is a quotation, the final point goes inside, eg, "Beauty is truth, truth beauty."
- **d Interrogation marks** never use with indirect questions or rhetorical questions, eg, "She asked why he did not laugh."
- **e Parentheses** use sparingly; try to use commas instead.
- **f Conjunctions** *And* and *but* may occasionally be used at the beginning of a sentence, especially for emphasis.
- **g Ellipses** use three points with full space after last word, then thin spacing between points, then full space before next word, eg, *not only … but also*

puns an enjoyable device for headline writers. Restrict their use to funny or light stories or features and if in doubt, avoid; but if irresistible, make sure they are in good taste

Puritan (16th/17th-century religious group); do not use as a contemporary adjective; *puritanical* is just permitted

putsch (military seizure of power, as in coup)

pygmy, pygmies

Pyramids the three main Pyramids at Giza (including the Great Pyramid) should be capped. But there are many other pyramids (l/c) throughout Egypt

pyrrhic l/c, as in *pyrrhic victory*

Qq

Qantas (not Quantas)

qat (hypnotic drug); preferable to *kat* or *khat*

QC, MP place commas each side when used after name

QCA Qualifications and Curriculum Authority; spell out at first mention. It is an amalgamation (from autumn 1997) of the *National Council for Vocational Qualifications* and the *School Curriculum and Assessment Authority*

QE2 normally spell out *Queen Elizabeth 2* at first mention, thereafter *QE2* or simply *the ship*

Qom, Iran (not Qum)

quadriplegia, quadriplegic (not quadra-)

quality press prefer *broadsheet.* See **broadsheet**

quango short for quasi-autonomous non-governmental organisation; no need to spell out or to quote

quantum leap avoid this cliché wherever possible

quarter sessions like assizes, no longer function, having been replaced by Crown Courts

Quebeckers rather than *Quebecois*

Queen, the aim at keeping *the* in headlines. Note caps for *the Queen's Speech* (to Parliament) and *the Queen's Birthday Honours.* See **Royal Family**, **New Year Honours**

Queen Elizabeth the Queen Mother no commas; always this style at first mention, thereafter *the Queen Mother*

Queen Elizabeth II Conference Centre, London (not QE2 or any other variant)

Queens, New York

Queensberry, Marquess of also *Queensberry Rules*

Queen's Club

Queens' College, Cambridge but note **The Queen's College, Oxford** (see **Cambridge University** and **Oxford University**); also note *The Queen's University of Belfast*, usually shortened to *Queen's University, Belfast* or simply *Queen's, Belfast*

Queens Park Rangers thereafter QPR

queueing note middle *e*

questionnaire

Question Time, Prime Minister's Questions caps, but note l/c *questions* to the Prime Minister, Foreign Secretary etc. See **Politics** special section (page 1853)

quicker never use as an adverb – always use *more quickly.* Confine *quicker* to adjectival comparison, eg, "he started at a quicker pace"

quid pro quo not italic

quiz show no hyphen; similarly *chat show, game show, talk show* etc

quotation marks (inverted commas); remember, single quotes in headlines, straps and display panels; double quotes in captions and keydecks. The only other use for single inverted commas is quotations within quotations.

Avoid inverted commas in sentences where they are clearly unnecessary, eg, *He described the attack as "outrageous".*

Quotation marks are no longer to be used for works of art. See **inverted commas, italics**

See also **punctuation** (paragraph c) for when punctuation goes inside or outside quotation marks

quotes direct quotes should be corrected only to remove the solecisms and other errors that occur in speech but look silly in print. Always take care that quotes are correctly attributed; and especially that literary or biblical quotations are 100 per cent accurate

Rr

race references to race should be used only when relevant to the sense of the story. The word is often better replaced by *people, nation, group* etc

racecourse, racehorse, racetrack see **horse**, and **Sports** special section (page 1854)

racked as in *racked by doubts, pain* etc; (not wracked)

racket (for tennis; not racquet); the game is *rackets*

RADA the Royal Academy of Dramatic Art; all caps

radio compounds are hyphenated in the wireless context (eg, *radio-telephone*); but one word when they concern rays (eg, *radioactive, radioisotope, radiotherapy*). Broadcasting frequencies are measured in *megahertz* (MHz) and *kilohertz* (kHz)

radio ham this term should strictly be applied only to licensed amateur radio operators, who are offended when it is used to apply to unlicensed "eavesdroppers" spying on private phone calls etc. Take care

Radio 1, 2, 3, 4, Radio 5 Live note also *Classic FM, BBC Radio*. But with foreign stations, usually l/c, eg, *Israel radio, Haiti radio, Moscow radio* etc; cap only if it is the specific name of the station or organisation

RAF Regiment (Corps within the Royal Air Force)

rail franchise director l/c; informal and acceptable short form of the *Director of Passenger Rail Franchising* (caps). The *Rail Regulator* takes caps; see **regulators**

rainforest one word

raison d'être use italics

Raleigh, Sir Walter (not Ralegh)

R&B abbreviation for rhythm and blues

ranging from overworked and often unnecessary phrase. There must be a scale in which the elements might be ranged: "ranging from 15 to 25 years" is correct, "a crowd ranging from priests to golfers" is not

ranks see **police ranks, Armed Forces** special section (page 1847)

Ranks Hovis McDougall but note *(The) Rank Organisation*

Rapid Reaction Force caps

rarefied, rarefy (not rarified)

rateable

rave acceptable in context as a musical event; see **gig.**

razzmatazz

re- whenever possible, run the prefix on to the word it qualifies, eg, *readmission, remake, reorganise, rework*, etc; but there are two main classes of exceptions:
a where the word after re- begins with *e*, eg, *re-election, re-emerge, re-examine, re-enter* etc;
b where there could be serious ambiguity in compounds such as *re-creation* (*recreation*), *re-cover* (*recover*), *re-dress* (*redress*). See **hyphens**

realpolitik not italic

rebut means to argue to the contrary, producing evidence; *to refute* is to win such an argument. Neither should be used as a synonym of *reject* or *deny*. Nor should they be used for *dispute* or *respond to*

receive "receiving an injury" is to be discouraged, though not banned. Prefer to say *sustained* or *suffered;* and never say someone received a broken leg etc – prefer *suffered a broken leg* or, better still, *broke a leg*. See **injure**

reckless (not wreckless); synonym for rash or foolhardy

record never write "set a new record", "was an all-time record" etc, where both the qualifiers are tautologous

recorders for when to cap, see **Courts** special section (page 1851)

recrudescence do not confuse with *resurgence* or *revival*. It means *worsening*, in the sense of reopening wounds or recurring diseases

redbrick (university); but note a *red-brick* building

Red Planet (informal name for Mars); caps

referendum plural *referendums*, as with *conundrums, stadiums, forums* and most words ending in *-um*. But note *millennia, strata*

refute take care with this word. See **rebut**

Regent's Park

regimen should be restricted to medical contexts – a prescribed course of exercise, way of life, diet etc. Do not use as a synonym of *regime* (government or administrative contexts)

register office (not registry office)

Register of Members' Interests caps; see **Politics** special section (page 1853)

Registrar (Oxford); but note *Registrary* (Cambridge)

Registrar-General

regulators of the privatised industries and the consumer watchdog should be styled as follows: *Director-General of Electricity and Gas Supply*, who heads Office of Gas Supply (Ofgas) and can be shortened to the *gas regulator*, and who also heads Office of Electricity Regulation (Offer) and can be shortened to the *electricity regulator*
Director-General of Water Services (heads Office of Water Services, Ofwat), or the *water regulator*
Director-General of Telecommunications (heads Office of Telecommunications, Oftel), or the *telecommunications regulator*
Rail Regulator (Office of the Rail Regulator) – cap as it is the official title; note that the *Office of Passenger Rail Franchising* (Opraf) is separate
Director-General of Fair Trading (Office of Fair Trading, OFT) best not to abbreviate – use *consumer watchdog* as alternative

Reith Lecture(s)

reject see **rebut**

relatively see **comparatively**

Religious Right (in American politics); caps. See **Right**

remainder avoid as a synonym of *the rest*

REME the Royal Electrical and Mechanical Engineers (never Reme). See **Armed Forces** special section (page 1847)

Remembrance Sunday prefer to Day

Renaissance, the but l/c *renaissance* as synonym of *revival* or *rebirth*

repellent (noun or adjective), not repellant

report l/c in titles of official documents such as *Taylor report*

reportedly avoid this slack word, which suggests that the material's source is not clear

Republic of Ireland, or **Irish Republic** see **Ireland**

republican l/c except when in an official name, such as *the Republican Party* or *Republicans* (US). See **Ireland**

rerun

Resolution cap in context of UN, eg, *Resolution 688*

respect of avoid "in respect of" whenever possible; never write "in respect to"

responsible people bear responsibility, things do not. Storms are not responsible for damage; they cause it. Avoid the phrase "the IRA *claimed responsibility for* the bombing"; say instead "the IRA *admitted causing* the bombing"

restaurateur (never restauranteur)

result in avoid this lazy phrase and always find an alternative, such as *cause, bring, create, evoke, lead to* etc

re-use one of the *re-* words where the hyphen is essential

Reuters use this form now in every context (no longer Reuter)

Reveille like Last Post, is *sounded,* not played

Revelation, Book of (not Revelations)

reverend at first mention, the style is *the Rev Tom Jones,* then *Mr Jones.* Never write "the Rev Jones" or (even worse) "Rev Jones" (which is as great a solecism as calling Sir Norman Fowler "Sir Fowler"). A parson and his wife are referred to as *the Rev Tom and Mrs Jones.* See **archbishops, Churches** special section (page 1850)

Review caps in names of government programmes such as *Strategic Defence Review, Comprehensive Spending Review*

Reykjavik, Iceland

rhinoceroses (plural)

Rhys-Jones, Sophie now the *Countess of Wessex* (subsequent mentions the *Countess*). See **Titles** special section (page 1855)

RIBA abbreviation of the Royal Institute of British Architects; all caps

Richter scale measures the energy released by an earthquake. It runs from 0 to 8; write "the earthquake measured 6 on the Richter scale"

RICS Royal Institution of Chartered Surveyors (not Institute); note caps

riffle, riffling as in flicking through papers or clothes on a rail; note *rifling* in the sense of ransacking

Right, the cap in the political context when referring to a group of like-minded individuals, eg, "The Right added to John Major's dilemma on the EU"; but l/c in "the party swung to the right". When the Right is qualified, generally keep the adjective l/c, eg, *the far Right* (but note *the Religious Right* in the US). Also, *the right wing, right-wing contenders, rightwingers.* See **Left**

rigmarole (not rigamarole)

ring-fence hyphen

Rio Tinto (no longer Rio Tinto-Zinc or RTZ)

riverbank one word

rivers cap in context of *River Thames, Mississippi River* (or simply *the Thames, the Mississippi* etc). Similarly, cap *estuary* when part of the name. See **Thames**

riveting try to avoid its clichéd use as a metaphor

roadblock, roadbuilding, roadbuilder etc

road rage wherever possible, quote at first mention (ie, "road rage"); but not thereafter, nor in headlines

roads as tautologous to write "the M5 motorway" as "the A435 road", but correct to say "the M40 London to Birmingham motorway". Unnecessary to define the M25 as London's orbital motorway, but generally, define a road geographically unless context is clear

Robert the Bruce prefer to Robert Bruce; subsequent mentions *the Bruce*

rock'n'roll

Rollerblade proprietary term, so cap. The American company's lawyers insist that even Rollerblading is capped; use *inline skates/skating* instead

rollerskate, rollercoaster

roll-on, roll-off (as in ferries); abbreviate to *ro-ro*

rollover (as in National Lottery); no hyphen

Rolls-Royce

Roman Catholic see **Catholic**

Romania (not Rumania); see **Ceausescu**

Roman numerals usually no full points, eg, *Edward VIII, Article XVI, Part II, Psalm xxiii.* But in official documents, to designate sub-sections, use the points, eg, *i., ii., iv.,* etc

roofs (not rooves)

rooms use *dining room, living room, drawing room, laundry room* (no hyphens except when adjectival, eg, *living-room carpet*); but note *bathroom, bedroom*

rottweiler l/c; see dogs

row be sparing in the use of this word, especially in headlines. Alternatives are *rift, split, clash* etc, and *dispute* in text. However, *row* is not banned

Rowntree be sure to distinguish between the *Joseph Rowntree Foundation,* a charity and independent funder of social policy research and development; and the *Joseph Rowntree Reform Trust,* not a charity and an entirely separate company that funds projects often with a political dimension

royal, royalty l/c for royalty but cap *the Royal Family*; royal is usually l/c when used adjectivally, as in *royal baby, royal approval, the royal wave,* but takes the cap in titles such as *Royal Assent, Royal Collection, Royal Household, Royal Yacht*

Royal College of Nursing (not Nurses)

royal commissions should be capped when the full title is given, eg, *Royal Commission on Environmental Pollution,* but otherwise l/c, eg, *the royal commission.* See **committee**

Royal Corps of Signals, or **Royal Signals** (not Royal Corps of Signallers); see **Armed Forces** special section (page 1847)

Royal Family takes caps, British and overseas; with names of the British Royal Family, give in full at first mention, eg, *the Duke of Edinburgh,* thereafter *the Duke* (cap) or occasionally *Prince Philip*; *Prince William,* thereafter *the Prince.* In royalty context, the cap after first mention should be confined to the British Royal Family and overseas heads of state. See **Queen, Duke, Prince, Diana, heads of state, Titles** special section (page 1855)

Royal Fine Art Commission

Royal Fleet Auxiliary ships are entitled RFA, not HMS; eg, *RFA Fort George.* See **Armed Forces** special section (page 1847)

Royal Institute of International Affairs (not Institution); often known as *Chatham House*

Royal Military Academy Sandhurst no commas; similarly *Royal Air Force College Cranwell* and *Royal Naval College Dartmouth*

Royal National Lifeboat Institution (not Life-Boat); abbreviate to RNLI

Royal Over-Seas League see **London clubs**

Royal Shakespeare Company thereafter the RSC; note also *Royal Opera House*; generally no need to include *Royal* with *Albert Hall, Festival Hall, National Theatre*

Royal Standard only for the Sovereign. Other members of the Royal Family have a *personal standard*; see **ensign**

Royal Train caps, as with the *Royal Yacht*

Royal Welch Fusiliers, The similarly, *Welch Regiment*; but note *Welsh Guards*; see **Armed Forces** special section (page 1847)

Royal Yacht *Britannia*, or **the *Britannia*** she is now decommissioned, so refer to her as the *former Royal Yacht*

RPI retail prices index; note plural and l/c

RPM (caps), resale price maintenance (not retail); and *rpm* (l/c) revolutions per minute

RSPCA does not exist in Scotland, which has the Scottish SPCA

rubbish do not use as a verb

Rubens (Flemish painter; not Reubens)

Rue Royale see **French names**

run-down adjective, as in *decaying* or *exhausted*; note noun *rundown* as in briefing; also verb *to run down*

running-mate hyphen

Rural England Council for the Protection of Rural England (not Preservation); abbreviate to CPRE

rush hour noun; but note hyphen for adjective, eg, *rush-hour traffic*

rushed to hospital avoid this cliché. Use *taken to* or *driven to;* similarly, write a victim was *flown to hospital* rather than *air-*

lifted to … Always avoid the American *hospitalise*

Russia take care not to designate parts of the former Soviet Union as Russia when they no longer are, eg, Ukraine, Georgia. The same applies to the people (though there are millions of ethnic Russians throughout the former Soviet Union). So always specify the republic concerned and do not use *Russian* in the inclusive sense except in the phrase *Russian vodka.* Use *Soviet* and the *Soviet Union* only in their historical contexts – and avoid USSR wherever possible. See **Soviet**

Russian names use *i* as first name ending, but *y* for surnames, eg, *Arkadi Volsky, Gennadi Yavlinsky* (but note the exception *Rutskoi*); and use *k* rather than *x* in the middle, eg, *Aleksei, Aleksandr,* also note *Viktor.* We should use the *-ya* rather than *-ia* in *Natalya* and *Tatyana* (not Natalia, Tatiana). But note that the styles of Garry Kasparov and Anatoly Karpov are sufficiently Westernised to be spelt thus. See **chess names**

Ss

saccharin (noun), **saccharine** (adjective)

sack avoid in the sense of *dismiss* except in headlines (and never use *axe* in this context)

sacrilegious (from sacrilege; not sacreligious)

Saddam Hussein, President write in full at first mention, then *Saddam*

Sadler's Wells

said prefer the construction *Mr Brown said* rather than *said Mr Brown*. See **writes**

sailing correspondent do not use yachting correspondent

Sainsbury the formal style is *J Sainsbury* (no point), especially in business stories, but *Sainsbury's* is permissible in general news stories. See **initials**

Saint nearly always abbreviated to *St*

St Albans

St Andrews (town and university in Fife)

St Catharine's College, Cambridge but note *St Catherine's College*, Oxford; see **Oxford University**, **Cambridge University**, **Catherine**

St David's (village and cathedral, Pembrokeshire); also St David's Head; but note the Bishop of St Davids does not take the apostrophe

St Giles' Cathedral, Edinburgh

St Helens, Merseyside

St James's Palace see **Court of...**

St John Ambulance Brigade/Association

St John's, Newfoundland but note **Saint John**, New Brunswick

St John's, Smith Square use comma

St John's Wood, London

St Katharine Docks, but *St Katharine's Yacht Haven*

St Martin-in-the-Fields

St Martins College of Art and Design see **Central St Martins**

St Neot, Cornwall but note **St Neots**, Cambridgeshire

St Paul's Cathedral

St Stephen's Green, Dublin (not Stephen's Green)

St Thomas' Hospital, London

Saint-Saëns (composer)

saleroom one word

Salonika, rather than Thessaloniki. See **foreign place names**

salutary not salutory

Salvadorean (not -ian)

Sam-7 (missiles)

Sanaa (capital of Yemen; not Sana'a, Sana, or other variants)

sanatorium (not sanitorium); note plural *sanatoriums*

sanction as a noun, define its use as trade, military etc

sandpit one word

SANE (schizophrenia charity); note caps

Santer, Jacques (former President of the European Commission); he is from Luxembourg, so call him Mr, not M; see **foreign appellations**

sarin (as in nerve gas); l/c

Sauchiehall Street, Glasgow

Saudi must never be used as short form for the country, Saudi Arabia. Confine its use to the adjectival, eg, *Saudi Royal Family*

Savile, Jimmy use *Sir James* in formal context only

Savile Row, Savile Club see **London clubs**

Saville Theatre

SBS Special Boat Service (not Squadron)

Sca Fell, Scafell Pike two separate mountains in the Lake District. Scafell Pike, at 3,206ft, is the highest in England

Scalextric (not Scalectrix)

Scandinavia (never Scandanavia)

Scarborough, North Yorkshire

scarify (to cut into, to cut skin from); its colloquial meaning of *to terrify* should be avoided wherever possible

scars do not heal (even metaphorically); *wounds* heal, *scars* remain

Schadenfreude (malicious enjoyment of another's misfortunes); note cap, italic

Schiphol airport, Amsterdam

schizophrenic never use as a term of abuse and avoid as a metaphor. See **medical terms**, **SANE**

Schleswig-Holstein

Schoenberg, Arnold

schools cap when full title is given (if in doubt, consult the *Independent Schools Year Book* or the state sector equivalent, the *Education Year Book*); nowadays use the classifications of *independent, state, grant-maintained, comprehensive, grammar, secondary modern* (rarely), etc, rather than public, private etc (except in historical context)

schoolchildren one word; note also *schoolgirl, schoolboy, schooldays, schoolmaster, schoolmistress* and *schoolteacher* (rarely), but *school-leaver*

School Curriculum and Assessment Authority (not Schools); but see **QCA**

Schwarzenegger, Arnold

Schweitzer, Albert

scientific measures write out first time with abbreviations in parentheses, shorten thereafter. The abbreviation takes no point and no *s* in the plural, eg, *14km* (not 14kms). Some basic international units and their abbreviations are: *metre* (*m*); *gram* (*g*); *litre* (*l*); *ampere* (*A*); *volt* (*V*); *watt* (*W*); note also *kilowatt-hour* (*kWh*).

Only abbreviate *mile* to *m* in *mph* and *mpg*; and *gallon* to *g* in *mpg* (otherwise *gal*). Beware of using *m* for million or for miles in any scientific context when it might be taken for metres. See **weights**

scientific names when employing the Latin terminology, use the internationally accepted convention of initial cap on the first (genus) word, then l/c for the second (species); eg, Homo sapiens, *Branta canadensis* (Canada goose) etc. Italicise all but the most common

Scilly, Isles of (not Scilly Isles); note spelling of *St Mary's* and *Tresco*

Scope new name for the former Spastics Society

Scotch (whisky); do not use as a substitute for the adjectives Scottish and Scots. But note *Scotch broth, Scotch mist, Scotch egg* and *Scotch terrier*; also *Scots pine*

Scottish National Party (SNP); now cap *Nationalists* in the Scottish party context, but l/c nationalists in the wider sense

Scottish Parliament now cap *P*. Note First Minister (not Secretary)

Scottish place names always write, eg, Motherwell, North Lanarkshire (never Motherwell, Scotland). Take care with new names under local government reorganisation; regions such as *Central, Grampian* and *Strathclyde* should now be referred to only in their historical context or if they persist in official titles such as *Strathclyde Police* or *the University of Strathclyde*. Permissible too to refer informally to the *Central belt* (between Edinburgh and Glasgow).

The same principle about counties applies to Wales and

Northern Ireland: give the county unless the town or city is big enough or well-known enough for the county to be unnecessary

ScottishPower

Scott Thomas, Kristin (no hyphen)

Scouts no longer Boy Scouts

scrapheap one word

scratchcard one word; similarly *smartcard, swipecard*

Scripture cap as in *Holy Scripture*; but note l/c *scriptural*

scriptwriter

sculptures set in italic. With photographs of sculptures, always give the sculptor's name. See **Arts** special section (page 1849)

seabed, seabird, seahorse, seagull, seasick no hyphens

seasonal, but **unseasonable** (not unseasonal). Note also *seasonal affective disorder* (l/c), abbreviated to SAD

seasons always l/c when unattached, ie, *spring, summer, autumn, winter*, but note *Winter Olympics* etc

seatbelt

second-hand hyphenated

Second World War (not World War II/Two etc)

Secret Intelligence Service abbreviate to SIS, or MI6; takes caps; see **Security Service** (MI5)

Secretary-General (of the United Nations, Nato)

Securities and Investments Board the SIB has now been replaced by the new City super-regulator, the *Financial Services Authority* (FSA)

Security Service (MI5); takes caps; but l/c for *security services* in non-specific use. See **Secret Intelligence Service**

seize (never sieze)

select committees as with parliamentary committees cap at first mention, or when full title is given, eg, *the Foreign Affairs Select Committee*; thereafter *the select committee*, or *the committee*

Selfridges

sell-off, sell-out but see **buyout**

Sellotape trade name, so cap; alternatively use *sticky tape* or *adhesive tape*

semiconductor

Semtex cap

Senate (US); write *Senator Edward Kennedy*, thereafter *the senator*, alternatively, *Mr Kennedy, the Massachusetts senator*

senior abbreviate to *Sr* (not Snr) in the American context, eg, *Henry Ramstein Sr*, see **junior**. Avoid the cliché *senior executive* when you mean *executive* – nine times out of ten the adjective is redundant (as *major*)

Senior Salaries Review Body caps; has replaced the Top Salaries Review Body

septuagenarian

Serb for the people, but *Serbian* can be used (sparingly) as an adjective

Serious Fraud Office abbreviate to SFO; but note *fraud squad*. See **Flying Squad**

Serjeant at Arms

Serps spell out at first mention as *state earnings related pension scheme (Serps)*

serve in a warship (but *on* a merchant ship), and serve in (not on) a submarine, even though subs are boats, not ships. Important to make this distinction. See **Armed Forces** special section (page 1847)

Services, Armed Services, or **Armed Forces, the** note caps; also cap *Service* when used adjectivally as in *a Service family* (where meaning might otherwise be ambiguous); but l/c *serviceman, servicewoman*

Session, Court of (supreme Scottish court; not Sessions). See **Courts** special section (page 1851)

setback noun; but note *to set back*

sett as with badgers

set-up try to find a synonym such as *arrangement, organisation, structure, system* etc

sewage (waste matter); note **sewerage** (disposal system)

sexism always be aware of sensitivities and be careful to avoid giving offence to women. It is often difficult to draw the line between sexism and political correctness

sex offenders register (l/c, no apostrophe)

Shadow cap in all cases, such as *Shadow Cabinet, Shadow Environment Secretary, Shadow Chief Whip, a Shadow spokesman*. See **Politics** special section (page 1853)

Shah, Eddy (not Eddie)

shake-out, shake-up but see **buyout**

Shakespearean (not -ian)

shall, should keep up the vigorous defence of these against the encroaching *will* and *would*. Good practice is that *shall* and *should* go with the first person singular and plural (I shall, we shall), *will* and *would* with the others (he will, they will). *Shall* with second and third persons singular, and plural has a slightly more emphatic meaning than *will*

shambles take care not to overwork this strong word, which means a *slaughterhouse* and, by extension, a *scene of carnage*

Shangri-La

Shankill Road, Belfast (not Shankhill); see **Ireland**

SHAPE Supreme Headquarters, Allied Powers, Europe; all caps

share a joke banned in captions on photographs showing people laughing

share shop(s) l/c, as jobcentre

Sharia (Islamic law); never use the tautology *Sharia law*

sheikh (not shaikh)

Shepherds Bush

Sherborne alumni of the Dorset public school are *Shirburnians*

sheriff (never sherrif)

Shetland, or **the Shetland Islands** (not the Shetlands). See **Orkney**

Shia (not Shiite or any such variation); write *Shia Muslims* (as opposed to *Sunni Muslims*)

ships italicise the HMS when first mention of warship, eg, *HMS Sheffield*. Ships should generally be treated as feminine; thus *she* and *her* rather than *it* and *its*. See **warships, boat, serve in**

ships' tonnage for passenger ships, give gross tonnage in *tonnes* (rather than tons); for cargo ships, deadweight tonnage. Check with *Lloyd's Register*

shock avoid in headlines unless in the electric context; in text, use the word as little as possible and never as a modifier, *shock revelations* etc (unless the context is ironic)

shock waves two words, but use sparingly as a metaphor as it is becoming a cliché

shopkeeper, shopowner, shopfront, shoplift etc but note *shop assistant* and *shop steward*

shortlist one word as noun or verb

short-lived, short-sighted

showbusiness one word; note *showbiz* is acceptable in quotes and informal context

showcase avoid use as a verb *to showcase something*. Use *display* or *exhibit* instead

showjumping should now be one word except when it appears in a title such as the *British Show Jumping Association*, or the name of an event using it as two words; similarly, *showjumper*

Shroud of Turin, or **the Turin Shroud** note caps; subsequently *the shroud* (l/c)

Siamese cats, twins for Siam use Thailand except in historical context; note the adjective Thai

Sichuan (not Szechuan, Setzuan, Szechwan or any other variant); see **Chinese names**

sickbed similarly *deathbed*

side-effects

siege (never seige)

Siena (not Sienna)

sign language (not deaf-and-dumb language)

Silicon Valley, silicon chips, but *silicone implants* (for breasts etc)

silk barristers *take silk* and *become silks* (all l/c); see **Courts** special section (page 1851)

Simon's Town, South Africa (not Simonstown); see **South Africa**

Sindy doll (not Cindy)

singeing (from *singe*), to distinguish it from *singing*

sink, sank the past participle is *sunk*, the adjective *sunken*

siphon (not syphon)

Sistine Chapel (not Cistine)

sitcom permissible abbreviation for *situation comedy*

sit-in

situation avoid wherever possible; such phrases as *crisis situation, ongoing situation* and *no-win situation* are banned unless a direct quote demands them

Six Nations Championship (rugby), no longer the Five Nations Championship (England, Wales, Scotland, Ireland, France and Italy)

sizeable

ski, skier, skied, skiing

skulduggery

Slavic must not be used; the noun and adjective are *Slav*

slay do not use this biblical word in headlines for *kill* or *murder*

slimline one word

Slovak (people and language); *Slovakian* is the general adjective. See **Croat**

smartcard one word; similarly *scratchcard, swipecard*

smelt (not smelled)

Smith, WH no points; see **companies**, **initials**

Smithsonian Institution, Washington (never Institute); can be shortened to *the Smithsonian*

snarl-up do not use as a synonym of *traffic jam, confusion* etc

sniffer dogs, tracker dogs avoid these clichés wherever possible; usually *dogs* is sufficient, but if the context is unclear, write *police dogs*

snowball, snowbound, snowdrift, snowfall, snowman etc

Soane's the museum in Lincoln's Inn Fields is *the Sir John Soane's Museum*

soap opera prefer to just *soap*, though the latter may have its place in less formal pieces

soccer an acceptable word. See **football** and **Sports** special section (page 1854)

social chapter l/c, as it is an informal title

Social Democratic and Labour Party (Northern Ireland); abbreviate to SDLP

socialism, socialist for when to cap, see **communism**

Solent, the note l/c *the*

Solicitor-General hyphen, as *Attorney-General*; similarly *Solicitor-General for Scotland*

Solicitors Complaints Bureau no apostrophes; has now been replaced by the *Office for the Supervision of Solicitors*

Solti, Sir Georg (not George)

Solzhenitsyn, Aleksandr no longer use Anglicised spelling; see **Russian names**

SOS

Sotheby's

soundbite

south, southeast, southern etc for when to cap, see **compass points**

South Africa never use the abbreviation SA, even in headlines.

The capital is Pretoria, which has the embassies (branches sometimes in Cape Town when Parliament is sitting) and government ministries. The legislature meets in Cape Town, and the Appeal Court sits in Bloemfontein. Pretoria can be referred to as the seat of government. Each of the new South African provinces has its own capital.

Note caps for *Northern Province* and the *Eastern/ Western/ Northern Cape, KwaZulu/ Natal* and *Simon's Town.*

Take care; several provinces have been renamed since the apartheid era, eg, *Mpumalanga* (formerly Eastern Transvaal). Use *southern Africa* when referring to Africa south of the Congo and Zambezi Rivers

South Asia encompasses Afghanistan, Bangladesh, Bhutan, India, the Maldives, Nepal, Pakistan and Sri Lanka

South-East Asia comprises the nine Asean states – Indonesia, Singapore, Malaysia, Thailand, the Philippines, Brunei, Vietnam, Burma and Laos – plus Cambodia. Avoid calling Burma *Myanmar* (except occasionally in direct quotes). See **Asean**

South of France

Southern Ocean caps

Sovereign, the cap; see **monarch**, **Royal Family**

Soviet Union never refer to *the Soviets* for the people or the Government, even in the historical context. The phrase is an Americanism often with disparaging overtones; a *soviet* is a *committee*, not a person. Refer instead to *the Soviet people* or *the Soviet Government* in historical context. See **Russia**, **USSR**

space avoid the phrase *outer space;* see **Earth**, **Moon**, **Sun**, **Universe**

Spanish regions use the Anglicised forms such as *Andalusia* (not Andalucía); *Catalonia* (not Cataluña), *Navarre* (not Navarra), *Majorca* (not Mallorca), *Minorca* (not Menorca) etc

spastic never use figuratively or as a term of abuse; see **medical terms**, **Scope**

Speaker always cap in parliamentary context

Special Branch caps, but no *the*; see **branch**

species both singular and plural in plant and animal sense. See **scientific names**

spelt (not spelled); note *misspelt*

Spiceworld: the Movie

spiders note they are not insects, although like insects they are arthropods

Spielberg, Steven

spilt (not spilled)

spin, spun (do not use *span* as past tense)

spin-doctor hyphen; see **Politics** special section (page 1853)

Spiritualism, Spiritualist

split infinitives do not use except in famous quotes such as "to boldly go where no man ..." or in limited emphatic constructions such as "I want to live – to really live"

spoilt (not spoiled); but note *despoiled*

spokesman, spokeswoman avoid where possible, eg, "the ministry said" rather than "a ministry spokesman said". *Official* is a useful alternative. Never use *spokesperson.* See **chairman**

sports clubs for when to use singular or plural, see **teams**

sportsmen, sportswomen omit the Mr, Mrs, Miss, Ms etc unless they are in news reports (eg, court hearings) in a specifically non-sporting context. See **appellations**

sprang (past tense of the verb *to spring*, eg, "she sprang into action"); note *sprung* (past participle, eg, "the wind has sprung up")

sprightly (not spritely)

spring-clean hyphen

squads in police context, usually l/c, but see **Flying Squad;** also note **Royal and Diplomatic Protection Squad**

Sri Lanka do not use Ceylon for the country except in historical context. But note *Ceylon tea* etc

SSSI site of special scientific interest, l/c

stadium plural *stadiums*; see **referendum**

stalemate try to avoid in the sense of *deadlock*. It should be confined to chess reports

Stalinist, Stalinism see **communism**

stanch verb, as in *to stanch a flow of blood*; note adjective *staunch* meaning *loyal* or *firm*

stand-off noun, hyphen; but note **standby**, noun, no hyphen

Stansted (airport; never Stanstead); see **airports**

stargazers, stargazing

Star Trek two words, italic

State cap; use sparingly in context of the State as a wide concept; but l/c in the *welfare state*, or when used adjectivally, eg, *state benefits*

stationary (not moving); but **stationery** (writing materials)

Stationery Office, The (TSO abbreviated); no longer HMSO

stations l/c in *Euston station, Waterloo station, Birmingham New Street station*, but where possible, simply *Euston, Waterloo* etc. See **airports**

statistic(s) do not use as a fancy word for *figure(s)* or *number(s)*. Note that the Central Statistical Office has been replaced by the *Office for National Statistics* (not of)

status quo roman; but note italics for the less familiar *status quo ante*

statute book

stay home avoid; use *stay at home* instead

Stealth bomber

steelworks, steelworker etc

stepfather, stepmother, stepson, stepdaughter but note *step-family, step-parents*

Stephenson, George (trains), **Robert** (bridges) note also **Stevenson**, Robert Louis, Adlai

still avoid writing the tautologous "still continues", "still remains" etc

Stock Exchange caps for *London Stock Exchange* and *New York Stock Exchange*, l/c for all others; note l/c for **stock market**

stony (not stoney)

storey (of a building); note plural *storeys*

storyteller, storytelling

straight be sparing in the use of this word to mean heterosexual. See **gay**

straight-faced but note **straightforward**

Strait of Hormuz, Strait of Gibraltar, Strait of Dover (not Straits)

straitjacket

strait-laced note also *in dire straits*

Stratford-upon-Avon except in the parliamentary constituency, which is *Stratford-on-Avon*

stratum plural *strata*

Streisand, Barbra

stress prefer *emphasise* as in "he emphasised the importance"

stricture means *adverse criticism* or *censure* (not constraint)

strippagram

stylebook one word, as with *guidebook, textbook* etc; but note *style guide*

sub- like *multi-*, the hyphen here is often a question of what looks better. A random sample gives us *subdivision, sublet, subnormal, subsection, substandard, subtext*; in contrast, *sub-committee, sub-editor, sub-postmaster, sub-post office* etc. See **hyphens, multi-**

Subbuteo

sub-continent, the (India, Pakistan and Bangladesh); note l/c

subjects, academic use l/c for most subjects studied at school or university, eg, "she was reading modern history with philosophy"; but where a proper name is involved, the cap is retained, eg, "he got a first in English literature and German after he dropped Latin in his second year"; and always cap Classics and PPE (short for philosophy, politics and economics). But note, eg, Professor of History when the phrase accompanies a name; see **Professor, university posts**

sub-let (as in property)

sub-machinegun see **machinegun**

submarine always a *boat*, not a ship. See **boat, ships, serve in**

subplot, subtext, subtitle

subpoena, subpoenas, subpoenaing, subpoenaed

sub-Saharan Africa

subsequently prefer *afterwards* or *later*, and never say *subsequent to* when the meaning is *after*

subtropical one word; see **Tropics**

such as do not confuse with *like;* see **like**

Sudan (not the Sudan, except occasionally in historical context)

suing (from *to sue;* not sueing)

summon the verb is *to summon*, the noun *a summons* (plural *summonses*). A person is *summoned* to appear before a tribunal etc; but a person in receipt of a specific summons can be said to have been *summonsed*. But see **Woolf reforms** and **Courts** special section (page 1851)

Sun see **Earth, Moon** and **Universe**

sunbathing, sunburn, sunglasses, suntan etc but note *suncare* (products etc)

superhighway (as in information superhighway); similarly *superconductor*

superlatives beware of calling any person, event or thing *the first, the biggest, the best* etc without firm evidence that this is correct. Also, never say *first-ever, best-ever* etc; see **ever, first, universal claims**

supersede (never supercede)

supersonic (of speeds); for waves use *ultrasonic*

supervisor (not superviser)

supine (lying face-up); see **prone**

Supreme Court (US)

Surinam (not Suriname)

surprising (not suprising)

Sussex always specify whether a place is in East Sussex or West Sussex, two separate counties

swap (not swop). Do not use unless a mutual exchange is involved and never for organ transplants

swaths (as in *cutting swaths through*; not *swathes)*; note **swathes** to be used only as bandages

swatting (flies), **swotting** (study)

swearword

swingeing (as in cuts), to distinguish it from *swinging*

Swinging London, Swinging Sixties caps

swipecard similarly *scratchcard, smartcard*

Symphony Hall, Birmingham (does not take *the*). See **Arts** special section (page 1849)

synod l/c on its own, but note caps for *General Synod*. See **Churches** special section (page 1850)

synthesizer (musical); but note **synthesise** (chemical etc)

Tt

-t in nearly all cases, where there is a choice of past tense between a final *-t* or *-ed*, use *-t*, as in *burnt, spelt* etc. But never *earnt*

tad heavily overworked as synonym of *a little* or *a bit*; avoid

tailback

Tajikistan

takeaway (meals)

take-off (aircraft)

takeover noun; but note verb *to take over*

takeover code but note caps for *Takeover Panel*

Taleban (Afghan Islamic rebel group) takes a singular verb; no need to say *the* Taleban unless appropriate; note that the singular is *a Taleb*, but prefer *a member of Taleban*

talk show similarly *chat show, game show, quiz show* etc

Tallinn (capital of Estonia)

Tangier no final *s*

Tannoy trade name, so cap; use *loudspeaker* as alternative

Taoiseach always cap; see **Ireland**

taramasalata (not taramo-); see **hoummos**

targeted

Tarmac trade name, but cap *T* is used only for the civil engineering company. Common usage allows the road surface or airport runway to be written as *tarmac*; *tarmacadam* is not a trade name

Tartars preferred to Tatars

task force (as in Falklands)

tattoos, tattooed, tattooing

taxman one word as colloquialism for *Inland Revenue*; similarly taxpayer

Tchaikovsky

teams normally plural, eg, "Manchester United were disappointing when they lost to Barcelona". But sports clubs usually take the singular, especially in news stories, eg, "Manchester City Football Club was fined heavily for crowd disturbances". There is some room for variation in this format, but whatever is decided, never mix singular and plural in the same story. Note hyphen in *team-mates*. See **Sports** special section (page 1854)

teargas

Technicolor trade name. It must not be used except in that company's context. Use *multicoloured* as the general alternative

Tecs short for training and enterprise councils; note initial cap only; see **Lecs**

Teesside no hyphen, double *s* in middle; but note *Deeside* in both Scotland and Wales

teetotal

Tehran (not Teheran)

telephone numbers with three groups of figures, hyphenate only the first two, eg, 0181-234 8464. With revised codes (introduced in June 1999, but not fully operational until April 2000) write, eg, 020-7782 5000, not 0207-782 5000.

Teletext replaced Oracle (at the end of 1992) as the text service for ITV and Channel 4; do not use Oracle any more

television use TV in headlines, but try to avoid in the text. ITV is an acceptable alternative for *independent television*. ITN (Independent Television News) is acceptable in its abbreviated form (in the same way as BBC). Note l/c in non-specific use, eg, *BBC Television, BBC1, BBC2* etc; but *Argentine television, Norwegian television* etc. See **BBC, ITV, Channel 4, Radio 1**

television and radio programmes italicise, except for first mention in reviews, when they go in bold. See **Arts** special section (page 1849)

temperatures the style is *16C (61F)*. See **celsius**

ten-minute rule (Bill) etc; see **Politics** special section (page 1853)

Tennessee

tenpin bowling

Teresa see **Mother**

Terminal 1 (Heathrow; also Terminal 2, 3, 4, 5 etc). See **airports, Heathrow**

Terre'Blanche, Eugene

Terrence Higgins Trust (not Terence)

Territorial Army, or **the Territorials** note cap *T*

terrorist take care with this word and the associated *terrorism; guerrilla* is a less loaded word in the context of violent political struggle. Never use as a synonym of any dissident group that uses violence, eg, *hunt saboteurs*, and always try to specify groups as *paramilitaries, gangster organisations* etc. Remember, one man's terrorist is another man's freedom fighter

Tessa(s) tax-exempt special savings account

Test match should apply only to *cricket* (not rugby); for other sports, use the term *international* (match). See **Sports** special section (page 1854)

textbook one word, similarly *guidebook, stylebook, rulebook* etc

TGV (*train à grande vitesse* – not *de*; French high-speed train)

thalidomide l/c

Thames Barrier, Thames Estuary caps; see **rivers**

Thamesmead, near Erith note *Thamesdown* (Wiltshire administrative district), but *Thames-side*

that do not be shy of this word after *said, denied, claimed* etc; eg, "he denied that the evidence was confusing" is more elegant than "he denied the evidence was confusing". *That* is almost always better than *which* in a defining clause, eg, "the train that I take stops at Slough". As a general rule, use *which* for descriptive clauses and place it between commas, eg, "the night train, which used to carry newspapers, stops at Crewe". See **ensure**

Thatcher at first mention Baroness Thatcher, thereafter Lady Thatcher. In historical context, preferable to say Mrs Thatcher or Margaret Thatcher, eg, "Mrs Thatcher took quick action in sending the task force to the Falklands". It would be wrong to say that her party forced Lady Thatcher from office in 1990. Note **Sir Denis Thatcher** (not Dennis)

theatre always attach *Theatre* (cap) to names at first mention, eg, *the Criterion Theatre* (thereafter *the Criterion* or simply *the theatre*). Some of the main London exceptions are *the Old Vic, Young Vic, Palladium, Coliseum, Apollo Victoria, Donmar Warehouse, Hackney Empire*; and outside London, many such as the *Birmingham Hippodrome, Oxford Playhouse, West Yorkshire Playhouse* etc. See **Arts** special section (page 1849)

theatregoer

the then avoid expressions such as "the then Prime Minister" or (worse) "the then Mr Callaghan"; write "then Prime Minister", "who was Prime Minister at the time" or "Lord Callaghan of Cardiff (then Mr Callaghan)"

The Times almost always use italics for the name of the newspaper, except in headlines. But Times Newspapers Ltd (roman), publisher of *The Times* and *The Sunday Times*, is the operating company of Times Newspapers Holdings.

Also (especially in features headlines, standfirsts etc) The Times Gardener etc is an acceptable style to avoid a mass of italics and apostrophes.

In text, in the difficult area of correspondents' and executive titles, it is permissible to say "the *Times* political correspondent", "the *Times* wine correspondent" etc, although "political editor of *The Times*", "wine correspondent of *The Times*" etc are preferable.

Always say "Editor of *The Times*", "deputy editor of *The Times*" etc.

It is permissible to say "a *Times* reader", "*Times* readers", but prefer "readers of *The Times*". Similarly, adjectival uses such as "a *Times* article", "a *Times* offer" are acceptable.

Also note Times Law Report (without *The*), but *The Times* Diary, *The Times* Crossword etc. Again, some flexibility – to avoid a proliferation of italics – can be used in puff material etc.

For sections of the paper, avoid italics: eg, *The Times* Magazine, Weekend, Interface.

Keep phrases such as "told *The Times*" to a minimum: *said* is usually preferable.

Note supplements: *The Times Educational Supplement, The Times Higher Education Supplement, The Times Literary Supplement,* and *Nursery World.*

See **correspondents**, **editor**, **exclusive**, **News International**

thermonuclear

Thermos trade name, so always cap

they should always agree with the subject. Avoid sentences such as "If someone loves animals, they should protect them". Say instead "If people love animals, they should protect them"

think-tanks take care in describing their ideological persuasions; we should call the Social Market Foundation (SMF), Demos and Politeia *independent think-tanks*; the Centre for Policy Studies (CPS) and the Institute of Economic Affairs (IEA) *free-market* or *right-wing think-tanks*; and the Institute for Public Policy Research (IPPR) a *left-wing think-tank*

Third Way (caps); new Labour's political stratagem

Third World (caps)

This Morning, the Richard (Madeley) and Judy (Finnegan) show (not *This Morning with Richard and Judy*)

threshold

throne cap sparingly, only in terms of the institution, eg, "he deferred to the wisdom of the Throne"; in other contexts, as with the chair itself, use l/c, eg, "The Queen came to the throne in 1952"

thunderbolts are mythological and do not exist; *lightning bolts* and *thunderclaps* do exist and can also be used metaphorically

thus far avoid; prefer *so far*

Tiananmen Square, Beijing

"tiger" economies (of South-East Asia and the Pacific); use quotes where possible for first mention, subsequently without quotes, and always l/c

time bomb but note *timescale, timeshare*

times never write 6pm last night, 9am tomorrow morning; instead write *6 o'clock last night* or (if the context allows) *6pm,* or *9am tomorrow*

Tinseltown (as in Hollywood); one word

titles the most common solecism is to write Lady Helen Brown etc when we should say simply *Lady Brown.* As a quick rule of thumb, no wife of a baronet or knight takes her Christian name in her title unless she is the daughter of a duke, marquess or earl.

Some titles include a place name, eg, Lord Callaghan of Cardiff, Lord Archer of Weston-super-Mare, while others do not. Follow *Who's Who,* where those whose place name must be included appear in bold caps.

Always check with *Debrett* or *Who's Who* if in doubt. See **Titles** special section (page 1855)

together with avoid; prefer simply *with;* also beware such tautology as *blend together, meet together, link together* etc

Tolkien, J.R.R. (not Tolkein)

tomatoes plural; similarly *potatoes*

tons, tonnes prefer to use *tonnes* in most contexts, though in historical passages *tons* would be more appropriate

Tontons Macoute (Haiti); plural, no final *s*

Top Salaries Review Body now called the *Senior Salaries Review Body*

Top Ten, Top 20, Top 40 etc (in musical or other lists)

tornado (storm); plural *tornados;* also *Tornado, Tornados* (aircraft)

torpedo but note plural *torpedoes*

Torvill (Jayne) **and Dean** (Christopher)

Tory, Tories acceptable alternative for *Conservative(s).* Note *Tory party* (l/c *p*) is permissible. See **Conservative**, **committee** (for 1922 Committee), **select committees**, and **Politics** special section (page 1853)

totalisator, tote take l/c, no quotes; note *the Tote* refers to the organisation

touchpaper

towards (not toward)

townhouse (one word)

tracker dogs, sniffer dogs avoid these clichés wherever possible; usually *dogs* is sufficient, but if the context is unclear, say *police dogs*

tracksuit one word

Trade Descriptions Act

trade-in noun or adjective; but note verb *to trade in*

trademark (one word)

trade names many names of products in common use are proprietary and must be given a capital letter (at risk of legal action if we fail to do so); eg, *Biro, CinemaScope, Dictaphone, Hoover, Jeep, Kodak, Land Rover, Lycra, Perspex, Polaroid, Rollerblade, Tannoy, Technicolor, Thermos, Walkman, Xerox, Yale lock.* Be especially careful about drugs: try to use non-proprietary words such as *aspirin, sleeping pills* etc

trade unions plural (not trades unions); but note *Trades Union Congress.* See **TUC**

trainspotter, trainspotting no hyphens

tranquilliser, tranquillity

transatlantic, transcontinental but note *cross-Channel*

transistor do not use on its own in sense of *transistor radio*

transpire (*to come to light* or *to leak out*). Do not use as an alternative of *to happen* or *occur*

transsexual no hyphen; but note *trans-ship*

Transvaal but note *a Transvaler,* see **South Africa**

trauma, traumatic avoid in the clichéd sense of *deeply upsetting, distressing* etc; it should be confined to its medical meaning of severe shock after an accident or stressful event

travellers, New Age travellers see **Gypsy**, **hippy**

traveller's cheques

Travellers Club no apostrophe; see **London clubs**

Triads cap in Chinese gangster context

Tricolour cap for the French flag, l/c in more general context

trillion American for *a thousand billion* (or *a million million, 1,000,000,000,000*), and should be explained as such in stories about overseas budgets, for example. Try to avoid in stories about Britain

Trinity College Dublin no comma

triple crown (rugby). See **Sports** special section (page 1854)

tripos l/c general context, but note *the History Tripos* etc

trolleys plural of trolley (not -ies)

Trooping the Colour (not *of* the Colour); note also *beating retreat*

Tropics, the cap; note also *the Tropic of Capricorn/ Cancer,* but l/c *tropical, subtropical*

Troubles, the see **Ireland**

troubleshooter one word; similarly *troublespot*

truck permissible in most contexts; see **lorry**

Truman, Harry S. (former US President), but **Fred Trueman**, cricketer

try to the verb *try* must be followed by *to* before the next verb, never by *and*, eg, "I will try to cross the road", not "I will try and cross the road"

TSA The Securities Association

Tsar (not czar); also *Tsarevich, Tsaritsa* (not czarina); caps with the name, l/c in general sense. But note the exception *drugs czar*

TSB formerly the Trustee Savings Bank, now part of Lloyds TSB

T-shirt

Tube cap; acceptable in context on its own for *London Tube*, or *London Underground*. Also cap the various lines such as *Central Line, Metropolitan Line, Victoria Line* etc

tuberculosis the adjective is *tuberculous* (not tubercular)

TUC Trades Union Congress. Note at first mention *General Council of the TUC*, thereafter *general council*. Cap also *General Secretary of the TUC* (as leader of the national body), but note l/c *general secretaries* of individual unions

tug-of-war

tunku (Malaysian prince); cap before name, otherwise l/c

turbo-jet, turbo-prop see **aircraft**

Turin Shroud subsequently *the shroud*

Turkey cap parties, as in *Motherland Party, Welfare Party, True Path Party* etc

turn down prefer *reject* or *refuse* (except of beds)

turnlines in bold, set right on the front page (and on inside pages where the story begins and spills) – eg, **Continued on page 2, col 7** – and set left on inside pages, eg, **Continued from page 1**

turn-off, turn-on nouns, but note no hyphens in *turnout, turnaround, turnabout*

Tussaud's, Madame but note *the Tussauds Group* (no apostrophe), which also includes *the London Planetarium, Warwick Castle, Alton Towers* and *Chessington World of Adventures.*

Tutankhamun never permit a break as Tutan-khamun; if the name has to be broken on a turn, it may be hyphenated as *Tut-ankhamun* or *Tutankh-amun*

Tutsis see **Hutus**

TV-am no longer exists

Twentieth Century Fox

twentysomething, thirtysomething, fortysomething etc if this modern cliché must be used

Twin Towers (of Wembley) (caps)

twofold, threefold, fourfold, tenfold etc

two minutes' silence, the see **Armistice, Remembrance**

two thirds, three quarters etc but hyphenate adjectival use, eg, *a two-thirds share*. Such expressions usually take the plural verb, eg, "three quarters of the children prefer horror films"; the same applies even in "a third of the children prefer blancmange". But note "two thirds of the bus was empty"

Tyne and Wear (not &)

typify, typified (not typefy)

Tyrol (no longer Tirol)

Uu

U no full point after Burmese prefix, eg, U Nu

Ucas Universities and Colleges Admissions Service (not UCAS)

Uefa, Uefa Cup (not UEFA); see **Cup**, **Sports** special section (page 1854)

UK acceptable abbreviation for *United Kingdom* in both text and headlines. But be careful that it is strictly applicable; see **Britain**

Ukraine (not *the* Ukraine)

Ulster permissible, especially in headlines, but use *Northern Ireland* or *the Province* when possible; see **Ireland**

ultimate use sparingly. *Ultimate limit* means *limit*

ultimatums (not ultimata); see **referendum**

ultraviolet

unchristian l/c; see **Christian**

uncoordinated but note *co-ordinate*; see **hyphens**

under-age hyphenated; similarly *over-age*

underestimate

Underground, London see **Tube**

underreact

undervalue

underwater one word as adjective, eg, *underwater exploration*; but two words as adverb, eg, the couple were married *under water*

under way always two words

Unesco United Nations Educational, Scientific, and Cultural Organisation. See **United Nations**

UNHCR United Nations High Commissioner for Refugees. See **United Nations** (paragraph d)

Unionist cap in Ulster political context; see **Ireland**

Union Jack except in most naval and some ceremonial contexts, when **Union Flag** is correct; note that in the Royal Navy, *Union Jack* only when flown at the jackstaff

unique (only one, having no like or equal); do not use except in this specific sense. Phrases such as *very unique, even more unique* are nonsense and are banned

unitary authorities since the abolition of Avon, Humberside, Cleveland, and now Hereford and Worcester, plus wholesale reorganisation of Welsh and Scottish local government, take care when locating towns in these areas.

Former county of Avon: should now be described as in either Gloucestershire or Somerset.

Former Hereford and Worcester County Council: from April 1998, replaced by a new Worcestershire County Council and a new unitary authority for Herefordshire.

Former Berkshire County Council: replaced by six unitary authorities (Bracknell Forest, Newbury, Reading, Slough, Windsor and Maidenhead, and Wokingham).

Former Humberside: should be located as either East Riding (north of the Humber) or Lincolnshire (south of the river).

Former Cleveland, reorganised Yorkshire: cap the West and South in West Yorkshire and South Yorkshire, even though they are not new unitary authorities (as North Yorkshire is). The reason is that they are still regarded by people living there as cohesive regions, similar to the West Midlands and Greater Manchester, two other metropolitan counties that no longer exist per se. Moreover, statutory bodies such as *West Yorkshire Police* and *West Yorkshire Passenger Transport Authority* still exist; so the best rule-of-thumb will be to use the cap in future in all cases.

Wales: note that Clwyd, Dyfed and Gwent no longer exist as authorities, so unless the new county has a traditional and generally familiar name (eg, Pembrokeshire, Carmarthenshire, Powys, Denbighshire etc), it will often be simpler to locate smaller towns and villages just as in North Wales, Mid Wales, West Wales, South Wales. Note that Gwynedd does still exist as a unitary authority (though smaller than when it was a county). If in doubt, use one of the North/Mid/West/South designations.

Scotland: regions such as Central, Grampian and Strathclyde should now be referred to only in their historical context or if they persist in titles such as *Strathclyde Police* or *University of Strathclyde*. Permissible too to refer informally to the *Central belt* (between Edinburgh and Glasgow), despite the scrapping of Central region

United Nations, or **UN, the** spell out at first mention where possible, though this can no longer be a hard and fast rule. Other points:

a *Secretary-General of the UN*; now Kofi Annan

b *UN Security Council, UN General Assembly* at first mention, and thereafter keep the caps, as in *the Security Council, the General Assembly*

c UN derivatives such as *Unesco, Unifil, Unprofor* etc are written thus where the word can be voiced. See **initials**

d *The UN High Commissioner for Refugees* (never Commission) is the organisation, as well as a person. Abbreviate to UNHCR after first mention

United Reformed Church (not Reform); see **Churches** special section (page 1850)

United States (of America); always followed by a singular verb. Common usage allows abbreviation to US in text as well as headlines, but do not ignore the word *America*. See **America(n)**, **New York**, **Washington**

universal claims always beware of claiming that something is the first or last of its kind, or that someone is the first person to ... or the last surviving member of ... or the oldest inhabitant etc. See **ever**, **first**, **superlatives**

Universe cap in planetary context, as *Sun, Earth, Moon* etc, but l/c in phrases such as "she became the centre of his universe"

universities always cap as in *Birmingham University* (or the *University of Birmingham*), *Sussex University, the University of East Anglia* etc; thereafter l/c *the university*. If in doubt about the proper title, consult *The Times Good University Guide*. See **Cambridge University**, **Oxford University**, **Vice-Chancellor**

University College London no comma

university posts at first mention, cap *Vice-Chancellor, Chancellor, Pro-Vice-Chancellor, Pro-Chancellor, Dean, Master, Professor, Fellow* etc; at subsequent mentions l/c; eg, "Dr Mark Blodkin, Professor of Modern History at Kent University, said ..." then later, "the professor said ..."

unlikeable, unloveable

unmistakable (not with the middle *e*)

unparalleled

unshakeable

Untouchables (in Indian caste system); cap

unveil take care with this word, which means to remove a covering from something, or (by extension) to disclose. It should not be used in phrases such as unveiling a ship, or unveiling a flag

up avoid unnecessary use after verbs, as in meet up, rest up, end up. See **down**

upbeat, upfront, upgrade

upmarket similarly *downmarket*

upon take care with use of *up, upon, up on,* and *on*, eg, "The cat jumped *on* the floor, *upon* the mouse, *up on* the table, then *up* the tree"

Upper House, Lower House see **Politics** special section (page 1853)

Uruguay Round (world trade deal); note caps. See **Gatt**, **World Trade Organisation**

US see **America(n)**, **United States**

USSR avoid wherever possible; write *Soviet Union* instead (and now only in historical context). See **Russia**

utilise almost always prefer *use*

Utopia, Utopian cap

U-turn overworked phrase, especially in the political context. Be sparing in its use, particularly when only a minor change of policy direction is involved

Vv

vacuum in common use as a verb, but avoid *Hoover*, a trade name. See **Hoover**, **trade names**

vagaries means *aimless wanderings* or *eccentric ideas*, not *vicissitudes* or *changes* (as in weather)

Valentine's Day (normally omit St); keep cap for *Valentine card* etc

Valium proprietary term, so cap

Valletta (Malta)

valley cap in full name, such as *the Thames Valley, the Wye Valley* etc. Note also the *Welsh Valleys*

Van cap in Dutch names when surname alone is given, eg, Van Gogh, but l/c when used in full, eg, Vincent van Gogh. Note Ludwig *van* Beethoven (not von), although the composer was German. See **von**

Van Dyck, Sir Anthony but note l/c *vandyke brown, vandyke beard* etc

various do not use as a pronoun as in "various of the countries protested"; write "several/ many of the countries ..."

Varsity match acceptable colloquialism for the Oxford-Cambridge rugby match

VAT value-added tax; no longer need to spell out fully

V-chip (electronic scramblers for TV)

VE-Day see **D-Day**, **VJ-Day**

Velázquez, Diego Rodríguez de Silva y Velázquez (17th-century Spanish artist; not Velasquez); normally last name on its own will suffice

Velcro (cap, proprietary)

veld (not veldt)

ventricles (anatomical; not ventricals)

veranda no final *h*

verbal (pertaining to words); do not confuse with *oral* (pertaining to the mouth). Sadly, corrupted phrases such as *verbal abuse* and *verbal warning* have permeated sports journalism to the point of our having to accept them occasionally, but always try to find an alternative. See **oral**

verbosity watch out for, and eliminate, wordy phrases such as "on the part of" (use *by*), "a large number of" (*many*), "numerous occasions" (*often*), "this day and age" (does not even demand an alternative)

verdict do not use for civil hearings – verdicts come at the end of criminal trials. See **employment tribunals**

verger, virger use the latter in context of St Paul's and Winchester Cathedrals

vermilion (not vermillion)

versus abbreviation is *v* (l/c, no point)

very one of the most overworked words in English. Always try to omit

vetoes plural

viable (capable of independent existence); do not use as a synonym of *feasible* or *practicable*

vicar take care not to use as a generic word for *priest, parson* or *clergyman. Vicar* means specifically the incumbent of a parish (unless a rector); if in doubt, *clergyman* is usually safer. See **Churches** special section (page 1850)

vice always hyphenate in its deputy context, eg, *vice-chairman, vice-president* etc but not in its depravity context, eg, *vice squad.* Do not confine the meaning of vice to sex: it is the opposite of virtue and has a correspondingly wide range of meaning

Vice-Chancellor (of a university); cap at first mention, then l/c. See **university posts**, **job titles**

vice versa roman, no hyphen

Victoria and Albert (Museum); use the ampersand only in the abbreviation *V&A*

videotape one word; but note *video cassette, video recorder/recording. Video* (for film recording) is now common usage and permissible

Vietcong (not Viet Cong)

Virgil (not Vergil)

Virtuality trade name, so cap; do not use as a synonym of virtual reality

vis-à-vis note roman, hyphens and accent

viscountcy (describes the rank); see **Titles** special section (page 1855)

vitamin A, B, C etc note l/c *v*

viz prefer *namely, that is,* or even *ie*

VJ-Day see **D-Day**, **VE-Day**

vocal cords (not chords)

voiceover no hyphen

volcanoes plural of volcano

volte-face roman, hyphenated

von (German); usually l/c in the middle of a name, and capped only at the beginning of a sentence. See **Van**

VP never use as abbreviation of *vice-president*

Ww

wagon

Wales cap *North Wales, South Wales, Mid Wales, West Wales.* For new counties under the local government reorganisation of 1996, see **unitary authorities**

Walkman trade name, so cap; in general sense, use *personal stereo*

walkout

Wall's (ice-cream etc)

Wan Azizah, wife of Anwar Ibrahim, Malaysian politician. At subsequent mentions, *Dr Azizah* (do not use the Ismail part of her name)

war crimes tribunal cap only when using the full title, *the International War Crimes Tribunal for the Former Yugoslavia.* It sits at The Hague and has a President and a Chief Prosecutor

war game(s) two words

warfarin not a trade name, so l/c

warn transitive verb that requires a direct personal object: ie, a person has to warn somebody about something. Do not write "The Chancellor warned that taxes would rise"; but "The Chancellor *gave warning that/issued a warning that* ...", or alternatively, "The Chancellor *warned MPs that* ...". However, we can afford some flexibility in headlines, eg, *Teachers warn of school closures* would be acceptable

wars cap the *First World War, Second World War, Cold War, Korean War, Vietnam War, Gulf War* etc; but prefer the *Falklands conflict* because war was never formally declared; if the phrase has to be used, write *Falklands war* (l/c)

warships take care with the following distinction: to serve *in* a warship, but *on* a merchant ship; a naval officer is *appointed* to serve *in HMS Sheffield,* not *posted* to serve. See **Armed Forces** special section (page 1847)

wartime

Washington not usually necessary to add DC (as in Washington DC), but occasionally useful to distinguish it from Washington State (caps). That and New York State are the only two states needing caps to avoid confusion. See **New York**

washout (one word)

waste usually better to write *waste* than *wastage,* which means process of loss, its amount or rate

wastepaper bin/basket

watchdog

watercolour, watercolourist but note *Royal Society of Painters in Water Colours*

Waterstone's (booksellers); note apostrophe

wear write *menswear, women's wear, children's wear, sportswear.* See **clothing**

weather stories (about floods, hurricanes, snow, record sunshine etc in the UK) always take a cross-reference to the back page weather forecast. Style is bold, set right, eg, **Forecast, page 24**

website, but cap **the Web:** see **World Wide Web**

week, weekend the week ends on Saturday night. Common sense will dictate whether to say *last week, this week, next week* etc. Beware of references to *at the weekend* in Monday papers: always make clear whether you mean the weekend just past or next Saturday and Sunday

weights and measures abbreviations context will determine when to abbreviate inches, stone, pounds, ounces etc. "He was 6ft 7in" (not ins, and no space between number and abbreviation); but "she stood two feet from the kerb". Similarly, "she weighed 8st 12lb" (not lbs); but "he was several pounds overweight". See **scientific measures**

weights and measures conversion no longer convert metric measures into their imperial counterpart. See **scientific measures, celsius**

Welch, Welsh note *The Royal Welch Fusiliers,* but *Welsh Guards* (part of The Guards Division). See **Armed Forces** special section (page1847)

welfare state l/c; but note the *Welfare to Work* programme (cap W twice, no hyphens). See **State**

wellbeing

wellington boots note l/c

wellwisher do not hyphenate

Welsh Assembly now capped; and note *First Secretary* (not First Minister) of the Assembly.

Welsh, Irvine (the playwright)

Welsh Valleys for the (former) mining valleys of South Wales

west, western etc for when to cap in geographical context, see **compass points**

West, the (in global political sense); similarly *Western leaders, Western Europe* etc

western (as in cowboy films); l/c

whereabouts singular, eg, "his whereabouts is not known". Prefer "nobody knows where he is"

whether rarely needs *or not* to follow it

which see **that**

while (not whilst)

whingeing with middle *e*

whips cap *Chief Whip, Whips' Office,* but l/c the unspecific, eg, **a government whip**. See **Politics** special section (page 1853)

whisky (from Scotland); *Scotch* is acceptable as alternative; but **whiskey** (from Ireland and America). See **Scotch**

whistle-blower

whistle-stop (tour etc)

Whitbread Round the World Race note caps, no hyphens

White Cliffs of Dover caps

white-collar workers

White Paper note caps, as with *Green Paper,* but cap only those issued by the Government. A "white paper" from the Opposition should be styled in quotes and l/c at first mention, thereafter just l/c. See **Green Paper, Politics** special section (page 1853)

whiz-kid note only one *z,* but use this colloquialism sparingly

WHO World Health Organisation; spell out at first mention, then *the WHO*

who, whom which of these to use is determined solely by its function in the relative clause. Remember that *whom* has to be the object of the verb in the relative clause. Thus, "she is the woman whom the police wish to interview" (ie, the police wish to interview *her,* not *she*); the other most common use of *whom* is after a preposition such as *by, with* or *from,* eg, "the person from whom he bought a ticket".

Beware of traps, however: "Who do you think did it?" is correct (not *whom,* because *who* is the subject of "did it", not the object of "do you think"); and "Give it to whoever wants it" is correct (not *whomever*) because *whoever* is the subject of the verb *wants.*

Beware too of constructions such as "he squirted ammonia at a van driver who [correct] he believed had cut him up". This is correct because "he believed" is simply an interjection; "who" is not the object of "he believed" but the subject of the subordinate clause, "who ... had cut him up"

whodunnit (not whodunit)

why usually superfluous after *reason,* eg, "the reason he did it was ...", not "the reason why he did it was ..."

wide no hyphen in compounds such as *countrywide, nationwide, worldwide*

wideawake always one word

widow (woman); note *widower* (man); never say "widow of the late John Jones"; she is the "widow of John Jones"

wildfowl, wildlife

Wild West

Wimbledon caps for the *Centre Court, No 1 Court, No 14 Court* etc. See **Sports** special section (page 1854)

Winchester College its pupils are *Wykehamists*

wind with strong winds, give a description as well as force number (in numerals), eg, *storm force 10* (add "on the Beaufort scale" where appropriate. The scale grades wind speeds from 0 to 12; Americans use the scale to 17). Never say "gale-force winds" when *gales* is meant

wines l/c in most cases, for both the type and the grape, except where it would look out of place, eg, *bordeaux, burgundy, champagne, claret, moselle, alsace, rioja*, but a *Côtes du Rhône*, a *Hunter Valley chardonnay.* Cap when referring specifically to the wine-growing region, eg, "I prefer a good burgundy to an alsace, but I think the best wines still come from Bordeaux"; "he preferred to buy his champagne only in Champagne"

wine bar two words

Winslet, Kate

Wirral (not Wirrall); permissible to refer to *The Wirral* (cap *T*), but note *the Wirral peninsula*

wistaria (not wisteria)

witch-hunt but note *witchcraft*

withhold (not withold)

witnesses in British courts witnesses go into the witness box and give evidence; they do not take the stand and testify. In the general sense, prefer *witness* to *eyewitness* wherever possible. See **eyewitness**

woebegone, woeful

Wolf Cubs now just Cubs; see **Boy Scouts**

women doctors, women teachers etc adopt the plural through common usage. See **feminine designations, lady**

Woolf reforms several important changes have been made in civil litigation rules and terminology since April 1999. Three of the commonest are: plaintiffs are now *claimants*; a writ is now a *claim form*; and *notices of application* will be served in the place of summonses. For fuller list, see **Courts** special section (page 1851)

Woolworths no apostrophe either in formal name for business contexts or colloquial use for the store and products

word-processor, word-processing note hyphens

workers *farmworkers, metalworkers, roadworkers* one word; note two for *car workers, oil workers, office workers* etc

workforce, workshop, work-to-rule

world avoid, wherever possible, phrases such as *the fashion world, the theatre world, the cricket world* etc

World Heritage Site (caps)

World Trade Organisation (successor body to Gatt); abbreviate to WTO; see **Gatt**, **Uruguay Round**

World Wide Fund for Nature (not Worldwide; nor World Wildlife Fund, its old name); abbreviate to WWF; note the general adjective *worldwide*

World Wide Web (Internet); caps and three words; and *the Web* for short. But keep *website* l/c. See **Internet**

Worrall Thompson, Antony (TV cook)

worthwhile one word; often used where simply *worth* would be better, eg, "the programme was worth recording"

wrack (seaweed or wreckage); do not confuse with *racked by doubts* etc. See **racked**

wreaked (havoc, heavy damage, vengeance etc; not wrought)

write-off noun, similarly the noun *write-up*, but note *a write-down* (in business context)

writes with written-in bylines, prefer the construction "Ann Bloggs writes" to "writes Ann Bloggs". Use the singular with, eg, (Our Foreign Staff writes). Normal style is to use brackets on news and sports pages, italics on features

wrongdoer, wrongdoing but note *wrong-footed, wrong-headed*

WWF abbreviation of the World Wide Fund for Nature and for legal reasons must not be used for the World Wrestling Federation (write *the federation* if a shorter form for the wrestling group is needed). See **World Wide Fund for Nature**

Wyndham's Theatre (London); note the apostrophe

Xx Yy Zz

xenophobe, xenophobia

Xerox trade name, so cap

Xhosa (Bantu tribe; not Khosa); note plural Xhosas

Xmas must not be used in *The Times* (unless part of special title or in a direct quote etc)

X-ray now an acceptable abbreviation of *X-ray examination*. Note also the verb *to X-ray someone*. But do not shorten when you mean *an X-ray photograph*

Yardies (West Indian criminal gangs)

Yarmouth (Isle of Wight); note *Great Yarmouth* on the Norfolk coast

Yellow Pages italics for the book, but roman for the organisation

Yemen (not *the* Yemen)

"yes" vote, "no" vote

yeti (abominable snowman); note l/c

YMCA, YWCA

yoghurt

yoke (oxen); do not confuse with **yolk** (egg)

Yorkshire since the reorganisation of 1996, see **unitary authorities** for how to locate places in the county. Specify the location for smaller towns and villages, eg, Thirsk, North Yorkshire, but not Bradford or Leeds. Note *the Yorkshire Dales*, or simply *the Dales*, and *the North York Moors* (not North Yorkshire Moors)

young offender institution l/c for general use, but cap for specific, eg, *Feltham Young Offender Institution*

Young Turks caps

youth courts not juvenile courts, which no longer exist. See **Courts** special section (page 1851)

yuan the Chinese currency (rather than *the renminbi*)

Yugoslav (not Yugoslavian); adjective from Yugoslavia

yuletide (l/c)

yuppie noun or adjective

Yves Saint Laurent (not St)

Zaire after the overthrow of President Mobutu in May 1997, call the country, at first mention, the Democratic Republic of Congo (formerly Zaire), and thereafter simply Congo. The former French Congo should be called Congo-Brazzaville

Zambezi (not Zambesi)

-ze in almost all cases use the *-ise* ending rather than *-ize*. Two of the main exceptions are *capsize* and *synthesizer*

Zeitgeist (the spirit of the times); note cap and italics

zeppelin (airship); note l/c

Zeta-Jones, Catherine (hyphen)

ziggurat

zigzag, zigzagging

Zimmer frame trademark, so cap

zodiac, zodiacal (as in signs of the zodiac); note l/c

zoo cap as in *London Zoo, Dudley Zoo*; thereafter *the zoo*

SPECIAL SECTIONS

THE ARMED FORCES

ROYAL NAVY

At first mention *the Royal Navy* (caps), thereafter *the Navy* (retain the cap); *naval* is l/c except in titles such as *Royal Naval Volunteer Reserve* (RNVR) etc.

Ships are styled *HMS Achilles* or the *Achilles*. They should generally be treated as feminine; thus *she* and *her* rather than *it* and *its*. Ships are *named*, not *christened*. Note that Royal Fleet Auxiliary ships are entitled RFA, eg, *RFA Fort George* (not HMS...)

General terms

alter course (not change)

Armed Forces, Armed Services, the Services caps, but l/c *serviceman, servicewoman*. Also cap *Service* and *Forces* when used adjectivally as in *a Service family*

astern (never behind or following); eg, the *Achilles* was astern of the *Ajax*

Britannia refer to her as the former Royal Yacht

company Royal Navy ships do not have crews, they have ship's company

embarked *in* (not on)

the Fleet cap

line ahead (not astern)

moored or **made fast** (never tied up)

on board preferable to aboard

pennant (not pendant)

ratings (not *other ranks*, in the Navy)

Royal Marines caps

SBS Special Boat Service (no longer Squadron)

serving *in* a warship (but on a merchant ship); an officer is *appointed* to serve *in HMS Sheffield*, not posted to serve ... Also note that sailors serve *in a submarine*, even though subs are boats

signalman (not signaller)

submarines called *boats* (not ships) in the Royal Navy

tow the towing ship has the towed ship *in* tow; the towed ship is *under* tow

Union Flag (not Union Jack in naval contexts, except when flown at the jackstaff)

under way

weigh anchor (not ship anchor, which would mean that a ship had left her anchor at the bottom of the sea)

Ranks

abbreviation prefer not to abbreviate ranks in text of news stories; however, in lists of promotions etc on the Court Page, the following abbreviations will apply: Adm, Cdre (Commodore), Capt, Cdr (Commander), Lt-Cdr, Lt, CPO (Chief Petty Officer), L/S (Leading Seaman)

hyphenation *Times* style is to hyphenate those ranks consisting of a compound of two individual designations, eg, *Lieutenant-Commander, Commandant-General, Surgeon-Captain*; also any rank with *vice* or *rear*, eg, *Vice-Admiral, Rear-Admiral*. We should also hyphenate *Commander-in-Chief*

flag ranks a flag officer is a rear-admiral or above, exercising command and authorised by the Admiralty to fly a flag. The following are flag ranks: *Admiral of the Fleet, Admiral, Vice-Admiral, Rear-Admiral*. Although the Duke of Edinburgh is an Admiral of the Fleet, the Fleet is actually commanded by an admiral whose job title is *Commander-in-Chief Fleet* (CinC Fleet)

THE ARMY

Cap *the Army* when referred to as *the Service*, eg, "Two hundred new tanks were bought by the Army yesterday", or "He denied that he hated the Army"; but l/c when used adjectivally, eg, "An army raid was launched yesterday on the front line... ", or "An army spokesman rejected the idea..."

Give soldiers their full title at first mention, eg, General Herbert Carruthers, thereafter General Carruthers or the general. Never refer to them as Mr in news stories.

General terms

beating retreat (not beating the retreat)

guards of honour (ceremonial troops used to greet visiting dignitaries); like all guards, they are *mounted*, as sentries are *posted*

The King's Own Royal Border Regiment (full title)

King's Troop RHA (Royal Horse Artillery), remains thus even though the Sovereign is the Queen

Last Post (not *the*); note it is *sounded* (not played)

parade troops *march* through the streets (not parade)

Royal Corps of Signals may be contracted to *Royal Signals* (not RCS)

Royal Electrical and Mechanical Engineers REME for short (never Reme)

Royal Engineers can be abbreviated to RE (not REs)

The Royal Welch Fusiliers, Welch Regiment but note *Welsh Guards*

SAS Special Air Service (regiment). See **SBS** under **Royal Navy**

Trooping the Colour (not Trooping *of* the Colour)

trumpeters, buglers cavalry regiments have *trumpeters*, infantry regiments have *buglers*. They are not interchangeable

Ranks and regiments

regimental names one of the trickiest areas is when to include *The* as part of the name of regiments. With defence cuts and the amalgamation of regiments in the past few years, titles have changed rapidly, so checking an up-to-date *Army List* is imperative. General styles as follows:

Companies A Company, B Battery, 94 (Locating) Battery, C Squadron
Battalions 1st, 2nd etc, and 1st/5th, 61 Field Regiment, RA
Brigades 24 Infantry Brigade, 5 Airborne Brigade
Divisions 7th Armoured Division
Corps X Corps, XII Corps
Armies First Army
Army Groups 21 Army Group

ranks the same guidance on abbreviation and hyphenation applies as to the Royal Navy:

abbreviation prefer not to abbreviate ranks in text of news stories; however, in lists of promotions etc on the Court Page, the following abbreviations will apply: Gen, Lt-Gen, Maj-Gen, Brig, Col, Lt-Col, Maj, Capt, Lt, 2nd Lt, WO1 (Warrant Officer Class 1), WO2, S Sgt (Staff Sergeant), Sgt, Cpl, Bdr (Bombardier), L Cpl, Pte (Private), Gdsmn (Guardsman), Gnr (Gunner), Rfn (Rifleman)

hyphenation hyphenate those ranks consisting of a compound of two individual designations, eg, *Major-General, Lieutenant-General, Lieutenant-Colonel, Sergeant-Major* etc, but not compounds such as *Staff Sergeant, Lance Corporal*. (Note that *Brigadier-General* does not exist in the British Army, though it does, eg, in the American and French.)

Chief of the Defence Staff a naval Chief of the Defence Staff becomes *Admiral of the Fleet Sir John Jones*; an army one is *Field Marshal Sir John Jones*; and an air force one is *Marshal of the Royal Air Force Sir John Jones*, in each case followed by *Chief of the Defence Staff*

field marshal either a peer or a knight, so at first mention, eg, *Field Marshal Sir Richard Potts*, subsequently *Sir Richard*

officers with personal titles describe in full at first mention, eg, *Lieutenant-General Sir Amos Burke*, subsequently *Sir Amos* or *General Burke*

ROYAL AIR FORCE

Use the *Royal Air Force* or the *RAF* in text, not the Air Force (see **air force** in main section).

Ranks

ranks with ranks, the same guidance on abbreviation applies as to the Royal Navy and the Army (see previous page)

hyphenation the only RAF rank to take a hyphen is *Air Vice-Marshal*

abbreviations in lists only, as follows: AVM (Air Vice-Marshal), Air Cdre (Air Commodore), Gp Capt (Group Captain), Wg Cdr (Wing Commander), Sqn Ldr (Squadron Leader), Flt Lt (Flight Lieutenant), FO (Flying Officer), PO (Pilot Officer), FS (Flight Sergeant), Chief Tech (Chief Technician), Sgt (Sergeant), Cpl (Corporal), SAC/SACW (Senior Aircraftman/Senior Aircraftwoman) etc. Note, never shorten Flight Lieutenant to Lieutenant at subsequent mentions.

Types of aircraft (not planes); *Harrier jump-jet*, *Tornado* (plural *Tornados*), *B52*, *F111* (no hyphens), etc

THE ARTS

ART

Titles of paintings, drawings, sculptures and exhibitions are now all in italic.

DANCE

ballets titles in italics

cha-cha-cha (not cha-cha)

Latin dancing cap *L*

pas de deux, corps de ballet roman

paso doble two words

pointe shoes (not point)

FILM

auteur roman

cinéma-vérité roman

8mm film, 16mm etc

films titles in italics

film-maker hyphen

film noir roman

Palme d'or roman

3-D

LITERATURE

Book titles including novels, plays, short stories, poems (short or long), magazine articles, chapter headings, textbooks, reference books, biographies etc take italics. But do not italicise the Bible, the Talmud, the Koran, Book of Genesis etc.

MUSIC

Song titles (classical or pop) take italics; no need to cap every word in the title, eg, *Bring it on Home to Me* rather than *Bring It On Home To Me.*

albums titles in italics

First Violin Concerto note roman and caps, because it is a genre

Mozart works use the numbering system of Köchel, eg, K527

Number abbreviate to No, eg, Symphony No 3

operas titles in italics, as arias

Opus write, eg, Op (Op28)

orchestral works those with non-genre titles take italics, eg, *Night on the Bare Mountain*

Proms, the no need to spell out Promenade Concerts; note also caps for *Promenaders; the Last Night of the Proms*

Requiem roman caps, because it is a genre

symphony style is roman caps, eg, Symphony No 3; but where symphonies have numbers and popular alternative titles, place the title in italics, eg, *Eroica.* Spell out ordinals, eg, Mahler's Fourth Symphony, but note Symphony No 4

tempos (not tempi)

virtuosos (not virtuosi)

THEATRE

Act I, scene 2 etc cap Act and use Roman numeral, l/c scene and Arabic numeral

dramatis personae roman

plays titles in italics

Wyndham's Theatre (London)

TV AND RADIO

Television and radio programmes take italics, except for first mention in reviews, when they go in bold.

GENERAL ARTS TERMS

a cappella

Albert Hall, Festival Hall, National Theatre generally omit *Royal*; but note *Royal Opera House, Royal Shakespeare Company, Royal Ballet* (which is different from the *Birmingham Royal Ballet*), etc

Arts Council thereafter l/c *the council* provided the context is clear

Bartók, Béla

the Beatles, the Rolling Stones etc no need to cap *the* unless at the start of a sentence; but prefer to keep cap *T* with *The Who* and *The The*

cinemagoer, dancegoer, theatregoer one word

commedia dell'arte

debut, decor, matinee, premiere note no accents

Dvořák, Antonin

hi-fi

Internet, the note cap; also *the Net, World Wide Web, the Web,* but lower case for *website*

Janáček, Leos

Janet Holmes à Court

mezzo-soprano hyphen

nightclub

subplot, subtext, subtitle

Symphony Hall, Birmingham omit *the*

3-D

THE CHURCHES

GENERAL STYLES

Anglican bishops note they are *consecrated*; Roman Catholic bishops are *ordained*

Archbishop of Canterbury is Primate of All England; note the *Archbishop of York* is Primate of England

biblical references write, eg, II Corinthians ii, 2; Luke iv, 5

Bible, the always cap and roman, similarly the Koran, the Talmud; but note l/c *biblical*. Also caps and roman for Books of the Bible, eg, Book of Job

caps or **l/c** use caps for Bible (note l/c *biblical*), Blessed Sacrament, (Holy) Communion, the Cross, the Crucifixion, Eucharist, the Gospels, (Requiem) Mass, the Resurrection etc; use l/c for baptism, confirmation, evensong, last rites, matins, ordination, psalms (but the *Book of Psalms*)

churches use caps with, eg, the Church of England, the Roman Catholic Church, the United Reformed Church, the Methodist Church, the Church Army. Also cap the Church in context of the institution (but not adjectivally, as in "the vicar accused church authorities yesterday ..."). For individual churches, write, eg, St James's Church, Bighampton, or simply St James's, Bighampton

Church Commissioners cap first mention, then l/c *the commissioners*; note there are three chief officers: the First (Second, Third) Church Estates Commissioner

churchgoer one word

Church of Ireland, Church in Wales (NB *in*), **Scottish Episcopal Church** note that these are Anglican but disestablished; the *Church of Scotland* is Presbyterian but established

Episcopal(ian) means Anglican in the United States, Scotland and elsewhere

General Synod cap at first mention, thereafter l/c *the synod*. It has three houses: bishops, clergy and laity

hymns names go in italics

Nonconformist and **Free Churches** caps; note that the *United Reformed Church* is composed of the former Congregational Church and the Presbyterian Church of England; but some "Congregational" congregations remain outside the reformed group

Pope, the not usually necessary to give his full name, eg, Pope John Paul II (unless several Popes are mentioned in a story), but always cap. Note l/c *papacy, pontiff*

Rev never ever write the solecism the Rev Brown or (even worse) Rev Brown. The correct style is *the Rev Joseph Brown*, thereafter *Mr Brown*

Roman Catholic at first mention in full; thereafter *Catholic* is acceptable

Scotland distinguish the *Free Church of Scotland* (the "Wee Frees") from the established *Church of Scotland* and also from the *Presbyterian Church of Scotland*, of which Lord Mackay of Clashfern is a member. Note the *Moderator of the General Assembly of the Church of Scotland* (not Moderator of the Church of Scotland)

Supreme Governor of the Church of England (the Queen; note not *head* of the Church of England)

Trinity note cap pronoun, eg, *Jesus's teachings, His example; God is He*

Vicar do not use as a generic word for *priest, parson, clergyman* etc. Vicar means specifically the incumbent of a parish (unless a rector). If in doubt, *clergyman* is usually a safer term

TITLES

Senior clergy, Anglicans

bishops and **archbishops** by convention, always follow the title of their office, eg, the Archbishop of Canterbury, Dr George Carey; the Archbishop of Barchester, the Most Rev John Smith; or (for diocesan bishops), the Bishop of Barchester, the Right Rev John Smith. Use Dr when appropriate, though not all high ecclesiastics have doctorates; eg, the Bishop of Lowchester, Dr John Smith; subsequent references, the archbishop (bishop), or Dr Smith (if so entitled) – never Mr Smith

archdeacons below archbishops and bishops, similar styles prevail, eg, Archdeacon of Barchester, the Ven John Smith (thereafter Mr Smith or, more commonly, Canon Smith)

cathedral deans and provosts write, eg, the Dean of Barchester, the Very Rev John Smith (Dean Smith)

rural deans just the Rev John Smith (Mr Smith)

canons and prebendaries write, eg, Canon/Prebendary John Smith, thereafter Canon Smith

Senior clergy, Roman Catholic

archbishops at first mention, the Roman Catholic Archbishop of Liverpool, the Most Rev Patrick Kelly; subsequent mention Archbishop Kelly or the archbishop

Archbishop of Westminster, Cardinal X – no need to say Roman Catholic Archbishop of Westminster, but note Roman Catholic Archdiocese of Westminster. Subsequent mentions, Cardinal X

bishops first mention the Roman Catholic Bishop of Plymouth, the Right Rev Christopher Budd, thereafter Bishop Budd or the bishop; very few Catholic archbishops or bishops have doctorates, but if so, write, eg, Dr Budd

Monsignor (abbreviate to Mgr); do not use for Roman Catholic archbishops or bishops in Britain, though it can be a convenient form in foreign stories

Junior clergy

Christian priests, deacons, ministers, rectors, vicars of all denominations except Roman Catholic or Orthodox write, eg, the Rev Frank Faith at first mention, thereafter Mr Faith (see General Styles, under Rev). For *women clergy*, write the Rev Joan Faith, thereafter Mrs Faith or Miss Faith

Roman Catholic and Orthodox clergy write, eg, Father Justin Hope at first mention (avoid the ugly Fr abbreviation), thereafter Father Hope for Catholics, but Father Justin for Orthodox. Also use Father with Benedictines, eg, Father Goode, not Dom Goode

nuns use Sister Charity, Mother Charity, Mother Teresa

Jesuits take designation SJ on first mention, eg, "the Rev Albert Leader, SJ, said yesterday ..."

Foreign prelates

Ireland, Africa, North America etc write Anglican Bishop of ..., Roman Catholic Bishop of ...; but in countries where, for example, Roman Catholicism is the overwhelming faith, the denomination may be superfluous (eg, the Archbishop of Warsaw ...) or supplied by context

South Africa

Church of the Province of Southern Africa (or Church of the Province, or the Anglican Church) is Anglican but sometimes uses incense, Stations of the Cross etc

The Church of England (in South Africa); separate entity from the Anglican Church. The Church of England split from the Anglican communion in the late 19th century; incense, Stations of the Cross etc are not used

THE COURTS

civil cases These are heard in magistrates' courts and county courts, the more serious in the High Court, which has three divisions – the Queen's Bench, Chancery, and Family Divisions (cap Division in full title). In London they are based at the Royal Courts of Justice in the Strand.

The Divisional Court of the Queen's Bench Division can quash decisions by magistrates' courts and hear appeals from lower courts on points of law. It is also the court for reviewing governmental bodies' or local authorities' decisions – judicial review. Distinguish between applications for leave and the main hearing

criminal cases Most of these are dealt with by magistrates' courts, presided over by magistrates, who are lay justices (JPs). The busiest have full-time paid magistrates, stipendiaries. The more serious criminal cases are heard in the Crown Court, of which the most famous (in the City of London) is the Central Criminal Court, or Old Bailey (either form acceptable)

Court of Appeal always use the full title at first mention and wherever possible thereafter, though *appeal court* (l/c) may be used sparingly. The court sits with three judges, who are Lords Justices of Appeal. The highest court in the land is the Judicial Committee of the House of Lords (though normally the *House of Lords* or simply l/c *the law lords* will suffice); they are the most senior judges, formally called the Lords of Appeal in Ordinary

Scottish courts Court of Session, Edinburgh (for civil actions); High Court of Justiciary (prosecution of serious crimes and criminal appeals); the senior judge is Lord President (of the Court of Session) and also Lord Justice-General (in High Court); others are Lord Justice-Clerk (in both) and, formally, Lords of Session and Lords Commissioners of Justiciary. Sheriff (not sheriff's) Courts deal with less serious criminal and civil cases. Other points in Scotland: advocate (equivalent of English barrister); the Crown prosecutors are the Lord Advocate and Advocates-Depute and (in each sheriffdom) the Procurator Fiscal (plural, Procurators Fiscal); in civil actions, pursuer (equivalent of plaintiff), defender (the defendant), summons (writ containing pursuer's case)

youth courts these have replaced the old juvenile courts

JUDGES

bench, the (in magistrates' courts) always l/c

circuit judge sits either in the Crown Court or in the county court and should be referred to as Judge Joe Bean, QC, (the QC where appropriate). Circuit judges may also sit in the High Court, in which case they should be described as "Judge Joe Bean, sitting as a High Court judge..."

Court of Appeal judges are Lords Justices of Appeal. Use Lord Justice Bean throughout, or out of court context, Sir John Bean. Note Lady Justice Butler-Sloss. Also Lord Justice Brooke (not Brook)

district judge replaced the old county court registrar and is referred to (at first mention) as District Judge Fred Brown

High Court judges should be referred to as Mr (or Mrs) Justice Bean throughout. First names are not normally necessary unless there are two or more High Court judges with the same surname, where it is essential to differentiate. These judges have a knighthood and may also be described as Sir John Bean, Dame Eleanor Bean etc, but generally only out of the court context. It is correct, however, to refer judicially to Sir Richard Scott, Vice-Chancellor of the Supreme Court, and Sir Stephen Brown, President of the Family Division

House of Lords, or **law lords** the most senior judges, they are the Lords of Appeal in Ordinary. Call them Lord Bean, in or out of court; first mention, give full title, eg, Lord Bean of Muckleflugga, thereafter Lord Bean. When writing about their judgments, say "the House of Lords ruled" or "the law lords ruled"

recorder at the Central Criminal Court, the Recorder of the City of London is usually referred to as "the Recorder". Note caps for the Common Serjeant. The Recorder of London, Recorder of Liverpool and Recorder of Manchester (and no other places) are *circuit judges* and are referred to at first mention as Judge Michael Bean, Recorder of Manchester etc (thereafter the recorder, not Mr Recorder)

retired judges refer to retired judges as follows:
retired High Court judges Sir Ivan Parsons
retired Crown Court judges George Vickers, QC, (first mention), then Mr Vickers

COURT REPORTING

appeals in criminal cases, the defendant becomes the appellant; the respondent is usually the Crown. Say "counsel for Mr Smith" rather than "counsel for the appellant". In civil appeals, either the claimant (plaintiff) or the defendant can be the appellant; it is always better to identify the parties and then avoid the phrase *counsel for the appellant/respondent* wherever possible

caps for courts cap when specific, eg Birmingham Crown Court, Clerkenwell County Court, Dawlish Magistrates' Court, Ashford Youth Court etc; in a general, unspecific context, always cap the High Court, and the Crown Court (it sits in about 90 centres); but l/c county court, magistrates' court, youth court etc

civil cases the parties in civil cases are *the claimant* (formerly the plaintiff) and *the defendant*. Write "counsel for Mrs Y" rather than "counsel for the claimant" etc. In judicial review, the person challenging the decision is *the applicant*

commercial court l/c, as not an official division of the High Court (unlike the Family Division, Queen's Bench Division etc)

coroner's court at inquests, the coroner is l/c unless specific, as in the Westminster Coroner. Juries *return* the verdict, the coroner *records* it. Be careful not to describe pathologists automatically as a Home Office pathologist – most are private consultants, so always check and use simply "the pathologist" if in doubt. There are no coroner's inquests in Scotland: sudden deaths are reported to the Procurator Fiscal, who may hold a fatal accident inquiry

Criminal Bar (caps); similarly, the *Commercial Bar* etc

criminal cases lawyers here appear "for the prosecution", "for the defence" (avoid "prosecuting", "defending"). To *admit* or *deny an offence* is preferred to "pleads guilty" or "pleads not guilty", though the latter form is not banned.

Do not report details of sex offences involving children and do not allow sex trial reports to become surreptitious pornography. Also, do not identify victims of alleged sexual offences.

At the end of a court report, say if the trial – or the hearing, in a civil case – continues. Always give the verdict at the end of a trial or hearing.

Defendants take their titles Mr, Mrs etc until they are convicted (see **appellations**, paragraph f)

Director of Public Prosecutions heads the Crown Prosecution Service (CPS), whose lawyers are Crown prosecutors; abbreviate to DPP

Inns of Court order of precedence is Lincoln's Inn, Inner Temple, Middle Temple, Gray's Inn

Latin phrases go in roman, eg, mandamus, habeas corpus, certiorari etc, but maxims take italic, eg, *caveat emptor*

Law Report cases cited go in italics, eg, *Gornall v Ritter* and in *Gornall's* case. In news reports and features, use roman

legal bodies or services (from 1999): *Legal Services Commission*; *Community Legal Service*; *Criminal Defence Service* (all caps)

legal officers cap Official Solicitor, Treasury Solicitor, Senior

Official Receiver; but note l/c *official receiver*, because there are several. These should be distinguished from the *law officers*, who are *the Attorney-General* and *the Solicitor-General*

"no win, no fee" legislation/agreement etc

Office for the Supervision of Solicitors (no longer the Solicitors Complaints Bureau)

President of the Law Society and **Chairman of the Bar Council** note now capped

prosecution, defence note *Times* style in court reports is *for the prosecution* and *for the defence* (not *prosecuting* and *defending)*

recorders when part-time judges, barristers or solicitors are sitting as recorders, refer to them as, eg, Donald Williams, QC, (where appropriate) the Recorder (later mentions, Mr Williams or the recorder); never write Mr Recorder Williams etc

silk barristers *take silk* and *become silks*; note l/c

small claims court l/c, as not its official title

solicitors never refer to a "company" of solicitors – they are always "firms". Always omit Messrs before the firm's name, eg, simply Sue, Grabbit & Run

titles in general, use l/c for titles etc except when in full or specific; thus, Anthony Bloggs, QC, the Recorder (thereafter the recorder), the West London Magistrate, Chelmsford Crown Court, Horseferry Road Magistrates' Court, Dawlish Magistrates' Court (caps on first mention), etc; but "the court was told", "the judge said", "the magistrate ordered" etc. *The Bench* is capped only when referring to the judges as a group; *a bench of magistrates* is always l/c. Always cap *the Bar* and *the Inn* (even when used on its own)

Woolf reforms In April 1999 new procedural rules for the conduct of civil litigation came into force, including important changes of terminology. These include:
a plaintiff is now a *claimant*
a writ is now a *claim form*
all pleadings are *statements of case*
affidavits become very rare; most written evidence will simply be verified by a *statement of truth*
notices of application will be served in the place of summonses
The means by which justice will be speeded up and administered is *allocation* to the appropriate track; the *small claims track* (up to £5,000), the *fast track* (up to £15,000), and the *multitrack* (the rest)

INTERNATIONAL COURTS

Court of Auditors sits in Luxembourg. It is the fifth institution of the EU, under the Maastricht treaty. (The others are the Council of the European Union, the European Commission, the European Court of Justice and the European Parliament.)

European Court of Human Rights sits in Strasbourg. It is the judicial body of the Council of Europe (not an EC or EU body); the human rights court rules on cases brought against states under the Convention for the Protection of Human Rights and Fundamental Freedoms, usually referred to as the **European Convention on Human Rights**. From November 1998, the European Court of Human Rights has incorporated the former European Commission of Human Rights.

In the Strasbourg context note that neither the Parliamentary Assembly of the Council of Europe nor the Committee of Ministers of the Council of Europe is an EU institution

European Court of Justice sits in Luxembourg. It is the shortened (and usual) form of the Court of Justice of the European Communities. The *Advocate General* (caps, no hyphen) sits in the European Court; he presents the case to the court and delivers an opinion, then the court makes its judgment

International Court of Justice sits in The Hague. It is the judicial organ of the UN and only states can be parties there

POLITICS

GENERAL POINTS

Always check the spelling of MPs and their constituencies if not entirely familiar: the best reference is *The Times Guide to the House of Commons*. Similarly, check *Vacher's Parliamentary Companion* or *Who's Who* for peers.

For guidance on when to cap or l/c Government, Opposition, Parliament, Party, see individual entries in the main section of this Style Guide.

Government, Cabinet, Opposition, Parliament, Party etc take the singular verb, eg, the Cabinet is considering ...

It is never necessary to say *Tony Blair, the Prime Minister*, etc: we may assume that *Times* readers know who the Prime Minister is. But it may be helpful to the flow of the story to write, eg, *the Prime Minister said* ... lower down the story, to avoid the endless repetition of *Mr Blair*.

PARLIAMENTARY TERMS

Act(s) always cap, whether fully identified or not

backbench, frontbench (adjective); similarly *backbenchers, frontbenchers, crossbench* (in the Lords); but note *the back benches, the front bench* and *the cross benches*

Bill(s) always cap (as with Acts above). Bills are read a first time without a debate. The second reading debate is the debate on the principle of the Bill. The Bill then goes to its committee stage, usually in a standing committee composed of about 20 MPs, but occasionally on the floor of the Commons. It then returns to the Commons chamber for its report stage and third reading, which is the final debate on the principle of the Bill. It then goes to the Lords, where similar procedures apply. Note that some legislation starts in the Lords and comes to the Commons thereafter

Cabinet always cap (as with Act and Bill), whether used as a noun or adjectivally, except in the informal *kitchen cabinet*. *Cabinet committees* should be capped

chamber l/c

Clause Four (as in Labour Party policy); but *Clause 4* permissible in headlines

closure as in *move the closure*

committees cap select committees when full title, such as the Select Committee on the Environment; Cabinet committees such as the Cabinet Committee on the Intelligence Services; the *Public Accounts Committee* (PAC); the *1922 Committee* (of Tory backbenchers); the *National Executive Committee* (NEC) of the Labour Party (or *Labour's national executive* as a shorter alternative)

crossbench, the cross benches see **backbench**

Cunningham through common usage, refer to him at first mention as Jack Cunningham (rather than John), then Dr Cunningham (though he is not a medical doctor)

deputy speakers there are three, and should appear thus: John Jones, the Deputy Speaker

dispatch box l/c

Downing Street policy unit; 10 Downing Street, or **No 10**

Duncan Smith, Iain no hyphen

early day motion l/c

elections always l/c *general election*; similarly *by-election, European elections* etc

frontbench (adjective); note *the front bench*; see **backbench**

galleries l/c, but note the *Press Gallery, Strangers' Gallery* etc

group cap in cases such as the *92 Group* (of Tory rightwingers)

guillotine l/c, no quotation marks

Hamilton, Sir Archibald (not Sir Archie)

Hansard italics

House of Lords officers note *the Clerk of the Parliaments, the Clerk Assistant* (of the Parliaments), *the Reading Clerk* (of the House of Lords)

leaders cap the *Leader of the House, Leader of the Opposition*, but l/c for *the Conservative/Labour/Liberal Democrat leader, the leader of the party* etc

Liberal Democrats permissible to use *Lib Dems* in either headlines or text (though sparingly in text). The term *Liberals* must not be used as a synonym of Liberal Democrats

Lower House caps

Members of Parliament note caps; in almost every case, MPs is the preferable form. But in the Political Sketch, and discursive or commentary articles, the term *Members* sometimes occurs for stylistic reasons and should be retained and capped; similarly in such articles, the Member for Billericay, the Hon Member etc

National Executive Committee of the Labour Party, or simply *Labour's national executive*; abbreviate to NEC

new Labour (as in Tony Blair's policies); l/c *n*, quotes not usually necessary, except when the writer or speaker is making a particular, perhaps ironic, point. But keep caps in slogans such as "New Labour, New Danger"; note *New Deal*

1922 Committee (of Tory backbenchers)

One Nation Tories, One Nation politics etc

Opposition the same cap or l/c rules apply as to Government, ie, cap as a noun but generally l/c as an adjective, eg, "He accused the Opposition of lying", but "He said it was an opposition lie"

order, order paper l/c

Parliament cap always in the British context (for when to cap foreign parliaments, see **Parliament** in main section). The cap rule now applies even to phrases such as *the lifetime of this Parliament* or *the Bill is unlikely to progress until the next Parliament*. The adjective *parliamentary* is usually l/c except when used as part of a title, eg, *Parliamentary Labour Party* (PLP)

parliamentary private secretary l/c, abbreviate to PPS

Part I, Part II (of Bill etc); caps also for *Section 2, Article 8* etc

party abbreviations in lists or political sketches or reports of debates where party affiliation is added after an MP's name – eg, Tony Benn (Lab, Chesterfield) – use *Lab* for Labour, *C* for Conservative (not Con), and *LD* for Liberal Democrat (not Lib Dem)

party conferences l/c, as in *Labour Party conference*

Private Member's Bill caps

Public Accounts Committee abbreviate to PAC

Queen's Speech caps

Question Time, Prime Minister's Questions also *Agriculture Questions, Treasury Questions* etc; but note l/c *questions* to the Prime Minister, the Foreign Secretary etc

Register of Members' Interests caps

Royal Assent caps

royal commissions see main section

select committees cap when giving full title, eg, *Treasury Select Committee*

Serjeant at Arms

Smith the widow of John Smith is Baroness Smith of Gilmorehill, thereafter Lady Smith; she is not Dame Elizabeth Smith

Speaker usual style is Betty Boothroyd, the Speaker, at first mention, thereafter the Speaker or Miss Boothroyd

spin-doctor hyphen

State Opening (of Parliament); note caps

ten-minute rule (Bill etc)

Treasury bench

Upper House caps

Vote (of money); takes cap

whips cap for the *Chief Whip, Opposition Chief Whip, Whips' Office*; but l/c as in *three-line whip, to lose the party whip, a government whip*

SPORTS

Sports writing is notoriously vulnerable to cliché and jargon. Apart from direct quotes, avoid the type of language used by players and TV commentators.

GENERAL STYLES

All England Club

baseball inning (not innings)

Blue (from Oxford, Cambridge, for the award or the sportsman or woman); note cap

cross country hyphenate only in adjectival use, as in *cross-country trials*

Cup Final cap *the FA Cup Final,* but note l/c *f* for *World Cup final, Worthington Cup final, Benson and Hedges Cup final* etc; also l/c for *FA Cup semi-final,* because by definition more than one

divisions, groups, sections etc in sporting context these always take l/c, eg, *World Cup group A, Nationwide League first division, European championship section D* etc

England Under-21 etc

first division, second division etc (not Division One, 2, etc or any variant)

hat-trick (cricket or football)

racecourse, racehorse but note *horse race, horse racing*

stretchered off avoid; instead use *carried off on a stretcher*

women's competitions, championships, events etc (not ladies')

World Cup caps; note l/c for *world championship* in all sports

BOXING

General terms featherweight, heavyweight, light-heavyweight etc; knockout(s)

CRICKET

General terms wicketkeeper, mid-off, mid-wicket; follow on (verb) but the follow-on; hat-trick; hit-wicket; mis-hit; third man; extra cover; off break; leg-before; no-ball; a four (not 4); AXA Life League; Benson and Hedges Cup

delivery in cricket this is a bowling action, not a ball, eg, "Qadir has a puzzling delivery", not "Warne bowled Gatting with his first delivery"

England and Wales Cricket Board from January 1, 1997, the ECB took control of all levels of the domestic game, and the Test and County Cricket Board (TCCB) is no more

First-Class Forum represents the views of the first-class counties; abbreviate to FCF

MCC Marylebone Cricket Club; concerned with the laws of cricket and matters at Lord's. Do not refer to *the* MCC

off spinner (bowler who bowls off breaks)

FOOTBALL

By itself, football means the association code. *Soccer* is now an acceptable alternative.

American football should always be described thus, unless the context is so obvious that football on its own is enough.

General terms goalkeeper, kick-off (noun), Arsenal (not *the*), midfield, offside

FA Carling Premiership at first mention write in full, thereafter *the Premiership.* Do not confuse with the *FA Premier League*

FA Premier League (organisation that runs the FA Carling Premiership); take care not to confuse the competition and the organisation

Fifa (football's governing body; not FIFA); similarly *Uefa* (not UEFA)

Football Association, or **FA** (never the English Football Association)

Nationwide League first division, second division etc (lower divisions; no longer Endsleigh); note l/c. This competition is run by the *Football League*

St Andrew's, Birmingham; do not confuse with St Andrews (golf)

St James' Park, Newcastle and Exeter

RUGBY UNION, RUGBY LEAGUE

General terms full back; scrum half; fly half; dropped goal; knock on (verb) but a knock-on (noun); scrummage; three-quarter; open-side flanker; wing (not winger); lineout(s); 22-metre line, the 22; touch judge; triple crown; grand slam; the British Isles, not the British Lions (though Lions on its own is acceptable at second mention)
Note stand-off half in rugby league

rugby union, rugby league both take l/c in general usage (though not, of course, in titles)

rugger do not use

Six Nations Championship note caps, and no longer Five Nations except in historical contexts

GOLF

The holes should appear in both text and results as 1st, 2nd, 10th, 18th, but write the "third extra hole" after that. In a match-play use, "Jones beat Brown 2 and 1" (not two and one). Usual *Times* style for numbers (spell out from one to ten, figures thereafter) in sentences such as "Faldo holed from eight feet/15 feet".

General terms the Open Championship (not British Open); bogey; birdie; eagle (no quotes); dormy, only if the match can be halved (a player cannot be dormy if the match can be taken to, say, the 19th hole to reach a decision)

MOTOR RACING

British Grand Prix, Japanese Grand Prix etc cap as specific; but note l/c for unspecific *grand prix racing* etc ; plural *grands prix*

Formula One motor racing two caps; spell out *One*

pitstop (one word)

SWIMMING

General terms freestyle, backstroke, breaststroke (no hyphens)

TENNIS

Flushing Meadows, New York (home of the US Open tennis championships; not Meadow)

Moyà, Carlos note accent

YACHTING

America's Cup

sailing correspondent (not yachting correspondent)

Whitbread Round the World Race caps, no hyphens

TITLES

Diana, Princess of Wales, at first mention; though since her death use the form *the late Princess* where appropriate. Never refer to her as Princess Diana or (even worse) Lady Di or Princess Di. Also, note one comma only for the *Diana, Princess of Wales Memorial Fund*

Duke of Edinburgh, the thereafter *the Duke* or (sparingly) *Prince Philip*

Duke of York, the thereafter *the Duke* or *Prince Andrew*. Note the *Duchess of York* is no longer a member of the Royal Family since her divorce. At first mention, refer to her as *the Duchess of York*, then l/c *the duchess* – never "Fergie" or any such vulgarity

Earl of Wessex, the thereafter *the Earl* or *Prince Edward*; similarly the *Countess of Wessex, the Countess*, or *the former Sophie Rhys-Jones*

Prince of Wales, the thereafter *the Prince* or (sparingly) *Prince Charles*

Princess Royal, the thereafter *the Princess*. Use *Princess Anne* only in historical context

Queen, the try to use *the* even in headlines

Queen Elizabeth the Queen Mother (no comma) first mention, thereafter the Queen Mother

Royal Dukes keep the cap at subsequent mentions (eg, the *Duke of Kent*, later *the Duke*); other dukes do not retain the cap (see below)

PEERAGE AND KNIGHTS

Titles of nobility in descending order as follows: *duke, marquess* (not marquis, except in foreign contexts and occasional Scottish titles), *earl, viscount* and *baron*. At first mention, give the formal title (as in *Who's Who*) eg, the Marquess of Paddington, the Earl of Waterloo, but then Lord Paddington, Lord Waterloo etc. This does not apply to *barons*, who are always Lord except in the announcement of new baronies. *Dukes* are always dukes and do not become Lord (eg, the Duke of Rutland). Note style of *the 2nd Earl, the 3rd Viscount* etc. Note a major difference from royalty is that these titles take l/c rather than cap after the first mention, (eg, the Duke of Argyll, thereafter the duke).

announcement of titles baronets, knights and dames take the appropriate title as soon as the honour is announced. Peers have to submit their choice of title for approval, so wait until the formal public announcement (usually in *The London Gazette*)

baron always Lord except in the announcement of new baronies

baronesses in their own right or life peeresses are *Baroness* at first mention, and then *Lady* (eg, Baroness Thatcher, then Lady Thatcher)

baronets, knights write, eg, Sir John Euston, thereafter Sir John. Note the wife of a baronet is called Lady from the start, eg, Lady Euston. Remember this essential point: no wife of a baronet or knight takes her first name in her title unless she is the daughter of a duke, a marquess or an earl. If a baronet has had more than one wife, the first wife is, eg, Mary Lady Smith (no commas) – the same form applies to the widow of a baron. If a knight has had more than one wife, the former wife puts her Christian name in brackets, eg, Lady (Alice) Brown, to distinguish her from the present wife, Lady Brown.

If two baronets or knights have the same name, their wives (when mentioned apart from their husbands) put his first name in brackets, eg, Lady (Stephen) Brown, Lady (Andrew) Brown

children of peers eldest sons of a duke, marquess or earl use the father's second title as a courtesy title (eg, the Duke of Bedford's son is the Marquess of Tavistock). These people are not peers, even in headlines. Younger sons of dukes and marquesses use their first names and the family surname (eg, Lord John Worthington; subsequent mention Lord John, never Lord Worthington; his wife is Lady John Worthington).

Daughters of dukes, marquesses or earls take their first names in their title, eg, Lady Olive York, and in subsequent mentions Lady Olive (never Lady York).

Younger sons of earls and all children of viscounts and barons have the style *the Hon*, but use this only in Court Page copy; normally, they are simply Mr, Miss, Ms etc (none is a peer)

countess (wife of an earl); use *Lady* at subsequent mentions

Dames (of an order of chivalry); dames take the same style as knights, eg, Dame Felicity Brown, thereafter Dame Felicity. A dame who is married may prefer to use her own style, eg, Dame Jennifer Jenkins, wife of Lord Jenkins of Hillhead; personal preferences should be respected

duchess (wife of a duke) always *Duchess*, eg, the Duchess of X

duke always described as duke so does not become Lord at subsequent mention. The wife of a duke is a *duchess*

earl at first mention, give the formal title, thereafter Lord. The wife of an earl is a *countess*

first names with titles take great care especially with the names of wives of peers, baronets and knights. No wife of a baronet or knight takes her first name in her title unless she is the daughter of a duke, a marquess or an earl. The wife of Lord St Pancras is simply Lady St Pancras. The wife of Sir John Fenchurch is simply Lady Fenchurch (together, Sir John and Lady Fenchurch). However, when the name is a common one and there is no other convenient identification, or where there is some other compelling reason, it is permissible to say Lady (John) Brown (brackets essential; see **baronets, knights**)

marchioness (wife of a marquess); use *Lady* at subsequent mentions

marquess (not marquis, except in foreign contexts and occasional Scottish titles). At first mention, give the formal title and thereafter Lord. The wife of a marquess is a *marchioness*

titles including place name some titles include a place name, eg, Lord Callaghan of Cardiff, Lord Archer of Weston-super-Mare, while others do not. Follow *Who's Who*, where those whose place name must be included appear in **bold caps.**

Always give the full title at first mention, thereafter the abbreviated form, eg, Lord Bingham of Cornhill, thereafter Lord Bingham. Among titles spelt differently from the place name are the Marquess of Ailesbury, Marquess of Donegall, Earl of Guilford, Earl of Scarbrough

viscount give formal title at first mention, thereafter Lord. The wife of a viscount is a *viscountess*

viscountess (wife of a viscount); give full title, then *Lady* at subsequent mentions

widows/former wives of titles those who have not remarried use their first name before the title, eg, Margaret Duchess of Argyll (no commas). A widow may also be known as the Dowager Duchess of Y, or the Dowager Lady Z

WORLD MAPS

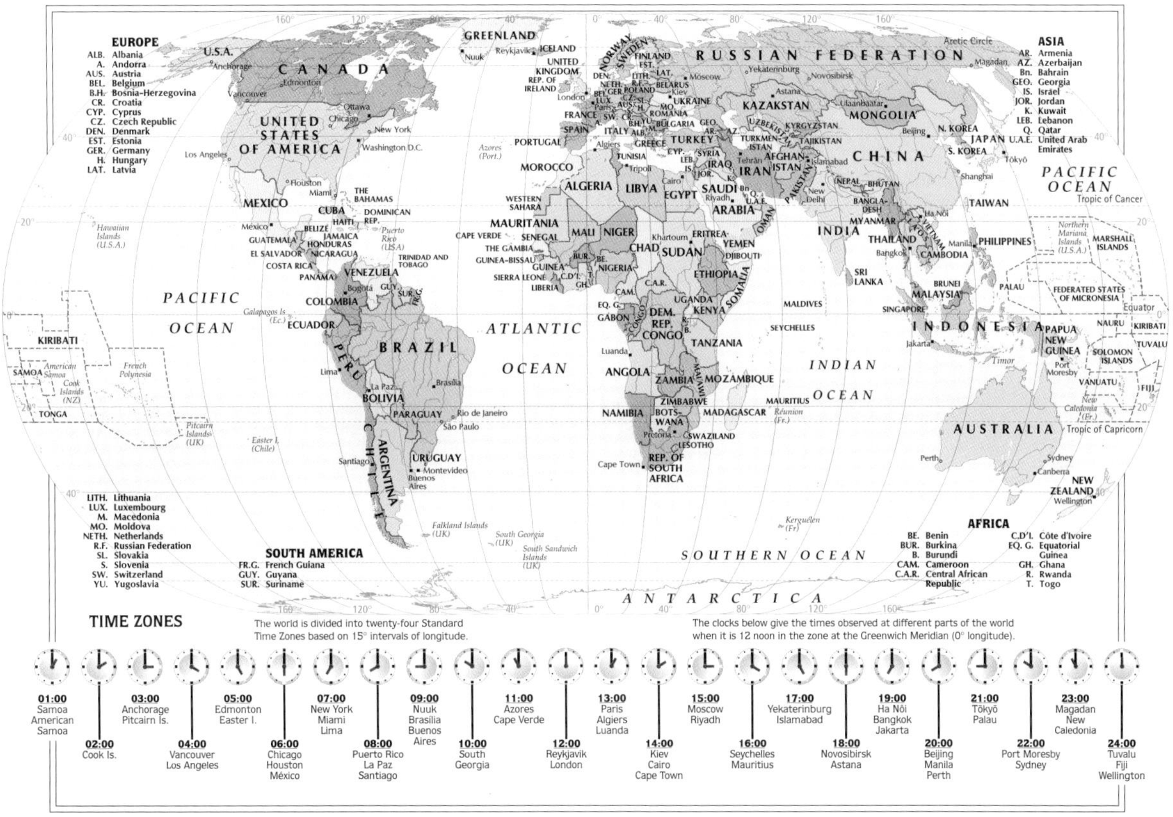

EUROPE

ALB. Albania
A. Andorra
AUS. Austria
BEL. Belgium
B.H. Bosnia-Herzegovina
CR. Croatia
CYP. Cyprus
CZ. Czech Republic
DEN. Denmark
EST. Estonia
GER. Germany
H. Hungary
LAT. Latvia
LITH. Lithuania
LUX. Luxembourg
M. Macedonia
MO. Moldova
NETH. Netherlands
R.F. Russian Federation
SL. Slovakia
S. Slovenia
SW. Switzerland
YU. Yugoslavia

SOUTH AMERICA

FR.G. French Guiana
GUY. Guyana
SUR. Suriname

ASIA

AR. Armenia
AZ. Azerbaijan
Bn. Bahrain
GEO. Georgia
IS. Israel
JOR. Jordan
K. Kuwait
LEB. Lebanon
Q. Qatar
U.A.E. United Arab Emirates

AFRICA

BE. Benin
BUR. Burkina
B. Burundi
CAM. Cameroon
C.A.R. Central African Republic
C.D'I. Côte d'Ivoire
EQ. G. Equatorial Guinea
GH. Ghana
R. Rwanda
T. Togo

TIME ZONES

The world is divided into twenty-four Standard Time Zones based on 15° intervals of longitude.

The clocks below give the times observed at different parts of the world when it is 12 noon in the zone at the Greenwich Meridian (0° longitude).

01:00 Samoa, American Samoa
02:00 Cook Is.
03:00 Anchorage, Pitcairn Is.
04:00 Vancouver, Los Angeles
05:00 Edmonton, Easter I.
06:00 Chicago, Houston, México
07:00 New York, Miami, Lima
08:00 Puerto Rico, La Paz, Santiago
09:00 Nuuk, Brasilia, Buenos Aires
10:00 South Georgia
11:00 Azores, Cape Verde
12:00 Reykjavik, London
13:00 Paris, Algiers, Luanda
14:00 Kiev, Cairo, Cape Town
15:00 Moscow, Riyadh
16:00 Seychelles, Mauritius
17:00 Yekaterinburg, Islamabad
18:00 Novosibirsk, Astana
19:00 Ha Nôi, Bangkok, Jakarta
20:00 Beijing, Manila, Perth
21:00 Tōkyō, Palau
22:00 Port Moresby, Sydney
23:00 Magadan, New Caledonia
24:00 Tuvalu, Fiji, Wellington

SETTLEMENTS

NATIONAL CAPITAL

Over 5 million	**Beijing**
1 to 5 million	**Seoul**
500000 to 1 million	**Bangui**
100000 to 500000	Wellington
50000 to 100000	Port of Spain
10000 to 50000	Malabo
Less than 10000	Roseau

ADMINISTRATIVE CAPITAL

Over 5 million	**Tianjin**
1 to 5 million	**Lagos**
500000 to 1 million	**Douala**
100000 to 500000	Mansa
50000 to 100000	Lubango
10000 to 50000	Chinhoyi
Less than 10000	Áti

CITY OR TOWN

Over 5 million	**New York**
1 to 5 million	**Barranquilla**
500000 to 1 million	**Memphis**
100000 to 500000	Mara
50000 to 100000	Arecibo
10000 to 50000	El Tigre
Less than 10000	Soledad

PHYSICAL FEATURES

- Freshwater lake
- Seasonal freshwater lake
- Saltwater lake *or* Lagoon
- Seasonal saltwater lake
- Dry salt lake *or* Saltpan
- Marsh
- River
- Waterfall
- Dam *or* Barrage
- Seasonal river *or* Wadi
- Canal
- Flood dyke
- Reef
- Volcano
- Lava field
- Sandy desert
- Rocky desert
- Oasis
- Escarpment
- 923 Mountain pass *height in metres*
- Ice cap *or* Glacier

COMMUNICATIONS

- Motorway
- Motorway *under construction*
- Motorway tunnel

Motorways are classified separately at scales greater than 1:5 million. At smaller scales motorways are classified with main roads.

- Main road
- Main road *under construction*
- Main road tunnel
- Other road
- Other road *under construction*
- Other road tunnel
- Track
- Main railway
- Main railway *under construction*
- Main railway tunnel
- Other railway
- Other railway *under construction*
- Other railway tunnel
- Main airport
- Other airport

BOUNDARIES

- International
- International *disputed*
- Ceasefire line
- Main administrative (U.K.)
- Main administrative
- Main administrative *through water*

OTHER FEATURES

- National park
- Reserve
- Ancient wall
- Historic *or* Tourist site
- Urban area

UNITED KINGDOM and REPUBLIC OF IRELAND

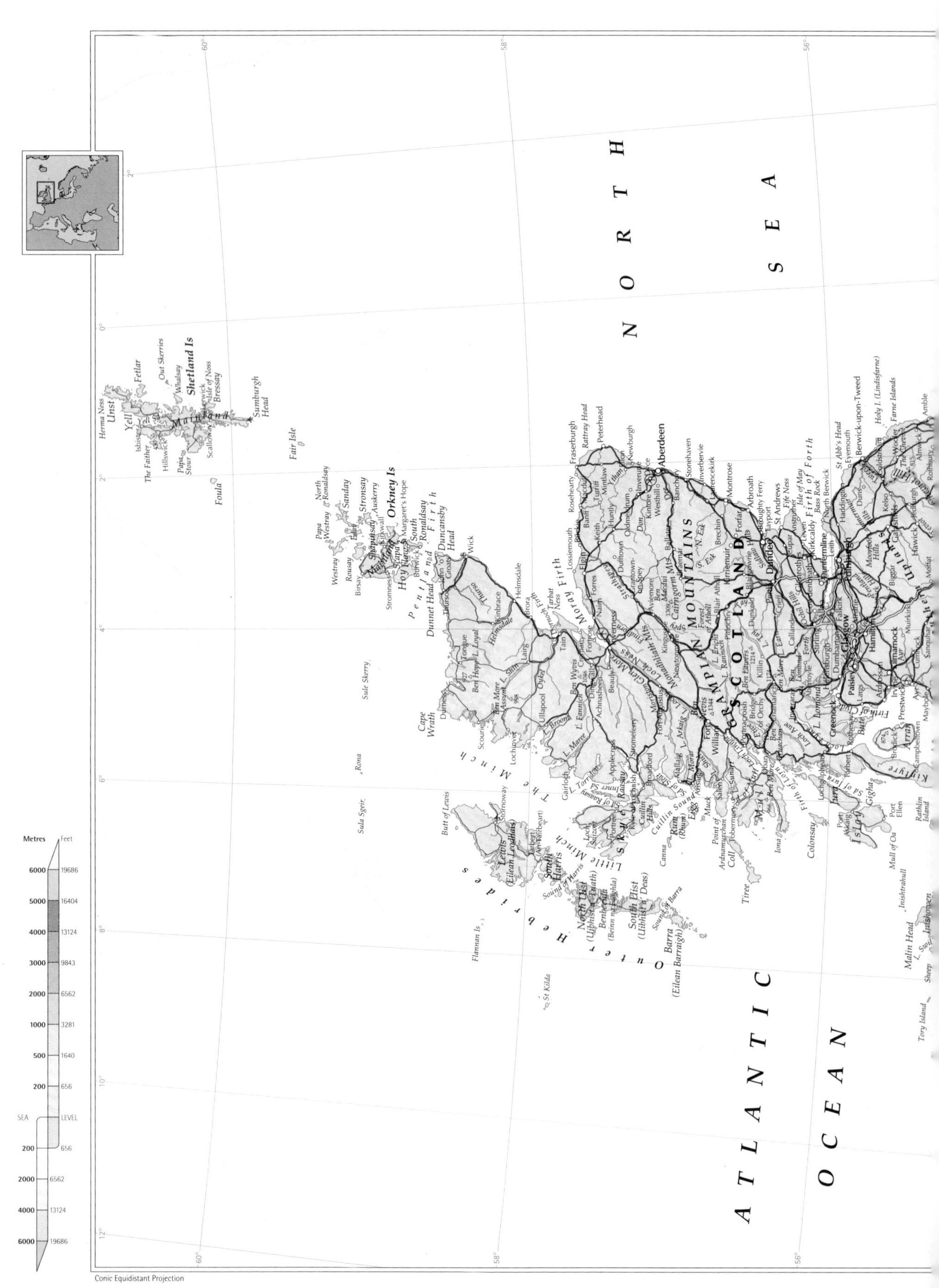

Conic Equidistant Projection

UNITED KINGDOM and REPUBLIC OF IRELAND

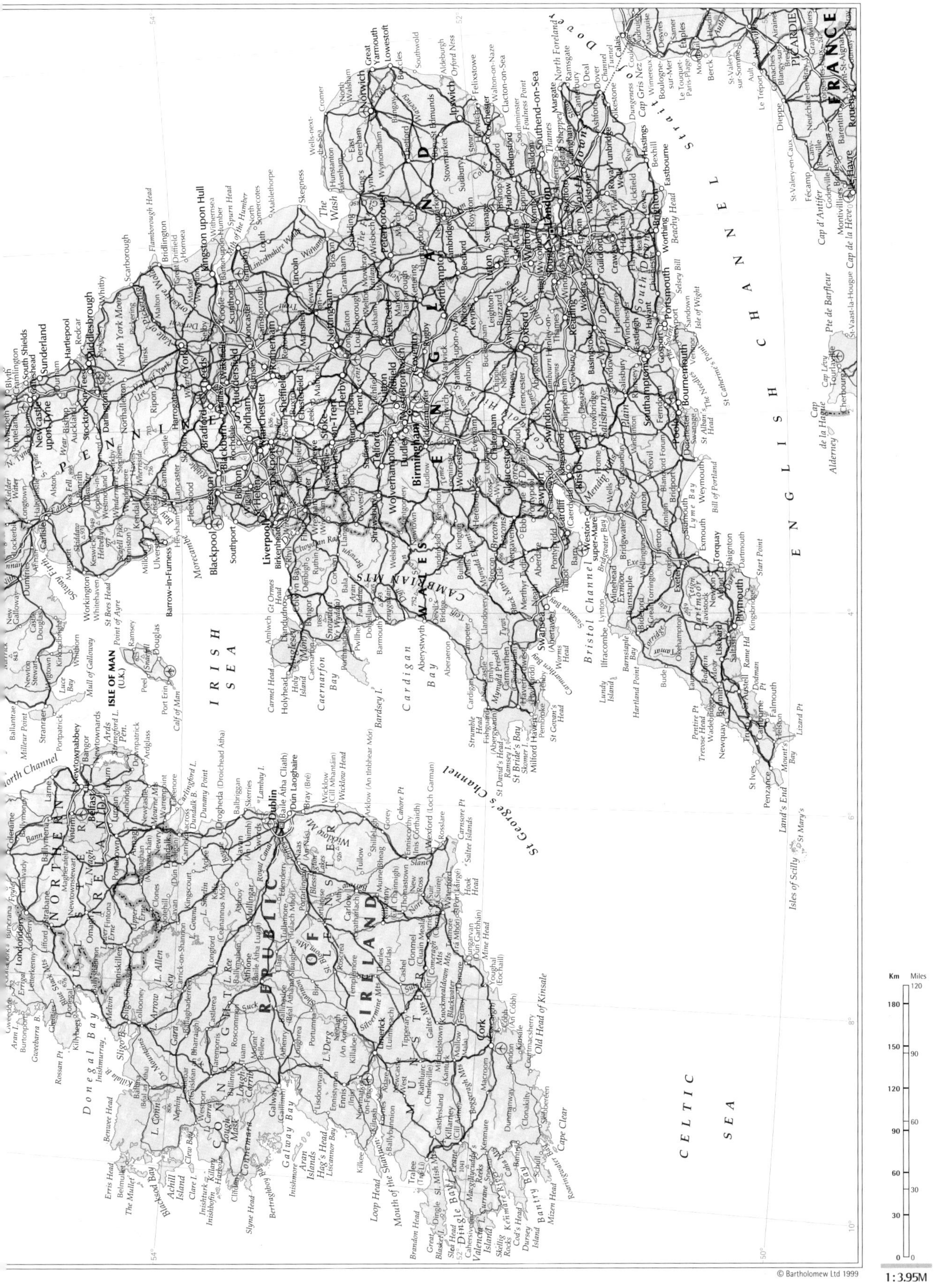

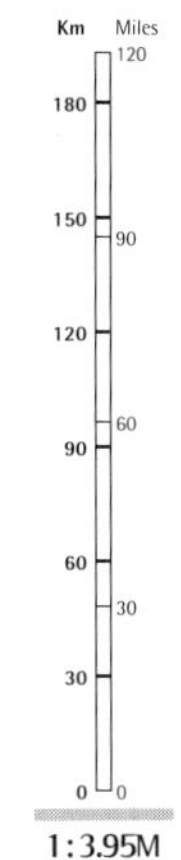

1:3.95M

Lambert Conformal Conic Projection

BLACK SEA
Adriatic Sea
Tyrrhenian Sea
Ionian Sea
Aegean Sea
MEDITERRANEAN SEA
POLAND
BELARUS
UKRAINE
CZECH REPUBLIC
SLOVAKIA
AUSTRIA
HUNGARY
ROMANIA
MOLDOVA
SLOVENIA
CROATIA
BOSNIA-HERZEGOVINA
YUGOSLAVIA
BULGARIA
MACEDONIA (F.Y.R.O.M.)
ALBANIA
GREECE
TURKEY
ITALY
LIBYA
EGYPT
MALTA
Berlin
Warsaw
Prague
Vienna
Budapest
Bucharest
Belgrade
Sofia
Athens
Istanbul
Rome
Naples
Kiev
Tripoli
Alexandria
Khalīj Surt (Gulf of Sirte)
Crete
Sicily
Km
Miles
1:11M
© Bartholomew Ltd 1999

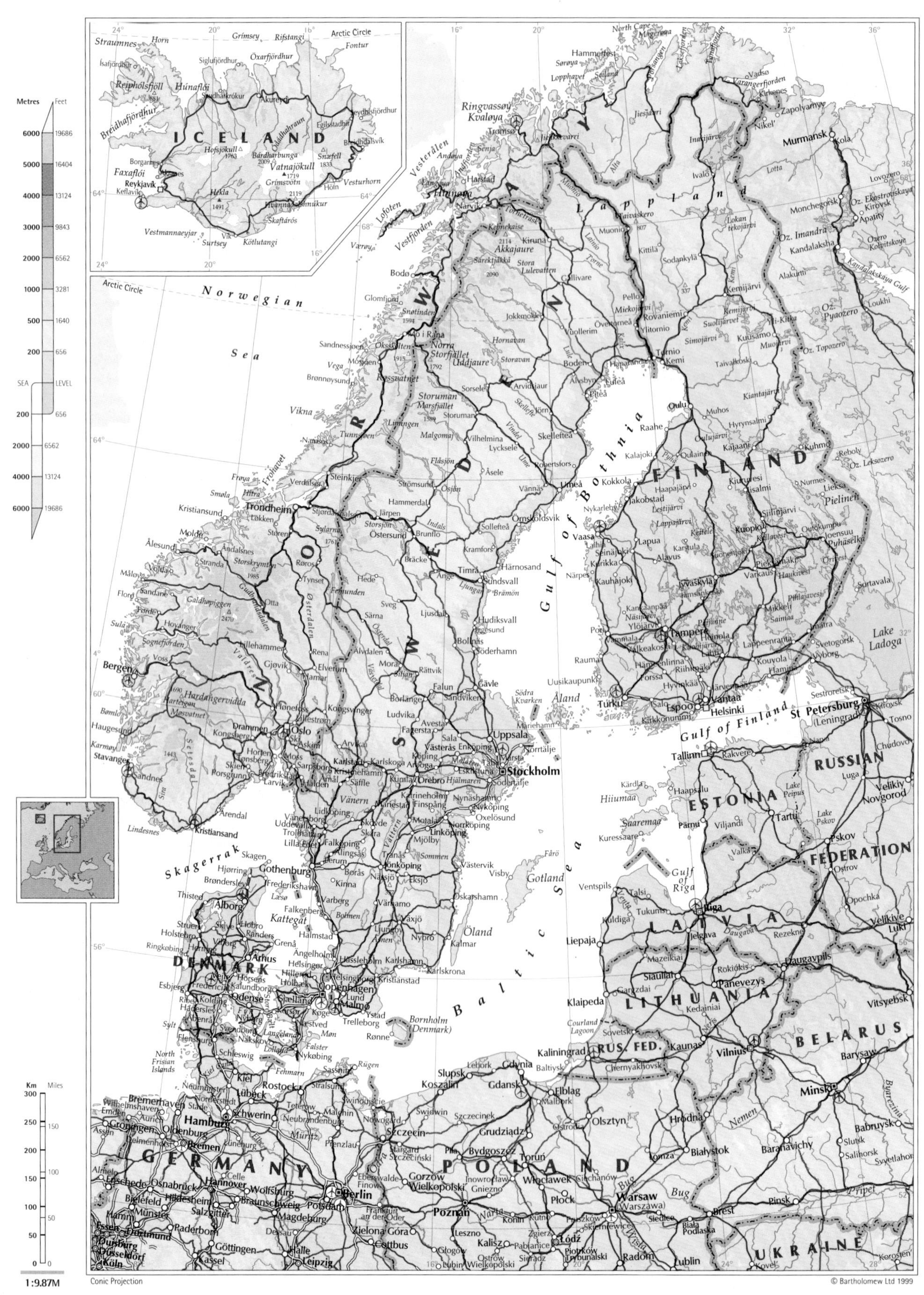
ICELAND
Reykjavík
Vatnajökull
Arctic Circle
Norwegian Sea
NORWAY
SWEDEN
FINLAND
Lappland
Gulf of Bothnia
Gulf of Finland
Baltic Sea
Gotland
Öland
Skagerrak
Kattegat
DENMARK
GERMANY
POLAND
RUSSIAN FEDERATION
ESTONIA
LATVIA
LITHUANIA
RUS. FED.
BELARUS
UKRAINE
Oslo
Stockholm
Helsinki
Copenhagen
Tallinn
Riga
Vilnius
Minsk
Warsaw (Warszawa)
Berlin
St Petersburg (Leningrad)
Bergen
Trondheim
Gothenburg
Murmansk
Lake Ladoga
Metres
Feet
SEA
LEVEL
Km
Miles
1:9.87M
Conic Projection
© Bartholomew Ltd 1999

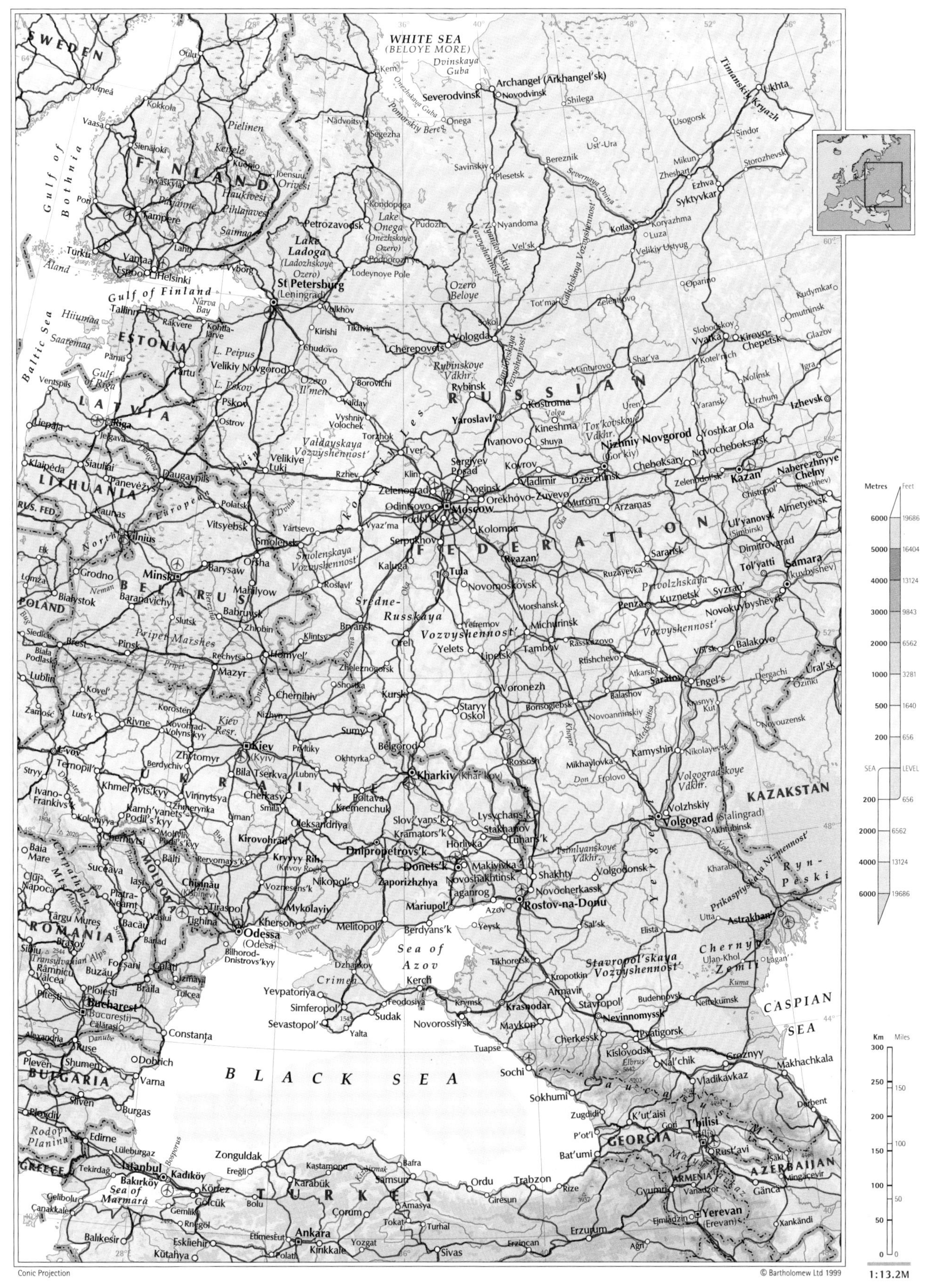
WHITE SEA
(BELOYE MORE)
SWEDEN
FINLAND
ESTONIA
LATVIA
LITHUANIA
BELARUS
POLAND
UKRAINE
MOLDOVA
ROMANIA
BULGARIA
GREECE
TURKEY
GEORGIA
ARMENIA
AZERBAIJAN
KAZAKSTAN
RUSSIAN FEDERATION
BLACK SEA
CASPIAN SEA
Sea of Azov
Gulf of Finland
Gulf of Bothnia
Baltic Sea
Gulf of Riga
Archangel (Arkhangel'sk)
St Petersburg
(Leningrad)
Moscow
Nizhniy Novgorod
(Gor'kiy)
Kazan'
Samara
(Kuybyshev)
Volgograd (Stalingrad)
Rostov-na-Donu
Kharkiv (Khar'kov)
Kiev
(Kyiv)
Minsk
Riga
Vilnius
Tallinn
Helsinki
Odessa
(Odesa)
Chişinău
(Kishinev)
Bucharest
(Bucureşti)
Istanbul
Ankara
T'bilisi
Yerevan
(Erevan)
Dnipropetrovs'k
Donets'k
Metres
Feet
6000
19686
5000
16404
4000
13124
3000
9843
2000
6562
1000
3281
500
1640
200
656
SEA LEVEL
Km
Miles
300
250
200
150
100
50
0
1:13.2M
Conic Projection
© Bartholomew Ltd 1999

Conic Equidistant Projection

OCEAN
East Siberian Sea
(Vostochno-Sibirskoye More)
Laptev Sea
(More Laptevykh)
Chukchi Sea
Bering Strait
BERING SEA
SEA OF OKHOTSK
(OKHOTSKOYE MORE)
Sea of Japan
Yellow Sea
Bo Hai
FEDERATION
SREDNE-SIBIRSKOYE PLOSKOGOR'YE
(CENTRAL SIBERIAN PLATEAU)
Khrebet Cherskogo
Verkhoyanskiy Khrebet
Stanovoy Khrebet
Stanovoye Nagor'ye
Khrebet Dzhugdzhur
Khrebet Kolymskiy
Koryakskiy Khrebet
Sredinnyy Khrebet
Sikhote-Alin'
Kamchatka Peninsula
Sakhalin
Kuril Islands
(Kuril'skiye Ostrova)
Hokkaidō
Honshū
Kyūshū
Shikoku
JAPAN
NORTH KOREA
SOUTH KOREA
MONGOLIA
GOBI
CHINA
U.S.A.
Lake Baikal
(Ozero Baykal)
Novosibirskiye Ostrova
(New Siberia Islands)
Severnaya Zemlya
Poluostrov Taymyr
Wrangell I.
Yakutsk
Magadan
Petropavlovsk-Kamchatskiy
Khabarovsk
Vladivostok
Irkutsk
Ulan-Ude
Chita
Blagoveshchensk
Komsomol'sk-na-Amure
Yuzhno-Sakhalinsk
Ulaanbaatar
(Ulan Bator)
Beijing
(Peking)
Tianjin
(Tientsin)
Shenyang
Harbin
Changchun
Dalian
P'yŏngyang
Seoul
(Soul)
Pusan
Sapporo
Tōkyō
Yokohama
Nagoya
Ōsaka
Kyōto
Kōbe
Hiroshima
Fukuoka
Kagoshima
Km
Miles
1200
1000
800
600
400
200
0
600
450
300
150
0
1:26M
© Bartholomew Ltd 1999

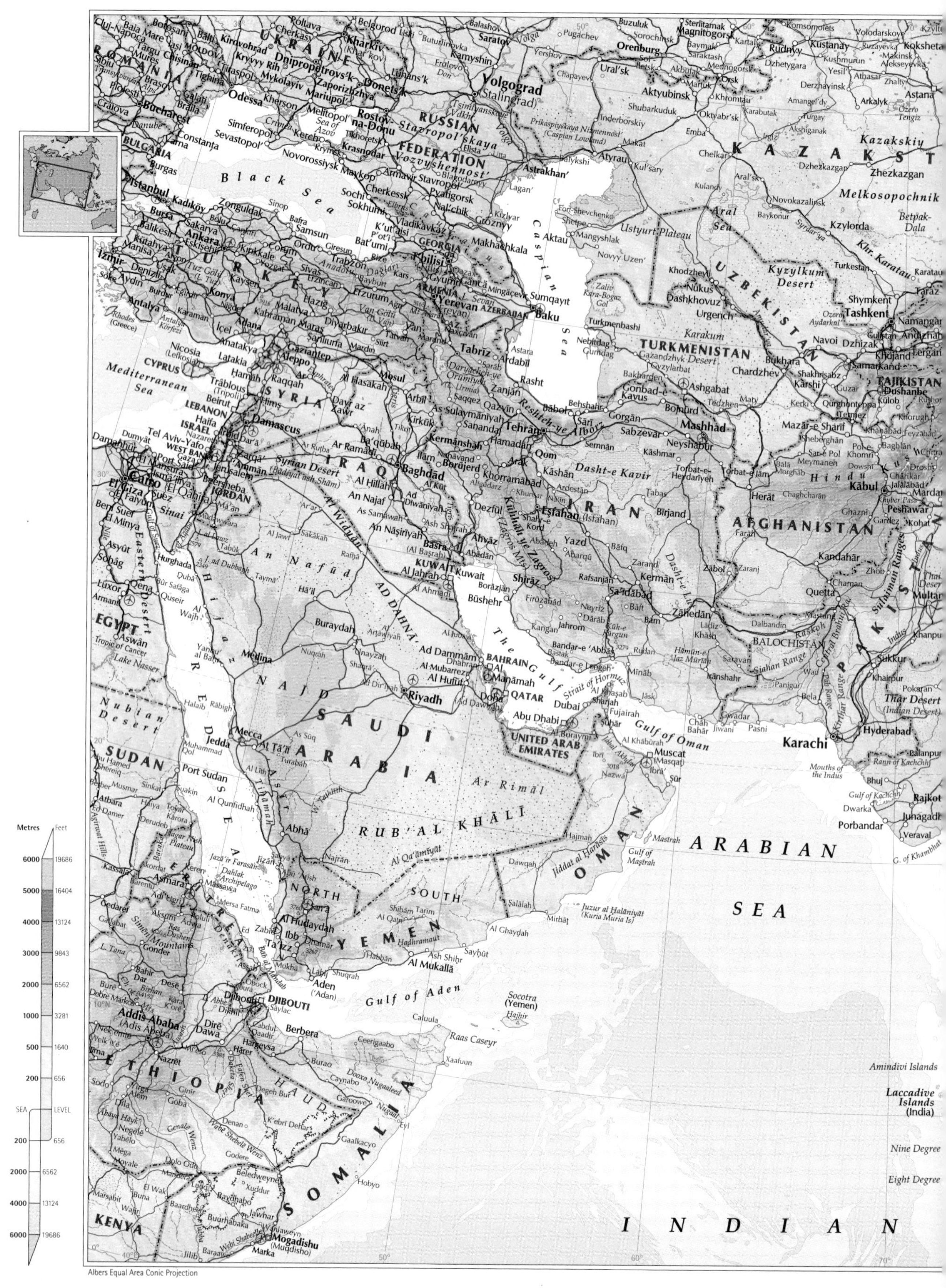

Albers Equal Area Conic Projection

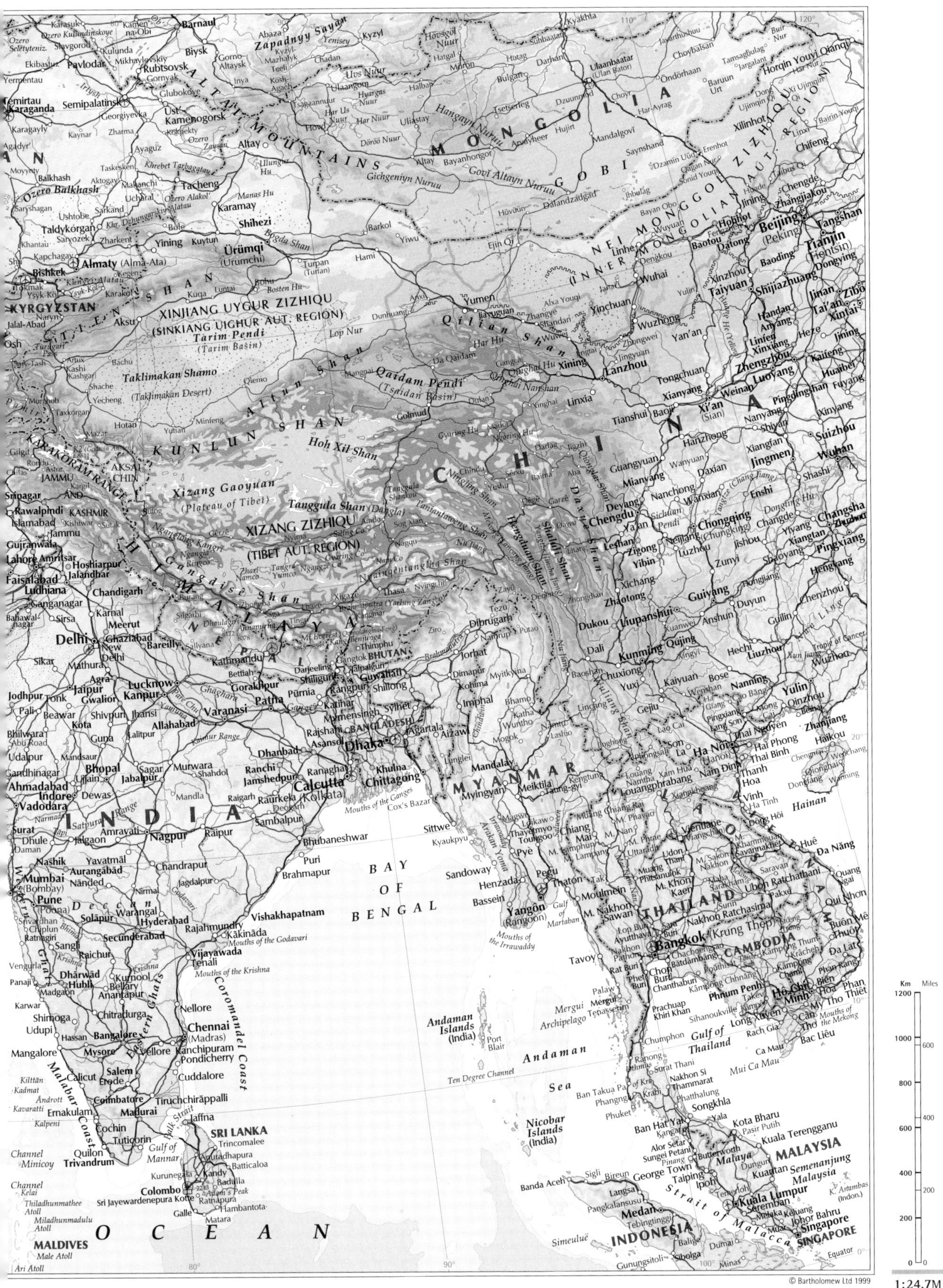
MONGOLIA
GOBI
ALTAI MOUNTAINS
NEI MONGGOL ZIZHIQU
(INNER MONGOLIAN AUT. REGION)
XINJIANG UYGUR ZIZHIQU
(SINKIANG UIGHUR AUT. REGION)
KYRGYZSTAN
TIEN SHAN
Taklimakan Shamo
(Taklimakan Desert)
Tarim Pendi
(Tarim Basin)
KUNLUN SHAN
Altun Shan
Qilian Shan
Qaidam Pendi
(Tsaidam Basin)
Hoh Xil Shan
Xizang Gaoyuan
(Plateau of Tibet)
Tanggula Shan
XIZANG ZIZHIQU
(TIBET AUT. REGION)
KARAKORAM RANGE
AKSAI CHIN
JAMMU AND KASHMIR
HIMALAYA
NEPAL
BHUTAN
BANGLADESH
INDIA
Deccan
Western Ghats
Eastern Ghats
Coromandel Coast
Malabar Coast
SRI LANKA
MALDIVES
CHINA
MYANMAR
THAILAND
LAOS
CAMBODIA
VIETNAM
MALAYSIA
SINGAPORE
INDONESIA
BAY OF BENGAL
Andaman Sea
Gulf of Thailand
Strait of Malacca
Andaman Islands (India)
Nicobar Islands (India)
Hainan
OCEAN
Beijing (Peking)
Tianjin (Tientsin)
Ürümqi (Urumchi)
Almaty (Alma-Ata)
Bishkek
Ulaanbaatar (Ulan Bator)
Lanzhou
Xi'an (Sian)
Chengdu
Chongqing (Chungking)
Kunming
Wuhan
Delhi
New Delhi
Calcutta (Kolkata)
Mumbai (Bombay)
Chennai (Madras)
Hyderabad
Bangalore
Dhaka
Kathmandu
Colombo
Yangôn (Rangoon)
Mandalay
Bangkok (Krung Thep)
Ha Noi (Hanoi)
Phnum Penh
Ho Chi Minh
Kuala Lumpur
Km Miles
1200
1000
800
600
400
200
0
© Bartholomew Ltd 1999

1:24.7M

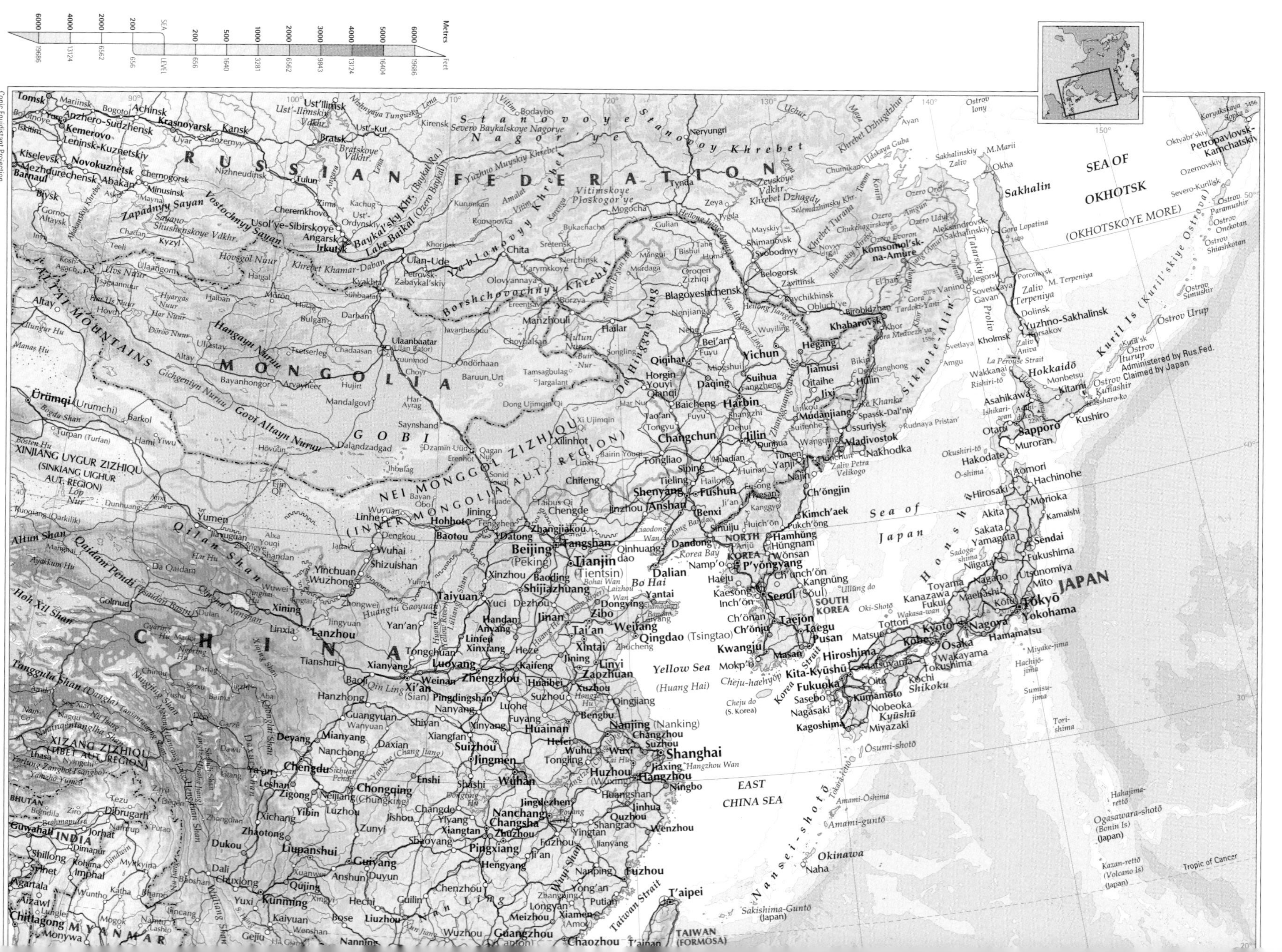
SEA OF
OKHOTSK
(OKHOTSKOYE MORE)
JAPAN
Sea of Japan
EAST
CHINA SEA
Yellow Sea
(Huang Hai)
RUSSIAN FEDERATION
MONGOLIA
GOBI
CHINA
Metres
Feet
6000
19686
5000
16404
4000
13124
3000
9843
2000
6562
1000
3281
500
1640
200
656
SEA
LEVEL
200
656
2000
6562
4000
13124
6000
19686
Conic Equidistant Projection

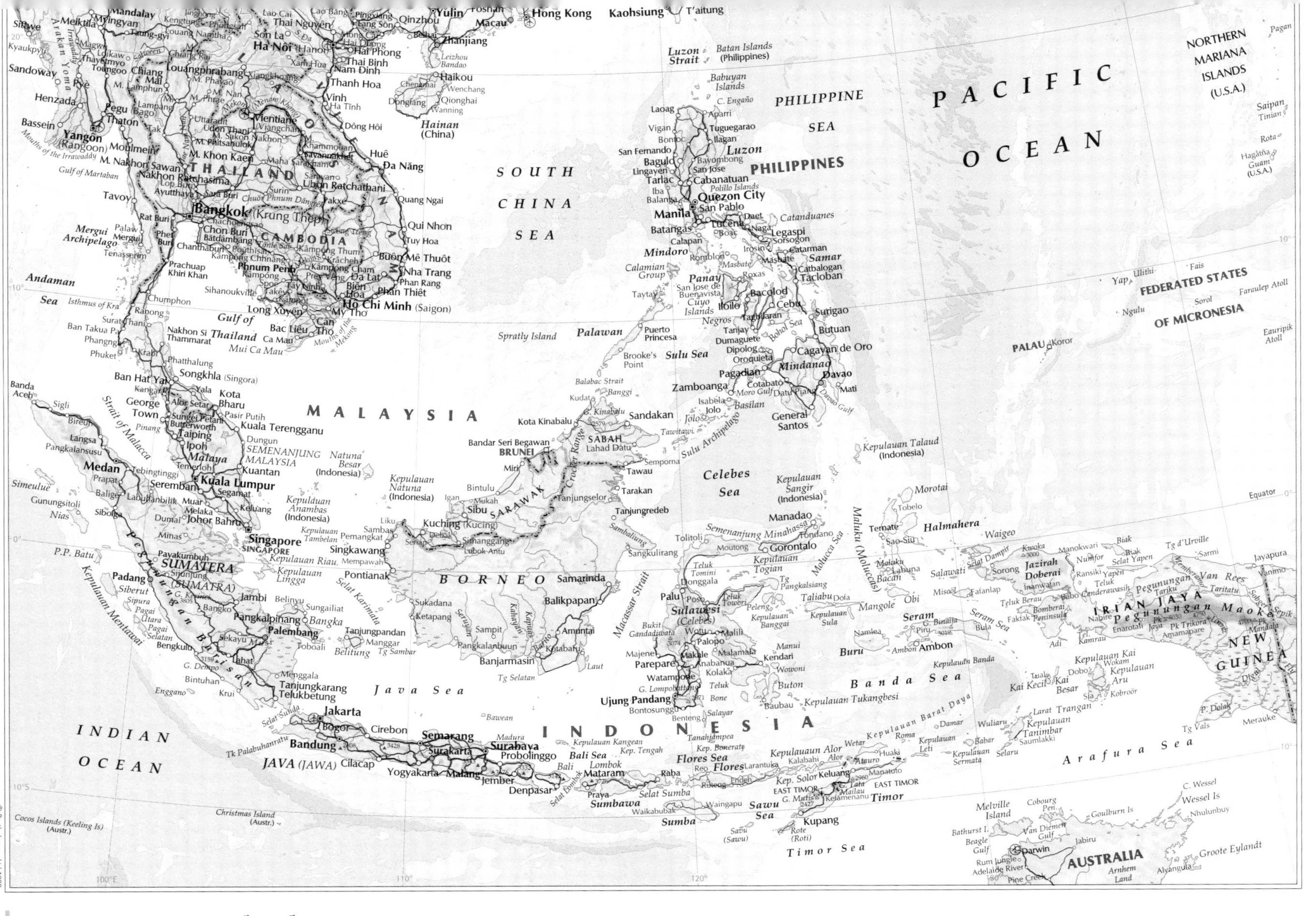

© Bartholomew Ltd 1999

1:24.7M

AUSTRALIA and Southwestern PACIFIC

1872

Lambert Azimuthal Equal Area Projection

AUSTRALIA and Southwestern PACIFIC

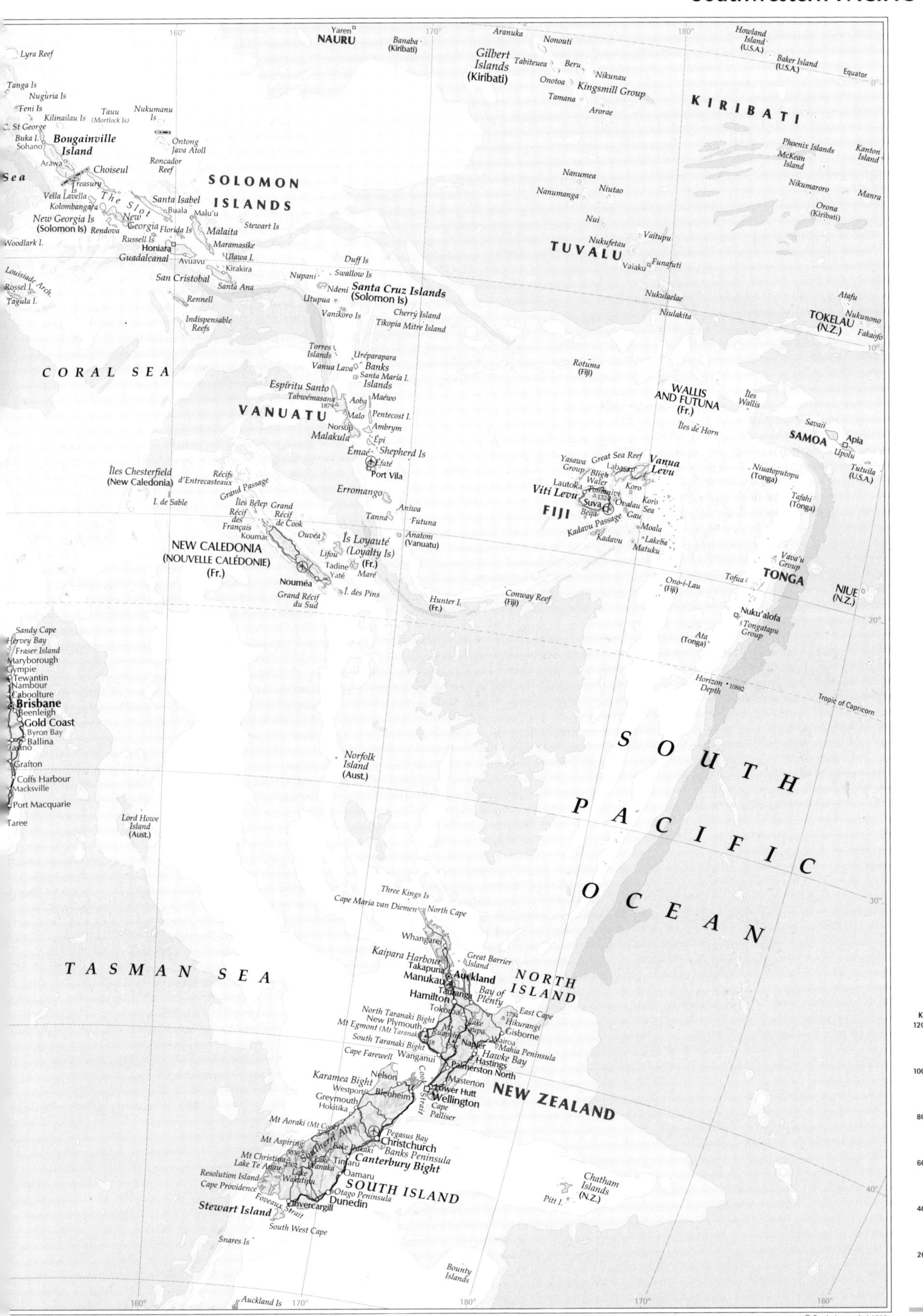

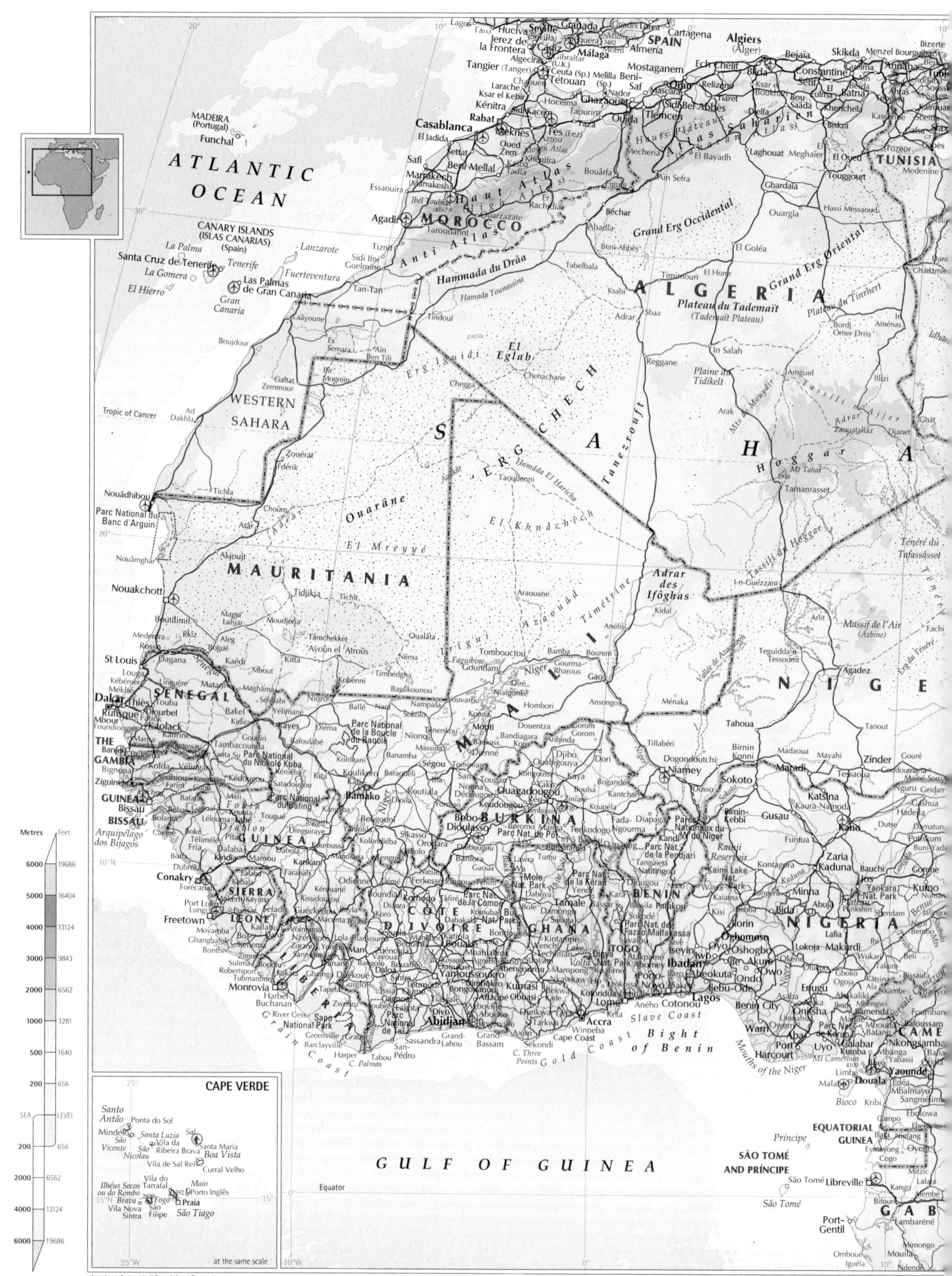
ATLANTIC OCEAN
MADEIRA (Portugal)
Funchal
CANARY ISLANDS (ISLAS CANARIAS) (Spain)
La Palma
Santa Cruz de Tenerife
Tenerife
La Gomera
El Hierro
Las Palmas de Gran Canaria
Gran Canaria
Lanzarote
Fuerteventura
SPAIN
Huelva
Sevilla
Granada
Jerez de la Frontera
Cádiz
Málaga
Almeria
Cartagena
Algeciras
Gibraltar (U.K.)
Tangier (Tanger)
Ceuta (Sp.)
Melilla (Sp.)
Tétouan
Larache
Ksar el Kebir
Kénitra
Rabat
Casablanca
El Jadida
Meknes
Fès (Fez)
Safi
Beni Mellal
Marrakech (Marrakesh)
Essaouira
Agadir
MOROCCO
Haut Atlas (High Atlas)
Moyen Atlas
Anti Atlas
Taroudannt
Ouarzazate
Tiznit
Sidi Ifni
Guelmine
Tan-Tan
Hammada du Drâa
Tindouf
Laâyoune
Es Semara
Boujdour
WESTERN SAHARA
Ad Dakhla
Tropic of Cancer
Algiers (Alger)
Oran
Mostaganem
Ech Chelif
Blida
Bejaïa
Skikda
Constantine
Sétif
Annaba
Batna
Biskra
Tlemcen
Sidi Bel Abbès
Oujda
Saida
Tiaret
Djelfa
Laghouat
Aïn Sefra
Béchar
El Bayadh
Ghardaïa
Ouargla
Touggourt
Hassi Messaoud
El Oued
Tebessa
TUNISIA
Medenine
Grand Erg Occidental
Grand Erg Oriental
El Goléa
Timimoun
Adrar
Reggane
In Salah
ALGERIA
Plateau du Tademaït (Tademaït Plateau)
Plateau du Tinrhert
Erg Iguidi
El Eglab
Erg Chech
Tanezrouft
Chegga
Tassili n'Ajjer
Illizi
Djanet
Hoggar
Mt Tahat 2918
Tamanrasset
Tassili du Hoggar
In-Guezzam
SAHARA
Nouâdhibou
Parc National du Banc d'Arguin
Zouérat
Fdérik
Atâr
Chinguetti
Akjoujt
Nouakchott
Ouarâne
El Mreyyé
El Khnâchîch
Taoudenni
MAURITANIA
Tidjikja
Tichit
Kiffa
'Ayoûn el 'Atroûs
Néma
Oualâta
Rosso
St Louis
Dakar
Thiès
Kaolack
SENEGAL
Tambacounda
Parc National du Niokolo Koba
THE GAMBIA
Banjul
Ziguinchor
GUINEA-BISSAU
Bissau
Arquipélago dos Bijagós
GUINEA
Conakry
Kindia
Labé
Kankan
SIERRA LEONE
Freetown
Bo
Kenema
LIBERIA
Monrovia
Buchanan
Grain Coast
Harper
C. Palmas
MALI
Araouane
Tombouctou
Gao
Kidal
Adrar des Ifôghas
Tilemsi
Mopti
Ségou
Bamako
Kayes
Sikasso
Parc National de la Boucle du Baoulé
Niger
BURKINA
Ouagadougou
Bobo Dioulasso
Koudougou
Fada-Ngourma
Parc National du W du Niger
CÔTE D'IVOIRE
Yamoussoukro
Bouaké
Abidjan
Korhogo
Daloa
Man
San-Pédro
Sassandra
Parc National de Taï
GHANA
Tamale
Kumasi
Accra
Sekondi
Cape Coast
C. Three Points
Gold Coast
TOGO
Lomé
BENIN
Cotonou
Porto-Novo
Parakou
Slave Coast
Bight of Benin
NIGER
Niamey
Agadez
Zinder
Maradi
Tahoua
Arlit
Massif de l'Aïr (Azbine)
Ténéré du Tafassasset
Erg du Ténéré
NIGERIA
Sokoto
Kano
Kaduna
Zaria
Jos
Abuja
Ilorin
Ibadan
Lagos
Abeokuta
Ogbomosho
Oshogbo
Benin City
Enugu
Onitsha
Port Harcourt
Calabar
Makurdi
Mouths of the Niger
CAMEROON
Douala
Yaoundé
Mt Cameroun 4100
Bioco
EQUATORIAL GUINEA
Príncipe
SÃO TOMÉ AND PRÍNCIPE
São Tomé
Libreville
GABON
Port-Gentil
Lambaréné
GULF OF GUINEA
Equator
CAPE VERDE
Santo Antão
Mindelo
São Vicente
Santa Luzia
São Nicolau
Sal
Boa Vista
Maio
Fogo
Brava
Praia
São Tiago
at the same scale
Metres
Feet
SEA LEVEL
Lambert Azimuthal Equal Area Projection

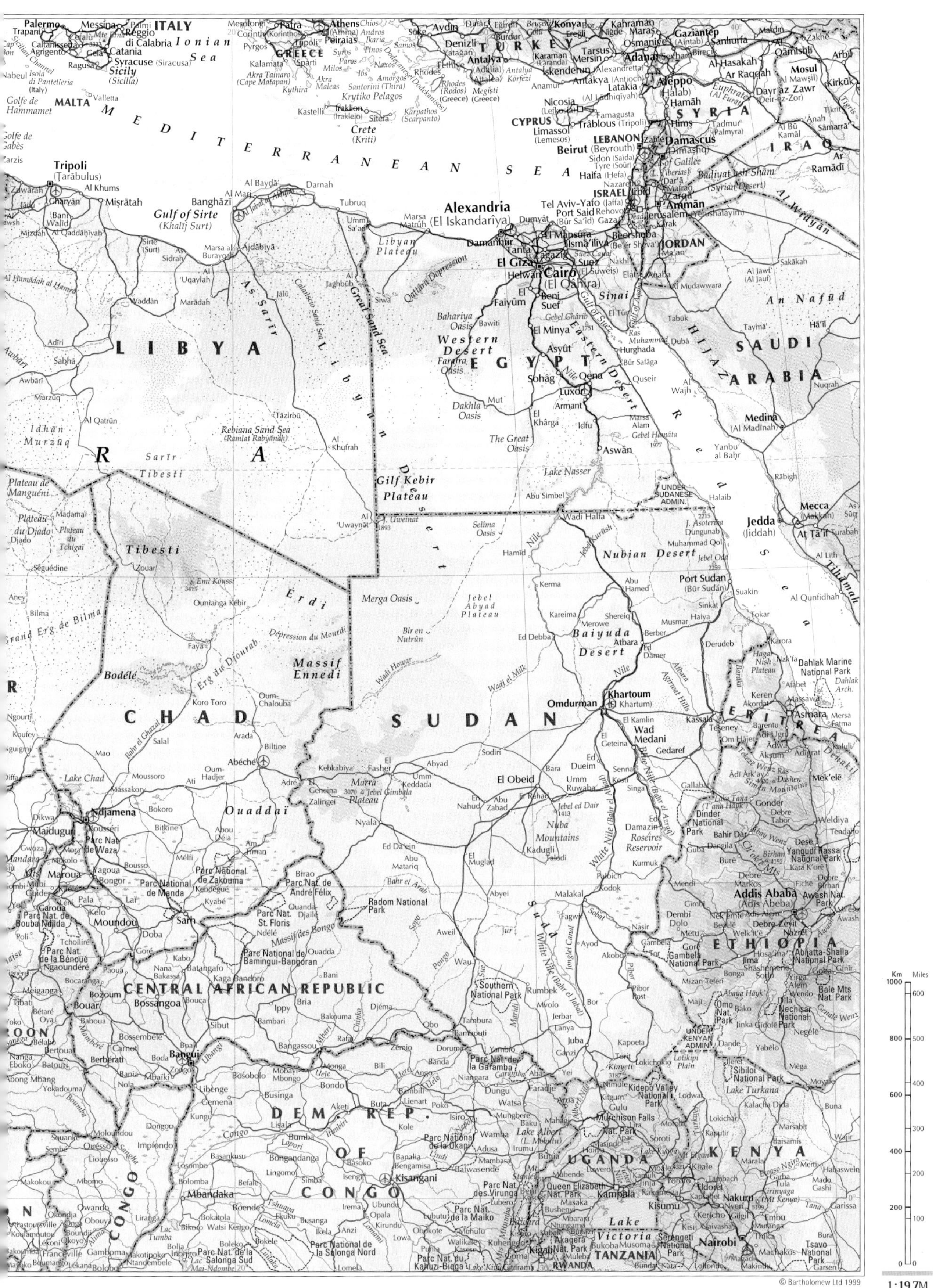

1:19.7M

Central and Southern AFRICA

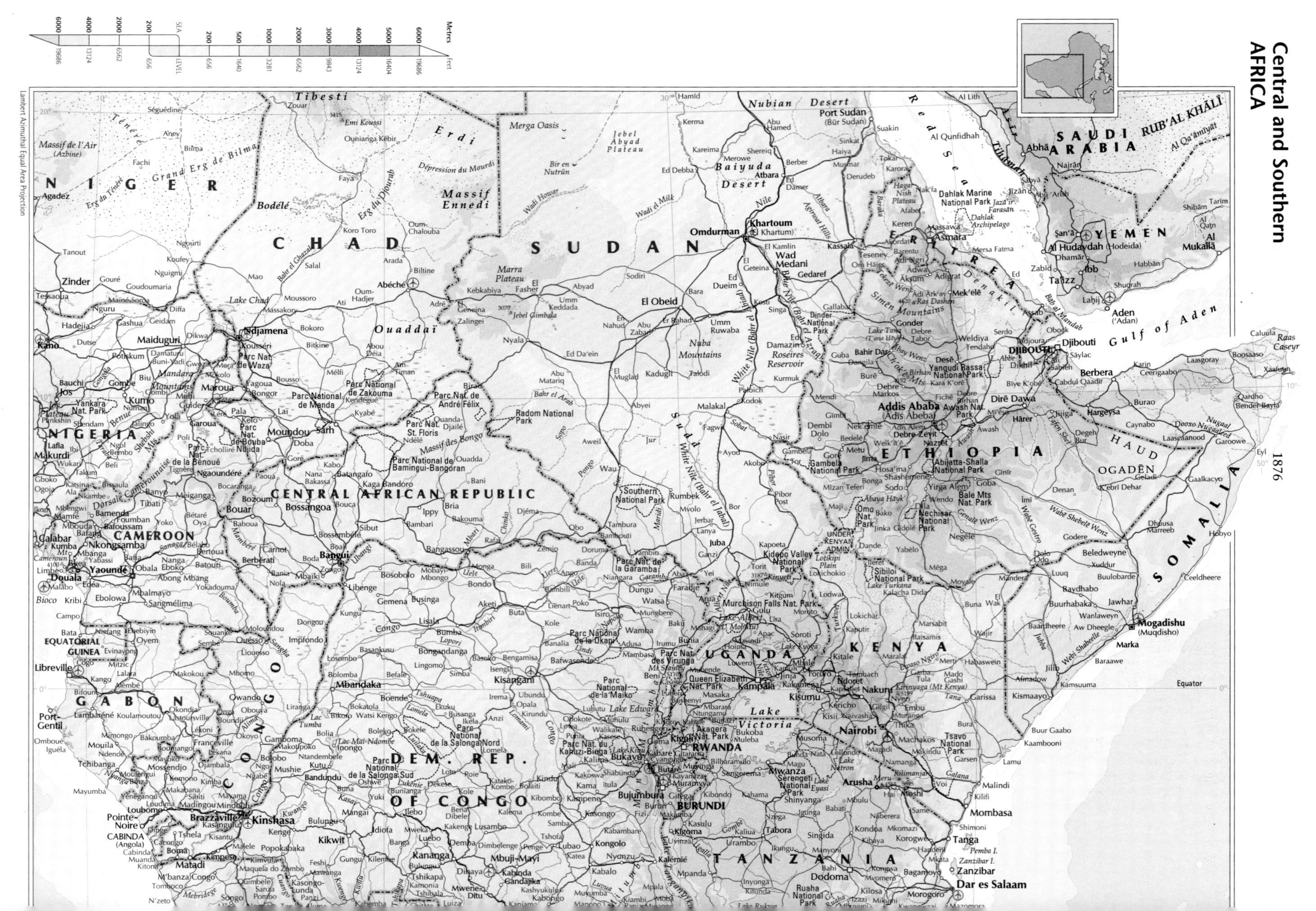

ANGOLA
ZAMBIA
MALAWI
MOZAMBIQUE
ZIMBABWE
BOTSWANA
NAMIBIA
REPUBLIC OF SOUTH AFRICA
LESOTHO
SWAZILAND
MADAGASCAR
COMOROS
MAYOTTE (France)
Mozambique Channel
INDIAN OCEAN
ATLANTIC OCEAN
Kalahari Desert
Namib Desert
Tropic of Capricorn
Luanda
Lusaka
Harare
Lilongwe
Maputo
Pretoria
Johannesburg
Windhoek
Gaborone
Maseru
Mbabane
Antananarivo
Moroni
Cape Town
Durban
Port Elizabeth
East London
Bulawayo
Beira
Km
Miles
1000
800
600
400
200
0
600
500
400
300
200
100
0

1:19.7M

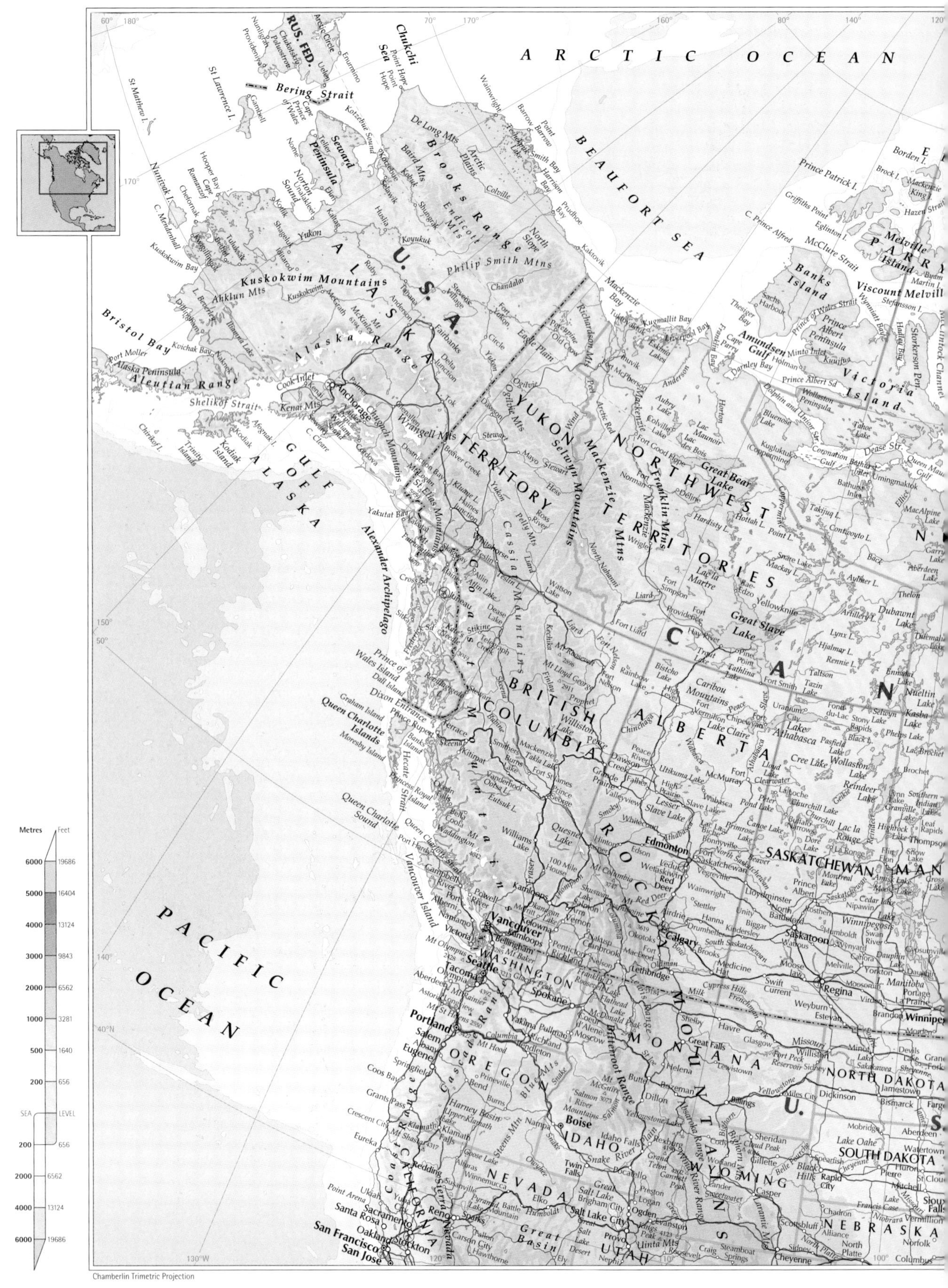
ARCTIC OCEAN
BEAUFORT SEA
PACIFIC OCEAN
GULF OF ALASKA
Bristol Bay
Bering Strait
Chukchi Sea
RUS. FED.
U.S.A.
ALASKA
Brooks Range
Alaska Range
Kuskokwim Mountains
Aleutian Range
Alaska Peninsula
Seward Peninsula
Anchorage
Fairbanks
Juneau
Alexander Archipelago
YUKON TERRITORY
NORTHWEST TERRITORIES
BRITISH COLUMBIA
ALBERTA
SASKATCHEWAN
CANADA
ROCKY MOUNTAINS
Coast Mountains
Mackenzie Mountains
Selwyn Mountains
Great Bear Lake
Great Slave Lake
Lake Athabasca
Banks Island
Victoria Island
Melville Island
Queen Charlotte Islands
Vancouver Island
Vancouver
Victoria
Edmonton
Calgary
Saskatoon
Regina
Winnipeg
Seattle
Portland
Spokane
Boise
Salt Lake City
Sacramento
San Francisco
San Jose
Oakland
WASHINGTON
OREGON
IDAHO
MONTANA
WYOMING
NEVADA
UTAH
CALIFORNIA
NORTH DAKOTA
SOUTH DAKOTA
NEBRASKA
Great Basin
Metres
Feet
6000 19686
5000 16404
4000 13124
3000 9843
2000 6562
1000 3281
500 1640
200 656
SEA LEVEL
200 656
2000 6562
4000 13124
6000 19686
Chamberlin Trimetric Projection

GREENLAND
(KALAALLIT NUNAAT)
(Denmark)
ICELAND
Reykjavík
Denmark Strait
BAFFIN BAY
DAVIS STRAIT
Labrador Sea
NEWFOUNDLAND
Baffin Island
Devon Island
Ellesmere Island
Axel Heiburg Island
Nares Strait
Smith Sound
Jones Sound
Lancaster Sound
Barrow Strait
Somerset Island
Prince of Wales Island
Boothia Peninsula
Gulf of Boothia
King William I.
Melville Peninsula
Foxe Basin
Foxe Chan.
Foxe Peninsula
Prince Charles Island
Nettilling Lake
Amadjuak Lake
Cumberland Peninsula
Cumberland Sound
Hall Pen.
Meta Incognita Pen.
Iqaluit
Southampton Island
Coats Island
Mansel Island
Hudson Strait
Ungava Bay
Péninsule d'Ungava
HUDSON BAY
Belcher Islands
James Bay
Akimiski Island
QUEBEC
LABRADOR
Smallwood Reservoir
Churchill Falls
Happy Valley-Goose Bay
Strait of Belle Isle
Newfoundland
Gander
St John's
Cabot Strait
Gulf of St Lawrence
Île d'Anticosti
PRINCE EDWARD ISLAND
Charlottetown
NOVA SCOTIA
Halifax
Cape Breton Island
Sable Island
NEW BRUNSWICK
Fredericton
Saint John
Bay of Fundy
ONTARIO
MANITOBA
Lake Winnipeg
Churchill
Thunder Bay
Lake Superior
Lake Michigan
Lake Huron
Sudbury
Sault Ste Marie
North Bay
Ottawa
Montreal
Québec
Trois Rivières
Sherbrooke
Toronto
Kingston
Hamilton
London
Detroit
Windsor
Chicago
Milwaukee
Minneapolis
St Paul
Duluth
Buffalo
Rochester
Syracuse
Albany
Boston
Providence
Hartford
New Haven
New York
Cleveland
MINNESOTA
WISCONSIN
MICHIGAN
IOWA
NEW YORK
PENNSYLVANIA
VERMONT
MAINE
N.H.
MASS.
CONN.
R.I.
ST PIERRE AND MIQUELON (France)
NORTH ATLANTIC OCEAN
Km
Miles
1:21M

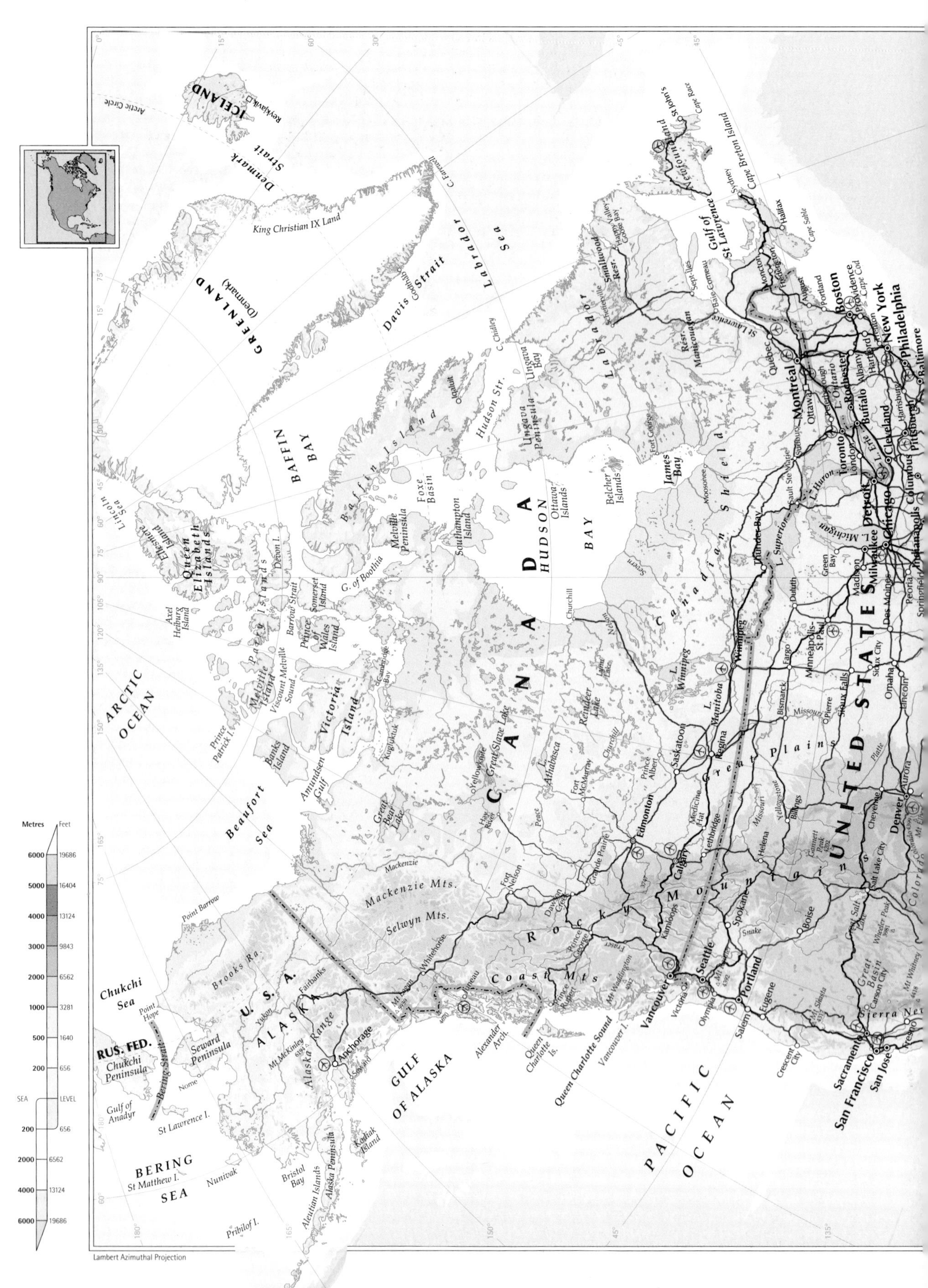
ARCTIC OCEAN
Beaufort Sea
BAFFIN BAY
GREENLAND (Denmark)
ICELAND
Labrador Sea
Davis Strait
Denmark Strait
HUDSON BAY
James Bay
CANADA
UNITED STATES
ALASKA
U.S.A.
RUS. FED.
Chukchi Sea
BERING SEA
GULF OF ALASKA
PACIFIC OCEAN
Rocky Mountains
Great Plains
Canadian Shield
Mackenzie Mts.
Selwyn Mts.
Coast Mts
Brooks Ra.
Alaska Range
Queen Elizabeth Islands
Baffin Island
Victoria Island
Gulf of St Lawrence
Anchorage
Vancouver
Seattle
Portland
San Francisco
Sacramento
San Jose
Edmonton
Calgary
Winnipeg
Regina
Saskatoon
Montreal
Toronto
Ottawa
Quebec
Boston
New York
Philadelphia
Baltimore
Chicago
Detroit
Cleveland
Milwaukee
Denver
Halifax
Lambert Azimuthal Projection
Metres
Feet
6000
19686
5000
16404
4000
13124
3000
9843
2000
6562
1000
3281
500
1640
200
656
SEA
LEVEL

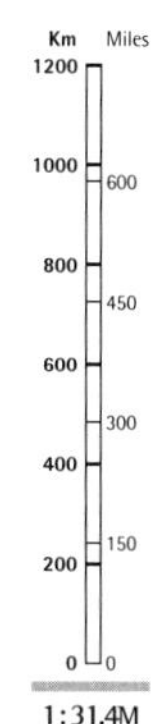

1:31.4M

CARIBBEAN SEA
ATLANTIC OCEAN
PACIFIC OCEAN
ATLANTIC OCEAN
Punta Gallinas
G. de Venezuela
Isla de Margarita
Barranquilla
Maracaibo
Caracas
Cumaná
TRINIDAD & TOBAGO
Golfo del Darién
Cartagena
L. Maracaibo
Barquisimeto
Valencia
Orinoco Delta
Waini Point
PANAMA
Montería
San Cristóbal
Orinoco
Ciudad Guayana
San Fernando de Apure
Georgetown
Medellín
VENEZUELA
Paramaribo
Pointe Isère
Cerro Yavi 2285
GUYANA
Cabo Corrientes
Cayenne
Cabo Orange
Manizales
SURINAME
FRENCH GUIANA
Buenaventura
Bogotá
I. de Malpelo (Col.)
Cali
Sa Pacaraima
Boa Vista
Guaviare
COLOMBIA
Ilha de Maracá
Pasto
Florencia
Macapa
Mouths of the Amazon
Cotopaxi 5896
Quito
Caquetá
Equator
Portoviejo
ECUADOR
I. de Marajó
Belém
Guayaquil
Chimborazo 6310
Japurá
Negro
Represa de Balbina
Baía de São Marcos
Cuenca
Putumayo
Amazon
São Luís
Parnaíba
Fortaleza
Golfo de Guayaquil
Manaus
Santarem
Altamira
Iquitos
Amazon
Itaituba
Ponta do Calcanhar
Marañón
Piura
Marabá
Bacabal
Codó
Teresina
Natal
Imperatriz
Represa Tucuruí
João Pessoa
Chiclayo
Araguaína
Juazeiro do Norte
Recife
Trujillo
Cruzeiro do Sul
SELVAS
BRAZIL
Pucallpa
Pôrto Velho
Barragem de Sobradinho
Petrolina
Maceió
Rio Branco
Ariquemes
Nevado de Huascarán 6768
PERU
Aracaju
Feira de Santana
Salvador
Cabo Santo Antônio
Lima
Callao
Serra dos Parecis
Serra Geral de Goiás
Chapada Diamantina
Bahía de Pisco
Ayacucho
Ica
Cusco
Lago de San Luis
Trinidad
Ilhéus
Cordillera Oriental
Cordillera Occidental
Cordillera Central
Brasília
Espinosa
Vitória da Conquista
Juliaca
Cáceres
Cuiabá
Lago Titicaca
La Paz
Goiânia
Arequipa
BOLIVIA
Cochabamba
Santa Cruz
Rio Verde
Montes Claros
Ponta da Baleia
Arica
Bañados del Izozog
Corumbá
Teófilo Otôni
Sucre
Potosí
Uberaba
Iquique
Belo Horizonte
Vitória
Campo Grande
Tarija
Dourados
Araçatuba
Nova Iguaçu
Campos
Cabo de São Tomé
Calama
Gran Chaco
Campinas
Rio de Janeiro
Pta Tetas
San Salvador de Jujuy
PARAGUAY
São Paulo
Tropic of Capricorn
Antofagasta
Santos
Ilha de São Sebastião
San Pedro
Asunción
Salta
Curitiba
Pta Ballena
Foz do Iguaçu
Iguaçu Falls
Islas de los Desventurados (Chile)
San Miguel de Tucumán
Pta Morro
Posadas
Florianopolis
Corrientes
Cerro Bonete 6872
Catamarca
Santa Maria
Porto Alegre
La Serena
Uruguaiana
San Juan
Córdoba
Santa Fé
Lagoa dos Patos
Juan Fernandez Islands (Chile)
Tacuarembó
Rio Grande
Valparaíso
Mendoza
Paraná
URUGUAY
Lagoa Mirim
Aconcagua
Santiago
Rosario
Buenos Aires
Rocha
Talca
La Plata
Montevideo
Río de la Plata
PAMPAS
Concepción
Santa Rosa
Olavarría
Mar del Plata
Temuco
Bahía Blanca
Neuquén
Bahía Blanca
Pta Galera
Negro
Puerto Montt
Viedma
Golfo San Matías
Isla de Chiloé
Esquel
Península Valdés
Rawson
Patagonia
Archipiélago de los Chonos
Comodoro Rivadavia
Golfo de San Jorge
Golfo de Penas
Cochrane
Deseado
Pta Medanosa
L. San Martín
L. Argentino
Bahía Grande
Falkland Islands (U.K.)
Río Gallegos
West Falkland
Stanley
East Falkland
Puerto Natales
Est. de Magallanes
Punta Arenas
Tierra del Fuego
I. de los Estados
Ushuaia
South Georgia (U.K.)
Cape Horn
ANDES
ARGENTINA
CHILE
Metres
Feet
6000
19686
5000
16404
4000
13124
3000
9843
2000
6562
1000
3281
500
1640
200
656
SEA LEVEL
Km
Miles
1800
1500
1200
900
600
300
0
1:35.3M
Sinusoidal Projection

Guide to the Text

Headword

Pronunciation

prenomen (priːˈnəʊmɛn) *n, pl* **-nomina** (-ˈnɒmɪnə) *or* **-nomens.** *U.S.* a less common spelling of **praenomen.**

prenominal (priːˈnɒmɪnᵊl) *adj* **1** placed before a noun, esp. (of an adjective or sense of an adjective) used only before a noun. **2** of or relating to a praenomen.

prenotion (priːˈnəʊʃən) *n* a rare word for **preconception.**

prentice (ˈprɛntɪs) *n* an archaic word for **apprentice.**

prenuptial agreement *n* a contract made between a man and woman before they marry, agreeing on the distribution of their assets in the event of divorce.

preoccupation (priːˌɒkjʊˈpeɪʃən) *or* **preoccupancy** (priːˈɒkjʊpənsɪ) *n* **1** the state of being preoccupied, esp. mentally. **2** something that holds the attention or preoccupies the mind.

preoccupied (priːˈɒkjʊˌpaɪd) *adj* **1** engrossed or absorbed in something, esp. one's own thoughts. **2** already or previously occupied. **3** *Biology.* (of a taxonomic name) already used to designate a genus, species, etc.

Inflected forms

preoccupy (priːˈɒkjʊˌpaɪ) *vb* **-pies, -pying, -pied.** (*tr*) **1** to engross the thoughts or mind of. **2** to occupy before or in advance of another. **[C16:** from Latin *praeoccupāre* to capture in advance, from *prae* before + *occupāre* to seize, take possession of**]**

preordain (ˌpriːɔːˈdeɪn) *vb* (*tr*) to ordain, decree, or appoint beforehand. ▸ **preordination** (ˌpriːɔːdɪˈneɪʃən) *n*

Part of speech

prep (prɛp) *n* **1** *Informal.* short for **preparation** (sense 5) or (chiefly U.S.) **preparatory school.** ◆ *vb* **preps, prepping, prepped. 2** (*tr*) to prepare (a patient) for a medical operation or procedure.

prep. *abbrev. for:* **1** preparation. **2** preparatory. **3** preposition.

Sense number

Example

Subject-field label

preparation (ˌprɛpəˈreɪʃən) *n* **1** the act or process of preparing. **2** the state of being prepared; readiness. **3** (*often pl*) a measure done in order to prepare for something; provision: *to make preparations for something.* **4** something that is prepared, esp. a medicine. **5** (esp. in a boarding school) **5a** homework. **5b** the period reserved for this. Usually shortened to **prep. 6** *Music.* **6a** the anticipation of a dissonance so that the note producing it in one chord is first heard in the preceding chord as a consonance. **6b** a note so employed. **7** (*often cap.*) the preliminary prayers at Mass or divine service.

preparative (prɪˈpærətɪv) *adj* **1** serving to prepare; preparatory. ◆ *n* **2** something that prepares. ▸ **preˈparatively** *adv*

preparatory (prɪˈpærətərɪ, -trɪ) *adj* **1** serving to prepare. **2** introductory or preliminary. **3** occupied in preparation. **4 preparatory to.** as a preparation to; before: *a drink preparatory to eating.* ▸ **preˈparatorily** *adv*

preparatory school *n* **1** (in Britain) a private school, usually single-sex and for children between the ages of 6 and 13, generally preparing pupils for public school. **2** (in the U.S.) a private secondary school preparing pupils for college. ◆ Often shortened to **prep school.**

Definition

Idiom or phrase

prepare (prɪˈpɛə) *vb* **1** to make ready or suitable in advance for a particular purpose or for some use, event, etc.: *to prepare a meal; to prepare to go.* **2** to put together using parts or ingredients; compose or construct. **3** (*tr*) to equip or outfit, as for an expedition. **4** (*tr*) *Music.* to soften the impact of (a dissonant note) by the use of preparation. **5 be prepared.** (*foll. by an infinitive*) to be willing and able (to do something): *I'm not prepared to reveal these figures.* **[C15:** from Latin *praeparāre,* from *prae* before + *parāre* to make ready**]** ▸ **preˈparer** *n*

preparedness (prɪˈpɛərɪdnɪs) *n* the state of being prepared or ready, esp. militarily ready for war. ▸ **preˈparedly** *adv*

prepared piano *n* a piano in which some strings have been damped by having objects placed between them or tuned differently from the rest for specific tonal effect. This process was pioneered by John Cage.

prepay (priːˈpeɪ) *vb* **-pays, -paying, -paid.** (*tr*) to pay for in advance. ▸ **preˈpayable** *adj* ▸ **preˈpayment** *n*

prepense (prɪˈpɛns) *adj* (*postpositive*) (usually in legal contexts) arranged in advance; premeditated (esp. in the phrase **malice prepense**). **[C18:** from Anglo-Norman *purpensé,* from Old French *purpenser* to consider in advance, from *penser* to think, from Latin *pēnsāre* to weigh, consider**]**

preponderant (prɪˈpɒndərənt) *adj* greater in weight, force, influence, etc. ▸ **preˈponderance** *or* **preˈponderancy** *n* ▸ **preˈponderantly** *adv*

Grammatical information

preponderate (prɪˈpɒndəˌreɪt) *vb* (*intr*) **1** (*often foll. by over*) to be more powerful, important, numerous, etc. (than). **2** to be of greater weight than something else. **[C17:** from Late Latin *praeponderāre* to be of greater weight, from *pondus* weight**]** ▸ **preˈponderately** *adv* ▸ **preˈponderˌating** *adj* ▸ **preˌponderˈation** *n*

preposition (ˌprɛpəˈzɪʃən) *n* a word or group of words used before a noun or pronoun to relate it grammatically or semantically to some other constituent of a sentence. Abbrev.: **prep. [C14:** from Latin *praepositiō* a putting before, from *pōnere* to place**]** ▸ **ˌprepoˈsitional** *adj* ▸ **ˌprepoˈsitionally** *adv*

Usage note

USAGE The practice of ending a sentence with a preposition (*Venice is a place I should like to go to*) was formerly regarded as incorrect, but is now acceptable and is the preferred form in many contexts.